Presented to ___English Dept.___

By _____

Date _____

WEBSTER'S
Ninth New
Collegiate
Dictionary

WEBSTER'S

Ninth New Collegiate Dictionary

A Merriam-Webster®

MERRIAM-WEBSTER INC., *Publishers*
Springfield, Massachusetts, U.S.A.

A GENUINE MERRIAM-WEBSTER

The name *Webster* alone is no guarantee of excellence. It is used by a number of publishers and may serve mainly to mislead an unwary buyer.

A Merriam-Webster® is the registered trademark you should look for when you consider the purchase of dictionaries or other fine reference books. It carries the reputation of a company that has been publishing since 1831 and is your assurance of quality and authority.

Copyright © 1991 by Merriam-Webster Inc.

Philippines Copyright 1991 by Merriam-Webster Inc.

Library of Congress Cataloging in Publication Data
Main entry under title:

Webster's ninth new collegiate dictionary.
      p.   cm.
  ISBN 0-87779-508-8. — ISBN 0-87779-509-6 (indexed). — ISBN 0-87779-510-X (deluxe)
   1. English language—Dictionaries. I. Merriam-Webster, Inc.
PE1628.W5638   1991
423—dc20   90-47350
                                       CIP

Webster's Ninth New Collegiate Dictionary principal copyright 1983

COLLEGIATE trademark Reg. U.S. Pat. Off.

Made in the United States of America

4142434445RMcN91

Contents

Preface

Webster's Ninth New Collegiate Dictionary is the latest in the Collegiate line of Merriam-Webster® dictionaries which began in 1898. Every entry and feature of the last edition has been reexamined so that this Collegiate offers the dictionary user much that is new and useful while preserving the best features of preceding editions. This dictionary is meant to serve the general public as its chief source of information about the words of our language. The school or college student, the office worker, the home user—all will find this Collegiate a reliable guide to understanding the English of our day and communicating in it.

While Webster's Ninth New Collegiate Dictionary holds no more pages than did the last edition, a change in the dimensions of the page and a different design of some elements on that page have allowed the editors to add thousands of new words and senses as well as to introduce several significant new features and other improvements.

The treatment of words in the A-Z vocabulary section is as nearly exhaustive as the compass of an abridged work permits. As in all Merriam-Webster® dictionaries, the information given is based on the unparalleled collection of citations maintained in the offices of this company. These citations show words used in a wide range of printed sources, and the collection is constantly augmented through the efforts of the editorial staff. Thus, the user of the dictionary may be confident that entries in the Collegiate are based on current as well as older material. The citation files hold 3,000,000 more examples than were available to the editors of Webster's Third New International Dictionary, published in 1961, the total now being 13,000,000.

Those entries known to be trademarks or service marks are so labeled and are treated in accordance with a formula approved by the United States Trademark Association. No entry in this dictionary, however, should be regarded as affecting the validity of any trademark or service mark.

Several features of the vocabulary section are worth special notice. The treatment of synonymy has been completely revised for this edition so that all the synonym articles now discriminate from one another words of closely associated meaning. Many of the articles are enriched with typical examples of usage based on—or sometimes quoted from—citations in our files.

Pictorial illustrations have been prominent in Collegiate dictionaries from the beginning. In this edition, as before, they have been selected chiefly for their ability to inform by supplementing and clarifying definitions. In many instances this function has been enhanced for this edition by increasing the size of the illustration so that significant details are more readily apparent.

In Webster's Ninth New Collegiate Dictionary two features make their first appearance in any Merriam-Webster® dictionary. Before the first entered sense of each entry for a generic word, the user of this Collegiate will find a date that indicates when the earliest example known to us of the use of that sense was written or printed. This date serves as a link, in the case of entries with several senses, between the etymology preceding it and the historically ordered senses following it. We believe that the date will often be a point of considerable interest in its own right as well.

A number of entries for words posing special problems of confused or disputed usage include for the first time brief articles that provide the dictionary user with suitable guidance on the usage in question. The guidance offered is never based merely on received opinion, though opinions are often noted, but typically on both a review of the historical background and a careful evaluation of what citations reveal about actual contemporary practice. These articles should prove a helpful complement to the usage information offered through the traditional devices of the usage label and the usage note.

The front matter of this book attempts to establish a context for understanding what this dictionary is and how it came to be, as well as how it may be used most effectively. The Explanatory Notes address themselves to the latter topic. They answer the user's questions about the conventions, devices, and techniques by which the editors have been able to compress mountains of information about English words into fewer than 1400 pages. All users of the dictionary are urged to read this section through and then consult it for special information as they need to. The brief essay on our language as it is recorded in Merriam-Webster® dictionaries, and this Collegiate in particular, is meant to satisfy an interest in lexicography often expressed in the correspondence which our editors receive. The Guide to Pronunciation serves both to show how the pronunciations recorded in this book are arrived at and to explain the mechanics of the respelling system in which they are set down.

The back matter retains all six sections from the last edition of the Collegiate. These are Foreign Words and Phrases that occur frequently in English texts but have not become part of the English vocabulary; thousands of proper names gathered under the separate headings Biographical Names and Geographical Names; a list of the degree-granting, two-year and four-year Colleges and Universities of the United States and Canada; a gathering of important Signs and Symbols that cannot readily be alphabetized; and a Handbook of Style in which various stylistic conventions (as of punctuation and capitalization) are summarized and exemplified. All these sections are expanded with new material in this edition. One section has been added: Abbreviations and Symbols for Chemical Elements, which were in the main vocabulary of the 1973 Collegiate, are now in the back matter.

Webster's Ninth New Collegiate Dictionary is the result of much patient labor by the trained staff of Merriam-Webster Incorporated, working in collaboration with each other and, in a sense, with the editors of earlier Collegiates and Internationals, who have left numberless, often indiscernible traces of their thought, insight, and care upon the pages of this dictionary. There is unfortunately no space to acknowledge former editors individually, but all the staff members who made substantial contributions to this edition are listed on the facing page. Many demonstrated their versatility by working in several widely separated parts of the book and in very different roles.

Webster's Ninth New Collegiate Dictionary is offered to the user in the same spirit as were earlier editions: it is the product of a company with a sustained tradition of excellence in the making of dictionaries, and we are confident that whoever comes to know it and use it carefully will be well served by it.

Frederick C. Mish
Editor in Chief

Editorial Staff

Editor in Chief

Frederick C. Mish

Managing Editor

E. Ward Gilman

Senior Editors

James G. Lowe · Robert D. McHenry
· Roger W. Pease, Jr.

Associate Editors

John K. Bollard · Julie A. Collier
· Robert D. Copeland · Kathleen M. Doherty
· William C. Hale · Grace A. Kellogg
· John M. Morse

Assistant Editors

Michael G. Belanger · Eileen M. Haraty
· Peter D. Haraty · Daniel J. Hopkins
· Karen J. Langridge · Madeline L. Novak
· Stephen J. Perrault

Editorial Assistants

Robin L. Easson · Elizabeth A. Johnson
Jeanne M. Julian · Amy L. Liston
Arden J. Lowe · Michele T. Plourde
· Dru A. Whitten

Editorial Advisor

Hubert P. Kelsey

Librarian

Francine A. Roberts

Departmental Secretary

Helene Gingold

Head of Typing Room

Gloria J. Afflitto

Senior General Clerk

Ruth W. Gaines

Clerks and Typists

Georgette B. Boucher · Karen L. Cormier
· Florence J. Cressotti · Jean M. Fitzgerald
· Patricia M. Jensen · Joan M. Lancour
· Frances W. Muldrew · Mildred C. Paquette
· Barbara A. Winkler

Merriam-Webster Incorporated

William A. Llewellyn, President and Publisher

Left-column feature labels:

- angle brackets
  PAGE 18
- binomial
  PAGES 20, 21
- boldface colon
  PAGE 19
- called also
  PAGE 18
- capitalization label
  PAGE 15
- centered dots
  PAGE 11
- cognate cross-reference
  PAGES 21, 22
- cutback inflected forms
  PAGES 13, 14
- date
  PAGE 17
- defined run-on entry
  PAGE 11
- definition
  PAGES 19, 20
- directional cross-reference
  PAGES 21, 22
- equal variant
  PAGE 11
- etymology
  PAGES 15, 16
- functional label
  PAGE 13
- guide phrase
  PAGE 18
- homographs
  PAGE 10
- illustrative quotation
  PAGE 18
- inflected forms
  PAGES 13, 14
- inflectional cross-reference
  PAGES 21, 22
- list of undefined words
  PAGE 22
- lowercase
  PAGE 15
- main entry
  PAGE 10
- often attrib
  PAGE 15

Dictionary text:

²**pet** *adj* (1584) **1** : kept or treated as a pet **2** : expressing fondness or endearment ⟨a ~ name⟩ **3** : FAVORITE ⟨his ~ project⟩

pharaoh ant *n* (ca. 1947) : a little red ant (*Monomorium pharaonis*) that is a common household pest

pher·o·mone \'fer-ə-ˌmōn\ *n* [ISV *phero-* (fr. Gk *pherein* to carry) + *-mone* (as in *hormone*) — more at BEAR] (1959) : a chemical substance that is produced by an animal and serves esp. as a stimulus to other individuals of the same species for one or more behavioral responses — **pher·o·mon·al** \ˌfer-ə-'mōn-ᵊl\ *adj*

phil·a·del·phus \ˌfil-ə-'del-fəs\ *n* [NL, fr. Gk *philadelphos* brotherly, fr. *phil-* + *adelphos* brother — more at -ADELPHOUS] (1950) : any of a genus of ornamental shrubs of the saxifrage family of which several are widely grown in temperate regions for their showy white flowers — **called also** *mock orange, syringa*

Phi·lis·tine \'fil-ə-ˌstēn, fə-'lis-tən, -ˌtēn; 'fil-ə-stən\ *n* (14c) **1** : a native or inhabitant of ancient Philistia **2** *often not cap* **a** : a crass prosaic often priggish individual guided by material rather than intellectual or artistic values : BABBITT **b** : one uninformed in a special area of knowledge — **philistine** *adj, often cap* — **phi·lis·tin·ism** \-ˌstē-ˌniz-əm, -tə-, -stə-\ *n, often cap*

pic·tur·esque \ˌpik-chə-'resk\ *adj* [F & It; F *pittoresque*, fr. It *pittoresco*, fr. *pittore* painter, fr. L *pictor*, fr. *pictus*, pp.] (1703) **1 a** : resembling a picture : suggesting a painted scene **b** : charming or quaint in appearance **2** : evoking mental images : VIVID *syn* see GRAPHIC — **pic·tur·esque·ly** *adv* — **pic·tur·esque·ness** *n*

³**pie** *var of* PI

²**pillory** *vt* **-ried; -ry·ing** (ca. 1600) **1** : to set in a pillory as punishment **2** : to expose to public contempt, ridicule, or scorn

pin·fold \-ˌfōld\ *n* [ME, fr. OE *pundfald*, fr. *pund-* enclosure + *fald* fold] (13c) **1** : ⁴POUND 1a **2** : a place of restraint

pins and needles *n pl* (1813) : a pricking tingling sensation in a limb growing numb or recovering from numbness — **on pins and needles** : in a nervous or jumpy state of anticipation

pi·ra·nha \pə-'ran-yə, -'rän-(yə)\ *n* [Pg, fr. Tupi] (1869) : a small So. American characin fish (genus *Serrasalmo*) that often attacks and inflicts dangerous wounds upon men and large animals — called also *caribe*

pis·til \'pis-tᵊl\ *n* [NL *pistillum*, fr. L, pestle — more at PESTLE] (1726) : the ovule-bearing organ of a seed plant that consists of the ovary with its appendages — **see FLOWER illustration**

pla·gal \'plā-gəl\ *adj* [ML *plagalis*, deriv. of Gk *plagios* oblique, sideways, fr. *plagos* side; akin to L *plaga* net, region, Gk *pelagos* sea — more at FLAKE] (1597) **1** *of a church mode* : having the keynote on the 4th scale step — compare AUTHENTIC 4a **2** *of a cadence* : progressing from the subdominant chord to the tonic — **compare AUTHENTIC 4b**

plagu·ey *or* **plaguy** \'plā-gē, 'pleg-ē\ *adj, chiefly dial* (1615) : causing irritation or annoyance : TROUBLESOME — **plaguey** *adv* — **plagu·i·ly** \'plā-gə-lē, 'pleg-ə-\ *adv*

plead \'plēd\ *vb* **plead·ed** \'plēd-əd\ *or* **pled** \'pled\; **plead·ing** [ME *plaiden* to institute a lawsuit, fr. MF *plaidier*, fr. *plaid* plea] *vi* (14c) **1** : to argue a case or cause in a court of law **2 a** : to make an allegation in an action or other legal proceeding; *esp* : to answer the previous pleading of the other party by denying facts therein stated or by alleging new facts **b** : to conduct pleadings **3** : to make a plea of a specified nature ⟨~ not guilty⟩ **4 a** : to argue for or against a claim **b** : to entreat or appeal earnestly : IMPLORE ~ *vt* **1** : to maintain (as a case or cause) in a court of law or other tribunal **2** : to allege in or by way of a legal plea **3** : to offer as a plea usu. in defense, apology, or excuse — **plead·able** \'plēd-ə-bəl\ *adj* — **plead·er** *n* — **plead·ing·ly** \'plēd-iŋ-lē\ *adv*

plo·ver \'pləv-ər, 'plō-vər\ *n, pl* **plover** *or* **plovers** [ME, fr. MF, fr. (assumed) VL *pluviarius*, fr. L *pluvia* rain — more at PLUVIAL] (14c) **1** : any of numerous shore-inhabiting birds (family Charadriidae) that differ from the sandpipers in having a short hard-tipped bill and usu. a stouter more compact build **2** : any of various birds (as a turnstone or sandpiper) related to the plovers

¹**plu·vi·al** \'plü-vē-əl\ *adj* [L *pluvialis*, fr. *pluvia* rain, fr. fem. of *pluvius* rainy, fr. *pluere* to rain — more at FLOW] (ca. 1656) **1 a** : of or relating to rain **b** : characterized by abundant rain **2** *of a geologic change* : resulting from the action of rain

¹**point·ed** \'point-əd\ *adj* (13c) **1 a** : having a point **b** : being an arch with a pointed crown; *also* : marked by the use of a pointed arch ⟨~ architecture⟩ **2 a** : being to the point : PERTINENT **b** : aimed at a particular person or group **3** : CONSPICUOUS, MARKED ⟨~ indifference⟩ — **point·ed·ly** *adv* — **point·ed·ness** *n*

²**pointed** *adj* [short for *appointed*] *obs* (1523) : SET, FIXED

³**poise** *n* [ME *poyse* weight, heaviness, fr. MF *pois*, fr. L *pensum*, fr. neut. of *pensus*, pp. of *pendere* to weigh — more at PENDANT] (1555) **1** : a stably balanced state : EQUILIBRIUM ⟨a ~ between widely divergent impulses —F. R. Leavis⟩ **2 a** : easy self-possessed assurance of manner : gracious tact in coping or handling; *also* : the pleasantly tranquil interaction between persons of poise ⟨no angry outbursts marred the ~ of the meeting⟩ **b** : a particular way of carrying oneself : BEARING, CARRIAGE *syn* see TACT

⁴**poise** *vt* **poled; pol·ing** (ca. 1753) **1** : to act upon with a pole **2** : to impel or push with a pole ~ *vi* **1** : to propel a boat with a pole **2** : to use ski poles to gain speed

poleis *pl of* POLIS

post- *prefix* [ME, fr. L, fr. *post*; akin to Skt *paśca* behind, after, Gk *apo* away from — more at OF] **1 a** : after : subsequent : later ⟨*post*date⟩ **b** : behind : posterior : following after ⟨*post*lude⟩ ⟨*post*consonantal⟩ **2 a** : subsequent to : later than ⟨*post*operative⟩ ⟨*post*-Pleistocene⟩ **b** : posterior to ⟨*post*orbital⟩

post·abor·tion	post·elec·tion	post·mat·ing
post·ac·ci·dent	post·em·bry·o·nal	post·me·di·eval
post·ad·o·les·cent	post·em·bry·on·ic	post·mid·night

posy \'pō-zē\ *n, pl* **posies** [alter. of *poesy*] (15c) **1** : a brief sentiment, motto, or legend **2 a** : BOUQUET, NOSEGAY **b** : FLOWER

po·tas·si·um \pə-'tas-ē-əm\ *n, often attrib* [NL, fr. *potassa* potash, fr. E *potash*] (ca. 1807) : a silver-white soft light low-melting univalent metallic element of the alkali metal group that occurs abundantly in nature esp. combined in minerals — see ELEMENT table

Explanatory Chart

po·ten·tate \'pōt-ᵊn-ˌtāt\ *n* (15c) : RULER, SOVEREIGN; *broadly* : one who wields great power or sway

po·tion \'pō-shən\ *n* [ME *pocioun*, fr. MF *potion*, fr. L *potion-*, *potio* drink, potion, fr. *potus*, pp. of *potare* to drink — more at POTABLE] (14c) : a mixture of liquids (as liquor or medicine)

²potlatch *n* [Chinook Jargon, fr. Nootka *patshatl* giving] (ca. 1861) **1** : a ceremonial feast of the Indians of the northwest coast marked by the host's lavish distribution of gifts requiring reciprocation **2** *Northwest* : a social event or celebration

pot·sherd \'pät-ˌshərd\ *n* [ME *pot-sherd*, fr. *pot* + *sherd* shard] (14c) : a pottery fragment

pouf *also* **pouff** *or* **pouffe** \'püf\ *n* [F *pouf*, something inflated, of imit. origin] (1893) **1** : PUFF 3b(3) **2** : a bouffant or fluffy part of a garment or accessory **3** : OTTOMAN — **poufed** *or* **pouffed** \'püft\ *adj*

poult \'pōlt\ *n* [ME *polet*, *pulte* young fowl — more at PULLET] (15c) : a young fowl; *esp* : a young turkey

²pounce *vi* **pounced; pounc·ing** (1744) **1 a** : to swoop upon and seize something with or as if with talons **b** : to seize upon and make capital of something (as another's blunder or an opportunity) **2** : to make a sudden assault or approach

prexy \'prek-sē\ *also* **prex** \'preks\ *n, pl* **prex·ies** *also* **prex·es** [*prexy* fr. *prex*, by shortening & alter. fr. *president*] *slang* (1871) : PRESIDENT used chiefly of a college president

proph·et \'präf-ət\ *n* [ME *prophete*, fr. OF, fr. L *propheta*, fr. Gk *prophētēs*, fr. *pro* for + *phanai* to speak — more at FOR, BAN] (12c) **1** : one who utters divinely inspired revelations; *specif, often cap* : the writer of one of the prophetic books of the Old Testament **2** : one gifted with more than ordinary spiritual and moral insight; *esp* : an inspired poet **3** : one who foretells future events : PREDICTOR **4** : an effective or leading spokesman for a cause, doctrine, or group **5** *Christian Science* **a** : a spiritual seer **b** : disappearance of material sense before the conscious facts of spiritual Truth

pro·pose \prə-'pōz\ *vb* **pro·posed; pro·pos·ing** [ME *proposen*, fr. MF *proposer*, fr. L *proponere* (perf. indic. *proposui*) — more at PROPOUND] *vi* (14c) **1** : to form or put forward a plan or intention ⟨man ~s, but God disposes⟩ **2** *obs* : to engage in talk or discussion **3** : to make an offer of marriage ~ *vt* **1 a** : to set before the mind (as for discussion, imitation, or action) ⟨*proposed* a plan for settling the dispute⟩ **b** : to set before someone and esp. oneself as an aim or intent ⟨*proposed* to spend the summer in study⟩ **2 a** : to set forth for acceptance or rejection ⟨~ terms for peace⟩ **b** : to recommend to fill a place or vacancy : NOMINATE ⟨agreed to ~ him for membership⟩ **c** : to offer as a toast ⟨~ the health of the ladies⟩ — **pro·pos·er** *n*

¹pros·pect \'präs-ˌpekt\ *n* [ME, fr. L *prospectus* view, prospect, fr. *prospectus*, pp. of *prospicere* to look forward, exercise foresight, fr. *pro-* forward + *specere* to look — more at PRO-, SPY] (15c) **1** : EXPOSURE 3b **2 a** (1) : an extensive view (2) : a mental consideration : SURVEY **b** : a place that commands an extensive view : LOOKOUT **c** : something extended to the view : SCENE **d** *archaic* : a sketch or picture of a scene **3** *obs* : ASPECT **4 a** : the act of looking forward **b** : a mental picture of something to come : VISION **c** : something that is awaited or expected : POSSIBILITY **d** *pl* (1) : financial expectations (2) : CHANCES

syn PROSPECT, OUTLOOK, ANTICIPATION, FORETASTE mean an advance realization of something to come. PROSPECT implies expectation of a particular event, condition, or development of definite interest or concern; OUTLOOK suggests a forecasting of the future; ANTICIPATION implies a prospect or outlook that involves advance suffering or enjoyment of what is foreseen; FORETASTE implies an actual though brief or partial experience of something forthcoming.

— **in prospect** : possible or likely for the future

¹pros·trate \'präs-ˌtrāt\ *adj* [ME *prostrat*, fr. L *prostratus*, pp. of *prosternere*, fr. *pro-* before + *sternere* to spread out, throw down — more at STREW] (14c) **1** : stretched out with face on the ground in adoration or submission; *also* : lying flat **2** : completely overcome and lacking vitality, will, or power to rise ⟨was ~ from the heat⟩ **3** : trailing on the ground : PROCUMBENT ⟨~ shrub⟩ **syn** see PRONE

pro·ten·sive \-'ten(t)-siv\ *adj* [L *protensus*, pp. of *protendere*] (1671) **1** *archaic* : having continuance in time **2** *archaic* : having lengthwise extent or extensiveness — **pro·ten·sive·ly** *adv*

Protestant ethic *n* (1926) : an ethic that stresses the virtue of hard work, thrift, and self-discipline

prove \'prüv\ *vb* **proved; proved** *or* **prov·en** \'prü-vən, *Brit also* 'prō-\; **prov·ing** \'prü-viŋ\ [ME *proven*, fr. OF *prover*, fr. L *probare* to test, approve, prove, fr. *probus* good, honest, fr. *pro-* for, in favor + *-bus* (akin to OE *bēon* to be)] *vt* (12c) **1** *archaic* : to learn or find out by experience **2 a** : to test the truth, validity, or genuineness of ⟨the exception ~s the rule⟩ ⟨~ a will at probate⟩ **b** : to test the worth or quality of; *specif* : to compare against a standard — sometimes used with *up* or *out* **c** : to check the correctness of (as an arithmetic result) **3** : to establish the existence, truth, or validity of (as by evidence or logic) ⟨~ a theorem⟩ ⟨the charges were never *proved* in court⟩ ⟨they *proved* their appeal at the box office⟩ **b** : to demonstrate as having a particular quality or worth ⟨the vaccine has been *proven* effective after years of tests⟩ ⟨*proved* herself a great actress⟩

usage The past participle *proven*, orig. the past participle of *preve*, a Middle English variant of *prove* that survived in Scotland, has gradually worked its way into standard English over the past three and a half centuries. It seems to have first become established in legal use and to have come only slowly into literary use. Tennyson was one of its earliest frequent users, prob. for metrical reasons. It was disapproved by 19th century grammarians, one of whom included it in a list of "words that are not words." Surveys made some 30 or 40 years ago indicated that *proved* was about four times as frequent as *proven*. But our evidence from the last 10 or 15 years shows this no longer to be the case. As a past participle *proven* is now about as frequent as *proved* in all contexts. As an attributive adjective ⟨*proved* or *proven* gas reserves⟩ *proven* is much more common than *proved*.

pro·vid·ed *conj* [pp. of *provide*] (15c) : on condition that : with the understanding that : IF *usage* see PROVIDING

prow·ess \'prau̇-əs *also* 'prō-\ *n* [ME *prouesse*, fr. OF *proesse*, fr. *prou* valiant — more at PROUD] (13c) **1** : distinguished bravery; *esp* : military valor and skill **2** : extraordinary ability ⟨his ~ on the football field⟩

Chart labels

Label	Reference
primary stress	PAGE 12
pronunciation	PAGES 12, 13
regional label	PAGES 17, 18
secondary stress	PAGE 12
secondary variants	PAGE 11
sense divider	PAGE 19
sense letter	PAGE 19
sense number	PAGE 19
stylistic label	PAGES 17, 18
subject label	PAGE 18
swung dash (boldface)	PAGE 13
swung dash (lightface)	PAGE 18
synonymous cross-reference	PAGES 21, 22
synonym paragraph	PAGE 22
syn see	PAGE 22
temporal label	PAGE 17
undefined run-on entry	PAGE 11
uppercase	PAGE 15
usage note	PAGES 18, 19
usage paragraph	PAGE 19
usage see	PAGE 19
verbal illustration	PAGE 18

Explanatory Notes

Entries

MAIN ENTRIES

A boldface letter or a combination of such letters set flush with the left-hand margin of each column of type is a main entry or entry word. The main entry may consist of letters set solid, of letters joined by a hyphen, or of letters separated by one or more spaces:

> **brass** . . . *n*
>
> **brass–collar** . . . *adj*
>
> **brass hat** . . . *n*

The material in lightface type that follows each main entry on the same line and on succeeding indented lines explains and justifies its inclusion in the dictionary.

Variation in the styling of compound words in English is frequent and widespread. It is often completely acceptable to choose freely among open, hyphenated, and closed alternatives (as *headwaiter, head-waiter,* or *head waiter*). However, to show all the stylings that are found for English compounds would require space that can be better used for other information. So this dictionary limits itself to a single styling for a compound:

> **ten·der·foot**
>
> **out–group**
>
> **future shock**

When a compound is widely used and one styling predominates, that styling is shown. When a compound is uncommon or when the evidence indicates that two or three stylings are approximately equal in frequency, the styling shown is based on the analogy of parallel compounds.

ORDER OF MAIN ENTRIES

The main entries follow one another in alphabetical order letter by letter without regard to intervening spaces or hyphens: *battle royal* follows *battlement* and *earth-shattering* follows *earthshaking.* Those containing an Arabic numeral are alphabetized as if the numeral were spelled out: *3-D* comes between *three-color* and *three-decker.* Those that often begin with the abbreviation *St.* in common usage have the abbreviation spelled out: *Saint Anthony's fire.*

Full words come before parts of words made up of the same letters. Solid compounds come first and are followed by hyphenated compounds and then open compounds. Lowercase entries come before entries that begin with a capital letter:

> **hy·per** . . . *adj*
>
> **hyper-** *prefix*
>
> **work–up** . . . . *n*

> **work–up** . . . *n*
>
> **work up** . . . *vt*
>
> **creek** . . . *n*
>
> **Creek** . . . *n*

HOMOGRAPHS

When one main entry has exactly the same written form as another, the two are distinguished by superscript numerals preceding each word:

> [1] **fence** . . . *n*   [1] **lore** . . . *n*
>
> [2] **fence** *vb*   [2] **lore** *n*

Sometimes such homographs are related: the two entries *fence* are derived from the same root. Sometimes there is no relationship: the two entries *lore* are unrelated beyond the accident of spelling. The order of homographs is usually historical: the one first used in English is entered first. A homograph derived from an earlier homograph by functional shift, however, follows its parent immediately, with the result that occasionally one homograph appears ahead of another that is older in usage. For example, of the three entries *kennel* the second (a verb) is derived from the first (a noun). Even though the unrelated third entry *kennel* was used in English many years before the second, it follows the two related entries.

GUIDE WORDS

A pair of guide words is printed at the top of each page. The entries that fall alphabetically between the guide words are found on that page.

It is important to remember that alphabetical order rather than position of an entry on the page determines the selection of guide words. The first guide word is the alphabetically first entry on the page. The second guide word is usually the alphabetically last entry on the page:

> **adjunct ● ado**

The entry need not be a main entry. Another boldface word—a variant, an inflected form, or a defined or undefined run-on—may be selected as a guide word. For this reason the last printed main entry on a page is not always the last entry alphabetically:

> **achromatic lens ● acquitting**

On the page where these guide words are used, *acquittance* is the last printed entry, but *acquitting,* an inflected form at *acquit,* is the last entry alphabetically and so has been chosen as the second guide word.

All guide words must themselves be in alphabetical order from page to page throughout the dictionary; thus, the alphabetically last entry on a page is not used if it follows alphabetically the first guide word on the next page:

> **aerostat ● affirmative**

On the page where these guide words are found, *affirmatively,* a run-on at the first entry *affirmative,* is the last entry alphabetically, but it is not used as the second guide word because it follows alphabetically the entry *affirmative action,* which is the first guide word on the next page. To use *affirmatively* would violate the alphabetical order of guide words from page to page, and so the entry *affirmative* is the second guide word instead.

END-OF-LINE DIVISION

The centered dots within entry words indicate division points at which a hyphen may be put at the end of a line of print or writing. Thus the noun *re·frig·er·a·tor* may be ended on one line with:

re-
refrig-
refriger-
refrigera-

and continued on the next with:

frigerator
erator
ator
tor

Centered dots are not shown after a single initial letter or before a single terminal letter because printers seldom cut off a single letter:

aplomb . . . *n*

hoary . . . *adj*

idea . . . *n*

Nor are they shown at second and succeeding homographs unless these differ among themselves:

¹mas·ter . . . *n*   ¹til·ler . . . *n*

²master *adj*   ²til·ler *vi*

³master *vt*   ³till·er . . . *n*

There are acceptable alternative end-of-line divisions just as there are acceptable variant spellings and pronunciations. It is, for example, all but impossible to produce a convincing argument that either of the divisions *aus·ter·i·ty, au·ster·i·ty* is better than the other. But space cannot be taken for entries like *aus·ter·i·ty* or *au·ster·i·ty,* and *au·s·ter·i·ty* would likely be confusing to many. No more than one division is, therefore, shown for an entry in this dictionary.

Many words have two or more common pronunciation variants, and the same end-of-line division is not always appropriate for each of them. The division *pi·an·ist,* for example, best fits the variant \pē-'an-əst\ whereas the division *pi·a·nist* best fits the variant \'pē-ə-nəst\. In instances like this, the division falling farther to the left is used, regardless of the order of the pronunciations:

pi·a·nist \pē-'an-əst, 'pē-ə-nəst\

A double hyphen at the end of a line in this dictionary (as in the definition at *indexation*) stands for a hyphen that belongs at that point in a hyphenated word and that is retained when the word is written as a unit on one line.

VARIANTS

When a main entry is followed by the word *or* and another spelling, the two spellings are equal variants. Both are standard, and either one may be used according to personal inclination:

mea·ger *or* mea·gre

If two variants joined by *or* are out of alphabetical order,

they remain equal variants. The one printed first is, however, slightly more common than the second:

judg·ment *or* judge·ment

When another spelling is joined to the main entry by the word *also,* the spelling after *also* is a secondary variant and occurs less frequently than the first:

quin·tet *also* quin·tette

Secondary variants belong to standard usage and may be used according to personal inclination. If there are two secondary variants, the second is joined to the first by *or.* Once the word *also* is used to signal a secondary variant, all following variants are joined by *or:*

¹Shake·spear·ean *or* Shake·spear·ian *also* Shak·sper·ean *or* Shak·sper·ian

Variants whose spelling places them alphabetically more than a column away from the main entry are entered at their own alphabetical places and usually not at the main entry:

Cha·nu·kah . . . *var of* HANUKKAH

rime, rimer, rimester *var of* RHYME, RHYMER, RHYMESTER

Variants having a usage label appear only at their own alphabetical places:

tyre *chiefly Brit var of* TIRE

agin . . . *dial var of* AGAINST

RUN-ON ENTRIES

A main entry may be followed by one or more derivatives or by a homograph with a different functional label. These are run-on entries. Each is introduced by a lightface dash and each has a functional label. They are not defined, however, since their meanings are readily derivable from the meaning of the root word:

¹praise . . . *vb* . . . —prais·er *n*

dole·ful . . . *adj* . . . —dole·ful·ly . . . *adv* —dole·ful·ness *n*

styp·tic . . . *adj* . . . —styptic *n*

A main entry may be followed by one or more phrases containing the entry word or an inflected form of it. These are also run-on entries. Each is introduced by a lightface dash but there is no functional label. They are, however, defined since their meanings are more than the sum of the meanings of their elements:

for·get . . . *vb* . . . —forget oneself : . . .

²take *n* . . . —on the take : . . .

Defined phrases of this sort are run on at the entry constituting the first major element in the phrase. The first major element is ordinarily a verb or a noun, but when these are absent another part of speech may serve instead:

¹be·tween . . . *prep* . . . —between you and me : . . .

When there are variants, however, the run-on appears at the entry constituting the first major invariable element in the phrase:

¹clock . . . *n* . . . —kill the clock *or* run out the clock : . . .

¹hand . . . *n* . . . —on all hands *or* on every hand : . . .

A run-on entry is an independent entry with respect to function and status. Labels at the main entry do not apply unless they are repeated.

Attention is called to the definition of *vocabulary entry* in this book. The term *dictionary entry* includes all vocabulary entries as well as all boldface entries in the separate sections of the back matter headed "Abbreviations and Symbols for Chemical Elements," "Foreign Words and Phrases," "Biographical Names," "Geographical Names," and "Colleges and Universities."

Pronunciation

Pronunciation is indicated between a pair of reversed virgules \ \ following the entry word. The symbols used are listed in the chart printed inside the back cover of this dictionary and on the page facing the first page of the dictionary proper. An abbreviated list appears at the bottom of the second column of each right-hand page of the vocabulary. Explanations of the symbols are given in the Guide to Pronunciation.

SYLLABLES

A hyphen is used in the pronunciation to show syllabic division. These hyphens sometimes coincide with the centered dots in the entry word that indicate end-of-line division; sometimes they do not:

> **dis·cov·er** \dis-'kəv-ər\
>
> [1] **met·ric** \'me-trik\

STRESS

A high-set mark \ ' \ indicates primary (strongest) stress or accent; a low-set mark \ ˌ \ indicates secondary (medium) stress or accent:

> [1] **rough·neck** \'rəf-ˌnek\

The stress mark stands at the beginning of the syllable that receives the stress.

In some cases the pronunciation of a word or compound shows no primary stress. One such class of words includes those that occur in main entries only as elements of an open compound. The stress shown for these words is the usual stress in the compound and may be less than primary:

> **clum·ber spaniel** \ˌkləm-bər-\

In other contexts the word may have primary stress, as in "Is that spaniel a clumber?"

VARIANT PRONUNCIATIONS

The presence of variant pronunciations indicates that not all educated speakers pronounce words the same way. A second-place pronunciation is not to be regarded as less acceptable than the pronunciation that is given first. It may, in fact, be used by as many educated speakers as the first variant, but the requirements of the printed page are such that one must precede the other:

> **apri·cot** \'ap-rə-ˌkät, 'ā-prə-\
>
> **for·eign** \'for-ən, 'fär-\

A variant that is appreciably less common than the preceding variant is preceded by the word *also*:

> **col·league** \'käl-ˌēg *also* -ig\

A variant preceded by *sometimes* is infrequent, though it does occur in educated speech:

> **in·vei·gle** \in-'vā-gəl *sometimes* -'vē-\

Sometimes a regional label precedes a variant:

> [1] **great** \'grāt, *Southern also* 'gre(ə)t\

The symbol \ ÷ \ is placed before a pronunciation variant that occurs in educated speech but that is considered by some to be unacceptable:

> **cu·po·la** \'kyü-pə-lə, ÷-ˌlō\

This symbol refers only to the immediately following variant and not to subsequent variants separated from it by a comma or a semicolon.

PARENTHESES IN PRONUNCIATIONS

Symbols enclosed by parentheses represent elements that are present in the pronunciation of some speakers but are absent from the pronunciation of other speakers, elements that are present in some but absent from other utterances of the same speaker, or elements whose presence or absence is uncertain:

> **hap·pen** . . . *vi* . . . **hap·pen·ing** \'hap-(ə-)niŋ\
>
> **sat·is·fac·to·ry** \ˌsat-əs-'fak-t(ə-)rē\
>
> **re·sponse** \ri-'spän(t)s\

Thus, the parentheses at *happening* mean that there are some who pronounce the \ə\ between \p\ and \n\ and others who do not pronounce it.

PARTIAL AND ABSENT PRONUNCIATIONS

When a main entry has less than a full pronunciation, the missing part is to be supplied from a pronunciation in a preceding entry or within the same pair of reversed virgules:

> **cham·pi·on·ship** \-ˌship\
>
> **Ma·dei·ra** \mə-'dir-ə, -'der-\

The pronunciation of the first three syllables of *championship* is found at the main entry *champion*:

> [1] **cham·pi·on** \'cham-pē-ən\

The hyphens before and after \'der\ in the pronunciation of *Madeira* indicate that both the first and the last parts of the pronunciation are to be taken from the immediately preceding pronunciation.

Partial pronunciations are usually shown when two or more variants have a part in common. When a variation of stress is involved, a partial pronunciation may be terminated at the stress mark which stands at the beginning of a syllable not shown:

> **di·verse** \dī-'vərs, də-', 'dī-,\
>
> **an·cho·vy** \'an-ˌchō-vē, an-'\

In general, no pronunciation is indicated for open compounds consisting of two or more English words that have own-place entry:

> **kangaroo court** *n*

A pronunciation is shown, however, for any element of an open compound that does not have entry at its own alphabetical place:

> **con·ger eel** \ˌkäŋ-gər-\
>
> **sieve of Er·a·tos·the·nes** \-ˌer-ə-'täs-thə-ˌnēz\

Only the first entry in a sequence of numbered homographs is given a pronunciation if their pronunciations are the same:

> [1] **re·ward** \ri-'wȯ(ə)rd\
>
> [2] **reward**

Pronunciations are shown for obsolete words only if they occur in Shakespeare:

clois·tress \ 'klôi-strəs\ *n, obs*

The pronunciation of unpronounced derivatives and compounds run on at a main entry is a combination of the pronunciation at the main entry and the pronunciation of the suffix or final element as given at its alphabetical place in the vocabulary:

— **oval·ness** *n*

— **shot in the dark**

Thus, the pronunciation of *ovalness* is the sum of the pronunciations given at *oval* and *-ness*; that of *shot in the dark,* the sum of the pronunciation of the four elements that make up the phrase.

Functional Labels

An italic label indicating a part of speech or some other functional classification follows the pronunciation or, if no pronunciation is given, the main entry. The eight traditional parts of speech are indicated as follows:

im·mense . . . *adj*	drag·on . . . *n*
tar·di·ly . . . *adv*	with . . . *prep*
and . . . *conj*	some·one . . . *pron*
²ouch *interj*	nes·tle . . . *vb*

If a verb is both transitive and intransitive, the labels *vt* and *vi* introduce the subdivisions:

mor·ti·fy . . . *vb* . . . *vt* . . . ~ *vi*

A boldface swung dash ~ is used to stand for the main entry (as *mortify*) and separate the subdivisions of the verb. If there is no subdivision, *vt* or *vi* takes the place of *vb*:

²fleece *vt*

ap·per·tain . . . *vi*

Labeling a verb as transitive, however, does not preclude occasional intransitive use (as in absolute constructions).

Other italicized labels used to indicate functional classifications that are not traditional parts of speech are:

pan- *comb form*	-ment . . . *n suffix*
-al·gia . . . *n comb form*	⁴-ate . . . *vb suffix*
-i·form . . . *adj comb form*	Ja·cuz·zi . . . *trademark*
extra- *prefix*	-nd *symbol*
Gram·my . . . *service mark*	¹may . . . *verbal auxiliary*
-ous . . . *adj suffix*	gid·dap . . . *vb imper*
²-ward *or* -wards *adv suffix*	me·thinks . . . *vb impersonal*

Two functional labels are sometimes combined:

zilch . . . *adj or n*

afloat . . . *adj or adv*

Inflected Forms

In comparison with some other languages English does not have many inflected forms. Of those which it has, several are inflected forms of words belonging to small, closed groups (as the personal pronouns or the demonstratives). These forms can readily be found at their own alphabetical places with a full entry (as *whom,* the objective case form of *who*) or with a cross-reference in small capital letters to another entry (as *those,* the plural form of *that*).

Most other inflected forms, however, are covered explicitly or by implication at the main entry for the base form. These are the plurals of nouns, the principal parts of verbs (the past tense, the past participle when it differs from the past tense, and the present participle), and the comparative and superlative forms of adjectives and adverbs. In general, it may be said that when these inflected forms are created in a manner considered regular in English (as by adding *-s* or *-es* to nouns, *-ed* and *-ing* to verbs, and *-er* and *-est* to adjectives and adverbs) and when it seems that there is nothing about the formation likely to give the dictionary user doubts, the inflected form is not shown in order to save space for information more likely to be sought. Inflected forms are also not shown at undefined run-ons or at some entries bearing a limiting label:

His·pan·ic . . . *adj* . . .	— His·pan·i·cize . . . *vt*
fe·cund . . . *adj* . . .	— fe·cun·di·ty . . . *n*
²lake *n* . . .	— laky . . . *adj*
²cote . . . *vt* . . . *obs* . . . : to pass by	
crouse . . . *adj* . . . *chiefly Scot* . . . : BRISK, LIVELY	

On the other hand, if the inflected form is created in an irregular way or if the dictionary user is likely to have doubts about it (even though it is formed regularly), the inflected form is shown in boldface, either in full or cut back to a convenient and easily recognizable point. Full details about the kinds of entries at which inflected forms are shown and the kinds at which they are not shown are given in the three following sections.

NOUNS

The plurals of nouns are shown in this dictionary when suffixation brings about a change of final *-y* to *-i-,* when the noun ends in a consonant plus *-o* or in *-ey,* when the noun ends in *-oo,* when the noun has an irregular plural or a zero plural or a foreign plural, when the noun is a compound that pluralizes any element but the last, when the noun has variant plurals, and when it is believed that the dictionary user might have reasonable doubts about the spelling of the plural or when the plural is spelled in a way contrary to expectations:

²fly *n, pl* flies
ego . . . *n, pl* egos
val·ley . . . *n, pl* valleys
²boo *n, pl* boos
¹tooth . . . *n, pl* teeth
sheep . . . *n, pl* sheep
bac·te·ri·um . . . *n, pl* -ria
moth·er-in-law . . . *n, pl* moth·ers-in-law
¹seed . . . *n, pl* seed *or* seeds
⁴pi *n, pl* pis
³dry *n, pl* drys
sta·tus . . . *n, pl-* sta·tus·es

Cutback inflected forms are used when the noun has three or more syllables:

in·fir·mi·ty . . . *n, pl* -ties

The plurals of nouns are usually not shown when the base word is unchanged by suffixation, when the noun is a compound whose second element is readily recognizable as a regular free form entered at its own place, or when the noun is unlikely to occur in the plural:

¹ fire . . . *n*

² wish *n*

gad·fly . . . *n*

big·a·my . . . *n*

Nouns that are plural in form and that regularly occur in plural construction are labeled *n pl*:

en·vi·rons . . . *n pl*

Nouns that are plural in form but that are not always construed as plurals are appropriately labeled:

ge·net·ics . . . *n pl but sing in constr*

forty winks *n pl but sing or pl in constr*

A noun that is singular in construction takes a singular verb when it is used as a subject; a noun that is plural in construction takes a plural verb when it is used as a subject.

VERBS

The principal parts of verbs are shown in this dictionary when suffixation brings about a doubling of a final consonant or an elision of a final -*e* or a change of final -*y* to -*i*-, when final -*c* changes to -*ck* in suffixation, when the verb ends in -*ey*, when the inflection is irregular, when there are variant inflected forms, and when it is believed that the dictionary user might have reasonable doubts about the spelling of an inflected form or when the inflected form is spelled in a way contrary to expectations:

³ brag *vb* bragged; brag·ging

² love *vb* loved; lov·ing

¹ spy . . . *vb* spied; spy·ing

² picnic *vi* pic·nicked; pic·nick·ing

² monkey *vb* mon·keyed; mon·key·ing

¹ swim . . . *vb* swam . . .; swum . . .; swim·ming

⁴ bias *vt* bi·ased *or* bi·assed; bi·as·ing *or* bi·as·sing

² visa *vt* vi·saed . . .; vi·sa·ing

² chagrin *vt* cha·grined . . .; cha·grin·ing

The principal parts of a regularly inflected verb are shown when it is desirable to indicate the pronunciation of one of the inflected forms:

³ spell *vb* spelled \'speld\; spell·ing

fat·ten . . . *vb* fat·tened; fat·ten·ing \'fat·niŋ, -ᵊn·iŋ\

Cutback inflected forms are often used when the verb has three or more syllables, when it is a disyllable that ends in -*l* and has variant spellings, and when it is a compound whose second element is readily recognized as an irregular verb:

² ded·i·cate . . . *vt* -cat·ed; -cat·ing

² carol *vb* -oled *or* -olled; -ol·ing *or* -ol·ling

be·speak . . . *vt* -spoke . . .; -spo·ken . . .; -speak·ing

The principal parts of verbs are usually not shown when the base word is unchanged by suffixation or when the verb is a compound whose second element is readily recognizable as a regular free form entered at its own place:

¹ walk . . . *vb*

dis·sat·is·fy . . . *vt*

Another inflected form of English verbs is the third person singular of the present tense, which is regularly formed by the addition of -*s* or -*es* to the base form of the verb. This inflected form is not shown except at a handful of entries (as *have* and *do*) for which it is in some way anomalous.

ADJECTIVES & ADVERBS

The comparative and superlative forms of adjectives and adverbs are shown in this dictionary when suffixation brings about a doubling of a final consonant or an elision of a final -*e* or a change of final -*y* to -*i*-, when the word ends in -*ey*, when the inflection is irregular, and when there are variant inflected forms:

¹ mad . . . *adj* mad·der; mad·dest

¹ bare . . . *adj* bar·er; bar·est

¹ pret·ty . . . *adj* pret·ti·er; -est

¹ ear·ly . . . *adv* ear·li·er; -est

hom·ey . . . *adj* hom·i·er; -est

¹ good . . . *adj* bet·ter . . .; best

² ill *adv* worse; worst

¹ shy . . . *adj* shi·er *or* shy·er . . .; shi·est *or* shy·est

The superlative forms of adjectives and adverbs of two or more syllables are usually cut back:

² timely *adj* time·li·er; -est

² easy *adv* eas·i·er; -est

The comparative and superlative forms of regularly inflected adjectives and adverbs are shown when it is desirable to indicate the pronunciation of the inflected forms:

¹ long \'lȯŋ\ *adj* lon·ger \'lȯŋ·gər *also* -ər\; lon·gest \'lȯŋ·gəst *also* -əst\

The inclusion of inflected forms in -*er* and -*est* at adjective and adverb entries means nothing more about the use of *more* and *most* with these adjectives and adverbs than that their comparative and superlative degrees may be expressed in either way: *lazier* or *more lazy*; *laziest* or *most lazy*.

At a few adjective entries only the superlative form is shown:

³ mere . . . *adj, superlative* mer·est

The absence of the comparative form indicates that there is no evidence of its use.

The comparative and superlative forms of adjectives and adverbs are not shown when the base word is unchanged by suffixation or when the word is a compound whose second element is readily recognizable as a regular free form entered at its own place:

crass . . . *adj*

un·hap·py . . . *adj*

The comparative and superlative forms of adverbs are not shown when they are identical with the inflected forms of a preceding adjective homograph:

¹ hot . . . *adj* hot·ter; hot·test

² hot *adv*

Capitalization

Most entries in this dictionary begin with a lowercase letter. A few of these have an italicized label *often cap*, which indicates that the word is as likely to be capitalized as not, that it is as acceptable with an uppercase initial as it is with one in lowercase. Some entries begin with an uppercase letter, which indicates that the word is usually capitalized. The absence of an initial capital or of an *often cap* label indicates that the word is not ordinarily capitalized:

> **sa·tir·ic** . . . *adj*
>
> **an·gli·cize** . . . *vt* . . . *often cap*
>
> **Hal·low·een** . . . *n*

The capitalization of entries that are open or hyphenated compounds is similarly indicated by the form of the entry or by an italicized label:

> **king cobra** *n*
>
> [2]**french fry** *vt, often cap 1st F*
>
> **neo·im·pres·sion·ism** . . . *n, often cap N&I*
>
> **un–Amer·i·can** . . . *adj*
>
> **Dutch oven** *n*
>
> **Gloria Pa·tri** . . . *n*

A word that is capitalized in some senses and lowercase in others shows variations from the form of the main entry by the use of italicized labels at the appropriate senses:

> **Gyp·sy** . . . *n* . . . 3 *not cap*
>
> **Sal·va·tion·ist** . . . *n* . . . 2 *often not cap*
>
> **har·py** . . . *n* . . . 1 *cap*
>
> **es·tab·lish·ment** . . . *n* . . . 2 . . . b *often cap*

Attributive Nouns

The italicized label *often attrib* placed after the functional label *n* indicates that the noun is often used as an adjective equivalent in attributive position before another noun:

> [1]**air** . . . *n, often attrib*
>
> **com·put·er** . . . *n, often attrib*

Examples of the attributive use of these nouns are *air traffic* and *computer printout*.

While any noun may occasionally be used attributively, the label *often attrib* is limited to those having broad attributive use. This label is not used when an adjective homograph (as *iron* or *paper*) is entered. And it is not used at open compounds (as *X ray*) that may be used attributively with an inserted hyphen (as in *X-ray therapy*).

Etymology

The matter in boldface square brackets preceding the definition is the etymology. Meanings given in roman type within these brackets are not definitions of the entry, but are meanings of the Middle English, Old English, or non-English words within the brackets.

The etymology traces a vocabulary entry as far back as possible in English (as to Old English), tells from what lan-

guage and in what form it came into English, and (except in the case of such words outside the general vocabulary of English as *dacha* and *zloty*) traces the pre-English source as far back as possible. These etyma are printed in italics.

OLD, MIDDLE, AND MODERN ENGLISH

The etymology usually gives the Middle English and the Old English forms of words in the following style:

> [1]**reed** . . . *n* [ME *rede,* fr. OE *hrēod* . . .]
>
> [1]**hate** . . . *n* [ME, fr. OE *hete* . . .]

An etymology in which a word is traced back to Middle English but not to Old English indicates that the word is found in Middle English but not in those texts that have survived from the Old English period:

> [1]**clog** . . . *n* [ME *clogge* short thick piece of wood]
>
> [1]**rub** . . . *vb* . . . [ME *rubben;* akin to Icel *rubba* to scrape]

An etymology in which a word is traced back directly to Old English with no intervening mention of Middle English indicates that the word has not survived continuously from Old English times to the present. Rather, it died out after the Old English period and has been revived in modern times:

> **Geat** . . . *n* [OE *Gēat*]
>
> **thegn** . . . *n* [OE . . .]

An etymology is not usually given for a word created in English by the combination of existing constituents or by functional shift. This indicates that the identity of the constituents is expected to be self-evident to the user:

> **an·ti·quark** . . . *n* . . . : the antiparticle of the quark
>
> **time·sav·ing** . . . *adj* . . . : intended or serving to expedite something
>
> **tooth·paste** . . . *n* . . . : a paste for cleaning the teeth
>
> **nose cone** *n* . . . : a protective cone constituting the forward end of a rocket or missile
>
> [2]**wheel** *vi* . . . 1 : to turn on or as if on an axis . . .

In the case of a family of words obviously related to a common English word but differing from it by containing various easily recognizable suffixes, an etymology is usually given only at the base word, even though some of the derivatives may have been formed in a language other than English:

> [1]**equal** . . . *adj* [ME, fr. L *aequalis,* fr. *aequus* level, equal] . . . 1 a (1) : of the same measure, quantity, amount, or number as another
>
> **equal·i·ty** . . . *n* . . . 1 : the quality or state of being equal
>
> **equal·ize** . . . *vt* . . . 1 : to make equal

While *equalize* was formed in Modern English, *equality* was actually borrowed into Middle English (via Middle French) from Latin *aequalitas.*

When an entry word is derived from an earlier Modern English word that is not entered in this dictionary, the meaning of such a word is given in parentheses:

> [3]**press** *vb* [alter. of obs. *prest* (to enlist by giving pay in advance)]

LANGUAGES OTHER THAN ENGLISH

The etymology gives the language from which words borrowed into English have come. It also gives the form or a transliteration of the word in that language if the form differs from that in English:

> [1]**fes·ti·val** . . . *adj* [ME, fr. MF, fr. L *festivus* festive]
>
> **sham·rock** . . . *n* [Ir Gael *seamrōg*]

¹**school** . . . *n* [ME *scole,* fr. OE *scōl,* fr. L *schola* . . .]

¹**yak** . . . *n* . . . [Tibetan *gyak*]

In a few cases the expression "deriv. of" replaces the more usual "fr." This expression indicates that one or more intermediate steps have been omitted in tracing the derivation of the form preceding the expression from the form following it:

gal·ley . . . *n* . . . [. . . OF *galie,* deriv. of MGk *galea*]

Small superscript figures following words or syllables in an etymology refer to the tone of the word or syllable which they follow. They are, accordingly, used only with forms cited from tone languages:

ty·coon . . . *n* [Jp *taikun,* fr. Chin (Pek) *ta*⁴ great + *chün*¹ ruler]

¹**voo·doo** . . . *n* . . . [LaF *voudou,* of African origin; akin to Ewe *vo*¹ *du*³ tutelary deity, demon]

WORDS OF UNKNOWN ORIGIN

When the source of a word appearing as a main entry is unknown, the expression "origin unknown" is usually used. Only in rare and exceptional circumstances (as with some ethnic names) does the absence of an etymology mean that it has not been possible to furnish any informative etymology. More often, it means that no etymology is believed to be necessary. This is the case, for instance, with most of the entries identified as variants and with many derivatives.

ETYMOLOGIES OF TECHNICAL WORDS

Much of the technical vocabulary of the sciences and other specialized studies consists of words or word elements that are current in two or more languages, with only such slight modifications as are necessary to adapt them to the structure of the individual language in each case. Many words and word elements of this kind have become sufficiently a part of the general vocabulary of English as to require entry in an abridged dictionary. Because of the vast extent of the relevant published material in many languages and in many scientific and other specialized fields, it is impracticable to ascertain the language of origin of every such term. Yet it would not be accurate to formulate a statement about the origin of any such term in a way that could be interpreted as implying that it was coined in English. Accordingly, whenever a term that is entered in this dictionary belongs recognizably to this class of internationally current terms and whenever no positive evidence is at hand to show that it was coined in English, the etymology recognizes its international status and the possibility that it originated elsewhere than in English by use of the label ISV (for International Scientific Vocabulary):

mega·watt . . . *n* [ISV]

phy·lo·ge·net·ic . . . *adj* [ISV, fr. NL *phylogenesis* . . .]

¹**-ol** . . . *n suffix* [ISV, fr. *alcohol*]

COMPRESSION OF INFORMATION

An etymology beginning with the name of a language (including ME or OE) and not giving the foreign (or Middle English or Old English) form indicates that this form is the same as that of the entry word:

ka·pok . . . *n* [Malay]

¹**po·grom** . . . *n* [Yiddish, fr. Russ . . .]

¹**fell** . . . *n* [ME, fr. OE . . .]

An etymology beginning with the name of a language (including ME or OE) and not giving the foreign (or Middle English or Old English) meaning indicates that this meaning is the same as that expressed in the first definition in the entry:

vig·or·ous . . . *adj* [ME, fr. MF, fr. OF, fr. *vigor*] . . . **1** : possessing vigor

When a word from a foreign language (or Middle English or Old English) is a key element in the etymologies of several related entries that are found close together, the meaning of the word is usually given at only one of the entries:

ve·lo·ce . . . *adv or adj* [It, fr. L *veloc-, velox*]

ve·loc·i·pede . . . *n* [F *vélocipède,* fr. L *veloc-, velox* + *ped-, pes* foot — more at FOOT]

ve·loc·i·ty . . . *n* . . . [MF *velocité,* fr. L *velocitat-, velocitas,* fr. *veloc-, velox* quick; akin to L *vehere* to carry — more at WAY]

When an etymology includes the expression "by alter." and the altered form is not cited, the form is the term given in small capital letters as the definition:

copse . . . *n* [by alter.]. . . : COPPICE 1

When the origin of a word is traced to the name of a person or place not further identified, additional information may be found in the Biographical Names or Geographical Names section in the back matter:

²**volt** . . . *n* [Alessandro *Volta*]

li·ma bean . . . *n* [*Lima,* Peru]

COGNATES

When a word has been traced back to the earliest language in which it is attested, and if this is an Indo-European language, selected cognates in other Indo-European languages (especially Old High German, Latin, and Greek) are usually given:

¹**one** . . . *adj* [ME *on, ān,* fr. OE *ān*; akin to OHG *ein* one, L *unus* (OL *oinos*), Skt *eka*]

equine . . . *adj* [L *equinus,* fr. *equus* horse; akin to OE *eoh* horse, Gk *hippos*]

Sometimes, however, to avoid space-consuming repetition, the expression "more at" directs the user to another entry where the cognates are given:

night·in·gale . . . *n* [ME, fr. OE *nihtegale,* fr. *niht* + *galan* to sing — more at YELL]

Besides the use of "akin to" to denote an ordinary cognate relationship, some etymologies make special use of "akin to" as part of a longer formula "of — origin; akin to —." This formula indicates that a word was borrowed from some language belonging to a group of languages whose name is inserted in the blank before the word *origin,* that it is impossible to say that the word in question is a borrowing of a particular attested word in a particular language of the source group, and that the form cited in the blank after the expression *akin to* is a cognate of the word in question as attested within the source group:

¹**ca·noe** . . . *n* [F, fr. NL *canoa,* fr. Sp, fr. Arawakan, of Cariban origin; akin to Galibi *canaoua*]

²**cant** *n* [ME, prob. fr. MD or ONF; MD, edge, corner, fr. ONF, fr. L *canthus, cantus* iron tire, perh. of Celt origin; akin to W *cant* rim; akin to Gk *kanthos* corner of the eye]

This last example shows the two contrasting uses of "akin to." The word cited immediately after "of Celt origin; akin to" is a Celtic cognate of the presumed Celtic source word from which the Latin word was borrowed. The word cited after the second "akin to" is a further cognate from another Indo-European language.

Dates

At most main entries and particularly at entries for complete generic words will be found a date enclosed in parentheses immediately preceding the boldface colon that introduces the first sense or preceding the boldface sense number, when one is present:

jal·ou·sie . . . *n* [F, lit., jealousy, fr. OF *jelous* jealous] (1783) **1 :** a blind with adjustable horizontal slats for admitting light and air while excluding sun and rain

This is the date of the earliest recorded use in English, as far as it could be determined, of the sense which the date precedes. Several caveats are appropriate at this point. First, a few classes of main entries that are not complete words (as prefixes, suffixes, combining forms, and letters of the English alphabet) or are not generic words (as trademarks and names of figures from mythology) are not given dates. Second, the date given is always for the first recorded use of the first entered sense and not necessarily of the word: many words, especially those with long histories, have obsolete, archaic, or uncommon senses that are not entered in this dictionary, and such senses have been excluded from consideration in determining the date:

²launder *n* [ME, launderer, fr. MF *lavandier*, fr. ML *lavandarius*, fr. L *lavandus*, gerundive of *lavare* to wash—more at LYE] (1667) **:** TROUGH; *esp* **:** a box conduit conveying a particulate material suspended in water in ore dressing

The date 1667 is for the sense of *launder* in which it is synonymous with *trough*; the word also has an obsolete sense "one who washes clothes" recorded as early as the fourteenth century, but as that sense is not entered it is ignored for the purpose of dating this main entry. Third, the printed date should not be taken to mark the very first time that the word—or even the sense—was used in English. Many words were certainly in spoken use for decades or even longer before they passed into the written language. The date is for the earliest written or printed use that the editors have been able to discover. This fact means further that any date is subject to change as evidence of still earlier use may emerge, and many dates given now can confidently be expected to yield to others in future printings and editions.

A date will appear in one of three different styles:

sans·cu·lotte . . . *n* [F *sans-culotte*, lit., without breeches] (1790) **1 :** an extreme radical republican in France at the time of the Revolution

cop·per·smith . . . *n* (14c) **:** a worker in copper

¹lid . . . *n* [ME, fr. OE *hlid*; akin to OHG *hlit* cover, OE *hlinian* to lean—more at LEAN] (bef. 12c) **1 :** a movable cover for the opening of a hollow container (as a vessel or box)

The style that names a year (as 1790) is the one used for the period from the sixteenth century to the present. The style that names only a century (as 14c) is the one used for the period from the twelfth century through the fifteenth century, a span that roughly approximates the period of Middle English. The style (bef. 12c) is used for the period before the twelfth century back to the earliest records of English, a span that approximates the period of Old English. For words from the Old and Middle English periods the examples of use on which the dates depend very often occur in manuscripts which are themselves of uncertain date and which may record a text whose date of composition is highly conjectural. To date words from these periods by year would frequently give a quite misleading impression of the state of our knowledge, and so the broader formulas involving centuries are used instead.

Each date reflects a particular instance of the use of a word, and examples from running text are considered the norm. In cases where the earliest appearance of a word dated by year is not from running text but from a source (as a dictionary or glossary) that defines or explains the word instead of simply using it, the year is preceded by an abbreviation for *circa*:

magnesium sulfate *n* (ca. 1890) **:** a sulfate of magnesium . . .

Ca. indicates that while the source providing the date attests that the word was in use in the relevant sense at that time, it does not offer an example of the normal use of the word and thus gives no better than an approximate date for such use. For the example above no use has so far been found that is earlier than its appearance (spelled *magnesium sulphate*) as an entry in Webster's International Dictionary, published in 1890, so the date is given with the qualifying abbreviation.

Usage

USAGE LABELS

Three types of status labels are used in this dictionary—temporal, regional, and stylistic—to signal that a word or a sense of a word is not part of the standard vocabulary of English.

The temporal label *obs* for "obsolete" means that there is no evidence of use since 1755:

egal . . . *adj* . . . *obs*

¹in·stance . . . *n* . . . **2** . . . **c** *obs*

The label *obs* is a comment on the word being defined. When a thing, as distinguished from the word used to designate it, is obsolete, appropriate orientation is usually given in the definition:

bal·lis·ta . . . *n* . . . **:** an ancient military engine often in the form of a crossbow for hurling large missiles

²ruff *n* . . . **1 :** a wheel-shaped stiff collar worn by men and women of the late 16th and early 17th centuries

The temporal label *archaic* means that a word or sense once in common use is found today only sporadically or in special contexts:

thorp . . . *n* . . . *archaic*

al·lege . . . *vt* . . . **2** *archaic*

A word or sense limited in use to a specific region of the U.S. has a regional label. Some regional labels correspond loosely to areas defined in Hans Kurath's *Word Geography of the Eastern United States*. The adverb *chiefly* precedes a label when the word has some currency outside the specified region, and a double label is used to indicate considerable currency in each of two specific regions:

²tonic *n* . . . **1** . . . **d** *chiefly NewEng*

ban·quette . . . *n* . . . **1** . . . **b** *Southern*

cal·cu·late . . . *vt* . . . **3** *chiefly Northern*

can·ti·na . . . *n* . . . **1** *Southwest*

em·bar·ca·de·ro . . . *n* . . . *West*

light bread . . . *n* . . . *chiefly Southern & Midland*

jolt–wag·on . . . *n*, *Midland*

²potlatch *n* . . . **2** *Northwest*

Words current in all regions of the U.S. have no label.

A word or sense limited in use to one of the other countries of the English-speaking world has an appropriate regional label:

¹syne . . . *adv* . . . *chiefly Scot*

be·gor·ra . . . *interj* . . . *Irish*

¹din·kum . . . *adj* . . . *Austral & New Zeal*

com·man·do . . . *n* . . . **1** *So Afr*

ze·bra crossing *n, Brit*

foot·ball . . . *n* . . . **1** . . . **e** *Canad*

³gang *vi* . . . *Scot*

him·self . . . *pron* . . . **3** *chiefly Irish & Scot*

The label *dial* for "dialect" indicates that the pattern of use of a word or sense is too complex for summary labeling: it usually includes several regional varieties of American English or of American and British English:

²larrup *vt* . . . **1** *dial*

The label *dial Brit* indicates currency in several dialects of the British Commonwealth; *dial Eng* indicates currency in one or more provincial dialects of England:

¹lair . . . *n* . . . **1** *dial Brit*

few·trils . . . *n pl* . . . *dial Eng*

The stylistic label *slang* is used with words or senses that are especially appropriate in contexts of extreme informality, that usually have a currency not limited to a particular region or area of interest, and that are composed typically of shortened forms or extravagant or facetious figures of speech:

clip joint *n* . . . **1** *slang* : a place of public entertainment (as a night-club) that makes a practice of defrauding patrons (as by over-charging)

hu·mon·gous . . . *adj* . . . *slang* . . . : extremely large : HUGE

natch . . . *adv* . . . *slang* . . . : of course : NATURALLY

There is no satisfactory objective test for slang, especially with reference to a word out of context. No word, in fact, is invariably slang, and many standard words can be given slang applications.

The stylistic label *nonstand* for "nonstandard" is used for a few words or senses that are disapproved by many but that have some currency in reputable contexts:

ir·re·gard·less . . . *adv* . . . *nonstand*

¹lay . . . *vi* . . . **2** *nonstand*

The stylistic label *substand* for "substandard" is used for those words or senses that conform to a widespread pattern of usage that differs in choice of word or form from that of the prestige group of the community:

ain't . . . **2** *substand*

learn . . . *vt* . . . **2 a** *substand*

A subject label or guide phrase is sometimes used to indicate the specific application of a word or sense:

ape·ri·od·ic . . . *adj* . . . **3** *cryptology*

hemi·he·dral . . . *adj* . . . *of a crystal*

¹scram·ble . . . *vi* . . . **5** *of a football quarterback*

In general, however, subject orientation is given in the definition:

Gun·ther . . . *n* . . . : a Burgundian king and husband of Brunhild in Germanic legend

plié . . . *n* . . . : a bending of the knees by a ballet dancer with the back held straight

ILLUSTRATIONS OF USAGE

Definitions are sometimes followed by verbal illustrations that show a typical use of the word in context. These illustrations are enclosed in angle brackets, and the word being illustrated is usually replaced by a lightface swung dash. The swung dash stands for the boldface entry word, and it may be followed by an italicized suffix:

kil·ter . . . *n* . . . < out of ~ >

³low *adj* . . . **11** . . . < had a ~ opinion of him >

¹join . . . *vt* . . . **4 a** . . . < ~ed us for lunch >

proud . . . *adj* . . . **2** . . . **b** . . . < the ~est moment in her life >

The swung dash is not used when the form of the boldface entry word is changed in suffixation, and it is not used for open compounds:

¹dare . . . *vt* **1 a** . . . < *dared* him to jump >

set down *vt* . . . **7 a** . . . < *set* him *down* as a liar >

Illustrative quotations are also used to show words in typical contexts:

¹eye . . . *n* . . . **3** . . . < the ~ of the problem — Norman Mailer >

Omissions in quotations are indicated by suspension points:

¹jog . . . *vi* **1** : . . . < his . . . holster *jogging* against his hip — Thomas Williams >

USAGE NOTES

Definitions are sometimes followed by usage notes that give supplementary information about such matters as idiom, syntax, semantic relationship, and status. A usage note is introduced by a lightface dash:

¹stead . . . *n* . . . **2** : . . . —used chiefly in the phrase *to stand one in good stead*

³zero *vt* . . . **2 a** : . . . —usu. used with *in*

¹as . . . *adv* . . . **3** : . . . —usu. used before a preposition or a participle

¹guide . . . *n* . . . **3** : . . . —used esp. in commands

¹lar·go . . . *adv or adj* . . . : . . . —used as a direction in music

dick . . . *n* . . . **2** : . . . —usu. considered vulgar

Kaf·fir *or* Kaf·ir . . . *n* . . . **2** . . . : . . . —usu. used disparagingly

Two or more usage notes are separated by a semicolon:

thank . . . *vt* . . . **1** : . . . —used in the phrase *thank you* usu. without a subject to politely express gratitude < ~ you for the loan > ; used in such phrases as *thank God, thank heaven* usu. without a subject to express gratitude or more often only the speaker's or writer's pleasure or satisfaction in something

Sometimes a usage note calls attention to one or more terms with the same denotation as the main entry:

wood louse *n* . . . : a terrestrial isopod crustacean (suborder Oniscoidea) with a flattened elliptical body often capable of being rolled into a ball — called also *pill bug, sow bug*

The called-also terms are shown in italic type. If such a term falls alphabetically more than a column away from the main entry, it is entered at its own place with the sole definition being a synonymous cross-reference to the entry where it appears in the usage note:

pill bug *n* . . . : WOOD LOUSE

sow bug . . . *n* . . . : WOOD LOUSE

Sometimes a usage note is used in place of a definition. Some function words (as conjunctions and prepositions) have little or no semantic content; most interjections express feelings but are otherwise untranslatable into meaning; and some other words (as oaths and honorific titles) are more amenable to comment than to definition:

¹if . . . *conj* . . . **3** —used as a function word to introduce an exclamation expressing a wish

with . . . *prep* . . . **7 a** —used as a function word to indicate manner of action

hey . . . *interj* . . . —used esp. to call attention or to express interrogation, surprise, or exultation

³**gad** *interj* . . . —used as a mild oath

¹**lord** . . . *n* . . . **4** —used as a British title

USAGE PARAGRAPHS

Brief usage paragraphs have been placed at a number of entries for terms that are considered to present problems of confused or disputed usage. A usage paragraph typically summarizes the historical background of the item and its associated body of opinion, compares these with available evidence of current usage, and often adds a few words of suitable advice for the dictionary user.

Each paragraph is signaled by an indented boldface italic *usage*. Where appropriate, discussion is keyed by sense number to the definition of the meaning in question. Most paragraphs incorporate appropriate verbal illustrations and illustrative quotations to clarify and exemplify the points being made:

ag·gra·vate . . . *vt* . . . **1** *obs* **a** : to make heavy : BURDEN **b** : INCREASE **2** : to make worse, more serious, or more severe : intensify unpleasantly < problems have been *aggravated* by neglect > **3 a** : to rouse to displeasure or anger by usu. persistent and often petty goading **b** : to produce inflammation in . . .
   usage Although *aggravate* has been used in sense 3a since the 17th century, it has been the object of disapproval only since about 1870. It is used in expository prose < declining to directly in the motorcade . . . greatly *aggravating* the President —W. F. Buckley *b*1925 > but seems to be more common in speech and casual writing < our two countries *aggravate* each other from time to time —O. W. Holmes †1935 (letter to Sir Frederick Pollock, 1895) > < times when we get *aggravated* and displeased, for instance, with the French —Jimmy Carter (press conference, 1980) > Sense 2 is far more common than sense 3a in published prose. Such is not the case, however, with *aggravation* and *aggravating*. *Aggravation* is used in sense 3 somewhat more than in its earlier senses; *aggravating* has practically no use other than to express annoyance.

When a second word is also discussed in a paragraph, the main entry for that word is followed by a run-on *usage* see—which refers to the entry where the paragraph may be found:

ag·gra·va·ting *adj* . . . *usage* see AGGRAVATE

Definitions

DIVISION OF SENSES

A boldface colon is used in this dictionary to introduce a definition:

equine . . . *adj* . . . : of, relating to, or resembling a horse or the horse family

It is also used to separate two or more definitions of a single sense:

²**imitation** *adj* . . . : resembling something else that is usu. genuine and of better quality : not real

Boldface Arabic numerals separate the senses of a word that has more than one sense:

pal·pa·ble . . . *adj* . . . **1** : capable of being touched or felt : TANGIBLE **2** : easily perceptible : NOTICEABLE **3** : easily perceptible by the mind : MANIFEST

Boldface lowercase letters separate the subsenses of a word:

¹**name** . . . *n* . . . **3 a** : REPUTATION . . . **b** : an illustrious record : FAME . . . **c** : a person or thing with a reputation

Lightface numerals in parentheses indicate a further division of subsenses:

¹**re·treat** . . . *n* . . . **1 a** (1) : an act or process of withdrawing . . . (2) : the process of receding . . . **b** (1) : the usu. forced withdrawal of troops . . . (2) : a signal for retreating . . .

A lightface colon following a definition and immediately preceding two or more subsenses indicates that the subsenses are subsumed by the preceding definition:

ven·om·ous . . . *adj* . . . **1** : full of venom: as **a** : POISONOUS, ENVENOMED **b** : NOXIOUS, PERNICIOUS . . . **c** : SPITEFUL, MALEVOLENT

¹**pe·cu·liar** . . . *adj* . . . **2** : different from the usual or normal: **a** : SPECIAL, PARTICULAR **b** : ODD, CURIOUS **c** : ECCENTRIC, QUEER

The word *as* may or may not follow the lightface colon. Its presence (as at *venomous*) indicates that the following subsenses are typical or significant examples. Its absence (as at *peculiar*) indicates that the subsenses which follow are exhaustive.

The system of separating the various senses of a word by numerals and letters is a lexical convenience. It reflects something of their semantic relationship, but it does not evaluate senses or set up a hierarchy of importance among them.

Sometimes a particular semantic relationship between senses is suggested by the use of one of four italic sense dividers: *esp, specif, also,* or *broadly.*

The sense divider *esp* (for *especially*) is used to introduce the most common meaning subsumed in the more general preceding definition:

tad . . . *n* . . . **1** : a small child; *esp* : BOY

The sense divider *specif* (for *specifically*) is used to introduce a common but highly restricted meaning subsumed in the more general preceding definition:

²**pitcher** *n* . . . : one that pitches; *specif* : the player that pitches in a game of baseball

The sense divider *also* is used to introduce a meaning that is closely related to but may be considered less important than the preceding sense:

equ·i·page . . . *n* . . . **3** : a horse-drawn carriage with its servants; *also* : such a carriage alone

The sense divider *broadly* is used to introduce an extended or wider meaning of the preceding definition:

pha·lanx . . . *n* . . . **1** : a body of heavily armed infantry in ancient Greece formed in close deep ranks and files; *broadly* : a body of troops in close array

ORDER OF SENSES

The order of senses within an entry is historical: the sense known to have been first used in English is entered first. This is not to be taken to mean, however, that each sense of a multisense word developed from the immediately preceding sense. It is altogether possible that sense 1 of a word has given rise to sense 2 and sense 2 to sense 3, but frequently senses 2 and sense 3 may have arisen independently of one another from sense 1.

When a numbered sense is further subdivided into lettered subsenses, the inclusion of particular subsenses within a sense is based upon their semantic relationship to one another, but their order is likewise historical: subsense 1a is earlier than 1b, 1b is earlier than 1c, and so forth. Divisions of subsenses indicated by lightface numerals in parentheses are also in historical order with respect to one another. Subsenses may be out of historical order, however, with respect to the broader numbered senses:

¹**job** . . . *n* . . . (1627) **1 a** : a piece of work; *esp* : a small miscellaneous piece of work taken on order at a stated rate **b** : the object or material on which work is being done **c** : something produced by or as if by work < do a better ~ next time > **d** : an

example of a usu. specified type : ITEM <this ~ is round-necked and sleeveless—Lois Long> **2 a :** something done for private advantage <suspected the whole incident was a put-up ~> **b :** a criminal enterprise; *specif* : ROBBERY **c :** a damaging or destructive bit of work <did a ~ on him> **3 a** (1) : something that has to be done : TASK (2) : an undertaking requiring unusual exertion <it was a real ~ to talk over that noise> **b :** a specific duty, role, or function **c :** a regular remunerative position **d** *chiefly Brit* : state of affairs—used with *bad* and *good* <it was a good ~ you didn't hit the old man—E. L. Thomas>

At *job* the date indicates that the earliest unit of meaning, sense 1a, was born in the seventeenth century, and it is readily apparent how the following subsenses are linked to it and to each other by the idea of work. Even subsense 1d is so linked, because while it does not apply exclusively to manufactured items, it often does so, as the illustrative quotation suggests. Yet 1d did not exist before the 1920s, while 2a and 3a (1) both belong to the seventeenth century, although they are later than 1a. Even the very last subsense, 3d, is earlier than 1d, as it is found in the works of Dickens.

Historical order also determines whether transitive or intransitive senses are given first at verbs which have both kinds. If the earliest sense is transitive, all the transitive senses precede all the intransitive senses.

OMISSION OF A SENSE

Occasionally the dictionary user, having turned to an entry, may not find a particular sense that was expected or hoped for. This usually means no more than that the editors judged the sense insufficiently common or otherwise important to include in a dictionary of this scope. Such a sense will frequently be found at the appropriate entry in a dictionary (as Webster's Third New International Dictionary) that has room for less common words and meanings. One special case is worth noting, however.

At times it would be possible to include the definition of a meaning at more than one entry (as at a simple verb and a verb-adverb collocation or at a verb and an adjective derived from a participle of that verb). To save space for other information such double coverage is avoided, and the meaning is generally defined only at the base form. For the derivative term the meaning is then considered to be essentially self-explanatory and is not defined. For example *cast off* has a sense "to get rid of" in such typical contexts as "cast off all restraint," and so has the simple verb *cast* in contexts like "cast all restraint to the winds." This meaning is defined as sense 1e(2) of *cast* and is omitted from the entry *cast off*, where the dictionary user will find a number of senses that cannot be considered self-explanatory in relation to the entries for *cast* and *off*. Likewise, the entry for the adjective *picked* gives only one sense—"CHOICE, PRIME"—which is not the meaning of *picked* in such a context as "the picked fruit lay stacked in boxes awaiting shipment." A definition suitable for this use is not given at *picked* because one is given at the first homograph *pick*, the verb from which the adjective *picked* is derived, as sense 3a—"to gather by plucking."

INFORMATION AT INDIVIDUAL SENSES

Information coming between the entry word and the first definition of a multisense word applies to all senses and subsenses. Information applicable only to some senses or subsenses is given between the appropriate boldface numeral or letter and the symbolic colon. A variety of kinds of information is offered in this way:

²**palm** *n* . . . **3** [L *palmus,* fr. *palma*]

ole·in . . . *n* . . . **2** *also* ole·ine \-ən, -,ēn\

¹**disk** *or* **disc** . . . *n* . . . **4** . . . **b** *usu disc*

cru·ci·fix·ion . . . *n* . . . **1 a** . . . **b** *cap*

¹**tile** . . . *n* . . . **1** *pl* tiles *or* tile **a** . . .

del·i·ca·tes·sen . . . *n pl* . . . **1** . . . **2** *sing, pl* **delicatessens**

fix·ing . . . *n* . . . **2** *pl*

²**die** . . . *n, pl* **dice** . . . *or* **dies** . . . **1** *pl* **dice** . . . **2** *pl usu* **dice** . . . **3** *pl* **dies** . . . **4** *pl* **dies**

¹**folk** . . . *n, pl* **folk** *or* **folks** . . . **4** *folks pl*

At *palm* the subetymology indicates that the third sense, while ultimately derived from the same source (Latin *palma*) as the other senses of the word, has a different immediate etymon (Latin *palmus*), from which it receives its meaning. At *olein* one is told that in the second sense the word has a variant spelling not used for other senses and that this variant is a secondary or less common one. At *disk* the italic label of sense 4b indicates that, while the spelling *disk* is overall somewhat the more common (since it precedes *disc* out of alphabetical order at the beginning of the entry), *disc* is the usual spelling for this particular sense. At *crucifixion* the label *cap* points out the one meaning of the word in which it is capitalized. At the first homograph *tile* no plural is shown at the beginning of the entry because the usual plural, *tiles,* is regular. The subsenses of sense 1, however, have a zero plural as well as the usual one, and so both plurals appear in boldface at sense 1. At *delicatessen* the situation is different: the entry as a whole is labeled a plural noun, but sense 2 is used as a singular. In this sense *delicatessen* can take the plural ending -*s* when needed, a fact that is indicated by the appearance of the plural in boldface at the sense. At *fixing* the italic abbreviation simply means that when used in this sense the word is always written in its plural form, *fixings.* At the second homograph *die* the actual distribution of the variant plurals can be given sense by sense in italic type because both variants are shown in boldface earlier in the entry. At the first homograph *folk* a singular noun is shown with variant plurals of nearly equal frequency, when all senses are taken into account. The fourth sense, however, is unique in being always plural in form and construction. The form of the plural for this sense is *folks,* as shown, and the placement of the form before the label instead of after it (as at the senses of *die*) means that this sense is always plural.

When an italicized label or guide phrase follows a boldface numeral, the label or phrase applies only to that specific numbered sense and its subsenses. It does not apply to any other boldface numbered senses:

²**conceit** *vt* . . . **1** *obs* . . . **2** *dial* . . . **3** *dial Brit* . . .

ro·man·ti·cism . . . *n* . . . **1** *often cap* **a** (1) . . . (2) . . . **b** . . . **2** . . .

At *conceit* the *obs* label applies only to sense 1, the *dial* label only to sense 2, and the *dial Brit* label only to sense 3. At *romanticism,* the *often cap* label applies to all the subsenses of sense 1 but not to sense 2.

When an italicized label or guide phrase follows a boldface letter, the label or phrase applies only to that specific lettered sense and its subsenses. It does not apply to any other boldface lettered senses:

¹**hearse** . . . *n* . . . **2 a** *archaic* . . . **b** *obs*

The *archaic* label applies to sense 2a but not to sense 2b. The *obs* label applies to sense 2b but not to sense 2a.

When an italicized label or guide phrase follows a parenthesized numeral, the label or phrase applies only to that specific numbered sense:

¹**mat·ter** . . . *n* . . . **1** . . . **h** (1) *obs* : REASON, CAUSE

The *obs* label applies to sense 1h(1) and to no other subsenses of the word.

Names of Plants & Animals

The entries that define the common or vernacular names (as *peach* and *lion*) of plants and animals or sometimes a related term (as *streptomycin*), if a common name is rare or does not exist, employ in part the formal, codified, New Latin vocabulary of biological systematics. This vocabulary has been developed and used by biologists in accordance with international codes of botanical and zoological nomenclature for the purpose of identifying and indicating the relationships of plants and animals. This system of names classifies organisms into a hierarchy of groups—taxa—with each kind of organism having one—and only one—correct name and belonging to one—and only one—taxon at each level of classification in the hierarchy.

This contrasts with the system of common or vernacular names which is determined by popular usage and in which one organism may have several names (as *mountain lion, cougar*, and *painter*), different organisms may have the same name (as *dolphin*), and there may be variation in meaning or overlapping of the categories denoted by the names (as *whale, dolphin*, and *porpoise*).

The fundamental taxon is the genus. It includes a group of closely related kinds of plants (as *Prunus*, which includes the wild and cultivated cherries, apricots, peaches, and almonds) or animals (as *Felis*, which includes domestic and wild cats, lions, tigers, and cougars). The genus name is a capitalized singular noun.

The unique name of each kind of organism or species—the binomial or species name—consists of a singular capitalized genus name combined with an uncapitalized specific epithet. The name for a variety or subspecies—the trinomial, variety name, or subspecies name—adds a similar varietal or subspecific epithet. The cultivated cabbage (*Brassica oleracea capitata*), the cauliflower (*Brassica oleracea botrytis*), and brussels sprouts (*Brassica oleracea gemmifera*) belong to the same species (*Brassica oleracea*) of cole.

Names of taxa higher than the genus (as family, order, and class) are capitalized plural nouns that are often used with singular verbs and that are not abbreviated in normal use. No two genera of animals in good standing are permitted to have the same name, nor are any two genera of plants in good standing. Since the botanical and zoological codes are independent, however, a plant genus and an animal genus may have the same name. Thus, a number of cabbage butterflies (as *Pieris rapae*) are placed in a genus of animals with the same name as the plant genus to which the Japanese andromeda (*Pieris japonica*) belongs. Although no two higher taxa of plants are permitted to have the same name, the rules of zoological nomenclature do not apply to taxa above the family so that rarely some widely separated groups may receive the same taxonomic name (as the ordinal name Decapoda in the entry *decapod*) from different specialists.

The taxonomic names of biological nomenclature used in this dictionary are enclosed in parentheses and usually come immediately after the primary orienting noun. Genus names as well as binomials and trinomials are italicized, but names of taxa above the genus are not italicized:

¹bee·tle . . . *n* . . . 1 : any of an order (Coleoptera) of insects having four wings of which the outer pair are modified into stiff elytra that protect the inner pair when at rest

rob·in . . . *n* . . . 1 a : a small European thrush (*Erithacus rubecula*) resembling a warbler and having a brownish olive back and yellowish red throat and breast b : any of various Old World songbirds that are related to or resemble the European robin 2 : a large No. American thrush (*Turdus migratorius*) with olivaceous gray upperparts, blackish head and tail, black and whitish streaked throat, and chiefly dull reddish breast and underparts

strep·to·my·cin . . . *n* . . . : an antibiotic organic base $C_{21}H_{39}N_7O_{12}$ produced by a soil actinomycete (*Streptomyces griseus*), active against many bacteria, and used esp. in the treatment of infections (as tuberculosis) by gram-negative bacteria

Taxonomic names are used in this dictionary to provide precise technical identifications through which defined terms may be pursued in technical writings. Because of their specialized nature taxonomic names do not have separate entry. However, many common names are derived directly from the names of taxa and especially genera with little or no modification. It is particularly important to distinguish between a common name and the genus name from which it is derived

without a change in spelling, as these names appear in print. The common name (as clostridium or drosophila) is not usually capitalized or italicized but does have a plural (as clostridia or drosophilas) which often has an ending different from that of the singular. In contrast the genus name (as *Clostridium* or *Drosophila*) is capitalized and italicized but never takes a plural. Occasionally a common name in plural form (as coleoptera) may be spelled like the name of a taxon, but it is not usually capitalized.

The entries defining the names of plants and animals are usually oriented to higher taxa by other vernaculars (as by *alga* at *seaweed* or *thrush* at *robin*) or by technical adjectives (as by *composite* at *daisy*, *leguminous* at *pea*, or *teleost* at *perch*) so that the name of a higher taxon may often be found by consulting an entry defining a more inclusive common name or a term related to it. Among the higher plants, except for the composites and legumes and a few obscure tropical groups, such orientation is by a vernacular family name that is linked at the corresponding taxonomic entry to its technical equivalent:

beech . . . *n* . . . : any of a genus (*Fagus* of the family Fagaceae, the beech family) of hardwood trees with smooth gray bark and small edible nuts; *also* : its wood

oak . . . *n* . . . 1 a : a tree or shrub (genera *Quercus* or *Lithocarpus*) of the beech family that produces a rounded one-seeded thin-shelled nut surrounded at the base by an indurated cup

A genus name may be abbreviated to its initial letter when it is used more than once in senses not separated by a boldface number:

nas·tur·tium . . . *n* . . . : any of a genus (*Tropaeolum* of the family Tropaeolaceae, the nasturtium family) of herbs with showy spurred flowers and pungent seeds; *esp* : either of two widely cultivated ornamentals (*T. majus* and *T. minus*)

Cross-Reference

Four different kinds of cross-references are used in this dictionary: directional, synonymous, cognate, and inflectional. In each instance the cross-reference is readily recognized by the lightface small capitals in which it is printed.

A cross-reference following a lightface dash and beginning with *see* or *compare* is a directional cross-reference. It directs the dictionary user to look elsewhere for further information. A *compare* cross-reference is regularly appended to a definition; a *see* cross-reference may stand alone:

²verbal *n* . . . —compare GERUND, INFINITIVE, PARTICIPLE

ngul·trum . . . *n* . . . —see MONEY table

A cross-reference immediately following a boldface colon is a synonymous cross-reference. It may stand alone as the only definitional matter for an entry or for a sense or subsense of an entry; it may follow an analytical definition; it may be one of two synonymous cross-references separated by a comma:

tran·sien·cy . . . *n* . . . : TRANSIENCE

drain·age . . . *n* . . . 2 : a device for draining : DRAIN

es·ti·ma·tion . . . *n* . . . 1 : JUDGMENT, OPINION

A synonymous cross-reference indicates that a definition at the entry cross-referred to can be substituted as a definition for the entry or the sense or subsense in which the cross-reference appears.

A cross-reference following an italic *var of* is a cognate cross-reference:

rou·ble *var of* RUBLE

Sometimes a cognate cross-reference has a limiting label preceding *var of* as a specific indication that the variant is not standard English:

> oe·soph·a·gus *chiefly Brit var of* ESOPHAGUS

> quare . . . *dial var of* [1]QUEER

> sher·ris . . . *archaic var of* SHERRY

A cross-reference following an italic label that identifies an entry as an inflected form of a noun, of an adjective or adverb, or of a verb is an inflectional cross-reference. Inflectional cross-references appear only when the inflected form falls at least a column away from the entry cross-referred to:

> lives *pl of* LIFE

> shone *past and past part of* SHINE

When guidance seems needed as to which one of several homographs or which sense of a multisense word is being referred to, a superscript numeral may precede the cross-reference or a sense number may follow it or both:

> fly ball *n* . . . : [2]FLY 5

Synonyms

Brief paragraphs discriminating words of closely associated meaning from one another have been placed at a number of entries. They are signaled by an indented boldface italic *syn*. Each paragraph begins with a list of the words to be discussed in it, followed by a concise statement of the element of meaning that the words have in common. The discriminations themselves are frequently amplified with verbal illustrations and illustrative quotations:

> [1]haste . . . *n* . . .
> *syn* HASTE, HURRY, SPEED, EXPEDITION, DISPATCH mean quickness in movement or action. HASTE applies to personal action and implies urgency and precipitancy and often rashness <marry in *haste* and repent at leisure — *Old Proverb* > HURRY often has a strong suggestion of agitated bustle or confusion <in the *hurry* of departure she forgot her toothbrush> SPEED suggests swift efficiency in movement or action <the more haste, the less *speed*—*Old Proverb* > <exercises to increase your reading *speed*> EXPEDITION and DISPATCH both imply speed and efficiency in handling affairs but EXPEDITION stresses ease or efficiency of performance and DISPATCH carries a stronger suggestion of promptness in bringing matters to a conclusion <put her things on with remarkable *expedition* — Arnold Bennett > <there was no task in all the household . . . which her mistress could not do far better and with more *dispatch* than she — Thomas Wolfe >

When a word is included in a synonym paragraph, the main entry for that word is followed by a run-on *syn* see — which refers to the entry where the synonym paragraph appears:

> [1]speed . . . *n* . . . *syn* SEE HASTE

When a word is a main entry at which there is a synonym paragraph and is also included in another paragraph else-where, the paragraph at the main entry is followed by a run-on *syn* see in addition — which refers to the entry where the other paragraph may be found:

> [3]let *vb* . . .
> *syn* LET, ALLOW, PERMIT mean not to forbid or prevent . . . . *syn* see in addition HIRE

> [2]hire *vb* . . .
> *syn* HIRE, LET, LEASE, RENT, CHARTER mean to engage or grant for use at a price . . . .

Combining Forms, Prefixes & Suffixes

An entry that begins or ends with a hyphen is a word element that forms part of an English compound:

> mini- *comb form* . . . < *mini*bus >

> -gram . . . *n comb form* . . . < tele*gram* >

> -lyze . . . *vb comb form* . . . < electro*lyze* >

> epi- *or* ep- *prefix* . . . 1 . . . < *epi*center >

> [1]-er . . . *adj suffix or adv suffix* . . . < hott*er* > < dri*er* >

> -ure *n suffix* . . . 2 . . . < legislat*ure* >

> [2]-en *vb suffix* . . . 1 a . . . < sharp*en* >

Combining forms, prefixes, and suffixes are entered in this dictionary for three reasons: to make easier the writing of etymologies of words in which these word elements occur over and over again; to make understandable the meaning of many undefined run-ons which for reasons of space would be omitted if they had to be given etymologies and definitions; and to make recognizable the meaningful elements of new words that are not well enough established in the language to warrant dictionary entry.

Lists of Undefined Words

Lists of undefined words occur after the entries of these prefixes and combining forms:

anti-	multi-	re-
co-	non-	self-
counter-	out-	sub-
hyper-	over-	super-
inter-	post-	ultra-
mis-	pre-	un-

These words are not defined because they are self-explanatory; their meanings are simply the sum of a meaning of the prefix or combining form and a meaning of the root word. Centered dots are shown to save the dictionary user the trouble of consulting another entry.

The English Language in the Dictionary

In the offices where Webster's Ninth New Collegiate Dictionary was edited, several thousand letters are received each year. The topics they articulate are enormously varied. Some letters merely ask for a particular bit of information about the English language that has been sought but not found in the dictionary. A few others are in hot pursuit of a special interest. Still others, their writers having come to think of the dictionary as an all-purpose reference book, ask questions about many other subjects besides words. A surprising number of correspondents, however, express considerable curiosity about how their dictionary—that formidably long and closely printed work with its many special abbreviations, symbols, and devices and its multitude of uses—came to be just the book it is.

They may ask quite directly such questions as how words make it into the dictionary or what it is that lexicographers do when they are editing or reediting a dictionary. But even questions of a very different sort on the surface may unwittingly reveal much the same interest. "Why did you fail to include word *x* in your book?" and "Why don't you still use the system of transcribing pronunciations with which I grew up instead of the present one with its 'upside-down *e*'?" may be in part expressions of annoyance at what is seen (not always accurately) as the dictionary's failure to do its job, but they are just as truly demands to know how dictionary editors make the decision to exclude some words from a given dictionary or to revise a long-standing feature of earlier editions. What follows is an effort to present a brief overview of the English language and its history and to provide brief and necessarily somewhat general answers to a few of the questions that users of this dictionary probably have about it, the processes that went into its making, and its relation to that fascinating and sometimes maddening marvel which we call the English language.

Language is the object of study of the academic discipline known as linguistics. Although the roots of linguistic science are found in earlier centuries, it is in most respects a modern creation, and the understanding of language that it offers us differs in a number of fundamental ways from the conceptions of language held by thinkers of the ancient and medieval worlds, the Renaissance, or the Enlightenment. This understanding does not differ, however, in every way. The use of language is still seen by linguists as a peculiarly human activity. We often use the word *language* to refer to the limited stock of movements or utterances by which some animals communicate a limited number of messages, but in doing so we recognize that we are speaking of something different in kind from our own language. Moreover, modern definitions of language are just as likely as earlier definitions to emphasize its functional aspect: language enables human beings, at least those who share a particular language, to communicate with each other by stating ideas, expressing feelings, and exchanging information.

Modern definitions of language, though, are more likely than older ones to stress some other aspects. One is the arbitrary nature of the relationship between the conventional sounds or other signs which serve as the vehicle of language and the meaning being conveyed by them. A few naive souls may believe that domestic swine are called pigs because their habits are so dirty, but it is clear to most that no inherent or necessary connection exists between the sequence of sounds \p\ plus \i\ plus \g\ and "any of various stout-bodied short-legged omnivorous mammals (family Suidae) with a thick bristly skin and a long mobile snout." A similarly naive Frenchman or German could insist with neither more nor less reason that *cochon* or *Schwein* is the word that naturally expresses the essential piggishness of the animal.

A linguistically oriented definition of language would also be likely to emphasize the systematic nature of language. Were it not for highly organized systems operating within any natural language—be it one with many millions of native speakers and enormous international importance like Spanish, Mandarin Chinese, or English or one spoken by a handful of people in a remote area—it could hardly be the subtle and effective tool of communication that it is. These systems are enormously complex both in themselves and in their mutual interaction, so complex indeed that no language has yet had its workings fully described; yet, paradoxically, and fortunately for the human race, any child with a normal ability to learn can, within a very few years, master at least the essentials of these systems for any one language with which it is in daily contact (or even two languages if the child's environment is bilingual). It is uncertain whether this is so because, as some linguists believe, at a profound level of structure the details that make English so different from other languages are unimportant and the systems of all languages are largely the same, but the fact that we learn our native language almost effortlessly up to a certain basic level of control is hardly to be denied.

The Systems of Language

The major systems that make up the broad comprehensive system of language itself are four in number: lexicon, grammar, semantics, and phonology. The one that dictionary editors and dictionary users are most directly concerned with is the vocabulary or *lexicon,* the collection of words and word elements which we put together in various ways to form larger units of discourse: phrases, clauses, sentences, paragraphs, and so forth. All languages have a lexicon, and all lexicons are governed by rules that permit some kinds of word formation, make others dubious, and render still others clearly impossible. In English we might say *versatileness* without hesitation if we needed such a word and could not for the moment think of *versatility*, even though the former is not normally part of our everyday working vocabulary; but *versatilize* might give us considerable pause, and *nessversatile* we would simply never utter. The size of the lexicon varies considerably from language to language. The language of an isolated people, for example, may be perfectly adequate with a relatively small and fixed vocabulary, since it has no need of the coinages attendant upon modern technology, while English and other major languages have enormous stocks of words, to which they add year by year at a great rate. Since the dictionary is concentrated upon the lexicon, our discussion of the other systems of language, as it proceeds, will be largely concerned with how they are related to the lexicon and thus are important within the dictionary.

The grammatical system of a language governs the way in which words are put together to form the larger units of discourse mentioned earlier. Grammar, of course, varies a great deal from language to language just as the lexicon does: in English, word order is a dominant factor in determining meaning, while the use of inflectional endings to mark the grammatical function of individual words within a sentence plays a clearly subordinate role, though important in some ways (as in indicating the number of a noun, the case of a personal pronoun, and the tense of a verb). Other languages show markedly different patterns, such as Latin with its elaborate set of paradigms for nouns, verbs, adjectives, and pronouns and its highly flexible word order. The semantic system of a language has to do with meanings and thus with the relation between the conventionalized symbols that constitute language and the external reality about which we need to communicate through language. The phonological system of a language is what allows a speaker of that language to transform a grammatical unit embodying a meaning into a flow of uttered sounds that can be heard and interpreted (accurately, if all goes well) by another speaker of the language. This system is always very tightly organized. The inventory of basic meaningful units of sound within a language (called *phonemes* by linguists) is never very large compared with the number of words and word elements in the lexicon; most speakers of English get by with about 40. Phonemes are identified by the fact that in some pairs of words they create a contrast that signals a difference in meaning: we consider the vowel sounds of *trip* and *trap* to be different phonemes because the difference in vowel sounds is the sole determinant of their being two distinct words. Their consonant sounds are identical. Similarly, the initial consonant sounds of *pull* and *bull*, *tie* and *die*, and *come* and *gum* are contrasting phonemes. On the other hand, the sound at the beginning of *pit* and at the end of *tip* are phonetically quite different, but as they do not contrast meaningfully we do not perceive them as distinct phonemes. The combinations of these phonemes permitted in a given language are severely restricted, as are the ways in which speech sounds occur in conjunction with other significant elements of the phonological system such as stress (force or intensity) and intonation (the rise and fall in pitch of the voice as it moves through an utterance). In English, for example, it is possible for the consonants \str\ to occur in succession, but only at the beginning of a word (as in *strict*) or in the middle (as in *monstrous*), not at the end, and the sequence \pgr\ cannot occur at either the beginning or the end of a word but may occur in the middle (as in *upgrade*).

Variation and Change in Language

All of the systems of language are constantly in operation, and in a given language at a given time they may seem almost to be monolithic or at least to have sufficient identity that it makes sense, for example, to talk of *the* grammar of English. And, indeed, how could it be otherwise? Language would be a far more imperfect tool of communication than it is if the speakers of a language were not functioning within a system sufficiently unified to permit almost constant mutual intelligibility. Yet the impression of unity which we receive when we take a broad descriptive look at a single language at a particular time (taking a *synchronic* point of view, as linguists say) is more than a little misleading because it has failed to take account of the enormous variation that exists within the language.

Each of us speaks a distinctive form of English which is not identical in every particular with the form spoken by anyone else; linguists call this individual variety of a language an *idiolect*. Those who speak idiolects sharing certain features of vocabulary, grammar, and phonology that are distinctively different from corresponding features shared by others who live in a different geographical area or belong to a different social group or who differ in some other way that affects their language are said to speak a *dialect* of the language. Researchers have identified a number of different geographical dialect areas within the United States, rather clearly marked on the Eastern seaboard but progressively less well defined as one moves west; yet, the dialects of American English do not differ overall very greatly from one another; some dialects of Great Britain are more strikingly divergent in phonology, for example, than are any two dialects within this country, and some dialects of other languages approach the condition of mutual unintelligibility that is often taken to divide separate dialects from separate languages.

Nor is variation in language by any means confined to matters of idiolect or dialect. Variation may also be related to the several functional varieties of a language that people take up and discard as their roles and relationships change from moment to moment throughout the day. Such variation can involve vocabulary, pronunciation, and even grammar. A worker who queries one colleague concerning the whereabouts of another with "Seen John?" from which both the auxiliary verb *have* and the subject *you* have been deleted may not put the question in the same informal way to a superior.

If variation is one of the most prominent aspects of language as one considers it at the present time, the inescapable fact that emerges from considering language historically (taking a *diachronic* point of view, as linguists say) is change. No living language stands still, however much we might wish at times that it would. Change over the short run is most readily noticed in the lexicon, as a comparison of successive editions of any modern dictionary will show; in grammar and phonology the forces of change typically operate much more slowly. Still, the cumulative effect of changes that are imperceptible as they occur can be impressive when measured across the centuries. The English of one's great-great-grandfather might not sound so very different from one's own. Perhaps it might seem a bit stiff and formal, a bit old-fashioned in its vocabulary, but the differences would not be dramatic. If we could somehow listen to an English-speaker of King Alfred's time, however, we would hear what all but a few scholars of historical English would take to be a foreign tongue.

The History of English

The history of English is conventionally, if perhaps too neatly, divided into three periods usually called Old English, (or Anglo-Saxon), Middle English, and Modern English. The earliest period begins with the migration of certain Germanic tribes from the continent to Britain in the fifth century A.D., though no records of their language survive from before the seventh century, and it continues until the end of the eleventh century or a bit later. By that time Latin, Old Norse (the language of the Viking invaders), and especially the Anglo-Norman French of the dominant class after the Norman Conquest in 1066 had begun to have a substantial impact on the lexicon, and the well-developed inflectional system that typifies the grammar of Old English had begun to break down. The following brief sample of Old English prose illustrates several of the significant ways in which change has so transformed English that we must look carefully to find points of resemblance between the language of the tenth century and our own. It is taken from Aelfric's "Homily on St. Gregory the Great" and concerns the famous story of how that pope came to send missionaries to convert the heathen Anglo-Saxons to Christianity after seeing Anglo-Saxon boys for sale as slaves in Rome:

Eft he axode, hu ðære ðeode nama wære þe hi of comon. Him wæs geandwyrd, þæt hi Angle genemnode wæron. þa cwæð he, "Rihtlice hi sind Angle gehatene, for ðan ðe hi engla wlite habbað, and swilcum gedafenað þæt hi on heofonum engla geferan beon."

A few of these words will be recognized as identical in spelling with their modern equivalents—*he, of, him, for, and, on*—and the resemblance of a few others to familiar words may be guessed—*nama* to *name, comon* to *come, wære* to *were, wæs* to *was*—but only those who have made a special study of Old English will be able to read the passage with understanding. The sense of it is as follows: "Again he [St. Gregory] asked what might be the name of the people from which they came. It was answered to him that they were named Angles. Then he said, 'Rightly are they called Angles because they have the beauty of angels, and it is fitting that such as they should be the angels' companions in heaven.'" Some of the words in the original have survived in altered form, including *axode (asked), hu (how), rihtlice (rightly), engla (angels), habbað (have), swilcum (such), heofonum (heaven),* and *beon (be)*. Others, however, have vanished from our lexicon, mostly without a trace, including several that were quite common words in Old English: *eft* "again," *ðeode* "people, nation," *cwæð* "said, spoke," *gehatene* "called, named," *wlite* "appearance, beauty," and *geferan* "companions." Recognition of some words is naturally hindered by the presence of two special characters, þ, called "thorn," and ð, called "edh," which served in Old English to represent the sounds now spelled with *th.*

Other points worth noting include the fact that the pronoun system did not yet, in the late tenth century, include the third person plural forms beginning with *th-: hi* appears where we would use *they.* Several aspects of word order will also strike the reader as oddly unlike ours. Subject and verb are inverted after an adverb—*þa cwæð he* "Then said he"—a phenomenon not unknown in modern English but now restricted to a few adverbs such as *never* and requiring the presence of an auxiliary verb like *do* or *have.* In subordinate clauses the main verb must be last, and so an object or a preposition may precede it in a way no longer natural: *þe hi of comon* "which they from came," *for ðan ðe hi engla wlite habbað* "because they angels' beauty have."

Perhaps the most distinctive difference between Old and Modern English reflected in Aelfric's sentences is the elaborate system of inflections, of which we now have only remnants. Nouns, adjectives, and even the definite article are inflected for gender, case, and number: *ðære ðeode* "(of) the people" is feminine, genitive, and singular, *Angle* "Angles" is masculine, accusative, and plural, and *swilcum* "such" is masculine, dative, and plural. The system of inflections for verbs was also more elaborate than ours: for example, *habbað* "have" ends with the *-að* suffix characteristic of plural present indicative verbs. In addition, there

were two imperative forms, four subjunctive forms (two for the present tense and two for the preterit, or past, tense), and several others which we no longer have. Even where Modern English retains a particular category of inflection, the form has often changed: Old English present participles ended in *-ende* not *-ing,* and past participles bore a prefix *ge-* (as *geandwyrd* "answered" in the passage above).

The period of Middle English extends roughly from the twelfth century through the fifteenth. The influence of French (and Latin, often by way of French) upon the lexicon continued throughout this period, the loss of some inflections and the reduction of others (often to a final unstressed vowel spelled *-e*) accelerated, and many changes took place within the phonological and grammatical systems of the language. A typical prose passage, especially one from the later part of the period, will not have such a foreign look to us as did Aelfric's prose; but it will not be mistaken for contemporary writing either. The following brief passage is drawn from a work of the late fourteenth century called *Mandeville's Travels.* It is fiction in the guise of travel literature, and, though it purports to be from the pen of an English knight, it was originally written in French and later translated into Latin and English. In this extract Mandeville describes the land of Bactria, apparently not an altogether inviting place, as it is inhabited by "full yuele [evil] folk and full cruell."

In þat lond ben trees þat beren wolle, as þogh it were of scheep; whereof men maken clothes, and all þing þat may ben made of wolle. In þat contree ben many ipotaynes, þat dwellen som tyme in the water, and somtyme on the lond: and þei ben half man and half hors, as I haue seyd before; and þei eten men, whan þei may take hem. And þere ben ryueres and watres þat ben fulle byttere, þree sithes more þan is the water of the see. In þat contré ben many griffounes, more plentee þan in ony other contree. Sum men seyn þat þei han the body vpward as an egle, and benethe as a lyoun: and treuly þei seyn soth þat þei ben of þat schapp. But o griffoun hath the body more gret, and is more strong, þanne eight lyouns, of suche lyouns as ben o this half; and more gret and strongere þan an hundred egles, suche as we han amonges vs. For o griffoun þere wil bere fleynge to his nest a gret hors, зif he may fynde him at the poynt, or two oxen зoked togidere, as þei gon at the plowgh.

The spelling is often peculiar by modern standards and even inconsistent within these few sentences (*contré* and *contree, o* [*griffoun*] and *a* [*gret hors*], *þanne* and *þan,* for example). Moreover, there is in addition to thorn another old character з, yogh, to make difficulty. It can represent several sounds but there may be thought of as equivalent to *y.* Even the older spellings (including those where *u* stands for *v*) are recognizable, however, and there are only a few words like *ipotaynes* "hippopotamuses" and *sithes* "times" that have dropped out of the language altogether. We may notice a few words and phrases that have meanings no longer common such as *byttere* "salty," *o this half* "on this side of the world," and *at the poynt* "to hand," and the effect of the centuries-long dominance of French on the vocabulary is evident in many familiar words which could not have occurred in Aelfric's writing even if his subject had allowed them, words like *contree, ryueres, plentee, egle,* and *lyoun.*

In general word order is now very close to that of our time, though we notice constructions like *hath the body more gret* and *three sithes more þan is the water of the see.* We also notice that present tense verbs still receive a plural inflection as in *beren, dwellen, han,* and *ben* and that while nominative *þei* has replaced Aelfric's *hi* in the third person plural, the form for objects is still *hem.* All the same, the number of inflections for nouns, adjectives, and verbs has been greatly reduced, and in most respects Mandeville is closer to Modern than to Old English.

The period of Modern English extends from the sixteenth century to our own day. The early part of this period saw the completion of a revolution in the phonology of English that had begun in late Middle English and that effectively redistributed the occurrence of the vowel phonemes to something approximating their present pattern. (Mandeville's English would have sounded even less familiar to us than it looks.) Other important early developments include the stabilizing effect on spelling of the printing press and the beginning of the direct influence of Latin and, to a lesser extent, Greek on the lexicon. Later, as English came into contact with other cultures around the world and distinctive dialects of English developed in the many areas which Britain had colonized, numerous other languages made small but interesting contributions to our word-stock.

The historical aspect of English really encompasses more than the three stages of development just under consideration. English has what might be called a prehistory as well. As we have seen, our language did not simply spring into existence; it was brought from the Continent by Germanic tribes who had no form of writing and hence left no records. Philologists know that they must have spoken a dialect of a language that can be called West Germanic and that other dialects of this unknown language must have included the ancestors of such languages as German, Dutch, Low German, and Frisian. They know this because of certain systematic similarities which these languages share with each other but do not share with, say, Danish. However, they have had somehow to reconstruct what that language was like in its lexicon, phonology, grammar, and semantics as best they can through sophisticated techniques of comparison developed chiefly during the last century. Similarly, because ancient and modern languages like Old Norse and Gothic or Icelandic and Norwegian have points in common with Old English and Old High German or Dutch and English that they do not share with French or Russian, it is clear that there was an earlier unrecorded language that can be called simply Germanic and that must be reconstructed in the same way. Still earlier, Germanic was just a dialect (the ancestors of Greek, Latin, and Sanskrit were three other such dialects) of a language conventionally designated Indo-European, and thus English is just one relatively young member of an ancient family of languages whose descendants cover a fair portion of the globe. (For more detail on the Indo-European languages and their relationships, see the table having that title in the dictionary.)

The Dictionary and the Systems of English

By far the largest part of this volume is called "A Dictionary of the English Language" and so is naturally concerned with the systems of English that we have cursorily surveyed in their synchronic and diachronic aspects. In fact, information related to all four systems is given at most entries in the dictionary, as well as information related to what could reasonably be considered a fifth system of English and many other (though not all) languages—writing. The writing system provides an alternative to speech that permits long-distance transmission and visual reception of a communication and also enables a record to be kept for much longer than human memory can keep it. The writing system of Modern English allows for considerable variation, as is shown by the persistence of variant spellings like *veranda* and *verandah* or *judgment* and *judgement* and by the fact that many compound words have solid, hyphenated, and open stylings all in common use (as *decision maker, decision-maker,* and *decisionmaker*). At the same time, however, it tends to be a force for standardization and unification because recorded language creates a precedent for future language use and provides a basis on which language use can be taught to the younger members of a community. This con-

servative effect is one reason why spelling reformers have so far met with but modest success in their efforts.

We may now begin to look at the ways in which the specific systems of our language are treated in the dictionary and at the processes of lexicography which produce the information about these systems that the dictionary user encounters. A dictionary is necessarily and obviously concerned with the lexicon above all, and the information it can convey about the language systems is confined to the level of the word or short phrase. The result is that no dictionary of English, however good it may be, can provide all of the information about the English language that one might wish to have at one time or another. Thus, for example, details about such important aspects of phonology as the patterns of sentence stress and sentence intonation cannot readily be accommodated in a work of reference organized in terms of discrete words, nor can grammatical topics such as word order in subordinate clauses or the structural relation of interrogative to declarative sentences.

The History of English in the Dictionary

A similar limitation applies to the treatment of the historical aspect of English; yet, Webster's Ninth New Collegiate Dictionary is able to offer a good deal of historical information about words. What we earlier called the prehistory of English is encountered in the etymologies that appear in square brackets ahead of the definitional material at many entries. An etymology tells us what is known of an English word before it became the word we enter in the dictionary; that is, if the word was created in English the etymology shows, to whatever extent is not already obvious from the shape of the word, what materials were used to form it, and if the word was borrowed into English the etymology traces the steps of the borrowing process backward from the point at which the word entered English to the earliest recorded ancestral language. Where it is most relevant, note is made of one or several words from other languages that are related ("akin") to the entry word but are not in the direct line of borrowing. Thus, a word like Aelfric's *heofon* (ignoring for the moment the dative plural inflection *-um* that it bears in the passage we looked at earlier) appears as part of this dictionary's etymology for the modern word *heaven:* [ME *heven,* fr. OE *heofon;* akin to OHG *himil*]. Since *heaven* is a native English word, it has only two recorded ancestors, Middle English *heven* and Old English *heofon.* Beyond those forms lie only the hypothetical, reconstructed forms of West Germanic, Germanic, and Indo-European. In this case one West Germanic cognate is shown, Old High German *himil,* which is the parent of Modern German *Himmel* but only a second cousin of our English word. Similarly Mandeville's *contree* appears as the first element in the etymology of its modern descendant *country:* [ME *contree,* fr. OF *contrée,* fr. ML *contrata,* fr. L *contra* against, on the opposite side]. Here we see that our word can be traced back through three nouns of Middle English, Old French, and Medieval Latin (all of which had the same basic meaning as the Modern English noun and so are not glossed) to a Latin preposition (which has a different meaning and so is glossed). The two etymological patterns are, as we would expect from what we know of the history of the English vocabulary, among the most common and are repeated with differing details at entry after entry throughout the book. Of course, borrowings that have occurred within the Modern English period are more various, and we find such exotic language names as Nahuatl (at *chocolate*), Taino (at ²*barbecue*), Tagalog (at *boondocks*), Malay (at ³*amok*), and Kimbundu (at *banjo*) as well as the more familiar Russian (at *troika*), Italian (at ¹*ballot*), Arabic (at *mullah*), Spanish (at ¹*macho*) and Japanese (at *tycoon*).

An etymologist must know a good deal about the history of English and also about the relationships of sound and meaning and their changes over time that underlie the reconstruction of the Indo-European family, but even that considerable learning is not enough to do all that must be done to provide etymologies of English words in a dictionary such as this. A knowledge is also needed of the various processes by which words are created within Modern English: among the most important processes are shortening, or clipping (see ¹*stereo*), functional shift (as the noun *commute* from the verb *commute*), back-formation (see *grid*), combination of initial letters (see *radar*), transfer of personal or place names (see *silhouette* and *denim*), imitation of sounds (see ¹*whiz*), folk etymology (see *Jerusalem artichoke*), and blending of two words (see *motel*). Also available to one who feels the need for a new word to name a new thing or express a new idea is the very considerable store of prefixes, suffixes, and combining forms that already exist in English. Some of these are native and others are borrowed from French, but the largest number have been taken directly from Latin or Greek, and they have been combined in many different ways often without any special regard for matching two elements from the same original language. The combination of these word elements has produced many scientific and technical terms of Modern English. Once in a while a word is created spontaneously out of the creative play of sheer imagination. (For examples of the latter sort of creation see the etymologies of *boondoggle* and *googol* in the dictionary. Such invention is common, as Merriam-Webster editors know from their mail, which frequently includes requests from coiners that their brand-new words be entered in the dictionary. Very few coinages of this kind ever come into common enough use to justify dictionary entry, however.)

An etymologist working on a new edition of the Collegiate Dictionary must review the etymologies at existing main entries and prepare such etymologies as are required for the main entries being added to the new edition. In the course of the former activity adjustments must sometimes be made either to incorporate a useful piece of information that has previously been overlooked or to revise the account of the word's origin in the light of new evidence. Such evidence may be unearthed by the etymologist or may be the product of published research by scholars of historical linguistics and others. In writing new etymologies this editor must, of course, be alive to the possible languages from which a new term may have been borrowed and to the possible ways in which one may have been created. New scientific and technical terms sometimes pose special difficulties. While they are most often formed from familiar word elements, occasionally a case like *methotrexate* presents itself in which one element (here *-trexate*) resists identification.

When all attempts to provide a satisfactory etymology have failed, the editor has recourse to the formula "origin unknown." This formula seldom means that the editor is unaware of various speculations about the origin of the term but instead usually means that no single theory conceived by the etymologist or proposed by others is well enough backed by evidence to include in a serious work of reference, even when qualified by "probably" or "perhaps." Thus, our editors frequently have to explain to correspondents that the dictionary fails to state that the origin of *posh* is in the initial letters of the phrase "port out, starboard home"—supposedly a shipping term for the cooler accommodations on steamships plying between Britain and India from the mid-nineteenth century on—not because the story is unknown to us but because no evidence to support it has yet been produced. Some evidence exists that casts strong doubt on it; the word is not known earlier than 1918 (in a source unrelated to shipping), and the acronymic explanation does not appear until 1935. It therefore seems reasonable to consider the acronymic explanation a modern invention and assign

posh the etymology [origin unknown]. The etymologist must sift such theories, often several conflicting theories of greater or lesser likelihood, and try to evaluate the evidence conservatively but fairly in arriving at the soundest possible etymology that the available information permits. Occasionally time will prove the result to be somewhat (or even quite) mistaken, and the etymology will need to be replaced by something better. This can happen even when the etymologist felt quite certain of the soundness of the original etymology, and it is just one among many reasons why dictionaries must be reedited from time to time if they are to remain reliable.

Historical information about words is also provided by the date appearing in parentheses just before the first or only definition at most main entries. The date given is for the earliest recorded use known to our editors of the first entered sense of that entry. In most cases the date is also, in effect, for the earliest use of the word itself that we know of. Some words, however, had early senses that later passed from common use without gaining special literary importance, and these senses are omitted from this dictionary. Because it would be misleading to give a date for a sense that the dictionary does not show, the date is always for the first sense actually defined at the entry. Because the senses of any word having more than one are always presented in historical order, with the one known to have been used first given first, the date serves as a link between the prehistory of the word shown in the etymology and its later recorded history of semantic development within the language, as reflected in the order of definitions.

Evidence for the dates has come from a number of sources. Especially for words that have been a part of the language since before this century, the most important sources have been the major historical dictionaries of English. These works include for each sense dated examples of use from one or several authors including the earliest one available to the editors. Chief among these dictionaries is the majestic thirteen-volume Oxford English Dictionary and its supplements. Also of great importance have been the Middle English Dictionary, A Dictionary of American English, A Dictionary of Americanisms, The Scottish National Dictionary, and A Dictionary of the Older Scottish Tongue. Other dictionaries that include a greater or lesser number of dated quotations and that have proved helpful in particular cases include Hobson-Jobson (a glossary of Anglo-Indian terms), The Stanford Dictionary of Anglicised Words and Phrases, Wright's English Dialect Dictionary, Cassidy and Le Page's Dictionary of Jamaican English, Branford's Dictionary of South African English, Avis's Dictionary of Canadianisms on Historical Principles, Wentworth's American Dialect Dictionary, Wentworth and Flexner's Dictionary of American Slang, The Barnhart Dictionary of New English Since 1963, and The Second Barnhart Dictionary of New English. The Century Dictionary and Cyclopedia and the successive editions of Merriam-Webster's unabridged dictionaries and their supplements of new words have also provided much assistance, for while these dictionaries do not incorporate dated quotations, an entry in one or another of them is sometimes earlier than any example of the word from running text that we have been able to find.

The other major source of dates, especially for the period from 1890 to the present, is the Merriam-Webster file of examples of words used in context, which are called citations. More will be said of this collection later. Here it need only be noted that among the 13,000,000 slips which the file contains frequently appear one or more examples of a given word that are earlier than any quoted in our reference sources. And, of course, our citations have been essential to the dating of a considerable number of entries not included in any of the dictionaries mentioned above. The date of 1949 at *classical conditioning* is a case of the first sort, the earliest example in a reference source being from 1964, while the date of 1974 at *earth tone* is of the second sort. Some of the older books in our editorial library and in other libraries to which our editors have access have occasionally supplemented the resources of the citation file in supplying dates.

Almost from the appearance of the first volume of The Oxford English Dictionary, scholars have been discovering earlier dates for particular words and senses by examining works not searched for examples by the dictionary's readers or by reading some works a second time and publishing the results of their findings in various journals. Many hundreds of entries in this dictionary include a date derived from one of these articles, and while far too many scholars and other interested students have participated in this work for a listing here to be practical, some collective acknowledgment of our debt to them is necessary. The date of 1676 at *menagerie* may be cited as an example of one derived from a source of this kind; the newly discovered quotation is 36 years older than the earliest example that had previously been found.

The style of the date is determined by the period of English to which the sense being dated belongs: for entries from Old English we indicate simply that the example is from the period before the twelfth century (bef. 12c); for those from Middle English we indicate their century, as (14c); for those from Modern English we give a single year, as (1742).

Some caution needs to be exercised in interpreting the significance of a date. It is never meant to indicate the exact point at which a word entered the language. For one thing, words have often been in spoken use for many years before they come to be written down. Then, too, not all surviving texts, even for the earlier periods, have been read to collect examples for any historical dictionary, and obviously for the modern era only a very small sample of all published material has been examined in that way. One can perhaps with some justification think of the date as indicating a time by which one can be sure that the word was in use, but it will be safest simply to remember that the date actually belongs to the earliest occurrence known to the editors of this dictionary of the first entered sense of the word.

Leaving the historical aspect of English aside now, we may consider how information about the systems of English as they presently exist is recorded in this dictionary. The phonological system needs little more than a mention here. Its role in this dictionary is discussed in some detail in the "Guide to Pronunciation," which immediately follows this section, as is the way in which the pronunciations shown in the dictionary have been determined.

Semantics in the Dictionary

In turning to consider the coverage of the semantic system in the dictionary, we face several difficult problems. If one function of a dictionary is more important than its many others, surely that function is to define the meaning of words. But while definition is central to the dictionary and quite obviously is involved with semantics, for the most part it deals with individual words in isolation from other words and thus ignores, to a considerable extent, the systematic, relational side of English semantics. Another problem is that although we know quite a lot about the system of English phonology and a good deal (though less) about the grammatical system, our understanding of the semantic system is very imperfect, and much of what we do know about it does not come very obviously into play in a dictionary. Still, we will have a glimpse of this system when we consider the dictionary treatment of synonyms, and in the meantime there is much to be said about the defining of words. Perhaps the first thing that we need to remind ourselves of is that when we speak of the meaning of a word we are employing an artificial, if highly useful, convention. Meaning does not truly reside within the word but in the minds of those who hear or read

it. This fact alone guarantees that meaning will be to a great degree amorphous: no two people have had exactly the same experience with what a word refers to and so the meaning of the word will be slightly or greatly different for each of us. It is obvious, then, that a dictionary which set itself the task of defining the meanings of words in their entirety would be a foolhardy enterprise. So dictionary editors invoke the traditional distinction between *denotation*—the direct and specific part of meaning which is sometimes indicated as the total of all the referents of a word and is shared by all or most people who use the word—and *connotation*—the more personal associations and shades of meaning that gather about a word as a result of individual experience and which may not be widely shared. The dictionary concerns itself essentially with the denotations of words.

For the editors of this dictionary the defining process began long before they actually sat down to examine critically the definitions of the last edition and to formulate trial definitions. It began with an activity that is called in our offices "reading and marking." Ordinarily each editor spends a portion of the working day reading a variety of newspapers, magazines, and books, looking for anything that might be useful to a definer of English words. Because both time and staff are limited and the scope of English seems nearly unlimited, changes in subject matter, geographical area covered, and individual publications must be made from time to time in a way carefully calculated to ensure the breadth and depth as well as the continuity of our coverage of the vocabulary of English. An editor who is reading and marking will, of course, be looking for examples of new words and for unusual applications of familiar words that suggest the possible emergence of a new meaning but will also be concerned to provide evidence of the current status of variant spellings, inflected forms, and the stylings of compound words, to collect examples that may be quotable as illustrations of typical use in the dictionary, and to record many other useful kinds of information. In each instance the reader will underline the word or phrase that is of interest and mark off as much context as is considered helpful in clarifying the meaning. This example of a word used in context is called a *citation* of the word. Ideally the editor would like all citations to illuminate the meaning of the word, but some passages will remain obscure no matter how far they extend, and sometimes one must mark a citation simply for the occurrence of the word or meaning (especially when it is new), trusting that the reading-and-marking process will yield more helpful examples in the long run. In the case of ephemeral words, of course, this may never happen, but truly ephemeral words will not need to be defined for a dictionary. At this early stage of the dictionary-making process editors do not make judgments about the likelihood of a word's establishing itself in the language. If a possible citation has even the barest potential to be useful at a later time, it is marked.

These samples of words in bracketed context are put onto 3×5 slips of paper, and the citation slips are placed in alphabetical order in rows of filing cabinets. They will be used, as needed, by the editors in their roles as writers of definitions and certain other parts of dictionary entries. The editors engaged in this ninth edition of the Collegiate reviewed every one of the million and a half citations that had been gathered since the eighth edition was prepared in the early 1970s. When necessary, they also drew upon the additional resources of what are called the "consolidated" files, those that contain all the citations (over eleven and a half million) that had been accumulated in our offices since the late nineteenth century and had been used in the editing of the many dictionaries this company published before the present one.

The actual defining process begins with a number of special assignments called "group defining projects," which may range from a small set of words like those for the days of the week or the letters of the English alphabet (for which parallel, formulaic definitions are required) to the vocabulary of a large subject area such as music or anthropology. When these assignments have been completed, defining proceeds alphabetically, with the editors responsible for the terminology of the life sciences or the physical sciences and related technologies working independently of the editors responsible for defining the general vocabulary.

If you were a definer, you would typically be working at a given moment with a group of citations covering a relatively short segment of the alphabet, *grio-* to *gror-*, for example, and with the entries of the dictionary being reedited that fall within the same segment. Your job would be to determine, under the guidance of the citations, which existing entries could remain in the new edition essentially unchanged because their usage showed no significant alteration, which entries needed to be revised either by modification of existing definitions or by the addition of new ones, which old entries were expendable for the new edition, and what new entries should be added to keep coverage of the lexicon up-to-date. You would begin by reading and sorting out the citation slips, first by grammatical function, in the case of a word like *groom* that is both noun and verb, and then by meaning within each part of speech. For each group of citations that was covered by an adequate existing definition, you would need only to indicate that you had examined them and would do nothing to the definition. For definitions needing adjustment, you would indicate the change to be made. In many cases, you would have some citations left over that were not covered by an existing definition, and it would then be your job to determine whether that segment of meaning was perhaps relatively uncommon and not backed by a sufficient range and number of citations and so not needed for the dictionary or whether in fact it was a sense that dictionary users are entitled to find suitably defined when they come looking for it. In the former case you would reject the citations, and eventually they would find their way back to the files to await review for another dictionary (by which time perhaps the citational backing would be stronger and a definition needed). In the latter case yours would be the responsibility to frame the kind of definition that will adequately convey that particular segment of meaning to the dictionary user.

In writing that definition, you could follow any of a number of paths marked out by the instructions given to each definer. These include both the general policies and practices that govern all Merriam-Webster dictionaries and the more specific directions and prohibitions contained in the "style file," as it is called, for this particular dictionary.

The kind of definition that you would write in most cases is called an analytical definition. It consists in its purest form of the statement of a class to which the term being defined is assigned and a number of characteristics which differentiate the individual from other members of the class. For example, the first sense of *grove* is defined in this Collegiate as "a small wood without underbrush," assigning a grove to the more general class of woods and using "small" and "without underbrush" to indicate in what ways a grove is unlike other kinds of woods. Another possibility would be for you to define a synonym, as is done at the sixth sense of the noun *grip*, where the definition is "STAGEHAND." Defining by synonym tends to be inexact because even true synonyms do not have just the same meaning and is perhaps most useful in cases like the one just mentioned where one kind of referent has two or more names, a situation that occurs frequently with the common names of plants and animals. For this reason we link any synonym definition to an analytical definition by making the synonym a cross-reference (in small capital letters) to another entry where an analytical definition suitable for both words is given: at *stagehand* is the definition "a stage worker who handles scenery,

properties, or lights," which is also a good definition of the sixth sense of *grip*.

Within these basic defining patterns many variations are permitted. Some analytical definitions may justifiably be truncated by the use of a related word within the definition in order to save precious space for more entries. For example, *grievance committee* can be defined as "a committee formed by a labor union or by employer and employees jointly to discuss and where possible to eliminate grievances" because the second sense of *grievance* is "a cause of distress (as an unsatisfactory working condition) felt to afford reason for complaint or resistance," and so the definition of *grievance committee* need not give that information a second time.

It is also possible to add a synonymous cross-reference to an analytical definition and thereby incorporate at little cost of space a second version of the meaning that looks at it from a slightly different aspect. It is possible, as in the definition of *grievance* just cited, to add a parenthetical element that specifies one or several of the typical referents of the word or that indicates the sole or a typical object of a transitive verb. One may begin an adjective definition with one of a wide variety of formulas but others are forbidden. It is clear already that definers' instructions are elaborately detailed, and it would be tedious to rehearse them here. Their purpose is to assist in developing the definer's native talent so that the definitions that he or she writes are consistently good ones. What is a good definition? Many qualities could be mentioned, and probably different definers would rank the relative importance of those on any list differently; but all definers want a sufficient range and number of their definitions to be objective in reflecting what the word means as it is actually used rather than what the definer or someone else thinks it ought to mean, and they want their definitions to be accurate, clear, informative, and concise. In short, they want their definitions to have the qualities that users have in mind when they call a dictionary they admire "authoritative."

In the course of your defining, you would have an opportunity fairly often to make another kind of decision: whether to include or omit a new candidate for main entry. Let us take as an example the word *gentrification,* which is one of many entries new to this edition of the Collegiate Dictionary. If you had been the definer who handled that word, you would have been faced with a group of 26 citations to read covering a span of five years and including extracts from such publications as *The New York Times, Scientific American, Playboy, American Demographics, The Boston Globe, Smithsonian, Money, The Christian Science Monitor, Saturday Review, The Wall Street Journal,* and *Harper's*. In reading the citations you would notice that while they varied in many details of context, they seemed (with only a single exception) to embody one meaning. There was a significant variable, however; in some citations the immigration was taking place in run-down areas and in others the process of restoring the neighborhood was already well advanced. You might then have produced the following definition incorporating that variation: "the immigration of middle-class people into a deteriorating or recently renewed city area."

The number and time span of the citations and the variety of the sources would already have told you that this was a very strong, and perhaps even an essential, candidate for entry in the new edition. There is no magic number of citations that guarantees entry and no particular span of years that must be reached. To a great extent the judgment made here must rest on your insight and experience as a definer who has seen the citational backing for many words, who has most likely defined words for other Merriam-Webster dictionaries in the past, and who thus has some sense of the relative importance and degree of establishment of new entries within the lexicon and of their likely staying power.

You would have noticed that in addition to the evidence

for *gentrification* there were also eight citations for a verb *gentrify,* and, seeing both that it was less important than the noun (though also well backed by citations) and that its meaning was easy to infer from the meaning of the noun, you would have added it to your new main entry as an undefined run-on.

To take one further example of a somewhat different kind, if you had been the life-sciences definer responsible for handling the term *Reye's syndrome,* you would have read 13 citations. Many of these would have been from sources such as *The Journal of the American Medical Association, Biological Abstracts, Science,* and *Emergency Medicine* likely to be seen chiefly by people with specialized interests; but you would also have seen examples from *Newsweek, Parade, The New York Times,* and an encyclopedia yearbook. In other words, the term is likely to be encountered by people with general interests and, given its nature, will probably be looked up in a dictionary fairly often. Such considerations would have led you to propose entry for the term and with a much higher priority than if the citational backing had been nearly all technical. You would also have noted several citations for the spelling *Reye syndrome* and would have appropriately added that as a secondary variant.

It is worth noting briefly that in the course of your work as a definer you would have been concerned with what the citations reveal about a word in addition to its meaning. The definer is initially responsible for most of the framework of the entry including not only spelling variants and run-ons but also inflected forms, usage notes, verbal illustrations and illustrative quotations, and temporal, regional, stylistic, and subject labels.

The other important part of the entries in this dictionary that is concerned with English semantics is the synonym paragraph. These paragraphs are not written by each individual definer as particular entries are encountered but are rather the special assignment of one, or sometimes several, editors who decide which words will be included in a single paragraph and at which entry the paragraph will be placed. The synonym editor has a number of responsibilities in addition to the actual writing or revising of the synonym paragraph. Each entry for a term discussed in a paragraph must be checked to ensure that the definition of a given sense is fully consonant with its treatment in the paragraph, and the editor has the authority to make small adjustments of definitions so that no discrepancies which might puzzle a user remain.

Like the definer, this editor must read citations very carefully to see that the opening statement of the core meaning shared by the synonyms includes neither too much nor too little, that each discrimination of one word from the others is accurate, and that where space permits typical examples may be selected to include as illustrative quotations or as verbal illustrations. It is particularly in these paragraphs that the dictionary user comes into contact with the systematic side of English semantics because here the concern is with the relationship of meanings instead of the meanings themselves as discrete entities. For example, the synonym paragraph at *splendid* in this dictionary states that *splendid, resplendent, gorgeous, glorious, sublime,* and *superb* mean "extraordinarily or transcendently impressive." This statement of meaning is at once too broad and too narrow to be a good definition for any of the words; it trims away the particular elements of meaning that make each word distinctive (the most important of which are stated in the following discussion). It does, however, give us an accurate notion of the point at which these words come into a precise semantic relationship with each other.

Grammar and Usage in the Dictionary

The last of the four systems of English whose reflection we may see, at least briefly and occasionally, in the dictionary is the grammatical system. As we saw earlier, this system involves chiefly the relationship between words as they form more complex units rather than individual words themselves. A descriptive grammar of English is a very different kind of book from a dictionary. Nevertheless, virtually every entry in this dictionary contains at least one piece of information about its grammatical nature and the kinds of relationships it can enter into, namely, the functional label which typically indicates the part of speech of the entry or, in the case of terminal word elements, the part of speech of the words that they form. If an entry is labeled *adv,* we know that it can describe the action of a verb but cannot itself be the main verb of a sentence, while an entry labeled *n* cannot link the subject of a sentence with a predicate adjective but can be the subject. Other parts of the entry also give us information that is grammatical in nature. One sort of information is offered by the boldface inflected forms that are shown at every entry for which they are irregular exceptions to the ordinary patterns of English inflection or may present some other sort of problem to the dictionary user. Another is offered by the undefined run-on entries. They illustrate the complex patterns by which one word or a number of words can be derived from a single base by means of affixation or functional shift. Certain kinds of usage notes following or standing in place of definitions also present grammatical information. Typical of the former kind of usage note is the one given at sense 2b of *boy,* "often used interjectionally," and the one given at sense 2b of the verb *conk,* "usu. used with *off* or *out.*" Typical of the latter are the several usage notes at the entry for the preposition *for,* "used as a function word to indicate duration of time or extent of space" at sense 9, for example.

Usage is a concept that embraces many aspects of and attitudes toward language. Grammar is certainly only a small part of what goes to make up usage, though some people use one term for the other, as when they label what is really a controversial point of usage a grammatical error. Usage guidance is offered in this dictionary in many ways; it would be little exaggeration to say that any information a user seeks and finds in this book can offer some guidance as to usage. But usage information is chiefly conveyed through three devices: usage notes; temporal, regional, and stylistic labels; and usage paragraphs. The first two are developed by definers from their examination of citations, including sometimes (and particularly in the case of the labels) citations found in historical, dialect, and slang dictionaries as well as those in Merriam-Webster's citation file. The usage paragraphs like the synonym paragraphs are the result of a special project chiefly in the hands of two editors with assistance from several others. The editors attempted to select particular problems of confused or disputed usage that would be of broad general interest and could be treated at individual entries in the dictionary. The great majority of them involve words that have traditionally been points of dispute (a few of these are now probably more traditional than truly the subjects of heated dispute), but some are relatively new items for this kind of consideration. Several paragraphs deal with pronunciation, a subject rarely treated in books about usage.

The editors who wrote the paragraphs used several kinds of material: books describing one or another aspect of the history of usage as a problem in English; books and articles ruling on particular points of usage, whether the product of one person or a group; historical and other dictionaries, and above all citations of usage itself from our file. In digesting this mass of information and presenting it in a very brief compass, the editors have typically combined information on the history of the controversy, the current state of expressed opinion, illustrations of both old and modern use (often quoted), and practical advice.

It has been close to 250 years since Dr. Johnson published his great dictionary and over 150 years since Noah Webster's *American Dictionary of the English Language* appeared.

Even the more modest Collegiate series will be approaching its hundredth birthday before many years have passed. It seems clear that the long tradition of English dictionaries is not likely to wither and die. Indeed, dictionaries are likely to become, if anything, even more important to the general public in the future, at least as long as the vocabulary of English continues the rapid growth which began earlier in this century and which seems now to intensify year by year. As long as they are edited with a proper regard for the right of the dictionary user to have accurate information about what English words actually mean and how they are actually used, those dictionaries will continue to serve a useful purpose and to be needed. Though they are incomplete as descriptions of the systems of English and are edited by fallible humans whose best intentions sometimes fall short of the mark, such dictionaries will continue to form, as the best dictionaries have always done, a helpful bridge between what we know about language and how we use it. Movement across such a bridge is, of course, in both directions: our use of language furnishes the basis for our knowledge of it, but our knowledge of it also helps us to use it more effectively.

Guide to Pronunciation

The English language has, of course, both a written form and a spoken form. Each of these is in a state of continual and inexorable change. The written language, however, is more stable than the spoken. With the rapid spread of printing, particularly from the 16th to the 18th centuries, printers and scholars gradually adopted an increasingly fixed set of spelling conventions. Most of these are adhered to today, though there is still some orthographic variation. Because the spoken language is more susceptible to change, we find ourselves now with spellings that often reveal more about the history of English than about current pronunciation. It has become necessary, therefore, for English dictionaries to indicate pronunciation in order to provide an adequate picture of the English vocabulary.

Just as present-day English is not static, it is also not completely uniform. The pronunciation, vocabulary, and grammar of people living in different areas differ in varying degrees. Similarly, people who have different levels of education, who hold different sorts of jobs, or who, for one reason or another, move only among certain segments of society may have distinct forms of speech. In fact, each person's speech is distinguishable in some ways from that of everyone else; thus, we are able to identify people by the sound of their voices. However, largely because speech is primarily a form of communication, certain patterns in pronunciation, vocabulary, and usage can be discerned among the members of regional or social groups that regularly communicate with one another. The more isolated a particular group is from other speakers of the same language, the greater the differences between the speech of that group and the speech of others will tend to become. As such isolation continues, these differences increase, eventually resulting in distinct dialects. Given a long enough time and sufficiently limited intercommunication, the speech of a particular group may become so incomprehensible to others that it can be classified as a separate language. The evolution of Latin into French, Italian, Portuguese, Rumanian, and Spanish is an example of this process.

As geographical and social barriers are overcome, a more widespread mutual comprehensibility becomes possible. Especially as a result of the technological developments in transportation and communication during the past century, many millions of people are crossing or communicating across dialect boundaries. We can therefore be assured that slowly and, for the most part, imperceptibly these boundaries will continue to shift; some may disappear and new ones may develop.

During this century researchers into differences in pronunciation, vocabulary, and grammar have been able to discern patterns that define three major geographical dialect areas in the U.S.—Northern, Southern, and Midland. Each of these areas also has recognizable subdivisions. These dialectal differences began with early settlers from Britain who brought their various dialects to different areas along the eastern coast. With the subsequent isolation from Britain the speech of the settlers in North America gradually diverged from that of the parts of Britain from which they came. When the population expanded and moved westward, the various dialects were carried westward in an increasingly complex pattern as migration paths crossed and as new lines of communication opened up. However, the pronunciation of English throughout the U.S. is still based on the three major dialects, which are most clearly defined in the eastern states. In Canada, which has had closer contact with and more recent settlement from Britain, greater similarity to British speech can be heard with a mixture of some Northern U.S. features. There are, of course, other aspects of pronunciation, grammar, and vocabulary that arose in or are confined to Canada itself.

There are several broad types or classes of pronunciation variation and these are covered in various ways in a general dictionary. In each dialect area the significant individual sounds (or *phonemes*) of the language may be articulated differently from those in other areas. Many of the features that we perceive as differences in accent fall into this class. In Southern speech, for example, the vowel of *tip* or *bit* is pronounced differently from the same vowel in Northern speech. A Southern speaker seeing the symbol \i\ in the pronunciation respelling of a word in this dictionary can turn to the chart of pronunciation symbols and find there the common words *tip, active,* and *banish* illustrating the pronunciation of that vowel. This speaker knows the sound native to his or her own dialect and can use it in the pronunciation of the word in question. A Northern or Midland speaker will do the same, reproducing the natural and appropriate variety of the sound. It is not necessary, therefore, that a general dictionary indicate these variations for every word. In effect, they are covered implicitly by the set of pronunciation symbols used in the book.

Some dialectal differences are the result not simply of variation in the sounds themselves but in the choice of sounds used. This type of variation is regularly shown in this dictionary. Research has revealed, for example, that south of a line running irregularly westward through Maryland, northern Virginia, and southern West Virginia the word *creek* is usually pronounced \'krēk\. North of this line the more frequent pronunciation is \'krik\, though the spelling pronunciation \'krēk\ is often heard as well. Another such line could be drawn just north of New York City, south along the western boundary of New Jersey, and northwestward through Pennsylvania. To the north of this line the great majority of people pronounce *greasy* as \'grē-sē\, while to the south most people say \'grē-zē\. Comparison of a large number of such items makes the boundaries of dialect areas apparent. For those cases in which the distribution of variants is restricted to a fairly simple pattern within one or two dialect areas, it is possible to label them appropriately, as the entries for *great* and *help* where a \\ *Southern* \\ label appears and for *figure* where a \\ *Brit* \\ label indicates a variant heard most frequently in British speech.

A third type of variation that figures widely in this dictionary may be called unpredictable variation. For many words the distribution of variants is either so widespread (if not random) or so complex in relation to the defined dialect areas that it is impossible to predict accurately which variant or variants a speaker from a particular area might use. This very common variation is represented in the pronunciation of such words as *economic, ration, envelope,* and *temperature,* to name only four out of thousands. Often when a foreign word is borrowed into English, a number of variants will coexist as people attempt either to reproduce its foreign pronunciation or perhaps to pronounce it according to the spelling, as if it were English in origin. Thus we hear a number of pronunciation variants for such well-established words as *junta* and *lingerie.*

A major problem that arises in editing a dictionary is how to determine the incidence and extent of pronunciation variants. Since the middle of the 1930's the Merriam-Webster pronunciation editors have been doing their best to solve this problem by carrying out an ongoing program of listening to, recording, and transcribing the pronunciation of educated native speakers of English, especially in the United States, Britain, and Canada. The result of this program is a unique and extensive file of transcriptions that provides the data on which decisions regarding pronunciation are based.

The Merriam-Webster pronunciation file consists primarily of a collection of 3×5 slips of paper (*citations*), each of which contains a transcription of the pronunciation of a word actually used by someone. Along with the transcription are included the name of the speaker, additional identifying information, and the date. These citations are collected by listening to radio, television, and live speech, and in these days of network and satellite broadcasting it is possible to hear a wide range of speakers from all over the English-speaking world. It is generally inadvisable, however, to transcribe the pronunciation of actors in performance, since they may not be using their natural speech. The best source of pronunciation is a native speaker of English who can be identified by name and whose geographical and educational background is known. When most people speak, whether privately or publicly, they concentrate more on the content of what they are saying than on the pronunciation of each word. This is ideal for the linguist (or pronunciation editor) who is interested in learning how people speak when communicating with others.

When an entry in a Merriam-Webster dictionary is written or revised, the pronunciation citations for that word are reviewed to determine whether it has any pronunciation variants that are sufficiently widespread to warrant inclusion. One fact that the evidence in our pronunciation file makes apparent, and that is reflected in our dictionaries, is that there is a considerable amount of perfectly acceptable pronunciation variation in the language. Unless restricted by a regional or other usage label, all of the variants shown in this book fall within the range of acceptable variation.

No system of indicating pronunciation is self-explanatory. The following discussion sets out the signification and use of the pronunciation symbols and devices in this book, with special attention to those areas where experience has shown that dictionary users may have questions. More detailed information can be found in the Guide to Pronunciation in Webster's Third New International Dictionary. The order of symbols discussed below is the same as the order on the page of Pronunciation Symbols,

with the exception that the symbols which are not letter characters are here listed first.

\\ \\ All pronunciation information is printed between reversed virgules. Pronunciation symbols are printed in roman type and all other information, such as labels and notes, is printed in italics.

\\ **ˈ** \\ A high-set stress mark precedes a syllable with primary (strongest) stress; a low-set mark precedes a syllable with secondary (medium) stress; a third level of weak stress requires no mark at all: \\ ˈpen-mən-ˌship \\.

Since the nineteenth century the International Phonetics Association has recommended that stress marks precede the stressed syllable, and linguists worldwide have adopted this practice on the basic principle that before a syllable can be uttered the speaker must know what degree of stress to give it. In accordance with the practice of French phoneticians, no stress marks are shown in the transcription of words borrowed from French whose pronunciations have not been anglicized, as at *ancien régime* and *émeute.*

\\ **-** \\ Hyphens are used to separate syllables in pronunciation transcriptions. In actual speech, of course, there is no pause between the syllables of a word. The placement of these hyphens is based on phonetic principles and may not match the end-of-line divisions indicated by centered dots in boldface entry words.

\\ **( )** \\ Parentheses are used in pronunciations to indicate that whatever is symbolized between them is present in some utterances but not in others; thus *factory* \\ ˈfak-t(ə-)rē \\ is pronounced both \\ ˈfak-tə-rē \\ and \\ ˈfak-trē \\, *industry* \\ ˈin-(ˌ)dəs-trē \\ is pronounced both \\ ˈin-dəs-trē \\ and \\ ˈin-ˌdəs-trē \\. In some phonetic environments, as in *fence* \\ ˈfen(t)s \\ and *more* \\ ˈmō(ə)r, ˈmȯ(ə)r \\, it may be difficult to determine whether the sound shown in parentheses is or is not present in a given utterance; even the usage of a single speaker may vary considerably.

\\ **,** **;** \\ Variant pronunciations are separated by commas; groups of variants are separated by semicolons. The order of variants does not mean that the first is in any way preferable to or more acceptable than the others. All of the variants in this book, except those restricted by a regional or usage label, are widely used in acceptable educated speech. If evidence reveals that a particular variant is used more frequently than another, the former will be given first. This should not, however, prejudice anyone against the second or subsequent variants. In many cases the numerical distribution of variants is equal but one of them, of course, must be printed first.

\\ **÷** \\ The obelus, or division sign, is placed before a pronunciation variant that occurs in educated speech but that is considered by some to be questionable or unacceptable. This symbol is used sparingly and primarily for variants that have been objected to over a period of time in print by commentators on usage, in schools by teachers, or in correspondence that has come to the Merriam-Webster editorial department. In most cases the objection is based on orthographic or etymological arguments. For instance, the second variant of *cupola* \\ ˈkyü-pə-lə, ÷-ˌlō \\, though used frequently in speech, is objected to because *a* is very rarely pronounced \\ ō \\ in English. The pronunciations \\ ˈfeb-yə-ˌwer-ē \\ and \\ ˈfeb-ə-ˌwer-ē \\ (indicated simultaneously by the use of parentheses) are similarly marked at the entry for *February*

\÷'feb-(y)ə-,wer-ē, 'feb-rə-\, even though they are the most frequently heard pronunciations, because some people insist that both *r*'s should be pronounced. The obelus applies only to that portion of the transcription which it immediately precedes and not to any other variants following.

\ə\ in unstressed syllables as in banana, collide, abut. This neutral vowel may be represented orthographically by any of the letters *a, e, i, o, u, y,* and by many combinations of letters. Unstressed \ə\ often intrudes between a stressed vowel and a following \l\ or \r\ though it is not represented in the spelling, as in *eel* \'ē(ə)l\, *wire* \'wī(ə)r\, *corn* \'kȯ(ə)rn\, *sour* \'saủ(ə)r\.

\'ə, ˌə\ in stressed syllables as in humdrum, abut.

\ᵊ\ immediately preceding \l\, \n\, \m\, \ŋ\, as in battle, cotton, and one pronunciation of open\'ōp-ᵊm\ and of and \ᵊŋ\ as in one pronunciation of the phrase *lock and key* \ˌläk-ᵊŋ-'kē\. The symbol \ᵊ\ preceding these consonants does not itself represent a sound. It signifies instead that the following consonant is syllabic; that is, the consonant itself forms the nucleus of a syllable that does not contain a vowel.

In the pronunciation of some French or French-derived words \ᵊ\ is placed immediately after \l\, \m\, \r\ to indicate one nonsyllabic pronunciation of these consonants, as in the French words table "table," prisme "prism," and titre "title," each of which in isolation and in some contexts is a one-syllable word.

\ər\ as in further, merger, bird. (See the section on \r\.) The anglicized pronunciation of the vowel \œ\ is represented in this book as \ə(r)\. (See the section on \œ\.)

\'ər-, 'ə-r\ as in two different pronunciations of *hurry*. Most U.S. speakers pronounce \'hər-ē\ with the \ər\ representing the same sounds as in *bird* \'bərd\. Usually in metropolitan New York and southern England and frequently in New England and the southeastern U.S. the vowel is much the same as the vowel of *hum* followed by a syllable-initial variety of \r\. This pronunciation of *hurry* is represented as \'hə-rē\ in this book. Both types of pronunciation are shown for words composed of a single meaningful unit (or *morpheme*) as in *current, hurry,* and *worry.* In words such as *furry, stirring,* and *purring* in which a vowel or vowel-initial suffix is added to a word ending in *r* or *rr* (as *fur, stir,* and *purr*), the second type of pronunciation outlined above is heard only occasionally and is not shown in this dictionary.

\a\ as in mat, map, mad, gag, snap, patch. Some variation in this vowel is occasioned by the consonant that follows it; thus, for some speakers *map, mad,* and *gag* have noticeably different vowel sounds. There is a very small number of words otherwise identical in pronunciation that these speakers may distinguish solely by variation of this vowel, as in the two words *can* (put into cans; be able) in the sentence "Let's can what we can." However, this distinction is sufficiently infrequent that the traditional practice of using a single symbol is followed in this book.

\ā\ as in day, fade, date, aorta, drape, cape. In most English speech this is actually a diph-

thong. In lowland South Carolina, in coastal Georgia and Florida, and occasionally elsewhere \ā\ is pronounced as a monophthong. As a diphthong \ā\ has a first element \e\ or monophthongal \ā\ and a second element \i\.

\ä\ as in bother, cot, and, with most American speakers, father, cart. The symbol \ä\ represents the vowel of *cot, cod,* and the stressed vowel of *collar* in the speech of those who pronounce this vowel differently from the vowel in *caught, cawed,* and *caller,* represented by \ȯ\. In U.S. speech \ä\ is pronounced with little or no rounding of the lips, and it is fairly long in duration, especially before voiced consonants. In southern England \ä\ is usually accompanied by some lip rounding and is relatively short in duration. The vowel \ȯ\ generally has appreciable lip rounding. Some U.S. speakers (a perhaps growing minority) do not distinguish between *cot—caught, cod—cawed,* and *collar—caller,* usually because they lack or have less lip rounding in the words transcribed with \ȯ\. Though the symbols \ä\ and \ȯ\ are used throughout this book to distinguish the members of the above pairs and similar words, the speakers who rhyme these pairs will automatically reproduce a sound that is consistent with their own speech.

In words such as *card* and *cart* most U.S. speakers have a sequence of sounds that we transcribe as \är\. Most speakers who do not pronounce \r\ before another consonant or a pause, however, do not rhyme *card* with either *cod* or *cawed* and do not rhyme *cart* with either *cot* or *caught.* The pronunciation of *card* and *cart* by such speakers, although not shown in this dictionary, would be transcribed as \'kȧd\ and \'kȧt\. Speakers of r-dropping dialects will automatically substitute \ȧ\ for the transcribed \är\. (See the sections on \ȧ\ and \r\.)

\ȧ\ as in father as pronounced by those who do not rhyme it with *bother.* The pronunciation of this vowel varies regionally. In eastern New England and southern England it is generally pronounced farther forward in the mouth than \ä\ but not as far forward as \a\. In New York City and the southeastern U.S. it may have much the same quality as \ä\ but somewhat greater duration.

In areas in which \r\ is not pronounced before another consonant or a pause, \ȧ\ occurs for the sequence transcribed in this book as \är\. (See the sections on \ä\ and \r\.) In these areas \ȧ\ also occurs with varying frequency in a small group of words in which *a* in the spelling is followed by a consonant letter other than *r* and is not preceded by *w* or *wh,* as in *father, calm, palm,* and *tomato* but not in *watch, what,* or *swap* (though \ȧ\ does sometimes occur in *waft*). Especially in southern England and, less consistently, in eastern New England \ȧ\ occurs in certain words in which \a\ is the usual American vowel and in most of which the vowel is followed by \f\, \th\, \s\, or by \n\ and another consonant. The following words and word elements are among the most susceptible to the \ȧ\ pronunciation. Where *a* appears in the spelling more than once, the vowel that may be pronounced \ȧ\ is marked with a dot.

advȧnce, advȧntage, aft, after, aghȧst, answer, ask, aunt, avalȧnche, bask, basket, bath, behalf, blanch, blast, branch, brass, calf, calve, can't, cask, casket, cast, caste, caster, castle, castor, chaff, chance, chancel, chancellor, chancery, chandler, chant, clasp, class, command, dance, demand, fancy, fast, fasten, flabbergȧst, flask, gasp, ghastly, giraffe, glance, glass, graft, graph, -graph, grass, grasp, half, halve, lance, last, lath, laugh, mask, mast, master, nasty, pass, past, pastor, path, plant, plaster, prance, raft, rafter, rȧscal, rasp, raspberry, re-

mand, repast, reprimand, salve (n), sample, sampler, shaft, shan't, slander, slant, staff, stanchion, supplant, task, trance, trans-, vántage, vast

The pronunciation with \å\ is to be understood as a variant for all of the words discussed in this paragraph, though \å\ is shown only for those few in which it occurs with especially high frequency.

The symbol \å\ is also used in the transcription of some foreign-derived words and names. This vowel, as in French *patte* "paw" and *chat* "cat," is intermediate between \a\ and \ä\ and is similar in quality to the \å\ heard in eastern New England.

\au̇** as in **now, **loud**, **out**. The initial element of this diphthong may vary from \a\ to \å\ or \ä\, the first being more common in Southern and south Midland speech than elsewhere. In coastal areas of the southern U.S. and in parts of Canada this diphthong is often realized as \əu̇\ when immediately preceding a voiceless consonant, as in the noun *house* and in *out*.

\b** as in **baby, **rib**.

\ch** as in **chin, **nature** \'nā-chər\. Actually, this sound is \t\ + \sh\. The distinction between the phrases *why choose* and *white shoes* is maintained by a difference in the juncture of the \t\ and the \sh\ in each case and the consequent use of different varieties (or *allophones*) of \t\.

\d** as in **did, **adder**.

\e** as in **bet, **bed**, **peck**.

\'ē,ˌē** in stressed syllables as in **beat, **nosebleed**, **evenly**, **easy**.

\ē** in unstressed syllables, as in **easy, **mealy**. Though the fact is not shown in this book, some dialects such as southern British and southern U.S. often, if not usually, pronounce \i\ instead of unstressed \ē\.

\f** as in **fifty, **cuff**.

\g** as in **go, **big**, **gift**.

\h** as in **hat, **ahead**.

\hw** as in **whale as pronounced by those who do not have the same pronunciation for both *whale* and *wail*. Most U.S. speakers distinguish these two words as \'hwā(ə)l\ and \'wā(ə)l\ respectively, though frequently in the U.S. and usually in southern England \'wā(ə)l\ is used for both. Some linguists consider \hw\ to be a single sound, a voiceless \w\.

\i** as in **tip, **banish**, **active**.

\ī** as in **site, **side**, **buy**, **tripe**. Actually, this sound is a diphthong, usually composed of \ä\ + \i\ or \å\ + \i\. In Southern speech, especially before a

pause or voiced consonant, as in *shy* and *five*, the second element \i\ may not be pronounced. Chiefly in eastern Virginia, coastal South Carolina, and parts of Canada the diphthong is approximately \ə\ + \i\ before voiceless consonants, as in *nice* and *write*.

\j** as in **job, **gem**, **edge**, **join**, **judge**. Actually, this sound is \d\ + \zh\. Assuming the anglicization of *Jeanne d'Arc* as \zhän-'därk\, the distinction between the sentences *They betray John Dark* and *They betrayed Jeanne d'Arc* is maintained by a difference in the juncture of the \d\ and the \zh\ in each case and the consequent use of different varieties (or *allophones*) of \d\.

\k** as in **kin, **cook**, **ache**.

\k** as in German ich** "I," Bu**ch** "book," and one pronunciation of English lo**ch**. Actually, there are two distinct sounds in German; the \k̲\ in *ich* is pronounced toward the front of the mouth and the \k̲\ in *Buch* is pronounced toward the back. In English, however, no two words otherwise identical are distinguished by these two varieties of \k̲\, and therefore only a single symbol is necessary. In English speech the front variety of \k̲\ is produced automatically to accompany a front vowel, such as \e\ or \i\, and the back variety to accompany a back vowel, such as \ä\ or \ü\.

\l** as in **lily, **pool**. In words such as *battle* and *fiddle* the \l\ is a syllabic consonant. (See the section on \ə\ above.)

\m** as in **murmur, **dim**, **nymph**. In pronunciation variants of some words, such as *open* and *happen*, \m\ is a syllabic consonant. (See the section on \ə\ above.)

\n** as in **no, **own**. In words such as *cotton* and *sudden*, the \n\ is a syllabic consonant. (See the section on \ə\ above.)

\ⁿ indicates that a preceding vowel or diphthong is pronounced with the nasal passages open, as in French *un bon vin blanc* \œn-bōⁿ-vaⁿ-bläⁿ\ "a good white wine."

\ŋ** as in **sing \'siŋ\, **singer** \'siŋ-ər\, **finger** \'fiŋ-gər\, **ink** \'iŋk\. In some contexts \ŋ\ may be a syllabic consonant. (See the section on \ə\ above.)

\ō** as in **bone, **know**, **beau**. Especially in positions of emphasis, such as when it is word final or when as primary stress, \ō\ tends to become diphthongal, moving from \ō\ toward a second element \u̇\. In southern England and in some U.S. speech, particularly in the Philadelphia area and in the Pennsylvania-Ohio-West Virginia border area, the first element is often approximately \ə\. In coastal South Carolina, Georgia, and Florida stressed \ō\ is often monophthongal when final, but when a consonant follows it is often a diphthong moving from \ō\ to \ə\. In this book the symbol \ō\ represents all of the above variants.

\ȯ** as in **saw, **all**, **gnaw**, **caught**. (See the section on \ä\.)

\œ** as in French **boeuf "beef," German H**ö**lle "hell." This vowel, which occurs only in foreign-derived terms and names, can be approximated by attempting to pronounce the vowel \e\ with the lips moderately rounded as for the vowel \u̇\. This vowel is often anglicized as the \ər\ of *bird* by those who do not "drop their r's" or as the corresponding vowel of *bird* used by those who do (see the section on \r\). Where this anglicization is shown, it is represented as \ə(r)\.

\œ̄\ as in French *feu* "fire," German *Höhle* "hole." This vowel, which occurs primarily in foreign=derived terms and names, can be approximated by attempting to pronounce a monophthongal vowel \ā\ with the lips fully rounded as for the vowel \ü\. This vowel also occurs in Scots and thus is used in the pronunciation of *guidwillie*, mainly restricted to Scotland.

\ȯi\ as in *coin*, *destroy*. In some Southern speech, especially before a consonant in the same word, the second element may disappear or be replaced by \ə\. Some utterances of *drawing* and *sawing* have a sequence of vowel sounds identical to that in *coin*, but because *drawing* and *sawing* are analyzed by many as two-syllable words they are transcribed with a parenthesized hyphen: \ˈdrȯ(-)iŋ\, \ˈsȯ(-)iŋ\.

\p\ as in *pepper*, *lip*.

\r\ as in *red*, *rarity*, *car*, *beard*. In some dialects, especially those of the southeastern U.S., eastern New England, New York City, and southern England, \r\ is not pronounced when another consonant or a pause follows immediately. This is often, if somewhat misleadingly, referred to as r-dropping. In these dialects *r* is pronounced as a nonsyllabic \ə\ when it occurs in these positions or there may be no sound corresponding to the *r*; thus *beard*, *corn*, and *assured* may be pronounced as \ˈbiəd\, \ˈkȯən\, and \ə-ˈshu̇əd\ or, usually with some lengthening of the vowel sound, as \ˈbid\, \ˈkȯn\, and \ə-ˈshu̇d\. In *car*, *card*, and *cart* those who do not pronounce \r\ generally have a vowel which we would transcribe as \ä\, usually pronounced with some lengthening and without a following \ə\. (See the sections on \ä\ and \a̤\.) The stressed vowel of *bird* and *hurt* in r-dropping speech is similar to the vowel used by r-keepers in the same words but without the simultaneous raising of the center and/or tip of the tongue. In the U.S. most speakers of r-dropping dialects will pronounce \r\ before consonants in some words or in some contexts. Because it is determined by the phonetic context, r-dropping is not explicitly represented in this dictionary; speakers of r-dropping dialects will automatically substitute the sounds appropriate to their own speech.

\s\ as in *source*, *less*.

\sh\ as in *shy*, *mission*, *machine*, *special*. Actually this is a single sound, not two. When the two sounds \s\ and \h\ occur in sequence, they are separated by a hyphen in this book, as in *grasshopper* \ˈgras-ˌhäp-ər\.

\t\ as in *tie*, *attack*, *late*, *later*, *latter*. In some contexts, as when a stressed or unstressed vowel precedes and an unstressed vowel or \ᵊl\ follows, the sound represented by *t* or *tt* is pronounced in much American speech the same as the sound represented by *d* or *dd* in similar contexts. Thus, the pairs *ladder* and *latter*, *leader* and *liter*, *parody* and *parity* are often homophones. In such instances this dictionary shows \d\ at the end of a syllable for those words spelled with *d* or *dd* (\ˈlad-ər\, \ˈlēd-ər\, \ˈpar-əd-ē\) and \t\ at the end

of a syllable for those with *t* or *tt* (\ˈlat-ər\, \ˈlēt-ər\, \ˈpar-ət-ē\).

\th\ as in *thin*, *ether*. Actually, this is a single sound, not two. When the two sounds \t\ and \h\ occur in sequence they are separated by a hyphen in this book, as in *knighthood* \ˈnīt-ˌhu̇d\.

\th\ as in *then*, *either*, *this*. Actually, this is a single sound, not two. The basic difference between \th\ and \th\ is that the former is pronounced without and the latter with vibration of the vocal cords.

\ü\ as in *rule*, *youth*, *union* \ˈyün-yən\, *few* \ˈfyü\.

\u̇\ as in *pull*, *wood*, *book*, *curable* \ˈkyu̇r-ə-bəl\, *fury* \ˈfyu̇(ə)r-ē\.

\ue\ as in German *füllen* "to fill," *hübsch* "handsome." This vowel, which occurs only in foreign-derived terms and names, can be approximated by attempting to pronounce the vowel \i\ with the lips moderately rounded as for the vowel \u̇\.

\ue̅\ as in French *rue* "street," German *fühlen* "to feel." This vowel, which occurs only in foreign=derived terms and names, can be approximated by attempting to pronounce the vowel \ē\ with the lips fully rounded as for the vowel \ü\.

\v\ as in *vivid*, *invite*.

\w\ as in *we*, *away*. In some words having final \(ˌ)ō\, as *follow*, \(ˌ)yü\, as *value*, or \(ˌ)ü\, as *statue*, an unstressed variant \ə\ or \yə\ may occur, especially before a consonant or a pause, as in \ˈfäl-əd\ or \ˈval-yəd\, and a variant \ə-w\ or \yə-w\ occurs before vowels, as in \ˈfäl-ə-wiŋ\ or \ˈval-yə-wiŋ\. These variants are transcribed \ə(-w)\ or \yə(-w)\ at the entry word.

\y\ as in *yard*, *young*, *cue* \ˈkyü\, *curable* \ˈkyu̇r-ə-bəl\, *few* \ˈfyü\, *fury* \ˈfyu̇(ə)r-ē\, *union* \ˈyün-yən\. The sequences \lyü\, \syü\, and \zyü\ in the same syllable, as in *lewd*, *suit*, and *presume*, are common in southern British speech but are rare in American speech and only \lü\, \sü\, and \zü\ are shown in this dictionary.

In English \y\ does not occur at the end of a syllable after a vowel. In a few words of French origin whose pronunciation has not been anglicized, a postvocalic \y\ is transcribed, as in *mille-feuille* \mēl-fœy\ and in *rouille* \ˈrü-ē, F rüy\. The sound represented is the consonantal \y\ of *yard*.

\ʸ\ indicates that during the articulation of the preceding consonant the tongue has substantially the position it has for the articulation of the \y\ of *yard*, as in French *digne* \dēnʸ\ "worthy." Thus \ʸ\ does not itself represent a sound but rather modifies the preceding symbol.

\z\ as in *zone*, *raise*.

\zh\ as in *vision*, *azure* \ˈazh-ər\. Actually, this is a single sound, not two. When the two sounds \z\ and \h\ occur in sequence, they are separated by a hyphen in this book, as in *hogshead* \ˈhȯgz-ˌhed, ˈhägz-\.

English Spelling and Sound Correspondences

The following lists are representative of the more common ways (and some less common ways) of spelling each sound. They are by no means exhaustive, but they should enable the user who is uncertain of the spelling to find most words in this book. In actual practice, knowing the first five letters of almost any word will get the user to within a few inches of the right place in even the largest unabridged dictionaries.

In these lists, ways of spelling each sound are indicated by boldface letters. Some words may be pronounced in more than one way; any such words on these lists are printed in italics if the relevant portion of the spelling is affected. The pronunciation transcription at the entry for the word will show the variation. If there is no letter in a word representative of a sound heard in that word, the word is given following a dash at the end of the appropriate section, with the pronunciation given in full as in the last two entries at \ə\:

— chasm \'kaz-əm\
— McCoy \mə-'kòi\

If it is difficult to tell which letter or letters stand for a particular sound in a word, that word appears at the end of the appropriate section, with the pronunciation given in full as in the last entry at \ch\:

nature \'nā-chər\

Vowels and Diphthongs

\ə\	a	abut
	e	silent
	i	maritime
	o	connect
	u	circus
	y	physician
	ah	verandah
	ai	*captain*
	ea	ocean
	ei	mullein
	eo	luncheon
	ia	collegiate
	io	fashion
	oa	*waistcoat*
	oe	Phoenician
	oi	porpoise
	ou	famous
	ow	*pillowcase*
	ue	guerrilla
	eau	bureaucrat
	—	chasm \'kaz-əm\
	—	McCoy \mə-'kòi\

\'ə, ˌə\	a	was
	o	above
	u	humdrum
	y	*Cymric*
	oe	does
	oo	flood
	ou	rough

\ər\	ar	liar
	er	batter
	ir	elixir
	or	honor
	re	ogre
	ur	injurer
	yr	martyr
	eur	*chauffeur*
	our	glamour

| \'ər\ | er | fern, *were* |

	ir	bird
	or	world
	ur	fur
	yr	myrtle
	ear	earth
	err	*err*
	eur	*chauffeur*
	irr	*squirrel*
	our	journal
	urr	hurry
	yrrh	myrrh
		colonel \'kərn-əl\

\a\	a	mat, *calf*
	e	*there*
	i	meringue
	ae	*aerial*
	ai	plaid, *air*
	au	*aunt*
	ay	*prayer*
	ea	*bear*
	ei	*their*
		chert \'chərt, 'chat\

\ā\	a	fade
	e	melee
	ae	maelstrom
	ai	main, straight
	ao	gaol
	au	gauge
	ay	day
	ea	steak
	ee	matinee
	ei	vein, reign, weigh
	ey	prey
	ie	*lingerie*
	ui	Uitlander

\ä\	a	farther, *father*, guard
	e	entree, sergeant
	i	*lingerie*
	o	cot

	aa	bazaar
	ah	shah
	au	*nautical*
	ea	heart
	ou	*nought*
	eau	bureaucracy
		patois \'pa-ˌtwä, 'pä-\

\à\	a	*father, calf*
	ar	*cart* (in the speech of so-called *r-droppers*)
	au	*aunt*
	aar	*bazaar* (in the speech of so-called *r-droppers*)

\au̇\	au	sauerkraut
	ou	loud, bough
	ow	now
	aou	caoutchouc

\e\	a	any
	e	bet, *err*, guess
	i	*vanilla*
	u	bury
	ae	aesthetic, *aerial*
	ai	said, *air*
	ay	says, *prayer*
	ea	bread, *bear*
	ei	heifer, *their*
	eo	leopard
	ie	friend
	oe	*foetid*
	ieu	*lieutenant*
	—	mbira \em-'bir-ə\

\ē\	e	me
	i	ski
	y	pretty
	ae	aeon

37

ay — Monday, quay
ea — easy
ee — see, beet
ei — receive
eo — people
ey — key
ie — grief
oe — phoebe, *foetid*
shillelagh, shillalah \shə-'lā-lē\
chamois \'sham-ē, . . . *also* sham-'wä\

\i\
a — homage, *catercorner*
e — England, *pretty, serious*
i — tip
o — women
u — busy
y — myth
ea — hear
ee — been, beer, *creek*
ei — counterfeit, weird
ia — carriage
ie — sieve
ui — building

\ī\
i — fine, sigh, guide
y — sly
ai — aisle, *aioli*
ay — bayou, papaya
ei — heist, height
ey — geyser
ie — lie
oy — coyote
uy — buy
ye — dye
aye — *aye*
eye — eye
choir \'kwī(-ə)r\

\ō\
a — *quahog, cupola*
o — bone, folk
ao — pharaoh
au — chauvinist
eo — yeoman
ew — sew
oa — coat
oe — doe
oh — oh, Noh
oo — *brooch*
ou — boulder, though
ow — know
ua — *quahog*
eau — plateau
— — burgh \'bər-(,)ō, 'bə-(,)rō\
ewe \'yü, 'yō\

\ȯ\
a — ball, talk
o — soft
ah — *Utah*
au — sausage, caught
aw — saw
eo — Georgian
oa — broad
ou — cough, thought
ow — toward

\ȯi\
aw — *lawyer*
eu — Freudian
oi — coin
oy — boy
uoy — *buoy*

---

sawing \'sȯ(-)iŋ\

\ü\
o — do, move, two
u — flu
w — crwth, cwm
eu — rheumatism, maneuver
ew — crew
oe — shoe
oo — school
ou — youth, through
ue — blue
ui — cruise
eew — *leeward*
ieu — *lieutenant*
oeu — manoeuvre
beauty \'byüt-ē\
ewe \'yü, 'yō\
peewit \'pē-,wit, 'pyü-ət\

\u̇\
o — woman, wolf
u — pull
oo — wood
ou — *could*

Consonants

\b\
b — baby
v — *government, seven*
bb — rubber
bh — bhang
pb — cupboard, raspberry

\ch\
c — cello
ch — chin
cz — Czech
si — tension
te — righteous
ti — question
tch — match
nature \'nā-chər\

\d\
d — did
dd — ladder
dh — dhow
ed — seemed
ld — would
(In the speech of most Americans t and tt between vowels are pronounced the same as d and dd.)

\f\
f — fan, safe
ff — offer
gh — laugh
lf — calf
ph — telephone
— — *lieutenant* \lü-'ten-ənt, *Brit* le(f)-'ten-\

\g\
g — go
gg — egg
gh — ghost
gu — guide, plague
example \ig-'zam-pəl\

\h\
g — Gila monster
h — hat
j — jai alai
ch — *Chanukah*

---

wh — who

\hw\
ju — *marijuana, San Juan*
wh — whale, when

\j\
g — gem
j — joy
ch — *Greenwich*
dg — budget, bridge
di — soldier
dj — adjective
gg — exaggerate
gi — region
jj — hajj
graduation \,graj-ə-'wā-shən\

\k\
c — catch
k — kid, take
q — quit
cc — account
ch — chaos, *loch, schism*
ck — pick
cq — acquire
cu — biscuit
gh — *lough*
kh — khaki
kk — chukka, pukka
lk — talk
qu — liquor, plaque, quay
cch — saccharine
cqu — lacquer
tax \'taks\

\k̲\
h — *Hanukkah, Hasid*
ch — *loch, Chasid*
gh — *lough*

\l\
l — low, sale
ll — filling, faille
lh — Lhasa apso
ln — *kiln*

\ᵊl\
l — *dirndl*
al — pedal
el — betel
le — battle
yl — phenyl

\m\
m — me, come
gm — phlegm
lm — *calm*
mb — comb
mh — mho
mm — dummy
mn — autumn
chm — drachm

\ᵊm\
en — *open, happen*
ain — *captain*
ernm — *government*

\n\
n — no, alone
gn — sign, gnat, reign
kn — knot
mn — mnemonic
mp — *comptroller*
nn — banner
pn — pneumonia

\ᵊn\
en — sudden
on — cotton
ain — certain

\ŋ\
n — ink, finger, *orangutan*

nd	handkerchief	
ng	sing, singer	
ngg	mah-jongg	
ngu	harangue	
\p\ **p**	port, stop, ape	
ph	shepherd, *diphthong*	
pp	supper	
\r\ **r**	red, care, card, car (Many people usually, some people occasionally, do not pronounce r followed by a consonant or a pause)	
rh	rhyme	
rr	merry	
wr	write	
rrh	diarrhea	
	colonel \'kərn-ᵊl\	
\s\ **c**	proceed, race	
s	say, loose	
z	pretzel	
ps	psalm	
sc	fascinate, scissors	
ss	mass	
st	listen, Christmas	
ts	*tsar*	
tz	*tzar*	
sch	*schism*	
sth	isthmus	
	tax \'taks\	
\sh\ **c**	oceanic	
s	sugar, sure	
ch	machine	
ci	special	
sc	fascism	
se	*nauseous*	
sh	shy	
si	emulsion	
sk	*ski*	
ss	tissue	
ti	nation	
chi	marchioness	
psh	pshaw	
sch	schist	
sci	conscious	
ssi	mission	
chsi	fuchsia	
\t\ **t**	tea, eat, late	
bt	debt	
ct	ctenoid	
ed	walked	
pt	ptomaine, receipt	
th	thyme, Thomas, Thai	
tt	button	

cht	yacht	
ght	night, straight	
phth	phthisic	
\th\ **gh**	*trough*	
th	thin, breath	
ght	*drought*	
chth	chthonic	
phth	phthalein	
\th\ **dd**	eisteddfod	
dh	edh	
th	this, teething, breathe	
\v\ **f**	of	
v	very, save	
w	wedeln	
ph	Stephen	
vv	savvy	
\w\ **u**	persuade, quit	
w	way	
ju	*San Juan, marijuana*	
ou	ouabain, *bivouac*	
wh	*whale, when*	
—	one \'wən\	
	choir \'kwī(-ə)r\	
	patois \'pa-ˌtwä, 'pä-\	
	strenuous \'stren-yə-wəs\	
\y\ **i**	opinion	
j	hallelujah	
y	yard	
	beauty \'byüt-ē\	
	cañon \'kan-yən\	
	cute \'kyüt\	
	feud \'fyüd\	
	few \'fyü\	
	strenuous \'stren-yə-wəs\	
	tortilla \tȯr-'tē-(y)ə\	
	unit \'yü-nət\	
\z\ **s**	days, was, please	
x	xylophone, *bateaux*	
z	zone, haze	
cz	czar	
sc	*discern*	
ss	scissors	
ts	*tsar*	
tz	*tzar*	
zz	buzz	
	example \ig-'zam-pəl\	
\zh\ **g**	regime, beige	
j	jongleur	
si	vision	
zi	glazier	
ssi	*fission*	

azure \'azh-ər\
measure \'mezh-ər, 'māzh-\

Silent Letters

The following letters often appear in the spelling but with no corresponding sound in the pronunciation of some words. Perhaps every letter of the alphabet is "silent" (by which we really mean "unpronounced") in some English word or other. For instance, *nc* is not pronounced in *blancmange*. Many such uncommon or rare instances are not included in this list.

b	comb, debt
c	Connecticut, ctenoid
ch	yacht, chthonic
e	date, live, battle, seemed, plague
g	gnat, sign, diaphragm
gh	night, straight, though, thought
h	hour, honor, rhyme, thyme
i	business, *parliament*
k	knot, know
l	talk, folk, would, *calm*
m	mnemonic
n	autumn, *government*, *kiln*
o	sophomore, *opossum*
p	cupboard, pneumonia, psalm, ptomaine, raspberry
ph	phthalein, phthisic
r	surprise \sə(r)-'prīz\ (Many people usually, most people occasionally, do not pronounce r when followed by a consonant or a pause.)
s	aisle, island, patois, demesne
t	beret, boatswain, Christmas, depot, listen
th	asthma, isthmus, *northeaster*
u	biscuit, build, guest, *pursuivant*, quay
ue	plague, plaque
w	who, write, two, sword, boatswain
x	faux pas, *bateaux*
y	*yeast*
z	rendezvous

Abbreviations in This Work

A.&M.	Agricultural and	*Braz*	Brazilian	*equiv*	equivalent	*Jav*	Javanese
	Mechanical	*Bret*	Breton	*Esk*	Eskimo	*Jp*	Japanese
ab	about	*Brit*	Britain, British	*esp*	especially	*L*	Latin
abbr	abbreviation	*bro*	brother	*est*	estimated	*LaF*	Louisiana
abl	ablative	*Bulg*	Bulgarian	*Eth*	Ethiopic		French
Acad	Academy	*c*	century	*ethnol*	ethnologist	*lat*	latitude
acc	accusative	*C*	centigrade, College	*exc*	except	*Lat*	Latin
act	active	*ca*	circa	*F*	Fahrenheit, French	*LG*	Low German
A.D.	anno Domini	*Canad*	Canadian	*fem*	feminine	*LGk*	Late Greek
adj	adjective	*CanF*	Canadian French	*Finn*	Finnish	*LHeb*	Late Hebrew
adv	adverb	*Cant*	Cantonese	*fl*	flourished	*lit*	literally,
AF	Anglo-French	*cap*	capital, capitalized	*Flem*	Flemish		literary
AFB	Air Force Base	*Catal*	Catalan	*fr*	from	*Lith*	Lithuanian
Afrik	Afrikaans	*caus*	causative	*Fr*	France, French	*LL*	Late Latin
Agric	Agriculture	*Celt*	Celtic	*freq*	frequentative	*long*	longitude
Alb	Albanian	*cen*	central	*Fris*	Frisian	*m*	meters
alter	alteration	*cent*	century	*ft*	feet	*manuf*	manufacturer
Am	America, American	*chem*	chemist	*fut*	future	*masc*	masculine
Amer	American	*Chin*	Chinese	*G*	German	*math*	mathematician
AmerF	American French	*comb*	combining	*Gael*	Gaelic	*MBret*	Middle Breton
AmerInd	American Indian	*Comm*	Community	*gen*	general, genitive	*MD*	Middle Dutch
AmerSp	American Spanish	*compar*	comparative	*Ger*	German	*ME*	Middle English
anc	ancient, anciently	*Confed*	Confederate	*Gk*	Greek	*Mech*	Mechanical
ant	antonym	*conj*	conjugation,	*Gmc*	Germanic	*Med*	Medical
anthropol	anthropologist,		conjunction	*Goth*	Gothic	*Mex*	Mexican, Mexico
	anthropology	*constr*	construction	*gov*	governor	*MexSp*	Mexican Spanish
aor	aorist	*contr*	contraction	*govt*	government	*MF*	Middle French
Ar	Arabic	*Copt*	Coptic	*Gr Brit*	Great Britain	*MFlem*	Middle Flemish
Arab	Arabian	*Corn*	Cornish	*Heb*	Hebrew	*MGk*	Middle Greek
Aram	Aramaic	*criminol*	criminologist	*hist*	historian	*MHG*	Middle High
archaeol	archaeologist	*d*	died	*Hitt*	Hittite		German
Arm	Armenian	*D*	Dutch	*Hung*	Hungarian	*mi*	miles
art	article	*Dan*	Daniel,	*Icel*	Icelandic	*mil*	military
Assyr	Assyrian		Danish	*IE*	Indo-European	*min*	minister
astron	astronomer,	*dat*	dative	*imit*	imitative	*MIr*	Middle Irish
	astronomy	*dau*	daughter	*imper*	imperative	*ML*	Medieval Latin
attrib	attributive,	*def*	definite	*incho*	inchoative	*MLG*	Middle Low
	attributively	*deriv*	derivative	*indef*	indefinite		German
atty	attorney	*dial*	dialect	*indic*	indicative	*modif*	modification
aug	augmentative	*dim*	diminutive	*infin*	infinitive	*MPer*	Middle Persian
Austral	Australian	*disc*	discovered	*Inst*	Institute	*MS*	manuscript
Av	Avestan	*Dor*	Doric	*instr*	instrumental	*mt*	mountain
AV	Authorized Version	*dram*	dramatist	*intens*	intensive	*Mt*	Mount
b	born	*Du*	Dutch	*interj*	interjection	*MW*	Middle Welsh
Bab	Babylonian	*DV*	Douay Version	*interrog*	interrogative	*n*	northern, noun
bacteriol	bacteriologist	*e*	eastern	*Ion*	Ionic	*N*	north, northern
B.C.	before Christ,	*E*	east, eastern,	*Ir*	Irish	*naut*	nautical
	British Columbia		English	*IrGael*	Irish Gaelic	*NE*	northeast
bef	before	*econ*	economist	*irreg*	irregular	*neut*	neuter
Belg	Belgian	*Ed*	Education	*Is*	island	*NewEng*	New England
Beng	Bengali	*educ*	educator	*ISV*	International	*NewZeal*	New Zealand
bet	between	*EGmc*	East Germanic		Scientific	*NGk*	New Greek
bib	biblical	*Egypt*	Egyptian		Vocabulary	*NGmc*	North Germanic
biochem	biochemist	*emp*	emperor	*It, Ital*	Italian	*NHeb*	New Hebrew
biol	biologist	*Eng*	England, English	*ital*	italic	*NL*	New Latin

40

No	North	*PaG*	Pennsylvania German	*R.C.*	Roman Catholic	*specif*	specifically
nom	nominative			*redupl*	reduplication	*spp*	species
nonstand	nonstandard	*part*	participle	*refl*	reflexive	*St*	Saint
Norw	Norwegian	*pass*	passive	*rel*	relative	*Ste*	Sainte
nov	novelist	*Pek*	Pekingese	*resp*	respectively	*subj*	subjunctive
n pl	noun plural	*Per, Pers*	Persian	*rev*	revolution	*substand*	substandard
NZ	New Zealand	*perf*	perfect	*Rom*	Roman,	*superl*	superlative
obs	obsolete	*perh*	perhaps		Romanian	*Sw, Swed*	Swedish
OCatal	Old Catalan	*pers*	person	*RSV*	Revised Standard	*syn*	synonym,
occas	occasionally	*Pg*	Portuguese		Version		synonymy
OE	Old English	*philos*	philosopher	*Rum*	Rumanian	*Syr*	Syriac
OF	Old French	*PhilSp*	Philippine Spanish	*Russ*	Russian	*Tag*	Tagalog
OFris	Old Frisian	*physiol*	physiologist	*S*	south, southern	*Tech*	Technology
OHG	Old High German	*pl*	plural	*Sc*	Scotch, Scots	*theol*	theologian
OIr	Old Irish	*Pol*	Polish	*Scand*	Scandinavian	*Theol*	Theological
OIt	Old Italian	*polit*	political, politician	*ScGael*	Scottish Gaelic	*Toch*	Tocharian
OL	Old Latin	*pop*	population	*Sch*	School	*trans*	translation
ON	Old Norse	*Port*	Portuguese	*Scot*	Scotland,	*treas*	treasury
ONF	Old North French	*pp*	past participle		Scottish	*Turk*	Turkish
OPer	Old Persian	*prec*	preceding	*secy*	secretary	*U*	University
OPg	Old Portuguese	*prep*	preposition	*Sem*	Seminary, Semitic	*usu*	usually
OProv	Old Provençal	*pres*	present, president	*Serb*	Serbian	*var*	variant
OPruss	Old Prussian	*prob*	probably	*Shak*	Shakespeare	*v, vb*	verb
orig	original,	*pron*	pronoun,	*sing*	singular	*vi*	verb intransitive
	originally		pronunciation	*Skt*	Sanskrit	*VL*	Vulgar Latin
ORuss	Old Russian	*pronunc*	pronunciation	*Slav*	Slavic	*voc*	vocative
OS	Old Saxon	*Prov*	Provençal	*So*	South	*vt*	verb transitive
OSlav	Old Church	*prp*	present participle	*So Afr*	South Africa,	*W*	Welsh, west,
	Slavonic	*Pruss*	Prussian		South African		western
OSp	Old Spanish	*pseud*	pseudonym	*sociol*	sociologist	*WGmc*	West Germanic
OW	Old Welsh	*psychol*	psychologist	*Sp, Span*	Spanish	*zool*	zoologist

Pronunciation Symbols

For more information see Guide to Pronunciation

ə . . . . banana, collide, abut

ˈə, ˌə . . . . humdrum, abut

ᵊ . . . . immediately preceding \l\, \n\, \m\, \ŋ\, as in battle, mitten, eaten, and sometimes open \ˈōp-ᵊm\, lock and key \-ᵊŋ\; immediately following \l\, \m\, \r\, as often in French table, prisme, titre

ər . . . . further, merger, bird

ˈər-
ˈə-r } . . . . as in two different pronunciations of hurry \ˈhər-ē, ˈhə-rē\

a . . . . mat, map, mad, gag, snap, patch

ā . . . . day, fade, date, aorta, drape, cape

ä . . . . bother, cot, and, with most American speakers, father, cart

ȧ . . . . father as pronounced by speakers who do not rhyme it with bother; French patte

au̇ . . . . now, loud, out

b . . . . baby, rib

ch . . . . chin, nature \ˈnā-chər\ (actually, this sound is \t\ + \sh\)

d . . . . did, adder

e . . . . bet, bed, peck

ˈē, ˌē . . . . beat, nosebleed, evenly, easy

ē . . . . easy, mealy

f . . . . fifty, cuff

g . . . . go, big, gift

h . . . . hat, ahead

hw . . . . whale as pronounced by those who do not have the same pronunciation for both whale and wail

i . . . . tip, banish, active

ī . . . . site, side, buy, tripe (actually, this sound is \ä\ + \i\, or \ȧ\ + \i\)

j . . . . job, gem, edge, join, judge (actually, this sound is \d\ + \zh\)

k . . . . kin, cook, ache

k̲ . . . . German ich, Buch; one pronunciation of loch

l . . . . lily, pool

m . . . . murmur, dim, nymph

n . . . . no, own

ⁿ . . . . indicates that a preceding vowel or diphthong is pronounced with the nasal passages open, as in French un bon vin blanc \œⁿ-bōⁿ-vaⁿ-bläⁿ\

ŋ . . . . sing \ˈsiŋ\, singer \ˈsiŋ-ər\, finger \ˈfiŋ-gər\, ink \ˈiŋk\

ō . . . . bone, know, \beau

ȯ . . . . saw, all, gnaw, caught

œ . . . . French bœuf, German Hölle

œ̄ . . . . French feu, German Höhle

ȯi . . . . coin, destroy

p . . . . pepper, lip

r . . . . red, car, rarity

s . . . . source, less

sh . . . . as in shy, mission, machine, special (actually, this is a single sound, not two); with a hyphen between, two sounds as in grasshopper \ˈgras-ˌhäp-ər\

t . . . . tie, attack, late, later, latter

th . . . . as in thin, ether (actually, this is a single sound, not two); with a hyphen between, two sounds as in knighthood \ˈnit-ˌhu̇d\

t̲h̲ . . . . then, either, this (actually, this is a single sound, not two)

ü . . . . rule, youth, union \ˈyün-yən\, few \ˈfyü\

u̇ . . . . pull, wood, book, curable \ˈkyu̇r-ə-bəl\, fury \ˈfyu̇(ə)r-ē\

ue . . . . German füllen, hübsch

ūe . . . . French rue, German fühlen

v . . . . vivid, give

w . . . . we, away; in some words having final \(ˌ)ō\, \(ˌ)yü\, or \(ˌ)ü\ a variant \ə-w\ occurs before vowels, as in \ˈfäl-ə-wiŋ\, covered by the variant \ə(-w)\ or \yə(-w)\ at the entry word

y . . . . yard, young, cue \ˈkyü\, mute \ˈmyüt\, union \ˈyün-yən\

ʸ . . . . indicates that during the articulation of the sound represented by the preceding character the front of the tongue has substantially the position it has for the articulation of the first sound of yard, as in French digne \dēnʸ\

z . . . . zone, raise

zh . . . . as in vision, azure \ˈazh-ər\ (actually, this is a single sound, not two); with a hyphen between, two sounds as in hogshead \ˈhȯgz-ˌhed, ˈhägz-\

\ . . . . slant line used in pairs to mark the beginning and end of a transcription: \ˈpen\

ˈ . . . . mark preceding a syllable with primary (strongest) stress: \ˈpen-mən-ˌship\

ˌ . . . . mark preceding a syllable with secondary (medium) stress: \ˈpen-mən-ˌship\

- . . . . mark of syllable division

( ) . . . . indicate that what is symbolized between is present in some utterances but not in others: factory \ˈfak-t(ə-)rē\

÷ . . . . indicates that many regard as unacceptable the pronunciation variant immediately following: cupola \ˈkyü-pə-lə, ÷-ˌlō\

A Dictionary of the English Language

A

¹a \'ā\ *n, pl* **a's** *or* **as** \'āz\ *often cap, often attrib* **1 a** : the 1st letter of the English alphabet **b** : a graphic representation of this letter **c** : a speech counterpart of orthographic *a* **2** : the 6th tone of a C-major scale **3** : a graphic device for reproducing the letter *a* **4** : one designated *a* esp. as the 1st in order or class **5 a** : a grade rating a student's work as superior in quality **b** : one graded or rated with an A **6** : something shaped like the letter A

²a \ə, (')ā\ *indefinite article* [ME, fr. OE *ān* one — more at ONE] (bef. 12c) **1** — used as a function word before singular nouns when the referent is unspecified ⟨*a* man overboard⟩ and before number collectives and some numbers ⟨*a* dozen⟩ **2** : the same ⟨birds of *a* feather⟩ ⟨swords all of *a* length⟩ **3 a** — used as a function word before a singular noun followed by a restrictive modifier ⟨*a* man who was here yesterday⟩ **b** : ANY ⟨*a* man who is sick can't work⟩ **c** — used as a function word before a mass noun to denote a particular type or instance ⟨*a* bronze made in ancient times⟩ ⟨glucose is *a* simple sugar⟩ **4** — used as a function word with nouns to form adverbial phrases of quantity, amount, or degree ⟨felt *a* little tired⟩

usage In speech and writing *a* is used before a consonant sound ⟨*a* door⟩ ⟨*a* human⟩ Before a vowel sound *an* is usual ⟨*an* icicle⟩ ⟨*an* honor⟩ but esp. in speech *a* is used occasionally, more often in some dialects than in others ⟨*a* apple⟩ ⟨*a* hour⟩ ⟨*a* obligation⟩ Before a consonant sound represented by a vowel letter *a* is usual ⟨*a* one⟩ ⟨*a* union⟩ but *an* also occurs though less frequently now than formerly ⟨*an* unique⟩ ⟨such *an* one⟩ Before unstressed or weakly stressed syllables with initial *h* both *a* and *an* are used in writing ⟨*a* historic⟩ ⟨*an* historic⟩ but in speech *an* is more frequent whether \h\ is pronounced or not. In the King James Version of the Old Testament and occasionally in writing and speech *an* is used before *h* in a stressed syllable ⟨*an* huntress⟩ ⟨*an* hundred⟩ ⟨children are *an* heritage of the Lord — Ps 127:3(AV)⟩

³a \ə *also* (')ā\ *prep* [ME, fr. OE *a-, an, on*] (bef. 12c) **1** *chiefly dial* : ON, IN, AT **2** : in, to, or for each ⟨twice *a* week⟩ ⟨five dollars a dozen⟩ *usage* see ²A

⁴a \ə, (')a\ *vb* [ME, contr. of *have*] *archaic* (14c) : HAVE ⟨I might *a* had husbands afore now — John Bunyan⟩

⁵a \ə\ *prep* [ME, by contr.] (1500) : OF — often attached to the preceding word ⟨kinda⟩ ⟨lotta⟩

¹a- \ə\ *prefix* [ME, fr. OE] **1** : on : in : at ⟨abed⟩ **2** : in (such) a state or condition ⟨afire⟩ **3** : in (such) a manner ⟨aloud⟩ **4** : in the act or process of ⟨gone *a*-hunting⟩ ⟨atingle⟩

²a- \(')ā *also* (')a *or* (')ä\ *or* **an-** \(')an\ *prefix* [L & Gk; L, fr. Gk — more at UN-] : not : without ⟨asexual⟩ — *a*- before consonants other than *h* and sometimes even before *h*, *an*- before vowels and usu. before *h* ⟨achromatic⟩ ⟨ahistorical⟩ ⟨anastigmatic⟩ ⟨anharmonic⟩

-a- *comb form* [ISV] : replacing carbon esp. in a ring ⟨aza-⟩

-a \ə\ *n suffix* [NL, fr. *-a* (as in *magnesia*)] : OXIDE ⟨thoria⟩

aah \'ä, often prolonged and/or followed by ə\ *vi* (1953) : to exclaim in amazement, joy, or surprise ⟨one finds oneself oohing and ∼ing over the exciting new TV commercials — Walter Goodman⟩ — **aah** *n*

aard·vark \'ärd-,värk\ *n* [obs. Afrik, fr. Afrik *aard* earth + *vark* pig] (1833) : a large burrowing nocturnal African mammal (*Orycteropus afer* of the order Tubulidentata) that has an extensile tongue, powerful claws, large ears, and heavy tail and feeds esp. on termites

aard·wolf \-,wu̇lf\ *n* [Afrik, fr. aard + *wolf*] (1833) : a maned striped mammal (*Proteles cristatus*) of southern and eastern Africa that resembles the related hyenas and feeds chiefly on carrion and insects

Aar·on \'ar-ən, 'er-\ *n* [LL, fr. Gk *Aarōn*, fr. Heb *Ahărōn*] : a brother of Moses and high priest of the Hebrews

Aa·ron·ic \a-'rän-ik, e-\ *adj* (ca. 1828) **1** : of or stemming from Aaron **2** : of or relating to the lower order of the Mormon priesthood

aardwolf

Ab \'äb, 'äv, 'ȯv\ *n* [Heb *Ābh*] (ca. 1769) : the 11th month of the civil year or the 5th month of the ecclesiastical year in the Jewish calendar — see MONTH table

ab- \(')ab, əb\ *prefix* [ME, fr. OF & L; OF, fr. L *ab-, abs-, a-*, fr. *ab, a* — more at OF] : from : away : off ⟨abaxial⟩ ⟨abstrict⟩

---

aba \ə-'bä, ä-'bä\ *n* [Ar '*abā*'] (1811) **1** : a loose sleeveless outer garment worn by Arabs **2** : a fabric woven from the hair of camels or goats

ab·a·ca \,ab-ə-'kä, 'ab-ə-,\ *n* [Sp *abacá*, fr. Tag *abaká*] (ca. 1818) **1** : a fiber obtained from the leafstalk of a banana (*Musa textilis*) native to the Philippines — called also *Manila hemp* **2** : the plant that yields abaca

aback \ə-'bak\ *adv* (bef. 12c) **1** *archaic* : BACKWARD, BACK **2** : in a position to catch the wind upon the forward surface of a square sail **3** : by surprise : UNAWARES ⟨was taken ∼ by her sharp retort⟩

abac·te·ri·al \,ā-(,)bak-'tir-ē-əl\ *adj* (ca. 1935) : not caused by or characterized by the presence of bacteria ⟨an ∼ inflammation⟩

aba·cus \'ab-ə-kəs, ə-'bak-əs\ *n, pl* **aba·ci** \'ab-ə-,sī, -,kē; ə-'bak-,ī\ *or* **aba·cus·es** [L, fr. Gk *abak-, abax*, lit., slab] (14c) **1** : an instrument for performing calculations by sliding counters along rods or in grooves **2** : a slab that forms the uppermost member or division of the capital of a column

¹abaft \ə-'baft\ *prep* [¹a- + *baft* (aft)] (1594) : to the rear of; *specif*: toward the stern from

²abaft *adv* (1628) : toward or at the stern : AFT

ab·a·lo·ne \,ab-ə-'lō-nē, 'ab-ə-,\ *n* [AmerSp *abulón*] (1850) : any of a genus (*Haliotis*) of rock-clinging gastropod mollusks that have a flattened shell slightly spiral in form, lined with mother-of-pearl, and with a row of apertures along its outer edge

¹aban·don \ə-'ban-dən\ *vt* [ME *abandounen*, fr. MF *abandoner*, fr. *abandon*, n., surrender, fr. *a bandon* in one's power] (14c) **1 a** : to give up to the control or influence of another person or agent ⟨∼ed her baby to fate⟩ **b** : to give up with the intent of never again claiming a right or interest in **2** : to withdraw from often in the face of danger or encroachment ⟨∼ ship⟩ **3** : to withdraw protection, support, or help from ⟨∼ed the candidate when the polls went against him⟩ **4** : to give (oneself) over unrestrainedly **5 a** : to cease from maintaining, practicing, or using ⟨immigrants slow to ∼ their native language⟩ **b** : to cease intending or attempting to perform ⟨∼ed their attempts to escape⟩ — **aban·don·er** *n* — **aban·don·ment** \-dən-mənt\ *n*

syn ABANDON, DESERT, FORSAKE mean to leave without intending to return. ABANDON suggests that the thing or person left may be helpless without protection; DESERT implies that the object left may be weakened but not destroyed by one's absence; FORSAKE suggests an action more likely to bring impoverishment or bereavement to that which is forsaken than its exposure to physical dangers. *syn* see in addition RELINQUISH

²abandon *n* (14c) : a thorough yielding to natural impulses; *esp* : ENTHUSIASM, EXUBERANCE

aban·doned \ə-'ban-dənd\ *adj* (14c) **1** : wholly free from restraint **2** : given up : FORSAKEN

à bas \ä-'bä\ [F] (ca. 1897) : down with ⟨*à bas* the profiteers⟩

abase \ə-'bās\ *vt* **abased; abas·ing** [ME *abassen*, fr. MF *abaisser*, fr. *a-* (fr. L *ad-*) + (assumed) VL *bassiare* to lower] (15c) **1** *archaic* : to lower physically **2** : to lower in rank, office, prestige, or esteem — **abase·ment** \-'bā-smənt\ *n*

syn ABASE, DEMEAN, DEBASE, DEGRADE, HUMILIATE mean to lower in one's own estimation or in that of others. ABASE suggests losing or voluntarily yielding up dignity or prestige; DEMEAN implies losing or injuring social standing by an unsuitable act or association; DEBASE implies a deterioration of moral standards or character; DEGRADE suggests the taking of a step downward sometimes in rank but more often on the road to moral degeneration; HUMILIATE implies the severe wounding of one's pride and the causing of deep shame.

abash \ə-'bash\ *vt* [ME *abaishen*, fr. (assumed) MF *abaiss-, abair* to astonish, alter. of MF *esbair*, fr. *ex-* + *baer* to yawn — more at ABEYANCE] (14c) : to destroy the self-possession or self-confidence of : DISCONCERT — **abash·ment** \-mənt\ *n*

abate \ə-'bāt\ *vb* **abat·ed; abat·ing** [ME *abaten*, fr. OF *abattre* to beat down — more at REBATE] *vt* (13c) **1 a** : to put an end to ⟨∼ a nuisance⟩ **b** : NULLIFY ⟨∼ a writ⟩ **2 a** : to reduce in degree or intensity : MODERATE **b** : to reduce in value or amount : make less esp. by way of relief ⟨∼ a tax⟩ **3** : DEDUCT, OMIT ⟨∼ part of the price⟩ **4 a** : to beat down or cut away so as to leave a figure in relief **b** *obs* : BLUNT **5** : DEPRIVE ∼ *vi* **1** : to decrease in force or intensity **2 a** : to become

---

\ə\ abut \ᵊ\ kitten, F table \ər\ further \a\ ash \ā\ ace \ä\ cot, cart
\au̇\ out \ch\ chin \e\ bet \ē\ easy \g\ go \i\ hit \ī\ ice \j\ job
\ŋ\ sing \ō\ go \ȯ\ law \oi\ boy \th\ thin \th\ the \ü\ loot \u̇\ foot
\y\ yet \zh\ vision \á, k̲, ⁿ, œ, œ̄, ᵫ, ᵫ̄, ᵫ̇\ see Guide to Pronunciation

defeated or become null or void **b :** to decrease in amount or value — **abat·er** *n*

syn ABATE, SUBSIDE, WANE, EBB mean to die down in force or intensity. ABATE stresses the idea of progressive diminishing; SUBSIDE implies the ceasing of turbulence or agitation; WANE suggests the fading or weakening of something good or impressive; EBB suggests the receding of something (as the tide) that commonly comes and goes. ***syn*** see in addition DECREASE

abate·ment \ə-'bāt-mənt\ *n* (14c) **1 :** the act or process of abating **:** the state of being abated **2 :** an amount abated; *esp* **:** a deduction from the full amount of a tax

ab·a·tis \'ab-ə-,tē, 'ab-ət-əs\ *n, pl* **ab·a·tis** \'ab-ə-,tēz\ *or* **ab·a·tis·es** \-ət-ə-səz\ [F, fr. *abattre*] (1766) **:** a defensive obstacle formed by felled trees with sharpened branches facing the enemy

A battery *n* (1922) **:** a battery used to heat the filaments or cathode heaters of electron tubes

ab·at·toir \'ab-ə-,twär, -,t(w)ȯr\ *n* [F, fr. *abattre*] (1820) **:** SLAUGHTERHOUSE

ab·ax·i·al \(')a-'bak-sē-əl\ *adj* (1857) **:** situated out of or directed away from the axis ⟨the ~ or lower surface of a leaf⟩

ab·ba·cy \'ab-ə-sē\ *n, pl* **-cies** [ME *abbatie*, fr. LL *abbatia*] (15c) **:** the office, dignity, jurisdiction, or tenure of an abbot

Ab·bas·id \ə-'bas-əd, 'ab-ə-səd\ *n* (1788) **:** a member of a dynasty of caliphs ruling the Muslim Empire (750–1258) and claiming descent from Abbas the uncle of Muhammad

ab·ba·tial \ə-'bā-shəl, a-\ *adj* (1642) **:** of or relating to an abbot, abbess, or abbey

ab·bé \a-'bā, 'ab-,ā\ *n* [F, fr. LL *abbat-, abbas*] (1530) **:** a member of the French secular clergy in major or minor orders — used as a title

ab·bess \'ab-əs\ *n* [ME *abbesse*, fr. OF, fr. LL *abbatissa*, fem. of *abbat-, abbas*] (13c) **:** a woman who is the superior of a convent of nuns

Abbe·vil·li·an \,ab-(ə-)'vil-ē-ən\ *adj* [*Abbeville, France*] (ca. 1934) **:** of or relating to an early lower Paleolithic culture characterized by bifacial stone hand axes

ab·bey \'ab-ē\ *n, pl* **abbeys** [ME, fr. OF *abaïe*, fr. LL *abbatia* abbey, fr. *abbat-, abbas*] (13c) **1 a :** a monastery ruled by an abbot **b :** a convent ruled by an abbess **2 :** an abbey church

ab·bot \'ab-ət\ *n* [ME *abbod*, fr. OE, fr. LL *abbat-, abbas*, fr. LGk *abbas*, fr. Aram *abbā* father] (bef. 12c) **:** the superior of a monastery for men

ab·bre·vi·ate \ə-'brē-vē-,āt\ *vt* **-at·ed; -at·ing** [ME *abbreviaten*, fr. LL *abbreviatus*, pp. of *abbreviare* — more at ABRIDGE] (15c) **:** to make briefer; *esp* **:** to reduce to a shorter form intended to stand for the whole ***syn*** see SHORTEN — **ab·bre·vi·a·tor** \-,āt-ər\ *n*

ab·bre·vi·a·tion \ə-,brē-vē-'ā-shən\ *n* (15c) **1 :** the act or result of abbreviating **:** ABRIDGMENT **2 :** a shortened form of a written word or phrase used in place of the whole ⟨*amt* is an ~ for *amount*⟩

ABC \,ā-(,)bē-'sē\ *n, pl* **ABC's** *or* **ABCs** \-'sēz\ (13c) **1 :** ALPHABET — usu. used in pl. **2 a :** the rudiments of reading, writing, and spelling — usu. used in pl. **b :** the rudiments of a subject

ABC soil *n* (1938) **:** a soil that has a well-differentiated profile with distinct A-, B-, and C-horizons

ABD \,ā-(,)bē-'dē\ *n* [*all but dissertation*] (1965) **:** a doctoral candidate who has completed required courses and examinations but not a dissertation

Ab·di·as \ab-'dī-əs\ *n* [LL, fr. Gk] **:** OBADIAH

ab·di·cate \'ab-di-,kāt\ *vb* **-cat·ed; -cat·ing** [L *abdicatus*, pp. *of abdicare*, fr. *ab-* + *dicare* to proclaim — more at DICTION] *vt* (1541) **1 :** to cast off **:** DISCARD **2 :** to relinquish (as sovereign power) formally ~ *vi* **:** to renounce a throne, high office, dignity, or function — **ab·di·ca·ble** \-kə-bəl\ *adj* — **ab·di·ca·tion** \,ab-di-'kā-shən\ *n* — **ab·di·ca·tor** \'ab-di-,kāt-ər\ *n*

syn ABDICATE, RENOUNCE, RESIGN mean to give up a position with no possibility of resuming it. ABDICATE implies a giving up of sovereign power or sometimes an evading of responsibility such as that of a parent; RENOUNCE may replace it but often implies additionally a sacrifice for a greater end; RESIGN applies to the giving up of an unexpired office or trust.

ab·do·men \'ab-də-mən, -,dō-; ab-'dō-mən, ab-\ *n* [MF & L; MF, fr. L] (1615) **1 :** the part of the body between the thorax and the pelvis; *also* **:** the cavity of this part of the trunk containing the chief viscera **2 :** the posterior section of the body behind the thorax in an arthropod — see INSECT illustration — **ab·dom·i·nal** \ab-'däm-ən-ᵊl, əb-, -'däm-nᵊl\ *adj* — **ab·dom·i·nal·ly** \-ē\ *adv*

ab·du·cens \ab-'d(y)ü-,senz\ *n, pl* **ab·du·cen·tes** \,ab-d(y)ü-'sent-(,)ēz\ (ca. 1909) **:** ABDUCENS NERVE

abducens nerve *n* [NL *abducent-, abducens*, fr. L, prp.] (ca. 1901) **:** either of the 6th pair of cranial nerves that are motor nerves supplying the rectus on the outer and lateral side of each eye — called also *abducent nerve*

ab·du·cent \ab-'d(y)üs-ᵊnt\ *adj* [L *abducent-, abducens*, prp. of *abducere*] (1713) **:** serving to abduct ⟨an ~ muscle⟩

ab·duct \ab-'dəkt, əb-; 2 *also* 'ab-,\ *vt* [L *abductus*, pp. of *abducere*, lit., to lead away, fr. *ab-* + *ducere* to lead — more at TOW] (1834) **1 :** to carry off (as a person) by force **2 :** to draw away (as a limb) from a position near or parallel to the median axis of the body; *also* **:** to move (similar parts) apart — **ab·duc·tor** \-'dək-tər\ *n*

ab·duc·tion \ab-'dək-shən, əb-\ *n* (1626) **1 :** the action of abducting **:** the condition of being abducted **2 :** the unlawful carrying away of a woman for marriage or intercourse

abeam \ə-'bēm\ *adv or adj* (1836) **:** on a line at right angles to a ship's keel

[1]**abe·ce·dar·i·an** \,ā-bē-(,)sē-'der-ē-ən\ *n* [ME *abecedary*, fr. ML *abecedarium* alphabet, fr. LL, neut. of *abecedarius* of the alphabet, fr. the letters *a* + *b* + *c* + *d*] (1603) **:** one learning the rudiments of something (as the alphabet)

[2]**abecedarian** *adj* (1665) **1 a :** of or relating to the alphabet **b :** alphabetically arranged **2 :** RUDIMENTARY

abed \ə-'bed\ *adv or adj* (bef. 12c) **:** in bed

Abel \'ā-bəl\ *n* [LL, fr. Gk, fr. Heb *Hebhel*] **:** a son of Adam and Eve killed by his brother Cain

abe·li·an \ə-'bē-lē-ən\ *adj, often cap* [Niels *Abel* †1829 Norw. mathematician] (ca. 1909) **:** COMMUTATIVE 2 ⟨~ group⟩ ⟨~ ring⟩

abel·mosk \'ā-bəl-,mäsk\ *n* [deriv. of Ar *abū-l-misk* father of the musk] (ca. 1771) **:** a bushy herb (*Hibiscus moschatus*) of the mallow family native to tropical Asia and the East Indies whose musky seeds are used in perfumery and in flavoring coffee

Ab·er·deen An·gus \,ab-ər-,dē-'naŋ-gəs\ *n* [*Aberdeen & Angus*, counties in Scotland] (1862) **:** any of a breed of usu. black hornless beef cattle originating in Scotland

[1]**ab·er·rant** \a-'ber-ənt, ə-; 'ab-ə-rənt, -,e(ə)r-ənt\ *adj* [L *aberrant-, aberrans*, prp. of *aberrare* to go astray, fr. *ab-* + *errare* to wander, err] (ca. 1798) **1 :** straying from the right or normal way **2 :** deviating from the usual or natural type **:** ATYPICAL — **ab·er·rance** \-ən(t)s\ *n* — **ab·er·ran·cy** \-ən-sē\ *n* — **ab·er·rant·ly** *adv*

[2]**aberrant** *n* (1938) **1 :** an aberrant natural group, individual, or structure **2 :** a person whose behavior departs substantially from the standard

ab·er·rat·ed \'ab-ə-,rāt-əd\ *adj* [L *aberratus*] (1950) **:** ABERRANT

ab·er·ra·tion \,ab-ə-'rā-shən\ *n* [L *aberratus*, pp. of *aberrare*] (1594) **1 :** the act of being aberrant esp. from a moral standard or normal state **2 :** failure of a mirror, refracting surface, or lens to produce exact point-to-point correspondence between an object and its image **3 :** unsoundness or disorder of the mind **4 :** a small periodic change of apparent position in celestial bodies due to the combined effect of the motion of light and the motion of the observer **5 :** an aberrant organ or individual **:** SPORT 5 — **ab·er·ra·tion·al** \-shnəl, -shən-ᵊl\ *adj*

abet \ə-'bet\ *vt* **abet·ted; abet·ting** [ME *abetten*, fr. MF *abeter*, fr. OF, fr. *a-* (fr. L *ad-*) + *beter* to bait, of Gmc origin; akin to OE *bǣtan* to bait] (14c) **1 :** to actively second and encourage (as an activity or plan) **:** FORWARD **2 :** to assist or support in the achievement of a purpose ⟨*abetted* the cause of justice⟩ ***syn*** see INCITE — **abet·ment** \-mənt\ *n* — **abet·tor** *or* **abet·ter** \-'bet-ər\ *n*

abey·ance \ə-'bā-ən(t)s\ *n* [MF *abeance* expectation, fr. *abaer* to desire, fr. *a-* + *baer* to yawn, fr. ML *batare*] (1528) **1 :** a lapse in succession during which there is no person in whom a title is vested **2 :** temporary inactivity **:** SUSPENSION

abey·ant \-ənt\ *adj* [back-formation fr. *abeyance*] (1866) **:** being in abeyance ***syn*** see LATENT

ab·hor \əb-'hȯ(ə)r, ab-\ *vt* **ab·horred; ab·hor·ring** [ME *abhorren*, fr. L *abhorrēre*, fr. *ab-* + *horrēre* to shudder — more at HORROR] (15c) **1 :** to regard with extreme repugnance **:** LOATHE **2 :** to turn aside or keep away from esp. in scorn or shuddering fear **:** REJECT ⟨the university should ~ mediocrity — Walter Moberly⟩ ***syn*** see HATE — **ab·hor·rer** \-'hȯr-ər\ *n*

ab·hor·rence \əb-'hȯr-ən(t)s, -'här-\ *n* (1660) **1 a :** the act or state of abhorring **b :** the feeling of one who abhors **2 :** one that is abhorred

ab·hor·rent \-ənt\ *adj* [L *abhorrent-, abhorrens*, prp. of *abhorrēre*] (1619) **1 a** *archaic* **:** strongly opposed **b :** feeling or showing abhorrence **2 :** not agreeable **:** CONTRARY ⟨a notion ~ to their philosophy⟩ **3 :** being so repugnant as to stir up positive antagonism ⟨acts ~ to every right-minded person⟩ ***syn*** see REPUGNANT — **ab·hor·rent·ly** *adv*

Abib \ä-'vēv\ *n* [Heb *Ābhībh*, lit., ear of grain] (1535) **:** the 1st month of the ancient Hebrew calendar corresponding to Nisan

abid·ance \ə-'bīd-ᵊn(t)s\ *n* (1647) **1 :** an act or state of abiding **:** CONTINUANCE **2 :** COMPLIANCE ⟨~ by the rules⟩

abide \ə-'bīd\ *vb* **abode** \-'bōd\ *or* **abid·ed; abid·ing** [ME *abiden*, fr. OE *ābīdan*, fr. *ā-*, perfective prefix + *bīdan* to bide; akin to OHG *ir-*, perfective prefix] *vt* (bef. 12c) **1 :** to wait for **:** AWAIT **2 a :** to endure without yielding **:** WITHSTAND **b :** to bear patiently **:** TOLERATE ⟨cannot ~ such bigots⟩ **3 :** to accept without objection ~ *vi* **1 :** to remain stable or fixed in a state **2 :** to continue in a place **:** SOJOURN ***syn*** see BEAR, CONTINUE — **abid·er** *n* — **abide by 1 :** to conform to **2 :** to acquiesce in

abid·ing \ə-'bīd-iŋ\ *adj* (14c) **:** ENDURING, CONTINUING ⟨an ~ interest in nature⟩ — **abid·ing·ly** *adv*

ab·i·gail \'ab-ə-,gāl\ *n* [*Abigail*, servant in *The Scornful Lady*, a play by Francis Beaumont & John Fletcher] (1671) **:** a lady's personal maid

abil·i·ty \ə-'bil-ət-ē\ *n, pl* **-ties** [ME *abilite*, fr. MF *habilité*, fr. L *habilitat-, habilitas*, fr. *habilis* apt, skillful — more at ABLE] (14c) **1 a :** the quality or state of being able; *esp* **:** physical, mental, or legal power to perform **b :** competence in doing **:** SKILL **2 :** natural talent or acquired proficiency **:** APTITUDE ⟨children whose *abilities* warrant higher education⟩

-abil·i·ty *also* **-ibil·i·ty** \ə-'bil-ət-ē\ *n suffix* [ME *-abilite, -ibilite*, fr. MF *-abilité, -ibilité*, fr. L *-abilitas, -ibilitas*, fr. *-abilis, -ibilis* -able + *-tas* -ty] **:** capacity, fitness, or tendency to act or be acted on in a (specified) way ⟨ensil*ability*⟩

ab in·i·tio \,ab-ə-'nish-ē-,ō\ *adv* [L] (1599) **:** from the beginning

abio·gen·e·sis \,ā-,bī-ō-'jen-ə-səs\ *n* [NL, fr. [2]*a-* + *bio-* + L *genesis*] (1870) **:** the supposed spontaneous origination of living organisms directly from lifeless matter — **abi·og·e·nist** \,ā-(,)bī-'äj-ə-nəst\ *or* **abio·gen·e·sist** \-,bī-ō-'jen-ə-səst\ *n*

abio·gen·ic \,ā-,bī-ō-'jen-ik\ *adj* (1912) **:** not produced by the action of living organisms — **abio·gen·i·cal·ly** \-i-k(ə-)lē\ *adv*

abi·o·log·i·cal \,ā-,bī-ə-'läj-i-kəl\ *adj* (1877) **:** not biological; *esp* **:** not involving or produced by organisms ⟨~ synthesis of amino acids⟩ — **abi·o·log·i·cal·ly** \-i-k(ə-)lē\ *adv*

abi·ot·ic \,ā-(,)bī-'ät-ik\ *adj* (ca. 1893) **:** not biotic **:** ABIOLOGICAL ⟨the ~ environment⟩ — **abi·ot·i·cal·ly** \-i-k(ə-)lē\ *adv*

ab·ject \'ab-,jekt\ *adj* [ME, fr. L *abjectus*, fr. pp. of *abicere* to cast off, fr. *ab-* + *jacere* to throw — more at JET] (15c) **1 :** sunk to or existing in a low state or condition ⟨to lowest pitch of ~ fortune thou art fallen — John Milton⟩ **2 a :** cast down in spirit **:** SERVILE, SPIRITLESS ⟨a man made ~ by suffering⟩ **b :** showing utter hopelessness or resignation ⟨~ surrender⟩ **3 :** expressing or offered in a humble and often ingratiating spirit ⟨~ flattery⟩ ⟨an ~ apology⟩ ***syn*** see MEAN — **ab·ject·ly** \'ab-,jek-(t)lē, ab-'\ *adv* — **ab·ject·ness** \-,jek(t)-nəs, -'jek(t)-\ *n*

ab·jec·tion \ab-'jek-shən\ *n* (15c) **1 :** a low or downcast state **:** DEGRADATION **2 :** the act of making abject **:** HUMBLING, REJECTION ⟨I protest . . . this vile ~ of youth to age — G. B. Shaw⟩

ab·ju·ra·tion \,ab-jə-'rā-shən\ *n* (15c) **1 :** the act or process of abjuring **2 :** an oath of abjuring

ab·jure \ab-'jù(ə)r\ *vt* **ab·jured; ab·jur·ing** [ME *abjuren*, fr. MF or L; MF *abjurer*, fr. L *abjurare*, fr. *ab-* + *jurare* to swear — more at JURY]

(15c) **1 a :** to renounce upon oath **b :** to reject solemnly **2 :** to abstain from : AVOID ⟨~ extravagance⟩ — **ab·jur·er** *n*

syn ABJURE, RENOUNCE, FORSWEAR, RECANT, RETRACT mean to withdraw one's word or professed belief. ABJURE implies a firm and final rejecting or abandoning often made under oath; RENOUNCE often equals ABJURE but may carry the meaning of disclaim or disown; FORSWEAR may add to ABJURE an implication of perjury or betrayal; RECANT stresses the withdrawing or denying of something professed or taught; RETRACT applies to the withdrawing of a promise, an offer, or an accusation.

ab·late \a-ˈblāt\ *vb* **ab·lat·ed; ab·lat·ing** [L *ablatus* (suppletive pp. of *auferre* to remove, fr. *au-* away + *ferre* to carry), fr. *ab-* + *latus,* suppletive pp. of *ferre* — more at UKASE, BEAR, TOLERATE] *vt* (1542) **:** to remove by cutting, erosion, melting, evaporation, or vaporization ~ *vi* **:** to become ablated

ab·la·tion \a-ˈblā-shən\ *n* (15c) **:** the process of ablating: as **a :** surgical removal **b :** removal of a part (as the outside of a nose cone) by melting or vaporization

1ab·la·tive \ˈab-lət-iv\ *adj* (15c) **:** of, relating to, or constituting a grammatical case expressing typically the relations of separation and source and also frequently such relations as cause or instrument — **ablative** *n*

2ab·la·tive \a-ˈblāt-iv\ *adj* (1567) **1 :** of or relating to ablation **2 :** tending to ablate ⟨~ material on a nose cone⟩ — **ab·la·tive·ly** *adv*

ablative absolute \ˌab-lət-iv-\ *n* (ca. 1828) **:** a construction in Latin in which a noun or pronoun and its adjunct both in the ablative case form together an adverbial phrase expressing generally the time, cause, or an attendant circumstance of an action

ab·laut \ˈäp-ˌlau̇t, ˈab-\ *n* [G, fr. *ab* away from + *laut* sound] (1849) **:** a systematic variation of vowels in the same root or affix or in related roots or affixes esp. in the Indo-European languages that is usu. paralleled by differences in use or meaning (as in *sing, sang, sung, song*)

ablaze \ə-ˈblāz\ *adj or adv* (14c) **1 :** being on fire **2 :** having radiant light or bright color : GLOWING ⟨his face all ~ with excitement — Bram Stoker⟩

able \ˈā-bəl\ *adj* **abler** \-b(ə-)lər\; **ablest** \-b(ə-)ləst\ [ME, fr. MF, fr. L *habilis* apt, fr. *habēre* to have — more at HABIT] (14c) **1 a :** having sufficient power, skill, or resources to accomplish an object **b :** susceptible to action or treatment **2 :** marked by intelligence, knowledge, skill, or competence

-able *also* **-ible** \ə-bəl\ *adj suffix* [ME, fr. OF, fr. L *-abilis, -ibilis,* fr. *-a-, -i-,* verb stem vowels + *-bilis* capable or worthy of] **1 :** capable of, fit for, or worthy of (being so acted upon or toward) — chiefly in adjectives derived from verbs ⟨break*able*⟩ ⟨collect*ible*⟩ **2 :** tending, given, or liable to ⟨knowledge*able*⟩ ⟨perish*able*⟩ — **-ably** *also* **-ibly** \ə-blē\ *adv suffix*

able–bod·ied \ˌā-bəl-ˈbäd-ēd\ *adj* (1622) **:** having a sound strong body

able–bodied seaman *n* (ca. 1909) **:** ABLE SEAMAN

able seaman *n* (1702) **:** an experienced deck-department seaman qualified to perform routine duties at sea

abloom \ə-ˈblüm\ *adj* (1855) **:** abounding with blooms : BLOOMING ⟨parks ~ with roses⟩

ab·lut·ed \ə-ˈblüt-əd, a-\ *adj* [back-formation fr. *ablution*] (1650) **:** washed clean

ab·lu·tion \ə-ˈblü-shən, a-\ *n* [ME, fr. MF or L; MF, fr. L *ablution-, ablutio,* fr. *ablutus,* pp. of *abluere* to wash away, fr. *ab-* + *luere* to wash; akin to L *lavere* to wash — more at LYE] (1533) **1 :** the washing of one's body or part of it (as in a religious rite) **2** *pl* **:** a building housing bathing and toilet facilities on a military base — **ab·lu·tion·ary** \-shə-ˌner-ē\ *adj*

ably \ˈā-b(ə-)lē\ *adv* (14c) **:** in an able manner

ABM \ˌā-(ˌ)bē-ˈem\ *n, pl* **ABM's** *or* **ABMs** \-ˈemz\ (1966) **:** ANTIBALLISTIC MISSILE

Ab·na·ki \ab-ˈnäk-ē\ *n, pl* **Abnaki** *or* **Abnakis** (1721) **1 :** a member of an American Indian people of Maine and southern Quebec **2 :** an Algonquian language of the Abnaki and Penobscot peoples

ab·ne·gate \ˈab-ni-ˌgāt\ *vt* **-gat·ed; -gat·ing** [back-formation fr. *abnegation*] (1657) **1 :** SURRENDER, RELINQUISH ⟨*abnegated* his powers⟩ **2 :** DENY, RENOUNCE ⟨*abnegated* his God⟩ — **ab·ne·ga·tor** \-ˌgāt-ər\ *n*

ab·ne·ga·tion \ˌab-ni-ˈgā-shən\ *n* [LL *abnegation-, abnegatio,* fr. L *abnegatus,* pp. of *abnegare* to refute, fr. *ab-* + *negare* to deny — more at NEGATE] (14c) **:** DENIAL; *esp* **:** SELF-DENIAL

1ab·nor·mal \(ˈ)ab-ˈnȯr-məl, əb-\ *adj* [alter. (influenced by L *abnormis*) of F *anormal,* fr. ML *anormalis,* fr. L *a-* + LL *normalis* normal] (1835) **1 :** deviating from the normal or average; *esp* **:** markedly irregular ⟨~ behavior⟩ **2 :** characterized by mental deficiency or disorder ⟨~ children⟩ — **ab·nor·mal·ly** \-mə-lē\ *adv*

2abnormal *n* (1927) **:** an abnormal person

ab·nor·mal·i·ty \ˌab-nər-ˈmal-ət-ē, -(ˌ)nȯr-\ *n, pl* **-ties** (1854) **1 :** the quality or state of being abnormal **2 :** something abnormal

abnormal psychology *n* (ca. 1903) **:** a branch of psychology concerned with mental and emotional disorders (as neuroses, psychoses, and mental deficiency) and with certain incompletely understood normal phenomena (as dreams and hypnosis)

abo \ˈab-(ˌ)ō\ *n, pl* **ab·os** *Austral* (1906) **:** ABORIGINE — often used disparagingly

1aboard \ə-ˈbō(ə)rd, -ˈbȯ(ə)rd\ *adv or adj* (14c) **1 :** ALONGSIDE **2 a :** on, onto, or within a vehicle (as a car or ship) **b :** in or into a group, association, or organization ⟨her second promotion since coming ~⟩ **3** *baseball* **:** on base

2aboard *prep* (15c) **:** ON, ONTO, WITHIN ⟨go ~ ship⟩ ⟨~ a plane⟩

ABO blood group \ˌā-(ˌ)bē-ˌō-\ *n* (1951) **:** one of the four blood groups A, B, AB, and O comprising the ABO system

abode \ə-ˈbōd\ *n* [ME *abod,* fr. *abiden* to abide] (13c) **1** *obs* **:** WAIT, DELAY **2 :** a temporary stay : SOJOURN **3 :** the place where one abides : HOME

aboil \ə-ˈbȯi(ə)l\ *adj or adv* (1858) **1 :** being at the boiling point : BOILING **2 :** intensely excited or stirred up ⟨the meeting was ~ with controversy⟩

abol·ish \ə-ˈbäl-ish\ *vt* [ME *abolisshen,* fr. MF *aboliss-,* stem of *abolir,* fr. L *abolēre,* prob. back-formation fr. *abolescere* to disappear, fr. *ab-* + *-olescere* (as in *adolescere* to grow up) — more at ADULT] (15c) **1 :** to do away with wholly : ANNUL **2 :** to destroy completely — **abol·ish·able** \-ə-bəl\ *adj* — **abol·ish·er** *n* — **abol·ish·ment** \-mənt\ *n*

ab·o·li·tion \ˌab-ə-ˈlish-ən\ *n* [MF, fr. L *abolition-, abolitio,* fr. *abolitus,* pp. of *abolēre*] (1529) **1 :** the act of abolishing : the state of being abolished **2 :** the abolishing of slavery — **ab·o·li·tion·ary** \-ˈlish-ə-ˌner-ē\ *adj*

ab·o·li·tion·ism \-ˈlish-ə-ˌniz-əm\ *n* (1808) **:** principles or measures fostering abolition esp. of slavery — **ab·o·li·tion·ist** \-ˈlish-(ə-)nəst\ *n or adj*

ab·oma·sum \ˌab-ō-ˈmā-səm\ *n, pl* **-sa** \-sə\ [NL, fr. L *ab-* + *omasum* tripe of a bullock] (ca. 1706) **:** the chamber of the ruminant stomach that is fourth and has a true digestive function — **ab·oma·sal** \-səl\ *adj*

A–bomb \ˈā-ˌbäm\ *n* (1945) **:** ATOM BOMB — **A–bomb** *vb*

abom·i·na·ble \ə-ˈbäm-(ə-)nə-bəl\ *adj* (14c) **1 :** worthy of or causing disgust or hatred : DETESTABLE ⟨the ~ treatment of the poor⟩ **2 :** quite disagreeable or unpleasant ⟨~ weather⟩ — **abom·i·na·bly** \-blē\ *adv*

abominable snow·man \-ˈsnō-mən, -ˌman\ *n, often cap A&S* (ca. 1921) **:** a mysterious animal reported as existing in the high Himalayas and usu. thought to be a bear — called also *yeti*

abom·i·nate \ə-ˈbäm-ə-ˌnāt\ *vt* **-nat·ed; -nat·ing** [L *abominatus,* pp. of *abominari,* lit., to deprecate as an ill omen, fr. *ab-* + *omin-, omen* omen] (1644) **:** to hate or loathe intensely : ABHOR ***syn*** see HATE — **abom·i·na·tor** \-ˌnāt-ər\ *n*

abom·i·na·tion \ə-ˌbäm-ə-ˈnā-shən\ *n* (14c) **1 :** something abominable **2 :** extreme disgust and hatred : LOATHING

ab·oral \(ˈ)a-ˈbōr-əl, -ˈbȯr-\ *adj* (1857) **:** situated opposite to or away from the mouth ⟨the ~ surface of a sea urchin⟩ — **ab·oral·ly** \-ə-lē\ *adv*

1ab·orig·i·nal \ˌab-ə-ˈrij-nəl, -ən-ᵊl\ *adj* (1667) **1 :** being the first of its kind present in a region and often primitive in comparison with more advanced types **2 :** of or relating to aborigines ***syn*** see NATIVE — **ab·orig·i·nal·ly** \-ē\ *adv*

2aboriginal *n* (1767) **:** ABORIGINE; *specif* **:** an Australian aborigine

ab·orig·i·ne \ˌab-ə-ˈrij-ə-(ˌ)nē\ *n* [L *aborigines,* pl., fr. *ab origine* from the beginning] (ca. 1533) **1 :** an aboriginal inhabitant esp. as contrasted with an invading or colonizing people **2** *pl* **:** the original fauna and flora of a geographical area

1aborn·ing \ə-ˈbȯ(ə)r-niŋ\ *adv* [1*a-* + E dial. *borning* (birth)] (1919) **:** while being born or produced ⟨a resolution that died ~⟩

2aborning *adj* (1943) **:** being born or produced ⟨the ~ fiasco⟩

1abort \ə-ˈbȯ(ə)rt\ *vb* [L *abortare,* fr. *abortus,* pp. of *aboriri* to miscarry, fr. *ab-* + *oriri* to rise, be born — more at RISE] *vi* (1580) **1 :** to bring forth premature or stillborn offspring **2 :** to become checked in development so as to remain rudimentary or to shrink away ~ *vt* **1 a :** to induce the abortion of or give birth to prematurely **b :** to terminate the pregnancy of before term **2 a :** to terminate prematurely : CANCEL ⟨~ a project⟩ ⟨~ a spaceflight⟩ **b :** to stop in the early stages ⟨~ a disease⟩ — **abort·er** *n*

2abort *n* (ca. 1944) **:** the premature termination of the flight of an aircraft on a combat or bombing mission; *also* **:** such termination of an action, procedure, or mission relating to a rocket or spacecraft ⟨a launch ~⟩

abor·ti·fa·cient \ə-ˌbȯrt-ə-ˈfā-shənt\ *adj* (1873) **:** inducing abortion — **abortifacient** *n*

abor·tion \ə-ˈbȯr-shən\ *n* (1547) **1 :** the expulsion of a nonviable fetus: as **a :** spontaneous expulsion of a human fetus during the first 12 weeks of gestation — compare MISCARRIAGE **b :** induced abortion **2 :** MONSTROSITY **3 a :** arrest of development (as of a part or process) resulting in imperfection **b :** a result of such arrest

abor·tion·ist \-sh(ə-)nəst\ *n* (1871) **:** one who induces abortions

abor·tive \ə-ˈbȯrt-iv\ *adj* (14c) **1** *obs* **:** prematurely born **2 :** FRUITLESS, UNSUCCESSFUL **3 :** imperfectly formed or developed **4 :** tending to cut short — **abor·tive·ly** *adv* — **abor·tive·ness** *n*

ABO system \ˌā-(ˌ)bē-ˈō-\ *n* (1944) **:** the basic system of antigens of human blood behaving in heredity as an allelic unit to produce any of the ABO blood groups

abound \ə-ˈbau̇nd\ *vi* [ME *abounden,* fr. MF *abonder,* fr. L *abundare,* fr. *ab-* + *unda* wave — more at WATER] (14c) **1 :** to be present in large numbers or in great quantity : be prevalent **2 :** to be copiously supplied ⟨life ~*ed* in mysteries — Norman Mailer⟩ ⟨institutions ~ with evidence of his success — *Johns Hopkins Mag.*⟩

1about \ə-ˈbau̇t\ *adv* [ME, fr. OE *abūtan,* fr. 1*a-* + *būtan* outside — more at BUT] (bef. 12c) **1 :** on all sides : AROUND **2 a :** in rotation **b :** around the outside **3 a :** reasonably close to ⟨~ a year ago⟩ **b :** ALMOST ⟨~ starved⟩ **4 :** here and there **5 :** in the vicinity : NEAR **6 :** in succession : ALTERNATELY ⟨turn ~ is fair play⟩ **7 :** in the opposite direction ⟨face ~⟩ ⟨the other way ~⟩

2about *prep* (bef. 12c) **1 :** in a circle around : on every side of : AROUND **2 a :** in the immediate neighborhood of : NEAR **b :** on or near the person of **c :** in the makeup of ⟨a mature wisdom ~ him⟩ **d :** at the command of ⟨has his wits ~ him⟩ **3 a :** engaged in **b :** on the verge of ⟨~ to join the army⟩ **4 a :** with regard to : CONCERNING **b :** concerned with **5 :** over or in different parts of **6** — used with the negative to express intention or determination ⟨is not ~ to quit⟩

3about *adj* (1815) **1 :** moving from place to place; *specif* **:** being out of bed **2 :** AROUND 2

about–face \ə-ˈbau̇t-ˈfās\ *n* [fr. the imper. phrase *about face*] (1861) **1 :** a 180° turn to the right from the position of attention **2 :** a reversal of direction **3 :** a reversal of attitude or point of view — **about–face** *vi*

1above \ə-ˈbəv\ *adv* [ME, fr. OE *abufan,* fr. *a-* + *bufan* above, fr. *be-* + *ufan* above; akin to OE *ofer* over] (bef. 12c) **1 a :** in the sky : OVERHEAD **b :** in or to heaven **2 a :** in or to a higher place **b :** higher on the same page or on a preceding page **c :** UPSTAIRS **d :** above zero ⟨10 degrees ~⟩ **3 :** in or to a higher rank or number ⟨30 and ~⟩ **4** *archaic* **:** in addition : BESIDES **5 :** UPSTAGE

2above *prep* (bef. 12c) **1 :** in or to a higher place than : OVER **2 a :** superior to (as in rank, quality, or degree) **b :** out of reach of **c :** in preference to **d :** too proud or honorable to stoop to **3 :** exceeding in number, quantity, or size : more than

³**above** *n, pl* **above** (13c) **1 a :** something that is above **b :** a person whose name is written above **2 a :** a higher authority **b :** HEAVEN *usage* Although still objected to by some, the use of *above* as a noun in sense 1a ⟨none of the *above*⟩ ⟨the *above* is Theseus's opinion — William Blake⟩ and as an adjective ⟨without the *above* reserve — O. W. Holmes †1935⟩ ⟨I was brought up on the *above* words — Viscount Montgomery⟩ has been long established as standard.

⁴**above** *adj* (1776) : written or discussed higher on the same page or on a preceding page *usage* see ³ABOVE

above all *adv* (14c) : before every other consideration : ESPECIALLY

¹**above·board** \ə-ˈbəv-ˌbō(ə)rd, -ˌbȯ(ə)rd\ *adv* [fr. the difficulty of cheating at cards when the hands are above the table] (1616) : in a straightforward manner : OPENLY

²**aboveboard** *adj* (1648) : free from all traces of deceit or duplicity

above-ground \ə-ˈbəv-ˌgraund\ *adj* (1617) **1 :** located or occurring on or above the surface of the ground **2 :** existing, produced, or published by or within the establishment ⟨~ movies⟩

ab ovo \ab-ˈō-(ˌ)vō\ *adv* [L, lit., from the egg] (1586) : from the beginning

ab·ra·ca·dab·ra \ˌab-rə-kə-ˈdab-rə\ *n* [LL] (ca. 1565) **1 :** a magical charm or incantation **2 :** unintelligible language

abrad·ant \ə-ˈbrād-ᵊnt\ *n* (1877) : ABRASIVE

abrade \ə-ˈbrād\ *vb* **abrad·ed; abrad·ing** [L *abradere* to scrape off, fr. *ab-* + *radere* to scrape — more at RAT] *vt* (1677) **1 a :** to rub or wear away esp. by friction : ERODE **b :** to irritate or roughen by rubbing **2 :** to wear down in spirit : IRRITATE, WEARY ~ *vi* : to undergo abrasion — **abrad·able** \-ə-bəl\ *adj* — **abrad·er** *n*

Abra·ham \ˈā-brə-ˌham\ *n* [LL, fr. Gk *Abraam*, fr. Heb *'Abrāhām*] : an Old Testament patriarch and founder of the Hebrew people

abra·sion \ə-ˈbrā-zhən\ *n* [ML *abrasion-, abrasio*, fr. L *abrasus*, pp. of *abradere*] (1656) **1 a :** a wearing, grinding, or rubbing away by friction **b :** IRRITATION **2 :** an abraded area of the skin or mucous membrane

¹**abra·sive** \ə-ˈbrā-siv, -ziv\ *n* (1853) : a substance (as emery or pumice) used for abrading, smoothing, or polishing

²**abrasive** *adj* (1875) **1 :** tending to abrade **2 :** causing irritation ⟨~ manners⟩ — **abra·sive·ly** *adv* — **abra·sive·ness** *n*

ab·re·ac·tion \ˌab-rē-ˈak-shən\ *n* [part trans. of G *abreagierung* catharsis, fr. *ab* (fr. OHG *aba*) off, away + *reagierung* reaction, fr. L *reagere* to react — more at OF, REACT] (1912) : the expression and emotional discharge of unconscious material (as a repressed idea or emotion) by verbalization esp. in the presence of a therapist — **ab·re·act** \-ˈakt\ *vb*

abreast \ə-ˈbrest\ *adv or adj* (15c) **1 :** beside one another with bodies in line ⟨columns of men five ~⟩ **2 :** up to a particular standard or level esp. of knowledge of recent developments ⟨keeps ~ of the latest trends⟩

abridge \ə-ˈbrij\ *vt* **abridged; abridg·ing** [ME *abregen*, fr. MF *abregier*, fr. LL *abbreviare*, fr. L *ad-* + *brevis* short — more at BRIEF] (14c) **1 a** *archaic* : DEPRIVE **b :** to reduce in scope : DIMINISH ⟨attempts to ~ the right of free speech⟩ **2 :** to shorten in duration or extent ⟨modern transportation that ~s distance⟩ **3 :** to shorten by omission of words without sacrifice of sense : CONDENSE *syn* see SHORTEN — **abridg·er** *n*

abridg·ment *or* **abridge·ment** \ə-ˈbrij-mənt\ *n* (15c) **1 :** the action of abridging : the state of being abridged **2 :** a shortened form of a work retaining the general sense and unity of the original

abroach \ə-ˈbrōch\ *adv or adj* (14c) **1 :** in a condition for letting out a liquid (as wine) ⟨a cask set ~⟩ **2 :** in action or agitation : ASTIR ⟨mischiefs that I set ~ —Shak.⟩

abroad \ə-ˈbrȯd\ *adv or adj* (13c) **1 :** over a wide area : WIDELY **2 :** away from one's home **3 :** beyond the boundaries of one's country **4 :** in wide circulation : ABOUT **5 :** wide of the mark : ASTRAY

ab·ro·gate \ˈab-rə-ˌgāt\ *vt* **-gat·ed; -gat·ing** [L *abrogatus*, pp. of *abrogare*, fr. *ab-* + *rogare* to ask, propose a law — more at RIGHT] (15c) **1 :** to abolish by authoritative action : ANNUL **2 :** to do away with *syn* see NULLIFY — **ab·ro·ga·tion** \ˌab-rə-ˈgā-shən\ *n*

abrupt \ə-ˈbrəpt\ *adj* [L *abruptus*, pp. of *abrumpere* to break off, fr. *ab-* + *rumpere* to break — more at REAVE] (1591) **1 a :** occurring without warning : UNEXPECTED ⟨~ weather changes⟩ **b :** unceremoniously curt ⟨an ~ manner⟩ **c :** marked by sudden changes in subject matter : DISCONNECTED **2 a :** broken off **b :** suddenly terminating as if cut or broken off ⟨~ plant filaments⟩ **3 :** rising or dropping sharply as if broken off ⟨a high ~ bank bounded the stream⟩ *syn* see PRECIPITATE, STEEP — **abrupt·ly** \ə-ˈbrəp-(t)lē\ *adv* — **abrupt·ness** \ə-ˈbrəp(t)-nəs\ *n*

abrup·tion \ə-ˈbrəp-shən\ *n* (1606) : a sudden breaking off or away

ABS \ˌā-(ˌ)bē-ˈes\ *n* [acrylonitrile-butadiene-styrene] (1966) : a tough rigid plastic used esp. for automobile parts and building materials

ab·scess \ˈab-ˌses\ *n, pl* **ab·scess·es** \ˈab-səs-ˌēz, -ˌses-, -əz\ [L *abscessus*, lit., act of going away, fr. *abscessus*, pp. of *abscedere* to go away, fr. *abs-, ab-* + *cedere* to go — more at CEDE] (1615) : a localized collection of pus surrounded by inflamed tissue — **ab·scessed** \-ˌsest\ *adj*

ab·scise \ab-ˈsīz\ *vb* **ab·scised; ab·scis·ing** [L *abscisus*, pp. of *abscidere*, fr. *abs-* + *caedere* to cut — more at CONCISE] *vt* (1612) : to cut off by abscission ~ *vi* : to separate by abscission

ab·scis·ic acid \ab-ˌsiz-ik-, -ˌsis-\ [*abscisin* (var. of *abscission*) + *-ic*] (1968) : a plant hormone $C_{15}H_{20}O_4$ that is widespread in nature and is made synthetically and that typically promotes leaf abscission and dormancy and has an inhibitory effect on cell elongation — called also *abscisin II*

ab·scis·in \ˈab-sə-sən, ab-ˈsis-ᵊn\ *n* [*abscision* + *-in*] (1961) : any of a group of plant regulatory substances orig. found in young cotton bolls that tend to promote leaf abscission and inhibit various growth processes — compare ABSCISIC ACID

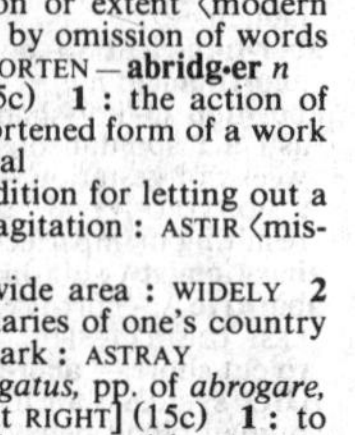

ab·scis·sa \ab-ˈsis-ə\ *n, pl* **abscissas** *also* **ab·scis·sae** \-ˈsis-(ˌ)ē\ [NL, fr. L, fem. of *abscissus*, pp. of *abscindere* to cut off, fr. *ab-* + *scindere* to cut — more at SHED] (1694) : the horizontal coordinate of a point in a plane Cartesian coordinate system obtained by measuring parallel to the x-axis — compare ORDINATE

ab·scis·sion \ab-ˈsizh-ən\ *n* [L *abscission-, abscissio*, fr. *abscissus*] (15c) **1 :** the act or process

of cutting off : REMOVAL **2 :** the natural separation of flowers, fruit, or leaves from plants at a special separation layer

ab·scond \ab-ˈskänd, əb-\ *vi* [L *abscondere* to hide away, fr. *abs-* + *condere* to store up, conceal — more at CONDIMENT] (1565) : to depart secretly and hide oneself — **ab·scond·er** *n*

ab·sence \ˈab-sən(t)s\ *n* (14c) **1 :** the state of being absent **2 :** the period of time that one is absent **3 :** WANT, LACK ⟨an ~ of detail⟩ **4 :** inattention to present surroundings or occurrences ⟨~ of mind⟩

¹**ab·sent** \ˈab-sənt\ *adj* [ME, fr. MF, fr. L *absent-, absens*, prp. of *abesse* to be absent, fr. *ab-* + *esse* to be — more at IS] (14c) **1 :** not present or attending : MISSING **2 :** not existing : LACKING ⟨danger in a situation where power is ~ —M. H. Trytten⟩ **3 :** INATTENTIVE, PREOCCUPIED — **ab·sent·ly** *adv*

²**ab·sent** \ab-ˈsent, ˈab-,\ *vt* (15c) : to keep (oneself) away

³**ab·sent** \ˈab-sənt\ *prep* (1945) : in the absence of : WITHOUT

ab·sen·tee \ˌab-sən-ˈtē\ *n* (1605) : one that is absent or that absents himself; *specif* : a proprietor that lives away from his estate or business — **absentee** *adj*

absentee ballot *n* (1932) : a ballot submitted (as by mail) in advance of an election by a voter who is unable to be present at the polls

ab·sen·tee·ism \ˌab-sən-ˈtē-ˌiz-əm\ *n* (1829) **1 :** prolonged absence of an owner from his property **2 :** chronic absence (as from work or school); *also* : the rate of such absence

ab·sent·mind·ed \ˌab-sənt-ˈmīn-dəd\ *adj* (1854) : lost in thought and unaware of one's surroundings or action : PREOCCUPIED; *also* : given to absence of mind — **ab·sent·mind·ed·ly** *adv* — **ab·sent·mind·ed·ness** *n*

absent without leave *adj* (ca. 1919) : absent without authority from one's place of duty in the armed forces

ab·sinthe *also* **ab·sinth** \ˈab-(ˌ)sin(t)th\ *n* [F *absinthe*, fr. L *absinthium*, fr. Gk *apsinthion*] (1612) **1 :** WORMWOOD 1; *esp* : a common European wormwood (*Artemisia absinthium*) **2 :** a green liqueur flavored with wormwood or a substitute, anise, and other aromatics

ab·so·lute \ˈab-sə-ˌlüt, ˌab-sə-ˈ\ *adj* [ME *absolut*, fr. L *absolutus*, fr. pp. of *absolvere* to set free, absolve] (14c) **1 a :** free from imperfection : PERFECT **b :** free or relatively free from mixture : PURE ⟨~ alcohol⟩ **c :** OUTRIGHT, UNMITIGATED ⟨an ~ lie⟩ **2 :** being, governed by, or characteristic of a ruler or authority completely free from constitutional or other restraint **3 a :** standing apart from a normal or usual syntactical relation with other words or sentence elements ⟨the ~ construction *this being the case* in the sentence "this being the case, let us go"⟩ **b** *of an adjective or possessive pronoun* : standing alone without a modified substantive ⟨*blind* in "help the blind" and *ours* in "your work and ours" are ~⟩ **c** *of a verb* : having no object in the particular construction under consideration though normally transitive ⟨*kill* in "if looks could kill" is an ~ verb⟩ **4 :** having no restriction, exception, or qualification ⟨an ~ requirement⟩ ⟨~ freedom⟩ **5 :** POSITIVE, UNQUESTIONABLE ⟨~ proof⟩ **6 a :** independent of arbitrary standards of measurement **b :** relating to or derived in the simplest manner from the fundamental units of length, mass, and time ⟨~ electric units⟩ **c :** relating to the absolute-temperature scale ⟨10° ~⟩ **7 :** FUNDAMENTAL, ULTIMATE ⟨~ knowledge⟩ **8 :** perfectly embodying the nature of a thing ⟨~ justice⟩ **9 :** being self-sufficient and free of external references or relationships ⟨an ~ term in logic⟩ ⟨~ music⟩ **10 :** measuring or representing the distance from an aircraft to the ground or water beneath — **absolute** *n* — **ab·so·lute·ness** *n*

absolute ceiling *n* (1920) : the maximum height above sea level at which a particular airplane can maintain horizontal flight under standard air conditions — called also *ceiling*

absolute convergence *n* (ca. 1909) : convergence of a mathematical series when the absolute values of the terms are taken

absolute humidity *n* (ca. 1867) : the amount of water vapor present in a unit volume of air

ab·so·lute·ly \ˈab-sə-ˌlüt-lē, ˌab-sə-ˈ\ *adv* (14c) **1 :** in an absolute manner or condition **2 :** with respect to absolute values ⟨an ~ convergent series⟩

absolute magnitude *n* (ca. 1902) : the intrinsic luminosity of a celestial body (as a star) if viewed from a distance of 10 parsecs

absolute pitch *n* (1864) **1 :** the position of a tone in a standard scale independently determined by its rate of vibration **2 :** the ability to recognize or sing a given isolated note

absolute scale *n* (ca. 1848) : a temperature scale based on absolute zero

absolute space *n* (ca. 1889) : SPACE 4b

absolute temperature *n* (1852) : temperature measured on a scale based on absolute zero; *esp* : temperature measured on the Kelvin scale

absolute value *n* (1907) **1 :** a nonnegative number equal in numerical value to a given real number ⟨6 is the *absolute value* of −6⟩ **2 :** the positive square root of the sum of the squares of the real and imaginary parts of a complex number

absolute zero *n* (1848) : a theoretical temperature characterized by complete absence of heat and equivalent to exactly −273.15°C or −459.67°F

ab·so·lu·tion \ˌab-sə-ˈlü-shən\ *n* (13c) : the act of absolving; *specif* : a remission of sins pronounced by a priest (as in the sacrament of penance)

ab·so·lut·ism \ˈab-sə-ˌlüt-ˌiz-əm\ *n* (1830) **1 a :** a political theory that absolute power should be vested in one or more rulers **b :** government by an absolute ruler or authority : DESPOTISM **2 :** advocacy of a rule by absolute standards or principles **3 :** an absolute standard or principle — **ab·so·lut·ist** \-ˌlüt-əst\ *n or adj* — **ab·so·lu·tis·tic** \ˌab-sə-(ˌ)lü-ˈtis-tik\ *adj*

ab·so·lut·ize \ˈab-sə-ˈsȯ(ə)lüt-ˌīz\ *vt* **-ized; -iz·ing** (1919) : to make absolute : convert into an absolute

ab·solve \əb-ˈzälv, -ˈsälv, -ˈzȯlv, -ˈsȯlv *also without* l\ *vt* **ab·solved; ab·solv·ing** [ME *absolven*, fr. L *absolvere*, fr. *ab-* + *solvere* to loosen — more at SOLVE] (15c) **1 :** to set free from an obligation or the consequences of guilt **2 :** to remit (a sin) by absolution *syn* see EXCULPATE — **ab·solv·er** *n*

ab·sorb \əb-ˈsȯ(ə)rb, -ˈzȯ(ə)rb\ *vt* [MF *absorber*, fr. L *absorbēre*, fr. *ab-* + *sorbēre* to suck up] (15c) **1 :** to take in and make part of an existent whole ⟨the capacity of China to ~ invaders⟩ **2 a :** to suck up or take up ⟨a sponge ~s water⟩ ⟨charcoal ~s gas⟩ ⟨plant roots ~ water⟩ **b :** to take in ⟨convictions ~ed in youth —M. R. Cohen⟩ **c :** USE UP, CONSUME ⟨the fever ~ed her strength⟩ **3 :** to engage or engross wholly ⟨~ed in thought⟩ **4 a** (1) **:** to receive without recoil or echo ⟨pro-

[diagram of Cartesian coordinate axes labeled y, x, P, A, O with:]
AP abscissa of point P

vided with a sound-*absorbing* surface⟩ (2) : ENDURE, SUSTAIN ⟨~*ing* hardships⟩ **b** : to transform (radiant energy) into a different form usu. with a resulting rise in temperature ⟨the earth ~*s* the sun's rays⟩ **5** : to take over (a cost) — **ab·sorb·abil·i·ty** \əb-ˌsȯr-bə-ˈbil-ət-ē, -ˌzȯr-\ *n* — **ab·sorb·able** \əb-ˈsȯr-bə-bəl, -ˈzȯr-\ *adj* — **ab·sorb·er** *n*

syn ABSORB, IMBIBE, ASSIMILATE mean to take something in so as to become imbued with it. ABSORB may connote a loss of identity in what is taken in or an enrichment of what takes in; IMBIBE implies a drinking in which may be unconscious but whose effect may be significant or profound; ASSIMILATE stresses an incorporation into the substance of the body or mind.

ab·sor·bance \əb-ˈsȯr-bən(t)s, -ˈzȯr-\ *n* (1948) : the ability of a layer of a substance to absorb radiation expressed mathematically as the negative common logarithm of transmittance

ab·sor·ben·cy \əb-ˈsȯr-bən-sē, -ˈzȯr-\ *n, pl* **-cies** (1859) **1** : the quality or state of being absorbent **2** *or* **ab·sor·ban·cy** : ABSORBANCE

ab·sor·bent *also* **ab·sor·bant** \-bənt\ *adj* [L *absorbent-, absorbens,* prp. of *absorbēre*] (1718) : able to absorb ⟨as ~ as a sponge⟩ — **absorbent** *also* **absorbant** *n*

ab·sorb·ing *adj* (1862) : fully taking one's attention : ENGROSSING ⟨an ~ novel⟩ — **ab·sorb·ing·ly** \-biŋ-lē\ *adv*

ab·sorp·tance \əb-ˈsȯrp-tən(t)s, -ˈzȯrp-\ *n* [*absorption* + *-ance*] (ca. 1931) : the ratio of the radiant energy absorbed by a body to that incident upon it

ab·sorp·tion \əb-ˈsȯrp-shən, -ˈzȯrp-\ *n* [F & L; F, fr. L *absorption-, absorptio,* fr. *absorptus,* pp. of *absorbēre*] (1741) **1 a** : the process of absorbing or of being absorbed — compare ADSORPTION **b** : interception of radiant energy or sound waves **2** : entire occupation of the mind ⟨~ in his work⟩ — **ab·sorp·tion·al** \-shnəl, -shən-ᵊl\ *adj* — **ab·sorp·tive** \-tiv\ *adj*

absorption spectrum *n* (1879) : an electromagnetic spectrum whose distribution of intensities by wavelength has been modified by passage through a selectively absorbing substance (as chlorophyll)

ab·sorp·tiv·i·ty \əb-ˌsȯrp-ˈtiv-ət-ē, -ˌzȯrp-\ *n, pl* **-ties** (ca. 1864) : the property of a body that determines the fraction of incident radiation absorbed by the body

ab·stain \əb-ˈstān, ab-\ *vi* [ME *absteinen,* fr. MF *abstenir,* fr. L *abstinēre,* fr. *abs-, ab-* + *tenēre* to hold — more at THIN] (14c) : to refrain deliberately and often with an effort of self-denial from an action or practice — **ab·stain·er** *n*

ab·ste·mi·ous \ab-ˈstē-mē-əs\ *adj* [L *abstemius,* fr. *abs-* + *temetum* mead — more at TEMERITY] (1610) **1** : sparing esp. in eating or drinking **2** : sparingly used or indulged in ⟨~ diet⟩ — **ab·ste·mi·ous·ly** *adv*

ab·sten·tion \əb-ˈsten-chən, ab-\ *n* [LL *abstention-, abstentio,* fr. L *abstentus,* pp. of *abstinēre*] (1521) : the act or practice of abstaining — **ab·sten·tious** \-chəs\ *adj*

ab·sti·nence \ˈab-stə-nən(t)s\ *n* [ME, fr. MF, fr. L *abstinentia,* fr. *abstinent-, abstinens,* prp. of *abstinēre*] (14c) **1** : voluntary forbearance esp. from indulgence of an appetite or craving or from eating some foods : ABSTENTION **2** : habitual abstaining from intoxicating beverages — **ab·sti·nent** \-nənt\ *adj* — **ab·sti·nent·ly** *adv*

[1]**ab·stract** \ab-ˈstrakt, ˈab-ˌ\ *adj* [ML *abstractus,* fr. L, pp. of *abstrahere* to draw away, fr. *abs-, ab-* + *trahere* to draw — more at DRAW] (15c) **1 a** : disassociated from any specific instance ⟨~ entity⟩ **b** : difficult to understand : ABSTRUSE ⟨~ problems⟩ **c** : IDEAL ⟨~ justice⟩ **d** : insufficiently factual : FORMAL ⟨possessed only an ~ right⟩ **2** : expressing a quality apart from an object ⟨the word *poem* is concrete, *poetry* is ~⟩ **3 a** : dealing with a subject in its abstract aspects : THEORETICAL ⟨~ science⟩ **b** : IMPERSONAL, DETACHED ⟨the ~ compassion of a surgeon —*Time*⟩ **4** : having only intrinsic form with little or no attempt at pictorial representation or narrative content ⟨~ painting⟩ — **ab·stract·ly** \ab-ˈstrak-(t)lē, ˈab-ˌ\ *adv* — **ab·stract·ness** \ab-ˈstrak(t)-nəs, ˈab-ˌ\ *n*

[2]**ab·stract** \ˈab-ˌstrakt, *in sense 2 also* ab-ˈ\ *n* [ME, fr. L *abstractus*] (15c) **1** : a summary of points (as of a writing) usu. presented in skeletal form **2** : an abstract thing or state **3** : ABSTRACTION 4

[3]**ab·stract** \ab-ˈstrakt, ˈab-ˌ, *in sense 3 usu* ˈab-ˌ\ *vt* (1542) **1** : REMOVE, SEPARATE **2** : to consider apart from application to or association with a particular instance **3** : to make an abstract of : SUMMARIZE **4** : to draw away the attention of **5** : STEAL, PURLOIN ~ *vi* : to make an abstraction — **ab·stract·able** \-ˈstrak-tə-bəl, -ˌstrak-\ *adj* — **ab·strac·tor** *or* **ab·stract·er** \-tər\ *n*

ab·stract·ed \ab-ˈstrak-təd, ˈab-ˌ\ *adj* (1643) **1** : PREOCCUPIED, ABSENT-MINDED ⟨the ~ look of a professor⟩ **2** : ABSTRACT 4 ⟨~ geometric shapes⟩ — **ab·stract·ed·ly** *adv* — **ab·stract·ed·ness** *n*

abstract expressionism *n* (1951) : art in which the artist attempts to convey his attitudes and emotions through nonrepresentational means — **abstract expressionist** *n*

ab·strac·tion \ab-ˈstrak-shən, əb-\ *n* (1549) **1 a** : the act or process of abstracting : the state of being abstracted **b** : an abstract idea or term **2** : absence of mind **3** : abstract quality or character **4** : an abstract composition or creation in art — **ab·strac·tion·al** \-shnəl, -shən-ᵊl\ *adj* — **ab·strac·tive** \ab-ˈstrak-tiv, ˈab-ˌ\ *adj*

ab·strac·tion·ism \ab-ˈstrak-shə-ˌniz-əm, əb-\ *n* (1926) : the principles or practice of creating abstract art — **ab·strac·tion·ist** \-sh(ə-)nəst\ *adj or n*

abstract of title (1858) : a summary statement of the successive conveyances and other facts on which a person's title to a piece of land rests

ab·struse \əb-ˈstrüs, ab-\ *adj* [L *abstrusus,* fr. pp. of *abstrudere* to conceal, fr. *abs-, ab-* + *trudere* to push — more at THREAT] (1599) : difficult to comprehend : RECONDITE ⟨the ~ calculations of mathematicians⟩ — **ab·struse·ly** *adv* — **ab·struse·ness** *n*

ab·stru·si·ty \-ˈstrü-sət-ē\ *n, pl* **-ties** (1646) **1** : the quality or state of being abstruse **2** : ABSTRUSENESS **2** : something that is abstruse

[1]**ab·surd** \əb-ˈsərd, -ˈzərd\ *adj* [MF *absurde,* fr. L *absurdus,* fr. *ab-* + *surdus* deaf, stupid — more at SURD] (1557) **1** : ridiculously unreasonable, unsound, or incongruous **2** : having no rational or orderly relationship to man's life : MEANINGLESS; *also* : lacking order or value **3** : dealing with the absurd or with absurdism — **ab·surd·ly** *adv* — **ab·surd·ness** *n*

[2]**absurd** *n* (1946) : the state or condition in which man exists in an irrational and meaningless universe and in which man's life has no meaning outside his own existence — usu. used with *the*

ab·surd·ism \-ˌiz-əm\ *n* (1946) : a philosophy based on the belief that man exists in an irrational and meaningless universe and that his search for order brings him into conflict with his universe — compare EXISTENTIALISM — **ab·surd·ist** \-əst\ *n or adj*

ab·sur·di·ty \əb-ˈsərd-ət-ē, -ˈzərd-\ *n, pl* **-ties** (1528) **1** : the quality or state of being absurd : ABSURDNESS **2** : something that is absurd

abub·ble \ə-ˈbəb-əl\ *adj* (1868) **1** : being in the process of bubbling : EFFERVESCENT **2** : being in a state of agitated activity or motion : ASTIR

abuild·ing \ə-ˈbil-diŋ\ *adj* (1535) : being in the process of building or of being built

abu·lia \ā-ˈb(y)ü-lē-ə, ə-\ *n* [NL, fr. [2]*a-* + Gk *boulē* will] (ca. 1864) : abnormal lack of ability to act or to make decisions — **abu·lic** \-lik\ *adj*

abun·dance \ə-ˈbən-dən(t)s\ *n* (14c) **1** : an ample quantity : PROFUSION **2** : AFFLUENCE, WEALTH **3** : relative degree of plentifulness ⟨low ~*s* of uranium and thorium —H. C. Urey⟩

abun·dant \-dənt\ *adj* [ME, fr. MF, fr. L *abundant-, abundans,* prp. of *abundare* to abound] (14c) **1 a** : marked by great plenty (as of resources) ⟨a fair and ~ land⟩ **b** : amply supplied : ABOUNDING ⟨~ with fly life and other natural trout food —Alexander MacDonald⟩ **2** : occurring in abundance : AMPLE ⟨~ rainfall⟩ ***syn*** see PLENTIFUL — **abun·dant·ly** *adv*

[1]**abuse** \ə-ˈbyüs\ *n* [ME, fr. MF *abus,* fr. L *abusus,* pp. of *abuti* to consume, fr. *ab-* + *uti* to use—more at USE] (15c) **1** : a corrupt practice or custom **2** : improper use or treatment : MISUSE ⟨drug ~⟩ **3** *obs* : a deceitful act : DECEPTION **4** : language that condemns or vilifies usu. unjustly, intemperately, and angrily **5** : physical maltreatment

syn ABUSE, VITUPERATION, INVECTIVE, OBLOQUY, SCURRILITY, BILLINGSGATE mean vehemently expressed condemnation or disapproval. ABUSE, the most general term, usu. implies the anger of the speaker and stresses the harshness of the language; VITUPERATION implies fluent and sustained abuse; INVECTIVE implies a comparable vehemence but suggests greater verbal and rhetorical skill and may apply to a public denunciation; OBLOQUY suggests defamation and consequent shame and disgrace; SCURRILITY implies viciousness of attack and coarseness or foulness of language; BILLINGSGATE implies practiced fluency and variety of profane or obscene abuse.

[2]**abuse** \ə-ˈbyüz\ *vt* **abused; abus·ing** (15c) **1** *obs* : DECEIVE **2** : to put to a wrong or improper use ⟨~ a privilege⟩ **3** : to use so as to injure or damage : MALTREAT ⟨~ a dog⟩ **4** : to attack in words : REVILE — **abus·able** \-ˈbyü-zə-bəl\ *adj* — **abus·er** *n*

abu·sive \ə-ˈbyü-siv, -ziv\ *adj* (1583) **1** : characterized by wrong or improper use or action : CORRUPT ⟨~ financial practices⟩ **2 a** : using harsh insulting language : characterized by or serving for abuse **b** : physically injurious ⟨~ treatment⟩ — **abu·sive·ly** *adv* — **abu·sive·ness** *n*

abut \ə-ˈbət\ *vb* **abut·ted; abut·ting** [ME *abutten,* partly fr. OF *aboter* to border on, fr. *a-* (fr. L *ad-*) + *bout* blow, end, fr. *boter* to strike; partly fr. OF *abuter* to come to an end, fr. *a-* + *but* end, aim — more at [1]BUTT, [4]BUTT] *vi* (15c) **1** : to touch along a border or with a projecting part ⟨land ~*s* on the road⟩ **2 a** : to terminate at a point of contact **b** : to lean for support ~ *vt* **1** : to border on : TOUCH **2** : to cause to abut — **abut·ter** *n*

abu·ti·lon \ə-ˈbyüt-ᵊl-ˌän, -ᵊl-ən\ *n* [NL, genus name, fr. Ar *awbūtīlūn* abutilon] (ca. 1578) : any of a genus (*Abutilon*) of plants of the mallow family with usu. lobed leaves and showy solitary bell-shaped flowers

abut·ment \ə-ˈbət-mənt\ *n* (1644) **1** : the place at which abutting occurs **2 a** : the part of a structure that directly receives thrust or pressure (as of an arch) **b** : an anchorage for the cables of a suspension bridge or aerial railway

abut·tals \ə-ˈbət-ᵊlz\ *n pl* (1630) : the boundaries of lands with respect to adjacent lands

abut·ting *adj* (1599) : that abuts or serves as an abutment : ADJOINING, BORDERING ***syn*** see ADJACENT

abuzz \ə-ˈbəz\ *adj* (1859) : filled or resounding with or as if with a buzzing sound ⟨a lake ~ with outboards⟩ ⟨a town ~ with excitement⟩

aby *or* **abye** \ə-ˈbī\ *vt* [ME *abien,* fr. OE *ābycgan,* fr. *ā-* + *bycgan* to buy — more at ABIDE, BUY] *archaic* (bef. 12c) : to suffer a penalty for

abysm \ə-ˈbiz-əm\ *n* [ME *abime,* fr. MF *abisme,* modif. of LL *abyssus*] (14c) : ABYSS ⟨the dark backward and ~ of time —Shak.⟩

abys·mal \ə-ˈbiz-məl, a-\ *adj* (ca. 1656) **1 a** : having immense or fathomless extension downward, backward, or inward ⟨an ~ cliff⟩ **b** : immeasurably great : PROFOUND ⟨~ ignorance⟩ **c** : immeasurably low or wretched ⟨~ living conditions of the poor⟩ **2** : ABYSSAL — **abys·mal·ly** \-mə-lē\ *adv*

abyss \ə-ˈbis, *a- also* ˈab-(ˌ)is\ *n* [ME *abissus,* fr. LL *abyssus,* fr. Gk *abyssos,* fr. *abyssos,* adj., bottomless, fr. *a-* + *byssos* depth; akin to Gk *bathys* deep — more at BATHY-] (14c) **1** : the bottomless gulf, pit, or chaos of the old cosmogonies **2 a** : an immeasurably deep gulf or great space **b** : intellectual or spiritual profundity

abys·sal \ə-ˈbis-əl\ *adj* (1691) **1** : UNFATHOMABLE **a** **2** : of or relating to the bottom waters of the ocean depths

Ab·ys·sin·i·an cat \ˌab-ə-ˌsin-ē-ən-, -ˌsin-yən-\ *n* [*Abyssinia,* kingdom in Africa] (1876) : any of a breed of small slender cats of African origin with short brownish hair ticked with bands of darker color — see CAT illustration

ac- — see AD-

-ac \ˌak, *in a few words* ik *or* ək\ *n suffix* [NL *-acus* of or relating to, fr. Gk *-akos*] : one affected with ⟨nostalgiac⟩

aca·cia \ə-ˈkā-shə\ *n* [NL, genus name, fr. L, acacia tree, fr. Gk *akakia* shittah] (14c) **1** : GUM ARABIC **2** : any of a genus (*Acacia*) of woody leguminous plants of warm regions with leaves pinnate or reduced to phyllodes and white or yellow flower clusters

ac·a·deme \'ak-ə-ˌdēm, ˌak-ə-'\ *n* [irreg. fr. NL *academia*] (1588) **1 a** : a place of instruction : SCHOOL **b** : the academic environment **c** (1) : the academic community (2) : academic life **2** : ACADEMIC; *esp* : PEDANT

ac·a·de·mia \ˌak-ə-'dē-mē-ə\ *n* [NL, fr. L, academy] (1946) : ACADEME 1c

1ac·a·dem·ic \ˌak-ə-'dem-ik\ *n* (1587) **1** : a member of an institution of learning **2** : one who is academic in background, outlook, or methods

2academic *also* **ac·a·dem·i·cal** \-i-kəl\ *adj* (1588) **1 a** : of, relating to, or associated with an academy or school esp. of higher learning **b** : of or relating to performance in academic courses **c** : very learned but inexperienced in practical matters ⟨~ thinkers⟩ **d** : based on formal study esp. at an institution of higher learning **2** : of or relating to literary or artistic rather than technical or professional studies **3** : conforming to the traditions or rules of a school (as of literature or art) or an official academy : CONVENTIONAL **4 a** : THEORETICAL, SPECULATIVE ⟨an ~ question⟩ **b** : having no practical or useful significance — **ac·a·dem·i·cal·ly** \-i-k(ə-)lē\ *adv*

academic freedom *n* (1901) : freedom to teach or to learn without interference (as by government officials)

ac·a·de·mi·cian \ˌak-əd-ə-'mish-ən, ə-ˌkad-ə-\ *n* (1748) **1 a** : a member of an academy for promoting science, art, or literature **b** : a follower of an artistic or philosophical tradition or a promoter of its ideas **2** : ACADEMIC

ac·a·dem·i·cism \ˌak-ə-'dem-ə-ˌsiz-əm\ *also* **acad·e·mism** \ə-'kad-ə-ˌmiz-əm\ *n* (1610) **1** : the doctrines of Plato's Academy; *specif* : the skeptical doctrines of the later Academy holding that nothing can be known — compare PYRRHONISM **2** : a formal academic quality (as in art or music) **3** : purely speculative thoughts and attitudes

academic year *n* (ca. 1934) : the annual period of sessions of an educational institution usu. beginning in September and ending in June

acad·e·my \ə-'kad-ə-mē\ *n, pl* **-mies** [L *academia,* fr. Gk *Akadēmeia,* fr. *Akadēmeia,* gymnasium where Plato taught, fr. *Akadēmos* Attic mythological hero] (15c) **1** *cap* **a** : the school for advanced education founded by Plato **b** : the philosophical doctrines associated with Plato's Academy **2 a** : a school usu. above the elementary level; *esp* : a private high school **b** : a high school or college in which special subjects or skills are taught **c** : higher education — used with *the* ⟨the functions of the ~ in modern society⟩ **3** : a society of learned persons organized to advance art, science, or literature **4** : a body of established opinion widely accepted as authoritative in a particular field

Aca·di·an \ə-'kād-ē-ən, a-\ *n* (1705) **1** : a native or inhabitant of Acadia **2 a** : CAJUN 1 **b** : a dialect of French spoken by Acadians — **Acadian** *adj*

acanth- *or* **acantho-** *comb form* [NL, fr. Gk *akanth-, akantho-,* fr. *akantha* — more at AWN] : thorn : spine ⟨*acanth*ous⟩ ⟨*acantho*cephalan⟩

acan·tho·ceph·a·lan \ə-ˌkan(t)-thə-'sef-ə-lən\ *n* [deriv. of *acanth-* + Gk *kephalē* head — more at CEPHALIC] (ca. 1909) : SPINY-HEADED WORM — **acanthocephalan** *adj*

ac·an·thop·ter·yg·i·an \ˌak-ən-ˌthäp-tə-'rij-ē-ən\ *n* [deriv. of *acanth-* + Gk *pteryg-, pteryx* wing, fin — more at PTERYGOID] (ca. 1835) : any of a major division (Acanthopterygii) of teleost fishes including most spiny-finned fishes (as basses, perches, and mackerels) and some soft-finned fishes — **acanthopterygian** *adj*

acan·thus \ə-'kan(t)-thəs\ *n, pl* **acan·thus·es** *also* **acan·thi** \-'kan-ˌthī\ [NL, genus name, fr. Gk *akanthos,* an acanthus, fr. *akantha*] (ca. 1616) **1** : any of a genus (*Acanthus* of the family Acanthaceae, the acanthus family) of prickly herbs of the Mediterranean region **2** : an ornamentation (as in a Corinthian capital) representing or suggesting the leaves of the acanthus

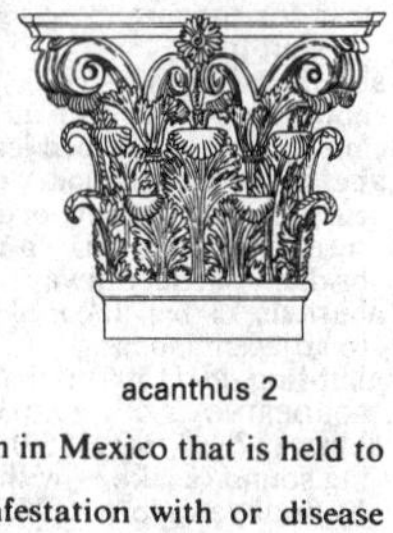
acanthus 2

a cap·pel·la *also* **a ca·pel·la** \ˌäk-ə-'pel-ə\ *adv or adj* [It *a cappella* in chapel style] (ca. 1864) : without instrumental accompaniment

Ac·a·pul·co gold \ˌak-ə-ˌpu̇l-(ˌ)kō-, ˌäk-\ *n* [*Acapulco,* Mexico] (1968) : marijuana grown in Mexico that is held to be very potent

ac·a·ri·a·sis \ˌak-ə-'rī-ə-səs\ *n* (ca. 1828) : infestation with or disease caused by mites

ac·a·rid \'ak-ə-rəd\ *n* (1881) : any of an order (Acarina) of arachnids including the mites and ticks; *esp* : a typical mite (family Acaridae) — **acarid** *adj*

ac·a·roid resin \ˌak-ə-ˌrȯid-\ *n* [NL *acaroides*] (1857) : an alcohol-soluble resin from Australian grass trees (genus *Xanthorrhoea,* esp. *X. australis*)

ac·a·rus \'ak-ə-rəs\ *n, pl* **-ri** \-ˌrī\ [NL, genus name, fr. Gk *akari,* a mite] (1658) : MITE; *esp* : one of a formerly extensive genus (*Acarus*)

acat·a·lec·tic \(ˌ)ā-ˌkat-ᵊl-'ek-tik\ *adj* [LL *acatalecticus,* fr. *acatalectus,* fr. Gk *akatalēktos,* fr. *a-* + *katalēgein* to leave off — more at CATALECTIC] (1589) : not catalectic ⟨~ verse⟩ — **acatalectic** *n*

acau·les·cent \ˌā-kȯ-'les-ᵊnt\ *adj* [*a-* + L *caulis* stem — more at HOLE] (ca. 1854) : having no stem or appearing to have none

ac·cede \ak-'sēd, ik-\ *vi* **ac·ced·ed; ac·ced·ing** [ME *acceden,* fr. L *accedere* to go to, be added, fr. *ad-* + *cedere* to go — more at CEDE] (15c) **1** *archaic* : APPROACH **2 a** : to become a party (as to an agreement) **b** : to express approval or give consent : give in to a request or demand **3** : to enter upon an office or position ***syn*** see ASSENT

ac·ce·le·ran·do \(ˌ)ä-ˌchel-ə-'rän-(ˌ)dō; ik-ˌsel-, (ˌ)ak-\ *adv or adj* [It, lit., accelerating, fr. L *accelerandum,* gerund of *accelerare*] (ca. 1842) : gradually faster — used as a direction in music

ac·cel·er·ant \ik-'sel-ə-rənt, ak-\ *n* (1916) : a substance used to accelerate a process (as the spreading of a fire)

ac·cel·er·ate \-ə-ˌrāt\ *vb* **-at·ed; -at·ing** [L *acceleratus,* pp. of *accelerare,* fr. *ad-* + *celer* swift — more at CELERITY] *vt* (1525) **1** : to bring about at an earlier time **2** : to cause to move faster; *also* : to cause to undergo acceleration **3 a** : to hasten the progress or development of **b** : INCREASE ⟨~ food production⟩ **4 a** : to enable (a student) to complete a course in less than usual time **b** : to speed up (as a course of study) ~ *vi* **1 a** : to move faster : gain speed **b** : GROW, INCREASE ⟨believed inflation was *accelerating*⟩ **2** : to follow a speeded-up educational program — **ac·cel·er·at·ing·ly** \-ˌrāt-iŋ-lē\ *adv*

ac·cel·er·a·tion \ik-ˌsel-ə-'rā-shən, (ˌ)ak-\ *n* (1531) **1** : the act or process of accelerating : the state of being accelerated **2** : the rate of change of velocity with respect to time; *broadly* : change of velocity

acceleration of gravity (ca. 1889) : the acceleration of a freely falling body under the influence of gravity expressed as the rate of increase of velocity per unit of time with the value at sea level in latitude 45 degrees being 980.616 centimeters per second per second

acceleration principle *n* (ca. 1941) : a theory in economics: an increase or decrease in income induces a corresponding but magnified change in investment

ac·cel·er·a·tive \ik-'sel-ə-ˌrāt-iv, ak-\ *adj* (1751) : of, relating to, or tending to cause acceleration : ACCELERATING

ac·cel·er·a·tor \ik-'sel-ə-ˌrāt-ər, ak-\ *n* (1611) : one that accelerates: as **a** : a muscle or nerve that speeds the performance of an action **b** : a device for increasing the speed of a motor vehicle engine; *esp* : a foot-operated throttle that varies the supply of fuel-air mixture to the combustion chamber **c** : a substance that speeds a chemical reaction **d** : an apparatus for imparting high velocities to charged particles (as electrons)

ac·cel·er·om·e·ter \ik-ˌsel-ə-'räm-ət-ər, ak-\ *n* [ISV *acceleration* + *-o-* + *-meter*] (ca. 1890) : an instrument for measuring acceleration or for detecting and measuring vibrations

1ac·cent \'ak-ˌsent, ak-'\ *vt* [MF *accenter,* fr. *accent* intonation, fr. L *accentus,* perh. fr. *ad-* + *cantus* song — more at CHANT] (1530) **1** : to give prominence to : make more prominent **2 a** : to pronounce with accent : STRESS **b** : to mark with a written or printed accent

2ac·cent \'ak-ˌsent, *chiefly Brit* -sənt\ *n* (1538) **1** : a distinctive manner of expression: as **a** : an individual's distinctive or characteristic inflection, tone, or choice of words — usu. used in pl. **b** : speech habits typical of a particular group of people and esp. of the natives or residents of a region **2** : an articulative effort giving prominence to one syllable over adjacent syllables; *also* : the prominence thus given a syllable **3** : rhythmically significant stress on the syllables of a verse usu. at regular intervals **4** *archaic* : UTTERANCE **5 a** : a mark (as ´, `, ˆ) used in writing or printing to indicate a specific sound value, stress, or pitch, to distinguish words otherwise identically spelled, or to indicate that an ordinarily mute vowel should be pronounced **b** : an accented letter **6 a** : greater stress given to one musical tone than to its neighbors **b** (1) : the principle of regularly recurring stresses which serve to distribute a succession of pulses into measures (2) : special emphasis placed exceptionally upon tones not subject to such accent **c** : ACCENT MARK 2 **7 a** : emphasis laid on a part of an artistic design or composition **b** : an emphasized detail or area; *esp* : a small detail in sharp contrast with its surroundings **c** : a substance or object used for emphasis **8** : a mark placed to the right of a letter or number and usu. slightly above it: **a** (1) : a double prime (2) : PRIME **b** : a mark used singly with numbers to denote minutes and doubly to denote seconds of time or to denote minutes and seconds of an angle or arc **c** : a mark used singly with numbers to denote feet and doubly to denote inches **9** : special concern or attention : EMPHASIS ⟨an ~ on youth⟩ — **ac·cent·less** \-ləs\ *adj*

accent mark *n* (ca. 1889) **1** : ACCENT 5a, 8 **2 a** : a symbol used to indicate musical stress **b** : a mark placed after a letter designating a note of music to indicate in which octave the note occurs

ac·cen·tu·al \ak-'sench-(ə-)wəl, ik-\ *adj* [L *accentus*] (1610) : of, relating to, or characterized by accent; *specif* : based on accent rather than on quantity or syllabic recurrence — **ac·cen·tu·al·ly** \-ē\ *adv*

ac·cen·tu·ate \ik-'sen-chə-ˌwāt, ak-\ *vt* **-at·ed; -at·ing** [ML *accentuatus,* pp. of *accentuare,* fr. L *accentus*] (ca. 1731) : ACCENT, EMPHASIZE; *also* : INTENSIFY ⟨~s the feeling of despair⟩ — **ac·cen·tu·a·tion** \ik-ˌsen-chə-'wā-shən, (ˌ)ak-\ *n*

ac·cept \ik-'sept, ak- *also* ek-\ *vb* [ME *accepten,* fr. MF *accepter,* fr. L *acceptare,* fr. *acceptus,* pp. of *accipere* to receive, fr. *ad-* + *capere* to take — more at HEAVE] *vt* (14c) **1 a** : to receive willingly ⟨~ a gift⟩ **b** : to be able or designed to take or hold (something applied or added) ⟨a surface that will not ~ ink⟩ **2** : to give admittance or approval to ⟨~ her as one of the group⟩ **3 a** : to endure without protest or reaction ⟨~ poor living conditions⟩ **b** : to regard as proper, normal, or inevitable ⟨the idea is widely ~*ed*⟩ **c** : to recognize as true : BELIEVE ⟨refused to ~ the explanation⟩ **d** : to regard as having a certain meaning : UNDERSTAND ⟨users of a language ~ words to mean certain things⟩ **4 a** : to make a favorable response to ⟨~ an offer⟩ **b** : to agree to undertake (a responsibility) ⟨~ a job⟩ **5** : to assume an obligation to pay; *also* : to take in payment ⟨we don't ~ personal checks⟩ **6** : to receive (a legislative report) officially ~ *vi* : to receive favorably something offered — usu. used with *of* — **ac·cept·ing·ly** \-'sep-tiŋ-lē\ *adv* — **ac·cept·ing·ness** \-iŋ-nəs\ *n*

ac·cept·able \ik-'sep-tə-bəl, ak- *also* ek-\ *adj* (14c) **1** : capable or worthy of being accepted ⟨no compromise would be ~⟩ **2 a** : WELCOME, PLEASING ⟨compliments are always ~⟩ **b** : barely satisfactory or adequate ⟨performances varied from excellent to ~⟩ — **ac·cept·abil·i·ty** \ik-ˌsep-tə-'bil-ət-ē, (ˌ)ak-, ek-\ *n* — **ac·cept·able·ness** \ik-'sep-tə-bəl-nəs, ak-\ *n* — **ac·cept·ably** \-blē\ *adv*

ac·cep·tance \ik-'sep-tən(t)s, ak-\ *n* (1574) **1** : an agreeing either expressly or by conduct to the act or offer of another so that a contract is concluded and the parties become legally bound **2** : the quality or state of being accepted or acceptable **3** : the act of accepting : the fact of being accepted : APPROVAL **4 a** : the act of accepting a time draft or bill of exchange for payment when due according to the specified terms **b** : an accepted draft or bill of exchange **5** : ACCEPTATION 2

ac·cep·tant \-tənt\ *adj* (1851) : willing to accept : RECEPTIVE

ac·cep·ta·tion \ˌak-ˌsep-'tā-shən\ *n* (15c) **1** : ACCEPTANCE; *esp* : favorable reception or approval **2** : a generally accepted meaning of a word or understanding of a concept

ac·cept·ed *adj* (15c) : generally approved or used — **ac·cept·ed·ly** *adv*

ac·cept·er \ik-'sep-tər, ak-\ *n* (1585) **1** : one that accepts **2** : ACCEPTOR 2

ac·cep·tive \ak-'sep-tiv\ *adj* (1596) **1** : RECEPTIVE **2** : ACCEPTABLE

ac·cep·tor \ik-'sep-tər, ak-\ *n* (14c) **1** : ACCEPTER 1 **2** : one that accepts an order or a bill of exchange **3** : a compound, atom, or subatomic particle capable of receiving another entity (as an atom, chemical group, or subatomic particle) to form a compound — compare DONOR 3a

[1]**ac·cess** \'ak-ˌses *also* ik-'ses\ *n* [ME, fr. MF & L; MF *acces* arrival, fr. L *accessus* approach, fr. *accessus,* pp. of *accedere* to approach — more at ACCEDE] (14c) **1 a :** ONSET 2 **b :** a fit of intense feeling : OUTBURST **2 a :** permission, liberty, or ability to enter, approach, communicate with, or pass to and from **b :** freedom or ability to obtain or make use of **c :** a way or means of access **d :** the action of going to or reaching **3 :** an increase by addition

[2]**access** *vt* (1966) **:** to get at : gain access to

ac·ces·si·ble \ik-'ses-ə-bəl, ak-, ek-\ *adj* (15c) **1 :** usable for access **2 a :** capable of being reached ⟨~ by rail⟩ **b :** easy to speak or deal with ⟨~ people⟩ **3 :** capable of being influenced : OPEN **4 :** capable of being used or seen : AVAILABLE **5 :** capable of being understood or appreciated ⟨the author's most ~ stories⟩ — **ac·ces·si·bil·i·ty** \-ˌses-ə-'bil-ət-ē\ *n* — **ac·ces·si·ble·ness** \-'ses-ə-bəl-nəs\ *n* — **ac·ces·si·bly** \-blē\ *adv*

[1]**ac·ces·sion** \ik-'sesh-ən, ak-\ *n* (1588) **1 :** something added : ACQUISITION **2 a :** the act of becoming joined : ADHERENCE **b :** the act by which one nation becomes party to an agreement already in force between other powers **3 a :** increase by something added **b :** acquisition of additional property (as by growth or increase of existing property) **4 :** the act of assenting or agreeing **5 a :** an act of coming near or to : APPROACH, ADMITTANCE **b :** the act of coming to high office or a position of honor or power **6 :** a sudden fit or outburst : ACCESS — **ac·ces·sion·al** \-'sesh-nəl, -ən-ᵊl\ *adj*

[2]**accession** *vt* (1892) **:** to record in order of acquisition

ac·ces·so·ri·al \ˌak-sə-'sōr-ē-əl, -'sȯr-\ *adj* (1726) **1 :** of or relating to an accessory ⟨~ liability⟩ **2 :** of, relating to, or constituting an accession : SUPPLEMENTARY ⟨~ services⟩

ac·ces·so·rize \ik-'ses-ə-ˌrīz, ak-\ *vb* **-rized; -riz·ing** *vt* (1939) **:** to furnish with accessories ~ *vi* **:** to wear clothing accessories

[1]**ac·ces·so·ry** *also* **ac·ces·sa·ry** \ik-'ses-(ə-)rē, ak-, ek- *also* ə-'ses-\ *n, pl* **-ries** (15c) **1 a :** a thing of secondary or subordinate importance : ADJUNCT **b :** an object or device not essential in itself but adding to the beauty, convenience, or effectiveness of something else ⟨auto *accessories*⟩ ⟨clothing *accessories*⟩ **2 a :** a person not actually or constructively present but contributing as an assistant or instigator to the commission of an offense — called also *accessory before the fact* **b :** one who knowing that a crime has been committed aids or shelters the offender with intent to defeat justice — called also *accessory after the fact*

[2]**accessory** *adj* (1607) **1 :** assisting as a subordinate; *esp* **:** contributing to a crime but not as the chief agent **2 :** aiding or contributing in a secondary way : SUPPLEMENTARY **3 :** present in a minor amount and not essential as a constituent ⟨an ~ mineral in a rock⟩

accessory fruit *n* (1900) **:** a fruit (as the apple) of which a conspicuous part consists of tissue other than that of the ripened ovary

accessory nerve *n* (1842) **:** either of a pair of motor nerves that are the 11th cranial nerves of higher vertebrates, arise from the medulla and the upper part of the spinal cord, and supply chiefly the pharynx and muscles of the upper chest, back, and shoulders

accessory shoe *n* (1967) **:** SHOE 5b

access time *n* (1950) **:** the time lag between the time stored information (as in a computer) is requested and the time it is delivered

ac·ciac·ca·tu·ra \(ˌ)ä-ˌchäk-ə-'tu̇r-ə\ *n* [It, lit., crushing] (ca. 1819) **:** a discordant note sounded with a principal note or chord and immediately released

ac·ci·dence \'ak-səd-ən(t)s, -sə-ˌden(t)s\ *n* [L *accidentia* inflections of words, nonessential qualities, pl. of *accident-, accidens,* n.] (15c) **:** a part of grammar that deals with inflections

ac·ci·dent \'ak-səd-ənt, -sə-ˌdent; 'aks-dənt\ *n* [ME, fr. MF, fr. L *accident-, accidens* nonessential quality, chance, fr. prp. of *accidere* to happen, fr. *ad-* + *cadere* to fall — more at CHANCE] (14c) **1 a :** an unforeseen and unplanned event or circumstance **b :** lack of intention or necessity : CHANCE ⟨met by ~ rather than by design⟩ **2 a :** an unfortunate event resulting esp. from carelessness or ignorance **b :** an unexpected happening causing loss or injury which is not due to any fault or misconduct on the part of the person injured but for which legal relief may be sought **3 :** a nonessential property or quality of an entity or circumstance ⟨the ~ of geographical distribution⟩

[1]**ac·ci·den·tal** \ˌak-sə-'dent-ᵊl\ *adj* (14c) **1 :** arising from extrinsic causes : INCIDENTAL, NONESSENTIAL **2 a :** occurring unexpectedly or by chance **b :** happening without intent or through carelessness and often with unfortunate results — **ac·ci·den·tal·ly** \-'dent-lē, -ᵊl-ē\ *also* **ac·ci·dent·ly** \-'dent-lē\ *adv* — **ac·ci·den·tal·ness** \-'dent-ᵊl-nəs\ *n*

syn ACCIDENTAL, FORTUITOUS, CASUAL, CONTINGENT mean not amenable to planning or prediction. ACCIDENTAL stresses chance; FORTUITOUS so strongly suggests chance that it often connotes entire absence of cause; CASUAL stresses lack of real or apparent premeditation or intent; CONTINGENT suggests possibility of happening but stresses uncertainty and dependence on other future events for existence or occurrence.

[2]**accidental** *n* (1651) **1 :** a nonessential property **2 a :** a note foreign to a key indicated by a signature **b :** a prefixed sign indicating an accidental

accident insurance *n* (1866) **:** insurance against loss through accidental bodily injury to the insured

accident–prone *adj* (1926) **1 :** having a greater than average number of accidents **2 :** having personality traits that predispose to accidents

ac·cid·ie \'ak-səd-ē\ *n* (13c) **:** ACEDIA

ac·cip·i·ter \ak-'sip-ət-ər, ik-\ *n* [NL, genus name, fr. L, hawk] (ca. 1828) **:** any of a genus (*Accipiter*) of medium-sized short-winged long-legged hawks with low darting flight; *broadly* **:** a hawk (as of the family Accipitridae, the accipiter family) of similar appearance or habit of flight — **ac·cip·i·trine** \-'sip-ə-ˌtrīn\ *adj or n*

[1]**ac·claim** \ə-'klām\ *vb* [L *acclamare,* lit., to shout at, fr. *ad-* + *clamare* to shout — more at CLAIM] *vt* (1633) **1 :** APPLAUD, PRAISE **2 :** to declare by acclamation ~ *vi* **:** to shout praise or applause — **ac·claim·er** *n*

[2]**acclaim** *n* (1667) **1 :** the act of acclaiming **2 :** PRAISE, APPLAUSE

ac·cla·ma·tion \ˌak-lə-'mā-shən\ *n* [L *acclamation-, acclamatio,* fr. *acclamatus,* pp. of *acclamare*] (1585) **1 :** a loud eager expression of approval, praise, or assent **2 :** an overwhelming affirmative vote by cheers, shouts, or applause rather than by ballot

ac·cli·mate \'ak-lə-ˌmāt; ə-'klī-mət, -ˌmāt\ *vb* **-mat·ed; -mat·ing** [F *acclimater,* fr. *a-* (fr. L *ad-*) + *climat* climate] (1792) **:** ACCLIMATIZE

ac·cli·ma·tion \ˌak-lə-'mā-shən, -ˌlī-\ *n* (1826) **:** ACCLIMATIZATION; *esp* **:** physiological adjustment by an organism to environmental change

ac·cli·ma·ti·za·tion \ə-ˌklī-mət-ə-'zā-shən\ *n* (1830) **:** the process or result of acclimatizing

ac·cli·ma·tize \ə-'klī-mə-ˌtīz\ *vb* **-tized; -tiz·ing** *vt* (1836) **:** to adapt to a new temperature, altitude, climate, environment, or situation ~ *vi* **:** to become acclimatized — **ac·cli·ma·tiz·er** *n*

ac·cliv·i·ty \ə-'kliv-ət-ē, a-\ *n, pl* **-ties** [L *acclivitas,* fr. *acclivis* ascending, fr. *ad-* + *clivus* slope — more at DECLIVITY] (1614) **:** an ascending slope (as of a hill)

ac·co·lade \'ak-ə-ˌlād, -ˌläd\ *n* [F, fr. *accoler* to embrace, fr. (assumed) VL *accollare,* fr. L *ad-* + *collum* neck — more at COLLAR] (1623) **1 a :** a ceremonial embrace **b :** a ceremony or salute conferring knighthood **2 a :** a mark of acknowledgment : AWARD **b :** an expression of praise **3 :** a brace or a line used in music to join two or more staffs carrying simultaneous parts

ac·com·mo·date \ə-'käm-ə-ˌdāt\ *vb* **-dat·ed; -dat·ing** [L *accommodatus,* pp. of *accommodare,* fr. *ad-* + *commodare* to make fit, fr. *commodus* suitable — more at COMMODE] *vt* (1550) **1 :** to make fit, suitable, or congruous **2 :** to bring into agreement or concord : RECONCILE **3 :** to provide with something desired, needed, or suited (as a helpful service, a loan, or lodgings) **4 a :** to make room for **b :** to hold without crowding or inconvenience **5 :** to give consideration to : allow for ⟨~ the special interests of various groups⟩ ~ *vi* **:** to adapt oneself; *also* **:** to undergo visual accommodation ***syn*** see ADAPT, CONTAIN — **ac·com·mo·da·tive** \-ˌdāt-iv\ *adj* — **ac·com·mo·da·tive·ness** *n*

ac·com·mo·dat·ing *adj* (1775) **:** HELPFUL, OBLIGING — **ac·com·mo·dat·ing·ly** \-ˌdāt-iŋ-lē\ *adv*

ac·com·mo·da·tion \ə-ˌkäm-ə-'dā-shən\ *n* (1616) **1 :** something supplied for convenience or to satisfy a need: as **a :** lodging, food, and services or traveling space and related services — usu. used in pl. ⟨tourist ~*s* on the boat⟩ ⟨overnight ~*s*⟩ **b :** a public conveyance (as a train) that stops at all or nearly all points **c :** LOAN **2 :** the act of accommodating : the state of being accommodated: as **a :** the providing of what is needed or desired for convenience **b :** ADAPTATION, ADJUSTMENT **c :** a reconciliation of differences : SETTLEMENT **d :** the automatic adjustment of the eye for seeing at different distances effected chiefly by changes in the convexity of the crystalline lens; *also* **:** the range over which such adjustment is possible — **ac·com·mo·da·tion·al** \-shnəl, -shən-ᵊl\ *adj*

ac·com·mo·da·tion·ist \-'dā-sh(ə-)nəst\ *n* (1964) **:** one who adapts to or compromises with an opposing viewpoint; *specif* **:** a black who adapts to the ideals or attitudes of whites ⟨making Uncle Toms, compromisers, and ~*s* . . . ashamed of the urbane and smiling hypocrisy we practice — Ossie Davis⟩

accommodation ladder *n* (1769) **:** a light ladder or stairway hung over the side of a ship for ascending from or descending to small boats

ac·com·mo·da·tor \ə-'käm-ə-ˌdāt-ər\ *n* (1630) **:** one that accommodates; *esp* **:** a part-time or special-occasion domestic worker

ac·com·pa·ni·ment \ə-'kəmp-(ə-)nē-mənt\ *n* (1744) **1 :** an instrumental or vocal part designed to support or complement a melody **2 a :** an addition (as an ornament) intended to give completeness or symmetry : COMPLEMENT **b :** an accompanying situation or occurrence : CONCOMITANT

ac·com·pa·nist \ə-'kəmp-(ə-)nəst\ *n* (ca. 1828) **:** one (as a pianist) who plays an accompaniment

ac·com·pa·ny \ə-'kəmp-(ə-)nē, -'kämp-\ *vb* **-nied; -ny·ing** [ME *accompanien,* fr. MF *acompaignier,* fr. *a-* (fr. L *ad-*) + *compaing* companion — more at COMPANION] *vt* (15c) **1 :** to go with as an associate or companion **2 :** to perform an accompaniment to or for **3 a :** to cause to be in association ⟨*accompanied* their advice with a warning⟩ **b :** to be in association with ⟨the pictures that ~ the text⟩ ~ *vi* **:** to perform an accompaniment

syn ACCOMPANY, ATTEND, ESCORT mean to go along with. When referring to persons, ACCOMPANY usu. implies equality of status; ATTEND implies a waiting upon in order to serve usu. as a subordinate; ESCORT adds to ACCOMPANY implications of protection, ceremony, or courtesy.

ac·com·plice \ə-'käm-pləs, -'kəm-\ *n* [alter. (fr. incorrect division of *a complice*) of *complice*] (15c) **:** one associated with another esp. in wrongdoing

ac·com·plish \ə-'käm-plish, -'kəm-\ *vt* [ME *accomplisshen,* fr. MF *acompliss-,* stem of *acomplir,* fr. (assumed) VL *accomplēre,* fr. L *ad-* + *complēre* to fill up — more at COMPLETE] (14c) **1 :** to bring about (a result) by effort ⟨have much to ~ today⟩ ⟨regretted that he had never ~*ed* a marriage for her — Francis Hackett⟩ **2 :** to bring to completion : FULFILL ⟨we can ~ the job in an hour⟩ **3 :** to succeed in reaching (a stage in a progression) ⟨would starve before ~*ing* half the distance — W. H. Hudson⟩ **4** *archaic* **a :** to equip thoroughly **b :** PERFECT ***syn*** see PERFORM — **ac·com·plish·able** \-ə-bəl\ *adj* — **ac·com·plish·er** *n*

ac·com·plished *adj* (15c) **1 a :** proficient as the result of practice or training ⟨an ~ dancer⟩ **b :** having many social accomplishments **2 :** established beyond doubt or dispute ⟨an ~ fact⟩

ac·com·plish·ment \ə-'käm-plish-mənt, -'kəm-\ *n* (15c) **1 :** the act of accomplishing : COMPLETION **2 :** something that has been accomplished : ACHIEVEMENT **3 a :** a quality or ability equipping one for society **b :** a special skill or ability acquired by training or practice ***syn*** see ACQUIREMENT

[1]**ac·cord** \ə-'kȯ(ə)rd\ *vb* [ME *accorden,* fr. OF *acorder,* fr. (assumed) VL *accordare,* fr. L *ad-* + *cord-, cor* heart — more at HEART] *vt* (12c) **1** *archaic* **:** to bring into agreement : RECONCILE **2 :** to grant esp. as appropriate, due, or earned ~ *vi* **1** *archaic* **:** to arrive at an agreement **2** *obs* **:** to give consent **3 :** to be consistent or in harmony : AGREE ***syn*** see GRANT

[2]**accord** *n* [ME, fr. OF *acort,* fr. *acorder*] (13c) **1 a :** AGREEMENT, CONFORMITY ⟨acted in ~ with the company's policy⟩ **b :** a formal reaching

\ə\ abut \ᵊ\ kitten, F table \ər\ further \a\ ash \ā\ ace \ä\ cot, cart \au̇\ out \ch\ chin \e\ bet \ē\ easy \g\ go \i\ hit \ī\ ice \j\ job \ŋ\ sing \ō\ go \ȯ\ law \ȯi\ boy \th\ thin \t͟h\ the \ü\ loot \u̇\ foot \y\ yet \zh\ vision \à, k̲, ⁿ, œ, œ̄, ue, ue̅, ʸ\ see Guide to Pronunciation

of agreement : COMPACT, TREATY **2** : balanced interrelationship : HARMONY **3** *obs* : ASSENT **4** : voluntary or spontaneous impulse to act ⟨gave generously of their own ~⟩
ac·cor·dance \ə-ˈkȯrd-^{ə}n(t)s\ *n* (14c) **1** : AGREEMENT, CONFORMITY ⟨in ~ with a rule⟩ **2** : the act of granting
ac·cor·dant \-^{ə}nt\ *adj* (14c) **1** : CONSONANT, AGREEING **2** : HARMONIOUS, CORRESPONDENT — **ac·cor·dant·ly** *adv*
ac·cord·ing as *conj* (1500) **1** : in accord with the way in which **2 a** : depending on how **b** : depending on whether : IF
ac·cord·ing·ly \ə-ˈkȯrd-iŋ-lē\ *adv* (14c) **1** : in accordance : CORRESPONDINGLY **2** : CONSEQUENTLY, SO
according to *prep* (14c) **1** : in conformity with **2** : as stated or attested by **3** : depending on
[1]**ac·cor·di·on** \ə-ˈkȯrd-ē-ən\ *n* [G *akkordion*, fr. *akkord* chord, fr. F *accord*, fr. OF *acort*] (1831) : a portable keyboard wind instrument in which the wind is forced past free reeds by means of a hand-operated bellows — **ac·cor·di·on·ist** \-ē-ə-nəst\ *n*
[2]**accordion** *adj* (1885) : folding or creased or hinged to fold like an accordion ⟨an ~ pleat⟩ ⟨an ~ door⟩
ac·cost \ə-ˈkȯst, -ˈkäst\ *vt* [MF *accoster*, deriv. of L *ad-* + *costa* rib, side — more at COAST] (1599) : to approach and speak to often in a challenging or aggressive way
ac·couche·ment \ˌa-ˌküsh-ˈmä^{n}, ə-ˈküsh-ˌ\ *n* [F — more at COUCH] (1803) : the time or act of giving birth

accordion

ac·cou·cheur \ˌa-ˌkü-ˈshər\ *n* [F] (1759) : one that assists at a birth; *esp* : OBSTETRICIAN
[1]**ac·count** \ə-ˈkau̇nt\ *n* (14c) **1** *archaic* : RECKONING, COMPUTATION **2 a** : a record of debit and credit entries to cover transactions involving a particular item or a particular person or concern **b** : a statement of transactions during a fiscal period and the resulting balance **3 a** : a statement explaining one's conduct **b** : a statement or exposition of reasons, causes, or motives ⟨no satisfactory ~ of these phenomena⟩ **c** : a reason for an action : BASIS ⟨on that ~ I must refuse⟩ **4 a** : a formal business arrangement providing for regular dealings or services (as banking, advertising, or store credit) and involving the establishment and maintenance of an account; *also* : CLIENT, CUSTOMER **b** : money deposited in a bank account and subject to withdrawal by the depositor **5 a** : VALUE, IMPORTANCE ⟨it's of no ~ to me⟩ **b** : ESTEEM ⟨stood high in their ~⟩ **6** : ADVANTAGE ⟨turned her wit to good ~⟩ **7 a** : careful thought : CONSIDERATION ⟨have to take many things into ~⟩ **b** : a usu. mental record : TRACK ⟨keep ~ of all you do⟩ **8** : a description of facts, conditions, or events : REPORT, NARRATIVE ⟨the newspaper ~ of the fire⟩ ⟨by all ~*s* they're well-off⟩; *also* : PERFORMANCE ⟨a straightforward ~ of the sonata⟩ — **on account** : with the price charged to one's account — **on account of** : for the sake of : by reason of : because of — **on no account** : under no circumstances — **on one's own account 1** : on one's own behalf **2** : at one's own risk **3** : by oneself : on one's own
[2]**account** *vb* [ME *accounten*, fr. MF *acompter*, fr. *a-* (fr. L *ad-*) + *compter* to count] *vt* (14c) **1** : to probe into : ANALYZE **2** : to think of as : CONSIDER ⟨~*s* himself lucky⟩ **~** *vi* **1** : to furnish a justifying analysis or explanation — used with *for* **2 a** : to be the sole or primary factor — used with *for* **b** : to bring about the capture, death, or destruction of something ⟨~*ed* for two rabbits⟩
ac·count·able \ə-ˈkau̇nt-ə-bəl\ *adj* (14c) **1** : subject to giving an account : ANSWERABLE **2** : capable of being accounted for : EXPLAINABLE *syn* see RESPONSIBLE — **ac·count·abil·i·ty** \-ˌkau̇nt-ə-ˈbil-ət-ē\ *n* — **ac·count·able·ness** \-ˈkau̇nt-ə-bəl-nəs\ *n* — **ac·count·ably** \-blē\ *adv*
ac·coun·tan·cy \ə-ˈkau̇nt-^{ə}n-sē\ *n* (1854) : the profession or practice of accounting
[1]**ac·coun·tant** \ə-ˈkau̇nt-^{ə}nt\ *n* (15c) **1** : one that gives an account or is accountable **2** : one who is skilled in the practice of accounting or who is in charge of public or private accounts — **ac·coun·tant·ship** \-^{ə}n(t)-ˌship\ *n*
[2]**accountant** *adj*, *obs* (15c) : ACCOUNTABLE, ANSWERABLE ⟨I stand ~ for as great a sin —*Shak.*⟩
account executive *n* (ca. 1941) : a business executive (as in an advertising agency) responsible for dealing with a client's account
ac·count·ing \ə-ˈkau̇nt-iŋ\ *n* (1802) **1** : the system of recording and summarizing business and financial transactions and analyzing, verifying, and reporting the results; *also* : the principles and procedures of accounting **2 a** : work done in accounting or by accountants **b** : an instance of applied accounting or of the settling or presenting of accounts
account payable *n*, *pl* **accounts payable** (ca. 1936) : the balance due to a creditor on a current account
account receivable *n*, *pl* **accounts receivable** (1936) : a balance due from a debtor on a current account
ac·cou·tre *or* **ac·cou·ter** \ə-ˈküt-ər\ *vt* **-cou·tred** *or* **-cou·tered; -cou·tring** *or* **-cou·ter·ing** \-ˈküt-ə-riŋ, -ˈkü-triŋ\ [F *accoutrer*, fr. MF *acoustrer*, fr. *a-* + *costure* seam, fr. (assumed) VL *consutura*, fr. L *consutus*, pp. of *consuere* to sew together, fr. *com-* + *suere* to sew — more at SEW] (1596) : to provide with equipment or furnishings : OUTFIT *syn* see FURNISH
ac·cou·tre·ment *or* **ac·cou·ter·ment** \ə-ˈkü-trə-mənt, -ˈküt-ər-mənt\ *n* (1591) **1** *archaic* : the act of accoutring **2 a** : an accessory item of clothing or equipment — usu. used in pl. **b** : EQUIPMENT, TRAPPINGS; *specif* : a soldier's outfit usu. not including clothes and weapons — usu. used in pl. **3** : an identifying and often superficial characteristic or device — usu. used in pl. ⟨~*s* of power that define our diplomacy —Elizabeth Drew⟩
ac·cred·it \ə-ˈkred-ət\ *vt* [F *accréditer*, fr. *ad-* + *crédit* credit] (1620) **1** : to consider or recognize as outstanding **2** : to give official authorization to or approval of: **a** : to provide with credentials; *esp* : to send (an envoy) with letters of authorization **b** : to recognize or vouch for as conforming with a standard **c** : to recognize (an educational institution) as maintaining standards that qualify the graduates for admission to higher or more specialized institutions or for professional practice **3** : ATTRIBUTE, CREDIT *syn* see APPROVE — **ac·cred·i·table** \-ə-bəl\ *adj* — **ac·cred·i·ta·tion** \ə-ˌkred-ə-ˈtā-shən, -ˈdā-\ *n*
ac·crete \ə-ˈkrēt\ *vb* **ac·cret·ed; ac·cret·ing** [back-formation fr. *accretion*] *vi* (1784) : to grow or become attached by accretion **~** *vt* : to cause to adhere or become attached; *also* : ACCUMULATE
ac·cre·tion \ə-ˈkrē-shən\ *n* [L *accretion-*, *accretio*, fr. *accretus*, pp. of *accrescere* — more at ACCRUE] (1615) **1** : the process of growth or enlargement by a gradual buildup: as **a** : increase by external addition or accumulation (as by adhesion of external parts or particles) **b** : the increase of land by the action of natural forces **2** : a product of accretion; *esp* : an extraneous addition ⟨~*s* of grime⟩ **3** : coherence of separate particles : CONCRETION — **ac·cre·tion·ary** \-shə-ˌner-ē\ *adj* — **ac·cre·tive** \ə-ˈkrēt-iv\ *adj*
ac·cru·al \ə-ˈkrü-əl\ *n* (1880) **1** : the action or process of accruing **2** : something that accrues or has accrued
ac·crue \ə-ˈkrü\ *vb* **ac·crued; ac·cru·ing** [ME *acreuen*, prob. fr. MF *acreue* increase, fr. *acreistre* to increase, fr. L *accrescere*, fr. *ad-* + *crescere* to grow — more at CRESCENT] *vi* (15c) **1** : to come into existence as a legally enforceable claim **2 a** : to come about as a natural growth, increase, or advantage ⟨the wisdom that ~*s* with age⟩ **b** : to come as a direct result of some state or action ⟨rewards due to the feminine will ~ to me — Germaine Greer⟩ **3** : to accumulate or be added periodically ⟨interest ~*s* on a daily basis⟩ **~** *vt* : to accumulate or have due after a period of time ⟨~ vacation time⟩ — **ac·cru·able** \-ˈkrü-ə-bəl\ *adj* — **ac·crue·ment** \-ˈkrü-mənt\ *n*
ac·cul·tur·ate \ə-ˈkəl-chə-ˌrāt, a-\ *vt* **-at·ed; -at·ing** [back-formation fr. *acculturation*] (1930) : to change through acculturation
ac·cul·tur·a·tion \ə-ˌkəl-chə-ˈrā-shən, a-\ *n* (1880) **1** : cultural modification of an individual, group, or people by adapting to or borrowing traits from another culture; *also* : a merging of cultures as a result of prolonged contact **2** : the process beginning at infancy by which a human being acquires the culture of his society — **ac·cul·tur·a·tion·al** \-shnəl, -shən-^{ə}l\ *adj* — **ac·cul·tur·a·tive** \ə-ˈkəl-chə-ˌrāt-iv, a-\ *adj*
ac·cu·mu·late \ə-ˈkyü-m(y)ə-ˌlāt\ *vb* **-lat·ed; -lat·ing** [L *accumulatus*, pp. of *accumulare*, fr. *ad-* + *cumulare* to heap up — more at CUMULATE] *vt* (1529) : to gather or pile up esp. little by little : AMASS ⟨~ a fortune⟩ **~** *vi* : to increase gradually in quantity or number
ac·cu·mu·la·tion \ə-ˌkyü-m(y)ə-ˈlā-shən\ *n* (1606) **1** : the action or process of accumulating : the state of being or having accumulated **2** : increase or growth by addition esp. when continuous or repeated ⟨~ of interest⟩ **3** : something that has accumulated or has been accumulated
ac·cu·mu·la·tive \ə-ˈkyü-m(y)ə-ˌlāt-iv, -lət-\ *adj* (1651) **1** : CUMULATIVE ⟨an age of rapid and ~ change⟩ **2** : tending or given to accumulation — **ac·cu·mu·la·tive·ly** *adv* — **ac·cu·mu·la·tive·ness** *n*
ac·cu·mu·la·tor \ə-ˈkyü-m(y)ə-ˌlāt-ər\ *n* (1691) : one that accumulates: as **a** : SHOCK ABSORBER **b** *Brit* : STORAGE CELL **c** : a part (as in a computer) where numbers are totaled or stored
ac·cu·ra·cy \ˈak-yə-rə-sē, ˈak-(ə-)rə-\ *n*, *pl* **-cies** (1662) **1** : freedom from mistake or error : CORRECTNESS **2 a** : conformity to truth or to a standard or model : EXACTNESS **b** : degree of conformity of a measure to a standard or a true value
ac·cu·rate \ˈak-yə-rət, ˈak-(ə-)rət\ *adj* [L *accuratus*, fr. pp. of *accurare* to take care of, fr. *ad-* + *cura* care — more at CURE] (1612) **1** : free from error esp. as the result of care ⟨an ~ diagnosis⟩ **2** : conforming exactly to truth or to a standard : EXACT ⟨providing ~ color⟩ **3** : able to give an accurate result ⟨an ~ gauge⟩ *syn* see CORRECT — **ac·cu·rate·ly** \ˈak-yə-rət-lē, ˈak-(ə-)rət-, ˈak-(y)ərt-\ *adv* — **ac·cu·rate·ness** \-yə-rət-nəs, -(ə-)rət-nəs\ *n*
ac·cursed \ə-ˈkərst, -ˈkər-səd\ *or* **ac·curst** \ə-ˈkərst\ *adj* [ME *acursed*, fr. pp. of *acursen* to consign to destruction with a curse, fr. *a-* (fr. OE *ā*, perfective prefix) + *cursen* to curse — more at ABIDE] (13c) **1** : being under or as if under a curse **2** : DAMNABLE — **ac·curs·ed·ly** \-ˈkər-səd-lē\ *adv* — **ac·curs·ed·ness** \-ˈkər-səd-nəs\ *n*
ac·cus·al \ə-ˈkyü-zəl\ *n* (1594) : ACCUSATION
ac·cu·sa·tion \ˌak-yə-ˈzā-shən, -yü-\ *n* (14c) **1** : the act of accusing : the state or fact of being accused **2** : a charge of wrongdoing
[1]**ac·cu·sa·tive** \ə-ˈkyü-zət-iv\ *adj* [ME, fr. MF or L; MF *accusatif*, fr. L *accusativus*, fr. *accusatus*, pp. of *accusare*] (15c) **1** : of, relating to, or being the grammatical case that marks the direct object of a verb or the object of any of several prepositions **2** : ACCUSATORY
[2]**accusative** *n* (1620) : the accusative case of a language : a form in the accusative case
ac·cu·sa·to·ry \ə-ˈkyü-zə-ˌtōr-ē, -ˌtȯr-\ *adj* (15c) : containing or expressing accusation : ACCUSING
ac·cuse \ə-ˈkyüz\ *vb* **ac·cused; ac·cus·ing** [ME *accusen*, fr. OF *acuser*, fr. L *accusare* to call to account, fr. *ad-* + *causa* lawsuit — more at CAUSE] *vt* (13c) **1** : to charge with a fault or offense : BLAME **2** : to charge with an offense judicially or by a public process **~** *vi* : to bring an accusation — **ac·cus·er** \ə-ˈkyü-zər\ *n* — **ac·cus·ing·ly** \-ˈkyü-ziŋ-lē\ *adv*
ac·cused *n*, *pl* **accused** (1593) : one charged with an offense; *esp* : the defendant in a criminal case
ac·cus·tom \ə-ˈkəs-təm\ *vt* [ME *accustomen*, fr. MF *acostumer*, fr. *a-* (fr. L *ad-*) + *costume* custom] (15c) : to make familiar with something through use or experience — **ac·cus·tom·ation** \-ˌkəs-tə-ˈmā-shən\ *n*
ac·cus·tomed \ə-ˈkəs-təmd\ *adj* (15c) **1** : CUSTOMARY, USUAL ⟨her ~ cheerfulness⟩ **2** : adapted to existing conditions ⟨eyes ~ to the dark⟩ **3** : being in the habit or custom ⟨~ to making decisions⟩ *syn* see USUAL — **ac·cus·tomed·ness** \-təm(d)-nəs\ *n*
AC/DC \ˈā-(ˌ)sē-ˈdē-(ˌ)sē\ *adj* [fr. the likening of a bisexual person to an electrical appliance which can operate on either alternating or direct current] (ca. 1960) : BISEXUAL 1b
[1]**ace** \ˈās\ *n* [ME *as*, fr. MF, fr. L, unit, a copper coin] (14c) **1 a** : a die face marked with one spot **b** : a playing card marked in its center with one pip **c** : a domino end marked with one spot **2** : a very small amount or degree : PARTICLE **3** : a point scored esp. on a service (as in tennis or handball) that an opponent fails to touch **4** : a golf score of one stroke on a hole; *also* : a hole made in one stroke **5** : a

combat pilot who has brought down at least five enemy airplanes **6** : one that excels at something — **ace in the hole 1** : an ace dealt face down to a player (as in stud poker) and not exposed until the showdown **2** : an effective and decisive argument or resource held in reserve — **within an ace of** : on the point of : very near to ⟨came *within an ace of* winning⟩

[2]**ace** *vt* **aced; ac·ing** (1923) **1** : to score an ace against (an opponent) **2** : to make (a hole in golf) in one stroke **3** : to defeat, displace, or dispose of : gain a decisive advantage over — usu. used with *out* **4** : to earn a high grade on (as an examination); *esp* : to get an A on

[3]**ace** *adj* (1930) : of first or high rank or quality

-a·ce·ae \ˈā-sē-ˌē\ *n pl suffix* [NL, fr. L, fem. pl. of *-aceus* -aceous] : plants of the nature of ⟨Ros*aceae*⟩ — in names of families of plants; formerly in names of orders of plants

ace·dia \ə-ˈsēd-ē-ə\ *n* [LL, fr. Gk *akēdeia,* fr. *a-* + *kēdos* care, grief — more at HATE] (13c) : APATHY, BOREDOM

Acel·da·ma \ə-ˈsel-də-mə\ *n* [Gk *Akeldama,* fr. Aram *ḥăqēl dĕmā,* lit., field of blood] (14c) : the potter's field bought with the money Judas had been paid for betraying Christ

acel·lu·lar \(ˈ)ā-ˈsel-yə-lər\ *adj* (1940) : containing no cells : not divided into cells

acen·tric \(ˈ)ā-ˈsen-trik\ *adj* (1937) : lacking a centromere ⟨~ chromosomes⟩

-a·ceous \ˈā-shəs\ *adj suffix* [L *-aceus*] **1 a** : characterized by : full of ⟨set*aceous*⟩ **b** : consisting of ⟨carbon*aceous*⟩ : having the nature or form of ⟨tuff*aceous*⟩ **2 a** : of or relating to a group of animals typified by (such) a form ⟨cet*aceous*⟩ or characterized by (such) a feature ⟨crust*aceous*⟩ **b** : of or relating to a plant family typified by (such) a genus ⟨ros*aceous*⟩

aceph·a·lous \(ˈ)ā-ˈsef-ə-ləs, ə-ˈsef-\ *adj* [Gk *akephalos,* fr. *a-* + *kephalē* head — more at CEPHALIC] (1731) **1** : lacking a head or having the head reduced **2** : lacking a governing head or chief

ace·quia \ə-ˈsā-kē-ə, ä-\ *n* [Sp, fr. Ar *as-sāqiyah* the irrigation stream] *Southwest* (1844) : an irrigation ditch or canal

acerb \ə-ˈsərb, a-\ *adj* [F or L; F *acerbe,* fr. L *acerbus,* fr. *acer*] (1657) : ACERBIC

ac·er·bate \ˈas-ər-ˌbāt\ *vt* **-bat·ed; -bat·ing** (ca. 1731) : IRRITATE, EXASPERATE

acer·bic \ə-ˈsər-bik, a-\ *adj* (1865) : acid in temper, mood, or tone — **acer·bi·cal·ly** \-bi-k(ə-)lē\ *adv*

acer·bi·ty \-bət-ē\ *n, pl* **-ties** (1572) : the quality of being acerbic

ac·er·o·la \ˌas-ə-ˈrō-lə\ *n* [Amer Sp, fr. Sp, fruit of a shrub (*Crataegus azarolus*), fr. Ar *az-zu'rūr*] (1945) : a West Indian shrub (genus *Malpighia*) with mildly acid cherrylike fruits very rich in vitamin C

acet- *or* **aceto-** *comb form* [F & L; F *acét-,* fr. L *acet-,* fr. *acetum*] : acetic acid : acetic ⟨*acetyl*⟩

ac·e·tab·u·lar·ia \ˌas-ə-ˌtab-yə-ˈlar-ē-ə, -ˈler-\ *n* [NL, genus name, fr. L *acetabulum*] (ca. 1903) : a large single-celled green alga (genus *Acetabularia*) of warm seas that resembles a small mushroom in form

ac·e·tab·u·lum \-ˈtab-yə-ləm\ *n, pl* **-lums** *or* **-la** \-lə\ [L, lit., vinegar cup, fr. *acetum* vinegar] (14c) **1 a** : the cup-shaped socket in the hipbone **b** : the cavity by which the leg of an insect articulates with the body **2** : a sucker of an invertebrate (as a trematode or leech) — **ac·e·tab·u·lar** \-lər\ *adj*

ac·e·tal \ˈas-ə-ˌtal\ *n* [G *azetal,* fr. *azet-* acet- + *al*kohol alcohol] (1853) : any of various compounds characterized by the grouping $C(OR)_2$ and obtained esp. by heating aldehydes or ketones with alcohols

ac·et·al·de·hyde \ˌas-ə-ˈtal-də-ˌhīd\ *n* [ISV] (ca. 1877) : a colorless volatile water-soluble liquid aldehyde C_2H_4O used chiefly in organic synthesis

acet·amide \ə-ˈset-ə-ˌmīd, ˌas-ət-ˈam-ˌīd\ *n* [G *azetamid,* fr. *azet-* + *amid* amide] (1873) : a white crystalline amide C_2H_5NO of acetic acid used esp. as a solvent and in organic synthesis

acet·amin·o·phen \ə-ˌsēt-ə-ˈmin-ə-fən, ˌas-ət-\ *n* [*acet-* + *amin-* + *phenol*] (1958) : a crystalline compound $C_8H_9NO_2$ that is a hydroxy derivative of acetanilide and is used in chemical synthesis and in medicine to relieve pain and fever

ac·et·an·i·lide *or* **ac·et·an·i·lid** \ˌas-ə-ˈtan-ᵊl-ˌīd, -ᵊl-əd\ *n* [ISV] (ca. 1864) : a white crystalline compound C_8H_9NO that is derived from aniline and acetic acid and is used esp. to check pain or fever

ac·e·tate \ˈas-ə-ˌtāt\ *n* (1827) **1** : a salt or ester of acetic acid **2** : cellulose acetate or any of its products **3** : a phonograph recording disk made of an acetate or coated with cellulose acetate

ac·et·azol·amide \ˌas-ət-ə-ˈzōl-ə-ˌmīd, -ˈzäl-, -məd\ *n* [*acet-* + *azole* + *amide*] (ca. 1929) : a diuretic drug $C_4H_6N_4O_3S_2$ used esp. in the treatment of edema associated with congestive heart failure and of glaucoma

ace·tic \ə-ˈsēt-ik\ *adj* [prob. fr. F *acétique,* fr. L *acetum* vinegar, fr. *acēre* to be sour, fr. *acer* sharp — more at EDGE] (1808) : of, relating to, or producing acetic acid or vinegar

acetic acid *n* (1808) : a colorless pungent liquid acid $C_2H_4O_2$ that is the chief acid of vinegar and that is used esp. in synthesis (as of plastics)

ace·ti·fy \ə-ˈsēt-ə-ˌfī, -ˈset-\ *vt* **-fied; -fy·ing** (ca. 1828) : to turn into acetic acid or vinegar — **ace·ti·fi·ca·tion** \-ˌsēt-ə-fə-ˈkā-shən, -ˌset-\ *n* — **ace·ti·fi·er** \-ˈsēt-ə-ˌfī(-ə)r, -ˈset-\ *n*

ace·to·ace·tic acid \ˌas-ə-(ˌ)tō-ə-ˌsēt-ik-, ə-ˌsēt-ō-\ *n* [part trans. of G *azetessigsäure,* fr. *azet-* acet- + *essigsäure* acetic acid] (ca. 1900) : an unstable acid $C_4H_6O_3$ that is a ketone body found in abnormal quantities in the blood and urine in some conditions (as diabetes)

ac·e·tone \ˈas-ə-ˌtōn\ *n* [G *azeton,* fr. L *acetum*] (1839) : a volatile fragrant flammable liquid ketone C_3H_6O used chiefly as a solvent and in organic synthesis and found in abnormal quantities in diabetic urine — **ac·e·ton·ic** \ˌas-ə-ˈtän-ik\ *adj*

ace·to·phe·net·i·din \ˌas-ə-(ˌ)tō-fə-ˈnet-əd-ən, ə-ˌsēt-ō-\ *n* [ISV] (1910) : PHENACETIN

ace·tous \ə-ˈsēt-əs, ˈas-ət-əs\ *adj* (1714) : relating to or producing vinegar ⟨~ fermentation⟩; *also* : SOUR, VINEGARY

ace·tyl \ə-ˈsēt-ᵊl, ˈas-ət-; ˈas-ə-ˌtēl\ *n* (ca. 1864) : the radical CH_3CO of acetic acid

acet·y·late \ə-ˈset-ᵊl-ˌāt\ *vt* **-lat·ed; -lat·ing** (ca. 1909) : to introduce the acetyl radical into (a compound) — **acet·y·la·tion** \-ˌset-ᵊl-ˈā-shən\ *n* — **acet·y·la·tive** \-ˈset-ᵊl-ˌāt-iv\ *adj*

ace·tyl·cho·line \ə-ˌset-ᵊl-ˈkō-ˌlēn, -ˌsēt-; ˈas-ə-ˌtēl-\ *n* [ISV] (1906) : a compound $C_7H_{17}NO_3$ released at autonomic nerve endings, active in the transmission of the nerve impulse, and formed enzymatically in the tissues from choline — **ace·tyl·cho·lin·ic** \-kō-ˈlin-ik\ *adj*

ace·tyl·cho·lin·es·ter·ase \-ˌkō-lə-ˈnes-tə-ˌrās, -ˌrāz\ *n* [*acetylcholine* + *esterase*] (ca. 1947) : an enzyme that occurs esp. in some nerve endings and in the blood and promotes the hydrolysis of acetylcholine

ace·tyl–coA \-ˌkō-ˈā\ *n* (ca. 1959) : ACETYL COENZYME A

acetyl coenzyme A *n* (ca. 1952) : a compound $C_{25}H_{38}N_7O_{17}P_3S$ formed as an intermediate in metabolism and active as a coenzyme in biological acetylations

acet·y·lene \ə-ˈset-ᵊl-ən, -ᵊl-ˌēn\ *n* (1864) : a colorless gaseous hydrocarbon $HC{\equiv}CH$ made esp. by the action of water on calcium carbide and used chiefly in organic synthesis and as a fuel (as in welding and soldering) — **acet·y·le·nic** \ə-ˌset-ᵊl-ˈē-nik, -ˈen-ik\ *adj*

ace·tyl·sa·lic·y·late \ə-ˌsēt-ᵊl-sə-ˈlis-ə-ˌlāt\ *n* (ca. 1960) : a salt or ester of acetylsalicylic acid

ace·tyl·sal·i·cyl·ic acid \ə-ˈsēt-ᵊl-ˌsal-ə-ˌsil-ik-\ *n* [ISV] (1897) : ASPIRIN 1

ac·ey–deuc·ey *also* **ac·ey–deu·cy** \ˌā-sē-ˈd(y)ü-sē\ *n* (1925) : a variation of backgammon in which a throw of a 1-2 gives the player extra turns

[1]**Achae·an** \ə-ˈkē-ən\ *or* **Achai·an** \-ˈkī-ən, -ˈkā-(y)ən\ *adj* (1567) : of, relating to, or characteristic of Achaea; *broadly* : of or relating to Greece

[2]**Achaean** *or* **Achaian** *n* (1607) : a native or inhabitant of Achaea; *broadly* : GREEK

Ach·ae·me·ni·an \ˌak-ə-ˈmē-nē-ən\ *adj* (1717) : of or relating to the Achaemenids

Achae·me·nid \ə-ˈkē-mə-nəd\ *n, pl* **-menids** *also* **-men·i·dae** \ˌak-ə-ˈmen-ə-ˌdē\ [Gk *Achaimenides,* fr. *Achaimenes,* 7th cent. B.C. Pers. king, founder of the dynasty + *-ides* (patronymic suffix)] (1900) : a member of the ruling house of ancient Persia generally considered historically important from the assumption of power by Cyrus the Great (559 B.C.) to the overthrow of Darius III (330 B.C.)

acha·la·sia \ˌā-kə-ˈlā-zh(ē-)ə\ *n* [NL, fr. *a-* + Gk *chalasis* slackening + NL *-ia*] (1914) : failure of a ring of muscle (as the anal sphincter or one of the esophagus) to relax

Acha·tes \ə-ˈkāt-ēz\ *n* [L] : a faithful companion of Aeneas in Vergil's *Aeneid*

[1]**ache** \ˈāk\ *vi* **ached; ach·ing** [ME *aken,* fr. OE *acan*] (bef. 12c) **1 a** : to suffer a usu. dull persistent pain **b** : to become distressed or disturbed (as with anxiety or regret) **c** : to feel compassion **2** : to experience a painful eagerness or yearning

[2]**ache** *n* (bef. 12c) **1** : a usu. dull persistent pain **2** : a condition marked by aching

achene \ə-ˈkēn\ *n* [NL *achaenium,* fr. *a-* + Gk *chainein* to yawn — more at YAWN] (ca. 1855) : a small dry indehiscent one-seeded fruit developing from a simple ovary and usu. having a thin pericarp attached to the seed at only one point — **ache·ni·al** \ə-ˈkē-nē-əl\ *adj*

Ach·er·on \ˈak-ə-ˌrän, -rən\ *n* [Gk *Acherōn*] : a river in Hades

Acheu·le·an *or* **Acheu·li·an** \ə-ˈshü-lē-ən\ *adj* [F *Acheuléen,* fr. St. Acheul, near Amiens, France] (ca. 1894) : of or relating to a lower Paleolithic culture characterized by bifacial tools with round cutting edges

à che·val \ˌäsh-ə-ˈväl\ *adv* [F, lit., on horseback] (1832) **1** : with a leg on each side : ASTRIDE **2** : in such a way as to be played or chanced simultaneously on two numbers or events (as in roulette)

achieve \ə-ˈchēv\ *vb* **achieved; achiev·ing** [ME *acheven,* fr. MF *achever* to finish, fr. *a-* (fr. L *ad-*) + *chief* end, head — more at CHIEF] *vt* (14c) **1** : to carry out successfully : ACCOMPLISH ⟨~ a gradual increase in production⟩ **2** : to get or attain as the result of exertion : REACH ⟨*achieved* a high degree of skill⟩ ⟨*achieved* greatness⟩ ~ *vi* : to attain a desired end or aim : become successful ***syn*** see PERFORM — **achiev·able** \-ˈchē-və-bəl\ *adj* — **achiev·er** *n*

achieve·ment \ə-ˈchēv-mənt\ *n* (15c) **1** : the act of achieving : ACCOMPLISHMENT **2 a** : a result brought about by effort **b** : a great or heroic deed **3** : the quality and quantity of a student's work ***syn*** see FEAT

Achil·les \ə-ˈkil-ēz\ *n* [L, fr. Gk *Achilleus*] : the greatest warrior among the Greeks at Troy and slayer of Hector

Achilles' heel *n* [fr. the story that Achilles was vulnerable only in the heel] (1864) : a vulnerable point

Achilles tendon *n* (1890) : the strong tendon joining the muscles in the calf of the leg to the bone of the heel

ach·ing \ˈā-kiŋ\ *adj* (13c) **1** : that aches ⟨an ~ back⟩ **2** : causing or reflecting distress, deep emotion, or longing ⟨~ country ballads⟩ — **ach·ing·ly** *adv*

achla·myd·e·ous \ˌak-lə-ˈmid-ē-əs, ˌā-klə-\ *adj* [*a-* + Gk *chlamyd-, chlamys* mantle] (1830) : lacking both calyx and corolla

achlor·hy·dria \ˌā-ˌklōr-ˈhid-rē-ə, -ˌklȯr-\ *n* [NL, fr. *a-* + *chlor*ine + *hydr*ogen] (ca. 1898) : absence of hydrochloric acid from the gastric juice — **achlor·hy·dric** \-ˈhid-rik, -ˈhī-drik\ *adj*

achon·drite \(ˈ)ā-ˈkän-ˌdrīt\ *n* (1904) : a stony meteorite without rounded grains — **achon·drit·ic** \ˌā-ˌkän-ˈdrit-ik\ *adj*

achon·dro·pla·sia \ˌā-ˌkän-drə-ˈplā-zh(ē-)ə\ *n* [NL] (ca. 1893) : failure of normal development of cartilage resulting in dwarfism — **achon·dro·plas·tic** \-ˈplas-tik\ *adj*

ach·ro·mat \ˈak-rə-ˌmat\ *n* (ca. 1909) : ACHROMATIC LENS

achromat- *or* **achromato-** *comb form* [Gk *achrōmatos* colorless, fr. *a-* + *chrōmat-, chrōma* color — more at CHROMATIC] : achromatic ⟨*achromat*ism⟩

ach·ro·mat·ic \ˌak-rə-ˈmat-ik\ *adj* (1766) **1** : refracting light without dispersing it into its constituent colors : giving images practically free from extraneous colors ⟨an ~ telescope⟩ **2** : not readily colored by the usual staining agents **3** : possessing no hue : being or involving black, gray, or white : NEUTRAL ⟨~ visual sensations⟩ **4** : being without accidentals or modulation : DIATONIC — **ach·ro·mat·i·cal·ly** \-i-k(ə-)lē\ *adv* — **ach·ro·ma·tic·i·ty** \ˌak-rō-mə-ˈtis-ət-ē\ *n* — **achro·ma·tize** \(ˈ)ā-ˈkrō-mə-ˌtīz, a-\ *vt*

\ə\ abut \ᵊ\ kitten, F table \ər\ further \a\ ash \ā\ ace \ä\ cot, cart \au̇\ out \ch\ chin \e\ bet \ē\ easy \g\ go \i\ hit \ī\ ice \j\ job \ŋ\ sing \ō\ go \ȯ\ law \ȯi\ boy \th\ thin \t͟h\ the \ü\ loot \u̇\ foot \y\ yet \zh\ vision \à, k̲, ⁿ, œ, œ̄, ue, ue̅, ʸ\ *see* Guide to Pronunciation

achromatic lens *n* (ca. 1864) **:** a lens made by combining lenses of different glasses having different focal powers so that the light emerging from the lens forms an image practically free from unwanted colors
achro·ma·tism \(ˈ)ā-ˈkrō-mə-ˌtiz-əm, a-\ *n* (1797) **:** the quality or state of being achromatic
achy \ˈā-kē\ *adj* **ach·i·er; ach·i·est** (1875) **:** afflicted with aches — **ach·i·ness** *n*
acic·u·lar \ə-ˈsik-yə-lər\ *adj* [LL *acicula* (dim. of L *acus* needle) + E *-ar* —more at ACUTE] (1794) **:** shaped like a needle ⟨~ leaves⟩ ⟨~ crystals⟩
1**ac·id** \ˈas-əd\ *adj* [F or L; F *acide,* fr. L *acidus,* fr. *acēre* to be sour — more at ACETIC] (1626) **1 a :** sour, sharp, or biting to the taste **b :** sharp, biting, or sour in manner, disposition, or nature ⟨an ~ individual⟩ **c :** sharply clear, discerning, or pointed ⟨an ~ wit⟩ **d :** piercingly intense and often jarring ⟨~ yellow⟩ **2 a :** of, relating to, or being an acid; *also* **:** having the reactions or characteristics of an acid ⟨~ soil⟩ ⟨an ~ solution⟩ **b** *of salts and esters* **:** derived by partial exchange of replaceable hydrogen ⟨~ sodium carbonate $NaHCO_3$⟩ **c :** marked by or resulting from an abnormally high concentration of acid ⟨~ indigestion⟩ **3 :** relating to or made by a process (as in making steel) in which the furnace is lined with acidic material and an acidic slag is used **4 :** rich in silica ⟨~ rocks⟩ — **ac·id·ly** *adv* — **ac·id·ness** *n*
2**acid** *n* (1696) **1 :** a sour substance; *specif* **:** any of various typically water-soluble and sour compounds that are capable of reacting with a base to form a salt, that redden litmus, that are hydrogen-containing molecules or ions able to give up a proton to a base, or that are substances able to accept an unshared pair of electrons from a base **2 :** something incisive, biting, or sarcastic ⟨a social satire dripping with ~⟩ **3 :** LSD — **ac·idy** \ˈas-əd-ē\ *adj*
ac·id–fast \ˈas-əd-ˌfast\ *adj* (1903) **:** not easily decolorized by acids
ac·id·head \-ˌhed\ *n* (1966) **:** an individual who uses LSD
acid·ic \ə-ˈsid-ik, a-\ *adj* (1880) **1 :** acid-forming **2 :** ACID
acid·i·fi·er \ə-ˈsid-ə-ˌfī(-ə)r, a-\ *n* (ca. 1828) **:** one that acidifies; *esp* **:** a substance used to increase soil acidity
acid·i·fy \-ˌfī\ *vb* **-fied; -fy·ing** *vt* (1797) **1 :** to make acid **2 :** to convert into an acid ~ *vi* **:** to become acid — **acid·i·fi·ca·tion** \-ˌsid-ə-fə-ˈkā-shən\ *n*
ac·i·dim·e·ter \ˌas-ə-ˈdim-ət-ər\ *n* (ca. 1828) **:** an apparatus for measuring the strength or the amount of acid present in a mixture or solution — **acid·i·met·ric** \ə-ˌsid-ə-ˈme-trik\ *adj* — **ac·i·dim·e·try** \ˌas-ə-ˈdim-ə-trē\ *n*
acid·i·ty \ə-ˈsid-ət-ē, a-\ *n, pl* **-ties** (1620) **1 :** the quality, state, or degree of being acid **2 :** the state of being excessively acid
acid·o·phil \ə-ˈsid-ə-ˌfil, a-\ *also* **acid·o·phile** \-ˌfīl\ *n* (ca. 1900) **:** a substance, tissue, or organism that stains readily with acid stains — **acidophil** *also* **acidophile** *adj*
ac·i·do·phil·ic \ˌas-ə-dō-ˈfil-ik\ *adj* (ca. 1900) **1 :** staining readily with acid stains **:** ACIDOPHIL **2 :** preferring or thriving in a relatively acid environment
ac·i·doph·i·lus milk \ˌas-ə-ˌdäf-(ə-)ləs-\ *n* [NL *Lactobacillus acidolphilus* lit., acidophilic lactobacillus] (1921) **:** milk fermented by any of several bacteria and used therapeutically to change the intestinal flora
ac·i·do·sis \ˌas-ə-ˈdō-səs\ *n* (1900) **:** an abnormal condition characterized by reduced alkalinity of the blood and of the body tissues — **ac·i·dot·ic** \-ˈdät-ik\ *adj*
acid phosphatase *n* (1949) **:** a phosphatase (as the phosphomonoesterase from the prostate gland) active in acid medium
acid precipitation *n* (1979) **:** precipitation (as rain or snow) whose increased acidity is caused by environmental factors (as atmospheric pollutants)
acid rain *n* (1858) **:** acid precipitation in the form of rain
acid rock *n* (1966) **:** rock music with lyrics and sound relating to or suggestive of drug-induced experiences
acid test *n* (1912) **:** a severe or crucial test
acid·u·late \ə-ˈsij-ə-ˌlāt\ *vt* **-lat·ed; -lat·ing** [L *acidulus*] (1732) **:** to make acid or slightly acid — **acid·u·la·tion** \-ˌsij-ə-ˈlā-shən\ *n*
acid·u·lent \ə-ˈsij-ə-lənt\ *adj* [F *acidulant,* fr. prp. of *aciduler* to acidulate, fr. L *acidulus*] (1834) **:** ACIDULOUS
acid·u·lous \ə-ˈsij-ə-ləs\ *adj* [L *acidulus* sourish, fr. *acidus*] (1769) **:** somewhat acid in taste or manner **:** HARSH
ac·i·nar \ˈas-ə-nər, -ˌnär\ *adj* (1936) **:** of, relating to, or comprising an acinus ⟨pancreatic ~ cells⟩
ac·i·nus \ˈas-ə-nəs\ *n, pl* **-ni** \-ˌnī\ [NL, fr. L, berry, berry seed] (ca. 1751) **:** any of the small sacs that terminate the ducts of a racemose gland and are lined with secreting cells — **ac·i·nous** \-nəs\ *adj*
ack–ack \ˈak-ˌak\ *n* [Brit. signalmen's former telephone pron. of *AA,* abbr. of *antiaircraft*] (1926) **:** an antiaircraft gun; *also* **:** antiaircraft fire
ac·knowl·edge \ik-ˈnäl-ij, ak-\ *vt* **-edged; -edg·ing** [*ac-* (as in *accord*) + *knowledge*] (15c) **1 :** to recognize the rights, authority, or status of **2 :** to own or admit knowledge of or agreement with **3 a :** to express gratitude or obligation for **b :** to take notice of **c :** to make known the receipt of **4 :** to recognize as genuine or valid ⟨~ a debt⟩ — **ac·knowl·edge·able** \-ə-bəl\ *adj*

syn ACKNOWLEDGE, ADMIT, OWN, AVOW, CONFESS mean to disclose against one's will or inclination. ACKNOWLEDGE implies the disclosing of something that has been or might be concealed; ADMIT implies reluctance to disclose, grant, or concede and refers usu. to facts rather than their implications; OWN implies acknowledging something in close relation to oneself; AVOW implies boldly declaring, often in the face of hostility, what one might be expected to be silent about; CONFESS may apply to an admission of a weakness, failure, omission, or guilt.

ac·knowl·edged \-ijd\ *adj* (1598) **:** generally recognized, accepted, or admitted — **ac·knowl·edged·ly** \-ij-(ə-)dlē\ *adv*
ac·knowl·edg·ment *also* **ac·knowl·edge·ment** \ik-ˈnäl-ij-mənt, ak-\ *n* (1594) **1 a :** the act of acknowledging **b :** recognition or favorable notice of an act or achievement **2 :** a thing done or given in recognition of something received **3 :** a declaration or avowal of one's act or of a fact to give it legal validity
aclin·ic line \(ˌ)ā-ˌklin-ik-\ *n* [2*a-* + *clinic*] (1850) **:** an imaginary line roughly parallel to the geographical equator and passing through those points where a magnetic needle has no dip
ac·me \ˈak-mē\ *n* [Gk *akmē* point, highest point — more at EDGE] (1620) **:** the highest point or stage; *also* **:** one that represents perfection of the thing expressed ⟨he was the ~ of courtesy⟩ ***syn*** see SUMMIT
ac·ne \ˈak-nē\ *n* [Gk *aknē* eruption of the face, MS var. of *akmē,* lit., point] (ca. 1828) **:** a disorder of the skin caused by inflammation of the skin glands and hair follicles; *specif* **:** one found chiefly in adolescents and marked by pimples esp. on the face — **ac·ned** \-nēd\ *adj*
acock \ə-ˈkäk\ *adj or adv* (1846) **:** being in a cocked position
acoe·lo·mate \(ˈ)ā-ˈsē-lə-ˌmāt\ *n* (ca. 1889) **:** an invertebrate lacking a coelom; *esp* **:** one belonging to the group comprising the flatworms and nemerteans and characterized by bilateral symmetry and a digestive cavity that is the only internal cavity — **acoelomate** *adj*
acold \ə-ˈkōld\ *adj* [ME] *archaic* (14c) **:** COLD, CHILLED ⟨the owl, for all his feathers, was ~ — John Keats⟩
ac·o·lyte \ˈak-ə-ˌlīt\ *n* [ME *acolite,* fr. MF & ML; OF, fr. ML *acoluthus,* fr. MGk *akolouthos,* fr. Gk, adj., following, fr. *a-, ha-* (akin to Gk *homos* same) + *keleuthos* path] (14c) **1 :** one who assists the clergyman in a liturgical service by performing minor duties **2 :** one who attends or assists **:** FOLLOWER ⟨helped by his admiring ~*s*⟩
ac·o·nite \ˈak-ə-ˌnīt\ *n* [MF or L; fr. L *aconitum,* fr. Gk *akoniton*] (1551) **1 :** MONKSHOOD **2 :** the dried tuberous root of a monkshood (*Aconitum napellus*) formerly used as a sedative and anodyne
acorn \ˈā-ˌkȯ(ə)rn, -kərn\ *n* [ME *akern,* fr. OE *æcern;* akin to OE *æcer* field, MHG *ackeran* acorns collectively — more at ACRE] (bef. 12c) **:** the nut of the oak usu. seated in or surrounded by a hard woody cupule of indurated bracts
acorn squash *n* (1937) **:** an acorn-shaped dark green winter squash with a ridged surface and sweet yellow to orange flesh
acorn tube *n* (1934) **:** a very small vacuum tube that resembles an acorn in shape and is used at extremely high frequencies
acorn worm *n* (ca. 1889) **:** any of a group (Enteropneusta) of burrowing wormlike marine animals having an acorn-shaped proboscis and usu. classified with the chordates
acous·tic \ə-ˈkü-stik\ *or* **acous·ti·cal** \-sti-kəl\ *adj* [Gk *akoustikos* of hearing, fr. *akouein* to hear — more at HEAR] (1605) **1 :** of or relating to the sense or organs of hearing, to sound, or to the science of sounds ⟨~ apparatus of the ear⟩ ⟨~ energy⟩: as **a :** deadening or absorbing sound ⟨~ tile⟩ **b :** operated by or utilizing sound waves **2 :** of, relating to, or being a musical instrument whose sound is not electronically modified — **acous·ti·cal·ly** \-k(ə-)lē\ *adv*
ac·ous·ti·cian \ˌak-ˌü-ˈstish-ən, ə-ˌkü-\ *n* (1859) **:** a specialist in acoustics
acous·tics \ə-ˈkü-stiks\ *n pl but sing or pl in constr* (1683) **1 :** a science that deals with the production, control, transmission, reception, and effects of sound **2** *also* **acoustic :** the qualities that determine the ability of an enclosure (as an auditorium) to reflect sound waves in such a way as to produce distinct hearing
ac·quaint \ə-ˈkwānt\ *vt* [ME *aquainten,* fr. OF *acointier,* fr. ML *accognitare,* fr. LL *accognitus,* pp. of *accognoscere* to know perfectly, fr. L *ad-* + *cognoscere* to know — more at COGNITION] (13c) **1 :** to cause to know personally ⟨was ~*ed* with the mayor⟩ **2 :** to make familiar **:** cause to know firsthand ***syn*** see INFORM
ac·quain·tance \ə-ˈkwānt-ᵊn(t)s\ *n* (14c) **1 a :** personal knowledge **:** FAMILIARITY **b :** the state of being acquainted **2 a :** the persons with whom one is acquainted ⟨should auld ~ be forgot — Robert Burns⟩ **b :** a person whom one knows but who is not a particularly close friend — **ac·quain·tance·ship** \-ˌship\ *n*
ac·qui·esce \ˌak-wē-ˈes\ *vi* **-esced; -esc·ing** [F *acquiescer,* fr. L *acquiescere,* fr. *ad-* + *quiescere* to be quiet — more at QUIET] (1620) **:** to accept or comply tacitly or passively ***syn*** see ASSENT
ac·qui·es·cence \-ˈes-ᵊn(t)s\ *n* (1631) **1 :** the act of acquiescing **:** the state of being acquiescent **2 :** an instance of acquiescing
ac·qui·es·cent \-ˈes-ᵊnt\ *adj* [L *acquiescent-, acquiescens,* prp. of *acquiescere*] (1753) **:** inclined to acquiesce — **ac·qui·es·cent·ly** *adv*
ac·quir·able \ə-ˈkwī-rə-bəl\ *adj* (1646) **:** capable of being acquired
ac·quire \ə-ˈkwī(ə)r\ *vt* **ac·quired; ac·quir·ing** [ME *aqueren,* fr. MF *aquerre,* fr. L *acquirere,* fr. *ad-* + *quaerere* to seek, obtain] (15c) **1 :** to get as one's own: **a :** to come into possession or control of often by unspecified means **b :** to come to have as a new or added characteristic, trait, or ability (as by sustained effort or natural selection) ⟨~ fluency in French⟩ ⟨bacteria that ~ tolerance to antibiotics⟩ **2 :** to locate and hold (a desired object) in a detector ⟨~ a target by radar⟩
acquired immune deficiency syndrome *n* (1982) **:** AIDS
acquired immunodeficiency syndrome *n* (1982) **:** AIDS
ac·quire·ment \ə-ˈkwī(ə)r-mənt\ *n* (1630) **1 :** an attainment of mind or body usu. resulting from continued endeavor **2 :** the act of acquiring

syn ACQUIREMENT, ACQUISITION, ATTAINMENT, ACCOMPLISHMENT mean a power or skill won through deliberate effort. ACQUIREMENT suggests the result of constant endeavor to cultivate oneself; ACQUISITION stresses the effort involved and the inherent value of what is gained; ATTAINMENT suggests a distinguished achievement; ACCOMPLISHMENT implies a socially useful skill.

ac·qui·si·tion \ˌak-wə-ˈzish-ən\ *n* [ME *acquisicioun,* fr. MF or L; MF *acquisition,* fr. L *acquisition-, acquisitio,* fr. *acquisitus,* pp. of *acquirere*] (14c) **1 :** the act of acquiring **2 :** something acquired or gained **3 :** the acquiring of library materials (as books and periodicals) by purchase, exchange, or gift ***syn*** see ACQUIREMENT — **ac·qui·si·tion·al** \-shnəl, -shən-ᵊl\ *adj* — **ac·quis·i·tor** \ə-ˈkwiz-ət-ər\ *n*
ac·quis·i·tive \ə-ˈkwiz-ət-iv\ *adj* (1846) **:** strongly desirous of acquiring and possessing ***syn*** see COVETOUS — **ac·quis·i·tive·ly** *adv* — **ac·quis·i·tive·ness** *n*
ac·quit \ə-ˈkwit\ *vt* **ac·quit·ted; ac·quit·ting** [ME *aquiten,* fr. OF *aquiter,* fr. *a-* (fr. L *ad-*) + *quite* free of — more at QUIT] (13c) **1 a** *archaic* **:** to pay off (as a claim or debt) **b** *obs* **:** REPAY, REQUITE **2 :** to discharge completely (as from an obligation or accusation) ⟨the court *acquitted* the prisoner⟩ **3 :** to conduct (oneself) usu. satisfactorily esp. under stress ⟨the recruits *acquitted* themselves like veterans⟩ ***syn*** see BEHAVE, EXCULPATE — **ac·quit·ter** *n*
ac·quit·tal \ə-ˈkwit-ᵊl\ *n* (15c) **:** a setting free from the charge of an offense by verdict, sentence, or other legal process
ac·quit·tance \ə-ˈkwit-ᵊn(t)s\ *n* (14c) **:** a document evidencing a discharge from an obligation; *esp* **:** a receipt in full

acr- *or* **acro-** *comb form* [MF or Gk; MF *acro-,* fr. Gk *akr-, akro-,* fr. *akros* topmost, extreme; akin to Gk *akmē* point — more at EDGE] **1** : beginning : end : tip ⟨*acro*nym⟩ **2 a** : top : peak : summit ⟨*acro*dont⟩ **b** : height ⟨*acro*phobia⟩ **c** : extremity of the body ⟨*acro*cyanosis⟩

acre \'ā-kər\ *n* [ME, fr. OE *æcer;* akin to OHG *ackar* field, L *ager,* Gk *agros,* L *agere* to drive — more at AGENT] (bef. 12c) **1 a** *archaic* : a field esp. of arable or pasture land **b** *pl* : LANDS, ESTATE **2** : any of various units of area; *esp* : a unit in the U.S. and England equal to 160 square rods ⟨a lake of 9 ~*s*⟩ — see WEIGHT table **3** : a broad expanse or great quantity ⟨~*s* of time devoted to trivia⟩

acre·age \'ā-k(ə-)rij\ *n* (1859) : area in acres : ACRES

acre–foot \'ā-kər-'fu̇t\ *n* (1900) : the volume (as of irrigation water) that would cover one acre to a depth of one foot

acre–inch \'ā-kə-'rinch\ *n* (ca. 1909) : one twelfth of an acre-foot

ac·rid \'ak-rəd\ *adj* [modif. of L *acr-, acer* sharp — more at EDGE] (1712) **1** : sharp and harsh or unpleasantly pungent in taste or odor : IRRITATING **2** : deeply or violently bitter : ACRIMONIOUS ⟨an ~ denunciation⟩ *syn* see CAUSTIC — **acrid·i·ty** \a-'krid-ət-ē, ə-\ *n* — **ac·rid·ly** \'ak-rəd-lē\ *adv* — **ac·rid·ness** *n*

ac·ri·dine \'ak-rə-,dēn\ *n* (ca. 1877) : a colorless crystalline compound $C_{13}H_9N$ occurring in coal tar and important as the parent compound of dyes and pharmaceuticals

acridine orange *n* (ca. 1909) : a basic orange dye structurally related to acridine and used esp. to stain nucleic acids

ac·ri·fla·vine \,ak-rə-'flā-,vēn, -vən\ *n* [*acridine* + *flavine*] (1917) : a yellow dye $C_{14}H_{14}N_3Cl$ used as an antiseptic esp. for wounds

Ac·ri·lan \'ak-rə-,lan, -lən\ *trademark* — used for an acrylic fiber

ac·ri·mo·ni·ous \,ak-rə-'mō-nē-əs\ *adj* (1775) : caustic, biting, or rancorous esp. in feeling, language, or manner ⟨an ~ dispute⟩ — **ac·ri·mo·ni·ous·ly** *adv* — **ac·ri·mo·ni·ous·ness** *n*

ac·ri·mo·ny \'ak-rə-,mō-nē\ *n, pl* **-nies** [MF or L; MF *acrimonie,* fr. L *acrimonia,* fr. *acr-, acer*] (1542) : harsh or biting sharpness esp. of words, manner, or disposition

ac·ro·bat \'ak-rə-,bat\ *n* [F & Gk; F *acrobate,* fr. Gk *akrobatēs,* fr. *akrobatos* walking up high, fr. *akros* + *bainein* to go — more at COME] (1825) **1** : one that performs gymnastic feats requiring skillful control of the body **2** : one adept at swiftly changing his position or viewpoint ⟨a political ~⟩ — **ac·ro·bat·ic** \,ak-rə-'bat-ik\ *adj* — **ac·ro·bat·i·cal·ly** \-i-k(ə-)lē\ *adv*

ac·ro·bat·ics \,ak-rə-'bat-iks\ *n pl but sing or pl in constr* (1882) **1** : the art, performance, or activity of an acrobat **2** : a spectacular, showy, or startling performance involving great agility

ac·ro·cen·tric \,ak-rō-'sen-trik\ *adj* [*acr-* + *-centric*] (1945) : having the centromere situated so that one chromosomal arm is much shorter than the other — **acrocentric** *n*

ac·ro·dont \'ak-rə-,dänt\ *adj* (1872) **1** *of teeth* : consolidated with the summit of the alveolar ridge without sockets **2** : having acrodont teeth

acro·le·in \ə-'krō-lē-ən\ *n* [ISV *acr-* (fr. L *acr-, acer*) + L *olēre* to smell — more at ODOR] (ca. 1864) : a colorless irritant pungent liquid aldehyde C_3H_4O obtained by dehydration of glycerol or oxidation of propylene or allyl alcohol

ac·ro·meg·a·ly \,ak-rō-'meg-ə-lē\ *n* [F *acromégalie,* fr. *acr-* + Gk *megal-, megas* large — more at MUCH] (1889) : chronic hyperpituitarism marked by progressive enlargement of hands, feet, and face — **ac·ro·me·gal·ic** \-mə-'gal-ik\ *adj or n*

ac·ro·nym \'ak-rə-,nim\ *n* [*acr-* + *-onym* (as in *homonym*)] (1943) : a word (as *radar* or *snafu*) formed from the initial letter or letters of each of the successive parts or major parts of a compound term — **ac·ro·nym·ic** \,ak-rə-'nim-ik\ *adj* — **ac·ro·nym·i·cal·ly** \-i-k(ə-)lē\ *adv*

acrop·e·tal \ə-'kräp-ət-ᵊl, a-\ *adj* [*acr-* + *-petal* (as in *centripetal*)] (1875) : proceeding from the base toward the apex or from below upward — **acrop·e·tal·ly** \-ᵊl-ē\ *adv*

ac·ro·pho·bia \,ak-rə-'fō-bē-ə\ *n* [NL] (1892) : abnormal dread of being at a great height — **ac·ro·phobe** \'ak-rə-,fōb\ *n*

acrop·o·lis \ə-'kräp-ə-ləs\ *n* [Gk *akropolis,* fr. *akr-* acr- + *polis* city — more at POLICE] (1662) : the upper fortified part of an ancient Greek city (as Athens)

ac·ro·some \'ak-rə-,sōm\ *n* [ISV] (1899) : an anterior prolongation of a spermatozoon that releases egg-penetrating enzymes — **ac·ro·so·mal** \,ak-rə-'sō-məl\ *adj*

¹across \ə-'krȯs, *chiefly dial* -'krȯst\ *adv* [ME *acros,* fr. AF *an crois,* fr. *an* in (fr. L *in*) + *crois* cross, fr. L *crux* — more at IN, CROSS] (14c) **1** : in a position reaching from one side to the other : CROSSWISE **2** : to or on the opposite side **3** : so as to be understandable, acceptable, or successful : OVER ⟨get an argument ~⟩

²across *prep* (1591) **1 a** : from one side to the opposite side of : OVER, THROUGH ⟨swam ~ the river⟩ **b** : on the opposite side of ⟨lives ~ the street from us⟩ **2** : so as to intersect or pass through at an angle ⟨sawed ~ the grain of the wood⟩ **3** : into transitory contact with ⟨ran ~ an old friend in the store⟩

³across *adj* (1646) : being in a crossed position

across–the–board *adj* (1945) **1** : placed to win if a competitor wins, places, or shows ⟨an ~ racing bet⟩ **2** : embracing or affecting all classes or categories : BLANKET ⟨an ~ pay raise⟩

acros·tic \ə-'krȯs-tik, -'kräs-\ *n* [MF & Gk; MF *acrostiche,* fr. Gk *akrostichis,* fr. *akr-* acr- + *stichos* line; akin to *steichein* to go — more at STAIR] (1530) **1** : a composition usu. in verse in which sets of letters (as the initial or final letters of the lines) taken in order form a word or phrase or a regular sequence of letters of the alphabet **2** : ACRONYM — **acrostic** *also* **acros·ti·cal** \-ti-kəl\ *adj* — **acros·ti·cal·ly** \-ti-k(ə-)lē\ *adv*

ac·ry·late \'ak-rə-,lāt\ *n* (1873) **1** : a salt or ester of acrylic acid **2** : ACRYLIC RESIN

¹acryl·ic \ə-'kril-ik\ *adj* [ISV *acrolein* + *-yl* + *-ic*] (ca. 1855) : of or relating to acrylic acid or its derivatives ⟨~ polymers⟩

²acrylic *n* (1942) **1 a** : ACRYLIC RESIN **b** : a paint in which the vehicle is an acrylic resin **c** : a painting done in an acrylic resin **2** : ACRYLIC FIBER

acrylic acid *n* (ca. 1855) : an unsaturated liquid acid $C_3H_4O_2$ that is obtained by synthesis and that polymerizes readily to form useful products (as constituents for varnishes and lacquers)

acrylic fiber *n* (1951) : a quick-drying synthetic textile fiber made by polymerization of acrylonitrile usu. with other monomers

acrylic resin *n* (1936) : a glassy thermoplastic made by polymerizing acrylic or methacrylic acid or a derivative of either and used for cast and molded parts or as coatings and adhesives

ac·ry·lo·ni·trile \,ak-rə-lō-'nī-trəl, -,trēl\ *n* (1893) : a colorless volatile flammable liquid nitrile C_3H_3N used chiefly in organic synthesis and for polymerization

¹act \'akt\ *n* [ME, partly fr. L *actus* doing, act, fr. *actus,* pp. of *agere* to drive, do; partly fr. L *actum* thing done, record, fr. neut. of *actus,* pp. — more at AGENT] (14c) **1 a** : the doing of a thing : DEED **b** : something done voluntarily **2** : a state of real existence rather than possibility **3** : the formal product of a legislative body : STATUTE; *also* : a decision or determination of a sovereign, a legislative council, or a court of justice **4** : the process of doing ⟨caught in the ~⟩ **5** *often cap* : a formal record of something done or transacted **6 a** : one of the principal divisions of a theatrical work (as a play or opera) **b** : one of the successive parts or major parts of a performance in a variety show or circus **7** : a display of affected behavior : PRETENSE

²act *vt* (15c) **1** *obs* : ACTUATE, ANIMATE **2 a** : to represent or perform by action esp. on the stage **b** : FEIGN, SIMULATE **c** : IMPERSONATE **3** : to play the part of as if in a play ⟨~ the man of the world⟩ **4** : to behave in a manner suitable to ⟨~ your age⟩ ~ *vi* **1 a** : to perform on the stage **b** : to behave as if performing on the stage : PRETEND **2** : to take action : MOVE ⟨think before ~*ing*⟩ ⟨~*ed* favorably on the recommendation⟩ **3** : to conduct oneself : BEHAVE ⟨~ like a fool⟩ **4** : to perform a specified function : SERVE ⟨trees ~*ing* as a windbreak⟩ **5** : to produce an effect : WORK ⟨wait for a medicine to ~⟩ **6** *of a play* : to be capable of being performed ⟨the play ~*s* well⟩ **7** : to give a decision or award ⟨adjourned without ~*ing* on the bill⟩ — **act·abil·i·ty** \,ak-tə-'bil-ət-ē\ *n* — **act·able** \'ak-tə-bəl\ *adj*

Ac·tae·on \ak-'tē-ən\ *n* [L, fr. Gk *Aktaiōn*] : a hunter turned into a stag and killed by his own hounds for having seen Artemis bathing

ACTH \,ā-,sē-(,)tē-'āch\ *n* [*a*drenocorti*c*o*t*ropic *h*ormone] (1947) : a protein hormone of the anterior lobe of the pituitary gland that stimulates the adrenal cortex — called also *adrenocorticotropic hormone*

ac·tin \'ak-tən\ *n* [ISV, fr. L *actus*] (1942) : a protein of muscle that is active in muscular contraction

actin- *or* **actini-** *or* **actino-** *comb form* [NL, ray, fr. Gk *aktin-, aktino-,* fr. *aktin-, aktis;* akin to OE *ūhte* morning twilight, L *noct-, nox* night — more at NIGHT] **1 a** : having a radiate form ⟨*Actino*myces⟩ **b** : actinian ⟨*actini*form⟩ **2 a** : actinic ⟨*actin*ium⟩ **b** : actinic radiation (as X rays) ⟨*actino*therapy⟩

¹act·ing \'ak-tiŋ\ *n* (1664) : the art or practice of representing a character on a stage or before cameras

²acting *adj* (1797) **1** : holding a temporary rank or position : performing services temporarily ⟨~ president⟩ **2 a** : suitable for stage performance ⟨an ~ play⟩ **b** : prepared with directions for actors ⟨an ~ text of a play⟩

ac·tin·i·an \ak-'tin-ē-ən\ *n* [NL *actinia,* fr. Gk *aktin-, aktis*] (1888) : SEA ANEMONE; *also* : a related animal — **actinian** *adj*

ac·tin·ic \ak-'tin-ik\ *adj* (1884) : of, relating to, or exhibiting actinism — **ac·tin·i·cal·ly** \-i-k(ə-)lē\ *adv*

actinic ray *n* (ca. 1845) : a radiation having marked photochemical action

ac·ti·nide \'ak-tə-,nīd\ *n* [ISV] (1945) : any element in a series of elements of increasing atomic numbers beginning with actinium (89) or thorium (90) and ending with element of atomic number 103 — see PERIODIC TABLE table

ac·ti·nism \'ak-tə-,niz-əm\ *n* (1844) : the property of radiant energy esp. in the visible and ultraviolet spectral regions by which chemical changes are produced

ac·tin·i·um \ak-'tin-ē-əm\ *n* [NL] (ca. 1900) : a radioactive trivalent metallic element that resembles lanthanum in chemical properties and that is found esp. in pitchblende — see ELEMENT table

ac·tin·o·lite \ak-'tin-ᵊl-,īt\ *n* (ca. 1828) : a bright or grayish green amphibole occurring in fibrous, radiate, or columnar forms

ac·ti·nom·e·ter \,ak-tə-'näm-ət-ər\ *n* (1833) **1** : an instrument for measuring the direct heating power of the sun's rays **2** : an instrument for measuring the actinic power of radiant energy or for determining photographic exposure to be given — **ac·ti·no·me·tric** \-nō-'me-trik\ *adj* — **ac·ti·nom·e·try** \-'näm-ə-trē\ *n*

ac·ti·no·mor·phic *adj* \,ak-(,)tin-ō-'mȯr-fik, -tə-nō-; ak-,tin-ō-\ [ISV] (1900) : being radially symmetrical and capable of division into essentially symmetrical halves by any longitudinal plane passing through the axis — **ac·ti·no·mor·phy** \'ak-tə-nō-,mȯr-fē, ak-'tin-ō-\ *n*

ac·ti·no·my·ces \,ak-(,)tin-ō-'mī-,sēz, -tə-nō-; ak-,tin-ō-\ *n, pl* **actinomyces** [NL, genus name, fr. *actin-* + Gk *mykēt-, mykēs* fungus; akin to Gk *myxa* mucus — more at MUCUS] (1882) : any of a genus (*Actinomyces*) of filamentous bacteria including both soil-inhabiting saprophytes and disease-producing parasites — **ac·ti·no·my·ce·tal** \-mī-'sēt-ᵊl\ *adj*

ac·ti·no·my·cete \-'mī-,sēt, -mī-'sēt\ *n* [deriv. of Gk *aktin-, aktis* + *mykēt-, mykēs*] (1911) : any of an order (Actinomycetales) of filamentous or rod-shaped bacteria including the actinomyces and streptomyces — **ac·ti·no·my·ce·tous** \-mī-'sēt-əs\ *adj*

ac·ti·no·my·cin \-'mīs-ᵊn\ *n* (1940) : any of various red or yellow-red mostly toxic polypeptide antibiotics isolated from soil bacteria (esp. *Streptomyces antibioticus*); *specif* : one used to inhibit DNA or RNA synthesis

ac·ti·no·my·co·sis \-mī-'kō-səs\ *n* (1882) : infection with or disease caused by actinomycetes; *esp* : a chronic disease of cattle, swine, and man characterized by hard granulomatous masses usu. in the mouth and jaw — **ac·ti·no·my·cot·ic** \-'kät-ik\ *adj*

ac·ti·non \'ak-tə-,nän\ *n* [NL, fr. *actinium*] (1926) : a gaseous radioactive isotope of radon that has a half-life of about 4 seconds

ac·ti·no·ura·ni·um \,ak-(,)tin-ō-yu̇-'rā-nē-əm, -tə-nō-, ak-,tin-ō-\ *n* [NL, fr. *actinium* + *uranium*] (1929) : the uranium isotope of mass 235

\ə\ abut \ᵊ\ kitten, F table \ər\ further \a\ ash \ā\ ace \ä\ cot, cart \au̇\ out \ch\ chin \e\ bet \ē\ easy \g\ go \i\ hit \ī\ ice \j\ job \ŋ\ sing \ō\ go \ȯ\ law \ȯi\ boy \th\ thin \t͟h\ the \ü\ loot \u̇\ foot \y\ yet \zh\ vision \à, k̟, ⁿ, œ, œ̄, ue, ue̅, ʸ\ *see* Guide to Pronunciation

ac·tion \'ak-shən\ *n* (14c) **1** : a proceeding in a court of justice by which one demands or enforces one's right **2** : the bringing about of an alteration by force or through a natural agency **3** : the manner or method of performing: **a** : the deportment of an actor or speaker or his expression by means of attitude, voice, and gesture **b** : the style of movement of the feet and legs (as of a horse) **c** : a function of the body or one of its parts **4** : an act of will **5 a** : a thing done : DEED **b** : the accomplishment of a thing usu. over a period of time, in stages, or with the possibility of repetition ⟨an ~, the product and expression of exerted force —Thomas Carlyle⟩ **c** *pl* : BEHAVIOR, CONDUCT ⟨unscrupulous ~*s*⟩ **d** : INITIATIVE, ENTERPRISE ⟨a man of ~⟩ **6 a** (1) : an engagement between troops or ships (2) : combat in war ⟨gallantry in ~⟩ **b** (1) : an event or series of events forming a literary composition (2) : the unfolding of the events of a drama or work of fiction : PLOT (3) : the movement of incidents in a plot **c** : the combination of circumstances that constitute the subject matter of a painting or sculpture **7 a** : an operating mechanism **b** : the manner in which a mechanism operates **8 a** : the price movement and trading volume of a commodity, security, or market **b** : the process of betting including the offering and acceptance of a bet and determination of a winner **9** : the most vigorous, productive, or exciting activity in a particular field, area, or group ⟨they itch to go where the ~ is —D. J. Henahan⟩

ac·tion·able \'ak-sh(ə-)nə-bəl\ *adj* (1591) : subject to or affording ground for an action or suit at law — **ac·tion·ably** \-blē\ *adv*

ac·tion·less \'ak-shən-ləs\ *adj* (1817) : marked by inaction : IMMOBILE

action painting *n* (1952) : abstract expressionism marked esp. by the use of spontaneous techniques (as dribbling, splattering, or smearing) — **action painter** *n*

action potential *n* (1926) : a momentary change in electrical potential (as between the inside of a nerve cell and the extracellular medium) that occurs when a cell or tissue has been activated by a stimulus

ac·ti·vate \'ak-tə-,vāt\ *vb* **-vat·ed; -vat·ing** *vt* (1626) : to make active or more active: as **a** (1) : to make (as molecules) reactive or more reactive (2) : to convert (as a provitamin) into a biologically active derivative **b** : to make (a substance) radioactive, luminescent, photosensitive, or photoconductive **c** : to treat (as carbon or alumina) so as to improve adsorptive properties **d** : to aerate (sewage) so as to favor the growth of organisms that decompose organic matter **e** (1) : to set up or formally institute (as a military unit) with the necessary personnel and equipment (2) : to put (an individual or unit) on active duty ~ *vi* : to become active — **ac·ti·va·tion** \,ak-tə-'vā-shən\ *n* — **ac·ti·va·tor** \'ak-tə-,vāt-ər\ *n*

activated carbon *n* (1921) : a highly adsorbent powdered or granular carbon made usu. by carbonization and chemical activation and used chiefly for purifying by adsorption — called also *activated charcoal*

activation analysis *n* (ca. 1949) : analysis to determine chemical elements in a material by bombarding it with neutrons to produce radioactive atoms whose radiations are characteristic of the elements present

activation energy *n* (1940) : the minimum amount of energy required to convert a normal stable molecule into a reactive molecule

ac·tive \'ak-tiv\ *adj* [ME, fr. MF or L; MF *actif*, fr. L *activus*, fr. *actus*, pp. of *agere* to drive, do — more at AGENT] (14c) **1** : characterized by action rather than by contemplation or speculation **2** : productive of action or movement **3 a** *of a verb form or voice* : asserting that the person or thing represented by the grammatical subject performs the action represented by the verb ⟨*hits* in "he hits the ball" is ~⟩ **b** : expressing action as distinct from mere existence or state **4** : quick in physical movement : LIVELY **5** : marked by vigorous activity : BUSY ⟨the stock market was ~⟩ **6** : requiring vigorous action or exertion ⟨~ sports⟩ **7** : having practical operation or results : EFFECTIVE ⟨an ~ law⟩ **8 a** : disposed to action : ENERGETIC ⟨~ interest⟩ **b** : engaged in an action or activity ⟨an ~ club member⟩ **9** : engaged in full-time service esp. in the armed forces ⟨~ duty⟩ **10** : marked by present operation, transaction, movement, or use ⟨~ account⟩ **11 a** : capable of acting or reacting : ACTIVATED ⟨~ nitrogen⟩ ⟨~ charcoal⟩ **b** : tending to progress or to cause degeneration ⟨~ tuberculosis⟩ **c** : exhibiting optical activity **d** *of an electronic element* : capable of controlling voltages or currents **e** : requiring the expenditure of energy ⟨~ calcium ion uptake⟩ **12** : still eligible to win the pot in poker **13** : moving down the line : visiting in the set — used of couples in contredanses or square dances — **active** *n* — **ac·tive·ly** *adv* — **ac·tive·ness** *n*

active immunity *n* (1911) : usu. long-lasting immunity that is acquired through production of antibodies within the organism in response to the presence of antigens — compare PASSIVE IMMUNITY

active transport *n* (ca. 1963) : movement of a chemical substance by the expenditure of energy through a gradient (as across a cell membrane) in concentration or electrical potential and opposite to the direction of normal diffusion

ac·tiv·ism \'ak-ti-,viz-əm\ *n* (1915) : a doctrine or practice that emphasizes direct vigorous action (as a mass demonstration) in support of or opposition to one side of a controversial issue — **ac·tiv·ist** \-vəst\ *n or adj* — **ac·tiv·is·tic** \,ak-ti-'vis-tik\ *adj*

ac·tiv·i·ty \ak-'tiv-ət-ē\ *n, pl* **-ties** (15c) **1** : the quality or state of being active **2** : vigorous or energetic action : LIVELINESS **3** : natural or normal function: as **a** : a process (as digestion) that an organism carries on or participates in by virtue of being alive **b** : a similar process actually or potentially involving mental function; *specif* : an educational procedure designed to stimulate learning by firsthand experience **4** : an active force **5 a** : a pursuit in which a person is active **b** : a form of organized, supervised, often extracurricular recreation **6** : an organizational unit for performing a specific function; *also* : its function or duties

act of God (1859) : an extraordinary interruption by a natural cause (as a flood or earthquake) of the usual course of events that experience, prescience, or care cannot reasonably foresee or prevent

ac·to·my·o·sin \,ak-tə-'mī-ə-sən\ *n* [ISV *actin* + *-o-* + *myosin*] (1942) : a viscous contractile complex of actin and myosin concerned together with ATP in muscular contraction

ac·tor \'ak-tər *also* -,tó(ə)r\ *n* (15c) **1** : one that acts : DOER **2 a** : one who represents a character in a dramatic production **b** : a theatrical performer **c** : one that behaves as if acting a part **3** : one that takes part in any affair — **ac·tor·ish** \-tə-rish\ *adj*

act out *vt* (1611) **1 a** : to represent in action ⟨children *act out* what they read⟩ **b** : to translate into action ⟨unwilling to *act out* their beliefs⟩ **2** : to express (as an impulse or a fantasy) directly in overt behavior without modification to comply with social norms

ac·tress \'ak-trəs\ *n* (1676) : a woman who is an actor

Acts \'akts\ *n pl but sing in constr* : a book in the New Testament narrating the beginnings of the Christian Church — called also *Acts of the Apostles*; see BIBLE table

ac·tu·al \'ak-ch(ə-w)əl, -sh(ə-w)əl\ *adj* [ME *actuel*, fr. MF, fr. LL *actualis*, fr. L *actus* act] (14c) **1** *obs* : ACTIVE **2 a** : existing in act and not merely potentially **b** : existing in fact or reality ⟨~ and imagined conditions⟩ **c** : not false or apparent ⟨~ costs⟩ **3** : existing or occurring at the time : CURRENT ⟨caught in the ~ commission of a crime⟩

actual cash value *n* (1946) : money equal to the cost of replacing lost, stolen, or damaged property after depreciation

ac·tu·al·i·ty \,ak-chə-'wal-ət-ē, ,ak-shə-\ *n, pl* **-ties** (1652) **1** : the quality or state of being actual **2** : something that is actual : FACT, REALITY ⟨possible risks which have been seized upon as *actualities* —T. S. Eliot⟩

ac·tu·al·ize \'ak-ch(ə-w)ə-,līz, -sh(ə-w)ə-,līz\ *vb* **-ized; -iz·ing** *vt* (1701) : to make actual ~ *vi* : to become actual — **ac·tu·al·iza·tion** \,ak-ch(ə-w)ə-lə-'zā-shən, -sh(ə-w)ə-lə-\ *n*

ac·tu·al·ly *adv* \'ak-ch(ə-w)ə-lē, -sh(ə-w)ə-lē; 'aks(h)-lē\ (15c) **1** : in act or in fact : REALLY ⟨nominally but not ~ independent —Karl Loewenstein⟩ **2** : in point of fact : in truth ⟨he ~ spoke Latin⟩

ac·tu·ar·i·al \,ak-chə-'wer-ē-əl, -shə-\ *adj* (1869) **1** : of or relating to actuaries **2** : relating to statistical calculation esp. of life expectancy — **ac·tu·ar·i·al·ly** \-ē-ə-lē\ *adv*

ac·tu·ary \'ak-chə-,wer-ē, -shə-\ *n, pl* **-ar·ies** [L *actuarius* shorthand writer, fr. *actum* record — more at ACT] (1553) **1** *obs* : CLERK, REGISTRAR **2** : one who calculates insurance and annuity premiums, reserves, and dividends

ac·tu·ate \'ak-chə-,wāt, -shə-\ *vt* **-at·ed; -at·ing** [ML *actuatus*, pp. of *actuare*, to execute, fr. L *actus* act] (1645) **1** : to put into mechanical action or motion **2** : to move to action ***syn*** see MOVE — **ac·tu·a·tion** \,ak-chə-'wā-shən, -shə-\ *n*

ac·tu·a·tor \'ak-chə-,wāt-ər, -shə-\ *n* (ca. 1864) : one that actuates; *specif* : a mechanism for moving or controlling something indirectly instead of by hand

act up *vi* (1903) **1** : to act in a way different from that which is normal or expected: as **a** : to behave in an unruly, recalcitrant, or capricious manner **b** : SHOW OFF **c** : to function improperly ⟨this typewriter is *acting up* again⟩ **2** : to become active or acute after being quiescent ⟨her rheumatism started to *act up*⟩

acu·ity \ə-'kyü-ət-ē, a-\ *n, pl* **-ities** [MF *acuité*, fr. OF *agüeté*, fr. *agu* sharp, fr. L *acutus*] (1543) : keenness of perception : SHARPNESS

acu·le·ate \ə-'kyü-lē-ət\ *adj* [L *aculeatus* having stings, fr. *aculeus*, dim. of *acus*] (1661) : having a sting ⟨~ insects⟩

acu·men \ə-'kyü-mən, 'ak-yə-mən\ *n* [L *acumin-*, *acumen*, lit., point, fr. *acuere*] (1531) : keenness and depth of perception, discernment, or discrimination esp. in practical matters : SHREWDNESS ***syn*** see DISCERNMENT

acu·mi·nate \ə-'kyü-mə-nət\ *adj* (1646) : tapering to a slender point

acu·pres·sure \'ak-(y)ə-,presh-ər\ *n* (1859) : SHIATSU

acu·punc·ture \-,pəŋ(k)-chər\ *n* [L *acus* + E *puncture*] (ca. 1860) : an orig. Chinese practice of puncturing the body (as with needles) at specific points to cure disease or relieve pain (as in surgery) — **acu·punc·tur·ist** \-,pəŋ(k)-chə-rəst\ *n*

acute \ə-'kyüt\ *adj* **acut·er; acut·est** [L *acutus*, pp. of *acuere* to sharpen, fr. *acus* needle; akin to L *acer* sharp — more at EDGE] (14c) **1 a** (1) : characterized by sharpness or severity ⟨~ pain⟩ ⟨an ~ infection⟩ (2) : having a sudden onset, sharp rise, and short course ⟨~ disease⟩ **b** : lasting a short time ⟨~ experiments⟩ **2** : ending in a sharp point: as **a** : being or forming an angle measuring less than 90 degrees ⟨~ angle⟩ **b** : composed of acute angles ⟨~ triangle⟩ **3 a** : marked by keen discernment or intellectual perception esp. of subtle distinctions : PENETRATING ⟨an ~ thinker⟩ **b** : responsive to slight impressions or stimuli ⟨~ observer⟩ **4** : felt, perceived, or experienced intensely ⟨~ distress⟩ **5** : seriously demanding urgent attention ⟨an ~ housing shortage⟩ **6 a** *of an accent mark* : having the form ´ **b** : marked with an acute accent **c** : of the variety indicated by an acute accent — **acute·ly** *adv* — **acute·ness** *n*

syn ACUTE, CRITICAL, CRUCIAL mean of uncertain outcome. ACUTE stresses intensification of conditions leading to a culmination or breaking point; CRITICAL adds to ACUTE implications of imminent change, of attendant suspense, and of decisiveness in the outcome; CRUCIAL suggests a dividing of the ways and often a test or trial involving the determination of a future course or direction. ***syn*** see in addition SHARP

acy·clic \(')ā-'sī-klik, -'sik-lik\ *adj* (1878) **1** : not cyclic; *esp* : not disposed in cycles or whorls **2** : having an open-chain structure; *esp* : ALIPHATIC ⟨an ~ compound⟩

ac·yl \'as-əl\ *n* [ISV, fr. *acid*] (1901) : a radical derived usu. from an organic acid by removal of the hydroxyl from all acid groups

¹ad \'ad\ *n, often attrib* (1841) **1** : ADVERTISEMENT 2 **2** : ADVERTISING

²ad *n* (1947) : ADVANTAGE 4

ad- *or* **ac-** *or* **af-** *or* **ag-** *or* **al-** *or* **ap-** *or* **as-** *or* **at-** *prefix* [ME, fr. MF, OF & L; MF, fr. OF, fr. L, fr. *ad* — more at AT] **1** : to : toward — usu. *ac-* before *c, k,* or *q* ⟨*ac*culturation⟩ and *af-* before *f* and *ag-* before *g* ⟨*ag*grade⟩ and *al-* before *l* ⟨*al*literation⟩ and *ap-* before *p* ⟨*ap*proximal⟩ and *as-* before *s* ⟨*as*suasive⟩ and *at-* before *t* ⟨*at*tune⟩ and *ad-* before other sounds but sometimes *ad-* even before one of the listed consonants ⟨*ad*sorb⟩ **2** : near : adjacent to — in this sense always in the form *ad-* ⟨*ad*renal⟩

-ad \,ad, əd\ *adv suffix* [L *ad*] : in the direction of : toward ⟨cephal*ad*⟩

ad·age \'ad-ij\ *n* [MF, fr. L *adagium*, fr. *ad-* + *-agium* (akin to *aio* I say)] (1548) : a saying often in metaphorical form that embodies a common observation

¹ada·gio \ə-'däj-(ē-,)ō, ä-, -'däzh-\ *adv or adj* [It, fr. *ad* to + *agio* ease, fr. LL *adjacens* near at hand — more at EASE] (1724) : in an easy graceful manner : SLOWLY — used chiefly as a direction in music

²adagio *n, pl* **-gios** (1754) **1** : a musical composition or movement in adagio tempo **2** : a ballet duet by a man and woman or a mixed trio displaying difficult feats of balance, lifting, or spinning

[1]**Ad·am** \'ad-əm\ *n* [ME, fr. LL, fr. Gk, fr. Heb *Ādhām*] **1 :** the first man and father by Eve of Cain and Abel **2 :** the unregenerate nature of man — used esp. in the phrase *the old Adam* — **Adam·ic** \ə-'dam-ik\ *or* **Adam·i·cal** \-i-kəl\ *adj*

[2]**Adam** *adj* [Robert *Adam* & James *Adam*] (1872) **:** of or relating to an 18th century decorative style (as of furniture) characterized by straight lines, surface decoration, and conventional designs (as festooned garlands and medallions)

ad·a·mance \'ad-ə-mən(t)s\ *n* (1968) **:** ADAMANCY

ad·a·man·cy \-mən-sē\ *n* [[2]*adamant* + *-cy*] (1937) **:** OBSTINACY

adam–and–eve \ˌad-ə-mən-'(d)ēv\ *n* (1807) **:** PUTTYROOT

[1]**ad·a·mant** \'ad-ə-mənt, -ˌmant\ *n* [ME, fr. MF, fr. L *adamant-, adamas* hardest metal, diamond, fr. Gk] (14c) **1 :** a stone (as a diamond) formerly believed to be of impenetrable hardness **2 :** an unbreakable or extremely hard substance

[2]**adamant** *adj* (1535) **:** unshakable or immovable esp. in opposition **:** UNYIELDING ***syn*** see INFLEXIBLE — **ad·a·mant·ly** *adv*

ad·a·man·tine \ˌad-ə-'man-ˌtēn, -ˌtīn, -'mant-ᵊn\ *adj* [ME, fr. L *adamantinus*, fr. Gk *adamantinos*, fr. *adamant-, adamas*] (13c) **1 :** made of or having the quality of adamant **2 :** rigidly firm **:** UNYIELDING **3 :** resembling the diamond in hardness or luster

Adam's apple *n* (ca. 1775) **:** the projection in the front of the neck formed by the largest cartilage of the larynx

Adam's needle *n* (1791) **:** any of several yuccas

adapt \ə-'dapt, a-\ *vb* [F or L; F *adapter*, fr. L *adaptare*, fr. *ad-* + *aptare* to fit, fr. *aptus* apt, fit] *vt* (15c) **:** to make fit (as for a specific or new use or situation) often by modification ~ *vi* **:** to become adapted — **adapt·ed·ness** *n*

syn ADAPT, ADJUST, ACCOMMODATE, CONFORM, RECONCILE mean to bring one thing into correspondence with another. ADAPT implies a modification according to changing circumstances ⟨they *adapted* themselves to the warmer climate⟩ ADJUST suggests bringing into a close and exact correspondence or harmony as exists between the parts of a mechanism ⟨*adjusted* the budget to allow for inflation⟩ ACCOMMODATE may suggest yielding or compromising in order to effect a correspondence ⟨*accommodated* his political beliefs in order to win⟩ CONFORM applies to bringing into harmony or accordance with a pattern, example, or principle ⟨refused to *conform* to society's idea of woman's proper role⟩ RECONCILE implies the demonstration of the underlying consistency or congruity of things that seem to be incompatible ⟨tried to *reconcile* what they said with what I knew⟩

adapt·able \ə-'dap-tə-bəl, a-\ *adj* (1800) **:** capable of being adapted **:** SUITABLE ***syn*** see PLASTIC — **adapt·abil·i·ty** \-ˌdap-tə-'bil-ət-ē\ *n*

ad·ap·ta·tion \ˌad-ˌap-'tā-shən, -əp-\ *n* (1610) **1 :** the act or process of adapting **:** the state of being adapted **2 :** adjustment to environmental conditions: as **a :** adjustment of a sense organ to the intensity or quality of stimulation **b :** modification of an organism or its parts that makes it more fit for existence under the conditions of its environment **3 :** something that is adapted; *specif* **:** a composition rewritten into a new form — **ad·ap·ta·tion·al** \-shnəl, -shən-ᵊl\ *adj* — **ad·ap·ta·tion·al·ly** \-ē\ *adv*

adapt·er *also* **adap·tor** \ə-'dap-tər, a-\ *n* (1801) **1 :** one that adapts **2 a :** a device for connecting two parts (as of different diameters) of an apparatus **b :** an attachment for adapting apparatus for uses not orig. intended

adap·tion \ə-'dap-shən, a-\ *n* (1704) **:** ADAPTATION

adap·tive \ə-'dap-tiv, a-\ *adj* (1824) **:** showing or having a capacity for or tendency toward adaptation — **adap·tive·ly** *adv* — **adap·tive·ness** *n* — **ad·ap·tiv·i·ty** \ˌad-ˌap-'tiv-ət-ē\ *n*

adaptive radiation *n* (1902) **:** evolutionary diversification of a generalized ancestral form with production of a number of adaptively specialized forms

Adar \ä-'där, 'ä-\ *n* [ME, fr. Heb *Ădhār*] (14c) **:** the 6th month of the civil year or the 12th month of the ecclesiastical year in the Jewish calendar — see MONTH table

Adar She·ni \ä-ˌdär-shā-'nē\ *n* [Heb *Ădhār Shēnī* second Adar] (ca. 1901) **:** VEADAR

ad·ax·i·al \(ˈ)a-'dak-sē-əl\ *adj* (1900) **:** situated on the same side as or facing the axis (as of an organ) ⟨the ~ or upper surface of a leaf⟩

add \'ad\ *vb* [ME *adden*, fr. L *addere*, fr. *ad-* + *-dere* to put — more at DO] *vt* (14c) **1 :** to join or unite so as to bring about an increase or improvement ⟨~*s* 60 acres to his land⟩ ⟨wine ~*s* a creative touch to cooking⟩ **2 :** to say further **:** APPEND **3 :** to combine (numbers) into an equivalent simple quantity or number **4 :** to include as a member of a group ⟨don't forget to ~ me in⟩ ~ *vi* **1 a :** to perform addition **b :** to come together or unite by addition **2 a :** to serve as an addition ⟨the movie will ~ to his fame⟩ **b :** to make an addition ⟨~*ed* to her savings⟩ — **add·able** *or* **add·ible** \'ad-ə-bəl\ *adj*

ad·dax \'ad-ˌaks\ *n, pl* **ad·dax·es** [L] (1693) **:** a large light-colored antelope (*Addax nasomaculata*) of No. Africa, Arabia, and Syria

ad·dend \'ad-ˌend, ə-'dend\ *n* [short for *addendum*] (ca. 1909) **:** a number to be added to another

ad·den·dum \ə-'den-dəm\ *n, pl* **-den·da** \-'den-də\ [L, neut. of *addendus*, gerundive of *addere*] (1684) **1 :** a thing added **:** ADDITION **2 :** a supplement to a book — often used in pl. but sing. in constr.

[1]**ad·der** \'ad-ər\ *n* [ME, alter. (by incorrect division of *a naddre*) of *naddre*, fr. OE *nǣdre*; akin to OHG *nātara* adder, L *natrix* water snake] (bef. 12c) **1 :** the common venomous viper (*Vipera berus*) of Europe; *broadly* **:** a terrestrial viper (family Viperidae) **2 :** any of several No. American snakes (as the hognose snakes) that are harmless but are popularly believed to be venomous

[2]**add·er** \'ad-ər\ *n* (1580) **:** one that adds; *esp* **:** a device (as in a computer) that performs addition

ad·der's–tongue \'ad-ərz-ˌtəŋ\ *n* (1578) **1 :** a fern (genus *Ophioglossum*, family Ophioglossaceae) whose fruiting spike resembles a serpent's tongue **2 :** DOGTOOTH VIOLET

[1]**ad·dict** \ə-'dikt\ *vt* [L *addictus*, pp. of *addicere* to favor, fr. *ad-* + *dicere* to say — more at DICTION] (1534) **1 :** to devote or surrender (oneself) to something habitually or obsessively ⟨~*ed* to gambling⟩ **2 :** to cause to become physiologically dependent upon a drug

[2]**ad·dict** \'ad-(ˌ)ikt\ *n* (1909) **1 :** one who is addicted to a drug **2 :** DEVOTEE ⟨a detective novel ~⟩

ad·dic·tion \ə-'dik-shən, a-\ *n* (1599) **1 :** the quality or state of being addicted ⟨~ to reading⟩ **2 :** compulsive physiological need for a habit-forming drug (as heroin) — compare HABITUATION

ad·dic·tive \-'dik-tiv\ *adj* (1939) **:** causing or characterized by addiction

Ad·di·son's disease \'ad-ə-sənz-\ *n* [Thomas *Addison* †1860 Eng. physician] (ca. 1856) **:** a destructive disease marked by deficient adrenocortical secretion and characterized by extreme weakness, loss of weight, low blood pressure, gastrointestinal disturbances, and brownish pigmentation of the skin and mucous membranes

ad·di·tion \ə-'dish-ən, a-\ *n* [ME, fr. MF, fr. L *addition-, additio*, fr. *additus*, pp. of *addere*] (14c) **1 :** the result of adding **:** INCREASE **2 :** the act or process of adding; *esp* **:** the operation of combining numbers so as to obtain an equivalent simple quantity **3 :** a part added (as to a building or residential section) **4 :** direct chemical combination of substances into a single product — **in addition :** [2]BESIDES, ALSO — **in addition to :** combined or associated with

ad·di·tion·al \-'dish-nəl, -'dish-ən-ᵊl\ *adj* (1646) **:** existing by way of addition **:** ADDED — **ad·di·tion·al·ly** \-ē\ *adv*

[1]**ad·di·tive** \'ad-ət-iv\ *adj* (1699) **1 :** of, relating to, or characterized by addition **2 :** produced by addition **3 :** characterized by, being, or producing effects (as drug responses or gene products) that are the sum when the causative factors act together of the effects produced when they act individually — **ad·di·tive·ly** *adv* — **ad·di·tiv·i·ty** \ˌad-ə-'tiv-ət-ē\ *n*

[2]**additive** *n* (1945) **:** a substance added to another in relatively small amounts to impart or improve desirable properties or suppress undesirable properties ⟨food ~*s*⟩

additive identity *n* (1960) **:** an identity element (as 0 in the group of whole numbers under the operation of addition) that in a given mathematical system leaves unchanged any element to which it is added

additive inverse *n* (1958) **:** a number that when added to a given number gives zero ⟨the *additive inverse* of 4 is −4⟩

[1]**ad·dle** \'ad-ᵊl\ *adj* [ME *adel* filth, fr. OE *adela*; akin to MLG *adele* liquid manure] (bef. 12c) **1** *of an egg* **:** ROTTEN **2 :** CONFUSED

[2]**addle** *vb* **ad·dled; ad·dling** \'ad-liŋ, -ᵊl-iŋ\ *vt* (1712) **:** to throw into confusion **:** CONFOUND ~ *vi* **1 :** to become rotten **:** SPOIL **2 :** to become confused

ad·dle·pat·ed \ˌad-ᵊl-'pāt-əd\ *adj* (1630) **1 :** being mixed up **:** CONFUSED **2 :** ECCENTRIC

add–on \'ad-ˌȯn, -ˌän\ *n* (1946) **:** something added as a supplement; *esp* **:** a component (as of a hi-fi or computer system) that increases capability

[1]**ad·dress** \ə-'dres, a- *also* 'ad-ˌres\ *vb* [ME *adressen*, fr. MF *adresser*, fr. *a-* (fr. L *ad-*) + *dresser* to arrange — more at DRESS] *vt* (14c) **1** *archaic* **a :** DIRECT, AIM **b :** to direct to go **:** SEND **2** *archaic* **:** to make ready; *esp* **:** DRESS **3 a :** to direct the efforts or attention of (oneself) ⟨will ~ himself to the problem⟩ **b :** to deal with **:** TREAT ⟨intrigued by the chance to ~ important issues — I. L. Horowitz⟩ **4 a :** to communicate directly ⟨~*es* his thanks to his host⟩ **b :** to speak or write directly to; *esp* **:** to deliver a formal speech to **5 a :** to mark directions for delivery on ⟨~ a letter⟩ **b :** to consign to the care of another (as an agent or factor) **6 :** to greet by a prescribed form **7 :** to adjust the club preparatory to hitting (a golf ball) **8 :** to identify (as a peripheral or memory location) by an address for information transfer ~ *vi, obs* **:** to direct one's speech or attentions — **ad·dress·er** *n*

[2]**ad·dress** \ə-'dres, *for 5 & 7 & 4 also* 'ad-ˌres\ *n* (1539) **1 :** dutiful and courteous attention esp. in courtship — usu. used in pl. **2 a :** readiness and capability for dealing (as with a person or problem) skillfully and smoothly **:** ADROITNESS **b** *obs* **:** a making ready; *also* **:** a state of preparedness **3 a :** manner of bearing onself ⟨a man of rude ~⟩ **b :** manner of speaking or singing **:** DELIVERY **4 :** a formal communication; *esp* **:** a prepared speech delivered to a special audience or on a special occasion **5 a :** a place where a person or organization may be communicated with **b :** directions for delivery on the outside of an object (as a letter or package) **c :** the designation of place of delivery placed between the heading and salutation on a business letter **6 :** a preparatory position of the player and club in golf **7 :** a location (as in the memory of a computer) where particular information is stored; *also* **:** the digits that identify such a location ***syn*** see TACT

ad·dress·able \ə-'dres-ə-bəl\ *adj* (1955) **1 :** able to be addressed **:** directly accessible ⟨~ registers in a computer⟩ **2 :** of or relating to a subscription television system that uses decoders addressable by the system operator

ad·dress·ee \ˌad-ˌres-'ē, ə-ˌdres-'ē\ *n* (1810) **:** one to whom something is addressed

ad·duce \ə-'d(y)üs\ *vt* **ad·duced; ad·duc·ing** [L *adducere*, lit., to lead to, fr. *ad-* + *ducere* to lead — more at TOW] (15c) **:** to offer as example, reason, or proof in discussion or analysis — **ad·duc·er** *n*

[1]**ad·duct** \ə-'dəkt, a-\ *vt* [L *adductus*, pp. of *adducere*] (1836) **:** to draw (as a limb) toward or past the median axis of the body; *also* **:** to bring together (similar parts) ⟨~ the fingers⟩ — **ad·duc·tive** \-'dək-tiv\ *adj*

[2]**ad·duct** \'ad-ˌəkt\ *n* [G *addukt*, fr. L *adductus*] (1941) **:** a chemical addition product

ad·duc·tion \ə-'dək-shən, a-\ *n* (14c) **1 :** the action of adducting **:** the state of being adducted **2 :** the act or action of adducing or bringing forward

ad·duc·tor \-'dək-tər\ *n* [NL, fr. L, one that draws to, fr. *adductus*] (1615) **1 :** a muscle that draws a part toward the median line of the body or toward the axis of an extremity **2 :** a muscle that closes the valves of a bivalve mollusk

add up *vi* (1850) **1 a :** to come to the expected total ⟨the bill doesn't *add up*⟩ **b :** to form an intelligible pattern **:** make sense ⟨her story just doesn't *add up*⟩ **2 :** AMOUNT — used with *to* ⟨the play *adds up* to a lot of laughs⟩ ~ *vt* **:** to form an opinion of ⟨*added* him *up* at a glance⟩

-ade \'ād, ˌād\ *n suffix* [ME, fr. MF, fr. OProv *-ada*, fr. LL *-ata*, fr. L, fem. of *-atus* -ate] **1 :** act **:** action ⟨block*ade*⟩ **2 :** product; *esp* **:** sweet drink ⟨lime*ade*⟩

Adé·lie penguin \ə-ˌdā-lē-\ *n* [*Adélie* Coast, Antarctica] (1907) **:** a small antarctic penguin (*Pygoscelis adeliae*) — called also *Adélie*

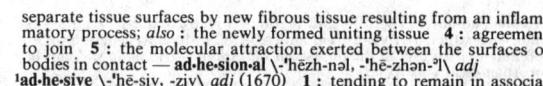

Adélie penguin

-adel·phous \ə-ˈdel-fəs\ *adj comb form* [prob. fr. NL *-adelphus,* fr. Gk *adelphos* brother, fr. *ha-, a-* (akin to *homos* same) + *delphys* womb — more at SAME, DOLPHIN] **:** having (such or so many) stamen fascicles ⟨mon*adelphous*⟩

aden- *or* **adeno-** *comb form* [NL, fr. Gk, fr. *aden-, adēn;* akin to L *inguen* groin, Gk *nephros* kidney — more at NEPHRITIS] **:** gland ⟨*aden*itis⟩

ad·e·nine \ˈad-ᵊn-ˌēn\ *n* [ISV, fr. its presence in glandular tissue] (1885) **:** a purine base $C_5H_5N_5$ that codes hereditary information in the genetic code in DNA and RNA — compare CYTOSINE, GUANINE, THYMINE, URACIL

ad·e·ni·tis \ˌad-ᵊn-ˈīt-əs\ *n* [NL] (ca. 1848) **:** inflammation of a gland; *esp* **:** LYMPHADENITIS

ad·e·no·car·ci·no·ma \ˌad-ᵊn-(ˌ)ō-ˌkärs-ᵊn-ˈō-mə\ *n* [NL] (ca. 1889) **:** a malignant tumor originating in glandular epithelium — **ad·e·no·car·ci·no·ma·tous** \-mət-əs\ *adj*

ad·e·no·hy·poph·y·sis \-hī-ˈpäf-ə-səs\ *n, pl* **-y·ses** \-ə-ˌsēz\ [NL] (1935) **:** the anterior glandular lobe of the pituitary gland — **ad·e·no·hy·poph·y·se·al** \-(ˌ)hī-ˌpäf-ə-ˈsē-əl\ *or* **ad·e·no·hy·po·phys·i·al** \-ˌhī-pə-ˈfiz-ē-əl\ *adj*

[1]**ad·e·noid** \ˈad-ᵊn-ˌȯid, ˈad-ˌnȯid\ *n* [Gk *adenoeidēs* glandular, fr. *adēn*] (ca. 1890) **:** an enlarged mass of lymphoid tissue at the back of the pharynx characteristically obstructing breathing — usu. used in pl.

[2]**adenoid** *adj* (1947) **1 :** of or relating to the adenoids **2 :** relating to, affected with, or associated with abnormally enlarged adenoids ⟨a severe ~ condition⟩ ⟨~ facies⟩

ad·e·noi·dal \ˌad-ᵊn-ˈȯid-ᵊl\ *adj* (1919) **:** typical or suggestive of one affected with abnormally enlarged adenoids **:** ADENOID ⟨an ~ tenor⟩ — not usu. used technically

ad·e·no·ma \ˌad-ᵊn-ˈō-mə\ *n, pl* **-mas** *or* **-ma·ta** \-mət-ə\ [NL *adenomat-, adenoma*] (1870) **:** a benign tumor of a glandular structure or of glandular origin — **ad·e·no·ma·tous** \-mət-əs\ *adj*

aden·o·sine \ə-ˈden-ə-ˌsēn, sən\ *n* [ISV, blend of *adenine* and *ribose*] (ca. 1909) **:** a nucleoside $C_{10}H_{13}N_5O_4$ that is a constituent of RNA yielding adenine and ribose on hydrolysis

adenosine diphosphate *n* (1938) **:** ADP

adenosine mo·no·phos·phate \-ˌmän-ə-ˈfäs-ˌfāt, -ˌmō-nə-\ *n* (1950) **:** AMP

adenosine 3′,5′–monophosphate \-ˌthrē-ˌfīv-\ *n* (1970) **:** CYCLIC AMP

adenosine tri·phos·pha·tase \-trī-ˈfäs-fə-ˌtās, -ˌtāz\ *n* (1943) **:** ATPASE

adenosine tri·phos·phate \-trī-ˈfäs-ˌfāt\ *n* (1938) **:** ATP

ad·e·no·vi·rus \ˌad-ᵊn-ō-ˈvī-rəs\ *n* [*adenoid* + *-o-* + *virus*] (ca. 1956) **:** any of a group of DNA-containing viruses orig. identified in human adenoid tissue, causing respiratory diseases (as catarrh), and including some capable of inducing malignant tumors in experimental animals — **ad·e·no·vi·ral** \-rəl\ *adj*

ad·e·nyl·ate cy·clase \ə-ˌden-ᵊl-ət-ˈsī-ˌklās, ˌad-ᵊn-(ˌ)il-, -ˌāt-, -ˌklāz\ *n* (1968) **:** an enzyme that catalyzes the formation of cyclic AMP from ATP

ad·e·nyl cyclase \ˌad-ᵊn-ˌil-\ *n* (1968) **:** ADENYLATE CYCLASE

ad·e·nyl·ic acid \ˌad-ᵊn-ˌil-ik-\ *n* (ca. 1894) **:** AMP

[1]**ad·ept** \ˈad-ˌept\ *n* [NL *adeptus* alchemist who has attained the knowledge of how to change base metals into gold, fr. L, pp. of *adipisci* to attain, fr. *ad-* + *apisci* to reach — more at APT] (1685) **:** a highly skilled or well-trained individual **:** EXPERT ⟨an ~ at chess⟩

[2]**adept** \ə-ˈdept, a-; ˈad-ˌept\ *adj* (1691) **:** thoroughly proficient **:** EXPERT ***syn*** see PROFICIENT — **adept·ly** \ə-ˈdep-(t)lē, a-\ *adv* — **adept·ness** \-ˈdep(t)-nəs\ *n*

ad·e·qua·cy \ˈad-i-kwə-sē\ *n, pl* **-cies** (1808) **:** the quality or state of being adequate

ad·e·quate \-kwət\ *adj* [L *adaequatus,* pp. of *adaequare* to make equal, fr. *ad-* + *aequare* to equal — more at EQUATE] (1617) **1 :** sufficient for a specific requirement ⟨~ taxation of goods⟩; *esp* **:** barely sufficient or satisfactory ⟨her first performance was merely ~⟩ **2 :** lawfully and reasonably sufficient ***syn*** see SUFFICIENT — **ad·e·quate·ly** *adv* — **ad·e·quate·ness** *n*

ad eun·dem \ˌad-ē-ˈən-dəm\ *or* **ad eundem gra·dum** \-ˈgrād-əm\ *adv or adj* [NL *ad eundem gradum*] (1711) **:** to, in, or of the same rank — used esp. of the honorary granting of academic standing or a degree by a university to one whose actual work was done elsewhere

[1]**à deux** \ä-ˈdə(r), à-dœ̄\ *adj* [F] (1886) **:** involving two people esp. in private ⟨a cozy evening *à deux*⟩

[2]**à deux** *adv* (1927) **:** privately or intimately with only two present ⟨dined *à deux*⟩

ad·here \ad-ˈhi(ə)r, əd-\ *vb* **ad·hered; ad·her·ing** [MF or L; MF *adhérer,* fr. L *adhaerēre,* fr. *ad-* + *haerēre* to stick — more at HESITATE] *vi* (1597) **1 :** to give support or maintain loyalty **2** *obs* **:** to be consistent **:** ACCORD **3 :** to hold fast or stick by or as if by gluing, suction, grasping, or fusing **4 :** to bind oneself to observance **~** *vt* **:** to cause to stick fast ***syn*** see STICK

ad·her·ence \-ˈhir-ən(t)s\ *n* (1531) **1 :** the act, action, or quality of adhering **2 :** steady or faithful attachment **:** FIDELITY

ad·her·end \-ˈhi(ə)r-ˌend, ˌad-ˌhi(ə)r-ˈ\ *n* [*adhere* + *-end* (as in *addend*)] (1946) **1 :** the surface to which an adhesive adheres **2 :** one of the bodies held to another by an adhesive

[1]**ad·her·ent** \ad-ˈhir-ənt, əd-\ *adj* [ME, fr. MF or L; MF *adhérent,* fr. L *adhaerent-, adhaerens,* prp. of *adhaerēre*] (14c) **1 :** able or tending to adhere **2 :** connected or associated with esp. by contract **3 :** ADNATE — **ad·her·ent·ly** *adv*

[2]**adherent** *n* (15c) **:** one that adheres: as **a :** a follower of a leader, party, or profession **b :** a believer in or advocate esp. of a particular idea or church ***syn*** see FOLLOWER

ad·he·sion \ad-ˈhē-zhən, əd-\ *n* [F or L; F *adhésion,* fr. L *adhaesion-, adhaesio,* fr. *adhaesus,* pp. of *adhaerēre*] (1624) **1 :** steady or firm attachment **:** ADHERENCE **2 :** the action or state of adhering; *specif* **:** a union of bodily parts by growth **3 :** the abnormal union of separate tissue surfaces by new fibrous tissue resulting from an inflammatory process; *also* **:** the newly formed uniting tissue **4 :** agreement to join **5 :** the molecular attraction exerted between the surfaces of bodies in contact — **ad·he·sion·al** \-ˈhēzh-nəl, -ˈhē-zhən-ᵊl\ *adj*

[1]**ad·he·sive** \-ˈhē-siv, -ziv\ *adj* (1670) **1 :** tending to remain in association or memory **2 :** tending to adhere or cause adherence **3 :** prepared for adhering — **ad·he·sive·ly** *adv* — **ad·he·sive·ness** *n*

[2]**adhesive** *n* (1912) **1 :** an adhesive substance (as glue or cement) **2 :** a postage stamp with a gummed back

adhesive binding *n* (1955) **:** PERFECT BINDING — **ad·he·sive–bound** \-ˌbau̇nd\ *adj*

adhesive tape *n* (ca. 1928) **:** tape coated on one side with an adhesive mixture; *esp* **:** one used for covering wounds

[1]**ad hoc** \(ˈ)ad-ˈhäk, -ˈhōk; (ˈ)äd-ˈhōk\ *adv* [L, for this] (1659) **:** for the particular end or case at hand without consideration of wider application

[2]**ad hoc** *adj* (1879) **1 a :** concerned with a particular end or purpose ⟨an *ad hoc* investigating committee⟩ **b :** formed or used for specific or immediate problems or needs ⟨*ad hoc* solutions⟩ **2 :** fashioned from whatever is immediately available **:** IMPROVISED ⟨large *ad hoc* parades and demonstrations —Nat Hentoff⟩

[1]**ad ho·mi·nem** \(ˈ)ad-ˈhäm-ə-ˌnem, -nəm\ *adj* [NL, lit., to the man] (1598) **1 :** appealing to a person's feelings or prejudices rather than his intellect **2 :** marked by an attack on an opponent's character rather than by an answer to his contentions

[2]**ad hominem** *adv* (1883) **:** in an ad hominem manner ⟨was arguing *ad hominem*⟩

adi·a·bat·ic \ˌad-ē-ə-ˈbat-ik, ˌā-ˌdī-ə-\ *adj* [Gk *adiabatos* impassable, fr. *a-* + *diabatos* passable, fr. *diabainein* to go across, fr. *dia-* + *bainein* to go — more at COME] (1870) **:** occurring without loss or gain of heat ⟨~ expansion of a body of air⟩ — **adi·a·bat·i·cal·ly** \-i-k(ə-)lē\ *adv*

adieu \ə-ˈd(y)ü, a-\ *n, pl* **adieus** *or* **adieux** \-ˈd(y)üz\ [ME, fr. MF, fr. *a* (fr. L *ad*) + *Dieu* God, fr. L *Deus* — more at DEITY] (14c) **:** FAREWELL — often used interjectionally

ad in·fi·ni·tum \ˌad-ˌin-fə-ˈnīt-əm *also* ˌäd-\ *adv or adj* [L] (1610) **:** without end or limit

[1]**ad in·ter·im** \(ˈ)ad-ˈin-tə-rəm, -ˌrim\ *adv* [L] (1787) **:** for the intervening time **:** TEMPORARILY

[2]**ad interim** *adj* (1818) **:** made or serving ad interim

adi·os \ˌad-ē-ˈōs, ˌäd-\ *interj* [Sp *adiós,* fr. *a* (fr. L *ad*) + *Dios* God, fr. L *Deus*] (1837) — used to express farewell

ad·i·pose \ˈad-ə-ˌpōs\ *adj* [NL *adiposus,* fr. L *adip-, adeps* fat, fr. Gk *aleipha;* akin to Gk *lipos* fat] (1743) **:** of or relating to animal fat; *broadly* **:** FAT — **ad·i·pos·i·ty** \ˌad-ə-ˈpäs-ət-ē\ *n*

adipose tissue *n* (1854) **:** connective tissue in which fat is stored and which has the cells distended by droplets of fat

ad·it \ˈad-ət\ *n* [L *aditus* approach, fr. *aditus,* pp. of *adire* to go to, fr. *ad-* + *ire* to go — more at ISSUE] (1602) **:** a nearly horizontal passage from the surface in a mine

ad·ja·cen·cy \ə-ˈjās-ᵊn-sē\ *n, pl* **-cies** (1646) **1 :** something that is adjacent **2 :** the quality or state of being adjacent **:** CONTIGUITY

ad·ja·cent \ə-ˈjās-ᵊnt\ *adj* [ME, fr. MF or L; MF, fr. L *adjacent-, adjacens,* prp. of *adjacēre* to lie near, fr. *ad-* + *jacēre* to lie; akin to L *jacere* to throw — more at JET] (15c) **1 a :** not distant **:** NEARBY ⟨the city and ~ suburbs⟩ **b :** having a common endpoint or border ⟨~ lots⟩ ⟨~ sides of a triangle⟩ **c :** immediately preceding or following **2** *of two angles* **:** having the vertex and one side in common — **ad·ja·cent·ly** *adv*

syn ADJACENT, ADJOINING, CONTIGUOUS, JUXTAPOSED mean being in close proximity. ADJACENT may or may not imply contact but always implies absence of anything of the same kind in between; ADJOINING definitely implies meeting and touching at some point or line; CONTIGUOUS implies having contact on all or most of one side; JUXTAPOSED means placed side by side esp. so as to permit comparison and contrast.

ad·jec·ti·val \ˌaj-ik-ˈtī-vəl\ *adj* (1797) **1 :** ADJECTIVE **2 :** characterized by the use of adjectives — **ad·jec·ti·val·ly** \-və-lē\ *adv*

[1]**ad·jec·tive** \ˈaj-ik-tiv *also* ˈaj-ət-iv\ *adj* [ME, fr. MF or LL; MF *adjectif,* fr. LL *adjectivus,* fr. L *adjectus,* pp. of *adjicere* to throw to, fr. *ad-* + *jacere* to throw — more at JET] (14c) **1 :** of, relating to, or functioning as an adjective ⟨an ~ clause⟩ **2 :** not standing by itself **:** DEPENDENT **3 :** requiring or employing a mordant ⟨~ dyes⟩ **4 :** PROCEDURAL ⟨~ law⟩ — **ad·jec·tive·ly** *adv*

[2]**adjective** *n* (14c) **:** a word belonging to one of the major form classes in any of numerous languages and typically serving as a modifier of a noun to denote a quality of the thing named, to indicate its quantity or extent, or to specify a thing as distinct from something else

ad·join \ə-ˈjȯin, a-\ *vb* [ME *adjoinen,* fr. MF *adjoindre,* fr. L *adjungere,* fr. *ad-* + *jungere* to join — more at YOKE] *vt* (14c) **1 :** to add or attach by joining **2 :** to lie next to or in contact with **~** *vi* **:** to be close to or in contact with one another

ad·join·ing *adj* (15c) **:** touching or bounding at a point or line ***syn*** see ADJACENT

ad·joint \ˈaj-ˌȯint\ *n* [F, fr. pp. of *adjoindre* to adjoin] (ca. 1909) **:** the transpose of a matrix in which each element is replaced by its cofactor

ad·journ \ə-ˈjərn\ *vb* [ME *ajournen,* fr. MF *ajourner,* fr. *a-* (fr. L *ad-*) + *jour* day — more at JOURNEY] *vt* (14c) **:** to suspend indefinitely or until a later stated time **~** *vi* **1 :** to suspend a session to another time or place or indefinitely **2 :** to move to another place

ad·journ·ment \-mənt\ *n* (1607) **1 :** the act of adjourning **2 :** the state or interval of being adjourned

ad·judge \ə-ˈjəj\ *vt* **ad·judged; ad·judg·ing** [ME *ajugen,* fr. MF *ajugier,* fr. L *adjudicare,* fr. *ad-* + *judicare* to judge — more at JUDGE] (14c) **1 a :** to decide or rule upon as a judge **:** ADJUDICATE **b :** to pronounce judicially **:** RULE **2** *archaic* **:** SENTENCE, CONDEMN **3 :** to hold or pronounce to be **:** DEEM ⟨~ the book a success⟩ **4 :** to award or grant judicially in a case of controversy

ad·ju·di·cate \ə-ˈjüd-i-ˌkāt\ *vb* **-cat·ed; -cat·ing** *vt* (1775) **:** to settle judicially **~** *vi* **:** to act as judge — **ad·ju·di·ca·tive** \-ˌkāt-iv, -kət-\ *adj* — **ad·ju·di·ca·tor** \-ˌkāt-ər\ *n*

ad·ju·di·ca·tion \ə-ˌjüd-i-ˈkā-shən\ *n* [F or LL; F, fr. LL *adjudicatio,* fr. L *adjudicatus,* pp. of *adjudicare*] (1691) **1 :** the act or process of adjudicating **2 a :** a judicial decision or sentence **b :** a decree in bankruptcy — **ad·ju·di·ca·to·ry** \-ˈjüd-i-kə-ˌtōr-ē, -ˌtȯr-\ *adj*

[1]**ad·junct** \ˈaj-ˌəŋ(k)t\ *n* [L *adjunctum*, fr. neut. of *adjunctus*, pp. of *adjungere*] (1588) **1 :** something joined or added to another thing but not essentially a part of it **2 :** a word or word group that qualifies or completes the meaning of another word or other words and is not itself a main structural element in its sentence **3 :** an associate or assistant of another — **ad·junc·tive** \a-ˈjəŋ(k)-tiv, ə-\ *adj*

[2]**adjunct** *adj* (1595) **1 :** added or joined as an accompanying object or circumstance **2 :** attached in a subordinate or temporary capacity to a staff ⟨an ~ psychiatrist⟩ — **ad·junct·ly** \ˈaj-ˌəŋ(k)-tlē, -ˌəŋ-klē\ *adv*

ad·junc·tion \a-ˈjəŋ(k)-shən\ *n* (1618) **:** the act or process of adjoining

ad·ju·ra·tion \ˌaj-ə-ˈrā-shən\ *n* (1611) **1 :** a solemn oath **2 :** an earnest urging or advising — **ad·jur·a·to·ry** \ə-ˈju̇r-ə-ˌtōr-ē, -ˌtȯr-\ *adj*

ad·jure \ə-ˈju̇(ə)r\ *vt* **ad·jured; ad·jur·ing** [ME *adjuren*, fr. MF & L; MF *ajurer*, fr. L *adjurare*, fr. *ad-* + *jurare* to swear — more at JURY] (14c) **1 :** to command solemnly under or as if under oath or penalty of a curse **2 :** to urge or advise earnestly ***syn*** see BEG

ad·just \ə-ˈjəst\ *vb* [ME *ajusten*, fr. MF *ajuster* to gauge, adjust, fr. *a-* (fr. L *ad-*) + *juste* right, exact — more at JUST] *vt* (14c) **1 a :** to bring to a more satisfactory state: (1) **:** SETTLE, RESOLVE (2) **:** RECTIFY **b :** to make correspondent or conformable **:** ADAPT **c :** to bring the parts of to a true or more effective relative position ⟨~ a carburetor⟩ **2 :** to reduce to a system **:** REGULATE **3 :** to determine the amount to be paid under an insurance policy in settlement of (a loss) ~ *vi* **1 :** to adapt or conform oneself (as to climate, food, or new working hours) **2 :** to achieve mental and behavioral balance between one's own needs and the demands of others ***syn*** see ADAPT — **adjust·abil·i·ty** \-ˌjəs-tə-ˈbil-ət-ē\ *n* — **ad·just·able** \-ˈjəs-tə-bəl\ *adj* — **adjus·tive** \-ˈjəs-tiv\ *adj*

ad·just·ed *adj* (1674) **1 :** accommodated to suit a particular set of circumstances or requirements **2 :** having achieved a harmonious relationship with the environment or with other individuals ⟨a well-*adjusted* schoolchild⟩

ad·just·er *also* **ad·jus·tor** \ə-ˈjəs-tər\ *n* (1673) **:** one that adjusts; *esp* **:** an insurance agent who investigates personal or property damage and makes estimates for effecting settlements

ad·just·ment \ə-ˈjəs(t)-mənt\ *n* (1644) **1 :** the act or process of adjusting **2 :** a settlement of a claim or debt in a case in which the amount involved is uncertain or in which full payment is not made **3 :** the state of being adjusted **4 :** a means (as a mechanism) by which things are adjusted one to another **5 :** a correction or modification to reflect actual conditions — **ad·just·men·tal** \ə-ˌjəs(t)-ˈment-ᵊl, ˌaj-ˌəs(t)-\ *adj*

ad·ju·tan·cy \ˈaj-ət-ən-sē\ *n* (1775) **:** the office or rank of an adjutant

ad·ju·tant \ˈaj-ət-ənt\ *n* [L *adjutant-, adjutans*, prp. of *adjutare* to help — more at AID] (1600) **1 :** a staff officer in the army, air force, or marine corps who assists the commanding officer and is responsible esp. for correspondence **2 :** one who helps **:** ASSISTANT

adjutant general *n, pl* **adjutants general** (1645) **1 :** the chief administrative officer of an army who is responsible esp. for the administration and preservation of personnel records **2 :** the chief administrative officer of a major military unit (as a division or corps)

[1]**ad·ju·vant** \ˈaj-ə-vənt\ *adj* [F or L; F, fr. L *adjuvant-, adjuvans*, prp. of *adjuvare* to aid — more at AID] (1574) **:** serving to aid or contribute **:** AUXILIARY

[2]**adjuvant** *n* (1609) **:** one that helps or facilitates: as **a :** an ingredient (as in a prescription or a solution) that modifies the action of the principal ingredient **b :** something (as a drug or method) that enhances the effectiveness of medical treatment

Ad·le·ri·an \äd-ˈlir-ē-ən, ad-\ *adj* [Alfred *Adler*] (1933) **:** of, relating to, or being a theory and technique of psychotherapy emphasizing the importance of feelings of inferiority, a will to power, and overcompensation in neurotic processes

[1]**ad–lib** \ˈad-ˈlib\ *vb* **ad–libbed; ad–lib·bing** [*ad lib*] *vt* (1919) **:** to deliver spontaneously ~ *vi* **:** to improvise esp. lines or a speech — **ad–lib** *n*

[2]**ad–lib** *adj* (1935) **:** spoken, composed, or performed without preparation

ad lib *adv* [NL *ad libitum*] (ca. 1811) **1 :** in accordance with one's wishes **2 :** without restraint or limit

[1]**ad li·bi·tum** \(ˈ)ad-ˈlib-ət-əm\ *adv* [NL, in accordance with desire] (1610) **:** AD LIB ⟨rats fed *ad libitum*⟩

[2]**ad libitum** *adj* (1769) **:** omissible according to a performer's wishes — used as a direction in music; compare OBBLIGATO

ad·man \ˈad-ˌman\ *n* (1909) **:** one who writes, solicits, or places advertisements

ad·mass \ˈad-ˌmas\ *adj* [*ad*vertising + *mass*] *chiefly Brit* (1955) **:** of, relating to, or characteristic of a society that devotes itself chiefly to the production, promotion, and consumption of material goods

ad·mea·sure \ad-ˈmezh-ər, -ˈmā-zhər\ *vt* **-sured; -sur·ing** [ME *amesuren*, fr. MF *amesurer*, fr. *a-* (fr. L *ad-*) + *mesurer* to measure] (14c) **:** to determine the proper share of **:** APPORTION

ad·mea·sure·ment \-ˈmezh-ər-mənt, -ˈmā-zhər-\ *n* (1598) **1 :** determination and apportionment of shares **2 :** determination or comparison of dimensions **3 :** DIMENSIONS, SIZE

Ad·me·tus \ad-ˈmēt-əs\ *n* [L, fr. Gk *Admētos*] **:** a king of Pherae who is saved by Apollo from his fated death when his wife Alcestis offers to die in his place

ad·min·is·ter \əd-ˈmin-ə-stər\ *vb* **ad·min·is·tered; ad·min·is·ter·ing** \-st(ə-)riŋ\ [ME *administren*, fr. MF *administrer*, fr. L *administrare*, fr. *ad-* + *ministrare* to serve, fr. *minister* servant — more at MINISTER] *vt* (14c) **1 :** to manage or supervise the execution, use, or conduct of ⟨~ a trust fund⟩ **2 a :** to mete out **:** DISPENSE ⟨~ punishment⟩ **b :** to give ritually ⟨~ the last rites⟩ **c :** to give remedially ⟨~ a dose of medicine⟩ ~ *vi* **1 :** to perform the office of administrator **2 :** to furnish a benefit **:** MINISTER ⟨~ to his ailing friend⟩ **3 :** to manage affairs ***syn*** see EXECUTE — **ad·min·is·tra·ble** \-strə-bəl\ *adj* — **ad·min·is·trant** \-strənt\ *n*

ad·min·is·trate \-ˌstrāt\ *vt* **-trat·ed; -trat·ing** [L *administratus*, pp. of *administrare*] (1651) **:** ADMINISTER

ad·min·is·tra·tion \əd-ˌmin-ə-ˈstrā-shən, (ˌ)ad-\ *n* (14c) **1 :** the act or process of administering **2 :** performance of executive duties **:** MANAGEMENT **3 :** the execution of public affairs as distinguished from policy-making **4 a :** a body of persons who administer **b** *cap* **:** a group constituting the political executive in a presidential government **c :** a governmental agency or board **5 :** the term of office of an administrative officer or body — **ad·min·is·tra·tion·al** \-shnəl, -shən-ᵊl\ *adj* — **ad·min·is·tra·tion·ist** \-sh(ə-)nəst\ *n*

ad·min·is·tra·tive \əd-ˈmin-ə-ˌstrāt-iv, -strət-\ *adj* (1731) **:** of or relating to administration or an administration **:** EXECUTIVE — **ad·min·is·tra·tive·ly** *adv*

administrative county *n* (1949) **:** a British local administrative unit often not coincident with an older county

administrative law *n* (ca. 1892) **:** law dealing with the establishment, duties, and powers of and available remedies against authorized agencies in the executive branch of the government

ad·min·is·tra·tor \əd-ˈmin-ə-ˌstrāt-ər, -ˌstrā-ˌtō(ə)r\ *n* (15c) **1 :** a person legally vested with the right of administration of an estate **2 a :** one that administers esp. business, school, or governmental affairs **b :** a priest appointed to administer a diocese or parish temporarily

ad·min·is·tra·trix \-ˌmin-ə-ˈstrā-triks\ *n, pl* **-tra·tri·ces** \-ˈstrā-trə-ˌsēz\ [NL] (1626) **:** a woman administrator esp. of an estate

ad·mi·ra·ble \ˈad-m(ə-)rə-bəl\ *adj* (15c) **1 :** deserving the highest esteem **:** EXCELLENT **2** *obs* **:** exciting wonder **:** SURPRISING — **ad·mi·ra·bil·i·ty** \ˌad-m(ə-)rə-ˈbil-ət-ē\ *n* — **ad·mi·ra·ble·ness** \ˈad-m(ə-)rə-bəl-nəs\ *n* — **ad·mi·ra·bly** \-blē\ *adv*

ad·mi·ral \ˈad-m(ə-)rəl\ *n* [ME, fr. MF *amiral* admiral & ML *admiralis* emir, *admirallus* admiral, fr. Ar *amīr-al-* commander of the (as in *amīr-al-baḥr* commander of the sea)] (15c) **1** *archaic* **:** the commander in chief of a navy **2 a :** FLAG OFFICER **b :** a commissioned officer in the navy or coast guard who ranks above a vice admiral and whose insignia is four stars — compare GENERAL **3** *archaic* **:** FLAGSHIP **4 :** any of several brightly colored butterflies (family Nymphalidae)

admiral of the fleet (1660) **:** the highest-ranking officer of the British navy

ad·mi·ral·ty \ˈad-m(ə-)rəl-tē\ *n* (15c) **1** *cap* **:** the executive department or officers formerly having general authority over British naval affairs **2 :** the court having jurisdiction of maritime questions; *also* **:** the system of law administered by admiralty courts

Admiralty mile *n* (ca. 1903) **:** NAUTICAL MILE a

ad·mi·ra·tion \ˌad-mə-ˈrā-shən\ *n* (15c) **1** *archaic* **:** WONDER **2 :** an object of esteem **3 a :** a feeling of delighted or astonished approbation **b :** the act or process of regarding with admiration

ad·mire \əd-ˈmī(ə)r\ *vt* **ad·mired; ad·mir·ing** [MF *admirer*, fr. L *admirari*, fr. *ad-* + *mirari* to wonder — more at SMILE] (1590) **1** *archaic* **:** to marvel at **2 :** to regard with admiration **3 :** to think highly of often in a somewhat impersonal manner ⟨~ a man's capacity for work⟩ ***syn*** see REGARD — **ad·mir·er** *n* — **ad·mir·ing·ly** \-ˈmī-riŋ-lē\ *adv*

ad·mis·si·ble \əd-ˈmis-ə-bəl, ad-\ *adj* [F, fr. ML *admissibilis*, fr. L *admissus*, pp. of *admittere*] (1611) **1 :** capable of being allowed or conceded **:** PERMISSIBLE ⟨behavior that was hardly ~⟩ **2 :** capable or worthy of being admitted ⟨foreign products ~ to a domestic market⟩ — **ad·mis·si·bil·i·ty** \-ˌmis-ə-ˈbil-ət-ē\ *n*

ad·mis·sion \əd-ˈmish-ən, ad-\ *n* (15c) **1 a :** the act or process of admitting **b :** the state or privilege of being admitted **c :** a fee paid at or for admission **2 a :** the granting of an argument or position not fully proved **b :** acknowledgment that a fact or statement is true ***syn*** see ADMITTANCE — **ad·mis·sive** \-ˈmis-iv\ *adj*

ad·mit \əd-ˈmit, ad-\ *vb* **ad·mit·ted; ad·mit·ting** [ME *admitten*, fr. L *admittere*, fr. *ad-* + *mittere* to send] *vt* (15c) **1 a :** to allow scope for **:** PERMIT **b :** to concede as true or valid ⟨compelled to ~ his failure⟩ **2 :** to allow entry (as to a place, fellowship, or privilege) ⟨each ticket ~*s* two persons⟩ ⟨*admitted* to the university⟩ ~ *vi* **1 :** to give entrance or access **2 a :** ALLOW, PERMIT ⟨this order ~*s* of two interpretations⟩ **b :** to make acknowledgment — used with *to* ***syn*** see ACKNOWLEDGE — **ad·mit·ted·ly** \-ˈmit-əd-lē\ *adv*

ad·mit·tance \əd-ˈmit-ᵊn(t)s, ad-\ *n* (1593) **1 :** permission to enter a place **:** ENTRANCE **2 :** the reciprocal of the impedance of a circuit

syn ADMITTANCE, ADMISSION mean permitted entrance. ADMITTANCE is usu. applied to mere physical entrance to a locality or a building; ADMISSION applies to entrance or formal acceptance (as into a club) that carries with it rights, privileges, standing, or membership.

ad·mix \ad-ˈmiks\ *vt* [back-formation fr. obs. *admixt* mingled (with), fr. ME, fr. L *admixtus*] (15c) **:** MINGLE, BLEND

ad·mix·ture \ad-ˈmiks-chər\ *n* [L *admixtus*, pp. of *admiscēre* to mix with, fr. *ad-* + *miscēre* to mix — more at MIX] (1605) **1 a :** the act of mixing **b :** the fact of being mixed **2 a :** something added by mixing **b :** a product of mixing **:** MIXTURE

ad·mon·ish \ad-ˈmän-ish\ *vt* [ME *admonesten*, fr. MF *admonester*, fr. (assumed) VL *admonestare*, alter. of L *admonēre* to warn, fr. *ad-* + *monēre* to warn — more at MENTAL] (14c) **1 a :** to indicate duties or obligations to **b :** to express warning or disapproval to esp. in a gentle, earnest, or solicitous manner **2 :** to give friendly earnest advice or encouragement to ***syn*** see REPROVE — **ad·mon·ish·er** *n* — **ad·mon·ish·ing·ly** \-ish-iŋ-lē\ *adv* — **ad·mon·ish·ment** \-mənt\ *n*

ad·mo·ni·tion \ˌad-mə-ˈnish-ən\ *n* [ME *amonicioun*, fr. MF *amonition*, fr. L *admonition-, admonitio*, fr. *admonitus*, pp. of *admonēre*] (14c) **1 :** gentle or friendly reproof **2 :** counsel or warning against fault or oversight

ad·mon·i·to·ry \əd-ˈmän-ə-ˌtōr-ē, -ˌtȯr-\ *adj* (1594) **:** expressing admonition **:** WARNING — **ad·mon·i·to·ri·ly** \-ˌmän-ə-ˈtōr-ə-lē, -ˈtȯr-\ *adv*

ad·nate \ˈad-ˌnāt\ *adj* [L *adgnatus*, pp. of *adgnasci* to grow on, fr. *ad-* + *nasci* to be born — more at NATION] (1661) **:** grown to a usu. unlike part esp. along a margin ⟨a calyx ~ to the ovary⟩ — **ad·na·tion** \ad-ˈnā-shən\ *n*

ad nau·se·am \ad-ˈnȯ-zē-əm *also* -ˌam\ *adv* [L] (1647) **:** to a sickening degree

ad·nexa \ad-ˈnek-sə\ *n pl* [NL, fr. L *annexa*, neut. pl. of *annexus*, pp. of *annectere* to bind to — more at ANNEX] (1899) **:** conjoined, subordinate, or associated anatomic parts; *specif* **:** the temporary structures and esp. the embryonic membranes of the embryo — **ad·nex·al** \-səl\ *adj*

ado \ə-ˈdü\ *n* [ME, fr. *at do*, fr. *at* + *don*, *do* to do] (14c) **1 :** fussy bustling excitement **:** TO-DO **2 :** time-wasting bother over trivial details ⟨wrote the paper without further ~⟩ **3 :** TROUBLE, DIFFICULTY

\ə\ abut \ᵊ\ kitten, F table \ər\ further \a\ ash \ā\ ace \ä\ cot, cart \au̇\ out \ch\ chin \e\ bet \ē\ easy \g\ go \i\ hit \ī\ ice \j\ job \ŋ\ sing \ō\ go \ȯ\ law \ȯi\ boy \th\ thin \t͟h\ the \ü\ loot \u̇\ foot \y\ yet \zh\ vision \á, k̲, ⁿ, œ, ᵫ, ue, u̅e̅, ʸ\ see Guide to Pronunciation

ado·be \ə-ˈdō-bē\ *n* [Sp, fr. Ar *aṭ-ṭub* the brick, fr. Copt *tōbe* brick] (1748) **1 :** a brick or building material of sun-dried earth and straw **2 :** a heavy clay used in making adobe bricks; *broadly* **:** alluvial or playa clay in desert or arid regions **3 :** a structure made of adobe bricks

ado·bo \ə-ˈdō-bō, ä-ˈt͟hō-bō\ *n, pl* **-bos** [Sp] (ca. 1951) **:** a Philippine dish of fish or meat marinated in a sauce usu. containing vinegar and garlic, browned in fat, and simmered in the marinade

ad·o·les·cence \ˌad-ᵊl-ˈes-ᵊn(t)s\ *n* (15c) **1 :** the state or process of growing up **2 :** the period of life from puberty to maturity terminating legally at the age of majority **3 :** a stage of development (as of a language or culture) prior to maturity

[1]**ad·o·les·cent** \-ᵊnt\ *n* [F, fr. L *adolescent-, adolescens,* prp. of *adolescere* to grow up — more at ADULT] (15c) **:** one that is in the state of adolescence

[2]**adolescent** *adj* (1785) **1 :** of, relating to, or being in adolescence **2 :** emotionally or intellectually immature — **ad·o·les·cent·ly** *adv*

Ado·nai \ˌäd-ə-ˈnȯi, -ˈnī\ *n* [Heb *ʼădhōnāy*] — used as a name of the God of the Hebrews

Ado·nis \ə-ˈdän-əs, -ˈdō-nəs\ *n* [L, fr. Gk *Adōnis*] **:** a youth loved by Aphrodite who is killed at hunting by a wild boar and restored to Aphrodite from Hades for a part of each year

adopt \ə-ˈdäpt\ *vt* [ME *adopten,* fr. MF or L; MF *adopter,* fr. L *adoptare,* fr. *ad-* + *optare* to choose — more at OPTION] (1500) **1 :** to take by choice into a relationship; *specif* **:** to take voluntarily (a child of other parents) as one's own child **2 :** to take up and practice or use as one's own ⟨~ another's mannerisms⟩ **3 :** to accept formally and put into effect ⟨~ a constitutional amendment⟩ **4 :** to choose (a textbook) for required study in a course — **adopt·abil·i·ty** \-ˌdäp-tə-ˈbil-ət-ē\ *n* — **adopt·able** \-ˈdäp-tə-bəl\ *adj* — **adopt·er** *n*

syn ADOPT, EMBRACE, ESPOUSE mean to take an opinion, policy, or practice as one's own. ADOPT implies accepting something created by another or foreign to one's nature; EMBRACE implies a ready or happy acceptance; ESPOUSE adds an implication of close attachment to a cause and a sharing of its fortunes.

adopt·ee \ə-ˌdäp-ˈtē\ *n* (1892) **:** one that is adopted

adop·tion \ə-ˈdäp-shən\ *n* (14c) **:** the act of adopting **:** the state of being adopted

adop·tion·ism *or* **adop·tian·ism** \-shə-ˌniz-əm\ *n, often cap* (1874) **:** the doctrine that Jesus of Nazareth became the Son of God by adoption — **adop·tion·ist** \-sh(ə-)nəst\ *n, often cap*

adop·tive \ə-ˈdäp-tiv\ *adj* (15c) **1 :** of or relating to adoption **2 :** made or acquired by adoption ⟨the ~ father⟩ **3 :** tending to adopt — **adop·tive·ly** *adv*

ador·able \ə-ˈdōr-ə-bəl, -ˈdȯr-\ *adj* (1611) **1 :** worthy of being adored **2 :** extremely charming ⟨an ~ child⟩ — **ador·abil·i·ty** \-ˌdōr-ə-ˈbil-ət-ē, -ˌdȯr-\ *n* — **ador·able·ness** \-ˈdōr-ə-bəl-nəs, -ˈdȯr-\ *n* — **ador·ably** \-blē\ *adv*

ad·o·ra·tion \ˌad-ə-ˈrā-shən\ *n* (1528) **:** the act of adoring **:** the state of being adored

adore \ə-ˈdō(ə)r, -ˈdȯ(ə)r\ *vt* **adored; ador·ing** [MF *adorer,* fr. L *adorare,* fr. *ad-* + *orare* to speak, pray — more at ORATION] (14c) **1 :** to worship or honor as a deity or as divine **2 :** to regard with reverent admiration and devotion ⟨at 40 he still *adored* his father⟩ **3 :** to be extremely fond of ⟨always ~*s* a good time⟩ ***syn*** see REVERE — **ador·er** *n*

adorn \ə-ˈdȯ(ə)rn\ *vt* [ME *adornen,* fr. MF *adorner,* fr. L *adornare,* fr. *ad-* + *ornare* to furnish — more at ORNATE] (15c) **:** to decorate esp. with ornaments

syn ADORN, DECORATE, ORNAMENT, EMBELLISH BEAUTIFY, DECK, GARNISH mean to enhance the appearance of something by adding something unessential. ADORN implies an enhancing by something beautiful in itself; DECORATE suggests relieving plainness or monotony by adding beauty of color or design; ORNAMENT and EMBELLISH imply the adding of something extraneous, ORNAMENT stressing the heightening or setting off of the original, EMBELLISH often stressing the adding of superfluous or adventitious ornament; BEAUTIFY adds to EMBELLISH a suggestion of counterbalancing plainness or ugliness; DECK implies the addition of something that contributes to gaiety, splendor, or showiness; GARNISH suggests decorating with a small final touch and is used esp. in referring to the serving of food.

adorn·ment \-mənt\ *n* (14c) **1 :** the action of adorning **:** the state of being adorned **2 :** something that adorns

ADP \ˌā-ˌdē-ˈpē, ā-ˈdē-ˌpē\ *n* [*a*denosine *d*i*p*hosphate] (1944) **:** an ester of adenosine that is reversibly converted to ATP for the storing of energy by the addition of a high-energy phosphate group — called also *adenosine diphosphate*

ad rem \(ˈ)ad-ˈrem\ *adv or adj* [L, to the thing] (1608) **:** to the point or purpose **:** RELEVANTLY

adren- *or* **adreno-** *comb form* [*adrenal*] **1 :** adrenal glands ⟨*adreno*cortical⟩ **2 :** adrenaline ⟨*adren*ergic⟩

[1]**ad·re·nal** \ə-ˈdrēn-ᵊl\ *adj* [*ad-* + *renal*] (1875) **1 :** adjacent to the kidneys **2 :** of, relating to, or derived from adrenal glands or secretion — **ad·re·nal·ly** \-ᵊl-ē\ *adv*

[2]**adrenal** *n* (1882) **:** ADRENAL GLAND

ad·re·nal·ec·to·my \ə-ˌdrēn-ᵊl-ˈek-tə-mē\ *n* (ca. 1910) **:** surgical removal of one or both adrenal glands — **ad·re·nal·ec·to·mized** \-ˌmīzd\ *adj*

adrenal gland *n* (1875) **:** either of a pair of complex endocrine organs near the anterior medial border of the kidney consisting of a mesodermal cortex that produces steroids like sex hormones and hormones concerned esp. with metabolic functions and an ectodermal medulla that produces adrenaline — called also *adrenal*

Adren·a·lin \ə-ˈdren-ᵊl-ən\ *trademark* — used for a preparation of levorotatory epinephrine

adren·a·line \ə-ˈdren-ᵊl-ən\ *n* (1901) **:** EPINEPHRINE

ad·ren·er·gic \ˌad-rə-ˈnər-jik\ *adj* [*adren-* + *ergic*] (1934) **1 :** liberating or activated by adrenaline or a substance like adrenaline ⟨an ~ nerve⟩ **2 :** resembling adrenaline esp. in physiological action ⟨~ drugs⟩ — **ad·ren·er·gi·cal·ly** \-ji-k(ə-)lē\ *adv*

ad·re·no·chrome \ə-ˈdrē-nō-ˌkrōm\ *n* (1940) **:** a red-colored mixture of quinones derived from epinephrine by oxidation

ad·re·no·cor·ti·cal \ə-ˌdrē-nō-ˈkȯrt-i-kəl\ *adj* (1936) **:** of, relating to, or derived from the cortex of the adrenal glands

ad·re·no·cor·ti·co·ste·roid \-ˌkȯrt-i-kō-ˈsti(ə)r-ˌȯid *also* -ˈste(ə)r-\ *n* (ca. 1961) **:** a steroid obtained from or resembling or having physiological effects like those of the adrenal cortex

ad·re·no·cor·ti·co·tro·pic \ə-ˈdrē-nō-ˌkȯrt-i-kō-ˈtrō-pik\ *or* **adre·no·cor·ti·co·tro·phic** \-ˈtrō-fik\ *adj* (1936) **:** acting on or stimulating the adrenal cortex ⟨~ activity⟩

adrenocorticotropic hormone *or* **adrenocorticotrophic hormone** *n* (1937) **:** ACTH

ad·re·no·cor·ti·co·tro·pin \-ˈtrō-pən\ *or* **ad·re·no·cor·ti·co·tro·phin** \-ˈtrō-fən\ *n* (1952) **:** ADRENOCORTICOTROPIC HORMONE

adria·my·cin \ˌā-drē-ə-ˈmīs-ᵊn, ˌad-rē-\ *n* [*Adria*tic sea + *-mycin*] (1973) **:** an antibiotic with antitumor activity obtained from a bacterium (*Streptomyces peucetius*) and administered as the hydrochloride $C_{27}H_{29}NO_{11}·HCl$ — called also *doxorubicin*

adrift \ə-ˈdrift\ *adv or adj* (1624) **1 :** without motive power and without anchor or mooring **2 :** without guidance or purpose

adroit \ə-ˈdrȯit\ *adj* [F, fr. OF, *a-* (fr. L *ad-*) + *droit* right, droit] (1652) **:** having or showing skill, cleverness, or resourcefulness in handling situations ⟨an ~ leader⟩ ***syn*** see CLEVER, DEXTEROUS — **adroit·ly** *adv* — **adroit·ness** *n*

ad·sci·ti·tious \ˌad-sə-ˈtish-əs\ *adj* [L *adscitus,* fr. pp. of *adsciscere* to receive, fr. *ad-* + *sciscere* to accept, fr. *scire* to know — more at SCIENCE] (1620) **:** derived or acquired from something extrinsic

ad·sorb \ad-ˈsȯ(ə)rb, -ˈzȯ(ə)rb\ *vb* [*ad-* + *-sorb* (as in *absorb*)] *vt* (1882) **:** to take up and hold by adsorption ~ *vi* **:** to become adsorbed — **ad·sorb·able** \-ˈsȯr-bə-bəl, -ˈzȯr-\ *adj*

ad·sor·bate \ad-ˈsȯr-bət, -ˈzȯr-, -ˌbāt\ *n* (1928) **:** an adsorbed substance

ad·sor·bent \-bənt\ *adj* (1924) **:** having the capacity or tendency to adsorb — **adsorbent** *n*

ad·sorp·tion \ad-ˈsȯrp-shən, -ˈzȯrp-\ *n* [irreg. fr. *adsorb*] (1882) **:** the adhesion in an extremely thin layer of molecules (as of gases, solutes, or liquids) to the surfaces of solid bodies or liquids with which they are in contact — compare ABSORPTION — **ad·sorp·tive** \-ˈsȯrp-tiv, -ˈzȯrp-\ *adj*

ad·u·lar·ia \ˌaj-ə-ˈlar-ē-ə, ˌad-yə-, -ˈler-\ *n* [It *adularia,* fr. F *adulaire,* fr. *Adula,* Swiss mountain group] (1798) **:** a transparent or translucent orthoclase

ad·u·late \ˈaj-ə-ˌlāt, ˈad-yə-; ˈad-ᵊl-ˌāt\ *vt* **-lat·ed; -lat·ing** [back-formation fr. *adulation,* fr. ME, fr. MF, fr. L *adulation-, adulatio,* fr. *adulatus,* pp. of *adulari* to flatter] (1777) **:** to flatter or admire excessively or slavishly — **ad·u·la·tion** \ˌaj-ə-ˈlā-shən, ˌad-yə-; ˌad-ᵊl-ˈā-\ *n* — **ad·u·la·tor** \ˈaj-ə-ˌlāt-ər, ˈad-yə-; ˈad-ᵊl-ˌāt-\ *n* — **ad·u·la·to·ry** \-lə-ˌtōr-ē, -ˌtȯr-\ *adj*

[1]**adult** \ə-ˈdəlt, ˈad-ˌəlt\ *adj* [L *adultus,* pp. of *adolescere* to grow up, fr. *ad-* + *-olescere* (fr. *alescere* to grow) — more at OLD] (1531) **1 :** fully developed and mature **:** GROWN-UP **2 :** of, relating to, intended for, or befitting adults ⟨an ~ approach to a problem⟩ **3 :** dealing in or with explicitly sexual material ⟨~ bookstores⟩ ⟨~ movies⟩ — **adult·hood** \ə-ˈdəlt-ˌhu̇d\ *n* — **adult·ly** \ə-ˈdəlt-lē, ˈad-ˌəlt-\ *adv* — **adult·ness** \ə-ˈdəlt-nəs, ˈad-ˌəlt-\ *n*

[2]**adult** *n* (1658) **:** one that is adult; *esp* **:** a human being after an age (as 21) specified by law — **adult·like** \ə-ˈdəlt-ˌlīk\ *adj*

adult education *n* (1851) **:** lecture or correspondence courses for adults usu. not otherwise engaged in formal study

adul·ter·ant \ə-ˈdəl-t(ə-)rənt\ *n* (ca. 1755) **:** an adulterating substance or agent — **adulterant** *adj*

[1]**adul·ter·ate** \ə-ˈdəl-tə-ˌrāt\ *vt* **-at·ed; -at·ing** [L *adulteratus,* pp. of *adulterare,* fr. *ad-* + *alter* other — more at ELSE] (1531) **:** to corrupt, debase, or make impure by the addition of a foreign or inferior substance; *esp* **:** to prepare for sale by replacing more valuable with less valuable or inert ingredients — **adul·ter·a·tor** \-ˌrāt-ər\ *n*

[2]**adul·ter·ate** \ə-ˈdəl-t(ə-)rət\ *adj* (1590) **1 :** tainted with adultery **:** ADULTEROUS **2 :** being adulterated **:** SPURIOUS

adul·ter·a·tion \ə-ˌdəl-tə-ˈrā-shən\ *n* (1506) **1 :** the process of adulterating **:** the condition of being adulterated **2 :** an adulterated product

adul·ter·er \ə-ˈdəl-tər-ər\ *n* (14c) **:** one that commits adultery; *esp* **:** a man who commits adultery

adul·ter·ess \ə-ˈdəl-t(ə-)rəs\ *n* (14c) **:** a woman who commits adultery

adul·ter·ine \ə-ˈdəl-tə-ˌrīn, -ˌrēn\ *adj* (1542) **1 a :** marked by adulteration **:** SPURIOUS **b :** ILLEGAL **2 :** born of adultery

adul·ter·ous \ə-ˈdəl-t(ə-)rəs\ *adj* (15c) **:** relating to, characterized by, or given to adultery — **adul·ter·ous·ly** *adv*

adul·tery \ə-ˈdəl-t(ə-)rē\ *n, pl* **-ter·ies** [ME, alter. of *avoutrie,* fr. MF, fr. L *adulterium,* fr. *adulter* adulterer, back-formation fr. *adulterare*] (14c) **:** voluntary sexual intercourse between a married man and someone other than his wife or between a married woman and someone other than her husband; *also* **:** an act of adultery

syn ADULTERY, FORNICATION, INCEST designate forms of illicit sexual intercourse that are clearly distinguished in legal use. ADULTERY can be applied only to sexual intercourse between a married person and a partner other than his or her wife or husband; FORNICATION designates sexual intercourse on the part of an unmarried person; INCEST refers to sexual intercourse between persons proscribed from marrying on the basis of kinship ties.

ad·um·brate \ˈad-əm-ˌbrāt, a-ˈdəm-\ *vt* **-brat·ed; -brat·ing** [L *adumbratus,* pp. of *adumbrare,* fr. *ad-* + *umbra* shadow — more at UMBRAGE] (1581) **1 :** to foreshadow vaguely **:** INTIMATE **2 a :** to give a sketchy representation or outline of **b :** to suggest or disclose partially **3 :** OVERSHADOW, OBSCURE — **ad·um·bra·tion** \ˌad-(ˌ)əm-ˈbrā-shən\ *n* — **ad·um·bra·tive** \a-ˈdəm-brət-iv\ *adj* — **ad·um·bra·tive·ly** *adv*

adust \ə-ˈdəst\ *adj* [ME, fr. L *adustus,* pp. of *adurere* to set fire to, fr. *ad-* + *urere* to burn — more at EMBER] (15c) **1 :** SCORCHED, BURNED **2** *archaic* **:** of a sunburned appearance **3** *archaic* **:** of a gloomy appearance or disposition

ad va·lo·rem \ˌad-və-ˈlōr-əm, -ˈlȯr-\ *adj* [L, according to the value] (1698) **:** imposed at a rate percent of value ⟨*ad valorem* tax on goods⟩

[1]**ad·vance** \əd-ˈvan(t)s\ *vb* **ad·vanced; ad·vanc·ing** [ME *advauncen,* fr. OF *avancier,* fr. (assumed) VL *abantiare,* fr. L *abante* before, fr. *ab-* + *ante* before — more at ANTE-] *vt* (13c) **1 :** to bring or move forward **2 :** to accelerate the growth or progress of **3 :** to raise to a higher rank **4 :** to supply or furnish in expectation of repayment **5** *archaic* **:** to lift up **:** RAISE **6 a :** to bring forward in time; *esp* **:** to make earlier ⟨~ the date of the meeting⟩ **b :** to place later in time **7 :** to bring forward for notice, consideration, or acceptance **:** PROPOSE **8 :** to raise in rate **:** INCREASE ⟨~ the rent⟩ ~ *vi* **1 :** to move forward **:** PROCEED **2**

: to make progress : INCREASE ⟨~ in age⟩ 3 : to rise in rank, position, or importance 4 : to rise in rate or price — **ad·vanc·er** *n*
syn ADVANCE, PROMOTE, FORWARD, FURTHER mean to help (someone or something) to move ahead. ADVANCE stresses effective assisting in hastening a process or bringing about a desired end; PROMOTE suggests an encouraging or fostering and may denote an increase in status or rank; FORWARD implies an impetus forcing something ahead; FURTHER suggests a removing of obstacles in the way of a desired advance.

[2]advance *n* (1668) 1 : a moving forward 2 a : progress in development : IMPROVEMENT ⟨an ~ in medical technique⟩ b : a progressive step ⟨the job meant a personal ~ forward⟩ 3 : a rise in price, value, or amount 4 : a first step or approach made : OFFER ⟨her attitude discouraged all ~*s*⟩ 5 : a provision of something (as money or goods) before a return is received; *also* : the money or goods supplied — **in advance** : before a deadline or an anticipated event — **in advance of** : AHEAD OF

[3]advance *adj* (1845) 1 : made, sent, or furnished ahead of time ⟨an ~ payment⟩ 2 : going or situated before ⟨an ~ party of soldiers⟩

ad·vanced *adj* (15c) 1 : far on in time or course ⟨a man ~ in years⟩ 2 a : beyond the elementary or introductory ⟨~ chemistry⟩ b : being beyond others in progress or development ⟨an ~ country⟩

advanced degree *n* (1928) : a university degree (as a master's or doctor's degree) higher than a bachelor's

Advanced level *n* (1949) : A LEVEL

advance man *n* (1926) 1 : a business representative (as of a theatrical company) who makes necessary arrangements for the public appearance of the company — called also *advance agent* 2 : an aide (as of a political candidate) who makes a security check or handles publicity in advance of his employer's personal appearances

ad·vance·ment \əd-ˈvan(t)-smənt\ *n* (13c) 1 : the action of advancing : the state of being advanced: a : promotion or elevation to a higher rank or position b : progression to a higher stage of development 2 : an advance of money or value

[1]ad·van·tage \əd-ˈvant-ij\ *n* [ME *avantage*, fr. MF, fr. *avant* before, fr. L *abante*] (14c) 1 : superiority of position or condition ⟨higher ground gave the enemy the ~⟩ 2 a : BENEFIT, GAIN; *esp* : benefit resulting from some course of action ⟨a mistake which turned out to his ~⟩ b *obs* : INTEREST 2a 3 : a factor or circumstance of benefit to its possessor ⟨lacked the ~*s* of an education⟩ 4 : the first point won in tennis after deuce — **to advantage** : so as to produce a favorable impression or effect

[2]advantage *vt* **-taged; -tag·ing** (15c) : to give an advantage to : BENEFIT

ad·van·ta·geous \ˌad-ˌvan-ˈtā-jəs, -vən-\ *adj* (1598) : giving an advantage : FAVORABLE — **ad·van·ta·geous·ly** *adv* — **ad·van·ta·geous·ness** *n*

ad·vec·tion \əd-ˈvek-shən\ *n* [L *advection-, advectio* act of bringing, fr. *advectus*, pp. of *advehere* to carry to, fr. *ad-* + *vehere* to carry — more at WAY] (1910) 1 : the horizontal movement of a mass of air that causes changes in the physical properties of the air (as temperature) 2 : the flow of a current of water (as in the sea); *also* : transport by such a flow — **ad·vect** \-ˈvekt\ *vt* — **ad·vec·tive** \-ˈvek-tiv\ *adj*

Ad·vent \ˈad-ˌvent, *chiefly Brit* -vənt\ *n* [ME, fr. ML *adventus*, fr. L, arrival, fr. *adventus*, pp.] (12c) 1 : the period beginning four Sundays before Christmas and observed by some Christians as a season of prayer and fasting 2 a : the coming of Christ at the Incarnation b : SECOND COMING 3 *not cap* : COMING, ARRIVAL ⟨the ~ of spring⟩ ***syn*** see ARRIVAL

Ad·vent·ism \ˈad-ˌvent-ˌiz-əm\ *n* (1874) 1 : the doctrine that the second coming of Christ and the end of the world are near at hand 2 : the principles and practices of Seventh-Day Adventists — **Ad·vent·ist** \əd-ˈvent-əst, ad-ˈ, ˈad-ˌ\ *adj or n*

ad·ven·ti·tia \ˌad-vən-ˈtish-ə, -(ˌ)ven-\ *n* [NL, alter. of L *adventicia*, neut. pl. of *adventicius* coming from outside, fr. *adventus*, pp.] (1876) : an external chiefly connective tissue covering of an organ; *esp* : the external coat of a blood vessel — **ad·ven·ti·tial** \-əl\ *adj*

ad·ven·ti·tious \ˌad-(ˌ)ven-ˈtish-əs, -vən-\ *adj* [L *adventicius*] (1603) 1 : added from another source and not inherent or innate 2 : arising or occurring sporadically or in other than the usual location ⟨~ buds⟩ — **ad·ven·ti·tious·ly** *adv*

ad·ven·tive \ad-ˈvent-iv\ *adj* (1605) 1 : introduced but not fully naturalized 2 : ADVENTITIOUS 2 — **adventive** *n*

Advent Sunday *n* (15c) : the first Sunday in Advent

[1]ad·ven·ture \əd-ˈven-chər\ *n* [ME *aventure*, fr. OF, fr. (assumed) VL *adventura*, fr. L *adventus*, pp. of *advenire* to arrive, fr. *ad-* + *venire* to come] (13c) 1 a : an undertaking involving danger and unknown risks b : the encountering of risks ⟨the spirit of ~⟩ 2 : an exciting or remarkable experience ⟨an ~ in exotic dining⟩ 3 : an enterprise involving financial risk

[2]adventure *vb* **ad·ven·tured; ad·ven·tur·ing** \-ˈvench-(ə-)riŋ\ *vt* (14c) 1 : to expose to danger or loss : VENTURE 2 : to venture upon : TRY ~ *vi* 1 : to proceed despite risk 2 : to take the risk

ad·ven·tur·er \əd-ˈvench-(ə-)rər\ *n* (1548) 1 : one that adventures: as a : SOLDIER OF FORTUNE b : one that engages in risky commercial enterprises for profit 2 : one who seeks unmerited wealth or position esp. by playing on the credulity or prejudice of others

ad·ven·ture·some \əd-ˈven-chər-səm\ *adj* (ca. 1731) : inclined to take risks : VENTURESOME — **ad·ven·ture·some·ness** *n*

ad·ven·tur·ess \əd-ˈvench-(ə-)rəs\ *n* (1754) : a female adventurer; *esp* : a woman who seeks position or livelihood by questionable means

ad·ven·tur·ism \əd-ˈven-chə-ˌriz-əm\ *n* (1843) : rash improvisation or experimentation esp. in politics or foreign affairs in the absence or in defiance of consistent plans or principles — **ad·ven·tur·ist** \-ˈvench-(ə-)rəst\ *n* — **ad·ven·tur·is·tic** \-ˌven-chə-ˈris-tik\ *adj*

ad·ven·tur·ous \əd-ˈvench-(ə-)rəs\ *adj* (14c) 1 : disposed to seek adventure or to cope with the new and unknown ⟨an ~ explorer⟩ 2 : characterized by unknown dangers and risks ⟨an ~ journey⟩ — **ad·ven·tur·ous·ly** *adv* — **ad·ven·tur·ous·ness** *n*
syn ADVENTUROUS, VENTURESOME, DARING, DAREDEVIL, RASH, RECKLESS, FOOLHARDY mean exposing oneself to danger more than required by good sense. ADVENTUROUS implies a willingness to accept risks but not necessarily imprudence; VENTURESOME implies a jaunty eagerness for perilous undertakings; DARING heightens the implication of fearlessness in courting danger; DAREDEVIL stresses ostentation in daring; RASH suggests imprudence and lack of forethought; RECKLESS implies heedlessness of probable consequences; FOOLHARDY suggests a recklessness that is inconsistent with good sense.

[1]ad·verb \ˈad-ˌvərb\ *n* [ME *adverbe*, fr. MF, fr. L *adverbium*, fr. *ad-* + *verbum* word — more at WORD] (14c) : a word belonging to one of the major form classes in any of numerous languages, typically serving as a modifier of a verb, an adjective, another adverb, a preposition, a phrase, a clause, or a sentence, and expressing some relation of manner or quality, place, time, degree, number, cause, opposition, affirmation, or denial

[2]adverb *adj* (1879) : ADVERBIAL

ad·ver·bi·al \ad-ˈvər-bē-əl\ *adj* (1611) : of, relating to, or having the function of an adverb — **adverbial** *n* — **ad·ver·bi·al·ly** \-ə-lē\ *adv*

ad ver·bum \(ˈ)ad-ˈvər-bəm\ *adv* [L] (1573) : to a word : VERBATIM

ad·ver·sar·i·al \ˌad-və(r)-ˈser-ē-əl\ *adj* (1967) : of, relating to, or characteristic of an adversary or adversary procedures : ADVERSARY

[1]ad·ver·sary \ˈad-və(r)-ˌser-ē\ *n, pl* **-sar·ies** (14c) : one that contends with, opposes, or resists : ENEMY — **ad·ver·sari·ness** *n*

[2]adversary *adj* (14c) 1 : of, relating to, or involving an adversary 2 : having or involving antagonistic parties or interests ⟨divorce can be an ~ proceeding⟩

ad·ver·sa·tive \əd-ˈvər-sət-iv, ad-\ *adj* (15c) : expressing antithesis, opposition, or adverse circumstance ⟨the ~ conjunction *but*⟩ — **adversative** *n* — **ad·ver·sa·tive·ly** *adv*

ad·verse \ad-ˈvərs, ˈad-ˌ\ *adj* [ME, fr. MF *advers*, fr. L *adversus*, pp. of *advertere*] (14c) 1 : acting against or in a contrary direction : HOSTILE ⟨hindered by ~ winds⟩ 2 : opposed to one's interests : UNFAVORABLE ⟨an ~ verdict⟩ 3 *archaic* : opposite in position — **ad·verse·ly** *adv* — **ad·verse·ness** *n*

ad·ver·si·ty \ad-ˈvər-sət-ē\ *n, pl* **-ties** (13c) 1 : a condition of suffering, destitution, or affliction 2 : a calamitous or disastrous experience ***syn*** see MISFORTUNE

[1]ad·vert \ad-ˈvərt\ *vi* [ME *adverten*, fr. MF & L; MF *advertir*, fr. L *advertere*, fr. *ad-* + *vertere* to turn] (15c) 1 : to pay heed or attention 2 : to make a usu. slight or glancing reference : refer casually (as by interpolation)

[2]ad·vert \ˈad-ˌvərt\ *n, chiefly Brit* (1860) : ADVERTISEMENT

ad·ver·tence \ad-ˈvərt-ᵊns\ *n* (14c) 1 : the action or process of adverting : ATTENTION 2 : ADVERTENCY 1

ad·ver·ten·cy \-ᵊn-sē\ *n, pl* **-cies** (1646) 1 : the quality or state of being advertent : HEEDFULNESS 2 : ADVERTENCE 1

ad·ver·tent \-ᵊnt\ *adj* [L *advertent-, advertens*, prp. of *advertere*] (1671) : giving attention : HEEDFUL — **ad·ver·tent·ly** *adv*

ad·ver·tise \ˈad-vər-ˌtīz\ *vb* **-tised; -tis·ing** [ME *advertisen*, fr. MF *advertiss-*, stem of *advertir*] *vt* (15c) 1 : to make something known to : NOTIFY 2 a : to make publicly and generally known ⟨*advertising* their readiness to make concessions⟩ b : to announce publicly esp. by a printed notice or a broadcast c : to call public attention to esp. by emphasizing desirable qualities so as to arouse a desire to buy or patronize ~ *vi* : to issue or sponsor advertising ⟨~ for a secretary⟩ — **ad·ver·tis·er** *n*

ad·ver·tise·ment \ˌad-vər-ˈtīz-mənt; əd-ˈvərt-əz-mənt, -ə-smənt\ *n* (15c) 1 : the act or process of advertising 2 : a public notice; *esp* : one published in the press or broadcast over the air

ad·ver·tis·ing *n* (1762) 1 : the action of calling something to the attention of the public esp. by paid announcements 2 : ADVERTISEMENTS ⟨the magazine contains much ~⟩ 3 : the business of preparing advertisements for publication or broadcast

ad·vice \əd-ˈvīs\ *n* [ME, fr. MF *avis* opinion, prob. fr. the phrase *ce m'est a vis* that appears to me, part trans. of L *mihi visum est* it seemed so to me, I decided] (14c) 1 : recommendation regarding a decision or course of conduct : COUNSEL ⟨he shall have power, by and with the ~ and consent of the Senate, to make treaties — *U.S. Constitution*⟩ 2 : information or notice given — usu. used in pl. 3 : an official notice concerning a business transaction
syn ADVICE, COUNSEL denote recommendation as to a decision or a course of conduct. ADVICE implies real or pretended knowledge or experience, often professional or technical, on the part of the one who advises; COUNSEL often stresses the fruit of wisdom or deliberation and may presuppose a weightier occasion, or more authority, or more personal concern on the part of the one giving counsel.

ad·vis·able \əd-ˈvī-zə-bəl\ *adj* (1647) : fit to be advised or done : PRUDENT ***syn*** see EXPEDIENT — **ad·vis·abil·i·ty** \-ˌvī-zə-ˈbil-ət-ē\ *n* — **ad·vis·able·ness** \-ˈvī-zə-bəl-nəs\ *n* — **ad·vis·ably** \-blē\ *adv*

ad·vise \əd-ˈvīz\ *vb* **ad·vised; ad·vis·ing** [ME *advisen, avisen*, fr. MF *aviser*, fr. *avis*] *vt* (14c) 1 a : to give advice to : COUNSEL ⟨~ her to try a drier climate⟩ b : CAUTION, WARN ⟨~ him of the danger⟩ c : RECOMMEND ⟨~ prudence⟩ 2 : to give information or notice to : INFORM ⟨~ his friends of his marriage⟩ ~ *vi* 1 : to give advice ⟨~ on legal matters⟩ 2 : to take counsel : CONSULT ⟨~ with one's parents⟩ — **ad·vis·er** *or* **ad·vi·sor** \-ˈvī-zər\ *n*

ad·vised \əd-ˈvīzd\ *adj* (14c) : thought out : CONSIDERED — usu. used in combination ⟨ill-*advised* plans⟩ — **ad·vis·ed·ly** \-ˈvī-zəd-lē\ *adv*

ad·vis·ee \əd-ˌvī-ˈzē\ *n* (1824) : one that is advised

ad·vise·ment \əd-ˈvīz-mənt\ *n* (14c) : careful consideration : DELIBERATION

[1]ad·vi·so·ry \əd-ˈvīz-(ə-)rē\ *adj* (1778) 1 : having or exercising power to advise 2 : containing or giving advice

[2]advisory *n, pl* **-ries** (ca. 1938) : a report giving information (as on the weather) and often recommending action to be taken

ad·vo·ca·cy \ˈad-və-kə-sē\ *n* (14c) : the act or process of advocating : SUPPORT

advocacy journalism *n* (1970) : journalism that advocates a cause or expresses a viewpoint

[1]ad·vo·cate \ˈad-və-kət, -ˌkāt\ *n* [ME *advocat*, fr. MF, fr. L *advocatus*, fr. pp. of *advocare* to summon, fr. *ad-* + *vocare* to call — more at VOICE] (14c) 1 : one that pleads the cause of another; *specif* : one that pleads the cause of another before a tribunal or judicial court **2 :** one that defends or maintains a cause or proposal

[2]**ad·vo·cate** \-ˌkāt\ *vt* **-cat·ed; -cat·ing** (1767) **:** to plead in favor of ***syn*** see SUPPORT — **ad·vo·ca·tion** \ˌad-və-ˈkā-shən\ *n* — **ad·vo·ca·tive** \ˈad-və-ˌkāt-iv\ *adj* — **ad·vo·ca·tor** \-ˌkāt-ər\ *n*

ad·vow·son \əd-ˈvau̇z-ᵊn\ *n* [ME, fr. OF *avoueson,* fr. ML *advocation-, advocatio,* fr. L, act of calling, fr. *advocatus,* pp.] (13c) **:** the right in English law of presenting a nominee to an ecclesiastical benefice

ady·nam·ic \ˌā-(ˌ)dī-ˈnam-ik, ˌad-ə-ˈnam-\ *adj* [Gk *adynamia* lack of strength, fr. *a-* + *dynamis* power, fr. *dynasthai* to be able] (1829) **:** characterized by or causing a loss of strength or function

ad·y·tum \ˈad-ə-təm\ *n, pl* **-ta** \-tə\ [L, fr. Gk *adyton,* neut. of *adytos* not to be entered, fr. *a-* + *dyein* to enter] (1611) **:** the innermost sanctuary in an ancient temple open only to priests **:** SANCTUM

adz *or* **adze** \ˈadz\ *n* [ME *adse,* fr. OE *adesa*] (bef. 12c) **:** a cutting tool that has a thin arched blade set at right angles to the handle and is used chiefly for shaping wood

ae \ˈā\ *adj* [ME (northern dial.) *a,* alter. of *an*] *chiefly Scot* (1737) **:** ONE

Ae·a·cus \ˈē-ə-kəs\ *n* [L, fr. Gk *Aiakos*] **:** a son of Zeus who is given the Myrmidons as followers and becomes on his death a judge of the underworld

ae·cio·spore \ˈē-s(h)ē-ə-ˌspō(ə)r, -ˌspȯ(ə)r\ *n* (1905) **:** one of the spores arranged within an aecium in a series like a chain

ae·ci·um \ˈē-s(h)ē-əm\ *n, pl* **-cia** \-s(h)ē-ə\ [NL, fr. Gk *aikia* assault, fr. *aeikēs* unseemly, fr. *a-* + *eikōs* seemly, fr. participle of *eikenai* to seem] (1905) **:** the fruiting body of a rust fungus in which the first binucleate spores are usu. produced — **ae·cial** \-sh(ē-)əl\ *adj*

aë·des \ā-ˈēd-(ˌ)ēz\ *n, pl* **aëdes** [NL, genus name, fr. Gk *aēdēs* unpleasant, fr. *a-* + *ēdos* pleasure; akin to Gk *hēdys* sweet — more at SWEET] (ca. 1909) **:** any of a genus (*Aëdes*) of mosquitoes including the vector of yellow fever, dengue, and other diseases — **ae·dine** \-ˈē-ˌdīn\ *adj*

ae·dile \ˈē-ˌdīl, ˈēd-ᵊl\ *n* [L *aedilis,* fr. *aedes* temple — more at EDIFY] (1540) **:** an official in ancient Rome in charge of public works and games, police, and the grain supply

Ae·ge·an \i-ˈjē-ən\ *adj* [L *Aegaeus,* fr. Gk *Aigaios*] (ca. 1889) **1 :** of or relating to the arm of the Mediterranean sea east of Greece **2 :** of or relating to the chiefly Bronze Age civilization of the islands of the Aegean sea and the countries adjacent to it

ae·gis \ˈē-jəs *also* ˈā-\ *n* [L, fr. Gk *aigis* goatskin, perh. fr. *aig-, aix* goat] (1611) **1 :** a shield or breastplate emblematic of majesty that was orig. associated chiefly with Zeus but later mainly with Athena **2 :** PROTECTION ⟨under the ~ of the law⟩ **3 :** AUSPICES, SPONSORSHIP ⟨under the ~ of the education department⟩

Ae·gis·thus \i-ˈjis-thəs\ *n* [L, fr. Gk *Aigisthos*] **:** a lover of Clytemnestra slain with her by her son Orestes

-aemia — see -EMIA

Ae·ne·as \i-ˈnē-əs\ *n* [L, fr. Gk *Aineias*] **:** a son of Anchises and Aphrodite, defender of Troy, and hero of Vergil's *Aeneid*

Aeneo·lith·ic \ā-ˌē-nē-ō-ˈlith-ik\ *adj* [L *aeneus* of copper or bronze, fr. *aes* copper, bronze — more at ORE] (1901) **:** of or relating to a transitional period between the Neolithic and Bronze ages in which some copper was used

[1]**ae·o·lian** \ē-ˈō-lē-ən, -ˈōl-yən\ *adj* (1603) **1** *often cap* **:** of or relating to Aeolus **2 :** giving forth or marked by a moaning or sighing sound or musical tone produced by or as if by the wind

[2]**aeolian** *var of* EOLIAN

[1]**Ae·o·lian** \ē-ˈō-lē-ən, ā-, -ˈōl-yən\ *adj* (1589) **:** of or relating to Aeolis or its inhabitants

[2]**Aeolian** *n* (ca. 1895) **1 :** a member of a group of Greek peoples of Thessaly and Boeotia that colonized Lesbos and the adjacent coast of Asia Minor **2 :** AEOLIC

aeolian harp *n* (1791) **:** a box-shaped musical instrument having stretched strings usu. tuned in unison on which the wind produces varying harmonics over the same fundamental tone

[1]**Ae·ol·ic** \ē-ˈäl-ik\ *adj* (1738) **:** AEOLIAN

[2]**Aeolic** *n* (ca. 1902) **:** a group of ancient Greek dialects used by the Aeolians

ae·o·lo·trop·ic \ˌē-ə-lō-ˈträp-ik\ *adj* [Gk *aiolos* variegated] (1867) **:** ANISOTROPIC 1 — **ae·o·lot·ro·py** \-ˈlä-trə-pē\ *n*

Ae·o·lus \ˈē-ə-ləs\ *n* [L, fr. Gk *Aiolos*] **:** the Greek god of the winds

ae·on \ˈē-ən, ˈē-ˌän\ *n* [L, fr. Gk *aiōn* — more at AYE] (1647) **1 :** an immeasurably or indefinitely long period of time **:** AGE **2 :** a unit of time equal to one billion years — used in geology

ae·o·ni·an \ē-ˈō-nē-ən\ *or* **ae·on·ic** \-ˈän-ik\ *adj* (ca. 1765) **:** lasting for an immeasurably or indefinitely long period of time

ae·py·or·nis \ˌē-pē-ˈȯr-nəs\ *n* [NL, genus name, fr. Gk *aipys* high + *ornis* bird — more at ERNE] (1851) **:** any of a group (genus *Aepyornis* or order Aepyornithiformes) of gigantic ratite birds known only from remains found in Madagascar

aer- *or* **aero-** *comb form* [ME *aero-,* fr. MF, fr. L, fr. Gk *aer-, aero-,* fr. *aēr*] **1 a :** air **:** atmosphere ⟨*aer*ate⟩ ⟨*aero*biology⟩ **b :** aerial and ⟨*aero*marine⟩ **2 :** gas ⟨*aero*sol⟩ **3 :** aviation ⟨*aero*drome⟩

aer·ate \ˈa(-ə)r-ˌāt, ˈe(-ə)r-\ *vt* **aer·at·ed; aer·at·ing** (1794) **1 :** to supply (the blood) with oxygen by respiration **2 :** to supply or impregnate (as the soil or a liquid) with air **3 a :** to combine or charge with a gas (as carbon dioxide) **b :** to make effervescent — **aer·a·tion** \ˌa(-ə)r-ˈā-shən, ˌe(-ə)r-\ *n*

aer·a·tor \ˈa(-ə)r-ˌāt-ər, ˈe(-ə)r-\ *n* (1861) **:** one that aerates; *esp* **:** an apparatus for aerating something (as sewage)

aer·en·chy·ma \ˌa(ə)r-ˈeŋ-kə-mə, ˌe(ə)r-\ *n* [NL] (ca. 1900) **:** the spongy modified cork tissue of many aquatic plants that facilitates gaseous exchange and maintains buoyancy

[1]**ae·ri·al** \ˈar-ē-əl, ˈer-, ā-ˈir-ē-əl\ *adj* [L *aerius,* fr. Gk *aerios,* fr. *aēr*] (1604) **1 a :** of, relating to, or occurring in the air or atmosphere **b :** consisting of air ⟨~ particles⟩ **c :** existing or growing in the air rather than in the ground or in water **d :** LOFTY ⟨~ spires⟩ **e :** operating or operated overhead on elevated cables or rails ⟨an ~ railroad⟩ **2 :** suggestive of air: as **a :** lacking substance **:** THIN ⟨fine and ~ distinctions⟩ **b :** IMAGINARY, ETHEREAL ⟨visions of ~ joy — P. B. Shelley⟩ **3 a :** of or relating to aircraft ⟨~ navigation⟩ **b :** designed for use in, taken from, or operating from or against aircraft ⟨~ photo⟩ **c :** effected by means of aircraft ⟨~ transportation⟩ **4 :** of, relating to, or gained by the forward pass in football — **ae·ri·al·ly** \-ə-lē\ *adv*

[2]**aer·i·al** \ˈar-ē-əl, ˈer-\ *n* (1902) **1 :** ANTENNA 2 **2 :** FORWARD PASS

ae·ri·al·ist \ˈar-ē-ə-ləst, ˈer-, ā-ˈir-\ *n* (1905) **:** one that performs feats in the air or above the ground esp. on the flying trapeze

aerial ladder *n* (1904) **:** a mechanically operated extensible ladder usu. mounted on a fire truck

aerial perspective *n* (1731) **:** the expression of space in painting by gradation of color and distinctness

ae·rie \ˈa(ə)r-ē, ˈe(ə)r-, ˈi(ə)r-, ˈā-(ə-)rē\ *n* [ML *aerea,* fr. OF *aire,* fr. L *area* area, feeding place for animals] (1581) **1 :** the nest of a bird on a cliff or a mountaintop **2** *obs* **:** a brood of birds of prey **3 :** an elevated dwelling, structure, or position

aero \ˈa(-ə)r-(ˌ)ō, ˈe(-ə)r-\ *adj* [*aero-*] (1900) **1 :** of or relating to aircraft or aeronautics ⟨an ~ engine⟩ **2 :** designed for aerial use ⟨an ~ lens⟩

aero·bal·lis·tics \ˌar-ō-bə-ˈlis-tiks, ˌer-\ *n pl but sing or pl in constr* (1949) **:** the ballistics of the flight of missiles and projectiles in the atmosphere — **aero·bal·lis·tic** \-tik\ *adj*

aer·o·bat·ics \ˌar-ə-ˈbat-iks, ˌer-\ *n pl but sing or pl in constr* [blend of *aer-* and *acrobatics*] (ca. 1911) **:** spectacular flying feats and maneuvers (as rolls and dives) — **aer·o·bat·ic** \-ik\ *adj*

aer·obe \ˈa(-ə)r-ˌōb, ˈe(-ə)r-\ *n* [F *aérobie,* fr. *aér-* aer- + *-bie* (fr. Gk *bios* life) — more at QUICK] (1886) **:** an organism (as a bacterium) that lives only in the presence of oxygen

aer·o·bic \ˌa(-ə)r-ˈō-bik, ˌe(-ə)r-\ *adj* (1884) **1 :** living, active, or occurring only in the presence of oxygen ⟨~ respiration⟩ **2 :** of, relating to, or induced by aerobes **3 :** involving or utilizing aerobics — **aer·o·bi·cal·ly** \-bi-k(ə-)lē\ *adv*

aer·o·bics \-biks\ *n pl but sing or pl in constr* (1967) **:** a system of physical conditioning designed to improve respiratory and circulatory function by exercises (as running, walking, or swimming) that increase oxygen consumption

aero·bi·ol·o·gy \ˌar-ō-bī-ˈäl-ə-jē\ *n* [*aer-* + *biology*] (ca. 1937) **:** the science dealing with the occurrence, transportation, and effects of airborne materials (as viruses, pollen, or pollutants) — **aero·bi·o·log·i·cal** \-ˌbī-ə-ˈläj-i-kəl\ *adj* — **aero·bi·o·log·i·cal·ly** \-k(ə-)lē\ *adv*

aero·bi·o·sis \ˌar-ō-bī-ˈō-səs, ˌer-, -bē-\ *n, pl* **-o·ses** \-ˌsēz\ (ca. 1900) **:** life in the presence of air or oxygen

aero·drome \ˈar-ə-ˌdrōm, ˈer-\ *n, chiefly Brit* (1908) **:** AIRFIELD, AIRPORT

aero·dy·nam·i·cist \-ˈnam-ə-səst\ *n* (1926) **:** one who specializes in aerodynamics

aero·dy·nam·ics \ˌar-ō-dī-ˈnam-iks, ˌer-\ *n pl but sing or pl in constr* (1837) **:** a branch of dynamics that deals with the motion of air and other gaseous fluids and with the forces acting on bodies in motion relative to such fluids — **aero·dy·nam·ic** \-ik\ *or* **aero·dy·nam·i·cal** \-i-kəl\ *adj* — **aero·dy·nam·i·cal·ly** \-i-k(ə-)lē\ *adv*

aero·dyne \ˈar-ə-ˌdīn, ˈer-\ *n* [*aerodynamic*] (ca. 1906) **:** a heavier-than-air aircraft that derives its lift in flight from forces resulting from its motion through the air

aero·em·bo·lism \ˌar-ō-ˈem-bə-ˌliz-əm, ˌer-\ *n* (ca. 1939) **1 :** a gaseous embolism **2 :** a condition equivalent to bends caused by rapid ascent to high altitudes and resulting exposure to rapidly lowered air pressure

aero·gram *or* **aero·gramme** \ˈar-ə-ˌgram, ˈer-\ *n* (1899) **:** AIR LETTER 2

aer·og·ra·pher \ˌa(-ə)r-ˈäg-rə-fər, ˌe(-ə)r-\ *n* (ca. 1929) **:** a navy warrant officer who observes and forecasts weather and surf conditions

aer·og·ra·phy \-fē\ *n* (1753) **:** METEOROLOGY

aer·o·lite \ˈar-ə-ˌlīt, ˈer-\ *also* **aero·lith** \-ˌlith\ *n* (ca. 1815) **:** a stony meteorite — **aer·o·lit·ic** \ˌar-ə-ˈlit-ik, ˌer-\ *adj*

aer·ol·o·gy \ˌa(-ə)r-ˈäl-ə-jē, ˌe(-ə)r-\ *n* (ca. 1736) **1 :** METEOROLOGY **2 :** a branch of meteorology that deals esp. with the air — **aer·o·log·i·cal** \ˌar-ə-ˈläj-i-kəl, ˌer-\ *adj* — **aer·ol·o·gist** \ˌa(-ə)r-ˈäl-ə-jəst, ˌe(-ə)r-\ *n*

aero·mag·net·ic \ˌar-ō-mag-ˈnet-ik, ˌer-\ *adj* (1948) **:** of, relating to, or derived from a study of the earth's magnetic field esp. from the air ⟨an ~ survey⟩

aero·me·chan·ics \-mə-ˈkan-iks\ *n pl but sing or pl in constr* (ca. 1900) **:** mechanics that deals with the equilibrium and motion of gases and of solid bodies immersed in them

aero·med·i·cine \-ˈmed-ə-sən\ *n* (1942) **:** a branch of medicine that deals with the diseases and disturbances arising from flying and the associated physiological and psychological problems — **aero·med·i·cal** \-ˈmed-i-kəl\ *adj*

aero·me·te·or·o·graph \ˌar-ō-ˌmēt-ē-ˈȯr-ə-ˌgraf, ˌer-\ *n* (ca. 1941) **:** METEOROGRAPH; *esp* **:** one adapted for use on an airplane

aer·om·e·ter \ˌa(-ə)r-ˈäm-ət-ər, ˌe(-ə)r-\ *n* [prob. fr. F *aéromètre,* fr. *aér-* + *mètre* -meter] (1794) **:** an instrument for ascertaining the weight or density of air or other gases

aero·naut \ˈar-ə-ˌnȯt, ˈer-, -ˌnät\ *n* [F *aéronaute,* fr. *aér-* aer- + Gk *nautēs* sailor — more at NAUTICAL] (1784) **:** one that operates or travels in an airship or balloon

aero·nau·tics \ˌar-ə-ˈnȯt-iks\ *n pl but sing in constr* (ca. 1824) **1 :** a science dealing with the operation of aircraft **2 :** the art or science of flight — **aero·nau·ti·cal** \-i-kəl\ *or* **aero·nau·tic** \-ik\ *adj* — **aero·nau·ti·cal·ly** \-i-k(ə-)lē\ *adv*

aer·on·o·my \ˌa(-ə)r-ˈän-ə-mē, ˌe(-ə)r-\ *n* (1957) **:** a science that deals with the physics and chemistry of the upper atmosphere of planets — **aer·on·o·mer** \-mər\ *n* — **aer·o·nom·ic** \ˌar-ə-ˈnäm-ik, ˌer-\ *or* **aer·o·nom·i·cal** \-i-kəl\ *adj* — **aer·o·nom·ics** \-iks\ *n pl but sing in constr* — **aer·on·o·mist** \ˌa(-ə)r-ˈän-ə-məst, ˌe(-ə)r-\ *n*

aero·pause \ˈar-ō-ˌpȯz, ˈer-\ *n* (1951) **:** the level above the earth's surface where the atmosphere becomes ineffective for human and aircraft functions

aero·plane \ˈar-ə-ˌplān, ˈer-\ *n, chiefly Brit* (1873) **:** AIRPLANE

aero·sol \ˈar-ə-ˌsäl, ˈer-, -ˌsȯl\ *n* (ca. 1923) **1 :** a suspension of fine solid or liquid particles in gas ⟨smoke, fog, and mist are ~*s*⟩ **2 :** a substance (as an insecticide or cosmetic) dispensed from a pressurized container as an aerosol; *also* **:** the container for this

aero·sol·ize \-ˌsäl-ˌīz, -ˌsȯl-, -səl-\ *vt* **-ized; -iz·ing** (1944) **:** to disperse as an aerosol — **aero·sol·iza·tion** \ˌar-ə-ˌsäl-ə-ˈzā-shən, -ˌsȯl-, -səl-\ *n*

[1]**aero·space** \ˈar-ō-ˌspās, ˈer-\ *n* (ca. 1958) **1 :** space comprising the earth's atmosphere and the space beyond **2 :** a physical science that deals with aerospace **3 :** the aerospace industry

[2]**aerospace** *adj* (ca. 1958) **:** of or relating to aerospace, to vehicles used in aerospace or the manufacture of such vehicles, or to travel in aerospace ⟨~ research⟩ ⟨~ profits⟩ ⟨~ medicine⟩

aero·sphere \ˈar-ō-ˌsfi(ə)r, ˈer-\ *n* [F *aérosphère,* fr. *aér-* aer- + *sphère* sphere, fr. L *sphaera*] (ca. 1884) **:** the body of air around the earth

aero·stat \-ˌstat\ *n* [F *aérostat,* fr. *aér-* + *-stat*] (1784) **:** an aircraft that embodies one or more containers filled with a gas lighter than air and that is supported chiefly by buoyancy derived from the surrounding air

aero·stat·ics \ˌar-ō-'stat-iks, ˌer-\ *n pl but sing or pl in constr* [modif. of NL *aerostatica,* fr. *aer-* + *statica* statics] (1784) **:** a branch of statics that deals with the equilibrium of gaseous fluids and of solid bodies immersed in them

aero·ther·mo·dy·nam·ics \-ˌthər-mə-(ˌ)dī-'nam-iks\ *n pl but sing or pl in constr* (1949) **:** the thermodynamics of gases and esp. of air

[1]**aery** \'a(ə)r-ē, 'e(ə)r-ē, 'ā-ə-rē\ *adj* **aer·i·er; -est** [L *aerius* — more at AERIAL] (14c) **:** having an aerial quality **:** ETHEREAL ⟨~ visions⟩ — **aer·i·ly** \'ar-ə-lē, 'er-\ *adv*

[2]**aery** *like* AERIE\ *var of* AERIE

Aes·cu·la·pi·an \ˌes-k(y)ə-'lā-pē-ən\ *adj* [*Aesculapius,* Greco-Roman god of medicine, fr. L, fr. Gk *Asklēpios*] (1605) **:** of or relating to Aesculapius or the healing art **:** MEDICAL

Ae·sir \'ā-ˌzi(ə)r, -ˌsi(ə)r\ *n pl* [ON *Æsir,* pl. of *āss* god] **:** the principal race of Norse gods

Ae·so·pi·an \ē-'sō-pē-ən, -'säp-ē-\ *also* **Ae·sop·ic** \-'säp-ik\ *adj* (1728) **1 :** of, relating to, or characteristic of Aesop or his fables **2 :** conveying an innocent meaning to an outsider but a hidden meaning to a member of a conspiracy or underground movement ⟨~ language⟩

aesthesio- — see ESTHESIO-

aes·thete \'es-ˌthēt, *Brit usu* 'ēs-\ *n* [back-formation fr. *aesthetic*] (1881) **:** one having or affecting sensitivity to the beautiful esp. in art

aes·thet·ic \es-'thet-ik, is-, *Brit usu* ēs-\ *or* **aes·thet·i·cal** \-i-kəl\ *adj* [G *ästhetisch,* fr. NL *aestheticus,* fr. Gk *aisthētikos* of sense perception, fr. *aisthanesthai* to perceive — more at AUDIBLE] (1798) **1 a :** of, relating to, or dealing with aesthetics or the beautiful ⟨~ theories⟩ **b :** ARTISTIC ⟨a work of ~ value⟩ **2 :** appreciative of, responsive to, or zealous about the beautiful — **aes·thet·i·cal·ly** \-i-k(ə-)lē\ *adv*

aesthetic distance *n* (1938) **:** the frame of reference that an artist creates by the use of technical devices in and around the work of art to differentiate it psychologically from reality

aes·the·ti·cian \ˌes-thə-'tish-ən\ *n* (1829) **:** a specialist in aesthetics

aes·thet·i·cism \es-'thet-ə-ˌsiz-əm, is-\ *n* (1855) **1 :** a doctrine that the principles of beauty are basic to other and esp. moral principles **2 :** devotion to or emphasis on beauty or the cultivation of the arts

aes·thet·ics \-'thet-iks\ *n pl but sing or pl in constr, also* **aes·thet·ic** \-ik\ (1825) **1 :** a branch of philosophy dealing with the nature of beauty, art, and taste and with the creation and appreciation of beauty **2 :** a particular theory or conception of beauty or art ⟨modernist ~⟩ **3 :** a pleasing appearance or effect **:** BEAUTY ⟨appreciated the ~ of the gemstones⟩

aes·ti·val \'es-tə-vəl\ *var of* ESTIVAL

aes·ti·vate, aes·ti·va·tion *var of* ESTIVATE, ESTIVATION

ae·ti·ol·o·gy *var of* ETIOLOGY

af- — see AD-

[1]**afar** \ə-'fär\ *adv* [ME *afer,* fr. *on fer* at a distance and *of fer* from a distance] (14c) **:** from, to, or at a great distance ⟨roamed ~⟩

[2]**afar** *n* (14c) **:** a great distance ⟨saw him from ~⟩

afeard *or* **afeared** \ə-'fi(ə)rd\ *adj* [ME *afered,* fr. OE *āfǣred,* pp. of *āfǣran* to frighten, fr. *ā-,* perfective prefix + *fǣran* to frighten — more at ABIDE, FEAR] *dial* (bef. 12c) **:** AFRAID

afe·brile \(ˈ)ā-'feb-ˌrīl *also* -'fēb-\ *adj* (1875) **:** not marked by fever

af·fa·ble \'af-ə-bəl\ *adj* [MF, fr. L *affabilis,* fr. *affari* to speak to, fr. *ad-* + *fari* to speak — more at BAN] (15c) **1 :** being pleasant and at ease in talking to others **2 :** characterized by ease and friendliness ***syn*** see GRACIOUS — **af·fa·bil·i·ty** \ˌaf-ə-'bil-ət-ē\ *n* — **af·fa·bly** \-blē\ *adv*

af·fair \ə-'fa(ə)r, -'fe(ə)r\ *n* [ME & MF; ME *affaire,* fr. MF, fr. *a faire* to do] (14c) **1 a** *pl* **:** commercial, professional, public, or personal business **b :** MATTER, CONCERN **2 :** a procedure, action, or occasion only vaguely specified; *also* **:** an object or collection of objects only vaguely specified ⟨his house was a 2-story ~⟩ **3** *also* **af·faire a :** a romantic or passionate attachment typically of limited duration **:** LIAISON 1b **b :** a matter occasioning public anxiety, controversy, or scandal **:** CASE

[1]**af·fect** \'af-ˌekt\ *n* [L *affectus*] (14c) **1** *obs* **:** FEELING, AFFECTION **2 :** the conscious subjective aspect of an emotion considered apart from bodily changes ***usage*** see EFFECT

[2]**af·fect** \ə-'fekt, a-\ *vb* [MF & L; MF *affecter,* fr. L *affectare,* fr. *affectus,* pp. of *afficere* to influence, fr. *ad-* + *facere* to do — more at DO] *vt* (15c) **1** *archaic* **:** to aim at **2 a** *archaic* **:** to have affection for **b :** to be given to **:** FANCY ⟨~ flashy clothes⟩ **3 :** to make a display of liking or using **:** CULTIVATE ⟨~ a worldly manner⟩ **4 :** to put on a pretense of **:** FEIGN ⟨~ indifference, though deeply hurt⟩ **5 :** to tend toward ⟨drops of water ~ roundness⟩ **6 :** FREQUENT ~ *vi, obs* **:** INCLINE 2 ***syn*** see ASSUME ***usage*** see EFFECT

[3]**affect** *vt* (15c) **:** to produce an effect upon: as **a :** to produce a material influence upon or alteration in ⟨paralysis ~*ed* his limbs⟩ **b :** to act upon (as a person or his mind or his feelings) so as to effect a response **:** INFLUENCE ***usage*** see EFFECT — **af·fect·abil·i·ty** \-ˌfek-tə-'bil-ət-ē\ *n* — **af·fect·able** \-'fek-tə-bəl\ *adj*

syn AFFECT, INFLUENCE, TOUCH, IMPRESS, STRIKE, SWAY mean to produce or have an effect upon. AFFECT implies the action of a stimulus that can produce a response or reaction ⟨the sight *affected* her to tears⟩ INFLUENCE implies a force that brings about a change (as in nature or behavior) ⟨our beliefs are *influenced* by our upbringing⟩ ⟨a drug that *influences* growth rates⟩ TOUCH may carry a vivid suggestion of close contact and may connote stirring, arousing, or harming ⟨plants *touched* by frost⟩ ⟨his emotions were *touched* by her distress⟩ IMPRESS stresses the depth and persistence of the effect ⟨only one of the plans *impressed* him⟩ STRIKE, similar to but weaker than *impress,* may convey the notion of sudden sharp perception or appreciation ⟨*struck* by the solemnity of the occasion⟩ SWAY implies the acting of influences that are not resisted or are irresistible, with resulting change in character or course of action ⟨he is *swayed* by fashion, by suggestion, by transient moods —H. L. Mencken⟩

af·fec·ta·tion \ˌaf-ˌek-'tā-shən\ *n* (1548) **1 a :** the act of taking on or displaying an attitude or mode of behavior not natural to oneself or not genuinely felt **b :** speech or conduct not natural to oneself **:** ARTIFICIALITY **2** *obs* **:** a striving after ***syn*** see POSE

af·fect·ed \ə-'fek-təd, a-\ *adj* (1587) **1 :** INCLINED, DISPOSED ⟨was well ~ toward her⟩ **2 a :** given to affection **b :** assumed artificially or falsely **:** PRETENDED ⟨an ~ interest in art⟩ — **af·fect·ed·ly** *adv* — **af·fect·ed·ness** *n*

af·fect·ing \ə-'fek-tiŋ, a-\ *adj* (1720) **:** evoking a strong emotional response ***syn*** see MOVING — **af·fect·ing·ly** \-tiŋ-lē\ *adv*

[1]**af·fec·tion** \ə-'fek-shən\ *n* [ME, fr. OF *affection,* fr. L *affection-, affectio,* fr. *affectus,* pp.] (13c) **1 :** a moderate feeling or emotion **2 :** tender attachment **:** FONDNESS ⟨she had a deep ~ for her parents⟩ **3** *obs* **:** PARTIALITY, PREJUDICE **4 :** the feeling aspect (as in pleasure) of consciousness **5 a :** PROPENSITY, DISPOSITION **b** *archaic* **:** AFFECTATION 1 ***syn*** see FEELING — **af·fec·tion·less** \-ləs\ *adj*

[2]**affection** *n* (1541) **1 a (1) :** a bodily condition **(2) :** DISEASE, MALADY **b :** ATTRIBUTE ⟨shape and weight are ~s of bodies⟩ **2 :** the action of affecting **:** the state of being affected

af·fec·tion·al \ə-'fek-shnəl, -shən-ᵊl\ *adj* (1859) **:** of or relating to the affections — **af·fec·tion·al·ly** \-ē\ *adv*

af·fec·tion·ate \ə-'fek-sh(ə-)nət\ *adj* (15c) **1** *obs* **:** INCLINED, DISPOSED **2 :** having affection or warm regard **:** LOVING **3 :** proceeding from affection **:** TENDER ⟨~ care⟩ — **af·fec·tion·ate·ly** *adv*

af·fec·tioned \-shənd\ *adj, archaic* (1555) **:** having a tendency, disposition, or inclination **:** DISPOSED

af·fec·tive \a-'fek-tiv\ *adj* (1623) **1 :** relating to, arising from, or influencing feelings or emotions **:** EMOTIONAL ⟨~ disorders⟩ **2 :** expressing emotion ⟨~ language⟩ — **af·fec·tive·ly** *adv* — **af·fec·tiv·i·ty** \ˌaf-ˌek-'tiv-ət-ē\ *n*

af·fect·less \'af-ˌek-tləs, a-'fek-\ *adj* (1967) **:** UNFEELING ⟨a ruthless ~ society⟩ — **af·fect·less·ness** *n*

af·fen·pin·scher \'af-ən-ˌpin-chər\ *n* [G, fr. *affe* ape + *pinscher,* a breed of hunting dog] (ca. 1903) **:** any of a breed of small dogs with a wiry black, red, or gray coat, pointed ears, and bushy eyebrows, chin tuft, and mustache

[1]**af·fer·ent** \'af-ə-rənt, -ˌer-ənt\ *adj* [L *afferent-, afferens,* prp. of *afferre* to bring to, fr. *ad-* + *ferre* to bear — more at BEAR] (ca. 1839) **:** bearing or conducting inward; *specif* **:** conveying impulses toward a nerve center (as the brain or spinal cord) — compare EFFERENT — **af·fer·ent·ly** *adv*

[2]**afferent** *n* (1949) **:** an afferent anatomical part (as a nerve)

[1]**af·fi·ance** \ə-'fī-ən(t)s\ *n* [ME, fr. MF, fr. *affier* to pledge, trust, fr. ML *affidare* to pledge, fr. L *ad-* + (assumed) VL *fidare* to trust — more at FIANCÉ] *archaic* (14c) **:** TRUST, CONFIDENCE

[2]**affiance** *vt* **-anced; -anc·ing** (1555) **:** to solemnly promise (oneself or another) in marriage **:** BETROTH

af·fi·ant \ə-'fī-ənt\ *n* [MF, fr. prp. of *affier*] (1807) **:** one that swears to an affidavit; *broadly* **:** DEPONENT

af·fi·cio·na·do *var of* AFICIONADO

af·fi·da·vit \ˌaf-ə-'dā-vət\ *n* [ML, he has made an oath, fr. *affidare*] (1598) **:** a sworn statement in writing made esp. under oath or on affirmation before an authorized magistrate or officer

[1]**af·fil·i·ate** \ə-'fil-ē-ˌāt\ *vb* **-at·ed; -at·ing** [ML *affiliatus,* pp. of *affiliare* to adopt as a son, fr. L *ad-* + *filius* son — more at FEMININE] *vt* (1761) **1 a :** to bring or receive into close connection as a member or branch **b :** to associate as a member ⟨~s himself with the local club⟩ **2 :** to trace the origin of ~ *vi* **:** to connect or associate oneself **:** COMBINE — **af·fil·i·a·tion** \-ˌfil-ē-'ā-shən\ *n*

[2]**af·fil·i·ate** \ə-'fil-ē-ət, -ˌāt\ *n* (1879) **:** an affiliated person or organization

af·fil·i·at·ed \-ē-ˌāt-əd\ *adj* (1795) **:** closely associated with another typically in a dependent or subordinate position ⟨the university and its ~ medical school⟩

[1]**af·fine** \a-'fīn, ə-\ *n* [MF *affin,* fr. L *affinis,* fr. *affinis* related] (1509) **:** a relative by marriage

[2]**affine** *adj* [L *affinis,* adj.] (1918) **:** of, relating to, or being a transformation (as a translation, a rotation, or a uniform stretching) that carries straight lines into straight lines and parallel lines into parallel lines but may alter distance between points and angles between lines ⟨~ geometry⟩ — **af·fine·ly** *adv*

af·fined \ə-'fīnd, ə-\ *adj* (1597) **1 :** joined in a close relationship **:** CONNECTED **2 :** bound by obligation

af·fin·i·ty \ə-'fin-ət-ē\ *n, pl* **-ties** [ME *affinite,* fr. MF or L; MF *afinité,* fr. L *affinitas,* fr. *affinis* bordering on, related by marriage, fr. *ad-* + *finis* end, border] (14c) **1 :** relationship by marriage **2 a :** sympathy marked by community of interest **:** KINSHIP **b :** ATTRACTION; *esp* **:** an attractive force between substances or particles that causes them to enter into and remain in chemical combination **c :** a person esp. of the opposite sex having a particular attraction for one **3 a :** likeness based on relationship or causal connection **b :** a relation between biological groups involving resemblance in structural plan and indicating community of origin ***syn*** see ATTRACTION, LIKENESS

af·firm \ə-'fərm\ *vb* [ME *affermen,* fr. MF *afermer,* fr. L *affirmare,* fr. *ad-* + *firmare* to make firm, fr. *firmus* firm — more at FIRM] *vt* (14c) **1 a :** VALIDATE, CONFIRM **b :** to state positively **2 :** to assert (as a judgment or decree) as valid or confirmed **3 :** to express dedication to ~ *vi* **1 :** to testify or declare by affirmation **2 :** to uphold a judgment or decree of a lower court ***syn*** see ASSERT — **af·firm·able** \ə-'fər-mə-bəl\ *adj* — **af·fir·mance** \ə-'fər-mən(t)s\ *n*

af·fir·ma·tion \ˌaf-ər-'mā-shən\ *n* (15c) **1 a :** the act of affirming **b :** something affirmed **:** a positive assertion **2 :** a solemn declaration made under the penalties of perjury by a person who conscientiously declines taking an oath

[1]**af·fir·ma·tive** \ə-'fər-mət-iv\ *adj* (15c) **1 :** asserting a predicate of a subject **2 :** asserting that the fact is so **3 :** POSITIVE ⟨~ approach⟩ **4 :** favoring or supporting a proposition or motion — **af·fir·ma·tive·ly** *adv*

[2]**affirmative** *n* (15c) **1 :** an expression (as the word *yes*) of affirmation or assent **2 :** an affirmative proposition **3 :** the side that upholds the proposition stated in a debate

affirmative action *n* (1965) : an active effort to improve the employment or educational opportunities of members of minority groups and women

1af·fix \ə-ˈfiks, a-\ *vt* [ME *affichen,* prob. fr. ML *affixare,* fr. L *affixus,* pp. of *affigere* to fasten to, fr. *ad-* + *figere* to fasten — more at DIKE] (14c) **1 :** to attach physically ⟨~ a stamp to a letter⟩ **2 :** to attach in any way : ADD, APPEND ⟨~ a signature to a document⟩ **3 :** IMPRESS ⟨~*ed* his seal⟩ ***syn*** see FASTEN — **af·fix·able** \-ˈfik-sə-bəl\ *adj* — **af·fix·a·tion** \ˌaf-ˌik-ˈsā-shən\ *n* — **af·fix·ment** \ə-ˈfik-smənt, a-\ *n*

2af·fix \ˈaf-ˌiks\ *n* (1612) **1 :** one or more sounds or letters occurring as a bound form attached to the beginning or end of a word, base, or phrase or inserted within a word or base and serving to produce a derivative word or an inflectional form **2 :** APPENDAGE — **af·fix·al** \-ˌik-səl\ *or* **af·fix·i·al** \a-ˈfik-sē-əl\ *adj*

af·fla·tus \ə-ˈflāt-əs, a-\ *n* [L, act of blowing or breathing on, fr. *afflatus,* pp. of *afflare* to blow on, fr. *ad-* + *flare* to blow — more at BLOW] (1660) : a divine imparting of knowledge or power : INSPIRATION

af·flict \ə-ˈflikt\ *vt* [ME *afflicten,* fr. L *afflictus,* pp. of *affligere* to cast down, fr. *ad-* + *fligere* to strike — more at PROFLIGATE] (14c) **1** *obs* **a :** HUMBLE **b :** OVERTHROW **2 a :** to distress so severely as to cause persistent suffering or anguish **b :** TROUBLE, INJURE

syn AFFLICT, TRY, TORMENT, TORTURE, RACK, GRILL mean to inflict on a person something that is hard to bear. AFFLICT is a general term and applies to the causing of pain or suffering or of acute annoyance, embarrassment, or any distress; TRY suggests imposing something that strains the powers of endurance or of self-control; TORMENT suggests persecution or the repeated inflicting of suffering or annoyance; TORTURE adds the implication of causing unbearable pain or suffering; RACK stresses straining or wrenching; GRILL suggests causing acute discomfort as by long and relentless questioning.

af·flic·tion \ə-ˈflik-shən\ *n* (14c) **1 :** the state of being afflicted **2 a :** the cause of persistent pain or distress **b :** great suffering

af·flic·tive \ə-ˈflik-tiv\ *adj* (1611) : causing affliction : DISTRESSING, TROUBLESOME — **af·flic·tive·ly** *adv*

af·flu·ence \ˈaf-(ˌ)lü-ən(t)s *also* a-ˈflü- *or* ə-\ *n* (14c) **1 a :** an abundant flow or supply : PROFUSION **b :** abundance of property : WEALTH **2 :** a flowing to or toward a point : INFLUX

af·flu·en·cy \-ən-sē\ *n, pl* **-cies** (1664) : AFFLUENCE

1af·flu·ent \-ənt\ *adj* [ME, fr. MF, fr. L *affluent-, affluens,* prp. of *affluere* to flow to, flow abundantly, fr. *ad-* + *fluere* to flow — more at FLUID] (15c) **1 a :** flowing in abundance : COPIOUS **b :** having a generously sufficient and typically increasing supply of material possessions ⟨our ~ society⟩ **2 :** flowing toward ***syn*** see RICH — **af·flu·ent·ly** *adv*

2affluent *n* (1833) **1 :** a tributary stream **2 :** an affluent person

af·flux \ˈaf-ˌləks\ *n* [F or L; F, fr. L *affluxus,* pp. of *affluere*] (1611) : AFFLUENCE 2

af·ford \ə-ˈfō(ə)rd, -ˈfȯ(ə)rd\ *vt* [ME *aforthen,* fr. OE *geforthian* to carry out, fr. *ge-,* perfective prefix + *forthian* to carry out, fr. *forth* — more at CO-, FORTH] (bef. 12c) **1 a :** to manage to bear without serious detriment ⟨you can't ~ to neglect your health⟩ **b :** to be able to bear the cost of ⟨he can't ~ to be out of work long⟩ ⟨~ a new coat⟩ **2 :** to make available, give forth, or provide naturally or inevitably ⟨the sun ~*s* warmth to the earth⟩ ⟨the roof ~*ed* a fine view⟩ ***syn*** see GIVE — **af·ford·able** \-ˈfōrd-ə-bəl, -ˈfȯrd-\ *adj*

af·for·es·ta·tion \(ˌ)a-ˌfȯr-ə-ˈstā-shən, ə-, -ˌfär-\ *n* [ML *afforestation-, afforestatio,* fr. *afforestare,* fr *ad-* + *foresta* forest — more at FOREST] (1615) : the act or process of establishing a forest esp. on land not previously forested — **af·for·est** \a-ˈfȯr-əst, -ˈfär-\ *vt*

1af·fray \ə-ˈfrā\ *n* [ME, fr. MF, fr. *affreer* to startle] (14c) : FRAY, BRAWL

2affray *vt* [ME *affraien,* fr. MF *affreer*] *archaic* (14c) : STARTLE, FRIGHTEN

af·fri·cate \ˈaf-ri-kət\ *n* [prob. fr. G *affrikata,* fr. L *affricata,* fem. of *affricatus,* pp. of *affricare* to rub against, fr. *ad-* + *fricare* to rub — more at FRICTION] (1880) : a stop and its immediately following release through the articulatory position for a continuant nonsyllabic consonant (as the \t\ and \sh\ that are the constituents of the \ch\ in *why choose*) — **af·fric·a·tive** \a-ˈfrik-ət-iv, ə-\ *n or adj*

1af·fright \ə-ˈfrīt\ *vt* [fr. ME *afyrht, afright* frightened, fr. OE *āfyrht,* pp. of *āfyrhtan* to frighten, fr. *ā-,* perfective prefix + *fyrhtan* to fear; akin to OE *fyrhto* fright — more at ABIDE, FRIGHT] (bef. 12c) : FRIGHTEN, ALARM

2affright *n* (1596) : sudden and great fear : TERROR

1af·front \ə-ˈfrənt\ *vt* [ME *afronten,* fr. MF *afronter* to defy, fr. (assumed) VL *affrontare,* fr. L *ad-* + *front-, frons* forehead — more at FRONT] (14c) **1 :** to insult esp. to the face by behavior or language **2 a :** to face in defiance : CONFRONT ⟨~ death⟩ **b** *obs* **:** to encounter face to face **3 :** to appear directly before ***syn*** see OFFEND

2affront *n* (1598) **1 :** a deliberate offense : INSULT ⟨an ~ to his dignity⟩ **2** *obs* **:** a hostile encounter

af·fu·sion \a-ˈfyü-zhən\ *n* [LL *affusion-, affusio,* fr. L *affusus,* pp. of *affundere* to pour on, fr. *ad-* + *fundere* to pour — more at FOUND] (1615) : an act of pouring a liquid on (as in baptism)

Af·ghan \ˈaf-ˌgan *also* -gən\ *n* [Pashto *afghānī*] (1609) **1 :** a native or inhabitant of Afghanistan **2 :** PASHTO **3** *not cap* **:** a blanket or shawl of colored wool knitted or crocheted in strips or squares **4** *not cap* **:** a Turkoman carpet of large size and long pile woven in geometric designs **5 :** AFGHAN HOUND — **Afghan** *adj*

Afghan hound *n* (1925) : any of a breed of tall slim swift hunting dogs native to the Near East with a coat of silky thick hair and a long silky topknot

Afghan hound

af·ghani \af-ˈgan-ē, -ˈgän-\ *n* [Pashto *afghānī,* lit., Afghan] (1927) — see MONEY table

afi·cio·na·da \ə-ˌfish(-ē)-ə-ˈnäd-ə, -ˌfis-ē-, -ˌfē-sē-, -ˈnäd-(ˌ)ä\ *n* [Sp, fem. of *aficionado*] (1952) : a female aficionado ⟨card-playing ~*s*⟩

afi·cio·na·do \-ˈnäd-(ˌ)ō\ *n, pl* **-dos** [Sp, fr. pp. of *aficionar* to inspire affection, fr. *afición* affection, fr. L *affection-, affectio* — more at AFFECTION] (1845) : DEVOTEE, FAN ⟨~*s* of the bullfight⟩ ⟨movie ~*s*⟩

afield \ə-ˈfē(ə)ld\ *adv or adj* (bef. 12c) **1 :** to, in, or on the field ⟨was weak at bat but strong ~⟩ **2 :** away from home : ABROAD **3 :** out of the way : ASTRAY ⟨irrelevant remarks that carried us far ~⟩

afire \ə-ˈfī(ə)r\ *adj or adv* (14c) : being on fire : BLAZING

aflame \ə-ˈflām\ *adj or adv* (1555) : AFIRE

af·la·tox·in \ˌaf-lə-ˈtäk-sən\ *n* [NL *Aspergillus flavus,* species of mold + E *toxin*] (1963) : any of several carcinogenic mycotoxins that are produced esp. in stored agricultural crops (as peanuts) by molds (as *Aspergillus flavus*)

afloat \ə-ˈflōt\ *adj or adv* [ME *aflot,* fr. OE *on flot,* fr. *on* + *flot,* fr. *flot* deep water, sea; akin to OE *flēotan* to float — more at FLEET] (bef. 12c) **1 a :** borne on or as if on the water **b :** being at sea **2 :** free of difficulties : SELF-SUFFICIENT ⟨the inheritance kept them ~ for years⟩ **3 a :** circulating about ⟨nasty stories were ~⟩ **b :** ADRIFT

aflut·ter \ə-ˈflət-ər\ *adj* (1830) **1 :** being in a flutter : FLUTTERING **2 :** nervously excited **3 :** filled with or marked by the presence of fluttering things ⟨roofs ~ with flags⟩

afoot \ə-ˈfu̇t\ *adv or adj* (13c) **1 :** on foot **2 :** in the process of development : UNDER WAY ⟨something out of the ordinary was ~ — Hamilton Basso⟩

afore \ə-ˈfō(ə)r, -ˈfȯ(ə)r\ *adv or conj or prep* [ME, fr. OE *onforan,* fr. *on* + *foran* before — more at BEFORE] *chiefly dial* (bef. 12c) : BEFORE

afore·men·tioned \-ˈmen-chənd\ *adj* (1587) : mentioned previously

afore·said \-ˌsed\ *adj* (14c) : said or named before or above

afore·thought \-ˌthȯt\ *adj* (1581) : previously in mind : PREMEDITATED, DELIBERATE ⟨with malice ~⟩

a for·ti·o·ri \ˌā-ˌfȯr-shē-ˈō(ə)r-ˌī, ˌä-ˌfȯr-shē-ˈō(ə)r-ē, -ˌfȯrt-ē-, -ˈō(ə)r-\ *adv* [NL, lit., from the stronger (argument)] (1588) : with greater reason or more convincing force — used in drawing a conclusion that is inferred to be even more certain than another ⟨the man of prejudice is, *a fortiori,* a man of limited mental vision⟩

afoul of \ə-ˈfau̇-ləv\ *prep* (1824) **1 :** in or into collision or entanglement with **2 :** in or into conflict with

Afr- *or* **Afro-** *comb form* [L *Afr-, Afer*] **:** African ⟨*Afr*american⟩ **:** African and ⟨*Afro*-Asiatic⟩

afraid \ə-ˈfrād, *Southern also* ə-ˈfre(ə)d\ *adj* [ME *affraied,* fr. pp. of *affraien* to frighten — more at AFFRAY] (14c) **1 :** filled with fear or apprehension ⟨~ of machines⟩ ⟨~ for his job⟩ **2 :** filled with concern or regret over an unwanted situation ⟨I'm ~ I won't be able to go⟩ **3 :** having a dislike for something ⟨~ of hard work⟩ ***syn*** see FEARFUL

A–frame \ˈā-ˌfrām\ *n* (1962) : a building typically having triangular front and rear walls and a roof reaching to the ground

afreet *or* **afrit** \ˈaf-ˌrēt, ə-ˈfrēt\ *n* [Ar *ʿifrīt*] (1786) : a powerful evil jinni, demon, or monstrous giant in Arabic mythology

afresh \ə-ˈfresh\ *adv* (15c) : from a fresh beginning : ANEW, AGAIN

1Af·ri·can \ˈaf-ri-kən\ *n* (bef. 12c) **1 :** a native or inhabitant of Africa **2 :** a person of immediate or remote African ancestry; *esp* **:** NEGRO

2African *adj* (bef. 12c) : of, relating to, or characteristic of the continent of Africa or its people — **Af·ri·can·ness** \-kən-nəs\ *n*

Af·ri·ca·na \ˌaf-ri-ˈkan-ə, -ˈkän-, -ˈkān-\ *n pl* (1908) : materials (as books, documents, or artifacts) relating to African history and culture

Af·ri·can–Amer·i·can \ˌaf-ri-kən-ə-ˈmer-ə-kən\ *n* (1984) : AFRO-AMERICAN — **African–American** *adj*

Af·ri·can·der *or* **Af·ri·kan·der** \ˌaf-ri-ˈkan-dər\ *n* [Afrik *Afrikaner, Afrikaander,* lit., Afrikaner] (1852) : any of a breed of tall red large-horned humped southern African cattle used chiefly for meat or draft

African elephant *n* (1948) : ELEPHANT 1 a

Af·ri·can·ism \ˈaf-ri-kə-ˌniz-əm\ *n* (1641) **1 :** a characteristic feature (as a custom or belief) of African culture **2 :** a characteristic feature of an African language occurring in a non-African language **3 :** allegiance to the traditions, interests, or ideals of Africa

Af·ri·can·ist \-nəst\ *n* (1895) : a specialist in African languages or cultures

Af·ri·can·ize \-ˌnīz\ *vt* **-ized; -iz·ing** (1853) **1 :** to cause to acquire a distinctively African trait **2 :** to bring under the influence, control, or cultural or civil supremacy of Africans and esp. Negroes — **Af·ri·can·iza·tion** \ˌaf-ri-kə-nə-ˈzā-shən\ *n*

African mahogany *n* (1842) : MAHOGANY 1b

African violet *n* (ca. 1902) : any of several tropical African plants (esp. *Saintpaulia ionantha*) of the gloxinia family widely grown as houseplants for their velvety fleshy leaves and showy purple, pink, or white flowers

1Af·ri·kaans \ˌaf-ri-ˈkän(t)s, -ˈkänz, ˈaf-ri-ˌ\ *n* [Afrik, fr. *afrikaans,* adj., African, fr. obs. Afrik *afrikanisch,* fr. L *africanus*] (1908) : a language developed from 17th century Dutch that is one of the official languages of the Republic of So. Africa

2Afrikaans *adj* (1923) : of or relating to Afrikaners or Afrikaans

Af·ri·ka·ner \ˌaf-ri-ˈkän-ər\ *n* [Afrik, lit., African, fr. L *africanus*] (1824) : a So. African native of European descent; *esp* **:** an Afrikaans-speaking descendant of the 17th century Dutch settlers

1Af·ro \ˈaf-(ˌ)rō\ *adj* [prob. fr. *Afro-American*] (1966) : having the hair shaped into a round bushy mass

2Afro *n, pl* **Afros** (1968) : an Afro hairstyle

Af·ro–Amer·i·can \ˌaf-rō-ə-ˈmer-ə-kən\ *n* (1853) : an American of African and esp. of Negroid descent — **Afro–American** *adj*

Af·ro–Asi·at·ic languages \ˌaf-rō-ˌā-z(h)ē-ˌat-ik- *also* -shē-\ *n pl* (ca. 1958) : a family of languages widely distributed over southwestern Asia and northern Africa comprising the Semitic, Egyptian, Berber, Cushitic, and Chad subfamilies

1aft \ˈaft\ *adv* [ME *afte* back, fr. OE *æftan* from behind, behind; akin to OE *æfter*] (bef. 12c) : near, toward, or in the stern of a ship or the tail of an aircraft : ABAFT ⟨called all hands ~⟩

2aft *adj* (13c) : REARWARD, 4AFTER 2 ⟨the ~ decks⟩

3aft *Scot var of* OFT

1af·ter \ˈaf-tər\ *adv* [ME, fr. OE *æfter;* akin to OHG *aftar* after] (bef. 12c) : following in time or place : AFTERWARD, BEHIND, LATER ⟨we arrived shortly ~⟩ ⟨returned 20 years ~⟩

Afro

[2]**after** *prep* (bef. 12c) **1 a :** behind in place **b** (1) **:** subsequent to in time or order (2) **:** subsequent to and in view of ⟨~ all our advice⟩ **2** — used as a function word to indicate the object of a stated or implied action ⟨go ~ gold⟩ **3 :** so as to resemble: as **a :** in accordance with **b :** with the name of or a name derived from that of **c :** in the characteristic manner of **d :** in imitation of

[3]**after** *conj* (bef. 12c) **:** subsequently to the time when

[4]**after** *adj* (bef. 12c) **1 :** later in time ⟨in ~ years⟩ **2 :** located toward the rear and esp. toward the stern of a ship or tail of an aircraft

[5]**after** *n* (1902) **:** AFTERNOON

after all *adv* (1846) **1 :** in spite of considerations or expectations to the contrary **:** NEVERTHELESS ⟨decided to take the train *after all*⟩ ⟨didn't rain *after all*⟩ **2** — used as a sentence modifier to emphasize something to be taken into consideration ⟨literature which is *after all* only a special department of reading —W. W. Watt⟩

af·ter·birth \ˈaf-tər-ˌbərth\ *n* (1587) **:** the placenta and fetal membranes that are expelled after delivery

af·ter·burn·er \-ˌbər-nər\ *n* (1947) **1 :** an auxiliary burner attached to the tail pipe of a turbojet engine for injecting fuel into the hot exhaust gases and burning it to provide extra thrust **2 :** a device for burning or catalytically destroying unburned or partially burned carbon compounds in exhaust (as from an automobile)

af·ter·care \-ˌke(ə)r, -ˌka(ə)r\ *n* (1894) **:** the care, treatment, help, or supervision given to persons discharged from an institution (as a hospital or prison)

af·ter·clap \-ˌklap\ *n* (14c) **:** an unexpected damaging or unsettling event following a supposedly closed affair

af·ter·damp \-ˌdamp\ *n* (1860) **:** a toxic gas mixture remaining after an explosion of firedamp in mines

af·ter·deck \-ˌdek\ *n* (1897) **:** the part of a deck abaft midships

af·ter·ef·fect \ˈaf-tə-rə-ˌfekt\ *n* (1817) **:** an effect that follows its cause after an interval

af·ter·glow \ˈaf-tər-ˌglō\ *n* (1871) **1 :** a glow remaining where a light has disappeared **2 :** a reflection of past splendor, success, or emotion

af·ter–hours \ˌaf-tə-ˈrau̇(-ə)rz\ *adj* (1955) **:** engaged in or operating after a legal or conventional closing time ⟨~ drinking⟩ ⟨an ~ nightclub⟩

af·ter·im·age \ˈaf-tə-ˌrim-ij\ *n* (1874) **:** a usu. visual sensation occurring after stimulation by its external cause has ceased

af·ter·life \ˈaf-tər-ˌlīf\ *n* (1593) **1 :** an existence after death **2 :** a later period in one's life

af·ter·mar·ket \-ˌmär-kət\ *n* (1940) **:** the market for parts and accessories used in the repair or enhancement of a product (as an automobile)

af·ter·math \-ˌmath\ *n* [[4]*after* + *math* (mowing, crop)] (1523) **1 :** a second-growth crop — called also *rowen* **2 :** CONSEQUENCE, RESULT ⟨stricken with guilt as an ~ of the accident⟩ **3 :** the period immediately following a usu. ruinous event ⟨in the ~ of the war⟩

af·ter·most \-ˌmōst\ *adj* (1773) **:** nearest the stern of a ship **:** farthest aft

af·ter·noon \ˌaf-tər-ˈnün\ *n* (14c) **1 :** the part of day between noon and sunset **2 :** a relatively late period (as of time or life) ⟨in the ~ of the 19th century⟩ — **afternoon** *adj*

af·ter·noons \-ˈnünz\ *adv* (1896) **:** in the afternoon repeatedly **:** on any afternoon

af·ter·piece \ˈaf-tər-ˌpēs\ *n* (1779) **:** a short usu. comic entertainment performed after a play

af·ters \ˈaf-tərz\ *n pl, Brit* (ca. 1909) **:** DESSERT

af·ter–shave \ˈaf-tər-ˌshāv\ *n* (1946) **:** a usu. scented lotion for use on the face after shaving

af·ter·shock \-ˌshäk\ *n* (1894) **:** a minor shock following the main shock of an earthquake

af·ter·taste \-ˌtāst\ *n* (ca. 1798) **:** persistence of a sensation (as of flavor or an emotion) after the stimulating agent or experience has gone

af·ter–tax \ˈaf-tər-ˌtaks\ *adj* (1954) **:** remaining after payment of taxes and esp. of income tax ⟨an ~ profit⟩

af·ter·thought \-ˌthȯt\ *n* (1661) **1 :** an idea occurring later **2 :** a part, feature, or device not thought of originally

af·ter·time \-ˌtīm\ *n* (1571) **:** FUTURE

af·ter·ward \ˈaf-tə(r)-wərd\ *or* **af·ter·wards** \-wərdz\ *adv* (13c) **:** at a later or succeeding time **:** SUBSEQUENTLY, THEREAFTER

af·ter·word \-ˌwərd\ *n* (1890) **:** EPILOGUE 1

af·ter·world \-ˌwərld\ *n* (1596) **:** a future world **:** a world after death

ag \ˈag\ *adj* (ca. 1918) **:** of or relating to agriculture ⟨~ schools⟩

ag- — see AD-

Ag·a·da \ə-ˈgäd-ə, -ˈgȯd-\ *var of* HAGGADAH

again \ə-ˈgen, -ˈgin, -ˈgān\ *adv* [ME, opposite, again, fr. OE *ongēan* opposite, back, fr. *on* + *gēn, gēan* still, again; akin to OE *gēan-* against, OHG *gegin* against, toward] (13c) **1 :** in return **:** BACK ⟨swore he would pay him ~ when he was able —Shak.⟩ **2 :** another time **:** once more **:** ANEW ⟨I shall not look upon his like ~ —Shak.⟩ **3 :** on the other hand ⟨he might go, and ~ he might not⟩ **4 :** in addition **:** BESIDES ⟨~, there is another matter to consider⟩

again and again *adv* (1604) **:** OFTEN, REPEATEDLY

[1]**against** \ə-ˈgen(t)st, -ˈgin(t)st, -ˈgān(t)st\ *prep* [ME, alter. of *againes,* fr. *again*] (12c) **1 a :** directly opposite **:** FACING **b** *obs* **:** exposed to **2 a :** in opposition or hostility to **b :** unfavorable to **c :** as a defense or protection from **3 :** compared or contrasted with **4 :** in preparation or provision for **5 a :** in the direction of and into contact with **b :** in contact with **6 :** in a direction opposite to the motion or course of **:** counter to **7 a :** as a counterbalance to **b :** in exchange for **c :** as a charge on **8 :** before the background of

[2]**against** *conj, archaic* (14c) **:** in preparation for the time when ⟨throw on another log of wood ~ father comes home —Charles Dickens⟩

Ag·a·mem·non \ˌag-ə-ˈmem-ˌnän, -nən\ *n* [L, fr. Gk *Agamemnōn*] **:** a king of Mycenae and leader of the Greeks in the Trojan War

aga·mete \ˌā-gə-ˈmēt, (ˈ)ā-ˈgam-ˌēt\ *n* [ISV, fr. Gk *agametos* unmarried, fr. *a-* + *gamein* to marry — more at GAMETE] (ca. 1920) **:** an asexual reproductive cell (as a spore)

agam·ic \(ˈ)ā-ˈgam-ik\ *adj* [Gk *agamos* unmarried, fr. *a-* + *gamos* marriage — more at BIGAMY] (1850) **:** ASEXUAL, PARTHENOGENETIC — **agam·i·cal·ly** \-i-k(ə-)lē\ *adv*

agam·ma·glob·u·lin·emia \ˌā-ˌgam-ə-ˌgläb-yə-lə-ˈnē-mē-ə\ *n* [NL, fr. *a-* + ISV *gamma globulin* + NL *-emia*] (ca. 1952) **:** a condition in which the body forms few or no gamma globulins or antibodies — **agam·ma·glob·u·lin·emic** \-ˈnē-mik\ *adj*

aga·mo·sper·my \(ˈ)ā-ˈgam-ə-ˌspər-mē, ˈag-ə-mō-ˌspər-\ *n* [Gk *agamos* + E *-spermy*] (1945) **:** APOGAMY; *specif* **:** apogamy in which sexual union is not completed and the embryo is produced from the innermost layer of the integument of the female gametophyte

ag·a·pan·thus \ˌag-ə-ˈpan(t)-thəs\ *n* [NL, genus name, fr. Gk *agapē* + *anthos* flower — more at ANTHOLOGY] (ca. 1789) **:** any of several African plants (genus *Agapanthus*) of the lily family cultivated for their umbels of showy blue or purple flowers

[1]**aga·pe** \ä-ˈgä-(ˌ)pā, ˈäg-ə-ˌpā\ *n* [LL, fr. Gk *agapē*, lit., love] (1607) **1 :** LOVE FEAST **2 :** LOVE 4a

[2]**agape** \ə-ˈgāp *also* -ˈgap\ *adj or adv* (1667) **1 :** wide open **:** GAPING **2 :** being in a state of wonder

agar \ˈäg-ər\ *n* [Malay *agar-agar*] (1889) **1 :** a gelatinous colloidal extractive of a red alga (as of the genera *Gelidium, Gracilaria,* and *Eucheuma*) used esp. in culture media or as a gelling and stabilizing agent in foods **2 :** a culture medium containing agar

agar–agar \ˌäg-ə-ˈräg-ər\ *n* [Malay] (ca. 1813) **:** AGAR

aga·ric \ˈag-ə-rik, ə-ˈgar-ik\ *n* [L *agaricum,* a fungus, fr. Gk *agarikon*] (15c) **1 a :** any of several pore fungi (genus *Fomes*) used esp. in the preparation of punk **b :** the dried fruiting body of a fungus (*F. officinalis*) formerly used in medicine **2 :** any of a family (Agaricaceae) of fungi with the sporophore usu. resembling an umbrella and with numerous lamellae on the underside of the cap

aga·rose \ˈag-ə-ˌrōs, ˈäg-, -ˌrōz\ *n* (1968) **:** a polysaccharide obtained from agar that is used esp. as a supporting medium in electrophoresis

ag·ate \ˈag-ət\ *n, often attrib* [MF, fr. L *achates,* fr. Gk *achatēs*] (1570) **1 :** a fine-grained variegated chalcedony having its colors arranged in stripes, blended in clouds, or showing mosslike forms **2 :** something made of or fitted with agate: as **a :** a drawplate used by gold-wire drawers **b :** a playing marble of agate **3 :** a size of type approximately $5^1/_2$ point

agate line *n* (ca. 1935) **:** a space one column wide and $^1/_{14}$ inch deep used as a unit of measurement in classified advertising

agate ware *n* (1857) **1 :** pottery veined and mottled to resemble agate **2 :** an enameled iron or steel ware for household utensils

aga·ve \ə-ˈgäv-ē\ *n* [NL *Agave,* genus name, fr. L, a daughter of Cadmus, fr. Gk *Agauē*] (ca. 1797) **:** any of a genus (*Agave*) of plants of the amaryllis family having spiny-margined leaves and flowers in tall spreading panicles and including some cultivated for their fiber or for ornament

agaze \ə-ˈgāz\ *adj* (ca. 1902) **:** engaged in the act of gazing

[1]**age** \ˈāj\ *n* [ME, fr. OF *aage,* fr. (assumed) VL *aetaticum,* fr. L *aetat-, aetas,* fr. *aevum* lifetime — more at AYE] (13c) **1 a :** the part of an existence extending from the beginning to any given time ⟨a boy 10 years of ~⟩ **b :** LIFETIME **c :** the time of life at which some particular qualification, power, or capacity arises or rests ⟨the voting ~ is 18⟩; *specif* **:** MAJORITY **d :** one of the stages of life **e :** an advanced stage of life **2 a :** the period contemporary with a person's lifetime or with his active life **b :** GENERATION **c :** a long time — usu. used in pl. ⟨haven't seen him in ~*s*⟩ **3 :** a period of time dominated by a central figure or prominent feature ⟨the ~ of Pericles⟩: as **a :** a period in history or human progress ⟨the ~ of reptiles⟩ ⟨the ~ of exploration⟩ **b :** a cultural period marked by the prominence of a particular item ⟨entering the atomic ~⟩ **c :** a division of geologic time that is usu. shorter than an epoch **4 :** an individual's development measured in terms of the years requisite for like development of an average individual ***syn*** see PERIOD

[2]**age** *vb* **aged; ag·ing** *or* **age·ing** *vi* (14c) **1 :** to become old **:** show the effects or the characteristics of increasing age **2 a :** to acquire a desirable quality by standing undisturbed for some time ⟨after flour is milled it ~*s* —S. C. Prescott & B. E. Proctor⟩ **b :** to become mellow or mature **:** RIPEN ⟨this cheese has *aged* for nearly two years⟩ ~ *vt* **1 :** to cause to become old **2 :** to bring to a state fit for use or to maturity

-age \ij\ *n suffix* [ME, fr. OF, fr. L *-aticum*] **1 :** aggregate **:** collection ⟨track*age*⟩ **2 a :** action **:** process ⟨haul*age*⟩ **b :** cumulative result of ⟨break*age*⟩ **c :** rate of ⟨dos*age*⟩ **3 :** house or place of ⟨orphan*age*⟩ **4 :** state **:** rank ⟨peon*age*⟩ **5 :** charge ⟨post*age*⟩

aged \ˈā-jəd, ˈājd; ˈājd *for 1b*\ *adj* (15c) **1 :** grown old: as **a :** of an advanced age **b :** having attained a specified age ⟨a man ~ 40 years⟩ **c :** well advanced toward reduction to base level — used of topographic features **2 :** typical of old age — **ag·ed·ness** \ˈā-jəd-nəs\ *n*

age–group \ˈāj-ˌgrüp\ *n* (1911) **:** a segment of a population that is of approximately the same age or is within a specified range of ages

age·ism \ˈā-(ˌ)jiz-əm\ *n* (1969) **:** prejudice or discrimination against a particular age-group and esp. the elderly — **age·ist** \-jist\ *adj*

age·less \ˈāj-ləs\ *adj* (1651) **1 :** not growing old or showing the effects of age **2 :** TIMELESS, ETERNAL ⟨~ truths⟩ — **age·less·ly** *adv* — **age·less·ness** *n*

age·long \ˈāj-ˌlȯŋ\ *adj* (1810) **:** lasting for an age **:** EVERLASTING

age–mate \-ˌmāt\ *n* (1583) **:** one who is of about the same age as another

agen·cy \ˈā-jən-sē\ *n, pl* **-cies** (1658) **1 :** the capacity, condition, or state of acting or of exerting power **:** OPERATION **2 :** a person or thing through which power is exerted or an end is achieved **:** INSTRUMENTALITY ⟨communicated through the ~ of his ambassador⟩ **3 a :** the office or function of an agent **b :** the relationship between a principal and his agent **4 :** an establishment engaged in doing business for another ⟨an advertising ~⟩ **5 :** an administrative division (as of a government) ⟨the ~ for consumer protection⟩

agency shop *n* (ca. 1946) **:** a shop in which the union serves as the agent for and receives dues and assessments from all employees in the bargaining unit regardless of union membership

agen·da \ə-ˈjen-də\ *n* [L, neut. pl. of *agendum,* gerundive of *agere*] (1657) **:** a list, outline, or plan of things to be considered or done ⟨~*s* of faculty meetings⟩ — **agen·da·less** \-də-ləs\ *adj*

agen·dum \-dəm\ *n, pl* **-da** \-də\ *or* **-dums** [L] (ca. 1847) **1** : AGENDA **2** : an item on an agenda

agene \'ā-,jēn\ *n* [fr. *Agene,* a trademark] (1932) : NITROGEN TRICHLORIDE

agen·e·sis \(')ā-'jen-ə-səs\ *n* [NL] (ca. 1879) : lack or failure of development (as of a body part)

age·nize \'ā-jə-,nīz\ *vt* **-nized; -niz·ing** (1947) : to treat (flour) with nitrogen trichloride

agent \'ā-jənt\ *n* [ME, fr. ML *agent-, agens,* fr. L, prp. of *agere* to drive, lead, act, do; akin to ON *aka* to travel in a vehicle, Gk *agein* to drive, lead] (15c) **1 a** : something that produces or is capable of producing an effect : an active or efficient cause **b** : a chemically, physically, or biologically active principle **2** : one who acts for or in the place of another by authority from him: as **a** : a representative, emissary, or official of a government ⟨crown ~⟩ ⟨federal ~⟩ **b** : one engaged in undercover activities (as espionage) : SPY ⟨secret ~⟩ **3** : a means or instrument by which a guiding intelligence achieves a result **4** : one that acts or exerts power **5** : a person responsible for his acts

agent–general *n, pl* **agents–general** (1914) : a chief agent; *specif* : the representative in England of a British dominion

Agent Orange *n* [so called fr. the identifying color stripe on its container] (1970) : an herbicide widely used as a defoliant in the Vietnam War that is composed of 2,4-D and 2,4,5-T and contains dioxin as a contaminant

agent pro·vo·ca·teur \'äzh-,äⁿ-prō-,väk-ə-'tər, 'ā-jənt-\ *n, pl* **agents provocateurs** \'äzh-,äⁿ-prō-,väk-ə-'tər, 'ā-jən(t)s-prō-\ [F, lit., provoking agent] (1877) : one employed to associate himself with suspected persons and by pretending sympathy with their aims to incite them to some incriminating action

agent·ry \'ā-jən-trē\ *n, pl* **-ries** (1925) : the office, duties, or activities of an agent

age of consent (ca. 1809) : the age at which one is legally competent to give consent (as to marriage)

age of reason (ca. 1794) **1** : a period characterized by a prevailing belief in the use of reason; *esp* : the 18th century in England and France **2** : the time of life when one begins to be able to distinguish right from wrong

age–old \'ā-'jōld\ *adj* (1904) : having existed for ages : ANCIENT

ag·er·a·tum \,aj-ə-'rāt-əm\ *n, pl* **-tums** [NL, genus name, fr. Gk *agēratos* ageless, fr. *a-* + *gēras* old age — more at CHURL] (1866) : any of a large genus (*Ageratum*) of tropical American composite herbs often cultivated for their small showy heads of blue or white flowers; *also* : any of several related blue-flowered plants (genus *Eupatorium*)

Ag·ge·us \a-'gē-əs\ *n* [LL *Aggaeus,* fr. Gk *Aggaios,* fr. Heb *Ḥaggai*] : HAGGAI

¹ag·gie \'ag-ē\ *n, often cap* [agricultural + *-ie*] (1902) : an agricultural school or college; *also* : a student at such an institution

²aggie *n* [agate + *-ie*] (1915) : a playing marble; *specif* : AGATE 2b

ag·gior·na·men·to \ə-,jór-nə-'men-(,)tō\ *n, pl* **-tos** [It, fr. *aggiornare* to bring up to date, fr. *a* to (fr. L *ad-*) + *giorno* day, fr. LL *diurnum* day — more at JOURNEY] (1964) : a bringing up to date : MODERNIZATION ⟨dedicated to the ~ of the church⟩

¹ag·glom·er·ate \ə-'gläm-ə-,rāt\ *vt* **-at·ed; -at·ing** [L *agglomeratus,* pp. of *agglomerare* to heap up, join, fr. *ad-* + *glomer-, glomus* ball — more at CLAM] (1684) : to gather into a ball, mass, or cluster

²ag·glom·er·ate \-rət\ *adj* (1828) : gathered into a ball, mass, or cluster; *specif* : clustered or growing together but not coherent ⟨an ~ flower head⟩

³ag·glom·er·ate \-rət\ *n* (1830) **1** : a jumbled mass or collection **2** : a rock composed of volcanic fragments of various sizes and degrees of angularity

ag·glom·er·a·tion \ə-,gläm-ə-'rā-shən\ *n* (1774) **1** : the action or process of collecting in a mass **2** : a heap or cluster of disparate elements ⟨urban ~s knit together by the new railways —*Times Lit. Supp.*⟩ — **ag·glom·er·a·tive** \-'gläm-ə-,rāt-iv\ *adj*

ag·glu·ti·na·bil·i·ty \ə-,glüt-ᵊn-ə-'bil-ət-ē\ *n* (1901) : capacity (as of red blood cells) to be agglutinated — **ag·glu·ti·na·ble** \ə-'glüt-ᵊn-ə-bəl\ *adj*

¹ag·glu·ti·nate \ə-'glüt-ᵊn-,āt\ *vb* **-nat·ed; -nat·ing** [L *agglutinatus,* pp. of *agglutinare* to glue to, fr. *ad-* + *glutinare* to glue, fr. *glutin-, gluten* glue — more at GLUTEN] *vt* (1586) **1** : to cause to adhere : FASTEN **2** : to combine into a compound : attach to a base as an affix **3** : to cause to undergo agglutination ~ *vi* **1** : to unite or combine into a group or mass **2** : to form words by agglutination

²ag·glu·ti·nate \-ᵊn-ət, -ᵊn-,āt\ *n* (1952) : a clump of agglutinated material (as blood cells or mineral particles in soil)

ag·glu·ti·na·tion \ə-,glüt-ᵊn-'ā-shən\ *n* (1541) **1** : the action or process of agglutinating **2** : a mass or group formed by the union of separate elements **3** : the formation of derivational or inflectional words by putting together constituents of which each expresses a single definite meaning **4** : a reaction in which particles (as red blood cells or bacteria) suspended in a liquid collect into clumps and which occurs esp. as a serologic response to a specific antibody

ag·glu·ti·na·tive \ə-'glüt-ᵊn-,āt-iv, -ət-\ *adj* (1634) **1** : ADHESIVE **2** : characterized by linguistic agglutination

ag·glu·ti·nin \ə-'glüt-ᵊn-ən\ *n* [ISV *agglutination* + *-in*] (1896) : a substance (as an antibody) producing agglutination

ag·glu·ti·no·gen \ə-'glüt-ᵊn-ə-jən\ *n* [*agglutinin* + *-o-* + *-gen*] (1904) : an antigen whose presence results in the formation of an agglutinin — **ag·glu·ti·no·gen·ic** \-,glüt-ᵊn-ə-'jen-ik\ *adj*

ag·gra·da·tion \,ag-rə-'dā-shən\ *n* (1898) : a modification of the earth's surface in the direction of uniformity of grade by deposition

ag·grade \ə-'grād\ *vt* [*ad-* + *grade*] (1896) : to fill with detrital material

ag·gran·dize \ə-'gran-,dīz *also* 'ag-rən-\ *vt* **-dized; -diz·ing** [F *agrandiss-,* stem of *agrandir,* fr. *a-* (fr. L *ad-*) + *grandir* to increase, fr. L *grandire,* fr. *grandis* great] (1634) **1** : to make great or greater : INCREASE, ENLARGE **2** : to make appear great or greater : praise highly ⟨*aggrandized* the one and disparaged the other⟩ **3** : to enhance the power, wealth, position, or reputation of ⟨exploited the situation to ~ himself⟩ — **ag·gran·dize·ment** \ə-'gran-dəz-mənt, -,dīz- *also* ,ag-rən-'dīz-\ *n* — **ag·gran·diz·er** \ə-'gran-,dī-zər *also* 'ag-rən-\ *n*

ag·gra·vate \'ag-rə-,vāt\ *vt* **-vat·ed; -vat·ing** [L *aggravatus,* pp. of *aggravare* to make heavier, fr. *ad-* + *gravare* to burden, fr. *gravis* heavy — more at GRIEVE] (1530) **1** *obs* **a** : to make heavy : BURDEN **b** : INCREASE **2** : to make worse, more serious, or more severe : intensify unpleasantly ⟨problems have been *aggravated* by neglect⟩ **3 a** : to rouse to displeasure or anger by usu. persistent and often petty goading **b** : to produce inflammation in ***syn*** see INTENSIFY

usage Although *aggravate* has been used in sense 3a since the 17th century, it has been the object of disapproval only since about 1870. It is used in expository prose ⟨declining to participate directly in the motorcade . . . greatly *aggravating* the President —W. F. Buckley *b* 1925⟩ but seems to be more common in speech and casual writing ⟨our two countries *aggravate* each other from time to time —O. W. Holmes †1935 (letter to Sir Frederick Pollock, 1895)⟩ ⟨times when we get *aggravated* and displeased, for instance, with the French —Jimmy Carter (press conference, 1980)⟩ Sense 2 is far more common than sense 3a in published prose. Such is not the case, however, with *aggravation* and *aggravating. Aggravation* is used in sense 3 somewhat more than in its earlier senses; *aggravating* has practically no use other than to express annoyance

aggravated assault *n* (1925) : an assault that is more serious than a common assault: as **a** : an assault combined with an intent to commit a crime **b** : any of various assaults so defined by statute

ag·gra·va·ting *adj* (1775) : arousing displeasure, impatience, or anger ***usage*** see AGGRAVATE

ag·gra·va·tion \,ag-rə-'vā-shən\ *n* (1615) **1** : the act, action, or result of aggravating; *esp* : an increasing in seriousness or severity **2** : an act or circumstance that intensifies or makes worse **3** : IRRITATION, PROVOCATION ***usage*** see AGGRAVATE

¹ag·gre·gate \'ag-ri-gət\ *adj* [ME *aggregat,* fr. L *aggregatus,* pp. of *aggregare* to add to, fr. *ad-* + *greg-, grex* flock — more at GREGARIOUS] (15c) : formed by the collection of units or particles into a body, mass, or amount : COLLECTIVE: as **a** (1) : clustered in a dense mass or head ⟨an ~ flower⟩ (2) : formed from the several ovaries of a single flower **b** : composed of mineral crystals of one or more kinds or of mineral rock fragments **c** : taking all units as a whole ⟨~ sales⟩ — **ag·gre·gate·ly** *adv* — **ag·gre·gate·ness** *n*

²ag·gre·gate \-,gāt\ *vt* **-gat·ed; -gat·ing** (15c) **1** : to collect or gather into a mass or whole **2** : to amount in the aggregate to : TOTAL

³ag·gre·gate \-gət\ *n* (15c) **1** : the whole sum or amount : SUM TOTAL **2** : a mass or body of units or parts somewhat loosely associated with one another **3 a** : an aggregate rock **b** : any of several hard inert materials (as sand, gravel, or slag) used for mixing with a cementing material to form concrete, mortar, or plaster **c** : a clustered mass of individual soil particles varied in shape, ranging in size from a microscopic granule to a small crumb, and considered the basic structural unit of soil **4** : SET 21 — **in the aggregate** : considered as a whole : COLLECTIVELY ⟨dividends for the year amounted *in the aggregate* to 25 million dollars⟩

ag·gre·ga·tion \,ag-ri-'gā-shən\ *n* (1547) **1** : a group, body, or mass composed of many distinct parts or individuals (as animals) **2 a** : the collecting of units or parts into a mass or whole **b** : the condition of being so collected — **ag·gre·ga·tion·al** \-shnəl, -shən-ᵊl\ *adj*

ag·gre·ga·tive \'ag-ri-,gāt-iv\ *adj* (1644) **1** : of or relating to an aggregate **2** : tending to aggregate — **ag·gre·ga·tive·ly** *adv*

ag·gress \ə-'gres\ *vi* (1714) : to commit aggression : act aggressively ⟨inmates always ~*ing* against their keepers —H. J. Mattick⟩

ag·gres·sion \ə-'gresh-ən\ *n* [L *aggressus,* pp. of *aggredi* to attack, fr. *ad-* + *gradi* to step, go — more at GRADE] (1611) **1** : a forceful action or procedure (as an unprovoked attack) esp. when intended to dominate or master **2** : the practice of making attacks or encroachments; *esp* : unprovoked violation by one country of the territorial integrity of another **3** : hostile, injurious, or destructive behavior or outlook esp. when caused by frustration

ag·gres·sive \ə-'gres-iv\ *adj* (1824) **1 a** : tending toward or exhibiting aggression ⟨~ behavior⟩ **b** : marked by combative readiness ⟨an ~ fighter⟩ **2 a** : marked by driving forceful energy or initiative : ENTERPRISING ⟨an ~ salesman⟩ **b** : marked by obtrusive energy **3** : HARSH, INTENSE ⟨~ colors⟩ — **ag·gres·sive·ly** *adv* — **ag·gres·sive·ness** *n* — **ag·gres·siv·i·ty** \,ag-,re-'siv-ət-ē\ *n*

syn AGGRESSIVE, MILITANT, ASSERTIVE, SELF-ASSERTIVE, PUSHING mean obtrusively energetic esp. in pursuing particular goals. AGGRESSIVE implies a disposition to dominate often in disregard of others' rights or in determined and energetic pursuit of one's ends; MILITANT also implies a fighting disposition but suggests not self-seeking but devotion to a cause, movement, or principle; ASSERTIVE suggests bold self-confidence in expression of opinion; SELF-ASSERTIVE connotes forwardness or brash self-confidence; PUSHING may apply to ambition or enterprise or to snobbish and crude intrusiveness or officiousness.

ag·gres·sor \ə-'gres-ər\ *n* (1646) : one that commits or practices aggression

ag·grieve \ə-'grēv\ *vt* **ag·grieved; ag·griev·ing** [ME *agreven,* fr. MF *agrever,* fr. L *aggravare* to make heavier] (14c) **1** : to give pain or trouble to : DISTRESS **2** : to inflict injury on ***syn*** see WRONG

ag·grieved \ə-'grēvd\ *adj* (14c) **1** : troubled or distressed in spirit **2 a** : showing or expressing grief, injury, or offense ⟨an ~ plea⟩ **b** : suffering from an infringement or denial of legal rights ⟨~ minority groups⟩ — **ag·griev·ed·ly** \-'grē-vəd-lē\ *adv*

ag·grieve·ment \ə-'grēv-mənt\ *n* (1847) : the quality or state of being aggrieved

ag·gro \'ag-(,)rō\ *n, pl* **aggros** [by shortening and alter. fr. *aggravation*] (1969) **1** *Brit* : EXASPERATION, IRRITATION **2** *Brit* : a rivalry or grievance and esp. one public in nature that is marked by mistrust, rancor, and often violence

aghast \ə-'gast\ *adj* [ME *agast,* fr. pp. of *agasten* to frighten, fr. *a-* (perfective prefix) + *gasten* to frighten — more at ABIDE, GAST] (13c) : struck with terror, amazement, or horror : SHOCKED

ag·ile \'aj-əl, -,īl\ *adj* [MF, fr. L *agilis,* fr. *agere* to drive, act — more at AGENT] (1577) **1** : marked by ready ability to move with quick easy grace **2** : mentally quick and resourceful — **ag·ile·ly** \-ə(l)-lē, -,ī(l)-lē\ *adv*

agil·i·ty \ə-'jil-ət-ē\ *n, pl* **-ties** (15c) : the quality or state of being agile : NIMBLENESS, DEXTERITY ⟨played with increasing ~⟩

agin \ə-'gin\ *dial var of* AGAINST

aging *pres part of* AGE

ag·i·tate \ˈaj-ə-ˌtāt\ *vb* **-tat·ed; -tat·ing** [L *agitatus,* pp. of *agitare,* freq. of *agere* to drive — more at AGENT] *vt* (15c) **1 a** *obs* : to give motion to **b** : to move with an irregular, rapid, or violent action ⟨the storm *agitated* the sea⟩ **2** : to excite and often trouble the mind or feelings of : DISTURB **3 a** : to discuss excitedly and earnestly **b** : to stir up public discussion of ~ *vi* : to attempt to arouse public feeling ⟨*agitated* for better schools⟩ ***syn*** see SHAKE, DISCOMPOSE — **ag·i·tat·ed·ly** *adv* — **ag·i·ta·tion** \ˌaj-ə-ˈtā-shən\ *n* — **ag·i·ta·tion·al** \-shnəl, -shən-ᵊl\ *adj*

ag·i·ta·tive \ˈaj-ə-ˌtāt-iv\ *adj* (1687) : causing or tending to cause agitation

ag·i·ta·to \ˌaj-ə-ˈtät-(ˌ)ō\ *adv or adj* [It, lit., agitated, fr. L *agitatus*] (ca. 1819) : in a restless and agitated manner — used as a direction in music

ag·i·ta·tor \ˈaj-ə-ˌtāt-ər\ *n* (1734) : one that agitates: as **a** : one who stirs up public feeling on controversial issues ⟨political ~*s*⟩ **b** : a device or an apparatus for stirring or shaking

ag·it·prop \ˈaj-ət-ˌpräp\ *n* [Russ, office of agitation and propaganda, fr. *agitatsiya* agitation + *propaganda*] (ca. 1926) **1** : PROPAGANDA; *esp* : political and typically pro-communist propaganda promulgated chiefly in literature, drama, music, or art **2** : the means (as a government department or a medium of communication) by which agitprop is disseminated — **agitprop** *adj*

Aglaia \ə-ˈglī-ə, -ˈglā-(y)ə\ *n* [L, fr. Gk] : one of the three Graces

aglare \ə-ˈgla(ə)r, -ˈgle(ə)r\ *adj* (1872) : GLARING ⟨his eyes ~ with fury⟩

agleam \ə-ˈglēm\ *adj* (1870) : reflecting light by gleaming

ag·let \ˈag-lət\ *n* [ME *aglet,* fr. MF *aguillette, aiguillette,* dim. of *aguille, aiguille* needle, fr. LL *acicula, acucula* ornamental pin, dim. of L *acus* needle, pin — more at ACUTE] (15c) **1** : the plain or ornamental tag covering the ends of a lace or point **2** : any of various ornamental studs, cords, or pins worn on clothing

agley \ə-ˈglā, -ˈglē, -ˈglī\ *adv* [Sc, lit., squintingly, fr. [1]*a-* + *gley* to squint] *chiefly Scot* (1785) : AWRY, WRONG ⟨the best-laid schemes o' mice an' men gang aft ~ —Robert Burns⟩

aglit·ter \ə-ˈglit-ər\ *adj* (1865) : reflecting light by glittering

aglow \ə-ˈglō\ *adj* (1817) : radiant with warmth or excitement

agly·cone \ag-ˈlī-ˌkōn\ *also* **agly·con** \-ˌkän\ *n* [ISV *a-* (fr. Gk *ha-, a-* together) + *glyc-* + *-one, -on*] (1925) : an organic compound (as a phenol or alcohol) combined with the sugar portion of a glycoside

[1]**ag·nate** \ˈag-ˌnāt\ *n* [L *agnatus,* fr. pp. of *agnasci* to be born in addition to, fr. *ad-* + *nasci* to be born — more at NATION] (1534) **1** : a relative whose kinship is traceable exclusively through males **2** : a paternal kinsman

[2]**agnate** *adj* (1782) **1** : ALLIED, AKIN **2** : related through male descent or on the father's side — **ag·nat·ic** \ag-ˈnat-ik\ *adj*

Ag·ne·an \ˈäg-nē-ən\ *n* [*Agni,* ancient kingdom in Turkestan] (1939) : TOCHARIAN A

ag·nize \ag-ˈnīz\ *vt* **ag·nized; ag·niz·ing** [L *agnoscere* to acknowledge (fr. *ad-* + *noscere* to know) + E *-ize* (as in *recognize*) — more at KNOW] *archaic* (1535) : RECOGNIZE, ACKNOWLEDGE

ag·no·men \ag-ˈnō-mən\ *n, pl* **-nom·i·na** \-ˈnäm-ə-nə\ *or* **-no·mens** [L, irreg. fr. *ad-* + *nomen* name — more at NAME] (1665) : an additional cognomen given to a person by the ancient Romans (as in honor of some achievement)

ag·no·sia \ag-ˈnō-zhə, -shə\ *n* [NL, fr. Gk *agnōsia* ignorance, fr. *a-* + *-gnosis* — more at KNOW] (ca. 1900) : loss or diminution of the ability to recognize familiar objects usu. as a result of brain damage

[1]**ag·nos·tic** \ag-ˈnäs-tik, əg-\ *n* [Gk *agnōstos* unknown, unknowable, fr. *a-* + *gnōstos* known, fr. *gignōskein* to know — more at KNOW] (1870) : one who holds the view that any ultimate reality (as God) is unknown and prob. unknowable — **ag·nos·ti·cism** \-tə-ˌsiz-əm\ *n*

[2]**agnostic** *adj* (1873) **1** : of, relating to, or being an agnostic or the beliefs of agnostics **2** : NONCOMMITTAL, UNDOGMATIC

Ag·nus Dei \ˌäg-ˌnu̇s-ˈdā-(ˌē), -ˌnüs-; ˌän-yu̇s-; ˌag-nəs-\ *n* [ME, fr. LL, lamb of God; fr. its opening words] (14c) **1** : a liturgical prayer addressed to Christ as Savior **2** : an image of a lamb often with a halo and a banner and cross used as a symbol of Christ

ago \ə-ˈgō\ *adj or adv* [ME *agon, ago,* fr. pp. of *agon* to pass away, fr. OE *āgān,* fr. *ā-* (perfective prefix) + *gān* to go — more at ABIDE, GO] (14c) : earlier than the present time ⟨10 years ~⟩

agog \ə-ˈgäg\ *adj* [MF *en gogues* in mirth] (1542) : full of intense interest or excitement : EAGER ⟨kids all ~ over new toys⟩

[1]**a-go-go** \ä-ˈgō-(ˌ)gō, ə-\ *n* [*Whisky à Gogo,* café and discotheque in Paris, France, from F *à gogo* galore, fr. MF] (1965) : a nightclub for dancing to pop music : DISCOTHEQUE

[2]**a-go-go** *adj* (1965) : GO-GO 1, 2

-a·gogue \ə-ˌgäg\ *n comb form* [F & NL; F, fr. LL *-agogus* promoting the expulsion of, fr. Gk *-agōgos,* fr. *agein* to lead; NL *-agogon,* fr. Gk, neut. of *-agōgos* — more at AGENT] : substance that promotes the secretion or expulsion of ⟨emmen*agogue*⟩

agon \ˈäg-ˌän, ä-ˈgōn\ *n* [Gk *agōn*] (1600) : CONTEST, CONFLICT; *specif* : the dramatic conflict between the chief characters in a literary work

ag·o·nal \ˈag-ən-ᵊl\ *adj* (ca. 1900) : of, relating to, or associated with agony and esp. the death agony

agone \ə-ˈgȯn *also* -ˈgän\ *adj or adv, archaic* (14c) : AGO

agon·ic line \(ˈ)ā-ˈgän-ik-, ə-\ *n* [Gk *agōnos* without angle, fr. *a-* + *gōnia* angle — more at -GON] (ca. 1859) : an imaginary line passing through points where there is no magnetic declination and where a freely suspended magnetic needle indicates true north

ag·o·nist \ˈag-ə-nəst\ *n* [LL *agonista* competitor, fr. Gk *agōnistēs,* fr. *agōnizesthai* to contend, fr. *agōn*] (ca. 1626) **1** : one that is engaged in a struggle **2** [back-formation fr. *antagonist*] **a** : a muscle that is controlled by the action of an antagonist with which it is paired **b** : a chemical substance capable of combining with a nervous receptor and initiating a reaction — compare ANTAGONIST 2b

ag·o·nis·tic \ˌag-ə-ˈnis-tik\ *adj* (1648) **1** : of or relating to the athletic contests of ancient Greece **2** : ARGUMENTATIVE **3** : striving for effect : STRAINED **4** : of, relating to, or being aggressive or defensive social interaction (as fighting, fleeing, or submitting) between individuals usu. of the same species — **ag·o·nis·ti·cal·ly** \-ti-k(ə-)lē\ *adv*

ag·o·nize \ˈag-ə-ˌnīz\ *vb* **-nized; -niz·ing** *vt* (1583) : to cause to suffer agony : TORTURE ~ *vi* **1** : to suffer agony, torture, or anguish ⟨~*s* over every decision⟩ **2** : STRUGGLE

ag·o·nized *adj* (1583) : characterized by, suffering, or expressing agony

ag·o·niz·ing *adj* (1686) : causing agony : PAINFUL — **ag·o·niz·ing·ly** *adv*

ag·o·ny \ˈag-ə-nē\ *n, pl* **-nies** [ME *agonie,* fr. LL *agonia,* fr. Gk *agōnia* struggle, anguish, fr. *agōn* gathering, contest for a prize, fr. *agein* to lead, celebrate — more at AGENT] (14c) **1 a** : intense pain of mind or body : ANGUISH, TORTURE **b** : the struggle that precedes death **2** : a violent struggle or contest **3** : a strong sudden display (as of joy or delight) : OUTBURST ***syn*** see DISTRESS

agony column *n* (1863) : a newspaper column of personal advertisements relating esp. to missing relatives or friends

[1]**ag·o·ra** \ˈag-ə-rə\ *n, pl* **-ras** *or* **-rae** \-ˌrē, -ˌrī\ [Gk — more at GREGARIOUS] (1589) : a gathering place; *esp* : the marketplace in ancient Greece

[2]**ago·ra** \ˌäg-ə-ˈrä\ *n, pl* **ago·rot** \-ˈrōt\ [NHeb *ăgōrāh,* fr. Heb, a small coin] (1963) — see *shekel* at MONEY table

ag·o·ra·pho·bia \ˌag(-ə)-rə-ˈfō-bē-ə\ *n* [NL, fr. Gk *agora* + NL *phobia*] (1873) : abnormal fear of crossing or of being in open or public places — **ag·o·ra·pho·bi·ac** \-ˈfō-bē-ˌak\ *n* — **ag·o·ra·pho·bic** \-ˈfō-bik\ *adj or n*

agou·ti \ə-ˈgüt-ē\ *n* [F, fr. Sp. *agutí,* fr. Guarani] (1625) **1** : a tropical American rodent (genus *Dasyprocta* or *Myoprocta*) about the size of a rabbit **2** : a grizzled color of fur resulting from the barring of each hair in several alternate dark and light bands

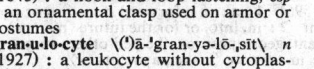

agouti 1

agrafe *or* **agraffe** \ə-ˈgraf\ *n* [F *agrafe*] (1643) : a hook-and-loop fastening; *esp* : an ornamental clasp used on armor or costumes

agran·u·lo·cyte \(ˈ)ā-ˈgran-yə-lō-ˌsīt\ *n* (1927) : a leukocyte without cytoplasmic granules

agran·u·lo·cy·to·sis \ˌā-ˌgran-yə-lō-ˌsī-ˈtō-səs\ *n, pl* **-to·ses** \-ˈtō-ˌsēz\ (ca. 1923) : an acute febrile condition marked by severe decrease in blood granulocytes and often associated with the use of certain drugs

ag·ra·pha \ˈag-rə-fə\ *n pl* [Gk, neut. pl. of *agraphos* unwritten, fr. *a-* + *graphein* to write — more at CARVE] (1890) : sayings of Jesus not in the canonical gospels but found in other New Testament or early Christian writings

agraph·ia \(ˈ)ā-ˈgraf-ē-ə\ *n* [NL, fr. [2]*a-* + Gk *graphein* to write] (1871) : the pathologic loss of the ability to write

[1]**agrar·i·an** \ə-ˈgrer-ē-ən, -ˈgrar-\ *adj* [L *agrarius,* fr. *agr-, ager* field — more at ACRE] (1618) **1** : of or relating to fields or lands or their tenure **2 a** : of, relating to, or characteristic of the farmer or his way of life **b** : organized or designed to promote agricultural interests ⟨an ~ political party⟩ ⟨~ reforms⟩

[2]**agrarian** *n* (1818) : a member of an agrarian party or movement

agrar·i·an·ism \-ē-ə-ˌniz-əm\ *n* (1830) : a social or political movement designed to bring about land reforms or to improve the economic status of the farmer

agree \ə-ˈgrē\ *vb* **agreed; agree·ing** [ME *agreen,* fr. MF *agreer,* fr. *a-* (fr. L *ad-*) + *gre* will, pleasure, fr. L *gratum,* neut. of *gratus* pleasing, agreeable — more at GRACE] *vt* (15c) **1** : ADMIT, CONCEDE **2** : to settle on by common consent : ARRANGE ~ *vi* **1** : to accept or concede something (as the views or wishes of another) typically after resolving points of disagreement **2 a** : to achieve or be in harmony (as of opinion, feeling, or purpose) **b** : to get along together **c** : to come to terms **3 a** : to be similar : CORRESPOND ⟨both copies ~⟩ **b** : to be consistent ⟨the story ~*s* with the facts⟩ **4** : to be fitting, pleasing, or healthful : SUIT ⟨this climate ~*s* with him⟩ **5** : to have an inflectional form denoting identity or a regular correspondence other than identity in a grammatical category (as gender, number, case, or person)

syn AGREE, CONCUR, COINCIDE mean to come into or be in harmony regarding a matter of opinion. AGREE implies complete accord usually attained by discussion and adjustment of differences ⟨on some points we all can *agree*⟩ CONCUR tends to suggest cooperative thinking or acting toward an end ⟨for the creation of a masterwork of literature two powers must *concur,* the power of the man and the power of the moment —Matthew Arnold⟩ but sometimes implies no more than approval (as of a decision reached by others). COINCIDE, used more often of opinions, judgments, wishes, or interests than of people, implies an agreement amounting to identity ⟨their wishes *coincide* exactly with my desire⟩ ***syn*** see in addition ASSENT

agree·able \ə-ˈgrē-ə-bəl\ *adj* (14c) **1** : pleasing to the mind or senses esp. as according well with one's tastes or needs ⟨an ~ companion⟩ ⟨an ~ change⟩ **2** : ready or willing to agree or consent **3** : being in harmony : CONSONANT — **agree·abil·i·ty** \-ˌgrē-ə-ˈbil-ət-ē\ *n* — **agree·able·ness** \-ˈgrē-ə-bəl-nəs\ *n* — **agree·ably** \-blē\ *adv*

agree·ment \ə-ˈgrē-mənt\ *n* (15c) **1 a** : the act or fact of agreeing **b** : harmony of opinion, action, or character : CONCORD **2 a** : an arrangement as to a course of action **b** : COMPACT, TREATY **3 a** : a contract duly executed and legally binding **b** : the language or instrument embodying such a contract

ag·ri·busi·ness \ˈag-rə-ˌbiz-nəs, -nəz\ *n* [*agriculture* + *business*] (ca. 1955) : a combination of the producing operations of a farm, the manufacture and distribution of farm equipment and supplies, and the processing, storage, and distribution of farm commodities

ag·ri·cul·tur·al \ˌag-ri-ˈkəlch-(ə-)rəl\ *adj* (1776) : of, relating to, used in, or concerned with agriculture — **ag·ri·cul·tur·al·ly** \-ē\ *adv*

ag·ri·cul·ture \ˈag-ri-ˌkəl-chər\ *n* [ME, fr. MF, fr. L *agricultura,* fr. *ager* field + *cultura* cultivation — more at ACRE, CULTURE] (15c) : the science or art of cultivating the soil, producing crops, and raising livestock and in varying degrees the preparation of these products for man's use and their disposal (as by marketing) : FARMING — **ag·ri·cul·tur·ist** \ˌag-ri-ˈkəlch-(ə-)rəst\ *or* **ag·ri·cul·tur·al·ist** \-(ə-)rə-ləst\ *n*

ag·ri·mo·ny \ˈag-rə-ˌmō-nē\ *n, pl* **-nies** [ME, fr. MF & L; MF *aigremoine,* fr. L *agrimonia,* MS var. of *argemonia,* fr. Gk *argemōnē*] (14c) : any of a genus (*Agrimonia* and esp. *A. eupatoria*) of herbs of the rose family with compound leaves that bear slender spikes of small yellow flowers and fruits like burs

\ə\ abut \ᵊ\ kitten, F table \ər\ further \a\ ash \ā\ ace \ä\ cot, cart
\au̇\ out \ch\ chin \e\ bet \ē\ easy \g\ go \i\ hit \ī\ ice \j\ job
\ŋ\ sing \ō\ go \ȯ\ law \ȯi\ boy \th\ thin \th\ the \ü\ loot \u̇\ foot
\y\ yet \zh\ vision \à, k, ⁿ, œ, ǣ, ue, ue̅, ʸ\ *see* Guide to Pronunciation

agro- *comb form* [F, fr. Gk, fr. *agros* field — more at ACRE] **1 :** of or belonging to fields or soil : agricultural ⟨*agro*chemical⟩ **2 :** agricultural and ⟨*agro*-industrial⟩
ag·ro·chem·i·cal \ˌag-rō-ˈkem-i-kəl\ *also* **ag·ri·chem·i·cal** \ˌag-ri-\ *n* (1956) : an agricultural chemical (as an herbicide or an insecticide)
ag·ro–in·dus·tri·al \ˌag-rō-in-ˈdəs-trē-əl\ *adj* (ca. 1940) : of or relating to production (as of power for industry and water for irrigation) for both industrial and agricultural purposes
agron·o·my \ə-ˈgrän-ə-mē\ *n* [prob. fr. F *agronomie,* fr. *agro-* + *-nomie* -nomy] (1814) : a branch of agriculture dealing with field-crop production and soil management — **ag·ro·nom·ic** \ˌag-rə-ˈnäm-ik\ *adj* — **ag·ro·nom·i·cal·ly** \-i-k(ə-)lē\ *adv* — **agron·o·mist** \ə-ˈgrän-ə-məst\ *n*
aground \ə-ˈgrau̇nd\ *adv or adj* (1500) **1 :** on or onto the shore or the bottom of a body of water ⟨a ship run ~⟩ **2 :** on the ground ⟨planes aloft and ~⟩
ague \ˈā-(ˌ)gyü\ *n* [ME, fr. MF *ague,* fr. ML (*febris*) *acuta,* lit., sharp fever, fr. L, fem. of *acutus* sharp — more at ACUTE] (14c) **1 :** a fever (as malaria) marked by paroxysms of chills, fever, and sweating that recur at regular intervals **2 :** a fit of shivering : CHILL — **agu·ish** \ˈā-gyü-ish\ *adj*
ah \ˈä\ *interj* [ME] (13c) — used to express delight, relief, regret, or contempt
aha \ä-ˈhä\ *interj* [ME] (14c) — used to express surprise, triumph, or derision
ahead \ə-ˈhed\ *adv or adj* (1596) **1 a :** in a forward direction or position : FORWARD **b :** in front **2 :** in, into, or for the future ⟨plan ~⟩ **3 :** in or toward a more advantageous position ⟨helped others to get ~⟩ **4 :** at or to an earlier time : in advance ⟨make payments ~⟩
ahead of *prep* (1748) **1 :** in front or advance of **2 :** in excess of
ahem *a throat-clearing sound; often read as* ə-ˈhem\ *interj* [imit.] (1763) — used esp. to attract attention
ahim·sa \ə-ˈhim-ˌsä\ *n* [Skt *ahiṁsā* noninjury] (1875) : the Hindu and Buddhist doctrine of refraining from harming any living being
ahis·tor·i·cal \ˌā-his-ˈtȯr-i-kəl, -ˈtär-\ *or* **ahis·tor·ic** \-ik\ *adj* (1945) : not concerned with or related to history, historical development, or tradition ⟨the ~ attitudes of the radicals⟩
ahold \ə-ˈhōld\ *n* [prob. fr. the phrase *a hold*] (1872) : HOLD ⟨if you could get ~ of a representative —Norman Mailer⟩
A–ho·ri·zon \ˈā-hə-ˌrīz-ᵊn\ *n* (1936) : the uppermost dark-colored layer of a soil consisting largely of partly disintegrated organic debris
ahoy \ə-ˈhȯi\ *interj* [*a-* (as in *aha*) + *hoy*] (1751) — used in hailing ⟨ship ~⟩
Ah·ri·man \ˈär-i-mən, -ˌmän\ *n* [Per, modif. of Av *aṅrō mainyuš* hostile spirit] : Ahura Mazda's antagonist who is a spirit of darkness and evil in Zoroastrianism
Ahu·ra Maz·da \ə-ˌhu̇r-ə-ˈmaz-də, ä-ˌhu̇r-\ *n* [Av *Ahuramazda,* lit., wise god] : the Supreme Being represented as a deity of goodness and light in Zoroastrianism
Ai·as \ˈī-əs\ *n* [Gk] : AJAX
ai·blins \ˈā-blənz\ *adv* [*able* + *-lings, -lins* -lings] *chiefly Scot* (1597) : PERHAPS
[1]**aid** \ˈād\ *vb* [ME *eyden,* fr. MF *aider,* fr. L *adjutare,* fr. *adjutus,* pp. of *adjuvare,* fr. *ad-* + *juvare* to help] *vt* (15c) : to provide with what is useful or necessary in achieving an end ~ *vi* : to give assistance ***syn*** see HELP — **aid·er** *n*
[2]**aid** *n* (15c) **1 :** a subsidy granted to the king by the English parliament until the 18th century for an extraordinary purpose **2 a :** the act of helping **b :** help given : ASSISTANCE; *specif* : tangible means of assistance (as money or supplies) **3 a :** an assisting person or group — compare AIDE **b :** something by which assistance is given : an assisting device ⟨an ~ to understanding⟩ ⟨a visual ~⟩; *specif* : HEARING AID **4 :** a tribute paid by a vassal to his lord
aide \ˈād\ *n* [short for *aide-de-camp*] (1777) : a person who acts as an assistant; *specif* : a military officer acting as assistant to a superior
aide–de–camp \ˌād-di-ˈkamp, -ˈkäⁿ\ *n, pl* **aides–de–camp** \ˌād(z)-di-\ [F *aide de camp,* lit., camp assistant] (1670) : a military aide; *also* : a civilian aide usu. to an executive
aide–mé·moire \ˌād-mām-ˈwär\ *n, pl* **aide–mémoire** [F, fr. *aider* to aid + *mémoire* memory] (1846) **1 :** an aid to the memory; *esp* : a mnemonic device **2 :** a written summary or outline of important items of a proposed agreement or diplomatic communication : MEMORANDUM
aid·man \ˈād-ˌman\ *n* (1944) : an army medical corpsman attached to a field unit
AIDS \ˈādz\ *n* [*a*cquired *i*mmuno*d*eficiency *s*yndrome] (1982) : a condition of acquired immunological deficiency associated with infection of the cells of the immune system by a retrovirus, occurring esp. in homosexual and bisexual men and in intravenous drug abusers, and recognized clinically usu. by a life-threatening infection (esp. pneumonia caused by the microorganism *Pneumocystis carinii*) or Kaposi's sarcoma or both in addition to marked depression of the immune system
AIDS–related complex *n* (1984) : a collection of symptoms that includes fever, weight loss, and lymphadenopathy, is associated with the presence of antibodies to the AIDS virus, and is followed by the development of AIDS in a certain proportion of cases
AIDS virus *n* (1985) : the retrovirus associated with AIDS and the AIDS-related complex — called also *HIV, human immunodeficiency virus*
ai·grette \ā-ˈgret, ˈā-ˌ\ *n* [F, plume, egret, fr. MF — more at EGRET] (1630) **1 :** a spray of feathers (as of the egret) for the head **2 :** a spray of gems worn on a hat or in the hair
ai·guille \ā-ˈgwē(ə)l, -ˈgwē\ *n* [F, lit., needle — more at AGLET] (1816) : a sharp-pointed pinnacle of rock
ai·guil·lette \ˌā-gwi-ˈlet\ *n* [F — more at AGLET] (1816) : AGLET; *specif* : a shoulder cord worn by designated military aides — compare FOURRAGÈRE
ai·ki·do \ˌī-ki-ˈdō, ī-ˈkē-(ˌ)dō\ *n* [Jp *aikidō,* fr. *ai-* match, coordinate + *ki* breath, spirit + *dō* art, way] (1963) : a Japanese art of self-defense employing locks and holds and utilizing the principle of nonresistance to cause an opponent's own momentum to work against him
[1]**ail** \ˈā(ə)l\ *vb* [ME *eilen,* fr. OE *eglan;* akin to MLG *egelen* to annoy] *vt* (bef. 12c) : to give physical or emotional pain, discomfort, or trouble to ~ *vi* : to have something the matter; *esp* : to suffer ill health
[2]**ail** *n* (13c) : AILMENT
ai·lan·thus \ā-ˈlan(t)-thəs\ *n* [NL, fr. Amboinese *ai lanto,* lit., tree (of) heaven] (ca. 1807) : any of a small Asian genus (*Ailanthus* of the family Simaroubaceae, the ailanthus family) of chiefly tropical trees and shrubs with bitter bark, pinnate leaves, and terminal panicles of ill-scented greenish flowers
ai·le·ron \ˈā-lə-ˌrän\ *n* [F, fr. dim. of *aile* wing — more at AISLE] (1909) : a movable part of an airplane wing or a movable airfoil external to the wing at the trailing edge for imparting a rolling motion and thus providing lateral control — see AIRPLANE illustration
ail·ment \ˈā(ə)l-mənt\ *n* (ca. 1706) **1 :** a bodily disorder or chronic disease **2 :** UNREST, UNEASINESS
ai·lu·ro·phile \ī-ˈlu̇r-ə-ˌfīl, ā-\ *n* [Gk *ailouros* cat] (1927) : a cat fancier : a lover of cats
ai·lu·ro·phobe \-ˌfōb\ *n* (1905) : one who hates or fears cats
[1]**aim** \ˈām\ *vb* [ME *aimen,* fr. MF *aesmer* & *esmer;* MF *aesmer,* fr. OF, fr. *a-* (fr. L *ad-*) + *esmer* to estimate, fr. L *aestimare* — more at ESTEEM] *vi* (14c) **1 :** to direct a course; *specif* : to point a weapon at an object **2 :** ASPIRE, INTEND ⟨~*s* to reform the government⟩ ~ *vt* **1** *obs* : GUESS, CONJECTURE **2 a :** POINT **b :** to direct to or toward a specified object or goal ⟨a program ~*ed* at reducing pollution⟩
[2]**aim** *n* (14c) **1** *obs* : MARK, TARGET **2 a :** the pointing of a weapon at a mark **b :** the ability to hit a target **c :** a weapon's accuracy or effectiveness **3** *obs* **a :** CONJECTURE, GUESS **b :** the directing of effort toward a goal **4 :** a clearly directed intent or purpose ***syn*** see INTENTION — **aim·less** \-ləs\ *adj* — **aim·less·ly** *adv* — **aim·less·ness** *n*
ain \ˈān\ *adj* [prob. fr. ON *eiginn*] *Scot* (bef. 12c) : OWN
ain't \ˈānt\ [prob. contr. of *are not*] **1 a :** are not **b :** is not **c :** am not **2** *substand* **a :** have not **b :** has not
usage Although disapproved by many and more common in less educated speech, *ain't* is used orally in most parts of the U.S. Its use by educated people is in sense 1 esp. orally in the phrase *ain't I.* At all levels of education it is used deliberately to catch attention or for emphasis both in speech ⟨makes me look half-witted, which I *ain't* —Sir Winston Churchill⟩ and in writing ⟨the wackiness of movies, once so deliciously amusing, *ain't* funny anymore —Richard Schickel⟩ and is found frequently in a few fixed phrases and constructions ⟨leftovers *ain't* what they used to be —*Apartment Life*⟩ ⟨well — class it *ain't* —Cleveland Amory⟩ ⟨and that *ain't* hay⟩ ⟨you *ain't* seen nothin' yet⟩ It is also used for metrical reasons in popular songs ⟨It *Ain't* Necessarily So⟩ ⟨*Ain't* She Sweet⟩ ⟨the old gray mare, she *ain't* what she used to be⟩
Ai·nu \ˈī-(ˌ)nü\ *n, pl* **Ainu** *or* **Ainus** [Ainu, lit., man] (1819) **1 :** a member of an indigenous Caucasoid people of Japan **2 :** the language of the Ainu people
ai·o·li \(ˈ)ī-ˈō-lē, (ˈ)ā-\ *n* [Prov, fr. *ai* garlic + *oli* oil—more at OIL] (ca. 1900) : a sauce made of crushed garlic, egg yolks, olive oil, and lemon juice and sometimes potato : garlic mayonnaise
[1]**air** \ˈa(ə)r, ˈe(ə)r\ *n, often attrib* [ME, fr. MF, fr. L *aer,* fr. Gk *aēr*] (14c) **1 a** *archaic* : BREATH **b :** the mixture of invisible odorless tasteless gases (as nitrogen and oxygen) that surrounds the earth **c :** a light breeze **2 a :** empty space **b :** NOTHINGNESS ⟨vanished into thin ~⟩ **c :** a sudden severance of relations ⟨she gave him the ~⟩ **3 :** COMPRESSED AIR **4 a (1) :** AIRCRAFT ⟨go by ~⟩ **(2) :** AVIATION ⟨~ safety⟩ ⟨~ rights⟩ **(3) :** AIR FORCE ⟨~ headquarters⟩ **b :** the medium of transmission of radio waves; *also* : RADIO, TELEVISION ⟨went on the ~⟩ **5 :** public utterance ⟨he gave ~ to his opinion⟩ **6 a :** the look, appearance, or bearing of a person esp. as expressive of some personal quality or emotion : DEMEANOR ⟨an ~ of dignity⟩ **b :** an artificial or affected manner ⟨to put on ~*s*⟩ **c :** outward appearance of a thing ⟨an ~ of luxury⟩ **d :** a surrounding or pervading influence : ATMOSPHERE ⟨an ~ of mystery⟩ **7** [prob. trans. of It *aria*] **a** *Elizabethan & Jacobean music* : an accompanied song or melody in usu. strophic form **b :** the chief voice part or melody in choral music **c :** TUNE, MELODY **8 :** a football offense utilizing primarily the forward pass ⟨trailing by 20 points, the team took to the ~⟩ **9 :** an air-conditioning system ***syn*** see POSE — **air·less** \-ləs\ *adj* — **air·less·ness** *n* — **in the air :** in wide circulation : ABOUT — **up in the air :** not yet settled
[2]**air** *vt* (1530) **1 :** to expose to the air for drying, purifying, or refreshing : VENTILATE — often used with *out* **2 :** to expose to public view or bring to public notice **3 :** to transmit by radio or television ⟨~ a program⟩ ~ *vi* **1 :** to become exposed to the open air **2 :** to become broadcast ⟨the program ~*s* daily⟩ ***syn*** see EXPRESS
air bag *n* (1969) : an automatically inflating bag in front of riders in an automobile to protect them from pitching forward into solid parts in case of an accident
air base *n* (1915) : a base of operations for military aircraft
air bladder *n* (1731) : a sac containing gas and esp. air; *esp* : a hydrostatic organ present in most fishes that serves as an accessory respiratory organ
air·boat \ˈa(ə)r-ˌbōt, ˈe(ə)r-\ *n* (1946) : a shallow-draft boat driven by an airplane propeller and steered by an airplane rudder
air·borne \-ˌbō(ə)rn, -ˌbȯ(ə)rn\ *adj* (1641) **1 :** supported wholly by aerodynamic and aerostatic forces **2 :** transported by air
air brake *n* (1871) **1 :** a brake operated by a piston driven by compressed air **2 :** a surface (as an aileron) that may be projected into the airstream for lowering the speed of an airplane
[1]**air·brush** \-ˌbrəsh\ *n* (ca. 1889) : an atomizer for applying by compressed air a fine spray (as of paint or liquid color)
[2]**airbrush** *vt* (1938) : to paint, treat, or alter with an airbrush
air·burst \-ˌbərst\ *n* (1917) : the burst of a shell or bomb in the air
air·bus \-ˌbəs\ *n* (1945) : a short-range or medium-range subsonic jet passenger airplane
air chief marshal *n* (ca. 1919) : a commissioned officer in the British air force who ranks with a general in the army
air coach *n* (1948) : a passenger airliner offering service at less than first-class rates usu. with curtailed accommodations
air commodore *n* (ca. 1919) : a commissioned officer in the British air force who ranks with a brigadier in the army
air–con·di·tion \ˌa(ə)r-kən-ˈdish-ən, ˌe(ə)r-\ *vt* [back-formation fr. *air conditioning*] (1933) : to equip (as a building) with an apparatus for washing air and controlling its humidity and temperature; *also* : to subject (air) to these processes — **air con·di·tion·er** \-ˈdish-(ə-)nər\ *n* — **air–con·di·tion·ing** \-ˈdish-(ə-)niŋ\ *n*

air–cool \'a(ə)r-'kül, 'e(ə)r-\ *vt* [back-formation fr. *air-cooled* & *air cooling*] (1899) : to cool the cylinders of (an internal-combustion engine) by air without the use of an intermediate medium — **air–cooled** *adj*

air·craft \'a(ə)r-ˌkraft, 'e(ə)r-\ *n, pl* **aircraft** *often attrib* (1850) : a weight-carrying structure for navigation of the air that is supported either by its own buoyancy or by the dynamic action of the air against its surfaces

aircraft carrier *n* (1919) : a warship with a flight deck on which airplanes can be launched and landed

air·crew \'a(ə)r-ˌkrü, 'e(ə)r-\ *n* (1921) : the crew manning an airplane

air–cushion vehicle *n* (ca. 1962) : GROUND-EFFECT MACHINE

air·date \-ˌdāt\ *n* (1971) : the scheduled date of a broadcast

air·drome \'a(ə)r-ˌdrōm, 'e(ə)r-\ *n* [alter. of *aerodrome*] (1917) : AIRPORT

air·drop \-ˌdräp\ *n* (ca. 1945) : delivery of cargo or personnel by parachute from an airplane in flight — **air–drop** *vt* — **air–drop·pa·ble** \-ˌdräp-ə-bəl\ *adj*

air–dry \-'drī\ *adj* (ca. 1889) : dry to such a degree that no further moisture is given up on exposure to air

Aire·dale terrier \ˌa(ə)r-ˌdāl-, ˌe(ə)r-\ *n* [*Airedale*, valley of the Aire river, England] (1880) : any of a breed of large terriers with a hard, wiry, black-and-tan coat — called also *Airedale*

air·er \'a(ə)r-ər, 'e(ə)r-\ *n, Brit* (ca. 1847) : a frame on which clothes are aired or dried

Air Express *service mark* — used for package transport by air

air·fare \'a(ə)r-ˌfa(ə)r, 'e(ə)r-, -ˌfe(ə)r\ *n* (1918) : fare for travel by airplane

air·field \-ˌfēld\ *n* (1927) **1** : the landing field of an airport **2** : AIRPORT

air·flow \-ˌflō\ *n* (ca. 1911) : a flow of air; *specif* : the motion of air (as around parts of an airplane in flight) relative to the surface of a body immersed in it

air·foil \-ˌfȯil\ *n* (ca. 1922) : a body (as an airplane wing or propeller blade) designed to provide a desired reaction force when in motion relative to the surrounding air

air force *n* (1917) **1** : the military organization of a nation for air warfare **2** : a unit of the U.S. Air Force higher than a division and lower than a command

air·frame \-ˌfrām\ *n* [*aircraft* + *frame*] (1931) : the structure of an aircraft, rocket vehicle, or missile without the power plant

air·freight \-'frāt\ *n* (1929) : freight transport by air in volume; *also* : the charge for this service — **airfreight** *vt*

air·glow \-ˌglō\ *n* (ca. 1950) : light that is observed esp. during the night, that originates in the high atmosphere of a planet (as the earth), and that is associated with photochemical reactions of gases caused by solar radiation

air gun *n* (ca. 1753) **1** : a gun from which a projectile is propelled by compressed air **2** : any of various hand tools that work by compressed air; *esp* : AIRBRUSH

air·head \-ˌhed\ *n* [*'air* + *-head* (as in *beachhead*)] (ca. 1944) : an area in hostile territory secured usu. by airborne troops for further use in bringing in troops and materiel by air

air hole *n* (15c) **1 a** : a hole to admit or discharge air **b** : a spot not frozen over in ice **2** : AIR POCKET

air·ing \'a(ə)r-iŋ, 'e(ə)r-\ *n* (1604) **1** : exposure to air or heat for drying or freshening **2** : exposure to or exercise in the open air esp. to promote health or fitness **3** : exposure to public view or notice **4** : a radio or television broadcast

air lane *n* (ca. 1910) : a path customarily followed by airplanes

air letter *n* (1920) **1** : an airmail letter **2** : a sheet of airmail stationery that can be folded and sealed with the message inside and the address outside

air·lift \'a(ə)r-ˌlift, 'e(ə)r-\ *n* (1945) : a system of transporting cargo or passengers by aircraft usu. to or from an otherwise inaccessible area — **airlift** *vt*

air·line \-ˌlīn\ *n* (ca. 1910) : an air transportation system including its equipment, routes, operating personnel, and management

air line *n* (1813) : a straight line through the air between two points

air·lin·er \-ˌlī-nər\ *n* (1908) : an airplane operated by an airline

air lock *n* (1857) **1** : an intermediate chamber between the outer air and the working chamber of a pneumatic caisson; *also* : a similar intermediate chamber between places of unequal atmospheric pressure or temperature **2** : a stoppage of flow caused by air being in a part where liquid ought to circulate

air·mail \'a(ə)r-ˌmā(ə)l, 'e(ə)r-, -ˌmäl\ *n* (1913) : the system of transporting mail by aircraft; *also* : the mail thus transported — **airmail** *vt*

air·man \-mən\ *n* (1873) **1** : a civilian or military pilot, aviator, or aviation technician **2** : an enlisted man in the air force: as **a** : an enlisted man of one of the three ranks below sergeant **b** : an enlisted man ranking above an airman basic and below an airman first class

airman basic *n* (ca. 1961) : an enlisted man of the lowest rank in the air force

airman first class *n* (1952) : an enlisted man in the air force ranking above an airman and below a sergeant

air·man·ship \'a(ə)r-mən-ˌship, 'e(ə)r-\ *n* (ca. 1908) : skill in piloting or navigating airplanes

air marshal *n* (1919) : a commissioned officer in the British air force who ranks with a lieutenant general in the army

air mass *n* (1893) : a body of air extending hundreds or thousands of miles horizontally and sometimes as high as the stratosphere and maintaining as it travels nearly uniform conditions of temperature and humidity at any given level

air mattress *n* (1926) : MATTRESS 1b

Air Medal *n* (1942) : a U.S. military decoration awarded for meritorious achievement while participating in an aerial flight

air mile *n* (1919) : a mile in air travel; *specif* : a unit equal to 6076.1154 feet

air–mind·ed \'a(ə)r-ˌmīn-dəd, 'e(ə)r-\ *adj* (1924) : interested in aviation or in air travel — **air–mind·ed·ness** *n*

air·mo·bile \-ˌmō-bəl, -ˌbēl, -ˌbil\ *adj* [*air* + *'mobile*] (1965) : of, relating to, or being a military unit whose members are transported to combat areas usu. by helicopter

air·park \-ˌpärk\ *n* (1929) : a small airport usu. near an industrial area

air piracy *n* (1948) : the hijacking of a flying airplane : SKYJACKING

air·plane \'a(ə)r-ˌplān, 'e(ə)r-\ *n* [alter. of *aeroplane*, prob. fr. LGk *aeroplanos* wandering in air, fr. Gk *aer-* + *planos* wandering, fr. *planasthai* to wander — more at PLANET] (1907) : a fixed-wing aircraft heavier than air that is driven by a propeller or by a high-velocity jet and supported by the dynamic reaction of the air against its wings

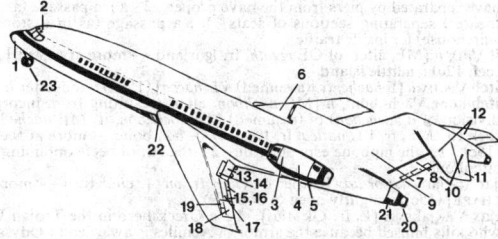

airplane: 1 weather radar, 2 cockpit, 3 jet engine, 4 engine pod, 5 pylon, 6 swept-back wing, 7 vertical stabilizer, 8 rudder, 9, 10 tabs, 11 elevator, 12 horizontal stabilizer, 13 inboard flap, 14 inboard spoiler, 15, 16 tabs, 17 aileron, 18 outboard flap, 19 outboard spoiler, 20 sound suppressor, 21 thrust reverser, 22 cabin air intake, 23 nose landing gear

air plant *n* (1842) **1** : EPIPHYTE **2** : BRYOPHYLLUM

air·play \-ˌplā\ *n* (1967) : the playing of a phonograph record on the air by a radio station

air pocket *n* (1912) : a condition of the atmosphere (as a local down current) that causes an airplane to drop suddenly

air police *n* (1944) : the military police of an air force

air·port \'a(ə)r-ˌpō(ə)rt, 'e(ə)r-, -ˌpȯ(ə)rt\ *n* (1907) : a tract of land or water that is maintained for the landing and takeoff of aircraft and for receiving and discharging passengers and cargo and that usu. has facilities for the shelter, supply, and repair of planes

air·post \-ˌpōst\ *n* (ca. 1926) : AIRMAIL

air power *n* (1908) : the military strength of a nation's air force

air pump *n* (1660) : a pump for exhausting air from a closed space or for compressing air or forcing it through other apparatus

air raid *n* (1914) : an attack by armed airplanes on a surface target

air rifle *n* (ca. 1897) : a rifle whose projectile (as a BB or pellet) is propelled by compressed air or carbon dioxide

air right *n* (ca. 1922) : a property right to the space above a surface area or object

air sac *n* (ca. 1828) **1** : one of the air-filled spaces in the body of a bird connected with the air passages of the lungs **2** : ALVEOLUS 1b **3** : a thin-walled dilation of a trachea occurring in many insects

air·screw \'a(ə)r-ˌskrü, 'e(ə)r-\ *n* (1894) **1** : a screw propeller designed to operate in air **2** *Brit* : an airplane propeller

air·ship \-ˌship\ *n* (1819) : a lighter-than-air aircraft having propulsion and steering systems

air·sick \-ˌsik\ *adj* (1785) : affected with motion sickness associated with flying — **air·sick·ness** *n*

air·space \-ˌspās\ *n* (1911) : the space lying above the earth or above a certain area of land or water; *esp* : the space lying above a nation and coming under its jurisdiction

air·speed \-ˌspēd\ *n* (ca. 1909) : the speed (as of an airplane) with relation to the air — compare GROUND SPEED

air·stream \-ˌstrēm\ *n* (1869) : a current of air; *specif* : AIRFLOW

air strike *n* (1945) : an air attack

air·strip \-ˌstrip\ *n* (1942) : a runway without normal air base or airport facilities

¹airt \'a(ə)rt, 'e(ə)rt\ *n* [ME *art*, fr. ScGael *àird*] *chiefly Scot* (15c) : compass point : DIRECTION

²airt *vt, chiefly Scot* (1782) : DIRECT, GUIDE

air·tight \'a(ə)r-ˌtīt, 'e(ə)r-\ *adj* (1760) **1** : impermeable to air or nearly so **2 a** : having no noticeable weakness, flaw, or loophole ⟨an ~ argument⟩ **b** : permitting no opportunity for an opponent to score ⟨an ~ defense⟩ — **air·tight·ness** *n*

air·time \-ˌtīm\ *n* (1942) **1** : the time at which a radio or television broadcast is scheduled to begin **2** : the time or any part thereof that a radio or television station is on the air

air–to–air \ˌa(ə)rt-ə-'(w)a(ə)r, ˌe(ə)rt-ə-'(w)e(ə)r\ *adj* (1941) : launched from one airplane in flight at another : involving aircraft in flight ⟨~ rockets⟩ ⟨~ combat⟩

air vice–marshal *n* (1919) : a commissioned officer in the British air force who ranks with a major general in the army

air·wave \'a(ə)r-ˌwāv, 'e(ə)r-\ *n* (1928) **1** : the medium of radio and television transmission — usu. used in pl. **2** : AIRWAY 4

air·way \-ˌwā\ *n* (1849) **1** : a passage for a current of air (as in a mine or to the lungs) **2** : a designated route along which airplanes fly from airport to airport; *esp* : such a route equipped with navigational aids **3** : AIRLINE **4** : a channel of a designated radio frequency for broadcasting or other radio communication

air·wor·thy \-ˌwər-ˌt͟hē\ *adj* (1829) : fit for operation in the air ⟨an ~ airplane⟩ — **air·wor·thi·ness** *n*

airy \'a(ə)r-ē, 'e(ə)r-\ *adj* **air·i·er; -est** (14c) **1 a** : of or relating to air : ATMOSPHERIC **b** : high in the air : LOFTY ⟨~ perches⟩ **c** : performed in air : AERIAL ⟨~ leaps⟩ **2** : UNREAL, ILLUSORY ⟨~ romances⟩ **3 a** : being light and graceful in movement or manner : SPRIGHTLY, VIVACIOUS **b** : ETHEREAL **4 a** : open to the free circulation of air **b** : having-ing openings or spaces ⟨~ lacework⟩ **5 :** AFFECTED, PROUD ⟨~ condescension⟩ — **air·i·ly** \'a(ə)r-ə-lē, 'e(ə)r-\ *adv* — **air·i·ness** \-ē-nəs\ *n*

airy–fairy \-'fa(ə)r-ē, -'fe(ə)r-ē\ *adj* (1869) **1** *chiefly Brit* **:** DELICATE, FAIRYLIKE **2** *chiefly Brit* **:** lacking substance or purpose ⟨in . . . an ~, unserious, insufficiently careful fashion — *Times Lit. Supp.*⟩

aisle \'ī(ə)l\ *n* [ME *ile,* fr. MF *aile* wing, fr. L *ala;* akin to OE *eaxl* shoulder, L *axilla* armpit — more at AXIS] (15c) **1 :** the side of a church nave separated by piers from the nave proper **2 a :** a passage (as in a theater) separating sections of seats **b :** a passage (as in a store or warehouse) for inside traffic

ait \'āt\ *n* [ME, alter. of OE *īggoth,* fr. *īg* island — more at ISLAND] *Brit* (bef. 12c) **:** a little island

aitch \'āch\ *n* [F *hache,* fr. (assumed) VL *hacca*] (1573) **:** the letter *h*

aitch·bone \'āch-,bōn\ *n* [ME *hachbon,* alter. (resulting from incorrect division of *a nachebon*) of (assumed) ME *nachebon,* fr. ME *nache* buttock (fr. MF, fr. LL *natica,* fr. L *natis*) + *bon* bone — more at NATES] (15c) **1 :** the hipbone esp. of cattle **2 :** the cut of beef containing the aitchbone

ajar \ə-'jär\ *adj or adv* [earlier *on char,* fr. *on* + *char* turn — more at CHARE] (15c) **:** slightly open ⟨a door ~⟩

Ajax \'ā-,jaks\ *n* [L, fr. Gk *Aias*] **1 :** a Greek hero in the Trojan War who kills himself because the armor of Achilles is awarded to Odysseus **2 :** a fleet-footed Greek hero in the Trojan War

Akan \'äk-,än\ *n, pl* **Akan** *or* **Akans** (1694) **1 :** a member of any of the Akan-speaking peoples **2 :** a language spoken over a wide area in Ghana and extending into the Ivory Coast

akim·bo \ə-'kim-(,)bō\ *adj or adv* [ME *in kenebowe*] (15c) **1 :** having the hand on the hip and the elbow turned outward **2 :** set in a bent position ⟨a tailor sitting with legs ~⟩

akin \ə-'kin\ *adj* (15c) **1 :** related by blood **:** descended from a common ancestor or prototype **2 :** essentially similar, related, or compatible ***syn*** see SIMILAR

Aki·ta \ə-'kēt-ə, ä-\ *n* [fr. *Akita,* Japan] (1928) **:** a large dog that belongs to a Japanese breed and resembles a spitz

Ak·ka·di·an \ə-'kād-ē-ən\ *n* (1855) **1 :** an ancient Semitic language of Mesopotamia used from about the 28th to the 1st century B.C. **2 :** a Semitic inhabitant of central Mesopotamia before 2000 B.C. — **Akkadian** *adj*

ak·va·vit \'äk-wə-,vēt, 'äk-vä-\ *var of* AQUAVIT

al- — see AD-

[1]-al \əl, [ə]l\ *adj suffix* [ME, fr. OF & L; OF, fr. L *-alis*] **:** of, relating to, or characterized by ⟨direction*al*⟩ ⟨fiction*al*⟩

[2]-al *n suffix* [ME *-aille,* fr. OF, fr. L *-alia,* neut. pl. of *-alis*] **:** action **:** process ⟨rehears*al*⟩

[3]-al \,al, ,ȯl, əl, [ə]l\ *n suffix* [F, fr. *alcool* alcohol, fr. ML *alcohol*] **1 :** aldehyde ⟨butan*al*⟩ **2 :** acetal ⟨butyr*al*⟩

ala \'ā-lə\ *n, pl* **alae** \-,lē\ [L — more at AISLE] (1738) **:** a wing or a winglike anatomic process or part — **alar** \'ā-lər\ *adj* — **ala·ry** \-lə-rē\ *adj*

à la *also* **a la** \,äl-(,)ä, ,äl-ə, ,al-ə\ *prep* [F *à la*] (1589) **:** in the manner of

al·a·bas·ter \'al-ə-,bas-tər\ *n* [ME *alabastre,* fr. MF, fr. L *alabaster* vase of alabaster, fr. Gk *alabastros*] (14c) **1 :** a compact fine-textured usu. white and translucent gypsum often carved into vases and ornaments **2 :** a hard compact calcite or aragonite that is translucent and sometimes banded — **alabaster** *or* **al·a·bas·trine** \,al-ə-'bas-trən\ *adj*

à la carte *also* **a la carte** \,äl-ə-'kärt, ,al-\ *adv or adj* [F, by the bill of fare] (1826) **:** according to a menu that prices each item separately

alack \ə-'lak\ *interj* [ME] (15c) — used to express sorrow or regret

alac·ri·ty \ə-'lak-rət-ē\ *n* [L *alacritas,* fr. *alacr-, alacer* lively, eager] (15c) **:** promptness in response **:** cheerful readiness ⟨accepted the invitation with ~⟩ ***syn*** see CELERITY — **alac·ri·tous** \-rət-əs\ *adj*

Alad·din \ə-'lad-[ə]n\ *n* **:** a youth in the *Arabian Nights' Entertainments* who comes into possession of a magic lamp

à la grecque \,äl-ə-'grek, ,al-\ *adj, often cap G* [F, in the Greek manner] (ca. 1925) **:** served in a sauce made of olive oil, lemon juice, and several seasonings (as fennel, coriander, sage, and thyme)

à la king \,äl-ə-'kiŋ, ,al-\ *adj* (1919) **:** served in a cream sauce with mushrooms and pimiento or green peppers ⟨chicken *à la king*⟩

al·a·me·da \,al-ə-'mēd-ə, -'mād-\ *n* [Sp, fr. *álamo* poplar] (ca. 1797) **:** a public promenade bordered with trees

à la mode *also* **a la mode** \,äl-ə-'mōd, ,al-\ *adj* [F, according to the fashion] (1649) **1 :** FASHIONABLE, STYLISH **2 :** topped with ice cream

al·a·nine \'al-ə-,nēn\ *n* [G *alanin,* irreg. fr. *aldehyd* aldehyde] (ca. 1863) **:** a white crystalline amino acid $C_3H_7NO_2$ formed esp. by the hydrolysis of proteins

al·a·nyl \'al-ə-,nil\ *n* [ISV *alanine* + *-yl*] (ca. 1919) **:** an acyl radical of alanine

[1]alarm \ə-'lärm\ *also* **ala·rum** \ə-'lär-əm, -'lar-, *Brit also* -'ler-\ *n* [ME *alarme, alarom,* fr. MF *alarme,* fr. OIt *all'arme,* lit., to the weapon] (14c) **1** *usu* ***alarum,*** *archaic* **:** a call to arms ⟨the angry trumpet sounds *alarum* —Shak.⟩ **2 :** a signal (as a loud noise or flashing light) that warns or alerts; *also* **:** a device that signals ⟨set the ~ to wake me at seven⟩ **3 :** sudden sharp apprehension and fear resulting from the perception of imminent danger **4 :** a warning notice ***syn*** see FEAR

[2]alarm *also* **alarum** *vt* (1605) **1 :** DISTURB, EXCITE **2 :** to give warning to **3 :** to strike with fear — **alarm·ing·ly** \-'lär-miŋ-lē\ *adv*

alarm clock *n* (1697) **:** a clock that can be set to sound an alarm at a desired time

alarm·ism \ə-'lär-,miz-əm\ *n* (1867) **:** the often unwarranted exciting of fears or warning of danger — **alarm·ist** \-məst\ *n or adj*

alarm reaction *n* (1936) **:** the initial reaction of an organism (as increased hormonal activity) to stress

alarums and excursions *n pl* (1592) **1 :** martial sounds and the movement of soldiers across the stage — used as a stage direction in Elizabethan drama **2 :** clamor, excitement, and feverish or disordered activity

alas \ə-'las\ *interj* [ME, fr. OF, fr. *a* ah + *las* weary, fr. L *lassus* — more at LET] (13c) — used to express unhappiness, pity, or concern

Alas·kan malamute \ə-,las-kən-\ *n* (1938) **:** any of a breed of powerful heavy-coated deep-chested dogs of Alaskan origin with erect ears, heavily cushioned feet, and plumy tail

Alas·ka time \ə-'las-kə-\ *n* (1945) **:** the time of the 9th time zone west of Greenwich that includes most of Alaska

[1]alate \'ā-,lāt\ *adj* [L *alatus,* fr. *ala*] (1668) **:** having wings or a winglike part

[2]alate *n* (1941) **:** a winged insect (as an aphid) of a kind having winged and wingless forms

alb \'alb\ *n* [ME *albe,* fr. OE, fr. ML *alba,* fr. L, fem. of *albus* white; akin to ON *elptr* swan, OE *ælf* elf] (bef. 12c) **:** a full-length white linen ecclesiastical vestment with long sleeves that is gathered at the waist with a cincture — see VESTMENT illustration

al·ba·core \'al-bə-,kō(ə)r, -,kȯ(ə)r\ *n, pl* **-core** *or* **-cores** [Pg *albacor,* fr. Ar *al-bakūrah* the albacore] (1579) **1 :** a large pelagic tuna (*Thunnus alalunga*) with long pectoral fins that is a source of canned tuna; *broadly* **:** any of various tunas (as a bonito) **2 :** any of several carangid fishes

Al·ba·nian \al-'bā-nē-ən, -nyən *also* ȯl-\ *n* (1579) **1 :** a native or inhabitant of Albania **2 :** the Indo-European language of the Albanian people — see INDO-EUROPEAN LANGUAGES table — **Albanian** *adj*

al·ba·tross \'al-bə-,trȯs, -,träs\ *n, pl* **-tross** *or* **-tross·es** [prob. alter. of *alcatras* (water bird), fr. Pg or Sp *alcatraz* pelican] (1564) **1 :** any of various large web-footed seabirds (family Diomedeidae) that are related to the petrels and include the largest seabirds **2 a :** something that causes persistent deep concern or anxiety **b :** something that greatly hinders accomplishment **:** ENCUMBRANCE

al·be·do \al-'bēd-(,)ō\ *n, pl* **-dos** [LL, whiteness, fr. L *albus*] (ca. 1859) **:** reflective power; *specif* **:** the fraction of incident light or electromagnetic radiation that is reflected by a surface or body (as the moon or a cloud)

al·be·it \ȯl-'bē-ət, al-\ *conj* [ME, lit., all though it be] (14c) **:** conceding the fact that **:** even though

Al·bi·gen·ses \,al-bə-'jen-,sēz\ *n pl* [ML, pl. of *Albigensis,* lit., inhabitant of Albi, fr. *Albiga* (Albi), France] (1625) **:** members of a Catharistic sect of southern France flourishing primarily in the 12th and 13th centuries — **Al·bi·gen·sian** \-'jen-chən, -'jen(t)-sē-ən \ *adj or n* — **Al·bi·gen·sian·ism** \-,iz-əm\ *n*

al·bi·nism \'al-bə-,niz-əm, al-'bī-\ *n* (1836) **:** the condition of an albino — **al·bi·nis·tic** \,al-bə-'nis-tik\ *adj*

al·bi·no \al-'bī-(,)nō\ *n, pl* **-nos** [Pg, fr. Sp, fr. *albo* white, fr. L *albus*] (1777) **:** an organism exhibiting deficient pigmentation; *esp* **:** a human being or lower animal that is congenitally deficient in pigment and usu. has a milky or translucent skin, white or colorless hair, and eyes with pink or blue iris and deep-red pupil

al·bi·not·ic \,al-bə-'nät-ik\ *adj* [*albino* + *-tic* (as in *melanotic*)] (1872) **1 :** of, relating to, or affected with albinism **2 :** tending toward albinism

Al·bi·on \'al-bē-ən\ *n* [L] (bef. 12c) **1 :** Great Britain **2 :** England

al·bite \'al-,bīt\ *n* [Sw *albit,* fr. L *albus*] (1843) **:** a triclinic usu. white feldspar consisting of a sodium aluminum silicate $NaAlSi_3O_8$ — **al·bit·ic** \al-'bit-ik\ *adj*

al·bum \'al-bəm\ *n* [L, a white tablet, fr. neut. of *albus*] (1612) **1 a :** a book with blank pages used for making a collection (as of autographs, stamps, or photographs) **b :** a paperboard container for a phonograph record **:** JACKET **c :** one or more long-playing phonograph records or tape recordings produced as a single unit ⟨a 2-record ~⟩ **2 :** a collection usu. in book form of literary selections, musical compositions, or pictures **:** ANTHOLOGY

al·bu·men \al-'byü-mən; 'al-,byü-, -byə-\ *n* [L, fr. *albus*] (1599) **1 :** the white of an egg — see EGG illustration **2 :** ALBUMIN

al·bu·min \al-'byü-mən; 'al-,byü-, -byə-\ *n* [ISV *albumen* + *-in*] (1869) **:** any of numerous simple heat-coagulable water-soluble proteins that occur in blood plasma or serum, muscle, the whites of eggs, milk, and other animal substances and in many plant tissues and fluids

al·bu·min·ous \al-'byü-mə-nəs\ *adj* (1791) **:** relating to, containing, or having the properties of albumen or albumin

al·bu·min·uria \(,)al-,byü-mə-'n(y)u̇r-ē-ə\ *n* [NL] (1842) **:** the presence of albumin in the urine often symptomatic of kidney disease — **al·bu·min·uric** \-'n(y)u̇(ə)r-ik\ *adj*

al·bu·mose \'al-byə-,mōs, -,mōz\ *n* [F, fr. *albumine* albumen + *-ose*] (1884) **:** any of various products of enzymatic protein hydrolysis

al·bur·num \al-'bər-nəm\ *n* [L, fr. *albus* white] (1664) **:** SAPWOOD

al·ca·ic \al-'kā-ik\ *adj, often cap* [LL *Alcaicus* of Alcaeus, fr. Gk *Alkaïkos,* fr. *Alkaios* Alcaeus, *fl ab* 600 B.C. Gk poet] (1696) **:** relating to or written in a verse or strophe marked by complicated variation of a dominant iambic pattern — **alcaic** *n, often cap*

al·cai·de *or* **al·cay·de** \al-'kīd-ē\ *n* [Sp *alcaide,* fr. Ar *al-qā'id* the captain] (1502) **:** a commander of a castle or fortress (as among Spaniards, Portuguese, or Moors)

al·cal·de \al-'käl-dē\ *n* [Sp, fr. Ar *al-qāḍī* the judge] (1565) **:** the chief administrative and judicial officer of a Spanish town

al·ca·zar \al-'käz-ər, -'kaz-\ *n* [Sp *alcázar,* fr. Ar *al-qaṣr* the castle] (1615) **:** a Spanish fortress or palace

Al·ces·tis \al-'ses-təs\ *n* [L, fr. Gk *Alkēstis*] **:** the wife of Admetus who dies for her husband and is restored to him by Hercules

al·che·mist \'al-kə-məst\ *n* (14c) **:** one who studies or practices alchemy — **al·che·mis·tic** \,al-kə-'mis-tik\ *or* **al·che·mis·ti·cal** \-ti-kəl\ *adj*

al·che·mize \'al-kə-,mīz\ *vt* **-mized; -miz·ing** (1603) **:** to change by alchemy **:** TRANSMUTE

al·che·my \'al-kə-mē\ *n* [ME *alkamie, alquemie,* fr. MF or ML; MF *alquemie,* fr. ML *alchymia,* fr. Ar *al-kīmiyā',* fr. *al* the + *kīmiyā'* alchemy, fr. LGk *chēmeia*] (14c) **1 :** a medieval chemical science and speculative philosophy aiming to achieve the transmutation of the base metals into gold, the discovery of a universal cure for disease, and the discovery of a means of indefinitely prolonging life **2 :** a power or process of transforming something common into something special **3 :** an inexplicable or mysterious transmuting — **al·chem·ic** \al-'kem-ik\ *or* **al·chem·i·cal** \-i-kəl\ *adj* — **al·chem·i·cal·ly** \-i-k(ə-)lē \ *adv*

Alc·me·ne \alk-'mē-nē\ *n* [Gk *Alkmēnē*] **:** the mother of Hercules by Zeus in the form of her husband Amphitryon

al·co·hol \'al-kə-,hȯl\ *n* [NL, fr. ML, powdered antimony, fr. OSp, fr. Ar *al-kuḥul* the powdered antimony, fr. *kuḥl* kohl] (1672) **1 :** a colorless volatile flammable liquid C_2H_6O that is the intoxicating agent in fermented and distilled liquors and is used also as a solvent — called also *ethyl alcohol* **2 :** any of various compounds that are analogous to ethyl alcohol in constitution and that are hydroxyl derivatives of hydrocarbons **3 :** drink (as whiskey or beer) containing alcohol

¹al·co·hol·ic \ˌal-kə-ˈhȯl-ik, -ˈhäl-\ *adj* (1790) **1 a :** of, relating to, or caused by alcohol **b :** containing alcohol **2 :** affected with alcoholism — **al·co·hol·i·cal·ly** \-i-k(ə-)lē\ *adv*

²alcoholic *n* (ca. 1890) **:** one affected with alcoholism

al·co·hol·ism \ˈal-kə-ˌhȯ-ˌliz-əm, -kə-hə- *also* ˈal-kə-ˌliz-\ *n* (1860) **1 :** continued excessive or compulsive use of alcoholic drinks **2 :** poisoning by alcohol; *esp* **:** a complex chronic psychological and nutritional disorder associated with excessive and usu. compulsive drinking

al·co·hol·om·e·ter \ˌal-kə-ˌhȯ-ˈläm-ət-ər\ *n* [F *alcoolomètre,* fr. *alcool* alcohol + *-o-* + *-mètre* -meter] (ca. 1846) **:** a device for determining the alcoholic strength of liquids — **al·co·hol·om·e·try** \-ˈläm-ə-trē\ *n*

Al·co·ran \ˌal-kə-ˈran\ *n* [ME, fr. MF or ML; MF & ML, fr. Ar *al-qurʼān,* lit., the reading] *archaic* (14c) **:** KORAN

al·cove \ˈal-ˌkōv\ *n* [F *alcôve,* fr. Sp *alcoba,* fr. Ar *al-qubbah* the arch] (1676) **1 a :** a small recessed section of a room **:** NOOK **b :** an arched opening (as in a wall) **:** NICHE **2 :** SUMMERHOUSE — **al·coved** \-ˌkōvd\ *adj*

al·cy·o·nar·ian \ˌal-sē-ə-ˈnar-ē-ən\ *n* [deriv. of Gk *alkyoneion* zoophyte, fr. neut. of *alkyoneios* of a kingfisher, fr. *alkyon* kingfisher; fr. its resemblance to a kingfisher's nest] (1878) **:** any of a subclass (Alcyonaria) of colonial anthozoans (as the sea pen) having polyps with eight branched tentacles and eight septa

Al·cy·o·ne \al-ˈsī-ə-(ˌ)nē\ *n* [L, fr. Gk *Alkyonē*] **:** the brightest star in the Pleiades

Al·deb·a·ran \al-ˈdeb-ə-rən\ *n* [Ar *al-dabarān,* lit., the follower] **:** a red star of the first magnitude that is seen in the eye of Taurus and is the brightest star in the Hyades

al·de·hyde \ˈal-də-ˌhīd\ *n* [G *aldehyd,* fr. NL *al. dehyd.,* abbr. of *alcohol dehydrogenatum* dehydrogenated alcohol] (ca. 1846) **:** ACETALDEHYDE; *broadly* **:** any of various highly reactive compounds typified by acetaldehyde and characterized by the group CHO — **al·de·hy·dic** \ˌal-də-ˈhīd-ik\ *adj*

al den·te \äl-ˈden-(ˌ)tā, al-\ *adj* [It; lit., to the tooth] (1947) **:** cooked just enough to retain a somewhat firm texture

al·der \ˈȯl-dər\ *n* [ME, fr. OE *alor;* akin to OHG *elira* alder, L *alnus*] (bef. 12c) **:** any of a genus (*Alnus*) of toothed-leaved trees or shrubs of the birch family growing in moist ground and having wood used by turners and bark used in dyeing and tanning

al·der·man \ˈȯl-dər-mən\ *n* [ME, fr. OE *ealdorman,* fr. *ealdor* parent (fr. *eald* old) + *man* — more at OLD] (bef. 12c) **1 :** a person governing a kingdom, district, or shire as viceroy for an Anglo-Saxon king **2 a :** a magistrate formerly ranking next below the mayor in an English or Irish city or borough **b :** a high-ranking member of a borough or county council in England or Ireland chosen by elected members **3 :** a member of a city legislative body — **al·der·man·ic** \ˌȯl-dər-ˈman-ik\ *adj*

al·der·wom·an \ˈȯl-dər-ˌwu̇m-ən\ *n* [*alder-* (as in *alderman*) + *woman*] (1768) **:** a female member of a city legislative body

al·dol \ˈal-ˌdȯl, -ˌdōl\ *n* [ISV *aldehyde* + *-ol*] (1874) **:** a colorless beta-hydroxy aldehyde $C_4H_8O_2$ used esp. in organic synthesis; *broadly* **:** any of various similar aldehydes — **al·dol·iza·tion** \ˌal-ˌdȯ-lə-ˈzā-shən, -ˌdō-\ *n*

al·dol·ase \ˈal-də-ˌlās, -ˌlāz\ *n* [*aldol* + *-ase*] (1940) **:** a crystalline enzyme that occurs widely in living systems and catalyzes reversibly the cleavage of a fructose ester into triose sugars

al·dose \ˈal-ˌdōs, -ˌdōz\ *n* [ISV *aldehyde* + *-ose*] (1894) **:** a sugar containing one aldehyde group per molecule

al·do·ste·rone \al-ˈdäs-tə-ˌrōn, ˌal-dō-stə-ˈrōn\ *n* [*ald*ehyde + *-o-* + *ster*ol + *-one*] (ca. 1954) **:** a steroid hormone $C_{21}H_{28}O_5$ of the adrenal cortex that functions in the regulation of the salt and water balance of the body

al·do·ste·ron·ism \-ˌrō-ˌniz-əm, -ˈrō-\ *n* (1955) **:** a condition that is characterized by excessive production and excretion of aldosterone and typically by loss of body potassium, muscular weakness, and elevated blood pressure

al·drin \ˈȯl-drən, ˈal-\ *n* [Kurt *Alder* †1958 G chemist + E *-in*] (ca. 1949) **:** an exceedingly poisonous cyclodiene insecticide $C_{12}H_8Cl_6$

ale \ˈā(ə)l\ *n* [ME, fr. OE *ealu;* akin to ON *öl* ale, L *alumen* alum] (bef. 12c) **1 :** an alcoholic beverage brewed esp. by rapid fermentation from an infusion of malt with the addition of hops **2 :** an English country festival at which ale is the principal beverage

ale·a·tor·ic \ˌā-lē-ə-ˈtȯr-ik, -ˈtär-\ *adj* [L *aleatorius* of a gambler] (1961) **:** improvisatory or random in character ⟨~ music⟩

ale·a·to·ry \ˈā-lē-ə-ˌtōr-ē, -ˌtȯr-\ *adj* [L *aleatorius* of a gambler, fr. *aleator* gambler, fr. *alea* a dice game] (1693) **1 :** depending on an uncertain event or contingency as to both profit and loss ⟨an ~ contract⟩ **2 :** relating to luck and esp. to bad luck **3 :** ALEATORIC

alee \ə-ˈlē\ *adv* (14c) **:** on or toward the lee — compare AWEATHER

ale·house \ˈā(ə)l-ˌhau̇s\ *n* (bef. 12c) **:** a place where ale is sold to be drunk on the premises

Al·e·man·nic \ˌal-ə-ˈman-ik\ *n* [LL *alemanni,* of Gmc origin; akin to Goth *alamans* totality of people] (ca. 1797) **:** the group of dialects of German spoken in Alsace, Switzerland, and southwestern Germany

alem·bic \ə-ˈlem-bik\ *n* [ME, fr. MF & ML; MF *alambic* & ML *alembicum,* fr. Ar *al-anbīq,* fr. *al* the + *anbīq* still, fr. LGk *ambik-, ambix* alembic, fr. Gk, cap of a still] (14c) **1 :** an apparatus formerly used in distillation **2 :** something that refines or transmutes as if by distillation ⟨philosophy . . . filtered through the ~ of Plato's mind — B. T. Shropshire⟩

alen·çon \ə-ˈlen-ˌsän, -ˈlen(t)-sən\ *n* [*Alençon,* France] (ca. 1858) **:** a delicate needlepoint lace

aleph \ˈäl-ˌef, -əf\ *n* [Heb *āleph,* prob. fr. *eleph* ox] (14c) **:** the 1st letter of the Hebrew alphabet — see ALPHABET table

aleph–null \-ˈnəl\ *n* (ca. 1909) **:** the cardinal number of the set of all integers which is the smallest transfinite cardinal number

¹alert \ə-ˈlərt\ *adj* [It *all' erta,* lit., on the ascent] (1712) **1 :** ACTIVE, BRISK **2 a :** watchful and prompt to meet danger or emergency **b :** quick to perceive and act ***syn*** see WATCHFUL, INTELLIGENT — **alert·ly** *adv* — **alert·ness** *n*

²alert *n* (1796) **1 :** the state of readiness of those warned by an alert **2 :** an alarm or other signal of danger **3 :** the period during which an alert is in effect — **on the alert :** on the lookout esp. for danger or opportunity

³alert *vt* (1868) **1 :** to call to a state of readiness **:** WARN **2 :** to make aware of ⟨~*ed* the public to the dangers of pesticides⟩

-a·les \ˈā-(ˌ)lēz\ *n pl suffix* [NL, fr. L, pl. of *-alis* -al] **:** plants consisting of or related to — in the names of taxonomic orders

al·eu·rone \ˈal-yə-ˌrōn\ *n* [G *aleuron,* fr. Gk, flour; akin to Arm *ałam* I grind] (ca. 1869) **:** protein matter in the form of minute granules or grains occurring in seeds in endosperm or in a special peripheral layer — **al·eu·ron·ic** \ˌal-yə-ˈrän-ik\ *adj*

Aleut \ˌal-ē-ˈüt, ˈal-ē-ˌ; ə-ˈlüt\ *n* [Russ] (1780) **1 :** a member of a people of the Aleutian and Shumagin islands and the western part of Alaska peninsula **2 :** the language of the Aleuts

A level *n* (1951) **:** the later of two standardized British examinations in a secondary school subject used as a qualification for university entrance; *also* **:** the level of knowledge required to pass such an examination — called also *Advanced level;* compare O LEVEL

al·e·vin \ˈal-ə-vən\ *n* [F, fr. OF, fr. *alever* to lift up, rear (offspring), fr. L *allevare,* fr. *ad-* + *levare* to raise — more at LEVER] (1868) **:** a young fish; *esp* **:** the newly hatched salmon when still attached to the yolk sac

¹ale·wife \ˈā(ə)l-ˌwīf\ *n* (15c) **:** a woman who keeps an alehouse

²alewife *n* (1633) **:** a food fish (*Alosa pseudoharengus*) of the herring family (Clupeidae) very abundant along the Atlantic coast; *also* **:** any of several related fishes (as the menhaden)

al·ex·an·der \ˌal-ig-ˈzan-dər, ˌel-\ *n, often cap* (1928) **:** an iced cocktail made from crème de cacao, sweet cream, and gin or brandy

Al·ex·an·dri·an \ˌal-ig-ˈzan-drē-ən, ˌel-\ *adj* (ca. 1864) **1 :** of or relating to Alexander the Great **2 :** HELLENISTIC

al·ex·an·drine \-ˈzan-ˌdrēn, -drən, -ˌdrīn\ *n, often cap* [MF *alexandrin,* adj., fr. *Alexandre* Alexander the Great; fr. its use in a poem on Alexander] (1667) **:** a line of verse of 12 syllables consisting regularly of 6 iambs with a caesura after the 3d iamb — **alexandrine** *adj*

al·ex·an·drite \-ˈzan-ˌdrīt\ *n* [G *alexandrit,* fr. *Alexander I* Russ emperor] (1837) **:** a grass-green chrysoberyl that shows a red color by transmitted or artificial light

alex·ia \ə-ˈlek-sē-ə\ *n* [NL, fr. *a-* + Gk *lexis* speech, fr. *legein* to speak — more at LEGEND] (1878) **:** aphasia marked by loss of ability to read

Al·fa \ˈal-fə\ (1952) — a communications code word for the letter *a*

al·fal·fa \al-ˈfal-fə\ *n* [Sp, modif. of Ar dial. *al-fasfaṣah* the alfalfa] (1845) **:** a deep-rooted European leguminous plant (*Medicago sativa*) widely grown for hay and forage

alfalfa weevil *n* (1912) **:** a small dark brown European weevil (*Hypera postica*) that is now a widespread pest of alfalfa in No. America

al·fil·a·ria \(ˌ)al-ˌfil-ə-ˈrē-ə\ *n* [AmerSp *alfilerillo,* fr. Sp, dim. of *alfiler* pin, modif. of Ar *al-khilāl* the thorn] (1868) **:** a European weed (*Erodium cicutarium*) of the geranium family grown for forage in western America

al·for·ja \al-ˈfȯr-(ˌ)hä\ *n* [Sp, fr. Ar *al-khurj*] *West* (1611) **:** SADDLEBAG

al·fres·co \al-ˈfres-(ˌ)kō\ *adj or adv* [It] (1753) **:** taking place in the open air **:** OUTDOOR, OUTDOORS ⟨an ~ lunch⟩

alg- *or* **algo-** *comb form* [NL, fr. Gk *alg-,* fr. *algos*] **:** pain ⟨algophobia⟩

al·ga \ˈal-gə\ *n, pl* **al·gae** \ˈal-(ˌ)jē\ *also* **algas** [L, seaweed] (1551) **:** any of a group (Algae) of chiefly aquatic nonvascular plants (as seaweeds, pond scums, and stoneworts) with chlorophyll often masked by a brown or red pigment — **al·gal** \-gəl\ *adj* — **al·goid** \-ˌgȯid\ *adj*

al·ga·ro·ba *also* **al·gar·ro·ba** \ˌal-gə-ˈrō-bə\ *n* [Sp *algarroba,* fr. Ar *al-kharrūbah* the carob] (1577) **1 :** CAROB **2** [MexSp, fr. Sp] **:** MESQUITE; *also* **:** its pods

al·ge·bra \ˈal-jə-brə\ *n* [ML, fr. Ar *al-jabr,* lit., the reduction] (1551) **1 a :** a generalization of arithmetic in which letters representing numbers are combined according to the rules of arithmetic **b :** a treatise on algebra **2 :** LINEAR ALGEBRA 2 **3 :** a logical or set calculus — **al·ge·bra·ist** \-ˌbrā-əst\ *n*

al·ge·bra·ic \ˌal-jə-ˈbrā-ik\ *adj* (1662) **1 :** relating to, involving, or according to the laws of algebra **2 :** involving only a finite number of repetitions of addition, subtraction, multiplication, division, extraction of roots, and raising to powers ⟨~ equation⟩ — compare TRANSCENDENTAL — **al·ge·bra·i·cal·ly** \-ˈbrā-ə-k(ə-)lē\ *adv*

algebraic number *n* (ca. 1904) **:** a root of an algebraic equation with rational coefficients

-al·gia \ˈal-j(ē-)ə\ *n comb form* [Gk, fr. *algos*] **:** pain ⟨neuralgia⟩

al·gi·cide *or* **al·gae·cide** \ˈal-jə-ˌsīd\ *n* [*alga* + *-i-* + *-cide*] (1904) **:** an agent used to kill algae — **al·gi·cid·al** \ˌal-jə-ˈsīd-ᵊl\ *adj*

al·gid \ˈal-jəd\ *adj* [L *algidus,* fr. *algēre* to feel cold] (ca.1626) **:** COLD

al·gin \ˈal-jən\ *n* (1883) **:** any of various colloidal substances from marine brown algae: as **a :** ALGINIC ACID **b :** a soluble salt of alginic acid used esp. as a stabilizer or emulsifier

al·gi·nate \ˈal-jə-ˌnāt\ *n* (ca. 1909) **:** a salt of alginic acid

al·gin·ic acid \(ˌ)al-ˌjin-ik-\ *n* [ISV *algin* + *-ic*] (1885) **:** an insoluble colloidal acid $(C_6H_8O_6)_n$ that in the form of its salts is a constituent of the cell walls of brown algae

Al·gol \ˈal-ˌgäl, -ˌgȯl\ *n* [Ar *al-ghūl,* lit., the ghoul] **:** a binary star in the constellation Perseus whose larger component revolves about and eclipses the smaller brighter star causing periodic variation in brightness

AL·GOL *or* **Al·gol** \ˈal-ˌgäl, -ˌgȯl\ *n* [*algo*rithmic *l*anguage] (1959) **:** an algebraic computer programming language in which problems are solved by use of algorithms and which is used esp. in mathematical and scientific applications

al·go·lag·nia \ˌal-gō-ˈlag-nē-ə\ *n* [NL, fr. *alg-* + Gk *lagneia* lust] (ca. 1901) **:** a perversion (as sadism) characterized by pleasure and esp. sexual gratification in inflicting or suffering pain — **al·go·lag·nic** \-ˈlag-nik\ *adj* — **al·go·lag·ni·ac** \-ˈlag-nē-ˌak\ *n*

al·gol·o·gy \al-ˈgäl-ə-jē\ *n* (1849) **:** the study or science of algae — **al·go·log·i·cal** \ˌal-gə-ˈläj-i-kəl\ *adj* — **al·go·log·i·cal·ly** \-k(ə-)lē\ *adv* — **al·gol·o·gist** \al-ˈgäl-ə-jəst\ *n*

Al·gon·ki·an \al-ˈgäŋ-kē-ən\ *adj* (1890) **:** PROTEROZOIC

Al·gon·qui·an \al-'gän-kwē-ən, -'gäŋ-\ *or* **Al·gon·quin** \-kwən\ *or* **Al·gon·ki·an** \-'gäŋ-kē-ən\ *or* **Al·gon·kin** \-'gäŋ-kən\ *n* [CanF *Algonquin*] (1625) **1** : an Indian people of the Ottawa river valley **2** *usu Algonquin* : a dialect of Ojibwa **3** *usu Algonquian* : a stock of Indian languages spoken from Labrador to Carolina and westward to the Great Plains **4** *usu Algonquian* : a member of the Indian peoples speaking Algonquian languages **5** *Algonkian* : the Algonkian era or system or group of systems

al·go·pho·bia \,al-gə-'fō-bē-ə\ *n* [NL] (ca. 1897) : morbid fear of pain

al·go·rithm \'al-gə-,rith-əm\ *n* [alter. of ME *algorisme*, fr. OF & ML; OF, fr. ML *algorismus*, fr. Ar *al-khuwārizmi*, fr. *al-Khuwārizmi fl* A.D. 825 Arab mathematician] (ca. 1894) : a procedure for solving a mathematical problem (as of finding the greatest common divisor) in a finite number of steps that frequently involves repetition of an operation; *broadly* : a step-by-step procedure for solving a problem or accomplishing some end — **al·go·rith·mic** \,al-gə-'rith-mik\ *adj*

Al·ham·bra \al-'ham-brə\ *n* [Sp, fr. Ar *al-ḥamrā'* the red house] (1612) : the palace of the Moorish kings at Granada, Spain

ali- *comb form* [L, fr. *ala* — more at AISLE] : wing ⟨*ali*form⟩

¹alias \'ā-lē-əs, 'āl-yəs\ *adv* [L, otherwise, fr. *alius* other — more at ELSE] (15c) : otherwise called : otherwise known as

²alias *n* (1605) : an assumed or additional name

Ali Ba·ba \,al-ē-'bäb-ə\ *n* : a woodcutter in the *Arabian Nights' Entertainments* who enters the cave of the Forty Thieves by using the password *Sesame*

¹al·i·bi \'al-ə-,bī\ *n* [L, elsewhere, fr. *alius*] (1743) **1** : the plea of having been at the time of the commission of an act elsewhere than at the place of commission; *also* : the fact or state of having been elsewhere at the time **2** : an excuse usu. intended to avert blame or punishment (as for failure or negligence) ***syn*** see APOLOGY

²alibi *vb* **-bied; -bi·ing** *vt* (1909) : to exonerate by an alibi ~ *vi* : to offer an excuse

Al·ice-in-Won·der·land \'al-ə-sən-'wən-dər-,land\ *adj* [fr. *Alice's Adventures in Wonderland* (1865) by Lewis Carroll] (1925) : suitable to a world of fantasy or illusion : UNREAL

ali·cy·clic \,al-ə-'sī-klik, -'sik-lik\ *adj* [ISV *ali*phatic + *cyclic*] (1891) : combining the properties of aliphatic and cyclic compounds

al·i·dade \'al-ə-,dād\ *n* [ME *allidatha*, fr. ML *alhidada*, fr. Ar *al-'idādah* the revolving radius of a circle] (15c) : a rule equipped with simple or telescopic sights and used for determination of direction: as **a** : a part of an astrolabe **b** : a part of a surveying instrument consisting of the telescope and its attachments

¹alien \'ā-lē-ən, 'āl-yən\ *adj* [ME, fr. MF, fr. L *alienus*, fr. *alius*] (14c) **1 a** : belonging or relating to another person, place, or thing : STRANGE **b** : relating, belonging, or owing allegiance to another country or government : FOREIGN **2** : differing in nature or character typically to the point of incompatibility ***syn*** see EXTRINSIC — **alienly** *adv* — **alien·ness** \-lē-ən-nəs, -yən-nəs\ *n*

²alien *n* (14c) **1** : a person of another family, race, or nation **2** : a foreign-born resident who has not been naturalized and is still a subject or citizen of a foreign country; *broadly* : a foreign-born citizen **3** : EXTRATERRESTRIAL

³alien *vt* (14c) **1** : ALIENATE, ESTRANGE **2** : to make over (as property)

alien·able \'āl-yə-nə-bəl, 'ā-lē-ə-nə-\ *adj* (1611) : transferable to another's ownership — **alien·abil·i·ty** \,āl-yə-nə-'bil-ət-ē, ,ā-lē-ə-nə-\ *n*

alien·age \'āl-yə-nij, 'ā-lē-ə-nij\ *n* (1809) : the status of an alien

alien·ate \'ā-lē-ə-,nāt, 'āl-yə-\ *vt* **-at·ed; -at·ing** (ca. 1509) **1** : to make unfriendly, hostile, or indifferent where attachment formerly existed **2** : to convey or transfer (as property or a right) usu. by a specific act rather than the due course of law **3** : to cause to be withdrawn or diverted ***syn*** see ESTRANGE — **alien·ator** \-,nāt-ər\ *n*

alien·ation \,ā-lē-ə-'nā-shən, ,āl-yə-\ *n* (14c) **1** : a withdrawing or separation of a person or his affections from an object or position of former attachment : ESTRANGEMENT ⟨~ . . . from the values of one's society and family — S. L. Halleck⟩ **2** : a conveyance of property to another

alien·ee \-'nē\ *n* (1531) : one to whom property is transferred

alien·ism \'ā-lē-ə-,niz-əm, 'āl-yə-\ *n* (1808) : ALIENAGE

alien·ist \-nəst\ *n* [F *aliéniste*, fr. *aliéné* insane, fr. L *alienatus*, pp. of *alienare* to estrange, fr. *alienus*] (1864) : PSYCHIATRIST; *esp* : one specializing in the legal aspects of psychiatry

alien·or \,ā-lē-ə-'nó(ə)r, ,āl-yə-\ *n* (ca. 1552) : one who transfers property to another

¹alight \ə-'līt\ *vi* **alight·ed** *also* **alit** \ə-'lit\; **alight·ing** [ME *alighten*, fr. OE *ālīhtan*, fr. *ā-* (perfective prefix) + *līhtan* to alight — more at ABIDE, LIGHT] (bef. 12c) **1** : to come down from something: as **a** : DISMOUNT **b** : DEPLANE **2** : to descend from the air and come to rest : LAND, SETTLE **3** *archaic* : to come by chance — **alight·ment** *n*

²alight *adj* (14c) **1** *chiefly Brit* : being on fire **2** : lighted up

align *also* **aline** \ə-'līn\ *vb* [F *aligner*, fr. OF, fr. *a-* (fr. L *ad-*) + *ligne* line, fr. L *linea*] *vt* (ca. 1693) **1** : to bring into line or alignment **2** : to array on the side of or against a party or cause ~ *vi* **1** : to get or fall into line **2** : to be in or come into precise adjustment or correct relative position — **align·er** *n*

align·ment *also* **aline·ment** \ə-'līn-mənt\ *n* (1790) **1** : the act of aligning or state of being aligned; *esp* : the proper positioning or state of adjustment of parts (as of a mechanical or electronic device) in relation to each other **2 a** : a forming in line **b** : the line thus formed **3** : the ground plan (as of a railroad or fieldwork) in distinction from the profile **4** : an arrangement of groups or forces in relation to one another ⟨new ~*s* within the political party⟩

¹alike \ə-'līk\ *adj* [ME *ilik* (alter. of *ilich*) & *alik*, alter. of OE *onlīc*, fr. *on* + *līc* body — more at LIKE] (bef. 12c) : exhibiting close resemblance without being identical ⟨~ in their beliefs⟩ ***syn*** see SIMILAR — **alike·ness** *n*

²alike *adv* (bef. 12c) : in the same manner, form, or degree : EQUALLY ⟨was denounced by teachers and students ~⟩

¹al·i·ment \'al-ə-mənt\ *n* [ME, fr. L *alimentum*, fr. *alere* to nourish — more at OLD] (15c) : FOOD, NUTRIMENT; *also* : SUSTENANCE

²al·i·ment \-,ment\ *vt* (15c) : to give aliment to : NOURISH, SUSTAIN

al·i·men·ta·ry \,al-ə-'ment-ə-rē, -'men-trē\ *adj* (1615) **1** : of or relating to nourishment or nutrition **2** : furnishing sustenance or maintenance

alimentary canal *n* (1764) : the tubular passage that extends from mouth to anus and functions in digestion and absorption of food and elimination of residual waste

al·i·men·ta·tion \,al-ə-mən-'tā-shən, -,men-\ *n* (ca. 1656) : the act or process of affording nutriment or nourishment ⟨intravenous ~⟩

al·i·mo·ny \'al-ə-,mō-nē\ *n, pl* **-nies** [L *alimonia* sustenance, fr. *alere*] (1656) **1** : an allowance made to one spouse by the other for support pending or after legal separation or divorce **2** : the means of living : MAINTENANCE

A-line \'ā-,līn\ *adj* (1964) : having a flared bottom and a close-fitting top — used of a garment ⟨an ~ skirt⟩

Al·i·oth \'al-ē-,äth, -,ōth\ *n* [Ar *alyat* fat tail of a sheep] : a star of the second magnitude in the handle of the Big Dipper

al·i·phat·ic \,al-ə-'fat-ik\ *adj* [ISV, fr. Gk *aleiphat-*, *aleiphar* oil, fr. *aleiphein* to smear; akin to Gk *lipos* fat — more at LEAVE] (1889) : of, relating to, or derived from fat; *specif* : belonging to a group of organic compounds having an open-chain structure and consisting of the paraffin, olefin, and acetylene hydrocarbons and their derivatives

al·i·quot \'al-ə-,kwät, -kwət\ *adj* [ML *aliquotus*, fr. L *aliquot* some, several, fr. *alius* other + *quot* how many — more at ELSE, QUOTA] (1570) **1** : contained an exact number of times in something else — used of a divisor or part ⟨5 is an ~ part of 15⟩ ⟨an ~ portion of a solution⟩ **2** : FRACTIONAL ⟨an ~ part of invested capital⟩ — **aliquot** *n*

A-list \'ā-,list\ *n* (1980) : a list or group of individuals of the highest level of society, excellence, or eminence

alive \ə-'līv\ *adj* [ME, fr. OE *on life*, fr. *on* + *līf* life] (bef. 12c) **1** : having life : not dead or inanimate **2** : still in existence, force, or operation : ACTIVE ⟨kept hope ~⟩ **3** : knowing or realizing the existence of : SENSITIVE ⟨~ to the danger⟩ **4** : marked by alertness, energy, or briskness **5** : marked by much life, animation, or activity : SWARMING ⟨streets ~ with traffic⟩ **6** — used as an intensive following the noun ⟨the proudest boy ~⟩ ***syn*** see AWARE — **alive·ness** *n*

ali·yah *or* **ali·ya** \ä-'lē-(,)yä, ,ä-lē-'yä\ *n* [NHeb *'alīyāh*, fr. Heb, ascent] (ca. 1934) : the immigration of Jews to Israel

aliz·a·rin \ə-'liz-ə-rən\ *n* [prob. fr. F *alizarine*] (ca. 1835) **1** : an orange or red crystalline compound $C_{14}H_8O_4$ formerly prepared from madder and now made synthetically and used esp. to dye Turkey reds and in making red pigments **2** : any of various acid, mordant, and solvent dyes derived like alizarin proper from anthraquinone

al·ka·hest \'al-kə-,hest\ *n* [NL *alchahest*] (1641) : the universal solvent believed by alchemists to exist — **al·ka·hes·tic** \,al-kə-'hes-tik\ *adj*

al·ka·li \'al-kə-,lī\ *n, pl* **-lies** *or* **-lis** [ME, fr. ML, fr. Ar *al-qili* the ashes of the plant saltwort] (14c) **1** : a soluble salt obtained from the ashes of plants and consisting largely of potassium or sodium carbonate; *broadly* : a substance (as a hydroxide or carbonate of an alkali metal) having marked basic properties — compare BASE 7 **2** : ALKALI METAL **3** : a soluble salt or a mixture of soluble salts present in some soils of arid regions in quantity detrimental to agriculture

alkali metal *n* (ca. 1885) : any of the univalent mostly basic metals of group I of the periodic table comprising lithium, sodium, potassium, rubidium, cesium, and francium

al·ka·lim·e·ter \,al-kə-'lim-ət-ər\ *n* [F *alcalimètre*, fr. *alcali* alkali + *-mètre* -meter] (ca. 1828) : an apparatus for measuring the strength or the amount of alkali in a mixture or solution — **al·ka·lim·e·try** \-'lim-ə-trē\ *n*

al·ka·line \'al-kə-lən, -,līn\ *adj* (1677) : of, relating to, or having the properties of an alkali; *esp* : having a pH of more than 7 — **al·ka·lin·i·ty** \,al-kə-'lin-ət-ē\ *n*

alkaline earth *n* (1816) **1** : an oxide of any of several bivalent strongly basic metals comprising calcium, strontium, and barium and sometimes also magnesium, radium, or less often beryllium **2** : ALKALINE-EARTH METAL

alkaline-earth metal *n* (ca. 1903) : any of the metals whose oxides are the alkaline earths

alkaline phosphatase *n* (1949) : a phosphatase (as the phosphomonoesterase from blood plasma or milk) active in alkaline medium

al·ka·lin·ize \'al-kə-lə-,nīz\ *vt* **-ized; -iz·ing** (1800) : to make alkaline — **al·ka·lin·iza·tion** \,al-kə-,lin-ə-'zā-shən, -lə-nə-\ *n*

al·ka·loid \'al-kə-,lȯid\ *n* (ca. 1831) : any of numerous usu. colorless, complex, and bitter organic bases (as morphine or codeine) containing nitrogen and usu. oxygen that occur esp. in seed plants — **al·ka·loi·dal** \,al-kə-'lȯid-ᵊl\ *adj*

al·ka·lo·sis \,al-kə-'lō-səs\ *n* (1911) : an abnormal condition of increased alkalinity of the blood and tissues — **al·ka·lot·ic** \-'lät-ik\ *adj*

al·kane \'al-,kān\ *n* [*alkyl* + *-ane*] (1899) : any of a series of open-chain saturated hydrocarbons C_nH_{2n+2} (as methane) — called also *paraffin*

al·ka·net \'al-kə-,net\ *n* [ME, fr. OSp *alcaneta*, dim. of *alcana* henna shrub, fr. ML *alchanna*, fr. Ar *al-ḥinnā'* the henna] (14c) **1 a** : a European plant (*Alkanna tinctoria*) of the borage family; *also* : its root **b** : a red dyestuff prepared from the root **2** : a plant (*Anchusa officinalis*) of the borage family with delicate usu. blue flowers

al·kene \'al-,kēn\ *n* [ISV *alkyl* + *-ene*] (1899) : OLEFIN; *specif* : any of a series of open-chain hydrocarbons C_nH_{2n} (as ethylene) having one double bond

alk·oxy \'al-,käk-sē\ *adj* [ISV *alkyl* + *oxygen*] (ca. 1925) : of, relating to, or containing a univalent radical composed of an alkyl group united with oxygen

al·kyd \'al-kəd\ *n* [blend of *alkyl* and *acid*] (1929) : any of numerous thermoplastic or thermosetting synthetic resins made by heating polyhydroxy alcohols with polybasic acids or their anhydrides and used esp. for protective coatings

al·kyl \'al-kəl\ *n* [prob. fr. G, fr. *alkohol* alcohol, fr. ML *alcohol*] (1882) **1 a** : a univalent aliphatic radical C_nH_{2n+1} (as methyl) **b** : any univalent aliphatic, aromatic-aliphatic, or alicyclic hydrocarbon radical **2** : a compound of alkyl radicals with a metal — **alkyl** *adj*

al·kyl·ate \'al-kə-,lāt\ *vt* **-at·ed; -at·ing** (1889) : to introduce one or more alkyl groups into (a compound)

al·kyl·ation \,al-kə-'lā-shən\ *n* (1900) : the act or process of alkylating esp. for producing high-octane fuel

al·kyne \'al-,kīn\ *n* [*alkyl* + *-yne*, alter. of *-ine*] (ca. 1909) : any of a series of open-chain hydrocarbons C_nH_{2n-2} (as acetylene) having one triple bond

¹all \'ȯl\ *adj* [ME *all*, *al*, fr. OE *eall*; akin to OHG *all* all] (bef. 12c) **1 a** : the whole amount or quantity of ⟨sat up ~ night⟩ **b** : as much as possible ⟨spoke in ~ seriousness⟩ **2** : every member or individual component of ⟨~ men will go⟩ ⟨~ five children were present⟩ **3 :** the whole number or sum of ⟨~ the angles of a triangle are equal to two right angles⟩ **4 :** EVERY ⟨~ manner of hardship⟩ **5 :** any whatever ⟨beyond ~ doubt⟩ **6 :** nothing but : ONLY: **a :** completely taken up with, given to, or absorbed by ⟨became ~ attention⟩ **b :** having or seeming to have (some physical feature) in conspicuous excess or prominence ⟨~ legs⟩ **c :** paying full attention with ⟨~ ears⟩ **7** *dial* **:** used up : entirely consumed — used esp. of food and drink **8 :** being more than one person or thing ⟨who ~ is coming⟩ ***syn*** see WHOLE — **all the :** as much of . . . as : as much of a . . . as ⟨*all the* home I ever had⟩

[2]all *adv* (bef. 12c) **1 :** WHOLLY, ALTOGETHER ⟨sat ~ alone⟩ — often used as an intensive ⟨~ out of proportion⟩ **2** *obs* **:** ONLY, EXCLUSIVELY **3** *archaic* **:** JUST **4 :** so much ⟨~ the better for it⟩ **5 :** for each side : APIECE ⟨the score is two ~⟩

[3]all *pron* (bef. 12c) **1 :** the whole number, quantity, or amount : TOTALITY ⟨~ that I have⟩ ⟨~ of us⟩ ⟨~ of the books⟩ **2 :** EVERYBODY, EVERYTHING ⟨gave equal attention to ~⟩ — **all in all :** on the whole : GENERALLY ⟨*all in all,* things might have been worse⟩ — **and all :** and everything else esp. of a kind suggested by a previous context ⟨cards to fill out with . . . numbers *and all* —Sally Quinn⟩

[4]all *n* (1593) **:** the whole of one's possessions, resources, or energy ⟨gave his ~ for the cause⟩

all- *or* **allo-** *comb form* [Gk, fr. *allos* other — more at ELSE] **1 :** other : different : atypical ⟨*allo*gamous⟩ ⟨*allo*merism⟩ **2** *allo-* **:** isomeric form or variety of (a specified chemical compound) **3** *allo-* **:** being one of a group whose members together constitute a structural unit esp. of a language ⟨*allo*phone⟩

[1]al·la bre·ve \ˌal-ə-ˈbrev, ˌäl-ə-ˈbrev-(ˌ)ā\ *n* [It, lit., according to the breve] (ca. 1740) **:** the sign marking a piece or passage to be played alla breve; *also* **:** a passage so marked

[2]alla breve *adv or adj* (ca. 1823) **:** in duple or quadruple time with the beat represented by the half note

Al·lah \ˈäl-ə, ˈal-ə, ˈäl-ˌä, ä-ˈlä\ *n* [Ar *allāh*] **:** the Supreme Being of Islam

all along *adv* (1670) **:** all the time ⟨knew the truth *all along*⟩

[1]all–Amer·i·can \ˌȯ-lə-ˈmer-ə-kən\ *adj* (1888) **1 :** composed wholly of American elements **2 :** representative or typical of the U.S. or its ideals ⟨an ~ boy⟩ ⟨her ~ optimism⟩ **3 a :** selected (as by a poll of journalists) as one of the best in the U.S. in a particular category at a particular time ⟨an ~ quarterback⟩ **b :** having only all-American participants ⟨an ~ basketball team⟩ **4 :** of or relating to the American nations as a group

[2]all–American *n* (1920) **:** one (as an athlete) that is voted all-American

al·lan·to·in \ə-ˈlan-tə-wən\ *n* [prob. fr. G, fr. NL *allantois* + G *-in*] (ca. 1845) **:** a crystalline oxidation product $C_4H_6N_4O_3$ of uric acid used to promote healing of local wounds and infections

al·lan·to·is \ə-ˈlant-ə-wəs\ *n, pl* **al·lan·to·ides** \ˌal-ən-ˈtō-ə-ˌdēz, ˌal-ˌan-\ [NL, deriv. of Gk *allant-, allas* sausage] (ca. 1646) **:** a vascular fetal membrane of reptiles, birds, and mammals that is formed as a pouch from the hindgut and that in placental mammals is intimately associated with the chorion in formation of the placenta — **al·lan·to·ic** \ˌal-ən-ˈtō-ik, ˌal-ˌan-\ *adj*

al·lar·gan·do \ˌäl-ˌär-ˈgän-(ˌ)dō\ *adj or adv* [It, widening, verbal of *allargare* to widen, fr. *al-* (fr. L *ad-*) + *largare* to widen] (ca. 1893) **:** becoming gradually slower and more stately — used as a direction in music

all–around \ˌȯ-lə-ˈrau̇nd\ *adj* (1867) **1 :** competent in many fields ⟨an ~ man of letters⟩ **2 :** having general utility or merit **3 :** considered in or encompassing all aspects : INCLUSIVE ⟨the best ~ performance so far⟩

al·lay \a-ˈlā, ə-\ *vb* [ME *alayen,* fr. OE *ālecgan,* fr. *ā-* (perfective prefix) + *lecgan* to lay — more at ABIDE, LAY] *vt* (bef. 12c) **1 :** to subdue or reduce in intensity or severity : ALLEVIATE ⟨expect a breeze to ~ the heat⟩ **2 :** to make quiet : CALM ~ *vi, obs* **:** to diminish in strength : SUBSIDE ***syn*** see RELIEVE

all but *adv* (1598) **:** very nearly : ALMOST ⟨would be *all but* impossible⟩

all clear *n* (1917) **:** a signal that a danger has passed

all–day \ˌȯl-ˌdā\ *adj* (1870) **:** lasting for, occupying, or appearing throughout an entire day ⟨an ~ trip⟩

al·le·ga·tion \ˌal-i-ˈgā-shən\ *n* (15c) **1 :** the act of alleging **2 :** a positive assertion; *specif* **:** a statement by a party to a legal action of what he undertakes to prove **3 :** an assertion unsupported and by implication regarded as unsupportable ⟨vague ~*s* of misconduct⟩

al·lege \ə-ˈlej\ *vt* **al·leged; al·leg·ing** [ME *alleggen,* fr. MF *alleguer,* fr. L *allegare* to dispatch, cite, fr. *ad-* + *legare* to depute — more at LEGATE] (14c) **1 :** to assert without proof or before proving ⟨the newspaper ~*s* the mayor's guilt⟩ **2** *archaic* **:** to adduce or bring forward as a source or authority **3 :** to bring forward as a reason or excuse

al·leged \ə-ˈlejd, -ˈlej-əd\ *adj* (1509) **1 :** asserted to be true or to exist ⟨an ~ miracle⟩ **2 :** questionably true or of a specified kind : SUPPOSED, SO-CALLED ⟨bought an ~ antique vase⟩ — **al·leg·ed·ly** \-ˈlej-əd-lē\ *adv*

Al·le·ghe·ny spurge \ˌal-ə-ˌgā-nē- *also* -ˌgen-ē-\ *n* [*Allegheny* mts., U.S.A.] (ca. 1936) **:** a low herb or subshrub (*Pachysandra procumbens*) of the box family widely grown as a ground cover

al·le·giance \ə-ˈlē-jən(t)s\ *n* [ME *allegeaunce,* modif. of MF *ligeance,* fr. OF, fr. *lige* liege] (14c) **1 a :** the obligation of a feudal vassal to his liege lord **b (1) :** the fidelity owed by a subject or citizen to his sovereign or government **(2) :** the obligation of an alien to the government under which he resides **2 :** devotion or loyalty to a person, group, or cause ***syn*** see FIDELITY

al·le·giant \-jənt\ *adj* (1613) **:** giving allegiance : LOYAL

al·le·gor·i·cal \ˌal-ə-ˈgȯr-i-kəl, -ˈgär-\ *adj* (1528) **1 :** of, relating to, or having the characteristics of allegory **2 :** having hidden spiritual meaning that transcends the literal sense of a sacred text — **al·le·gor·i·cal·ly** \-k(ə-)lē\ *adv* — **al·le·gor·i·cal·ness** \-kəl-nəs\ *n*

al·le·go·rist \ˈal-ə-ˌgōr-əst, -ˌgȯr-\ *n* (1684) **:** a writer of allegory

al·le·go·ri·za·tion \ˌal-ə-ˌgōr-ə-ˈzā-shən, -ˌgȯr-, -gər-\ *n* (1847) **:** allegorical representation or interpretation

al·le·go·rize \ˈal-ə-ˌgōr-ˌīz, -ˌgȯr-, -gər-\ *vb* **-rized; -riz·ing** *vt* (15c) **1 :** to treat or explain as an allegory **2 :** to make into allegory ~ *vi* **1 :** to give allegorical explanations **2 :** to compose or use allegory — **al·le·go·riz·er** *n*

al·le·go·ry \ˈal-ə-ˌgōr-ē, -ˌgȯr-\ *n, pl* **-ries** [ME *allegorie,* fr. L *allegoria,* fr. Gk *allēgoria,* fr. *allēgorein* to speak figuratively, fr. *allos* other + *-agorein* to speak publicly, fr. *agora* assembly — more at ELSE, GREGARIOUS] (14c) **1 :** the expression by means of symbolic fictional figures and actions of truths or generalizations about human existence; *also* **:** an instance (as in a story or painting) of such expression **2 :** a symbolic representation : EMBLEM

[1]al·le·gret·to \ˌal-ə-ˈgret-(ˌ)ō, ˌäl-\ *adv or adj* [It, dim. of *allegro*] (ca. 1740) **:** faster than andante but not so fast as allegro — used as a direction in music

[2]allegretto *n, pl* **-tos** (ca. 1807) **:** a musical composition or movement in allegretto tempo

[1]al·le·gro \ə-ˈleg-(ˌ)rō, -ˈlā-(ˌ)grō\ *adv or adj* [It, merry, fr. (assumed) VL *alecrus* lively, alter. of L *alacr-, alacer* — more at ALACRITY] (1683) **:** in a brisk lively manner — used as a direction in music

[2]allegro *n, pl* **-gros** (1683) **:** a musical composition or movement in allegro tempo

al·lele \ə-ˈlē(ə)l\ *n* [G *allel,* short for *allelomorph*] (1928) **1 :** one of a group of genes that occur alternatively at a given locus **2 :** either of a pair of alternative Mendelian characters (as smooth and wrinkled seed in the pea) — **al·le·lic** \-ˈlē-lik, -ˈlel-ik\ *adj* — **al·lel·ism** \-ˈlē(ə)l-ˌiz-əm, -ˈlel-ˌiz-\ *n*

al·le·lo·morph \ə-ˈlē-lə-ˌmȯrf, -ˈlel-ə-\ *n* [Gk *allēlōn* of each other (fr. *allos . . . allos* one . . . the other, fr. *allos* other) + *morphē* form — more at ELSE] (1902) **:** ALLELE — **al·le·lo·mor·phic** \ə-ˌlē-lə-ˈmȯr-fik, -ˌlel-ə-\ *adj* — **al·le·lo·mor·phism** \ə-ˈlē-lə-ˌmȯr-ˌfiz-əm, -ˈlel-ə-\ *n*

al·le·lop·a·thy \ə-ˈlē-lə-ˌpath-ē, -ˈlel-ə-; *also* ˌal-ə-ˈläp-ə-thē\ *n* [ISV *allelo-* of or for each other, reciprocal + *-pathy*] (1948) **:** the suppression of growth of one plant species by another due to the release of toxic substances — **al·le·lo·path·ic** \ə-ˌlē-lə-ˈpath-ik, -ˌləl-ə-\ *adj*

al·le·lu·ia \ˌal-ə-ˈlü-yə\ *interj* [ME, fr. LL, fr. Gk *allēlouia,* fr. Heb *hallĕlūyāh* praise ye Jehovah] (13c) **:** HALLELUJAH

al·le·mande \ˈal-ə-ˌman(d), -mən, -ˌmänd, *1a & 2 also* ˌal-ə-ˈ\ *n, often cap* [F, fr. fem. of *allemand* German] (1685) **1 :** a musical composition or movement (as in a baroque suite) in moderate tempo and duple or quadruple time **2 a :** a 17th and 18th century court dance developed in France from a German folk dance **b :** a dance step with arms interlaced

all–em·brac·ing \ˌȯ-lim-ˈbrā-siŋ\ *adj* (ca. 1828) **:** COMPLETE, SWEEPING ⟨an ~ charity toward his fellowmen⟩

al·ler·gen \ˈal-ər-jən\ *n* (1910) **:** a substance that induces allergy — **al·ler·gen·ic** \ˌal-ər-ˈjen-ik\ *adj*

al·ler·gic \ə-ˈlər-jik\ *adj* (1911) **1 :** of, relating to, inducing, or affected by allergy **2 :** having an aversion ⟨~ to work⟩

al·ler·gist \ˈal-ər-jəst\ *n* (1928) **:** a specialist in allergy

al·ler·gy \ˈal-ər-jē\ *n, pl* **-gies** [G *allergie,* fr. *all-* + Gk *ergon* work — more at WORK] (1910) **1 :** altered bodily reactivity (as anaphylaxis) to an antigen in response to a first exposure ⟨his bee-venom ~ may render a second sting fatal⟩ **2 :** exaggerated or pathological reaction (as by sneezing, respiratory embarrassment, itching, or skin rashes) to substances, situations, or physical states that are without comparable effect on the average individual **3 :** medical practice concerned with allergies **4 :** a feeling of antipathy or repugnance

al·le·thrin \ˈal-ə-thrən\ *n* [*all*yl + pyr*ethrin*] (ca. 1950) **:** a light yellow viscous oily synthetic insecticide $C_{19}H_{26}O_3$ used esp. in household aerosols

al·le·vi·ate \ə-ˈlē-vē-ˌāt\ *vt* **-at·ed; -at·ing** [LL *alleviatus,* pp. of *alleviare,* fr. L *ad-* + *levis* light — more at LIGHT] (15c) **:** RELIEVE, LESSEN: as **a :** to make (as suffering) more bearable ⟨her sympathy *alleviated* his distress⟩ **b :** to partially remove or correct ***syn*** see RELIEVE — **al·le·vi·a·tion** \-ˌlē-vē-ˈā-shən\ *n* — **al·le·vi·a·tor** \-ˈlē-vē-ˌāt-ər\ *n*

[1]al·ley \ˈal-ē\ *n, pl* **alleys** [ME, fr. MF *alee,* fr. OF, fr. *aler* to go] (14c) **1 :** a garden or park walk bordered by trees or bushes **2 a (1) :** a grassed enclosure for bowling or skittles **(2) :** a hardwood lane for bowling; *also* **:** a room or building housing a group of such lanes **b :** the space on each side of a tennis doubles court between the sideline and the service sideline **3 :** a narrow street; *esp* **:** a thoroughfare through the middle of a block giving access to the rear of lots or buildings — **up one's alley** *also* **down one's alley :** suited to one's own tastes or abilities

[2]alley *n, pl* **alleys** [by shortening and alter. fr. *alabaster*] (1720) **:** a playing marble; *esp* **:** one of superior quality

al·ley·way \ˈal-ē-ˌwā\ *n* (1788) **1 :** a narrow passageway **2 :** ALLEY 3

All Fools' Day *n* (1712) **:** APRIL FOOLS' DAY

all fours *n pl* (14c) **1 a :** all four legs of a quadruped **b :** the two legs and two arms of a person when used to support the body **2** *sing in constr* **:** any of various card games in which points are scored for the high trump, low trump, jack of trumps, and game

all get–out \ˌȯl-ˈget-ˌau̇t; -get-ˈau̇t, -git-\ *n* (1884) **:** the utmost conceivable degree — used in comparisons to suggest something superlative ⟨is handsome as *all get-out* and has a deft way with the ladies — John McCarten⟩

all hail *interj* (14c) — used to express greeting, welcome, or acclamation

All·hal·lows \ȯl-ˈhal-(ˌ)ōz, -əz\ *n, pl* **Allhallows** [short for *All Hallows' Day*] (12c) **:** ALL SAINTS' DAY

all·heal \ˈȯl-ˌhēl\ *n* (1597) **:** any of several plants (as valerian or self-heal) used esp. in folk medicine

al·li·a·ceous \ˌal-ē-ˈā-shəs\ *adj* [L *allium*] (1792) **:** resembling garlic or onion esp. in smell or taste

al·li·ance \ə-ˈlī-ən(t)s\ *n* (13c) **1 a :** the state of being allied : the action of allying **b :** a bond or connection between families, states, parties, or individuals ⟨a closer ~ between government and industry⟩ **2 :** an association to further the common interests of the members; *specif* **:** a confederation of nations by treaty **3 :** union by relationship in qualities : AFFINITY **4 :** a treaty of alliance

al·lied \ə-ˈlīd, ˈal-ˌīd\ *adj* (13c) **1 :** having or being in close association : CONNECTED ⟨a strong personal pride ~ with the utmost probity⟩ ⟨two families ~ by marriage⟩ **2 :** joined in alliance by compact or treaty; *specif, cap* **:** of or relating to the nations united against the Central

\ə\ abut \ᵊ\ kitten, F table \ər\ further \a\ ash \ā\ ace \ä\ cot, cart \au̇\ out \ch\ chin \e\ bet \ē\ easy \g\ go \i\ hit \ī\ ice \j\ job \ŋ\ sing \ō\ go \ȯ\ law \ȯi\ boy \th\ thin \t͟h\ the \ü\ loot \u̇\ foot \y\ yet \zh\ vision \ȧ, k̲, ⁿ, œ, œ̄, ue, ue̅, ʸ\ see Guide to Pronunciation

European powers in World War I or those united against the Axis powers in World War II **3 a :** related esp. by common properties or qualities ⟨heraldry and ~ subjects⟩ **b :** related genetically
allies *pl of* ALLY
al·li·ga·tor \'al-ə-ˌgāt-ər\ *n* [Sp *el lagarto* the lizard, fr. *el* the (fr. L *ille* that) + *lagarto* lizard, fr. (assumed) VL *lacartus,* fr. L *lacertus, lacerta* — more at LIZARD] (1568) **1 a :** either of two crocodilians (genus *Alligator)* having broad heads not tapering to the snout and a special pocket in the upper jaw for reception of the enlarged lower fourth tooth **b :** CROCODILIAN **2 :** leather made from alligator hide

alligator 1a

alligator clip *n* (ca. 1941) **:** a spring-loaded clip that has jaws resembling an alligator's and is used for making temporary electrical connections
alligator pear *n* [prob. by folk etymology fr. Sp *aguacate* — more at AVOCADO] (1763) **:** AVOCADO
alligator snapper *n* (1884) **:** a snapping turtle (*Macrochelys temminckii)* of the rivers of the Gulf states that may reach nearly 150 pounds (68 kilograms) in weight and 5 feet (1.5 meters) in length
all–im·por·tant \ˌȯ-lim-'pȯrt-ᵊnt, -ənt\ *adj* (1839) **:** of very great or greatest importance ⟨an ~ question⟩
all–in \ˌȯ-'lin\ *adj, chiefly Brit* (1890) **:** ALL-INCLUSIVE
all in *adj* (1902) **:** TIRED, EXHAUSTED ⟨after a day of wood-splitting he was *all in*⟩
all–in·clu·sive \ˌȯ-lin-'klü-siv, -ziv\ *adj* (ca. 1855) **:** including everything ⟨a broader and more nearly ~ view⟩ — **all–in·clu·sive·ness** *n*
al·lit·er·ate \ə-'lit-ə-ˌrāt\ *vb* **-at·ed; -at·ing** [back-formation fr. *alliteration*] *vi* (1816) **1 :** to form an alliteration **2 :** to write or speak alliteratively ~ *vt* **:** to arrange or place so as to make alliteration ⟨~ syllables in a sentence⟩
al·lit·er·a·tion \ə-ˌlit-ə-'rā-shən\ *n* [*ad-* + L *littera* letter] (ca. 1656) **:** the repetition of usu. initial consonant sounds in two or more neighboring words or syllables (as *w*ild and *w*oolly, *thr*eatening *thr*ongs) — called also *head rhyme, initial rhyme*
al·lit·er·a·tive \ə-'lit-ə-ˌrāt-iv, -rət-\ *adj* (1764) **:** of, relating to, or marked by alliteration — **al·lit·er·a·tive·ly** *adv*
al·li·um \'al-ē-əm\ *n* [NL, genus name, fr. L, garlic] (ca. 1823) **:** any of a large genus (*Allium)* of bulbous herbs of the lily family including the onion, garlic, chive, leek, and shallot
all–night \ˌȯl-ˌnīt\ *adj* (1888) **1 :** lasting throughout the night ⟨an ~ poker game⟩ **2 :** open throughout the night ⟨an ~ diner⟩
allo- — see ALL-
al·lo·an·ti·body \ˌal-ō-'ant-i-ˌbäd-ē\ *n* (1967) **:** ISOANTIBODY
al·lo·an·ti·gen \ˌal-ō-'ant-i-jən\ *n* (1966) **:** an antigen present only in some individuals (as of a particular blood group) of a species and capable of inducing the production of an isoantibody by individuals which lack it — called also *isoantigen*
al·lo·ca·ble \'al-ə-kə-bəl\ *adj* (1916) **:** capable of being allocated
al·lo·cate \'al-ə-ˌkāt\ *vt* **-cat·ed; -cat·ing** [ML *allocatus,* pp. of *allocare,* fr. L *ad-* + *locare* to place, fr. *locus* place — more at STALL] (1640) **1 :** to apportion for a specific purpose or to particular persons or things **:** DISTRIBUTE ⟨~ tasks among human and automated components⟩ **2 :** to set apart or earmark **:** DESIGNATE ⟨~ a section of the building for special research purposes⟩ — **al·lo·cat·able** \-ˌkāt-ə-bəl\ *adj* — **al·lo·ca·tion** \ˌal-ə-'kā-shən\ *n* — **al·lo·ca·tor** \'al-ə-ˌkāt-ər\ *n*
al·lo·cu·tion \ˌal-ə-'kyü-shən\ *n* [L *allocution-, allocutio,* fr. *allocutus,* pp. of *alloqui* to speak to, fr. *ad-* + *loqui* to speak] (1615) **:** a formal speech; *esp* **:** an authoritative or hortatory address
al·log·a·mous \ə-'läg-ə-məs\ *adj* (ca. 1890) **:** reproducing by cross-fertilization — **al·log·a·my** \-mē\ *n*
al·lo·ge·ne·ic \ˌal-ō-jə-'nē-ik\ *adj* [*all-* + *-geneic* (as in *syngeneic*)] (1963) **:** involving or derived from individuals of the same species that are sufficiently unlike genetically to interact antigenically
al·lo·graft \'al-ə-ˌgraft\ *n* (1964) **:** a homograft between allogeneic individuals — **allograft** *vt*
al·lo·graph \'al-ə-ˌgraf\ *n* (1951) **1 :** a letter of an alphabet in a particular shape (as A or a) **2 :** a letter or combination of letters that is one of several ways of representing one phoneme (as *pp* in *hopping* representing the phoneme \p\) — **al·lo·graph·ic** \ˌal-ə-'graf-ik\ *adj*
al·lom·er·ism \ə-'läm-ə-ˌriz-əm\ *n* (ca. 1885) **:** variability in chemical constitution without variation in crystalline form — **al·lom·er·ous** \-rəs\ *adj*
al·lom·e·try \ə-'läm-ə-trē\ *n* (1936) **:** relative growth of a part in relation to an entire organism or to a standard; *also* **:** the measure and study of such growth — **al·lo·met·ric** \ˌal-ə-'me-trik\ *adj*
¹al·lo·morph \'al-ə-ˌmȯrf\ *n* [ISV] (1866) **1 :** any of two or more distinct crystalline forms of the same substance **2 :** a pseudomorph that has undergone change or substitution of material — **al·lo·mor·phic** \ˌal-ə-'mȯr-fik\ *adj* — **al·lo·mor·phism** \'al-ə-ˌmȯr-ˌfiz-əm\ *n*
²allomorph *n* [*allo-* + *morpheme*] (1945) **:** one of two or more forms of a morpheme ⟨the *-es* \əz\ of *dishes,* the *-s* \z\ of *dreams,* the *-s* \s\ of *traps,* the *-en* \ən\ of *oxen,* the vowel modification distinguishing *teeth* from *tooth,* and the zero suffix of *sheep* in *those sheep* are ~s of the same morpheme⟩ — **al·lo·mor·phic** \ˌal-ə-'mȯr-fik\ *adj* — **al·lo·mor·phism** \'al-ə-ˌmȯr-ˌfiz-əm\ *n*
al·longe \a-'lōⁿzh\ *n* [F, lit., lengthening] (ca. 1859) **:** RIDER 2a
al·lo·pat·ric \ˌal-ə-'pa-trik\ *adj* [*all-* + Gk *patra* fatherland, fr. *patēr* father — more at FATHER] (1942) **:** occurring in different areas or in isolation ⟨~ speciation⟩ — compare SYMPATRIC — **al·lo·pat·ri·cal·ly** \-tri-k(ə-)lē\ *adv* — **al·lop·a·try** \ə-'läp-ə-trē\ *n*
al·lo·phane \'al-ə-ˌfān\ *n* [Gk *allophanēs* appearing otherwise, fr. *all-* + *phainesthai* to appear, pass. of *phainein* to show — more at FANCY] (ca. 1821) **:** an amorphous translucent mineral of various colors often occurring in incrustations or stalactite forms and consisting of a hydrous aluminum silicate
al·lo·phone \'al-ə-ˌfōn\ *n* [*allo-* + *phone*] (1938) **:** one of two or more variants of the same phoneme ⟨the aspirated \p\ of *pin* and the unaspirated \p\ of *spin* are ~s of the phoneme \p\⟩ — **al·lo·phon·ic** \ˌal-ə-'fän-ik\ *adj*
al·lo·poly·ploid \ˌal-ō-'päl-i-ˌplȯid\ *n* (1928) **:** an individual or strain whose chromosomes are composed of more than two genomes each of which has been derived more or less complete but possibly modified from one of two or more species — **allopolyploid** *adj* — **al·lo·poly·ploi·dy** \-ˌplȯid-ē\ *n*
al·lo·pu·ri·nol \ˌal-ō-'pyůr-ə-ˌnȯl, -ˌnōl\ *n* [*all-* + *purine* + *-ol*] (ca. 1964) **:** a drug $C_5H_4N_4O$ used to promote excretion of uric acid
all–or–none \ˌȯ-lər-'nən\ *adj* (1900) **:** marked either by entire or complete operation or effect or by none at all ⟨~ response of a nerve cell⟩
all–or–noth·ing \-'nəth-iŋ\ *adj* (1765) **1 :** ALL-OR-NONE **2 a :** accepting no less than everything ⟨he's an ~ perfectionist⟩ **b :** risking everything ⟨playing an ~ game⟩
al·lo·ste·ric \ˌal-ō-'ster-ik, -'sti(ə)r-\ *adj* [*all-* + *steric*] (1963) **:** of, relating to, or being alteration of the activity of a protein (as an enzyme) by combination with another substance at a point other than the chemically active site — **al·lo·ste·ri·cal·ly** \-i-k(ə-)lē\ *adv* — **al·lo·ste·ry** \'al-ō-ˌster-ē, -ˌsti(ə)r-\ *n*
al·lot \ə-'lät\ *vt* **al·lot·ted; al·lot·ting** [ME *alotten,* fr. MF *aloter,* fr. *a-* (fr. L *ad-*) + *lot,* of Gmc origin; akin to OE *hlot* lot] (15c) **1 :** to assign as a share or portion ⟨~ 10 minutes for the speech⟩ **2 :** to distribute by or as if by lot ⟨~ hotel rooms to members of the delegation⟩ — **al·lot·ter** *n*
al·lo·te·tra·ploid \ˌal-ō-'te-trə-ˌplȯid\ *n* (1930) **:** AMPHIDIPLOID — **al·lo·te·tra·ploi·dy** \-ˌplȯid-ē\ *n*
al·lot·ment \ə-'lät-mənt\ *n* (1574) **1 :** the act of allotting **:** APPORTIONMENT **2 :** something that is allotted
al·lo·trans·plant \ˌal-ō-tran(t)s-'plant\ *vt* (1968) **:** to transplant between genetically different individuals — **al·lo·trans·plant** \-'tran(t)s-ˌ\ *n* — **al·lo·trans·plan·ta·tion** \-ˌtran(t)s-ˌplan-'tā-shən\ *n*
al·lo·trope \'al-ə-ˌtrōp\ *n* [ISV, back-formation fr. *allotropy*] (ca. 1889) **:** a form showing allotropy
al·lot·ro·py \ə-'lä-trə-pē\ *n, pl* **-pies** (1850) **:** the existence of a substance and esp. an element in two or more different forms (as of crystals) usu. in the same phase — **al·lo·trop·ic** \ˌal-ə-'träp-ik\ *adj* — **al·lo·trop·i·cal·ly** \-i-k(ə-)lē\ *adv*
all' ot·ta·va \ˌal-ə-'täv-ə, ˌäl-ō-\ *adv or adj* [It, at the octave] (ca. 1823) **:** OTTAVA
al·lot·tee \ə-ˌlät-'ē\ *n* (1846) **:** one to whom an allotment is made
al·lo·type \'al-ə-ˌtīp\ *n* (ca. 1920) **:** an alloantigen that is part of a plasma protein (as an immunoglobulin) — **al·lo·typ·ic** \ˌal-ə-'tip-ik\ *adj* — **al·lo·typ·i·cal·ly** \-i-k(ə-)lē\ *adv* — **al·lo·typy** \'al-ə-ˌtī-pē\ *n*
all–out \'ȯ-'lau̇t\ *adj* (1908) **:** made with maximum effort **:** THOROUGHGOING ⟨an ~ effort to win the contest⟩
all out *adv* (1895) **:** with full determination or enthusiasm **:** with maximum effort — used chiefly in the phrase *go all out*
¹all·over \'ȯ-ˌlō-vər\ *adj* (1859) **:** covering the whole extent or surface ⟨a sweater with an ~ pattern⟩
²allover *n* (1899) **1 :** an embroidered, printed, or lace fabric with a design covering most of the surface **2 :** a pattern or design in which a single unit is repeated so as to cover an entire surface
all over *adv* (1577) **1 :** over the whole extent ⟨decorated *all over* with a flower pattern⟩ **2 :** EVERYWHERE ⟨looked *all over* for the book⟩ **3 :** in every respect **:** THOROUGHLY ⟨she is her mother *all over*⟩
al·low \ə-'lau̇\ *vb* [ME *allowen,* fr. MF *alouer* to place, (fr. ML *allocare)* & *allouer* to approve, fr. L *adlaudare* to extol, fr. *ad-* + *laudare* to praise — more at ALLOCATE, LAUD] *vt* (14c) **1 a :** to assign as a share or suitable amount (as of time or money) ⟨~ an hour for lunch⟩ **b :** to reckon as a deduction or an addition ⟨~ a gallon for leakage⟩ **2 :** ADMIT, CONCEDE ⟨must ~ that money causes problems in marriage⟩ **3 a :** PERMIT ⟨doesn't ~ people to smoke in his home⟩ **b :** to forbear or neglect to restrain or prevent ⟨~ the dog to roam⟩ **4 a :** to be of the opinion **:** THINK **b :** SAY, STATE **5** *dial* **:** INTEND, PLAN ~ *vi* **1 :** to make a possibility **:** ADMIT — used with *of* ⟨evidence that ~s of only one conclusion⟩ **2 :** to give consideration to circumstances or contingencies — used with *for* ⟨~ for expansion⟩ **3** *dial* **:** SUPPOSE, CONSIDER ***syn*** see LET
al·low·able \ə-'lau̇-ə-bəl\ *adj* (15c) **:** PERMISSIBLE — **al·low·able·ness** *n* — **al·low·ably** \-blē\ *adv*
¹al·low·ance \ə-'lau̇-ən(t)s\ *n* (14c) **1 a :** a share or portion allotted or granted **b :** a sum granted as a reimbursement or bounty or for expenses ⟨salary includes cost-of-living ~⟩; *esp* **:** a sum regularly provided for personal or household expenses ⟨each child has an ~⟩ **c :** a fixed or available amount ⟨provide an ~ of time for recreation⟩ **d :** a reduction from a list price or stated price ⟨a trade-in ~⟩ **2 :** an imposed handicap (as in a race) **3 :** an allowed dimensional difference between mating parts of a machine **4 :** the act of allowing **:** PERMISSION **5 :** an allowing for mitigating circumstances or contingencies
²allowance *vt* **-anced; -anc·ing** (ca. 1828) **1 :** to put on a fixed allowance (as of food and drink) **2 :** to supply in a fixed or regular quantity
al·low·ed·ly \ə-'lau̇-əd-lē\ *adv* (1602) **:** by allowance **:** ADMITTEDLY
al·lox·an \ə-'läk-sən\ *n* [G, fr. *all*antoin + *ox*alsäure oxalic acid + *-an*] (1853) **:** a crystalline compound $C_4H_2N_2O_4$ causing diabetes mellitus when injected into experimental animals; *also* **:** one of its similarly acting derivatives
¹al·loy \'al-ˌȯi, ə-'lȯi\ *n* [F *aloi,* fr. *aloier* to combine, fr. L *alligare* to bind — more at ALLY] (14c) **1 :** the degree of mixture with base metals **:** FINENESS **2 :** a substance composed of two or more metals or of a metal and a nonmetal intimately united usu. by being fused together and dissolving in each other when molten; *also* **:** the state of union of the components **3** *archaic* **:** a metal mixed with a more valuable metal to give durability or some other desired quality **4 a :** an admixture that lessens value **b :** an impairing alien element **5 :** a compound, mixture, or union of different things **:** AMALGAM ⟨an ethnic ~ of many peoples⟩
²al·loy \ə-'lȯi, 'al-ˌȯi\ *vt* (15c) **1 :** to reduce the purity of by mixing with a less valuable metal **2 :** to mix so as to form an alloy **3 a :** to impair or debase by admixture **b :** TEMPER, MODERATE ~ *vi* **:** to lend itself to being alloyed ⟨iron ~s well⟩
all–pow·er·ful \'ȯl-'pau̇(-ə)r-fəl\ *adj* (1692) **:** having complete or sole power
all–pur·pose \-'pər-pəs\ *adj* (1928) **:** suited for many purposes or uses
¹all right \(')ȯl-'rīt, *esp for 2* 'ȯl-ˌ\ *adv* (14c) **1 :** beyond doubt **:** CERTAINLY ⟨she has pneumonia *all right*⟩ **2 :** well enough ⟨does *all right* in school⟩ **3 :** very well **:** YES ⟨*all right,* let's go⟩ ***usage*** see ALRIGHT

[2]**all right** \(ˈ)ȯl-ˈ\ *adj* (15c) **1 :** SATISFACTORY ⟨the film is *all right* for children⟩ **2 :** SAFE, WELL ⟨he was ill but he's *all right* now⟩ **3 :** AGREEABLE, PLEASING — usu. used as a generalized term of approval ***usage*** see ALRIGHT
all–round \ˈȯl-ˈrau̇nd\ *var of* ALL-AROUND
all–round·er \(ˈ)ȯl-ˈrau̇n-dər\ *n, Brit* (1875) **:** one that is all-around
All Saints' Day *n* (ca. 1755) **:** November 1 observed in Western liturgical churches as a Christian feast in honor of all the saints
all·seed \ˈȯl-ˌsēd\ *n* (ca. 1825) **:** any of several many-seeded plants; *esp* **:** a tiny annual (*Millegrana radiola*) of the flax family
All Souls' Day *n* (14c) **:** November 2 observed as a day of prayer for the souls of the faithful departed
all·spice \ˈȯl-ˌspīs\ *n* (1621) **1 :** the berry of a West Indian tree (*Pimenta dioica*) of the myrtle family; *also* **:** the allspice tree **2 :** a mildly pungent and aromatic spice prepared from allspice berries
[1]**all–star** \ˌȯl-ˌstär\ *adj* (1889) **:** composed wholly or chiefly of stars or of outstanding performers or participants ⟨an ~ cast⟩
[2]**all–star** \ˈȯl-ˌstär\ *n* (ca. 1934) **:** a member of an all-star team
all that \(ˈ)ȯl-ˈt͟hat\ *adv* (1945) **:** to an indicated or suggested extent or degree **:** SO ⟨didn't take his threats *all that* seriously⟩
all the same *adv* (1803) **:** NEVERTHELESS ⟨she was very tired but enjoyed the play *all the same*⟩
all–time \ˌȯl-ˌtīm\ *adj* (1914) **1 :** FULL-TIME **2 :** exceeding all others of all time ⟨an ~ best-seller⟩
all told *adv* (1850) **:** with everything taken into account **:** in all
al·lude \ə-ˈlüd\ *vi* **al·lud·ed; al·lud·ing** [L *alludere,* lit., to play with, fr. *ad-* + *ludere* to play — more at LUDICROUS] (1533) **:** to make indirect reference
[1]**al·lure** \ə-ˈlu̇(ə)r\ *vt* **al·lured; al·lur·ing** [ME *aluren,* fr. MF *alurer,* fr. OF, fr. *a-* (fr. L *ad-*) + *loire* lure — more at LURE] (15c) **:** to entice by charm or attraction ***syn*** see ATTRACT — **al·lure·ment** \-ˈlu̇(ə)r-mənt\ *n* — **al·lur·ing·ly** *adv*
[2]**allure** *n* (1548) **:** power of attraction or fascination **:** CHARM
al·lu·sion \ə-ˈlü-zhən\ *n* [LL *allusion-, allusio,* fr. L *allusus,* pp. of *alludere*] (1548) **1 :** the act of alluding or hinting at **2 :** an implied or indirect reference esp. when used in literature; *also* **:** the use of such references — **al·lu·sive** \-ˈlü-siv, -ziv\ *adj* — **al·lu·sive·ly** *adv* — **al·lu·sive·ness** *n*
[1]**al·lu·vi·al** \ə-ˈlü-vē-əl\ *adj* (1802) **:** relating to, composed of, or found in alluvium ⟨~ soil⟩ ⟨~ diamonds⟩
[2]**alluvial** *n* (1866) **:** an alluvial deposit
alluvial fan *n* (1873) **:** the alluvial deposit of a stream where it issues from a gorge upon a plain or of a tributary stream at its junction with the main stream
al·lu·vi·on \ə-ˈlü-vē-ən\ *n* [L *alluvion-, alluvio,* fr. *alluere* to wash against, fr. *ad-* + *luere* to wash — more at LYE] (1536) **1 :** the wash or flow of water against a shore **2 :** FLOOD, INUNDATION **3 :** ALLUVIUM **4 :** an accession to land by the gradual addition of matter (as by deposit of alluvium) that then belongs to the owner of the land to which it is added; *also* **:** the land so added
al·lu·vi·um \-vē-əm\ *n, pl* **-vi·ums** *or* **-via** \-vē-ə\ [LL, neut. of *alluvius* alluvial, fr. L *alluere*] (1665) **:** clay, silt, sand, gravel, or similar detrital material deposited by running water
[1]**al·ly** \ə-ˈlī, ˈal-ˌī\ *vb* **al·lied; al·ly·ing** [ME *allien,* fr OF *alier,* fr. L *alligare* to bind to, fr. *ad-* + *ligare* to bind — more at LIGATURE] *vt* (13c) **1 :** to unite or form a connection between **:** ASSOCIATE ⟨*allied* himself with a wealthy family by marriage⟩ **2 :** to connect or form a relation between (as by likeness or compatibility) **:** RELATE ~ *vi* **:** to form or enter into an alliance
[2]**al·ly** \ˈal-ˌī, ə-ˈlī\ *n, pl* **allies** (14c) **1 :** a sovereign or state associated with another by treaty or league **2 :** a plant or animal linked to another by genetic or evolutionary relationship **3 :** one that is associated with another as a helper **:** AUXILIARY
-al·ly \(ə-)lē\ *adv suffix* [[1]-*al* + *-ly*] **:** [2]-LY ⟨terrific*ally*⟩ — in adverbs formed from adjectives in *-ic* with no alternative form in *-ical*
al·lyl \ˈal-əl\ *n* [ISV, fr. L *allium* garlic] (1854) **:** an unsaturated univalent radical C_3H_5 compounds of which are found in the oils of garlic and mustard — **al·lyl·ic** \ə-ˈlil-ik, a-\ *adj*
al·ma·gest \ˈal-mə-ˌjest\ *n* [ME *almageste,* fr. MF & ML, fr. Ar *almajusti* the almagest, fr. *al* the + Gk *megistē,* fem. of *megistos,* superl. of *megas* great — more at MUCH] (14c) **:** any of several early medieval treatises on a branch of knowledge
al·ma ma·ter \ˌal-mə-ˈmät-ər\ *n* [L, fostering mother] (1696) **1 :** a school, college, or university which one has attended or from which one has graduated **2 :** the song or hymn of a school, college, or university
al·ma·nac \ˈȯl-mə-ˌnak, ˈal-\ *n* [ME *almenak,* fr. ML *almanach,* prob. fr. Ar *al-manākh* the almanac] (14c) **1 :** a publication containing astronomical and meteorological data arranged according to the days, weeks, and months of a given year and often including a miscellany of other information **2 :** a usu. annual publication containing statistical, tabular, and general information
al·man·dine \ˈal-mən-ˌdēn, -ˌdīn\ *n* [ME *alabandine,* fr. ML *alabandina,* fr. *Alabanda,* ancient city in Asia Minor] (14c) **:** ALMANDITE
al·man·dite \ˈal-mən-ˌdīt\ *n* [alter. of *almandine*] (ca. 1837) **:** a deep red garnet consisting of an iron aluminum silicate $Fe_3Al_2(SiO_4)_3$
[1]**al·mighty** \ȯl-ˈmīt-ē\ *adj* [ME, fr. OE *ealmihtig,* fr. *eall* all + *mihtig* mighty] (bef. 12c) **1** *often cap* **:** having absolute power over all ⟨*Almighty* God⟩ **2 :** relatively unlimited in power **3 :** great in magnitude or seriousness — **al·mighti·ness** *n, often cap*
[2]**almighty** *adv* (1833) **:** to a great degree **:** EXTREMELY ⟨although he did not precisely starve, he was ~ hungry — W. A. Swanberg⟩
Almighty *n* (bef. 12c) **:** GOD 1 — used with *the*
al·mond \ˈäm-ənd, ˈam-; ˈäl-mənd, ˈal-\ *n* [ME *almande,* fr. MF, fr. LL *amandula,* alter. of L *amygdala,* fr. Gk *amygdalē*] (14c) **1 a :** a small tree (*Prunus amygdalus*) of the rose family with flowers and young fruit resembling those of the peach **b :** the drupaceous fruit of the almond; *esp* **:** its ellipsoidal edible kernel used as a nut **2 :** any of several fruits similar to the almond; *also* **:** the trees producing them
al·mond–eyed \ˌäm-ən-ˈdīd, ˌam-; ˌäl-mən-, ˌal-\ *adj* (1870) **:** having narrow slant almond-shaped eyes
al·mo·ner \ˈal-mə-nər, ˈäm-ə-\ *n* [ME *almoiner,* fr. MF *almosnier,* fr. *almosne* alms, fr. LL *eleemosyna*] (14c) **1 :** one who distributes alms **2** *Brit* **:** a social-service worker in a hospital
al·most \ˈȯl-ˌmōst, ȯl-ˈ\ *adv* [ME, fr. OE *ealmǣst,* fr. *eall* + *mǣst* most] (bef. 12c) **:** very nearly but not exactly or entirely
alms \ˈä(l)mz, *NewEng also* ˈamz\ *n, pl* **alms** [ME *almesse, almes,* fr. OE *ælmesse, ælmes,* fr. LL *eleemosyna* alms, fr. Gk *eleēmosynē* pity, alms, fr. *eleēmōn* merciful, fr. *eleos* pity] (bef. 12c) **1** *archaic* **:** CHARITY **2 :** something (as money or food) given freely to relieve the poor — **alms·giv·er** \-ˌgiv-ər\ *n* — **alms·giv·ing** \-ˌgiv-iŋ\ *n*
alms·house \-ˌhau̇s\ *n* (14c) **1** *Brit* **:** a privately financed home for the poor **2 :** POORHOUSE
alms·man \-mən\ *n* (bef. 12c) **:** a recipient of alms
al·ni·co \ˈal-ni-ˌkō\ *n* [*al*uminum + *ni*ckel + *co*balt] (1935) **:** a powerful permanent-magnet alloy containing iron, nickel, aluminum, and one or more of the elements cobalt, copper, and titanium
al·oe \ˈal-(ˌ)ō\ *n* [ME, fr. LL, fr. L, dried juice of aloe leaves, fr. Gk *aloē*] (bef. 12c) **1** *pl* **:** the fragrant wood of an East Indian tree (*Aquilaria agallocha*) of the mezereon family **2 a :** any of a large genus (*Aloe*) of succulent chiefly southern African plants of the lily family with basal leaves and spicate flowers **b :** the dried juice of the leaves of various aloes used as a purgative and tonic — usu. used in pl. but sing. in constr. **3 :** any of a genus (*Furcraea*) of American plants of the amaryllis family somewhat like the African aloes
[1]**aloft** \ə-ˈlȯft\ *adv* [ME, fr. ON *ā lopt,* fr. *ā* on, in + *lopt* air — more at ON, LOFT] (13c) **1 :** at or to a great height **2 :** in the air; *esp* **:** in flight (as in an airplane) ⟨meals served ~⟩ **3 :** at, on, or to the masthead or the higher rigging
[2]**aloft** *prep* (14c) **:** on top of **:** ABOVE ⟨bright signs ~ hotels⟩
alog·i·cal \(ˈ)ā-ˈläj-i-kəl\ *adj* (1694) **:** being outside the bounds of that to which logic can apply — **alog·i·cal·ly** \-k(ə-)lē\ *adv*
alo·ha \ə-ˈlō-(h)ə, ä-, -ˌ(h)ä\ *interj* [Hawaiian, fr. *aloha* love] (ca. 1892) — used as a greeting or farewell
aloha shirt *n* (1940) **:** a loose brightly colored Hawaiian sport shirt
al·o·in \ˈal-ə-wən\ *n* (1841) **:** a bitter yellow crystalline cathartic obtained from the aloe
[1]**alone** \ə-ˈlōn\ *adj* [ME, fr. *al* all + *one* one] (13c) **1 :** separated from others **:** ISOLATED **2 :** exclusive of anyone or anything else **:** ONLY **3 a :** considered without reference to any other ⟨the children ~ would eat that much⟩ **b :** INCOMPARABLE, UNIQUE ⟨~ in his ability to solve fiscal problems⟩ — **alone·ness** \-ˈlōn-nəs\ *n*
syn ALONE, SOLITARY, LONELY, LONESOME, LONE, FORLORN, DESOLATE mean isolated from others. ALONE stresses the objective fact of being by oneself with slighter notion of emotional involvement than most of the remaining terms ⟨everyone needs to be *alone* sometimes⟩ SOLITARY may indicate isolation as a chosen course ⟨glorying in the calm of her *solitary* life⟩ but more often it suggests sadness and a sense of loss ⟨left *solitary* by the death of his wife⟩ LONELY adds to SOLITARY a suggestion of longing for companionship ⟨felt *lonely* and forsaken⟩ LONESOME heightens the suggestion of sadness and poignancy ⟨an only child often leads a *lonesome* life⟩ LONE may replace LONELY or LONESOME but typically is as objective as ALONE ⟨a *lone* robin pecking at the lawn⟩ FORLORN stresses dejection, woe, and listlessness at separation from one held dear ⟨a *forlorn* lost child⟩ DESOLATE implies inconsolable grief at loss or bereavement.
[2]**alone** *adv* (13c) **1 :** SOLELY, EXCLUSIVELY **2 :** without aid or support
[1]**along** \ə-ˈlȯŋ\ *prep* [ME, fr. OE *andlang,* fr. *and-* against + *lang* long — more at ANTE-] (bef. 12c) **1 :** in a line parallel with the length or direction of **2 :** in the course of **3 :** in accordance with **:** IN
[2]**along** *adv* (14c) **1 :** FORWARD, ON ⟨move ~⟩ **2 :** from one to another ⟨word was passed ~⟩ **3 a :** in company **:** as a companion ⟨brought his wife ~⟩ — often used with *with* ⟨walked to school ~ with her friends⟩ **b :** in association — used with *with* ⟨work ~ with colleagues⟩ **4 :** at or to an advanced point ⟨plans are far ~⟩ **5 :** in addition **:** ALSO — often used with *with* ⟨a bill came ~ with the package⟩ **6 :** at hand **:** as a necessary or useful item ⟨had his gun ~⟩ **7 :** on hand **:** THERE ⟨tell him I'll be ~ to see him⟩
along of *prep* [ME *ilong on,* fr. OE *gelang on,* fr. *ge-,* associative prefix + *lang* — more at CO-] *dial* (bef. 12c) **:** BECAUSE OF
along·shore \ə-ˈlȯŋ-ˈshō(ə)r, -ˈshȯ(ə)r\ *adv or adj* (1779) **:** along the shore or coast ⟨walked ~⟩ ⟨~ currents⟩
[1]**along·side** \-ˌsīd\ *adv* (1707) **1 :** along the side **:** in parallel position **2 :** at the side **:** close by ⟨a guard with a prisoner ~⟩
[2]**alongside** *prep* (1793) **:** side by side with; *specif* **:** parallel to
alongside of *prep* (1781) **:** ALONGSIDE
[1]**aloof** \ə-ˈlüf\ *adv* [obs. *aloof* (to windward)] (1540) **:** at a distance **:** out of involvement
[2]**aloof** *adj* (1872) **:** removed or distant in interest or feeling **:** RESERVED ***syn*** see INDIFFERENT — **aloof·ly** *adv* — **aloof·ness** *n*
al·o·pe·cia \ˌal-ə-ˈpē-sh(ē-)ə\ *n* [ME *allopicia,* fr. L *alopecia,* fr. Gk *alōpekia,* fr. *alōpek-, alōpēx* fox — more at VULPINE] (14c) **:** loss of hair, wool, or feathers **:** BALDNESS — **al·o·pe·cic** \-ˈpē-sik\ *adj*
aloud \ə-ˈlau̇d\ *adv* [ME, fr. [1]*a-* + *loud*] (13c) **1** *archaic* **:** in a loud manner **:** LOUDLY **2 :** with the speaking voice
alow \ə-ˈlō\ *adv* [ME, fr. [1]*a-* + *low*] (13c) **:** BELOW ⟨~ in the ship's hold⟩
alp \ˈalp\ *n* [back-formation fr. *Alps,* mountain system of Europe] (15c) **1 :** a high rugged mountain **2 :** something suggesting an alp in height, size, or ruggedness
al·paca \al-ˈpak-ə\ *n* [Sp, fr. Aymara *allpaca*] (1604) **1 :** a mammal with fine long woolly hair that is domesticated in Peru and is prob. a variety of the guanaco **2 a :** wool of the alpaca **b (1) :** a thin cloth made of or containing this wool **(2) :** a rayon or cotton imitation of this cloth

alpaca 1

al·pen·glow \ˈal-pən-ˌglō\ *n* [prob. part

ALPHABET TABLE

Showing the letters of five non-Roman alphabets and the transliterations used in the etymologies

HEBREW[1,4]		ARABIC[3,4]		GREEK[7]	RUSSIAN[8]	SANSKRIT[11]	
א aleph ' [2]	ا ا	ٮ ٮ ٮ alif [5]	A α alpha a	А а a	अ a	ञ ñ
ב beth b, bh	ب ب ٮ ب bā b	B β beta b	Б б b	आ ā	ट ṭ
ג gimel g, gh	ت ت ـت ت tā t		В в v	इ i	ठ ṭh
ד daleth d, dh	ث ث ـث ث thā th	Γ γ gamma g, n	Г г g	ई ī	ड ḍ
ה he h	ج ج ـج ج jīm j	Δ δ delta d	Д д d	उ u	ढ ḍh
ו waw w	ح ح ـح ح ḥā ḥ	E ε epsilon e	Е е e	ऊ ū	ण ṇ
ז zayin z	خ خ ـخ خ khā kh	Z ζ zeta z	Ж ж zh	ऋ ṛ	त t
ח heth ḥ	د د dāl d	H η eta ē	З з z	ॠ ṝ	थ th
ט teth ṭ	ذ ذ dhāl dh	Θ θ theta th	И и Й й i, ĭ	ऌ ḷ	द d
י yod y	ر ر rā r	I ι iota i	К к k	ॡ ḹ	ध dh
כ ך kaph k, kh	ز ز zāy z	K κ kappa k	Л л l	ए e	न n
ל lamed l	س س ـس ـس sīn s	Λ λ lambda l	М м m	ऐ ai	प p
מ ם mem m	ش ش ـش ـش shīn sh	M μ mu m	Н н n	ओ o	फ ph
נ ן nun n	ص ص ـص ـص ṣād ṣ	N ν nu n	О о o	औ au	ब b
ס samekh s	ض ض ـض ـض ḍād ḍ	Ξ ξ xi x	П п p	ं ṃ	भ bh
ע ayin '	ط ط ـط ـط ṭā ṭ	O o omicron o	Р р r	ः ḥ	म m
פ ף pe p, ph	ظ ظ ـظ ـظ ẓā ẓ	Π π pi p	С с s	क k	य y
צ ץ sadhe ṣ	ع ع ـع ـع 'ayn '	P ρ rho r, rh	Т т t	ख kh	र r
ק qoph q	غ غ ـغ ـغ ghayn gh	Σ σ ς sigma s	У у u	ग g	ल l
ר resh r	ف ف ـف ـف fā f	T τ tau t	Ф ф f	घ gh	व v
ש sin ś	ق ق ـق ـق qāf q	Υ υ upsilon y, u	Х х kh	ङ ṅ	श ś
ש shin sh	ك ك ـك ـك kāf k	Φ φ phi ph	Ц ц ts	च c	ष ṣ
ת taw t, th	ل ل ـل ـل lām l	X χ chi ch	Ч ч ch	छ ch	स s
	م م ـم ـم mīm m	Ψ ψ psi ps	Ш ш sh	ज j	ह h
	ن ن ـن ـن nūn n	Ω ω omega ō	Щ щ shch	झ jh	
	ه ه ـه ـه hā h[5]		Ъ ъ[9] "		
	و و wāw w		Ы ы y		
	ي ي ـي ـي yā y		Ь ь[10] '		
			Э э e		
			Ю ю yu		
			Я я ya		

trans. of G *Alpenglühen,* fr. *Alpen* Alps + *glühen* glow] (1871) : a reddish glow seen near sunset or sunrise on the summits of mountains

al·pen·horn \'al-pən-,hȯrn\ *or* **alp·horn** \'alp-,hȯrn\ *n* [G, fr. *Alpen* + *horn* horn] (1864) : a straight wooden horn 5 to 14 feet in length used chiefly by Swiss herdsmen

al·pen·stock \'al-pən-,stäk\ *n* [G, fr. *Alpen* + *stock* staff] (1829) : a long iron-pointed staff used in mountain climbing

1al·pha \'al-fə\ *n* [ME, fr. L, fr. Gk, of Sem origin; akin to Heb *āleph* aleph] (13c) **1** : the 1st letter of the Greek alphabet — see ALPHABET table **2** : something that is first : BEGINNING **3** : the chief or brightest star of a constellation **4** : ALPHA WAVE

2alpha *or* α- *adj* (1863) : closest in the structure of an organic molecule to a particular group or atom ⟨α-substitution⟩ ⟨α-naphthol⟩

3alpha *adj* (1949) **1** : socially dominant esp. in a group of animals **2** : ALPHABETIC

al·pha–ad·ren·er·gic \,al-fə-,ad-rə-'nər-jik\ *adj* (1966) : of, relating to, or being an alpha-receptor ⟨~ blocking action⟩

alpha and omega *n* [fr. the fact that alpha and omega are respectively the first and last letters of the Greek alphabet] (14c) **1** : the beginning and ending **2** : the principal element

al·pha·bet \'al-fə-,bet, -bət\ *n* [ME *alphabete,* fr. LL *alphabetum,* fr. Gk *alphabētos,* fr. *alpha* + *bēta* beta] (15c) **1 a** : a set of letters or other characters with which one or more languages are written esp. if arranged in a customary order **b** : a system of signs or signals that serve as equivalents for letters **2** : RUDIMENTS, ELEMENTS

al·pha·bet·ic \,al-fə-'bet-ik\ *or* **al·pha·bet·i·cal** \-i-kəl\ *adj* (1642) **1** : arranged in the order of the letters of the alphabet **2** : of, relating to, or employing an alphabet — **al·pha·bet·i·cal·ly** \-i-k(ə-)lē\ *adv*

al·pha·bet·iza·tion \,al-fə-,bet-ə-'zā-shən\ *n* (1889) **1** : the act or process of alphabetizing **2** : an alphabetically arranged series, list, or file

al·pha·bet·ize \'al-fə-bə-,tīz\ *vt* **-ized; -iz·ing** (1796) **1** : to arrange alphabetically **2** : to furnish with an alphabet — **al·pha·bet·iz·er** *n*

alphabet soup *n* (1934) : a hodgepodge esp. of initials (as of the names of organizations)

alpha globulin *n* [ISV] (1923) : any of several globulins of plasma or serum that have at alkaline pH the greatest electrophoretic mobility next to albumin — compare BETA GLOBULIN, GAMMA GLOBULIN

al·pha–he·lix \,al-fə-'hē-liks\ *n* (1955) : the coiled structural arrangement of many proteins consisting of a single chain of amino acids stabilized by hydrogen bonds — **al·pha–he·li·cal** \-'hel-i-kəl, -'hē-li-\ *adj*

alpha iron *n* (1902) : the form of iron stable below 910°C

al·pha·mer·ic \,al-fə-'mer-ik\ *adj* [*alpha*bet + nu*meric*] (ca. 1952) : ALPHANUMERIC

al·pha·nu·mer·ic \-n(y)ü-'mer-ik\ *also* **al·pha·nu·mer·i·cal** \-i-kəl\ *adj* [*alpha*bet + *numeric, numerical*] (ca. 1950) **1** : consisting of both letters and numbers and often other symbols (as punctuation marks and mathematical symbols) ⟨an ~ code⟩; *also* : being a character in an alphanumeric system **2** : capable of using or displaying alphanumeric characters — **al·pha·nu·mer·i·cal·ly** \-i-k(ə-)lē\ *adv* — **al·pha·nu·mer·ics** \-iks\ *n pl*

alpha particle *n* (1903) : a positively charged nuclear particle identical with the nucleus of a helium atom that consists of two protons and two neutrons and is ejected at high speed in certain radioactive transformations

alpha privative *n* (1590) : the prefix *a-* or *an-* expressing negation in Greek and in English

alpha ray *n* (1902) **1** : an alpha particle moving at high speed (as in radioactive emission) **2** : a stream of alpha particles — called also *alpha radiation*

al·pha–re·cep·tor \'al-fə-ri-,sep-tər\ *n* (1961) : any of a group of receptors on cell membranes that are held to be associated with vasoconstriction, relaxation of intestinal muscle, and contraction of the nictitating membrane, iris dilator muscle, splenic smooth muscle, and muscular layer of the wall of the uterus

alpha wave *n* (1936) : an electrical rhythm of the brain with a frequency of 8 to 13 cycles per second that is often associated with a state of wakeful relaxation — called also *alpha, alpha rhythm*

Al·phe·us \al-'fē-əs\ *n* [L, fr. Gk *Alpheios*] : a Greek river-god who pursues the nymph Arethusa and is finally united with her

al·pine \'al-,pīn\ *n* (ca. 1828) **1** : a plant native to alpine or boreal regions that is often grown for ornament **2** *cap* : a person possessing Alpine physical characteristics

Alpine *adj* (15c) **1** *often not cap* : of, relating to, or resembling the Alps or any mountains **2** *often not cap* : of, relating to, or growing in the biogeographic zone including the elevated slopes above timberline **3** : of or relating to a type of stocky broad-headed white men of medium height with brown hair or eyes often regarded as constituting a branch of the Caucasian race **4** : of or relating to competitive ski events consisting of slalom and downhill racing — compare NORDIC

al·pin·ism \'al-pə-,niz-əm\ *n, often cap* (1884) : mountain climbing in the Alps or other high mountains — **al·pin·ist** \-nəst\ *n*

al·ready \ȯl-'red-ē, ȯl-,\ *adv* [ME *al redy,* fr. *al redy,* adj., wholly ready, fr. *al* all + *redy* ready] (14c) **1** : prior to a specified or implied past, present, or future time : by this time : PREVIOUSLY ⟨he had ~ left when I called⟩ **2** — used as an intensive ⟨all right ~⟩ ⟨enough ~⟩

al·right \(')ȯl-'rīt, 'ȯl-,\ *adv or adj* [ME, fr. OE *ealriht*] (14c) : ALL RIGHT

usage In now obsolete senses *all right* or *alright* was formed in Old English as *ealriht.* Variation in early scribal and printing practices and in spoken stress patterns has given us this and similar pairs in *all ready, already* and *all together, altogether.* Since the 19th century some have insisted that *alright* is wrong, but, though it is less frequent than *all right,* it remains in common use and appears in the work of reputable writers ⟨the first two years of medical school were *alright* —Gertrude Stein⟩ ⟨it is doing a bit of *alright* —P. H. Dougherty, *N.Y. Times*⟩

Al·sa·tian \al-'sā-shən\ *n* [ML *Alsatia* Alsace] (1917) : GERMAN SHEPHERD

al·sike clover \,al-,sak-, -,sīk-\ *n* [*Alsike,* Sweden] (1852) : a European perennial clover (*Trifolium hybridum*) much used as a forage plant

al·so \'ȯl(t)-(,)sō, 'ȯ-\ *adv* [ME, fr. OE *eallswā,* fr. *eall* all + *swā* so — more at SO] (bef. 12c) **1** : LIKEWISE **2** : BESIDES : in addition : TOO

al·so–ran \-,ran\ *n* (1896) **1** : a horse or dog that finishes out of the money in a race **2** : a contestant that does not win **3** : one that is of little importance esp. competitively ⟨was just an ~ in the scramble for . . . privileges — C. A. Buss⟩

Al·ta·ic \al-'tā-ik\ *adj* (ca. 1828) **1** : of or relating to the Altai mountains **2** : of, relating to, or constituting a language family comprising the Turkic, Tungusic, and Mongolic subfamilies

Al·tair \al-'tī(ə)r, -'ta(ə)r, -'te(ə)r, 'al-,\ *n* [Ar *al-ṭā'ir,* lit., the flier] : the first magnitude star Alpha (α) Aquilae

al·tar \'ȯl-tər\ *n, often attrib* [ME *alter,* fr. OE *altar,* fr. L *altare;* akin to L *adolēre* to burn up] (bef. 12c) **1** : a usu. raised structure or place on which sacrifices are offered or incense is burned in worship **2** : a table on which the eucharistic elements are consecrated or which serves as a center of worship or ritual

altar boy *n* (1772) : a boy who assists the celebrant in a liturgical service

altar call *n* (1946) : an appeal by an evangelist to worshipers to come forward to signify their decision to commit their lives to Christ

altar of repose *often cap A&R* (ca. 1872) : REPOSITORY 2

al·tar·piece \'ȯl-tər-,pēs\ *n* (1644) : a work of art that decorates the space above and behind an altar

altar rail *n* (1860) : a railing in front of an altar separating the chancel from the body of the church

altar stone *n* (14c) : a stone slab with a compartment containing the relics of martyrs that forms an essential part of a Roman Catholic altar

alt·az·i·muth \(')al-'taz-(ə-)məth\ *n* [ISV *al*titude + *azimuth*] (1860) : a telescope mounted so that it can swing horizontally and vertically; *also* : any of several other similarly mounted instruments

al·ter \'ȯl-tər\ *vb* **al·tered; al·ter·ing** \-t(ə-)riŋ\ [ME *alteren,* fr. MF *alterer,* fr. ML *alterare,* fr. L *alter* other (of two); akin to L *alius* other — more at ELSE] *vt* (14c) **1** : to make different without changing into something else **2** : CASTRATE, SPAY ~ *vi* : to become different ***syn*** see CHANGE — **al·ter·abil·i·ty** \,ȯl-t(ə-)rə-'bil-ət-ē\ *n* — **al·ter·able** \'ȯl-t(ə-)rə-bəl\ *adj* — **al·ter·ably** \-blē\ *adv* — **al·ter·er** \-tər-ər\ *n*

al·ter·ation \,ȯl-tə-'rā-shən\ *n* (14c) **1** : the act or process of altering : the state of being altered **2** : the result of altering : MODIFICATION

al·ter·ative \'ȯl-tə-,rāt-iv, -rət-\ *n* (14c) : a drug used empirically to alter favorably the course of an ailment

al·ter·cate \'ȯl-tər-,kāt\ *vi* **-cat·ed; -cat·ing** [L *altercatus,* pp. of *altercari,* fr. *alter*] (1530) : to dispute angrily or noisily : WRANGLE

al·ter·ca·tion \,ȯl-tər-'kā-shən\ *n* (14c) : a noisy heated angry dispute; *also* : noisy controversy

al·ter ego \,ȯl-tə-'rē-(,)gō *also* -'reg-(,)ō\ *n* [L, lit., second I] (1537) : a second self: as **a** : a trusted friend **b** : the opposite side of a personality **c** : COUNTERPART 3

1al·ter·nate \'ȯl-tər-,nāt *also* 'al-\ *vb* **-nat·ed; -nat·ing** *vt* (15c) **1** : to perform by turns or in succession **2** : to cause to alternate ~ *vi* : to change from one to another repeatedly ⟨storms *alternated* with sunshine⟩

2al·ter·nate *US & Canad* 'ȯl-tər-nət *also* 'al-; *chiefly Brit* ȯl-'tər-\ *adj* [L *alternatus,* pp. of *alternare,* fr. *alternus* alternate, fr. *alter*] (1513) **1** : occurring or succeeding by turns ⟨a day of ~ sunshine and rain⟩ **2 a** : arranged first on one side and then on the other at different levels or points along an axial line ⟨~ leaves⟩ — compare OPPOSITE **b** : arranged one above or alongside the other **3** : every other : every second ⟨he works on ~ days⟩ **4** : constituting an alternative ⟨took the ~ route home⟩ **5** : ALTERNATIVE 3 — **al·ter·nate·ly** *adv*

3al·ter·nate *like*²\ *n* (1718) **1** : ALTERNATIVE **2** : one that substitutes for or alternates with another

alternate angle *n* (1660) : one of a pair of angles with different vertices and on opposite sides of a transversal at its intersection with two other lines: **a** : one of a pair of angles inside the two intersected lines — called also *alternate interior angle* **b** : one of a pair of angles outside the two intersected lines — called also *alternate exterior angle*

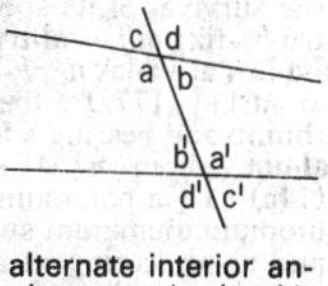

alternate interior angles *a, a', b, b'*; alternate exterior angles *c, c', d, d'*

alternating current *n* (1839) : an electric current that reverses its direction at regularly recurring intervals — abbr. *AC*

alternating group *n* (ca. 1909) : a permutation group whose elements comprise those permutations of *n* objects which can be formed from the original order by making consecutively an even number of interchanges of pairs of objects

alternating series *n* (ca. 1909) : a mathematical series in which consecutive terms are alternatively positive and negative

al·ter·na·tion \,ȯl-tər-'nā-shən *also* ,al-\ *n* (15c) **1 a** : the act or process of alternating or causing to alternate **b** : alternating occurrence : SUCCESSION **2** : INCLUSIVE, DISJUNCTION **3** : the occurrence of different allomorphs or allophones

alternation of generations (1858) : the occurrence of two or more forms differently produced in the life cycle of a plant or animal usu. involving the regular alternation of a sexual with an asexual generation but not infrequently consisting of alternation of a dioecious generation with one or more parthenogenetic generations

1al·ter·na·tive \ȯl-'tər-nət-iv, al-\ *adj* (1540) **1** : ALTERNATE **2** : offering or expressing a choice ⟨several ~ plans⟩ **3** : existing or functioning outside the established cultural, social, or economic system ⟨~ newspaper⟩ ⟨~ life-style⟩ — **al·ter·na·tive·ly** *adv* — **al·ter·na·tive·ness** *n*

2alternative *n* (1624) **1 a** : a proposition or situation offering a choice between two or more things only one of which may be chosen **b** : an opportunity for deciding between two or more courses or propositions **2 a** : one of two or more things, courses, or propositions to be chosen **b** : something which can be chosen instead ⟨the only ~ to intervention⟩ ***syn*** see CHOICE

alternative school *n* (1972) : an elementary or secondary school with a nontraditional curriculum

al·ter·na·tor \'ȯl-tər-,nāt-ər *also* 'al-\ *n* (1892) : an electric generator for producing alternating current

\ə\ abut \ᵊ\ kitten, F table \ər\ further \a\ ash \ā\ ace \ä\ cot, cart \au̇\ out \ch\ chin \e\ bet \ē\ easy \g\ go \i\ hit \ī\ ice \j\ job \ŋ\ sing \ō\ go \ȯ\ law \ȯi\ boy \th\ thin \th\ the \ü\ loot \u̇\ foot \y\ yet \zh\ vision \à, k, ⁿ, œ, œ̄, ue, ue̅, ʸ\ *see* Guide to Pronunciation

al·thaea *or* **al·thea** \al-'thē-ə\ *n* [L *althaea* marsh mallow, fr. Gk *althaia*] (1526) **1 :** a hollyhock or related plant (genus *Althaea*) **2 :** ROSE OF SHARON
alt·horn \'alt-ˌhȯ(ə)rn\ *n* [G, fr. *alt* alto + *horn* horn] (1859) **:** an alto saxhorn
al·though *also* **al·tho** \ȯl-'thō\ *conj* [ME *although,* fr. *al* all + *though*] (14c) **:** in spite of the fact that **:** even though
al·tim·e·ter \al-'tim-ət-ər, 'al-tə-ˌmēt-ər\ *n* [L *altus* + E *-meter*] (ca. 1828) **:** an instrument for measuring altitude; *specif* **:** an aneroid barometer designed to register changes in atmospheric pressure accompanying changes in altitude — **al·tim·e·try** \al-'tim-ə-trē\ *n*
al·ti·pla·no \ˌal-ti-'plän-(ˌ)ō\ *n, pl* **-nos** [AmerSp, fr. L *altus* + *planum* plain] (1919) **:** a high plateau or plain **:** TABLELAND
al·ti·tude \'al-tə-ˌt(y)üd\ *n* [ME, fr. L *altitudo* height, depth, fr. *altus* high, deep — more at OLD] (14c) **1 a :** the angular elevation of a celestial object above the horizon **b :** the vertical elevation of an object above a surface (as sea level or land) of a planet or natural satellite **c** (1) **:** a perpendicular line segment from a vertex of a geometric figure (as a triangle or a pyramid) to the opposite side or the opposite side extended or from a side or face to a parallel side or face or the side or face extended (2) **:** the length of an altitude **2 :** the highest level of a quality or feeling ⟨the ~ of passion⟩ **3 a :** vertical distance or extent **b :** position at a height **c :** an elevated region **:** EMINENCE — usu. used in pl. ***syn*** see HEIGHT — **al·ti·tu·di·nal** \ˌal-tə-'t(y)üd-nəl, -ᵊn-əl\ *adj* — **al·ti·tu·di·nous** \-'t(y)üd-nəs, -ᵊn-əs\ *adj*
altitude sickness *n* (1920) **:** the effects (as nosebleed or nausea) of oxygen deficiency in the blood and tissues developed in rarefied air at high altitudes
[1]**al·to** \'al-(ˌ)tō\ *n, pl* **altos** [It, lit., high, fr. L *altus*] (ca. 1724) **1 a :** COUNTERTENOR **b :** CONTRALTO **2 :** the second highest voice part in a 4-part chorus **3 :** a member of a family of instruments having a range lower than that of the treble or soprano; *esp.* **:** an alto saxophone
[2]**alto** *adj* (ca. 1724) **:** relating to or having the range or part of an alto
al·to·cu·mu·lus \ˌal-tō-'kyü-myə-ləs\ *n, pl* **-li** \-ˌlī, -ˌlē\ [NL, fr. L *altus* + NL *-o-* + *cumulus*] (1894) **:** a fleecy cloud formation consisting of large whitish globular cloudlets with shaded portions — see CLOUD illustration
[1]**al·to·geth·er** \ˌȯl-tə-'geth-ər\ *adv* [ME *altogedere,* fr. *al* all + *togedere* together] (13c) **1 :** WHOLLY, COMPLETELY ⟨an ~ different problem⟩ ⟨stopped crying ~⟩ **2 :** in all **:** ALL TOLD ⟨spent a hundred dollars ~⟩ **3 :** on the whole **:** in the main ⟨~ their efforts were successful⟩
[2]**altogether** *n* (1894) **:** NUDE — used with *the* ⟨posed in the ~⟩
al·to–re·lie·vo *or* **al·to–ri·lie·vo** \ˌal-(ˌ)tō-ri-'lē-(ˌ)vō, ˌäl-(ˌ)tō-rēl-'yā-(ˌ)vō\ *n, pl* **alto–relievos** *or* **al·to–ri·lie·vi** \ˌäl-(ˌ)tō-rēl-'yā-(ˌ)vē\ [It *altorilievo*] (1664) **1 :** HIGH RELIEF **2 :** a sculpture in high relief
al·to·stra·tus \ˌal-tō-'strāt-əs, -'strat-\ *n, pl* **-ti** \-ˌī\ [NL, fr. L *altus* + NL *-o-* + *stratus*] (1894) **:** a cloud formation similar to cirrostratus but darker and at a lower level — see CLOUD illustration
al·tri·cial \al-'trish-əl\ *adj* [L *altric-, altrix* fem. of *altor* one who nourishes, fr. *altus* pp. of *alere* to nourish — more at OLD] (1872) **:** being hatched or born or having the young hatched or born in a very immature and helpless condition so as to require care for some time ⟨~ birds⟩ — compare PRECOCIAL
al·tru·ism \'al-trü-ˌiz-əm\ *n* [F *altruisme,* fr. *autrui* other people, fr. OF, oblique case form of *autre* other, fr. L *alter*] (1853) **1 :** unselfish regard for or devotion to the welfare of others **2 :** behavior by an animal that is not beneficial to or may be harmful to itself but that benefits the survival of its species — **al·tru·ist** \-trü-əst\ *n* — **al·tru·is·tic** \ˌal-trü-'is-tik\ *adj* — **al·tru·is·ti·cal·ly** \-ti-k(ə-)lē\ *adv*
al·u·la \'al-yə-lə\ *n, pl* **-lae** \-ˌlē, -ˌlī\ [NL, fr. L, dim. of *ala* wing — more at AISLE] (1772) **:** the process of a bird's wing corresponding to the thumb and bearing a few short quills — called also *bastard wing*
[1]**al·um** \'al-əm\ *n* [ME, fr. MF *alum, alun,* fr. L *alumen* — more at ALE] (14c) **1 :** a potassium aluminum sulfate $KAl(SO_4)_2 \cdot 12H_2O$ or an ammonium aluminum sulfate $NH_4Al(SO_4)_2 \cdot 12H_2O$ used esp. as an emetic and as an astringent and styptic **2 :** any of various double salts isomorphous with potassium aluminum sulfate **3 :** ALUMINUM SULFATE
[2]**alum** \ə-'ləm\ *n* [by shortening] (1930) **:** ALUMNUS, ALUMNA
alu·mi·na \ə-'lü-mə-nə\ *n* [NL, fr. L *alumin-, alumen* alum] (1801) **:** aluminum oxide Al_2O_3 occurring native as corundum and in hydrated forms (as in bauxite)
alu·mi·nate \-nət\ *n* (1841) **:** a compound of alumina with a metallic oxide
al·u·min·i·um \ˌal-yə-'min-ē-əm\ *n* [NL, fr. *alumina*] *chiefly Brit* (1812) **:** ALUMINUM
alu·mi·nize \ə-'lü-mə-ˌnīz\ *vt* **-nized; -niz·ing** (1934) **:** to treat or coat with aluminum
alu·mi·no·sil·i·cate \ə-ˌlü-mə-nō-'sil-ə-ˌkāt, -'sil-i-kət\ *n* [L *alumin-, alumen* + *-o-* + ISV *silicate*] (1907) **:** a combined silicate and aluminate
alu·mi·nous \ə-'lü-mə-nəs\ *adj* (15c) **:** of, relating to, or containing alum or aluminum
alu·mi·num \ə-'lü-mə-nəm\ *n, often attrib* [NL, fr. *alumina*] (1812) **:** a bluish silver-white malleable ductile light trivalent metallic element with good electrical and thermal conductivity, high reflectivity, and resistance to oxidation that is the most abundant metal in the earth's crust occurring always in combination — see ELEMENT table
aluminum sulfate *n* (1873) **:** a white salt $Al_2(SO_4)_3$ usu. made by treating bauxite with sulfuric acid and used in making paper, in water purification, and in tanning
alum·na \ə-'ləm-nə\ *n, pl* **-nae** \-(ˌ)nē *also* -ˌnī\ [L, fem. of *alumnus*] (1882) **:** a girl or woman who has attended or has graduated from a particular school, college, or university
alum·nus \ə-'ləm-nəs\ *n, pl* **-ni** \-ˌnī\ [L, foster son, pupil, fr. *alere* to nourish — more at OLD] (1645) **1 :** one who has attended or has graduated from a particular school, college, or university **2 :** one who is a former member, employee, contributor, or inmate
al·um·root \'al-əm-ˌrüt, -ˌrut\ *n* (1813) **:** any of several No. American herbs (genus *Heuchera*) of the saxifrage family; *esp* **:** one (*H. americana*) with an astringent root
al·u·nite \'al-(y)ə-ˌnīt\ *n* [F, fr. *alun* alum] (1868) **:** a mineral $K(AlO)_3(SO_4)_2 \cdot 3H_2O$ consisting of a hydrous potassium aluminum sulfate and occurring in massive form or in rhombohedral crystals
al·ve·o·lar \al-'vē-ə-lər\ *adj* (1799) **1 :** of, relating to, resembling, or having alveoli **2 :** of, relating to, or constituting the part of the jaws where the teeth arise, the air cells of the lungs, or glands with secretory cells about a central space **3 :** articulated with the tip of the tongue touching or near the teethridge — **al·ve·o·lar·ly** *adv*
al·ve·o·late \-lət\ *adj* (ca. 1823) **:** pitted like a honeycomb ⟨~ pollen⟩ — **al·ve·o·la·tion** \(ˌ)al-ˌvē-ə-'lā-shən\ *n*
al·ve·o·lus \al-'vē-ə-ləs\ *n, pl* **-li** \-ˌlī, -(ˌ)lē\ [NL, fr. L, dim. of *alveus* cavity, hollow, fr. *alvus* belly] (ca. 1706) **1 :** a small cavity or pit: as **a :** a socket for a tooth **b :** an air cell of the lungs **c :** an acinus of a compound gland **d :** a cell or compartment of a honeycomb **2 :** TEETHRIDGE
al·way \'ȯl-(ˌ)wā\ *adv* [ME] *archaic* (bef. 12c) **:** ALWAYS
al·ways \'ȯl-wēz, -wəz, -(ˌ)wāz *also* 'ȯ-\ *adv* [ME *alway, alwayes,* fr. OE *ealne weg,* lit., all the way, fr. *ealne* (acc. of *eall* all) + *weg* (acc.) way — more at WAY] (13c) **1 :** at all times **:** INVARIABLY **2 :** FOREVER, PERPETUALLY **3 :** at any rate **:** in any event ⟨as a last resort one can ~ work⟩
Al·yce clover \'al-əs-\ *n* [prob. by folk etymology fr. NL *Alysicarpus,* genus name, fr. Gk *halysis* chain + *karpos* fruit] (1941) **:** a low spreading annual Old World legume (*Alysicarpus vaginalis*) used in the southern U.S. as a cover crop and for hay and pasturage
alys·sum \ə-'lis-əm\ *n* [NL, fr. Gk *alysson,* plant believed to cure rabies, fr. neut. of *alyssos* curing rabies, fr. *a-* + *lyssa* rabies] (ca. 1548) **1 :** any of a genus (*Alyssum*) of Old World herbs of the mustard family with small yellow racemose flowers **2 :** SWEET ALYSSUM
Alz·hei·mer's disease \'älts-ˌhī-mərz-\ *n* [Alois *Alzheimer* †1915 Ger. physician] (1912) **:** a degenerative disease of the central nervous system characterized esp. by premature senile mental deterioration
am [ME, fr. OE *eom;* akin to ON *em* am, L *sum,* Gk *eimi*] *pres 1st sing of* BE
AM \'ā-ˌem\ *n* [*a*mplitude *m*odulation] (1940) **:** a broadcasting system using amplitude modulation; *also* **:** a radio receiver of such a system — **AM** *adj*
ama \'äm-(ˌ)ä\ *n, pl* **amas** *or* **ama** [Jp] (1946) **:** a Japanese diver esp. for pearls
amah \'äm-(ˌ)ä\ *n* [Pg *ama* wet nurse, fr. ML *amma*] (1839) **:** an Oriental female servant; *esp* **:** a Chinese nurse
amain \ə-'mān\ *adv* (1540) **1** *archaic* **:** with all one's might ⟨down came the storm, and smote ~ the vessel — H. W. Longfellow⟩ **2** *archaic* **a :** at full speed **b :** in great haste **3** *archaic* **:** to a high degree **:** EXCEEDINGLY ⟨they whom I favour thrive in wealth ~ — John Milton⟩
Am·a·le·kite \'am-ə-ˌlek-ˌīt, ə-'mal-ə-ˌkīt\ *n* [Heb *ʽĂmālēqī,* pl. fr. *ʽĂmālēq* Amalek, grandson of Esau] (1609) **:** a member of an ancient nomadic people living south of Canaan
amal·gam \ə-'mal-gəm\ *n* [ME *amalgame,* fr. MF, fr. ML *amalgama*] (15c) **1 :** an alloy of mercury with another metal that is solid or liquid at room temperature according to the proportion of mercury present and is used esp. in making tooth cements **2 :** a mixture of different elements **:** COMBINATION
amal·gam·ate \-gə-ˌmāt\ *vt* **-at·ed; -at·ing** (1660) **:** to unite in or as if in an amalgam; *esp* **:** to merge into a single body ***syn*** see MIX — **amal·gam·ator** \-ˌmāt-ər\ *n*
amal·gam·ation \ə-ˌmal-gə-'mā-shən\ *n* (ca. 1612) **1 a :** the action or process of amalgamating **:** UNITING **b :** the state of being amalgamated **2 :** the result of amalgamating **:** AMALGAM **3 :** CONSOLIDATION, MERGER ⟨~ of two corporations⟩
aman·dine \ˌä-ˌmän-'dēn\ *adj* [F] (1925) **:** prepared or served with almonds
am·a·ni·ta \ˌam-ə-'nīt-ə, -'nēt-\ *n* [NL, genus name, fr. Gk *amanitai,* pl., a kind of fungus] (ca. 1909) **:** any of various mostly poisonous white-spored fungi (genus *Amanita*) with the volva separate from the cap
am·a·ni·tin \-'nīt-ᵊn, -'nēt-\ *n* [*amanita* + *-in*] (ca. 1847) **:** a highly toxic peptide produced by the death cap that selectively inhibits mammalian RNA polymerase
aman·ta·dine \ə-'mant-ə-ˌdēn\ *n* [ISV *adamant*ane ($C_{10}H_{16}$) + *amine*] (1964) **:** a drug used esp. as the hydrochloride $C_{10}H_{17}N \cdot HCl$ to prevent infection (as by an influenza virus) by interfering with virus penetration into host cells
aman·u·en·sis \ə-ˌman-yə-'wen(t)-səs\ *n, pl* **-en·ses** \-(ˌ)sēz\ [L, fr. (*servus*) *a manu* slave with secretarial duties] (1619) **:** one employed to write from dictation or to copy manuscript
am·a·ranth \'am-ə-ˌran(t)th\ *n* [L *amarantus,* a flower, fr. Gk *amaranton,* fr. neut. of *amarantos* unfading, fr. *a-* + *marainein* to waste away] (1548) **1 :** any of a large genus (*Amaranthus* of the family Amaranthaceae, the amaranth family) of coarse herbs including pigweeds and various forms cultivated as food crops **2 :** a flower that never fades **3 :** a red azo dye
am·a·ran·thine \ˌam-ə-'ran(t)-thən, -'ran-ˌthīn\ *adj* (1667) **1 a :** of or relating to an amaranth **b :** UNDYING **2 :** of the color amaranth
am·a·ret·to \ˌam-ə-'ret-(ˌ)ō, ˌäm-\ *n, often cap* [It, dim. of *amaro* bitter, fr. L *amarus*] (1973) **:** an almond-flavored liqueur
am·a·ryl·lis \ˌam-ə-'ril-əs\ *n* [NL, genus name, prob. fr. L, name of a shepherdess in Vergil's *Eclogues*] (1789) **:** any of a genus (*Amaryllis* of the family Amaryllidaceae, the amaryllis family) of bulbous African herbs with showy umbellate flowers; *also* **:** a plant of any of several related genera (as *Hippeastrum* or *Sprekelia*)
amass \ə-'mas\ *vb* [MF *amasser,* fr. OF, fr. *a-* (fr. L *ad-*) + *masser* to gather into a mass, fr. *masse* mass] *vt* (15c) **1 :** to collect for oneself **:** ACCUMULATE ⟨~ a great fortune⟩ **2 :** to collect into a mass **:** GATHER ⟨~ the wool into a large ball⟩ ~ *vi* **:** to come together **:** ASSEMBLE — **amass·er** *n* — **amass·ment** \-mənt\ *n*
am·a·teur \'am-ə-ˌtər, -ət-ər, -ə-ˌt(y)u̇(ə)r, -ə-ˌchu̇(ə)r, -ə-chər\ *n* [F, fr. L *amator* lover, fr. *amatus,* pp. of *amare* to love] (1784) **1 :** DEVOTEE, ADMIRER **2 :** one who engages in a pursuit, study, science, or sport as a pastime rather than as a profession **3 :** one lacking in experience and competence in an art or science — **amateur** *adj* — **am·a·teur·ish** \ˌam-ə-'tər-ish, -'t(y)u̇(ə)r-\ *adj* — **am·a·teur·ish·ly** *adv* — **am·a·teur·ish·ness** *n* — **am·a·teur·ism** \'am-ə-ˌtər-ˌiz-əm, -ət-ə-ˌriz-, -ə-ˌt(y)u̇(ə)r-ˌiz-, -ˌchu̇(ə)r-ˌiz-, -chə-ˌriz-\ *n*
syn AMATEUR, DILETTANTE, DABBLER, TYRO mean a person who follows a pursuit without attaining proficiency or professional status. AMATEUR often applies to one practicing an art without mastery of its essentials; in sports it may also suggest not so much lack of skill but avoidance of direct remuneration; DILETTANTE may apply to the lover of an art rather than its skilled practitioner but usu. implies elegant

trifling in the arts and an absence of serious commitment; DABBLER suggests desultory habits of work and lack of persistence; TYRO implies inexperience often combined with audacity with resulting crudeness or blundering.

Ama·ti \ä-ˈmät-ē, ə-\ *n, pl* **Amatis** (1829) **:** a violin made by a member of the Amati family of Cremona

am·a·tive \ˈam-ət-iv\ *adj* [ML *amativus,* fr. L *amatus*] (1636) **:** disposed or disposing to love **:** AMOROUS — **am·a·tive·ly** *adv* — **am·a·tive·ness** *n*

am·a·tol \ˈam-ə-ˌtȯl, -ˌtäl, -ˌtōl\ *n* [ISV *ammonium* + connective *-a-* + trinitro*toluene*] (1918) **:** an explosive consisting of ammonium nitrate and trinitrotoluene

am·a·to·ry \ˈam-ə-ˌtōr-ē, -ˌtȯr-\ *adj* (1599) **:** of, relating to, or expressing sexual love

am·au·ro·sis \ˌam-ȯ-ˈrō-səs\ *n, pl* **-ro·ses** \-ˌsēz\ [NL, fr. Gk *amaurōsis,* lit., dimming, fr. *amauroun* to dim, fr. *amauros* dim] (1603) **:** decay of sight occurring without externally perceptible change in the eye — **am·au·rot·ic** \-ˈrät-ik\ *adj*

amaurotic family idiocy *n* (1896) **:** AMAUROTIC IDIOCY

amaurotic idiocy *n* (1896) **:** any of several recessive genetic conditions characterized by the accumulation of lipid-containing cells in the viscera and nervous system, mental deficiency, and impaired vision or blindness; *esp* **:** TAY-SACHS DISEASE

[1]**amaze** \ə-ˈmāz\ *vb* **amazed; amaz·ing** [ME *amasen,* fr. OE *āmasian,* fr. *ā-* (perfective prefix) + (assumed) *masian* to confuse — more at ABIDE] *vt* (bef. 12c) *1 obs* **:** BEWILDER, PERPLEX **2 :** to fill with wonder **:** ASTOUND ~ *vi* **:** to show or cause astonishment ⟨his calmness continues to ~⟩ *syn* see SURPRISE — **amaz·ing·ly** \-ˈmā-ziŋ-lē\ *adv*

[2]**amaze** *n* (15c) **:** AMAZEMENT

amaze·ment \ə-ˈmāz-mənt\ *n* (1595) *1 obs* **:** CONSTERNATION, BEWILDERMENT **2 :** the quality or state of being amazed

am·a·zon \ˈam-ə-ˌzän, -ə-zən\ *n* [ME, fr. L, fr. Gk *Amazōn,* prob. fr. *a-* without + *mazos* (alter. of *mastos*) breast; fr. their habit of removing a breast to facilitate drawing the bow — more at MEAT] (14c) **1** *cap* **:** a member of a race of female warriors repeatedly battling the Greeks of mythology **2 :** a tall strong masculine woman

Am·a·zo·nian \ˌam-ə-ˈzō-nē-ən, -nyən\ *adj* (1594) **1 a :** relating to, resembling, or befitting an Amazon **b** *not cap* **:** MASCULINE, WARLIKE ⟨an *amazonian* woman⟩ **2 :** of or relating to the Amazon river or its valley

am·a·zon·ite \ˈam-ə-zə-ˌnīt\ *n* [*Amazon* river] (ca. 1879) **:** an apple-green or bluish-green microcline

am·a·zon·stone \-zən-ˌstōn\ *n* (1836) **:** AMAZONITE

am·bage \ˈam-bij\ *n, pl* **am·ba·ges** \am-ˈbā-(ˌ)jēz, ˈam-bij-əz\ [back-formation fr. ME *ambages,* fr. MF or L; MF, fr. L, fr. *ambi-* + *agere* to drive — more at AGENT] (14c) **1** *archaic* **:** AMBIGUITY, CIRCUMLOCUTION — usu. used in pl. **2** *pl, archaic* **:** indirect ways or proceedings — **am·ba·gious** \am-ˈbā-jəs\ *adj*

am·bas·sa·dor \am-ˈbas-əd-ər, əm-, im-, -ˈbas-ə-ˌdȯ(ə)r, -ˈbas-dər\ *n* [ME *ambassadour,* fr. MF *ambassadeur,* of Gmc origin; akin to OHG *ambaht* service] (14c) **1 :** an official envoy; *esp* **:** a diplomatic agent of the highest rank accredited to a foreign government or sovereign as the resident representative of his own government or sovereign or appointed for a special and often temporary diplomatic assignment **2 a :** an authorized representative or messenger **b :** an unofficial representative ⟨traveling abroad as ~s of goodwill⟩ — **am·bas·sa·do·ri·al** \-ˌbas-ə-ˈdōr-ē-əl, -ˈdȯr-\ *adj* — **am·bas·sa·dor·ship** \-ˈbas-əd-ər-ˌship\ *n*

ambassador-at-large *n, pl* **ambassadors-at-large** (1908) **:** a minister of the highest rank not accredited to a particular foreign government or sovereign

am·bas·sa·dress \am-ˈbas-ə-drəs, əm-, im-\ *n* (1594) **1 :** a female ambassador **2 :** the wife of an ambassador

am·beer \ˈam-ˌbi(ə)r\ *n* [prob. alter. of *amber;* fr. its color] *chiefly Southern & Midland* (1763) **:** TOBACCO JUICE

[1]**am·ber** \ˈam-bər\ *n* [ME *ambre,* fr. MF, fr. ML *ambra,* fr. Ar *ʿanbar* ambergris] (14c) **1 :** a hard yellowish to brownish translucent fossil resin that takes a fine polish and is used chiefly in making ornamental objects (as beads) **2 :** a variable color averaging a dark orange yellow

[2]**amber** *adj* (15c) **1 :** consisting of amber **2 :** resembling amber; *esp* **:** having the color amber

am·ber·gris \ˈam-bər-ˌgris, -ˌgrē(s)\ *n* [ME *ambregris,* fr. MF *ambre gris,* fr. *ambre* + *gris* gray — more at GRIZZLE] (15c) **:** a waxy substance found floating in or on the shores of tropical waters, believed to originate in the intestines of the sperm whale, and used in perfumery as a fixative

am·ber·jack \-ˌjak\ *n* [fr. its color] (ca. 1893) **:** any of several carangid fishes (genus *Seriola*); *esp* **:** a large vigorous sport fish (*S. dumerili*) of the western Atlantic

ambi- *prefix* [L *ambi-, amb-* both, around; akin to L *ambo* both, Gk *amphō* both, *amphi* around — more at BY] **:** both ⟨*ambi*valent⟩

am·bi·dex·ter·i·ty \ˌam-bi-(ˌ)dek-ˈster-ət-ē\ *n* (1652) **:** the quality or state of being ambidextrous

am·bi·dex·trous \ˌam-bi-ˈdek-strəs\ *adj* [LL *ambidexter,* fr. L *ambi-* + *dexter* right hand] (1646) **1 :** using both hands with equal ease **2 :** unusually skillful **:** VERSATILE **3 :** characterized by duplicity **:** DOUBLE-DEALING — **am·bi·dex·trous·ly** *adv*

am·bi·ence *or* **am·bi·ance** \ˈam-bē-ən(t)s, äⁿ-byäⁿs\ *n* [F *ambiance,* fr. *ambiant* ambient] (1889) **:** a feeling or mood associated with a particular place, person, or thing **:** ATMOSPHERE

[1]**am·bi·ent** \ˈam-bē-ənt\ *adj* [L *ambient-, ambiens,* prp. of *ambire* to go around, fr. *ambi-* + *ire* to go — more at ISSUE] (1596) **:** surrounding on all sides **:** ENCOMPASSING

[2]**ambient** *n* (1624) **:** an encompassing atmosphere **:** ENVIRONMENT

am·bi·gu·ity \ˌam-bə-ˈgyü-ət-ē\ *n, pl* **-ities** (15c) **1 a :** the quality or state of being ambiguous esp. in meaning ⟨~ is often a feature of poetry⟩ **b :** an ambiguous word or expression **2 :** UNCERTAINTY

am·big·u·ous \am-ˈbig-yə-wəs\ *adj* [L *ambiguus,* fr. *ambigere* to wander about, fr. *ambi-* + *agere* to drive — more at AGENT] (1528) **1 a :** doubtful or uncertain esp. from obscurity or indistinctness ⟨eyes of an ~ color⟩ **b :** INEXPLICABLE **2 :** capable of being understood in two or more possible senses or ways *syn* see OBSCURE — **am·big·u·ous·ly** *adv* — **am·big·u·ous·ness** *n*

am·bi·sex·u·al \ˌam-bi-ˈseksh-(ə-)wəl, -ˈsek-shəl\ *adj* (1939) **:** BISEXUAL — **ambisexual** *n* — **am·bi·sex·u·al·i·ty** \-ˌsek-shə-ˈwal-ət-ē\ *n*

am·bit \ˈam-bət\ *n* [ME, fr. L *ambitus,* fr. *ambitus,* pp. of *ambire*] (14c) **1 :** CIRCUIT, COMPASS **2 :** the bounds or limits of a place or district **3 :** a sphere of action, expression, or influence **:** SCOPE

[1]**am·bi·tion** \am-ˈbish-ən\ *n* [ME, fr. MF or L; MF, fr. L *ambition-, ambitio,* lit., going around, fr. *ambitus,* pp.] (14c) **1 a :** an ardent desire for rank, fame, or power **b :** desire to achieve a particular end **2 :** the object of ambition **3 :** a desire for activity or exertion ⟨felt sick and had no ~⟩ — **am·bi·tion·less** \-ləs\ *adj*

syn AMBITION, ASPIRATION, PRETENSION mean strong desire for advancement. AMBITION applies to the desire for personal advancement or preferment and may suggest equally a praiseworthy or an inordinate desire; ASPIRATION implies a striving after something higher than oneself and usu. implies that the striver is thereby ennobled; PRETENSION suggests ardent desire for recognition of accomplishment without actual possession of the necessary ability and therefore implies presumption.

[2]**ambition** *vt* (1664) **:** to have as one's ambition **:** DESIRE

am·bi·tious \am-ˈbish-əs\ *adj* (14c) **1 a :** having or controlled by ambition **b :** having a desire to achieve a particular goal **:** ASPIRING **2 :** resulting from, characterized by, or showing ambition — **am·bi·tious·ly** *adv* — **am·bi·tious·ness** *n*

am·biv·a·lence \am-ˈbiv-ə-lən(t)s\ *n* [ISV] (1918) **1 :** simultaneous and contradictory attitudes or feelings (as attraction and repulsion) toward an object, person, or action **2 a :** continual fluctuation (as between one thing and its opposite) **b :** uncertainty as to which approach to follow — **am·biv·a·lent** \-lənt\ *adj* — **am·biv·a·lent·ly** *adv*

am·bi·ver·sion \ˌam-bi-ˈvər-zhən, -shən\ *n* [*ambi-* + *-version* (as in *introversion*)] (ca. 1927) **:** the personality configuration of an ambivert — **am·bi·ver·sive** \-ˈvər-siv, -ziv\ *adj*

am·bi·vert \ˈam-bi-ˌvərt\ *n* [*ambi-* + *-vert* (as in *introvert*)] (ca. 1927) **:** a person having characteristics of both extrovert and introvert

[1]**am·ble** \ˈam-bəl\ *vi* **am·bled; am·bling** \-b(ə-)liŋ\ [ME *amblen,* fr. MF *ambler,* fr. L *ambulare* to walk] (14c) **:** to go at or as if at an amble **:** SAUNTER — **am·bler** \-b(ə-)lər\ *n*

[2]**amble** *n* (14c) **1 a :** an easy gait of a horse in which the legs on the same side of the body move together **b :** [7]RACK b **2 :** an easy gait **3 :** a leisurely walk

am·blyg·o·nite \am-ˈblig-ə-ˌnīt\ *n* [G *amblygonit,* fr. Gk *amblygōnios* obtuse-angled, fr. *amblys* blunt, dull + *gōnia* angle] (ca. 1828) **:** a mineral $(Li,Na)AlPO_4(F,OH)$ consisting of basic lithium aluminum phosphate commonly containing sodium and fluorine and occurring in white cleavable masses

am·bly·opia \ˌam-blē-ˈō-pē-ə\ *n* [NL, fr. Gk *amblyōpia,* fr. *amblys* + *-ōpia* -opia] (ca. 1706) **:** dimness of sight esp. in one eye without apparent change in the eye structures — called also *lazy eye* — **am·bly·opic** \-ˈō-pik, -ˈäp-ik\ *adj*

am·bo·cep·tor \ˈam-bō-ˌsep-tər\ *n* [ISV *ambi-* + *receptor*] (1902) **:** an antibody that lyses an antigen in combination with complement

Am·boi·nese \ˌam-ˌbȯi-ˈnēz, -ˈnēs, am-ˈbȯi-ˌ\ *or* **Am·bo·nese** \ˌam-bə-ˈnēz, -ˈnēs\ *n, pl* **Amboinese** *or* **Ambonese** [*Amboina* (*Ambon*) + *-ese*] (ca. 1864) **1 :** a native or inhabitant of Ambon **2 :** the language of the people of Ambon

am·boy·na *or* **am·boi·na** \am-ˈbȯi-nə\ *n* [*Amboina,* Moluccas, Indonesia] (ca. 1864) **:** a mottled curly-grained wood of a leguminous tree (*Pterocarpus indicus*) of southeastern Asia

am·bro·sia \am-ˈbrō-zh(ē-)ə\ *n* [L, fr. Gk, lit., immortality, fr. *ambrotos* immortal, fr. *a-* + *-mbrotos* (akin to *brotos* mortal) — more at MURDER] (1555) **1 a :** the food of the Greek and Roman gods **b :** the ointment or perfume of the gods **2 :** something extremely pleasing to taste or smell **3 :** a dessert made of oranges and shredded coconut — **am·bro·sial** \-zh(ē-)əl\ *adj* — **am·bro·sial·ly** \-ē\ *adv*

ambrosia beetle *n* (ca. 1900) **:** any of various small wood-boring beetles (family Scolytidae) that cultivate a fungus on which they feed and raise their larvae

am·bro·type \ˈam-brə-ˌtīp\ *n* [Gk *ambrotos* + E *type*] (1855) **:** a positive picture made of a photographic negative on glass backed by a dark surface

am·bry \ˈam-brē; ˈäm-rē, ˈȯm-\ *n, pl* **ambries** [ME *armarie,* fr. MF, fr. L *armarium,* fr. *arma* weapons — more at ARM] (14c) **1** *dial chiefly Brit* **:** PANTRY **2 :** a recess in a church wall (as for holding sacramental vessels)

ambs·ace \ˈām-ˌzās\ *n* [ME *ambes as,* fr. OF, fr. *ambes* both + *as* aces] *archaic* (13c) **:** the lowest throw at dice; *also* **:** something worthless or unlucky

am·bu·la·cral \ˌam-byə-ˈlak-rəl, -ˈlāk-\ *adj* (1836) **:** of, relating to, or being any of the radial areas of echinoderms along which run the principal nerves, blood vessels, and elements of the water-vascular system ⟨~ grooves⟩

am·bu·la·crum \-rəm\ *n, pl* **-cra** \-rə\ [NL, fr. L, alley, fr. *ambulare* to walk] (1837) **:** an ambulacral area or part

am·bu·lance \ˈam-b(y)ə-lən(t)s *also* -ˌlan(t)s\ *n* [F, fr. (*hôpital*) *ambulant,* lit., ambulant field hospital, fr. *ambulant* itinerant, fr. L *ambulant-, ambulans,* prp. of *ambulare*] (1809) **:** a vehicle equipped for transporting the injured or sick

ambulance chaser *n* (1897) **:** a lawyer or lawyer's agent who incites accident victims to sue for damages — **ambulance chasing** *n*

am·bu·lant \ˈam-byə-lənt\ *adj* (1619) **:** moving about **:** AMBULATORY

am·bu·late \-ˌlāt\ *vi* **-lat·ed; -lat·ing** [L *ambulatus,* pp. of *ambulare*] (ca. 1623) **:** to move from place to place **:** WALK — **am·bu·la·tion** \ˌam-byə-ˈlā-shən\ *n*

[1]**am·bu·la·to·ry** \ˈam-byə-lə-ˌtōr-ē, -ˌtȯr-\ *adj* (1622) **1 :** of, relating to, or adapted to walking; *also* **:** occurring during a walk **2 :** moving from place to place **:** ITINERANT **3 :** capable of being altered ⟨a will is ~ until the testator's death⟩ **4 a :** able to walk about and not bedridden **b :** involving an individual who is able to walk about ⟨~ medical care⟩ — **am·bu·la·to·ri·ly** \ˌam-byə-lə-ˈtōr-ə-lē, -ˈtȯr-\ *adv*

\ə\ abut \ᵊ\ kitten, F table \ər\ further \a\ ash \ā\ ace \ä\ cot, cart
\au̇\ out \ch\ chin \e\ bet \ē\ easy \g\ go \i\ hit \ī\ ice \j\ job
\ŋ\ sing \ō\ go \ȯ\ law \ȯi\ boy \th\ thin \t͟h\ the \ü\ loot \u̇\ foot
\y\ yet \zh\ vision \à, k̲, ⁿ, œ, œ̄, ue, ue̅, ʸ\ *see* Guide to Pronunciation

[2]**ambulatory** *n, pl* **-ries** (ca. 1623) **:** a sheltered place (as in a cloister or church) for walking

am·bus·cade \'am-bə-ˌskād, ˌam-bə-'\ *n* [MF *embuscade,* modif. of OIt *imboscata,* fr. *imboscare* to place in ambush, fr. *in* (fr. L) + *bosco* forest, perh. of Gmc origin; akin to OHG *busc* forest — more at IN, BUSH] (1582) **:** AMBUSH — **ambuscade** *vb* — **am·bus·cad·er** *n*

[1]**am·bush** \'am-ˌbu̇sh\ *vb* [ME *embushen,* fr. MF *embuschier,* fr. *en* in (fr. L *in*) + *busche* stick of firewood] *vt* (14c) **1 :** to station in ambush **2 :** to attack from an ambush **:** WAYLAY ~ *vi* **:** to lie in wait **:** LURK — **am·bush·er** *n* — **am·bush·ment** \-mənt\ *n*

[2]**ambush** *n* (15c) **1 :** a trap in which concealed persons lie in wait to attack by surprise **2 :** the persons stationed in ambush; *also* **:** their concealed position **3 :** an attack esp. from an ambush

am·bys·to·ma \am-'bis-tə-mə\ *n* [NL, irreg. fr. LL *ambly-* blunt, fr. Gk *amblys* + *stoma* stoma, mouth] (1931) **:** any of an American genus (*Ambystoma*) of salamanders comprising the axolotls and the tiger salamander

ame·ba, ame·bic, ame·boid *var of* AMOEBA, AMOEBIC, AMOEBOID

am·e·bi·a·sis \ˌam-i-'bī-ə-səs\ *n, pl* **-a·ses** \-ˌsēz\ (1905) **:** infection with or disease caused by amoebas

ame·bic dysentery \ə-ˌmē-bik-\ *n* (1891) **:** acute intestinal amebiasis of man caused by an amoeba (*Entamoeba histolytica*) and marked by dysentery, gripes, and erosion of the intestinal wall

ame·bo·cyte *var of* AMOEBOCYTE

ameer *var of* EMIR

ame·lio·rate \ə-'mēl-yə-ˌrāt, -'mē-lē-ə-\ *vb* **-rat·ed; -rat·ing** [alter. of *meliorate*] *vt* (1790) **:** to make better or more tolerable ~ *vi* **:** to grow better — **ame·lio·ra·tion** \-ˌmēl-yə-'rā-shən, -ˌmē-lē-ə-\ *n* — **ame·lio·ra·tive** \-'mēl-yə-ˌrāt-iv, -'mē-lē-ə-\ *adj* — **ame·lio·ra·tor** \-ˌrāt-ər\ *n* — **ame·lio·ra·to·ry** \-rə-ˌtōr-ē, -ˌtȯr-\ *adj*

am·e·lo·blast \'am-ə-lō-ˌblast\ *n* [*amel* (fr. ME *amel,* fr. MF *esmail*) + *-o-* + *-blast* — more at ENAMEL] (1882) **:** one of a group of columnar cells that produce and deposit enamel on the surface of a developing vertebrate tooth

amen \(ˈ)ä-'men, (ˈ)ā-; 'ä- *when sung*\ *interj* [ME, fr. OE, fr. LL, fr. Gk *amēn,* fr. Heb *āmēn*] (bef. 12c) — used to express solemn ratification (as of an expression of faith) or hearty approval (as of an assertion)

ame·na·ble \ə-'mē-nə-bəl, -'men-ə-\ *adj* [prob. fr. (assumed) AF, fr. MF *amener* to lead up, fr. OF, fr. *a-* (fr. L *ad-*) + *mener* to lead, fr. L *minare* to drive, fr. *minari* to threaten — more at MOUNT] (1596) **1 :** liable to be brought to account **:** ANSWERABLE ⟨citizens ~ to the law⟩ **2 a :** capable of submission (as to judgment or test) **:** SUITED ⟨the data is ~ to analysis⟩ **b :** readily brought to yield or submit **:** TRACTABLE ⟨a child ~ to discipline⟩ ***syn*** see RESPONSIBLE, OBEDIENT — **ame·na·bil·i·ty** \-ˌmē-nə-'bil-ət-ē, -ˌmen-ə-\ *n* — **ame·na·bly** \-'mē-nə-blē, -'men-ə-\ *adv*

amen corner \ˌā-ˌmen-\ *n* (1860) **:** a conspicuous corner in a church occupied by fervent worshipers

amend \ə-'mend\ *vb* [ME *amenden,* fr. OF *amender,* modif. of L *emendare,* fr. *e, ex* out + *menda* fault; akin to L *mendax* lying, *mendicus* beggar, Skt *mindā* physical defect] *vt* (13c) **1 :** to put right; *specif* **:** to make emendations in (as a text) **2 a :** to change or modify for the better **:** IMPROVE ⟨~ the situation⟩ **b :** to alter esp. in phraseology; *specif* **:** to alter formally by modification, deletion, or addition ⟨~ the constitution⟩ ~ *vi* **:** to reform oneself ***syn*** see CORRECT — **amend·able** \-'men-də-bəl\ *adj* — **amend·er** *n*

amen·da·to·ry \ə-'men-də-ˌtōr-ē, -ˌtȯr-\ *adj* [*amend* + *-atory* (as in *emendatory*)] (ca. 1828) **:** CORRECTIVE

amend·ment \ə-'men(d)-mənt\ *n* (13c) **1 :** the act of amending **:** CORRECTION **2 :** a substance that aids plant growth indirectly by improving the condition of the soil **3 a :** the process of amending by parliamentary or constitutional procedure **b :** an alteration proposed or effected by this process ⟨the 18th ~⟩

amends \ə-'men(d)z\ *n pl but sing or pl in constr* [ME *amendes,* fr. MF, pl. of *amende* reparation, fr. *amender*] (14c) **:** compensation for a loss or injury **:** RECOMPENSE ⟨make ~⟩

ame·ni·ty \ə-'men-ət-ē, -'mē-nət-\ *n, pl* **-ties** [ME *amenite,* fr. L *amoenitat-, amoenitas,* fr. *amoenus* pleasant] (14c) **1 a :** the quality of being pleasant or agreeable **b** (1) **:** the attractiveness and value of real estate or of a residential structure (2) **:** a feature conducive to such attractiveness and value **2 :** something that conduces to material comfort or convenience **3 :** something (as a conventional social gesture) that conduces to smoothness or pleasantness of social relationships

amen·or·rhea \ˌā-ˌmen-ə-'rē-ə, ˌäm-ˌen-\ *n* [NL, fr. *a-* + Gk *mēn* month + NL *-o-* + *-rrhea* — more at MOON] (1804) **:** abnormal absence or suppression of the menstrual discharge — **amen·or·rhe·ic** \-'rē-ik\ *adj*

ament \'am-ənt, 'ā-mənt\ *n* [NL *amentum,* fr. L, thong, strap] (1791) **:** an indeterminate spicate inflorescence (as in the willow) bearing scaly bracts and apetalous unisexual flowers — **amen·ta·ceous** \ˌam-ən-'tā-shəs, ˌā-mən-\ *adj* — **amen·tif·er·ous** \-'tif-(ə-)rəs\ *adj*

amen·tia \(ˈ)ā-'men-ch(ē-)ə, (ˈ)ä-\ *n* [NL, fr. L, madness, fr. *ament-, amens* mad, fr. *a-* (fr. *ab-*) + *ment-, mens* mind — more at MIND] (14c) **:** mental deficiency; *specif* **:** a condition of lack of development of intellectual capacity

Am·er·asian \ˌam-ə-'rā-zhən, -shən\ *n* [*Amer*ican + *Asian*] (1953) **:** a person of mixed American and Asian descent; *esp* **:** one whose mother is Asian and whose father is American

amerce \ə-'mərs\ *vt* **amerced; amerc·ing** [ME *amercien,* fr. AF *amercier,* fr. OF *a merci* at (one's) mercy] (14c) **:** to punish by a fine whose amount is fixed by the court; *broadly* **:** PUNISH — **amerce·ment** \-'mərs-mənt\ *n* — **amer·cia·ble** \-'mər-sē-ə-bəl, -'mər-shə-bəl\ *adj*

[1]**Amer·i·can** \ə-'mer-ə-kən, -'mər-, -'mar-, -i-kən\ *n* (1578) **1 :** an Indian of No. America or So. America **2 :** a native or inhabitant of No. America or So. America **3 :** a citizen of the U.S. **4 :** AMERICAN ENGLISH

[2]**American** *adj* (1598) **1 :** of or relating to America **2 :** of or relating to the U.S. or its possessions or original territory **3 :** of or relating to the division of mankind that comprises the Indians of No. America and So. America — **Amer·i·can·ness** \-kən-nəs\ *n*

Amer·i·ca·na \ə-ˌmer-ə-'kän-ə, -ˌmər-, -ˌmar-, -'kan-ə\ *n pl* (1841) **1 :** materials concerning or characteristic of America, its civilization, or its culture; *broadly* **:** things typical of America **2 :** American culture

American chameleon *n* (1881) **:** a lizard (*Anolis carolinensis*) of the southeastern U.S.

American cheese *n* (1804) **:** a process cheese made from American cheddar

American dream *n, often cap D* (1933) **:** an American social ideal that stresses egalitarianism and esp. material prosperity

American elm *n* (1813) **:** a large elm (*Ulmus americana*) with gradually spreading branches and pendulous branchlets that is common in eastern No. America

American English *n* (1806) **:** the native language of most inhabitants of the U.S. — used esp. with the implication that it is clearly distinguishable from British English yet not so divergent as to be a separate language

American foxhound *n* (ca. 1891) **:** any of an American breed of foxhounds that are smaller than the English foxhound but with longer ears and that have a dense hard glossy coat usu. of black, tan, and white

American Indian *n* (1732) **:** a member of any of the aboriginal peoples of the western hemisphere except usu. the Eskimos constituting one of the divisions of the Mongoloid stock

Amer·i·can·ism \ə-'mer-ə-kə-ˌniz-əm, -'mər-, -'mar-\ *n* (1781) **1 :** a characteristic feature of American English esp. as contrasted with British English **2 :** attachment or allegiance to the traditions, interests, or ideals of the U.S. **3 a :** a custom or trait peculiar to America **b :** the political principles and practices essential to American culture

Amer·i·can·ist \-kə-nəst\ *n* (1881) **1 :** a specialist in the languages or cultures of the aboriginal inhabitants of America **2 :** a specialist in American culture or history

American ivy *n* (1785) **:** VIRGINIA CREEPER

Amer·i·can·iza·tion \ə-ˌmer-ə-kə-nə-'zā-shən, -ˌmər-, -ˌmar-\ *n* (1858) **1 :** the act or process of Americanizing **2 :** instruction of foreigners (as immigrants) in English and in U.S. history, government, and culture

Amer·i·can·ize \ə-'mer-ə-kə-ˌnīz, -'mər-, -'mar-\ *vb* **-ized; -iz·ing** *vt* (1797) **1 :** to cause to acquire or conform to American characteristics **2 :** to bring (as an area) under the political, cultural, or commercial influence of the U.S. ~ *vi* **:** to acquire or conform to American traits

American plan *n* (1856) **:** a hotel plan whereby the daily rates cover the costs of the room and meals — compare EUROPEAN PLAN

American saddle horse *n* (1921) **:** a 3-gaited or 5-gaited saddle horse of a breed developed chiefly in Kentucky from Thoroughbreds and native stock

American Sign Language *n* (1965) **:** a sign language for the deaf in which meaning is conveyed by a system of articulated hand gestures and their placement relative to the upper body

American Staffordshire terrier *n* (1970) **:** a strong stocky terrier of a breed orig. developed for dogfighting

American Standard Version *n* (1901) **:** an American version of the Bible based on the Revised Version and published in 1901 — called also *American Revised Version*

American saddle horse

American trotter *n* (ca. 1894) **:** STANDARDBRED

American water spaniel *n* (1947) **:** any of a breed of medium-sized spaniels of American origin with a thick curly chocolate or liver-colored coat

am·er·i·ci·um \ˌam-ə-'ris(h)-ē-əm\ *n* [NL, fr. *America* + NL *-ium*] (1946) **:** a radioactive metallic element produced by bombardment of plutonium with high-energy neutrons — see ELEMENT table

Am·er·in·di·an \ˌam-ə-'rin-dē-ən\ *n* [*Amer*ican + *Indian*] (1897) **:** AMERICAN INDIAN — **Am·er·ind** \'am-ə-ˌrind\ *n or adj* — **Amerindian** *adj*

Ame·slan \'am-əs-ˌlan, 'am-ˌslan\ *n* (1974) **:** AMERICAN SIGN LANGUAGE

am·e·thop·ter·in \ˌam-ə-'thäp-tə-rən\ *n* [*amin-* + *meth-* + *pterin*] (1948) **:** METHOTREXATE

am·e·thyst \'am-ə-thəst, -(ˌ)thist\ *n* [ME *amatiste,* fr. OF & L; OF, fr. L *amethystus,* fr. Gk *amethystos,* lit., remedy against drunkenness, fr. *a-* + *methyein* to be drunk, fr. *methy* wine — more at MEAD] (13c) **1 a :** a clear purple or bluish violet variety of crystallized quartz that is much used as a jeweler's stone **b :** a deep purple variety of corundum **2 :** a variable color averaging a moderate purple — **am·e·thys·tine** \ˌam-ə-'this-tən\ *adj*

am·e·tro·pia \ˌam-ə-'trō-pē-ə\ *n* [NL, fr. Gk *ametros* without measure (fr. *a-* + *metron* measure) + NL *-opia* — more at MEASURE] (1875) **:** an abnormal refractive condition of the eye in which images fail to focus upon the retina — **am·e·tro·pic** \-'trō-pik, -'träp-ik\ *adj*

Am·har·ic \am-'har-ik\ *n* (1813) **:** the Semitic language that is the official language of Ethiopia — **Amharic** *adj*

ami·a·ble \'ā-mē-ə-bəl\ *adj* [ME, fr. MF, fr. LL *amicabilis* friendly, fr. L *amicus* friend; akin to L *amare* to love] (14c) **1** *archaic* **:** PLEASING, ADMIRABLE **2 a :** generally agreeable ⟨an ~ musical comedy⟩ **b :** being friendly, sociable, and congenial — **ami·a·bil·i·ty** \ˌā-mē-ə-'bil-ət-ē\ *n* — **ami·a·ble·ness** \'ā-mē-ə-bəl-nəs\ *n* — **ami·a·bly** \-blē\ *adv*

syn AMIABLE, GOOD-NATURED, OBLIGING, COMPLAISANT mean having the desire or disposition to please. AMIABLE implies having qualities that make one liked and easy to deal with; GOOD-NATURED implies cheerfulness or helpfulness and sometimes a willingness to be imposed upon; OBLIGING stresses a friendly readiness to be helpful; COMPLAISANT often implies passivity or a yielding to others because of weakness.

am·i·an·thus \ˌam-ē-'an(t)-thəs\ *or* **am·i·an·tus** \-'ant-əs\ *n* [L *amiantus,* fr. Gk *amiantos,* fr. *amiantos* unpolluted, fr. *a-* + *miainein* to pollute] (1600) **:** fine silky asbestos

am·i·ca·ble \'am-i-kə-bəl\ *adj* [ME, fr. LL *amicabilis*] (15c) **:** characterized by friendly goodwill **:** PEACEABLE — **am·i·ca·bil·i·ty** \ˌam-i-kə-'bil-ət-ē\ *n* — **am·i·ca·ble·ness** \'am-i-kə-bəl-nəs\ *n* — **am·i·ca·bly** \-blē\ *adv*

syn AMICABLE, NEIGHBORLY, FRIENDLY mean exhibiting goodwill and an absence of antagonism. AMICABLE implies a state of peace and a desire on the part of the parties not to quarrel; NEIGHBORLY implies a disposition to live on good terms with others and to be helpful on principle; FRIENDLY stresses cordiality and often warmth or intimacy of personal relations.

am·ice \ˈam-əs\ *n* [ME *amis,* prob. fr. MF, pl. of *amit,* fr. ML *amictus,* fr. L, cloak, fr. *amictus,* pp. of *amicire* to wrap around, fr. *am-, amb-* around + *jacere* to throw — more at AMBI-, JET] (13c) **:** a liturgical vestment made of an oblong piece of cloth usu. of white linen and worn about the neck and shoulders and partly under the alb — see VESTMENT illustration

ami·cus cu·ri·ae \ə-ˌmē-kə-ˈsk(y)u̇r-ē-ˌī\ *n, pl* **ami·ci curiae** \-ˌmē-(ˌ)kē-ˈk(y)u̇r-\ [NL, lit., friend of the court] (1612) **:** one (as a professional person or organization) that is not a party to a particular litigation but that is permitted by the court to advise it in respect to some matter of law that directly affects the case in question

amid \ə-ˈmid\ *or* **amidst** \-ˈmidst, -ˈmitst\ *prep* [*amid* fr. ME *amidde,* fr. OE *onmiddan,* fr. *on* + *middan,* dat. of *midde* mid; *amidst* fr. ME *amiddes,* fr. *amidde* + *-es* -s] (bef. 12c) **1 :** in or into the middle of **:** surrounded by **:** AMONG **2 a :** DURING **b :** with the accompaniment of ⟨resigned ~ rumors of misconduct⟩

amid- *or* **amido-** *comb form* [ISV, fr. *amide*] **1 :** containing the group NH_2 characteristic of amides united to a radical of acid character ⟨*amido*sulfuric⟩ **2 :** AMIN- ⟨*amido*phenol⟩

am·i·dase \ˈam-ə-ˌdās, -ˌdāz\ *n* [ISV *amide* + *-ase*] (1921) **:** an enzyme that hydrolyzes acid amides usu. with the liberation of ammonia

am·ide \ˈam-ˌīd, -əd\ *n* [ISV, fr. NL *ammonia*] (ca. 1847) **:** a compound resulting from replacement of an atom of hydrogen in ammonia by an element or radical or of one or more atoms of hydrogen in ammonia by univalent acid radicals — compare IMIDE — **amid·ic** \ə-ˈmid-ik, a-\ *adj*

ami·do \ə-ˈmēd-(ˌ)ō, ˈam-ə-ˌdō\ *adj* [*amid-*] (1877) **1 :** relating to or containing the group NH_2 or a substituted group NHR or NR_2 united to an acid radical — compare AMINO **2 :** AMINO

am·i·dol \ˈam-ə-ˌdȯl, -ˌdōl\ *n* [G, fr. *Amidol,* a trademark] (1892) **:** a colorless crystalline salt $C_6H_8N_2O{\cdot}2HCl$ used chiefly as a photographic developer

amid·ships \ə-ˈmid-ˌships\ *adv* (1692) **1 :** in or toward the part of a ship midway between bow and stern **2 :** in or toward the middle

ami·go \ə-ˈmē-(ˌ)gō, ä-\ *n, pl* **-gos** [Sp, fr. L *amicus* — more at AMIABLE] (1837) **:** FRIEND

amin- *or* **amino-** *comb form* [ISV, fr. *amine*] **:** containing the group NH_2 united to a radical other than an acid radical ⟨*amino*benzoic acid⟩

amine \ə-ˈmēn, ˈam-ˌēn\ *n* [ISV, fr. NL *ammonia*] (1863) **1 :** any of various basic compounds derived from ammonia by replacement of hydrogen by one or more univalent hydrocarbon radicals **2 :** a compound containing one or more halogen atoms attached to nitrogen

ami·no \ə-ˈmē-(ˌ)nō\ *adj* [*amin-*] (1904) **:** relating to or containing the group NH_2 or a substituted group NHR or NR_2 united to a radical other than an acid radical — compare AMIDO

amino acid *n* (1898) **:** an amphoteric organic acid containing the amino group NH_2; *esp* **:** any of the alpha-amino acids that are the chief components of proteins and are synthesized by living cells or are obtained as essential components of the diet

ami·no·ac·id·uria \ə-ˌmē-nō-ˌas-ə-ˈd(y)u̇r-ē-ə\ *n* [NL] (ca. 1923) **:** a condition in which one or more amino acids are excreted in excessive amounts

ami·no·ben·zo·ic acid \ə-ˌmē-nō-ben-ˌzō-ik-\ *n* [ISV] (1904) **:** any of three crystalline derivatives $C_7H_7NO_2$ of benzoic acid of which the yellowish para-substituted acid is a growth factor of the vitamin B complex and of folic acids

ami·no·pep·ti·dase \ə-ˌmē-nō-ˈpep-tə-ˌdās, -ˌdāz\ *n* (ca. 1940) **:** an enzyme that hydrolyzes peptides by acting on the peptide bond next to a terminal amino acid containing a free amino group

am·i·noph·yl·line \ˌam-ə-ˈnäf-ə-lən\ *n* [*amin-* + theo*phylline*] (1934) **:** a theophylline derivative $C_{16}H_{24}N_{10}O_4$ used esp. to stimulate the heart in congestive heart failure and to dilate the air passages in respiratory disorders

am·i·nop·ter·in \ˌam-ə-ˈnäp-tə-rən\ *n* [*amin-* + *pter-* + *-in*] (1948) **:** a derivative of glutamic acid $C_{19}H_{20}N_8O_5$ used as a rodenticide and antimetabolite

ami·no·py·rine \ə-ˌmē-nō-ˈpī(ə)r-ˌēn\ *n* [ISV, fr. *amin-* + anti*pyrine*] (ca. 1936) **:** a white crystalline compound $C_{13}H_{17}N_3O$ formerly used to relieve pain and fever but now largely abandoned for this purpose because of the occurrence of fatal agranulocytosis as a side effect in some users

ami·no·sal·i·cyl·ic acid \ə-ˌmē-nō-ˌsal-ə-ˌsil-ik-\ *n* (ca. 1922) **:** any of four isomeric derivatives $C_7H_7NO_3$ of salicylic acid that have a single amino group; *esp* **:** PARA-AMINOSALICYLIC ACID

ami·no·trans·fer·ase \-ˈtran(t)s-fə-ˌrās, -ˌrāz\ *n* (ca. 1965) **:** TRANSAMINASE

amir *var of* EMIR

Amish \ˈäm-ish, ˈam-, ˈām-\ *adj* [prob. fr. G *amisch,* fr. Jacob *Amman* or *Amen fl* 1693 Swiss Mennonite bishop] (1844) **:** of or relating to a strict sect of Mennonite followers of Amman that settled in America chiefly in the 18th century — **Amish** *n*

[1]amiss \ə-ˈmis\ *adv* (13c) **1 a :** in a mistaken way **:** WRONGLY ⟨if you think he is guilty, you judge ~⟩ **b :** ASTRAY ⟨something had gone ~⟩ **2 :** in a faulty way **:** IMPERFECTLY

[2]amiss *adj* (14c) **1 :** not being in accordance with right order **2 :** FAULTY, IMPERFECT **3 :** out of place in given circumstances — usu. used with a negative ⟨a few remarks may not be ~ here⟩

ami·to·sis \ˌā-mī-ˈtō-səs\ *n* [NL, fr. [2]*a-* + *mitosis*] (1894) **:** cell division by simple cleavage of the nucleus and division of the cytoplasm without spindle formation or appearance of chromosomes — **ami·tot·ic** \-ˈtät-ik\ *adj* — **ami·tot·i·cal·ly** \-i-k(ə-)lē\ *adv*

am·i·trip·ty·line \ˌam-ə-ˈtrip-tə-ˌlēn\ *n* [origin unknown] (1961) **:** a tricyclic antidepressant drug $C_{20}H_{23}N$

am·i·trole \ˈam-ə-ˌtrōl\ *n* [*amin-* + tr*iazole*] (ca. 1960) **:** a systemic herbicide $C_2H_4N_4$ used in areas other than food croplands

am·i·ty \ˈam-ət-ē\ *n, pl* **-ties** [ME *amite,* fr. MF *amité,* fr. ML *amicitas,* fr. L *amicus* friend — more at AMIABLE] (15c) **:** FRIENDSHIP; *esp* **:** friendly relations between nations

am·me·ter \ˈam-ˌēt-ər\ *n* [*ampere* + *-meter*] (1882) **:** an instrument for measuring electric current in amperes

am·mine \ˈam-ˌēn, a-ˈmēn\ *n* [ISV *ammonia* + *-ine*] (1897) **1 :** a molecule of ammonia as it exists in a coordination complex ⟨hex*ammine*cobalt chloride $CoN_6H_{18}Cl_3$⟩ **2 :** an ammino compound

am·mi·no \ˈam-ə-ˌnō, a-ˈmē-(ˌ)nō\ *adj* [ISV *ammino-,* fr. *ammine*] (ca. 1920) **:** of, relating to, or being an ammine

am·mo \ˈam-(ˌ)ō\ *n* [by shortening & alter.] (1911) **:** AMMUNITION

am·mo·nia \ə-ˈmō-nyə\ *n* [NL, fr. L *sal ammoniacus* sal ammoniac, lit., salt of Ammon, fr. Gk *ammōniakos* of Ammon, fr. *Ammōn* Ammon, Amen, an Egyptian god near one of whose temples it was prepared] (ca. 1799) **1 :** a pungent colorless gaseous alkaline compound of nitrogen and hydrogen NH_3 that is very soluble in water and can easily be condensed to a liquid by cold and pressure **2 :** AMMONIA WATER

am·mo·ni·ac \ə-ˈmō-nē-ˌak\ *n* [ME & L; ME, fr. L *ammoniacum,* fr. Gk *ammōniakon,* fr. neut. of *ammōniakos* of Ammon] (14c) **:** the aromatic gum resin of a Persian herb (*Dorema ammoniacum*) of the carrot family used as an expectorant and stimulant and in plasters

am·mo·ni·a·cal \ˌam-ə-ˈnī-ə-kəl\ *also* **am·mo·ni·ac** \ə-ˈmō-nē-ˌak\ *adj* (1732) **:** of, relating to, containing, or having the properties of ammonia

am·mo·ni·ate \ə-ˈmō-nē-ˌāt\ *vt* **-at·ed; -at·ing** (ca. 1923) **1 :** to combine or impregnate with ammonia or an ammonium compound **2 :** to subject to ammonification — **am·mo·ni·a·tion** \-ˌmō-nē-ˈā-shən\ *n*

ammonia water *n* (ca. 1903) **:** a water solution of ammonia

am·mo·ni·fi·ca·tion \ə-ˌmän-ə-fə-ˈkā-shən, -ˌmō-nə-\ *n* (1886) **1 :** the act or process of ammoniating **2 :** decomposition with production of ammonia or ammonium compounds esp. by the action of bacteria on nitrogenous organic matter — **am·mo·ni·fy** \-ˌfī\ *vb*

am·mo·nite \ˈam-ə-ˌnīt\ *n* [NL *ammonites,* fr. L *cornu Ammonis,* lit., horn of Ammon] (1609) **:** any of numerous flat spiral fossil shells of extinct cephalopods (order Ammonoidea) esp. abundant in the Mesozoic age — **am·mo·nit·ic** \ˌam-ə-ˈnit-ik\ *adj*

Am·mon·ite \ˈam-ə-ˌnīt\ *n* [LL *Ammonites,* fr. Heb *ʽAmmōn,* Ammon (son of Lot), descendant of Ammon] (1611) **:** a member of a Semitic people who in Old Testament times lived east of the Jordan between the Jabbok and the Arnon — **Ammonite** *adj*

am·mo·ni·um \ə-ˈmō-nē-əm\ *n* [NL, fr. *ammonia*] (1808) **:** an ion NH_4^+ or radical NH_4 derived from ammonia by combination with a hydrogen ion or atom and known in compounds (as salts) that resemble in properties the compounds of the alkali metals and in organic compounds (as quaternary ammonium compounds)

ammonium carbonate *n* (ca. 1881) **:** a carbonate of ammonium; *specif* **:** the commercial mixture of the bicarbonate and carbamate used esp. in smelling salts

ammonium chloride *n* (1869) **:** a white crystalline volatile salt NH_4Cl that is used in dry cells and as an expectorant — called also *sal ammoniac*

ammonium cyanate *n* (ca. 1881) **:** an inorganic white crystalline salt N_2H_4OC that can be converted into organic urea

ammonium hydroxide *n* (ca. 1903) **:** a weakly basic compound NH_5O that is formed when ammonia dissolves in water and that exists only in solution

ammonium nitrate *n* (ca. 1881) **:** a colorless crystalline salt $N_2H_4O_3$ used in explosives and fertilizers and in veterinary medicine

ammonium phosphate *n* (ca. 1881) **:** a phosphate of ammonium; *esp* **:** a white crystalline compound $N_2H_9PO_4$ used esp. as a fertilizer and as a fire retardant

ammonium sulfate *n* (ca. 1881) **:** a colorless crystalline salt $N_2H_8SO_4$ used chiefly as a fertilizer

am·mo·noid \ˈam-ə-ˌnȯid\ *n* (1884) **:** AMMONITE

am·mu·ni·tion \ˌam-yə-ˈnish-ən\ *n* [obs. F *amunition,* fr. MF, alter. of *munition*] (1626) **1 a :** the projectiles with their fuses, propelling charges, or primers fired from guns **b :** CARTRIDGES **c :** explosive military items (as grenades or bombs) **2 :** material for use in attacking or defending a position ⟨facts that were the ~ for their argument⟩

am·ne·sia \am-ˈnē-zhə\ *n* [NL, fr. Gk *amnēsia* forgetfulness, prob. alter. of *amnēstia*] (1786) **1 :** loss of memory due usu. to brain injury, shock, fatigue, repression, or illness **2 :** a gap in one's memory — **am·ne·si·ac** \-z(h)ē-ˌak\ *or* **am·ne·sic** \-zik, -sik\ *adj or n*

am·nes·ty \ˈam-nə-stē\ *n, pl* **-ties** [Gk *amnēstia* forgetfulness, fr. *a-* + *mnēstis* remembrance — more at MENTAL] (1580) **:** the act of an authority (as a government) by which pardon is granted to a large group of individuals — **amnesty** *vt*

am·nio·cen·te·sis \ˌam-nē-ō-(ˌ)sen-ˈtē-səs\ *n, pl* **-te·ses** \-ˌsēz\ [NL, fr. *amnion* + *centesis* puncture, fr. Gk *kentēsis,* fr. *kentein* to prick — more at CENTER] (1957) **:** the surgical insertion of a hollow needle through the abdominal wall and into the uterus of a pregnant female esp. to obtain amniotic fluid for the determination of fetal sex or chromosomal abnormality

am·ni·on \ˈam-nē-ˌän, -ən\ *n, pl* **amnions** *or* **am·nia** \-nē-ə\ [NL, fr. Gk, caul, prob. fr. dim. of *amnos* lamb — more at YEAN] (1667) **1 :** a thin membrane forming a closed sac about the embryos of reptiles, birds, and mammals and containing a serous fluid in which the embryo is immersed **2 :** a membrane analogous to the amnion and occurring in various invertebrates — **am·ni·ot·ic** \ˌam-nē-ˈät-ik\ *adj*

am·ni·ote \ˈam-nē-ˌōt\ *n* [modif. of NL *amniota* (after such pairs as *chordata: chordate*), irreg. fr. *amnion*] (ca. 1909) **:** any of a group (Amniota) of vertebrates that develop an amnion in the embryo and include the birds, reptiles, and mammals — **amniote** *adj*

amo·bar·bi·tal \ˌam-ō-ˈbär-bə-ˌtȯl\ *n* [*amyl* + *-o-* + *barbital*] (ca. 1949) **:** a barbiturate $C_{11}H_{18}N_2O_3$ used as a hypnotic and sedative; *also* **:** its sodium salt

amoe·ba \ə-ˈmē-bə\ *n, pl* **-bas** *or* **-bae** \-(ˌ)bē\ [NL, genus name, fr. Gk *amoibē* change, fr. *ameibein* to change — more at MIGRATE] (1878) **:** any of a large genus (*Amoeba*) of naked rhizopod protozoans with lobed and never anastomosing pseudopodia, without permanent organelles or supporting structures, and of wide distribution in fresh and

\ə\ abut \ᵊ\ kitten, F table \ər\ further \a\ ash \ā\ ace \ä\ cot, cart \au̇\ out \ch\ chin \e\ bet \ē\ easy \g\ go \i\ hit \ī\ ice \j\ job \ŋ\ sing \ō\ go \ȯ\ law \ȯi\ boy \th\ thin \t͟h\ the \ü\ loot \u̇\ foot \y\ yet \zh\ vision \á, k̲, ⁿ, œ, ᵫ, ue, ᵫ̄, ʸ\ see Guide to Pronunciation

salt water and moist terrestrial environments; *broadly* : a naked rhizopod or other amoeboid protozoan — **amoe·bic** \-bik\ *adj*

am·oe·bi·a·sis *var of* AMEBIASIS

amoe·bo·cyte \ə-'mē-bə-,sīt\ *n* (1892) : a cell (as a phagocyte) having amoeboid form or movements

amoe·boid \-,bȯid\ *adj* (1856) : resembling an amoeba specif. in moving or changing in shape by means of protoplasmic flow

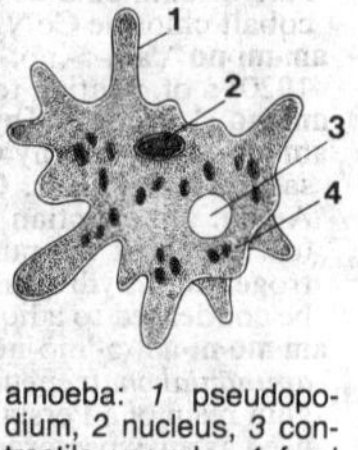

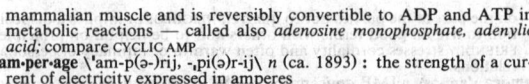

amoeba: *1* pseudopodium, *2* nucleus, *3* contractile vacuole, *4* food vacuole

¹amok \ə-'mək, -'mäk\ *n* (1665) : a murderous frenzy that occurs chiefly among Malays

²amok *adv* [Malay *amok*] (1672) **1** : in a murderously frenzied state **2** **a** : in a violently raging manner ⟨a virus that had run ~⟩ **b** : in an undisciplined or faulty manner

³amok *adj* (1944) : possessed with or motivated by a murderous or violently uncontrollable frenzy

amo·le \ə-'mō-lē\ *n* [Sp. fr. Nahuatl *amolli* soap] (1831) : a plant part (as a root) possessing detergent properties and serving as a substitute for soap; *also* : a plant so used

among \ə-'məŋ\ *also* **amongst** \-'məŋ(k)st\ *prep* [*among* fr. ME, fr. OE *on gemonge,* fr. *on* + *gemonge,* dat. of *gemong* crowd, fr. *ge-* (associative prefix) + *-mong* (akin to OE *mengan* to mix); *amongst* fr. ME *amonges,* fr. *among* + *-es* -s — more at CO-, MINGLE] (bef. 12c) **1** : in or through the midst of : surrounded by **2** : in company or association with ⟨living ~ artists⟩ **3** : by or through the aggregate of ⟨discontent ~ the poor⟩ **4** : in the number or class of ⟨wittiest ~ poets⟩ ⟨~ other things she was president of her college class⟩ **5** : in shares to each of ⟨divided ~ the heirs⟩ **6** **a** : through the reciprocal acts of ⟨quarrel ~ themselves⟩ **b** : through the joint action of ⟨made a fortune ~ themselves⟩ ***usage*** see BETWEEN

amon·til·la·do \ə-,män-tə-'läd-(,)ō, -ti(l)-'yäth-(,)ō\ *n, pl* **-dos** [Sp, fr. *a* to + *montilla* a wine from Montilla, Spain] (1825) : a medium dry sherry

amor·al \(')ā-'mȯr-əl, (')a-, -'mär-\ *adj* (1882) **1** **a** : being neither moral nor immoral; *specif* : lying outside the sphere to which moral judgments apply ⟨science as such is completely ~ —W.S. Thompson⟩ **b** : lacking moral sensibility ⟨infants are ~⟩ **2** : being outside or beyond the moral order or a particular code of morals ⟨~ customs⟩ — **amor·al·ism** \-ə-,liz-əm\ *n* — **amo·ral·i·ty** \,ā-mə-'ral-ət-ē, ,a-, -(,)mȯ-\ *n* — **amor·al·ly** \(')ā-'mȯr-ə-lē, (')a-, -'mär-\ *adv*

amo·ret·to \,am-ə-'ret-(,)ō, ,äm-\ *n, pl* **-ti** \-(,)ē\ *or* **-tos** [It, dim. of *amore* love, cupid, fr. L *amor*] (1873) : CUPID, CHERUB 2

am·or·ist \'am-ə-rəst\ *n* (1581) **1** : a devotee of love and esp. sexual love : GALLANT **2** : one that writes about romantic love — **am·or·is·tic** \,am-ə-'ris-tik\ *adj*

Am·o·rite \'am-ə-,rīt\ *n* [Heb *Ĕmōrī*] (1560) : a member of one of various Semitic peoples living in Mesopotamia, Syria, and Palestine during the 3d and 2d millennia B.C. — **Amorite** *adj*

am·o·rous \'am-(ə-)rəs\ *adj* [ME, fr. MF, fr. ML *amorosus,* fr. L *amor* love, fr. *amare* to love] (14c) **1** : strongly moved by love and esp. sexual love ⟨~ women⟩ **2** : being in love : ENAMORED — usu. used with *of* ⟨~ of the girl⟩ **3** **a** : indicative of love ⟨received ~ glances from her partner⟩ **b** : of or relating to love ⟨an ~ novel⟩ — **am·o·rous·ly** *adv* — **am·o·rous·ness** *n*

amor·phism \ə-'mȯr-,fiz-əm\ *n* (ca. 1852) : amorphous quality

amor·phous \-fəs\ *adj* [Gk *amorphos,* fr. *a-* + *morphē* form] (ca. 1731) **1** **a** : having no definite form : SHAPELESS ⟨an ~ cloud mass⟩ **b** : being without definite character or nature : UNCLASSIFIABLE ⟨an ~ segment of society⟩ **c** : lacking organization or unity ⟨an ~ style⟩ **2** : having no real or apparent crystalline form : UNCRYSTALLIZED ⟨an ~ mineral⟩ — **amor·phous·ly** *adv* — **amor·phous·ness** *n*

amort \ə-'mȯ(ə)rt\ *adj* [short for *all-a-mort,* by folk etymology fr. MF *a la mort* to the death] *archaic* (1590) : being at the point of death

am·or·ti·za·tion \,am-ərt-ə-'zā-shən *also* ə-,mȯrt-\ *n* (ca. 1859) **1** : the act or process of amortizing **2** : the result of amortizing

am·or·tize \'am-ər-,tīz *also* ə-'mȯr-\ *vt* **-tized; -tiz·ing** [ME *amortisen* to deaden, alienate in mortmain, modif. of MF *amortiss-,* stem of *amortir,* fr. (assumed) VL *admortire* to deaden, fr. L *ad-* + *mort-, mors* death — more at MURDER] (1882) **1** : to provide for the gradual extinguishment of (as a mortgage) usu. by contribution to a sinking fund at the time of each periodic interest payment **2** : to amortize an expenditure for ⟨~ intangibles⟩ ⟨~ the new factory⟩ — **am·or·tiz·able** \-,tī-zə-bəl\ *adj*

Amos \'ā-məs\ *n* [Heb *'Āmōs*] **1** : a Hebrew prophet of the 8th century B.C. **2** : a prophetic book of canonical Jewish and Christian Scripture — see BIBLE table

¹amount \ə-'maůnt\ *vi* [ME *amounten,* fr. MF *amonter,* fr. *amont* upward, fr. *a-* (fr. L *ad-*) + *mont* mountain — more at MOUNT] (14c) **1** : to be equivalent ⟨acts that ~ to treason⟩ **2** : to add up ⟨the bill ~*s* to $10⟩

²amount *n* (1710) **1** **a** : the total number or quantity : AGGREGATE **b** : the quantity at hand or under consideration ⟨has an enormous ~ of energy⟩ **2** : the whole effect, significance, or import **3** : a principal sum and the interest on it

usage *Number* is regularly used with count nouns ⟨a large *number* of mistakes⟩ ⟨any *number* of times⟩ while *amount* is usu. used with mass nouns ⟨annual *amount* of rainfall⟩ ⟨a substantial *amount* of money⟩ The less common use of *amount* with count nouns has been frequently criticized; it seems to occur most often when the number of things can be visualized as a mass ⟨glad to furnish any *amount* of black pebbles —*New Yorker*⟩ or when money is involved ⟨a substantial *amount* of loans —E. R. Black⟩

amour \ə-'mů(ə)r, ä-, a-\ *n* [ME, love, affection, fr. MF, fr. OProv *amor,* fr. L, fr. *amare* to love] (14c) : a usu. illicit love affair

amour pro·pre \,am-,ůr-'prȯprᵊ, ,äm-, -'prȯpr\ *n* [F *amour-propre,* lit., love of oneself] (1808) : SELF-ESTEEM

Amoy \ä-'mȯi, a-, ə-\ *n* (ca. 1904) : the dialect of Chinese spoken in and near Amoy in southeastern China

amp \'amp\ *n* [by shortening] (1962) : AMPLIFIER; *also* : a unit consisting of an electronic amplifier and a loudspeaker

AMP \,ā-,em-'pē\ *n* [*a*denosine *m*ono*p*hosphate] (ca. 1951) : a mononucleotide of adenine $C_{10}H_{12}N_5O_3H_2PO_4$ that was orig. isolated from mammalian muscle and is reversibly convertible to ADP and ATP in metabolic reactions — called also *adenosine monophosphate, adenylic acid;* compare CYCLIC AMP

am·per·age \'am-p(ə-)rij, -,pi(ə)r-ij\ *n* (ca. 1893) : the strength of a current of electricity expressed in amperes

am·pere \'am-,pi(ə)r *also* -,pe(ə)r\ *n* [André-Marie *Ampère*] (ca. 1881) **1** : the practical mks unit of electric current that is equivalent to a flow of one coulomb per second or to the steady current produced by one volt applied across a resistance of one ohm **2** : a unit of electric current equal to a constant current that when maintained in two straight parallel conductors of infinite length and negligible circular sections one meter apart in a vacuum produces between the conductors a force equal to 2×10^{-7} newton per meter of length

ampere–hour *n* (1885) : a unit quantity of electricity equal to the quantity carried past any point of a circuit in one hour by a steady current of one ampere

ampere–turn *n* (1884) : the mks unit of magnetomotive force equal to the magnetomotive force around a path that links with one turn of wire carrying an electric current of one ampere

am·per·sand \'am-pər-,sand\ *n* [alter. of *and* (&)*per se and,* lit., (the character) & by itself (is the word) *and*] (1828) : a character typically & standing for the word *and*

am·phet·amine \am-'fet-ə-,mēn, -mən\ *n* [ISV *a*lpha + *m*ethyl + *phe*n- + *et*hyl + *amine*] (1938) **1** : a compound $C_9H_{13}N$ used esp. as an inhalant and in solution as a spray in head colds and hay fever **2** : any of various derivatives of amphetamine used as stimulants for the central nervous system: as **a** : a white crystalline compound $C_{18}H_{28}N_2O_4S$ — called also *amphetamine sulfate* **b** : DEXTROAMPHETAMINE

amphi- *or* **amph-** *prefix* [L *amphi-* around, on both sides, fr. Gk *amphi-, amph-,* fr. *amphi* — more at AMBI-] : on both sides : of both kinds : both ⟨*amphi*biotic⟩ ⟨*amphi*stylar⟩

am·phib·ia \am-'fib-ē-ə\ *n pl* (1607) : AMPHIBIANS

am·phib·i·an \-ē-ən\ *n* [deriv. of Gk *amphibion* amphibious being, fr. neut. of *amphibios*] (1657) **1** : an amphibious organism; *esp* : any of a class (Amphibia) of cold-blooded vertebrates (as frogs, toads, or newts) intermediate in many characters between fishes and reptiles and having gilled aquatic larvae and air-breathing adults **2** : an airplane designed to take off from and land on either land or water **3** : a flat-bottomed vehicle that moves on tracks having finlike extensions by means of which it is propelled on land or water — **amphibian** *adj*

am·phib·i·ous \am-'fib-ē-əs\ *adj* [Gk *amphibios,* lit., living a double life, fr. *amphi-* + *bios* mode of life — more at QUICK] (1643) **1** : able to live both on land and in water ⟨~ plants⟩ **2** **a** : relating to or adapted for both land and water ⟨~ vehicles⟩ **b** : executed by coordinated action of land, sea, and air forces organized for invasion; *also* : trained or organized for such action ⟨~ forces⟩ **3** : combining two characteristics — **am·phib·i·ous·ly** *adv* — **am·phib·i·ous·ness** *n*

am·phi·bole \'am(p)-fə-,bōl\ *n* [F, fr. LL *amphibolus,* fr. Gk *amphibolos* ambiguous, fr. *amphiballein* to throw round, doubt, fr. *amphi-* + *ballein* to throw — more at DEVIL] (ca. 1823) **1** : HORNBLENDE **2** : any of a group of complex silicate minerals with like crystal structures that contain calcium, sodium, magnesium, aluminum, and iron ions or a combination of them

am·phib·o·lite \am-'fib-ə-,līt\ *n* (ca. 1833) : a usu. metamorphic rock consisting essentially of amphibole — **am·phib·o·lit·ic** \(,)am-,fib-ə-'lit-ik\ *adj*

am·phi·brach \'am(p)-fə-,brak\ *n* [L *amphibrachys,* fr. Gk, lit., short at both ends, fr. *amphi-* + *brachys* short — more at BRIEF] (1589) : a metrical foot consisting of a long syllable between two short syllables in quantitative verse or of a stressed syllable between two unstressed syllables in accentual verse ⟨*romantic* is an accentual ~⟩ — **am·phi·brach·ic** \,am(p)-fə-'brak-ik\ *adj*

am·phic·ty·o·ny \am-'fik-tē-ə-nē\ *n, pl* **-nies** [Gk *amphiktyonia*] (ca. 1835) : an association of neighboring states in ancient Greece to defend a common religious center; *broadly* : an association of neighboring states for their common interest — **am·phic·ty·on·ic** \(,)am-,fik-tē-'än-ik\ *adj*

am·phi·dip·loid \,am(p)-fi-'dip-,lȯid\ *n* (1930) : an interspecific hybrid having a complete diploid chromosome set from each parent form — called also *allotetraploid* — **amphidiploid** *adj* — **am·phi·dip·loi·dy** \-,lȯid-ē\ *n*

am·phim·a·cer \am-'fim-ə-sər\ *n* [L *amphimacrus,* fr. Gk *amphimakros,* lit., long at both ends, fr. *amphi-* + *makros* long — more at MEAGER] (1589) : a metrical foot consisting of a short syllable between two long syllables in quantitative verse or of an unstressed syllable between two stressed syllables in accentual verse ⟨*twenty-two* is an accentual ~⟩

am·phi·mic·tic \,am(p)-fi-'mik-tik\ *adj* [ISV *amphi-* + Gk *miktos* blended, fr. *mignynai*] (ca. 1944) : capable of interbreeding freely and of producing fertile offspring — **am·phi·mic·ti·cal·ly** \-ti-k(ə-)lē\ *adv*

am·phi·mix·is \-'mik-səs\ *n, pl* **-mix·es** \-,sēz\ [NL, fr. *amphi-* + Gk *mixis* mingling, fr. *mignynai* to mix — more at MIX] (ca. 1893) : the union of germ cells in sexual reproduction

Am·phi·on \am-'fī-ən\ *n* [L, fr. Gk *Amphiōn*] : a musician of Greek myth who builds the walls of Thebes by charming the stones into place with his lyre

am·phi·ox·us \,am(p)-fē-'äk-səs\ *n, pl* **-oxi** \-,sī\ *or* **-ox·us·es** [NL, fr. *amphi-* + Gk *oxys* sharp] (ca. 1890) : any of a genus (*Branchiostoma*) of lancelets; *broadly* : LANCELET

am·phi·ploid \'am(p)-fi-,plȯid\ *adj, of an interspecific hybrid* (1945) : having at least one complete diploid set of chromosomes derived from each ancestral species — **amphiploid** *n* — **am·phi·ploi·dy** \-,plȯid-ē\ *n*

am·phi·pod \-,päd\ *n* [deriv. of Gk *amphi-* + *pod-, pous* foot — more at FOOT] (1835) : any of a large group (Amphipoda) of small crustaceans (as the sand flea) with a laterally compressed body — **amphipod** *adj*

am·phi·pro·style \,am(p)-fi-'prō-,stīl\ *adj* [L *amphiprostylos,* fr. Gk, fr. *amphi-* + *prostylos* having pillars in front, fr. *pro-* + *stylos* pillar — more at STEER] (1850) : having columns at each end only ⟨an ~ building⟩ — **amphiprostyle** *n*

am·phis·bae·na \,am(p)-fəs-'bē-nə\ *n* [L, fr. Gk *amphisbaina,* fr. *amphis* on both sides (fr. *amphi* around) + *bainein* to walk, go — more at BY, COME] (14c) : a serpent in classical mythology having a head at each end and capable of moving in either direction — **am·phis·bae·nic** \-nik\ *adj*

am·phi·sty·lar \ˌam(p)-fi-ˈstī-lər\ *adj* (ca. 1901) **:** having columns at both ends or on both sides ⟨an ~ building⟩
am·phi·the·ater \ˈam(p)-fə-ˌthē-ət-ər *also* ˈam-pə-ˌthē-\ *n* [L *amphitheatrum,* fr. Gk *amphitheatron,* fr. *amphi-* + *theatron* theater] (14c) **1 :** an oval or circular building with rising tiers of seats ranged about an open space and used in ancient Rome esp. for contests and spectacles **2 a :** a very large auditorium **b :** a room with a gallery from which doctors and students may observe surgical operations **c :** a rising gallery in a modern theater **d :** a flat or gently sloping area surrounded by abrupt slopes **3 :** a place of public games or contests — **am·phi·the·at·ric** \ˌam(p)-fə-thē-ˈa-trik *also* ˌam-pə-thē-\ *or* **am·phi·the·at·ri·cal** \-tri-kəl\ *adj* — **am·phi·the·at·ri·cal·ly** \-tri-k(ə-)lē\ *adv*
Am·phit·ry·on \am-ˈfi-trē-ən\ *n* [Gk *Amphitryōn*] **:** the husband of Alcmene
am·pho·ra \ˈam(p)-fə-rə\ *n, pl* **-rae** \-ˌrē, -ˌrī\ *or* **-ras** [L, modif. of Gk *amphoreus, amphiphoreus,* fr. *amphi-* + *phoreus* bearer, fr. *pherein* to bear — more at BEAR] (14c) **1 :** an ancient Greek jar or vase with a large oval body, narrow cylindrical neck, and two handles that rise almost to the level of the mouth **2 :** a 2-handled vessel shaped like an amphora

amphora 1

am·pho·ter·ic \ˌam(p)-fə-ˈter-ik\ *adj* [ISV, fr. Gk *amphoteros* each of two, fr. *amphō* both — more at AMBI-] (ca. 1849) **:** partly one and partly the other; *specif* **:** capable of reacting chemically either as an acid or as a base
am·pho·ter·i·cin \-ˈter-ə-sən\ *n* [*amphoteric* + *-in*] (1955) **:** either of two antibiotic drugs obtained from a soil actinomycete (*Streptomyces nodosus*); *esp* **:** AMPHOTERICIN B
amphotericin B *n* (1955) **:** the amphotericin that is useful against deep-seated and systemic fungal infections
am·pi·cil·lin \ˌam-pə-ˈsil-ən\ *n* [*amin-* + *penicillin*] (1962) **:** a penicillin that is effective against gram-negative and gram-positive bacteria and is used to treat various infections of the urinary, respiratory, and intestinal tracts
am·ple \ˈam-pəl\ *adj* **am·pler** \-p(ə-)lər\; **am·plest** \-p(ə-)ləst\ [MF, fr. L *amplus*] (15c) **1 :** generous or more than adequate in size, scope, or capacity ⟨there was room for an ~ garden⟩ **2 :** generously sufficient to satisfy a requirement or need ⟨they had ~ money for the trip⟩ **3 :** BUXOM, PORTLY ⟨an ~ figure⟩ ***syn*** see SPACIOUS, PLENTIFUL — **am·ple·ness** \-pəl-nəs\ *n* — **am·ply** \-plē\ *adv*
am·plex·us \am-ˈplek-səs\ *n* [NL, fr. L, embrace, fr. *amplexus,* pp.] (ca. 1927) **:** the mating embrace of a frog or toad during which eggs are shed into the water and there fertilized
am·pli·dyne \ˈam-plə-ˌdīn\ *n* [*ampli*fier + Gk *dyn*amis power — more at DYNAMIC] (ca. 1940) **:** a direct-current generator that by the use of compensating coils and a short circuit across two of its brushes precisely controls a large power output whenever a small power input is varied in the field winding of the generator
am·pli·fi·ca·tion \ˌam-plə-fə-ˈkā-shən\ *n* (1546) **1 :** an act, example, or product of amplifying **2 a :** the particulars by which a statement is expanded **b :** an expanded statement
am·pli·fi·er \ˈam-plə-ˌfī(-ə)r\ *n* (1542) **:** one that amplifies; *specif* **:** a device (as in a computer or sound-reproducing system) usu. employing electron tubes or transistors to obtain amplification of voltage, current, or power
am·pli·fy \-ˌfī\ *vb* **-fied; -fy·ing** [ME *amplifien,* fr. MF *amplifier,* fr. L *amplificare,* fr. *amplus*] *vt* (15c) **1 :** to expand (as a statement) by the use of detail or illustration or by closer analysis **2 :** to make larger or greater (as in amount, importance, or intensity) **:** INCREASE **3 :** to utilize (an input of power) so as to obtain an output of greater magnitude through the relay action of a transducer ~ *vi* **:** to expand one's remarks or ideas ***syn*** see EXPAND
am·pli·tude \-ˌt(y)üd\ *n* (1555) **1 :** the quality or state of being ample **:** FULLNESS **2 :** the extent or range of a quality, property, process, or phenomenon: as **a :** the extent of a vibratory movement (as of a pendulum) measured from the mean position to an extreme **b :** the maximum departure of the value of an alternating current or wave from the average value **3 :** the arc of the horizon between the true east or west point and the foot of the vertical circle passing through any star or object
amplitude modulation *n* (1921) **1 :** modulation of the amplitude of a radio carrier wave in accordance with the strength of the audio or other signal **2 :** a broadcasting system using amplitude modulation — compare FREQUENCY MODULATION
am·poule *or* **am·pule** *also* **am·pul** \ˈam-ˌpyü(ə)l, -ˌpül\ *n* [MF *ampulle* flask, fr. OE & OF; OE *ampulle* & OF *ampoule,* fr. L *ampulla*] (1886) **1 :** a hermetically sealed small bulbous glass vessel that is used to hold a solution for hypodermic injection **2 :** a vial resembling an ampoule
am·pul·la \am-ˈpu̇l-ə, ˈam-ˌpyü-lə\ *n, pl* **-lae** \-(ˌ)ē, -ˌī\ [ME, fr. OE, fr. L, dim. of *amphora*] (bef. 12c) **1 :** a glass or earthenware flask with a globular body and two handles used esp. by the ancient Romans to hold ointment, perfume, or wine **2 :** a saccular anatomic swelling or pouch — **am·pul·la·ry** \am-ˈpu̇l-ə-rē, ˈam-pyə-ˌler-ē\ *adj*
am·pu·tate \ˈam-pyə-ˌtāt\ *vt* **-tat·ed; -tat·ing** [L *amputatus,* pp. of *amputare,* fr. *am-, amb-* around + *putare* to cut, prune — more at AMBI-] (1638) **:** to cut or lop off; *esp* **:** to cut (as a limb) from the body — **am·pu·ta·tion** \ˌam-pyə-ˈtā-shən\ *n*
am·pu·tee \ˌam-pyə-ˈtē\ *n* (1910) **:** one that has had a limb amputated
am·trac *or* **am·track** \ˈam-ˌtrak\ *n* [*am*phibious + *trac*tor] (ca. 1944) **:** AMPHIBIAN 3
amuck \ə-ˈmək\ *var of* AMOK
am·u·let \ˈam-yə-lət\ *n* [L *amuletum*] (15c) **:** a charm (as an ornament) often inscribed with a magic incantation or symbol to protect the wearer against evil (as disease or witchcraft) or to aid him
amuse \ə-ˈmyüz\ *vb* **amused; amus·ing** [MF *amuser,* fr. OF, fr. *a-* (fr. L *ad-*) + *muser* to muse] *vt* (15c) **1 a** *archaic* **:** to divert the attention of so as to deceive **b** *obs* **:** to occupy the attention of **:** ABSORB **c** *obs* **:** DISTRACT, BEWILDER **2 a :** to entertain or occupy in a light, playful, or pleasant manner ⟨~ the child with a story⟩ **b :** to appeal to the sense of humor of ⟨the joke doesn't ~ me⟩ ~ *vi, obs* **:** MUSE — **amus·ed·ly** \-ˈmyü-zəd-lē\ *adv* — **amus·er** *n*
syn AMUSE, DIVERT, ENTERTAIN mean to pass or cause to pass the time pleasantly. AMUSE suggests that one's attention is engaged lightly or frivolously; DIVERT implies the distracting of the attention from worry or routine occupation esp. by something funny; ENTERTAIN suggests supplying amusement or diversion by specially prepared or contrived methods.
amuse·ment \ə-ˈmyüz-mənt\ *n* (1603) **1 :** a means of amusing or entertaining ⟨what are her favorite ~s⟩ **2 :** the condition of being amused ⟨his ~ knew no bounds⟩ **3 :** pleasurable diversion **:** ENTERTAINMENT ⟨plays the piano for ~⟩
amus·ing \ə-ˈmyü-ziŋ\ *adj* (1712) **:** giving amusement **:** DIVERTING — **amus·ing·ly** \-ziŋ-lē\ *adv* — **amus·ing·ness** *n*
amu·sive \ə-ˈmyü-ziv, -siv\ *adj* (1728) **:** tending to amuse or arouse mirth **:** AMUSING
amyg·da·la \ə-ˈmig-də-lə\ *n, pl* **-lae** \-ˌlē, -ˌlī\ [NL, fr. L, almond, fr. Gk *amygdalē*] (ca. 1860) **:** the one of the four basal ganglia in each cerebral hemisphere that consists of an almond-shaped mass of gray matter in the anterior extremity of the temporal lobe — called also *amygdaloid nucleus*
amyg·da·lin \-lən\ *n* [NL *Amygdalus,* genus name, fr. LL, almond tree, fr. Gk *amygdalos;* akin to Gk *amygdalē*] (1651) **:** a white crystalline cyanogenetic glucoside $C_{20}H_{27}NO_{11}$ found esp. in the bitter almond (*Amygdalus communis amara*)
1**amyg·da·loid** \-ˌlȯid\ *n* [Gk *amygdaloeidēs,* adj., fr. *amygdalē* almond] (1791) **:** an igneous and usu. volcanic rock orig. containing small cavities filled with deposits of different minerals (as chalcedony or calcite) — **amyg·da·loi·dal** \-ˌmig-də-ˈlȯid-ᵊl\ *adj*
2**amygdaloid** *adj* (1836) **1 :** almond-shaped **2 :** of, relating to, or affecting an amygdala
am·yl \ˈam-əl\ *n* [blend of *amyl-* and *-yl*] (1850) **:** a univalent hydrocarbon radical C_5H_{11} that occurs in various isomeric forms and is derived from pentane — called also *pentyl*
amyl- *or* **amylo-** *comb form* [LL *amyl-,* fr. L *amylum,* fr. Gk *amylon,* fr. neut. of *amylos* not ground at the mill, fr. *a-* + *mylē* mill — more at MEAL] **:** starch ⟨*amylase*⟩
amyl acetate *n* (ca. 1868) **:** BANANA OIL 1
amyl alcohol *n* (1863) **:** any of eight isomeric alcohols $C_5H_{12}O$ used esp. as solvents and in making esters; *also* **:** either of two commercially produced mixtures of amyl alcohols obtained from fusel oil or derived from pentanes and used esp. as solvents
am·y·lase \ˈam-ə-ˌlās, -ˌlāz\ *n* (1893) **:** any of the enzymes (as amylopsin) that accelerate the hydrolysis of starch and glycogen or their intermediate hydrolysis products
am·y·loid \-ˌlȯid\ *n* (1859) **:** a waxy translucent substance consisting of protein in combination with polysaccharides that is deposited in some animal organs under abnormal conditions — **amyloid** *adj*
am·y·loid·osis \ˌam-ə-ˌlȯi-ˈdō-səs\ *n* [NL] (ca. 1900) **:** a condition characterized by the deposition of amyloid in bodily organs and tissues
am·y·lo·lyt·ic \ˌam-ə-lō-ˈlit-ik\ *adj* [NL *amylolysis,* fr. *amyl-* + *lysis*] (ca. 1868) **:** characterized by or capable of the enzymatic splitting of starch into soluble products ⟨~ enzymes⟩ ⟨~ activity⟩
am·y·lo·pec·tin \ˌam-ə-lō-ˈpek-tən\ *n* (1905) **:** a component of starch that has a high molecular weight and branched structure and does not tend to gel in aqueous solutions
am·y·lo·plast \ˈam-ə-(ˌ)lō-ˌplast\ *n* (1886) **:** a colorless starch-forming plastid
am·y·lop·sin \ˌam-ə-ˈläp-sən\ *n* [*amyl-* + *-psin* (as in *trypsin*)] (ca. 1868) **:** the amylase of the pancreatic juice
am·y·lose \ˈam-ə-ˌlōs, -ˌlōz\ *n* (ca. 1868) **1 :** any of various polysaccharides (as starch or cellulose) **2 :** a component of starch characterized by its straight chains of glucose units and by the tendency of its aqueous solutions to set to a stiff gel **3 :** any of various compounds $(C_6H_{10}O_5)_x$ obtained by the hydrolysis of starch
am·y·lum \-ləm\ *n* [L — more at AMYL-] (1558) **:** STARCH
amyo·to·nia \ˌā-ˌmī-ə-ˈtō-nē-ə\ *n* [NL] (ca. 1919) **:** deficiency of muscle tone
amyo·tro·phic lateral sclerosis \ˌā-ˌmī-ə-ˌtrō-fik-, -ˌträf-ik-\ *n* (ca. 1889) **:** a rare progressive degenerative fatal disease affecting the spinal cord, usu. beginning in middle age, and characterized esp. by increasing and spreading muscular weakness — called also *Lou Gehrig's disease*
Am·y·tal \ˈam-ə-ˌtȯl\ *trademark* — used for amobarbital
1**an** \ən, (ˈ)an\ *indefinite article* [ME, fr. OE *ān* one — more at ONE] (bef. 12c) **:** 2A ***usage*** see 2A
2**an** \ən, an\ *prep* (bef. 12c) **:** 3A 2 ***usage*** see 2A
3**an** *or* **an'** *conj* (12c) **1** *see* AND\ **:** AND **2** \(ˈ)an\ *archaic* **:** IF
an- — see 2A-
1**-an** *or* **-ian** *also* **-ean** *n suffix* [*-an* & *-ian* fr. ME *-an, -ian,* fr. OF & L; OF *-ien,* fr. L *-ianus,* fr. *-i-* + *-anus,* fr. *-anus,* adj. suffix; *-ean* fr. such words as *Mediterranean, European*] **1 :** one that is of or relating to ⟨*American*⟩ ⟨*Bostonian*⟩ **2 :** one skilled in or specializing in ⟨*phonetician*⟩
2**-an** *or* **-ian** *also* **-ean** *adj suffix* **1 :** of or belonging to ⟨*American*⟩ ⟨*Floridian*⟩ **2 :** characteristic of **:** resembling ⟨*Mozartean*⟩
3**-an** *n suffix* [ISV *-an, -ane,* alter. of *-ene, -ine,* & *-one*] **1 :** unsaturated carbon compound ⟨*tolan*⟩ **2 :** anhydride of a carbohydrate ⟨*dextran*⟩
1**ana** \ˈan-ə\ *adv* [ME, fr. ML, fr. Gk, at the rate of, lit., up] (15c) **:** of each an equal quantity — used in prescriptions
2**ana** \ˈan-ə, ˈän-ə, ˈā-nə\ *n, pl* **ana** *or* **anas** [*-ana*] (1727) **1 :** a collection of the memorable sayings of a person **2 :** a collection of anecdotes or interesting information about a person or a place
ana- *or* **an-** *prefix* [L, fr. Gk, up, back, again, fr. *ana* up — more at ON] **1 :** up **:** upward ⟨*anabolism*⟩ **2 :** back **:** backward ⟨*anatropous*⟩

\ə\ abut \ᵊ\ kitten, F table \ər\ further \a\ ash \ā\ ace \ä\ cot, cart \au̇\ out \ch\ chin \e\ bet \ē\ easy \g\ go \i\ hit \ī\ ice \j\ job \ŋ\ sing \ō\ go \ȯ\ law \ȯi\ boy \th\ thin \th\ the \ü\ loot \u̇\ foot \y\ yet \zh\ vision \à, k, ⁿ, œ, œ̄, ue, ue̅, ʸ\ *see* Guide to Pronunciation

-ana \'än-ə, 'an-ə, *also* 'ā-nə\ *or* **-i·ana** \ē-'\ *n pl suffix* [NL, fr. L, neut. pl. of *-anus* -an & *-ianus* -ian] : collected items of information esp. anecdotal or bibliographical concerning ⟨*Americana*⟩ ⟨*Johnsoniana*⟩

ana·bap·tism \ˌan-ə-'bap-ˌtiz-əm\ *n* [NL *anabaptismus,* fr. LGk *anabaptismos* rebaptism, fr. *anabaptizein* to rebaptize, fr. *ana-* again + *baptizein* to baptize] (1577) **1** *cap* **a :** the doctrine or practices of the Anabaptists **b :** the Anabaptist movement **2 :** the baptism of one previously baptized

Ana·bap·tist \-'bap-təst\ *n* (1532) **:** a Protestant sectarian of a radical movement arising in the 16th century and advocating the baptism and church membership of adult believers only, nonresistance, and the separation of church and state — **Anabaptist** *adj*

anab·a·sis \ə-'nab-ə-səs\ *n, pl* **-a·ses** \-ˌsēz\ [Gk, inland march, fr. *anabainein* to go up or inland, fr. *ana-* + *bainein* to go — more at COME] (1706) **1 :** a going or marching up **:** ADVANCE; *esp* **:** a military advance **2** [fr. the retreat of Gk mercenaries in Asia Minor described in the *Anabasis* of Xenophon] **:** a difficult and dangerous military retreat

an·a·bat·ic \ˌan-ə-'bat-ik\ *adj* [Gk *anabatos,* verbal of *anabainein*] (ca. 1853) **:** moving upward **:** RISING ⟨an ~ wind⟩

anabolic steroid *n* (1961) **:** any of a group of usu. synthetic hormones that increase constructive metabolism and are sometimes taken by athletes in training to increase temporarily the size of their muscles

anab·o·lism \ə-'nab-ə-ˌliz-əm\ *n* [ISV *ana-* + *-bolism* (as in *metabolism*)] (1886) **:** the constructive part of metabolism concerned esp. with macromolecular synthesis — **an·a·bol·ic** \ˌan-ə-'bäl-ik\ *adj*

anach·ro·nism \ə-'nak-rə-ˌniz-əm\ *n* [prob. fr. MGk *anachronismos,* fr. *anachronizesthai* to be an anachronism, fr. LGk *anachronizein* to be late, fr. Gk *ana-* + *chronos* time] (ca. 1646) **1 :** an error in chronology; *esp* **:** a chronological misplacing of persons, events, objects, or customs in regard to each other **2 :** a person or a thing that is chronologically out of place; *esp* **:** one from a former age that is incongruous in the present — **anach·ro·nis·tic** \ə-ˌnak-rə-'nis-tik\ *also* **ana·chron·ic** \ˌan-ə-'krän-ik\ *or* **anach·ro·nous** \ə-'nak-rə-nəs\ *adj* — **anach·ro·nis·ti·cal·ly** \ə-ˌnak-rə-'nis-ti-k(ə-)lē\ *also* **anach·ro·nous·ly** *adv*

an·a·clit·ic \ˌan-ə-'klit-ik\ *adj* [Gk *anaklitos,* verbal of *anaklinein* to lean upon, fr. *ana-* + *klinein* to lean — more at LEAN] (1922) **:** characterized by dependence of libido on a nonsexual instinct

an·a·co·lu·thon \ˌan-ə-kə-'lü-ˌthän\ *n, pl* **-tha** \-thə\ *also* **-thons** [LL, fr. LGk *anakolouthon* inconsistency in logic, fr. Gk, neut. of *anakolouthos,* inconsistent, fr. *an-* + *akolouthos* following, fr. *ha-, a-* together + *keleuthos* path] (ca. 1706) **:** syntactical inconsistency or incoherence within a sentence; *esp* **:** the shift from one construction to another (as in "you really ought — well, do it your own way") — **an·a·co·lu·thic** \-thik\ *adj* — **an·a·co·lu·thi·cal·ly** \-thi-k(ə-)lē\ *adv*

an·a·con·da \ˌan-ə-'kän-də\ *n* [prob. modif. of Sinhalese *henakandayā,* a slender green snake] (1768) **:** a large semiaquatic snake (*Eunectes murinus*) of the boa family of tropical So. America that kills by constriction; *broadly* **:** a large constricting snake

anaconda

anac·re·on·tic \ə-ˌnak-rē-'änt-ik\ *n* (1656) **:** a poem in the manner of Anacreon; *esp* **:** a drinking song or light lyric

Anacreontic *adj* [L *anacreonticus,* fr. *Anacreont-, Anacreon* Anacreon, fr. Gk *Anakreont-, Anakreōn*] (1611) **1 :** of, relating to, or resembling the poetry of Anacreon **2 :** convivial or amatory in tone or theme

an·a·cru·sis \ˌan-ə-'krü-səs\ *n, pl* **-cru·ses** \-ˌsēz\ [NL, fr. Gk *anakrousis* beginning of a song, fr. *anakrouein* to begin a song, fr. *ana-* + *krouein* to strike, beat] (1830) **1 :** one or more syllables at the beginning of a line of poetry that are regarded as preliminary to and not a part of the metrical pattern **2 :** UPBEAT; *specif* **:** one or more notes or tones preceding the first downbeat of a musical phrase

an·a·dem \'an-ə-ˌdem\ *n* [L *anadema,* fr. Gk *anadēma,* fr. *anadein* to wreathe, fr. *ana-* + *dein* to bind — more at DIADEM] *archaic* (1604) **:** a wreath for the head **:** GARLAND

ana·di·plo·sis \ˌan-əd-ə-'plō-səs, ˌan-ə-(ˌ)dī-'plō-\ *n, pl* **-plo·ses** \-ˌsēz\ [LL, fr. Gk *anadiplōsis,* lit., repetition, fr. *anadiploun* to double, fr. *ana-* + *diploun* to double — more at DIPLOMA] (1589) **:** repetition of a prominent and usu. the last word in one phrase or clause at the beginning of the next (as in "rely on his honor — honor such as his?")

anad·ro·mous \ə-'nad-rə-məs\ *adj* [Gk *anadromos* running upward, fr. *anadramein* to run upward, fr. *ana-* + *dramein* to run — more at DROMEDARY] (ca. 1753) **:** ascending rivers from the sea for breeding ⟨shad are ~⟩

anae·mia, anae·mic *var of* ANEMIA, ANEMIC

an·aer·obe \'an-ə-ˌrōb; (ˈ)an-'a(-ə)r-ˌōb, -'e(-ə)r-\ *n* [ISV] (1884) **:** an anaerobic organism

an·aer·o·bic \ˌan-ə-'rō-bik; ˌan-ˌa(-ə)r-'ō-, -ˌe(-ə)r-\ *adj* (ca. 1881) **1 :** living, active, or occurring in the absence of free oxygen ⟨~ respiration⟩ **2 :** relating to or induced by anaerobes — **an·aer·o·bi·cal·ly** \-bi-k(ə-)lē\ *adv*

an·aero·bi·o·sis \ˌan-ə-rō-(ˌ)bī-'ō-səs, -bē-; ˌan-ˌa(-ə)r-ō-, -ˌe(-ə)r-\ *n, pl* **-o·ses** \-'ō-ˌsēz\ (ca. 1889) **:** life in the absence of air or free oxygen

an·aes·the·sia, an·aes·thet·ic *var of* ANESTHESIA, ANESTHETIC

ana·gen·e·sis \ˌan-ə-'jen-ə-səs\ *n* [NL] (1889) **:** evolutionary change involving a continuous succession of forms replacing one another without branching **:** phyletic evolution — compare CLADOGENESIS

ana·glyph \'an-ə-ˌglif\ *n* [LL *anaglyphus* embossed, fr. Gk *anaglyphos,* fr. *anaglyphein* to emboss, fr. *ana-* + *glyphein* to carve — more at CLEAVE] (1651) **1 :** a sculptured, chased, or embossed ornament worked in low relief **2 :** a stereoscopic motion or still picture in which the right component of a composite image usu. red in color is superposed on the left component in a contrasting color to produce a three-dimensional effect when viewed through correspondingly colored filters in the form of spectacles — **ana·glyph·ic** \ˌan-ə-'glif-ik\ *adj*

an·a·go·ge *or* **an·a·go·gy** \'an-ə-ˌgō-jē\ *n, pl* **-ges** *or* **-gies** [LL *anagoge,* fr. LGk *anagōgē,* fr. Gk, reference, fr. *anagein* to refer, fr. *ana-* + *agein* to lead — more at AGENT] (15c) **:** interpretation of a word, passage, or text (as of Scripture or poetry) that finds beyond the literal, allegorical, and moral senses a fourth and ultimate spiritual or mystical sense — **an·a·gog·ic** \ˌan-ə-'gäj-ik\ *or* **an·a·gog·i·cal** \-i-kəl\ *adj* — **an·a·gog·i·cal·ly** \-i-k(ə-)lē\ *adv*

[1]ana·gram \'an-ə-ˌgram\ *n* [prob. fr. MF *anagramme,* fr. NL *anagrammat-, anagramma,* modif. of Gk *anagrammatismos,* fr. *anagrammatizein* to transpose letters, fr. *ana-* + *grammat-, gramma* letter — more at GRAM] (1589) **1 :** a word or phrase made by transposing the letters of another word or phrase **2** *pl but sing in constr* **:** a game in which words are formed by rearranging the letters of other words or by arranging letters taken (as from a stock of cards or blocks) at random — **ana·gram·mat·ic** \ˌan-ə-grə-'mat-ik\ *also* **ana·gram·mat·i·cal** \-i-kəl\ *adj* — **ana·gram·mat·i·cal·ly** \-i-k(ə-)lē\ *adv*

[2]anagram *vt* **-grammed; -gram·ming** (1630) **1 :** ANAGRAMMATIZE **2 :** to rearrange (the letters of a text) in order to discover a hidden message

ana·gram·ma·tize \ˌan-ə-'gram-ə-ˌtīz\ *vt* **-tized; -tiz·ing** (1588) **:** to transpose (as letters in a word) so as to form an anagram — **ana·gram·ma·ti·za·tion** \-ˌgram-ət-ə-'zā-shən\ *n*

anal \'ān-ᵊl\ *adj* (1769) **1 :** of, relating to, or situated near the anus **2 a :** of, relating to, characterized by, or being the stage of psychosexual development in psychoanalytic theory during which the child is concerned esp. with its feces **b :** of, relating to, characterized by, or being personality traits (as parsimony, meticulousness, and ill humor) considered typical of fixation at the anal stage of development — **anal·ly** \-ᵊl-ē\ *adv*

anal·cime \ə-'nal-ˌsēm\ *n* [F, fr. Gk *analkimos* weak, fr. *an-* + *alkimos* strong, fr. *alkē* strength] (1803) **:** a white or slightly colored mineral $NaAlSi_2O_6{\cdot}H_2O$ occurring in various igneous rocks in massive form or in crystals — **anal·ci·mic** \-ˌnal-'sē-mik, -'sim-ik\ *adj*

anal·cite \ə-'nal-ˌsīt\ *n* (1868) **:** ANALCIME

an·a·lects \'an-ᵊl-ˌek(t)s\ *also* **an·a·lec·ta** \ˌan-ᵊl-'ek-tə\ *n pl* [NL *analecta,* fr. Gk *analekta,* neut. pl. of *analektos,* verbal of *analegein* to collect, fr. *ana-* + *legein* to gather — more at LEGEND] (1652) **:** selected miscellaneous written passages

an·a·lem·ma \ˌan-ᵊl-'em-ə\ *n* [L, sundial on a pedestal, fr. Gk *analēmma,* lofty structure, sundial, fr. *analambanein* to take up, restore, fr. *ana-* + *lambanein* to take — more at LATCH] (1832) **:** a graduated scale having the shape of a figure 8 and showing the sun's declination and the equation of time for each day of the year — **an·a·lem·mat·ic** \ˌan-ə-le-'mat-ik, -lə-\ *adj*

an·a·lep·tic \ˌan-ᵊl-'ep-tik\ *n* [Gk *analēptikos,* fr. *analambanein*] (1671) **:** a drug that stimulates the central nervous system — **analeptic** *adj*

an·al·ge·sia \ˌan-ᵊl-'jē-zhə, -z(h)ē-ə\ *n* [NL, fr. Gk *analgēsia,* fr. *an-* + *algēsis* sense of pain, fr. *algein* to suffer pain, fr. *algos* pain] (ca. 1706) **:** insensibility to pain without loss of consciousness — **an·al·ge·sic** \-'jē-zik, -sik\ *adj or n* — **an·al·get·ic** \-'jet-ik\ *adj or n*

anal·i·ty \ā-'nal-ət-ē\ *n, pl* **-ties** (1939) **:** the psychological state or quality of being anal

[1]an·a·log *var of* ANALOGUE

[2]an·a·log \'an-ᵊl-ˌȯg, -ˌäg\ *adj* (1946) **1 :** of, relating to, or being an analogue **2 a :** being or relating to a mechanism in which data is represented by continuously variable physical quantities **b :** of or relating to an analog computer **c :** being a watch having hour and minute hands

analog computer *n* (1948) **:** a computer that operates with numbers represented by directly measurable quantities (as voltages or rotations) — compare DIGITAL COMPUTER, HYBRID COMPUTER

an·a·log·i·cal \ˌan-ᵊl-'äj-i-kəl\ *also* **an·a·log·ic** \-ik\ *adj* (1609) **1 :** of, relating to, or based on analogy **2 :** expressing or implying analogy — **an·a·log·i·cal·ly** \-i-k(ə-)lē\ *adv*

anal·o·gist \ə-'nal-ə-jəst\ *n* (ca. 1828) **:** one who searches for or reasons from analogies

anal·o·gize \-ˌjīz\ *vb* **-gized; -giz·ing** *vi* (1655) **:** to use or exhibit analogy ~ *vt* **:** to compare by analogy

anal·o·gous \ə-'nal-ə-gəs\ *adj* [L *analogus,* fr. Gk *analogos,* lit., proportionate, fr. *ana-* + *logos* reason, ratio, fr. *legein* to gather, speak — more at LEGEND] (1646) **1 :** showing an analogy or a likeness that permits one to draw an analogy **2 :** being or related to as an analogue ***syn*** see SIMILAR — **anal·o·gous·ly** *adv* — **anal·o·gous·ness** *n*

an·a·logue \'an-ᵊl-ˌȯg, -ˌäg\ *n* [F *analogue,* fr. *analogue* analogous, fr. Gk *analogos*] (1826) **1 :** something that is analogous or similar to something else **2 :** an organ similar in function to an organ of another animal or plant but different in structure and origin **3 :** a chemical compound structurally similar to another but differing often by a single element of the same valence and group of the periodic table as the element it replaces **4 :** a synthetic food product made of vegetable matter (as soybeans) and used as a meat substitute

anal·o·gy \ə-'nal-ə-jē\ *n, pl* **-gies** (15c) **1 :** inference that if two or more things agree with one another in some respects they will prob. agree in others **2 a :** resemblance in some particulars between things otherwise unlike **:** SIMILARITY **b :** comparison based on such resemblance **3 :** correspondence between the members of pairs or sets of linguistic forms that serves as a basis for the creation of another form **4 :** correspondence in function between anatomical parts of different structure and origin — compare HOMOLOGY ***syn*** see LIKENESS

an·al·pha·bet \(ˈ)an-'al-fə-ˌbet, -bət\ *n* [Gk *analphabētos* not knowing the alphabet, fr. *an-* + *alphabētos* alphabet] (1881) **:** one who cannot read **:** ILLITERATE — **an·al·pha·bet·ic** \ˌan-ˌal-fə-'bet-ik\ *adj or n* — **an·al·pha·bet·ism** \(ˈ)an-'al-fə-bə-ˌtiz-əm\ *n*

anal·y·sand \ə-'nal-ə-ˌsand\ *n* [*analyse* + *-and* (as in *multiplicand*)] (1917) **:** one who is undergoing psychoanalysis

an·a·lyse *chiefly Brit var of* ANALYZE

anal·y·sis \ə-'nal-ə-səs\ *n, pl* **-y·ses** \-ˌsēz\ [NL, fr. Gk, fr. *analyein* to break up, fr. *ana-* + *lyein* to loosen — more at LOSE] (1581) **1 :** separation of a whole into its component parts **2 a :** an examination of a complex, its elements, and their relations **b :** a statement of such an analysis **3 :** the use of function words instead of inflectional forms as a characteristic device of a language **4 a :** the identification or separation of ingredients of a substance **b :** a statement of the constituents of a mixture **5 a :** proof of a mathematical proposition by assuming the result and deducing a valid statement by a series of reversible steps **b (1) :** a branch of mathematics concerned mainly with functions and limits **(2) :** CALCULUS 1b **6 a :** a method in philosophy of resolving complex expressions into simpler or more basic ones **b :** clarification of an expression by an elucidation of its use in discourse **7** : PSYCHOANALYSIS

analysis of variance (ca. 1939) : analysis of variation in an experimental outcome and esp. of a statistical variance in order to determine the contributions of given factors or variables to the variance

analysis si·tus \-'sīt-əs, -'sēt-; -'sī-ˌtüs, -'sē-\ *n* [NL, lit., analysis of situation] (ca. 1909) : TOPOLOGY 2a(1)

an·a·lyst \'an-ᵊl-əst\ *n* [prob. fr. *analyze*] (1656) **1** : a person who analyzes or who is skilled in analysis **2** : PSYCHOANALYST

an·a·lyt·ic \ˌan-ᵊl-'it-ik\ *adj* [LL *analyticus*, fr. Gk *analytikos*, fr. *analyein*] (1601) **1** : of or relating to analysis or analytics; *esp* : separating something into component parts or constituent elements **2** : skilled in or using analysis esp. in thinking or reasoning ⟨a keenly ~ man⟩ **3** : being a proposition (as "no bachelor is married") whose truth is evident from the meaning of the words it contains — compare SYNTHETIC **4** : characterized by analysis rather than inflection ⟨~ languages⟩ **5** : PSYCHOANALYTIC **6** : treated or treatable by or using the methods of algebra and calculus **7 a** *of a function of a real variable* : capable of being expanded in a Taylor's series in powers of *x* – *h* in some neighborhood of the point *h* **b** *of a function of a complex variable* : differentiable at every point in some neighborhood of a given point or points — **an·a·ly·tic·i·ty** \ˌan-ᵊl-ə-'tis-ət-ē\ *n*

an·a·lyt·i·cal \ˌan-ᵊl-'it-i-kəl\ *adj* (1525) : ANALYTIC — **an·a·lyt·i·cal·ly** \-i-k(ə-)lē\ *adv*

analytic geometry *n* (ca. 1886) : the study of geometric properties by means of algebraic operations upon symbols defined in terms of a coordinate system — called also *coordinate geometry*

analytic philosophy *n* (1936) : PHILOSOPHICAL ANALYSIS

an·a·lyt·ics \ˌan-ᵊl-'it-iks\ *n pl but sing or pl in constr* (1590) : the method of logical analysis

an·a·ly·za·tion \ˌan-ᵊl-ə-'zā-shən\ *n* (1742) : ANALYSIS

an·a·lyze \'an-ᵊl-ˌīz\ *vt* **-lyzed; -lyz·ing** [prob. irreg. fr. *analysis*] (1587) **1** : to study or determine the nature and relationship of the parts of by analysis ⟨~ a traffic pattern⟩ **2** : to subject to scientific or grammatical analysis **3** : PSYCHOANALYZE — **an·a·lyz·abil·i·ty** \ˌan-ᵊl-ˌī-zə-'bil-ət-ē\ *n* — **an·a·lyz·able** \'an-ᵊl-ˌī-zə-bəl\ *adj* — **an·a·lyz·er** \-ˌī-zər\ *n*

syn ANALYZE, DISSECT, BREAK DOWN mean to divide a complex whole into its parts or elements. ANALYZE suggests separating or distinguishing the component parts of something (as a substance, a process, a situation) so as to discover its true nature or inner relationships; DISSECT suggests a searching analysis by laying bare parts or pieces for individual scrutiny; BREAK DOWN implies a reducing to simpler parts or divisions.

an·am·ne·sis \ˌan-ˌam-'nē-səs\ *n, pl* **-ne·ses** \-ˌsēz\ [NL, fr. Gk *anamnēsis*, fr. *anamimnēskesthai* to remember, fr. *ana-* + *mimnēskesthai* to remember — more at MIND] (ca. 1593) **1** : a recalling to mind : REMINISCENCE **2** : a preliminary case history of a medical or psychiatric patient

an·am·nes·tic \-'nes-tik\ *adj* [Gk *anamnēstikos* easily recalled, fr. *anamimnēskesthai*] (ca. 1753) **1** : of or relating to an anamnesis **2** : of or relating to a secondary response to an immunogenic substance after serum antibodies can no longer be detected in the blood

ana·mor·phic \ˌan-ə-'mȯr-fik\ *adj* [NL *anamorphosis* distorted optical image] (ca. 1925) : producing or having different magnification of the image in each of two perpendicular directions — used of an optical device or its image

An·a·ni·as \ˌan-ə-'nī-əs\ *n* [Gk, prob. fr. Heb *Ḥănanyāh*] **1** : an early Christian struck dead for lying **2** : LIAR

an·a·pest \'an-ə-ˌpest\ *n* [L *anapaestus*, fr. Gk *anapaistos*, lit., struck back (a dactyl reversed), fr. (assumed) Gk *anapaiein* to strike back, fr. Gk *ana-* + *paiein* to strike — more at PAVE] (ca. 1678) : a metrical foot consisting of two short syllables followed by one long syllable or of two unstressed syllables followed by one stressed syllable (as *unabridged*) — **an·a·pes·tic** \ˌan-ə-'pes-tik\ *adj or n*

ana·phase \'an-ə-ˌfāz\ *n* [ISV] (1887) : the stage of mitosis and meiosis in which the chromosomes move toward the poles of the spindle — **anaphase** *or* **ana·pha·sic** \ˌan-ə-'fā-zik\ *adj*

anaph·o·ra \ə-'naf-ə-rə\ *n* [LL, fr. LGk, fr. Gk, act of carrying back, reference, fr. *anapherein* to carry back, refer, fr. *ana-* + *pherein* to carry — more at BEAR] (ca. 1589) **1** : repetition of a word or expression at the beginning of successive phrases, clauses, sentences, or verses esp. for rhetorical or poetic effect ⟨Lincoln's "we cannot dedicate — we cannot consecrate — we cannot hallow — this ground" is an example of ~⟩ — compare EPISTROPHE **2** : use of a grammatical substitute (as a pronoun or a pro-verb) to refer to a preceding word or group of words

an·a·phor·ic \ˌan-ə-'fȯr-ik, -'fär-\ *adj* (1904) : referring to a preceding word or group of words ⟨the ~ *do* in "you run faster than I do"⟩

ana·phy·lac·tic \ˌan-ə-fə-'lak-tik\ *adj* (1907) : of, relating to, affected by, or causing anaphylaxis or anaphylactic shock — **ana·phy·lac·ti·cal·ly** \-ti-k(ə-)lē\ *adv* — **ana·phy·lac·toid** \-'lak-ˌtȯid\ *adj*

anaphylactic shock *n* (1910) : an often severe and sometimes fatal systemic reaction in a susceptible individual upon exposure to a specific antigen (as wasp venom or penicillin) after previous sensitization that is characterized esp. by respiratory symptoms, fainting, itching, and urticaria

ana·phy·lax·is \-'lak-səs\ *n, pl* **-lax·es** \-ˌsēz\ [NL, fr. *ana-* + *-phylaxis* (as in *prophylaxis*)] (1907) **1** : hypersensitivity (as to foreign proteins or drugs) resulting from sensitization following prior contact with the causative agent **2** : ANAPHYLACTIC SHOCK

an·a·pla·sia \ˌan-ə-'plā-zh(ē-)ə\ *n* [NL] (ca. 1909) : reversion of cells to a more primitive or undifferentiated form — **an·a·plas·tic** \-'plas-tik\ *adj*

an·arch \'an-ˌärk\ *n* [back-formation fr. *anarchy*] (1667) : a leader or advocate of revolt or anarchy

an·ar·chic \a-'när-kik, ə-\ *adj* (1790) **1 a** : of, relating to, or advocating anarchy **b** : likely to bring about anarchy ⟨~ violence⟩ **2** : lacking order, regularity, or definiteness ⟨~ art forms⟩

an·ar·chism \'an-ər-ˌkiz-əm, -ˌär-\ *n* (1642) **1** : a political theory holding all forms of governmental authority to be unnecessary and undesirable and advocating a society based on voluntary cooperation and free association of individuals and groups **2** : the advocacy or practice of anarchistic principles

an·ar·chist \'an-ər-kəst, -ˌär-\ *n* (1678) **1** : one who rebels against any authority, established order, or ruling power **2** : one who believes in, advocates, or promotes anarchism or anarchy; *esp* : one who uses violent means to overthrow the established order — **anarchist** *or* **an·ar·chis·tic** \ˌan-ər-'kis-tik, -(ˌ)är-\ *adj*

anarcho- *comb form* [ML *anarch-*, fr. Gk, fr. *anarchos*] **1** : anarchism and ⟨*anarcho*-pragmatism⟩ **2** : anarchist and ⟨*anarcho*-individualist⟩

an·ar·cho–syn·di·cal·ism \a-ˌnär-kō-'sin-di-kə-ˌliz-əm, ˌan-ər-kō-\ *n* (ca. 1928) : SYNDICALISM — **an·ar·cho–syn·di·cal·ist** \-kə-ləst\ *n or adj*

an·ar·chy \'an-ər-kē, -ˌär-\ *n* [ML *anarchia*, fr. Gk, fr. *anarchos* having no ruler, fr. *an-* + *archos* ruler — more at ARCH-] (1539) **1 a** : absence of government **b** : a state of lawlessness or political disorder due to the absence of governmental authority **c** : a utopian society of individuals who enjoy complete freedom without government **2** : absence of order : DISORDER **3** : ANARCHISM

ana·sar·ca \ˌan-ə-'sär-kə\ *n* [NL, fr. *ana-* + Gk *sark-*, *sarx* flesh — more at SARCASM] (14c) : generalized edema with accumulation of serum in the connective tissue — **ana·sar·cous** \-kəs\ *adj*

An·a·sa·zi \ˌän-ə-'säz-ē\ *n, pl* **Anasazi** [Navaho *a-naa-sázi* alien ancient one] (1938) **1** : a group of American Indian cliff dwellers of the southwestern U.S. **2** : BASKET MAKER 2 **3** : PUEBLO 2b

an·astig·mat \a-'nas-tig-ˌmat, ˌan-ə-'stig-\ *n* [G, back-formation fr. *anastigmatisch* anastigmatic] (1890) : an anastigmatic lens

an·astig·mat·ic \ˌan-ə-(ˌ)stig-'mat-ik, ˌan-ˌas-tig-\ *adj* [ISV] (1890) : not astigmatic — used esp. of lenses that are able to form approximately point images of object points

anas·to·mose \ə-'nas-tə-ˌmōz, -ˌmōs\ *vb* **-mosed; -mos·ing** [prob. back-formation fr. *anastomosis*] *vt* (1697) : to connect or join by anastomosis ~ *vi* : to communicate by anastomosis

anas·to·mo·sis \ə-ˌnas-tə-'mō-səs\ *n, pl* **-mo·ses** \-ˌsēz\ [LL, fr. Gk *anastomōsis*, fr. *anastomoun* to provide with an outlet, fr. *ana-* + *stoma* mouth, opening — more at STOMACH] (1541) **1** : the union of parts or branches (as of streams, blood vessels, or leaf veins) so as to intercommunicate : INOSCULATION **2** : a product of anastomosis : NETWORK — **anas·to·mot·ic** \-'mät-ik\ *adj*

anas·tro·phe \ə-'nas-trə-(ˌ)fē\ *n* [ML, fr. Gk *anastrophē*, lit., turning back, fr. *anastrephein* to turn back, fr. *ana-* + *strephein* to turn — more at STROPHE] (ca. 1577) : inversion of the usual syntactical order of words for rhetorical effect — compare HYSTERON PROTERON

an·a·tase \'an-ə-ˌtās, -ˌtāz\ *n* [F, fr. Gk *anatasis* extension, fr. *anateinein* to extend, fr. *ana-* + *teinein* to stretch — more at THIN] (ca. 1821) : a tetragonal titanium dioxide used esp. as a white pigment

anath·e·ma \ə-'nath-ə-mə\ *n* [LL *anathemat-*, *anathema*, fr. Gk, thing devoted to evil, curse, fr. *anatithenai* to set up, dedicate, fr. *ana-* + *tithenai* to place, set — more at DO] (1526) **1 a** : one that is cursed by ecclesiastical authority **b** : one that is intensely disliked : something or someone odious ⟨ideas that are ~ to him⟩ **2 a** : a ban or curse solemnly pronounced by ecclesiastical authority and accompanied by excommunication **b** : the denunciation of something as accursed **c** : a vigorous denunciation : CURSE

anath·e·ma·tize \-ˌtīz\ *vt* **-tized; -tiz·ing** (1566) : to pronounce an anathema upon ***syn*** see EXECRATE

An·a·to·lian \ˌan-ə-'tō-lē-ən, -'tōl-yən\ *n* (1590) **1** : a native or inhabitant of Anatolia and specif. of the western plateau lands of Turkey in Asia **2** : a branch of the Indo-European language family that includes a group of extinct languages of ancient Anatolia — see INDO-EUROPEAN LANGUAGES table — **Anatolian** *adj*

an·a·tom·i·co- \ˌan-ə-'täm-i-(ˌ)kō\ *or* **anat·o·mo-** \ə-'nat-ə-(ˌ)mō\ *comb form* : anatomical and : anatomical ⟨*anatomico*pathological⟩ ⟨*anatomo*clinical⟩

anat·o·mist \ə-'nat-ə-məst\ *n* (1543) **1** : a student of anatomy; *esp* : one skilled in dissection **2** : one who analyzes minutely and critically ⟨an ~ of urban society⟩

anat·o·mize \-ˌmīz\ *vt* **-mized; -miz·ing** (15c) **1** : to cut in pieces in order to display or examine the structure and use of the parts : DISSECT **2** : ANALYZE

anat·o·my \ə-'nat-ə-mē\ *n, pl* **-mies** [LL *anatomia* dissection, fr. Gk *anatomē*, fr. *anatemnein* to dissect, fr. *ana-* + *temnein* to cut — more at TOME] (14c) **1** : a branch of morphology that deals with the structure of organisms **2** : a treatise on anatomic science or art **3** : the art of separating the parts of an organism in order to ascertain their position, relations, structure, and function : DISSECTION **4** *obs* : a body dissected or to be dissected **5** : structural makeup esp. of an organism or any of its parts **6** : a separating or dividing into parts for detailed examination : ANALYSIS **7 a** (1) : SKELETON (2) : MUMMY **b** : the human body — **an·a·tom·ic** \ˌan-ə-'täm-ik\ *or* **an·a·tom·i·cal** \-i-kəl\ *adj* — **an·a·tom·i·cal·ly** \-i-k(ə-)lē\ *adv*

ana·tox·in \ˌan-ə-'täk-sən\ *n* [ISV *ana-* + *toxin*] (ca. 1925) : TOXOID

anat·ro·pous \ə-'na-trə-pəs\ *adj* (ca. 1846) : having or being an ovule inverted so that the micropyle is bent down to the funiculus to which the body of the ovule is united

-ance \ən(t)s, ᵊn(t)s\ *n suffix* [ME, fr. OF, fr. L *-antia*, fr. *-ant-*, *-ans* -ant + *-ia* -y] **1** : action or process ⟨further*ance*⟩ : instance of an action or process ⟨perform*ance*⟩ **2** : quality or state : instance of a quality or state ⟨protuber*ance*⟩ **3** : amount or degree ⟨conduct*ance*⟩

an·ces·tor \'an-ˌses-tər *also* -səs-\ *n* [ME *ancestre*, fr. OF, fr. L *antecessor* one that goes before, fr. *antecessus*, pp. of *antecedere* to go before, fr. *ante-* + *cedere* to go — more at CEDE] (13c) **1 a** : one from whom a person is descended and who is usu. more remote in the line of descent than a grandparent **b** : FOREFATHER 2 **2** : FORERUNNER, PROTOTYPE **3** : a progenitor of a more recent or existing species or group

ancestor worship *n* (1854) : the custom of venerating deceased ancestors who are considered still a part of the family and whose spirits are believed to have the power to intervene in the affairs of the living

an·ces·tral \an-'ses-trəl\ *adj* (15c) : of, relating to, or inherited from an ancestor ⟨~ estates⟩ — **an·ces·tral·ly** \-trə-lē\ *adv*

an·ces·tress \'an-ˌses-trəs\ *n* (1580) : a female ancestor

\ə\ abut \ᵊ\ kitten, F table \ər\ further \a\ ash \ā\ ace \ä\ cot, cart
\aů\ out \ch\ chin \e\ bet \ē\ easy \g\ go \i\ hit \ī\ ice \j\ job
\ŋ\ sing \ō\ go \ȯ\ law \ȯi\ boy \th\ thin \th\ the \ü\ loot \ů\ foot
\y\ yet \zh\ vision \à, k, ⁿ, œ, œ̄, ue, uē, ʸ\ see Guide to Pronunciation

an·ces·try \'an-,ses-trē\ n (14c) 1 : line of descent : LINEAGE: specif : honorable, noble, or aristocratic descent 2 : persons initiating or comprising a line of descent : ANCESTORS

An·chi·ses \an-'ki-(,)sēz, aŋ-\ n [L. fr. Gk Anchisēs] : the father of Aeneas rescued by his son from the burning city of Troy

¹**an·chor** \'aŋ-kər\ n, often attrib [ME ancre, fr. OE ancor, fr. L anchora, fr. Gk ankyra — more at ANGLE] (bef. 12c) 1 : a device usu. of metal attached to a ship or boat by a cable and cast overboard to hold it in a particular place by means of a fluke that digs into the bottom 2 : a reliable or principal support : MAINSTAY 3 : something that serves to hold an object firmly 4 : an object shaped like a ship's anchor 5 : an anchorman or anchorwoman 6 pl, slang : the brakes of a motor vehicle — **an·chor·less** \-ləs\ adj

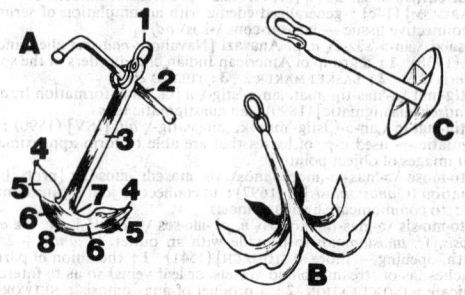

anchor 1: A yachtsman's: *1* ring, *2* stock, *3* shank, *4* bill, *5* fluke, *6* arm, *7* throat, *8* crown, *B* grapnel, *C* mushroom

²**anchor** vb **an·chored; an·chor·ing** \-k(ə-)riŋ\ vt (13c) 1 : to hold in place in the water by an anchor 2 : to secure firmly : FIX 3 : to act or serve as an anchor for ⟨need a large store to ~ the mall⟩ ⟨~ ing the evening news⟩ ~ vi 1 : to cast anchor 2 : to become fixed

an·chor·age \'aŋ-k(ə-)rij\ n (1587) 1 a : a place where vessels anchor : a place suitable for anchoring b : the act of anchoring : the condition of being anchored 2 : a means of securing : a source of reassurance ⟨this ~ of Christian hope —T. O. Wedel⟩ 3 : something that provides a secure hold

an·cho·ress \'aŋ-k(ə-)rəs\ or **an·cress** \'aŋ-krəs\ n [ME ankeresse, fr. anker hermit, fr. OE ancor, fr. OIr anchara, fr. LL anachoreta] (14c) : a female anchorite

an·cho·rite \'aŋ-kə-,rīt\ also **an·cho·ret** \-,ret\ n [ME, fr. ML anchorita, alter. of LL anachoreta, fr. LGk anachōrētēs, fr. Gk anachōrein to withdraw, fr. ana- + chōrein to make room, fr. chōros place; akin to Gk chēros left, bereaved — more at HEIR] (15c) : one who lives in seclusion usu. for religious reasons — **an·cho·rit·ic** \,aŋ-kə-'rit-ik\ adj — **an·cho·rit·i·cal·ly** \-i-k(ə-)lē\ adv

an·chor·man \'aŋ-kər-,man\ n (1911) 1 : one who is last: as a : the member of a team who competes last ⟨the ~ on a relay team⟩ b : one who has the lowest scholastic standing in his graduating class 2 : a broadcaster (as on a news program) who introduces reports by other broadcasters and usu. reads the news 3 : MODERATOR 2c

an·chor·peo·ple \-,pē-pəl\ n pl (1974) : ANCHORPERSONS

an·chor·per·son \-,pərs-ᵊn\ n (1973) : an anchorman or anchorwoman

an·chor·wom·an \-,wům-ən\ n (1973) : a woman who anchors a broadcast

an·cho·veta also **an·cho·vet·ta** \,an-chō-'vet-ə\ n [Sp anchoveta, dim. of anchova] (1940) : a small anchovy (Cetengraulis mysticetus) of the Pacific coast of No. America

an·cho·vy \'an-,chō-vē, an-'\ n, pl **-vies** or **-vy** [Sp anchova] (1596) : any of numerous small fishes (family Engraulidae) resembling herrings; esp : a common Mediterranean one (Engraulis encrasicholus) used esp. in appetizers, as a garnish, and for making sauces and relishes

an·cien ré·gime \,äⁿs-yaⁿ-rā-zhēm\ n [F, lit., old regime] (1794) 1 : the political and social system of France before the Revolution of 1789 2 : a system or mode no longer prevailing

¹**an·cient** \'ān-shənt, -chənt, 'āŋ(k)-shənt\ adj [ME ancien, fr. MF, fr. (assumed) VL anteanus, fr. L ante before — more at ANTE-] (14c) 1 : having had an existence of many years 2 : of or relating to a remote period, to a time early in history, or to those living in such a period or time; specif : of or relating to the historical period beginning with the earliest known civilizations and extending to the fall of the western Roman Empire in A.D. 476 3 : having the qualities of age or long existence: a : VENERABLE b : OLD-FASHIONED, ANTIQUE syn see OLD — **an·cient·ness** n

²**ancient** n (1502) 1 : an aged living being ⟨a penniless ~⟩ 2 : one who lived in ancient times: a pl : the civilized people of antiquity; esp : those of the classical nations b : one of the classical authors ⟨Plutarch and other ~s⟩ 3 : an ancient coin

³**ancient** n [alter. of ensign] (1554) 1 archaic : ENSIGN, STANDARD, FLAG 2 obs : the bearer of an ensign

ancient history n (1595) 1 : the history of ancient times 2 : knowledge or information that is widespread and has lost its initial freshness or importance : common knowledge

an·cient·ly adv (1502) : in ancient times : long ago

an·cient·ry \-rē\ n (1580) 1 : ANTIQUITY, ANCIENTNESS

an·cil·la \an-'sil-ə\ n, pl **-lae** \-(,)ē\ [L, female servant] (1871) : AID, HELPER

an·cil·lary \'an(t)-sə-,ler-ē, esp Brit an-'sil-ə-rē\ adj (1667) 1 : SUBORDINATE, SUBSIDIARY ⟨the main factory and its ~ plants⟩ 2 : AUXILIARY, SUPPLEMENTARY ⟨the need for ~ evidence⟩ — **ancillary** n

an·con \'aŋ-,kän\ n, pl **an·co·nes** \aŋ-'kō-nēz\ [L, fr. Gk ankōn elbow; akin to L uncus hook] (ca. 1706) : a bracket, elbow, or console used as an architectural support

-an·cy \ən-sē, ᵊn-\ n suffix [L -antia — more at -ANCE] : quality or state ⟨piquancy⟩

an·cy·lo·sto·mi·a·sis \,aŋ-ki-,lō-stə-'mī-ə-səs, ,an(t)-sə-\ n, pl **-a·ses** \-,sēz\ [NL, fr. Ancylostoma, genus of hookworms, fr. Gk ankylos hooked + stoma mouth — more at ANGLE, STOMACH] (1887) : infestation with or disease caused by hookworms; esp : a lethargic anemic state in man due to blood loss from hookworms feeding in the small intestine

and \ən(d), (ᵊ)an(d), usu ²n(d) after t, d, s or z, often ²m after p or b, sometimes ᵊŋ after k or g\ conj [ME, fr. OE; akin to OHG unti and] (bef. 12c) 1 — used as a function word to indicate connection or addition esp. of items within the same class or type; used to join sentence elements of the same grammatical rank or function 2 — used as a function word to express logical modification, consequence, antithesis, or supplementary explanation 3 obs : IF 4 — used in logic to form a conjunction — **and how** \'and-'haů\ — used to emphasize the preceding idea — **and so forth** \ən-'sō-,förth, -,förth\ 1 : and others or more of the same or similar kind 2 : further in the same or similar manner 3 : and the rest 4 : and other things — **and so on** \ən-'sō-,ón, -,än\ : and so forth

AND \'and\ n (1949) : a logical operator equivalent to the sentential connective and ⟨~ gate in a computer⟩

an·da·lu·site \,an-də-'lü-,sīt\ n [F andalousite, fr. Andalousie Andalusia, region in Spain] (ca. 1828) : a mineral Al_2SiO_5 consisting of a silicate of aluminum usu. in thick orthorhombic prisms of various colors

¹**an·dan·te** \än-'dän-(,)tā, -'dänt-ē; an-'dant-ē\ adv or adj [It, lit., going, prp. of andare to go] (1724) : moderately slow — used as a direction in music

²**andante** n (1784) : a musical composition or movement in andante tempo

¹**an·dan·ti·no** \,än-,dän-'tē-(,)nō\ adv or adj [It, dim. of andante] (1819) : slightly faster than andante — used as a direction in music

²**andantino** n, pl **-nos** (1845) : a musical composition or movement in andantino tempo

an·des·ite \'an-di-,zīt\ n [G andesit, fr. Andes] (1850) : an extrusive usu. dark grayish rock consisting essentially of oligoclase or feldspar — **an·des·it·ic** \,an-di-'zit-ik\ adj

and·iron \'an-,di(-ə)rn\ n [ME aundiren, modif. of MF andier] (14c) : one of a pair of metal supports for firewood used on a hearth and made of a horizontal bar mounted on short legs with usu. a vertical shaft surmounting the front end

and/or \'an-'dó(ə)r\ conj (1853) — used as a function word to indicate that two words or expressions are to be taken together or individually ⟨punishable by a fine and/or a term in jail⟩

an·douille \än-'dü-ē, ,än-dü-'ē\ n [F, prob. fr. ML inductilia sausage, deriv. of L inducere to insert, bring in — more at INDUCE] (1605) : a highly spiced smoked pork sausage

andr- or **andro-** comb form [MF, fr. L, fr. Gk, fr. andr-, anēr man (male); akin to Oscan ner man, Skt nr, OIr nert strength] 1 : man ⟨androphobia⟩ 2 : male ⟨androecium⟩

an·dra·dite \an-'dräd-,īt, 'an-drə-,dīt\ n [José B. de Andrada e Silva †1838 Brazilian geologist] (1868) : a garnet $Ca_3Fe_2(SiO_4)_3$ of any of various colors ranging from yellow and green to brown and black

An·dro·cles \'an-drə-,klēz\ n [L, fr. Gk Androklēs] : a fabled Roman slave spared in the arena by a lion from whose foot he had years before extracted a thorn

an·droe·ci·um \an-'drē-s(h)ē-əm\ n, pl **-cia** \-s(h)ē-ə\ [NL, fr. andr- + Gk oikion, dim. of oikos house — more at VICINITY] (ca. 1839) : the aggregate of microsporophylls in the flower of a seed plant

an·dro·gen \'an-drə-jən\ n [ISV] (1936) : a male sex hormone (as testosterone) — **an·dro·gen·ic** \,an-drə-'jen-ik\ adj

an·dro·gen·e·sis \,an-drō-'jen-ə-səs\ n (ca. 1900) : development in which the embryo contains only paternal chromosomes due to failure of the egg to participate in fertilization — **an·dro·ge·net·ic** \-jə-'net-ik\ adj

an·dro·gyne \'an-drə-,jīn\ n [MF, fr. L androgynus] (1552) : one that is androgynous

an·drog·y·nous \an-'dräj-ə-nəs\ adj [L androgynus hermaphrodite, fr. Gk androgynos, fr. andr- + gynē woman — more at QUEEN] (1651) 1 : having the characteristics or nature of both male and female 2 a : neither specifically feminine or masculine ⟨the ~ pronoun them⟩ b : suitable to or for either sex ⟨~ clothing⟩ 3 : having traditional male and female roles obscured or reversed ⟨an ~ marriage⟩ — **an·drog·y·ny** \-nē\ n

an·droid \'an-,dróid\ n [LGk androeidēs manlike, fr. Gk andr- + -oeidēs -oid] (1727) : an automaton with a human form

An·drom·a·che \an-'dräm-ə-(,)kē\ n [L, fr. Gk Andromachē] : the wife of Hector

An·drom·e·da \an-'dräm-əd-ə\ n [L, fr. Gk Andromedē] 1 : a mythological Ethiopian princess rescued from a monster by her future husband Perseus 2 [L (gen. Andromedae)] : a northern constellation directly south of Cassiopeia between Pegasus and Perseus

an·dros·ter·one \an-'dräs-tə-,rōn\ n [ISV andr- + sterol + -one] (1934) : an androgenic hormone that is a hydroxy ketone $C_{19}H_{30}O_2$ found in human male and female urine

-an·drous \an-drəs\ adj comb form [NL -andrus, fr. Gk -andros having (such or so many) men, fr. andr-, anēr] : having (such or so many) stamens ⟨monandrous⟩

ane \'ān\ adj or n or pron, chiefly Scot (bef. 12c) : ONE

-ane \,ān\ n suffix [ISV -an, -ane, alter. of -ene, -ine, & -one] 1 : ³,¹AN 1 ⟨tolane⟩ 2 : saturated or completely hydrogenated carbon compound (as a hydrocarbon) ⟨methane⟩

an·ec·dot·age \'an-ik-,dōt-ij\ n (1823) : the telling of anecdotes; also : ANECDOTES

an·ec·dot·al \,an-ik-'dōt-ᵊl\ adj (1836) 1 : relating to, characteristic of, or containing anecdotes 2 : having the form or style of anecdotes 3 : depicting an anecdote ⟨~ art⟩ — **an·ec·dot·al·ly** \-ᵊl-ē\ adv

an·ec·dot·al·ist \,an-ik-'dōt-ᵊl-əst\ or **an·ec·dot·ist** \,an-ik-,dōt-əst\ n (1837) : one who is given to or is skilled in telling anecdotes

an·ec·dote \'an-ik-,dōt\ n [F, fr. Gk anekdota unpublished items, fr. neut. pl. of anekdotos unpublished, fr. a- + ekdidonai to publish, fr. ex out + didonai to give — more at EX-, DATE] (1721) : a usu. short narrative of an interesting, amusing, or biographical incident

an·ec·dot·ic \,an-ik-'dät-ik\ or **an·ec·dot·i·cal** \-'dät-i-kəl\ adj (1786) 1 : ANECDOTAL 2 : given to or skilled in telling anecdotes — **an·ec·dot·i·cal·ly** \-'dät-i-k(ə-)lē\ adv

an·echo·ic \,an-i-'kō-ik\ adj (1946) : free from echoes and reverberations ⟨an ~ chamber⟩

an·elas·tic \ˌan-ᵊl-ˈas-tik\ *adj* (1947) **:** relating to the property of a substance in which there is no definite relation between stress and strain — **an·elas·tic·i·ty** \-ᵊl-ˌas-ˈtis-ət-ē, -ˈtis-tē\ *n*

anem- *or* **anemo-** *comb form* [prob. fr. F *anémo-*, fr. Gk *anem-*, *anemo-*, fr. *anemos* — more at ANIMATE] **:** wind ⟨*anemo*meter⟩

ane·mia \ə-ˈnē-mē-ə\ *n* [NL, fr. Gk *anaimia* bloodlessness, fr. *a-* + *-aimia* -emia] (1807) **1 a :** a condition in which the blood is deficient in red blood cells, in hemoglobin, or in total volume **b :** ISCHEMIA **2 :** lack of vitality — **ane·mic** \ə-ˈnē-mik\ *adj* — **ane·mi·cal·ly** \-mi-k(ə-)lē\ *adv*

anemo·graph \ə-ˈnem-ə-ˌgraf\ *n* (1865) **:** a recording anemometer

an·e·mom·e·ter \ˌan-ə-ˈmäm-ət-ər\ *n* (ca. 1727) **:** an instrument for measuring and indicating the force or speed of the wind

an·e·mom·e·try \ˌan-ə-ˈmäm-ə-trē\ *n* (ca. 1847) **:** the act or process of ascertaining the force, speed, and direction of wind

anem·o·ne \ə-ˈnem-ə-nē\ *n* [L, fr. Gk *anemōnē*] (1548) **1 :** any of a large genus (*Anemone*) of the buttercup family having lobed or divided leaves and showy flowers without petals but with conspicuous often colored sepals **2 :** SEA ANEMONE

an·e·moph·i·lous \ˌan-ə-ˈmäf-ə-ləs\ *adj* (1874) **:** normally wind-pollinated

an·en·ceph·a·ly \ˌan-(ˌ)en-ˈsef-ə-lē\ *n, pl* **-lies** (ca. 1889) **:** congenital absence of all or a major part of the brain — **an·en·ce·phal·ic** \-ˌen(t)-sə-ˈfal-ik\ *adj*

anent \ə-ˈnent\ *prep* [ME *onevent, anent,* fr. OE *on efen* alongside, fr. *on* + *efen* even] (12c) **:** ABOUT, CONCERNING

an·er·oid \ˈan-ə-ˌrȯid\ *adj* [F *anéroïde,* fr. Gk *a-* + LGk *nēron* water, fr. Gk, neut. of *nearos, nēros* fresh; akin to Gk *neos* new — more at NEW] (1848) **:** containing no liquid or actuated without the use of liquid

aneroid barometer *n* (1849) **:** a barometer in which the action of atmospheric pressure in bending a metallic surface is made to move a pointer

an·es·the·sia \ˌan-əs-ˈthē-zhə\ *n* [NL, fr. Gk *anaisthēsia* insensibility, fr. *a-* + *aisthēsis* perception, fr. *aisthanesthai* to perceive — more at AUDIBLE] (ca. 1721) **:** loss of sensation with or without loss of consciousness

an·es·the·si·ol·o·gist \-ˌthē-zē-ˈäl-ə-jəst\ *n* (1942) **:** ANESTHETIST; *specif* **:** a physician specializing in anesthesiology

an·es·the·si·ol·o·gy \-jē\ *n* (ca. 1914) **:** a branch of medical science dealing with anesthesia and anesthetics

[1]**an·es·thet·ic** \ˌan-əs-ˈthet-ik\ *adj* (1846) **1 :** of, relating to, or capable of producing anesthesia **2 :** lacking awareness or sensitivity ⟨unmoved and quite ~ to his presence —S. J. Perelman⟩ — **an·es·thet·i·cal·ly** \-i-k(ə-)lē\ *adv*

[2]**anesthetic** *n* (1848) **1 :** a substance that produces anesthesia **2 :** something that brings relief **:** PALLIATIVE

anes·the·tist \ə-ˈnes-thət-əst, *Brit* -ˈnēs-\ *n* (1882) **:** one who administers anesthetics

anes·the·tize \-thə-ˌtīz\ *vt* **-tized; -tiz·ing** (1848) **:** to subject to anesthesia

an·es·trous \(ˈ)an-ˈes-trəs\ *adj* (ca. 1909) **1 :** not exhibiting estrus **2 :** of or relating to anestrus

an·es·trus \-trəs\ *n* [NL, fr. *a-* + *estrus*] (1927) **:** the period of sexual quiescence between two periods of sexual activity in cyclically breeding mammals

an·eu·ploid \ˈan-yu̇-ˌplȯid\ *adj* [*an-* + *euploid*] (1926) **:** having or being a chromosome number that is not an exact multiple of the usu. haploid number — compare EUPLOID — **aneuploid** *n* — **an·eu·ploi·dy** \-ˌplȯid-ē\ *n*

an·eu·rysm *also* **an·eu·rism** \ˈan-yə-ˌriz-əm\ *n* [Gk *aneurysma,* fr. *aneurynein* to dilate, fr. *ana-* + *eurynein* to stretch, fr. *eurys* wide — more at EURY-] (15c) **:** a permanent abnormal blood-filled dilatation of a blood vessel resulting from disease of the vessel wall — **an·eu·rys·mal** \ˌan-yə-ˈriz-məl\ *adj*

anew \ə-ˈn(y)ü\ *adv* [ME *of newe,* fr. OE *of nīwe,* fr. *of* + *nīwe* new] (bef. 12c) **1 :** for an additional time **:** AFRESH **2 :** in a new or different form

an·frac·tu·os·i·ty \(ˌ)an-ˌfrak-chə-ˈwäs-ət-ē, -shə-\ *n, pl* **-ties** (1596) **1 :** the quality or state of being anfractuous **2 :** a winding channel or course; *esp* **:** an intricate path or process (as of the mind)

an·frac·tu·ous \an-ˈfrak-chə-wəs, -shə-\ *adj* [F *anfractueux,* fr. LL *anfractuosus,* fr. L *anfractus* coil, bend, fr. *anfractus* crooked, fr. *an-* (fr. *ambi-* around) + *fractus,* pp. of *frangere* to break — more at AMBI-, BREAK] (1621) **:** full of windings and intricate turnings **:** TORTUOUS

an·ga·ry \ˈaŋ-gə-rē\ *n* [LL *angaria* service to a lord, fr. Gk *angareia* compulsory public service, fr. *angaros* Persian courier] (1880) **:** the right in international law of a belligerent to seize, use, or destroy property of neutrals

an·gel \ˈān-jəl\ *n* [ME, fr. OE *engel* & OF *angele;* both fr. LL *angelus,* fr. Gk *angelos,* lit., messenger] (bef. 12c) **1 a :** a spiritual being superior to man in power and intelligence; *specif* **:** one in the lowest rank in the celestial hierarchy **b** *pl* **:** an order of angels —see CELESTIAL HIERARCHY **2 :** an attendant spirit or guardian **3 :** a white-robed winged figure of human form in fine art **4 :** MESSENGER, HARBINGER ⟨~ of death⟩ **5 :** a person believed to resemble an angel **6** *Christian Science* **:** inspiration from God **7 :** one (as a backer of a theatrical venture) who aids or supports with money or influence **8 :** ANGELFISH — **an·gel·ic** \an-ˈjel-ik\ *or* **an·gel·i·cal** \-i-kəl\ *adj* — **an·gel·i·cal·ly** \-i-k(ə-)lē\ *adv*

angel dust *n* (ca. 1968) **:** PHENCYCLIDINE

An·ge·le·no \ˌan-jə-ˈlē-(ˌ)nō\ *n, pl* **-nos** [AmSp *angeleño,* fr. Los *Angeles,* Calif. + Sp *-eño* (suffix denoting residence)] (1888) **:** a native or resident of Los Angeles, Calif.

an·gel·fish \ˈān-jəl-ˌfish\ *n* (1668) **1 :** any of several compressed brightcolored teleost fishes (family Chaetodontidae) of warm seas **2 :** SCALARE

angel food cake *n* (1920) **:** a usu. white sponge cake made of flour, sugar, and whites of eggs

an·gel·i·ca \an-ˈjel-i-kə\ *n* [NL, genus name, fr. ML, fr. LL, fem. of *angelicus* angelic, fr. LGk *angelikos,* fr. Gk, of a messenger, fr. *angelos*] (1527) **1 a :** any of a genus (*Angelica*) of herbs of the carrot family; *esp* **:** a biennial (*A. archangelica*) whose roots and fruit furnish a flavoring oil **b :** a confection prepared from angelica **2** *cap* **:** a sweet fortified wine produced in California

angelica tree *n* (1785) **:** HERCULES'-CLUB 1

an·ge·lol·o·gy \ˌān-jə-ˈläl-ə-jē\ *n* (ca. 1828) **:** a belief in or doctrine of angels

An·ge·lus \ˈan-jə-ləs\ *n* [ML, fr. LL, angel; fr. the first word of the opening versicle] (1658) **1 :** a devotion of the Western church that commemorates the Incarnation and is said in the morning, at noon, and in the evening **2 :** a bell announcing the time for the Angelus

[1]**an·ger** \ˈaŋ-gər\ *n* [ME, affliction, anger, fr. ON *angr* grief; akin to OE *enge* narrow, L *angere* to strangle, Gk *anchein*] (13c) **1 :** a strong feeling of displeasure and usu. of antagonism **2 :** RAGE 2 — **an·ger·less** \-ləs\ *adj*

syn ANGER, IRE, RAGE, FURY, INDIGNATION, WRATH mean an intense emotional state induced by displeasure. ANGER, the most general term, names the reaction but in itself conveys nothing about intensity or justification or manifestation of the emotional state ⟨tried to hide his *anger*⟩ ⟨Moses' *anger* waxed hot —Exod 32:19 (AV)⟩ IRE, more frequent in literary contexts, may suggest greater intensity than *anger,* often with an evident display of feeling ⟨cheeks flushed dark with *ire*⟩ RAGE suggests loss of self-control from violence of emotion ⟨screaming with *rage*⟩ FURY is overmastering destructive rage verging on madness ⟨in his *fury* made sudden decisions which would prove utterly disastrous —W. L. Shirer⟩ INDIGNATION stresses righteous anger at what one considers unfair, mean, or shameful ⟨behavior that caused general *indignation*⟩ WRATH is likely to suggest a desire or intent to revenge or punish ⟨rose in his *wrath* and struck his tormentor to the floor⟩

[2]**anger** *vb* **an·gered; an·ger·ing** \-g(ə-)riŋ\ *vt* (13c) **:** to make angry ~ *vi* **:** to become angry

An·ge·vin \ˈan-jə-vən\ *adj* [F, fr. OF, fr. ML *andegavinus,* fr. *Andegavia* Anjou] (1769) **:** of, relating to, or characteristic of Anjou or the Plantagenets — **Angevin** *n*

angi- *or* **angio-** *comb form* [NL, fr. Gk *angei-, angeio-,* fr. *angeion* vessel, blood vessel, dim. of *angos* vessel] **1 :** blood or lymph vessel **:** blood vessels and ⟨*angi*oma⟩ ⟨*angio*cardiography⟩ **2 :** pericarp ⟨*angio*sperm⟩

an·gi·na \an-ˈjī-nə, ˈan-jə-\ *n* [L, quinsy, fr. *angere*] (1578) **:** a disease marked by spasmodic attacks of intense suffocative pain: as **a :** a severe inflammatory or ulcerated condition of the mouth or throat **b :** ANGINA PECTORIS — **an·gi·nal** \an-ˈjīn-ᵊl, ˈan-jən-\ *adj*

angina pec·to·ris \-ˈpek-t(ə-)rəs\ *n* [NL, lit., angina of the chest] (1744) **:** a disease marked by brief paroxysmal attacks of chest pain precipitated by deficient oxygenation of the heart muscles

an·gio·car·di·og·ra·phy \ˈan-jē-ō-ˌkärd-ē-ˈäg-rə-fē\ *n* (1938) **:** the roentgenographic visualization of the heart and its blood vessels after injection of a radiopaque substance — **an·gio·car·dio·graph·ic** \-ē-ə-ˈgraf-ik\ *adj*

an·gio·gram \ˈan-jē-ə-ˌgram\ *n* (1933) **:** a roentgenogram made by angiography

an·gi·og·ra·phy \ˌan-jē-ˈäg-rə-fē\ *n* (1933) **:** the roentgenographic visualization of the blood vessels after injection of a radiopaque substance — **an·gio·graph·ic** \ˌan-jē-ə-ˈgraf-ik\ *adj*

an·gi·ol·o·gy \ˌan-jē-ˈäl-ə-jē\ *n* (ca. 1706) **:** the study of blood vessels and lymphatics

an·gi·o·ma \ˌan-jē-ˈō-mə\ *n* (1871) **:** a tumor composed chiefly of blood vessels or lymph vessels — **an·gi·o·ma·tous** \-mət-əs\ *adj*

an·gio·sperm \ˈan-jē-ə-ˌspərm\ *n* [deriv. of NL *angi-* + Gk *sperma* seed — more at SPERM] (ca. 1828) **:** any of a class (Angiospermae) of vascular plants (as orchids or roses) having the seeds in a closed ovary — **an·gio·sper·mous** \ˌan-jē-ə-ˈspər-məs\ *adj*

an·gio·ten·sin \ˌan-jē-ō-ˈten(t)-sən\ *n* [*angi-* + hyper*tension* + *-in*] (ca. 1961) **:** either of two forms of a kinin of which one has marked vasoconstrictive action; *also* **:** a synthetic amide derivative of the physiologically active form used to treat some forms of hypotension

an·gio·ten·sin·ase \-sə-ˌnās, -ˌnāz\ *n* (ca. 1961) **:** any of several enzymes in the blood that hydrolyze angiotensin

[1]**an·gle** \ˈaŋ-gəl\ *n* [ME, fr. MF, fr. L *angulus;* akin to OE *anclēow* ankle] (14c) **1 :** a corner whether constituting a projecting part or a partially enclosed space ⟨they sheltered in an ~ of the building⟩ **2 a :** the figure formed by two lines extending from the same point; *also* **:** DIHEDRAL ANGLE **b :** a measure of an angle or of the amount of turning necessary to bring one line or plane into coincidence with or parallel to another **3 a :** the precise viewpoint from which something is observed or considered; *also* **:** the aspect seen from such an angle **b (1) :** a special approach, point of attack, or technique for accomplishing an objective **(2) :** an often improper or illicit method of obtaining advantage ⟨he always had an ~ to beat the other fellow⟩ **4 :** a sharply divergent course ⟨the road went off at an ~⟩ **5 :** a position to the side of an opponent in football from which a player may block his opponent more effectively or without penalty — usu. used in the phrases *get an angle* or *have an angle* — **an·gled** \-gəld\ *adj*

[2]**angle** *vb* **an·gled; an·gling** \-g(ə-)liŋ\ *vt* (14c) **1 :** to turn, move, or direct at an angle **2 :** to present (as a news story) from a particular or prejudiced point of view **:** SLANT ~ *vi* **:** to turn or proceed at an angle

[3]**angle** *vi* **an·gled; an·gling** \-g(ə-)liŋ\ [ME *angelen,* fr. *angel* fishhook, fr. OE, fr. *anga* hook; akin to OHG *ango* hook, L *uncus,* Gk *onkos* barbed hook, *ankos* glen] (15c) **1 :** to fish with a hook **2 :** to use artful means to attain an objective ⟨*angled* for an invitation⟩

angle bracket *n* (ca. 1956) **:** BRACKET 3b

angle iron *n* (ca. 1853) **1 :** an iron cleat for joining parts of a structure at an angle **2 :** a piece of structural steel rolled with an L-shaped section

angle of attack (ca. 1908) **:** the acute angle between the direction of the relative wind and the chord of an airfoil

angle of depression (1790) **:** the angle formed by the line of sight and the horizontal plane for an object below the horizontal

angle of elevation (1790) **:** the angle formed by the line of sight and the horizontal plane for an object above the horizontal

angle of incidence (1628) **:** the angle that a line (as a ray of light) falling on a surface makes with a perpendicular to the surface at the point of incidence

\ə\ abut \ᵊ\ kitten, F table \ər\ further \a\ ash \ā\ ace \ä\ cot, cart \au̇\ out \ch\ chin \e\ bet \ē\ easy \g\ go \i\ hit \ī\ ice \j\ job \ŋ\ sing \ō\ go \ȯ\ law \ȯi\ boy \th\ thin \th̲\ the \ü\ loot \u̇\ foot \y\ yet \zh\ vision \à, k̲, ⁿ, œ, œ̄, ue, ue̅, ʸ\ *see* Guide to Pronunciation

angle of reflection (1638) : the angle between a reflected ray and the normal drawn at the point of incidence to a reflecting surface

angle of refraction (ca. 1737) : the angle between a refracted ray and the normal drawn at the point of incidence to the interface at which refraction occurs

an·gler \'aŋ-glər\ *n* (15c) **1** : one that angles **2** : ANGLERFISH

an·gler·fish \-,fish\ *n* (ca. 1889) : any of several pediculate fishes; *esp* : one (*Lophius piscatorius*) having a large flattened head and wide mouth with a lure on the head and fleshy mouth appendages used to attract smaller fishes as prey

An·gles \'aŋ-gəlz\ *n pl* [L *Angli*, of Gmc origin; akin to OE *Engle* Angles] (bef. 12c) : a Germanic people that invaded England along with the Saxons and Jutes in the 5th century A.D. and merged with them to form the Anglo-Saxon peoples

angle shot *n* (1937) : a picture taken with the camera pointed at an angle from the horizontal

an·gle·site \'aŋ-gəl-,sīt, -glə-\ *n* [F *anglésite*, fr. *Anglesey* island, Wales] (1837) : a mineral $PbSO_4$ consisting of lead sulfate formed by the oxidation of galena

an·gle·worm \'aŋ-gəl-,wərm\ *n* (1832) : EARTHWORM

An·gli·an \'aŋ-glē-ən\ *n* (1726) **1** : a member of the Angles **2** : the Old English dialects of Mercia and Northumbria — **Anglian** *adj*

An·gli·can \'aŋ-gli-kən\ *adj* [ML *anglicanus*, fr. *anglicus* English, fr. LL *Angli* English people, fr. L, Angles] (1635) **1** : of or relating to the established episcopal Church of England and churches of similar faith and order in communion with it **2** : of or relating to England or the English nation — **Anglican** *n* — **An·gli·can·ism** \-kə-,niz-əm\ *n*

an·gli·ce \'aŋ-glə-(,)sē\ *adv, often cap* [ML, adv. of *anglicus*] (1602) : in English; *esp* : in readily understood English ⟨the city of Napoli, ~ Naples⟩

an·gli·cism \'aŋ-glə-,siz-əm\ *n, often cap* [ML *anglicus* English] (1642) **1** : a characteristic feature of English occurring in another language **2** : adherence or attachment to English customs or ideas

An·gli·cist \'aŋ-glə-səst\ *n* (1930) : a specialist in English linguistics

an·gli·cize \'aŋ-glə-,sīz\ *vt* **-cized**; **-ciz·ing** *often cap* (1710) **1** : to make English in quality or characteristics **2** : to adapt (a foreign word or phrase) to English usage; *esp* : to borrow into English without alteration of form or spelling and with or without change in pronunciation — **an·gli·ci·za·tion** \,aŋ-glə-sə-'zā-shən\ *n, often cap*

an·gling \'aŋ-gliŋ\ *n* (15c) : the act of one who angles; *esp* : the act or sport of fishing with hook and line

An·glist \'aŋ-gləst\ *n* (1888) : ANGLICIST

An·glo \'aŋ-(,)glō\ *n, pl* **Anglos** [in sense 2, fr. MexSp, fr. Sp *anglo-americano* Anglo-American] (1800) **1** : ANGLO-AMERICAN **2** : a Caucasian inhabitant of the U.S. of non-Latin extraction — **Anglo** *adj*

An·glo- *comb form* [NL, fr. LL *Angli*] **1** \'aŋ-(,)glō, -glə\ : English ⟨*Anglo*-Norman⟩ **2** \-(,)glō\ : English and ⟨*Anglo*-Japanese⟩

An·glo–Amer·i·can \,aŋ-glō-ə-'mer-ə-kən\ *n* (1781) **1** : a North American whose native language is English and whose culture is of English origin **2** : an inhabitant of the U.S. of English origin or descent — **Anglo–American** *adj*

An·glo–Cath·o·lic \-'kath-(ə-)lik\ *adj* (1838) : of or relating to a High Church movement in Anglicanism emphasizing its continuity with historic Catholicism and fostering Catholic dogmatic and liturgical traditions — **Anglo–Catholic** *n* — **An·glo–Cathol·i·cism** \-kə-'thäl-ə-,siz-əm\ *n*

An·glo–French \-'french\ *n* (ca. 1885) : the French language used in medieval England

An·glo·ma·nia \-'mā-nē-ə, -nyə\ *n* (1787) : an absorbing or pervasive interest in England or things English

An·glo–Nor·man \-'nȯr-mən\ *n* (1811) **1** : one of the Normans living in England after the Conquest **2** : the form of Anglo-French used by Anglo-Normans

An·glo·phile \'aŋ-glə-,fīl\ *also* **An·glo·phil** \-,fil\ *n* [F, fr. *anglo-* + *-phile*] (1883) : one who greatly admires or favors England and things English — **Anglophile** *or* **An·glo·phil·ic** \,aŋ-glə-'fil-ik\ *adj*

An·glo·phil·ia \,aŋ-glə-'fil-ē-ə\ *n* (1896) : unusual admiration or partiality for England, English ways, or things English — **An·glo·phil·i·ac** \-ē-,ak\ *adj*

An·glo·phobe \'aŋ-glə-,fōb\ *n* [prob. fr. F, fr. *anglo-* + *-phobe*] (1866) : one who is averse to or dislikes England and things English — **An·glo·pho·bia** \,aŋ-glə-'fō-bē-ə\ *n* — **An·glo·pho·bic** \-bik\ *adj*

an·glo·phone \'aŋ-glə-,fōn\ *adj, often cap* (1971) : consisting of or belonging to an English-speaking population — **Anglophone** *n*

An·glo–Sax·on \,aŋ-glō-'sak-sən\ *n* [NL *Anglo-Saxones*, pl., alter. of ML *Angli Saxones*, fr. L *Angli* Angles + LL *Saxones* Saxons] (bef. 12c) **1** : a member of the Germanic peoples conquering England in the 5th century A.D. and forming the ruling class until the Norman conquest — compare ANGLES, JUTE, SAXON **2** **a** : ENGLISHMAN; *specif* : a person descended from the Anglo-Saxons **b** : a white gentile of an English-speaking nation **3** : OLD ENGLISH 1 **4** : direct plain English; *esp* : English using words considered crude or vulgar — **Anglo–Saxon** *adj*

an·go·ra \aŋ-'gōr-ə, an-, -'gȯr-\ *n* (1839) **1** : the hair of the Angora rabbit or Angora goat — called also *angora wool* **2** : a yarn of Angora rabbit hair used esp. for knitting **3** *cap* **a** : ANGORA CAT **b** : ANGORA GOAT **c** : ANGORA RABBIT

Angora cat *n* [*Angora* (Ankara), Turkey] (1819) : a long-haired domestic cat; *specif* : any of a breed that differs from the Persian in having a narrower head and slighter body

Angora goat *n* (1833) : any of a breed or variety of the domestic goat raised for its long silky hair which is the true mohair

Angora rabbit *n* (1849) : any of a breed of long-haired usu. white rabbits with red eyes that is raised for fine wool

an·gos·tu·ra bark \,aŋ-gə-'st(y)u̇r-ə-\ *n* [*Angostura* (now Ciudad Bolivar), Venezuela] (1791) : the aromatic bitter bark of either of two So. American trees (*Galipea officinalis* and *Cusparia trifoliata*) of the rue family that is used as a tonic and antipyretic

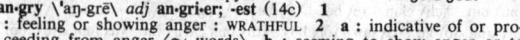

Angora goat

an·gry \'aŋ-grē\ *adj* **an·gri·er**; **-est** (14c) **1** : feeling or showing anger : WRATHFUL **2** **a** : indicative of or proceeding from anger ⟨~ words⟩ **b** : seeming to show anger or to threaten in an angry manner ⟨an ~ sky⟩ **3** : painfully inflamed ⟨an ~ rash⟩ — **an·gri·ly** \-grə-lē\ *adv* — **an·gri·ness** \-grē-nəs\ *n*

angry young man *n* (1941) **1** : an outspoken critic of or protester against an economic condition or social injustice **2** : one of a group of mid-20th century British authors whose works express the bitterness of the lower classes toward the established sociopolitical system and toward the mediocrity and hypocrisy of the middle and upper classes

angst \'äŋ(k)st, 'aŋ(k)st\ *n* [Dan & G; Dan, fr. G; akin to L *angustus*] (ca. 1942) : a feeling of anxiety, apprehension, or insecurity

ang·strom \'aŋ-strəm *also* 'ȯŋ-\ *n* [Anders J. *Ångström*] (1897) : a unit of length equal to one ten-billionth of a meter — used esp. for wavelengths of light

[1]**an·guish** \'aŋ-gwish\ *n* [ME *angwisshe*, fr. OF *angoisse*, fr. L *angustiae*, pl., straits, distress fr. *angustus* narrow; akin to OE *enge* narrow — more at ANGER] (13c) : extreme pain, distress, or anxiety ***syn*** see SORROW

[2]**anguish** *vi* (14c) : to suffer anguish ~ *vt* : to cause to suffer anguish

an·guished *adj* (14c) **1** : suffering anguish : TORMENTED ⟨the ~ martyrs⟩ **2** : expressing anguish : AGONIZED ⟨~ cries⟩

an·gu·lar \'aŋ-gyə-lər\ *adj* [MF or L; MF *angulaire*, fr. L *angularis*, fr. *angulus* angle] (15c) **1** **a** : having one or more angles **b** : forming an angle : sharp-cornered **2** : measured by an angle ⟨~ distance⟩ **3** **a** : stiff in character or manner : lacking smoothness or grace **b** : lean and having prominent bone structure — **an·gu·lar·ly** *adv*

an·gu·lar·i·ty \,aŋ-gyə-'lar-ət-ē\ *n, pl* **-ties** (1642) **1** : the quality of being angular **2** *pl* : angular outlines or characteristics

angular momentum *n* (1870) : a vector quantity that is the measure of the intensity of rotational motion, that is equal in classical physics to the product of the angular velocity of a rotating body or system and its moment of inertia with respect to the rotation axis, and that is directed along the rotation axis

angular velocity *n* (1819) : the time rate of change of angular displacement

an·gu·la·tion \,aŋ-gyə-'lā-shən\ *n* (1869) **1** : the action of making angular **2** : an angular position, formation, or shape

An·gus \'aŋ-gəs\ *n* [*Angus*, county in Scotland] (1842) : ABERDEEN ANGUS

an·hin·ga \an-'hiŋ-gə\ *n* [Pg, fr. Tupi] (1769) : any of a genus (*Anhinga*) of fish-eating birds related to the cormorants but distinguished by a long slender neck and sharp pointed bill; *esp* : one (*A. anhinga*) occurring from the southern U.S. to northern Argentina

an·hy·dride \(')an-'hī-,drīd\ *n* (1863) : a compound derived from another (as an acid) by removal of the elements of water

an·hy·drite \-,drīt\ *n* [G *anhydrit*, fr. Gk *anydros*] (ca. 1823) : a mineral $CaSO_4$ consisting of an anhydrous calcium sulfate that is usu. massive and white or slightly colored

an·hy·drous \-drəs\ *adj* [Gk *anydros*, fr. *a-* + *hydōr* water — more at WATER] (1819) : free from water and esp. water of crystallization

ani \ä-'nē\ *n* [Sp *aní*, or Pg *ani*, fr. Tupi *ani*] (ca. 1823) : any of several black cuckoos (genus *Crotophaga*) of the warmer parts of America

anile \'an-,īl, 'ā-,nīl\ *adj* [L *anilis*, fr. *anus* old woman] (1652) : of or resembling a doddering old woman; *esp* : SENILE — **anil·i·ty** \a-'nil-ət-ē, ā-, ə-\ *n*

an·i·line \'an-ᵊl-ən\ *n* [G *anilin*, fr. *anil* indigo, fr. F, fr. Pg, fr. Ar *an-nīl* the indigo plant, fr. Skt *nīlī* indigo, fr. fem. of *nīla* dark blue] (1850) : an oily liquid poisonous amine $C_6H_5NH_2$ obtained esp. by the reduction of nitrobenzene and used chiefly in organic synthesis (as of dyes)

aniline dye *n* (1864) : a dye made by the use of aniline or one chemically related to such a dye; *broadly* : a synthetic organic dye

ani·lin·gus \,ā-ni-'liŋ-gəs\ *or* **ani·linc·tus** \-'liŋ(k)-təs\ *n* [NL, fr. *anus* + *-i-* + *-lingus*, *-linctus* (as in *cunnilingus*, *cunnilinctus*)] (1949) : erotic stimulation achieved by contact between mouth and anus

an·i·ma \'an-ə-mə\ *n* [NL, fr. L, soul] (1923) : an individual's true inner self that in the analytic psychology of C. G. Jung reflects archetypal ideals of conduct; *also* : an inner feminine part of the male personality — compare ANIMUS 3, PERSONA 2

an·i·mad·ver·sion \,an-ə-,mad-'vər-zhən, -məd-, -'vər-shən\ *n* [L *animadversion-*, *animadversio*, fr. *animadversus*, pp. of *animadvertere*] (1599) **1** : a critical and usu. censorious remark — often used with *on* **2** : adverse criticism

an·i·mad·vert \-'vərt\ *vb* [L *animadvertere* to pay attention to, censure, fr. *animum advertere*, lit., to turn the mind to] *vt, archaic* (15c) : NOTICE, OBSERVE ~ *vi* : to make an animadversion

[1]**an·i·mal** \'an-ə-məl\ *n* [L, fr. *animale*, neut. of *animalis* animate, fr. *anima* soul — more at ANIMATE] (14c) **1** : any of a kingdom (Animalia) of living beings typically differing from plants in capacity for spontaneous movement and rapid motor response to stimulation **2** **a** : one of the lower animals as distinguished from human beings **b** : MAMMAL **3** : a human being considered chiefly with regard to his physical or nonrational nature; *also* : this nature **4** : an individual with a particular interest or aptitude ⟨a political ~⟩ **5** : MATTER, THING ⟨the theater . . . is an entirely different ~ —Arthur Miller⟩ — **an·i·mal·like** \-məl-(l)īk\ *adj* — **an·i·mal·ness** \-məl-nəs\ *n*

[2]**animal** *adj* (1615) **1** : of, relating to, or derived from animals **2** **a** : of or relating to the physical or sentient as contrasted with the intellectual or rational **b** : SENSUAL, FLESHLY **3** : of or relating to the animal pole of an egg or to the part from which ectoderm normally develops ***syn*** see CARNAL — **an·i·mal·ly** \-mə-lē\ *adv*

animal control *n* (1957) : an office or department responsible for enforcing ordinances relating to the control, impoundment, and disposition of animals

animal cracker *n* (1898) : a small animal-shaped cookie

an·i·mal·cule \,an-ə-'mal-(,)kyü(ə)l\ *also* **an·i·mal·cu·lum** \-'mal-kyə-ləm\ *n, pl* **-cules** *also* **-cu·la** \-kyə-lə\ [NL *animalculum*, dim. of L *animal*] (1599) : a minute usu. microscopic organism

animal heat *n* (1779) : heat produced in the body of a living animal by functional chemical and physical activities

animal husbandry *n* (1919) : a branch of agriculture concerned with the production and care of domestic animals

an·i·mal·ism \'an-ə-mə-,liz-əm\ *n* (1831) : ANIMALITY 1, 2 — **an·i·mal·is·tic** \,an-ə-mə-'lis-tik\ *adj*

an·i·mal·i·ty \,an-ə-'mal-ət-ē\ *n* (1615) **1** : qualities associated with animals: **a** : VITALITY **b** : a natural unrestrained unreasoned response to physical drives or stimuli **2** : the animal nature of human beings

an·i·mal·ize \'an-ə-mə-ˌlīz\ *vt* **-ized; -iz·ing** (1741) **1 :** to represent in animal form **2 :** to cause to be or act like an animal — **an·i·mal·iza·tion** \ˌan-ə-mə-lə-'zā-shən\ *n*
animal kingdom *n* (1847) **:** the one of the three basic groups of natural objects that includes all living and extinct animals — compare MINERAL KINGDOM, PLANT KINGDOM
animal magnetism *n* (1784) **1 :** a mysterious force claimed by Mesmer to enable him to hypnotize patients **2 :** a magnetic charm or appeal; *esp* **:** SEX APPEAL
animal pole *n* (1887) **:** the point on the surface of an egg that is diametrically opposite to the vegetal pole and usu. marks the most active part of the protoplasm or the part containing least yolk
animal spirits *n pl* (15c) **1** *sometimes* **animal spirit** *obs* **:** the nervous energy that is the source of physical sensation and movement **2 :** vivacity arising from physical health and energy
animal starch *n* (ca. 1860) **:** GLYCOGEN
[1]**an·i·mate** \'an-ə-mət\ *adj* [ME, fr. L *animatus,* pp. of *animare* to give life to, fr. *anima* breath, soul; akin to OE *ōthian* to breathe, L *animus* spirit, mind, courage, Gk *anemos* wind] (15c) **1 :** possessing or characterized by life **:** ALIVE **2 :** of or relating to animal life as opposed to plant life **3 :** full of life **:** ANIMATED **4 :** referring to a living thing ⟨an ~ noun⟩ — **an·i·mate·ly** *adv* — **an·i·mate·ness** *n*
[2]**an·i·mate** \-ˌmāt\ *vt* **-mat·ed; -mat·ing** (1538) **1 :** to give spirit and support to **:** ENCOURAGE **2 a :** to give life to **b :** to give vigor and zest to **3 :** to move to action **4 a :** to make or design in such a way as to create apparently spontaneous lifelike movement **b :** to produce in the form of an animated cartoon ***syn*** see QUICKEN
an·i·mat·ed \-ˌmāt-əd\ *adj* (1534) **1 a :** endowed with life or the qualities of life **:** ALIVE ⟨viruses that can behave as ~ bodies or inert crystals⟩ **b :** full of movement and activity **c :** full of vigor and spirit **:** LIVELY ⟨an ~ discussion⟩ **2 :** having the appearance of something alive **3 :** made in the form of an animated cartoon ***syn*** see LIVELY — **an·i·mat·ed·ly** *adv*
animated cartoon *n* (1915) **1 :** a motion picture made from a series of drawings simulating motion by means of slight progressive changes in the drawings **2 :** ANIMATION 2a
an·i·ma·tion \ˌan-ə-'mā-shən\ *n* (1597) **1 :** the act of animating **:** the state of being animate or animated **2 a :** a motion picture made by photographing successive positions of inanimate objects (as puppets or mechanical parts) **b :** ANIMATED CARTOON 1 **3 :** the preparation of animated cartoons
an·i·ma·to \ˌän-ə-'mät-(ˌ)ō, ˌan-\ *adv or adj* [It, fr. L *animatus*] (ca. 1724) **:** with animation — used as a direction in music
an·i·ma·tor \'an-ə-ˌmāt-ər\ *n* (1611) **1 :** one that animates ⟨the chief ~ of the movement⟩ **2 :** an artist who creates drawings for an animated cartoon
an·i·mism \'an-ə-ˌmiz-əm\ *n* [G *animismus,* fr. L *anima* soul] (1832) **1 :** a doctrine that the vital principle of organic development is immaterial spirit **2 :** attribution of conscious life to nature or natural objects **3 :** belief in the existence of spirits separable from bodies — **an·i·mist** \-məst\ *n* — **an·i·mis·tic** \ˌan-ə-'mis-tik\ *adj*
an·i·mos·i·ty \ˌan-ə-'mäs-ət-ē\ *n, pl* **-ties** [ME *animosite,* fr. MF or LL; MF *animosité,* fr. LL *animositat-, animositas,* fr. L *animosus* spirited, fr. *animus*] (1605) **:** ill will or resentment tending toward active hostility **:** an antagonistic attitude ***syn*** see ENMITY
an·i·mus \'an-ə-məs\ *n* [L, spirit, mind, courage, anger] (1816) **1 :** basic attitude or governing spirit **:** DISPOSITION, INTENTION **2 :** a usu. prejudiced and often spiteful or malevolent ill will **3 :** an inner masculine part of the female personality in the analytic psychology of C. G. Jung — compare ANIMA ***syn*** see ENMITY
an·ion \'an-ˌī-ən\ *n* [Gk, neut. of *aniōn,* prp. of *anienai* to go up, fr. *ana-* + *ienai* to go — more at ISSUE] (1834) **:** the ion in an electrolyzed solution that migrates to the anode; *broadly* **:** a negatively charged ion
an·ion·ic \ˌan-(ˌ)ī-'än-ik\ *adj* (ca. 1920) **1 :** of or relating to anions **2 :** characterized by an active and esp. surface-active anion — **an·ion·i·cal·ly** \-i-k(ə-)lē\ *adv*
anis- *or* **aniso-** *comb form* [NL, fr. Gk, fr. *anisos,* fr. *a-* + *isos* equal] **:** unequal ⟨*anis*eikonia⟩ ⟨*aniso*dactylous⟩
an·ise \'an-əs\ *n* [ME *anis,* fr. MF, fr. L *anisum,* fr. Gk *annēson, anison*] (14c) **:** an herb (*Pimpinella anisum*) of the carrot family having carminative and aromatic seeds; *also* **:** ANISEED
ani·seed \'an-ə(s)-ˌsēd\ *n* [ME *anis seed,* fr. *anis* + *seed*] (14c) **:** the seed of anise often used as a flavoring in liqueurs and in cooking
an·is·ei·ko·nia \ˌan-ˌī-ˌsī-'kō-nē-ə\ *n* [NL, fr. *anis-* + Gk *eikōn* image — more at ICON] (1934) **:** a defect of binocular vision in which the two retinal images of an object differ in size — **an·is·ei·kon·ic** \-'kän-ik\ *adj*
an·is·ette \ˌan-ə-'set, -'zet\ *n* [F, fr. *anis*] (1837) **:** a usu. colorless sweet liqueur flavored with aniseed
an·isog·a·mous \ˌan-(ˌ)ī-'säg-ə-məs\ *also* **an·iso·gam·ic** \-ˌī-sə-'gam-ik\ *adj* (1891) **:** characterized by fusion of heterogamous gametes or of individuals that usu. differ chiefly in size ⟨~ reproduction⟩ — **an·isog·a·my** \-(ˌ)ī-'säg-ə-mē\ *n*
an·iso·me·tro·pia \ˌan-ˌī-sə-mə-'trō-pē-ə\ *n* [NL, fr. Gk *anisometros* of unequal measure (fr. *anis-* + *metron* measure) + NL *-opia* — more at MEASURE] (ca. 1880) **:** unequal refractive power in the two eyes — **an·iso·me·tro·pic** \-'träp-ik, -'trō-pik\ *adj*
an·iso·trop·ic \ˌan-ˌī-sə-'träp-ik\ *adj* (1879) **1 :** exhibiting properties with different values when measured along axes in different directions ⟨an ~ crystal⟩ **2 :** assuming different positions in response to external stimuli — **an·iso·trop·i·cal·ly** \-i-k(ə-)lē\ *adv* — **an·isot·ro·py** \-(ˌ)ī-'sä-trə-pē\ *or* **an·isot·ro·pism** \-ˌpiz-əm\ *n*
an·ker·ite \'aŋ-kə-ˌrīt\ *n* [G *ankerit,* fr. M. J. Anker †1843 Austrian mineralogist] (ca. 1843) **:** a dolomitic iron-containing mineral $Ca(Fe,Mg,Mn)(CO_3)_2$
ankh \'äŋk\ *n* [Egypt *'nh*] (1888) **:** a cross having a loop for its upper vertical arm and serving esp. in ancient Egypt as an emblem of life

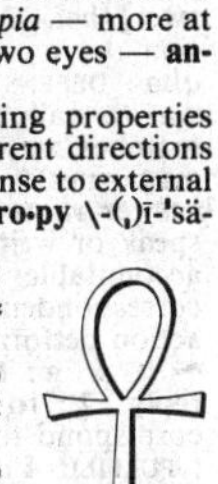
ankh

an·kle \'aŋ-kəl\ *n* [ME *ankel,* fr. OE *anclēow;* akin to OHG *anchlāo* ankle, L *angulus* angle] (bef. 12c) **1 :** the joint between the foot and the leg; *also* **:** the region of this joint **2 :** the joint between the cannon bone and pastern (as in the horse)
an·kle·bone \ˌaŋ-kəl-'bōn, 'aŋ-kəl-ˌ\ *n* (14c) **:** TALUS 1
an·klet \'aŋ-klət\ *n* (1819) **1 :** something (as an ornament) worn around the ankle **2 :** a short sock reaching slightly above the ankle **3 :** a woman's or child's low shoe having one or more ankle straps
an·ky·lose \'aŋ-ki-ˌlōs, -ˌlōz\ *vb* **-losed; -los·ing** [back-formation fr. *ankylosis*] *vt* (1787) **:** to unite or stiffen by ankylosis ~ *vi* **:** to undergo ankylosis
an·ky·lo·sis \ˌaŋ-ki-'lō-səs\ *n, pl* **-lo·ses** \-ˌsēz\ [NL, fr. Gk *ankylōsis,* fr. *ankyloun* to make crooked, fr. *ankylos* crooked — more at ANGLE] (1713) **1 :** stiffness or fixation of a joint by disease or surgery **2 :** union of separate bones or hard parts to form a single bone or part — **an·ky·lot·ic** \-'lät-ik\ *adj*
an·ky·lo·sto·mi·a·sis \ˌaŋ-ki-lō-stə-'mī-ə-səs\ *var of* ANCYLOSTOMIASIS
an·la·ge \'än-ˌläg-ə\ *n, pl* **-gen** \-ən\ *also* **-ges** \-əz\ [G, lit., act of laying on] (1892) **:** the foundation of a subsequent development; *esp* **:** PRIMORDIUM
an·na \'än-ə\ *n* [Hindi *ānā*] (1708) **1 :** a former monetary unit of Burma, India, and Pakistan equal to $^1/_{16}$ rupee **2 :** a coin representing one anna
an·nal·ist \'an-ᵊl-əst\ *n* (ca. 1611) **:** a writer of annals **:** HISTORIAN — **an·nal·is·tic** \ˌan-ᵊl-'is-tik\ *adj*
an·nals \'an-ᵊlz\ *n pl* [L *annales,* fr. pl. of *annalis* yearly — more at ANNUAL] (1542) **1 :** a record of events arranged in yearly sequence **2 :** historical records **:** CHRONICLES **3 :** records of the activities of an organization
An·nam·ese \ˌan-ə-'mēz, -'mēs\ *n, pl* **Annamese** [*Annam,* region of Vietnam] (1826) **1 a :** a Mongolian people inhabiting Vietnam **b** *or* **An·nam·ite** \'an-ə-ˌmīt\ **:** a member of this people **2 :** the language of the Annamese people **:** VIETNAMESE — **Annamese** *adj* — **Annamite** *adj*
an·nat·to \ə-'nät-(ˌ)ō\ *n* [of Cariban origin; akin to Galibi *annoto* tree producing annatto] (1629) **:** a yellowish red dyestuff made from the pulp around the seeds of a tropical tree (*Bixa orellana,* family Bixaceae); *also* **:** the tree that yields annatto
an·neal \ə-'nē(ə)l\ *vb* [ME *anelen,* fr. OE *onǣlan,* fr. *on* + *ǣlan* to set on fire, burn, fr. *āl* fire; akin to OE *ād* funeral pyre — more at EDIFY] *vt* (1580) **1 :** to heat (as glass) in order to fix laid-on colors **2 a :** to heat and then cool (as steel or glass) usu. for softening and making less brittle **b :** to heat and then cool (nucleic acid) in order to separate strands and induce combination at lower temperature esp. with complementary strands of a different species **3 :** STRENGTHEN, TOUGHEN ~ *vi* **:** to be capable of combining with complementary nucleic acid by a process of heating and cooling
an·ne·lid \'an-ᵊl-əd, 'an-ə-ˌlid\ *n* [deriv. of L *anellus* little ring — more at ANNULET] (1834) **:** any of a phylum (Annelida) of coelomate and usu. elongated segmented invertebrates (as earthworms, various marine worms, and leeches) — **annelid** *adj* — **an·nel·i·dan** \ə-'nel-əd-ᵊn, a-\ *adj or n*
[1]**an·nex** \ə-'neks, 'an-ˌeks\ *vt* [ME *annexen,* fr. MF *annexer,* fr. OF, fr. *annexe* joined, fr. L *annexus,* pp. of *annectere* to bind to, fr. *ad-* + *nectere* to bind] (14c) **1 :** to attach as a quality, consequence, or condition **2** *archaic* **:** to join together materially **:** UNITE **3 :** to add to something earlier, larger, or more important **4 :** to incorporate (a country or other territory) within the domain of a state **5 :** to obtain or take for oneself — **an·nex·ation** \ˌan-ˌek-'sā-shən\ *n* — **an·nex·ation·al** \-shnəl, -shən-ᵊl\ *adj* — **an·nex·ation·ist** \-sh(ə-)nəst\ *n*
[2]**an·nex** \'an-ˌeks, -iks\ *n* (1501) **:** something annexed as an expansion or supplement: as **a :** an added stipulation or statement **:** APPENDIX **b :** a subsidiary or supplementary structure **:** WING
an·nexe \'an-ˌeks, -iks\ *chiefly Brit var of* [2]ANNEX
An·nie Oak·ley \ˌan-ē-'ō-klē\ *n, pl* **Annie Oakleys** [*Annie Oakley* †1926 Am. markswoman; fr. the resemblance of a punched pass to a playing card with bullet holes through the spots] (ca. 1910) **:** a free ticket
an·ni·hi·late \ə-'nī-ə-ˌlāt\ *vb* **-lat·ed; -lat·ing** [LL *annihilatus,* pp. of *annihilare* to reduce to nothing, fr. L *ad-* + *nihil* nothing — more at NIL] *vt* (1525) **1 a :** to cause to be of no effect **:** NULLIFY **b :** to destroy the substance or force of **2 :** to regard as of no consequence **3 :** to cause to cease to exist **4 a :** to destroy a considerable part of ⟨the army was *annihilated*⟩ **b :** to vanquish completely **:** ROUT ~ *vi* **:** to cease to exist **:** VANISH — used of a particle and its antiparticle upon coming together and converting into other energy forms (as particles or radiation) — **an·ni·hi·la·tion** \-ˌnī-ə-'lā-shən\ *n* — **an·ni·hi·la·tive** \ə-'nī-ə-ˌlāt-iv\ *adj* — **an·ni·hi·la·tor** \-ˌlāt-ər\ *n* — **an·ni·hi·la·to·ry** \-'nī-ə-lə-ˌtōr-ē, -ˌtȯr-\ *adj*
an·ni·ver·sa·ry \ˌan-ə-'vərs-(ə-)rē\ *n, pl* **-ries** [ME *anniversarie,* fr. ML *anniversarium,* fr. L, neut. of *anniversarius* returning annually, fr. *annus* year + *versus,* pp. of *vertere* to turn — more at ANNUAL] (13c) **1 :** the annual recurrence of a date marking a notable event **2 :** the celebration of an anniversary
an·no Do·mi·ni \ˌan-(ˌ)ō-'däm-ə-nē, -'dō-mə-, -ˌnī\ *adv, often cap A* [ML, in the year of the Lord] (1530) — used to indicate that a time division falls within the Christian era
an·no he·gi·rae \-hi-'jī(ə)r-(ˌ)ē, -'hej-ə-ˌrē\ *adv, often cap A&H* [NL, in the year of the Hegira] (ca. 1889) — used to indicate that a time division falls within the Islamic era
an·no·tate \'an-ə-ˌtāt\ *vb* **-tat·ed; -tat·ing** [L *annotatus,* pp. of *annotare,* fr. *ad-* + *notare* to mark — more at NOTE] *vi* (1733) **:** to make or furnish critical or explanatory notes or comment ~ *vt* **:** to make or furnish annotations for (a literary work or subject) — **an·no·ta·tive** \-ˌtāt-iv\ *adj* — **an·no·ta·tor** \-ˌtāt-ər\ *n*
an·no·ta·tion \ˌan-ə-'tā-shən\ *n* (15c) **1 :** a note added by way of comment or explanation **2 :** the act of annotating
an·nounce \ə-'nau̇n(t)s\ *vb* **-nounced; -nounc·ing** [ME *announcen,* fr. MF *annoncer,* fr. L *annuntiare,* fr. *ad-* + *nuntiare* to report, fr. *nuntius* messenger] *vt* (15c) **1 :** to make known publicly **:** PROCLAIM ⟨*announced* their engagement⟩ **2 a :** to give notice of the arrival, presence, or readiness of ⟨~ dinner⟩ **b :** to indicate beforehand **:** FORETELL **3 :** to serve as an announcer of ~ *vi* **1 :** to serve as an

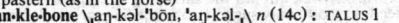

announcer 2 : to declare one's candidacy : give one's political support ***syn*** see DECLARE

an·nounce·ment \ə-'naủn(t)-smənt\ *n* (1798) **1 :** the act of announcing or of being announced **2 :** a public notification or declaration **3 :** a piece of formal stationery designed for a social or business announcement

an·nounc·er \ə-'naủn(t)-sər\ *n* (ca. 1611) : one that announces: as **a :** one who introduces television or radio programs, makes commercial announcements, or gives station identification **b :** one who describes and comments on the action in a broadcast sports event

an·noy \ə-'nȯi\ *vb* [ME *anoien,* fr. MF *enuier,* fr. LL *inodiare* to make loathsome, fr. L *in* + *odium* hatred — more at ODIUM] *vt* (13c) **1 :** to disturb or irritate esp. by repeated acts **2 :** to harass esp. by quick brief attacks ~ *vi* : to cause annoyance — **an·noy·er** *n*

syn ANNOY, VEX, IRK, BOTHER mean to upset a person's composure. ANNOY implies a wearing on the nerves by persistent petty unpleasantness; VEX implies greater provocation and stronger disturbance and usu. connotes anger but sometimes perplexity or anxiety; IRK stresses difficulty in enduring and the resulting weariness or impatience of spirit; BOTHER suggests interference with comfort or peace of mind. ***syn*** see in addition WORRY

an·noy·ance \ə-'nȯi-ən(t)s\ *n* (14c) **1 :** the act of annoying or of being annoyed **2 :** the state or feeling of being annoyed : VEXATION **3 :** a source of vexation or irritation : NUISANCE

an·noy·ing *adj* (14c) : causing vexation : IRRITATING — **an·noy·ing·ly** \-iŋ-lē\ *adv*

[1]**an·nu·al** \'an-yə(-wə)l\ *adj* [ME, fr. MF & LL; MF *annuel,* fr. LL *annualis,* blend of L *annuus* yearly (fr. *annus* year) and L *annalis* yearly (fr. *annus* year); akin to Goth *athnam* (dat. pl.) years, Skt *atati* he walks, goes] (14c) **1 :** covering the period of a year ⟨~ rainfall⟩ **2 :** occurring or happening every year or once a year : YEARLY ⟨an ~ reunion⟩ **3 :** completing the life cycle in one growing season — **an·nu·al·ly** \-ē\ *adv*

[2]**annual** *n* (14c) **1 :** an event that occurs yearly **2 :** a publication appearing yearly **3 :** something that lasts one year or season; *specif* : an annual plant

an·nu·al·ize \'an-yə(-wə)-,līz\ *vt* **-ized; iz·ing** (1918) : to calculate or adjust to reflect a rate based on a full year ⟨quarterly returns yielding at an *annualized* rate of 7 percent⟩

annual ring *n* (ca. 1879) : the layer of wood produced by a single year's growth of a woody plant

an·nu·itant \ə-'n(y)ü-ət-ənt\ *n* (1720) : a beneficiary of an annuity

an·nu·ity \ə-'n(y)ü-ət-ē\ *n, pl* **-ities** [ME *annuite,* fr. MF *annuité,* fr. ML *annuitat-, annuitas,* fr. L *annuus* yearly] (15c) **1 :** a sum of money payable yearly or at other regular intervals **2 :** the right to receive an annuity **3 :** a contract or agreement providing for the payment of an annuity

an·nul \ə-'nəl\ *vt* **an·nulled; an·nul·ling** [ME *annullen,* fr. MF *annuller,* fr. LL *annullare,* fr. L *ad-* + *nullus* not any — more at NULL] (15c) **1 :** to reduce to nothing : OBLITERATE **2 :** to make ineffective or inoperative : NEUTRALIZE ⟨~ the drug's effect⟩ **3 :** to declare or make legally invalid or void ⟨wants the marriage *annulled*⟩ ***syn*** see NULLIFY

an·nu·lar \'an-yə-lər\ *adj* [MF or L; MF *annulaire,* fr. L *annularis,* fr. *annulus*] (1571) : of, relating to, or forming a ring

annular eclipse *n* (1771) : an eclipse in which a thin outer ring of the sun's disk is not covered by the apparently smaller dark disk of the moon

an·nu·late \'an-yə-lət, -,lāt\ *adj* (ca. 1823) : furnished with or composed of rings : RINGED

an·nu·la·tion \,an-yə-'lā-shən\ *n* (1829) : a ringlike anatomical structure

an·nu·let \'an-yə-lət\ *n* [modif. of MF *annelet,* dim. of *anel,* fr. L *anellus,* dim. of *annulus*] (1572) **1 :** a little ring **2 :** a small architectural molding or ridge forming a ring

an·nul·ment \ə-'nəl-mənt\ *n* (15c) **1 :** the act of annulling : the state of being annulled **2 :** a judicial pronouncement declaring a marriage invalid

an·nu·lus \'an-yə-ləs\ *n, pl* **-li** \-,lī, -(,)lē\ *also* **-lus·es** [ML, fr. L *anulus* finger ring, fr. *anus* ring] (1563) **1 :** RING **2 :** a part, structure, or marking resembling a ring; as **a :** a line of cells around a fern sporangium that ruptures the sporangium by contracting **b :** a growth ring (as on the scale of a fish) that is used in estimating age

an·nun·ci·ate \ə-'nən(t)-sē-,āt\ *vt* **-at·ed; -at·ing** (1536) : ANNOUNCE

an·nun·ci·a·tion \ə-,nən(t)-sē-'ā-shən\ *n* [ME *annunciacioun,* fr. MF *anunciation,* fr. LL *annuntiation-, annuntiatio,* fr. L *annuntiatus,* pp. of *annuntiare* — more at ANNOUNCE] (14c) **1 :** the act of announcing or of being announced : ANNOUNCEMENT **2** *cap* : March 25 observed as a church festival in commemoration of the announcement of the Incarnation to the Virgin Mary

an·nun·ci·a·tor \ə-'nən(t)-sē-,āt-ər\ *n* (ca. 1753) : one that annunciates; *specif* : a usu. electrically controlled signal board or indicator — **an·nun·ci·a·to·ry** \-sē-ə-,tōr-ē, -,tȯr-\ *adj*

an·nus mi·ra·bi·lis \,an-ə-smə-'räb-ə-ləs, ,än-\ *n, pl* **an·ni mi·ra·bi·les** \'an-,ī-mə-'räb-ə-,lēz, 'än-(,)ē-mə-'räb-ə-,lās\ [NL, lit., wonderful year] (1660) : a remarkable or notable year

an·ode \'an-,ōd\ *n* [Gk *anodos* way up, fr. *ana-* + *hodos* way] (1834) **1 :** the positive terminal of an electrolytic cell — compare CATHODE **2 :** the negative terminal of a primary cell or of a storage battery that is delivering current **3 :** the electron-collecting electrode of an electron tube — **an·od·ic** \a-'näd-ik\ *or* **an·od·al** \-'nōd-ᵊl\ *adj* — **an·od·i·cal·ly** \-i-k(ə-)lē\ *or* **an·od·al·ly** \-ᵊl-ē\ *adv*

an·od·ize \'an-ə-,dīz\ *vt* **-ized; -iz·ing** (1931) : to subject (a metal) to electrolytic action as the anode of a cell in order to coat with a protective or decorative film — **an·od·iza·tion** \,an-,ōd-ə-'zā-shən, -əd-\ *n*

[1]**an·o·dyne** \'an-ə-,dīn\ *adj* [L *anodynos,* fr. Gk *anōdynos,* fr. *a-* + *odynē* pain] (1543) **1 :** serving to assuage pain **2 :** not likely to offend or arouse tensions : BLAND, INNOCUOUS

[2]**anodyne** *n* (1578) **1 :** a drug that allays pain **2 :** something that soothes, calms, or comforts ⟨the ~ of bridge, a comfortable book, or sport — Harrison Smith⟩

anoint \ə-'nȯint\ *vt* [ME *anointen,* fr. MF *enoint,* pp. of *enoindre,* fr. L *inunguere,* fr. *in-* + *unguere* to smear — more at OINTMENT] (14c) **1 :** to smear or rub with oil or an oily substance **2 a :** to apply oil to as a sacred rite esp. for consecration **b :** to choose by or as if by divine election — **anoint·er** *n* — **anoint·ment** \-mənt\ *n*

anointing of the sick (ca. 1885) : EXTREME UNCTION

anom·a·lis·tic \ə-,näm-ə-'lis-tik\ *adj* (1767) : of or relating to the astronomical anomaly — **anom·a·lis·ti·cal** \-ti-kəl\ *adj*

anom·a·lous \ə-'näm-ə-ləs\ *adj* [LL *anomalus,* fr. Gk *anōmalos,* lit., uneven, fr. *a-* + *homalos* even, fr. *homos* same — more at SAME] (1655) **1 :** inconsistent with or deviating from what is usual, normal, or expected : IRREGULAR, UNUSUAL **2 :** of uncertain nature or classification : EQUIVOCAL, PARADOXICAL ***syn*** see IRREGULAR — **anom·a·lous·ly** *adv* — **anom·a·lous·ness** *n*

anom·a·ly \ə-'näm-ə-lē\ *n, pl* **-lies** (1664) **1 :** deviation from the common rule : IRREGULARITY **2 :** the angular distance of a planet from its perihelion as seen from the sun **3 :** something different, abnormal, peculiar, or not easily classified

an·o·mie *also* **an·o·my** \'an-ə-mē\ *n* [MF *anomie,* fr. Gk *anomia* lawlessness, fr. *anomos* lawless, fr. *a-* + *nomos* law, fr. *nemein* to distribute — more at NIMBLE] (1591) : social instability resulting from a breakdown of standards and values; *also* : personal unrest, alienation, and uncertainty that comes from a lack of purpose or ideals — **ano·mic** \ə-'näm-ik, -'nō-mik\ *adj*

anon \ə-'nän\ *adv* [ME, fr. OE *on ān,* fr. *on* in + *ān* one — more at ON, ONE] (bef. 12c) **1** *archaic* : at once : IMMEDIATELY **2 :** SOON, PRESENTLY **3 :** after a while : LATER

an·o·nym \'an-ə-,nim\ *n* (1812) **1 :** one who is anonymous **2 :** PSEUDONYM

an·o·nym·i·ty \,an-ə-'nim-ət-ē\ *n, pl* **-ties** (1820) **1 :** the quality or state of being anonymous **2 :** one that is anonymous

anon·y·mous \ə-'nän-ə-məs\ *adj* [LL *anonymus,* fr. Gk *anōnymos,* fr. *a-* + *onyma* name — more at NAME] (1601) **1 :** not named or identified ⟨an ~ author⟩ ⟨they wish to remain ~⟩ **2 :** of unknown authorship or origin ⟨an ~ tip⟩ **3 :** lacking individuality, distinction, or recognizability ⟨the ~ faces in the crowd⟩ ⟨the gray ~ streets —William Styron⟩ — **anon·y·mous·ly** *adv* — **anon·y·mous·ness** *n*

anoph·e·les \ə-'näf-ə-,lēz\ *n* [NL, genus name, fr. Gk *anōphelēs* useless, fr. *a-* + *ōphelos* advantage, help] (1899) : any of a genus (*Anopheles*) of mosquitoes that includes all mosquitoes which transmit malaria to man — **anoph·e·line** \-,līn\ *adj or n*

an·o·rak \'an-ə-,rak\ *n* [Greenland Esk *ánorâq*] *chiefly Brit* (1922) : PARKA

[1]**an·o·rec·tic** \,an-ə-'rek-tik\ *or* **an·o·ret·ic** \-'ret-ik\ *adj* [Gk *anorektos,* fr. *an-* [2]*a-* + *oregein* to reach after — more at RIGHT] (ca. 1900) **1 :** lacking appetite **2 :** causing loss of appetite

[2]**anorectic** *or* **anoretic** *n* (ca. 1957) : an anorectic agent

an·orex·ia \,an-ə-'rek-sē-ə, -'rek-shə\ *n* [NL, fr. Gk, fr. *a-* + *orexis* appetite, fr. *oregein*] (ca. 1626) : loss of appetite esp. when prolonged

anorexia ner·vo·sa \-(,)nər-'vō-sə, -zə\ *n* [NL, nervous anorexia] (1873) : a psychological and endocrine disorder primarily of young women in their teens that is characterized esp. by a pathological fear of weight gain leading to faulty eating patterns, malnutrition, and usu. excessive weight loss

an·orex·ic \,an-ə-'rek-sik\ *adj* (ca. 1965) : ANORECTIC; *also* : affected with anorexia nervosa — **anorexic** *n*

an·orex·i·gen·ic \,an-ə-,rek-sə-'gen-ik\ *adj* (1948) : ANORECTIC 2

an·or·thite \ə-'nȯr-,thīt\ *n* [F, fr. *a-* + Gk *orthos* straight] (1833) : a white, grayish, or reddish feldspar $CaAl_2Si_2O_8$ occurring in many igneous rocks — **an·or·thit·ic** \,an-ȯr-'thit-ik\ *adj*

an·or·tho·site \ə-'nȯr-thə-,sīt\ *n* [F *anorthose,* a feldspar, fr. *a-* + Gk *orthos*] (1863) : a granular plutonic igneous rock composed almost exclusively of a soda-lime feldspar (as labradorite) — **an·or·tho·si·tic** \ə-,nȯr-thə-'sit-ik\ *adj*

an·os·mia \a-'näz-mē-ə\ *n* [NL, fr. *a-* + Gk *osmē* smell — more at ODOR] (ca. 1811) : loss or impairment of the sense of smell — **an·os·mic** \-mik\ *adj*

[1]**an·oth·er** \ə-'nət͟h-ər *also* a- *or* ā-\ *adj* (12c) **1 :** different or distinct from the one first considered ⟨the same scene viewed from ~ angle⟩ **2 :** some other : LATER ⟨do it ~ time⟩ **3 :** being one more in addition to one or more of the same kind : NEW ⟨have ~ piece of pie⟩

[2]**another** *pron* (12c) **1 :** an additional one of the same kind : one more **2 :** one that is different from the first or present one **3 :** one of a group of unspecified or indefinite things ⟨in one way or ~⟩

anoth·er–guess \ə-'nət͟h-ər-,ges\ *adj* [alter. of *anothergates,* fr. [1]*another* + *gate*] *archaic* (1625) : of another sort

an·ovu·lant \a-'näv-yə-lənt, -'nōv-\ *n* [[2]*a-* + *ovulate* + *-ant*] (1968) : a drug that suppresses ovulation — **anovulant** *adj*

an·ovu·la·to·ry \(')an-'äv-yə-lə-,tōr-ē, -'ōv-, -,tȯr-\ *adj* [[2]*a-* + *ovulate* + *-ory*] (ca. 1935) **1 :** not involving or associated with ovulation ⟨~ bleeding⟩ **2 :** suppressing ovulation

an·ox·emia \,an-,äk-'sē-mē-ə\ *n* [NL] (ca. 1881) : a condition of subnormal oxygenation of the arterial blood — **an·ox·emic** \-mik\ *adj*

an·ox·ia \a-'näk-sē-ə\ *n* [NL] (1931) : hypoxia esp. of such severity as to result in permanent damage — **an·ox·ic** \-sik\ *adj*

an·ser·ine \'an(t)-sə-,rīn\ *adj* [L *anserinus,* fr. *anser* goose — more at GOOSE] (ca. 1828) : of, relating to, or resembling a goose

[1]**an·swer** \'an(t)-sər\ *n* [ME, fr. OE *andswaru;* akin to ON *andsvar* answer] (bef. 12c) **1 a :** something spoken or written in reply to a question **b :** a correct response **2 :** a reply to a legal charge or suit : PLEA; *also* : DEFENSE **3 :** something done in response or reaction ⟨his only ~ was to walk out⟩ **4 :** a solution of a problem **5 :** one that imitates, matches, or corresponds to another ⟨it's television's ~ to the news magazines⟩

[2]**answer** *vb* **an·swered; an·swer·ing** \'an(t)s-(ə-)riŋ\ *vi* (bef. 12c) **1 :** to speak or write in reply **2 a :** to be or make oneself responsible or accountable **b :** to make amends : ATONE **3 :** to be in conformity or correspondence ⟨~*ed* to the description⟩ **4 :** to act in response to an action performed elsewhere or by another **5 :** to be adequate : SERVE ~ *vt* **1 a :** to speak or write in reply to **b :** to say or write by way of reply **2 :** to reply in rebuttal, justification, or explanation **3 a :** to correspond to ⟨~*s* the description⟩ **b :** to be adequate or usable for : FULFILL **4** *obs* : to atone for **5 :** to act in response to ⟨~*ed* the call to arms⟩ **6 :** to offer a solution for; *esp* : SOLVE — **an·swer·er** \'an(t)-sər-ər\ *n*

syn ANSWER, RESPOND, REPLY, REJOIN, RETORT mean to say, write, or do something in return. ANSWER implies the satisfying of a question, demand, call, or need; RESPOND may suggest an immediate or quick reaction; REPLY implies making a return commensurate with the original question or demand; REJOIN often implies sharpness or quickness in answering; RETORT suggests responding to an explicit charge or criticism by way of retaliation.

an·swer·able \ˈan(t)s-(ə-)rə-bəl\ *adj* (1548) **1** : liable to be called to account : RESPONSIBLE **2** *archaic* : SUITABLE, ADEQUATE **3** *archaic* : CORRESPONDING, SIMILAR **4** : capable of being refuted ***syn*** see RESPONSIBLE

answering service *n* (1961) : a commercial service that answers telephone calls for its clients

ant \ˈant\ *n* [ME *ante, emete,* fr. OE *æmette;* akin to OHG *āmeiza* ant] (bef. 12c) : any of a family (Formicidae) of colonial hymenopterous insects with a complex social organization and various castes performing special duties — **ants in one's pants** : impatience for action or activity : RESTLESSNESS

ant- — see ANTI-

[1]**-ant** \ənt, ᵊnt\ *n suffix* [ME, fr. OF, fr. *-ant,* prp. suffix, fr. L *-ant-, -ans,* prp. suffix of first conjugation, fr. *-a-* (stem vowel of first conjugation) + *-nt-, -ns,* prp. suffix; akin to OE *-nde,* prp. suffix, Gk *-nt-, -n,* part. suffix] **1 a** : one that performs (a specified action) : personal or impersonal agent ⟨claim*ant*⟩ ⟨cool*ant*⟩ **b** : thing that promotes (a specified action or process) ⟨expector*ant*⟩ **2** : one connected with ⟨annuit*ant*⟩ **3** : thing that is acted upon (in a specified manner) ⟨inhal*ant*⟩

[2]**-ant** *adj suffix* **1** : performing (a specified action) or being (in a specified condition) ⟨somnambul*ant*⟩ **2** : promoting (a specified action or process) ⟨expector*ant*⟩

an·ta \ˈant-ə\ *n, pl* **antas** *or* **an·tae** \ˈan-ˌtē, -ˌtī\ [L; akin to ON *önd* anteroom] (1598) : a pier produced by thickening a wall at its termination

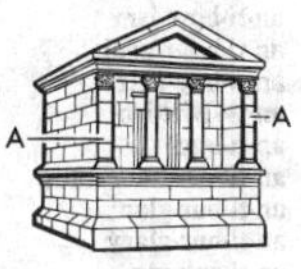

A anta

ant·ac·id \(ˈ)ant-ˈas-əd\ *n* (1732) : an agent that counteracts or neutralizes acidity — **antacid** *adj*

An·tae·an \an-ˈtē-ən\ *adj* [*Antaeus,* a giant overcome by Hercules] (1921) **1** : having superhuman strength **2** : MAMMOTH

an·tag·o·nism \an-ˈtag-ə-ˌniz-əm\ *n* (1928) **1 a** : opposition of a conflicting force, tendency, or principle ⟨the ~ of democracy to dictatorship⟩ **b** : actively expressed opposition or hostility ⟨~ between factions⟩ **2** : opposition in physiological action; *esp* : interaction of two or more substances such that the action of any one of them on living cells or tissues is lessened ***syn*** see ENMITY

an·tag·o·nist \-nəst\ *n* (1599) **1** : one that contends with or opposes another : ADVERSARY, OPPONENT **2** : an agent of physiological antagonism: as **a** : a muscle that contracts with and limits the action of an agonist with which it is paired — called also *antagonistic muscle* **b** : a chemical that acts within the body to reduce the physiological activity of another chemical substance (as an opiate); *esp* : one that opposes the action on the nervous system of a drug or a substance occurring naturally in the body by combining with and blocking its nervous receptor — compare AGONIST 2b

an·tag·o·nis·tic \(ˌ)an-ˌtag-ə-ˈnis-tik\ *adj* (1632) : marked by or resulting from antagonism — **an·tag·o·nis·ti·cal·ly** \-ti-k(ə-)lē\ *adv*

an·tag·o·nize \an-ˈtag-ə-ˌnīz\ *vt* **-nized; -niz·ing** [Gk *antagōnizesthai,* fr. *anti-* + *agōnizesthai* to struggle, fr. *agōn* contest — more at AGONY] (1634) **1** : to act in opposition to : COUNTERACT **2** : to incur or provoke the hostility of ***syn*** see OPPOSE

ant·arc·tic \(ˈ)ant-ˈärk-tik, -ˈärt-ik\ *adj, often cap* [ME *antartik,* fr. L *antarcticus,* fr. Gk *antarktikos,* fr. *anti-* + *arktikos* arctic] (14c) : of or relating to the south pole or to the region near it

antarctic circle *n, often cap A&C* (1556) : the parallel of latitude that is approximately 66½ degrees south of the equator and that circumscribes the southern frigid zone

An·tar·es \an-ˈta(ə)r-(ˌ)ēz, -ˈte(ə)r-\ *n* [Gk *Antarēs*] : a giant red star of very low density that is the brightest star in Scorpio

ant bear *n* (1555) : a large anteater (*Myrmecophaga jubata*) of So. America with shaggy gray fur, a black band across the breast, and a white stripe on the shoulder

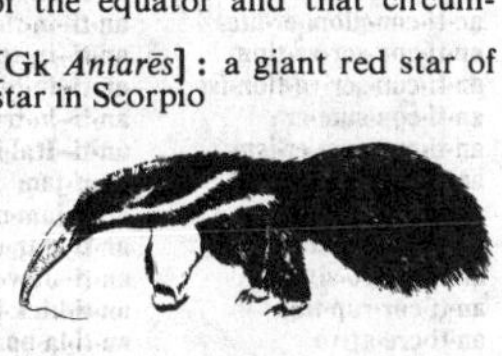
ant bear

ant cow *n* (1875) : an aphid from which ants obtain honeydew

[1]**an·te** \ˈant-ē\ *n* [*ante-*] (ca. 1838) **1** : a poker stake usu. put up before the deal to build the pot ⟨the dealer called for a dollar ~⟩ **2** : COST, PRICE ⟨these improvements would raise the ~⟩

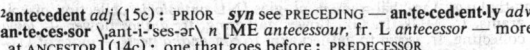

[2]**ante** *vb* **an·ted; an·te·ing** *vt* (1845) : to put up (an ante); *also* : PAY, PRODUCE — often used with *up* ~ *vi* : PAY UP — often used with *up*

ante- *prefix* [ME, fr. L, fr. *ante* before, in front of; akin to OE *and-* against, Gk *anti* before, against — more at END] **1 a** : prior : earlier ⟨*ante*type⟩ **b** : anterior : forward ⟨*ante*room⟩ **2 a** : prior to : earlier than ⟨*ante*diluvian⟩ **b** : in front of ⟨*ante*choir⟩

ant·eat·er \ˈant-ˌēt-ər\ *n* (1764) : any of several mammals that feed largely or entirely on ants or termites: as **a** : any of various edentates (as the pangolin) with a long narrow snout, a long tongue, and enormous salivary glands **b** : ECHIDNA **c** : AARDVARK

an·te·bel·lum \ˌant-i-ˈbel-əm\ *adj* [L *ante bellum* before the war] (ca. 1847) : existing before a war; *esp* : existing before the Civil War

an·te·cede \ˌant-ə-ˈsēd\ *vt* **-ced·ed; -ced·ing** [L *antecedere*] (1624) : PRECEDE

an·te·ced·ence \-ˈsēd-ᵊn(t)s\ *n* (1535) : PRIORITY, PRECEDENCE

[1]**an·te·ced·ent** \ˌant-ə-ˈsēd-ᵊnt\ *n* [ME, fr. ML & L; ML *antecedent-, antecedens,* fr. L, logical antecedent, lit., one that goes before, fr. neut. of *antecedent-, antecedens,* prp. of *antecedere,* fr. *ante-* + *cedere* to go — more at CEDE] (14c) **1** : a substantive word, phrase, or clause referred to by a pronoun (as *John* in "Mary saw John and spoke to him"); *broadly* : a word or group of words replaced and referred to by a substitute **2** : the conditional element in a proposition (as *if A* in "if A, then B") **3** : the first term of a mathematical ratio **4 a** : a preceding event, condition, or cause **b** *pl* : the significant events, conditions, and traits of one's earlier life **5 a** : PREDECESSOR; *esp* : a model or stimulus for later developments **b** *pl* : ANCESTORS, PARENTS ***syn*** see CAUSE

[2]**antecedent** *adj* (15c) : PRIOR ***syn*** see PRECEDING — **an·te·ced·ent·ly** *adv*

an·te·ces·sor \ˌant-i-ˈses-ər\ *n* [ME *antecessour,* fr. L *antecessor* — more at ANCESTOR] (14c) : one that goes before : PREDECESSOR

an·te·cham·ber \ˈant-i-ˌchām-bər\ *n* [F *antichambre,* fr. MF, fr. It *anti-* (fr. L *ante-*) + MF *chambre* room] (ca. 1656) : ANTEROOM

an·te·choir \ˈant-i-ˌkwī(ə)r\ *n* (ca. 1889) : a space enclosed or reserved for the clergy and choristers at the entrance to a choir

[1]**an·te·date** \ˈant-i-ˌdāt\ *n* (15c) : a date assigned to an event or document earlier than the actual date of the event or document

[2]**an·te·date** \ˈant-i-ˌdāt, ˌant-i-ˈ\ *vt* (1572) **1 a** : to date as of a time prior to that of execution **b** : to assign to a date prior to that of actual occurrence **2** *archaic* : ANTICIPATE **3** : to precede in time

an·te·di·lu·vi·an \ˌant-i-də-ˈlü-vē-ən, -(ˌ)dī-\ *adj* [*ante-* + L *diluvium* flood — more at DELUGE] (1646) **1** : of or relating to the period before the flood described in the Bible **2** : made, evolved, or developed a long time ago ⟨an ~ automobile⟩ — **antediluvian** *n*

an·te·fix \ˈant-i-ˌfiks\ *n* [L *antefixum,* fr. neut. of *antefixus,* pp. of *antefigere* to fasten before, fr. *ante-* + *figere* to fasten — more at DIKE] (1832) **1** : an ornament at the eaves of a classical building concealing the ends of the joint tiles of the roof **2** : an ornament of the molding of a classic cornice — **an·te·fix·al** \ˌant-i-ˈfik-səl\ *adj*

an·te·lope \ˈant-ᵊl-ˌōp\ *n, pl* **-lope** *or* **-lopes** [ME, fabulous heraldic beast, prob. fr. MF *antelop* savage animal with sawlike horns, fr. ML *anthalopus,* fr. LGk *antholop-, antholops*] (15c) **1 a** : any of various Old World ruminant mammals (family Bovidae) that differ from the true oxen esp. in lighter racier build and horns directed upward and backward **b** : PRONGHORN **2** : leather from antelope hide

an·te me·ri·di·em \ˌant-i-mə-ˈrid-ē-əm, -ē-ˌem\ *adj* [L] (1563) : being before noon — abbr. *a.m.*

an·te·mor·tem \-ˈmȯrt-əm\ *adj* [L *ante mortem*] (1883) : preceding death

an·te·na·tal \-ˈnāt-ᵊl\ *adj* (1817) : PRENATAL ⟨~ diagnosis of birth defects⟩ — **an·te·na·tal·ly** \-ē\ *adv*

an·ten·na \an-ˈten-ə\ *n, pl* **-nae** \-(ˌ)ē\ *or* **-nas** [ML, fr. L, sail yard] (1646) **1** : a movable segmented organ of sensation on the head of insects, myriapods, and crustaceans — see INSECT illustration **2** *pl usu* **-nas** : a usu. metallic device (as a rod or wire) for radiating or receiving radio waves — **an·ten·nal** \-ˈten-ᵊl\ *adj*

an·ten·nule \an-ˈten-(ˌ)yü(ə)l\ *n* (1845) : a small antenna or similar appendage — **an·ten·nu·lar** \-ˈten-yə-lər\ *adj*

an·te·pen·di·um \ˌant-i-ˈpen-dē-əm\ *n, pl* **-di·ums** *or* **-dia** \-dē-ə\ [ML, fr. L *ante-* + *pendēre* to hang — more at PENDANT] (ca. 1696) : a hanging for the front of an altar, pulpit, or lectern

an·te·pe·nult \ˌant-i-ˈpē-ˌnəlt, -pi-ˈ\ *also* **an·te·pen·ul·ti·ma** \-pi-ˈnəl-tə-mə\ *n* [LL *antepaenultima,* fem. of *antepaenultimus* preceding the next to last, fr. L *ante-* + *paenultimus* penultimate] (1581) : the third syllable of a word counting from the end (as *cu* in *accumulate*) — **an·te·pen·ul·ti·mate** \-pi-ˈnəl-tə-mət\ *adj or n*

an·te–post \ˈant-i-ˌpōst\ *adj, Brit* (1902) : relating to or being a wager on a horse race made esp. before the day of the race

an·te·ri·or \an-ˈtir-ē-ər\ *adj* [L, compar. of *ante* before — more at ANTE-] (1541) **1 a** : situated before or toward the front **b** : situated near or toward the head or part most nearly corresponding to a head **2** : coming before in time or development ***syn*** see PRECEDING — **an·te·ri·or·ly** *adv*

an·tero- \ˌant-ə-(ˌ)rō\ *comb form* [NL, fr. L *anterior*] : anterior ⟨*antero*parietal⟩ : anterior and ⟨*antero*lateral⟩ : from front to ⟨*antero*posterior⟩

an·te·room \ˈant-i-ˌrüm, -ˌru̇m\ *n* (1762) : an outer room that leads to another room and that is often used as a waiting room

anth- — see ANTI-

an·the·lion \ant-ˈhēl-yən, an-ˈthēl-\ *n, pl* **-lia** \-yə\ *or* **-lions** [Gk *anthēlion,* fr. neut. of *anthēlios* opposite the sun, fr. *anti-* + *hēlios* sun — more at SOLAR] (1670) : a somewhat bright white spot appearing on the parhelic circle opposite the sun

an·thel·min·tic \ˌant-ˌhel-ˈmint-ik, ˌan-ˌthel-\ *adj* [*anti-* + Gk *helminth-, helmis* worm — more at HELMINTH] (1684) : expelling or destroying parasitic worms esp. of the intestine — **anthelmintic** *n*

an·them \ˈan(t)-thəm\ *n* [ME *antem,* fr. OE *antefn,* fr. LL *antiphona,* fr. LGk *antiphōna,* pl. of *antiphōnon,* fr. Gk, neut. of *antiphōnos* responsive, fr. *anti-* + *phōnē* sound — more at BAN] (bef. 12c) **1 a** : a psalm or hymn sung antiphonally or responsively **b** : a sacred vocal composition with words usu. from the Scriptures **2** : a song or hymn of praise or gladness

an·the·mi·on \an-ˈthē-mē-ən\ *n, pl* **-mia** \-mē-ə\ [Gk, fr. dim. of *anthemon* flower, fr. *anthos* — more at ANTHOLOGY] (1865) : a flat ornament of floral form (as in relief sculpture or in painting)

an·ther \ˈan(t)-thər\ *n* [NL *anthera,* fr. L, medicine made fr. flowers, fr. Gk *anthēra,* fr. fem. of *anthēros* flowery, fr. *anthos*] (ca. 1706) : the part of a stamen that develops and contains pollen and is usu. borne on a stalk — see FLOWER illustration — **an·ther·al** \-thə-rəl\ *adj*

an·ther·id·i·um \ˌan(t)-thə-ˈrid-ē-əm\ *n, pl* **-id·ia** \-ē-ə\ [NL, fr. *anthera*] (1854) : the male reproductive organ of a cryptogamous plant — **an·ther·id·i·al** \-ē-əl\ *adj*

an·the·sis \an-ˈthē-səs\ *n* [NL, fr. Gk *anthēsis* bloom, fr. *anthein* to flower, fr. *anthos*] (ca. 1823) : the action or period of opening of a flower

ant·hill \ˈant-ˌhil\ *n* (13c) : a mound thrown up by ants or termites in digging their nest

an·tho·cy·a·nin \ˌan(t)-thə-ˈsī-ə-nən\ *also* **an·tho·cy·an** \-ˈsī-ən, -ˌan\ *n* [Gk *anthos* + *kyanos* dark blue] (1839) : any of various soluble glycoside pigments producing blue to red coloring in flowers and plants

an·thol·o·gist \an-ˈthäl-ə-jəst\ *n* (1805) : a compiler of an anthology

an·thol·o·gize \-ˌjīz\ *vt* **-gized; -giz·ing** (1892) : to compile, publish, or include in an anthology — **an·thol·o·giz·er** \-ˌjī-zər\ *n*

an·thol·o·gy \an-ˈthäl-ə-jē\ *n, pl* **-gies** [NL *anthologia* collection of epigrams, fr. MGk, fr. Gk, flower gathering, fr. *anthos* flower + *logia* collecting, fr. *legein* to gather; akin to Skt *andha* herb — more at LEGEND] (1640) **1 :** a collection of selected literary pieces or passages or works of art or music **2 :** ASSORTMENT ⟨an ~ of threadbare clichés of . . . bistro cuisine —Jay Jacobs⟩ — **an·tho·log·i·cal** \ˌan(t)-thə-ˈläj-i-kəl\ *adj*

an·thoph·i·lous \an-ˈthäf-ə-ləs\ *adj* [ISV, fr. Gk *anthos* + E *-philous*] (1883) **:** feeding upon or living among flowers ⟨~ insects⟩

an·tho·zo·an \ˌan(t)-thə-ˈzō-ən\ *n* [deriv. of Gk *anthos* + *zōion* animal; akin to Gk *zōē* life — more at QUICK] (ca. 1889) **:** any of a class (Anthozoa) of marine coelenterates (as the corals and sea anemones) having polyps with radial partitions — **anthozoan** *adj*

an·thra·cene \ˈan(t)-thrə-ˌsēn\ *n* (1863) **:** a crystalline cyclic hydrocarbon $C_{14}H_{10}$ obtained from coal-tar distillation

an·thra·cite \ˈan(t)-thrə-ˌsīt\ *n* [Gk *anthrakitis,* fr. *anthrak-, anthrax* coal] (1812) **:** a hard natural coal of high luster differing from bituminous coal in containing little volatile matter — **an·thra·cit·ic** \ˌan(t)-thrə-ˈsit-ik\ *adj*

an·thrac·nose \an-ˈthrak-ˌnōs\ *n* [F, fr. Gk *anthrak-, anthrax* + *nosos* disease] (ca. 1886) **:** any of numerous destructive plant diseases caused by imperfect fungi and characterized by often dark sunken lesions or blisters

an·thra·ni·late \an-ˈthran-ᵊl-ˌāt, ˌan-thrə-ˈnil-ˌāt\ *n* (1921) **:** a salt or ester of anthranilic acid

an·thra·nil·ic acid \ˌan(t)-thrə-ˌnil-ik-\ *n* [ISV *anthracene* + *aniline*] (ca. 1901) **:** a crystalline acid $NH_2C_6H_4COOH$ used as an intermediate in the manufacture of dyes (as indigo), pharmaceuticals, and perfumes

an·thra·qui·none \ˌan(t)-thrə-kwin-ˈōn, -ˈkwin-ˌōn\ *n* [prob. fr. F, fr. *anthracene* + *quinone*] (ca. 1885) **:** a yellow crystalline ketone $C_{14}H_8O_2$ often derived from anthracene and used esp. in the manufacture of dyes

an·thrax \ˈan-ˌthraks\ *n* [ME *antrax* carbuncle, fr. L *anthrax,* fr. Gk, coal, carbuncle] (1876) **:** an infectious disease of warm-blooded animals (as cattle and sheep) caused by a spore-forming bacterium (*Bacillus anthracis*), transmissible to man esp. by the handling of infected products (as hair), and characterized by external ulcerating nodules or by lesions in the lungs

anthrop- *or* **anthropo-** *comb form* [L *anthropo-,* fr. Gk *anthrōp-, anthrōpo-,* fr. *anthrōpos*] **:** human being ⟨*anthropo*genesis⟩

an·throp·ic \an-ˈthräp-ik\ *or* **an·throp·i·cal** \-i-kəl\ *adj* [Gk *anthrōpikos,* fr. *anthrōpos*] (1804) **:** of or relating to human beings or the period of their existence on earth

an·thro·po·cen·tric \ˌan(t)-thrə-pə-ˈsen-trik\ *adj* (1863) **1 :** considering human beings as the most significant entity of the universe **2 :** interpreting or regarding the world in terms of human values and experiences — **an·thro·po·cen·tri·cal·ly** \-tri-k(ə-)lē\ *adv* — **an·thro·po·cen·tric·i·ty** \-pō-(ˌ)sen-ˈtris-ət-ē\ *n*

an·thro·po·gen·ic \-pə-ˈjen-ik\ *adj* (ca. 1890) **:** of, relating to, or resulting from the influence of human beings on nature ⟨~ sources of pollution⟩

an·thro·pog·ra·phy \ˌan(t)-thrə-ˈpäg-rə-fē\ *n* (1834) **:** a branch of anthropology dealing with the distribution of man as distinguished by physical character, language, institutions, and customs

[1]**an·thro·poid** \ˈan(t)-thrə-ˌpȯid\ *n* (1832) **:** APE 1b

[2]**anthropoid** *adj* [Gk *anthrōpoeidēs,* fr. *anthrōpos*] (1837) **1 :** resembling a person esp. in shape **2 :** resembling an ape esp. in action ⟨~ gangster⟩

anthropoid ape *n* (1837) **:** APE 1b

an·thro·pol·o·gy \ˌan(t)-thrə-ˈpäl-ə-jē\ *n* [NL *anthropologia,* fr. *anthrop-* + *-logia* -logy] (1593) **1 :** the science of human beings; *esp* **:** the study of human beings in relation to distribution, origin, classification, and relationship of races, physical character, environmental and social relations, and culture **2 :** a part of Christian teaching that concerns the origin, nature, and destiny of human beings — **an·thro·po·log·i·cal** \-pə-ˈläj-i-kəl\ *adj* — **an·thro·po·log·i·cal·ly** \-i-k(ə-)lē\ *adv* — **an·thro·pol·o·gist** \ˌan(t)-thrə-ˈpäl-ə-jəst\ *n*

an·thro·pom·e·try \ˌan(t)-thrə-ˈpäm-ə-trē\ *n* [F *anthropométrie,* fr. *anthrop-* + *-métrie* -metry] (ca. 1839) **:** the study of human body measurements esp. on a comparative basis — **an·thro·po·met·ric** \-pə-ˈme-trik\ *adj*

an·thro·po·mor·phic \ˌan(t)-thrə-pə-ˈmȯr-fik\ *adj* [LL *anthropomorphus* of human form, fr. Gk *anthrōpomorphos,* fr. *anthrōp-* + *-morphos* -morphous] (1827) **1 :** described or thought of as having a human form or human attributes ⟨~ deities⟩ **2 :** ascribing human characteristics to nonhuman things ⟨~ supernaturalism⟩ — **an·thro·po·mor·phi·cal·ly** \-fi-k(ə-)lē\ *adv*

an·thro·po·mor·phism \-ˌfiz-əm\ *n* (1753) **:** an interpretation of what is not human or personal in terms of human or personal characteristics **:** HUMANIZATION — **an·thro·po·mor·phist** \-fəst\ *n*

an·thro·po·mor·phize \-ˌfīz\ *vb* **-phized; -phiz·ing** *vt* (1845) **:** to attribute human form or personality to ~ *vi* **:** to attribute human form or personality to things not human

an·thro·po·pa·thism \ˌan(t)-thrə-ˈpäp-ə-ˌthiz-əm, -pō-ˈpath-ˌiz-\ *n* [LGk *anthrōpopatheia* humanity, fr. Gk *anthrōpopathēs* having human feelings, fr. *anthrōp-* + *pathos* experience — more at PATHOS] (1847) **:** the ascription of human feelings to something not human

an·thro·poph·a·gous \ˌan(t)-thrə-ˈpäf-ə-gəs\ *adj* (ca. 1828) **:** feeding on human flesh — **an·thro·poph·a·gy** \-ə-jē\ *n*

an·thro·poph·a·gus \-ə-gəs\ *n, pl* **-a·gi** \-ə-ˌgī, -ˌjī, -ˌgē\ [L, fr. Gk *anthrōpophagos,* fr. *anthrōp-* + *-phagos* -phagous] (1552) **:** MAN-EATER, CANNIBAL

an·thro·pos·o·phy \ˌan(t)-thrə-ˈpäs-ə-fē\ *n* (1916) **:** a 20th century religious system growing out of theosophy and centering on human development

an·thur·i·um \an-ˈth(y)u̇r-ē-əm\ *n* [NL, fr. Gk *anthos* flower + *-urium,* fr. *oura* tail; akin to Gk *orrhos* — more at ASS] (ca. 1839) **:** any of a genus (*Anthurium,* family Araceae) of tropical American plants with large often highly colored leaves, a cylindrical spadix, and a colored spathe

[1]**an·ti** \ˈan-ˌtī, ˈant-ē\ *n, pl* **antis** [*anti-*] (1788) **:** one that is opposed

[2]**anti** *adj* (1857) **:** OPPOSED

[3]**anti** *prep* (1953) **:** opposed to **:** AGAINST

anti- *or* **ant-** *or* **anth-** *prefix* [*anti-* fr. ME, fr. MF & L; MF, fr. L, against, fr. Gk, fr. *anti; ant-* fr. ME, fr. L, against, fr. Gk, fr. *anti; anth-* fr. L, against, fr. Gk, fr. *anti* — more at ANTE-] **1 a :** of the same kind but situated opposite, exerting energy in the opposite direction, or pursuing an opposite policy ⟨*anti*clinal⟩ **b :** one that is opposite in kind to ⟨*anti*climax⟩ **2 a :** opposing or hostile to in opinion, sympathy, or practice ⟨*anti*-Semite⟩ **b :** opposing in effect or activity ⟨*ant*acid⟩ ⟨*anti*catalyst⟩ **3 :** serving to prevent, cure, or alleviate ⟨*anti*anxiety⟩ **4 :** combating or defending against ⟨*anti*aircraft⟩ ⟨*anti*missile⟩

an·ti·ac·a·dem·ic
an·ti·ad·min·is·tra·tion
an·ti·ag·gres·sion
an·ti·ag·ing
an·ti·alien
an·ti·al·ler·gen·ic
an·ti·apart·heid
an·ti·aris·to·crat·ic
an·ti·ar·thrit·ic
an·ti·as·sim·i·la·tion
an·ti·au·thor·i·tar·i·an
an·ti·au·thor·i·tar·i·an·ism
an·ti·au·thor·i·ty
an·ti·back·lash
an·ti·bi·as
an·ti·bill·board
an·ti–Bol·she·vik
an·ti·boss
an·ti·boss·ism
an·ti·bour·geois
an·ti·boy·cott
an·ti–Brit·ish
an·ti·bug
an·ti·bu·reau·crat·ic
an·ti·bur·glar
an·ti·bur·glary
an·ti·cak·ing
an·ti·cap·i·tal·ism
an·ti·cap·i·tal·ist
an·ti·car
an·ti·car·cin·o·gen
an·ti·car·ci·no·gen·ic
an·ti·car·ies
an·ti–Cath·o·lic
an·ti·cen·sor·ship
an·ti–Chris·tian
an·ti–Chris·tian·i·ty
an·ti·church
an·ti·cig·a·rette
an·ti·city
an·ti·clas·si·cal
an·ti·cling
an·ti·clot·ting
an·ti·cold
an·ti·col·li·sion
an·ti·co·lo·nial
an·ti·co·lo·nial·ism
an·ti·co·lo·nial·ist
an·ti·com·mer·cial
an·ti·com·mer·cial·ism
an·ti·com·mu·nism
an·ti·com·mu·nist
an·ti·con·glom·er·ate
an·ti·con·ser·va·tion
an·ti·con·ser·va·tion·ist
an·ti·con·sum·er
an·ti·con·sum·er·ism
an·ti·con·ven·tion·al
an·ti·cor·po·rate
an·ti·cor·ro·sion
an·ti·cor·ro·sive
an·ti·cor·rup·tion
an·ti·cre·ative
an·ti·crime
an·ti·cru·el·ty
an·ti·cult
an·ti·cul·tur·al
an·ti–Dar·win·ian
an·ti–Dar·win·ism
an·ti·de·pres·sion
an·ti·de·seg·re·ga·tion
an·ti·des·ic·cant
an·ti·di·a·bet·ic
an·ti·di·ar·rhe·al
an·ti·di·lu·tion
an·ti·dis·crim·i·na·tion
an·ti·dis·si·dent
an·ti·dog·mat·ic
an·ti·draft
an·ti·eaves·drop·ping
an·ti·eco·nom·ic
an·ti·ed·u·ca·tion·al
an·ti·egal·i·tar·i·an
an·ti·elite
an·ti·elit·ism
an·ti·elit·ist
an·ti·emet·ic
an·ti–En·glish
an·ti·en·tro·pic
an·ti·ep·i·lep·sy
an·ti·ep·i·lep·tic
an·ti·erot·ic
an·ti·es·tab·lish·ment
an·ti·evo·lu·tion
an·ti·evo·lu·tion·ary
an·ti·evo·lu·tion·ism
an·ti·evo·lu·tion·ist
an·ti·fam·i·ly
an·ti·fas·cism
an·ti·fas·cist
an·ti·fash·ion
an·ti·fash·ion·able
an·ti·fa·tigue
an·ti·fe·male
an·ti·fem·i·nine
an·ti·fem·i·nism
an·ti·fem·i·nist
an·ti·fil·i·bus·ter
an·ti·foam
an·ti·foam·ing
an·ti·fog·ging
an·ti·fore·clo·sure
an·ti·for·eign
an·ti·for·eign·er
an·ti·for·mal·ist
an·ti·fraud
an·ti–French
an·ti·fric·tion
an·ti·gam·bling
an·ti·gay
an·ti–Ger·man
an·ti·glare
an·ti·gov·ern·ment
an·ti·growth
an·ti·guer·ril·la
an·ti·gun
an·ti·hi·er·ar·chi·cal
an·ti·hi·jack
an·ti·his·tor·i·cal
an·ti·ho·mo·sex·u·al
an·ti·ho·mo·sex·u·al·i·ty
an·ti·hu·man·ism
an·ti·hu·man·is·tic
an·ti·hu·man·i·tar·i·an
an·ti·hu·man·i·ty
an·ti·hunt·er
an·ti·hunt·ing
an·ti·hys·ter·ic
an·ti·ic·ing
an·ti–ideo·log·i·cal
an·ti–im·mu·no·glob·u·lin
an·ti–im·pe·ri·al·ism
an·ti–im·pe·ri·al·ist
an·ti–in·cum·bent
an·ti–in·fec·tive
an·ti–in·fla·tion
an·ti–in·fla·tion·ary
an·ti–in·sti·tu·tion·al
an·ti–in·te·gra·tion
an·ti–in·tru·sion
an·ti–Ital·ian
an·ti·jam
an·ti·jam·ming
an·ti–Jap·a·nese
an·ti–Jew·ish
an·ti·kick·back
an·ti·la·bor
an·ti·leak
an·ti·left
an·ti·lep·ro·sy
an·ti·lib·er·al
an·ti·lib·er·al·ism
an·ti·lib·er·tar·i·an
an·ti·lit·er·a·cy
an·ti·lit·er·ate
an·ti·lit·ter
an·ti·lit·ter·ing
an·ti·log·i·cal
an·ti·lot·tery
an·ti·lynch·ing
an·ti·ma·cho
an·ti·male
an·ti·man
an·ti·man·age·ment
an·ti·mar·i·jua·na
an·ti·mar·ket
an·ti·ma·te·ri·al·ism
an·ti·ma·te·ri·al·ist
an·ti·mech·a·nist
an·ti·merg·er
an·ti·met·a·bol·ic
an·ti·meta·phys·i·cal
an·ti·mil·i·ta·rism
an·ti·mil·i·ta·rist
an·ti·mil·i·tary
an·ti·mis·ce·ge·na·tion
an·ti·mo·nar·chi·cal
an·ti·mon·ar·chist
an·ti·mo·nop·o·list
an·ti·mo·nop·o·ly
an·ti·mos·qui·to
an·ti·mouse
an·ti·mu·sic
an·ti·mu·si·cal
an·ti·nar·ra·tive
an·ti·na·tion·al
an·ti·na·tion·a·list
an·ti·na·ture
an·ti–Na·zi
an·ti–Ne·gro
an·ti·nep·o·tism
an·ti·noise
an·ti·obe·si·ty
an·ti·ob·scen·i·ty
an·ti·or·ga·ni·za·tion
an·ti·pa·pal
an·ti·par·ty
an·ti·pes·ti·cide
an·ti·pill
an·ti·pi·ra·cy
an·ti·plague
an·ti·plant
an·ti·plea·sure
an·ti·poach·ing
an·ti·po·lice
an·ti·po·lit·i·cal
an·ti·pol·i·tics
an·ti·pop·u·lar
an·ti·porn
an·ti·por·no·graph·ic
an·ti·por·nog·ra·phy
an·ti·pot
an·ti·pov·er·ty
an·ti·pred·a·tor
an·ti·prof·i·teer·ing
an·ti·pro·gres·sive
an·ti·pros·ti·tu·tion
an·ti·ra·bies
an·ti·rac·ism
an·ti·rac·ist
an·ti·rack·e·teer·ing
an·ti·ra·dar
an·ti·rad·i·cal
an·ti·rad·i·cal·ism
an·ti·rape
an·ti·ra·tio·nal
an·ti·ra·tio·nal·ism
an·ti·ra·tio·nal·ist
an·ti·ra·tio·nal·i·ty
an·ti·re·al·ism
an·ti·re·al·is·tic
an·ti·re·ces·sion
an·ti·re·ces·sion·ary
an·ti·red
an·ti·re·duc·tion·ist
an·ti·re·flec·tion
an·ti·re·flec·tive
an·ti·re·form
an·ti·reg·u·la·tory
an·ti·re·li·gion
an·ti·re·li·gious
an·ti·re·sis·tant
an·ti·res·o·nance
an·ti·re·verse
an·ti·rev·o·lu·tion·ary
an·ti·rights
an·ti·ri·ot
an·ti·rit·u·al·ism
an·ti·roll
an·ti·ro·man·tic
an·ti·ro·man·ti·cism
an·ti·roy·al·ist
an·ti–Rus·sian
an·ti·rust
an·ti·sag
an·ti·sat·el·lite
an·ti·schizo·phre·nia
an·ti·sci·ence
an·ti·sci·en·tif·ic
an·ti·se·cre·cy
an·ti·seg·re·ga·tion
an·ti·sen·ti·men·tal
an·ti·sep·a·rat·ist
an·ti·sex
an·ti·sex·ist
an·ti·sex·u·al
an·ti·sex·u·al·i·ty
an·ti·shark
an·ti·ship
an·ti·shock
an·ti·shop·lift·ing
an·ti·sky·jack·ing

an·ti·slav·ery
an·ti·sleep
an·ti·slip
an·ti·smog
an·ti·smoke
an·ti·smok·er
an·ti·smok·ing
an·ti·smug·gling
an·ti·smut
an·ti·snob
an·ti·so·lar
an·ti–So·vi·et
an·ti·spec·u·la·tion
an·ti·spec·u·la·tive
an·ti·spend·ing
an·ti·state
an·ti·stat·ism
an·ti·ste·ril·i·ty
an·ti·stick
an·ti·sto·ry
an·ti·stress
an·ti·strike
an·ti·stu·dent
an·ti·sub·ma·rine
an·ti·sub·si·dy
an·ti·sub·ver·sion
an·ti·sub·ver·sive
an·ti·sui·cide
an·ti·syph·i·lit·ic
an·ti·take·over
an·ti·tank
an·ti·tar·nish
an·ti·tax
an·ti·tech·no·log·i·cal
an·ti·tech·nol·o·gy
an·ti·ter·ror·ism
an·ti·ter·ror·ist
an·ti·theft
an·ti·the·o·ret·i·cal
an·ti·to·bac·co
an·ti·to·tal·i·tar·i·an
an·ti·tra·di·tion·al
an·ti·tu·ber·cu·lar
an·ti·tu·ber·cu·lo·sis
an·ti·tu·ber·cu·lous
an·ti·tu·mor
an·ti·tu·mor·al
an·ti·ty·phoid
an·ti·ul·cer
an·ti·un·em·ploy·ment
an·ti·union
an·ti·uni·ver·si·ty
an·ti·ur·ban
an·ti·vi·o·lence
an·ti·vi·ral
an·ti·vivi·sec·tion
an·ti·vivi·sec·tion·ist
an·ti·war
an·ti·wear
an·ti·weed
an·ti·wel·fare
an·ti–West
an·ti–West·ern
an·ti·wom·an
an·ti·wrin·kle
an·ti–Zi·on·ist

an·ti·abor·tion \ˌant-ē-ə-ˈbȯr-shən, ˌan-ˌtī-\ *adj* (ca. 1966) **:** opposed to abortion ⟨~ lobbyists⟩ — **an·ti·abor·tion·ist** \-sh(ə-)nəst\ *n*

¹an·ti·air·craft \-ˈa(ə)r-ˌkraft, -ˈe(ə)r-\ *adj* (1914) **:** designed for or concerned with defense against air attack

²antiaircraft *n* (1926) **:** an antiaircraft weapon

an·ti–Amer·i·can \-ə-ˈmer-ə-kən, -ˈmər-, -ˈmar-, -i-kən\ *adj* (1773) **:** opposed or hostile to the people or the government policies of the U.S. — **an·ti–Amer·i·can·ism** \-kə-ˌniz-əm\ *n*

an·ti·anx·i·ety \-(ˌ)aŋ-ˈzī-ət-ē\ *adj* (1962) **:** tending to prevent or relieve anxiety ⟨~ drugs⟩

an·ti·ar·rhyth·mic \ˌant-ē-(ˌ)ā-ˈrit͟h-mik, ˌan-ˌtī-\ *adj* (1954) **:** tending to prevent or relieve cardiac arrhythmia ⟨an ~ agent⟩

an·ti–art \-ˈärt\ *n* (1937) **:** art based on premises antithetical to traditional or popular art forms; *specif* **:** DADA

an·ti·aux·in \-ˈȯk-sən\ *n* (1949) **:** a plant substance that opposes or suppresses the natural effect of an auxin

an·ti·bac·te·ri·al \ˌant-i-bak-ˈtir-ē-əl, ˌan-ˌtī-\ *adj* (ca. 1897) **:** directed or effective against bacteria — **antibacterial** *n*

an·ti·bal·lis·tic missile \ˌant-i-bə-ˌlis-tik-, ˌan-ˌtī-\ *n* (1959) **:** a missile for intercepting and destroying ballistic missiles

an·ti·bi·o·sis \-bī-ˈō-səs, -bē-\ *n* [NL] (ca. 1899) **:** antagonistic association between organisms to the detriment of one of them or between one organism and a metabolic product of another

¹an·ti·bi·ot·ic \ˌant-i-bī-ˈät-ik, ˌan- ˌtī-; ˌant-i-bē-\ *adj* (1894) **1 :** tending to prevent, inhibit, or destroy life **2 :** of or relating to antibiotics or to antibiosis — **an·ti·bi·ot·i·cal·ly** \-i-k(ə-)lē\ *adv*

²antibiotic *n* (1943) **:** a substance produced by or a semisynthetic substance derived from a microorganism and able in dilute solution to inhibit or kill another microorganism

an·ti·black \-ˈblak\ *adj* (1952) **:** opposed or hostile to people belonging to the Negro race ⟨his ~ attitude⟩ — **an·ti·black·ism** \-ˌiz-əm\ *n*

an·ti·body \ˈant-i-ˌbäd-ē\ *n* (1900) **:** any of the body immunoglobulins that are produced in response to specific antigens and that counteract their effects esp. by neutralizing toxins, agglutinating bacteria or cells, and precipitating soluble antigens

an·ti·busi·ness \-ˈbiz-nəs, -nəz\ *adj* (1938) **:** antagonistic toward business and esp. big business

an·ti·bus·ing \-ˈbəs-iŋ\ *adj* (ca. 1969) **:** opposed to the busing of schoolchildren ⟨~ parents⟩ ⟨~ campaign⟩

¹an·tic \ˈant-ik\ *n* [It *antico* ancient thing or person, fr. *antico* ancient, fr. L *antiquus* — more at ANTIQUE] (1529) **1 :** an attention-drawing often wildly playful or funny act or action **:** CAPER ⟨childish ~*s*⟩ **2** *archaic* **:** a performer of a grotesque or ludicrous part **:** BUFFOON

²antic *adj* (1548) **1** *archaic* **:** GROTESQUE, BIZARRE **2 a :** characterized by clownish extravagance or absurdity **b :** whimsically gay **:** FROLICSOME — **an·ti·cal·ly** \-i-k(ə-)lē\ *adv*

an·ti·can·cer \ˌant-i-ˈkan(t)-sər, ˌan-ˌtī-\ *adj* (1926) **:** used or effective against cancer ⟨~ drugs⟩

an·ti·cat·a·lyst \-ˈkat-ᵊl-əst\ *n* (ca. 1922) **1 :** an agent that retards a chemical reaction **2 :** a catalytic poison

an·ti·cho·lin·er·gic \-ˌkō-lə-ˈnər-jik\ *adj* (1942) **:** opposing or blocking the physiological action of acetylcholine — **anticholinergic** *n*

an·ti·cho·lin·es·ter·ase \-ˈnes-tə-ˌrās, -ˌrāz\ *n* (1942) **:** a substance (as neostigmine) that inhibits a cholinesterase by combination with it

An·ti·christ \ˈant-i-ˌkrīst\ *n* [ME *anticrist,* fr. OE & LL; OE *antecrist*, fr. LL *Antichristus,* fr. Gk *Antichristos,* fr. *anti-* + *Christos* Christ] (bef. 12c) **1 :** one who denies or opposes Christ; *specif* **:** a great antagonist expected to fill the world with wickedness but to be conquered forever by Christ at his second coming **2 :** a false Christ

an·tic·i·pant \an-ˈtis-ə-pənt\ *adj* (1626) **:** EXPECTANT, ANTICIPATING — usu. used with *of* — **anticipant** *n*

an·tic·i·pate \an-ˈtis-ə-ˌpāt\ *vb* **-pat·ed; -pat·ing** [L *anticipatus,* pp. of *anticipare,* fr. *ante-* + *-cipare* (fr. *capere* to take) — more at HEAVE] *vt* (1532) **1 :** to give advance thought, discussion, or treatment to **2 :** to meet (an obligation) before a due date **3 :** to foresee and deal with in advance **:** FORESTALL **4 :** to use or expend in advance of actual possession **5 :** to act before (another) often so as to check or counter **6 :** to look forward to as certain **:** EXPECT ~ *vi* **:** to speak or write in knowledge or expectation of later matter ***syn*** see FORESEE, PREVENT — **an·tic·i·pat·able** \-ˌpāt-ə-bəl\ *adj* — **an·tic·i·pa·tor** \-ˌpāt-ər\ *n*

an·tic·i·pa·tion \(ˌ)an-ˌtis-ə-ˈpā-shən\ *n* (14c) **1 a :** a prior action that takes into account or forestalls a later action **b :** the act of looking forward; *specif* **:** pleasurable expectation **2 :** the use of money before it is available **3 a :** visualization of a future event or state **b :** an object or form that anticipates a later type **4 :** the early sounding of one or more tones of a succeeding chord to form a temporary dissonance — compare SUSPENSION ***syn*** see PROSPECT

an·tic·i·pa·to·ry \an-ˈtis-ə-pə-ˌtōr-ē, -ˌtȯr-\ *adj* (1669) **:** characterized by anticipation **:** ANTICIPATING

an·ti·cler·i·cal \ˌant-i-ˈkler-i-kəl, ˌan-ˌtī-\ *adj* (1845) **:** opposed to clericalism or to the interference or influence of the clergy in secular affairs — **anticlerical** *n* — **an·ti·cler·i·cal·ism** \-kə-ˌliz-əm\ *n*

an·ti·cli·mac·tic \-klī-ˈmak-tik, -klə-\ *also* **an·ti·cli·mac·ti·cal** \-ti-kəl\ *adj* (1898) **:** of, relating to, or marked by anticlimax — **an·ti·cli·mac·ti·cal·ly** \-ti-k(ə-)lē\ *adv*

an·ti·cli·max \-ˈklī-ˌmaks\ *n* (1710) **1 :** the usu. sudden transition in discourse from a significant idea to a trivial or ludicrous idea; *also* **:** an instance of this transition **2 :** an event (as at the end of a series) that is strikingly less important than what has preceded it

an·ti·cli·nal \ˌant-i-ˈklīn-ᵊl\ *adj* [*anti-* + Gk *klinein* to lean — more at LEAN] (1833) **:** inclining in opposite directions: **a :** of or relating to a geological anticline **b :** occurring at right angles to the surface or circumference of a plant organ

an·ti·cline \ˈant-i-ˌklīn\ *n* [back-formation fr. *anticlinal*] (ca. 1861) **:** an arch of stratified rock in which the layers bend downward in opposite directions from the crest — compare SYNCLINE

cross section of strata showing anticline

an·ti·clock·wise \ˌant-i-ˈkläk-ˌwīz, ˌan-ˌtī-\ *adj or adv* (1898) **:** COUNTERCLOCKWISE

an·ti·co·ag·u·lant \-kō-ˈag-yə-lənt\ *n* (ca. 1905) **:** a substance that hinders the clotting of blood — **anticoagulant** *adj*

an·ti·co·don \-ˈkō-ˌdän\ *n* [*anti-* + *codon*] (1965) **:** a triplet of nucleotide bases in transfer RNA that identifies the amino acid carried and binds to a complementary codon in messenger RNA during protein synthesis at a ribosome

an·ti·com·pet·i·tive \-kəm-ˈpet-ət-iv\ *adj* (1952) **:** tending to reduce or discourage competition

an·ti·con·vul·sant \-kən-ˈvəl-sənt\ *also* **an·ti·con·vul·sive** \-siv\ *adj* (1734) **:** used or tending to control or to prevent convulsions (as in epilepsy) — **anticonvulsant** *also* **anticonvulsive** *n*

an·ti·cy·clone \ˌant-i-ˈsī-ˌklōn\ *n* (1877) **1 :** a system of winds that rotates about a center of high atmospheric pressure clockwise in the northern hemisphere and counterclockwise in the southern, that usu. advances at 20 to 30 miles per hour, and that usu. has a diameter of 1500 to 2500 miles **2 :** HIGH 2 — **an·ti·cy·clon·ic** \-sī-ˈklän-ik\ *adj*

an·ti·dem·o·crat·ic \ˌant-i-ˌdem-ə-ˈkrat-ik, ˌan-ˌtī-\ *adj* (1837) **:** opposed or hostile to the theories or policies of democracy

¹an·ti·de·pres·sant \-di-ˈpres-ᵊnt\ *adj* (1961) **:** used or tending to relieve or prevent psychic depression

²antidepressant *n* (1962) **:** an antidepressant drug — called also *energizer, psychic energizer*

an·ti·de·riv·a·tive \-di-ˈriv-ət-iv\ *n* (ca. 1942) **:** INDEFINITE INTEGRAL

an·ti·di·uret·ic hormone \ˌant-i-ˌdī-yü-ˌret-ik-\ *n* (1942) **:** VASOPRESSIN

an·ti·dot·al \ˌant-i-ˈdōt-ᵊl\ *adj* (1646) **:** of, relating to, or acting as an antidote — **an·ti·dot·al·ly** \-ᵊl-ē\ *adv*

an·ti·dote \ˈant-i-ˌdōt\ *n* [ME *antidot,* fr. L *antidotum,* fr. Gk *antidotos,* fr. fem. of *antidotos* given as an antidote, fr. *antididonai* to give as an antidote, fr. *anti-* + *didonai* to give — more at DATE] (15c) **1 :** a remedy to counteract the effects of poison **2 :** something that relieves, prevents, or counteracts ⟨an ~ to the mechanization of our society⟩ — **antidote** *vt*

an·ti·drom·ic \ˌant-i-ˈdräm-ik\ *adj* [*anti* + *dromic,* fr. Gk *dromikos* relating to the form of a racecourse, fr. *dromos* racecourse, running — more at DROMEDARY] (ca. 1909) **:** proceeding or conducting in a direction opposite to the usual one — used esp. of a nerve impulse or fiber — **an·ti·drom·i·cal·ly** \-i-k(ə-)lē\ *adv*

an·ti·dump·ing \ˌant-i-ˈdəm-piŋ, ˌan-ˌtī-\ *adj* (1915) **:** designed to discourage the importation and sale of foreign goods at prices well below domestic prices ⟨~ tariffs⟩

an·ti·elec·tron \ˌant-ē-ə-ˈlek-ˌträn, ˌan-ˌtī-\ *n* (1931) **:** POSITRON

an·ti–fed·er·al·ist \ˌant-i-ˈfed-(ə-)rə-ləst, ˌan-ˌtī-\ *n, often cap A&F* (1787) **:** a member of the group that opposed the adoption of the U.S. Constitution

an·ti·fer·ro·mag·net·ic \-ˌfer-ō-mag-ˈnet-ik\ *adj* (1936) **:** FERRIMAGNETIC — **an·ti·fer·ro·mag·net** \-ˈmag-nət\ *n* — **an·ti·fer·ro·mag·net·ism** \-ˈmag-nə-ˌtiz-əm\ *n*

an·ti·fer·til·i·ty \-fər-ˈtil-ət-ē\ *adj* (1953) **:** capable of or tending to reduce or destroy fertility **:** CONTRACEPTIVE ⟨~ agents⟩

an·ti·flu·o·ri·da·tion·ist \-ˌflu̇r-ə-ˈdā-sh(ə-)nəst, -ˌflōr-, -ˌflȯr-\ *n* (1961) **:** a person vigorously opposed to the fluoridation of public water supplies

an·ti·foul·ing \-ˈfau̇-liŋ\ *adj* (1869) **:** intended to prevent fouling of underwater structures (as the bottoms of ships) ⟨~ paint⟩

an·ti·freeze \ˈant-i-ˌfrēz\ *n* (1924) **:** a substance added to a liquid (as the water in an automobile engine) to lower its freezing point

an·ti·fun·gal \ˌant-i-ˈfəŋ-gəl, ˌan-ˌtī-\ *adj* (1945) **:** FUNGICIDAL ⟨~ drugs⟩ — **antifungal** *n*

an·ti·gen \ˈant-i-jən, -ˌjen\ *n* [ISV] (1908) **:** a usu. protein or carbohydrate substance (as a toxin or enzyme) capable of stimulating an immune response — **an·ti·gen·ic** \ˌant-i-ˈjen-ik\ *adj* — **an·ti·gen·i·cal·ly** \-i-k(ə-)lē\ *adv* — **an·ti·ge·nic·i·ty** \-jə-ˈnis-ət-ē\ *n*

an·ti·glob·u·lin \ˌant-i-ˈgläb-yə-lən, ˌan-ˌtī-\ *n* (ca. 1909) **:** an antibody that combines with and precipitates globulin

An·tig·o·ne \an-ˈtig-ə-(ˌ)nē\ *n* [Gk *Antigonē*] **:** a daughter of Oedipus and Jocasta who buries her brother Polynices' body against the order of her uncle Creon

¹an·ti·grav·i·ty \ˌant-i-ˈgrav-ət-ē, ˌan-ˌtī-\ *adj* (1944) **:** reducing or canceling the effect of gravity or protecting against it

²antigravity *n* (1959) **:** a hypothetical effect resulting from or in cancelation or reduction of a gravitational field

an·ti·he·mo·phil·ic factor \-ˌhē-mə-ˌfil-ik-\ *n* (1947) **:** a glycoprotein of blood plasma that is essential for blood clotting and is absent or inactive in hemophilia — called also *antihemophilic globulin, factor VIII*

\ə\ abut \ᵊ\ kitten, F table \ər\ further \a\ ash \ā\ ace \ä\ cot, cart \au̇\ out \ch\ chin \e\ bet \ē\ easy \g\ go \i\ hit \ī\ ice \j\ job \ŋ\ sing \ō\ go \ȯ\ law \ȯi\ boy \th\ thin \t͟h\ the \ü\ loot \u̇\ foot \y\ yet \zh\ vision \å, k̲, ⁿ, œ, œ̄, ue, ue̅, ʸ\ *see* Guide to Pronunciation

an·ti·he·ro \'ant-i-ˌhē-(ˌ)rō, 'an-ˌtī-, -ˌhi(ə)r-(ˌ)ō\ *n* (1714) **:** a protagonist who is notably lacking in heroic qualities — **an·ti·he·ro·ic** \ˌant-i-hi-'rō-ik, ˌan-ˌtī-\ *adj*

an·ti·her·o·ine \ˌant-i-'her-ə-wən, ˌan-ˌtī-\ *n* (1907) **:** a female antihero

an·ti·his·ta·mine \-'his-tə-ˌmēn, -mən\ *n* (1946) **:** any of various compounds that counteract histamine in the body and that are used for treating allergic reactions (as hay fever) and cold symptoms — **antihistamine** *adj* — **an·ti·his·ta·min·ic** \-ˌhis-tə-'min-ik\ *adj or n*

an·ti·hu·man \-'hyü-mən, 'yü-\ *adj* (1854) **:** acting or being against man; *also* **:** reacting strongly with human antigens

an·ti·hy·per·ten·sive \-ˌhī-pər-'ten(t)-siv\ *n* (ca. 1957) **:** a substance that is effective against high blood pressure — **antihypertensive** *adj*

an·ti–in·flam·ma·to·ry \-in-'flam-ə-ˌtōr-ē, -ˌtȯr-\ *adj* (1957) **:** counteracting inflammation — **anti–inflammatory** *n*

an·ti–in·tel·lec·tu·al \-ˌint-ᵊl-'ek-ch(ə-w)əl, -'eksh-wəl\ *adj* (1936) **:** opposing or hostile to intellectuals or to an intellectual view or approach — **anti–intellectual** *n* — **an·ti–in·tel·lec·tu·al·ism** \-'ek-chə(-wə)-ˌliz-əm, -'eksh-wə-\ *n*

an·ti·knock \ˌant-i-'näk, ˌan-ˌtī-\ *n* (1921) **:** a substance used as a fuel or fuel additive to prevent knocking in an internal-combustion engine

an·ti·leu·ke·mic \-lü-'kē-mik\ *adj* (1951) **:** counteracting the effects of leukemia

an·ti·life \-'līf\ *adj* (1929) **:** antipathetic to normal, full, or healthy life; *also* **:** favoring birth control

an·ti·log \'ant-i-ˌlȯg, 'an-ˌtī-, -ˌläg\ *n* (1910) **:** ANTILOGARITHM

an·ti·log·a·rithm \ˌant-i-'lȯg-ə-ˌrith-əm, ˌan-ˌtī-, -'läg-\ *n* (1675) **:** the number corresponding to a given logarithm

an·ti·ma·cas·sar \ˌant-i-mə-'kas-ər\ *n* [*anti-* + *Macassar (oil)* (a hairdressing)] (1852) **:** a cover to protect the back or arms of furniture

an·ti·mag·net·ic \ˌant-i-mag-'net-ik, ˌan-ˌtī-\ *adj, of a watch* (1946) **:** having a balance unit composed of alloys that will not remain magnetized

an·ti·ma·lar·i·al \-mə-'ler-ē-əl\ *adj* (ca. 1893) **:** serving to prevent, check, or cure malaria — **antimalarial** *n*

an·ti·mat·ter \'ant-i-ˌmat-ər\ *n* (1950) **:** matter composed of the counterparts of ordinary matter (as antiprotons instead of protons, positrons instead of electrons, and antineutrons instead of neutrons)

an·ti·me·tab·o·lite \ˌant-i-mə-'tab-ə-ˌlīt, ˌan-ˌtī-\ *n* (1945) **:** a substance that replaces or inhibits the utilization of a metabolite

an·ti·mi·cro·bi·al \ˌant-i-mī-'krō-bē-əl\ *adj* (ca. 1910) **:** destroying or inhibiting the growth of microorganisms — **antimicrobial** *n*

an·ti·mis·sile missile \ˌant-i-'mis-əl-, ˌan-ˌtī-; *chiefly Brit* ˌant-i-'mis-ˌīl-\ *n* (ca. 1956) **:** ANTIBALLISTIC MISSILE

an·ti·mi·tot·ic \ˌant-i-mī-'tät-ik, ˌan-ˌtī-\ *adj* (1970) **:** inhibiting or disrupting mitosis ⟨~ agents⟩ ⟨~ activity⟩ — **antimitotic** *n*

an·ti·mo·ni·al \ˌant-ə-'mō-nē-əl\ *adj* (1605) **:** of, relating to, or containing antimony — **antimonial** *n*

an·ti·mon·ic \-'män-ik\ *adj* (ca. 1828) **:** of, relating to, or containing antimony with a valence of five

an·ti·mo·ni·ous \-'mō-nē-əs\ *adj* (ca. 1828) **:** of, relating to, or containing antimony with a valence of three

an·ti·mo·ny \'ant-ə-ˌmō-nē\ *n* [ME *antimonie*, fr. ML *antimonium*] (15c) **1 :** STIBNITE **2 :** a trivalent and pentavalent metalloid commonly metallic silvery white, crystalline, and brittle element that is used esp. as a constituent of alloys and in medicine — see ELEMENT table

an·ti·my·cin A \ˌant-i-ˌmīs-ᵊn-'ā\ *n* [*anti-* + *-mycin*] (1949) **:** a crystalline antibiotic $C_{28}H_{40}N_2O_9$ used esp. as a fungicide, insecticide, and miticide — called also *antimycin*

an·ti·neo·plas·tic \ˌant-i-ˌnē-ə-'plas-tik, ˌan-ˌtī-\ *adj* (1969) **:** inhibiting or preventing the growth and spread of neoplasms or malignant cells

an·ti·neu·tri·no \-n(y)ü-'trē-(ˌ)nō\ *n* (1934) **:** the antiparticle of the neutrino

an·ti·neu·tron \-'n(y)ü-ˌträn\ *n* (1942) **:** an uncharged particle of mass equal to that of the neutron but having a magnetic moment in the opposite direction

ant·ing \'ant-iŋ\ *n* (1936) **:** behavior by birds in which ants are rubbed against their feathers

an·ti·node \'ant-i-ˌnōd, 'an-ˌtī-\ *n* [ISV] (1882) **:** a region of maximum amplitude situated between adjacent nodes in a vibrating body — **an·ti·nod·al** \ˌant-i-'nōd-ᵊl, ˌan-ˌtī-\ *adj*

an·ti·no·mi·an \ˌant-i-'nō-mē-ən\ *n* [ML *antinomus*, fr. L *anti-* + Gk *nomos* law] (1645) **1 :** one who holds that under the gospel dispensation of grace the moral law is of no use or obligation because faith alone is necessary to salvation **2 :** one who rejects a socially established morality — **antinomian** *adj* — **an·ti·no·mi·an·ism** \-mē-ə-ˌniz-əm\ *n*

an·tin·o·my \an-'tin-ə-mē\ *n, pl* **-mies** [G *antinomie*, fr. L *antinomia* conflict of laws, fr. Gk, fr. *anti-* + *nomos* law — more at NIMBLE] (1592) **1 :** a contradiction between two apparently equally valid principles or between inferences correctly drawn from such principles **2 :** a fundamental and apparently unresolvable conflict or contradiction ⟨*antinomies* of beauty and evil, freedom and slavery —Stephen Holden⟩ — **an·ti·nom·ic** \ˌant-i-'näm-ik\ *adj*

an·ti·nov·el \'ant-i-ˌnäv-əl, 'an-ˌtī-\ *n* (1958) **:** a work of fiction that lacks most or all of the traditional features of the novel — **an·ti·nov·el·ist** \-ˌnäv-(ə-)ləst\ *n*

an·ti·nu·cle·ar \ˌant-i-'n(y)ü-klē-ər, ˌan-ˌtī-, ÷-kyə-lər\ *adj* (1958) **1 :** tending to react with cell nuclei or their components (as DNA) ⟨~ antibodies⟩ **2 :** opposing the use or production of nuclear power plants

an·ti·nu·cle·on \-'n(y)ü-klē-ˌän\ *n* (1946) **:** the antiparticle of a nucleon

an·ti·nuke \-'n(y)ük\ *adj* (1975) **:** ANTINUCLEAR 2

an·ti·ox·i·dant \ˌant-ē-'äk-səd-ənt, ˌan-ˌtī-\ *n* (1926) **:** a substance that opposes oxidation or inhibits reactions promoted by oxygen or peroxides — **antioxidant** *adj*

an·ti·ozon·ant \-'ō-(ˌ)zō-nənt\ *n* (1954) **:** a substance that opposes ozonization or protects against it

an·ti·par·al·lel \ˌant-i-'par-ə-ˌlel, ˌan-ˌtī-, -ləl\ *adj* (ca. 1828) **:** parallel but oppositely directed or oriented ⟨~ electron spins⟩ ⟨two ~ chains of nucleotides comprise DNA⟩

an·ti·par·a·sit·ic \ˌant-i-ˌpar-ə-'sit-ik, ˌan-ˌtī-\ *adj* (1899) **:** acting against parasites

an·ti·par·ti·cle \'ant-i-ˌpärt-i-kəl, 'an-ˌtī-\ *n* (1934) **:** a subatomic particle identical to another subatomic particle in mass but opposite to it in electric and magnetic properties that when brought together with its counterpart produces mutual annihilation

an·ti·pas·to \ˌant-i-'pas-(ˌ)tō, ˌänt-i-'päs-\ *n, pl* **-ti** \-(ˌ)tē\ [It, fr. *anti-* (fr. L *ante-*) + *pasto* food, fr. L *pastus*, fr. *pastus*, pp. of *pascere* to feed — more at FOOD] (1590) **:** any of various typically Italian hors d'oeuvres; *also* **:** a plate of these served esp. as the first course of a meal

an·ti·pa·thet·ic \ˌant-i-pə-'thet-ik\ *adj* (1640) **1 :** having a natural aversion **2 :** arousing or showing antipathy ⟨the . . . Congress was ~ to his new stance —*Current Biog.*⟩ — **an·ti·pa·thet·i·cal·ly** \-i-k(ə-)lē\ *adv*

an·tip·a·thy \an-'tip-ə-thē\ *n, pl* **-thies** [L *antipathia*, fr. Gk *antipatheia*, fr. *antipathēs* of opposite feelings, fr. *anti-* + *pathos* experience — more at PATHOS] (1601) **1** *obs* **:** opposition in feeling **2 :** settled aversion or dislike **:** DISTASTE **3 :** an object of aversion ***syn*** see ENMITY

an·ti·per·son·nel \ˌant-i-ˌpərs-ᵊn-'el, ˌan-ˌtī-\ *adj* (1939) **:** designed for use against military personnel ⟨an ~ mine⟩

an·ti·per·spi·rant \-'pər-sp(ə-)rənt\ *n* (1943) **:** a cosmetic preparation used to check excessive perspiration

an·ti·phlo·gis·tic \-flə-'jis-tik\ *adj* (1769) **:** ANTI-INFLAMMATORY — **antiphlogistic** *n*

an·ti·phon \'ant-ə-fən, -ˌfän\ *n* [LL *antiphona* — more at ANTHEM] (1500) **1 :** a psalm, anthem, or verse sung responsively **2 :** a verse usu. from Scripture said or sung before and after a canticle, psalm, or psalm verse as part of the liturgy

[1]**an·tiph·o·nal** \an-'tif-ən-ᵊl\ *n* (1537) **:** ANTIPHONARY

[2]**antiphonal** *adj* (1719) **:** of or relating to an antiphon or antiphony — **an·tiph·o·nal·ly** \-ᵊl-ē\ *adv*

an·tiph·o·nary \an-'tif-ə-ˌner-ē\ *n, pl* **-nar·ies** (14c) **1 :** a book containing a collection of antiphons **2 :** a book containing the choral parts of the Divine Office

an·tiph·o·ny \an-'tif-ə-nē\ *n, pl* **-nies** (1592) **:** responsive alternation between two groups esp. of singers

an·tiph·ra·sis \an-'tif-rə-səs\ *n, pl* **-ra·ses** \-ˌsēz\ [LL, fr. Gk, fr. *anti-* + *phrasis* diction — more at PHRASE] (1533) **:** the usu. ironic or humorous use of words in senses opposite to the generally accepted meanings ⟨"this giant of 3 feet 4 inches" is an example of ~⟩

[1]**an·tip·o·dal** \an-'tip-əd-ᵊl\ *adj* (1646) **1 :** of or relating to the antipodes; *specif* **:** situated at the opposite side of the earth or moon ⟨an ~ meridian⟩ ⟨an ~ continent⟩ **2 :** diametrically opposite ⟨an ~ point on a sphere⟩ **3 :** OPPOSED ⟨a system ~ to democracy⟩

[2]**antipodal** *n* (1919) **:** any of three cells in the female gametophyte of most angiosperms that are grouped at the end of the embryo sac farthest from the micropyle — called also *antipodal cell*

an·ti·pode \'ant-ə-ˌpōd\ *n, pl* **an·tip·o·des** \an-'tip-ə-ˌdēz\ [ME *antipodes*, pl., persons dwelling at opposite points on the globe, fr. L, fr. Gk, fr. pl. of *antipod-*, *antipous* with feet opposite, fr. *anti-* + *pod-*, *pous* foot — more at FOOT] (1549) **1 :** the parts of the earth diametrically opposite — usu. used in pl. **2 :** the exact opposite or contrary — **an·tip·o·de·an** \(ˌ)an-ˌtip-ə-'dē-ən\ *adj*

an·ti·po·et·ic \ˌant-i-pō-'et-ik, ˌan-ˌtī-\ *adj* (1847) **:** of, relating to, or characterized by opposition to traditional poetic technique or style

an·ti·pol·lu·tion \-pə-'lü-shən\ *adj* (1924) **:** designed to prevent, reduce, or eliminate pollution ⟨~ laws⟩ — **antipollution** *n*

an·ti·pope \'ant-i-ˌpōp\ *n* [MF *antipape*, fr. ML *antipapa*, fr. *anti-* + *papa* pope] (15c) **:** one elected or claiming to be pope in opposition to the pope canonically chosen

an·ti·pro·ton \ˌant-i-'prō-ˌtän, ˌan-ˌtī-\ *n* (1940) **:** the antiparticle of the proton

an·ti·psy·chot·ic \ˌant-i-sī-'kät-ik\ *adj* (1955) **:** tending to alleviate psychosis or psychotic states ⟨an ~ drug⟩ — **antipsychotic** *n*

an·ti·py·ret·ic \-pī-'ret-ik\ *n* (1681) **:** an agent that reduces fever — **antipyretic** *adj*

an·ti·py·rine \-'pī(ə)r-ˌēn\ *n* [fr. *Antipyrine*, a trademark] (1884) **:** a white crystalline compound $C_{11}H_{12}N_2O$ formerly widely used to relieve fever, pain, or rheumatism but now largely replaced in oral use by less toxic substances (as aspirin)

[1]**an·ti·quar·i·an** \ˌant-ə-'kwer-ē-ən\ *n* (1610) **:** one who collects or studies antiquities

[2]**antiquarian** *adj* (1771) **1 :** of or relating to antiquarians or antiquities **2 :** dealing in old or rare books — **an·ti·quar·i·an·ism** \-ē-ə-ˌniz-əm\ *n*

an·ti·quark \'ant-i-ˌkwärk, 'an-ˌtī-\ *n* (1965) **:** the antiparticle of the quark

an·ti·quary \'ant-ə-ˌkwer-ē\ *n, pl* **-quar·ies** (1586) **:** ANTIQUARIAN

an·ti·quate \'ant-ə-ˌkwāt\ *vt* **-quat·ed; -quat·ing** [LL *antiquatus*, pp. of *antiquare*, fr. L *antiquus*] (1596) **:** to make old or obsolete — **an·ti·qua·tion** \ˌant-ə-'kwā-shən\ *n*

an·ti·quat·ed *adj* (1623) **1 :** OBSOLETE ⟨a calendar becomes ~ —A. L. Kroeber⟩ **2 :** outmoded or discredited by reason of age **:** being out of style or fashion ⟨~ methods of farming⟩ **3 :** advanced in age ***syn*** see OLD

[1]**an·tique** \an-'tēk\ *n* (1530) **1 :** a relic or object of ancient times or of an earlier period than the present **2 :** a work of art, piece of furniture, or decorative object made at an earlier period and according to various customs laws at least 100 years ago

[2]**an·tique** \(')an-'tēk, *in verse often* 'ant-ik\ *adj* [MF, fr. L *antiquus*, fr. *ante* before — more at ANTE-] (1536) **1 :** existing since or belonging to earlier times **:** ANCIENT ⟨~ trade routes to the Orient⟩ **2 a :** being in the style or fashion of former times ⟨~ manners and graces⟩ **b :** made in or representative of the work of an earlier period ⟨~ mirrors⟩; *also* **:** being an antique **3 :** selling or exhibiting antiques ⟨an ~ show⟩ ***syn*** see OLD

[3]**an·tique** \an-'tēk\ *vt* **-tiqued; -tiqu·ing** (1923) **:** to finish or refinish in antique style **:** give an appearance of age to

an·tiq·ui·ty \an-'tik-wət-ē\ *n, pl* **-ties** (13c) **1 :** ancient times; *esp* **:** those before the Middle Ages **2 :** the quality of being ancient **3** *pl* **a :** relics or monuments (as coins, statues, or buildings) of ancient times **b :** matters relating to the life or culture of ancient times **4 :** the people of ancient times

an·ti·ra·chit·ic \ˌant-i-rə-'kit-ik, ˌan-ˌtī-\ *adj* (1853) **:** opposing or preventing the development of rickets ⟨an ~ vitamin⟩

an·ti·rheu·mat·ic \-rü-'mat-ik\ *adj* (1817) **:** alleviating or preventing rheumatism ⟨~ therapy⟩ — **antirheumatic** *n*

an·tir·rhi·num \ˌant-ə-'rī-nəm\ *n* [NL, genus name, fr. L, snapdragon, fr. Gk *antirrhinon*, fr. *anti-* like (fr. *anti* against, equivalent to) + *rhin-*,

rhis nose — more at ANTI-] (1548) **:** any of a large genus (*Antirrhinum*) of herbs (as the snapdragon) of the figwort family with bright-colored irregular flowers
antis *pl of* ANTI
an·ti·scor·bu·tic \ˌant-i-skȯr-ˈbyüt-ik, ˌan-ˌtī-\ *adj* (1725) **:** counteracting scurvy ⟨the ~ vitamin is vitamin C⟩ — **antiscorbutic** *n*
an·ti–Sem·i·tism \ˌant-i-ˈsem-ə-ˌtiz-əm, ˌan-ˌtī-\ *n* (1881) **:** hostility toward or discrimination against Jews as a religious or racial group — **an·ti–Se·mit·ic** \-sə-ˈmit-ik\ *adj* — **an·ti–Sem·ite** \-ˈsem-ˌīt\ *n*
an·ti·sep·sis \ˌant-ə-ˈsep-səs\ *n* (1875) **:** the inhibiting of the growth and multiplication of microorganisms by antiseptic means
¹an·ti·sep·tic \ˌant-ə-ˈsep-tik\ *adj* [*anti-* + Gk *sēptikos* putrefying, septic] (1751) **1 a :** opposing sepsis, putrefaction, or decay; *esp* **:** preventing or arresting the growth of microorganisms (as on living tissue) **b :** acting or protecting like an antiseptic **2 :** relating to or characterized by the use of antiseptics **3 a :** scrupulously clean **:** ASEPTIC **b :** extremely neat or orderly; *esp* **:** neat to the point of being bare or uninteresting **c :** free from what is held to be contaminating **4 :** IMPERSONAL, DETACHED; *esp* **:** coldly impersonal ⟨"acceptable losses on the battlefield" is another ~ phrase⟩ — **an·ti·sep·ti·cal·ly** \-ti-k(ə-)lē\ *adv*
²antiseptic *n* (1751) **:** a substance that checks the growth or action of microorganisms esp. in or on living tissue; *also* **:** GERMICIDE
an·ti·se·rum \ˈant-i-ˌsir-əm, ˈan-ˌtī-, -ˌser-\ *n* [ISV] (1901) **:** a serum containing antibodies
an·ti·so·cial \-ˈsō-shəl\ *adj* (1797) **1 :** averse to the society of others **:** UNSOCIABLE **2 :** hostile or harmful to organized society; *esp* **:** being or marked by behavior deviating sharply from the social norm
an·ti·spas·mod·ic \-spaz-ˈmäd-ik\ *adj* (ca. 1755) **:** capable of preventing or relieving spasms or convulsions — **antispasmodic** *n*
an·ti·stat \-ˈstat\ *or* **an·ti·stat·ic** \-ˈstat-ik\ *adj* (1952) **:** reducing, removing, or preventing the buildup of static electricity
an·tis·tro·phe \an-ˈtis-trə-(ˌ)fē\ *n* [LL, fr. Gk *antistrophē,* fr. *anti-* + *strophē* strophe] (ca. 1550) **1 a :** the repetition of words in reversed order **b :** the repetition of a word or phrase at the end of successive clauses **2 a :** a returning movement in Greek choral dance exactly answering to a previous strophe **b :** the part of a choral song delivered during the antistrophe — **an·ti·stroph·ic** \ˌant-ə-ˈsträf-ik\ *adj* — **an·ti·stroph·i·cal·ly** \-i-k(ə-)lē\ *adv*
an·ti·sym·met·ric \-sə-ˈme-trik\ *adj* (1923) **:** relating to or being a relation (as "is a subset of") that implies equality of any two quantities for which it holds in both directions ⟨the relation *R* is ~ if *aRb* and *bRa* implies *a* = *b*⟩
an·tith·e·sis \an-ˈtith-ə-səs\ *n, pl* **-e·ses** \-ˌsēz\ [LL, fr. Gk, lit., opposition, fr. *antitithenai* to oppose, fr. *anti-* + *tithenai* to set — more at DO] (1529) **1 a (1) :** the rhetorical contrast of ideas by means of parallel arrangements of words, clauses, or sentences (as in "action, not words" or "they promised freedom and provided slavery") **(2) :** OPPOSITION, CONTRAST ⟨the ~ of prose and verse⟩ **b (1) :** the second of two opposing constituents of an antithesis **(2) :** the direct opposite **2 :** the second stage of a dialectic process
an·ti·thet·i·cal \ˌant-ə-ˈthet-i-kəl\ *also* **an·ti·thet·ic** \-ˈthet-ik\ *adj* (1583) **1 :** constituting or marked by antithesis **2 :** being in direct and unequivocal opposition ***syn*** see OPPOSITE — **an·ti·thet·i·cal·ly** \-i-k(ə-)lē\ *adv*
an·ti·thy·roid \ˌant-i-ˈthī-ˌrȯid\ *adj* (1908) **:** able to counteract excessive thyroid activity ⟨~ drugs⟩
an·ti·tox·ic \-ˈtäk-sik\ *adj* (ca. 1890) **1 :** counteracting toxins ⟨~ versus antibacterial immunity⟩ **2 :** being or containing antitoxins ⟨~ serum⟩
an·ti·tox·in \ˌant-i-ˈtäk-sən\ *n* [ISV] (ca. 1890) **:** an antibody that is capable of neutralizing the specific toxin (as a specific causative agent of disease) that stimulated its production in the body and is produced in animals for medical purposes by injection of a toxin or toxoid with the resulting serum being used to counteract the toxin in other individuals; *also* **:** a serum containing antitoxins
an·ti·trades \ˈant-i-ˌtrādz, ˈan-ˌtī-\ *n pl* (1853) **1 :** the prevailing westerly winds of middle latitudes **2 :** the westerly winds above the trade winds
an·ti·trust \ˌant-i-ˈtrəst, ˌan-ˌtī-\ *adj* (1890) **:** of or relating to legislation or opposition to trusts or combinations; *specif* **:** consisting of laws to protect trade and commerce from unlawful restraints and monopolies or unfair business practices
an·ti·trust·er \-ˈtrəs-tər\ *n* (1947) **:** one who advocates or enforces antitrust provisions of the law
an·ti·tus·sive \-ˈtəs-iv\ *n* (ca. 1909) **:** a cough suppressant — **antitussive** *adj*
an·ti–utopia \ˌant-i-yu̇-ˈtō-pē-ə, ˌan-ˌtī-\ *n* (1966) **1 :** DYSTOPIA **2 :** a work describing an anti-utopia
¹an·ti–uto·pi·an \-pē-ən\ *adj* (1947) **:** of, relating to, or having the characteristics of an anti-utopia
²anti–utopian *n* (1966) **:** one that believes in or predicts an anti-utopia
an·ti·ven·in \ˌant-i-ˈven-ən, ˌan-ˌtī-\ *n* [ISV] (1895) **:** an antitoxin to a venom; *also* **:** an antiserum containing such antitoxin
an·ti·vi·ta·min \ˈant-i-ˌvīt-ə-mən\ *n* (1927) **:** a substance that makes a vitamin metabolically ineffective
an·ti·white \ˌant-i-ˈhwīt, ˌan-ˌtī-, -ˈwīt\ *adj* (1906) **:** opposed or hostile to people belonging to a light-skinned race
ant·ler \ˈant-lər\ *n* [ME *aunteler,* fr. MF *antoillier,* fr. (assumed) VL *anteoculare,* fr. neut. of *anteocularis* located before the eye, fr. L *ante-* + *oculus* eye — more at EYE] (14c) **:** the solid deciduous horn of an animal of the deer family; *also* **:** a branch of this horn — **ant·lered** \-lərd\ *adj*
ant lion *n* (1815) **:** any of various neuropterous insects (as of the genus *Myrmeleon*) having a long-jawed larva that digs a conical pit in which it lies in wait to catch insects (as ants) on which it feeds

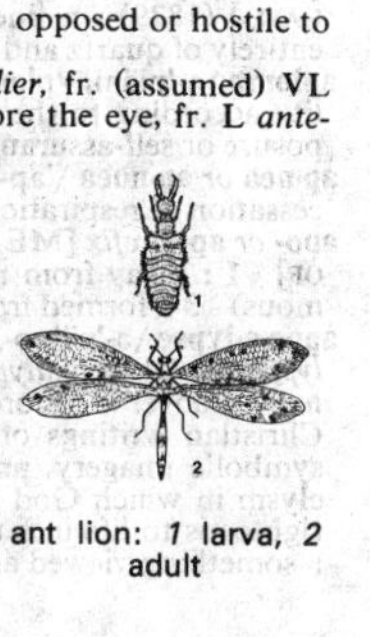

ant lion: *1* larva, *2* adult

An·to·ni·an \an-ˈtō-nē-ən\ *n* [L *Antonius* Anthony] (ca. 1907) **:** a member of one of several monastic communities (as the Armenian Antonians) that follow a rule derived from St. Anthony

ant·onym \ˈant-ə-ˌnim\ *n* (1870) **:** a word of opposite meaning ⟨the usual ~ of *good* is *bad*⟩ — **ant·onym·ic** \ˌant-ə-ˈnim-ik\ *adj* — **an·ton·y·mous** \an-ˈtän-ə-məs\ *adj* — **an·ton·y·my** \-mē\ *n*
an·tre \ˈant-ər\ *n* [F, fr. L *antrum*] (1604) **:** CAVE 1
an·trum \ˈan-trəm\ *n, pl* **an·tra** \-trə\ [LL, fr. L, cave, fr. Gk *antron*] (ca. 1727) **:** the cavity of a hollow organ or a sinus — **an·tral** \-trəl\ *adj*
ant·sy \ˈant-sē\ *adj* (1951) **:** FIDGETY
an·uran \ə-ˈn(y)u̇r-ən, a-\ *adj or n* [deriv. of *a-* + Gk *oura* tail — more at ASS] (1900) **:** SALIENTIAN
an·uria \ə-ˈn(y)u̇r-ē-ə, a-\ *n* [NL] (1838) **:** absence or defective excretion of urine — **an·uric** \-ˈn(y)u̇r-ik\ *adj*
anus \ˈā-nəs\ *n* [L; perh. akin to OIr *áinne* anus] (15c) **:** the posterior opening of the alimentary canal
an·vil \ˈan-vəl\ *n* [ME *anfilt,* fr. OE; akin to OHG *anafalz* anvil; akin to L *pellere* to beat — more at ON, FELT] (bef. 12c) **1 :** a heavy usu. steel-faced iron block on which metal is shaped (as by hand hammering) **2 :** INCUS
anx·i·ety \aŋ-ˈzī-ət-ē\ *n, pl* **-eties** [L *anxietas,* fr. *anxius*] (1525) **1 a :** painful or apprehensive uneasiness of mind usu. over an impending or anticipated ill **b :** fearful concern or interest **c :** a cause of anxiety **2 :** an abnormal and overwhelming sense of apprehension and fear often marked by physiological signs (as sweating, tension, and increased pulse), by doubt concerning the reality and nature of the threat, and by self-doubt about one's capacity to cope with it ***syn*** see CARE
an·xi·o·lyt·ic \ˌaŋ-zē-ō-ˈlit-ik, ˌaŋ(k)-sē-\ *n* [*anxiety* + *-o-* + *-lytic*] (1965) **:** a drug that relieves anxiety — **anxiolytic** *adj*
anx·ious \ˈaŋ(k)-shəs\ *adj* [L *anxius;* akin to L *angere* to strangle, distress — more at ANGER] (1623) **1 :** characterized by extreme uneasiness of mind or brooding fear about some contingency **:** WORRIED **2 :** characterized by, resulting from, or causing anxiety **:** WORRYING **3 :** ardently or earnestly wishing ***syn*** see EAGER — **anx·ious·ly** *adv* — **anx·ious·ness** *n*
¹any \ˈen-ē\ *adj* [ME, fr. OE *ǣnig;* akin to OHG *einag* any, OE *ān* one — more at ONE] (bef. 12c) **1 :** one or some indiscriminately of whatever kind: **a :** one or another taken at random ⟨ask ~ man you meet⟩ **b :** EVERY — used to indicate one selected without restriction ⟨~ child would know that⟩ **2 :** one, some, or all indiscriminately of whatever quantity: **a :** one or more — used to indicate an undetermined number or amount ⟨have you ~ money⟩ **b :** ALL — used to indicate a maximum or whole ⟨needs ~ help he can get⟩ **c :** a or some without reference to quantity or extent ⟨grateful for ~ favor at all⟩ **3 a :** unmeasured or unlimited in amount, number, or extent ⟨~ quantity you desire⟩ **b :** appreciably large or extended ⟨could not endure it ~ length of time⟩
²any *pron, sing or pl in constr* (bef. 12c) **1 :** any person or persons **:** ANYONE **2 a :** any thing or things **b :** any part, quantity, or number
³any *adv* (14c) **:** to any extent or degree **:** AT ALL ⟨was never ~ good⟩
any·body \-ˌbäd-ē, -bəd-\ *pron* (14c) **:** any person **:** ANYONE
any·how \-ˌhau̇\ *adv* (1694) **1 a :** in any manner whatever **b :** in a haphazard manner **2 a :** at any rate **b :** in any event
any·more \ˌen-ē-ˈmō(ə)r, -ˈmȯ(ə)r\ *adv* (14c) **1 :** any longer ⟨I was not moving ~ with my feet — Anaïs Nin⟩ **2 :** at the present time **:** NOW ⟨hardly a day passes without rain ~⟩
usage Although both *anymore* and *any more* are found in written use, in the 20th century *anymore* is the more common styling. *Anymore* is regularly used in negative ⟨no one can be natural *anymore* —May Sarton⟩, interrogative ⟨do you read much *anymore?*⟩, and conditional ⟨if you do that *anymore,* I'll leave⟩ contexts and in certain positive constructions ⟨the Washingtonian is too sophisticated to believe *any more* in solutions —Russell Baker⟩ In some regions the use of *anymore* in sense 2 is quite common in positive constructions ⟨listening is a rare art *anymore!* —Alma Holland (*Writer's Digest*)⟩ ⟨in a way he almost felt sorry for him, *any more* —James Jones⟩ While most common in Midland settlement areas of the U.S., this usage is also found in other areas. It has been noted at least since the 19th century in England and may be of British dialectal origin ⟨'Quite absurd,' he said. 'Suffering bores me, *any more.*' —D.H. Lawrence⟩
any·one \ˈen-ē-(ˌ)wən\ *pron* (1711) **:** any person at all
any·place \-ˌplās\ *adv* (1916) **:** in any place **:** ANYWHERE
¹any·thing \-ˌthiŋ\ *pron* (bef. 12c) **:** any thing whatever
²anything *adv* (bef. 12c) **:** AT ALL
any·time \ˈen-ē-ˌtīm\ *adv* (1926) **:** at any time whatever
any·way \-ˌwā\ *adv* (13c) **1 :** ANYWISE **2 :** in any case **:** ANYHOW
any·ways \-ˌwāz\ *adv* (13c) **1** *archaic* **:** ANYWISE **2** *chiefly dial* **:** in any case
¹any·where \-ˌ(h)we(ə)r, -ˌ(h)wa(ə)r, -(h)wər\ *adv* (14c) **1 :** at, in, or to any place or point **2 :** to any extent **:** AT ALL **3** — used as a function word to indicate limits of variation ⟨~ from 40 to 60 students⟩
²anywhere *n* (1924) **:** any place
any·wise \ˈen-ē-ˌwīz\ *adv* (bef. 12c) **:** in any way whatever **:** AT ALL
An·zac \ˈan-ˌzak\ *n* [*A*ustralian and *N*ew *Z*ealand *A*rmy *C*orps] (1915) **:** a soldier from Australia or New Zealand
A–OK \ˌā-(ˌ)ō-ˈkā\ *adv or adj* (1959) **:** very definitely OK
A1 \ˈā-ˈwən\ *adj* (1837) **1 :** having the highest possible classification — used of a ship **2 :** of the finest quality **:** FIRST-RATE
ao·rist \ˈā-ə-rəst, ˈe-ə-\ *n* [LL & Gk; LL *aoristos,* fr. Gk, fr. *aoristos* undefined, fr. *a-* + *horistos* definable, fr. *horizein* to define — more at HORIZON] (1581) **:** an inflectional form of a verb typically denoting simple occurrence of an action without reference to its completeness, duration, or repetition — **aorist** *or* **ao·ris·tic** \ˌā-ə-ˈris-tik, ˌe-ə-\ *adj* — **ao·ris·ti·cal·ly** \-ti-k(ə-)lē\ *adv*
aort- *or* **aorto-** *comb form* **:** aorta **:** aortic and ⟨*aorto*esophageal⟩
aor·ta \ā-ˈȯrt-ə\ *n, pl* **-tas** *or* **-tae** \-ē\ [NL, fr. Gk *aortē,* fr. *aeirein* to lift] (1578) **:** the great arterial trunk that carries blood from the heart to be distributed by branch arteries through the body — see HEART illustration — **aor·tic** \-ˈȯrt-ik\ *adj*

aortic arch *n* (1903) **:** one of the arterial branches in vertebrate embryos that exist in a series of pairs with one on each side of the embryo, connect the ventral arterial system lying anterior to the heart to the dorsal arterial system above the alimentary tract, and persist in adult fishes but are reduced or much modified in the adult of higher forms

aor·tog·ra·phy \ˌā-ˌȯr-ˈtäg-rə-fē\ *n* (ca. 1935) **:** arteriography of the aorta — **aor·to·graph·ic** \(ˌ)ā-ˌȯrt-ə-ˈgraf-ik\ *adj*

aou·dad \ˈau̇-ˌdad, ˈä-ü-\ *n* [F, fr. Berber *audad*] (1861) **:** a wild sheep (*Ammotragus lervia*) of No. Africa

à ou·trance \ˌä-ˌü-ˈträ^ns\ *adv* [F] (1600) **:** to the limit **:** UNSPARINGLY

1ap- — see AD-

2ap- — see APO-

apace \ə-ˈpās\ *adv* [ME, prob. fr. MF *à pas* on step] (14c) **1 :** at a quick pace **:** SWIFTLY **2 :** ABREAST — used with *of* or *with*

Apache \ə-ˈpach-ē, *in sense 3* ə-ˈpash\ *n, pl* **Apache** *or* **Apach·es** \-ˈpach-ēz, -ˈpash(-əz)\ [Sp] (1745) **1 a :** a group of American Indian peoples of the southwestern U.S. **b :** a member of any of these peoples **2 :** any of the Athapaskan languages of the Apache people **3** *not cap* [F, fr. *Apache* Apache Indian] **a :** a member of a gang of criminals esp. in Paris **b :** RUFFIAN

ap·a·nage *var of* APPANAGE

ap·a·re·jo \ˌap-ə-ˈrā-(ˌ)(h)ō\ *n, pl* **-jos** [AmerSp] (1844) **:** a packsaddle of stuffed leather or canvas

1apart \ə-ˈpärt\ *adv* [ME, fr. MF *a part*, lit., to the side] (14c) **1 a :** at a little distance ⟨tried to keep ~ from the family squabbles⟩ **b :** away from one another in space or time ⟨towns 20 miles ~⟩ **2 a :** as a separate unit **:** INDEPENDENTLY ⟨viewed ~, his arguments were unsound⟩ **b :** so as to separate one from another ⟨found it hard to tell the twins ~⟩ **3 :** excluded from consideration **:** ASIDE ⟨a few blemishes ~, the novel is excellent⟩ **4 :** in or into two or more parts **:** to pieces ⟨had to take the engine ~⟩

2apart *adj* (1786) **1 :** SEPARATE, ISOLATED **2 :** holding different opinions **:** DIVIDED — **apart·ness** *n*

apart from *prep* (1617) **:** other than **:** BESIDES

apart·heid \ə-ˈpär-ˌtāt, -ˌtīt\ *n* [Afrik, fr. D, fr. *apart* apart + *-heid* -hood] (1947) **1 :** racial segregation; *specif* **:** a policy of segregation and political and economic discrimination against non-European groups in the Republic of So. Africa **2 :** SEPARATION, SEGREGATION ⟨I favor ~ of smokers —L.E. Bellin⟩ ⟨sexual ~⟩

apart·ment \ə-ˈpärt-mənt\ *n* [F *appartement*, fr. It *appartamento*] (1641) **1 :** a room or set of rooms fitted esp. with housekeeping facilities and usu. leased as a dwelling **2 :** a building containing several individual apartments — **apart·men·tal** \ə-ˌpärt-ˈment-ᵊl\ *adj*

apartment hotel *n* (1909) **:** a hotel containing apartments as well as accommodations for transients

apartment house *n* (1874) **:** a building containing separate residential apartments — called also *apartment building*

ap·a·thet·ic \ˌap-ə-ˈthet-ik\ *adj* (1744) **1 :** having or showing little or no feeling or emotion **:** SPIRITLESS **2 :** having little or no interest or concern **:** INDIFFERENT ***syn*** see IMPASSIVE — **ap·a·thet·i·cal·ly** \-i-k(ə-)lē\ *adv*

ap·a·thy \ˈap-ə-thē\ *n* [Gk *apatheia*, fr. *apathēs* without feeling, fr. *a-* + *pathos* emotion] (1603) **1 :** lack of feeling or emotion **:** IMPASSIVENESS **2 :** lack of interest or concern **:** INDIFFERENCE

ap·a·tite \ˈap-ə-ˌtīt\ *n* [G *apatit*, fr. Gk *apatē* deceit] (1803) **:** any of a group of calcium phosphate minerals of the approximate general formula $Ca_5(F,Cl,OH,{}^1/_2CO_3)(PO_4)_3$ occurring variously as hexagonal crystals, as granular masses, or in fine-grained masses as the chief constituent of phosphate rock and of bones and teeth; *specif* **:** calcium phosphate fluoride $Ca_5F(PO_4)_3$

1ape \ˈāp\ *n* [ME, fr. OE *apa*; akin to OHG *affo* ape] (bef. 12c) **1 a :** MONKEY; *esp* **:** one of the larger tailless or short-tailed Old World forms **b :** any of a family (Pongidae) of large tailless semierect primates (as the chimpanzee, gorilla, orangutan, or gibbon) — called also *anthropoid, anthropoid ape* **2 a :** MIMIC **b :** a large uncouth person — **ape·like** \ˈā-ˌplīk\ *adj*

2ape *vt* **aped; ap·ing** (1632) **:** to copy closely but often clumsily and ineptly ⟨servants *aping* their betters⟩ ***syn*** see COPY — **ap·er** *n*

3ape *adj* (ca. 1955) **:** being beyond restraint **:** CRAZY, WILD — usu. used in the phrase *go ape*

apeak \ə-ˈpēk\ *adj or adv* [alter. of earlier *apike*, prob. fr. F *à pic* vertically] (1596) **:** being in a vertical position ⟨with oars ~⟩

ape–man \ˈāp-ˈman, -ˌman\ *n* (1879) **:** a primate (as pithecanthropine) intermediate in character between Homo sapiens and the higher apes

aper·çu \ȧ-per-sü̅e, ˌap-ər-ˈsü\ *n, pl* **aperçus** \-sü̅e(z), -ˈsüz\ [F, fr. *aperçu*, pp. of *apercevoir* to perceive, fr. OF *aperceivre*, fr. *a-* (fr. L *ad-*) + *perceivre* to perceive — more at PERCEIVE] (1828) **1 :** an immediate impression; *esp* **:** INSIGHT 2 **2 :** a brief survey or sketch **:** OUTLINE

ape·ri·ent \ə-ˈpir-ē-ənt\ *adj* [L *aperient-, aperiens*, prp. of *aperire*] (1626) **:** gently moving the bowels **:** LAXATIVE — **aperient** *n*

ape·ri·od·ic \ˌā-ˌpir-ē-ˈäd-ik\ *adj* (1879) **1 :** of irregular occurrence ⟨~ floods⟩ **2 :** not having periodic vibrations **:** not oscillatory **3** *cryptology* **:** not repeating or not repeating with a short or easily discoverable period ⟨an ~ key⟩ — **ape·ri·od·i·cal·ly** \-i-k(ə-)lē\ *adv* — **ape·ri·o·dic·i·ty** \-ē-ə-ˈdis-ət-ē\ *n*

aper·i·tif \ˌäp-ˌer-ə-ˈtēf, ə-ˈper-ə-ˌ\ *n* [F *apéritif* aperient, aperitif, fr. MF *aperitif*, adj., aperient, fr. ML *aperitivus*, irreg. fr. L *aperire*] (1894) **:** an alcoholic drink taken before a meal as an appetizer

ap·er·ture \ˈap-ə(r)-ˌchu̇(ə)r, -chər, -ˌt(y)u̇(ə)r\ *n* [ME, fr. L *apertura*, fr. *apertus*, pp. of *aperire* to open] (15c) **1 :** an opening or open space **:** HOLE **2 a :** the opening in a photographic lens that admits the light **b :** the diameter of the stop in an optical system that determines the diameter of the bundle of rays traversing the instrument **c :** the diameter of the objective lens or mirror of a telescope

apet·al·ous \(ˈ)ā-ˈpet-ᵊl-əs\ *adj* (ca. 1706) **:** having no petals

apex \ˈā-ˌpeks\ *n, pl* **apex·es** *or* **api·ces** \ˈā-pə-ˌsēz, ˈap-ə-\ [L; akin to L *apsis* — more at APSIS] (1601) **1 a :** the uppermost point **:** VERTEX ⟨the ~ of a mountain⟩ **b :** the narrowed or pointed end **:** TIP ⟨the ~ of the tongue⟩ **2 :** the highest or culminating point ⟨the ~ of his career⟩ ***syn*** see SUMMIT

aphaer·e·sis *or* **apher·e·sis** \ə-ˈfer-ə-səs\ *n, pl* **-e·ses** \-ˌsēz\ [LL, fr. Gk *aphairesis*, lit., taking off, fr. *aphairein* to take away, fr. *apo-* + *hairein* to take] (ca. 1550) **:** the loss of one or more sounds or letters at the beginning of a word (as in *round* for *around* and *coon* for *raccoon*) — **aph·ae·ret·ic** \ˌaf-ə-ˈret-ik\ *adj*

aph·a·nite \ˈaf-ə-ˌnīt\ *n* [F, fr. Gk *aphanēs* invisible, fr. *a-* + *phainesthai* to appear — more at PHENOMENON] (ca. 1828) **:** a dark rock of such close texture that its separate grains are invisible to the naked eye — **aph·a·nit·ic** \ˌaf-ə-ˈnit-ik\ *adj*

apha·sia \ə-ˈfā-zh(ē-)ə\ *n* [NL, fr. Gk, fr. *a-* + *-phasia*] (1867) **:** loss or impairment of the power to use or comprehend words usu. resulting from a brain lesion — **apha·si·ac** \-zē-ˌak\ *n* — **apha·sic** \-zik\ *n or adj*

aph·elion \a-ˈfēl-yən\ *n, pl* **-elia** \-yə\ [NL, fr. Gk *apo-* + Gk *hēlios* sun — more at SOLAR] (1656) **:** the point in the path of a celestial body (as a planet) that is farthest from the sun — compare PERIHELION

aph·e·sis \ˈaf-ə-səs\ *n, pl* **-e·ses** \-ˌsēz\ [NL, fr. Gk, release, fr. *aphienai* to let go, fr. *apo-* + *hienai* to send — more at JET] (1880) **:** aphaeresis consisting of the loss of a short unaccented vowel (as in *lone* for *alone*) — **aphet·ic** \ə-ˈfet-ik\ *adj* — **aphet·i·cal·ly** \-i-k(ə-)lē\ *adv*

aphid \ˈā-fəd *also* ˈaf-əd\ *n* (1884) **:** any of numerous small sluggish homopterous insects (superfamily Aphidoidea) that suck the juices of plants

aphis \ˈā-fəs *also* ˈaf-əs\ *n, pl* **aphi·des** \ˈā-fə-ˌdēz, ˈaf-ə-\ [NL *Aphid-, Aphis*, genus name] (1771) **:** an aphid of a common genus (*Aphis*); *broadly* **:** APHID

aphis lion *n* (1870) **:** any of several insect larvae (as a lacewing or ladybug larva) that feed on aphids — called also *aphid lion*

apho·nia \(ˈ)ā-ˈfō-nē-ə\ *n* [NL, fr. Gk *aphōnia*, fr. *aphōnos* voiceless, fr. *a-* + *phōnē* sound — more at BAN] (1778) **:** loss of voice and of all but whispered speech — **apho·nic** \-ˈfän-ik, -ˈfō-nik\ *adj*

aph·o·rism \ˈaf-ə-ˌriz-əm\ *n* [MF *aphorisme*, fr. LL *aphorismus*, fr. Gk *aphorismos* definition, aphorism, fr. *aphorizein* to define, fr. *apo-* + *horizein* to bound — more at HORIZON] (1528) **1 :** a concise statement of a principle **2 :** a terse formulation of a truth or sentiment **:** ADAGE — **aph·o·rist** \-rəst\ *n* — **aph·o·ris·tic** \ˌaf-ə-ˈris-tik\ *adj* — **aph·o·ris·ti·cal·ly** \-ti-k(ə-)lē\ *adv*

aph·o·rize \ˈaf-ə-ˌrīz\ *vi* **-rized; -riz·ing** (1669) **:** to write or speak in or as if in aphorisms

apho·tic \(ˈ)ā-ˈfōt-ik\ *adj* (ca. 1900) **:** lacking light ⟨the ~ zone in the ocean⟩

aph·ro·di·si·ac \ˌaf-rə-ˈdē-zē-ˌak, -ˈdiz-ē-\ *also* **aph·ro·di·si·a·cal** \ˌaf-rə-di-ˈsī-ə-kəl, -ˈzī-\ *adj* [Gk *aphrodisiakos* sexual, fr. *aphrodisia* sexual pleasures, fr. neut. pl. of *aphrodisios* of Aphrodite, fr. *Aphroditē*] (ca. 1828) **:** exciting sexual desire — **aphrodisiac** *n*

Aph·ro·di·te \ˌaf-rə-ˈdīt-ē\ *n* [Gk *Aphroditē*] **:** the Greek goddess of love and beauty — compare VENUS

api·ar·i·an \ˌā-pē-ˈer-ē-ən\ *adj* (1801) **:** of or relating to beekeeping or bees

api·a·rist \ˈā-pē-ə-rəst, -pē-ˌer-əst\ *n* (1816) **:** BEEKEEPER

api·ary \ˈā-pē-ˌer-ē\ *n, pl* **-ar·ies** [L *apiarium*, fr. *apis* bee] (1654) **:** a place where bees are kept; *esp* **:** a collection of hives or colonies of bees kept for their honey

api·cal \ˈā-pi-kəl *also* ˈap-i-\ *adj* [prob. fr. NL *apicalis*, fr. L *apic-, apex*] (1828) **1 :** of, relating to, or situated at an apex **2 :** of, relating to, or formed with the tip of the tongue ⟨*n, l,* and *r* are ~ consonants⟩ — **api·cal·ly** \-k(ə-)lē\ *adv*

apical dominance *n* (1947) **:** inhibition of the growth of lateral buds by the terminal bud of a shoot

apical meristem *n* (ca. 1934) **:** a meristem at the apex of a root or shoot that is responsible for increase in length

apic·u·late \ə-ˈpik-yə-lət, ā-\ *adj* [NL *apiculus*, dim. of L *apic-, apex*] (1830) **:** ending abruptly in a small distinct point ⟨an ~ leaf⟩

api·cul·ture \ˈā-pə-ˌkəl-chər\ *n* [prob. fr. F, fr. L *apis* bee + F *culture*] (1864) **:** the keeping of bees esp. on a large scale — **api·cul·tur·al** \ˌā-pə-ˈkəlch(-ə)-rəl\ *adj* — **api·cul·tur·ist** \-rəst\ *n*

apiece \ə-ˈpēs\ *adv* (15c) **:** for each one **:** INDIVIDUALLY

Apis \ˈā-pəs\ *n* [L, fr. Gk, fr. Egypt *ḥp*] **:** a sacred bull worshiped by the ancient Egyptians

ap·ish \ˈā-pish\ *adj* (1532) **:** resembling an ape: as **a :** given to slavish imitation **b :** extremely silly or affected — **ap·ish·ly** *adv* — **ap·ish·ness** *n*

APL \ˌā-(ˌ)pē-ˈel\ *n* [*a p*rogramming *l*anguage] (1969) **:** a computer programming language designed esp. for the concise representation of algorithms

apla·cen·tal \ˌā-plə-ˈsent-ᵊl\ *adj* (1857) **:** having or developing no placenta

ap·la·nat·ic \ˌap-lə-ˈnat-ik\ *adj* [*a-* + Gk *planasthai* to wander — more at PLANET] (1794) **:** free from or corrected for spherical aberration ⟨an ~ lens⟩

aplas·tic anemia \(ˌ)ā-ˌplas-tik-\ *n* (ca. 1934) **:** anemia that is characterized by defective function of the blood-forming organs (as the bone marrow) and is caused by toxic agents (as chemicals or X rays) or is idiopathic in origin

1aplen·ty \ə-ˈplent-ē\ *adj* (1830) **:** being in plenty or abundance ⟨money ~ for all his needs⟩

2aplenty *adv* (1846) **1 :** in abundance **:** PLENTIFULLY **2 :** very much **:** EXTREMELY ⟨scared ~⟩

ap·lite \ˈap-ˌlīt\ *n* [prob. fr. G *aplit*, fr. Gk *haploos* simple — more at HAPL-] (1879) **:** a fine-grained light-colored granite consisting almost entirely of quartz and feldspar — **ap·lit·ic** \a-ˈplit-ik\ *adj*

aplomb \ə-ˈpläm, -ˈpləm\ *n* [F, lit., perpendicularity, fr. MF, fr. *a plomb*, lit., according to the plummet] (1828) **:** complete and confident composure or self-assurance **:** POISE ***syn*** see CONFIDENCE

ap·nea *or* **ap·noea** \ˈap-nē-ə\ *n* [NL, fr. *a-* + *pnea*] (1719) **1 :** transient cessation of respiration **2 :** ASPHYXIA — **ap·ne·ic** \-nē-ik\ *adj*

apo- *or* **ap-** *prefix* [ME, fr. MF & L; MF, fr. L, fr. Gk, fr. *apo* — more at OF] **1 :** away from **:** off ⟨*aphelion*⟩ **2 :** detached **:** separate ⟨*apogamous*⟩ **3 :** formed from **:** related to ⟨*apomorphine*⟩

apoc·a·lypse \ə-ˈpäk-ə-ˌlips\ *n* [ME, revelation, Revelation, fr. LL *apocalypsis*, fr. Gk *apokalypsis*, fr. *apokalyptein* to uncover, fr. *apo-* + *kalyptein* to cover — more at HELL] (13c) **1 a :** one of the Jewish and Christian writings of 200 B.C. to A.D. 150 marked by pseudonymity, symbolic imagery, and the expectation of an imminent cosmic cataclysm in which God destroys the ruling powers of evil and raises the righteous to life in a messianic kingdom **b** *cap* **:** REVELATION 2 **2 a :** something viewed as a prophetic revelation **b :** ARMAGEDDON

apoc·a·lyp·tic \ə-ˌpäk-ə-ˈlip-tik\ *also* **apoc·a·lyp·ti·cal** \-ti-kəl\ *adj* (1633) **1** : of, relating to, or resembling an apocalypse **2** : forecasting the ultimate destiny of the world : PROPHETIC **3** : foreboding imminent disaster or final doom : TERRIBLE **4** : wildly unrestrained in making predictions : GRANDIOSE **5** : ultimately decisive : CLIMACTIC — **apoc·a·lyp·ti·cal·ly** \-ti-k(ə-)lē\ *adv*

apoc·a·lyp·ti·cism \-tə-ˌsiz-əm\ *or* **apoc·a·lyp·tism** \ə-ˈpäk-ə-ˌlip-ˌtiz-əm\ *n* (1884) : apocalyptic expectation; *esp* : a doctrine concerning an imminent end of the world and an ensuing general resurrection and final judgment

apoc·a·lyp·tist \ə-ˈpäk-ə-ˌlip-təst\ *n* (ca. 1859) : the writer of an apocalypse

apo·chro·mat·ic \ˌap-ə-krō-ˈmat-ik\ *adj* [ISV] (1887) : free from chromatic and spherical aberration ⟨an ~ lens⟩

apoc·o·pe \ə-ˈpäk-ə-(ˌ)pē\ *n* [LL, fr. Gk *apokopē*, lit., cutting off, fr. *apokoptein* to cut off, fr. *apo-* + *koptein* to cut — more at CAPON] (1591) : the loss of one or more sounds or letters at the end of a word (as in *sing* from Old English *singan*)

apo·crine \ˈap-ə-krən, -ˌkrīn, -ˌkrēn\ *adj* [ISV *apo-* + Gk *krinein* to separate — more at CERTAIN] (1926) : producing a fluid secretion by pinching off one end of the secreting cell while leaving the rest intact ⟨an ~ gland⟩; *also* : produced by an apocrine gland

apoc·ry·pha \ə-ˈpäk-rə-fə\ *n pl but sing or pl in constr* [ML, fr. LL, neut. pl. of *apocryphus* secret, not canonical, fr. Gk *apokryphos* obscure, fr. *apokryptein* to hide away, fr. *apo-* + *kryptein* to hide — more at CRYPT] (14c) **1** : writings or statements of dubious authenticity **2** *cap* **a** : books included in the Septuagint and Vulgate but excluded from the Jewish and Protestant canons of the Old Testament — see BIBLE table **b** : early Christian writings not included in the New Testament

apoc·ry·phal \-fəl\ *adj* (1590) **1** : of doubtful authenticity : SPURIOUS **2** *often cap* : of or resembling the Apocrypha ***syn*** see FICTITIOUS — **apoc·ry·phal·ly** \-fə-lē\ *adv* — **apoc·ry·phal·ness** *n*

apo·cyn·thi·on \ˌap-ə-ˈsin(t)-thē-ən\ *n* [NL, fr. *apo-* + *Cynthia*] (ca. 1960) : APOLUNE

apo·dic·tic \ˌap-ə-ˈdik-tik\ *also* **apo·deic·tic** \-ˈdīk-tik\ *adj* [L *apodicticus*, fr. Gk *apodeiktikos*, fr. *apodeiknynai* to demonstrate, fr. *apo-* + *deiknynai* to show — more at DICTION] (ca. 1645) : expressing or of the nature of necessary truth or absolute certainty — **apo·dic·ti·cal·ly** \-ti-k(ə-)lē\ *adv*

apod·o·sis \ə-ˈpäd-ə-səs\ *n, pl* **-o·ses** \-ˌsēz\ [NL, fr. Gk, fr. *apodidonai* to give back, deliver, fr. *apo-* + *didonai* to give — more at DATE] (1638) : the main clause of a conditional sentence — compare PROTASIS

apo·en·zyme \ˌap-ō-ˈen-ˌzīm\ *n* [ISV] (ca. 1936) : a protein that forms an active enzyme system by combination with a coenzyme and determines the specificity of this system for a substrate

apog·a·my \ə-ˈpäg-ə-mē\ *n* [ISV] (1878) : development of a sporophyte from a gametophyte without fertilization — **apog·a·mous** \ə-ˈpäg-ə-məs\ *adj* — **apog·a·mous·ly** \-lē\ *adv*

apo·gee \ˈap-ə-(ˌ)jē\ *n* [F *apogée*, fr. NL *apogaeum*, fr. Gk *apogaion*, fr. neut. of *apogeios*, *apogaios* far from the earth, fr. *apo-* + *gē* earth] (1594) **1** : the point in the orbit of a satellite of the earth or of a vehicle orbiting the earth that is at the greatest distance from the center of the earth; *also* : the point farthest from a planet or a satellite (as the moon) reached by an object orbiting it — compare PERIGEE **2** : the farthest or highest point : CULMINATION ⟨Aegean civilization reached its ~ in Crete⟩ — **apo·ge·an** \ˌap-ə-ˈjē-ən\ *adj*

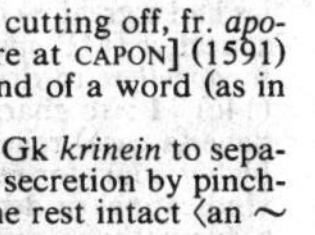

apogee 1

apo·lit·i·cal \ˌā-pə-ˈlit-i-kəl\ *adj* (1935) **1** : having an aversion for or no interest or involvement in political affairs **2** : having no political significance — **apo·lit·i·cal·ly** \-k(ə-)lē\ *adv*

Ap·ol·lin·i·an \ˌap-ə-ˈlin-ē-ən\ *adj* (1924) : APOLLONIAN

Apol·lo \ə-ˈpäl-(ˌ)ō\ *n* [L *Apollin-*, *Apollo*, fr. Gk *Apollōn*] : the Greek and Roman god of sunlight, prophecy, music, and poetry

Ap·ol·lo·ni·an \ˌap-ə-ˈlō-nē-ən\ *adj* (1663) **1** : of, relating to, or resembling the god Apollo **2** : harmonious, measured, ordered, or balanced in character — compare DIONYSIAN

Apol·lyon \ə-ˈpäl-yən, -ˈpäl-ē-ən\ *n* [Gk *Apollyōn*] : the angel of the bottomless pit in the Book of Revelation

[1]**apol·o·get·ic** \ə-ˌpäl-ə-ˈjet-ik\ *n* (15c) : APOLOGETICS 1

[2]**apologetic** *adj* [Gk *apologētikos*, fr. *apologeisthai* to defend, fr. *apo-* + *logos* speech] (1649) **1 a** : offered in defense or vindication ⟨the ~ writings of the early Christians⟩ **b** : offered by way of excuse or apology ⟨an ~ smile⟩ **2** : regretfully acknowledging fault or failure : CONTRITE ⟨was ~ about his mistake⟩ — **apol·o·get·i·cal·ly** \-i-k(ə-)lē\ *adv*

apol·o·get·ics \-iks\ *n pl but sing or pl in constr* (1733) **1** : systematic argumentative discourse in defense (as of a doctrine) **2** : a branch of theology devoted to the defense of the divine origin and authority of Christianity

ap·o·lo·gia \ˌap-ə-ˈlō-j(ē-)ə\ *n* [LL] (1784) : a defense esp. of one's opinions, position, or actions ⟨the finest ~ or explanation of what drives a man to devote his life to pure mathematics —*Brit. Book News*⟩ ***syn*** see APOLOGY

apol·o·gist \ə-ˈpäl-ə-jəst\ *n* (1640) : one who speaks or writes in defense of a faith, a cause, or an institution

apol·o·gize \-ˌjīz\ *vi* **-gized; -giz·ing** (1597) : to make an apology — **apol·o·giz·er** *n*

ap·o·logue \ˈap-ə-ˌlȯg, -ˌläg\ *n* [F, fr. L *apologus*, fr. Gk *apologos*, fr. *apo-* + *logos* speech, narrative] (1552) : an allegorical narrative usu. intended to convey a moral

apol·o·gy \ə-ˈpäl-ə-jē\ *n, pl* **-gies** [MF or LL; MF *apologie*, fr. LL *apologia*, fr. Gk, fr. *apo-* + *logos* speech — more at LEGEND] (1533) **1 a** : a formal justification : DEFENSE **b** : EXCUSE 2a **2** : an admission of error or discourtesy accompanied by an expression of regret **3** : a poor substitute : MAKESHIFT

syn APOLOGY, APOLOGIA, EXCUSE, PLEA, PRETEXT, ALIBI mean matter offered in explanation or defense. APOLOGY usu. applies to an expression of regret for a mistake or wrong with implied admission of guilt or fault and with or without reference to palliating circumstances ⟨said by way of *apology* that he would have met them if he could⟩ Sometimes *apology*, like APOLOGIA, implies not admission of guilt or regret but a desire to make clear the grounds for some course, belief, or position ⟨the speech was an effective *apology* for his foreign policy⟩ EXCUSE implies an intent to avoid or remove blame or censure ⟨used his illness as an *excuse* for missing the meeting⟩ PLEA stresses argument or appeal for understanding or sympathy or mercy ⟨their *pleas* for help were ignored⟩ PRETEXT suggests subterfuge and the offering of false reasons or motives in excuse or explanation ⟨used any *pretext* to get out of work⟩ ALIBI implies a desire to shift blame or evade punishment and imputes plausibility rather than truth to the explanation offered ⟨his *alibi* failed to stand scrutiny⟩

apo·lune \ˈap-ə-ˌlün\ *n* [*apo-* + L *luna* moon — more at LUNAR] (ca. 1968) : the point in the path of a body orbiting the moon that is farthest from the center of the moon — compare PERILUNE

apo·mict \ˈap-ə-ˌmikt\ *n* [prob. back-formation fr. ISV *apomictic*, fr. *apo-* + Gk *mignynai* to mix — more at MIX] (1938) : one produced or reproducing by apomixis — **apo·mic·tic** \ˌap-ə-ˈmik-tik\ *adj* — **apo·mic·ti·cal·ly** \-ti-k(ə-)lē\ *adv*

apo·mix·is \ˌap-ə-ˈmik-səs\ *n, pl* **-mix·es** \-ˌsēz\ [NL, fr. *apo-* + Gk *mixis* act of mixing, fr. *mignynai*] (1913) : reproduction (as apogamy or parthenogenesis) involving specialized generative tissues but not dependent on fertilization

apo·mor·phine \ˌap-ə-ˈmȯr-ˌfēn\ *n* [ISV] (ca. 1885) : a crystalline morphine derivative $C_{17}H_{17}NO_2$ that is a dopamine agonist and is administered as the hydrochloride for its powerful emetic action

apo·neu·ro·sis \ˌap-ə-n(y)ü-ˈrō-səs\ *n* [NL, fr. Gk *aponeurōsis*, fr. *aponeurousthai* to pass into a tendon, fr. *apo-* + *neuron* sinew — more at NERVE] (1676) : any of the thicker and denser of the deep fasciae that cover, invest, and form the terminations and attachments of various muscles and differ from tendons in being broad, flat, and thin — **apo·neu·rot·ic** \-ˈrät-ik\ *adj*

ap·o·phthegm \ˈap-ə-ˌthem\ *var of* APOTHEGM

apo·phyl·lite \ˌap-ə-ˈfil-ˌīt, ə-ˈpäf-ə-ˌlīt\ *n* [F, fr. *apo-* + Gk *phyllon* leaf — more at BLADE] (1810) : a mineral $KCa_4Si_8O_{20}(F,OH)\cdot 8H_2O$ composed of a hydrous potassium calcium silicate related to the zeolites and usu. found in transparent square prisms or white or grayish masses

apoph·y·sis \ə-ˈpäf-ə-səs\ *n, pl* **-y·ses** \-ˌsēz\ [NL, fr. Gk, fr. *apo-* + *phyein* to bring forth — more at BE] (1611) : an expanded or projecting part esp. of an organism — **apoph·y·se·al** \-ˌpäf-ə-ˈsē-əl\ *adj*

ap·o·plec·tic \ˌap-ə-ˈplek-tik\ *adj* [F or LL; F *apoplectique*, fr. LL *apoplecticus*, fr. Gk *apoplēktikos*, fr. *apoplēssein*] (1611) **1** : of, relating to, or causing stroke **2** : affected with, inclined to, or showing symptoms of stroke **3** : of a kind to cause stroke; *esp* : highly excited ⟨flew into an ~ rage⟩ — **ap·o·plec·ti·cal·ly** \-ti-k(ə-)lē\ *adv*

ap·o·plexy \ˈap-ə-ˌplek-sē\ *n* [ME *apoplexie*, fr. MF & LL; MF, fr. LL *apoplexia*, fr. Gk *apoplēxia*, fr. *apoplēssein* to cripple by a stroke, fr. *apo-* + *plēssein* to strike — more at PLAINT] (14c) : STROKE 5

aport \ə-ˈpō(ə)rt, -ˈpȯ(ə)rt\ *adv* (1627) : on or toward the left side of a ship ⟨put the helm hard ~⟩

apo·se·mat·ic \ˌap-ə-si-ˈmat-ik\ *adj* (1890) : being conspicuous and serving to warn ⟨~ coloration⟩ — **apo·se·mat·i·cal·ly** \-i-k(ə-)lē\ *adv*

ap·o·si·o·pe·sis \ˌap-ə-ˌsī-ə-ˈpē-səs\ *n, pl* **-pe·ses** \-ˌsēz\ [LL, fr. Gk *aposiōpēsis*, fr. *aposiōpan* to be quite silent, fr. *apo-* + *siōpan* to be silent, fr. *siōpē* silence] (1578) : the leaving of a thought incomplete usu. by a sudden breaking off (as in "his behavior was — but I blush to mention that") — **ap·o·si·o·pet·ic** \-ˈpet-ik\ *adj*

apos·po·ry \ˈap-ə-ˌspōr-ē, -ˌspȯr-; ə-ˈpäs-pə-rē\ *n* (1884) : production of gametophytes directly from somatic cells of the sporophytes without spore formation (as in certain ferns and mosses) — **ap·o·spo·ric** \ˌap-ə-ˈspōr-ik, -ˈspȯr-\ *or* **apos·po·rous** \ˈap-ə-ˌspōr-əs, -ˌspȯr-; ə-ˈpäs-pə-rəs\ *adj*

apos·ta·sy \ə-ˈpäs-tə-sē\ *n, pl* **-sies** [ME *apostasie*, fr. LL *apostasia*, fr. Gk, lit., revolt, fr. *aphistasthai* to revolt, fr. *apo-* + *histasthai* to stand — more at STAND] (14c) **1** : renunciation of a religious faith **2** : abandonment of a previous loyalty : DEFECTION

apos·tate \ə-ˈpäs-ˌtāt, -tət\ *n* (14c) : one who commits apostasy — **apostate** *adj*

apos·ta·tize \ə-ˈpäs-tə-ˌtīz\ *vi* **-tized; -tiz·ing** (1611) : to commit apostasy

a pos·te·ri·o·ri \ˌä-(ˌ)pō-ˌstir-ē-ˈō(ə)r-ē, -ˌster-; ˌā-(ˌ)pä-ˌstir-ē-ˈō(ə)r-ˌī, -(ˌ)pō-, -ˈȯ(ə)r-ē; -ˈȯ(ə)r-\ *adj* [L, lit., from the latter] (1588) **1** : INDUCTIVE **2** : relating to or derived by reasoning from observed facts — compare A PRIORI — **a posteriori** *adv*

apos·tle \ə-ˈpäs-əl\ *n* [ME, fr. OF & OE; OF *apostle* & OE *apostol*, both fr. LL *apostolus*, fr. Gk *apostolos*, fr. *apostellein* to send away, fr. *apo-* + *stellein* to send — more at STALL] (bef. 12c) **1** : one sent on a mission: as **a** : one of an authoritative New Testament group sent out to preach the gospel and made up esp. of Christ's 12 original disciples and Paul **b** : the first prominent Christian missionary to a region or group **2 a** : one who initiates a great moral reform or who first advocates an important belief or system **b** : an ardent supporter : ADHERENT ⟨an ~ of liberty⟩ **3** : the highest ecclesiastical official in some church organizations **4** : one of a Mormon administrative council of 12 men — **apos·tle·ship** \-ˌship\ *n*

Apostles' Creed *n* (15c) : a Christian statement of belief ascribed to the Twelve Apostles and used esp. in public worship

apos·to·late \ə-ˈpäs-tə-ˌlāt, -lət\ *n* [LL *apostolatus*, fr. *apostolus*] (15c) **1** : the office or mission of an apostle **2** : an association of persons dedicated to the propagation of a religion or a doctrine

ap·os·tol·ic \ˌap-ə-ˈstäl-ik\ *adj* (13c) **1 a** : of or relating to an apostle **b** : of, relating to, or conforming to the teachings of the New Testament apostles **2 a** : of or relating to a succession of spiritual authority from the apostles held (as by Roman Catholics, Anglicans, and Eastern Orthodox) to be perpetuated by successive ordinations of bishops and to be necessary for valid sacraments and orders **b** : PAPAL — **apos·to·lic·i·ty** \ə-ˌpäs-tə-ˈlis-ət-ē\ *n*

apostolic delegate *n* (ca. 1909) : an ecclesiastical representative of the Holy See in a country that has no formal diplomatic relations with it

Apostolic Father *n* (1828) : a church father of the first or second century A.D.

\ə\ **abut** \ᵊ\ **kitten**, F **table** \ər\ **further** \a\ **ash** \ā\ **ace** \ä\ **cot, cart** \au̇\ **out** \ch\ **chin** \e\ **bet** \ē\ **easy** \g\ **go** \i\ **hit** \ī\ **ice** \j\ **job** \ŋ\ **sing** \ō\ **go** \ȯ\ **law** \ȯi\ **boy** \th\ **thin** \t͟h\ **the** \ü\ **loot** \u̇\ **foot** \y\ **yet** \zh\ **vision** \á, k̲, ⁿ, œ, œ̄, ue, ue̅, ʸ\ *see* Guide to Pronunciation

[1]apos·tro·phe \ə-ˈpäs-trə-(ˌ)fē\ *n* [L, fr. Gk *apostrophē*, lit., act of turning away, fr. *apostrephein* to turn away, fr. *apo-* + *strephein* to turn — more at STROPHE] (1533) : the addressing of a usu. absent person or a usu. personified thing rhetorically ⟨Carlyle's "O Liberty, what things are done in thy name!" is an example of ~⟩ — **ap·os·troph·ic** \ˌap-ə-ˈsträf-ik\ *adj*

[2]apostrophe *n* [MF & LL; MF, fr. LL *apostrophus*, fr. Gk *apostrophos*, fr. *apostrophos* turned away, fr. *apostrephein*] (1588) : a mark ' used to indicate the omission of letters or figures, the possessive case, or the plural of letters or figures — **apostrophic** *adj*

apos·tro·phize \ə-ˈpäs-trə-ˌfīz\ *vb* **-phized; -phiz·ing** *vt* (1718) : to address by or in apostrophe ~ *vi* : to make use of apostrophe

apothecaries' measure *n* (ca. 1900) : a measure of capacity used chiefly by pharmacists

apothecaries' weight *n* (1765) : a system of weights used chiefly by pharmacists — see WEIGHT table

apoth·e·cary \ə-ˈpäth-ə-ˌker-ē\ *n, pl* **-car·ies** [ME *apothecarie*, fr. ML *apothecarius*, fr. LL, shopkeeper, fr. L *apotheca* storehouse, fr. Gk *apothēkē*, fr. *apotithenai* to put away, fr. *apo-* + *tithenai* to put — more at DO] (14c) **1** : one who prepares and sells drugs or compounds for medicinal purposes **2** : PHARMACY

apo·the·ci·um \ˌap-ə-ˈthē-s(h)ē-əm\ *n, pl* **-cia** \-s(h)ē-ə\ [NL, fr. L *apotheca*] (1830) : a spore-bearing structure in many lichens and fungi consisting of a discoid or cupped body bearing asci on the exposed flat or concave surface — **apo·the·cial** \-sh(ē-)əl, -sē-əl\ *adj*

ap·o·thegm \ˈap-ə-ˌthem\ *n* [Gk *apophthegmat-*, *apophthegma*, fr. *apophthengesthai* to speak out, fr. *apo-* + *phthengesthai* to utter] (1553) : a short, pithy, and instructive saying or formulation : APHORISM — **ap·o·theg·mat·ic** \ˌap-ə-theg-ˈmat-ik\ *adj*

ap·o·them \ˈap-ə-ˌthem\ *n* [ISV *apo-* + *-them* (fr. Gk *thema* something laid down, theme)] (ca. 1856) : the perpendicular from the center of a regular polygon to one of the sides

apo·the·o·sis \ə-ˌpäth-ē-ˈō-səs, ˌap-ə-ˈthē-ə-səs\ *n, pl* **-o·ses** \-ˌsēz\ [LL, fr. Gk *apotheōsis*, fr. *apotheoun* to deify, fr. *apo-* + *theos* god] (1573) **1** : elevation to divine status : DEIFICATION **2** : the perfect example : QUINTESSENCE ⟨she is the ~ of womanhood⟩ — **apo·the·o·size** \ˌap-ə-ˈthē-ə-ˌsīz, ə-ˈpäth-ē-ə-\ *vt*

apo·tro·pa·ic \ˌap-ə-trō-ˈpā-ik\ *adj* [Gk *apotropaios*, fr. *apotrepein* to avert, fr. *apo-* + *trepein* to turn — more at TROPE] (1883) : designed to avert evil ⟨an ~ ritual⟩ — **apo·tro·pa·i·cal·ly** \-ˈpā-ə-k(ə-)lē\ *adv*

Ap·pa·la·chian \ˌap-ə-ˈlā-ch(ē-)ən, -sh(ē-)ən; -ˈlach-(ē-)ən\ *n* (1949) : a white native or resident of the Appalachian mountain area

ap·pal *also* **ap·pall** \ə-ˈpȯl\ *vb* **ap·palled; ap·pall·ing** [ME *appallen*, fr. MF *apalir*, fr. OF, fr. *a-* (fr. L *ad-*) + *palir* to grow pale, fr. L *pallescere*, incho. of *pallēre* to be pale — more at FALLOW] *vi, obs* (14c) : WEAKEN, FAIL ~ *vt* : to overcome with consternation, shock, or dismay ***syn*** see DISMAY

ap·pall·ing *adj* (1817) : inspiring horror, dismay, or disgust ⟨living under ~ conditions⟩ — **ap·pall·ing·ly** *adv*

Ap·pa·loo·sa \ˌap-ə-ˈlü-sə\ *n* [prob. fr. *Palouse*, an Indian people of Wash. and Idaho] (ca. 1849) : any of a breed of rugged saddle horses developed in western No. America and having small dark spots or blotches on a white coat

Appaloosa

ap·pa·nage \ˈap-ə-nij\ *n* [F *apanage*, fr. OF, fr. *apaner* to provide for a younger offspring, fr. OProv *apanar* to support, fr. *a-* (fr. L *ad-*) + *pan* bread, fr. L *panis* — more at FOOD] (1602) **1 a** : a grant (as of land or revenue) made by a sovereign or a legislative body to a dependent member of the royal family or a principal liege man **b** : a property or privilege appropriated to or by a person as his share **2** : a rightful endowment or adjunct

ap·pa·rat \ˈap-ə-ˌrat, ˌäp-ə-ˈrät\ *n* [Russ] (1941) : APPARATUS 2

ap·pa·rat·chik \ˌäp-ə-ˈrä(t)-chik\ *n, pl* **-chiks** *or* **-chi·ki** \-chi-kē\ [Russ, fr. *apparat*] (1941) **1** : a member of a Communist apparat **2** : an official blindly devoted to his superiors or organization

ap·pa·ra·tus \ˌap-ə-ˈrat-əs, -ˈrāt-\ *n, pl* **-tus·es** *or* **-tus** [L, fr. *apparatus*, pp. of *apparare* to prepare, fr. *ad-* + *parare* to prepare — more at PARE] (1628) **1 a** : a set of materials or equipment designed for a particular use **b** : an instrument or appliance designed for a specific operation **c** : a group of bodily parts and esp. organs having a common function **2** : the functional processes by means of which a systematized activity is carried out: as **a** : the machinery of government **b** : the organization of a political party or an underground movement

[1]ap·par·el \ə-ˈpar-əl\ *vt* **-eled** *or* **-elled; -el·ing** *or* **-el·ling** [ME *appareilen*, fr. MF *apareillier* to prepare, fr. (assumed) VL *appariculare*, irreg. fr. L *apparare*] (14c) **1** : to put clothes on : DRESS **2** : ADORN, EMBELLISH

[2]apparel *n* (14c) **1** : the equipment (as sails and rigging) of a ship **2** : personal attire : CLOTHING **3** : something that clothes or adorns ⟨the bright ~ of spring⟩

ap·par·ent \ə-ˈpar-ənt, -ˈper-\ *adj* [ME, fr. MF *aparent*, fr. L *apparent-*, *apparens*, prp. of *apparēre* to appear] (14c) **1** : open to view : VISIBLE **2** : clear or manifest to the understanding **3** : appearing as actual to the eye or mind **4** : having an indefeasible right to succeed to a title or estate **5** : manifest to the senses or mind as real or true on the basis of evidence that may or may not be factually valid ⟨his ~ absorption was belied by his rigid pose⟩ — **ap·par·ent·ly** \-ˈpar(-ə)nt-lē, -ˈper(-ə)nt-\ *adv* — **ap·par·ent·ness** \-ˈpar-ənt-nəs, -ˈper-\ *n*

syn APPARENT, ILLUSORY, SEEMING, OSTENSIBLE mean not actually being what appearance indicates. APPARENT suggests appearance to unaided senses that is not or may not be borne out by more rigorous examination or greater knowledge; ILLUSORY implies a false impression based on deceptive resemblance or faulty observation, or influenced by emotions that prevent a clear view; SEEMING implies a character in the thing observed that gives it the appearance, sometimes through intent, of something else; OSTENSIBLE suggests a discrepancy between an openly declared or naturally implied aim or reason and the true one. ***syn*** see in addition EVIDENT

apparent horizon *n* (ca. 1828) : HORIZON 1a

apparent time *n* (1694) : the time of day indicated by the hour angle of the sun or by a sundial

ap·pa·ri·tion \ˌap-ə-ˈrish-ən\ *n* [ME *apparicioun*, fr. LL *apparition-*, *apparitio* appearance, fr. L *apparitus*, pp. of *apparēre*] (15c) **1 a** : an unusual or unexpected sight : PHENOMENON **b** : a ghostly figure **2** : the act of becoming visible : APPEARANCE — **ap·pa·ri·tion·al** \-ˈrish-nəl, -ən-ᵊl\ *adj*

ap·par·i·tor \ə-ˈpar-ət-ər\ *n* [L, fr. *apparitus*] (15c) : an official formerly sent to carry out the orders of a magistrate, judge, or court

[1]ap·peal \ə-ˈpē(ə)l\ *n* (13c) **1** : a legal proceeding by which a case is brought from a lower to a higher court for rehearing **2** : a criminal accusation **3 a** : an application (as to a recognized authority) for corroboration, vindication, or decision **b** : an earnest plea : ENTREATY **4** : the power of arousing a sympathetic response : ATTRACTION ⟨movies had a great ~ for him⟩

[2]appeal *vb* [ME *appelen* to accuse, appeal, fr. MF *apeler*, fr. L *appellare*, fr. *appellere* to drive to, fr. *ad-* + *pellere* to drive — more at FELT] *vt* (14c) **1** : to charge with a crime : ACCUSE **2** : to take proceedings to have (a case) reheard in a higher court ~ *vi* **1** : to take a case to a higher court for rehearing **2** : to call upon another for corroboration, vindication, or decision **3** : to make an earnest request **4** : to arouse a sympathetic response — **ap·peal·abil·i·ty** \-ˌpē-lə-ˈbil-ət-ē\ *n* — **ap·peal·able** \-ˈpē-lə-bəl\ *adj* — **ap·peal·er** *n*

ap·peal·ing \ə-ˈpē-liŋ\ *adj* (1813) **1** : marked by earnest entreaty : IMPLORING **2** : having appeal : PLEASING — **ap·peal·ing·ly** \-liŋ-lē\ *adv*

ap·pear \ə-ˈpi(ə)r\ *vi* [ME *apperen*, fr. OF *aparoir*, fr. L *apparēre*, fr. *ad-* + *parēre* to show oneself] (13c) **1 a** : to be or come in sight ⟨the sun ~s on the horizon⟩ **b** : to show up ⟨~s promptly at eight each day⟩ **2** : to come formally before an authoritative body ⟨must ~ in court today⟩ **3** : to have an outward aspect ⟨~s happy enough⟩ **4** : to become evident or manifest ⟨there ~s to be evidence to the contrary⟩ **5** : to come into public view ⟨first ~*ed* on a television variety show⟩ **6** : to come into existence ⟨man ~s late in the evolutionary chain⟩

ap·pear·ance \ə-ˈpir-ən(t)s\ *n* (14c) **1 a** : the act, action, or process of appearing **b** : the coming into court of a party in an action or his attorney **2 a** : outward aspect : LOOK ⟨had a fierce ~⟩ **b** : external show : SEMBLANCE ⟨although hostile, he tried to preserve an ~ of neutrality⟩ **c** *pl* : outward indication ⟨would do anything to keep up ~*s*⟩ **3 a** : a sense impression or aspect of a thing ⟨the blue of distant hills is only an ~⟩ **b** : the world of sensible phenomena **4 a** : something that appears : PHENOMENON **b** : an instance of appearing : OCCURRENCE

ap·pease \ə-ˈpēz\ *vt* **ap·peased; ap·peas·ing** [ME *appesen*, fr. MF *apaisier*, fr. *a-* (fr. L *ad-*) + *pais* peace — more at PEACE] (14c) **1** : to bring to a state of peace or quiet : CALM **2** : to cause to subside : ALLAY ⟨~ his hunger⟩ **3** : PACIFY, CONCILIATE; *esp* : to buy off (an aggressor) by concessions usu. at the sacrifice of principles ***syn*** see PACIFY — **ap·peas·able** \-ˈpē-zə-bəl\ *adj* — **ap·pease·ment** \-ˈpēz-mənt\ *n* — **ap·peas·er** *n*

[1]ap·pel·lant \ə-ˈpel-ənt\ *adj* (14c) : of or relating to an appeal : APPELLATE

[2]appellant *n* (15c) : one that appeals; *specif* : one that appeals from a judicial decision or decree

ap·pel·late \ə-ˈpel-ət\ *adj* [L *appellatus*, pp. of *appellare*] (1768) : of, relating to, or recognizing appeals; *specif* : having the power to review the judgment of another tribunal ⟨an ~ court⟩

ap·pel·la·tion \ˌap-ə-ˈlā-shən\ *n* (15c) **1** : an identifying name or title : DESIGNATION **2** *archaic* : the act of calling by a name

ap·pel·la·tive \ə-ˈpel-ət-iv\ *adj* (15c) **1** : of or relating to a common noun **2** : of, relating to, or inclined to the giving of names — **ap·pel·la·tive** *n* — **ap·pel·la·tive·ly** *adv*

ap·pel·lee \ˌap-ə-ˈlē\ *n* (1531) : one against whom an appeal is taken

ap·pend \ə-ˈpend\ *vt* [ME *appenden*, fr. MF *appendre*, fr. LL *appendere*, fr. L, to weigh, fr. *ad-* + *pendere* to weigh — more at PENDANT] (14c) **1** : ATTACH, AFFIX **2** : to add as a supplement or appendix (as in a book)

ap·pend·age \ə-ˈpen-dij\ *n* (1649) **1** : an adjunct to something larger or more important : APPURTENANCE **2** : a dependent or subordinate person **3** : a subordinate or derivative body part; *esp* : a limb or analogous part (as a seta)

ap·pen·dant \ə-ˈpen-dənt\ *adj* (15c) **1** : belonging as a right — used of annexed land in English law **2** : associated as an attendant circumstance **3** : attached as an appendage ⟨a seal ~ to a document⟩ — **appendant** *n*

ap·pen·dec·to·my \ˌap-ən-ˈdek-tə-mē, ˌap-ˌen-\ *n, pl* **-mies** [L *appendic-*, *appendix* + E *-ectomy*] (1894) : surgical removal of the vermiform appendix

ap·pen·di·cec·to·my \ə-ˌpen-də-ˈsek-tə-mē\ *n, pl* **-mies** *Brit* (1894) : APPENDECTOMY

ap·pen·di·ci·tis \ə-ˌpen-də-ˈsīt-əs\ *n* (1886) : inflammation of the vermiform appendix

ap·pen·dic·u·lar \ˌap-ən-ˈdik-yə-lər\ *adj* (1651) : of or relating to an appendage and esp. a limb ⟨the ~ skeleton⟩

ap·pen·dix \ə-ˈpen-diks\ *n, pl* **-dix·es** *or* **-di·ces** \-də-ˌsēz\ [L *appendic-*, *appendix*, fr. *appendere*] (1542) **1 a** : APPENDAGE **b** : supplementary material usu. attached at the end of a piece of writing **2** : a bodily outgrowth or process; *specif* : VERMIFORM APPENDIX

ap·per·ceive \ˌap-ər-ˈsēv\ *vt* **-ceived; -ceiv·ing** [ME *apperceiven*, fr. MF *aperceivre*, fr. *a-* (fr. L *ad-*) + *perceivre* to perceive] (14c) : to have apperception of

ap·per·cep·tion \-ˈsep-shən\ *n* [F *aperception*, fr. *apercevoir*, fr. MF *aperceivre*] (1753) **1** : introspective self-consciousness **2** : mental perception; *esp* : the process of understanding something perceived in terms of previous experience — **ap·per·cep·tive** \-ˈsep-tiv\ *adj*

ap·per·tain \ˌap-ər-ˈtān\ *vi* [ME *apperteinen*, fr. MF *apartenir*, fr. LL *appertinēre*, fr. L *ad-* + *pertinēre* to belong — more at PERTAIN] (14c) : to belong or be connected as a rightful part or attribute : PERTAIN

ap·pe·tence \ˈap-ət-ən(t)s\ *n* (1610) : APPETENCY

ap·pe·ten·cy \-ən-sē\ *n, pl* **-cies** [L *appetentia*, fr. *appetent-*, *appetens*, prp. of *appetere*] (1627) **1** : a natural affinity (as between chemicals) **2** : a fixed and strong desire : APPETITE — **ap·pe·tent** \-ənt\ *adj*

ap·pe·tite \ˈap-ə-ˌtīt\ *n* [ME *apetit*, fr. MF, fr. L *appetitus*, fr. *appetitus*, pp. of *appetere* to strive after, fr. *ad-* + *petere* to go to — more at

FEATHER] (14c) **1 :** any of the instinctive desires necessary to keep up organic life; *esp* **:** the desire to eat **2 a :** an inherent craving ⟨an insatiable ~ for work⟩ **b :** TASTE, PREFERENCE ⟨the cultural ~s of the time —J. D. Hart⟩ — **ap·pe·ti·tive** \-ˌtīt-iv\ *adj*

ap·pe·tiz·er \'ap-ə-ˌtī-zər\ *n* (1862) **:** a food or drink that stimulates the appetite and is usu. served before a meal

ap·pe·tiz·ing \-ˌtī-ziŋ\ *adj* (1653) **:** appealing to the appetite esp. in appearance or aroma ***syn*** see PALATABLE — **ap·pe·tiz·ing·ly** \-ziŋ-lē\ *adv*

ap·plaud \ə-'plȯd\ *vb* [ME *applauden,* fr. MF or L; MF *applaudir,* fr. L *applaudere,* fr. *ad-* + *plaudere* to applaud] *vi* (15c) **:** to express approval esp. by clapping the hands ~ *vt* **1 :** to express approval of **:** PRAISE ⟨~ her efforts to lose weight⟩ **2 :** to show approval of esp. by clapping the hands — **ap·plaud·able** \-ə-bəl\ *adj* — **ap·plaud·ably** \-blē\ *adv* — **ap·plaud·er** *n*

ap·plause \ə-'plȯz\ *n* [ML *applausus,* fr. L, clashing noise, fr. *applausus,* pp. of *applaudere*] (15c) **1 :** marked commendation **:** ACCLAIM ⟨the kind of ~ every really creative writer wants—Robert Tallant⟩ **2 :** approval publicly expressed (as by clapping the hands)

ap·ple \'ap-əl\ *n, often attrib* [ME *appel,* fr. OE *æppel;* akin to OHG *apful* apple] (bef. 12c) **1 :** the fleshy usu. rounded and red or yellow edible pome fruit of a tree (genus *Malus*) of the rose family; *also* **:** an apple tree **2 :** a fruit or other vegetable production suggestive of an apple — compare OAK APPLE — **apple of one's eye :** one that is highly cherished ⟨his daughter is the *apple of his eye*⟩

ap·ple·cart \-ˌkärt\ *n* (1788) **:** a plan, system, situation, or undertaking that may be disrupted or terminated ⟨upset the legislative ~ with a long filibuster⟩

ap·ple·jack \-ˌjak\ *n* (1816) **:** brandy distilled from hard cider; *also* **:** an alcoholic beverage traditionally made by freezing hard cider

ap·ple–knock·er \-ˌnäk-ər\ *n* (1919) **:** RUSTIC

apple maggot *n* (1867) **:** a two-winged fly (*Rhagoletis pomonella*) whose larva burrows in and feeds esp. on apples

ap·ple–pie \ˌap-əl-ˌpī\ *adj* (1780) **1 :** EXCELLENT, PERFECT ⟨~ order⟩ **2 :** of, relating to, or characterized by traditionally American values (as honesty or simplicity) ⟨is the epitome of ~ wholesomeness⟩

ap·ple–pol·ish \'ap-əl-ˌpäl-ish\ *vb* [fr. the traditional practice of schoolchildren bringing a shiny apple as a gift to their teacher] *vi* (1935) **:** to attempt to ingratiate oneself **:** TOADY ~ *vt* **:** to curry favor with (as by flattery) — **ap·ple–pol·ish·er** *n*

ap·ple·sauce \-ˌsȯs\ *n* (1739) **1 :** a relish or dessert made of apples stewed to a pulp and sweetened **2** *slang* **:** BUNKUM, NONSENSE

apple scab *n* (ca. 1899) **:** a disease of apple trees caused by a fungus (*Venturia inaequalis*) producing dark blotches or lesions on the leaves, fruit, and sometimes the young twigs

ap·pli·ance \ə-'plī-ən(t)s\ *n* (1561) **1 :** an act of applying **2 a :** a piece of equipment for adapting a tool or machine to a special purpose **:** ATTACHMENT **b :** an instrument or device designed for a particular use; *specif* **:** a household or office device (as a stove, fan, or refrigerator) operated by gas or electric current **3** *obs* **:** COMPLIANCE ***syn*** see IMPLEMENT

ap·pli·ca·ble \'ap-li-kə-bəl *also* ə-'plik-ə-\ *adj* (1660) **:** capable of or suitable for being applied **:** APPROPRIATE ⟨statutes ~ to the case⟩ ***syn*** see RELEVANT — **ap·pli·ca·bil·i·ty** \ˌap-li-kə-'bil-ət-ē *also* ə-ˌplik-ə-\ *n*

ap·pli·cant \'ap-li-kənt\ *n* (15c) **:** one who applies ⟨a job ~⟩

ap·pli·ca·tion \ˌap-lə-'kā-shən\ *n* [ME *applicacioun,* fr. L *application-, applicatio* inclination, fr. *applicatus,* pp. of *applicare*] (15c) **1 :** an act of applying: **a (1) :** an act of putting to use ⟨~ of new techniques⟩ **(2) :** a use to which something is put ⟨new ~s for old remedies⟩ **b :** an act of administering or superposing ⟨~ of paint to a house⟩ **c :** assiduous attention ⟨succeeds by ~ to his studies⟩ **2 a :** REQUEST, PETITION ⟨an ~ for financial aid⟩ **b :** a form used in making a request **3 :** the practical inference to be derived from a discourse (as a moral tale) **4 :** a medicated or protective layer or material ⟨an oily ~ for dry skin⟩ **5 :** capacity for practical use ⟨words of varied ~⟩

ap·pli·ca·tive \'ap-lə-ˌkāt-iv, ə-'plik-ət-\ *adj* (1638) **1 :** APPLICABLE, PRACTICAL **2 :** put to use **:** APPLIED — **ap·pli·ca·tive·ly** *adv*

ap·pli·ca·tor \'ap-lə-ˌkāt-ər\ *n* (1659) **:** one that applies; *specif* **:** a device for applying a substance (as medicine or polish)

ap·pli·ca·to·ry \'ap-li-kə-ˌtōr-ē, -ˌtȯr-, ə-'plik-ə-\ *adj* (1649) **:** capable of being applied

ap·plied \ə-'plīd\ *adj* (1656) **:** put to practical use; *esp* **:** applying general principles to solve definite problems ⟨~ sciences⟩

¹ap·pli·qué \ˌap-lə-'kā\ *n* [F, pp. of *appliquer* to put on, fr. L *applicare*] (1801) **:** a cutout decoration fastened to a larger piece of material

²appliqué *vt* **-quéd; -qué·ing** (1881) **:** to apply (as a decoration or ornament) to a larger surface **:** OVERLAY

ap·ply \ə-'plī\ *vb* **ap·plied; ap·ply·ing** [ME *applien,* fr. MF *aplier,* fr. L *applicare,* fr. *ad-* + *plicare* to fold — more at PLY] *vt* (14c) **1 a :** to put to use esp. for some practical purpose ⟨*applies* pressure to get what he wants⟩ **b :** to bring into action ⟨~ the brakes⟩ **c :** to lay or spread on ⟨~ varnish to a table⟩ **d :** to put into operation or effect ⟨~ a law⟩ **2 :** to employ diligently or with close attention ⟨should ~ himself to his work⟩ ~ *vi* **1 :** to have relevance or a valid connection ⟨this rule *applies* to freshmen only⟩ **2 :** to make an appeal or request esp. in the form of a written application ⟨~ for a job⟩ — **ap·pli·er** \-'plī(-ə)r\ *n*

ap·pog·gia·tu·ra \ə-ˌpäj-ə-'tu̇r-ə\ *n* [It, lit., support] (ca. 1753) **:** an embellishing note or tone preceding an essential melodic note or tone and usu. written as a note of smaller size

ap·point \ə-'pȯint\ *vb* [ME *appointen,* fr. MF *apointier* to arrange, fr. *a-* (fr. L *ad-*) + *point* point] *vt* (14c) **1 a :** to fix or set officially ⟨~ a trial date⟩ **b :** to name officially ⟨will ~ him director of the program⟩ **c** *archaic* **:** ARRANGE **d :** to determine the disposition of (an estate) to someone by virtue of a power of appointment **2 :** to provide with complete and usu. appropriate or elegant furnishings or equipment ~ *vi* **:** to exercise a power of appointment ***syn*** see FURNISH

ap·poin·tee \ə-ˌpȯin-'tē, ˌa-\ *n* (1768) **1 :** one who is appointed **2 :** one to whom an estate is appointed

ap·point·ive \ə-'pȯint-iv\ *adj* (1881) **:** of, relating to, or filled by appointment ⟨an ~ office⟩

ap·point·ment \ə-'pȯint-mənt\ *n* (15c) **1 a :** an act of appointing **:** DESIGNATION **b :** the designation by virtue of a vested power of a person to enjoy an estate **2 :** a nonelective office or position ⟨holds an academic ~⟩ **3 :** an arrangement for a meeting **:** ENGAGEMENT **4 :** EQUIPMENT, FURNISHINGS — usu. used in pl.

ap·por·tion \ə-'pōr-shən, -'pȯr-\ *vt* **-tioned; -tion·ing** \-sh(ə-)niŋ\ [MF *apportionner,* fr. *a-* (fr. L *ad-*) + *portionner* to portion] (1574) **:** to divide and share out according to a plan; *esp* **:** to make a proportionate division or distribution of

ap·por·tion·ment \-shən-mənt\ *n* (1628) **:** an act or result of apportioning; *esp* **:** the apportioning of representatives or taxes among the states according to U.S. law

ap·pose \a-'pōz\ *vt* **ap·posed; ap·pos·ing** [MF *aposer,* fr. OF, fr. *a-* + *poser* to put — more at POSE] (1593) **1** *archaic* **:** to put before **:** apply (one thing) to another **2 :** to place in juxtaposition or proximity

ap·po·site \'ap-ə-zət\ *adj* [L *appositus,* fr. pp. of *apponere* to place near, fr. *ad-* + *ponere* to put — more at POSITION] (1621) **:** highly pertinent or appropriate **:** APT ***syn*** see RELEVANT — **ap·po·site·ly** *adv* — **ap·po·site·ness** *n*

ap·po·si·tion \ˌap-ə-'zish-ən\ *n* (15c) **1 a :** a grammatical construction in which two usu. adjacent nouns having the same referent stand in the same syntactical relation to the rest of a sentence (as *the poet* and *Burns* in "a biography of the poet Burns") **b :** the relation of one of such a pair of nouns or noun equivalents to the other **2 a :** an act or instance of apposing; *specif* **:** the deposition of successive layers upon those already present (as in cell walls) **b :** the state of being apposed — **ap·po·si·tion·al** \-'zish-nəl, -ən-ᵊl\ *adj*

ap·pos·i·tive \ə-'päz-ət-iv, a-\ *adj* (1693) **:** of, relating to, or standing in grammatical apposition — **appositive** *n* — **ap·pos·i·tive·ly** *adv*

ap·prais·al \ə-'prā-zəl\ *n* (1817) **:** an act or instance of appraising; *esp* **:** a valuation of property by the estimate of an authorized person

ap·praise \ə-'prāz\ *vt* **ap·praised; ap·prais·ing** [ME *appreisen,* fr. MF *aprisier* to apprize] (14c) **1 :** to set a value on **:** estimate the amount of **2 :** to evaluate the worth, significance, or status of; *esp* **:** to give an expert judgment of the value or merit of ***syn*** see ESTIMATE — **ap·praise·ment** \-'prāz-mənt\ *n* — **ap·prais·er** *n* — **ap·prais·ing** *adj* — **ap·prais·ing·ly** \-'prā-ziŋ-lē\ *adv*

ap·pre·cia·ble \ə-'prē-shə-bəl, -'prish(-ē)-ə-bəl\ *adj* (1818) **:** capable of being perceived or measured ***syn*** see PERCEPTIBLE — **ap·pre·cia·bly** \-blē\ *adv*

ap·pre·ci·ate \ə-'prē-shē-ˌāt, -'prish-ē- *also* 'prē-sē-\ *vb* **-at·ed; -at·ing** [LL *appretiatus,* pp. of *appretiare,* fr. L *ad-* + *pretium* price — more at PRICE] *vt* (1655) **1 a :** to grasp the nature, worth, quality, or significance of ⟨can't ~ the difference between right and wrong⟩ **b :** to value or admire highly ⟨thinks no one ~s his endeavors⟩ **c :** to judge with heightened perception or understanding **:** be fully aware of ⟨must experience it to ~ it⟩ **d :** to recognize with gratitude ⟨certainly ~s your kindness⟩ **2 :** to increase the value of ~ *vi* **:** to increase in number or value — **ap·pre·ci·a·tor** \-ˌāt-ər\ *n* — **ap·pre·cia·to·ry** \-'prē-shə-ˌtōr-ē, -'prish-ə-, -ˌtȯr-\ *adj*

syn APPRECIATE, VALUE, PRIZE, TREASURE, CHERISH mean to hold in high estimation. APPRECIATE often connotes sufficient understanding to enjoy or admire a thing's excellence; VALUE implies rating a thing highly for its intrinsic worth; PRIZE implies taking a deep pride in something one possesses; TREASURE emphasizes jealously safeguarding something considered precious; CHERISH implies a special love and care for something. ***syn*** see in addition UNDERSTAND

ap·pre·ci·a·tion \ə-ˌprē-shē-'ā-shən, -ˌprish-ē- *also* -ˌprē-sē-\ *n* (1604) **1 a :** JUDGMENT, EVALUATION; *esp* **:** a favorable critical estimate **b :** sensitive awareness; *esp* **:** recognition of aesthetic values **c :** an expression of admiration, approval, or gratitude **2 :** increase in value

ap·pre·cia·tive \ə-'prē-shət-iv, -'prish-ət- *also* -'prē-shē-ˌāt-\ *adj* (1698) **:** having or showing appreciation — **ap·pre·cia·tive·ly** *adv* — **ap·pre·cia·tive·ness** *n*

ap·pre·hend \ˌap-ri-'hend\ *vb* [ME *apprehenden,* fr. L *apprehendere,* lit., to seize, fr. *ad-* + *prehendere* to seize — more at PREHENSILE] *vt* (1513) **1 :** ARREST, SEIZE ⟨~ a thief⟩ **2 a :** to become aware of **:** PERCEIVE **b :** to anticipate esp. with anxiety, dread, or fear **3 :** to grasp with the understanding **:** recognize the meaning of ~ *vi* **:** UNDERSTAND, GRASP ***syn*** see FORESEE

ap·pre·hen·si·ble \ˌap-ri-'hen(t)-sə-bəl\ *adj* (15c) **:** capable of being apprehended — **ap·pre·hen·si·bly** \-blē\ *adv*

ap·pre·hen·sion \ˌap-ri-'hen-chən\ *n* [ME, fr. LL *apprehension-, apprehensio,* fr. L *apprehensus,* pp. of *apprehendere*] (14c) **1 a :** the act or power of perceiving or comprehending ⟨a man of dull ~⟩ **b :** the result of apprehending mentally **:** CONCEPTION ⟨according to popular ~⟩ **2 :** seizure by legal process **:** ARREST **3 :** suspicion or fear esp. of future evil **:** FOREBODING

ap·pre·hen·sive \-'hen(t)-siv\ *adj* (14c) **1 :** capable of apprehending or quick to do so **:** DISCERNING **2 :** having apprehension **:** COGNIZANT **3 :** viewing the future with anxiety or alarm ***syn*** see FEARFUL — **ap·pre·hen·sive·ly** *adv* — **ap·pre·hen·sive·ness** *n*

¹ap·pren·tice \ə-'prent-əs\ *n* [ME *aprentis,* fr. MF, fr. OF, fr. *aprendre* to learn, fr. L *apprendere, apprehendere*] (14c) **1 a :** one bound by indenture to serve another for a prescribed period with a view to learning an art or trade **b :** one who is learning by practical experience under skilled workers a trade, art, or calling **2 :** an inexperienced person **:** NOVICE ⟨an ~ in cooking⟩ — **ap·pren·tice·ship** \-ə(sh)-ˌship, -əs-ˌship\ *n*

²apprentice *vb* **-ticed; -tic·ing** *vt* (1631) **:** to set at work as an apprentice; *esp* **:** to bind to an apprenticeship by contract or indenture ~ *vi* **:** to serve as an apprentice

ap·pressed \a-'prest\ *adj* [L *appressus,* pp. of *apprimere* to press to, fr. *ad-* + *premere* to press — more at PRESS] (1791) **:** pressed close to or lying flat against something ⟨leaves ~ against the stem⟩

ap·pres·so·ri·um \ˌa-pres-'ōr-ē-əm, -'ȯr-\ *n, pl* **-ria** \-ē-ə\ [NL, fr. L *appressus* + *-orium*] (1897) **:** the flattened thickened tip of a hyphal branch by which some parasitic fungi are attached to their host

ap·prise \ə-'prīz\ *vt* **ap·prised; ap·pris·ing** [F *appris,* pp. of *apprendre* to learn, teach, fr. OF *aprendre*] (1694) **:** to give notice to **:** TELL ***syn*** see INFORM

ap·prize \ə-'prīz\ *vt* **ap·prized; ap·priz·ing** [ME *apprisen,* fr. MF *aprisier,* fr. OF, fr. *a-* (fr. L *ad-*) + *prisier* to appraise — more at PRIZE] (15c) : VALUE, APPRECIATE

1ap·proach \ə-'prōch\ *vb* [ME *approchen,* fr. OF *aprochier,* fr. LL *appropiare,* fr. L *ad-* + *prope* near; akin to L *pro* before — more at PROXIMATE] *vt* (13c) **1 a** : to draw closer to : NEAR ⟨~ the podium⟩ **b** : to come very near to : be almost the same as ⟨its mathematics *~es* mysticism —Theodore Sturgeon⟩ ⟨as the quantity *x ~es* zero⟩ **2 a** : to make advances to esp. in order to create a desired result ⟨was *~ed* by several Broadway producers⟩ **b** : to take preliminary steps toward accomplishment or full knowledge or experience of ⟨~ the subject with an open mind⟩ ~ *vi* **1** : to draw nearer ⟨dawn *~es*⟩ **2** : to make an approach in golf

2approach *n* (15c) **1 a** : an act or instance of approaching ⟨the ~ of summer⟩ **b** : APPROXIMATION ⟨in this book he makes his closest ~ to greatness⟩ **2 a** : the taking of preliminary steps toward a particular purpose ⟨experimenting with new lines of ~⟩ **b** : a particular manner of taking such steps ⟨a highly individual ~ to language⟩ **3** : a means of access : AVENUE **4 a** : a golf shot from the fairway toward the green **b** : the steps taken by a bowler before he delivers the ball; *also* : the part of the alley behind the foul line from which the bowler delivers the ball

ap·proach·able \ə-'prō-chə-bəl\ *adj* (1571) : capable of being approached : ACCESSIBLE; *specif* : easy to meet or deal with — **ap·proach·abil·i·ty** \-,prō-chə-'bil-ət-ē\ *n*

ap·pro·bate \'ap-rə-,bāt\ *vt* **-bat·ed; -bat·ing** [ME *approbaten,* fr. L *approbatus,* pp. of *approbare* — more at APPROVE] (15c) : APPROVE, SANCTION — **ap·pro·ba·to·ry** \'ap-rə-bə-,tōr-ē, ə-'prō-bə-, -,tȯr-\ *adj*

ap·pro·ba·tion \,ap-rə-'bā-shən\ *n* (14c) **1** *obs* : PROOF **2 a** : an act of approving formally or officially **b** : COMMENDATION, PRAISE

1ap·pro·pri·ate \ə-'prō-prē-,āt\ *vt* **-at·ed; -at·ing** [ME *appropriaten,* fr. LL *appropriatus,* pp. of *appropriare,* fr. L *ad-* + *proprius* own] (15c) **1** : to take exclusive possession of : ANNEX ⟨no one should ~ a common benefit⟩ **2** : to set apart for or assign to a particular purpose or use ⟨~ money for the research program⟩ **3** : to take or make use of without authority or right — **ap·pro·pri·a·ble** \-prē-ə-bəl\ *adj* — **ap·pro·pri·a·tor** \-prē-,āt-ər\ *n*

2ap·pro·pri·ate \ə-'prō-prē-ət\ *adj* (15c) : especially suitable or compatible : FITTING ***syn*** see FIT — **ap·pro·pri·ate·ly** *adv* — **ap·pro·pri·ate·ness** *n*

ap·pro·pri·a·tion \ə-,prō-prē-'ā-shən\ *n* (14c) **1** : an act or instance of appropriating **2** : something that has been appropriated; *specif* : money set aside by formal action for a specific use — **ap·pro·pri·a·tive** \-'prō-prē-,āt-iv\ *adj*

ap·prov·able \ə-'prü-və-bəl\ *adj* (15c) : capable or worthy of being approved — **ap·prov·ably** \-blē\ *adv*

ap·prov·al \ə-'prü-vəl\ *n* (1616) : an act or instance of approving : APPROBATION — **on approval** : subject to a prospective buyer's acceptance or refusal ⟨took the suit home *on approval*⟩

ap·prove \ə-'prüv\ *vb* **ap·proved; ap·prov·ing** [ME *approven,* fr. MF *aprover,* fr. L *approbare,* fr. *ad-* + *probare* to prove — more at PROVE] *vt* (14c) **1** *obs* : PROVE, ATTEST **2** : to have or express a favorable opinion of ⟨couldn't ~ his conduct⟩ **3 a** : to accept as satisfactory ⟨hopes she will ~ the date of the meeting⟩ **b** : to give formal or official sanction to : RATIFY ⟨Congress *approved* the proposed budget⟩ ~ *vi* : to take a favorable view ⟨doesn't ~ of fighting⟩ — **ap·prov·ing·ly** \-'prü-viŋ-lē\ *adv*

syn APPROVE, ENDORSE, SANCTION, ACCREDIT, CERTIFY mean to have or express a favorable opinion of. APPROVE often implies no more than this but may suggest considerable esteem or admiration; ENDORSE suggests an explicit statement of support; SANCTION implies both approval and authorization; ACCREDIT and CERTIFY usu. imply official endorsement attesting to conformity to set standards.

approved school *n, Brit* (1932) : a school for juvenile delinquents

1ap·prox·i·mate \ə-'präk-sə-mət\ *adj* [LL *approximatus,* pp. of *approximare* to come near, fr. L *ad-* + *proximare* to come near — more at PROXIMATE] (15c) **1** : nearly correct or exact ⟨an ~ solution⟩ **2** : located close together ⟨~ leaves⟩ — **ap·prox·i·mate·ly** *adv*

2ap·prox·i·mate \-,māt\ *vb* **-mat·ed; -mat·ing** *vt* (15c) **1 a** : to bring near or close **b** : to bring (cut edges of tissue) together **2** : to come near to or be close to in position, value, or characteristics ⟨a child tries to ~ his parents' speech⟩ ~ *vi* : to come close

ap·prox·i·ma·tion \ə-,präk-sə-'mā-shən\ *n* (15c) **1** : the act or process of drawing together **2** : the quality or state of being close or near ⟨an ~ to the truth⟩ **3** : something that is approximate; *esp* : a mathematical quantity that is close in value to but not the same as a desired quantity — **ap·prox·i·ma·tive** \-'präk-sə-,māt-iv\ *adj*

ap·pur·te·nance \ə-'pərt-nən(t)s, -ᵊn-ən(t)s\ *n* (14c) **1** : an incidental right (as a right-of-way) attached to a principal property right and passing in possession with it **2** : a subordinate part or adjunct ⟨the ~ of welcome is fashion and ceremony—Shak.⟩ **3** *pl* : accessory objects : APPARATUS

ap·pur·te·nant \ə-'pərt-nənt, -ᵊn-ənt\ *adj* [ME *apertenant,* fr. MF, fr. OF, prp. of *apartenir* to belong — more at APPERTAIN] (14c) **1** : constituting a legal accompaniment **2** : AUXILIARY, ACCESSORY — **appurtenant** *n*

aprax·ia \(')ā-'prak-sē-ə\ *n* [NL, fr. Gk, inaction, fr. *a-* + *praxis* action, fr. *prassein* to do — more at PRACTICAL] (1888) : loss or impairment of the ability to execute complex coordinated movements without impairment of the muscles or senses — **aprac·tic** \-'prak-tik\ *or* **aprax·ic** \-'prak-sik\ *adj*

après \(,)äp-,rā, (,)ap-\ *prep* [prob. back-formation fr. *après-ski*] (1954) : AFTER ⟨~ tennis⟩ — usu. used in combination ⟨*après*-theater party⟩

après–ski \,äp-,rā-'skē, ,ap-\ *n* [F *après* after + *ski* ski, skiing] (1954) : social activity (as at a ski lodge) after a day's skiing — **après–ski** *adj*

apri·cot \'ap-rə-,kät, 'ā-prə-\ *n, often attrib* [alter. of earlier *abrecock,* deriv. of Ar *al-birqūq* the apricot] (1551) **1 a** : the oval orange-colored fruit of a temperate-zone tree (*Prunus armeniaca*) resembling the related peach and plum in flavor **b** : a tree that bears apricots **2** : a variable color averaging a moderate orange

April \'ā-prəl\ *n* [ME, fr. OF & L; OF *avrill,* fr. L *Aprilis*] (bef. 12c) : the 4th month of the Gregorian calendar

April fool *n* (1687) : the butt of a joke or trick played on April Fools' Day; *also* : such a joke or trick

April Fools' Day *n* (1832) : April 1 characteristically marked by the playing of practical jokes

a pri·o·ri \,ä-prē-'ō(ə)r-ē, ,ap-rē-; ,ā-(,)prī-'ō(ə)r-,ī, ,-prē-'ō(ə)r-ē; -'ȯ(ə)r-\ *adj* [L, lit., from the former] (1651) **1 a** : DEDUCTIVE **b** : relating to or derived by reasoning from self-evident propositions — compare A POSTERIORI **c** : presupposed by experience **2 a** : being without examination or analysis : PRESUMPTIVE **b** : formed or conceived beforehand — **a priori** *adv* — **apri·or·i·ty** \-'ór-ət-ē\ *n*

apron \'ā-prən, -pərn\ *n, often attrib* [ME, alter. (resulting fr. incorrect division of *a napron*) of *napron,* fr. MF *naperon,* dim. of *nape* cloth, modif. of L *mappa* napkin — more at MAP] (14c) **1** : a garment usu. of cloth, plastic, or leather usu. tied around the waist and used to protect clothing or adorn a costume **2** : something that suggests or resembles an apron in shape, position, or use: as **a** : the lower member under the sill of the interior casing of a window **b** : an upward or downward vertical extension of a sink or lavatory **c** : a piece of waterproof cloth spread out (as before the seat of a vehicle) as a protection from rain or mud **d** : a covering (as of sheet metal) for protecting parts of machinery **e** : an endless belt for carrying material **f** : an extensive fan-shaped deposit of detritus **g** : the part of the stage in front of the proscenium arch **h** : the area along the waterfront edge of a pier or wharf **i** : a shield (as of concrete, planking, or brushwood) along the bank of a river, along a seawall, or below a dam **j** : the extensive paved part of an airport immediately adjacent to the terminal area or hangars

apron string *n* (1542) : the string of an apron — usu. used in pl. as a symbol of dominance or complete control ⟨though 40 years old he was still tied to his mother's *apron strings*⟩

1ap·ro·pos \,ap-rə-'pō, 'ap-rə-,\ *adv* [F *à propos,* lit., to the purpose] (1668) **1** : at an opportune time : SEASONABLY **2** : BY THE WAY

2apropos *adj* (1686) : being both relevant and opportune ***syn*** see RELEVANT

3apropos *prep* (1910) : APROPOS OF

apropos of *prep* (1746) : with regard to : CONCERNING

apse \'aps\ *n* [ML & L; ML *apsis,* fr. L] (1822) **1** : APSIS 1 **2** : a projecting part of a building (as a church) that is usu. semicircular in plan and vaulted

ap·si·dal \'ap-səd-ᵊl\ *adj* (1846) : of or relating to an apse

ap·sis \'ap-səs\ *n, pl* **ap·si·des** \-sə-,dēz\ [NL *apsid-, apsis,* fr. L, arch, orbit, fr. Gk *hapsid-, hapsis,* fr. *haptein* to fasten] (1658) **1** : the point in an astronomical orbit at which the distance of the body from the center of attraction is either greatest or least **2** : APSE 2

apt \'apt\ *adj* [ME, fr. L *aptus,* lit., fastened, fr. pp. of *apere* to fasten; akin to L *apisci* to reach, *apud* near, Gk *hapsis* fastened, Skt *āpta* fit] (14c) **1** : unusually fitted or qualified : READY ⟨proved an ~ tool in the hands of the conspirators⟩ **2 a** : having a tendency : LIKELY ⟨plants ~ to suffer from drought⟩ **b** : ordinarily disposed : INCLINED ⟨~ to accept what is plausible as true⟩ **3** : suited to a purpose; *esp* : being to the point ⟨an ~ quotation⟩ **4** : keenly intelligent and responsive ***syn*** see FIT, QUICK ***usage*** see LIABLE — **apt·ly** \'ap-(t)lē\ *adv* — **apt·ness** \'ap(t)-nəs\ *n*

ap·ter·ous \'ap-tə-rəs\ *adj* [Gk *apteros,* fr. *a-* + *pteron* wing — more at FEATHER] (1775) : lacking wings ⟨~ insects⟩

ap·ter·yx \'ap-tə-riks\ *n* [NL, fr. *a-* + Gk *pteryx* wing; akin to Gk *pteron*] (1813) : KIWI

ap·ti·tude \'ap-tə-,t(y)üd\ *n* [ME, fr. ML *aptitudo,* fr. LL, fitness, fr. L *aptus*] (15c) **1 a** : INCLINATION, TENDENCY **b** : a natural ability : TALENT **2** : capacity for learning : APTNESS **3** : general suitability ***syn*** see GIFT — **ap·ti·tu·di·nal** \,ap-tə-'t(y)üd-nəl, -ᵊn-əl\ *adj* — **ap·ti·tu·di·nal·ly** \-ē\ *adv*

aptitude test *n* (1923) : a standardized test designed to predict an individual's ability to learn certain skills

ap·y·rase \'ap-ə-,rās, -,rāz\ *n* [*a*denosine + *pyro*phosphate + *-ase*] (1945) : any of several enzymes that hydrolyze ATP with the liberation of phosphate and energy

aqua \'ak-wə, 'äk-\ *n, pl* **aquae** \'ak-(,)wē, 'äk-,wī\ *or* **aquas** [L— more at ISLAND] (14c) **1** : WATER; *esp* : an aqueous solution (as of a volatile substance) **2** : a light greenish blue color

aqua·cade \'ak-wə-,kād, 'äk-\ *n* [*Aquacade,* a water entertainment spectacle orig. at Cleveland, Ohio (1937)] (1937) : a water spectacle that consists usu. of exhibitions of swimming and diving with musical accompaniment

aqua·cul·ture *also* **aqui·cul·ture** \'ak-wə-,kəl-chər, 'äk-\ *n* [L *aqua* + E *-culture* (as in *agriculture*)] (1867) : the cultivation of the natural produce of water (as fish or shellfish) — **aqua·cul·tur·al** \,ak-wə-'kəlch-(ə-)rəl, ,äk-\ *adj* — **aqua·cul·tur·ist** \-(ə-)rəst\ *n*

Aqua·dag \'ak-wə-,dag, 'äk-\ *trademark* — used for a colloidal suspension of fine particles of graphite in water for use as a lubricant

aqua·for·tis \,ak-wə-'fȯrt-əs, ,äk-\ *n* [NL *aqua fortis,* lit., strong water] (15c) : NITRIC ACID

aqua·lung·er \'ak-wə-,ləŋ-ər, 'äk-\ *n* [fr. *Aqua-lung,* a trademark] (1952) : SCUBA DIVER

aqua·ma·rine \,ak-wə-mə-'rēn, ,äk-\ *n* [NL *aqua marina,* fr. L, sea water] (1598) **1** : a transparent beryl that is blue, blue-green, or green in color **2** : a pale blue to light greenish blue

aqua·naut \'ak-wə-,nȯt, 'äk-, -,nät\ *n* [L *aqua* + E *-naut* (as in *aeronaut*)] (1881) : a scuba diver who lives and operates both inside and outside an underwater shelter for an extended period

aqua·plane \'ak-wə-,plān, 'äk-\ *n* (1914) : a board towed behind a speeding motorboat and ridden by a person standing on it — **aquaplane** *vi* — **aqua·plan·er** *n*

aqua pu·ra \,ak-wə-'pyùr-ə, ,äk-\ *n* [L] (ca. 1934) : pure water

aqua re·gia \-'rē-j(ē-)ə\ *n* [NL, lit., royal water] (1610) : a mixture of nitric and hydrochloric acids that dissolves gold or platinum

aqua·relle \,ak-wə-'rel, ,äk-\ *n* [F, fr. obs. It *acquarella* (now *acquerello*), fr. *acqua* water, fr. L *aqua*] (1869) : a drawing usu. in transparent watercolor — **aqua·rell·ist** \-'rel-əst\ *n*

Aquar·i·an \ə-'kwar-ē-ən, -'kwer-\ *n* (1968) : AQUARIUS 2b

aquar·ist \ə-'kwar-əst, -'kwer-\ *n* (ca. 1893) : one who keeps an aquarium

aquar·i·um \ə-'kwar-ē-əm, -'kwer-\ *n, pl* **-i·ums** *or* **-ia** \-ē-ə\ [L, watering place for cattle, fr. neut. of *aquarius* of water, fr. *aqua*] (ca. 1847) **1** : a container (as a glass tank) or an artificial pond in which living aquatic animals or plants are kept **2** : an establishment where aquatic collections of living organisms are kept and exhibited

Aquar·i·us \-ē-əs\ *n* [L (gen. *Aquarii*), lit., water carrier] **1 :** a constellation south of Pegasus pictured as a man pouring water **2 a :** the 11th sign of the zodiac in astrology — see ZODIAC table **b :** one born under this sign

[1]aquat·ic \ə-ˈkwät-ik, -ˈkwat-\ *adj* (1642) **1 :** growing or living in or frequenting water ⟨~ mosquito larvae⟩ **2 :** taking place in or on water ⟨~ sports⟩ — **aquat·i·cal·ly** \-i-k(ə-)lē\ *adv*

[2]aquatic *n* (1600) **1 :** an aquatic animal or plant **2** *pl but sing or pl in constr* **:** water sports

aqua·tint \ˈak-wə-ˌtint, ˈäk-\ *n* [It *acqua tinta* dyed water] (1782) **:** a method of etching a printing plate so that tones similar to watercolor washes can be reproduced; *also* **:** a print made from a plate so etched — **aquatint** *vt* — **aqua·tint·er** *n* — **aqua·tint·ist** \-əst\ *n*

aqua·vit \ˈäk-wə-ˌvēt\ *n* [Sw, Dan, & Norw *akvavit,* fr. ML *aqua vitae*] (1890) **:** a clear Scandinavian liquor flavored with caraway seeds

aqua vi·tae \ˌak-wə-ˈvīt-ē, ˌäk-\ *n* [ME, fr. ML, lit., water of life] (15c) **:** ARDENT SPIRITS; *esp* **:** a strong alcoholic liquor (as brandy)

aq·ue·duct \ˈak-wə-ˌdəkt\ *n* [L *aquaeductus,* fr. *aquae* (gen. of *aqua*) + *ductus* act of leading — more at DUCT] (1538) **1 a :** a conduit for water; *esp* **:** one for carrying a large quantity of flowing water **b :** a structure for conveying a canal over a river or hollow **2 :** a canal or passage in a part or organ

aque·ous \ˈā-kwē-əs, ˈak-wē-\ *adj* [ML *aqueus,* fr. L *aqua*] (1646) **1 a :** of, relating to, or resembling water **b :** made from, with, or by water **2 :** of or relating to the aqueous humor

aqueous humor *n* (1643) **:** a transparent fluid occupying the space between the crystalline lens and the cornea of the eye

aqui·fer \ˈak-wə-fər, ˈäk-\ *n* [NL, fr. L *aqua* + *-fer*] (1901) **:** a water-bearing stratum of permeable rock, sand, or gravel — **aquif·er·ous** \a-ˈkwif-ə-rəs, ä-\ *adj*

aq·ui·le·gia \ˌak-wə-ˈlē-j(ē-)ə\ *n* [NL] (1871) **:** COLUMBINE

aq·ui·line \ˈak-wə-ˌlīn, -lən\ *adj* [L *aquilinus,* fr. *aquila* eagle] (1646) **1 :** of, relating to, or resembling an eagle **2 :** curving like an eagle's beak ⟨an ~ nose⟩ — **aq·ui·lin·i·ty** \ˌak-wə-ˈlin-ət-ē\ *n*

aquiv·er \ə-ˈkwiv-ər\ *adj* (1883) **:** marked by trembling or quivering ⟨all ~ with excitement⟩

ar \ˈär\ *n* [ME] (14c) **:** the letter *r*

-ar \ər *also* ˌär\ *adj suffix* [ME, fr. L *-aris,* alter. of *-alis* -al] **:** of or relating to ⟨molecul*ar*⟩ **:** being ⟨spectacul*ar*⟩ **:** resembling ⟨ocul*ar*⟩

Ar·ab \ˈar-əb\ *n* [ME, fr. L *Arabus, Arabs,* fr. Gk *Arab-, Araps,* fr. Ar *ʿArab*] (14c) **1 a :** a member of the Semitic people of the Arabian peninsula **b :** a member of an Arabic-speaking people **2 :** ARABIAN HORSE — **Arab** *adj*

[1]ar·a·besque \ˌar-ə-ˈbesk\ *adj* [F, fr. It *arabesco* Arabian in fashion, fr. *Arabo* Arab, fr. L *Arabus*] (ca. 1611) **:** of, relating to, or being in the style of arabesque

[2]arabesque *n* (1786) **1 :** an ornament or style that employs flower, foliage, or fruit and sometimes animal and figural outlines to produce an intricate pattern of interlaced lines **2 :** a posture in ballet in which the body is bent forward from the hip on one leg with one arm extended forward and the other arm and leg backward **3 :** a contrived intricate pattern of verbal expression ⟨~s of alliteration —C. E. Montague⟩

arabesque 1

Ara·bi·an horse \ə-ˌrā-bē-ən-\ *n* (1737) **1 :** a horse of the stock used by the natives of Arabia and adjacent regions **2 :** a horse of a breed noted for its graceful build, stamina, intelligence, and spirit — called also *Arabian*

[1]Ar·a·bic \ˈar-ə-bik\ *n* (14c) **:** a Semitic language orig. of the Arabs of the Hejaz and Nejd that is now the prevailing speech of Arabia, Jordan, Lebanon, Syria, Iraq, Egypt, and parts of northern Africa

[2]Arabic *adj* (1526) **1 :** of, relating to, or characteristic of Arabia or the Arabs **2 :** of, relating to, or constituting Arabic **3 :** expressed in or utilizing Arabic numerals

Arabic alphabet *n* (1946) **:** the alphabet of 28 letters derived from the Aramaic which is used for writing Arabic and also with adaptations for several other languages of Islam

arab·i·cize \ə-ˈrab-ə-ˌsīz\ *vt* **-cized; -ciz·ing** *often cap* (1872) **1 :** to adapt (a language or elements of a language) to the phonetic or structural pattern of Arabic **2 :** ARABIZE 1

Arabic numeral *n* (ca. 1847) **:** one of the number symbols 0, 1, 2, 3, 4, 5, 6, 7, 8, 9 — see NUMBER table

arab·i·nose \ə-ˈrab-ə-ˌnōs, -ˌnōz\ *n* [ISV *arabin* (the solid principle in gum arabic, fr. *gum arabic* + *-in*) + *-ose*] (ca. 1884) **:** a crystalline aldose sugar $C_5H_{10}O_5$ of the pentose class

ara·bi·no·side \ˌar-ə-ˈbin-ə-ˌsīd, ə-ˈrab-ə-nō-ˌsīd\ *n* (1927) **:** a glycoside that yields arabinose on hydrolysis

Ar·ab·ist \ˈar-ə-bəst\ *n* (ca. 1753) **1 :** a specialist in the Arabic language or in Arabic culture **2 :** one who favors Arab interests and positions in international affairs

ar·ab·ize \ˈar-ə-ˌbīz\ *vt* **-ized; -iz·ing** *often cap* (1883) **1 a :** to cause to acquire Arabic customs, manners, speech, or outlook **b :** to modify (a racial or national stock) by an admixture of Arab blood **2 :** ARABICIZE 1

[1]ar·a·ble \ˈar-ə-bəl\ *adj* [MF or L; MF, fr. L *arabilis,* fr. *arare* to plow; akin to OE *erian* to plow, Gk *aroun*] (15c) **:** fit for or cultivated by plowing or tillage — **ar·a·bil·i·ty** \ˌar-ə-ˈbil-ət-ē\ *n*

[2]arable *n* (1576) **:** land that is tilled or tillable

ar·a·chi·don·ic acid \ˌar-ə-kə-ˌdän-ik-\ *n* [ISV, fr. NL *Arachid-, Arachis,* genus name + *-onic* (as in *gluconic acid*) containing carboxyl] (1913) **:** a liquid unsaturated acid $C_{20}H_{32}O_2$ that occurs in most animal fats, is a precursor of some prostaglandins, and is considered essential in animal nutrition

ar·a·chis oil \ˈar-ə-kəs-\ *n* [NL *Arachis,* genus name, prob. fr. Gk *arakis,* dim. of *arakos,* a legume] (ca. 1889) **:** PEANUT OIL

arach·nid \ə-ˈrak-nəd, -ˌnid\ *n* [deriv. of Gk *arachnē* spider] (1869) **:** any of a class (Arachnida) of arthropods comprising mostly air-breathing invertebrates, including the spiders and scorpions, mites, and ticks, and having a segmented body divided into two regions of which the anterior bears four pairs of legs but no antennae — **arachnid** *adj*

[1]arach·noid \ə-ˈrak-ˌnȯid\ *n* [NL *arachnoides,* fr. Gk *arachnoeidēs,* like a cobweb, fr. *arachnē* spider, spider's web] (1751) **:** a thin membrane of the brain and spinal cord that lies between the dura mater and the pia mater

[2]arachnoid *adj* (1789) **1 :** of or relating to the arachnoid ⟨the ~ membrane⟩ **2 :** covered with or composed of soft loose hairs or fibers

[3]arachnoid *adj* [deriv. of Gk *arachnē*] (1852) **:** resembling or related to the arachnids

ara·go·nite \ə-ˈrag-ə-ˌnīt, ˈar-ə-gə-\ *n* [G *aragonit,* fr. *Aragon,* Spain] (1803) **:** a mineral $CaCO_3$ consisting like calcite of calcium carbonate but differing from calcite in its orthorhombic crystallization, greater density, and less distinct cleavage — **ara·go·nit·ic** \ə-ˌrag-ə-ˈnit-ik, ˌar-ə-gə-\ *adj*

Ar·a·mae·an \ˌar-ə-ˈmē-ən\ *n* [L *Aramaeus,* fr. Gk *Aramaios,* fr. Heb *ʾĂrām* Aram, ancient name for Syria] (1839) **1 :** ARAMAIC **2 :** a member of a Semitic people of the second millennium B.C. in Syria and Upper Mesopotamia — **Aramaean** *adj*

Ar·a·ma·ic \ˌar-ə-ˈmā-ik\ *n* (1882) **:** a Semitic language known since the ninth century B.C. as the speech of the Aramaeans and later used extensively in southwest Asia as a commercial and governmental language and adopted as their customary speech by various non-Aramaean peoples including the Jews after the Babylonian exile

Aramaic alphabet *n* (1925) **1 :** an extinct North Semitic alphabet dating from the ninth century B.C. which was for several centuries the commercial alphabet of southwest Asia and the parent of other alphabets (as Syriac and Arabic) **2 :** the square Hebrew alphabet as distinguished from the early Hebrew alphabet

ar·a·mid \ˈar-ə-məd, -ˌmid\ *n* [*ar*omatic poly*amide*] (1972) **:** any of a group of lightweight but very strong heat-resistant synthetic aromatic polyamide materials that are fashioned into fibers, filaments, or sheets and used esp. in textiles and plastics

Arap·a·ho *or* **Arap·a·hoe** \ə-ˈrap-ə-ˌhō\ *n, pl* **Arapaho** *or* **Arapahos** *or* **Arapahoe** *or* **Arapahoes** (1854) **:** a member of an American Indian people of the plains region ranging from Saskatchewan and Manitoba to New Mexico and Texas

Arau·ca·ni·an \ə-ˌrau̇-ˈkän-ē-ən, ˌar-ˌȯ-ˈkän-\ *also* **Arau·can** \ə-ˈrau̇-kən\ *n* [Sp *araucano,* fr. *Arauco,* province in Chile] (1903) **1 :** a member of a group of Indian peoples of south central Chile and adjacent regions of Argentina **2 :** the language of the Araucanian people that constitutes an independent language family — **Araucanian** *adj*

ar·au·car·ia \ˌar-ˌȯ-ˈkar-ē-ə\ *n* [NL, fr. *Arauco*] (1809) **:** any of a genus (*Araucaria*) of So. American or Australian trees of the pine family — **ar·au·car·i·an** \-ē-ən\ *adj*

Ar·a·wak \ˈar-ə-ˌwäk, -ˌwak\ *n, pl* **Arawak** *or* **Arawaks** (1769) **1 :** a member of an Indian people of the Arawakan group now living chiefly along the coast of Guyana **2 :** the language of the Arawak people

Ar·a·wak·an \ˌar-ə-ˈwäk-ən, -ˈwak-\ *n, pl* **Arawakan** *or* **Arawakans** (1901) **1 :** a member of a group of Indian peoples of South America and the West Indies **2 :** the language family of the Arawakan peoples

arb \ˈärb\ *n* (1979) **:** ARBITRAGEUR

ar·ba·lest *or* **ar·ba·list** \ˈär-bə-ləst\ *n* [ME *arblast,* fr. OE, fr. OF *arbaleste,* fr. LL *arcuballista,* fr. L *arcus* bow + *ballista* — more at ARROW] (bef. 12c) **:** CROSSBOW; *esp* **:** a medieval military weapon with a steel bow used to throw balls, stones, and quarrels — **ar·ba·lest·er** \-ˌles-tər\ *n*

ar·bi·ter \ˈär-bət-ər\ *n* [ME *arbitre,* fr. MF, fr. L *arbitr-, arbiter*] (14c) **1 :** a person with power to decide a dispute **:** JUDGE **2 :** a person or agency having absolute power of judging and determining

arbiter el·e·gan·ti·a·rum \-ˌel-ə-ˌgan-shē-ˈar-əm, -ˈer-\ *n* [L, lit., arbiter of refinements] (1818) **:** one who prescribes, rules on, or is a recognized authority on matters of social behavior and taste

ar·bi·tra·ble \ˈär-bə-trə-bəl, är-ˈbi-\ *adj* (1531) **:** subject to decision by arbitration

[1]ar·bi·trage \ˈär-bə-ˌträzh\ *n* [F, fr. MF, arbitration, fr. OF, fr. *arbitrer* to render judgment, fr. L *arbitrari,* fr. *arbitr-, arbiter*] (ca. 1879) **:** the often simultaneous purchase and sale of the same or equivalent security (as in different markets) in order to profit from price discrepancies

[2]arbitrage *vi* **-traged; -trag·ing** (1900) **:** to engage in arbitrage

ar·bi·tra·geur \ˌär-bə-(ˌ)trä-ˈzhər\ *or* **ar·bi·trag·er** \ˈär-bə-ˌträzh-ər\ *n* [F *arbitrageur,* fr. *arbitrage* + *-eur* -or] (1870) **:** one that practices arbitrage

ar·bi·tral \ˈär-bə-trəl\ *adj* (1609) **:** of or relating to arbiters or arbitration

ar·bit·ra·ment \är-ˈbi-trə-mənt\ *n* [ME, fr. MF *arbitrement,* fr. *arbitrer*] (15c) **1** *archaic* **:** the right or power of deciding **2 :** the settling of a dispute by an arbiter **3 :** the judgment given by an arbitrator

ar·bi·trary \ˈär-bə-ˌtrer-ē\ *adj* (15c) **1 :** depending on individual discretion (as of a judge) and not fixed by law ⟨the manner of punishment is ~⟩ **2 a :** not restrained or limited in the exercise of power **:** ruling by absolute authority ⟨an ~ government⟩ **b :** marked by or resulting from the unrestrained and often tyrannical exercise of power ⟨protection from ~ arrest and detention⟩ **3 a :** based on or determined by individual preference or convenience rather than by necessity or the intrinsic nature of something ⟨an ~ standard⟩ ⟨take any ~ positive number⟩ ⟨~ division of historical studies into watertight compartments —A.M. Toynbee⟩ **b :** existing or coming about seemingly at random or by chance or as a capricious and unreasonable act of will ⟨when a task is not seen in a meaningful context it is experienced as being ~ —Nehemiah Jordan⟩ — **ar·bi·trari·ly** \ˌär-bə-ˈtrer-ə-lē\ *adv* — **ar·bi·trari·ness** \ˈär-bə-ˌtrer-ē-nəs\ *n*

ar·bi·trate \ˈär-bə-ˌtrāt\ *vb* **-trat·ed; -trat·ing** *vi* (15c) **:** to act as arbitrator ~ *vt* **1 :** to act as arbiter upon **2 :** to submit or refer for decision to an arbiter ⟨agreed to ~ their differences⟩ **3** *archaic* **:** DECIDE, DETERMINE — **ar·bi·tra·tive** \-ˌtrāt-iv\ *adj*

ar·bi·tra·tion \ˌär-bə-ˈtrā-shən\ *n* (15c) **:** the act of arbitrating; *esp* **:** the hearing and determination of a case in controversy by a person chosen by the parties or appointed under statutory authority — **ar·bi·tra·tion·al** \-shnəl, -shən-ᵊl\ *adj*

ar·bi·tra·tor \ˈär-bə-ˌtrāt-ər\ *n* (15c) **1 :** a person chosen to settle differences between two parties in controversy **2 :** ARBITER 2

¹ar·bor \ˈär-bər\ *n* [ME *erber* plot of grass, arbor, fr. MF *herbier* plot of grass, fr. *herbe* herb, grass] (14c) **:** a shelter of vines or branches or of latticework covered with climbing shrubs or vines

²arbor *n* [L, tree, shaft] (1659) **1 a :** a main shaft or beam **b :** a spindle or axle of a wheel **c :** a shaft on which a revolving cutting tool is mounted **d :** a spindle on a cutting machine that holds the work to be cut **2** *pl* **ar·bo·res** \ˈär-bə-ˌrēz\ **:** a tree as distinguished from a shrub

Arbor Day *n* [L *arbor* tree] (1872) **:** a day designated for planting trees

ar·bo·re·al \är-ˈbōr-ē-əl, -ˈbȯr-\ *adj* [L *arboreus* of a tree, fr. *arbor*] (1667) **1 :** of, relating to, or resembling a tree **2 :** inhabiting or frequenting trees ⟨~ monkeys⟩ — **ar·bo·re·al·ly** \-ə-lē\ *adv*

ar·bo·re·ous \-ē-əs\ *adj* (1646) **1 :** ARBOREAL ⟨an ~ palm⟩ ⟨an ~ bird⟩ **2 :** WOODED

ar·bo·res·cent \ˌär-bə-ˈres-ᵊnt\ *adj* (1675) **:** resembling a tree in properties, growth, structure, or appearance — **ar·bo·res·cence** \-ᵊn(t)s\ *n*

ar·bo·re·tum \ˌär-bə-ˈrēt-əm\ *n, pl* **-retums** *or* **-re·ta** \-ˈrēt-ə\ [NL, fr. L, place grown with trees, fr. *arbor*] (1838) **:** a place where trees, shrubs, and herbaceous plants are cultivated for scientific and educational purposes

ar·bor·ist \ˈär-bə-rəst\ *n* (1578) **:** a specialist in the care and maintenance of trees

ar·bo·ri·za·tion \ˌär-bə-rə-ˈzā-shən\ *n* (1794) **:** formation of or into an arborescent figure or arrangement; *also* **:** such a figure or arrangement (as a dendritic process of a nerve cell)

ar·bo·rize \ˈär-bə-ˌrīz\ *vi* **-rized; -riz·ing** (1907) **:** to branch freely and repeatedly

ar·bor·vi·tae \ˌär-bər-ˈvīt-ē\ *n* [NL *arbor vitae*, lit., tree of life] (1646) **:** any of various evergreen trees (esp. genus *Thuja*) of the pine family that usu. have closely overlapping or compressed scale leaves and are often grown for ornament and in hedges

ar·bour *chiefly Brit var of* ARBOR

ar·bo·vi·rus \ˌär-bə-ˈvī-rəs\ *n* [*ar*thropod-*bo*rne *virus*] (1957) **:** any of various viruses transmitted by arthropods and including the causative agents of encephalitis, yellow fever, and dengue

ar·bu·tus \är-ˈbyüt-əs\ *n* [NL, fr. L, strawberry tree] (1548) **1 :** any of a genus (*Arbutus*) of shrubs and trees of the heath family with white or pink flowers and scarlet berries **2 :** a trailing plant (*Epigaea repens*) of the heath family that occurs in eastern No. America and bears fragrant pinkish flowers in early spring

¹arc \ˈärk\ *n* [ME *ark*, fr. MF *arc* bow, arch, arc, fr. L *arcus* bow, arch, arc — more at ARROW] (14c) **1 :** the apparent path described above and below the horizon by a celestial body (as the sun) **2 :** something arched or curved **3 :** a sustained luminous discharge of electricity across a gap in a circuit or between electrodes; *also* **:** ARC LAMP **4 :** a continuous portion (as of a circle or ellipse) of a curved line

²arc *vi* (1893) **1 :** to form an electric arc **2 :** to follow an arc-shaped course

³arc *adj* [*arc sine* arc or angle (corresponding to the) sine (of so many degrees)] (ca. 1909) **:** INVERSE 2 — used with the trigonometric functions and hyperbolic functions

ar·cade \är-ˈkād\ *n* [F, fr. It *arcata*, fr. *arco* arch, fr. L *arcus*] (1725) **1 :** a long arched building or gallery **2 :** an arched covered passageway or avenue (as between shops) **3 :** a series of arches with their columns or piers **4 :** an amusement center having coin-operated games

ar·cad·ed \-ˈkād-əd\ *adj* (1805) **:** formed in or furnished or decorated with arches or arcades

ar·ca·dia \är-ˈkād-ē-ə\ *n, often cap* [*Arcadia*, region of ancient Greece frequently chosen as background for pastoral poetry] (ca. 1890) **:** a region or scene of simple pleasure and quiet

Ar·ca·di·an \är-ˈkād-ē-ən\ *n* (1590) **1** *often not cap* **:** a person who lives a simple quiet life **2 :** a native or inhabitant of Arcadia **3 :** the dialect of ancient Greek used in Arcadia — **arcadian** *adj, often cap*

ar·cad·ing \är-ˈkād-iŋ\ *n* (1849) **:** a series of arches or arcades used in the construction or decoration esp. of a building

Ar·ca·dy \ˈär-kəd-ē\ *n* (14c) **:** ARCADIA

ar·cane \är-ˈkān\ *adj* [L *arcanus*] (1547) **:** known or knowable only to one having the key **:** SECRET ⟨~ rites⟩

ar·ca·num \är-ˈkā-nəm\ *n, pl* **-na** \-nə\ [L, fr. neut. of *arcanus* secret, fr. *arcēre* to enclose, defend — more at ARK] (15c) **1 :** mysterious knowledge known only to the initiate **2 :** ELIXIR 1

arc·co·se·cant \-ˌärk-(ˈ)kō-ˈsē-ˌkant, -kənt\ *n* (ca. 1942) **:** the inverse function to the cosecant ⟨if *y* is the cosecant of *θ*, then *θ* is the ~ of *y*⟩

arc·co·sine \-ˈkō-ˌsīn\ *n* (ca. 1942) **:** the inverse function to the cosine ⟨if *y* is the cosine of *θ*, then *θ* is the ~ of *y*⟩

arc·co·tan·gent \-(ˈ)kō-ˈtan-jənt\ *n* (ca. 1942) **:** the inverse function to the cotangent ⟨if *y* is the cotangent of *θ*, then *θ* is the ~ of *y*⟩

¹arch \ˈärch\ *n* [ME *arche*, fr. MF, fr. (assumed) VL *arca*, fr. L *arcus* — more at ARROW] (14c) **1 :** a typically curved structural member spanning an opening and serving as a support (as for the wall or other weight above the opening) **2 a :** something resembling an arch in form or function; *esp* **:** either of two vaulted portions of the bony structure of the foot that impart elasticity to it **b :** a curvature having the form of an arch **3 :** ARCHWAY

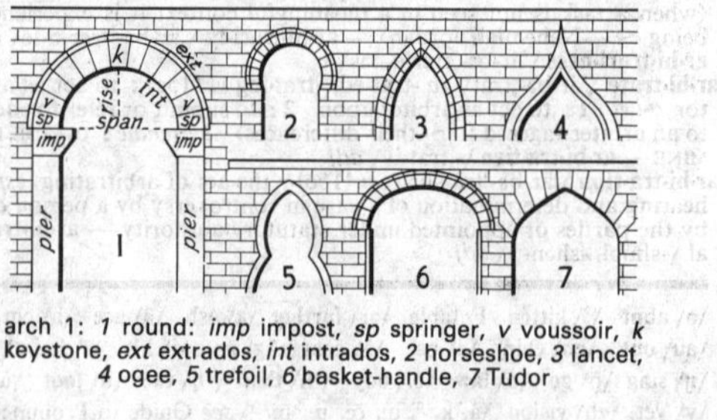

arch 1: *1* round: *imp* impost, *sp* springer, *v* voussoir, *k* keystone, *ext* extrados, *int* intrados, *2* horseshoe, *3* lancet, *4* ogee, *5* trefoil, *6* basket-handle, *7* Tudor

²arch *vt* (15c) **1 :** to cover or provide with an arch **2 :** to form into an arch ~ *vi* **1 :** to form an arch **2 :** to take an arch-shaped course

³arch *adj* [*arch-*] (1547) **1 :** PRINCIPAL, CHIEF ⟨an *arch*-villain⟩ **2 a :** MISCHIEVOUS, SAUCY **b :** marked by a deliberate and often forced irony, brashness, or impudence — **arch·ly** *adv* — **arch·ness** *n*

¹arch- *prefix* [ME *arche-*, *arch-*, fr. OE & OF; OE *arce-*, fr. LL *arch-* & L *archi-*; OF *arch-*, fr. LL *arch-* & L *archi-*, fr. Gk *arch-*, *archi-*, fr. *archein* to begin, rule; akin to Gk *archē* beginning, rule, *archos* ruler] **1 :** chief **:** principal ⟨*arch*rival⟩ **2 :** extreme **:** most fully embodying the qualities of his or its kind ⟨*arch*conservative⟩

²arch- — see ARCHI-

¹-arch \ˌärk, *in a few words also* ərk\ *n comb form* [ME *-arche*, fr. OF & LL & L; OF *-arche*, fr. LL *-archa*, fr. L *-arches*, *-archus*, fr. Gk *-archēs*, *-archos*, fr. *archein*] **:** ruler **:** leader ⟨matri*arch*⟩

²-arch \ˌärk\ *adj comb form* [prob. fr. G, fr. Gk *archē* beginning] **:** having (such) a point or (so many) points of origin ⟨end*arch*⟩

archae- *or* **archaeo-** *also* **archeo-** *comb form* [Gk *archaio-*, fr. *archaios* ancient, fr. *archē* beginning] **:** ancient **:** primitive ⟨*Archaeo*pteryx⟩ ⟨*Archeo*zoic⟩

ar·chaeo·as·tron·o·my \ˌär-kē-(ˌ)ō-ə-ˈsträn-ə-mē\ *n* (1973) **:** the study of the astronomy of ancient cultures

ar·chae·ol·o·gy *or* **ar·che·ol·o·gy** \ˌär-kē-ˈäl-ə-jē\ *n* [F *archéologie*, fr. LL *archaeologia* antiquarian lore, fr. Gk *archaiologia*, fr. *archaio-* + *-logia* -logy] (1837) **1 :** the scientific study of material remains (as fossil relics, artifacts, and monuments) of past human life and activities **2 :** remains of the culture of a people **:** ANTIQUITIES — **ar·chae·o·log·i·cal** \ˌär-kē-ə-ˈläj-i-kəl\ *adj* — **ar·chae·o·log·i·cal·ly** \-k(ə-)lē\ *adv* — **ar·chae·ol·o·gist** \ˌär-kē-ˈäl-ə-jəst\ *n*

ar·chae·op·ter·yx \ˌär-kē-ˈäp-tə-riks\ *n* [NL, fr. *archae-* + Gk *pteryx* wing; akin to Gk *pteron* wing — more at FEATHER] (1859) **:** a primitive bird (genus *Archaeopteryx*) of the Upper Jurassic period of Europe with reptilian characteristics

ar·cha·ic \är-ˈkā-ik\ *adj* [F or Gk; F *archaïque*, fr. Gk *archaïkos*, fr. *archaios*] (1832) **1 :** having the characteristics of the language of the past and surviving chiefly in specialized uses **2 :** of, relating to, or characteristic of an earlier or more primitive time **:** ANTIQUATED ⟨~ legal traditions⟩ **3 :** surviving from an earlier period; *specif* **:** typical of a previously dominant evolutionary stage ***syn*** see OLD — **ar·cha·i·cal·ly** \-i-k(ə-)lē\ *adv*

archaic smile *n* (1902) **:** an expression that resembles a smile and is characteristic of early Greek sculpture

ar·cha·ism \ˈär-kē-ˌiz-əm, -(ˌ)kā-ˌiz-\ *n* [NL *archaïsmus*, fr. Gk *archaïsmos*, fr. *archaios*] (1643) **1 :** the use of archaic diction or style **2 :** an instance of archaic usage **3 :** something (as a practice or custom) that is outmoded or old-fashioned — **ar·cha·ist** \-əst\ *n* — **ar·cha·is·tic** \ˌär-kē-ˈis-tik, -(ˌ)kā-\ *adj* — **ar·cha·ize** \ˈär-kē-ˌīz, -(ˌ)kā-\ *vb*

arch·an·gel \ˈär-ˌkān-jəl\ *n* [ME, fr. OF or LL; OF *archangele*, fr. LL *archangelus*, fr. Gk *archangelos*, fr. *arch-* + *angelos* angel] (12c) **1 :** a chief angel **2** *pl* **:** an order of angels — see CELESTIAL HIERARCHY — **arch·an·gel·ic** \ˌär-(ˌ)kan-ˈjel-ik\ *adj*

arch·bish·op \(ˈ)ärch-ˈbish-əp\ *n* [ME, fr. OE *arcebiscop*, fr. LL *archiepiscopus*, fr. LGk *archiepiskopos*, fr. Gk *archi-* + *episkopos* bishop — more at BISHOP] (bef. 12c) **:** a bishop at the head of an ecclesiastical province or one of equivalent honorary rank — **arch·bish·op·ric** \-ə-(ˌ)prik\ *n*

arch·dea·con \(ˈ)ärch-ˈdē-kən\ *n* [ME *archedeken*, fr. OE *arcediacon*, fr. LL *archidiaconus*, fr. LGk *archidiakonos*, fr. Gk *archi-* + *diakonos* deacon] (bef. 12c) **:** a clergyman having the duty of assisting a diocesan bishop in ceremonial functions or administrative work — **arch·dea·con·ate** \-kə-nət\ *n*

arch·dea·con·ry \-kən-rē\ *n, pl* **-ries** (15c) **:** the district or residence of an archdeacon

arch·di·o·cese \(ˈ)ärch-ˈdī-ə-səs, -ˌsēz, -ˌsēs\ *n, pl* **-ces·es** \-ˈdī-ə-ˌsēz, -ˌsē-zəz, -sə-səz, -sə-ˌsēz\ (1844) **:** the diocese of an archbishop — **arch·di·oc·e·san** \ˌärch-dī-ˈäs-ə-sən\ *adj*

arch·du·cal \(ˈ)ärch-ˈd(y)ü-kəl\ *adj* [F *archiducal*, fr. *archiduc*] (1665) **:** of or relating to an archduke or archduchy

arch·duch·ess \-ˈdəch-əs\ *n* [F *archiduchesse*, fem. of *archiduc* archduke, fr. MF *archeduc*] (1618) **1 :** the wife or widow of an archduke **2 :** a woman having in her own right a rank equal to that of an archduke

arch·duchy \-ˈdəch-ē\ *n* [F *archiduché*, fr. MF *archeduché*, fr. *arche-* arch- + *duché* duchy] (1680) **:** the territory of an archduke or archduchess

arch·duke \-ˈd(y)ük\ *n* [MF *archeduc*, fr. *arche-* arch- + *duc* duke] (ca. 1530) **1 :** a sovereign prince **2 :** a prince of the imperial family of Austria — **arch·duke·dom** \-dəm\ *n*

Ar·che·an *or* **Ar·chae·an** \är-ˈkē-ən\ *adj* [Gk *archaios*] (ca. 1879) **:** of, relating to, or being the earlier part of the Precambrian era or the oldest known group of rocks; *also* **:** PRECAMBRIAN — **Archean** *n*

arched \ˈärcht\ *adj* (14c) **:** made with, formed in, or covered with an arch ⟨an ~ beam⟩ ⟨an ~ door⟩

ar·che·go·ni·al \ˌär-ki-ˈgō-nē-əl\ *adj* (1865) **:** of or relating to an archegonium; *also* **:** ARCHEGONIATE

¹ar·che·go·ni·ate \-nē-ət\ *adj* (1897) **:** bearing archegonia

²archegoniate *n* (1902) **:** a plant (as a moss, fern, horsetail, or club moss) that bears archegonia

ar·che·go·ni·um \-nē-əm\ *n, pl* **-nia** \-nē-ə\ [NL, fr. Gk *archegonos* originator, fr. *archein* to begin + *gonos* procreation; akin to Gk *gignesthai* to be born — more at ARCH-, KIN] (1854) **:** the flask-shaped female sex organ of mosses, ferns, and some gymnosperms

arch·en·e·my \(ˈ)är-ˈchen-ə-mē\ *n, pl* **-mies** (1550) **:** a principal enemy

arch·en·ter·on \är-ˈkent-ə-ˌrän, -rən\ *n* [NL] (1877) **:** the cavity of the gastrula of an embryo

Ar·cheo·zo·ic *also* **Ar·chaeo·zo·ic** \ˌär-kē-ə-ˈzō-ik\ *adj* (1872) **:** of, relating to, or being the earliest era of geological history; *also* **:** relating to the system of rocks formed in this era — see GEOLOGIC TIME table — **Archeozoic** *n*

ar·cher \ˈär-chər\ *n* [ME, fr. OF, fr. LL *arcarius*, alter. of *arcuarius*, fr. *arcuarius* of a bow, fr. L *arcus* bow — more at ARROW] (13c) **1 :** one who uses a bow and arrow **2** *cap* **:** SAGITTARIUS

ar·cher·fish \ˈär-chər-ˌfish\ *n* (ca. 1889) **:** a small East Indian fish (*Toxotes jaculator*) that catches insects by stunning them with drops of water ejected from its mouth; *also* **:** any of various related fish of similar habits

ar·chery \\'ärch-(ə-)rē\\ n (15c) **1** : the art, practice, or skill of shooting with bow and arrow **2** : an archer's weapons **3** : a body of archers

ar·che·spo·ri·um \\,är-ki-'spōr-ē-əm, -'spȯr-\\ n, pl **-spo·ria** \\-ē-ə\\ [NL, fr. arche- (as in archegonium) + -sporium (fr. spora spore)] (1882) : the cell or group of cells from which spore mother cells develop — **ar·che·spo·ri·al** \\-är-ki-'spōr-ē-əl, -'spȯr-\\ adj

ar·che·type \\'är-ki-,tīp\\ n [L archetypum, fr. Gk archetypon, fr. neut. of archetypos archetypal, fr. archein + typos type] (1605) **1** : the original pattern or model of which all things of the same type are representations or copies : PROTOTYPE; also : a perfect example **2** : IDEA 1a **3** : an inherited idea or mode of thought in the psychology of C. G. Jung that is derived from the experience of the race and is present in the unconscious of the individual — **ar·che·typ·al** \\,är-ki-'tī-pəl\\ also **ar·che·typ·i·cal** \\-'tip-i-kəl\\ adj — **ar·che·typ·al·ly** \\-ə-lē\\ adv

arch·fiend \\(')ärch-'fēnd\\ n (1667) : a chief fiend; esp : SATAN

archi- or **arch-** prefix [F or L; F, fr. L, fr. Gk — more at ARCH-] **1** : chief : principal ⟨archiblast⟩ **2** : primitive : original : primary ⟨archenteron⟩ ⟨archicarp⟩

ar·chi·carp \\'är-ki-,kärp\\ n (ca. 1887) : the female sex organ in ascomycetous fungi consisting usu. of a filamentous trichogyne and a basal fertile ascogonium

ar·chi·di·ac·o·nal \\,är-ki-dī-'ak-ən-'l\\ adj [LL archidiaconus archdeacon] (15c) : of or relating to an archdeacon

ar·chi·epis·co·pal \\,är-kē-ə-'pis-kə-pəl\\ adj [ML archiepiscopalis, fr. LL archiepiscopus archbishop — more at ARCHBISHOP] (1611) : of or relating to an archbishop — **ar·chi·epis·co·pal·ly** \\-p(ə-)lē\\ adv — **ar·chi·epis·co·pate** \\-pət, -,pāt\\ n

ar·chil \\'är-chəl\\ n [ME orchell] (15c) **1** : a violet dye obtained from lichens (genera Roccella and Lecanora) **2** : a lichen that yields archil

ar·chi·man·drite \\,är-kə-'man-,drīt\\ n [LL archimandrites, fr. LGk archimandritēs, fr. Gk archi- + LGk mandra monastery, fr. Gk, fold, pen] (1591) : a dignitary in an Eastern church ranking below a bishop; specif : the superior of a large monastery or group of monasteries

Ar·chi·me·des' screw \\,är-kə-,mēd-ēz-\\ n [Archimedes] (ca. 1864) : a device made of a tube bent spirally around an axis or of a broad-threaded screw encased by a cylinder and used to raise water

ar·chi·pe·lag·ic \\,är-kə-pə-'laj-ik, ,är-chə-\\ adj (1841) : of, relating to, or located in an archipelago

ar·chi·pel·a·go \\,är-kə-'pel-ə-,gō, ,är-chə-\\ n, pl **-goes** or **-gos** [Archipelago Aegean sea, fr. It Arcipelago, lit., chief sea, fr. arci- (fr. L archi-) + Gk pelagos sea — more at FLAKE] (1589) **1** : an expanse of water with many scattered islands **2** : a group of islands

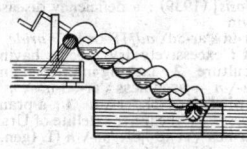

Archimedes' screw

ar·chi·tect \\'är-kə-,tekt\\ n [MF architecte, fr. L architectus, fr. Gk architektōn master builder, fr. archi- + tektōn builder, carpenter — more at TECHNICAL] (1563) **1** : one who designs buildings and advises in their construction **2** : one who plans and achieves a difficult objective ⟨the great ~ of the military victory —Time⟩

ar·chi·tec·ton·ic \\,är-kə-,tek-'tän-ik\\ adj [L architectonicus, fr. Gk architektonikos, fr. architektōn] (1645) **1** : of, relating to, or according with the principles of architecture : ARCHITECTURAL **2** : having an organized and unified structure or concept that suggests an architectural design — **ar·chi·tec·ton·i·cal·ly** \\-i-k(ə-)lē\\ adv

ar·chi·tec·ton·ics \\-'tän-iks\\ n pl but sing or pl in constr, also **ar·chi·tec·ton·ic** \\-ik\\ (1660) **1** : the science of architecture **2 a** : the unifying structural design of something **b** : the system of structure

ar·chi·tec·tur·al \\,är-kə-'tek-chə-rəl, -'tek-shrəl\\ adj (1762) **1** : of, relating to, or conforming to the rules of architecture **2** : having or conceived of as having a single unified overall design, form, or structure — **ar·chi·tec·tur·al·ly** \\-ē\\ adv

ar·chi·tec·ture \\'är-kə-,tek-chər\\ n (1555) **1** : the art or science of building; specif : the art or practice of designing and building structures and esp. habitable ones **2 a** : formation or construction as or as if as the result of conscious act **b** : a unifying or coherent form or structure ⟨the novel lacks ~⟩ **3** : architectural product or work **4** : a method or style of building

ar·chi·trave \\'är-kə-,trāv\\ n [MF, fr. OIt, fr. archi- + trave beam, fr. L trabs — more at THORP] (1563) **1** : the lowest division of an entablature resting in classical architecture immediately on the capital of the column — see ENTABLATURE illustration **2** : the molding around a rectangular opening (as a door)

ar·chi·val \\är-'kī-vəl\\ adj (ca. 1828) : relating to, contained in, or constituting archives

¹ar·chive \\'är-,kīv\\ n [F & L; F, fr. L archivum, fr. Gk archeion government house (in pl., official documents), fr. archē rule, government — more at ARCH-] (1603) **1** : a place in which public records or historical documents are preserved; also : the material preserved — often used in pl.

²archive vt **ar·chived; ar·chiv·ing** (ca. 1934) : to file or collect (as records or documents) in or as if in an archive

ar·chi·vist \\'är-kə-vəst, -,kī-\\ n (1753) : a person in charge of archives

ar·chi·volt \\'är-kə-,vōlt\\ n [It archivolto, fr. ML archivoltum] (ca. 1731) : an ornamental molding around an arch corresponding to an architrave

ar·chon \\'är-,kän, -kən\\ n [L, fr. Gk archōn, fr. prp. of archein] (1579) **1** : a chief magistrate in ancient Athens **2** : a presiding officer

arch·priest \\(')ärch-'prēst\\ n (14c) : a priest of preeminent rank

arch·way \\'ärch-,wā\\ n (1802) : a way or passage under an arch; also : an arch over a passage

-ar·chy \\,är-kē, in a few words also ər-kē\\ n comb form, pl **-ar·chies** [ME -archie, fr. MF, fr. L -archia, fr. Gk, fr. archein to rule — more at ARCH-] : rule : government ⟨squirearchy⟩

arc lamp n (1882) : an electric lamp that produces light by an arc made when a current passes between two incandescent electrodes surrounded by gas — called also arc light

ar·co \\'är-(,)kō\\ adv or adj [It, fr. arco bow, fr. L arcus] (1806) : with the bow — usu. used as a direction in music for players of stringed instruments; compare PIZZICATO

arc·se·cant \\(,)ärk-'sē-,kant, -kənt\\ n (ca. 1961) : the inverse function to the secant ⟨if y is the secant of θ, then θ is the ~ of y⟩

arc·sine \\-'sīn\\ n (ca. 1909) : the inverse function to the sine ⟨if y is the sine of θ, then θ is the ~ of y⟩

arc·tan·gent \\-'tan-jənt\\ n (ca. 1909) : the inverse function to the tangent ⟨if y is the tangent of θ, then θ is the ~ of y⟩

¹arc·tic \\'ärk-tik, 'ärt-ik\\ adj [ME artik, fr. L arcticus, fr. Gk arktikos, fr. arktos bear, Ursa Major, north; akin to L ursus bear] (14c) **1** often cap : of or relating to the region around the north pole to approximately 65° N **2 a** : bitter cold : FRIGID **b** : cold in temper or mood ⟨an ~ smile⟩ — **arc·ti·cal·ly** \\-(t)i-k(ə-)lē\\ adv

²arc·tic \\'ärt-ik, 'ärk-tik\\ n (1867) : a rubber overshoe reaching to the ankle or above

arctic char n (1902) : a char (Salvelinus alpinus) esp. of arctic lakes and streams of No. America

arctic circle n, often cap A&C (1622) : the parallel of latitude that is approximately 66½ degrees north of the equator and that circumscribes the northern frigid zone

arctic fox n (1772) : a small fox (Alopex lagopus) of the arctic regions

arctic tern n (1844) : a tern (Sterna paradisaea) that breeds in arctic regions and migrates to southern Africa and So. America

Arc·tu·rus \\ärk-'t(y)ùr-əs\\ n [L, fr. Gk Arktouros, lit., bear watcher] : a giant fixed star of the first magnitude in Boötes

ar·cu·ate \\'är-kyə-wət, -,wāt\\ adj [L arcuatus, pp. of arcuare to bend like a bow, fr. arcus bow] (1626) : curved like a bow ⟨an ~ cloud⟩ ⟨an ~ view of a leaf⟩ — **ar·cu·ate·ly** adv

-ard \\ərd\\ also **-art** \\ərt\\ n suffix [ME, fr. OF, of Gmc origin; akin to OHG -hart (in personal names such as Gērhart Gerard), OE heard hard] : one that is characterized by performing some action, possessing some quality, or being associated with some thing esp. conspicuously or excessively ⟨braggart⟩ ⟨dullard⟩ ⟨pollard⟩

ar·deb \\'är-,deb\\ n [Ar ardabb, irdabb] (1836) : any of numerous Egyptian units of capacity; esp : the customs unit equal to 5.44 imperial or 5.619 U.S. bushels or 198.0 liters

ar·dent \\'ärd-ᵊnt\\ adj [ME, fr. MF, fr. L ardent-, ardens, prp. of ardēre] (14c) **1** : characterized by warmth of feeling typically expressed in eager zealous support or activity **2** : FIERY, HOT ⟨an ~ sun⟩ **3** : SHINING, GLOWING ⟨~ eyes⟩ syn see IMPASSIONED — **ar·den·cy** \\-ᵊn-sē\\ n — **ar·dent·ly** adv

ardent spirits n pl (1833) : strong distilled liquors

ar·dor \\'ärd-ər\\ n [ME ardour, fr. MF & L; MF, fr. L ardor, fr. ardēre to burn; akin to OHG essa forge, L aridus dry] (14c) **1 a** : an often restless or transitory warmth of feeling ⟨the sudden ~s of youth⟩ **b** : extreme vigor or energy : INTENSITY **c** : ZEAL, LOYALTY **2** : strong or burning heat syn see PASSION

ar·dour chiefly Brit var of ARDOR

ar·du·ous \\'ärj-(ə-)wəs\\ adj [L arduus high, steep, difficult; akin to ON örthigr high, steep] (1538) **1 a** : hard to accomplish or achieve : DIFFICULT ⟨years of ~ training⟩ **b** : marked by great labor or effort : STRENUOUS ⟨a life of ~ toil —A. C. Cole⟩ **2** : hard to climb : STEEP syn see HARD — **ar·du·ous·ly** adv — **ar·du·ous·ness** n

¹are [ME, fr. OE earun; akin to ON eru, erum are, OE is is] pres 2d sing or pres pl of BE

²are \\'a(ə)r, 'e(ə)r, 'är\\ n [F, fr. L area] (ca. 1819) — see METRIC SYSTEM table

ar·ea \\'ar-ē-ə, 'er-; 'ä-rē-ä\\ n [L, piece of level ground, threshing floor, fr. arēre to be dry; akin to L ardor] (1538) **1** : a level piece of ground **2** : the surface included within a set of lines; specif : the number of unit squares equal in measure to the surface — see METRIC SYSTEM table, WEIGHT table **3** : AREAWAY ⟨went down the steps into the ~ of a house —James Joyce⟩ **4** : a particular extent of space or surface or one serving a special function **5** : the scope of a concept, operation, or activity : FIELD ⟨the whole ~ of foreign policy⟩ **6** : a part of the cerebral cortex having a particular function — **ar·e·al** \\-ē-əl\\ adj — **ar·e·al·ly** \\-ə-lē\\ adv

area code n (1964) : a 3-digit number that identifies each telephone service area in a country (as the U.S. or Canada)

area·way \\'ar-ē-ə-,wā, 'er-; ä-rē-\\ n (1899) : a sunken space affording access, air, and light to a basement

are·ca \\ə-'rē-kə, 'ar-i-kə\\ n [NL, fr. Pg, fr. Malayalam atekka] (1510) : any of several tropical Asian palms (Areca and related genera); esp : BETEL PALM

arec·o·line \\ə-'rek-ə-,lēn\\ n [ISV areca + -ol + -ine] (1899) : a toxic parasympathomimetic alkaloid $C_8H_{13}NO_2$ that is used as a veterinary anthelmintic and occurs naturally in betel nuts

are·na \\ə-'rē-nə\\ n [L harena, arena sand, sandy place] (1600) **1** : an area in a Roman amphitheater for gladiatorial combats **2 a** : an enclosed area used for public entertainment **b** : a building containing an arena **3** : a sphere of interest, activity, or competition : SCENE ⟨the political ~⟩

are·na·ceous \\,ar-ə-'nā-shəs\\ adj [L arenaceus, fr. arena] (1646) **1** : resembling, made of, or containing sand or sandy particles **2** : growing in sandy places

arena theater n (1943) : a theater in which the stage is located in the center of the auditorium — called also theater-in-the-round

are·nic·o·lous \\,ar-ə-'nik-ə-ləs\\ adj [L arena + E -i- + -colous] (ca. 1851) : living, burrowing, or growing in sand

aren't \\(')ärnt, 'är-ənt\\ **1** : are not **2** : am not — used in questions

ar·eo·cen·tric \\,ar-ē-ō-'sen-trik\\ adj [Gk Areios of Ares, fr. Arēs] (1877) : having or relating to the planet Mars as a center

are·o·la \\ə-'rē-ə-lə\\ n, pl **-lae** \\-,lē\\ or **-las** [NL, fr. L, small open space, dim. of area] (1664) **1** : a small area between things or about something; esp : a colored ring (as about the nipple, a vesicle, or a pustule) — **are·o·lar** \\-lər\\ adj — **are·o·late** \\-lət\\ adj

are·ole \\'ar-ē-,ōl\\ n (ca. 1934) : a small pit or cavity

Ar·e·op·a·gite \\,ar-ē-'äp-ə-,jīt, -,git\\ n (14c) : a member of the Areopagus — **Ar·e·op·a·git·ic** \\-,äp-ə-'jit-ik\\ adj

---

\\ə\\ abut \\ᵊ\\ kitten, F table \\ər\\ further \\a\\ ash \\ā\\ ace \\ä\\ cot, cart \\aù\\ out \\ch\\ chin \\e\\ bet \\ē\\ easy \\g\\ go \\i\\ hit \\ī\\ ice \\j\\ job \\ŋ\\ sing \\ō\\ go \\ò\\ law \\òi\\ boy \\th\\ thin \\t̲h̲\\ the \\ü\\ loot \\ù\\ foot \\y\\ yet \\zh\\ vision \\ə, k, ⁿ, œ, œ̄, ᵫ, ᵫ̄, �\\ see Guide to Pronunciation

Ar·e·op·a·gus \ˌar-ē-ˈäp-ə-gəs\ *n* [L, fr. Gk *Areios pagos,* fr. *Areios pagos* (lit., hill of Ares), a hill in Athens where the tribunal met] (1586) **:** the supreme tribunal of Athens

Ar·es \ˈa(ə)r-(ˌ)ēz, ˈe(ə)r-\ *n* [Gk *Arēs*] **:** the Greek god of war — compare MARS

arête \ə-ˈrāt\ *n* [F, lit., fish bone, fr. LL *arista,* fr. L, beard of grain] (1838) **:** a sharp-crested ridge in rugged mountains

Ar·e·thu·sa \ˌar-ə-ˈth(y)ü-zə\ *n* [L, fr. Gk *Arethousa*] **:** a wood nymph who is changed into a spring while fleeing the advances of the river-god Alpheus

ar·ga·li \ˈär-gə-lē\ *n* [Mongolian] (1774) **:** a large wild sheep (*Ovis ammon*) of Asia that is noted for its large horns; *also* **:** any of several other large wild sheep (as the bighorn)

Ar·gand diagram \ˌär-ˌgän-, -ˌgan-\ *n* [John Robert *Argand* †1825 Fr. mathematician] (1908) **:** a conventional diagram in which the complex number $x + iy$ is represented by the point whose rectangular coordinates are x and y

ar·gent \ˈär-jənt\ *n* [ME, fr. MF & L; MF, fr. L *argentum;* akin to L *arguere* to make clear, Gk *argyros* silver, *argos* white] (15c) **1** *archaic* **:** the metal silver; *also* **:** WHITENESS **2 :** the heraldic color silver or white — **argent** *adj*

ar·gen·tic \är-ˈjent-ik\ *adj* (1868) **:** of, relating to, or containing silver esp. when bivalent

ar·gen·tif·er·ous \ˌär-jən-ˈtif-(ə-)rəs\ *adj* (1801) **:** producing or containing silver

[1]**ar·gen·tine** \ˈär-jən-ˌtīn, -ˌtēn\ *adj* (15c) **:** SILVER, SILVERY

[2]**argentine** *n* (1577) **:** SILVER; *also* **:** any of various materials resembling it

ar·gen·tite \ˈär-jən-ˌtīt\ *n* (1837) **:** native silver sulfide Ag_2S having a metallic luster and dark lead-gray color and constituting a valuable ore of silver

ar·gen·tous \är-ˈjent-əs\ *adj* (1869) **:** of, relating to, or containing silver esp. when univalent

ar·gil \ˈär-jəl\ *n* [ME, fr. L *argilla,* fr. Gk *argillos;* akin to Gk *argos* white] (14c) **:** CLAY; *esp* **:** POTTER'S CLAY

ar·gil·la·ceous \ˌär-jə-ˈlā-shəs\ *adj* (ca. 1731) **:** of, relating to, or containing clay or clay minerals **:** CLAYEY

ar·gil·lite \ˈär-jə-ˌlīt\ *n* (1795) **:** a compact argillaceous rock differing from shale in being cemented by silica and from slate in having no slaty cleavage

ar·gi·nase \ˈär-jə-ˌnās, -ˌnāz\ *n* [ISV] (1904) **:** a crystalline enzyme that converts naturally occurring arginine into ornithine and urea

ar·gi·nine \ˈär-jə-ˌnēn\ *n* [G *arginin*] (1886) **:** a crystalline basic amino acid $C_6H_{14}N_4O_2$ derived from guanidine

Ar·give \ˈär-ˌjīv, -ˌgīv\ *adj* [L *Argivus,* fr. Gk *Argeios,* lit., of Argos, fr. *Argos* city-state of ancient Greece] (1598) **:** of or relating to the Greeks or Greece and esp. the Achaean city of Argos or the surrounding territory of Argolis — **Argive** *n*

ar·gle–bar·gle \ˌär-gəl-ˈbär-gəl\ *n* [redupl. of Sc & E *argle,* alter. of *argue*] *chiefly Brit* (1872) **:** ARGY-BARGY

Ar·go \ˈär-(ˌ)gō\ *n* [L (gen. *Argus*), fr. Gk *Argō*] **:** a large constellation in the southern hemisphere lying principally between Canis Major and the Southern Cross

ar·gol \ˈär-ˌgȯl\ *n* [ME *argoile,* fr. AF *argoil*] (14c) **:** crude tartar deposited in wine casks during aging

ar·gon \ˈär-ˌgän\ *n* [Gk, neut. of *argos* idle, lazy, fr. *a-* + *ergon* work; fr. its relative inertness — more at WORK] (ca. 1890) **:** a colorless odorless inert gaseous element found in the air and in volcanic gases and used esp. as a filler for electric bulbs — see ELEMENT table

ar·go·naut \ˈär-gə-ˌnȯt, -ˌnät\ *n* [L *Argonautes,* fr. Gk *Argonautēs,* fr. *Argō,* ship in which the Argonauts sailed + *nautēs* sailor — more at NAUTICAL] (14c) **1 a** *cap* **:** any of a band of heroes sailing with Jason in quest of the Golden Fleece **b :** an adventurer engaged in a quest **2 :** PAPER NAUTILUS

ar·go·sy \ˈär-gə-sē\ *n, pl* **-sies** [modif. of It *ragusea* Ragusan vessel, fr. *Ragusa,* Dalmatia (now Dubrovnik, Yugoslavia)] (1577) **1 :** a large ship; *esp* **:** a large merchant ship ⟨three of your *argosies* are . . . come to harbor—Shak.⟩ **2 :** a fleet of ships **3 :** a rich supply ⟨an ~ of railway folklore —F.P. Donovan⟩

ar·got \ˈär-gət, -(ˌ)gō\ *n* [F] (1860) **:** an often more or less secret vocabulary and idiom peculiar to a particular group ⟨the American Negro has . . . developed his own ~, partly to put the white man off, partly to put him down —Daniel Stern⟩

ar·gu·able \ˈär-gyə-wə-bəl\ *adj* (ca. 1611) **1 :** open to argument, dispute, or question **2 :** that can be plausibly or convincingly argued — **ar·gu·ably** \-blē\ *adv*

ar·gue \ˈär-(ˌ)gyü, -gyə(-w)\ *vb* **ar·gued; ar·gu·ing** [ME *arguen,* fr. MF *arguer* to accuse, reason & L *arguere* to make clear; MF *arguer,* fr. L *argutare* to prate, fr. *argutus* clear, noisy, fr. pp. of *arguere* — more at ARGENT] *vi* (14c) **1 :** to give reasons for or against something **:** REASON **2 :** to contend or disagree in words **:** DISPUTE ~ *vt* **1 :** to give evidence of **:** INDICATE **2 :** to consider the pros and cons of **:** DISCUSS **3 :** to prove or try to prove by giving reasons **:** MAINTAIN **4 :** to persuade by giving reasons **:** INDUCE ***syn*** see DISCUSS — **ar·gu·er** \-gyə-wər\ *n*

ar·gu·fy \ˈär-gyə-ˌfī\ *vb* **-fied; -fy·ing** *vt* (1771) **:** DISPUTE, DEBATE ~ *vi* **:** WRANGLE — **ar·gu·fi·er** \-ˌfī(-ə)r\ *n*

ar·gu·ment \ˈär-gyə-mənt\ *n* [ME, fr. MF, fr. L *argumentum,* fr. *arguere*] (14c) **1** *obs* **:** an outward sign **:** INDICATION **2 a :** a reason given in proof or rebuttal **b :** discourse intended to persuade **3 a :** the act or process of arguing **:** ARGUMENTATION **b :** a coherent series of statements leading from a premise to a conclusion **c :** QUARREL, DISAGREEMENT **4 :** an abstract or summary esp. of a literary work ⟨a later editor added an ~ to the poem⟩ **5 :** the subject matter esp. of a literary work **6 a :** one of the independent variables upon whose value that of a function depends **b :** the angle that fixes the direction of a complex number ⟨if $a + bi$ is written as $re^{i\theta} = r(\cos\theta + i\sin\theta)$ then θ is the ~⟩

ar·gu·men·ta·tion \ˌär-gyə-mən-ˈtā-shən, -ˌmen-\ *n* (15c) **1 :** the act or process of forming reasons and of drawing conclusions and applying them to a case in discussion **2 :** DEBATE, DISCUSSION

ar·gu·men·ta·tive \ˌär-gyə-ˈment-ət-iv\ *also* **ar·gu·men·tive** \-ˈment-iv\ *adj* (15c) **1 :** characterized by argument **:** CONTROVERSIAL **2 :** given to argument **:** DISPUTATIOUS — **ar·gu·men·ta·tive·ly** *adv*

ar·gu·men·tum \ˌär-gyə-ˈment-əm\ *n, pl* **-men·ta** \-ˈment-ə\ [L] (1690) **:** ARGUMENT 3b

Ar·gus \ˈär-gəs\ *n* [L, fr. Gk *Argos*] **1 :** a hundred-eyed monster of Greek legend **2 :** a watchful guardian

Ar·gus–eyed \ˌär-gə-ˈsīd\ *adj* (1603) **:** vigilantly observant

ar·gy–bar·gy \ˌär-jē-ˈbär-jē, ˌär-gē-ˈbär-gē\ *n* [redupl. of Sc & E dial. *argy,* alter. of *argue*] *chiefly Brit* (ca. 1887) **:** a lively discussion **:** ARGUMENT, DISPUTE

ar·gyle *also* **ar·gyll** \ˈär-ˌgīl, är-ˈ\ *n, often cap* [*Argyle, Argyll,* branch of the Scottish clan of Campbell, fr. whose tartan the design was adapted] (1899) **:** a geometric knitting pattern of varicolored diamonds in solid and outline shapes on a single background color; *also* **:** a sock knit in this pattern

Ar·gy·rol \ˈär-jə-ˌrȯl, -ˌrōl\ *trademark* — used for a silver-protein compound whose aqueous solution is used as a local antiseptic esp. for mucous membranes

ar·hat \ˈär-(ˌ)hət\ *n* [Skt, fr. prp. of *arhati* he deserves; akin to Gk *alphein* to gain] (1850) **:** a Buddhist who has reached the stage of enlightenment — **ar·hat·ship** \-ˌship\ *n*

aria \ˈär-ē-ə\ *n* [It, lit., atmospheric air, modif. of L *aer*] (ca. 1724) **1 :** AIR, MELODY, TUNE; *specif* **:** an accompanied elaborate melody sung (as in an opera) by a single voice **2 :** a striking solo performance (as in a movie)

Ar·i·ad·ne \ˌar-ē-ˈad-nē\ *n* [L, fr. Gk *Ariadnē*] **:** a daughter of Minos who helps Theseus escape from the labyrinth

[1]**Ar·i·an** \ˈar-ē-ən, ˈer-\ *adj* (14c) **:** of or relating to Arius or his doctrines esp. that the Son is not of the same substance as the Father but was created as an agent for creating the world — **Ar·i·an·ism** \-ə-ˌniz-əm\ *n*

[2]**Arian** *n* (14c) **:** a supporter of Arian doctrines

[3]**Ar·i·an** \ˈer-ē-ən, ˈar-\ *n* (1967) **:** ARIES 2b

-ar·i·an \ˈer-ē-ən, ˈar-\ *n suffix* [L *-arius* -ary] **1 :** believer ⟨necessit*arian*⟩ **:** advocate ⟨latitudin*arian*⟩ **2 :** producer ⟨disciplin*arian*⟩

ari·bo·fla·vin·osis \ˌā-ˌrī-bə-ˌflā-və-ˈnō-səs\ *n* [NL, fr. *a-* + *riboflavin* + *-osis*] (1939) **:** a deficiency disease due to inadequate intake of riboflavin

ar·id \ˈar-əd\ *adj* [F or L; F *aride,* fr. L *aridus* — more at ARDOR] (1642) **1 :** excessively dry; *specif* **:** having insufficient rainfall to support agriculture **2 :** lacking in interest and life **:** JEJUNE — **arid·i·ty** \ə-ˈrid-ət-ē, a-\ *n* — **ar·id·ness** \ˈar-əd-nəs\ *n*

Ar·i·el \ˈar-ē-əl, ˈer-\ *n* **1 :** a prankish spirit in Shakespeare's *The Tempest* **2 :** the inner satellite of Uranus

Ar·i·es \ˈer-(ˌē-)ˌēz, ˈar-\ *n* [L (gen. *Arietis*), lit., ram; akin to Gk *eriphos* kid, OIr *heirp* doe] **1 :** a constellation between Pisces and Taurus pictured as a ram **2 a :** the first sign of the zodiac in astrology — see ZODIAC table **b :** one born under this sign

ari·et·ta \ˌär-ē-ˈet-ə, ˌar-\ *n* [It, dim. of *aria*] (ca. 1724) **:** a short aria

aright \ə-ˈrīt\ *adv* [ME, fr. OE *arihtt,* fr. [1]*a-* + *riht* right] (bef. 12c) **:** RIGHTLY, CORRECTLY ⟨if I remember ~⟩

ar·il \ˈar-əl\ *n* [prob. fr. NL *arillus,* fr. ML, raisin, grape seed] (1794) **:** an exterior covering or appendage of some seeds that develops after fertilization as an outgrowth from the ovule stalk — **ar·iled** \ˈar-əld\ *adj* — **ar·il·late** \ˈar-ə-ˌlāt\ *adj*

ari·o·so \ˌär-ē-ˈō-(ˌ)sō, -(ˌ)zō\ *n, pl* **-sos** *also* **-si** \-(ˌ)sē, -(ˌ)zē\ [It, fr. *aria*] (ca. 1724) **:** a musical passage or composition having a mixture of free recitative and metrical song

arise \ə-ˈrīz\ *vi* **arose** \-ˈrōz\; **aris·en** \-ˈriz-ᵊn\; **aris·ing** \-ˈrī-ziŋ\ [ME *arisen,* fr. OE *ārīsan,* fr. *ā-,* perfective prefix + *rīsan* to rise — more at ABIDE] (bef. 12c) **1 :** to get up **:** RISE **2 a :** to originate from a source **b :** to come into being or to attention **3 :** ASCEND ***syn*** see SPRING

aris·ta \ə-ˈris-tə\ *n, pl* **-tae** \-(ˌ)tē, -ˌtī\ *or* **-tas** [NL, fr. L, beard of grain] (1691) **:** a bristlelike structure or appendage — **aris·tate** \-ˌtāt\ *adj*

aris·to \ə-ˈris-(ˌ)tō\ *n, pl* **-tos** [by shortening] *chiefly Brit* (1864) **:** ARISTOCRAT

ar·is·toc·ra·cy \ˌar-ə-ˈstäk-rə-sē\ *n, pl* **-cies** [MF & LL; MF *aristocratie,* fr. LL *aristocratia,* fr. Gk *aristokratia,* fr. *aristos* best + *-kratia* -cracy] (1561) **1 :** government by the best individuals or by a small privileged class **2 a :** a government in which power is vested in a minority consisting of those believed to be best qualified **b :** a state with such a government **3 :** a governing body or upper class usu. made up of an hereditary nobility **4 :** the aggregate of those believed to be superior

aris·to·crat \ə-ˈris-tə-ˌkrat, a-; ˈar-ə-stə-\ *n* (1789) **1 :** a member of an aristocracy; *esp* **:** NOBLE **2 a :** one who has the bearing and viewpoint typical of the aristocracy **b :** one who favors aristocracy **3 :** one believed to be superior of its kind ⟨the ~ of Southern resorts —*Southern Living*⟩

aris·to·crat·ic \ə-ˌris-tə-ˈkrat-ik, (ˌ)a-ˌris-tə-, ˌar-ə-stə-\ *adj* [MF *aristocratique,* fr. ML *aristocraticus,* fr. Gk *aristokratikos,* fr. *aristos* + *-kratikos* -cratic] (1602) **1 :** belonging to, having the qualities of, or favoring aristocracy **2 a :** socially exclusive ⟨an ~ neighborhood⟩ **b :** SNOBBISH — **aris·to·crat·i·cal·ly** \-i-k(ə-)lē\ *adv*

Ar·is·to·te·lian *or* **Ar·is·to·te·lean** \ˌar-ə-stə-ˈtēl-yən\ *adj* [L *Aristoteles* Aristotle, fr. Gk *Aristotelēs*] (1607) **:** of or relating to the Greek philosopher Aristotle or his philosophy — **Aristotelian** *n* — **Ar·is·to·te·lian·ism** \-yə-ˌniz-əm\ *n*

arith·me·tic \ə-ˈrith-mə-ˌtik\ *n* [ME *arsmetrik,* fr. OF *arismetique,* fr. L *arithmetica,* fr. Gk *arithmētikē,* fr. fem. of *arithmētikos* arithmetical, fr. *arithmein* to count, fr. *arithmos* number; akin to OE *rīm* number, Gk *arariskein* to fit] (13c) **1 a :** a branch of mathematics that deals usu. with the nonnegative real numbers including sometimes the transfinite cardinals and with the application of the operations of addition, subtraction, multiplication, and division to them **b :** a treatise on arithmetic **2 :** COMPUTATION, CALCULATION — **ar·ith·met·ic** \ˌar-ith-ˈmet-ik\ *or* **ar·ith·met·i·cal** \-i-kəl\ *adj* — **ar·ith·met·i·cal·ly** \-i-k(ə-)lē\ *adv* — **arith·me·ti·cian** \ə-ˌrith-mə-ˈtish-ən\ *n*

arithmetic mean *n* (1767) **:** a value that is computed by dividing the sum of a set of terms by the number of terms

arithmetic progression *n* (1594) **:** a progression (as 3, 5, 7, 9) in which the difference between any term and its predecessor is constant

-ar·i·um \ˈar-ē-əm, ˈer-\ *n suffix, pl* **-ariums** *or* **-ar·ia** \-ē-ə\ [L, fr. neut. of *-arius* -ary] **:** thing or place relating to or connected with ⟨planet*arium*⟩

ark \ˈärk\ *n* [ME, fr. OE *arc,* fr. L *arca* chest; akin to L *arcēre* to hold off, defend, Gk *arkein*] (bef. 12c) **1 a :** a boat or ship held to resemble that in which Noah and his family were preserved from the Deluge **b :** something that affords protection and safety **2 a :** the sacred chest representing to the Hebrews the presence of God among them **b :** a repository traditionally in or against the wall of a synagogue for the scrolls of the Torah

¹arm \ˈärm\ *n* [ME, fr. OE *earm;* akin to L *armus* shoulder, Gk *harmos* joint, L *arma* weapons, *ars* skill, Gk *arariskein* to fit] (bef. 12c) **1 :** a human upper limb; *esp* **:** the part between the shoulder and the wrist **2 :** something like or corresponding to an arm: as **a :** the forelimb of a vertebrate **b :** a limb of an invertebrate animal **c :** a branch or lateral shoot of a plant **d :** a slender part of a structure, machine, or an instrument projecting from a main part, axis, or fulcrum **e :** the end of a ship's yard; *also* **:** the part of an anchor from the crown to the fluke **3 :** an inlet of water (as from the sea) **4 :** a narrow extension of a larger area, mass, or group **5 :** POWER, MIGHT ⟨the long ~ of the law⟩ **6 :** a support (as on a chair) for the elbow and forearm **7 :** SLEEVE **8 :** a functional division of a group or activity ⟨the logistical ~ of the air force⟩ — **armed** \ˈärmd\ *adj* — **arm·less** \ˈärm-ləs\ *adj* — **arm·like** \-ˌlīk\ *adj*

²arm *vb* [ME *armen,* fr. OF *armer,* fr. L *armare,* fr. *arma* weapons, tools] *vt* (13c) **1 :** to furnish or equip with weapons **2 :** to furnish with something that strengthens or protects **3 :** to fortify morally **4 :** to equip or ready for action or operation ⟨~ a bomb⟩ ~ *vi* **:** to prepare oneself for struggle or resistance ***syn*** see FURNISH

³arm *n* [ME *armes* (pl.) weapons, fr. OF, fr. L *arma*] (13c) **1 a :** a means (as a weapon) of offense or defense; *esp* **:** FIREARM **b :** a combat branch (as of an army) **c :** an organized branch of national defense (as the navy) **2** *pl* **a :** the hereditary heraldic devices of a family **b :** heraldic devices adopted by a government **3** *pl* **a :** active hostilities **:** WARFARE **b :** military service — **up in arms :** aroused and ready to undertake hostilities

ar·ma·da \ˌär-ˈmäd-ə, -ˈmād-, -ˈmad-\ *n* [Sp, fr. ML *armata* army, fleet, fr. L, fem. of *armatus,* pp. of *armare* to arm, fr. *arma*] (1533) **1 :** a fleet of warships **2 :** a large force or group of usu. moving things ⟨an ~ of fishing boats⟩

ar·ma·dil·lo \ˌär-mə-ˈdil-(ˌ)ō\ *n, pl* **-los** [Sp, fr. dim. of *armado* armed one, fr. L *armatus*] (1577) **:** any of several burrowing chiefly nocturnal edentate mammals (family Dasypodidae) of warm parts of the Americas having body and head encased in an armor of small bony plates in which many of them can curl up into a ball when attacked

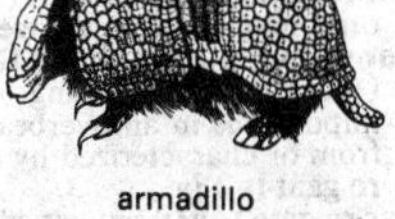

armadillo

Ar·ma·ged·don \ˌär-mə-ˈged-ᵊn\ *n* [Gk *Armageddōn, Harmagedōn,* scene of the battle foretold in Rev 16:14–16] (1611) **1 a :** the site or time of a final and conclusive battle between the forces of good and evil **b :** the battle taking place at Armageddon **2 :** a usu. vast decisive conflict or confrontation

Ar·ma·gnac \ˈär-mən-ˌyak\ *n* [F, fr. *Armagnac,* region in southwest France] (1850) **:** a brandy produced in the Gers district of France

ar·ma·ment \ˈär-mə-mənt *also* ˈärm-mənt\ *n* [F *armement,* fr. L *armamenta* (pl.) utensils, military or naval equipment, fr. *armare*] (1699) **1 :** a military or naval force **2 a :** the aggregate of a nation's military strength **b :** arms and equipment (as of a combat unit) **c :** means of protection or defense **:** ARMOR **3 :** the process of preparing for war

ar·ma·men·tar·i·um \ˌär-mə-ˌmen-ˈter-ē-əm, -mən-\ *n, pl* **-tar·ia** \-ē-ə\ [L, armory, fr. *armamenta*] (ca. 1860) **1 :** the equipment and methods used esp. in medicine **2 :** matter available or utilized for an undertaking or field of activity ⟨a whole ~ of devices to create an illusion of real life —Kenneth Rexroth⟩

arm and a leg *n* (1967) **:** an exorbitant price

ar·ma·ture \ˈär-mə-ˌchu̇(ə)r, -chər, -ˌt(y)u̇(ə)r\ *n* [L *armatura* armor, equipment, fr. *armatus*] (15c) **1 :** an organ or structure (as teeth or thorns) for offense or defense **2 a :** a piece of soft iron or steel that connects the poles of a magnet or of adjacent magnets **b :** a part which consists essentially of coils of wire around a metal core and in which electric current is induced in a generator or in which the input current interacts with a magnetic field to produce torque in a motor **c :** the movable part of an electromagnetic device (as a loudspeaker) **d :** a framework used by a sculptor to support a figure being modeled in a plastic material **e :** FRAMEWORK 1b ⟨the ~ of the book derives from fourteenth century England —Stanley Kauffmann⟩

¹arm·chair \ˈärm-ˌche(ə)r, -ˌcha(ə)r, ˈärm-ˈ\ *n* (1633) **:** a chair with armrests

²armchair *adj* (1886) **1 :** remote from direct dealing with problems **:** theoretical rather than practical ⟨~ strategists⟩ **2 :** sharing vicariously in another's experiences ⟨an ~ traveler⟩

armed forces *n pl* (1943) **:** the combined military, naval, and air forces of a nation

Ar·me·nian \är-ˈmē-nē-ən, -nyən\ *n* (1598) **1 :** a member of a people dwelling chiefly in Armenia **2 :** the Indo-European language of the Armenians — see INDO-EUROPEAN LANGUAGES table — **Armenian** *adj*

arm·ful \ˈärm-ˌfu̇l\ *n, pl* **arm·fuls** \-ˌfu̇lz\ *or* **arms·ful** \ˈärmz-ˌfu̇l\ (1579) **:** as much as the arm can hold

arm·hole \ˈärm-ˌhōl\ *n* (ca. 1775) **:** an opening for the arm in a garment

ar·mi·ger \ˈär-mi-jər\ *n* [ML, fr. L, armor-bearer, fr. *armiger* bearing arms, fr. *arma* arms + *-ger* -gerous] (1598) **1 :** SQUIRE **2 :** one entitled to bear heraldic arms — **ar·mig·er·al** \är-ˈmij-ə-rəl\ *adj*

ar·mig·er·ous \är-ˈmij-ə-rəs\ *adj* (ca. 1731) **:** bearing heraldic arms

ar·mil·la·ry sphere \ˌär-mə-ˌler-ē-, är-ˌmil-ə-rē-\ *n* [F *sphère armillaire,* fr. ML *armilla,* fr. L, bracelet, iron ring, fr. *armus* arm, shoulder; akin to OE *earm* arm] (1664) **:** an old astronomical instrument composed of rings showing the positions of important circles of the celestial sphere

Ar·min·i·an \är-ˈmin-ē-ən\ *adj* (1598) **:** of or relating to Arminius or his doctrines opposing the absolute predestination of strict Calvinism and maintaining the possibility of salvation for all — **Arminian** *n* — **Ar·min·i·an·ism** \-ē-ə-ˌniz-əm\ *n*

ar·mi·stice \ˈär-mə-stəs\ *n* [F or NL; F, fr. NL *armistitium,* fr. L *arma* + *-stitium* (as in *solstitium* solstice)] (ca. 1707) **:** temporary suspension of hostilities by agreement between the opponents **:** TRUCE

Armistice Day *n* [fr. the armistice terminating World War I on November 11, 1918] (1919) **:** VETERANS DAY — used before the official adoption of *Veterans Day* in 1954

arm·let \ˈärm-lət\ *n* (1535) **1 :** a band (as of cloth or metal) worn around the upper arm **2 :** a small arm (as of the sea)

ar·moire \ärm-ˈwär, ˈär-mər\ *n* [MF, fr. OF *armaire,* fr. L *armarium,* fr. *arma*] (1571) **:** a usu. tall cupboard or wardrobe

ar·mor \ˈär-mər\ *n* [ME *armure,* fr. OF, fr. L *armatura* — more at ARMATURE] (13c) **1 :** defensive covering for the body; *esp* **:** covering (as of metal) used in combat **2 :** a quality or circumstance that affords protection ⟨the ~ of prosperity⟩ **3 a :** a usu. metallic protective covering (as for a ship, fort, airplane, or automobile) **b :** a protective covering (as a diver's suit, the covering of a plant or animal, or a sheathing for wire, cordage, or hose) **4 :** armored forces and vehicles (as tanks) — **armor** *vt* — **ar·mored** \-mərd\ *adj* — **ar·mor·less** \-mər-ləs\ *adj*

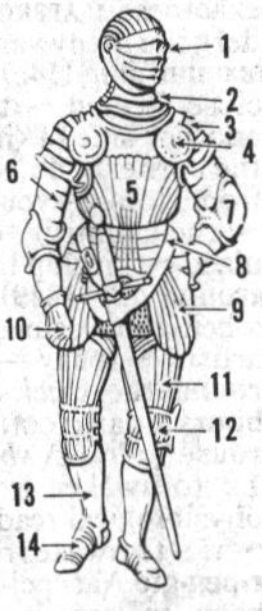

armor 1: *1* helmet, *2* gorget, *3* shoulder piece, *4* pallette, *5* breastplate, *6* brassard, *7* elbow piece, *8* skirt of tasses, *9* tuille, *10* gauntlet, *11* cuisse, *12* knee piece, *13* jambeau, *14* solleret

¹ar·mor–clad \ˈär-mər-ˌklad\ *adj* (1862) **:** sheathed in or protected by armor

²armor–clad *n* (1881) **:** an armor-clad warship

armored scale *n* (ca. 1903) **:** any of numerous scale insects constituting a family (Diaspididae) and having a firm covering of wax best developed in the female

ar·mor·er \ˈär-mər-ər\ *n* (14c) **1 :** one that makes armor or arms **2 :** one that repairs, assembles, and tests firearms

ar·mo·ri·al \är-ˈmōr-ē-əl, -ˈmȯr-\ *adj* [*armory* (heraldry)] (1576) **:** of, relating to, or bearing heraldic arms — **ar·mo·ri·al·ly** \-ē-ə-lē\ *adv*

Ar·mor·i·can \är-ˈmȯr-i-kən, -ˈmär-\ *or* **Ar·mor·ic** \-ik\ *n* (1645) **:** a native or inhabitant of Armorica; *esp* **:** BRETON — **Armorican** *or* **Armoric** *adj*

ar·mory \ˈärm-(ə-)rē\ *n, pl* **ar·mor·ies** (14c) **1 a :** a supply of arms for defense or attack **b :** a collection of available resources **2 :** a place where arms and military equipment are stored; *esp* **:** one used for training military reserve personnel **3 :** a place where arms are manufactured

ar·mour \ˈär-mər\ *chiefly Brit var of* ARMOR

arm·pit \ˈärm-ˌpit\ *n* (14c) **:** the hollow beneath the junction of the arm and shoulder

arm·rest \-ˌrest\ *n* (ca. 1889) **:** a support for the arm

arm's length *n* (ca. 1909) **1 :** a distance discouraging personal contact or familiarity ⟨kept former friends at *arm's length* now⟩ **2 :** the condition or fact that the parties to a transaction are independent and on an equal footing

arm–twist·ing \-ˌtwis-tiŋ\ *n* (1948) **:** the use of direct personal pressure in order to achieve a desired end ⟨for all the ~, the . . . vote on the measure was unexpectedly tight —*Newsweek*⟩

arm wrestling *n* (1973) **:** a form of wrestling in which two opponents sit face to face gripping usu. their right hands, set corresponding elbows firmly on a surface (as a tabletop), and attempt to force each other's arm down — called also *Indian wrestling*

ar·my \ˈär-mē\ *n, pl* **armies** [ME *armee,* fr. MF, fr. ML *armata* — more at ARMADA] (14c) **1 a :** a large organized body of men armed and trained for war esp. on land **b :** a unit capable of independent action and consisting usu. of a headquarters, two or more corps, and auxiliary troops **c** *often cap* **:** the complete military organization of a nation for land warfare **2 :** a great multitude ⟨an ~ of bicycles —Norm Fruchter⟩ **3 :** a body of persons organized to advance a cause

army ant *n* (1874) **:** any of various nomadic social ants (subfamily Dorylinae)

ar·my·worm \ˈär-mē-ˌwərm\ *n* (1816) **:** any of numerous moths whose larvae travel in multitudes from field to field destroying grass, grain, and other crops; *esp* **:** the common armyworm (*Pseudaletia unipuncta*) of the northern U.S.

ar·ni·ca \ˈär-ni-kə\ *n* [NL] (ca. 1753) **1 :** any of many composite herbs (genus *Arnica*) including some with bright yellow ray flowers **2 :** the dried flower heads of an arnica (esp. *Arnica montana*) used esp. in the form of a tincture as a liniment (as for sprains or bruises); *also* **:** this tincture

ar·oid \ˈa(ə)r-ˌȯid, ˈe(ə)r-\ *adj* [NL *Arum*] (ca. 1890) **:** of or relating to the arum family — **aroid** *n*

aroint \ə-ˈrȯint\ *vb imper* [origin unknown] *archaic* (1605) **:** BEGONE ⟨~ thee, witch —Shak.⟩

aro·ma \ə-ˈrō-mə\ *n* [ME *aromat* spice, fr. OF, fr. L *aromat-, aroma,* fr. Gk *arōmat-, arōma*] (1814) **1 a :** a distinctive pervasive and usu. pleasant or savory smell; *broadly* **:** ODOR **b :** the bouquet of a wine **2 :** a distinctive quality or atmosphere **:** FLAVOR ⟨the ~ of enjoyment —Stella D. Gibbons⟩ ***syn*** see SMELL

¹ar·o·mat·ic \ˌar-ə-ˈmat-ik\ *adj* (14c) **1 :** of, relating to, or having aroma: **a :** FRAGRANT **b :** having a strong smell **c :** having a distinctive quality **2 :** of, relating to, or characterized by the presence of at least one benzene ring — used of cyclic hydrocarbons and their derivatives — **ar·o·mat·i·cal·ly** \-i-k(ə-)lē\ *adv* — **aro·ma·tic·i·ty** \ˌar-ə-mə-ˈtis-ət-ē, ə-ˌrō-mə-\ *n* — **ar·o·mat·ic·ness** \ˌar-ə-ˈmat-ik-nəs\ *n* ***syn*** see ODOROUS

²aromatic *n* (15c) **1 :** an aromatic plant, drug, or medicine **2 :** an aromatic organic compound

aro·ma·tize \ə-ˈrō-mə-ˌtīz\ *vt* **-tized; -tiz·ing** (15c) **1 :** to make aromatic **:** FLAVOR **2 :** to convert into one or more aromatic compounds — **aro·ma·ti·za·tion** \-ˌrō-mət-ə-ˈzā-shən\ *n*

arose *past of* ARISE

[1]**around** \ə-'rau̇nd\ *adv* [ME, fr. [1]*a-* + *round*] (14c) **1 a :** in circumference ⟨a tree five feet ~⟩ **b :** in, along, or through a circuit ⟨the road goes ~ by the lake⟩ **2 a :** on all or various sides ⟨papers lying ~⟩ **b :** in close from all sides so as to surround **c :** in or near one's present place or situation ⟨wait ~ awhile⟩ **3 a :** here and there : from one place to another **b :** to a particular place **4 a :** in rotation or succession **b :** from beginning to end : THROUGH ⟨mild the year ~⟩ **5 :** in or to an opposite direction or position **6 :** with some approach to exactness : APPROXIMATELY ⟨cost ~ $5⟩ — **been around :** having undergone many varied experiences : become worldly-wise

[2]**around** *prep* (14c) **1 a :** on all sides of **b :** so as to encircle or enclose ⟨seated ~ the table⟩ **c :** so as to avoid or get past : on or to another side of ⟨find a way ~ their objections⟩ ⟨went ~ the lake⟩ ⟨~ the corner⟩ **d :** NEAR ⟨lives ~ Chicago⟩ **2 :** in all directions outward from ⟨look ~ you⟩ **3 :** here and there in or throughout ⟨barnstorming ~ the country⟩ **4 :** so as to have a center or basis in ⟨a society organized ~ kinship ties⟩

[3]**around** *adj* (1849) **1 :** ABOUT 1 ⟨has been up and ~ for two days⟩ **2 :** being in existence, evidence, or circulation ⟨the most intelligent of the artists ~ today —R. M. Coates⟩

around–the–clock *adj* (1943) **:** being in effect, continuing, or lasting 24 hours a day : CONSTANT

arouse \ə-'rau̇z\ *vb* **aroused; arous·ing** [*a-* (as in *arise*) + *rouse*] *vt* (1593) **1 :** to awaken from sleep **2 :** to rouse or stimulate to action or to physiological readiness for activity : EXCITE ⟨the book *aroused* debate⟩ ~ *vi* **:** to awake from sleep : STIR — **arous·al** \-'rau̇-zəl\ *n*

ar·peg·gio \är-'pej-(ē-ˌ)ō\ *n, pl* **-gios** [It, fr. *arpeggiare* to play on the harp, fr. *arpa* harp, of Gmc origin; akin to OHG *harpha* harp] (ca. 1724) **1 :** production of the tones of a chord in succession and not simultaneously **2 :** a chord played in arpeggio

ar·pent \är-'pä^{n}\ *n, pl* **ar·pents** \-'pä^{n}(z)\ [MF] (1580) **1 :** any of various old French units of land area; *esp* **:** one used in French sections of Canada and the U.S. equal to about 0.85 acre **2 :** a unit of length equal to one side of a square arpent

arquebus \'är-\ *var of* HARQUEBUS

ar·rack \'ar-ək, ə-'rak\ *n* [Ar *'araq* sweet juice, liquor] (1516) **:** an Asian alcoholic beverage like rum that is distilled from a fermented mash of malted rice with toddy or molasses

ar·raign \ə-'rān\ *vt* [ME *arreinen,* fr. MF *araisner,* fr. OF, fr. *a-* (fr. L *ad-*) + *raisnier* to speak, fr. (assumed) VL *rationare,* fr. L *ration-, ratio* reason — more at REASON] (14c) **1 :** to call (a defendant) before a court to answer to an indictment : CHARGE **2 :** to accuse of wrong, inadequacy, or imperfection — **ar·raign·ment** \-mənt\ *n*

ar·range \ə-'rānj\ *vb* **-ranged; -rang·ing** [ME *arangen,* fr. MF *arangier,* fr. OF, fr. *a-* + *rengier* to set in a row, fr. *reng* row — more at RANK] *vt* (14c) **1 :** to put into a proper order or into a correct or suitable sequence, relationship, or adjustment ⟨~ flowers in a vase⟩ ⟨~ cards alphabetically⟩ **2 :** to make preparations for : PLAN ⟨*arranged* a reception for the visitor⟩ **3 :** to bring about an agreement or understanding concerning : SETTLE ⟨~ an exchange of war prisoners⟩ **4 a :** to adapt (a musical composition) by scoring for voices or instruments other than those for which orig. written **b :** ORCHESTRATE ~ *vi* **1 :** to bring about an agreement or understanding ⟨*arranged* to have a table at the restaurant⟩ **2 :** to make preparations : PLAN ⟨*arranged* for a vacation with his family⟩ ***syn*** see ORDER — **ar·rang·er** \ə-'rān-jər\ *n*

ar·range·ment \ə-'rānj-mənt\ *n* (1690) **1 a :** the state of being arranged : ORDER ⟨everything in neat ~⟩ **b :** the act of arranging ⟨the ~ of the details was quickly accomplished⟩ **2 :** something arranged: as **a :** a preliminary measure : PREPARATION ⟨travel ~*s*⟩ **b :** an adaptation of a musical composition by rescoring **c :** an informal agreement or settlement esp. on personal, social, or political matters ⟨~*s* under the new regime⟩ **3 :** something made by arranging parts or things together ⟨a floral ~⟩

ar·rant \'ar-ənt\ *adj* [alter. of *errant*] (14c) **:** being notoriously without moderation : EXTREME ⟨we are ~ knaves, all; believe none of us —Shak.⟩ — **ar·rant·ly** *adv*

ar·ras \'ar-əs\ *n, pl* **arras** [ME, fr. *Arras,* France] (15c) **1 :** a tapestry of Flemish origin used esp. for wall hangings and curtains **2 :** a wall hanging or screen of tapestry

[1]**ar·ray** \ə-'rā\ *vt* [ME *arrayen,* fr. OF *arayer,* fr. (assumed) VL *arredare,* fr. L *ad-* + a base of Gmc origin; akin to Goth *garaiths* arranged — more at READY] (13c) **1 :** to dress or decorate esp. in splendid or impressive attire : ADORN **2 a :** to set or place in order : DRAW UP, MARSHAL **b :** to set or set forth in order (as a jury) for the trial of a cause — **ar·ray·er** *n*

[2]**array** *n* (14c) **1 a :** a regular and imposing grouping or arrangement : ORDER ⟨lined up . . . in soldierly ~ —Donald Barthelme⟩ **b :** an orderly listing of jurors impaneled **2 a :** CLOTHING, ATTIRE **b :** rich or beautiful apparel : FINERY **3 :** a body of soldiers : MILITIA ⟨the baron and his feudal ~⟩ **4 :** an imposing group : large number ⟨faced a whole ~ of problems⟩ **5 a :** a number of mathematical elements arranged in rows and columns **b :** a series of statistical data arranged in classes in order of magnitude **6 :** a group of elements forming a complete unit ⟨an antenna ~⟩

ar·rear \ə-'ri(ə)r\ *n* [ME *arrere* behind, backward, fr. MF, fr. (assumed) VL *ad retro* backward, fr. L *ad* to + *retro* backward, behind — more at AT, RETRO-] (1620) **1 :** the state of being behind in the discharge of obligations — usu. used in pl. ⟨in ~*s* with his payments⟩ **2 a :** an unfinished duty — usu. used in pl. ⟨~*s* of work that have piled up⟩ **b :** an unpaid and overdue debt — usu. used in pl. ⟨paying off the ~*s* of the past several months⟩

ar·rear·age \-ij\ *n* (14c) **1 :** the condition of being in arrears **2 :** something that is in arrears; *esp* **:** something unpaid and overdue

[1]**ar·rest** \ə-'rest\ *vt* [ME *aresten,* fr. MF *arester* to rest, arrest, fr. (assumed) VL *arrestare,* fr. L *ad-* + *restare* to remain — more at REST] (14c) **1 a :** to bring to a stop ⟨sickness ~*ed* his activities⟩ **b :** CHECK, SLOW **c :** to make inactive ⟨an ~*ed* tumor⟩ **2 :** SEIZE, CAPTURE; *specif* **:** to take or keep in custody by authority of law **3 :** to catch suddenly and engagingly — **ar·rest·er** *or* **ar·res·tor** \-'res-tər\ *n* — **ar·rest·ment** \-'res(t)-mənt\ *n*

[2]**arrest** *n* (14c) **1 a :** the act of stopping **b :** the condition of being stopped or inactive **2 :** the taking or detaining in custody by authority of law **3 :** a device for arresting motion — **under arrest :** in legal custody

ar·res·tant \ə-'res-tənt\ *n* (1962) **:** a substance or stimulus that causes an insect to stop locomotion

ar·rest·ee \ə-ˌres-'tē\ *n* (1944) **:** one that is under arrest

ar·rest·ing \ə-'res-tiŋ\ *adj* (1792) **:** catching the attention : STRIKING, IMPRESSIVE — **ar·rest·ing·ly** \-tiŋ-lē\ *adv*

ar·rhyth·mia \ā-'rit͟h-mē-ə\ *n* [NL, fr. Gk, lack of rhythm, fr. *arrhythmos* unrhythmical, fr. *a-* + *rhythmos* rhythm] (ca. 1888) **:** an alteration in rhythm of the heartbeat either in time or force

ar·rhyth·mic \-mik\ *adj* [Gk *arrhythmos*] (1853) **:** lacking rhythm or regularity ⟨~ locomotor activity⟩

ar·ri·ère–ban \ˌar-ē-ˌe(ə)r-'bän, -'ban\ *n* [F] (1553) **:** a proclamation of a king (as of France) calling his vassals to arms; *also* **:** the body of vassals summoned

ar·ri·ère–pen·sée \-pä^{n}-'sā\ *n* [F, fr. *arrière* in back + *pensée* thought] (1823) **:** mental reservation

ar·ris \'ar-əs\ *n, pl* **arris** *or* **ar·ris·es** [prob. modif. of MF *areste,* lit., fishbone, fr. LL *arista* — more at ARÊTE] (1677) **:** the sharp edge or salient angle formed by the meeting of two surfaces esp. in moldings

ar·riv·al \ə-'rī-vəl\ *n* (14c) **1 :** the act of arriving **2 :** the attainment of an end or state **3 :** one that has recently reached a destination

syn ARRIVAL, ADVENT mean the reaching of a destination. ARRIVAL emphasizes the preceding travel or movement; ADVENT applies to a momentous or conspicuous arrival, an appearance upon a scene esp. for the first time, or a beginning.

ar·rive \ə-'rīv\ *vi* **ar·rived; ar·riv·ing** [ME *ariven,* fr. OF *ariver,* fr. (assumed) VL *arripare* to come to shore, fr. L *ad-* + *ripa* shore — more at RIVE] (13c) **1 a :** to reach a destination **b :** to make an appearance ⟨all the guests have *arrived*⟩ **2 a** *archaic* **:** HAPPEN **b :** to be near in time : COME ⟨the moment has *arrived*⟩ **3 :** to achieve success — **ar·riv·er** *n* — **arrive at :** to reach by effort or thought ⟨have *arrived at* a decision⟩

ar·ri·vé \ˌar-i-'vā\ *n* [F, fr. pp. of *arriver* to arrive, fr. OF *ariver*] (1925) **:** one who has risen rapidly to success, power, or fame

ar·ri·viste \-'vēst\ *n* [F, fr. *arriver*] (1901) **:** one that is a new and uncertain arrival (as in social position or artistic endeavor)

ar·ro·ba \ə-'rō-bə\ *n* [Sp & Pg, fr. Ar *ar-rub'*, lit., the quarter] (1555) **1 :** an old Spanish unit of weight equal to about 25 pounds used in some Spanish-American countries **2 :** an old Portuguese unit of weight equal to about 32 pounds used in Brazil

ar·ro·gance \'ar-ə-gən(t)s\ *n* (14c) **:** a feeling or an impression of superiority manifested in an overbearing manner or presumptuous claims

ar·ro·gant \-gənt\ *adj* [ME, fr. L *arrogant-, arrogans,* prp. of *arrogare*] (14c) **1 :** exaggerating or disposed to exaggerate one's own worth or importance in an overbearing manner ⟨an ~ official⟩ **2 :** proceeding from or characterized by arrogance ⟨~ manners⟩ ***syn*** see PROUD — **ar·ro·gant·ly** *adv*

ar·ro·gate \-ˌgāt\ *vt* **-gat·ed; -gat·ing** [L *arrogatus,* pp. of *arrogare,* fr. *ad-* + *rogare* to ask — more at RIGHT] (1537) **1 a :** to claim or seize without justification **b :** to make undue claims to having : ASSUME **2 :** to claim on behalf of another : ASCRIBE — **ar·ro·ga·tion** \ˌar-ə-'gā-shən\ *n*

ar·ron·disse·ment \ə-'rän-də-smənt, 'ar-ˌō^{n}-(ˌ)dē-'smä^{n}\ *n* [F] (1807) **1 :** the largest division of a French department **2 :** an administrative district of some large French cities

ar·row \'ar-(ˌ)ō, -ə(-w)\ *n* [ME *arwe,* fr. OE; akin to Goth *arhwazna* arrow, L *arcus* bow, arch, arc] (bef. 12c) **1 :** a missile weapon shot from a bow and usu. having a slender shaft, a pointed head, and feathers at the butt **2 :** something shaped like an arrow; *esp* **:** a mark (as on a map or signboard) to indicate direction

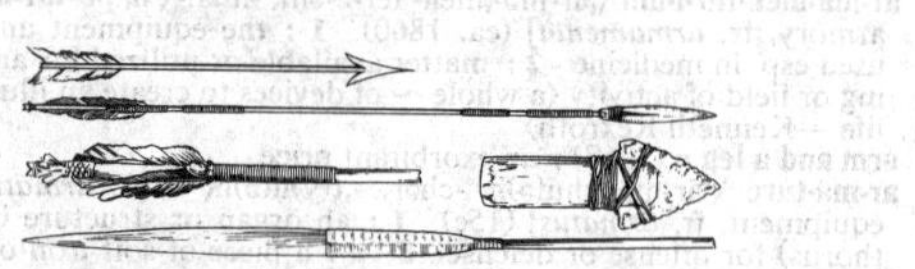

arrow 1

ar·row·head \'ar-ō-ˌhed, 'ar-ə-\ *n* (14c) **1 :** a usu. wedge-shaped piercing tip fixed to an arrow **2 :** something resembling an arrowhead **3 :** any of a genus (*Sagittaria*) of plants of the water-plantain family with leaves shaped like arrowheads

ar·row·root \-ˌrüt, -ˌru̇t\ *n* (1696) **1 a :** any of a genus (*Maranta* of the family Marantaceae, the arrowroot family) of tropical American plants with tuberous roots; *esp* **:** one (*M. arundinacea*) whose roots yield a nutritive starch **b :** any of several plants (as coontie) that yield starch **2 :** starch yielded by an arrowroot

ar·row·wood \-ˌwu̇d\ *n* (1709) **:** any of several shrubs (as several viburnums) having tough pliant shoots formerly used to make arrows

ar·row·worm \-ˌwərm\ *n* (ca. 1889) **:** CHAETOGNATH

ar·rowy \'ar-ə-wē\ *adj* (1637) **1 :** consisting of arrows **2 :** resembling or suggesting an arrow; *esp* **:** swiftly moving

ar·royo \ə-'rȯi-ə, -(ˌ)ō\ *n, pl* **-royos** [Sp] (1843) **1 :** a watercourse (as a creek or stream) in an arid region **2 :** a water-carved gully or channel

ar·roz con po·llo \ä-'rōth-(ˌ)kōn-'pōl-(ˌ)yō, -'pō-(ˌ)yō\ *n* [Sp, lit., rice with chicken] (1938) **:** chicken cooked with rice and usu. flavored with saffron

arse *var of* ASS

ar·se·nal \'ärs-nəl, -ᵊn-əl\ *n* [It *arsenale,* modif. of Ar *dār ṣinā'ah* house of manufacture] (1555) **1 a :** an establishment for the manufacture or storage of arms and military equipment **b :** a collection of weapons **2 :** STORE, REPERTORY ⟨the team's ~ of veteran players⟩

ar·se·nate \'ärs-nət, -ᵊn-ət, -ᵊn-ˌāt\ *n* (1800) **:** a salt or ester of an arsenic acid

[1]**ar·se·nic** \'ärs-nik, -ᵊn-ik\ *n* [ME, yellow orpiment, fr. MF & L; MF, fr. L *arsenicum,* fr. Gk *arsenikon, arrhenikon,* fr. Syr *zarnīg;* akin to Av *zaranya* gold, Skt *hari* yellowish — more at YELLOW] (14c) **1 :** a trivalent and pentavalent solid poisonous element that is commonly metallic steel-gray, crystalline, and brittle — see ELEMENT table **2 :** a poi-

sonous trioxide As_2O_3 or As_4O_6 of arsenic used esp. as an insecticide or weed killer — called also *arsenic trioxide*

²**ar·sen·ic** \är-ˈsen-ik\ *adj* (1801) : of, relating to, or containing arsenic esp. with a valence of five

ar·sen·i·cal \är-ˈsen-i-kəl\ *adj* (1605) : of, relating to, or containing arsenic ⟨an ~ drug⟩ — **arsenical** *n*

ar·se·nic trisulfide \ˌärs-nik-, -ᵊn-ik-\ *n* (ca. 1909) : a yellow compound As_2S_3 occurring native as orpiment or prepared artificially and used in fireworks and as a pigment

ar·se·nide \ˈärs-ᵊn-ˌīd\ *n* (1863) : a binary compound of arsenic with a more positive element

ar·se·ni·ous \är-ˈsē-nē-əs\ *adj* (1818) : of, relating to, or containing arsenic esp. when trivalent

ar·se·nite \ˈärs-ᵊn-ˌīt\ *n* (1800) : a salt or ester of an arsenious acid

ar·se·no·py·rite \ˌärs-ᵊn-ō-ˈpī(ə)r-ˌīt\ *n* (1881) : a mineral FeAsS consisting of a combined sulfide and arsenide of iron occurring in prismatic orthorhombic crystals or in masses or grains

ar·sine \är-ˈsēn, ˈär-ˌ\ *n* [ISV, fr. *arsenic*] (1876) : a colorless flammable extremely poisonous gas AsH_3 with an odor like garlic; *also* : a derivative of arsine

ar·sis \ˈär-səs\ *n, pl* **ar·ses** \-ˌsēz\ [LL & Gk; LL, raising of the voice, accented part of foot, fr. Gk, upbeat, less important part of foot, lit., act of lifting, fr. *aeirein, airein* to lift] (14c) **1 a** : the lighter or shorter part of a poetic foot esp. in quantitative verse **b** : the accented or longer part of a poetic foot esp. in accentual verse **2** : the unaccented part of a musical measure — compare THESIS

ar·son \ˈärs-ᵊn\ *n* [obs. F, fr. OF, fr. *ars,* pp. of *ardre* to burn, fr. L *ardēre* — more at ARDOR] (1680) : the malicious or fraudulent burning of property (as a building) — **ar·son·ist** \-əst\ *n* — **ar·son·ous** \-əs\ *adj*

ars·phen·a·mine \ärs-ˈfen-ə-ˌmēn, -mən\ *n* [ISV *arsenic* + *phenamine*] (1917) : a light-yellow toxic hygroscopic powder $C_{12}CL_2H_{14}As_2N_2$-O_2·$2H_2O$ formerly used in the treatment esp. of syphilis and yaws

¹**art** \(ˈ)ärt, ərt\ [ME, fr. OE *eart;* akin to ON *est, ert* (thou) art, OE *is* is] *archaic pres 2d sing of* BE

²**art** \ˈärt\ *n* [ME, fr. OF, fr. L *art-, ars* — more at ARM] (13c) **1** : skill acquired by experience, study, or observation ⟨the ~ of making friends⟩ **2 a** : a branch of learning: (1) : one of the humanities (2) *pl* : LIBERAL ARTS **b** *archaic* : LEARNING, SCHOLARSHIP **3** : an occupation requiring knowledge or skill ⟨the ~ of organ building⟩ **4 a** : the conscious use of skill and creative imagination esp. in the production of aesthetic objects; *also* : works so produced **b** (1) : FINE ARTS (2) : one of the fine arts (3) : a graphic art **5 a** *archaic* : a skillful plan **b** : the quality or state of being artful **6** : decorative or illustrative elements in printed matter

syn ART, SKILL, CUNNING, ARTIFICE, CRAFT mean the faculty of executing well what one has devised. ART implies a personal, unanalyzable creative power; SKILL stresses technical knowledge and proficiency; CUNNING suggests ingenuity and subtlety in devising, inventing, or executing; ARTIFICE suggests mechanical skill esp. in imitating things in nature; CRAFT may imply expertness in workmanship.

-art — see -ARD

art de·co \ˌär(t)-dā-ˈkō, (ˈ)är(t)-ˈdā-(ˌ)-\ *n, often cap A&D* [F *Art Déco,* fr. *Exposition Internationale des Arts Décoratifs et Industriels Modernes,* an exposition of modern decorative and industrial arts held in Paris, France, in 1925] (1966) : a popular decorative style of the 1920s and 1930s characterized esp. by bold outlines, streamlined and rectilinear forms, and the use of new materials (as plastic)

ar·te·fact *chiefly Brit var of* ARTIFACT

ar·tel \är-ˈtel(-yə)\ *n* [Russ *artel'*, fr. It *artieri,* pl. of *artiere* artisan, fr. *arte* art] (1884) : a workers' or peasants' cooperative in the U.S.S.R.

Ar·te·mis \ˈärt-ə-məs\ *n* [Gk] : a Greek moon goddess often portrayed as a virgin huntress — compare DIANA

ar·te·mi·sia \ˌärt-ə-ˈmizh-(ē-)ə, -ˈmiz-ē-ə\ *n* [NL, fr. L, artemisia, fr. Gk, wormwood] (12c) : any of a genus (*Artemisia*) of composite herbs and shrubs with strong-smelling foliage

arteri- *or* **arterio-** *comb form* [MF, fr. LL, fr. Gk *artēri-, artērio-,* fr. *artēria* artery] **1** : artery ⟨*arterio*logy⟩ **2** : arterial and ⟨*arterio*venous⟩

¹**ar·te·ri·al** \är-ˈtir-ē-əl\ *adj* (15c) **1 a** : of or relating to an artery **b** : relating to or being the bright red blood present in most arteries that has been oxygenated in lungs or gills **2** : of, relating to, or constituting through-traffic facilities — **ar·te·ri·al·ly** \-ē-ə-lē\ *adv*

²**arterial** *n* (1932) : a through street or arterial highway

ar·te·rio·gram \är-ˈtir-ē-ə-ˌgram\ *n* [ISV] (1929) : a roentgenogram of an artery made by arteriography

ar·te·ri·og·ra·phy \är-ˌtir-ē-ˈäg-rə-fē\ *n, pl* **-phies** [ISV] (1929) : the roentgenographic visualization of an artery after injection of a radiopaque substance — **ar·te·rio·graph·ic** \-ē-ə-ˈgraf-ik\ *adj*

ar·te·ri·ole \är-ˈtir-ē-ˌōl\ *n* [F or NL; F *artériole,* prob. fr. NL *arteriola,* dim. of L *arteria*] (ca. 1839) : any of the small terminal twigs of an artery that ends in capillaries — **ar·te·ri·o·lar** \-ˌtir-ē-ˈō-ˌlär, -lər\ *adj*

ar·te·rio·scle·ro·sis \är-ˌtir-ē-ō-sklə-ˈrō-səs\ *n* [NL] (1886) : a chronic disease characterized by abnormal thickening and hardening of the arterial walls with resulting loss of elasticity — **ar·te·rio·scle·rot·ic** \-ˈrät-ik\ *adj or n*

ar·te·rio·ve·nous \-ˈvē-nəs\ *adj* [ISV] (ca. 1880) : of, relating to, or connecting the arteries and veins ⟨an ~ fistula⟩

ar·ter·i·tis \ˌärt-ə-ˈrīt-əs\ *n* [NL] (1836) : arterial inflammation

ar·tery \ˈärt-ə-rē, ˈär-trē\ *n, pl* **-ter·ies** [ME *arterie,* fr. L *arteria,* fr. Gk *artēria;* akin to Gk *aortē* aorta] (14c) **1** : any of the tubular branching muscular- and elastic-walled vessels that carry blood from the heart through the body **2** : a channel (as a river or highway) of transportation or communication; *esp* : the main channel in a branching system

ar·te·sian well \är-ˌtē-zhən-\ *n* [F *artésien,* lit., of Artois, fr. OF, fr. *Arteis* Artois, France] (1842) **1** : a well made by boring into the earth until water is reached which from internal pressure flows up like a fountain **2** : a deep-bored well

art film *n* (1926) : a motion picture produced as an artistic effort

art form *n* (1868) **1** : a recognized form (as a symphony) or medium (as sculpture) of artistic expression **2** : an unconventional form or medium in which impulses regarded as artistic may be expressed ⟨describe pinball as a great American *art form* —Tom Buckley⟩

art·ful \ˈärt-fəl\ *adj* (1615) **1** : performed with or showing art or skill ⟨an ~ performance on the violin⟩ **2 a** : using or characterized by art and skill : DEXTEROUS ⟨an ~ prose stylist⟩ **b** : adroit in attaining an end often by insinuating or indirect means : WILY ⟨an ~ cross-examiner⟩ **3** : ARTIFICIAL ⟨trim walks and ~ bowers —William Wordsworth⟩ ***syn*** see SLY — **art·ful·ly** \-fə-lē\ *adv* — **art·ful·ness** *n*

art glass *n* (1926) : articles of glass designed primarily for decorative purposes; *esp* : novelty glassware

art–historical *adj, chiefly Brit* (1933) : of or relating to the history of art

art house *n* (1951) : ART THEATER

arthr- *or* **arthro-** *comb form* [L, fr. Gk, fr. *arthron;* akin to Gk *arthroun* to articulate, *arariskein* to fit — more at ARM] : joint ⟨*arthr*algia⟩

ar·thral·gia \är-ˈthral-j(ē-)ə\ *n* [NL] (ca. 1848) : neuralgic pain in one or more joints — **ar·thral·gic** \-jik\ *adj*

ar·thrit·ic \är-ˈthrit-ik\ *adj* (14c) **1** : of, relating to, or affected with arthritis **2** : being or showing effects associated with aging ⟨~ anxiety⟩ — **arthritic** *n* — **ar·thrit·i·cal·ly** \-i-k(ə-)lē\ *adv*

ar·thri·tis \är-ˈthrīt-əs\ *n, pl* **-thrit·i·des** \-ˈthrit-ə-ˌdēz\ [L, fr. Gk, fr. *arthron*] (14c) : inflammation of joints due to infectious, metabolic, or constitutional causes

ar·throd·e·sis \är-ˈthräd-ə-səs\ *n, pl* **-e·ses** \-ˌsēz\ [NL, fr. *arthr-* + Gk *desis* binding, fr. *dein* to bind] (ca. 1901) : the surgical immobilization of a joint so that the bones grow solidly together : artificial ankylosis

ar·throp·a·thy \är-ˈthräp-ə-thē\ *n, pl* **-thies** (ca. 1860) : a disease of a joint

ar·thro·pod \ˈär-thrə-ˌpäd\ *n* [NL *Arthropoda,* group name, fr. *arthr-* + Gk *pod-, pous* foot — more at FOOT] (1877) : any of a phylum (Arthropoda) of invertebrate animals (as insects, arachnids, and crustaceans) that have a jointed body and limbs, usu. a chitinous shell molted at intervals, and the brain dorsal to the alimentary canal and connected with a ventral chain of ganglia — **arthropod** *adj* — **ar·throp·o·dan** \är-ˈthräp-əd-ən\ *also* **ar·throp·o·dous** \-əd-əs\ *adj*

ar·thros·co·py \är-ˈthräs-kə-pē\ *n* [ISV *arthr-* + *-scope* + *-y* activity] (ca. 1935) : visual examination of the interior of a joint (as the knee) with a special surgical instrument — **ar·thro·scope** \ˈär-thrə-ˌskōp\ *n* — **ar·thro·scop·ic** \ˌär-thrə-ˈskäp-ik\ *adj*

ar·thro·sis \är-ˈthrō-səs\ *n, pl* **-thro·ses** \-ˌsēz\ [NL, fr. Gk *arthrōsis* jointing, articulation, fr. *arthroun* to articulate, fr. *arthron*] (1634) : an articulation or line of juncture between bones

ar·thro·spore \ˈär-thrə-ˌspō(ə)r, -ˌspȯ(ə)r\ *n* (1895) : OIDIUM 1b

Ar·thur \ˈär-thər\ *n* : a legendary king of the Britons whose story is based on traditions of a 6th century military leader

Ar·thu·ri·an \är-ˈth(y)u̇r-ē-ən\ *adj* (1612) : of or relating to King Arthur and his court

ar·ti·choke \ˈärt-ə-ˌchōk\ *n* [It dial. *articiocco,* fr. Ar *al-khurshūf* the artichoke] (1530) **1** : a tall composite herb (*Cynara scolymus*) like a thistle with coarse pinnately incised leaves; *also* : its edible flower head which is cooked as a vegetable **2** : JERUSALEM ARTICHOKE

¹**ar·ti·cle** \ˈärt-i-kəl\ *n* [ME, fr. OF, fr. L *articulus* joint, division, dim. of *artus* joint; akin to Gk *arariskein* to fit — more at ARM] (13c) **1 a** : a distinct often numbered section of a writing **b** : a separate clause **c** : a stipulation in a document (as a contract or a creed) **d** : a nonfictional prose composition usu. forming an independent part of a publication (as a magazine) **2** : an item of business : MATTER **3** : any of a small set of words or affixes (as *a, an,* and *the*) used with nouns to limit or give definiteness to the application **4** : a member of a class of things; *esp* : a piece of goods ⟨~*s* of value⟩ **5** : a thing of a particular and distinctive kind ⟨the genuine ~⟩

²**article** *vt* **ar·ti·cled; ar·ti·cling** \-k(ə-)liŋ\ (1820) : to bind by articles (as of apprenticeship)

article of faith (15c) : a basic belief

ar·tic·u·la·ble \är-ˈtik-yə-lə-bəl\ *adj* (1833) : capable of being articulated

ar·tic·u·lar \är-ˈtik-yə-lər\ *adj* [ME *articuler,* fr. L *articularis,* fr. *articulus*] (15c) : of or relating to a joint ⟨~ cartilage⟩

¹**ar·tic·u·late** \är-ˈtik-yə-lət\ *adj* [L *articulatus* jointed, pp. of *articulare,* fr. *articulus*] (1586) **1 a** : divided into syllables or words meaningfully arranged : INTELLIGIBLE **b** : able to speak **c** : expressing oneself readily, clearly, or effectively; *also* : expressed in this manner **2 a** : consisting of segments united by joints : JOINTED ⟨~ animals⟩ **b** : distinctly marked off — **ar·tic·u·late·ly** *adv* — **ar·tic·u·late·ness** *n*

²**ar·tic·u·late** \-ˌlāt\ *vb* **-lat·ed; -lat·ing** *vt* (1691) **1 a** : to utter distinctly ⟨*articulating* each note in the musical phrase⟩ **b** : to give clear and effective utterance to ⟨ ~ one's grievances⟩ **2 a** : to unite by means of a joint : JOINT **b** : to make of parts united by flexible joints **c** : to form or fit into a systematic whole ⟨*articulating* a program for all school grades⟩ ~ *vi* **1** : to utter articulate sounds **2** : to become united or connected by or as if by a joint — **ar·tic·u·la·tive** \-lət-iv, -ˌlāt-\ *adj* — **ar·tic·u·la·tor** \-ˌlāt-ər\ *n*

ar·tic·u·la·tion \(ˌ)är-ˌtik-yə-ˈlā-shən\ *n* (15c) **1 a** : the action or manner of jointing or interrelating **b** : the state of being jointed or interrelated **2 a** (1) : a joint or juncture between bones or cartilages in the skeleton of a vertebrate (2) : a movable joint between rigid parts of an animal **b** (1) : a joint between two separable plant parts (as the base of a leafstalk) (2) : a plant stem node or internode **3 a** : the act of giving utterance or expression **b** : the act or manner of articulating sounds **c** : an articulated utterance or sound; *specif* : CONSONANT **4** : OCCLUSION 1b

ar·tic·u·la·to·ry \är-ˈtik-yə-lə-ˌtōr-ē, -ˌtȯr-\ *adj* (1818) : of or relating to articulation

ar·ti·fact \ˈärt-i-ˌfakt\ *n* [L *arte* by skill (abl. of *art-, ars* skill) + *factum,* neut. of *factus,* pp. of *facere* to do — more at ARM, DO] (1821) **1** : a characteristic product of human activity: as **a** : a usu. hand-made object (as a tool or ornament) representing a particular culture or stage of technological development **b** : a mass-produced item ⟨~*s* of industrial society⟩ **c** : a usu. inferior artistic work **d** : someone or something held to be a typical product (as of social forces) **2** : a product (as a structure on a prepared microscope slide) of artificial character due to extraneous (as human) agency — **ar·ti·fac·tu·al** \ˌärt-i-ˈfak-chə(-wə)l, -ˈfaksh-wəl\ *adj*

ar·ti·fice \'ärt-ə-fəs\ *n* [MF, fr. L *artificium,* fr. *artific-, artifex* artificer, fr. L *art-, ars* + *facere*] (1620) **1 a :** an artful stratagem **:** TRICK **b :** false or insincere behavior ⟨social ~⟩ **2 a :** an ingenious device or expedient **b :** clever or artful skill **:** INGENUITY ⟨believing that characters had to be created from within rather than with ~ —Garson Kanin⟩ ***syn*** see TRICK, ART

ar·ti·fi·cer \är-'tif-ə-sər, 'ärt-ə-fə-sər\ *n* (14c) **1 :** a skilled or artistic worker or craftsman **2 :** one that makes or contrives **:** DEVISER ⟨had been the ~ of his own fortunes —*Times Lit. Supp.*⟩

ar·ti·fi·cial \,ärt-ə-'fish-əl\ *adj* (14c) **1 :** humanly contrived often on a natural model **:** MAN-MADE ⟨an ~ limb⟩ ⟨~ diamonds⟩ **2 a :** having existence in legal, economic, or political theory **b :** caused or produced by a human and esp. social or political agency ⟨an ~ price advantage⟩ ⟨~ barriers of discrimination —R.C. Weaver⟩ **3** *obs* **:** ARTFUL, CUNNING **4 a :** lacking in natural or spontaneous quality ⟨an ~ smile⟩ ⟨an ~ excitement⟩ **c :** IMITATION, SHAM ⟨~ flavor⟩ **5 :** based on differential morphological characters not necessarily indicative of natural relationships ⟨an ~ key for plant identification⟩ — **ar·ti·fi·ci·al·i·ty** \,ärt-ə-,fish-ē-'al-ət-ē\ *n* — **ar·ti·fi·cial·ly** \-'fish-(ə-)lē\ *adv* — **ar·ti·fi·cial·ness** \-'fish-əl-nəs\ *n*

artificial horizon *n* (1833) **1 :** HORIZON 1c **2 :** an aeronautical instrument based on a gyroscope and designed to furnish a surface constantly perpendicular to the vertical and therefore parallel to the horizon

artificial insemination *n* (1897) **:** introduction of semen into the uterus or oviduct by other than natural means

artificial intelligence *n* (ca. 1961) **:** the capability of a machine to imitate intelligent human behavior

artificial respiration *n* (1852) **:** the rhythmic forcing of air into and out of the lungs of a person whose breathing has stopped

ar·til·ler·ist \är-'til-ə-rəst\ *n* (1781) **:** GUNNER, ARTILLERYMAN

ar·til·lery \är-'til-(ə-)rē\ *n, pl* **-ler·ies** [ME *artillerie,* fr. MF] (14c) **1 :** weapons (as bows, slings, and catapults) for discharging missiles **2 :** large caliber crew-served mounted firearms (as guns, howitzers, and rockets) **:** ORDNANCE **3 :** a branch of an army armed with artillery **4 :** means of impressing, arguing, or persuading ⟨the ~ of satire⟩ ⟨a soprano's vocal ~⟩

ar·til·lery·man \-(ə-)rē-mən\ *n* (1635) **:** a soldier in the artillery

ar·tio·dac·tyl \,ärt-ē-ō-'dak-tᵊl\ *n* [deriv. of Gk *artios* fitting, even-numbered + *daktylos* finger, toe; akin to Gk *arariskein* to fit — more at ARM] (ca. 1879) **:** any of an order (Artiodactyla) of hoofed mammals (as the camel or ox) with an even number of functional toes on each foot — **artiodactyl** *adj*

ar·ti·san \'ärt-ə-zən, -sən, *chiefly Brit* ,ärt-ə-'zan\ *n* [MF, fr. OIt *artigiano,* fr. *arte* art, fr. L *art-, ars*] (1538) **:** one (as a carpenter, plumber, or tailor) trained to manual dexterity or skill in a trade; *broadly* **:** a skilled worker ⟨literary ~s⟩ — **ar·ti·san·al** \-ᵊl\ *adj* — **ar·ti·san·ship** \-,ship\ *n*

art·ist \'ärt-əst\ *n* (1581) **1 a :** one who professes and practices an imaginative art **b :** a person skilled in one of the fine arts **2 :** a skilled performer; *esp* **:** ARTISTE **3 a** *obs* **:** one skilled or versed in learned arts **b** *archaic* **:** PHYSICIAN **c** *archaic* **:** ARTISAN **4 :** one who is adept at deception

ar·tiste \är-'tēst\ *n* [F] (1712) **:** a skilled adept public performer; *specif* **:** a musical or theatrical entertainer

ar·tis·tic \är-'tis-tik\ *adj* (1753) **1 :** of, relating to, or characteristic of art or artists ⟨~ subjects⟩ ⟨an ~ success⟩ **2 :** showing imaginative skill in arrangement or execution ⟨~ photography⟩ — **ar·tis·ti·cal·ly** \-ti-k(ə-)lē\ *adv*

art·ist·ry \'ärt-ə-strē\ *n* (1868) **1 :** artistic quality of effect or workmanship ⟨the ~ of his novel⟩ **2 :** artistic ability ⟨the ~ of the violinist⟩ ⟨a lawyer's ~ in persuading juries⟩

art·less \'ärt-ləs\ *adj* (1589) **1 :** lacking art, knowledge, or skill **:** UNCULTURED **2 a :** made without skill **:** CRUDE **b :** free from artificiality **:** NATURAL ⟨~ grace⟩ **3 :** free from guile or craft **:** sincerely simple ***syn*** see NATURAL — **art·less·ly** *adv* — **art·less·ness** *n*

art nou·veau \,är(t)-nü-'vō\ *n, often cap A & N* [F, lit., new art] (1901) **:** a decorative style of late 19th century origin characterized esp. by sinuous lines and foliate forms

art song *n* (ca. 1910) **:** a usu. through-composed lyric song with melody and accompaniment

art·sy \'ärt-sē\ *adj* (1902) **:** ARTY

artsy–craftsy \,ärt-sē-'kraf(t)-sē\ *also* **arty–crafty** \ärt-ē-'kraf-tē\ *adj* [fr. the phrase *arts and crafts*] (1902) **:** ARTY

art theater *n* (1923) **:** a theater that specializes in the presentation of art films

art·work \'ärt-,wərk\ *n* (1877) **1 a :** an artistic production ⟨an 8-foot metal ~⟩ **b :** artistic work ⟨~ being sold on the sidewalk⟩ **2 a :** ART 6 **b :** material (as a drawing or photograph) prepared for reproduction in printed matter

arty \'ärt-ē\ *adj* **art·i·er; -est** (1901) **:** showily or pretentiously artistic ⟨~ lighting and photography⟩ — **art·i·ly** \'ärt-ᵊl-ē\ *adv* — **art·i·ness** \'ärt-ē-nəs\ *n*

aru·gu·la \ə-'rü-g(y)ə-lə\ *n* [prob. fr. It dial. *arugula,* fr. L *eruca* colewort; akin to F *roquette* rocket] (1967) **:** GARDEN ROCKET

ar·um \'ar-əm, 'er-\ *n* [NL, fr. L *arum,* fr. Gk *aron*] (14c) **:** any of a genus (*Arum* of the family Araceae, the arum family) of Old World plants with flowers in a fleshy spathe subtended by a leafy bract; *broadly* **:** a plant of the arum family

1-ary *US usu* ,er-ē *when an unstressed syllable precedes,* ə-rē *or* rē *when a stressed syllable precedes; Brit usu* ə-rē *or* rē *in all cases*\ *n suffix* [ME *-arie,* fr. OF & L; OF *-aire, -arie,* fr. L *-arius, -aria, -arium,* fr. *-arius,* adj. suffix] **1 :** thing belonging to or connected with; *esp* **:** place of ⟨ov*ary*⟩ **2 :** person belonging to, connected with, or engaged in ⟨function*ary*⟩

2-ary *adj suffix* [ME *-arie,* fr. MF & L; MF *-aire,* fr. L *-arius*] **:** of, relating to, or connected with ⟨budget*ary*⟩

1Ary·an \'ar-ē-ən, 'er-; 'är-yən\ *adj* [Skt *ārya* noble, belonging to the people speaking an Indo-European dialect who migrated into northern India] (1839) **1 :** of or relating to the Indo-European family of languages or to their hypothetical prototype **2 :** of or relating to speakers of Indo-European languages **3 a :** of or relating to a hypothetical ethnic type illustrated by or descended from early speakers of Indo-European languages **b :** NORDIC **4 :** of or relating to Indo-Iranian or its speakers

2Aryan *n* (1851) **1 :** a member of the Indo-European-speaking people early occupying the Iranian plateau or entering India and conquering and amalgamating with the earlier non-Indo-European inhabitants **2 a :** a member of the people speaking the language from which the Indo-European languages are derived **b :** an individual of any of those peoples speaking these languages since prehistoric times **:** INDO-EUROPEAN **c :** NORDIC **d :** GENTILE

ar·yl \'ar-əl\ *n* [ISV *ar*omatic + *-yl*] (1906) **:** a radical (as phenyl) derived from an aromatic hydrocarbon by the removal of one hydrogen atom

ar·y·te·noid \,ar-ə-'tē-,nȯid, ə-'rit-ᵊn-,ȯid\ *adj* [NL *arytaenoides,* fr. Gk *arytainoeidēs,* lit., ladle-shaped, fr. *arytaina* ladle] (ca. 1727) **1 :** relating to or being either of two small laryngeal cartilages to which the vocal cords are attached **2 :** relating to or being either of a pair of small muscles or an unpaired muscle of the larynx — **arytenoid** *n*

1as \əz, (,)az\ *adv* [ME, fr. OE *eallswā* likewise, just as — more at ALSO] (bef. 12c) **1 :** to the same degree or amount ⟨~ deaf as a post⟩ ⟨twice ~ long⟩ **2 :** for instance ⟨various trees, ~ oak or pine⟩ **3 :** when considered in a specified form or relation — usu. used before a preposition or a participle ⟨my opinion ~ distinguished from his⟩

2as *conj* (12c) **1 :** AS IF ⟨looks ~ he had seen a ghost — S. T. Coleridge⟩ **2 :** in or to the same degree in which ⟨deaf ~ a post⟩ — usu. used as a correlative after an adjective or adverb modified by adverbial *as* or *so* ⟨as cool ~ a cucumber⟩ **3 :** in the way or manner that ⟨do ~ I do⟩ **4 :** in accordance with what or the way in which ⟨quite good ~ boys go⟩ **5 :** WHILE, WHEN ⟨spilled the milk ~ she got up⟩ **6 :** regardless of the degree to which **:** THOUGH ⟨improbable ~ it seems, it's true⟩ **7 :** for the reason that **:** BECAUSE, SINCE ⟨stayed home ~ she had no car⟩ **8 :** that the result is ⟨so clearly guilty ~ to leave no doubt⟩ ***usage*** see LIKE — **as is :** in the presently existing condition without modification ⟨bought the clock at an auction *as is*⟩ — **as it were :** as if it were so **:** in a manner of speaking

3as *pron* (12c) **1 :** THAT, WHO, WHICH — used after *same* or *such* ⟨in the same building ~ my brother⟩ ⟨tears such ~ angels weep — John Milton⟩ and chiefly dial. after a substantive not modified by *same* or *such* ⟨that kind of fruit ~ maids call medlars — Shak.⟩ **2 :** a fact that ⟨is a foreigner, ~ is evident from his accent⟩

4as *prep* (13c) **1 a :** LIKE 2 ⟨all rose ~ one man⟩ **b :** LIKE 1a ⟨his face was ~ a mask — Max Beerbohm⟩ **2 :** in the capacity, character, condition, or role of ⟨works ~ an editor⟩

5as \'as\ *n, pl* **as·ses** \'as-,ēz, 'as-əz\ [L] (1540) **1 :** LIBRA 2a **2 a :** a bronze coin of the ancient Roman republic **b :** a unit of value equivalent to an as coin

as- — see AD-

asa·fet·i·da *or* **asa·foe·ti·da** \,as-ə-'fit-əd-ē, -'fet-əd-ə\ *n* [ME *asafetida,* fr. ML *asafoetida,* fr. Per *azā* mastic + L *foetida,* fem. of *foetidus* fetid] (14c) **:** the fetid gum resin of various oriental plants (genus *Ferula*) of the carrot family formerly used in medicine as an antispasmodic and in folk medicine as a general prophylactic against disease

as·bes·tos *also* **as·bes·tus** \as-'bes-təs, az-\ *n* [ME *albestron* mineral supposed to be inextinguishable when set on fire, prob. fr. MF, fr. ML *asbeston,* alter. of L *asbestos,* fr. Gk, unslaked lime, fr. *asbestos* inextinguishable, fr. *a-* + *sbennynai* to quench] (1607) **:** any of several minerals (as chrysotile) that readily separate into long flexible fibers suitable for use as a noncombustible, nonconducting, or chemically resistant material

as·bes·to·sis \,as-,bes-'tō-səs, ,az-\ *n, pl* **-to·ses** \-,sēz\ (1927) **:** a pneumoconiosis due to asbestos particles

asc- *or* **asco-** *comb form* [NL, fr. *ascus*] **:** ascus ⟨*asco*carp⟩

as·ca·ri·a·sis \,as-kə-'rī-ə-səs\ *n, pl* **-a·ses** \-,sēz\ (ca. 1888) **:** infestation with or disease caused by ascarids

as·ca·rid \'as-kə-rəd\ *n* [deriv. of LL *ascarid-, ascaris* intestinal worm, fr. Gk *askarid-, askaris;* akin to Gk *skairein* to gambol — more at CARDINAL] (ca. 1890) **:** any of a family (Ascaridae) of nematode worms that includes the common roundworm (*Ascaris lumbricoides*) parasitic in the human intestine

as·ca·ris \'as-kə-rəs\ *n, pl* **as·car·i·des** \ə-'skar-ə-,dēz\ (14c) **:** ASCARID

as·cend \ə-'send\ *vb* [ME *ascenden,* fr. L *ascendere,* fr. *ad-* + *scandere* to climb — more at SCAN] *vi* (14c) **1 a :** to move gradually upward **b :** to slope upward **2 a :** to rise from a lower level or degree **b :** to go back in time or in order of genealogical succession ~ *vt* **1 :** to go or move up or toward **2 :** to succeed to **:** OCCUPY — **as·cend·able** *or* **as·cend·ible** \-'sen-də-bəl\ *adj*

as·cen·dance *also* **as·cen·dence** \ə-'sen-dən(t)s\ *n* (1742) **:** ASCENDANCY

as·cen·dan·cy *also* **as·cen·den·cy** \ə-'sen-dən-sē\ *n* (1712) **:** governing or controlling influence **:** DOMINATION

1as·cen·dant *also* **as·cen·dent** \ə-'sen-dənt\ *n* [ME *ascendent,* fr. ML *ascendent-, ascendens,* fr. L, prp. of *ascendere*] (1591) **1 :** the point of the ecliptic or degree of the zodiac that rises above the eastern horizon at any moment **2 :** a state or position of dominant power or importance **3 :** a lineal or collateral relative in the ascending line

2ascendant *also* **ascendent** *adj* (14c) **1 a :** moving upward **:** RISING **b :** directed upward ⟨an ~ stem⟩ **2 a :** SUPERIOR **b :** DOMINANT — **as·cen·dant·ly** *adv*

as·cend·er \ə-'sen-dər, 'a-\ *n* (ca. 1867) **:** the part of a lowercase letter (as b) that rises above the main body of the letter; *also* **:** a letter that has such a part

as·cend·ing \ə-'sen-diŋ\ *adj* (1616) **1 a :** mounting or sloping upward **b :** rising or increasing to higher levels, values, or degrees ⟨~ powers of x⟩ **2 :** rising upward usu. from a more or less prostrate base or point of attachment

ascending rhythm *n* (ca. 1903) **:** RISING RHYTHM

as·cen·sion \ə-'sen-chən\ *n* [ME, fr. L *ascension-, ascensio,* fr. *ascensus,* pp. of *ascendere*] (14c) **:** the act or process of ascending

as·cen·sion·al \ə-'sench-nəl, -ən-ᵊl\ *adj* (1594) **:** of or relating to ascension or ascent

Ascension Day *n* (14c) **:** the Thursday 40 days after Easter observed in commemoration of Christ's ascension into Heaven

as·cen·sive \ə-'sen(t)-siv\ *adj* (1646) **:** rising or tending to rise

as·cent \ə-'sent, a-\ *n* [irreg. fr. *ascend*] (1614) **1 a :** the act of rising or mounting upward **:** CLIMB **b :** an upward slope or rising grade

: ACCLIVITY **c** : the degree of elevation : INCLINATION, GRADIENT **2** : an advance in social status or reputation : PROGRESS **3** : a going back in time or upward in order of genealogical succession

as·cer·tain \ˌas-ər-'tān\ *vt* [ME *acertainen,* fr. MF *acertainer,* fr. *a-* (fr. L *ad-*) + *certain*] (15c) **1** *archaic* : to make certain, exact, or precise **2** : to find out or learn with certainty ***syn*** see DISCOVER — **as·cer·tain·able** \-'tā-nə-bəl\ *adj* — **as·cer·tain·ment** \-'tān-mənt\ *n*

as·ce·sis \ə-'sē-səs\ *n, pl* **-ce·ses** \-'sē-(ˌ)sēz\ [LL or Gk; LL, fr. Gk *askēsis,* lit., exercise, fr. *askein*] (1873) : SELF-DISCIPLINE, ASCETICISM

as·cet·ic \ə-'set-ik, a-\ *adj also* **as·cet·i·cal** \-i-kəl\ *adj* [Gk *askētikos,* lit., laborious, fr. *askētēs* one that exercises, hermit, fr. *askein* to work, exercise] (1646) **1** : practicing strict self-denial as a measure of personal and esp. spiritual discipline **2** : austere in appearance, manner, or attitude ***syn*** see SEVERE — **ascetic** *n* — **as·cet·i·cal·ly** \-i-k(ə-)lē\ *adv* — **as·cet·i·cism** \-'set-ə-ˌsiz-əm\ *n*

as·cid·i·an \ə-'sid-ē-ən\ *n* (1856) : any of an order (Ascidiacea) of simple or compound tunicates; *broadly* : TUNICATE

as·cid·i·um \ə-'sid-ē-əm\ *n, pl* **-cid·ia** \-ē-ə\ [NL, fr. Gk *askidion,* dim. of *askos* wineskin, bladder] (1830) : a pitcher-shaped or flask-shaped organ or appendage of a plant

ASCII \'as-(ˌ)kē\ *n* [*A*merican *S*tandard *C*ode for *I*nformation *I*nterchange] (ca. 1966) : a code for representing alphanumeric information

as·ci·tes \ə-'sīt-ēz\ *n, pl* **ascites** [ME *aschytes,* fr. LL *ascites,* fr. Gk *askitēs,* fr. *askos*] (14c) : accumulation of serous fluid in the spaces between tissues and organs in the cavity of the abdomen — **as·cit·ic** \-'sit-ik\ *adj*

as·cle·pi·ad \ə-'sklē-pē-əd, a-, -ˌad\ *n* [deriv. of Gk *asklēpiad-, asklēpias* swallowwort] (1859) : MILKWEED

as·co·carp \'as-kə-ˌkärp\ *n* (1887) : the mature fruiting body of an ascomycetous fungus; *broadly* : such a body with its enclosed asci, spores, and paraphyses — **as·co·car·pic** \ˌas-kə-'kär-pik\ *adj*

as·co·go·ni·um \ˌas-kə-'gō-nē-əm\ *n, pl* **-nia** \-nē-ə\ [NL, fr. *asc-* + Gk *gonos* procreation — more at KIN] (1875) : the fertile basal often one-celled portion of an archicarp; *broadly* : ARCHICARP

as·co·my·cete \ˌas-kō-'mī-ˌsēt, -ˌmī-'sēt\ *n* [deriv. of Gk *askos* + *mykēt-, mykēs* fungus; akin to L *mucus*] (1875) : any of a class (Ascomycetes) of higher fungi (as yeasts or molds) with septate hyphae and spores formed in asci — **as·co·my·ce·tous** \-ˌmī-'sēt-əs\ *adj*

ascor·bate \ə-'skȯr-ˌbāt, -bət\ *n* (1941) : a salt of ascorbic acid

ascor·bic acid \ə-ˌskȯr-bik-\ *n* [ISV *a-* + NL *scorbutus* scurvy — more at SCORBUTIC] (1933) : VITAMIN C

as·co·spore \'as-kə-ˌspō(ə)r, -ˌspȯ(ə)r\ *n* (1875) : one of the spores contained in an ascus — **as·co·spor·ic** \ˌas-kə-'spōr-ik, -'spȯr-\ *adj*

as·cot \'as-kət, -ˌkät\ *n* [*Ascot* Heath, racetrack near Ascot, England] (1900) : a broad neck scarf that is looped under the chin

as·cribe \ə-'skrīb\ *vt* **as·cribed; as·crib·ing** [ME *ascriven,* fr. MF *ascrivre,* fr. L *ascribere,* fr. *ad-* + *scribere* to write — more at SCRIBE] (14c) : to refer to a supposed cause, source, or author — **as·crib·able** \-'skrī-bə-bəl\ *adj*

syn ASCRIBE, ATTRIBUTE, ASSIGN, IMPUTE, CREDIT mean to lay something to the account of a person or thing. ASCRIBE suggests an inferring or conjecturing of cause, quality, authorship; ATTRIBUTE suggests less tentativeness than ASCRIBE, less definiteness than ASSIGN; ASSIGN implies ascribing with certainty or after deliberation; IMPUTE suggests ascribing something that brings discredit by way of accusation or blame; CREDIT implies ascribing a thing or esp. an action to a person or other thing as its agent, source, or explanation.

as·cribed *adj* (1972) : acquired or assigned arbitrarily (as at birth) ⟨~ social status⟩

as·crip·tion \ə-'skrip-shən\ *n* [LL *ascription-, ascriptio,* fr. L, written addition, fr. *ascriptus,* pp. of *ascribere*] (ca. 1619) **1** : the act of ascribing : ATTRIBUTION **2** : arbitrary placement (as at birth) in a particular social status

as·crip·tive \-'skrip-tiv\ *adj* (1650) : relating to, marked by, or involving ascription

as·cus \'as-kəs\ *n, pl* **as·ci** \'as-ˌ(k)ī, -ˌkē\ [NL, fr. Gk *askos* wineskin, bladder] (1830) : the membranous oval or tubular spore case of an ascomycete

as·dic \'az-(ˌ)dik\ *n* [*A*nti-*S*ubmarine *D*etection *I*nvestigation *C*ommittee] (1940) : SONAR

-ase \ˌās, ˌāz\ *n suffix* [F, fr. *diastase*] : enzyme ⟨prote*ase*⟩

asep·sis \(ˌ)ā-'sep-səs, ə-\ *n* [NL] (1892) **1** : the condition of being aseptic **2** : the methods of making or keeping aseptic

asep·tic \-'sep-tik\ *adj* [ISV] (ca. 1859) **1 a** : preventing infection ⟨~ techniques⟩ **b** : free or freed from pathogenic microorganisms ⟨an ~ operating room⟩ **2 a** : lacking vitality, emotion, or warmth ⟨~ essays⟩ **b** : DETACHED, OBJECTIVE ⟨an ~ view of civilization⟩ — **asep·ti·cal·ly** \-ti-k(ə-)lē\ *adv*

asex·u·al \(ˌ)ā-'seksh-(ə-)wəl, -'sek-shəl\ *adj* (1830) **1** : lacking sex or functional sex organs ⟨~ plants⟩ **2 a** : involving or reproducing by reproductive processes (as cell division, spore formation, fission, or budding) that do not involve the union of individuals or germ cells ⟨~ reproduction⟩ ⟨an ~ generation⟩ **b** : produced by asexual reproduction ⟨~ spores⟩ **3** : devoid of sexuality ⟨an ~ relationship⟩ — **asex·u·al·i·ty** \ˌā-ˌsek-shə-'wal-ət-ē\ *n* — **asex·u·al·ly** \(ˌ)ā-'seksh-(ə-)wə-lē, -ˌseksh-(ə-)lē\ *adv*

[1]**as far as** *conj* (14c) : to the extent or degree that ⟨is safe, *as far as* we know⟩

[2]**as far as** *prep* (1523) : with regard to : CONCERNING ⟨neatly groomed and, *as far as* clothes, casual looking — *N.Y. Times*⟩ ⟨*as far as* being mentioned in the Ten Commandments, I think it is —Billy Graham⟩ — chiefly in oral use

as for *prep* (15c) : with regard to : CONCERNING ⟨*as for* the others, they'll arrive later⟩

As·gard \'as-ˌgärd, 'az-\ *n* [ON *āsgarthr,* fr. *āss* the Norse gods + *garthr* court, stronghold; akin to OE *geard*— more at YARD] : the home of the Norse gods

[1]**ash** \'ash\ *n* [ME *asshe,* fr. OE *æsc;* akin to OHG *ask* ash, L *ornus* wild mountain ash] (bef. 12c) **1** : any of a genus (*Fraxinus*) of trees of the olive family with pinnate leaves, thin furrowed bark, and gray branchlets **2** : the tough elastic wood of an ash **3** [OE *æsc,* name of the corresponding runic letter] : the ligature æ used in Old English and some phonetic alphabets to represent a low front vowel \a\

[2]**ash** *n, often attrib* [ME *asshe,* fr. OE *asce;* akin to OHG *asca* ash, L *aridus* dry — more at ARDOR] (bef. 12c) **1 a** : the solid residue left when combustible material is thoroughly burned or is oxidized by chemical means **b** : fine particles of mineral matter from a volcanic vent **2** *pl* : RUINS **3** *pl* : the remains of the dead human body after cremation or disintegration **4** : something that symbolizes grief, repentance, or humiliation **5** *pl* : deathly pallor ⟨the lip of ~*es* and the cheek of flame —Lord Byron⟩ — **ash·less** \-ləs\ *adj*

[3]**ash** *vt* (1894) : to convert into ash

ashamed \ə-'shāmd\ *adj* [ME, fr. OE *āscamod,* pp. of *āscamian* to shame, fr. *ā-* (perfective prefix) + *scamian* to shame — more at ABIDE, SHAME] (bef. 12c) **1 a** : feeling shame, guilt, or disgrace **b** : feeling inferior or unworthy **2** : restrained by anticipation of shame ⟨was ~ to beg⟩ — **asham·ed·ly** \-'shā-məd-lē\ *adv*

Ashan·ti \ə-'shant-ē, -'shänt-\ *n, pl* **Ashanti** *or* **Ashantis** [Ashanti *A*[1]*san*[3]*te*[1]] (1705) **1** : a West African people of Ghana **2** : the dialect of Akan spoken by the Ashanti people

ash·can \'ash-ˌkan\ *adj, often cap* (1939) : of or relating to a group of 20th century American painters who depicted city life realistically ⟨~ school⟩

ash can *n* (1899) **1** : a metal receptacle for refuse **2** *slang* : DEPTH CHARGE

[1]**ash·en** \'ash-ən\ *adj* (14c) : of, relating to, or made from ash wood

[2]**ashen** *adj* (14c) : resembling ashes (as in color); *esp* : deadly pale ⟨a face ~ and haggard⟩

Ash·er \'ash-ər\ *n* [Heb *Āshēr*] : a son of Jacob and the traditional eponymous ancestor of one of the tribes of Israel

Ash·ke·nazi \ˌash-kə-'naz-ē\ *n, pl* **-naz·im** \-'naz-əm\ [Heb *Ashkĕnāzī,* fr. *Ashkĕnāz,* medieval rabbinical name for Germany] (1839) : a member of one of the two great divisions of Jews comprising the eastern European Yiddish-speaking Jews — **Ash·ke·naz·ic** \-'naz-ik\ *adj*

ash·lar \'ash-lər\ *n* [ME *asheler,* fr. MF *aisselier* traverse beam, fr. OF, fr. *ais* board, fr. L *axis,* alter. of *assis*] (14c) **1** : hewn or squared stone; *also* : masonry of such stone **2** : a thin squared and dressed stone for facing a wall of rubble or brick

ashore \ə-'shō(ə)r, -'shȯ(ə)r\ *adv* (1586) : on or to the shore

as how *conj* (1821) : THAT ⟨allowed *as how* she was glad to be here⟩

ash·ram \'äsh-rəm, 'ash-ˌram; 'äsh-ˌräm\ *n* [Skt *āśrama,* fr. *ā* toward + *śrama* religious exercise] (1917) **1 a** : a secluded dwelling of a Hindu sage **b** : the group of disciples instructed there **2** : a religious retreat

Ash·to·reth \'ash-tə-ˌreth\ *n* [Heb *'Ashtōreth*] : ASTARTE

ash·tray \'ash-ˌtrā\ *n* (1887) : a receptacle for tobacco ashes and for cigar and cigarette butts

Ashur \'ä-ˌshu̇(ə)r\ *n* [Assyrian *Ashūr*] : the chief deity of the Assyrians

Ash Wednesday *n* (13c) : the first day of Lent — see EASTER table

ashy \'ash-ē\ *adj* **ash·i·er; -est** (15c) **1** : of or relating to ashes **2** : ASHEN

Asi·a·go \ˌäzh-ē-'ä-(ˌ)gō, ˌäs(h)-\ *n* [*Asiago,* commune in province of Vicenza, It.] (1938) : a pungent hard yellow cheese of Italian origin suitable for grating

Asian \'ā-zhən, -shən\ *adj* (1599) : of, relating to, or characteristic of the continent of Asia or its people — **Asian** *n*

Asian influenza *n* (1957) : influenza caused by a mutant strain of the influenza virus isolated during the 1957 epidemic in Asia — called also *Asian flu*

Asi·at·ic \ˌā-z(h)ē-'at-ik\ *adj* (1602) : ASIAN — sometimes taken to be offensive — **Asiatic** *n*

Asiatic cholera *n* (1831) : an acute infectious epidemic cholera of Asian origin caused by a bacterium (*Vibrio comma*)

Asiatic elephant *n* (1930) : ELEPHANT 1b

[1]**aside** \ə-'sīd\ *adv* (14c) **1** : to or toward the side ⟨stepped ~⟩ **2** : out of the way : AWAY ⟨brushed ~ all objections to his views⟩ **3** : set to one side ⟨jesting ~⟩

[2]**aside** *prep, obs* (1592) : BEYOND, PAST

[3]**aside** *n* (ca. 1727) **1** : an utterance meant to be inaudible to someone; *esp* : an actor's speech heard by the audience but supposedly not by other characters **2** : a straying from the theme : DIGRESSION

aside from *prep* (1818) **1** : in addition to : BESIDES **2** : EXCEPT FOR

as if *conj* (13c) **1** : as it would be if ⟨it was *as if* he had lost his last friend⟩ **2** : as one would do if ⟨he ran *as if* ghosts were chasing him⟩ **3** : THAT ⟨it seemed *as if* the day would never end⟩

as·i·nine \'as-ᵊn-ˌīn\ *adj* [L *asininus,* fr. *asinus* ass; akin to Gk *onus*] (15c) **1** : marked by inexcusable failure to exercise intelligence or sound judgment ⟨an ~ excuse⟩ **2** : of, relating to, or resembling an ass ***syn*** see SIMPLE — **as·i·nine·ly** *adv* — **as·i·nin·i·ty** \ˌas-ᵊn-'in-ət-ē\ *n*

ask \'ask, 'ȧsk\ *vb* **asked** \'as(k)t, 'ȧs(k)t, 'ask\; **ask·ing** [ME *asken,* fr. OE *āscian;* akin to OHG *eiscōn* to ask, L *aeruscare* to beg] *vt* (bef. 12c) **1 a** : to call on for an answer **b** : to put a question about **c** : SPEAK, UTTER ⟨~ a question⟩ **2 a** : to make a request of ⟨she ~*ed* her teacher for help⟩ **b** : to make a request for ⟨she ~*ed* help from her teacher⟩ **3** : to call for : REQUIRE **4** : to set as a price ⟨~*ed* $3000 for the car⟩ **5** : INVITE ~ *vi* **1** : to seek information **2** : to make a request ⟨~*ed* for food⟩ **3** : LOOK — often used in the phrase *ask for trouble* — **ask·er** *n*

syn ASK, QUESTION, INTERROGATE, QUERY, INQUIRE mean to address a person in order to gain information. ASK implies no more than the putting of a question; QUESTION usu. suggests the asking of series of questions; INTERROGATE suggests formal or official systematic questioning; QUERY implies a desire for authoritative information or confirmation; INQUIRE implies a searching for facts or for truth often specifically by asking questions.

syn ASK, REQUEST, SOLICIT mean to seek to obtain by making one's wants known. ASK implies no more than the statement of the desire; REQUEST implies greater formality and courtesy; SOLICIT suggests a calling attention to one's wants or desires by public announcement or advertisement.

\ə\ abut \ᵊ\ kitten, F table \ər\ further \a\ ash \ā\ ace \ä\ cot, cart \au̇\ out \ch\ chin \e\ bet \ē\ easy \g\ go \i\ hit \ī\ ice \j\ job \ŋ\ sing \ō\ go \ȯ\ law \ȯi\ boy \th\ thin \t͟h\ the \ü\ loot \u̇\ foot \y\ yet \zh\ vision \ȧ, k̲, ⁿ, œ, œ̄, ue, u̅e, ʸ\ *see* Guide to Pronunciation

askance \ə-ˈskan(t)s\ *also* **askant** \-ˈskant\ *adv* [origin unknown] (ca. 1530) **1 :** with a side-glance **:** OBLIQUELY **2 :** with disapproval or distrust **:** SCORNFULLY
as·ke·sis \ə-ˈskē-səs\ *var of* ASCESIS
askew \ə-ˈskyü\ *adv or adj* [prob. fr. *a-* + *skew*] (1573) **:** out of line **:** AWRY ⟨the picture hung ~⟩ — **askew·ness** *n*
asking price *n* (1755) **:** the price at which something is offered for sale
[1]**aslant** \ə-ˈslant\ *adv or adj* (14c) **:** in a slanting direction **:** OBLIQUELY
[2]**aslant** *prep* (1602) **:** over or across in a slanting direction
[1]**asleep** \ə-ˈslēp\ *adj* [ME *aslepe,* fr. OE *on slæpe*] (13c) **1 :** being in a state of sleep **2 :** DEAD **3 :** lacking sensation **:** NUMB **4 a :** INACTIVE, DORMANT **b :** not alert **:** INDIFFERENT
[2]**asleep** *adv* (13c) **1 :** into a state of sleep **2 :** into the sleep of death **3 :** into a state of inactivity, sluggishness, or indifference
as long as *conj* (15c) **1 :** provided that ⟨can do as they like *as long as* they have a B average⟩ **2 :** INASMUCH AS, SINCE ⟨*as long as* you're going, I'll go too⟩
aslope \ə-ˈslōp\ *adj or adv* (14c) **:** being in a sloping or slanting position or direction
aso·cial \(ˈ)ā-ˈsō-shəl\ *adj* (1883) **:** not social: as **a :** rejecting or lacking the capacity for social interaction **b :** ANTISOCIAL
as of *prep* (1900) **:** ON, AT, FROM ⟨takes effect *as of* July 1⟩
[1]**asp** \ˈasp\ *n* [ME, fr. OE *æspe*] (bef. 12c) **:** ASPEN
[2]**asp** *n* [ME *aspis,* fr. L, fr. Gk] (14c) **:** a small venomous snake of Egypt variously identified as the cerastes or a small cobra (*Naja haje*)
as·par·a·gine \ə-ˈspar-ə-ˌjēn\ *n* [F, fr. L *asparagus*] (1813) **:** a white crystalline amino acid $C_4H_8N_2O_3$ that is an amide of aspartic acid and serves as a storage depot for amino groups in many plants
as·par·a·gus \ə-ˈspar-ə-gəs\ *n* [NL, genus name, fr. L, asparagus plant, fr. Gk *asparagos;* akin to Gk *spargan* to swell — more at SPARK] (1548) **:** any of a genus (*Asparagus*) of Old World perennial plants of the lily family having much-branched stems, minute scalelike leaves, and linear cladophylls; *esp* **:** one (*A. officinalis*) widely cultivated for its edible young shoots
as·par·tame \ˈas-pər-ˌtām, ə-ˈspär-ˌtām\ *n* (1972) **:** a crystalline low-calorie sweetener $C_{14}H_{18}N_2O_5$ that is a protein rather than a carbohydrate and is formed from the amino acids phenylalanine and aspartic acid
as·par·tate \ə-ˈspär-ˌtāt\ *n* (1863) **:** a salt or ester of aspartic acid
as·par·tic acid \ə-ˌspärt-ik-\ *n* [ISV, irreg. fr. L *asparagus*] (1863) **:** a crystalline amino acid $C_4H_7NO_4$ found esp. in plants
as·pect \ˈas-ˌpekt\ *n* [ME, fr. L *aspectus,* fr. *aspectus,* pp. of *aspicere* to look at, fr. *ad-* + *specere* to look — more at SPY] (14c) **1 a :** the position of planets or stars with respect to one another held by astrologers to influence human affairs; *also* **:** the apparent position (as conjunction) of a body in the solar system with respect to the sun **b :** a position facing a particular direction **:** EXPOSURE **c :** the manner of presentation of a plane to a fluid through which it is moving or to a current **2 a (1) :** appearance to the eye or mind **(2) :** a particular appearance of countenance **:** MIEN **b :** a particular status or phase in which something appears or may be regarded ⟨studied every ~ of the question⟩ **3** *archaic* **:** an act of looking **:** GAZE **4 a :** the nature of the action of a verb as to its beginning, duration, completion, or repetition and without reference to its position in time **b :** a set of inflected verb forms that indicate aspect — **as·pec·tu·al** \a-ˈspek-chə(-wə)l\ *adj*
aspect ratio *n* (1907) **:** a ratio of one dimension to another: as **a :** the ratio of span to mean chord of an airfoil **b :** the ratio of the width of a television or motion-picture image to its height
as·pen \ˈas-pən\ *n* [alter. of ME *asp,* fr. OE *æspe;* akin to OHG *aspa* aspen] (14c) **:** any of several poplars (esp. *Populus tremula* of Europe and *P. tremuloides* and *P. grandidentata* of No. America) with leaves that flutter in the lightest wind because of their flattened petioles
as·per·ges \ə-ˈspər-(ˌ)jēz\ *n* [L, thou wilt sprinkle, fr. *aspergere*] (ca. 1533) **:** a ceremony of sprinkling altar and people with holy water
as·per·gil·lo·sis \ˌas-pər-(ˌ)jil-ˈō-səs\ *n, pl* **-lo·ses** \-ˌsēz\ (1898) **:** infection with or disease caused (as in poultry) by molds (genus *Aspergillus*)
as·per·gil·lum \ˌas-pər-ˈjil-əm\ *n, pl* **-la** \-ə\ *or* **-lums** [NL, fr. L *aspergere*] (1649) **:** a brush or small perforated container with a handle that is used for sprinkling holy water in a liturgical service

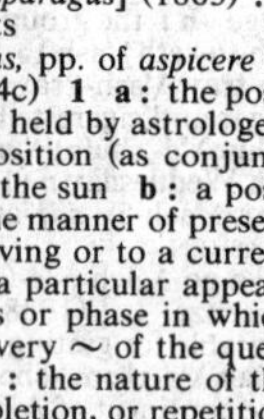
aspergillum

as·per·gil·lus \-ˈjil-əs\ *n, pl* **-gil·li** \-ˈjil-ˌī\ [NL, genus name, fr. *aspergillum*] (ca. 1847) **:** any of a genus (*Aspergillus*) of ascomycetous fungi with branched radiate sporophores including many common molds
as·per·i·ty \a-ˈsper-ət-ē, ə-\ *n, pl* **-ties** [ME *asprete,* fr. OF *aspreté,* fr. *aspre* rough, fr. L *asper;* akin to L *spernere* — more at SPURN] (13c) **1 :** RIGOR, SEVERITY **2 a :** roughness of surface **:** UNEVENNESS; *also* **:** a tiny projection from a surface **b :** roughness of sound **3 :** roughness of manner or of temper **:** HARSHNESS
as·perse \ə-ˈspərs, a-\ *vt* **as·persed; as·pers·ing** [L *aspersus,* pp. of *aspergere,* fr. *ad-* + *spargere* to scatter — more at SPARK] (15c) **1 :** SPRINKLE; *esp* **:** to sprinkle with holy water **2 :** to attack with evil reports or false or injurious charges ***syn*** see MALIGN
as·per·sion \ə-ˈspər-zhən, -shən\ *n* (ca. 1553) **1 :** a sprinkling with water esp. in religious ceremonies **2 a :** the act of calumniating **:** DEFAMATION **b :** a calumnious expression ⟨he cast ~*s* on her integrity⟩
as·phalt \ˈas-ˌfȯlt, *esp Brit* -ˌfalt\ *or* **as·phal·tum** \as-ˈfȯl-təm, *esp Brit* -ˈfal-\ *n* [ME *aspalt,* fr. LL *aspaltus,* fr. Gk *asphaltos*] (14c) **1 :** a brown to black bituminous substance that is found in natural beds and is also obtained as a residue in petroleum refining and that consists chiefly of hydrocarbons **2 :** an asphaltic composition used for pavements and as a waterproof cement — **as·phal·tic** \as-ˈfȯl-tik, *esp Brit* -ˈfal-\ *adj*
as·phalt·ite \ˈas-ˌfȯl-ˌtīt, *esp Brit* -ˌfal-\ *n* (ca. 1899) **:** a native asphalt occurring in vein deposits below the surface of the ground
asphalt jungle *n* (ca. 1920) **:** a big city or a specified part of a big city
aspher·ic \(ˈ)ā-ˈsfi(ə)r-ik, -ˈsfer-\ *or* **aspher·i·cal** \-i-kəl\ *adj* (ca. 1922) **1 :** departing slightly from the spherical form ⟨~ optical surface⟩ **2 :** free from spherical aberration ⟨an ~ lens⟩
as·pho·del \ˈas-fə-ˌdel\ *n* [L *asphodelus,* fr. Gk *asphodelos*] (15c) **:** any of various Old World usu. perennial herbs (esp. genera *Asphodelus* and *Asphodeline*) of the lily family with flowers in long erect racemes
as·phyx·ia \as-ˈfik-sē-ə, əs-\ *n* [NL, fr. Gk, stopping of the pulse, fr. *a-* + *sphyzein* to throb] (1802) **:** a lack of oxygen or excess of carbon dioxide in the body that is usu. caused by interruption of breathing and that causes unconsciousness
as·phyx·i·ate \-sē-ˌāt\ *vb* **-at·ed; -at·ing** *vt* (1836) **:** to cause asphyxia in; *also* **:** to kill or make unconscious through want of adequate oxygen, presence of noxious agents, or other obstruction to normal breathing ~ *vi* **:** to become asphyxiated — **as·phyx·i·a·tion** \-ˌfik-sē-ˈā-shən\ *n* — **as·phyx·i·a·tor** \-ˈfik-sē-ˌāt-ər\ *n*
[1]**as·pic** \ˈas-pik\ *n* [MF, alter. of *aspe,* fr. L *aspis*] *obs* (1530) **:** [2]ASP
[2]**aspic** *n* [F, lit., asp] (1789) **:** a clear savory jelly (as of fish or meat stock) used as a garnish or to make a meat, fish, or vegetable mold
as·pi·dis·tra \ˌas-pə-ˈdis-trə\ *n* [NL, irreg. fr. Gk *aspid-, aspis* shield] (1822) **:** an Asian plant (*Aspidistra lurida*) of the lily family that has large basal leaves and is often grown as a foliage plant
[1]**as·pi·rant** \ˈas-p(ə-)rənt, ə-ˈspī-rənt\ *n* (1738) **:** one who aspires ⟨presidential ~*s*⟩
[2]**aspirant** *adj* (1814) **:** seeking to attain a desired position or status
[1]**as·pi·rate** \ˈas-pə-ˌrāt\ *vt* **-rat·ed; -rat·ing** [L *aspiratus,* pp. of *aspirare*] (1700) **1 :** to pronounce (a vowel, a consonant, or a word) with an accompanying *h*-sound **2 a :** to draw by suction **b :** to remove (as blood) by aspiration **c :** INHALE
[2]**as·pi·rate** \ˈas-p(ə-)rət\ *n* (1725) **1 :** an independent sound \h\ or a character (as the letter *h*) representing it **2 :** a consonant having aspiration as its final component ⟨in English the *p* of *pit* represents an ~⟩ **3 :** material removed by aspiration
as·pi·ra·tion \ˌas-pə-ˈrā-shən\ *n* (14c) **1 :** the pronunciation or addition of an aspirate; *also* **:** the aspirate or its symbol **2 :** a drawing of something in, out, up, or through by or as if by suction: as **a :** the act of breathing and esp. of breathing in **b :** the withdrawal of fluid from the body **c :** the taking of foreign matter into the lungs with the respiratory current **3 a :** a strong desire to achieve something high or great **b :** an object of such desire ***syn*** see AMBITION — **as·pi·ra·tion·al** \-ˈrāsh-nəl, -ˈrā-shən-ᵊl\ *adj*
as·pi·ra·tor \ˈas-pə-ˌrāt-ər\ *n* (1804) **:** an apparatus for producing suction or moving or collecting materials by suction; *esp* **:** a hollow tubular instrument connected with a partial vacuum and used to remove fluid or tissue or foreign bodies from the body
as·pire \ə-ˈspī(ə)r\ *vi* **as·pired; as·pir·ing** [ME *aspiren,* fr. MF or L; MF *aspirer,* fr. L *aspirare,* lit., to breathe upon, fr. *ad-* + *spirare* to breathe — more at SPIRIT] (15c) **1 :** to seek to attain or accomplish a particular goal ⟨*aspired* to a career in medicine⟩ **2 :** ASCEND, SOAR — **as·pir·er** *n*
as·pi·rin \ˈas-p(ə-)rən\ *n, pl* **aspirin** *or* **aspirins** [ISV, fr. acetyl + *spira*eic acid (former name of salicylic acid), fr. NL *Spiraea,* genus of shrubs — more at SPIREA] (1899) **1 :** a white crystalline derivative $C_9H_8O_4$ of salicylic acid used for relief of pain and fever **2 :** a tablet of aspirin
as regards *or* **as respects** *prep* (1867) **:** in regard to **:** with respect to
[1]**ass** \ˈas\ *n* [ME, fr. OE *assa,* perh. fr. OIr *asan,* fr. L *asinus*] (bef. 12c) **1 :** any of several hardy gregarious mammals (genus *Equus*) that are smaller than the horse, have long ears, and include the donkey **2 :** a stupid, obstinate, or perverse person
[2]**ass** \ˈas\ *or* **arse** \ˈas, ˈärs\ *n* [ME *ars, ers,* fr. OE *ærs, ears;* akin to OHG & ON *ars* buttocks, Gk *orrhos, oura* tail] (bef. 12c) **1 a :** BUTTOCKS — often considered vulgar **b :** ANUS — often considered vulgar **2 :** SEXUAL INTERCOURSE — usu. considered vulgar
[1]**-ass** \ˌas\ *adj or adv comb form* [[2]*ass*] — used as a derogatory intensive ⟨fancy-*ass*⟩; often considered vulgar
[2]**-ass** *n comb form* [[2]*ass*] **:** a contemptible person ⟨smart-*ass*⟩ — often considered vulgar
as·sai \ä-ˈsī\ *adv* [It, fr. (assumed) VL *ad satis* enough — more at ASSET] (ca. 1724) **:** VERY — used with tempo direction in music ⟨allegro ~⟩
as·sail \ə-ˈsā(ə)l\ *vt* [ME *assailen,* fr. OF *asaillir,* fr. (assumed) VL *assalire,* alter. of L *assilire* to leap upon, fr. *ad-* + *salire* to leap — more at SALLY] (13c) **:** to attack violently with blows or words ***syn*** see ATTACK — **as·sail·able** \-ˈsā-lə-bəl\ *adj* — **as·sail·ant** \-ˈsā-lənt\ *n*
As·sam·ese \ˌas-ə-ˈmēz, -ˈmēs\ *n, pl* **Assamese** (1826) **1 :** a native or inhabitant of Assam, India **2 :** the Indic language of Assam
as·sas·sin \ə-ˈsas-ᵊn\ *n* [ML *assassinus,* fr. Ar *ḥashshāshīn,* pl. of *ḥashshāsh* one who smokes or chews hashish, fr. *ḥashīsh* hashish] (1603) **1** *cap* **:** one of a secret order of Muslims that at the time of the Crusades terrorized Christians and other enemies by secret murder committed under the influence of hashish **2 :** one who commits murder; *esp* **:** one that murders a politically important person either for hire or from fanatical motives
as·sas·si·nate \ə-ˈsas-ᵊn-ˌāt\ *vt* **-nat·ed; -nat·ing** (1618) **1 :** to murder by sudden or secret attack usu. for impersonal reasons ⟨~ a senator⟩ **2 :** to injure or destroy unexpectedly and treacherously ***syn*** see KILL — **as·sas·si·na·tion** \-ˌsas-ᵊn-ˈā-shən\ *n* — **as·sas·si·na·tor** \-ˈsas-ᵊn-ˌāt-ər\ *n*
assassin bug *n* (1895) **:** any of a family (Reduviidae) of bugs that are usu. predatory on insects though some suck the blood of mammals **:** CONENOSE
[1]**as·sault** \ə-ˈsȯlt\ *n* [ME *assaut,* fr. OF, fr. (assumed) VL *assaltus,* fr. *assaltus,* pp. of *assalire*] (13c) **1 :** a violent physical or verbal attack **2 a :** an apparently violent attempt or a willful offer with force or violence to do hurt to another without the actual doing of the hurt threatened (as by lifting the fist in a threatening manner) — compare BATTERY 1b **b :** RAPE
[2]**assault** *vt* (15c) **1 :** to make an assault on **2 :** RAPE ~ *vi* **:** to make an assault ***syn*** see ATTACK — **as·sault·er** *n* — **as·saul·tive** \-ˈsȯl-tiv\ *adj* — **as·saul·tive·ly** *adv* — **as·saul·tive·ness** *n*
assault boat *n* (1941) **:** a small portable boat used in an amphibious military attack or in land warfare for crossing rivers or lakes
[1]**as·say** \ˈas-ˌā, a-ˈsā\ *n* [ME, fr. OF *essai, assai* test, effort — more at ESSAY] (14c) **1** *archaic* **:** TRIAL, ATTEMPT **2 :** examination and determination as to characteristics (as weight, measure, or quality) **3 :** analysis (as of an ore or drug) to determine the presence, absence, or quantity of one or more components **4 :** a substance to be assayed; *also* **:** the tabulated result of assaying

[2]as·say \a-'sā, 'as-,ā\ *vt* (14c) **1 :** TRY, ATTEMPT **2 a :** to analyze (as an ore) for one or more specific components **b :** to judge the worth of **:** ESTIMATE ~ *vi* **:** to prove up in an assay — **as·say·er** *n*

-assed \'ast\ *adj or adv comb form* **:** [1]-ASS — often considered vulgar

as·se·gai *or* **as·sa·gai** \'as-i-,gī\ *n* [deriv. of Ar *az-zaghāya* the assegai, fr. *al-* the + *zaghāya* assegai] (1523) **:** a slender hardwood spear or light javelin usu. tipped with iron and used in southern Africa

as·sem·blage \ə-'sem-blij, *for 3 also* ,as-,äm-'bläzh\ *n* (1690) **1 :** a collection of persons or things **:** GATHERING **2 :** the act of assembling **:** the state of being assembled **3 a :** an artistic composition made from scraps, junk, and odds and ends (as of paper, cloth, wood, stone, or metal) **b :** the art of making assemblages

as·sem·blag·ist \-blij-əst, -'bläzh-əst\ *n* (1965) **:** an artist who specializes in assemblages

as·sem·ble \ə-'sem-bəl\ *vb* **as·sem·bled; as·sem·bling** \-b(ə-)liŋ\ [ME *assemblen,* fr. OF *assembler,* fr. (assumed) VL *assimulare,* fr. L *ad-* + *simul* together] *vt* (13c) **1 :** to bring together (as in a particular place or for a particular purpose) **2 :** to fit together the parts of ~ *vi* **:** to meet together **:** CONVENE ***syn*** see GATHER

as·sem·bler \-b(ə-)lər\ *n* (1635) **1 :** one that assembles **2 a :** a computer program that automatically converts instructions written in a symbolic code into the equivalent machine code **b :** ASSEMBLY LANGUAGE

as·sem·bly \ə-'sem-blē\ *n, pl* **-blies** [ME *assemblee,* fr. MF, fr. OF, fr. *assembler*] (14c) **1 :** a company of persons gathered for deliberation and legislation, worship, or entertainment **2** *cap* **:** a legislative body; *specif* **:** the lower house of a legislature **3 :** ASSEMBLAGE 1, 2 **4 :** a signal for troops to assemble or fall in **5 a :** the fitting together of manufactured parts into a complete machine, structure, or unit of a machine **b :** a collection of parts so assembled **6 :** the translation of symbolic code to machine code by an assembler

assembly language *n* (1964) **:** a symbolic language for programming a computer that is a close approximation of machine language

assembly line *n* (1914) **1 :** an arrangement of machines, equipment, and workers in which work passes from operation to operation in direct line until the product is assembled **2 :** a process for turning out a finished product in a mechanically efficient manner ⟨academic *assembly lines*⟩

as·sem·bly·man \ə-'sem-blē-mən\ *n* (1647) **:** a member of an assembly

Assembly of God (1914) **:** a congregation belonging to a Pentecostal body founded in the U.S. in 1914

as·sem·bly·wom·an \-,wu̇m-ən\ *n* (1969) **:** a female member of an assembly

[1]as·sent \ə-'sent, a-\ *vi* [ME *assenten,* fr. OF *assenter,* fr. L *assentari,* fr. *assentire,* fr. *ad-* + *sentire* to feel — more at SENSE] (13c) **:** to agree to something esp. after thoughtful consideration **:** CONCUR — **as·sen·tor** *or* **as·sent·er** \-'sent-ər\ *n*

syn ASSENT, CONSENT, ACCEDE, ACQUIESCE, AGREE, SUBSCRIBE mean to concur with what has been proposed. ASSENT implies an act involving the understanding or judgment and applies to propositions or opinions; CONSENT involves the will or feelings and indicates compliance with what is requested or desired; ACCEDE implies a yielding, often under pressure, of assent or consent; ACQUIESCE implies tacit acceptance or forbearance of opposition; AGREE sometimes implies previous difference of opinion or attempts at persuasion; SUBSCRIBE implies not only consent or assent but hearty approval and active support.

[2]assent *n* (14c) **:** an act of assenting **:** ACQUIESCENCE, AGREEMENT

as·sen·ta·tion \,as-ᵊn-'tā-shən, ,as-,en-\ *n* (15c) **:** ready assent esp. when insincere or obsequious

as·sert \ə-'sərt, a-\ *vt* [L *assertus,* pp. of *asserere,* fr. *ad-* + *serere* to join — more at SERIES] (1604) **1 :** to state or declare positively and often forcefully or aggressively **2 a :** to demonstrate the existence of ⟨~ his manhood —James Joyce⟩ **b :** POSIT, POSTULATE

syn ASSERT, DECLARE, AFFIRM, PROTEST, AVOW mean to state positively usu. in anticipation of denial or objection. ASSERT implies stating confidently without need for proof or regard for evidence; DECLARE stresses open or public statement; AFFIRM implies conviction based on evidence, experience, or faith; PROTEST emphasizes affirming in the face of denial or doubt; AVOW stresses frank declaration and acknowledgment of personal responsibility for what is declared. ***syn*** see in addition MAINTAIN

— **assert oneself :** to compel recognition esp. of one's rights

as·sert·ed·ly \ə-'sərt-əd-lē, a-\ *adv* (1937) **:** by positive and usu. unsubstantiated assertion **:** ALLEGEDLY

as·ser·tion \ə-'sər-shən, a-\ *n* (15c) **:** the act of asserting; *also* **:** DECLARATION, AFFIRMATION

as·ser·tive \ə-'sərt-iv, a-\ *adj* (1562) **1 :** disposed to or characterized by bold or confident assertion **2 :** having a strong or distinctive flavor or aroma ⟨~ wines⟩ ***syn*** see AGGRESSIVE — **as·ser·tive·ly** *adv* — **as·ser·tive·ness** *n*

asses *pl of* AS *or of* ASS

as·sess \ə-'ses, a-\ *vt* [ME *assessen,* prob. fr. ML *assessus,* pp. of *assidēre,* fr. L, to sit beside, assist in the office of a judge — more at ASSIZE] (15c) **1 :** to determine the rate or amount of (as a tax) **2 a :** to impose (as a tax) according to an established rate **b :** to subject to a tax, charge, or levy **3 :** to make an official valuation of (property) for the purposes of taxation **4 :** to determine the importance, size, or value of ***syn*** see ESTIMATE — **as·sess·able** \-'ses-ə-bəl\ *adj*

as·sess·ment \ə-'ses-mənt, a-\ *n* (1540) **1 :** the act or an instance of assessing **:** APPRAISAL **2 :** the amount assessed

as·ses·sor \ə-'ses-ər\ *n* (14c) **1 :** an official who assists a judge or magistrate **2 :** an official who assesses property for taxation

as·set \'as-,et *also* 'as-ət\ *n* [back-formation fr. *assets,* sing., sufficient property to pay debts and legacies, fr. AF *asetz,* fr. OF *assez* enough, fr. (assumed) VL *ad satis,* fr. L *ad* to + *satis* enough — more at AT, SAD] (1531) **1** *pl* **a :** the property of a deceased person subject by law to the payment of his debts and legacies **b :** the entire property of all sorts of a person, association, corporation, or estate applicable or subject to the payment of his or its debts **2 :** ADVANTAGE, RESOURCE ⟨his wit is his chief ~⟩ **3** *pl* **:** the items on a balance sheet showing the book value of property owned

as·sev·er·ate \ə-'sev-ə-,rāt\ *vt* **-at·ed; -at·ing** [L *asseveratus,* pp. of *asseverare,* fr. *ad-* + *severus* severe] (1791) **:** to affirm or aver positively or earnestly — **as·sev·er·a·tion** \-,sev-ə-'rā-shən\ *n* — **as·sev·er·a·tive** \-'sev-ə-,rāt-iv\ *adj*

ass·hole \'as-,(h)ōl\ *n* (14c) **1 :** ANUS — usu. considered vulgar **2 :** a stupid, incompetent, or detestable person — usu. considered vulgar

as·si·du·ity \,as-ə-'d(y)ü-ət-ē\ *n, pl* **-ities** (15c) **1 :** the quality or state of being assiduous **:** DILIGENCE **2 :** solicitous or obsequious attention to a person

as·sid·u·ous \ə-'sij-(ə-)wəs\ *adj* [L *assiduus,* fr. *assidēre*] (1538) **:** marked by careful unremitting attention or persistent application ⟨~ patrons of the opera⟩ ***syn*** see BUSY — **as·sid·u·ous·ly** *adv* — **as·sid·u·ous·ness** *n*

[1]as·sign \ə-'sīn\ *vt* [ME *assignen,* fr. OF *assigner,* fr. L *assignare,* fr. *ad-* + *signare* to mark, fr. *signum* mark, sign] (13c) **1 :** to transfer (property) to another esp. in trust or for the benefit of creditors **2 a :** to appoint to a post or duty **b :** PRESCRIBE ⟨~ the lesson⟩ **3 :** to fix or specify in correspondence or relationship ⟨~ counsel to the defendant⟩ ⟨~ a unique real number to each point⟩ **4 :** to ascribe with assurance esp. as motive or reason ***syn*** see ASCRIBE — **as·sign·abil·i·ty** \-,sī-nə-'bil-ət-ē\ *n* — **as·sign·able** \-'sī-nə-bəl\ *adj* — **as·sign·er** \ə-'sī-nər\ *or* **as·sign·or** \,as-ə-'nȯ(ə)r, ,as-,ī-, ə-,sī-\ *n*

[2]assign *n* (15c) **:** ASSIGNEE

as·si·gnat \,as-(,)ēn-'yä, 'as-ig-,nat\ *n* [F, fr. L *assignatus,* pp. of *assignare*] (1790) **:** a bill issued as currency by the French Revolutionary government (1789–96) on the security of expropriated lands

as·sig·na·tion \,as-ig-'nā-shən\ *n* (15c) **1 :** the act of assigning or the assignment made; *esp* **:** ALLOTMENT **2 :** TRYST ⟨returned from an ~ with his mistress —W. B. Yeats⟩

assigned risk *n* (1946) **:** a poor risk (as an accident-prone motorist) that insurance companies would normally reject but are forced to insure by state law

as·sign·ee \,as-ə-'nē, ,as-,ī-, ə-,sī-\ *n* (14c) **1 :** a person to whom an assignment is made **2 :** a person appointed to act for another **3 :** a person to whom a right or property is legally transferred

as·sign·ment \ə-'sīn-mənt\ *n* (14c) **1 :** the act of assigning **2 a :** a position, post, or office to which one is assigned **b :** a specified task or amount of work assigned or undertaken as if assigned by authority **3 :** the transfer of property; *esp* **:** the transfer of property to be held in trust or to be used for the benefit of creditors ***syn*** see TASK

as·sim·i·la·ble \ə-'sim-ə-lə-bəl\ *adj* (1667) **:** capable of being assimilated — **as·sim·i·la·bil·i·ty** \-,sim-ə-lə-'bil-ət-ē\ *n*

[1]as·sim·i·late \ə-'sim-ə-,lāt\ *vb* **-lat·ed; -lat·ing** [ML *assimilatus,* pp. of *assimilare,* fr. L *assimulare* to make similar, fr. *ad-* + *simulare* to make similar, simulate] *vt* (15c) **1 a :** to take in and appropriate as nourishment **:** absorb into the system **b :** to take into the mind and thoroughly comprehend **2 a :** to make similar **b :** to alter by assimilation **c :** to absorb into the cultural tradition of a population or group ⟨the community *assimilated* many immigrants⟩ **3 :** COMPARE, LIKEN ~ *vi* **:** to become assimilated ***syn*** see ABSORB — **as·sim·i·la·tor** \-,lāt-ər\ *n*

[2]as·sim·i·late \-lət, -,lāt\ *n* (1935) **:** something that is assimilated

as·sim·i·la·tion \ə-,sim-ə-'lā-shən\ *n* (15c) **1 a :** an act, process, or instance of assimilating **b :** the state of being assimilated **2 :** the incorporation or conversion of nutrients into protoplasm that in animals follows digestion and absorption and in higher plants involves both photosynthesis and root absorption **3 :** change of a sound in speech so that it becomes identical with or similar to a neighboring sound ⟨in the word *cupboard* the \p\ sound of the word *cup* has undergone complete ~⟩

as·sim·i·la·tion·ism \-shə-,niz-əm\ *n* (1952) **:** a policy of assimilating differing racial or cultural groups — **as·sim·i·la·tion·ist** \-sh(ə-)nəst\ *n or adj*

as·sim·i·la·tive \ə-'sim-ə-,lāt-iv, -lət-\ *adj* (14c) **:** of, relating to, or causing assimilation

as·sim·i·la·to·ry \ə-'sim-ə-lə-,tōr-ē, -,tȯr-\ *adj* (ca. 1847) **:** ASSIMILATIVE

As·sin·i·boin *or* **As·sin·i·boine** \ə-'sin-ə-,bȯin\ *n, pl* **-boin** *or* **-boins** *or* **-boine** *or* **-boines** [Ojibwa *ŭsini-ŭpwäwᵃ,* lit., one who cooks by use of stones] (1681) **:** a member of an American Indian people orig. of the area between the upper Missouri and middle Saskatchewan rivers

[1]as·sist \ə-'sist\ *vb* [MF or L; MF *assister* to help, stand by, fr. L *assistere,* fr. *ad-* + *sistere* to cause to stand; akin to L *stare* to stand — more at STAND] *vt* (15c) **:** to give usu. supplementary support or aid to ⟨~ a lame man up the stairs⟩ ~ *vi* **1 :** to give support or aid **2 :** to be present as a spectator ***syn*** see HELP

[2]assist *n* (1597) **1 :** an act of assistance **:** AID **2 :** the action of a player who by passing a ball or puck enables a teammate to make a putout or score a goal; *also* **:** official credit given for such an action **3 :** a mechanical device that provides assistance

as·sis·tance \ə-'sis-tən(t)s\ *n* (14c) **:** the act of assisting or the help supplied **:** AID ⟨financial and technical ~⟩

as·sis·tant \-tənt\ *n* (15c) **:** one who assists **:** HELPER; *also* **:** an auxiliary device or substance — **assistant** *adj*

assistant professor *n* (1851) **:** a member of a college or university faculty who ranks above an instructor and below an associate professor — **assistant professorship** *n*

as·sis·tant·ship \ə-'sis-tən(t)-,ship\ *n* (1948) **:** a paid appointment awarded annually to a qualified graduate student that requires part-time teaching, research, or residence hall duties

as·size \ə-'sīz\ *n* [ME *assise,* fr. OF, session, settlement, fr. *asseoir* to seat, fr. (assumed) VL *assedēre,* fr. L *assidēre* to sit beside, assist in the office of a judge, fr. *ad-* + *sedēre* to sit — more at SIT] (14c) **1 :** an enactment made by a legislative assembly **:** ORDINANCE **2 a :** a statute regulating weights and measures of articles sold in the market **b :** the regulation of the price of bread or ale by the price of grain **3 :** a fixed or customary standard **4 a :** a judicial inquest **b :** an action to be decided by such an inquest, the writ for instituting it, or the verdict or finding rendered by the jury **5 a :** the former periodical sessions of the superior courts in English counties for trial of civil and criminal cases — usu. used in pl. **b :** the time or place of holding such a court, the court itself, or a session of it — usu. used in pl.

\ə\ **abut** \ᵊ\ **kitten,** F **table** \ər\ **further** \a\ **ash** \ā\ **ace** \ä\ **cot, cart**
\au̇\ **out** \ch\ **chin** \e\ **bet** \ē\ **easy** \g\ **go** \i\ **hit** \ī\ **ice** \j\ **job**
\ŋ\ **sing** \ō\ **go** \ȯ\ **law** \ȯi\ **boy** \th\ **thin** \t͟h\ **the** \ü\ **loot** \u̇\ **foot**
\y\ **yet** \zh\ **vision** \à, k̟, ⁿ, œ, ǣ, ue, ue̅, ʸ\ *see* Guide to Pronunciation

as·so·cia·ble \ə-ˈsō-sh(ē-)ə-bəl, -sē-ə-\ *adj* (1855) **:** capable of being associated, joined, or connected in thought

¹as·so·ci·ate \ə-ˈsō-s(h)ē-ˌāt\ *vb* **-at·ed; -at·ing** [ME *associat* associated, fr. L *associatus*, pp. of *associare* to unite, fr. *ad-* + *sociare* to join, fr. *socius* companion — more at SOCIAL] *vt* (14c) **1 :** to join as a partner, friend, or companion **2** *obs* **:** to keep company with **:** ATTEND **3 :** to join or connect together **:** COMBINE; *specif* **:** to subject to chemical association **4 :** to bring together or into relationship in any of various intangible ways (as in memory or imagination) ~ *vi* **1 :** to come or be together as partners, friends, or companions **2 :** to combine or join with other parts **:** UNITE ***syn*** see JOIN

²as·so·ciate \ə-ˈsō-s(h)ē-ət, -shət, -s(h)ē-ˌāt\ *adj* (14c) **1 :** closely connected (as in function or office) with another **2 :** closely related esp. in the mind **3 :** having secondary or subordinate status ⟨~ membership in a society⟩

³as·so·ciate *like* ²\ *n* (1533) **1 :** one associated with another: as **a :** PARTNER, COLLEAGUE **b :** COMPANION, COMRADE **2** *often cap* **:** a degree conferred esp. by a junior college ⟨~ in arts⟩ — **as·so·ciate·ship** \-ˌship\ *n*

associate professor *n* (1822) **:** a member of a college or university faculty who ranks above an assistant professor and below a professor — **associate professorship** *n*

as·so·ci·a·tion \ə-ˌsō-sē-ˈā-shən, -shē-\ *n* (1535) **1 a :** the act of associating **b :** the state of being associated **:** COMBINATION, RELATIONSHIP **2 :** an organization of persons having a common interest **:** SOCIETY **3 :** something linked in memory or imagination with a thing or person **4 :** the process of forming mental connections or bonds between sensations, ideas, or memories **5 :** the aggregation of chemical species to form (as with hydrogen bonds) loosely bound complexes **6 :** a major unit in ecological community organization characterized by essential uniformity and usu. by two or more dominant species — **as·so·ci·a·tion·al** \-shnəl, -shən-ᵊl\ *adj*

association area *n* (ca. 1909) **:** an area of the cerebral cortex that functions in linking and coordinating the sensory and motor areas

association football *n* (1873) **:** SOCCER

as·so·ci·a·tion·ism \ə-ˌsō-sē-ˈā-shə-ˌniz-əm, -ˌsō-shē-\ *n* (1875) **:** a reductionist school of psychology that holds that the content of consciousness can be explained by the association and reassociation of irreducible sensory and perceptual elements — **as·so·ci·a·tion·ist** \-ˈā-sh(ə-)nəst\ *n* — **as·so·ci·a·tion·is·tic** \-ˌā-shə-ˈnis-tik\ *adj*

as·so·cia·tive \ə-ˈsō-s(h)ē-ˌāt-iv, -shət-iv\ *adj* (1812) **1 :** of or relating to association esp. of ideas or images **2 :** dependent on or acquired by association or learning **3 :** combining elements such that when the order of the elements is preserved the result is independent of the grouping ⟨addition is ~ since $(a + b) + c = a + (b + c)$⟩ — **as·so·cia·tive·ly** *adv* — **as·so·cia·tiv·i·ty** \-ˌsō-s(h)ē-ə-ˈtiv-ət-ē, -shə-ˈtiv-\ *n*

associative learning *n* (1957) **:** a learning process in which discrete ideas and percepts become linked to one another

associative neuron *n* (1935) **:** a neuron that conveys impulses from one neuron to another

as·soil \ə-ˈsȯi(ə)l\ *vt* [ME *assoilen*, fr. OF *assoldre*, fr. L *absolvere* to absolve] (13c) **1** *archaic* **:** ABSOLVE, PARDON **2** *archaic* **:** ACQUIT, CLEAR **3** *archaic* **:** EXPIATE — **as·soil·ment** \-mənt\ *n, archaic*

as·so·nance \ˈas-ə-nən(t)s\ *n* [F, fr. L *assonare* to answer with the same sound, fr. *ad-* + *sonare* to sound — more at SOUND] (1727) **1 :** resemblance of sound in words or syllables **2 a :** relatively close juxtaposition of similar sounds esp. of vowels **b :** repetition of vowels without repetition of consonants (as in *stony* and *holy*) used as an alternative to rhyme in verse — **as·so·nant** \-nənt\ *adj or n*

as soon as *conj* (14c) **:** immediately at or just after the time that

as·sort \ə-ˈsȯ(ə)rt\ *vb* [MF *assortir*, fr. *a-* (fr. L *ad-*) + *sorte* sort] *vt* (15c) **1 :** to distribute into groups of a like kind **:** CLASSIFY **2 :** to supply with an assortment (as of goods) ~ *vi* **1 :** to agree in kind **:** HARMONIZE **2 :** to keep company **:** ASSOCIATE — **as·sort·er** *n*

as·sor·ta·tive \ə-ˈsȯrt-ət-iv\ *adj* (1897) **:** being nonrandom mating based on like or unlike characteristics

as·sort·ed \-ˈsȯrt-əd\ *adj* (ca. 1797) **1 :** suited by nature, character, or design ⟨an ill-*assorted* pair⟩ **2 :** consisting of various kinds

as·sort·ment \-ˈsȯ(ə)rt-mənt\ *n* (ca. 1611) **1 a :** the act of assorting **b :** the state of being assorted **2 :** a collection of assorted things or persons

as·suage \ə-ˈswāj *also* -ˈswāzh *or* -ˈswäzh\ *vt* **as·suaged; as·suag·ing** [ME *aswagen*, fr. OF *assouagier*, fr. (assumed) VL *assuaviare*, fr. L *ad-* + *suavis* sweet — more at SWEET] (14c) **1 :** to lessen the intensity of (something that pains or distresses) **:** EASE **2 :** PACIFY, QUIET **3 :** to put an end to by satisfying **:** APPEASE, QUENCH ⟨he *assuaged* his hunger with a sandwich⟩ ***syn*** see RELIEVE — **as·suage·ment** \-mənt\ *n*

as·sua·sive \ə-ˈswā-siv, -ziv\ *adj* (1708) **:** SOOTHING, CALMING

as·sume \ə-ˈsüm\ *vt* **as·sumed; as·sum·ing** [ME *assumen*, fr. L *assumere*, fr. *ad-* + *sumere* to take — more at CONSUME] (15c) **1 a :** to take up or in **:** RECEIVE **b :** to take into partnership, employment, or use **2 a :** to take to or upon oneself **:** UNDERTAKE **b :** PUT ON, DON **3 :** SEIZE, USURP **4 :** to pretend to have or be **:** FEIGN ⟨*assumed* an air of confidence in spite of her dismay⟩ **5 :** to take as granted or true **:** SUPPOSE **6 :** to take over (the debts of another) as one's own — **as·sum·abil·i·ty** \-ˌsü-mə-ˈbil-ət-ē\ *n* — **as·sum·able** \-ˈsü-mə-bəl\ *adj* — **as·sum·ably** \-blē\ *adv*

syn ASSUME, AFFECT, PRETEND, SIMULATE, FEIGN, COUNTERFEIT, SHAM mean to put on a false or deceptive appearance. ASSUME often implies a justifiable motive rather than an intent to deceive; AFFECT implies making a false show of possessing, using, or feeling; PRETEND implies an overt and sustained false appearance; SIMULATE suggests a close imitation of the appearance of something; FEIGN implies more artful invention than PRETEND, less specific mimicry than SIMULATE; COUNTERFEIT implies achieving the highest degree of verisimilitude of any of these words; SHAM implies an obvious falseness that fools only the gullible.

as·sum·ing *adj* (1695) **:** PRETENTIOUS, PRESUMPTUOUS

as·sump·sit \ə-ˈsəm(p)-sət\ *n* [NL, he undertook, fr. L *assumere* to undertake] (1590) **1 a :** a common-law action alleging damage from a breach of agreement **b :** an action to recover damages for breach of contract or promise **2 :** a promise or contract not under seal on which an action of assumpsit may be brought

as·sump·tion \ə-ˈsəm(p)-shən\ *n* [ME, fr. LL *assumption-*, *assumptio* taking up, fr. L *assumptus*, pp. of *assumere*] (13c) **1 a :** the taking up of a person into heaven **b** *cap* **:** August 15 observed in commemoration of the Assumption of the Virgin Mary **2 :** a taking to or upon oneself ⟨a delay in the ~ of his new position⟩ **3 :** the act of laying claim to or taking possession of something ⟨the ~ of power⟩ **4 :** ARROGANCE, PRETENSION **5 a :** the supposition that something is true **b :** a fact or statement (as a proposition, axiom, postulate, or notion) taken for granted **6 :** the taking over of another's debts

as·sump·tive \ə-ˈsəm(p)-tiv\ *adj* (1611) **1 :** taken as one's own **2 :** taken for granted ⟨~ beliefs⟩ **3 :** making undue claims **:** ASSUMING ⟨an ~ person⟩

as·sur·ance \ə-ˈshu̇r-ən(t)s\ *n* (14c) **1 :** the act or action of assuring: as **a :** PLEDGE, GUARANTEE **b :** the act of conveying real property; *also* **:** the instrument by which it is conveyed **c** *chiefly Brit* **:** INSURANCE **2 :** the state of being assured: as **a :** SECURITY **b :** a being certain in the mind ⟨the puritan's ~ of salvation⟩ **c :** confidence of mind or manner **:** easy freedom from self-doubt or uncertainty; *also* **:** excessive self-confidence **:** BRASHNESS, PRESUMPTION **3 :** something that inspires or tends to inspire confidence ⟨gave repeated ~*s* of his goodwill⟩ ***syn*** see CERTAINTY, CONFIDENCE

as·sure \ə-ˈshu̇(ə)r\ *vt* **as·sured; as·sur·ing** [ME *assuren*, fr. MF *assurer*, fr. ML *assecurare*, fr. L *ad-* + *securus* secure] (14c) **1 :** to make safe (as from risks or against overthrow) **:** INSURE **2 :** to give confidence to **:** REASSURE **3 :** to make sure or certain **:** CONVINCE **4 :** to inform positively ⟨*assured* her of his fidelity⟩ **5 :** to make certain the coming or attainment of **:** GUARANTEE ⟨worked hard to ~ accuracy⟩ ***syn*** see ENSURE

¹as·sured \ə-ˈshu̇(ə)rd\ *adj* (15c) **1 :** characterized by certainty or security **:** GUARANTEED ⟨an ~ market⟩ **2 a :** SELF-ASSURED ⟨an ~ dancer⟩ **b :** SELF-SATISFIED, COMPLACENT **3 :** satisfied as to the certainty or truth of a matter **:** CONVINCED — **as·sured·ly** \-ˈshu̇r-əd-lē, -ˈshu̇(ə)rd-\ *adv* — **as·sured·ness** \-ˈshu̇r-əd-nəs, -ˈshu̇(ə)rd-\ *n*

²assured *n, pl* **assured** *or* **assureds** (1755) **:** INSURED

as·sur·er \ə-ˈshu̇r-ər\ *or* **as·sur·or** \ə-ˈshu̇r-ər, ə-ˌshu̇r-ˈȯ(ə)r\ *n* (1607) **:** one that assures **:** INSURER

as·sur·gent \ə-ˈsər-jənt\ *adj* [L *assurgent-*, *assurgens*, prp. of *assurgere* to rise, fr. *ad-* + *surgere* to rise — more at SURGE] (1578) **:** moving upward **:** RISING; *esp* **:** ASCENDANT 1b

As·syr·i·an \ə-ˈsir-ē-ən\ *n* (1604) **1 :** a member of an ancient Semitic race forming the Assyrian nation **2 :** the Semitic language of the Assyrians — **Assyrian** *adj*

As·syr·i·ol·o·gist \ə-ˌsir-ē-ˈäl-ə-jəst\ *n* (1865) **:** a specialist in Assyriology

As·syr·i·ol·o·gy \-jē\ *n* (1828) **:** the science or study of the history, language, and antiquities of ancient Assyria and Babylonia — **As·syr·i·o·log·i·cal** \-ˌsir-ē-ə-ˈläj-i-kəl\ *adj*

-ast \ˌast, əst\ *n suffix* [ME, fr. L *-astes*, fr. Gk *-astēs*, fr. verbs in *-azein*] **:** one connected with ⟨ecdysi*ast*⟩

astar·board \ə-ˈstär-bərd\ *adv* (1627) **:** toward or on the starboard side of a ship ⟨put the helm hard ~⟩

As·tar·te \ə-ˈstärt-ē\ *n* [L, fr. Gk *Astartē*] **:** the Phoenician goddess of fertility and of sexual love

astat·ic \(ˈ)ā-ˈstat-ik\ *adj* (1827) **1 :** not static **:** not stable or steady **2 :** having little or no tendency to take a fixed or definite position or direction — **astat·i·cal·ly** \-i-k(ə-)lē\ *adv* — **astat·i·cism** \-ˈstat-ə-ˌsiz-əm\ *n*

as·ta·tine \ˈas-tə-ˌtēn\ *n* [Gk *astatos* unsteady, fr. *a-* + *statos* standing, fr. *histanai* to cause to stand — more at STAND] (1947) **:** a radioactive halogen element discovered by bombarding bismuth with helium nuclei and also formed by radioactive decay — see ELEMENT table

as·ter \ˈas-tər\ *n* (1664) **1** [NL, fr. L, aster, fr. Gk *aster-*, *astēr* star, aster — more at STAR] **a :** any of various chiefly fall-blooming leafy-stemmed composite herbs (*Aster* and closely related genera) with often showy heads containing tubular flowers or both tubular and ray flowers **b :** CHINA ASTER **2** [NL, fr. Gk *aster-*, *astēr*] **:** a system of gelated cytoplasmic rays arranged radially about a centrosome at either end of the mitotic or meiotic spindle

-as·ter \ˌas-tər, ˈas-\ *n suffix* [ME, fr. L, suffix denoting partial resemblance] **:** one that is inferior or not genuine ⟨critic*aster*⟩

as·te·ria \a-ˈstir-ē-ə\ *n* [L, a precious stone, fr. Gk, fem. of *asterios* starry, fr. *aster-*, *astēr*] (1903) **:** a gemstone cut to show asterism

as·te·ri·at·ed \-ē-ˌāt-əd\ *adj* [Gk *asterios*] (1816) **:** exhibiting asterism ⟨~ sapphire⟩

¹as·ter·isk \ˈas-tə-ˌrisk\ *n* [ME, fr. LL *asteriscus*, fr. Gk *asteriskos*, lit., little star, dim. of *aster-*, *astēr*] (14c) **:** the character * used in printing or writing as a reference mark, as an indication of the omission of letters or words, or to denote a hypothetical or unattested linguistic form — **as·ter·isk·less** \-ləs\ *adj*

²asterisk *vt* (ca. 1733) **:** to mark with an asterisk **:** STAR

as·ter·ism \ˈas-tə-ˌriz-əm\ *n* [Gk *asterismos*, fr. *asterizein* to arrange in constellations, fr. *aster-*, *astēr*] (1598) **1 a :** CONSTELLATION **b :** a small group of stars **2 :** a star-shaped figure exhibited by some crystals by reflected light (as in a star sapphire) or by transmitted light (as in some mica)

astern \ə-ˈstərn\ *adv or adj* (1627) **1 :** behind a ship **2 :** at or toward the stern of a ship **3 :** STERNFOREMOST, BACKWARD

¹as·ter·oid \ˈas-tə-ˌrȯid\ *n* [Gk *asteroeidēs* starlike, fr. *aster-*, *astēr*] (1802) **1 :** one of thousands of small planets between Mars and Jupiter with diameters from a fraction of a mile to nearly 500 miles **2 :** STARFISH — **as·ter·oi·dal** \ˌas-tə-ˈrȯid-ᵊl\ *adj*

²asteroid *adj* (1854) **1 :** resembling a star **2 :** of or resembling a starfish

aster yellows *n pl* (1922) **:** a widespread virus disease that affects more than 40 families of plants, is characterized esp. by yellowing and dwarfing, and is transmitted by leafhoppers

as·the·nia \as-ˈthē-nē-ə\ *n* [NL, fr. Gk *astheneia*, fr. *asthenēs* weak, fr. *a-* + *sthenos* strength] (1802) **:** lack or loss of strength **:** DEBILITY

as·then·ic \as-ˈthen-ik\ *adj* (1789) **1 :** of, relating to, or exhibiting asthenia **:** WEAK **2 :** ECTOMORPHIC 2

as·theno·sphere \as-ˈthen-ə-ˌsfi(ə)r\ *n* [Gk *asthenēs* weak + E *-o-* + *sphere*] (1914) **:** a hypothetical zone of the earth which lies beneath the lithosphere and within which the material is believed to yield readily to persistent stresses

asth·ma \ˈaz-mə, *Brit* ˈas-\ *n* [ME *asma*, fr. ML, modif. of Gk *asthma;* akin to L *anima* — more at ANIMATE] (14c) **:** a condition often of allergic origin that is marked by continuous or paroxysmal labored breathing accompanied by wheezing, by a sense of constriction in the chest, and often by attacks of coughing or gasping — **asth·mat·ic** \az-ˈmat-ik, *Brit* as-\ *adj or n* — **asth·mat·i·cal·ly** \-i-k(ə-)lē\ *adv*

as though *conj* (13c) **:** AS IF

as·tig·mat·ic \ˌas-tig-ˈmat-ik\ *adj* [*a-* + Gk *stigmat-, stigma* mark] (1849) **1 :** affected with, relating to, or correcting astigmatism **2 :** showing incapacity for observation or discrimination ⟨an ~ fanaticism, a disregard for the facts—*N. Y. Herald Tribune*⟩ — **astigmatic** *n*

astig·ma·tism \ə-ˈstig-mə-ˌtiz-əm\ *n* (1849) **1 :** a defect of an optical system (as a lens) in consequence of which rays from a point fail to meet in a focal point resulting in a blurred and imperfect image **2 :** a defect of vision due to astigmatism of the refractive system of the eye and esp. to corneal irregularity **3 :** distorted understanding suggestive of the blurred vision of an astigmatic person

astir \ə-ˈstər\ *adj* (1823) **1 :** exhibiting activity **2 :** being out of bed **:** UP

as to *prep* (14c) **1 :** AS FOR, ABOUT ⟨at a loss *as to* how to explain the error⟩ **2 :** ACCORDING TO, BY ⟨graded *as to* size and color⟩

as·ton·ied \ə-ˈstän-ēd\ *adj* [ME, fr. pp. of *astonien*] (14c) **1** *archaic* **:** deprived briefly of the power to act **:** DAZED **2** *archaic* **:** filled with consternation or dismay

as·ton·ish \ə-ˈstän-ish\ *vt* [prob. fr. earlier *astony* (fr. ME *astonen, astonien*, fr. OF *estoner*, fr. — assumed — VL *extonare*, fr. L *ex-* + *tonare* to thunder) + *-ish* (as in *abolish*) — more at THUNDER] (1535) **1** *obs* **:** to strike with sudden fear **2 :** to strike with sudden and usu. great wonder or surprise ***syn*** see SURPRISE

as·ton·ish·ing \-iŋ\ *adj* (1612) **:** causing astonishment **:** SURPRISING — **as·ton·ish·ing·ly** \-iŋ-lē\ *adv*

as·ton·ish·ment \ə-ˈstän-ish-mənt\ *n* (1586) **1 a :** the state of being astonished **b :** CONSTERNATION **c :** AMAZEMENT **2 :** a cause of amazement or wonder

1**as·tound** \ə-ˈstau̇nd\ *adj* [ME *astoned*, fr. pp. of *astonen*] *archaic* (14c) **:** overwhelmed with astonishment or amazement **:** ASTOUNDED

2**astound** *vt* (14c) **:** to fill with bewilderment or wonder ***syn*** see SURPRISE

as·tound·ing \ə-ˈstau̇n-diŋ\ *adj* (1586) **:** causing astonishment or amazement — **as·tound·ing·ly** \-diŋ-lē\ *adv*

astr- *or* **astro-** *comb form* [ME *astro-*, fr. OF, fr. L *astr-, astro-*, fr. Gk, fr. *astron* — more at STAR] **:** star **:** heavens **:** outer space **:** astronomical ⟨*astro*physics⟩

1**astrad·dle** \ə-ˈstrad-ᵊl\ *adv* (1703) **:** on or above and extending onto both sides **:** ASTRIDE

2**astraddle** *prep* (1935) **:** with one leg on each side of **:** ASTRIDE

as·tra·gal \ˈas-tri-gəl\ *n* [L *astragalus*, fr. Gk *astragalos* anklebone, molding] (1563) **1 :** a narrow half-round molding **2 :** a projecting strip on the edge of a folding door

as·trag·a·lus \ə-ˈstrag-ə-ləs\ *n, pl* **-li** \-ˌlī, -ˌlē\ [NL, fr. Gk *astragalos;* akin to Gk *osteon* — more at OSSEOUS] (1541) **:** one of the proximal bones of the tarsus of the higher vertebrates — compare TALUS 1

as·tra·khan *or* **as·tra·chan** \ˈas-trə-kən, -ˌkan\ *n, often cap* [*Astrakhan*, U.S.S.R.] (1766) **1 :** karakul of Russian origin **2 :** a cloth with a usu. wool, curled, and looped pile resembling karakul

as·tral \ˈas-trəl\ *adj* [LL *astralis*, fr. L *astrum* star, fr. Gk *astron* — more at STAR] (1605) **1 a :** of or relating to the stars **b :** consisting of stars **:** STARRY **2 :** of or relating to a mitotic or meiotic aster **3 :** of or consisting of a supersensible substance held in theosophy to be next above the tangible world in refinement **4 a :** VISIONARY **b :** elevated in station or position **:** EXALTED — **as·tral·ly** \-trə-lē\ *adv*

astray \ə-ˈstrā\ *adv or adj* [ME, fr. MF *estraié* wandering, fr. *estraier* to stray — more at STRAY] (14c) **1 :** off the right path or route **:** STRAYING **2 :** in error **:** away from what is proper or desirable

1**astride** \ə-ˈstrīd\ *adv* (1664) **1 :** with one leg on each side ⟨rode her horse ~⟩ **2 :** with the legs stretched wide apart ⟨standing ~⟩

2**astride** *prep* (1713) **1 :** on or above and with one leg on each side of **2 :** placed or lying on both sides of **3 :** extending over or across **:** SPANNING, BRIDGING

1**as·trin·gent** \ə-ˈstrin-jənt\ *adj* [prob. fr. MF, fr. L *astringent-, astringens*, prp. of *astringere* to bind fast, fr. *ad-* + *stringere* to bind tight — more at STRAIN] (1541) **1 :** able to draw together the soft organic tissues **:** STYPTIC, PUCKERY ⟨~ lotions⟩ ⟨an ~ fruit⟩ **2 :** suggestive of an astringent effect upon tissue **:** rigidly severe **:** AUSTERE ⟨dry ~ comments⟩; *also* **:** PUNGENT — **as·trin·gen·cy** \-jən-sē\ *n* — **as·trin·gent·ly** *adv*

2**astringent** *n* (1626) **:** an astringent agent or substance

as·tro·bi·ol·o·gy \ˌas-trō-(ˌ)bī-ˈäl-ə-jē\ *n* (1955) **:** EXOBIOLOGY — **as·tro·bi·o·log·i·cal** \-ˌbī-ə-ˈläj-i-kəl\ *adj* — **as·tro·bi·ol·o·gist** \-(ˌ)bī-ˈäl-ə-jəst\ *n*

as·tro·cyte \ˈas-trə-ˌsīt\ *n* [ISV] (1898) **:** a star-shaped cell (as of the neuroglia) — **as·tro·cyt·ic** \ˌas-trə-ˈsit-ik\ *adj*

as·tro·cy·to·ma \ˌas-trə-sī-ˈtō-mə\ *n, pl* **-mas** *or* **-ma·ta** \-mət-ə\ [NL] (ca. 1923) **:** a nerve-tissue tumor composed of astrocytes

as·tro·dome \ˈas-trə-ˌdōm\ *n* [ISV] (1941) **:** a transparent dome in the upper surface of an airplane from within which the navigator makes celestial observations

as·tro·labe \ˈas-trə-ˌlāb *also* -ˌlab\ *n* [ME, fr. MF & ML; MF, fr. ML *astrolabium*, fr. LGk *astrolabion*, dim. of Gk *astrolabos*, fr. *astr-* + *lambanein* to take — more at LATCH] (14c) **:** a compact instrument used to observe and calculate the position of celestial bodies before the invention of the sextant

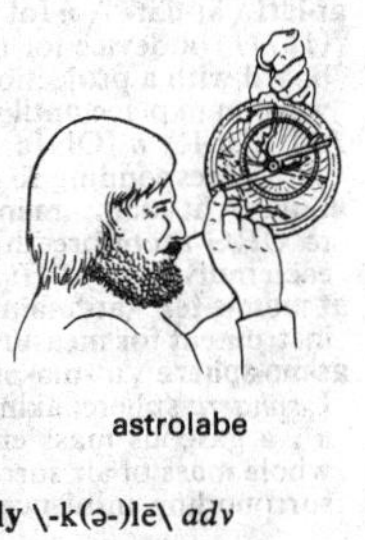
astrolabe

as·trol·o·ger \ə-ˈsträl-ə-jər\ *n* (14c) **:** one who practices astrology

as·trol·o·gy \ə-ˈsträl-ə-jē\ *n* [ME *astrologie*, fr. MF, fr. L *astrologia*, fr. Gk, fr. *astr-* + *-logia* -logy] (14c) **1** *obs* **:** ASTRONOMY **2 :** the divination of the supposed influences of the stars and planets on human affairs and terrestrial events by their positions and aspects — **as·tro·log·i·cal** \ˌas-trə-ˈläj-i-kəl\ *adj* — **as·tro·log·i·cal·ly** \-k(ə-)lē\ *adv*

as·tro·naut \ˈas-trə-ˌnȯt, -ˌnät\ *n* [*astr-* + *-naut* (as in *aeronaut*)] (1929) **:** a person who travels beyond the earth's atmosphere; *also* **:** a trainee for spaceflight

as·tro·nau·tics \ˌas-trə-ˈnȯt-iks, -ˈnät-\ *n pl but sing or pl in constr* (1928) **1 :** the science of the construction and operation of vehicles for travel in space beyond the earth's atmosphere **2 :** navigation in space beyond the earth's atmosphere — **as·tro·nau·tic** \-ik\ *or* **as·tro·nau·ti·cal** \-i-kəl\ *adj* — **as·tro·nau·ti·cal·ly** \-i-k(ə-)lē\ *adv*

as·tro·nav·i·ga·tion \ˌas-trō-ˌnav-ə-ˈgā-shən\ *n* (1942) **:** CELESTIAL NAVIGATION

as·tron·o·mer \ə-ˈsträn-ə-mər\ *n* (14c) **:** one who is skilled in astronomy or who makes observations of celestial phenomena

as·tro·nom·i·cal \ˌas-trə-ˈnäm-i-kəl\ *also* **as·tro·nom·ic** \-ik\ *adj* (1556) **1 :** of or relating to astronomy **2 :** enormously or inconceivably large ⟨~ numbers⟩ — **as·tro·nom·i·cal·ly** \-i-k(ə-)lē\ *adv*

astronomical unit *n* (1903) **:** a unit of length used in astronomy equal to the mean distance of the earth from the sun or about 93 million miles (150 million kilometers)

as·tron·o·my \ə-ˈsträn-ə-mē\ *n, pl* **-mies** [ME *astronomie*, fr. OF, fr. L *astronomia*, fr. Gk, fr. *astr-* + *-nomia* -nomy] (13c) **1 :** the science of the celestial bodies and of their magnitudes, motions, and constitution **2 :** a treatise on astronomy

as·tro·pho·tog·ra·phy \ˌas-(ˌ)trō-fə-ˈtäg-rə-fē\ *n* [ISV] (ca. 1858) **:** photography as used in astronomical investigations

as·tro·phys·ics \ˌas-trə-ˈfiz-iks\ *n pl but sing or pl in constr* [ISV] (1890) **:** a branch of astronomy dealing with the physical and chemical constitution of celestial matter — **as·tro·phys·i·cal** \-i-kəl\ *adj* — **as·tro·phys·i·cist** \-ˈfiz-(ə-)səst\ *n*

as·tute \ə-ˈst(y)üt, a-\ *adj* [L *astutus*, fr. *astus* craft] (ca. 1611) **:** having or showing shrewdness and perspicacity ⟨an ~ observer⟩ ⟨~ remarks⟩; *also* **:** CRAFTY, WILY ***syn*** see SHREWD — **as·tute·ly** *adv* — **as·tute·ness** *n*

As·ty·a·nax \ə-ˈstī-ə-ˌnaks\ *n* [Gk] **:** a son of Hector and Andromache hurled by the Greeks from the walls of Troy

asun·der \ə-ˈsən-dər\ *adv or adj* (14c) **1 :** into parts ⟨torn ~⟩ **2 :** apart from each other in position ⟨wide ~⟩

aswarm \ə-ˈswȯ(ə)rm\ *adj* (1868) **:** filled to overflowing **:** SWARMING ⟨streets ~ with people⟩

1**as well as** *conj* (14c) **:** and in addition **:** AND ⟨brave *as well as* loyal⟩

2**as well as** *prep* (15c) **:** in addition to **:** BESIDES ⟨the coach, *as well as* the team, is ready⟩

aswirl \ə-ˈswər(-ə)l\ *adj* (1877) **:** being in a swirl **:** SWIRLING

aswoon \ə-ˈswün\ *adj* (14c) **:** being in a swoon **:** DAZED

asy·lum \ə-ˈsī-ləm\ *n* [ME, fr. L, fr. Gk *asylon*, neut. of *asylos* inviolable, fr. *a-* + *sylon* right of seizure] (14c) **1 :** an inviolable place of refuge and protection giving shelter to criminals and debtors **:** SANCTUARY **2 :** a place of retreat and security **:** SHELTER **3 a :** the protection or inviolability afforded by an asylum **:** REFUGE **b :** protection from arrest and extradition given esp. to political refugees by a nation or by an embassy or other agency enjoying diplomatic immunity **4 :** an institution for the relief or care of the destitute or afflicted and esp. the insane

asym·met·ri·cal \ˌā-sə-ˈme-tri-kəl\ *or* **asym·met·ric** \-trik\ *adj* [Gk *asymmetria* lack of proportion, fr. *asymmetros* ill-proportioned, fr. *a-* + *symmetros* symmetrical] (1690) **1 :** not symmetrical **2 :** characterized by being bonded to different atoms or groups — **asym·met·ri·cal·ly** \-tri-k(ə-)lē\ *adv* — **asym·me·try** \(ˈ)ā-ˈsim-ə-trē\ *n*

asymp·tom·at·ic \ˌā-ˌsim(p)-tə-ˈmat-ik\ *adj* (1927) **:** presenting no symptoms of disease — **asymp·tom·at·i·cal·ly** \-i-k(ə-)lē\ *adv*

as·ymp·tote \ˈas-əm(p)-ˌtōt\ *n* [prob. fr. (assumed) NL *asymptotus*, fr. Gk *asymptōtos* not meeting, fr. *a-* + *sympiptein* to meet — more at SYMPTOM] (1656) **:** a straight line associated with a curve such that as a point moves along an infinite branch of the curve the distance from the point to the line approaches zero and the slope of the curve at the point approaches the slope of the line — **as·ymp·tot·ic** \ˌas-əm(p)-ˈtät-ik\ *adj* — **as·ymp·tot·i·cal·ly** \-i-k(ə-)lē\ *adv*

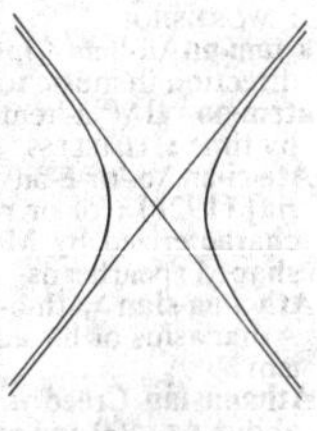
asymptotes to the hyperbola

asyn·ap·sis \ˌā-sə-ˈnap-səs\ *n, pl* **-ap·ses** \-ˌsēz\ [NL 2*a-* + *synapsis*] (1930) **:** failure of pairing of homologous chromosomes in meiosis

asyn·chro·nous \(ˈ)ā-ˈsiŋ-krə-nəs, -ˈsin-\ *adj* (1748) **:** not synchronous — **asyn·chro·nous·ly** *adv*

asyn·chro·ny \-krə-nē\ *or* **asyn·chro·nism** \-krə-ˌniz-əm\ *n* (1875) **:** the quality or state of being asynchronous **:** absence or lack of concurrence in time

as·yn·det·ic \ˌas-ᵊn-ˈdet-ik\ *adj* (ca. 1864) **:** marked by asyndeton — **as·yn·det·i·cal·ly** \-i-k(ə-)lē\ *adv*

asyn·de·ton \ə-ˈsin-də-ˌtän, (ˈ)ā-ˈsin-\ *n, pl* **-tons** *or* **-ta** \-dət-ə\ [LL, fr. Gk, fr. neut. of *asyndetos* unconnected, fr. *a-* + *syndetos* bound together, fr. *syndein* to bind together, fr. *syn-* + *dein* to bind — more at DIADEM] (1589) **:** omission of the conjunctions that ordinarily join coordinate words or clauses (as in "I came, I saw, I conquered")

1**at** \ət, (ˈ)at\ *prep* [ME, fr. OE *æt;* akin to OHG *az* at, L *ad*] (bef. 12c) **1 —** used as a function word to indicate presence or occurrence in, on, or near ⟨staying ~ a hotel⟩ ⟨~ a party⟩ ⟨sick ~ heart⟩ **2 —** used as a function word to indicate the goal of an indicated or implied action or motion ⟨aim ~ the target⟩ ⟨creditors are ~ him again⟩ **3 —** used as a function word to indicate that with which one is occupied or employed ⟨~ work⟩ ⟨~ the controls⟩ ⟨good ~ chess⟩ **4 —** used as a function word to indicate situation in an active or passive state or condition ⟨~ liberty⟩ ⟨~ rest⟩ **5 —** used as a function word to indicate the means, cause, or manner ⟨sold ~ auction⟩ ⟨laughed ~ his joke⟩ ⟨act ~ your own discretion⟩ **6 a —** used as a function word to indicate the rate, degree, or position in a scale or series ⟨the temperature ~ 90⟩ ⟨~ first⟩

\ə\ abut \ᵊ\ kitten, F table \ər\ further \a\ ash \ā\ ace \ä\ cot, cart \au̇\ out \ch\ chin \e\ bet \ē\ easy \g\ go \i\ hit \ī\ ice \j\ job \ŋ\ sing \ō\ go \ȯ\ law \ȯi\ boy \th\ thin \th\ the \ü\ loot \u̇\ foot \y\ yet \zh\ vision \à, k̲, ⁿ, œ, œ̄, ue, ue̅, ʸ\ see Guide to Pronunciation

b — used as a function word to indicate age or position in time ⟨will retire ~ 65⟩

²at \'ät\ *n, pl* **at** [Siamese] (1955) — see *kip* at MONEY table

at- — see AD-

At·a·brine \'at-ə-brən, -ˌbrēn\ *trademark* — used for quinacrine

At·a·lan·ta \ˌat-ᵊl-'ant-ə\ *n* [L, fr. Gk *Atalantē*] : a fleet-footed huntress in Greek mythology who challenges her suitors to a race and is defeated by Hippomenes when she stops to pick up three golden apples he has dropped

at all \ət-'ȯl, ə-'tȯl, at-'ȯl\ *adv* (14c) : in any way or respect : to the least extent or degree : under any circumstances ⟨doesn't smoke *at all*⟩

at·a·man \ˌat-ə-'man\ *n* [Russ] (1835) : HETMAN

at·a·mas·co lily \ˌat-ə-'mas-(ˌ)kō-\ *n* [*attamusco*, lit., it is red (in some Algonquian language of Virginia)] (1743) : any of a genus (*Zephyranthes*) of American bulbous herbs of the amaryllis family with pink, white, or yellowish flowers

at·a·rac·tic \ˌat-ə-'rak-tik\ *or* **at·a·rax·ic** \-'rak-sik\ *n* [*ataractic* fr. Gk *ataraktos* calm, fr. *a-* + *tarassein* to disturb; *ataraxic* fr. Gk *ataraxia* calmness, fr. *a-* + *tarassein* — more at DREG] (1955) : TRANQUILIZER 2 — **ataractic** *or* **ataraxic** *adj*

at·a·vism \'at-ə-ˌviz-əm\ *n* [F *atavisme*, fr. L *atavus* ancestor] (1833) **1** : recurrence in an organism or in any of its parts of a form typical of ancestors more remote than the parents usu. due to genetic recombination **2** : an individual or character manifesting atavism : THROWBACK — **at·a·vis·tic** \ˌat-ə-'vis-tik\ *adj* — **at·a·vis·ti·cal·ly** \-ti-k(ə-)lē\ *adv*

atax·ia \ə-'tak-sē-ə, (ˈ)ā-\ *n* [Gk, fr. *a-* + *tassein* to put in order — more at TACTICS] (1670) : an inability to coordinate voluntary muscular movements that is symptomatic of some nervous disorders — **atax·ic** \-sik\ *adj*

at bat \ət-'bat\ *n* (1884) : an official time at bat charged to a baseball batter except when he walks, sacrifices, is hit by a pitched ball, or is interfered with by the catcher ⟨three hits in five *at bats*⟩

ate *past of* EAT

Ate \'ät-ē, 'āt-; 'ä-ˌtā, 'ā-ˌtē\ *n* [Gk *Atē*] : a Greek goddess personifying foolhardy and ruinous impulse

¹-ate \ət, ˌāt\ *n suffix* [ME *-at*, fr. OF, fr. L *-atus, -atum*, masc. & neut. of *-atus*, pp. ending] **1** : one acted upon (in a specified way) ⟨distil*late*⟩ **2** [NL *-atum*, fr. L] : chemical compound or complex anion derived from a (specified) compound or element ⟨phenol*ate*⟩ ⟨ferr*ate*⟩; *esp* : salt or ester of an acid with a name ending in *-ic* and not beginning with *hydro-* ⟨bor*ate*⟩

²-ate *n suffix* [ME *-at*, fr. OF, fr. L *-atus*, fr. *-atus*, pp. ending] **1** : office : function : rank : group of persons holding a (specified) office or rank or having a (specified) function ⟨vicar*ate*⟩ **2** : state : dominion : jurisdiction ⟨emir*ate*⟩ ⟨khan*ate*⟩

³-ate *adj suffix* [ME *-at*, fr. L *-atus*, fr. pp. ending of 1st conj. verbs, fr. *-a-*, stem vowel of 1st conj. + *-tus*, pp. suffix — more at -ED] : marked by having ⟨crani*ate*⟩

⁴-ate \ˌāt\ *vb suffix* [ME *-aten*, fr. L *-atus*, pp. ending] : act on (in a specified way) ⟨insul*ate*⟩ : cause to be modified or affected by ⟨camphor*ate*⟩ : cause to become ⟨activ*ate*⟩ : furnish with ⟨capacit*ate*⟩

At·e·brin \'at-ə-brən\ *trademark* — used for quinacrine

-at·ed \ˌāt-əd\ *adj suffix* : ³-ATE ⟨locul*ated*⟩

at·el·ec·ta·sis \ˌat-ᵊl-'ek-tə-səs\ *n, pl* **-ta·ses** \-ˌsēz\ [NL, fr. Gk *atelēs* incomplete, defective (fr. *a-* ²*a-* + *telos* end) + *ektasis* extension, fr. *ekteinein* to stretch out, fr. *ex-* + *teinein* to stretch — more at WHEEL, THIN] (1859) : collapse of the expanded lung; *also* : defective expansion of the pulmonary alveoli at birth

ate·lier \ˌat-ᵊl-'yā\ *n* [F, fr. MF *astelier* woodpile, fr. *astele* splinter, fr. LL *astella*] (1699) **1** : an artist's or designer's studio or workroom **2** : WORKSHOP

a tem·po \ä-'tem-(ˌ)pō\ *adv or adj* [It] (ca. 1740) : in time — used as a direction in music to return to the original rate of speed

atem·po·ral \(ˈ)ā-'tem-p(ə-)rəl\ *adj* (1870) : independent of or unaffected by time : TIMELESS

Ate·ri·an \ə-'tir-ē-ən\ *adj* [F *atérien*, fr. Bir el-Ater (Constantine), Algeria] (1928) : of or relating to a Paleolithic culture of northern Africa characterized by Mousterian features, tanged arrow points, and leaf-shaped spearheads

Ath·a·na·sian \ˌath-ə-'nā-zhən, -'nā-shən\ *adj* (1586) : of or relating to Athanasius or his advocacy of the homoousian doctrine against Arianism

Athanasian Creed *n* (1586) : a Christian creed originating in Europe about A.D. 400 and relating esp. to the Trinity and Incarnation

Ath·a·pas·kan *or* **Ath·a·pas·can** \ˌath-ə-'pas-kən\ *or* **Ath·a·bas·can** *or* **Ath·a·bas·kan** \-'bas-\ *n* [Cree *Athap-askaw*, an Athapaskan people, lit., grass or reeds here and there] (1846) **1** : a language stock of the Na-dene group in No. America **2** : a member of a people speaking an Athapaskan language

athe·ism \'ā-thē-ˌiz-əm\ *n* [MF *athéisme*, fr. *athée* atheist, fr. Gk *atheos* godless, fr. *a-* + *theos* god] (1546) **1 a** : a disbelief in the existence of deity **b** : the doctrine that there is no deity **2** : UNGODLINESS, WICKEDNESS

athe·ist \'ā-thē-əst\ *n* (1571) : one who denies the existence of God — **athe·is·tic** \ˌā-thē-'is-tik\ *or* **athe·is·ti·cal** \ˌā-thē-'is-ti-kəl\ *adj* — **athe·is·ti·cal·ly** \-ti-k(ə-)lē\ *adv*

ath·e·ling \'ath-ə-liŋ, 'at͟h-\ *n* [ME, fr. OE *ætheling*, fr. *æthelu* nobility, akin to OHG *adal* nobility] (bef. 12c) : an Anglo-Saxon prince or nobleman; *esp* : the heir apparent or a prince of the royal family

Athe·na \ə-'thē-nə\ *or* **Athe·ne** \-nē\ *n* [L *Athena*, fr. Gk *Athēnē*] : the Greek goddess of wisdom — compare MINERVA

ath·e·nae·um *or* **ath·e·ne·um** \ˌath-ə-'nē-əm\ *n* [L *Athenaeum*, a school in ancient Rome for the study of arts, fr. Gk *Athēnaion*, a temple of Athena, fr. *Athēnē*] (1799) **1** : a building or room in which books, periodicals, and newspapers are kept for use **2** : a literary or scientific association

athe·o·ret·i·cal \ˌā-ˌthē-ə-'ret-i-kəl, -ˌthi(-ə)r-'et-\ *adj* (1969) : not based on or concerned with theory

ath·ero·gen·e·sis \ˌath-ə-rō-'jen-ə-səs\ *n* (1953) : the production of atheroma

ath·ero·gen·ic \-'jen-ik\ *adj* [*atheroma* + *-genic*] (1954) : relating to or producing degenerative changes in arterial walls ⟨~ diet⟩

ath·er·o·ma \ˌath-ə-'rō-mə\ *n* [NL *atheromat-, atheroma*, fr. L, a tumor containing matter resembling gruel, fr. Gk *athērōma*, fr. *athēra* gruel] (1875) : fatty degeneration of the inner coat of the arteries — **ath·er·o·ma·tous** \-'rō-mət-əs\ *adj*

ath·ero·scle·ro·sis \ˌath-ə-ˌrō-sklə-'rō-səs\ *n* [NL, fr. *atheroma* + *sclerosis*] (1910) : an arteriosclerosis characterized by the deposition of fatty substances in and fibrosis of the inner layer of the arteries — **ath·ero·scle·rot·ic** \-sklə-'rät-ik\ *adj* — **ath·ero·scle·rot·i·cal·ly** \-i-k(ə-)lē\ *adv*

athirst \ə-'thərst\ *adj* [ME, fr. OE *ofthyrst*, pp. of *ofthyrstan* to suffer from thirst, fr. *of* off, from + *thyrstan* to thirst — more at OF] (bef. 12c) **1** *archaic* : THIRSTY **2** : having a strong eager desire ⟨I that for ever feel ~ for glory —John Keats⟩ ***syn*** see EAGER

ath·lete \'ath-ˌlēt, ÷'ath-ə-ˌlēt\ *n* [ME, fr. L *athleta*, fr. Gk *athlētēs*, fr. *athlein* to contend for a prize, fr. *athlon* prize, contest] (15c) : one who is trained or skilled in exercises, sports, or games requiring physical strength, agility, or stamina

athlete's foot *n* (1928) : ringworm of the feet

ath·let·ic \ath-'let-ik, ÷ˌath-ə-'let-\ *adj* (1636) **1** : of or relating to athletes or athletics **2** : characteristic of an athlete; *esp* : VIGOROUS, ACTIVE **3** : MESOMORPHIC **4** : used by athletes — **ath·let·i·cal·ly** \-i-k(ə-)lē\ *adv* — **ath·let·i·cism** \-'let-ə-ˌsiz-əm\ *n*

ath·let·ics \ath-'let-iks, ÷ˌath-ə-'let-\ *n pl but sing or pl in constr* (1727) **1** : exercises, sports, or games engaged in by athletes **2** : the practice or principles of athletic activities

athletic supporter *n* (1927) : a supporter for the genitals worn by men participating in sports or strenuous activities

ath·o·dyd \'ath-ə-ˌdid\ *n* [*aero-thermodynamic duct*] (1945) : a jet engine (as a ramjet engine) consisting essentially of a continuous duct of varying diameter which admits air at the forward end, adds heat to it by the combustion of fuel, and discharges it from the after end

at–home \ət-ˌhōm\ *adj* (1951) **1** : intended or suitable for one's home ⟨an ~ dress⟩ **2** : being or occurring at one's home ⟨~ entertainment⟩

at home \ət-'hōm\ *n* (1745) : a reception given at one's home

-athon \ə-ˌthän\ *n comb form* [*marathon*] : event or activity lasting a long time ⟨talk*athon*⟩ ⟨sale*athon*⟩

ath·ro·cyte \'ath-rə-ˌsīt\ *n* [Gk *athroos* together, collected + ISV *-cyte*] (1938) : a cell capable of picking up foreign material and storing it in granular form in its cytoplasm

¹athwart \ə-'thwȯ(ə)rt, *naut often* -'thȯ(ə)rt\ *prep* (15c) **1** : ACROSS **2** : in opposition to ⟨a procedure directly ~ the New England prejudices —R. G. Cole⟩

²athwart *adv* (1500) **1** : across esp. in an oblique direction **2** : in opposition to the right or expected course ⟨and quite ~ goes all decorum —Shak.⟩

athwart·ship \-ˌship\ *adj* (1879) : being across the ship from side to side ⟨~ and longitudinal framing⟩

athwart·ships \-ˌships\ *adv* (1718) : across the ship from side to side

atilt \ə-'tilt\ *adv or adj* (1562) **1** : in a tilted position **2** : with lance in hand ⟨run ~ at death—Shak.⟩

atin·gle \ə-'tiŋ-gəl\ *adj* (1855) : tingling esp. with excitement

-a·tion \'ā-shən\ *n suffix* [ME *-acioun*, fr. OF *-ation*, fr. L *-ation-, -atio*, fr. *-atus* -ate + *-ion-, -io* -ion] : action or process ⟨flirt*ation*⟩ : something connected with an action or process ⟨discolor*ation*⟩

-a·tive \ˌāt-iv, ət-\ *adj suffix* [ME, fr. MF *-atif*, fr. L *-ativus*, fr. *-atus* + *-ivus* -ive] : of, relating to, or connected with ⟨authorit*ative*⟩ : tending to ⟨talk*ative*⟩

At·ka mackerel \ˌat-kə-, ˌät-\ *n* [*Atka* Island, Alaska] (1893) : a greenling (*Pleurogrammus monopterygius*) of Alaska and adjacent regions valued as a food fish

¹At·lan·te·an \ˌat-ˌlan-'tē-ən, ət-'lant-ē-\ *adj* (1667) : of, relating to, or resembling Atlas : STRONG

²Atlantean *adj* (ca. 1828) : of or relating to Atlantis

At·lan·tic \ət-'lant-ik, at-\ *adj* (1579) **1 a** : of, relating to, or found in, on, or near the Atlantic ocean **b** : of, relating to, or found on or near the east coast of the U.S. **2** : of or relating to the nations that border the Atlantic ocean ⟨the ~ community⟩

Atlantic croaker *n* (ca. 1949) : a small but important food fish (*Micropogan undulatus*) of the Gulf coast and the Atlantic coast south of Cape Cod — called also *hardhead*

At·lan·ti·cism \-'lant-ə-ˌsiz-əm\ *n* [*Atlantic (ocean)*] (1950) : a policy of military cooperation between European powers and the U.S. — **At·lan·ti·cist** \-səst\ *n*

Atlantic salmon *n* (1902) : SALMON 1a

Atlantic time *n* [*Atlantic (ocean)*] (ca. 1909) : the time of the fourth time zone west of Greenwich that includes the Canadian Maritime Provinces, Puerto Rico, and the Virgin Islands — called also *Atlantic standard time*

At·lan·tis \ət-'lant-əs, at-\ *n* [L, fr. Gk, fr. *Atlas*] : a fabled island in the Atlantic that according to legend sank beneath the sea

at·las \'at-ləs\ *n* [L *Atlant-, Atlas*, fr. Gk] **1** *cap* : a Titan who for his part in the Titans' revolt against the gods is forced by Zeus to support the heavens on his shoulders **2** *cap* : one who bears a heavy burden **3 a** : a bound collection of maps often including illustrations, informative tables, or textual matter **b** : a bound collection of tables, charts, or plates **4** : the first vertebra of the neck **5** *pl usu* **at·lan·tes** \ət-'lant-(ˌ)ēz, at-\ : a figure or half figure of a man used as a column to support an entablature

at·latl \'ät-ˌlät-ᵊl\ *n* [of Uto-Aztecan origin; akin to Nahuatl *atlatl* atlatl] (1871) : a device for throwing a spear or dart that consists of a rod or board with a projection (as a hook or thong) at the rear end to hold the weapon in place until released

At·li \'ät-lē\ *n* [ON] : a king of the Huns figuring in Germanic legend and corresponding to the historical Attila

at·man \'ät-mən, -ˌmän\ *n, often cap* [Skt *ātman*, lit., breath, soul; akin to OHG *ātum* breath] (1785) **1** *Hinduism* : the innermost essence of each individual **2** *Hinduism* : the supreme universal self : BRAHMA 1

at·mom·e·ter \at-'mäm-ət-ər\ *n* [Gk *atmos* + E *-meter*] (1815) : an instrument for measuring the evaporating capacity of the air

at·mo·sphere \'at-mə-ˌsfi(ə)r\ *n* [NL *atmosphaera*, fr. Gk *atmos* vapor + L *sphaera* sphere; akin to Gk *aenai* to blow — more at WIND] (1638) **1 a** : a gaseous mass enveloping a celestial body (as a planet) **b** : the whole mass of air surrounding the earth **2** : the air of a locality **3** : a surrounding influence or environment ⟨an ~ of mutual trust⟩ **4** : a unit of pressure equal to the pressure of the air at sea level or approximately 14.7 pounds to the square inch **5 a :** the overall aesthetic effect of a work of art **b :** a dominant aesthetic or emotional effect or appeal — **at·mo·sphered** \-ˌsfi(ə)rd\ *adj*

at·mo·spher·ic \ˌat-mə-ˈsfi(ə)r-ik, -ˈsfer-\ *adj* (1783) **1 a :** of or relating to the atmosphere **b :** resembling the atmosphere : AIRY **c :** occurring in or actuated by the atmosphere **2 :** having, marked by, or contributing aesthetic or emotional atmosphere — **at·mo·spher·i·cal·ly** \-i-k(ə-)lē\ *adv*

at·mo·spher·ics \-iks\ *n pl* (1915) **1 :** audible disturbances produced in radio receiving apparatus by atmospheric electrical phenomena (as lightning); *also* **:** the electrical phenomena causing these disturbances **2 :** actions (as official statements) intended to create or suggest a particular atmosphere or mood in international relations; *also* **:** the mood so created or suggested

atmospheric tide *n* (ca. 1864) **:** TIDE 2a(5)

at·mo·sphe·ri·um \ˌat-mə-ˈsfir-ē-əm\ *n* [*atmosphere* + *-ium* (as in *planetarium*)] (1967) **:** an optical device for projecting images of meteorological phenomena (as clouds) on the inside of a dome; *also* **:** a room housing this device

atoll \ˈa-ˌtȯl, -ˌtäl, -ˌtōl, ˈā-\ *n* [*atolu,* native name in the Maldive islands] (1625) **:** a coral island consisting of a reef surrounding a lagoon

at·om \ˈat-əm\ *n* [ME, fr. L *atomus,* fr. Gk *atomos,* fr. *atomos* indivisible, fr. *a-* + *temnein* to cut — more at TOME] (15c) **1 :** one of the minute indivisible particles of which according to ancient materialism the universe is composed **2 :** a tiny particle : BIT **3 :** the smallest particle of an element that can exist either alone or in combination **4 :** the atom considered as a source of vast potential energy

atom bomb *n* (1944) **1 :** a bomb whose violent explosive power is due to the sudden release of atomic energy resulting from the splitting of nuclei of a heavy chemical element (as plutonium or uranium) by neutrons in a very rapid chain reaction — called also *atomic bomb, fission bomb* **2 :** a bomb whose explosive power is due to the release of atomic energy — **atom–bomb** *vt*

atom·ic \ə-ˈtäm-ik\ *adj* (1678) **1 :** of, relating to, or concerned with atoms, atomic energy, or atom bombs **2 :** MINUTE **3** *of a chemical element* **:** existing in the state of separate atoms — **atom·i·cal·ly** \-i-k(ə-)lē\ *adv*

atomic clock *n* (1938) **:** a precision clock that depends for its operation on an electrical oscillator regulated by the natural vibration frequencies of an atomic system (as a beam of cesium atoms)

atomic energy *n* (1906) **:** energy that can be liberated by changes in the nucleus of an atom (as by fission of a heavy nucleus or fusion of light nuclei into heavier ones with accompanying loss of mass)

at·o·mic·i·ty \ˌat-ə-ˈmis-ət-ē\ *n* (1865) **1 :** VALENCE 1 **2 :** the state of consisting of atoms

atomic mass *n* (1898) **:** the mass of any species of atom usu. expressed in atomic mass units

atomic mass unit *n* (ca. 1942) **:** a unit of mass for expressing masses of atoms, molecules, or nuclear particles equal to $^1/_{12}$ of the atomic mass of the most abundant carbon isotope $_6C^{12}$

atomic number *n* (1821) **:** an experimentally determined number characteristic of a chemical element that represents the number of protons in the nucleus which in a neutral atom equals the number of electrons outside the nucleus and that determines the place of the element in the periodic table — see ELEMENT table

atomic pile *or* **atomic reactor** *n* (1945) **:** REACTOR 3b

atom·ics \ə-ˈtäm-iks\ *n pl but sing in constr* (1920) **:** the science of atoms esp. when involving atomic energy

atomic theory *n* (ca. 1847) **1 :** a theory of the nature of matter: all material substances are composed of minute particles or atoms of a comparatively small number of kinds and all the atoms of the same kind are uniform in size, weight, and other properties — called also *atomic hypothesis* **2 :** any of several theories of the structure of the atom; *esp* **:** one based on experimentation and theoretical considerations holding that the atom is composed essentially of a small positively charged comparatively heavy nucleus surrounded by a comparatively large arrangement of electrons

atomic weight *n* (1820) **:** the average atomic mass of an element compared to $^1/_{12}$ the mass of carbon 12 — see ELEMENT table

at·om·ism \ˈat-ə-ˌmiz-əm\ *n* (1678) **1 :** a doctrine that the universe is composed of simple indivisible minute particles **2 :** INDIVIDUALISM 1 — **at·om·ist** \-məst\ *n*

at·om·is·tic \ˌat-ə-ˈmis-tik\ *adj* (1809) **1 :** of or relating to atoms or atomism **2 :** composed of many simple elements; *also* **:** divided into unconnected or antagonistic fragments ⟨an ~ society⟩ — **at·om·is·ti·cal·ly** \-ti-k(ə-)lē\ *adv*

at·om·is·tics \-tiks\ *n pl but sing in constr* (1928) **:** a science dealing with the atom or with the use of atomic energy

at·om·ize \ˈat-ə-ˌmīz\ *vt* **-ized; -iz·ing** (1865) **1 :** to reduce to minute particles or to a fine spray **2 :** to treat as made up of many discrete units **3 :** to subject to atom bombing **4 :** DIVIDE, FRAGMENT — **at·om·iza·tion** \ˌat-ə-mə-ˈzā-shən\ *n*

at·om·iz·er \ˈat-ə-ˌmī-zər\ *n* (1865) **:** an instrument for atomizing usu. a perfume, disinfectant, or medicament

atom smasher *n* (1937) **:** ACCELERATOR d

at·o·my \ˈat-ə-mē\ *n, pl* **-mies** [irreg. fr. L *atomi,* pl. of *atomus* atom] (1591) **:** a tiny particle : ATOM, MITE

aton·al \(ˈ)ā-ˈtōn-ᵊl, (ˈ)a-\ *adj* [²*a-* + *tonal*] (1922) **:** marked by avoidance of traditional musical tonality; *esp* **:** organized without reference to key or tonal center and using the tones of the chromatic scale impartially — **aton·al·ism** \-ᵊl-ˌiz-əm\ *n* — **aton·al·ist** \-ᵊl-əst\ *n* — **ato·nal·i·ty** \ˌā-tō-ˈnal-ət-ē, ˌa-\ *n* — **aton·al·ly** \(ˈ)ā-ˈtōn-ᵊl-ē, (ˈ)a-\ *adv*

atone \ə-ˈtōn\ *vb* **atoned; aton·ing** [ME *atonen* to become reconciled, fr. *at on* in harmony, fr. *at* + *on* one] *vt* (1593) **1** *obs* **:** RECONCILE **2 :** to supply satisfaction for : EXPIATE ~ *vi* **:** to make amends

atone·ment \ə-ˈtōn-mənt\ *n* (1513) **1** *obs* **:** RECONCILIATION **2 :** the reconciliation of God and man through the sacrificial death of Jesus Christ **3 :** reparation for an offense or injury : SATISFACTION ⟨made ~ for his cruelty⟩ **4** *Christian Science* **:** the exemplifying of man's oneness with God

aton·ic \(ˈ)ā-ˈtän-ik, (ˈ)a-\ *adj* (1792) **1 :** characterized by atony **2 :** uttered without accent or stress

at·o·ny \ˈat-ᵊn-ē\ *n* [LL *atonia,* fr. Gk, fr. *atonos* without tone, fr. *a-* + *tonos* tone] (1693) **:** lack of physiological tone esp. of a contractile organ

¹**atop** \ə-ˈtäp\ *prep* (1655) **:** on top of

²**atop** *adv or adj* (1658) **:** on, to, or at the top

at·o·py \ˈat-ə-pē\ *n* [Gk *atopia* uncommonness, fr. *atopos* out of the way, uncommon, fr. *a-* + *topos* place — more at TOPIC] (1923) **:** a probably hereditary allergy characterized by symptoms (as asthma, hay fever, or hives) produced upon exposure to the exciting antigen without inoculation — **atop·ic** \(ˈ)ā-ˈtäp-ik, -ˈtō-pik\ *adj*

-a·tor *n suffix* [ME *-atour,* fr. OF & L; OF, fr. L *-ator,* fr. *-atus* -ate + *-or*] **:** one that does ⟨totalizator⟩

ATP \ˌā-ˌtē-ˈpē, ā-ˈtē-ˌpē\ *n* [adenosine *triphosphate*] (1944) **:** a phosphorylated nucleoside $C_{10}H_{16}N_5O_{13}P_3$ of adenine that supplies energy for many biochemical cellular processes by undergoing enzymatic hydrolysis esp. to ADP — called also *adenosine triphosphate*

ATPase \ˌā-ˌtē-ˈpē-ˌās, -ˌāz\ *n* (1946) **:** an enzyme that hydrolyzes ATP; *esp* **:** one that hydrolyzes ATP to ADP and inorganic phosphate

at·ra·bil·ious \ˌa-trə-ˈbil-yəs\ *adj* [L *atra bilis* black bile] (1651) **1 :** given to or marked by melancholy : GLOOMY **2 :** ILL-NATURED, PEEVISH — **at·ra·bil·ious·ness** *n*

at·ra·zine \ˈa-trə-ˌzēn\ *n* [ISV *atr-* (prob. fr. L *atr-, ater* black, dark) + *triazine*] (1962) **:** a photosynthesis-inhibiting persistent herbicide $C_8H_{14}ClN_5$ used esp. to kill annual weeds and quack grass

atrem·ble \ə-ˈtrem-bəl\ *adj* (1862) **:** shaking involuntarily : TREMBLING ⟨he was white as death and all ~ —Robert Coover⟩

atre·sia \ə-ˈtrē-zhə\ *n* [NL, fr. ²*a-* + Gk *trēsis* perforation, fr. *tetrainein* to pierce — more at THROW] (ca. 1807) **1 :** absence or closure of a natural passage of the body **2 :** absence or disappearance of an anatomical part (as an ovarian follicle) by degeneration

Atreus \ˈā-ˌtrüs, -trē-əs\ *n* [Gk] **:** a king of Mycenae and father of Agamemnon and Menelaus

atrio·ven·tric·u·lar \ˌā-trē-ō-ven-ˈtrik-yə-lər, -vən-\ *adj* [NL *atrium* + E *ventricular*] (ca. 1860) **:** of, relating to, or located between an atrium and ventricle of the heart

atrioventricular node *n* (ca. 1934) **:** a small mass of tissue in the right atrioventricular region of higher vertebrates through which impulses from the sinoatrial node are passed to the ventricles

atrip \ə-ˈtrip\ *adj, of an anchor* (1796) **:** AWEIGH

atri·um \ˈā-trē-əm\ *n, pl* **atria** \-trē-ə\ *also* **atri·ums** [L] (1557) **1 :** the central hall of a Roman house **2** [NL, fr. L] **:** an anatomical cavity or passage; *esp* **:** the chamber or either of the chambers of the heart that receives blood from the veins and forces it into the ventricle or ventricles — see HEART illustration **3** *pl usu* **atriums :** a rectangularly shaped open patio around which a house is built; *also* **:** a many-storied court in a building (as a hotel) usu. with a skylight — **atri·al** \-trē-əl\ *adj*

atro·cious \ə-ˈtrō-shəs\ *adj* [L *atroc-, atrox* gloomy, atrocious, fr. *atr-, ater* black + *-oc-, -ox* (akin to Gk *ōps* eye) — more at EYE] (1669) **1 :** extremely wicked, brutal, or cruel : BARBARIC **2 :** APPALLING, HORRIFYING ⟨the ~ weapons of modern war⟩ **3 a :** utterly revolting : ABOMINABLE ⟨~ working conditions⟩ **b :** of very poor quality ⟨~ handwriting⟩ — **atro·cious·ly** *adv* — **atro·cious·ness** *n*

atroc·i·ty \ə-ˈträs-ət-ē\ *n, pl* **-ties** (1534) **1 :** the quality or state of being atrocious **2 :** an atrocious act, object, or situation ⟨the . . . sufferings and *atrocities* of trench warfare —Aldous Huxley⟩

at·ro·phy \ˈa-trə-fē\ *n, pl* **-phies** [LL *atrophia,* fr. Gk, fr. *atrophos* ill fed, fr. *a-* + *trephein* to nourish; akin to Gk *thrombos* clot, curd] (1601) **1 :** decrease in size or wasting away of a body part or tissue; *also* **:** arrested development or loss of a part or organ incidental to the normal development or life of an animal or plant **2 :** a wasting away or progressive decline : DEGENERATION ⟨the ~ of freedom⟩ ⟨was not a solitude of ~, of negation, but of perpetual flowering —Willa Cather⟩ — **atro·phic** \(ˈ)ā-ˈtrō-fik\ *adj* — **atrophy** \ˈa-trə-fē, -ˌfī\ *vb*

at·ro·pine \ˈa-trə-ˌpēn\ *n* [G *atropin,* fr. NL *Atropa,* genus name of belladonna, fr. Gk *Atropos,* one of the three Fates] (1836) **:** a racemic mixture of hyoscyamine from belladonna and related plants used esp. in the form of its sulfate to inhibit the actions of acetylcholine in the parasympathetic nervous system (as by relieving spasms of smooth muscle or dilating the pupil of the eye)

at·tach \ə-ˈtach\ *vb* [ME *attachen,* fr. MF *attacher,* fr. OF *estachier,* fr. *estache* stake, of Gmc origin; akin to OE *staca* stake] *vt* (14c) **1 :** to take by legal authority esp. under a writ ⟨the court's sheriffs ~*ed* his property⟩ **2 a :** to bring (oneself) into an association **b :** to assign temporarily **3 :** to bind by personal ties (as of affection or sympathy) ⟨was strongly ~*ed* to his family⟩ **4 :** to make fast (as by tying or gluing) ⟨~ a label to a package⟩ **5 :** to associate esp. as a property : ATTRIBUTE ⟨~*ed* great importance to public opinion polls⟩ ~ *vi* **:** to become attached : ADHERE ***syn*** see FASTEN — **at·tach·able** \-ˈtach-ə-bəl\ *adj*

at·ta·ché \ˌat-ə-ˈshā, ˌa-ˌta-, ə-ˌta-\ *n* [F, pp. of *attacher*] (1829) **1 :** a technical expert on the diplomatic staff of his country at a foreign capital ⟨a military ~⟩ **2 :** ATTACHÉ CASE

at·ta·ché case \ˌa-ˌta-ˈshā-, ˌat-ə-; ə-ˈtash-(ˌ)ā-\ *n* (1904) **:** a small thin suitcase used esp. for carrying business papers

at·tached \ə-ˈtacht\ *adj* (1854) **:** permanently fixed when adult ⟨~ barnacles⟩

at·tach·ment \ə-ˈtach-mənt\ *n* (15c) **1 :** a seizure by legal process; *also* **:** the writ or precept commanding such seizure **2 a :** the state of being personally attached : FIDELITY ⟨~ to a cause⟩ **b :** affectionate regard ⟨a deep ~ to nature⟩ **3 :** a device attached to a machine or implement **4 :** the physical connection by which one thing is attached to another **5 :** the process of physically attaching

¹**at·tack** \ə-ˈtak\ *vb* [MF *attaquer,* fr. (assumed) OIt *estaccare* to attach, fr. *stacca* stake, of Gmc origin; akin to OE *staca*] *vt* (1600) **1 :** to set upon forcefully **2 :** to threaten (a piece in chess) with immediate capture **3 :** to assail with unfriendly or bitter words **4 :** to begin to af-

\ə\ abut \ᵊ\ kitten, F table \ər\ further \a\ ash \ā\ ace \ä\ cot, cart \au̇\ out \ch\ chin \e\ bet \ē\ easy \g\ go \i\ hit \ī\ ice \j\ job \ŋ\ sing \ō\ go \ȯ\ law \ȯi\ boy \th\ thin \t͟h\ the \ü\ loot \u̇\ foot \y\ yet \zh\ vision \à, k̟, ⁿ, œ, œ̄, ue, ue̅, ʸ\ *see* Guide to Pronunciation

fect or to act on injuriously **5 :** to set to work on ~ *vi* **:** to make an attack — **at·tack·er** *n*

syn ATTACK, ASSAIL, ASSAULT, BOMBARD, STORM mean to make an onslaught upon. ATTACK implies taking the initiative in a struggle; ASSAIL implies attempting to break down resistance by repeated blows or shots; ASSAULT suggests a direct attempt to overpower by suddenness and violence of onslaught; BOMBARD applies to attacking with bombs or shells; STORM implies attempting to break into a defended position.

[2]**attack** *n* (1661) **1 :** the act of attacking **:** ASSAULT **2 :** a belligerent or antagonistic action **3 :** the beginning of destructive action ⟨as by a chemical agent⟩ **4 :** the setting to work on some undertaking ⟨made a new ~ on the problem⟩ **5 :** the act or manner of beginning a musical tone or phrase **6 a :** a fit of sickness; *esp* **:** an active episode of a chronic or recurrent disease **b :** a period of being strongly affected by something ⟨as a desire or mood⟩ **7 a :** an offensive or scoring action ⟨won the game with an eight-hit ~⟩ **b :** offensive players or the positions taken up by them

at·tack·man \-ˌman\ *n* (1940) **:** a player (as in lacrosse) assigned to an offensive zone or position

at·tain \ə-ˈtān\ *vb* [ME *atteynen,* fr. OF *ataindre,* fr. (assumed) VL *attangere,* fr. L *attingere,* fr. *ad-* + *tangere* to touch — more at TANGENT] *vt* (14c) **1 :** to reach as an end **:** GAIN, ACHIEVE ⟨~ a goal⟩ **2 :** to come into possession of **:** OBTAIN ⟨he ~*ed* preferment over his fellows⟩ **3 :** to come to as the end of a progression or course of movement ⟨they ~*ed* the top of the hill⟩ ⟨~ a ripe old age⟩ ~ *vi* **:** to come or arrive by motion, growth, or effort — **at·tain·abil·i·ty** \-ˌtā-nə-ˈbil-ət-ē\ *n* — **at·tain·able** \-ˈtā-nə-bəl\ *adj*

at·tain·der \ə-ˈtān-dər\ *n* [ME *attaynder,* fr. MF *ataindre* to accuse, attain] (15c) **1 :** extinction of the civil rights and capacities of a person upon sentence of death or outlawry usu. after a conviction of treason **2** *obs* **:** DISHONOR

at·tain·ment \ə-ˈtān-mənt\ *n* (1549) **1 :** the act of attaining **:** the condition of being attained **2 :** something attained **:** ACCOMPLISHMENT ⟨scientific ~*s*⟩ ***syn*** see ACQUIREMENT

[1]**at·taint** \ə-ˈtānt\ *vt* [ME *attaynten,* fr. MF *ataint,* pp. of *ataindre*] (14c) **1 :** to affect by attainder **2 a :** INFECT, CORRUPT **b** *archaic* **:** TAINT, SULLY **3** *archaic* **:** ACCUSE

[2]**attaint** *n, obs* (1592) **:** a stain upon honor or purity **:** DISGRACE

at·tar \ˈat-ər, ˈa-ˌtär\ *n* [Per *ʽaṭir* perfumed, fr. Ar, fr. *ʽiṭr* perfume] (1798) **:** a fragrant essential oil (as from rose petals); *also* **:** FRAGRANCE

[1]**at·tempt** \ə-ˈtem(p)t\ *vt* [L *attemptare,* fr. *ad-* + *temptare* to touch, try — more at TEMPT] (14c) **1 :** to make an effort to do, accomplish, solve, or effect ⟨~*ed* to swim the swollen river⟩ **2** *archaic* **:** TEMPT **3** *archaic* **:** to try to subdue **:** ATTACK — **at·tempt·able** \-ˈtem(p)-tə-bəl\ *adj*

syn ATTEMPT, TRY, ENDEAVOR, ESSAY, STRIVE mean to make an effort to accomplish an end. ATTEMPT stresses the initiation or beginning of an effort; TRY stresses effort or experiment made in the hope of testing or proving something; ENDEAVOR heightens the implications of exertion and difficulty; ESSAY implies difficulty but also suggests tentative trying or experimenting; STRIVE implies great exertion against great difficulty and specifically suggests persistent effort.

[2]**attempt** *n* (1534) **1 :** the act or an instance of attempting; *esp* **:** an unsuccessful effort **2 :** ATTACK, ASSAULT ⟨an ~ on the life of the president⟩

at·tend \ə-ˈtend\ *vb* [ME *attenden,* fr. OF *atendre,* fr. L *attendere,* lit., to stretch to, fr. *ad-* + *tendere* to stretch — more at THIN] *vt* (14c) **1 :** to give heed to **2 :** to look after **:** take charge of **3** *archaic* **a :** to wait for **b :** to be in store for **4 a :** to go or stay with as a companion, nurse, or servant **b :** to visit professionally as a physician **5 :** to be present with **:** ACCOMPANY **6 :** to be present at **:** go to ⟨~ law school⟩ ~ *vi* **1 :** to apply oneself ⟨~ to your work⟩ **2 :** to apply the mind or pay attention **:** HEED **3 a :** to be ready for service ⟨ministers who ~ upon the king⟩ **b :** to be present **4** *obs* **:** WAIT, STAY **5 :** to take charge **:** SEE ⟨I'll ~ to that⟩ ***syn*** see ACCOMPANY — **at·tend·er** *n*

at·ten·dance \ə-ˈten-dən(t)s\ *n* (14c) **1 :** the act or fact of attending ⟨a physician in ~⟩ **2 a :** the persons or number of persons attending ⟨daily ~ at the fair dwindled⟩ **b :** the number of times a person attends

attendance officer *n* (1884) **:** one employed by a public-school system to investigate the continued absences of pupils

[1]**at·ten·dant** \ə-ˈten-dənt\ *n* (15c) **1 :** one who attends another to perform a service; *esp* **:** an employee who waits on customers ⟨a parking-lot ~⟩ **2 :** something that accompanies **:** CONCOMITANT **3 :** ATTENDEE

[2]**attendant** *adj* (1617) **:** accompanying or following as a consequence ⟨problems ~ upon pollution⟩

at·tend·ee \ə-ˌten-ˈdē, ˌa-\ *n* (1937) **:** one who is present on a given occasion or at a given place ⟨~*s* at a convention⟩

at·tend·ing \ə-ˈten-diŋ\ *adj* (ca. 1923) **:** serving as a physician on the staff of a teaching hospital ⟨~ surgeon⟩

at·ten·tion \ə-ˈten-chən\ *n* [ME *attencioun,* fr. L *attention-, attentio,* fr. *attentus,* pp. of *attendere*] (14c) **1 a :** the act or state of attending esp. through applying the mind to an object of sense or thought **b :** a condition of readiness for such attention involving esp. a selective narrowing or focusing of consciousness and receptivity **2 :** OBSERVATION, NOTICE; *esp* **:** consideration with a view to action ⟨a problem requiring prompt ~⟩ **3 a :** an act of civility or courtesy esp. in courtship **b :** sympathetic consideration of the needs and wants of others **:** ATTENTIVENESS **4 :** a position assumed by a soldier with heels together, body erect, arms at the sides, and eyes to the front — often used as a command — **at·ten·tion·al** \-ˈtench-nəl, -ˈten-chən-ᵊl\ *adj*

attention line *n* (1925) **:** a line usu. placed above the salutation in a business letter directing the letter to one specified

attention span *n* (1934) **:** the length of time during which an individual is able to concentrate

at·ten·tive \ə-ˈtent-iv\ *adj* (14c) **1 :** MINDFUL, OBSERVANT ⟨~ to what he is doing⟩ **2 :** heedful of the comfort of others **:** SOLICITOUS **3 :** offering attentions in or as if in the role of a suitor — **at·ten·tive·ly** *adv* — **at·ten·tive·ness** *n*

[1]**at·ten·u·ate** \ə-ˈten-yə-ˌwāt\ *vb* **-at·ed; -at·ing** [L *attenuatus,* pp. of *attenuare* to make thin, fr. *ad-* + *tenuis* thin — more at THIN] *vt* (15c) **1 :** to make thin in consistency **:** RAREFY **2 :** to make thin or slender **3 :** to lessen the amount, force, magnitude, or value of **:** WEAKEN **4 :** to reduce the severity, virulence, or vitality of ~ *vi* **:** to become thin, fine, or less — **at·ten·u·a·tion** \-ˌten-yə-ˈwā-shən\ *n*

[2]**at·ten·u·ate** \ə-ˈten-yə-wət\ *adj* (15c) **1 :** attenuated esp. in thickness, density, or force **2 :** tapering gradually usu. to a long slender point ⟨~ leaves⟩

at·ten·u·a·tor \-yə-ˌwāt-ər\ *n* (1924) **:** a device for attenuating; *esp* **:** one for reducing the amplitude of an electrical signal without appreciable distortion

at·test \ə-ˈtest\ *vb* [MF *attester,* fr. L *attestari,* fr. *ad-* + *testis* witness — more at TESTAMENT] *vt* (1596) **1 a :** to affirm to be true or genuine; *specif* **:** to authenticate by signing as a witness **b :** to authenticate officially **2 :** to establish or verify the usage of **3 :** to be proof of **:** MANIFEST ⟨her record ~*s* her integrity⟩ **4 :** to put on oath ~ *vi* **:** to bear witness **:** TESTIFY ⟨~ to a belief⟩ ***syn*** see CERTIFY — **at·tes·ta·tion** \ˌa-ˌtes-ˈtā-shən, ˌat-ə-ˈstā-\ *n* — **at·test·er** \ə-ˈtes-tər\ *n*

at·tic \ˈat-ik\ *n* [F *attique,* fr. *attique* of Attica, fr. L *Atticus*] (ca. 1696) **1 :** a low story or wall above the main order of a facade in the classical styles **2 :** a room behind an attic **3 :** a room or a space immediately below the roof of a building **:** GARRET

[1]**At·tic** \ˈat-ik\ *adj* [L *Atticus,* fr. Gk *Attikos,* fr. *Attikē* Attica, Greece] (1599) **1 :** Athenian **2 :** marked by simplicity, purity, and refinement ⟨an ~ prose style⟩

[2]**Attic** *n* (ca. 1771) **:** a dialect of ancient Greek orig. used in Attica and later the literary language of the Greek-speaking world

at·ti·cism \ˈat-ə-ˌsiz-əm\ *n, often cap* (1612) **1 :** a witty or well-turned phrase **2 :** a characteristic feature of Attic Greek occurring in another language or dialect

[1]**at·tire** \ə-ˈtī(ə)r\ *vt* **-tired; -tir·ing** [ME *attiren,* fr. OF *atirier,* fr. *a-* (fr. L *ad-*) + *tire* order, rank] (14c) **:** to put garments on **:** DRESS, ARRAY; *esp* **:** to clothe in fancy or rich garments

[2]**attire** *n* (14c) **1 :** DRESS, CLOTHES; *esp* **:** splendid or decorative clothing **2 :** the antlers or antlers and scalp of a stag or buck

at·ti·tude \ˈat-ə-ˌt(y)üd\ *n* [F, fr. It *attitudine,* fr. *attitudine* aptitude, fr. LL *aptitudin-, aptitudo* fitness — more at APTITUDE] (1668) **1 :** the arrangement of the parts of a body or figure **:** POSTURE **2 a :** a mental position with regard to a fact or state **b :** a feeling or emotion toward a fact or state **3 :** a position assumed for a specific purpose ⟨a threatening ~⟩ **4 :** a ballet position similar to the arabesque in which the raised leg is bent at the knee **5 :** the position of an aircraft or spacecraft determined by the relationship between its axes and a reference datum (as the horizon or a particular star) **6 :** an organismic state of readiness to respond in a characteristic way to a stimulus (as an object, concept, or situation)

at·ti·tu·di·nal \ˌat-ə-ˈt(y)üd-nəl, -ᵊn-əl\ *adj* [*attitude* + *-inal* (as in *aptitudinal,* fr. L *aptitudin-, aptitudo*)] (1831) **:** relating to, based on, or expressive of personal attitudes or feelings ⟨~ judgment⟩

at·ti·tu·di·nize \ˌat-ə-ˈt(y)üd-ᵊn-ˌīz\ *vi* **-nized; -niz·ing** (1784) **:** to assume an affected mental attitude **:** POSE

at·to- \ˈat-(ˌ)ō\ *comb form* [ISV, fr. Dan or Norw *atten* eighteen, fr. ON *āttjān;* akin to OE *eahtatiene* eighteen] **:** one quintillionth (10^{-18}) part of ⟨*atto*gram⟩

at·torn \ə-ˈtərn\ *vi* [ME *attournen,* fr. MF *atorner,* fr. OF, fr. *a-* (fr. L *ad-*) + *torner* to turn] (15c) **:** to agree to be tenant to a new owner or landlord of the same property — **at·torn·ment** \-mənt\ *n*

at·tor·ney \ə-ˈtər-nē\ *n, pl* **-neys** [ME *attourney,* fr. MF *atorné,* pp. of *atorner*] (14c) **:** one who is legally appointed by another to transact business for him; *specif* **:** a legal agent qualified to act for suitors and defendants in legal proceedings — **at·tor·ney·ship** \-ˌship\ *n*

attorney–at–law *n, pl* **attorneys–at–law** (1768) **:** a practitioner in a court of law who is legally qualified to prosecute and defend actions in such court on the retainer of clients

attorney general *n, pl* **attorneys general** *or* **attorney generals** (1585) **:** the chief law officer of a nation or state who represents the government in litigation and serves as its principal legal adviser

at·tract \ə-ˈtrakt\ *vb* [ME *attracten,* fr. L *attractus,* pp. of *attrahere,* fr. *ad-* + *trahere* to draw — more at DRAW] *vt* (15c) **:** to cause to approach or adhere: as **a :** to pull to or toward oneself or itself ⟨a magnet ~*s* iron⟩ **b :** to draw by appeal to natural or excited interest, emotion, or aesthetic sense **:** ENTICE ⟨~ attention⟩ ~ *vi* **:** to exercise attraction — **at·tract·able** \-ˈtrak-tə-bəl\ *adj* — **at·trac·tor** \-ˈtrak-tər\ *n*

syn ATTRACT, ALLURE, CHARM, CAPTIVATE, FASCINATE, ENCHANT mean to draw another by exerting a powerful influence. ATTRACT applies to any degree or kind of ability to exert influence over another; ALLURE implies an enticing by what is fair, pleasing, or seductive; CHARM implies the power of casting a spell over the person or thing affected and so compelling a response, but it may, like CAPTIVATE, suggest no more than evoking delight or admiration; FASCINATE suggests a magical influence and tends to stress the ineffectiveness of attempts to resist; ENCHANT is perhaps the strongest of these terms in stressing the appeal of the agent and the degree of delight evoked in the subject.

at·trac·tan·cy \ə-ˈtrak-tən-sē\ *also* **at·trac·tance** \-tən(t)s\ *n* (1948) **:** the quality or capacity of attracting

at·trac·tant \ə-ˈtrak-tənt\ *n* (1920) **:** a substance (as a pheromone) that attracts insects or other animals

at·trac·tion \ə-ˈtrak-shən\ *n* (15c) **1 a :** the act, process, or power of attracting **b :** personal charm **2 :** the action or power of drawing forth a response **:** an attractive quality **3 :** a force acting mutually between particles of matter, tending to draw them together, and resisting their separation **4 :** something that attracts or is intended to attract people by appealing to their desires and tastes ⟨~*s* at the local theater⟩

syn ATTRACTION, AFFINITY, SYMPATHY mean the relationship existing between things or persons that are naturally or involuntarily drawn together. ATTRACTION implies the possession by one thing of a quality that pulls another to it; AFFINITY implies a susceptibility or predisposition on the part of the one drawn; SYMPATHY implies a reciprocal or natural relation between two things that are both susceptible to the same influence.

at·trac·tive \ə-ˈtrak-tiv\ *adj* (14c) **1 :** having or relating to the power to attract ⟨~ forces between molecules⟩ ⟨an ~ offer⟩ **2 :** arousing interest or pleasure **:** CHARMING ⟨an ~ smile⟩ — **at·trac·tive·ly** *adv* — **at·trac·tive·ness** *n*

[1]at·tri·bute \'a-trə-ˌbyüt\ *n* [ME, fr. L *attributus,* pp. of *attribuere* to attribute, fr. *ad-* + *tribuere* to bestow — more at TRIBUTE] (14c) **1** : an inherent characteristic; *also* : an accidental quality **2** : an object closely associated with or belonging to a specific person, thing, or office ⟨a scepter is the ~ of power⟩; *esp* : such an object used for identification in painting or sculpture **3** : a word ascribing a quality; *esp* : ADJECTIVE ***syn*** see QUALITY

[2]at·trib·ute \ə-'trib-yət, -ˌyüt\ *vt* **-ut·ed; -ut·ing** (15c) **1** : to explain by indicating a cause ⟨*attributed* his success to his coach⟩ **2 a** : to regard as a characteristic of a person or thing **b** : to reckon as made or originated in an indicated fashion ⟨*attributed* the invention to a Russian⟩ **c** : CLASSIFY, DESIGNATE ***syn*** see ASCRIBE — **at·trib·ut·able** \-yət-ə-bəl\ *adj*

at·tri·bu·tion \ˌa-trə-'byü-shən\ *n* (1596) **1** : the act of attributing; *esp* : the ascribing of a work (as of literature or art) to a particular author or artist **2** : an ascribed quality, character, or right — **at·tri·bu·tion·al** \-shnəl, -shən-ᵊl\ *adj*

at·trib·u·tive \ə-'trib-yət-iv\ *adj* (1606) **1** : relating to or of the nature of an attribute : ATTRIBUTING **2** : joined directly to a modified noun without a linking verb ⟨*city* in *city streets* is an ~ noun⟩ — **attributive** *n* — **at·trib·u·tive·ly** *adv*

at·trit·ed \ə-'trīt-əd\ *adj* (1760) : worn by attrition

at·tri·tion \ə-'trish-ən, a-\ *n* [L *attrition-, attritio,* fr. *attritus,* pp. of *atterere* to rub against, fr. *ad-* + *terere* to rub — more at THROW] (14c) **1** [ME *attricioun,* fr. (assumed) ML *attrition-, attritio,* fr. L] : sorrow for one's sins that arises from a motive other than that of the love of God **2** : the act of rubbing together : FRICTION; *also* : the act of wearing or grinding down by friction **3** : the act of weakening or exhausting by constant harassment or abuse **4** : a reduction in numbers usu. as a result of resignation, retirement, or death — **at·tri·tion·al** \-'trish-nəl, -'trish-ən-ᵊl\ *adj*

at·tune \ə-'t(y)ün\ *vt* (1596) **1** : to bring into harmony : TUNE **2** : to make aware or responsive ⟨~ businesses to changing trends⟩ — **at·tune·ment** \-mənt\ *n*

atwit·ter \ə-'twit-ər\ *adj* (1833) : nervously concerned : EXCITED ⟨gossips ~ with speculation —*Time*⟩

atyp·i·cal \(')ā-'tip-i-kəl\ *adj* (1885) : not typical : IRREGULAR, UNUSUAL — **atyp·i·cal·i·ty** \ˌā-ˌtip-ə-'kal-ət-ē\ *n* — **atyp·i·cal·ly** \(')ā-'tip-i-k(ə-)lē\ *adv*

au·bade \ō-'bäd\ *n* [F, fr. MF, fr. (assumed) OProv *aubada,* fr. OProv *alba, auba* dawn, fr. (assumed) VL *alba,* fr. L, fem. of *albus* white — more at ALB] (ca. 1678) **1** : a song or poem greeting the dawn **2 a** : a morning love song **b** : a song or poem of lovers parting at dawn **3** : morning music — compare NOCTURNE

au·ber·gine \'ō-bər-ˌzhēn\ *n* [F, fr. Catal *albergínia,* fr. Ar *al-bādhinjān* the eggplant] (1794) : EGGPLANT

[1]au·burn \'ȯ-bərn\ *adj* [ME *auborne* blond, fr. MF, fr. ML *alburnus* whitish, fr. L *albus*] (15c) **1** : of the color auburn **2** : of a reddish brown color

[2]auburn *n* (1634) : a moderate brown

Au·bus·son \ˌō-bə-'sōⁿ\ *n* [*Aubusson,* France] (1851) **1** : a figured scenic tapestry used for wall hangings and upholstery **2** : a rug woven to resemble Aubusson tapestry

au cou·rant \ˌō-kü-'räⁿ\ *adj* [F, lit., in the current] (1762) **1** : fully informed : UP-TO-DATE **2** : fully familiar : CONVERSANT

[1]auc·tion \'ȯk-shən\ *n* [L *auction-, auctio,* lit., increase, fr. *auctus,* pp. of *augēre* to increase — more at EKE] (1595) **1** : a sale of property to the highest bidder **2** : the act or process of bidding in some card games

[2]auction *vt* **auc·tioned; auc·tion·ing** \-sh(ə-)niŋ\ (1807) : to sell at auction ⟨~*ed* off his library⟩

auction bridge *n* (1908) : a bridge game differing from contract bridge in that tricks made in excess of the contract are scored toward game

auc·tion·eer \ˌȯk-shə-'ni(ə)r\ *n* (ca. 1708) : an agent who sells goods at auction

auc·to·ri·al \ȯk-'tōr-ē-əl, -'tȯr-\ *adj* [L *auctor* author — more at AUTHOR] (1821) : of or relating to an author

au·da·cious \ȯ-'dā-shəs\ *adj* [MF *audacieux,* fr. *audace* boldness, fr. L *audacia,* fr. *audac-, audax* bold, fr. *audēre* to dare, fr. *avidus* eager — more at AVID] (1550) **1 a** : intrepidly daring : ADVENTUROUS ⟨an ~ mountain climber⟩ **b** : recklessly bold : RASH **2** : contemptuous of law, religion, or decorum : INSOLENT **3** : marked by originality and verve — **au·da·cious·ly** *adv* — **au·da·cious·ness** *n*

au·dac·i·ty \ȯ-'das-ət-ē\ *n, pl* **-ties** [ME *audacite,* fr. L *audac-, audax*] (15c) **1** : the quality or state of being audacious: as **a** : intrepid boldness **b** : bold or arrogant disregard of normal restraints **2** : an audacious act — usu. used in pl. ***syn*** see TEMERITY

[1]au·di·ble \'ȯd-ə-bəl\ *adj* [LL *audibilis,* fr. L *audire* to hear; akin to Gk *aisthanesthai* to perceive, Skt *āvis* evidently] (1529) : heard or capable of being heard — **au·di·bil·i·ty** \ˌȯd-ə-'bil-ət-ē\ *n* — **au·di·bly** \'ȯd-ə-blē\ *adv*

[2]audible *n* (1962) : AUTOMATIC 3

au·di·ence \'ȯd-ē-ən(t)s, 'äd-\ *n* [ME, fr. MF, fr. L *audientia,* fr. *audient-, audiens,* prp. of *audire*] (14c) **1** : the act or state of hearing **2 a** : a formal hearing or interview ⟨an ~ with the pope⟩ **b** : an opportunity of being heard ⟨he would succeed if he were once given ~⟩ **3 a** : a group of listeners or spectators **b** : the reading, viewing, or listening public **4** : FOLLOWING

au·dile \'ȯ-ˌdīl\ *adj* [L *audire* to hear] (1897) : AUDITORY

aud·ing \'ȯd-iŋ\ *n* [L *audire* + E *-ing*] (ca. 1949) : the process of hearing, recognizing, and interpreting spoken language

[1]au·dio \'ȯd-ē-ˌō\ *adj* [*audio-*] (1916) **1** : of or relating to acoustic, mechanical, or electrical frequencies corresponding to normally audible sound waves which are of frequencies approximately from 15 to 20,000 cycles per second **2 a** : of or relating to sound or its reproduction and esp. high-fidelity reproduction **b** : relating to or used in the transmission or reception of sound — compare VIDEO **c** : of, relating to, or utilizing recorded sound

[2]audio *n* (ca. 1937) **1** : an audio signal; *broadly* : SOUND **2** : the section of television or motion-picture equipment that deals with sound **3** : the transmission, reception, or reproduction of sound

audio- *comb form* [L *audire* to hear] **1** : hearing ⟨*audio*meter⟩ **2** : sound ⟨*audio*phile⟩ **3** : auditory and ⟨*audio*visual⟩

au·dio·cas·sette \ˌȯd-ē-(ˌ)ō-kə-'set, -ka-\ *n* (1972) : an audiotape recording mounted in a cassette

au·dio·gen·ic \ˌȯd-ē-ō-'jen-ik\ *adj* (1941) : produced by frequencies corresponding to sound waves — used esp. of epileptoid responses

au·dio·gram \'ȯd-ē-ō-ˌgram\ *n* (1927) : a graphic representation of the relation of vibration frequency and the minimum sound intensity for hearing

au·dio–lin·gual \ˌȯd-ē-ō-'liŋ-g(yə-)wəl\ *adj* (ca. 1957) : involving a drill routine of listening and speaking in language learning

au·di·ol·o·gy \ˌȯd-ē-'äl-ə-jē\ *n* (1946) : a branch of science dealing with hearing; *specif* : therapy of individuals having impaired hearing — **au·di·o·log·i·cal** \-ē-ə-'läj-i-kəl\ *also* **au·di·o·log·ic** \-ē-ə-'läj-ik\ *adj* — **au·di·ol·o·gist** \-ē-'äl-ə-jəst\ *n*

au·di·om·e·ter \ˌȯd-ē-'äm-ət-ər\ *n* (1879) : an instrument used in measuring the acuity of hearing — **au·dio·met·ric** \-ē-ō-'me-trik\ *adj* — **au·di·om·e·try** \-ē-'äm-ə-trē\ *n*

au·dio·phile \'ȯd-ē-ō-ˌfīl\ *n* (1951) : one who is enthusiastic about high-fidelity sound reproduction

au·dio·tape \ˌȯd-ē-ō-'tāp\ *n* (1963) : a tape recording of sound

au·dio·vi·su·al \ˌȯd-ē-(ˌ)ō-'vizh-(ə-)wəl, -'vizh-əl\ *adj* (1937) **1** : designed to aid in learning or teaching by making use of both hearing and sight **2** : of or relating to both hearing and sight

au·dio·vi·su·als \-wəlz, -əlz\ *n pl* (1955) : teaching materials (as filmstrips accompanied by recordings) that make use of both sight and sound

[1]au·dit \'ȯd-ət\ *n* [ME, fr. L *auditus* act of hearing, fr. *auditus,* pp.] (15c) **1 a** : a formal examination of an organization's or individual's accounts or financial situation **b** : the final report of an audit **2** : a methodical examination and review — **au·dit·able** \-ə-bəl\ *adj*

[2]audit *vt* (15c) **1** : to perform an audit on or for ⟨~ the books⟩ ⟨~ the company⟩ **2** : to attend (a course) without working for or expecting to receive formal credit

[1]au·di·tion \ȯ-'dish-ən\ *n* [MF or L; MF, fr. L *audition-, auditio,* fr. *auditus,* pp. of *audire*] (1599) **1** : the power or sense of hearing **2** : the act of hearing; *esp* : a critical hearing ⟨an ~ of new recordings⟩ **3** : a trial performance to appraise an entertainer's merits

[2]audition *vb* **au·di·tioned; au·di·tion·ing** \-'dish-(ə-)niŋ\ *vt* (1934) : to test esp. in an audition ~ *vi* : to give a trial performance

au·di·tive \'ȯd-ət-iv\ *adj* (15c) : AUDITORY

au·di·tor \'ȯd-ət-ər\ *n* (14c) **1** : one that hears or listens; *esp* : one that is a member of an audience **2** : one authorized to examine and verify accounts **3** : one that audits a course of study **4** : one that hears (as a court case) in the capacity of judge

au·di·to·ri·um \ˌȯd-ə-'tōr-ē-əm, -'tȯr-\ *n, pl* **-riums** *also* **-ria** \-ē-ə\ [L, lit., lecture room] (ca. 1727) **1** : the part of a public building where an audience sits **2** : a room, hall, or building used for public gatherings

[1]au·di·to·ry \'ȯd-ə-ˌtōr-ē, -ˌtȯr-\ *n* [ME *auditorie,* fr. L *auditorium*] (14c) **1** *archaic* : AUDIENCE **2** *archaic* : AUDITORIUM

[2]au·di·to·ry *adj* [LL *auditorius*] (1578) : of, relating to, or experienced through hearing

auditory nerve *n* (1724) : either of the 8th pair of cranial nerves connecting the inner ear with the brain and transmitting impulses concerned with hearing and balance — see EAR illustration

Auf·klä·rung \'au̇f-ˌklā-rəŋ, -ˌkler-əŋ\ *n* [G] (1842) : ENLIGHTENMENT 2

auf Wie·der·seh·en \au̇f-'vēd-ər-ˌzā(-ə)n\ *interj* [G, lit., till seeing again] (1885) — used to express farewell

Au·ge·an \ȯ-'jē-ən\ *adj* [L *Augeas,* king of Elis, fr. Gk *Augeias;* fr. the legend that his stable, left neglected for 30 years, was finally cleaned by Hercules] (1599) : extremely formidable or difficult and occas. distasteful ⟨an ~ task⟩

Augean stable *n* (1635) : a condition or place marked by great accumulation of filth or corruption ⟨every government should attend to cleaning its own *Augean stables*⟩

au·gend \'ȯ-ˌjend\ *n* [L *augendus,* gerundive of *augēre* to increase — more at EKE] (ca. 1909) : a quantity to which an addend is added

au·ger \'ȯ-gər\ *n* [ME, alter. (resulting from incorrect division of *a nauger*) of *nauger,* fr. OE *nafogār;* akin to OHG *nabugēr* auger, OE *gār* spear — more at GORE] (bef. 12c) **1** : a tool for boring holes in wood consisting of a shank with a crosswise handle for turning, a central tapered screw, and a pair of cutting lips **2** : any of various instruments or devices made like an auger and used for boring (as in soil), forcing (as through a meat grinder), or for moving material (as in a snow thrower)

[1]aught \'ȯt, 'ät\ *pron* [ME, fr. OE *āwiht,* fr. *ā* ever + *wiht* creature, thing — more at AYE, WIGHT] (bef. 12c) **1** : ANYTHING **2** : ALL ⟨for ~ I care⟩

[2]aught *adv, archaic* (13c) : AT ALL

[3]aught *n* [alter. (resulting from incorrect division of *a naught*) of *naught*] (1872) **1** : ZERO, CIPHER **2** *archaic* : NONENTITY, NOTHING

au·gite \'ȯ-ˌjīt\ *n* [L *augites,* a precious stone, fr. Gk *augitēs*] (1804) **1** : a mineral consisting of an aluminous usu. black or dark green pyroxene that is found in igneous rocks **2** : PYROXENE — **au·git·ic** \ȯ-'jit-ik\ *adj*

aug·ment \ȯg-'ment\ *vb* [ME *augmenten,* fr. MF *augmenter,* fr. LL *augmentare,* fr. *augmentum* increase, fr. *augēre* to increase — more at EKE] *vi* (15c) : to become augmented ~ *vt* **1** : to make greater, more numerous, larger, or more intense ⟨the impact of the report was ~*ed* by its timing⟩ **2** : to add an augment to **3** : SUPPLEMENT ⟨~*ed* her scholarship by working nights⟩ ***syn*** see INCREASE — **aug·ment·er** *or* **aug·men·tor** \-'ment-ər\ *n*

[2]aug·ment \'ȯg-ˌment\ *n* (1771) : a vowel prefixed or a lengthening of the initial vowel to mark past time esp. in Greek and Sanskrit verbs

aug·men·ta·tion \ˌȯg-mən-'tā-shən, -ˌmen-\ *n* (14c) **1 a** : the act or process of augmenting **b** : the state of being augmented **2** : something that augments : ADDITION

[1]aug·men·ta·tive \ȯg-'ment-ət-iv\ *adj* (15c) **1** : able to augment **2** : indicating large size and sometimes awkwardness or unattractiveness — used of words and affixes; compare DIMINUTIVE

[2]augmentative *n* (1804) : an augmentative word or affix

\ə\ abut \ᵊ\ kitten, F table \ər\ further \a\ ash \ā\ ace \ä\ cot, cart
\au̇\ out \ch\ chin \e\ bet \ē\ easy \g\ go \i\ hit \ī\ ice \j\ job
\ŋ\ sing \ō\ go \ȯ\ law \ȯi\ boy \th\ thin \t͟h\ the \ü\ loot \u̇\ foot
\y\ yet \zh\ vision \à, k̲, ⁿ, œ, œ̄, ue, ue̅, ʸ\ *see* Guide to Pronunciation

aug·ment·ed \ȯg-ˈment-əd\ *adj, of a musical interval* (ca. 1825) **:** made one half step greater than major or perfect ⟨an ~ fifth⟩
augmented matrix *n* (ca. 1942) **:** a matrix whose elements are the coefficients of a set of simultaneous linear equations with the constant terms of the equations entered in an added column
au gra·tin \ō-ˈgrät-ᵊn, ȯ-, -ˈgrat-\ *adj* [F, lit., with the burnt scrapings from the pan] (1806) **:** covered with bread crumbs or grated cheese and browned (as under a broiler)
¹au·gur \ˈȯ-gər\ *n* [L; prob. akin to L *augēre*] (14c) **1 :** an official diviner of ancient Rome **2 :** one held to foretell events by omens
²augur *vt* (1601) **1 :** to foretell esp. from omens **2 :** to give promise of **:** PRESAGE ⟨higher pay ~*s* a better future⟩ ~ *vi* **:** to predict the future esp. from omens
au·gu·ry \ˈȯ-gyə-rē, -gə-\ *n, pl* **-ries** (14c) **1 :** divination from omens or portents or from chance events (as the fall of lots) **2 :** OMEN, PORTENT
au·gust \ȯ-ˈgəst, ˈȯ-(ˌ)gəst\ *adj* [L *augustus;* akin to L *augēre* to increase] (1664) **:** marked by majestic dignity or grandeur — **au·gust·ly** *adv* — **au·gust·ness** \ȯ-ˈgəs(t)-nəs, ˈȯ-(ˌ)gəs(t)-\ *n*
Au·gust \ˈȯ-gəst\ *n* [ME, fr. OE, fr. L *Augustus,* fr. *Augustus* Caesar] (bef. 12c) **:** the 8th month of the Gregorian calendar
Au·gus·tan \ȯ-ˈgəs-tən, ə-\ *adj* (1704) **1 :** of, relating to, or characteristic of Augustus Caesar or his age **2 :** of, relating to, or characteristic of the neoclassical period in England — **Augustan** *n*
¹Au·gus·tin·i·an \ˌȯ-gə-ˈstin-ē-ən\ *n* (1602) **1 :** a follower of St. Augustine **2 :** a member of an Augustinian order; *specif* **:** a friar of the Hermits of St. Augustine founded in 1256 and devoted to educational, missionary, and parish work
²Augustinian *adj* (1674) **1 :** of or relating to St. Augustine or his doctrines **2 :** of or relating to any of several orders under a rule ascribed to St. Augustine — **Au·gus·tin·i·an·ism** \-ē-ə-ˌniz-əm\ *n*
au jus \ō-ˈzhü(s), -ˈjüs; ō-zhü̅\ *adj* [F, lit., with juice] *of meat* (ca. 1919) **:** served in the juice obtained from roasting
auk \ˈȯk\ *n* [Norw or Icel *alk, alka,* fr. ON *ālka;* akin to L *olor* swan] (ca. 1674) **:** any of several black-and-white short-necked diving seabirds (family Alcidae) that breed in colder parts of the northern hemisphere

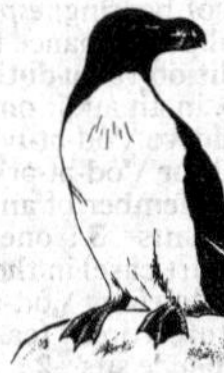
auk

auk·let \ˈȯ-klət\ *n* (1886) **:** any of several small auks of the No. Pacific coasts
auld \ˈȯl(d), ˈäl(d)\ *adj, chiefly Scot* (14c) **:** OLD
auld lang syne \ˌōl-ˌ(d)aŋ-ˈzīn, ˌōl-ˌ(d)laŋ-, ˌȯl-\ *n* [Sc, lit., old long ago] (1692) **:** the good old times
au na·tu·rel \ˌō-ˌnat-ə-ˈrel, -ˌnach-\ *adj* [F] (1817) **1 :** cooked or served plainly **2 a :** being in natural style or condition **b :** NUDE
aunt \ˈant, ˈänt\ *n* [ME, fr. OF *ante,* fr. L *amita;* akin to OHG *amma* mother, nurse, Gk *amma* nurse] (13c) **1 :** the sister of one's father or mother **2 :** the wife of one's uncle — **aunt·hood** \-ˌhu̇d\ *n* — **aunt·like** \-ˌlīk\ *adj* — **aunt·ly** *adj*
Aunt Sal·ly \-ˈsal-ē\ *n, pl* **Aunt Sallies** [*Aunt Sally,* name given to an effigy of a woman smoking a pipe set up as an amusement attraction at English fairs for patrons to throw missiles at] *Brit* (1898) **:** an object of criticism or contention; *esp* **:** one that is set up to invite criticism or be easily refuted
au pair \ˈō-ˈpa(ə)r, -ˈpe(ə)r\ *n* [F *au pair,* on even terms] (1960) **:** a foreign girl who does domestic work for a family in return for room and board and the opportunity to learn the family's language
aur- *or* **auri-** *comb form* [L, fr. *auris* — more at EAR] **1 :** ear ⟨*aural*⟩ ⟨*auri*scope⟩ **2 :** aural and ⟨*auri*nasal⟩
au·ra \ˈȯr-ə\ *n* [ME, fr. L, air, breeze, fr. Gk; akin to Gk *aēr* air] (1732) **1 a :** a subtle sensory stimulus (as an aroma) **b :** a distinctive atmosphere surrounding a given source ⟨the place had an ~ of mystery⟩ **2 :** a luminous radiation **:** NIMBUS **3 :** a subjective sensation (as of lights) experienced before an attack of some nervous disorders
au·ral \ˈȯr-əl\ *adj* (1847) **:** of or relating to the ear or to the sense of hearing — **au·ral·ly** \-ə-lē\ *adv*
aurar *pl of* EYRIR
au·re·ate \ˈȯr-ē-ət\ *adj* [ME *aureat,* fr. ML *aureatus* decorated with gold, fr. L *aureus* — more at ORIOLE] (15c) **1 :** of a golden color or brilliance **2 :** marked by grandiloquent and rhetorical style
au·re·ole \ˈȯr-ē-ˌōl\ *or* **au·re·o·la** \ȯ-ˈrē-ə-lə, ə-\ *n* [ME *aureole* heavenly crown worn by saints, fr. ML *aureola,* fr. L, fem. of *aureolus* golden — more at ORIOLE] (13c) **1 :** a radiant light around the head or body of a representation of a sacred personage **2 :** RADIANCE, AURA ⟨had about him an ~ of youth and health⟩ **3 :** the luminous area surrounding the sun or other bright light when seen through thin cloud or mist **:** CORONA **4 :** a ring-shaped zone around an igneous intrusion — **aureole** *vt*
Au·reo·my·cin \ˌȯr-ē-ō-ˈmīs-ᵊn\ *trademark* — used for chlortetracycline
au·re·us \ˈȯr-ē-əs\ *n, pl* **-rei** \-ē-ˌī\ [L, lit., golden] (1609) **:** a gold coin of ancient Rome varying in weight from $^1/_{30}$ to $^1/_{70}$ libra
au re·voir \ˌōr-əv-ˈwär, ˌȯr-, *F* ōr(-ə)-vwȧr\ *n* [F, lit., till seeing again] (1694) **:** GOOD-BYE — often used interjectionally
au·ric \ˈȯr-ik\ *adj* [L *aurum* gold — more at ORIOLE] (ca. 1828) **:** of, relating to, or derived from gold esp. when trivalent
au·ri·cle \ˈȯr-i-kəl\ *n* [L *auricula,* fr. dim. of *auris* ear — more at EAR] (15c) **1 a :** an atrium of a heart **b :** PINNA 2b **c :** an anterior ear-shaped pouch in each atrium of the human heart **2 :** an angular or ear-shaped anatomic lobe or process
au·ric·u·la \ȯ-ˈrik-yə-lə\ *n* [NL, fr. L, external ear] (1655) **:** a yellow-flowered Alpine primrose (*Primula auricula*)
au·ric·u·lar \ȯ-ˈrik-yə-lər\ *adj* (15c) **1 :** told privately ⟨an ~ confession⟩ **2 :** understood or recognized by the sense of hearing **3 :** of, relating to, or using the ear or the sense of hearing **4 :** of or relating to an auricle
au·ric·u·late \ȯ-ˈrik-yə-lət\ *adj* (1713) **:** having ears or auricles
au·rif·er·ous \ȯ-ˈrif-(ə-)rəs\ *adj* [L *aurifer,* fr. *aurum* + *-fer* -ferous] (1727) **:** gold-bearing
Au·ri·ga \ȯ-ˈrī-gə\ *n* [L, lit., charioteer] **:** a constellation between Perseus and Gemini
Au·ri·gna·cian \ˌȯr-ēn-ˈyā-shən\ *adj* [F *aurignacien,* fr. *Aurignac,* France] (1909) **:** of or relating to an Upper Paleolithic culture marked by finely made artifacts of stone and bone, paintings, and engravings
au·rochs \ˈau̇(ə)r-ˌäks, ˈȯ(ə)r-\ *n, pl* **aurochs** [G, fr. OHG *ūrohso,* fr. *ūro* aurochs + *ohso* ox; akin to OE *ūr* aurochs — more at OX] (ca. 1766) **1 :** URUS **2 :** WISENT
au·ro·ra \ə-ˈrōr-ə, ȯ-, -ˈrȯr-\ *n, pl* **auroras** *or* **au·ro·rae** \-(ˌ)ē\ [L — more at EAST] (14c) **1 :** DAWN **2** *cap* **:** the Roman goddess of dawn — compare EOS **3 :** a luminous phenomenon that consists of streamers or arches of light appearing in the upper atmosphere of a planet's polar regions and is caused by the emission of light from atoms excited by electrons accelerated along the planet's magnetic field lines — **au·ro·ral** \-əl\ *adj* — **au·ro·re·an** \-ē-ən\ *adj*
aurora aus·tra·lis \-ȯ-ˈstrā-ləs, -ä-ˈstrā-\ *n* [NL, lit., southern dawn] (1741) **:** an aurora that occurs in earth's southern hemisphere — called also *southern lights*
aurora bo·re·al·is \-ˌbōr-ē-ˈal-əs, -ˌbȯr-\ *n* [NL, lit., northern dawn] (1717) **:** an aurora that occurs in earth's northern hemisphere — called also *northern lights*
au·rous \ˈȯr-əs\ *adj* [ISV, fr. L *aurum* gold — more at ORIOLE] (1862) **:** of, relating to, or containing gold esp. when univalent
aus·cul·tate \ˈȯ-skəl-ˌtāt\ *vt* **-tat·ed; -tat·ing** [back-formation fr. *auscultation*] (ca. 1860) **:** to examine by auscultation — **aus·cul·ta·to·ry** \ȯ-ˈskəl-tə-ˌtōr-ē, -ˌtȯr-\ *adj*
aus·cul·ta·tion \ˌȯ-skəl-ˈtā-shən\ *n* [L *auscultation-, auscultatio* act of listening, fr. *auscultatus,* pp. of *auscultare* to listen; akin to L *auris* ear — more at EAR] (ca. 1828) **:** the act of listening to sounds arising within organs (as the lungs) as an aid to diagnosis and treatment
aus·land·er \ˈau̇-ˌslen-dər, -ˌslan-\ *n* [G *ausländer,* lit., outlander] (1936) **:** OUTSIDER, FOREIGNER
aus·pice \ˈȯ-spəs\ *n, pl* **aus·pic·es** \-spə-səz, -ˌsēz\ [L *auspicium,* fr. *auspic-, auspex* diviner by birds, fr. *avis* bird + *specere* to look, look at — more at AVIARY, SPY] (1533) **1 :** observation by an augur esp. of the flight and feeding of birds to discover omens **2 :** a prophetic sign; *esp* **:** a favorable sign **3** *pl* **:** kindly patronage and guidance
aus·pi·cious \ȯ-ˈspish-əs\ *adj* (1601) **1 :** affording a favorable auspice **:** PROPITIOUS ⟨made an ~ beginning by getting an A⟩ **2 :** attended by good auspices **:** PROSPEROUS ⟨an ~ year⟩ ***syn*** see FAVORABLE — **aus·pi·cious·ly** *adv* — **aus·pi·cious·ness** *n*
Aus·sie \ˈȯ-sē, ˈäs-ē, *Brit & Austral usu* ˈȯ-zē\ *n* [Australian + *-ie*] (1917) **:** a native or inhabitant of Australia
aus·ten·ite \ˈȯs-tə-ˌnīt, ˈäs-\ *n* [F, fr. Sir W. C. Roberts-*Austen* †1902 Eng. metallurgist] (1902) **:** a solid solution in iron of carbon and sometimes other solutes that occurs as a constituent of steel under certain conditions — **aus·ten·it·ic** \ˌȯs-tə-ˈnit-ik, ˌäs-\ *adj*
aus·tere \ȯ-ˈsti(ə)r *also* -ˈste(ə)r\ *adj* [ME, fr. MF, fr. L *austerus,* fr. Gk *austēros* harsh, severe; akin to Gk *hauos* dry — more at SERE] (14c) **1 a :** stern and cold in appearance or manner **b :** SOMBER, GRAVE ⟨an ~ critic⟩ **2 :** morally strict **:** ASCETIC **3 :** simple and unadorned ⟨an ~ office⟩ ⟨an ~ style of writing⟩ **4 :** giving little or no scope for pleasure ⟨~ diets⟩ ***syn*** see SEVERE — **aus·tere·ly** *adv* — **aus·tere·ness** *n*
aus·ter·i·ty \ȯ-ˈster-ə-tē *also* -ˈstir-\ *n, pl* **-ties** (14c) **1 :** the quality or state of being austere **2 a :** an austere act, manner, or attitude **b :** an ascetic practice **3 :** enforced or extreme economy
¹Austr- *or* **Austro-** *comb form* [ME *austr-,* fr. L, fr. *Austr-, Auster* south wind; akin to L *aurora* dawn — more at EAST] **1 :** south **:** southern ⟨*Austro*asiatic⟩ **2 :** Australian and ⟨*Austro*-Malayan⟩
²Austr- *or* **Austro-** *comb form* [prob. fr. NL, fr. *Austria*] **:** Austrian and ⟨*Austro*-Hungarian⟩
¹aus·tral \ˈȯs-trəl, ˈäs-\ *adj* (1541) **1 :** SOUTHERN **2** *cap* **:** AUSTRALIAN
²aus·tral \au̇-ˈsträl\ *n, pl* **aus·tral·es** \-ˈsträl-ās\ *also* **australs** [Sp] (1985) — see MONEY table
Aus·tra·lia Day \ȯ-ˈstrāl-yə-, ä-, ə-\ *n* (1925) **:** a national holiday in Australia observed in commemoration of the landing of the British at Sydney Cove in 1788 and observed on Jan. 26 if a Monday and otherwise on the next Monday
¹Aus·tra·lian \ȯ-ˈstrāl-yən, ä-, ə-\ *adj* (1814) **1 :** of, relating to, or characteristic of the continent or commonwealth of Australia, its inhabitants, or the languages spoken there **2 :** of, relating to, or being a biogeographic region that comprises Australia and the islands north of it from the Celebes eastward, Tasmania, New Zealand, and Polynesia
²Australian *n* (1815) **1 :** a native or inhabitant of the Australian commonwealth **2 :** the speech of the aboriginal inhabitants of Australia
Australian ballot *n* (1888) **:** an official ballot printed at public expense on which the names of all the candidates and proposals appear and which is distributed only at the polling place and marked in secret
Australian cattle dog *n* (1926) **:** any of a medium-sized compact breed of dogs developed in Australia to herd cattle and having upright ears and a red or blue mottled coat
Australian pine *n* (1919) **:** any of several casuarinas (esp. *Casuarina equisetifolia*) now widely grown as ornamentals in warm regions
Australian Rules football *n* (1933) **:** a game resembling rugby that is played between two teams of 18 players on a field 180–190 yards long that has four goalposts at each end
Australian terrier *n* (1903) **:** any of a breed of small rather short-legged usu. grayish wirehaired terriers of Australian origin
Aus·tra·loid \ˈȯs-trə-ˌlȯid, ˈäs-\ *adj* [*Australia* + E *-oid*] (1864) **:** of or relating to an ethnic group including the Australian aborigines and other peoples of southern Asia and Pacific islands sometimes including the Ainu — **Australoid** *n*

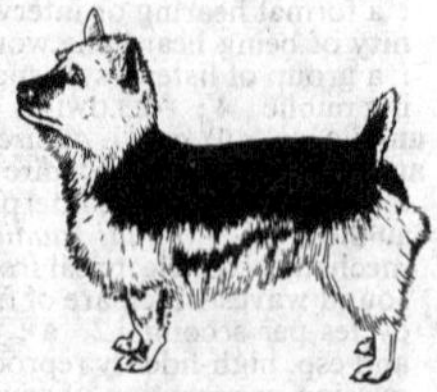
Australian terrier

aus·tra·lo·pith·e·cine \ȯ-ˌstrā-lō-ˈpith-ə-ˌsīn, ä-; ˌȯs-trə-, ˌäs-\ *n* [deriv. of L *australis* southern (fr. *Austr-, Auster*) + Gk *pithēkos* ape — more at PITHECANTHROPUS] (1938) **:** any of a genus (*Australopithecus*) of extinct southern African hominids with near-human dentition and a relatively small brain — **australopithecine** *adj*
Aus·tral·orp \ˈȯs-trə-ˌlȯ(ə)rp, ˈäs-\ *n* [*Australian* + *Orpington*] (1922) **:** a usu. black domestic fowl developed in Australia and valued for egg production

Aus·tro·asi·at·ic \ˌös-(ˌ)trō-ˌā-z(h)ē-ˈat-ik, ˈäs- *also* -ˌā-shē-\ *adj* (1922) : of, relating to, or constituting a family of languages once widespread over northeastern India and Indochina

Aus·tro·ne·sian \ˌös-trə-ˈnē-zhən, ˌäs-, -shən\ *adj* [*Austronesia*, islands of the southern Pacific] (1925) : of, relating to, or constituting a family of agglutinative languages spoken in the area extending from Madagascar eastward through the Malay peninsula and archipelago to Hawaii and Easter Island and including practically all the native languages of the Pacific Islands with the exception of the Australian, Papuan, and Ne-grito languages

aut- *or* **auto-** *comb form* [Gk, fr. *autos* same, -self, self] 1 : self : same one ⟨*autism*⟩ ⟨*autobiography*⟩ 2 : automatic : self-acting : self-regulating ⟨*autodyne*⟩

au·ta·coid \ˈöt-ə-ˌkȯid\ *n* [*aut-* + Gk *akos* remedy] (1914) : a specific organic substance (as a hormone) forming in one part of the body, moving in the body fluid or the sap, and modifying the activity of the cells of another part

au·tar·chic \ȯ-ˈtär-kik\ *adj* (1883) : AUTARKIC — **au·tar·chi·cal** \-ki-kəl\ *adj*

¹au·tar·chy \ˈȯ-ˌtär-kē\ *n* [by alter.] (1617) : AUTARKY

²autarchy *n, pl* **-chies** [Gk *autarchia*, fr. *aut-* + *-archia* -archy] (1665) 1 : absolute sovereignty 2 : absolute or autocratic rule

au·tar·kic \ȯ-ˈtär-kik\ *adj* (1936) : of, relating to, or marked by autarky — **au·tar·ki·cal** \-ki-kəl\ *adj*

au·tar·ky \ˈȯ-ˌtär-kē\ *n* [G *autarkie*, fr. Gk *autarkeia*, fr. *autarkēs* self-sufficient, fr. *aut-* + *arkein* to defend, suffice — more at ARK] (1657) 1 : SELF-SUFFICIENCY, INDEPENDENCE; *specif* : national economic self-sufficiency and independence 2 : a policy of establishing a self-sufficient and independent national economy

aut·ecol·o·gy \ˌȯt-i-ˈkäl-ə-jē, ˌȯt-ē-\ *n* [ISV] (ca. 1910) : ecology dealing with individual organisms or individual kinds of organisms — **aut·eco·log·i·cal** \ˌȯt-ˌē-kə-ˈläj-i-kəl, -ˌek-ə-\ *adj*

au·teur theory \ō-ˈtər-\ *n* [part trans. of F *politique des auteurs*, fr. *auteur* author; fr. the view that directors are the true authors of a film] (ca. 1962) : a view of film making in which the director is considered the primary creative force in a motion picture

au·then·tic \ə-ˈthent-ik, ȯ-\ *adj* [ME *autentik*, fr. MF *autentique*, fr. LL *authenticus*, fr. Gk *authentikos*, fr. *authentēs* perpetrator, master, fr. *aut-* + *-hentēs* (akin to Gk *anyein* to accomplish, Skt *sanoti* he gains)] (14c) 1 *obs* : AUTHORITATIVE 2 : worthy of acceptance or belief as conforming to fact or reality : TRUSTWORTHY 3 a : not imaginary, false, or imitation ⟨one of the few remaining ~ colonial buildings⟩ b : conforming to an original so as to reproduce essential features ⟨an ~ reproduction of a colonial farmhouse⟩ 4 a *of a church mode* : ranging upward from the keynote — compare PLAGAL 1 b *of a cadence* : progressing from the dominant chord to the tonic — compare PLA-GAL 2 — **au·then·ti·cal·ly** \-i-k(ə-)lē\ *adv* — **au·then·tic·i·ty** \ˌȯ-ˌthen-ˈtis-ət-ē, -thən-\ *n*

syn AUTHENTIC, GENUINE, VERITABLE, BONA FIDE mean being actually and exactly what is claimed. AUTHENTIC implies being fully trustworthy as according with fact or actuality ⟨the *authentic* story⟩ GENUINE implies accordance with an original or a type without counterfeiting, admixture, or adulteration ⟨*genuine* maple syrup⟩ or it may stress sincerity ⟨*genuine* piety⟩ VERITABLE may stress true existence or actual identity ⟨*veritable* offspring⟩ but more commonly merely asserts the suitability of a metaphor ⟨*veritable* hail of questions⟩ BONA FIDE can apply when sincerity of intention is in question ⟨*bona fide* sale of securities⟩

au·then·ti·cate \ə-ˈthent-i-ˌkāt, ȯ-\ *vt* **-cat·ed; -cat·ing** (1653) : to prove or serve to prove the authenticity of *syn* see CONFIRM — **au·then·ti·ca·tion** \-ˌthent-i-ˈkā-shən\ *n* — **au·then·ti·ca·tor** \-ˈthent-i-ˌkāt-ər\ *n*

¹au·thor \ˈȯ-thər\ *n* [ME *auctour*, fr. ONF, fr. L *auctor* promoter, originator, author, fr. *auctus*, pp. of *augēre* to increase — more at EKE] (14c) 1 : the writer of a literary work (as a book) 2 a : one that originates or gives existence : SOURCE ⟨trying to track down the ~ of the rumor⟩ ⟨the ~ of a theory⟩ b *cap* : GOD 1 — **au·tho·ri·al** \ȯ-ˈthȯr-ē-əl, -ˈthōr-\ *adj*

²author *vt* (1596) : to be the author of

au·thor·ess \ˈȯ-th(ə-)rəs\ *n* (15c) : a woman author

au·thor·i·tar·i·an \ə-ˌthär-ə-ˈter-ē-ən, ȯ-, -ˌthȯr-\ *adj* (1879) 1 : of, relating to, or favoring blind submission to authority ⟨had ~ parents⟩ 2 : of, relating to, or favoring a concentration of power in a leader or an elite not constitutionally responsible to the people — **authoritarian** *n* — **au·thor·i·tar·i·an·ism** \-ē-ə-ˌniz-əm\ *n*

au·thor·i·ta·tive \ə-ˈthär-ə-ˌtāt-iv, ȯ-, -ˈthȯr-\ *adj* (1605) 1 a : having or proceeding from authority : OFFICIAL ⟨~ church doctrine⟩ b : entitled to credit or acceptance : CONCLUSIVE ⟨a most ~ literary critique⟩ 2 : DICTATORIAL, PEREMPTORY — **au·thor·i·ta·tive·ly** *adv* — **au·thor·i·ta·tive·ness** *n*

au·thor·i·ty \ə-ˈthär-ət-ē, ȯ-, -ˈthȯr-\ *n, pl* **-ties** [ME *auctorite*, fr. OF *auctorité*, fr. L *auctoritat-, auctoritas* opinion, decision, power, fr. *auctor*] (13c) 1 a (1) : a citation (as from a book or file) used in defense or support (2) : the source from which the citation is drawn b (1) : a conclusive statement or set of statements (as an official decision of a court) (2) : a decision taken as a precedent (3) : TESTIMONY c : an individual cited or appealed to as an expert 2 a : power to influence or command thought, opinion, or behavior b : freedom granted by one in authority : RIGHT 3 a : persons in command; *specif* : GOVERNMENT b : a governmental agency or corporation to administer a revenue-producing public enterprise ⟨the transit ~⟩ 4 a : GROUNDS, WARRANT ⟨had excellent ~ for his strange actions⟩ b : convincing force : WEIGHT ⟨his strong tenor lent ~ to the performance⟩ *syn* see INFLUENCE, POWER

au·tho·ri·za·tion \ˌȯ-th(ə-)rə-ˈzā-shən\ *n* (15c) 1 : the act of authorizing 2 : an instrument that authorizes : SANCTION

au·tho·rize \ˈȯ-thə-ˌrīz\ *vt* **-rized; -riz·ing** (14c) 1 : to establish by or as if by authority : SANCTION ⟨a custom *authorized* by time⟩ 2 : to invest esp. with legal authority : EMPOWER ⟨*authorized* to act for her husband⟩ 3 *archaic* : to furnish a ground for : JUSTIFY — **au·tho·riz·er** *n*

Authorized Version *n* (ca. 1613) : a revision of the English Bishops' Bible carried out under James I, published in 1611, and widely used by Protestants

au·thor·ship \ˈȯ-thər-ˌship\ *n* (1710) 1 : the profession of writing 2 a : the source (as the author) of a piece of writing, music, or art b : the state or act of writing, creating, or causing

au·tism \ˈȯ-ˌtiz-əm\ *n* (1912) : absorption in self-centered subjective mental activity (as daydreams, fantasies, delusions, and hallucinations) esp. when accompanied by marked withdrawal from reality — **au·tis·tic** \ȯ-ˈtis-tik\ *adj* — **au·tis·ti·cal·ly** \-ti-k(ə-)lē\ *adv*

au·to \ˈȯt-(ˌ)ō, ˈät-\ *n, pl* **autos** (1899) : AUTOMOBILE

¹auto- — see AUT-

²auto- *comb form* [¹*automobile*] : self-propelling : automotive ⟨*autotruck*⟩

au·to·an·ti·body \ˌȯt-ō-(ˌ)ō-ˈant-i-ˌbäd-ē\ *n* (ca. 1910) : an antibody active against a tissue constituent of the individual producing it

au·to·bahn \ˈȯt-ō-ˌbän, ˈaut-\ *n* [G, fr. *auto* + *bahn* road] (1937) : a German expressway

au·to·bi·o·graph·i·cal \ˌȯt-ə-ˌbī-ə-ˈgraf-i-kəl\ *also* **au·to·bio·graph·ic** \-ik\ *adj* (1829) : of, relating to, or of the nature of an autobiography — **au·to·bio·graph·i·cal·ly** \-i-k(ə-)lē\ *adv*

au·to·bi·og·ra·phy \ˌȯt-ə-bī-ˈäg-rə-fē, -bē-\ *n* (1771) : the biography of a person narrated by himself — **au·to·bi·og·ra·pher** \-fər\ *n*

au·to·bus \ˈȯt-ō-ˌbəs\ *n* [*auto* + *bus*] (1899) : OMNIBUS 1

au·to·cade \ˈȯt-ō-ˌkād\ *n* (ca. 1931) : MOTORCADE

au·to·ca·tal·y·sis \ˌȯt-ō-kə-ˈtal-ə-səs\ *n, pl* **-y·ses** \-ˌsēz\ [NL] (1891) : catalysis of a reaction by one of its products — **au·to·cat·a·lyt·ic** \-ˌkat-ᵊl-ˈit-ik\ *adj* — **au·to·cat·a·lyt·i·cal·ly** \-i-k(ə-)lē\ *adv*

au·to·ceph·a·lous \ˌȯt-ō-ˈsef-ə-ləs\ *adj* [LGk *autokephalos*, fr. Gk *aut-* + *kephalē* head — more at CEPHALIC] (1863) : being independent of external and esp. patriarchal authority — used esp. of Eastern national churches

au·toch·thon \ȯ-ˈtäk-thən\ *n, pl* **-thons** *or* **-tho·nes** \-thə-ˌnēz\ [Gk *autochthōn*, fr. *aut-* + *chthōn* earth — more at HUMBLE] (ca. 1579) : one (as a person, plant, or animal) that is autochthonous

au·toch·tho·nous \ȯ-ˈtäk-thə-nəs\ *adj* (1805) 1 : INDIGENOUS, NATIVE ⟨an ~ people⟩ 2 : formed or originating in the place where found ⟨~ rock⟩ ⟨an ~ infection⟩ — **au·toch·tho·nous·ly** *adv*

¹au·to·clave \ˈȯt-ō-ˌklāv\ *n* [F, fr. *aut-* + L *clavis* key — more at CLAVICLE] (1876) : an apparatus (as for sterilizing) using superheated steam under pressure

²autoclave *vt* **-claved; -clav·ing** (1911) : to subject to the action of an autoclave

au·toc·ra·cy \ȯ-ˈtäk-rə-sē\ *n, pl* **-cies** (1655) 1 : the authority or rule of an autocrat 2 : government in which one person possesses unlimited power 3 : a community or state governed by autocracy

au·to·crat \ˈȯt-ə-ˌkrat\ *n* [F *autocrate*, fr. Gk *autokratēs* ruling by oneself, absolute, fr. *aut-* + *-kratēs* ruling — more at -CRAT] (1803) 1 : a person (as a monarch) ruling with unlimited authority 2 : one who has undisputed influence or power

au·to·crat·ic \ˌȯt-ə-ˈkrat-ik\ *adj* (1823) 1 : of, relating to, or being an autocracy : ABSOLUTE ⟨an ~ government⟩ 2 : characteristic of or resembling an autocrat : DESPOTIC ⟨an ~ ruler⟩ — **au·to·crat·i·cal** \-i-kəl\ *adj* — **au·to·crat·i·cal·ly** \-i-k(ə-)lē\ *adv*

au·to·cross \ˈȯt-ō-ˌkrȯs, ˈät-\ *n* [*auto*] (1963) : an automobile gymkhana

au·to–da–fé \ˌaut-ō-də-ˈfā, ˌȯt-\ *n, pl* **au·tos–da–fé** \-ōz-də-\ [Pg *auto da fé*, lit., act of the faith] (1723) : the ceremony accompanying the pronouncement of judgment by the Inquisition and followed by the execution of sentence by the secular authorities; *broadly* : the burning of a heretic

au·to·di·dact \ˌȯt-ō-ˈdī-ˌdakt, -dī-ˈ, -də-ˈ\ *n* [Gk *autodidaktos* self-taught, fr. *aut-* + *didaktos* taught, fr. *didaskein* to teach] (1748) : a self-taught person — **au·to·di·dac·tic** \-dī-ˈdak-tik, -də-ˈ\ *adj*

au·to·dyne \ˈȯt-ə-ˌdīn\ *n* [ISV *aut-* + *heterodyne*] (1911) : a heterodyne in which the auxiliary current is generated in the device used for rectification

au·toe·cious \ȯ-ˈtē-shəs\ *adj* [*aut-* + Gk *oikia* house — more at VICINITY] (ca. 1882) : passing through all life stages on the same host ⟨~ rusts⟩ — **au·toe·cious·ly** *adv* — **au·toe·cious·ness** \-siz-əm\ *n*

au·to·er·o·tism \ˌȯt-ō-ˈer-ə-ˌtiz-əm\ *or* **au·to·erot·i·cism** \-i-ˈrät-ə-ˌsiz-əm\ *n* (1898) 1 : sexual feeling arising without known external stimulation 2 : sexual gratification obtained solely through stimulation by oneself of one's own body — **au·to·erot·ic** \-i-ˈrät-ik\ *adj*

au·tog·a·my \ȯ-ˈtäg-ə-mē\ *n* (1877) : SELF-FERTILIZATION: as a : pollination of a flower by its own pollen b : conjugation of two sister cells or sister nuclei of protozoans or fungi — **au·tog·a·mous** \-məs\ *adj*

au·tog·e·nous \ȯ-ˈtäj-ə-nəs\ *also* **au·to·gen·ic** \ˌȯt-ə-ˈjen-ik\ *adj* [Gk *autogenēs*, fr. *aut-* + *-genēs* born, produced — more at -GEN] (1846) 1 : produced independently of external influence or aid : ENDOGENOUS 2 : originating or derived from sources within the same individual ⟨an ~ graft⟩ ⟨~ vaccine⟩ 3 : not requiring a meal of blood to produce eggs ⟨~ mosquitoes⟩ — **au·tog·e·nous·ly** *adv* — **au·tog·e·ny** \ȯ-ˈtäj-ə-nē\ *n*

au·to·gi·ro *also* **au·to·gy·ro** \ˌȯt-ō-ˈjī(ə)r-(ˌ)ō\ *n, pl* **-ros** [fr. *Autogiro*, a trademark] (1923) : a rotary-wing aircraft that employs a propeller for forward motion and a freely rotating rotor for lift

au·to·graft \ˈȯt-ō-ˌgraft\ *n* (ca. 1913) : a tissue or organ that is transplanted from one part to another of the same body — **autograft** *vt*

¹au·to·graph \ˈȯt-ə-ˌgraf\ *n* [LL *autographum*, fr. L, neut. of *autographus* written with one's own hand, fr. Gk *autographos*, fr. *aut-* + *-graphos* written — more at -GRAPH] (1640) 1 : something written or made with one's own hand: a : an original manuscript or work of art b : a person's handwritten signature 2 : a representation or trace of an object produced in a photographic emulsion by the mechanical, electrical, chemical, or radiation effects of the object itself — **au·tog·ra·phy** \ȯ-ˈtäg-rə-fē\ *n*

²autograph *vt* (1818) 1 : to write with one's own hand 2 : to write one's signature in or on

---

\ə\ abut \ᵊ\ kitten, F table \ər\ further \a\ ash \ā\ ace \ä\ cot, cart
\au̇\ out \ch\ chin \e\ bet \ē\ easy \g\ go \i\ hit \ī\ ice \j\ job
\ŋ\ sing \ō\ go \ȯ\ law \ȯi\ boy \th\ thin \t̲h̲\ the \ü\ loot \u̇\ foot
\y\ yet \zh\ vision \ā, ᵏ, ⁿ, œ, œ̄, ᵫ, ᵫ̄, ᵋ\ see Guide to Pronunciation

au·to·graph·ic \ˌȯt-ə-ˈgraf-ik\ *adj* (1810) **1 :** of, relating to, or constituting an autograph **2 a** *of an instrument* **:** SELF-RECORDING **b** *of a record* **:** recorded by a self-recording instrument — **au·to·graph·i·cal·ly** \-i-k(ə-)lē\ *adv*

Au·to·harp \ˈȯt-ō-ˌhärp\ *trademark* — used for a zither with button-controlled dampers for selected strings

au·to·hyp·no·sis \ˌȯt-ō-hip-ˈnō-səs\ *n* [NL] (1903) **:** self-induced and usu. automatic hypnosis — **au·to·hyp·not·ic** \-ˈnät-ik\ *adj*

au·to·im·mune \-im-ˈyün\ *adj* (1952) **:** of, relating to, or caused by autoantibodies or lymphocytes that attack molecules, cells, or tissues of the organism producing them ⟨~ diseases⟩ — **au·to·im·mu·ni·ty** \-ˈyü-nət-ē\ *n* — **au·to·im·mu·ni·za·tion** \-ˌim-yə-nə-ˈzā-shən *also* -im-ˌyü-\ *n*

au·to·in·fec·tion \-in-ˈfek-shən\ *n* [ISV] (ca. 1903) **:** reinfection with larvae produced by parasitic worms already in the body

au·to·in·tox·i·ca·tion \-in-ˌtäk-sə-ˈkā-shən\ *n* [ISV] (1887) **:** a state of being poisoned by toxic substances produced within the body

au·to·load·ing \ˌȯt-ō-ˈlōd-iŋ\ *adj* (1923) **:** SEMIAUTOMATIC b

au·tol·o·gous \ȯ-ˈtäl-ə-gəs\ *adj* [*aut-* + *-ologous* (as in *homologous*)] (ca. 1921) **:** derived from the same individual ⟨~ grafts⟩

au·tol·y·sate \ȯ-ˈtäl-ə-ˌsāt, -ˌzāt\ *also* **au·tol·y·zate** \-ˌzāt\ *n* (1910) **:** a product of autolysis

au·tol·y·sis \-ə-səs\ *n* [NL] (1902) **:** breakdown of all or part of a cell or tissue by self-produced enzymes — **au·to·lyt·ic** \ˌȯt-ᵊl-ˈit-ik\ *adj*

au·to·mak·er \ˈȯt-ō-ˌmā-kər, ˈät-\ *n* (ca. 1905) **:** a manufacturer of automobiles

au·to·man \ˈȯt-ō-ˌman, ˈät-\ *n* (1952) **:** AUTOMAKER

au·to·ma·nip·u·la·tion \ˌȯt-ō-mə-ˌnip-yə-ˈlā-shən\ *n* (1964) **:** physical stimulation of the genital organs by oneself — **au·to·ma·nip·u·la·tive** \-ˈnip-yə-ˌlāt-iv\ *adj*

Au·to·mat \ˈȯt-ə-ˌmat\ *service mark* — used for a cafeteria in which food is obtained esp. from vending machines

au·to·mate \ˈȯt-ə-ˌmāt\ *vb* **-mat·ed; -mat·ing** [back-formation fr. *automation*] *vt* (1952) **1 :** to operate by automation **2 :** to convert to largely automatic operation **:** AUTOMATIZE ~ *vi* **:** to undergo automation — **au·to·mat·able** \-ˌmāt-ə-bəl\ *adj*

[1]**au·to·mat·ic** \ˌȯt-ə-ˈmat-ik\ *adj* [Gk *automatos* self-acting, fr. *aut-* + *-matos* (akin to L *ment-, mens* mind) — more at MIND] (1748) **1 a :** largely or wholly involuntary; *esp* **:** REFLEX 5 ⟨~ blinking of the eyelids⟩ **b :** acting or done spontaneously or unconsciously **c :** resembling an automaton **:** MECHANICAL ⟨knew the lesson so well that her answers were ~⟩ **2 :** having a self-acting or self-regulating mechanism **3** *of a firearm* **:** using either gas pressure or force of recoil and mechanical spring action for repeatedly ejecting the empty cartridge shell, introducing a new cartridge, and firing it ***syn*** see SPONTANEOUS — **au·to·mat·i·cal·ly** \-i-k(ə-)lē\ *adv* — **au·to·ma·tic·i·ty** \-mə-ˈtis-ət-ē, -ma-\ *n*

[2]**automatic** *n* (1902) **1 :** a machine or apparatus that operates automatically: as **a :** an automatic firearm **b :** an automatic gear-shifting mechanism **2 :** a semiautomatic firearm **3 :** a substitute offensive or defensive play called at the line of scrimmage in football — called also *audible*

automatic pilot *n* (1916) **:** a device for automatically steering ships, aircraft, and spacecraft — called also *autopilot*

automatic writing *n* (1883) **:** writing performed without conscious intention and sometimes without awareness as if of telepathic or spiritualistic origin

au·to·ma·tion \ˌȯt-ə-ˈmā-shən\ *n* [[1]*automatic*] (1948) **1 :** the technique of making an apparatus, a process, or a system operate automatically **2 :** the state of being operated automatically **3 :** automatically controlled operation of an apparatus, process, or system by mechanical or electronic devices that take the place of human organs of observation, effort, and decision

au·tom·a·tism \ȯ-ˈtäm-ə-ˌtiz-əm\ *n* [F *automatisme*, fr. *automate* automaton, fr. L *automaton*] (1838) **1 a :** the quality or state of being automatic **b :** an automatic action **2 :** a theory that views the body as a machine and consciousness as a noncontrolling adjunct of the body **3 :** the power or fact of moving or functioning independently of external stimuli (as in the beating of the heart) or under the influence of external stimuli but independent of conscious control **4 :** suspension of the conscious mind to release subconscious images — **au·tom·a·tist** \-ˈtäm-ət-əst\ *n*

au·tom·a·ti·za·tion \ȯ-ˌtäm-ət-ə-ˈzā-shən\ *n* (1924) **:** AUTOMATION

au·tom·a·tize \ȯ-ˈtäm-ə-ˌtīz\ *vt* **-tized; -tiz·ing** [[1]*automatic*] (1837) **:** to make automatic

au·tom·a·ton \ȯ-ˈtäm-ət-ən, -ə-ˌtän\ *n, pl* **-atons** *or* **-a·ta** \-ət-ə, -ə-ˌtä\ [L, fr. Gk, neut. of *automatos*] (1645) **1 :** a mechanism that is relatively self-operating; *esp* **:** ROBOT **2 :** a machine or control mechanism designed to follow automatically a predetermined sequence of operations or respond to encoded instructions **3 :** an individual who acts in a mechanical fashion

[1]**au·to·mo·bile** \ˈȯt-ə-mō-ˌbēl, ˌȯt-ə-mō-ˈbē(ə)l, ˌȯt-ə-ˈmō-ˌbēl\ *adj* [F, fr. *aut-* + *mobile*] (1883) **:** AUTOMOTIVE

[2]**automobile** *n* (ca. 1890) **:** a usu. four-wheeled automotive vehicle designed for passenger transportation and commonly propelled by an internal-combustion engine using a volatile fuel — **automobile** *vi* — **au·to·mo·bil·ist** \-ˈbē-ləst, -ˌbē-\ *n*

au·to·mor·phism \ˌȯt-ə-ˈmȯr-ˌfiz-əm\ *n* [*aut-* + *isomorphism*] (1903) **:** an isomorphism of a set (as a group) with itself

au·to·mo·tive \ˌȯt-ə-ˈmōt-iv\ *adj* (1898) **1 :** of, relating to, or concerned with self-propelled vehicles or machines **2 :** SELF-PROPELLED

au·to·nom·ic \ˌȯt-ə-ˈnäm-ik\ *adj* (1898) **1 a :** acting or occurring involuntarily ⟨~ reflexes⟩ **b :** relating to, affecting, or controlled by the autonomic nervous system or its effects or activity ⟨~ drugs⟩ **2 :** due to causes internal to the plant ⟨~ movements⟩ — **au·to·nom·i·cal·ly** \-i-k(ə-)lē\ *adv*

autonomic nervous system *n* (ca. 1898) **:** a part of the vertebrate nervous system that innervates smooth and cardiac muscle and glandular tissues and governs involuntary actions (as secretion and peristalsis) and that consists of the sympathetic nervous system and the parasympathetic nervous system

au·ton·o·mist \ȯ-ˈtän-ə-məst\ *n* (1865) **:** one who advocates autonomy

au·ton·o·mous \ȯ-ˈtän-ə-məs\ *adj* [Gk *autonomos* independent, fr. *aut-* + *nomos* law — more at NIMBLE] (1800) **1 :** of, relating to, or marked by autonomy **2 a :** having the right or power of self-government **b :** undertaken or carried on without outside control **:** SELF-CONTAINED ⟨an ~ school system⟩ **3 a :** existing or capable of existing independently ⟨an ~ zooid⟩ **b :** responding, reacting, or developing independently of the whole ⟨an ~ growth⟩ **4 :** controlled by the autonomic nervous system ***syn*** see FREE — **au·ton·o·mous·ly** *adv*

au·ton·o·my \-mē\ *n, pl* **-mies** (ca. 1623) **1 :** the quality or state of being self-governing; *esp* **:** the right of self-government **2 :** a self-governing state **3 :** self-directing freedom and esp. moral independence

au·to·pi·lot \ˈȯt-ō-ˌpī-lət\ *n* (1935) **:** AUTOMATIC PILOT

au·to·poly·ploid \ˌȯt-ō-ˈpäl-i-ˌplȯid\ *n* (1928) **:** an individual or strain whose chromosome complement consists of more than two complete copies of the genome of a single ancestral species — **autopolyploid** *adj* — **au·to·poly·ploi·dy** \-ˌplȯid-ē\ *n*

au·top·sy \ˈȯ-ˌtäp-sē, ˈȯt-əp-\ *n, pl* **-sies** [Gk *autopsia* act of seeing with one's own eyes, fr. *aut-* + *opsis* sight, fr. *opsesthai* to be going to see — more at OPTIC] (1678) **1 :** POSTMORTEM EXAMINATION **2 :** a critical examination, evaluation, or assessment of a past event, institution, work, or personality ⟨a detailed ~ on the loser's campaign⟩ — **autopsy** *vt*

au·to·ra·dio·gram \ˌȯt-ō-ˈrād-ē-ə-ˌgram\ *n* (1949) **:** AUTORADIOGRAPH

au·to·ra·dio·graph \ˌȯt-ō-ˈrād-ē-ə-ˌgraf\ *n* [ISV] (1903) **:** an image produced on a photographic film or plate by the radiations from a radioactive substance in an object which is in close contact with the emulsion — **au·to·ra·dio·graph·ic** \-ˌrād-ē-ə-ˈgraf-ik\ *adj* — **au·to·ra·di·og·ra·phy** \-ˌrād-ē-ˈäg-rə-fē\ *n*

au·to·ro·ta·tion \-rō-ˈtā-shən\ *n* (1918) **:** the turning of the rotor of an autogiro or a helicopter with the resulting lift caused solely by the aerodynamic forces induced by motion of the rotor along its flight path — **au·to·ro·tate** \-ˈrō-ˌtāt\ *vi* — **au·to·ro·ta·tion·al** \-rō-ˈtā-shnəl, -shən-ᵊl\ *adj*

autos–da–fé *pl of* AUTO-DA-FÉ

au·to·sex·ing \ˈȯt-ō-ˌsek-siŋ\ *adj* (1936) **:** exhibiting different characters in the two sexes at birth or hatching

au·to·some \ˈȯt-ə-ˌsōm\ *n* (ca. 1906) **:** a chromosome other than a sex chromosome — **au·to·so·mal** \ˌȯt-ə-ˈsō-məl\ *adj* — **au·to·so·mal·ly** \-mə-lē\ *adv*

au·to·stra·da \ˌau̇t-ō-ˈsträd-ə, ˌȯt-ō-\ *n, pl* **-stradas** *or* **-stra·de** \-ˈsträd-(ˌ)ā\ [It, fr. *auto*mobile + *strada* street, fr. LL *strata* paved road — more at STREET] (1927) **:** a high-speed multilane highway first developed in Italy

au·to·sug·ges·tion \ˌȯt-ō-sə(g)-ˈjes(h)-chən\ *n* [ISV] (1890) **:** an influencing of one's own attitudes, behavior, or physical condition by mental processes other than conscious thought **:** SELF-HYPNOSIS — **au·to·sug·gest** \-sə(g)-ˈjest\ *vt*

au·to·te·lic \ˌȯt-ō-ˈtel-ik, -ˈtē-lik\ *adj* [Gk *autotelēs*, fr. *aut-* + *telos* end — more at WHEEL] (ca. 1901) **:** having a purpose in itself

au·to·tet·ra·ploid \ˌȯt-ō-ˈte-trə-ˌplȯid\ *n* (1930) **:** an individual or strain whose chromosome complement consists of four copies of a single genome due to doubling of an ancestral chromosome complement — **autotetraploid** *adj* — **au·to·tet·ra·ploi·dy** \-ē\ *n*

au·tot·o·mize \ȯ-ˈtät-ə-ˌmīz\ *vb* **-mized; -miz·ing** *vt* (1901) **:** to effect autotomy of ~ *vi* **:** to undergo autotomy

au·tot·o·my \-mē\ *n* [ISV] (ca. 1897) **:** reflex separation of a part from the body **:** division of the body into two or more pieces — **au·tot·o·mous** \ȯ-ˈtät-ə-məs\ *adj*

au·to·trans·form·er \ˌȯt-ō-tran(t)s-ˈfȯr-mər\ *n* (ca. 1895) **:** a transformer in which the primary and secondary coils have part or all of their turns in common

au·to·troph \ˈȯt-ə-ˌtrōf, -ˌträf\ *n* [G, fr. *autotroph*, adj.] (1938) **:** an autotrophic organism

au·to·tro·phic \ˌȯt-ə-ˈtrō-fik\ *adj* [prob. fr. G *autotroph*, fr. Gk *autotrophos* supplying one's own food, fr. *aut-* + *trephein* to nourish — more at ATROPHY] (ca. 1900) **1 :** needing only carbon dioxide or carbonates as a source of carbon and a simple inorganic nitrogen compound for metabolic synthesis **2 :** not requiring a specified exogenous factor for normal metabolism — **au·to·tro·phi·cal·ly** \-fi-k(ə-)lē\ *adv* — **au·tot·ro·phy** \ȯ-ˈtä-trə-fē\ *n*

au·to·wor·ker \ˈȯt-ō-ˌwər-kər, ˈät-\ *n* (1941) **:** a person employed in the automobile manufacturing industry

au·tumn \ˈȯt-əm\ *n* [ME *autumpne*, fr. L *autumnus*] (14c) **1 :** the season between summer and winter comprising in the northern hemisphere usu. the months of September, October, and November or as reckoned astronomically extending from the September equinox to the December solstice — called also *fall* **2 :** a period of maturity or incipient decline ⟨in the ~ of her life⟩ — **au·tum·nal** \ȯ-ˈtəm-nəl\ *adj* — **au·tum·nal·ly** \-nə-lē\ *adv*

autumn crocus *n* (ca. 1909) **:** an autumn-blooming colchicum

au·tun·ite \ō-ˈtən-ˌīt, ˈȯt-ᵊn-\ *n* [*Autun*, France] (ca. 1852) **:** a radioactive lemon-yellow mineral $Ca(UO_2)(PO_4)_2{\cdot}10–12H_2O$ occurring in tabular crystals with basal cleavage and in scales like mica

aux·e·sis \ȯg-ˈzē-səs, ȯk-ˈsē-\ *n* [NL, fr. Gk *auxēsis* increase, growth, fr. *auxein* to increase — more at EKE] (ca. 1848) **:** GROWTH; *specif* **:** increase of cell size without cell division — **aux·et·ic** \-ˈzet-ik, -ˈset-\ *adj or n*

[1]**aux·il·ia·ry** \ȯg-ˈzil-yə-rē, -ˈzil-(ə-)rē\ *adj* [L *auxiliaris*, fr. *auxilium* help; akin to L *augēre* — more at EKE] (15c) **1 a :** offering or providing help **b :** functioning in a subsidiary capacity ⟨an ~ branch of the state university⟩ **2** *of a verb* **:** accompanying another verb and typically expressing person, number, mood, or tense **3 a :** SUPPLEMENTARY **b :** constituting a reserve ⟨an ~ power plant⟩ **4 :** equipped with sails and a supplementary inboard engine

[2]**auxiliary** *n, pl* **-ries** (1601) **1 a :** an auxiliary person, group, or device; *specif* **:** a member of a foreign force serving a nation at war **b :** a Roman Catholic titular bishop assisting a diocesan bishop and not having the right of succession **2 :** an auxiliary boat or ship **3 :** an auxiliary verb

aux·in \ˈȯk-sən\ *n* [ISV, fr. Gk *auxein*] (1934) **:** an organic substance that is able in low concentrations to promote elongation of plant shoots and usu. to control other specific growth effects; *broadly* **:** PLANT HORMONE — **aux·in·ic** \ȯk-ˈsin-ik\ *adj*

auxo·troph \ˈȯk-sə-ˌtrōf, -ˌträf\ *n* (1953) **:** an auxotrophic strain or individual

auxo•tro•phic \ˌȯk-sə-ˈtrō-fik\ *adj* [Gk *auxein* to increase + *-o-* + E *-trophic*] (1944) **:** requiring a specific growth substance beyond the minimum required for normal metabolism and reproduction by the parental or wild-type strain ⟨~ mutants of bacteria⟩ — **aux•ot•ro•phy** \ȯk-ˈsä-trə-fē\ *n*

¹avail \ə-ˈvā(ə)l\ *vb* [ME *availen*, prob. fr. *a-* (as in *abaten* to abate) + *vailen* to avail, fr. OF *valoir* to be of worth, fr. L *valēre* — more at WIELD] *vi* (14c) **:** to be of use or advantage **:** SERVE ⟨our best efforts did not ~⟩ ~ *vt* **1 :** to be of use or advantage to **:** PROFIT **2 :** to result in **:** bring about ⟨his efforts ~*ed* him nothing⟩ — **avail oneself of** *also* **avail of :** to make use of **:** take advantage of

²avail *n* (15c) **1 :** advantage toward attainment of a goal or purpose **:** USE ⟨effort was of little ~⟩ **2** *pl, archaic* **:** profits or proceeds esp. from a business or from the sale of property

avail•abil•i•ty \ə-ˌvā-lə-ˈbil-ət-ē\ *n, pl* **-ties** (1803) **1 :** the quality or state of being available **2 :** an available person or thing

avail•able \ə-ˈvā-lə-bəl\ *adj* (15c) **1** *archaic* **:** having a beneficial effect **2 :** VALID — used of a legal plea or charge **3 :** present or ready for immediate use **4 :** ACCESSIBLE, OBTAINABLE ⟨articles ~ in any drugstore⟩ **5 :** qualified or willing to do something or to assume a responsibility ⟨~ candidates⟩ **6 :** present in such chemical or physical form as to be usable (as by a plant) ⟨~ nitrogen⟩ ⟨~ water⟩ — **avail•able•ness** *n* — **avail•ably** \-blē\ *adv*

¹av•a•lanche \ˈav-ə-ˌlanch\ *n* [F, fr. F dial. *lavantse, avalantse*] (1788) **1 :** a large mass of snow, ice, earth, rock, or other material in swift motion down a mountainside or over a precipice **2 :** a sudden great or overwhelming rush or accumulation of something ⟨office workers tied down with an ~ of paperwork⟩ **3 :** a cumulative process in which photons or accelerated charge carriers produce additional photons or charge carriers through collisions (as with gas molecules)

²avalanche *vb* **-lanched; -lanch•ing** *vi* (1872) **:** to descend in an avalanche ~ *vt* **:** OVERWHELM, FLOOD

Av•a•lon \ˈav-ə-ˌlän\ *n* **:** a paradise to which Arthur is carried after his death

¹avant–garde \ˌäv-ˌän(t)-ˈgärd, ˌav-, ˌäv-; ə-ˈvänt-ˌ; ˌav-ˌōⁿ-ˈ, ˌav-ˌȯn(t)-ˈ\ *n* [F, vanguard] (1910) **:** an intelligentsia that develops new or experimental concepts esp. in the arts — **avant–gard•ism** \-ˈgärd-ˌiz-əm\ *n* — **avant–gard•ist** \-ˈgärd-əst\ *n*

²avant–garde *adj* (1925) **:** of or relating to an avant-garde ⟨~ writers⟩

av•a•rice \ˈav-(ə-)rəs\ *n* [ME, fr. OF, fr. L *avaritia*, fr. *avarus* avaricious, fr. *avēre* to covet — more at AVID] (14c) **:** excessive or insatiable desire for wealth or gain **:** GREEDINESS, CUPIDITY

av•a•ri•cious \ˌav-ə-ˈrish-əs\ *adj* (14c) **:** greedy of gain **:** excessively acquisitive esp. in seeking to hoard riches ***syn*** see COVETOUS — **av•a•ri•cious•ly** *adv* — **av•a•ri•cious•ness** *n*

avas•cu•lar \(ˈ)ā-ˈvas-kyə-lər\ *adj* (ca. 1900) **:** having few or no blood vessels ⟨~ tissue⟩ — **avas•cu•lar•i•ty** \ˌā-ˌvas-kyə-ˈlar-ət-ē\ *n*

avast \ə-ˈvast\ *vb imper* [perh. fr. D *houd vast* hold fast] (1681) — a nautical command to stop or cease

av•a•tar \ˈav-ə-ˌtär\ *n* [Skt *avatāra* descent, fr. *avatarati* he descends, fr. *ava-* away + *tarati* he crosses over — more at UKASE, THROUGH] (1784) **1 :** the incarnation of a Hindu deity (as Vishnu) **2 a :** an incarnation in human form **b :** an embodiment (as of a concept or philosophy) usu. in a person **3 :** a variant phase or version of a continuing basic entity

avaunt \ə-ˈvȯnt, -ˈvänt\ *adv* [ME, fr. MF *avant*, fr. L *abante* forward, before, fr. *ab* from + *ante* before — more at OF, ANTE-] (15c) **:** AWAY, HENCE

ave \ˈäv-(ˌ)ā\ *n* [ME, fr. L, hail] (13c) **1 :** an expression of greeting or of leave-taking **:** HAIL, FAREWELL **2** *often cap* **:** AVE MARIA

avel•lan \ə-ˈvel-ən\ *or* **avel•lane** \ə-ˈvel-ˌān, ˈav-ə-ˌlān\ *adj* [L *abellana, avellana* filbert, fr. fem. of *Abellanus* of Abella, fr. *Abella*, ancient town in Italy] *of a heraldic cross* (1611) **:** having the four arms shaped like conventionalized filberts — see CROSS illustration

Ave Ma•ria \ˌäv-(ˌ)ā-mə-ˈrē-ə\ *n* [ME, fr. ML, hail, Mary] (13c) **:** HAIL MARY

avenge \ə-ˈvenj\ *vt* **avenged; aveng•ing** [ME *avengen*, prob. fr. *a-* (as in *abaten* to abate) + *vengen* to avenge, fr. OF *vengier* — more at VENGEANCE] (14c) **1 :** to take vengeance for or on behalf of **2 :** to exact satisfaction for (a wrong) by punishing the wrongdoer — **aveng•er** *n*

av•ens \ˈav-ənz\ *n, pl* **avens** [ME *avence*, fr. OF] (13c) **:** any of a genus (*Geum*) of perennial herbs of the rose family with white, purple, or yellow flowers

av•en•tail \ˈav-ən-ˌtāl\ *n* [ME, modif. of OF *ventaille*] (14c) **:** VENTAIL

aven•tu•rine \ə-ˈven-chə-ˌrēn, -rən\ *n* [F, fr. *aventure* chance — more at ADVENTURE] (1811) **1 :** glass containing opaque sparkling particles of foreign material usu. copper or chromic oxide **2 :** a translucent quartz spangled throughout with scales of mica or other mineral

av•e•nue \ˈav-ə-ˌn(y)ü\ *n* [MF, fr. fem. of *avenu*, pp. of *avenir* to come to, fr. L *advenire* — more at ADVENTURE] (1600) **1 :** a way of access **:** ROUTE **2 :** a channel for pursuing a desired object ⟨~*s* of communication⟩ **3 a** *chiefly Brit* **:** the principal walk or driveway to a house situated off a main road **b :** a broad passageway bordered by trees **4 :** an often broad street or road

aver \ə-ˈvər\ *vt* **averred; aver•ring** [ME *averren*, fr. MF *averer*, fr. ML *adverare* to confirm as authentic, fr. L *ad-* + *verus* true — more at VERY] (15c) **1 a :** to verify or prove to be true in pleading a cause **b :** to allege or assert in pleading **2 :** to declare positively

¹av•er•age \ˈav-(ə-)rij\ *n* [fr. earlier *average* proportionally-distributed charge for damage at sea, modif. of MF *avarie* damage to ship or cargo, fr. OIt *avaria*, fr. Ar *ʽawārīyah* damaged merchandise] (1735) **1 a :** a single value (as a mean, mode, or median) that summarizes or represents the general significance of a set of unequal values **b :** MEAN 1b **2 a :** an estimation of or approximation to an arithmetic mean **b :** a level (as of intelligence) typical of a group, class, or series ⟨above the ~⟩ **3 :** a ratio expressing the average performance esp. of an athletic team or an athlete computed according to the number of opportunities for successful performance

syn AVERAGE, MEAN, MEDIAN, NORM mean something that represents a middle point. AVERAGE is exactly or approximately the quotient obtained by dividing the sum total of a set of figures by the number of figures; MEAN may be the simple average or it may represent value midway between two extremes ⟨a high of 70° and a low of 50° give a *mean* of 60°⟩ MEDIAN applies to the value that represents the point at which there are as many instances above as there are below ⟨*average* of a group of persons earning 3, 4, 5, 8, and 10 dollars a day is 6 dollars, whereas the *median* is 5 dollars⟩ NORM means the computed or estimated average of performance of a significantly large group, class, or grade ⟨scores about the *norm* for 5th grade arithmetic⟩

²average *adj* (1770) **1 :** equaling an arithmetic mean **2 a :** being about midway between extremes ⟨a man of ~ height⟩ **b :** not out of the ordinary **:** COMMON ⟨the ~ person⟩ — **av•er•age•ly** *adv* — **av•er•age•ness** *n*

³average *vb* **av•er•aged; av•er•ag•ing** *vi* (1769) **1 a :** to be or come to an average ⟨the gain *averaged* out to 20 percent⟩ **b :** to have a medial value of ⟨a color *averaging* a pale purple⟩ **2 :** to buy on a falling market or sell on a rising market additional shares or commodities so as to obtain a more favorable average price — usu. used with *down* or *up* ~ *vt* **1 :** to do, get, or have on the average or as an average sum or quantity ⟨~*s* 12 hours of work a day⟩ **2 :** to find the arithmetic mean of (a series of unequal quantities) **3 a :** to bring toward the average **b :** to divide among a number proportionately

aver•ment \ə-ˈvər-mənt\ *n* (15c) **1 :** the act of averring **2 :** something that is averred **:** AFFIRMATION

averse \ə-ˈvərs\ *adj* [L *aversus*, pp. of *avertere*] (1597) **:** having an active feeling of repugnance or distaste ⟨~ to strenuous exercise⟩ ***syn*** see DISINCLINED — **averse•ly** *adv* — **averse•ness** *n*

aver•sion \ə-ˈvər-zhən, -shən\ *n* (1596) **1** *obs* **:** the act of turning away **2 a :** a feeling of repugnance toward something with a desire to avoid or turn from it ⟨regards drunkenness with ~⟩ **b :** a settled dislike **:** ANTIPATHY ⟨expressed an ~ to parties⟩ **c :** a tendency to extinguish a behavior or to avoid a thing or situation and esp. a usu. pleasurable one because it is or has been associated with a noxious stimulus **3 :** one that is the object of aversion

aversion therapy *n* (1946) **:** therapy intended to change habits or antisocial behavior by inducing dislike for them through association with a noxious stimulus

aver•sive \ə-ˈvər-siv, -ziv\ *adj* (1923) **:** tending to avoid or causing avoidance of a noxious or punishing stimulus ⟨behavior modification by ~ stimulation⟩ — **aver•sive•ly** *adv* — **aver•sive•ness** *n*

avert \ə-ˈvərt\ *vt* [ME *averten*, fr. MF *avertir*, fr. L *avertere*, fr. *ab-* + *vertere* to turn — more at WORTH] (15c) **1 :** to turn away or aside (as the eyes) in avoidance **2 :** to see coming and ward off **:** AVOID

Aves•ta \ə-ˈves-tə\ *n* [MPer *Avastāk*, lit., original text] (1856) **:** the book of the sacred writings of Zoroastrianism

Aves•tan \-tən\ *n* (1856) **:** one of the two ancient languages of Old Iranian and that in which the sacred books of Zoroastrianism were written — see INDO-EUROPEAN LANGUAGES table — **Avestan** *adj*

av•gas \ˈav-ˌgas\ *n* [*aviation gasoline*] (1943) **:** gasoline for airplanes

av•go•lem•o•no \ˌäv-gō-ˈlem-ə-(ˌ)nō\ *n* [NGk *augolemono*, fr. *augon* egg + *lemonion* lemon] (1961) **:** a soup made of chicken stock, rice, egg yolks, and lemon sauce

avi•an \ˈā-vē-ən\ *adj* [L *avis*] (1870) **:** of, relating to, or derived from birds

avi•ary \ˈā-vē-ˌer-ē\ *n, pl* **-ar•ies** [L *aviarium*, fr. *avis* bird; akin to Gk *aetos* eagle] (1577) **:** a place for keeping birds confined

avi•ate \ˈā-vē-ˌāt, ˈav-ē-\ *vi* **-at•ed; -at•ing** [back-formation fr. *aviation*] (1887) **:** to navigate the air (as in an airplane)

avi•a•tion \ˌā-vē-ˈā-shən, ˌav-ē-\ *n, often attrib* [F, fr. L *avis*] (1866) **1 :** the operation of heavier-than-air aircraft **2 :** military airplanes **3 :** airplane manufacture, development, and design

aviation cadet *n* (1941) **:** one in training for a military or naval commission with an aeronautical rating

avi•a•tor \ˈā-vē-ˌāt-ər, ˈav-ē-\ *n* (1887) **:** the operator or pilot of an airplane

aviator glasses *n* [fr. the resemblance of their shape to goggles] (1968) **:** eyeglasses having a lightweight metal frame and usu. tinted lenses

avi•a•tress \-ˌā-trəs\ *n* (ca. 1909) **:** AVIATRIX

avi•a•trix \ˌā-vē-ˈā-triks, ˌav-ē-\ *n, pl* **-trix•es** \-trik-səz\ *or* **-tri•ces** \-trə-ˌsēz\ (1910) **:** a woman aviator

avi•cul•ture \ˈā-və-ˌkəl-chər, ˈav-ə-\ *n* [L *avis* + E *culture*] (ca. 1879) **:** the raising and care of birds and esp. of wild birds in captivity — **avi•cul•tur•ist** \ˌā-və-ˈkəlch-(ə-)rəst, ˌav-ə-\ *n*

av•id \ˈav-əd\ *adj* [F or L; F *avide*, fr. L *avidus*, fr. *avēre* to covet; akin to OE *ēathe* easily, willingly] (1769) **1 :** desirous to the point of greed **:** urgently eager **:** GREEDY ⟨~ fondness for publicity⟩ **2 :** characterized by enthusiasm and vigorous pursuit ⟨~ readers⟩ ***syn*** see EAGER — **av•id•ly** *adv* — **av•id•ness** *n*

av•i•din \ˈav-əd-ən\ *n* [fr. its avidity for biotin] (1941) **:** a protein found in white of egg that combines with biotin and makes it inactive

avid•ity \ə-ˈvid-ət-ē, a-\ *n, pl* **-ities** (15c) **1 :** the quality or state of being avid: **a :** keen eagerness **b :** consuming greed **2 a :** the strength of an acid or base dependent on its degree of dissociation **b :** AFFINITY 2b

avi•fau•na \ˌā-və-ˈfȯn-ə, ˌav-ə-, -ˈfän-ə\ *n* [NL, fr. L *avis* + NL *fauna*] (1874) **:** the birds or the kinds of birds of a region, period, or environment — **avi•fau•nal** \-ˈfȯn-ᵊl, -ˈfän-\ *adj*

avi•on•ics \ˌā-vē-ˈän-iks, ˌav-ē-\ *n pl* [*aviation electronics*] (ca. 1949) **:** the development and production of electrical and electronic devices for use in aviation, missilery, and astronautics; *also* **:** the devices and systems so developed — **avi•on•ic** \-ik\ *adj*

avir•u•lent \(ˈ)ā-ˈvir-(y)ə-lənt\ *adj* [ISV] (ca. 1900) **:** not virulent — compare NONPATHOGENIC

avi•ta•min•osis \ˌā-ˌvīt-ə-mə-ˈnō-səs\ *n, pl* **-o•ses** \-ˌsēz\ (1919) **:** disease (as pellagra) resulting from a deficiency of one or more vitamins — **avi•ta•min•ot•ic** \-mə-ˈnät-ik\ *adj*

avo \ˈav-(ˌ)ü\ *n, pl* **avos** [Pg, fr. *avo* fractional part, fr. *-avo* ordinal suffix (as in *oitavo* eighth, fr. L *octavus*) — more at OCTAVE] (ca. 1909) — see *pataca* at MONEY table

av·o·ca·do \ˌav-ə-ˈkäd-(ˌ)ō, ˌäv-\ *n, pl* **-dos** *also* **-does** [modif. of Sp *aguacate,* fr. Nahuatl *ahuacatl,* lit., testicle] (1697) **:** the pulpy green or purple edible fruit of various tropical American trees (genus *Persea*) of the laurel family; *also* **:** a tree bearing avocados — called also *alligator pear, avocado pear*

av·o·ca·tion \ˌav-ə-ˈkā-shən\ *n* [L *avocation-, avocatio,* fr. *avocatus,* pp. of *avocare* to call away, fr. *ab-* + *vocare* to call, fr. *voc-, vox* voice — more at VOICE] (1617) **1** *archaic* **:** DIVERSION, DISTRACTION **2 :** a subordinate occupation pursued in addition to one's vocation esp. for enjoyment **:** HOBBY **3 :** customary employment **:** VOCATION — **av·o·ca·tion·al** \-shnəl, -shən-ᵊl\ *adj* — **av·o·ca·tion·al·ly** \-ē\ *adv*

av·o·cet \ˈav-ə-ˌset\ *n* [F & It; F *avocette,* fr. It *avocetta*] (1766) **:** any of several rather large long-legged shorebirds (genus *Recurvirostra*) with webbed feet and slender upward-curving bill

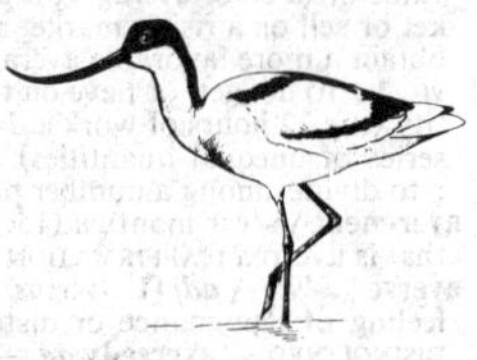

avocet

Avo·ga·dro number \ˌav-ə-ˌgäd-(ˌ)rō-, ˌäv-, -ˌgad-\ *n* [Count Amedeo *Avogadro*] (1924) **:** the number 6.023 × 10^{23} indicating the number of atoms or molecules in a mole of any substance

avoid \ə-ˈvȯid\ *vt* [ME *avoiden,* fr. MF *esvuidier,* fr. *es-* (fr. L *ex-*) + *vuidier* to empty — more at VOID] (14c) **1** *obs* **:** VOID, EXPEL **2** *archaic* **:** to depart or withdraw from **:** LEAVE **3 :** to make legally void **:** ANNUL ⟨~ a plea⟩ **4 a :** to keep away from **:** SHUN **b :** to prevent the occurrence or effectiveness of **c :** to refrain from *syn* see ESCAPE — **avoid·able** \-ə-bəl\ *adj* — **avoid·ably** \-blē\ *adv* — **avoid·er** *n*

avoid·ance \ə-ˈvȯid-ᵊn(t)s\ *n* (14c) **1** *obs* **a :** an action of emptying, vacating, or clearing away **b :** OUTLET **2 :** ANNULMENT 1 **3 :** an act or practice of avoiding or withdrawing from something

av·oir·du·pois \ˌav-ərd-ə-ˈpȯiz, ˈav-ərd-ə-ˌ\ *n* [ME *avoir de pois* goods sold by weight, fr. OF, lit., goods of weight] (15c) **1 :** AVOIRDUPOIS WEIGHT **2 :** WEIGHT, HEAVINESS; *esp* **:** personal weight

avoirdupois weight *n* (1619) **:** the series of units of weight based on the pound of 16 ounces and the ounce of 16 drams — see WEIGHT table

avouch \ə-ˈvau̇ch\ *vt* [ME *avouchen* to cite as authority, fr. MF *avochier* to summon, fr. L *advocare* — more at ADVOCATE] (15c) **1 :** to declare as a matter of fact or as a thing that can be proved **:** AFFIRM **2 :** to vouch for **:** CORROBORATE **3 a :** to acknowledge (as an act) as one's own **b :** CONFESS, AVOW

avouch·ment \-mənt\ *n* (1574) **:** an act of avouching **:** AVOWAL

avow \ə-ˈvau̇\ *vt* [ME *avowen,* fr. MF *avouer,* fr. L *advocare*] (14c) **1 :** to declare assuredly **2 :** to declare openly, bluntly, and without shame ⟨ever ready to ~ his reactionary outlook⟩ — **avow·ed·ly** \-ˈvau̇-əd-lē\ *adv* — **avow·er** \-ˈvau̇(-ə)r\ *n*

avow·al \-ˈvau̇(-ə)l\ *n* (ca. 1732) **:** an open declaration or acknowledgment

avulse \ə-ˈvəls\ *vt* **avulsed; avuls·ing** [L *avulsus,* pp. of *avellere* to tear off, fr. *ab-* + *vellere* to pluck — more at VULNERABLE] (1765) **:** to separate by avulsion

avul·sion \ə-ˈvəl-shən\ *n* (1622) **:** a forcible separation or detachment: as **a :** a tearing away of a body part accidentally or surgically **b :** a sudden cutting off of land by flood, currents, or change in course of a body of water; *esp* **:** one separating land from one person's property and joining it to another's

avun·cu·lar \ə-ˈvəŋ-kyə-lər\ *adj* [L *avunculus* maternal uncle — more at UNCLE] (1831) **1 :** of or relating to an uncle **2 :** suggestive of an uncle esp. in kindliness or geniality ⟨~ indulgence⟩

aw \ˈȯ\ *interj* (1852) — used to express mild sympathy, remonstrance, incredulity, or disgust

await \ə-ˈwāt\ *vb* [ME *awaiten,* fr. ONF *awaitier,* fr. *a-* (fr. L *ad-*) + *waitier* to watch — more at WAIT] *vt* (13c) **1** *obs* **:** to lie in wait for **2 a :** to wait for **b :** to remain in abeyance until ⟨a treaty ~*ing* ratification⟩ **3 :** to be in store for ⟨wondered what ~*ed* him at the end of his journey⟩ ~ *vi* **1** *obs* **:** ATTEND **2 :** to stay or be in waiting **:** WAIT **3 :** to be in store

[1]**awake** \ə-ˈwāk\ *vb* **awoke** \-ˈwōk\ *also* **awaked** \-ˈwākt\; **awaked** *or* **awo·ken** \-ˈwō-kən\ *also* **awoke; awak·ing** *vi* (bef. 12c) **1 :** to cease sleeping **2 :** to become aroused or active again **3 :** to become conscious or aware of something ⟨*awoke* to their danger⟩ ~ *vt* **1 :** to arouse from sleep or a sleeplike state **2 :** to make active **:** stir up ⟨*awoke* old memories⟩

[2]**awake** *adj* (13c) **:** fully conscious and alert and aware **:** not asleep *syn* see AWARE

awak·en \ə-ˈwā-kən\ *vb* **awak·ened; awak·en·ing** \-ˈwāk-(ə-)niŋ\ [ME *awakenen,* fr. OE *awæcnian,* fr. *a-* + *wæcnian* to waken] (bef. 12c) **:** AWAKE — **awak·en·er** \-ˈwāk-(ə-)nər\ *n*

[1]**award** \ə-ˈwȯ(ə)rd\ *vt* [ME *awarden* to decide, fr. ONF *eswarder,* fr. *es-* (fr. L *ex-*) + *warder* to guard, of Gmc origin; akin to OHG *wartēn* to watch — more at WARD] (14c) **1 :** to give by judicial decree or after careful consideration **2 :** to confer or bestow as being deserved or merited or needed ⟨~ scholarships to ghetto students⟩ *syn* see GRANT — **award·able** \-ˈwȯrd-ə-bəl\ *adj* — **award·ee** \-ˌwȯrd-ˈē\ *n* — **award·er** \-ˈwȯrd-ər\ *n*

[2]**award** *n* (14c) **1 a :** a judgment or final decision; *esp* **:** the decision of arbitrators in a case submitted to them **b :** the document containing the decision of arbitrators **2 :** something that is conferred or bestowed esp. on the basis of merit or need

aware \ə-ˈwa(ə)r, -ˈwe(ə)r\ *adj* [ME *iwar,* fr. OE *gewær,* fr. *ge-* (associative prefix) + *wær* wary — more at CO-, WARY] (bef. 12c) **1** *archaic* **:** WATCHFUL, WARY **2 :** having or showing realization, perception, or knowledge — **aware·ness** *n*

syn AWARE, COGNIZANT, CONSCIOUS, SENSIBLE, ALIVE, AWAKE mean having knowledge of something. AWARE implies vigilance in observing or alertness in drawing inferences from what one experiences; COGNIZANT implies having special or certain knowledge as from firsthand sources; CONSCIOUS implies that one is focusing one's attention on something or is even preoccupied by it; SENSIBLE implies direct or intuitive perceiving esp. of intangibles or of emotional states or qualities; ALIVE adds to SENSIBLE the implication of acute sensitivity to something; AWAKE implies that one has become alive to something and is on the alert.

awash \ə-ˈwȯsh, -ˈwäsh\ *adj* (1833) **1 a :** alternately covered and exposed by waves or tide **b :** washing about **:** AFLOAT **c :** covered with water **:** FLOODED **2 :** filled, covered, or completely overrun as if by a flood

[1]**away** \ə-ˈwā\ *adv* (bef. 12c) **1 :** on the way **:** ALONG ⟨get ~ early⟩ **2 :** from this or that place **:** HENCE, THENCE ⟨go ~⟩ **3 a :** in a secure place or manner ⟨locked ~⟩ ⟨tucked ~⟩ **b :** in another direction ⟨look ~⟩ **4 :** out of existence **:** to an end ⟨echoes dying ~⟩ **5 :** from one's possession ⟨gave ~ a fortune⟩ **6 :** in or into an ongoing state ⟨clocks ticking ~⟩ **7 :** by a long distance or interval **:** FAR ⟨~ back in 1910⟩

[2]**away** *adj* (14c) **1 :** absent from a place **:** GONE ⟨~ for the weekend⟩ **2 :** distant in space or time ⟨a lake 10 miles ~⟩ ⟨the season is two months ~⟩ **3 :** played on an opponent's grounds ⟨home and ~ games⟩ **4** *baseball* **:** OUT ⟨two ~ in the ninth⟩ — **away·ness** *n*

[1]**awe** \ˈȯ\ *n* [ME, fr. ON *agi;* akin to OE *ege* awe, Gk *achos* pain] (bef. 12c) **1** *archaic* **a :** DREAD, TERROR **b :** the power to inspire dread **2 :** emotion in which dread, veneration, and wonder are variously mingled: as **a :** fearful reverence inspired by deity or by something sacred or mysterious **b :** submissive and admiring fear inspired by authority or power ⟨they stood in ~ of the king⟩ **c :** wondering reverence tinged with fear inspired by the sublime

[2]**awe** *vt* **awed; aw·ing** (13c) **:** to inspire with awe

awea·ry \ə-ˈwi(ə)r-ē\ *adj, archaic* (1552) **:** being weary

aweath·er \ə-ˈwet͟h-ər\ *adv* (1599) **:** on or toward the weather or windward side — compare ALEE

awed \ˈȯd\ *adj* (15c) **:** showing awe ⟨~ respect⟩

aweigh \ə-ˈwā\ *adj* (ca. 1627) **:** raised just clear of the ground — used of an anchor

awe·less *or* **aw·less** \ˈȯ-ləs\ *adj* (bef. 12c) **1 :** feeling no awe **2** *obs* **:** inspiring no awe

awe·some \ˈȯ-səm\ *adj* (1598) **1 :** expressive of awe ⟨~ tribute⟩ **2 a :** inspiring awe ⟨an ~ sight⟩ **b :** better than usual **:** EXTRAORDINARY — **awe·some·ly** *adv* — **awe·some·ness** *n*

awe·struck \-ˌstrək\ *also* **awe·strick·en** \-ˌstrik-ən\ *adj* (1634) **:** filled with awe

[1]**aw·ful** \ˈȯ-fəl\ *adj* (bef. 12c) **1 :** inspiring awe **2 :** filled with awe: as **a** *obs* **:** AFRAID, TERRIFIED **b :** deeply respectful or reverential **3 :** extremely disagreeable or objectionable **4 :** exceedingly great — used as an intensive ⟨they took an ~ chance⟩ — **aw·ful·ly** \ˈȯ-fə-lē, *esp as adv of adj senses 3 & 4* -flē\ *adv* — **aw·ful·ness** \-fəl-nəs\ *n*

usage Many grammarians take issue with the senses of *awful* and *awfully* that do not convey the etymological connection with *awe.* However, senses 3 and 4 of the adjective were used in speech and casual writing by the late 18th century ⟨it is an *awful* while since you have heard from me — John Keats (letter)⟩ ⟨there was an *awful* crowd — Sir Walter Scott (letter)⟩ ⟨this is an *awful* thing to say to oil painters — William Blake⟩ Adverbial use of *awful* as an intensifier began to appear in print in the early 19th century, as did the senses of *awfully* corresponding to senses 3 and 4 of the adjective. Both adverbs remain in widespread use ⟨a sad state of affairs and *awful* tough on art —H.L. Mencken⟩ ⟨the *awfully* rich young American —Henry James⟩ ⟨sorry that . . . he also decided to play it so *awfully* safe —A.M. Schlesinger *b*1917⟩

[2]**awful** *adv* (1818) **:** VERY, EXTREMELY ⟨~ tired⟩

awhile \ə-ˈhwī(ə)l, ə-ˈwī(ə)l\ *adv* (bef. 12c) **:** for a while

usage Although considered a solecism by many commentators, *awhile* is often used in place of *a while* as the object of a preposition ⟨for *awhile* there is a silence —Lord Dunsany⟩

awhirl \ə-ˈhwər(-ə)l, -ˈwər(-ə)l\ *adj* (1883) **:** being in a whirl

awk·ward \ˈȯ-kwərd\ *adj* [ME *awkeward* in the wrong direction, fr. *awke* turned the wrong way, fr. ON *öfugr;* akin to OHG *abuh* turned the wrong way] (15c) **1** *obs* **:** PERVERSE **2** *archaic* **:** UNFAVORABLE, ADVERSE **3 a :** lacking dexterity or skill (as in the use of hands) ⟨~ with a needle and thread⟩ **b :** showing the result of a lack of expertness ⟨~ pictures⟩ **4 a :** lacking ease or grace (as of movement or expression) **b :** lacking the right proportions, size, or harmony of parts **:** UNGAINLY **5 a :** lacking social grace and assurance **b :** causing embarrassment ⟨an ~ moment⟩ **6 :** not easy to handle or deal with **:** requiring great skill, ingenuity, or care ⟨an ~ load⟩ ⟨an ~ diplomatic situation⟩ — **awk·ward·ly** *adv* — **awk·ward·ness** *n*

syn AWKWARD, CLUMSY, MALADROIT, INEPT, GAUCHE mean not marked by ease (as of performance or movement). AWKWARD is widely applicable and may suggest unhandiness, inconvenience, lack of muscular control, embarrassment, or lack of tact; CLUMSY implies stiffness and heaviness and so may connote inflexibility, unwieldiness, or lack of ordinary skill; MALADROIT, INEPT, and GAUCHE imply lack of mental or social dexterity; MALADROIT suggests a tendency to create awkward situations; INEPT often implies complete failure or inadequacy; GAUCHE implies the effects of shyness, inexperience, or ill breeding.

awl \ˈȯl\ *n* [ME *al,* fr. ON *alr;* akin to OHG *āla* awl] (bef. 12c) **:** a pointed tool for marking surfaces or piercing small holes (as in leather or wood)

awn \ˈȯn\ *n* [ME, fr. OE *agen,* fr. ON *ögn;* akin to OHG *agana* awn, OE *ecg* edge — more at EDGE] (bef. 12c) **:** one of the slender bristles that terminate the glumes of the spikelet in some cereal and other grasses — **awned** \ˈȯnd\ *adj* — **awn·less** \ˈȯn-ləs\ *adj*

aw·ning \ˈȯ-niŋ, ˈä-\ *n* [origin unknown] (1624) **:** a rooflike cover extending over or in front of a place (as over the deck or in front of a door or window) as a shelter — **aw·ninged** \-iŋd\ *adj*

awoke *past and past part of* AWAKE

awoken *past part of* AWAKE

[1]**AWOL** \ˈā-ˌwȯl, ˌā-ˌdəb-əl-yü-ˌō-ˈel\ *adj or adv, sometimes not cap* [absent without leave] (1919) **:** ABSENT WITHOUT LEAVE

[2]**AWOL** *n, sometimes not cap* (1919) **:** one who is AWOL

awry \ə-ˈrī\ *adv or adj* (14c) **1 :** in a turned or twisted position or direction **:** ASKEW **2 :** out of the right or hoped-for course **:** AMISS

aw–shucks \ˌȯ-ˌshəks\ *adj* (1951) **:** being or marked by an unsophisticated, self-conscious, or self-effacing manner

[1]**ax** *or* **axe** \ˈaks\ *n* [ME, fr. OE *æcs;* akin to OHG *ackus* ax, L *ascia,* Gk *axinē*] (bef. 12c) **1 :** a cutting tool that consists of a heavy edged head

fixed to a handle with the edge parallel to the handle and that is used esp. for felling trees and chopping and splitting wood   **2** : a hammer with a sharp edge for dressing or spalling stone   **3** : abrupt removal (as from employment or from a budget) — sometimes used in the phrase *get the ax*   **4** : a musical instrument (as a guitar or a saxophone) — **ax to grind** : an ulterior often selfish purpose to further

²**ax** *or* **axe** *vt* **axed; ax•ing** (1679)   **1 a** : to shape, dress, or trim with an ax   **b** : to chop, split, or sever with an ax   **2** : to remove abruptly (as from employment or from a budget)

ax•el \'ak-səl, 'äk-\ *n* [*Axel* Paulsen *fl* 1890 Norw. figure skater] (1930) : a jump in figure skating from the outer forward edge of one skate with 1¹/₂ turns taken in the air and a return to the outer backward edge of the other skate

axe•nic \(')ā-'zen-ik, -'zēn-\ *adj* [*a-* + Gk *xenos* strange] (ca. 1942) : free from other living organisms — **axe•ni•cal•ly** \-i-k(ə-)lē\ *adv*

ax•i•al \'ak-sē-əl\ *adj* (ca. 1847)   **1** : of, relating to, or having the characteristics of an axis   **2 a** : situated around, in the direction of, on, or along an axis   **b** : extending in a direction essentially perpendicular to the plane of a cyclic structure (as of cyclohexane) ⟨∼ hydrogens⟩ — compare EQUATORIAL — **ax•i•al•i•ty** \ak-sē-'al-ət-ē\ *n* — **ax•i•al•ly** \'ak-sē-ə-lē\ *adv*

axial skeleton *n* (ca. 1872) : the skeleton of the trunk and head

ax•il \'ak-səl, -,sil\ *n* [NL *axilla*, fr. L — more at AXIS] (1794) : the angle between a branch or leaf and the axis from which it arises

ax•ile \-,sil\ *adj* (1845) : relating to or situated in an axis of a plant

ax•il•la \ag-'zil-ə, ak-'sil-\ *n, pl* **-lae** \-(,)ē, -,ī\ *or* **-las** [L] (1616) : ARMPIT

ax•il•lar \ag-'zil-ər, ak-'sil-, 'ag-zəl-, 'ak-səl-, -,är\ *n* (1541) : an axillary part (as a vein, nerve, or feather)

¹**ax•il•lary** \'ak-sə-,ler-ē\ *adj* (1615)   **1** : of, relating to, or located near the axilla   **2** : situated in or growing from an axil ⟨∼ buds⟩

²**axillary** *n, pl* **-lar•ies** (ca. 1890) : AXILLAR; *esp* : one of the feathers arising from the axilla and closing the space between the flight feathers and body of a flying bird

ax•i•ol•o•gy \ak-sē-'äl-ə-jē\ *n* [Gk *axios* + ISV *-logy*] (1908) : the study of the nature, types, and criteria of values and of value judgments esp. in ethics — **ax•i•o•log•i•cal** \ak-sē-ə-,läj-i-kəl\ *adj* — **ax•i•o•log•i•cal•ly** \-i-k(ə-)lē\ *adv*

ax•i•om \'ak-sē-əm\ *n* [L *axioma*, fr. Gk *axiōma*, lit., honor, fr. *axioun* to think worthy, fr. *axios* worth, worthy; akin to Gk *agein* to drive — more at AGENT] (15c)   **1** : a maxim widely accepted on its intrinsic merit   **2** : a statement accepted as true as the basis for argument or inference : POSTULATE 1   **3** : an established rule or principle or a self-evident truth

ax•i•om•at•ic \ak-sē-ə-'mat-ik\ *adj* [MGk *axiōmatikos*, fr. Gk, honorable, fr. *axiōmat-, axiōma*] (1797)   **1** : taken for granted : SELF-EVIDENT   **2** : based on or involving an axiom or system of axioms ⟨∼ set theory⟩ — **ax•i•om•at•i•cal•ly** \-i-k(ə-)lē\ *adv*

ax•i•om•a•ti•za•tion \ak-sē-ə-,mat-ə-'zā-shən, -sē-,äm-ət-ə-\ *n* (1931) : the act or process of reducing to a system of axioms — **ax•i•om•a•tize** \-sē-'äm-ə-,tīz\ *vt*

ax•is \'ak-səs\ *n, pl* **ax•es** \-,sēz\ [L, axis, axle; akin to OE *eax* axis, axle, Gk *axōn*, L *axilla* armpit, *agere* to drive — more at AGENT] (14c)   **1 a** : a straight line about which a body or a geometric figure rotates or may be supposed to rotate   **b** : a straight line with respect to which a body or figure is symmetrical — called also *axis of symmetry*   **c** : a straight line that bisects at right angles a system of parallel chords of a curve and divides the curve into two symmetrical parts   **d** : one of the reference lines of a coordinate system   **2 a** : the second vertebra of the neck on which the head and first vertebra turn as on a pivot   **b** : any of various central, fundamental, or axial parts   **3** : a plant stem   **4** : one of several imaginary lines assumed in describing the positions of the planes by which a crystal is bounded and the positions of atoms in the structure of the crystal   **5** : a main line of direction, motion, growth, or extension   **6 a** : an implied line in painting or sculpture through a composition to which elements in the composition are referred   **b** : a line actually drawn and used as the basis of measurements in an architectural or other working drawing   **7** : any of three fixed lines of reference in an airplane which usu. pass through the center of mass and are mutually perpendicular and of which the first is the principal longitudinal line in the plane of symmetry, the second is perpendicular to the first in the plane of symmetry, and the third is perpendicular to the other two — called also respectively *longitudinal axis, normal axis, lateral axis*   **8** : PARTNERSHIP, ALLIANCE

Axis *adj* (1938) : of or relating to the three powers Germany, Italy, and Japan engaged against the Allied nations in World War II

axi•sym•met•ric \ak-si-sə-'me-trik\ *also* **axi•sym•met•ri•cal** \-tri-kəl\ *adj* [*axis* + *symmetric*] (1893) : symmetric in respect to an axis — **axi•sym•me•try** \-'sim-ə-trē\ *n*

ax•le \'ak-səl\ *n* [ME *axel-* (as in *axeltre*)] (14c)   **1 a** : a pin or shaft on or with which a wheel or pair of wheels revolves   **b** (1) : the spindle of an axletree   (2) : AXLETREE   **2** *archaic* : AXIS

axle•tree \-,(,)trē\ *n* [ME *axeltre*, fr. ON *öxultrē*, fr. *öxull* axle + *trē* tree] (14c) : a fixed bar or beam with bearings at its ends on which wheels (as of a cart) revolve

ax•man \'ak-smən\ *n* (1671) : one who wields an ax

Ax•min•ster \'ak-,smin(t)-stər\ *n* [*Axminster*, England] (1818) : a machine-woven carpet with pile tufts inserted mechanically in a variety of textures and patterns

ax•o•lotl \'ak-sə-,lät-ᵊl\ *n* [Nahuatl, lit., water doll] (ca. 1768) : any of several salamanders (genus *Ambystoma*) of mountain lakes of Mexico and the western U.S. that ordinarily live and breed without metamorphosing

ax•on \'ak-,sän\ *also* **ax•one** \-,sōn\ *n* [NL *axon*, fr. Gk *axōn*] (ca. 1899) : a usu. long and single nerve-cell process that usu. conducts impulses away from the cell body — **ax•o•nal** \'ak-sən-ᵊl; 'ak-'sän-, -'sōn-\ *adj*

ax•o•neme \'ak-sə-,nēm\ *n* [NL, fr. Gk *axōn* + NL *-neme* (as in *treponeme*)] (1901) : the fibrillar bundle of a flagellum or cilium that usu. consists of nine double fibrils surrounding two single central fibrils — **ax•o•ne•mal** \,ak-sə-'nē-məl\ *adj*

ax•o•no•met•ric \,ak-sə-nō-,me-trik\ *adj* [Gk *axōn* axis + E *-metric*] (1908) : being or prepared by the projection of objects on the drawing surface so that they appear inclined with three sides showing and with horizontal and vertical distances drawn to scale but diagonal and curved lines distorted ⟨an ∼ drawing⟩

axo•plasm \'ak-sə-,plaz-əm\ *n* [*axon* + *-plasm*] (ca. 1900) : the protoplasm of an axon — **axo•plas•mic** \,ak-sə-'plaz-mik\ *adj*

ay \(')ī\ *interj* [MF *aymi* ay me] (14c) — usu. used with following *me* to express sorrow or regret

ayah \'ī-ə; 'ä-yə, -,(,)yä\ *n* [Hindi *āyā*, fr. Pg *aia*, fr. L *avia* grandmother] (1779) : a nurse or maid native to India

aya•hua•sca \,ī-(y)ə-'(h)wäs-kə\ *n* [AmerSp *ayahuasca*, fr. Quechua *ayawáskha*, lit., vine of the dead] (1949) : an hallucinogenic beverage prepared from the root of a So. American vine (*Banisteriopsis caapi* of the family Malpighiaceae)

aya•tol•lah \,ī-ə-'tō-lə, -'täl-ə, -'təl-ə, 'ī-ə-,; ,ī-ə-tə-'lä\ *n* [Per, lit., sign of God, fr. Ar *āyat* sign, miracle + *allāh* God] (1953) : a religious ¹eader among Shiite Muslims — used as a title of respect esp. for one who is not an imam

¹**aye** *also* **ay** \'ā\ *adv* [ME, fr. ON *ei;* akin to OE *ā* always, L *aevum* age, lifetime, Gk *aiōn* age] (13c) : ALWAYS, CONTINUALLY, EVER ⟨love that will ∼ endure —W. S. Gilbert⟩

²**aye** *also* **ay** \'ī\ *adv* [perh. fr. ME *ye, yie* — more at YEA] (1576) : YES ⟨∼, ∼, sir⟩

³**aye** *also* **ay** \'ī\ *n, pl* **ayes** (1589) : an affirmative vote or voter ⟨the ∼s have it⟩

aye–aye \'ī-,ī\ *n* [F, fr. Malagasy *aiay*] (ca. 1781) : a nocturnal lemur (*Daubentonia madagascariensis*) of Madagascar

ayin \'ī-ən\ *n* [Heb *'ayin*, lit., eye] (1823) : the 16th letter of the Hebrew alphabet — see ALPHABET table

Ay•ma•ra \,ī-mə-'rä\ *n, pl* **Aymara** *or* **Aymaras** [Sp *aymará*] (1860)   **1** : a member of an Indian people of Bolivia and Peru   **2 a** : the language of the Aymara people   **b** : a language family of the Kechumaran stock comprising Aymara

Ayr•shire \'a(ə)r-,shi(ə)r, 'e(ə)r-, -shər; 'ash-,i(ə)r\ *n* [*Ayrshire*, Scotland] (1856) : any of a breed of hardy dairy cattle originated in Ayr and marked with blotches of red or brown with white

az- *or* **azo-** *comb form* [ISV, fr. *azote*] : containing nitrogen esp. as the bivalent group N=N ⟨*azine*⟩

aza- *or* **az-** *comb form* [ISV *az-* + *-a-*] : containing nitrogen in place of carbon and usu. the bivalent group NH for the group CH₂ or a single trivalent nitrogen atom for the group CH ⟨*azaguanine*⟩

aza•lea \ə-'zāl-yə\ *n* [NL, genus name, fr. Gk, fem. of *azaleos* dry; akin to L *aridus* dry — more at ARDOR] (1767) : any of a genus or subgenus (*Azalea*) of rhododendrons with funnel-shaped corollas and usu. deciduous leaves including many species and hybrid forms cultivated as ornamentals

aza•thi•o•prine \,az-ə-'thī-ə-,prēn\ *n* [*aza-* + *thio-* + *purine*] (1962) : a purine antimetabolite C₉H₇N₇O₂S used esp. as an immunosuppressant

Aza•zel \ə-'zā-zəl, 'az-ə-,zel\ *n* [Heb *'ăzāzēl*] : an evil spirit of the wilderness to which a scapegoat was sent by the ancient Hebrews in a ritual of atonement

azeo•trope \'ā-zē-ə-,trōp\ *n* [²*a-* + *zeo-* (fr. Gk *zein* to boil) + Gk *tropos* turn — more at YEAST, TROPE] (1938) : a liquid mixture that is characterized by a constant minimum or maximum boiling point which is lower or higher than that of any of the components

azide \'ā-,zīd, 'az-,īd\ *n* (ca. 1904) : a compound containing the group N₃ combined with an element or radical — **az•i•do** \'az-ə-,dō\ *adj*

az•i•do•thy•mi•dine \ə-,zid-ō-'thī-mə-,dēn\ *n* [*azido* + *thymidine*] (1974) : an antiviral drug C₁₀H₁₃N₅O₄ used to treat AIDS — called also *AZT, zidovudine*

az•i•muth \'az-(ə-)məth\ *n* [ME, fr. MF, fr. Ar *as-sumūt*, pl. of *as-samt* the way] (14c)   **1** : an arc of the horizon measured between a fixed point (as true north) and the vertical circle passing through the center of an object usu. in astronomy and navigation clockwise from the north point through 360 degrees   **2** : horizontal direction expressed as the angular distance between the direction of a fixed point (as the observer's heading) and the direction of the object — **az•i•muth•al** \,az-ə-'məth-əl\ *adj* — **az•i•muth•al•ly** \-'məth-ə-lē\ *adv*

azimuthal equidistant projection *n* (1942) : a map projection of the

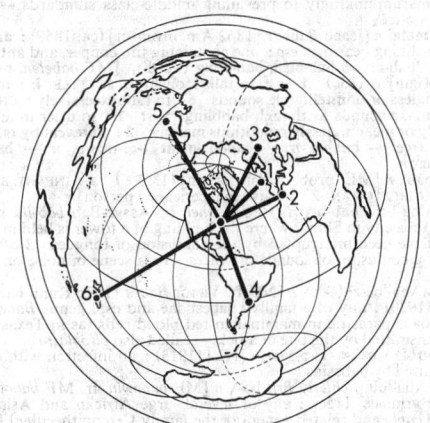

azimuthal equidistant projection, centered on Washington, D.C.: *1* London, *2* Algiers, *3* Moscow, *4* Rio de Janeiro, *5* Tokyo, *6* Auckland

---

surface of the earth so centered at any given point that a straight line radiating from the center to any other point represents the shortest distance and can be measured to scale

az·ine \'ā-,zēn, 'az-,ēn\ *n* (1887) **1** : any of numerous organic compounds with a nitrogenous 6-membered ring **2** : a compound of the general formula RCH=NN=CHR or R$_2$C=NN=CR$_2$ formed by the action of hydrazine on aldehydes or ketones

azo \'ā-(,)zō, 'az-(,)ō\ *adj* [*az-*] (ca. 1879) : relating to or containing the bivalent group N=N united at both ends to carbon

azo dye *n* (1884) : any of numerous versatile dyes containing azo groups

azo·ic \(')ā-'zō-ik\ *adj* [*a-* + Gk *zōē* life — more at QUICK] (ca. 1847) : having no life; *specif* : of or relating to the part of geologic time that antedates life — compare ARCHEAN

azole \'ā-,zōl, 'az-,ōl\ *n* (ca. 1899) : any of numerous compounds characterized by a 5-membered ring containing at least one atom of nitrogen

azon·al \(')ā-'zōn-ºl\ *adj* (1896) : of, relating to, or being a soil or a major soil group marked by soils lacking well-developed horizons often because of immaturity — compare INTRAZONAL, ZONAL

azote \'ā-,zōt, 'az-,ōt\ *n* [F, irreg. fr. *a-* + Gk *zōē* life] (1791) : NITROGEN

azo·te·mia \,ā-zō-'tē-mē-ə\ *n* [ISV *azote* + NL *-emia*] (ca. 1900) : an excess of nitrogenous bodies in the blood as a result of kidney insufficiency — compare UREMIA — **azo·te·mic** \-mik\ *adj*

az·oth \'az-,ōth\ *n* [Ar *az-zā'ūq* the mercury] (15c) **1** : mercury regarded by alchemists as the first principle of metals **2** : the universal remedy of Paracelsus

azo·to·bac·ter \ā-'zōt-ə-,bak-tər\ *n* [NL, genus name, fr. ISV *azote* + NL *bacterium*] (1910) : any of a genus (*Azotobacter*) of large rod= shaped or spherical bacteria occurring in soil and sewage and fixing atmospheric nitrogen

azo·tu·ria \,ā-zō-'t(y)ur-ē-ə\ *n* [ISV *azote* + NL *-uria*] (ca. 1838) : an excess of urea or other nitrogenous substances in the urine

AZT \,ā-,zē-'tē\ *n* (1985) : AZIDOTHYMIDINE

Az·tec \'az-,tek\ *n* [Sp *azteca*, fr. Nahuatl, pl. of *aztecatl*] (1787) **1 a** : a member of a Nahuatlan people that founded the Mexican empire conquered by Cortes in 1519 **b** : a member of any people under Aztec influence **2 a** : the language of the Aztec people **b** : NAHUATL — **Az·tec·an** \-ən\ *adj*

azure \'azh-ər\ *n* [ME *asur*, fr. OF *azur*, prob. fr. OSp, modif. of Ar *lāzaward*, fr. Per *lāzhuward*] (14c) **1** *archaic* : LAPIS LAZULI **2 a** : the blue color of the clear sky **b** : the heraldic color blue **3** : the unclouded sky — **azure** *adj*

azur·ite \'azh-ə-,rīt\ *n* [F, fr. *azur* azure] (ca. 1868) **1** : a mineral Cu$_3$(OH)$_2$(CO$_3$)$_2$ consisting of blue basic carbonate of copper, occurring in monoclinic crystals, in mass, and in earthy form, and constituting an ore of copper **2** : a semiprecious stone derived from azurite

azygo- *comb form* [ISV, fr. Gk *azygos*] : azygos

¹azy·gos \ā-'zī-gəs\ *n* [NL, fr. Gk, unyoked, fr. *a-* + *zygon* yoke — more at YOKE] (1646) : an azygos anatomical part

²azy·gos *also* **azy·gous** \(')ā-'zī-gəs\ *adj* (1681) : not being one of a pair : SINGLE ⟨an ~ vein⟩

---

b \'bē\ *n, pl* **b's** *or* **bs** \'bēz\ *often cap, often attrib* **1 a** : the 2d letter of the English alphabet **b** : a graphic representation of this letter **c** : a speech counterpart of orthographic *b* **2** : the 7th tone of a C-major scale **3** : a graphic device for reproducing the letter *b* **4** : one designated *b* esp. as the 2d in order or class **5 a** : a grade rating a student's work as good but short of excellent **b** : one graded or rated with a B **6** : something shaped like the letter B

baa *or* **ba** \'ba, 'bä\ *n* [imit.] (1589) : the bleat of a sheep — **baa** *vi*

baal \'bā-(ə)l\ *n, pl* **baals** *or* **baa·lim** \'bā-(ə)ləm, 'bä-ə-,lim\ *often cap* [Heb *ba'al* lord] (14c) : any of numerous Canaanite and Phoenician local deities — **baal·ism** \'bā-(ə-),liz-əm\ *n, often cap*

ba·ba \'bäb-(,)ä, -ə\ *n* [F, fr. Pol, lit., old woman] (1827) : a rich cake soaked in a rum and sugar syrup

ba·bas·su \,bäb-ə-'sü\ *n* [Pg *babaçú*] (1917) : a tall pinnate-leaved palm (*Orbignya speciosa* or *O. martiana*) of northeastern Brazil with hard= shelled nuts yielding a valuable oil

¹bab·bitt \'bab-ət\ *vt* (1874) : to line or furnish with babbitt metal

²babbitt *n* (1901) : a babbitt-metal lining for a bearing

Bab·bitt \'bab-ət\ *n* [George F. *Babbitt*, character in the novel *Babbitt* (1922) by Sinclair Lewis] (1923) : a business or professional man who conforms unthinkingly to prevailing middle-class standards — **Bab·bitt·ry** \-ə-trē\ *n*

babbitt metal *n* [Isaac *Babbitt* †1862 Am. inventor] (ca. 1859) : an alloy used for lining bearings; *esp* : one containing tin, copper, and antimony

bab·ble \'bab-əl\ *vb* **bab·bled; bab·bling** \-(ə-)liŋ\ [ME *babelen*, prob. of imit. origin] *vi* (13c) **1 a** : to talk foolishly : PRATTLE **b** : to utter meaningless or unintelligible sounds **c** : to talk excessively : CHATTER **2** : to make sounds as though babbling ~ *vt* **1** : to utter in an incoherently or meaninglessly repetitious manner **2** : to reveal by talk that is too free — **babble** *n* — **bab·ble·ment** \-əl-mənt\ *n* — **bab·bler** \-(ə-)lər\ *n*

babe \'bāb\ *n* [ME, prob. of imit. origin] (13c) **1 a** : INFANT, BABY **b** *slang* : GIRL, WOMAN **2** : a naive inexperienced person

Ba·bel \'bā-bəl, 'bab-əl\ *n* [Heb *Bābhel*, fr. Assyr-Bab *bāb-ilu* gate of god] **1** : a city in Shinar where the building of a tower is held in Genesis to have been interrupted by the confusion of tongues **2** *often not cap* **a** : a confusion of sounds or voices **b** : a scene of noise or confusion

ba·be·sia \bə-'bē-zh(ē-)ə\ *n* [NL, fr. Victor *Babeş* †1926 Rum. bacteriologist] (1920) : any of a family (Babesiidae and esp. genus *Babesia*) of sporozoans parasitic in mammalian red blood cells (as in Texas fever) and transmitted by the bite of a tick — called also *piroplasm*

bab·e·si·o·sis \,bab-ə-'zī-ə-səs\ *n* [NL] (1913) : an infection with or disease caused by babesias

ba·boon \ba-'bün, *chiefly Brit* bə-\ *n* [ME *babewin*, fr. MF *babouin*, fr. *baboue* grimace] (15c) : any of several large African and Asian primates (*Papio* and related genera of the family Cercopithecidae) having doglike muzzles and usu. short tails

ba·bu \'bäb-(,)ü\ *n* [Hindi *bābū*, lit., father] (1776) **1** : a Hindu gentleman — a form of address corresponding to *Mr.* **2 a** : an Indian clerk who writes English **b** : an Indian having some education in English — often used disparagingly

ba·bul \bə-'bül\ *n* [Per *babūl*] (1780) : an acacia tree (*Acacia arabica*) widespread in northern Africa and across Asia that yields gum arabic and tannins as well as fodder and timber

ba·bush·ka \bə-'büsh-kə, -'bush-\ *n* [Russ, grandmother, dim. of *baba* old woman] (1938) **1** : a usu. triangularly folded kerchief for the head **2** : a head covering resembling a babushka

¹ba·by \'bā-bē\ *n, pl* **babies** [ME, fr. *babe*] (13c) **1 a** (1) : an extremely young child; *esp* : INFANT (2) : an extremely young animal **b** : the youngest of a group **2** : an infantile person **3 a** *slang* : GIRL, WOMAN — often used in address **b** : PERSON, THING **c** *slang* : BOY, MAN — often used in address — **ba·by·hood** \-bē-,hùd\ *n* — **ba·by·ish** \-ish\ *adj*

²baby *adj* (1605) **1** : of or relating to a baby **2** : much smaller than usual ⟨~ corn⟩ ⟨a ~ flattop⟩

³baby *vt* **ba·bied; ba·by·ing** (1742) **1** : to tend or indulge with often excessive or inappropriate care and solicitude ⟨parents must resist the urge to ~ an only child⟩ **2** : to operate or treat with care ⟨~ a new motor⟩ *syn* see INDULGE

baby blue–eyes \-'blü-,īz\ *n pl but sing or pl in constr* (1887) : a delicate blue-flowered California herb (*Nemophila menziesii*)

baby boom *n* (1953) : a marked rise in birthrate (as in the U.S. immediately following the end of World War II) — **baby boom·er** *n*

baby carriage *n* (1866) : a small four-wheeled carriage often with a folding top for pushing a baby around in — called also *baby buggy*

baby farm *n* (1868) : a place where care of babies is provided for a fee

baby grand *n* (ca. 1903) : a small grand piano

Bab·y·lon \'bab-ə-lən, -,län\ *n* [*Babylon*, ancient city of Babylonia] (14c) : a city devoted to materialism and the pursuit of sensual pleasure

¹Bab·y·lo·nian \,bab-ə-'lō-nyən, -nē-ən\ *n* (1564) **1** : a native or inhabitant of ancient Babylonia or Babylon **2** : the form of the Akkadian language used in ancient Babylonia

²Babylonian *adj* (1612) **1** : of, relating to, or characteristic of Babylonia or Babylon, the Babylonians, or Babylonian **2** : LUXURIOUS

baby's breath *n* (ca. 1890) **1** : GYPSOPHILA **2** : a bedstraw (*Galium sylvaticum*) with thin lanceolate leaves and white flowers

ba·by–sit \'bā-bē-,sit\ *vb* **-sat** \-,sat\; **-sit·ting** [back-formation fr. *baby-sitter*] *vi* (1947) : to care for children usu. during a short absence of the parents ~ *vt* : to baby-sit for — **ba·by–sit·ter** *n*

baby talk *n* (1836) **1** : the syntactically imperfect speech or phonetically modified forms used by small children learning to talk **2** : the consciously imperfect or mutilated speech or prattle often used by adults in speaking to small children

bac·ca·lau·re·ate \,bak-ə-'lòr-ē-ət, -'lär-\ *n* [ML *baccalaureatus*, fr. *baccalaureus* bachelor, alter. of *baccalarius*] (1625) **1** : the degree of bachelor conferred by universities and colleges **2** : a sermon to a graduating class **b** : the service at which this sermon is delivered

bac·ca·rat \,bäk-ə-'rä, ,bak-\ *n* [F *baccara*] (1865) : a card game resembling chemin de fer in which three hands are dealt and players may bet either or both hands against the dealer's; *also* : a two-handed version in which players may bet on or against the dealer

Bac·chae \'bak-,ē, -,ī\ *n pl* [L, fr. Gk *Bakchai*, pl. of *Bakchē*] **1** : the female attendants or priestesses of Bacchus **2** : the women participating in the Bacchanalia

¹bac·cha·nal \'bak-ən-ºl\ *adj* [L *bacchanalis* of Bacchus] (1550) : of, relating to, or suggestive of the Bacchanalia : BACCHANALIAN

²bac·cha·nal \'bak-ən-ºl, ,bak-ə-'nal, ,bäk-ə-'näl\ *n* (1590) **1 a** : a devotee of Bacchus; *esp* : one who celebrates the Bacchanalia **b** : REVELER **2** : drunken revelry : BACCHANALIA

bac·cha·na·lia \,bak-ə-'nāl-yə\ *n, pl* **bacchanalia** [L, pl., fr. neut. pl. of *bacchanalis*] (1591) **1** *pl, cap* : a Roman festival of Bacchus celebrated with dancing, song, and revelry **2** : a drunken feast : ORGY — **bac·cha·na·lian** \-'nāl-yən\ *adj or n*

bac·chant \bə-'kant, -'känt\ *'bak-ənt\ *n, pl* **bacchants** *or* **bacchantes** \bə-'kants, -'känts, -'kant-ēz, -'känt-ēz\ [L *bacchant-, bacchans*, fr. prp. of *bacchari* to take part in the orgies of Bacchus] (1699) : BACCHANAL — **bacchant** *adj* — **bac·chan·tic** \bə-'kant-ik, -'känt-\ *adj*

bac·chante \bə-'kant-(ē), -'känt-(ē)\ *n* [F, fr. L *bacchant-, bacchans*] (1579) : a priestess or female follower of Bacchus : MAENAD

bac·chic \ˈbak-ik\ *adj, often cap* (1669) **1 :** of or relating to Bacchus **2 :** of or relating to the Bacchanalia : BACCHANALIAN

Bac·chus \ˈbak-əs\ *n* [L, fr. Gk *Bakchos*] : the Greek god of wine — called also *Dionysus*

bach \ˈbach\ *vi* (1870) : to live as a bachelor — **bach** *n*

bach·e·lor \ˈbach-(ə-)lər\ *n* [ME *bacheler,* fr. OF, fr. ML *baccalarius* tenant farmer, squire, advanced student, of Celtic origin; akin to IrGael *bachlach* shepherd, peasant, fr. OIr *bachall* staff, fr. L *baculum* — more at BACTERIUM] (13c) **1 :** a young knight who follows the banner of another **2 :** a person who has received what is usu. the lowest degree conferred by a four-year college, university, or professional school ⟨~ of arts⟩ **3 a :** an unmarried man **b :** a male animal (as a fur seal) without a mate during breeding time — **bach·e·lor·hood** \-ˌhu̇d\ *n*

bach·e·lor·ette \ˌbach(-ə)-lə-ˈret\ *n* (1938) : a young unmarried woman

bachelor's button *n* (1847) : a European composite (*Centaurea cyanus*) having flower heads with blue, pink, or white rays that is often cultivated in No. America — called also *cornflower*

ba·cil·la·ry \ˈbas-ə-ˌler-ē, bə-ˈsil-ə-rē\ *or* **ba·cil·lar** \bə-ˈsil-ər, ˈbas-ə-lər\ *adj* [ML & NL *bacillus*] (1865) **1 :** shaped like a rod; *also* : consisting of small rods **2 :** of, relating to, or caused by bacilli

ba·cil·lus \bə-ˈsil-əs\ *n, pl* **-li** \-ˌī *also* -ē\ [NL, fr. ML, small staff, rod, dim. of L *baculus* staff, alter. of *baculum* — more at PEG] (ca. 1879) **1 :** any of a genus (*Bacillus*) of aerobic rod-shaped bacteria producing endospores that do not thicken the rod and including many saprophytes and some parasites (as *B. anthracis* of anthrax); *broadly* : a straight rod-shaped bacterium **2 :** BACTERIUM; *esp* : a disease-producing bacterium

bac·i·tra·cin \ˌbas-ə-ˈtrās-ᵊn\ *n* [NL *Bacillus subtilis* (species of bacillus producing the toxin) + Margaret *Tracy b ab* 1936 Am. child in whose tissues it was found] (1945) : a toxic polypeptide antibiotic isolated from a bacillus (*Bacillus subtilis*) and usu. used topically against cocci

[1]**back** \ˈbak\ *n* [ME, fr. OE *bæc;* akin to OHG *bah* back] (bef. 12c) **1 a :** the rear part of the human body esp. from the neck to the end of the spine **b :** the corresponding part of a lower animal (as a quadruped) **c :** SPINAL COLUMN **d :** BACKBONE 4 **2 a :** the side or surface opposite the front or face : the rear part; *also* : the farther or reverse side **b :** something at or on the back for support ⟨~ of a chair⟩ **3 :** a position in some games (as football or soccer) behind the front line of players; *also* : a player in this position — **backed** \ˈbakt\ *adj* — **back·less** \ˈbak-ləs\ *adj*

[2]**back** *adv* (bef. 12c) **1 a :** to, toward, or at the rear **b :** in or into the past : AGO **c :** in or into a reclining position **d** (1) **:** under restraint (2) **:** in a delayed or retarded condition **2 a :** to, toward, or in a place from which a person or thing came **b :** to or toward a former state **c :** in return or reply — **back and forth :** backward and forward : from one place to another

[3]**back** *adj* (15c) **1 a :** being at or in the back ⟨~ door⟩ **b :** distant from a central or main area : REMOTE **c :** articulated at or toward the back of the oral passage **2 :** having returned or been returned ⟨men ~ from the war⟩ **3 :** being in arrears : OVERDUE **4 :** moving or operating backward **5 :** not current ⟨~ number of a magazine⟩ **6 :** constituting the final 9 holes of an 18-hole golf course

[4]**back** *vt* (1548) **1 a :** to support by material or moral assistance — often used with *up* **b :** SUBSTANTIATE **c :** to assume financial responsibility for **2 :** to cause to go back or in reverse **3 a :** to furnish with a back **b :** to be at the back of ~ *vi* **1 :** to move backward **2** *of the wind* **:** to shift counterclockwise — compare VEER **3 :** to have the back in the direction of something ***syn*** see SUPPORT, RECEDE — **back and fill 1 :** to manage the sails of a ship so as to keep it clear of obstructions as it floats down with the current of a river or channel **2 :** to take opposite positions alternately : SHILLY-SHALLY

[5]**back** *n* [D *bak*] (1682) : a shallow vat or tub used esp. by brewers or dyers

back·ache \ˈbak-ˌāk\ *n* (1601) : a pain in the lower back

back away *vi* (1919) : to move back (as from a theoretical position) : WITHDRAW

back·beat \ˈbak-ˌbēt\ *n* (1928) : a steady pronounced rhythm that is the characteristic driving force esp. of rock music

back bench *n* (1874) : a bench in a British legislature (as the House of Commons) occupied by rank-and-file members — compare FRONT BENCH — **back·bench·er** \-ˈben-chər\ *n*

back·bite \-ˌbīt\ *vb* **-bit; -bitten; -biting** *vt* (12c) : to say mean or spiteful things about ~ *vi* : to backbite a person — **back·bit·er** *n*

back·block \-ˌbläk\ *n, Austral & New Zeal* (1872) : OUTBACK

back·board \-ˌbō(ə)rd, -ˌbȯ(ə)rd\ *n* (1761) : a board placed at or serving as the back of something; *specif* : a rounded or rectangular board that is behind the basket on a basketball court and that serves to keep missed shots from going out-of-bounds and as a surface from which the ball can be made to rebound into the basket

back·bone \-ˈbōn, -ˌbōn\ *n* (14c) **1 :** SPINAL COLUMN, SPINE **2 a :** a chief mountain ridge, range, or system **b :** the foundation or most substantial or sturdiest part of something **3 :** firm and resolute character **4 :** the back of a book usu. lettered with the title and the author's and publisher's names

back·break·ing \-ˌbrāk-iŋ\ *adj* (1870) : extremely tiring or demanding : OPPRESSIVE ⟨~ labor⟩ ⟨~ rents⟩ — **back·break·er** \-ər\ *n*

back burner *n* (1969) : the condition of being out of active consideration or development ⟨put the project on the *back burner*⟩

back–check \-ˌchek\ *vi* (1937) : to skate back toward one's own goal while closely defending against the offensive rushes of an opposing player in ice hockey

back·cloth \-ˌklȯth\ *n, chiefly Brit* (1879) : BACKDROP

back·coun·try \-ˌkən-trē\ *n* (1746) : a thinly settled rural area

back·court \-ˈkō(ə)rt, -ˈkȯ(ə)rt\ *n* (1890) **1 :** the area near or nearest the back boundary lines or back wall of the playing area in a net or court game **2 :** a basketball team's defensive half of the court; *also* : the part of the offensive half of the court farthest from the goal

back·court·man \-mən\ *n* (1954) : a guard on a basketball team

[1]**back·cross** \ˈbak-ˌkrȯs\ *vt* (1904) : to cross (a first-generation hybrid) with one of the parental types

[2]**backcross** *n* (1918) : a mating that involves backcrossing; *also* : an individual produced by backcrossing

back dive *n* (ca. 1934) : a dive from a position facing the diving board

back·door \ˌbak-ˌdō(ə)r, -ˌdȯ(ə)r\ *adj* (1805) : INDIRECT, CONCEALED, DEVIOUS

back down *vi* (1849) : to withdraw from a commitment or position

back·drop \ˈbak-ˌdräp\ *n* (1913) **1 :** a painted cloth hung across the rear of a stage **2 :** BACKGROUND

back·er \ˈbak-ər\ *n* (1583) **1 :** one that supports **2 :** one who works with backs or backing

back·field \-ˌfēld\ *n* (1920) : the football players whose positions are behind the line of scrimmage; *also* : the positions themselves

back·fill \-ˌfil\ *vt* (1926) : to refill (as an excavation) usu. with excavated material ~ *vi* : to backfill an excavation — **backfill** *n*

[1]**back·fire** \-ˌfī(ə)r\ *n* (1784) **1 :** a fire started to check an advancing forest or prairie fire by clearing an area **2 :** an improperly timed explosion of fuel mixture in the cylinder of an internal-combustion engine

[2]**backfire** *vi* (1886) **1 :** to make or undergo a backfire **2 :** to have the reverse of the desired or expected effect

back–formation *n* (1889) **1 :** a word formed by subtraction of a real or supposed affix from an already existing longer word (as *burgle* from *burglar*) **2 :** the formation of a back-formation

back·gam·mon \ˈbak-ˌgam-ən, bak-ˈ\ *n* [perh. fr. [3]*back* + ME *gamen, game* game] (1645) : a board game played with dice and counters in which each player tries to be the first to gather his pieces into one corner and then systematically remove them from the board

[1]**back·ground** \ˈbak-ˌgrau̇nd\ *n* (1672) **1 a :** the scenery or ground behind something **b :** the part of a painting representing what lies behind objects in the foreground **2 :** an inconspicuous position **3 a :** the conditions that form the setting within which something is experienced **b** (1) **:** the circumstances or events antecedent to a phenomenon or development (2) **:** information essential to understanding of a problem or situation **c :** the total of a person's experience, knowledge, and education **4 a :** a somewhat steady level of radiation in the natural environment (as from cosmic rays or radioactivity) **b :** intrusive sound or radiation that interferes with received or recorded electronic signals

[2]**background** *vt* (1768) : to provide with background

background music *n* (1928) : music to accompany the dialogue or action of a motion picture or radio or television drama

[1]**back·hand** \ˈbak-ˌhand\ *n* (1657) **1 a :** a stroke (as in tennis) made with the back of the hand turned in the direction of movement; *also* : the side on which such strokes are made **b :** a catch (as in baseball) made to the side of the body opposite the hand being used **2 :** handwriting whose strokes slant downward from left to right

[2]**backhand** *adj* (1695) : made with a backhand ⟨a ~ tennis stroke⟩

[3]**backhand** *or* **back·hand·ed** \-ˈhan-dəd\ *adv* (1889) : with a backhand

[4]**backhand** *vt* (1935) : to do, hit, or catch backhand

back·hand·ed \ˈbak-ˈhan-dəd\ *adj* (1800) **1 :** INDIRECT, DEVIOUS; *esp* : SARCASTIC **2 :** using or made with a backhand — **back·hand·ed·ly** *adv*

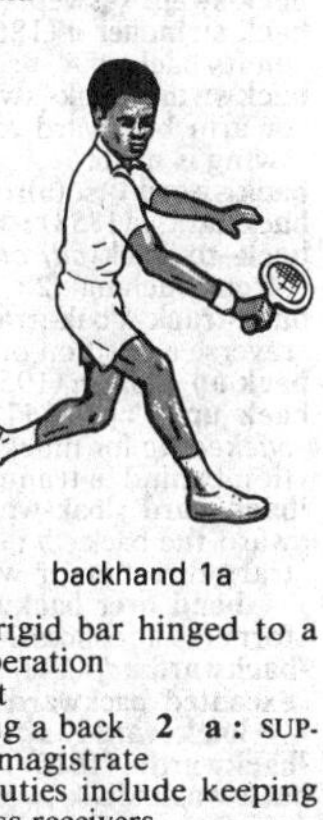

backhand 1a

back·hoe \-ˌhō\ *n* (1942) : an excavating machine having a bucket that is attached to a rigid bar hinged to a boom and that is drawn toward the machine in operation

back·house \-ˌhau̇s\ *n* (ca. 1847) : an outdoor toilet

back·ing \ˈbak-iŋ\ *n* (1793) **1 :** something forming a back **2 a :** SUPPORT, AID **b :** endorsement esp. of a warrant by a magistrate

back judge *n* (1966) : a football official whose duties include keeping the game's official time and identifying eligible pass receivers

back·lash \ˈbak-ˌlash\ *n* (1815) **1 a :** a sudden violent backward movement or reaction **b :** the play between adjacent movable parts (as in a series of gears); *also* : the jar caused by this when the parts are put into action **2 :** a snarl in that part of a fishing line wound on the reel **3 :** a strong adverse reaction (as to a recent political or social development) — **back·lash·er** *n*

back·light \-ˌlīt\ *vt* (1952) : to illuminate (an object) from behind

[1]**back·log** \-ˌlȯg, -ˌläg\ *n* (1684) **1 :** a large log at the back of a hearth fire **2 :** an accumulation of tasks unperformed or materials not processed

[2]**backlog** *vb* (1963) : ACCUMULATE

back matter *n* (1947) : matter following the main text of a book

back mutation *n* (1939) : mutation of a previously mutated gene to its former condition

back of *prep* (1694) : BEHIND

back off *vi* (1954) : BACK DOWN

back out *vi* (1807) : to withdraw esp. from a commitment or contest

[1]**back·pack** \ˈbak-ˌpak\ *n* (1914) **1 a :** a load carried on the back **b :** a camping pack (as of canvas or nylon) supported by a usu. aluminum frame and carried on the back **2 :** a piece of equipment designed for use while being carried on the back

[2]**backpack** *vt* (1916) : to carry (food or equipment) on the back esp. in hiking ~ *vi* : to hike with a backpack — **back·pack·er** *n*

back·ped·al \ˈbak-ˌped-ᵊl\ *vi* (1901) : to retreat or move backward (as in boxing)

back·rest \-ˌrest\ *n* (1859) : a rest for the back

back room *n* (1592) **1 :** a room situated in the rear **2 :** the meeting place of a directing group that exercises its authority in an inconspicuous and indirect way

back·saw \ˈbak-ˌsȯ\ *n* (ca. 1877) : a saw with a metal rib along its back

back·scat·ter \-ˌskat-ər\ *or* **back·scat·ter·ing** \-ə-riŋ\ *n* (1940) : the scattering of radiation (as X rays) in a direction opposite to that of the incident radiation due to reflection from particles of the medium traversed; *also* : the radiation so reversed in direction

\ə\ **abut** \ᵊ\ **kitten,** F **table** \ər\ **further** \a\ **ash** \ā\ **ace** \ä\ **cot, cart**
\au̇\ **out** \ch\ **chin** \e\ **bet** \ē\ **easy** \g\ **go** \i\ **hit** \ī\ **ice** \j\ **job**
\ŋ\ **sing** \ō\ **go** \ȯ\ **law** \ȯi\ **boy** \th\ **thin** \t͟h\ **the** \ü\ **loot** \u̇\ **foot**
\y\ **yet** \zh\ **vision** \à, k̲, ⁿ, œ, œ̄, ue, u̅e, ʸ\ *see* Guide to Pronunciation

back·seat \-ˈsēt\ *n* (1829) **1 :** a seat in the back (as of an automobile) **2 :** an inferior position ⟨won't take a ~ to anyone⟩

back·set \ˈbak-ˌset\ *n* (1721) **:** SETBACK

back·side \-ˈsīd\ *n* (1500) **:** BUTTOCKS — often used in pl.

back·slap \-ˌslap\ *vt* (1926) **:** to display excessive or effusive goodwill for ~ *vi* **:** to display excessive cordiality or goodwill — **back·slap·per** *n*

back·slide \-ˌslīd\ *vi* **-slid** \-ˌslid\; **-slid** *or* **-slid·den** \-ˌslid-ᵊn\; **-slid·ing** \-ˌslīd-iŋ\ (1581) **:** to lapse morally or in the practice of religion — **back·slid·er** \-ˌslīd-ər\ *n*

back·space \-ˌspās\ *vi* (1911) **:** to move the carriage of a typewriter back one space with each depression of a key — **backspace** *n*

back·spin \-ˌspin\ *n* (ca. 1909) **:** a backward rotary motion of a ball

[1]**back·stage** \ˈbak-ˌstāj\ *adj* (1916) **1 :** of, relating to, or occurring in the area behind the proscenium and esp. in the dressing rooms **2 :** of or relating to the private lives of theater people **3 :** of or relating to the inner working or operation (as of an organization)

[2]**back·stage** \ˈbak-ˈstāj\ *adv* (1923) **1 :** in or to a backstage area **2 :** in private **:** SECRETLY

back·stairs \-ˌsta(ə)rz, -ˌste(ə)rz\ *adj* (1663) **1 :** SECRET, FURTIVE ⟨~ political deals⟩ **2 :** SORDID, SCANDALOUS ⟨~ gossip⟩

back·stay \-ˌstā\ *n* (1626) **1 :** a stay extending from the mastheads to the side of a ship and slanting aft **2 :** a strengthening or supporting device at the back (as of a carriage or a shoe)

back·stitch \-ˌstich\ *n* (1611) **:** a hand stitch sewn one stitch length backward on the front side of the fabric and two stitch lengths forward on the reverse side to form a solid line of stitching on both sides — **backstitch** *vb*

[1]**back·stop** \-ˌstäp\ *n* (1851) **1 :** something at the back serving as a stop: as **a :** a screen or fence for keeping a ball from leaving the field of play **b :** a stop (as a pawl) that prevents a backward movement (as of a wheel) **2 :** a player (as the catcher) whose position is behind the batter

[2]**backstop** *vt* (1941) **1 :** to serve as a backstop to **2 :** SUPPORT, BOLSTER

back·stretch \ˈbak-ˈstrech\ *n* (1839) **:** the side opposite the homestretch on a racecourse

back·stroke \-ˌstrōk\ *n* (1879) **:** a swimming stroke executed on the back

back·swept \-ˌswept\ *adj* (ca. 1918) **:** swept or slanting backward

back swimmer *n* (1862) **:** a water bug (family Notonectidae) that swims on its back

back·swing \ˈbak-ˌswiŋ\ *n* (1899) **:** the movement of a club, racket, bat, or arm backward to a position from which the forward or downward swing is made

back·sword \-ˌsō(ə)rd, -ˌsȯ(ə)rd\ *n* (1611) **:** a single-edged sword

back talk *n* (1858) **:** an impudent, insolent, or argumentative reply

back–to–back *adj or adv* (15c) **1 :** facing in opposite directions and often touching **2 :** coming one after the other **:** CONSECUTIVE

back·track \ˈbak-ˌtrak\ *vi* (1904) **1 :** to retrace one's course **2 :** to reverse a position or stand

back·up \-ˌəp\ *n* (1951) **:** one that serves as a substitute or support

back up \-ˈəp\ *vi* (1842) **:** to accumulate in a congested state ⟨traffic *backed up* for miles⟩ ~ *vt* **1 :** HOLD BACK 1 **2 :** to move into a position behind (a teammate) in order to assist on a play

[1]**back·ward** \ˈbak-wərd\ *or* **back·wards** \-wərdz\ *adv* (14c) **1 a :** toward the back **b :** with the back foremost **2 a :** in a reverse or contrary direction or way **b :** toward the past **c :** toward a worse state — **bend over backward** *or* **lean over backward :** to make extreme efforts (as at concession)

[2]**backward** *adj* (14c) **1 a :** directed or turned backward **b :** done or executed backward **2 :** DIFFIDENT, SHY **3 :** retarded in development — **back·ward·ly** *adv* — **back·ward·ness** *n*

[3]**backward** *n* (1610) **:** the part behind or past

back·wash \ˈbak-ˌwȯsh, -ˌwäsh\ *n* (1876) **1 :** backward movement (as of water or air) produced by a propelling force (as the motion of oars) **2 :** a consequence or by-product of an event **:** AFTERMATH

back·wa·ter \-ˌwȯt-ər, -ˌwät-\ *n* (14c) **1 a :** water turned back in its course by an obstruction, an opposing current, or the tide **b :** a body of water turned back **2 :** an isolated or backward place or condition

back·woods \-ˈwu̇dz\ *n pl but sing or pl in constr* (1709) **1 :** wooded or partly cleared areas far from cities **2 :** a remote or culturally backward area

back·wrap \-ˌrap\ *n* (1951) **:** a wraparound garment (as a skirt) that fastens in the back

back·yard \-ˈyärd\ *n* (1659) **1 :** an area at the rear of a house **2 :** an area that is one's special domain

ba·con \ˈbā-kən\ *n* [ME, fr. MF, of Gmc origin; akin to OHG *bahho* side of bacon, *bah* back] (14c) **:** a side of a pig cured and smoked

Ba·co·ni·an \bā-ˈkō-nē-ən\ *adj* (1812) **1 :** of, relating to, or characteristic of Francis Bacon or his doctrines **2 :** of or relating to those who believe that Francis Bacon wrote the works usu. attributed to Shakespeare — **Baconian** *n*

bac·ter·emia \ˌbak-tə-ˈrē-mē-ə\ *n* [NL, alter. of *bacteriemia,* fr. *bacteri-* + *-emia*] (ca. 1890) **:** the usu. transient presence of bacteria in the blood — **bac·ter·emic** \-mik\ *adj*

bacteri- *or* **bacterio-** *comb form* [NL *bacterium*] **:** bacteria ⟨*bacteri*al⟩

bacteria *pl of* BACTERIUM

bac·te·ri·al \bak-ˈtir-ē-əl\ *adj* (1871) **:** of, relating to, or caused by bacteria ⟨a ~ chromosome⟩ ⟨~ infection⟩ — **bac·te·ri·al·ly** \-ə-lē\ *adv*

bac·te·ri·cid·al \bak-ˌtir-ə-ˈsīd-ᵊl\ *adj* (1878) **:** destroying bacteria — **bac·te·ri·cid·al·ly** \-ᵊl-ē\ *adv* — **bac·te·ri·cide** \-ˈtir-ə-ˌsīd\ *n*

bac·ter·in \ˈbak-tə-rən\ *n* (ca. 1912) **:** a suspension of killed or attenuated bacteria for use as a vaccine

bac·te·rio·chlo·ro·phyll \bak-ˌtir-ē-ō-ˈklōr-ə-ˌfil, -ˈklȯr-, -fəl\ *n* (1938) **:** a pyrrole derivative in photosynthetic bacteria related to the chlorophyll of higher plants

bac·te·rio·cin \bak-ˈtir-ē-ə-sən\ *n* [ISV *bacteri-* + *-cin* (as in *colicin*)] (ca. 1954) **:** an antibiotic (as colicin) produced by bacteria

bac·te·ri·ol·o·gy \(ˌ)bak-ˌtir-ē-ˈäl-ə-jē\ *n* [ISV] (1884) **1 :** a science that deals with bacteria and their relations to medicine, industry, and agriculture **2 :** bacterial life and phenomena — **bac·te·ri·o·log·ic** \bak-ˌtir-ē-ə-ˈläj-ik\ *or* **bac·te·ri·o·log·i·cal** \-ˈläj-i-kəl\ *adj* — **bac·te·ri·o·log·i·cal·ly** \-i-k(ə-)lē\ *adv* — **bac·te·ri·ol·o·gist** \(ˌ)bak-ˌtir-ē-ˈäl-ə-jəst\ *n*

bac·te·ri·ol·y·sis \(ˌ)bak-ˌtir-ē-ˈäl-ə-səs\ *n* [NL] (1900) **:** destruction or dissolution of bacterial cells — **bac·te·ri·o·lyt·ic** \bak-ˌtir-ē-ə-ˈlit-ik\ *adj*

bac·te·rio·phage \bak-ˈtir-ē-ə-ˌfāj, -ˌfäzh\ *n* [ISV] (1920) **:** any of various specific bacteriolytic viruses normally present in sewage and in body products — **bac·te·ri·oph·a·gy** \(ˌ)bak-ˌtir-ē-ˈäf-ə-jē\ *n*

bac·te·rio·sta·sis \bak-ˌtir-ē-ō-ˈstā-səs\ *n* [NL] (ca. 1920) **:** inhibition of the growth of bacteria without destruction

bac·te·rio·stat \-ˈtir-ē-ō-ˌstat\ *n* (ca. 1920) **:** an agent that causes bacteriostasis — **bac·te·rio·stat·ic** \-ˌtir-ē-ō-ˈstat-ik\ *adj* — **bac·te·rio·stat·i·cal·ly** \-i-k(ə-)lē\ *adv*

bac·te·ri·um \bak-ˈtir-ē-əm\ *n, pl* **-ria** \-ē-ə\ [NL, fr. Gk *baktērion* staff — more at PEG] (1847) **:** any of a class (Schizomycetes) of microscopic plants having round, rodlike, spiral, or filamentous single-celled or noncellular bodies often aggregated into colonies or motile by means of flagella, living in soil, water, organic matter, or the bodies of plants and animals, and being autotrophic, saprophytic, or parasitic in nutrition and important to man because of their chemical effects and as pathogens

bac·te·ri·uria \bak-ˌtir-ē-ˈ(y)u̇r-ē-ə\ *n* [NL] (1889) **:** the presence of bacteria in the urine

bac·te·rize \ˈbak-tə-ˌrīz\ *vt* **-rized; -riz·ing** (1914) **:** to subject to bacterial action — **bac·te·ri·za·tion** \ˌbak-tə-rə-ˈzā-shən\ *n*

bac·te·roid \ˈbak-tə-ˌrȯid\ *n* (1878) **1 :** an irregularly shaped bacterium (as a rhizobium) found esp. in root nodules of legumes **2 :** a bacterium or a microorganism like a bacterium found in cells of the fat body esp. of roaches

Bac·tri·an camel \ˌbak-trē-ən-\ *n* [fr. its habitat in ancient Bactria] (1609) **:** CAMEL 1b

[1]**bad** \ˈbad\ *adj* **worse** \ˈwərs\; **worst** \ˈwərst\ [ME] (13c) **1 a :** failing to reach an acceptable standard **:** POOR **b :** UNFAVORABLE ⟨make a ~ impression⟩ **c :** not fresh **:** SPOILED ⟨~ fish⟩ **d :** not sound **:** DILAPIDATED ⟨the house was in ~ condition⟩ **2 a :** morally objectionable **b :** MISCHIEVOUS, DISOBEDIENT **3 :** inadequate or unsuited to a purpose ⟨a ~ plan⟩ ⟨~ lighting⟩ **4 :** DISAGREEABLE, UNPLEASANT ⟨~ news⟩ **5 a :** INJURIOUS, HARMFUL **b :** SEVERE ⟨a ~ cold⟩ **6 :** INCORRECT, FAULTY ⟨~ grammar⟩ **7 a :** suffering pain or distress ⟨felt generally ~⟩ **b :** UNHEALTHY, DISEASED ⟨~ teeth⟩ **8 :** SORROWFUL, SORRY **9 :** INVALID, VOID ⟨a ~ check⟩ **10 bad·der; bad·dest** *slang* **:** GOOD, GREAT — **bad·ness** *n*

syn BAD, EVIL, ILL, WICKED, NAUGHTY mean not morally good. BAD may apply to any degree of reprehensibility; EVIL is a stronger term than BAD and usu. carries a baleful or sinister connotation; ILL is a less emphatic synonym of EVIL and may imply malevolence or vice; WICKED usu. connotes malice and malevolence; NAUGHTY applies either to trivial misdeeds or to matters impolite or amusingly risqué.

[2]**bad** *n* (15c) **1 :** something that is bad **2 :** an evil or unhappy state

[3]**bad** *adv* (1681) **:** BADLY

bad·ass \-ˌas\ *adj, slang* (1962) **:** ready to cause or get into trouble **:** MEAN ⟨pretending to be a ~ gunslinger —L. L. King⟩ — **badass** *n*

bad blood *n* (1825) **:** ill feeling **:** BITTERNESS

bad·die *or* **bad·dy** \ˈbad-ē\ *n, pl* **baddies** (1937) **:** one that is bad; *esp* **:** an opponent of the hero (as in fiction or motion pictures)

bade *past and past part of* BID

badge \ˈbaj\ *n* [ME *bage, bagge*] (14c) **1 :** a device or token esp. of membership in a society or group **2 :** a characteristic mark **3 :** an emblem awarded for a particular accomplishment — **badge** *vt*

[1]**bad·ger** \ˈbaj-ər\ *n* [prob. fr. *badge;* fr. the white mark on its forehead] (1523) **1 a :** any of several sturdy burrowing mammals (genera *Meles* and *Taxidea* of the family Mustelidae) widely distributed in the northern hemisphere **b :** the pelt or fur of a badger **2** *cap* **:** a native or resident of Wisconsin — used as a nickname

[2]**badger** *vt* **bad·gered; bad·ger·ing** \ˈbaj-(ə-)riŋ\ [fr. the sport of baiting badgers] (1794) **:** to harass or annoy persistently

ba·di·nage \ˌbad-ᵊn-ˈäzh\ *n* [F] (ca. 1658) **:** playful repartee **:** BANTER

bad·land \ˈbad-ˌland\ *n* (1851) **:** a region marked by intricate erosional sculpturing, scanty vegetation, and fantastically formed hills — usu. used in pl.

bad·ly \ˈbad-lē\ *adv* (14c) **1 :** in a bad manner **2 :** to a great or intense degree ⟨want something ~⟩

bad·min·ton \ˈbad-ˌmint-ᵊn\ *n* [*Badminton,* residence of the Duke of Beaufort, England] (1874) **:** a court game played with light long-handled rackets and a shuttlecock volleyed over a net

bad–mouth \ˈbad-ˌmau̇th, -ˌmau̇t͟h\ *vt* (1942) **:** to criticize severely

Bae·de·ker \ˈbād-i-kər, ˈbed-\ *n* [Karl *Baedeker* †1859 Ger. publisher of guidebooks] (1924) **:** GUIDEBOOK

[1]**baf·fle** \ˈbaf-əl\ *vt* **baf·fled; baf·fling** \-(ə-)liŋ\ [prob. alter. of ME (Sc) *bawchillen* to denounce, discredit publicly] (1590) **1 :** to defeat or check (as a person) by confusing or puzzling **:** DISCONCERT **2 a :** to check or break the force or flow of by or as if by a baffle **b :** to prevent (sound waves) from interfering with each other (as by a baffle) ***syn*** see FRUSTRATE — **baf·fle·ment** \-əl-mənt\ *n* — **baf·fler** \-(ə-)lər\ *n* — **baf·fling·ly** \ˈbaf-liŋ-lē\ *adv*

[2]**baffle** *n* (ca. 1900) **:** a device (as a plate, wall, or screen) to deflect, check, or regulate flow (as of a fluid, light, or sound)

[1]**bag** \ˈbag\ *n* [ME *bagge,* fr. ON *baggi*] (13c) **1 :** a usu. flexible container that may be closed for holding, storing, or carrying something: as **a :** PURSE; *esp* **:** HANDBAG **b :** a bag for game **c :** TRAVELING BAG **2 :** something resembling a bag: as **a :** a pouched or pendulous bodily part or organ; *esp* **:** UDDER **b :** a puffed-out sag or bulge in cloth **c :** a square white stuffed canvas bag to mark a base in baseball **3 :** the amount contained in a bag **4 a :** a quantity of game taken; *also* **:** the maximum legal quantity of game **b :** an assortment or collection esp. of nonmaterial things ⟨a ~ of tricks⟩ **5 :** a slovenly unattractive woman **6 :** something one likes or does regularly or well; *also* **:** one's characteristic way of doing things — **in the bag :** SURE, CERTAIN

[2]**bag** *vb* **bagged; bag·ging** *vi* (15c) **1 :** to swell out **:** BULGE **2 :** to hang loosely ~ *vt* **1 :** to cause to swell **2 :** to put into a bag **3 a :** to take (animals) as game **b :** to get possession of esp. by strategy or stealth **c :** CAPTURE, SEIZE **d :** to shoot down **:** DESTROY ***syn*** see CATCH — **bag·ger** *n*

ba·gasse \bə-ˈgas\ *n* [F] (1826) **:** plant residue (as of sugarcane or grapes) left after a product (as juice) has been extracted

bag·a·telle \ˌbag-ə-ˈtel\ *n* [F, fr. It *bagattella*] (1633) **1 :** TRIFLE 1 **2 :** any of various games involving the rolling of balls into scoring areas

ba·gel \ˈbā-gəl\ *n* [Yiddish *beygel,* deriv. of OHG *boug* ring; akin to OE *bēag* ring — more at BEE] (1932) **:** a hard glazed doughnut-shaped roll

bag·ful \'bag-ˌfu̇l\ *n* (14c) **1 :** as much or as many as a bag will hold **2 :** a large number or amount ⟨had a ~ of tricks⟩

1bag·gage \'bag-ij\ *n* [ME *bagage,* fr. MF, fr. *bague* bundle] (15c) **1 :** suitcases, trunks, and personal belongings of travelers : LUGGAGE **2 :** transportable equipment esp. of a military force **3 :** things that get in the way : IMPEDIMENTA

2baggage *n* [prob. modif. of MF *bagasse,* fr. OProv *bagassa*] (1596) **1 :** a contemptible woman; *esp* : PROSTITUTE **2 :** a young woman

bag·ging \'bag-iŋ\ *n* (1732) **:** material (as cloth) for bags

bag·gy \'bag-ē\ *adj* **bag·gi·er; -est** (1831) **:** loose, puffed out, or hanging like a bag ⟨~ trousers⟩ — **bag·gi·ly** \'bag-ə-lē\ *adv* — **bag·gi·ness** \'bag-ē-nəs\ *n*

bag lady *n* (1979) **:** SHOPPING-BAG LADY

bag·man \'bag-mən\ *n* (1765) **1** *chiefly Brit* **:** TRAVELING SALESMAN **2 :** a person who on behalf of another collects or distributes illicitly gained money

ba·gnio \'ban-(ˌ)yō\ *n, pl* **bagnios** [It *bagno,* lit., public baths (fr. the use of Roman baths at Constantinople for imprisonment of Christian prisoners by the Turks), fr. L *balneum,* fr. Gk *balaneion;* akin to OHG *quellan* to gush — more at DEVIL] (1599) **1** *obs* **:** PRISON **2 :** BROTHEL

bag of waters (ca. 1881) **:** the double-walled fluid-filled sac that encloses and protects the fetus in the womb and that breaks releasing its fluid during the birth process

bag·pipe \'bag-ˌpīp\ *n* (14c) **:** a wind instrument consisting of a reed melody pipe and from one to five drones with air supplied continuously either by a bag with valve-stopped mouth tube or by bellows — often used in pl. — **bag·pip·er** \-ˌpī-pər\ *n*

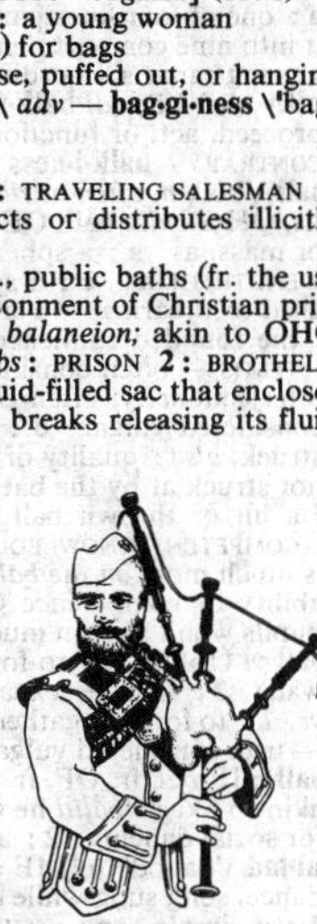

bagpipe

ba·guette \ba-'get\ *n* [F, lit., rod] (ca. 1738) **1 :** a small molding like but smaller than the astragal **2 :** a gem having the shape of a narrow rectangle; *also* **:** the shape itself **3 :** a long thin loaf of French bread

bag·wig \'bag-ˌwig\ *n* (1717) **:** an 18th century wig with the back hair enclosed in a small silk bag

bag·worm \-ˌwərm\ *n* (1862) **:** any of a family (Psychidae) of moths with wingless females and plant-feeding larvae that live in a silk case covered with plant debris; *esp* **:** one (*Thyridopteryx ephemeraeformis*) often destructive to deciduous and evergreen trees of the eastern U.S.

bah \'bä, 'ba\ *interj* (1600) — used to express disdain or contempt

Ba·ha'i \bä-'hä-ˌē, -'hī\ *n, pl* **Baha'is** [Per *bahā'ī,* lit., of glory, fr. *bahā* glory] (1889) **:** an adherent of a religious movement originating in Iran in the 19th century and emphasizing the spiritual unity of mankind — **Baha'i** *adj* — **Ba·ha·ism** \-'hä-ˌiz-əm, -'hī-ˌiz-\ *n* — **Ba·ha·ist** \-'hä-(ˌ)ist\ *n*

Ba·ha·sa In·do·ne·sia \bə-ˌhäs-ə-ˌin-də-'nē-zhə, -shə\ *n* [Indonesian *bahasa indonésia,* lit., Indonesian language] (1952) **:** INDONESIAN 2b

Ba·hia grass \bə-'hē-ə-\ *n* [*Bahia,* state in Brazil] (ca. 1927) **:** a perennial tropical American grass (*Paspalum notatum*) used in the southern U.S. as a pasture grass

baht \'bät\ *n, pl* **baht** *also* **bahts** [Thai *bāt*] (1828) — see MONEY table

1bail \'bā(ə)l\ *n* [ME *baille,* fr. MF, bucket, fr. ML *bajula* water vessel, fr. fem. of L *bajulus*] (14c) **:** a container used to remove water from a boat

2bail *vt* (1613) **1 :** to clear (water) from a boat by dipping and throwing over the side — usu. used with *out* **2 :** to clear water from by dipping and throwing — usu. used with *out* ~ *vi* **:** to parachute from an airplane — usu. used with *out* — **bail·er** *n*

3bail *n* [ME, custody, security for appearance, fr. MF, custody, fr. *bailler* to have in charge, deliver, fr. ML *bajulare* to control, fr. L, to carry a load, fr. *bajulus* porter] (15c) **1 :** security given for the due appearance of a prisoner in order to obtain his release from imprisonment **2 :** the temporary release of a prisoner on bail **3 :** one who provides bail

4bail *vt* (1548) **1 :** to release under bail **2 :** to procure the release of by giving bail — often used with *out* **3 :** to help from a predicament — used with *out* ⟨~*ing* out impoverished countries⟩ — **bail·able** *adj*

5bail *n* [ME *beil, baile,* prob. of Scand origin; akin to Sw *bygel* bow, hoop; akin to OE *būgan* to bend — more at BOW] (15c) **1** **a :** a supporting half hoop **b :** a hinged bar for holding paper against the platen of a typewriter **2 :** the usu. arched handle of a kettle or pail

6bail *vt* [AF *baillier,* fr. F] (1768) **:** to deliver (property) in trust to another for a special purpose and for a limited period

7bail *n* [ME *baille* bailey, fr. OF] *chiefly Brit* (1844) **:** a device for confining or separating animals

bail·ee \bā-'lē\ *n* (1528) **:** the person to whom property is bailed

bai·ley \'bā-lē\ *n, pl* **baileys** [ME *bailli,* fr. OF *baille, balie* palisade, bailey] (13c) **1 :** the outer wall of a castle or any of several walls surrounding the keep **2 :** the space immediately within the external wall or between two outer walls of a castle

Bai·ley bridge \ˌbā-lē-\ *n* [Sir Donald *Bailey* b1901 Eng. engineer] (1944) **:** a bridge designed for rapid construction from interchangeable latticed steel panels that are coupled with steel pins

bai·lie \'bā-lē\ *n* [ME] (14c) **1** *chiefly dial* **:** BAILIFF **2 :** a Scottish municipal magistrate corresponding to an English alderman

bai·liff \'bā-ləf\ *n* [ME *baillif, bailie,* fr. OF *baillif,* fr. *bail* custody, jurisdiction — more at BAIL] (14c) **1** **a :** an official employed by a British sheriff to serve writs and make arrests and executions **b :** a minor officer of some U.S. courts usu. serving as a messenger or usher **2** *chiefly Brit* **:** one who manages an estate or farm — **bai·liff·ship** \-ˌship\ *n*

bai·li·wick \'bā-li-ˌwik\ *n* [ME *baillifwik,* fr. *baillif* + *wik* dwelling place, village, fr. OE *wīc,* fr. L *vicus* village — more at VICINITY] (15c) **1 :** the office or jurisdiction of a bailiff **2 :** a special domain

bail·ment \'bā(ə)l-mənt\ *n* (1554) **:** the act of bailing a person or property

bail·or \bā-'lȯ(ə)r, 'bā-lər\ *or* **bail·er** \'bā-lər\ *n* (1602) **:** one who delivers goods or money to another in trust

bail·out \'bā-ˌlau̇t\ *n* (1951) **:** a rescue (as of a corporation) from financial distress

bail out \'bā-'lau̇t\ *vi* (1951) **:** to get oneself out of harm's way; *also* **:** LEAVE, DEPART

bails·man \'bā(ə)lz-mən\ *n* (1862) **:** one who gives bail for another

bairn \'ba(ə)rn, 'be(ə)rn\ *n* [ME *bern, barn,* fr. OE *bearn* & ON *barn;* akin to OHG *barn* child] *chiefly Scot* (bef. 12c) **:** CHILD

1bait \'bāt\ *vb* [ME *baiten,* fr. ON *beita;* akin to OE *bǣtan* to bait, *bītan* to bite] *vt* (13c) **1** **a :** to persecute or exasperate with unjust, malicious, or persistent attacks **b :** TEASE **2** **a :** to harass (as a chained animal) with dogs usu. for sport **b :** to attack by biting and tearing **3** **a :** to furnish with bait **b :** ENTICE, LURE **4 :** to give food and drink to (an animal) esp. on the road ~ *vi, archaic* **:** to stop for food and rest when traveling — **bait·er** *n*

2bait *n* [ME, fr. ON *beit* pasturage & *beita* food; akin to OE *bītan* to bite] (14c) **1** **a :** something used in luring esp. to a hook or trap **b :** a poisonous material placed where it will be eaten by pests **2 :** LURE, TEMPTATION ⟨the ~ of high commissions⟩

bait and switch *n* (1967) **:** a sales tactic in which a customer is attracted by the advertisement of a low-priced item but is then encouraged to buy a higher-priced one

bai·za \'bī-(ˌ)zä\ *n, pl* **baiza** *or* **baizas** [colloq. Ar, fr. Hindi *paisā*] (1970) — see *rial* at MONEY table

baize \'bāz\ *n* [MF *baies,* pl. of *baie* baize, fr. fem. of *bai* bay-colored] (1578) **:** a coarse woolen or cotton fabric napped to imitate felt

1bake \'bāk\ *vb* **baked; bak·ing** [ME *baken,* fr. OE *bacan;* akin to OHG *bahhan* to bake, Gk *phōgein* to roast] *vt* (bef. 12c) **1 :** to cook (as food) by dry heat esp. in an oven **2 :** to dry or harden by subjecting to heat ~ *vi* **1 :** to prepare food by baking it **2 :** to become baked **3 :** to become extremely hot — **bak·er** *n*

2bake *n* (1565) **1 :** the act or process of baking **2 :** a social gathering at which a baked food is served **3 :** baked food ⟨a ~ sale⟩

Ba·ke·lite \'bā-kə-ˌlīt, -ˌklīt\ *trademark* — used for any of various synthetic resins and plastics

baker's dozen *n* (1599) **:** THIRTEEN

baker's yeast *n* (1854) **:** a yeast (as *Saccharomyces cerevisiae*) used or suitable for use as leaven

bak·ery \'bā-k(ə-)rē\ *n, pl* **-er·ies** (ca. 1820) **:** a place for baking or selling baked goods

bake·shop \'bāk-ˌshäp\ *n* (1789) **:** BAKERY

baking powder *n* (1850) **:** a powder used as a leavening agent in making baked goods (as quick breads) that consists of a carbonate, an acid substance, and starch or flour

baking soda *n* (1881) **:** SODIUM BICARBONATE

bak·la·va \ˌbäk-lə-'vä\ *n* [Turk, lit., lozenge] (1824) **:** a dessert made of thin pastry, nuts, and honey

bak·sheesh \'bak-ˌshēsh, bak-'\ *n* [Per *bakhshish,* fr. *bakhshidan* to give; akin to Gk *phagein* to eat, Skt *bhajati* he allots] (1775) **:** payment (as a tip or bribe) to expedite service

BAL \ˌbē-ˌā-'el\ *n* [*B*ritish *A*nti-*L*ewisite] (1942) **:** DIMERCAPROL

Ba·laam \'bā-ləm\ *n* [Gk, fr. Heb *Bil'ām*] **:** an Old Testament prophet who is reproached by the ass he is riding and rebuked by God's angel while on the way to meet with an enemy of Israel

bal·a·cla·va \ˌbal-ə-'kläv-ə, -'klav-\ *n* [fr. *Balaclava,* village in the Crimea where a battle of the Crimean War was fought] (1881) **:** a knit cap for the head and neck — called also *balaclava helmet*

bal·a·lai·ka \ˌbal-ə-'lī-kə\ *n* [Russ] (1788) **:** a usu. 3-stringed instrument with a triangular body used esp. in the U.S.S.R.

1bal·ance \'bal-ən(t)s\ *n* [ME, fr. OF, fr. (assumed) VL *bilancia,* fr. LL *bilanc-, bilanx* having two scalepans, fr. L *bi-* + *lanc-, lanx* plate] (13c) **1 :** an instrument for weighing: as **a :** a beam that is supported freely in the center and has two pans of equal weight suspended from its ends **b :** a device that uses the elasticity of a spiral spring for measuring weight or force **c** *cap* **:** LIBRA **2 :** a means of judging or deciding **3 :** a counterbalancing weight, force, or influence **4 :** a vibrating wheel operating with a hairspring to regulate the movement of a timepiece **5** **a :** stability produced by even distribution of weight on each side of the vertical axis **b :** equipoise between contrasting, opposing, or interacting elements **c :** equality between the totals of the two sides of an account **6** **a :** an aesthetically pleasing integration of elements **b :** the juxtaposition in writing of syntactically parallel constructions containing similar or contrasting ideas **7** **a :** physical equilibrium **b :** the ability to retain one's balance **8** **a :** weight or force of one side in excess of another **b :** something left over : REMAINDER **c :** an amount in excess esp. on the credit side of an account **9 :** mental and emotional steadiness — **bal·anced** \-ən(t)st\ *adj* — **in the balance** *or* **in balance :** with the fate or outcome about to be determined — **on balance :** all things considered

2balance *vb* **bal·anced; bal·anc·ing** *vt* (1588) **1** **a** (1) **:** to compute the difference between the debits and credits of (an account) (2) **:** to pay the amount due on : SETTLE **b** (1) **:** to arrange so that one set of elements exactly equals another ⟨~ a mathematical equation⟩ (2) **:** to complete (a chemical equation) so that the same number of atoms and electric charges of each kind appears on each side **2** **a :** COUNTERBALANCE, OFFSET **b :** to equal or equalize in weight, number, or proportion **3 :** to weigh in or as if in a balance **4** **a :** to bring to a state or position of equipoise **b :** to poise in or as if in balance **c :** to bring into harmony or proportion ~ *vi* **1 :** to become balanced or established in balance **2 :** to be an equal counterpoise **3 :** WAVER 1 ⟨~*s* and temporizes on matters that demand action⟩

balance beam *n* (ca. 1949) **1 :** a narrow wooden beam supported in a horizontal position approximately four feet above the floor and used for balancing feats in gymnastics **2 :** an event in gymnastics competition in which the balance beam is used

balance of payments (1844) **:** a summary of the international transactions of a country or region over a period of time including commodity and service transactions, capital transactions, and gold movements

balance of power (1579) **:** an equilibrium of power sufficient to discourage or prevent one nation or party from imposing its will on or interfering with the interests of another

balance of terror (1960) **:** an equilibrium of military power (as nuclear capability) between potentially opposing nations sufficient to deter one nation from waging war on another

balance of trade (1668) **:** the difference in value over a period of time between a country's imports and exports

bal·anc·er \'bal-ən-sər\ *n* (15c) **:** one that balances; *specif* **:** HALTERE

balance sheet *n* (1838) **:** a statement of financial condition at a given date

balance wheel *n* (1669) **1 :** a wheel that regulates or stabilizes the motion of a mechanism **2 :** a balancing or stabilizing force

Ba·lante \bə-'länt\ *n, pl* **Balante** *or* **Balantes** [F, fr. Balante *Bulanda*] (ca. 1895) **1 :** a member of a Negro people of Senegal and Angola **2 :** the language of the Balante people

bal·as \'bal-əs\ *n* [ME, fr. MF *balais,* fr. Ar *balakhsh,* fr. *Balakhshān,* ancient region of Afghanistan] (15c) **:** a ruby spinel of a pale rose-red or orange

ba·la·ta \bə-'lät-ə\ *n* [Sp, of Cariban origin; akin to Galibi *balata*] (1860) **:** a substance like gutta-percha that is the dried juice of tropical American trees (esp. *Manilkara bidentata*) of the sapodilla family and is used esp. in belting and golf balls; *also* **:** a tree yielding it

bal·boa \bal-'bō-ə\ *n* [Sp, fr. Vasco Núñez de *Balboa*] (ca. 1909) — see MONEY table

bal·brig·gan \bal-'brig-ən\ *n* [*Balbriggan,* Ireland] (1885) **:** a knitted cotton fabric used esp. for underwear or hosiery

bal·co·ny \'bal-kə-nē\ *n, pl* **-nies** [It *balcone,* fr. OIt, scaffold, of Gmc origin; akin to OHG *balko* beam — more at BALK] (1618) **1 :** a platform that projects from the wall of a building and is enclosed by a parapet or railing **2 :** an interior projecting gallery in a public building (as a theater) — **bal·co·nied** \-nēd\ *adj*

[1]**bald** \'bȯld\ *adj* [ME *balled;* prob. akin to OE *bǣl* fire, pyre, Dan *bældet* bald, L *fulica* coot, Gk *phalios* having a white spot] (14c) **1 a :** lacking a natural or usual covering (as of hair, vegetation, or nap) **b :** having little or no tread ⟨~ tires⟩ **2 :** UNADORNED **3 :** UNDISGUISED, PALPABLE **4 :** marked with white ***syn*** see BARE — **bald·ish** \'bȯl-dish\ *adj* — **bald·ly** \'bȯl-(d)lē\ *adv* — **bald·ness** \'bȯl(d)-nəs\ *n*

[2]**bald** *vi* (1938) **:** to become bald ⟨is ~*ing* on top⟩

bal·da·chin \'bȯl-də-kən, 'bal-\ *or* **bal·da·chi·no** \,bal-də-'kē-(,)nō, ,bäl-\ *n, pl* **baldachins** *or* **baldachinos** [It *baldacchino,* fr. *Baldacco* Baghdad, Iraq] (1598) **1 :** a rich embroidered fabric of silk and gold **2 :** a cloth canopy fixed or carried over an important person or a sacred object **3 :** an ornamental structure resembling a canopy used esp. over an altar

bald cypress *n* (1709) **1 :** either of two large swamp trees (*Taxodium distichum* and *T. ascendens*) of the southern U.S. that are related to the sequoias **2 :** the hard red wood of bald cypress that is much used for shingles

bald eagle *n* (1688) **:** the common eagle (*Haliaeetus leucocephalus*) of No. America that is wholly brown when young but in full adult plumage has white head and neck feathers and a white tail

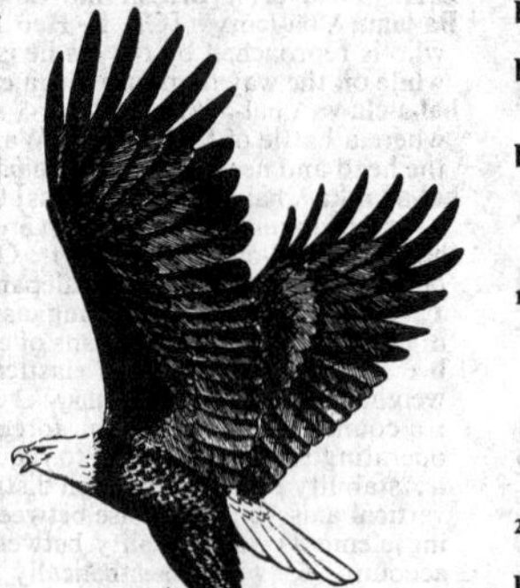
bald eagle

Bal·der \'bȯl-dər\ *n* [ON *Baldr*] **:** the son of Odin and Frigga and Norse god of light and peace slain through the trickery of Loki by a mistletoe sprig

bal·der·dash \'bȯl-dər-,dash\ *n* [origin unknown] (1674) **:** NONSENSE

bald–faced \'bȯl(d)-'fāst\ *adj* (1943) **:** BAREFACED

bald·head \'bȯld-,hed\ *n* (1535) **:** a bald-headed person

bald·pate \'bȯl(d)-,pāt\ *n* (1601) **1 :** BALDHEAD **2 :** a No. American wigeon (*Anas americana*) with a large white patch on each wing and in the male a white crown

bal·dric \'bȯl-drik\ *n* [ME *baudry, baudrik*] (14c) **:** an often ornamented belt worn over one shoulder to support a sword or bugle

[1]**bale** \'bā(ə)l\ *n* [ME, fr. OE *bealu;* akin to OHG *balo* evil, OSlav *bolŭ* sick man] (bef. 12c) **1 :** great evil **2 :** WOE, SORROW

[2]**bale** *n* [ME, fr. MF, of Gmc origin; akin to OHG *balla* ball] (14c) **:** a large bundle of goods; *specif* **:** a large closely pressed package of merchandise bound and usu. wrapped ⟨a ~ of paper⟩ ⟨a ~ of hay⟩

[3]**bale** *vt* **baled; bal·ing** (1760) **:** to make up into a bale — **bal·er** *n*

ba·leen \bə-'lēn\ *n* [ME *baleine* whale, baleen, fr. L *balaena* whale, fr. Gk *phallaina;* akin to Gk *phallos* penis — more at BLOW] (14c) **:** WHALEBONE

baleen whale *n* (1874) **:** WHALEBONE WHALE

bale·fire \'bā(ə)l-,fī(ə)r\ *n* [ME, fr. OE *bǣlfȳr* funeral fire, fr. *bǣl* pyre + *fȳr* fire — more at BALD] (bef. 12c) **:** an outdoor fire often used as a signal fire

bale·ful \-fəl\ *adj* (bef. 12c) **1 :** deadly or pernicious in influence **2 :** foreboding evil **:** OMINOUS ***syn*** see SINISTER — **bale·ful·ly** \-fə-lē\ *adv* — **bale·ful·ness** \-fəl-nəs\ *n*

Ba·li·nese \,bäl-i-'nēz, ,bal-, -'nēs\ *n* [D *Balinees,* fr. *Bali* island of Indonesia] (ca. 1963) **:** any of a breed of slender long-haired cats that originated as a spontaneous mutation of the Siamese

[1]**balk** \'bȯk\ *n* [ME *balke,* fr. OE *balca;* akin to OHG *balko* beam, L *fulcire* to prop, Gk *phalanx* log, phalanx] (bef. 12c) **1 :** a ridge of land left unplowed as a dividing line or through carelessness **2 :** BEAM, RAFTER **3 :** HINDRANCE, CHECK **4 a :** the space behind the balkline on a billiard table **b :** any of the outside divisions made by the balklines **5 :** failure of a player to complete a motion; *esp* **:** an illegal motion of the pitcher in baseball while in position

[2]**balk** *vt* (15c) **1** *archaic* **:** to pass over or by **2 :** to check or stop by or as if by an obstacle **:** BLOCK ~ *vi* **1 :** to stop short and refuse to proceed **2 :** to refuse abruptly — used with *at* **3 :** to commit a balk in sports ***syn*** see FRUSTRATE — **balk·er** *n*

bal·kan·ize \'bȯl-kə-,nīz\ *vt* **-ized; -iz·ing** *often cap* [*Balkan* peninsula] (1919) **:** to break up (as a region or group) into smaller and often hostile units — **bal·kan·iza·tion** \,bȯl-kə-nə-'zā-shən\ *n, often cap*

balk·line \'bȯ-,klīn\ *n* (1839) **1 :** a line across a billiard table near one end behind which the cue balls are placed in making opening shots **2 a :** one of four lines parallel to the cushions of a billiard table dividing it into nine compartments **b :** a billiards game that sets restrictions in scoring caroms according to these lines

balky \'bȯ-kē\ *adj* **balk·i·er; -est** (1847) **:** refusing or likely to refuse to proceed, act, or function as directed or expected ⟨a ~ mule⟩ ***syn*** see CONTRARY — **balk·i·ness** *n*

[1]**ball** \'bȯl\ *n, often attrib* [ME *bal,* fr. ON *böllr;* akin to OE *bealluc* testis, OHG *balla* ball, OE *bula* bull] (13c) **1 :** a round or roundish body or mass: as **a :** a spherical or ovoid body used in a game or sport **b :** EARTH, GLOBE **c :** a spherical or conical projectile; *also* **:** projectiles used in firearms **d :** a roundish protuberant anatomic structure; *esp* **:** the rounded eminence at the base of the thumb or great toe **2 a :** TESTIS — often considered vulgar **b** *pl* (1) **:** NONSENSE — often used interjectionally; often considered vulgar (2) **:** NERVE 3a, 3b — often considered vulgar **3 :** a game in which a ball is thrown, kicked, or struck; *also* **:** quality of play in such a game **4 a :** a pitched baseball not struck at by the batter that fails to pass through the strike zone **b :** a hit or thrown ball in various games ⟨foul ~⟩ — **on the ball 1 :** COMPETENT, KNOWLEDGEABLE, ALERT ⟨the other introductory essay . . . is much more *on the ball* —*Times Lit. Supp.*⟩ ⟨keep *on the ball*⟩ **2 :** of ability or competence ⟨if the teacher has something *on the ball,* the pupils won't squirm much —*New Yorker*⟩

[2]**ball** *vt* (1658) **1 :** to form or gather into a ball ⟨~*ed* the paper into a wad⟩ **2 :** to have sexual intercourse with — usu. considered vulgar ~ *vi* **1 :** to form or gather into a ball **2 :** to engage in sexual intercourse — usu. considered vulgar

[3]**ball** *n* [F *bal,* fr. OF, fr. *baller* to dance, fr. LL *ballare,* fr. Gk *ballizein;* akin to Skt *balbalīti* he whirls] (ca. 1632) **1 :** a large formal gathering for social dancing **2 :** a very pleasant experience **:** a good time

bal·lad \'bal-əd\ *n* [ME *balade* ballade, song, fr. MF, fr. OProv *balada* dance, song sung while dancing, fr. *balar* to dance, fr. LL *ballare*] (14c) **1 :** a simple song **:** AIR **2 a :** a narrative composition in rhythmic verse suitable for singing **b :** an art song accompanying a traditional ballad **3 :** a popular song; *esp* **:** a slow romantic or sentimental song — **bal·lad·ic** \bə-'lad-ik, ba-\ *adj*

bal·lade \bə-'läd, ba-\ *n* [ME *balade,* fr. MF, ballad, ballade] (14c) **1 :** a fixed verse form consisting usu. of three stanzas with recurrent rhymes, an envoi, and an identical refrain for each part **2 :** a musical composition usu. for piano suggesting the epic ballad

bal·lad·eer \,bal-ə-'di(ə)r\ *n* (1830) **:** a singer of ballads

bal·lad·ist \'bal-əd-əst\ *n* (1858) **:** one who writes or sings ballads

bal·lad·ry \'bal-ə-drē\ *n* (1598) **:** the composing or performing of ballads

ballad stanza *n* (1934) **:** a stanza consisting of four lines with the first and third lines unrhymed iambic tetrameters and the second and fourth lines rhymed iambic trimeters

ball–and–socket joint *n* (1669) **1 :** a joint in which a ball moves within a socket so as to allow rotary motion in every direction within certain limits **2 :** an articulation (as the hip joint) in which the rounded head of one bone fits into a cuplike cavity of the other and admits movement in any direction — called also *enarthrosis*

[1]**bal·last** \'bal-əst\ *n* [prob. fr. LG; perh. akin to OE *bær* bare & to OE *hlæst* load, *hladan* to load — more at LADE] (1530) **1 :** a heavy substance used to improve the stability and control the draft of a ship or the ascent of a balloon **2 :** something that gives stability (as in character or conduct) **3 :** gravel or broken stone laid in a railroad bed or used in making concrete **4 :** a device used to provide the starting voltage or to stabilize the current in a circuit (as of a fluorescent lamp) — **in ballast** *of a ship* **:** having only ballast for a load

[2]**ballast** *vt* (1538) **1 :** to steady or equip with or as if with ballast **2 :** to fill in (as a railroad bed) with ballast

ball bearing *n* (1883) **:** a bearing in which the journal turns upon loose hardened steel balls that roll easily in a race; *also* **:** one of the balls in such a bearing

ball boy *n* (1903) **:** a tennis court attendant who retrieves balls for the players

ball·car·ri·er \'bȯl-,kar-ē-ər\ *n* (1935) **:** the football player carrying the ball on an offensive play

ball cock *n* (1790) **:** an automatic valve whose opening and closing are controlled by a spherical float at the end of a lever

bal·le·ri·na \,bal-ə-'rē-nə\ *n* [It, fr. *ballare* to dance, fr. LL] (1792) **:** a female ballet dancer **:** DANSEUSE

bal·let \'ba-,lā, ba-'\ *n* [F, fr. It *balletto,* dim. of *ballo* dance, fr. *ballare*] (1667) **1 a :** dancing in which conventional poses and steps are combined with light flowing figures (as leaps and turns) **b :** a theatrical art form using ballet dancing, music, and scenery to convey a story, theme, or atmosphere **2 :** music for a ballet **3 :** a group that performs ballets — **bal·let·ic** \ba-'let-ik\ *adj*

bal·let·o·mane \ba-'let-ə-,mān\ *n* [*ballet* + *-o-* + *-mane* (fr. *mania*)] (1930) **:** a devotee of ballet — **bal·let·o·ma·nia** \-,let-ə-'mā-nē-ə, -nyə\ *n*

ball–flow·er \'bȯl-,flau̇(-ə)r\ *n* (1845) **:** an architectural ornament consisting of a ball placed in the flower-shaped hollow of a circular mold

ball game *n* (1848) **1 :** a game played with a ball **2 a :** a set of circumstances **:** SITUATION ⟨a whole new *ball game*⟩ **b :** CONTEST, COMPETITION

ball girl *n* (1926) **:** a tennis court attendant who retrieves balls for the players

bal·lis·ta \bə-'lis-tə\ *n, pl* **-tae** \-,tē\ [L, fr. (assumed) Gk *ballistēs,* fr. *ballein* to throw — more at DEVIL] (14c) **:** an ancient military engine often in the form of a crossbow for hurling large missiles

bal·lis·tic \bə-'lis-tik\ *adj* [L *ballista*] (ca. 1775) **:** of or relating to ballistics or to a body in motion according to the laws of ballistics — **bal·lis·ti·cal·ly** \-ti-k(ə-)lē\ *adv*

ballistic missile *n* (1954) **:** a self-propelled missile guided in the ascent of a high-arch trajectory and freely falling in the descent

bal·lis·tics \bə-ˈlis-tiks\ *n pl but sing or pl in constr* (ca. 1753) **1 a :** the science of the motion of projectiles in flight **b :** the flight characteristics of a projectile **2 a :** the study of the processes within a firearm as it is fired **b :** the firing characteristics of a firearm or cartridge
bal·lis·to·car·dio·gram \bə-ˈlis-tō-ˈkärd-ē-ə-ˌgram\ *n* (1938) **:** the record made by a ballistocardiograph
bal·lis·to·car·dio·graph \-ˌgraf\ *n* [*ballistic* + *-o-* + *cardiograph*] (1937) **:** a device for measuring the amount of blood passing through the heart in a specified time by recording the recoil movements of the body that result from contraction of the heart muscle in ejecting blood from the ventricles — **bal·lis·to·car·dio·graph·ic** \-ˌkärd-ē-ə-ˈgraf-ik\ *adj* — **bal·lis·to·car·di·og·ra·phy** \-ē-ˈäg-rə-fē\ *n*
ball lightning *n* (1857) **:** a rare form of lightning consisting of luminous balls that may move along solid objects or float in the air
ball of fire (ca. 1900) **:** a person of unusual energy, vitality, or drive
ball of wax (1953) **:** AFFAIR, CONCERN ⟨the whole *ball of wax*⟩
bal·lon \ba-ˈlōⁿ\ *n* [F, lit., balloon] (1830) **:** lightness of movement that exaggerates the duration of a ballet dancer's jump
bal·lo·net \ˌbal-ə-ˈnā\ *n* [F *ballonnet,* dim. of *ballon*] (1902) **:** a compartment of variable volume within the interior of a balloon or airship used to control ascent and descent
[1]**bal·loon** \bə-ˈlün\ *n* [F *ballon* large football, balloon, fr. It dial. *ballone* large football, aug. of *balla* ball, of Gmc origin] (1783) **1 :** a nonporous bag of tough light material filled with heated air or a gas lighter than air so as to rise and float in the atmosphere **2 :** a toy consisting of an inflatable rubber bag **3 :** the outline enclosing words spoken or thought by a figure esp. in a cartoon
[2]**balloon** *adj* (ca. 1783) **1 :** relating to, resembling, or suggesting a balloon ⟨a ~ sleeve⟩ **2 :** being or having a final installment that is much larger than preceding ones in a term or installment note
[3]**balloon** *vi* (1792) **1 :** to ascend or travel in a balloon **2 :** to swell or puff out **:** EXPAND **3 :** to increase rapidly ~ *vt* **:** INFLATE, INCREASE
bal·loon·ing \bə-ˈlü-niŋ\ *n* (1784) **:** the act or sport of riding in a balloon
bal·loon·ist \-nəst\ *n* (1784) **:** one who ascends in a balloon
balloon tire *n* (1923) **:** a pneumatic tire with a flexible carcass and large cross section designed to provide cushioning through low pressure
balloon vine *n* (1836) **:** a tropical American vine (*Cardiospermum halicacabum*) of the soapberry family bearing large ornamental pods
[1]**bal·lot** \ˈbal-ət\ *n* [It *ballotta,* fr. It dial., dim. of *balla* ball] (1549) **1 a :** a small ball used in secret voting **b :** a sheet of paper used to cast a secret vote **2 a :** the action or system of secret voting **b :** the right to vote **c :** VOTE 1a **3 :** the number of votes cast
[2]**ballot** *vi* (1549) **:** to vote or decide by ballot — **bal·lot·er** *n*
ballot box *n* (ca. 1680) **1 :** a box for receiving ballots **2 :** BALLOT 2a
bal·lotte·ment \bə-ˈlät-mənt\ *n* [F, lit., act of tossing, fr. *ballotter* to toss, fr. MF *baloter,* fr. *balotte* little ball, fr. It dial. *ballotta*] (ca. 1839) **:** a sharp upward pushing with a finger against the uterine wall for diagnosing pregnancy by feeling the return impact of the displaced fetus; *also* **:** a similar procedure for detecting a floating kidney
[1]**ball·park** \ˈbȯl-ˌpärk\ *n* (1899) **1 :** a park in which ball games are played **2 :** a range (as of prices or views) within which comparison or compromise is possible — **in the ballpark :** approximately correct
[2]**ballpark** *adj* [fr. the expression *in the ballpark*] (1969) **:** approximately correct ⟨a ~ estimate⟩
ball·point \-ˌpȯint\ *n* (1936) **:** a pen having as the writing point a small rotating metal ball that inks itself by contact with an inner magazine
ball·room \ˈbȯl-ˌrüm, -ˌru̇m\ *n* (1736) **:** a large room for dances
balls–up \ˈbȯl-ˌzəp\ *n, Brit* (1939) **:** FOUL-UP
ball·sy \ˈbȯl-zē\ *adj* **ball·si·er; -est** [ˈ*ball*] (1960) **:** aggressively tough **:** GUTSY
ball up *vt* (1885) **:** to make a mess of **:** CONFUSE, MUDDLE ⟨incompetents who *balled up* the whole program⟩ ~ *vi* **:** to become badly muddled or confused
ball valve *n* (1839) **:** a valve in which a ball regulates the aperture by its rise and fall due to fluid pressure, a spring, or its own weight
bal·ly·hoo \ˈbal-ē-ˌhü\ *n, pl* **-hoos** [origin unknown] (1901) **1 :** a noisy attention-getting demonstration or talk **2 :** flamboyant, exaggerated, or sensational advertising or propaganda — **ballyhoo** *vt*
bal·ly·rag \-ˌrag\ *var of* BULLYRAG
balm \ˈbä(l)m, *NewEng also* ˈbȧm\ *n* [ME *basme, baume,* fr. OF, fr. L *balsamum* balsam] (13c) **1 :** a balsamic resin; *esp* **:** one from small tropical evergreen trees (genus *Commiphora* of the family Burseraceae) **2 :** an aromatic preparation (as a healing ointment) **3 :** any of various aromatic plants (as of the genera *Melissa* or *Monarda*) of the mint family **4 :** a spicy aromatic odor **5 :** a soothing restorative agency
bal·ma·caan \ˌbal-mə-ˈkan, -ˈkän\ *n* [*Balmacaan,* estate near Inverness, Scotland] (1919) **:** a loose single-breasted overcoat usu. having raglan sleeves and a short turnover collar
balm of Gil·e·ad \-ˈgil-ē-əd\ [*Gilead,* region of ancient Palestine known for its balm] (1703) **1 :** a small evergreen African and Asian tree (*Commiphora meccanensis* of the family Burseraceae) with aromatic leaves; *also* **:** a fragrant oleoresin from this tree **2 :** an agency that soothes, relieves, or heals **3 :** either of two poplars: **a :** a hybrid northern tree (*Populus gileadensis*) with broadly cordate leaves that are pubescent esp. on the underside **b :** BALSAM POPLAR
bal·mor·al \bal-ˈmȯr-əl, -ˈmär-\ *n* [*Balmoral* Castle, Scotland] (1857) **1 :** a laced boot or shoe **2** *often cap* **:** a round flat cap with a top projecting all around
balmy \ˈbäm-ē, ˈbäl-mē, *NewEng also* ˈbȧm-ē\ *adj* **balm·i·er; -est** (15c) **1 a :** having the qualities of balm **:** SOOTHING **b :** MILD **2 :** CRAZY, FOOLISH — **balm·i·ly** \-ə-lē\ *adv* — **balm·i·ness** \-ē-nəs\ *n*
bal·ne·ol·o·gy \ˌbal-nē-ˈäl-ə-jē\ *n* [ISV, fr. L *balneum* bath — more at BAGNIO] (ca. 1879) **:** the science of the therapeutic use of baths
[1]**ba·lo·ney** \bə-ˈlō-nē\ *var of* BOLOGNA
[2]**baloney** *n* [*bologna*] (ca. 1926) **:** pretentious nonsense **:** BUNKUM — often used as a generalized expression of disagreement ⟨it is a wish-gratifying intellectual toy. And a lot of ~ —H. D. Scott⟩
bal·sa \ˈbȯl-sə\ *n* [Sp] (1588) **1 :** RAFT; *specif* **:** one made of two cylinders of metal or wood joined by a framework **2 :** a tropical American tree (*Ochroma lagopus*) of the silk-cotton family with extremely light strong wood used esp. for floats; *also* **:** its wood
bal·sam \ˈbȯl-səm\ *n* [L *balsamum,* fr. Gk *balsamon*] (bef. 12c) **1 a :** an aromatic and usu. oily and resinous substance flowing from various plants; *esp* **:** any of several resinous substances containing benzoic or cinnamic acid and used esp. in medicine **b :** a preparation containing resinous substances and having a balsamic odor **2 a :** a balsam-yielding tree; *esp* **:** BALSAM FIR **b :** IMPATIENS; *esp* **:** a common garden ornamental (*Impatiens balsamina*) **3 :** BALM 5 — **bal·sam·ic** \bȯl-ˈsam-ik\ *adj*
balsam fir *n* (1805) **:** a resinous American evergreen tree (*Abies balsamea*) that is widely used for pulpwood and as a Christmas tree and is the source of Canada balsam
balsam poplar *n* (1786) **:** a No. American poplar (*Populus balsamifera*) that is often cultivated as a shade tree and has buds thickly coated with an aromatic resin — called also *balm of Gilead, tacamahac*
Bal·ti \ˈbəl-tē, ˈbȯl-\ *n* (1901) **:** a Tibeto-Burman language of northern Kashmir
Bal·tic \ˈbȯl-tik\ *adj* [ML (*mare*) *balticum* Baltic sea] (1590) **1 :** of or relating to the Baltic sea or to the states of Lithuania, Latvia, and Estonia **2 :** of or relating to a branch of the Indo-European languages containing Latvian, Lithuanian, and Old Prussian — see INDO-EUROPEAN LANGUAGES table
Bal·ti·more oriole \ˌbȯl-tə-ˌmō(ə)r-, -ˌmȯ(ə)r-, -mər-\ *n* [George Calvert, Lord *Baltimore*] (1808) **:** a common American oriole (*Icterus galbula*) in which the male is brightly colored with orange, black, and white and the female is primarily brown and greenish yellow — called also *Baltimore* \ˈbȯl-\
Bal·to–Slav·ic \ˌbȯl-(ˌ)tō-ˈslav-ik, -ˈsläv-\ *n* (1896) **:** a subfamily of Indo-European languages consisting of the Baltic and the Slavic branches — see INDO-EUROPEAN LANGUAGES table
Ba·lu·chi \bə-ˈlü-chē\ *n, pl* **Baluchi** *or* **Baluchis** [Per *Balūchī*] (1616) **1 a :** an Indo-Iranian people of Baluchistan **b :** a member of this people **2 :** the Iranian language of the Baluchi people
bal·us·ter \ˈbal-ə-stər\ *n* [F *balustre,* fr. It *balaustro,* fr. *balaustra* wild pomegranate flower, fr. L *balaustium,* fr. Gk *balaustion;* fr. its shape] (1602) **1 :** an upright often vase-shaped support for a rail **2 :** an object or vertical member (as the leg of a table, a round in the back of a chair, or the stem of a glass) having a vaselike or turned outline
bal·us·trade \-ə-ˌsträd\ *n* [F, fr. It *balaustrata,* fr. *balaustro*] (1644) **:** a row of balusters topped by a rail; *also* **:** a low parapet or barrier
Bam·ba·ra \bam-ˈbär-ə\ *n, pl* **Bambara** *or* **Bambaras** (1883) **1 :** a member of a Negroid people of the upper Niger **2 :** a Mande language of the Bambara people
bam·bi·no \bam-ˈbē-(ˌ)nō, bäm-\ *n, pl* **-nos** *or* **-ni** \-(ˌ)nē\ [It, dim. of *bambo* child] (1722) **1** *pl usu bambini* **:** a representation of the infant Christ **2 :** CHILD, BABY
bam·boo \(ˈ)bam-ˈbü\ *n, pl* **bamboos** [Malay *bambu*] (1586) **:** any of various chiefly tropical woody or arborescent grasses (as of the genera *Bambusa, Arundinaria,* and *Dendrocalamus*) including some with hollow stems used for building, furniture, or utensils and young shoots used for food — **bamboo** *adj*
bamboo curtain *n, often cap B&C* (1949) **:** a political, military, and ideological barrier in the Orient
bam·boo·zle \bam-ˈbü-zəl\ *vt* **-boo·zled; -boo·zling** \-ˈbüz-(ə-)liŋ\ [origin unknown] (1703) **:** to deceive by underhand methods **:** DUPE, HOODWINK — **bam·boo·zle·ment** \-ˈbü-zəl-mənt\ *n*
[1]**ban** \ˈban\ *vb* **banned; ban·ning** [ME *bannen* to summon, curse, fr. OE *bannan* to summon; akin to OHG *bannan* to command, L *fari* to speak, Gk *phanai* to say, *phōnē* sound, voice] *vt* (12c) **1** *archaic* **:** CURSE **2 :** to prohibit esp. by legal means ⟨~ discrimination⟩; *also* **:** to prohibit the use, performance, or distribution of ⟨~ a book⟩ ⟨~ a pesticide⟩ ~ *vi* **:** to utter curses or maledictions
[2]**ban** *n* [ME, partly fr. *bannen* & partly fr. OF *ban,* of Gmc origin; akin to OHG *bannan* to command] (14c) **1 :** the summoning in feudal times of the king's vassals for military service **2 :** ANATHEMA, EXCOMMUNICATION **3 :** MALEDICTION, CURSE **4 :** legal or formal prohibition **5 :** censure or condemnation esp. through social pressure
[3]**ban** \ˈbän\ *n, pl* **ba·ni** \ˈbän-(ˌ)ē\ [Rom] (1880) — see *leu* at MONEY table
Ba·nach space \ˈbä-ˌnäk-, -nək-\ *n* [Stefan *Banach* †1945 Pol. mathematician] (1949) **:** a normed vector space for which the field of multipliers comprises the real or complex numbers and in which every Cauchy sequence converges to a point in the space
ba·nal \bə-ˈnal, ba-, -ˈnäl; bā-ˈnal; ˈbān-ᵊl\ *adj* [F, fr. MF, of compulsory feudal service, possessed in common, commonplace, fr. *ban*] (1840) **:** lacking originality, freshness, or novelty **:** TRITE ***syn*** see INSIPID — **ba·nal·i·ty** \bə-ˈnal-ət-ē *also* bā- *or* ba-\ *n* — **ba·nal·ize** \bə-ˈnal-ˌīz, ba-, -ˈnäl-; bā-ˈnal-; ˈbān-ᵊl-\ *vt* — **ba·nal·ly** \bə-ˈnal-lē, ba-, -ˈnäl-; bā-ˌnal-; ˈbān-ᵊl-(l)ē\ *adv*
ba·nana \bə-ˈnan-ə, *esp Brit* -ˈnän-\ *n, often attrib* [Sp or Pg; Sp, fr. Pg, of African origin; akin to Wolof *banäna* banana] (1597) **1 :** an elongated usu. tapering tropical fruit with soft pulpy flesh enclosed in a soft usu. yellow rind **2 :** a widely cultivated perennial herb (genus *Musa* of the family Musaceae, the banana family) bearing bananas in compact pendent bunches
banana oil *n* (1926) **1 :** a colorless liquid acetate $C_7H_{14}O_2$ of amyl alcohol that has a pleasant fruity odor and is used as a solvent and in the manufacture of artificial fruit essences **2 :** a lacquer containing banana oil
banana republic *n* (1935) **:** a small dependent country; *esp* **:** one run despotically
ba·nan·as \bə-ˈnan-əz, *esp Brit* -ˈnän-\ *adj* (1968) **:** CRAZY ⟨go ~⟩ ⟨drives me ~⟩
banana seat *n* (1965) **:** an elongated bicycle saddle
banana split *n* (1920) **:** ice cream served on a banana sliced in half lengthwise and usu. garnished with flavored syrups, fruits, nuts, and whipped cream
ba·nau·sic \bə-ˈnȯ-sik, -zik\ *adj* [Gk *banausikos* of an artisan, nonintellectual, vulgar, fr. *banausos* artisan] (1845) **:** relating to or concerned

\ə\ abut \ᵊ\ kitten, F table \ər\ further \a\ ash \ā\ ace \ä\ cot, cart
\au̇\ out \ch\ chin \e\ bet \ē\ easy \g\ go \i\ hit \ī\ ice \j\ job
\ŋ\ sing \ō\ go \ȯ\ law \ȯi\ boy \th\ thin \th\ the \ü\ loot \u̇\ foot
\y\ yet \zh\ vision \á, k, ⁿ, œ, œ̄, ue, ue̅, ʸ\ *see* Guide to Pronunciation

with earning a living — used pejoratively ⟨contempt for the ~ occupations —T.S. Eliot⟩; *also* : UTILITARIAN, PRACTICAL ⟨disdains such mundane and ~ considerations as comfort and durability —G.B. Boyer⟩

[1]band \'band\ *n* [in senses 1 & 2, fr. ME *band, bond* something that constricts, fr. ON *band;* akin to OE *bindan* to bind; in other senses, fr. ME *bande* strip, fr. MF, fr. (assumed) VL *binda,* of Gmc origin; akin to OHG *binta* fillet; akin to OE *bindan* to bind, *bend* fetter] (12c) **1** : something that confines or constricts while allowing a degree of movement **2** : something that binds or restrains legally, morally, or spiritually **3** : a strip serving to join or hold things together: as **a** : BELT 2 **b** : a cord or strip across the back of a book to which the sections are sewn **4** : a thin flat encircling strip esp. for binding: as **a** : a close-fitting strip that confines material at the waist, neck, or cuff of clothing **b** : a strip of cloth used to protect a newborn baby's navel — called also *bellyband* **c** : a ring of elastic **5** : an elongated surface or section with parallel or roughly parallel sides: as **a** : a strip (as of living tissue or rock) or a stripe (as on an animal) differentiable (as by color, texture, or structure) from adjacent material **b** : a more or less well-defined range of wavelengths, frequencies, or energies of optical, electric, or acoustic radiation **6** : a narrow strip serving chiefly as decoration: as **a** : a narrow strip of material applied as trimming to an article of dress **b** *pl* : a pair of strips hanging at the front of the neck as part of a clerical, legal, or academic dress **c** : a ring without raised portions **7** : a group of grooves on a phonograph record containing recorded sound

[2]band *vt* (13c) **1** : to affix a band to or tie up with a band **2** : to finish with a band **3** : to gather together : UNITE ⟨~*ed* themselves together for protection⟩ ~ *vi* : to unite for a common purpose — often used with *together* ⟨have ~*ed* together in hopes of attacking the blight that is common to them all —J.B. Conant⟩ — **band·er** *n*

[3]band *n* [MF *bande* troop] (15c) : a group of persons, animals, or things; *esp* : a group of musicians organized for ensemble playing and using chiefly woodwinds, brass, and percussion instruments — compare ORCHESTRA

[1]ban·dage \'ban-dij\ *n* [MF, fr. *bande*] (1599) **1** : a strip of fabric used esp. to dress and bind up wounds **2** : a flexible strip or band used to cover, strengthen, or compress something

[2]bandage *vt* **ban·daged; ban·dag·ing** (1774) : to bind, dress, or cover with a bandage

Band–Aid \'ban-'dād\ *trademark* — used for a small adhesive strip with a gauze pad for covering minor wounds

ban·dan·na *or* **ban·dana** \ban-'dan-ə\ *n* [Hindi *bā̃dhnū* tie-dyeing, cloth so dyed, fr. *bā̃dhnā* to tie, fr. Skt *badhnāti* he ties; akin to OE *bindan*] (1741) : a large figured handkerchief

band·box \'ban(d)-,bäks\ *n* (1631) **1** : a usu. cylindrical box of paperboard or thin wood for holding light articles of attire **2** : a structure (as a theater or baseball park) having relatively small interior dimensions

ban·deau \ban-'dō\ *n, pl* **ban·deaux** \-'dōz\ [F, dim. of *bande*] (1706) **1** : a fillet or band esp. for the hair **2** : BRASSIERE; *also* : a band–shaped covering for the breasts

band·ed \'ban-dəd\ *adj* (1787) : having or marked with bands

ban·de·ri·lla \,ban-də-'rē(l)-yə\ *n* [Sp, dim. of *bandera* banner] (1797) : a decorated barbed dart that the banderillero thrusts into the neck or shoulders of the bull in a bullfight

ban·de·ril·le·ro \,ban-də-(,)rē(l)-'ye(ə)r-(,)ō\ *n, pl* **-ros** [Sp, fr. *banderilla*] (1797) : one who thrusts in the banderillas in a bullfight

ban·de·role *or* **ban·de·rol** \'ban-də-,rōl\ *n* [F *banderole,* fr. It *banderuola,* dim. of *bandiera* banner, of Gmc origin; akin to Goth *bandwo* sign — more at FANCY] (1562) **1** : a long narrow forked flag or streamer **2** : a long scroll bearing an inscription or a device

ban·di·coot \'ban-di-,küt\ *n* [Telugu *pandikokku*] (1789) **1** : any of several very large rats (*Nesokia* and related genera) of India and Ceylon destructive to rice fields and gardens **2** : any of various small insectivorous and herbivorous marsupial mammals (family Peramelidae) of Australia, Tasmania, and New Guinea

ban·dit \'ban-dət\ *n* [It *bandito,* fr. pp. of *bandire* to banish, of Gmc origin; akin to OHG *bannan* to command — more at BAN] (1591) **1** *pl also* **ban·dit·ti** \ban-'dit-ē\ : an outlaw who lives by plunder; *esp* : a member of a band of marauders **2** : ROBBER — **ban·dit·ry** \'ban-də-trē\ *n*

band·lead·er \'ban-,dlēd-ər\ *n* (1894) : the conductor of a band (as a dance band)

band·mas·ter \'ban(d)-,mas-tər\ *n* (1858) : a conductor of a military or concert band

ban·dog \'ban-,dȯg\ *n* [ME *bandogge,* fr. *band* + *dogge* dog] (14c) : a dog kept tied to serve as a watchdog or because of its ferocity

ban·do·lier *or* **ban·do·leer** \,ban-də-'li(ə)r\ *n* [MF *bandouliere,* deriv. of OSp *bando* band, of Gmc origin; akin to Goth *bandwo*] (ca. 1577) : a belt worn over the shoulder and across the breast often for the suspending or supporting of some article (as cartridges) or as a part of an official or ceremonial dress

ban·dore \'ban-,dō(ə)r, -,dȯ(ə)r\ *or* **ban·do·ra** \ban-'dōr-ə, -'dȯr-\ *n* [Sp *bandurria* or Pg *bandurra,* fr. LL *pandura* 3-stringed lute, fr. Gk *pandoura*] (1566) : a bass stringed instrument resembling a guitar

band saw *n* (ca. 1864) : a saw in the form of an endless steel belt running over pulleys; *also* : a power sawing machine using this device

band shell *n* (1926) : a bandstand having at the rear a sounding board shaped like a huge concave seashell

bands·man \'ban(d)z-mən\ *n* (1842) : a member of a musical band

band·stand \'ban(d)-,stand\ *n* (1859) **1** : a usu. roofed platform on which a band or orchestra performs outdoors **2** : a platform in a ballroom or nightclub on which musicians perform

band·wag·on \'ban-,dwag-ən\ *n* (1855) **1** : a usu. ornate and high wagon for a band of musicians esp. in a circus parade **2** : a party, faction, or cause that attracts adherents or amasses power by its timeliness, showmanship, or momentum **3** : a current or fashionable trend

band·width \'ban-,dwidth\ *n* (ca. 1937) : a range within a band of wavelengths, frequencies, or energies; *esp* : a range of radio frequencies which is occupied by a modulated carrier wave, which is assigned to a service, or over which a device can operate

[1]ban·dy \'ban-dē\ *vb* **ban·died; ban·dy·ing** [prob. fr. MF *bander* to be tight, to bandy, fr. *bande* strip — more at BAND] *vt* (1577) **1** : to bat (as a tennis ball) to and fro **2 a** : to toss from side to side or pass about from one to another often in a careless or inappropriate manner **b** : EXCHANGE; *esp* : to exchange (words) argumentatively **c** : to discuss lightly or banteringly **d** : to use in a glib or offhand manner — often used with *about* ⟨~ these statistics about with considerable bravado —Richard Pollak⟩ **3** *archaic* : to band together ~ *vi* **1** *obs* : CONTEND **2** *archaic* : UNITE

[2]bandy *n* [perh. fr. MF *bandé,* pp. of *bander*] (1693) : a game similar to hockey and believed to be its prototype

[3]bandy *adj* [prob. fr. *bandy* (hockey stick)] (1687) **1** *of legs* : BOWED **2** : BOWLEGGED — **ban·dy–legged** \,ban-dē-'leg(-ə)d, -'lāg(-ə)d\ *adj*

[1]bane \'bān\ *n* [ME, fr. OE *bana;* akin to OHG *bano* death, Av *banta* ill] (bef. 12c) **1 a** *obs* : KILLER, SLAYER **b** : POISON **c** : DEATH, DESTRUCTION ⟨money, thou ~ of bliss, and source of woe —George Herbert⟩ **d** : WOE **2** : a source of harm or ruin : CURSE ⟨national frontiers have been more of a ~ than a boon for mankind —D. C. Thomson⟩

[2]bane *vt* **baned; ban·ing** *obs* (1578) : to kill esp. with poison

[3]bane *n* [ME (northern dial.) *ban,* fr. OE *bān*] *chiefly Scot* (bef. 12c) : BONE

bane·ber·ry \'bān-,ber-ē\ *n* (1755) : the acrid poisonous berry of any plant of a genus (*Actaea*) of the buttercup family; *also* : one of the plants

bane·ful \'bān-fəl\ *adj* (1579) **1** : productive of destruction or woe : seriously harmful ⟨a ~ influence⟩ **2** *archaic* : POISONOUS ***syn*** see PERNICIOUS — **bane·ful·ly** \-fə-lē\ *adv*

[1]bang \'baŋ\ *vb* [prob. of Scand origin; akin to Icel *banga* to hammer] *vt* (1550) **1** : to strike sharply : BUMP ⟨fell and ~*ed* his knee⟩ **2** : to knock, beat, or thrust vigorously often with a sharp noise **3** : to have sexual intercourse with — often considered vulgar ~ *vi* **1** : to strike with a sharp noise or thump ⟨the falling chair ~*ed* against the wall⟩ **2** : to produce a sharp often metallic explosive or percussive noise or series of such noises

[2]bang *n* (1550) **1** : a resounding blow **2** : a sudden loud noise — often used interjectionally **3 a** : a sudden striking effect **b** : a quick burst of energy ⟨start off with a ~⟩ **c** : THRILL ⟨I get a ~ out of all this —W. H. Whyte⟩

[3]bang *adv* (1828) : RIGHT, DIRECTLY ⟨ran ~ up against more trouble⟩

[4]bang *n* [prob. short for *bangtail* (short tail)] (1878) : a fringe of banged hair — usu. used in pl.

[5]bang *vt* (1878) : to cut (as front hair) short and squarely across

ban·ga·lore torpedo \,baŋ-gə-,lō(ə)r-, -,lȯ(ə)r-\ *n* [*Bangalore,* India] (1913) : a metal tube that contains explosives and a firing mechanism and is used to cut barbed wire and detonate buried mines

bang away *vi* (ca. 1889) **1** : to work with determined effort ⟨students *banging away* at their homework⟩ **2** : to attack persistently ⟨police are going to keep *banging away* at you —Erle Stanley Gardner⟩

bang·er \'baŋ-ər\ *n, Brit* (ca. 1919) : SAUSAGE

bang·kok \'baŋ-,käk, baŋ-'\ *n* [earlier *bangkok,* a fine straw, fr. *Bangkok,* Thailand] (1916) : a hat woven of fine palm fiber in the Philippines

ban·gle \'baŋ-gəl\ *n* [Hindi *bangli*] (1787) **1** : a stiff usu. ornamental bracelet or anklet slipped or clasped on **2** : an ornamental disk that hangs loosely (as on a bracelet)

Bang's disease \'baŋz-\ *n* [Bernhard L. F. *Bang* †1932 Dan. veterinarian] (ca. 1929) : BRUCELLOSIS; *specif* : contagious abortion of cattle caused by a brucella (*Brucella abortus*)

bang·tail \'baŋ-,tāl\ *n* [*bangtail* (short tail)] (1921) : RACEHORSE

bang–up \'baŋ-,əp\ *adj* [[3]*bang*] (1810) : FIRST-RATE, EXCELLENT ⟨a ~ job⟩

bang up \-'əp\ *vt* [[1]*bang*] (1886) : to cause extensive damage to

bani *pl of* BAN

ban·ish \'ban-ish\ *vt* [ME *banishen,* fr. MF *baniss-,* stem of *banir,* of Gmc origin; akin to OHG *bannan* to command — more at BAN] (14c) **1** : to require by authority to leave a country **2** : to drive out or remove from a home or place of usual resort or continuance **3** : to clear away : DISPEL ⟨his discovery ~*es* anxiety —Stringfellow Barr⟩ — **ban·ish·er** *n* — **ban·ish·ment** \-ish-mənt\ *n*

syn BANISH, EXILE, DEPORT, TRANSPORT mean to remove by authority from a state or country. BANISH implies compulsory removal from a country not necessarily one's own; EXILE may imply compulsory removal or an enforced or voluntary absence from one's own country; DEPORT implies sending out of the country an alien who has illegally entered or whose presence is judged inimical to the public welfare; TRANSPORT implies sending a convicted criminal to an overseas penal colony.

ban·is·ter \'ban-ə-stər\ *n* [alter. of *baluster*] (1667) **1** : one of the upright supports of a handrail alongside a staircase **2 a** : a handrail with its supporting posts **b** : HANDRAIL

ban·jo \'ban-(,)jō\ *n, pl* **banjos** *also* **banjoes** [prob. of African origin; akin to Kimbundu *mbanza,* a similar instrument] (1739) : a musical instrument with a drum-like body, a fretted neck, and usu. four or five strings which may be plucked or strummed — **ban·jo·ist** \-jō-əst\ *n*

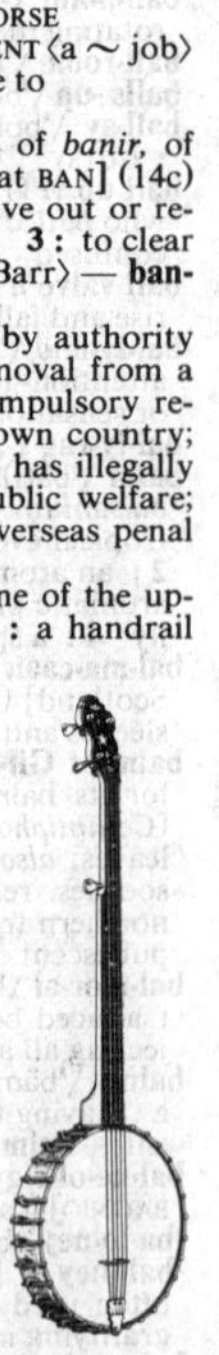

banjo

[1]bank \'baŋk\ *n* [ME, prob. of Scand origin; akin to ON *bakki* bank; akin to OE *benc* bench — more at BENCH] (13c) **1** : a mound, pile, or ridge raised above the surrounding level: as **a** : a piled-up mass of cloud or fog **b** : an undersea elevation rising esp. from the continental shelf **2** : the rising ground bordering a lake, river, or sea or forming the edge of a cut or hollow **3 a** : a steep slope (as of a hill) **b** : the lateral inward tilt of a surface along a curve or of a vehicle (as an airplane) when taking a curve **4** : a protective or cushioning rim or piece

[2]bank *vt* (1590) **1 a** : to raise a bank about **b** : to cover (as a fire) with fresh fuel and adjust the draft of air so as to keep in an inactive state **c** : to build (a curve) with the roadbed or track inclined laterally upward from the inside edge **2** : to heap or pile in a bank **3** : to drive (a ball in billiards) into a cushion **4** : to form or group in a tier ~ *vi* **1** : to rise in or form a bank — often used with *up* ⟨clouds would ~ up about midday, and showers fall —William Beebe⟩ **2 a** : to incline an airplane laterally **b** (1) : to incline laterally (2) : to follow a curve or incline ⟨skiers ~*ing* around the turn⟩

[3]bank *n* [ME, fr. MF or OIt; MF *banque,* fr. OIt *banca,* lit., bench, of Gmc origin; akin to OE *benc*] (15c) **1 a** *obs* : the table, counter, or place of business of a money changer **b** : an establishment for the custody, loan, exchange, or issue of money, for the extension of credit, and for facilitating the transmission of funds **2** : a person conducting a gambling house or game; *specif* : DEALER **3** : a supply of something held in reserve: as **a** : the fund of supplies (as money, chips, or pieces) held by the banker or dealer for use in a game **b** : a fund of pieces belonging to a game (as dominoes) from which the players draw **4** : a place where something is held available; *esp* : a depot for the collection and storage of a biological product of human origin for medical use

[4]bank *vi* (ca. 1727) **1** : to keep a bank **2** : to deposit money or have an account in a bank ~ *vt* : to deposit in a bank — **bank on** : to depend or rely on

[5]bank *n* [ME, fr. OF *banc* bench, of Gmc origin; akin to OE *benc*] (1599) **1** : a bench for the rowers of a galley **2** : a group or series of objects arranged together in a row or a tier: as **a** : a row of keys on a typewriter **b** : a set of two or more elevators **3** : one of the horizontal and usu. secondary or lower divisions of a headline

bank·able \'baŋ-kə-bəl\ *adj* (1818) **1** : acceptable to or at a bank **2** : sure to bring in a profit ⟨Hollywood's most ~ star —Sidney Sheldon⟩

bank·book \'baŋk-,bu̇k\ *n* (1714) : the depositor's book in which a bank records deposits and withdrawals — called also *passbook*

bank·card \-,kärd\ *n* (1970) : a credit card issued by a bank

bank discount *n* (1841) : the interest discounted in advance on a note and computed on the face value of the note

[1]bank·er \'baŋ-kər\ *n* (1534) **1** : one that engages in the business of banking **2** : the player who keeps the bank in various games

[2]banker *n* (1666) : a man or boat employed in the cod fishery on the Newfoundland banks

[3]banker *n* (1677) : a sculptor's or mason's workbench

banker's acceptance *n* (ca. 1913) : a short-term credit instrument issued by an importer's bank that guarantees payment of an exporter's invoice

banker's bill *n* (ca. 1902) : BANKER'S ACCEPTANCE

bank holiday *n* (1871) **1** *Brit* : LEGAL HOLIDAY **2** : a period when banks in general are closed often by government fiat

bank·ing *n* (1735) : the business of a bank or a banker

bank line *n* [[1]*bank*] (1939) : a fishing line attached to the shore and not constantly tended by a fisherman

bank money *n* (1904) : a medium of exchange consisting chiefly of checks and drafts

bank note *n* (1695) : a promissory note issued by a bank payable to bearer on demand without interest and acceptable as money

bank rate *n, Brit* (1876) : DISCOUNT RATE

[1]bank·roll \'baŋ-,krōl\ *n* (1887) : supply of money : FUNDS

[2]bankroll *vt* (1928) : to supply the capital for or pay the cost of (a business or project) — **bank·roll·er** *n*

[1]bank·rupt \'baŋ-(,)krəpt\ *n* [modif. of MF & OIt; MF *banqueroute* bankruptcy, fr. OIt *bancarotta,* fr. *banca* bank + *rotta* broken, fr. L *rupta,* fem. of *ruptus,* pp. of *rumpere* to break — more at BANK, REAVE] (1533) **1 a** : a person who has done any of the acts that by law entitle his creditors to have his estate administered for their benefit **b** : a person judicially declared subject to having his estate administered under the bankrupt laws for the benefit of his creditors **c** : a person who becomes insolvent **2** : one who is destitute of a particular thing ⟨a moral ~⟩

[2]bankrupt *adj* (1570) **1 a** : reduced to a state of financial ruin : IMPOVERISHED; *specif* : legally declared a bankrupt ⟨the company went ~⟩ **b** : of or relating to bankrupts or bankruptcy ⟨~ laws⟩ **2 a** : BROKEN, RUINED ⟨a ~ professional career⟩ **b** : exhausted of valuable qualities : STERILE ⟨a ~ old culture⟩ **c** : DESTITUTE — used with *of* or *in* ⟨~ of all merciful feelings⟩

[3]bankrupt *vt* (1588) **1** : to reduce to bankruptcy **2** : IMPOVERISH ⟨war had ~*ed* the nation's natural resources⟩ ***syn*** see DEPLETE

bank·rupt·cy \'baŋ-(,)krəp-(t)sē\ *n, pl* **-cies** (1700) **1** : the quality or state of being bankrupt **2** : utter failure or impoverishment

bank shot *n* (1897) **1** : a shot in billiards and pool in which a player banks the cue ball or the object ball **2** : a shot in basketball played to rebound from the backboard into the basket

bank·sia \'baŋ(k)-sē-ə\ *n* [NL, genus name, fr. Sir Joseph *Banks*] (1803) : any of a genus (*Banksia*) of Australian evergreen trees or shrubs of the protea family with alternate leathery leaves and flowers in dense cylindrical heads

bank·side \'baŋk-,sīd\ *n* (15c) **1** : the slope of a bank esp. of a stream **2** *cap* : the bank of the Thames at Southwark

[1]ban·ner \'ban-ər\ *n* [ME *banere,* fr. OF, of Gmc origin; akin to Goth *bandwo* sign — more at FANCY] (13c) **1 a** : a piece of cloth attached by one edge to a staff and used by a leader (as a monarch or feudal lord) as his standard **b** : [2]FLAG 1 **c** : an ensign displaying a distinctive or symbolic device or legend; *esp* : one presented as an award of honor or distinction **2** : a headline in large type running across a newspaper page **3** : a strip of cloth on which a sign is painted ⟨welcome ~s stretched across the street⟩ **4** : a name, slogan, or goal associated with a particular group or ideology ⟨the new ~ is "community control" —F. M. Hechinger⟩ — often used with *under* ⟨every new administration arrives . . . under the ~ of change —John Cogley⟩

[2]banner *adj* (1840) **1** : prominent in support of a political party ⟨a ~ Democratic county⟩ **2** : distinguished from all others esp. in excellence ⟨a ~ year for business⟩

[1]ban·ner·et \'ban-ə-rət, ,ban-ə-'ret\ *n, often cap* [ME *baneret,* fr. OF, fr. *banere*] (14c) : a knight leading his vassals into the field under his own banner

[2]banneret *also* **ban·ner·ette** *n* (14c) : a small banner

ban·ne·rol *also* **ban·ner roll** \'ban-ə-,rōl\ *n* (1548) : BANDEROLE

bannister *var of* BANISTER

ban·nock \'ban-ək\ *n* [ME *bannok,* fr. OE *bannuc*] (bef. 12c) **1** : a usu. unleavened flat bread or biscuit made with oatmeal or barley meal **2** *NewEng* : CORN BREAD; *esp* : a thin cake baked on a griddle

banns \'banz\ *n pl* [pl. of *bann,* fr. ME *bane, ban* proclamation, ban] (14c) : public announcement esp. in church of a proposed marriage

[1]ban·quet \'baŋ-kwət, 'ban- *also* -,kwet\ *n* [MF, fr. OIt *banchetto,* fr. dim. of *banca* bench, bank] (15c) : an elaborate and often ceremonious meal for numerous people often in honor of a person

[2]banquet *vi* (ca. 1500) : to partake of a banquet ~ *vt* : to treat with a banquet : FEAST — **ban·quet·er** *n*

banquet room *n* (1837) : a large room (as in a restaurant or hotel) suitable for banquets

ban·quette \baŋ-'ket, ban-, *1b is also* 'baŋ-kət\ *n* [F, fr. Prov *banqueta,* dim. of *banc* — more at BANK] (1629) **1 a** : a raised way along the inside of a parapet or trench for gunners or guns **b** *Southern* : SIDEWALK **2 a** : a long upholstered bench **b** : a sofa having one roll-over arm **c** : a built-in upholstered bench along a wall

Ban·quo \'baŋ-(,)kwō, 'ban-\ *n* : a murdered Scottish thane in Shakespeare's *Macbeth* whose ghost appears to Macbeth

ban·shee \'ban-(,)shē, ban-'\ *n* [ScGael *bean-sìth,* fr. or akin to OIr *ben síde* woman of fairyland] (1771) : a female spirit in Gaelic folklore whose appearance or wailing warns a family that one of them will soon die

[1]ban·tam \'bant-əm\ *n* [*Bantam,* former residency in Java] (1749) **1** : any of numerous small domestic fowls that are often miniatures of members of the standard breeds **2** : a person of diminutive stature and often combative disposition

[2]bantam *adj* (1782) **1** : SMALL, DIMINUTIVE **2** : pertly combative : SAUCY

ban·tam·weight \-,wāt\ *n* (1884) : a boxer in a weight division having a maximum limit of 118 pounds for professionals and 119 pounds for amateurs — compare FEATHERWEIGHT, FLYWEIGHT

[1]ban·ter \'bant-ər\ *vb* [origin unknown] *vt* (1676) **1** : to speak to or address in a witty and teasing manner **2** *archaic* : DELUDE **3** *chiefly Southern & Midland* : CHALLENGE ~ *vi* : to speak or act playfully or wittily — **ban·ter·er** \-ər-ər\ *n* — **ban·ter·ing·ly** \'bant-ə-riŋ-lē\ *adv*

[2]banter *n* (1690) : good-natured and usu. witty and animated joking ⟨exchanged ~ with newsmen⟩

bant·ling \'bant-liŋ\ *n* [perh. modif. of G *bänkling* bastard, fr. *bank* bench, fr. OHG — more at BENCH] (1593) : a very young child

Ban·tu \'ban-(,)tü, 'bän-\ *n, pl* **Bantu** *or* **Bantus** (1862) **1** : a group of African languages spoken generally south of a line from Cameroons to Kenya **2 a** : a family of Negroid peoples who occupy equatorial and southern Africa **b** : a member of any of these peoples

Ban·tu·stan \,ban-tu̇-'stan, ,bän-tu̇-'stän\ *n* [*Bantu* + *-stan* land (as in *Hindustan*)] (1956) : any of several all-black enclaves in the Republic of So. Africa that have a limited degree of self-government

ban·yan \'ban-yən\ *n* [earlier *banyan* Hindu merchant, fr. Hindi *baniyā,* fr. Skt *vāṇija* merchant] (1634) : an East Indian tree (*Ficus bengalensis*) of the mulberry family with branches that send out shoots which grow down to the soil and root to form secondary trunks

ban·zai \(')bän-'zī\ *n* [Jp] (1893) : a Japanese cheer or war cry

bao·bab \'bau̇-,bab, 'bā-ə-\ *n* [prob. native name in Africa] (1640) : a broad-trunked Old World tropical tree (*Adansonia digitata*) of the silk-cotton family with an edible acid fruit resembling a gourd and bark used in making paper, cloth, and rope

bap·ti·sia \bap-'tizh-(ē-)ə\ *n* [NL, genus name, fr. Gk *baptisis* a dipping, fr. *baptein*] (1888) : any of a genus (*Baptisia*) of No. American leguminous plants with showy papilionaceous flowers

bap·tism \'bap-,tiz-əm, *esp Southern* 'bab-\ *n* [ME *baptisme*] (14c) **1 a** : a Christian sacrament marked by ritual use of water and admitting the recipient to the Christian community **b** : a non-Christian rite using water for ritual purification **c** *Christian Science* : purification by or submergence in Spirit **2** : an act, experience, or ordeal by which one is purified, sanctified, initiated, or named — **bap·tis·mal** \bap-'tiz-məl, *esp Southern* bab-\ *adj* — **bap·tis·mal·ly** \-mə-lē\ *adv*

baptismal name *n* (1869) : a name given at christening or confirmation

baptism of fire (1857) **1** : an introductory or initial experience that is a severe ordeal; *specif* : a soldier's first exposure to enemy fire **2** : a spiritual baptism by a gift of the Holy Spirit — often used in allusion to Acts 2:3-4; Mt 3:11 (RSV)

bap·tist \'bap-təst, *esp Southern* 'bab-\ *n* (13c) **1** : one that baptizes **2** *cap* : a member or adherent of an evangelical Protestant denomination marked by congregational polity and baptism by immersion of believers only — **Baptist** *adj*

bap·tis·tery *or* **bap·tis·try** \'bap-tə-strē, *esp Southern* 'bab-\ *n, pl* **-ter·ies** *or* **-tries** (14c) : a part of a church or formerly a separate building used for baptism

bap·tize \bap-'tīz, 'bap-,, *esp Southern* bab- *or* 'bab-\ *vb* **bap·tized; bap·tiz·ing** [ME *baptizen,* fr. OF *baptiser,* fr. LL *baptizare,* fr. Gk *baptizein* to dip, baptize, fr. *baptos* dipped, fr. *baptein* to dip; akin to ON *kvefja* to quench] *vt* (13c) **1** : to administer baptism to **2 a** : to purify or cleanse spiritually esp. by a purging experience or ordeal **b** : INITIATE **3** : to give a name to (as at baptism) : CHRISTEN ~ *vi* : to administer baptism — **bap·tiz·er** *n*

[1]bar \'bär\ *n, often attrib* [ME *barre,* fr. MF] (12c) **1 a** : a straight piece (as of wood or metal) that is longer than it is wide and has any of various uses (as for a lever, support, barrier, or fastening) **b** : a solid piece or block of material that is usu. rectangular and considerably longer than it is wide **c** : a usu. rigid piece (as of wood or metal) longer than it is wide that is used as a handle or support; *esp* : a handrail used by ballet dancers to maintain balance while exercising **2** : something that obstructs or prevents passage, progress, or action: as **a** : the complete and permanent destruction of an action or claim in law; *also* : a plea or objection that effects such destruction **b** : an intangible or nonphysical impediment **c** : a submerged or partly submerged bank (as of sand) along a shore or in a river often obstructing navigation **3 a** (1) : the railing in a courtroom that encloses the place about the judge where prisoners are stationed or where the business of the court is transacted in civil cases (2) : COURT, TRIBUNAL (3) : a particular system of courts (4) : an authority or tribunal that hands down judgment **b** (1) : the barrier in the English Inns of Court that formerly separated the seats of the benchers or readers from the body of the hall occupied by the students (2) : the whole body of

\ə\ abut \ᵊ\ kitten, F table \ər\ further \a\ ash \ā\ ace \ä\ cot, cart
\au̇\ out \ch\ chin \e\ bet \ē\ easy \g\ go \i\ hit \ī\ ice \j\ job
\ŋ\ sing \ō\ go \ȯ\ law \ȯi\ boy \th\ thin \th\ the \ü\ loot \u̇\ foot
\y\ yet \zh\ vision \à, k, ⁿ, œ, œ̄, ue, uē, ʸ\ see Guide to Pronunciation

barristers or lawyers qualified to practice in any jurisdiction (3) : the profession of barrister or lawyer **4** : a straight stripe, band, or line much longer than it is wide: as **a** : one of two or more horizontal stripes on a heraldic shield **b** : a metal or embroidered strip worn on a military uniform esp. to indicate rank or service **5 a** : a counter at which food or esp. alcoholic beverages are served **b** : BARROOM **c** : SHOP 2b **6 a** : a vertical line across the musical staff before the initial measure accent **b** : MEASURE **7** : a lace and embroidery joining covered with buttonhole stitch for connecting various parts of the pattern in needlepoint lace and cutwork — **behind bars** : in jail

2bar *vt* **barred; bar·ring** (13c) **1 a** : to fasten with a bar **b** : to place bars across to prevent ingress or egress **2** : to mark with bars : STRIPE **3 a** : to confine or shut in by or as if by bars **b** : to set aside : RULE OUT **c** : to keep out : EXCLUDE **4 a** : to interpose legal objection to or to the claim of **b** : PREVENT, FORBID

3bar *prep* (1714) : EXCEPT

4bar *n* [G, fr. Gk *baros*] (1903) **1** : a unit of pressure equal to one million dynes per square centimeter **2** : the absolute cgs unit of pressure equal to one dyne per square centimeter

bar- *or* **baro-** *comb form* [Gk *baros;* akin to Gk *barys* heavy — more at GRIEVE] : weight : pressure ⟨*barometer*⟩

Ba·rab·bas \bə-ˈrab-əs\ *n* [Gk, fr. Aram *Bar-abba*] : a Jewish prisoner according to Matthew, Mark, and John released in preference to Christ at the demand of the multitude

bar·a·thea \ˌbar-ə-ˈthē-ə\ *n* [fr. *Barathea,* a trademark] (1862) : a fabric that has a broken rib weave and a pebbly texture and that is made of silk, worsted, or synthetic fiber or a combination of these

1barb \ˈbärb\ *n* [ME *barbe* barb, beard, fr. MF, fr. L *barba* — more at BEARD] (14c) **1** : a medieval cloth headdress passing over or under the chin and covering the neck **2 a** : a sharp projection extending backward (as from the point of an arrow or fishhook) and preventing easy extraction; *also* : a sharp projection with its point similarly oblique to something else **b** : a biting or pointedly critical remark or comment **3** : 2BARBEL **4** : any of the side branches of the shaft of a feather — see FEATHER illustration **5** : a plant hair or bristle ending in a hook

2barb *vt* (1759) : to furnish with a barb

3barb *n* [F *barbe,* fr. It *barbero,* fr. *barbero* of Barbary, fr. *Barberia* Barbary, coastal region in Africa] (1636) : any of a northern African breed of horses that are noted for speed and endurance and are related to Arabians

4barb *n, slang* (1967) : BARBITURATE

bar·bar·i·an \bär-ˈber-ē-ən, -ˈbar-\ *adj* [L *barbarus*] (14c) **1** : of or relating to a land, culture, or people alien and usu. believed to be inferior to one's own **2** : lacking refinement, learning, or artistic or literary culture — **barbarian** *n* — **bar·bar·i·an·ism** \-ē-ə-ˌniz-əm\ *n*

bar·bar·ic \bär-ˈbar-ik\ *adj* (15c) **1 a** : of, relating to, or characteristic of barbarians **b** : possessing or characteristic of a cultural level more complex than primitive savagery but less sophisticated than advanced civilization **2 a** : marked by a lack of restraint : WILD **b** : having a bizarre, primitive, or unsophisticated quality — **bar·bar·i·cal·ly** \-i-k(ə-)lē\ *adv*

bar·ba·rism \ˈbär-bə-ˌriz-əm\ *n* (15c) **1 a** : a barbarian or barbarous social or intellectual condition : BACKWARDNESS **b** : the practice or display of barbarian acts, attitudes, or ideas **2** : an idea, act, or expression that in form or use offends against contemporary standards of good taste or acceptability

bar·bar·i·ty \bär-ˈbar-ət-ē\ *n, pl* **-ties** (ca. 1570) **1** : BARBARISM **2 a** : barbarous cruelty : INHUMANITY **b** : an act or instance of such cruelty

bar·ba·ri·za·tion \ˌbär-bə-rə-ˈzā-shən\ *n* (1822) : the act or process of barbarizing : the state of being barbarized

bar·ba·rize \ˈbär-bə-ˌrīz\ *vb* **-rized; -riz·ing** *vt* (1602) : to make barbarian or barbarous ~ *vi* : to become barbarous

bar·ba·rous \ˈbär-b(ə-)rəs\ *adj* [L *barbarus,* fr. Gk *barbaros* foreign, ignorant] (15c) **1 a** : UNCIVILIZED **b** : lacking culture or refinement : PHILISTINE **2** : characterized by the occurrence of barbarisms **3** : mercilessly harsh or cruel ***syn*** see FIERCE — **bar·ba·rous·ly** *adv* — **bar·ba·rous·ness** *n*

Bar·ba·ry ape \ˌbär-b(ə-)rē-\ *n* [*Barbary, Africa*] (ca. 1864) : a tailless monkey (*Macaca sylvana*) of No. Africa and Gibraltar

Barbary Coast *n* (1880) : a district or section of a city noted as a center of gambling, prostitution, and riotous nightlife

Barbary sheep *n* (ca. 1898) : AOUDAD

barbe \ˈbärb\ *n* [ME, fr. MF, lit., beard] (14c) : 1BARB 2

1bar·be·cue \ˈbär-bi-ˌkyü\ *vt* **-cued; -cu·ing** (1690) **1** : to roast or broil on a rack over hot coals or on a revolving spit before or over a source of heat **2** : to cook in a highly seasoned vinegar sauce — **bar·be·cu·er** *n*

2barbecue *n* [AmerSp *barbacoa,* prob. fr. Taino] (1709) **1** : a large animal (as a steer) roasted whole or split over an open fire or barbecue pit; *also* : smaller pieces of barbecued meat **2** : a social gathering esp. in the open air at which barbecued food is eaten **3** : an often portable fireplace over which meat and fish are roasted

barbed \ˈbärbd\ *adj* (15c) **1** : having barbs **2** : characterized by pointed and biting criticism ⟨~ witticisms⟩

barbed wire \ˈbä(r)b-ˈ(d)wī(ə)r\ *n* (1881) : twisted wires armed with barbs or sharp points — called also *barbwire*

1bar·bel \ˈbär-bəl\ *n* [ME, fr. MF, fr. (assumed) VL *barbellus,* dim. of L *barbus* barbel, fr. *barba* beard — more at BEARD] (15c) : a European freshwater cyprinid fish (*Barbus barbus*) with four barbels on its upper jaw; *also* : any of various other fishes of this genus

2barbel *n* [obs. F, fr. MF, dim. of *barbe* barb, beard] (1601) : a slender tactile process on the lips of certain fishes (as catfishes)

bar·bell \ˈbär-ˌbel\ *n* (1887) : a bar with adjustable weighted disks attached to each end that is used for exercise and in weight lifting

1bar·ber \ˈbär-bər\ *n* [ME, fr. MF *barbeor,* fr. *barbe* beard — more at BARB] (14c) : one whose business is cutting and dressing hair, shaving and trimming beards, and performing related services

2barber *vb* **bar·bered; bar·ber·ing** \-b(ə-)riŋ\ *vt* (1606) : to perform the services of a barber for ~ *vi* : to perform the services of a barber

bar·ber·ry \ˈbär-ˌber-ē\ *n* [ME *barbere,* fr. MF *barbarin,* fr. Ar *barbārīs*] (15c) : any of a genus (*Berberis* of the family Berberidaceae, the barberry family) of shrubs having spines, yellow flowers, and oblong red berries

1bar·ber·shop \ˈbär-bər-ˌshäp\ *n* (1579) : a barber's place of business

2barbershop *adj* [fr. the old custom of men in barbershops forming quartets for impromptu singing of sentimental songs] (1910) : of a style of unaccompanied group singing of popular songs usu. marked by highly conventionalized close harmony

barber's itch *n* (ca. 1860) : ringworm of the face and neck

bar·bet \ˈbär-bət\ *n* [prob. fr. 1*barb*] (1824) : any of numerous nonpasserine tropical birds (family Capitonidae) with a stout bill bearing bristles and usu. swollen at the base

bar·bette \bär-ˈbet\ *n* [F, dim. of *barbe* headdress] (1772) **1** : a mound of earth or a protected platform from which guns fire over a parapet **2** : a cylinder of armor protecting a gun turret on a warship

bar·bi·can \ˈbär-bi-kən\ *n* [ME, fr. MF *barbacane,* fr. ML *barbacana*] (13c) : an outer defensive work; *esp* : a tower at a gate or bridge

bar·bi·cel \ˈbär-bə-ˌsel\ *n* [NL *barbicella,* dim. of L *barba*] (1869) : any of the small hook-bearing processes on a barbule of a feather

bar·bi·tal \ˈbär-bə-ˌtȯl\ *n* [*barbit*uric + *-al* (as in *Veronal*)] (1919) : a white crystalline addictive hypnotic $C_8H_{12}N_2O_3$ often administered in the form of its soluble sodium salt

bar·bi·tone \ˈbär-bə-ˌtōn\ *n* [*barbit*uric + *-one*] *Brit* (1914) : BARBITAL

bar·bi·tu·rate \bär-ˈbich-ə-rət, -ˌrāt; ˌbär-bə-ˈt(y)u̇r-ət, -ˈt(y)u̇(ə)r-ˌāt\ *n* (1928) **1** : a salt or ester of barbituric acid **2** : any of various derivatives of barbituric acid used esp. as sedatives, hypnotics, and antispasmodics

bar·bi·tu·ric acid \ˌbär-bə-ˌt(y)u̇r-ik-\ *n* [part trans. of G *barbitursäure,* irreg. fr. the name *Barbara* + ISV *uric* + G *säure* acid] (1866) : a synthetic crystalline acid $C_4H_4N_2O_3$ derived from pyrimidine

bar·bule \ˈbär-(ˌ)byü(ə)l\ *n* (1835) : a minute barb; *esp* : one of the processes that fringe the barbs of a feather — see FEATHER illustration

barb·wire \(ˈ)bä(r)b-ˈwī(ə)r\ *n* (1880) : BARBED WIRE

bar car *n* (1945) : a railroad car with facilities for preparing and serving refreshments and esp. drinks

bar·ca·role *or* **bar·ca·rolle** \ˈbär-kə-ˌrōl\ *n* [F *barcarolle,* fr. It *barcarola,* fr. *barcarolo* gondolier, fr. *barca* bark, fr. LL] (ca. 1779) **1** : a Venetian boat song usu. in 6/8 or 12/8 time characterized by the alternation of a strong and weak beat that suggests a rowing rhythm **2** : music imitating a barcarole

Bar·ce·lo·na chair \ˌbär-sə-ˌlō-nə-\ *n* [*Barcelona, Spain*] (ca. 1965) : an armless chair with leather-covered cushions on a stainless steel frame

bar chart *n* (1923) : BAR GRAPH

bar code *n* (1972) : a code consisting of a group of printed and variously patterned bars and spaces and sometimes numerals that is designed to be scanned and read into computer memory as identification for the object it labels

1bard \ˈbärd\ *n* [ME, fr. ScGael & IrGael] (15c) **1 a** : a tribal poet-singer skilled in composing and reciting verses on heroes and their deeds **b** : a composer, singer, or declaimer of epic or heroic verse **2** : POET — **bard·ic** \-ik\ *adj*

2bard *or* **barde** \ˈbärd\ *n* [MF *barde,* fr. OSp *barda,* fr. Ar *barda'ah*] (15c) : a piece of armor or ornament for a horse's neck, breast, or flank

3bard *vt* (1501) : to furnish with bards

bard·ol·a·ter \bär-ˈdäl-ət-ər\ *n* [*Bard (of Avon),* epithet of Shakespeare + *idolater*] (1903) : one who idolizes Shakespeare — **bard·ol·a·try** \-ə-trē\ *n*

Bar·do·li·no \ˌbärd-ᵊl-ˈē-(ˌ)nō\ *n* [*Bardolino,* village on Lake Garda, Italy] (1934) : a light red Italian wine

1bare \ˈba(ə)r, ˈbe(ə)r\ *adj* **bar·er; bar·est** [ME, fr. OE *bær;* akin to OHG *bar* naked, Lith *basas* barefoot] (bef. 12c) **1 a** : lacking a natural, usual, or appropriate covering **b (1)** : lacking clothing **(2)** *obs* : BAREHEADED **c** : UNARMED **2** : open to view : EXPOSED **3 a** : unfurnished or scantily supplied **b** : DESTITUTE ⟨~ of all safeguards⟩ **4 a** : having nothing left over or added ⟨the ~ necessities of life⟩ **b** : MERE ⟨a ~ two hours away⟩ **c** : devoid of amplification or adornment **5** *obs* : WORTHLESS — **bare·ness** *n*

syn BARE, NAKED, NUDE, BALD, BARREN mean deprived of naturally or conventionally appropriate covering. BARE implies the removal of what is additional, superfluous, ornamental, or dispensable; NAKED suggests absence of protective or ornamental covering but may imply a state of nature, of destitution, of defenselessness, of simple beauty; NUDE applies esp. to the unclothed human figure; BALD implies actual or seeming absence of natural covering and may suggest a conspicuous bareness; BARREN often suggests aridity or impoverishment or sterility.

2bare *vt* **bared; bar·ing** (bef. 12c) : to make or lay bare : UNCOVER

3bare *archaic past of* BEAR

bare·back \-ˌbak\ *or* **bare·backed** \-ˈbakt\ *adv or adj* (1562) : on the bare back of a horse : without a saddle ⟨a young boy riding ~⟩ ⟨~ riding⟩

bare bones *n pl* (1915) : the barest essentials, facts, or elements

bare·faced \ˈba(ə)r-ˈfāst, ˈbe(ə)r-\ *adj* (1590) **1** : having the face uncovered: **a** : having no beard or whiskers : BEARDLESS **b** : wearing no mask **2 a** : OPEN, UNCONCEALED **b** : lacking scruples — **bare·faced·ly** \-ˈfā-səd-lē, -ˈfāst-lē\ *adv* — **bare·faced·ness** \-ˈfā-səd-nəs, -ˈfās(t)-nəs\ *n*

bare·foot \-ˌfu̇t\ *or* **bare·foot·ed** \-ˈfu̇t-əd\ *adv or adj* (bef. 12c) : with the feet bare : UNSHOD ⟨went ~ most of the summer⟩ ⟨~ boy, with cheek of tan —J. G. Whittier⟩

barefoot doctor *n* (ca. 1970) : an auxiliary medical worker trained to provide health care in rural areas of China

ba·rege \bə-ˈrezh\ *n* [F *barège,* fr. *Barèges,* town in the Pyrenees, France] (1828) : a sheer fabric of open weave for women's clothing usu. made of wool in combination with silk or cotton

bare–hand·ed \ˈba(ə)r-ˈhan-dəd, ˈbe(ə)r-\ *adv or adj* (15c) **1** : without gloves **2** : without tools or weapons ⟨fight an animal ~⟩

bare·head·ed \-ˈhed-əd\ *adv or adj* (14c) : without a covering for the head ⟨go ~ in the hot sun⟩ ⟨a ~ boy who had lost his cap⟩ — **bare·head·ed·ness** *n*

bare–knuck·le \-ˈnək-əl\ *or* **bare–knuck·led** \-əld\ *adj or adv* (1903) **1** : not using boxing gloves ⟨champion ~ prizefighter of England —Dennis Craig⟩ ⟨the days in which men fought ~⟩ **2** : having a fierce unrelenting character ⟨a . . . ~ polemic —*Nat'l Review*⟩ ⟨fighting ~ in congress for his beliefs⟩

bare·ly *adv* (bef. 12c) **1** : in a meager manner : PLAINLY ⟨a ~ furnished room⟩ **2** : SCARCELY, HARDLY ⟨~ enough money to cover expenses⟩

barf \ˈbärf\ *vi* [origin unknown] (1957) : VOMIT

bar·fly \ˈbär-ˌflī\ *n* (1910) : a drinker who frequents bars

[1]**bar·gain** \ˈbär-gən\ *n, often attrib* (14c) **1 :** an agreement between parties settling what each gives or receives in a transaction between them or what course of action or policy each pursues in respect to the other **2 :** something acquired by or as if by bargaining; *esp* **:** an advantageous purchase **3 :** a transaction, situation, or event regarded in the light of its results — **in the bargain** *or* **into the bargain :** BESIDES

[2]**bargain** *vb* [ME *bargainen,* fr. MF *bargaignier,* fr. ML *barcaniare,* prob. of Gmc origin; prob. akin to OE *borgian* to borrow — more at BURY] *vi* (14c) **1 :** to negotiate over the terms of a purchase, agreement, or contract **:** HAGGLE **2 :** to come to terms **:** AGREE ~ *vt* **1 :** to bring to a desired level by bargaining ⟨~ a price down⟩ **2 :** to sell or dispose of by bargaining — **bar·gain·er** *n* — **bargain for :** EXPECT

bargain basement *n* (1899) **:** a section of a store (as the basement) where merchandise is sold at reduced prices

bargain counter *n* (1888) **:** a counter where merchandise is sold at bargain prices

[1]**barge** \ˈbärj\ *n* [ME, fr. MF, fr. LL *barca*] (14c) **:** any of various boats: as **a :** a roomy usu. flat-bottomed boat used chiefly for the transport of goods on inland waterways and usu. propelled by towing **b :** a large motorboat supplied to the flag officer of a flagship **c :** a roomy pleasure boat; *esp* **:** a boat of state elegantly furnished and decorated

[2]**barge** *vb* **barged; barg·ing** *vt* (1649) **:** to carry by barge ~ *vi* **1 :** to move ponderously or clumsily **2 :** to thrust oneself heedlessly or unceremoniously

barge·board \ˈbärj-ˌbō(ə)rd, -ˌbȯ(ə)rd\ *n* [origin unknown] (1833) **:** an often ornamented board that conceals roof timbers projecting over gables

barg·ee \bär-ˈjē\ *n, Brit* (1666) **:** BARGEMAN

bar·gel·lo \bär-ˈjel-(ˌ)ō\ *n* [the *Bargello,* museum in Florence, Italy; fr. the use of this stitch in the upholstery of 17th cent. chairs at the Bargello] (ca. 1924) **:** a needlepoint stitch that produces a zigzag pattern

barge·man \ˈbärj-mən\ *n* (14c) **:** the master or a deckhand of a barge

bar graph *n* (1924) **:** a graphic means of quantitative comparison by rectangles with lengths proportional to the measure of the data or things being compared — called also *bar chart*

bar·hop \ˈbär-ˌhäp\ *vi* (1947) **:** to visit and drink at a series of bars in the course of an evening

ba·ri·lla \bə-ˈrē(l)-yə\ *n* [Sp *barrilla*] (1622) **:** an impure sodium carbonate made from plant ashes esp. of two European saltworts (*Salsola kali* and *S. soda*) and formerly used esp. in making soap and glass

bar·ite \ˈba(ə)r-ˌīt, ˈbe(ə)r-\ *n* [Gk *barytēs* weight, fr. *barys*] (1868) **:** barium sulfate $BaSO_4$ occurring as a mineral

[1]**bari·tone** \ˈbar-ə-ˌtōn\ *n* [F *baryton* or It *baritono,* fr. Gk *barytonos* deep sounding, fr. *barys* heavy + *tonos* tone — more at GRIEVE] (1609) **1 :** a male singing voice of medium compass between bass and tenor; *also* **:** a person having this voice **2 :** a member of a family of instruments having a range between tenor and bass; *esp* **:** the baritone saxhorn or baritone saxophone — **bari·tonal** \ˌbar-ə-ˈtōn-ᵊl\ *adj*

[2]**baritone** *adj* (1729) **:** relating to or having the range or part of a baritone

bar·i·um \ˈbar-ē-əm, ˈber-\ *n* [NL, fr. *bar-*] (1808) **:** a silver-white malleable toxic bivalent metallic element of the alkaline-earth group that occurs only in combination — see ELEMENT table

barium sulfate *n* (ca. 1904) **:** a colorless crystalline insoluble compound $BaSO_4$ that occurs in nature as barite, is obtained artificially by precipitation, and is used as a pigment and extender, as a filler, and as a substance opaque to X rays in medical photography of the alimentary canal

[1]**bark** \ˈbärk\ *vb* [ME *berken,* fr. OE *beorcan;* akin to ON *berkja* to bark, Lith *burgėti* to growl] *vi* (bef. 12c) **1 a :** to make the characteristic short loud cry of a dog **b :** to make a noise resembling a bark **2 :** to speak in a curt loud and usu. angry tone **:** SNAP ~ *vt* **1 :** to utter in a curt loud usu. angry tone **2 :** to advertise by persistent outcry ⟨newsboys ~*ed* their wares persistently⟩ — **bark up the wrong tree :** to proceed under a misapprehension

[2]**bark** *n* (bef. 12c) **1 a :** the sound made by a barking dog **b :** a similar sound **2 :** a short sharp peremptory tone of speech or utterance — **bark·less** \ˈbär-kləs\ *adj*

[3]**bark** *n* [ME, fr. ON *bark-, börkr;* akin to MD & MLG *borke* bark] (14c) **1 :** the tough exterior covering of a woody root or stem **2 :** CINCHONA 2 — **bark·less** \ˈbär-kləs\ *adj*

[4]**bark** *vt* (14c) **1 :** to treat with an infusion of tanbark **2 a :** to strip the bark from **b :** to rub off or abrade the skin of

[5]**bark** *n* [ME, fr. MF *barque,* fr. OProv *barca,* fr. LL] (15c) **1 a :** a small sailing ship **b :** a 3-masted ship with foremast and mainmast square-rigged and mizzenmast fore-and-aft rigged **2 :** a craft propelled by sails or oars

bark beetle *n* (1862) **:** any of numerous beetles (family Scolytidae) that bore under the bark of trees both as a larva and as an adult

bar·keep \ˈbär-ˌkēp\ *or* **bar·keep·er** \-ˌkē-pər\ *n* (1712) **:** BARTENDER

bar·ken·tine \ˈbär-kən-ˌtēn\ *n* [[5]*bark* + *-entine,* alter. of *-antine* (as in *brigantine*)] (1693) **:** a 3-masted ship having the foremast square-rigged and the mainmast and mizzenmast fore-and-aft rigged

[1]**bark·er** \ˈbär-kər\ *n* (1611) **:** one that removes or prepares bark

[2]**barker** *n* (1699) **:** one that barks; *esp* **:** a person who advertises by hawking at an entrance to a show

barky \ˈbär-kē\ *adj* **bark·i·er; -est** (1590) **:** covered with or resembling bark

bar·ley \ˈbär-lē\ *n* [ME *barly,* fr. OE *bærlic* of barley; akin to OE *bere* barley, L *far* spelt] (bef. 12c) **:** a cereal grass (genus *Hordeum,* esp. *H. vulgare*) having the flowers in dense spikes with long awns and three spikelets at each joint of the rachis; *also* **:** its seed used in malt beverages and in breakfast foods and stock feeds

bar·ley–bree \-ˌbrē\ *also* **bar·ley–broo** \-ˌbrü\ *n* [*barley* + Sc *bree* or *broo* (bree)] (1724) **1** *chiefly Scot* **:** WHISKEY **2** *chiefly Scot* **:** BEER, ALE

bar·ley·corn \-ˌkȯ(ə)rn\ *n* (1500) **1 :** a grain of barley **2 :** an old unit of length equal to the third part of an inch

bar·low \ˈbär-ˌlō\ *n* [Russell *Barlow* 18th cent. Eng. knife maker] (1779) **:** a sturdy inexpensive jackknife

barm \ˈbärm\ *n* [ME *berme,* fr. OE *beorma;* akin to L *fermentum* yeast, *fervēre* to boil] (bef. 12c) **:** yeast formed on fermenting malt liquors

bar·maid \ˈbär-ˌmād\ *n* (1658) **:** a female bartender

bar·man \-mən\ *n* (1837) **:** BARTENDER

Bar·me·cid·al \ˌbär-mə-ˈsīd-ᵊl\ *or* **Bar·me·cide** \ˈbär-mə-ˌsīd\ *adj* [*Barmecide,* a wealthy Persian, who, in a tale of *The Arabian Nights' Entertainments,* invited a beggar to a feast of imaginary food] (1845) **:** providing only the illusion of plenty or abundance ⟨a ~ feast⟩

[1]**bar mitz·vah** \bär-ˈmits-və\ *n, often cap B&M* [Heb *bar miṣwāh,* lit., son of the (divine) law] (1816) **1 :** a Jewish boy who reaches his 13th birthday and attains the age of religious duty and responsibility **2 :** the initiatory ceremony recognizing a boy as a bar mitzvah

[2]**bar mitzvah** *vt* **bar mitz·vahed; bar mitz·vah·ing** (1947) **:** to administer the ceremony of bar mitzvah to

[1]**barmy** \ˈbär-mē\ *adj* **barm·i·er; -est** (1535) **:** full of froth or ferment

[2]**barmy** *adj* **barmier; -est** [alter. of *balmy*] (1892) **:** BALMY 2

barn \ˈbärn\ *n* [ME *bern,* fr. OE *beręrn,* fr. *bere* barley + *ærn* place; akin to OE *ræst* — more at REST] (bef. 12c) **1 a :** a usu. large building for the storage of farm products, for feed, and usu. for the housing of farm animals or farm equipment **b :** an unusually large and usu. bare building ⟨a great ~ of a hotel —W. A. White⟩ **2 :** a large building for the housing of a fleet of vehicles (as trolley cars or trucks) — **barn·like** \-ˌlīk\ *adj* — **barny** \ˈbär-nē\ *adj*

Bar·na·bas \ˈbär-nə-bəs\ *n* [Gk, fr. Aram *Barnebhūʼāh*] **:** a companion of the apostle Paul on his first missionary journey

bar·na·cle \ˈbär-ni-kəl\ *n* [ME *barnakille,* alter. of *bernake,* of Celt origin; akin to Corn *brennyk* limpet] (13c) **1 :** a European goose (*Branta leucopsis*) that breeds in the arctic and is larger than the related brant — called also *barnacle goose* **2 :** any of numerous marine crustaceans (subclass Cirripedia) with feathery appendages for gathering food that are free-swimming as larvae but fixed to rocks or floating objects as adults — **bar·na·cled** \-kəld\ *adj*

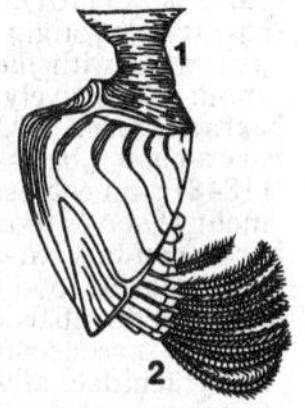

barnacle 2: *1* peduncle, *2* cirri

barn dance *n* (1894) **:** an American social dance orig. held in a barn and featuring several dance forms (as square dancing)

barn lot *n, chiefly Southern & Midland* (1724) **:** BARNYARD

barn owl *n* (1674) **:** a widely distributed owl (*Tyto alba*) that has plumage mottled buff brown and gray above and chiefly white below, frequents barns and other buildings, and preys esp. on rodents

barn raising *n* (1856) **:** a gathering for the purpose of erecting a barn — compare [4]BEE

barn·storm \ˈbärn-ˌstȯrm\ *vi* (1883) **1 :** to tour through rural districts staging usu. theatrical performances **2 :** to travel from place to place making brief stops (as in a political campaign or a promotional tour) **3 :** to pilot one's airplane in sightseeing flights with passengers or in exhibition stunts in an unscheduled itinerant course esp. in rural districts ~ *vt* **:** to travel across while barnstorming — **barn·storm·er** *n*

[1]**barn·yard** \-ˌyärd\ *n* (14c) **:** a usu. fenced area adjoining a barn

[2]**barnyard** *adj* (1927) **:** EARTHY, SMUTTY, SCATOLOGICAL ⟨~ humor⟩

barnyard grass *n* (1843) **:** a coarse annual grass (*Echinochloa crusgalli*) with terminal spikelike panicles of one-sided flower clusters that is nearly cosmopolitan as a weed in cultivated ground

baro- — see BAR-

baro·gram \ˈbar-ə-ˌgram\ *n* [ISV] (1884) **:** a barographic tracing

baro·graph \-ˌgraf\ *n* [ISV] (ca. 1864) **:** a recording barometer — **baro·graph·ic** \ˌbar-ə-ˈgraf-ik\ *adj*

Ba·ro·lo \bär-ˈō-(ˌ)lō, bə-ˈrō-\ *n* [*Barolo,* village in the Piedmont region, Italy] (1875) **:** a dry red Italian wine

ba·rom·e·ter \bə-ˈräm-ət-ər\ *n* (1665) **1 :** an instrument for determining the pressure of the atmosphere and hence for assisting in judgment as to probable weather changes and for determining the height of an ascent **2 :** one that indicates fluctuations (as in public opinion) — **baro·met·ric** \ˌbar-ə-ˈme-trik\ *or* **baro·met·ri·cal** \-tri-kəl\ *adj* — **baro·met·ri·cal·ly** \-tri-k(ə-)lē\ *adv* — **ba·rom·e·try** \bə-ˈräm-ə-trē\ *n*

barometric pressure *n* (1827) **:** the pressure of the atmosphere usu. expressed in terms of the height of a column of mercury

bar·on \ˈbar-ən\ *n* [ME, fr. OF, of Gmc origin; akin to OHG *baro* freeman] (13c) **1 a :** one of a class of tenants holding his rights and title by military or other honorable service directly from a feudal superior (as a king) **b :** a lord of the realm **:** NOBLE, PEER **2 a :** a member of the lowest grade of the peerage in Great Britain **b :** a nobleman on the continent of Europe of varying rank **c :** a member of the lowest order of nobility in Japan **3 :** a man of great power or influence in some field of activity ⟨cattle ~⟩

bar·on·age \-ə-nij\ *n* (13c) **:** the whole body of barons or peers **:** NOBILITY 2

bar·on·ess \ˈbar-ə-nəs, -ˌnes, *US also* ˌbar-ə-ˈnes\ *n* (15c) **1 :** the wife or widow of a baron **2 :** a woman who holds a baronial title in her own right

bar·on·et \ˈbar-ə-nət, *US also* ˌbar-ə-ˈnet\ *n* (1614) **:** the holder of a rank of honor below a baron and above a knight

bar·on·et·age \-ij\ *n* (1760) **1 :** BARONETCY **2 :** the whole body of baronets

bar·on·et·cy \-sē\ *n* (1812) **:** the rank of a baronet

ba·rong \bə-ˈrȯŋ, -ˈräŋ\ *n* [native name in the Philippines] (1898) **:** a thick-backed thin-edged knife or sword used by the Moro

ba·ro·ni·al \bə-ˈrō-nē-əl\ *adj* (1767) **1 :** of or relating to a baron or the baronage **2 :** STATELY, AMPLE ⟨a ~ room⟩

bar·ony \ˈbar-ə-nē\ *n, pl* **-on·ies** (13c) **1 :** the domain, rank, or dignity of a baron **2 :** a vast private landholding **3 :** a field of activity under the sway of an individual or a special group

[1]**ba·roque** \bə-ˈrōk, ba-, -ˈräk, -ˈrȯk\ *adj* [F, fr. It *barocco* baroque, adj. or Pg *barrôco* baroque, n.; It *barocco* fr. Pg *barrôco,* perh. fr. *barroca* rocky, mountainous country] (1765) **1 :** of, relating to, or having the characteristics of a style of artistic expression prevalent esp. in the 17th

century that is marked generally by extravagant forms and elaborate and sometimes grotesque ornamentation and specifically also in architecture by dynamic opposition and the use of curved and plastic figures, in music by improvisation, contrasting effects, and the use of continuo and in literature by complexity of form and bizarre, ingenious, and often ambiguous imagery **2 :** characterized by grotesqueness, extravagance, or flamboyance — **ba·roque·ly** *adv*

²baroque *n* [F, fr. Pg *barrôco*] (1926) **:** an irregularly shaped pearl

baro·re·cep·tor \ˌbar-ō-ri-ˈsep-tər\ *also* **baro·cep·tor** \ˈbar-ō-ˌsep-tər\ *n* [*bar-* + *receptor*] (1948) **:** a neural receptor (as of the arterial walls) sensitive to changes in pressure

ba·rouche \bə-ˈrüsh\ *n* [G *barutsche,* fr. It *biroccio,* deriv. of LL *birotus* two-wheeled, fr. L *bi-* + *rota* wheel — more at ROLL] (1801) **:** a four-wheeled carriage with a driver's seat high in front, two double seats inside facing each other, and a folding top over the back seat

bar pilot *n* (1944) **:** a pilot who navigates a ship from a pilot station over a bar and often into a harbor or to the harbor docks

barque \ˈbärk\, **bar·quen·tine** \ˈbär-kən-ˌtēn\ *var of* BARK, BARKENTINE

¹bar·rack \ˈbar-ək, -ik\ *n* [F *baraque* hut, fr. Catal *barraca*] (1686) **1 :** a building or set of buildings used esp. for lodging soldiers in garrison **2 a :** a structure resembling a shed or barn that provides temporary housing **b :** housing characterized by extreme plainness or dreary uniformity — usu. used in pl. in all senses

²barrack *vt* (1701) **:** to lodge in barracks

³barrack *vb* [origin unknown] *vi* (1890) **1** *chiefly Brit* **:** ROOT, CHEER — usu. used with *for* **2** *chiefly Brit* **:** JEER, SCOFF ~ *vt, chiefly Brit* **:** to shout at derisively or sarcastically — **bar·rack·er** *n*

barracks bag *n* (1938) **:** a fabric bag for carrying personal equipment

bar·ra·coon \ˌbar-ə-ˈkün\ *n* [Sp *barracón,* aug. of *barraca* hut, fr. Catal] (1848) **:** an enclosure or barracks formerly used for temporary confinement of slaves or convicts — often used in pl.

bar·ra·cou·ta \ˌbar-ə-ˈküt-ə\ *n* [modif. of AmerSp *barracuda*] (1839) **:** a large marine food fish (*Thyrsites atun*)

bar·ra·cu·da \ˌbar-ə-ˈküd-ə\ *n, pl* **-da** *or* **-das** [AmerSp] (1678) **:** any of several predaceous marine fishes (genus *Sphyraena* of the family Sphyraenidae) of warm seas that include excellent food fishes as well as forms regarded as toxic

¹bar·rage \ˈbär-ij\ *n* [F, fr. *barrer* to bar, fr. *barre* bar] (1859) **:** an artificial dam placed in a watercourse to increase the depth of water or to divert it into a channel for navigation or irrigation

²bar·rage \bə-ˈräzh, -ˈräj\ *n* [F *(tir de) barrage* barrier fire] (1916) **1 :** artillery fire laid on a line close to friendly troops to screen and protect them **2 :** a vigorous expulsion or projection of many things at once ⟨a ~ of protests⟩

³bar·rage \bə-ˈräzh, -ˈräj\ *vt* **bar·raged; bar·rag·ing** (1918) **:** to deliver a barrage against

barrage balloon *n* (1920) **:** a small captive balloon used to support wires or nets as protection against air attacks

bar·ra·mun·di \ˌbar-ə-ˈmən-dē\ *also* **bar·ra·mun·da** \-də\ *n* [native name in Australia] (1864) **:** any of several Australian fishes (esp. *Lates calcarifer* of the family Centropomidae) used for food

bar·ran·ca \bə-ˈraŋ-kə\ *or* **bar·ran·co** \-(ˌ)kō\ *n, pl* **-cas** *or* **-cos** [Sp] (1691) **1 :** a deep gully or arroyo with steep sides **2 :** a steep bank or bluff

bar·ra·tor *also* **bar·ra·ter** \ˈbar-ət-ər\ *n* (15c) **:** one who engages in barratry

bar·ra·try \ˈbar-ə-trē\ *n, pl* **-tries** [ME *barratrie,* fr. MF *baraterie* deception, fr. *barater* to deceive, exchange] (15c) **1 :** the purchase or sale of office or preferment in church or state **2 :** a fraudulent breach of duty on the part of a master of a ship or of the mariners to the injury of the owner of the ship or cargo **3 :** the persistent incitement of litigation

Barr body \ˈbär-\ *n* [Murray Llewellyn *Barr b*1908 Canad. anatomist] (1964) **:** material from the inactivated X chromosome present in each somatic cell of most mammals that is used as a test of genetic femaleness (as in a fetus or an athlete) — called also *sex chromatin*

barre \ˈbär\ *n* [F, fr. ML *barra*] (1936) **:** BAR 1c

barred \ˈbärd\ *adj* (14c) **:** marked by or divided off by bars; *specif* **:** having alternate bands of different color ⟨~ feather⟩

¹bar·rel \ˈbar-əl\ *n* [ME *barel,* fr. MF *baril*] (14c) **1 :** a round bulging vessel of greater length than breadth that is usu. made of staves bound with hoops and has flat ends of equal diameter **2 a :** the amount contained in a barrel; *esp* **:** the amount (as 31 gal. of fermented beverage or 42 gal. of petroleum) fixed for a certain commodity used as a unit of measure **b :** a great quantity **3 :** a drum or cylindrical part: as **a :** the discharging tube of a gun **b :** the cylindrical metal box enclosing the mainspring of a timepiece **c :** the part of a fountain pen or of a pencil containing the ink or lead **d :** a cylindrical or tapering housing containing the optical components of a photographic-lens system and the iris diaphragm **e :** TUMBLING BARREL **f :** the fuel outlet from the carburetor on a gasoline engine **4 :** the trunk of a quadruped — see COW illustration — **bar·reled** \-əld\ *adj* — **on the barrel :** asking for or granting no credit **:** in cash — **over a barrel :** at a disadvantage **:** in an awkward position

²barrel *vb* **-reled** *or* **-relled; -rel·ing** *or* **-rel·ling** *vt* (15c) **:** to put or pack in a barrel ~ *vi* **:** to move at a high speed

bar·rel·age \ˈbar-ə-lij\ *n* (1890) **:** amount (as of beer) in barrels

barrel cactus *n* (1881) **:** any of a genus (*Ferocactus*) of nearly globular deeply ribbed spiny cacti of Mexico and the adjacent U.S.

bar·rel·ful \ˈbar-əl-ˌfu̇l\ *n, pl* **barrelfuls** \-ˌfu̇lz\ *or* **bar·rels·ful** \-əlz-ˌfu̇l\ (14c) **1 :** as much or as many as a barrel will hold **2 :** a large number or amount

bar·rel·house \ˈbar-əl-ˌhau̇s\ *n* (1883) **1 :** a cheap drinking and usu. dancing establishment **2 :** a strident, uninhibited, and forcefully rhythmic style of jazz or blues

barrel organ *n* (1772) **:** an instrument for producing music by the action of a revolving cylinder studded with pegs on a series of valves that admit air from a bellows to a set of pipes

barrel roll *n* (ca. 1920) **:** an airplane maneuver in which a complete revolution about the longitudinal axis is made

¹bar·ren \ˈbar-ən\ *adj* [ME *bareine,* fr. OF *baraine*] (13c) **1 :** not reproducing: as **a :** incapable of producing offspring — used esp. of females or matings **b :** not yet or not recently pregnant **c :** habitually failing to fruit **2 :** not productive: as **a :** producing little or no vegetation **:** DESOLATE ⟨~ deserts⟩ **b :** producing inferior crops ⟨~ soil⟩ **c :** unproductive of results or gain **:** FRUITLESS ⟨a ~ scheme⟩ **3 :** DEVOID, LACKING — used with *of* ⟨~ of excitement⟩ **4 :** lacking interest, information, or charm **5 :** DULL, UNRESPONSIVE ***syn*** see BARE — **bar·ren·ly** *adv* — **bar·ren·ness** \-ən-nəs\ *n*

²barren *n* (1651) **1** *pl* **:** an extent of usu. level land having an inferior growth of trees or little vegetation **2 :** a tract of barren land

bar·rette \bä-ˈret, bə-\ *n* [F, dim. of *barre* bar] (1901) **:** a clip or bar for holding a woman's hair in place

¹bar·ri·cade \ˈbar-ə-ˌkād, ˌbar-ə-ˈ\ *vt* **-cad·ed; -cad·ing** (1592) **1 :** to block off or stop up with a barricade **2 :** to prevent access to by means of a barricade

²barricade *n* [F, fr. MF, fr. *barriquer* to barricade, fr. *barrique* barrel] (1642) **1 :** an obstruction or rampart thrown up across a way or passage to check the advance of the enemy **2 :** BARRIER, OBSTACLE **3** *pl* **:** a field of combat or dispute

bar·ri·ca·do \ˌbar-ə-ˈkād-(ˌ)ō\ *n, pl* **-does** [modif. of F *barricade*] *archaic* (1590) **:** BARRICADE — **barricado** *vt, archaic*

bar·ri·er \ˈbar-ē-ər\ *n* [ME *barrere,* fr. MF *barriere,* fr. *barre*] (14c) **1 a :** a material object or set of objects that separates, demarcates, or serves as a barricade **b :** an extension of the antarctic continental ice cap into the sea resting partly on the bottom **2** *pl, often cap* **:** a medieval war game in which combatants fight on foot with a fence or railing between them **3 :** the movable gate or device at the starting line in a racetrack **4 :** something immaterial that impedes or separates ⟨~s of reserve⟩ **5 :** a factor that tends to restrict the free movement, mingling, or interbreeding of individuals or populations ⟨behavioral and geographic ~s to hybridization⟩

barrier reef *n* (1805) **:** a coral reef roughly parallel to a shore and separated from it by a lagoon

bar·ring \ˈbär-iŋ\ *prep* (15c) **:** excluding by exception **:** EXCEPTING

bar·rio \ˈbär-ē-ˌō, ˈbar-\ *n, pl* **-ri·os** [Sp, fr. Ar *barrī* of the open country, fr. *barr* outside, open country] (1892) **1 :** a ward, quarter, or district of a city or town in Spanish-speaking countries **2 :** a Spanish-speaking quarter or neighborhood in a city or town in the U.S. esp. in the Southwest

bar·ris·ter \ˈbar-ə-stər\ *n* [¹*bar* + *-i-* + *-ster*] (15c) **:** a counsel admitted to plead at the bar and undertake the public trial of causes in an English superior court — compare SOLICITOR

bar·room \ˈbär-ˌrüm, -ˌru̇m\ *n* (1797) **:** a room or establishment whose main feature is a bar for the sale of liquor

¹bar·row \ˈbar-(ˌ)ō, -ə(-w)\ *n* [ME *bergh,* fr. OE *beorg;* akin to OHG *berg* mountain, Skt *bṛhant* high] (bef. 12c) **1 :** MOUNTAIN, MOUND — used only in the names of hills in England **2 :** a large mound of earth or stones over the remains of the dead **:** TUMULUS

²barrow *n* [ME *barow,* fr. OE *bearg;* akin to OHG *barug* barrow, OE *borian* to bore] (bef. 12c) **:** a male hog castrated before sexual maturity

³barrow *n* [ME *barew,* fr. OE *bearwe;* akin to OE *beran* to carry — more at BEAR] (bef. 12c) **1 a :** HANDBARROW **b :** WHEELBARROW **2 :** a cart with a shallow box body, two wheels, and shafts for pushing it **:** PUSHCART

barrow boy *n, Brit* (1939) **:** COSTERMONGER

bar sinister *n* (1823) **1 :** a heraldic charge held to be a mark of bastardy **2 :** the fact or condition of being of illegitimate birth

bar·tend·er \ˈbär-ˌten-dər\ *n* (1836) **:** one that serves liquor at a bar

¹bar·ter \ˈbärt-ər\ *vb* [ME *bartren,* fr. MF *barater* deceive, exchange] *vi* (15c) **:** to trade by exchanging one commodity for another ~ *vt* **:** to trade or exchange by or as if by bartering — **bar·ter·er** \-ər-ər\ *n*

²barter *n* (15c) **1 :** the act or practice of carrying on trade by bartering **2 :** the thing given in exchange in bartering

Bar·tho·lin's gland \ˌbär-thə-lənz-, ˌbärt-ᵊl-ənz-\ *n* [Kaspar *Bartholin* †1738 Dan. physician] (1901) **:** either of two oval racemose glands lying one to each side of the lower part of the vagina and secreting a lubricating mucus — compare COWPER'S GLAND

bar·ti·zan \ˈbärt-ə-zən, ˌbärt-ə-ˈzan\ *n* [ME *bretasinge,* fr. *bretais* parapet — more at BRATTICE] (14c) **:** a small structure (as a turret) projecting from a building and serving esp. for lookout or defense

Ba·ruch \bə-ˈrük, ˈbär-ˌük\ *n* [LL, fr. Gk *Barouch,* fr. Heb *Bārūkh*] **:** a homiletic book included in the Roman Catholic canon of the Old Testament and in the Protestant Apocrypha — see BIBLE table

bar·ware \ˈbär-ˌwa(ə)r, -ˌwe(ə)r\ *n* (1941) **:** glassware or utensils used in serving alcoholic beverages

bary·on \ˈbar-ē-ˌän\ *n* [ISV *bary-* (fr. Gk *barys* heavy) + ²*-on* — more at GRIEVE] (1953) **:** any of a group of subatomic particles (as nucleons) that undergo strong interactions and are held to be a combination of three quarks — **bary·on·ic** \ˌbar-ē-ˈän-ik\ *adj*

ba·ry·ta \bə-ˈrīt-ə\ *n* [NL, modif. of Gk *barytēs* weight — more at BARITE] (1809) **:** any of several compounds of barium: as **a :** barium monoxide **b :** barium hydroxide **c :** BARIUM SULFATE

bar·yte \ˈba(ə)r-ˌīt, ˈbe(ə)r-\ *or* **ba·ry·tes** \bə-ˈrīt-ēz\ *var of* BARITE

bary·tone \ˈbar-ə-ˌtōn\ *var of* BARITONE

bas·al \ˈbā-səl, -zəl\ *adj* (1645) **1 a :** relating to, situated at, or forming the base **b :** arising from the base of a stem ⟨~ leaves⟩ **2 a :** of or relating to the foundation, base, or essence **:** FUNDAMENTAL **b :** of, relating to, or being essential for maintaining the fundamental vital activities of an organism **:** MINIMAL **c :** used for teaching beginners ⟨~ readers⟩ — **ba·sal·ly** \-ē\ *adv*

basal body *n* (1902) **:** a minute distinctively staining cell organelle found at the base of a flagellum or cilium and identical to a centriole in structure — called also *basal granule, kinetosome*

basal cell *n* (ca. 1903) **:** one of the innermost cells of the deeper epidermis of the skin

basal ganglion *n* (ca. 1889) **:** any of four deeply placed masses of gray matter (as the amygdala) in each cerebral hemisphere

basal metabolic rate *n* (1922) **:** the rate at which heat is given off by an organism at complete rest

basal metabolism *n* (1913) **:** the turnover of energy in a fasting and resting organism using energy solely to maintain vital cellular activity, respiration, and circulation as measured by the basal metabolic rate

ba·salt \bə-ˈsȯlt, ˈbā-ˌ\ *n* [L *basaltes,* MS var. of *basanites* touchstone, fr. Gk *basanitēs* (*lithos*), fr. *basanos* touchstone, fr. Egypt *bḫnw*] (1601) **:** a dark gray to black dense to fine-grained igneous rock that consists of basic plagioclase, augite, and usu. magnetite — **ba·sal·tic** \bə-ˈsȯl-tik\ *adj*

bas·cule \ˈbas-(ˌ)kyü(ə)l\ *n* [F, seesaw] (1678) **:** an apparatus or structure (as a drawbridge) in which one end is counterbalanced by the other on the principle of the seesaw or by weights

[1]**base** \ˈbās\ *n, pl* **bas·es** \ˈbā-səz\ [ME, fr. MF, fr. L *basis,* fr. Gk, step, base, fr. *bainein* to go — more at COME] (13c) **1 a** (1) **:** the lower part of a wall, pier, or column considered as a separate architectural feature (2) **:** the lower part of a complete architectural design **b :** the bottom of something considered as its support **:** FOUNDATION **c** (1) **:** a side or face of a geometrical figure from which an altitude can be constructed; *esp* **:** one on which the figure stands (2) **:** the length of a base **d :** that part of a bodily organ by which it is attached to another more central structure of the organism **2 a :** a main ingredient ⟨paint having a latex ~⟩ **b :** a supporting or carrying ingredient (as of a medicine) **3 a :** the fundamental part of something **:** GROUNDWORK **b :** the economic factors on which in Marxist theory all legal, social, and political relations are formed **4 :** the lower part of a heraldic field **5 a :** the starting point or line for an action or undertaking **b :** a line in a survey which serves as the origin for computations **c :** a center of operations; *specif* **:** the locality or the installations on which a military force relies for supplies or from which it initiates operations **d** (1) **:** a number (as 5 in $5^{6.44}$ or 5^7) that is raised to a power; *esp* **:** the number that when raised to a power equal to the logarithm of a number yields the number itself ⟨the logarithm of 100 to the ~ 10 is 2 since $10^2 = 100$⟩ (2) **:** a number equal to the number of units in a given digit's place that for a given system of writing numbers is required to give the numeral 1 in the next higher place ⟨the decimal system uses a ~ of 10⟩; *also* **:** such a system of writing numbers using an indicated base ⟨convert from ~ 10 to ~ 2⟩ **e :** ROOT 6 **6 a :** the starting place or goal in various games **b :** any one of the four stations at the corners of a baseball infield **c :** a point to be considered ⟨his opening remarks touched every ~⟩ **7 :** any of various typically water-soluble and bitter tasting compounds capable of reacting with an acid to form a salt that are molecules or ions able to take up a proton from an acid or substances able to give up an unshared pair of electrons to an acid **8 :** a number that is multiplied by a rate or of which a percentage or fraction is calculated ⟨to find the interest on $90 at 10% multiply the ~ 90 by .10⟩ **9 :** a price level at which a security previously actively declining in price resists further price decline **10 :** the part of a transformational grammar that consists of rules and a lexicon and generates the deep structures of a language — **based** \ˈbāst\ *adj* — **base·less** \ˈbā-sləs\ *adj* — **off base 1 :** WRONG, MISTAKEN **2 :** UNAWARES

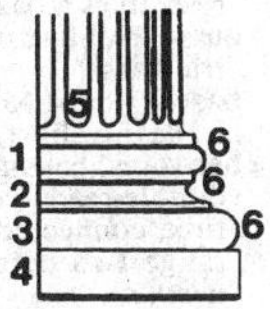

base of column: *1* upper torus, *2* scotia, *3* lower torus, *4* plinth, *5* shaft, *6* fillets

[2]**base** *adj* (15c) **:** constituting or serving as a base ⟨are now setting up a string of ~ camps —*Time*⟩

[3]**base** *vt* **based; bas·ing** (1587) **1 :** to make, form, or serve as a base for **2 :** to find a base or basis for — usu. used with *on* or *upon*

[4]**base** *adj* [ME *bas,* fr. MF, fr. ML *bassus* short, low] (14c) **1** *archaic* **:** of little height **2** *obs* **:** low in place or position **3** *obs* **:** BASS **4** *archaic* **:** BASEBORN **5 a :** resembling a villein **:** SERVILE ⟨a ~ tenant⟩ **b :** held by villenage ⟨~ tenure⟩ **6 a :** being of comparatively low value and having relatively inferior properties (as lack of resistance to corrosion) ⟨a ~ metal such as iron⟩ — compare NOBLE **b :** containing a larger than usual proportion of base metals ⟨~ silver denarii⟩ **7 a :** lacking or indicating the lack of higher qualities of mind or spirit **:** IGNOBLE ⟨a ~ betrayal⟩ **b :** lacking higher values **:** DEGRADING ⟨a drab ~ way of life⟩ **8 :** of relatively little value — **base·ly** *adv* — **base·ness** *n*

syn BASE, LOW, VILE mean deserving of contempt because of the absence of higher values. BASE stresses the ignoble and may suggest cruelty, treachery, greed, or grossness ⟨*base* self-centered indulgence and selfish ambition —W. R. Inge⟩ LOW may connote crafty cunning, vulgarity, or immorality and regularly implies an outraging of one's sense of decency or propriety ⟨refused to listen to such *low* talk⟩ VILE, the strongest of these words, tends to suggest disgusting depravity or filth ⟨a *vile* remark⟩ ⟨matricide, the *vilest* of crimes⟩

base angle *n* (1925) **:** either of the angles of a triangle that have one side in common with the base

base·ball \ˈbās-ˌbȯl\ *n, often attrib* (1815) **:** a game played with a bat and ball between two teams of nine players each on a large field having four bases that mark the course a runner must take to score; *also* **:** the ball used in this game

base·board \-ˌbō(ə)rd, -ˌbȯ(ə)rd\ *n* (1853) **:** a board situated at or forming the base of something; *specif* **:** a molding covering the joint of a wall and the adjoining floor

base·born \-ˈbȯ(ə)rn\ *adj* (1591) **1 :** MEAN, IGNOBLE **2 a :** of humble birth **b :** of illegitimate birth

base burner *n* (1874) **:** a stove in which the fuel is fed from a hopper as the lower layer is consumed

base component *n* (1965) **:** BASE 10

base exchange *n* (1956) **:** a post exchange at a naval or air force base

base hit *n* (1874) **:** a hit in baseball that enables the batter to reach base safely without benefit of an error or fielder's choice

base·lev·el \ˈbā-ˌslev-əl\ *n* (1875) **:** the level below which a land surface cannot be reduced by running water

base·line \ˈbā-ˌslīn\ *n* (1750) **1 :** a line serving as a basis; *esp* **:** one of known measure or position used (as in surveying or navigation) to calculate or locate something **2 :** the area within which a baseball player must keep when running between bases **3 :** the back line at each end of a court in various games (as tennis) **4 :** a set of critical observations or data used for comparison or a control

base·ment \ˈbā-smənt\ *n* [prob. fr. [1]*base*] (1730) **1 :** the part of a building that is wholly or partly below ground level **2 :** the ground floor facade or interior in Renaissance architecture **3 :** the lowest or fundamental part of something; *specif* **:** the rocks underlying stratified rocks **4** *chiefly NewEng* **:** TOILET, WASHROOM — **base·ment·less** \-ləs\ *adj*

basement membrane *n* (1847) **:** a usu. single-layered connective-tissue membrane underlying the epithelial cells of many organs

ba·sen·ji \bə-ˈsen-jē, -ˈzen-\ *n* [of Bantu origin; akin to Lingala *basenji,* pl. of *mosenji* native] (1933) **:** any of an African breed of small compact curly-tailed chestnut-brown dogs that do not bark

base on balls (ca. 1891) **:** an advance to first base awarded a baseball player who during his turn at bat takes four pitches that are balls

base pair *n* (1962) **:** one of the pairs of chemical bases composed of a purine on one strand of DNA joined by hydrogen bonds to a pyrimidine on the other that hold together the two complementary strands much like the rungs of a ladder and include adenine linked to thymine or sometimes to uracil and guanine linked to cytosine

base path *n* (1935) **:** the area between the bases of a baseball field used by a base runner

base pay *n* (1920) **:** a rate or amount of pay for a standard work period, job, or position exclusive of additional payments or allowances

base runner *n* (1867) **:** a baseball player of the team at bat who is on base or is attempting to reach a base — **base-run·ning** *n*

bases *pl of* BASE *or of* BASIS

[1]**bash** \ˈbash\ *vb* [origin unknown] *vt* (1750) **1 :** to strike violently **:** HIT; *also* **:** to injure or damage by striking **:** SMASH — often used with *in* **2 :** to attack physically or verbally ~ *vi* **:** CRASH — **bash·er** *n*

[2]**bash** *n* (1805) **1 :** a forceful blow **2 :** a festive social gathering **:** PARTY **3 :** TRY, ATTEMPT ⟨have a ~ at it⟩

ba·shaw \bə-ˈshȯ\ *var of* PASHA

bash·ful \ˈbash-fəl\ *adj* [obs. *bash* (to be abashed)] (1548) **1 :** socially shy or timid **:** DIFFIDENT, SELF-CONSCIOUS ⟨an awkward and ~ adolescent⟩ **2 :** resulting from or typical of a bashful nature ⟨a ~ smile⟩ ***syn*** see SHY — **bash·ful·ly** \-fə-lē\ *adv* — **bash·ful·ness** \-fəl-nəs\ *n*

[1]**ba·sic** \ˈbā-sik, -zik\ *adj* (1842) **1 :** of, relating to, or forming the base or essence **:** FUNDAMENTAL **2 :** constituting or serving as the basis or starting point **3 a :** of, relating to, containing, or having the character of a chemical base **b :** having an alkaline reaction **4** *of rocks* **:** containing relatively little silica **5 :** of, relating to, or made by a basic process — **ba·si·cal·ly** \-si-k(ə-)lē, -zi-\ *adv* — **ba·sic·i·ty** \bā-ˈsis-ət-ē\ *n*

[2]**basic** *n* (1926) **1 :** something that is basic **:** FUNDAMENTAL ⟨get back to ~*s*⟩ **2 :** BASIC TRAINING

BA·SIC \ˈbā-sik, -zik\ *n* [*B*eginner's *A*ll-purpose *S*ymbolic *I*nstruction *C*ode] (1964) **:** a simplified language for programming and interacting with a computer

basic process *n* (1883) **:** a process of making steel carried on in a furnace lined with basic material and under a slag that is dominantly basic

basic slag *n* (1888) **:** a slag low in silica and high in base-forming oxides that is used in the basic process of steelmaking and that is then useful as a fertilizer

basic training *n* (1943) **:** the initial period of training of a military recruit

ba·sid·io·my·cete \bə-ˌsid-ē-ō-ˈmī-ˌsēt, -ˌmī-ˈsēt\ *n* [deriv. of NL *basidium* + Gk *mykēt-, mykēs* fungus — more at MYC-] (ca. 1899) **:** any of a large class (Basidiomycetes) of higher fungi having septate hyphae, bearing spores on a basidium, and including rusts, smuts, mushrooms, and puffballs — **ba·sid·io·my·ce·tous** \-ē-ō-ˌmī-ˈsēt-əs\ *adj*

ba·sid·io·spore \bə-ˈsid-ē-ə-ˌspō(ə)r, -ˌspȯ(ə)r\ *n* [NL *basidium* + E *-o-* + *spore*] (1859) **:** a spore produced by a basidium

ba·sid·i·um \bə-ˈsid-ē-əm\ *n, pl* **-ia** \-ē-ə\ [NL, fr. L *basis*] (1859) **:** a structure on a basidiomycete in which nuclear fusion occurs followed by meiosis and on which usu. four basidiospores are borne

ba·si·fy \ˈbā-sə-ˌfī\ *vt* **-fied; -fy·ing** (ca. 1847) **:** to convert into a base or make alkaline — **ba·si·fi·ca·tion** \ˌbā-sə-fə-ˈkā-shən\ *n*

ba·sil \ˈbaz-əl, ˈbāz-, ˈbas-, ˈbās-\ *n* [MF *basile,* fr. LL *basilicum,* fr. Gk *basilikon,* fr. neut. of *basilikos*] (15c) **:** any of several plants of the mint family: as **a :** SWEET BASIL **b :** BUSH BASIL

bas·i·lar \ˈbaz-(ə-)lər, ˈbas- *also* ˈbāz- *or* ˈbās-\ *adj* [irreg. fr. *basis*] (1541) **:** of, relating to, or situated at the base

basilar membrane *n* (1867) **:** a membrane extending from the bony shelf of the cochlea to the outer wall and supporting the organ of Corti

Ba·sil·i·an \bə-ˈzil-ē-ən, -ˈsil-\ *n* (1780) **:** a member of the monastic order founded by St. Basil in the 4th century in Cappadocia — **Basilian** *adj*

ba·sil·i·ca \bə-ˈsil-i-kə, -ˈzil-\ *n* [L, fr. Gk *basilikē,* fr. fem. of *basilikos* royal, fr. *basileus* king] (1540) **1 :** an oblong building ending in a semicircular apse used in ancient Rome esp. for a court of justice and place of public assembly **2 :** an early Christian church building consisting of nave and aisles with clerestory and a large high transept from which an apse projects **3 :** a Roman Catholic church given ceremonial privileges — **ba·sil·i·can** \-kən\ *adj*

bas·i·lisk \ˈbas-ə-ˌlisk, ˈbaz-\ *n* [ME, fr. L *basiliscus,* fr. Gk *basiliskos,* fr. dim. of *basileus*] (14c) **1 :** a legendary reptile with fatal breath and glance **2 :** any of several crested tropical American lizards (genus *Basiliscus*) related to the iguanas and noted for their ability to run on their hind legs — **basilisk** *adj*

ba·sin \ˈbās-ᵊn\ *n* [ME, fr. OF *bacin,* fr. LL *bacchinon*] (13c) **1 a :** an open usu. circular vessel with sloping or curving sides used typically for holding water for washing **b :** the quantity contained in a basin **2 a :** a dock built in a tidal river or harbor **b :** an enclosed or partly enclosed water area **3 a :** a large or small depression in the surface of the land or in the ocean floor **b :** the entire tract of country drained by a river and its tributaries **c :** a great depression in the surface of the lithosphere occupied by an ocean **4 :** a broad area of the earth beneath which the strata dip usu. from the sides toward the center — **ba·sin·al** \-ᵊn-əl\ *adj* — **ba·sined** \-ᵊnd\ *adj*

bas·i·net \ˌbas-ə-ˈnet\ *n* [ME *bacinet,* fr. MF, dim. of OF *bacin*] (14c) **:** a light often pointed steel helmet

ba·sip·e·tal \bā-ˈsip-ət-ᵊl, -ˈzip-\ *adj* [L *basis* + *petere* to go toward — more at FEATHER] (1869) **:** proceeding from the apex toward the base or from above downward — **ba·sip·e·tal·ly** \-ᵊl-ē\ *adv*

\ə\ abut \ᵊ\ kitten, F table \ər\ further \a\ ash \ā\ ace \ä\ cot, cart \au̇\ out \ch\ chin \e\ bet \ē\ easy \g\ go \i\ hit \ī\ ice \j\ job \ŋ\ sing \ō\ go \ȯ\ law \ȯi\ boy \th\ thin \t͟h\ the \ü\ loot \u̇\ foot \y\ yet \zh\ vision \ȧ, k͟, ⁿ, œ, œ̄, ue, ue̅, ʸ\ see Guide to Pronunciation

ba·sis \'bā-səs\ *n, pl* **ba·ses** \-ˌsēz\ [L — more at BASE] (1571) **1 :** the bottom of something considered as its foundation **2 :** the principal component of something **3 a :** something on which something else is established or based **b :** an underlying condition or state of affairs ⟨hired on a trial ~⟩ **4 :** the basic principle **5 :** a set of linearly independent vectors in a vector space such that any vector in the vector space can be expressed as a linear combination of them with appropriately chosen coefficients

basis point *n* (1967) **:** one hundredth of one percent in the yield of an investment

bask \'bask\ *vb* [ME *basken,* perh. fr. ON *bathask,* refl. of *batha* to bathe; akin to OE *bæth* bath] *vi* (14c) **1 :** to lie in or expose oneself to a pleasant warmth or atmosphere **2 :** to take pleasure or derive enjoyment ~ *vt, obs* **:** to warm by continued exposure to heat

bas·ket \'bas-kət\ *n* [ME, prob. fr. (assumed) ONF *baskot;* akin to OF *baschoue* wooden vessel; both fr. L *bascauda* dishpan, of Celt origin; akin to MIr *basc* necklace — more at FASCIA] (13c) **1 a :** a receptacle made of interwoven material (as osiers) **b :** any of various lightweight usu. wood containers **c :** the quantity contained in a basket **2 :** something that resembles a basket esp. in shape or use **3 a :** a net open at the bottom and suspended from a metal ring that constitutes the goal in basketball **b :** a field goal in basketball **4 :** a ring around the lower end of a ski pole that keeps the pole from sinking too deep in snow — **bas·ket·ful** \-ˌfu̇l\ *n* — **bas·ket·like** \-ˌlīk\ *adj*

bas·ket·ball \-ˌbȯl\ *n, often attrib* (1892) **:** a usu. indoor court game between two teams of usu. five players each who score by tossing an inflated ball through a raised goal; *also* **:** the ball used in this game

basket case *n* (1919) **1 :** one who has all four limbs amputated **2 :** one that is totally worn-out, incapacitated, or inoperative

basket hilt *n* (1663) **:** a hilt with a basket-shaped guard to protect the hand — **bas·ket–hilt·ed** \ˌbas-kət-'hil-təd\ *adj*

Basket Maker *n* (1897) **1 :** any of three stages of an ancient culture of the plateau area of southwestern U.S. that preceded and formed one cultural development with the Pueblo **2 :** a member of the people who produced the Basket Maker culture

basket–of–gold *n* (1930) **:** a European perennial herb (*Alyssum saxatile*) widely cultivated for its grayish foliage and yellow flowers

bas·ket·ry \'bas-kə-trē\ *n, pl* **-ries** (1851) **1 :** the art or craft of making baskets or objects woven like baskets **2 :** objects produced by basketry

basket star *n* (1923) **:** an echinoderm (order Euryalida) resembling a starfish with slender complexly branched interlacing arms

basket weave *n* (ca. 1915) **:** a textile weave resembling the checkered pattern of a plaited basket

bas·ket·work \'bas-kət-ˌwərk\ *n* (1769) **:** BASKETRY 2

bask·ing shark \ˌbas-kiŋ-\ *n* (1769) **:** a large plankton-feeding shark (*Cetorhinus maximus*) that has an oil-rich liver and sometimes attains a length of 40 feet

bas mitz·vah \bä-'smits-və\ *n, often cap B&M* [Heb *bath miṣwāh,* lit., daughter of the (divine) law] (1952) **1 :** a Jewish girl who at about 13 years of age assumes religious responsibilities **2 :** the initiatory ceremony recognizing a girl as a bas mitzvah

ba·so·phil \'bā-sə-ˌfil, -zə-\ *or* **ba·so·phile** \-ˌfīl\ *n* (1890) **:** a basophilic substance or structure; *esp* **:** a white blood cell with basophilic granules

ba·so·phil·ia \ˌbā-sə-'fil-ē-ə, -zə-\ *n* [NL] (1905) **1 :** tendency to stain with basic dyes **2 :** an abnormal condition in which some tissue element has increased basophilia

ba·so·phil·ic \-'fil-ik\ *adj* [ISV *base* + *-o-* + *-philic*] (1894) **:** staining readily with basic stains

Basque \'bask\ *n* [F, fr. L *Vasco*] (1835) **1 :** one of a people of obscure origin inhabiting the western Pyrenees on the Bay of Biscay **2 :** the language of the Basques of unknown relationship **3** *not cap* **:** a tight-fitting bodice for women — **Basque** *adj*

bas–re·lief \ˌbä-ri-'lēf, 'bä-ri-ˌ\ *n* [F, fr. *bas* low + *relief* raised work] (1667) **1 :** sculptural relief in which the projection from the surrounding surface is slight and no part of the modeled form is undercut **2 :** sculpture executed in bas-relief

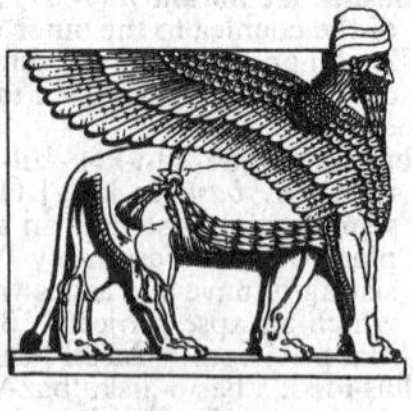
bas-relief

¹bass \'bas\ *n, pl* **bass** *or* **bass·es** [ME *base,* alter. of OE *bærs;* akin to OHG *bersich* perch] (bef. 12c) **:** any of numerous edible spiny-finned fishes (esp. families Centrarchidae and Serranidae)

²bass \'bās\ *adj* [ME *bas* base] (15c) **1 :** deep or grave in tone **2 a :** of low pitch **b :** relating to or having the range or part of a bass

³bass \'bās\ *n* (15c) **1 :** a deep or grave tone **:** a low-pitched sound **2 a :** the lowest voice part in a 4-part chorus **b :** the lower half of the whole vocal or instrumental tonal range — compare TREBLE **c :** the lowest adult male singing voice; *also* **:** a person having this voice **d :** a member of a family of instruments having the lowest range; *esp* **:** DOUBLE BASS

⁴bass \'bas\ *n* [alter. of *bast*] (1691) **1 :** a coarse tough fiber from palms **2 :** BASSWOOD 1

bass clef *n* (1903) **1 :** a clef placing the F below middle C on the fourth line of the staff **2 :** the bass staff

bass drum *n* (1804) **:** a large drum having two heads and giving a booming sound of low indefinite pitch — see DRUM illustration

bas·set hound \'bas-ət-\ *n* [F *basset,* fr. MF, fr. *basset* short, fr. *bas* low — more at BASE] (1883) **:** any of an old French breed of short-legged slow-moving hunting dogs with very long ears and crooked front legs — called also *basset*

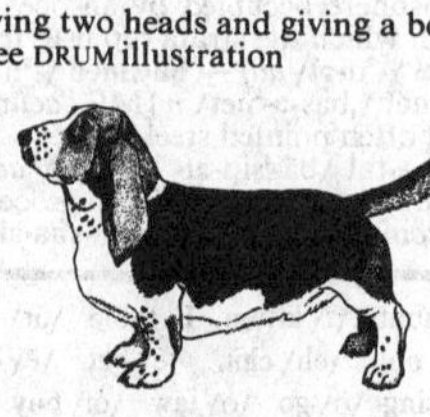
basset hound

bass fiddle *n* (1951) **:** DOUBLE BASS

bass horn *n* (1852) **:** an obsolete wind instrument shaped like a bassoon but with a cup-shaped mouthpiece

bas·si·net \ˌbas-ə-'net\ *n* [prob. modif. of F *barcelonnette,* dim. of *berceau* cradle] (1854) **1 :** a baby's basketlike bed (as of wickerwork or plastic) often with a hood over one end **2 :** a perambulator that resembles a bassinet

bass·ist \'bā-səst\ *n* (ca. 1909) **:** a person who plays an acoustic or electric bass

bas·so \'bas-(ˌ)ō, 'bäs-\ *n, pl* **bassos** *or* **bas·si** \'bäs-ˌē\ [It, fr. ML *bassus,* fr. *bassus* short, low] (1817) **:** a bass singer; *esp* **:** an operatic bass

bas·soon \bə-'sün, ba-\ *n* [F *basson,* fr. It *bassone,* fr. *basso*] (ca. 1727) **:** a double-reed woodwind instrument having a long U-shaped conical tube connected to the mouthpiece by a thin metal tube and a usual range two octaves lower than that of the oboe — **bas·soon·ist** \-'sü-nəst\ *n*

bas·so pro·fun·do \ˌbas(ˌ)ō-prə-'fən-(ˌ)dō, ˌbäs-, -'fün-\ *n, pl* **basso profundos** [It, lit., deep bass] (1860) **:** a deep heavy bass voice with an exceptionally low range; *also* **:** a person having this voice

bas·so–re·lie·vo *also* **bas·so–ri·lie·vo** \ˌbas-(ˌ)ō-ri-'lē-(ˌ)vō, ˌbäs-(ˌ)ō-rēl-'yā-(ˌ)vō\ *n* [It *bassorilievo,* fr. *basso* low + *rilievo* relief] (1666) **:** BAS-RELIEF

bass viol *n* (1590) **1 :** VIOLA DA GAMBA **2 :** DOUBLE BASS

bass·wood \'bas-ˌwu̇d\ *n* (1670) **1 :** any of several New World lindens; *esp* **:** LINDEN 1b **2 :** the straight-grained white wood of a basswood

bast \'bast\ *n* [ME, fr. OE *bæst;* akin to OHG & ON *bast*] (bef. 12c) **1 :** PHLOEM **2 :** BAST FIBER

¹bas·tard \'bas-tərd\ *n* [ME, fr. OF] (13c) **1 :** an illegitimate child **2 :** something that is spurious, irregular, inferior, or of questionable origin **3 a :** an offensive or disagreeable person — used as a generalized term of abuse **b :** MAN, FELLOW — **bas·tard·ly** *adj*

²bastard *adj* (13c) **1 :** ILLEGITIMATE **2 :** of inferior breed or stock **:** MONGREL **3 :** of abnormal shape or irregular size **4 :** of a kind similar to but inferior to or less typical than some standard ⟨~ measles⟩ **5 :** lacking genuineness or authority **:** FALSE

bas·tard·ize \'bas-tər-ˌdīz\ *vt* **-ized; -iz·ing** (ca. 1611) **1 :** to declare or prove to be a bastard **2 :** to reduce from a higher to a lower state or condition **:** DEBASE — **bas·tard·iza·tion** \ˌbas-tərd-ə-'zā-shən\ *n*

bastard wing *n* (1772) **:** ALULA

bas·tardy \'bas-tərd-ē\ *n, pl* **-tard·ies** (15c) **1 :** the quality or state of being a bastard **:** ILLEGITIMACY **2 :** the begetting of an illegitimate child

¹baste \'bāst\ *vt* **bast·ed; bast·ing** [ME *basten,* fr. MF *bastir,* of Gmc origin; akin to OHG *besten* to patch, OE *bæst* bast] (15c) **:** to sew with long loose stitches in order to hold something in place temporarily — **bas·ter** *n*

²baste *vt* **bast·ed; bast·ing** [origin unknown] (15c) **:** to moisten (as meat) at intervals with a liquid (as melted butter, fat, or pan drippings) esp. during cooking — **bast·er** *n*

³baste *vt* **bast·ed; bast·ing** [prob. fr. ON *beysta;* akin to OE *bēatan* to beat] (1533) **1 :** to beat severely or soundly **:** THRASH **2 :** to scold vigorously **:** BERATE

bast fiber *n* (ca. 1885) **:** a strong woody fiber obtained chiefly from the phloem of plants and used esp. in cordage, matting, and fabrics

bas·tille \ba-'stē(ə)l\ *n* [F *bastille,* fr. the *Bastille,* fortress in Paris used as a prison] (1790) **:** PRISON, JAIL

Bastille Day *n* (1920) **:** July 14 observed in France as a national holiday in commemoration of the fall of the Bastille in 1789

¹bas·ti·na·do \ˌbas-tə-'nād-(ˌ)ō, -'näd-\ *or* **bas·ti·nade** \ˌbas-tə-'nād, -'näd\ *n, pl* **-na·does** *or* **-nades** [Sp *bastonada,* fr. *bastón* stick, fr. LL *bastum*] (1577) **1 :** a blow with a stick or cudgel **2 a :** a beating esp. with a stick **b :** a punishment consisting of beating the soles of the feet with a stick **3 :** STICK, CUDGEL

²bastinado *vt* **-doed; -do·ing** (1599) **:** to subject to repeated blows

¹bast·ing \'bā-stiŋ\ *n* (15c) **1 :** the action of a sewer who bastes **2 a :** the thread used in basting **b :** the stitching made by basting

²basting *n* (1530) **1 :** the action of one that bastes food **2 :** the liquid used in basting

³basting *n* (1590) **:** a severe beating

bas·tion \'bas-chən\ *n* [MF, fr. *bastille* fortress, modif. of OProv *bastida,* fr. *bastir* to build, of Gmc origin; akin to OHG *besten* to patch] (1562) **1 :** a projecting part of a fortification **2 :** a fortified area or position **3 :** something that is considered a stronghold **:** BULWARK — **bas·tioned** \-chənd\ *adj*

Ba·su·to \bə-'süt-(ˌ)ō\ *n, pl* **Basuto** *or* **Basutos** (1835) **:** one of the Bantu-speaking people of Lesotho

¹bat \'bat\ *n* [ME, fr. OE *batt,* prob. of Celt origin; akin to Gaulish *andabata,* a gladiator — more at BATTLE] (bef. 12c) **1 :** a stout solid stick **:** CLUB **2 :** a sharp blow **:** STROKE **3 a :** a wooden implement used for hitting the ball in various games **b :** a paddle used in various games (as table tennis) **c :** the short whip used by a jockey **4 a :** BATSMAN **b :** a turn at batting — usu. used in the phrase *at bat* **5 :** BATT **6** *Brit* **:** rate of speed **:** GAIT **7 :** BINGE — **off one's own bat :** through one's own efforts — **off the bat :** without delay **:** IMMEDIATELY

²bat *vb* **bat·ted; bat·ting** *vt* (14c) **1 :** to strike or hit with or as if with a bat **2 a :** to advance (a base runner) by batting **b :** to have a batting average of **3 :** to discuss at length **:** consider in detail ~ *vi* **1 a :** to strike or hit a ball with a bat **b :** to take one's turn at bat **2 :** to wander aimlessly

³bat *n* [alter. of ME *bakke,* prob. of Scand origin; akin to OSw *natt-bakka* bat] (14c) **:** any of an order (Chiroptera) of nocturnal placental flying mammals with forelimbs modified to form wings

⁴bat *vt* **bat·ted; bat·ting** [prob. alter of ²*bate*] (1838) **:** to wink esp. in surprise or emotion ⟨never *batted* an eye⟩

bat·boy \'bat-ˌbȯi\ *n* (1925) **:** a boy employed to look after the equipment (as bats) of a baseball team

¹batch \'bach\ *n* [ME *bache;* akin to OE *bacan* to bake] (15c) **1 :** the quantity baked at one time **:** BAKING **2 a :** the quantity of material prepared or required for one operation; *specif* **:** a mixture of raw materials ready for fusion into glass **b :** the quantity produced at one operation **c :** a group of jobs to be run on a computer at one time with the same program ⟨~ processing⟩ **3 :** a group of persons or things **:** LOT

²batch *vt* (ca. 1804) **:** to bring together or process as a batch — **batch·er** *n*

³batch *var of* BACH

[1]bate \ˈbāt\ *vb* **bat·ed; bat·ing** [ME *baten,* short for *abaten* to abate] *vt* (14c) **1 :** to reduce the force or intensity of **:** RESTRAIN ⟨with *bated* breath⟩ **2 :** to take away **:** DEDUCT **3** *archaic* **:** to lower esp. in amount or estimation **4** *archaic* **:** BLUNT **~** *vi, obs* **:** DIMINISH, DECREASE

[2]bate *vi* **bat·ed; bat·ing** [ME *baten,* fr. MF *batre* to beat — more at DEBATE] *of a falcon* (14c) **:** to beat the wings impatiently

ba·teau \ba-ˈtō\ *n, pl* **ba·teaux** \-ˈtō(z)\ [CanF, fr. F, fr. OF *batel,* fr. OE *bāt* boat — more at BOAT] (1711) **:** any of various small craft; *esp* **:** a flat-bottomed boat with raked bow and stern and flaring sides

Bates·ian \ˌbāt-sē-ən\ *adj* [Henry Walter *Bates* †1892 Eng. naturalist] (1896) **:** characterized by or being mimicry involving resemblance of an innocuous species to another that is protected from predators by repellent qualities (as unpalatability) ⟨~ mimic⟩

bat·fish \ˈbat-ˌfish\ *n* (ca. 1889) **:** any of several fishes with winglike processes; *esp* **:** any of a family (Ogcocephalidae) of flattened pediculate fishes (as a common West Indian form *Ogcocephalus vespertillo*)

bat·fowl \-ˌfau̇l\ *vi* (15c) **:** to catch birds at night by blinding them with a light and knocking them down with a stick or netting them

[1]bath \ˈbath, ˈbȧth\ *n, pl* **baths** \ˈbat͟hz, ˈbaths, ˈbȧt͟hz, ˈbȧths\ [ME, fr. OE *bæth;* akin to OHG *bad* bath, OE *bacan* to bake] (bef. 12c) **1 :** a washing or soaking (as in water or steam) of all or part of the body **2 a :** water used for bathing **b** (1) **:** a contained liquid for a special purpose (2) **:** a receptacle holding the liquid **c** (1) **:** a medium for regulating the temperature of something placed in or on it (2) **:** a vessel containing this medium **3 a :** BATHROOM **b :** a building containing an apartment or a series of rooms designed for bathing **c :** SPA — usu. used in pl. **4 a :** the quality or state of being covered with a liquid **b :** FLOOD 3 **5 :** BATHTUB

[2]bath *vt, Brit* (15c) **:** to give a bath to **~** *vi, Brit* **:** to take a bath

[3]bath *n* [Heb] (14c) **:** an ancient Hebrew liquid measure corresponding to the ephah of dry measure

bath- *or* **batho-** *comb form* [ISV, fr. Gk *bathos,* fr. *bathys* deep — more at BATHY-] **:** depth ⟨*batho*meter⟩

bath chair \ˈbath-, ˈbȧth-\ *n, often cap B* [*Bath,* England] (1823) **:** a hooded and sometimes glassed wheeled chair used esp. by invalids; *broadly* **:** WHEELCHAIR

[1]bathe \ˈbāt͟h\ *vb* **bathed; bath·ing** [ME *bathen,* fr. OE *bathian;* akin to OE *bæth* bath] *vt* (bef. 12c) **1 :** to wash in a liquid (as water) **2 :** MOISTEN, WET **3 :** to apply water or a liquid medicament to **4 :** to flow along the edge of **:** LAVE **5 :** to suffuse with or as if with light **~** *vi* **1 :** to take a bath **2 :** to go swimming **3 :** to become immersed or absorbed — **bath·er** \ˈbā-t͟hər\ *n*

[2]bathe *n* (1831) **1** *Brit* **:** [1]BATH 1 **2** *Brit* **:** SWIM, DIP

ba·thet·ic \bə-ˈthet-ik\ *adj* [*bathos* + *-etic* (as in *pathetic*)] (ca. 1864) **:** characterized by bathos — **ba·thet·i·cal·ly** \-i-k(ə-)lē\ *adv*

bath·house \ˈbath-ˌhau̇s, ˈbȧth-\ *n* (14c) **1 :** a building equipped for bathing **2 :** a building containing dressing rooms for bathers

bathing beauty *n* (1920) **:** a woman in a bathing suit who is a contestant in a beauty contest

bathing suit *n* (1873) **:** SWIMSUIT

bath mat *n* (1895) **:** a usu. washable mat used in a bathroom

batho·lith \ˈbath-ə-ˌlith\ *n* [ISV] (1903) **:** a great mass of intruded igneous rock that for the most part stopped in its rise a considerable distance below the surface — **batho·lith·ic** \ˌbath-ə-ˈlith-ik\ *adj*

ba·thom·e·ter \bə-ˈthäm-ət-ər\ *n* (1875) **:** an instrument for measuring depths in water

ba·thos \ˈbā-ˌthäs\ *n* [Gk, lit., depth] (1727) **1 a :** the sudden appearance of the commonplace in otherwise elevated matter or style **b :** ANTICLIMAX **2 :** exceptional commonplaceness **:** TRITENESS **3 :** insincere or overdone pathos **:** SENTIMENTALISM

bath·robe \ˈbath-ˌrōb, ˈbȧth-\ *n* (1902) **:** a loose usu. absorbent robe worn before and after bathing or as a dressing gown

bath·room \-ˌrüm, -ˌru̇m\ *n* (1780) **1 :** a room containing a bathtub or shower and usu. a washbowl and toilet **2 :** LAVATORY 2

bath salts *n pl* (1907) **:** a usu. colored crystalline compound for perfuming and softening bathwater

bath·tub \-ˌtəb\ *n* (1869) **:** a usu. fixed tub for bathing

bathtub gin *n* (1930) **:** a homemade spirit concocted from raw alcohol, water, essences, and essential oils

bath·wa·ter \ˈbath-ˌwȯt-ər, ˈbȧth-, -ˌwät-ər\ *n* (1912) **:** water for a bath

bathy- *comb form* [ISV, fr. Gk, fr. *bathys* deep; akin to Skt *gāhate* he dives into] **1 :** deep **:** depth ⟨*bathy*al⟩ **2 :** deep-sea ⟨*bathy*sphere⟩

bathy·al \ˈbath-ē-əl\ *adj* (1921) **:** of or relating to the ocean depths or floor usu. from 600 to 6000 feet (180 to 1800 meters)

ba·thym·e·try \bə-ˈthim-ə-trē\ *n, pl* **-tries** [ISV] (ca. 1864) **:** the measurement of depths of water in oceans, seas, and lakes; *also* **:** the information derived from such measurements — **bathy·met·ric** \ˌbath-i-ˈme-trik\ *also* **bathy·met·ri·cal** \-tri-kəl\ *adj* — **bathy·met·ri·cal·ly** \-tri-k(ə-)lē\ *adv*

bathy·pe·lag·ic \ˌbath-i-pə-ˈlaj-ik\ *adj* [*bathy-* + *pelagic*] (ca. 1909) **:** of, relating to, or living in the ocean depths esp. between 2000 and 12,000 feet (600 and 3600 meters)

bathy·scaphe \ˈbath-i-ˌskaf, -ˌskāf\ *also* **bathy·scaph** \-ˌskaf\ *n* [ISV *bathy-* + Gk *skaphē* light boat] (1947) **:** a navigable submersible ship for deep-sea exploration having a spherical watertight cabin attached to its underside

bathy·sphere \-ˌsfi(ə)r\ *n* (1930) **:** a strongly built steel diving sphere for deep-sea observation

bathy·ther·mo·graph \-ˈthər-mə-ˌgraf\ *n* (1938) **:** an instrument designed to record water temperature as a function of depth

ba·tik \bə-ˈtēk, ˈbat-ik\ *n* [Malay] (1880) **1 a :** an Indonesian method of hand-printing textiles by coating with wax the parts not to be dyed **b :** a design so executed **2 :** a fabric printed by batik

bat·ing \ˈbāt-iŋ\ *prep* (1647) **:** with the exception of **:** EXCEPTING

ba·tiste \bə-ˈtēst, ba-\ *n* [F] (1697) **:** a fine soft sheer fabric of plain weave made of various fibers

bat·man \ˈbat-mən\ *n* [deriv. of Gk *bastazein* to carry] (1755) **:** an orderly of a British military officer

bat mitz·vah \bät-ˈmits-və\ *often cap B&M, var of* BAS MITZVAH

ba·ton \bə-ˈtän, ba-, -ˈtō^{n} *also* ˈbat-^{ə}n\ *n* [F *bâton,* fr. OF *baston,* fr. LL *bastum* stick] (1520) **1 :** CUDGEL, TRUNCHEON **2 :** a staff borne as a symbol of office **3 :** a narrow heraldic bend **4 :** a slender rod with which a leader directs a band or orchestra **5 :** a hollow cylinder carried by each member of a relay team and passed to the succeeding runner **6 :** a hollow metal rod with a weighted bulb at one or both ends that is flourished or twirled by a drum major or drum majorette

bat out *vt* (1941) **:** to compose esp. in a casual, careless, or hurried manner

ba·tra·chi·an \bə-ˈtrā-kē-ən\ *n* [deriv. of Gk *batrachos* frog] (ca. 1828) **:** FROG, TOAD, SALIENTIAN; *broadly* **:** a vertebrate amphibian — **batrachian** *adj*

bats \ˈbats\ *adj* (1919) **:** BATTY 2

bats·man \ˈbat-smən\ *n* (1756) **:** a batter esp. in cricket

batt \ˈbat\ *n* (1871) **:** BATTING 2; *also* **:** an often square piece of batting

bat·tai·lous \ˈbat-^{ə}l-əs\ *adj* [ME *bataillous,* fr. MF *bataillos,* fr. *bataille* battle] *archaic* (14c) **:** ready for battle **:** WARLIKE

bat·ta·lia \bə-ˈtāl-yə, -ˈtal-\ *n* [It *battaglia*] (1569) **1** *archaic* **:** order of battle **2** *obs* **:** a large body of men in battle array

bat·tal·ion \bə-ˈtal-yən\ *n* [MF *bataillon,* fr. OIt *battaglione,* aug. of *battaglia* company of soldiers, battle, fr. LL *battalia* combat — more at BATTLE] (1579) **1 :** a considerable body of troops organized to act together **:** ARMY **2 :** a military unit composed of a headquarters and two or more companies, batteries, or similar units **3 :** a large group ⟨a ~ of holiday shoppers⟩

batteau *var of* BATEAU

bat·te·ment \ˌbat-(ə-)ˈmä^{n}\ *n* [F, fr. *battre* to beat (fr. L *battuere*) + *-ment* — more at BATTLE] (1830) **:** a ballet movement in which the foot is extended in any direction usu. followed by a beat against the supporting foot

[1]bat·ten \ˈbat-^{ə}n\ *vb* **bat·tened; bat·ten·ing** \ˈbat-niŋ, -^{ə}n-iŋ\ [prob. fr. ON *batna* to improve; akin to OE *betera* better] *vi* (1591) **1 a :** to grow fat **b :** to feed gluttonously **2 :** to grow prosperous esp. at the expense of another **~** *vt* **:** FATTEN

[2]batten *n* [F *bâton*] (1658) **1 a** *Brit* **:** a piece of lumber used esp. for flooring **b :** a thin narrow strip of lumber used esp. to seal or reinforce a joint **2 :** a strip, bar, or support resembling or used similarly to a batten

[3]batten *vt* **bat·tened; bat·ten·ing** \ˈbat-niŋ, -^{ə}n-iŋ\ (1663) **:** to furnish or fasten with battens — often used with *down*

[1]bat·ter \ˈbat-ər\ *vb* [ME *bateren,* prob. freq. of *batten* to bat, fr. *bat*] *vt* (14c) **1 a :** to beat with successive blows so as to bruise, shatter, or demolish **b :** BOMBARD **2 :** to subject to strong, overwhelming, or repeated attack **3 :** to wear or damage by hard usage or blows ⟨a ~*ed* old hat⟩ **~** *vi* **:** to strike heavily and repeatedly **:** BEAT *syn* see MAIM

[2]batter *n* [ME *bater,* prob. fr. *bateren*] (14c) **1 :** a mixture consisting chiefly of flour, egg, and milk or water and being thin enough to pour or drop from a spoon **2 :** an instance of battering

[3]batter *n* (1743) **:** a receding upward slope of the outer face of a structure

[4]batter *vt* [origin unknown] (ca. 1909) **:** to give a receding upward slope to (as a wall)

[5]batter *n* (1773) **:** one that bats; *esp* **:** the player whose turn it is to bat

bat·te·rie \ˌbat-ə-ˈrē\ *n* [F, lit., beating — more at BATTERY] (1712) **:** a ballet movement consisting of beating together the feet or calves of the legs during a leap

battering ram *n* (1611) **1 :** a military siege engine consisting of a large wooden beam with a head of iron used in ancient times to beat down the walls of a besieged place **2 :** a heavy metal bar with handles used (as by firemen) to batter down doors and walls

bat·tery \ˈbat-ə-rē, ˈba-trē\ *n, pl* **-ter·ies** [MF *batterie,* fr. OF, fr. *battre* to beat, fr. L *battuere* — more at BATTLE] (1531) **1 a :** the act of battering or beating **b :** the unlawful beating or use of force on a person without his consent — compare ASSAULT 2a **2 a :** a grouping of artillery pieces for tactical purposes **b :** the guns of a warship **3 :** an artillery unit in the army equivalent to a company **4 a :** a combination of apparatus for producing a single electrical effect **b :** a group of two or more cells connected together to furnish electric current; *also* **:** a single cell that furnishes electric current ⟨a flashlight ~⟩ **5 a :** a number of similar articles, items, or devices arranged, connected, or used together **:** SET, SERIES ⟨a ~ of tests⟩ **b :** an impressive or imposing group **:** ARRAY **6 :** the position of readiness of a gun for firing **7 :** the pitcher and catcher of a baseball team

bat·ting \ˈbat-iŋ\ *n* (1611) **1 a :** the action of one who bats **b :** the use of or ability with a bat **2 :** layers or sheets of raw cotton or wool or of synthetic fibrous material used for lining quilts or for stuffing or packaging; *also* **:** a blanket of thermal insulation (as fiberglass)

batting average *n* (1867) **1 :** a ratio (as a rate per thousand) of base hits to official times at bat for a baseball player **2 :** a record of achievement or accomplishment

[1]bat·tle \ˈbat-^{ə}l\ *n, often attrib* [ME *batel,* fr. OF *bataille* battle, fortifying tower, battalion, fr. LL *battalia* combat, alter. of *battualia* fencing exercises, fr. L *battuere* to beat, of Celt origin; akin to Gaulish *andabata,* a gladiator; akin to L *fatuus* foolish, Russ *bat* cudgel] (13c) **1 :** a general encounter between armies, ships of war, or airplanes **2 :** a combat between two persons **3** *archaic* **:** BATTALION **4 :** an extended contest, struggle, or controversy

[2]battle *vb* **bat·tled; bat·tling** \ˈbat-liŋ, -^{ə}l-iŋ\ *vi* (14c) **1 :** to engage in battle **:** FIGHT **2 :** to contend with full strength, vigor, craft, or resources **:** STRUGGLE **~** *vt* **1 :** to fight against **2 :** to force (as one's way) by battling — **bat·tler** \-lər, -^{ə}l-ər\ *n*

[3]battle *vt* **bat·tled; bat·tling** [ME *batailen,* fr. MF *bataillier* to fortify, fr. OF, fr. *bataille*] *archaic* (14c) **:** to fortify with battlements

bat·tle–ax \ˈbat-^{ə}l-ˌaks\ *n* (14c) **1 :** a broadax formerly used as a weapon of war **2 :** a quarrelsome domineering woman

battle cruiser *n* (1911) **:** a large heavily armed warship that is lighter, faster, and more maneuverable than a battleship

battle cry *n* (1814) **:** WAR CRY

battle fatigue *n* (1945) **:** COMBAT FATIGUE — **bat·tle–fa·tigued** *adj*

bat·tle·field \'bat-ᵊl-ˌfēld\ *n* (1812) **1** : a place where a battle is fought **2** : an area of conflict
bat·tle·front \-ˌfrənt\ *n* (1914) : the military sector in which actual combat takes place
bat·tle·ground \-ˌgrau̇nd\ *n* (1815) : BATTLEFIELD
battle group *n* (1954) : a military unit normally made up of five companies
bat·tle·ment \'bat-ᵊl-mənt\ *n* [ME *batelment,* fr. MF *bataille*] (14c) : a parapet with open spaces that surmounts a wall and is used for defense or decoration — **bat·tle·ment·ed** \-ˌment-əd\ *adj*

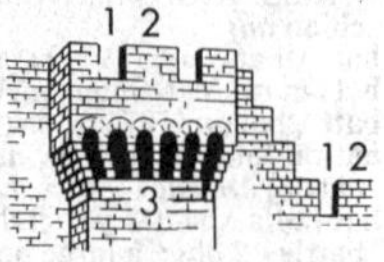

battlement: *1* crenels, *2* merlons, *3* machicolations

battle royal *n, pl* **battles royal** *or* **battle royals** (1672) **1 a** : a fight participated in by more than two combatants; *esp* : one in which the last man in the ring or on his feet is declared the winner **b** : a violent struggle **2** : a heated dispute
bat·tle·ship \'bat-ᵊl-ˌship\ *n* [short for *line-of-battle ship*] (1794) : a warship of the largest and most heavily armed and armored class
bat·tle·wag·on \-ˌwag-ən\ *n* (ca. 1927) : BATTLESHIP
bat·tu \ba-'t(y)ü\ *adj* [F, fr. pp. of *battre* to beat] *of a ballet movement* (1947) : performed with a striking together of the legs
bat·tue \ba-'t(y)ü\ *n* [F, fr. *battre* to beat] (1816) : the beating of woods and bushes to flush game; *also* : a hunt in which this procedure is used
bat·ty \'bat-ē\ *adj* **bat·ti·er; -est** (1590) **1** : of, relating to, or resembling a bat **2** : mentally unstable : CRAZY — **bat·ti·ness** *n*
bau·ble \'bȯ-bəl, 'bäb-əl\ *n* [ME *babel,* fr. MF] (14c) **1** : TRINKET **2** : a fool's scepter **3** : TRIFLE
Bau·cis \'bȯ-səs\ *n* [L, fr. Gk *Baukis*] : the wife of Philemon
baud \'bȯd, *Brit* 'bōd\ *n, pl* **baud** *also* **bauds** [*baud* (telegraphic transmission speed unit), fr. J. M. E. *Baudot* †1903 Fr. inventor] (1931) : a variable unit of data transmission speed sometimes equal to one bit per second
bau·drons \'bȯd-rənz, 'bȯth-\ *n* [ME] *Scot* (15c) : CAT
Bau·haus \'bau̇-ˌhau̇s\ *adj* [G *Bauhaus,* lit., architecture house, school founded by Gropius] (1923) : of, relating to, or influenced by a school of design noted esp. for a program that synthesized technology, craftsmanship, and design aesthetics
baulk *chiefly Brit var of* BALK
Bau·mé \bō-'mā\ *adj* [Antoine *Baumé*] (1844) : being, calibrated in accordance with, or according to either of two arbitrary hydrometer scales for liquids lighter than water or for liquids heavier than water that indicate specific gravity in degrees
baux·ite \'bȯk-ˌsīt, 'bäk-\ *n* [F *bauxite,* fr. Les *Baux,* near Arles, France] (1861) : an impure mixture of earthy hydrous aluminum oxides and hydroxides that commonly contains similar compounds of iron and occas. of silicon, usu. has a concretionary or oolitic structure, and is the principal source of aluminum — **baux·it·ic** \bȯk-'sit-ik, bäk-\ *adj*
Ba·var·i·an \bə-'ver-ē-ən, -'var-\ *n* (1638) **1** : a native or inhabitant of Bavaria **2** : the High German dialect of Bavaria and Austria — **Bavarian** *adj*
baw·bee \'bȯ-(ˌ)bē, bȯ-'\ *n* [prob. fr. Alexander Orrok, laird of Sillebawbe *fl* 1538 Scot. master of the mint] (1542) **1** : any of various Scottish coins of small value **2** : an English halfpenny
baw·cock \'bȯ-ˌkäk\ *n* [F *beau coq,* fr. *beau* fine + *coq* fellow, cock] *archaic* (1599) : a fine fellow
bawd \'bȯd\ *n* [ME *bawde*] (14c) **1** *obs* : PANDER **2 a** : one who keeps a house of prostitution : MADAM **b** : PROSTITUTE
bawd·ry \'bȯ-drē\ *n* [ME *bawderie,* fr. *bawde*] (15c) **1** *obs* : UNCHASTITY **2** : suggestive, coarse, or obscene language
1**bawdy** \'bȯd-ē\ *adj* **bawd·i·er; -est** [*bawd*] (1513) **1** : OBSCENE, LEWD **2** : boisterously or humorously indecent — **bawd·i·ly** \'bȯd-ᵊl-ē\ *adv* — **bawd·i·ness** \'bȯd-ē-nəs\ *n*
2**bawdy** *n* [prob. fr. 1*bawdy*] (1656) : BAWDRY 2
1**bawl** \'bȯl\ *vb* [ME *baulen,* prob. of Scand origin; akin to Icel *baula* to low] *vi* (15c) **1** : to cry out loudly and unrestrainedly : YELL, BELLOW **2** : to cry loudly : WAIL ~ *vt* : to cry out at the top of one's voice — **bawl·er** *n*
2**bawl** *n* (1792) : a loud prolonged cry : OUTCRY
bawl out *vt* (1905) : to reprimand loudly or severely
1**bay** \'bā\ *adj* [ME, fr. MF *bai,* fr. L *badius;* akin to OIr *buide* yellow] (14c) : reddish brown ⟨a ~ mare⟩
2**bay** *n* (15c) **1** : a bay-colored animal; *specif* : a horse with a bay-colored body and black mane, tail, and points — compare 1CHESTNUT 4, 1SORREL 1 **2** : a reddish brown
3**bay** *n* [ME, berry, fr. MF *baie,* fr. L *baca*] (15c) **1 a** : the European laurel (*Laurus nobilis*) **b** : any of several shrubs or trees (as of the genera *Magnolia, Myrica,* and *Gordonia*) resembling the laurel **2 a** : a garland or crown esp. of laurel given as a prize for victory or excellence **b** : HONOR, FAME — usu. used in pl.
4**bay** *n* [ME, fr. MF *baee* opening, fr. OF, fr. fem. of *baé,* pp. of *baer* to gape, yawn — more at ABEYANCE] (14c) **1** : a principal compartment of the walls, roof, or other part of a building or of the whole building **2** : a main division of a structure **3** : BAY WINDOW **4** : SICK BAY **5** : any of various compartments or sections used for a special purpose (as in an airplane, spacecraft, automobile service station, or paved area) ⟨bomb ~⟩ **6** : a support or housing for electronic equipment
5**bay** *vb* [ME *baien, abaien,* fr. OF *abaiier,* of imit. origin] *vi* (14c) **1** : to bark with prolonged tones **2** : to cry out : SHOUT ~ *vt* **1** : to bark at **2** : to bring to bay **3** : to pursue with barking **4** : to utter in deep prolonged tones
6**bay** *n* (14c) **1** : the position of one unable to retreat and forced to face danger ⟨brought his quarry to ~⟩ **2** : the position of one checked ⟨police kept the rioters at ~⟩ **3** : a baying of dogs
7**bay** *n, often attrib* [ME *baye,* fr. MF *baie*] (14c) **1** : an inlet of the sea or other body of water usu. smaller than a gulf **2** : a small body of water set off from the main body **3** : any of various terrestrial formations resembling a bay of the sea
ba·ya·dere \'bī-ə-ˌdi(ə)r, -ˌde(ə)r\ *n* [F *bayadère* Hindu dancing girl] (1856) : a fabric with horizontal stripes in strongly contrasted colors
bay·ber·ry \'bā-ˌber-ē\ *n* (1687) **1 a** : any of several wax myrtles; *esp* : a hardy shrub (*Myrica pensylvanica*) of coastal eastern No. America bearing dense clusters of small globular nuts covered with grayish white wax **b** : the fruit of a bayberry **2** : a West Indian tree (*Pimenta racemosa*) of the myrtle family yielding a yellow aromatic oil
Bayes·ian \'bā-zē-ən, -zhən\ *adj* [Thomas *Bayes* †1761 Eng. mathematician] (1961) : being or relating to a theory (as of decision or statistical inference) in which probabilities are associated with individual events or statements and not merely with sequences of events (as in frequency theories)
bay leaf *n* (15c) : the dried leaf of the European laurel used in cooking
1**bay·o·net** \'bā-ə-nət, -ˌnet, ˌbā-ə-'net\ *n* [F *baïonnette,* fr. *Bayonne,* France] (1672) : a steel blade attached at the muzzle end of a shoulder arm (as a rifle) and used in hand-to-hand combat
2**bayonet** *vb* **-net·ed** *also* **-net·ted; -net·ing** *also* **net·ting** *vt* (1700) **1** : to stab with a bayonet **2** : to compel or drive by or as if by the bayonet ~ *vi* : to use a bayonet
bay·ou \'bī-(ˌ)(y)ō, -(ˌ)(y)ü, -(y)ə\ *n* [LaF, fr. Choctaw *bayuk*] (1763) **1** : a creek, secondary watercourse, or minor river that is tributary to another body of water **2** : any of various usu. marshy or sluggish bodies of water
bay rum *n* (1840) : a fragrant cosmetic and medicinal liquid distilled from the leaves of the West Indian bayberry or usu. prepared from essential oils, alcohol, and water
Bay Stat·er \'bā-ˌstāt-ər\ *n* (1845) : a native or resident of Massachusetts — used as a nickname
bay window *n* (15c) **1** : a window or series of windows forming a bay or recess in a room and projecting outward from the wall **2** : POTBELLY
ba·zaar \bə-'zär\ *n* [Per *bāzār*] (1588) **1** : an oriental market consisting of rows of shops or stalls selling miscellaneous goods **2 a** : a place for the sale of goods **b** : DEPARTMENT STORE **3** : a fair for the sale of articles esp. for charitable purposes
ba·zoo·ka \bə-'zü-kə\ *n* [*bazooka* (a crude musical instrument made of pipes and a funnel)] (1943) : a light portable weapon consisting of an open-breech smoothbore firing tube that launches armor-piercing rockets and is fired from the shoulder
BB \'bē-(ˌ)bē\ *n* (1874) **1** : a shot pellet 0.18 inch in diameter for use in a shotgun cartridge **2** : a shot pellet 0.175 inch in diameter for use in an air gun
B battery *n* (1920) : an electric battery connected in the plate circuit of an electron tube to cause flow of electron current in the tube
BCD \ˌbē-(ˌ)sē-'dē\ *n* [*binary coded decimal*] (ca. 1962) : a computer code for representing alphanumeric information
B cell *n* [*bone-marrow-derived cell*] (1971) : any of the lymphocytes that have immunoglobulin molecules on the surface and comprise the antibody-secreting plasma cells when mature — called also *B lymphocyte;* compare T CELL
BCG vaccine \ˌbē-(ˌ)sē-'jē-\ *n* [*bacillus, Calmette-Guérin* (an attenuated strain of tubercle bacilli), fr. Albert *Calmette* †1933 and Camille *Guérin* †1961 Fr. bacteriologists] (1925) : a vaccine prepared from a living attenuated strain of tubercle bacilli and used to vaccinate human beings against tuberculosis — called also *BCG*
B complex *n* (1938) : VITAMIN B COMPLEX
BC soil \'bē-'sē-\ *n* (1938) : a soil whose profile has only B-horizons and C-horizons
bdel·li·um \'del-ē-əm\ *n* [ME, fr. L, fr. Gk *bdellion*] (14c) : a gum resin similar to myrrh obtained from various trees (genus *Commiphora*) of the East Indies and Africa
be \(')bē\ *vb, past 1st & 3d sing* **was** \(')wəz, 'wäz\; *2d sing* **were** \(')wər\; *pl* **were;** *past subjunctive* **were;** *past part* **been** \(')bin, *chiefly Brit* (')bēn\; *pres part* **be·ing** \'bē(-i)ŋ\; *pres 1st sing* **am** \əm, (')am\; *2d sing* **are** \ər, (')är\; *3d sing* **is** \(')iz, əz\; *pl* **are;** *pres subjunctive* **be** [ME *been,* fr. OE *bēon;* akin to OHG *bim* am, L *fui* I have been, *futurus* about to be, *fieri* to become, be done, Gk *phynai* to be born, be by nature, *phyein* to bring forth] *vi* (bef. 12c) **1 a** : to equal in meaning : have the same connotation as : SYMBOLIZE ⟨God *is* love⟩ ⟨January *is* the first month⟩ ⟨let *x* ~ 10⟩ **b** : to have identity with ⟨the first person I met *was* my brother⟩ **c** : to constitute the same class as **d** : to have a specified qualification or characterization ⟨the leaves *are* green⟩ **e** : to belong to the class of ⟨the fish *is* a trout⟩ — used regularly in senses 1a through 1e as the copula of simple predication **2 a** : to have an objective existence : have reality or actuality : LIVE ⟨I think, therefore I *am*⟩ ⟨once upon a time there *was* a knight⟩ **b** : to have, maintain, or occupy a place, situation, or position ⟨the book *is* on the table⟩ **c** : to remain unmolested, undisturbed, or uninterrupted — used only in infinitive form ⟨let him ~⟩ **d** : to take place : OCCUR ⟨the concert *was* last night⟩ **e** *archaic* : BELONG, BEFALL ~ *verbal auxiliary* **1** — used with the past participle of transitive verbs as a passive-voice auxiliary ⟨the money *was* found⟩ ⟨the house is *being* built⟩ **2** — used as the auxiliary of the present participle in progressive tenses expressing continuous action ⟨he *is* reading⟩ ⟨I have *been* sleeping⟩ **3** — used with the past participle of some intransitive verbs as an auxiliary forming archaic perfect tenses ⟨Christ *is* risen from the dead — 1 Cor 15:20 (DV)⟩ **4** — used with the infinitive with *to* to express futurity, arrangement in advance, or obligation ⟨I *am* to interview him today⟩ ⟨he *was* to become famous⟩
be- *prefix* [ME, fr. OE *bi-, be-;* akin to OE *bī* by, near — more at BY] **1** : on : around : over ⟨*bedaub*⟩ ⟨*besmear*⟩ **2** : to a great or greater degree : thoroughly ⟨*befuddle*⟩ ⟨*berate*⟩ **3** : excessively : ostentatiously — in intensive verbs formed from simple verbs ⟨*bedeck*⟩ and in adjectives based on adjectives ending in *-ed* ⟨*beribboned*⟩ **4** : about : to : at : upon : against : across ⟨*bestride*⟩ ⟨*bespeak*⟩ **5** : make : cause to be : treat as ⟨*belittle*⟩ ⟨*befool*⟩ ⟨*befriend*⟩ **6** : call or dub esp. excessively ⟨*bedoctor*⟩ **7** : affect, afflict, treat, provide, or cover with esp. excessively ⟨*bedevil*⟩ ⟨*befog*⟩
1**beach** \'bēch\ *n* [origin unknown] (1535) **1** : shore pebbles : SHINGLE **2 a** : a shore of an ocean, sea, or lake or the bank of a river covered by sand, gravel, or larger rock fragments **b** : a seashore area
2**beach** *vt* (1840) **1** : to run or drive ashore **2** : to make (a person) incapable or ineffective : DISABLE
beach ball *n* (1940) : a large inflated ball for use at the beach
beachboy *n* (1939) : a male beach attendant (as at a club or hotel)
beach break *n* (1965) : a wave that breaks close to the shore
beach buggy *n* (1943) : a motor vehicle with oversize tires for use on sand beaches

beach·comb·er \'bēch-ˌkō-mər\ *n* (1840) **1 :** a white man living as a drifter or loafer esp. on the islands of the So. Pacific **2 :** one who searches along a shore for useful or salable flotsam and refuse — **beach·comb** \-ˌkōm\ *vb*
beach flea *n* (1843) **:** any of numerous amphipod crustaceans (family Orchestiidae) living on ocean beaches and leaping like fleas
beach·front \'bēch-ˌfrənt\ *n* (1921) **:** a strip of land that fronts a beach — called also *shorefront*
beach grass *n* (1681) **:** any of several tough strongly rooted grasses that grow on exposed sandy shores; *esp* **:** a rhizomatous perennial (genus *Ammophila*) widely planted to bind sandy slopes
beach·head \'bēch-ˌhed\ *n* (1940) **1 :** an area on a hostile shore occupied to secure further landing of troops and supplies **2 :** FOOTHOLD
beach pea *n* (1802) **:** a wild pea (*Lathyrus maritimus*) with tough roots and purple flowers found along sandy seashores
beach plum *n* (1784) **:** a shrubby plum (*Prunus maritima*) having showy white flowers and growing along the northeastern coast of No. America; *also* **:** its dark purple edible fruit that is often used in jams and jellies
beach·side \'bēch-ˌsīd\ *adj* (1952) **:** located on a beach
beach wagon *n* (1935) **:** STATION WAGON
beach·wear \'bēch-ˌwa(ə)r, -ˌwe(ə)r\ *n* (1928) **:** clothing for wear at a beach
beachy \'bē-chē\ *adj* (1597) **:** covered with pebbles or shingle
[1]bea·con \'bē-kən\ *n* [ME *beken*, fr. OE *bēacen* sign; akin to OHG *bouhhan* sign] (bef. 12c) **1 :** a signal fire commonly on a hill, tower, or pole **2 a :** a lighthouse or other signal for guidance **b :** a radio transmitter emitting signals for guidance of aircraft **3 :** a source of light or inspiration
[2]beacon *vt* (1821) **:** to furnish with a beacon ~ *vi* **:** to shine as a beacon
[1]bead \'bēd\ *n* [ME *bede* prayer, prayer bead, fr. OE *bed, gebed* prayer; akin to OE *biddan* to entreat, pray — more at BID] (bef. 12c) **1 a** *obs* **:** PRAYER — usu. used in pl. **b** *pl* **:** a series of prayers and meditations made with a rosary **2 :** a small piece of material pierced for threading on a string or wire (as in a rosary) **3** *pl* **a :** ROSARY **b :** a necklace of beads or pearls **4 :** a small ball-shaped body: as **a :** a drop of sweat or blood **b :** a bubble formed in or on a beverage **c :** a small metal knob on a firearm used as a front sight **d :** a blob or a line of weld metal **e :** a glassy drop of flux (as borax) used as a solvent and color test for several metallic oxides and salts **5 :** a projecting rim, band, or molding
[2]bead *vt* (1577) **1 :** to furnish, adorn, or cover with beads or beading **2 :** to string together like beads ~ *vi* **:** to form into a bead
bead·ing *n* (1845) **1 :** a beaded molding **2 :** material or a part or a piece consisting of a bead **3 :** an openwork trimming **4 :** BEADWORK
bea·dle \'bēd-ᵊl\ *n* [ME *bedel* messenger, fr. OE *bydel*; akin to OHG *butil* bailiff, OE *bēodan* to command — more at BID] (1581) **:** a minor parish official whose duties include ushering and preserving order at services and sometimes civil functions
bead·roll \'bē-ˌdrōl\ *n* [fr. the reading in church of a list of names of persons for whom prayers are to be said] (1529) **1 :** a list of names **:** CATALOG **2 :** ROSARY
beads·man \'bēdz-mən\ *n, archaic* (13c) **:** one who prays for another
bead·work \'bē-ˌdwərk\ *n* (1751) **1 :** ornamental work in beads **2 :** joinery beading
beady \'bēd-ē\ *adj* **bead·i·er; -est** (1826) **1 a :** resembling beads **b :** small, round, and shiny with interest or greed ⟨~ eyes⟩ **2 :** marked by bubbles or beads ⟨a ~ liquor⟩
bea·gle \'bē-gəl\ *n* [ME *begle*] (15c) **:** a small short-legged smooth-coated hound
beak \'bēk\ *n* [ME *bec*, fr. OF, fr. L *beccus*, of Gaulish origin] (13c) **1 a :** the bill of a bird; *esp* **:** the bill of a bird of prey adapted for striking and tearing **b** (1) **:** any of various rigid projecting mouth structures (as of a turtle) (2) **:** the elongated sucking mouth of some insects (as the typical bugs) **c :** the human nose **2 :** a pointed structure or formation: **a :** a metal-pointed beam projecting from the bow of an ancient galley for piercing an enemy ship **b :** the spout of a vessel **c :** a continuous slight architectural projection ending in an arris — see MOLDING illustration **d :** a process suggesting the beak of a bird **3** *chiefly Brit* **a :** MAGISTRATE **b :** HEADMASTER — **beaked** \'bēkt\ *adj*
bea·ker \'bē-kər\ *n* [ME *biker*, fr. ON *bikarr*, prob. fr. OS *bikeri*, fr. ML *bicarius* beaker — more at PITCHER] (14c) **1 :** a large drinking cup that has a wide mouth and is sometimes supported on a standard **2 :** a deep widemouthed and often projecting-lipped thin vessel used esp. by chemists and pharmacists
be–all and end–all \'bē-ˌȯ-lən-'(d)en-ˌdȯl\ *n* (1605) **:** prime cause **:** essential element
[1]beam \'bēm\ *n* [ME *beem*, fr. OE *bēam* tree, beam; akin to OHG *boum* tree] (bef. 12c) **1 a :** a long piece of heavy often squared timber suitable for use in construction **b :** a wood or metal cylinder in a loom on which the warp is wound **c :** the part of a plow to which handles, standard, and colter are attached **d :** the bar of a balance from which scales hang **e :** one of the principal horizontal supporting members of a building or ship ⟨a steel ~ supporting a floor⟩; *also* **:** BOOM, SPAR ⟨the ~ of a crane⟩ **f :** the extreme width of a ship at the widest part **g :** an oscillating lever on a central axis receiving motion at one end from an engine piston rod and transmitting it at the other **2 a :** a ray or shaft of light **b :** a collection of nearly parallel rays (as X rays) or a stream of particles (as electrons) **c :** a constant directional radio signal transmitted for the guidance of pilots; *also* **:** the course indicated by a radio beam **3 :** the main stem of a deer's antler **4 :** the width of the buttocks — **on the beam 1 :** following a guiding beam **2 :** proceeding or operating correctly
[2]beam *vt* (15c) **1 :** to emit in beams or as a beam **2 :** to support with beams **3 a :** to aim (a broadcast) by directional antennas **b :** to direct to a particular audience ~ *vi* **1 :** to send out beams of light **2 :** to smile with joy
beam–ends \'bē-'men(d)z\ *n pl* (1773) **:** the ends of a ship's beams — **on her beam–ends :** inclined so much on one side that the beams approach a vertical position
beam·ish \'bē-mish\ *adj* (1870) **:** beaming and bright with optimism, promise, or achievement — **beam·ish·ly** *adv*
beamy \'bē-mē\ *adj* (14c) **1 :** emitting beams of light **:** RADIANT **2 :** broad in the beam ⟨a ~ cargo ship⟩
[1]bean \'bēn\ *n* [ME *bene*, fr. OE *bēan*; akin to OHG *bōna* bean] (bef. 12c) **1 a :** BROAD BEAN **b :** the seed of any of various erect or climbing leguminous plants (esp. genera *Phaseolus, Dolichos,* and *Vigna*) other than the broad bean **c :** a plant bearing beans **d :** a bean pod used when immature as a vegetable **2 a :** a valueless item **b** *pl* **:** a small amount ⟨didn't know ~*s* about it⟩ **3 :** any of various seeds or fruits that resemble beans or bean pods; *also* **:** a plant producing these **4 :** a protuberance on the upper mandible of waterfowl **5 :** HEAD, BRAIN **6** *pl* **:** EXUBERANCE — used in the phrase *full of beans*
[2]bean *vt* (1910) **:** to strike (a person) on the head with an object
bean·bag \'bēn-ˌbag\ *n* (1871) **1 :** a cloth bag partially filled typically with dried beans and used as a toy **2 :** any of various pellet-filled bags used as furniture (as a chair) or household articles (as an ashtray base)
bean·ball \-ˌbȯl\ *n* (1905) **:** a pitched baseball thrown at a batter's head
bean curd *n* (ca. 1889) **:** a soft vegetable cheese prepared by treating soybean milk with coagulants (as magnesium chloride or dilute acids) — called also *tofu*
bean·ery \'bēn-(ə-)rē\ *n, pl* **-er·ies** (1887) **:** RESTAURANT
bean·ie \'bē-nē\ *n* (1940) **:** a small round tight-fitting skullcap worn esp. by schoolboys and college freshmen
beano \'bē-(ˌ)nō\ *n, pl* **beanos** [by alter.] (1935) **:** BINGO
bean sprouts *n pl* (1923) **:** the sprouts of bean seeds esp. of the mung bean used as a vegetable
[1]bear \'ba(ə)r, 'be(ə)r\ *n, pl* **bears** *often attrib* [ME *bere*, fr. OE *bera*; akin to OE *brūn* brown — more at BROWN] (bef. 12c) **1** *or pl* **bear :** any of a family (Ursidae of the order Carnivora) of large heavy mammals having long shaggy hair, rudimentary tail, and plantigrade feet and feeding largely on fruit and insects as well as on flesh **2 :** a surly, uncouth, or shambling person **3** [prob. fr. the proverb about *selling the bearskin before catching the bear*] **:** one that sells securities or commodities in expectation of a price decline — compare BULL
[2]bear *vb* **bore** \'bō(ə)r, 'bȯ(ə)r\; **borne** \'bō(ə)rn, 'bȯ(ə)rn\ *also* **born** \'bȯ(ə)rn\; **bear·ing** [ME *beren*, fr. OE *beran*; akin to OHG *beran* to carry, L *ferre*, Gk *pherein*] *vt* (bef. 12c) **1 a :** to move while holding up and supporting **b :** to be equipped or furnished with **c :** to hold in the mind **d :** DISSEMINATE **e :** BEHAVE, CONDUCT ⟨~*ing* himself well⟩ **f :** to have as a feature or characteristic **g :** to give as testimony ⟨~ false witness⟩ **h :** to have as an identification ⟨*bore* the name of John⟩ **i :** LEAD, ESCORT **j :** RENDER, GIVE **2 a :** to give birth to **b :** to produce as yield **c** (1) **:** to permit growth of (2) **:** CONTAIN ⟨oil-*bearing* shale⟩ **3 a :** to support the weight of **:** SUSTAIN **b :** to put up with esp. without giving way ⟨couldn't ~ his wife's family⟩ **c :** ASSUME, ACCEPT **d :** to hold above, on top, or aloft **e :** to admit of **:** ALLOW **f :** to call for as suitable or essential ⟨his odd behavior ~*s* watching⟩ **4 :** THRUST, PRESS ~ *vi* **1 a :** to force one's way **b :** to be situated **:** LIE **c :** to extend in a direction indicated or implied **d :** to become directed **e :** to go or incline in an indicated direction **2 a :** APPLY, PERTAIN **b :** to exert influence or force **3 :** to support a weight or strain — often used with *up* **4 :** to produce fruit **:** YIELD
syn BEAR, SUFFER, ENDURE, ABIDE, TOLERATE, STAND mean to put up with something trying or painful. BEAR usu. implies the power to sustain without flinching or breaking; SUFFER often suggests acceptance or passivity rather than courage or patience in bearing; ENDURE implies continuing firm or resolute through trials and difficulties; ABIDE suggests acceptance without resistance or protest; TOLERATE suggests overcoming or successfully controlling an impulse to resist, avoid, or resent something injurious or distasteful; STAND emphasizes even more strongly the ability to bear without discomposure or flinching.
— **bear a hand :** to join in and help out — **bear arms 1 :** to carry or possess arms **2 :** to serve as a soldier — **bear fruit :** to come to satisfying fruition, production, or development — **bear in mind :** to think of esp. as a warning **:** REMEMBER — **bear with :** to be indulgent, patient, or forbearing with
bear·able \'bar-ə-bəl, 'ber-\ *adj* (ca. 1550) **:** capable of being borne — **bear·abil·i·ty** \ˌbar-ə-'bil-ət-ē, ˌber-\ *n* — **bear·ably** \-blē\ *adv*
bear·bait·ing \'ba(ə)r-ˌbāt-iŋ, 'be(ə)r-\ *n* (14c) **:** the practice of setting dogs on a chained bear
bear·ber·ry \-ˌber-ē\ *n* (1625) **:** a trailing evergreen plant (*Arctostaphylos uva-ursi*) of the heath family with astringent foliage and red berries
[1]beard \'bi(ə)rd\ *n* [ME *berd*, fr. OE *beard*; akin to OHG *bart* beard, L *barba*] (bef. 12c) **1 :** the hair that grows on a man's face often excluding the mustache **2 :** a hairy or bristly appendage or tuft — **beard·ed** \-əd\ *adj* — **beard·ed·ness** *n* — **beard·less** \-ləs\ *adj*
[2]beard *vt* (14c) **1 :** to furnish with a beard **2 :** to confront and oppose with boldness, resolution, and often effrontery **:** DEFY
bearded collie *n* (1880) **:** any of a breed of large working dogs that originated in Scotland and that have a long rough coat and drooping ears
bear down *vt* (14c) **:** OVERCOME, OVERWHELM ~ *vi* **:** to exert full strength and concentrated attention — **bear down on 1 :** EMPHASIZE **2 :** to weigh heavily on **:** BURDEN
beard·tongue \'bi(ə)rd-ˌtəŋ\ *n* (1821) **:** PENTSTEMON
bear·er \'bar-ər, 'ber-\ *n* (13c) **:** one that bears: as **a :** PORTER 1 **b :** a plant yielding fruit **c :** PALLBEARER **d :** one holding a check, draft, or other order for payment esp. if marked payable to bearer
bear grass *n* (1750) **:** any of several plants (genera *Yucca, Nolina,* or *Xerophyllum*) of the lily family chiefly of the southern and western U.S. with foliage resembling coarse blades of grass
bear hug *n* (1921) **:** a rough tight embrace
bear·ing *n* (13c) **1 :** the manner in which one bears or comports oneself ⟨a man of erect and soldierly ~⟩ **2 a :** the act, power, or time of bringing forth offspring or fruit **b :** a product of bearing **:** CROP **3 :** PRESSURE, THRUST **4 a :** an object, surface, or point that supports **b :** a machine part in which another part (as a journal or pin) turns or slides **5 :** a figure borne on a heraldic field **6 a :** the situation or horizontal direction of one point with respect to another or to the compass **b :** a determination of position **c** *pl* **:** comprehension of one's position, environment, or situation **d :** RELATION, CONNECTION; *also*

: PURPORT **7** : the part of a structural member that rests on its supports

syn BEARING, DEPORTMENT, DEMEANOR, MIEN, MANNER, CARRIAGE mean the outward manifestation of personality or attitude. BEARING is the most general of these words but now usu. implies characteristic posture; DEPORTMENT suggests actions or behavior as formed by breeding or training; DEMEANOR suggests one's attitude toward others as expressed in outward behavior; MIEN is a literary term referring both to bearing and demeanor; MANNER implies characteristic or customary way of moving and gesturing and addressing others; CARRIAGE applies chiefly to habitual posture in standing or walking.

bearing rein n (1794) : CHECKREIN 1
bear·ish \'ba(ə)r-ish, 'be(ə)r-\ adj (1744) **1** : resembling a bear in roughness, gruffness, or surliness **2 a** : marked by, tending to cause, or fearful of falling prices (as in a stock market) **b** : PESSIMISTIC — **bear·ish·ly** adv — **bear·ish·ness** n
bé·ar·naise sauce \,bā-är-'nāz-, -ər-; ,be(ə)r-\ n [F *béarnaise*, fem. of *béarnais* of Béarn, France] (1877) : a sauce of egg yolks and butter flavored with shallots, wine, vinegar, and seasonings
bear out vt (15c) : CONFIRM, SUBSTANTIATE ⟨research *bore out* his theory⟩
bear·skin \'ba(ə)r-,skin, 'be(ə)r-\ n (1752) : an article made of the skin of a bear; esp : a military hat made of the skin of a bear
bear up vt (13c) : SUPPORT, ENCOURAGE ~ vi : to summon up courage, resolution, or strength ⟨*bearing up* under the strain⟩
beast \'bēst\ n [ME *beste*, fr. OF, fr. L *bestia*] (13c) **1 a** : an animal as distinguished from a plant **b** : a lower animal as distinguished from man **c** : a four-footed mammal as distinguished from man, lower vertebrates, and invertebrates **d** : an animal under human control **2** : a contemptible person
beast epic n (1889) : a poem with epic conventions in which animals speak and act like human beings
beast fable n (1865) : a usu. didactic prose or verse fable in which animals speak and act like human beings
beast·ie \'bē-stē\ n (1773) : BEAST; esp : one that is wild or strange
beas·tings var of BEESTINGS
¹**beast·ly** \'bēst-lē\ adj **beast·li·er; -est** (13c) **1** : BESTIAL 1 **2** : ABOMINABLE, DISAGREEABLE ⟨~ weather⟩ — **beast·li·ness** n
²**beastly** adv (1834) : VERY ⟨a ~ cold day⟩
beast of burden (1740) : an animal employed to carry heavy material or to perform other heavy work (as pulling a plow)
¹**beat** \'bēt\ vb **beat; beat·en** \'bēt-ⁿn\ or **beat; beat·ing** [ME *beten*, fr. OE *bēatan*; akin to OHG *bōzan* to beat, L *-futare* to beat, *fustis* club] vt (bef. 12c) **1** : to strike repeatedly: **a** : to hit repeatedly so as to inflict pain — often used with *up* **b** : to walk on : TREAD **c** : to strike directly against forcefully and repeatedly : dash against **d** : to flap or thrash at vigorously **e** : to strike at in order to rouse game; *also* : to range over in or as if in quest of game **f** : to mix by stirring : WHIP — often used with *up* **g** : to strike repeatedly in order to produce music or a signal ⟨~ a drum⟩ **2 a** : to drive or force by blows **b** : to pound into a powder, paste, or pulp **c** : to make by repeated treading or driving over **d** (1) : to dislodge by repeated hitting (2) : to lodge securely by repeated striking **e** : to shape by beating ⟨~ swords into plowshares⟩; *esp* : to flatten thin by blows **f** : to sound or express esp. by drumbeat **3** : to cause to strike or flap repeatedly **4 a** : OVERCOME, DEFEAT; *also* : SURPASS — often used with *out* **b** : to prevail despite ⟨~ the odds⟩ **c** : BEWILDER, BAFFLE **d** (1) : FATIGUE, EXHAUST (2) : to leave dispirited, irresolute, or hopeless **e** : CHEAT, SWINDLE **5 a** (1) : to act ahead of usu. so as to forestall **c** : to report a news item in advance of **b** : to come or arrive before **c** : CIRCUMVENT ⟨~ the system⟩ **6** : to indicate by beating ⟨~ the tempo⟩ ~ vi **1 a** : to become forcefully impelled : DASH **b** : to glare or strike with oppressive intensity **c** : to sustain distracting activity **d** : to beat a drum **2 a** (1) : PULSATE, THROB (2) : TICK **b** : to sound upon being struck **3 a** : to strike repeated blows **b** : to strike the air : FLAP **c** : to strike cover in order to rouse game; *also* : to range or scour for or as if for game **4** : to progress with much difficulty — **beat about the bush** or **beat around the bush** : to fail or refuse to come to the point in discourse — **beat a retreat** : to leave in haste — **beat it 1** : to hurry away : SCRAM **2** : HURRY, RUSH — **beat one's brains out** : to try intently to resolve something difficult by thinking — **beat the bushes** : to search thoroughly through all possible areas — **beat the drum** : to proclaim as meritorious or significant : publicize vigorously — **beat the rap** : to escape or evade the penalties connected with an accusation or charge
²**beat** n (1615) **1 a** : a single stroke or blow esp. in a series; *also* : PULSATION, TICK **b** : a sound produced by or as if by beating **c** : a driving impact or force **2** : one swing of the pendulum or balance of a timepiece **3** : each of the pulsations of amplitude produced by the union of sound or radio waves or electric currents having different frequencies **4** : an accented stroke (as of one leg or foot against the other) in dancing **5 a** : a metrical or rhythmic stress in poetry or music or the rhythmic effect of these stresses **b** : the tempo indicated (as by a conductor) to a musical performer **c** : the pronounced rhythm that is the characteristic driving force in jazz or rock music; *also* : ²ROCK 2 **6 a** : a regularly traversed round ⟨the cop on the ~⟩ **7 a** : something that excels ⟨I've never seen the ~ of it⟩ **b** : the reporting of a news story ahead of competitors **8** : DEADBEAT **9** : an act of beating to windward **a** : one of the reaches so traversed : TACK — **beat·less** \-ləs\ adj
³**beat** adj [ME *beten*, fr. pp. of *beten*] (1746) **1 a** : being in a state of exhaustion : EXHAUSTED **b** : sapped of resolution or morale **2** often cap : of, relating to, or being beatniks ⟨~ poets⟩
⁴**beat** n, often cap (1958) : BEATNIK
beat·en \'bēt-ⁿn\ adj (13c) **1** : hammered into a desired shape ⟨~ gold⟩ **2** : much trodden and worn smooth; *also* : FAMILIAR ⟨a ~ path⟩ **3** : being in a state of exhaustion : EXHAUSTED
beat·er \'bēt-ər\ n (14c) **1** : one that beats: as **a** : EGGBEATER **b** : a rotary blade attached to an electric mixer **c** : DRUMSTICK 1 **2** : one that strikes bushes or other cover to rouse game
be·atif·ic \,bē-ə-'tif-ik\ adj [L *beatificus* making happy, fr. *beatus* happy, fr. pp. of *beare* to bless; akin to L *bonus* good — more at BOUNTY] (1639) **1** : of, possessing, or imparting beatitude **2** : having a blissful or benign appearance ⟨a ~ smile⟩ — **be·atif·i·cal·ly** \-i-k(ə-)lē\ adv
beatific vision n (1639) : the direct knowledge of God enjoyed by the blessed in heaven

be·at·i·fy \bē-'at-ə-,fī\ vt **-fied; -fy·ing** [MF *beatifier*, fr. LL *beatificare*, fr. L *beatus* + *facere* to make — more at DO] (1535) **1** : to make supremely happy **2** : to declare to have attained the blessedness of heaven and authorize the title "Blessed" and limited public religious honor — **be·at·i·fi·ca·tion** \-,at-ə-fə-'kā-shən\ n
beat·ing \'bēt-iŋ\ n (14c) **1** : an act of striking with repeated blows so as to injure or damage; *also* : the injury or damage thus inflicted **2** : PULSATION **3** : DEFEAT, SETBACK
beating reed n (1879) : a reed in a musical instrument that vibrates against the edges of an air opening (as in a clarinet or organ pipe) to which it is attached — compare FREE REED
be·at·i·tude \bē-'at-ə-,t(y)üd\ n [L *beatitudo*, fr. *beatus*] (15c) **1 a** : a state of utmost bliss **b** — used as a title for a primate esp. of an Eastern church **2** : any of the declarations made in the Sermon on the Mount (Mt 5:3–12) beginning in the AV "Blessed are"
beat·nik \'bēt-nik\ n [³*beat* + *-nik*] (1958) : a person who rejects the mores of established society (as by dressing and behaving unconventionally) and indulges in exotic philosophizing and self-expression
beat off vt (15c) : REPEL ~ vi : MASTURBATE — usu. considered vulgar
beat out vt (1577) **1** : to make or perform by or as if by beating **2** : to mark or accompany by beating **3** : to turn (a routine ground ball) into a hit in baseball by fast running to first base
Be·atrice \,bā-ä-'trē-(,)chä, 'bē-ə-trəs\ n [It] : a Florentine woman idealized in Dante's *Vita Nuova* and *Divina Commedia*
beat-up \'bēt-'əp\ adj (ca. 1946) : DILAPIDATED, SHABBY
beau \'bō\ n, pl **beaux** \'bōz\ or **beaus** [F, fr. *beau* beautiful, fr. L *bellus* pretty] (1684) **1** : DANDY 1 **2** : BOYFRIEND 2
Beau Brum·mell \bō-'brəm-əl\ n [nickname of G. B. *Brummell*] (1920) : DANDY 1
beau·coup \'bō-(')kü\ adj, slang [F] (1918) : great in quantity or amount : MANY, MUCH ⟨spent ~ dollars⟩
Beau·fort scale \'bō-fərt-\ n [Sir Francis *Beaufort*] (1858) : a scale in which the force of the wind is indicated by numbers from 0 to 12

BEAUFORT SCALE

BEAUFORT NUMBER	NAME	MILES PER HOUR	DESCRIPTION
0	calm	less than 1	calm; smoke rises vertically
1	light air	1–3	direction of wind shown by smoke but not by wind vanes
2	light breeze	4–7	wind felt on face; leaves rustle; ordinary vane moved by wind
3	gentle breeze	8–12	leaves and small twigs in constant motion; wind extends light flag
4	moderate breeze	13–18	raises dust and loose paper; small branches are moved
5	fresh breeze	19–24	small trees in leaf begin to sway; crested wavelets form on inland waters
6	strong breeze	25–31	large branches in motion; telegraph wires whistle; umbrellas used with difficulty
7	moderate gale (or near gale)	32–38	whole trees in motion; inconvenience in walking against wind
8	fresh gale (or gale)	39–46	breaks twigs off trees; generally impedes progress
9	strong gale	47–54	slight structural damage occurs; chimney pots and slates removed
10	whole gale (or storm)	55–63	trees uprooted; considerable structural damage occurs
11	storm (or violent storm)	64–72	very rarely experienced; accompanied by widespread damage
12	hurricane*	73–136	devastation occurs

*The U.S. uses 74 statute mph as the speed criterion for hurricane.

beau geste \bō-'zhest\ n, pl **beaux gestes** or **beau gestes** \bō-'zhest\ [F, lit., beautiful gesture] (1914) **1** : a graceful or magnanimous gesture **2** : an ingratiating conciliatory gesture
beau ide·al \,bō-ī-'dē(-ə)l, ,bō-,ēd-ā-'äl\ n, pl **beau ideals** [F *beau idéal* ideal beauty] (1809) : the perfect type or model
Beau·jo·lais \,bō-zhō-'lā, -zhə-\ n [F, fr. *Beaujolais*, region of central France] (1863) : a light fruity red Burgundy wine
Beau·mé var of BAUMÉ
beau monde \bō-'mänd, -'mōⁿd\ n, pl **beau mondes** \-'män(d)z\ or **beaux mondes** \bō-'mōⁿd\ [F, lit., fine world] (1673) : the world of high society and fashion
beaut \'byüt\ n (1896) : BEAUTY 3
beau·te·ous \'byüt-ē-əs\ adj [ME, fr. *beaute*] (15c) : BEAUTIFUL — **beau·te·ous·ly** adv — **beau·te·ous·ness** n
beau·ti·cian \byü-'tish-ən\ n [*beauty* + *-ician*] (1924) : COSMETOLOGIST
beau·ti·ful \'byüt-i-fəl\ adj (15c) **1** : having qualities of beauty : exciting aesthetic pleasure **2** : generally pleasing : EXCELLENT — **beau·ti·ful·ly** \-f(ə-)lē\ adv — **beau·ti·ful·ness** \-fəl-nəs\ n
syn BEAUTIFUL, LOVELY, HANDSOME, COMELY, FAIR mean exciting sensuous or aesthetic pleasure. BEAUTIFUL applies to whatever excites the

keenest of pleasure to the senses and stirs emotion through the senses; LOVELY is close to BEAUTIFUL but applies to a narrower range of emotional excitation in suggesting the graceful, delicate, or exquisite; HANDSOME suggests aesthetic pleasure due to proportion, symmetry, or elegance; PRETTY applies to superficial or insubstantial attractiveness; COMELY is like HANDSOME in suggesting what is coolly approved rather than emotionally responded to; FAIR suggests beauty because of purity, flawlessness, or freshness.

beautiful people *n pl, often cap B & P* (1966) **:** people who are identified with international society

beau·ti·fy \ˈbyüt-ə-ˌfī\ *vb* **-fied; -fy·ing** *vt* (1526) **:** to make beautiful or add beauty to **:** EMBELLISH ~ *vi* **:** to grow beautiful ***syn*** see ADORN — **beau·ti·fi·ca·tion** \ˌbyüt-ə-fə-ˈkā-shən\ *n* — **beau·ti·fi·er** \ˈbyüt-ə-ˌfī(-ə)r\ *n*

beau·ty \ˈbyüt-ē\ *n, pl* **beauties** [ME *beaute*, fr. OF *biauté*, fr. *bel, biau* beautiful, fr. L *bellus* pretty; akin to L *bonus* good — more at BOUNTY] (14c) **1 :** the quality or aggregate of qualities in a person or thing that gives pleasure to the senses or pleasurably exalts the mind or spirit **:** LOVELINESS **2 :** a beautiful person or thing; *esp* **:** a beautiful woman **3 :** a brilliant, extreme, or egregious example or instance ⟨that mistake was a ~⟩ **4 :** a particularly graceful, ornamental, or excellent quality

beauty bush *n* (1926) **:** a Chinese shrub (*Kolkwitzia amabilis*) of the honeysuckle family with pinkish flowers and bristly fruit

beauty contest *n* (1899) **1 :** an assemblage of girls or women at which judges select the most beautiful **2 :** a presidential primary election in which the popular vote does not determine the number of convention delegates a candidate receives

beauty part *n* (1951) **:** the most desirable or beneficial aspect of something

beauty shop *n* (1901) **:** an establishment or department where hairdressing, facials, and manicures are done — called also *beauty parlor, beauty salon*

beauty spot *n* (1657) **1 :** 1PATCH 2 **2 a :** NEVUS **b :** a minor blemish

beaux arts \bō-ˈzär\ *n pl* [F] (1821) **:** FINE ARTS

1**bea·ver** \ˈbē-vər\ *n, pl* **beavers** [ME *bever*, fr. OE *beofor*; akin to OHG *bibar* beaver, OE *brūn* brown — more at BROWN] (bef. 12c) **1** *or pl* **beaver a :** either of two large semiaquatic rodents (genus *Castor*) having webbed hind feet and a broad flat tail, constructing dams and underwater lodges, and yielding valuable fur and castoreum **b :** the fur or pelt of the beaver **2 a :** a hat made of beaver fur or a fabric imitation **b :** SILK HAT **3 :** a heavy fabric of felted wool or of cotton napped on both sides **4 :** the pudenda of a woman — often considered vulgar

2**beaver** *n* [ME *baviere*, fr. MF] (15c) **1 :** a piece of armor protecting the lower part of the face **2 :** a helmet visor

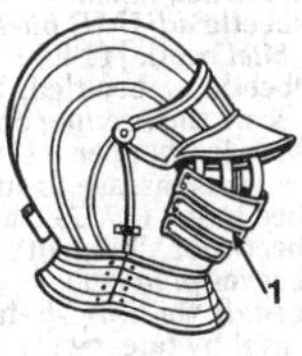

beaver 1

3**beaver** *vi* (1946) **:** to work energetically ⟨~*ing* away at the problem⟩

bea·ver·board \ˈbē-vər-ˌbō(ə)rd, -ˌbȯ(ə)rd\ *n* [fr. *Beaver Board*, a trademark] (1909) **:** a fiberboard used for partitions and ceilings

be·bop \ˈbē-ˌbäp\ *n* [imit.] (1944) **:** 3BOP — **be·bop·per** *n*

be·calm \bi-ˈkä(l)m, *NewEng also* -ˈkȧm\ *vt* (1595) **1 :** to keep motionless by lack of wind **2 :** to make calm **:** SOOTHE

be·cause \bi-ˈkȯz, -(ˈ)kəz\ *conj* [ME *because that*, *because*, fr. *by cause that*] (14c) **1 :** for the reason that **:** SINCE ⟨rested ~ he was tired⟩ **2 :** the fact that **:** THAT ⟨the reason I am here is ~ I wish to bring a voice from the wilderness —J.C. Snyder⟩

because of *prep* (14c) **:** by reason of **:** on account of

bé·cha·mel \ˌbā-shə-ˈmel\ *n* [F *sauce béchamelle*, fr. Louis de *Béchamel* †1703 Fr. courtier] (1796) **:** a white sauce sometimes enriched with cream

be·chance \bi-ˈchan(t)s\ *vb, archaic* (1530) **:** BEFALL

bêche–de–mer \ˌbesh-də-ˈme(ə)r, ˌbāsh-\ *n* [F, lit., sea grub] (1783) **1** *pl* **bêche–de–mer** *or* **bêches–de–mer** \ˌbesh-(əz-)də-, ˌbāsh-\ **:** TREPANG **2** *cap B&M* **:** a lingua franca based on English and used esp. in New Guinea, the Bismarck archipelago, and the Solomon islands

1**beck** \ˈbek\ *n* [ME *bek*, fr. ON *bekkr*; akin to OE *bæc* brook, OHG *bah*, MIr *búal* flowing water] *Brit* (12c) **:** CREEK 2

2**beck** *vt* [ME *becken*, alter. of *beknen*] *archaic* (13c) **:** BECKON

3**beck** *n* (14c) **1** *chiefly Scot* **:** BOW, CURTSY **2 a :** a beckoning gesture **b :** SUMMONS, BIDDING — **at one's beck and call :** in obedient readiness to obey any command

beck·et \ˈbek-ət\ *n* [origin unknown] (1769) **:** a device for holding something in place: as **a :** a grommet or a loop of rope with a knot at one end to catch in an eye at the other **b :** a ring of rope or metal **c :** a loop of rope (as for a handle)

becket bend *n* (1884) **:** SHEET BEND

beck·on \ˈbek-ən\ *vb* **beck·oned; beck·on·ing** \ˈbek-(ə-)niŋ\ [ME *beknen*, fr. OE *bīecnan*, fr. *bēacen* sign — more at BEACON] *vi* (bef. 12c) **1 :** to summon or signal typically with a wave or nod **2 :** to appear inviting **:** ATTRACT ~ *vt* **:** to beckon to — **beckon** *n*

be·cloud \bi-ˈklau̇d\ *vt* (1598) **1 :** to obscure with or as if with a cloud **2 :** to prevent clear perception or realization of **:** MUDDLE ⟨prejudices that ~ his judgment⟩

be·come \bi-ˈkəm\ *vb* **-came** \-ˈkām\; **-come; -com·ing** [ME *becomen* to come to, become, fr. OE *becuman*, fr. *be-* + *cuman* to come] *vi* (bef. 12c) **1 a :** to come into existence **b :** to come to be ⟨~ sick⟩ **2 :** to undergo change or development ~ *vt* **:** to suit or be suitable to ⟨her clothes ~ her⟩ — **become of :** to happen to

be·com·ing \-ˈkəm-iŋ\ *adj* (15c) **:** SUITABLE, FITTING; *esp* **:** attractively suitable — **be·com·ing·ly** \-iŋ-lē\ *adv*

1**bed** \ˈbed\ *n* [ME, fr. OE *bedd*; akin to OHG *betti* bed, L *fodere* to dig] (bef. 12c) **1 a :** a piece of furniture on or in which one may lie and sleep **b** (1) **:** a place of marital sex relations (2) **:** marital relationship **c :** a place for sleeping **d :** SLEEP; *also* **:** a time for sleeping ⟨took a walk before ~⟩ **e** (1) **:** a mattress filled with soft material (2) **:** BEDSTEAD **f :** the equipment and services needed to care for one hospitalized patient or hotel guest **2 :** a flat or level surface: as **a :** a plot of ground prepared for plants; *also* **:** the plants grown in such a plot **b :** the bottom of a body of water; *esp* **:** an area of sea bottom supporting a heavy growth of a particular organism ⟨an oyster ~⟩ **3 :** a supporting surface or structure **:** FOUNDATION; *esp* **:** the earthwork that supports the ballast and track of a railroad **4 :** LAYER, STRATUM **5 a :** the place or material in which a block or brick is laid **b :** the lower surface of a brick, slate, or tile **6 :** a mass or heap resembling a bed ⟨a ~ of ashes⟩ — **in bed :** in the act of sexual intercourse

2**bed** *vb* **bed·ded; bed·ding** *vt* (bef. 12c) **1 a :** to furnish with a bed or bedding **:** settle in sleeping quarters — often used with *down* **b :** to put, take, or send to bed **2 a :** EMBED **b :** to plant or arrange in beds **c :** BASE, ESTABLISH **3 a :** to lay flat or in a layer **b :** to make a bed in or of **4 :** to have sexual intercourse with — often used with *down* ~ *vi* **1 a :** to find or make sleeping accommodations **b :** to go to bed **2 :** to form a layer **3 :** to lie flat or flush

be·dab·ble \bi-ˈdab-əl\ *vt* (1590) **:** to wet or soil by dabbling

bed–and–breakfast *adj* (1930) **:** offering lodging and breakfast ⟨a ~ place⟩

be·daub \bi-ˈdȯb, -ˈdäb\ *vt* (1553) **1 :** to daub over **:** BESMEAR **2 :** to ornament with vulgar excess

be·daz·zle \bi-ˈdaz-əl\ *vt* (1596) **1 :** to confuse by a strong light **:** DAZZLE **2 :** to impress forcefully **:** ENCHANT — **be·daz·zle·ment** \-mənt\ *n*

bed board *n* (1946) **:** a stiff thin wide board inserted usu. between bedspring and mattress esp. to give support to one's back or to protect a mattress from sagging springs

bed·bug \ˈbed-ˌbəg\ *n* (1808) **:** a wingless bloodsucking bug (*Cimex lectularius*) sometimes infesting houses and esp. beds and feeding on human blood

bed·cham·ber \-ˌchām-bər\ *n* (14c) **:** BEDROOM

bed check *n* (1927) **:** a night inspection to check the presence of persons (as soldiers) required by regulations to be in bed or in quarters

bed·clothes \ˈbed-ˌklō(th)z\ *n pl* (14c) **:** the covering (as sheets and blankets) used on a bed

bed·ded \ˈbed-əd\ *adj* (1831) **:** having a bed or beds of a specified kind or number — used in combination ⟨a twin-*bedded* room⟩

bed·der \ˈbed-ər\ *n* (1612) **1 :** one that makes up beds **2 :** a bedding plant

1**bed·ding** \ˈbed-iŋ\ *n* [ME, fr. OE, fr. *bedd*] (bef. 12c) **1 :** BEDCLOTHES **2 :** a bottom layer **:** FOUNDATION **3 :** material to provide a bed for livestock **4 :** STRATIFICATION

2**bedding** *adj* [fr. gerund of 2*bed*] (1856) **:** appropriate or adapted for culture in open-air beds

be·deck \bi-ˈdek\ *vt* (1566) **:** to clothe with finery **:** deck out

be·dev·il \bi-ˈdev-əl\ *vt* (1574) **1 :** to change for the worse **:** SPOIL **2 :** to possess with or as if with a devil **3 :** to cause distress **:** TROUBLE **4 :** to confuse utterly **:** BEWILDER — **be·dev·il·ment** \-mənt\ *n*

be·dew \bi-ˈd(y)ü\ *vt* (14c) **:** to wet with or as if with dew

bed·fast \ˈbed-ˌfast\ *adj* (1639) **:** BEDRIDDEN

bed·fel·low \-ˌfel-(ˌ)ō, -ə(-w)\ *n* (15c) **1 :** one who shares a bed with another **2 :** a close associate **:** ALLY ⟨political ~*s*⟩

Bed·ford cord \ˌbed-fərd-\ *n* [perh. fr. New *Bedford*, Massachusetts] (1862) **:** a clothing fabric with lengthwise ribs that resembles corduroy; *also* **:** the weave used in making this fabric

be·dight \bi-ˈdīt\ *vt* **be·dight·ed** *or* **bedight; be·dight·ing** *archaic* (14c) **:** EQUIP, ARRAY

be·dim \bi-ˈdim\ *vt* (1583) **1 :** to make less bright **2 :** to make indistinct **:** OBSCURE

Bed·i·vere \ˈbed-ə-ˌvi(ə)r\ *n* **:** a knight of the Round Table

be·di·zen \bi-ˈdīz-ᵊn, -ˈdiz-\ *vt* (1661) **:** to dress or adorn gaudily — **be·di·zen·ment** \-mənt\ *n*

bed·lam \ˈbed-ləm\ *n* [*Bedlam*, popular name for the Hospital of St. Mary of Bethlehem, London, an insane asylum, fr. ME *Bedlem* Bethlehem] (1522) **1** *obs* **:** MADMAN, LUNATIC **2** *often cap* **:** a lunatic asylum **3 :** a place, scene, or state of uproar and confusion — **bedlam** *adj*

bed·lam·ite \-lə-ˌmīt\ *n* (1621) **:** MADMAN, LUNATIC — **bedlamite** *adj*

Bed·ling·ton terrier \ˌbed-liŋ-tən-\ *n* [*Bedlington*, England] (1867) **:** a swift lightly built terrier with a narrow head and arched back — called also *Bedlington*

bed·mate \ˈbed-ˌmāt\ *n* (1583) **:** one who shares one's bed; *esp* **:** a sexual partner

bed molding *n* (1703) **:** the molding of a cornice below the corona and above the frieze; *also* **:** a molding below a deep projection

bed of roses (1648) **:** a place or situation of agreeable ease

bed·ou·in *or* **bed·u·in** \ˈbed(-ə)-wən\ *n, pl* **bedouin** *or* **bedouins** *or* **beduin** *or* **beduins** *often cap* [F *bédouin*, fr. Ar *badāwi, bidwān*, pl. of *badawi* desert dweller] (15c) **:** a nomadic Arab of the Arabian, Syrian, or No. African deserts

bed·pan \ˈbed-ˌpan\ *n* (1678) **:** a shallow vessel used by a person in bed for urination or defecation

bed·plate \-ˌplāt\ *n* (1850) **:** a plate or framing used as a support

bed·post \-ˌpōst\ *n* (1598) **:** the usu. turned or carved post of a bed

be·drag·gle \bi-ˈdrag-əl\ *vt* (1727) **:** to wet thoroughly

be·drag·gled \bi-ˈdrag-əld\ *adj* (1727) **1 :** left wet and limp by or as if by rain **2 :** soiled and stained by or as if by trailing in mud **3 :** DILAPIDATED ⟨~ buildings⟩

bed rest *n* (1944) **:** confinement of a sick person to bed

bed·rid·den \ˈbed-ˌrid-ᵊn\ *also* **bed·rid** \-ˌrid\ *adj* [alter. of ME *bedrede, bedreden*, fr. OE *bedreda*, fr. *bedreda* one confined to bed, fr. *bedd* bed + *-rida, -reda* rider, fr. *rīdan* to ride] (bef. 12c) **:** confined (as by illness) to bed

bed·rock \-ˈräk, -ˌräk\ *n* (1850) **1 :** the solid rock underlying unconsolidated surface materials (as soil) **2 a :** lowest point **:** NADIR **b :** BASIS — **bedrock** *adj*

bed·roll \-ˌrōl\ *n* (1910) **:** bedding rolled up for carrying

1**bed·room** \-ˌrüm, -ˌru̇m\ *n* (1616) **:** a room furnished with a bed and intended primarily for sleeping

2**bed·room** *adj* (1915) **1 :** dealing with, suggestive of, or inviting to sexual relations ⟨a ~ farce⟩ ⟨~ eyes⟩ **2 :** inhabited or used by commuters ⟨~ suburbs⟩

\ə\ abut \ᵊ\ kitten, F table \ər\ further \a\ ash \ā\ ace \ä\ cot, cart \au̇\ out \ch\ chin \e\ bet \ē\ easy \g\ go \i\ hit \ī\ ice \j\ job \ŋ\ sing \ō\ go \ȯ\ law \ȯi\ boy \th\ thin \th\ the \ü\ loot \u̇\ foot \y\ yet \zh\ vision \à, k, ⁿ, œ, ᵫ, ue, ue, ʸ\ see Guide to Pronunciation

[1]**bed·side** \'bed-,sīd\ *n* (14c) **:** the side of a bed **:** a place beside a bed
[2]**bedside** *adj* (1837) **1 :** of, relating to, or conducted at the bedside ⟨a ~ diagnosis⟩ **2 :** suitable for a bedridden person ⟨~ reading⟩
bedside manner *n* (1869) **:** the manner that a physician assumes toward his patients
bed–sit·ter \'bed-,sit-ər\ *n* [*bed*room + *sitt*ing room + *-er*] *Brit* (1927) **:** a one-room apartment serving as both bedroom and sitting room — called also *bed-sit, bed-sitting-room*
bed·sore \'bed-,sō(ə)r, -,sȯ(ə)r\ *n* (1861) **:** an ulceration of tissue deprived of nutrition by prolonged pressure
bed·spread \-,spred\ *n* (1845) **:** a usu. ornamental cloth cover for a bed
bed·spring \-,spriŋ\ *n* (1897) **:** a spring supporting a mattress
bed·stead \'bed-,sted\ *n* [ME *bedstede*, fr. *bed* + *stede* stead, place — more at STEAD] (15c) **:** the framework of a bed
bed·straw \-,strȯ\ *n* [fr. its use for mattresses] (1527) **:** any of a genus (*Galium*) of herbs of the madder family having angled stems, opposite or whorled leaves, and small flowers
bed table *n* (1811) **1 :** an adjustable table used (as for eating or writing) by a person in bed **2 :** a small table used beside a bed
bed·time \-,tīm\ *n* (13c) **:** a time for going to bed
bedtime story *n* (1899) **:** a story read or recounted to someone (as a child) at bedtime
bed warmer *n* (1922) **:** a covered pan containing hot coals used to warm a bed
bed–wet·ting \-,wet-iŋ\ *n* (1890) **:** enuresis esp. when occurring in bed during sleep —**bed wetter** *n*
[1]**bee** \'bē\ *n* [ME, fr. OE *bēo;* akin to OHG *bīa* bee, Lith *bitis*] (bef. 12c) **1 :** a social colonial hymenopterous insect (*Apis mellifera*) often kept in hives for the honey that it produces; *broadly* **:** any of numerous insects (superfamily Apoidea) that differ from the related wasps esp. in the heavier hairier body and in having sucking as well as chewing mouthparts, that feed on pollen and nectar, and that store both and often also honey **2 :** an eccentric notion **:** FANCY — **bee·like** \-,līk\ *adj* — **bee in one's bonnet :** [1]BEE 2
[2]**bee** *n* [ME *beghe* metal ring, fr. OE *bēag;* akin to OE *būgan* to bend — more at BOW] (ca. 1864) **:** a piece of hard wood at the side of a bowsprit to reeve fore-topmast stays through
[3]**bee** *n* (bef. 12c) **:** the letter *b*
[4]**bee** *n* [perh. fr. E dial. *been* help given by neighbors, fr. ME *bene* prayer, boon, fr. OE *bēn* prayer — more at BOON] (1769) **:** a gathering of people for a specific purpose ⟨quilting ~⟩
bee balm *n* (1847) **:** any of several mints (as monarda) attractive to bees; *esp* **:** OSWEGO TEA
bee·bee *var of* BB
bee·bread \'bē-,bred\ *n* (1657) **:** bitter yellowish brown pollen stored up in honeycomb cells and used mixed with honey by bees as food
beech \'bēch\ *n, pl* **beech·es** *or* **beech** [ME *beche,* fr. OE *bēce;* akin to OE *bōc* beech, OHG *buohha,* L *fagus,* Gk *phēgos* oak] (bef. 12c) **:** any of a genus (*Fagus* of the family Fagaceae, the beech family) of hardwood trees with smooth gray bark and small edible nuts; *also* **:** its wood — **beech·en** \'bē-chən\ *adj*
beech·drops \'bēch-,dräps\ *n pl but sing or pl in constr* (1815) **:** a low wiry plant (*Epifagus virginiana*) of the broomrape family parasitic on the roots of beeches
beech·nut \-,nət\ *n* (1739) **:** the nut of the beech
bee eater *n* (1668) **:** any of a family (Meropidae) of brightly colored slender-billed insectivorous chiefly tropical Old World birds
[1]**beef** \'bēf\ *n, pl* **beefs** \'bēfs\ *or* **beeves** \'bēvz\ [ME, fr. OF *buef* ox, beef, fr. L *bov-, bos* head of cattle — more at COW] (13c) **1 :** the flesh of an adult domestic bovine (as a steer or cow) used as food **2 a :** an ox, cow, or bull in a full-grown or nearly full-grown state; *esp* **:** a steer or cow fattened for food ⟨quality Texas *beeves*⟩ ⟨a herd of good ~⟩ **b :** a dressed carcass of a beef animal **3 :** muscular flesh **:** BRAWN **4** *pl* **beefs :** COMPLAINT
[2]**beef** *vt* (1860) **:** to add weight, strength, or power to — usu. used with *up* ⟨money to ~ up its staff of professional economists —John Fischer⟩ ~ *vi* **:** COMPLAIN

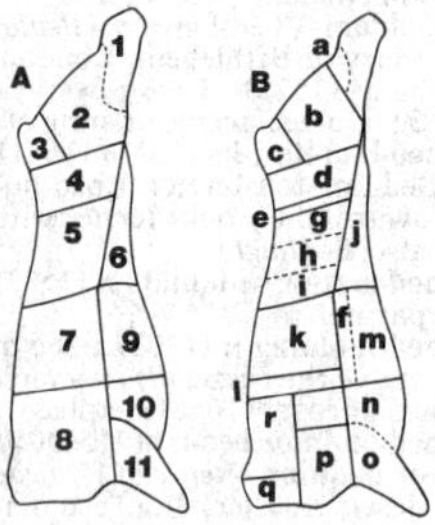

beef 2b: *A* wholesale cuts: *1* shank, *2* round with rump and shank cut off, *3* rump, *4* sirloin, *5* short loin, *6* flank, *7* rib, *8* chuck, *9* plate, *10* brisket, *11* shank; *B* retail cuts: *a* heel pot roast, *b* round steak, *c* rump roast, *d* sirloin steak, *e* pinbone steak, *f* short ribs, *g* porterhouse steak, *h* T-bone steak, *i* club steak, *j* flank steak, *k* rib roast, *l* blade rib roast, *m* plate, *n* brisket, *o* crosscut shank, *p* arm pot roast, *q* boneless neck, *r* blade roast

beef·alo \'bē-fə-,lō\ *n, pl* **-alos** *or* **-aloes** [[1]*beef* + buff*alo*] (1973) **:** any of a breed of beef cattle developed in No. America that is genetically 3/8 American bison and 5/8 domestic bovine
beef·cake \'bēf-,kāk\ *n* (1949) **:** a usu. photographic display of muscular male physiques — compare CHEESECAKE
beef cattle *n pl* (1758) **:** cattle developed primarily for the efficient production of meat and marked by capacity for rapid growth, heavy well-fleshed body, and stocky build
beef·eat·er \'bē-,fēt-ər\ *n* (1671) **:** a yeoman of the guard of an English monarch
bee fly *n* (1852) **:** any of numerous two-winged flies (family Bombyliidae) many of which resemble bees
beef·steak \'bēf-,stāk\ *n* (1711) **:** a steak of beef usu. from the hindquarter
beef Stro·ga·noff \-'strȯ-gə-,nȯf, -'strō-\ *n* [Count Paul *Stroganoff,* 19th cent. Russ. diplomat] (1944) **:** beef sliced thin and cooked in a sour-cream sauce
beef Wel·ling·ton \-'wel-iŋ-tən\ *n* [prob. fr. the name *Wellington*] (1965) **:** a fillet of beef covered with pâté de foie gras and baked in a casing of pastry
beef·wood \'bēf-,wu̇d\ *n* (1756) **:** any of several hard heavy reddish chiefly tropical woods used esp. for cabinetwork; *also* **:** an Australian pine (*Casuarina equisetifolia*)
beefy \'bē-fē\ *adj* **beef·i·er; -est** (1743) **1 a :** heavily and powerfully built **b :** SUBSTANTIAL, STURDY ⟨~ fabrics for sportswear⟩ **2 :** full of beef
bee·hive \'bē-,hīv\ *n* (14c) **1 :** HIVE 1 **2 :** something resembling a hive for bees: as **a :** a scene of crowded activity **b :** a woman's hairdo that is conical in shape — **beehive** *adj*
bee·keep·er \-,kē-pər\ *n* (1817) **:** one who raises bees — **bee·keep·ing** *n*
bee·line \-,līn\ *n* [fr. the belief that nectar-laden bees return to their hives in a direct line] (1830) **:** a straight direct course
Beel·ze·bub \bē-'el-zi-,bəb, 'bēl-zi-, 'bel-\ *n* [*Beelzebub,* prince of devils, fr. L, fr. Gk *Beelzeboub,* fr. Heb *Ba'al zĕbhūbh,* a Philistine god, lit., lord of flies] (bef. 12c) **1 :** DEVIL **2 :** a fallen angel in Milton's *Paradise Lost* ranking next to Satan
been *past part of* BE
[1]**beep** \'bēp\ *n* [imit.] (1929) **:** a sound (as from a horn or an electronic device) that serves as a signal or warning
[2]**beep** *vi* (1936) **1 :** to sound a horn **2 :** to make a beep ~ *vt* **:** to cause (as a horn) to sound
beep·er \'bē-pər\ *n* (1970) **:** a portable electronic device used to page the person carrying it that beeps when it receives a special radio signal
beer \'bi(ə)r\ *n* [ME *ber,* fr. OE *bēor;* akin to OHG *bior* beer] (bef. 12c) **1 :** an alcoholic beverage usu. made from malted cereal grain (as barley), flavored with hops, and brewed by slow fermentation **2 :** a carbonated nonalcoholic or a fermented slightly alcoholic beverage with flavoring from roots or other plant parts ⟨birch ~⟩
beery \'bi(ə)r-ē\ *adj* **beer·i·er; -est** (1848) **1 :** smelling or tasting of beer ⟨~ tavern⟩ **2 :** affected or caused by beer ⟨~ voices⟩
bees·tings \'bē-stiŋz\ *n pl but sing or pl in constr* [ME *bestynge,* fr. OE *bȳsting,* fr. *bēost* beestings] (bef. 12c) **:** the colostrum esp. of a cow
bees·wax \'bēz-,waks\ *n* (1676) **:** WAX 1
beet \'bēt\ *n* [ME *bete,* fr. OE *bēte,* fr. L *beta*] (bef. 12c) **:** a biennial garden plant (genus *Beta*) of the goosefoot family with thick long-stalked edible leaves and swollen root used as a vegetable, as a source of sugar, or for forage; *also* **:** its root
beet armyworm *n* (1902) **:** an armyworm (*Spodoptera exigua*) that eats the foliage of beets, alfalfa, and vegetables
[1]**bee·tle** \'bēt-ᵊl\ *n* [ME *betylle,* fr. OE *bitula,* fr. *bītan* to bite] (bef. 12c) **1 :** any of an order (Coleoptera) of insects having four wings of which the outer pair are modified into stiff elytra that protect the inner pair when at rest **2 :** any of various insects resembling a beetle
[2]**beetle** *n* [ME *betel,* fr. OE *bīetel;* akin to OE *bēatan* to beat] (bef. 12c) **1 :** a heavy wooden hammering or ramming instrument **2 :** a wooden pestle or bat for domestic tasks **3 :** a machine for giving fabrics a lustrous finish
[3]**beetle** *adj* [ME *bitel-browed* having overhanging brows, prob. fr. *betylle, bitel* beetle] (14c) **:** being prominent and overhanging ⟨~ brows⟩
[4]**beetle** *vi* **bee·tled; bee·tling** \'bēt-liŋ, -ᵊl-iŋ\ (1602) **:** PROJECT, JUT ⟨to scale the *beetling* crags —R. L. Stevenson⟩
beet leafhopper *n* (1919) **:** a leafhopper (*Eutettix tenellus*) that transmits a virus disease to sugar beets and other plants in the western U.S.
bee tree *n* (1782) **:** a hollow tree in which honeybees nest
beet·root \'bē-,trüt\ *n, chiefly Brit* (1579) **:** the root of the beet
beeves *pl of* BEEF
be·fall \bi-'fȯl\ *vb* **-fell** \-'fel\; **-fall·en** \-'fȯ-lən\ *vi* (13c) **:** to happen esp. as if by fate ~ *vt* **:** to happen to
be·fit \bi-'fit\ *vt* **be·fit·ted; be·fit·ting** (15c) **:** to be proper or becoming to
be·fit·ting \-'fit-iŋ\ *adj* (1564) **1 :** SUITABLE, APPROPRIATE **2 :** PROPER, DECENT — **be·fit·ting·ly** \-iŋ-lē\ *adv*
be·fog \bi-'fȯg, -'fäg\ *vt* (1601) **1 :** CONFUSE **2 :** FOG, OBSCURE
be·fool \bi-'fül\ *vt* (14c) **1 :** to make a fool of **2 :** DELUDE, DECEIVE
[1]**be·fore** \bi-'fō(ə)r, -'fȯ(ə)r\ *adv or adj* [ME, adv. & prep., fr. OE *beforan,* fr. *be-* + *foran* before, fr. *fore*] (bef. 12c) **1 :** in advance **:** AHEAD **2 :** at an earlier time **:** PREVIOUSLY ⟨the night ~⟩
[2]**before** *prep* (bef. 12c) **1 a (1) :** in front of **(2) :** in the presence of **b :** under the jurisdiction or consideration of ⟨the case ~ the court⟩ **c (1) :** at the disposal of **(2) :** in store for **2 :** preceding in time **:** earlier than **3 :** in a higher or more important position than ⟨put quantity ~ quality⟩
[3]**before** *conj* (13c) **1 :** earlier than the time when **2 :** sooner than
be·fore·hand \bi-'fō(ə)r-,hand, -'fȯ(ə)r-\ *adv or adj* (13c) **1 a :** in anticipation **b :** in advance **2 :** ahead of time **:** EARLY
be·fore·time \-,tīm\ *adv, archaic* (14c) **:** FORMERLY
be·foul \bi-'fau̇(ə)l\ *vt* (bef. 12c) **:** to make foul with or as if with dirt
be·friend \bi-'frend\ *vt* (1559) **:** to act as a friend to
be·fud·dle \bi-'fəd-ᵊl\ *vt* (ca. 1879) **1 :** to muddle or stupefy with or as if with drink **2 :** CONFUSE, PERPLEX — **be·fud·dle·ment** \-mənt\ *n*
beg \'beg\ *vb* **begged; beg·ging** [ME *beggen*] *vt* (13c) **1 :** to ask for as a charity **2 a :** to ask earnestly for **:** ENTREAT **b :** to require as necessary or appropriate **3 a :** EVADE, SIDESTEP ⟨*begged* the real problems⟩ **b :** to assume as established or proved ⟨~ the question⟩ ~ *vi* **1 :** to ask for alms **2 :** to ask earnestly ⟨*begged* for mercy⟩

syn BEG, ENTREAT, BESEECH, IMPLORE, SUPPLICATE, ADJURE, IMPORTUNE mean to ask urgently. BEG suggests earnestness or insistence esp. in asking for a favor; ENTREAT implies an effort to persuade or to overcome resistance; BESEECH implies great eagerness or anxiety; IMPLORE adds to BESEECH a suggestion of greater urgency or anguished appeal; SUPPLICATE suggests a posture of humility; ADJURE implies advising as well as pleading and suggests the involving of something sacred; IMPORTUNE suggests an annoying persistence in trying to break down resistance to a request.

— **beg off :** to ask to be released from something
be·get \bi-'get\ *vt* **-got** \-'gät\ *also* **-gat** \-'gat\; **-got·ten** \-'gät-ᵊn\ *or* **-got; -get·ting** [ME *begeten,* alter. of *beyeten,* fr. OE *bigietan* — more at GET] (13c) **1 :** to procreate as the father **:** SIRE **2 :** to produce as an effect or outgrowth **:** CAUSE — **be·get·ter** *n*
[1]**beg·gar** \'beg-ər\ *n* [ME *beggere, beggare,* fr. *beggen* to beg + *-ere, -are* -er] (13c) **1 :** one that begs; *esp* **:** one that lives by asking for gifts **2 :** PAUPER **3 :** FELLOW 4c
[2]**beggar** *vt* **beg·gared; beg·gar·ing** \'beg-(ə-)riŋ\ (15c) **1 :** to reduce to beggary **2 :** to exceed the resources or abilities of **:** DEFY ⟨~s description⟩
beg·gar·ly \'beg-ər-lē\ *adj* (1526) **1 :** contemptibly mean, scant, petty, or paltry **2 :** befitting or resembling a beggar; *esp* **:** marked by extreme poverty — **beg·gar·li·ness** *n*

beg·gar's–lice \'beg-ərz-ˌlīs\ *or* **beg·gar–lice** \-ər-ˌlīs\ *n pl but sing or pl in constr* (1847) **:** any of several plants (as of the genera *Lappula, Hackelia,* and *Desmodium*) with prickly or adhesive fruits; *also* **:** one of these fruits

beg·gar's–ticks *also* **beg·gar's–ticks** \-ˌtiks\ *n pl but sing or pl in constr* (ca. 1817) **1 :** BUR MARIGOLD; *also* **:** its prickly achenes **2 :** BEGGAR'S-LICE

beg·gar·weed \'beg-ər-ˌwēd\ *n* (ca. 1809) **1 :** any of various plants (as a knotgrass, spurrey, or dodder) that grow in waste ground **2 :** any of several tick trefoils (genus *Desmodium*); *esp* **:** a West Indian forage plant (*D. tortuosum*) cultivated in the southern U.S.

beg·gary \'beg-(ə-)rē\ *n, pl* **-gar·ies** (14c) **1 :** POVERTY, PENURY **2 :** the class or occupation of beggars **3 :** the practice of begging **:** MENDICANCY

be·gin \bi-'gin\ *vb* **be·gan** \-'gan\; **be·gun** \-'gən\; **be·gin·ning** [ME *beginnen,* fr. OE *beginnan;* akin to OHG *biginnan* to begin, OE *onginnan*] *vi* (bef. 12c) **1 a :** to do the first part of an action **:** START **b :** to undergo initial steps **2 a :** to come into existence **:** ARISE **b :** to have a starting point **3 :** to do or succeed in the least degree ~ *vt* **1 :** to set about the activity of **:** START **2 a :** to bring into being **:** FOUND **b :** ORIGINATE, INVENT **3 :** to come first in

syn BEGIN, COMMENCE, START, INITIATE, INAUGURATE mean to take the first step in a course, process, or operation. BEGIN and COMMENCE are practically identical in meaning but COMMENCE suggests greater formality; START, opposed to *stop,* suggests a getting or setting into motion or setting out on a journey; INITIATE implies the taking of a first step of a process or series that is to continue; INAUGURATE implies a ceremonious beginning.

be·gin·ner \bi-'gin-ər\ *n* (14c) **:** one that begins something; *specif* **:** an inexperienced person

¹be·gin·ning \bi-'gin-iŋ\ *n* (12c) **1 :** the point at which something begins **:** START **2 :** the first part **3 :** ORIGIN, SOURCE **4 a :** a rudimentary stage or early period — usu. used in pl. **b :** something undeveloped or incomplete

²beginning *adj* (1576) **1 :** just created or formed **:** INCIPIENT **2 :** INTRODUCTORY, EARLY **3 :** BASIC ⟨~ chemistry⟩ **4 :** just becoming familiar with the rudiments or practice ⟨a ~ machinist⟩

beginning rhyme *n* (1913) **1 :** rhyme at the beginning of successive lines of verse **2 :** ALLITERATION

be·gird \bi-'gərd\ *vt* (bef. 12c) **1 :** GIRD 1a **2 :** SURROUND, ENCOMPASS

be·gone \bi-'gȯn *also* -'gän\ *vi* [ME, fr. *be gone* (imper.)] (14c) **:** to go away **:** DEPART — used esp. in the imperative

be·go·nia \bi-'gōn-yə\ *n* [NL, genus name, fr. Michel *Bégon* †1710 Fr. governor of Santo Domingo] (1751) **:** any of a large genus (*Begonia* of the family Begoniaceae, the begonia family) of tropical herbs having asymmetrical leaves and being widely cultivated as ornamentals

be·gor·ra \bi-'gȯr-ə, -'gär-\ *interj* [euphemism for *by God*] *Irish* (1839) — used as a mild oath

be·grime \bi-'grīm\ *vt* **be·grimed; be·grim·ing** (1553) **1 :** to make dirty with grime **2 :** SULLY, CORRUPT

be·grudge \bi-'grəj\ *vt* (14c) **1 :** to give or concede reluctantly **2 a :** to look upon with reluctance or disapproval **b :** to take little pleasure in **:** be annoyed by **3 :** to envy the pleasure or enjoyment of — **be·grudg·ing·ly** \-'grəj-iŋ-lē\ *adv*

be·guile \bi-'gī(ə)l\ *vb* **be·guiled; be·guil·ing** *vt* (13c) **1 :** to lead by deception **2 a :** HOODWINK **b :** to deprive by guile **:** CHEAT **3 :** to while away esp. by some agreeable occupation **4 :** to please or persuade by the use of wiles **:** CHARM ~ *vi* **:** to deceive by wiles ***syn*** see DECEIVE — **be·guile·ment** \-'gī(ə)l-mənt\ *n* — **be·guil·er** \-'gī-lər\ *n* — **be·guil·ing·ly** \-'gī-liŋ-lē\ *adv*

be·guine \bi-'gēn\ *n* [AmerF *béguine,* fr. F *béguin* flirtation] (1935) **:** a vigorous popular dance of the islands of Saint Lucia and Martinique that somewhat resembles the rumba

Be·guine \'bā-ˌgēn, ˌbā-'\ *n* [MF] (15c) **:** a member of one of various ascetic and philanthropic communities of women not under vows founded chiefly in the Netherlands in the 13th century

be·gum \'bā-gəm, 'bē-\ *n* [Hindi *begam*] (1617) **:** a Muslim woman of high rank

be·half \bi-'haf, -'háf\ *n* [ME, fr. *by* + *half* half, side] (14c) **:** INTEREST, BENEFIT; *also* **:** SUPPORT, DEFENSE ⟨argued in his ~⟩ — **on behalf of** *or* **in behalf of :** in the interest of **:** as a representative of

be·have \bi-'hāv\ *vb* **be·haved; be·hav·ing** [ME *behaven,* fr. *be-* + *haven* to have, hold] *vt* (15c) **1 :** to bear or comport (oneself) in a particular way **2 :** to conduct (oneself) in a proper manner ~ *vi* **1 :** to act, function, or react in a particular way **2 :** to conduct oneself properly — **be·hav·er** *n*

syn BEHAVE, CONDUCT, DEPORT, COMPORT, ACQUIT mean to act or to cause oneself to do something in a certain way. BEHAVE may apply to the meeting of a standard of what is proper or decorous; CONDUCT implies action or behavior that shows the extent of one's power to control or direct oneself; DEPORT implies behaving so as to show how far one conforms to conventional rules of discipline or propriety; COMPORT suggests conduct measured by what is expected or required of one in a certain class or position; ACQUIT applies to action under stress that deserves praise or meets expectations.

be·hav·ior \bi-'hā-vyər\ *n* [alter. of ME *behavour,* fr. *behaven*] (15c) **1 :** the manner of conducting oneself **2 a :** anything that an organism does involving action and response to stimulation **b :** the response of an individual, group, or species to its environment **3 :** the way in which something (as a machine) behaves — **be·hav·ior·al** \-vyə-rəl\ *adj* — **be·hav·ior·al·ly** \-rə-lē\ *adv*

behavioral science *n* (1951) **:** a science (as psychology, sociology, or anthropology) that deals with human action and seeks to generalize about human behavior in society — **behavioral scientist** *n*

be·hav·ior·ism \bi-'hā-vyə-ˌriz-əm\ *n* (1913) **:** a school of psychology that takes the objective evidence of behavior (as measured responses to stimuli) as the only concern of its research and the only basis of its theory without reference to conscious experience — compare INTROSPECTIONISM — **be·hav·ior·ist** \-vyə-rəst\ *adj or n* — **be·hav·ior·is·tic** \-ˌhā-vyə-'ris-tik\ *adj*

be·hav·iour *chiefly Brit var of* BEHAVIOR

be·head \bi-'hed\ *vt* (bef. 12c) **:** to cut off the head of **:** DECAPITATE

be·he·moth \bi-'hē-məth, 'bē-ə-məth, -ˌmäth, -ˌmȯth\ *n* [ME, fr. L, fr. Heb *bĕhēmōth*] (14c) **1** *often cap* **:** an animal described in Job 40:15–24 that is prob. the hippopotamus **2 :** something of oppressive or monstrous size or power

be·hest \bi-'hest\ *n* [ME, promise, command, fr. OE *behǣs* promise, fr. *behātan* to promise, fr. *be-* + *hātan* to command, promise — more at HIGHT] (12c) **1 :** an authoritative order **:** COMMAND **2 :** an urgent prompting ⟨returned home at the ~ of his friends⟩

¹be·hind \bi-'hīnd\ *adv or adj* [ME *behinde,* fr. OE *behindan,* fr. *be-* + *hindan* from behind; akin to OE *hinder* behind — more at HIND] (bef. 12c) **1 a :** in the place, situation, or time that is being or has been departed from ⟨stay ~⟩ **b :** in, to, or toward the back ⟨look ~⟩ **2 a :** in a secondary or inferior position **b :** in arrears ⟨~ in his payments⟩ **c :** SLOW **3** *archaic* **:** still to come

²behind *prep* (bef. 12c) **1 a** (1) **:** in or to a place or situation in back of or to the rear of ⟨look ~ you⟩ (2) **:** beyond in past time ⟨left a great name ~ him⟩ **b** — used as a function word to indicate something that lies between one thing (as an observer) and another ⟨malice ~ the mask of friendship⟩ **2** — used as a function word to indicate backwardness ⟨~ his classmates in performance⟩, delay ⟨~ schedule⟩, or deficiency ⟨lagged ~ last year's sales⟩ **3 a :** in the background of ⟨the conditions ~ the strike⟩ **b :** in a supporting position at the back of ⟨solidly ~ their candidate⟩

³behind *n* [ˈ*behind*] (13c) **:** BUTTOCKS

be·hind·hand \bi-'hīnd-ˌhand\ *adj* (14c) **1 :** being in arrears **2 a :** lagging behind the times **:** BACKWARD **b :** being in an inferior position **c :** being behind schedule

behind–the–scenes *adj* (1711) **1 :** being or working out of public view or in secret ⟨~ organizers⟩ **2 :** revealing or reporting the hidden workings ⟨a ~ account⟩

be·hold \bi-'hōld\ *vb* **-held** \-'held\; **-hold·ing** [ME *beholden* to keep, behold, fr. OE *behealdan,* fr. *be-* + *healdan* to hold] *vt* (bef. 12c) **1 :** to perceive through sight or apprehension **:** SEE **2 :** to gaze upon **:** OBSERVE ~ *vi* — used in the imperative esp. to call attention — **be·hold·er** *n*

be·hold·en \bi-'hōl-dən\ *adj* [ME, fr. pp. of *beholden*] (14c) **:** being under obligation for a favor or gift **:** INDEBTED

be·hoof \bi-'hüf\ *n* [ME *behof,* fr. OE *behōf* profit, need; akin to OE *hebban* to raise — more at HEAVE] (bef. 12c) **:** ADVANTAGE, PROFIT ⟨for his own ~⟩

be·hoove \bi-'hüv\ *or* **be·hove** \-'hōv\ *vb* **be·hooved** *or* **be·hoved; be·hoov·ing** *or* **be·hov·ing** [ME *behoven,* fr. OE *behōfian,* fr. *behōf*] *vt* (bef. 12c) **:** to be necessary, proper, or advantageous for ⟨it ~*s* us to fight⟩ ~ *vi* **:** to be necessary, fit, or proper

beige \'bāzh\ *n* [F] (ca. 1858) **1 :** cloth made of natural undyed wool **2 a :** a variable color averaging light grayish yellowish brown **b :** a pale to grayish yellow — **beige** *adj* — **beigy** \'bā-zhē\ *adj*

¹be·ing \'bē(-i)ŋ\ *n* (14c) **1 a :** the quality or state of having existence **b** (1) **:** something conceivable as existing (2) **:** something that actually exists (3) **:** the totality of existing things **c :** conscious existence **:** LIFE **2 :** the qualities that constitute an existent thing **:** ESSENCE; *esp* **:** PERSONALITY **3 :** a living thing; *esp* **:** PERSON

²being *adj* [prp. of *be*] (14c) **:** PRESENT — used in the phrase *for the time being*

Be·ja \'bā-jə\ *n, pl* **Beja** (1819) **1 a :** a nomadic pastoral people living between the Nile and the Red sea **b :** a member of this people **2 :** the Cushitic language of the Beja people

be·je·sus \bi-'jē-zəs, -'jā-, -zəz\ *interj* [alter. of *by Jesus*] (ca. 1908) — used as a mild oath; used as a noun for emphasis ⟨whipped the ~ out of him⟩

be·jew·eled \bi-'jü-əld, -'jüld *also* -'jů(ə)ld\ *adj* (1557) **:** ornamented with or as if with jewels

bel \'bel\ *n* [Alexander Graham *Bell*] (1929) **:** ten decibels

be·la·bor \bi-'lā-bər\ *vt* (1596) **1 a :** ASSAIL, ATTACK **b :** to beat soundly **2 :** to work on or at to absurd lengths ⟨~ the obvious⟩

be·la·bour *chiefly Brit var of* BELABOR

be·lat·ed \bi-'lāt-əd\ *adj* [pp. of *belate* (to make late)] (1670) **1 :** delayed beyond the usual time **2 :** existing or appearing past the normal or proper time — **be·lat·ed·ly** *adv* — **be·lat·ed·ness** *n*

be·laud \bi-'lȯd\ *vt* (1849) **:** to praise usu. to excess

¹be·lay \bi-'lā\ *vb* [ME *beleggen* to beset, fr. OE *belecgan,* fr. *be-* + *lecgan* to lay] *vt* (bef. 12c) **1 a :** to secure (as a rope) by turns around a cleat, pin, or bitt **b :** to make fast **2 :** STOP **3 a :** to secure (a person) at the end of a rope **b :** to secure (a rope) to a person or object ~ *vi* **1 :** to be made fast **2 :** STOP, QUIT — used in the imperative ⟨~ there⟩ **3 :** to make a line fast by turns around a cleat, pin, or bitt

²belay *n* (1908) **1 :** the obtaining of a hold (as for a rope) during mountain climbing; *also* **:** a method of obtaining such a hold **2 :** something (as a projection of rock) to which a mountain climber's rope is anchored

bel can·to \bel-'kän-(ˌ)tō, -'kan-\ *n* [It, lit., beautiful singing] (1894) **:** operatic singing originating in 17th century and 18th century Italy and stressing ease, purity, and evenness of tone production and an agile and precise vocal technique

belch \'belch\ *vb* [ME *belchen,* fr. OE *bealcan*] *vi* (bef. 12c) **1 :** to expel gas suddenly from the stomach through the mouth **2 :** to erupt, explode, or detonate violently **3 :** to issue forth spasmodically **:** GUSH ~ *vt* **1 :** to eject or emit violently **2 :** to expel (gas) from the stomach suddenly **:** ERUCT — **belch** *n*

bel·dam *or* **bel·dame** \'bel-dəm\ *n* [ME *beldam* grandmother, fr. MF *bel* beautiful + ME *dam*] (1580) **:** an old woman; *esp* **:** HAG

be·lea·guer \bi-'lē-gər\ *vt* **-guered; -guer·ing** \-g(ə-)riŋ\ [D *belegeren,* fr. *be-* (akin to OE *be-*) + *leger* camp; akin to OHG *legar* bed — more at LAIR] (1587) **1 :** to surround with an army so as to prevent escape **:** BESIEGE **2 :** TROUBLE, HARASS ⟨~*ed* parents⟩

bel·em·nite \'bel-əm-ˌnīt\ *n* [F *bélemnite,* fr. Gk *belemnon* dart; akin to Gk *ballein* to throw — more at DEVIL] (1646) **:** a conical fossil shell of an extinct cephalopod (family Belemnitidae) — **bel·em·nit·ic** \ˌbel-əm-'nit-ik\ *adj*

\ə\ abut \ᵊ\ kitten, F table \ər\ further \a\ ash \ā\ ace \ä\ cot, cart \au̇\ out \ch\ chin \e\ bet \ē\ easy \g\ go \i\ hit \ī\ ice \j\ job \ŋ\ sing \ō\ go \ȯ\ law \ȯi\ boy \th\ thin \t͟h\ the \ü\ loot \u̇\ foot \y\ yet \zh\ vision \à, k̲, ⁿ, œ, œ̄, ue, uē, ʸ\ see Guide to Pronunciation

bel·fry \'bel-frē\ *n, pl* **belfries** [ME *belfrey,* alter. of *berfrey,* fr. MF *berfrei,* fr. MHG *bervrit,* fr. ML *berfredus,* deriv. of Gk *pyrgos phorētos* movable war tower] (15c) **1 :** a bell tower; *esp* **:** one surmounting or attached to another structure **2 :** a room in which a bell is hung in a tower **3 :** a cupola, turret, or framework for enclosing a bell
bel·ga \'bel-gə\ *n* [F, fr. L *Belga* Belgian] (1926) **:** a former Belgian monetary unit for use in foreign exchange equal to five francs
Bel·gae \'bel-,gī, -jē\ *n pl* [L, pl. of *Belga*] (ca. 1895) **:** a people occupying northern France, Belgium, and England in Caesar's time — **Bel·gic** \-jik\ *adj*
Bel·gian \'bel-jən\ *n* (ca. 1623) **1 :** a native or inhabitant of Belgium **2 :** any of a Belgian breed of heavy usu. roan or chestnut draft horses — **Belgian** *adj*
Belgian hare *n* (1900) **:** any of a breed of slender dark-red domestic rabbits
Belgian Ma·li·nois \-,mal-ən-'wä\ *n* (1968) **:** any of a breed of squarely built working dogs closely related to the Belgian sheepdog and having relatively short straight hair with a dense undercoat — called also *Malinois*
Belgian sheepdog *n* (1929) **:** any of a breed of hardy black dogs developed in Belgium esp. for herding sheep
Belgian Ter·vu·ren \-(,)tər-'vyu̇r-ən, -ter-\ *n* [*Tervuren,* commune in Brabant, Belgium] (1964) **:** any of a breed of working dogs closely related to the Belgian sheepdog but having abundant long straight fawn-colored hair with black tips
Bel·go- \'bel-(,)gō\ *comb form* [*Belgian*] **:** Belgian and ⟨*Belgo*-English⟩
Be·lial \'bē-lē-əl, 'bēl-yəl\ *n* [Gk, fr. Heb *bəlīya'al* worthlessness] **1** — a biblical name of the devil or one of the fiends **2 :** one of the fallen angels in Milton's *Paradise Lost*
be·lie \bi-'lī\ *vt* **-lied; -ly·ing** (bef. 12c) **1 a :** to give a false impression of **b :** to contrast with **2 a :** to prove (something) false **b :** to run counter to **:** CONTRADICT — **be·li·er** \-'lī(-ə)r\ *n*
be·lief \bə-'lēf\ *n* [ME *beleave,* prob. alter. of OE *gelēafa,* fr. *ge-,* associative prefix + *lēafa;* akin to OE *lēof* dear] (bef. 12c) **1 :** a state or habit of mind in which trust or confidence is placed in some person or thing **2 :** something believed; *specif* **:** a tenet or body of tenets held by a group **3 :** conviction of the truth of some statement or the reality of some being or phenomenon esp. when based on examination of evidence
syn BELIEF, FAITH, CREDENCE, CREDIT mean assent to the truth of something offered for acceptance. BELIEF and FAITH are often used interchangeably but BELIEF may or may not imply certitude in the believer whereas FAITH always does even where there is no evidence or proof; CREDENCE suggests intellectual assent without implying anything about grounds for assent; CREDIT implies assent on grounds other than direct proof. ***syn*** see in addition OPINION
be·liev·able \-'lē-və-bəl\ *adj* (14c) **:** capable of being believed esp. as within the range of known possibility or probability — **be·liev·abil·i·ty** \-,lē-və-'bil-ət-ē\ *n* — **be·liev·ably** \-'lē-və-blē\ *adv*
be·lieve \bə-'lēv\ *vb* **be·lieved; be·liev·ing** [ME *beleven,* fr. OE *belēfan,* fr. *be-* + *lȳfan, lēfan* to allow, believe; akin to OHG *gilouben* to believe, OE *lēof* dear — more at LOVE] *vi* (bef. 12c) **1 a :** to have a firm religious faith **b :** to accept trustfully and on faith ⟨people who ~ in the natural goodness of man⟩ **2 :** to have a firm conviction as to the reality or goodness of something ⟨~ in exercise⟩ **3 :** to hold an opinion **:** THINK ~ *vt* **1 :** to consider to be true or honest ⟨~ the reports⟩ **2 :** to hold as an opinion **:** SUPPOSE ⟨I ~ it will rain soon⟩ — **be·liev·er** *n*
be·like \bi-'līk\ *adv, archaic* (1533) **:** most likely **:** PROBABLY
be·lit·tle \bi-'lit-ᵊl\ *vt* **-lit·tled; -lit·tling** \-'lit-ᵊl-iŋ, -'lit-liŋ\ (1797) **1 :** DISPARAGE 2 ⟨~*s* her efforts⟩ **2 :** to cause (a person or thing) to seem little or less ***syn*** see DECRY — **be·lit·tle·ment** \-'lit-ᵊl-mənt\ *n* — **be·lit·tler** \-'lit-ᵊl-ər, -'lit-lər\ *n*
be·live \bi-'līv\ *adv* [ME *bilive,* fr. *by* + *live,* dat. of *lif* life] *Scot* (15c) **:** in due time **:** BY AND BY
[1]**bell** \'bel\ *n* [ME *belle,* fr. OE; akin to OE *bellan* to roar — more at BELLOW] (bef. 12c) **1 :** a hollow metallic device that vibrates and gives forth a ringing sound when struck **2 :** the sounding of a bell as a signal **3 a :** a bell rung to tell the hour **b :** a stroke of such a bell esp. on shipboard **c :** the time so indicated **d :** a half hour period of a watch on shipboard indicated by the strokes of a bell — see SHIP'S BELLS table below **4 :** something having the form of a bell: as **a :** the corolla of a flower **b :** the part of the capital of a column between the abacus and neck molding **c :** the flared end of a wind instrument **5 a :** a percussion instrument consisting of metal bars or tubes that when struck give out tones resembling bells — usu. used in pl. **b :** GLOCKENSPIEL

SHIP'S BELLS

NO. OF BELLS	HOUR (A.M. OR P.M.)		
1	12:30	4:30	8:30
2	1:00	5:00	9:00
3	1:30	5:30	9:30
4	2:00	6:00	10:00
5	2:30	6:30	10:30
6	3:00	7:00	11:00
7	3:30	7:30	11:30
8	4:00	8:00	12:00

[2]**bell** *vt* (14c) **1 :** to provide with a bell **2 :** to make bell-mouthed ~ *vi* **:** to take the form of a bell **:** FLARE — **bell the cat :** to do a daring or risky deed
[3]**bell** *vi* [ME *bellen,* fr. OE *bellan*] (bef. 12c) **:** to make a resonant bellowing or baying sound ⟨the wild buck ~*s* from ferny brake —Sir Walter Scott⟩
[4]**bell** *n* (1862) **:** BELLOW, ROAR
bel·la·don·na \,bel-ə-'dän-ə\ *n* [It, lit., beautiful lady] (1597) **1 :** a European poisonous plant (*Atropa belladonna*) of the nightshade family having reddish bell-shaped flowers, shining black berries, and root and leaves that yield atropine — called also *deadly nightshade* **2 :** a medicinal extract (as atropine) from the belladonna plant
bell·bird \'bel-,bərd\ *n* (1802) **:** any of several birds whose notes suggest the sound of a bell
bell–bot·toms \'bel-'bät-əmz\ *n pl* (1898) **:** pants with wide flaring bottoms — **bell–bottom** *adj*
bell·boy \'bel-,bȯi\ *n* (1861) **:** BELLHOP
bell buoy *n* (1838) **:** a buoy with a bell rung by the action of the waves
bell captain *n* (1926) **:** CAPTAIN 2c
bell curve *n* [fr. the shape] (ca. 1941) **:** NORMAL CURVE
belle \'bel\ *n* [F, fr. fem. of *beau* beautiful — more at BEAU] (1622) **:** a popular and attractive girl or woman; *esp* **:** a girl or woman whose charm and beauty make her a favorite ⟨the ~ of the ball⟩
Bel·leek \bə-'lēk\ *n* [*Belleek,* town in Northern Ireland] (1869) **:** a very thin translucent porcelain with a lustrous pearly glaze first produced in Ireland in the mid-nineteenth century — called also *Belleek china, Belleek ware*
Bel·ler·o·phon \bə-'ler-ə-fən, -,fän\ *n* [L, fr. Gk *Bellerophōn*] **:** a legendary Greek hero noted for killing the Chimera
belles let·tres \bel-letrᵊ\ *n pl but sing in constr* [F, lit., fine letters] (1710) **:** literature that is an end in itself and not practical or purely informative; *specif* **:** light, entertaining, and often sophisticated literature
bel·le·trist \bel-'le-trəst\ *n* [*belles lettres*] (1816) **:** a writer of belles lettres — **bel·le·tris·tic** \,bel-ə-'tris-tik\ *adj*
bell·flow·er \'bel-,flau̇(-ə)r\ *n* (1578) **:** any of several plants having bell-shaped flowers; *esp* **:** any of a genus (*Campanula* of the family Campanulaceae, the bellflower family) having an acrid juice, alternate leaves, and usu. showy flowers
bell·hop \-,häp\ *n* [short for *bell-hopper*] (1910) **:** a hotel or club employee who escorts guests to rooms, assists them with luggage, and runs errands
bel·li·cose \'bel-i-,kōs\ *adj* [ME, fr. L *bellicosus,* fr. *bellicus* of war, fr. *bellum* war] (15c) **:** favoring or inclined to start quarrels or wars ***syn*** see BELLIGERENT — **bel·li·cos·i·ty** \,bel-i-'käs-ət-ē\ *n*
-bel·lied \'bel-ēd\ *adj comb form* **:** having (such) a belly ⟨a big-*bellied* man⟩
bel·lig·er·ence \bə-'lij(-ə)-rən(t)s\ *n* (1814) **:** an aggressive or truculent attitude, atmosphere, or disposition
bel·lig·er·en·cy \-rən-sē\ *n* (1863) **1 :** the state of being at war or in conflict; *specif* **:** the status of a legally recognized belligerent **2 :** BELLIGERENCE
bel·lig·er·ent \-rənt\ *adj* [modif. of L *belligerant-, belligerans,* prp. of *belligerare* to wage war, fr. *belliger* waging war, fr. *bellum* + *gerere* to wage — more at CAST] (1577) **1 :** waging war; *specif* **:** belonging to or recognized as a state at war and protected by and subject to the laws of war **2 :** inclined to or exhibiting assertiveness, hostility, or combativeness — **belligerent** *n* — **bel·lig·er·ent·ly** *adv*
syn BELLIGERENT, BELLICOSE, PUGNACIOUS, QUARRELSOME, CONTENTIOUS mean having an aggressive or fighting attitude. BELLIGERENT implies being actually at war or engaged in hostilities; BELLICOSE suggests a disposition to fight; PUGNACIOUS suggests a disposition that takes pleasure in personal combat; QUARRELSOME stresses an ill-natured readiness to fight without good cause; CONTENTIOUS implies perverse and irritating fondness for arguing and quarreling.
bell jar *n* (ca. 1864) **:** a bell-shaped usu. glass vessel designed to cover objects or to contain gases or a vacuum
bell–ly·ra \'bel-'lī-rə\ *or* **bell lyre** \-,lī(ə)r\ *n* [*lyra* fr. L, lyre] (ca. 1943) **:** a glockenspiel mounted in a portable lyre-shaped frame and used esp. in marching bands
bell·man \'bel-mən\ *n* (14c) **1 :** a man (as a town crier) who rings a bell **2 :** BELLHOP
bell metal *n* (1541) **:** bronze that consists usu. of three to four parts of copper to one of tin and that is used for making bells
Bel·lo·na \bə-'lō-nə\ *n* [L] **:** the Roman goddess of war
bel·low \'bel-(,)ō, -ə(-w)\ *vb* [ME *belwen,* fr. OE *bylgian;* akin to OE & OHG *bellan* to roar, Skt *bhāṣate* he talks] *vi* (bef. 12c) **1 :** to make the loud deep hollow sound characteristic of a bull **2 :** to shout in a deep voice ~ *vt* **:** BAWL ⟨~*s* the orders⟩ — **bellow** *n*
bel·lows \'bel-(,)ōz, -əz\ *n pl but sing or pl in constr* [ME *bely,* fr. OE *belg* — more at BELLY] (bef. 12c) **1 :** an instrument or machine that by alternate expansion and contraction draws in air through a valve or orifice and expels it through a tube; *also* **:** any of various other blowers **2 :** LUNGS **3 :** the pleated expansible part in a camera; *also* **:** a metallic or plastic flexible and expansible vessel
bell·pull \'bel-,pu̇l\ *n* (1832) **:** a handle or knob attached to a cord by which one rings a bell; *also* **:** the cord itself
bell push *n* (1884) **:** a button that is pushed to ring a bell
bells \'belz\ *n pl* (1969) **:** BELL-BOTTOMS
Bell's palsy \'belz-\ *n* [Sir Charles *Bell* †1842 Scot. anatomist] (ca. 1860) **:** paralysis of the facial nerve producing distortion on one side of the face
bell tower *n* (1614) **:** a tower that supports or shelters a bell
bell·weth·er \'bel-'weth-ər, -,weth-\ *n* [ME, leading sheep of a flock, leader, fr. *belle* bell + *wether;* fr. the practice of belling the leader of a flock] (15c) **:** one that takes the lead or initiative **:** LEADER; *also* **:** an indicator of trends
bell·wort \'bel-,wərt, -,wȯ(ə)rt\ *n* (1784) **:** any of a small genus (*Uvularia*) of herbs of the lily family with yellow drooping bell-shaped flowers
[1]**bel·ly** \'bel-ē\ *n, pl* **bellies** [ME *bely* bellows, belly, fr. OE *belg* bag, skin; akin to OHG *balg* bag, skin, OE *blāwan* to blow — more at BLOW] (bef. 12c) **1 a :** ABDOMEN 1 **b :** the undersurface of an animal's body; *also* **:** hide from this part **c :** WOMB, UTERUS **d :** the stomach and its adjuncts **2 :** an internal cavity **:** INTERIOR **3 :** appetite for food **4 :** a surface or object curved or rounded like a human belly **5 a :** the part of a sail that swells out when filled with wind **b :** the enlarged fleshy body of a muscle
[2]**belly** *vb* **bel·lied; bel·ly·ing** (1606) **:** SWELL, FILL
[1]**bel·ly·ache** \'bel-ē-,āk\ *n* (1881) **:** pain in the abdomen and esp. in the bowels **:** COLIC
[2]**bellyache** *vi* (1888) **:** to complain whiningly or peevishly **:** find fault — **bel·ly·ach·er** *n*
bel·ly·band \'bel-ē-,band\ *n* (15c) **:** a band around or across the belly: as **a :** GIRTH 1 **b :** BAND 4b
belly button *n* (ca. 1877) **:** NAVEL 1
belly dance *n* (1899) **:** a usu. solo dance emphasizing movements of the belly — **belly dance** *vi* — **belly dancer** *n*

belly flop *n* (1895) **:** a dive (as into water or in coasting prone on a sled) in which the front of the body strikes flat against another surface — called also *belly flopper* — **belly flop** *vi*
bel·ly·ful \ˈbel-ē-ˌfu̇l\ *n* (1535) **:** an excessive amount ⟨a ~ of advice⟩
bel·ly–land \-ˌland\ *vi* (1943) **:** to land an airplane on its undersurface without use of landing gear — **belly landing** *n*
belly laugh *n* (1921) **:** a deep hearty laugh
bel·ly–up \-ˈəp\ *adj* [fr. the belly-up floating position of a dead fish] (1939) **:** DONE FOR; *esp* **:** BANKRUPT ⟨the business went ~⟩
belly up *vi* (1948) **:** to move close or next to ⟨he *bellied up* to the bar⟩
be·long \bi-ˈlȯŋ\ *vi* [ME *belongen,* fr. *be-* + *longen* to be suitable — more at LONG] (14c) **1 a :** to be suitable, appropriate, or advantageous ⟨a dictionary ~*s* in every home⟩ **b :** to be in a proper situation ⟨a man of his ability ~*s* in teaching⟩ **2 a :** to be the property of a person or thing — used with *to* **b :** to be attached or bound by birth, allegiance, or dependency **c :** to be a member of a club, organization, or set **3 :** to be an attribute, part, adjunct, or function of a person or thing ⟨nuts and bolts ~ to a car⟩ **4** *chiefly Southern & Midland* **:** OUGHT **5 :** to be properly classified
be·long·ing \-ˈlȯŋ-iŋ\ *n* (1603) **1 :** POSSESSION — usu. used in pl. **2 :** close or intimate relationship ⟨a sense of ~⟩
Belo·rus·sian \ˌbel-ō-ˈrəsh-ən\ *n* (1943) **1 :** a native or inhabitant of Belorussia, U.S.S.R. **2 :** the Slavic language of the Belorussians — **Belorussian** *adj*
be·loved \bi-ˈləv(-ə)d\ *adj* [ME, fr. pp. of *beloven* to love, fr. *be-* + *loven* to love] (14c) **:** dearly loved **:** dear to the heart — **beloved** *n*
[1]**be·low** \bi-ˈlō\ *adv* [*be-* + *low,* adj.] (14c) **1 :** in or to a lower place **2 a :** on earth **b :** in or to Hades or hell **3 :** on or to a lower floor or deck **4 a :** in, to, at, or by a lower rank or number **b :** below zero ⟨20 degrees ~⟩ **5 :** lower on the same page or on a following page **6 :** under the surface of the water
[2]**below** *prep* (1575) **1 :** in or to a lower place than **:** UNDER **2 :** inferior to (as in rank) **3 :** not suitable to the rank of **:** BENEATH
[3]**below** *adj* (1697) **:** written or discussed lower on the same page or on a following page
[4]**below** *n* (1939) **:** something that is below
Bel Pa·ese \ˌbel-pä-ˈā-zə, -zē\ *trademark* — used for a mild soft creamy cheese in a firm rind
Bel·shaz·zar \bel-ˈshaz-ər\ *n* [Heb *Bēlshaṣṣar*] **:** a son of Nebuchadnezzar and king of Babylon
[1]**belt** \ˈbelt\ *n* [ME, fr. OE; akin to OHG *balz* belt; both fr. L *balteus* belt] (bef. 12c) **1 a :** a strip of flexible material worn esp. around the waist **b :** a similar article worn as a corset or for protection or safety **2 :** a continuous band of tough flexible material for transmitting motion and power or conveying materials **3 :** an area characterized by some distinctive feature (as of culture, habitation, geology, or life forms); *esp* **:** one suited to a particular crop ⟨the corn ~⟩ — **belt·ed** \ˈbel-təd\ *adj* — **belt·less** \ˈbelt-ləs\ *adj* — **below the belt :** UNFAIRLY — **under one's belt :** in one's possession **:** as part of one's experience
[2]**belt** *vt* (14c) **1 a :** to encircle or fasten with a belt **b :** to strap on **2 a :** to beat with or as if with a belt **:** THRASH **b :** STRIKE, HIT **3 :** to mark with a band **4 :** to sing in a forceful manner or style ⟨~*ing* out popular songs⟩ ~ *vi* **:** to move or act in a vigorous or violent manner
[3]**belt** *n* (1899) **1 :** a jarring blow **:** WHACK **2 :** DRINK ⟨a ~ of gin⟩
belt·ed–bi·as tire \ˌbel-təd-ˌbī-əs-\ *n* (1968) **:** a pneumatic tire with a hooplike belt of cord or steel around the tire underneath the tread and on top of the ply-cords laid at an acute angle to the center line of the tread
belt highway *n* (1945) **:** BELTWAY
belt·ing \ˈbel-tiŋ\ *n* (1567) **1 :** BELTS **2 :** material for belts
belt–tight·en·ing \ˈbelt-ˌtīt-niŋ, -ᵊn-iŋ\ *n* (1937) **:** a reduction in spending
belt up *vi, Brit* (1949) **:** SHUT UP
belt·way \ˈbelt-ˌwā\ *n* (ca. 1951) **:** a highway skirting an urban area
be·lu·ga \bə-ˈlü-gə\ *n* [Russ, fr. *belyĭ* white; akin to Gk *phainein* to show — more at FANCY] (1591) **1 a :** a white sturgeon (*Acipenser huso*) of the Black sea, Caspian sea, and their tributaries **b :** caviar processed from beluga roe **2** [Russ *belukha,* fr. *belyĭ*] **:** WHITE WHALE

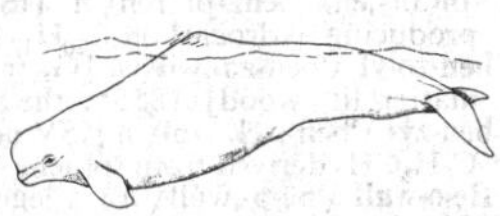
beluga 2

bel·ve·dere \ˈbel-və-ˌdi(ə)r\ *n* [It, lit., beautiful view] (1596) **:** a structure (as a cupola or a summerhouse) designed to command a view
be·ma \ˈbē-mə\ *n* [LL & LGk; LL, fr. LGk *bēma,* fr. Gk, step, tribunal, fr. *bainein* to go — more at COME] (1683) **:** the part of an Eastern church containing the altar
Bem·ba \ˈbem-bə\ *n, pl* **Bemba** *or* **Bembas** (1940) **1 :** a member of a primarily agricultural Bantu-speaking people of northern Rhodesia **2 :** a Bantu language of the Bemba people
be·med·aled *or* **be·med·alled** \bi-ˈmed-ᵊld\ *adj* (1880) **:** wearing or decorated with medals
be·mire \bi-ˈmī(ə)r\ *vt* (1532) **1 :** to soil with mud or dirt **2 :** to drag through or sink in mire
be·moan \bi-ˈmōn\ *vt* (bef. 12c) **1 :** to express deep grief or distress over **2 :** to regard with displeasure, disapproval, or regret ***syn*** see DEPLORE
be·mock \bi-ˈmäk, -ˈmȯk\ *vt, archaic* (1607) **:** MOCK
be·muse \bi-ˈmyüz\ *vt* (1735) **1 :** to make confused **:** BEWILDER **2 :** to cause to become lost in thought — **be·mus·ed·ly** \-ˈmyü-zəd-lē\ *adv* — **be·muse·ment** \-ˈmyüz-mənt\ *n*
[1]**ben** \ˈben\ *adv* [ME, fr. OE *binnan,* fr. *be-* + *innan* within, from within, fr. *in*] *Scot* (bef. 12c) **:** WITHIN
[2]**ben** \(ˈ)ben\ *prep, Scot* (bef. 12c) **:** WITHIN
[3]**ben** \ˈben\ *n, Scot* (ca. 1791) **:** the inner room or parlor of a 2-room cottage
Bence–Jones protein \ˌben(t)s-ˌjōnz-\ *n* [Henry *Bence-Jones* †1873 Eng. physician and chemist] (ca. 1923) **:** a globulin or a group of globulins found in the blood serum and urine in multiple myeloma and occas. in other bone diseases
[1]**bench** \ˈbench\ *n* [ME, fr. OE *benc;* akin to OHG *bank* bench] (bef. 12c) **1 a :** a long seat for two or more persons **b :** a thwart in a boat **c** (1) **:** a seat on which the members of an athletic team await a turn or opportunity to play (2) **:** the reserve players on a team **2 a :** the seat where a judge sits in court **b :** the office or dignity of a judge **c :** the place where justice is administered **:** COURT **d :** the persons who sit as judges **3 a :** a seat for an official **b :** the office or dignity of such an official **c :** the officials occupying such a bench **4 a :** a long worktable; *also* **:** LABORATORY ⟨~ chemist⟩ ⟨~ test⟩ **b :** a table forming part of a machine **5 :** TERRACE, SHELF; *esp* **:** a former wave-cut shore of a sea or lake or floodplain of a river **6 :** a compartmented platform on which dogs or cats are kept at a show when not being judged
[2]**bench** *vt* (14c) **1 :** to furnish with benches **2 a :** to seat on a bench **b** (1) **:** to remove from or keep out of a game (2) **:** to remove from the starting lineup **3 :** to exhibit (dogs or cats) to the public on a bench ~ *vi* **:** to form a bench by natural processes
bench·er \ˈben-chər\ *n* (15c) **:** one who sits on or presides at a bench
bench mark *n* (ca. 1842) **1 :** a mark on a permanent object indicating elevation and serving as a reference in topographical surveys and tidal observations **2** *usu* **benchmark a :** a point of reference from which measurements may be made **b :** something that serves as a standard by which others may be measured
bench warrant *n* (1696) **:** a warrant issued by a presiding judge or by a court against a person guilty of contempt or indicted for a crime
[1]**bend** \ˈbend\ *vb* **bent** \ˈbent\; **bend·ing** [ME *bendan,* fr. OE *bendan;* akin to OE *bend* fetter — more at BAND] *vt* (bef. 12c) **1 :** to constrain or strain to tension by curving ⟨~ a bow⟩ **2 a :** to turn or force from straight or even to curved or angular **b :** to force back to an original straight or even condition **c :** to force from a proper shape **3 :** FASTEN ⟨~ a sail to its yard⟩ **4 :** to make submissive **:** SUBDUE **5 a :** to cause to turn from a straight course **:** DEFLECT **b :** to guide or turn toward **:** DIRECT **c :** INCLINE, DISPOSE **d :** to adapt to one's purpose **:** DISTORT ⟨~ the rules⟩ **6 :** to direct strenuously or with interest **:** APPLY ~ *vi* **1 :** to curve out of a straight line or position; *specif* **:** to incline the body in token of submission **2 :** INCLINE, TEND **3 :** to apply oneself vigorously ⟨~*ing* to their work⟩ **4 :** to make concessions **:** COMPROMISE — **bend one's ear :** to talk to someone at length
[2]**bend** *n* [ME, fr. MF *bende,* of Gmc origin; akin to OHG *binta, bant* band — more at BAND] (15c) **1 :** a diagonal band that runs from the dexter chief to the sinister base on a heraldic shield **2 :** the half of a butt or a hide trimmed of the thinner parts **3** [ME, band, fr. OE *bend* fetter — more at BAND] **:** a knot by which one rope is fastened to another or to some object
[3]**bend** *n* (15c) **1 :** the act or process of bending **:** the state of being bent **2 :** something that is bent: as **a :** a curved part of a stream **b :** [1]WALE 2 — usu. used in pl. **3** *pl but sing or pl in constr* **:** a sometimes fatal disorder that is marked by neuralgic pains and paralysis, distress in breathing, and often collapse and that is caused by the release of gas bubbles in tissue upon too rapid decrease in air pressure after a stay in a compressed atmosphere — called also *caisson disease;* compare AEROEMBOLISM 2 — **around the bend :** MAD, CRAZY ⟨afraid his friend was going *around the bend*⟩
ben·day \ˈben-ˈdā\ *adj, often cap* [*Ben*jamin *Day* †1916 Am. printer] (1903) **:** involving a process for adding shaded or tinted areas made up of dots for reproduction by line engraving — **benday** *vt*
bend·er \ˈben-dər\ *n* (15c) **1 :** one that bends **2 :** SPREE
bend sinister *n* (1612) **:** a diagonal bend that runs from the sinister chief to the dexter base on a heraldic shield
[1]**be·neath** \bi-ˈnēth\ *adv* [ME *benethe,* fr. OE *beneothan,* fr. *be-* + *neothan* below; akin to OE *nithera* nether] (bef. 12c) **1 :** in or to a lower position **:** BELOW **2 :** directly under **:** UNDERNEATH
[2]**beneath** *prep* (bef. 12c) **1 a :** in or to a lower position than **:** BELOW **b :** directly under **c :** at the foot of **2 :** not suitable to the rank of **:** unworthy of **3 :** under the control, pressure, or influence of
ben·e·dict \ˈben-ə-ˌdikt\ *n* [alter. of *Benedick,* character in Shakespeare's *Much Ado about Nothing*] (1821) **:** a newly married man who has long been a bachelor
Ben·e·dic·tine \ˌben-ə-ˈdik-tən, -ˌtēn\ *n* (15c) **:** a monk or a nun of one of the congregations following the rule of St. Benedict and devoted esp. to scholarship and liturgical worship — **Benedictine** *adj*
bene·dic·tion \ˌben-ə-ˈdik-shən\ *n* [ME *benediccioun,* fr. LL *benediction-, benedictio,* fr. *benedictus,* pp. of *benedicere* to bless, fr. L, to speak well of, fr. *bene* well + *dicere* to say — more at BOUNTY, DICTION] (15c) **1 :** an expression of good wishes **2 :** the invocation of a blessing; *esp* **:** the short blessing with which public worship is concluded **3** *often cap* **:** a Roman Catholic or Anglo-Catholic devotion including the exposition of the eucharistic Host in the monstrance and the blessing of the people with it **4 :** something that promotes goodness or well-being
bene·dic·to·ry \-ˈdik-t(ə-)rē\ *adj* (1710) **:** of or expressing benediction
Ben·e·dict's solution \ˌben-ə-ˌdik(t)(s)-\ *n* [Stanley Rossiter *Benedict* †1936 Am. chemist] (1921) **:** a blue solution containing a carbonate, citrate, and sulfate which yields a red, yellow, or orange precipitate upon warming with a sugar that is a mild oxidizing agent
Bene·dic·tus \-ˈdik-təs\ *n* [LL, blessed, fr. pp. of *benedicere;* fr. its first word] (1880) **1 :** a canticle from Mt 21:9 beginning "Blessed is he that cometh in the name of the Lord" **2 :** a canticle from Lk 1:68 beginning "Blessed be the Lord God of Israel"
bene·fac·tion \ˌben-ə-ˈfak-shən\ *n* [LL *benefaction-, benefactio,* fr. L *bene factus,* pp. of *bene facere* to do good to, fr. *bene* + *facere* to do — more at DO] (1662) **1 :** the act of benefiting **2 :** a benefit conferred; *esp* **:** a charitable donation
bene·fac·tor \ˈben-ə-ˌfak-tər\ *n* (15c) **:** one that confers a benefit; *esp* **:** one that makes a gift or bequest — **bene·fac·tress** \-trəs\ *n*
be·nef·ic \bə-ˈnef-ik\ *adj* [L *beneficus,* fr. *bene* + *facere*] (1641) **:** BENEFICENT
ben·e·fice \ˈben-ə-fəs\ *n* [ME, fr. MF, fr. ML *beneficium,* fr. L, favor, promotion, fr. *beneficus*] (14c) **1 :** an ecclesiastical office to which the

revenue from an endowment is attached **2 :** a feudal estate in lands **:** FIEF — **benefice** *vt*

be·nef·i·cence \bə-ˈnef-ə-sən(t)s\ *n* [L *beneficentia,* fr. *beneficus*] (15c) **1 :** the quality or state of being beneficent **2 :** BENEFACTION

be·nef·i·cent \-sənt\ *adj* [back-formation fr. *beneficence*] (1616) **1 :** doing or producing good; *esp* **:** performing acts of kindness and charity **2 :** BENEFICIAL — **be·nef·i·cent·ly** *adv*

ben·e·fi·cial \ˌben-ə-ˈfish-əl\ *adj* [L *beneficium* favor, benefit] (15c) **1 :** conferring benefits **:** conducive to personal or social well-being **2 :** receiving or entitling one to receive advantage, use, or benefit ⟨the ~ owner of an estate⟩ ⟨a ~ legacy⟩ — **ben·e·fi·cial·ly** \-ˈfish-ə-lē\ *adv* — **ben·e·fi·cial·ness** *n*

ben·e·fi·cia·ry \ˌben-ə-ˈfish-ē-ˌer-ē, -ˈfish-(ə-)rē\ *n, pl* **-ries** (1611) **1 :** one that benefits from something ⟨*beneficiaries* of government programs⟩ **2 a :** the person designated to receive the income of a trust estate **b :** the person named (as in an insurance policy) to receive proceeds or benefits — **beneficiary** *adj*

ben·e·fi·ci·ate \-ˈfish-ē-ˌāt\ *vt* **-at·ed; -at·ing** (1871) **:** to treat (a raw material) so as to improve properties; *esp* **:** to prepare (iron ore) for smelting — **ben·e·fi·ci·a·tion** \-ˌfish-ē-ˈā-shən\ *n*

[1]**ben·e·fit** \ˈben-ə-ˌfit\ *n* [ME, fr. AF *benfet,* fr. L *bene factum,* fr. neut. of *bene factus*] (14c) **1** *archaic* **:** an act of kindness **:** BENEFACTION **2 a :** something that promotes well-being **:** ADVANTAGE **b :** useful aid **:** HELP **3 a :** financial help in time of sickness, old age, or unemployment **b :** a payment or service provided for under an annuity, pension plan, or insurance policy **4 :** an entertainment or social event to raise funds for a person or cause

[2]**benefit** *vb* **-fit·ed** \-ˌfit-əd\ *also* **-fit·ted; -fit·ing** *also* **-fit·ting** *vt* (15c) **:** to be useful or profitable to ⟨medicines that ~ mankind⟩ ~ *vi* **:** to receive benefit — **ben·e·fit·er** \-ˌfit-ər\ *n*

benefit of clergy (15c) **1 :** clerical exemption from trial in a civil court **2 :** the ministration or sanction of the church

be·nev·o·lence \bə-ˈnev-(ə-)lən(t)s\ *n* (14c) **1 :** disposition to do good **2 a :** an act of kindness **b :** a generous gift **3 :** a compulsory levy by certain English kings with no other authority than the claim of prerogative

be·nev·o·lent \-lənt\ *adj* [ME, fr. L *benevolent-, benevolens,* fr. *bene* + *volent-, volens,* prp. of *velle* to wish — more at WILL] (15c) **1 a :** marked by or disposed to doing good ⟨a ~ donor⟩ **b :** organized for the purpose of doing good ⟨a ~ society⟩ **2 :** marked by or suggestive of goodwill ⟨~ smiles⟩ — **be·nev·o·lent·ly** *adv* — **be·nev·o·lent·ness** *n*

Ben·gal·ee \ben-ˈgȯ-lē, beŋ-\ *n* [Hindi *Baṅgālī* Bengali] (1972) **:** a native or resident of Bangladesh — **Bengalee** *adj*

Ben·gali \ben-ˈgȯ-lē, beŋ-\ *n* [Hindi *Baṅgālī,* fr. *Baṅgāl* Bengal] (1848) **1 :** a native or resident of Bengal **2 :** BENGALEE **3 :** the modern Indic language of Bengal — **Bengali** *adj*

ben·ga·line \ˈbeŋ-gə-ˌlēn\ *n* [F, fr. *Bengal*] (1884) **:** a fabric with a crosswise rib made from textile fibers (as rayon, nylon, cotton, or wool) often in combination

Ben·gal light \ˌben-ˌgȯl-, ˌbeŋ-\ *n* (1791) **1 :** a blue light used formerly for signaling and illumination **2 :** any of various colored lights or flares

be·night·ed \bi-ˈnīt-əd\ *adj* (1560) **1 :** overtaken by darkness or night **2 :** existing in a state of intellectual, moral, or social darkness **:** UNENLIGHTENED — **be·night·ed·ly** *adv* — **be·night·ed·ness** *n*

be·nign \bi-ˈnīn\ *adj* [ME *benigne,* fr. MF, fr. L *benignus,* fr. *bene* well, after such pairs as L *malus* bad: *malignus* malign — more at BOUNTY, MALIGN] (14c) **1 :** of a gentle disposition **:** GRACIOUS ⟨a ~ teacher⟩ **2 a :** showing kindness and gentleness ⟨~ faces⟩ **b :** FAVORABLE ⟨a ~ climate⟩ **3 :** of a mild type or character that does not threaten health or life ⟨~ tumor⟩ — **be·nig·ni·ty** \-ˈnig-nət-ē\ *n* — **be·nign·ly** \-ˈnīn-lē\ *adv*

be·nig·nan·cy \bi-ˈnig-nən-sē\ *n* (1876) **:** benignant quality

be·nig·nant \-nənt\ *adj* [*benign* + *-ant* (as in *malignant*)] (1782) **1 :** serenely mild and kindly **:** BENIGN **2 :** FAVORABLE, BENEFICIAL ⟨a ~ power⟩ — **be·nig·nant·ly** *adv*

ben·i·son \ˈben-ə-sən, -zən\ *n* [ME *beneson,* fr. MF *beneiçon,* fr. LL *benediction-, benedictio*] (14c) **:** BLESSING, BENEDICTION

Ben·ja·min \ˈbenj-(ə-)mən\ *n* [Heb *Binyāmīn*] **:** a son of Jacob and the traditional eponymous ancestor of one of the tribes of Israel

ben·ne *or* **bene** \ˈben-ē\ *n* [of African origin; akin to Mandingo *bĕne* sesame] (1769) **:** SESAME 1

ben·ny \ˈben-ē\ *n, pl* **bennies** [*Benzedrine* + *-ie*] *slang* (1949) **:** a tablet of amphetamine taken as a stimulant

ben·o·myl \ˈben-ə-ˌmil\ *n* [*benz-* + *-o-* + *-myl* (by shortening & alter. fr. *methyl*)] (1969) **:** a derivative $C_{14}H_{18}N_4O_3$ of carbamate and benzimidazole used esp. as a systemic agricultural fungicide

[1]**bent** \ˈbent\ *n* [ME, grassy place, bent grass, fr. OE *beonot-;* akin to OHG *binuz* rush] (bef. 12c) **1 :** unenclosed grassland **2 a (1) :** a reedy grass **(2) :** a stalk of stiff coarse grass **b :** BENT GRASS

[2]**bent** *adj* [ME, fr. pp. of *benden* to bend] (14c) **1 :** changed by bending out of an original straight or even condition ⟨~ twigs⟩ **2 :** strongly inclined **:** DETERMINED ⟨was ~ on winning⟩ **3** *slang* **a :** different from the normal or usual **b** *chiefly Brit* **:** DISHONEST, CORRUPT

[3]**bent** *n* [irreg. fr. [1]*bend*] (1586) **1 a :** a strong inclination or interest **:** BIAS **b :** a special inclination or capacity **:** TALENT **2 :** capacity of endurance **3 :** a transverse framework (as in a bridge) to carry lateral as well as vertical loads ***syn*** see GIFT

bent grass *n* (1791) **:** any of a genus (*Agrostis*) including important chiefly perennial and rhizomatous pasture and lawn grasses with fine velvety or wiry herbage

Ben·tham·ism \ˈben(t)-thə-ˌmiz-əm\ *n* (1829) **:** the utilitarian philosophy of Jeremy Bentham and his followers — **Ben·tham·ite** \-ˌmīt\ *n*

ben·thic \ˈben(t)-thik\ *adj* [*benthos*] (1902) **1 :** of, relating to, or occurring at the bottom of a body of water **2 :** of, relating to, or occurring in the depths of the ocean

ben·thon·ic \ben-ˈthän-ik\ *adj* [irreg. fr. *benthos*] (1897) **:** BENTHIC

ben·thos \ˈben-ˌthäs\ *n* [NL, fr. Gk, depth, deep sea; akin to Gk *bathys* deep — more at BATHY-] (1891) **:** organisms that live on or in the bottom of bodies of water

ben·ton·ite \ˈbent-ᵊn-ˌīt\ *n* [Fort *Benton,* Mont.] (ca. 1898) **:** an absorptive and colloidal clay used esp. as a filler (as in paper) or carrier (as of drugs) — **ben·ton·it·ic** \ˌbent-ᵊn-ˈit-ik\ *adj*

ben tro·va·to \ˌben-trō-ˈvät-(ˌ)ō\ *adj* [It, lit., well found] (1883) **:** characteristic or appropriate even if not true ⟨the story may be *ben trovato*⟩

bent·wood \ˈbent-ˌwu̇d\ *adj* (1862) **:** made of wood that is bent and not cut into shape ⟨~ furniture⟩ — **bentwood** *n*

be·numb \bi-ˈnəm\ *vt* [ME *benomen, benome,* pp. of *benimen* to deprive, fr. OE *beniman,* fr. *be-* + *niman* to take — more at NIMBLE] (bef. 12c) **1 :** to make inactive **:** DEADEN **2 :** to make numb esp. by cold

benz- *or* **benzo-** *comb form* [ISV, fr. *benzoin*] **:** related to benzene or benzoic acid ⟨*benzo*phenone⟩ ⟨*benz*yl⟩

benz·al·de·hyde \ben-ˈzal-də-ˌhīd\ *n* [G *benzaldehyd,* fr. *benz-* + *aldehyd* aldehyde] (1866) **:** a colorless nontoxic aromatic liquid C_6H_5CHO found in essential oils (as in peach kernels) and used in flavoring and perfumery, in pharmaceuticals, and in synthesis of dyes

benz·an·thra·cene \ben-ˈzan(t)-thrə-ˌsēn\ *n* [ISV] (1938) **:** a crystalline feebly carcinogenic cyclic hydrocarbon $C_{18}H_{12}$ that is found in small amounts in coal tar

Ben·ze·drine \ˈben-zə-ˌdrēn\ *trademark* — used for amphetamine

ben·zene \ˈben-ˌzēn, ben-ˈ\ *n* [ISV *benz-* + *-ene*] (1872) **:** a colorless volatile flammable toxic liquid aromatic hydrocarbon C_6H_6 used in organic synthesis, as a solvent, and as a motor fuel — called also *benzol* — **ben·ze·noid** \ˈben-zə-ˌnȯid\ *adj*

benzene hexachloride *n* (1884) **:** BHC

benzene ring *n* (1877) **:** a structural arrangement of atoms held to exist in benzene and other aromatic compounds and marked by six carbon atoms linked in a planar symmetrical hexagon with each carbon attached to hydrogen in benzene itself or to other atoms or groups in substituted benzenes — called also *benzene nucleus;* compare META- 4b, ORTH- 4b, PARA- 2b

ben·zi·dine \ˈben-zə-ˌdēn\ *n* [prob. fr. G *benzidin,* fr. *benzin* + *-idin* -idine] (1878) **:** a crystalline base $C_{12}H_{12}N_2$ prepared from nitrobenzene and used esp. in making dyes

benz·imid·azole \ˌben-ˌzim-ə-ˈdaz-ˌōl, ˌben-zə-ˈmid-ə-ˌzōl\ *n* [ISV *benz-* + *imidazole*] (ca. 1929) **:** a crystalline base $C_7H_6N_2$ that inhibits the growth of various organisms (as some viruses); *also* **:** one of its derivatives

ben·zine \ˈben-ˌzēn, ben-ˈ\ *n* [G *benzin,* fr. *benz-*] (1835) **:** any of various volatile flammable petroleum distillates used esp. as solvents or as motor fuels

ben·zo·ate \ˈben-zə-ˌwāt\ *n* (1806) **:** a salt or ester of benzoic acid

ben·zo·caine \ˈben-zə-ˌkān\ *n* [ISV] (1922) **:** a white crystalline ester $C_9H_{11}NO_2$ used as a local anesthetic

ben·zo·di·az·e·pine \ˌben-zō-dī-ˈaz-ə-ˌpēn\ *n* [*benz-* + *diazepam* + *-ine*] (1966) **:** any of a group of aromatic lipophilic amines (as diazepam and chlordiazepoxide) used as tranquilizers

ben·zo·fu·ran \ˌben-zō-ˈfyu̇(ə)r-ˌan, -fyu̇-ˈran\ *n* [*benz-* + *furan*] (1946) **:** COUMARONE

ben·zo·ic acid \ben-ˌzō-ik-\ *n* [ISV, fr. *benzoin*] (1791) **:** a white crystalline acid $C_7H_6O_2$ found naturally (as in benzoin or in cranberries) or made synthetically and used esp. as a preservative of foods, in medicine, and in organic synthesis

ben·zo·in \ˈben-zə-wən, -ˌwēn; -ˌzȯin\ *n* [MF *benjoin,* fr. OCatal *benjuí,* fr. Ar *lubān jāwī,* lit., frankincense of Java] (1561) **1 :** a hard fragrant yellowish balsamic resin from trees (genus *Styrax*) of southeastern Asia used esp. in medication, as a fixative in perfumes, and as incense **2 :** a white crystalline hydroxy ketone $C_{14}H_{12}O_2$ made from benzaldehyde **3 a :** a tree yielding benzoin **b :** SPICEBUSH

ben·zol \ˈben-ˌzȯl, -ˌzōl\ *n* [G, fr. *benz-* + *-ol*] (1838) **:** BENZENE; *also* **:** a mixture of benzene and other aromatic hydrocarbons

ben·zo·phe·none \ˌben-zō-fi-ˈnōn, -ˈfē-ˌnōn\ *n* [ISV] (ca. 1885) **:** a colorless crystalline ketone $C_{13}H_{10}O$ used chiefly in perfumery and sunscreens

ben·zo·py·rene \ˌben-zō-ˈpī(ə)r-ˌēn, -pī-ˈrēn\ *or* **benz·py·rene** \benz-ˈpī(ə)r-ˌēn, ˌbenz-pī-ˈrēn\ *n* [ISV] (1927) **:** a yellow crystalline cancer-producing hydrocarbon $C_{20}H_{12}$ found in coal tar

ben·zo·yl \ˈben-zə-ˌwil\ *n* [G, fr. *benzoësäure* benzoic acid + Gk *hylē* matter, lit., wood] (1855) **:** the radical C_6H_5CO of benzoic acid

ben·zyl \ˈben-ˌzēl, -zəl\ *n* [ISV *benz-* + *-yl*] (1869) **:** a univalent radical $C_6H_5CH_2$ derived from toluene — **ben·zyl·ic** \ben-ˈzil-ik\ *adj*

Be·o·wulf \ˈbā-ə-ˌwu̇lf\ *n* **:** a legendary Geatish warrior and hero of the Old English poem *Beowulf*

be·paint \bi-ˈpānt\ *vt, archaic* (1555) **:** TINGE

be·queath \bi-ˈkwēth, -ˈkwē<u>th</u>\ *vt* [ME *bequethen,* fr. OE *becwethan,* fr. *be-* + *cwethan* to say — more at QUOTH] (bef. 12c) **1 :** to give or leave by will — used esp. of personal property **2 :** to hand down **:** TRANSMIT — **be·queath·al** \-əl\ *n*

be·quest \bi-ˈkwest\ *n* [ME, irreg. fr. *bequethen*] (14c) **1 :** the act of bequeathing **2 :** something bequeathed **:** LEGACY

be·rate \bi-ˈrāt\ *vt* (1548) **:** to scold or condemn vehemently and at length ***syn*** see SCOLD

Ber·ber \ˈbər-bər\ *n* [Ar *Barbar*] (1732) **1 :** a member of a Caucasoid people of northern Africa west of Tripoli **2 a :** a branch of the Afro-Asiatic language family comprising languages spoken by various tribal groups (as the Tuareg or the Kabyle) in northern Africa **b :** any one of these languages

ber·ber·ine \ˈbər-bə-ˌrēn\ *n* [G *berberin,* fr. NL *berberis* barberry root, fr. ML *barbaris,* fr. Ar *barbāris*] (ca. 1847) **:** a bitter crystalline yellow alkaloid $C_{20}H_{19}NO_5$ obtained from the roots of various plants (as barberry) and used as a tonic in medicine

ber·ceuse \be(ə)r-ˈsə(r)z\ *n, pl* **ber·ceuses** \-ˈsə(r)z(-əz)\ [F, fr. *bercer* to rock] (1876) **1 :** LULLABY **2 :** a musical composition usu. in $^6/_8$ time that resembles a lullaby

be·reave \bi-ˈrēv\ *vt* **-reaved** *or* **-reft** \-ˈreft\; **-reav·ing** [ME *bereven,* fr. OE *berēafian,* fr. *be-* + *rēafian* to rob — more at REAVE] (bef. 12c) **1** *archaic* **:** to deprive of something — usu. used with *of* ⟨madam, you have *bereft* me of all words —Shak.⟩ **2** *archaic* **:** to take away (a valued or necessary possession) esp. by force

[1]**be·reaved** \bi-ˈrēvd\ *adj* (1828) **:** suffering the death of a loved one ⟨~ parents⟩

[2]**bereaved** *n, pl* **bereaved** (1943) **:** one who is bereaved

be·reave·ment \bi-ˈrēv-mənt\ *n* (ca. 1731) **:** the state or fact of being bereaved; *esp* **:** the loss of a loved one by death

be·reft \-'reft\ *adj* (1586) **1 a :** deprived or robbed of the possession or use of something — usu. used with *of* ⟨both players are instantly ~ of their poise —A. E. Wier⟩ **b :** lacking something needed, wanted, or expected — used with *of* ⟨the book is . . . completely ~ of an index —*Times Lit. Supp.*⟩ **2 :** BEREAVED ⟨a ~ mother⟩

Ber·e·ni·ce's Hair \ˌber-ə-ˌnī-sēz-\ *n* **:** COMA BERENICES

be·ret \bə-'rā\ *n* [F *béret,* fr. Prov *berret — more at* BIRETTA] (1827) **:** a visorless usu. woolen cap with a tight headband and a soft full flat top

berg \'bərg\ *n* (1823) **:** ICEBERG

ber·ga·mot \'bər-gə-ˌmät\ *n* [F *bergamote,* fr. It *bergamotta,* of Turkic origin; akin to Turk *bey-armudu* prince's pear] (1696) **1 :** a pear-shaped orange (*Citrus bergamia*) whose rind yields an essential oil used in perfumery **2 :** any of several mints (genus *Monarda*) — compare WILD BERGAMOT

be·rib·boned \bi-'rib-ənd\ *adj* (1863) **:** adorned with ribbons

beri·beri \ˌber-ē-'ber-ē\ *n* [Sinhalese *bæribæri*] (1703) **:** a deficiency disease marked by inflammatory or degenerative changes of the nerves, digestive system, and heart and caused by a lack of or inability to assimilate thiamine

Berke·le·ian *or* **Berke·ley·an** \'bär-klē-ən, 'bər-; bär-', ˌbər-'\ *adj* (1842) **:** of, relating to, or suggestive of Bishop Berkeley or his system of philosophical idealism — **Berkeleian** *n* — **Berke·le·ian·ism** \-ə-ˌniz-əm\ *n*

berke·li·um \'bər-klē-əm\ *n* [NL, fr. *Berkeley,* Calif.] (ca. 1950) **:** a radioactive metallic element produced by bombarding americium 241 with helium ions — see ELEMENT table

Berk·shire \'bərk-ˌshi(ə)r, -shər\ *n* [*Berkshire,* England] (1811) **:** any of a breed of medium-sized black swine with white markings

berm *or* **berme** \'bərm\ *n* [F *berme,* fr. D *berm* strip of ground along a dike; akin to ME *brimme* brim] (1729) **:** a narrow shelf, path, or ledge typically at the top or bottom of a slope; *also* **:** a mound or wall of earth ⟨a landscaped ~⟩

Ber·mu·da bag \(ˌ)bər-'myüd-ə-, *esp Southern* -'müd-\ *n* [*Bermuda* islands, No. Atlantic] (1979) **:** a round or oval-shaped handbag with a wooden handle and removable cloth covers

Bermuda grass *n* (1808) **:** a trailing stoloniferous southern European grass (*Cynodon dactylon*)

Bermuda rig *n* (1853) **:** a fore-and-aft rig marked by a triangular sail and a mast with an extreme rake

Ber·mu·das \(ˌ)bər-'myüd-əz, *esp Southern* -'müd-\ *n pl* (1961) **:** BERMUDA SHORTS

Bermuda shorts *n pl* (1951) **:** knee-length walking shorts

Ber·nese mountain dog \ˌbər-ˌnēz-, -ˌnēs-\ *n* [*Bern,* Switzerland] (1938) **:** any of a Swiss breed of large powerful long-coated black dogs with tan and white markings formerly used for draft

Ber·noul·li trial \bər-'nü-lē-, ˌber-ˌnü-'lē-\ *n* [Jacques *Bernoulli* †1705 Swiss mathematician] (1951) **:** one of the repetitions of a statistical experiment having two mutually exclusive outcomes with constant probability of occurrence

ber·ried \'ber-ēd\ *adj* (1794) **1 :** furnished with berries **2 :** bearing eggs ⟨a ~ lobster⟩

[1]**ber·ry** \'ber-ē, *esp in compounds in which a stressed syllable immediately precedes, Brit often & US sometimes* b(ə-)rē\ *n, pl* **berries** [ME *berye,* fr. OE *berie;* akin to OHG *beri* berry] (bef. 12c) **1 a :** a pulpy and usu. edible fruit (as a strawberry, raspberry, or checkerberry) of small size irrespective of its structure **b :** a simple fruit (as a currant, grape, tomato, or banana) with a pulpy or fleshy pericarp **c :** the dry seed of some plants (as coffee) **2 :** an egg of a fish or lobster

[2]**berry** \'ber-ē\ *vi* **ber·ried; ber·ry·ing** (1798) **1 :** to bear or produce berries ⟨a ~*ing* shrub⟩ **2 :** to gather or seek berries

ber·ry·like \'ber-ē-ˌlīk\ *adj* (1964) **1 :** resembling a berry esp. in size or structure **2 :** being small and rounded **:** COCCOID

ber·seem \(ˌ)bər-'sēm\ *n* [Ar *barsīm,* fr. Copt *bersīm*] (1901) **:** a succulent clover (*Trifolium alexandrinum*) cultivated as a forage plant and green-manure crop esp. in the alkaline soils of the Nile valley and in the southwestern U.S. — called also *Egyptian clover*

[1]**ber·serk** \bə(r)-'sərk, ˌbər-, -'zərk, 'bər-ˌ\ *or* **ber·serk·er** \-ər\ *n* [ON *berserkr,* fr. *björn* bear + *serkr* shirt; akin to OE *bera* — more at BEAR] (1818) **1 :** an ancient Scandinavian warrior frenzied in battle and held to be invulnerable **2 :** one whose actions are recklessly defiant

[2]**berserk** *adj* (1851) **:** FRENZIED, CRAZED — usu. used in the phrase *go berserk* ⟨sinister ravings of an imagination gone ~ —John Gruen⟩ — **berserk** *adv* — **ber·serk·ly** *adv*

[1]**berth** \'bərth\ *n* [prob. fr. [2]*bear* + *-th*] (15c) **1 a :** sufficient distance for maneuvering a ship **b :** safe distance — used esp. with *wide* **2 a :** the place where a ship lies when at anchor or at a wharf **b :** a space for an automotive vehicle at rest ⟨a truck-loading ~⟩ **3 :** a place to sit or sleep esp. on a ship or vehicle **:** ACCOMMODATION **4 a :** a billet on a ship **b :** JOB, POSITION, PLACE ⟨won a starting ~ on the varsity basketball team —*Current Biog.*⟩

[2]**berth** *vt* (1667) **1 :** to bring into a berth **2 :** to allot a berth to ~ *vi* **:** to come into a berth

ber·tha \'bər-thə\ *n* [F *berthe,* fr. *Berthe* (Bertha) †783 queen of the Franks] (1842) **:** a wide round collar covering the shoulders

Ber·til·lon system \'bərt-ᵊl-ˌän-, 'bert-ē-ˌ(y)ōⁿ-\ *n* [Alphonse *Bertillon* †1914 Fr. criminologist] (1896) **:** a system of identification of persons by a description based on anthropometric measurements, standardized photographs, notation of markings, color, thumb line impressions, and other data

ber·yl \'ber-əl\ *n* [ME, fr. MF *beril,* fr. L *beryllus,* fr. Gk *bēryllos,* of Indic origin; akin to Skt *vaidūrya* cat's-eye] (14c) **:** a mineral $Be_3Al_2Si_6O_{18}$ consisting of a silicate of beryllium and aluminum of great hardness and occurring in green, bluish green, yellow, pink, or white hexagonal prisms

be·ryl·li·um \bə-'ril-ē-əm\ *n* [NL, fr. Gk *bēryllion,* dim. of *bēryllos*] (ca. 1847) **:** a steel-gray light strong brittle toxic bivalent metallic element used chiefly as a hardening agent in alloys — see ELEMENT table

be·seech \bi-'sēch\ *vb* **-sought** \-'sȯt\ *or* **-seeched; -seech·ing** [ME *besechen,* fr. *be-* + *sechen* to seek] *vt* (12c) **1 :** to beg for urgently or anxiously **2 :** to request earnestly **:** IMPLORE ~ *vi* **:** to make supplication *syn* see BEG — **be·seech·ing·ly** \-'sē-chiŋ-lē\ *adv*

be·seem \bi-'sēm\ *vi, archaic* (13c) **:** to be fitting or becoming ~ *vt, archaic* **:** to be suitable to **:** BEFIT

be·set \bi-'set\ *vt* **-set; -set·ting** [ME *besetten,* fr. OE *besettan,* fr. *be-* + *settan* to set] (bef. 12c) **1 :** to set or stud with or as if with ornaments **2 :** TROUBLE, HARASS ⟨inflation ~*s* the economy⟩ **3 a :** to set upon **:** ASSAIL ⟨the settlers were ~ by savages⟩ **b :** to hem in **:** SURROUND — **be·set·ment** \-mənt\ *n*

be·set·ting *adj* (1795) **:** constantly present or attacking **:** OBSESSIVE

be·shrew \bi-'shrü, *esp Southern* -'srü\ *vt, archaic* (14c) **:** CURSE

[1]**be·side** \bi-'sīd\ *adv* [ME, adv. & prep., fr. OE *be sīdan* at or to the side, fr. *be* at (fr. *bī*) + *sīdan,* dat. & acc. of *sīde* side — more at BY] (bef. 12c) **1** *archaic* **:** NEARBY **2** *archaic* **:** BESIDES

[2]**beside** *prep* (13c) **1 a :** by the side of ⟨walk ~ me⟩ **b :** in comparison with **c :** on a par with **2 :** BESIDES **3 :** not relevant to ⟨~ the point⟩ — **beside oneself :** in a state of extreme excitement

[1]**be·sides** \bi-'sīdz\ *prep* (14c) **1 :** other than **:** EXCEPT **2 :** together with

[2]**besides** *adv* (1564) **1 :** as well **:** ALSO **2 :** MOREOVER, FURTHERMORE

[3]**besides** *adj* (1954) **:** ELSE

be·siege \bi-'sēj\ *vt* **-sieged; -sieg·ing** (13c) **1 :** to surround with armed forces **2 a :** to press with requests **:** IMPORTUNE **b :** to cause worry or distress to **:** BESET ⟨doubts that *besieged* him⟩ — **be·sieg·er** *n*

be·smear \bi-'smi(ə)r\ *vt* (bef. 12c) **:** SMEAR

be·smirch \bi-'smərch\ *vt* (1598) **:** SULLY, SOIL

[1]**be·som** \'bē-zəm\ *n* [ME *beseme,* fr. OE *besma;* akin to OHG *besmo* broom] (bef. 12c) **:** BROOM 2; *esp* **:** one made of twigs

[2]**besom** *n* [origin unknown] (1965) **:** an edging or reinforcement around a pocket opening

be·sot \bi-'sät\ *vt* **be·sot·ted; be·sot·ting** [*be-* + *sot* (to stultify)] (1581) **:** to make dull or stupid; *esp* **:** to muddle with drunkenness or infatuation

be·spat·ter \bi-'spat-ər\ *vt* (1640) **:** SPATTER

be·speak \bi-'spēk\ *vt* **-spoke** \-'spōk\; **-spo·ken** \-'spō-kən\; **-speak·ing** (1583) **1 :** to hire, engage, or claim beforehand **2 :** to speak to esp. with formality **:** ADDRESS **3 :** REQUEST ⟨~ a favor⟩ **4 a :** INDICATE, SIGNIFY ⟨her performance ~*s* considerable practice⟩ **b :** to show beforehand **:** FORETELL

be·spec·ta·cled \bi-'spek-ti-kəld, -ˌtik-əld\ *adj* (1742) **:** wearing spectacles

be·spoke \bi-'spōk\ *or* **be·spo·ken** \-'spō-kən\ *adj* [pp. of *bespeak*] (1607) **1 a :** CUSTOM-MADE **b :** dealing in or producing custom-made articles **2** *dial* **:** ENGAGED

be·sprent \bi-'sprent\ *adj* [ME *bespreynt,* fr. pp. of *besprengen* to besprinkle, fr. OE *besprengan*] *archaic* (14c) **:** sprinkled over

be·sprin·kle \bi-'spriŋ-kəl\ *vt* [ME *besprengeln,* freq. of *besprengen*] (15c) **:** SPRINKLE

Bes·se·mer converter \ˌbes-ə-mər-\ *n* (1926) **:** the furnace used in the Bessemer process

Bessemer process *n* [Sir Henry *Bessemer*] (ca. 1887) **:** a process of making steel from pig iron by burning out carbon and other impurities by means of a blast of air forced through the molten metal

[1]**best** \'best\ *adj, superlative of* GOOD [ME, fr. OE *betst;* akin to OE *bōt* remedy — more at BETTER] (bef. 12c) **1 :** excelling all others ⟨the ~ student⟩ **2 :** most productive of good or of advantage, utility, or satisfaction ⟨what is the ~ thing to do⟩ **3 :** MOST, LARGEST ⟨it rained for the ~ part of their vacation⟩

[2]**best** *adv, superlative of* WELL (bef. 12c) **1 :** in the best way **:** to greatest advantage ⟨some things are ~ left unsaid⟩ **2 :** MOST ⟨those ~ able will provide needed support⟩

[3]**best** *n, pl* **best** (bef. 12c) **1 :** the best state or part **2 :** one that is best ⟨the ~ falls short⟩ **3 :** the greatest degree of good or excellence **4 :** one's maximum effort ⟨do your ~⟩ **5 :** best clothes ⟨Sunday ~⟩ — **at best :** under the most favorable circumstances

[4]**best** *vt* (1863) **:** to get the better of **:** OUTDO

best–ball \'bes(t)-'bȯl\ *adj* (1909) **:** relating to or being a golf match in which one player competes against the best individual score of two or more players for each hole — compare FOUR-BALL

best boy *n* (1937) **:** the chief assistant to the gaffer in motion-picture or television production

[1]**be·stead** *also* **be·sted** \bi-'sted\ *adj* [ME *bested,* fr. *be-* + *sted,* pp. of *steden* to place, fr. *stede* place — more at STEAD] *archaic* (14c) **:** SITUATED

[2]**bestead** *vt* **be·stead·ed; be·stead; be·stead·ing** [*be-* + *stead*] (1581) **1** *archaic* **:** HELP **2** *archaic* **:** to be useful to **:** AVAIL

bes·tial \'bes(h)-chəl, 'bēs(h)-\ *adj* [ME, fr. MF, fr. L *bestialis,* fr. *bestia* beast] (14c) **1 a :** of or relating to beasts **b :** resembling a beast **2 a :** lacking intelligence or reason **b :** marked by base or inhuman instincts or desires **:** BRUTAL — **bes·tial·ize** \-chə-ˌlīz\ *vt* — **bes·tial·ly** \-chə-lē\ *adv*

bes·ti·al·i·ty \ˌbes(h)-chē-'al-ət-ē, ˌbēs(h)-\ *n, pl* **-ties** (14c) **1 :** the condition or status of a lower animal **2 :** display or gratification of bestial traits or impulses **3 :** sexual relations between a human being and a lower animal

bes·ti·ary \'bes(h)-chē-ˌer-ē, 'bēs(h)-\ *n, pl* **-ar·ies** [ML *bestiarium,* fr. L, neut. of *bestiarius* of beasts, fr. *bestia*] (1840) **1 :** a medieval allegorical or moralizing work on the appearance and habits of real or imaginary animals **2 :** a collection of descriptions of real or imaginary animals

be·stir \bi-'stər\ *vt* (14c) **:** to rouse to action **:** get going

best man *n* (1782) **:** the principal groomsman at a wedding

be·stow \bi-'stō\ *vt* [ME *bestowen,* fr. *be-* + *stowe* place — more at STOW] (14c) **1 :** to put to use **:** APPLY ⟨~*ed* his spare time on study⟩ **2 :** to put in a particular or appropriate place **:** STOW **3 :** to provide with quarters **:** PUT UP **4 :** to convey as a gift — usu. used with *on* or *upon* *syn* see GIVE — **be·stow·al** \-'stō-əl\ *n*

be·strew \bi-'strü\ *vt* **-strewed** *or* **-strewn** \-'strün\; **-strew·ing** (bef. 12c) **1 :** STREW **2 :** to lie scattered over

be·stride \bi-'strīd\ *vt* **-strode** \-'strōd\; **-strid·den** \-'strid-ᵊn\; **-strid·ing** \-'strīd-iŋ\ (bef. 12c) **1 :** to ride, sit, or stand astride **:** STRADDLE **2 :** to tower over **:** DOMINATE ⟨the bloated bureaucracy that ~*s* us all —Edward Ney⟩ **3** *archaic* **:** to stride across

best–sell·er \ˈbes(t)-ˈsel-ər\ *n* (1889) **:** an article (as a book) whose sales are among the highest of its class — **best·sell·er·dom** \-dəm\ *n* — **best–sell·ing** \-ˈsel-iŋ\ *adj*

¹bet \ˈbet\ *n* [origin unknown] (1592) **1 a :** something that is laid, staked, or pledged typically between two parties on the outcome of a contest or a contingent issue **:** WAGER **b :** the act of giving such a pledge **2 :** something to wager on **3 :** a choice made by consideration of probabilities ⟨your best ~ is the back road⟩

²bet *vb* **bet** *also* **bet·ted; bet·ting** *vt* (1597) **1 a :** to stake on the outcome of an issue **b :** to be able to be sure that — usu. used in the expression *you bet* ⟨you ~ I'll be there⟩ **2 a :** to maintain with or as if with a bet **b :** to make a bet with ~ *vi* **:** to lay a bet

¹be·ta \ˈbāt-ə, *chiefly Brit* ˈbē-tə\ *n* [Gk *bēta*, of Sem origin; akin to Heb *bēth* beth] (14c) **1 :** the 2d letter of the Greek alphabet — see ALPHABET table **2 :** the second brightest star of a constellation **3 a :** BETA PARTICLE **b :** BETA RAY

²beta *or* **β-** *adj* (1899) **:** second in position in the structure of an organic molecule from a particular group or atom ⟨~ substitution⟩

³beta *n* (1971) **:** a measure of a stock's or a portfolio's volatility that is expressed numerically as deviation from the market's volatility taken as unity

be·ta–ad·ren·er·gic \-ˌad-rə-ˈnər-jik\ *adj* (1968) **:** of, relating to, or being a beta-receptor ⟨~ blocking action⟩

beta cell *n* (1926) **:** any of the insulin-secreting pancreatic cells in the islets of Langerhans

beta globulin *n* [ISV] (1947) **:** any of several globulins of plasma or serum that have at alkaline pH electrophoretic mobilities intermediate between those of the alpha globulins and gamma globulins

be·ta·ine \ˈbēt-ə-ˌēn\ *n* [ISV, fr. L *beta* beet] (1879) **:** a sweet crystalline quaternary ammonium salt $C_5H_{11}NO_2$ occurring esp. in beet juice; *also* **:** its hydrate $C_5H_{13}NO_3$ or the chloride of this

be·take \bi-ˈtāk\ *vt* **-took** \-ˈtu̇k\; **-tak·en** \-ˈtā-kən\; **-tak·ing** (13c) **1** *archaic* **:** COMMIT **2 :** to cause (oneself) to go

be·ta–ox·i·da·tion \ˈbāt-ə-ˌäk-sə-ˈdā-shən\ *n* (ca. 1935) **:** stepwise catabolism of fatty acids in which two-carbon fragments are successively removed from the carboxyl end of the chain

beta particle *n* (1904) **:** an electron or positron ejected from the nucleus of an atom during radioactive decay; *also* **:** a high-speed electron or positron

beta ray *n* (1902) **1 :** BETA PARTICLE **2 :** a stream of beta particles

be·ta–re·cep·tor \ˈbāt-ə-ri-ˈsep-tər\ *n* (1964) **:** any of a group of receptors on cell membranes that are held to be associated esp. with positive effects on the beat and muscular contractility of the heart, with vasodilation, and with inhibition of smooth muscle in the bronchi, intestine, and muscular layer of the wall of the uterus

be·ta·tron \ˈbāt-ə-ˌträn\ *n* [ISV] (1941) **:** an accelerator in which electrons are propelled by the inductive action of a rapidly varying magnetic field

beta wave *n* (1936) **:** an electrical rhythm of the brain with a frequency of 13 to 30 cycles per second that is associated with normal conscious waking experience — called also *beta, beta rhythm*

be·tel \ˈbē-ᵊl\ *n* [Pg, fr. Tamil *verrilai*] (1553) **:** a climbing pepper (*Piper betle*) whose leaves are chewed together with betel nut and lime as a stimulant masticatory esp. by southeastern Asians

Be·tel·geuse \ˈbēt-ᵊl-ˌjüs, ˈbet-, -ˌjüz, -ˌjə(r)z\ *n* [F *Bételgeuse*, fr. Ar *bayt al-jawzā'* Gemini, lit., the house of the twins (confused with Orion & Betelgeuse)] **:** a variable red giant star of the first magnitude near one shoulder of Orion

betel nut *n* [fr. its being chewed with betel leaves] (1681) **:** the astringent seed of the betel palm

betel palm *n* [*betel* nut] (1875) **:** an Asian pinnate-leaved palm (*Areca catechu*) that has an orange-colored drupe with an outer fibrous husk

bête noire \ˌbet-n(ə-)ˈwär, ˌbāt-\ *n, pl* **bêtes noires** \ˌbet-n(ə-)ˈwär(z), ˌbāt-\ [F, lit., black beast] (1844) **:** a person or thing strongly detested or avoided **:** BUGBEAR

beth \ˈbāt(h), ˈbās\ *n* [Heb *bēth*, fr. *bayith* house] (1823) **:** the 2d letter of the Hebrew alphabet — see ALPHABET table

beth·el \ˈbeth-əl\ *n* [Heb *bēth' ēl* house of God] (1617) **1 :** a hallowed spot **2 a :** a chapel for Nonconformists **b :** a place of worship for seamen

be·think \bi-ˈthiŋk\ *vt* **-thought** \-ˈthȯt\; **-think·ing** (bef. 12c) **1 a :** REMEMBER, RECALL **b :** to cause (oneself) to be reminded **2 :** to cause (oneself) to consider

be·tide \bi-ˈtīd\ *vt* (bef. 12c) **:** to happen to **:** BEFALL ~ *vi* **:** to happen esp. as if by fate

be·times \bi-ˈtīmz\ *adv* (13c) **1 :** in good time **:** EARLY **2** *archaic* **:** in a short time **:** SPEEDILY **3 :** at times **:** OCCASIONALLY

bê·tise \bā-ˈtēz\ *n, pl* **bê·tises** \-ˈtēz\ [F, fr. OF *beste* beast] (1827) **1 :** an act of foolishness or stupidity **2 :** lack of good sense **:** STUPIDITY

be·to·ken \bi-ˈtō-kən\ *vt* **-to·kened; -to·ken·ing** \-ˈtōk-(ə-)niŋ\ (15c) **1 :** to give evidence of **:** SHOW **2 :** to typify beforehand **:** PRESAGE

be·tray \bi-ˈtrā\ *vb* [ME *betrayen*, fr. *be-* + *trayen* to betray, fr. OF *trair*, fr. L *tradere* — more at TRAITOR] *vt* (13c) **1 :** to lead astray; *esp* **:** SEDUCE **2 :** to deliver to an enemy by treachery **3 :** to fail or desert esp. in time of need **4 a :** to reveal unintentionally **b :** SHOW, INDICATE **c :** to disclose in violation of confidence ~ *vi* **:** to prove false ***syn*** see REVEAL — **be·tray·al** \-ˈtrā-(ə)l\ *n* — **be·tray·er** \-ˈtrā-ər\ *n*

be·troth \bi-ˈtrōth, -ˈtrȯth\ *vt* [ME *betrouthen*, fr. *be-* + *trouthe* truth, troth] (14c) **:** to promise to marry or to give in marriage

be·troth·al \-ˈtrōth-əl, -ˈtrȯth-, -ˈtrōth-\ *n* (1844) **1 :** the act of betrothing or fact of being betrothed **2 :** a mutual promise or contract for a future marriage

be·trothed \bi-ˈtrōthd, -ˈtrȯtht\ *n* (1588) **:** the person to whom one is betrothed

bet·ta \ˈbet-ə\ *n* [NL] (1927) **:** any of a genus (*Betta*) of small brilliantly colored long-finned freshwater fishes of southeastern Asia

¹bet·ter \ˈbet-ər\ *adj, comparative of* GOOD [ME *bettre*, fr. OE *betera*; akin to OE *bōt* remedy, Skt *bhadra* fortunate] (bef. 12c) **1 :** more than half **2 :** improved in health or mental attitude **3 :** more attractive, favorable, or commendable **4 :** more advantageous or effective **5 :** improved in accuracy or performance

²better *vt* (bef. 12c) **1 :** to make better: as **a :** to make more tolerable or acceptable ⟨trying to ~ the lot of slum dwellers⟩ **b :** to make more complete or perfect ⟨looked forward to ~*ing* her acquaintance with the new neighbors⟩ **2 :** to surpass in excellence **:** EXCEL ~ *vi* **:** to become better

³better *adv, comparative of* WELL (12c) **1 a :** in a more excellent manner **b :** to greater advantage **:** PREFERABLY ⟨some things are ~ left unsaid⟩ **2 a :** to a higher or greater degree ⟨he knows the story ~ than you do⟩ **b :** MORE ⟨it is ~ than nine miles to the next town⟩

⁴better *n* (12c) **1 a :** something better **b :** a superior esp. in merit or rank **2 :** ADVANTAGE, VICTORY ⟨get the ~ of him⟩

bet·ter·ment \ˈbet-ər-mənt\ *n* (1598) **1 :** a making or becoming better **2 :** an improvement that adds to the value of a property or facility

better–off \ˌbet-ə-ˈrȯf\ *adj* (1865) **1 :** being in comfortable economic circumstances ⟨the ~ people live in the older section of town⟩ **2 :** being in a more advantageous position

betting shop *n, Brit* (1952) **:** a shop where bets are taken

bet·tor *or* **bet·ter** \ˈbet-ər\ *n* (1609) **:** one that bets

¹be·tween \bi-ˈtwēn\ *prep* [ME *betwene*, prep. & adv., fr. OE *betwēonum*, fr. *be-* + *-twēonum* (dat. pl.) (akin to Goth *tweihnai* two each); akin to OE *twā* two] (bef. 12c) **1 a :** by the common action of **:** jointly engaging ⟨shared the work ~ the two of them⟩ ⟨talks ~ the three —*Time*⟩ **b :** in common to **:** shared by ⟨divided ~ his four grandchildren⟩ **2 a :** in the time, space, or interval that separates **b :** in intermediate relation to **3 a :** from one to the other of ⟨air service ~ Miami and Chicago⟩ **b :** serving to connect or unite in a relationship (as difference, likeness, or proportion) ⟨a one-to-one correspondence ~ sets⟩ **c :** separating from ⟨the line ~ fact and fancy⟩ **4 :** in point of comparison of ⟨not much to choose ~ the two coats⟩

usage There is a persistent but unfounded notion that *between* can be used only of two items and that *among* must be used for more than two. *Between* has been used of more than two since Old English; it is esp. appropriate to denote a one-to-one relationship, regardless of the number of items. It can be used when the number is unspecified ⟨economic cooperation *between* nations⟩, when more than two are enumerated ⟨*between* you and me and the lamppost⟩ ⟨partitioned *between* Austria, Prussia, and Russia —Nathaniel Benchley⟩, and even when only one item is mentioned (but repetition is implied) ⟨pausing *between* every sentence to rap the floor —George Eliot⟩ *Among* is more appropriate where the emphasis is on distribution rather than individual relationships ⟨discontent *among* the peasants⟩ When *among* is automatically chosen for more than two, some strain on English idiom can result ⟨a worthy book that nevertheless falls *among* many stools —John Simon⟩ ⟨the author alternates *among* mod slang, clichés and quotes from literary giants —A. H. Johnson⟩

— **between you and me :** in confidence

²between *adv* (bef. 12c) **:** in an intermediate space or interval

be·tween·brain \-ˌbrān\ *n* (ca. 1909) **:** DIENCEPHALON

be·tween·ness \bi-ˈtwēn-nəs\ *n* (1892) **:** the quality or state of being between two others in an ordered mathematical set

be·tween·times \bi-ˈtwēn-ˌtīmz\ *adv* (1907) **:** at or during intervals

be·tween·whiles \-ˌhwīlz, -ˌwīlz\ *adv* (1678) **:** BETWEENTIMES

be·twixt \bi-ˈtwikst\ *adv or prep* [ME, fr. OE *betwux*, fr. *be-* + *-twux* (akin to Goth *tweihnai*)] (bef. 12c) **:** BETWEEN

betwixt and between *adv or adj* (1832) **:** in a midway position **:** neither one thing nor the other

Beu·lah \ˈbyü-lə\ *n* **:** an idyllic land near the end of life's journey in Bunyan's *Pilgrim's Progress*

beurre blanc \ˈbər-ˈbläⁿ\ *n* [F, lit., white butter] (1931) **:** a butter sauce flavored with vinegar or lemon juice that is usu. served hot with fish

beurre ma·nié \-män-ˈyā\ *n* [F, lit., handled butter] (1939) **:** flour and butter kneaded together used as a thickener in sauces

beurre noir \-nə-ˈwär\ *n* [F, lit., black butter] (1856) **:** butter heated until brown or black and often flavored with vinegar or lemon juice

¹bev·el \ˈbev-əl\ *adj* (1600) **:** OBLIQUE, BEVELED

²bevel *n* [(assumed) MF, fr. OF *baïf* with open mouth, fr. *baer* to yawn — more at ABEYANCE] (1611) **1 :** an instrument consisting of two rules or arms jointed together and opening to any angle for drawing angles or adjusting surfaces to be cut at an angle **2 a :** the angle that one surface or line makes with another when they are not at right angles **b :** the slant of such a surface or line **3 :** the part of printing type extending from face to shoulder

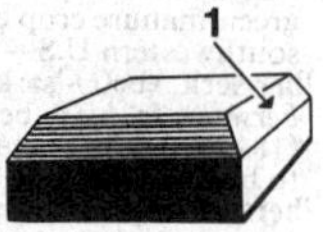

bevel 2

³bevel *vb* **-eled** *or* **-elled; -el·ing** *or* **-el·ling** \ˈbev-(ə-)liŋ\ *vt* (1677) **:** to cut or shape to a bevel ~ *vi* **:** INCLINE, SLANT

bevel gear *n* (1833) **:** one of a pair of toothed wheels whose working surfaces are inclined to nonparallel axes

bev·er·age \ˈbev-(ə-)rij\ *n* [ME, fr. MF *bevrage*, fr. *beivre* to drink, fr. L *bibere* — more at POTABLE] (14c) **:** a drinkable liquid

bevy \ˈbev-ē\ *n, pl* **bev·ies** [ME *bevey*] (15c) **1 :** a large group or collection ⟨a ~ of girls⟩ **2 :** a group of animals and esp. quail together

be·wail \bi-ˈwā(ə)l\ *vt* (14c) **1 :** to wail over **2 :** to express deep sorrow for usu. by wailing and lamentation ⟨wringing her hands and ~*ing* her fate⟩ ***syn*** see DEPLORE

be·ware \bi-ˈwa(ə)r, -ˈwe(ə)r\ *vb* [ME *been war*, fr. *been* to be + *war* careful — more at BE, WARE] *vi* (13c) **:** to be on one's guard ⟨~ of the dog⟩ ~ *vt* **1 :** to take care of **2 :** to be wary of

be·whis·kered \-ˈhwis-kərd, -ˈwis-\ *adj* (1762) **:** wearing whiskers

be·wigged \bi-ˈwigd\ *adj* (1774) **:** wearing a wig

be·wil·der \bi-ˈwil-dər\ *vt* **-wil·dered; -wil·der·ing** \-d(ə-)riŋ\ (1684) **1 :** to cause to lose one's bearings **2 :** to perplex or confuse esp. by a complexity, variety, or multitude of objects or considerations ***syn*** see PUZZLE — **be·wil·dered·ly** *adv* — **be·wil·dered·ness** *n* — **be·wil·der·ing·ly** \-d(ə-)riŋ-lē\ *adv*

be·wil·der·ment \-dər-mənt\ *n* (1820) **1 :** the quality or state of being bewildered **2 :** a bewildering tangle or confusion

be·witch \bi-ˈwich\ *vt* (13c) **1 a :** to influence or affect esp. injuriously by witchcraft **b :** to cast a spell over **2 :** to attract as if by the power of witchcraft ⟨~*ed* by her beauty⟩ ~ *vi* **:** to bewitch someone or something — **be·witch·ery** \-(ə-)rē\ *n* — **be·witch·ing·ly** \-iŋ-lē\ *adv*

be·witch·ment \-ˈwich-mənt\ *n* (1607) **1 a :** the act or power of bewitching **b :** a spell that bewitches **2 :** the state of being bewitched

be·wray \bi-ˈrā\ *vt* [ME *bewreyen*, fr. *be-* + *wreyen* to accuse, fr. OE *wrēgan*] *archaic* (13c) **:** DIVULGE, BETRAY

bey \'bā\ n [Turk, gentleman, chief] (1599) **1 a :** a provincial governor in the Ottoman Empire **b :** the former native ruler of Tunis or Tunisia **2** — formerly used as a courtesy title in Turkey and Egypt

[1]**be·yond** \bē-'änd\ adv [ME, prep. & adv., fr. OE begeondan, fr. be- + geondan beyond, fr. geond yond — more at YOND] (bef. 12c) **1 :** on or to the farther side : FARTHER **2 :** in addition : BESIDES

[2]**beyond** prep (bef. 12c) **1 :** on or to the farther side of : at a greater distance than **2 a :** out of the reach or sphere of **b :** in a degree or amount surpassing **c :** out of the comprehension of **3 :** in addition to : BESIDES

[3]**beyond** n (14c) **1 :** something that lies beyond **2 :** something that lies outside the scope of ordinary experience; specif : [2]HEREAFTER

be·zant \'bez-ʰnt, bə-'zant\ n [ME besant, fr. OF, fr. ML Byzantius Byzantine, fr. Byzantium, ancient name of Istanbul] (13c) **1 :** SOLIDUS 1 **2 :** a flat disk used in architectural ornament

be·zel \'bē-zəl, 'bez-əl\ n [prob. F dial., alter. of F biseau] (1611) **1 :** a sloping edge or face esp. on a cutting tool **2 :** the oblique side or face of a cut gem; specif : the upper faceted portion of a brilliant projecting from the setting — see BRILLIANT illustration **3 :** a rim that holds a transparent covering (as on a watch, clock, or headlight) or that is rotatable and has special markings (as on a watch)

be·zique \bə-'zēk\ n [F bésique] (1861) : a card game similar to pinochle that is played with a pack of 64 cards

be·zoar \'bē-ˌzō(ə)r, -ˌzó(ə)r\ n [F bézoard, fr. Sp bezoar, fr. Ar bāzahr, fr. Per pād-zahr, fr. pād protecting (against) + zahr poison] (15c) : any of various concretions found chiefly in the alimentary organs of ruminants and formerly believed to possess magical properties

B–girl n [prob. fr. bar + girl] (1936) : a woman who entertains bar patrons and encourages them to spend freely

BHA \ˌbē-(ˌ)ā-'chā\ n [butylated hydroxyanisole, fr. hydroxy + anisole (fr. F anisole, fr. L anisum anise + ISV -ol)] (1950) : a phenolic antioxidant $C_{11}H_{16}O_2$ used to preserve fats and oils in food, some cosmetics, and pharmaceuticals

Bha·ga·vad Gi·ta \ˌbäg-ə-ˌväd-'gēt-ə\ n [Skt Bhagavadgītā, lit., song of the blessed one (Krishna)] (ca. 1785) : a Hindu devotional work in poetic form

bhak·ti \'bək-tē\ n [Skt, lit., portion] (1832) : devotion to a deity constituting a way to salvation in Hinduism

bhang \'baŋ, 'bäŋ\ n [Hindi bhāg] (1563) **1 a :** HEMP 1 **b :** the leaves and flowering tops of uncultivated hemp : CANNABIS — compare MARIJUANA **2 :** an intoxicant product obtained from bhang — compare HASHISH

BHC \ˌbē-ˌäch-'sē\ n [benzene hexachloride] (1947) : a compound $C_6H_6Cl_6$ that occurs in several stereoisomeric forms and is used as an insecticide — compare LINDANE

Bhoj·puri \'bōj-ˌpur-ē, 'bäj-, -pə-rē\ n [Hindi Bhojpurī, fr. Bhojpur, village in Bihar] (1901) : the dialect of Bihari spoken in Western Bihar and the eastern United Provinces, India

B–horizon n (1938) : a subsurface soil layer that is immediately beneath the A-horizon from which it obtains organic matter chiefly by illuviation and is usu. distinguished by less weathering

BHT \ˌbē-ˌäch-'tē\ n [butylated hydroxytoluene] (1961) : a crystalline phenol $C_{15}H_{24}O$ used esp. to preserve fats and oils in food, some cosmetics, and pharmaceuticals

bi \'bī\ n or adj (ca. 1965) : BISEXUAL

[1]**bi-** prefix [ME, fr. L — more at TWI-] **1 a :** two ⟨biparous⟩ **b :** coming or occurring every two ⟨bimonthly⟩ ⟨biweekly⟩ **c :** into two parts ⟨bisect⟩ **2 a :** twice : doubly : on both sides ⟨biconvex⟩ ⟨biserrate⟩ **b :** coming or occurring two times ⟨biweekly⟩ — often disapproved in this sense because of the likelihood of confusion with sense 1b; compare SEMI- **3 :** between, involving, or affecting two (specified) symmetrical parts ⟨biaural⟩ **4 a :** containing one (specified) constituent in double the proportion of the other constituent or in double the ordinary proportion ⟨bicarbonate⟩ **b :** DI- 2 ⟨biphenyl⟩

[2]**bi-** or **bio-** comb form [Gk, fr. bios mode of life — more at QUICK] : life : living organisms or tissue ⟨bioecology⟩ ⟨bioluminescence⟩

Bi·a·fran \bē-'af-rən, bē-, -'äf-\ n [Biafra, name adopted by Eastern Region of Nigeria during its secession, 1967–70] (1967) : a native or inhabitant of the secessionist Republic of Biafra — **Biafran** adj

bi·aly \bē-'äl-ē\ n, pl **bialys** [Yiddish, short for bialystoker, fr. bialystoker of Bialystok, city in Poland] (1965) : a flat breakfast roll that has a depressed center and is usu. covered with onion flakes

bi·an·nu·al \(')bī-'an-yə(-wə)l\ adj (1877) : occurring twice a year; sometimes : BIENNIAL 1 — **bi·an·nu·al·ly** \-ē\ adv

[1]**bi·as** \'bī-əs\ n [MF biais] (1530) **1 :** a line diagonal to the grain of a fabric; esp : a line at a 45° angle to the selvage often utilized in the cutting of garments for smoother fit **2 a :** an inclination of temperament or outlook; esp : a highly personal and unreasoned distortion of judgment : PREJUDICE **b :** BENT, TENDENCY **c** (1) : deviation of the expected value of a statistical estimate from the quantity it estimates (2) : systematic error introduced into sampling or testing by selecting or encouraging one outcome or answer over others **3 a :** a peculiarity in the shape of a bowl that causes it to swerve when rolled on the green **b :** the tendency of a bowl to swerve; also : the impulse causing this tendency **c :** the swerve of the bowl **4 a :** a voltage applied to a device (as a transistor control electrode) to establish a reference level for operation **b :** a high-frequency voltage combined with an audio signal to reduce distortion in tape recording **syn** see PREDILECTION — **on the bias** : ASKEW, OBLIQUELY

[2]**bias** adj (1551) : DIAGONAL, SLANTING — used chiefly of fabrics and their cut — **bi·as·ness** n

[3]**bias** adv (1575) **1 :** DIAGONALLY ⟨cut cloth ∼⟩ **2** obs : AWRY

[4]**bias** vt **bi·ased** or **bi·assed; bi·as·ing** or **bi·as·sing** (1628) **1 :** to give a settled and often prejudiced outlook ⟨his background ∼es him against history⟩ **2 :** to apply a slight negative or positive voltage to (as an electron-tube grid) **syn** see INCLINE

bi·ased adj (1649) **1 :** exhibiting or characterized by bias **2 :** tending to yield one outcome more frequently than others in a statistical experiment ⟨a ∼ coin⟩ **3 :** having an expected value different from the quantity or parameter estimated ⟨a ∼ estimate⟩

bi·as-ply tire \ˌbī-ə-ˌsplī-\ n (1971) : a pneumatic tire having crossed layers of ply-cord set diagonally to the center line of the tread

bias tape n (1926) : a narrow strip of cloth cut on the bias, folded, and used for finishing or decorating clothing

bi·ath·lon \bī-'ath-lən, -ˌlän\ n [[1]bi- + Gk athlon contest — more at ATHLETE] (1958) : a composite athletic contest consisting of cross-country skiing and rifle sharpshooting

bi·ax·i·al \(')bī-'ak-sē-əl\ adj (1854) : having or relating to two axes or optic axes ⟨a ∼ crystal⟩ — **bi·ax·i·al·ly** \-ə-lē\ adv

[1]**bib** \'bib\ vb **bibbed; bib·bing** [ME bibben] (14c) : DRINK

[2]**bib** n (1580) **1 :** a cloth or plastic shield tied under the chin to protect the clothes **2 :** the part of an apron or of overalls extending above the waist — **bibbed** \'bibd\ adj — **bib·less** \'bib-ləs\ adj

bib and tucker n (1747) : an outfit of clothing — usu. used in the phrase best bib and tucker

bibb \'bib\ n [alter. of [2]bib] (ca. 1779) : a side piece of timber bolted to the hounds of a ship's mast to support the trestletrees

bib·ber \'bib-ər\ n (1536) : one addicted to drinking : TIPPLER — **bib·bery** \'bib-ə-rē\ n

Bibb lettuce \'bib-\ n [Major John Bibb, 19th cent. Am. grower] (1961) : lettuce of a variety that has a small head and dark green color

bib·cock \'bib-ˌkäk\ also **bibb cock** n (ca. 1853) : a faucet having a bent-down nozzle

bi·be·lot \'bē-bə-ˌlō\ n, pl **bibelots** \-ˌlō(z)\ [F] (1873) **1 :** a small household ornament or decorative object : TRINKET **2 :** a miniature book esp. of elegant design or format

bi·ble \'bī-bəl\ n [ME, fr. OF, fr. ML biblia, fr. Gk, pl. of biblion book, dim. of byblos papyrus, book, fr. Byblos, ancient Phoenician city from which papyrus was exported] (14c) **1** cap **a :** the sacred scriptures of Christians comprising the Old Testament and the New Testament **b :** the sacred scriptures of some other religion (as Judaism) **2** obs : BOOK **3** cap : a particular edition or copy of the Bible **4 :** a publication that is preeminent esp. in authoritativeness ⟨the fisherman's ∼⟩

BOOKS OF THE OLD TESTAMENT

ROMAN CATHOLIC CANON	PROTESTANT CANON	ROMAN CATHOLIC CANON	PROTESTANT CANON
Genesis	Genesis	Wisdom	
Exodus	Exodus	Ecclesiasticus	
Leviticus	Leviticus	Isaias	Isaiah
Numbers	Numbers	Jeremias	Jeremiah
Deuteronomy	Deuteronomy	Lamentations	Lamentations
Josue	Joshua	Baruch	
Judges	Judges	Ezechiel	Ezekiel
Ruth	Ruth	Daniel	Daniel
1 & 2 Kings	1 & 2 Samuel	Osee	Hosea
3 & 4 Kings	1 & 2 Kings	Joel	Joel
1 & 2 Paralipomenon	1 & 2 Chronicles	Amos	Amos
		Abdias	Obadiah
1 Esdras	Ezra	Jonas	Jonah
2 Esdras	Nehemiah	Micheas	Micah
Tobias		Nahum	Nahum
Judith		Habacuc	Habakkuk
Esther	Esther	Sophonias	Zephaniah
Job	Job	Aggeus	Haggai
Psalms	Psalms	Zacharias	Zechariah
Proverbs	Proverbs	Malachias	Malachi
Ecclesiastes	Ecclesiastes	1 & 2 Machabees	
Canticle of Canticles	Song of Solomon		

JEWISH SCRIPTURE

Law	1 & 2 Kings	Nahum	Song of Songs
Genesis	Isaiah	Habakkuk	Ruth
Exodus	Jeremiah	Zephaniah	Lamentations
Leviticus	Ezekiel	Haggai	Ecclesiastes
Numbers	Hosea	Zechariah	Esther
Deuteronomy	Joel	Malachi	Daniel
Prophets	Amos	Hagiographa	Ezra
Joshua	Obadiah	Psalms	Nehemiah
Judges	Jonah	Proverbs	1 & 2 Chronicles
1 & 2 Samuel	Micah	Job	

PROTESTANT APOCRYPHA

1 & 2 Esdras	Wisdom of Solomon	Baruch	Susanna
Tobit	Ecclesiasticus or the Wisdom of Jesus Son of Sirach	Prayer of Azariah and the Song of the Three Holy Children	Bel and the Dragon
Judith			The Prayer of Manasses
Additions to Esther			1 & 2 Maccabees

BOOKS OF THE NEW TESTAMENT

Matthew	Romans	1 & 2 Thessalonians	1 & 2 Peter
Mark	1 & 2 Corinthians		1, 2, 3 John
Luke	Galatians	1 & 2 Timothy	Jude
John	Ephesians	Titus	Revelation (Roman Catholic canon: Apocalypse)
Acts of the Apostles	Philippians	Philemon	
	Colossians	Hebrews	
		James	

Bible Belt n (1925) : an area chiefly in the southern U.S. believed to hold uncritical allegiance to the literal accuracy of the Bible; broadly : an area characterized by ardent religious fundamentalism

bib·li·cal \'bib-li-kəl\ *adj* [ML *biblicus*, fr. *biblia*] (1790) **1 :** of, relating to, or being in accord with the Bible **2 :** suggestive of the Bible or Bible times — **bib·li·cal·ly** \-k(ə-)lē\ *adv*

bib·li·cism \'bib-lə-,siz-əm\ *n, often cap* (1851) **:** adherence to the letter of the Bible — **bib·li·cist** \-lə-səst\ *n, often cap*

biblio- *comb form* [MF, fr. L, fr. Gk, fr. *biblion*] **:** book ⟨*biblio*film⟩

bib·li·og·ra·pher \,bib-lē-'äg-rə-fər\ *n* (1775) **1 :** an expert in bibliography **2 :** a compiler of bibliographies

bib·li·og·ra·phy \,bib-lē-'äg-rə-fē\ *n, pl* **-phies** [prob. fr. NL *bibliographia*, fr. Gk, the copying of books, fr. *biblio-* + *-graphia* -graphy] (1802) **1 :** the history, identification, or description of writings or publications **2 a :** a list often with descriptive or critical notes of writings relating to a particular subject, period, or author **b :** a list of works written by an author or printed by a publishing house **3 :** the works or a list of the works referred to in a text or consulted by the author in its production — **bib·lio·graph·ic** \,bib-lē-ə-'graf-ik\ *also* **bib·lio·graph·i·cal** \-i-kəl\ *adj* — **bib·lio·graph·i·cal·ly** \-k(ə-)lē\ *adv*

bib·li·ol·a·ter \,bib-lē-'äl-ət-ər\ *n* (1847) **1 :** one overly devoted to books **2 :** one having excessive reverence for the letter of the Bible — **bib·li·ol·a·trous** \-'äl-ə-trəs\ *adj* — **bib·li·ol·a·try** \-trē\ *n*

bib·li·ol·o·gy \,bib-lē-'äl-ə-jē\ *n* (1806) **1 :** the history and science of books as physical objects **:** BIBLIOGRAPHY **2** *often cap* **:** the study of the theological doctrine of the Bible

bib·lio·ma·nia \,bib-lē-ə-'mā-nē-ə, -nyə\ *n* [F *bibliomanie*, fr. *biblio-* + *manie* mania, fr. LL *mania*] (1734) **:** extreme preoccupation with collecting books — **bib·lio·ma·ni·ac** \-nē-,ak\ *n or adj* — **bib·lio·ma·ni·a·cal** \-lē-ō-mə-'nī-ə-kəl\ *adj*

bib·li·op·e·gy \,bib-lē-'äp-ə-jē\ *n* [deriv. of Gk *biblio-* + *pēgnynai* to fasten together — more at PACT] (ca. 1864) **:** the art of binding books — **bib·li·o·pe·gic** \,bib-lē-ə-'pej-ik, -'pēj-\ *adj* — **bib·li·o·pe·gi·cal·ly** \-i-k(ə-)lē\ *adv* — **bib·li·op·e·gist** \,bib-lē-'äp-ə-jəst\ *n* — **bib·li·op·e·gis·tic** \-,äp-ə-'jis-tik\ *adj*

bib·lio·phile \'bib-lē-ə-,fīl\ *n* [F, fr. *biblio-* + *-phile*] (1824) **:** a lover of books esp. for qualities of format; *also* **:** a book collector — **bib·lio·phil·ic** \,bib-lē-ə-'fil-ik\ *adj* — **bib·li·oph·i·lism** \-äf-ə-,liz-əm\ *n* — **bib·li·oph·i·list** \-ləst\ *n* — **bib·li·oph·i·ly** \-lē\ *n*

bib·li·o·pole \'bib-lē-ə-,pōl\ *or* **bib·li·op·o·list** \,bib-lē-'äp-ə-ləst\ *n* [L *bibliopola* bookseller, fr. Gk *bibliopōlēs*, fr. *biblio-* + *pōlein* to sell] (1775) **:** a dealer esp. in rare or curious books — **bib·li·o·po·lic** \,bib-lē-ə-'pō-lik, -'päl-ik\ *adj*

bib·lio·the·ca \,bib-lē-ə-'thē-kə\ *n, pl* **-cas** *or* **-cae** \-,sē, -,kē\ [L, fr. Gk *bibliothēkē*, fr. *biblio-* + *thēkē* case; akin to Gk *tithenai* to put, place — more at DO] (1824) **1 :** a collection of books **2 :** a list of books — **bib·lio·the·cal** \-'thē-kəl\ *adj*

bib·lio·ther·a·py \,bib-lē-ə-'ther-ə-pē\ *n* (1919) **:** the use of reading materials for help in solving personal problems or for psychiatric therapy

bib·li·ot·ics \,bib-lē-'ät-iks\ *n pl but sing in constr* [*biblio-* + connective *-t-* + *-ics*] (1901) **:** the study of handwriting, documents, and writing materials esp. for determining genuineness or authorship — **bib·li·ot·ic** \-ik\ *adj* — **bib·li·o·tist** \'bib-lē-ə-təst\ *n*

bib·u·lous \'bib-yə-ləs\ *adj* [L *bibulus*, fr. *bibere* to drink — more at POTABLE] (1675) **1 :** highly absorbent **2 a :** fond of alcoholic beverages **b :** of or relating to the consumption of alcoholic beverages — **bib·u·lous·ly** *adv* — **bib·u·lous·ness** *n*

bi·cam·er·al \(')bī-'kam-(ə-)rəl\ *adj* (1863) **:** having, consisting of, or based on two legislative chambers ⟨a ~ legislature⟩ — **bi·cam·er·al·ism** \-,iz-əm\ *n*

bi·car·bon·ate \(')bī-'kär-bə-,nāt, -nət\ *n* [ISV] (1819) **:** an acid carbonate

bicarbonate of soda (1887) **:** SODIUM BICARBONATE

bi·car·pel·late \(')bī-'kär-pə-,lāt, -lət\ *adj* (ca. 1900) **:** having two carpels

bi·cen·te·na·ry \,bī-(,)sen-'ten-ə-rē, (')bī-'sent-ᵊn-,er-ē, ,bī-(,)sen-'tē-nə-rē\ *n* (1872) **:** BICENTENNIAL — **bicentenary** *adj*

bi·cen·ten·ni·al \,bī-(,)sen-'ten-ē-əl\ *n* (1883) **:** a 200th anniversary or its celebration — **bicentennial** *adj*

bi·ceps \'bī-,seps\ *n, pl* **biceps** *also* **bi·ceps·es** [NL *bicipit-*, *biceps*, fr. L, two-headed, fr. *bi-* + *capit-*, *caput* head — more at HEAD] (1650) **:** a muscle having two heads: as **a :** the large flexor muscle of the front of the upper arm **b :** the large flexor muscle of the back of the upper leg

biceps bra·chii \-'brā-kē-,ī, -kē-,ē\ *n* [NL, lit., biceps of the arm] (ca. 1860) **:** BICEPS a

biceps fe·mo·ris \-'fem-ə-rəs\ *n* [NL, lit., biceps of the femur] (ca. 1860) **:** BICEPS b

bi·chlo·ride \(')bī-'klō(ə)r-,īd, -'klȯ(ə)r-\ *n* [ISV] (1810) **:** MERCURIC CHLORIDE

bichloride of mercury (1810) **:** MERCURIC CHLORIDE

bi·chon fri·se \bē-,shōⁿ-frē-'zā\ *n, pl* **bi·chons fri·ses** \-,shōⁿ-frē-'zā(z)\ [modif. of F *bichon à poil frisé* curly-haired lapdog] (1966) **:** any of a small sturdy breed of dogs of Mediterranean origin having a thick wavy white coat

bi·chro·mate \(')bī-'krō-,māt, 'bī-krō-\ *n* (1836) **:** DICHROMATE; *esp* **:** one of sodium or potassium — **bi·chro·mat·ed** \-,māt-əd\ *adj*

bi·chrome \'bī-,krōm\ *adj* (1924) **:** two-colored

bi·cip·i·tal \bī-'sip-ət-ᵊl\ *adj* (1646) **:** of, relating to, or being a biceps

1**bick·er** \'bik-ər\ *n* [ME *biker*] (14c) **1 :** petulant quarreling **:** ALTERCATION **2 :** a sound of or as if of bickering

2**bicker** *vi* **bick·ered; bick·er·ing** \-(ə-)riŋ\ (15c) **1 :** to contend in petulant or petty altercation **2 a :** to move quickly and unsteadily with a rapidly repeated noise **b :** QUIVER, FLICKER — **bick·er·er** \-ər-ər\ *n*

bi·col·ored \'bī-,kəl-ərd\ *also* **bi·col·or** \-ər\ *adj* [L *bicolor*, fr. *bi-* + *color*] (ca. 1847) **:** two-colored — **bicolor** *n*

bicolor lespedeza *n* (1948) **:** an Asian leguminous shrub (*Lespedeza bicolor*) with purple flowers in axillary racemes widely used as an ornamental, as a source of wild-bird food, and in erosion control

bi·con·cave \,bī-(,)kän-'kāv, (')bī-'kän-,\ *adj* [ISV] (1833) **:** concave on both sides — **bi·con·cav·i·ty** \,bī-(,)kän-'kav-ət-ē\ *n*

bi·con·di·tion·al \,bī-kən-'dish-nəl, -ən-ᵊl\ *n* (1940) **:** a relation between two propositions that is true only when both propositions are simultaneously true or false

bi·con·vex \,bī-(,)kän-'veks, (')bī-'kän-,, ,bī-kən-'\ *adj* [ISV] (ca. 1849) **:** convex on both sides — **bi·con·vex·i·ty** \,bī-kən-'vek-sət-ē, -(,)kän-\ *n*

bi·corne \'bī-,kȯ(ə)rn\ *n* [F, fr. L *bicornis* two-horned, fr. *bi-* + *cornu* horn — more at HORN] (1936) **:** COCKED HAT 2

bi·cor·nu·ate \(')bī-'kȯr-nyə-wət\ *adj* [*bi-* + L *cornu*] (ca. 1889) **:** having two horns or horn-shaped processes ⟨a ~ uterus⟩

bi·cul·tur·al·ism \(')bī-'kəlch(-ə)-rə-,liz-əm\ *n* (1953) **:** the existence of two distinct cultures in one nation — **bi·cul·tur·al** \-rəl\ *adj*

1**bi·cus·pid** \(')bī-'kəs-pəd\ *adj* [NL *bicuspid-*, *bicuspis*, fr. *bi-* + L *cuspid-*, *cuspis* point] (ca. 1836) **:** having or ending in two points ⟨~ teeth⟩

2**bicuspid** *n* (1852) **:** a human premolar tooth — see TOOTH illustration

bicuspid valve *n* (ca. 1900) **:** a cardiac valve that consists of two triangular flaps and guards the orifice between the left atrium and ventricle — called also *mitral valve*

1**bi·cy·cle** \'bī-,sik-əl, -,sīk-\ *n* [F, fr. *bi-* + *-cycle* (as in *tricycle*)] (1868) **:** a vehicle with two wheels tandem, a steering handle, a saddle seat, and pedals by which it is propelled

2**bicycle** *vi* **bi·cy·cled; bi·cy·cling** \-(ə-)liŋ\ (1869) **:** to ride a bicycle — **bi·cy·cler** \-lər\ *n* — **bi·cy·clist** \-ləst\ *n*

bi·cy·clic \(')bī-'sī-klik, -'sik-lik\ *adj* [ISV] (ca. 1889) **1 :** consisting of or arranged in two cycles **2 :** containing two usu. fused rings in the structure of the molecule

1**bid** \'bid\ *vb* **bade** \'bad, 'bād\ *or* **bid; bid·den** \'bid-ᵊn\ *or* **bid** *also* **bade; bid·ding** [partly fr. ME *bidden*, fr. OE *biddan*; akin to OHG *bitten* to entreat, Skt *bādhate* he harasses; partly fr. ME *beden* to offer, command, fr. OE *bēodan*; akin to OHG *biotan* to offer, Gk *pynthanesthai* to learn by inquiry, Skt *bodhi* enlightenment] *vt* (bef. 12c) **1 a** *obs* **:** BESEECH, ENTREAT **b :** to issue an order to **:** TELL **c :** to request to come **:** INVITE **2 :** to give expression to ⟨*bade* a tearful farewell⟩ **3 a :** OFFER — usu. used in the phrase *to bid defiance* **b** *past* **bid** (1) **:** to offer (a price) whether for payment or acceptance (2) **:** to make a bid of or in (a suit at cards) ~ *vi* **:** to make a bid ***syn*** see COMMAND — **bid·der** *n* — **bid fair :** to seem likely

2**bid** *n* (1788) **1 a :** the act of one who bids **b :** a statement of what one will give or take for something; *esp* **:** an offer of a price **c :** something offered as a bid **2 :** an opportunity to bid **3 :** INVITATION **4 a :** an announcement of what a cardplayer proposes to undertake **b :** the amount of such a bid **c :** a biddable bridge hand **5 :** an attempt or effort to win, achieve, or attract

bid·da·ble \'bid-ə-bəl\ *adj* (ca. 1768) **1 :** easily led, taught, or controlled **:** DOCILE **2 :** capable of being bid — **bid·da·bil·i·ty** \,bid-ə-'bil-ət-ē\ *n* — **bid·da·bly** \'bid-ə-blē\ *adv*

1**bid·dy** \'bid-ē\ *n, pl* **biddies** [perh. imit.] (1601) **:** HEN 1a; *also* **:** a young chicken

2**biddy** *n, pl* **biddies** [dim. of the name *Bridget*] (1861) **1 :** a hired girl or cleaning woman **2 :** WOMAN ⟨an eccentric old ~⟩

bide \'bīd\ *vb* **bode** \'bōd\ *or* **bid·ed; bided; bid·ing** [ME *biden*, fr. OE *bīdan*; akin to OHG *bītan* to wait, L *fidere* to trust, Gk *peithesthai* to believe] *vi* (bef. 12c) **1 :** to continue in a state or condition **2 :** to wait awhile **:** TARRY **3 :** to continue in a place **:** SOJOURN ~ *vt* **1** *past usu* **bided :** to wait for — used chiefly in the phrase *bide one's time* **2** *archaic* **:** to await confidently or defiantly **:** WITHSTAND ⟨two men . . . might ~ the winter storm — W. C. Bryant⟩ **3** *chiefly dial* **:** to put up with **:** TOLERATE — **bid·er** *n*

bi·det \bi-'dā\ *n* [F, small horse, bidet, fr. MF, fr. *bider* to trot] (1766) **:** a fixture about the height of the seat of a chair used esp. for bathing the external genitals and the posterior parts of the body

bi·di·a·lec·tal·ism \,bī-,dī-ə-'lek-tᵊl-,iz-əm\ *n* (1958) **:** the constant oral use of two dialects of the same language — **bi·di·a·lec·tal** *adj*

bi·di·rec·tion·al \,bī-də-'rek-shnəl, -dī-, -shən-ᵊl\ *adj* (1928) **:** involving, moving, or taking place in two usu. opposite directions ⟨~ flow⟩ ⟨~ replication of DNA⟩ — **bi·di·rec·tion·al·ly** \-ē\ *adv*

bi·don·ville \,bē-,dōⁿ-'vē(ə)l\ *n* [F, fr. *bidon* tin can + *ville* city] (1952) **:** a settlement of jerry-built dwellings on the outskirts of a city (as in France or No. Africa)

bid up *vt* (1864) **:** to raise the price of (as property at auction) by a succession of offers

Bie·der·mei·er \'bēd-ər-,mī(-ə)r\ *adj* [after Gottlieb *Biedermeier*, satirical name for an uninspired Ger. bourgeois] (1905) **:** of a style of furniture and interior decoration popular esp. with the middle class in early 19th century Germany that is similar to but considered aesthetically inferior to Empire

bield \'bē(ə)ld\ *vt or n* [ME *belden* to encourage, protect, fr. OE *bieldan* to encourage; akin to OE *beald* bold] *chiefly Scot* (bef. 12c) **:** SHELTER

bi·en·ni·al \(')bī-'en-ē-əl\ *adj* (1562) **1 :** occurring every two years **2 :** continuing or lasting for two years; *specif* **:** growing vegetatively during the first year and fruiting and dying during the second — **biennial** *n* — **bi·en·ni·al·ly** \-ə-lē\ *adv*

bi·en·ni·um \bī-'en-ē-əm\ *n, pl* **-ni·ums** *or* **-nia** \-ē-ə\ [L, fr. *bi-* + *annus* year — more at ANNUAL] (1899) **:** a period of two years

bier \'bi(ə)r\ *n* [ME *bere*, fr. OE *bǣr*; akin to OE *beran* to carry — more at BEAR] (bef. 12c) **1** *archaic* **:** a framework for carrying **2 :** a stand on which a corpse or coffin is placed; *also* **:** a coffin together with its stand

bi·face \'bī-,fās\ *n* (1934) **:** a bifacial stone tool

bi·fa·cial \(')bī-'fā-shəl\ *adj* (ca. 1847) **:** having opposite sides or faces worked on to form an edge for cutting or scraping — **bi·fa·cial·ly** \-ē\ *adv*

biff \'bif\ *n* [prob. imit.] (1889) **:** WHACK, BLOW — **biff** *vt*

bi·fid \'bī-,fid, -fəd\ *adj* [L *bifidus*, fr. *bi-* + *-fidus* -fid] (1661) **:** divided into two equal lobes or parts by a median cleft ⟨a ~ leaf⟩

bi·fi·lar \(')bī-'fī-lər\ *adj* [ISV *bi-* + L *filum* thread — more at FILE] (1846) **1 :** involving two threads or wires ⟨~ suspension of a pendulum⟩ **2 :** involving a single thread or wire doubled back upon itself ⟨a ~ resistor⟩ — **bi·fi·lar·ly** *adv*

bi·fla·gel·late \(')bī-'flaj-ə-lət, -,lāt; ,bī-flə-'jel-ət\ *adj* (1856) **:** having two flagella ⟨~ gametes⟩

1**bi·fo·cal** \(')bī-'fō-kəl\ *adj* [ISV] (1888) **1 :** having two focal lengths **2 :** having one part that corrects for near vision and one for distant vision ⟨a ~ eyeglass lens⟩

2**bifocal** *n* (ca. 1909) **1 :** a bifocal glass or lens **2** *pl* **:** eyeglasses with bifocal lenses

bi·func·tion·al \(')bī-'fəŋ(k)-shnəl, -shən-ᵊl\ *adj* (1936) **:** having two functions

bi·fur·cate \'bī-(,)fər-,kāt, bī-'fər-\ *vi* **-cat·ed; -cat·ing** [ML *bifurcatus*, pp. of *bifurcare*, fr. L *bifurcus* two-pronged, fr. *bi-* + *furca* fork] (1615) **:** to divide into two branches or parts — **bi·fur·cate** \(')bī-'fər-kət, -,kāt; 'bī-(,)fər-,kāt\ *adj*

bi·fur·ca·tion \ˌbī-(ˌ)fər-ˈkā-shən\ *n* (1615) **1 a :** the point at which bifurcating occurs **b :** BRANCH **2 :** the act of bifurcating **:** the state of being bifurcated

[1]**big** \ˈbig\ *adj* **big·ger; big·gest** [ME, prob. of Scand origin; akin to Norw dial. *bugge* important man; akin to OE *bȳl* boil, Skt *bhūri* abundant] (14c) **1 a** *obs* **:** of great strength **b :** of great force ⟨a ~ storm⟩ **2 a :** large in dimensions, bulk, or extent ⟨a ~ house⟩; *also* **:** large in quantity, number, or amount ⟨a ~ fleet⟩ **b :** conducted on a large scale ⟨~ government⟩ **c :** UPPERCASE **3 a :** PREGNANT; *esp* **:** nearly ready to give birth **b :** full to bursting **:** SWELLING ⟨~ with rage⟩ **c** *of the voice* **:** full and resonant **4 a :** CHIEF, PREEMINENT ⟨the ~ issue of the campaign⟩ **b :** outstandingly worthy or able ⟨a truly ~ man⟩ **c :** of great importance or significance ⟨the ~ moment⟩ **d :** IMPOSING, PRETENTIOUS; *also* **:** marked by or given to boasting ⟨~ talk⟩ **e :** MAGNANIMOUS, GENEROUS ⟨a ~ heart⟩ **5 :** POPULAR ⟨soft drinks are very ~ in Mexico —Russ Leadabrand⟩ **6 :** full-bodied and flavorful — used of wine — **big·ly** *adv* — **big·ness** *n* — **big on :** strongly in favor of; *also* **:** noted for ⟨she is *big on* blushing —Arnold Hano⟩

[2]**big** *adv* (1912) **1 :** to a large amount or extent ⟨eats ~ at noon⟩ **2 a :** in an outstanding manner ⟨made it ~ in New York⟩ **b :** in a pretentious manner ⟨he talks ~⟩ **c :** in a magnanimous manner ⟨took his defeat ~⟩

[3]**big** *n* (1965) **:** an individual or organization of outstanding importance or power; *esp* **:** MAJOR LEAGUE ⟨a chance to play in the ~*s*⟩

big·a·mous \ˈbig-ə-məs\ *adj* (1864) **1 :** guilty of bigamy **2 :** involving bigamy — **big·a·mous·ly** *adv*

big·a·my \ˈbig-ə-mē\ *n* [ME *bigamie*, fr. ML *bigamia*, fr. L *bi-* + LL *-gamia* -gamy, fr. Gk, fr. *gamos* marriage; akin to L *gener* son-in-law] (13c) **:** the act of entering into a marriage with one person while still legally married to another — **big·a·mist** \-məst\ *n*

bi·ga·rade \ˌbē-gä-ˈräd\ *n* [F, fr. Prov *bigarrado*, fr. pp. of *bigarra* to variegate] (1703) **1 :** SOUR ORANGE **2 :** a brown sauce flavored with the juice and grated rind of oranges

big band *n* (1926) **:** a jazz, dance, or rock band that is larger than a combo and that usu. features a mixture of ensemble playing and solo improvisation

big bang theory *n* (1955) **:** a theory in astronomy: the universe originated billions of years ago in an explosion from a single point of nearly infinite energy density — compare STEADY STATE THEORY

big beat *n, often cap both Bs* (1958) **:** music (as rock and roll) characterized by a heavy persistent beat

Big Ben \-ˈben\ *n* [after Sir *Benjamin* Hall †1867 Eng. Chief Commissioner of Works] (ca. 1895) **1 :** a large bell in the clock tower of the Houses of Parliament in London **2 :** the tower that houses Big Ben; *also* **:** the clock in the tower

big boy *n* (1926) **:** BIG GUN

big brother *n* (1863) **1 :** an older brother **2 :** a man who befriends a delinquent or friendless boy **3** *cap both Bs* [*Big Brother*, personification of the power of the state in *1984* (1949) by George Orwell] **a :** the leader of an authoritarian state or movement **b :** a seemingly benevolent but actually ruthless and all-powerful government or organization ⟨data banks that tell *Big Brother* all about us —Herbert Brucker⟩

Big Broth·er·ism \-ˈbrəth-ə-ˌriz-əm\ *n* (1950) **:** authoritarian attempts at complete control (as of a person or a nation)

big business *n* (1905) **:** an economic group consisting of large profit-making corporations esp. with regard to their influence on social or political policy

big daddy *n, often cap B&D* (1958) **:** one preeminent esp. by reason of power, size, or seniority **:** one representing paternalistic authority

big deal *n* (1949) **:** something of special importance

Big Dipper *n* (1869) **:** DIPPER 3a

bi·gem·i·ny \bī-ˈjem-ə-nē\ *n* [*bigeminal* (double, paired), fr. LL *bigeminus*, fr. *bi-* + *geminus* twin] (ca. 1923) **:** the state of having a pulse characterized by two beats close together with a pause following each pair of beats — **bi·gem·i·nal** \-ən-ᵊl\ *adj*

bi·ge·ner·ic \ˌbī-jə-ˈner-ik\ *adj* (1885) **:** of, relating to, or involving two genera ⟨a ~ hybrid⟩

big·eye \ˈbig-ˌī\ *n* (ca. 1889) **:** either of two small widely distributed reddish to silvery percoid fishes (*Priacanthus cruentatus* and *P. arenatus*) of tropical seas

big·foot \ˈbig-ˌfu̇t\ *n, often cap* [fr. the size of the footprints ascribed to it] (1962) **:** SASQUATCH

big game *n* (1864) **1 :** large animals sought or taken by hunting or fishing for sport **2 :** an important objective esp. when involving risk

big·ge·ty *or* **big·gi·ty** \ˈbig-ət-ē\ *adj* [prob. fr. *big* + *-ety* (as in *persnickety*)] (1880) **1** *Southern & Midland* **:** CONCEITED, VAIN **2** *Southern & Midland* **:** rudely self-important **:** IMPUDENT ⟨Mama never acted ~ in court, but she would bow her head only so low —Claude Brown⟩

big·gie \ˈbig-ē\ *n* [*big* + *-ie*] (ca. 1931) **:** one that is big

[1]**big·gin** *or* **big·ging** \ˈbig-ən\ *n* [ME *bigging*, fr. *biggen* to dwell, fr. ON *byggja*; akin to OE *bēon* to be] *archaic* (14c) **:** BUILDING

[2]**biggin** *n* [MF *beguin*] *archaic* (1530) **:** CAP: **a :** a child's cap **b :** NIGHTCAP

big·gish \ˈbig-ish\ *adj* (1626) **:** somewhat big

big gun *n* (1834) **:** one having preeminent status or power in a field

big·head \ˈbig-ˌhed\ *n* (1805) **1 :** any of several diseases of animals marked by swelling about the head **2 :** an exaggerated opinion of one's importance **:** CONCEIT — **big·head·ed** \-ˈhed-əd\ *adj*

big·heart·ed \-ˈhärt-əd\ *adj* (1868) **:** GENEROUS, CHARITABLE — **big·heart·ed·ly** *adv* — **big·heart·ed·ness** *n*

big·horn \ˈbig-ˌhȯ(ə)rn\ *n, pl* **bighorn** *or* **bighorns** (ca. 1784) **:** a usu. grayish brown wild sheep (*Ovis canadensis*) of mountainous western No. America

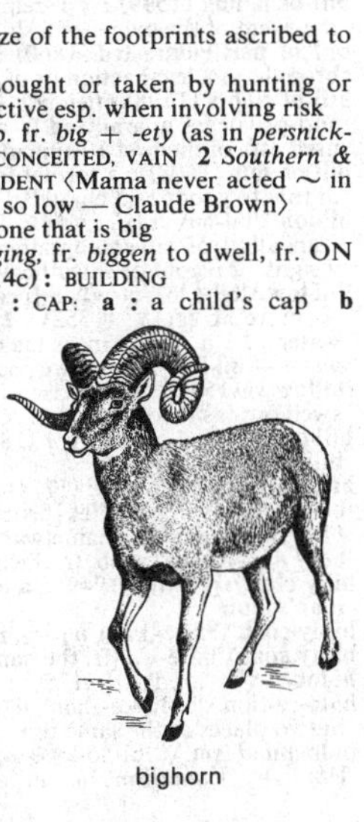
bighorn

big house *n, slang* (1916) **:** PENITENTIARY

bight \ˈbīt\ *n* [ME, fr. OE *byht* bend, bay; akin to OE *būgan* to bend — more at BOW] (15c) **1 :** a bend in a coast forming an open bay; *also* **:** a bay formed by such a bend **2 :** a slack part or loop in a rope

big league *n* (1899) **1 :** MAJOR LEAGUE **2 :** an enterprise or group at the top of its field — often used in pl. — **big–league** *adj* — **big leaguer** *n*

big lie *n, sometimes cap B&L* [trans. of G *grosse lüge*] (1949) **:** a gross distortion of the truth used esp. as a propaganda tactic

big·mouthed \ˈbig-ˈmau̇thd, -ˈmau̇tht\ *adj* (1642) **1 :** having a large mouth **2 :** LOUDMOUTHED

big name *n* (1926) **:** a performer or personage of top rank in popular recognition — **big–name** *adj*

big·no·nia \big-ˈnō-nē-ə\ *n* [NL, genus name, fr. J. P. *Bignon* †1743 Fr. royal librarian] (1785) **:** any of a genus (*Bignonia*) of American and Japanese woody vines of the trumpet-creeper family with compound leaves and tubular flowers

big·ot \ˈbig-ət\ *n* [MF, hypocrite, bigot] (1661) **:** one obstinately or intolerantly devoted to his own opinions and prejudices — **big·ot·ed** \-ət-əd\ *adj* — **big·ot·ed·ly** *adv*

big·ot·ry \ˈbig-ə-trē\ *n, pl* **-ries** (1674) **1 :** the state of mind of a bigot **2 :** acts or beliefs characteristic of a bigot

big shot \ˈbig-ˌshät\ *n* (1929) **:** a person of consequence or prominence

big stick *n* (1900) **:** threat esp. of military or political intervention

big–tick·et \ˈbig-ˈtik-ət\ *adj* (1945) **:** high-priced

big time \-ˌtīm\ *n* (1910) **1 :** a high-paying vaudeville circuit requiring only two performances a day **2 :** the top rank of an activity or enterprise — **big–time** *adj* — **big–tim·er** \-ˌtī-mər\ *n*

big toe *n* (ca. 1887) **:** the innermost and largest toe of the foot

big top *n* (1895) **1 :** the main tent of a circus **2 :** CIRCUS 2a, 2b, 2c

big tree *n* (1853) **:** a California evergreen (*Sequoiadendron giganteum*) of the pine family that sometimes exceeds 270 feet in height — called also *giant sequoia, sequoia*

big wheel *n* (1942) **:** BIGWIG

big·wig \ˈbig-ˌwig\ *n* (1703) **:** an important person

Bi·ha·ri \bi-ˈhär-ē\ *n* (1882) **1 :** a native or inhabitant of Bihar, India **2 :** a group of Indic dialects spoken by the Biharis

bi·jec·tion \(ˌ)bī-ˈjek-shən\ *n* [[1]*bi-* + *-jection* (as in *injection*)] (1966) **:** a mathematical function that is a one-to-one and onto mapping — compare INJECTION, SURJECTION — **bi·jec·tive** \-ˈjek-tiv\ *adj*

bi·jou \ˈbē-ˌzhü\ *n, pl* **bijous** *or* **bi·joux** \-ˌzhü(z)\ [F, fr. Bret *bizou* ring, fr. *biz* finger] (1668) **1 :** a small dainty usu. ornamental piece of delicate workmanship **:** JEWEL **2 :** something delicate, elegant, or highly prized — **bijou** *adj*

bi·jou·te·rie \bi-ˈzhüt-ə-(ˌ)rē\ *n* [F, fr. *bijou*] (1815) **:** a collection of trinkets or ornaments **:** JEWELS; *also* **:** DECORATION

[1]**bike** \ˈbīk\ *n* [ME] (14c) **1** *chiefly Scot* **:** a nest of wild bees, wasps, or hornets **2** *chiefly Scot* **:** a crowd or swarm of people

[2]**bike** *n* [by shortening & alter.] (1882) **1 :** BICYCLE **2 :** MOTORCYCLE **3 :** MOTORBIKE

[3]**bike** *vi* **biked; bik·ing** (1895) **:** to ride a bike

bik·er \ˈbī-kər\ *n* (1883) **1 :** BICYCLIST **2 :** MOTORCYCLIST; *esp* **:** one who is a member of an organized gang

bike·way \ˈbī-ˌkwā\ *n* (1965) **:** a thoroughfare for bicycles

bik·ie \ˈbīk-ē\ *n* [[2]*bike* + *-ie*] *chiefly Austral* (1967) **:** BIKER 2

bi·ki·ni \bə-ˈkē-nē\ *n* [F, fr. *Bikini*, atoll of the Marshall islands] (1947) **1 a :** a woman's scanty two-piece bathing suit **b :** a man's brief swimsuit **2 :** a man's or woman's low-cut briefs — **bi·ki·nied** \-nēd\ *adj*

[1]**bi·la·bi·al** \(ˈ)bī-ˈlā-bē-əl\ *n* (1889) **:** a bilabial consonant

[2]**bilabial** *adj* [ISV] *of a consonant* (1894) **:** produced with both lips

bi·la·bi·ate \-bē-ət\ *adj* (1794) **:** having two lips ⟨a ~ corolla of a mint⟩

bi·lat·er·al \(ˈ)bī-ˈlat-ə-rəl, -ˈla-trəl\ *adj* (1775) **1 :** having two sides **2 :** affecting reciprocally two sides or parties ⟨a ~ treaty⟩ ⟨a ~ trade agreement⟩ **3 :** having bilateral symmetry — **bi·lat·er·al·ly** \-ē\ *adv*

bilateral symmetry *n* (ca. 1889) **:** symmetry in which similar anatomical parts are arranged on opposite sides of a median axis so that one and only one plane can divide the individual into essentially identical halves

bi·lay·er \ˈbī-ˌlā-ər, -ˌle(-ə)r\ *n* (1963) **:** a film or membrane with two molecular layers ⟨a ~ of phospholipid molecules⟩ — **bilayer** *adj*

bil·ber·ry \ˈbil-ˌber-ē\ *n* [*bil-* (prob. of Scand origin; akin to Dan *bølle* whortleberry) + *berry*] (1577) **:** any of several plants (genus *Vaccinium*) that differ from the typical blueberries in having their flowers arise solitary or in very small clusters from axillary buds; *also* **:** its sweet edible bluish fruit

[1]**bil·bo** \ˈbil-(ˌ)bō\ *n* [perh. fr. *Bilboa*, Spain] (1551) **:** a long bar of iron with sliding shackles used to confine the feet of prisoners esp. on shipboard

[2]**bilbo** *or* **bil·boa** \ˈbil-(ˌ)bō\ *n* [*Bilboa, Bilbao*, Spain] (1584) **:** SWORD

bil·dungs·ro·man \ˈbil-du̇ŋ(k)s-rō-ˌmän, -du̇ŋz-\ *n* [G, fr. *bildung* education + *roman* novel] (1910) **:** a novel about the moral and psychological growth of the main character

bile \ˈbī(ə)l\ *n* [F, fr. L *bilis*, of Celtic origin; akin to W *bustl* bile] (1665) **1 a :** a yellow or greenish viscid alkaline fluid secreted by the liver and passed into the duodenum where it aids esp. in the emulsification and absorption of fats **b :** either of two humors associated in old physiology with irascibility and melancholy **2 :** inclination to anger

bile acid *n* (ca. 1881) **:** any of several steroid acids (as cholic acid) of or derived from bile

bile duct *n* (1774) **:** a duct by which bile passes from the liver or gallbladder to the duodenum

bile salt *n* (1881) **1 :** a salt of bile acid **2** *pl* **:** a dry mixture of the principal salts of the gall of the ox used as a liver stimulant and as a laxative

[1]**bi–lev·el** \ˈbī-ˈlev-əl\ *adj* (1960) **1 :** having two levels of freight or passenger space **2 :** divided vertically into two ground-floor levels

[2]**bi–level** \ˈbī-ˌ\ *n* (1966) **:** a bi-level house

[1]bilge \'bilj\ *n* [prob. modif. of MF *boulge, bouge* leather bag, curved part — more at BUDGET] (1513) **1 :** the bulging part of a cask or barrel **2 a :** the part of the underwater body of a ship between the flat of the bottom and the vertical topsides **b :** the lowest point of a ship's inner hull **3 :** stale or worthless remarks or ideas
[2]bilge *vi* **bilged; bilg·ing** (1728) **1 :** to become damaged in the bilge **2 :** to rest on the bilge
bilge keel *n* (1850) **:** a projection like a fin extending from the hull near the turn of the bilge on either side to check rolling
bilge water *n* (1706) **:** water that collects in the bilge of a ship
bil·har·zia \bil-'här-zē-ə, -'härt-sē-\ *n* [NL, fr. Theodor *Bilharz* †1862 Ger. zoologist] (1883) **1 :** SCHISTOSOMIASIS **2 :** SCHISTOSOME — **bil·har·zi·al** \-zē-əl, -sē-\ *adj*
bil·har·zi·a·sis \ˌbil-ˌhär-'zī-ə-səs, -ˌhärt-'sī-\ *n, pl* **-a·ses** \-ˌsēz\ [NL, fr. *bilharzia* + *-iasis*] (ca. 1900) **:** SCHISTOSOMIASIS
bil·i·ary \'bil-ē-ˌer-ē\ *adj* [F *biliare,* fr. L *bilis*] (1731) **:** of, relating to, or conveying bile; *also* **:** affecting the bile-conveying structures
bi·lin·ear \(')bī-'lin-ē-ər\ *adj* (1886) **:** linear with respect to each of two mathematical variables; *specif* **:** of or relating to an algebraic form each term of which involves one variable to the first degree from each of two sets of variables
bi·lin·gual \(')bī-'liŋ-g(yə-)wəl\ *adj* [L *bilinguis,* fr. *bi-* + *lingua* tongue — more at TONGUE] (1847) **1 :** having or expressed in two languages **2 :** using or able to use two languages esp. with equal fluency — **bilingual** *n* — **bi·lin·gual·ly** \-ē\ *adv*
bilingual education *n* (1972) **:** education in an English-language school system in which minority students with little fluency in English are taught in their native language
bi·lin·gual·ism \-ˌiz-əm\ *n* (1873) **:** the ability to speak two languages **:** the constant oral use of two languages
bil·ious \'bil-yəs\ *adj* [MF *bilieux,* fr. L *biliosus,* fr. *bilis*] (1541) **1 a :** of or relating to bile **b :** marked by or suffering from disordered liver function and esp. excessive secretion of bile **c :** appearing as if affected by a bilious disorder **2 :** of a peevish ill-natured disposition — **bil·ious·ly** *adv* — **bil·ious·ness** *n*
bil·i·ru·bin \ˌbil-i-'rü-bən, 'bil-i-ˌ\ *n* [L *bilis* + *ruber* red — more at RED] (1871) **:** a reddish yellow pigment $C_{33}H_{36}N_4O_6$ occurring in bile, blood, urine, and gallstones
bil·i·ver·din \-'vərd-ᵊn, -ˌvərd-\ *n* [Sw, fr. L *bilis* + obs. F *verd* green] (ca. 1845) **:** a green pigment $C_{33}H_{34}N_4O_6$ occurring in bile
[1]bilk \'bilk\ *vt* [perh. alter. of [2]*balk*] (1651) **1 :** to block the free development of **:** FRUSTRATE ⟨fate ~*s* their hopes⟩ **2 a :** to cheat out of what is due **b :** to evade payment of or to ⟨~*s* his creditors⟩ **3 :** to slip away from **:** ELUDE ⟨~ his pursuers⟩ — **bilk·er** *n*
[2]bilk *n* (1790) **:** an untrustworthy tricky individual **:** CHEAT
[1]bill \'bil\ *n* [ME *bile,* fr. OE; akin to OE *bill*] (bef. 12c) **1 :** the jaws of a bird together with their horny covering **2 :** a mouthpart (as the beak of a turtle) that resembles a bird's bill **3 :** a projection of land like a beak **4 :** the point of an anchor fluke **5 :** the visor of a cap or hood

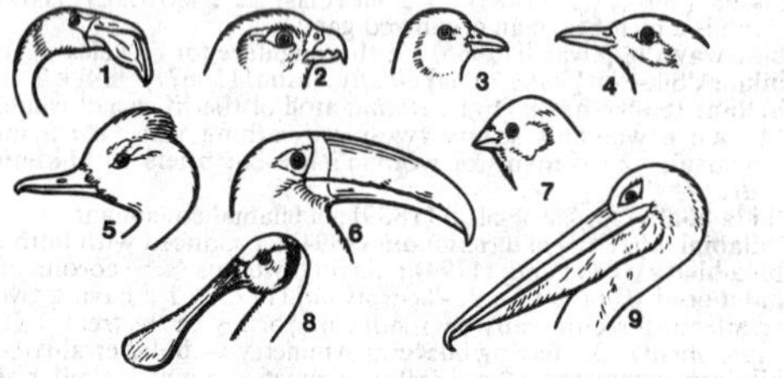

bill 1: *1* flamingo, *2* falcon, *3* pigeon, *4* thrush, *5* merganser, *6* toucan, *7* finch, *8* spoonbill, *9* pelican

[2]bill *vi* (1592) **1 :** to touch and rub bill to bill **2 :** to caress affectionately ⟨~*ing* and cooing⟩
[3]bill *n* [ME *bil,* fr. OE *bill;* akin to OHG *bill* pickax, Gk *phitros* log] (bef. 12c) **1 :** a weapon in use up to the 18th century that consists of a long staff ending in a hook-shaped blade **2 :** BILLHOOK
[4]bill *n* [ME, fr. ML *billa.* seal, alter. of *bulla,* fr. L, bubble, boss] (14c) **1 :** a written document or note **2** *obs* **:** a formal petition **3 :** a draft of a law presented to a legislature for enactment; *also* **:** the law itself ⟨the GI ~⟩ **4 :** a declaration in writing stating a wrong a complainant has suffered from a defendant or stating a breach of law by some person ⟨a ~ of complaint⟩ **5 :** an itemized list or a statement of particulars (as a list of materials or of members of a ship's crew) **6 a :** an itemized account of the separate cost of goods sold, services performed, or work done **:** INVOICE **b :** an amount expended or owed **c :** a statement of charges for food or drink **:** CHECK **7 a :** a written or printed advertisement posted or otherwise distributed to announce an event of interest to the public; *esp* **:** an announcement of a theatrical entertainment **b :** a programmed presentation (as a motion picture, play, or concert) **8 a :** a piece of paper money **b :** an individual or commercial note ⟨~*s* receivable⟩ **c** *slang* **:** one hundred dollars — **fill the bill** *or* **fit the bill :** to be exactly what is needed **:** be suitable
[5]bill *vt* (14c) **1 a :** to enter in an accounting system **:** prepare a bill of (charges) **b :** to submit a bill of charges to **c :** to enter (as freight) in a waybill **d :** to issue a bill of lading to or for **2 :** to announce (as a performance) esp. by posters or placards **3 :** ADVERTISE, PROMOTE ⟨the book is ~*ed* as a "report" —P. G. Altbach⟩ — **bill·able** *adj*
bil·la·bong \'bil-ə-ˌbȯŋ, -ˌbäŋ\ *n* [native name in Australia] (1865) **1** *Austral* **a :** a blind channel leading out from a river **b :** a usu. dry streambed that is filled seasonally **2** *Austral* **:** a backwater forming a stagnant pool
[1]bill·board \'bil-ˌbō(ə)rd, -ˌbȯ(ə)rd\ *n* [[4]*bill* + *board*] (1851) **:** a flat surface (as of a panel, wall, or fence) on which bills are posted; *specif* **:** a large panel designed to carry outdoor advertising
[2]billboard *vt* (1970) **:** to promote by a conspicuous display on or as if on a billboard
[3]billboard *n* (ca. 1860) **:** a projection or ledge fixed on the bow of a vessel for the anchor to rest on
bill·bug \'bil-ˌbəg\ *n* [[1]*bill* + *bug*] (1861) **:** any of various weevils (as of the genus *Sphenophorus*) having larvae that eat the roots of cereal and other grasses
-billed \'bild\ *adj comb form* **:** having (such) a bill ⟨hard-*billed*⟩
bill·er \'bil-ər\ *n* (1920) **:** one that bills; *esp* **:** one that makes out bills
[1]bil·let \'bil-ət\ *n* [ME *bylet,* fr. MF *billette,* dim. of *bulle* document, fr. ML *bulla*] (15c) **1** *archaic* **:** a brief letter **:** NOTE **2 a :** an official order directing that a member of a military force be provided with board and lodging (as in a private home) **b :** quarters assigned by or as if by a billet **3 :** POSITION, JOB ⟨a lucrative ~⟩
[2]billet *vt* (1595) **1 :** to assign lodging to (as soldiers) by a billet **:** QUARTER **2 :** to serve with a billet ⟨~ a householder⟩ ~ *vi* **:** to have quarters
[3]billet *n* [ME *bylet,* fr. MF *billete,* dim. of *bille* log, of Celt origin; akin to OIr *bile* sacred tree] (15c) **1 a :** a chunky piece of wood (as for firewood) **b** *obs* **:** CUDGEL **2 a :** a bar of metal **b :** a piece of semifinished iron or steel nearly square in section made by rolling an ingot or bloom **c :** a section of nonferrous metal ingot hot-worked by forging, rolling, or extrusion **:** a nonferrous casting suitable for rolling or extrusion
bil·let–doux \ˌbil-ē-'dü, ˌbil-(ˌ)ā-\ *n, pl* **bil·lets–doux** \-'dü(z)\ [F *billet doux,* lit., sweet letter] (1673) **:** a love letter
bill·fish \'bil-ˌfish\ *n* (1782) **:** a fish (as a marlin or gar) with long slender jaws
bill·fold \-ˌfōld\ *n* [short for earlier *billfolder*] (1895) **:** a folding pocketbook for paper money; *esp* **:** one with various compartments for cards, photographs, or loose change
bill·hook \-ˌhu̇k\ *n* (1611) **:** a cutting or pruning tool with a hooked blade
bil·liard \'bi(l)-yərd\ *n* [back-formation fr. *billiards*] (1580) — used as an attributive form of *billiards* ⟨~ ball⟩
bil·liards \-yərdz\ *n pl but sing in constr* [MF *billard* billiard cue, billiards, fr. *bille*] (1580) **:** any of several games played on an oblong table by driving small balls against one another or into pockets with a cue; *specif* **:** a game in which one scores by causing a cue ball to hit in succession two object balls — compare POOL
bil·li–bi *also* **bil·ly–bi** \'bil-ē-ˌbē, ˌbil-ē-'\ *n* [F, alter. of *Billy B.,* William B. Leeds, Jr. †1972 Am. industrialist; fr. his partiality for it] (1961) **:** a soup made of mussel stock, white wine, and cream and served hot or cold
bill·ing \'bil-iŋ\ *n* [[5]*bill*] (1875) **1 :** advertising or public promotion (as of a product or personality); *also* **:** relative prominence of a name in such promotion ⟨got top ~⟩ **2 :** total amount of business or investments (as of an advertising agency) within a given period
bil·lings·gate \'bil-iŋz-ˌgāt, *Brit usu* -git\ *n* [*Billingsgate,* old gate and fish market, London, England] (1652) **:** coarsely abusive language **syn** see ABUSE
bil·lion \'bi(l)-yən\ *n* [F, fr. *bi-* + *-illion* (as in *million*)] (1834) **1** — see NUMBER table **2 :** a very large number — **billion** *adj* — **bil·lionth** \-yən(t)th\ *adj or n*
bil·lion·aire \ˌbi(l)-yə-'na(ə)r, -'ne(ə)r, 'bi(l)-yə-ˌ\ *n* [*billion* + *-aire* (as in *millionaire*)] (1860) **:** one whose wealth is estimated at a billion or more (as of dollars or pounds)
bill of exchange (1579) **:** an unconditional written order from one person to another to pay a specified sum of money to a designated person
bill of fare (1636) **1 :** MENU **2 :** PROGRAM
bill of goods (1920) **1 :** a consignment of merchandise **2 :** something intentionally misrepresented **:** something passed off in a deception or fraud — often used in the phrase *sell a bill of goods*
bill of health (1644) **1 :** a certificate given to the ship's master at the time of leaving port that indicates the state of health of a ship's company and of a port with regard to infectious diseases **2 :** a usu. favorable report about a condition or situation ⟨gave the criticized textbook a clean *bill of health*⟩
bill of indictment (1530) **:** an indictment before it is found or ignored by the grand jury
bill of lading (1599) **:** a receipt listing goods shipped that is signed by the agent of the owner of a ship or issued by a common carrier
bill of particulars (ca. 1860) **:** a detailed listing of charges or claims brought in a legal action or of a defendant's response or counterclaim
bill of rights (1798) *often cap B&R* **:** a summary of fundamental rights and privileges guaranteed to a people against violation by the state — used esp. of the first 10 amendments to the U.S. Constitution
bill of sale (1608) **:** a formal instrument for the conveyance or transfer of title to goods and chattels
bil·lon \'bil-ən\ *n* [F, fr. MF, fr. *bille* log — more at BILLET] (1819) **1 :** an alloy of silver containing more than 50 percent of copper by weight **2 :** gold or silver heavily alloyed with a less valuable metal
[1]bil·low \'bil-(ˌ)ō, -ə(-w)\ *n* [prob. fr. ON *bylgja;* akin to OHG *balg* bag — more at BELLY] (1552) **1 :** WAVE; *esp* **:** a great wave or surge of water **2 :** a rolling mass (as of flame or smoke) that resembles a high wave — **bil·lowy** \'bil-ə-wē\ *adj*
[2]billow *vi* (1597) **1 :** to rise or roll in waves or surges **2 :** to bulge or swell out (as through action of the wind) ~ *vt* **:** to cause to billow
bill·post·er \'bil-ˌpō-stər\ *n* (1809) **:** one that posts advertising bills — **bill·post·ing** \-stiŋ\ *n*
bill·stick·er \-ˌstik-ər\ *n* (1774) **:** BILLPOSTER
[1]bil·ly \'bil-ē\ *n, pl* **billies** [prob. short for *billycan* (billy)] *chiefly Austral* (1839) **:** a metal or enamelware pail or pot with a lid and wire bail
[2]billy *n, pl* **billies** [prob. fr. the name *Billy*] (1848) **:** BILLY CLUB
billy club *n* [[2]*billy*] (1949) **:** a heavy usu. wooden club; *specif* **:** a policeman's club
bil·ly·cock \'bil-ē-ˌkäk\ *n* [origin unknown] *Brit* (1721) **:** DERBY 3
bil·ly goat \'bil-ē-\ *n* [fr. the name *Billy*] (1861) **:** a male goat
bi·lobed \'bī-'lōbd\ *adj* (1756) **:** divided into two lobes ⟨a ~ nucleus⟩
bi·lo·ca·tion \ˌbī-lō-'kā-shən\ *n* (1858) **:** the state of being or ability to be in two places at the same time
bi·lo·qui·al·ism \(')bī-'lō-kwē-ə-ˌliz-əm\ *also* **bi·lo·qui·lism** \-kwə-ˌliz-\ *n* [*'bi-* + *-loquialism* (as in *colloquialism*)] (1972) **:** BIDIALECTALISM

bil·tong \ˈbil-ˌtȯŋ, -ˌtäŋ\ *n* [Afrik, fr. *bil* buttock + *tong* tongue] *chiefly So Afr* (1815) : jerked meat

bi·man·u·al \(ˈ)bī-ˈman-yə(-wə)l\ *adj* (ca. 1889) : done with or requiring the use of both hands — **bi·man·u·al·ly** \-ē\ *adv*

bim·bo \ˈbim-(ˌ)bō\ *n, pl* **bimbos** [prob. fr. It *bimbo* baby] *slang* (1919) : MAN, WOMAN — used esp. as a generalized term of disparagement ⟨telling a thickheaded pitcher that the ~ at the plate hasn't hit a curve in three seasons —Jay Stuller⟩; *also* : TRAMP 1c ⟨evidence of how her hubby's been cheating on her with various ~*s* —Dan Greenburg⟩

bi·met·al \ˈbī-ˌmet-ᵊl\ *adj* (1924) : BIMETALLIC — **bimetal** *n*

bi·me·tal·lic \ˌbī-mə-ˈtal-ik\ *adj* (1876) **1 :** relating to, based on, or using bimetallism **2 :** composed of two different metals — often used of devices having a part in which two metals that expand differently are bonded together — **bimetallic** *n*

bi·met·al·lism \(ˈ)bī-ˈmet-ᵊl-ˌiz-əm\ *n* [F *bimétallisme,* fr. *bi-* + *métal* metal] (1876) : the use of two metals (as gold and silver) jointly as a monetary standard with both constituting legal tender at a predetermined ratio — **bi·met·al·list** \-ᵊl-əst\ *n* — **bi·met·al·lis·tic** \ˌbī-ˌmet-ᵊl-ˈis-tik\ *adj*

bi·mil·le·na·ry \(ˈ)bī-ˈmil-ə-ˌner-ē, ˌbī-mə-ˈlen-ə-rē\ *or* **bi·mil·len·ni·al** \ˌbī-mə-ˈlen-ē-əl\ *n* (1850) **1 :** a period of 2000 years **2 :** a 2000th anniversary — **bimillenary** *adj*

bi·mod·al \(ˈ)bī-ˈmōd-ᵊl\ *adj* (1903) : having or relating to two modes; *esp* : having or occurring with two statistical modes — **bi·mo·dal·i·ty** \ˌbī-mō-ˈdal-ət-ē\ *n*

bi·mo·lec·u·lar \ˌbī-mə-ˈlek-yə-lər\ *adj* [ISV] (1899) **1 :** relating to or formed from two molecules **2 :** being two molecules thick ⟨~ lipid layers⟩ — **bi·mo·lec·u·lar·ly** *adv*

[1]**bi·month·ly** \(ˈ)bī-ˈmən(t)th-lē\ *adj* (1846) **1 :** occurring every two months **2 :** occurring twice a month : SEMIMONTHLY

[2]**bimonthly** *adv* (1864) **1 :** once every two months **2 :** twice a month

[3]**bimonthly** *n* (1890) : a bimonthly publication

bi·mor·phe·mic \ˌbī-mȯr-ˈfē-mik\ *adj* (1942) : consisting of two morphemes

[1]**bin** \ˈbin\ *n* [ME *binn,* fr. OE] (bef. 12c) : a box, frame, crib, or enclosed place used for storage

[2]**bin** *vt* **binned; bin·ning** (1841) : to put into a bin

bin- *prefix* [ME, fr. LL, fr. L *bini* two by two; akin to OE *twīn* twine] : [1]BI- ⟨*bin*aural⟩

[1]**bi·na·ry** \ˈbī-nə-rē\ *n, pl* **-ries** (15c) : something made of two things or parts

[2]**binary** *adj* [LL *binarius,* fr. L *bini*] (1597) **1 :** compounded or consisting of or marked by two things or parts **2 a :** composed of two chemical elements, an element and a radical that acts as an element, or two such radicals **b :** utilizing two harmless ingredients that upon combining form a lethal substance (as a gas) ⟨~ weapon⟩ **3 a :** relating to, being, or belonging to a system of numbers having 2 as its base ⟨the ~ digits 0 and 1⟩ **b :** involving a choice or condition of two alternatives (as on-off or yes-no) **4 :** relating two logical or mathematical elements ⟨~ operation⟩ **5 a :** having two musical subjects or two complementary sections **b :** DUPLE — used of measure or rhythm

binary fission *n* (1897) : reproduction of a cell by division into two approximately equal parts ⟨the *binary fission* of protozoans⟩

binary star *n* (ca. 1847) : a system of two stars that revolve around each other under their mutual gravitation —called also *binary system*

bi·na·tion·al \(ˈ)bī-ˈnash-nəl, -ən-ᵊl\ *adj* (1888) : of or relating to two nations ⟨a ~ board of directors⟩

bin·au·ral \(ˈ)bī-ˈnȯr-əl, (ˈ)bin-ˈȯr-\ *adj* [ISV] (1878) **1 :** of, relating to, or involving two or both ears **2 :** of, relating to, or constituting sound reproduction involving the use of two separated microphones and two transmission channels to achieve a stereophonic effect — **bin·au·ral·ly** \-ə-lē\ *adv*

[1]**bind** \ˈbīnd\ *vb* **bound** \ˈbau̇nd\; **bind·ing** [ME *binden,* fr. OE *bindan;* akin to OHG *bintan* to bind, Gk *peisma* cable] *vt* (bef. 12c) **1 a :** to make secure by tying **b :** to confine, restrain, or restrict as if with bonds **c :** to put under an obligation ⟨~*s* himself with an oath⟩ **d :** to constrain with legal authority **2 a :** to wrap around with something so as to enclose or cover **b :** BANDAGE **3 :** to fasten round about **4 :** to tie together (as stocks of wheat) **5 a :** to cause to stick together **b :** to take up and hold (as by chemical forces) : combine with **6 :** CONSTIPATE **7 :** to make a firm commitment for ⟨a handshake ~*s* the deal⟩ **8 :** to protect, strengthen, or decorate by a band or binding **9 :** to apply the parts of the cover to (a book) **10 :** to set at work as an apprentice : INDENTURE **11 :** to cause or bring about an emotional attachment **12 :** to fasten together ~ *vi* **1 :** to form a cohesive mass **2 :** to hamper free movement or natural action **3 :** to become hindered from free operation **4 :** to exert a restraining or compelling effect ⟨a promise that ~*s*⟩

[2]**bind** *n* (bef. 12c) **1 a :** something that binds **b :** the act of binding : the state of being bound **c :** a place where binding occurs **2 :** TIE 3 **3 :** a position or situation in which one is hampered, constrained, or prevented from free movement or action — **in a bind :** in trouble

bind·er \ˈbīn-dər\ *n* (bef. 12c) **1 :** a person that binds something (as books) **2 a :** something used in binding **b :** a usu. detachable cover (as for holding sheets of paper) **3 :** something (as tar or cement) that produces or promotes cohesion in loosely assembled substances **4 :** SURETY BOND

bind·ery \ˈbīn-d(ə-)rē\ *n, pl* **-er·ies** (1810) : a place where books are bound

[1]**bind·ing** \ˈbīn-diŋ\ *n* (13c) **1 :** the action of one that binds **2 :** a material or device used to bind: as **a :** the cover and materials that hold a book together **b :** a narrow fabric used to finish raw edges **c :** a set of ski fastenings for holding the boot firm on the ski

[2]**binding** *adj* (14c) **1 :** that binds **2 :** imposing an obligation — **bind·ing·ly** \-diŋ-lē\ *adv* — **bind·ing·ness** *n*

binding energy *n* (1932) : the energy required to break up a molecule, atom, or atomic nucleus completely into its constituent particles

bin·dle stiff \ˈbin-dᵊl-ˌstif\ *n* [*bindle,* alter. of *bundle*] (1901) : HOBO; *esp* : one who carries his clothes or bedding in a bundle

bind off *vt* (ca. 1939) : to cast off in knitting

bind over *vt* (1610) : to put under a bond to do something (as to appear in court)

bind·weed \ˈbīn-ˌdwēd\ *n* (1548) : any of various twining plants (esp. genus *Convolvulus* of the morning-glory family) that mat or interlace with plants among which they grow

bine \ˈbīn\ *n* [alter. of [2]*bind*] (1807) : a twining stem or flexible shoot (as of the hop); *also* : a plant (as woodbine) whose shoots are bines

Bi·net–Si·mon scale \bi-ˌnā-sē-ˈmō^{n}-\ *n* [Alfred *Binet* †1911 and Théodore *Simon* †1961 Fr. psychologists] (1914) : an intelligence test consisting orig. of tasks graded from the level of the average 3-year-old to that of the average 12-year-old but later extended in range

binge \ˈbinj\ *n* [E dial. *binge* (to drink heavily)] (1854) **1 a :** a drunken revel : SPREE **b :** an unrestrained indulgence ⟨a buying ~⟩ **2 :** a social gathering : PARTY

[1]**bin·go** \ˈbiŋ-(ˌ)gō\ *interj* [alter. of *bing* interj., of imit. origin] (1925) **1** — used as if in imitation of the sound of a bell to announce an unexpected event or instantaneous result **2** — used to announce a winning position in bingo

[2]**bingo** *n, pl* **bingos** (1932) : a game of chance played with cards having numbered squares corresponding to numbered balls drawn at random and won by covering five such squares in a row

bin·na·cle \ˈbin-i-kəl\ *n* [alter. of ME *bitakle,* fr. OPg or OSp; OPg *bitácola* & OSp *bitácula,* fr. L *habitaculum* dwelling place, fr. *habitare* to inhabit — more at HABITATION] (15c) : a housing for a ship's compass and a lamp

[1]**bin·oc·u·lar** \bī-ˈnäk-yə-lər, bə-\ *adj* (1738) : of, relating to, using, or adapted to the use of both eyes ⟨~ vision⟩ — **bin·oc·u·lar·i·ty** \(ˌ)bī-ˌnäk-yə-ˈlar-ət-ē, bə-\ *n* — **bin·oc·u·lar·ly** \bī-ˈnäk-yə-lər-lē, bə-\ *adv*

[2]**bin·oc·u·lar** \bə-ˈnäk-yə-lər, bī-\ *n* (1871) **1 :** a binocular optical instrument **2 :** a hand-held optical instrument composed of two telescopes and a focusing device and usu. having prisms to increase magnifying ability — usu. used in pl.

bi·no·mi·al \bī-ˈnō-mē-əl\ *n* [NL *binomium,* fr. ML, neut. of *binomius* having two names, alter. of L *binominis,* fr. *bi-* + *nomin-, nomen* name — more at NAME] (1557) **1 :** a mathematical expression consisting of two terms connected by a plus sign or minus sign **2 :** a biological species name consisting of two terms — **binomial** *adj* — **bi·no·mi·al·ly** \-mē-ə-lē\ *adv*

binomial coefficient *n* (ca. 1889) : a coefficient of a term in the expansion of the binomial $(x + y)^n$ according to the binomial theorem

binomial distribution *n* (1911) : a probability function each of whose values gives the probability that an outcome with constant probability of occurrence in a statistical experiment will occur a given number of times in a succession of repetitions of the experiment

binomial nomenclature *n* (1880) : a system of nomenclature in which each species of animal or plant receives a name of two terms of which the first identifies the genus to which it belongs and the second the species itself

binomial theorem *n* (1870) : a theorem that specifies the expansion of a binomial of the form $(x + y)^n$ as the sum of $n + 1$ terms of which the general term is of the form

$$\frac{n!}{(n-k)!k!}x^{(n-k)}y^k$$

where k takes on values from 0 to n

bint \ˈbint\ *n* [Ar, girl, daughter] *Brit* (1855) : GIRL, WOMAN

bi·nu·cle·ate \(ˈ)bī-ˈn(y)ü-klē-ət\ *also* **bi·nu·cle·at·ed** \-klē-ˌāt-əd\ *adj* (1881) : having two cellular nuclei

bio \ˈbī-(ˌ)ō\ *n, pl* **bi·os** (1947) : a biography or biographical sketch

bio- — see BI-

bio·acous·tics \ˌbī-(ˌ)ō-ə-ˈkü-stiks\ *n pl but sing in constr* (1957) : a branch of science concerned with the production of sound by and its effects on living systems

bio·as·say \ˌbī-(ˌ)ō-ˈas-ˌā, -a-ˈsā\ *n* [[2]*bio-* + *assay*] (1912) : determination of the relative strength of a substance (as a drug) by comparing its effect on a test organism with that of a standard preparation — **bio·as·say** \-a-ˈsā, -ˈas-ˌā\ *vt*

bio·as·tro·nau·tics \ˌbī-ō-ˌas-trə-ˈnȯt-iks, -ˈnät-\ *n pl but sing or pl in constr* (ca. 1957) : the medical and biological aspect of astronautics — **bio·as·tro·nau·ti·cal** \-i-kəl\ *adj*

bio·ce·no·sis *or* **bio·coe·no·sis** \-sə-ˈnō-səs\ *n, pl* **-no·ses** \-ˌsēz\ [NL, fr. [2]*bi-* + Gk *koinōsis* sharing, fr. *koinos* common — more at CO-] (ca. 1883) : an ecological community (as an oyster bed) esp. when forming a self-regulating unit — **bio·ce·not·ic** *or* **bio·coe·not·ic** \-ˈnät-ik\ *adj*

bio·chem·i·cal \ˌbī-ō-ˈkem-i-kəl\ *adj* [ISV] (1867) **1 :** of or relating to biochemistry **2 :** characterized by, produced by, or involving chemical reactions in living organisms — **biochemical** *n* — **bio·chem·i·cal·ly** \-k(ə-)lē\ *adv*

biochemical oxygen demand *n* (ca. 1927) : the oxygen used in meeting the metabolic needs of aerobic microorganisms in water rich in organic matter (as water polluted with sewage) — called also *biological oxygen demand*

bio·chem·is·try \ˌbī-ō-ˈkem-ə-strē\ *n* [ISV] (1881) **1 :** chemistry that deals with the chemical compounds and processes occurring in organisms **2 :** the chemical characteristics and reactions of a particular living system or biological substance (as chlorophyll) ⟨a change in the patient's ~ accompanied her psychological depression⟩ — **bio·chem·ist** \-əst\ *n*

bio·cid·al \ˌbī-ə-ˈsīd-ᵊl\ *adj* (1949) : destructive to life

bio·cide \ˈbī-ə-ˌsīd\ *n* (1947) : a substance (as DDT) that is destructive to many different organisms

bio·cli·mat·ic \ˌbī-ō-klī-ˈmat-ik\ *adj* (1918) : of or relating to the relations of climate and living matter ⟨~ adaptations⟩

bio·con·ver·sion \ˌbī-(ˌ)ō-kən-ˈvər-zhən, ˈbī-(ˌ)ō-kən-ˌ, -shən\ *n* (1960) : the conversion of organic materials (as wastes) into an energy source (as methane) by processes (as fermentation) involving living organisms

bio·de·grad·able \-di-ˈgrād-ə-bəl\ *adj* [[2]*bi-* + *degrade* + *-able*] (1961) : capable of being broken down esp. into innocuous products by the action of living things (as microorganisms) — **bio·de·grad·abil·i·ty** \-ˌgrād-ə-'bil-ət-ē\ n — **bio·deg·ra·da·tion** \-ˌdeg-rə-'dā-shən\ n — **bio·de·grade** \-di-'grād\ vb

bio·ecol·o·gy \ˌbī-ō-i-'käl-ə-jē\ n (1927) : ecology dealing with the interrelation of plants and animals with their common environment — **bio·eco·log·i·cal** \-ˌē-kə-'läj-i-kəl, -ˌek-ə-\ adj — **bio·ecol·o·gist** \-i-'käl-ə-jəst\ n

bio·elec·tric \-i-'lek-trik\ also **bio·elec·tri·cal** \-tri-kəl\ adj (1918) : of or relating to electric phenomena in animals and plants — **bio·elec·tric·i·ty** \-ˌlek-'tris-ət-ē, -'tris-tē\ n

bio·en·er·get·ics \-ˌen-ər-'jet-iks\ n pl but sing in constr (1912) **1** : the biology of energy transformations and energy exchanges (as in photosynthesis) within and between living things and their environments **2** : a system of therapy that combines breathing and body exercises, psychological therapy, and the free expression of impulses and emotions and that is held to increase well-being by releasing blocked physical and psychic energy — **bio·en·er·get·ic** \-'jet-ik\ adj

bio·en·gi·neer·ing \-ˌen-jə-'ni(ə)r-iŋ\ n (ca. 1954) : application to biological or medical science of engineering principles (as the theory of control systems in models of the nervous system) or engineering equipment (as in the construction of artificial organs)

bio·eth·ics \-'eth-iks\ n pl but sing in constr (1971) : a discipline dealing with the ethical implications of biological research and applications esp. in medicine — **bio·eth·i·cal** \-'eth-i-kəl\ adj — **bio·eth·i·cist** \-'eth-ə-səst\ n

bio·feed·back \-'fēd-ˌbak\ n (1971) : the technique of making unconscious or involuntary bodily processes (as heartbeat or brain waves) perceptible to the senses (as by the use of an oscilloscope) in order to manipulate them by conscious mental control

bio·gen·e·sis \ˌbī-ō-'jen-ə-səs\ n [NL] (1870) **1** : the development of life from preexisting life **2** : a supposed tendency for stages in the evolutionary history of a race to briefly recur during the development and differentiation of an individual of that race **3** : BIOSYNTHESIS — **bio·ge·net·ic** \-jə-'net-ik\ adj — **bio·ge·net·i·cal·ly** \-i-k(ə-)lē\ adv

biogenetic law n (1882) : a theory of development much disputed in biology: an organism passes through successive stages resembling the series of ancestral types from which it has descended so that the ontogeny of the individual is a recapitulation of the phylogeny of the group

bio·gen·ic \-'jen-ik\ also **bi·og·e·nous** \bī-'äj-ənəs\ adj (1913) : produced by living organisms

bio·geo·chem·is·try \-ˌjē-ō-'kem-ə-strē\ n [²bio- + geochemistry] (1938) : a science that deals with the relation of earth chemicals to plant and animal life in an area — **bio·geo·chem·i·cal** \-'kem-i-kəl\ adj

bio·ge·og·ra·phy \-jē-'äg-rə-fē\ n [ISV] (1895) : a branch of biology that deals with the geographical distribution of animals and plants — **bio·ge·og·ra·pher** \-rə-fər\ n — **bio·geo·graph·ic** \-ˌjē-ə-'graf-ik\ or **bio·geo·graph·i·cal** \-i-kəl\ adj

bi·og·ra·phee \bī-ˌäg-rə-'fē, bē-\ n (1841) : a person about whom a biography is written

bi·og·ra·pher \-'äg-rə-fər\ n (1715) : a writer of a biography

bio·graph·i·cal \ˌbī-ə-'graf-i-kəl\ also **bio·graph·ic** \-ik\ adj (1738) **1** : of, relating to, or constituting biography **2** : consisting of biographies ⟨a ~ dictionary⟩ **3** : relating to a list briefly identifying persons ⟨~ notes⟩ — **bio·graph·i·cal·ly** \-i-k(ə-)lē\ adv

bi·og·ra·phy \bī-'äg-rə-fē, bē-\ n, pl **-phies** [LGk biographia, fr. Gk bi- + -graphia -graphy] (1683) **1** : a usu. written history of a person's life **2** : biographical writings in general **3** : an account of the life of some-

thing (as an animal, a coin, or a building)

bio·haz·ard \'bī-ō-ˌhaz-ərd\ n (1967) : a biological agent or condition (as an infectious organism or insecure laboratory conditions) that constitutes a hazard to man or his environment; also : a hazard posed by such an agent or condition

bio·in·stru·men·ta·tion \'bī-ō-ˌin-strə-mən-'tā-shən, -ˌmen-\ n (1962) : the development and use of instruments for recording and transmitting physiological data (as from astronauts in flight)

bi·o·log·ic \ˌbī-ə-'läj-ik\ or **bi·o·log·i·cal** \-i-kəl\ n (1921) : a biological product used in medicine

biological also **biologic** adj (1859) **1** : of or relating to biology or to life and living processes **2** : used in or produced by applied biology — **bi·o·log·i·cal·ly** \-i-k(ə-)lē\ adv

biological clock n (1955) : an inherent timing mechanism that is inferred to exist in some living systems (as a cell) in order to explain various cyclical behaviors and physiological processes

biological control n (1923) : reduction in numbers or elimination of pest organisms by interference with their ecology (as by the introduction of parasites or diseases)

biological oxygen demand n (1945) : BIOCHEMICAL OXYGEN DEMAND

biological warfare n (1946) : warfare involving the use of living organisms (as disease germs) or their toxic products against men, animals, or plants; also : warfare involving the use of synthetic chemicals harmful to plants

bi·ol·o·gism \bī-'äl-ə-ˌjiz-əm\ n (1924) : preoccupation with biological explanations in the analysis of social situations — **bi·ol·o·gis·tic** \-ˌäl-ə-'jis-tik\ adj

bi·ol·o·gy \bī-'äl-ə-jē\ n [G biologie, fr. bi- + -logie -logy] (1813) **1** : a branch of knowledge that deals with living organisms and vital processes **2 a** : the plant and animal life of a region or environment **b** : the life processes of an organism or group; broadly : ECOLOGY — **bi·ol·o·gist** \-jəst\ n

bio·lu·mi·nes·cence \ˌbī-ō-ˌlü-mə-'nes-ⁿ(t)s\ n [ISV] (1916) : the emission of light from living organisms; also : the light so produced — **bio·lu·mi·nes·cent** \-ⁿt\ adj

bio·mass \'bī-ō-ˌmas\ n (1934) **1** : the amount of living matter (as in a unit area or volume of habitat) **2** : plant materials and animal waste used as a source of fuel

bio·ma·te·ri·al \ˌbī-ō-mə-'tir-ē-əl\ n (1966) : material used for or suitable for use in prostheses that come in direct contact with living tissues

bio·math·e·mat·ics \-ˌmath-ə-'mat-iks, -math-'mat-\ n pl but usu sing in constr (1923) : mathematics of special use in biology and medicine — **bio·math·e·mat·i·cal** \-i-kəl\ adj — **bio·math·e·ma·ti·cian** \-ˌmath-(ə-)mə-'tish-ən\ n

bi·ome \'bī-ˌōm\ n [²bi- + -ome] (1916) : a major ecological community type (as grassland or desert)

bio·me·chan·ics \'bī-ō-mə-'kan-iks\ n pl but sing or pl in constr (1933) : the mechanics of biological and esp. muscular activity (as in locomotion or exercise) — **bio·me·chan·i·cal** \-i-kəl\ adj — **bio·me·chan·i·cal·ly** \-i-k(ə-)lē\ adv

bio·med·i·cal \ˌbī-ō-'med-i-kəl\ adj (1955) **1** : of or relating to biomedicine **2** : of, relating to, or involving biological, medical, and physical science

bio·med·i·cine \-'med-ə-sən, Brit usu -'med-sən\ n (1947) : a branch of medical science concerned esp. with the capacity of human beings to survive and function in abnormally stressing environments and with the protective modification of such environments

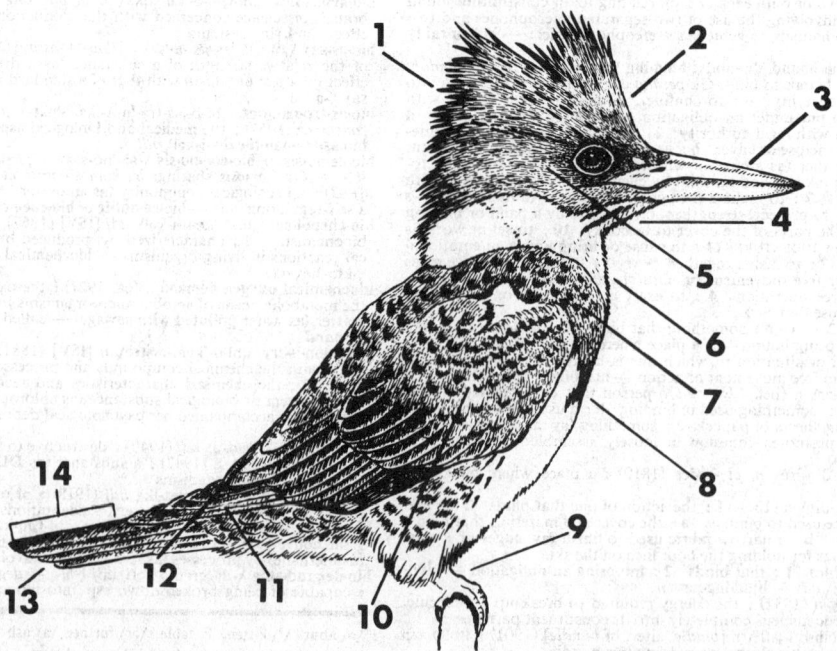

bird 2 (kingfisher): 1 crest, 2 crown, 3 bill, 4 throat, 5 auricular region, 6 breast, 7 scapulars, 8 abdomen, 9 tarsus, 10 upper wing coverts, 11 primaries, 12 secondaries, 13 rectrix, 14 tail

bio·me·te·o·rol·o·gy \-ˌmēt-ē-ə-ˈräl-ə-jē\ *n* (1946) **:** a science that deals with the relationship between living beings and atmospheric phenomena

bio·met·rics \-ˈme-triks\ *n pl but sing or pl in constr* (1902) **:** BIOMETRY

bi·om·e·try \bī-ˈäm-ə-trē\ *n* [ISV] (1831) **:** the statistical analysis of biological observations and phenomena — **bio·met·ric** \ˌbī-ō-ˈme-trik\ *or* **bio·met·ri·cal** \-tri-kəl\ *adj* — **bio·me·tri·cian** \-me-ˈtrish-ən\ *n*

bio·mor·phic \ˌbī-ō-ˈmȯr-fik\ *adj* (1895) **:** resembling or suggesting the forms of living organisms ⟨~ sculptures⟩ ⟨~ images⟩

bi·on·ic \bī-ˈän-ik\ *adj* (1973) **1 :** of or relating to bionics **2 :** having normal biological capability or performance enhanced by or as if by electronic or electromechanical devices

bi·on·ics \bī-ˈän-iks\ *n pl but sing or pl in constr* [²*bi-* + *-onics* (as in *electronics*)] (1960) **:** a science concerned with the application of data about the functioning of biological systems to the solution of engineering problems

bi·o·nom·ics \ˌbī-ə-ˈnäm-iks\ *n pl but sing or pl in constr* [*bionomic,* adj., prob. fr. F *bionomique,* fr. *bionomie* ecology, fr. *bi-* + *-nomie* -nomy] (1888) **:** ECOLOGY — **bi·o·nom·ic** \-ik\ *adj* — **bi·o·nom·i·cal** \-i-kəl\ *adj*

-bi·ont \ˈbī-ˌänt\ *n comb form* [prob. fr. G, modif. of Gk *biount-, biōn,* prp. of *bioun* to live, fr. *bios* life] **:** one having a (specified) mode of life ⟨haplo*biont*⟩

bio·phys·ics \ˌbī-ō-ˈfiz-iks\ *n pl but sing or pl in constr* (1892) **:** a branch of science concerned with the application of physical principles and methods to biological problems — **bio·phys·i·cal** \-i-kəl\ *adj* — **bio·phys·i·cist** \-ˈfiz-(ə-)səst\ *n*

bio·poly·mer \ˌbī-ō-ˈpäl-ə-mər\ *n* (1963) **:** a polymeric substance (as a protein or polysaccharide) formed in a biological system

bi·op·sy \ˈbī-ˌäp-sē\ *n, pl* **-sies** [ISV *bi-* + Gk *opsis* appearance — more at OPTIC] (1895) **:** the removal and examination of tissue, cells, or fluids from the living body

bio·rhythm \ˈbī-ō-ˌrith-əm\ *n* (1961) **:** an inherent rhythm that appears to control or initiate various biological processes — **bio·rhyth·mic** \-ˈrith-mik\ *adj*

bio·sat·el·lite \ˌbī-ō-ˈsat-ᵊl-ˌīt\ *n* (1957) **:** an artificial satellite for carrying a living human being, animal, or plant

bio·sci·ence \-ˈsī-ən(t)s\ *n* (1941) **:** BIOLOGY 1; *also* **:** LIFE SCIENCE — **bio·sci·en·tif·ic** \-ˌsī-ən-ˈtif-ik\ *adj* — **bio·sci·en·tist** \-ˈsī-ənt-əst\ *n*

-bi·o·sis \(ˌ)bī-ˈō-səs, bē-\ *n comb form, pl* **-bi·o·ses** \-ˌsēz\ [NL, fr. Gk *biōsis,* fr. *bioun* to live, fr. *bios*] **:** mode of life ⟨para*biosis*⟩

bio·so·cial \ˌbī-ō-ˈsō-shəl\ *adj* (1897) **:** of, relating to, or concerned with the interaction of the biological aspects and social relationships of living organisms — **bio·so·cial·ly** \-ˈsōsh-(ə-)lē\ *adv*

bio·sphere \ˈbī-ə-ˌsfi(ə)r\ *n* (1899) **1 :** the part of the world in which life can exist **2 :** living beings together with their environment — **bio·spher·ic** \ˌbī-ə-ˈsfi(ə)r-ik, -ˈsfer-\ *adj*

bio·sta·tis·tics \ˌbī-ō-stə-ˈtis-tiks\ *n pl but sing in constr* (1950) **:** statistical processes and methods applied to the analysis of biological data — **bio·sta·tis·ti·cal** \-ti-kəl\ *adj* — **bio·stat·is·ti·cian** \-ˌstat-ə-ˈstish-ən\ *n*

bio·strati·graph·ic \-ˌstrat-ə-ˈgraf-ik\ *adj* (1947) **:** of or relating to the branch of paleontology dealing with the conditions and order of deposition of sedimentary rocks — **bio·stra·tig·ra·phy** \-strə-ˈtig-rə-fē\ *n*

bio·syn·the·sis \-ˈsin(t)-thə-səs\ *n* [NL] (1930) **:** the production of a chemical compound by a living organism — **bio·syn·thet·ic** \-sin-ˈthet-ik\ *adj* — **bio·syn·thet·i·cal·ly** \-i-k(ə-)lē\ *adv*

bio·sys·te·mat·ics \-ˌsis-tə-ˈmat-iks\ *n pl but sing or pl in constr* (1945) **:** experimental taxonomy esp. as based on cytogenetics — **bio·sys·te·mat·ic** \-ik\ *adj* — **bio·sys·tem·atist** \-ˈsis-tə-mət-əst, -sis-ˈtem-ət-\ *n*

bi·o·ta \bī-ˈōt-ə\ *n* [NL, fr. Gk *biotē* life; akin to Gk *bios*] (ca. 1901) **:** the flora and fauna of a region

bio·tech·nol·o·gy \ˌbī-ō-tek-ˈnäl-ə-jē\ *n* (1941) **1 :** applied biological science (as bioengineering or recombinant DNA technology) **2 :** ERGONOMICS — **bio·tech·no·log·i·cal** \-ˌtek-nə-ˈläj-i-kəl\ *adj*

bio·te·lem·e·try \-tə-ˈlem-ə-trē\ *n* (1963) **:** the remote detection and measurement of a condition, activity, or function relating to a man or animal — **bio·tel·e·met·ric** \-ˌtel-ə-ˈme-trik\ *adj*

bi·ot·ic \bī-ˈät-ik\ *adj* [Gk *biōtikos,* fr. *bioun*] (1868) **:** of or relating to life; *esp* **:** caused or produced by living beings

-bi·ot·ic \(ˌ)bī-ˈät-ik, bē-\ *adj comb form* [prob. fr. NL *-bioticus,* fr. Gk *biōtikos*] **:** having a (specified) mode of life ⟨endo*biotic*⟩

biotic potential *n* (1935) **:** the inherent capacity of an organism or species to reproduce and survive

bi·o·tin \ˈbī-ə-tən\ *n* [ISV, fr. Gk *biotos* life, sustenance; akin to Gk *bios*] (1936) **:** a colorless crystalline growth vitamin $C_{10}H_{16}N_2O_3S$ of the vitamin B complex found esp. in yeast, liver, and egg yolk

bi·o·tite \ˈbī-ə-ˌtīt\ *n* [G *biotit,* fr. Jean B. *Biot* †1862 Fr. mathematician] (1862) **:** a generally black or dark green form of mica $K_2(Mg,Fe,Al)_6(Si,Al)_8O_{20}(OH)_4$ forming a constituent of crystalline rocks and consisting of a silicate of iron, magnesium, potassium, and aluminum — **bi·o·tit·ic** \ˌbī-ə-ˈtit-ik\ *adj*

bio·tope \ˈbī-ə-ˌtōp\ *n* [²*bi-* + Gk *topos* place — more at TOPIC] (1927) **:** a region uniform in environmental conditions and in its populations of animals and plants for which it is the habitat

bio·trans·for·ma·tion \ˈbī-ō-ˌtran(t)s-fər-ˈmā-shən, -ˌfȯr-\ *n* (1955) **:** the transformation of chemical compounds within a living system

bio·type \-ˌtīp\ *n* [ISV] (1906) **:** the organisms sharing a specified genotype; *also* **:** the genotype shared or its distinguishing peculiarity — **bio·typ·ic** \ˌbī-ə-ˈtip-ik\ *adj*

bi·pa·ren·tal \ˌbī-pə-ˈrent-ᵊl\ *adj* (1900) **:** of, relating to, involving, or derived from two parents — **bi·pa·ren·tal·ly** \-ᵊl-ē\ *adv*

bi·par·ti·san \(ˈ)bī-ˈpärt-ə-zən, -sən, -ˌzan, *chiefly Brit* ˌbī-ˌpärt-ə-ˈzan\ *adj* (ca. 1909) **:** of, relating to, or involving members of two parties ⟨a ~ commission⟩ — **bi·par·ti·san·ism** \-zə-ˌniz-əm, -sə-\ *n* — **bi·par·ti·san·ship** \-zən-ˌship, -sən-\ *n*

bi·par·tite \(ˈ)bī-ˈpär-ˌtīt\ *adj* [L *bipartitus,* pp. of *bipartire* to divide in two, fr. *bi-* + *partire* to divide, fr. *part-, pars* part] (1574) **1 a :** being in two parts **b :** having two correspondent parts one for each party ⟨a ~ contract⟩ **c :** shared by two ⟨a ~ treaty⟩ **2 :** divided into two parts almost to the base ⟨a ~ leaf⟩ — **bi·par·tite·ly** *adv* — **bi·par·ti·tion** \ˌbī-(ˌ)pär-ˈtish-ən\ *n*

bi·ped \ˈbī-ˌped\ *n* [L *biped-, bipes,* fr. *bi-* + *ped-, pes* foot — more at FOOT] (1646) **:** a two-footed animal — **bi·ped·al** \(ˈ)bī-ˈped-ᵊl\ *adj*

bi·ped·al·ism \(ˈ)bī-ˈped-ᵊl-ˌiz-əm\ *n* (1907) **:** the condition of having two feet or of using only two feet for locomotion

bi·phe·nyl \(ˈ)bī-ˈfen-ᵊl, -ˈfēn-\ *n* [ISV] (1922) **:** a white crystalline hydrocarbon $C_6H_5{\cdot}C_6H_5$ used esp. as a heat-transfer medium

bi·pin·nate \-ˈpin-ˌāt\ *adj* (1794) **:** twice pinnate — **bi·pin·nate·ly** *adv*

bi·plane \ˈbī-ˌplān\ *n* (1874) **:** an airplane with two main supporting surfaces usu. placed one above the other

bi·pod \ˈbī-ˌpäd\ *n* [*bi-* + *-pod* (as in *tripod*)] (1922) **:** a two-legged support

bi·po·lar \(ˈ)bī-ˈpō-lər\ *adj* (1810) **1 :** having or marked by two mutually repellent forces or diametrically opposed natures or views **2 :** having or involving the use of two poles **3 :** relating to, associated with, or occurring in both polar regions ⟨~ species of birds⟩ — **bi·po·lar·i·ty** \ˌbī-pō-ˈlar-ət-ē\ *n* — **bi·po·lar·iza·tion** \(ˌ)bī-ˌpō-lə-rə-ˈzā-shən\ *n* — **bi·po·lar·ize** \(ˈ)bī-ˈpō-lə-ˌrīz\ *vt*

bi·pro·pel·lant \ˌbī-prə-ˈpel-ənt\ *n* (1947) **:** a rocket propellant consisting of separate fuel and oxidizer that come together only in a combustion chamber

bi·qua·drat·ic \ˌbī-kwä-ˈdrat-ik\ *adj or n* (1668) **:** QUARTIC

bi·ra·cial \(ˈ)bī-ˈrā-shəl\ *adj* (1922) **:** of, relating to, or involving members of two races — **bi·ra·cial·ism** \-shə-ˌliz-əm\ *n*

bi·ra·di·al \(ˈ)bī-ˈrād-ē-əl\ *adj* (ca. 1909) **:** having both bilateral and radial symmetry

bi·ra·mous \(ˈ)bī-ˈrā-məs\ *adj* (1877) **:** having two branches

¹**birch** \ˈbərch\ *n* [ME, fr. OE *beorc;* akin to OHG *birka* birch, L *fraxinus* ash tree, OE *beorht* bright — more at BRIGHT] (bef. 12c) **1 :** any of a genus (*Betula* of the family Betulaceae, the birch family) of monoecious deciduous usu. short-lived trees or shrubs having simple petioled leaves and typically a layered membranous outer bark that peels readily **2 :** the hard pale close-grained wood of a birch **3 :** a birch rod or bundle of twigs for flogging — **birch** *or* **birch·en** \ˈbər-chən\ *adj*

²**birch** *vt* (1830) **:** to beat with or as if with a birch **:** WHIP

birch·bark \ˈbərch-ˌbärk\ *n* (1868) **:** a canoe made of birch bark

Birch·er \ˈbər-chər\ *n* (1961) **:** a member or adherent of the John Birch Society — **Birch·ism** \ˈbər-ˌchiz-əm\ *n* — **Birch·ist** \-chəst\ *or* **Birch·ite** \-ˌchīt\ *n or adj*

¹**bird** \ˈbərd\ *n, often attrib* [ME, fr. OE *bridd*] (bef. 12c) **1** *archaic* **:** the young of a feathered vertebrate **2 :** any of a class (Aves) of warm-blooded vertebrates distinguished by having the body more or less completely covered with feathers and the forelimbs modified as wings **3 :** a game bird **4 :** CLAY PIGEON **5 a :** FELLOW; *esp* **:** a peculiar person **b** *chiefly Brit* **:** GIRL **6 :** SHUTTLECOCK **7 a :** a hissing or jeering expressive of disapproval **b :** dismissal from employment **8 :** something (as an aircraft, rocket, or satellite) resembling a bird esp. by flying or being aloft **9 :** an obscene gesture of contempt made by pointing the middle finger upward while keeping the other fingers down — usu. used with *the;* called also *finger* — **bird·like** \-ˌlīk\ *adj* — **for the birds :** WORTHLESS, RIDICULOUS

²**bird** *vi* (1918) **:** to observe or identify wild birds in their natural environment

bird·bath \ˈbərd-ˌbath, -ˌbȧth\ *n* (1895) **:** a usu. ornamental basin set up for birds to bathe in

bird·brain \-ˌbrān\ *n* (1943) **1 :** a stupid person **2 :** SCATTERBRAIN — **bird·brained** \-ˌbrānd\ *adj*

bird·call \-ˌkȯl\ *n* (1625) **1 :** a device for imitating the cry of a bird **2 :** the note or cry of a bird; *also* **:** a sound imitative of it

bird colonel *n* [fr. the eagle serving as insignia for this rank] *slang* (ca. 1947) **:** COLONEL 1a

bird–dog \ˈbərd-ˌdȯg\ *vi* (1943) **:** to watch closely ~ *vt* **:** to seek out **:** FOLLOW, DETECT

bird dog *n* (1888) **1 :** a gundog trained to hunt or retrieve birds **2 a :** one (as a canvasser or talent scout) who seeks out something for another **b :** one who steals another's date

bird–dog·ging *n* (ca. 1944) **1 :** the stealing of another's date (as at a party) **2 :** the action of one that bird-dogs

bird·er \ˈbərd-ər\ *n* (15c) **1 :** a catcher or hunter of birds esp. for market **2 :** a person who birds

bird·house \ˈbərd-ˌhau̇s\ *n* (1870) **:** an artificial nesting site for birds; *also* **:** AVIARY

¹**bird·ie** \ˈbərd-ē\ *n* (1792) **1 :** a little bird **2 :** a golf score of one stroke less than par on a hole — compare EAGLE

²**birdie** *vt* **bird·ied; bird·ie·ing** (1948) **:** to shoot in one stroke under par

bird·lime \ˈbərd-ˌlīm\ *n* (15c) **1 :** a sticky substance usu. made from the bark of a holly (*Ilex aquifolium*) that is smeared on twigs to snare small birds **2 :** something that ensnares — **birdlime** *vt*

bird louse *n* (1826) **:** BITING LOUSE

bird·man \ˈbərd-mən, *esp for 1 also* -ˌman\ *n* (1697) **1 :** one who deals with birds **2 :** a person (as an aviator, helicopter pilot, or hang glider operator) resembling a bird esp. by flying or being aloft

bird of paradise (1638) **:** any of numerous brilliantly colored plumed oscine birds (family Paradiseidae) of the New Guinea area

bird of passage (1732) **1 :** a person who leads a wandering or unsettled life **2 :** a migratory bird

bird of prey (14c) **:** a carnivorous bird (as a hawk, falcon, or vulture) that feeds wholly or chiefly on carrion or on meat taken by hunting

bird pepper *n* (ca. 1696) **:** a capsicum (*Capsicum frutescens*) having very small oblong extremely pungent red fruits

bird·seed \ˈbərd-ˌsēd\ *n* (1840) **:** a mixture of seeds (as of hemp, millet, and sunflowers) used for feeding caged and wild birds

¹**bird's–eye** \ˈbərd-ˌzī\ *n* (1597) **1 :** any of numerous plants with small bright-colored flowers; *esp* **:** a speedwell (*Veronica chamaedrys*) **2 a :** an allover pattern for textiles consisting of a small diamond with a center dot **b :** a fabric woven with this pattern **3 :** a small spot in wood surrounded with an ellipse of concentric fibers

²**bird's–eye** *adj* (1665) **1 :** marked with spots resembling birds' eyes **2 a :** seen from above as if by a flying bird ⟨a ~ view⟩ **b :** CURSORY **3 :** of or relating to wood (as maple) containing bird's-eyes

\ə\ abut \ᵊ\ kitten, F table \ər\ further \a\ ash \ā\ ace \ä\ cot, cart
\au̇\ out \ch\ chin \e\ bet \ē\ easy \g\ go \i\ hit \ī\ ice \j\ job
\ŋ\ sing \ō\ go \ȯ\ law \ȯi\ boy \th\ thin \th\ the \ü\ loot \u̇\ foot
\y\ yet \zh\ vision \à, ḵ, ⁿ, œ, œ̄, ue, ue̅, ʸ\ see Guide to Pronunciation

bird's–foot \'bərdz-ˌfu̇t\ *n, pl* **bird's–foots** (1578) **:** any of numerous plants with leaves or flowers resembling the foot of a bird; *esp* **:** any of several legumes (as of the genera *Ornithopus, Lotus,* and *Trigonella*) with bent and jointed pods

bird's–foot trefoil *n* (1833) **:** a European legume (*Lotus corniculatus*) having claw-shaped pods and widely used esp. in the U.S. as a forage and fodder plant

bird–watch \'bərd-ˌwäch\ *vi* [back-formation fr. *bird-watcher*] (1948) **:** BIRD

bird–watch·er \-ər\ *n* (1905) **:** BIRDER 2

birdy·back *or* **bird·ie·back** \'bərd-ē-ˌbak\ *n* [*birdie* + *-back* (as in *piggyback*)] (1967) **:** the movement of loaded truck trailers by airplane

bi·re·frin·gence \ˌbī-ri-'frin-jən(t)s\ *n* [ISV] (1898) **:** the refraction of light in two slightly different directions to form two rays — **bi·re·frin·gent** \-jənt\ *adj*

bi·reme \'bī-ˌrēm\ *n* [L *biremis,* fr. *bi-* + *remus* oar — more at ROW] (1662) **:** a galley with two banks of oars common in the early classical period

bi·ret·ta \bə-'ret-ə\ *n* [It *berretta,* fr. OProv *berret* cap, irreg. fr. LL *birrus* cloak with a hood, of Celt origin; akin to MIr *berr* short] (1598) **:** a square cap with three ridges on top worn by clergymen esp. of the Roman Catholic Church

birk \'bi(ə)rk\ *n* [ME *birch, birk*] *chiefly Scot* (14c) **:** BIRCH

birk·ie \'bi(ə)r-kē, 'bər-\ *n* [origin unknown] (1724) **1** *Scot* **:** a lively smart assertive person **2** *Scot* **:** FELLOW, BOY

birl \'bər(-ə)l, *Scot also* 'bir(-ə)l\ *vb* [ME *birlen,* fr. OE *byrelian;* akin to OE *beran* to carry — more at BEAR] *vt* (bef. 12c) **1** *chiefly Scot* **a :** POUR **b :** to ply with drink **2 a :** to cause (a floating log) to rotate by treading **b :** SPIN ~ *vi* **1** *chiefly Scot* **:** CAROUSE **2 :** to progress by whirling — **birl·er** \'bər-lər, 'bi(ə)r-lər\ *n*

Bi·ro \'bī-(ˌ)rō\ *trademark* — used for a ballpoint pen

[1]**birr** \'bər, 'bi(ə)r\ *n* [ME, strong wind, attack, fr. OE *byre* strong wind & ON *byrr* favoring wind; both akin to OE *beran*] (bef. 12c) **1 a :** force or onward rush (as of the wind) **b :** VIGOR **2 :** WHIR

[2]**birr** *vi, chiefly Scot* (1513) **:** to make a whirring sound

[3]**birr** *n, pl* **birr** [Ar] (1976) — see MONEY table

birse \'bi(ə)rs, 'bərs\ *n* [(assumed) ME *birst,* fr. OE *byrst* — more at BRISTLE] (bef. 12c) **1** *chiefly Scot* **:** a bristle or tuft of bristles **2** *chiefly Scot* **:** ANGER

[1]**birth** \'bərth\ *n, often attrib* [ME, fr. ON *byrth;* akin to OE *beran*] (13c) **1 a :** the emergence of a new individual from the body of its parent **b :** the act or process of bringing forth young from the womb **2 :** a state resulting from being born esp. at a particular time or place ⟨a Southerner by ~⟩ **3 a :** LINEAGE, EXTRACTION ⟨marriage between equals in ~⟩ **b :** high or noble birth **4 a** *archaic* **:** one that is born **b :** BEGINNING, START ⟨the ~ of an idea⟩

[2]**birth** *vt* (1906) **1** *chiefly dial* **:** to bring forth **2 :** to give rise to **:** ORIGINATE ~ *vi, dial* **:** to bring forth a child or young

birth certificate *n* (1900) **:** a copy of an official record of a person's date and place of birth and parentage

birth control *n* (1914) **:** control of the number of children born esp. by preventing or lessening the frequency of conception

birth·day \'bərth-ˌdā\ *n* (14c) **1 a :** the day of a person's birth **b :** a day of origin **2 :** an anniversary of a birth ⟨her 21st ~⟩

birthday suit *n* (1753) **:** unclothed skin **:** NAKEDNESS ⟨a small tribe all dressed in their *birthday suits* —*Bulletin* (Australia)⟩

birth defect *n* (1971) **:** a physical or biochemical defect (as cleft palate or phenylketonuria) that is present at birth and may be inherited or environmentally induced

birth·mark \'bərth-ˌmärk\ *n* (1580) **:** an unusual mark or blemish on the skin at birth **:** NEVUS

birth pang *n* (ca. 1887) **1 :** one of the regularly recurrent pains that are characteristic of childbirth — usu. used in pl. **2** *pl* **:** disorder and distress incident esp. to a major social change

birth·place \'bərth-ˌplās\ *n* (1607) **:** place of birth or origin

birth·rate \'bər-ˌthrāt\ *n* (1859) **:** the ratio between births and individuals in a specified population and time often expressed as number of live births per hundred or per thousand population per year

birth·right \'bər-ˌthrīt\ *n* (1535) **:** a right, privilege, or possession to which a person is entitled by birth

birth·root \'bər-ˌthrüt, -ˌthru̇t\ *n* (1822) **:** any of several trilliums with astringent roots used in folk medicine

birth·stone \'bərth-ˌstōn\ *n* (ca. 1909) **:** a gemstone associated symbolically with the month of one's birth

birth·wort \-ˌwərt, -ˌwȯ(ə)rt\ *n* (1551) **:** any of several plants (genus *Aristolochia* of the family Aristolochiaceae, the birthwort family) of herbs or woody vines with aromatic roots used in folk medicine to aid childbirth

bis \'bis\ *adv* [L, fr. OL *dvis;* akin to OHG *zwiro* twice, L *duo* two — more at TWO] (1819) **1 :** AGAIN — used in music as a direction to repeat **2 :** TWICE

bis- \(ˌ)bis, 'bis\ *comb form* [L *bis*] **:** twice **:** doubled — esp. in complex chemical expressions ⟨*bis*-dithiocarbamate⟩

Bi·sa·yan \bə-'sī-ən\ *n* [Bisayan *Bisayâ*] (1951) **1 :** a member of any of several peoples in the Visayan islands, Philippines **2 :** the Austronesian language of the Bisayans

bis·cuit \'bis-kət\ *n* [ME *bisquite,* fr. MF *bescuit,* fr. (*pain*) *bescuit* twice-cooked bread] (14c) **1 a :** any of various hard or crisp dry baked products: as (1) *Brit* **:** CRACKER 4 (2) *Brit* **:** COOKIE **b :** a small quick bread made from dough that has been rolled out and cut or dropped from a spoon **2 :** earthenware or porcelain after the first firing and before glazing **:** [3]BISQUE **3 a :** a light grayish yellowish brown **b :** a grayish yellow

bise \'bēz\ *n* [ME, fr. OF, of Gmc origin; akin to OHG *bisa* north wind] (14c) **:** a cold dry north wind of southern France, Switzerland, and Italy

bi·sect \'bī-ˌsekt, bī-'\ *vt* (ca. 1645) **:** to divide into two usu. equal parts ~ *vi* **:** CROSS, INTERSECT — **bi·sec·tion** \'bī-ˌsek-shən, bī-'\ *n* — **bi·sec·tion·al** \-shnəl, -shən-ᵊl\ *adj* — **bi·sec·tion·al·ly** \-ē\ *adv*

bi·sec·tor \'bī-ˌsek-tər, bī-'\ *n* (1864) **:** one that bisects; *esp* **:** a straight line that bisects an angle or a line segment

bi·sex·u·al \(')bī-'seksh-(ə-)wəl, -'sek-shəl\ *adj* (1824) **1 a :** possessing characters of both sexes **:** HERMAPHRODITIC **b :** sexually oriented toward both sexes ⟨a ~ person who participates in both heterosexual and homosexual relationships⟩ **2 :** of, relating to, or involving two sexes — **bisexual** *n* — **bi·sex·u·al·i·ty** \ˌbī-ˌsek-shə-'wal-ət-ē\ *n* — **bi·sex·u·al·ly** \(')bī-'seksh-(ə-)wə-lē, -(ə-)lē\ *adv*

bish·op \'bish-əp\ *n* [ME *bisshop,* fr. OE *bisceop,* fr. LL *episcopus,* fr. Gk *episkopos,* lit., overseer, fr. *epi-* + *skopos* watcher; akin to Gk *skeptesthai* to look — more at SPY] (bef. 12c) **1 :** one having spiritual or ecclesiastical supervision: as **a :** an Anglican, Eastern Orthodox, or Roman Catholic clergyman ranking above a priest, having authority to ordain and confirm, and typically governing a diocese **b :** any of various Protestant clerical officials who superintend other clergy **c :** a Mormon high priest presiding over a ward or over all other bishops and over the Aaronic priesthood **2 :** either of two pieces of each color in a set of chessmen having the power to move diagonally across any number of adjoining unoccupied squares **3 :** mulled port wine flavored with roasted oranges and cloves

bish·op·ric \'bish-ə-(ˌ)prik\ *n* [ME *bisshopriche,* fr. OE *bisceoprīce,* fr. *bisceop* + *rīce* kingdom — more at RICH] (bef. 12c) **1 :** DIOCESE **2 :** the office of bishop **3 :** the administrative body of a Mormon ward consisting of a bishop and two high priests as counselors

Bishops' Bible *n* [fr. its production by a number of bishops] (1835) **:** an officially commissioned English translation of the Bible published in 1568

bis·muth \'biz-məth\ *n* [obs. G *bismut* (now *wismut*), modif. of *wismut,* fr. *wise* meadow + *mut* claim to a mine] (1668) **:** a heavy brittle grayish white chiefly trivalent metallic element that is chemically like arsenic and antimony and that is used in alloys and pharmaceuticals — see ELEMENT table — **bis·mu·thic** \biz-'məth-ik, -'myü-thik\ *adj*

bi·son \'bīs-ᵊn, 'bīz-\ *n, pl* **bison** [L *bisont-, bison,* of Gmc origin; akin to OHG *wisant* aurochs] (14c) **:** any of several large shaggy-maned usu. gregarious recent or extinct bovine mammals (genus *Bison*) having a large head with short horns and heavy forequarters surmounted by a large fleshy hump: as **a :** WISENT **b :** BUFFALO b — **bi·son·tine** \-ᵊn-ˌtīn\ *adj*

[1]**bisque** \'bisk\ *n* [F] (1647) **1 a :** a thick cream soup made with shellfish or game **b :** a cream soup of pureed vegetables **2 :** ice cream containing powdered nuts or macaroons

[2]**bisque** *n* [F] (ca. 1656) **:** odds allowed an inferior player: as **a :** a point taken when desired in a set of tennis **b :** an extra turn in croquet **c :** one or more strokes off a golf score

[3]**bisque** *n* [by shortening & alter.] (1664) **:** BISCUIT 2; *esp* **:** unglazed china that is not to be glazed but is hard-fired and vitreous

bi·state \'bī-ˌstāt\ *adj* (1920) **:** of or relating to two states ⟨a ~ agency⟩

bis·ter *or* **bis·tre** \'bis-tər\ *n* [F *bistre*] (ca. 1727) **1 :** a yellowish brown to dark brown pigment used in art **2 :** a grayish to yellowish brown — **bis·tered** \-tərd\ *adj*

bis·tort \'bis-ˌtȯ(ə)rt, bis-'\ *n* [MF *bistorte,* fr. (assumed) ML *bistorta,* fr. L *bis-* + *torta,* fem. of *tortus,* pp. of *torquēre* to twist — more at TORTURE] (1578) **:** any of several polygonums; *esp* **:** a European herb (*Polygonum bistorta*) or a related American plant (*P. bistortoides*) with twisted roots used as astringents

bis·tro \'bēs-(ˌ)trō, 'bis-\ *n, pl* **bistros** [F] (1921) **1 :** a small or unpretentious European restaurant **2 a :** a small bar or tavern **b :** NIGHTCLUB — **bis·tro·ic** \bēs-'trō-ik, bis-\ *adj*

bi·sul·fate \(')bī-'səl-ˌfāt\ *n* [ISV] (1864) **:** an acid sulfate

bi·sul·fide \-ˌfīd\ *n* [ISV] (1863) **:** DISULFIDE

bi·sul·fite \-ˌfīt\ *n* [F, fr. *bi-* + *sulfite*] (ca. 1890) **:** an acid sulfite

bi–swing \ˌbī-ˌswiŋ\ *adj* [[1]*bi-* + *swing;* perh. fr. the freedom of movement allowed by this jacket] (1968) **:** made with a pleat or gusset at the back of the arms ⟨~ jacket⟩

[1]**bit** \'bit\ *n* [ME *bitt,* fr. OE *bite* act of biting; akin to OE *bītan*] (bef. 12c) **1 :** something bitten or held with the teeth: **a :** the usu. steel part of a bridle inserted in the mouth of a horse **b :** the rimmed mouth end on the stem of a pipe or cigar holder **2 a** (1) **:** the biting or cutting edge or part of a tool (2) **:** a replaceable part of a compound tool that actually performs the function (as drilling or boring) for which the whole tool is designed **b** *pl* **:** the jaws of tongs or pincers **3 :** something that curbs or restrains **4 :** the part of a key that enters the lock and acts on the bolt and tumblers

[2]**bit** *vt* **bit·ted; bit·ting** (1583) **1 a :** to put a bit in the mouth of (a horse) **b :** to control as if with a bit **:** CURB **2 :** to form a bit on (a key)

[3]**bit** *n* [ME, fr. OE *bita;* akin to OE *bītan*] (bef. 12c) **1 :** a small quantity of food; *esp* **:** a small delicacy **2 a :** a small piece or quantity of some material thing **b** (1) **:** a small coin (2) **:** a unit of value equal to $1/8$ of a dollar ⟨four ~*s*⟩ **3 :** something small or unimportant of its kind: as **a :** a brief period **:** WHILE **b :** an indefinite usu. small degree, extent, or amount ⟨a ~ of a rascal⟩ ⟨every ~ as powerful⟩ **c** (1) **:** a small part usu. with spoken lines in a theatrical performance (2) **:** a usu. short theatrical routine ⟨a corny comedy ~⟩ **4 :** the aggregate of items, situations, or activities appropriate to a given style, genre, or role ⟨rejected the whole ~ about love-marriage-motherhood —Vance Packard⟩ — **a bit :** SOMEWHAT, RATHER ⟨the play was *a bit* dull⟩ — **a bit much :** a little more than one wants to endure — **bit by bit :** by degrees **:** LITTLE BY LITTLE

[4]**bit** *n* [*b*inary dig*it*] (1948) **1 :** a unit of computer information equivalent to the result of a choice between two alternatives (as *yes* or *no, on* or *off*) **2 :** the physical representation (as in a computer tape or memory) of a bit by an electrical pulse, a magnetized spot, or a hole whose presence or absence indicates data

bi·tar·trate \(')bī-'tär-ˌtrāt\ *n* [ISV] (1879) **:** an acid tartrate

[1]**bitch** \'bich\ *n* [ME *bicche,* fr. OE *bicce*] (bef. 12c) **1 :** the female of the dog or some other carnivorous mammals **2 a :** a lewd or immoral woman **b :** a malicious, spiteful, and domineering woman **3 :** COMPLAINT **4 :** something that is highly objectionable or unpleasant

[2]**bitch** *vt* (1823) **1 :** SPOIL, BOTCH ⟨I must have ~*ed* up my life —Mavis Gallant⟩ **2 :** to complain of or about ⟨was occasionally quite talkative about his wife . . . mostly he ~*ed* her, but not vehemently —Chandler Brossard⟩ **3 :** CHEAT, DOUBLECROSS ~ *vi* **:** COMPLAIN ⟨wives ~ theatrically at their shrimpy husbands —Fred Powledge⟩

bitch·ery \'bich-ə-rē\ *n, pl* **-er·ies** (1936) **:** malicious, spiteful, or domineering behavior; *also* **:** an instance of such behavior

bitch goddess *n* (1906) **:** SUCCESS; *esp* **:** material or worldly success

bitchy \'bich-ē\ *adj* **bitch·i·er; -est** (1937) **:** characterized by malicious, spiteful, or arrogant behavior — **bitch·i·ly** \'bich-ə-lē\ *adv* — **bitch·i·ness** \'bich-ē-nəs\ *n*

[1]**bite** \'bīt\ *vb* **bit** \'bit\; **bit·ten** \'bit-ᵊn\ *also* **bit; bit·ing** \'bīt-iŋ\ [ME *biten,* fr. OE *bītan;* akin to OHG *bīzan* to bite, L *findere* to split] *vt* (bef. 12c) **1 a :** to seize esp. with teeth or jaws so as to enter, grip, or wound **b :** to wound, pierce, or sting esp. with a fang or a proboscis **2 :** to cut or pierce with or as if with an edged weapon **3 :** to cause sharp pain or stinging discomfort to **4 :** to take hold of **5 :** to eat into **:** CORRODE **6** *archaic* **:** to take in **:** CHEAT ~ *vi* **1 :** to bite or have the habit of biting something **2** *of a weapon or tool* **:** to cut, pierce, or take hold **3 :** to cause irritation or smarting **4 :** CORRODE **5 a** *of fish* **:** to take a bait **b :** to respond so as to be caught (as by a trick) **6 :** to take or maintain a firm hold — **bit·er** \'bīt-ər\ *n* — **bite off more than one can chew :** to undertake more than one can perform — **bite the bullet :** to enter with resignation upon a difficult or distressing course of action — **bite the dust 1 :** to fall dead esp. in battle **2 :** to suffer humiliation or defeat — **bite the hand that feeds one :** to injure a benefactor maliciously

[2]**bite** *n* (bef. 12c) **1 :** the act or manner of biting **2 :** FOOD: as **a :** the amount of food taken at a bite **:** MORSEL **b :** a small amount of food **:** SNACK **3** *archaic* **a :** CHEAT, TRICK **b :** SHARPER **4 :** a wound made by biting **5 :** the hold or grip by which friction is created or purchase is obtained **6 :** a surface that creates friction or is brought into contact with another for the purpose of obtaining a hold **7 a :** a keen incisive quality ⟨the ~ of sharp analysis⟩ **b :** a sharp penetrating effect ⟨the ~ of raw whiskey⟩ **8 :** the corroding of an etcher's plate by acid **9 :** an amount taken usu. in one operation for one purpose **:** CUT

bite·wing \'bīt-,wiŋ\ *n* (1938) **:** a dental X-ray film designed to show the crowns of the upper and lower teeth simultaneously

bit·ing \'bīt-iŋ\ *adj* (14c) **:** having the power to bite ⟨a ~ wind⟩; *esp* **:** able to grip and impress deeply ⟨the report is ~ in its intolerance of deceit⟩ — **bit·ing·ly** \-iŋ-lē\ *adv*

biting louse *n* (1896) **:** any of numerous wingless insects (order Mallophaga) that are mostly parasitic on birds — called also *bird louse*

biting midge *n* (1945) **:** any of a family (Ceratopogonidae) of tiny biting two-winged flies of which some are vectors of filarial worms

bit·stock \'bit-,stäk\ *n* (ca. 1887) **:** a device for turning a bit by hand **:** BRACE

bit·sy \'bit-sē\ *adj* [*itsy-bitsy*] (1905) **:** TINY

[1]**bitt** \'bit\ *n* [perh. fr. ON *biti* beam; akin to OE *bōt* boat] (1593) **1 :** a post or pair of posts fixed on the deck of a ship for securing lines **2 :** BOLLARD 1

[2]**bitt** *vt* (1769) **:** to make (a cable) fast about a bitt

[1]**bit·ter** \'bit-ər\ *adj* [ME, fr. OE *biter;* akin to OHG *bittar* bitter, OE *bītan*] (bef. 12) **1 a :** being or inducing the one of the four basic taste sensations that is peculiarly acrid, astringent, or disagreeable and suggestive of an infusion of hops — compare SALT, SOUR, SWEET **b :** distasteful or distressing to the mind **:** GALLING ⟨a ~ sense of shame⟩ **2 :** marked by intensity or severity: **a :** accompanied by severe pain or suffering ⟨a ~ death⟩ **b :** being relentlessly determined **:** VEHEMENT ⟨a ~ partisan⟩ **c :** exhibiting intense animosity ⟨~ enemies⟩ **d (1) :** harshly reproachful ⟨~ complaints⟩ **(2) :** marked by cynicism and rancor ⟨~ contempt⟩ **e :** intensely unpleasant esp. in coldness or rawness **3 :** expressive of severe pain, grief, or regret ⟨~ tears⟩ — **bit·ter·ish** \'bit-ə-rish\ *adj* — **bit·ter·ly** *adv* — **bit·ter·ness** *n*

[2]**bitter** *n* (bef. 12c) **1 :** bitter quality **2 a** *pl* **:** a usu. alcoholic solution of bitter and often aromatic plant products used esp. in preparing mixed drinks or as a mild tonic **b** *Brit* **:** a very dry heavily hopped ale

[3]**bitter** *vt* (12c) **:** to make bitter ⟨~*ed* ale⟩

[4]**bitter** *adv* (1749) **:** in a bitter manner ⟨it's ~ cold⟩

bit·ter·brush \'bit-ər-,brəsh\ *n* (1910) **:** a much-branched silvery shrub (*Purshia tridentata*) of arid western No. America that has 3-toothed leaves and yellow flowers and is valuable for forage

bitter cress *n* (ca. 1890) **:** any of a genus (*Cardamine*) of cruciferous herbs that produce flat pods and wingless seeds and grow in temperate regions

[1]**bit·ter end** \,bit-ə-'rend\ *n* (1849) **:** the last extremity however painful or calamitous — **bit·ter–end·er** \-'ren-dər\ *n*

[2]**bitter end** *n* [*bitter* (a turn of cable around the bitts)] (1867) **:** the inboard end of a ship's anchoring cable

[1]**bit·tern** \'bit-ərn\ *n* [ME *bitoure,* fr. MF *butor*] (14c) **:** any of various small or medium-sized nocturnal herons (*Botaurus* and related genera) with a characteristic booming cry

[2]**bittern** *n* [irreg. fr. [1]*bitter*] (1682) **:** the bitter water solution of salts that remains after sodium chloride has crystallized out of a brine

bitter principle *n* (ca. 1934) **:** any of various neutral substances of strong bitter taste (as aloin) extracted from plants

bit·ter·root \'bit-ə(r)-,rüt, -,ru̇t\ *n* (1838) **:** a succulent Rocky mountain herb (*Lewisia rediviva*) of the purslane family with fleshy farinaceous roots and pink or white flowers

[1]**bit·ter·sweet** \'bit-ər-,swēt\ *n* (14c) **1 :** something that is bittersweet; *esp* **:** pleasure alloyed with pain **2 a :** a sprawling poisonous weedy nightshade (*Solanum dulcamara*) with purple flowers and oval reddish orange berries **b :** a No. American woody climbing plant (*Celastrus scandens* of the family Celastraceae) having clusters of small greenish flowers succeeded by yellow capsules that open when ripe and disclose the scarlet aril

[2]**bittersweet** *adj* (1611) **1 :** being at once bitter and sweet; *esp* **:** pleasant but including or marked by elements of suffering or regret ⟨a ~ ballad⟩ **2 :** of or relating to a prepared chocolate containing little sugar — **bit·ter·sweet·ly** *adv* — **bit·ter·sweet·ness** *n*

bit·ter·weed \'bit-ər-,wēd\ *n* (1819) **:** any of several American plants containing a bitter principle: as **a :** HORSEWEED **b :** a sneezeweed (genus *Helenium*) **c :** an erect composite herb (*Actinea odorata*) of the southwestern U.S. having chiefly yellow terminal flowerheads and causing poisoning of livestock

bit·tock \'bit-ək\ *n, chiefly Scot* (ca. 1802) **:** a little bit

[1]**bit·ty** \'bit-ē\ *adj* (1892) **:** made up of or containing bits ⟨the contributors are given space to develop their thoughts, and it is not a ~ anthology —*Times Lit. Supp.*⟩

[2]**bitty** *adj* (1905) **:** SMALL, TINY

bi·tu·men \bə-'t(y)ü-mən, bī-, *esp Brit also* 'bit-yə-\ *n* [ME *bithumen* mineral pitch, fr. L *bitumin-, bitumen*] (15c) **1 :** an asphalt of Asia Minor used in ancient times as a cement and mortar **2 :** any of various mixtures of hydrocarbons (as tar) often together with their nonmetallic derivatives that occur naturally or are obtained as residues after heat-refining naturally occurring substances (as petroleum); *specif* **:** such a mixture soluble in carbon disulfide — **bi·tu·mi·ni·za·tion** \bə-,t(y)ü-mə-nə-'zā-shən, bī-\ *n* — **bi·tu·mi·nize** \-'t(y)ü-mə-,nīz\ *vt* — **bi·tu·mi·noid** \-,nȯid\ *adj*

bi·tu·mi·nous \bə-'t(y)ü-mə-nəs, bī-\ *adj* (1620) **1 :** resembling, containing, or impregnated with bitumen **2 :** of or relating to bituminous coal

bituminous coal *n* (1879) **:** a coal that when heated yields considerable volatile bituminous matter — called also *soft coal*

bi·unique \,bī-yü-'nēk\ *adj* [[1]*bi-* + *unique*] (1949) **:** being a correspondence between two sets that is one-to-one in both directions ⟨the ~ correspondence between the points on a straight line and the real numbers⟩ ⟨a phonemic transcription should be ~⟩ — **bi·unique·ness** *n*

[1]**bi·va·lent** \(')bī-'vā-lənt\ *adj* (1869) **1 :** having a valence of two **2 :** associated in pairs in synapsis

[2]**bivalent** *n* (ca. 1934) **:** a pair of synaptic chromosomes

[1]**bi·valve** \'bī-,valv\ *adj* (1661) **:** having a shell composed of two valves

[2]**bivalve** *n* (1683) **:** an animal (as a clam) with a 2-valved shell

bi·var·i·ate \(')bī-'ver-ē-ət, -'var-\ *adj* (1920) **:** of, relating to, or involving two variables ⟨a ~ frequency distribution⟩

[1]**biv·ouac** \'biv-(ə-),wak\ *n* [F, fr. LG *biwake,* fr. *bi* at + *wake* guard] (ca. 1702) **1 :** a usu. temporary encampment under little or no shelter **2 a :** a camping out for a night **b :** a temporary shelter or settlement

[2]**bivouac** *vi* **-ouacked; -ouack·ing** (1809) **:** to make a bivouac **:** CAMP

[1]**bi·week·ly** \(')bī-'wē-klē\ *adj* (ca. 1864) **1 :** occurring every two weeks **:** FORTNIGHTLY **2 :** occurring twice a week — **biweekly** *adv*

[2]**biweekly** *n* (ca. 1890) **1 :** a publication issued every two weeks **2 :** SEMIWEEKLY

bi·year·ly \(')bī-'yi(ə)r-lē\ *adj* (ca. 1961) **1 :** BIENNIAL **2 :** BIANNUAL

biz \'biz\ *n* (1862) **:** BUSINESS

[1]**bi·zarre** \bə-'zär\ *adj* [F, fr. It *bizzarro*] (ca. 1648) **:** strikingly out of the ordinary: as **a :** odd, extravagant, or eccentric in style or mode ⟨appears out of a ~ frog-shaped tent —Henry Hewes⟩ **b :** involving sensational contrasts or incongruities ***syn*** see FANTASTIC — **bi·zarre·ly** *adv* — **bi·zarre·ness** *n*

[2]**bizarre** *n* (ca. 1743) **:** a flower with atypical striped marking

bi·zar·re·rie \bi-,zär-ə-'rē\ *n* [F] (1747) **1 :** a bizarre quality **2 :** something bizarre

bi·zon·al \(')bī-'zōn-ᵊl\ *adj* (1946) **:** of or relating to the affairs of a zone governed or administered by two powers acting together — **bi·zone** \'bī-,zōn\ *n*

[1]**blab** \'blab\ *n* [ME *blabbe;* akin to ME *blaberen*] (14c) **1** *archaic* **:** one that blabs **:** TATTLETALE **2 :** idle or excessive talk **:** CHATTER — **blab·by** \'blab-ē\ *adj*

[2]**blab** *vb* **blabbed; blab·bing** *vt* (15c) **:** to reveal esp. by talking without reserve or discretion ⟨*blabbed* the whole affair to the press⟩ ~ *vi* **1 :** to talk idly or thoughtlessly **:** PRATTLE **2 :** to reveal a secret esp. by indiscreet chatter

[1]**blab·ber** \'blab-ər\ *vb* **blab·bered; blab·ber·ing** \-(ə-)riŋ\ [ME *blaberen*] *vi* (14c) **:** to talk foolishly or excessively ~ *vt* **:** to say indiscreetly

[2]**blabber** *n* (ca. 1913) **:** idle talk **:** BABBLE

[3]**blabber** *n* [[2]*blab*] (1557) **:** one that blabs

blab·ber·mouth \'blab-ər-,mau̇th\ *n* (1936) **:** one who talks too much; *esp* **:** TATTLETALE

[1]**black** \'blak\ *adj* [ME *blak,* fr. OE *blæc;* prob. akin to OHG *blah* black, L *flagrare* to burn, Gk *phlegein*] (bef. 12c) **1 a :** of the color black **b (1) :** very dark in color ⟨his face was ~ with rage⟩ **(2) :** having a very deep or low register ⟨a bass with a ~ voice⟩ **(3) :** HEAVY, SERIOUS ⟨the play was a ~ intrigue⟩ **2 a :** having dark skin, hair, and eyes **:** SWARTHY ⟨a ~ Irishman⟩ **b (1) :** of or relating to a group or race characterized by dark pigmentation; *esp* **:** of or relating to the Negro race ⟨~ Americans⟩ **(2) :** of or relating to the Afro-American people or culture ⟨~ literature⟩ ⟨~ theater⟩ ⟨~ pride⟩ **3 :** dressed in black **4 :** DIRTY, SOILED ⟨hands ~ with grime⟩ **5 a :** characterized by the absence of light ⟨a ~ night⟩ **b :** reflecting or transmitting little or no light ⟨~ water⟩ **c :** served without milk or cream ⟨~ coffee⟩ **6 a :** thoroughly sinister or evil **:** WICKED ⟨a ~ deed⟩ **b :** indicative of condemnation or discredit ⟨got a ~ mark for being late⟩ **7 :** connected with or invoking the supernatural and esp. the devil ⟨ ~ magic⟩ **8 a :** very sad, gloomy, or calamitous ⟨~ despair⟩ **b :** marked by the occurrence of disaster ⟨~ Friday⟩ **9 :** characterized by hostility or angry discontent **:** SULLEN ⟨~ resentment filled his heart⟩ **10** *chiefly Brit* **:** subject to boycott by trade-union members as employing or favoring nonunion workers or as operating under conditions considered unfair by the trade union ⟨declare a fish market ~⟩ **11 a** *of propaganda* **:** conducted so as to appear to originate within an enemy country and designed to weaken enemy morale **b :** characterized by or connected with the use of black propaganda ⟨~ radio⟩ **12 :** characterized by grim, distorted, or grotesque satire ⟨~ humor⟩ — **black·ish** \'blak-ish\ *adj* — **black·ly** *adv* — **black·ness** *n*

[2]**black** *n* (bef. 12c) **1 :** a black pigment or dye; *esp* **:** one consisting largely of carbon **2 :** the achromatic color of least lightness characteristically perceived to belong to objects that neither reflect nor transmit light **3 :** something that is black: as **a :** black clothing ⟨looks good in ~⟩ **b :** a black animal (as a horse) **4 a :** a person belonging to a dark-skinned race or one stemming in part from such a race; *esp* **:** NEGRO **b :** AFRO-AMERICAN **5 :** the pieces of a dark color in a two-handed board game (as chess) **6 :** total or nearly total absence of light ⟨the ~ of night⟩ **7 :** the condition of making a profit — usu. used with *the* ⟨operating in the ~⟩ — compare RED

\ə\ abut \ᵊ\ kitten, F table \ər\ further \a\ ash \ā\ ace \ä\ cot, cart \au̇\ out \ch\ chin \e\ bet \ē\ easy \g\ go \i\ hit \ī\ ice \j\ job \ŋ\ sing \ō\ go \ȯ\ law \ȯi\ boy \th\ thin \t͟h\ the \ü\ loot \u̇\ foot \y\ yet \zh\ vision \à, k̲, ⁿ, œ, œ̄, ue, ue̅, ʸ\ see Guide to Pronunciation

[3]**black** *vi* (13c) : to become black ~ *vt* **1** : to make black **2** *chiefly Brit* : to declare (as a business or industry) subject to boycott by trade-union members
black alder *n* (1805) : WINTERBERRY 1
black·a·moor \'blak-ə-,mu̇(ə)r\ *n* [irreg. fr. *black* + *Moor*] (1547) : a dark-skinned person; *esp* : NEGRO
black–and–blue \,blak-ən-'blü\ *adj* (14c) : darkly discolored from blood effused by bruising
black–and–tan \-ən-'tan\ *adj* (1863) **1** : having a predominantly black color pattern with deep red or rusty tan on the feet, breeching, and cheek patches, above the eyes, and inside the ears **2** : favoring or practicing proportional representation of whites and blacks in politics — compare LILY-WHITE **3** : frequented by both blacks and whites ⟨a ~ bar⟩
black and tan *n* (1857) **1** : a black-and-tan animal (as a dog) **2** : a member of a black-and-tan political organization (as in the southern U.S.) — compare LILY-WHITE **3** *cap B&T* [fr. the color of his uniform] : a recruit enlisted in England in 1920–21 for service in the Royal Irish Constabulary against the armed movement for Irish independence
black–and–tan coonhound *n* (1948) : any of an American breed of strong vigorous coonhounds that have black-and-tan markings
black–and–white \,blak-ən-'hwīt, -'wīt\ *adj* (1612) **1** : being in writing or print ⟨a ~ statement of the problem⟩ **2** : partly black and partly white in color ⟨a ~ cat⟩ **3** : executed in dark pigment on a light background or in light pigment on a dark ground ⟨a ~ drawing⟩ **4** : characterized by the reproduction or transmission of visual images in tones of gray rather than in colors ⟨~ film⟩ ⟨~ television⟩ **5** **a** : sharply divided into good and evil groups, sides, or ideas **b** : evaluating or viewing things as either all good or all bad ⟨~ morality⟩ ⟨~ thinkers⟩
black and white *n* (1599) **1** : WRITING, PRINT **2** : a drawing or print done in black and white or in monochrome **3** : monochrome reproduction of visual images (as by photography or television)
black art *n* (1590) : magic practiced by or as if by conjurers and witches
black–a–vised \'blak-ə-,vīst\ *adj* [*black* + F *à vis* as to face] (1758) : dark-complexioned
[1]**black·ball** \'blak-,bȯl\ *vt* (1770) **1** : to vote against; *esp* : to exclude from membership by casting a negative vote **2** **a** : to exclude socially : OSTRACIZE **b** : BOYCOTT
[2]**blackball** *n* (ca. 1847) **1** : a small black ball for use as a negative vote in a ballot box **2** : an adverse vote esp. against admitting someone to membership in an organization
black bass *n* (1815) : any of several highly prized freshwater sunfishes (genus *Micropterus*) native to eastern and central No. America — compare LARGEMOUTH BASS, SMALLMOUTH BASS
black bear *n* (1781) : the common American bear (*Euarctos americanus*) ranging in color from brown or typical black to white
black beast *n* (1926) : BÊTE NOIRE
[1]**black belt** \'blak-,belt\ *n* (1870) **1** : an area characterized by rich black soil **2** *often cap both Bs* : an area densely populated by blacks
[2]**black belt** \-'belt\ *n* (1954) **1** : a rating of expert in various arts of self-defense (as judo and karate) **2** : one who holds a black belt
black·ber·ry \'blak-,ber-ē\ *n* (bef. 12c) **1** : the usu. black or dark purple juicy but seedy edible fruit of various brambles (genus *Rubus*) of the rose family **2** : a plant that bears blackberries
black bile *n* (1797) : a humor of medieval physiology believed to be secreted by the kidneys or spleen and to cause melancholy
[1]**black·bird** \'blak-,bərd\ *n* (14c) **1** : any of various birds of which the males are largely or entirely black: as **a** : a common and familiar British thrush (*Turdus merula*) that is black with orange bill and eye rim **b** : any of several American birds (family Icteridae) **2** : a Pacific islander kidnapped for use as a plantation laborer
[2]**blackbird** *vi* (1928) : to engage in the slave trade esp. in the So. Pacific
black·bird·er *n* (1883) **1** : a person that blackbirds **2** : a ship used in blackbirding
black·board \'blak-,bō(ə)rd, -,bȯ(ə)rd\ *n* (1823) : a hard smooth usu. dark surface used esp. in a classroom for writing or drawing on with chalk
black·body \'blak-'bäd-ē\ *n* (1710) : an ideal body or surface that completely absorbs all radiant energy falling upon it with no reflection
black book *n* (1592) : a book containing a blacklist
black box *n* (1945) : a usu. complicated electronic device that functions and is packaged as a unit and whose internal mechanism is usu. hidden from or mysterious to the user; *broadly* : something that has mysterious or unknown internal functions or mechanisms
black·cap \'blak-,kap\ *n* (1847) **1** : BLACK RASPBERRY **2** : any of several birds with black heads or crowns: as **a** : a small European warbler (*Sylvia atricapilla*) with a black crown **b** : CHICKADEE
black–capped \-'kapt\ *adj, of a bird* (1781) : having the top of the head black
black·cock \-,käk\ *n* (15c) : BLACK GROUSE; *specif* : the male black grouse
black cohosh *n* (1830) : a bugbane (*Cimicifuga racemosa*) of the eastern U.S.
black crappie *n* (ca. 1926) : a silvery black-mottled sunfish (*Pomoxis nigro-maculatus*) of the Mississippi drainage and eastern U.S. having seven or eight protruding spines on the dorsal fins
black·damp \'blak-'damp\ *n* (1836) : a carbon dioxide mixture occurring as a mine gas and incapable of supporting life or flame
black death *n, often cap B&D* [fr. the black patches formed on the skin of its victims] (1758) **1** : PLAGUE 2b **2** : a severe epidemic of plague that occurred in Asia and Europe in the 14th century
black diamond *n* (ca. 1915) **1** *pl* : COAL 3a **2** : [3]CARBONADO **3** : dense black hematite
black duck *n* (1637) : any of various ducks that are dark in color; *esp* : a common brown duck (*Anas rubripes*) of the northeastern U.S. and Canada
black·en \'blak-ən\ *vb* **black·ened; black·en·ing** \-(ə-)niŋ\ *vi* (14c) : to become dark or black ⟨the sky ~*s*⟩ ~ *vt* **1** : to make black **2** : DEFAME, SULLY — **black·en·er** \-(ə-)nər\ *n*
Black English *n* (1969) : a nonstandard dialect of English held to be spoken by many American blacks
black·en·ing \-(ə-)niŋ\ *n* (ca. 1934) : BLACKING
black eye *n* (1604) **1** : a discoloration of the skin around the eye from bruising **2** : a bad reputation
black–eyed pea \,blak-,īd-\ *n* (1728) : COWPEA
black–eyed Su·san \-'süz-ᵊn\ *n* (1891) : either of two No. American coneflowers (*Rudbeckia hirta* and *R. serotina*) having flower heads with deep yellow to orange rays and dark conical disks
black·face \'blak-,fās\ *n* (1869) : makeup for a Negro role esp. in a minstrel show; *also* : an actor who plays this role
black·fish \-,fish\ *n* (1754) **1** : any of numerous dark-colored fishes: as **a** : TAUTOG **b** : a small food fish (*Dallia pectoralis*) of Alaska and Siberia that is noted for its resistance to cold **2** : any of several small toothed whales (genus *Globicephala*) related to the dolphins and found in the warmer seas
black–flag \-'flag\ *vt* (1963) : to signal (a race-car driver) to go immediately to the pits
black flag *n* (1720) : a pirate's flag usu. bearing a skull and crossbones
black·fly \'blak-,flī\ *n, pl* **-flies** *or* **-fly** (1608) : any of several small dark-colored insects; *esp* : a two-winged bloodsucking fly (*Simulium* or related genera) whose larvae usu. live in clear flowing streams
Black·foot \'blak-,fu̇t\ *n, pl* **Blackfeet** *or* **Blackfoot** (1834) **1** **a** *pl* : an American Indian confederacy of Montana, Alberta, and Saskatchewan **b** : a member of any of the Blackfoot peoples **2** : the Algonquian language of the Blackfeet
black–foot·ed albatross \,blak-,fu̇t-əd-\ *n* (1839) : an albatross (*Diomedea nigripes*) of the Pacific that is chiefly blackish with dusky bill and black feet and legs — called also *gooney, gooney bird*
black–footed ferret *n* (1846) : an American weasel (*Mustela nigripes*) that is related to the European polecat and resembles a yellow mink with dark feet, tail, and mask
black gold *n* (1910) : PETROLEUM
black grouse *n* (ca. 1828) : a large grouse (*Lyrurus tetrix*) of western Asia and Europe of which the male is black with white wing patches and the female is barred and mottled

black-footed ferret

[1]**black·guard** \'blag-ərd, -,ärd; 'blak-,gärd\ *n* (1535) **1** *obs* : the kitchen servants of a household **2** **a** : a rude or unscrupulous person **b** : one who uses foul or abusive language — **black·guard·ism** \-,iz-əm\ *n* — **black·guard·ly** \-lē\ *adj or adv*
[2]**blackguard** *vt* (1823) : to talk about or address in abusive terms
black gum *n* (1709) : a tupelo (*Nyssa sylvatica*) of the eastern U.S. with light and soft but tough wood
black hand *n, often cap B&H* [*Black Hand,* a Sicilian and Italian-American society of the late 19th and 20th centuries] (1898) : a lawless secret society engaged in criminal activities (as terrorism or extortion) — **black·hand·er** \'blak-,han-dər\ *n*
black·head \'blak-,hed\ *n* (1837) **1** : a small plug of sebum blocking the duct of a sebaceous gland esp. on the face **2** : a destructive disease of turkeys and related birds caused by a protozoan (*Histomonas meleagridis*) that invades the intestinal ceca and liver **3** : a larval clam or mussel attached to the skin or gills of a freshwater fish
black·heart \-,härt\ *n* (ca. 1927) : a plant disease in which the central tissues blacken
black hole *n* (1968) : a hypothetical invisible region in space with a small diameter and intense gravitational field that is held to be caused by the collapse of a massive star
black·ing \'blak-iŋ\ *n* (1571) : a substance (as a paste or polish) that is applied to an object to make it black
[1]**black·jack** \-,jak\ *n* (1591) **1** [*black* + *jack* (vessel)] : a tankard for beer or ale usu. of tar-coated leather **2** : SPHALERITE **3** : a hand weapon typically consisting of a piece of leather-enclosed metal with a strap or springy shaft for a handle **4** : a common often scrubby oak (*Quercus marilandica*) of the southeastern and southern U.S. with black bark **5** : a card game the object of which is to be dealt cards having a higher count than those of the dealer up to but not exceeding 21 — called also *twenty-one, vingt-et-un*
[2]**blackjack** *vt* (1905) **1** : to strike with a blackjack **2** : to coerce with threats or pressure
black·land \'blak-,land\ *n* (1803) **1** : a heavy sticky black soil such as that covering large areas in Texas **2** *pl* : a region of blackland
black lead *n* (1583) : GRAPHITE
black·leg \'blak-,leg, -,lāg\ *n* (1722) **1** : an enzootic usu. fatal toxemia esp. of young cattle **2** : a cheating gamester : SWINDLER **3** *chiefly Brit* : a worker hostile to trade unionism or acting in opposition to union policies : SCAB
black letter *n* (ca. 1640) : a heavy angular condensed typeface used esp. by the earliest European printers and based on handwriting used chiefly in the 13th to 15th centuries; *also* : this style of handwriting
black light *n* (1927) : invisible ultraviolet or infrared light
black·light trap \,blak-,līt-\ *n* (1961) : a trap for insects that uses a form of black light perceptible to particular insects as an attractant
[1]**black·list** \'blak-,list\ *n* (1692) : a list of persons who are disapproved of or are to be punished or boycotted
[2]**blacklist** *vt* (1718) : to put on a blacklist — **black·list·er** *n*
black locust *n* (1787) : a tall tree (*Robinia pseudoacacia*) of eastern No. America with pinnately compound leaves, drooping racemes of fragrant white flowers, and strong stiff wood
black lung *n* (ca. 1909) : a disease of the lungs caused by habitual inhalation of coal dust
black·mail \'blak-,māl\ *n* [*black* + [1]*mail*] (1552) **1** : a tribute anciently exacted on the Scottish border by freebooting chiefs for immunity from pillage **2** **a** : extortion by threats esp. of public exposure or criminal prosecution **b** : the payment that is extorted — **blackmail** *vt* — **black·mail·er** *n*
Black Ma·ria \,blak-mə-'rī-ə\ *n* (1847) : PATROL WAGON
black–mar·ket *vi* (1943) : to buy or sell goods in the black market ~ *vt* : to sell in the black market — **black marketer** *or* **black marketeer** \-,mär-kə-'ti(ə)r\ *n*
black market *n* (1931) : illicit trade in goods or commodities in violation of official regulations; *also* : a place where such trade is carried on
Black Mass *n* (1893) : a travesty of the Christian mass ascribed to the reputed worshipers of Satan

Black Muslim *n* (1960) : a member of a chiefly black group that professes Islamic religious belief
black nationalist *n, often cap B&N* (1964) : a member of a group of militant blacks who advocate separatism from the whites and the formation of self-governing black communities — **black nationalism** *n, often cap B&N*
black·out \'blak-,au̇t\ *n* (1913) **1 a :** a turning off of the stage lighting to separate scenes in a play, indicate that the play is over, or end a skit; *also* **:** a skit that ends with a blackout **b :** a period of darkness enforced as a precaution against air raids **c :** a period of darkness (as in a city) caused by a lack of illumination due to a failure of electrical power **2 :** a transient dulling or loss of vision, consciousness, or memory ⟨an alcoholic ~⟩ **3 a :** a wiping out or erasure : OBLITERATION ⟨a sudden ~ of his policy by the insurance company⟩ **b :** a blotting out by censorship : SUPPRESSION ⟨a ~ of news about the invasion⟩ **4 :** a usu. temporary loss of radio signal due to a magnetic storm or to a local effect at the transmitter of a spacecraft upon reentry **5 :** the prohibition or restriction of the telecasting of sports events to ensure ticket sales
black out \(')blak-'au̇t\ *vi* (1921) **1 :** to become enveloped in darkness **2 :** to undergo a temporary loss of vision, consciousness, or memory **3 :** to extinguish or screen all lights for protection esp. against air attack ~ *vt* **1 :** to cause to black out ⟨*black out* the stage⟩ **2 :** to make inoperative or temporarily nonexistent : DESTROY ⟨falling trees *blacked out* electric power lines⟩ **3 a :** to blot out or erase ⟨*blacked out* the event from his mind⟩ **b :** to suppress by censorship ⟨*black out* the news⟩ **4 :** to impose a blackout on
Black Panther *n* (1965) : a member of an organization of militant American blacks
black pepper *n* (bef. 12c) : a condiment that consists of the fruit of an East Indian plant (*Piper nigrum*) ground with the black husk still on
black·poll \'blak-,pōl\ *n* (1783) : a No. American warbler (*Dendroica striata*) having the top of the head of the male bird black when in full plumage
black power *n, often cap B&P* (1966) : the mobilization of the political and economic power of American blacks esp. to further racial equality
black pudding *n, chiefly Brit* (1568) : BLOOD SAUSAGE
black racer *n* (1849) : an American blacksnake (*Coluber constrictor constrictor*) common in the eastern U.S.
black raspberry *n* (1781) : a raspberry (*Rubus occidentalis*) with a purplish black fruit that is native to eastern No. America and is the source of several cultivated varieties — called also *blackcap*
Black Rod *n* (1646) : the principal usher of the House of Lords
black rot *n* (1849) : a bacterial or fungous rot of plants marked by dark brown discoloration
black sheep *n* (1792) : a discreditable member of a respectable group
Black·shirt \'blak-,shərt\ *n* (1922) : a member of a fascist organization having a black shirt as a distinctive part of its uniform; *esp* **:** a member of the Italian Fascist party
black·smith \'blak-,smith\ *n* [fr. his working with iron, known as black metal] (15c) : a smith who forges iron — **black·smith·ing** \-iŋ\ *n*
black·snake \-,snāk\ *n* (1634) **1 :** any of several snakes that are largely black or very dark in color; *esp* **:** either of two harmless snakes (*Coluber constrictor* and *Elaphe obsoleta*) of the U.S. **2 :** a long tapering braided whip of rawhide or leather
black spot *n* (ca. 1889) : any of several plant diseases characterized by black spots or blotches
black studies *n pl* (1969) : studies (as in history and literature) relating to American black culture
black·tail \'blak-,tāl\ *n* (1828) : BLACK-TAILED DEER
black–tailed deer \,blak-,tāl-'di(ə)r\ *n* (1806) : MULE DEER; *specif* **:** one of a subspecies (*Odocoileus hemionus columbianus*) esp. of British Columbia, Oregon, and Washington
black tea *n* (1789) : tea that is dark in color from complete fermentation of the leaf before firing
black·thorn \'blak-,thȯ(ə)rn\ *n* (14c) **1 :** a European spiny plum (*Prunus spinosa*) with hard wood and small white flowers **2 :** any of several American hawthorns
black–tie *adj* (1933) : characterized by or requiring the wearing of semiformal evening dress by men ⟨a ~ dinner⟩ — compare WHITE-TIE
black·top \'blak-,täp\ *n* (1931) : a bituminous material used esp. for surfacing roads; *also* **:** a surface paved with blacktop — **blacktop** *vt*
Blackwall hitch \,blak-,wȯl-\ *n* [*Blackwall*, shipyard in London, England] (ca. 1862) : a hitch for securing a rope to a hook — see KNOT illustration
black walnut *n* (1612) : a walnut (*Juglans nigra*) of eastern No. America with hard strong heavy dark brown wood and oily edible nuts; *also* **:** its wood or nut
black·wash \'blak-,wȯsh, -,wäsh\ *vt* [*black* + *-wash* (as in *whitewash*)] (1967) : to uncover or bring to light : EXPOSE
black·wa·ter \'blak-,wȯt-ər, -,wät-\ *n* (1800) : any of several diseases (as blackwater fever) of lower animals or man characterized by dark-colored urine
blackwater fever *n* (1884) : a febrile complication of repeated malarial attacks that is characterized esp. by extensive kidney damage and dark-colored urine caused by heme from blood
black widow *n* (1915) : a venomous New World spider (*Latrodectus mactans*) the female of which is black with an hourglass-shaped red mark on the underside of the abdomen
blad·der \'blad-ər\ *n* [ME, fr. OE *blǣdre;* akin to OHG *blātara* bladder, OE *blāwan* to blow] (bef. 12c) **1 a :** a membranous sac in animals that serves as the receptacle of a liquid or contains gas; *esp* **:** URINARY BLADDER **b :** VESICLE **2 :** something (as the rubber bag inside a football) resembling a bladder — **blad·der·like** \-,līk\ *adj*
blad·der·nut \'blad-ər-,nət\ *n* (1578) : an ornamental shrub or small tree (genus *Staphylea* of the family Staphyleaceae, the bladdernut family) with panicles of small white flowers followed by inflated capsules; *also* **:** one of the capsules
bladder worm *n* (1858) : a bladderlike larval tapeworm (as a cysticercus)
blad·der·wort \'blad-ər-,wərt, -,wȯ(ə)rt\ *n* (ca. 1815) : any of a genus (*Utricularia* of the family Lentibulariaceae, the bladderwort family) of chiefly aquatic plants with vesicular floats or insect traps
bladder wrack *n* (1810) : a common black rockweed (*Fucus vesiculosus*) used in preparing kelp and as a manure
blade \'blād\ *n* [ME, fr. OE *blæd;* akin to OHG *blat* leaf, L *folium*, Gk *phyllon*, OE *blōwan* to blossom — more at BLOW] (bef. 12c) **1 a :** LEAF 1a(1); *esp* **:** the leaf of an herb or a grass **b :** the flat expanded part of a leaf as distinguished from the petiole **2 :** something resembling the blade of a leaf: as **a :** the broad flattened part of an oar or paddle **b :** an arm of a screw propeller, electric fan, or steam turbine **c :** the broad flat or concave part of a machine (as a bulldozer or snowplow) that comes into contact with the material to be moved **d :** a broad flat body part; *specif* **:** SCAPULA — used chiefly in naming cuts of meat **e :** the flat portion of the tongue immediately behind the tip; *also* **:** this portion together with the tip **f :** the expanded rear portion of the comb of a single-comb fowl — see COCK illustration **3 a :** the cutting part of an implement **b** (1) **:** SWORD (2) **:** SWORDSMAN (3) **:** a dashing lively man **c :** the runner of an ice skate
blad·ed \'blād-əd\ *adj* (1578) : having blades — often used in combination ⟨broad-*bladed* leaves⟩
blae \'blā\ *adj* [ME *bla, blo*, fr. ON *blār;* akin to OHG *blāo* blue — more at BLUE] *chiefly Scot* (13c) : dark blue or bluish gray
¹blah \'blä\ *n* [imit.] (1918) **1** *also* **blah–blah** \-,blä\ **:** silly or pretentious chatter or nonsense **2** *pl* [perh. influenced in meaning by *blasé*] **:** a feeling of boredom, discomfort, or general dissatisfaction
²blah *adj* (1927) : lacking interest : MEDIOCRE ⟨a ~ winter day⟩
blain \'blān\ *n* [ME, fr. OE *blegen;* akin to MLG *bleine* blain, OE *blāwan* to blow] (bef. 12c) : an inflammatory swelling or sore
blam·able \'blā-mə-bəl\ *adj* (14c) : deserving blame : REPREHENSIBLE *syn* see BLAMEWORTHY — **blam·ably** \-blē\ *adv*
¹blame \'blām\ *vt* **blamed; blam·ing** [ME *blamen*, fr. OF *blamer*, fr. LL *blasphemare* to blaspheme, fr. Gk *blasphēmein*] (13c) **1 :** to find fault with : CENSURE ⟨the right to praise or ~ a literary work⟩ **2 a :** to hold responsible ⟨~ him for everything⟩ **b :** to place responsibility for ⟨~s it on me⟩ *syn* see CRITICIZE — **blam·er** *n*

usage Use of *blame* in sense 2b with *on* has occas. been disparaged as wrong. Such disparagement is without basis; *blame on* occurs as frequently in carefully edited prose as *blame for.* Both forms are standard.

— **to blame :** at fault : RESPONSIBLE
²blame *n* (13c) **1 :** an expression of disapproval or reproach : CENSURE **2 a :** a state of being blameworthy : CULPABILITY **b** *archaic* **:** FAULT, SIN **3 :** responsibility for something believed to deserve censure ⟨they must share the ~ for the crime⟩ — **blame·less** \-ləs\ *adj* — **blame·less·ly** *adv* — **blame·less·ness** *n*
blame·ful \'blām-fəl\ *adj* (14c) : BLAMABLE — **blame·ful·ly** \-fə-lē\ *adv*
blame·wor·thy \-,wər-t͟hē\ *adj* (14c) : being at fault : deserving blame — **blame·wor·thi·ness** *n*

syn BLAMEWORTHY, BLAMABLE, GUILTY, CULPABLE mean deserving reproach or punishment. BLAMEWORTHY and BLAMABLE apply to any degree of reprehensibility; GUILTY implies responsibility for or consciousness of crime, sin, or, at the least, grave error or misdoing; CULPABLE is weaker than *guilty* and is likely to connote malfeasance or errors of ignorance, omission, or negligence.

blanc fixe \'blaŋk-'fiks\ *n* [F, lit., fixed white] (1866) : barium sulfate prepared as a heavy white powder and used esp. as a filler in paper, rubber, and linoleum or as a pigment
blanch \'blanch\ *vb* [ME *blaunchen*, fr. MF *blanchir*, fr. OF *blanche*, fem. of *blanc*, adj., white — more at BLANK] *vt* (15c) **1 :** to take the color out of: **a :** to bleach by excluding light ⟨~ celery⟩ **b :** to scald or parboil in water or steam in order to remove the skin from, whiten, or stop enzymatic action in (as food for freezing) **c :** to clean (a coin blank) in an acid solution **d :** to cover (sheet iron or steel) with a coating of tin **2 :** to make ashen or pale ⟨fear ~es the cheek⟩ ~ *vi* **:** to become white or pale — **blanch·er** *n*
blanc·mange \blə-'mänj, -'mänzh\ *n* [ME *blancmanger*, fr. MF *blanc manger*, lit., white food] (14c) : a usu. sweetened and flavored dessert made from gelatinous or starchy ingredients (as cornstarch) and milk
bland \'bland\ *adj* [L *blandus*] (1661) **1 a :** smooth and soothing in manner or quality ⟨a ~ smile⟩ **b :** exhibiting no personal concern or embarrassment : UNPERTURBED ⟨a ~ confession of guilt⟩ **2 a :** not irritating, stimulating, or invigorating : SOOTHING **b :** DULL, INSIPID ⟨~ stories with little plot or action⟩ *syn* see SUAVE — **bland·ly** \'blan-(d)lē\ *adv* — **bland·ness** \'blan(d)-nəs\ *n*
blan·dish \'blan-dish\ *vb* [ME *blandishen*, fr. MF *blandiss-*, stem of *blandir*, fr. L *blandiri*, fr. *blandus* mild, flattering; akin to *L mollis* soft — more at MOLLIFY] *vt* (14c) : to coax with flattery : CAJOLE ~ *vi* **:** to act or speak in a flattering or coaxing manner — **blan·dish·er** *n*
blan·dish·ment \-dish-mənt\ *n* (1591) : something that tends to coax or cajole : ALLUREMENT — often used in pl.
¹blank \'blaŋk\ *adj* [ME, fr. MF *blanc*, of Gmc origin; akin to OHG *blanch* white; akin to L *flagrare* to burn — more at BLACK] (14c) **1** *archaic* **:** COLORLESS **2 a :** appearing or causing to appear dazed, confounded, or nonplussed ⟨stared in ~ dismay⟩ **b :** EXPRESSIONLESS ⟨a ~ stare⟩ **3 a :** lacking interest, variety, or change ⟨~ hours⟩ **b :** devoid of covering or content; *esp* **:** free from writing or marks ⟨~ paper⟩ **c :** having spaces to be filled in **d :** lacking any card : VOID ⟨a ~ suit at cards⟩ **4 :** ABSOLUTE, UNQUALIFIED ⟨a ~ refusal⟩ **5 :** UNFINISHED; *esp* **:** having a plain or unbroken surface where an opening is usual ⟨a ~ key⟩ ⟨a ~ arch⟩ *syn* see EMPTY — **blank·ly** *adv* — **blank·ness** *n*
²blank *n* (1570) **1 a :** an empty space (as on a paper) **b :** a paper with spaces for the entry of data ⟨a subscription ~⟩ **2 a :** an empty or featureless place or space ⟨my mind was a ~ during the test⟩ **b :** a vacant or uneventful period ⟨a long ~ in history⟩ **c :** something useless, valueless, or undesirable ⟨drew a ~⟩ **3 :** the bull's-eye of a target **4 :** a dash substituting for an omitted word **5 a :** a piece of material prepared to be made into something (as a key) by a further operation

b : a cartridge loaded with propellant and a wad but no projectile **6** : VOID 4

[3]**blank** *vt* (1763) **1 a :** OBSCURE, OBLITERATE ⟨~ out a line⟩ **b :** to stop access to : SEAL ⟨~ off a tunnel⟩ **2 :** to keep (an opposing team) from scoring ⟨were ~*ed* for eight innings⟩ **3 :** to cut with a die from a piece of stock ~ *vi* **1 :** FADE — usu. used with *out* ⟨the music ~*ed* out⟩ **2** : to become confused or abstracted — often used with *out* ⟨his mind ~*ed* out momentarily⟩

blank check *n* (ca. 1887) **1 :** a signed check with the amount unspecified **2 :** complete freedom of action or control : CARTE BLANCHE

[1]**blan·ket** \'blaŋ-kət\ *n* [ME, fr. OF *blankete,* fr. *blanc*] (14c) **1 a :** a large usu. oblong piece of woven fabric used as a bed covering **b :** a similar piece of fabric used as a body covering (as for an animal) ⟨a horse ~⟩ **2 :** something that resembles a blanket; *esp* : a covering or enclosing layer ⟨a ~ of fog⟩ ⟨a ~ of gloom⟩ — **blan·ket·like** \-ˌlīk\ *adj*

[2]**blanket** *vt* (1605) **1 :** to cover with a blanket ⟨new grass ~*s* the slope⟩ **2 a :** to cover so as to obscure, interrupt, suppress, or extinguish ⟨~ a fire with foam⟩ **b :** to apply or cause to apply to uniformly despite wide separation or diversity among the elements included ⟨freight rates that ~ a region⟩ **c :** to cause to be included ⟨automatically ~*ed* into the insurance program⟩

[3]**blanket** *adj* (1886) **1 :** covering all members of a group or class ⟨a ~ wage increase⟩ **2 :** effective or applicable in all instances

blan·ket·flow·er \'blaŋ-kət-ˌflau̇(-ə)r\ *n* (1879) : GAILLARDIA

blanket stitch *n* (1880) : a buttonhole stitch with spaces of variable width used on materials too thick to hem — **blanket–stitch** *vt*

blank verse *n* (1589) : unrhymed verse; *specif* : unrhymed iambic pentameter verse

[1]**blare** \'bla(ə)r, 'ble(ə)r\ *vb* **blared; blar·ing** [ME *bleren;* akin to OE *blǣtan* to bleat] *vi* (15c) : to sound loud and strident ⟨radios *blaring*⟩ ~ *vt* **1 :** to sound or utter raucously ⟨sat *blaring* the car horn⟩ **2 :** to proclaim flamboyantly ⟨headlines *blared* his defeat⟩

[2]**blare** *n* (1809) **1 :** a loud strident noise **2 :** dazzling often garish brilliance **3 :** FLAMBOYANCE

blar·ney \'blär-nē\ *n* [*Blarney stone,* a stone in Blarney Castle, near Cork, Ireland, held to bestow skill in flattery on those who kiss it] (1796) **1 :** skillful flattery : BLANDISHMENT **2 :** NONSENSE, HUMBUG ⟨gave her some ~ about why he was late⟩ — **blarney** *vb*

bla·sé \blä-'zā\ *adj* [F] (1819) **1 :** apathetic to pleasure or excitement as a result of excessive indulgence or enjoyment : WORLD-WEARY **2** : SOPHISTICATED, WORLDLY-WISE **3 :** UNCONCERNED *syn* see SOPHISTICATED

blas·pheme \blas-'fēm, 'blas-ˌ\ *vb* **blas·phemed; blas·phem·ing** [ME *blasfemen,* fr. LL *blasphemare* — more at BLAME] *vt* (14c) **1 :** to speak of or address with irreverence **2 :** REVILE, ABUSE ~ *vi* **:** to utter blasphemy — **blas·phem·er** \-'fē-mər; 'blas-ˌfē-mər, -fə-mər\ *n*

blas·phe·mous \'blas-fə-məs\ *adj* (15c) : impiously irreverent : PROFANE — **blas·phe·mous·ly** *adv* — **blas·phe·mous·ness** *n*

blas·phe·my \'blas-fə-mē\ *n, pl* **-mies** (13c) **1 a :** the act of insulting or showing contempt or lack of reverence for God **b :** the act of claiming the attributes of deity **2 :** irreverence toward something considered sacred or inviolable

[1]**blast** \'blast\ *n* [ME, fr. OE *blǣst;* akin to OHG *blāst* blast, OE *blāwan* to blow] (bef. 12c) **1 a :** a violent gust of wind **b :** the effect or accompaniment (as sleet) of such a gust **2 :** the sound produced by an impulsion of air through a wind instrument or whistle **3 :** something resembling a gust of wind: as **a :** a stream of air or gas forced through a hole **b :** a violent outburst ⟨leveled a ~ at special interests⟩ **c :** the continuous blowing to which a charge of ore or metal is subjected in a blast furnace **4 a :** a sudden pernicious influence or effect ⟨the ~ of a huge epidemic⟩ **b :** a disease that suggests the effects of a noxious wind; *esp* : one of plants that causes the foliage or flowers to wither **5 a :** an explosion or violent detonation **b :** an explosive charge **c :** the violent effect produced in the vicinity of an explosion that consists of a wave of increased atmospheric pressure followed by a wave of decreased atmospheric pressure **6 :** SPEED, CAPACITY, OPERATION ⟨go full ~⟩ ⟨in full ~⟩ **7 :** an enjoyably exciting experience, occasion, or event; *esp* : PARTY

[2]**blast** *vi* (14c) **1 :** BLARE ⟨music ~*ing* from the radio⟩ **2 a :** to use an explosive **b :** SHOOT **3 :** to make a vigorous attack **4 :** to hit a golf ball out of a sand trap with explosive force ~ *vt* **1 a :** to injure by or as if by the action of wind **b :** BLIGHT **2 :** to attack vigorously **3 a** : to shatter by or as if by an explosive **b :** to remove, open, or form by or as if by an explosive **c :** SHOOT **4 :** to apply a forced draft to **5** : to cause to blast off ⟨will ~ themselves from the moon's surface⟩ **6** : to hit vigorously and effectively — **blast·er** *n* — **blast·ing** *n or adj*

blast- *or* **blasto-** *comb form* [G, fr. Gk, fr. *blastos*] : bud : budding : germ ⟨*blasto*disc⟩ ⟨*blast*ula⟩

-blast \ˌblast\ *n comb form* [NL *-blastus,* fr. Gk *blastos* bud, shoot; akin to OE *molda* top of the head, Skt *mūrdhan* head] : formative unit esp. of living matter : germ : cell : cell layer ⟨epi*blast*⟩

blast·ed *adj* (1552) **1 :** damaged by or as if by an explosive, lightning, wind, or supernatural force ⟨upon this ~ heath—Shak.⟩ ⟨a ~ apple tree⟩ **2 :** DAMNED, DETESTABLE ⟨this ~ weather⟩

blas·te·ma \bla-'stē-mə\ *n, pl* **-mas** *or* **-ma·ta** \-mət-ə\ [NL, fr. Gk *blastēma* offshoot, fr. *blastos*] (1849) : a mass of living substance capable of growth and differentiation — **blas·te·mal** \-məl\ *or* **blas·te·mat·ic** \ˌblas-tə-'mat-ik\ *adj*

blast furnace *n* (1706) : a furnace in which combustion is forced by a current of air under pressure; *esp* : one for the reduction of iron ore

-blas·tic \'blas-tik\ *adj comb form* [ISV, fr. *-blast*] : having (such or so many) buds, germs, cells, or cell layers ⟨diplo*blastic*⟩

blast·ie \'blas-tē\ *n* [Sc *blast* to wither, fr. [2]*blast*] *Scot* (1787) : an ugly little creature

blast·ment \'blas(t)-mənt\ *n, archaic* (1602) : a blighting influence

blas·to·coel *or* **blas·to·coele** \'blas-tə-ˌsēl\ *n* [ISV] (1877) : the cavity of a blastula — see BLASTULA illustration — **blas·to·coe·lic** \ˌblas-tə-'sē-lik\ *adj*

blas·to·cyst \'blas-tə-ˌsist\ *n* (ca. 1890) : the modified blastula of a placental mammal

blas·to·derm \-ˌdərm\ *n* [G, fr. *blast-* + *-derm*] (1859) : a blastodisc after completion of cleavage and formation of the blastocoel

blas·to·der·mic vesicle \ˌblas-tə-ˌdər-mik-\ *n* (1836) : BLASTOCYST

blas·to·disc \'blas-tə-ˌdisk\ *n* (ca. 1887) : the embryo-forming portion of an egg with discoidal cleavage usu. appearing as a small disc on the upper surface of the yolk mass — see EGG illustration

blast–off \'blas-ˌtȯf\ *n* (1951) : a blasting off (as of a rocket)

blast off \(')blas-'tȯf\ *vi* (1951) : TAKE OFF 2d — used esp. of rocket-propelled missiles and vehicles

blas·to·mere \'blas-tə-ˌmi(ə)r\ *n* [ISV] (1877) : a cell produced during cleavage of an egg — **blas·to·mer·ic** \ˌblas-tə-'mi(ə)r-ik, -'mer-\ *adj*

blas·to·my·cete \ˌblas-tə-'mī-ˌsēt, -ˌmī-'sēt\ *n* [deriv. of *blast-* + Gk *mykēt-, mykēs* fungus — more at MYC-] (ca. 1900) : any of a group (Blastomycetes) of pathogenic fungi growing typically like yeasts

blas·to·my·co·sis \-ˌmī-'kō-səs\ *n* (ca. 1900) : a disease caused by a blastomycete — **blas·to·my·cot·ic** \-'kät-ik\ *adj*

blas·to·pore \'blas-tə-ˌpō(ə)r, -ˌpȯ(ə)r\ *n* (1880) : the opening of the archenteron — **blas·to·por·ic** \-'pōr-ik, -'pȯr-\ *adj*

blas·to·spore \'blas-tə-ˌspō(ə)r, -ˌspȯ(ə)r\ *n* [*blast-* + *spore*] (ca. 1923) : a fungous spore produced by budding

blas·tu·la \'blas-chə-lə\ *n, pl* **-las** *or* **-lae** \-ˌlē\ [NL, fr. Gk *blastos*] (1887) : an early metazoan embryo typically having the form of a hollow fluid-filled rounded cavity bounded by a single layer of cells — compare GASTRULA, MORULA — **blas·tu·la·tion** \ˌblas-chə-'lā-shən\ *n*

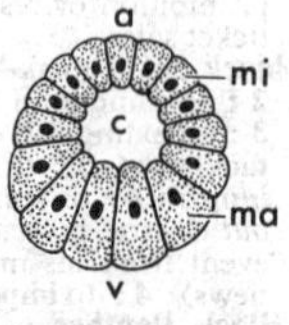

section of blastula: *c* blastocoel, *ma* macromere, *mi* micromere, *a* animal pole, *v* vegetal pole

blat \'blat\ *vb* **blat·ted; blat·ting** [perh. alter. of *bleat*] *vi* (1846) **1 :** to cry like a calf or sheep : BLEAT **2 a :** to make a raucous noise **b :** BLAB ~ *vt* **:** to utter loudly or foolishly : BLURT — **blat** *n*

bla·tan·cy \'blāt-ᵊn-sē\ *n, pl* **-cies** (1610) **1 :** the quality or state of being blatant **2 :** something that is blatant

bla·tant \'blāt-ᵊnt\ *adj* [perh. fr. L *blatire* to chatter] (1596) **1 :** noisy esp. in a vulgar or offensive manner : CLAMOROUS **2 :** completely obvious, conspicuous, or obtrusive esp. in a crass or offensive manner : BRAZEN *syn* see VOCIFEROUS — **bla·tant·ly** *adv*

blate \'blāt\ *adj* [ME] *chiefly Scot* (1535) : TIMID, SHEEPISH

[1]**blath·er** \'blath-ər\ *vi* **blath·ered; blath·er·ing** \-(ə-)riŋ\ [ON *blathra;* akin to MHG *blōdern* to chatter] (1524) : to talk foolishly — **blath·er·er** \-ər-ər\ *n*

[2]**blather** *n* (1719) **1 :** voluble or nonsensical talk **2 :** STIR, COMMOTION

blath·er·skite \'blath-ər-ˌskīt\ *n* [*blather* + Sc dial. *skate* a contemptible person] (ca. 1650) **1 :** a person who blathers and blusters **2 :** NONSENSE, BLATHER

blat·ter \'blat-ər\ *vi* [perh. fr. L *blaterare* to chatter — more at BLATANT] *dial* (1555) : to talk noisily and fast

blaw \'blȯ\ *vb* **blawed; blawn** \'blȯn\; **blaw·ing** \'blȯ(-)iŋ\ [ME (northern dial.) *blawen,* fr. OE *blāwan*] *chiefly Scot* (15c) : BLOW

[1]**blaze** \'blāz\ *n* [ME *blase,* fr. OE *blæse* torch] (bef. 12c) **1 a :** an intensely burning fire **b :** intense direct light often accompanied by heat ⟨the ~ of TV lights⟩ **c :** an active burning; *esp* : a sudden bursting forth of flame **2 :** something that resembles the blaze of a fire: as **a :** a dazzling display **b :** a sudden outburst ⟨a ~ of fury⟩ **c** *pl* : HELL ⟨go to ~*s*⟩

[2]**blaze** *vi* **blazed; blaz·ing** (13c) **1 a :** to burn brightly ⟨the sun *blazed* overhead⟩ **b :** to flare up : FLAME ⟨inflation *blazed* up⟩ **2 :** to be conspicuously brilliant or resplendent ⟨fields *blazing* with flowers⟩ **3** : to shoot rapidly and repeatedly — usu. used with *away*

[3]**blaze** *vt* **blazed; blaz·ing** [ME *blasen,* fr. MD *blāsen* to blow; akin to OHG *blāst* blast] (14c) : to make public or conspicuous : PROCLAIM

[4]**blaze** *n* [G *blas,* fr. OHG *plas;* akin to OE *blæse*] (1639) **1 a :** a white mark on the face of an animal **b :** a white or gray streak in the hair of the head **2 :** a trail marker; *esp* : a mark made on a tree by chipping off a piece of the bark

[5]**blaze** *vt* **blazed; blaz·ing** (1750) **1 :** to mark (as a trail) with blazes **2** : to lead or pioneer in some direction or activity ⟨~ new trails in education⟩

blaz·er \'blā-zər\ *n* (1635) **1 :** one that blazes **2 :** a sports jacket often with notched collar and patch pockets

blaz·ing *adj* (1596) : of outstanding power, speed, heat, or intensity ⟨~ eyes⟩ ⟨a ~ fastball⟩ ⟨~ gunfire⟩ — **blaz·ing·ly** *adv*

blazing star *n* (15c) **1** *archaic* : COMET **2 :** any of several plants having conspicuous flower clusters: as **a :** a plant (*Chamaelirium luteum*) of the lily family **b :** BUTTON SNAKEROOT 1

[1]**bla·zon** \'blāz-ᵊn\ *n* [ME *blason,* fr. MF] (14c) **1 a :** armorial bearings : COAT OF ARMS **b :** the proper description or representation of heraldic or armorial bearings **2 :** ostentatious display

[2]**blazon** *vt* **bla·zoned; bla·zon·ing** \'blāz-niŋ, -ᵊn-iŋ\ (1534) **1 :** to publish widely : PROCLAIM **2 a :** to describe (heraldic or armorial bearings) in technical terms **b :** to represent (armorial bearings) in drawing or engraving **3 a :** DISPLAY **b :** DECK, ADORN ⟨the town was ~*ed* with flags⟩ — **bla·zon·er** \-nər, -ᵊn-ər\ *n* — **blazoning** *n*

bla·zon·ry \'blāz-ᵊn-rē\ *n, pl* **-ries** (1622) **1 a :** BLAZON 1b **b :** BLAZON 1a **2 :** a dazzling display

[1]**bleach** \'blēch\ *vb* [ME *blechen,* fr. OE *blǣcean;* akin to OE *blāc* pale] *vt* (bef. 12c) **1 :** to remove color or stains from **2 :** to make whiter or lighter esp. by physical or chemical removal of color ~ *vi* **:** to grow white or lose color — **bleach·able** \'blē-chə-bəl\ *adj*

[2]**bleach** *n* (1887) **1 :** the act or process of bleaching **2 :** a preparation used in bleaching **3 :** the degree of whiteness obtained by bleaching

bleach·er \'blē-chər\ *n* (1550) **1 :** one that bleaches or is used in bleaching **2 :** a usu. uncovered stand of tiered planks providing seating space for spectators — usu. used in pl. — **bleach·er·ite** \-chə-ˌrīt\ *n*

bleaching powder *n* (1847) : a white powder consisting chiefly of calcium hydroxide, calcium chloride, and calcium hypochlorite and used as a bleach, disinfectant, or deodorant

bleak \'blēk\ *adj* [ME *bleke* pale; prob. akin to OE *blāc*] (1538) **1 :** exposed and barren and often windswept **2 :** COLD, RAW ⟨a ~ November evening⟩ **3 a :** lacking in warmth or kindliness **b :** not hopeful or encouraging : DEPRESSING, DISCOURAGING ⟨a ~ outlook⟩ **c :** severely simple or austere — **bleak·ish** \'blē-kish\ *adj* — **bleak·ly** *adv* — **bleak·ness** *n*

[1]**blear** \'bli(ə)r\ *vt* [ME *bleren*] (14c) **1 :** to make (the eyes) sore or watery **2 :** DIM, BLUR

[2]**blear** *adj* (14c) **1 :** dim with water or tears **2 :** obscure to the view or imagination

blear–eyed \-'īd\ *adj* (14c) **:** BLEARY-EYED

bleary \'bli(ə)r-ē\ *adj* (14c) **1** *of the eyes or vision* **:** dull or dimmed esp. from fatigue or sleep **2 :** poorly outlined or defined **:** DIM **3 :** tired to the point of exhaustion — **blear·i·ly** \'blir-ə-lē\ *adv* — **blear·i·ness** \'blir-ē-nəs\ *n*

bleary–eyed \-'īd\ *adj* (ca. 1927) **:** having the eyes dimmed and watery (as from fatigue, drink, or emotion)

[1]**bleat** \'blēt, *Northern also* 'blat, *Southern usu* 'blāt\ *vb* [ME *bleten,* fr. OE *blǣtan;* akin to L *flēre* to weep, OE *bellan* to roar — more at BELLOW] *vi* (bef. 12c) **1 a :** to utter the natural cry of a sheep or goat **b :** to make a sound resembling this cry **c :** WHIMPER **2 a :** to talk complainingly or with a whine **b :** BLATHER ~ *vt* **:** to utter in a bleating manner — **bleat·er** *n*

[2]**bleat** *n* (1590) **1 a :** the cry of a sheep or goat **b :** a sound resembling this cry **2 :** a feeble outcry, protest, or complaint

bleb \'bleb\ *n* [perh. alter. of *blob*] (1607) **1 :** a small blister **2 :** BUBBLE; *also* **:** a small particle — **bleb·by** \'bleb-ē\ *adj*

[1]**bleed** \'blēd\ *vb* **bled** \'bled\; **bleed·ing** [ME *bleden,* fr. OE *blēdan,* fr. *blōd* blood] *vi* (bef. 12c) **1 a :** to emit or lose blood **b :** to sacrifice one's blood esp. in battle **2 :** to feel anguish, pain, or sympathy ⟨a heart that ~*s* at a friend's misfortune⟩ **3 :** to escape by oozing or flowing (as from a wound) **4 :** to give up some constituent (as sap or dye) by exuding or diffusing it **5 a :** to pay out or give money **b :** to have money extorted **6 :** to be printed so as to run off one or more edges of the page after trimming ~ *vt* **1 :** to remove or draw blood from **2 :** to get or extort money from **3 :** to draw sap from (a tree) **4 a :** to extract or let out some or all of a contained substance from ⟨~ a tire⟩ **b :** to extract or cause to escape from a container **5 :** to cause (as a printed illustration) to bleed — **bleed white :** to drain of blood or resources

[2]**bleed** *n* (ca. 1937) **:** an illustration or a page that bleeds or is bled; *also* **:** the part trimmed off in bleeding

bleed·er *n* (1803) **1 :** one that bleeds; *esp* **:** HEMOPHILIAC **2** *Brit* **:** ROTTER; *also* **:** BLOKE

bleed·ing \'blēd-iŋ, -ᵊn\ *adj or adv, chiefly Brit* (1858) **:** BLOODY — used as an intensive

bleeding heart *n* (1691) **1 :** a garden plant (*Dicentra spectabilis*) of the fumitory family with racemes of deep pink drooping heart-shaped flowers; *broadly* **:** any of several plants (genus *Dicentra*) **2 :** one who shows extravagant sympathy esp. for an object of alleged persecution

[1]**bleep** \'blēp\ *n* [imit.] (1953) **:** a short high-pitched sound (as from electronic equipment)

[2]**bleep** *vt* (1968) **:** BLIP

[3]**bleep** *interj* (1970) — used in place of an expletive

blel·lum \'blel-əm\ *n* [perh. blend of Sc *bleber* to babble and *skellum* rascal] *Scot* (1790) **:** a lazy talkative person

[1]**blem·ish** \'blem-ish\ *vt* [ME *blemisshen,* fr. MF *blesmiss-,* stem of *blesmir* to make pale, wound] (14c) **:** to spoil by a flaw

[2]**blemish** *n* (1535) **:** a noticeable imperfection; *esp* **:** one that seriously impairs appearance

syn BLEMISH, DEFECT, FLAW mean an imperfection that mars or damages. BLEMISH suggests something that affects only the surface or appearance; DEFECT implies a lack, often hidden, of something that is essential to completeness or perfect functioning; FLAW suggests a small defect in continuity or cohesion that is likely to cause failure under stress.

[1]**blench** \'blench\ *vi* [ME *blenchen* to deceive, blench, fr. OE *blencan* to deceive; akin to ON *blekkja* to impose on] (bef. 12c) **:** to draw back or turn aside from lack of courage **:** FLINCH *syn* see RECOIL

[2]**blench** *vb* [alter. of *blanch*] (1813) **:** BLEACH, WHITEN

[1]**blend** \'blend\ *vb* **blend·ed** *also* **blent** \'blent\; **blend·ing** [ME *blenden,* modif. of ON *blanda;* akin to OE *blandan* to mix] *vt* (13c) **1 :** MIX; *esp* **:** to combine or associate so that the separate constituents or the line of demarcation cannot be distinguished **2 :** to prepare by thoroughly intermingling different varieties or grades ~ *vi* **1 a :** to mingle intimately **b :** to combine into an integrated whole **2 :** to produce a harmonious effect *syn* see MIX

[2]**blend** *n* (1883) **1 :** something produced by blending: as **a :** a product prepared by blending **b :** a word (as *brunch*) produced by combining other words or parts of words **2 :** a group of two or more consecutive consonants that begin a syllable

blende \'blend\ *n* [G, fr. *blenden* to blind, fr. OHG *blenten;* akin to OE *blind*] (1753) **1 :** SPHALERITE **2 :** any of several minerals (as metallic sulfides) with somewhat bright but nonmetallic luster

blended whiskey *n* (1940) **:** whiskey consisting of either a blend of two or more straight whiskeys or a blend of whiskey and neutral spirits

blend·er \'blen-dər\ *n* (1798) **:** one that blends; *esp* **:** an electric appliance for grinding or mixing ⟨a food ~⟩

blending inheritance *n* (ca. 1922) **:** inheritance by the progeny of characters intermediate between those of the parents

blen·ny \'blen-ē\ *n, pl* **blennies** [L *blennius,* a sea fish, fr. Gk *blennos*] (1774) **:** any of numerous usu. small and elongated and often scaleless fishes (Blenniidae and related families) living about rocky shores

blephar- *or* **blepharo-** *comb form* [NL, fr. Gk, fr. *blepharon*] **1 :** eyelid ⟨*blepharo*spasm⟩ **2 :** cilium **:** flagellum ⟨*blepharo*plast⟩

bleph·a·ro·plast \'blef-ə-rō-ˌplast\ *n* (1897) **:** a basal body esp. of a flagellated cell

bles·bok \'bles-ˌbäk\ *n* [Afrik, fr. *bles* blaze + *bok* male antelope] (1824) **:** a So. African antelope (*Damaliscus albifrons*) having a large white spot on the face

bless \'bles\ *vt* **blessed** \'blest\ *also* **blest** \'blest\; **bless·ing** [ME *blessen,* fr. OE *blētsian,* fr. *blōd* blood; fr. the use of blood in consecration] (bef. 12c) **1 :** to hallow or consecrate by religious rite or word **2 :** to hallow with the sign of the cross **3 :** to invoke divine care for **4 a :** PRAISE, GLORIFY ⟨~ his holy name⟩ **b :** to speak gratefully of ⟨~*ed* him for his kindness⟩ **5 :** to confer prosperity or happiness upon **6** *archaic* **:** PROTECT, PRESERVE

bless·ed \'bles-əd\ *also* **blest** \'blest\ *adj* (13c) **1 a :** held in reverence **:** VENERATED ⟨the ~ saints⟩ **b :** honored in worship **:** HALLOWED ⟨the ~ Trinity⟩ **c :** BEATIFIC ⟨a ~ visitation⟩ **2 :** of or enjoying happiness; *specif* **:** enjoying the bliss of heaven — used as a title for a beatified person **3 :** bringing pleasure or contentment **4** — used as an intensive ⟨no one gave us a ~ penny — *Saturday Rev.*⟩ — **bless·ed·ly** *adv* — **bless·ed·ness** *n*

Bless·ed Sacrament \ˌbles-əd-\ *n* (1556) **:** the Communion elements; *specif* **:** the consecrated host

bless·ing *n* (bef. 12c) **1 a :** the act or words of one that blesses **b :** APPROVAL, ENCOURAGEMENT **2 :** a thing conducive to happiness or welfare **3 :** grace said at a meal

bleth·er \'bleth-ər\ *var of* BLATHER

blew *past of* BLOW

[1]**blight** \'blīt\ *n* [origin unknown] (1669) **1 a :** a disease or injury of plants resulting in withering, cessation of growth, and death of parts without rotting **b :** an organism that causes blight **2 :** something that frustrates plans or hopes **3 :** something that impairs or destroys **4 :** an impaired condition ⟨urban ~⟩

[2]**blight** *vt* (1695) **1 :** to affect (as a plant) with blight **2 :** to cause to deteriorate ~ *vi* **:** to suffer from or become affected with blight

blight·er \'blīt-ər\ *n* (1822) **1 :** one that blights **2** *chiefly Brit* **a :** one who is held in low esteem **b :** FELLOW, GUY

blimp \'blimp\ *n* [imit.; perh. fr. the sound made by striking the gas bag with the thumb] (1916) **1 :** a nonrigid airship **2** *cap* **:** COLONEL BLIMP

blimp·ish \'blim-pish\ *adj, often cap* (1938) **:** of, relating to, or suggesting a Colonel Blimp — **blimp·ish·ly** *adv* — **blimp·ish·ness** *n*

blin \'blin\ *n, pl* **bli·ni** \'blē-nē, 'blin-ē, blə-'nē\ *or* **bli·nis** \'blē-nēz, 'blin-ēz, blə-'nēz\ [Russ] (1888) **:** a thin pancake usu. filled (as with sour cream) and folded

[1]**blind** \'blīnd\ *adj* [ME, fr. OE; akin to OHG *blint* blind and prob. to OE *blandan* to mix] (bef. 12c) **1 a** (1) **:** SIGHTLESS (2) **:** having less than $^1/_{10}$ of normal vision in the more efficient eye when refractive defects are fully corrected by lenses **b :** of or relating to sightless persons **2 a :** unable or unwilling to discern or judge ⟨~ to a lover's faults⟩ **b :** UNQUESTIONING ⟨~ loyalty⟩ ⟨~ faith⟩ **3 a :** having no regard to rational discrimination, guidance, or restriction ⟨~ choice⟩ **b :** lacking a directing or controlling consciousness ⟨~ chance⟩ **c :** DRUNK **4 :** made or done without sight of certain objects or knowledge of certain facts that could serve for guidance ⟨a ~ taste test⟩; *esp* **:** performed solely by the aid of instruments within an airplane ⟨a ~ landing⟩ **5 :** DEFECTIVE: as **a :** lacking a growing point or producing leaves instead of flowers **b :** lacking a complete or legible address ⟨~ mail⟩ **6 a :** difficult to discern, make out, or discover **b :** hidden from sight **:** COVERED ⟨~ seam⟩ **7 :** having but one opening or outlet ⟨~ sockets⟩ **8 :** having no opening for light or passage **:** BLANK ⟨~ wall⟩ — **blind·ly** \'blīn-(d)lē\ *adv* — **blind·ness** \'blīn(d)-nəs\ *n*

[2]**blind** *vt* (bef. 12c) **1 a :** to make blind **b :** DAZZLE **2 a :** to withhold light from **b :** HIDE, CONCEAL — **blind·ing·ly** \'blīn-diŋ-lē\ *adv*

[3]**blind** *n* (1702) **1 :** something to hinder sight or keep out light: as **a :** a window shutter **b :** a roller window shade **c :** VENETIAN BLIND **d :** BLINDER **2 :** a place of concealment; *esp* **:** a concealing enclosure from which one may shoot game or observe wildlife **3 a :** something put forward for the purpose of misleading **:** SUBTERFUGE **b** (1) **:** a person serving as an agent for another who keeps under cover (2) **:** one who acts as a decoy or distraction

[4]**blind** *adv* (1840) **1 :** BLINDLY: as **a :** to the point of insensibility ⟨~ drunk⟩ **b :** without seeing outside an airplane ⟨fly ~⟩ **2** — used as an intensive ⟨was robbed ~⟩

blind alley *n* (1583) **:** a fruitless or mistaken course or direction

blind date *n* (1925) **1 :** a date between two persons who have not previously met **2 :** either participant in a blind date

blind·er \'blīn-dər\ *n* (1809) **1 :** either of two flaps on a horse's bridle to prevent sight of objects at his sides **2** *pl* **:** an obstruction to sight or discernment

blind·fish \'blīn(d)-ˌfish\ *n* (1843) **:** any of several small fishes with vestigial functionless eyes found usu. in the waters of caves

[1]**blind·fold** \-ˌfōld\ *vt* [ME *blindfellen, blindfelden* to strike blind, blindfold, fr. *blind* + *fellen* to fell] (13c) **1 :** to cover the eyes of with or as if with a bandage **2 :** to hinder from seeing; *esp* **:** to keep from comprehension — **blindfold** *adj*

[2]**blindfold** *n* (1880) **1 :** a bandage for covering the eyes **2 :** something that obscures mental or physical vision

blind gut *n* (15c) **:** a digestive cavity open at only one end; *esp* **:** the cecum of the large intestine

blind·man's buff \ˌblīn(d)-ˌmanz-\ *n* (1600) **:** a group game in which a blindfolded player tries to catch and identify another player

blind pig *n* (1887) **:** BLIND TIGER

blind·side \'blīn(d)-ˌsīd\ *vt* (1972) **:** to hit unexpectedly from or as if from the blind side

blind side *n* (1655) **1 :** the side on which one that is blind in one eye cannot see **2 :** the side away from which one is looking

blind spot *n* (1864) **1 a :** the nearly circular light-colored area at the back of the retina where the optic nerve enters the eyeball and which is not sensitive to light — called also *optic disk;* see EYE illustration **b :** a portion of a field that cannot be seen or inspected with available equipment **2 :** an area in which one fails to exercise judgment or discrimination **3 :** a locality in which radio reception is markedly poorer than in the surrounding area

blind tiger *n* (1857) **:** a place that sells intoxicants illegally

blind trust *n* (1970) **:** an arrangement by which a person in a sensitive position protects himself from possible conflict of interest charges by placing his financial affairs in the hands of a fiduciary and giving up all right to know about or intervene in their handling

blind·worm \'blīn-ˌdwərm\ *n* (15c) **:** SLOWWORM

[1]**blink** \'bliŋk\ *vb* [ME *blinken* to open one's eyes] *vi* (14c) **1 a** *obs* **:** to look glancingly **:** PEEP **b :** to look with half-shut eyes **c :** to close and open the eyes involuntarily (as when struggling against drowsiness or

\ə\ abut \ᵊ\ kitten, F table \ər\ further \a\ ash \ā\ ace \ä\ cot, cart \au̇\ out \ch\ chin \e\ bet \ē\ easy \g\ go \i\ hit \ī\ ice \j\ job \ŋ\ sing \ō\ go \ȯ\ law \ȯi\ boy \th\ thin \th\ the \ü\ loot \u̇\ foot \y\ yet \zh\ vision \à, k, ⁿ, œ, œ̄, ue, ue̅, ʸ\ *see* Guide to Pronunciation

when dazzled) **2 :** to shine dimly or intermittently **3 a :** to look with too little concern **b :** to look with surprise or dismay ~ *vt* **1 a :** to cause to blink **b :** to remove (as tears) from the eye by blinking **2 :** to deny recognition to

[2]blink *n* (1594) **1** *chiefly Scot* **:** GLIMPSE, GLANCE **2 :** GLIMMER, SPARKLE **3 :** a usu. involuntary shutting and opening of the eye **4 :** ICEBLINK — **on the blink :** in or into a disabled or useless condition

[1]blink·er \'bliŋ-kər\ *n* (1636) **1 :** one that blinks; *esp* **:** a light that flashes off and on (as for the directing of traffic or the coded signaling of messages) **2 a :** BLINDER 1 **b :** a cloth hood with shades projecting at the sides of the eye openings used on skittish racehorses — usu. used in pl. **3** *pl* **:** BLINDER 2

[2]blinker *vt* (1865) **:** to put blinders on

blin·tze \'blin(t)-sə\ *or* **blintz** \'blin(t)s\ *n* [Yiddish *blintse,* fr. Russ *blinets,* dim. of *blin* pancake] (1903) **:** a wheat-flour blin folded to form a casing and then sautéed or baked

[1]blip \'blip\ *n* [imit.] (1953) **1 :** a short crisp sound **2 :** a trace on an oscilloscope; *esp* **:** an image on a radar screen **3 :** an interruption of the sound received in a radio or television program or occurring in a recording as a result of blipping **4 :** ABERRATION 1

[2]blip *vt* **blipped; blip·ping** (1968) **:** to remove (recorded sound) from a recording so that there is an interruption of the sound in the reproduction 〈a censor *blipped* the swearwords〉

bliss \'blis\ *n* [ME *blisse,* fr. OE *bliss;* akin to OE *blīthe* blithe] (bef. 12c) **1 :** complete happiness **2 :** PARADISE, HEAVEN

bliss·ful \'blis-fəl\ *adj* (13c) **:** full of, marked by, or causing bliss — **bliss·ful·ly** \-fə-lē\ *adv* — **bliss·ful·ness** *n*

[1]blis·ter \'blis-tər\ *n* [ME, modif. of OF or MD; OF *blostre* boil, fr. MD *bluyster* blister; akin to OE *blǣst* blast] (14c) **1 :** an elevation of the epidermis containing watery liquid **2 :** an enclosed raised spot (as in paint) resembling a blister **3 :** an agent that causes blistering **4 :** a disease of plants marked by large swollen patches on the leaves **5 :** any of various structures (as a gunner's compartment on an airplane) that bulge out — **blis·tery** \-t(ə-)rē\ *adj*

[2]blister *vb* **blis·tered; blis·ter·ing** \-t(ə-)riŋ\ *vi* (15c) **:** to become affected with a blister ~ *vt* **1 :** to raise a blister on **2 :** to deal with severely 〈~*ed* his opponent with charges of fraud〉

blister beetle *n* (1816) **:** a beetle (as the Spanish fly) used medicinally dried and powdered to raise blisters on the skin; *broadly* **:** any of numerous soft-bodied beetles (family Meloidae)

blister copper *n* (1861) **:** metallic copper of a black blistered surface that is the product of converting copper matte and is about 98.5 to 99.5 percent pure

blis·ter·ing *adj* (1542) **:** extremely intense or severe — **blistering** *adv* — **blis·ter·ing·ly** \-t(ə-)riŋ-lē\ *adv*

blister pack *n* (1955) **:** a package holding and displaying merchandise in a clear plastic case sealed to a sheet of cardboard

blister rust *n* (1916) **:** any of several diseases of pines that are caused by rust fungi (genus *Cronartium*) in the aecial stage and that affect the sapwood and inner bark and produce blisters externally

blithe \'blīth, 'blīth\ *adj* **blith·er; blith·est** [ME, fr. OE *blīthe;* akin to OHG *blīdi* joyous] (bef. 12c) **1 :** of a happy lighthearted character or disposition **2 :** CASUAL, HEEDLESS 〈~ unconcern〉 *syn* see MERRY — **blithe·ly** *adv*

blith·er \'blith-ər\ *vi or n* (1868) **:** BLATHER

blithe·some \'blīth-səm, 'blīth-\ *adj* (1724) **:** GAY, MERRY — **blithe·some·ly** *adv*

blitz \'blits\ *n* (1939) **1 a :** BLITZKRIEG 1 **b** (1) **:** an intensive aerial campaign (2) **:** AIR RAID **2 a :** an intensive nonmilitary campaign **:** a sudden overpowering bombardment **b :** a rush of the passer by the defensive linebackers in football — **blitz** *vb*

blitz·krieg \-ˌkrēg\ *n* [G, lit., lightning war, fr. *blitz* lightning + *krieg* war] (1939) **1 :** war conducted with great speed and force; *specif* **:** a violent surprise offensive by massed air forces and mechanized ground forces in close coordination **2 :** BLITZ 2a

bliz·zard \'bliz-ərd\ *n* [origin unknown] (1859) **1 :** a long severe snowstorm **2 :** an intensely strong cold wind filled with fine snow **3 :** an overwhelming rush or deluge 〈the ~ of mail at Christmas〉 — **blizzardy** \-ē\ *adj*

[1]bloat \'blōt\ *adj* [alter. of ME *blout*] (14c) **:** BLOATED, PUFFY

[2]bloat *vt* (1677) **1 :** to make turgid or swollen **2 :** to fill to capacity or overflowing ~ *vi* **:** SWELL

[3]bloat *n* (1860) **1 :** one that is bloated **2 :** a flatulent digestive disturbance of domestic animals and esp. cattle marked by abdominal bloating

bloat·ed *adj* (1711) **1 :** being much larger than what is warranted 〈a ~ estimate〉 **2 :** obnoxiously vain

[1]bloat·er \'blōt-ər\ *n* [obs. *bloat* (to cure)] (1832) **:** a large fat herring or mackerel lightly salted and briefly smoked

[2]bloater *n* [[2]*bloat*] (ca. 1934) **:** a small but common cisco (*Coregonus hoyi*) of the Great Lakes

[1]blob \'bläb\ *n* [ME] (15c) **1 a :** a small drop or lump of something viscid or thick **b :** a daub or spot of color **2 :** something ill-defined or amorphous

[2]blob *vt* **blobbed; blob·bing** (15c) **:** to mark with blobs **:** SPLOTCH

bloc \'bläk\ *n* [F, lit., block] (1903) **1 a :** a temporary combination of parties in a legislative assembly **b :** a group of legislators (as in a U.S. legislative assembly) who act together for some common purpose irrespective of party lines **2 a :** a combination of persons, groups, or nations forming a unit with a common interest or purpose **b :** a group of nations united by treaty or agreement for mutual support or joint action

[1]block \'bläk\ *n, often attrib* [ME *blok,* fr. MF *bloc,* fr. MD *blok;* akin to OHG *bloh* block, MIr *blog* fragment] (14c) **1 :** a compact usu. solid piece of substantial material esp. when worked or altered from its natural state to serve a particular purpose: as **a :** the piece of wood on which a person condemned to be beheaded lays his neck for execution **b :** a mold or form on which articles are shaped or displayed **c :** a hollow rectangular building unit usu. of artificial material **d :** a lightweight usu. cubical and solid wooden or plastic building toy that is usu. provided in sets **e :** the casting that contains the cylinders of an internal-combustion engine **2** *slang* **:** HEAD 1 **3 a :** OBSTACLE **b :** an obstruction of an opponent's play in sports; *esp* **:** a halting or impeding of the progress or movement of an opponent in football by use of the body **c :** interruption of normal physiological function (as of a tissue or organ); *esp* **:** HEART BLOCK **d :** an instance or the result of psychological blockage or blocking **4 :** a wooden or metal case enclosing one or more pulleys and having a hook, eye, or strap by which it may be attached **5 :** a platform from which property is sold at auction; *broadly* **:** sale at auction **6 a :** a quantity, number, or section of things dealt with as a unit **b** (1) **:** a large building divided into separate functional units (2) **:** a line of row houses (3) **:** a part of a building or integrated group of buildings distinctive in some respect **c** (1) **:** a usu. rectangular space (as in a city) enclosed by streets and occupied by or intended for buildings (2) **:** the distance along one of the sides of such a block **d :** a length of railroad track of defined limits the use of which is governed by block signals **7 :** a piece of material (as wood or linoleum) having on its surface a hand-cut design from which impressions are to be printed

[2]block *vt* (1580) **1 a :** to make unsuitable for passage or progress by obstruction **b** *archaic* **:** BLOCKADE **c :** to hinder the passage, progress, or accomplishment of by or as if by interposing an obstruction **d :** to shut off from view 〈forest canopy ~*ing* the sun〉 **e :** to interfere usu. legitimately with (as an opponent) in various games or sports **f :** to prevent normal functioning of **g :** to restrict the exchange of (as currency or checks) **2 :** to mark or indicate the outline or chief lines of 〈~ out a design〉 〈~ in a sketched figure〉 **3 :** to shape on, with, or as if with a block 〈~ a hat〉 **4 :** to make (two or more lines of writing or type) flush at the left or at both left and right **5 :** to secure, support, or provide with a block **6 :** to work out or chart the movements of (as stage performers) ~ *vi* **:** to block an opponent in sports *syn* see HINDER — **block·er** *n*

[1]block·ade \blä-'kād\ *vt* **block·ad·ed; block·ad·ing** (1680) **1 :** to subject to a blockade **2 :** BLOCK, OBSTRUCT — **block·ad·er** *n*

[2]blockade *n* (1693) **1 :** the isolation by a warring nation of a particular enemy area (as a harbor) by means of troops or warships to prevent passage of persons or supplies; *broadly* **:** a restrictive measure designed to obstruct the commerce and communications of an unfriendly nation **2 :** something that constitutes an obstacle **3 :** interruption of normal physiological function (as transmission of nerve impulses) of a tissue or organ

block·ade–run·ner \-'kād-ˌrən-ər\ *n* (1863) **:** a ship or person that runs through a blockade — **block·ade–run·ning** \-ˌrən-iŋ\ *n*

block·age \'bläk-ij\ *n* (1874) **:** an act or instance of obstructing **:** the state of being blocked 〈a ~ in the saltshaker〉

block and tackle *n* (1838) **:** pulley blocks with associated rope or cable for hoisting or hauling

block·bust·er \'bläk-ˌbəs-tər\ *n* (1942) **1 :** a huge high-explosive demolition bomb **2 :** one that is notably effective, successful, large, or violent **3 :** one who engages in blockbusting

block·bust·ing \-tiŋ\ *n* (1954) **:** profiteering by inducing property owners to sell hastily and often at a loss by appeals to fears of depressed values because of threatened minority encroachment and then reselling at inflated prices

block diagram *n* (1944) **:** a diagram (as of a system, process, or program) in which labeled figures (as rectangles) and interconnecting lines represent the relationship of parts

block grant *n* (1924) **:** an unrestricted federal grant

block·head \'bläk-ˌhed\ *n* (1589) **:** a stupid person

block·house \-ˌhau̇s\ *n* (1512) **1 a :** a structure of heavy timbers formerly used for military defense with sides loopholed and pierced for gunfire and often with a projecting upper story **b :** a small easily defended building for protection from enemy fire **2 :** a building usu. of reinforced concrete serving as an observation point for an operation likely to be accompanied by heat, blast, or radiation hazard

blockhouse 1a

block·ish \-ish\ *adj* (1565) **:** resembling a block

block letter *n* (1908) **:** an often hand-drawn simple capital letter composed of strokes of uniform thickness

block plane *n* (1884) **:** a small plane made with the blade set at a lower pitch than other planes and used chiefly on end grains of wood

block signal *n* (1882) **:** a fixed signal at the entrance of a block to govern railroad trains entering and using that block

block system *n* (1864) **:** a system by which a railroad track is divided into short sections and trains are run by guidance signals

blocky \'bläk-ē\ *adj* **block·i·er; -est** (1879) **1 :** resembling a block in form or massiveness **:** CHUNKY **2 :** filled with or made up of blocks or patches

bloke \'blōk\ *n* [origin unknown] *chiefly Brit* (1851) **:** MAN, FELLOW

[1]blond *or* **blonde** \'bländ\ *adj* [MF *blond,* masc., *blonde,* fem.] (15c) **1 a :** of a flaxen, golden, light auburn, or pale yellowish brown color 〈~ hair〉 **b :** of a pale white or rosy white color 〈~ skin〉 **c :** being a blond 〈a pretty ~ secretary〉 **2 a :** of a light color **b :** of the color blond **c :** made light-colored by bleaching 〈a table of ~ walnut〉 — **blond·ish** \'blän-dish\ *adj*

[2]blond *or* **blonde** *n* (1822) **1 :** a person having blond hair and usu. a light complexion and blue or gray eyes **2 :** a light yellowish brown to dark grayish yellow

[1]blood \'bləd\ *n, often attrib* [ME, fr. OE *blōd;* akin to OHG *bluot* blood; akin to OE *blāwan* to blow] (bef. 12c) **1 a :** the fluid that circulates in the heart, arteries, capillaries, and veins of a vertebrate animal carrying nourishment and oxygen to and bringing away waste products from all parts of the body **b :** a comparable fluid of an invertebrate **c :** a fluid resembling blood **2 a :** LIFEBLOOD; *broadly* **:** LIFE **b :** human stock or lineage; *esp* **:** royal lineage 〈a prince of the ~〉 **c :** relationship by descent from a common ancestor **:** KINSHIP **d :** persons related through common descent **:** KINDRED **e** (1) **:** honorable or high birth or descent (2) **:** descent from parents of recognized breed or pedigree **3 :** the shedding of blood; *also* **:** the taking of life **4 a :** blood regarded as the seat of the emotions **:** TEMPER **b** *obs* **:** LUST **c :** a showy foppish man **:** RAKE **5 :** PERSONNEL **6 :** a black American — used esp. among blacks

[2]**blood** *vt* (1633) **1** *archaic* **:** BLEED 1 **2 :** to stain or wet with blood **3 :** to expose (a hunting dog) to sight, scent, or taste of the blood of its prey **4 :** to give experience to ⟨troops ~*ed* in battle⟩
blood bank *n* (1938) **:** a place for storage of or an institution storing blood or plasma; *also* **:** blood so stored
blood·bath \ˈbləd-ˌbath, -ˌbäth\ *n* (1867) **:** a great slaughter **:** MASSACRE
blood–brain barrier \ˌbləd-ˌbrān-\ *n* (1944) **:** a barrier postulated to exist between brain capillaries and brain tissue to explain the relative inability of many substances to leave the blood and cross the capillary walls into the brain tissues
blood brother *n* (1890) **1 :** a brother by birth **2 :** one of two men pledged to mutual loyalty by a ceremonial use of each other's blood — **blood brotherhood** *n*
blood cell *n* (1846) **:** a cell normally present in blood
blood count *n* (ca. 1900) **:** the determination of the blood cells in a definite volume of blood; *also* **:** the number of cells so determined
blood·cur·dling \ˈbləd-ˌkərd-liŋ, -ᵊl-iŋ\ *adj* (1904) **:** arousing horror ⟨~ screams⟩
blood·ed \ˈbləd-əd\ *adj* (1858) **:** being entirely or largely purebred ⟨a herd of ~ stock⟩
-blooded *adj comb form* **:** having (such) blood or temperament ⟨cold-*blooded*⟩ ⟨warm-*blooded*⟩
blood feud *n* (1858) **:** a feud between different clans or families
blood fluke *n* (1872) **:** SCHISTOSOME
blood group *n* (1916) **:** one of the classes (as those designated A, B, or O) into which individuals or their blood can be separated on the basis of the presence or absence of specific antigens in the blood — called also *blood type*
blood·guilt \ˈbləd-ˌgilt\ *n* (1882) **:** guilt resulting from bloodshed — **blood·guilt·i·ness** \-ˌgil-tē-nəs\ *n* — **blood·guilty** \-tē\ *adj*
blood heat *n* (1812) **:** a temperature approximating that of the human body
blood·hound \ˈbləd-ˌhau̇nd\ *n* (14c) **1 :** a large powerful hound of a breed of European origin remarkable for acuteness of smell **2 :** a person keen in pursuit
blood·less \ˈbləd-ləs\ *adj* (bef. 12c) **1 :** deficient in or free from blood **2 :** not accompanied by loss or shedding of blood ⟨a ~ victory⟩ **3 :** lacking in spirit or vitality ⟨a ~ man with no sense of humor⟩ **4 :** lacking in human feeling ⟨~ statistics⟩ — **blood·less·ly** *adv* — **blood·less·ness** *n*
blood·let·ting \-ˌlet-iŋ\ *n* (13c) **1 :** PHLEBOTOMY **2 :** BLOODSHED **3 :** elimination of personnel or resources
blood·line \-ˌlīn\ *n* (ca. 1909) **:** a sequence of direct ancestors esp. in a pedigree; *also* **:** FAMILY, STRAIN
blood·mo·bile \-mō-ˌbēl\ *n* [*blood* + auto*mobile*] (1948) **:** an automotive vehicle staffed and equipped for collecting blood from donors
blood money *n* (1535) **1 :** money obtained at the cost of another's life **2 :** money paid by a manslayer or members of his family, clan, or tribe to the next of kin of a person killed by him
blood platelet *n* (1898) **:** one of the minute protoplasmic disks of vertebrate blood that assist in blood clotting
blood poisoning *n* (1863) **:** SEPTICEMIA
blood pressure *n* (1874) **:** pressure that is exerted by the blood upon the walls of the blood vessels and esp. arteries and that varies with the muscular efficiency of the heart, the blood volume and viscosity, the age and health of the individual, and the state of the vascular wall
blood·red \ˈbləd-ˈred\ *adj* (bef. 12c) **:** having the color of blood
blood·root \-ˌrüt, -ˌru̇t\ *n* (1578) **:** a plant (*Sanguinaria canadensis*) of the poppy family having a red root and sap and bearing a solitary lobed leaf and white flower in early spring
blood sausage *n* (1868) **:** very dark sausage containing a large proportion of blood — called also *blood pudding*
blood serum *n* (ca. 1909) **:** blood from which the fibrin and suspended material (as cells) have been removed
blood·shed \ˈbləd-ˌshed\ *n* (15c) **1 :** the shedding of blood **2 :** the taking of life **:** SLAUGHTER
blood·shot \-ˌshät\ *adj, of an eye* (15c) **:** inflamed to redness
blood·stain \-ˌstān\ *n* (1820) **:** a discoloration caused by blood
blood·stained \-ˌstānd\ *adj* (1596) **1 :** stained with blood **2 :** involved with slaughter ⟨a ~ chronicle of war⟩
blood·stock \-ˌstäk\ *n* (1830) **:** horses of Thoroughbred breeding esp. when used for racing
blood·stone \-ˌstōn\ *n* (1551) **:** a green chalcedony sprinkled with red spots resembling blood
blood·stream \-ˌstrēm\ *n* (1873) **1 :** the flowing blood in a circulatory system **2 :** a mainstream of power or vitality ⟨introduce into the economic ~ a large amount of money — *Harper's*⟩
blood·suck·er \-ˌsək-ər\ *n* (14c) **1 :** an animal that sucks blood; *esp* **:** LEECH **2 :** a person who sponges or preys on another — **blood·suck·ing** \-iŋ\ *adj*
blood sugar *n* (1918) **:** the glucose in the blood; *also* **:** its concentration (as in milligrams per 100 milliliters)
blood test *n* (1912) **:** a test of the blood; *esp* **:** a serologic test for syphilis
blood·thirsty \ˈbləd-ˌthər-stē\ *adj* (1535) **:** eager for or marked by the shedding of blood — **blood·thirst·i·ly** \-stə-lē\ *adv* — **blood·thirst·i·ness** \-stē-nəs\ *n*
blood–typ·ing \-ˌtī-piŋ\ *n* (1928) **:** the action or process of determining the blood group of someone
blood vessel *n* (1694) **:** any of the vessels through which blood circulates in an animal
blood·worm \ˈbləd-ˌwərm\ *n* (1714) **:** any of various reddish annelid worms often used as bait
[1]**bloody** \ˈbləd-ē\ *adj* **blood·i·er; -est** (bef. 12c) **1 a :** containing or made up of blood **b :** of or contained in the blood **2 :** smeared or stained with blood **3 :** accompanied by or involving bloodshed; *esp* **:** marked by great slaughter **4 a :** MURDEROUS **b :** MERCILESS, CRUEL **5 :** BLOODRED **6** — used as an intensive; sometimes considered vulgar — **blood·i·ly** \ˈbləd-ᵊl-ē\ *adv* — **blood·i·ness** \ˈbləd-ē-nəs\ *n*
[2]**bloody** *vt* **blood·ied; bloody·ing** (bef. 12c) **:** to make bloody or bloodred
[3]**bloody** *adv* (1676) — used as an intensive; sometimes considered vulgar
Bloody Mary *n, pl* **Bloody Marys** [prob. fr. *Bloody Mary,* appellation of Mary I of England] (1952) **:** a cocktail consisting essentially of vodka and tomato juice
bloody–mind·ed \ˌbləd-ē-ˈmīn-dəd\ *adj* (1584) **1 :** willing to accept violence or bloodshed **2** *chiefly Brit* **:** CONTRARY, CANTANKEROUS — **bloody–mind·ed·ness** *n*
bloody shirt *n* (1875) **:** a means employed to stir up or revive party or sectional animosity
[1]**bloom** \ˈblüm\ *n* [ME *blome* lump of metal, fr. OE *blōma*] (bef. 12c) **1 :** a mass of wrought iron from the forge or puddling furnace **2 :** a bar of iron or steel hammered or rolled from an ingot
[2]**bloom** *n* [ME *blome,* fr. ON *blōm;* akin to OE *blōwan* to blossom — more at BLOW] (13c) **1 a :** FLOWER **b :** the flowering state ⟨the roses in ~⟩ **c :** a period of flowering ⟨the spring ~⟩ **d :** an excessive growth of plankton **2 :** a state or time of beauty, freshness, and vigor **3 :** a surface coating or appearance: as **a :** a delicate powdery coating on some fruits and leaves **b :** a rosy appearance of the cheeks; *broadly* **:** an outward evidence of freshness or healthy vigor **c :** the grainy or powdery surface of a newly minted coin **d :** a cloudiness on a film of varnish or lacquer **e :** glare caused by an object reflecting too much light into a television camera
[3]**bloom** *vi* (13c) **1 a :** to produce or yield flowers **b :** to support abundant plant life ⟨make the desert ~⟩ **2 a :** to flourish in youthful beauty, freshness or excellence **b :** to shine out **:** GLOW **3 :** to appear or occur unexpectedly or in surprising quantity or degree **4 :** to become densely populated with microorganisms and esp. plankton — used of bodies of water ~ *vt* **1** *obs* **:** to cause to bloom **2 :** to give bloom to
[1]**bloom·er** \ˈblü-mər\ *n* (ca. 1730) **1 :** a plant that blooms **2 :** a person who reaches full competence or maturity **3 :** a stupid blunder
[2]**bloo·mer** \ˈblü-mər\ *n* [Amelia *Bloomer*] (1851) **1 :** a costume for women consisting of a short skirt and long loose trousers gathered closely about the ankles **2** *pl* **a :** full loose trousers gathered at the knee formerly worn by women for athletics **b :** underpants of similar design worn chiefly by girls
bloom·ing \ˈblü-mən, -miŋ\ *adj or adv* [prob. euphemism for *bloody*] *chiefly Brit* (1882) — used as a generalized intensive ⟨~ fool⟩
bloomy \ˈblü-mē\ *adj* (1593) **1 :** full of bloom **2 :** covered with bloom ⟨~ plums ⟩ **3 :** showing freshness or vitality ⟨all the ~ flush of life is fled —Oliver Goldsmith⟩
[1]**bloop** \ˈblüp\ *adj, of a baseball* (1952) **:** hit in the air just beyond the infield
[2]**bloop** *vt* [prob. fr. *bloop* (an unpleasing sound)] (1953) **:** to hit (a fly ball) usu. just beyond the infield in baseball ⟨~*ed* a single to center field⟩
bloop·er \ˈblü-pər\ *n* [*bloop* (an unpleasing sound)] (1945) **1 :** an embarrassing public blunder **2 a :** a high baseball pitch lobbed to the batter **b :** a fly ball hit barely beyond a baseball infield
[1]**blos·som** \ˈbläs-əm\ *n* [ME *blosme,* fr. OE *blōstm;* akin to OE *blōwan*] (bef. 12c) **1 a :** the flower of a seed plant **b :** the mass of bloom on a single plant; *also* **:** the state of bearing flowers **2 :** a peak period or stage of development — **blos·somy** \-ə-mē\ *adj*
[2]**blossom** *vi* (bef. 12c) **1 :** BLOOM **2 a :** to come into one's own **:** DEVELOP ⟨a ~*ing* talent⟩ **b :** to become evident **:** make an appearance
[1]**blot** \ˈblät\ *n* [ME] (14c) **1 :** a soiling or disfiguring mark **:** SPOT **2 :** a mark of reproach **:** moral flaw
[2]**blot** *vb* **blot·ted; blot·ting** *vt* (15c) **1 :** to spot, stain, or spatter with a discoloring substance **2** *obs* **:** MAR; *esp* **:** to stain with infamy **3 a :** to dry with an absorbing agent (as blotting paper) **b :** to remove by blotting the surface ~ *vi* **1 :** to make a blot **2 :** to become marked with a blot
[3]**blot** *n* [origin unknown] (1595) **1 :** a backgammon man exposed to capture **2** *archaic* **:** a weak or exposed point
[1]**blotch** \ˈbläch\ *vt* (1604) **:** to mark or mar with blotches
[2]**blotch** *n* [prob. alter. of *botch*] (1669) **1 :** IMPERFECTION, BLEMISH **2 :** a spot or mark (as of color or ink) esp. when large or irregular — **blotch·i·ly** \ˈbläch-ə-lē\ *adv* — **blotchy** \ˈbläch-ē\ *adj*
blot out *vt* (1530) **1 :** to make obscure, insignificant, or inconsequential ⟨this one good act *blots out* many bad ones⟩ **2 :** to wipe out **:** DESTROY ⟨one such bomb can *blot out* a city⟩
blot·ter \ˈblät-ər\ *n* (1591) **1 :** a piece of blotting paper **2 :** a book in which entries (as of transactions or occurrences) are made temporarily pending their transfer to permanent record books ⟨police ~⟩
blotting paper *n* (15c) **:** a soft spongy unsized paper used to absorb ink
blot·to \ˈblät-(ˌ)ō\ *adj* [prob. irreg. fr. [2]*blot*] (1917) **:** DRUNK
[1]**blouse** \ˈblau̇s *also* ˈblau̇z\ *n, pl* **blous·es** \ˈblau̇-səz, -zəz\ [F] (1828) **1 :** a loose overgarment that resembles a shirt or smock, varies from hip-length to calf-length, and is worn esp. by workmen, artists, and peasants **2 :** a usu. loose-fitting garment that covers the body from the neck to the waist and is worn esp. by women
[2]**blouse** \ˈblau̇s, ˈblau̇z\ *vb* **bloused; blous·ing** *vi* (1904) **:** to fall in a fold ⟨coats that ~ above the hip⟩ ~ *vt* **:** to cause to blouse ⟨trousers are *bloused* over the boots⟩
blou·son \ˈblau̇-ˌsän, ˈblü-ˌzän\ *n* [F, fr. *blouse*] (1904) **:** a garment (as a dress or blouse) having a close waistband with blousing of material over it
[1]**blow** \ˈblō\ *vb* **blew** \ˈblü\; **blown** \ˈblōn\; **blow·ing** [ME *blowen,* fr. OE *blāwan;* akin to OHG *blāen* to blow, L *flare,* Gk *phallos* penis] *vi* (bef. 12c) **1** *of air* **:** to move with speed or force **2 :** to send forth a current of air or other gas **3 a :** to make a sound by or as if by blowing **b** *of a wind instrument* **:** SOUND **4 a :** BOAST **b :** to talk windily **5 a :** PANT, GASP ⟨the horse *blew* heavily⟩ **b** *of a cetacean* **:** to eject moisture-laden air from the lungs through the blowhole **6 :** to move or be carried by or as if by wind **7** *of an electric fuse* **:** to melt when overloaded — usu. used with *out* **8** *of a tire* **:** to release the contained air through a spontaneous rupture — usu. used with *out* ~ *vt* **1 a :** to set (gas or vapor) in motion **b :** to act on with a current of gas or vapor **2 :** to play or sound on (a wind instrument) **3 a :** to spread by report **b :** DAMN, DISREGARD ⟨~ the expense⟩ **4 a :** to drive with a current of gas or vapor **b :** to clear of contents by forcible passage of

a current of air 5 a : to distend with or as if with gas b : to produce or shape by the action of blown or injected air ⟨~*ing* bubbles⟩ ⟨~*ing* glass⟩ 6 *of insects* : to deposit eggs or larvae on or in 7 : to shatter, burst, or destroy by explosion 8 a : to put out of breath with exertion b : to let (as a horse) pause to catch the breath 9 a : to spend (money) recklessly b : to treat with unusual expenditure ⟨I'll ~ you to a steak⟩ 10 : to cause (a fuse) to blow 11 : to rupture by too much pressure ⟨*blew* a gasket⟩ 12 : to lose by failing to use an advantage : MUFF ⟨*blew* his chance⟩ 13 : to leave hurriedly ⟨*blew* town⟩ 14 : to propel with great force or speed ⟨*blew* a fastball by the batter⟩ — **blow hot and cold** : to be favorable at one moment and adverse the next — **blow into** : to appear or arrive at casually or unexpectedly ⟨*blew into* town today⟩ — **blow one's cool** : to lose one's composure — **blow one's cover** : to reveal one's real identity — **blow one's mind** : to overwhelm one with wonder or bafflement — **blow one's top** *or* **blow one's stack** 1 : to become violently angry 2 : to go crazy — **blow the whistle** 1 : to bring into the open something kept secret 2 : INFORM *vi* 2

²blow *n* (1660) 1 : a blowing of wind esp. when strong or violent 2 : BRAG, BOASTING 3 : an act or instance of blowing 4 a : the time during which air is forced through molten metal to refine it b : the quantity of metal refined during that time

³blow *vi* **blew** \'blü\; **blown** \'blōn\; **blow·ing** [ME *blowen*, fr. OE *blōwan*; akin to OHG *bluoen* to bloom, L *florēre* to bloom, *flor-, flos* flower] (bef. 12c) : FLOWER, BLOOM

⁴blow *n* (1744) 1 : ²BLOOM 1b ⟨lilacs in full ~⟩ 2 : BLOSSOMS

⁵blow *n* [ME (northern dial.) *blaw*; prob. akin to OE *bealu* — more at BALE] (15c) 1 : a forcible stroke delivered with a part of the body or with an instrument 2 : a hostile act or state : COMBAT ⟨come to ~*s*⟩ 3 : a forcible or sudden act or effort : ASSAULT 4 : an unfortunate or calamitous happening ⟨failure to land the job came as a ~⟩

blow away *vt* (1776) 1 : to kill by gunfire : shoot dead 2 : to overwhelm emotionally : STUN

blow·by \'blō-,bī\ *n* (1926) : leakage of combustion gases between a piston and the cylinder wall into the crankcase in an automobile

blow–by–blow \-bī-, -bə-\ *adj* (1933) : minutely detailed ⟨a ~ account⟩

blow–dry \'blō-,drī\ *vt* (1973) : to dry and usu. style (hair) with a hand-held hair dryer — **blow–dry** *n*

blow·er \'blō(-ə)r\ *n* (bef. 12c) 1 : one that blows 2 : BRAGGART 3 : a device for producing a current of air or gas ⟨a vacuum-cleaner ~⟩

blow·fish \'blō-,fish\ *n* (ca. 1893) : PUFFER 2a

blow·fly \-,flī\ *n* (1821) : any of various two-winged flies (family Calliphoridae) that deposit their eggs or maggots esp. on meat or in wounds; *esp* : a widely distributed bluebottle (*Calliphora vicina*)

blow·gun \-,gən\ *n* (1864) : a tube through which a projectile (as a dart) may be impelled by the force of the breath

blow·hard \-,härd\ *n* (1857) : BRAGGART

blow·hole \-,hōl\ *n* (1691) 1 : a hole in metal caused by a bubble of gas captured during solidification 2 : a nostril in the top of the head of a whale or other cetacean 3 : a hole in the ice to which aquatic mammals (as seals) come to breathe

blow in *vi* (1895) : to arrive casually or unexpectedly

blown \'blōn\ *adj* [ME *blowen*, fr. pp. of *blowen* to blow] (15c) 1 : SWOLLEN; *esp* : afflicted with bloat 2 : FLYBLOWN 3 : being out of breath

blow off *vt* (1837) : to relieve by vigorous speech or action — **blow off steam** : to release pent-up emotions

blow·out \'blō-,au̇t\ *n* (1824) 1 : a festive social affair 2 a : a bursting of a container (as a tire) by pressure of the contents on a weak spot b : a hole made in a container by such bursting 3 : an uncontrolled eruption of an oil or gas well

blow out \(')blō-'au̇t\ *vi* (14c) 1 : to become extinguished by a gust 2 : to erupt out of control — used of an oil or gas well ~ *vt* 1 : to extinguish by a gust 2 : to dissipate (itself) by blowing — used of storms

blow over *vi* (1617) : to pass away without effect

blow·pipe \'blō-,pīp\ *n* (1685) 1 : a small tubular instrument for directing a jet of air or other gas into a flame so as to concentrate and increase the heat 2 : a tubular instrument used for revealing or cleaning a bodily cavity by forcing air into it 3 : BLOWGUN 4 : a long metal tube on the end of which a glassmaker gathers a quantity of molten glass and through which he blows to expand and shape it

blow·sy *also* **blow·zy** \'blau̇-zē\ *adj* [E dial. *blowse, blowze* (wench)] (1778) 1 : being coarse and ruddy of complexion 2 : having a sloppy appearance or aspect : FROWSY

blow·torch \'blō-,tȯrch\ *n* (1897) : a small burner having a device to intensify combustion by means of a blast of air or oxygen, usu. including a fuel tank pressurized by a hand pump, and used esp. in plumbing

blow·tube \-,t(y)üb\ *n* (1871) 1 : BLOWGUN 2 : BLOWPIPE 4

blow·up \'blō-,əp\ *n* (1807) : a blowing up: as a : EXPLOSION b : an outburst of temper c : a photographic enlargement

blow up \(')blō-'əp\ *vt* (1599) 1 : to rend apart, shatter, or destroy by explosion 2 : to build up or tout to an unreasonable extent ⟨advertisers *blowing up* their products⟩ 3 : to fill up with a gas and esp. air ⟨*blow up* a balloon⟩ 4 : to bring into existence by blowing of wind ⟨it may *blow up* a storm⟩ 5 : to make a photographic enlargement of ~ *vi* 1 a : EXPLODE b : to be disrupted or destroyed (as by explosion) c : to lose self-control; *esp* : to become violently angry 2 a : to become filled with a gas and esp. air b : to become expanded to unreasonable proportions 3 : to become or come into being by or as if by blowing of wind

blowy \'blō-ē\ *adj* (1830) 1 : WINDY ⟨a ~ March day⟩ 2 : readily blown about ⟨~ desert sand⟩

BLT *n* (1952) : a bacon, lettuce, and tomato sandwich

¹blub·ber \'bləb-ər\ *vb* **blub·bered; blub·ber·ing** \'bləb-(ə-)riŋ\ [ME *blubren* to make a bubbling sound, fr. *bluber*] *vi* (15c) : to weep noisily ~ *vt* 1 : to swell, distort, or wet with weeping 2 : to utter while weeping

²blubber *n* [ME *bluber* bubble, foam, prob. of imit. origin] (15c) 1 a : the fat of whales and other large marine mammals b : excessive fat on the body 2 : the action of blubbering

³blubber *adj* (1667) : puffed out : THICK ⟨~ lips⟩

blub·bery \'bləb-(ə-)rē\ *adj* (1791) 1 : having or characterized by blubber 2 : puffed out : THICK

blu·cher \'blü-chər *also* -kər\ *n* [G. L. von *Blücher*] (1831) : a shoe having the tongue and vamp cut in one piece and the quarters lapped over the vamp and laced together for closing

¹blud·geon \'bləj-ən\ *n* [origin unknown] (ca. 1730) 1 : a short stick that usu. has one thick or loaded end and is used as a weapon 2 : something used to attack or bully ⟨the ~ of satire⟩

²bludgeon *vt* (1868) 1 : to hit with heavy impact 2 : to overcome by aggressive argument

¹blue \'blü\ *adj* **blu·er; blu·est** [ME, fr. OF *blou*, of Gmc origin; akin to OHG *blāo* blue; akin to L *flavus* yellow, OE *bǣl* fire — more at BALD] (13c) 1 : of the color blue 2 a : BLUISH b : LIVID ⟨~ with cold⟩ c : bluish gray ⟨~ cat⟩ 3 a : low in spirits : MELANCHOLY b : marked by low spirits : DEPRESSING ⟨a ~ funk⟩ ⟨things looked ~⟩ 4 : wearing blue 5 *of a woman* : LEARNED, INTELLECTUAL 6 : PURITANICAL 7 a : PROFANE, INDECENT ⟨~ movie⟩ b : OFF-COLOR, RISQUÉ ⟨~ jokes⟩ 8 : of or relating to blues singing ⟨a ~ song⟩ — **blue·ly** *adv* — **blue·ness** *n* — **blue in the face** : extremely exasperated

²blue *n* (13c) 1 : a color whose hue is that of the clear sky or that of the portion of the color spectrum lying between green and violet 2 a : a pigment or dye that colors blue b : BLUING 3 a : blue clothing or cloth b *pl* : a blue costume or uniform 4 : one who wears a blue uniform: as a : a soldier in the Union army during the American Civil War b : the Union army 5 a (1) : SKY (2) : the far distance b : SEA 6 : a blue object 7 : BLUESTOCKING 8 : any of numerous small chiefly blue butterflies (family Lycaenidae) 9 : BLUEFISH — **out of the blue** : without advance notice : UNEXPECTEDLY ⟨a job offer that came *out of the blue*⟩

³blue *vb* **blued; blue·ing** *or* **blu·ing** *vt* (1606) : to make blue ~ *vi* : to turn blue

blue baby *n* (1903) : an infant with a bluish tint usu. from a congenital defect of the heart in which mingling of venous and arterial blood occurs

blue·beard \'blü-,bi(ə)rd\ *n* [*Bluebeard*, a fairy-tale character] (1822) : a man who marries and kills one wife after another

blue·bell \-,bel\ *n* (1578) 1 : any of various bellflowers; *esp* : HAREBELL 2 : any of various plants bearing blue bell-shaped flowers: as a : a European squill (*Scilla nonscripta*) having scapose racemes of drooping bell-shaped flowers — called also *wild hyacinth* b *pl* : a smooth erect eastern No. American herb (*Mertensia virginica*) of the borage family with entire leaves and showy blue flowers pink in the bud — called also *Virginia bluebells*

blue·ber·ry \'blü-,ber-ē, -b(ə-)rē\ *n* (1709) : the edible blue or blackish berry of any of several plants (genus *Vaccinium*) of the heath family; *also* : a low or tall shrub producing these berries

blue·bird \-,bərd\ *n* (1688) : any of several small No. American songbirds (genus *Sialia*) related to the robin but more or less blue above

blue–black \-'blak\ *adj* (1853) : being of a dark bluish hue

blue blood *n* (1834) 1 \'blü-'bləd\ : membership in a noble or socially prominent family 2 \-,bləd\ : a member of a noble or socially prominent family — **blue–blood·ed** \-'bləd-əd\ *adj*

blue·bon·net \'blü-,bän-ət\ *n* (1682) 1 a : a wide flat round cap of blue wool formerly worn in Scotland b : one that wears such a cap; *specif* : SCOT 2 : a low-growing annual lupine of Texas with silky foliage and blue flowers usu. classified as a single variable species (*Lupinus subcarnosus*)

blue book *n* (1836) 1 : a register esp. of socially prominent persons 2 : a book of specialized information often published under government auspices 3 : a blue-covered booklet used for writing examinations

blue·bot·tle \'blü-,bät-ᵊl\ *n* (15c) 1 : BACHELOR'S BUTTON 2 : any of several blowflies that have the abdomen or the whole body iridescent blue in color and that make a loud buzzing noise in flight

blue catfish *n* (1835) : a large bluish catfish (*Ictalurus furcatus*) of the Mississippi valley that may exceed 100 pounds in weight

blue cheese *n* (1925) : cheese having veins of greenish blue mold

blue chip *n* (1929) 1 a : a stock issue of high investment quality that usu. pertains to a substantial well-established company and enjoys public confidence in its worth and stability b : a consistently successful and profitable venture or enterprise 2 : an outstandingly worthwhile or valuable property or asset — **blue–chip** *adj*

blue·coat \'blü-,kōt\ *n* (1593) : one that wears a blue coat: as a : a Union soldier during the Civil War b : POLICEMAN

blue cohosh *n* (1821) : a perennial herb (*Caulophyllum thalictroides*) of the barberry family that has greenish yellow or purplish flowers and large blue fruits like berries

blue–col·lar \'blü-'käl-ər\ *adj* (1946) : of, relating to, or constituting the class of wage earners whose duties call for the wearing of work clothes or protective clothing — compare WHITE-COLLAR

blue crab *n* (1883) : any of several largely blue swimming crabs; *esp* : an edible crab (*Callinectes sapidus*) of the Atlantic and Gulf coasts

blue curls *n pl but sing or pl in constr* (ca. 1817) : any of several mints (genus *Trichostema*) with irregular blue flowers

blue devils *n pl* (1781) : low spirits : DESPONDENCY

blue–eyed grass \,blü-,īd-\ *n* (ca. 1784) : any of several plants (genus *Sisyrinchium*) of the iris family with grasslike foliage and delicate blue flowers

blue·fin tuna \,blü-,fin-\ *n* (1922) : a very large tuna (*Thunnus thynnus*) — called also *bluefin*

blue·fish \-,fish\ *n* (1622) 1 : an active voracious fish (*Pomatomus saltatrix*) related to the pompanos that is bluish above and silvery below 2 : any of various dark or bluish fishes (as the pollack)

blue flag *n* (1784) : a blue-flowered iris; *esp* : a common iris (*Iris versicolor*) of the eastern U.S. with a root formerly used medicinally

blue flu *n* [fr. the color of a police uniform] (ca. 1968) : a sick-out staged by police officers

blue·gill \'blü-,gil\ *n* (1881) : a common sunfish (*Lepomis macrochirus*) of the eastern and central U.S. sought for food and sport

blue·grass \-,gras\ *n* (1751) 1 : any of several grasses (genus *Poa*) of which some have bluish green culms; *esp* : KENTUCKY BLUEGRASS 2 [fr. the *Blue Grass Boys*, performing group, fr. *Bluegrass state*, nickname of Kentucky] : country music played on unamplified stringed instruments (as banjo, fiddle, guitar, and mandolin) and characterized by free improvisation and close usu. high-pitched harmony

blue–green alga \ˌblü-ˌgrēn-\ *n* (1899) **:** any of a class (Myxophyceae) of algae having the chlorophyll masked by bluish green pigments
blue gum *n* (ca. 1801) **:** any of several Australian timber trees (genus *Eucalyptus*)
blue heron *n* (ca. 1730) **:** any of various herons with bluish or slaty plumage; *esp* **:** GREAT BLUE HERON
blue·jack·et \-ˌjak-ət\ *n* (1830) **:** an enlisted man in the navy **:** SAILOR
blue jay \-ˌjā\ *n* (1709) **:** JAY 1b
blue jeans *n pl* (1901) **:** pants usu. made of blue denim
blue law *n* (1781) **1 :** one of numerous extremely rigorous laws designed to regulate morals and conduct in colonial New England **2 :** a statute regulating work, commerce, and amusements on Sundays
blue line *n* (1927) **:** either of two blue lines that divide an ice-hockey rink into three equal zones and that separate the offensive and defensive zones from the center-ice neutral zone
blue mold *n* (1664) **:** a fungus (genus *Penicillium*) that produces blue or blue-green surface growths
blue moon *n* (1821) **:** a very long period of time ⟨such people happen along only once in a *blue moon* —*Saturday Rev.*⟩
blue·nose \ˈblü-ˌnōz\ *n* (1903) **:** one who advocates a rigorous moral code
blue note *n* [fr. its frequent use in blues music] (1926) **:** a variable microtonal lowering of the third, seventh, and occas. fifth degrees of the major scale
blue–pen·cil \ˌblü-ˈpen(t)-səl\ *vt* (1888) **:** to edit esp. by shortening or deletion — **blue pen·cil·er** *n*
blue pencil *n* (1893) **:** the act or practice of blue-penciling
blue pe·ter \-ˈpēt-ər\ *n* (1823) **:** a blue signal flag with a white square in the center used to indicate that a merchant vessel is ready to sail
blue pike *n* (1842) **:** PIKE PERCH; *esp* **:** WALLEYE
blue plate *adj* (1926) **:** being a main course (as of a meat with vegetables) usu. offered at a special price in a restaurant ⟨*blue plate* luncheon⟩
blue·point \ˈblü-ˌpȯint\ *n* [*Blue Point*, Long Island] (1789) **:** a small oyster typically from the south shore of Long Island
blue point \-ˌpȯint\ *adj, of a domestic cat* (1944) **:** having a bluish cream body coat with dark gray points — **blue point** *n*
blue·print \-ˌprint\ *n* (1886) **1 :** a photographic print in white on a bright blue ground or blue on a white ground used esp. for copying maps, mechanical drawings, and architects' plans **2 :** something resembling a blueprint; *esp* **:** a program of action ⟨a ~ for victory⟩ — **blueprint** *vt*
blue racer *n* (1886) **:** a blacksnake of a bluish green subspecies (*Coluber constrictor flaviventris*) occurring from Ohio to Texas
blue–ribbon *adj* (1926) **:** selected for quality, reputation, or authority ⟨a ~ committee⟩
blue ribbon *n* (1651) **1 :** a blue ribbon awarded as an honor (as to the first-place winner in a competition) **2 :** an honor or award gained for preeminence
blue–ribbon jury *n* (1936) **:** SPECIAL JURY
blues \ˈblüz\ *n pl but sing or pl in constr* [*blue devils*] (1807) **1 :** low spirits **:** MELANCHOLY **2 :** a song often of lamentation characterized by usu. 12-bar phrases, 3-line stanzas in which the words of the second line usu. repeat those of the first, and continual occurrence of blue notes in melody and harmony **3 :** jazz or popular music using harmonic and phrase structures of blues
blue shark *n* (ca. 1672) **:** a voracious pelagic shark (*Prionace glauca*) that is found in all tropical and temperate seas and occas. attacks man
blue·shift \(ˈ)blü-ˈshift\ *n* (1951) **:** the displacement of the spectrum of an approaching celestial body toward shorter wavelengths — **blue-shift·ed** *adj*
blue–sky \ˈblü-ˈskī\ *adj* (1906) **1 :** having little or no value ⟨~ stock⟩ **2 :** having no practical application ⟨~ thinking⟩
blue–sky law *n* (1912) **:** a law providing for the regulation of the sale of securities (as stock)
blues·man \ˈblüz-mən\ *n* (1966) **:** one who plays or sings the blues
blue·stem \ˈblü-ˌstem\ *n* (1864) **1 :** an important hay and forage grass (*Andropogon furcatus*) of the western U.S. with smooth bluish leaf sheaths and slender spikes borne in pairs or clusters **2 :** LITTLE BLUESTEM
blue·stock·ing \-ˌstäk-iŋ\ *n* [*Bluestocking* society, 18th cent. literary clubs] (1790) **:** a woman having intellectual or literary interests
blue·stone \-ˌstōn\ *n* (1709) **:** a building or paving stone of bluish gray color; *specif* **:** a sandstone quarried near the Hudson river
blue streak *n* (1830) **1 :** something that moves very fast **2 :** a constant stream of words ⟨talked a *blue streak*⟩
bluesy \ˈblü-zē\ *adj* **blues·i·er; -est** (1946) **:** resembling, characteristic of, or suited to the blues
blu·et \ˈblü-ət\ *n* [prob. fr. 1*blue*] (ca. 1821) **:** an American plant (*Houstonia caerulea*) of the madder family with bluish flowers and tufted stems
blue·tongue \ˈblü-ˌtəŋ\ *n* (1863) **:** a serious virus disease esp. of sheep characterized by hyperemia, cyanosis, and punctate hemorrhages and by swelling and sloughing of the epithelium esp. about the mouth and tongue
blue vitriol *n* (1728) **:** a hydrated copper sulfate $CuSO_4{\cdot}5H_2O$
blue·weed \ˈblü-ˌwēd\ *n* (ca. 1843) **1 :** VIPER'S BUGLOSS **2 :** a small weedy sunflower (*Helianthus ciliaris*) of the southwestern U.S. with blue-green or gray-green foliage
blue whale *n* (1851) **:** a very large whalebone whale (*Sibbaldus musculus*) that may reach a weight of 100 tons (90 metric tons) and a length of 100 feet (30 meters) and is generally considered the largest living animal

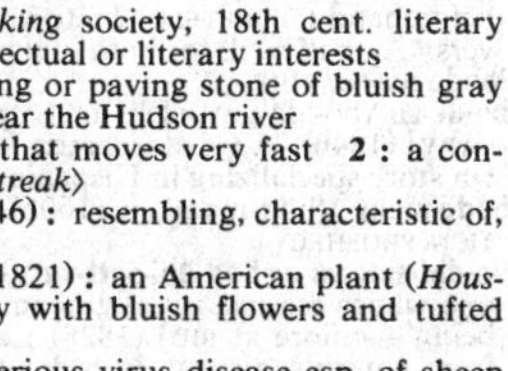
blue whale

bluey \ˈblü-ē\ *n* [fr. the blue blanket commonly used to wrap the bundle] *Austral* (ca. 1887) **:** a swagman's bundle of personal effects; *broadly* **:** a bag of clothing carried in travel
1bluff \ˈbləf\ *adj* [obs. D *blaf* flat; akin to MLG *blaff* smooth] (1627) **1 a :** having a broad flattened front **b :** rising steeply with a broad flat or rounded front **2 :** good-naturedly frank and outspoken — **bluff·ly** *adv* — **bluff·ness** *n*
syn BLUFF, BLUNT, BRUSQUE, CURT, CRUSTY, GRUFF mean abrupt and unceremonious in speech and manner. BLUFF connotes good-natured outspokenness and unconventionality; BLUNT suggests directness of expression in disregard of others' feelings; BRUSQUE applies to a sharpness or ungraciousness; CURT implies disconcerting shortness or rude conciseness; CRUSTY suggests a harsh or surly manner sometimes concealing an inner kindliness; GRUFF suggests a hoarse or husky speech which may imply bad temper but more often implies embarrassment or shyness.
2bluff *n* (1666) **:** a high steep bank **:** CLIFF
3bluff *vb* [prob. fr. D *bluffen* to boast, play a kind of card game] *vt* (1839) **1 a :** to deter or frighten by pretense or a mere show of strength **b :** DECEIVE **c :** FEIGN **2 :** to deceive (an opponent) in cards by a bold bet on an inferior hand with the result that the opponent withdraws a winning hand ~ *vi* **:** to bluff someone — **bluff·er** *n*
4bluff *n* (1845) **1 a :** an act or instance of bluffing **b :** the practice of bluffing **2 :** one who bluffs
blu·ing *or* **blue·ing** \ˈblü-iŋ\ *n* (1669) **:** a preparation used in laundering to counteract yellowing of white fabrics
blu·ish \ˈblü-ish\ *adj* (14c) **:** somewhat blue **:** having a tinge of blue — **blu·ish·ness** *n*
1blun·der \ˈblən-dər\ *vb* **blun·dered; blun·der·ing** \-d(ə-)riŋ\ [ME *blundren*] *vi* (14c) **1 :** to move unsteadily or confusedly **2 :** to make a mistake through stupidity, ignorance, or carelessness ~ *vt* **1 :** to utter stupidly, confusedly, or thoughtlessly **2 :** to make a stupid, careless, or thoughtless mistake in — **blun·der·er** \-dər-ər\ *n* — **blun·der·ing·ly** \-d(ə-)riŋ-lē\ *adv*
2blunder *n* (ca. 1706) **:** a gross error or mistake resulting usu. from stupidity, ignorance, or carelessness ***syn*** see ERROR
blun·der·buss \ˈblən-dər-ˌbəs\ *n* [by folk etymology fr. obs. D *donderbus*, fr. D *donder* thunder + obs. D *bus* gun] (1654) **1 :** a muzzle-loading firearm with a short barrel and flaring muzzle to facilitate loading **2 :** a blundering person
1blunt \ˈblənt\ *adj* [ME] (13c) **1 a :** slow or deficient in feeling **:** INSENSITIVE **b :** obtuse in understanding or discernment **:** DULL **2 :** having an edge or point that is not sharp **3 a :** abrupt in speech or manner **b :** being straight to the point **:** DIRECT ***syn*** see DULL, BLUFF — **blunt·ly** *adv* — **blunt·ness** *n*
2blunt *vt* (14c) **:** to make less sharp or definite ~ *vi* **:** to become blunt
1blur \ˈblər\ *n* [perh. akin to ME *bleren* to blear] (1548) **1 :** a smear or stain that obscures **2 :** something that is vague or lacking definite outline or distinct character
2blur *vb* **blurred; blur·ring** *vt* (1581) **1 :** to obscure or blemish by smearing **2 :** SULLY **3 :** to make dim, indistinct, or vague in outline or character **4 :** to make cloudy or confused ~ *vi* **1 :** to make blurs **2 :** to become vague, indistinct, or indefinite — **blur·ring·ly** \ˈblər-iŋ-lē\ *adv*
blurb \ˈblərb\ *n* [coined by Gelett Burgess] (ca. 1907) **:** a short publicity notice (as on a book jacket)
blur·ry \ˈblər-ē\ *adj* **blur·ri·er; -est** (1884) **:** marked by blurring — **blur·ri·ly** \ˈblər-ə-lē\ *adv* — **blur·ri·ness** \ˈblər-ē-nəs\ *n*
blurt \ˈblərt\ *vt* [prob. imit.] (1573) **:** to utter abruptly and impulsively — usu. used with *out* — **blurt·er** *n*
1blush \ˈbləsh\ *vi* [ME *blusshen*, fr. OE *blyscan* to redden; akin to OE *blȳsa* flame, OHG *bluhhen* to burn brightly] (15c) **1 :** to become red in the face esp. from shame, modesty, or confusion **2 :** to feel shame or embarrassment **3 :** to have a rosy or fresh color **:** BLOOM — **blush·ing·ly** \-iŋ-lē\ *adv*
2blush *n* [ME, prob. fr. *blusshen*] (14c) **1 :** APPEARANCE, VIEW ⟨at first ~⟩ **2 :** a reddening of the face esp. from shame, modesty, or confusion **3 :** a red or rosy tint — **blush·ful** \-fəl\ *adj*
blush·er \ˈbləsh-ər\ *n* (1665) **1 :** one that blushes **2 :** a cosmetic applied to the face to give a usu. pink color or to accent the cheekbones
1blus·ter \ˈbləs-tər\ *vb* **blus·tered; blus·ter·ing** \-t(ə-)riŋ\ [ME *blustren*, prob. fr. MLG *blüsteren*] *vi* (15c) **1 a :** to blow in stormy noisy gusts **b :** to be windy and boisterous **2 :** to talk or act with noisy swaggering threats ~ *vt* **1 :** to utter with noisy self-assertiveness **2 :** to drive or force by blustering — **blus·ter·er** \-tər-ər\ *n* — **blus·ter·ing·ly** \-t(ə-)riŋ-lē\ *adv*
2bluster *n* (1583) **1 :** a violent boisterous blowing **2 :** violent commotion **3 :** loudly boastful or threatening speech — **blus·ter·ous** \-t(ə-)rəs\ *adj* — **blus·tery** \-t(ə-)rē\ *adj*
B lymphocyte *n* (1971) **:** B CELL
boa \ˈbō-ə, *Brit also* ˈbȯ(-ə)\ *n* [L, a water snake] (14c) **1 :** a large snake (as the boa constrictor, anaconda, or python) that kills by constriction **2 :** a long fluffy scarf of fur, feathers, or delicate fabric
boa constrictor *n* (1809) **:** a tropical American boa (*Constrictor constrictor*) that is light brown barred or mottled with darker brown and reaches a length of 10 feet or more; *broadly* **:** BOA 1
boar \ˈbō(ə)r, ˈbȯ(ə)r\ *n* [ME *bor*, fr. OE *bār*; akin to OHG & OS *bēr* boar] (bef. 12c) **1 a :** an uncastrated male swine **b :** the male of any of several mammals (as a guinea pig or raccoon) **2 :** the Old World wild hog (*Sus scrofa*) from which most domestic swine derive — **boar·ish** \-ish\ *adj*

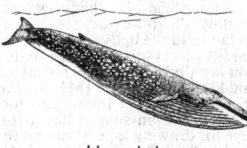

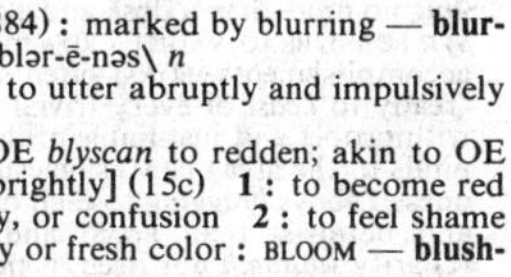
boar 2

1board \ˈbō(ə)rd, ˈbȯ(ə)rd\ *n* [ME *bord* piece of sawed lumber, border, ship's side, fr. OE; akin to OHG *bort* ship's side, Skt *bardhaka* carpenter] (bef. 12c) **1** *obs* **:** BORDER, EDGE **2 a :** the side of a ship **b :** the stretch that a ship makes on one tack in beating to windward **3 a :** a piece of sawed lumber of little thickness and a length greatly exceeding its width **b** *pl* **:** STAGE 2a(2) **4 a** *archaic* **:** TABLE 3a **b :** a table spread with a meal

c : daily meals esp. when furnished for pay **d :** a table at which a council or magistrates sit **e :** a group of persons having managerial, supervisory, investigatory, or advisory powers ⟨~ of directors⟩ ⟨~ of examiners⟩ **f :** LEAGUE, ASSOCIATION **g** (1) **:** the exposed hands of all the players in a stud poker game (2) **:** an exposed dummy hand in bridge **5 a :** a flat usu. rectangular piece of material (as wood) designed for a special purpose: as (1) **:** BACKBOARD (2) **:** a diving board (3) **:** SURFBOARD **b :** a surface, frame, or device for posting notices **c :** BLACKBOARD **d :** SWITCHBOARD **6 a :** PAPERBOARD **b :** the stiff foundation piece for the side of a book cover **7 :** a securities or commodities exchange **8** *pl* **:** the low wooden wall enclosing a hockey rink **9 :** a sheet of insulating material carrying circuit elements and terminals so that it can be inserted in an electronic apparatus — **board·like** \-ˌlīk\ *adj* — **on board :** ABOARD

[2]board *vt* (15c) **1** *archaic* **:** to come up against or alongside (a ship) usu. to attack **2 :** ACCOST, ADDRESS **3 :** to go aboard (as a ship, train, airplane, or bus) **4 :** to cover with boards ⟨~ up a window⟩ **5 :** to provide with regular meals and often also lodging usu. for compensation **6 :** to check (a player) against the rink boards in hockey ~ *vi* **:** to take one's meals usu. as a paying customer

board check *n* (ca. 1936) **:** a body check of an opposing player against the rink boards in ice hockey

board·er \ˈbōrd-ər, ˈbȯrd-\ *n* (ca. 1530) **:** one that boards; *esp* **:** one that is provided with regular meals or regular meals and lodging

board foot *n* (1896) **:** a unit of quantity for lumber equal to the volume of a board 12 x 12 x 1 inches — abbr. *bd ft*

board game *n* (1934) **:** a game of strategy (as checkers, chess, or backgammon) played by moving pieces on a board

board·ing·house \ˈbōrd-iŋ-ˌhau̇s, ˈbȯrd-\ *n* (1728) **:** a lodging house at which meals are provided

boarding school *n* (1677) **:** a school at which meals and lodging are provided

board·man \ˈbō(ə)rd-ˌman, ˈbȯ(ə)rd-, *esp for 2* -mən\ *n* (ca. 1923) **1 :** a member of a board **2 :** one who works at a board

board measure *n* (1656) **:** measurement in board feet

board of trade (1780) **1** *cap B&T* **:** a British governmental department concerned with commerce and industry **2 :** a commodities exchange

board·room \ˈbō(ə)rd-ˌrüm, ˈbȯ(ə)rd-, -ˌru̇m\ *n* (1836) **:** a room that is designated for meetings of a board

board·walk \ˈbō(ə)rd-ˌwȯk, ˈbȯ(ə)rd-\ *n* (1872) **1 :** a walk constructed of planking **2 :** a walk constructed along a beach

boart \ˈbō(ə)rt, ˈbȯ(ə)rt\ *var of* BORT

[1]boast \ˈbōst\ *n* [ME *boost*] (14c) **1 :** the act or an instance of boasting **:** BRAG **2 :** a cause for pride — **boast·ful** \ˈbōst-fəl\ *adj* — **boast·ful·ly** \-fə-lē\ *adv* — **boast·ful·ness** *n*

[2]boast *vi* (14c) **1 :** to puff oneself up in speech **:** speak vaingloriously **2** *archaic* **:** GLORY, EXULT ~ *vt* **1 :** to speak of or assert with excessive pride **2 a :** to possess and often call attention to (something that is a source of pride) ⟨~*s* a new sports car⟩ **b :** HAVE, CONTAIN ⟨a room ~*ing* no more than a desk and a chair⟩ — **boast·er** *n*

syn BOAST, BRAG, VAUNT, CROW mean to express pride in oneself or one's accomplishments. BOAST often suggests ostentation and exaggeration ⟨ready to *boast* of every trivial success⟩ but it may imply a claiming with proper and justifiable pride ⟨the town *boasts* one of the best hospitals in the area⟩ BRAG suggests crudity and artlessness in glorifying oneself ⟨boys *bragging* to each other⟩ VAUNT usu. connotes more pomp and bombast than BOAST and less crudity or naïveté than BRAG ⟨charity *vaunteth* not itself, is not puffed up —1 Cor 13:4(AV)⟩ CROW usu. implies exultant boasting or bragging ⟨loved to ~ about his ancestors⟩

[3]boast *vt* [origin unknown] (1823) **:** to shape (stone) roughly with a broad chisel in sculpture and stonecutting as a preliminary to finer work

[1]boat \ˈbōt\ *n* [ME *boot,* fr. OE *bāt;* akin to ON *beit* boat] (bef. 12c) **1 :** a small vessel propelled by oars or paddles or by sail or power **2 :** SHIP **3 :** a boat-shaped utensil or device ⟨a gravy ~⟩ ⟨a laboratory ~⟩ — **in the same boat :** in the same situation or predicament

[2]boat *vt* (1613) **:** to place in or bring into a boat ~ *vi* **:** to go by boat

boa·tel \bō-ˈtel\ *n* [blend of *boat* and *hotel*] (1956) **:** a waterside hotel having docks to accommodate persons traveling by boat

boat·er \ˈbōt-ər\ *n* (1605) **1 :** one who travels in a boat **2 :** a stiff hat usu. made of braided straw with a brim, hatband, and flat crown

boat hook *n* (ca. 1611) **:** a pole-handled hook with a point or knob on the back used esp. to pull or push a boat, raft, or log into place

boat·house \-ˌhau̇s\ *n* (1722) **:** a building to house and protect boats

boat·load \ˈbōt-ˌlōd\ *n* (1680) **1 :** a load that fills a boat **2 :** an indefinitely large number

boat·man \ˈbōt-mən\ *n* (14c) **:** a man who works on, deals in, or operates boats

boat people *n pl* (1977) **:** refugees fleeing by boat

boat·swain \ˈbōs-ᵊn\ *n* [ME *bootswein,* fr. *boot* boat + *swein* boy, servant — more at SWAIN] (14c) **1 :** a petty officer on a merchant ship having charge of hull maintenance and related work **2 :** a naval warrant officer in charge of the hull and all related equipment

boat train *n* (1884) **:** an express train for transporting passengers between a port and a city

[1]bob \ˈbäb\ *vb* **bobbed; bob·bing** [ME *boben*] *vt* (13c) **1 :** to strike with a quick light blow **:** RAP **2 :** to move up and down in a short quick movement ⟨~ the head⟩ **3 :** to polish with a bob **:** BUFF ~ *vi* **1 a :** to move up and down briefly or repeatedly ⟨a cork *bobbed* in the water⟩ **b :** to emerge, arise, or appear suddenly or unexpectedly ⟨the question *bobbed* up again⟩ **2 :** to nod or curtsy briefly **3 :** to try to seize a suspended or floating object with the teeth ⟨~ for apples⟩

[2]bob *n* (1550) **1 a :** a short quick down-and-up motion **b** *Scot* **:** any of several folk dances **2** *obs* **:** a blow or tap esp. with the fist **3 a :** a modification of the order in change ringing **b :** a method of change ringing using a bob **4 :** a small polishing wheel of solid felt or leather with rounded edges

[3]bob *vt* **bobbed; bob·bing** [ME *bobben,* fr. MF *bober*] (14c) **1** *obs* **:** DECEIVE, CHEAT **2** *obs* **:** to take by fraud **:** FILCH

[4]bob *n* [ME *bobbe*] (14c) **1 a** (1) **:** BUNCH, CLUSTER (2) *Scot* **:** NOSEGAY **b :** a knob, knot, twist, or curl esp. of ribbons, yarn, or hair **c :** a short haircut on a woman or child **2 :** FLOAT 2a **3 :** a hanging ball or weight (as on a plumb line or on the tail of a kite) **4 :** TRIFLE 1

[5]bob *vt* **bobbed; bob·bing** (1675) **1 :** to cut shorter **:** CROP ⟨~ a horse's tail⟩ **2 :** to cut (hair) in the style of a bob

[6]bob *n, pl* **bob** [perh. fr. the name *Bob*] *slang Brit* (1789) **:** SHILLING

[7]bob *n* (1856) **:** BOBSLED

bob·ber \ˈbäb-ər\ *n* (1837) **1 :** one that bobs **2 :** one who rides or races on a bobsled

bob·bery \ˈbäb-ə-rē\ *n, pl* **-ber·ies** [Hindi *bāp re,* lit., oh father!] (1803) **:** HUBBUB

bob·bin \ˈbäb-ən\ *n* [origin unknown] (1530) **1 a :** any of various small round devices on which threads are wound for working handmade lace **b :** a cylinder or spindle on which yarn or thread is wound (as in a sewing machine) **c :** a coil of insulated wire or the reel it is wound on **2 :** a cotton cord formerly used by dressmakers for piping

bob·bi·net \ˌbäb-ə-ˈnet\ *n* [blend of *bobbin* and *net*] (1814) **:** a machine-made net of cotton, silk, or nylon usu. with hexagonal mesh

[1]bob·ble \ˈbäb-əl\ *vb* **bob·bled; bob·bling** \-(ə-)liŋ\ [freq. of [1]*bob*] (1812) **1 :** [1]BOB **2 :** FUMBLE

[2]bobble *n* (1880) **1 :** a repeated bobbing movement **2 :** a small ball of fabric; *esp* **:** one in a series used on an edging ⟨curtains with ~*s*⟩ **3 :** ERROR, MISTAKE; *esp* **:** a fumble in baseball or football

bob·by \ˈbäb-ē\ *n, pl* **bobbies** [*Bobby,* nickname for *Robert,* after Sir *Robert* Peel, who organized the London police force] *Brit* (1844) **:** POLICEMAN

bob·by pin \ˈbäb-ē-\ *n* [perh. fr. [4]*bob*] (1932) **:** a flat wire hairpin with prongs that press close together

bob·by socks *or* **bobby sox** \ˈbäb-ē-\ *n pl* [perh. fr *bobby* pin] (1943) **:** girls' socks reaching above the ankle

bob·by–sox·er \-ˌsäk-sər\ *n* (1944) **:** an adolescent girl

bob·cat \ˈbäb-ˌkat\ *n* [[4]*bob;* fr. the stubby tail] (1888) **:** a common No. American lynx (*Lynx rufus*) typically rusty or reddish in base color

bo·beche \bō-ˈbesh, -ˈbāsh\ *n* [F *bobèche*] (ca. 1897) **:** a usu. glass collar on a candle socket to catch drippings or on a candlestick or chandelier to hold suspended glass prisms

bob·o·link \ˈbäb-ə-ˌliŋk\ *n* [imit.] (1774) **:** an American migratory songbird (*Dolichonyx oryzivorus*)

bob·sled \ˈbäb-ˌsled\ *n* [perh. fr. [4]*bob*] (1839) **1 :** a short sled usu. used as one of a pair joined by a coupling **2 :** a large usu. metal sled used in racing and equipped with two pairs of runners in tandem, a long seat for two or more people, a steering wheel, and a hand brake — **bobsled** *vi* — **bob·sled·der** *n*

bob·sled·ding \-ˌsled-iŋ\ *n* (1883) **:** the act, skill, or sport of riding or racing on a bobsled

bob·stay \ˈbäb-ˌstā\ *n* [prob. fr. [2]*bob*] (1758) **:** a stay to hold a ship's bowsprit down

bob·tail \ˈbäb-ˌtāl\ *n* [[4]*bob*] (1605) **1 a :** a bobbed tail **b :** a horse, dog, or cat with a bobbed or very short tail; *esp* **:** OLD ENGLISH SHEEPDOG **2 :** something curtailed — **bobtail** *or* **bob·tailed** \-ˌtāld\ *adj*

bob veal \ˈbäb-\ *n* [E dial. *bob* young calf] (1855) **:** the veal of a very young or unborn calf

bob·white \(ˈ)bäb-ˈhwīt, -ˈwīt\ *n* [imit.] (1819) **:** any of a genus (*Colinus*) of quail; *esp* **:** a favorite game bird (*C. virginianus*) of the eastern and central U.S.

bo·cac·cio \bə-ˈkäch-(ē-ˌ)ō\ *n* [perh. deriv. of Sp *bocacha,* aug. of *boca* mouth] (ca. 1890) **:** a large rockfish (*Sebastes paucispinis*) of the Pacific coast locally important as a market fish

boc·cie *or* **boc·ci** *or* **boc·ce** \ˈbäch-ē\ *n* [It *bocce,* pl. of *boccia* ball, fr. (assumed) VL *bottia* boss] (1902) **:** a game of Italian origin similar to lawn bowling played on a long narrow usu. dirt court

bock \ˈbäk\ *n* [G, short for *bockbier,* by shortening & alter. fr. *Einbecker bier,* lit., beer from Einbeck, fr. *Einbeck,* Germany] (1856) **:** a heavy dark rich beer usu. sold in the early spring

bod \ˈbäd\ *n* (1788) **1** *Brit* **:** FELLOW, GUY **2 :** BODY

bo·da·cious \bō-ˈdā-shəs\ *adj* [back-formation fr. earlier *bodaciously* (thoroughly), alter. of earlier *bodyaciously,* perh. fr. *body* + *-aciously* (as in *graciously*)] (1845) **1** *Southern & Midland* **:** OUTRIGHT, UNMISTAKABLE **2** *Southern & Midland* **:** REMARKABLE, NOTEWORTHY ⟨I got some ~ gossip —Fred Lasswell⟩ — **bo·da·cious·ly** *adv*

[1]bode \ˈbōd\ *vt* **bod·ed; bod·ing** [ME *boden,* fr. OE *bodian;* akin to OE *bēodan* to proclaim — more at BID] (bef. 12c) **1** *archaic* **:** to announce beforehand **:** FORETELL **2 :** to indicate by signs **:** PRESAGE ⟨this controversy . . . will ~ ill for both of us —A. H. Lowe⟩

[2]bode *past of* BIDE

bo·de·ga \bō-ˈdā-gə\ *n* [Sp, fr. L *apotheca* storehouse — more at APOTHECARY] (1846) **1 :** a storehouse for maturing wine **2 a :** WINESHOP **b :** a store specializing in Hispanic groceries **c :** [1]BAR 5a, b

bode·ment \ˈbōd-mənt\ *n* (1605) **1 :** OMEN, FOREBODING **2 :** PREDICTION, PROPHECY

bo·dhi·satt·va *or* **bod·dhi·satt·va** \ˌbōd-i-ˈsət-və, -ˈsät-\ *n* [Skt *bodhisattva* one whose essence is enlightenment, fr. *bodhi* enlightenment + *sattva* being — more at BID] (1828) **:** a being that compassionately refrains from entering nirvana in order to save others and is worshiped as a deity in Mahayana Buddhism

bodh·ran \ˈbȯ-(ˌ)rän, -rən\ *n* [IrGael] (1972) **:** an Irish goatskin drum

bod·ice \ˈbäd-əs\ *n* [alter. of *bodies,* pl. of [1]*body*] (1566) **1 :** the upper part of a woman's dress **2** *archaic* **:** CORSET, STAYS

bodice ripper *n* (1980) **:** a historical or Gothic romance typically featuring scenes in which a woman is physically humiliated and assaulted

-bod·ied \ˈbäd-ēd\ *adj comb form* **:** having a body of a specified nature ⟨full-*bodied*⟩ ⟨glass-*bodied*⟩

bodi·less \ˈbäd-i-ləs, ˈbäd-ᵊl-əs\ *adj* (14c) **:** having no body

[1]bodi·ly \ˈbäd-ᵊl-ē\ *adj* (14c) **1 :** having a body **:** PHYSICAL **2 :** of or relating to the body ⟨~ comfort⟩ ⟨~ organs⟩

[2]bodily *adv* (14c) **1 :** in the flesh **2 :** as a whole **:** ALTOGETHER

bod·ing \ˈbōd-iŋ\ *n* (13c) **:** FOREBODING

bod·kin \ˈbäd-kən\ *n* [ME *bodekin*] (14c) **1 a :** DAGGER, STILETTO **b :** a sharp slender instrument for making holes in cloth **c :** an ornamental hairpin shaped like a stiletto **2 :** a blunt needle with a large eye for drawing tape or ribbon through a loop or hem

[1]body \ˈbäd-ē\ *n, pl* **bod·ies** [ME, fr. OE *bodig;* akin to OHG *botah* body] (bef. 12c) **1 a :** the organized physical substance of an animal or plant either living or dead: as (1) **:** the material part or nature of a human being (2) **:** the dead organism **:** CORPSE (3) **:** the person of a human being before the law **b :** a human being **:** PERSON **2 a :** the main part of a plant or animal body esp. as distinguished from limbs and head : TRUNK **b :** the main, central, or principal part: as **(1) :** the nave of a church **(2) :** the bed or box of a vehicle on or in which the load is placed **3 a :** the part of a garment covering the body or trunk **b :** the main part of a literary or journalistic work : TEXT 2b **c :** the sound box or pipe of a musical instrument **4 a :** a mass of matter distinct from other masses ⟨a ~ of water⟩ **b :** one of the seven planets of the old astronomy **c :** something that embodies or gives concrete reality to a thing; *specif* **:** a sensible object in physical space **d :** AGGREGATE, QUANTITY ⟨a ~ of evidence⟩ **5 :** a group of persons or things: as **a :** a fighting unit : FORCE **b :** a group of individuals organized for some purpose : CORPORATION ⟨a legislative ~⟩ **6 a :** VISCOSITY, CONSISTENCY — used esp. of oils and grease **b :** compactness or firmness of texture **c :** fullness or resonance of a musical tone **d :** fullness and richness of flavor — used of a beverage (as wine)

[2]**body** *vt* **bod·ied; body·ing** (15c) **1 a :** to give form or shape to : EMBODY **b :** REPRESENT, SYMBOLIZE — usu. used with *forth* **2 :** to increase the viscosity of (an oil)

body·build·ing \-ˌbil-diŋ\ *n* (1904) **:** the developing of the body through exercise and diet; *specif* **:** the developing of the physique for competitive exhibition — **body·build·er** *n*

body cavity *n* (1875) **:** a cavity within an animal body; *specif* **:** COELOM

body check *n* (ca. 1892) **:** a blocking of an opposing player with the body (as in ice hockey or lacrosse) — **body·check** \'bäd-ē-ˌchek\ *vt*

body corporate *n* (15c) **:** CORPORATION

body count *n* (1967) **:** a count of or as if of the bodies of killed enemy soldiers

body English *n* (1908) **:** bodily motions made in a usu. unconscious effort to influence the progress of a propelled object (as a ball)

body·guard \'bäd-ē-ˌgärd\ *n* (1735) **:** a man or group of men whose duty is to protect a person from bodily harm

body language *n* (1926) **:** the gestures and mannerisms by which a person communicates with others

body louse *n* (1575) **:** a louse feeding primarily on the body; *esp* **:** a sucking louse (*Pediculus humanus*) feeding on the body and living in the clothing of man — called also *cootie*

body mechanics *n pl but sing or pl in constr* (ca. 1969) **:** systematic exercises designed esp. to develop coordination, endurance, and poise

body politic *n* (15c) **1 :** a group of persons politically organized under a single governmental authority **2** *archaic* **:** CORPORATION 2 **3 :** a people considered as a collective unit

body shirt *n* (1967) **1 :** a close-fitting shirt or blouse **2 :** a woman's close-fitting top made with a sewn-in or snapped crotch

body shop *n* (1954) **:** a shop where automotive bodies are made or repaired

body snatcher *n* (1812) **:** one that steals corpses from graves

body stocking *n* (1965) **:** a sheer close-fitting one-piece garment for the torso that often has sleeves and legs

body·suit \'bäd-ē-ˌsüt\ *n* (1970) **:** a close-fitting one-piece garment for the torso

body·surf \'bäd-ē-ˌsərf\ *vi* (1943) **:** to ride on a wave without a surfboard by planing on the chest and stomach — **body·surf·er** *n*

body wall *n* (1888) **:** the external surface of the animal body consisting of ectoderm and mesoderm and enclosing the body cavity

body·work \'bäd-ē-ˌwərk\ *n* (1908) **1 :** a vehicle body **2 :** the act or process of making or repairing vehicle bodies

boehm·ite \'bām-ˌīt, 'bə(r)m-\ *n* [G *böhmit,* fr. J. *Böhm* (*Boehm*), 20th cent. Ger. scientist] (ca. 1929) **:** a mineral consisting of an orthorhombic form of aluminum oxide and hydroxide AlO(OH) found in bauxite

Boer \'bō(ə)r, 'bȯ(ə)r, 'bu̇(ə)r\ *n* [D, lit., farmer — more at BOOR] (1834) **:** a South African of Dutch or Huguenot descent

boff \'bäf\ *or* **bof·fo** \'bäf-(ˌ)ō\ *n, pl* **boffs** *or* **boffos** [prob. fr. box office] (1946) **1 :** a hearty laugh **2 :** a gag or line that produces a hearty laugh **3 :** something that is conspicuously successful : HIT

bof·fin \'bäf-ən\ *n* [origin unknown] *chiefly Brit* (1945) **:** a scientific expert

bof·fo \'bäf-(ˌ)ō\ *adj* (ca. 1945) **:** extremely successful : SENSATIONAL

bof·fo·la \bä-'fō-lə\ *n* [irreg. fr. *boff*] (1947) **:** BOFF

Bo·fors gun \'bō-ˌfȯrz-, 'bü-\ *n* [*Bofors,* munition works in Sweden] (1939) **:** a double-barreled automatic antiaircraft gun

[1]**bog** \'bäg, 'bȯg\ *n* [prob. fr. IrGael *bogach* (fr. *bog* soft, fr. OIr *bocc*) & ScGael *boglach* (fr. *bog* soft); akin to OE *būgan* to bend — more at BOW] (14c) **:** wet spongy ground; *esp* **:** a poorly drained usu. acid area rich in plant residues, frequently surrounding a body of open water, and having a characteristic flora (as of sedges, heaths, and sphagnum) — **bog·gy** \'bäg-ē, 'bȯg-\ *adj*

[2]**bog** *vb* **bogged; bog·ging** *vt* (1599) **:** to cause to sink into or as if into a bog : IMPEDE, MIRE — usu. used with *down* ~ *vi* **:** to become impeded or stuck — usu. used with *down*

bog asphodel *n* (ca. 1857) **:** either of two bog herbs (*Narthecium ossifragum* of Europe and *N. americanum* of the U.S.) of the lily family

[1]**bo·gey** *also* **bo·gie** *or* **bo·gy** *n, pl* **bogeys** *also* **bogies** [prob. alter. of *bogle*] (1857) **1** \'bu̇g-ē, 'bō-gē, 'bü-gē\ **:** SPECTER, PHANTOM **2** \'bō-gē *also* 'bu̇g-ē *or* 'bü-gē\ **:** a source of fear, perplexity, or harassment **3** \'bō-gē\ **a** *chiefly Brit* **:** an average golfer's score used as a standard for a particular hole or course **b :** one stroke over par on a hole in golf **4** \'bō-gē\ **:** a numerical standard of performance set up as a mark to be aimed at in competition

[2]**bogey** \'bō-gē\ *vt* **bo·geyed; bo·gey·ing** (1950) **:** to shoot (a hole in golf) in one over par

bo·gey·man *also* **bo·gy·man** \'bu̇g-ē-ˌman, 'bō-gē-, 'bü-gē-, 'bu̇g-ər-\ *n* (ca. 1890) **1 :** a monstrous imaginary figure used in threatening children **2 :** a terrifying or dreaded person or thing : BUGBEAR

bog·gle \'bäg-əl\ *vb* **bog·gled; bog·gling** \-(ə-)liŋ\ [perh. fr. Brit. dial. *bogle* goblin, object of fear] *vi* (1598) **1 :** to start with fright or amazement : be overwhelmed ⟨the mind ~s at the research needed⟩ **2 :** to hesitate because of doubt, fear, or scruples **3 :** BUNGLE ~ *vt* **:** to overwhelm with wonder or bewilderment — **boggle** *n*

bo·gie *also* **bo·gey** *or* **bo·gy** \'bō-gē\ *n, pl* **bogies** *also* **bogeys** [origin unknown] (1835) **1 :** a low strongly built cart **2 a** *chiefly Brit* **:** a swiveling railway truck **b :** the driving-wheel assembly consisting of the rear four wheels of a 6-wheel automotive truck **3 :** a small supporting or aligning wheel (as on the inside perimeter of the tread of a tank)

bo·gle \'bō-gəl\ *also* **bog·gle** \'bäg-əl\ *n* [origin unknown] *dial Brit* (ca. 1505) **:** GOBLIN, SPECTER; *also* **:** an object of fear or loathing

Bo·go·mil *also* **Bo·go·mile** \ˌbəg-ə-'mē(ə)l\ *n* [Russ *bogomil,* fr. OSlav *Bogomilŭ* Bogomil, 10th cent. Bulg. priest, founder of the sect] (1574) **:** a member of a medieval Bulgarian sect holding that God has two sons, the rebellious Satan and the obedient Jesus

bo·gus \'bō-gəs\ *adj* [*bogus* (a machine for making counterfeit money)] (1825) **:** not genuine : COUNTERFEIT, SHAM

bo·hea \bō-'hē\ *n, often cap* [Chin (Pek) *wu³-i²,* hills in China where it was grown] (1701) **:** a black tea

bo·he·mia \bō-'hē-mē-ə\ *n, often cap* [trans. of F *bohème*] (1861) **:** a community of bohemians **:** the world of bohemians

Bo·he·mi·an \-mē-ən\ *n* (1603) **1 a :** a native or inhabitant of Bohemia **b :** the group of Czech dialects used in Bohemia **2** *often not cap* **a :** VAGABOND, WANDERER; *esp* **:** GYPSY **b :** a person (as a writer or an artist) living an unconventional life usu. in a colony with others — **bohemian** *adj, often cap*

Bohemian Brethren *n pl* (1863) **:** a Christian body originating in Bohemia in 1467 and forming a parent body of the Moravian Church

bo·he·mi·an·ism \bō-'hē-mē-ə-ˌniz-əm\ *n, often cap* (1861) **:** the unconventional way of life of bohemians

Bohr effect \'bō(ə)r-, 'bȯ(ə)r-\ *n* [Christian *Bohr* †1911 Dan. physiologist] (1939) **:** the decrease in oxygen affinity of hemoglobins and some invertebrate respiratory pigments in response to increased carbon dioxide concentration in the blood

Bohr theory *n* [Niels *Bohr*] (1922) **:** a theory in early quantum physics: an atom consists of a positively charged nucleus about which revolves one or more electrons

[1]**boil** \'bȯi(ə)l\ *n* [alter. of ME *bile,* fr. OE *bӯl* — more at BIG] (bef. 12c) **:** a localized swelling and inflammation of the skin resulting from infection in a skin gland, having a hard central core, and forming pus

[2]**boil** *vb* [ME *boilen,* fr. OF *boillir,* fr. L *bullire* to bubble, fr. *bulla* bubble] *vi* (13c) **1 a :** to generate bubbles of vapor when heated — used of a liquid **b :** to come to the boiling point **2 :** to become agitated like boiling water : SEETHE **3 :** to be moved, excited, or stirred up ⟨made his blood ~⟩ **4 a :** to rush headlong **b :** to burst forth : ERUPT ⟨water ~*ing* from a spring⟩ **5 :** to undergo the action of a boiling liquid ~ *vt* **1 :** to subject to the action of a boiling liquid ⟨~ eggs⟩ **2 :** to heat to the boiling point ⟨~ water⟩ **3 :** to form or separate (as sugar or salt) by boiling

[3]**boil** *n* (15c) **1 :** the act or state of boiling **2 :** a swirling upheaval (as of water)

boil down *vt* (1845) **1 :** to reduce in bulk by boiling **2 :** CONDENSE, SUMMARIZE ⟨*boil down* a report⟩ ~ *vi* **1 :** to undergo reduction in bulk by boiling **2 :** to be equivalent in summary : AMOUNT ⟨his speech *boiled down* to a plea for more money⟩

boiled oil *n* (ca. 1858) **:** a fatty oil (as linseed oil) whose drying properties have been improved by heating usu. with driers

boil·er \'bȯi-lər\ *n* (1540) **1 :** one that boils **2 a :** a vessel used for boiling **b :** the part of a steam generator in which water is converted into steam and which consists usu. of metal shells and tubes **c :** a tank in which water is heated or hot water is stored

boil·er·mak·er \'bȯi-lər-ˌmā-kər\ *n* (1865) **1 :** a worker who makes, assembles, or repairs boilers **2 :** whiskey with a beer chaser

boil·er·plate \-ˌplāt\ *n* (1893) **1 :** syndicated material supplied esp. to weekly newspapers in matrix or plate form **2 :** standardized, formulaic, or hackneyed language ⟨bureaucratic ~⟩

boil·er·suit \-ˌsüt\ *n* (1928) **:** COVERALL

[1]**boil·ing** \'bȯi-liŋ\ *adj* (14c) **1 a :** heated to the boiling point **b :** TORRID ⟨a ~ sun⟩ **2 :** intensely agitated ⟨a ~ sea⟩ ⟨~ with anger⟩

[2]**boiling** *adv* (1607) **:** to an extreme degree : VERY ⟨~ mad⟩ ⟨~ hot⟩

boiling point *n* (1773) **1 :** the temperature at which a liquid boils **2 a :** the point at which a person loses his temper **b :** the point of crisis : HEAD 17b ⟨matters had reached the *boiling point*⟩

boil over *vi* (15c) **1 :** to overflow while boiling or during boiling **2 :** to become so incensed as to lose one's temper

bois d'arc \'bō-ˌdä(r)k\ *n, pl* **bois d'arcs** *or* **bois d'arc** [F, lit., bow wood] (1805) **:** OSAGE ORANGE; *also* **:** its wood

bois·ter·ous \'bȯi-st(ə-)rəs\ *adj* [ME *boistous* rough] (14c) **1** *obs* **a :** DURABLE, STRONG **b :** COARSE **c :** MASSIVE **2 a :** noisily turbulent : ROWDY **b :** marked by or expressive of exuberance and high spirits **3 :** STORMY, TUMULTUOUS ***syn*** see VOCIFEROUS — **bois·ter·ous·ly** *adv* — **bois·ter·ous·ness** *n*

boîte \'bwät\ *n* [F, lit., box] (1922) **:** NIGHTCLUB

bok choy \'bäk-'chȯi\ *n* [modif. of Chin (Cant) *paâk ts'òi,* lit., white vegetable] (1938) **:** a Chinese cabbage (*Brassica chinensis*) forming an open head with long white stalks and green leaves

Bok·mål \'bu̇k-ˌmȯl, 'bōk-\ *n* [Norw, lit., book language] (1931) **:** a literary form of Norwegian developed by the gradual reform of written Danish — compare NYNORSK

bo·la \'bō-lə\ *or* **bo·las** \-ləs\ *n, pl* **bolas** \-ləz\ *also* **bo·las·es** [AmerSp *bolas,* fr. Sp *bola* ball] (1818) **:** a cord with weights attached to the ends for throwing at and entangling an animal

bold \'bōld\ *adj* [ME, fr. OE *beald;* akin to OHG *bald* bold] (bef. 12c) **1 a :** fearless before danger : INTREPID **b :** showing or requiring a fearless daring spirit ⟨a ~ plan⟩ **2 :** IMPUDENT, PRESUMPTUOUS **3** *obs* **:** ASSURED, CONFIDENT **4 :** SHEER, STEEP ⟨~ cliffs⟩ **5 :** ADVENTUROUS, FREE ⟨a ~ thinker⟩ **6 :** standing out prominently **7 :** being or set in boldface — **bold·ly** \'bōl-(d)lē\ *adv* — **bold·ness** \'bōl(d)-nəs\ *n*

bold·face \'bōl(d)-ˌfās\ *n* (ca. 1889) **:** a heavy-faced type; *also* **:** printing in boldface

bold–faced \'bōl(d)-'fāst\ *adj* (1591) **1 :** bold in manner or conduct : IMPUDENT **2** *usu* **bold·faced :** being or set in boldface

bole \'bōl\ *n* [ME, fr. ON *bolr*] (14c) **:** the trunk of a tree

bo·le·ro \bə-'le(ə)r-(ˌ)ō\ *n, pl* **-ros** [Sp] (1787) **1 :** a Spanish dance characterized by sharp turns, stamping of the feet, and sudden pauses in a position with one arm arched over the head; *also* **:** music in $^3/_4$ time for or suitable for a bolero **2 :** a loose waist-length jacket open at the front

\ə\ abut \ᵊ\ kitten, F table \ər\ further \a\ ash \ā\ ace \ä\ cot, cart \au̇\ out \ch\ chin \e\ bet \ē\ easy \g\ go \i\ hit \ī\ ice \j\ job \ŋ\ sing \ō\ go \ȯ\ law \ȯi\ boy \th\ thin \t͟h\ the \ü\ loot \u̇\ foot \y\ yet \zh\ vision \à, k̲, ⁿ, œ, œ̄, ue, ue̅, ʸ\ see Guide to Pronunciation

bo·le·tus \bō-ˈlēt-əs\ *n, pl* **-tus·es** *or* **-ti** \-ˈlēt-ˌī\ [NL, genus name, fr. L, a fungus, fr. Gk *bōlitēs*] (1601) : any of a genus (*Boletus*) of soft pore fungi some of which are poisonous and others edible

bo·li·var \bə-ˈlē-ˌvär, ˈbäl-ə-vər\ *n, pl* **-va·res** \ˌbäl-ə-ˈvär-ˌās, ˌbō-li-\ *or* **-vars** [AmerSp *bolívar*, fr. Simón *Bolívar*] (ca. 1885) — see MONEY table

bo·li·vi·a·no \bə-ˌliv-ē-ˈän-(ˌ)ō\ *n, pl* **-nos** [Sp] (ca. 1872) **1 :** a former monetary unit of Bolivia replaced in 1963 by the peso **2** — see MONEY table

boll \ˈbōl\ *n* [ME] (15c) **:** the pod or capsule of a plant (as cotton)

bol·lard \ˈbäl-ərd, *Brit also* -ˌärd\ *n* [perh. irreg. fr. *bole*] (ca. 1795) **1 :** a post of metal or wood on a wharf around which to fasten mooring lines **2 :** BITT 1 **3** *chiefly Brit* **:** any of a series of short posts set at intervals to delimit an area (as a traffic island) or to exclude vehicles

bol·lix \ˈbäl-iks\ *vt* [alter. of *ballocks*, pl. of *ballock* (testis), fr. ME, fr. OE *bealluc* — more at BALL] (1937) **:** to throw into disorder; *also* **:** BUNGLE — usu. used with *up* — **bollix** *n*

boll weevil *n* (1895) **:** a grayish weevil (*Anthonomus grandis*) about ¼ inch long that infests the cotton plant and feeds on the squares and bolls both as a larva and an adult

boll·worm \ˈbōl-ˌwərm\ *n* (1847) **:** CORN EARWORM; *also* **:** any of several other moths or their immature stages which feed on cotton bolls as larvae

bo·lo \ˈbō-(ˌ)lō\ *n, pl* **bolos** [Sp] (ca. 1899) **:** a long heavy single-edged knife of Philippine origin used to cut vegetation and as a weapon

bo·lo·gna \bə-ˈlō-nē *also* -n(y)ə\ *n* [short for *Bologna sausage*, fr. *Bologna*, Italy] (1596) **:** a large smoked sausage of beef, veal, and pork

bo·lom·e·ter \bō-ˈläm-ət-ər\ *n* [Gk *bolē* stroke, beam of light (fr. *ballein* to throw) + E *-o-* + *-meter*] (1881) **:** a very sensitive thermometer whose electrical resistance varies with temperature and which is used in the detection and measurement of feeble thermal radiation and is esp. adapted to the study of infrared spectra — **bo·lo·met·ric** \ˌbō-lə-ˈme-trik\ *adj* — **bo·lo·met·ri·cal·ly** \-tri-k(ə-)lē\ *adv*

bo·lo·ney \bə-ˈlō-nē\ *var of* BALONEY

bo·lo tie \ˌbō-lō-\ *or* **bo·la tie** \-lə-\ *n* [prob. fr. *bola*] (1964) **:** a cord fastened around the neck with an ornamental clasp and worn as a necktie

Bol·she·vik \ˈbōl-shə-ˌvik, ˈbȯl-, ˈbäl-, -ˌvēk\ *n, pl* **Bolsheviks** *also* **Bol·she·vi·ki** \ˌbōl-shə-ˈvik-ē, ˌbȯl-, ˌbäl-, -ˈvē-kē\ [Russ *bol'shevik*, fr. *bol'she* larger] (1917) **1 :** a member of the extremist wing of the Russian Social Democratic party that seized supreme power in Russia by the Revolution of November 1917 **2 :** COMMUNIST 3 — **Bolshevik** *adj*

bol·she·vism \ˈbōl-shə-ˌviz-əm, ˈbȯl-, ˈbäl-\ *n, often cap* (1917) **1 :** the doctrine or program of the Bolsheviks advocating violent overthrow of capitalism **2 :** Russian communism

Bol·she·vist \-vəst\ *n or adj* (1917) **:** BOLSHEVIK

bol·she·vize \-ˌvīz\ *vt* **-vized; -viz·ing** (1919) **:** to make Bolshevist — **Bol·she·vi·za·tion** \ˌbōl-shə-və-ˈzā-shən, ˌbȯl-, ˌbäl-\ *n*

bol·shie *or* **bol·shy** \ˈbōl-shē, ˈbȯl-, ˈbäl-\ *n or adj, often cap* (1918) **:** BOLSHEVIK

¹bol·ster \ˈbōl-stər\ *n* [ME, fr. OE; akin to OE *belg* bag — more at BELLY] (bef. 12c) **1 :** a long pillow or cushion **2 :** a structural part designed to eliminate friction or provide support or bearing; *esp* **:** the horizontal connection between the volutes of an Ionic capital

²bolster *vt* **bol·stered; bol·ster·ing** \-st(ə-)riŋ\ (1508) **1 :** to support with or as if with a bolster **:** REINFORCE **2 :** to give a boost to ⟨news that ~*ed* his spirits⟩ — **bol·ster·er** \-stər-ər\ *n*

¹bolt \ˈbōlt\ *n* [ME, fr. OE; akin to OHG *bolz* crossbow bolt, Lith *beldėti* to beat] (bef. 12c) **1 a :** a shaft or missile designed to be shot from a crossbow or catapult; *esp* **:** a short stout usu. blunt-headed arrow **b :** a lightning stroke **:** THUNDERBOLT **2 a :** a wood or metal bar or rod used to fasten a door **b :** the part of a lock that is shot or withdrawn by the key **3 a :** a roll of cloth of specified length **b :** a roll of wallpaper of specified length **4 :** a metal rod or pin for fastening objects together that usu. has a head at one end and a screw thread at the other and is secured by a nut **5 a :** a block of timber to be sawed or cut **b :** a short round section of a log **6 :** a metal cylinder that drives the cartridge into the chamber of a firearm, locks the breech, and usu. contains the firing pin and extractor

²bolt *vi* (13c) **1 :** to move suddenly or nervously **:** START **2 :** to move rapidly **:** DASH **3 a :** to dart off or away **:** FLEE **b :** to break away from control or a set course **4 :** to break away from or oppose one's political party or candidate ~ *vt* **1 a** *archaic* **:** SHOOT, DISCHARGE **b :** FLUSH, START ⟨~ rabbits⟩ **2 :** to say impulsively **:** BLURT **3 :** to secure with a bolt **4 :** to attach or fasten with bolts **5 :** to swallow hastily or without chewing **6 :** to break away from or refuse to support (as a political party)

³bolt *adv* (14c) **1 :** in an erect or straight-backed position **:** RIGIDLY ⟨sat ~ upright⟩ **2** *archaic* **:** DIRECTLY, STRAIGHT

⁴bolt *n* (1550) **:** the act or an instance of bolting

⁵bolt *vt* [ME *bulten*, fr. OF *buleter*, of Gmc origin; akin to MHG *biuteln* to sift, fr. *biutel* bag, fr. OHG *būtil*] (13c) **1 :** to sift (as flour) usu. through fine-meshed cloth **2** *archaic* **:** SIFT 2

bolt–ac·tion \ˈbōl-ˈtak-shən\ *adj, of a firearm* (1896) **:** loaded by means of a manually operated bolt

¹bolt·er \ˈbōl-tər\ *n* (15c) **:** a machine for bolting flour; *also* **:** the operator of such a machine

²bolter *n* (ca. 1699) **:** one that bolts: as **a :** as horse given to running away **b :** a voter who breaks away from or opposes his party

bolt·rope \ˈbōlt-ˌrōp\ *n* (ca. 1626) **:** a strong rope stitched to the edges of a sail to strengthen it

bo·lus \ˈbō-ləs\ *n* [LL, fr. Gk *bōlos* lump; akin to L *bulbus* bulb] (1562) **:** a rounded mass: as **a :** a large pill **b :** a soft mass of chewed food

¹bomb \ˈbäm\ *n* [F *bombe*, fr. It *bomba*, prob. fr. L *bombus* deep hollow sound, fr. Gk *bombos*, of imit. origin] (1684) **1 a :** an explosive device fused to detonate under specified conditions **b :** ATOM BOMB; *also* **:** nuclear weapons in general — usu. used with *the* **2 :** a vessel for compressed gases: as **a :** a pressure vessel for conducting chemical experiments **b :** a small dispenser for a substance (as paint or an insecticide) stored under pressure **3 :** a rounded mass of lava exploded from a volcano **4 :** a lead-lined container for radioactive material **5 :** FAILURE, FLOP ⟨the play was a ~⟩ **6** *Brit* **:** a large sum of money **7** *Brit* **:** a great success **:** HIT **8 :** a long pass in football

²bomb *vt* (1688) **1 :** to attack with or as if with bombs **:** BOMBARD **2 :** to defeat decisively ~ *vi* **1 :** to fall flat **:** FAIL **2** *slang* **:** to move rapidly ⟨~*ed* down the hill⟩ — **bomb·ing** *n*

¹bom·bard \ˈbäm-ˌbärd\ *n* [ME *bombarde*, fr. MF, prob. fr. L *bombus*] (15c) **:** a late medieval cannon used to hurl large stones

²bom·bard \bäm-ˈbärd *also* bəm-\ *vt* (1686) **1 :** to attack esp. with artillery or bombers **2 :** to assail vigorously or persistently (as with questions) **3 :** to subject to the impact of rapidly moving particles (as electrons or alpha rays) ***syn*** see ATTACK — **bom·bard·ment** \-mənt\ *n*

bom·bar·dier \ˌbäm-bə(r)-ˈdi(ə)r\ *n* (1560) **1 a** *archaic* **:** ARTILLERYMAN **b :** a noncommissioned officer in the British artillery **2 :** a bomber-crew member who uses the bombsight and releases the bombs

bom·bar·don \ˈbäm-bər-ˌdōn, bäm-ˈbärd-ᵊn\ *n* [F, fr. It *bombardone*] (1856) **1 :** the bass member of the shawm family **2 :** a bass tuba

bom·bast \ˈbäm-ˌbast\ *n* [ME *bombast* cotton padding, fr. MF *bombace*, fr. ML *bombac-*, *bombax* cotton, alter. of L *bombyc-*, *bombyx* silkworm, silk, fr. Gk *bombyk-*, *bombyx*] (1589) **:** pretentious inflated speech or writing

bom·bas·tic \bäm-ˈbas-tik\ *adj* (1704) **:** marked by or given to bombast **:** POMPOUS, OVERBLOWN — **bom·bas·ti·cal·ly** \-ti-k(ə-)lē\ *adv*

bom·ba·zine \ˌbäm-bə-ˈzēn\ *n* [MF *bombasin*, fr. ML *bombacinum*, *bombycinum* silken texture, fr. L, neut. of *bombycinus* of silk, fr. *bombyc-*, *bombyx*] (1572) **1 :** a twilled fabric with silk warp and worsted filling **2 :** a silk fabric in twill weave dyed black

bombe \ˈbäm, ˈbōⁿ(m)b\ *n* [F, lit., bomb] (1892) **:** a frozen dessert usu. containing ice cream and formed in layers in a round or cone-shaped mold

bombed \ˈbämd\ *adj* (1969) **:** affected by alcohol or drugs **:** DRUNK, HIGH

bomb·er \ˈbäm-ər\ *n* (1915) **:** one that bombs; *specif* **:** an airplane designed for bombing

bom·bi·nate \ˈbäm-bə-ˌnāt\ *vi* **-nat·ed; -nat·ing** [NL *bombinatus*, pp. of *bombinare*, alter. of L *bombilare*, fr. *bombus*] (1880) **:** BUZZ, DRONE — **bom·bi·na·tion** \ˌbäm-bə-ˈnā-shən\ *n*

bomb·proof \ˈbäm-ˈprüf\ *adj* (1702) **:** safe from the force of bombs

bomb·shell \ˈbäm-ˌshel\ *n* (1708) **1 :** BOMB 1a **2 :** one that is stunning, amazing, or devastating ⟨the book was a political ~⟩

bomb·sight \-ˌsīt\ *n* (1917) **:** a sighting device for aiming bombs

bo·na fide \ˈbō-nə-ˌfīd, ˈbän-ə-; ˌbō-nə-ˈfīd-ē, -ˈfīd-ə\ *adj* [L, lit., in good faith] (1788) **1 :** made in good faith without fraud or deceit ⟨a *bona fide* offer to buy a farm⟩ **2 :** made with earnest intent **:** SINCERE **3 :** neither specious nor counterfeit **:** GENUINE ***syn*** see AUTHENTIC

bo·na fi·des \ˌbō-nə-ˈfīd-ˌēz, ÷ˈbō-nə-ˌfīdz\ *n* [L, lit., good faith] (1798) **1 :** lack of fraud or deceit **:** SINCERITY ⟨a man on whom suspicion had never rested and whose *bona fides* was unshakable —Victor Canning⟩ **2 :** evidence of one's good faith — usu. pl. in constr. **3 :** evidence of one's qualifications or achievements — usu. pl. in constr.

bo·nan·za \bə-ˈnan-zə\ *n* [Sp, lit., fair weather, fr. ML *bonacia*, alter. (influenced by L *bonus* good) of L *malacia* calm at sea, fr. Gk *malakia*, lit., softness, fr. *malakos* soft] (1842) **1 :** an exceptionally large and rich ore shoot or pocket in veins carrying gold and silver **2 a :** something that is very valuable, profitable, or rewarding ⟨a box-office ~⟩ **b :** an extremely large amount ⟨expected a ~ of sympathy⟩

Bo·na·part·ism \ˈbō-nə-ˌpärt-ˌiz-əm\ *n* (1815) **1 :** support of the French emperors Napoleon I, Napoleon III, or their dynasty **2 :** a political movement associated chiefly with authoritarian rule usu. by a military leader ostensibly supported by a popular mandate — **Bo·na·part·ist** \-ˌpärt-əst\ *n or adj*

bon·bon \ˈbän-ˌbän\ *n* [F, (baby talk), redupl. of *bon* good, fr. L *bonus* — more at BOUNTY] (1796) **:** a candy with chocolate or fondant coating and fondant center that sometimes contains fruits and nuts

¹bond \ˈbänd\ *n* [ME *band, bond* — more at BAND] (12c) **1 :** something that binds or restrains **:** FETTER **2 :** a binding agreement **:** COVENANT **3 a :** a band or cord used to tie something **b :** a material or device for binding **c :** an attractive force that holds together the atoms, ions, or groups of atoms in a molecule or crystal — usu. represented in formulas by a line or two dots **d :** an adhesive, cementing material, or fusible ingredient that combines, unites, or strengthens **4 :** a uniting or binding element or force **:** TIE ⟨the ~*s* of friendship⟩ **5 a :** an obligation made binding by a money forfeit; *also* **:** the amount of the money guarantee **b :** one who acts as bail or surety **c :** an interest-bearing certificate of public or private indebtedness ⟨a 20-year ~ issue to finance a new courthouse⟩ **d :** an insurance agreement pledging surety for financial loss caused to another by the act or default of a third person or by some contingency over which the third person may have no control **6 :** the systematic lapping of brick in a wall **7 :** the state of goods made, stored, or transported under the care of bonded agencies until the duties or taxes on them are paid **8 :** a 100-proof straight whiskey aged at least four years under government supervision before being bottled — called also *bonded whiskey*

²bond *vt* (1677) **1 :** to lap (as brick) for solidity of construction **2 a :** to secure payment of duties and taxes on (goods) by giving a bond **b :** to convert into a debt secured by bonds **c :** to provide a bond for or cause to provide such a bond ⟨~ an employee⟩ **3 a :** to cause to adhere firmly **b :** to embed in a matrix **c :** to hold together in a molecule or crystal by chemical bonds ~ *vi* **:** to hold together or solidify by or as if by means of a bond or binder **:** COHERE — **bond·able** \ˈbän-də-bəl\ *adj* — **bond·er** *n*

³bond *adj* [ME *bonde*, fr. *bonde* peasant, serf, fr. OE *bōnda* householder, fr. ON *bōndi*] *archaic* (14c) **:** bound in slavery

bond·age \ˈbän-dij\ *n* (14c) **1 :** the tenure or service of a villein, serf, or slave **2 :** a state of being bound usu. by compulsion (as of law or mastery): as **a :** CAPTIVITY, SERFDOM ⟨the ~ of the Israelites in Egypt⟩ **b :** servitude or subjugation to a controlling person or force ⟨young people in ~ to drugs⟩

bond·ed \ˈbänd-əd\ *adj* (1945) **:** composed of two or more layers of the same or different fabrics held together by an adhesive ⟨~ jersey⟩

bond·hold·er \ˈbänd-ˌhōl-dər\ *n* (1823) **:** one that holds a government or corporation bond

bond·ing *n* (1976) **:** the formation of a close personal relationship (as between a mother and child) esp. through frequent or constant association

bond·maid \'bän(d)-ˌmād\ *n, archaic* (1526) **:** a female slave or bond servant
bond·man \'bän(d)-mən\ *n* (13c) **:** SLAVE, SERF
bond paper *n* (ca. 1877) **:** a strong durable paper orig. used for documents
bond servant *n* (15c) **:** one bound to service without wages; *also* **:** SLAVE
[1]bonds·man \'bän(d)z-mən\ *n* (14c) **:** BONDMAN
[2]bondsman *n* (1713) **:** one who assumes the responsibility of a bond **:** SURETY
bond·stone \'bän(d)-ˌstōn\ *n* (1845) **:** a stone long enough to extend through the full thickness of a wall to bind it together
bond·wom·an \'bän-ˌdwu̇m-ən\ *n* (14c) **:** a female slave
[1]bone \'bōn\ *n, often attrib* [ME *bon,* fr. OE *bān;* akin to OHG & ON *bein* bone] (bef. 12c) **1 a :** one of the hard parts of the skeleton of a vertebrate **b :** any of various hard animal substances or structures (as baleen or ivory) akin to or resembling bone **c :** the hard largely calcareous connective tissue of which the adult skeleton of most vertebrates is chiefly composed **2 a :** ESSENCE, CORE ⟨cut costs to the ~⟩ ⟨a liberal to the ~⟩ **b :** the most deeply ingrained part **:** HEART — usu. used in pl. ⟨knew in his ~*s* that it was wrong⟩ **3** *pl* **a** (1) **:** SKELETON (2) **:** BODY ⟨rested his weary ~*s*⟩ (3) **:** CORPSE ⟨inter a person's ~*s*⟩ **b :** the basic design or framework (as of a play or novel) **4 :** MATTER, SUBJECT ⟨a ~ of contention⟩ **5 a** *pl* **:** thin bars of bone, ivory, or wood held in pairs between the fingers and used to produce musical rhythms **b :** a strip of whalebone or steel used to stiffen a corset or dress **c** *pl* **:** DICE **6 :** something that is designed to placate **:** SOP ⟨throw a ~ to angry workers with a small raise⟩ **7 :** a light beige — **boned** \'bōnd\ *adj* — **bone·less** \'bōn-ləs\ *adj* — **bone to pick :** a matter to argue or complain about
[2]bone *vb* **boned; bon·ing** *vt* (15c) **1 :** to remove the bones from ⟨~ a fish⟩ **2 :** to provide (a garment) with stays ~ *vi* **:** to study hard **:** GRIND ⟨~ through medical school⟩
[3]bone *adv* (1825) **:** EXTREMELY, VERY ⟨~ tired⟩; *also* **:** TOTALLY
bone ash *n* (1622) **:** the white porous residue chiefly of tribasic calcium phosphate from bones calcined in air used esp. in making pottery and glass and in cleaning jewelry
bone black *n* (1815) **:** the black residue chiefly of tribasic calcium phosphate and carbon from bones calcined in closed vessels used esp. as a pigment or as a decolorizing adsorbent in sugar manufacturing — called also *bone char*
bone china *n* (ca. 1895) **:** translucent white china made with bone ash or calcium phosphate and characterized by whiteness
bone–dry \'bōn-'drī\ *adj* (ca. 1825) **1 :** very dry **2 :** DRY 5
bone·fish \'bōn-ˌfish\ *n* (1734) **1 a :** a slender silvery small-scaled fish *(Albula vulpes)* that is a notable sport and food fish of warm seas **b :** any of several fish of the same family (Albulidae) as the bonefish **2 :** LADYFISH 2 — **bone·fish·ing** *n*
[1]bone·head \-ˌhed\ *n* (1908) **:** a stupid person **:** NUMSKULL — **bone·head·ed** \-'hed-əd\ *adj* — **bone·head·ed·ness** *n*
[2]bonehead *adj* (1926) **:** being a college course for students lacking fundamental skills ⟨teaches ~ English⟩
bone·meal \'bōn-ˌmē(ə)l\ *n* (1850) **:** fertilizer or feed made of crushed or ground bone
bon·er \'bō-nər\ *n* (ca. 1899) **1 :** one that bones **2 :** BLUNDER, HOWLER
bone·set \'bōn-ˌset\ *n* (1764) **:** any of several composite herbs (genus *Eupatorium*); *esp* **:** a perennial (*E. perfoliatum*) with opposite perfoliate leaves and white-rayed flower heads used in folk medicine
bone·set·ter \-ˌset-ər\ *n* (15c) **:** a person who sets broken or dislocated bones usu. without being a licensed physician
bone up *vi* (1887) **1 :** to try to master necessary information quickly **:** CRAM ⟨had to *bone up* on math for the exam⟩ **2 :** to renew one's skill or refresh one's memory ⟨*boned up* on his speech just before giving it⟩
bone·yard \-ˌyärd\ *n* (1866) **1 :** CEMETERY **2 :** a place where worn-out or damaged objects (as cars) are collected to await disposal
bon·fire \'bän-ˌfī(ə)r\ *n* [ME *bonefire* a fire of bones, fr. *bon* bone + *fire*] (15c) **:** a large fire built in the open air
[1]bong \'bäŋ, 'bȯŋ\ *n* [imit.] (1860) **:** the deep resonant sound esp. of a bell
[2]bong *vb* (1936) **:** RING
[3]bong *n* [perh. alter. of *bhang*] (1972) **:** a simple water pipe consisting of a bottle or vertical tube partially filled with a liquid (as water or liqueur) and a smaller offset tube ending in a bowl
[1]bon·go \'bäŋ-(ˌ)gō, 'bȯŋ-\ *n, pl* **bongos** *also* **bongoes** [AmerSp *bongó*] (1920) **:** one of a pair of small connected drums of different sizes and pitches that are played with the hands — **bon·go·ist** \-ˌgō-əst\ *n*
[2]bongo *n, pl* **bongo** *or* **bongos** [of African origin; akin to Bobangi *mbangani* an antelope] (1861) **:** a chestnut-red forest antelope (*Boocercus euryceros*) of central Africa with narrow white stripes
bon·ho·mie \ˌbän-ə-'mē, ˌbō-nə-\ *n* [F *bonhomie,* fr. *bonhomme* good-natured man, fr. *bon* good + *homme* man] (1779) **:** good-natured easy friendliness **:** GENIALITY — **bon·ho·mous** \'bän-ə-məs\ *adj*
bon·i·face \'bän-ə-fəs, -ˌfās\ *n* [*Boniface,* innkeeper in *The Beaux' Stratagem* (1707) by George Farquhar] (1803) **:** the proprietor of a hotel, nightclub, or restaurant
bo·ni·to \bə-'nēt-(ˌ)ō, -'nēt-ə\ *n, pl* **-tos** *or* **-to** [Sp, fr. *bonito* pretty, fr. L *bonus* good] (1565) **:** any of various medium-sized tunas (esp. genera *Sarda* and *Euthynnus*) intermediate between the smaller mackerels and the larger tunas
bon·kers \'bäŋ-kərz, 'bȯŋ-\ *adj* [origin unknown] (ca. 1948) **:** CRAZY, MAD ⟨if I don't work, I go ~ —Zoe Caldwell⟩
bon mot \bōⁿ-'mō\ *n, pl* **bons mots** \bōⁿ-'mō(z)\ *or* **bon mots** \-'mō(z)\ [F, lit., good word] (ca. 1730) **:** a clever remark **:** WITTICISM
bonne \'bȯn\ *n* [F, fr. fem. of *bon*] (1771) **:** a French nursemaid or maidservant
[1]bon·net \'bän-ət\ *n* [ME *bonet,* fr. MF, fr. ML *abonnis*] (14c) **1 a** (1) *chiefly Scot* **:** a man's or boy's cap (2) **:** a brimless Scotch cap of seamless woolen fabric — compare TAM-O'-SHANTER 2 **b :** a cloth or straw hat tied under the chin and worn by women and children **2 a :** an additional piece of canvas laced to the foot of a jib or foresail **b** *Brit* **:** an automobile hood **c :** a cover for an open fireplace or a cowl or hood to increase the draft of a chimney **d :** a metal covering for valve chambers, hydrants, or ventilators
[2]bonnet *vt* (1824) **:** to provide with or dress in a bonnet
bon·ny \'bän-ē\ *adj* **bon·ni·er; -est** [ME *bonie,* fr. MF *bon* good, fr. L *bonus* — more at BOUNTY] *chiefly Brit* (14c) **:** ATTRACTIVE, FAIR; *also* **:** FINE, EXCELLENT — **bon·ni·ly** \'bän-ə-lē\ *adv*
bon·ny·clab·ber \'bän-ē-ˌklab-ər\ *n* [IrGael *bainne clabair,* fr. *bainne* milk + *clabair,* gen. of *clabar* sour thick milk] *Northern & Midland* (1631) **:** [1]CLABBER
bon·sai \(ˌ)bōn-'sī, 'bōn-ˌ, 'bän-ˌ, *also* 'bän-ˌzī\ *n, pl* **bonsai** [Jp] (ca. 1929) **:** a potted plant (as a tree) dwarfed by special methods of culture; *also* **:** the art of growing such a plant

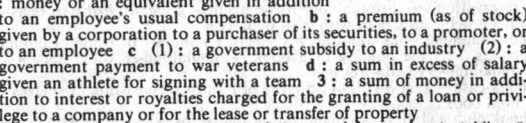

bonsai

bon·spiel \'bän-ˌspēl\ *n* [perh. fr. D *bond* league + *spel* game] (1772) **:** a match or tournament between curling clubs
bon ton \(ˌ)bän-'tän, 'bän-ˌ\ *n* [F, lit., good tone] (1747) **1 a :** fashionable manner or style **b :** the fashionable or proper thing ⟨it was considered *bon ton* to go⟩ **2 :** high society
bo·nus \'bō-nəs\ *n* [L, lit., good — more at BOUNTY] (1773) **1 :** something in addition to what is expected or strictly due **2 a :** money or an equivalent given in addition to an employee's usual compensation **b :** a premium (as of stock) given by a corporation to a purchaser of its securities, to a promoter, or to an employee **c** (1) **:** a government subsidy to an industry (2) **:** a government payment to war veterans **d :** a sum in excess of salary given an athlete for signing with a team **3 :** a sum of money in addition to interest or royalties charged for the granting of a loan or privilege to a company or for the lease or transfer of property
bon vi·vant \ˌbän-vē-'vänt, ˌbōⁿ-vē-'väⁿ\ *n, pl* **bons vivants** \ˌbän-vē-'vän(t)s, ˌbōⁿ-vē-'väⁿ(z)\ *or* **bon vivants** *same*\ [F, lit., good living] (1695) **:** a person having cultivated, refined, and sociable tastes esp. in respect to food and drink ***syn*** see EPICURE
bon voy·age \ˌbōⁿv-ˌwī-'äzh, -ˌwä-'yäzh; ˌbōⁿ-ˌvȯi-'äzh, ˌbän-\ *n* [F, lit., good journey!] (15c) **:** FAREWELL — often used interjectionally
bony *also* **bon·ey** \'bō-nē\ *adj* **bon·i·er; -est** (14c) **1 a :** consisting of bone **b :** resembling bone **2 a :** full of bones ⟨a ~ piece of fish⟩ **b :** having prominent bones ⟨a rugged ~ face⟩ **3 a :** SKINNY, SCRAWNY **b :** BARREN, LEAN
bony fish *n* (ca. 1890) **:** TELEOST
bonze \'bänz\ *n* [F, fr. Pg *bonzo,* fr. Jp *bonsō*] (1588) **:** a Buddhist monk
[1]boo \'bü\ *interj* [ME *bo*] (15c) — used to express contempt or disapproval or to startle or frighten
[2]boo *n, pl* **boos** (1575) **1 :** a shout of disapproval or contempt **2 :** any sound at all — usu. used in negative constructions ⟨never said ~⟩
[3]boo *vi* (1884) **:** to deride esp. by uttering *boo* ~ *vt* **:** to express disapproval of by booing ⟨the crowd ~*ed* the referee⟩
[4]boo *n* [origin unknown] (ca. 1959) **:** MARIJUANA
[1]boob \'büb\ *n* [short for *booby*] (1909) **1 :** a stupid awkward person **:** SIMPLETON **2 :** BOOR, PHILISTINE **3 :** BREAST — sometimes considered vulgar — **boob·ish** \'bü-bish\ *adj*
[2]boob *vi, Brit* (1935) **:** GOOF 1
boob·oi·sie \ˌbüb-ˌwä-'zē\ *n* [*boob* + *-oisie* (as in *bourgeoisie*)] (1922) **:** a segment of the general public regarded as consisting of boobs
boo–boo \'bü-(ˌ)bü\ *n, pl* **boo–boos** [prob. baby-talk alter. of *boohoo,* imitation of the sound of weeping] (1954) **1 :** a usu. trivial injury (as a bruise or scratch) esp. on a child **2 :** MISTAKE, BLUNDER
boob tube *n* (1966) **:** TELEVISION
[1]boo·by \'bü-bē\ *n, pl* **boobies** [modif. of Sp *bobo,* fr. L *balbus* stammering, prob. of imit. origin] (1599) **1 :** an awkward foolish person **:** DOPE **2 :** any of several small gannets (genus *Sula*) of tropical seas
[2]boo·by \'bu̇b-ē, 'büb-\ *n, pl* **boobies** [alter. of *bubby*] (1934) **:** BREAST — sometimes considered vulgar
booby hatch *n* (1840) **1 :** a raised framework with a sliding cover over a small hatch on a ship **2 :** an insane asylum
booby prize *n* (1889) **1 :** an award for the poorest performance in a game or competition **2 :** an acknowledgment of notable inferiority
booby trap *n* (1850) **1 :** a trap for the unwary or unsuspecting **:** PITFALL **2 :** a concealed explosive device contrived to go off when some harmless-looking object is touched — **boo·by–trap** *vt*
boo·dle \'büd-ᵊl\ *n* [D *boedel* estate, lot, fr. MD; akin to ON *būth* booth] (1625) **1 :** a collection or lot of persons **:** CABOODLE **2 a :** bribe money **b :** a large amount esp. of money
boog·er \'bu̇g-ər\ *n* [alter. of E dial. *buggard, boggart,* fr. [1]*bug* + *-ard*] (1866) **:** BOGEYMAN
boo·gey·man \'bu̇g-ē-ˌman, 'bü-gē-\ *also* **boog·er·man** \'bu̇g-ər-\ *n* [*boogey,* alter. of *booger* + *man*] (ca. 1850) **:** BOGEYMAN
[1]boo·gie \'bu̇g-ē, 'bü-gē\ *n* (1941) **1 :** BOOGIE-WOOGIE **2 :** earthy and strongly rhythmic rock music conducive to dancing
[2]boogie *also* **boo·gy** \'bu̇g-ē, 'bü-gē\ *vi* **boo·gied; boo·gy·ing** (1955) **:** to dance to rock music
boo·gie–woo·gie \ˌbu̇g-ē-'wu̇g-ē, ˌbü-gē-'wü-gē\ *n* [origin unknown] (1928) **:** a percussive style of playing blues on the piano characterized by a steady rhythmic ground bass of eighth notes in quadruple time and a series of improvised melodic variations
[1]book \'bu̇k\ *n* [ME, fr. OE *bōc;* akin to OHG *buoh* book; perh. akin to OE *bōc* beech (prob. fr. the early Germanic practice of carving runic characters on beech wood tablets) — more at BEECH] (bef. 12c) **1 a :** a set of written sheets of skin or paper or tablets of wood or ivory **b :** a set of written, printed, or blank sheets bound together into a volume **c :** a long written or printed literary composition **d :** a major division of a treatise or literary work **e :** a record of a business's financial transactions or financial condition — often used in pl. ⟨their ~*s* show a profit⟩ **2** *cap* **:** BIBLE **3 :** something that yields knowledge or understanding ⟨the great ~ of nature⟩ ⟨her face was an open ~⟩ **4 a :** the total available knowledge and experience that can be brought to

bear on a task or problem ⟨tried every trick in the ~ to win the election⟩ ⟨the ~ on that batter was that he couldn't hit a curveball⟩ **b** : the standards or authority relevant in a situation ⟨the factory is run according to the ~⟩ **5 a** : all the charges that can be made against an accused person ⟨they threw the ~ at him⟩ **b** : a position from which one must answer for certain acts : ACCOUNT ⟨the police try to bring criminals to ~⟩ **6 a** : LIBRETTO **b** : the script of a play **c** : a book of arrangements for a musician or dance orchestra : musical repertory **7** : a packet of items bound together like a book ⟨a ~ of stamps⟩ ⟨a ~ of matches⟩ **8 a** : BOOKMAKER **b** : the bets registered by a bookmaker; *also* : the business or activity of giving odds and taking bets **9** : the number of tricks a cardplayer or side must win before any trick can have scoring value — **book·ful** \-,fu̇l\ *n* — **in one's book** : in one's own opinion — **in one's good books** : in favor with one — **one for the book** : an act or occurrence worth noting — **on the books** : on the records

[2]book *adj* (13c) **1** : derived from books and not from practical experience ⟨~ learning⟩ **2** : shown by books of account ⟨~ assets⟩

[3]book *vt* (1807) **1 a** : to register (as a name) so as to engage transportation or reserve lodgings ⟨~*ed* to sail on Monday⟩ **b** : to schedule engagements for ⟨~ the band for a week⟩ **c** : to set aside time for **d** : to reserve in advance ⟨~ two seats at the theater⟩ ⟨were all ~*ed* up⟩ **2** : to enter charges against in a police register ~ *vi* **1** : to make a reservation ⟨~ through your travel agent⟩ **2** *chiefly Brit* : to register in a hotel — usu. used with *in* — **book·er** *n*

book·bind·ing \'bu̇k-,bīn-diŋ\ *n* (1771) **1** : the art or trade of binding books **2** : the binding of a book — **book·bind·er** \-,bīn-dər\ *n* — **book·bind·ery** \-d(ə-)rē\ *n*

book·case \-,kās\ *n* (1726) : a piece of furniture consisting of shelves to hold books

book club *n* (1905) : an organization that ships selected books to members usu. on a regular schedule and often at discount prices

book·end \-,end\ *n* (1907) : a support placed at the end of a row of books

book·ie \'bu̇k-ē\ *n* [by shortening & alter.] (ca. 1884) : BOOKMAKER 2

book·ing \'bu̇k-iŋ\ *n* (1836) **1** : the act of one that books **2** : an engagement or scheduled performance **3** : RESERVATION 1c

booking office *n, chiefly Brit* (1836) : a ticket office; *esp* : one in a railroad station

book·ish \'bu̇k-ish\ *adj* (1567) **1 a** : of or relating to books **b** : fond of books and reading **2 a** : inclined to rely on book knowledge rather than practical experience **b** *of words* : literary and formal as opposed to colloquial and informal **c** : given to literary or scholarly pursuits; *also* : affectedly learned — **book·ish·ly** *adv* — **book·ish·ness** *n*

book·keep·er \'bu̇k-,kē-pər\ *n* (1555) : one who records the accounts or transactions of a business — **book·keep·ing** \-piŋ\ *n*

book·let \'bu̇k-lət\ *n* (1859) : a little book; *esp* : PAMPHLET

book louse *n* (1867) : a minute wingless insect (order Corrodentia); *esp* : an insect (as *Liposcelis divinatorius*) injurious esp. to books

book lung *n* (1879) : a saccular breathing organ in many arachnids containing numerous thin folds of membrane arranged like the leaves of a book

book·mak·er \'bu̇k-,mā-kər\ *n* (15c) **1** : a printer, binder, or designer of books **2** : one who determines odds and receives and pays off bets — **book·mak·ing** \-kiŋ\ *n*

book·man \-mən\ *n* (1583) **1** : one who has a love of books and esp. of reading **2** : one who is involved in the writing, publishing, or selling of books

book·mark \-,märk\ *or* **book·mark·er** \-,mär-kər\ *n* (1838) : a marker for finding a place in a book

book–match \-,mach\ *vt* (1942) : to match the grains of (as two sheets of veneer) so that one sheet seems to be the mirrored image of the other

book·mo·bile \'bu̇k-mō-,bēl\ *n* [*book* + auto*mobile*] (1926) : a truck that serves as a traveling library

Book of Common Prayer (1549) : the service book of the Anglican Communion

book·plate \'bu̇k-,plāt\ *n* (1791) : a book owner's identification label that is usu. pasted to the inside front cover of a book

book·sell·er \'bu̇k-,sel-ər\ *n* (15c) : one who sells books; *esp* : the proprietor of a bookstore — **book·sell·ing** \-,sel-iŋ\ *n*

book·shelf \-,shelf\ *n* (1818) : an open shelf for holding books

book·shop \-,shäp\ *n* (1862) : BOOKSTORE

book·stall \-,stȯl\ *n* (1800) **1** : a stall where books are sold **2** *chiefly Brit* : NEWSSTAND

book·store \-,stō(ə)r, -,stȯ(ə)r\ *n* (ca. 1763) : a place of business where books are the main item offered for sale — called also *bookshop*

book value *n* (1899) : the value of something as shown on bookkeeping records as distinguished from market value: **a** : the value of an asset equal to cost less depreciation **b** : the value of a corporation's capital stock equal to its book value less its liabilities (as debt or preferred stock)

book·worm \'bu̇k-,wərm\ *n* (1599) **1** : a person unusually devoted to reading and study **2** : any of various insect larvae (as of a beetle) that feed on the binding and paste of books

Bool·ean \'bü-lē-ən\ *adj* [George *Boole* †1864 Eng. mathematician] (1851) : of, relating to, or being a logical combinatorial system (as Boolean algebra) that represents symbolically relationships (as those implied by the logical operators AND, OR, and NOT) between entities (as sets, propositions, or on-off computer circuit elements) ⟨~ expression⟩ ⟨~ search strategy for information retrieval⟩

Boolean algebra *n* (1889) : a set that is closed under two commutative binary operations and that can be described by any of various systems of postulates all of which can be deduced from the postulates that an identity element exists for each operation, that each operation is distributive over the other, and that for every element in the set there is another element which when combined with the first under one of the operations yields the identity element of the other operation ⟨under the operations of taking intersections and unions, the subsets of a given set form a *Boolean algebra*⟩

[1]boom \'büm\ *n* [D, tree, beam; akin to OHG *boum* tree — more at BEAM] (1627) **1** : a long spar used to extend the foot of a sail **2 a** : a long beam projecting from the mast of a derrick to support or guide cargo **b** : a long more or less horizontal supporting arm or brace (as for holding a microphone or for supporting the elements of a television antenna) **3 a** : a chain cable or line of connected floating timbers extended across a river, lake, or harbor (as to obstruct passage or catch floating objects) **b** : a temporary floating barrier used to contain an oil spill **4** : a spar or outrigger connecting the tail surfaces and the main supporting structure of an airplane

[2]boom *vb* [imit.] *vi* (15c) **1** : to make a deep hollow sound **2 a** : to increase in importance or esteem **b** : to experience a sudden rapid growth and expansion usu. with an increase in prices ⟨business was ~*ing*⟩ **c** : to develop rapidly in population and importance ⟨California ~*ed* when gold was discovered there⟩ ~ *vt* **1** : to cause to resound — often used with *out* ⟨his voice ~*s* out the lyrics⟩ **2** : to cause a rapid growth or increase of : BOOST

[3]boom *n* (1500) **1** : a booming sound or cry **2** : a rapid expansion or increase: as **a** : a general movement in support of a candidate for office **b** : rapid settlement and development of a town or district **c** : a rapid widespread expansion of economic activity

boom·er *n* (1858) **1** : one that booms **2** : one that joins a rush of settlers to a boom area **3** : a transient worker (as a bridge builder)

boo·mer·ang \'bü-mə-,raŋ\ *n* [native name in Australia] (1827) **1** : a bent or angular throwing club typically flat on one side and rounded on the other so that it soars or curves in flight; *esp* : one designed to return near the thrower **2** : an act or utterance that backfires on its originator — **boomerang** *vi*

boom·let \'büm-lət\ *n* (1880) : a small boom; *specif* : a sudden increase in business activity ⟨a stock market ~⟩

boom·town \'büm-,tau̇n\ *n* (1896) : a town enjoying a business and population boom

boomy \'bü-mē\ *adj* **boom·i·er; -est** (ca. 1930) **1** : of, relating to, or characterized by an economic boom **2** : having an excessive accentuation on the tones of lower pitch in reproduced sound

[1]boon \'bün\ *n* [ME, fr. ON *bōn* petition; akin to OE *bēn* prayer, *bannan* to summon — more at BAN] (12c) **1** : BENEFIT, FAVOR; *esp* : one that is given in answer to a request **2** : a timely benefit : BLESSING

[2]boon *adj* [ME *bon*, fr. MF, good — more at BONNY] (14c) **1** *archaic* : FAVORABLE **2** : CONVIVIAL ⟨a ~ companion⟩

boon·docks \'bün-,däks\ *n pl* [Tag *bundok* mountain] (1925) **1** : rough country filled with dense brush : JUNGLE **2** : a rural area : STICKS

boon·dog·gle \'bün-,däg-əl, -,dȯg-\ *n* [coined by Robert H. Link †1957 Am. scoutmaster] (ca. 1930) **1** : a handicraft article made of leather or wicker **2** : a trivial, useless, or wasteful project or activity — **boondoggle** *vi* — **boon·dog·gler** \-(ə-)lər\ *n*

boon·ies \'bü-nēz\ *n pl, slang* (ca. 1967) : BOONDOCKS 2

boor \'bu̇(ə)r\ *n* [D *boer;* akin to OE *būan* to dwell — more at BOWER] (1551) **1** : PEASANT **2** : a rude or insensitive person

boor·ish \'bu̇(ə)r-ish\ *adj* (1562) : resembling or befitting a boor (as in crude insensitivity) — **boor·ish·ly** *adv* — **boor·ish·ness** *n*

syn BOORISH, CHURLISH, LOUTISH, CLOWNISH mean uncouth in manners or appearance. BOORISH implies rudeness of manner due to insensitiveness to others' feelings and unwillingness to be agreeable; CHURLISH suggests surliness, unresponsiveness, and ungraciousness; LOUTISH implies bodily awkwardness together with stupidity; CLOWNISH suggests ill-bred awkwardness, ignorance or stupidity, ungainliness, and often a propensity for absurd antics.

[1]boost \'büst\ *vb* [origin unknown] *vt* (ca. 1815) **1** : to push or shove up from below **2 a** : INCREASE, RAISE ⟨plans to ~ production by 30 percent next year⟩ **b** : to aid or assist esp. toward progress or increase ⟨an extra holiday to ~ morale⟩ **3** : to promote the cause or interests of : PLUG ⟨a campaign to ~ the new fashions⟩ **4** : to raise the voltage of or across (an electric circuit) **5** *slang* : STEAL, SHOPLIFT ~ *vi, slang* : SHOPLIFT ***syn*** see LIFT

[2]boost *n* (1825) **1** : a push upward **2** : an increase in amount **3** : an act that brings help or encouragement

boost·er \'bü-stər\ *n* (1890) : one that boosts: as **a** : an enthusiastic supporter **b** : an auxiliary device for increasing force, power, pressure, or effectiveness **c** *slang* : SHOPLIFTER **d** : a radio-frequency amplifier for a radio or television receiving set **e** : a substance that increases the effectiveness of a medicament; *esp* : BOOSTER SHOT **f** : the first stage of a multistage rocket providing thrust for the launching and the initial part of the flight

boost·er·ism \-stə-,riz-əm\ *n* (ca. 1913) : the activities and attitudes characteristic of boosters

booster shot *n* (1944) : a supplementary dose of an immunizing agent — called also *booster, booster dose*

[1]boot \'büt\ *n* [ME, fr. OE *bōt* remedy; akin to OE *betera* better] (bef. 12c) **1** *archaic* : DELIVERANCE **2** *chiefly dial* : something to equalize a trade **3** *obs* : AVAIL — **to boot** : BESIDES

[2]boot *vb, archaic* (15c) : AVAIL, PROFIT

[3]boot *n* [ME, fr. MF *bote*] (14c) **1** : a fitted covering of leather or rubber for the foot and usu. reaching above the ankle **2** : an instrument of torture used to crush the leg and foot **3** : something that resembles or is likened to a boot; *esp* : an enclosing or protective casing or sheath (as for a rifle or over an electrical or mechanical connection) **4** : a sheath enclosing the inflorescence **5** *Brit* : an automobile trunk **6 a** : a kick with the foot **b** : summary dismissal — used with *the* **c** : momentary pleasure or enjoyment : BANG ⟨got a big ~ out of the joke⟩ **7** : a navy or marine corps recruit undergoing basic training

[4]boot *vt* (15c) **1** : to put boots on **2 a** : KICK **b** : to eject or discharge summarily — often used with *out* ⟨was ~*ed* out of office⟩ **3** : to make an error on (a grounder in baseball); *broadly* : BOTCH **4** : to ride (a horse) in a race ⟨~*ed* home three winners⟩

[5]boot *n* ['boot] *archaic* (1593) : BOOTY, PLUNDER

boot·black \'büt-,blak\ *n* (1817) : one who shines shoes

boot camp *n* (ca. 1942) : a Navy or Marine Corps camp for basic training

boot·ed \'büt-əd\ *adj* (1552) : wearing boots

boo·tee *or* **boo·tie** \bü-'tē, *of infants' footwear* 'büt-ē\ *n* (1799) : a usu. ankle-length boot, slipper, or sock; *esp* : an infant's knitted or crocheted sock

Bo·ö·tes \bō-'ōt-ēz\ *n* [L (gen. *Boötis*), fr. Gk *Boōtēs*, lit., plowman, fr. *bous* head of cattle — more at COW] : a northern constellation containing the bright star Arcturus

booth \'büth, *esp Brit* 'büth\ *n, pl* **booths** \'büthz, 'büths\ [ME *bothe,* of Scand origin; akin to ON *būth* booth; akin to OE *būan* to dwell — more at BOWER] (13c) **1 :** a temporary shelter for livestock or field workers **2 a :** a stall or stand (as at a fair) for the sale or exhibition of goods **b** (1) **:** a small enclosure affording privacy for one person at a time ⟨a telephone ~⟩ ⟨polling ~⟩ (2) **:** a small enclosure that isolates its occupant esp. from patrons or customers ⟨a ticket ~⟩ **c :** a restaurant seating arrangement consisting of a table between two high-back benches

boot·jack \'büt-ˌjak\ *n* (1841) **:** a device with a V-shaped notch for pulling off boots

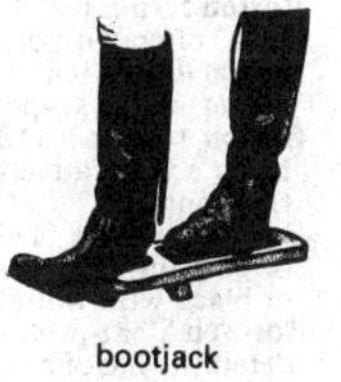

bootjack

boot·lace \-ˌlās\ *n, Brit* (ca. 1887) **:** SHOELACE

[1]boot·leg \-ˌleg, -ˌlāg\ *n* (1634) **1 :** the upper part of a boot **2 :** something bootlegged; *specif* **:** MOONSHINE **3 :** a football play in which the quarterback fakes a handoff, hides the ball against his hip, and rolls out — compare DRAW 8 — **bootleg** *adj*

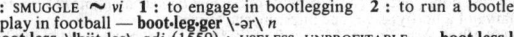

[2]bootleg *vt* (1900) **1 a :** to carry (alcoholic liquor) on one's person illegally **b :** to manufacture, sell, or transport for sale (alcoholic liquor) illegally **2 a :** to produce, reproduce, or distribute illicitly or without authorization **b :** SMUGGLE ~ *vi* **1 :** to engage in bootlegging **2 :** to run a bootleg play in football — **boot·leg·ger** \-ər\ *n*

boot·less \'büt-ləs\ *adj* (1559) **:** USELESS, UNPROFITABLE — **boot·less·ly** *adv* — **boot·less·ness** *n*

boot·lick \-ˌlik\ *vt* (1845) **:** to try to gain favor with through a servile or obsequious manner ~ *vi* **:** to act obsequiously — **bootlick** *n* — **boot·lick·er** *n*

boots \'büts\ *n pl but sing or pl in constr* [fr. pl. of [3]*boot*] *Brit* (1798) **:** a servant who shines shoes esp. in a hotel

[1]boot·strap \'büt-ˌstrap\ *n* (1908) **1 :** a looped strap sewed at the side or the rear top of a boot to help in pulling it on **2** *pl* **:** unaided efforts — often used in the phrase *by one's own bootstraps*

[2]bootstrap *adj* (1926) **1 :** designed to function independently of outside direction **:** capable of using one internal function or process to control another ⟨a ~ operation to load a computer⟩ **2 :** carried out with minimum resources or advantages **:** SELF-RELIANT ⟨the city recovered from the flood by the ~ method⟩

[3]bootstrap *vt* (1951) **:** to promote or develop by individual initiative and effort with a minimum of outside assistance — often used reflexively

boo·ty \'büt-ē\ *n, pl* **booties** [modif. of MF *butin,* fr. MLG *būte* exchange] (15c) **1 :** plunder taken (as in war); *esp* **:** plunder taken on land as distinguished from prizes taken at sea **2 :** a rich gain or prize *syn* see SPOIL

[1]booze \'büz\ *vi* **boozed; booz·ing** [ME *bousen,* fr. MD or MFlem *būsen;* akin to MHG *būs* swelling] (14c) **:** to drink intoxicating liquor to excess — often used in the phrase *booze it up* — **booz·er** \'bü-zər\ *n*

[2]booze *n* (14c) **:** intoxicating drink; *esp* **:** hard liquor — **booz·i·ly** \-zə-lē\ *adv* — **boozy** \-zē\ *adj*

[1]bop \'bäp\ *vt* **bopped; bop·ping** [imit.] (1931) **:** HIT, SOCK

[2]bop *n* (1947) **:** a blow (as with the fist or a club) that strikes a person

[3]bop *n* [short for *bebop*] (1947) **1 :** jazz characterized by harmonic complexity, convoluted melodic lines, and constant shifting of accent and often played at very rapid tempos **2 :** JIVE 2 — **bop·per** *n*

[4]bop *vi* **bopped; bop·ping** (1952) **1 :** to go quickly or unceremoniously **:** POP ⟨~ into the corner store⟩ — often used with *off* **2 :** to dance or shuffle along to or as if to bop music

bo·ra \'bōr-ə, 'bȯr-\ *n* [It. dial., fr. L *boreas*] (1864) **:** a violent cold northerly wind of the Adriatic

bo·rac·ic acid \bə-ˌras-ik-\ *n* [ML *borac-, borax* borax] (1801) **:** BORIC ACID

bor·age \'bȯr-ij, 'bär-\ *n* [ME, fr. OF *bourage*] (13c) **:** a coarse hairy blue-flowered European herb (*Borago officinalis* of the family Boraginaceae, the borage family) used medicinally and in salads

bo·rane \'bō(ə)r-ˌān, 'bȯ(ə)r-\ *n* [ISV, fr. *boron*] (1916) **:** a compound of boron and hydrogen or a derivative of such a compound

bo·rate \-ˌāt\ *n* (1816) **:** a salt or ester of a boric acid

bo·rat·ed \-ˌāt-əd\ *adj* (ca. 1901) **:** mixed or impregnated with borax or boric acid

[1]bo·rax \'bō(ə)r-ˌaks, 'bȯ(ə)r-, -əks\ *n* [ME *boras,* fr. MF, fr. ML *borac-, borax,* fr. Ar *būraq,* fr. Per *būrah*] (14c) **:** a white crystalline compound that consists of a hydrated sodium borate $Na_2B_4O_7·10H_2O$, that occurs as a mineral or is prepared from other minerals, and that is used esp. as a flux, cleansing agent, and water softener and as a preservative

[2]borax *n* [prob. fr. Yiddish; perh. akin to OHG *boragen* to protect — more at BORROW] (1932) **:** cheap shoddy merchandise

Bo·ra·zon \'bōr-ə-ˌzän, 'bȯr-\ *trademark* — used for a boron nitride abrasive

bor·bo·ryg·mus \ˌbȯr-bə-'rig-məs\ *n, pl* **-mi** \-ˌmī\ [NL, fr. Gk *borborygmos,* fr. *borboryzein* to rumble] (1794) **:** intestinal rumbling caused by moving gas

Bor·deaux \bȯr-'dō\ *n, pl* **Bor·deaux** \-'dōz\ *often not cap* (1510) **:** white or red wine of the Bordeaux region of France

bor·deaux mixture \bȯr-'dō-, 'bȯrd-ˌō-\ *n, often cap B* (1892) **:** a fungicide made by reaction of copper sulfate, lime, and water

bor·de·laise sauce \ˌbȯrd-ᵊl-'āz-\ *n, often cap B* [F *bordelaise,* fem. of *bordelais* of Bordeaux] (1902) **:** a sauce consisting of stock thickened with roux and flavored typically with red Bordeaux wine and shallots

bor·del·lo \bȯr-'del-(ˌ)ō\ *n, pl* **-los** [It, fr. OF *bordel,* fr. *borde* hut, of Gmc origin; akin to OE *bord* board] (1598) **:** BROTHEL

[1]bor·der \'bȯrd-ər\ *n* [ME *bordure,* fr. MF, fr. OF, fr. *border* to border, fr. *bort* border, of Gmc origin; akin to OE *bord* — more at BOARD] (14c) **1 :** an outer part or edge **2 :** BOUNDARY ⟨crossed the ~ into Italy⟩ **3 :** a narrow bed of planted ground along the edge of a garden or walk ⟨a ~ of tulips⟩ **4 :** an ornamental design at the edge of a fabric or rug **5 :** a plain or decorative margin around printed matter — **bor·dered** \-ərd\ *adj*

[2]border *vb* **bordered; bor·der·ing** \'bȯrd-(ə-)riŋ\ *vt* (15c) **1 :** to put a border on ⟨~ a bedspread with fringe⟩ **2 :** to touch at the edge or boundary **:** BOUND ⟨an airport ~*s* the city on the south⟩ ~ *vi* **1 :** to lie on the border ⟨the U.S. ~*s* on Canada⟩ **2 :** to approach the nature of a specified thing **:** VERGE ⟨his devotion to his dog ~*s* on the ridiculous⟩ — **bor·der·er** \-ər-ər\ *n*

Border collie *n* (1941) **:** a medium-sized sheepdog of British origin noted for its herding abilities

bor·de·reau \ˌbȯrd-ə-'rō\ *n, pl* **-reaux** \-'rō(z)\ [F, fr. MF *bord* border, fr. OF *bort*] (ca. 1858) **:** a detailed note or memorandum of account; *esp* **:** one containing an enumeration of documents

bor·der·land \'bȯrd-ər-ˌland\ *n* (1813) **1 a :** territory at or near a border **b :** FRINGE 3a ⟨lives on the ~ of society⟩ **2 :** a vague intermediate state or region ⟨the ~ between fantasy and reality⟩

bor·der·line \-ˌlīn\ *adj* (1907) **1 :** being in an intermediate position or state **:** not fully classifiable as one thing or its opposite ⟨~ homosexuals⟩; *esp* **:** not quite up to what is usual, standard or expected ⟨~ intelligence⟩ **2 :** situated at or near a border — **borderline** *n*

Border terrier *n* (1894) **:** a small terrier of British origin with a harsh dense coat and close undercoat

bor·dure \'bȯr-jər\ *n* [ME] (14c) **:** a border surrounding a heraldic shield

[1]bore \'bō(ə)r, 'bȯ(ə)r\ *vb* **bored; bor·ing** [ME *boren,* fr. OE *borian;* akin to OHG *borōn* to bore, L *forare* to bore, *ferire* to strike] *vt* (bef. 12c) **1 :** to pierce with a turning or twisting movement of a tool **2 :** to make (as a cylindrical hole) by boring or digging away material ⟨*bored* a tunnel⟩ ~ *vi* **1 a :** to make a hole by or as if by boring **b :** to sink a mine shaft or well **2 a :** to make one's way laboriously ⟨we *bored* through the jostling crowd⟩ **b :** to move ahead steadily against resistance ⟨the sturdy ship continued to ~ through towering waves⟩

[2]bore *n* (14c) **1 :** a usu. cylindrical hole made by or as if by boring **2 :** the long usu. cylindrical hollow part of something (as a tube or gun barrel) **3 :** the size of a bore: as **a :** the interior diameter of a gun barrel; *specif, chiefly Brit* **:** GAUGE 6 **b :** the diameter of an engine cylinder

[3]bore *past of* BEAR

[4]bore *n* [(assumed) ME *bore* wave, fr. ON *bāra*] (1601) **:** a tidal flood with a high abrupt front

[5]bore *n* [origin unknown] (ca. 1766) **:** one that causes boredom: as **a :** a tiresome person **b :** something that is devoid of interest

[6]bore *vt* **bored; bor·ing** (1768) **:** to make weary and restless by being uninteresting

bo·re·al \'bōr-ē-əl, 'bȯr-\ *adj* [ME *boriall,* fr. LL *borealis,* fr. L *boreas* north wind, north, fr. Gk, fr. *Boreas*] (15c) **1 :** of, relating to, or located in northern regions ⟨~ waters⟩ **2 :** of, relating to, or comprising the northern biotic area characterized esp. by dominance of coniferous forests

Bo·re·as \-ē-əs\ *n* [L, fr. Gk] **1 :** the Greek god of the north wind **2 :** the north wind personified

bore·dom \'bō(ə)rd-əm, 'bȯ(ə)rd-\ *n* (1852) **:** the state of being bored

bo·reen \bōr-'ēn, bȯr-\ *n* [IrGael *bōthrīn,* dim. of *bōthar* road] *Irish* (1836) **:** a narrow country lane

bore·hole \'bō(ə)r-ˌhōl, 'bȯ(ə)r-\ *n* (1708) **:** a hole bored or drilled in the earth; *esp* **:** an exploratory well

bor·er \'bōr-ər, 'bȯr-\ *n* (14c) **1 :** a tool used for boring **2 a :** SHIPWORM **b :** an insect that as larva or adult bores in the woody parts of plants

bo·ric \'bōr-ik, 'bȯr-\ *adj* (1869) **:** of or containing boron

boric acid *n* (1869) **:** a white crystalline acid H_3BO_3 easily obtained from its salts and used esp. as a weak antiseptic

bo·ride \'bō(ə)r-ˌīd, 'bȯ(ə)r-\ *n* (1863) **:** a binary compound of boron usu. with a more electropositive element or radical

bor·ing \'bō(ə)r-iŋ, 'bȯ(ə)r-\ *adj* (1841) **:** causing boredom **:** TIRESOME — **bor·ing·ly** \-iŋ-lē\ *adv* — **bor·ing·ness** *n*

born \'bȯ(ə)rn\ *adj* [ME, fr. OE *boren,* pp. of *beran* to carry — more at BEAR] (bef. 12c) **1 a :** brought forth by or as if by birth **b :** NATIVE — usu. used in combination ⟨American-*born*⟩ **c :** deriving or resulting from — usu. used in combination ⟨poverty-*born* crime⟩ **2 a :** having from birth specified qualities ⟨a ~ leader⟩ **b :** being in specified circumstances from birth ⟨nobly ~⟩ **3 :** destined from or as if from birth ⟨~ to succeed⟩

born–again *adj* [fr. the statement "Except a man be *born again,* he cannot see the Kingdom of God" —John 3:3 (AV)] (1967) **:** relating to or having experienced a profound revival of a particular personal faith or conviction or of a former activity ⟨~ Christians⟩ ⟨a ~ conservative⟩ ⟨a ~ bicyclist⟩

borne *past part of* BEAR

bor·ne·ol \'bȯr-nē-ˌȯl, -ˌōl\ *n* [ISV, fr. *Borneo,* island in the Malay archipelago] (1876) **:** a crystalline cyclic alcohol $C_{10}H_{17}OH$ that occurs in two enantiomeric forms, is found in essential oils, and is used esp. in perfumery

born·ite \'bȯ(ə)r-ˌnīt\ *n* [G *bornit,* fr. Ignaz von *Born* †1791 Austrian mineralogist] (ca. 1847) **:** a brittle metallic-looking mineral Cu_5FeS_4 consisting of a sulfide of copper and iron and constituting a valuable ore of copper

bo·ron \'bō(ə)r-ˌän, 'bȯ(ə)r-\ *n* [*borax* + *-on* (as in *carbon*)] (1812) **:** a trivalent metalloid element found in nature only in combination and used in metallurgy and in nucleonics — see ELEMENT table — **bo·ron·ic** \bȯr-'än-ik, bōr-\ *adj*

bo·ro·sil·i·cate \ˌbōr-ō-'sil-ə-ˌkāt, ˌbȯr-, -'sil-i-kət\ *n* [ISV *boron* + *silicate*] (1817) **:** a silicate containing boron in the anion and occurring naturally

bor·ough \'bər-(ˌ)ō, 'bə-(ˌ)rō, -ə(-w), -rə(-w)\ *n* [ME *burgh,* fr. OE *burg* fortified town; akin to OHG *burg* fortified place, OE *beorg* mountain — more at BARROW] (bef. 12c) **1 a :** a medieval fortified group of houses forming a town with special duties and privileges **b :** a town or urban constituency in Great Britain that sends a member to Parliament **c :** an urban area in Great Britain incorporated for purposes of self-government **2 a :** a municipal corporation proper in some states (as New Jersey and Minnesota) corresponding to the incorporated town or village of the other states **b :** one of the five constituent political divi-

sions of New York City **3 :** a civil division of the state of Alaska corresponding to a county in most other states
borough English *n* (14c) **:** a custom formerly existing in parts of England by which the lands of a tenant intestate descend to the youngest son
borough hall *n* (1939) **:** the chief administrative building of a borough
bor·row \'bär-(,)ō, 'bȯr-, -ə(-w)\ *vb* [ME *borwen,* fr. OE *borgian;* akin to OHG *boragen* to guard, protect, OE *beorgan* to preserve — more at BURY] *vt* (bef. 12c) **1 :** to receive with the implied or expressed intention of returning the same or an equivalent ⟨~ a book⟩ ⟨~*ed* a dollar⟩ **2 a :** to appropriate for one's own use ⟨~ a metaphor⟩ **b :** DERIVE, ADOPT **3 :** to take (one) from a digit of the minuend in arithmetical subtraction in order to add as 10 to the digit holding the next lower place **4 :** to introduce into one language from another **5** *dial* **:** LEND ~ *vi* **:** to borrow something — **bor·row·er** \-ə-wər\ *n* — **borrow trouble :** to do something unnecessarily that may result in adverse reaction or repercussions
bor·rowed time *n* (1898) **:** an uncertain and usu. uncontrolled postponement of something inevitable — used with *on* ⟨many a shooter has been living on *borrowed time* because he has been shooting ammunition which should blow up his gun —R. R. Camp⟩
bor·row·ing \'bär-ə-wiŋ, 'bȯr-\ *n* (1630) **:** something borrowed; *esp* **:** a word or phrase adopted from one language into another
borrow pit *n* (1893) **:** an excavated area where material has been dug for use as fill at another location
Bors \'bȯ(ə)rz\ *n* [ME, fr. MF *Bohort*] **:** a knight of the Round Table and nephew of Lancelot
borscht *or* **borsch** \'bȯ(ə)rsh(t)\ *n* [Russ *borshch*] (1884) **:** a soup made primarily of beets and served hot or cold often with sour cream
borscht belt *also* **borsch belt** *n* (1938) **:** BORSCHT CIRCUIT
borscht circuit *or* **borsch circuit** *n, often cap B&C* [fr. the popularity of borscht on menus of the resorts] (1939) **:** the theaters and nightclubs associated with the Jewish summer resorts in the Catskills
Bor·stal \'bȯr-stᵊl\ *n* [*Borstal,* Eng. village where the first such institution was set up] *Brit* (1907) **:** REFORMATORY
bort \'bȯ(ə)rt\ *n* [prob. fr. D *boort*] (1622) **:** imperfectly crystallized diamond or diamond fragments used as an abrasive
bor·zoi \'bȯr-,zȯi\ *n* [Russ *borzoĭ,* fr. *borzoĭ* swift; akin to L *festinare* to hasten] (1887) **:** any of a breed of large long-haired dogs of greyhound type developed in Russia esp. for pursuing wolves — called also *Russian wolfhound*
bos·cage *also* **bosk·age** \'bäs-kij\ *n* [ME *boskage,* fr. MF *boscage,* fr. OF, fr. *bois, bosc* forest, of Gmc origin; akin to ME *bush*] (14c) **:** a growth of trees or shrubs **:** THICKET
bosh \'bäsh\ *n* [Turk *boş* empty] (1834) **1 :** foolish talk or activity **:** NONSENSE — often used interjectionally **2 :** something worthless or trifling
bosk *or* **bosque** \'bäsk\ *n* [prob. back-formation fr. *bosky*] (1814) **:** a small wooded area
Bos·kop man \,bäs-,käp-\ *n* [*Boskop,* locality in the Transvaal] (1915) **:** a late Pleistocene southern African man prob. ancestral to modern Bushmen and Hottentots — **bos·kop·oid** \'bäs-kə-,pȯid\ *adj*
bosky \'bäs-kē\ *adj* [E dial. *bosk* bush, fr. ME *bush, bosk*] (1593) **1 :** having abundant trees or shrubs **2 :** of or relating to a woods
bo·s'n *or* **bo'·s'n** *or* **bo·sun** *or* **bo'·sun** \'bōs-ᵊn\ *var of* BOATSWAIN
1bo·som \'bu̇z-əm *also* 'büz-\ *n* [ME, fr. OE *bōsm;* akin to OHG *buosam* bosom — more at BIG] (bef. 12c) **1 a :** the human chest and esp. the front part of the chest ⟨hugged the child to his ~⟩ **b :** the female breasts — often used in pl. ⟨the future Congresswoman with ~*s* which spoke of . . . carnal abundance —Norman Mailer⟩ **2 a :** the chest conceived of as the seat of the emotions and intimate feelings ⟨a story you will take to your ~⟩ **b :** the security and intimacy of or like that of being hugged to someone's bosom ⟨lived in the ~ of her family⟩ **3 :** the part of a garment that covers the chest or the breasts ⟨tucked the note into the ~ of her dress⟩
2bosom *vt* (1590) **1 :** to enclose or carry in the bosom **2 :** EMBRACE
3bosom *adj* (1596) **:** CLOSE, INTIMATE ⟨~ friends⟩
-bo·somed \-əmd\ *adj comb form* **:** having (such) a bosom ⟨flat-*bosomed*⟩
bo·somy \-ə-mē\ *adj* (1860) **1 :** swelling upward or outward ⟨~ hills⟩ **2 :** having prominent breasts
bo·son \'bō-,sän\ *n* [Satyendranath *Bose* †1974 Indian physicist + E *²-on*] (1947) **:** a particle (as a photon, meson, or alpha particle) whose spin is zero or an integral number
bos·quet \'bäs-kət\ *n* [F, fr. It *boschetto,* dim. of *bosco* forest, of Gmc origin; akin to ME *bush*] (ca. 1737) **:** THICKET
1boss \'bäs, 'bȯs\ *n* [ME *boce,* fr. MF, fr. (assumed) VL *bottia*] (14c) **1 a :** a protuberant part or body ⟨a ~ of granite⟩ ⟨a ~ on an animal's horn⟩ **b :** a raised ornamentation **:** STUD **c :** an ornamental projecting block used in architecture **2 :** a soft pad used in ceramics and glassmaking **3 a :** the enlarged part of a shaft on which a wheel is mounted **b :** the hub of a propeller

boss 1c

2boss *vt* (15c) **1 :** to ornament with bosses **:** EMBOSS **2 :** to treat (as the surface of porcelain) with a boss
3boss \'bȯs\ *n* [D *baas* master] (1649) **1 :** one who exercises control or authority; *specif* **:** one who directs or supervises workers **2 :** a politician who controls votes in a party organization or dictates appointments or legislative measures — **boss·dom** \-dəm\ *n* — **boss·ism** \-,iz-əm\ *n*
4boss \'bȯs\ *adj, slang* (1836) **:** EXCELLENT, FIRST-RATE ⟨a beautiful blazer, a ~ piece of stitching —*N. Y. Times*⟩
5boss \'bȯs\ *vt* (1856) **1 :** to act as boss of **2 :** to give arbitrary orders to — usu. used with *around*
6boss \'bȯs, 'bäs\ *n* [E dial., young cow] (1790) **:** COW, CALF
bos·sa no·va \,bäs-ə-'nō-və\ *n* [Pg, lit., new trend] (1962) **1 :** popular music of Brazilian origin that is rhythmically related to the samba but with complex harmonies and improvised jazzlike passages **2 :** a dance performed to bossa nova music
boss man *n* (1934) **:** ³BOSS
1bossy \'bäs-ē, 'bȯ-sē\ *adj* (1543) **1 :** marked by a swelling or roundness **2 :** marked by bosses **:** STUDDED
2bossy \'bȯ-sē, 'bäs-ē\ *n, pl* **boss·ies** (1843) **:** COW, CALF
3bossy \'bȯ-sē\ *adj* **boss·i·er; -est** (1882) **:** inclined to domineer **:** DICTATORIAL — **boss·i·ness** *n*
Bos·ton \'bȯ-stən\ *n* [F, fr. *Boston,* Mass.] (1800) **1 :** a variation of whist played with two decks of cards **2** [*Boston,* Mass.] **:** a dance somewhat like a waltz
Boston bag *n* (1922) **:** a traveling bag or utility bag that is held together at the top opening by two handles
Boston cream pie *n* (ca. 1933) **:** a round cake that is split and filled with a custard or cream filling
Boston fern *n* (ca. 1900) **:** a luxuriant fern (*Nephrolepis exaltata bostoniensis*) often with drooping much-divided fronds
Boston ivy *n* (ca. 1900) **:** a woody Asian vine (*Parthenocissus tricuspidata*) of the grape family with 3-lobed leaves
Boston rocker *n* (1856) **:** a wooden rocking chair with a high spindle back, a decorative top panel, and a seat and arms that curve down at the front
Boston terrier *n* (1894) **:** any of a breed of small smooth-coated terriers originating as a cross of the bulldog and bullterrier and being brindled or black with white markings — called also *Boston bull*
Bos·well \'bäz-,wel, -wəl\ *n* [James *Boswell*] (1858) **:** one who records in detail the life of a usu. famous contemporary — **Bos·well·ian** \bäz-'wel-ē-ən\ *adj* — **Bos·well·ize** \'bäz-wəl-,īz, -,wel-\ *vb*
bot *also* **bott** \'bät\ *n* [perh. modif. of ScGael *boiteag* maggot] (15c) **:** the larva of a botfly; *esp* **:** one infesting the horse
bo·ta \'bōt-ə\ *n* [Sp, fr. LL *buttis* cask, flask — more at BOTTLE] (1832) **:** a leather bottle (as for wine)
bo·tan·i·ca \bə-'tan-i-kə\ *n* [Sp, fr. Gk *botanikos*] (1969) **:** a shop that deals in herbs and magic charms
1bo·tan·i·cal \bə-'tan-i-kəl\ *adj* [F *botanique,* fr. Gk *botanikos* of herbs, fr. *botanē* pasture, herb, fr. *boskein* to feed] (1658) **1 :** of or relating to plants or botany **2 :** derived from plants **3 :** SPECIES ⟨~ tulips⟩ — **bo·tan·i·cal·ly** \-k(ə-)lē\ *adv*
2botanical *n* (ca. 1925) **:** a vegetable drug esp. in the crude state
botanical garden *or* **bo·tan·ic garden** \bə-'tan-ik-\ *n* (1785) **:** a garden often with greenhouses for the culture, study, and exhibition of special plants
bot·a·nist \'bät-ᵊn-əst, 'bät-nəst\ *n* (1682) **:** a specialist in botany or in a branch of botany
bot·a·nize \-ᵊn-,īz\ *vb* **-nized; -niz·ing** *vi* (1767) **:** to collect plants for botanical investigation; *also* **:** to study plants esp. on a field trip ~ *vt* **:** to explore for botanical purposes
bot·a·ny \'bät-ᵊn-ē, 'bät-nē\ *n, pl* **-nies** [back-formation fr. *botanical*] (1696) **1 :** a branch of biology dealing with plant life **2 a :** plant life **b :** the properties and life phenomena exhibited by a plant, plant type, or plant group **3 :** a botanical treatise or study; *esp* **:** a particular system of botany
1botch \'bäch\ *n* [ME *boche,* fr. ONF, fr. (assumed) VL *bottia* boss] (14c) **:** an inflammatory sore
2botch *vt* [ME *bocchen*] (1530) **1 :** to foul up hopelessly **:** BUNGLE — often used with *up* **2 :** to put together in a makeshift way — **botch·er** *n*
3botch *n* (1605) **1 :** something that is botched **:** MESS **2 :** PATCHWORK, HODGEPODGE — **botchy** \-ē\ *adj*
bo·tel \bō-'tel\ *var of* BOATEL
bot·fly \'bät-,flī\ *n* (1819) **:** any of various stout two-winged flies (group Oestroidea) with larvae parasitic in cavities or tissues of various mammals including man
1both \'bōth\ *adj* [ME *bothe,* fr. ON *bāthir;* akin to OHG *beide* both] (12c) **:** being the two **:** affecting or involving the one and the other ⟨~ feet⟩ ⟨~ his eyes⟩ ⟨~ these armies⟩
2both *pron, pl in constr* (12c) **:** the one as well as the other ⟨~ of us⟩ ⟨we are ~ well⟩ ⟨$1000 fine or 30 days in jail, or ~⟩
3both *conj* (12c) — used as a function word to indicate and stress the inclusion of each of two or more things specified by coordinated words, phrases, or clauses ⟨~ New York and London⟩ ⟨prized ~ for its beauty and for its utility⟩
1both·er \'bäth-ər\ *vb* **both·ered; both·er·ing** \-(ə-)riŋ\ [perh. fr. IrGael *bodhar* bothered] *vt* (1745) **1 :** to annoy esp. by petty provocation **:** IRK **2 :** to intrude upon **:** PESTER **3 :** to cause to be anxious or concerned **:** TROUBLE — often used interjectionally ~ *vi* **1 :** to become concerned **2 :** to take pains **:** take the trouble ***syn*** see ANNOY
2bother *n* (1834) **1 a :** a state of petty discomfort, annoyance, or worry **b :** something that causes petty annoyance or worry **2 :** FUSS
both·er·ation \,bäth-ə-'rā-shən\ *n* (1797) **1 :** the act of bothering **:** the state of being bothered **2 :** something that bothers — often used interjectionally
both·er·some \'bäth-ər-səm\ *adj* (1834) **:** causing bother **:** VEXING
bo·thy \'bäth-ē, 'bōth-\ *n* [Sc, prob. fr. obs. Sc *both* booth] *chiefly Scot* (1771) **:** HUT
bot·o·née *or* **bot·on·née** \,bät-ᵊn-'ā\ *adj* [MF *botonné*] *of a heraldic cross* (15c) **:** having a cluster of three balls or knobs at the end of each arm — see CROSS illustration
bo tree \'bō-\ *n* [Sinhalese *bō,* fr. Skt *bodhi* enlightenment; fr. Buddha receiving enlightenment under this tree — more at BID] (1862) **:** PIPAL
bot·ry·oi·dal \,bä-trē-'ȯid-ᵊl\ *adj* [Gk *botryoeidēs,* fr. *botrys* bunch of grapes] (1816) **:** having the form of a bunch of grapes ⟨~ garnets⟩
1bot·tle \'bät-ᵊl\ *n, often attrib* [ME *botel,* fr. MF *bouteille,* fr. ML *butticula,* dim. of LL *buttis* cask; akin to Gk *pytinē* a kind of wine bottle] (14c) **1 a :** a rigid or semirigid container typically of glass or plastic having a comparatively narrow neck or mouth and usu. no handle **b :** a usu. bottle-shaped container made of skin for storing a liquid (as water or wine) **2 :** the quantity held by a bottle **3 a :** intoxicating drink **:** the practice of drinking ⟨took to the ~⟩ **b :** liquid food (as milk) used in place of mother's milk — **bot·tle·ful** \-,fu̇l\ *n*
2bottle *vt* **bot·tled; bot·tling** \'bät-liŋ, -ᵊl-iŋ\ (1622) **1 :** to confine as if in a bottle **:** RESTRAIN — usu. used with *up* ⟨*bottling* up their anger⟩ **2 :** to put into a bottle — **bot·tler** \-lər, -ᵊl-ər\ *n*
bot·tle·brush \'bät-ᵊl-,brəsh\ *n* [fr. the shape of the flowers] (ca. 1883) **:** any of a genus (*Callistemon*) of Australian trees and shrubs of the myrtle family widely cultivated in warm regions esp. for their spikes of brightly colored flowers

bottle club *n* (1943) **:** a club that serves patrons alcoholic drinks after normal legal closing hours from supplies they have previously purchased or reserved
bottled gas *n* (1930) **:** gas under pressure in portable cylinders
bot·tle–feed \ˈbät-ᵊl-ˌfēd\ *vt* **-fed; -feed·ing** (1865) **:** to feed (as an infant) with a bottle
bottle gourd *n* (ca. 1828) **:** a common cultivated gourd (*Lagenaria siceraria*) with a variably shaped fruit that is sometimes used as a container
bottle green *n* (1816) **:** a dark green
[1]**bot·tle·neck** \ˈbät-ᵊl-ˌnek\ *adj* (1896) **:** NARROW ⟨~ harbors⟩
[2]**bottleneck** *n* (1907) **1 a :** a narrow route **b :** a point of traffic congestion **2 a :** a condition or situation that retards or halts free movement and progress **b :** IMPASSE **3 :** a style of guitar playing in which glissando effects are produced by sliding an object (as a knife blade or the neck of a bottle) along the strings
[3]**bottleneck** *vt* (1937) **:** to slow or halt by causing a bottleneck
bot·tle–nosed dolphin \ˌbät-ᵊl-ˌnōz-\ *n* (ca. 1909) **:** any of various moderately large stout-bodied toothed whales (genus *Tursiops* and esp. *T. truncatus*) with a prominent beak and falcate dorsal fin
bottlenose dolphin *n* (1940) **:** BOTTLE-NOSED DOLPHIN
bot·tling \ˈbät-liŋ, -ᵊl-iŋ\ *n* (1954) **:** a beverage and esp. a wine that is bottled
[1]**bot·tom** \ˈbät-əm\ *n* [ME *botme,* fr. OE *botm;* akin to OHG *bodam* bottom, L *fundus,* Gk *pythmēn*] (bef. 12c) **1 a :** the underside of something **b :** a surface designed to support something resting on it **c :** the posterior end of the trunk **:** BUTTOCKS, RUMP **2 :** the surface on which a body of water lies **3 a :** the part of a ship's hull lying below the water **b :** BOAT, SHIP **4 a :** the lowest part or place **b :** the remotest or inmost point **c :** the lowest or last place in point of precedence ⟨started work at the ~⟩ **d :** the trousers or short pants of pajamas — usu. used in pl. **e :** the last half of an inning of baseball **f :** the bass or baritone instruments of a band **5 :** low-lying land along a watercourse — usu. used in pl. **6 :** BASIS, SOURCE **7 :** capacity (as of a horse) to endure strain **8 :** the main plowing mechanism of a plow **9 :** a foundation color applied to textile fibers before dyeing **10 :** a quantum characteristic ascribed to certain massive fundamental particles that accounts for the existence and lifetime of upsilon particles and has a value of zero for most known particles — **bot·tomed** \-əmd\ *adj* — **at bottom :** REALLY, BASICALLY
[2]**bottom** *adj* (14c) **1 :** of, relating to, or situated at the bottom ⟨~ rock⟩ **2 :** frequenting the bottom ⟨~ fish⟩
[3]**bottom** *vt* (1544) **1 :** to furnish with a bottom **2 :** to provide a foundation for **3 :** to bring to the bottom **4 :** to get to the bottom of ~ *vi* **1 :** to become based **2 :** to reach the bottom — **bot·tom·er** *n*
bot·tom·land \ˈbät-əm-ˌland\ *n* (1728) **:** BOTTOM 5
bot·tom·less \-ləs\ *adj* (14c) **1 :** having no bottom ⟨a ~ chair⟩ **2 a :** extremely deep **b :** impossible to comprehend **:** UNFATHOMABLE ⟨a ~ mystery⟩ **c :** BOUNDLESS, UNLIMITED **3 a** [fr. the absence of lower as well as upper garments] **:** NUDE ⟨~ dancers⟩ **b :** featuring nude entertainers — **bot·tom·less·ly** *adv* — **bot·tom·less·ness** *n*
bottom–line \ˈbät-əm-ˌlīn\ *adj* (1972) **1 :** concerned only with cost or profits **2 :** PRAGMATIC, REALISTIC
bottom line *n* (1967) **1 a :** the essential or salient point **:** CRUX **b :** the primary or most important consideration **2 a :** the line at the bottom of a financial report that shows the net profit or loss **b :** financial considerations (as cost or profit or loss) **c :** the final result **:** OUTCOME, UPSHOT
bot·tom·most \ˈbät-əm-ˌmōst\ *adj* (1861) **1 a :** situated at the very bottom **:** LOWEST, DEEPEST **b :** LAST ⟨the ~ part of the day —Alfred Kazin⟩ **2 :** most basic ⟨the ~ problems facing the world⟩
bottom out *vi* (1958) **:** to reach a low point before rebounding ⟨the market will *bottom out* in July⟩
bottom round *n* (1923) **:** meat (as steak) from the outer part of a round of beef
bot·u·lin \ˈbäch-ə-lən\ *n* [prob. fr. NL *botulinum*] (ca. 1900) **:** a toxin that is formed by the botulinum and is the direct cause of botulism
bot·u·li·num \ˌbäch-ə-ˈlī-nəm\ *also* **bot·u·li·nus** \-nəs\ *n* [NL, fr. L *botulus* sausage] (1902) **:** a spore-forming bacterium (*Clostridium botulinum*) that secretes botulin — **bot·u·li·nal** \-ˈlīn-ᵊl\ *adj*
bot·u·lism \ˈbäch-ə-ˌliz-əm\ *n* (1887) **:** acute food poisoning caused by botulin in food
bou·bou \ˈbü-ˌbü\ *n* [native name in Mali] (1961) **:** a long flowing garment worn in parts of Africa
bou·chée \bü-ˈshā\ *n* [F, lit., mouthful, fr. (assumed) VL *buccata,* fr. L *bucca* cheek, mouth — more at POCK] (1846) **:** a small patty shell usu. containing a creamed filling
bou·clé *or* **bou·cle** \bü-ˈklā\ *n* [F *bouclé* curly, fr. pp. of *boucler* to curl, fr. *bocle* buckle, curl] (1895) **1 :** an uneven yarn of three plies one of which forms loops at intervals **2 :** a textile fabric of bouclé yarn
bou·doir \ˈbüd-ˌwär, ˈbu̇d-\ *n* [F, fr. *bouder* to pout] (1781) **:** a woman's dressing room, bedroom, or private sitting room
bouf·fant \bü-ˈfänt, ˈbü-ˌ\ *adj* [F, fr. MF, fr. prp. of *bouffer* to puff] (1880) **:** puffed out ⟨~ hairdos⟩ ⟨a ~ veil⟩
bou·gain·vil·lea *also* **bou·gain·vil·laea** \ˌbüg-ən-ˈvil-yə, ˌbōg-, ˌbu̇g-, -ˈvē-(y)ə\ *n* [NL, fr. Louis Antoine de *Bougainville*] (1881) **:** any of a genus (*Bougainvillaea*) of the four-o'clock family of ornamental tropical American woody vines with brilliant purple or red floral bracts
bough \ˈbau̇\ *n* [ME, shoulder, bough, fr. OE *bōg;* akin to OHG *buog* shoulder, Gk *pēchys* forearm] (bef. 12c) **:** a branch of a tree; *esp* **:** a main branch — **boughed** \ˈbau̇d\ *adj*
bought \ˈbȯt\ *adj* [pp. of *buy*] (1599) **:** STORE 2 ⟨~ clothes⟩
bought·en \-ᵊn\ *adj* [*bought* + *-en* (as in *forgotten*)] *chiefly dial* (1793) **:** BOUGHT ⟨the only ~ carpet in the region —H. W. Thompson⟩
bou·gie \ˈbü-ˌzhē, -ˌjē\ *n* [F, fr. *Bougie,* seaport in Algeria] (1755) **1 :** a wax candle **2 a :** a tapering cylindrical instrument for introduction into a tubular passage of the body **b :** SUPPOSITORY
bouil·la·baisse \ˌbü-yə-ˈbās, ˈbü-yə-ˌ\ *n* [F] (1855) **1 :** a highly seasoned fish stew made with at least two kinds of fish **2 :** POTPOURRI
bouil·lon \ˈbü(l)-ˌyän, ˈbu̇(l)-; ˈbu̇l-yən; ˈbü-ˌyō^{n}\ *n* [F, fr. OF *boillon,* fr. *boillir* to boil] (ca. 1656) **:** a clear seasoned soup made usu. from lean beef
bouillon cube *n* (ca. 1922) **:** a cube of evaporated seasoned meat extract
boul·der \ˈbōl-dər\ *n* [short for *boulder stone,* fr. ME *bulder ston,* part trans. of a word of Scand origin; akin to Sw dial. *bullersten* large stone in a stream, fr. *buller* noise + *sten* stone] (1617) **:** a detached and rounded or much-worn mass of rock — **boul·dered** \-dərd\ *adj* — **boul·dery** \-d(ə-)rē\ *adj*
[1]**bou·le** \ˈbü-(ˌ)lē, bü-ˈlā\ *n* [Gk *boulē,* lit., will, fr. *boulesthai* to wish] (1846) **:** a legislative council of ancient Greece consisting first of an aristocratic advisory body and later of a representative senate
[2]**boule** \ˈbül\ *n* [F, ball — more at BOWL] (1918) **:** a pear-shaped mass (as of sapphire) formed synthetically in a special furnace with the atomic structure of a single crystal
bou·le·vard \ˈbu̇l-ə-ˌvärd, ˈbül-\ *n* [F, modif. of MD *bolwerc* bulwark] (1769) **:** a broad often landscaped thoroughfare
bou·le·vard·ier \ˌbu̇l-ə-ˌvär-ˈdyā, ˌbül-, -ˈdi(ə)r\ *n* [F, fr. *boulevard* + *-ier* -er] (1879) **:** a frequenter of the Parisian boulevards; *broadly* **:** MAN-ABOUT-TOWN
bou·le·ver·se·ment \bül-(ə-)ver-sə-mä^{n}\ *n* [F] (1782) **1 :** REVERSAL **2 :** a violent disturbance **:** DISORDER
boulle \ˈbül, ˈbyü(ə)l\ *n* [André Charles *Boulle* †1732 Fr. cabinetmaker] (1823) **:** inlaid decoration of tortoiseshell, yellow metal, and white metal in cabinetwork
[1]**bounce** \ˈbau̇n(t)s\ *vb* **bounced; bounc·ing** [ME *bounsen*] *vt* (13c) **1** *obs* **:** BEAT, BUMP **2 :** to cause to rebound ⟨~ a ball⟩ **3 a :** DISMISS, FIRE **b :** to expel precipitately from a place **4 :** to issue (a check) drawn on an account with insufficient funds ~ *vi* **1 :** to rebound after striking **2 :** to recover from a blow or a defeat quickly — usu. used with *back* **3 :** to be returned by a bank because of insufficient funds in a checking account ⟨his checks ~⟩ **4 a :** to leap suddenly **:** BOUND **b :** to walk with springing steps **5 :** to hit a baseball so that it hits the ground before it reaches an infielder
[2]**bounce** *n* (1523) **1 a :** a sudden leap or bound **b :** REBOUND **2 :** BLUSTER **3 :** VERVE, LIVELINESS
bounc·er \ˈbau̇n(t)-sər\ *n* (1865) **:** one that bounces: as **a :** one employed to restrain or eject disorderly persons **b :** a batted baseball that bounces
bounc·ing \-siŋ\ *adj* (1563) **1 :** LIVELY, ANIMATED **2 :** enjoying good health **:** ROBUST — **bounc·ing·ly** \-siŋ-lē\ *adv*
bouncing bet \-ˈbet\ *n, often cap 2d B* [fr. *Bet,* nickname for *Elizabeth*] (ca. 1817) **:** a European perennial herb (*Saponaria officinalis*) of the pink family that is widely naturalized in the U.S. and has pink or white flowers and leaves which yield a detergent when bruised — called also *soapwort*
bouncy \ˈbau̇n(t)-sē\ *adj* **bounc·i·er; -est** (1921) **1 :** BUOYANT, EXUBERANT **2 :** RESILIENT **3 :** marked by or producing bounces — **bounc·i·ly** \-sə-lē\ *adv*
[1]**bound** \ˈbau̇nd\ *adj* [ME *boun,* fr. ON *būinn,* pp. of *būa* to dwell, prepare; akin to OHG *būan* to dwell — more at BOWER] (13c) **1** *archaic* **:** READY **2 :** intending to go **:** GOING ⟨~ for home⟩ ⟨college-*bound*⟩
[2]**bound** *n* [ME, fr. OF *bodne,* fr. ML *bodina*] (13c) **1 a :** a limiting line **:** BOUNDARY — usu. used in pl. **b :** something that limits or restrains ⟨beyond the ~*s* of decency⟩ **2** *usu pl* **a :** BORDERLAND **b :** the land within certain bounds **3 :** a number greater than or equal to every number in a set (as the range of a function); *also* **:** a number less than or equal to every number in a set
[3]**bound** *vt* (14c) **1 :** to set limits or bounds to **:** CONFINE **2 :** to form the boundary of **:** ENCLOSE **3 :** to name the boundaries of
[4]**bound** *adj* [ME *bounden,* fr. pp. of *binden* to bind — more at BIND] (13c) **1 a :** fastened by or as if by a band **:** CONFINED ⟨desk-*bound*⟩ **b :** very likely **:** SURE ⟨~ to rain soon⟩ **2 :** placed under legal or moral restraint or obligation **:** OBLIGED ⟨duty-*bound*⟩ **3 :** made costive **:** CONSTIPATED **4** *of a book* **:** secured to the covers by cords, tapes, or glue **5 :** DETERMINED, RESOLVED **6 :** held in chemical or physical combination ⟨~ water in a molecule⟩ **7 :** always occurring in combination with another linguistic form ⟨*un-* in *unknown* and *-er* in *speaker* are ~ forms⟩ — compare [1]FREE 11d
[5]**bound** *n* [MF *bond,* fr. *bondir* to leap, fr. (assumed) VL *bombitire* to hum, fr. L *bombus* deep hollow sound — more at BOMB] (1553) **1 :** LEAP, JUMP **2 :** the action of rebounding **:** BOUNCE
[6]**bound** *vi* (1592) **1 :** to move by leaping **2 :** REBOUND, BOUNCE
bound·ary \ˈbau̇n-d(ə-)rē\ *n, pl* **-aries** (1626) **:** something that indicates or fixes a limit or extent; *specif* **:** a bounding or separating line, point, or plane
boundary layer *n* (ca. 1921) **:** a region of retarded fluid near the surface of a body which moves through a fluid or past which a fluid moves
bound·en \ˈbau̇n-dən\ *adj* [ME] (14c) **1** *archaic* **:** being under obligation **:** BEHOLDEN **2 :** made obligatory **:** BINDING ⟨our ~ duty⟩
bound·er \-dər\ *n* (1505) **1 :** one that bounds **2 :** a man of objectionable social behavior **:** CAD
bound·less \ˈbau̇n-dləs\ *adj* (1592) **:** having no boundaries **:** VAST — **bound·less·ly** *adv* — **bound·less·ness** *n*
bound up *adj* (1611) **:** closely involved or associated — usu. used with *with*
boun·te·ous \ˈbau̇nt-ē-əs\ *adj* [ME *bountevous,* fr. MF *bontif* kind, fr. OF, fr. *bonté*] (14c) **1 :** giving or disposed to give freely **2 :** liberally bestowed — **boun·te·ous·ly** *adv* — **boun·te·ous·ness** *n*
boun·tied \ˈbau̇nt-ēd\ *adj* (1788) **1 :** having the benefit of a bounty **2 :** rewarded or rewardable by a bounty
boun·ti·ful \ˈbau̇nt-i-fəl\ *adj* (1508) **1 :** liberal in bestowing gifts or favors **2 :** given or provided abundantly ⟨a ~ harvest⟩ ***syn*** see LIBERAL — **boun·ti·ful·ly** \-f(ə-)lē\ *adv* — **boun·ti·ful·ness** \-fəl-nəs\ *n*
boun·ty \ˈbau̇nt-ē\ *n, pl* **bounties** [ME *bounte* goodness, fr. OF *bonté,* fr. L *bonitat-, bonitas,* fr. *bonus* good, fr. OL *duenos;* akin to MHG *zwīden* to grant, L *bene* well] (13c) **1 :** something that is given generously **2 :** liberality in giving **:** GENEROSITY **3 :** yield esp. of a crop **4 :** a reward, premium, or subsidy esp. when offered or given by a government: as **a :** an extra allowance to induce entry into the armed services **b :** a grant to encourage an industry **c :** a payment to encourage the destruction of noxious animals **d :** a payment for the capturing or assisting in capturing an outlaw

\ə\ abut \ᵊ\ kitten, F table \ər\ further \a\ ash \ā\ ace \ä\ cot, cart \au̇\ out \ch\ chin \e\ bet \ē\ easy \g\ go \i\ hit \ī\ ice \j\ job \ŋ\ sing \ō\ go \ȯ\ law \ȯi\ boy \th\ thin \t͟h\ the \ü\ loot \u̇\ foot \y\ yet \zh\ vision \à, k̲, ^{n}, œ, ǣ, ue, ue̅, ʸ\ see Guide to Pronunciation

bounty hunter *n* (1957) **1 :** one that hunts predatory animals for the reward offered **2 :** one that tracks down and captures outlaws for whom a reward is offered

bou·quet \bō-ˈkā, bü-\ *n* [F, fr. MF, thicket, fr. ONF *bosquet,* fr. OF *bosc* forest — more at BOSCAGE] (1716) **1 a :** flowers picked and fastened together in a bunch : NOSEGAY **b :** MEDLEY ⟨~ of songs⟩ **2 :** COMPLIMENT **3 a :** a distinctive and characteristic fragrance (as of wine) **b :** a subtle aroma or quality (as of an artistic performance or a piece of writing)

bou·quet gar·ni \-gär-ˈnē\ *n, pl* **bou·quets gar·nis** \-ˈkā(z)-gär-ˈnē\ [F, lit., garnished bouquet] (1852) **:** an herb mixture that is either tied together or enclosed in a porous container and is removed from a dish at the completion of cooking

bour·bon \ˈbu̇(ə)r-bən, ˈbō(ə)r-, ˈbȯ(ə)r-; *usu* ˈbər- *in sense 4*\ *n* [*Bourbon,* seigniory in France] (1600) **1** *cap* **:** a member of a French family founded in 1272 to which belong the rulers of France from 1589 to 1793 and from 1814 to 1830, of Spain from 1700 to 1808, from 1814 to 1868, from 1875 to 1931, and from 1975, of Naples from 1735 to 1805, and of the Two Sicilies from 1815 to 1860 **2** *often cap* **:** a person who clings obstinately to the social and political ideas of the old order of things; *specif* **:** an extremely conservative member of the U.S. Democratic party usu. from the South **3** [*Bourbon* (now Réunion), French island in the Indian ocean] **:** a rose (*Rosa borboniana*) of compact upright growth with shining leaves, prickly branches, and clustered flowers **4** [*Bourbon* county, Kentucky] **:** a whiskey distilled from a mash made up of not less than 51 percent corn plus malt and rye — compare CORN WHISKEY — **bour·bon·ism** \-bə-ˌniz-əm\ *n, often cap*

bourg \ˈbu̇(ə)r(g)\ *n* [ME, fr. MF, fr. OF *borc,* fr. L *burgus* fortified place, of Gmc origin; akin to OHG *burg* fortified place — more at BOROUGH] (12c) **:** TOWN, VILLAGE; as **a :** one neighboring a castle **b :** a market town

1bour·geois \ˈbu̇(ə)rzh-ˌwä *also* ˈbu̇zh- *or* ˈbüzh- *or* bu̇rzh-ˈ\ *adj* [MF, fr. OF *borjois,* fr. *borc*] (1564) **1 :** of, relating to, or characteristic of the townsman or of the social middle class **2 :** marked by a concern for material interests and respectability and a tendency toward mediocrity — usu. used disparagingly **3 :** dominated by commercial and industrial interests **:** CAPITALISTIC — **bour·geois·ifi·ca·tion** \ˌbu̇(r)zh-ˌwäz-ə-fə-ˈkā-shən\ *n* — **bour·geois·ify** \bu̇(r)zh-ˈwäz-ə-ˌfī\ *vb*

2bourgeois *n, pl* **bourgeois** \-ˌwä(z), -ˈwä(z)\ (1674) **1 a :** BURGHER **b :** a middle-class person **2 :** one with social behavior and political views held to be influenced by private-property interest **:** CAPITALIST **3** *pl* **:** BOURGEOISIE

bour·geoise \ˈbu̇(ə)rzh-ˌwäz *also* ˈbu̇zh- *or* ˈbüzh- *or* bu̇rzh-ˈ\ *n* [F, fem. of *bourgeois*] (1794) **:** a woman of the middle class

bour·geoi·sie \ˌbu̇(r)zh-ˌwä-ˈzē\ *n* [F, fr. *bourgeois*] (1707) **1 :** MIDDLE CLASS **2 :** a social order dominated by bourgeois

bour·geon \ˈbər-jən\ *var of* BURGEON

bour·gui·gnonne \ˌbu̇r-gēn-ˈyȯn\ *also* **bour·gui·gnon** \-ˈyōⁿ\ *adj, often cap* [F, fr. *Bourgogne* Burgundy, region in France] (ca. 1919) **:** prepared or served in the manner of Burgundy (as with a sauce made with red Burgundy wine)

1bourn *or* **bourne** \ˈbō(ə)rn, ˈbȯ(ə)rn, ˈbu̇(ə)rn\ *n* [ME *burn, bourne* — more at BURN] (12c) **:** STREAM, BROOK

2bourn *or* **bourne** *n* [MF *bourne,* fr. OF *bodne* — more at BOUND] (1523) **1** *archaic* **:** BOUNDARY, LIMIT **2** *archaic* **:** GOAL, DESTINATION

bour·rée \bu̇-ˈrā, ˈbü-ˌ\ *n* [F] (1706) **1 :** a 17th century French dance usu. in quick duple time; *also* **:** a musical composition with the rhythm of this dance **2 :** PAS DE BOURRÉE

bour·ride \bu̇-ˈrēd, bə-\ *n* [Prov *bourrido, boulido* something boiled; akin to OF *boillir* to boil — more at BOIL] (ca. 1919) **:** a fish stew similar to bouillabaisse that is usu. thickened with egg yolks and strongly flavored with garlic

bourse \ˈbu̇(ə)rs\ *n* [MF, lit., purse, fr. ML *bursa* — more at PURSE] (1597) **1 :** EXCHANGE 5a; *specif* **:** a European stock exchange **2 :** a sale of numismatic or philatelic items on tables (as at a convention)

bour·tree \ˈbu̇(ə)r-(ˌ)trē\ *n* [ME *bourtre*] *Brit* (15c) **:** the common large black-fruited elder (*Sambucus nigra*) of Europe and Asia

bouse \ˈbau̇z\ *vb* **boused; bous·ing** [origin unknown] *vt* (1593) **:** to haul by means of a tackle ~ *vi* **:** to bouse something

bou·stro·phe·don \ˌbü-strə-ˈfēd-ˌän, -ᵊn\ *n* [Gk *boustrophēdon,* adv., lit., turning like oxen in plowing, fr. *bous* ox, cow + *strephein* to turn — more at COW, STROPHE] (1699) **:** the writing of alternate lines in opposite directions (as from left to right and from right to left) — **boustrophedon** *adj or adv* — **bou·stro·phe·don·ic** \-fē-ˈdän-ik\ *adj*

bout \ˈbau̇t\ *n* [E dial., a trip going and returning in plowing, fr. ME *bought* bend] (1575) **:** a spell of activity: as **a :** an athletic match (as of boxing) **b :** OUTBREAK, ATTACK **c :** SESSION

bou·tique \bü-ˈtēk\ *n, often attrib* [F, shop, prob. fr. OProv *botica,* fr. Gk *apothēkē* storehouse — more at APOTHECARY] (1767) **:** a small fashionable specialty shop or business; *also* **:** a small shop within a large department store

bou·ton·niere \ˌbüt-ᵊn-ˈi(ə)r, ˌbü-tən-ˈye(ə)r\ *n* [F *boutonnière* buttonhole, fr. MF, fr. *bouton* button] (1867) **:** a flower or bouquet worn in a buttonhole

Bou·vi·er des Flan·dres \ˌbü-vē-ˌād-ə-ˈflan-dərz, -ˈflaⁿdrᵊ\ *n* [F, lit., cowherd of Flanders] (1929) **:** any of a breed of large powerfully built rough-coated dogs originating in Belgium and used esp. for herding and in guard work

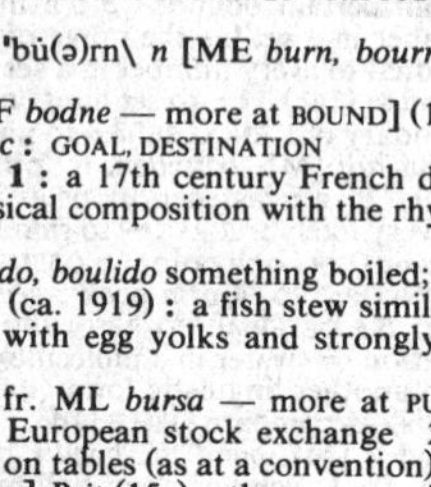

Bouvier des Flandres

bou·zou·ki \bu̇-ˈzü-kē\ *n* [NGk *mpouzouki*] (1952) **:** a long-necked stringed instrument of Greek origin that resembles a mandolin

1bo·vine \ˈbō-ˌvīn, -ˌvēn\ *adj* [LL *bovinus,* fr. L *bov-, bos* ox, cow — more at COW] (1817) **1 :** of, relating to, or resembling the ox or cow **2 :** having qualities (as sluggishness or patience) characteristic of oxen or cows — **bo·vine·ly** *adv* — **bo·vin·i·ty** \bō-ˈvin-ət-ē\ *n*

2bovine *n* (1865) **:** an ox (genus *Bos*) or a closely related animal

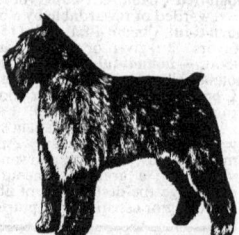

1bow \ˈbau̇\ *vb* [ME *bowen,* fr. OE *būgan;* akin to OHG *biogan* to bend, Skt *bhujati* he bends] *vi* (bef. 12c) **1 :** to suffer defeat in a contest **:** SUBMIT, YIELD **2 :** to bend the head, body, or knee in reverence, submission, or shame **3 :** to incline the head or body in salutation or assent or to acknowledge applause ~ *vt* **1 :** to cause to incline **2 :** to incline (as the head) esp. in respect or submission **3 :** to crush with a heavy burden **4 a :** to express by bowing **b :** to usher in or out with a bow

2bow *n* (1656) **:** a bending of the head or body in respect, submission, assent, or salutation

3bow \ˈbō\ *n* [ME *bowe,* fr. OE *boga;* akin to OE *būgan*] (bef. 12c) **1 a :** something bent into a simple curve **:** BEND, ARCH **b :** RAINBOW **2 :** a weapon that is made of a strip of flexible material (as wood) with a cord connecting the two ends and holding the strip bent and that is used to propel an arrow **3 :** ARCHER **4 a :** a metal ring or loop forming a handle (as of a key) **b :** a knot formed by doubling a ribbon or string into two or more loops **c :** BOW TIE **d :** a frame for the lenses of eyeglasses; *also* **:** the curved sidepiece of the frame passing over the ear **5 a :** a resilient wooden rod with horsehairs stretched from end to end used in playing an instrument of the viol or violin family **b :** a stroke of such a bow

4bow \ˈbō\ *vi* (bef. 12c) **1 :** to bend into a curve **2 :** to play a stringed musical instrument with a bow ~ *vt* **1 :** to cause to bend into a curve **2 :** to play (a stringed instrument) with a bow

5bow \ˈbau̇\ *n* [prob. fr. Dan *bov* shoulder, bow; akin to ON *bōgr* bow, OE *bōg* bough] (15c) **1 :** the forward part of a ship **2 :** 2BOWMAN

Bow bells \ˈbō-\ *n pl* (1600) **:** the bells of the Church of St. Mary-le-Bow in London

bowd·ler·iza·tion \ˌbōd-lə-rə-ˈzā-shən, ˌbau̇d-\ *n* (1882) **:** the act or result of bowdlerizing

bowd·ler·ize \ˈbōd-lə-ˌrīz, ˈbau̇d-\ *vt* **-ized; -iz·ing** [Thomas *Bowdler* †1825 Eng. editor] (1836) **1 :** to expurgate (as a book) by omitting or modifying parts considered vulgar **2 :** to modify by abridging, simplifying, or distorting in style or content — **bowd·ler·iz·er** *n*

1bowed \ˈbau̇d\ *adj* [pp. of 1*bow*] (14c) **1 :** bent downward and forward ⟨listened with ~ heads⟩ **2 :** having the back and head inclined

2bowed \ˈbōd\ *adj* [partly fr. 3*bow* + *-ed;* partly fr. pp. of 4*bow*] (15c) **:** furnished with or shaped like a bow

bow·el \ˈbau̇(-ə)l\ *n* [ME, fr. MF *boel,* fr. ML *botellus,* fr. L, dim. of *botulus* sausage] (14c) **1 :** INTESTINE **:** one of the divisions of the intestines **:** GUT — usu. used in pl. except in medical use ⟨the large ~⟩ ⟨move your ~s⟩ **2** *archaic* **:** the seat of pity, tenderness, or courage — usu. used in pl. **3** *pl* **:** the interior parts; *esp* **:** the deep or remote parts ⟨~s of the earth⟩ — **bow·el·less** \ˈbau̇(-ə)l-ləs\ *adj*

1bow·er \ˈbau̇(-ə)r\ *n* [ME *bour* dwelling, fr. OE *būr;* akin to OE & OHG *būan* to dwell, OE *bēon* to be — more at BE] (bef. 12c) **1 :** an attractive dwelling or retreat **2 :** a lady's private apartment in a medieval hall or castle **3 :** a shelter (as in a garden) made with tree boughs or vines twined together **:** ARBOR — **bow·ery** \-ē\ *adj*

2bower *vt* (1592) **:** EMBOWER, ENCLOSE

3bower *n* (1652) **:** an anchor carried at the bow of a ship

bow·er·bird \ˈbau̇(-ə)r-ˌbərd\ *n* (1845) **:** any of various passerine birds (family Paradisaeidae) of the Australian region in which the male builds a chamber or passage arched over with twigs and grasses, often adorned with bright-colored objects, and used esp. to attract the female

bow·ery \ˈbau̇(ə-)rē\ *n, pl* **-er·ies** [D *bouwerij,* fr. *bouwer* farmer, fr. *bouwen* to till; akin to OHG *būan* to dwell] (1650) **1 :** a colonial Dutch plantation or farm **2** [*Bowery,* street in New York City] **:** a city district notorious for cheap bars and homeless derelicts

bow·fin \ˈbō-ˌfin\ *n* (1845) **:** a predaceous dull-green iridescent American freshwater ganoid fish (*Amia calva*) of little value for food or sport

bow·front \-ˌfrənt\ *adj* (1925) **1 :** having an outward curving front ⟨~ furniture⟩ **2 :** having a bow window in front ⟨~ houses⟩

bow·head whale \-ˌhed-\ *n* (1887) **:** the whalebone whale (*Balaena mysticetus*) of the Arctic — called also *bowhead*

bow·ie knife \ˈbü-ē-, ˈbō-\ *n* [James *Bowie*] (1836) **:** a stout single-edged hunting knife with part of the back edge curved concavely to a point and sharpened

bow·ing \ˈbō-iŋ\ *n* (1838) **:** the technique of managing the bow in playing a stringed musical instrument

bow·knot \ˈbō-ˌnät, -ˈnät\ *n* (ca. 1547) **:** a knot with decorative loops

1bowl \ˈbōl\ *n* [ME *bolle,* fr. OE *bolla;* akin to OHG *bolla* blister, OE *blāwan* to blow] (bef. 12c) **1 :** a concave usu. hemispherical vessel used esp. for holding liquids; *specif* **:** a drinking vessel (as for wine) **2 :** the contents of a bowl **3 :** a bowl-shaped or concave part: as **a :** the hollow of a spoon or tobacco pipe **b :** the receptacle of a toilet **4 a :** a natural formation or geographical region shaped like a bowl **b :** a bowl-shaped structure; *esp* **:** an athletic stadium **5 :** a postseason football game between specially invited teams — **bowled** \ˈbōld\ *adj* — **bowl·ful** \-ˌfu̇l\ *n*

2bowl *n* [ME *boule,* fr. MF, fr. L *bulla* bubble] (15c) **1 a :** a ball (as of lignum vitae) weighted or shaped to give it a bias when rolled in lawn bowling **b** *pl but sing in constr* **:** LAWN BOWLING **2 :** a delivery of the ball in bowling **3 :** a cylindrical roller or drum (as for a mechanical device)

3bowl *vi* (15c) **1 a :** to participate in a game of bowling **b :** to roll a ball in bowling **2 :** to travel smoothly and rapidly (as in a wheeled vehicle) ~ *vt* **1 a :** to roll (a ball) in bowling **b** (1) **:** to complete by bowling ⟨~ a string⟩ (2) **:** to score by bowling ⟨~s 150⟩ **2 :** to strike with a swiftly moving object **3 :** to overwhelm with surprise

bowlder *var of* BOULDER

bow·leg \ˈbō-ˌleg, -ˌlāg, ˈbō-ˈ\ *n* (ca. 1864) **:** a leg bowed outward at or below the knee — **bow·legged** \ˈbō-ˈleg(-ə)d, -ˈlāg(-ə)d\ *adj*

1bowl·er \ˈbō-lər\ *n* (1500) **:** one that bowls; *specif* **:** the player that delivers the ball to the batsman in cricket

2bow·ler \ˈbō-lər\ *n* [*Bowler,* 19th cent. family of Eng. hatters] (1861) **:** a derby hat

bow·line \ˈbō-lən, -ˌlīn\ *n* [ME *bouline,* perh. fr. *bowe* bow + *line*] (13c) **1 :** a rope used to keep the weather edge of a square sail taut forward **2 :** a knot used to form a loop that neither slips nor jams — see KNOT illustration

bowl·ing \ˈbō-liŋ\ *n* (1535) **:** any of several games in which balls are rolled on a green or down an alley at an object or group of objects

bowl over *vt* (1867) **1 :** to take unawares **2 :** [1]IMPRESS 2
[1]**bow·man** \'bō-mən\ *n* (13c) **:** ARCHER 1
[2]**bow·man** \'bau̇-mən\ *n* (1829) **:** a boatman, oarsman, or paddler stationed in the front of a boat
Bow·man's capsule \ˌbō-mənz-\ *n* [Sir William *Bowman* †1892 Eng. surgeon] (ca. 1860) **:** a thin membranous double-walled capsule surrounding the glomerulus of a vertebrate nephron
bow out \(ˈ)bau̇-\ *vi* (ca. 1947) **:** RETIRE, WITHDRAW
bow saw \'bō-\ *n* (1677) **:** a saw having a narrow blade held under tension by a light bow-shaped frame
bowse \'bau̇z\ *var of* BOUSE
bow shock \'bau̇-\ *n* (1950) **:** an abrupt deflection of the solar wind caused by collision with the magnetic field of a planet
bow·sprit \'bau̇-ˌsprit, *Brit usu* 'bō-\ *n* [ME *bouspret*, prob. fr. MLG *bōchsprēt*, fr. *bōch* bow + *sprēt* pole — more at SPRIT] (13c) **:** a large spar projecting forward from the stem of a ship
bow·string \'bō-ˌstriŋ\ *n* (14c) **:** a waxed or sized cord joining the ends of a shooting bow
bowstring hemp *n* (ca. 1858) **:** any of various Asian and African sansevierias; *also* **:** its soft tough leaf fiber used esp. in cordage
bow tie \'bō-\ *n* (1897) **:** a short necktie tied in a bowknot
bow window \'bō-\ *n* (1753) **:** a usu. curved bay window
bow·wow \'bau̇-ˌwau̇, bau̇-'\ *n* [imit.] (1576) **1 :** the bark of a dog; *also* **:** DOG **2 :** noisy clamor **3 :** arrogant dogmatic manner
bow·yer \'bō-yər\ *n* [ME *bowyere*] (13c) **:** one that makes shooting bows
[1]**box** \'bäks\ *n, pl* **box** *or* **box·es** [ME, fr. OE, fr. L *buxus*, fr. Gk *pyxos*] (bef. 12c) **:** an evergreen shrub or small tree (genus *Buxus* of the family Buxaceae, the box family) with opposite entire leaves and capsular fruits; *esp* **:** a widely cultivated shrub (*B. sempervirens*) used for hedges, borders, and topiary figures
[2]**box** *n* [ME, fr. OE, fr. LL *buxis*, fr. Gk *pyxis*, fr. *pyxos* box tree] (bef. 12c) **1 a :** a rigid typically rectangular receptacle often with a cover **b :** something having a flat bottom and four upright sides **c :** the contents of a box as a measure of quantity **d :** the driver's seat on a carriage or coach **e** *slang* **:** GUITAR **f** *slang* **:** RECORD PLAYER **2** *Brit* **:** a gift in a box **3 a :** a small compartment (as for a group of spectators in a theater) **b :** PENALTY BOX **4 a :** a boxlike receptacle (as for a bearing); *also* **:** an automobile transmission ⟨four-speed automatic ~⟩ **b :** a signaling apparatus with its enclosing case ⟨a police ~⟩ **c :** TELEVISION **5 :** a square or oblong division or compartment **6 :** a square or oblong hollow space or recess **7 :** a small simple sheltering or enclosing structure **8 a :** a rectangular space for printed matter enclosed in rules or borders **b :** FRAME 6b(1) **9 :** any of six spaces on a baseball diamond where the batter, coaches, pitcher, and catcher stand **10 :** PREDICAMENT, FIX — **box·ful** \-ˌfu̇l\ *n* — **box·like** \'bäk-ˌslīk\ *adj*
[3]**box** *vt* (15c) **1 :** to furnish (as a wheel hub) with a box **2 :** to enclose in or as if in a box **3 :** BOXHAUL **4 :** to enclose with boarding or lathing so as to bring to a required form **5 :** to mix (paint) by pouring back and forth between two containers **6 :** to hem in (as an opponent) — usu. used with *in, out,* or *up* ⟨~*ed* out the opposing tackle⟩ — **box the compass 1 :** to name the 32 points of the compass in their order **2 :** to make a complete reversal
[4]**box** *n* [ME] (14c) **:** a punch or slap esp. on the ear
[5]**box** *vt* (1519) **1 :** to hit (as the ears) with the hand **2 :** to engage in boxing with ~ *vi* **:** to fight with the fists **:** engage in boxing
box·board \'bäks-ˌbō(ə)rd, -ˌbȯ(ə)rd\ *n* (1841) **:** paperboard used for making boxes and cartons
box camera *n* (1902) **:** a camera of simple box shape with a simple lens and rotary shutter
box·car \'bäk-ˌskär\ *n* (1856) **:** a roofed freight car usu. with sliding doors in the sides
box coat *n* (1822) **1 :** a heavy overcoat formerly worn for driving **2 :** a loose coat usu. fitted at the shoulders
box elder *n* (1787) **:** a No. American maple (*Acer negundo*) with compound leaves
[1]**box·er** \'bäk-sər\ *n* (1742) **:** one that engages in the sport of boxing
[2]**boxer** *n* (1871) **:** one that makes boxes or packs things in boxes
[3]**boxer** *n* [G, fr. E [1]*boxer*] (ca. 1904) **:** a compact medium-sized short-haired usu. fawn or brindled dog of a breed originating in Germany
Box·er \'bäk-sər\ *n* [approx. trans. of Chin (Pek.) *i⁴ho²ch'üan²*, lit., righteous harmonious fist] (1899) **:** a member of a Chinese secret society that in 1900 attempted by violence to drive foreigners out of China and to force native converts to renounce Christianity
boxer shorts *n pl* (1948) **:** SHORT 4b
box·haul \'bäks-ˌhȯl\ *vt* (1769) **:** to put (a square-rigged ship) on the other tack by luffing and then veering short round on the heel
[1]**box·ing** \'bäk-siŋ\ *n* (1607) **1 :** an act of enclosing in a box **2 :** a boxlike enclosure **:** CASING **3 :** material used for boxes and casings
[2]**boxing** *n* (1711) **:** the art of attack and defense with the fists practiced as a sport
Boxing Day *n* (1833) **:** the first weekday after Christmas observed as a legal holiday in parts of the British Commonwealth and marked by the giving of Christmas boxes to service workers (as postmen)
boxing glove *n* (1875) **:** one of a pair of leather mittens heavily padded on the back and worn in boxing
box kite *n* (1897) **:** a tailless kite consisting of two or more open-ended connected boxes
box lunch *n* (1950) **:** a lunch packed in a container (as a box)
box office *n* (1786) **1 :** an office (as in a theater) where tickets of admission are sold **2 :** success (as of a show) in attracting ticket buyers; *also* **:** something that enhances such success
box pleat *n* (1883) **:** a pleat made by forming two folded edges one facing right and the other left
box score *n* [fr. its arrangement in a newspaper box] (1913) **:** a printed score of a game (as baseball) giving the names and positions of the players and a record of the play arranged in tabular form; *broadly* **:** total count **:** SUMMARY
box seat *n* (1849) **1 :** the driver's seat on a coach **2 a :** a seat in a box (as in a theater or grandstand) **b :** a position favorable for viewing something
box social *n* (1929) **:** a fund-raising affair at which box lunches are auctioned to the highest bidder
box spring *n* (1895) **:** a bedspring that consists of spiral springs attached to a foundation and enclosed in a cloth-covered frame
box stall *n* (1885) **:** an individual enclosure within a barn or stable in which an animal may move about freely without a restraining device (as a tether)
box·thorn \'bäks-ˌthȯ(ə)rn\ *n* (ca. 1678) **:** MATRIMONY VINE
box turtle *n* (ca. 1804) **:** any of several No. American land turtles (genus *Terrapene*) capable of withdrawing into its shell and closing it by hinged joints in the lower half — called also *box tortoise*

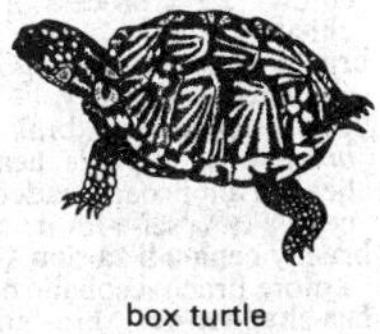
box turtle

box·wood \'bäk-ˌswu̇d\ *n* (1652) **1 :** the very close-grained heavy tough hard wood of the box (*Buxus*); *also* **:** a wood of similar properties **2 :** a plant producing boxwood
boxy \'bäk-sē\ *adj* **box·i·er; -est** (1861) **:** resembling a box — **box·i·ness** *n*
boy \'bȯi\ *n, often attrib* [ME; akin to Fris *boi* boy] (14c) **1 a :** a male child from birth to puberty **b :** SON **c :** an immature male **:** YOUTH **d :** SWEETHEART, BEAU **2 a :** one native to a given place ⟨local ~⟩ **b :** FELLOW, PERSON ⟨the ~*s* at the office⟩ — often used interjectionally ⟨~, what a game⟩ **3 :** a male servant — sometimes taken to be offensive — **boy·hood** \-ˌhu̇d\ *n* — **boy·ish** \-ish\ *adj* — **boy·ish·ly** *adv* — **boy·ish·ness** *n*
bo·yar *also* **bo·yard** \bō-'yär\ *n* [Russ *boyarin*, fr. OSlav *boljarinŭ*] (1591) **:** a member of a Russian aristocratic order next in rank below the ruling princes until its abolition by Peter the Great
[1]**boy·cott** \'bȯi-ˌkät\ *vt* [Charles C. *Boycott* †1897 Eng. land agent in Ireland who was ostracized for refusing to reduce rents] (1880) **:** to engage in a concerted refusal to have dealings with (as a person, store, or organization) usu. to express disapproval or to force acceptance of certain conditions — **boy·cot·ter** *n*
[2]**boycott** *n* (1880) **:** the process or an instance of boycotting
boy·friend \'bȯi-ˌfrend\ *n* (1896) **1 :** a male friend **2 :** a frequent or regular male companion of a girl or woman **3 :** a male lover
boyo \'bȯi-(ˌ)ō\ *n, pl* **boy·os** [*boy* + *-o*] *Irish* (1870) **:** BOY, LAD
Boy Scout *n* (1910) **1 :** a member of the scouting program of the Boy Scouts of America for boys 11 through 17 years of age **2 :** one who follows a simplistic moral or behavioral code
boy·sen·ber·ry \'bȯiz-ᵊn-ˌber-ē, 'bȯis-\ *n* [Rudolph *Boysen* †1950 Am. horticulturist + E *berry*] (1935) **:** a large bramble fruit with a raspberry flavor; *also* **:** the trailing hybrid bramble yielding this fruit and developed by crossing several blackberries and raspberries
boy wonder *n* (1946) **:** a young man whose achievements arouse admiration
bo·zo \'bō-(ˌ)zō\ *n, pl* **bozos** [origin unknown] *slang* (1920) **:** FELLOW, GUY
B picture *n* (1953) **:** a small-budget motion picture
bra \'brä\ *n* (1936) **:** BRASSIERE — **bra·less** *adj*
brab·ble \'brab-əl\ *vi* **brab·bled; brab·bling** \-(ə-)liŋ\ [perh. fr. MD *brabbelen*, of imit. origin] (1500) **:** SQUABBLE — **brabble** *n*
[1]**brace** \'brās\ *vb* **braced; brac·ing** [ME *bracen*, fr. MF *bracier* to embrace, fr. *brace*] *vt* (14c) **1** *archaic* **:** to fasten tightly **:** BIND **2 a :** to prepare for use by making taut **b :** PREPARE, STEEL ⟨~ yourself for the shock⟩ **c :** INVIGORATE, FRESHEN **3 :** to turn (a sail yard) by means of a brace **4 a :** to furnish or support with a brace ⟨heavily *braced* because of polio⟩ **b :** to make stronger **:** REINFORCE **5 :** to put or plant firmly ⟨~*s* his foot in the stirrup⟩ **6 :** to waylay esp. with demands or questions ~ *vi* **1 :** to take heart — used with *up* **2 :** to get ready (as for an attack)
[2]**brace** *n, pl* **brac·es** [ME, clasp, pair, fr. MF, two arms, fr. L *bracchia*, pl. of *bracchium* arm, fr. Gk *brachiōn*, fr. compar. of *brachys* short — more at BRIEF] (14c) **1 :** something (as a clasp) that connects or fastens **2** *or pl* **brace :** two of a kind ⟨several ~ of quail⟩ **3 :** a crank-shaped instrument for turning a bit **4 :** something that transmits, directs, resists, or supports weight or pressure: as **a :** a diagonal piece of structural material that serves to strengthen something (as a framework) **b :** a rope rove through a block at the end of a ship's yard to swing it horizontally **c** *pl* **:** SUSPENDERS **d :** an appliance for supporting a body part **e** *pl* **:** dental appliances used to exert pressure to straighten misaligned teeth **5 a :** a mark { or } used to connect words or items to be considered together **b** (1) **:** this mark connecting two or more musical staffs the parts on which are to be performed simultaneously (2) **:** the staffs so connected **c :** BRACKET 3a **6 :** an exaggerated position of rigidly erect bearing **7 :** something that arouses energy or strengthens morale
brace·let \'brā-slət\ *n* [ME, fr. MF, dim. of *bras* arm, fr. L *bracchium*] (15c) **1 :** an ornamental band or chain worn around the wrist **2 :** something (as handcuffs) resembling a bracelet
[1]**bra·cer** \'brā-sər\ *n* [ME, fr. MF *braciere*, fr. OF, fr. *braz* arm, fr. L *bracchium*] (14c) **:** an arm or wrist protector esp. for use by an archer
[2]**brac·er** \'brā-sər\ *n* (1579) **1 :** one that braces, binds, or makes firm **2 :** a drink (as of liquor) taken as a stimulant
bra·ce·ro \brä-'se(ə)r-(ˌ)ō\ *n, pl* **-ros** [Sp, laborer, fr. *brazo* arm, fr. L *brachium*] (1920) **:** a Mexican laborer admitted to the U.S. esp. for seasonal contract labor in agriculture — compare WETBACK
brace root *n* (1892) **:** PROP ROOT
brachial plexus *n* (ca. 1860) **:** a network of nerves lying mostly in the armpit and supplying nerves to the chest, shoulder, and arm
bra·chi·ate \'brā-kē-ˌāt\ *vi* **-at·ed; -at·ing** [L *bracchium*] (1932) **:** to progress by swinging from one hold to another by the arms ⟨*brachiating* gibbon⟩ — **bra·chi·a·tion** \ˌbrā-kē-'ā-shən\ *n*
bra·chio·ce·phal·ic artery \ˌbrā-kē-(ˌ)ō-sə-ˌfal-ik-\ *n* [NL *brachio-* (fr. L *bracchium* arm) + E *cephalic* — more at BRACE] (ca. 1836) **:** INNOMINATE ARTERY
brachiocephalic trunk *n* (ca. 1961) **:** INNOMINATE ARTERY
brachiocephalic vein *n* (ca. 1852) **:** INNOMINATE VEIN

\ə\ abut \ᵊ\ kitten, F table \ər\ further \a\ ash \ā\ ace \ä\ cot, cart
\au̇\ out \ch\ chin \e\ bet \ē\ easy \g\ go \i\ hit \ī\ ice \j\ job
\ŋ\ sing \ō\ go \ȯ\ law \ȯi\ boy \th\ thin \th\ the \ü\ loot \u̇\ foot
\y\ yet \zh\ vision \à, k̲, ⁿ, œ, œ̄, ue, ue̅, ʸ\ *see* Guide to Pronunciation

bra·chio·pod \'brā-kē-ə-,päd\ *n* [deriv. of L *bracchium* + Gk *pod-, pous* foot — more at FOOT] (1836) **:** any of a phylum (Brachiopoda) of marine invertebrates with bivalve shells within which is a pair of arms bearing tentacles by which a current of water is made to bring microscopic food to the mouth — **brachiopod** *adj*

bra·chi·um \'brā-kē-əm\ *n, pl* **-chia** \-kē-ə\ [L *bracchium, brachium* arm] (ca. 1731) **1 :** the upper part of the arm or forelimb from shoulder to elbow **2 :** a process of an invertebrate comparable to an arm — **bra·chi·al** \-əl\ *adj*

brachy- *comb form* [Gk, fr. *brachys* — more at BRIEF] **:** short ⟨*brachy*dactylous⟩

brachy·ce·phal·ic \,brak-i-sə-'fal-ik\ *adj* [NL *brachycephalus,* fr. Gk *brachy-* + *kephalē* head — more at CEPHALIC] (ca. 1849) **:** short-headed or broad-headed with a cephalic index of over 80 — **brachy·ceph·a·ly** \-'sef-ə-lē\ *n*

brachy·ceph·a·li·za·tion \-,sef-ə-lə-'zā-shən\ *n* (1923) **:** transition toward a more brachycephalic condition ⟨the increasing ~ of Europe⟩

bra·chyp·ter·ous \bra-'kip-tə-rəs\ *adj* [Gk *brachypteros,* fr. *brachy-* + *pteron* wing — more at FEATHER] (ca. 1847) **:** having rudimentary or abnormally small wings ⟨~ insects⟩

brac·ing \'brā-siŋ\ *adj* (1750) **:** giving strength, vigor, or freshness ⟨a ~ breeze⟩ — **brac·ing·ly** *adv*

bra·ci·o·la \,bräch(-ē)-'ō-lə\ *or* **bra·ci·o·le** \-'ō-,lā\ *n* [It, fr. *brace* live coal + *-ola* -ole; akin to OF *brese* coals — more at BRAZE] (ca. 1945) **:** a thin slice of meat wrapped around a seasoned filling and often cooked in wine

brack·en \'brak-ən\ *n* [ME *braken,* prob. of Scand origin; akin to OSw *brækne* fern] (14c) **1 :** a large coarse fern; *esp* **:** a common brake (*Pteridium aquilinum*) **2 :** a growth of brakes

[1]**brack·et** \'brak-ət\ *n* [MF *braguette* codpiece, fr. dim. of *brague* breeches, fr. OProv *braga,* fr. L *braca,* fr. Gaulish *brāca,* of Gmc origin; akin to OHG *bruoh* breeches — more at BREECH] (1580) **1 :** an overhanging member that projects from a structure (as a wall) and is usu. designed to support a vertical load or to strengthen an angle **2 :** a fixture (as for holding a lamp) projecting from a wall or column **3 a :** one of a pair of marks [ ] used in writing and printing to enclose matter or in mathematics and logic as signs of aggregation — called also *square bracket* **b :** one of the pair of marks ⟨ ⟩ used to enclose matter — called also *angle bracket* **c :** PARENTHESIS 3 **d :** BRACE 5b **4 :** a pair of shots fired (as in front of and beyond a target) to aid in determining the exact distance from gun to target **5 a :** a section of a continuously numbered or graded series ⟨the 18 to 22 age ~⟩ **b :** one of a graded series of income groups ⟨the $20,000 income ~⟩

[2]**bracket** *vt* (ca. 1847) **1 a :** to place within or as if within brackets ⟨the editor's comments are ~*ed*⟩ ⟨the players who ~ the action with a prologue and an epilogue —John McCarten⟩ **b :** to eliminate from consideration ⟨his approach to moral questions ~*s* off religion⟩ **c :** to extend around so as to encompass **:** INCLUDE ⟨test pressures . . . which ~ virtually the entire range of passenger-car tire pressures —*Consumer Reports*⟩ **2 :** to furnish or fasten with brackets **3 :** to put in the same category or group ⟨expressing a general distaste for troublemakers, and ~*ing* the civil-rights marchers with those who stoned them —C.C. O'Brien⟩ ⟨those ~*ed* in a seven-way tie for third —Dan Jenkins⟩ **4 a :** to get the range on (a target) by firing over and short ⟨there were mortar rounds ~*ing* the area —Ed Bradley⟩ **b :** to establish the limits of ⟨~*ed* the problem exactly by drawing the obvious connection between economic development and social development —K.E. Fry⟩

brack·et·ed *adj, of a serif* (1885) **:** joined to the stroke by a curved line

bracket fungus *n* (1899) **:** a basidiomycete that forms shelflike sporophores

brack·ish \'brak-ish\ *adj* [D *brac* salty; akin to MLG *brac* salty] (1538) **1 :** somewhat salty **2 a :** not appealing to the taste ⟨~ tea⟩ **b :** REPULSIVE — **brack·ish·ness** *n*

brac·o·nid \'brak-ə-(,)nid\ *n* [deriv. of Gk *brachys*] (ca. 1893) **:** any of a large family (Braconidae) of ichneumon flies — **braconid** *adj*

bract \'brakt\ *n* [NL *bractea,* fr. L, thin metal plate] (1770) **1 :** a leaf from the axil of which a flower or floral axis arises **2 :** a leaf borne on a floral axis; *esp* **:** one subtending a flower or flower cluster — **brac·te·al** \'brak-tē-əl\ *adj* — **brac·te·ate** \-tē-ət, -,āt\ *adj* — **bract·ed** \-təd\ *adj*

brac·te·ole \'brak-tē-,ōl\ *n* [NL *bracteola,* fr. L, dim. of *bractea*] (ca. 1828) **:** a small bract esp. on a floral axis

[1]**brad** \'brad\ *n* [ME, fr. ON *broddr* spike; akin to OE *byrst* bristle — more at BRISTLE] (13c) **1 :** a thin nail of the same thickness throughout but tapering in width and having a slight projection at the top of one side instead of a head **2 :** a slender wire nail with a small barrel-shaped head

[2]**brad** *vt* **brad·ded; brad·ding** (1794) **:** to fasten with brads

brad·awl \'brad-,ȯl\ *n* (1823) **:** an awl with chisel edge used to make holes for brads or screws

bra·dy·car·dia \,brād-i-'kärd-ē-ə *also* ,brad-\ *n* [NL, fr. Gk *bradys* slow + NL *-cardia*] (ca. 1890) **:** relatively slow heart action whether physiological or pathological — compare TACHYCARDIA

bra·dy·ki·nin \-'kī-nən\ *n* [Gk *bradys* slow] (1949) **:** a kinin that is formed locally in injured tissue, acts in vasodilation of small arterioles, is considered to play a part in inflammatory processes, and is composed of a chain of nine amino-acid residues

brae \'brā\ *n* [ME *bra,* fr. ON *brā* eyelid; akin to OE *brǣw* eyebrow, *bredgan* to move quickly — more at BRAID] *chiefly Scot* (13c) **:** a hillside esp. along a river

[1]**brag** \'brag\ *adj* **brag·ger; brag·gest** [ME] (1836) **:** FIRST-RATE

[2]**brag** *n* (14c) **1 :** a pompous or boastful statement **2 :** arrogant talk or manner **:** COCKINESS **3 :** BRAGGART

[3]**brag** *vb* **bragged; brag·ging** *vi* (14c) **:** to talk boastfully **:** engage in self-glorification ~ *vt* **:** to assert boastfully ***syn*** see BOAST — **brag·ger** \'brag-ər\ *n* — **brag·gy** \'brag-ē\ *adj*

brag·ga·do·cio \,brag-ə-'dō-s(h)ē-,ō, -(,)shō\ *n, pl* **-cios** [*Braggadochio,* personification of boasting in *Faerie Queene* by Edmund Spenser] (1594) **1 :** BRAGGART **2 a :** empty boasting **b :** arrogant pretension **:** COCKINESS

brag·gart \'brag-ərt\ *n* (1577) **:** a loud arrogant boaster — **braggart** *adj*

[1]**Brah·ma** \'bräm-ə\ *n* [Skt *brahman*] (1690) **1 :** the ultimate ground of all being in Hinduism **2 :** the creator god of the Hindu sacred triad — compare SIVA, VISHNU

[2]**Brah·ma** \'brā-mə, 'bräm-ə, 'bram-\ *n* (1938) **:** BRAHMAN 2

Brah·man *or* **Brah·min** \'bräm-ən; *2 is* 'brām-, 'bräm-, 'bram-\ *n* [Skt *brāhmaṇa,* lit., having to do with prayer, fr. *brahman,* neut., prayer] (14c) **1 a :** a Hindu of the highest caste traditionally assigned to the priesthood **b :** [1]BRAHMA 1 **2 :** any of an Indian breed of humped cattle **:** ZEBU; *esp* **:** a large vigorous heat-resistant and tick-resistant usu. silvery gray animal developed in the southern U.S. by interbreeding Indian cattle and used chiefly for crossbreeding **3** *usu* **Brahmin :** a person of high social standing and cultivated intellect and taste ⟨Boston ~*s*⟩ — **Brah·man·ic** \brä-'man-ik\ *adj*

Brah·man·ism \'bräm-ə-,niz-əm\ *n* (1816) **:** orthodox Hinduism adhering to the pantheism of the Vedas and to the ancient sacrifices and family ceremonies

[1]**braid** \'brād\ *vt* [ME *breyden,* lit., to move suddenly, fr. OE *bregdan;* akin to OHG *brettan* to draw (a sword), Gk *phorkon* something white or wrinkled] (bef. 12c) **1 a :** to form (three or more strands) into a braid **b :** to make by braiding **2 :** to do up (the hair) by interweaving three or more strands **3 :** MIX, INTERMINGLE ⟨~ fact with fiction⟩ **4 :** to ornament esp. with ribbon or braid — **braid·er** *n*

[2]**braid** *n* (1530) **1 a :** a cord or ribbon having usu. three or more component strands forming a regular diagonal pattern down its length; *esp* **:** a narrow fabric of intertwined threads used esp. for trimming **b :** a length of braided hair **2 :** high-ranking naval officers

braid·ed *adj* (15c) **1 a :** made by intertwining three or more strands **b :** ornamented with braid **2 :** forming an interlacing network of channels ⟨a ~ river⟩

braid·ing \'brād-iŋ\ *n* (15c) **:** something made of braided material

[1]**brail** \'brā(ə)l\ *n* [ME *brayle,* fr. AF *braiel,* fr. OF, strap] (15c) **1 :** a rope fastened to the leech of a sail and used for hauling the sail up or in **2 :** a dip net with which fish are hauled aboard a boat from a purse seine or trap

[2]**brail** *vt* (1625) **1 :** to take in (a sail) by the brails **2 :** to hoist (fish) by means of a brail

braille \'brā(ə)l\ *n, often cap* [Louis *Braille*] (1853) **:** a system of writing for the blind that uses characters made up of raised dots — **braille** *vt*

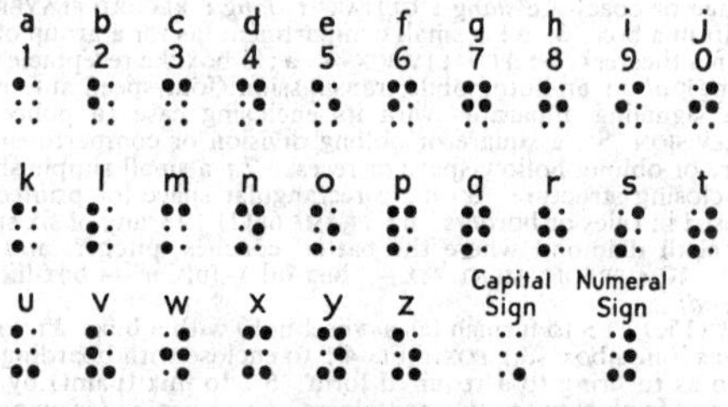
a b c d e f g h i j
1 2 3 4 5 6 7 8 9 0
k l m n o p q r s t
u v w x y z
Capital Sign
Numeral Sign
braille alphabet

braille·writ·er \-,rīt-ər\ *n, often cap* (1942) **:** a machine for writing braille

[1]**brain** \'brān\ *n* [ME, fr. OE *brægen;* akin to MLG *bregen* brain, Gk *brechmos* front part of the head] (bef. 12c) **1 a :** the portion of the vertebrate central nervous system that constitutes the organ of thought and neural coordination, includes all the higher nervous centers receiving stimuli from the sense organs and interpreting and correlating them to formulate the motor impulses, is made up of neurons and supporting and nutritive structures, is enclosed within the skull, and is continuous with the spinal cord through the foramen magnum **b :** a nervous center in invertebrates comparable in position and function to the vertebrate brain **2 a** (1) **:** INTELLECT, MIND ⟨has a clever ~⟩ (2) **:** intellectual endowment **:** INTELLIGENCE — often used in pl. ⟨plenty of ~*s* in that family⟩ **b** (1) **:** a very intelligent or intellectual person (2) **:** the chief planner of an organization or enterprise — usu. used in pl.

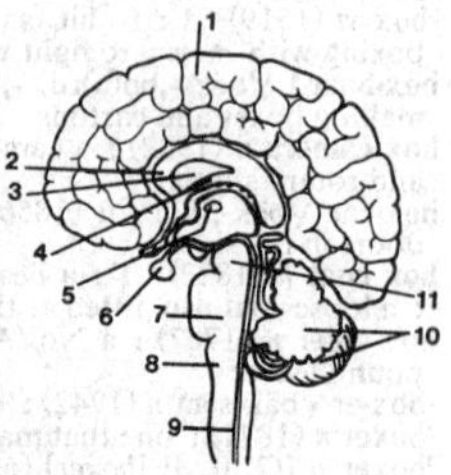
1
2
3
4
5
6
7
8
9
10
11
brain 1a: *1* cerebral hemisphere, *2* corpus callosum, *3* ventricle, *4* fornix, *5* thalamus, *6* pituitary gland, *7* pons, *8* medulla oblongata, *9* spinal cord, *10* cerebellum, *11* midbrain

[2]**brain** *vt* (14c) **1 :** to kill by smashing the skull **2 :** to hit on the head

brain·case \'brān-,kās\ *n* (1741) **:** the cranium enclosing the brain

brain·child \-,chīld\ *n* (1881) **:** a product of one's creative imagination

brain death *n* (1968) **:** final cessation of activity in the central nervous system esp. as indicated by a flat electroencephalogram for a predetermined length of time — **brain–dead** *adj*

brain drain *n* (1963) **:** a migration of professional people (as scientists, professors, or physicians) from one country to another usu. for higher salaries or better living conditions

-brained \'brānd\ *adj comb form* **:** having (such) a brain ⟨big-*brained*⟩ ⟨feather*brained*⟩

brain hormone *n* (1957) **:** a hormone that is secreted by neurosecretory cells of the insect brain and that stimulates the prothoracic glands to secrete ecdysone

brain·ish \'brā-nish\ *adj, archaic* (ca. 1530) **:** IMPETUOUS, HOTHEADED ⟨and in this ~ apprehension kills the unseen good old man —Shak.⟩

brain·less \'brān-ləs\ *adj* (15c) **:** devoid of intelligence **:** STUPID — **brain·less·ly** *adv* — **brain·less·ness** *n*

brain·pan \'brān-,pan\ *n* (14c) **:** BRAINCASE

brain–pick·ing \-,pik-iŋ\ *n* (1954) **:** the act of picking information from another's mind — **brain–pick·er** \-ər\ *n*

brain·pow·er \-,pau̇(-ə)r\ *n* (1878) **1 :** intellectual ability **2 :** people with developed intellectual ability

brain·sick \-,sik\ *adj* (15c) **1 :** mentally disordered **2 :** arising from mental disorder ⟨a ~ frenzy⟩ — **brain·sick·ly** *adv*

brain stem *n* (1879) : the part of the brain composed of the mesencephalon, pons, and medulla oblongata and connecting the spinal cord with the forebrain and cerebrum

brain·storm \-ˌstȯ(ə)rm\ *n* (ca. 1894) **1 :** a violent transient fit of insanity **2 a :** a sudden bright idea **b :** a harebrained idea

brain·storm·ing \-ˌstȯr-miŋ\ *n* (ca. 1955) : a group problem-solving technique that involves the spontaneous contribution of ideas from all members of the group — **brain·storm** *vt* — **brain·storm·er** *n*

brains trust *n, chiefly Brit* (ca. 1932) : BRAIN TRUST

brain·teas·er \-ˌtē-zər\ *n* (1923) : something (as a puzzle) that demands mental effort and acuity for its solution

brain trust *n* (1910) : expert advisers concerned esp. with planning and strategy who often lack official or acknowledged status — **brain trust·er** \-ˌtrəs-tər\ *n*

brain·wash·ing \ˈbrān-ˌwȯsh-iŋ, -ˌwäsh-\ *n* [trans. of Chin (Pek) *hsi³ nao³*] (1950) **1 :** a forcible indoctrination to induce someone to give up basic political, social, or religious beliefs and attitudes and to accept contrasting regimented ideas **2 :** persuasion by propaganda or salesmanship — **brain·wash** *vt* — **brainwash** *n* — **brain·wash·er** *n*

brain wave *n* (1890) **1 :** BRAINSTORM 2a **2 a :** rhythmic fluctuations of voltage between parts of the brain resulting in the flow of an electric current **b :** a current produced by brain waves

brainy \ˈbrā-nē\ *adj* **brain·i·er; -est** (1874) : having or showing a well-developed intellect : INTELLIGENT ⟨he was ~ enough to outmaneuver the intransigents —W. V. Shannon⟩ — **brain·i·ness** *n*

braise \ˈbrāz\ *vt* **braised; brais·ing** [F *braiser,* fr. *braise* charcoal — more at BRAZE] (1797) : to cook slowly in fat and little moisture in a closed pot

[1]**brake** \ˈbrāk\ *archaic past of* BREAK

[2]**brake** \ˈbrāk\ *n* [ME, fern] (14c) : any of a genus (*Pteridium*) of tall ferns with ternately compound fronds

[3]**brake** *n* [ME, fr. MLG; akin to OE *brecan* to break] (15c) **1 :** a toothed instrument or machine for separating out the fiber of flax or hemp by breaking up the woody parts **2 :** a machine for bending, flanging, folding, and forming sheet metal

[4]**brake** *n* [ME *-brake*] (1563) : rough or marshy land overgrown usu. with one kind of plant — **braky** \ˈbrā-kē\ *adj*

[5]**brake** *n* [ME] (1772) **1 :** a device for arresting the motion of a mechanism usu. by means of friction **2 :** something used to slow down or stop movement or activity ⟨interest rates acting as a ~ on expenditures⟩ — **brake·less** \ˈbrā-kləs\ *adj*

[6]**brake** *vb* **braked; brak·ing** *vt* (1868) : to retard or stop by a brake ~ *vi* **1 :** to operate or manage a brake; *esp* : to apply the brake on a vehicle **2 :** to become checked by a brake

brake·man \ˈbrāk-mən\ *n* (1833) **1 :** a freight or passenger train crew member who inspects the train and assists the conductor **2 :** the end man on a bobsled team who operates the brake

bram·ble \ˈbram-bəl\ *n* [ME *brembel,* fr. OE *brēmel;* akin to OE *brōm* broom] (bef. 12c) : any of a genus (*Rubus*) of usu. prickly shrubs of the rose family including the raspberries and blackberries; *broadly* : a rough prickly shrub or vine — **bram·bly** \-b(ə-)lē\ *adj*

bran \ˈbran\ *n* [ME, fr. MF] (14c) : the broken coats of the individual seeds of a cereal grain separated from the flour or meal by sifting or bolting

[1]**branch** \ˈbranch\ *n, often attrib* [ME, fr. MF *branche,* fr. LL *branca* paw] (14c) **1 :** a natural subdivision of a plant stem; *esp* : a secondary shoot or stem (as a bough) arising from a main axis (as of a tree) **2 :** something that extends from or enters into a main body or source: as **a** (1) **:** a stream that flows into another usu. larger stream : TRIBUTARY (2) *Southern & Midland* : CREEK 2 **b :** a side road or way **c :** a slender projection (as the tine of an antler) **d :** a distinctive part of a mathematical curve **e :** a part of a computer program executed as a result of a program decision **3 :** a part of a complex body: as **a :** a division of a family descending from a particular ancestor **b :** an area of knowledge that may be considered apart from related areas ⟨pathology is a ~ of medicine⟩ **c** (1) **:** a division of an organization (2) **:** a separate but dependent part of a central organization ⟨the neighborhood ~ of the city library⟩ **d :** a language group less inclusive than a family ⟨the Germanic ~ of the Indo-European language family⟩ — **branched** \ˈbrancht\ *adj* — **branch·less** \ˈbranch-ləs\ *adj* — **branchy** \ˈbran-chē\ *adj*

[2]**branch** *vi* (14c) **1 :** to put forth branches : RAMIFY **2 :** to spring out (as from a main stem) : DIVERGE **3 :** to be an outgrowth — used with *from* ⟨poetry that *~ed* from religious prose⟩ **4 :** to extend activities — usu. used with *out* ⟨the business is *~ing* out all over the state⟩ **5 :** to follow one of two or more branches (as in a computer program) ~ *vt* **1 :** to ornament with designs of branches **2 :** to divide up : SECTION

bran·chi·al \ˈbraŋ-kē-əl\ *adj* [deriv. of Gk *branchion* gill; akin to Gk *bronchos* trachea — more at CRAW] (1801) : of, relating to, or supplying the gills or associated structures or their embryonic precursors ⟨~ arteries⟩

bran·chio·pod \ˈbraŋ-kē-ə-ˌpäd\ *n* [deriv. of Gk *branchia* gills + *pod-, pous* foot — more at FOOT] (1824) : any of a group (Branchiopoda) of aquatic crustaceans (as a fairy shrimp or a water flea) typically having a long body, a carapace, and many pairs of leaflike appendages — **branchiopod** *adj*

branch·let \ˈbranch-lət\ *n* (ca. 1731) : a small usu. terminal branch

branch water *n* [[1]*branch* (creek)] (1850) : plain water ⟨bourbon and *branch water*⟩

[1]**brand** \ˈbrand\ *n* [ME, torch, sword, fr. OE; akin to OE *bærnan* to burn] (bef. 12c) **1 a :** a charred piece of wood **b :** FIREBRAND 1 **c :** something (as lightning) that resembles a firebrand **2 :** SWORD **3 a** (1) **:** a mark made by burning with a hot iron to attest manufacture or quality or to designate ownership (2) **:** a mark made with a stamp or stencil for similar purposes : TRADEMARK **b** (1) **:** a mark put on criminals with a hot iron (2) **:** a mark of disgrace : STIGMA ⟨the ~ of poverty⟩ **4 a :** a class of goods identified by name as the product of a single firm or manufacturer : MAKE **b :** a characteristic or distinctive kind : VARIETY ⟨a lively ~ of theater⟩ **5 :** a tool used to produce a brand

[2]**brand** *vt* (15c) **1 :** to mark with a brand **2 :** to mark with disapproval : STIGMATIZE **3 :** to impress indelibly ⟨~ the lesson on his mind⟩ — **brand·er** *n*

[1]**bran·dish** \ˈbran-dish\ *vt* [ME *braundisshen,* fr. MF *brandiss-,* stem of *brandir,* fr. OF, fr. *brand* sword, of Gmc origin; akin to OE *brand*] (14c) **1 :** to shake or wave (as a weapon) menacingly **2 :** to exhibit in an ostentatious or aggressive manner **syn** see SWING

[2]**brandish** *n* (1599) : an act or instance of brandishing

[1]**brand name** *n* (1922) : TRADE NAME 1b

[2]**brand name** *adj, often cap B&N* (1922) : having a reputation and a loyal following ⟨*brand name* authors⟩

brand–new \ˈbran-ˈn(y)ü\ *adj* [[1]*brand*] (1570) : conspicuously new and unused

[1]**bran·dy** \ˈbran-dē\ *n, pl* **brandies** [short for *brandywine,* fr. D *brandewijn,* fr. MD *brantwijn,* fr. *brant* distilled + *wijn* wine] (1657) : an alcoholic beverage distilled from wine or fermented fruit juice (as of apples)

[2]**brandy** *vt* **bran·died; bran·dy·ing** (1848) : to flavor, blend, or preserve with brandy

brank \ˈbraŋk\ *n* [origin unknown] (1559) : an instrument made of an iron frame surrounding the head and a sharp metal bit entering the mouth and formerly used to punish scolds — usu. used in pl.

bran·ni·gan \ˈbran-i-gən\ *n* [prob. fr. the name *Brannigan*] (1927) **1 :** a drinking spree **2 :** SQUABBLE

brant \ˈbrant\ *n, pl* **brant** *or* **brants** [origin unknown] (14c) : any of several wild geese (esp. genus *Branta*); *esp* : a small black-necked goose (*Branta bernicla*) about the size of a mallard

[1]**brash** \ˈbrash\ *adj* [origin unknown] (1566) **1 :** BRITTLE ⟨~ wood⟩ **2 a :** tending to act in headlong fashion : IMPETUOUS ⟨the ~ young man darted into the traffic⟩ **b :** done in haste without regard for consequences : RASH ⟨~ acts⟩ **3 :** uninhibitedly energetic or demonstrative : BUMPTIOUS ⟨a delightfully ~ comedian⟩ **4 a :** lacking restraint and discernment : TACTLESS ⟨made a ~ speech about his wife's bad habits⟩ **b :** aggressively self-assertive : IMPUDENT ⟨a man ~ to the point of arrogance⟩ **5 :** piercingly sharp : HARSH ⟨a ~ squeal of brakes⟩ — **brash·ly** *adv* — **brash·ness** *n*

[2]**brash** *n* [obs. E *brash* to breach a wall] (1787) : a mass of fragments (as of ice)

brass \ˈbras\ *n* [ME *bras,* fr. OE *bræs;* akin to MLG *bras* metal] (bef. 12c) **1 :** an alloy consisting essentially of copper and zinc in variable proportions **2 a :** the brass instruments of an orchestra or band — often used in pl. **b :** a usu. brass memorial tablet **c :** bright metal fittings, utensils, or ornaments **d :** a brass, bronze, or gunmetal lining for a bearing **e :** empty cartridge shells **3 :** brazen self-assurance : GALL **4 :** BRASS HATS — **brass** *adj*

bras·sard \brə-ˈsärd, ˈbras-ˌärd\ *n* [F *brassard,* fr. MF *brassal,* fr. OIt *bracciale,* fr. *braccio* arm, fr. L *bracchium* — more at BRACE] (1830) **1 :** armor for protecting the arm — see ARMOR illustration **2 :** a cloth band worn around the upper arm usu. bearing an identifying mark

brass band *n* (1834) : a band consisting chiefly or solely of brass and percussion instruments

brass·bound \ˈbras-ˌbau̇nd, -ˈbau̇nd\ *adj* (1867) **1 :** having trim made of brass or a metal resembling brass **2 a** (1) **:** tradition-bound and opinionated (2) **:** making no concessions : INFLEXIBLE **b :** BRAZEN, PRESUMPTUOUS

brass–collar \-ˈkäl-ər\ *adj* (1951) : invariably voting the straight party ticket ⟨~ Democrats⟩

bras·se·rie \ˌbras-(ə-)ˈrē\ *n* [F, fr. MF *brasser* to brew, fr. OF *bracier,* fr. L *braces* spelt] (1864) : an informal usu. French restaurant serving simple hearty food

brass hat *n* (1893) **1 :** a high-ranking military officer **2 :** a person in a high position in civilian life

bras·si·ca \ˈbras-i-kə\ *n* [NL, genus name, fr. L, cabbage] (1832) : any of a large genus (*Brassica*) of Old World temperate zone herbs (as cabbages) of the mustard family with beaked cylindrical pods

bras·siere \brə-ˈzi(ə)r *also* ˌbras-ē-ˈe(ə)r\ *n* [obs. F *brassière* bodice, fr. OF *braciere* arm protector, fr. *bras* arm — more at BRACELET] (1911) : a woman's close-fitting undergarment with cups for bust support

brass instrument *n* (1854) : one of a group of wind instruments (as a French horn, trombone, trumpet, or tuba) that is usu. characterized by a long cylindrical or conical metal tube commonly curved two or more times and ending in a flared bell, that produces tones by the vibrations of the player's lips against a usu. cup-shaped mouthpiece, and that usu. has valves or a slide by which the player may produce all the tones within the instrument's range

brass knuckles *n pl but sing or pl in constr* (1855) : KNUCKLE 4

brass tacks *n pl* (1897) : details of immediate practical importance — usu. used in the phrase *get down to brass tacks*

brassy \ˈbras-ē\ *adj* **brass·i·er; -est** (1576) **1 a :** being shamelessly bold **b :** OBSTREPEROUS **2 :** resembling brass esp. in color **3 :** resembling the sound of a brass instrument — **brass·i·ly** \ˈbras-ə-lē\ *adv* — **brass·i·ness** \ˈbras-ē-nəs\ *n*

brat \ˈbrat\ *n* [perh. fr. E dial. *brat* (coarse garment)] (1505) : CHILD; *specif* : an ill-mannered annoying child — **brat·ti·ness** \ˈbrat-ē-nəs\ *n* — **brat·tish** \ˈbrat-ish\ *adj* — **brat·ty** \-ē\ *adj*

brat·tice \ˈbrat-əs, ˈbrat-ish\ *n* [ME *bretais* parapet, fr. OF *bretesche,* fr. ML *breteschia*] (ca. 1846) : an often temporary partition of planks or cloth used esp. in a mine to control ventilation — **brattice** *vt*

[1]**brat·tle** \ˈbrat-ᵊl\ *n* [prob. imit.] *chiefly Scot* (1500) : CLATTER, SCAMPER

[2]**brattle** *vi* **brat·tled; brat·tling** *chiefly Scot* (1513) : to make a clattering or rattling sound

brat·wurst \ˈbrät-(ˌ)wərst, -ˌvu̇(ə)rst, -ˌvu̇s(h)t\ *n* [G, fr. OHG *brātwurst,* fr. *brāt* meat without waste + *wurst* sausage] (ca. 1888) : fresh pork sausage for frying

braun·schweig·er \ˈbrau̇n-ˌs(h)wī-gər\ *n* [G *Braunschweiger* (*wurst*), lit., Brunswick sausage] (ca. 1930) : smoked liverwurst

bra·va \ˈbräv-(ˌ)ä, brä-ˈvä\ *n* [It, fem. of *bravo*] (1877) : BRAVO — used interjectionally in applauding a woman

\ə\ abut \ᵊ\ kitten, F table \ər\ further \a\ ash \ā\ ace \ä\ cot, cart \au̇\ out \ch\ chin \e\ bet \ē\ easy \g\ go \i\ hit \ī\ ice \j\ job \ŋ\ sing \ō\ go \ȯ\ law \ȯi\ boy \th\ thin \t͟h\ the \ü\ loot \u̇\ foot \y\ yet \zh\ vision \á, k̲, ⁿ, œ, œ̄, ue, ue̅, ʸ\ see Guide to Pronunciation

bra·va·do \brə-ˈväd-(ˌ)ō\ *n, pl* **-does** *or* **-dos** [MF *bravade* & OSp *bravata,* fr. OIt *bravata,* fr. *bravare* to challenge, show off, fr. *bravo*] (1573) **1 a :** blustering swaggering conduct **b :** a pretense of bravery **2 :** the quality or state of being foolhardy

1brave \ˈbrāv\ *adj* **brav·er; brav·est** [MF, fr. OIt & OSp *bravo* courageous, wild, perh. fr. L *barbarus* barbarous] (15c) **1 :** having courage : DAUNTLESS **2 :** making a fine show : COLORFUL ⟨~ banners flying in the wind⟩ **3 :** EXCELLENT, SPLENDID ⟨the ~ fire I soon had going —J. F. Dobie⟩ — **brave·ly** *adv*

2brave *vb* **braved; brav·ing** *vt* (1546) **1 :** to face or endure with courage **2** *obs* **:** to make showy ~ *vi, archaic* **:** to make a brave show — **brav·er** *n*

3brave *n* (1590) **1** *archaic* **:** BRAVADO **2 :** one who is brave; *specif* **:** an American Indian warrior **3** *archaic* **:** BULLY, ASSASSIN

brave new world *n* [fr. the dystopian novel *Brave New World* (1932) by Aldous Huxley] (1933) **:** the world of the future; *esp* **:** a future society marked by an advanced technology and a totalitarian political system

brav·ery \ˈbrāv-(ə-)rē\ *n, pl* **-er·ies** (1562) **1 a :** fine clothes **b :** showy display **2 :** the quality or state of being brave : COURAGE

1bra·vo \ˈbräv-(ˌ)ō\ *n, pl* **bravos** *or* **bravoes** [It, fr. *bravo* brave] (1597) **:** VILLAIN, DESPERADO; *esp* **:** a hired assassin

2bra·vo \ˈbräv-(ˌ)ō, brä-ˈvō\ *vt* **bra·voed; bra·vo·ing** (1831) **:** to applaud by shouts of *bravo*

3bra·vo \ˈbräv-(ˌ)ō, brä-ˈvō\ *n, pl* **bravos** (1761) **:** a shout of approval — often used interjectionally in applauding a performance

Bra·vo \ˈbräv-(ˌ)ō\ (1952) — a communications code word for the letter *b*

bra·vu·ra \brə-ˈv(y)u̇r-ə, brä-\ *n, often attrib* [It, lit., bravery, fr. *bravare*] (1757) **1 :** a musical passage requiring exceptional agility and technical skill in execution **2 :** a florid brilliant style **3 :** a show of daring or brilliance

braw \ˈbrȯ, ˈbrä\ *adj* [modif. of MF *brave*] (1565) **1** *chiefly Scot* **:** GOOD, FINE **2** *chiefly Scot* **:** well dressed

1brawl \ˈbrȯl\ *vi* [ME *brawlen*] (14c) **1 :** to quarrel or fight noisily : WRANGLE **2 :** to make a loud confused noise ⟨the river ~*ing* by⟩ — **brawl·er** *n*

2brawl *n* (15c) **1 :** a noisy quarrel or fight **2 :** a loud tumultuous noise

brawly \ˈbrȯ-lē\ *adj* **brawl·i·er; -est** (1940) **1 :** inclined to brawl **2 :** characterized by brawls or brawling

brawn \ˈbrȯn\ *n* [ME, fr. MF *braon* muscle, of Gmc origin; akin to OE *brǣd* flesh] (13c) **1 a** *Brit* **:** the flesh of a boar **b :** HEADCHEESE **2 a :** full strong muscles esp. of the arm or leg **b :** muscular strength

brawny \ˈbrȯ-nē\ *adj* **brawn·i·er; -est** (1599) **1 :** MUSCULAR, STRONG **2 :** being swollen and hard ⟨a ~ infected foot⟩ — **brawn·i·ly** \-nə-lē\ *adv* — **brawn·i·ness** \-nē-nəs\ *n*

1bray \ˈbrā\ *vb* [ME *brayen,* fr. MF *braire* to cry, fr. (assumed) VL *bragere,* perh. of Celt origin; akin to MIr *braigid* he breaks wind — more at BREAK] *vi* (14c) **:** to utter the characteristic loud harsh cry of a donkey ~ *vt* **:** to utter or play loudly, harshly, or discordantly — **bray** *n*

2bray *vt* [ME *brayen,* fr. MF *broiier,* of Gmc origin; akin to OHG *brehhan* to break — more at BREAK] (14c) **1 :** to crush or grind fine ⟨~ seeds in a mortar⟩ **2 :** to spread thin ⟨~ printing ink⟩

bray·er \ˈbrā-ər\ *n* (1688) **:** a printer's hand inking roller

1braze \ˈbrāz\ *vt* **brazed; braz·ing** [irreg. fr. *brass*] *archaic* (1602) **:** HARDEN

2braze *vt* **brazed; braz·ing** [prob. fr. F *braser,* fr. *braise* charcoal, fr. *brese* live coals] (1677) **:** to solder with a nonferrous alloy that melts at a lower temperature than that of the metals being joined — **braz·er** *n*

1bra·zen \ˈbrāz-ᵊn\ *adj* [ME *brasen,* fr. OE *bræsen,* fr. *bræs* brass] (bef. 12c) **1 :** made of brass **2 a :** sounding harsh and loud like struck brass **b :** of the color of polished brass **3 :** marked by contemptuous boldness — **bra·zen·ly** *adv* — **bra·zen·ness** \ˈbrāz-ᵊn-(n)əs\ *n*

2brazen *vt* **bra·zened; bra·zen·ing** \ˈbrāz-niŋ, -ᵊn-iŋ\ (1555) **:** to face with defiance or impudence — usu. used in the phrase *brazen it out*

bra·zen–faced \ˌbrāz-ᵊn-ˈfāst\ *adj* (1571) **:** marked by insolence and bold disrespect ⟨~ assertions⟩

1bra·zier \ˈbrā-zhər\ *n* [ME *brasier,* fr. *bras* brass] (14c) **:** one that works in brass

2brazier *n* [F *brasier,* fr. OF, fire of hot coals, fr. *brese*] (ca. 1690) **1 :** a pan for holding burning coals **2 :** a utensil in which food is exposed to heat through a wire grill

Bra·zil nut \brə-ˈzil-\ *n* [*Brazil,* So. America] (1830) **:** a tall So. American tree (*Bertholletia excelsa* of the family Lecythidaceae) that bears large globular capsules each containing several closely packed roughly triangular oily edible nuts; *also* **:** its nut

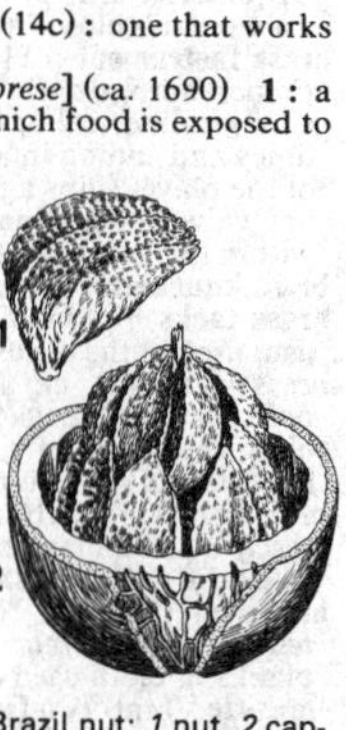

1
2
Brazil nut: *1* nut, *2* capsule with nuts

bra·zil·wood \brə-ˈzil-ˌwu̇d\ *n* [Sp *brasil,* fr. *brasa* live coals; fr. its color] (1559) **:** the heavy wood of any of various tropical leguminous trees (esp. genus *Caesalpinia*) that is used as red and purple dyewood and in cabinetwork

1breach \ˈbrēch\ *n* [ME *breche,* fr. OE *bryce;* akin to OE *brecan* to break] (bef. 12c) **1 :** infraction or violation of a law, obligation, tie, or standard **2 a :** a broken, ruptured, or torn condition or area **b :** a gap (as in a wall) made by battering **3 a :** a break in accustomed friendly relations **b :** a temporary gap in continuity : HIATUS **4 :** a leap esp. of a whale out of water

2breach *vt* (1547) **1 :** to make a breach in ⟨~ the city walls⟩ **2 :** BREAK, VIOLATE ⟨~ an agreement⟩ ~ *vi* **:** to leap out of water ⟨a whale ~*ing*⟩

breach of promise (1590) **:** violation of a promise esp. to marry

1bread \ˈbred\ *n* [ME *breed,* fr. OE *brēad;* akin to OHG *brōt* bread, OE *brēowan* to brew — more at BREW] (bef. 12c) **1 :** a usu. baked and leavened food made of a mixture whose basic constituent is flour or meal **2 :** FOOD, SUSTENANCE ⟨our daily ~⟩ **3 a :** LIVELIHOOD ⟨earns his ~ as a laborer⟩ **b** *slang* **:** MONEY — **bread upon the waters :** resources risked or charitable deeds performed without expectation of return

2bread *vt* (1629) **:** to cover with bread crumbs ⟨a ~*ed* pork chop⟩

bread–and–butter *adj* (1836) **1 a :** being as basic as the earning of one's livelihood ⟨~ economic issues⟩ **b :** that can be depended on ⟨the ~ repertoire of an orchestra⟩ **2 :** sent or given as thanks for hospitality ⟨a ~ letter⟩

bread and butter *n* (1732) **:** a means of sustenance or livelihood

bread and circuses *n pl* [trans. of L *panis et circenses*] (1914) **:** a palliative offered esp. to avert potential discontent

bread·bas·ket \ˈbred-ˌbas-kət\ *n* (1753) **1** *slang* **:** STOMACH **2 :** a major cereal-producing region

1bread·board \ˈbred-ˌbō(ə)rd, -ˌbȯ(ə)rd\ *n* (1857) **1 :** a board on which dough is kneaded or bread cut **2 :** a board on which components are mounted for breadboarding

2breadboard *vt* (1956) **:** to make an experimental arrangement of (as an electronic circuit or a mechanical system) to test feasibility

bread·fruit \ˈbred-ˌfrüt\ *n* (1697) **:** a round usu. seedless fruit that resembles bread in color and texture when baked; *also* **:** a tall tropical tree (*Artocarpus altilis*) of the mulberry family that bears this fruit

bread·line \-ˌlīn\ *n* (1900) **:** a line of people waiting to receive free food (as from a charity or welfare agency)

bread mold *n* (1914) **:** any of various molds found esp. on bread; *esp* **:** a rhizopus (*Rhizopus nigricans*)

bread·stuff \-ˌstəf\ *n* (1793) **1 :** a cereal product (as grain or flour) **2 :** BREAD

breadth \ˈbretth, ˈbreth, ˈbredth\ *n* [obs. E *brede* breadth (fr. ME, fr. OE *brǣdu,* fr. *brād* broad) + *-th* (as in *length*)] (1523) **1 :** distance from side to side : WIDTH **2 :** something of full width **3 a :** comprehensive quality : SCOPE ⟨~ of his learning⟩ **b :** liberality of views or taste ⟨~ of mind⟩

breadth·ways \-ˌwāz\ *adv or adj* (1677) **:** in the direction of the breadth ⟨a course of bricks laid ~⟩

breadth·wise \-ˌwīz\ *adv or adj* (1864) **:** BREADTHWAYS

bread·win·ner \ˈbred-ˌwin-ər\ *n* (1818) **1 :** a means (as a tool or craft) of livelihood **2 :** a member of a family whose wages supply its livelihood — **bread·win·ning** \-ˌwin-iŋ\ *n*

1break \ˈbrāk\ *vb* **broke** \ˈbrōk\; **bro·ken** \ˈbrō-kən\; **break·ing** [ME *breken,* fr. OE *brecan;* akin to OHG *brehhan* to break, L *frangere,* MIr *braigid* he breaks wind] *vt* (bef. 12c) **1 a :** to separate into parts with suddenness or violence **b :** FRACTURE ⟨~ an arm⟩ **c :** RUPTURE ⟨~ the skin⟩ **d :** to cut into and turn over the surface of **2 a :** VIOLATE, TRANSGRESS ⟨~ the law⟩ **b :** to invalidate (a will) by action at law **3 a** *archaic* **:** to force entry into **b :** to burst and force a way through ⟨~ the sound barrier⟩ ⟨~ a racial barrier⟩ **c :** to escape by force from ⟨~ jail⟩ **d :** to make or effect by cutting, forcing, or pressing through ⟨~ a trail through the woods⟩ **4 :** to make ineffective as a binding force ⟨~*ing* his chains⟩ **5 :** to disrupt the order or compactness of ⟨~ ranks⟩ **6 a :** to defeat utterly and end as an effective force : DESTROY **b :** to crush the spirit of **c :** to make tractable or submissive: as (1) **:** to train (an animal) to adjust to the service or convenience of man (2) **:** INURE, ACCUSTOM **d :** to exhaust in health, strength, or capacity **7 a :** to ruin financially **b :** to reduce in rank **8 a :** to check the force or intensity of ⟨the bushes will ~ his fall⟩ **b :** to cause failure and discontinuance of (a strike) by measures outside bargaining processes **9 a :** EXCEED, SURPASS ⟨~ the record⟩ **b :** to score less than (a specified total) ⟨golfer trying to ~ 90⟩ **10 :** to ruin the prospects of ⟨could make or ~ her career⟩ **11 :** to demonstrate the falsity of ⟨~ an alibi⟩ **12 :** to cause a sudden significant decrease in the price, value, or volume of ⟨news likely to ~ the market sharply⟩ **13 a :** to stop or bring to an end suddenly : HALT ⟨~ a deadlock⟩ **b :** INTERRUPT, SUSPEND ⟨~ the silence with a cry⟩ **c :** to open and bring about suspension of operation ⟨~ an electric circuit⟩ **d :** to destroy unity or completeness of ⟨~ a dining room set by buying a chair⟩ **e :** to change the appearance of uniformity of ⟨a dormer ~*s* the level roof⟩ **f :** to split the surface of ⟨fish ~*ing* water⟩ **g :** to cause to discontinue a habit ⟨tried to ~ him of smoking⟩ **14 :** to make known : TELL ⟨~ the bad news gently⟩ ⟨~ a news story⟩ **15 a :** to find an explanation or solution for : SOLVE ⟨the detective will ~ the case⟩ **b :** to discover the essentials of (a code or cipher system) **16 :** to split into smaller units, parts, or processes : DIVIDE ⟨~ a $5 bill⟩ — often used with *into, up,* or *down* **17 :** to open the action of (a breechloader) ~ *vi* **1 a :** to escape with sudden forceful effort — often used with *out* ⟨~ out of jail⟩ **b :** to come into being by or as if by bursting forth ⟨day was ~*ing*⟩ **c :** to effect a penetration ⟨~ through security lines⟩ **d :** to emerge through the surface of the water **e :** to start abruptly ⟨when the storm *broke*⟩ **f :** to become known or published ⟨when the news *broke*⟩ **g :** to make a sudden dash ⟨~ for cover⟩ **h :** to separate after a clinch in boxing **2 a :** to come apart or split into pieces : BURST, SHATTER **b :** to open spontaneously or by pressure from within ⟨his boil finally *broke*⟩ **c** *of a wave* **:** to curl over and fall apart in surf or foam **3 :** to become fair : CLEAR ⟨when the weather ~*s*⟩ **4 :** to give way in disorderly retreat **5 a :** to fail in health, strength, vitality, or control ⟨may ~ under questioning⟩ — often used with *down* **b :** to become inoperative because of damage, wear, or strain **6 :** to undergo a sudden significant decrease in price, value, or volume ⟨transportation stocks may ~ sharply⟩ **7 :** to end a relationship, connection, or agreement — usu. used with *with* **8 a :** to swerve suddenly **b :** to curve, drop, or rise sharply ⟨a fastball that ~*s* away from the batter⟩ **9 :** to alter sharply in tone, pitch, or intensity ⟨a voice ~*ing* with emotion⟩ **10 :** to fail to keep a prescribed gait — used of a horse **11 :** to interrupt one's activity or occupation for a brief period ⟨~ for lunch⟩ **12 :** to make the opening shot of a game of pool **13 a :** to divide into classes, categories, or types — usu. used with *into* and often with *down* ⟨the topic *breaks* into three questions⟩ ⟨the topic *breaks* down into three questions⟩ **b :** to fold, bend, lift, or come apart at a seam, groove, or joint **c** *of cream* **:** to separate during churning into liquid and fat **14 :** HAPPEN, DEVELOP ⟨for the team to succeed, everything has to ~ right⟩ — **break a leg** — used to wish good luck esp. to a performer — **break bread :** to dine together — **break camp :** to pack up gear and leave a camp or campsite — **break cover** *or* **break covert :** to start from a covert or lair — **break even :** to achieve a balance; *esp* **:** to operate a business or enterprise without either loss or profit — **break ground** *or* **break new ground :** to make or show discoveries : PIONEER — **break into 1 :** to begin with or as if with a sudden throwing off of restraint ⟨*broke into* tears⟩ ⟨face *breaking into* a smile⟩ ⟨the horse *breaks into* a gallop⟩ **2 :** to make entry or entrance ⟨trying to *break into* show business⟩ **3 :** INTERRUPT ⟨*break into* a TV program with a news flash⟩ — **break one's heart :** to crush emotionally with sorrow — **break one's wrists :** to turn the wrists as part of the swing of a club or bat — **break service** *or* **break one's service :** to win a game served by an opponent esp. in tennis — **break the back of :** to subdue the main force of ⟨*break the back of* inflation⟩ — **break the ice** **1 :** to make a beginning **2 :** to get through the first difficulties in starting a conversation or discussion — **break wind :** to expel gas from the intestine

[2]**break** *n* (14c) **1** **a :** an act or action of breaking **b :** the opening shot in a game of pool or billiards **c :** the process of opening a gap in an electrical circuit **2** **a :** a condition produced by or as if by breaking **:** GAP ⟨a ~ in the clouds⟩ **b :** a gap in an otherwise continuous electric circuit **3 :** the action or act of breaking in, out, or forth ⟨at ~ of day⟩ ⟨a jail ~⟩ **4** **a :** DASH, RUSH ⟨a base runner making a ~ for home⟩ **b :** FAST BREAK **5** **a :** the start of a race **b :** the act of separating after a clinch in boxing **6 :** an interruption in continuity ⟨a ~ in the weather⟩: as **a :** a notable change of subject matter, attitude, or treatment **b** (1) **:** an abrupt, significant, or noteworthy change or interruption in a continuous process, trend, or surface (2) **:** a respite from work or duty (3) **:** a planned interruption in a radio or television program ⟨a ~ for the commercial⟩ **c :** deviation of a pitched baseball from a straight line **d** *mining* **:** FAULT, DISLOCATION **e :** failure of a horse to maintain the prescribed gait **f :** an abrupt change in musical or vocal pitch or quality **g :** the action or an instance of breaking service **h :** a usu. solo instrumental passage in jazz, folk, or popular music **7** **a :** a rupture in previously agreeable relations ⟨a ~ between the two countries⟩ **b :** an abrupt split or difference with something previously adhered to or followed ⟨a sharp ~ with tradition⟩ **8 :** a place or situation at which a break occurs; *esp* **:** the place at which a word is divided esp. at the end of a line of print or writing **9 :** a sudden and abrupt decline of prices or values **10** **a :** a stroke of luck and esp. of good luck ⟨a bad ~⟩ ⟨got the ~*s* ⟩ **b :** a favorable or opportune situation **:** CHANCE ⟨waiting for a big ~ in show business⟩ **c :** favorable consideration or treatment ⟨a tax ~⟩ ⟨a ~ on the price⟩ **11 :** BREAKDOWN 1b ⟨suffered a mental ~⟩

break·able \ˈbrā-kə-bəl\ *adj* (1570) **:** capable of being broken — **breakable** *n*

break·age \ˈbrā-kij\ *n* (1813) **1** **a :** the action of breaking **b :** a quantity broken **2 :** loss due to things broken

[1]**break·away** \ˈbrā-kə-ˌwā\ *n* (1891) **1** **a :** one that breaks away **b :** an act or instance of breaking away (as from a group or tradition) **2 :** an object made to shatter or collapse under pressure or impact

[2]**breakaway** *adj* (1927) **1 :** favoring independence from an affiliation **:** SECEDING ⟨a ~ faction formed a new party⟩ **2 :** made to break, shatter, or bend easily ⟨~ road signs for highway safety⟩

break away *vi* (1535) **1 :** to detach oneself esp. from a group **:** get away **2 :** to depart from former or accustomed ways **3 :** to pull away with a burst of speed

break·bone fever \ˌbrāk-ˌbōn-\ *n* (ca. 1860) **:** DENGUE

break dancing *n* [perh. fr. [2]*break* 6h] (1983) **:** dancing in which individual dancers perform a series of often acrobatic moves

break·down \ˈbrāk-ˌdau̇n\ *n* (1832) **1 :** the action or result of breaking down: as **a :** a failure to function **b :** a physical, mental, or nervous collapse **c :** failure to progress or have effect **:** DISINTEGRATION ⟨a ~ of negotiations⟩ **d :** the process of decomposing **e :** division into categories **:** CLASSIFICATION; *also* **:** an account analyzed into categories **2 :** a fast shuffling dance; *also* **:** music for such a dance

break down \(ˈ)brāk-ˈdau̇n\ *vt* (14c) **1** **a :** to cause to fall or collapse by breaking or shattering **b :** to make ineffective ⟨*break down* legal barriers⟩ **2** **a :** to divide into parts or categories **b :** to separate (as a chemical compound) into simpler substances **:** DECOMPOSE **c :** to take apart esp. for storage or shipment and for later reassembling **~** *vi* **1** **a :** to stop functioning because of breakage or wear **b :** to become inoperative or ineffective **:** FAIL ⟨negotiations *broke down*⟩ **2** **a :** to be susceptible to analysis or subdivision ⟨the statistics *break down* like this⟩ **b :** to undergo decomposition ***syn*** see ANALYZE

[1]**break·er** \ˈbrā-kər\ *n* (12c) **1** **a :** one that breaks **b :** a machine or plant for breaking rocks or coal **2 :** a wave breaking into foam (as against the shore) **3 :** a strip of fabric under the tread of a tire for extra protection of the carcass

[2]**brea·ker** \ˈbrā-kər\ *n* [by folk etymology fr. Sp *barrica*] (1833) **:** a small water cask

break–even \brā-ˈkē-vən\ *adj* (1931) **:** having equal cost and income

break·fast \ˈbrek-fəst\ *n* (15c) **1 :** the first meal of the day esp. when taken in the morning **2 :** the food prepared for a breakfast ⟨eat your ~⟩ — **breakfast** *vb* — **break·fast·er** *n*

break·front \ˈbrāk-ˌfrənt\ *n* (1928) **:** a large cabinet or bookcase whose center section projects beyond the flanking end sections

break–in \ˈbrā-ˌkin\ *n* (1856) **1 :** the act or action of breaking in ⟨a rash of ~*s* at the new apartment house⟩ **2 :** a performance or a series of performances serving as a trial run **3 :** an initial period of operation during which working parts begin to function efficiently

break in \(ˈ)brā-ˈkin\ *vi* (ca. 1552) **1 :** to enter a house or building by force **2** **a :** to interrupt in a conversation **b :** INTRUDE ⟨*break in* upon his privacy⟩ **3 :** to start in an activity or enterprise ⟨*breaking in* as a cub reporter⟩ **~** *vt* **1 :** to accustom to a certain activity or occurrence ⟨*break in* the new quarterback⟩ **2 :** to overcome the stiffness or newness of

breaking and entering *n* (1797) **:** the act of forcing a passage into and entering another's building (as a house or store)

breaking point *n* (1908) **1 :** the point at which a person gives way under stress **2 :** the point at which a situation becomes crucial

break·neck \ˌbrāk-ˌnek\ *adj* (1562) **:** very fast or dangerous ⟨~ speed⟩

break off *vi* (14c) **:** to stop abruptly ⟨*break off* in the middle of a sentence⟩ **~** *vt* **:** DISCONTINUE ⟨*break off* diplomatic relations⟩

break·out \ˈbrā-ˌkau̇t\ *n* (1820) **:** a violent or forceful break from a restraining condition or situation; *esp* **:** a military attack to break from encirclement

break out \(ˈ)brā-ˈkau̇t\ *vi* (bef. 12c) **1 :** to develop or emerge with suddenness and force ⟨fire *broke out* ⟩ ⟨a riot *broke out*⟩ **2 :** to become affected with a skin eruption **3 :** to make a break from a restraining condition or situation ⟨*broke out* of a slump⟩ **~** *vt* **1** **a :** to make ready for action or use ⟨*break out* the tents and make camp⟩ **b :** to produce for consumption ⟨*break out* a bottle⟩ **2 :** to display flying and unfurled **3 :** to separate from a mass of data ⟨*break out* newsstand sales⟩

break·through \ˈbrāk-ˌthrü\ *n* (1918) **1 :** an act or instance of breaking through an obstruction **2 :** an offensive thrust that penetrates and carries beyond a defensive line in warfare **3 :** a sudden advance esp. in knowledge or technique ⟨a medical ~⟩

break through \(ˈ)brāk-ˈthrü\ *vi* (1968) **:** to make a breakthrough

break·up \ˈbrā-ˌkəp\ *n* (1794) **1 :** an act or instance of breaking up **2 :** the breaking, melting, and loosening of ice in the spring

break up \(ˈ)brā-ˈkəp\ *vt* (15c) **1 :** to disrupt the continuity or flow of ⟨*break up* a dull routine⟩ **2 :** DECOMPOSE ⟨*break up* a chemical⟩ **3 :** to bring to an end ⟨*broke up* the fight⟩ **4 :** to break into pieces **5 :** to do away with **:** DESTROY ⟨*break up* a monopoly⟩ **6 :** to cause to laugh heartily ⟨that joke *breaks* me *up*⟩ **~** *vi* **1** **a :** to cease to exist as a unified whole ⟨their partnership *broke up*⟩ **b :** to end a romance **2 :** to lose morale, composure, or resolution; *esp* **:** to become abandoned to laughter ⟨*breaks up* completely, laughing himself into a coughing fit —Gene Williams⟩

break·wa·ter \ˈbrā-ˌkwȯt-ər, -ˌkwät-\ *n* (ca. 1769) **:** an offshore structure (as a wall) used to protect a harbor or beach from the force of waves

[1]**bream** \ˈbrim, ˈbrēm\ *n, pl* **bream** *or* **breams** [ME *breme*, fr. MF, of Gmc origin; akin to OHG *brahsima* bream — more at BRAID] (14c) **1 :** a European freshwater cyprinid fish (*Abramis brama*); *broadly* **:** any of various related fishes **2** **a :** a porgy or related fish (family Sparidae) **b :** any of various freshwater sunfishes (*Lepomis* and related genera); *esp* **:** BLUEGILL

[2]**bream** \ˈbrēm\ *vt* [prob. fr. D *brem* furze] (1626) **:** to clean (a ship's bottom) by heating and scraping

[1]**breast** \ˈbrest\ *n* [ME *brest*, fr. OE *brēost*; akin to OHG *brust* breast] (bef. 12c) **1 :** either of two protuberant milk-producing glandular organs situated on the front of the chest in the human female and some other mammals; *broadly* **:** a discrete mammary gland **2 :** the fore or ventral part of the body between the neck and the abdomen **3 :** the seat of emotion and thought **:** BOSOM **4** **a :** something (as a front, swelling, or curving part) resembling a breast **b :** FACE 6 — **breast·ed** *adj*

[2]**breast** *vt* (1599) **1 :** to contend with resolutely **:** CONFRONT ⟨~ the rush traffic⟩ **2** *chiefly Brit* **:** CLIMB, ASCEND **3 :** to thrust the chest against ⟨the sprinter ~*ed* the tape⟩

breast–beat·ing \ˈbres(t)-ˌbēt-iŋ\ *n* (1940) **:** noisy demonstrative protestation (as of grief, anger, or self-recrimination)

breast·bone \ˈbres(t)-ˈbōn, -ˌbōn\ *n* (bef. 12c) **:** STERNUM

breast drill *n* (1865) **:** a portable drill with a plate that is pressed by the breast in forcing the drill against the work

breast–feed \ˈbrest-ˌfēd\ *vt* (1903) **:** to feed (a baby) from a mother's breast rather than from a bottle

breast·plate \ˈbres(t)-ˌplāt\ *n* (14c) **1 :** a metal plate worn as defensive armor for the breast — see ARMOR illustration **2 :** a vestment worn in ancient times by a Jewish high priest and set with 12 gems bearing the names of the tribes of Israel **3 :** a piece against which the workman presses his breast in operating a breast drill or similar tool

breast·stroke \ˈbres(t)-ˌstrōk\ *n* (1867) **:** a swimming stroke executed in a prone position by extending the arms in front of the head while drawing the knees forward and outward and then sweeping the arms back with palms out while kicking outward and backward — **breast·strok·er** \-ˌstrō-kər\ *n*

breast·work \ˈbres-ˌtwərk\ *n* (1642) **:** a temporary fortification

breath \ˈbreth\ *n* [ME *breth*, fr. OE *brǣth*; akin to OHG *brādam* breath, OE *beorma* yeast —more at BARM] (bef. 12c) **1** **a :** air filled with a fragrance or odor **b :** a slight indication **:** SUGGESTION ⟨the faintest ~ of scandal⟩ **2** **a :** the faculty of breathing ⟨recovering his ~ after the race⟩ **b :** an act of breathing ⟨fought to the last ~⟩ **c :** opportunity or time to breathe **:** RESPITE **3 :** a slight breeze **4** **a :** air inhaled and exhaled in breathing ⟨bad ~⟩ **b :** something (as moisture on a cold surface) produced by breath or breathing **5 :** a spoken sound **:** UTTERANCE **6 :** SPIRIT, ANIMATION **7 :** expiration of air with the glottis wide open (as in the formation of \f\ and \s\ sounds) — **in one breath** *or* **in the same breath :** almost simultaneously — **out of breath :** breathing very rapidly (as from strenuous exercise)

breath·able \ˈbrē-t͟hə-bəl\ *adj* (ca. 1731) **1 :** suitable for breathing ⟨~ air⟩ **2 :** allowing air to pass through **:** POROUS ⟨a ~ synthetic fabric⟩ —**breath·abil·i·ty** \ˌbrē-t͟hə-ˈbil-ət-ē\ *n*

Breath·a·ly·zer \ˈbreth-ə-ˌlī-zər\ *trademark* — used for a device that is used to determine the alcohol content of a breath sample

breathe \ˈbrēt͟h\ *vb* **breathed; breath·ing** [ME *brethen*, fr. *breth*] *vi* (13c) **1 :** to pause and rest before continuing **2** **a :** to draw air into and expel it from the lungs **:** RESPIRE; *broadly* **:** to take in oxygen and give out carbon dioxide through natural processes **b :** to inhale and exhale freely **3 :** LIVE **4** **a** *obs* **:** to emit a fragrance or aura **b :** to become perceptible **5 :** to blow softly **6** **a :** to permit passage of air or vapor ⟨a fabric that ~*s*⟩ **b** *of an internal-combustion engine* **:** to use air to support combustion **7** *of wine* **:** to develop flavor and bouquet by exposure to air **~** *vt* **1** **a :** to send out by exhaling **b :** to instill by or as if by breathing ⟨~ new life into the movement⟩ **2** **a :** UTTER, EXPRESS ⟨don't ~ a word of it to anyone⟩ **b :** to make manifest **:** EVINCE ⟨the novel ~*s* despair⟩ **3 :** to give rest from exertion to **4 :** to take in in breathing ⟨~ the scent of pines⟩ **5 :** to inhale and exhale ⟨~ air⟩ — **breathe down one's neck** **1 :** to threaten esp. in attack or pursuit **2 :** to keep one under close or constant surveillance ⟨parents always *breathing down his neck*⟩ — **breathe easily** *or* **breathe freely :** to enjoy relief (as from pressure or danger)

breathed \ˈbretht\ *adj* (1877) **1 :** having breath esp. of a specified kind — usu. used in combination ⟨sweet-*breathed*⟩ **2 :** VOICELESS 2

\ə\ **abut** \ᵊ\ **kitten**, **F table** \ər\ **further** \a\ **ash** \ā\ **ace** \ä\ **cot, cart**
\au̇\ **out** \ch\ **chin** \e\ **bet** \ē\ **easy** \g\ **go** \i\ **hit** \ī\ **ice** \j\ **job**
\ŋ\ **sing** \ō\ **go** \ȯ\ **law** \ȯi\ **boy** \th\ **thin** \t͟h\ **the** \ü\ **loot** \u̇\ **foot**
\y\ **yet** \zh\ **vision** \à, k̲, ⁿ, œ, œ̄, ue, uē, ʸ\ *see* Guide to Pronunciation

breath·er \'brē-thər\ *n* (14c) **1 :** one that breathes **2 :** a break in activity for rest or relief **3 :** a small vent in an otherwise airtight enclosure

breath·ing \'brē-thiŋ\ *n* (1598) **:** either of the marks ʻ and ʼ used in writing Greek to indicate aspiration or its absence

breathing space *n* (1650) **:** some time in which to recover, get organized, or get going — called also *breathing room, breathing spell*

breath·less \'breth-ləs\ *adj* (14c) **1 a :** not breathing **b :** DEAD **2 a :** panting or gasping for breath **b :** leaving one breathless **:** very rapid or strenuous ⟨go at a ~ pace⟩ **c :** holding one's breath from emotion ⟨~ in anticipation⟩ **d :** INTENSE, GRIPPING ⟨~ tension⟩ **3 :** oppressive because of no fresh air or breeze — **breath·less·ly** *adv* — **breath·less·ness** *n*

breath·tak·ing \'breth-,tā-kiŋ\ *adj* (1880) **1 :** making one out of breath **2 a :** EXCITING, THRILLING ⟨a ~ stock car race⟩ **b :** ASTONISHING ⟨his ~ ignorance⟩ — **breath·tak·ing·ly** \-kiŋ-lē\ *adv*

breathy \'breth-ē\ *adj* **breath·i·er; -est** (1883) **:** characterized or accompanied by or as if by the audible passage of breath — **breath·i·ness** \-nəs\ *n*

brec·cia \'brech-(ē-)ə\ *n* [It] (1774) **:** a rock consisting of sharp fragments embedded in a fine-grained matrix (as sand or clay)

brec·ci·ate \'brech-ē-,āt\ *vt* **-at·ed; -at·ing** (1772) **1 :** to form (rock) into breccia **2 :** to break (rock) into fragments — **brec·ci·a·tion** \,brech-ē-'ā-shən\ *n*

brede \'brēd\ *n* [alter. of *braid*] *archaic* (1640) **:** EMBROIDERY

bred–in–the–bone \,bred-ᵊn-thə-'bōn\ *adj* (15c) **1 :** DEEP-ROOTED ⟨~ honesty⟩ **2 :** INVETERATE ⟨a ~ gambler⟩

breech \'brēch\ *n* [ME, breeches, fr. OE *brēc,* pl. of *brōc* leg covering; akin to OHG *bruoh* breeches, OE *brecan* to break] (bef. 12c) **1** *pl* \'brich-əz *also* 'brē-chəz\ **a :** short pants covering the hips and thighs and fitting snugly at or just below the knee **b :** PANTS **2 :** the hind end of the body **:** BUTTOCKS **3 a :** the part of a firearm at the rear of the barrel **b :** the bottom of a pulley block

breech·block \'brēch-,bläk\ *n* (1881) **:** the block in breech-loading firearms that closes the rear of the barrel against the force of the charge and prevents gases from escaping

breech·cloth \'brēch-,klȯth, 'brich-\ *n* (1841) **:** LOINCLOTH

breech·clout \-,klau̇t\ *n* (1757) **:** LOINCLOTH

breech·es buoy \'brē-chəz- *also* 'brich-əz-\ *n* (1880) **:** a canvas seat in the form of breeches hung from a life buoy running on a hawser and used to haul persons from one ship to another or from ship to shore esp. in rescue operations

breech·ing \'brē-chiŋ, 'brich-iŋ\ *n* (1515) **1 :** the part of a harness that passes around the rump of a draft animal **2 :** the short coarse wool on the rump and hind legs of a sheep or goat; *also* **:** the hair on the corresponding part of a dog

breech·load·er \'brēch-'lōd-ər\ *n* (1858) **:** a firearm that loads at the breech — **breech–load·ing** \-'lōd-iŋ\ *adj*

[1]**breed** \'brēd\ *vb* **bred** \'bred\; **breed·ing** [ME *breden,* fr. OE *brēdan;* akin to OE *brōd* brood — more at BROOD] *vt* (bef. 12c) **1 :** to produce (offspring) by hatching or gestation **2 a :** BEGET 1 **b :** PRODUCE, ENGENDER ⟨despair often ~*s* violence⟩ **3 :** to propagate (plants or animals) sexually and usu. under controlled conditions ⟨*bred* several strains of corn together to produce a new high-lysine variety⟩ **4 a :** BRING UP, NURTURE ⟨born and *bred* in the country⟩ **b :** to inculcate by training ⟨~ good manners into one's children⟩ **5 a :** to mate with **:** INSEMINATE **b :** IMPREGNATE **6 :** to produce (a fissionable element) by bombarding a nonfissionable element with neutrons from a radioactive element so that more fissionable material is produced than is used up ~ *vi* **1 :** to produce offspring by sexual union **2 :** to propagate animals or plants

[2]**breed** *n* (1553) **1 :** a group of animals or plants presumably related by descent from common ancestors and visibly similar in most characters; *esp* **:** such a group differentiated from the wild type under the influence of man **2 :** a number of persons of the same stock **3 :** CLASS, KIND ⟨a new ~ of newswomen⟩ ⟨a new ~ of motel⟩

breed·er *n* (1531) **:** one that breeds: as **a :** an animal or plant kept for propagation **b :** one engaged in the breeding of a specified organism **c :** a reactor for breeding fissionable material — called also *breeder reactor*

breed·ing *n* (14c) **1 :** the action or process of bearing or generating **2 :** ANCESTRY **3 a** *archaic* **:** EDUCATION ⟨she had her ~ at my father's charge —Shak.⟩ **b :** training in or observance of the proprieties **4 :** the sexual propagation of plants or animals

breeding ground *n* (1856) **1 :** the place to which animals go to breed **2 :** a place or set of circumstances suitable for or favorable to growth and development ⟨hurricane *breeding grounds*⟩ ⟨a *breeding ground* for new values⟩

breeks \'brēks, 'briks\ *n pl* [ME (northern dial.) *breke,* fr. OE *brēc*] *chiefly Scot* (14c) **:** BREECHES

[1]**breeze** \'brēz\ *n* [ME *brise*] (1626) **1 a :** a light gentle wind **b :** a wind of from 4 to 31 miles an hour **2 :** something easily done **:** CINCH — **breeze·less** \-ləs\ *adj* — **in a breeze :** EASILY ⟨won the talent contest *in a breeze*⟩

[2]**breeze** *vi* **breezed; breez·ing** (1907) **1 :** to move swiftly and airily ⟨she *breezed* in wearing chiffon⟩ **2 :** to make progress quickly and easily ⟨*breezed* through the exam⟩

[3]**breeze** *n* [prob. modif. of F *braise* cinders — more at BRAISE] (1726) **:** residue from the making of coke or charcoal

breeze·way \'brēz-,wā\ *n* (1931) **:** a roofed often open passage connecting two buildings (as a house and garage) or halves of a building

breezy \'brē-zē\ *adj* **breez·i·er; -est** (1718) **1 :** swept by breezes **2 a :** briskly informal **b :** AIRY, NONCHALANT — **breez·i·ly** \-zə-lē\ *adv* — **breez·i·ness** \-zē-nəs\ *n*

breg·ma \'breg-mə\ *n, pl* **-ma·ta** \-mət-ə\ [NL *bregmat-, bregma,* fr. LL, front part of the head, fr. Gk; akin to Gk *brechmos* front part of the head — more at BRAIN] (1578) **:** the point of junction of the coronal and sagittal sutures of the skull — **breg·mat·ic** \breg-'mat-ik\ *adj*

brems·strah·lung \'brem(p)sh-,shträl-əŋ\ *n* [G, lit., decelerated radiation] (1939) **:** the electromagnetic radiation produced by the sudden retardation of a charged particle in an intense electric field

brent goose \,brent-\ *n, chiefly Brit* (1570) **:** BRANT

breth·ren \'breth-(ə-)rən, -ərn\ *pl of* BROTHER (bef. 12c) — used chiefly in formal or solemn address or in referring to the members of a profession, society, or sect

Brethren *n pl* (1822) **:** members of various sects originating chiefly in 18th century German Pietism; *esp* **:** DUNKERS

Bret·on \'bret-ᵊn\ *n* [F, fr. ML *Briton-, Brito,* fr. L, Briton] (14c) **1 :** a native or inhabitant of Brittany **2 :** the Celtic language of the Breton people — **Breton** *adj*

breve \'brēv, 'brev\ *n* [L, neut. of *brevis* brief — more at BRIEF] (15c) **1 :** a note equivalent to two whole notes **2 :** a curved mark ˘ used to indicate a short vowel or a short or unstressed syllable

[1]**bre·vet** \bri-'vet, *chiefly Brit* 'brev-it\ *n* [ME, an official message, fr. MF, fr. OF, dim. of *brief* letter — more at BRIEF] (1689) **:** a commission giving a military officer higher nominal rank than that for which he receives pay

[2]**brevet** *vt* **bre·vet·ted** *or* **brev·et·ed; bre·vet·ting** *or* **brev·et·ing** (1824) **:** to confer rank upon by brevet

bre·via·ry \'brē-v(y)ə-rē, -vē-,er-ē\ *n, pl* **-ries** [ME *breviarie,* fr. ML *breviarium,* fr. L, summary, fr. *brevis*] (15c) **1** *often cap* **a :** a book containing the prayers, hymns, psalms, and readings for the canonical hours **b :** DIVINE OFFICE **2** [L *breviarium*] **:** a brief summary **:** ABRIDGMENT

brev·i·ty \'brev-ət-ē\ *n, pl* **-ties** [L *brevitas,* fr. *brevis*] (1509) **:** shortness of duration; *esp* **:** shortness or conciseness of expression

[1]**brew** \'brü\ *vb* [ME *brewen,* fr. OE *brēowan;* akin to L *fervēre* to boil — more at BURN] *vt* (bef. 12c) **1 :** to prepare (as beer or ale) by steeping, boiling, and fermentation or by infusion and fermentation **2 a :** to bring about **:** FOMENT ⟨~ trouble⟩ **b :** CONTRIVE, PLOT **3 :** to prepare (as tea) by infusion in hot water ~ *vi* **1 :** to brew beer or ale **2 :** to be in the process of formation ⟨a storm is ~*ing* in the east⟩ — **brew·er** \'brü-ər, 'bru̇(-ə)r\ *n*

[2]**brew** *n* (1510) **1 a :** a brewed beverage **b :** a serving of a brewed beverage **c :** something produced by or as if by brewing **2 :** the process of brewing

brew·age \'brü-ij\ *n* (1542) **:** BREW

brewer's yeast *n* (1871) **:** a yeast used or suitable for use in brewing; *specif* **:** the dried pulverized cells of such a yeast (*Saccharomyces cerevisiae*) used esp. as a source of B-complex vitamins

brew·ery \'brü-ə-rē, 'bru̇(-ə)r-ē\ *n, pl* **-er·ies** (14c) **:** a plant where malt liquors are produced

[1]**bri·ar** \'brī(-ə)r\ *var of* BRIER

[2]**briar** *n* (1882) **:** a tobacco pipe made from the root of a brier

bri·ard \brē-'är(d)\ *n* [F, fr. *Brie,* district in France] (ca. 1929) **:** any of an old French breed of large long-coated sheepdogs

[1]**bribe** \'brīb\ *n* [ME, something stolen, fr. MF, bread given to a beggar] (15c) **1 :** money or favor given or promised to a person in a position of trust to influence his judgment or conduct **2 :** something that serves to induce or influence

[2]**bribe** *vb* **bribed; brib·ing** *vt* (1528) **:** to induce or influence by or as if by bribery ~ *vi* **:** to practice bribery — **brib·able** \'brī-bə-bəl\ *adj* — **brib·ee** \brī-'bē\ *n* — **brib·er** *n*

brib·ery \'brī-b(ə-)rē\ *n, pl* **-er·ies** (1549) **:** the act or practice of giving or taking a bribe

bric–a–brac \'brik-ə-,brak\ *n, pl* **bric–a–brac** [F *bric-à-brac*] (1840) **1 :** a miscellaneous collection of small articles commonly of ornamental or sentimental value **:** CURIOS **2 :** something suggesting bric-a-brac esp. in extraneous decorative quality

[1]**brick** \'brik\ *n, often attrib* [ME *bryke,* fr. MF *brique,* fr. MD *bricke;* akin to OE *brecan* to break] (15c) **1** *pl* **bricks** *or* **brick :** a handy-sized unit of building or paving material typically being rectangular and about $2^{1}/_{4}$ x $3^{3}/_{4}$ x 8 inches and of moist clay hardened by heat **2 :** a good-hearted person **3 :** a rectangular compressed mass (as of ice cream) **4 :** a semisoft cheese with numerous small holes, smooth texture, and usu. mild flavor **5 :** GAFFE, BLUNDER — used esp. in the phrase *drop a brick*

[2]**brick** *vt* (1648) **:** to close, face, or pave with bricks — usu. used with *up*

brick·bat \'brik-,bat\ *n* [*brick* + *bat* (lump, fragment)] (1563) **1 :** a fragment of a hard material (as a brick); *esp* **:** one used as a missile **2 :** an uncomplimentary remark

brick·field \-,fēld\ *n, Brit* (1801) **:** BRICKYARD

brick·lay·er \'brik-,lā-ər, -,le(-ə)r\ *n* (15c) **:** one who lays brick — **brick·lay·ing** \-,lā-iŋ\ *n*

brick·le \'brik-əl\ *adj* [ME *brekyl*] *dial* (13c) **:** BRITTLE

brick red *n* (1810) **:** a variable color averaging a moderate reddish brown

brick·work \'brik-,wərk\ *n* (ca. 1580) **:** work of or with bricks and mortar

brick·yard \-,yärd\ *n* (1731) **:** a place where bricks are made

bri·co·lage \,brē-kō-'läzh, ,brik-ō-\ *n* [F, fr. *bricoler* to putter about] (1966) **:** construction or something constructed by using whatever comes to hand

[1]**brid·al** \'brīd-ᵊl\ *n* [ME *bridale,* fr. OE *brȳdealu,* fr. *brȳd* + *ealu* ale — more at ALE] (bef. 12c) **:** a nuptial festival or ceremony **:** MARRIAGE

[2]**bridal** *adj* (13c) **1 :** of or relating to a bride or a wedding **:** NUPTIAL **2 :** intended for a newly married couple ⟨a ~ suite⟩

bridal wreath *n* (ca. 1889) **:** a spirea (*Spiraea prunifolia*) widely grown for its umbels of small white flowers borne in spring

bride \'brīd\ *n* [ME, fr. OE *brȳd;* akin to OHG *brūt* bride] (bef. 12c) **:** a woman just married or about to be married

bride·groom \'brīd-,grüm, -,gru̇m\ *n* [by folk etymology fr. ME *bridegome,* fr. OE *brȳdguma,* fr. *brȳd* + *guma* man; akin to OHG *brūtgomo* bridegroom — more at HOMAGE] (bef. 12c) **:** a man just married or about to be married

bride–price \'brīd-,prīs\ *n* (1876) **:** a payment (as of money or property) given by or in behalf of a prospective husband to the bride's family in many cultures

brides·maid \'brīdz-,mād\ *n* (ca. 1552) **1 :** a woman attendant of a bride **2 :** one that finishes just behind the winner

bride·well \'brī-,dwel, -dwəl\ *n* [*Bridewell,* London jail] (1589) **:** PRISON

[1]**bridge** \'brij\ *n* [ME *brigge,* fr. OE *brycg;* akin to OHG *brucka* bridge, OSlav *brŭvŭno* beam] (bef. 12c) **1 a :** a structure carrying a pathway or roadway over a depression or obstacle **b :** a time, place, or means of connection or transition **2 :** something resembling a bridge in form or function: as **a :** the upper bony part of the nose; *also* **:** the part of a

pair of glasses that rests upon it **b** : an arch serving to raise the strings of a musical instrument — see VIOLIN illustration **c** : a raised transverse platform on a ship from which it is navigated **d** : GANTRY 2b **e** : the hand as a rest for a billiards or pool cue; *also* : a device used as a cue rest **3 a** : a musical passage linking two sections of a song or composition **b** : a partial denture anchored to adjacent teeth **c** : a connection (as an atom or bond) that joins two different parts of a molecule (as opposite sides of a ring) **4** : an electrical instrument or network for measuring or comparing resistances, inductances, capacitances, or impedances by comparing the ratio of two opposing voltages to a known ratio — **bridge·less** \-ləs\ *adj*

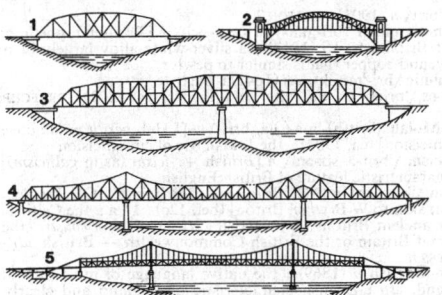

bridge 1a: *1* simple truss, *2* steel arch, *3* continuous truss, *4* cantilever, *5* suspension

²**bridge** *vt* **bridged; bridg·ing** (bef. 12c) **1** : to make a bridge over or across ⟨~ the gap⟩; *also* : to join by a bridge **2** : to provide with a bridge — **bridge·able** \-ə-bəl\ *adj*
³**bridge** *n* [alter. of earlier *biritch*, of unknown origin] (1843) : any of various card games for usu. four players in two partnerships that bid for the right to name a trump suit, score points for tricks made in excess of six, and play with the hand of declarer's partner exposed and played by declarer; *compare* CONTRACT BRIDGE
bridge·board \'brij-ˌbō(ə)rd, -ˌbȯ(ə)rd\ *n* (ca. 1864) : STRING 7a
bridge·head \-ˌhed\ *n* (1812) **1 a** : a fortification protecting the end of a bridge nearest an enemy **b** : an area around the end of a bridge **2** : an advanced position seized in hostile territory as a foothold for further advance
bridge·work \-ˌwərk\ *n* (1883) : dental bridges
¹**bri·dle** \'brīd-ᵊl\ *n* [ME *bridel*, fr. OE *bridel*; akin to MHG *brīdel* bridle, OE *bregdan* to move quickly — more at BRAID] (bef. 12c) **1 a** : the headgear with which a horse is governed and which carries a bit and reins **b** : a strip of metal joining two parts of a machine esp. for limiting or restraining motion **2** : something resembling a bridle in shape or function: as **a** : a length of secured cable with a second cable attached to the bight to which force is applied **b** : rigging on a kite for attaching line **c** : CURB, RESTRAINT ⟨set a ~ on his power⟩
²**bridle** *vb* **bri·dled; bri·dling** \'brīd-liŋ, -ᵊl-iŋ\ *vt* (bef. 12c) **1** : to put a bridle on **2** : to restrain, check, or control with or as if with a bridle; *esp* : to get and keep under restraint ⟨you must learn to ~ your tongue⟩ ~ *vi* : to show hostility or resentment (as to an affront to one's pride or dignity) esp. by drawing back the head and chin *syn* see RESTRAIN
bridle path *n* (1811) : a trail suitable for horseback riding
Brie \'brē\ *n* [F, fr. *Brie*, district in France] (ca. 1876) : a soft surface-ripened cheese with a whitish rind and a pale yellow interior
¹**brief** \'brēf\ *adj* [ME *bref, breve*, fr. MF *brief*, fr. L *brevis*; akin to OHG *murg* short, Gk *brachys*] (14c) **1** : short in duration, extent, or length **2 a** : CONCISE ⟨a ~ report⟩ **b** : CURT, ABRUPT ⟨a cold and ~ welcome⟩ — **brief·ness** *n*
syn BRIEF, SHORT mean lacking length. BRIEF applies primarily to duration and may imply condensation, conciseness, or occas. intensity; SHORT may imply sudden stoppage or incompleteness.
²**brief** *n* [ME *bref*, fr. MF, fr. ML *brevis*, fr. L *brevis*, adj.] (14c) **1** : an official letter or mandate; *esp* : a papal letter less formal than a bull **2** : a brief written item or document: as **a** : a concise article **b** : SYNOPSIS, SUMMARY **c** : a concise statement of a client's case made out for the instruction of counsel in a trial at law **3** : an outline of an argument; *esp* : a formal outline esp. in law that sets forth the main contentions with supporting statements or evidence **4** *pl* : short snug pants or underpants — **in brief** : in a few words : BRIEFLY
³**brief** *vt* (1601) **1** : to make an abstract or abridgment of **2 a** : to give final precise instructions to **b** : to coach thoroughly in advance **c** : to give essential information to — **brief·er** *n*
brief·case \'brēf-ˌkās\ *n* (1917) : a flat flexible case for carrying papers or books
brief·ing \'brē-fiŋ\ *n* (1910) : an act or instance of giving precise instructions or essential information
brief·less \'brēf-ləs\ *adj* (1824) : having no legal clients
brief·ly \'brē-flē\ *adv* (14c) **1 a** : in a brief way **b** : in brief **2** : for a short time
¹**bri·er** \'brī-(ə)r\ *n* [ME *brere*, fr. OE *brēr*] (bef. 12c) **1** : a plant (as of the genera *Rosa, Rubus*, and *Smilax*) with a woody and thorny or prickly stem; *also* : a mass or twig of these — **bri·ery** \'brī-(ə)r-ē\ *adj*
²**brier** *n* [F *bruyère* heath, fr. MF *bruiere*, fr. (assumed) VL *brucaria*, fr. LL *brucus* heather, of Celt origin; akin to OIr *froech* heather] (1868) : a heath (*Erica arborea*) of southern Europe with a root used for tobacco pipes
bri·er·root \'brī-(ə)r-ˌrüt, -ˌrut\ *n* (1869) : a root (as of the brier *Erica arborea*) used for tobacco pipes
¹**brig** \'brig\ *n* [short for *brigantine*] (1712) : a 2-masted square-rigged ship — *compare* HERMAPHRODITE BRIG

²**brig** *n* [prob. fr. ¹*brig*] (1852) **1** : a place (as on a ship) for temporary confinement of offenders in the U.S. Navy **2** : GUARDHOUSE, PRISON
¹**bri·gade** \brig-'ād\ *n* [F, fr. It *brigata*, fr. *brigare*] (1637) **1 a** : a large body of troops **b** : a tactical and administrative unit composed of a headquarters, one or more units of infantry or armor, and supporting units **2** : a group of people organized for special activity
²**brigade** *vt* **bri·gad·ed; bri·gad·ing** (1781) : to form or unite into a brigade
brig·a·dier \ˌbrig-ə-'di(ə)r\ *n* [F, fr. *brigade*] (1678) **1** : an officer in the British army commanding a brigade and ranking immediately below a major general **2** : BRIGADIER GENERAL
brigadier general *n* (1776) : a commissioned officer in the army, air force, or marine corps who ranks above a colonel and whose insignia is one star
brig·and \'brig-ənd\ *n* [ME *brigaunt*, fr. MF *brigand*, fr. OIt *brigante*, fr. *brigare* to fight, fr. *briga* strife, of Celt origin; akin to OIr *brig* strength] (14c) : one who lives by plunder usu. as a member of a band : BANDIT — **brig·and·age** \-ən-dij\ *n*
brig·an·dine \'brig-ən-ˌdēn\ *n* [ME, fr. MF, fr. *brigand*] (15c) : medieval body armor of scales or plates
brig·an·tine \'brig-ən-ˌtēn\ *n* [MF *brigantin*, fr. OIt *brigantino*, fr. *brigante*] (1525) **1** : a 2-masted square-rigged ship differing from a brig in not carrying a square mainsail **2** : HERMAPHRODITE BRIG
bright \'brīt\ *adj* [ME, fr. OE *beorht*; akin to OHG *beraht* bright, Skt *bhrājate* it shines] (bef. 12c) **1 a** : radiating or reflecting light : SHINING, SPARKLING ⟨~ lights⟩ ⟨~ eyes⟩ **b** : SUNNY ⟨a ~ day⟩; *also* : radiant with happiness ⟨~ smiling faces⟩ **2** : ILLUSTRIOUS, GLORIOUS ⟨~est star of the opera⟩ **3** : BEAUTIFUL **4** : of high saturation or brilliance ⟨~ colors⟩ **5 a** : LIVELY, CHEERFUL ⟨be ~ and jovial among your guests —Shak.⟩ **b** : INTELLIGENT, CLEVER ⟨a ~ idea⟩ ⟨~ children⟩ **6** : AUSPICIOUS, PROMISING ⟨~ prospects for the future⟩ — **bright** *adv* — **bright·ly** *adv*
syn BRIGHT, BRILLIANT, RADIANT, LUMINOUS, LUSTROUS mean shining or glowing with light. BRIGHT implies emitting or reflecting a high degree of light; BRILLIANT implies intense often sparkling brightness; RADIANT stresses the emission or seeming emission of rays of light; LUMINOUS implies emission of steady, suffused, glowing light by reflection or in surrounding darkness; LUSTROUS stresses an even, rich light from a surface that reflects brightly without sparkling or glittering.
bright·en \'brīt-ᵊn\ *vb* **bright·ened; bright·en·ing** \'brīt-niŋ, -ᵊn-iŋ\ *vi* (14c) : to become bright or brighter ~ *vt* : to make bright or brighter — **bright·en·er** \-nər, -ᵊn-ər\ *n*
bright·ness *n* (bef. 12c) **1** : the quality or state of being bright; *also* : an instance of such a quality or state **2** : the one of the three psychological dimensions of color perception by which visual stimuli are ordered continuously from light to dark and which is correlated with light intensity — *compare* HUE 2c, SATURATION
Bright's disease \'brīts-\ *n* [Richard *Bright* †1858 Eng. physician] (1831) : any of several kidney diseases marked by albumin in the urine
bright·work \'brīt-ˌwərk\ *n* (1841) : polished or plated metalwork
brill \'bril\ *n, pl* **brill** [perh. fr. Corn *brythel* mackerel] (15c) : a European flatfish (*Bothus rhombus*) related to the turbot; *broadly* : TURBOT
bril·liance \'bril-yən(t)s\ *n* (1755) : the quality or state of being brilliant
bril·lian·cy \-yən-sē\ *n, pl* **-cies** (1747) **1** : BRILLIANCE **2** : an instance of brilliance
¹**bril·liant** \'bril-yənt\ *adj* [F *brillant*, prp. of *briller* to shine, fr. It *brillare*, fr. *brillo* beryl, fr. L *beryllus* — more at BERYL] (ca. 1681) **1** : very bright : GLITTERING ⟨a ~ light⟩ **2 a** : STRIKING, DISTINCTIVE ⟨a ~ example⟩ **b** : distinguished by unusual mental keenness or alertness *syn* see BRIGHT — **bril·liant·ly** *adv*
²**brilliant** *n* (1690) : a gem (as a diamond) cut in a particular form with numerous facets so as to have special brilliance
bril·lian·tine \'bril-yən-ˌtēn\ *n* (1873) **1** : a light lustrous fabric that is similar to alpaca and is woven usu. with a cotton warp and mohair or worsted filling **2** : a preparation for making hair glossy
¹**brim** \'brim\ *n* [ME *brimme*; akin to MHG *brem* edge] (13c) **1 a** (1) : an upper or outer margin : VERGE (2) *archaic* : the upper surface of a body of water **b** : the edge or rim of a hollow vessel, a natural depression, or a cavity **2** : the projecting rim of a hat — **brim·less** \-ləs\ *adj*

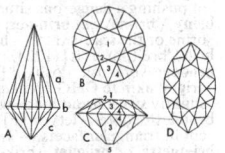

brilliant: *A* briolette; *B, C* American cut, top and side view; *D* marquise: *a* bezel, *b* girdle, *c* pavilion: *1* table, *2* star facet, *3* main facet, *4* corner facet, *5* culet

²**brim** *vb* **brimmed; brim·ming** *vt* (1611) : to fill to the brim ~ *vi* **1** : to be or become full often to overflowing **2** : to reach or overflow a brim
brim·ful \'brim-'fül\ *adj* (ca. 1530) : full to the brim : ready to overflow
-brimmed \'brimd\ *adj comb form* : having a brim of a specified nature ⟨a wide-*brimmed* hat⟩
brim·mer \'brim-ər\ *n* (1663) : a brimming cup or glass
brim·stone \'brim-ˌstōn\ *n* [ME *brinston*, prob. fr. *birnen* to burn + *ston* stone — more at BURN] (12c) : SULFUR
brind·ed \'brin-dəd\ *adj* [ME *brended*] *archaic* (15c) : BRINDLED
¹**brin·dle** \'brin-dᵊl\ *n* [*brindle*, adj.] (1676) **1** : a brindled color **2 a** : a brindled animal
brin·dled \-dᵊld\ *or* **brindle** *adj* [alter. of *brinded*] (1679) : having obscure dark streaks or flecks on a gray or tawny ground
¹**brine** \'brīn\ *n* [ME, fr. OE *brȳne*; akin to MD *brīne* brine, L *fricare* to rub — more at FRICTION] (bef. 12c) **1 a** : water saturated or strongly impregnated with common salt **b** : a strong saline solution (as of calcium chloride) **2** : the water of a sea or salt lake
²**brine** *vt* **brined; brin·ing** (1552) : to treat (as by steeping) with brine — **brin·er** *n*

Bri·nell hardness \brə-ˌnel-\ *n* [Johann A. *Brinell* †1925 Swed. engineer] (1915) : the hardness of a metal or alloy measured by hydraulically pressing a hard ball under a standard load into the specimen

Brinell number *n* (1915) : a number expressing Brinell hardness and denoting the load applied in testing in kilograms divided by the spherical area of indentation produced in the specimen in square millimeters

brine shrimp *n* (1836) : any of a genus (*Artemia*) of branchiopod crustaceans

bring \ˈbriŋ\ *vb* **brought** \ˈbrȯt\; **bring·ing** \ˈbriŋ-iŋ\ [ME *bringen*, fr. OE *bringan*; akin to OHG *bringan* to bring, W *hebrwng* to accompany] *vt* (bef. 12c) **1 a** : to convey, lead, carry, or cause to come along with one toward the place from which the action is being regarded **b** : to cause to be, act, or move in a special way: as (1) : ATTRACT ⟨her screams *brought* the neighbors⟩ (2) : PERSUADE, INDUCE (3) : FORCE, COMPEL (4) : to cause to come into a particular state or condition ⟨~ water to a boil⟩ **c** *dial* : ESCORT, ACCOMPANY **2** : to cause to exist or occur: as **a** : PRODUCE ⟨winter ~*s* snow⟩ **b** : to result in : EFFECT **c** : INSTITUTE ⟨~ legal action⟩ **d** : ADDUCE ⟨~ an argument⟩ **3** : PREFER ⟨~ a charge⟩ **4** : to procure in exchange : sell for ~ *vi, chiefly Midland* : YIELD, PRODUCE — **bring·er** *n* — **bring forth 1** : BEAR ⟨*brought forth* fruit⟩ **2** : to give birth to : PRODUCE **3** : ADDUCE ⟨*bring forth* persuasive arguments⟩ — **bring forward 1** : to produce to view : INTRODUCE ⟨*brought* new evidence *forward* to prove her innocence of the accusations⟩ **2** : to carry (a total) forward — **bring home** : to make unmistakably clear — **bring to account 1** : to bring to book **2** : REPRIMAND — **bring to bear 1** : to put to use ⟨*bring* knowledge *to bear*⟩ **2** : APPLY, EXERT ⟨*bring* pressure *to bear*⟩ — **bring to book** : to compel to give an account — **bring to light** : DISCLOSE, REVEAL — **bring to mind** : to cause to be recalled — **bring to terms** : to compel to agree, assent, or submit — **bring up the rear** : to come last or behind

bring about *vt* (14c) : to cause to take place : EFFECT

bring around *vt* (1862) **1** : to restore to consciousness : REVIVE **2** : to cause (someone) to adopt a particular opinion or course of action : PERSUADE

bring·down \ˈbriŋ-ˌdau̇n\ *n* (ca. 1944) : COMEDOWN, LETDOWN

bring down \(ˈ)briŋ-ˈdau̇n\ *vt* (14c) **1** : to cause to fall by or as if by shooting **2** : to carry (a total) forward — **bring down the house** : to win the enthusiastic approval of the audience

bring in *vt* (14c) **1** : INCLUDE, INTRODUCE **2** : to produce as profit or return ⟨each sale *brought in* $5⟩ **3** : to enable (a man on base) to reach home plate by a hit **4** : to report to a court ⟨jury *brought in* a verdict⟩ **5 a** : to cause (as an oil well) to be productive **b** : to win tricks with the cards of (a long suit) in bridge **6** : EARN ⟨he *brings in* a good salary⟩

bring off *vt* (13c) **1** : to cause to escape : RESCUE **2** : to carry to a successful conclusion : ACHIEVE, ACCOMPLISH

bring on *vt* (1671) : to cause to appear or occur

bring out *vt* (1605) **1 a** : to make apparent **b** : to effectively develop (as a quality) **2 a** : to present to the public **b** : to introduce formally to society **3** : UTTER

bring to *vt* (1753) **1** : to cause (a boat) to lie to or come to a standstill **2** : to restore to consciousness : REVIVE

bring up *vt* (14c) **1** : to bring (a person) to maturity through nurturing care and education **2** : to cause to stop suddenly **3** : to bring to attention : INTRODUCE **4** : VOMIT ~ *vi* : to stop suddenly

brink \ˈbriŋk\ *n* [ME, prob. of Scand origin; akin to ON *brekka* slope; akin to L *front-, frons* forehead] (13c) **1** : EDGE; *esp* : the edge at the top of a steep place **2** : a bank esp. of a river **3** : the point of onset : VERGE ⟨on the ~ of war⟩ **4** : the threshold of danger

brink·man·ship \ˈbriŋk-mən-ˌship\ *also* **brinks·man·ship** \ˈbriŋ(k)-smən-\ *n* [*brink* + *-manship* (as in *horsemanship*)] (1956) : the art or practice of pushing a dangerous situation to the limit of safety before stopping

briny \ˈbrī-nē\ *adj* **brin·i·er; -est** (1604) : of, relating to, or resembling brine or the sea : SALTY — **brin·i·ness** *n*

brio \ˈbrē-(ˌ)ō\ *n* [It] (1734) : enthusiastic vigor : VIVACITY, VERVE

bri·oche \brē-ˈōsh, -ˈȯsh\ *n* [F, fr. MF dial., fr. *brier* to knead, of Gmc origin; akin to OHG *brehhan* to break — more at BREAK] (1826) : light slightly sweet bread made with a rich yeast dough

bri·o·lette \ˌbrē-ə-ˈlet\ *n* [F] (1865) : an oval or pear-shaped diamond cut in triangular facets — see BRILLIANT illustration

bri·quette *or* **bri·quet** \brik-ˈet\ *n* [F *briquette*, dim. of *brique* brick] (1883) : a compacted often brick-shaped mass of usu. fine material ⟨a charcoal ~⟩ — **briquette** *vt*

bri·sance \bri-ˈzän(t)s, -ˈzäⁿs\ *n* [F, fr. *brisant*, prp. of *briser* to break, fr. OF *brisier*, of Celt origin; akin to OIr *brissim* I break; akin to L *fricare* to rub — more at FRICTION] (1915) : the shattering or crushing effect of an explosive — **bri·sant** \-ˈzänt, -ˈzäⁿ\ *adj*

¹brisk \ˈbrisk\ *adj* [prob. modif. of MF *brusque*] (1560) **1** : keenly alert : LIVELY **2 a** : pleasingly tangy ⟨~ tea⟩ **b** : FRESH, INVIGORATING ⟨~ weather⟩ **3** : sharp in tone or manner **4** : ENERGETIC, QUICK ⟨a ~ pace⟩ — **brisk·ly** *adv* — **brisk·ness** *n*

²brisk *vt* (1628) : to make brisk ~ *vi* : to become brisk — usu. used with *up* ⟨business ~*ed* up⟩

bris·ket \ˈbris-kət\ *n* [ME *brusket*; akin to OE *brēost* breast] (14c) : the breast or lower chest of a quadruped animal — see BEEF illustration

bris·ling *or* **bris·tling** \ˈbriz-liŋ, ˈbris-\ *n* [Norw *brisling*, fr. LG *bretling*, fr. *bret* broad; akin to OE *brād* broad] (ca. 1868) : a small herring (*Clupea sprattus*) that resembles and is processed like a sardine

¹bris·tle \ˈbris-əl\ *n* [ME *bristil*, fr. *brust* bristle, fr. OE *byrst*; akin to OE *brord* point, OHG *burst* bristle, L *fastigium* top] (bef. 12c) : a short stiff coarse hair or filament — **bris·tle·like** \ˈbris-əl-ˌ(l)īk\ *adj*

²bristle *vb* **bris·tled; bris·tling** \ˈbris-(ə-)liŋ\ *vt* (13c) **1** : to furnish with bristles **2** : to make bristly : RUFFLE ~ *vi* **1 a** : to rise and stand stiffly erect ⟨quills *bristling*⟩ **b** : to raise the bristles (as in anger) **2** : to take on an aggressive attitude or appearance (as in response to a slight) **3** : to be full of or covered with esp. something suggestive of bristles ⟨roofs *bristled* with chimneys⟩

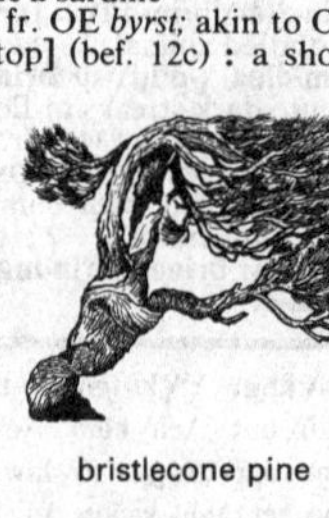

bristlecone pine

bris·tle·cone pine \ˌbris-əl-ˌkōn-\ *n* (1894) : a pine (*Pinus aristata*) of the western U.S. that includes the oldest living trees

bris·tle·tail \ˈbris-əl-ˌtāl\ *n* (1706) : any of various wingless insects (orders Thysanura and Entotrophi) with two or three slender caudal bristles

bris·tly \ˈbris-(ə-)lē\ *adj* **bris·tli·er; -est** (ca. 1591) **1 a** : consisting of or resembling bristles **b** : thickly set with bristles **2** : tending to bristle easily : BELLIGERENT

bris·tol board \ˈbris-tᵊl-\ *n* [*Bristol*, England] (1809) : a paperboard with a smooth surface suitable esp. for artwork — called also *bristol*

Bristol fashion *adj* [*Bristol*, England] (1823) : being in good order : SHIPSHAPE

brit *also* **britt** \ˈbrit\ *n* [Corn *brȳthel* mackerel] (ca. 1890) : minute marine animals (as crustaceans and pteropods) on which right whales feed

Brit \ˈbrit\ *n* (1901) : BRITON 2

Bri·tan·nia metal \bri-ˌtan-yə-, -ˌtan-ē-ə-\ *n* [*Britannia*, poetic name for Great Britain, fr. L] (1817) : a silver-white alloy largely of tin, antimony, and copper that is similar to pewter

Bri·tan·nic \bri-ˈtan-ik\ *adj* (1641) : BRITISH

britch·es \ˈbrich-əz\ *n pl* [alter. of *breeches*] (ca. 1803) : BREECHES, TROUSERS

Brith Mi·lah \brit(h)-ˈmē-(ˌ)lä, bris-\ *n* [LHeb *bĕrīth mīlāh* covenant of circumcision] (ca. 1902) : the Jewish rite of circumcision

Brit·i·cism \ˈbrit-ə-ˌsiz-əm\ *n* [*British* + *-icism* (as in *gallicism*)] (1868) : a characteristic feature of British English

Brit·ish \ˈbrit-ish\ *n* [ME *Bruttische* of Britain, fr. OE *Brettisc*, of Celt origin; akin to W *Brython* Briton] (bef. 12c) **1 a** : the Celtic language of the ancient Britons **b** : BRITISH ENGLISH **2** *pl in constr* : the people of Great Britain or the British Commonwealth — **British** *adj* — **Brit·ish·ness** *n*

British English *n* (1869) : the native language of most inhabitants of England; *esp* : English characteristic of England and clearly distinguishable from that used elsewhere (as in the U.S. or Australia)

Brit·ish·er \ˈbrit-ish-ər\ *n* (1829) : BRITON 2

British thermal unit *n* (ca. 1876) : the quantity of heat required to raise the temperature of one pound of water one degree Fahrenheit at a specified temperature (as 39°F)

Brit·on \ˈbrit-ᵊn\ *n* [ME *Breton*, fr. MF & L; MF, fr. L *Briton-, Brito*, of Celt origin; akin to W *Brython*] (13c) **1** : a member of one of the peoples inhabiting Britain prior to the Anglo-Saxon invasions **2** : a native or subject of Great Britain; *esp* : ENGLISHMAN

Brit·ta·ny spaniel \ˌbrit-ᵊn-ē-\ *n* [*Brittany*, region in France] (ca. 1935) : any of a French breed of long-legged medium-sized pointing spaniels

¹brit·tle \ˈbrit-ᵊl\ *adj* **brit·tler** \ˈbrit-lər, -ᵊl-ər\; **brit·tlest** \-ləst, -ᵊl-əst\ [ME *britil*; akin to OE *brēotan* to break, Skt *bhrūṇa* embryo] (14c) **1 a** : easily broken, cracked, or snapped ⟨~ clay⟩ ⟨~ glass⟩ **b** : easily disrupted, overthrown, or damaged : FRAIL ⟨a ~ friendship⟩ **2** : easily hurt or offended : SENSITIVE ⟨a ~ personality⟩ **3** : SHARP ⟨~ staccato of snare drums⟩ **4 a** : PERISHABLE, MORTAL **b** : TRANSITORY, EVANESCENT **5** : lacking warmth, depth, or generosity of spirit : COLD ⟨a ~ selfish person⟩ ***syn*** see FRAGILE — **brit·tle·ly** \ˈbrit-lē, -ᵊl-(l)ē\ *adv* — **brit·tle·ness** \ˈbrit-ᵊl-nəs\ *n*

²brittle *n* (1913) : a candy made with caramelized sugar and nuts spread in thin sheets ⟨peanut ~⟩

³brittle *vi* **brit·tled; brit·tling** \ˈbrit-liŋ, -ᵊl-iŋ\ (1920) : to become brittle : CRUMBLE, DETERIORATE

brittle star *n* (1843) : any of a subclass or class (Ophiuroidea) of echinoderms that have slender flexible arms

Brit·ton·ic \bri-ˈtän-ik\ *adj* [L *Britton-, Britto* Briton] (1923) : BRYTHONIC 2

Brix \ˈbriks\ *adj* (1897) : of or relating to a Brix scale

Brix scale *n* [Adolf F. *Brix* †1870 Austrian scientist] (1897) : a hydrometer scale for sugar solutions so graduated that its readings at a specified temperature represent percentages by weight of sugar in the solution — called also *Brix*

¹broach \ˈbrōch\ *n* [ME *broche*, fr. MF, fr. (assumed) VL *brocca*, fr. L, fem. of *broccus* projecting] (13c) **1** : BROOCH **2** : any of various pointed or tapered tools, implements, or parts: as **a** : a spit for roasting meat **b** : a tool for tapping casks **c** : a cutting tool for removing material from metal or plastic to shape an outside surface or a hole

²broach *vt* (15c) **1 a** : to pierce (as a cask) in order to draw the contents : TAP **b** : to open up or break into (as a mine or stores) **2** : to shape or enlarge (a hole) with a broach **3 a** : to make known for the first time **b** : to open up (a subject) for discussion ~ *vi* : to break the surface from below ***syn*** see EXPRESS — **broach·er** *n*

³broach *vb* [perh. fr. ²*broach*] *vi* (1705) : to veer or yaw dangerously so as to lie broadside to the waves — used chiefly with *to* ~ *vt* : to cause (a boat) to broach

¹broad \ˈbrȯd\ *adj* [ME *brood*, fr. OE *brād*; akin to OHG *breit* broad] (bef. 12c) **1 a** : having ample extent from side to side or between limits ⟨~ shoulders⟩ **b** : having a specified extension from side to side ⟨made the path 10 feet ~⟩ **2** : extending far and wide : SPACIOUS ⟨the ~ plains⟩ **3 a** : OPEN, FULL ⟨~ daylight⟩ **b** : PLAIN, OBVIOUS ⟨a ~ hint⟩ **4** : marked by lack of restraint, delicacy, or subtlety: **a** *obs* : OUTSPOKEN **b** : COARSE, RISQUÉ ⟨~ humor⟩ **5 a** : LIBERAL, TOLERANT ⟨~ views⟩ **b** : widely applicable or applied : GENERAL **6** : relating to the main or essential points ⟨~ outlines⟩ **7** : dialectal esp. in pronunciation **8** *of a vowel* : OPEN — used specif. of *a* pronounced as in *father* — **broad·ly** *adv* — **broad·ness** *n*

syn BROAD, WIDE, DEEP mean having horizontal extent. BROAD and WIDE apply to a surface measured or viewed from side to side ⟨a *broad* avenue⟩ WIDE is more common when units of measurement are mentioned ⟨rugs eight feet *wide*⟩ or applied to unfilled space between limits ⟨*wide* doorway⟩ BROAD is preferred when full horizontal extent is considered ⟨*broad* shoulders⟩ DEEP may indicate horizontal extent away from the observer or from a front or peripheral point ⟨a *deep* cupboard⟩ ⟨*deep* woods⟩

²broad *adv* (bef. 12c) : in a broad manner : FULLY

³broad *n* (1659) **1** *Brit* : an expansion of a river — often used in pl. **2** *slang* : WOMAN

broad arrow *n* (14c) **1** : an arrow with a flat barbed head **2** *Brit* : a mark shaped like a broad arrow that identifies government property including clothing formerly worn by convicts

broad·ax \ˈbrȯ-ˌdaks\ *n* (bef. 12c) : a large ax with a broad blade

broad·band \'brȯd-ˌband\ *adj* (1960) **:** of, having, or involving operation with uniform efficiency over a wide band of frequencies ⟨a ~ radio antenna⟩

broad bean *n* (1783) **:** the large flat edible seed of an Old World upright vetch (*Vicia faba*); *also* **:** this plant widely grown for its seeds and as fodder

broad·brush \'brȯd-ˌbrəsh\ *adj* (1967) **:** GENERAL, NONSPECIFIC

[1]**broad·cast** \'brȯd-ˌkast\ *adj* (1767) **1 :** cast or scattered in all directions **2 :** made public by means of radio or television **3 :** of or relating to radio or television broadcasting

[2]**broadcast** *vb* **broadcast** *also* **broad·cast·ed; broad·cast·ing** *vt* (1813) **1 :** to scatter or sow (as seed) broadcast **2 :** to make widely known **3 :** to transmit as a broadcast ~ *vi* **1 :** to transmit a broadcast **2 :** to speak or perform on a broadcast program — **broad·cast·er** *n*

[3]**broadcast** *adv* (1814) **:** to or over a broad area

[4]**broadcast** *n* (1922) **1 :** the act of transmitting sound or images by radio or television **2 :** a single radio or television program

Broad Church *adj* (1853) **:** of or relating to a liberal party in the Anglican communion esp. in the later 19th century — **Broad Churchman** *n*

broad·cloth \'brȯd-ˌklȯth\ *n* (15c) **1 :** a twilled napped woolen or worsted fabric with smooth lustrous face and dense texture **2 :** a fabric usu. of cotton, silk, or rayon made in plain and rib weaves with soft semigloss finish

broad·en \'brȯd-ᵊn\ *vb* **broad·ened; broad·en·ing** \'brȯd-niŋ, -ᵊn-iŋ\ *vt* (1726) **:** to make broader ~ *vi* **:** to become broad

broad gauge *n* (1844) **:** a railroad gauge wider than standard gauge — **broad–gauged** \'brȯd-'gājd\ *adj*

broad jump *n* (1872) **:** LONG JUMP — **broad jumper** *n*

broad–leaved \-'lēvd\ *or* **broad·leaf** \-'lēf\ *also* **broad–leafed** \-'lēft\ *adj* (ca. 1552) **1 :** having broad leaves; *specif* **:** having leaves that are not needles **2 :** composed of broad-leaved plants ⟨~ forests⟩

[1]**broad·loom** \-ˌlüm\ *adj* (1925) **:** woven on a wide loom; *also* **:** so woven in solid color

[2]**broadloom** *n* (1926) **:** a broadloom carpet

broad–mind·ed \'brȯd-'mīn-dəd\ *adj* (1882) **1 :** tolerant of varied views **2 :** inclined to condone minor departures from conventional behavior — **broad–mind·ed·ly** *adv* — **broad–mind·ed·ness** *n*

broad·sheet \-ˌshēt\ *n* (1705) **:** BROADSIDE 1

[1]**broad·side** \-ˌsīd\ *n* (1575) **1 a** (1) **:** a sizable sheet of paper printed on one side (2) **:** a sheet printed on one or both sides and folded **b :** something (as a ballad or an advertisement) printed on a broadside **2 :** the side of a ship above the waterline **3 a :** all the guns on one side of a ship; *also* **:** their simultaneous discharge **b :** a volley of verbal abuse or denunciation **4 :** a broad or unbroken surface

[2]**broadside** *adj* (1646) **:** directed or placed broadside ⟨a ~ attack⟩

[3]**broadside** *adv* (1870) **1 a :** with the side forward or toward a given point **:** SIDEWAYS ⟨turned ~⟩ **b :** directly from the side ⟨the car was hit ~⟩ **2 :** in one volley **3 :** at random

broad–spectrum *adj* (1952) **:** effective against various insects or microorganisms

broad·sword \'brȯd-ˌsō(ə)rd, -ˌsȯ(ə)rd\ *n* (bef. 12c) **:** a sword with a broad blade for cutting rather than thrusting

broad·tail \-ˌtāl\ *n* (1892) **1 :** KARAKUL 1 **2 :** the fur or skin of a very young or premature karakul lamb having a flat and wavy appearance resembling moiré silk

Broad·way \'brȯd-ˌwā, -'wā\ *n* [*Broadway*, street in New York on or near which were once located the majority of the city's legitimate theaters] (1835) **:** the New York commercial theater and amusement world; *specif* **:** playhouses located in the area between the Avenue of the Americas and Ninth Avenue and from W. 41st Street to W. 53d Street — **Broadway** *adj* — **Broad·way·ite** \-ˌīt\ *n*

Brob·ding·nag·ian \ˌbräb-diŋ-'nag-ē-ən, -dig-'nag-\ *adj* [*Brobdingnag*, imaginary land of giants in *Gulliver's Travels*, by Jonathan Swift] (1728) **:** marked by tremendous size **:** GIGANTIC — **Brobdingnagian** *n*

bro·cade \brō-'kād\ *n* [Sp *brocado*, fr. Catal *brocat*, fr. It *broccato*, fr. *broccare* to spur, brocade, fr. *brocco* small nail, fr. L *broccus* projecting] (1563) **1 :** a rich oriental silk fabric with raised patterns in gold and silver **2 :** a fabric characterized by raised designs — **brocade** *vt* — **bro·cad·ed** *adj*

Bro·ca's area \(ˌ)brō-'käz-, 'brō-kəz-\ *n* [Paul P. *Broca* †1880 Fr. surgeon] (ca. 1898) **:** a brain center associated with the motor control of speech and usu. located in the left side but sometimes in the right side of the frontal lobe

broc·a·telle \ˌbräk-ə-'tel\ *n* [F, fr. It *broccatello*, dim. of *broccato*] (1669) **:** a stiff decorating fabric with patterns in high relief

broc·co·li \'bräk-(ə-)lē\ *n* [It, pl. of *broccolo* flowering top of a cabbage, dim. of *brocco* small nail, sprout] (1699) **1 :** a large hardy cauliflower **2 :** a branching cauliflower with a head of functional florets at the end of each branch that is cut for food while the florets are tight green or purplish buds — called also *sprouting broccoli*

bro·chette \brō-'shet\ *n* [F, fr. OF *brochete*, fr. *broche* pointed tool — more at BROACH] (15c) **:** SKEWER; *also* **:** food broiled on a skewer

bro·chure \brō-'shu̇(ə)r *also* 'brō-ˌ\ *n* [F, fr. *brocher* to sew, fr. MF, to prick, fr. OF *brochier*, fr. *broche*] (1748) **:** PAMPHLET, BOOKLET; *esp* **:** one containing descriptive or advertising material

brock \'bräk\ *n* [ME, fr. OE *broc*, of Celt origin; akin to W *broch* badger] (bef. 12c) **:** BADGER

brock·age \'bräk-ij\ *n* [E dial. *brock* rubbish + E *-age*] (1879) **:** an imperfectly minted coin

brock·et \'bräk-ət\ *n* [ME *broket*, fr. ONF *broquard*; akin to OF *broche* tine of an antler, pointed tool — more at BROACH] (15c) **1 :** a male red deer two years old — compare PRICKET **2 :** any of several small So. American deer (genus *Mazama*) with unbranched horns

bro·gan \'brō-gən, -ˌgan; brō-'gan\ *n* [IrGael *brōgan*, dim. of *brōg*] (1835) **:** a heavy shoe; *esp* **:** a coarse work shoe reaching to the ankle

[1]**brogue** \'brōg\ *n* [IrGael & ScGael *brōg*, fr. MIr *brōc*, fr. ON *brōk* leg covering; akin to OE *brōc* leg covering — more at BREECH] (1586) **1 :** a stout coarse shoe worn formerly in Ireland and the Scottish Highlands **2 :** a heavy shoe often with a hobnailed sole **:** BROGAN **3 :** a stout oxford shoe with perforations and usu. a wing tip

[2]**brogue** *n* [perh. fr. IrGael *barrōg* wrestling hold; fr. the idea that unfamiliar features of pronunciation must be the result of a physical impediment of the tongue] (1705) **:** a dialect or regional pronunciation; *esp* **:** an Irish accent

broi·der \'brȯid-ər\ *vt* [ME *broideren*, modif. of MF *broder* — more at EMBROIDER] (14c) **:** EMBROIDER — **broi·dery** \'brȯid-(ə-)rē\ *n*

[1]**broil** \'brȯi(ə)l\ *vb* [ME *broilen*, fr. MF *bruler* to burn, prob. modif. of L *ustulare* to singe, fr. *ustus*, pp. of *urere* to burn] *vt* (14c) **:** to cook by direct exposure to radiant heat **:** GRILL ~ *vi* **:** to become broiled

[2]**broil** *n* (1583) **:** the act or state of broiling

[3]**broil** *vb* [ME *broilen*, fr. MF *brouiller* to mix, broil, fr. OF *brooilier*, fr. *breu* broth] *vt* (15c) **:** EMBROIL ~ *vi* **:** BRAWL

[4]**broil** *n* (1525) **:** a noisy disturbance **:** TUMULT; *esp* **:** BRAWL ⟨a tavern row . . . widens into a general ~ —J.R. Green⟩

broil·er \'brȯi-lər\ *n* (14c) **1 :** one that broils **2 :** a bird fit for broiling; *esp* **:** a young chicken of up to 2½ pounds dressed weight

[1]**broke** \'brōk\ *past of* BREAK

[2]**broke** *adj* [ME, alter. of *broken*] (1716) **:** PENNILESS

bro·ken \'brō-kən\ *adj* [ME, fr. OE *brocen*, fr. pp. of *brecan* to break] (bef. 12c) **1 :** violently separated into parts **:** SHATTERED **2 :** damaged or altered by breaking: as **a :** having undergone or been subjected to fracture ⟨a ~ leg⟩ **b** *of land surfaces* **:** being irregular, interrupted, or full of obstacles **c :** violated by transgression ⟨a ~ promise⟩ **d :** DISCONTINUOUS, INTERRUPTED **e :** disrupted by change **f** *of a flower* **:** having an irregular, streaked, or blotched pattern esp. from virus infection **3 a :** made weak or infirm **b :** subdued completely **:** CRUSHED ⟨a ~ spirit⟩ **c :** BANKRUPT **d :** reduced in rank **4 a :** cut off **:** DISCONNECTED **b :** imperfectly spoken or written ⟨~ English⟩ **5 :** not complete or full **6 :** disunited by divorce, separation, or desertion of one parent ⟨children from ~ homes⟩ ⟨a ~ family⟩ — **bro·ken·ly** *adv* — **bro·ken·ness** \-kən-(n)əs\ *n*

bro·ken–down \ˌbrō-kən-'dau̇n\ *adj* (1817) **:** WORN-OUT, DEBILITATED

bro·ken–field \-ˌfēld\ *adj* (1923) **:** accomplished (as by a ballcarrier in football) against widely scattered opposition

bro·ken·heart·ed \-'härt-əd\ *adj* (1526) **:** overcome by grief or despair

bro·ken–wind·ed \-'win-dəd\ *adj* (1523) **:** affected with or as if with heaves

bro·ker \'brō-kər\ *n* [ME, negotiator, fr. (assumed) AF *brocour*; akin to OF *broche* pointed tool, tap of a cask — more at BROACH] (14c) **1 :** one who acts as an intermediary: as **a :** an agent who arranges marriages **b :** an agent who negotiates contracts of purchase and sale (as of real estate, commodities, or securities) **2 :** POWER BROKER — **broker** *vb* — **bro·ker·ing** \'brō-k(ə-)riŋ\ *n*

bro·ker·age \'brō-k(ə-)rij\ *n* (15c) **1 :** the business or establishment of a broker **2 :** a broker's fee or commission

brol·ly \'bräl-ē\ *n, pl* **brollies** [by shortening & alter.] *chiefly Brit* (ca. 1874) **:** UMBRELLA

brom- *or* **bromo-** *comb form* [prob. fr. F *brome*, fr. Gk *brōmos* bad smell] **:** bromine ⟨*bromide*⟩

[1]**bro·mate** \'brō-ˌmāt\ *n* (1836) **:** a salt of bromic acid

[2]**bromate** *vt* **bro·mat·ed; bro·mat·ing** (ca. 1890) **:** to treat with a bromate; *broadly* **:** BROMINATE

brome·grass \'brōm-ˌgras\ *n* [NL *Bromus*, fr. L *bromos* oats, fr. Gk] (ca. 1759) **:** any of a large genus (*Bromus*) of tall grasses often having drooping spikelets

bro·me·lain \'brō-mə-lən, -ˌlān\ *also* **bro·me·lin** \'brō-mə-lən, brō-'mē-\ *n* [*bromelain* by alter. (influenced by *papain*) of *bromelin*, fr. NL *Bromelia*, genus name of the pineapple in some classifications + E *-in*] (1894) **:** a proteinase obtained from the juice of the pineapple

bro·me·li·ad \brō-'mē-lē-ˌad\ *n* [NL *Bromelia*, genus of tropical American plants, fr. Olaf *Bromelius* †1705 Swed. botanist] (1866) **:** any of a family (Bromeliaceae) of chiefly tropical American and epiphytic herbaceous plants including the pineapple, Spanish moss, and various ornamentals

bro·mic acid \ˌbrō-mik-\ *n* (1828) **:** an unstable strongly oxidizing acid $HBrO_3$ known only in solution or in the form of its salts

bro·mide \'brō-ˌmīd\ *n* (1836) **1 :** a binary compound of bromine with another element or a radical including some (as potassium bromide) used as sedatives **2 a :** a commonplace or tiresome person **:** BORE **b :** a commonplace or hackneyed statement or notion

bro·mid·ic \brō-'mid-ik\ *adj* (1906) **:** lacking in originality **:** DULL, TRITE

bro·mi·nate \'brō-mə-ˌnāt\ *vt* **-nat·ed; -nat·ing** (1873) **:** to treat or cause to combine with bromine or a compound of bromine — **bro·mi·na·tion** \ˌbrō-mə-'nā-shən\ *n*

bro·mine \'brō-ˌmēn\ *n* [F *brome* bromine + E *-ine*] (1827) **:** a nonmetallic halogen element that is isolated as a deep red corrosive toxic volatile liquid of disagreeable odor — see ELEMENT table

bro·mism \'brō-ˌmiz-əm\ *n* (1867) **:** an abnormal state due to excessive or prolonged use of bromides

bro·mo \'brō-(ˌ)mō\ *n, pl* **bromos** [*brom-*] (1923) **:** a proprietary effervescent mixture used as a headache remedy, sedative, and alkalinizing agent; *also* **:** a dose of such a mixture

bro·mo·ura·cil \ˌbrō-mō-'yu̇r-ə-ˌsil, -səl\ *n* [*bromo-* + *uracil*] (1960) **:** a mutagenic uracil derivative $C_4H_3N_2O_2Br$ that is an analogue of thymine and pairs readily with adenine and sometimes with guanine during bacterial or phage DNA synthesis

brom·thy·mol blue \'brōm-'thī-ˌmȯl-\ *n* [*brom-* + *thymol*] (1920) **:** a dye derived from thymol that is an acid-base indicator

bronc \'bräŋk\ *n* [short for *bronco*] (1893) **:** an unbroken or imperfectly broken range horse of western No. America; *broadly* **:** MUSTANG

bronch- *or* **broncho-** *comb form* [prob. fr. F, throat, fr. LL, fr. Gk, fr. *bronchos* — more at CRAW] **:** bronchial tube **:** bronchial ⟨*bronchitis*⟩

bronchi- *or* **bronchio-** *comb form* [NL, fr. *bronchia*, pl. of *bronchium* a branch of the bronchi, fr. LL, fr. Gk, dim. of *bronchos* bronchus] **:** bronchial tubes ⟨*bronchiectasis*⟩

bron·chi·al \'bräŋ-kē-əl\ *adj* (1735) **:** of or relating to the bronchi or their ramifications in the lungs — **bron·chi·al·ly** \-ə-lē\ *adv*

bronchial asthma *n* (ca. 1885) **:** asthma resulting from spasmodic contraction of bronchial muscles

bronchial tube *n* (1847) **:** a primary bronchus or any of its branches

\ə\ abut \ᵊ\ kitten, F table \ər\ further \a\ ash \ā\ ace \ä\ cot, cart \au̇\ out \ch\ chin \e\ bet \ē\ easy \g\ go \i\ hit \ī\ ice \j\ job \ŋ\ sing \ō\ go \ȯ\ law \ȯi\ boy \th\ thin \t͟h\ the \ü\ loot \u̇\ foot \y\ yet \zh\ vision \á, k̲, ⁿ, œ, œ̄, ue, ue̅, ʸ\ *see* Guide to Pronunciation

bron·chi·ec·ta·sis \ˌbräŋ-kē-'ek-tə-səs\ *n* [NL, fr. *bronchi-* + *ectasis* (as in *atelectasis*)] (ca. 1860) : a chronic dilatation of bronchi or bronchioles
bron·chi·ole \'bräŋ-kē-ˌōl\ *n* [NL *bronchiolum*, dim. of *bronchium*] (ca. 1860) : a minute thin-walled branch of a bronchus — **bron·chi·o·lar** \ˌbräŋ-kē-'ō-lər\ *adj*
bron·chi·tis \brän-'kīt-əs, bräŋ-\ *n* (ca. 1808) : acute or chronic inflammation of the bronchial tubes; *also* : a disease marked by this — **bron·chit·ic** \-'kit-ik\ *adj*
bron·cho·di·la·tor \ˌbräŋ-(ˌ)kō-dī-'lāt-ər, -'dī-ˌ\ *n* (1903) : a drug that relaxes bronchial muscle resulting in expansion of the bronchial air passages — **bronchodilator** *adj*
bron·cho·gen·ic \ˌbräŋ-kə-'jen-ik\ *adj* (1927) : of, relating to, or arising in or by way of the air passages of the lungs ⟨~ carcinoma⟩
bron·cho·pneu·mo·nia \ˌbräŋ-(ˌ)kō-n(y)u̇-'mō-nyə\ *n* [NL] (1858) : pneumonia involving many relatively small areas of lung tissue
bron·cho·scope \'bräŋ-kə-ˌskōp\ *n* [ISV] (1899) : a tubular illuminated instrument used for inspecting or passing instruments into the bronchi — **bron·cho·scop·ic** \ˌbräŋ-kə-'skäp-ik\ *adj* — **bron·chos·co·pist** \brän-'käs-kə-pəst, bräŋ-\ *n* —**bron·chos·co·py** \-pē\ *n*
bron·cho·spasm \'bräŋ-kə-ˌspaz-əm\ *n* (ca. 1901) : constriction of the air passages of the lung (as in asthma) by spasmodic contraction of the bronchial muscles — **bron·cho·spas·tic** \ˌbräŋ-kə-'spas-tik\ *adj*
bron·chus \'bräŋ-kəs\ *n, pl* **bron·chi** \'bräŋ-ˌkī, -ˌkē\ [NL, fr. Gk *bronchos*] (ca. 1706) : either of the two primary divisions of the trachea that lead respectively into the right and the left lung; *broadly* : BRONCHIAL TUBE
bron·co *also* **bron·cho** \'bräŋ-(ˌ)kō\ *n, pl* **broncos** *also* **bronchos** [MexSp, fr. Sp. lit., rough, wild] (1850) : BRONC
bron·co·bust·er \-kō-ˌbəs-tər\ *n* (1887) : one who breaks wild horses to the saddle
bron·to·sau·rus \ˌbränt-ə-'sȯr-əs\ *or* **bron·to·saur** \'bränt-ə-ˌsȯ(ə)r\ *n* [deriv. of Gk *brontē* thunder + *sauros* lizard — more at SAURIAN] (1905) : any of various large quadrupedal and prob. herbivorous dinosaurs (genus *Apatosaurus*)
Bronx cheer \'bräŋ(k)s-\ *n* [*Bronx*, borough of New York City] (1929) : RASPBERRY 2
[1]**bronze** \'bränz\ *vt* **bronzed; bronz·ing** (1645) : to give the appearance of bronze to — **bronz·er** *n*
[2]**bronze** *n, often attrib* [F, fr. It *bronzo*] (1739) **1 a** : an alloy of copper and tin and sometimes other elements **b** : any of various copper-base alloys with little or no tin **2** : a sculpture or artifact of bronze **3** : a moderate yellowish brown — **bronzy** \'brän-zē\ *adj*
Bronze Age *n* (1865) : the period of human culture characterized by the use of bronze that began between 4000 and 3000 B.C.
Bronze Star Medal *n* (1944) : a U.S. military decoration awarded for heroic or meritorious service not involving aerial flights
bronz·ing *n* (1868) : a bronze coloring or discoloration (as of leaves)
brooch \'brōch, 'brüch\ *n* [ME *broche* pointed tool, brooch — more at BROACH] (13c) : an ornament that is held by a pin or clasp and is worn at or near the neck
[1]**brood** \'brüd\ *n* [ME, fr. OE *brōd*; akin to OE *beorma* yeast — more at BARM] (bef. 12c) **1** : the young of an animal or a family of young; *esp* : the young (as of a bird or insect) hatched or cared for at one time **2** : a group having a common nature or origin
[2]**brood** *adj* (14c) : kept for breeding ⟨a ~ mare⟩ ⟨a ~ flock⟩
[3]**brood** *vt* (15c) **1 a** : to sit on or incubate (eggs) **b** : to produce by or as if by incubation : HATCH **2** *of a bird* : to cover (young) with the wings **3** : to think anxiously or gloomily about : PONDER **~** *vi* **1 a** *of a bird* : to brood eggs or young **b** : to sit quietly and thoughtfully : MEDITATE **2** : HOVER, LOOM **3 a** : to dwell gloomily on a subject : WORRY **b** : to be in a state of depression — **brood·ing·ly** \-iŋ-lē\ *adv*
brood·er \'brüd-ər\ *n* (1599) **1** : one that broods **2** : a heated structure used for raising young fowl
broody \'brüd-ē\ *adj* (1513) **1 a** : suitable for producing offspring ⟨a strong ~ mare⟩ **b** : being in a state of readiness to brood eggs that is characterized by cessation of laying and by marked changes in behavior and physiology **2** : given or conducive to introspection : CONTEMPLATIVE, MOODY — **brood·i·ness** *n*
[1]**brook** \'bru̇k\ *vt* [ME *brouken* to use, enjoy, fr. OE *brūcan*; akin to OHG *brūhhan* to use, L *frui* to enjoy] (15c) : to stand for : TOLERATE ⟨he would ~ no interference with his plans⟩
[2]**brook** *n* [ME, fr. OE *brōc*; akin to OHG *bruoh* marshy ground] (bef. 12c) : CREEK 2
brook·ite \'bru̇k-ˌīt\ *n* [Henry J. *Brooke* †1857 Eng. mineralogist] (1825) : titanium dioxide TiO_2 occurring as a mineral in orthorhombic crystals commonly translucent brown or opaque brown to black
brook·let \'bru̇k-lət\ *n* (1813) : a small brook
Brook·lyn·ese \ˌbru̇k-lə-'nēz, -'nēs\ *n* [*Brooklyn*, borough of New York City + *-ese*] (1939) : the vernacular speech of greater New York City and environs
brook trout *n* (1836) : the common speckled cold-water char (*Salvelinus fontinalis*) of No. America
[1]**broom** \'brüm, 'bru̇m\ *n* [ME, fr. OE *brōm*; akin to OHG *brāmo* bramble, ME *brimme* brim] (bef. 12c) **1** : any of various leguminous shrubs (esp. genera *Cytisus Genista*) with long slender branches, small leaves, and usu. showy yellow flowers; *esp* : SCOTCH BROOM **2** : a bundle of firm stiff twigs or fibers bound together on a long handle for sweeping and brushing
[2]**broom** *vt* (1838) **1** : to sweep with or as if with a broom **2** : to finish (as a concrete surface) by means of a broom
broom·ball \-ˌbȯl\ *n* (1935) : a variation of ice hockey played on ice without skates and with brooms and a soccer ball used instead of sticks and a puck — **broom·ball·er** \-ˌbȯ-lər\ *n*
broom·corn \-ˌkȯ(ə)rn\ *n* (1781) : any of several tall cultivated sorghums whose stiff-branched panicle is used in brooms and brushes
broom·rape \-ˌrāp\ *n* (ca. 1578) : any of various leafless herbs (family Orobanchaceae, the broomrape family) growing as parasites on the roots of other plants
broom·stick \-ˌstik\ *n* (1683) : the long thin handle of a broom
brose \'brōz\ *n* [perh. alter. of Sc *bruis* broth, fr. ME *brewes* — more at BREWIS] (1515) : a chiefly Scottish dish made with a boiling liquid and meal
broth \'brȯth\ *n, pl* **broths** \'brȯths, 'brȯt͟hz\ [ME, fr. OE; akin to OHG *brod* broth, L *fervēre* to boil — more at BURN] (bef. 12c) **1** : liquid in which meat, fish, cereal grains, or vegetables have been cooked : STOCK **2** : a fluid culture medium
broth·el \'bräth-əl, 'brȯth-\ *n* [ME, worthless fellow, prostitute, fr. *brothen*, pp. of *brethen* to waste away, go to ruin, fr. OE *brēothan* to waste away; akin to OE *brēotan* to break — more at BRITTLE] (1593) : WHOREHOUSE
broth·er \'brət͟h-ər\ *n, pl* **brothers** *also* **breth·ren** \'bret͟h-(ə-)rən, 'bret͟h-ərn\ [ME, fr. OE *brōthor*; akin to OHG *bruodor* brother, L *frater*, Gk *phratēr* member of the same clan] (bef. 12c) **1** : a male who has the same parents as another or one parent in common with another **2 a** : KINSMAN **b** : one who shares with another a common national or racial origin; *esp* : SOUL BROTHER **3** : a fellow member — used as a title for ministers in some evangelical denominations **4** : one related to another by common ties or interests **5** : one of a type similar to another **6 a** *cap* : a member of a congregation of men not in holy orders and usu. in hospital or school work **5 b** : a member of a men's religious order who is not preparing for or is not ready for holy orders ⟨a lay ~⟩
broth·er·hood \'brət͟h-ər-ˌhu̇d\ *n* [ME *brotherhede, brotherhod*, alter. (influenced by ME *-hod* -hood) of *brotherrede*, fr. OE *brōthorrǣden*, fr. *brōthor* + *rǣden* condition — more at KINDRED] (bef. 12c) **1** : the quality or state of being brothers **2** : FELLOWSHIP, ALLIANCE **3** : an association (as a labor union) for a particular purpose **4** : the whole body of persons engaged in business or profession
broth·er–in–law \'brət͟h-(ə-)rən-ˌlȯ, 'brət͟h-ərn-ˌlȯ\ *n, pl* **broth·ers–in–law** \'brət͟h-ər-zən-\ (14c) **1** : the brother of one's spouse **2 a** : the husband of one's sister **b** : the husband of one's spouse's sister
broth·er·ly \'brət͟h-ər-lē\ *adj* (bef. 12c) **1** : of or relating to brothers **2** : natural or becoming to brothers : AFFECTIONATE ⟨~ love⟩ — **broth·er·li·ness** *n* — **brotherly** *adv*
brougham \'brü(-ə)m, 'brō(-ə)m\ *n* [Henry Peter *Brougham*, Baron Brougham and Vaux †1868 Scot. jurist] (1851) **1** : a light closed horse-drawn carriage with the driver outside in front **2** : a coupe automobile; *esp* : one driven electrically **3** : a sedan automobile having no roof over the driver's seat
brought *past and past part of* BRING
brou·ha·ha \'brü-ˌhä-ˌhä, ˌbrü-ˌhä-'hä, brü-'hä-ˌhä\ *n* [F] (1890) : HUBBUB, UPROAR
brow \'brau̇\ *n* [ME, fr. OE *brū*; akin to ON *brūn* eyebrow, Gk *ophrys*] (bef. 12c) **1 a** : EYEBROW **b** : FOREHEAD **2** : the projecting upper part or margin of a steep place **3** : EXPRESSION, MIEN ⟨a contemptuous ~⟩
brow·beat \'brau̇-ˌbēt\ *vt* **-beat; -beat·en** \-ˌbēt-ᵊn\ *or* **-beat; -beat·ing** (1581) : to intimidate or disconcert by a stern manner or arrogant speech : BULLY
-browed \'brau̇d\ *adj comb form* : having brows of a specified nature ⟨smooth-*browed*⟩
[1]**brown** \'brau̇n\ *adj* [ME *broun*, fr. OE *brūn*; akin to OHG *brūn* brown, Gk *phrynē* toad] (bef. 12c) : of the color brown; *esp* : of dark or tanned complexion
[2]**brown** *n* (13c) **1** : any of a group of colors between red and yellow in hue, of medium to low lightness, and of moderate to low saturation **2** : a brown-skinned person — **brown·ish** \'brau̇-nish\ *adj* — **browny** \-nē\ *adj*
[3]**brown** *vi* (14c) : to become brown **~** *vt* : to make brown
brown alga *n* (ca. 1899) : any of a division (Phaeophyta) of variable mostly marine algae with chlorophyll masked by brown pigment
brown bag·ging \-'bag-iŋ\ *n* (1959) **1** : the practice of carrying (as to work) one's lunch usu. in a brown paper bag **2** : the practice of carrying a bottle of liquor into a restaurant or club where setups are available — **brown–bag** \(ˈ)brau̇n-'bag\ *vb or adj* — **brown bag·ger** \-'bag-ər\ *n*
brown bear *n* (1805) : any of several bears predominantly brown in color that are sometimes lumped in a single species (*Ursus arctos*) including the grizzly bear and that formerly inhabited western No. America from the barrens of Alaska to northern Mexico and much of Europe and Asia but are now much restricted in range
brown Bet·ty \-'bet-ē\ *n* (1864) : a baked pudding of apples, bread crumbs, and spices
brown bread \-ˌbred\ *n* (14c) **1** : bread made of whole wheat flour **2** : a dark brown steamed bread made usu. of cornmeal, white or whole wheat flours, molasses, soda, and milk or water
brown coal *n* (ca. 1828) : LIGNITE
brown earth *n* (1932) : any of a group of intrazonal soils developed in temperate humid regions under deciduous forests and characterized by a dark brown mull horizon that grades through lighter colored soil into parent material
brown–eyed Su·san \ˌbrau̇-ˌnīd-'süz-ᵊn\ *n* [*brown-eyed* + *Susan* (as in black-eyed *Susan*)] (ca. 1900) : a dark-centered coneflower (*Rudbeckia triloba*) of eastern No. America with tripartite lower leaves
brown fat *n* (1951) : a mammalian heat-producing tissue occurring esp. in human embryos and newborn infants and in hibernators
Brown·ian movement \ˌbrau̇-nē-ən-\ *n* [Robert *Brown* †1858 Scot. botanist] (1874) : a random movement of microscopic particles suspended in liquids or gases resulting from the impact of molecules of the fluid surrounding the particles — called also *Brownian motion*
brown·ie \'brau̇-nē\ *n* [[1]*brown*] (ca. 1500) **1** : a legendary good-natured elf that performs helpful services at night **2** *cap* : a member of the Girl Scouts of the United States of America from 6 through 8 years of age **3** : a small square or rectangle of rich usu. chocolate cake often containing nuts
brownie point *n, often cap B* (ca. 1962) : a credit regarded as earned esp. by currying favor with a superior
Brow·ning automatic rifle \'brau̇-niŋ-\ *n* [John M. *Browning* †1926 Am. designer of firearms] (1920) : a .30 caliber gas-operated air-cooled magazine-fed automatic rifle often provided with a rest for the barrel and used by U.S. troops in World War II and the Korean war
Browning machine gun *n* (1918) : a .30 or .50 caliber recoil-operated air- or water-cooled machine gun fed by a cartridge belt and used by U.S. troops in World War II and the Korean war

brown·nose \ˈbrau̇n-ˌnōz\ *vt* [fr. the implication that servility is equivalent to kissing the hinder parts of the person from whom advancement is sought] *slang* (ca. 1939) : to ingratiate oneself with : curry favor with — **brownnose** *n* — **brown·nos·er** *n*
brown·out \ˈbrau̇-ˌnau̇t\ *n* [*brown* + *-out* (as in *blackout*)] (1942) : a curtailment of the use of electric power; *also* : a period of reduced illumination resulting from such curtailment
brown rat *n* (1826) : the common domestic rat (*Rattus norvegicus*) — called also *Norway rat*
brown recluse spider *n* (1964) : a venomous spider (*Loxosceles reclusa*) introduced into the southern U.S. that has a violin-shaped mark on the cephalothorax and produces a dangerous neurotoxin
brown rice *n* (1916) : hulled but unpolished rice that retains most of the bran layers, endosperm, and germ
brown rot *n* (1894) : a disease of stone and pome fruits caused by fungi (genus *Sclerotinia*, esp. *S. fructicola*)
brown sauce *n* (1878) : a sauce consisting typically of stock thickened with flour browned in fat
brown·shirt \ˈbrau̇n-ˌshərt\ *n, often cap* (1932) : NAZI; *esp* : STORM TROOPER
brown·stone \-ˌstōn\ *n* (1836) **1** : a reddish brown sandstone used for building **2** : a dwelling faced with brownstone
brown study *n* (1532) : a state of serious absorption or abstraction
brown sugar *n* (1704) : soft sugar whose crystals are covered by a film of refined dark syrup
Brown Swiss *n* (ca. 1902) : any of a breed of large hardy brown dairy cattle originating in Switzerland
brown–tail moth \ˌbrau̇n-ˌtāl-\ *n* (1782) : a tussock moth (*Nygmia phaeorrhoea*) whose larvae feed on foliage and are irritating to the skin
brown trout *n* (1886) : a speckled European trout (*Salmo trutta*) widely introduced as a game fish
brow·ridge \ˈbrau̇-ˌrij\ *n* (1898) : a prominence of the frontal bone above the eye caused by the projection of the frontal air sinuses
1browse \ˈbrau̇z\ *vb* **browsed; brows·ing** *vt* (15c) **1 a** : to consume as browse **b** : GRAZE **2** : to look over casually : SKIM ~ *vi* **1 a** : to feed on or as if on browse **b** : GRAZE **2 a** : to skim through a book reading at random passages that catch the eye **b** : to look over or through an aggregate of things casually esp. in search of something of interest — **brows·er** *n*
2browse *n* [prob. modif. of MF *brouts*, pl. of *brout* sprout, fr. OF *brost*, of Gmc origin; akin to OS *brustian* to spout, OE *brēost* breast] (1523) **1** : tender shoots, twigs, and leaves of trees and shrubs used by animals for food **2** : an act or instance of browsing
bru·cel·la \brü-ˈsel-ə\ *n, pl* **-cel·lae** \-ˈsel-(ˌ)ē\ *or* **-cel·las** [NL, fr. Sir David *Bruce*] (1930) : any of a genus (*Brucella*) of nonmotile capsulated bacteria that cause disease in man and domestic animals
bru·cel·lo·sis \ˌbrü-sə-ˈlō-səs\ *n, pl* **-lo·ses** \-ˌsēz\ (1930) : infection with or disease caused by brucellae esp. in man or cattle
bru·cine \ˈbrü-ˌsēn\ *n* [prob. fr. F, fr. NL *Brucea* (genus name of *Brucea antidysenterica*, a shrub)] (ca. 1823) : a poisonous alkaloid $C_{23}H_{26}N_2O_4$ found with strychnine esp. in nux vomica
bru·in \ˈbrü-ən\ *n* [D, name of the bear in *Reynard the Fox*] (15c) : BEAR
1bruise \ˈbrüz\ *vb* **bruised; bruis·ing** [ME *brusen, brisen*, fr. AF & OE; AF *bruisier* to break, of Celt origin; akin to OIr *brūu* I shatter; OE *brȳsan* to bruise; akin to OIr *brūu*, L *frustum* piece] *vt* (bef. 12c) **1 a** *archaic* : DISABLE **b** : BATTER, DENT **2** : to inflict a bruise on : CONTUSE **3** : to break down (as leaves or berries) by pounding : CRUSH **4** : WOUND, INJURE; *esp* : to inflict psychological hurt on ~ *vi* **1** : to inflict a bruise **2** : to undergo bruising ⟨tomatoes ~ easily⟩
2bruise *n* (1541) **1 a** : an injury involving rupture of small blood vessels and discoloration without a break in the overlying skin : CONTUSION **b** : a similar injury to plant tissue **2** : ABRASION, SCRATCH **3** : an injury esp. to the feelings
bruis·er \ˈbrü-zər\ *n* (1744) : a big husky man
1bruit *n* [ME, fr. MF, fr. OF, noise] (15c) **1** \ˈbrüt\ *archaic* **a** : NOISE, DIN **b** : REPORT, RUMOR **2** \ˈbrü-ē\ [F, lit., noise] : any of several generally abnormal sounds heard on auscultation
2bruit \ˈbrüt\ *vt* (1525) : to noise abroad : REPORT
bru·mal \ˈbrü-məl\ *adj* [L *brumalis*, fr. L *bruma* winter] *archaic* (1513) : indicative of or occurring in the winter
brum·by \ˈbrəm-bē\ *n, pl* **brumbies** [prob. native name in Queensland, Australia] *Austral* (1880) : a wild or unbroken horse
brume \ˈbrüm\ *n* [F, mist, winter, fr. OProv *bruma*, fr. L, winter; akin to L *brevis* short — more at BRIEF] (1808) : MIST, FOG — **bru·mous** \ˈbrü-məs\ *adj*
brum·ma·gem \ˈbrəm-i-jəm\ *adj* [alter. of *Birmingham*, England, the source in the 17th cent. of counterfeit groats] (1637) : SPURIOUS; *also* : cheaply showy : TAWDRY — **brummagem** *n*
brunch \ˈbrənch\ *n* [*b*reakfast + l*unch*] (1896) : a meal usu. taken late in the morning that combines a late breakfast and an early lunch
1bru·net *or* **bru·nette** \brü-ˈnet\ *n* (ca. 1534) : a person having brown or black hair and usu. a relatively dark complexion
2brunet *or* **brunette** *adj* [F *brunet*, masc., *brunette*, fem., brownish, fr. OF, fr. *brun* brown, fr. ML *brunus*, of Gmc origin; akin to OHG *brūn*, brown — more at BROWN] (1712) **1** : being a brunet ⟨his ~ wife⟩ **2** : of a dark-brown or black color ⟨~ hair⟩
Brun·hild \ˈbrün-ˌhilt\ *n* [G] : a queen in Germanic legend won by Siegfried for Gunther
bru·ni·zem \ˌbrü-nə-ˈzem, -ˈzhȯm\ *n* [*bruni-* (fr. ML *brunus* brown) + *-zem* earth (as in *chernozem*)] (1954) : any of a zonal group of deep dark prairie soils developed from loess
Bruns·wick stew \ˌbrənz-(ˌ)wik-\ *n* [*Brunswick* county, Va.] (1856) : a stew made of vegetables and usu. of two meats (as chicken and squirrel)
brunt \ˈbrənt\ *n* [ME] (15c) **1** : the principal force, shock, or stress (as of an attack) **2** : the greater part : BURDEN
1brush \ˈbrəsh\ *n* [ME *brusch*, fr. MF *broce*] (14c) **1** : BRUSHWOOD **2 a** : scrub vegetation **b** : land covered with scrub vegetation
2brush *n* [ME *brusshe*, fr. MF *broisse*, fr. OF *broce*] (14c) **1** : a device composed of bristles set into a handle and used esp. for sweeping, smoothing, scrubbing, or painting **2** : something resembling a brush: as **a** : a bushy tail **b** : a feather tuft worn on a hat **3 a** : an electrical conductor (as of copper strips or carbon) that makes sliding contact between a stationary and a moving part of a generator or a motor **b** : BRUSH DISCHARGE **4 a** : an act of brushing **b** : a quick light touch or momentary contact in passing
3brush *vt* (15c) **1 a** : to apply a brush to **b** : to apply with a brush **2 a** : to remove with passing strokes (as of a brush) **b** : to dispose of in an offhand way : DISMISS ⟨~*ed* him off⟩ **3** : to pass lightly over or across : touch gently against in passing — **brush·er** *n*
4brush *n* [ME *brusche* rush, hostile collision, fr. *bruschen*] (14c) : a brief encounter or skirmish
5brush *vi* [ME *bruschen* to rush, fr. MF *brosser* to dash through underbrush, fr. *broce*] (1674) : to move lightly or heedlessly ⟨~*ed* past the well-wishers waiting to greet him⟩
brush·abil·i·ty \ˌbrəsh-ə-ˈbil-ət-ē\ *n* (1936) : ease of application with a brush ⟨~ of a paint⟩
brush·back \ˈbrəsh-ˌbak\ *n* (1954) : a fastball thrown near the batter's head in baseball in an attempt to make him move back from home plate — **brush back** \(ˈ)brəsh-ˈbak\ *vt*
brush border *n* (1903) : a stria of microvilli on the plasma membrane of an epithelial cell (as in a kidney tubule) that is specialized for absorption
brush discharge *n* (1849) : a faintly luminous relatively slow electrical discharge having no spark
brushed \ˈbrəsht\ *adj* (1711) : finished with a nap ⟨a ~ fabric⟩
brush·fire \ˈbrəsh-ˌfī(ə)r\ *adj* [*brush fire* (a fire involving brush but not full-sized trees)] (1954) : involving mobilization only on a small and local scale ⟨~ border wars⟩
brush·land \-ˌland\ *n* (1853) : an area covered with brush growth
brush–off \-ˌȯf\ *n* (1941) : a quietly curt or disdainful dismissal
brush up \(ˈ)brəsh-ˈəp\ *vt* (1600) **1** : to polish by eliminating small imperfections **2** : to renew one's skill in ~ *vi* : to refresh one's memory : renew one's skill ⟨*brush up* on math⟩ — **brush·up** \ˈbrəsh-ˌəp\ *n*
brush·wood \ˈbrəsh-ˌwu̇d\ *n* (1613) **1** : wood of small branches esp. when cut or broken **2** : a thicket of shrubs and small trees
brush·work \-ˌwərk\ *n* (1868) : work done with a brush (as in painting); *esp* : the characteristic work of an artist using a brush
1brushy \ˈbrəsh-ē\ *adj* **brush·i·er; -est** (1658) : covered with or abounding in brush or brushwood
2brushy *adj* **brush·i·er; -est** (1687) : SHAGGY, ROUGH
brusque *also* **brusk** \ˈbrəsk\ *adj* [F *brusque*, fr. It *brusco*, fr. ML *bruscus* butcher's-broom (plant with bristly twigs)] (1651) **1** : markedly short and abrupt **2** : blunt in manner or speech often to the point of ungracious harshness *syn* see BLUFF — **brusque·ly** *adv* — **brusque·ness** *n*
brus·que·rie \ˌbrəs-kə-ˈrē\ *n* [F, fr. *brusque*] (1752) : abruptness of manner
Brus·sels carpet \ˌbrəs-əlz-\ *n* [*Brussels*, Belgium] (1799) : a carpet made of colored worsted yarns first fixed in a foundation web of strong linen thread and then drawn up in loops to form the pattern
Brussels griffon *n* (1904) : any of a breed of short-faced compact rough- or smooth-coated toy dogs of Belgian origin — called also *griffon*

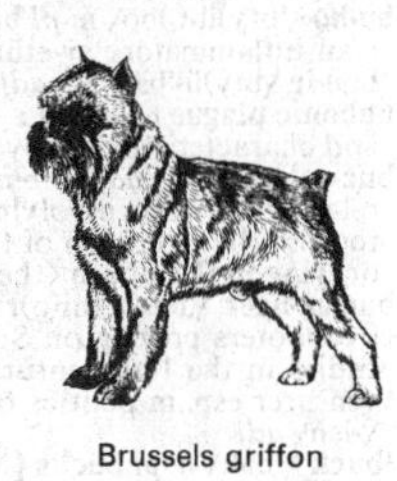
Brussels griffon

Brussels lace *n* (1748) **1** : any of various fine needlepoint or bobbin laces with floral designs made orig. in or near Brussels **2** : a machine-made net of hexagonal mesh
brus·sels sprout \ˌbrəs-əl-\ *n, often cap B* (1796) **1** *pl* : a plant (*Brassica oleracea gemmifera*) of the mustard family that bears small edible green heads on its stem **2** : any of the edible green heads borne on brussels sprouts — usu. used in pl.
brut \ˈbrüt, ˈbrüᵉt\ *adj* [F, lit., rough] *of champagne* (1891) : very dry; *specif* : being the driest made by the producer
bru·tal \ˈbrüt-ᵊl\ *adj* [ME, fr. MF or ML; MF, fr. ML *brutalis*, fr. L *brutus*] (15c) **1** *archaic* : typical of beasts : ANIMAL **2** : befitting a brute: as **a** : grossly ruthless or unfeeling ⟨a ~ slander⟩ **b** : CRUEL, COLD-BLOODED ⟨a ~ attack⟩ **c** : HARSH, SEVERE ⟨~ weather⟩ **d** : unpleasantly accurate and incisive ⟨the ~ truth⟩ — **bru·tal·ly** \-ᵊl-ē\ *adv*
bru·tal·i·ty \brü-ˈtal-ət-ē\ *n, pl* **-ties** (1549) **1** : the quality or state of being brutal **2** : a brutal act or course of action
bru·tal·ize \ˈbrüt-ᵊl-ˌīz\ *vt* **-ized; -iz·ing** (1704) **1** : to make brutal, unfeeling, or inhuman ⟨temperaments *brutalized* by poverty and disease⟩ **2** : to treat brutally ⟨an accord not to ~ prisoners of war⟩ — **bru·tal·iza·tion** \ˌbrüt-ᵊl-ə-ˈzā-shən\ *n*
1brute \ˈbrüt\ *adj* [ME, fr. MF *brut* rough, fr. L *brutus* stupid, lit., heavy; akin to L *gravis* heavy — more at GRIEVE] (15c) **1** : of or relating to beasts ⟨the ways of the ~ world⟩ **2** : INANIMATE 1a **3** : characteristic of an animal in quality, action, or instinct: as **a** : CRUEL, SAVAGE ⟨~ force⟩ **b** : not working by reason ⟨~ instinct⟩ **4** : purely physical ⟨~ strength⟩ **5** : being of unrelieved severity ⟨~ necessity⟩
2brute *n* (1611) **1** : BEAST **2** : a brutal person
brut·ish \ˈbrüt-ish\ *adj* (1534) **1** : befitting beasts ⟨lived a short and ~ life as a slave⟩ **2 a** : strongly and grossly sensual ⟨~ gluttony⟩ **b** : showing little intelligence or sensibility ⟨a ~ lack of understanding⟩ — **brut·ish·ly** *adv* — **brut·ish·ness** *n*
brux·ism \ˈbrək-ˌsiz-əm\ *n* [irreg. fr. Gk *brychein* to gnash the teeth + E *-ism*] (ca. 1940) : the habit of unconsciously gritting or grinding the teeth esp. in situations of stress or during sleep
Bryn·hild \ˈbrin-ˌhild\ *n* [ON *Brynhildr*] : a Valkyrie who is waked from an enchanted sleep by Sigurd and later has him killed when he forgets her
bry·ol·o·gy \brī-ˈäl-ə-jē\ *n* [Gk *bryon* moss + ISV *-logy*] (1863) **1** : moss life or biology **2** : a branch of botany that deals with the bryophytes
bry·o·ny \ˈbrī-ə-nē\ *n, pl* **-nies** [ME, fr. L *bryonia*, fr. Gk *bryōnia*; akin to Gk *bryon*] (14c) : any of a genus (*Bryonia*) of tendril-bearing vines of the gourd family with large leaves and red or black fruit

bryo·phyl·lum \ˌbrī-ə-ˈfil-əm\ *n* [NL, fr. Gk *bryon* + Gk *phyllon* leaf — more at BLADE] (1897) **:** any of various kalanchoes; *esp* **:** a succulent kalanchoe (*Kalanchoe pinnata*) often grown as a foliage plant that propagates new plants from its leaves

bryo·phyte \ˈbrī-ə-ˌfīt\ *n* [deriv. of Gk *bryon* + *phyton* plant; akin to Gk *phyein* to bring forth — more at BE] (1878) **:** any of a division (Bryophyta) of nonflowering plants comprising the mosses and liverworts — **bryo·phyt·ic** \ˌbrī-ə-ˈfit-ik\ *adj*

bryo·zo·an \ˌbrī-ə-ˈzō-ən\ *n* [NL *Bryozoa*, fr. Gk *bryon* + NL *-zoa*] (ca. 1864) **:** any of a phylum or class (Bryozoa) of aquatic mostly marine invertebrate animals that reproduce by budding and usu. form permanently attached branched or mossy colonies — **bryozoan** *adj*

Bryth·on \ˈbrith-ˌän, -ən\ *n* (ca. 1884) **1 :** a member of the British branch of Celts **2 :** a speaker of a Brythonic language

[1]**Bry·thon·ic** \brith-ˈän-ik\ *adj* (ca. 1884) **1 :** of, relating to, or characteristic of the Brythons **2 :** of, relating to, or characteristic of the division of the Celtic languages that includes Welsh, Cornish, and Breton

[2]**Brythonic** *n* (ca. 1884) **:** the Brythonic branch of the Celtic languages — see INDO-EUROPEAN LANGUAGES table

[1]**bub·ble** \ˈbəb-əl\ *n* [ME *bobel*] *often attrib* (14c) **1 :** a small globule typically hollow and light: as **a :** a small body of gas within a liquid **b :** a thin film of liquid inflated with air or gas **c :** a globule in a transparent solid **d :** something that is hemispherical or semicylindrical **2 a :** something that lacks firmness, solidity, or reality **b :** a delusive scheme **3 :** a sound like that of bubbling **4 :** MAGNETIC BUBBLE

[2]**bubble** *vb* **bub·bled; bub·bling** \ˈbəb-(ə-)liŋ\ *vi* (15c) **1 :** to form or produce bubbles **2 :** to flow with a gurgling sound ⟨a brook *bubbling* over rocks⟩ **3 a :** to become lively or effervescent ⟨*bubbling* with good humor⟩ **b :** to speak in a lively and fluent manner ~ *vt* **1 :** to utter (as words) effervescently **2 :** to cause to bubble

bubble and squeak *n, chiefly Brit* (1772) **:** a dish consisting of usu. leftover potatoes, cabbage, and sometimes meat fried together

bubble chamber *n* (1953) **:** a chamber of superheated liquid in which the path of an ionizing particle is made visible by a string of vapor bubbles

bubble gum *n* (1939) **1 :** a chewing gum that can be blown into large bubbles **2 :** rock music characterized by simple repetitive phrasings and intended esp. for young teenagers

bub·ble·head \ˈbəb-əl-ˌhed\ *n* (1949) **:** a foolish or stupid person — **bub·ble·head·ed** \-ˈhed-əd\ *adj*

bub·bler \ˈbəb-(ə-)lər\ *n* (1720) **1 :** one that bubbles **2 :** a drinking fountain from which a stream of water bubbles upward

[1]**bub·bly** \ˈbəb-(ə-)lē\ *adj* **bub·bli·er; -est** (1599) **1 :** full of bubbles **:** EFFERVESCENT ⟨a ~ bottle of pop⟩ **2 :** showing lively good spirits ⟨a ~ group at the party⟩ **3 :** resembling a bubble ⟨a ~ dome⟩

[2]**bubbly** *n* (1920) **:** CHAMPAGNE

bubby *var of* BOOBY

bu·bo \ˈb(y)ü-(ˌ)bō\ *n, pl* **buboes** [ML *bubon-, bubo*, fr. Gk *boubōn*] (14c) **:** an inflammatory swelling of a lymph gland esp. in the groin — **bu·bon·ic** \b(y)ü-ˈbän-ik\ *adj*

bubonic plague *n* (1885) **:** plague caused by a bacterium (*Yersinia pestis*) and characterized esp. by the formation of buboes

buc·cal \ˈbək-əl\ *adj* [L *bucca* cheek — more at POCK] (ca. 1771) **1 :** of, relating to, near, involving, or supplying a cheek ⟨the ~ surface of a tooth⟩ ⟨the ~ branch of the facial nerve⟩ **2 :** of, relating to, involving, or lying in the mouth ⟨the ~ cavity⟩ — **buc·cal·ly** \-ē\ *adv*

buc·ca·neer \ˌbək-ə-ˈni(ə)r\ *n* [F *boucanier*] (ca. 1690) **1 :** one of the freebooters preying on Spanish ships and settlements esp. in the West Indies in the 17th century; *broadly* **:** PIRATE **2 :** an unscrupulous adventurer esp. in politics or business — **buccaneer** *vi* — **buc·ca·neer·ish** \-ish\ *adj*

[1]**buck** \ˈbək\ *n, pl* **bucks** [ME, fr. OE *bucca* stag, he-goat; akin to OHG *boc* he-goat, MIr *bocc*] (bef. 12c) **1** *or pl* **buck :** a male animal; *esp* **:** a male deer or antelope **2 a :** a male human being **:** MAN **b :** a dashing fellow **:** DANDY **3** *or pl* **buck :** ANTELOPE **4 a :** BUCKSKIN; *also* **:** an article (as a shoe) made of buckskin **b (1) :** DOLLAR 3b **(2) :** a sum of money ⟨make a quick ~⟩; *also* **:** MONEY — usu. used in pl. ⟨big ~s⟩ **5** [short for *sawbuck*] **:** SAWHORSE **6 a :** a supporting rack or frame **b :** a short thick leather-covered block for gymnastic vaulting

[2]**buck** *vt* (1750) **1 a** *archaic* **:** [1]BUTT **b :** OPPOSE, RESIST ⟨~*ing* a trend⟩ **2 :** to throw (as a rider) by bucking **3 :** to charge into (as the opponent's line in football) **4 a :** to pass esp. from one person to another **b :** to move or load (as heavy objects) esp. with mechanical equipment ~ *vi* **1** *of a horse or mule* **:** to spring into the air with the back arched **2 :** to charge against something (as an obstruction) **3 a :** to move or react jerkily **b :** to refuse assent **:** BALK **4 :** to strive for advancement sometimes without regard to ethical behavior — **buck·er** *n*

[3]**buck** *n* (1877) **:** an act or instance of bucking

[4]**buck** *n* [short for earlier *buckhorn knife*] (1865) **1 :** an object formerly used in poker to mark the next player to deal; *broadly* **:** a token used as a mark or reminder **2 :** RESPONSIBILITY — used esp. in the phrases *pass the buck* and *the buck stops here*

[5]**buck** *adj* [prob. fr. [1]*buck*] (1918) **:** of the lowest grade within a military category ⟨~ private⟩

[6]**buck** *adv* [origin unknown] *Southern & Midland* (1928) **:** STARK ⟨~ naked⟩

buck-and-wing \ˌbək-ən-ˈwiŋ\ *n* (1895) **:** a solo tap dance with sharp foot accents, springs, leg flings, and heel clicks

buck·a·roo *also* **buck·er·oo** \ˌbək-ə-ˈrü, ˈbək-ə-ˌ\ *n, pl* **-aroos** *or* **-eroos** [by folk etymology fr. Sp *vaquero*, fr. *vaca* cow, fr. L *vacca* — more at VACCINE] (1827) **1 :** COWBOY **2 :** BRONCOBUSTER

buck·bean \ˈbək-ˌbēn\ *n* (1578) **:** a plant (*Menyanthes trifoliata* of the family Menyanthaceae) growing in bogs and having racemes of white or purplish flowers

buck·board \-ˌbō(ə)rd, -ˌbȯ(ə)rd\ *n* [obs. E *buck* body of a wagon + E *board*] (1839) **:** a four-wheeled vehicle with a springy platform

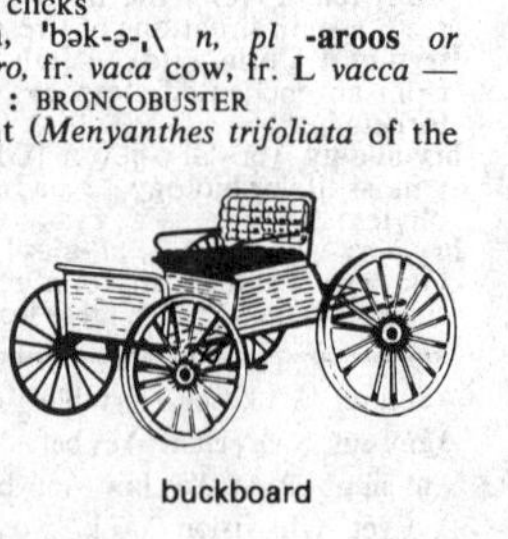
buckboard

[1]**buck·et** \ˈbək-ət\ *n* [ME, fr. AF *buket*, fr. OE *būc* pitcher, belly; akin to OHG *būh* belly, Skt *bhūri* abundant — more at BIG] (13c) **1 :** a typically round vessel for catching, holding, or carrying liquids or solids **2 :** something resembling a bucket: as **a :** the scoop of an excavating machine **b :** one of the receptacles on the rim of a waterwheel **c :** one of the cups of an endless-belt conveyor **d :** one of the vanes of a turbine rotor **3 :** a large quantity **4 :** BUCKET SEAT

[2]**bucket** *vt* (1649) **1 :** to draw or lift in buckets **2** *Brit* **a :** to ride (a horse) hard **b :** to drive hurriedly or roughly **3 :** to deal with in a bucket shop ~ *vi* **1 :** HUSTLE, HURRY **2 a :** to move about haphazardly or irresponsibly **b :** to move roughly or jerkily

bucket brigade *n* (1911) **:** a chain of persons acting to put out a fire by passing buckets of water from hand to hand

buck·et·ful \ˈbək-ət-ˌfu̇l\ *n, pl* **bucketfuls** \-ˌfu̇lz\ *or* **buck·ets·ful** \-əts-ˌfu̇l\ (1563) **:** as much as a bucket will hold

bucket seat *n* (1908) **:** a low separate seat for one person (as in automobiles and airplanes)

bucket shop *n* (1875) **1 :** a saloon in which liquor was formerly sold from or dispensed in open containers (as buckets or pitchers) **2 a :** a gambling establishment that formerly used market fluctuations (as in securities or commodities) as a basis for gaming **b :** a dishonest brokerage firm; *esp* **:** one that formerly failed to execute customers' margin orders in expectation of market fluctuations adverse to their interests

buck·eye \ˈbək-ˌī\ *n* (1763) **1 :** a shrub or tree (genus *Aesculus*) of the horse-chestnut family; *also* **:** its large nutlike seed **2** *cap* **:** a native or resident of Ohio — used as a nickname

buck fever *n* (1841) **:** nervous excitement of an inexperienced hunter at the sight of game

[1]**buck·le** \ˈbək-əl\ *n* [ME *bocle*, fr. MF, boss of a shield, buckle, fr. L *buccula*, dim. of *bucca* cheek — more at POCK] (14c) **1 :** a fastening for two loose ends that is attached to one and holds the other by a catch **2 :** an ornamental device that suggests a buckle **3** *archaic* **:** a crisp curl

[2]**buckle** *vb* **buck·led; buck·ling** \ˈbək-(ə-)liŋ\ *vt* (14c) **1 :** to fasten with a buckle **2 :** to prepare with vigor ⟨*buckled* himself to the task⟩ **3 :** to cause to bend, give way, or crumple ~ *vi* **1 :** to become fastened with a buckle **2 :** to apply oneself with vigor ⟨~*s* down to the job⟩ **3 :** to bend, heave, warp, or kink usu. under the influence of some external agency ⟨wheat *buckling* in the wind⟩ **4 :** COLLAPSE ⟨the props *buckled* under the strain⟩ **5 :** to give way **:** YIELD ⟨he *buckled* under pressure⟩

[3]**buckle** *n* (ca. 1876) **:** a product of buckling

[1]**buck·ler** \ˈbək-lər\ *n* [ME *bocler*, fr. MF, shield with a boss, fr. *bocle*] (14c) **1 a :** a small round shield held by a handle at arm's length **b :** a shield worn on the left arm **2 :** one that shields and protects

[2]**buckler** *vt* (1590) **:** to shield or defend with a buckler

bucko \ˈbək-(ˌ)ō\ *n, pl* **buck·oes** (1883) **1 :** one who is domineering and bullying **:** SWAGGERER **2** *chiefly Irish* **:** young fellow **:** LAD

buck passer *n* [[4]*buck*] (1920) **:** a person who habitually passes the buck — **buck–pass·ing** \ˈbək-ˌpas-iŋ\ *n*

[1]**buck·ram** \ˈbək-rəm\ *n* [ME *bukeram*, fr. OF *boquerant*, fr. OProv *bocaran*, prob. fr. *Bokhara*, city of central Asia] (15c) **1 :** a stiff-finished heavily sized fabric of cotton or linen used for interlinings in garments, for stiffening in millinery, and in bookbinding **2** *archaic* **:** STIFFNESS, RIGIDITY

[2]**buckram** *adj* (1589) **:** suggesting buckram esp. in stiffness or formality

[3]**buckram** *vt* (1783) **1 :** to give strength or stiffness to (as with buckram) **2** *archaic* **:** to make pretentious

buck·saw \ˈbək-ˌsȯ\ *n* (1856) **:** a saw set in a usu. H-shaped frame that is used for sawing wood

buck·shee \ˈbək-(ˌ)shē, ˌbək-ˈ\ *n* [Hindi *bakhśīś*] (1755) **1** *Brit* **:** something extra obtained free; *esp* **:** extra rations **2** *Brit* **:** WINDFALL, GRATUITY

buck·shot \ˈbək-ˌshät\ *n* (1775) **:** lead shot that is from .24 to .33 inches in diameter

buck·skin \-ˌskin\ *n* (13c) **1 a :** the skin of a buck **b :** a soft pliable usu. suede-finished leather **2 a** *pl* **:** buckskin breeches **b** *archaic* **:** a person dressed in buckskin; *esp* **:** an early American backwoodsman **3 :** a horse of a light yellowish dun color with black mane and tail — **buckskin** *adj*

buck·tail \-ˌtāl\ *n* (1911) **:** an angler's lure made typically of hairs from the tail of a deer

buck·thorn \-ˌthȯ(ə)rn\ *n* (1578) **1 :** any of a genus (*Rhamnus* of the family Rhamnaceae, the buckthorn family) of often thorny trees or shrubs some of which yield purgatives or pigments **2 :** a tree (*Bumelia lycioides*) of the sapodilla family of the southern U.S.

buck·tooth \-ˈtüth\ *n* (1753) **:** a large projecting front tooth — **buck–toothed** \-ˈtütht\ *adj*

buck up *vb* [[2]*buck*] *vi* (1844) **:** to become encouraged ~ *vt* **1 :** IMPROVE, SMARTEN **2 :** to raise the morale of

buck·wheat \ˈbək-ˌ(h)wēt\ *n* [D *boekweit*, fr. MD *boecweit*, fr. *boec-* (akin to OHG *buohha* beech tree) + *weit* wheat — more at BEECH] (1548) **1 :** any of a genus (*Fagopyrum* of the family Polygonaceae, the buckwheat family) of herbs with alternate leaves, clusters of apetalous pinkish white flowers and triangular seeds; *esp* **:** either of two plants (*F. esculentum* and *F. tartaricum*) cultivated for their edible seeds **2 :** the seed of a buckwheat used as a cereal grain

bu·col·ic \byü-ˈkäl-ik\ *adj* [L *bucolicus*, fr. Gk *boukolikos*, fr. *boukolos* cowherd, fr. *bous* head of cattle + *-kolos* (akin to L *colere* to cultivate) — more at COW, WHEEL] (ca. 1613) **1 :** of or relating to shepherds or herdsmen **:** PASTORAL **2 :** relating to or typical of rural life — **bu·col·i·cal·ly** \-i-k(ə-)lē\ *adv*

[1]**bud** \ˈbəd\ *n* [ME *budde*; akin to OE *budda* beetle, Skt *bhūri* abundant — more at BIG] (14c) **1 :** a small lateral or terminal protuberance on the stem of a plant that may develop into a flower, leaf, or shoot **2 :** something not yet mature or at full development: as **a :** an incompletely opened flower **b :** CHILD, YOUTH **c :** an outgrowth of an organism that differentiates into a new individual **:** GEMMA; *also* **:** PRIMORDIUM — **in the bud :** in an early stage of development ⟨nipped the rebellion *in the bud*⟩

[2]**bud** *vb* **bud·ded; bud·ding** *vi* (14c) **1** *of a plant* **a :** to set or put forth buds **b :** to commence growth from buds **2 :** to develop by way of outgrowth **3 :** to reproduce asexually esp. by the pinching off of a small part of the parent ~ *vt* **1 :** to produce or develop from buds **2 :** to cause (as a plant) to bud **3 :** to insert a bud from a plant of one

kind into an opening in the bark of (a plant of another kind) usu. in order to propagate a desired variety — **bud·der** *n*

Bud·dha \'büd-ə, 'bu̇d-\ *n* [Skt, enlightened; akin to Skt *bodhi* enlightenment — more at BID] (1681) **1 :** a person who has attained Buddhahood **2 :** a representation of Gautama Buddha

Bud·dha·hood \-,hu̇d\ *n* (1837) **:** a state of perfect enlightenment sought in Buddhism

Bud·dhism \'bü-,diz-əm, 'bu̇d-,iz-\ *n* (1801) **:** a religion of eastern and central Asia growing out of the teaching of Gautama Buddha that suffering is inherent in life and that one can be liberated from it by mental and moral self-purification — **Bud·dhist** \'büd-əst, 'bu̇d-\ *n or adj* — **Bud·dhis·tic** \bü-'dis-tik, bu̇-\ *adj*

bud·ding \'bəd-iŋ\ *adj* (1581) **:** being in an early stage of development ⟨~ novelists⟩

bud·dle \'bəd-ᵊl\ *n* [origin unknown] (1531) **:** an apparatus on which crushed ore is washed

bud·dle·ia \'bəd-lē-ə, ,bəd-'lē-\ *n* [NL, genus name, fr. Adam *Buddle* †1715 Eng. botanist] (1924) **:** any of a genus (*Buddleia* of the family Loganiaceae) of shrubs or trees of warm regions with showy terminal clusters of usu. yellow or violet flowers

1**bud·dy** \'bəd-ē\ *n, pl* **buddies** [prob. baby talk alter. of *brother*] (1850) **1 :** COMPANION, PARTNER **2 :** FELLOW — used esp. in informal address

2**buddy** *vi* **bud·died bud·dy·ing** (1918) **:** to become friendly — often used with *up* or *with*

buddy system *n* (1942) **:** an arrangement in which two individuals are paired (as for mutual safety in a hazardous situation)

1**budge** \'bəj\ *n* [ME *bugee,* fr. AF *bogee*] (14c) **:** a fur formerly prepared from lambskin dressed with the wool outward

2**budge** *vb* **budged; budg·ing** [MF *bouger,* fr. (assumed) VL *bullicare,* fr. L *bullire* to boil — more at BOIL] *vi* (1590) **1 :** MOVE, SHIFT ⟨the mule wouldn't ~⟩ **2 :** to give way **:** YIELD ⟨wouldn't ~ on the issue⟩ ~ *vt* **:** to cause to move or change

3**budge** *adj* [origin unknown] *archaic* (1634) **:** POMPOUS, SOLEMN

bud·ger·i·gar \'bəj-(ə-)rē-,gär\ *n* [native name in Australia] (1847) **:** a small Australian parrot (*Melopsittacus undulatus*) usu. light green with black and yellow markings in the wild but bred under domestication in many colors

1**bud·get** \'bəj-ət\ *n* [ME *bowgette,* fr. MF *bougette,* dim. of *bouge* leather bag, fr. L *bulga,* of Gaulish origin; akin to MIr *bolg* bag; akin to OE *bælg* bag — more at BELLY] (15c) **1** *chiefly dial* **:** a usu. leather pouch, wallet, or pack; *also* **:** its contents **2 :** STOCK, SUPPLY **3 :** a quantity (as of energy or water) involved in, available for, or assignable to a particular situation; *also* **:** an account of gains and losses of such a quantity **4 a :** a statement of the financial position of an administration for a definite period of time based on estimates of expenditures during the period and proposals for financing them **b :** a plan for the coordination of resources and expenditures **c :** the amount of money that is available for, required for, or assigned to a particular purpose — **bud·get·ary** \'bəj-ə-,ter-ē\ *adj*

2**budget** *vt* (1618) **1 a :** to put or allow for in a budget **b :** to require to adhere to a budget ⟨~*ed* shoppers⟩ **2 a :** to allocate funds for in a budget ⟨~*ing* a new hospital⟩ **b :** to plan or provide for the use of in detail ⟨~*ing* manpower in a tight labor market⟩ ~ *vi* **:** to put oneself on a budget ⟨~*ing* for a vacation⟩

3**budget** *adj* (1941) **:** suitable for one on a budget **:** INEXPENSIVE

bud·ge·teer \,bəj-ə-'ti(ə)r\ *or* **bud·get·er** \'bəj-ət-ər\ *n* (1845) **1 :** one who prepares a budget **2 :** one who is restricted to a budget

bud·gie \'bəj-ē\ *n* [by shortening and alter.] (1936) **:** BUDGERIGAR

bud scale *n* (ca. 1880) **:** one of the leaves resembling scales that form the sheath of a plant bud

1**buff** \'bəf\ *n* [MF *buffle* wild ox, fr. OIt *bufalo*] (1580) **1 :** a garment (as a uniform) made of buff leather **2 :** the bare skin **3 a :** a moderate orange yellow **b :** a light to moderate yellow **4 :** a device (as a stick or block) having a soft absorbent surface (as of cloth) by which polishing material is applied **5** [earlier *buff* (an enthusiast about going to fires); perh. fr. the buff overcoats worn by volunteer firemen in New York City *ab*1820] **:** FAN, ENTHUSIAST

2**buff** *adj* (1695) **:** of the color buff

3**buff** *vt* (1885) **1 :** POLISH, SHINE ⟨waxed and ~*ed* the floor⟩ **2 :** to give a velvety surface to (leather)

1**buf·fa·lo** \'bəf-ə-,lō\ *n, pl* **-lo** *or* **-loes** *also* **-los** [It *bufalo* & Sp *búfalo,* fr. LL *bufalus,* alter. of L *bubalus,* fr. Gk *boubalos* African gazelle, irreg. fr. *bous* head of cattle — more at COW] (1562) **1 :** any of several wild oxen: as **a :** WATER BUFFALO **b :** any of a genus (*Bison*); *esp* **:** a large shaggy-maned No. American wild ox (*B. bison*) with short horns and heavy forequarters with a large muscular hump **2 :** any of several suckers (genus *Ictiobus*) found mostly in the Mississippi valley — called also *buffalofish*

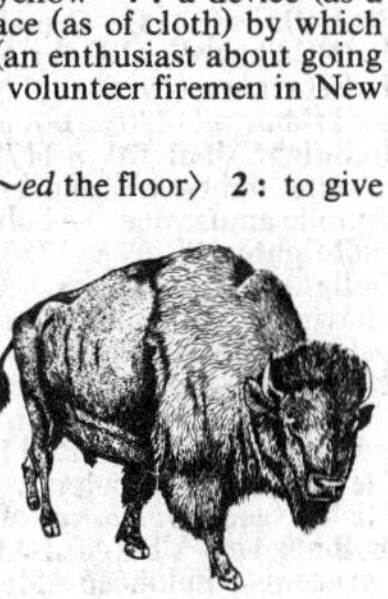

buffalo 1b

2**buffalo** *vt* **-loed; -lo·ing** (1903) **:** BEWILDER, BAFFLE

buffalo berry *n* (1805) **:** either of two western U.S. shrubs (*Shepherdia argentea* and *S. canadensis*) of the oleaster family with silvery foliage; *also* **:** their edible scarlet berry

buffalofish *n* (1768) **:** BUFFALO 2

buffalo grass *n* (1784) **:** a low-growing grass (*Buchloë dactyloides*) of former feeding grounds of the American buffalo; *also* **:** GRAMA

buffalo robe *n* (1804) **:** the hide of an American buffalo lined on the skin side with fabric and used as a coverlet or rug

1**buff·er** \'bəf-ər\ *n* [*buff* (to react like a soft body when struck)] (1835) **1 :** any of various devices or pieces of material for reducing shock due to contact **2 :** a means or device used as a cushion against the shock of fluctuations in business or financial activity **3 :** something that serves as a protective barrier: as **a :** BUFFER STATE **b :** a person who shields another esp. from annoying routine matters **4 :** a substance capable in solution of neutralizing both acids and bases and thereby maintaining the original acidity or basicity of the solution; *also* **:** such a solution **5 :** a temporary storage unit (as in a computer); *esp* **:** one that accepts information at one rate and delivers it at another

2**buffer** *vt* **buf·fered; buf·fer·ing** \-(ə-)riŋ\ (1894) **1 :** to lessen the shock of **:** CUSHION **2 :** to treat (as a solution or its acidity) with a buffer; *also* **:** to prepare (aspirin) with an antacid **3 a :** to supply with a buffer **b :** to collect (as data) in a buffer

3**buffer** *n* (1854) **:** one that buffs

buffer state *n* (1883) **:** a usu. neutral state lying between two larger potentially rival powers

buffer zone *n* (1908) **:** a neutral area separating conflicting forces; *broadly* **:** an area designed to separate

1**buf·fet** \'bəf-ət\ *n* [ME, fr. OF, dim. of *buffe*] (13c) **1 :** a blow esp. with the hand **2 :** something that strikes with telling force

2**buffet** *vt* (13c) **1 :** to strike sharply esp. with the hand **:** CUFF **2 :** to strike repeatedly **:** BATTER ⟨the waves ~*ed* the shore⟩ **3 :** to drive, force, or move by or as if by repeated blows ~ *vi* **:** to make one's way esp. under difficult conditions

3**buf·fet** \(,)bə-'fā, bü-', 'bü-,\ *n* [F] (1718) **1 :** SIDEBOARD **2 a :** a counter for refreshments **b** *chiefly Brit* **:** a restaurant operated as a public convenience (as in a railway station) **c :** a meal set out on a buffet or table for ready access and informal service

4**buf·fet** *like*³\ *adj* (1906) **:** served informally (as from a buffet)

buffing wheel *n* (ca. 1889) **:** a wheel covered with material for polishing

buff leather *n* (1580) **:** a strong supple oil-tanned leather produced chiefly from cattle hides

buf·fle·head \'bəf-əl-,hed\ *n* [archaic E *buffle* buffalo + E *head*] (1731) **:** a small No. American diving duck (*Bucephala albeola*)

buf·fo \'bü-(,)fō\ *n, pl* **buf·fi** \-(,)fē\ *or* **buffos** [It, fr. *buffone*] (1764) **:** CLOWN, BUFFOON; *specif* **:** a male singer of comic roles in opera

buf·foon \(,)bə-'fün\ *n* [MF *bouffon,* fr. OIt *buffone,* fr. ML *bufon-, bufo,* fr. L, toad] (1585) **1 :** a ludicrous figure **:** CLOWN **2 :** a gross and usu. ill-educated or stupid person — **buf·foon·ish** \-ish\ *adj*

buf·foon·ery \-'fün-(ə-)rē\ *n, pl* **-er·ies** (1621) **:** foolish or playful behavior or practice

1**bug** \'bəg\ *n* [ME *bugge* scarecrow; akin to Norw dial. *bugge* important man — more at BIG] *obs* (14c) **:** BOGEY, BUGBEAR

2**bug** *n* [origin unknown] (1622) **1 a :** an insect or other creeping or crawling invertebrate **b :** any of several insects commonly considered esp. obnoxious: as (1) **:** BEDBUG (2) **:** COCKROACH (3) **:** HEAD LOUSE **c :** any of an order (Hemiptera and esp. its suborder Heteroptera) of insects that have sucking mouthparts, forewings thickened at the base, and incomplete metamorphosis and are often economic pests — called also *true bug* **2 :** an unexpected defect, fault, flaw, or imperfection **3 :** a disease-producing germ; *also* **:** a disease caused by it **4 :** a sudden enthusiasm **5 :** ENTHUSIAST ⟨a camera ~⟩ **6 :** a prominent person **7 :** a concealed listening device **8** [fr. its designation by an asterisk on race programs] **:** a weight allowance given apprentice jockeys

3**bug** *vt* **bugged; bug·ging** (1949) **1 :** BOTHER, ANNOY ⟨don't ~ me with petty details⟩ **2 :** to plant a concealed microphone in

bug·a·boo \'bəg-ə-,bü\ *n, pl* **-boos** [origin unknown] (1740) **1 :** an imaginary object of fear **2** BUGBEAR 2; *also* **:** something that causes fear or distress out of proportion to its importance

bug·bane \'bəg-,bān\ *n* (1804) **:** any of several perennial herbs (esp. genus *Cimicifuga*) of the buttercup family that have two or three ternately divided serrate leaves and white flowers in long racemes; *esp* **:** BLACK COHOSH

bug·bear \-,ba(ə)r, -,be(ə)r\ *n* (1581) **1 :** an imaginary goblin or specter used to excite fear **2 a :** an object or source of dread **b :** a continuing source of irritation **:** PROBLEM

bug·eye \-,ī\ *n* (1881) **:** a small boat with a flat bottom, a centerboard, and two raked masts

bug–eyed \-,īd\ *adj* (1922) **:** having the eyes bulging (as with astonishment)

1**bug·ger** \'bəg-ər, 'bu̇g-ər\ *n* [ME *bougre* heretic, sodomite, fr. MF, fr. ML *Bulgarus,* lit., Bulgarian] (1555) **1 :** SODOMITE **2 a :** a worthless person **:** RASCAL **b :** FELLOW, CHAP

2**bug·ger** \'bəg-ər\ *vt* (1598) **1 :** to commit sodomy with — usu. considered vulgar **2 :** DAMN

3**bugger** *n* (1967) **:** one who plants electronic bugs

bug·gery \'bəg-ə-rē\ *n* (1514) **:** SODOMY

1**bug·gy** \'bəg-ē\ *adj* **bug·gi·er; -est** (1714) **:** infested with bugs

2**buggy** *n, pl* **buggies** [origin unknown] (1773) **1 :** a light one-horse carriage made with two wheels in England and with four wheels in the U.S. **2 :** a small cart or truck for short transportations of heavy materials **3 :** BABY CARRIAGE

1**bug·house** \'bəg-,hau̇s\ *adj* (1895) **:** mentally deranged **:** CRAZY

2**bughouse** *n* (1902) **:** an insane asylum

1**bu·gle** \'byü-gəl\ *n* [ME, fr. OF, fr. LL *bugula*] (13c) **:** any of a genus (*Ajuga*) of plants of the mint family; *esp* **:** a European annual (*A. reptans*) that has spikes of blue flowers and is naturalized in the U.S.

2**bugle** *n* [ME, bugle, instrument made of buffalo horn, bugle, fr. MF, fr. L *buculus,* dim. of *bos* head of cattle — more at COW] (14c) **:** a valveless brass instrument that resembles a trumpet and is used esp. for military calls

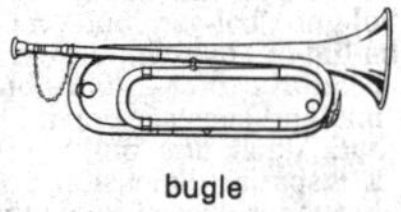

bugle

3**bugle** *vi* **bu·gled; bu·gling** \-g(ə-)liŋ\ (1862) **1 :** to sound a bugle **2 :** to utter the characteristic rutting call of the bull elk

4**bugle** *n* [perh. fr. 2*bugle*] (1579) **:** a small cylindrical bead of glass or plastic used for trimming esp. on women's clothing

bu·gler \'byü-glər\ *n* (1840) **:** one who sounds a bugle

bu·gle·weed \'byü-gəl-,wēd\ *n* (ca. 1817) **1 :** any of a genus (*Lycopus*) of mints; *esp* **:** one (*L. virginicus*) that is mildly narcotic and astringent **2 :** 1BUGLE

bu·gloss \'byü-,gläs, -,glȯs\ *n* [MF *buglosse,* fr. L *buglossa,* irreg. fr. Gk *bouglōssos,* fr. *bous* head of cattle + *glōssa* tongue — more at COW, GLOSS] (14c) **:** any of several coarse hairy plants (genera *Anchusa, Lycopsis,* and *Echium*) of the borage family — compare VIPER'S BUGLOSS

\ə\ abut \ᵊ\ kitten, F table \ər\ further \a\ ash \ā\ ace \ä\ cot, cart \au̇\ out \ch\ chin \e\ bet \ē\ easy \g\ go \i\ hit \ī\ ice \j\ job \ŋ\ sing \ō\ go \ȯ\ law \ȯi\ boy \th\ thin \t͟h\ the \ü\ loot \u̇\ foot \y\ yet \zh\ vision \à, k̲, ⁿ, œ, œ̄, ue, ue̅, ʸ\ *see* Guide to Pronunciation

bug·seed \'bəg-,sēd\ *n* (ca. 1889) **:** a fleshy annual herb (*Corispermum hyssopifolium*) of the goosefoot family with flat oval seeds
buhl \'bül, 'byü(ə)l\ *var of* BOULLE
buhr \'bər\ *n* (1834) **:** BUHRSTONE 2
buhr·stone \-,stōn\ *n* [prob. fr. *burr* + *stone*] (1821) **1 :** a siliceous rock used for millstones **2 :** a millstone cut from buhrstone
¹build \'bild\ *vb* **built** \'bilt\; **build·ing** [ME *bilden*, fr. OE *byldan*; akin to OE *būan* to dwell — more at BOWER] *vt* (bef. 12c) **1 :** to form by ordering and uniting materials by gradual means into a composite whole **:** CONSTRUCT **2 :** to cause to be constructed **3 :** to develop according to a systematic plan, by a definite process, or on a particular base **4 :** INCREASE, ENLARGE ~ *vi* **1 :** to engage in building **2 a :** to progress toward a peak (as of intensity) ⟨~ to a climax⟩ **b :** to develop in extent ⟨a crowd ~*ing*⟩ — **build a fire under :** to stimulate to vigorous action — **build into :** to make an integral part of ⟨*build* quality *into* the product⟩ — **build on :** to use as a foundation ⟨*building on* past experience⟩
²build *n* (1667) **:** form or mode of structure **:** MAKE; *esp* **:** bodily conformation of a person or lower animal
build·able \'bil-də-bəl\ *adj* (1927) **:** suitable for building ⟨~ land⟩
build·ed *archaic past of* BUILD
build·er \'bil-dər\ *n* (13c) **1 :** one that builds; *esp* **:** one that contracts to build and supervises building operations **2 :** a substance added to or used with detergents to increase their cleansing action
build in *vt* (1933) **:** to construct or develop as an integral part of something
build·ing \'bil-diŋ\ *n* (13c) **1 :** a usu. roofed and walled structure built for permanent use (as for a dwelling) **2 :** the art or business of assembling materials into a structure
building block *n* (1846) **:** a unit of construction or composition
build·up \'bil-,dəp\ *n* (1926) **1 :** the act or process of building up **2 :** something produced by building up
build up \(')bil-'dəp\ *vt* (1726) **1 :** to develop gradually by increments ⟨*building up* endurance⟩ ⟨*built up* a library⟩ **2 :** to promote the health, strength, esteem, or reputation of ~ *vi* **:** to accumulate or develop appreciably ⟨clouds *building up* on the horizon⟩
built \'bilt\ *adj* (1621) **:** formed as to physique or bodily contours ⟨ slimly ~⟩; *esp* **:** well or attractively formed
¹built–in \'bil-'tin\ *adj* (1898) **1 :** forming an integral part of a structure; *esp* **:** constructed as or in a recess in a wall **2 :** INHERENT
²built–in \-,tin\ *n* (1930) **:** a built-in piece of furniture
built–up \'bil-'təp\ *adj* (1829) **1 :** made of several sections or layers fastened together **2 :** covered with buildings
buird·ly \'bu̇(ə)r(d)-lē\ *adj* [prob. alter. of *burly*] *Scot* (1773) **:** STURDY
bulb \'bəlb\ *n* [L *bulbus*, fr. Gk *bolbos* bulbous plant] (1664) **1 a :** a resting stage of a plant (as the lily, onion, hyacinth, or tulip) that is usu. formed underground and consists of a short stem base bearing one or more buds enclosed in overlapping membranous or fleshy leaves **b :** a fleshy structure (as a tuber or corm) resembling a bulb in appearance **c :** a plant having or developing from a bulb **2 :** a bulb-shaped part; *specif* **:** a rounded glass envelope enclosing the light source of an electric lamp or such an envelope together with the light source it encloses **3 :** a rounded or swollen anatomical structure **4 :** a camera setting that indicates that the shutter can be opened by pressing on the release and closed by ending the pressure — **bulbed** \'bəlbd\ *adj*
bul·bar \'bəl-bər, -,bär\ *adj* (1878) **:** of or relating to a bulb; *specif* **:** involving the medulla oblongata
bul·bil \'bəl-bəl, -,bil\ *n* [F *bulbille*, dim. of *bulbe* bulb, fr. L *bulbus*] (1831) **:** BULBLET
bulb·let \'bəl-blət\ *n* (1842) **:** a small or secondary bulb; *esp* **:** an aerial deciduous bud produced in a leaf axil or replacing the flowers and capable when separated of producing a new plant
bul·bous \'bəl-bəs\ *adj* (1578) **1 :** having a bulb **:** growing from or bearing bulbs **2 :** resembling a bulb esp. in roundness ⟨a ~ nose⟩ — **bul·bous·ly** *adv*
bul·bul \'bu̇l-,bu̇l\ *n* [Per, fr. Ar] (1665) **1 :** a Persian songbird frequently mentioned in poetry that is prob. a nightingale (*Luscinia golzii*) **2 :** any of a group of gregarious passerine birds (family Pycnonotidae) of Asia and Africa
Bul·gar \'bəl-,gär, 'bu̇l-\ *n* [ML *Bulgarus*] (1759) **:** BULGARIAN
Bul·gar·i·an \,bəl-'gar-ē-ən, bu̇l-, -'ger-\ *n* (1555) **1 :** a native or inhabitant of Bulgaria **2 :** the Slavic language of the Bulgarians — **Bulgarian** *adj*
¹bulge \'bəlj\ *vb* **bulged; bulg·ing** *vt* (15c) **:** to cause to bulge ~ *vi* **1** *archaic* **:** BILGE 1 **2 a :** to jut out **:** SWELL **b :** to bend outward **c :** to become swollen or protuberant **3 :** to be filled to overflowing
²bulge *n* [MF *boulge, bouge* leather bag, curved part — more at BUDGET] (1622) **1 :** BILGE 1, 2 **2 :** a protuberant or swollen part or place **3 :** ADVANTAGE, UPPER HAND **4 :** sudden expansion ***syn*** see PROJECTION — **bulgy** \'bəl-jē\ *adj*
bul·gur \'bəl-gər, 'bu̇l-\ *n* [Turk] (1926) **:** parched cracked wheat
bu·lim·ia \byü-'lim-ē-ə\ *n* [NL, fr. Gk *boulimia* great hunger, fr. *bous* head of cattle + *limos* hunger — more at COW, LESS] (14c) **:** an abnormal and constant craving for food — **bu·lim·ic** \-'lim-ik\ *adj or n*
¹bulk \'bəlk *also* 'bu̇lk\ *n* [ME, heap, bulk, fr. ON *bulki* cargo] (15c) **1 a :** spatial dimension **:** MAGNITUDE **b :** material (as indigestible fibrous residues of food) that forms a mass in the intestine **2 a :** BODY; *esp* **:** a large or corpulent human body **b :** an organized structure esp. when viewed primarily as a mass of material **c :** a ponderous shapeless mass **3 :** the main or greater part
syn BULK, MASS, VOLUME mean the aggregate that forms a body or unit. BULK implies an aggregate that is impressively large, heavy, or numerous; MASS suggests an aggregate made by piling together things of the same kind; VOLUME applies to an aggregate without shape or outline and capable of flowing or fluctuating.
— **in bulk 1 :** not divided into parts or packaged in separate units **2 :** in large quantities
²bulk *vt* (1540) **1 :** to cause to swell or bulge **:** STUFF **2 :** to gather into a mass or aggregate ~ *vi* **1 :** SWELL, EXPAND **2 :** to appear as a factor **:** LOOM ⟨a consideration that ~*s* large in everyone's thinking⟩
³bulk *adj* (1693) **1 :** being in bulk ⟨~ cement⟩ **2 :** of or relating to materials in bulk
bulk·head \'bəlk-,hed, 'bəl-,ked\ *n* [*bulk* (structure projecting from a building) + *head*] (15c) **1 :** an upright partition separating compartments **2 :** a structure or partition to resist pressure or to shut off water, fire, or gas **3 :** a retaining wall along a waterfront **4 :** a projecting framework with a sloping door giving access to a cellar stairway or a shaft
bulky \'bəl-kē *also* 'bu̇l-\ **bulk·i·er; -est** *adj* (15c) **1 a :** having bulk **b** (1) **:** large of its kind (2) **:** CORPULENT **2 :** having great volume in proportion to weight ⟨a ~ knit sweater⟩ — **bulk·i·ly** \-kə-lē\ *adv* — **bulk·i·ness** \-kē-nəs\ *n*
¹bull \'bu̇l\ *n* [ME *bule*, fr. OE *bula*; akin to OE *blāwan* to blow] (bef. 12c) **1 a :** a male bovine; *esp* **:** an adult uncastrated male ox **b :** a usu. adult male of various large animals (as elephants, whales, or seals) **2 :** one who buys securities or commodities in expectation of a price rise or who acts to effect such a rise — compare BEAR **3 :** one that resembles a bull (as in brawny physique) **4 :** BULLDOG **5** *slang* **:** POLICEMAN, DETECTIVE **6** *cap* **:** TAURUS
²bull *adj* (12c) **1 a :** of or relating to a bull **b :** MALE **c :** suggestive of a bull **2 :** large of its kind
³bull *vt* (1842) **1 :** to try to raise the price of (as stocks) or in (a market) **2 a :** to act on with violence **b :** FORCE ⟨~*ed* his way through the crowd⟩ ~ *vi* **:** to advance forcefully
⁴bull *n* [ME *bulle*, fr. ML *bulla*, fr. L, bubble, amulet] (13c) **1 :** a solemn papal letter sealed with a bulla or with a red-ink imprint of the device on the bulla **2 :** EDICT, DECREE
⁵bull *vb* [origin unknown] *vt*, *slang* (1609) **:** to fool esp. by fast boastful talk ~ *vi*, *slang* **:** to engage in idle and boastful talk
⁶bull *n* (1640) **:** a grotesque blunder in language
⁷bull *n* [short for *bullshit*] (1914) **1** *slang* **:** empty boastful talk **2** *slang* **:** NONSENSE
bul·la \'bu̇l-ə\ *n*, *pl* **bul·lae** \'bu̇l-,ē, -,ī\ (14c) **1** [ML] **:** the round usu. lead seal attached to a papal bull **2** [NL, fr. L] **:** a hollow thin-walled rounded bony prominence **3 :** a large vesicle or blister
bul·lace \'bu̇l-əs\ *n* [ME *bolace*, fr. MF *beloce*, fr. ML *bolluca*] (14c) **:** a European plum (*Prunus domestica insititia*) with small ovoid fruit in clusters
bull·bait·ing \'bu̇l-,bāt-iŋ\ *n* (ca. 1580) **:** the former practice of baiting bulls with dogs
bull·bat \'bu̇l-,bat\ *n* (1838) **:** NIGHTHAWK 1a
¹bull·dog \'bu̇l-,dȯg\ *n* (1500) **1 :** any of a breed of compact muscular short-haired dogs having widely separated forelegs and an undershot lower jaw that were developed in England to fight bulls **2 :** a handgun with a thick usu. short barrel **3 :** a proctor's attendant at an English university
²bulldog *vt* (1907) **:** to throw (a steer) by seizing the horns and twisting the neck — **bull·dog·ger** *n*
³bulldog *adj* (1848) **:** suggestive of a bulldog ⟨~ tenacity⟩
bull·doze \'bu̇l-,dōz\ *vt* [perh. fr. ¹*bull* + alter. of *dose*] (1876) **1 :** BULLY **2 :** to move, clear, gouge out, or level off by pushing with or as if with a bulldozer **3 :** to force insensitively or ruthlessly ⟨*bulldozed* his program through the legislature⟩
bull·doz·er \-,dō-zər\ *n* (1876) **1 :** one that bulldozes **2 :** a tractor-driven machine having a broad blunt horizontal blade or ram for clearing land, road building, or comparable activities
bul·let \'bu̇l-ət\ *n*, *often attrib* [MF *boulette* small ball & *boulet* missile, dims. of *boule* ball — more at BOWL] (1579) **1 :** a round or elongated missile (as of lead) to be fired from a firearm; *broadly* **:** CARTRIDGE 1a **2 :** something resembling a bullet (as in curved form) **3 :** a very fast and accurately thrown ball — **bul·let·proof** \,bu̇l-ət-'prüf\ *adj*
¹bul·le·tin \'bu̇l-ət-ᵊn\ *n* [F, OF *bullette*, dim. of *bulle* papal edict, fr. ML] (1765) **1 :** a brief public notice issuing usu. from an authoritative source; *specif* **:** a brief news item intended for immediate publication or broadcast **2 :** PERIODICAL; *esp* **:** the organ of an institution or association
²bulletin *vt* (1838) **:** to make public by bulletin
bulletin board *n* (1831) **:** a board for posting notices (as at a school)
bullet train *n* (1966) **:** a high-speed passenger train
bull fiddle *n* (1880) **:** DOUBLE BASS — **bull fiddler** *n*
bull·fight \'bu̇l-,fīt\ *n* (1788) **:** a spectacle in which men ceremonially excite, fight with, and in Hispanic tradition kill bulls in an arena for public amusement — **bull·fight·er** \-ər\ *n*
bull·fight·ing \-iŋ\ *n* (1753) **:** the action involved in a bullfight
bull·finch \'bu̇l-,finch\ *n* (13c) **:** a European finch (*Pyrrhula pyrrhula*) having in the male rosy red underparts, blue-gray back, and black cap, chin, tail, and wings; *also* **:** any of several other finches
bull·frog \-,frȯg, -,fräg\ *n* (1698) **:** FROG; *esp* **:** a heavy-bodied deep-voiced frog (as of the genus *Rana*)
bull·head \-,hed\ *n* (15c) **:** any of various large-headed fishes (as a miller's-thumb or sculpin); *esp* **:** any of several common freshwater catfishes (genus *Ictalurus*) of the U.S.
bull·head·ed \'bu̇l-'hed-əd\ *adj* (1818) **:** stupidly stubborn **:** HEADSTRONG — **bull·head·ed·ly** *adv* — **bull·head·ed·ness** *n*
bull·horn \'bu̇l-,hȯ(ə)rn\ *n* (1942) **1 :** a loudspeaker on a naval ship **2 :** a hand-held combined microphone and loudspeaker
bul·lion \'bu̇l-yən\ *n* [ME, fr. AF, mint] (14c) **1 a :** gold or silver considered as so much metal; *specif* **:** uncoined gold or silver in bars or ingots **b :** metal in the mass ⟨lead ~⟩ **2 :** lace, braid, or fringe of gold or silver threads
bull·ish \'bu̇l-ish\ *adj* (1565) **1 :** suggestive of a bull (as in brawniness) **2 a :** marked by, tending to cause, or hopeful of rising prices (as in a stock market) **b :** OPTIMISTIC — **bull·ish·ly** *adv* — **bull·ish·ness** *n*
bull·mas·tiff \'bu̇l-,mas-təf\ *n* (ca. 1901) **:** any of a breed of large powerful dogs developed by crossing bulldogs with mastiffs
Bull Moose *n* [*bull moose*, emblem of the Progressive party of 1912] (1912) **:** a follower of Theodore Roosevelt in the U.S. presidential campaign of 1912
Bull Moos·er \-'mü-sər\ *n* (1912) **:** BULL MOOSE
bull neck *n* (13c) **:** a thick short powerful neck — **bull·necked** \'bu̇l-'nekt\ *adj*
bull·ock \'bu̇l-ək\ *n* (bef. 12c) **1 :** a young bull **2 :** a castrated bull **:** STEER — **bull·ocky** \-ə-kē\ *adj*
bul·lous \'bu̇l-əs\ *adj* (ca. 1860) **:** resembling or characterized by bullae **:** VESICULAR ⟨~ lesions⟩

bull pen *n* (1809) **1 :** a large cell where prisoners are detained until brought into court **2 a :** a place on a baseball field where relief pitchers warm up during a game **b :** the relief pitchers of a baseball team
bull·pout \ˈbu̇l-ˌpau̇t\ *n* [*bull*head + *pout*] (1823) **:** BULLHEAD; *esp* **:** the common dark bullhead (*Ictalurus nebulosus*)
bull·ring \ˈbu̇l-ˌriŋ\ *n* (1802) **:** an arena for bullfights
bull session *n* [7*bull*] (1920) **:** an informal discursive group discussion
bull's–eye \ˈbu̇l-ˌzī\ *n, pl* **bull's–eyes** (1825) **1 :** a very hard globular candy **2 :** a small thick disk of glass inserted (as in a deck) to let in light **3 a :** the center of a target; *also* **:** something central or crucial **b :** a shot that hits the bull's-eye; *broadly* **:** something that precisely attains a desired end **4 :** a simple lens of short focal distance; *also* **:** a lantern with such a lens **5 :** a circular opening for air or light
bull's–eye window *n* (1926) **:** a circular window or one filling a bull's-eye
1bull·shit \ˈbu̇l-ˌshit\ *n* [1*bull* + *shit*] (1915) **:** NONSENSE; *esp* **:** foolish insolent talk — usu. considered vulgar
2bullshit *vi* (1942) **1 :** to talk foolishly, boastfully, or idly — usu. considered vulgar **2 :** to engage in a discursive discussion — usu. considered vulgar ~ *vt* **:** to talk nonsense to esp. with the intention of deceiving or misleading — usu. considered vulgar
bull·shot \-ˌshät\ *n* (1964) **:** a drink made of vodka and bouillon
bull snake *n* (1784) **:** any of several large harmless No. American snakes (genus *Pituophis*) that feed chiefly on rodents — called also *gopher snake, pine snake*
bull·ter·ri·er \ˈbu̇l-ˈter-ē-ər\ *n* [*bull*dog + *terrier*] (1848) **:** any of a breed of short-haired terriers originated in England by crossing the bulldog with terriers
bull thistle *n* (1863) **:** a European thistle (*Cirsium vulgare*) with rather large heads and prickly leaves that is naturalized as a weed in the U.S.
bull tongue *n* (1831) **:** a wide blade attached to a cultivator or plow to stir the soil, kill weeds, or mark furrows
bull·whip \ˈbu̇l-ˌ(h)wip\ *n* (1852) **:** a rawhide whip with plaited lash 15 to 25 feet long
1bul·ly \ˈbu̇l-ē\ *n, pl* **bullies** [prob. modif. of D *boel* lover, fr. MHG *buole*] (1538) **1** *archaic* **a :** SWEETHEART **b :** a fine chap **2 a :** a blustering browbeating fellow; *esp* **:** one habitually cruel to others weaker than himself **b :** the protector of a prostitute **:** PIMP **3 :** a hired ruffian
2bully *adj* (1681) **1 :** EXCELLENT, FIRST-RATE — often used in interjectional expressions ⟨~ for you⟩ **2 :** resembling or characteristic of a bully
3bully *vb* **bul·lied; bul·ly·ing** *vt* (1710) **:** to treat abusively ~ *vi* **:** to use browbeating language or behavior **:** BLUSTER
4bully *n* [prob. modif. of F (*bœuf*) *boulli* boiled beef] (1753) **:** pickled or canned usu. corned beef
bul·ly·boy \ˈbu̇l-ē-ˌbȯi\ *n* (1609) **:** a swaggering tough
bully pulpit *n* (1976) **:** a prominent public position (as a political office) that provides an opportunity for expounding one's views; *also* **:** such an opportunity
bul·ly·rag \-ˌrag\ *vt* [origin unknown] (1760) **1 :** to intimidate by bullying **2 :** to vex by teasing **:** BADGER
bul·rush *also* **bull·rush** \ˈbu̇l-ˌrəsh\ *n* [ME *bulrysche*] (15c) **:** any of several large rushes or sedges growing in wetlands: as **a :** any of a genus of annual or perennial sedges (*Scirpus*, esp. *S. lacustris*) that bear solitary or much-clustered spikelets containing perfect flowers with a perianth of six bristles **b** *Brit* **:** either of two cattails (*Typha latifolia* and *T. angustifolia*) **c :** PAPYRUS
1bul·wark \ˈbu̇l-(ˌ)wərk, -ˌwȯrk; ˈbəl-(ˌ)wərk\ *n* [ME *bulwerke*, fr. MD *bolwerc*, fr. MHG, fr. *bole* plank + *werc* work] (15c) **1 a :** a solid wall-like structure raised for defense **:** RAMPART **b :** BREAKWATER, SEAWALL **2 :** a strong support or protection **3 :** the side of a ship above the upper deck — usu. used in pl.
2bulwark *vt* (15c) **:** to fortify or safeguard with a bulwark
1bum \ˈbəm\ *n* [ME *bom*] *chiefly Brit* (14c) **:** BUTTOCKS — sometimes considered vulgar
2bum *adj* (1859) **1 a :** INFERIOR, WORTHLESS ⟨~ advice⟩ **b :** acutely disagreeable ⟨a ~ trip⟩ **2 :** not functioning because of damage or injury **:** DISABLED ⟨a ~ knee⟩
3bum *vb* **bummed; bum·ming** [prob. back-formation fr. 1*bummer*] *vi* (1863) **1 :** LOAF **2 :** to spend time unemployed and often wandering ~ *vt* **:** to obtain by begging **:** CADGE
4bum *n* [prob. short for *bummer*] (1864) **1 a :** one who sponges off others and avoids work **b :** one who performs a function poorly ⟨called the umpire a ~⟩ **c :** one who devotes his time to a recreational activity ⟨a beach ~⟩ ⟨ski ~*s*⟩ **2 :** VAGRANT, TRAMP
5bum *n* [prob. fr. 3*bum*] (1879) **:** a drinking spree **:** BENDER — **on the bum :** with no settled residence or means of support
bum·ber·shoot \ˈbəm-bər-ˌshüt\ *n* [*bumber-* (alter. of *umbr-* in *umbrella*) + *-shoot* (alter. of *-chute* in *parachute*)] (ca. 1896) **:** UMBRELLA
1bum·ble \ˈbəm-bəl\ *vi* **bum·bled; bum·bling** \-b(ə-)liŋ\ [ME *bomblen* to boom, of imit. origin] (15c) **1 :** BUZZ **2 :** DRONE, RUMBLE
2bumble *vb* **bumbled; bumbling** [prob. alter. of *bungle*] *vi* (1532) **1 :** BLUNDER; *specif* **:** to speak ineptly in a stuttering and faltering manner **2 :** to proceed unsteadily **:** STUMBLE ~ *vt* **:** BUNGLE — **bum·bler** \-b(ə-)lər\ *n* — **bum·bling·ly** \-b(ə-)liŋ-lē\ *adv*
bum·ble·bee \ˈbəm-bəl-ˌbē\ *n* (1530) **:** any of numerous large robust hairy social bees (genus *Bombus*)
bum·boat \ˈbəm-ˌbōt\ *n* [prob. fr. LG *bumboot*, fr. *bum* tree + *boot* boat; akin to OE *bēam* tree] (1769) **:** a boat that brings provisions and commodities for sale to larger ships in port or offshore
bumf \ˈbəm(p)f\ *n* [Brit. slang *bumf* toilet paper, short for *bumfodder*, fr. 1*bum*] *Brit* (ca. 1889) **:** PAPERWORK
1bum·mer \ˈbəm-ər\ *n* [prob. modif. of G *bummler* loafer, fr. *bummel* to dangle, loaf] (1855) **:** one that bums
2bummer *n* [2*bum* + *-er*] (1967) **1 :** an unpleasant experience (as a bad reaction to a hallucinogenic drug) **2 :** FAILURE, FLOP
1bump \ˈbəmp\ *n* [prob. imit. of the sound of a blow] (1592) **1 :** a relatively abrupt convexity or protuberance on a surface: as **a :** a swelling of tissue **b :** a cranial protuberance **2 a :** a sudden forceful blow, impact, or jolt **b :** DEMOTION **3 :** an act of thrusting the hips forward in an erotic manner
2bump *vt* (ca. 1611) **1 :** to strike or knock with force or violence **2 :** to collide with **3 a** (1) **:** to dislodge with a jolt (2) **:** to subject to a scalar change ⟨rates being ~*ed* up⟩ **b :** to oust usu. by virtue of seniority or priority ⟨was ~*ed* from the flight⟩ **4 :** to apply pressure to (as sheet metal) so as to make or remove a concavity or convexity ~ *vi* **1 :** to knock against something with a forceful jolt **2 :** to proceed in a series of bumps — **bump into :** to encounter esp. by chance
1bum·per \ˈbəm-pər\ *n* [prob. fr. *bump* (to bulge)] (1676) **1 :** a brimming cup or glass **2 :** something unusually large
2bumper *adj* (1885) **:** unusually large ⟨a ~ crop⟩
3bump·er \ˈbəm-pər\ *n* (1839) **1 :** a device for absorbing shock or preventing damage (as in collision); *specif* **:** a usu. metal bar at either end of an automobile **2 :** one that bumps
bumper car *n* (1959) **:** a small electric car made to be driven around in an enclosure and to be bumped into others (as at an amusement park)
bumper sticker *n* (1967) **:** a strip of adhesive paper or plastic bearing a printed message (as a candidate's name or a slogan) and designed to be stuck on a vehicle's bumper
bumper–to–bumper *adj* (1951) **:** marked by long closed lines of cars
1bump·kin \ˈbəm(p)-kən\ *n* [perh. fr. Flem *bommekijn* small cask, fr. MD, fr. *bomme* cask] (ca. 1570) **:** an awkward and unsophisticated rustic — **bump·kin·ish** \-kə-nish\ *adj* — **bump·kin·ly** \-kən-lē\ *adj*
2bump·kin *or* **bum·kin** \ˈbəm(p)-kən\ *n* [prob. fr. Flem *boomken*, dim. of *boom* tree] (ca. 1632) **:** a spar projecting from the stern of a ship
bump off *vt* (1910) **:** to murder casually or cold-bloodedly
bump·tious \ˈbəm(p)-shəs\ *adj* [1*bump* + *-tious* (as in *fractious*)] (1803) **:** presumptuously, obtusely, and often noisily self-assertive **:** OBTRUSIVE — **bump·tious·ly** *adv* — **bump·tious·ness** *n*
bumpy \ˈbəm-pē\ *adj* **bump·i·er; -est** (1865) **1 a :** having or covered with bumps ⟨a ~ road⟩ **b :** marked by ups and downs **:** UNEVEN **2 a :** marked by bumps or jolts ⟨a ~ ride⟩ **b :** rhythmically jerky ⟨~ dance music⟩ — **bump·i·ly** \-pə-lē\ *adv* — **bump·i·ness** \-pē-nəs\ *n*
1bun \ˈbən\ *n* [ME *bunne*] (14c) **1 :** any of various small breads; *esp* **:** a round roll **2 :** a knot of hair shaped like a bun **3** *pl* **:** BUTTOCKS
2bun *n* [perh. alter. of E dial. *bung* (intoxicated)] (1901) **:** LOAD 4
Bu·na \ˈb(y)ü-nə\ *trademark* — used for any of several rubbers made by polymerization or copolymerization of butadiene
1bunch \ˈbənch\ *n* [ME *bunche*] (14c) **1 :** PROTUBERANCE, SWELLING **2 a :** a number of things of the same kind ⟨a ~ of grapes⟩ **b :** a homogeneous group — **bunch·i·ly** \ˈbən-chə-lē\ *adv* — **bunchy** \-chē\ *adj*
2bunch *vi* (14c) **1 :** SWELL, PROTRUDE **2 :** to form a group or cluster — often used with *up* ~ *vt* **:** to form into a bunch
bunch·ber·ry \ˈbənch-ˌber-ē\ *n* (1845) **:** a creeping perennial herb (*Cornus canadensis*) that has whorled leaves and white floral bracts and bears red berries in capitate cymes
bunch·flow·er \ˈbənch-ˌflau̇(-ə)r\ *n* (ca. 1817) **:** a tall summer-blooming herb (*Melanthium virginicum*) of the lily family that is found in the eastern and southern U.S. and bears a panicle of small greenish flowers
bunch·grass \-ˌgras\ *n* (1839) **:** any of several grasses (as of the genus *Andropogon*) esp. of the western U.S. that grow in tufts
bun·co *or* **bun·ko** \ˈbəŋ-(ˌ)kō\ *n, pl* **buncos** *or* **bunkos** [perh. alter. of Sp *banca* bench, banking, bank in gambling, fr. It — more at BANK] (1872) **:** a swindling game or scheme — **bunco** *vt*
1bund \ˈbənd\ *n* [Hindi *band*, fr. Per] (1810) **1 :** an embankment used esp. in India to control the flow of water **2 :** an embanked thoroughfare along a river or the sea esp. in the Far East
2bund \ˈbu̇nd, ˈbənd\ *n, often cap* [G, fr. MHG *bunt*; akin to OE *byndel*] (1850) **:** a political association; *specif* **:** a pro-Nazi German-American organization of the 1930s — **bund·ist** \-əst\ *n, often cap*
1bun·dle \ˈbən-dᵊl\ *n* [ME *bundel*, fr. MD; akin to OE *byndel* bundle, *bindan* to bind] (14c) **1 a :** a group of things fastened together for convenient handling **b :** PACKAGE, PARCEL **c :** a considerable number of things **:** LOT ⟨a ~ of contradictions⟩ **d :** a sizable sum of money **2 a :** a small band of mostly parallel fibers (as of nerve or muscle) **b :** VASCULAR BUNDLE
2bundle *vb* **bun·dled; bun·dling** \ˈbən-(d)liŋ, -dᵊl-iŋ\ *vt* (1628) **1 :** to make into a bundle or package **:** WRAP **2 :** to hustle or hurry unceremoniously ⟨*bundled* the children off to school⟩ ~ *vi* **1 :** HURRY, HUSTLE **2 :** to practice bundling — **bun·dler** \-dlər, -dᵊl-ər\ *n*
bundle of nerves (1936) **:** a very nervous person
bundle up *vt* (1918) **:** to dress (someone) warmly ~ *vi* **:** to dress warmly
bun·dling \ˈbən-(d)liŋ, -dᵊl-iŋ\ *n* (1781) **:** a former custom of an unmarried couple's occupying the same bed without undressing esp. during courtship
1bung \ˈbəŋ\ *n* [ME, fr. MD *bonne, bonghe*, perh. fr. LL *puncta* puncture, fr. L, fem. of *punctus*, pp. of *pungere* to prick — more at PUNGENT] (15c) **1 :** the stopper esp. in the bunghole of a cask; *also* **:** BUNGHOLE **2 :** the cecum or anus esp. of a slaughtered animal
2bung *vt* (1589) **:** to plug with or as if with a bung
bun·ga·low \ˈbəŋ-gə-ˌlō\ *n* [Hindi *baṅglā*, lit., (house) in the Bengal style] (1676) **:** a usu. one-storied house with a low-pitched roof
bung·hole \ˈbəŋ-ˌhōl\ *n* (1571) **:** a hole for emptying or filling a cask
bun·gle \ˈbəŋ-gəl\ *vb* **bun·gled; bun·gling** \-g(ə-)liŋ\ [perh. of Scand origin; akin to Icel *banga* to hammer] *vi* (1549) **:** to act or work clumsily and awkwardly ~ *vt* **:** MISHANDLE, BOTCH — **bun·gler** \-g(ə-)lər\ *n* — **bun·gling** *adj or n* — **bun·gling·ly** \-g(ə-)liŋ-lē\ *adv*
bun·gle·some \-gəl-səm\ *adj* (ca. 1889) **:** AWKWARD, CLUMSY
bung up *vt* (1829) **:** BATTER
bun·ion \ˈbən-yən\ *n* [prob. irreg. fr. *bunny* (swelling)] (1718) **:** an inflamed swelling of the small sac on the first joint of the big toe
1bunk \ˈbəŋk\ *n* [prob. short for *bunker*] (1758) **1 a :** BUNK BED **b :** a built-in bed (as on a ship) that is often one of a tier of berths **c :** a sleeping place **2 :** a feeding trough for cattle
2bunk *vi* (1840) **:** to occupy a bunk or bed **:** stay the night ⟨~*ed* with a friend for the night⟩ ~ *vt* **:** to provide with a bunk or bed
3bunk *n* (1900) **:** BUNKUM, NONSENSE
bunk bed *n* (1924) **:** one of two single beds usu. placed one above the other

\ə\ abut \ᵊ\ kitten, F table \ər\ further \a\ ash \ā\ ace \ä\ cot, cart \au̇\ out \ch\ chin \e\ bet \ē\ easy \g\ go \i\ hit \ī\ ice \j\ job \ŋ\ sing \ō\ go \ȯ\ law \ȯi\ boy \th\ thin \t͟h\ the \ü\ loot \u̇\ foot \y\ yet \zh\ vision \à, k̲, ⁿ, œ, œ̄, ue, ue̅, ʸ\ *see* Guide to Pronunciation

[1]**bun·ker** \'bəŋ-kər\ *n* [Sc *bonker* chest, box] (ca. 1718) **1 :** a bin or compartment for storage; *esp* **:** one on shipboard for the ship's fuel **2 a :** a protective embankment or dugout; *esp* **:** a fortified chamber mostly below ground often built of reinforced concrete and provided with embrasures **b :** a sand trap or embankment constituting a hazard on a golf course

[2]**bunker** *vb* **bun·kered; bun·ker·ing** \-k(ə-)riŋ\ *vi* (1891) **:** to fill a ship's bunker with coal or oil ~ *vt* **:** to place or store in a bunker

bunker mentality *n* (1976) **:** a state of mind esp. among members of a group that is characterized by chauvinistic defensiveness and self-righteous intolerance of criticism

bunk·house \'bəŋk-,haùs\ *n* (1876) **:** a rough simple building providing sleeping quarters

bun·kum *or* **bun·combe** \'bəŋ-kəm\ *n* [*Buncombe* county, N.C.; fr. the defense of a seemingly irrelevant speech made by its congressional representative that he was making a speech for Buncombe] (1845) **:** insincere or foolish talk **:** NONSENSE

bun·ny \'bən-ē\ *n, pl* **bunnies** [E dial. *bun* (rabbit)] (ca. 1690) **:** RABBIT; *esp* **:** a young rabbit

Bun·ra·ku \bün-'räk-(,)ü\ *n* [Jp] (1920) **:** Japanese puppet theater featuring large costumed wooden puppets, puppeteers who are onstage, and a chanter who speaks all the lines

Bun·sen burner \,bən(t)-sən-\ *n* [Robert W. *Bunsen*] (1870) **:** a gas burner consisting typically of a straight tube with small holes at the bottom where air enters and mixes with the gas to produce an intensely hot blue flame

[1]**bunt** \'bənt\ *n* [perh. fr. LG, bundle, fr. MLG; akin to OE *byndel* bundle] (1582) **1 a :** the middle part of a square sail **b :** the part of a furled sail gathered up in a bunch at the center of the yard **2 :** the bagging part of a fishing net

[2]**bunt** *vb* [alter. of *butt*] *vt* (1584) **1 :** to strike or push with or as if with the head **:** BUTT **2 :** to push or tap (a baseball) lightly without swinging the bat ~ *vi* **:** to bunt a baseball — **bunt·er** *n*

[3]**bunt** *n* (1767) **1 :** an act or instance of bunting **2 :** a bunted ball

[4]**bunt** *n* [origin unknown] (ca. 1790) **:** a destructive covered smut of wheat caused by a fungus (*Tilletia foetida* or *T. caries*)

[1]**bun·ting** \'bənt-iŋ\ *n* [ME] (13c) **:** any of various stout-billed birds (*Emberiza* and related genera) usu. included with the finches

[2]**bunting** *n* [perh. fr. E dial. *bunt* (to sift)] (1711) **1 :** a lightweight loosely woven fabric used chiefly for flags and festive decorations **2 a :** FLAGS **b :** decorations esp. in the colors of the national flag

[3]**bunting** *n* [term of endearment in the nursery rhyme "Bye, baby bunting"] (1922) **:** an infant's hooded sleeping bag made of napped fabric

bunt·line \'bənt-,līn, -lən\ *n* (1627) **:** one of the ropes attached to the foot of a square sail to haul the sail up to the yard for furling

Bun·yan·esque \,bən-yə-'nesk\ *adj* (1888) **1** [John *Bunyan*] **:** of, relating to, or suggestive of the allegorical writings of John Bunyan **2** [Paul *Bunyan*, legendary giant lumberjack of U.S. & Canada] **a :** of, relating to, or suggestive of the tales of Paul Bunyan **b :** of fantastically large size

[1]**buoy** \'bü-ē, 'bȯi\ *n* [ME *boye*, fr. (assumed) MF *boie*, fr. OF, fetter, buoy, of Gmc origin; akin to OHG *bouhhan* sign — more at BEACON] (13c) **1 :** FLOAT 2; *esp* **:** a floating object moored to the bottom to mark a channel or something (as a shoal) lying under the water **2 :** LIFE BUOY

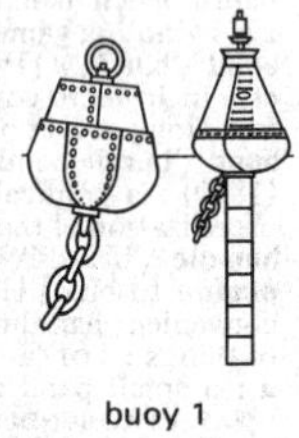

buoy 1

[2]**buoy** *vt* (1596) **1 :** to mark by or as if by a buoy **2 a :** to keep afloat **b :** SUPPORT, SUSTAIN ⟨an economy ~*ed* by the dramatic postwar growth of industry—*Time*⟩ **3 :** to raise the spirits of — usu. used with *up* ⟨hope ~*s* him up⟩ ~ *vi* **:** FLOAT

buoy·ance \'bȯi-ən(t)s, 'bü-yən(t)s\ *n* (1821) **:** BUOYANCY

buoy·an·cy \'bȯi-ən-sē, 'bü-yən-\ *n* (1713) **1 a :** the tendency of a body to float or to rise when submerged in a fluid **b :** the power of a fluid to exert an upward force on a body placed in it **2 :** the ability to recover quickly from depression or discouragement **:** RESILIENCE, VIVACITY

buoy·ant \'bȯi-ənt, 'bü-yənt\ *adj* (1578) **:** having buoyancy: as **a :** capable of floating **b :** CHEERFUL, GAY — **buoy·ant·ly** *adv*

buq·sha \'bük-shə\ *n* [Ar] (1963) **:** a unit of value of the Yemen Arab Republic equal to $^1/_{40}$ rial

bur *var of* BURR

Bur·ber·ry \'bər-bə-rē, 'bər-,ber-ē\ *trademark* — used for various fabrics used esp. for coats for outdoor wear

[1]**bur·ble** \'bər-bəl\ *vi* **bur·bled; bur·bling** \-b(ə-)liŋ\ [ME *burblen*] (14c) **1 :** BUBBLE **2 :** BABBLE, PRATTLE — **bur·bler** \-b(ə-)lər\ *n*

[2]**burble** *n* (1898) **1 :** PRATTLE **2 :** the breaking up of the streamline flow of air about a body (as an airplane wing) — **bur·bly** \-b(ə-)lē\ *adj*

bur·bot \'bər-bət\ *n, pl* **burbot** *also* **burbots** [ME *borbot*, fr. MF *bourbotte*, fr. *bourbeter* to burrow in the mud] (14c) **:** a freshwater fish (*Lota lota*) of the cod family having barbels on the nose and chin and existing in the northern parts of the New and the Old World

[1]**bur·den** \'bərd-ᵊn\ *n* [ME, fr. OE *byrthen*; akin to OE *beran* to carry — more at BEAR] (bef. 12c) **1 a :** something that is carried **:** LOAD **b :** DUTY, RESPONSIBILITY **2 :** something oppressive or worrisome **3 a :** the bearing of a load — usu. used in the phrase *beast of burden* **b :** capacity for carrying cargo ⟨a ship of a hundred tons ~⟩

[2]**burden** *vt* **bur·dened; bur·den·ing** \'bərd-niŋ, -ᵊn-iŋ\ (1541) **:** LOAD, OPPRESS ⟨I will not ~ you with a lengthy account⟩

[3]**burden** *n* [alter. of *bourdon*] (14c) **1** *archaic* **:** a bass or accompanying part **2 a :** CHORUS, REFRAIN **b :** a central topic **:** THEME

burden of proof (1593) **:** the duty of proving a disputed assertion or charge

bur·den·some \'bərd-ᵊn-səm\ *adj* (1578) **:** imposing or constituting a burden **:** OPPRESSIVE ⟨~ restrictions⟩ ***syn*** see ONEROUS

bur·dock \'bər-,däk\ *n* (15c) **:** any of a genus (*Arctium*) of coarse composite herbs bearing globular flower heads with prickly bracts

bu·reau \'byu̇(ə)r-(,)ō\ *n, pl* **bureaus** *also* **bu·reaux** \-(,)ōz\ [F, desk, cloth covering for desks, fr. OF *burel* woolen cloth, fr. (assumed) OF *bure*, fr. LL *burra* shaggy cloth] (1699) **1 a** *Brit* **:** WRITING DESK; *esp* **:** one having drawers and a slant top **b :** a low chest of drawers for use in a bedroom **2 a :** a specialized administrative unit; *esp* **:** a subdivision of an executive department of a government **b :** a branch of a newspaper, newsmagazine, or wire service in an important news center

bu·reau·cra·cy \byu̇-'räk-rə-sē\ *n, pl* **-cies** [F *bureaucratie*, fr. *bureau* + *-cratie* -cracy] (1818) **1 a :** a body of nonelective government officials **b :** an administrative policy-making group **2 :** government characterized by specialization of functions, adherence to fixed rules, and a hierarchy of authority **3 :** a system of administration marked by officialism, red tape, and proliferation

bu·reau·crat \'byu̇r-ə-,krat\ *n* (1842) **:** a member of a bureaucracy; *esp* **:** a government official who follows a narrow rigid formal routine or who is established with great authority in his own department

bu·reau·crat·ic \,byu̇r-ə-'krat-ik\ *adj* (1836) **:** of, relating to, or having the characteristics of a bureaucracy or a bureaucrat ⟨~ government⟩ — **bu·reau·crat·i·cal·ly** \-i-k(ə-)lē\ *adv*

bu·reau·crat·ism \'byu̇r-ə-,krat-,iz-əm\ *n* (1880) **:** a bureaucratic system **:** BUREAUCRACY

bu·reau·cra·tize \byu̇-'räk-rə-,tīz\ *vt* **-tized; -tiz·ing** (1892) **:** to make bureaucratic **:** subject to bureaucracy — **bu·reau·cra·ti·za·tion** \-,räk-rət-ə-'zā-shən\ *n*

bu·rette *or* **bu·ret** \byu̇-'ret\ *n* [MF, cruet, fr. *buire* pitcher, perh. alter. of OF *buie*, of Gmc origin; akin to OE *būc* pitcher — more at BUCKET] (1836) **:** a graduated glass tube with a small aperture and stopcock for delivering measured quantities of liquid or for measuring the liquid or gas received or discharged

burg \'bərg\ *n* [OE — more at BOROUGH] (1753) **1 :** an ancient or medieval fortress or walled town **2 :** CITY, TOWN

bur·gage \'bər-gij\ *n* [ME, property held by burgage tenure, fr. MF *bourgage*, fr. OF, fr. *bourg*, *borc* town — more at BOURG] (15c) **:** a tenure by which real property in England and Scotland was held under the king or a lord for a yearly rent or for watching and warding

bur·gee \,bər-'jē, 'bər-,\ *n* [perh. fr. F dial. *bourgeais* shipowner] (1750) **:** a swallow-tailed flag used esp. by ships for signals or identification

bur·geon \'bər-jən\ *vi* [ME *burjonen*, fr. *burjon* bud, fr. OF, fr. (assumed) VL *burrion-*, *burrio*, fr. LL *burra* shaggy cloth] (14c) **1 a :** to send forth new growth (as buds or branches) **:** SPROUT **b :** BLOOM **2 :** to grow and expand rapidly **:** FLOURISH

-burg·er \,bər-gər\ *n comb form* [*hamburger*] **:** a fried or grilled patty usu. served in a sandwich

bur·gess \'bər-jəs\ *n* [ME *burgeis*, fr. OF *borjois*, fr. *borc*, fr. L *burgus*] (13c) **1 a :** a citizen of a British borough **b :** a representative of a borough, corporate town, or university in the British Parliament **2 :** a representative in the popular branch of the legislature of colonial Maryland and Virginia

burgh \'bər-(,)ō, -ə(-w); 'bə-(,)rō, -rə(-w)\ *n* [ME — more at BOROUGH] (12c) **:** BOROUGH; *specif* **:** an incorporated town in Scotland having local jurisdiction of certain services

burgh·er \'bər-gər\ *n* (13c) **1 :** an inhabitant of a borough or a town **2 :** a member of the middle class **:** a prosperous solid citizen

bur·glar \'bər-glər\ *n* [AF *burgler*, fr. ML *burglator*, prob. alter. of *burgator*, fr. *burgatus*, pp. of *burgare* to commit burglary, fr. L *burgus* fortified place — more at BOURG] (1541) **:** one who commits burglary

bur·glar·i·ous \,bər-'glar-ē-əs, -'gler-\ *adj* (1769) **:** of, relating to, or resembling burglary — **bur·glar·i·ous·ly** *adv*

bur·glar·ize \'bər-glə-,rīz\ *vb* **-ized; -iz·ing** *vt* (1871) **1 :** to break into and steal from **2 :** to commit burglary against ~ *vi* **:** to commit burglary

bur·glar·proof \,bər-glər-'prüf\ *adj* (1856) **:** protected against or designed to afford protection against burglary

bur·glary \'bər-glə-rē\ *n, pl* **-glar·ies** (1532) **:** the act of breaking into a building esp. with intent to steal; *specif* **:** the act of breaking into and entering the dwelling house of another at night with intent to commit a felony

bur·gle \'bər-gəl\ *vt* **bur·gled; bur·gling** \-g(ə-)liŋ\ [back-formation fr. *burglar*] (1870) **:** BURGLARIZE

bur·go·mas·ter \'bər-gə-,mas-tər\ *n* [part modif., part trans. of D *burgemeester*, fr. *burg* town + *meester* master] (1562) **:** the chief magistrate of a town in some European countries **:** MAYOR

bur·go·net \'bər-gə-nət, ,bər-gə-'net\ *n* [modif. of MF *bourguignotte*] (1563) **:** a helmet of either of two 16th century styles

bur·goo \'bər-,gü, (,)bər-'\ *n, pl* **burgoos** [origin unknown] (1700) **1 :** oatmeal gruel **2 :** hardtack and molasses cooked together **3 a :** a stew or thick soup of meat and vegetables orig. served at outdoor gatherings **b :** a picnic at which burgoo is served

bur·gun·dy \'bər-gən-dē\ *n, pl* **-dies** [*Burgundy*, region in France] (1668) **1** *often cap* **:** a red or white unblended wine from Burgundy; *also* **:** a blended red wine produced elsewhere (as California) **2 :** a reddish purple color

buri·al \'ber-ē-əl\ *n, often attrib* [ME *beriel*, *berial*, back-formation fr. *beriels* (taken as a plural), fr. OE *byrgels*; akin to OS *burgisli* tomb, OE *byrgan* to bury — more at BURY] (bef. 12c) **1 :** GRAVE, TOMB **2 :** the act or process of burying

buri·er \'ber-ē-ər\ *n* (bef. 12c) **:** one that buries

bu·rin \'byu̇r-ən, 'bər-\ *n* [F] (1662) **1 :** an engraver's steel cutting tool having the blade ground obliquely to a sharp point **2 :** a prehistoric flint tool with a beveled point

burke \'bərk\ *vt* **burked; burking** [earlier *burke* to suffocate, fr. William *Burke* †1829 Irish strangler] (1840) **1 :** to suppress quietly or indirectly ⟨~ an inquiry⟩ **2 :** BYPASS, AVOID ⟨~ an issue⟩

Bur·kitt's lymphoma \'bər-kəts-\ *also* **Bur·kitt lymphoma** \-kət-\ *n* [Denis Parsons *Burkitt* *b*1911 Brit. surgeon] (1965) **:** a malignant lymphoma that occurs esp. in children of central Africa and is associated with Epstein-Barr virus

burl \'bər(-ə)l\ *n* [ME *burle*, fr. (assumed) OF *bourle* tuft of wool, fr. (assumed) VL *burrula*, dim. of LL *burra* shaggy cloth] (15c) **1 :** a knot or lump in thread or cloth **2 a :** a hard woody often flattened hemispherical outgrowth on a tree **b :** veneer made from burls

bur·la·de·ro \,bu̇r-lə-'de(ə)r-(,)ō, ,bər-\ *n, pl* **-ros** [Sp, fr. *burlar* to make fun of, elude, fr. *burla* joke] (1938) **:** a wooden shield set parallel to the wall in a bullring for bullfighters to take shelter behind if pursued

bur·lap \'bər-,lap\ *n* [origin unknown] (1695) **1 :** a coarse heavy plain-woven fabric usu. of jute or hemp used for bagging and wrapping and in furniture and linoleum manufacture **2 :** a lightweight material resembling burlap used in interior decoration or for clothing

burled \'bər(-ə)ld\ *adj* (1924) **:** having a distorted grain due to burls

[1]**bur•lesque** \(ˌ)bər-ˈlesk\ *n* [*burlesque,* adj. (comic, droll), fr. F, fr. It *burlesco,* fr. *burla* joke, fr. Sp] (1667) **1 :** a literary or dramatic work that seeks to ridicule by means of grotesque exaggeration or comic imitation **2 :** mockery usu. by caricature **3 :** theatrical entertainment of a broadly humorous often earthy character consisting of short turns, comic skits, and sometimes striptease acts ***syn*** see CARICATURE — **burlesque** *adj* — **bur•lesque•ly** *adv*

[2]**burlesque** *vb* **bur•lesqued; bur•lesqu•ing** *vt* (1676) **:** to imitate in a humorous or derisive manner **:** MOCK ~ *vi* **:** to employ burlesque — **bur•lesqu•er** *n*

bur•ley \ˈbər-lē\ *n* [prob. fr. the name *Burley*] (1881) **:** a thin-bodied air-cured tobacco grown mainly in Kentucky

bur•ly \ˈbər-lē\ *adj* **bur•li•er; -est** [ME] (13c) **1 :** strongly and heavily built **:** HUSKY **2 :** heartily direct and frank **:** BLUFF, FORTHRIGHT ⟨an evocative story less ~ than the real thing but entertaining—E. A. Weeks⟩ — **bur•li•ly** \-lə-lē\ *adv* — **bur•li•ness** \-lē-nəs\ *n*

bur marigold *n* (ca. 1817) **:** any of a genus (*Bidens*) of coarse composite herbs with prickly flattened achenes that adhere to clothing

Bur•mese \ˌbər-ˈmēz, -ˈmēs\ *n, pl* **Burmese** (1824) **1 :** a native or inhabitant of Burma **2 :** the Tibeto-Burman language of the Burmese people — **Burmese** *adj*

Burmese cat *n* (1939) **:** any of a U.S.-developed breed of slender short-haired cats having gold eyes and a usu. dark brown coat — see CAT illustration

[1]**burn** \ˈbərn\ *n* [ME, fr. OE; akin to OHG *brunno* spring of water] *Brit* (bef. 12c) **:** CREEK 2

[2]**burn** \ˈbərn\ *vb* **burned** \ˈbərnd, ˈbərnt \ *or* **burnt** \ˈbərnt\; **burn•ing** [ME *birnan,* fr. OE *byrnan,* v.i., *bærnan,* v.t.; akin to OHG *brinnan* to burn, L *fervēre* to boil] *vi* (bef. 12c) **1 a :** to consume fuel and give off heat, light, and gases ⟨a small fire ~*s* on the hearth⟩ **b :** to undergo combustion; *also* **:** to undergo nuclear fission or nuclear fusion **c :** to contain a fire ⟨little stove ~*ing* in the corner⟩ **d :** to give off light **:** SHINE, GLOW ⟨a light ~*ing* in the window⟩ **2 a :** to be hot ⟨the ~*ing* sand⟩ **b :** to produce or undergo discomfort or pain ⟨iodine ~*s* so⟩ ⟨ears ~*ing* from the cold⟩ **c :** to become emotionally excited or agitated: as **(1) :** to yearn ardently ⟨~*ing* to tell the story⟩ **(2) :** to be or become very angry or disgusted ⟨that remark really made him ~⟩ **3 a :** to undergo alteration or destruction by the action of fire or heat ⟨watched their house ~ down⟩ ⟨the potatoes ~*ed* to a crisp⟩ **b :** to die in the electric chair **4 :** to force or make a way by or as if by burning ⟨her words ~*ed* into his heart⟩ **5 :** to receive sunburn ⟨she ~*s* easily⟩ ~ *vt* **1 a :** to cause to undergo combustion; *esp* **:** to destroy by fire ⟨~*ed* the trash⟩ **b :** to use as fuel ⟨this furnace ~*s* gas⟩ **2 a :** to transform by exposure to heat or fire ⟨~ clay to bricks⟩ **b :** to produce by burning ⟨~*ed* a hole in his sleeve⟩ **3 a :** to injure or damage by or as if by exposure to fire, heat, or radiation **:** SCORCH ⟨~*ed* his hand⟩ **b :** to execute by burning ⟨~*ed* heretics at the stake⟩; *also* **:** ELECTROCUTE **4 a :** IRRITATE, ANNOY — usu. used with *up* ⟨really ~*s* me up⟩ **b :** to take advantage of **:** DECEIVE, CHEAT — often used in passive **5 :** to wear out **:** EXHAUST — **burn•able** \ˈbər-nə-bəl\ *adj* — **burn one's bridges** *also* **burn one's boats :** to cut off all means of retreat — **burn one's ears :** to rebuke strongly — **burn the candle at both ends :** to use one's resources or energies to excess — **burn the midnight oil :** to work or study far into the night

[3]**burn** *n* (1594) **1 :** the act, process, or result of burning: as **a :** injury or damage resulting from exposure to fire, heat, caustics, electricity, or certain radiations **b :** a burned area ⟨a ~ on the tabletop⟩ **c :** an abrasion (as of the skin) having the appearance of a burn ⟨rope ~*s*⟩ **d :** a burning sensation ⟨the ~ of iodine on a cut⟩ **2 :** the firing of a spacecraft rocket engine in flight **3 :** ANGER; *esp* **:** increasing fury — used chiefly in the phrase *slow burn*

burned–out \ˈbərn-ˈdau̇t, ˈbərnt-ˈau̇t\ *or* **burnt–out** \ˈbərnt-ˈau̇t\ *adj* (1837) **:** worn out by excessive or improper use ⟨~ bearings⟩; *also* **:** EXHAUSTED ⟨died a ~ man⟩

burn•er \ˈbər-nər\ *n* (14c) **:** one that burns; *esp* **:** the part of a fuel-burning or heat-producing device (as a furnace or stove) where the flame or heat is produced

bur•net \(ˌ)bər-ˈnet, ˈbər-nət\ *n* [ME, fr. MF *burnete,* fr. *brun* brown — more at BRUNET] (14c) **:** any of a genus (*Sanguisorba*) of herbs of the rose family with odd-pinnate stipulate leaves and spikes of apetalous flowers

burn in *vt* (ca. 1939) **:** to increase the density of (portions of a photographic print) during enlarging by giving extra exposure — compare DODGE

burn•ing \ˈbər-niŋ\ *adj* (bef. 12c) **1 a :** being on fire **b :** ARDENT, INTENSE ⟨~ enthusiasm⟩ **2 a :** affecting with or as if with heat ⟨a ~ fever⟩ **b :** resembling that produced by a burn ⟨a ~ sensation on the tongue⟩ **3 :** of fundamental importance **:** URGENT ⟨one of the ~ issues of our time⟩ — **burn•ing•ly** \-niŋ-lē\ *adv*

burning bush *n* (1785) **:** any of several plants associated with fire (as by redness): as **a :** [2]WAHOO **b :** SUMMER CYPRESS

burning ghat *n* (ca. 1877) **:** a level space at the head of a ghat for cremation

[1]**bur•nish** \ˈbər-nish\ *vt* [ME *burnischen,* fr. MF *bruniss-,* stem of *brunir,* lit., to make brown, fr. *brun* — more at BRUNETTE] (14c) **1 :** to make shiny or lustrous esp. by rubbing **:** POLISH **2 :** to rub (a material) with a tool for compacting or smoothing or for turning an edge — **bur•nish•er** *n* — **bur•nish•ing** *adj or n*

[2]**burnish** *n* (1647) **:** LUSTER, GLOSS

bur•noose *or* **bur•nous** \(ˌ)bər-ˈnüs\ *n* [F *burnous,* fr. Ar *burnus*] (1600) **:** a one-piece hooded cloak worn by Arabs and Berbers

burn•out \ˈbər-ˌnau̇t\ *n* (1940) **1 :** the cessation of operation of a jet or rocket engine; *also* **:** the point at which burnout occurs **2 :** exhaustion of physical or emotional strength

burn•sides \ˈbərn-ˌsīdz\ *n pl* [Ambrose E. *Burnside*] (1875) **:** SIDEWHISKERS; *esp* **:** full muttonchop whiskers

[1]**burp** \ˈbərp\ *n* [imit.] (ca. 1932) **:** BELCH

[2]**burp** *vi* (ca. 1932) **:** BELCH ~ *vt* **:** to help (a baby) expel gas from the stomach esp. by patting or rubbing the back

burp gun *n* (1944) **:** a small submachine gun

[1]**burr** \ˈbər\ *n* [ME *burre;* akin to OE *byrst* bristle — more at BRISTLE] (14c) **1** *usu* **bur a :** a rough or prickly envelope of a fruit **b :** a plant that bears burs **2 a :** something that sticks or clings ⟨a ~ in the throat⟩ **b :** HANGER-ON **3 :** an irregular rounded mass; *esp* **:** a tree burl **4 :** a thin ridge or area of roughness produced in cutting or shaping metal **5 a :** a trilled uvular \r\ as used by some speakers of English esp. in northern England and in Scotland **b :** a tongue-point trill that is the usual Scottish \r\ **6 a :** a small rotary cutting tool **b** *usu* **bur :** a bit used on a dental drill **7 :** a rough humming sound **:** WHIR — **burred** \ˈbərd\ *adj*

[2]**burr** *vi* (1798) **1 :** to speak with a burr **2 :** to make a whirring sound ~ *vt* **1 :** to pronounce with a burr **2 a :** to form into a projecting edge **b :** to remove burrs from — **burr•er** *n*

[3]**burr** *n* [ME *burwhe* circle] (1627) **:** a small washer put on the end of a rivet before swaging it down

[4]**burr** *n* [perh. fr. [1]*burr*] (1652) **:** BUHRSTONE

bur reed *n* (1597) **:** any of a genus (*Sparganium,* family Sparganiaceae) of plants with globose fruits resembling burs

bur•ri•to \bə-ˈrē-(ˌ)tō\ *n, pl* **-tos** [AmerSp, fr. Sp, lit., little donkey, dim. of *burro*] (1945) **:** a flour tortilla rolled or folded around a filling (as of meat, beans, or cheese) and usu. baked

bur•ro \ˈbər-(ˌ)ō, ˈbu̇r-, -ə(-w); ˈbə-(ˌ)rō, -rə(-w)\ *n, pl* **burros** [Sp, irreg. fr. *borrico,* fr. LL *burricus* small horse] (1800) **:** DONKEY; *esp* **:** a small one used as a pack animal

[1]**bur•row** \ˈbər-(ˌ)ō, -ə(-w); ˈbə-(ˌ)rō, -rə(-w)\ *n* [ME *borow*] (13c) **:** a hole or excavation in the ground made by an animal (as a rabbit) for shelter and habitation

[2]**burrow** *vt* (1602) **1** *archaic* **:** to hide in or as if in a burrow **2 a :** to construct by tunneling **b :** to penetrate by means of a burrow **3 :** to make a motion suggestive of burrowing with **:** NESTLE ⟨she ~*s* her grubby hand into mine⟩ ~ *vi* **1 :** to conceal oneself in or as if in a burrow **2 a :** to make a burrow **b :** to progress by or as if by digging **3 :** to make a motion suggestive of burrowing **:** SNUGGLE, NESTLE ⟨~*ed* against his back for warmth⟩ — **bur•row•er** *n*

burrstone *var of* BUHRSTONE

bur•ry \ˈbər-ē\ *adj* **bur•ri•er; -est** (15c) **1 :** containing burs **2 :** PRICKLY **3** *of speech* **:** characterized by a burr

bur•sa \ˈbər-sə\ *n, pl* **bur•sas** \-səz\ *or* **bur•sae** \-ˌsē, -ˌsī\ [NL, fr. ML, bag, purse — more at PURSE] (1803) **:** a bodily pouch or sac: as **a :** a small serous sac between a tendon and a bone **b :** BURSA OF FABRICIUS — **bur•sal** \-səl\ *adj*

bursa of Fa•bri•cius \-fə-ˈbrish(-ē)-əs\ [Johan C. Fabricius †1808 Dan. entomologist] (1945) **:** a lymphoid organ that opens into the cloaca of birds and functions in B cell production

bur•sar \ˈbər-sər, -ˌsär\ *n* [ML *bursarius,* fr. *bursa*] (13c) **:** an officer (as of a monastery or college) in charge of funds **:** TREASURER

bur•sa•ry \-s(ə-)rē\ *n, pl* **-ries** [ML *bursaria,* fr. *bursa*] (1695) **1 :** the treasury of a college or monastery **2** *Brit* **:** a monetary grant to a needy student **:** SCHOLARSHIP

burse \ˈbərs\ *n* [MF *bourse,* fr. ML *bursa*] (15c) **1 a :** PURSE **b :** a square cloth case used to carry the corporal in a Communion service **2** *obs* **:** EXCHANGE, BOURSE

bur•si•tis \(ˌ)bər-ˈsīt-əs\ *n* [NL, fr. *bursa*] (1857) **:** inflammation of a bursa esp. of the shoulder or elbow

[1]**burst** \ˈbərst\ *vb* **burst** *also* **burst•ed; burst•ing** [ME *bersten,* fr. OE *berstan;* akin to OHG *brestan* to burst, MIr *brosc* noise] *vi* (bef. 12c) **1 :** to break open, apart, or into pieces usu. from impact or from pressure from within **2 a :** to give way from an excess of emotion ⟨his heart will ~ with grief⟩ **b :** to give vent suddenly to a repressed emotion ⟨~ into tears⟩ ⟨~ out laughing⟩ **3 a :** to emerge or spring suddenly ⟨~ out of a house⟩ **b :** LAUNCH, PLUNGE ⟨~ into song⟩ **4 :** to be filled to the breaking point ~ *vt* **1 :** to cause to burst **2 :** to force open (as a door) by strong or vigorous action **3 :** to produce by or as if by bursting — **burst•er** *n* — **burst at the seams :** to be larger, fuller, or more crowded than could reasonably have been anticipated

[2]**burst** *n* (1610) **1 a :** a sudden outbreak; *esp* **:** a vehement outburst (as of emotion) **b :** EXPLOSION, ERUPTION **c :** a sudden intense effort ⟨a ~ of speed⟩ **d :** the duration of fire in one engagement of the mechanism of an automatic firearm **2 :** an act of bursting **3 :** a result of bursting; *specif* **:** a visible puff accompanying the explosion of a shell

bur•then \ˈbər-t͟hən\ *var of* BURDEN

bur•ton \ˈbərt-ᵊn\ *n* [origin unknown] (ca. 1704) **:** any of several arrangements of hoisting tackle; *esp* **:** one with a single and a double block

bur•weed \ˈbər-ˌwēd\ *n* (ca. 1783) **:** any of various plants (as a cocklebur or burdock) having burry fruit

bury \ˈber-ē *also* ˈbər-\ *vt* **bur•ied; bury•ing** [ME *burien,* fr. OE *byrgan;* akin to OHG *bergan* to shelter, Russ *berech'* to save] (bef. 12c) **1 :** to dispose of by depositing in or as if in the earth; *esp* **:** to inter with funeral ceremonies **2 a :** to conceal by or as if by covering with earth ⟨~ a treasure⟩ ⟨the report was *buried* under miscellaneous papers⟩ **b :** to cover from view ⟨*buried* her face in her hands⟩ **3 a :** to put completely out of mind **:** have done with ⟨~*ing* their differences⟩ **b :** to conceal in obscurity ⟨*buried* the retraction among the classified ads⟩ **c :** SUBMERGE, ENGROSS — usu. used with *in* ⟨*buried* himself in his books⟩ **4 :** to put (a playing card) out of play by placing it in or under the dealer's pack ***syn*** see HIDE — **bury the hatchet :** to settle a disagreement **:** become reconciled

[1]**bus** \ˈbəs\ *n, pl* **bus•es** *or* **bus•ses** *often attrib* [short for *omnibus*] (1832) **1 a :** a large motor-driven passenger vehicle operating usu. according to a schedule along a fixed route **b :** AUTOMOBILE **2 :** a small hand truck **3 a :** a conductor or an assembly of conductors for collecting electric currents and distributing them to outgoing feeders — called also *bus bar* **b :** a set of parallel conductors in a computer system that forms a main transmission path

[2]**bus** *vb* **bused** *or* **bussed; bus•ing** *or* **bus•sing** *vi* (1838) **1 :** to travel by bus **2 :** to work as a busboy ~ *vt* **:** to transport by bus

bus•boy \ˈbəs-ˌbȯi\ *n* [*omnibus* (busboy)] (1913) **:** a waiter's assistant; *specif* **:** one who removes dirty dishes and resets tables in a restaurant

bus·by \ˈbəz-bē\ *n, pl* **busbies** [prob. fr. the name *Busby*] (1853) : a military full-dress fur hat with a pendent bag on one side usu. of the color of regimental facings

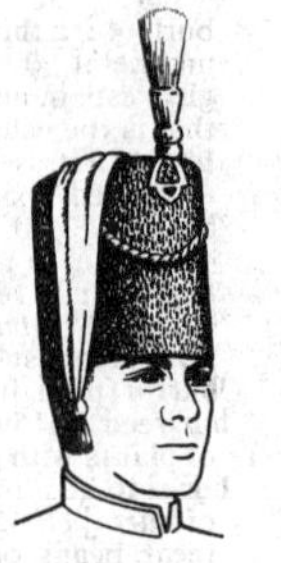

busby

[1]bush \ˈbu̇sh\ *n, often attrib* [ME; akin to OHG *busc* forest] (13c) **1 a :** SHRUB; *esp* **:** a low densely branched shrub **b :** a close thicket of shrubs suggesting a single plant **2 :** a large uncleared or sparsely settled area (as in Australia) usu. scrub-covered or forested **:** WILDERNESS **3 a** (1) *archaic* **:** a bunch of ivy formerly hung outside a tavern to indicate wine for sale (2) *obs* **:** TAVERN **b :** ADVERTISING ⟨good wine needs no ~ —Shak.⟩ **4 :** a bushy tuft or mass ⟨a ~ of hair —Roger Senhouse⟩; *esp* **:** [2]BRUSH 2a

[2]bush *vt* (15c) **:** to support, mark, or protect with bushes ~ *vi* **:** to extend like a bush **:** resemble a bush

[3]bush *adj* (ca. 1597) **:** having a low-growing compact bushy habit — used esp. of cultivated beans ⟨~ snap beans⟩

[4]bush *n* [D *bus* bushing, box, fr. MD *busse* box, fr. LL *buxis* — more at BOX] (1566) **1 :** BUSHING **2 :** a threaded socket

[5]bush *vt* (1566) **:** to furnish with a bushing

bush baby *n* (1901) **:** GALAGO

bush basil *n* (1597) **:** a small cultivated annual herb (*Ocimum minimum*) with nearly entire leaves

bush·buck \ˈbu̇sh-ˌbək\ *n, pl* **bushbuck** *or* **bushbucks** [trans. of Afrik *bosbok*] (1852) **:** a small southern African striped antelope (*Strepsiceros scriptus* or *Tragelaphus scriptus*) having spirally twisted horns and frequenting forests; *also* **:** any of several related antelopes

bush clover *n* (ca. 1817) **:** any of several usu. shrubby lespedezas

bushed \ˈbu̇sht\ *adj* (14c) **1 :** covered with or as if with a bushy growth **2** *chiefly Austral* **a :** lost esp. in the bush **b :** perplexed or confused esp. by a complexity or variety of considerations ⟨adapting his language to my ~ comprehension —Henry Lawson⟩ **3 :** TIRED, EXHAUSTED

[1]bush·el \ˈbu̇sh-əl\ *n* [ME *busshel,* fr. OF *boissel,* fr. (assumed) OF *boisse* one sixth of a bushel, of Celt origin; akin to MIr *boss* palm of the hand] (14c) **1 :** any of various units of dry capacity — see WEIGHT table **2 :** a container holding a bushel **3 :** a large quantity **:** LOTS ⟨always sends them a ~ of love⟩ — **bush·el·age** \-ə-lij\ *n*

[2]bushel *vb* **bush·eled; bush·el·ing** \-(ə-)liŋ\ [prob. fr. G *bosseln* to do poor work, to patch; akin to OE *bēatan* to beat] (ca. 1877) **:** REPAIR, RENOVATE — **bush·el·er** \-(ə-)lər\ *n*

bush·fire \ˈbu̇sh-ˌfī(ə)r\ *n, Austral* (1868) **:** an uncontrolled fire in a wooded area

Bu·shi·do \ˈbü-shi-ˌdō, ˈbüsh-\ *n* [Jp *bushidō*] (1898) **:** a feudal-military Japanese code of chivalry valuing honor above life

bush·ing \ˈbu̇sh-iŋ\ *n* (1839) **1 :** a usu. removable cylindrical lining for an opening (as of a mechanical part) used to limit the size of the opening, resist abrasion, or serve as a guide **2 :** an electrically insulating lining for a hole to protect a through conductor

bush jacket *n* [fr. its use in rough country] (1939) **:** a long cotton jacket resembling a shirt and having four patch pockets, a belt, and a notched collar

bush–league *adj* (1914) **:** belonging to an inferior class or group of its kind **:** MEDIOCRE

bush league *n* (1909) **:** MINOR LEAGUE — **bush leaguer** *n*

bush·man \ˈbu̇sh-mən\ *n* (1785) **1** *cap* [modif. of obs. Afrik *boschjesman,* fr. *boschje* (dim. of *bosch* forest) + Afrik *man*] **a :** a member of a race of nomadic hunters of southern Africa **b :** a Khoisan language of the Bushmen **2 a :** WOODSMAN **b** *chiefly Austral* **:** one that lives in the bush; *specif* **:** HICK

bush·mas·ter \-ˌmas-tər\ *n* (1826) **:** a tropical American pit viper (*Lachesis mutus*) that is the largest New World venomous snake

bush pilot *n* (1936) **:** a pilot who flies a small plane into remote areas

bush·rang·er \-ˌrān-jər\ *n* (1758) **1 :** FRONTIERSMAN, WOODSMAN **2** *Austral* **:** an outlaw living in the bush — **bush·rang·ing** \-jiŋ\ *n*

bush shirt *n* [fr. its use in rough country] (1909) **:** a usu. loose-fitting cotton shirt with patch pockets

bush·tit \-ˌtit\ *n* (ca. 1889) **:** any of several titmice (genus *Psaltriparus*) of western No. America

bush·whack \ˈbu̇sh-ˌ(h)wak\ *vb* [back-formation fr. *bushwhacker*] *vi* (1834) **1 a :** to propel a boat by pulling on bushes along the bank **b :** to clear a path through thick woods esp. by chopping down bushes and low branches **2 a :** to live or hide out in the woods **b :** to fight in or attack from the bush ~ *vt* **:** AMBUSH — **bush·whack·er** *n* — **bush·whack·ing** *n*

bushy \ˈbu̇sh-ē\ *adj* **bush·i·er; -est** (14c) **1 :** full of or overgrown with bushes **2 :** resembling a bush; *esp* **:** being thick and spreading — **bush·i·ly** \ˈbu̇sh-ə-lē\ *adv* — **bush·i·ness** \ˈbu̇sh-ē-nəs\ *n*

busi·ness \ˈbiz-nəs, -nəz\ *n, often attrib* (14c) **1** *archaic* **:** purposeful activity **:** BUSYNESS **2 a :** ROLE, FUNCTION ⟨how the human mind went about its ~ of learning —H. A. Overstreet⟩ **b :** an immediate task or objective **:** MISSION ⟨what is your ~ here at this hour⟩ **c :** a particular field of endeavor ⟨the best in the ~⟩ **3 a :** a usu. commercial or mercantile activity engaged in as a means of livelihood **:** TRADE, LINE ⟨in the ~ of supplying emergency services to industry⟩ **b :** a commercial or sometimes an industrial enterprise ⟨sold his ~ and retired⟩; *also* **:** such enterprises **c :** usu. economic dealings **:** PATRONAGE ⟨ready to take his ~ elsewhere unless service improved⟩ **4 :** AFFAIR, MATTER ⟨a strange ~⟩ **5 :** movement or action (as lighting a cigarette) by an actor intended esp. to establish atmosphere, reveal character, or explain a situation — called also *stage business* **6 a :** personal concern ⟨none of your ~⟩ **b :** RIGHT ⟨you have no ~ hitting her⟩ **7 a :** serious activity requiring time and effort and usu. the avoidance of distractions ⟨immediately got down to ~⟩ **b :** maximum effort **8 a :** a damaging assault **b :** REBUKE, TONGUE-LASHING **c :** DOUBLE CROSS

syn BUSINESS, COMMERCE, TRADE, INDUSTRY, TRAFFIC mean activity concerned with the supplying and distribution of commodities. BUSINESS may be an inclusive term but specifically designates the activities of those engaged in the purchase or sale of commodities or in related financial transactions; COMMERCE and TRADE imply the exchange and transportation of commodities; INDUSTRY applies to the producing of commodities, esp. by manufacturing or processing, usu. on a large scale; TRAFFIC applies to the operation and functioning of public carriers of goods and persons. ***syn*** see in addition WORK

business administration *n* (ca. 1908) **:** a program of studies in a college or university providing general knowledge of business principles and practices

business cycle *n* (1919) **:** a cycle of economic activity usu. consisting of recession, recovery, growth, and decline

busi·ness·like \ˈbiz-nə-ˌslīk, -nəz-ˌlīk\ *adj* (1791) **1 :** exhibiting qualities believed to be advantageous in business **2 :** SERIOUS, PURPOSEFUL

busi·ness·man \ˈbiz-nə-ˌsman, -nəz-ˌman\ *n* (1826) **:** a man who transacts business; *esp* **:** a business executive

busi·ness·peo·ple \ˈbiz-nə-ˌspē-pəl, -nəz-ˌpē-pəl\ *n pl* (1865) **:** persons active in business

busi·ness·per·son \ˈbiz-nə-ˌspərs-ᵊn, -nəz-ˌpərs-ᵊn\ *n* (1974) **:** a businessman or businesswoman

busi·ness·wom·an \ˈbiz-nə-ˌswu̇m-ən, -nəz-ˌwu̇m-\ *n* (1844) **:** a woman active in business; *esp* **:** a female business executive

bus·ing *or* **bus·sing** \ˈbəs-iŋ\ *n* (1889) **:** the act of transporting by bus; *specif* **:** the transporting of children to a school outside their residential area as a means of establishing racial balance in that school

busk·er \ˈbəs-kər\ *n* [origin unknown] *chiefly Brit* (1857) **:** one who entertains esp. by singing or reciting on the street, in pubs, or in subway passages

bus·kin \ˈbəs-kən\ *n* [perh. modif. of Sp *borcegui*] (1503) **1 :** a laced boot reaching halfway or more to the knee **2 a :** COTHURNUS 1 **b :** TRAGEDY; *esp* **:** tragedy resembling that of ancient Greek drama

bus·man's holiday \ˌbəs-mənz-\ *n* (1893) **:** a holiday spent in following or observing the practice of one's usual occupation

buss \ˈbəs\ *n* [perh. fr. ME *bassen* to kiss, fr. MF, fr. OF *baisier,* fr. L *bassiare*] (1570) **:** KISS — **buss** *vt*

[1]bust \ˈbəst\ *n* [F *buste,* fr. It *busto,* fr. L *bustum* tomb] (1645) **1 :** a sculptured representation of the upper part of the human figure including the head and neck and usu. part of the shoulders and breast **2 :** the upper part of the human torso between neck and waist; *esp* **:** the breasts of a woman

[2]bust *vb* **bust·ed** *also* **bust; bust·ing** *vt* [alter. of *burst*] (1860) **1 :** HIT, SLUG **2 a :** to break or smash esp. with force; *also* **:** to make inoperative ⟨~*ed* my watch this morning⟩ **b :** to bring an end to **:** BREAK UP ⟨helped ~ trusts —*Newsweek*⟩ — often used with *up* ⟨better not try to ~ up his happy marriage —*Forbes*⟩ **c :** to ruin financially **3 :** DEMOTE **4 :** TAME ⟨bronco ~*ing*⟩ **5** *slang* **a :** ARREST ⟨~*ed* for carrying guns — Saul Gottlieb⟩ **b :** RAID ⟨~*ed* the flat below . . . and found a sizable quantity of pot — Robert Courtney⟩ ~ *vi* **1 a :** BURST ⟨laughing fit to ~⟩ **b :** BREAK DOWN **2 :** to go broke **3 a :** to fail to complete a straight or flush in poker **b :** to lose at cards by exceeding a limit (as the count of 21 in blackjack)

[3]bust *n* (1840) **1 a :** SPREE **b :** a hearty drinking session ⟨a beer ~⟩ **2 a :** a complete failure **:** FLOP **b :** a business depression **3 :** PUNCH, SOCK **4** *slang* **:** a police raid

bus·tard \ˈbəs-tərd\ *n* [ME, modif. of MF *bistarde,* fr. OIt *bistarda,* fr. L *avis tarda,* lit., slow bird] (13c) **:** any of a family (Otididae) of Old World and Australian game birds

bust·er \ˈbəs-tər\ *n* (1848) **1** *chiefly Austral* **:** a sudden violent wind often coming from the south **2 a :** an unusually sturdy child **b** *often cap* **:** FELLOW — usu. used as a noun of address ⟨hey ~, come here⟩ **3 :** one that breaks or breaks up ⟨crime ~*s*⟩ **:** as **a :** PLOW **b** [short for *broncobuster*] **:** one who breaks horses **4 :** something having unusual destructive force: as **a :** a jarring fall **b :** BLOCKBUSTER

[1]bus·tle \ˈbəs-əl\ *vi* **bus·tled; bus·tling** \ˈbəs-(ə-)liŋ\ [prob. alter. of obs. *buskle* to prepare, freq. of *busk,* fr. ON *būask* to prepare oneself] (1580) **1 :** to move briskly and often ostentatiously **2 :** to be busily astir **:** TEEM — **bustling** *adj* — **bus·tling·ly** \-(ə-)liŋ-lē\ *adv*

[2]bustle *n* (1634) **:** noisy, energetic, and often obtrusive activity ⟨the hustle and ~ of the big city⟩

[3]bustle *n* [origin unknown] (1786) **:** a pad or framework expanding and supporting the fullness and drapery of the back of a woman's skirt

busty \ˈbəs-tē\ *adj* **bust·i·er; -est** (1944) **:** having a large bust

bu·sul·fan \byü-ˈsəl-fən\ *n* [*butane* + *sulfonyl*] (ca. 1958) **:** an antineoplastic agent $C_6H_{14}O_6S_2$ used in the treatment of chronic myelogenous leukemia

[1]busy \ˈbiz-ē\ *adj* **busi·er; -est** [ME *bisy,* fr. OE *bisig;* akin to MD & MLG *besich* busy] (bef. 12c) **1 a :** engaged in action **:** OCCUPIED **b :** being in use ⟨found the telephone ~⟩ **2 :** full of activity **:** BUSTLING ⟨a ~ seaport⟩ **3 :** foolishly or intrusively active **:** MEDDLING **4 :** full of distracting detail ⟨a ~ design⟩ — **busi·ly** \ˈbiz-ə-lē\ *adv* — **busy·ness** \ˈbiz-ē-nəs\ *n*

syn BUSY, INDUSTRIOUS, DILIGENT, ASSIDUOUS, SEDULOUS mean actively engaged or occupied. BUSY chiefly stresses activity as opposed to idleness or leisure; INDUSTRIOUS implies characteristic or habitual devotion to work; DILIGENT suggests earnest application to some specific object or pursuit; ASSIDUOUS stresses careful and unremitting application; SEDULOUS implies painstaking and persevering application.

[2]busy *vb* **bus·ied; busy·ing** *vt* (bef. 12c) **:** to make busy **:** OCCUPY ~ *vi* **:** BUSTLE ⟨small boats *busied* to and fro —Quentin Crewe⟩

busy·body \ˈbiz-ē-ˌbäd-ē\ *n* (1526) **:** an officious or inquisitive person

busy·work \-ˌwərk\ *n* (1911) **:** work that usu. appears productive or of intrinsic value but actually only keeps one occupied

[1]but \(ˈ)bət\ *conj* [ME, fr. OE *būtan,* prep. & conj., outside, without, except, except that; akin to OHG *būzan* without, except, OE *be* by, and OE *ūt* out — more at BY, OUT] (bef. 12c) **1 a :** except for the fact ⟨would have protested ~ that he was afraid⟩ **b :** THAT — used after a negative ⟨there is no doubt ~ he won⟩ **c :** without the concomitant that ⟨it never rains ~ it pours⟩ **d :** if not **:** UNLESS **e** *substand* **:** THAN ⟨no sooner started ~ it stopped⟩ **2 a :** on the contrary **:** on the other hand **:** NOTWITHSTANDING — used to connect coordinate elements ⟨he was called ~ he did not answer⟩ ⟨not peace ~ a sword⟩ **b :** YET ⟨poor ~ proud⟩ **c :** with the exception of — used before a word often taken to be the subject of a clause ⟨none ~ the brave deserves the fair —John Dryden⟩ — **but what :** that . . . not — used to indicate possibility or uncertainty ⟨I don't know *but what* I will go⟩

[2]but *prep* (bef. 12c) **1** *Scot* **a :** WITHOUT, LACKING **b :** OUTSIDE **2 a :** with the exception of **:** BARRING ⟨no one there ~ me⟩ — compare [1]BUT 2c **b :** other than ⟨this letter is nothing ~ an insult⟩

³but *adv* (12c) **1 :** ONLY, MERELY ⟨he is ~ a child⟩ **2** *Scot* **:** OUTSIDE **3 :** to the contrary ⟨who knows ~ that he may succeed⟩ **4** — used as an intensive ⟨get there ~ fast⟩
⁴but *pron* (1556) **:** that not **:** who not ⟨nobody ~ has his fault —Shak.⟩
⁵but \'bət\ *n* [Sc *but,* adj. (outer)] *Scot* (1724) **:** the kitchen or living quarters of a 2-room cottage
bu·ta·di·ene \ˌbyüt-ə-'dī-ˌēn, -ˌdī-'\ *n* [ISV *butane* + *di-* + *-ene*] (ca. 1900) **:** a flammable gaseous hydrocarbon C_4H_6 used in making synthetic rubbers
bu·tane \'byü-ˌtān\ *n* [ISV *butyric* + *-ane*] (1875) **:** either of two isomeric flammable gaseous paraffin hydrocarbons C_4H_{10} obtained usu. from petroleum or natural gas and used as a fuel
bu·ta·nol \'byüt-ᵊn-ˌòl, -ˌōl\ *n* (1894) **:** either of two butyl alcohols $C_4H_{10}O$ derived from normal butane
butch \'bu̇ch\ *adj* (1941) **1 :** playing the male role in a homosexual relationship **2 :** very masculine in appearance or manner
¹butch·er \'bu̇ch-ər\ *n* [ME *bocher,* fr. OF *bouchier,* fr. *bouc* he-goat, prob. of Celt origin; akin to MIr *bocc* he-goat — more at BUCK] (14c) **1 a :** one who slaughters animals or dresses their flesh **b :** a dealer in meat **2 :** one that kills ruthlessly or brutally **3 :** one that bungles or botches **4 :** a vendor esp. on trains or in theaters
²butcher *vt* **butch·ered; butch·er·ing** \-(ə-)riŋ\ (1562) **1 :** to slaughter and dress for market ⟨~ hogs⟩ **2 :** to kill in a barbarous manner **3 :** BOTCH ⟨~*ed* the play beyond recognition⟩
butch·er–bird \'bu̇ch-ər-ˌbərd\ *n* (1668) **:** any of various shrikes
butcher block *n* (1967) **:** a block made with thick strips of usu. laminated hardwood so as to form a durable working surface — **butcher–block** *adj*
butch·er·ly \'bu̇ch-ər-lē\ *adj* (1513) **:** resembling a butcher **:** SAVAGE
butch·ery \'bu̇ch-(ə-)rē\ *n, pl* **-er·ies** (14c) **1** *chiefly Brit* **:** SLAUGHTERHOUSE **2 :** the preparation of meat for sale **3 :** cruel and ruthless slaughter of human beings **4 :** BOTCH
bu·tene \'byü-ˌtēn\ *n* [ISV *butyl* + *-ene*] (1885) **:** a normal butylene
bu·teo \'byüt-ē-ˌō\ *n, pl* **-te·os** [NL, genus name, fr. L, a hawk — more at BUZZARD] (1940) **:** any of a genus (*Buteo*) of hawks with broad rounded wings and soaring flight; *broadly* **:** a hawk of similar appearance or habit of flight — **bu·te·o·nine** \byü-'tē-ə-ˌnīn, 'byüt-ē-\ *adj or n*
but·ler \'bət-lər\ *n* [ME *buteler,* fr. OF *bouteillier* bottle bearer, fr. *bouteille* bottle — more at BOTTLE] (13c) **1 :** a manservant having charge of the wines and liquors **2 :** the chief male servant of a household who has charge of other employees, receives guests, directs the serving of meals, and performs various personal services
butler's pantry *n* (1816) **:** a service room between kitchen and dining room
¹butt \'bət\ *vb* [ME *butten,* fr. OF *boter,* of Gmc origin; akin to OHG *bōzan* to beat — more at BEAT] *vi* (13c) **:** to thrust or push head foremost **:** strike with the head or horns ~ *vt* **:** to strike or shove with the head or horns
²butt *n* (1647) **:** a blow or thrust usu. with the head or horns
³butt *n* [ME, fr. MF *botte,* fr. OProv *bota,* fr. LL *buttis — more at* BOTA] (14c) **1 :** a large cask esp. for wine, beer, or water **2 :** any of various units of liquid capacity; *esp* **:** a measure equal to 108 imperial gallons
⁴butt *n* [ME, partly fr. MF *but* target, end, of Gmc origin; akin to ON *būtr* log, LG *butt* blunt; partly fr. MF *bute* backstop, fr. *but* target] (14c) **1 a :** a backstop (as a mound or bank) for catching missiles shot at a target **b :** TARGET **c** *pl* **:** RANGE 5c **d :** a blind for shooting birds **2 a** *obs* **:** LIMIT, BOUND **b** *archaic* **:** GOAL ⟨here is my journey's end, here is my ~ —Shak.⟩ **3 :** an object of abuse or ridicule **:** VICTIM ⟨he was the ~ of all their jokes⟩
⁵butt *n* [ME; prob. akin to ME *buttok* buttock, LG *butt* blunt] (15c) **1 :** BUTTOCKS **2 :** the large or thicker end part of something: **a :** a lean upper cut of the pork shoulder — see PORK illustration **b :** the base of a plant from which the roots spring **c :** the thicker or handle end of a tool or weapon **3 :** an unused remainder **4 :** the part of a hide or skin corresponding to the animal's back and sides
⁶butt *vb* [partly fr. ⁴*butt,* partly fr. ⁵*butt*] *vi* (14c) **:** ABUT — used with *on* or *against* ~ *vt* **1 :** to place end to end or side to side without overlapping **2 :** to trim or square off (as a log) at the end **3 :** to reduce (as a cigarette) to a butt by stubbing or stamping
butte \'byüt\ *n* [F, knoll, fr. MF *bute*] (1805) **:** an isolated hill or mountain with steep or precipitous sides usu. having a smaller summit area than a mesa
¹but·ter \'bət-ər\ *n* [ME, fr. OE *butere,* fr. L *butyrum,* fr. Gk *boutyron,* fr. *bous* cow + *tyros* cheese — more at COW] (bef. 12c) **1 :** a solid emulsion of fat globules, air, and water made by churning milk or cream and used as food **2 :** a buttery substance: as **a :** any of various fatty oils remaining nearly solid at ordinary temperatures **b :** a creamy food spread; *esp* **:** one made of ground roasted nuts ⟨peanut ~⟩ **3 :** FLATTERY — **but·ter·less** \-ləs\ *adj*
²butter *vt* (15c) **:** to spread with or as if with butter
but·ter–and–eggs \ˌbət-ə-rə-'negz, -'nāgz\ *n pl but sing or pl in constr* (1776) **:** a common European perennial herb (*Linaria vulgaris*) of the snapdragon family that has showy yellow and orange flowers and is a naturalized weed in much of No. America — called also *toadflax*
but·ter·ball \'bət-ər-ˌbòl\ *n* (1813) **1 :** BUFFLEHEAD **2 :** a chubby person
butter bean *n* (ca. 1819) **1 :** LIMA BEAN: as **a** *chiefly Southern & Midland* **:** a large dried lima bean **b :** SIEVA BEAN **2 :** WAX BEAN **3 :** a green shell bean esp. as opposed to a snap bean
butter clam *n* (1936) **:** either of two delicately flavored clams (*Saxidomus nuttallii* and *S. giganteus*) of the Pacific coast of No. America
but·ter·cup \'bət-ər-ˌkəp\ *n* (ca. 1777) **:** any of numerous plants (genus *Ranunculus* of the family Ranunculaceae, the buttercup family) with yellow flowers and lobed leaves
but·ter·fat \-ˌfat\ *n* (1889) **:** the natural fat of milk and chief constituent of butter consisting essentially of a mixture of glycerides (as olein and palmitin)
but·ter·fin·gered \-ˌfiŋ-gərd\ *adj* (1615) **:** apt to let things fall or slip through the fingers **:** CARELESS — **but·ter·fin·gers** \-gərz\ *n pl but sing or pl in constr*
but·ter·fish \-ˌfish\ *n* (1674) **:** any of numerous mostly percoid fishes (esp. family Stromateidae) with a slippery coating of mucus
¹but·ter·fly \-ˌflī\ *n, often attrib* [ME *butterflie,* fr. OE *buterflēoge,* fr. *butere* + *flēoge* fly; prob. fr. the belief that witches in this shape stole milk and butter] (bef. 12c) **1 :** any of numerous slender-bodied diurnal insects (order Lepidoptera) with broad often brightly colored wings **2 :** something that resembles or suggests a butterfly; *esp* **:** a person chiefly occupied with the pursuit of pleasure **3 :** a swimming stroke executed in a prone position by moving both arms in a circular motion while kicking the legs up and down simultaneously **4** *pl* **:** a feeling of hollowness or queasiness caused esp. by emotional or nervous tension or anxious anticipation
²butterfly *vt* **-flied; -fly·ing** (1954) **:** to split almost entirely and spread apart ⟨a *butterflied* steak⟩ ⟨*butterflied* shrimp⟩
butterfly bush *n* (1924) **:** BUDDLEIA
butterfly chair *n* (1953) **:** a chair for lounging consisting of a cloth sling supported by a frame of metal tubing or bars
but·ter·fly·er \'bət-ər-ˌflī(-ə)r\ *n* (1967) **:** a swimmer who specializes in the butterfly
butterfly fish *n* (1740) **:** a fish having variegated colors, broad expanded fins, or both: as **a :** any of a family (Chaetodontidae) of small brilliantly colored spiny-finned fishes of tropical seas with a narrow deep body and fins partly covered with scales **b :** a small brown freshwater fish (*Pantodon buchholzi*) of western Africa that has elongate winglike pectoral fins
butterfly valve *n* (1846) **1 :** a valve that acts as a clack valve and consists of two semicircular clappers hinged to a cross rib **2 :** a damper or valve in a pipe consisting of a disk turning on a diametral axis
butterfly weed *n* (ca. 1816) **:** an orange-flowered showy milkweed (*Asclepias tuberosa*) of eastern No. America
but·ter·milk \'bət-ər-ˌmilk\ *n* (15c) **1 :** the liquid left after butter has been churned from milk or cream **2 :** cultured milk made by the addition of suitable bacteria to sweet milk
but·ter·nut \-ˌnət\ *n* (1741) **1 a :** the edible oily nut of an American tree (*Juglans cinerea*) of the walnut family **b :** a tree that bears butternuts **2 a :** a light yellowish brown **b** *pl* **:** homespun overalls dyed brown with a butternut extract **c :** a soldier or partisan of the Confederacy during the Civil War
but·ter·scotch \-ˌskäch\ *n* (1855) **1 :** a candy made from brown sugar, butter, corn syrup, and water; *also* **:** the flavor of such candy **2 :** a moderate yellowish brown
butter up *vt* (1819) **:** to charm or beguile with lavish flattery or praise
but·ter·weed \'bət-ər-ˌwēd\ *n* (ca. 1845) **:** any of several plants having yellow flowers or smooth soft foliage: as **a :** HORSEWEED 1 **b :** an American ragwort (*Senecio glabellus*)
but·ter·wort \-ˌwərt, -ˌwȯ(ə)rt\ *n* (1597) **:** any of a genus (*Pinguicula*) of herbs of the bladderwort family with fleshy greasy leaves that produce a viscid secretion serving to capture and digest insects
¹but·tery \'bət-ə-rē, 'bə-trē\ *n, pl* **-ter·ies** [ME *boterie,* fr. MF, fr. *botte* cask, butt — more at BUTT] (14c) **1 :** a storeroom for liquors **2 a** *chiefly dial* **:** PANTRY **b :** a room (as in an English college) stocking provisions for sale to students
²but·tery \'bət-ə-rē\ *adj* (14c) **1 a :** having the qualities of butter **b :** containing or spread with butter **2 :** marked by flattery
butt hinge *n* (1815) **:** a hinge usu. mortised flush into the edge of a door
butt in *vi* (1900) **:** to meddle in the affairs of others **:** INTERFERE
butt·in·sky *also* **butt·in·ski** \ˌbət-'in-skē\ *n, pl* **-skies** [*butt in* + *-sky, -ski* (last element in many Slavic names)] (1902) **:** one given to butting in **:** a troublesome meddler
butt joint *n* (1823) **:** a joint made by fastening the parts together end-to-end without overlap and often with reinforcement
but·tock \'bət-ək\ *n* [ME *buttok* — more at BUTT] (14c) **1 :** the back of a hip that forms one of the fleshy parts on which a person sits **2** *pl* **a :** the seat of the body **b :** RUMP
¹but·ton \'bət-ᵊn\ *n, often attrib* [ME *boton,* fr. MF, fr. OF, fr. *boter* to thrust — more at BUTT] (14c) **1 a :** a small knob or disk secured to an article (as of clothing) and used as a fastener by passing it through a buttonhole or loop **b :** a usu. circular metal or plastic badge bearing a stamped design or printed slogan ⟨campaign ~⟩ **2 :** something that resembles a button: as **a :** any of various parts or growths of a plant or of an animal: as **(1) :** an immature whole mushroom **(2) :** the terminal segment of a rattlesnake's rattle **b :** a small globule of metal remaining after fusion in assaying **c :** a guard on the tip of a fencing foil **3 :** PUSH BUTTON **4 :** the point of the chin esp. as a target for a knockout blow — **on the button :** EXACTLY
²button *vb* **but·toned; but·ton·ing** \'bət-niŋ, -ᵊn-iŋ\ *vt* (14c) **1 :** to furnish or decorate with buttons **2 :** to close or fasten with buttons — often used with *up* ⟨~ up your overcoat⟩ **3 :** to close (the lips) to prevent speech ⟨~ your lip⟩ ~ *vi* **:** to have buttons for fastening ⟨this dress ~s at the back⟩ — **but·ton·er** \-nər, -ᵊn-ər\ *n*
but·ton·ball \'bət-ᵊn-ˌbȯl\ *n* (1821) **:** ²PLANE
but·ton·bush \-ˌbu̇sh\ *n* (1754) **:** a No. American shrub (*Cephalanthus occidentalis*) of the madder family with globular flower heads
but·ton–down \-ˌdau̇n\ *adj* (1934) **1 a** *of a collar* **:** having the ends fastened to the garment with buttons **b** *of a garment* **:** having a button-down collar **2** *also* **but·toned–down** \-ᵊn-ˌdau̇n\ **:** lacking originality and imagination and adhering to conventional ideals esp. in dress and behavior ⟨~ traditionalists⟩
¹but·ton·hole \'bət-ᵊn-ˌhōl\ *n* (1561) **:** a slit or loop through which a button is passed
²buttonhole *vt* (1828) **1 :** to furnish with buttonholes **2 :** to work with buttonhole stitch — **but·ton·hol·er** *n*
³buttonhole *vt* [alter. of earlier *buttonhold*] (1862) **:** to detain in conversation by or as if by holding on to the outer garments of
buttonhole stitch *n* (ca. 1885) **:** a closely worked loop stitch used to make a firm edge (as on a buttonhole)
but·ton·hook \'bət-ᵊn-ˌhu̇k\ *n* (1870) **1 :** a hook for drawing small buttons through buttonholes **2 :** an offensive play in football in which the pass receiver runs straight downfield and then abruptly cuts back toward the line of scrimmage — **buttonhook** *vi*

button quail *n* (1885) **:** any of various small terrestrial Old World birds (family Turnicidae) that resemble quails, have only three toes on a foot with the hind toe being absent, and are related to the cranes and bustards

button snakeroot *n* (1775) **1 :** any of a genus (*Liatris*) of composite plants with spikes of rosy-purple rayless flower heads **2 :** any of several usu. prickly herbs (genus *Eryngium*) of the carrot family

but·ton·wood \'bət-ᵊn-ˌwu̇d\ *n* (1674) **:** [2]PLANE

[1]**but·tress** \'bə-trəs\ *n* [ME *butres,* fr. MF *bouterez,* fr. OF *boterez,* fr. *boter* — more at BUTT] (14c) **1 :** a projecting structure of masonry or wood for supporting or giving stability to a wall or building **2 :** something that resembles a buttress: as **a :** a projecting part of a mountain or hill **b :** a horny protuberance on a horse's hoof at the heel — see HOOF illustration **c :** the broadened base of a tree trunk or a thickened vertical part of it **3 :** something that supports or strengthens ⟨a ~ of the cause of peace⟩ — **but·tressed** \-trəst\ *adj*

[2]**buttress** *vt* (14c) **:** to furnish or shore up with a buttress; *also* **:** SUPPORT, STRENGTHEN ⟨arguments ~*ed* by solid facts⟩

butt shaft *n* (1588) **:** a target arrow without a barb

butt·stock \'bət-ˌstäk\ *n* (ca. 1909) **:** the stock of a firearm in the rear of the breech mechanism

butt weld *n* (ca. 1864) **:** a butt joint made by welding — **butt–weld** *vt* — **butt weld·ing** *n*

but·ty \'bət-ē\ *n, pl* **butties** [origin unknown] *chiefly Brit* (ca. 1790) **:** a fellow worker **:** CHUM, PARTNER

bu·tut \bü-'tüt\ *n, pl* **bututs** *or* **butut** [native word in Gambia] (1971) — see *dalasi* at MONEY table

bu·tyl \'byüt-ᵊl\ *n* [ISV *butyric* + *-yl*] (ca. 1868) **:** any of four isomeric univalent radicals C_4H_9 derived from butanes

Butyl *trademark* — used for any of various synthetic rubbers made by polymerizing isobutylene

butyl alcohol *n* (ca. 1869) **:** any of four flammable alcohols C_4H_9OH derived from butanes and used in organic synthesis and as solvents

bu·tyl·ate \'byüt-ᵊl-ˌāt\ *vt* **-at·ed; -at·ing** (1942) **:** to introduce the butyl group into (a compound) — **bu·tyl·ation** \ˌbyüt-ᵊl-'ā-shən\ *n*

butylated hy·droxy·an·i·sole \-(ˌ)hī-ˌdräk-sē-'an-ə-ˌsōl\ *n* [*hydroxy* + *anisole,* fr. L *anisum* anise + E *-ol* — more at ANISE] (1950) **:** BHA

butylated hy·droxy·tol·u·ene \-'täl-yə-ˌwēn\ *n* (1961) **:** BHT

bu·tyl·ene \'byüt-ᵊl-ˌēn\ *n* (1877) **:** any of three isomeric hydrocarbons C_4H_8 of the ethylene series obtained usu. by cracking petroleum

butyr- *or* **butyro-** *comb form* [ISV, fr. *butyric*] **:** butyric ⟨*butyr*al⟩

bu·ty·ra·ceous \ˌbyüt-ə-'rā-shəs\ *adj* [L *butyrum* butter — more at BUTTER] (1668) **1 :** resembling or having the qualities of butter **2 :** yielding a buttery substance

bu·ty·ral \'byüt-ə-ˌral\ *n* (1888) **:** an acetal of butyraldehyde

bu·tyr·al·de·hyde \ˌbyüt-ə-'ral-də-ˌhīd\ *n* [ISV] (ca. 1888) **:** either of two aldehydes C_4H_8O used esp. in making polyvinyl butyral resins

bu·ty·rate \'byüt-ə-ˌrāt\ *n* (1873) **:** a salt or ester of butyric acid

bu·tyr·ic \byü-'tir-ik\ *adj* [F *butyrique,* fr. L *butyrum*] (1826) **:** relating to or producing butyric acid ⟨~ fermentation⟩

butyric acid *n* (1826) **:** either of two isomeric fatty acids $C_4H_8O_2$; *esp* **:** a normal acid of unpleasant odor found in perspiration and rancid butter

bu·ty·ro·phe·none \ˌbyüt-ə-(ˌ)rō-fə-'nōn\ *n* [*butyr-* + *phen-* + *-one*] (1945) **:** any of a class of neuroleptic drugs (as haloperidol) used esp. in the treatment of schizophrenia

bux·om \'bək-səm\ *adj* [ME *buxsum,* fr. (assumed) OE *būhsum;* akin to OE *būgan* to bend — more at BOW] (12c) **1** *obs* **a :** OBEDIENT, TRACTABLE **b :** offering little resistance **:** FLEXIBLE, PLIANT ⟨wing silently the ~ air —John Milton⟩ **2** *archaic* **:** full of gaiety **:** BLITHE **3 :** vigorously or healthily plump; *specif* **:** full-bosomed — **bux·om·ly** *adv* — **bux·om·ness** *n*

[1]**buy** \'bī\ *vb* **bought** \'bȯt\; **buy·ing** [ME *byen,* fr. OE *bycgan;* akin to Goth *bugjan* to buy] *vt* (bef. 12c) **1 :** to acquire possession, ownership, or rights to the use or services of by payment esp. of money **:** PURCHASE **2 a :** to obtain in exchange for something often at a sacrifice ⟨they *bought* peace with their freedom⟩ **b :** REDEEM 6 **3 :** BRIBE, HIRE **4 :** to be the purchasing equivalent of ⟨the dollar ~*s* less today than it used to⟩ **5 :** ACCEPT, BELIEVE ⟨I don't ~ that hooey⟩ ~ *vi* **:** to make a purchase — **buy·er** \'bī(-ə)r\ *n* — **buy time :** to delay an imminent action or decision **:** STALL ⟨*buying time* against the day when air pollution . . . reaches critical and dangerous proportions —*Plainsman*⟩

[2]**buy** *n* (1879) **1 :** something of value at a favorable price; *esp* **:** BARGAIN ⟨it's a real ~ at that price⟩ **2 :** an act of buying **:** PURCHASE

buyer's market *n* (1926) **:** a market in which goods are plentiful, buyers have a wide range of choice, and prices tend to be low — compare SELLER'S MARKET

buy off *vt* (1629) **1 :** to induce to refrain (as from prosecution) by a payment or other consideration **2 :** to free (as from military service) by payment

buy·out \'bī-ˌau̇t\ *n* (1971) **:** an act or instance of buying out

buy out *vt* (1644) **1 :** to purchase the share or interest of **2 :** to purchase the entire stock-in-trade and the goodwill of (a business)

buy up *vt* (1533) **1 :** to buy freely or extensively **2 :** to buy the entire available supply of

[1]**buzz** \'bəz\ *vb* [ME *bussen,* of imit. origin] *vi* (14c) **1 :** to make a low continuous humming sound like that of a bee **2 a :** MURMUR, WHISPER **b :** to be filled with a confused murmur ⟨the room ~*ed* with excitement⟩ **3 :** to make a signal with a buzzer **4 :** to go quickly **:** HURRY; *also* **:** SCRAM — usu. used with *off* ~ *vt* **1 :** to utter covertly by or as if by whispering **2 :** to cause to buzz **3 :** to fly low and fast over ⟨planes ~ the crowd⟩ **4 :** to summon or signal with a buzzer **5** *dial Eng* **:** to drink to the last drop ⟨get some more port whilst I ~ this bottle —W. M. Thackeray⟩

[2]**buzz** *n* (1605) **1 a :** RUMOR, GOSSIP **b :** a confused murmur or flurry of activity **2 :** a persistent vibratory sound **3 :** a signal conveyed by buzzer; *specif* **:** a telephone call

buz·zard \'bəz-ərd\ *n* [ME *busard,* fr. OF, alter. of *buison,* fr. L *buteon-, buteo* hawk; akin to Gk *byas* eagle-owl] (13c) **1** *chiefly Brit* **:** BUTEO **2 :** any of various usu. large birds of prey (as the turkey vulture) **3 :** a contemptible or rapacious person

buzz bomb *n* (1944) **:** ROBOT BOMB

buzz·er \'bəz-ər\ *n* (1606) **1 :** one that buzzes; *specif* **:** an electric signaling device that makes a buzzing sound **2 :** the sound of a buzzer ⟨sank a 20-foot jump shot at the ~⟩

buzz saw *n* (1858) **:** CIRCULAR SAW

buzz·word \'bəz-ˌwərd\ *n* (1967) **:** an important-sounding usu. technical word or phrase often of little meaning used chiefly to impress laymen

B.V.D. \ˌbē-(ˌ)vē-'dē\ *trademark* — used for underwear

B vitamin *n* (1940) **:** any vitamin of the vitamin B complex

bwa·na \'bwän-ə\ *n* [Swahili, fr. Ar *abūna* our father] (1878) **:** MASTER, BOSS

[1]**by** \(')bī, *esp before consonants* bə\ *prep* [ME, prep. & adv., fr. OE, prep., *be, bī;* akin to OHG *bī* by, near, L *ambi-* on both sides, around, Gk *amphi*] (bef. 12c) **1 :** in proximity to **:** NEAR ⟨standing ~ the window⟩ **2 a :** through or through the medium of **:** VIA ⟨enter ~ the door⟩ **b :** in the direction of **:** TOWARD ⟨north ~ east⟩ **c :** into the vicinity of and beyond **:** PAST ⟨went right ~ him⟩ **3 a :** during the course of ⟨studied ~ night⟩ **b :** not later than ⟨~ 2 p.m.⟩ **4 a :** through the agency or instrumentality of ⟨~ force⟩ **b :** sired or borne by **5 :** with the witness or sanction of ⟨swear ~ all that is holy⟩ **6 a :** in conformity with ⟨acted ~ the rules⟩ **b :** ACCORDING TO ⟨always bought ~ brand⟩ ⟨called her ~ name⟩ **7 :** with respect to **8 a :** in or to the amount or extent of ⟨win ~ a nose⟩ **b** *chiefly Scot* **:** in comparison with **:** BESIDE **9** — used as a function word to indicate successive units or increments ⟨succeeded little ~ little⟩ ⟨walk two ~ two⟩ **10** — used as a function word in multiplication, in division, and in measurements ⟨divide *a* ~ *b*⟩ ⟨multiply 10 ~ 4⟩ ⟨a room 15 feet ~ 20 feet⟩

[2]**by** \'bī\ *adv* (bef. 12c) **1 a :** close at hand **:** NEAR **b :** at or to another's home ⟨stop ~ for a chat⟩ **2 :** PAST ⟨saw him go ~⟩ **3 :** ASIDE, AWAY

[3]**by** *or* **bye** \'bī\ *adj* (14c) **1 :** being off the main route **:** SIDE **2 :** INCIDENTAL

[4]**by** *or* **bye** \'bī\ *n, pl* **byes** \'bīz\ (1567) **:** something of secondary importance **:** a side issue — **by the by :** BY THE WAY, INCIDENTALLY

[5]**by** *or* **bye** \'bī\ *interj* [short for *goodbye*] (1709) — used to express farewell; often used with following *now*

by–and–by \ˌbī-ən-'bī\ *n* (1591) **:** a future time or occasion

by and by \ˌbī-ən-'bī\ *adv* (1526) **:** before long **:** SOON

by and large \ˌbī-ən-'lärj\ *adv* (1669) **:** on the whole **:** in general

by–blow \'bī-ˌblō\ *n* (1594) **1 :** an indirect blow **2 :** an illegitimate child

bye \'bī\ *n* [alter. of [2]*by*] (1883) **:** the position of a participant in a tournament who has no opponent after pairs are drawn and advances to the next round without playing

[1]**bye–bye** *or* **by–by** \'bī-ˌbī, bī-'bī\ *interj* [baby-talk redupl. of *goodbye*] (1736) — used to express farewell

[2]**bye–bye** *or* **by–by** \'bī-ˌbī\ *adv* (1917) **:** out esp. for a walk or ride — used with the verb *go* ⟨if he wants to go ~ the baby may pat his head to indicate his desire for a hat —A.L. Gesell & Frances L. Ilg⟩

[3]**bye–bye** *or* **by–by** \'bī-ˌbī\ *n* (1867) **:** BED, SLEEP ⟨lie down . . . and go to ~ —Rudyard Kipling⟩

[4]**bye–bye** *or* **by–by** \'bī-ˌbī\ *adv* (1920) **:** to bed or sleep — used with the verb *go* ⟨I'll run in and read for just a second . . . and then perhaps I'll go ~ —Sinclair Lewis⟩

by–elec·tion *also* **bye–election** \'bī-ə-ˌlek-shən\ *n* (1880) **:** a special election held between regular elections in order to fill a vacancy

by·gone \'bī-ˌgȯn *also* -ˌgän\ *adj* (15c) **:** gone by **:** PAST; *esp* **:** OUTMODED — **bygone** *n*

by·law *or* **bye·law** \'bī-ˌlȯ\ *n* [ME *bilawe,* prob. fr. (assumed) ON *bȳlǫg,* fr. ON *bȳr* town + *lǫg* law] (13c) **:** a rule adopted by an organization chiefly for the government of its members and the regulation of its affairs

[1]**by·line** \'bī-ˌlīn\ *n* (1916) **1 :** a secondary line **:** SIDELINE **2 :** a line at the beginning of a news story, magazine article, or book giving the writer's name

[2]**byline** *vt* (1938) **:** to write (an article) under a byline — **by·lin·er** \-ˌlī-nər\ *n*

by·name \'bī-ˌnām\ *n* (14c) **1 :** a secondary name **2 :** NICKNAME

[1]**by·pass** \'bī-ˌpas\ *n* (1848) **1 :** a passage to one side; *esp* **:** a deflected route usu. around a town **2 a :** a channel carrying a fluid around a part and back to the main stream **b :** SHUNT 1b, 1c

[2]**bypass** *vt* (1886) **1 a :** to avoid by means of a bypass **b :** to cause to follow a bypass **2 a :** to neglect or ignore usu. intentionally **b :** CIRCUMVENT

by·past \'bī-ˌpast\ *adj* (15c) **:** BYGONE

by·path \-ˌpath, -ˌpȧth\ *n* (14c) **:** BYWAY

by·play \-ˌplā\ *n* (1812) **:** action engaged in on the side while the main action proceeds (as during a dramatic production)

by–prod·uct \-ˌpräd-(ˌ)əkt\ *n* (1857) **1 :** something produced in a usu. industrial process in addition to the principal product **2 :** a secondary and sometimes unexpected or unintended result ⟨unpleasant ~*s* of civilization⟩

byre \'bī(ə)r\ *n* [ME, fr. OE *bȳre;* akin to OE *būr* dwelling — more at BOWER] *chiefly Brit* (bef. 12c) **:** a cow barn

by·road \'bī-ˌrōd\ *n* (1673) **:** BYWAY

By·ron·ic \bī-'rän-ik\ *adj* (1823) **:** of, relating to, or having the characteristics of the poet Byron or his writings — **By·ron·i·cal·ly** \-i-k(ə-)lē\ *adv* — **By·ron·ism** \'bī-rə-ˌniz-əm\ *n*

bys·si·no·sis \ˌbis-ə-'nō-səs\ *n, pl* **-no·ses** \-ˌsēz\ [NL, fr. L *byssinus* of fine linen, fr. Gk *byssinos,* fr. *byssos*] (ca. 1890) **:** an occupational respiratory disease associated with inhalation of cotton, flax, or hemp dust and characterized initially by chest tightness, shortness of breath, and cough and eventually by irreversible lung disease

bys·sus \'bis-əs\ *n, pl* **bys·sus·es** *or* **bys·si** \-ˌī, -(ˌ)ē\ [ME *bissus,* fr. ML *byssus,* fr. L, fr. Gk *byssos* flax, of Sem origin; akin to Heb *būṣ* linen cloth] (14c) **1 :** a fine prob. linen cloth of ancient times **2** [NL, fr. L] **:** a tuft of long tough filaments by which some bivalve mollusks (as mussels) adhere to a surface

by·stand·er \'bī-ˌstan-dər\ *n* (1619) **:** one present but not taking part in a situation or event **:** a chance spectator

by·street \-ˌstrēt\ *n* (1672) **:** a street off a main thoroughfare **:** side street

byte \'bīt\ *n* [perh. alter. of [2]*bite*] (ca. 1962) **:** a group of adjacent binary digits often shorter than a word that a computer processes as a unit ⟨an 8-bit ~⟩

by the way *adv* (1548) **:** in passing **:** INCIDENTALLY

by·way \'bī-,wā\ *n* (14c) **1** : a little traveled side road **2** : a secondary or little known aspect or field ⟨meandering more and more in the fascinating ~s of learning —*Times Lit. Supp.*⟩

by·word \-,word\ *n* (bef. 12c) **1** : a proverbial saying : PROVERB **2 a** : one that personifies a type **b** : one that is noteworthy or notorious **3** : EPITHET **4** : a frequently used word or phrase

¹Byz·an·tine \'biz-ᵊn-,tēn, 'biz-, -,tīn; bə-'zan-,, bī-\ *adj* (1794) **1** : of, relating to, or characteristic of the ancient city of Byzantium **2** : of, relating to, or having the characteristics of a style of architecture developed in the Byzantine Empire esp. in the 5th and 6th centuries featuring the dome carried on pendentives over a square and incrustation

with marble veneering and with colored mosaics on grounds of gold **3** : of or relating to the churches using a traditional Greek rite and subject to Eastern canon law **4 a** : of, relating to, or characterized by a devious and usu. surreptitious manner of operation ⟨fits a pattern of ~ firings and near-firings that have long kept . . . executives looking over their shoulders —Paul Ingrassia⟩ **b** : LABYRINTHINE ⟨searching in the ~ complexity of the record for leads, defenses, and, in the case of Government lawyers, evidence of perjured testimony —B. L. Collier⟩

²Byzantine *n* (1836) : a native or inhabitant of Byzantium

By·zan·tin·ist \-,tē-nəst, -,tī-\ *n* (1892) : a student of Byzantine culture

---

c \'sē\ *n*, *pl* **c's** *or* **cs** \'sēz\ *often cap, often attrib* **1 a** : the 3d letter of the English alphabet **b** : a graphic representation of this letter **c** : a speech counterpart of orthographic *c* **2 a** : one hundred — see NUMBER table **b** *slang* : a sum of $100 **3** : the keynote of a C-major scale **4** : a graphic device for reproducing the letter *c* **5** : one designated *c* esp. as the 3d in order or class **6 a** : a grade rating a student's work as fair or mediocre in quality **b** : one graded or rated with a C **7** : something shaped like the letter C **8** : a structured programming language designed to produce a compact and efficient translation of a program into machine language

ca' \'kȯ, 'kä\ *Scot var of* CALL

¹cab \'kab\ *n* [Heb *qabh*] (1535) : an ancient Hebrew unit of capacity equal to about two quarts

²cab \'kab\ *n* [short for *cabriolet*] (1827) **1 a** (1) : CABRIOLET (2) : a similar light closed carriage (as a hansom) **b** : a carriage for hire **2** : TAXICAB **3** [short for *cabin*] **a** : the part of a locomotive that houses the engineer and operating controls **b** : a comparable shelter on a truck, tractor, or crane

¹ca·bal \kə-'bal, -'bäl\ *n* [F *cabale* cabala, intrigue, cabal, fr. ML *cabbala* cabala, fr. LHeb *qabbālāh*, lit., received (lore)] (1614) **1** : a number of persons secretly united to bring about an overturn or usurpation esp. in public affairs **2** : the artifices and intrigues of such a group *syn* see PLOT

²cabal *vi* **ca·balled; ca·bal·ling** (1680) : to unite in or form a cabal

ca·ba·la *or* **cab·ba·la** *or* **cab·ba·lah** \'kab-ə-lə, kə-'bäl-ə\ *n, often cap* [ML *cabbala*] (1521) **1** : a medieval and modern system of Jewish theosophy, mysticism, and thaumaturgy marked by belief in creation through emanation and a cipher method of interpreting Scripture **2 a** : a traditional, esoteric, occult, or secret matter **b** : esoteric doctrine or mysterious art — **cab·a·lism** \'kab-ə-,liz-əm\ *n* — **cab·a·lis·tic** \,kab-ə-'lis-tik\ *adj*

ca·ba·let·ta \,kab-ə-'let-ə, ,käb-\ *n* [It] (1842) **1** : an operatic song in simple popular style characterized by a uniform rhythm **2** : the lively bravura concluding section of an extended aria or duet

¹ca·ba·list \'kab-ə-ləst, kə-'bäl-əst\ *n* (1533) **1** *often cap* : a student, interpreter, or devotee of the Jewish cabala **2** : one skilled in esoteric doctrine or mysterious art

²ca·bal·ist \kə-'bal-əst\ *n* (1569) : a member of a cabal

ca·bal·le·ro \,kab-ə-'le(ə)r-(,)ō, -ə(l)-'ye(ə)r-\ *n, pl* **-ros** [Sp, fr. LL *caballarius* hostler — more at CAVALIER] (1749) **1** : KNIGHT, CAVALIER **2** *chiefly Southwest* : HORSEMAN

ca·ba·na \kə-'ban-(y)ə\ *n* [Sp *cabaña*, lit., hut, fr. ML *capanna*] (1890) **1** : a shelter resembling a cabin usu. with an open side facing a beach or swimming pool **2** : a lightweight structure with living facilities

cab·a·ret \,kab-ə-'rā, 'kab-ə-,\ *n* [F, fr. ONF] (1655) **1** *archaic* : a shop selling wines and liquors **2 a** : a restaurant serving liquor and providing entertainment (as by singers or dancers) : NIGHTCLUB **b** : the show provided at a cabaret

¹cab·bage \'kab-ij\ *n, often attrib* [ME *caboche*, fr. ONF, head, deriv. of L *caput* — more at HEAD] (15c) **1** : a leafy garden plant (*Brassica oleracea capitata*) of European origin with a short stem and a dense globular head of usu. green leaves that is used as a vegetable **2** : the terminal bud of a palm tree that resembles a head of cabbage and is eaten as a vegetable **3** *slang* : PAPER MONEY, BANK NOTES

²cabbage *n* [perh. by folk etymology fr. MF *cabas* cheating, theft] *Brit* (1663) : pieces of cloth left in cutting out garments and traditionally kept by tailors as perquisites

³cabbage *vt* **cab·baged; cab·bag·ing** (1712) : STEAL, FILCH

cabbage butterfly *n* (1816) : any of several largely white butterflies (family Pieridae) whose green larvae are cabbageworms; *esp* : a small cosmopolitan butterfly (*Pieris rapae*) that is a universal pest on cabbage

cabbage looper *n* (ca. 1902) : a noctuid moth (*Trichoplusia ni*) whose pale green white-striped larva is a measuring worm that feeds on cruciferous plants (as the cabbage)

cabbage palm *n* (ca. 1772) : a palm with terminal buds eaten as a vegetable

cabbage palmetto *n* (1802) : a fan-leaved cabbage palm (*Sabal palmetto*) native to coastal southern U.S. and the Bahamas

cab·bage·worm \'kab-ij-,wərm\ *n* (1688) : an insect larva (as of a cabbage butterfly) that feeds on cabbages

cab·bie *or* **cab·by** \'kab-ē\ *n, pl* **cabbies** (1859) : CABDRIVER

cab·driv·er \'kab-,drī-vər\ *n* (1830) : a driver of a cab

ca·ber \'kā-bər, 'käb-ər\ *n* [ScGael *cabar*] (1505) : POLE; *esp* : a young tree trunk used for tossing as a trial of strength in a Scottish sport

cab·er·net sau·vi·gnon \,kab-ər-'nā-sō-vēn-'yōⁿ\ *n* [F] (1941) : a dry red wine made from a single variety of black grape that is widely cultivated (as in Bordeaux, California, and Argentina) — called also *cabernet*

¹cab·in \'kab-ən\ *n* [ME *cabane*, fr. MF, fr. OProv *cabana* hut, fr. ML *capanna*] (14c) **1 a** : a private room on a ship for one or a few persons — compare CABIN CLASS **b** : a compartment below deck on a small boat for passengers or crew **c** : an airplane, airship, or space-craft compartment for cargo, crew, or passengers **2 a** : a small one-story dwelling usu. of simple construction **3 a** *chiefly Brit* : CAB 3 **b** : any of various enclosures for people (as automobile passengers)

²cabin *vi* (1586) : to live in or as if in a cabin ~ *vt* : CONFINE

cabin boy *n* (1726) : a boy working as servant on a ship

cabin car *n* (1879) : CABOOSE

cabin class *n* (1929) : a class of accommodations on a passenger ship superior to tourist class and inferior to first class

cabin cruiser *n* (1921) : CRUISER 3

¹cab·i·net \'kab-(ə-)nət\ *n* [MF, small room, dim. of ONF *cabine* gambling house] (1550) **1 a** : a case or cupboard usu. having doors and shelves **b** : a collection of specimens esp. of mineralogical, biological, or numismatic interest **c** : an upright case housing a device (as a television) : CONSOLE **d** : a chamber having temperature and humidity controls and used esp. for incubating biological samples **2 a** *archaic* : a small room providing seclusion **b** : a small exhibition room in a museum **3 a** *archaic* (1) : the private room serving as council chamber of the chief councillors or ministers of a sovereign (2) : the consultations and actions of these councillors **b** *often cap* : a body of advisers of a head of state (2) : a similar advisory council of a governor of a state or a mayor **c** *Brit* : a meeting of a cabinet

²cabinet *adj* (1696) **1** : suitable by reason of size for a small room or by reason of attractiveness or perfection for preservation and display in a cabinet **2** : of or relating to a governmental cabinet **3 a** : used or adapted for cabinetmaking **b** : done or used by a cabinetmaker

cab·i·net·mak·er \-,mā-kər\ *n* (1681) : a skilled woodworker who makes fine furniture — **cab·i·net·mak·ing** \-,mā-kiŋ\ *n*

cab·i·net·work \-,wərk\ *n* (1732) : finished woodwork made by a cabinetmaker

cabin fever *n* (1918) : extreme irritability and restlessness resulting from living in isolation or within a confined indoor area for a prolonged time

¹ca·ble \'kā-bəl\ *n, often attrib* [ME, fr. ONF, fr. ML *capulum* lasso, fr. L *capere* to take — more at HEAVE] (13c) **1 a** : a strong rope esp. of 10 or more inches in circumference **b** : a cable-laid rope **c** : a wire rope or metal chain of great tensile strength **d** : a wire or wire rope by which force is exerted to control or operate a mechanism **2** : CABLE LENGTH **3 a** : an assembly of electrical conductors insulated from each other but laid up together usu. by being twisted around a central core **b** : CABLEGRAM **4** : something resembling or fashioned like a cable ⟨a fiber-optic ~⟩ **5** : CABLE TELEVISION

²cable *vb* **ca·bled; ca·bling** \'kā-b(ə-)liŋ\ *vt* (1500) **1** : to fasten with or as if with a cable **2** : to provide with cables **3** : to telegraph by submarine cable **4** : to make into a cable or into a form resembling a cable ~ *vi* : to communicate by a submarine cable

cable car *n* (1887) : a vehicle moved by an endless cable : **a** : one suspended from an overhead cable **b** : one that moves along tracks

ca·ble·gram \'kā-bəl-,gram\ *n* (1868) : a message sent by a submarine telegraph cable

ca·ble-laid \,kā-bəl-'lād\ *adj* (1723) : composed of three ropes laid together left-handed with each containing three strands twisted together

cable length *n* (1555) : a maritime unit of length variously reckoned as 100 fathoms, 120 fathoms, or 608 feet

ca·blet \'kā-blət\ *n* (1575) : a small cable; *specif* : a cable-laid rope less than 10 inches in circumference

cable television *n* (1965) : a system of television reception in which signals from distant stations are picked up by a master antenna and sent by cable to the individual receivers of paying subscribers — called also *cable TV*

\ə\ abut \ᵊ\ kitten, F table \ər\ further \a\ ash \ā\ ace \ä\ cot, cart
\aů\ out \ch\ chin \e\ bet \ē\ easy \g\ go \i\ hit \ī\ ice \j\ job
\ŋ\ sing \ō\ go \ȯ\ law \ȯi\ boy \th\ thin \t͟h\ the \ü\ loot \ů\ foot
\y\ yet \zh\ vision \ä, k̲, ⁿ, œ, œ̄, ue, ūe, ᵞ\ see Guide to Pronunciation

ca·ble·way \'kā-bəl-,wā\ *n* (1899) **:** a suspended cable used as a track along which carriers can be pulled
cab·man \'kab-mən\ *n* (1834) **:** CABDRIVER
cab·o·chon \'kab-ə-,shän\ *n* [MF, aug. of ONF *caboche* head] (1578) **:** a gem or bead cut in convex form and highly polished but not faceted; *also* **:** this style of cutting — **cabochon** *adv*
ca·boo·dle \kə-'büd-ᵊl\ *n* [prob. fr. *ca-* (intensive prefix, prob. of imit. origin) + *boodle*] (1848) **:** COLLECTION, LOT ⟨sell the whole ~⟩
ca·boose \kə-'büs\ *n* [prob fr. D *kabuis*, fr. MLG *kabūse*] (1769) **1 :** a ship's galley **2 :** a freight-train car attached usu. to the rear mainly for the use of the train crew **3 :** one that follows or brings up the rear
cab·o·tage \'kab-ə-,täzh\ *n* [F, fr. *caboter* to sail along the coast] (1831) **1 :** trade or transport in coastal waters or airspace or between two points within a country **2 :** the right to engage in cabotage
ca·bret·ta \kə-'bret-ə\ *n* [modif. of Pg and Sp *cabra* goat] (1920) **:** a light soft leather from skins of hairy sheep
ca·bril·la \kə-'brē-(y)ə, -'bril-ə\ *n* [Sp, dim. of *cabra* goat, fr. L *capra* she-goat, fem. of *caper* he-goat — more at CAPRIOLE] (1859) **:** any of various sea basses (esp. of the genera *Epinephelus* and *Paralabrax*) of the Mediterranean, the California coast, and the warmer parts of the western Atlantic
cab·ri·ole \'kab-rē-,ōl\ *n* [F, caper] (1805) **1 :** a ballet leap in which one leg is extended in midair and the other struck against it **2 :** a curved furniture leg ending in an ornamental foot
cab·ri·o·let \,kab-rē-ə-'lā\ *n* [F, fr. dim. of *cabriole* caper, alter. of MF *capriole*] (1763) **1 :** a light 2-wheeled one-horse carriage with a folding leather hood, a large apron, and upward-curving shafts **2 :** a convertible coupe
cab·stand \'kab-,stand\ *n* (1848) **:** a place where cabs await hire
cac- *or* **caco-** *comb form* [NL, fr. Gk *kak-*, *kako-*, fr. *kakos* bad] **:** bad ⟨*cacography*⟩
ca' can·ny \kō-'kan-ē\ *n* [Sc, vb., to proceed cautiously, fr. *ca'* (call) + *canny* careful] *Brit* (1886) **:** SLOWDOWN — **ca' canny** *vi*, *Brit*
ca·cao \kə-'kaů, kə-'kā-(,)ō\ *n*, *pl* **cacaos** [Sp, fr. Nahuatl *cacahuatl* cacao beans] (1555) **1 :** a So. American tree (*Theobroma cacao* of the family Sterculiaceae) with small yellowish flowers followed by fleshy yellow pods with many seeds **2 :** the dried partly fermented fatty seeds of the cacao used in making cocoa, chocolate, and cocoa butter — called also *cacao bean*, *cocoa bean*
cacao butter *var of* COCOA BUTTER
cac·cia·to·re \,käch-ə-'tōr-ē, -'tȯr-\ *adj* [It, fr. *cacciatore* hunter] (1942) **:** cooked with tomatoes and herbs and sometimes wine ⟨veal ~⟩
cach·a·lot \'kash-ə-,lät, -,lō\ *n* [F] (1747) **:** SPERM WHALE
[1]**cache** \'kash\ *n* [F, fr. *cacher* to press, hide, fr. (assumed) VL *coacticare* to press together, fr. L *coactare* to compel, fr. *coactus*, pp. of *cogere* to compel — more at COGENT] (1797) **1 a :** a hiding place esp. for concealing and preserving provisions or implements **b :** a secure place of storage **2 :** something hidden or stored in a cache
[2]**cache** *vt* **cached; cach·ing** (1805) **:** to place, hide, or store in a cache
ca·chec·tic \kə-'kek-tik, ka-\ *adj* [F *cachectique*, fr. L *cachecticus*, fr. Gk *kachektikos*, fr. *kak-* + *echein*] (1634) **:** affected by cachexia
cache·pot \'kash-,pät, 'kash-(ə-),pō\ *n* [F, fr. *cacher* to hide + *pot* pot] (1872) **:** an ornamental receptacle to hold and usu. to conceal a flowerpot
ca·chet \ka-'shā\ *n* [F, fr. *cacher*] (1639) **1 a :** a seal used esp. as a mark of official approval **b :** an indication of approval carrying great prestige **2 a :** a characteristic feature or quality conferring prestige **b :** PRESTIGE **3 :** a medicinal preparation for swallowing consisting of a case usu. of rice-flour paste containing an unpleasant-tasting medicine **4 a :** a design or inscription on an envelope to commemorate a postal or philatelic event **b :** an advertisement forming part of a postage meter impression **c :** a motto or slogan included in a postal cancellation
ca·chex·ia \kə-'kek-sē-ə, ka-\ *n* [LL *cachexia*, fr. Gk *kachexia* bad condition, fr. *kak-* cac- + *hexis* condition, fr. *echein* to have, be disposed — more at SCHEME] (1541) **:** general physical wasting and malnutrition usu. associated with chronic disease
cach·in·nate \'kak-ə-,nāt\ *vi* **-nat·ed; -nat·ing** [L *cachinnatus*, pp. of *cachinnare*, of imit. origin] (1824) **:** to laugh loudly or immoderately — **cach·in·na·tion** \,kak-ə-'nā-shən\ *n*
ca·chou \ka-'shü, 'kash-(,)ü\ *n* [F, fr. Pg *cachu*, fr. Malayalam *kāccu*] (1704) **:** a pill or pastille used to sweeten the breath
ca·chu·cha \kə-'chü-chə\ *n* [Sp] (1840) **:** a lively Andalusian solo dance in triple time done with castanets
ca·cique \kə-'sēk\ *n* [Sp, of Arawakan origin; akin to Taino *cacique* chief] (1555) **1 :** a native Indian chief in areas dominated primarily by a Spanish culture **2 :** a local political boss in Spain and Latin America — **ca·ciqu·ism** \-'sē-,kiz-əm\ *n*
cack·le \'kak-əl\ *vi* **cack·led; cack·ling** \-(ə-)liŋ\ [ME *cakelen*, of imit. origin] (13c) **1 :** to make the sharp broken noise or cry characteristic of a hen esp. after laying **2 :** to laugh esp. in a harsh or sharp manner **3 :** CHATTER — **cackle** *n* — **cack·ler** \-(ə-)lər\ *n*
caco·de·mon \,kak-ə-'dē-mən\ *n* [Gk *kakodaimōn*, fr. *kak-* cac- + *daimōn* spirit] (14c) **:** DEMON — **caco·de·mon·ic** \-di-'män-ik\ *adj*
cac·o·dyl \'kak-ə-,dil\ *n* [ISV, fr. G *kakodyl*, fr. Gk *kakōdēs* ill smelling, fr. *kak-* + *-ōdēs* (akin to Gk *ozein* to smell) — more at ODOR] (1850) **1 :** an arsenical radical $As(CH_3)_2$ whose compounds have a vile smell and are usu. poisonous **2 :** a colorless liquid $As_2(CH_3)_4$ consisting of two cacodyl radicals
cac·o·dyl·ic acid \,kak-ə-,dil-ik-\ *n* (1850) **:** a toxic crystalline compound of arsenic $C_2H_7AsO_2$ used esp. as an herbicide
caco·ë·thes \,kak-ə-'wē-(,)thēz\ *n* [L, fr. Gk *kakoēthes* wickedness, fr. neut. of *kakoēthēs* malignant, fr. *kak-* cac- + *ēthos* character — more at ETHICAL] (1563) **:** an insatiable desire **:** MANIA
ca·cog·ra·phy \ka-'käg-rə-fē\ *n* (1656) **1 :** bad handwriting — compare CALLIGRAPHY **2 :** bad spelling — compare ORTHOGRAPHY — **caco·graph·i·cal** \,kak-ə-'graf-i-kəl\ *adj*
cac·o·mis·tle \'kak-ə-,mis-əl, ,kak-ə-'mis(t)-lē\ *n* [MexSp, fr. Nahuatl *tlacomiztli*, fr. *tlaco* half + *miztli* mountain lion] (1869) **:** a carnivore (*Bassariscus astutus*) related to and resembling the raccoon; *also* **:** its fur or pelt
ca·coph·o·nous \ka-'käf-ə-nəs\ *adj* [Gk *kakophōnos*, fr. *kak-* + *phōnē* voice, sound — more at BAN] (1797) **:** marked by cacophony **:** harsh-sounding — **ca·coph·o·nous·ly** *adv*
ca·coph·o·ny \-nē\ *n*, *pl* **-nies** (1656) **:** harsh or discordant sound **:** DISSONANCE; *specif* **:** harshness in the sound of words or phrases
cac·tus \'kak-təs\ *n*, *pl* **cac·ti** \-,tī, -(,)tē\ *also* **cac·tus·es** *or* **cactus** [NL, genus name, fr. L, cardoon, fr. Gk *kaktos*] (1767) **:** any of a family (Cactaceae, the cactus family) of plants that have fleshy stems and branches with scales or spines instead of leaves and are found esp. in dry areas (as deserts)
ca·cu·mi·nal \ka-'kyü-mən-ᵊl, kə-\ *adj* [ISV, fr. L *cacumin-*, *cacumen* top, point] (1862) **:** RETROFLEX 2
cad \'kad\ *n* [E dial., unskilled assistant, short for Sc *caddie*] (1833) **1 :** an omnibus conductor **2 :** a person without gentlemanly instincts
ca·das·tral \kə-'das-trəl\ *adj* (1858) **1 :** of or relating to a cadastre **2 :** showing or recording property boundaries, subdivision lines, buildings, and related details — **ca·das·tral·ly** \-trə-lē\ *adv*
ca·das·tre \kə-'das-tər\ *n* [F, fr. It *catastro*, fr. OIt *catastico*, fr. LGk *katastichon* notebook, fr. Gk *kata* by + *stichos* row, line — more at CATA-, DISTICH] (1804) **:** an official register of the quantity, value, and ownership of real estate used in apportioning taxes
ca·dav·er \kə-'dav-ər\ *n* [L, fr. *cadere* to fall] (14c) **:** a dead body; *specif* **:** one intended for dissection — **ca·dav·er·ic** \-(ə-)rik\ *adj*
ca·dav·er·ine \kə-'dav-ə-,rēn\ *n* (1887) **:** a syrupy colorless poisonous ptomaine $C_5H_{14}N_2$ formed by decarboxylation of lysine esp. in putrefaction of flesh
ca·dav·er·ous \kə-'dav-(ə-)rəs\ *adj* (ca. 1620) **1 a :** of or relating to a corpse **b :** suggestive of corpses or tombs **2 a :** PALLID, LIVID **b :** GAUNT, EMACIATED — **ca·dav·er·ous·ly** *adv*
cad·die *or* **cad·dy** \'kad-ē\ *n*, *pl* **caddies** [F *cadet* military cadet] (1730) **1** *Scot* **:** one that waits about for odd jobs **2 a :** one that assists a golfer esp. by carrying his clubs **b :** a wheeled device for conveying things not readily carried by hand — **caddie** *or* **caddy** *vi*
[1]**cad·dis** *also* **cad·dice** \'kad-əs\ *n* [ME *cadas* cotton wool, prob. fr. MF *cadaz*, fr. OProv *cadarz*] (1530) **:** worsted yarn; *specif* **:** a worsted ribbon or binding formerly used for garters and girdles
[2]**caddis** *n* (1651) **:** CADDIS WORM
caddis fly *also* **caddice fly** *n* (1787) **:** any of an order (Trichoptera) of insects with four membranous wings, vestigial mouthparts, slender many-jointed antennae, and aquatic larvae — compare CADDIS WORM
cad·dish \'kad-ish\ *adj* (1868) **:** of, relating to, or resembling a cad — **cad·dish·ly** *adv* — **cad·dish·ness** *n*
cad·dis·worm \'kad-ə-,swərm\ *n* [prob. alter. of obs. *codworm*; fr. the case or tube in which it lives] (1622) **:** the larva of a caddis fly that lives in and carries around a silken case covered with bits of debris
Cad·do \'kad-(,)ō\ *n*, *pl* **Caddo** *or* **Caddos** (1807) **:** a member of an American Indian people ranging from No. Dakota south to Texas
cad·dy \'kad-ē\ *n*, *pl* **caddies** [Malay *kati* catty] (1792) **1 :** a small box, can, or chest used esp. to keep tea in **2 :** a container or device for storing or holding objects when they are not in use
cade \'kād\ *adj* [E dial. *cade* pet lamb, fr. ME *cad*] (15c) **:** left by its mother and reared by hand **:** PET ⟨a ~ lamb⟩ ⟨a ~ colt⟩

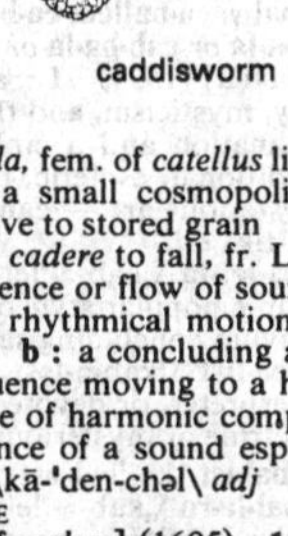
caddisworm

-cade \,kād, 'kād\ *n comb form* [*cavalcade*] **:** procession ⟨*motorcade*⟩
ca·delle \kə-'del\ *n* [F, fr. Prov *cadello*, fr. L *catella*, fem. of *catellus* little dog, dim. of *catulus* young animal] (1861) **:** a small cosmopolitan black beetle (*Tenebroides mauritanicus*) destructive to stored grain
ca·dence \'kād-ᵊn(t)s\ *n* [ME, fr. OIt *cadenza*, fr. *cadere* to fall, fr. L — more at CHANCE] (14c) **1 a :** a rhythmic sequence or flow of sounds in language **b :** the beat, time, or measure of rhythmical motion or activity **2 a :** a falling inflection of the voice **b :** a concluding and usu. falling strain; *specif* **:** a musical chord sequence moving to a harmonic close or point of rest and giving the sense of harmonic completion **3 :** the modulated and rhythmic recurrence of a sound esp. in nature — **ca·denced** \-ᵊn(t)st\ *adj* — **ca·den·tial** \kā-'den-chəl\ *adj*
ca·den·cy \'kād-ᵊn-sē\ *n*, *pl* **-cies** (1627) **:** CADENCE
ca·dent \'kād-ᵊnt\ *adj* [L *cadent-*, *cadens*, prp. of *cadere*] (1605) **1** *archaic* **:** being in the process of falling ⟨with ~ tears fret channels in her cheeks—Shak.⟩ **2 :** having rhythmic cadence
ca·den·za \kə-'den-zə\ *n* [It, cadence, cadenza] (1753) **1 :** a parenthetic flourish in an aria or other solo piece commonly just before a final or other important cadence **2 :** a technically brilliant sometimes improvised solo passage toward the close of a concerto
cade oil \'kād-\ *n* [E *cade* juniper, fr. MF, fr. OProv, fr. ML *catanus*] (1880) **:** JUNIPER TAR
ca·det \kə-'det\ *n*, *often attrib* [F, fr. F dial. *capdet* chief, fr. LL *capitellum*, dim. of L *capit-*, *caput* head — more at HEAD] (1610) **1 a :** a younger brother or son **b :** youngest son **c :** a younger branch of a family or a member of it **2 :** one in training for a military or naval commission; *esp* **:** a student in a service academy **3** *slang* **:** PIMP — **ca·det·ship** \-,ship\ *n*
Ca·dette scout \kə-,det-\ *n* [fr. *cadet*, after such pairs as F *brunet* male brunet: *brunette* female brunet] (1963) **:** a member of the Girl Scouts of the United States of America from 12 through 14 years of age
cadge \'kaj\ *vb* **cadged; cadg·ing** [back-formation fr. Sc *cadger* carrier, huckster, fr. ME *cadgear*, fr. *caggen* to tie] (1812) **:** BEG, SPONGE — **cadg·er** *n*
cad·mi·um \'kad-mē-əm\ *n* [NL, fr. L *cadmia* calamine, fr. Gk *kadmeia*, lit., Theban (earth), fr. fem. of *kadmeios* Theban, fr. *Kadmos*; fr. the occurrence of its ores together with calamine] (1822) **:** a bluish white malleable ductile toxic bivalent metallic element used esp. in protective platings and in bearing metals — see ELEMENT table
cadmium sulfide *n* (ca. 1888) **:** a yellow-brown poisonous salt CdS used esp. as a pigment, in electronic parts, in photoelectric cells, and in medicine
Cad·mus \'kad-məs\ *n* [L, fr. Gk *Kadmos*] **:** the legendary founder of Thebes
cad·re \'kad-rē, 'käd-, -,rā\ *n* [F, fr. It *quadro*, fr. L *quadrum* square — more at QUARREL] (1830) **1 :** FRAME, FRAMEWORK **2 :** a nucleus or

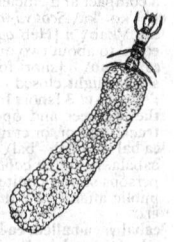

core group esp. of trained personnel able to assume control and to train others **3** **a** : a cell of indoctrinated leaders active in promoting the interests of a revolutionary party **b** : a member of a cadre, esp. a political cadre

ca·du·ceus \kə-ˈd(y)ü-sē-əs, -shəs\ *n, pl* **-cei** \-sē-ˌī\ [L, modif. of Gk *karykeion,* fr. *karyx, kēryx* herald; akin to OE *hrēth* glory] (1591) **1** : the symbolic staff of a herald; *specif* : a representation of a staff with two entwined snakes and two wings at the top **2** : an insignia bearing a caduceus and symbolizing a physician

ca·du·ci·ty \kə-ˈd(y)ü-sət-ē\ *n* [F *caducité,* fr. *caduc* transitory, fr. L *caducus*] (1769) **1** : SENILITY **2** : the quality of being transitory or perishable

ca·du·cous \kə-ˈd(y)ü-kəs\ *adj* [L *caducus* tending to fall, transitory, fr. *cadere* to fall — more at CHANCE] (1808) : falling off easily or before the usual time — used esp. of floral organs

cae·cal, cae·cum *var of* CECAL, CECUM

cae·ci·lian \si-ˈsil-yən, -ˈsēl-, -ē-ən\ *n* [deriv. of L *caecilia,* a lizard, fr. *caecus* blind] (ca. 1879) : any of an order (Gymnophiona) of chiefly tropical burrowing amphibians resembling worms — **caecilian** *adj*

caen- *or* **caeno-** — see CEN-

Caer·phil·ly \kär-ˈfil-ē\ *n* [*Caerphilly,* urban district in Wales] (1893) : a mild white friable cheese of Welsh origin

Cae·sar \ˈsē-zər\ *n* [Gaius Julius *Caesar*] (bef. 12c) **1** : any of the Roman emperors succeeding Augustus Caesar — used as a title **2** **a** *often not cap* : a powerful ruler: (1) : EMPEROR (2) : AUTOCRAT, DICTATOR **b** [fr. the reference in Mt 22:21] : the civil power : a temporal ruler — **Cae·sar·e·an** *or* **Cae·sar·i·an** \si-ˈzar-ē-ən, -zer-\ *adj*

cae·sar·e·an *or* **cae·sar·i·an** *var of* CESAREAN

Cae·sar·ism \ˈsē-zə-ˌriz-əm\ *n* (1857) : imperial authority or system : political absolutism : DICTATORSHIP — **Cae·sar·ist** \-zə-rəst\ *n*

Cae·sar salad \ˌsē-zər-\ *n* [*Caesar's,* restaurant in Tijuana, Mexico] (1950) : a tossed salad made typically with romaine, garlic, anchovies, and croutons and served with a dressing of olive oil, coddled egg, lemon juice, and grated cheese

cae·si·um *var of* CESIUM

caes·pi·tose \ˈses-pə-ˌtōs\ *adj* [NL *caespitosus,* fr. L *caespit-, caespes* turf] (1830) **1** : forming a dense turf **2** : growing in clusters or tufts

cae·su·ra \si-ˈz(h)u̇r-ə\ *n, pl* **-suras** *or* **-su·rae** \-ˈz(h)u̇(ə)r-(ˌ)ē\ [LL, fr. L, act of cutting, fr. *caedere* to cut] (1556) **1** *in Greek and Latin prosody* : a break in the flow of sound in a verse caused by the ending of a word within a foot **2** *in modern prosody* : a usu. rhetorical break in the flow of sound in the middle of a line of verse **3** : BREAK, INTERRUPTION **4** : a pause marking a rhythmic point of division in a melody — **cae·su·ral** \-ˈz(h)u̇r-əl\ *adj*

ca·fé *also* **ca·fe** \ka-ˈfā, kə-\ *n, often attrib* [F *café* coffee, café, fr. Turk *kahve* — more at COFFEE] (1802) **1** : a usu. small and informal establishment serving various refreshments (as coffee); *broadly* : RESTAURANT **2** : BARROOM **3** : CABARET, NIGHTCLUB

ca·fé au lait \(ˌ)ka-ˌfā-ō-ˈlā\ *n* [F, coffee with milk] (1763) **1** : coffee with usu. hot milk in about equal parts **2** : the color of coffee with milk

ca·fé noir \(ˌ)ka-ˌfān-(ə-)ˈwär\ *n* [F, black coffee] (1841) : coffee without milk or cream; *also* : DEMITASSE

caf·e·te·ria \ˌkaf-ə-ˈtir-ē-ə\ *n* [AmerSp *cafetería* retail coffee store, fr. Sp *café* coffee] (1839) : a restaurant in which the customers serve themselves or are served at a counter and take the food to tables to eat

caf·e·to·ri·um \-ˈtōr-ē-əm, -ˈtȯr-\ *n* [blend of *cafeteria* and *auditorium*] (1952) : a large room (as in a school building) designed for use both as a cafeteria and an auditorium

caf·feine \ka-ˈfēn, ˈka-ˌ\ *n* [G *kaffein,* fr. *kaffee* coffee, fr. F *café*] (ca. 1828) : a bitter alkaloid $C_8H_{10}N_4O_2$ found esp. in coffee, tea, and kola nuts and used medicinally as a stimulant and diuretic — **caf·fein·ic** \ka-ˈfē-nik, ˌkaf-ē-ˈin-ik\ *adj*

caf·tan \kaf-ˈtan, ˈkaf-ˌ\ *n* [Russ *kaftan,* fr. Turk, fr. Per *qaftān*] (1591) : a usu. cotton or silk ankle-length garment with long sleeves that is common throughout the Levant

[1]**cage** \ˈkāj\ *n* [ME, fr. OF, fr. L *cavea* cavity, cage, fr. *cavus* hollow — more at CAVE] (13c) **1** : a box or enclosure having some openwork for confining or carrying animals (as birds) **2** **a** : a barred cell for confining prisoners **b** : a fenced area for prisoners of war **3** : a framework serving as support ⟨the steel ~ of a skyscraper⟩ **4** : an enclosure resembling a cage in form or purpose ⟨a cashier's ~⟩ **5** **a** : a screen placed behind home plate to stop baseballs during batting practice **b** : a goal consisting of posts or a frame with a net attached (as in ice hockey) **6** : a large building with area for practicing outdoor sports and often adapted for indoor events : FIELD HOUSE 2 **7** : a sheer one-piece dress that has no waistline, is often gathered at the neck, and is worn over a close-fitting under dress or slip — **cage·ful** \-ˌfu̇l\ *n*

[2]**cage** *vt* **caged; cag·ing** (1577) **1** : to confine or keep in or as if in a cage **2** : to put (as a puck) into a cage and score a goal

cage·ling \ˈkāj-liŋ\ *n* (1859) : a caged bird

ca·gey *also* **ca·gy** \ˈkā-jē\ *adj* **ca·gi·er; -est** [origin unknown] (1893) **1** : hesitant about committing oneself **2** : wary of being trapped or deceived : SHREWD — **ca·gi·ly** \-jə-lē\ *adv* — **ca·gi·ness** *also* **ca·gey·ness** \-jē-nəs\ *n*

ca·hier \kä-ˈyā, kī-ˈā\ *n* [F, fr. MF *quaer, caier* quire — more at QUIRE] (1789) : a report or memorial concerning policy esp. of a parliamentary body

ca·hoot \kə-ˈhüt\ *n* [perh. fr. F *cahute* cabin, hut] (1829) : PARTNERSHIP, LEAGUE — usu. used in pl. ⟨in ~s with the devil⟩

ca·how \kə-ˈhau̇\ *n* [imit.] (1615) : a brown-and-white earth-burrowing nocturnal bird (*Pterodroma cahow*) formerly abundant in Bermuda but now nearly extinct

cai·man \ˈkā-mən; kā-ˈman, kī-\ *n* [Sp *caimán,* prob. fr. Carib *caymán*] (1577) : any of several Central and So. American crocodilians similar to alligators but often superficially resembling crocodiles

Cain \ˈkān\ *n* [Heb *Qayin*] : the brother and murderer of Abel

-caine \ˌkān, ˈkān\ *n comb form* [G *-kain,* fr. *kokain* cocaine] : synthetic alkaloid anesthetic ⟨*procaine*⟩

ca·ïque \kä-ˈēk, ˈkīk\ *n* [Turk *kayık*] (1625) **1** : a light skiff used on the Bosporus **2** : a Levantine sailing vessel

caird \ˈke(ə)rd\ *n* [ScGael *ceard;* akin to Gk *kerdos* profit] *Scot* (1663) : a traveling tinker; *also* : TRAMP, GYPSY

cairn \ˈka(ə)rn, ˈke(ə)rn\ *n* [ME *carne,* fr. ScGael *carn;* akin to OIr & W *carn* cairn] (14c) : a heap of stones piled up as a memorial or as a landmark — **cairned** \ˈka(ə)rnd, ˈke(ə)rnd\ *adj*

cairn·gorm \ˈka(ə)rn-ˌgȯ(ə)rm, ˈke(ə)rn-\ *n* [*Cairngorm,* mountain in Scotland] (1794) : a yellow or smoky-brown crystalline quartz

cairn terrier *n* [fr. its use in hunting among cairns] (1910) : a small compactly built hard-coated terrier of Scottish origin

cais·son \ˈkā-ˌsän, ˈkās-ᵊn, *Brit often* kə-ˈsün\ *n* [F, aug. of *caisse* box, fr. OProv *caisa,* fr. L *capsa* chest, case — more at CASE] (1702) **1** **a** : a chest to hold ammunition **b** : a usu. 2-wheeled vehicle for artillery ammunition attachable to a horse-drawn limber; *also* : a limber with its attached caisson **2** **a** : a watertight chamber used in construction work under water or as a foundation **b** : a float for raising a sunken vessel **c** : a hollow floating box or a boat used as a floodgate for a dock or basin **3** : COFFER 4

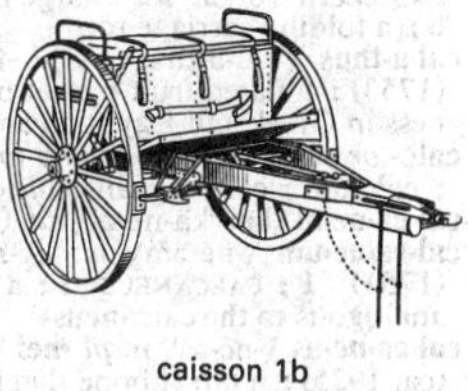
caisson 1b

caisson disease *n* (1883) : [3]BEND 3

cai·tiff \ˈkāt-əf\ *adj* [ME *caitif,* fr. ONF, captive, vile, fr. L *captivus* captive] (14c) : being base, cowardly, or despicable — **caitiff** *n*

caj·e·put \ˈkaj-ə-pət, -ˌpu̇t\ *n* [Malay *kayu puteh,* fr. *kayu* wood, tree + *puteh* white] (1876) : an East Indian tree (*Melaleuca leucadendron*) of the myrtle family that yields a pungent medicinal oil and has been introduced into Florida

ca·jole \kə-ˈjōl\ *vt* **ca·joled; ca·jol·ing** [F *cajoler* to chatter like a jay in a cage, cajole, alter. of MF *gaioler,* fr. ONF *gaiole* bird cage, fr. LL *caveola,* dim. of L *cavea* cage — more at CAGE] (1645) **1** : to persuade with flattery or gentle urging esp. in the face of reluctance : COAX ⟨had to ~ them into going⟩ **2** : to deceive with soothing words or false promises — **ca·jole·ment** \-ˈjōl-mənt\ *n* — **ca·jol·er** *n* — **ca·jol·ery** \-ˈjōl-(ə-)rē\ *n*

Ca·jun *also* **Ca·jan** \ˈkā-jən\ *n* [by alter. of *Acadian*] (1868) **1** : a Louisianian descended from French-speaking immigrants from Acadia **2** *usu Cajan* : one of a people of mixed white, Indian, and Negro ancestry in southwest Alabama and southeast Mississippi

[1]**cake** \ˈkāk\ *n* [ME, fr. ON *kaka;* akin to OHG *kuocho* cake] (13c) **1** **a** : a breadlike food made from a dough or batter that is usu. fried or baked in small flat shapes and is often unleavened **b** : a sweet baked food made from a dough or thick batter usu. containing flour and sugar and often shortening, eggs, and a raising agent (as baking powder) **c** : a flattened usu. round mass of food that is baked or fried ⟨a fish ~⟩ **2** **a** : a block of compacted or congealed matter ⟨a ~ of ice⟩ **b** : a hard or brittle layer or deposit — **cak·ey** \ˈkā-kē\ *adj*

[2]**cake** *vb* **caked; cak·ing** *vt* (1607) **1** : ENCRUST ⟨*caked* with dust⟩ **2** : to fill (a space) with a packed mass ~ *vi* : to form or harden into a mass

cake·walk \ˈkā-ˌkwȯk\ *n* (1879) **1** : an American Negro entertainment having a cake as prize for the most accomplished steps and figures in walking **2** : a stage dance developed from walking steps and figures typically involving a high prance with backward tilt **3** : a one-sided contest — **cakewalk** *vi* — **cake·walk·er** *n*

Cal·a·bar bean \ˌkal-ə-ˌbär-\ *n* [*Calabar,* Nigeria] (1876) : the dark brown highly poisonous seed of a tropical African woody vine (*Physostigma venenosum*) that is used as a source of physostigmine and as an ordeal poison in native witchcraft trials

cal·a·bash \ˈkal-ə-ˌbash\ *n* [F & Sp; F *calebasse* gourd, fr. Sp *calabaza,* prob. fr. Ar *qar'ah yābisah* dry gourd] (1596) **1** : GOURD; *esp* : one whose hard shell is used for a utensil **2** : a tropical American tree (*Crescentia cujete*) of the trumpet-creeper family; *also* : its hard globose fruit **3** : a utensil (as a bottle or dipper) made from the shell of a calabash

cal·a·boose \ˈkal-ə-ˌbüs\ *n* [Sp *calabozo* dungeon] *dial* (1792) : JAIL; *esp* : a local jail

ca·la·di·um \kə-ˈlād-ē-əm\ *n* [NL, genus name, fr. Malay *kĕladi,* an aroid plant] (1845) : any of a genus (*Caladium,* esp. *C. bicolor*) of tropical American ornamental plants of the arum family with showy variously colored leaves

cal·a·man·der \ˈkal-ə-ˌman-dər, ˌkal-ə-ˈ\ *n* [prob. fr. D *kalamanderhout* calamander wood] (1804) : the hazel-brown black-striped wood of an East Indian tree (genus *Diospyros,* esp. *D. quaesita*) that is used in furniture manufacturing

cal·a·mari \ˌkäl-ə-ˈmär-ē, ˈkal-ə-ˌmer-ē\ *n* [It, pl. of *calamaro,* fr. L *calamarius* pen-case, fr. *calamus;* fr. the inky substance the squid secretes] (1972) : squid used as food

cal·a·mary \ˈkal-ə-ˌmer-ē\ *n, pl* **-mar·ies** [L *calamarius*] (1567) : SQUID

cal·a·mine \ˈkal-ə-ˌmīn, -mən\ *n* [F, ore of zinc, fr. ML *calamina,* alter. of L *cadmia* — more at CADMIUM] (15c) : a mixture of zinc oxide with a small amount of ferric oxide used in lotions, liniments, and ointments

cal·a·mint \ˈkal-ə-ˌmint\ *n* [ME *calament,* fr. OF, fr. ML *calamentum,* fr. Gk *kalaminthē*] (13c) : any of a genus (*Satureja,* esp. *S. calamintha*) of mints

cal·a·mite \ˈkal-ə-ˌmīt\ *n* [NL *Calamites,* genus of fossil plants, fr. L *calamus*] (1837) : a Paleozoic fossil plant (esp. genus *Calamites*) resembling a giant horsetail

ca·lam·i·tous \kə-ˈlam-ət-əs\ *adj* (1545) : causing or accompanied by calamity — **ca·lam·i·tous·ly** *adv* — **ca·lam·i·tous·ness** *n*

ca·lam·i·ty \kə-ˈlam-ət-ē\ *n, pl* **-ties** [MF *calamité,* fr. L *calamitat-, calamitas;* akin to L *clades* destruction — more at HALT] (14c) **1** : a state of deep distress or misery caused by major misfortune or loss **2** : an extraordinarily grave event marked by great loss and lasting distress and affliction ***syn*** see DISASTER

cal·a·mon·din \ˌkal-ə-ˈmän-dən\ *n* [Tag *kalamunding*] (ca. 1928) : a small spiny citrus tree (*Citrus mitis*) of the Philippines; *also* : its fruit

cal·a·mus \ˈkal-ə-məs\ *n, pl* **-mi** \-ˌmī, -ˌmē\ [L, reed, reed pen, fr. Gk *kalamos* — more at HAULM] (14c) **1 a :** SWEET FLAG **b :** the aromatic peeled and dried rhizome of the sweet flag that is the source of a carcinogenic essential oil **2 :** the hollow basal portion of a feather below the vane : QUILL

ca·lash \kə-ˈlash\ *n* [F *calèche,* fr. G *kalesche,* fr. Czech *kolesa* wheels, carriage; akin to Gk *kyklos* wheel — more at WHEEL] (1679) **1 a :** a light small-wheeled 4-passenger carriage with a folding top **b :** CALÈCHE 1b **2 a :** a large hood worn by women in the 18th century **b :** a folding carriage top

cal·a·thus \ˈkal-ə-thəs\ *n, pl* **-thi** \-ˌthī, -ˌthē\ [L, fr. *kalathos* basket] (1753) **:** a flared fruit basket borne on the head as a symbol of fruitfulness in Greek and Egyptian art

calc- *or* **calci-** *or* **calco-** *comb form* [L *calc-, calx* lime — more at CHALK] **:** calcium **:** calcium salt ⟨*calc*ic⟩ ⟨*calci*fy⟩

cal·ca·ne·al \kal-ˈkā-nē-əl\ *adj* (1847) **:** relating to the heel or calcaneus

cal·ca·ne·um \-nē-əm\ *n, pl* **-nea** \-nē-ə\ [L, heel — more at CALK] (1751) **1 :** CALCANEUS **2 :** a process of the tarsometatarsus of a bird analogous to the calcaneus

cal·ca·ne·us \-nē-əs\ *n, pl* **-nei** \-nē-ˌī\ [LL, heel, alter. of L *calcaneum*] (ca. 1925) **:** a tarsal bone that in man is the great bone of the heel

cal·car \ˈkal-ˌkär\ *n, pl* **cal·car·ia** \kal-ˈkar-ē-ə, -ˈker-\ [L, fr. *calc-, calx* heel — more at CALK] (1836) **:** a spurred anatomical prominence (as of the calcaneum of a bat)

cal·car·e·ous \kal-ˈkar-ē-əs, -ˈker-\ *adj* [L *calcarius* of lime, fr. *calc-, calx* lime] (1677) **1 a :** resembling calcite or calcium carbonate esp. in hardness **b :** consisting of or containing calcium carbonate; *also* **:** containing calcium **2 :** growing on limestone or in soil impregnated with lime — **cal·car·e·ous·ly** *adv*

calces *pl of* CALX

cal·cic \ˈkal-sik\ *adj* (1871) **:** derived from or containing calcium or lime **:** rich in calcium

cal·ci·cole \ˈkal-sə-ˌkōl\ *n* [F, calcicolous, fr. *calc-* + *-cole* -colous] (1882) **:** a plant normally growing on calcareous soils — **cal·cic·o·lous** \kal-ˈsik-ə-ləs\ *adj*

cal·cif·er·ol \kal-ˈsif-ə-ˌrȯl, -ˌrōl\ *n* [*calci*ferous + ergost*erol*] (1931) **:** an alcohol $C_{28}H_{43}OH$ usu. prepared by irradiation of ergosterol and used as a dietary supplement in nutrition and medicinally in the control of rickets and related disorders — called also *vitamin* D_2

cal·cif·er·ous \kal-ˈsif-(ə-)rəs\ *adj* (1799) **:** producing or containing calcium carbonate

cal·cif·ic \kal-ˈsif-ik\ *adj* [*calcify*] (1861) **:** involving or caused by calcification ⟨~ lesions⟩

cal·ci·fuge \ˈkal-sə-ˌfyüj\ *n* [F, calcifugous, fr. *calc-* + L *fugere* to flee — more at FUGITIVE] (1926) **:** a plant not normally growing on calcareous soils — **calcifuge** *also* **cal·cif·u·gous** \kal-ˈsif-yə-gəs\ *adj*

cal·ci·fy \ˈkal-sə-ˌfī\ *vb* **-fied; -fy·ing** *vt* (1854) **1 :** to make calcareous by deposit of calcium salts **2 :** to make inflexible or unchangeable ~ *vi* **1 :** to become calcareous **2 :** to become inflexible and changeless **:** HARDEN — **cal·ci·fi·ca·tion** \ˌkal-sə-fə-ˈkā-shən\ *n*

cal·ci·mine \ˈkal-sə-ˌmīn\ *n* [alter. of *kalsomine,* of unknown origin] (1864) **:** a white or tinted wash that consists of glue, whiting or zinc white, and water and that is used esp. on plastered surfaces — **calcimine** *vt*

cal·ci·na·tion \ˌkal-sə-ˈnā-shən\ *n* (14c) **:** the act or process of calcining **:** the state of being calcined

[1]**cal·cine** \kal-ˈsīn, ˈkal-ˌ\ *vb* **cal·cined; cal·cin·ing** [ME *calcenen,* fr. MF *calciner,* fr. L *calc-, calx* lime — more at CHALK] *vt* (14c) **:** to heat (as inorganic materials) to a high temperature but without fusing in order to drive off volatile matter or to effect changes (as oxidation or pulverization) ~ *vi* **:** to undergo calcination

[2]**cal·cine** \ˈkal-ˌsīn\ *n* (ca. 1909) **:** a product (as a metal oxide) of calcination or roasting

cal·ci·no·sis \ˌkal-sə-ˈnō-səs\ *n, pl* **-no·ses** \-ˌsēz\ [NL, irreg. (influenced by ISV *calcine*) fr. *calc-* + *-osis*] (ca. 1929) **:** the abnormal deposition of calcium salts in a part or tissue of the body

cal·cite \ˈkal-ˌsīt\ *n* (1849) **:** a mineral $CaCO_3$ consisting of calcium carbonate crystallized in hexagonal form and including common limestone, chalk, and marble — **cal·cit·ic** \kal-ˈsit-ik\ *adj*

cal·ci·to·nin \ˌkal-sə-ˈtō-nən\ *n* [*calci-* + [1]*tonic* + *-in*] (1961) **:** a polypeptide hormone esp. from the thyroid gland that tends to lower the level of calcium in the blood plasma — called also *thyrocalcitonin*

cal·ci·um \ˈkal-sē-əm\ *n, often attrib* [NL, fr. L *calc-, calx* lime] (1808) **:** a silver-white bivalent metallic element of the alkaline-earth group occurring only in combination — see ELEMENT table

calcium carbide *n* (ca. 1889) **:** a usu. dark gray crystalline compound CaC_2 used esp. for the generation of acetylene and for making calcium cyanamide

calcium carbonate *n* (1873) **:** a compound $CaCO_3$ found in nature as calcite and aragonite and in plant ashes, bones, and shells and used in making lime and portland cement and as a gastric antacid

calcium chloride *n* (ca. 1885) **:** a white deliquescent salt $CaCl_2$ used in its anhydrous state as a drying and dehumidifying agent and in a hydrated state for controlling dust and ice on roads

calcium cyanamide *n* (ca. 1909) **:** a compound $CaCN_2$ used as a fertilizer and a weed killer and as a source of other nitrogen compounds

calcium gluconate *n* (1884) **:** a white powdery salt $CaC_{12}H_{22}O_{14}$ used esp. as a source of bodily calcium

calcium hydroxide *n* (ca. 1890) **:** a strong alkali $Ca(OH)_2$ commonly sold in water solution and as an ingredient of bleaching powder

calcium hypochlorite *n* (ca. 1889) **:** a white powder $CaCl_2O_2$ used esp. as a bleaching agent and disinfectant

calcium light *n* (1864) **:** LIMELIGHT 1a, 1b

calcium phosphate *n* (1869) **:** any of various phosphates of calcium: as **a :** the phosphate $CaH_4P_2O_8$ used as a fertilizer and in baking powder **b :** the phosphate $CaHPO_4$ used in pharmaceutical preparations and animal feeds **c :** the phosphate $Ca_3P_2O_8$ used as a fertilizer **d :** a naturally occurring phosphate of calcium $Ca_5(F,Cl,OH,{}^1\!/_2CO_3)(PO_4)_3$ that contains other elements or radicals and is the chief constituent of phosphate rock, bones, and teeth

calcium silicate *n* (ca. 1888) **:** any of several silicates of calicum; *esp* **:** either of two Ca_3SiO_5 or Ca_2SiO_4 that are essential constituents of portland cement

calc·spar \ˈkalk-ˌspär\ *n* [part trans. of Sw *kalkspat,* fr. *kalk* lime + *spat* spar] (1822) **:** CALCITE

cal·cu·la·ble \ˈkal-kyə-lə-bəl\ *adj* (1734) **1 :** subject to or ascertainable by calculation **2 :** that may be counted on **:** DEPENDABLE

cal·cu·late \ˈkal-kyə-ˌlāt\ *vb* **-lat·ed; -lat·ing** [L *calculatus,* pp. of *calculare,* fr. *calculus* pebble (used in reckoning), dim. of *calc-, calx* stone used in gaming, lime — more at CHALK] *vt* (1570) **1 a :** to determine by mathematical processes **b :** to reckon by exercise of practical judgment **:** ESTIMATE **c :** to solve or probe the meaning of **:** FIGURE OUT ⟨trying to ~ his expression —Hugh MacLennan⟩ **2 :** to design or adapt for a purpose **3** *chiefly Northern* **a :** to judge to be true or probable **b :** INTEND ~ *vi* **1 a :** to make a calculation **b :** to forecast consequences **2 :** COUNT, RELY

cal·cu·lat·ed \-ˌlāt-əd\ *adj* (1722) **1 :** APT, LIKELY **2 a :** worked out by mathematical calculation **b :** engaged in, undertaken, or displayed after reckoning or estimating the statistical probability of success or failure ⟨a ~ risk⟩ **3 :** planned or contrived to accomplish a purpose **4 :** brought about by deliberate intent — **cal·cu·lat·ed·ly** *adv* — **cal·cu·lat·ed·ness** *n*

cal·cu·lat·ing \-ˌlāt-iŋ\ *adj* (1710) **1 :** making calculations ⟨~ machine⟩ **2 :** marked by prudent and deliberate analysis or by shrewd consideration of self-interest **:** SCHEMING — **cal·cu·lat·ing·ly** \-iŋ-lē\ *adv*

cal·cu·la·tion \ˌkal-kyə-ˈlā-shən\ *n* (14c) **1 a :** the process or an act of calculating **b :** the result of an act of calculating **2 a :** studied care in analyzing or planning **b :** cold heartless planning to promote self-interest — **cal·cu·la·tion·al** \-ˈlāsh-nəl, -ˈlā-shən-ᵊl\ *adj*

cal·cu·la·tor \ˈkal-kyə-ˌlāt-ər\ *n* (14c) **1 :** one that calculates: as **a :** a mechanical or electronic device for performing mathematical calculations automatically **b :** a person who operates a calculator **2 :** a set or book of tables for facilitating computations

cal·cu·lous \ˈkal-kyə-ləs\ *adj* (1605) **:** caused or characterized by a calculus or calculi

cal·cu·lus \-ləs\ *n, pl* **-li** \-ˌlī, -ˌlē\ *also* **-lus·es** [L, stone (used in reckoning)] (1666) **1 a :** a method of computation or calculation in a special notation (as of logic or symbolic logic) **b :** the mathematical methods comprising differential and integral calculus **2 :** CALCULATION **3 a :** a concretion usu. of mineral salts around organic material found esp. in hollow organs or ducts **b :** TARTAR 2

calculus of variations (1837) **:** a branch of mathematics dealing with maxima and minima of definite integrals which have an integrand that is a function of independent variables and of dependent variables and their derivatives

cal·de·ra \kal-ˈder-ə, kȯl-, -ˈdir-\ *n* [Sp, lit., caldron, fr. LL *caldaria*] (1691) **:** a crater with a diameter many times that of the volcanic vent formed by collapse of the central part of a volcano or by explosions of extraordinary violence

cal·dron \ˈkȯl-drən\ *n* [ME, alter. of *cauderon,* fr. ONF, dim. of *caudiere,* fr. LL *caldaria,* fr. L, warm bath, fr. fem. of *caldarius* suitable for warming, fr. *calidus* warm, fr. *calēre* to be warm — more at LEE] (14c) **1 :** a large kettle or boiler **2 :** something resembling a boiling caldron ⟨a ~ of intense emotions⟩

ca·lèche *or* **ca·leche** \kə-ˈlesh, -ˈlash\ *n* [F *calèche* — more at CALASH] (1666) **1 a :** CALASH 1a **b :** a 2-wheeled horse-drawn vehicle with a driver's seat on the splashboard used in Quebec **2 :** CALASH 2a

cal·e·fac·to·ry \ˌkal-ə-ˈfak-t(ə-)rē\ *n, pl* **-ries** [ML *calefactorium,* fr. L *calefactus,* pp. of *calefacere* to warm — more at CHAFE] (1681) **:** a monastery room warmed and used as a sitting room

[1]**cal·en·dar** \ˈkal-ən-dər\ *n* [ME *calender,* fr. AF or ML; AF *calender,* fr. ML *kalendarium,* fr. L, moneylender's account book, fr. *kalendae* calends] (13c) **1 :** a system for fixing the beginning, length, and divisions of the civil year and arranging days and longer divisions of time (as weeks and months) in a definite order — see MONTH table **2 :** a tabular register of days according to a system usu. covering one year and referring the days of each month to the days of the week **3 :** an orderly list: as **a :** a list of cases to be tried in court **b :** a list of bills or other items reported out of committee for consideration by a legislative assembly **c :** a list of events giving dates and details **4** *Brit* **:** a university catalog

[2]**calendar** *vt* **-dared; -dar·ing** \-d(ə-)riŋ\ (15c) **:** to enter in a calendar

calendar year *n* (ca. 1909) **1 :** a period of a year beginning and ending with the dates that are conventionally accepted as marking the beginning and end of a numbered year (as January 1 and December 31 in the Gregorian calendar) **2 :** a period of time equal in length to that of the year in the calendar conventionally in use (as 365 days in the Gregorian calendar or when a Feb. 29 is included 366 days)

[1]**cal·en·der** \ˈkal-ən-dər\ *vt* **-dered; -der·ing** \-d(ə-)riŋ\ [MF *calandrer,* fr. *calandre* machine for calendering, modif. of Gk *kylindros* cylinder — more at CYLINDER] (1513) **:** to press (as cloth, rubber, or paper) between rollers or plates in order to smooth and glaze or to thin into sheets — **cal·en·der·er** \-dər-ər\ *n*

[2]**calender** *n* (1688) **:** a machine for calendering something

[3]**calender** *n* [Per *qalandar,* fr. Ar, fr. Per *kalandar* uncouth man] (1614) **:** one of a Sufic order of wandering mendicant dervishes

ca·len·dri·cal \kə-ˈlen-dri-kəl, ka-\ *also* **ca·len·dric** \-drik\ *adj* (ca. 1847) **:** of, relating to, characteristic of, or used in a calendar

cal·ends \ˈkal-ən(d)z, ˈkāl-\ *n pl but sing or pl in constr* [ME *kalendes,* fr. L *kalendae, calendae*] (14c) **:** the first day of the ancient Roman month from which days were counted backward to the ides

ca·len·du·la \kə-ˈlen-jə-lə\ *n* [NL, genus name, fr. ML, fr. L *calendae* calends] (ca. 1864) **:** any of a small genus (*Calendula*) of yellow-rayed composite herbs of temperate regions

cal·en·ture \ˈkal-ən-ˌchu̇(ə)r\ *n* [Sp *calentura,* fr. *calentar* to heat, fr. L *calent-, calens,* prp. of *calēre* to be warm — more at LEE] (1593) **:** a tropical fever caused by exposure to heat

[1]**calf** \ˈkaf, ˈkȧf\ *n, pl* **calves** \ˈkavz, ˈkȧvz\ *also* **calfs** *often attrib* [ME, fr. OE *cealf;* akin to OHG *kalb* calf, ON *kālfi* calf of the leg, L *galba* paunch] (bef. 12c) **1 a :** the young of the domestic cow; *also* **:** that of a closely related mammal (as a bison or water buffalo) **b :** the young of various large animals (as the elephant and whale) **2** *pl* **calfs :** the hide of the domestic calf; *esp* **:** CALFSKIN **3 :** an awkward or silly youth **4 :** a small mass of ice set free from a coast glacier or from an iceberg or floe — **calf·like** \ˈkaf-ˌlīk, ˈkȧf-\ *adj* — **in calf :** PREGNANT — used of a cow

[2]**calf** *n, pl* **calves** \ˈkavz, ˈkävz\ [ME, fr. ON *kālfi*] (14c) **:** the fleshy hinder part of the leg below the knee

calf love *n* (1823) **:** PUPPY LOVE

calf's–foot jelly \ˌkavz-ˌfu̇t-, ˌkafs-, ˌkävz-, ˌkäfs-\ *n* (1775) **:** jelly made from gelatin obtained by boiling calves' feet

calf•skin \ˈkaf-ˌskin, ˈkäf-\ *n* (15c) **:** leather made of the skin of a calf

Cal•gon \ˈkal-ˌgän\ *trademark* — used for a water softener

Cal•i•ban \ˈkal-ə-ˌban\ *n* **:** a savage and deformed slave in Shakespeare's *The Tempest*

cal•i•ber *or* **cal•i•bre** \ˈkal-ə-bər, *Brit also* kə-ˈlē-\ *n* [MF *calibre*, fr. OIt *calibro*, fr. Ar *qālib* shoemaker's last] (1568) **1 a :** the diameter of a bullet or other projectile **b :** the diameter of a bore of a gun usu. expressed in hundredths or thousandths of an inch and typically written as a decimal fraction ⟨.32 ~⟩ **2 :** the diameter of a round body; *esp* **:** the internal diameter of a hollow cylinder **3 a :** degree of mental capacity or moral quality **b :** degree of excellence or importance

cal•i•brate \ˈkal-ə-ˌbrāt\ *vt* **-brat•ed; -brat•ing** (1864) **1 :** to ascertain the caliber of (as a thermometer tube) **2 :** to determine, rectify, or mark the graduations of (as a thermometer tube) **3 :** to standardize (as a measuring instrument) by determining the deviation from a standard so as to ascertain the proper correction factors **4 :** ADJUST, TUNE — **cal•i•bra•tor** \-ˌbrāt-ər\ *n*

cal•i•bra•tion \ˌkal-ə-ˈbrā-shən\ *n* (1871) **1 :** the act or process of calibrating **:** the state of being calibrated **2 :** a set of graduations to indicate values or positions — usu. used in pl. ⟨~*s* on a gauge⟩

ca•li•che \kə-ˈlē-chē\ *n* [AmerSp, fr. Sp, flake of lime, fr. *cal* lime, fr. L *calx* — more at CHALK] (1858) **1 :** the nitrate-bearing gravel or rock of the sodium nitrate deposits of Chile and Peru **2 :** a crust of calcium carbonate that forms on the stony soil of arid regions

cal•i•co \ˈkal-i-ˌkō\ *n, pl* **-coes** *or* **-cos** [*Calicut*, India] (1540) **1 a :** cotton cloth imported from India **b** *Brit* **:** a plain white cotton fabric that is heavier than muslin **c :** any of various cheap cotton fabrics with figured patterns **2 :** a blotched or spotted animal; *esp* **:** one that is predominantly white with red and black patches — **calico** *adj*

calico bass *n* (1884) **:** BLACK CRAPPIE

calico bush *n* (1814) **:** MOUNTAIN LAUREL

Cal•i•for•nia condor \ˌkal-ə-ˌfȯr-nyə-\ *n* [*California*, state of U.S.] (1833) **:** a large nearly extinct vulture (*Gymnogyps californianus*) that is related to the condor of So. America and is found in the mountains of southern California

California condor

California laurel *n* (1871) **:** a Pacific coast tree (*Umbellularia californica*) of the laurel family with evergreen foliage and small umbellate flowers

California poppy *n* (1845) **:** any of a genus (*Eschscholtzia*) of herbs of the poppy family; *esp* **:** one (*E. californica*) widely cultivated for its pale yellow to red flowers

Cal•i•for•nio \ˌkal-ə-ˈfȯr-nē-ˌō\ *n, pl* **-nios** [Sp, fr. *California*] (1923) **:** one of the original Spanish colonists of California or their descendants

cal•i•for•ni•um \ˌkal-ə-ˈfȯr-nē-əm\ *n* [NL, fr. *California*, U.S.] (1950) **:** a radioactive element discovered by bombarding curium 242 with alpha particles — see ELEMENT table

ca•lig•i•nous \kə-ˈlij-ə-nəs\ *adj* [MF or L; MF *caligineux*, fr. L *caliginosus*, fr. *caligin-*, *caligo* darkness; akin to Gk *kelainos* black — more at COLUMBINE] (1548) **:** MISTY, DARK

Ca•li•na•go \ˌkal-ə-ˈnä-(ˌ)gō\ *n* (ca. 1972) **:** an Arawakan language of the Lesser Antilles and Central America

[1]**cal•i•per** *or* **cal•li•per** \ˈkal-ə-pər\ *n* [alter. of *caliber*] (1588) **1 a :** a measuring instrument with two legs or jaws that can be adjusted to determine thickness, diameter, and distance between surfaces — usu. used in pl. ⟨a pair of ~*s*⟩ **b :** an instrument for measuring diameters (as of logs or trees) consisting of a graduated beam and at right angles to it a fixed arm and a movable arm **c :** a device consisting of two plates lined with a frictional material that press against the sides of a rotating wheel or disc in certain brake systems **2 :** thickness esp. of paper, paperboard, or a tree

[2]**caliper** *or* **calliper** *vt* **-pered; -per•ing** \-p(ə-)riŋ\ (1876) **:** to measure by or as if by calipers

ca•liph *or* **ca•lif** \ˈkā-ləf, ˈkal-əf\ *n* [ME *caliphe*, fr. MF *calife*, fr. Ar *khalīfah* successor] (14c) **:** a successor of Muhammad as temporal and spiritual head of Islam — used as a title — **ca•liph•al** \-əl\ *adj*

ca•liph•ate \-ˌāt, -ət\ *n* (1614) **:** the office or dominion of a caliph

cal•is•then•ic \ˌkal-əs-ˈthen-ik\ *adj* (1842) **:** of or relating to calisthenics

cal•is•then•ics \-iks\ *n pl but sing or pl in constr* [Gk *kalos* beautiful + *sthenos* strength — more at CALLIGRAPHY] (1847) **1 :** systematic rhythmic bodily exercises performed usu. without apparatus **2** *usu sing in constr* **:** the art or practice of calisthenics

ca•lix \ˈkā-liks, ˈkal-iks\ *n, pl* **ca•li•ces** \ˈkā-lə-ˌsēz, ˈkal-ə-\ [L *calic-*, *calix* — more at CHALICE] (1698) **:** CUP

[1]**calk** \ˈkȯk\, **calk•er** \ˈkȯ-kər\ *var of* CAULK, CAULKER

[2]**calk** \ˈkȯk\ *n* [prob. alter. of *calkin*, fr. ME *kakun*, fr. MD or ONF; MD *calcoen* horse's hoof, fr. ONF *calcain* heel, fr. L *calcaneum*, fr. *calc-*, *calx* heel; akin to Gk *kōlon* limb, *skelos* leg] (1587) **:** a tapered piece projecting downward on the shoe of a horse to prevent slipping; *also* **:** a similar device worn on the sole of a shoe

[3]**calk** *vt* (1624) **1 :** to furnish with calks **2 :** to wound with a calk

[1]**call** \ˈkȯl\ *vb* [ME *callen*, fr. ON *kalla*; akin to OE *hildecalla* battle herald, OHG *kallōn* to talk loudly, OSlav *glasŭ* voice] *vi* (bef. 12c) **1 a :** to speak in a loud distinct voice so as to be heard at a distance **:** SHOUT ⟨~ for help⟩ **b :** to make a request or demand ⟨~ for an investigation⟩ **c** *of an animal* **:** to utter a characteristic note or cry **d :** to get or try to get into communication by telephone — often used with *up* **e :** to make a demand in card games (as for a particular card or for a show of hands) **f :** to give the calls for a square dance **2 :** to make a brief visit ⟨~*ed* to pay his respects⟩ ⟨~*ed* on a friend⟩ ~ *vt* **1 a (1) :** to utter in a loud distinct voice — often used with *out* ⟨~ out a number⟩ **(2) :** to announce or read loudly or authoritatively ⟨~ the roll⟩ ⟨~ off a row of figures⟩ **b (1) :** to command or request to come or be present ⟨~*ed* to testify⟩ **(2) :** to cause to come **:** BRING ⟨~*s* to mind an old saying⟩ **c :** to summon to a particular activity, employment, or office ⟨was ~*ed* to active duty⟩ **d :** to invite or command to meet **:** CONVOKE ⟨~ a meeting⟩ **e :** to rouse from sleep or summon to get up **f (1) :** to give the order for **:** bring into action ⟨~ a strike against the company⟩ **(2) :** to manage (as an offensive game) by giving the signals or orders ⟨that catcher ~*s* a good game⟩ **g (1) :** to make a demand in bridge for (a card or suit) **(2) :** to require (a player) to show the hand in poker by making an equal bet **(3) :** to challenge to make good on a statement **(4) :** to charge with or censure for an offense ⟨deserves to be ~*ed* on that⟩ **h :** to attract (as game) by imitating the characteristic cry **i :** to halt (as a baseball game) because of unsuitable conditions **j :** to rule on the status of (as a pitched ball or a player's action) ⟨~ balls and strikes⟩ ⟨~ a base runner safe⟩ **k :** to give the calls for (a square dance) — often used with *off* **l (1) :** to get or try to get in communication with by telephone **(2) :** to deliver (a message) by telephone **(3) :** to make a signal to in order to transmit a message ⟨~ the flagship⟩ **m (1) :** to demand payment of esp. by formal notice ⟨~ a loan⟩ **(2) :** to demand presentation of (as a bond or option) for redemption **2 a :** to speak of or address by a specified name **:** give a name to ⟨~ her Kitty⟩ **b (1) :** to regard or characterize as of a certain kind **:** CONSIDER ⟨can hardly be ~*ed* generous⟩ **(2) :** to estimate or consider for purposes of an estimate or for convenience ⟨~ it an even dollar⟩ **c (1) :** to describe correctly in advance of or without knowledge of the event **:** PREDICT **(2) :** to name or specify in advance ⟨~ the toss of a coin⟩ **3 :** to temporarily transfer control of computer processing to (as a subroutine) ***syn*** see SUMMON — **call a spade a spade :** to speak frankly — **call for 1 :** to call (as at one's house) to get ⟨I'll *call for* you after dinner⟩ **2 a :** to require as necessary or appropriate ⟨the job *calls for* typing skills⟩ **b :** to make necessary **3 a :** to give an order for **:** DIRECT ⟨legislation *calling for* new schools⟩ **b :** to provide for ⟨the design *calls for* three windows⟩ — **call forth :** ELICIT, EVOKE ⟨these events *call forth* great emotions⟩ — **call in question** *or* **call into question :** to cast doubt upon — **call it a day :** to stop for the remainder of the day or for the present whatever one has been doing — **call it quits :** to call it a day **:** QUIT — **call names :** to address or speak of a person or thing contemptuously or offensively — **call on 1 :** to call upon **2 :** to elicit a response from (as a student) ⟨the teacher *called on* her first⟩ — **call one's bluff :** to challenge in order to expose an empty pretense or threat — **call the shots :** to be in charge or control **:** determine the policy or procedure — **call the tune :** to call the shots — **call to account :** to hold responsible **:** REPRIMAND — **call upon 1 :** REQUIRE, OBLIGE ⟨may be *called upon* to do several jobs⟩ **2 :** to make a demand on **:** depend on ⟨universities are *called upon* to produce trained men⟩

[2]**call** *n* (14c) **1 a :** an act of calling with the voice **:** SHOUT **b :** an imitation of the cry of a bird or other animal made to attract it **c :** an instrument used for calling ⟨a duck ~⟩ **d :** the cry of an animal (as a bird) **2 a :** a request or command to come or assemble **b :** a summons or signal on a drum, bugle, or pipe **c :** admission to the bar as a barrister **d :** an invitation to become the minister of a church or to accept a professional appointment **e :** a divine vocation or strong inner prompting to a particular course of action **f :** a summoning of actors to rehearsal ⟨the ~ is for 11 o'clock⟩ **g :** the attraction or appeal of a particular activity, condition, or place ⟨the ~ of the wild⟩ **h :** an order specifying the number of men to be inducted into the armed services during a specified period **i :** the selection of a play in football **3 a :** DEMAND, CLAIM **b :** NEED, JUSTIFICATION **c :** a demand for payment of money **d :** an option to buy a specified amount of a security (as stock) or commodity (as wheat) at a fixed price at or within a specified time — compare [2]PUT 2 **e :** an instance of asking for something **:** REQUEST ⟨many ~*s* for Christmas stories⟩ **4 :** ROLL CALL **5 :** a short usu. formal visit **6 :** the name or thing called ⟨the ~ was heads⟩ **7 :** the act of calling in a card game **8 :** the act of calling on the telephone **9 :** a direction or a succession of directions for a square dance rhythmically called to the dancers **10 :** a decision or ruling made by an official of a sports contest **11 :** a temporary transfer of control of computer processing to a particular set of instructions (as a subroutine) — **at call** *or* **on call 1 a :** available for use **:** at the service of ⟨thousands of men *at* his *call*⟩ **b :** ready to respond to a summons or command ⟨a doctor *on call*⟩ **2 :** subject to demand for payment or return without previous notice ⟨money lent *at call*⟩ — **within call :** within hearing or reach of a summons **:** subject to summons

call•able \ˈkȯ-lə-bəl\ *adj* (1826) **:** capable of being called; *specif* **:** subject to a demand for presentation for payment ⟨~ bond⟩

cal•la lily \ˈkal-ə-\ *n* [NL, genus name, modif. of Gk *kallaia* rooster's wattles] (1805) **1 :** a house or greenhouse plant (*Zantedeschia aethiopica*) of the arum family with a white showy spathe and yellow spadix — called also *calla* **2 :** a plant resembling the calla lily

cal•la•loo \ˌkal-ə-ˈlü, ˈkal-ə-ˌ\ *n* [AmSp, fr. *calalú* tropical American plant] (1892) **:** a soup or stew made with greens, onions, and crabmeat

cal•lant \ˈkal-ənt, ˈkäl-\ *n* [D or ONF; D *kalant* customer, fellow, fr. ONF *calland* customer, fr. L *calent-*, *calens*, prp. of *calēre* to be warm — more at LEE] *chiefly Scot* (1597) **:** BOY, LAD

call•back \ˈkȯl-ˌbak\ *n* (1926) **:** a return call; *specif* **:** [2]RECALL 5

call–board \-ˌbō(ə)rd, -ˌbȯ(ə)rd\ *n* (1886) **:** BULLETIN BOARD

call box *n* (1885) **1** *Brit* **:** a public telephone booth **2 :** a telephone usu. located on the side of a road for reporting emergencies (as fires or automobile breakdowns)

call•boy \ˈkȯl-ˌbȯi\ *n* (1794) **:** BELLHOP, PAGE

\ə\ abut \ᵊ\ kitten, F table \ər\ further \a\ ash \ā\ ace \ä\ cot, cart \au̇\ out \ch\ chin \e\ bet \ē\ easy \g\ go \i\ hit \ī\ ice \j\ job \ŋ\ sing \ō\ go \ȯ\ law \ȯi\ boy \th\ thin \t͟h\ the \ü\ loot \u̇\ foot \y\ yet \zh\ vision \à, k̟, ⁿ, œ, œ̄, ue, ue̅, ʸ\ see Guide to Pronunciation

call down *vt* (1810) **1 :** to cause or entreat to descend ⟨*call down* a blessing on the crops⟩ **2 :** REPRIMAND ⟨*called* me *down* for being late⟩

called strike *n* (1887) **:** a pitched baseball not struck at by the batter that passes through the strike zone

¹cal·ler \'käl-ər\ *adj* [ME *callour*] (14c) **1** *Scot* **:** FRESH **2** *Scot* **:** COOL

²call·er \'kȯ-lər\ *n* (15c) **:** one that calls

cal·let \'kal-ət\ *n* [perh. fr. MF *caillette* frivolous person, fr. *Caillette fl* 1500 Fr. court fool] *chiefly Scot* (15c) **:** PROSTITUTE

call girl *n* (ca. 1940) **:** a prostitute with whom an appointment may be made by telephone

call house *n* (1929) **:** a house or apartment where call girls may be procured

cal·lig·ra·pher \kə-'lig-rə-fər\ *n* (1753) **1 :** one that writes a beautiful hand **2 :** PENMAN ⟨a fair ∼⟩ **3 :** a professional copyist or engrosser

cal·lig·ra·phist \-fəst\ *n* (1816) **:** CALLIGRAPHER

cal·lig·ra·phy \-fē\ *n* [F or Gk; F *calligraphie,* fr. Gk *kalligraphia,* fr. *kalli-* beautiful (fr. *kallos* beauty) + *-graphia* -graphy; akin to Gk *kalos* beautiful, Skt *kalya* healthy] (1613) **1 a :** beautiful or elegant handwriting — compare CACOGRAPHY **b :** the art of producing such writing **2 :** PENMANSHIP — **cal·li·graph·ic** \ˌkal-ə-'graf-ik\ *adj* — **cal·li·graph·i·cal·ly** \-i-k(ə-)lē\ *adv*

call in *vt* (1597) **1 :** to order to return or to be returned: as **a :** to withdraw from an advanced position ⟨*call in* the outposts⟩ **b :** to withdraw from circulation ⟨*call in* bank notes and issue new ones⟩ **2 :** to summon to one's aid or for consultation ⟨*call in* a mediator⟩ ∼ *vi* **:** to communicate with a person by telephone — **call in sick :** to report by telephone that one will be absent because of illness

call·ing \'kȯ-liŋ\ *n* (14c) **1 :** a strong inner impulse toward a particular course of action esp. when accompanied by conviction of divine influence **2 :** the vocation or profession in which one customarily engages **3 :** the characteristic cry of a female cat in heat; *also* **:** the period of heat ***syn*** see WORK

calling card *n* (1896) **:** VISITING CARD

cal·li·ope \kə-'lī-ə-(ˌ)pē, *in sense 2 also* 'kal-ē-ˌōp\ *n* [L, fr. Gk *Kalliopē*] **1** *cap* **:** the Greek Muse of heroic poetry **2 :** a keyboard musical instrument resembling an organ and consisting of a series of whistles sounded by steam or compressed air

cal·li·pyg·ian \ˌkal-ə-'pij-(ē-)ən\ *or* **cal·li·py·gous** \-'pī-gəs\ *adj* [Gk *kallipygos,* fr. *kalli-* + *-pygos,* fr. *pygē* buttocks; akin to Gk *physan* to blow, inflate — more at FOG] (1800) **:** having shapely buttocks

Cal·lis·to \kə-'lis-(ˌ)tō\ *n* [L, fr. Gk *Kallistō*] **1 :** a nymph loved by Zeus, changed into a she-bear by Hera, and subsequently changed into the Great Bear constellation **2 :** the so-called fourth but really fifth satellite of Jupiter

cal·li·thump \'kal-ə-ˌthəmp\ *n* [back-formation fr. *callithumpian,* adj., alter. of E dial. *gallithumpian* disturber of order at elections in 18th cent.] (1856) **:** a noisy boisterous parade — **cal·li·thump·ian** \ˌkal-ə-'thəm-pē-ən\ *adj*

call letters *n pl* (1913) **:** CALL SIGN

call loan *n* (1852) **:** a loan payable at the discretion of the borrower or on demand of the lender

call number *n* (1876) **:** a combination of characters assigned to a library book to indicate its place on a shelf

call off *vt* (1633) **1 :** to draw away **:** DIVERT ⟨her attention was *called off* by a new arrival⟩ **2 :** CANCEL ⟨*call* the trip *off*⟩

call of nature (1763) **:** the need to expel body wastes

cal·los·i·ty \ka-'läs-ət-ē, kə-\ *n, pl* **-ties** (1578) **1 :** the quality or state of being callous: as **a :** marked or abnormal hardness and thickness **b :** lack of feeling or capacity for emotion **2 :** CALLUS 1

¹cal·lous \'kal-əs\ *adj* [MF *calleux,* fr. L *callosus,* fr. *callum, callus* callous skin; akin to Skt *kiṇa* callosity] (15c) **1 a :** being hardened and thickened **b :** having calluses **2 a :** feeling no emotion **b :** feeling no sympathy for others — **cal·lous·ly** *adv* — **cal·lous·ness** *n*

²callous *vt* (1834) **:** to make callous

call out *vt* (15c) **1 :** to summon into action ⟨*call out* troops⟩ **2 :** to challenge to a duel **3 :** to order on strike ⟨*call out* the workers⟩

cal·low \'kal-(ˌ)ō, -ə(-w)\ *adj* [ME *calu* bald, fr. OE; akin to OHG *kalo* bald] (1580) **:** lacking adult sophistication **:** IMMATURE ⟨∼ youth⟩ — **cal·low·ness** \'kal-ō-nəs, -ə-nəs\ *n*

call sign *n* (ca. 1919) **:** the combination of identifying letters or letters and numbers assigned to an operator, office, activity, or station for use in communication (as in the address of a message sent by radio)

call slip *n* (1881) **:** a form filled out by a library patron for a desired book

call to quarters (ca. 1918) **:** a bugle call usu. shortly before taps that summons soldiers to their quarters

call–up \'kȯ-ˌləp\ *n* (1940) **:** an order to report for military service

call up \(')kȯ-'ləp\ *vt* (1632) **1 :** to bring to mind **:** EVOKE **2 :** to summon before an authority **3 :** to summon together or collect (as for a united effort) ⟨*call up* all his forces for the attack⟩ **4 :** to summon for active military duty **5 :** to bring forward for consideration or action

¹cal·lus \'kal-əs\ *n* [L] (1563) **1 :** a thickening of or a hard thickened area on skin or bark **2 :** a mass of exudate and connective tissue that forms around a break in a bone and is converted into bone in the healing of the break **3 :** soft tissue that forms over a wounded or cut plant surface

²callus *vi* (1864) **:** to form callus ∼ *vt* **:** to cause callus to form on

¹calm \'kä(l)m, *NewEng also* 'kȧm\ *adj* (14c) **1 :** marked by calm **:** STILL ⟨a ∼ sea⟩ **2 :** free from agitation, excitement, or disturbance ⟨a ∼ manner⟩ — **calm·ly** *adv* — **calm·ness** *n*

syn CALM, TRANQUIL, SERENE, PLACID, PEACEFUL mean quiet and free from disturbance. CALM often implies a contrast with a foregoing or nearby state of agitation or violence; TRANQUIL suggests a very deep quietude or composure; SERENE stresses an unclouded and lofty tranquillity; PLACID suggests an undisturbed appearance and often implies a degree of complacency; PEACEFUL implies a state of repose in contrast with or following strife or turmoil.

²calm *vi* (14c) **:** to become calm ∼ *vt* **:** to make calm

³calm *n* [ME *calme,* fr. MF, fr. OIt *calma,* fr. LL *cauma* heat, fr. Gk *kauma,* fr. *kaiein* to burn — more at CAUSTIC] (15c) **1 a :** a period or condition of freedom from storms, high winds, or rough activity of water **b :** complete absence of wind or presence of wind having a speed no greater than one mile per hour **2 :** a state of tranquillity

calm·ative \'käm-ət-iv, 'käl-mət-, *NewEng also* 'kȧm-ət-\ *n or adj* [²*calm* + *-ative* (as in *sedative*)] (1870) **:** SEDATIVE

cal·o·mel \'kal-ə-məl, -ˌmel\ *n* [prob. fr. (assumed) NL *calomelas,* fr. Gk *kalos* beautiful + *melas* black — more at CALLIGRAPHY, MULLET] (1676) **:** a white tasteless compound Hg_2Cl_2 used in medicine esp. as a purgative and fungicide — called also *mercurous chloride*

¹ca·lo·ric \kə-'lȯr-ik, -'lōr-, -'lär-; 'kal-ə-rik\ *n* [F *calorique,* fr. L *calor*] (1791) **1 :** a supposed form of matter formerly held responsible for the phenomena of heat and combustion **2** *archaic* **:** HEAT

²caloric *adj* (ca. 1828) **1 :** of or relating to heat **2 :** of or relating to calories — **ca·lo·ri·cal·ly** \kə-'lȯr-i-k(ə-)lē, -'lōr-, -'lär-\ *adv*

cal·o·rie *also* **cal·o·ry** \'kal-(ə-)rē\ *n, pl* **-ries** [F *calorie,* fr. L *calor* heat, fr. *calēre* to be warm — more at LEE] (1870) **1 a :** the amount of heat required at a pressure of one atmosphere to raise the temperature of one gram of water one degree Celsius that is equal to about 4.19 joules — called also *gram calorie, small calorie;* abbr. *cal* **b :** the amount of heat required to raise the temperature of one kilogram of water one degree Celsius **:** 1000 gram calories or 3.968 Btu — called also *kilogram calorie, large calorie;* abbr. *Cal* **2 a :** a unit equivalent to the large calorie expressing heat-producing or energy-producing value in food when oxidized in the body **b :** an amount of food having an energy-producing value of one large calorie

cal·o·rif·ic \ˌkal-ə-'rif-ik\ *adj* [F or L; F *calorifique,* fr. L *calorificus,* fr. *calor*] (1812) **1 :** CALORIC **2 :** of or relating to the production of heat

cal·o·rim·e·ter \ˌkal-ə-'rim-ət-ər\ *n* [ISV, fr. L *calor*] (1794) **:** any of several apparatuses for measuring quantities of absorbed or evolved heat or for determining specific heats — **ca·lo·ri·met·ric** \ˌkal-ə-rə-'me-trik; kə-ˌlȯr-ə-, -ˌlōr-, -ˌlär-\ *adj* — **ca·lo·ri·met·ri·cal·ly** \-tri-k(ə-)lē\ *adv* — **cal·o·rim·e·try** \ˌkal-ə-'rim-ə-trē\ *n*

ca·lotte \kə-'lät\ *n* [F] (1632) **:** SKULLCAP; *esp* **:** ZUCCHETTO

ca·loy·er \kə-'lȯi(-ə)r, 'kal-ə-yər\ *n* [It & F; F *caloyer,* fr. obs. It *caloiero,* fr. MGk *kalogēros* venerable, fr. *kalos* beautiful + *gēras* old age] (1599) **:** a monk of the Eastern Church

cal·pac *or* **cal·pack** \'kal-ˌpak, kal-'\ *n* [Turk *kalpak*] (1598) **:** a high-crowned cap worn in Turkey, Iran, and neighboring countries

calque \'kalk\ *n* [F, lit., copy, fr. *calquer* to trace, fr. It *calcare* to trample, trace, fr. L, to trample — more at CAULK] (1937) **:** LOAN TRANSLATION

cal·trop \'kal-trəp, 'kȯl-\ *also* **cal·throp** \-thrəp\ *n* [ME *calketrappe* star thistle, fr. OE *calcatrippe,* fr. ML *calcatrippa*] (bef. 12c) **1 a** *pl but sing or pl in constr* **:** STAR THISTLE 1 **b :** PUNCTURE VINE; *also* **:** any of various related herbs (genera *Tribulus* and *Kallstroemia*) **2 :** a device with four metal points so arranged that when any three are on the ground the fourth projects upward as a hazard to the hoofs of horses or to pneumatic tires

cal·u·met \'kal-yə-ˌmet, -mət\ *n* [AmerF, fr. F dial., straw, fr. LL *calamellus,* dim. of L *calamus* reed — more at CALAMUS] (1673) **:** a highly ornamented ceremonial pipe of the American Indians

ca·lum·ni·ate \kə-'ləm-nē-ˌāt\ *vt* **-at·ed; -at·ing** (1554) **1 :** to utter maliciously false statements, charges, or imputations about **2 :** to injure the reputation of by calumny ***syn*** see MALIGN — **ca·lum·ni·a·tion** \-ˌləm-nē-'ā-shən\ *n* — **ca·lum·ni·a·tor** \-'ləm-nē-ˌāt-ər\ *n*

ca·lum·ni·ous \kə-'ləm-nē-əs\ *adj* (15c) **:** constituting or marked by calumny **:** SLANDEROUS — **ca·lum·ni·ous·ly** *adv*

cal·um·ny \'kal-əm-nē *also* -yəm-\ *n, pl* **-nies** [MF & L; MF *calomnie,* fr. L *calumnia,* prob. fr. *calvi* to deceive; akin to OE *hōl* calumny, Gk *kēlein* to beguile] (15c) **1 :** the act of uttering false charges or misrepresentations maliciously calculated to damage another's reputation **2 :** a misrepresentation intended to blacken another's reputation

cal·va·dos \ˌkal-və-'dōs\ *n, often cap* [F, fr. *Calvados,* Normandy, France] (1906) **:** an applejack made in the department of Calvados, France

cal·var·i·um \kal-'var-ē-əm, -'ver-\ *n, pl* **-ia** \-ē-ə\ [NL, fr. L *calvaria* skull, fr. *calvus* bald] (14c) **:** a skull lacking the lower jaw or lower jaw and facial portion

cal·va·ry \'kalv-(ə-)rē\ *n, pl* **-ries** [*Calvary,* the hill near Jerusalem where Jesus was crucified] (1738) **1 :** an open-air representation of the crucifixion of Christ **2 :** an experience of usu. intense mental suffering

Calvary cross *n* (1826) **:** a Latin cross usu. mounted on three steps — see CROSS illustration

calve \'kav, 'kȧv\ *vb* **calved; calv·ing** [ME *calven,* fr. OE *cealfian,* fr. *cealf* calf] *vi* (bef. 12c) **1 :** to give birth to a calf; *also* **:** to produce offspring **2** *of an ice mass* **:** to separate or break so that a part becomes detached ∼ *vt* **1 :** to produce by birth **2** *of an ice mass* **:** to let become detached

calves *pl of* CALF

Cal·vin·ism \'kal-və-ˌniz-əm\ *n* [John *Calvin*] (1570) **:** the theological system of Calvin and his followers marked by strong emphasis on the sovereignty of God and esp. by the doctrine of predestination — **Cal·vin·ist** \-və-nəst\ *n or adj* — **Cal·vin·is·tic** \ˌkal-və-'nis-tik\ *adj* — **Cal·vin·is·ti·cal·ly** \-ti-k(ə-)lē\ *adv*

calx \'kalks\ *n, pl* **calx·es** *or* **cal·ces** \'kal-ˌsēz\ [ME *cals,* fr. L *calx* lime — more at CHALK] (15c) **:** the crumbly residue left when a metal or mineral has been subjected to calcination or combustion

¹ca·lyp·so \kə-'lip-(ˌ)sō\ *n* [L, fr. Gk *Kalypsō*] **1** *cap* **:** a sea nymph in Homer's *Odyssey* who keeps Odysseus seven years on the island of Ogygia **2** *pl* **calypsos** [NL, genus name, prob. fr. L] **:** a bulbous bog orchid (genus *Calypso*) of northern regions bearing a single flower variegated with white, purple, pink, and yellow

²calypso *n, pl* **-sos** *also* **-soes** [prob. fr. *Calypso*] (1934) **:** a style of music originating in the West Indies, marked by lively duple meter, and having lyrics that are often improvised and usu. satirize local personalities and events — **ca·lyp·so·ni·an** \kə-ˌlip-'sō-nē-ən, ˌkal-(ˌ)ip-\ *n or adj*

ca·lyp·tra \kə-'lip-trə\ *n* [NL, fr. Gk *kalyptra* veil, fr. *kalyptein* to cover — more at HELL] (ca. 1753) **:** the archegonium of a liverwort or moss; *esp* **:** one forming a membranous hood over the capsule in a moss

ca·lyx \'kā-liks *also* 'kal-iks\ *n, pl* **ca·lyx·es** *or* **ca·ly·ces** \'kā-lə-ˌsēz *also* 'kal-ə-\ [L *calyc-, calyx,* fr. Gk *kalyx* — more at CHALICE] (1693) **1 :** the external usu. green or leafy part of a flower consisting of sepals **2 :** a cuplike animal structure (as the body of a crinoid or a division of the kidney pelvis)

cal·zo·ne \kal-'zō-(ˌ)nā, -'zō-\ *n, pl* **calzone** *or* **calzones** [It, fr. *calzone,* sing. of *calzoni* pants, slacks] (ca. 1950) **:** a turnover stuffed with savory fillings (as cheese and ham)

cam \ˈkam\ *n* [perh. fr. F *came,* fr. G *kamm,* lit., comb, fr. OHG *kamb*] (1777) **:** a rotating or sliding piece that imparts motion to a roller moving against its edge or to a pin free to move in a groove on its face or that receives motion from such a roller or pin

ca·ma·ra·de·rie \ˌkäm(-ə)-ˈräd-ə-rē, ˌkam(-ə)-, -ˈrad-\ *n* [F, fr. *camarade* comrade] (1840) **:** a spirit of friendly good-fellowship

cam·a·ril·la \ˌkam-ə-ˈril-ə, -ˈrē-(y)ə\ *n* [Sp, lit., small room] (1839) **:** a group of unofficial often secret and scheming advisers; *also* **:** CABAL

cam·as *also* **cam·ass** \ˈkam-əs\ *n* [Chinook Jargon *kamass*] (1805) **:** any of a genus (*Camassia* esp. *C. quamash*) of plants of the lily family of the western U.S. with edible bulbs — compare DEATH CAMAS

[1]**cam·ber** \ˈkam-bər\ *vb* **cam·bered; cam·ber·ing** \-b(ə-)riŋ\ [F *cambrer,* fr. MF *cambre* curved, fr. L *camur* — more at CHAMBER] *vi* (1627) **:** to curve upward in the middle ~ *vt* **1 :** to arch slightly **2 :** to impart camber to

[2]**camber** *n* (1823) **1 :** a slight convexity, arching, or curvature (as of a beam, deck, or road) **2 :** the convexity of the curve of an airfoil from the leading edge to the trailing edge **3 :** a setting of the wheels of an automotive vehicle closer together at the bottom than at the top

cam·bi·um \ˈkam-bē-əm\ *n, pl* **-bi·ums** *or* **-bia** \-bē-ə\ [NL, fr. ML, exchange, fr. L *cambire* to exchange — more at CHANGE] (1671) **:** a thin formative layer between the xylem and phloem of most vascular plants that gives rise to new cells and is responsible for secondary growth — **cam·bi·al** \-bē-əl\ *adj*

Cam·bo·di·an \kam-ˈbōd-ē-ən\ *n* (1770) **1 :** a native or inhabitant of Cambodia **2 :** KHMER 2 — **Cambodian** *adj*

Cam·bri·an \ˈkam-brē-ən, ˈkām-\ *adj* [ML *Cambria* Wales, fr. MW *Cymry* Wales, Welshmen] (1656) **1 :** WELSH **2 :** of, relating to, or being the earliest geologic period of the Paleozoic era or the corresponding system of rocks marked by fossils of every great animal type except the vertebrate and by scarcely recognizable plant fossils — **Cambrian** *n*

cam·bric \ˈkām-brik\ *n* [obs. Flem *Kameryk* Cambrai, city of France] (1530) **1 :** a fine thin white linen fabric **2 :** a cotton fabric that resembles cambric

cambric tea *n* (1888) **:** a hot drink of water, milk, sugar, and often a small amount of tea

cam·cord·er \ˈkam-ˌkȯrd-ər\ *n* [*camera* + *recorder*] (1982) **:** a small portable combined videocassette camera and recorder

[1]**came** *past of* COME

[2]**came** \ˈkām\ *n* [origin unknown] (1688) **:** a slender grooved lead rod used to hold together panes of glass esp. in a stained-glass window

cam·el \ˈkam-əl\ *n* [ME, fr. OE & ONF, fr. L *camelus,* fr. Gk *kamēlos,* of Sem origin; akin to Heb & Phoenician *gāmāl* camel] (bef. 12c) **1 :** either of two large ruminant mammals used as draft and saddle animals in desert regions esp. of Africa and Asia: **a :** the one-humped camel (*Camelus dromedarius*) of western Asia and northern Africa — called also *dromedary* **b :** the two-humped camel (*C. bactrianus*) of Chinese Turkestan and Mongolia — called also *Bactrian camel* **2 :** a watertight structure used esp. to lift submerged ships **3 :** a variable color averaging a light yellowish brown

camel 1: *1* Arabian, *2* Bactrian

cam·el·back \ˈkam-əl-ˌbak\ *n* (1860) **1 :** the back of a camel **2 :** an uncured compound chiefly of reclaimed or synthetic rubber used for retreading or recapping pneumatic tires

cam·el·eer \ˌkam-ə-ˈli(ə)r\ *n* (1808) **:** a camel driver

camel hair *also* **camel's hair** *n* (14c) **1 :** the hair of the camel or a substitute for it (as hair from squirrels' tails) **2 :** cloth made of camel hair or a mixture of camel hair and wool usu. light tan and of soft silky texture

ca·mel·lia \kə-ˈmēl-yə\ *n* [NL *Camellia,* fr. *Camellus* (Georg Josef Kamel †1706 Moravian Jesuit missionary)] (1753) **:** any of several shrubs or trees (genus *Camellia*) of the tea family; *esp* **:** an ornamental greenhouse shrub (*C. japonica*) with glossy evergreen leaves and showy roselike flowers

ca·mel·o·pard \kə-ˈmel-ə-ˌpärd\ *n* [LL *camelopardus,* alter. of L *camelopardalis,* fr. Gk *kamēlopardalis,* fr. *kamēlos* + *pardalis* leopard] (14c) **1 :** GIRAFFE **2** *cap* **:** CAMELOPARDALIS

Ca·mel·o·par·da·lis \kə-ˌmel-ə-ˈpärd-ᵊl-əs\ *n* [L (gen. *Camelopardalis*), camelopard] **:** a northern constellation between Cassiopeia and Ursa Major

Cam·e·lot \ˈkam-ə-ˌlät\ *n* **1 :** the site of King Arthur's palace and court **2 :** a time, place, or atmosphere of idyllic happiness

Cam·em·bert \ˈkam-əm-ˌbe(ə)r\ *n* [F, fr. *Camembert,* Normandy, France] (1878) **:** a soft surface-ripened cheese with a thin grayish white rind and a yellow interior

cam·eo \ˈkam-ē-ˌō\ *n, pl* **-eos** [It] (15c) **1 a :** a gem carved in relief; *esp* **:** a small piece of sculpture on a stone or shell cut in relief in one layer with another contrasting layer serving as background **b :** a small medallion with a profiled head in relief **2 :** a carving or sculpture made in the manner of a cameo **3 :** a usu. brief literary or filmic piece that brings into delicate or sharp relief the character of a person, place, or event **4 :** a small theatrical role (as in television) performed by a well-known actor and often limited to a single scene — **cameo** *adj* — **cameo** *vt*

cam·era \ˈkam-(ə-)rə\ *n* [LL, room — more at CHAMBER] (1712) **1 :** the treasury department of the papal curia **2 a :** CAMERA OBSCURA **b :** a lightproof box fitted with a lens through the aperture of which the image of an object is recorded on a light-sensitive material **c :** an electronic device for capturing images and converting them into electrical impulses (as for television broadcast) — **on camera :** before a live televising camera

cam·era lu·ci·da \ˌkam-(ə-)rə-ˈlü-səd-ə\ *n* [NL, lit., light chamber] (1831) **:** an instrument that by means of a prism or mirrors and often a microscope causes a virtual image of an object to appear as if projected upon a plane surface so that an outline may be traced

cam·era·man \ˈkam-(ə-)rə-ˌman, -mən\ *n* (1908) **1 :** one who operates a camera **2 :** one who sells photographic equipment

cam·era ob·scu·ra \ˌkam-(ə-)rə-əb-ˈskyu̇r-ə\ *n* [NL, lit., dark chamber] (1725) **:** a darkened enclosure having an aperture usu. provided with a lens through which light from external objects enters to form an image of the objects on the opposite surface

cam·er·len·go \ˌkam-ər-ˈleŋ-(ˌ)gō\ *n, pl* **-gos** [It *camarlingo*] (1625) **:** a cardinal who heads the Apostolic Camera

ca·mion \kä-myōⁿ\ *n* [F] (1885) **:** MOTORTRUCK; *also* **:** BUS

cam·i·sa·do \ˌkam-ə-ˈsäd-(ˌ)ō, -ˈsäd-\ *n, pl* **-does** [prob. fr. obs. Sp. *camisada*] *archaic* (1548) **:** an attack by night

ca·mise \kə-ˈmēz, -ˈmēs\ *n* [Ar *qamīṣ,* perh. fr. LL *camisia*] (1812) **:** a light loose long-sleeved shirt, gown, or tunic

cam·i·sole \ˈkam-ə-ˌsōl\ *n* [F, prob. fr. OProv *camisolla,* dim. of *camisa* shirt, fr. LL *camisia*] (1795) **1 :** a short negligee jacket for women **2 :** a short sleeveless undergarment for women

cam·let \ˈkam-lət\ *n* [ME *cameloit,* fr. MF *camelot,* fr. Ar *khamlat* woolen plush] (15c) **1 a :** a medieval Asian fabric of camel hair or angora wool **b :** a European fabric of silk and wool **c :** a fine lustrous woolen **2 :** a garment made of camlet

camomile *var of* CHAMOMILE

ca·mor·ra \kə-ˈmȯr-ə, -ˈmär-\ *n* [It] (1865) **:** a group of persons united for dishonest or dishonorable ends; *esp* **:** a secret organization formed about 1820 at Naples, Italy

ca·mor·ris·ta \ˌkäm-ō-ˈrē-stə\ *n, pl* **-ti** \-(ˌ)stē\ [It, fr. *camorra* + *-ista* -ist] (1897) **:** a member of a camorra

[1]**cam·ou·flage** \ˈkam-ə-ˌfläzh, -ˌfläj\ *n* [F, fr. *camoufler* to disguise, fr. It *camuffare*] (1917) **1 :** the disguising esp. of military equipment or installations with paint, nets, or foliage; *also* **:** the disguise so applied **2 a :** concealment by means of disguise **b :** behavior or artifice designed to deceive or hide — **cam·ou·flag·ic** \ˌkam-ə-ˈfläzh-ik, -ˈfläj-\ *adj*

[2]**camouflage** *vb* **-flaged; -flag·ing** *vt* (1917) **:** to conceal or disguise by camouflage ~ *vi* **:** to practice camouflage — **cam·ou·flage·able** \ˈkam-ə-ˌfläzh-ə-bəl, -ˈfläj-\ *adj*

[1]**camp** \ˈkamp\ *n, often attrib* [MF, prob. fr. ONF or OProv, fr. L *campus* plain, field; akin to OHG *hamf* crippled, Gk *kampē* bend] (1528) **1 a :** ground on which temporary shelters (as tents) are erected **b :** a group of shelters erected on such ground **c :** a temporary shelter (as a cabin or tent) **d :** an open-air location where one or more persons camp **e :** a settlement newly sprung up in a lumbering or mining region **2 a :** a body of persons encamped **b (1) :** a group of persons; *esp* **:** a group engaged in promoting or defending a theory, doctrine, or position **(2) :** an ideological position **3 :** military service or life

[2]**camp** *vi* (1543) **1 :** to make camp or occupy a camp **2 :** to live temporarily in a camp or outdoors — often used with *out* **3 :** to take up one's quarters **:** LODGE **4 :** to take up one's position **:** settle down ~ *vt* **:** to put into a camp; *also* **:** ACCOMMODATE

[3]**camp** *n* [origin unknown] (ca. 1909) **1 :** exaggerated effeminate mannerisms exhibited esp. by homosexuals **2 :** HOMOSEXUAL **3 :** something so outrageously artificial, affected, inappropriate, or out-of-date as to be considered amusing — **camp·i·ly** \ˈkam-pə-lē\ *adv* — **camp·i·ness** \-pē-nəs\ *n* — **campy** \ˈkam-pē\ *adj*

[4]**camp** *adj* (1909) **:** of, relating to, being, or displaying camp ⟨~ send-ups of the songs of the fifties and sixties —John Elsom⟩

[5]**camp** *vi* (1925) **:** to engage in camp **:** exhibit the qualities of camp ⟨he . . . was ~*ing,* hands on hips, with a quick eye to notice every man who passed by —R. M. McAlmon⟩

[1]**cam·paign** \(ˈ)kam-ˈpān\ *n* [F *campagne,* prob. fr. It *campagna* level country, campaign, fr. LL *campania* level country, fr. L, the level country around Naples] (1652) **1 :** a connected series of military operations forming a distinct phase of a war **2 :** a connected series of operations designed to bring about a particular result ⟨election ~⟩

[2]**campaign** *vi* (1701) **:** to go on, engage in, or conduct a campaign — **cam·paign·er** *n*

cam·pa·ni·le \ˌkam-pə-ˈnē-lē, ˌkäm-, -(ˌ)lā, *esp of US structures also* ˌkam-pə-ˈnē(ə)l\ *n, pl* **-ni·les** *or* **-ni·li** \-ˈnē-lē\ [It, fr. *campana* bell, fr. LL] (1640) **:** a usu. freestanding bell tower

cam·pa·nol·o·gist \ˌkam-pə-ˈnäl-ə-jəst\ *n* (1857) **:** one that practices or is skilled in campanology

cam·pa·nol·o·gy \-jē\ *n* [NL *campanologia,* fr. LL *campana* + NL *-o-* + *-logia* -logy] (ca. 1841) **:** the art of bell ringing

cam·pan·u·la \kam-ˈpan-yə-lə\ *n* [NL, dim. of LL *campana*] (1664) **:** any of a genus (*Campanula*) of bellflowers

cam·pan·u·late \-lət, -ˌlāt\ *adj* [NL *campanulatus,* deriv. of LL *campana*] (1668) **:** shaped like a bell

Camp·bell·ite \ˈkam-(b)ə-ˌlīt\ *n* [Alexander *Campbell*] (1830) **:** DISCIPLE 2 — often taken to be offensive

camp·craft \ˈkamp-ˌkraft\ *n* (ca. 1888) **:** skill and practice in the activities relating to camping

camp·er \ˈkam-pər\ *n* (1856) **1 :** one that camps **2 :** a portable dwelling (as a specially equipped trailer or automotive vehicle) for use during casual travel and camping

camp·er·ship \-ˌship\ *n* [*camper* + *ship* (as in *scholarship*)] (1947) **:** a grant that enables a youngster to attend a summer camp

cam·pe·si·no \ˌkam-pə-ˈsē-(ˌ)nō\ *n, pl* **-nos** [Sp, fr. *campo* field, country, fr. L *campus* field — more at CAMP] (1898) **:** a native of a Latin-American rural area; *esp* **:** a Latin-American Indian farmer or farm laborer

cam·pes·tral \kam-ˈpes-trəl\ *adj* [L *campestr-, campester,* fr. *campus*] (ca. 1736) **:** of or relating to fields or open country **:** RURAL

Camp Fire girl *n* [fr. *Camp Fire Girls,* Inc., former name of Camp Fire, Inc.] (1912) **:** a girl who is a member of a national organization of young people from 5 to 18

camp follower *n* (1810) **1 :** a civilian who follows a military unit to attend or exploit military personnel; *specif* **:** PROSTITUTE **2 :** a disciple or follower who is not of the main body of members or adherents; *esp* **:** a politician who joins the party or movement solely for personal gain

\ə\ abut \ᵊ\ kitten, F table \ər\ further \a\ ash \ā\ ace \ä\ cot, cart \au̇\ out \ch\ chin \e\ bet \ē\ easy \g\ go \i\ hit \ī\ ice \j\ job \ŋ\ sing \ō\ go \ȯ\ law \ȯi\ boy \th\ thin \t͟h\ the \ü\ loot \u̇\ foot \y\ yet \zh\ vision \à, k̲, ⁿ, œ, œ̄, ue, ue̅, ʸ\ *see* Guide to Pronunciation

camp·ground \'kamp-ˌgrau̇nd\ *n* (1806) **:** the area or place (as a field or grove) used for a camp, for camping, or for a camp meeting
cam·phene \'kam-ˌfēn\ *n* (ca. 1839) **:** any of several terpenes related to camphor; *esp* **:** a colorless crystalline terpene $C_{10}H_{16}$ used in insecticides
cam·phine *or* **cam·phene** \'kam-ˌfēn\ *n* [ISV, fr. *camphor*] (1842) **:** an explosive mixture of turpentine and alcohol formerly used as an illuminant
cam·phor \'kam(p)-fər\ *n* [ME *caumfre,* fr. AF, fr. ML *camphora,* fr. Ar *kāfūr,* fr. Malay *kāpūr*] (14c) **:** a tough gummy volatile fragrant crystalline compound $C_{10}H_{16}O$ obtained esp. from the wood and bark of the camphor tree and used as a liniment and mild analgesic in medicine esp. externally, as a plasticizer, and as an insect repellent; *also* **:** any of several similar compounds (as some terpene alcohols and ketones) — **cam·pho·ra·ceous** \ˌkam(p)-fə-'rā-shəs\ *adj*
cam·phor·ate \'kam(p)-fə-ˌrāt\ *vt* **-at·ed; -at·ing** (1641) **:** to impregnate or treat with camphor
camphor tree *n* (1607) **:** a large evergreen tree (*Cinnamomum camphora*) of the laurel family grown in most warm countries
cam·pi·on \'kam-pē-ən\ *n* [prob. fr. obs. *campion* (champion)] (1576) **:** any of various plants (genera *Lychnis* and *Silene*) of the pink family
camp meeting *n* (1803) **:** a series of evangelistic meetings usu. held outdoors and attended by persons who often camp nearby
cam·po \'kam-(ˌ)pō, 'käm-\ *n, pl* **campos** [AmerSp, fr. Sp, field, fr. L *campus*] (1820) **:** a grassland plain in So. America with scattered perennial herbs
campong *var of* KAMPONG
camp·o·ree \ˌkam-pə-'rē\ *n* [*camp* + jambo*ree*] (1927) **:** a gathering of Boy Scouts or Girl Scouts from a given geographic area
camp·site \'kamp-ˌsīt\ *n* (1910) **:** a place suitable for or used as the site of a camp
cam·pus \'kam-pəs\ *n* [L, plain — more at CAMP] (1774) **:** the grounds and buildings of a university, college, or school
cam·py·lot·ro·pous \ˌkam-pi-'lä-trə-pəs\ *adj* [Gk *kampylos* bent + ISV *-tropous* -tropous; akin to Gk *kampē* bend — more at CAMP] (1835) **:** having the ovule curved
cam·shaft \'kam-ˌshaft\ *n* (ca. 1877) **:** a shaft to which a cam is fastened or of which a cam forms an integral part
cam wheel *n* (ca. 1864) **:** a wheel set or shaped to act as a cam
[1]**can** \kən, (ˈ)kan *sometimes* kᵊŋ\ *vb, past* **could** \kəd, (ˈ)ku̇d\; *pres sing & pl* **can** [ME (1st & 3d sing. pres. indic.), fr. OE; akin to OHG *kan* (1st & 3d sing. pres. indic.) know, am able, OE *cnāwan* to know — more at KNOW] *vt* (bef. 12c) **1** *obs* **:** KNOW, UNDERSTAND **2** *archaic* **:** to be able to do, make, or accomplish **~** *vi, archaic* **:** to have knowledge or skill **~** *verbal auxiliary* **1 a :** know how to ⟨he ~ read⟩ **b :** be physically or mentally able to ⟨he ~ lift 200 pounds⟩ **c** — used to indicate possibility ⟨do you think he ~ still be alive⟩ ⟨those things ~ happen⟩; sometimes used interchangeably with *may* **d :** be permitted by conscience or feeling to ⟨~ hardly blame him⟩ **e :** be made possible or probable by circumstances to ⟨he ~ hardly have meant that⟩ **f :** be inherently able or designed to ⟨everything that money ~ buy⟩ **g :** be logically or axiologically able to ⟨2 + 2 ~ also be written 3 + 1⟩ **h :** be enabled by law, agreement, or custom to **2 :** have permission to — used interchangeably with *may* ⟨you ~ go now if you like⟩
usage *Can* and *may* are most frequently interchangeable in senses denoting possibility; because the possibility of one's doing something may depend on another's acquiescence, they have also become interchangeable in the sense denoting permission. The use of *can* to ask or grant permission has been common since the 19th century and is well established, although some commentators feel *may* is more appropriate in formal contexts. *May* is relatively rare in negative constructions (few people use *mayn't*); *cannot* and *can't* are therefore usual in such contexts.
[2]**can** \'kan\ *n* [ME *canne,* fr. OE; akin to OHG *channa*] (bef. 12c) **1 :** a usu. cylindrical receptacle: **a :** a vessel for holding liquids; *specif* **:** a drinking vessel **b :** a typically cylindrical metal receptacle usu. with an open top, often with a removable cover, and sometimes with a spout or side handles (as for holding milk, oil, coffee, tobacco, ashes, or garbage) **c :** a container (as of tinplate) in which perishable foods or other products are hermetically sealed for preservation until use **d :** a jar for packing or preserving fruit or vegetables **2 :** JAIL **3 :** TOILET **4 :** BUTTOCKS **5 :** DEPTH CHARGE **6 :** DESTROYER 2 **7** *slang* **:** an ounce of marijuana — **can·ful** \'kan-ˌfu̇l\ *n* — **in the can** *of a film or videotape* **:** completed and ready for release
[3]**can** \'kan\ *vt* **canned; can·ning** (1861) **1 a :** to put in a can **:** preserve by sealing in airtight cans or jars **b :** to hit (a golf ball) into the cup **2** *slang* **:** to expel from school **:** discharge from employment **3** *slang* **:** to put a stop or end to ⟨~ that racket —Nathaniel Burt⟩ **4 :** to record on discs or tape — **can·ner** *n*
Ca·naan·ite \'kā-nə-ˌnīt\ *n* [Gk *Kananitēs,* fr. *Kanaan* Canaan, fr. Heb *Kena'an*] (1535) **:** a member of a Semitic people inhabiting ancient Palestine and Phoenicia from about 3000 B.C. — **Canaanite** *adj*
Can·a·da balsam \ˌkan-əd-ə-\ *n* [Canada, country in No. America] (1818) **:** a viscid yellowish to greenish oleoresin exudate of the balsam fir (*Abies balsmea*) that solidifies to a transparent mass and is used as a transparent cement esp. in microscopy
Canada goose *n* (1772) **:** the common wild goose (*Branta canadensis*) of No. America that is chiefly gray and brownish with black head and neck and a white patch running from the sides of the head under the throat
Canada thistle *n* (1799) **:** a European thistle (*Cirsium arvense*) with pinkish purple or white flowers that is a naturalized weed in No. America
Ca·na·di·an \kə-'nād-ē-ən\ *n* (1568) **:** a native or inhabitant of Canada — **Canadian** *adj*
Canadian bacon \kə-ˌnād-ē-ən-\ *n* (1938) **:** bacon cut from the loin
Canadian football *n* (1944) **:** a game resembling American football that is played on a turfed field between two teams of 12 players each
Canadian French *n* (1846) **:** the language of the French Canadians
Canadian lynx *or* **Canada lynx** *n* (1840) **:** LYNX c
ca·naille \kə-'nī, -'nā(ə)l\ *n* [F, fr. It *canaglia,* fr. *cane* dog, fr. L *canis* — more at HOUND] (1661) **1 :** RABBLE, RIFFRAFF **2 :** PROLETARIAN
[1]**ca·nal** \kə-'nal\ *n* [ME, fr. L *canalis* pipe, channel, fr. *canna* reed — more at CANE] (15c) **1 :** a tubular anatomical passage or channel **:** DUCT **2 :** CHANNEL, WATERCOURSE **3 :** an artificial waterway for navigation or for draining or irrigating land **4 :** any of various faint narrow markings held to exist on the planet Mars
[2]**canal** *vt* **-nalled** *or* **-naled; -nal·ling** *or* **-nal·ing** (1819) **:** to construct a canal through or across
can·a·lic·u·lus \ˌkan-ᵊl-'ik-yə-ləs\ *n, pl* **-li** \-ˌlī, -ˌlē\ [L, dim. of *canalis*] (ca. 1727) **:** a minute canal in a bodily structure — **can·a·lic·u·lar** \-lər\ *adj*
can·a·li·za·tion \ˌkan-ᵊl-ə-'zā-shən\ *n* (1844) **1 :** an act or instance of canalizing **2 :** a system of channels
can·a·lize \'kan-ᵊl-ˌīz\ *vb* **-lized; -liz·ing** *vt* (1860) **1 a :** to provide with a canal or channel **b :** to make into or similar to a canal **2 :** to provide with an outlet; *esp* **:** to direct into preferred channels **~** *vi* **1 :** to flow in or into a channel **2 :** to establish new channels
can·a·pé \'kan-ə-pē, -ˌpā\ *n* [F, lit., sofa, fr. ML *canopeum, canapeum* mosquito net — more at CANOPY] (1890) **:** an appetizer consisting of a piece of bread or toast or a cracker topped with a savory spread (as caviar or cheese) — compare HORS D'OEUVRE
ca·nard \kə-'närd *also* -'när\ *n* [F, lit., duck, fr. MF *vendre des canards à moitié* to cheat, lit., to half-sell ducks] (ca. 1864) **1 :** a false or unfounded report or story; *esp* **:** a fabricated report **2 :** an airplane with horizontal stabilizing and control surfaces in front of supporting surfaces
ca·nary \kə-'ne(ə)r-ē\ *n, pl* **ca·nar·ies** [MF *canarie,* fr. OSp *canario,* fr. *Islas Canarias* Canary islands] (1584) **1 :** a Canary islands usu. sweet wine similar to Madeira **2 :** a lively 16th century court dance **3 :** a small finch (*Serinus canarius*) of the Canary islands that is usu. greenish to yellow and is kept as a cage bird and singer **4** *slang* **:** INFORMER 2
canary seed *n* (1597) **:** seed of a Canary island grass (*Phalaris canariensis*) used as food for cage birds
canary yellow *n* (1865) **:** a light to a moderate or vivid yellow
ca·nas·ta \kə-'nas-tə\ *n* [Sp, lit., basket; fr. the large number of cards in a meld] (1948) **1 :** a form of rummy using two full decks in which players or partnerships try to meld groups of three or more cards of the same rank and score bonuses for 7-card melds **2 :** a meld of seven cards of the same rank in canasta
can·can \'kan-ˌkan\ *n* [F] (1848) **:** a woman's dance of French origin characterized by high kicking usu. while holding up the front of a full ruffled skirt
[1]**can·cel** \'kan(t)-səl\ *vb* **-celed** *or* **-celled; -cel·ing** *or* **-cel·ling** \-s(ə-)liŋ\ [ME *cancellen,* fr. MF *canceller,* fr. LL *cancellare,* fr. L, to make like a lattice, fr. *cancelli* (pl.), dim. of *cancer* lattice, prob. alter. of *carcer* prison] *vt* (14c) **1 a :** to destroy the force, effectiveness, or validity of **:** ANNUL ⟨~ a magazine subscription⟩ ⟨a ~*ed* check⟩ **b :** to bring to nothingness **:** DESTROY **c :** to match in force or effect **:** OFFSET — often used with *out* ⟨his irritability ~*ed* out his natural kindness — Osbert Sitwell⟩ **d :** to call off usu. without expectation of conducting or performing at a later time ⟨~ a football game⟩ **2 a :** to mark or strike out for deletion **b :** OMIT, DELETE **3 a :** to remove (a common divisor) from numerator and denominator **b :** to remove (equivalents) on opposite sides of an equation or account **4 :** to deface (a postage or revenue stamp) esp. with a set of parallel lines so as to invalidate for reuse **~** *vi* **:** to neutralize each other's strength or effect **:** COUNTERBALANCE — **can·cel·able** *or* **can·cel·la·ble** \-s(ə-)lə-bəl\ *adj* — **can·cel·er** *or* **can·cel·ler** \-s(ə)lər\ *n*
[2]**cancel** *n* (1806) **1 :** CANCELLATION **2 a :** a deleted part or passage **b** (1) **:** a leaf containing matter to be deleted (2) **:** a new leaf or slip substituted for matter already printed
can·cel·la·tion *also* **can·cel·ation** \ˌkan(t)-sə-'lā-shən\ *n* (1535) **1 :** the act or an instance of canceling **2 :** a released accommodation **3 :** a mark made to cancel something (as a postage stamp)
can·cel·lous \kan-'sel-əs, 'kan(t)-sə-ləs\ *adj* [NL *cancelli* intersecting osseous plates and bars in cancellous bone, fr. L, lattice] *of bone* (1836) **:** having a porous structure
can·cer \'kan(t)-sər\ *n* [ME, fr. L (gen. *Cancri*), lit., crab; akin to Gk *karkinos* crab, cancer] **1** *cap* **a :** a northern zodiacal constellation between Gemini and Leo **b** (1) **:** the 4th sign of the zodiac in astrology — see ZODIAC table (2) **:** one born under this sign **2** [L, crab, cancer] **a :** a malignant tumor of potentially unlimited growth that expands locally by invasion and systemically by metastasis **b :** an abnormal state marked by such tumors **3 :** something evil or malignant that spreads destructively ⟨the ~ of hidden resentment — *Irish Digest*⟩ **4 a :** an enlarged tumorlike growth **b :** a disease marked by such growths — **can·cer·ous** \'kan(t)s-(ə-)rəs\ *adj* — **can·cer·ous·ly** *adv*
can·cha \'kän-(ˌ)chä\ *n* [Sp, yard, court, fr. Quechua, yard] (ca. 1922) **:** a jai alai court
can·de·la \kan-'dē-lə, -'del-ə\ *n* [L, candle] (1949) **:** an international unit of luminous intensity in a given direction of a source that emits monochromatic radiation of frequency 540 × 10^{12} hertz and has a radiant intensity in that direction of $^1/_{683}$ watt per unit solid angle — called also *candle*
can·de·la·bra \ˌkan-də-'läb-rə *also* -'lab-\ *n* (1815) **:** a branched candlestick or lamp with several lights
usage Orig. the plural of *candelabrum, candelabra* has been used as a singular with the plural *candelabras* since the early 19th century. Unlike *criteria, candelabra* is well established as a singular and its use goes almost entirely unnoticed.
can·de·la·brum \-rəm\ *n, pl* **-bra** \-rə\ *also* **-brums** [L, fr. *candela*] (1811) **:** CANDELABRA
can·dent \'kan-dənt\ *adj* [L *candent-, candens,* prp. of *candēre*] (1577) **:** heated to whiteness **:** GLOWING
can·des·cence \kan-'des-ᵊn(t)s\ *n* (ca. 1864) **:** a candescent state **:** glowing whiteness
can·des·cent \-ᵊnt\ *adj* [L *candescent-, candescens,* prp. of *candescere* incho. of *candēre*] (1824) **:** glowing or dazzling esp. from great heat
can·did \'kan-dəd\ *adj* [F & L; F *candide,* fr. L *candidus* bright, white, fr. *candēre* to shine, glow; akin to LGk *kandaros* ember] (1630) **1 :** WHITE ⟨~ flames⟩ **2 :** free from bias, prejudice, or malice **:** FAIR ⟨a ~ observer⟩ **3 a :** marked by hon-

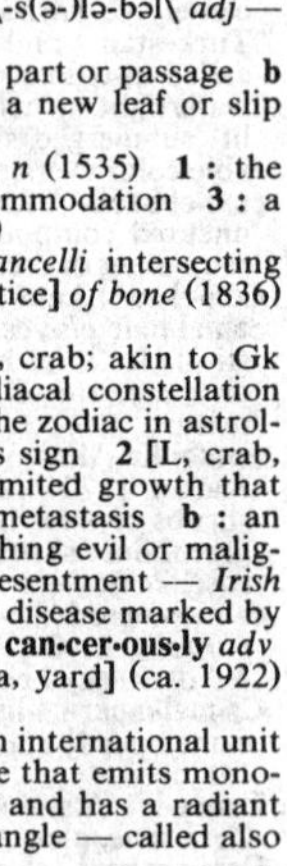
candelabrum

est sincere expression **b :** indicating or suggesting sincere honesty and absence of deception **c :** disposed to criticize severely : BLUNT **4 :** relating to photography of subjects acting naturally or spontaneously without being posed ⟨~ picture⟩ ***syn*** see FRANK — **can·did·ly** *adv* — **can·did·ness** *n*

can·di·da \'kan-dəd-ə\ *n* [NL, genus name, fr. L, fem. of *candidus*, white] (ca. 1944) : any of a genus (*Candida*) of parasitic imperfect fungi that resemble yeasts, produce small amounts of mycelium, and include the causative agent of thrush

can·di·da·cy \'kan-(d)əd-ə-sē\ *n, pl* **-cies** (1864) : the state of being a candidate

can·di·date \'kan-(d)ə-,dāt, -(d)əd-ət\ *n* [L *candidatus*, fr. *candidatus* clothed in white, fr. *candidus* white; fr. the white toga worn by candidates for office in ancient Rome] (1600) **1 :** one that aspires to or is nominated or qualified for an office, membership, or award **2 :** a student in the process of meeting final requirements for a degree

can·di·da·ture \'kan-(d)əd-ə-,chu̇(ə)r, -chər\ *n, chiefly Brit* (1851) : CANDIDACY

candid camera *n* (1929) **1 :** a usu. small camera equipped with a fast lens and used for taking informal photographs of unposed subjects often without their knowledge **2 :** a miniature camera

can·di·di·a·sis \,kan-də-'dī-ə-səs\ *n, pl* **-a·ses** \-,sēz\ (1949) : infection with or disease caused by a candida

can·died \'kan-dēd\ *adj* (ca. 1604) **1 :** encrusted or coated with sugar **2 :** baked with sugar or syrup until translucent

[1]**can·dle** \'kan-dᵊl\ *n* [ME *candel*, fr. OE, fr. L *candela*, fr. *candēre*] (bef. 12c) **1 :** a usu. molded or dipped mass of wax or tallow containing a wick that may be burned (as to give light, heat, or scent or for celebration or votive purposes) **2 :** something resembling a candle in shape or use ⟨a sulfur ~ for fumigating⟩ **3 :** CANDELA

[2]**candle** *vt* **can·dled; can·dling** \'kan-(d)liŋ, -dᵊl-iŋ\ (1879) : to examine by holding between the eye and a light; *esp* : to test (eggs) in this way for staleness, blood clots, fertility, and growth — **can·dler** \-(d)lər, -dᵊl-ər\ *n*

can·dle·ber·ry \'kan-dᵊl-,ber-ē\ *n* (1730) : a wax myrtle (*Myrica cerifera*); *also* : a bayberry (*Myrica pensylvanica*)

can·dle·fish \-,fish\ *n* (1881) : EULACHON

can·dle–foot \-'fu̇t\ *n* (1892) : FOOTCANDLE

can·dle·light \'kan-dᵊl-(l)īt\ *n* (bef. 12c) **1 a :** the light of a candle **b :** a soft artificial light **2 :** the time for lighting candles : TWILIGHT

can·dle·light·er \-ər\ *n* (15c) **1 :** one who lights the candles for a ceremony (as a wedding) **2 :** a long-handled implement with a taper and a snuffer that is used for the ceremonial lighting and extinguishing of candles

Can·dle·mas \'kan-dᵊl-məs\ *n* [ME *candelmasse*, fr. OE *candelmæsse*, fr. *candel* + *mæsse* mass, feast; fr. the candles blessed and carried in celebration of the feast] (bef. 12c) : February 2 observed as a church festival in commemoration of the presentation of Christ in the temple and the purification of the Virgin Mary

can·dle·nut \-,nət\ *n* (ca. 1835) : the oily seed of a tropical tree (*Aleurites moluccana*) of the spurge family used locally to make candles and commercially as a source of oil; *also* : this tree

can·dle·pin \-,pin\ *n* (ca. 1901) **1 :** a slender bowling pin tapering toward top and bottom **2** *pl but sing in constr* : a bowling game using candlepins and a smaller ball than that used in tenpins

can·dle·pow·er \-,pau̇(-ə)r\ *n* (1877) : luminous intensity expressed in candles or candelas

can·dle·snuff·er \-,snəf-ər\ *n* (1552) : an implement for snuffing candles that consists of a small hollow cone attached to a handle

can·dle·stick \-,stik\ *n* (bef. 12c) : a holder with a socket for a candle

can·dle·wick \-,wik\ *n* (bef. 12c) **1 :** the wick of a candle **2 :** a soft cotton embroidery yarn; *also* : embroidery made with this yarn usu. in tufts

can·dle·wood \-,wu̇d\ *n* (1712) **1 :** any of several trees or shrubs (as ocotillo) chiefly of resinous character **2 :** slivers of resinous wood burned for light

can·dor \'kan-dər, -,dȯ(ə)r\ *n* [F & L; F *candeur*, fr. L *candor*, fr. *candēre* — more at CANDID] (14c) **1 a :** WHITENESS, BRILLIANCE **b** *obs* : unstained purity **2 :** freedom from prejudice or malice : FAIRNESS **3** *archaic* : KINDLINESS **4 :** unreserved, honest, or sincere expression : FORTHRIGHTNESS ⟨the ~ with which he acknowledged a weakness in his own case —Aldous Huxley⟩

can·dour \'kan-dər\ *chiefly Brit var of* CANDOR

[1]**can·dy** \'kan-dē\ *n, pl* **candies** [ME *sugre candy*, part trans. of MF *sucre candi*, part trans. of OIt *zucchero candi*, fr. *zucchero* sugar + Ar *qandī* candied, fr. *qand* cane sugar] (15c) **1 :** crystallized sugar formed by boiling down sugar syrup **2 a :** a confection made with sugar and often flavoring and filling **b :** a piece of such confection — **candy** *adj*

[2]**candy** *vb* **can·died; can·dy·ing** *vt* (1533) **1 :** to encrust in or coat with sugar; *specif* : to cook (as fruit or fruit peel) in a heavy syrup until glazed **2 :** to make attractive : SWEETEN **3 :** to crystallize into sugar ~ *vi* : to become coated or encrusted with sugar crystals : become crystallized into sugar

candy strip·er \-,strī-pər\ *n* [fr. the striped uniform worn suggesting the stripes on some sticks of candy] (1963) : a teenage volunteer worker at a hospital

can·dy·tuft \'kan-dē-,təft\ *n* [*Candy* (now *Candia*) Crete, Greek island + E *tuft*] (1664) : any of a genus (*Iberis*) of plants of the mustard family cultivated for their white, pink, or purple flowers

[1]**cane** \'kān\ *n* [ME, fr MF, fr. OProv *cana*, fr. L *canna*, fr. Gk *kanna*, of Sem origin; akin to Ar *qanāh* hollow stick, reed] (14c) **1 a (1) :** a hollow or pithy and usu. slender and flexible jointed stem (as of a reed) **(2) :** any of various slender woody stems; *esp* : an elongated flowering or fruiting stem (as of a rose) usu. arising directly from the ground **b :** any of various tall woody grasses or reeds: as **(1) :** any of a genus (*Arundinaria*) of coarse grasses **(2) :** SUGARCANE **(3) :** SORGHUM **2 :** cane dressed for use: as **a :** a cane walking stick; *broadly* : WALKING STICK **b :** a cane or rod for flogging **c :** RATTAN; *esp* : split rattan for wickerwork or basketry

[2]**cane** *vt* **caned; can·ing** (1667) **1 :** to beat with a cane ⟨he sat in a professor's chair and *caned* sophomores for blowing spitballs —H. L. Mencken⟩ **2 :** to weave or furnish with cane ⟨~ the seat of a chair⟩

cane·brake \'kān-,brāk\ *n* (1769) : a thicket of cane

can·er \'kā-nər\ *n* (1868) : one that weaves cane seats and backs of chairs

ca·nes·cent \kə-'nes-ᵊnt, ka-\ *adj* [L *canescent-*, *canescens*, prp. of *canescere*, incho. of *canēre* to be gray, be white, fr. *canus* white, hoary — more at HARE] (ca. 1828) : growing white, whitish, or hoary; *esp* : having a fine grayish white pubescence ⟨~ leaves⟩

cane sugar *n* (1848) : sugar from sugarcane

cane·ware \'kān-,wa(ə)r, -,we(ə)r\ *n* [fr. its color] (1878) : a buff or yellowish stoneware

ca·nic·o·la fever \kə-,nik-ə-lə-\ *n* [NL *canicola*, fr. L *canis* dog + *-cola* inhabitant — more at HOUND, -COLOUS] (1943) : an acute disease in man and dogs characterized by gastroenteritis and mild jaundice and caused by a spirochete (*Leptospira canicola*)

Ca·nic·u·la \kə-'nik-yə-lə\ *n* [L, dim. of *canis*] : SIRIUS

ca·nic·u·lar \kə-'nik-yə-lər\ *adj* (12c) **1 :** of or relating to Sirius or Procyon or the rising of either **2 :** of or relating to the dog days

ca·nid \'kan-əd, 'kā-nəd\ *n* [NL *Canidae*, fr. L *canis* + *-idae*, pl. of *-ides* -id] (1889) : any of a family (Canidae) of carnivorous animals that includes the wolves, jackals, foxes, coyote, and the domestic dog

[1]**ca·nine** \'kā-,nīn\ *n* (14c) **1 :** a conical pointed tooth; *esp* : one situated between the lateral incisor and the first premolar — see TOOTH illustration **2 :** CANID, DOG 1a

[2]**canine** *adj* [L *caninus*, fr. *canis* dog — more at HOUND] (1623) **1 :** of or relating to dogs or to the family (Canidae) including the canids **2 :** of or resembling that of a dog ⟨~ loyalty⟩

Ca·nis Ma·jor \,kā-nə-'smā-jər, ,kan-ə-\ *n* [L (gen. *Canis Majoris*), lit., greater dog] : a constellation to the southeast of Orion containing Sirius

Canis Mi·nor \-'smī-nər\ *n* [L (gen. *Canis Minoris*), lit., lesser dog] : a constellation to the east of Orion containing Procyon

can·is·ter *also* **can·nis·ter** \'kan-ə-stər\ *n* [L *canistrum* basket, fr. Gk *kanastron* wicker basket, fr. *kanna* reed — more at CANE] (1711) **1 :** a small box or can for holding a dry product **2 :** encased shot for close-range artillery fire **3 :** a perforated metal box for gas masks with material to adsorb, filter, or detoxify airborne poisons and irritants

[1]**can·ker** \'kaŋ-kər\ *n* [ME, fr. ONF *cancre*, fr. L *cancer* crab, cancer] (13c) **1 a (1) :** an erosive or spreading sore **(2) :** an area of necrosis in a plant; *also* : a plant disease characterized by cankers **b :** any of various disorders of animals marked by chronic inflammatory changes **2** *archaic* : a caterpillar destructive to plants **3** *chiefly dial* **a :** RUST **b :** VERDIGRIS 2 **4 :** a source of corruption or debasement **5** *chiefly dial* : DOG ROSE — **can·ker·ous** \'kaŋ-k(ə-)rəs\ *adj*

[2]**canker** *vb* **can·kered; can·ker·ing** \'kaŋ-k(ə-)riŋ\ *vt* (14c) **1** *obs* : to infect with a spreading sore **2 :** to corrupt the spirit of ~ *vi* **1 :** to become infested with canker **2 :** to become corrupted

canker sore *n* (ca. 1909) : a small painful ulcer esp. of the mouth

can·ker·worm \'kaŋ-kər-,wərm\ *n* (1530) : either of two geometrid moths (*Alsophila pometaria* and *Paleacrita vernata*) and esp. their larvae which are serious pests of forest and shade trees

can·na \'kan-ə\ *n* [NL, genus name, fr. L, reed — more at CANE] (1664) : any of a genus (*Canna* of the family Cannaceae) of tropical herbs with simple stems, large leaves, and a terminal raceme of irregular flowers

can·na·bi·noid \'kan-ə-bə-,nȯid, kə-'nab-ə-\ *n* [L *cannabis* + *-n-* + [1]*-oid*] (1970) : any of various chemical constituents (as THC or cannabinol) of cannabis or marijuana

can·na·bi·nol \-,nȯl, -,nōl\ *n* [L *cannabis* + *-n-* + *-ol*] (ca. 1896) : a physiologically inactive crystalline cannabinoid $C_{21}H_{26}O_2$

can·na·bis \'kan-ə-bəs\ *n* [L, hemp, fr. Gk *kannabis*; akin to OE *hænep* hemp] (1728) **1 :** any of the preparations (as marijuana or hashish) or chemicals (as THC) that are derived from the hemp and are psychoactive **2 :** HEMP 1a

canned \'kand\ *adj* (1893) **1 a :** prepared or recorded in advance; *esp* : prepared in standardized form for nonspecific use or wide distribution ⟨~ laughter⟩ ⟨~ term papers⟩ ⟨~ news stories⟩ **b :** lacking originality or individuality as if mass-produced ⟨~ sales pitch⟩ **2** *slang* : DRUNK

can·nel coal \,kan-ᵊl-\ *n* [prob. fr. E dial. *cannel* candle, fr. ME *candel*] (1610) : a bituminous coal containing much volatile matter that burns brightly

can·nel·lo·ni \,kan-ᵊl-'ō-nē\ *n pl but sing or pl in constr* [It, pl. of *cannellone*, aug. of *cannello* segment of cane stalk, fr. *canna* reed, tube, fr. L — more at CANE] (1906) : a roll of boiled pasta filled with a meat, fish, cheese, or vegetable mixture and baked in a sauce

can·nery \'kan-(ə-)rē\ *n, pl* **-ner·ies** (1870) : a factory for the canning of foods

can·ni·bal \'kan-ə-bəl\ *n* [NL *Canibalis* Carib, fr. Sp *Caníbal*, fr. Arawakan *Caniba*, *Carib*, of Cariban origin; akin to Carib *Galibi* Caribs, lit., strong men] (1553) : one that eats the flesh of its own kind — **cannibal** *adj*

can·ni·bal·ism \'kan-ə-bə-,liz-əm\ *n* (1796) **1 :** the usu. ritualistic eating of human flesh by a human being **2 :** the eating of the flesh of an animal by another animal of the same kind — **can·ni·bal·is·tic** \,kan-ə-bə-'lis-tik\ *adj*

can·ni·bal·ize \'kan-ə-bə-,līz\ *vb* **-ized; -iz·ing** *vt* (1943) **1 :** to take salvageable parts from (as a disabled machine) for use in building or repairing another machine **2 :** to deprive of an essential part or element in creating or sustaining another facility or enterprise ⟨the energy system has begun *cannibalizing* the economic system it is supposed to fuel —Barry Commoner⟩ **3 :** to use or draw on material of (as another writer or an earlier work) ⟨a volume . . . that not only ~s previous publications but is intended itself to be *cannibalized* —R. M. Adams⟩ **4 :** to make use of (a part taken from one thing) in building or repairing something else ~ *vi* **1 :** to practice cannibalism **2 :** to cannibalize one unit for the sake of another of the same kind — **can·ni·bal·iza·tion** \,kan-ə-bə-lə-'zā-shən\ *n*

can·ni·kin \'kan-i-kən\ *n* [prob. fr. obs. D *kanneken*, fr. MD *canneken*, dim. of *canne* can; akin to OE *canne* can] (1570) **:** a small can or drinking vessel

can·no·li \kə-'nō-lē, ka-\ *n pl but sing or pl in constr* [It, pl. of *cannolo* small tube, dim. of *canna*] (1943) **:** a tube of pastry fried in deep fat and filled with a mixture of ricotta cheese, cream, sweetening, and flavoring

[1]can·non \'kan-ən\ *n, pl* **cannons** *or* **cannon** [MF *canon*, fr. It *cannone*, lit., large tube, aug. of *canna* reed, tube, fr. L, cane, reed — more at CANE] (15c) **1** *pl usu cannon* **a :** an artillery piece **:** big gun **b :** a heavy-caliber automatic aircraft gun firing explosive shells **2** *or* **can·on :** the projecting part of a bell by which it is hung **:** EAR **3 :** the part of the leg in which the cannon bone is found

[2]cannon *vi* (1691) **:** to discharge cannon ~ *vt* **:** CANNONADE

[1]can·non·ade \,kan-ə-'nād\ *n* (1562) **1 :** a heavy fire of artillery **2 :** an attack (as with words) likened to artillery fire **:** BOMBARDMENT

[2]cannonade *vb* **-ad·ed; -ad·ing** *vt* (1670) **:** to attack with or as if with artillery ~ *vi* **:** to deliver artillery fire

[1]can·non·ball \'kan-ən-,bȯl\ *n* (1663) **1 :** a usu. round solid missile made for firing from a cannon **2 :** a jump into water made with the arms holding the knees tight against the chest **3 :** a hard flat tennis service **4 :** an express train

[2]cannonball *vi* (1951) **:** to travel with great speed

cannon bone *n* [F *canon*, lit., cannon] (1834) **:** a bone in hoofed mammals that extends from the knee or hock to the fetlock

can·non·eer \,kan-ə-'ni(ə)r\ *n* (1562) **:** an artillery gunner

cannon fodder *n* (1891) **:** soldiers subject to the risk of being wounded or killed by artillery fire

can·non·ry \'kan-ən-rē\ *n, pl* **-ries** (ca. 1839) **:** a battery of cannons or cannon fire

can·not \'kan-(,)ät; kə-'nät, ka-'\ (14c) **:** can not — **cannot but :** to be unable to do otherwise than

can·nu·la \'kan-yə-lə\ *n, pl* **-las** *or* **-lae** \-,lē, -,lī\ [NL, fr. L, dim. of *canna* reed — more at CANE] (1684) **:** a small tube for insertion into a body cavity or into a duct or vessel

can·nu·lar \'kan-yə-lər\ *adj* (1823) **:** TUBULAR

[1]can·ny \'kan-ē\ *adj* **can·ni·er; -est** [[1]*can*] (1607) **1 :** CLEVER, SHREWD; *also* **:** PRUDENT **2 a** *Scot* **:** GENTLE, STEADY; *also* **:** RESTRAINED **b** *Scot* **:** QUIET, SNUG ⟨then ~, in some cozy place, they close the day — Robert Burns⟩ — **can·ni·ly** \'kan-ᵊl-ē\ *adv* — **can·ni·ness** \'kan-ē-nəs\ *n*

[2]canny *adv, Scot* (1816) **:** in a canny manner **:** CAREFULLY

[1]ca·noe \kə-'nü\ *n* [F, fr. NL *canoa*, fr. Sp, fr. Arawakan, of Cariban origin; akin to Galibi *canaoua*] (1555) **:** a light narrow boat with both ends sharp that is usu. propelled by paddling

[2]canoe *vb* **ca·noed; ca·noe·ing** *vi* (1841) **:** to go or travel in a canoe ~ *vt* **:** to transport in a canoe — **ca·noe·ist** *n*

can of worms (1969) **:** PANDORA'S BOX

[1]can·on \'kan-ən\ *n* [ME, fr. OE, fr. LL, fr. L, ruler, rule, model, standard, fr. Gk *kanōn*] (bef. 12c) **1 a :** a regulation or dogma decreed by a church council **b :** a provision of canon law **2** [ME, prob. fr. OF, fr. LL, fr. L, model] **:** the most solemn and unvarying part of the Mass including the consecration of the bread and wine **3** [ME, fr. LL, fr. L, standard] **a :** an authoritative list of books accepted as Holy Scripture **b :** the authentic works of a writer; *also* **:** a usu. specified group or a body of related works ⟨assimilating him into the ~ of standard modern authors — J. W. Aldridge⟩ **4 a :** an accepted principle or rule **b :** a criterion or standard of judgment **c :** a body of principles, rules, standards, or norms **5** [LGk *kanōn*, fr. Gk, model] **:** a contrapuntal musical composition in two or more voice parts in which the melody is imitated exactly and completely by the successive voices though not always at the same pitch ***syn*** see LAW

[2]canon *n* [ME *canoun*, fr. AF *canunie*, fr. LL *canonicus* one living under a rule, fr. L, according to rule, fr. Gk *kanonikos*, fr. *kanōn*] (13c) **1 :** a clergyman belonging to the chapter or the staff of a cathedral or collegiate church **2 :** CANON REGULAR

ca·ñon \'kan-yən\ *var of* CANYON

can·on·ess \'kan-ə-nəs\ *n* (1682) **1 :** a woman living in community under a religious rule but not under a perpetual vow **2 :** a member of a Roman Catholic congregation of women corresponding to canons regular

ca·non·ic \kə-'nän-ik\ *adj* (15c) **1 :** CANONICAL **2 :** of or relating to musical canon

ca·non·i·cal \-i-kəl\ *adj* (15c) **1 :** of, relating to, or forming a canon **2 :** conforming to a general rule or acceptable procedure **:** ORTHODOX **3 :** of or relating to a clergyman who is a canon **4 :** reduced to the simplest or clearest schema possible ⟨a ~ matrix⟩ — **ca·non·i·cal·ly** \-k(ə-)lē\ *adv*

canonical form *n* (1851) **:** the simplest form of something; *specif* **:** the form of a square matrix that has zero elements everywhere except along the principal diagonal

canonical hour *n* (15c) **1 :** a time of day canonically appointed for an office of devotion **2 :** one of the daily offices of devotion that compose the Divine Office and include matins with lauds, prime, terce, sext, none, vespers, and compline

ca·non·i·cals \kə-'nän-i-kəlz\ *n pl* (1748) **:** the vestments prescribed by canon for an officiating clergyman

can·on·ic·i·ty \,kan-ə-'nis-ət-ē\ *n* (1797) **:** the quality or state of being canonical

can·on·ist \'kan-ə-nəst\ *n* (14c) **:** a specialist in canon law

can·on·ize \'kan-ə-,nīz\ *vt* **can·on·ized** \-,nīzd; *in "Hamlet", usu* kə-'nän-,īzd\; **can·on·iz·ing** [ME *canonizen*, fr. ML *canonizare*, fr. LL *canon* catalog of saints, fr. L, standard] (14c) **1 :** to declare (a deceased person) an officially recognized saint **2 :** to make canonical **3 :** to sanction by ecclesiastical authority **4 :** to attribute authoritative sanction or approval to **5 :** to treat as illustrious, preeminent, or sacred — **can·on·iza·tion** \,kan-ə-nə-'zā-shən\ *n*

canon law *n* (14c) **:** the usu. codified law governing a church

canon lawyer *n* (ca. 1910) **:** CANONIST

canon regular *n, pl* **canons regular** (14c) **:** a member of one of several Roman Catholic religious institutes of regular priests living in community under a usu. Augustinian rule

can·on·ry \'kan-ən-rē\ *n, pl* **-ries** (15c) **:** the office of a canon; *also* **:** the endowment that financially supports a canon

ca·no·pic jar \kə-,nō-pik-, -,näp-ik-\ *n, often cap C* [*Canopus*, Egypt] (1893) **:** a jar in which the ancient Egyptians preserved the viscera of a deceased person usu. for burial with the mummy

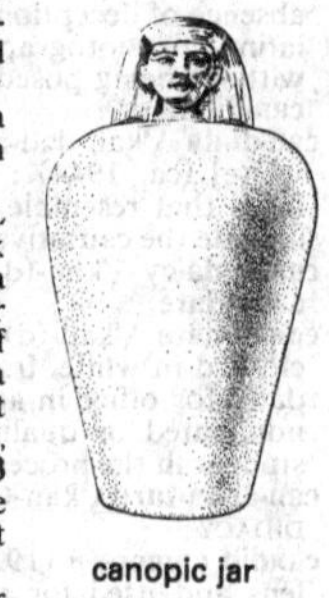

canopic jar

Ca·no·pus \kə-'nō-pəs\ *n* [L, fr. Gk *Kanōpos*] **:** a star of the first magnitude in the constellation Carina not visible north of 37° latitude

[1]can·o·py \'kan-ə-pē\ *n, pl* **-pies** [ME *canope*, fr. ML *canopeum* mosquito net, fr. L *conopeum*, fr. Gk *kōnōpion*, fr. *kōnōps* mosquito] (14c) **1 a :** a cloth covering suspended over a bed **b :** a cover (as of cloth) fixed or carried above a person of high rank or a sacred object **:** BALDACHIN **c :** a protective covering: as (1) **:** the uppermost spreading branchy layer of a forest (2) **:** AWNING, MARQUEE **2 :** an ornamental rooflike structure **3 a :** the transparent enclosure over an airplane cockpit **b :** the fabric part of a parachute that catches the air

[2]canopy *vt* **-pied; -py·ing** (1600) **:** to cover with or as if with a canopy

ca·no·rous \kə-'nōr-əs, -'nȯr-; 'kan-ə-rəs\ *adj* [L *canorus*, fr. *canor* melody, fr. *canere* to sing — more at CHANT] (1646) **:** pleasant sounding **:** MELODIOUS — **ca·no·rous·ly** *adv* — **ca·no·rous·ness** *n*

canst \kən(t)st, (')kan(t)st\ *archaic pres 2d sing of* CAN

[1]cant \'kant\ *adj* [ME, prob. fr. (assumed) MLG *kant*] *dial Eng* (14c) **:** LIVELY, LUSTY

[2]cant *n* [ME, prob. fr. MD or ONF; MD, edge, corner, fr. ONF, fr. L *canthus, cantus* iron tire, perh. of Celt origin; akin to W *cant* rim; akin to Gk *kanthos* corner of the eye] (15c) **1** *obs* **:** CORNER, NICHE **2 :** an external angle (as of a building) **3 :** a log with one or more squared sides **4 a :** an oblique or slanting surface **b :** INCLINATION, SLOPE

[3]cant *vt* (ca. 1542) **1 :** to give a cant or oblique edge to **:** BEVEL **2 :** to set at an angle **:** TILT **3** *chiefly Brit* **:** PITCH, TOSS ~ *vi* **1 :** to pitch to one side **:** LEAN **2 :** SLOPE

[4]cant *adj* (1663) **1 :** having canted corners or sides **2 :** INCLINED 2

[5]cant *vi* [prob. fr. ONF *canter* to tell, lit., to sing, fr. L *cantare* — more at CHANT] (1567) **1 :** talk or beg in a whining or singsong manner **2 :** to speak in cant or technical terms **3 :** to talk hypocritically

[6]cant *n* (1640) **1 :** affected singsong or whining speech **2 a :** the special private language of the underworld **b** *obs* **:** the phraseology peculiar to a religious class or sect **c :** JARGON 2 **3 :** a set or stock phrase **4 :** the expression or repetition of conventional, trite, or unconsidered opinions or sentiments; *esp* **:** the insincere use of pious words

can't \(')kant, (')kant, (')känt, *esp Southern* (')kānt\ **:** can not

Can·tab \'kan-,tab\ *n* [by shortening] (1750) **:** CANTABRIGIAN

can·ta·bi·le \kän-'täb-ə-,lā, kan-'tab-ə-lē\ *adv or adj* [It, fr. LL *cantabilis* worthy to be sung, fr. L *cantare*] (1724) **:** in a singing manner — often used as a direction in music

Can·ta·bri·gian \,kant-ə-'brij-(ē-)ən\ *n* [ML *Cantabrigia* Cambridge] (1540) **1 :** a student or graduate of Cambridge University **2 :** a native or resident of Cambridge, Mass. — **Cantabrigian** *adj*

can·ta·la \kan-'täl-ə\ *n* [origin unknown] (1911) **:** a hard fiber produced from the leaves of an agave (*Agave cantala*)

can·ta·loupe *also* **can·ta·loup** \'kant-ᵊl-,ōp\ *n* [*Cantalupo*, former papal villa near Rome, Italy] (1739) **1 :** a muskmelon (*Cucumis melo reticulatus*) having rind with netted tracery and reddish orange flesh **2 :** any of several muskmelons resembling the cantaloupe; *broadly* **:** MUSKMELON

can·tan·ker·ous \kan-'taŋ-k(ə-)rəs, kən-\ *adj* [perh. irreg. fr. obs. *contack* (contention)] (1772) **:** difficult or irritating to deal with — **can·tan·ker·ous·ly** *adv* — **can·tan·ker·ous·ness** *n*

can·ta·ta \kən-'tät-ə\ *n* [It, fr. L, fr. fem. of *cantatus*, pp. of *cantare*] (1724) **:** a composition for one or more voices usu. comprising solos, duets, recitatives, and choruses and sung to an instrumental accompaniment

can·ta·trice \,känt-ə-'trē-(,)chā, ,käⁿ-tə-'trēs\ *n, pl* **-trices** \-'trē-(,)chāz, -'trēs(-əz)\ *or* **-tri·ci** \,känt-ə-'trē-(,)chē\ [It & F, fr. It, fr. LL *cantatric-, cantatrix*, fem. of L *cantator* singer, fr. *cantatus*, pp.] (1803) **:** a female singer; *esp* **:** an opera singer

cant dog *n* [[2]*cant*] (1850) **:** PEAVEY

can·teen \kan-'tēn\ *n* [F *cantine* bottle case, sutler's shop, fr. It *cantina* wine cellar] (1744) **1 a :** a flask for carrying liquids (as on a hike) **b :** a portable chest with compartments for carrying bottles or for cooking and eating utensils **c :** MESS KIT **d** *Brit* **:** a chest for storing silverware **2 a :** a bar at a military post or camp **b :** a general store at a military post **:** EXCHANGE **c :** an establishment that serves as an informal social club (as for soldiers or a community's teenagers) **d :** a small cafeteria or snack bar

canteloupe, canteloup *var of* CANTALOUPE

[1]can·ter \'kant-ər\ *n* (1609) **:** one that uses cant: as **a :** BEGGAR, VAGABOND **b :** a user of professional or religious cant

[2]can·ter \'kant-ər\ *vb* [short for obs. *canterbury* n. (canter), fr. *Canterbury*, England; fr. the supposed gait of pilgrims riding to Canterbury] *vi* (1706) **1 :** to move at or as if at a canter **:** LOPE **2 :** to ride a horse at a canter ~ *vt* **:** to cause to go at a canter

[3]can·ter *n* (1755) **1 :** a 3-beat gait resembling but smoother and slower than the gallop **2 :** a ride at a canter

Can·ter·bury bell \,kant-ə(r)-,ber-ē-\ *n* [*Canterbury*, England] (1578) **:** any of several bellflowers (as *Campanula medium*) cultivated for their showy flowers

can·tha·ris \'kan(t)-thə-rəs\ *n, pl* **can·thar·i·des** \kan-'thar-ə-,dēz\ [ME & L; ME *cantharide*, fr. L *cantharid-, cantharis*, fr. Gk *kantharid-, kantharis*] (14c) **1 :** SPANISH FLY 1 **2** *pl but sing or pl in constr* **:** a preparation of dried beetles (as Spanish flies) used in medicine as a counterirritant and formerly as an aphrodisiac

cant hook *n* [[2]*cant*] (1848) **:** a lumberman's lever that has a pivoting hooked arm and a blunt often toothed metal cap at one end — compare PEAVEY

can·thus \'kan(t)-thəs\ *n, pl* **can·thi** \'kan-,thī, -,thē\ [LL, fr. Gk *kanthos* — more at CANT] (1646) **:** either of the angles formed by the meeting of the upper and lower eyelids

can·ti·cle \ˈkant-i-kəl\ *n* [ME, fr. L *canticulum,* dim. of *canticum* song, fr. *cantus,* pp. of *canere* to sing] (13c) **:** SONG; *specif* **:** one of several liturgical songs (as the Magnificat) taken from the Bible
Canticle of Canticles (ca. 1934) **:** SONG OF SOLOMON
Canticles *n pl but sing in constr* (15c) **:** SONG OF SOLOMON
can·ti·le·na \ˌkant-ᵊl-ˈā-nə, -ˈē-nə\ *n* [It, fr. L, song, fr. *cantillare*] (1740) **:** a vocal or instrumental passage of sustained lyricism
[1]**can·ti·le·ver** \ˈkant-ᵊl-ˌē-vər *also* -ˌev-ər\ *n* [perh. fr. [2]*cant* + *-i-* + *lever*] (1667) **:** a projecting beam or member supported at only one end: as **a :** a bracket-shaped member supporting a balcony or a cornice **b :** either of the two beams or trusses that project from piers toward each other and that when joined directly or by a suspended connecting member form a span of a cantilever bridge — see BRIDGE illustration
[2]**cantilever** *vi* (1902) **:** to project as a cantilever ~ *vt* **1 :** to build as a cantilever **2 :** to support by a cantilever ⟨a ~*ed* shelf⟩
can·til·late \ˈkant-ᵊl-ˌāt\ *vt* **-lat·ed; -lat·ing** [L *cantillatus,* pp. of *cantillare* to sing low, fr. *cantare* to sing — more at CHANT] (ca. 1828) **:** to recite with musical tones — **can·til·la·tion** \ˌkant-ᵊl-ˈā-shən\ *n*
can·ti·na \kan-ˈtē-nə\ *n* [AmerSp, fr. Sp, canteen, fr. It, wine cellar — more at CANTEEN] (1844) **1** *Southwest* **:** a pouch or bag at the pommel of a saddle **2** *Southwest* **:** a small barroom **:** SALOON
cant·ing \ˈkant-iŋ\ *adj* [[5]*cant*] (1663) **:** affectedly pious or righteous
can·tle \ˈkant-ᵊl\ *n* [ME *cantel,* fr. ONF, dim. of *cant* edge, corner — more at CANT] (14c) **1 :** a segment cut off or out of something **:** PART, PORTION **2 :** the upward projecting rear part of a saddle
can·to \ˈkan-(ˌ)tō\ *n, pl* **cantos** [It, fr. L *cantus* song, fr. *cantus,* pp. of *canere* to sing — more at CHANT] (1590) **:** one of the major divisions of a long poem
can·ton \ˈkant-ᵊn, ˈkan-ˌtän\ *n* [MF, fr. OProv, fr. *cant* edge, corner, fr. L *canthus* iron tire — more at CANT] (1572) **1** *obs* **:** DIVISION, SECTION **2** [MF, fr. It *cantone,* fr. *canto* corner, fr. L *canthus*] **:** a small territorial division of a country: as **a :** one of the states of the Swiss confederation **b :** a division of a French arrondissement **3 :** the top inner quarter of a flag **4 :** the dexter chief region of a heraldic field — **can·ton·al** \ˈkant-ᵊn-əl, kan-ˈtän-ᵊl\ *adj*
can·ton crepe \ˌkan-ˌtän-\ *n, often cap 1st C* [*Canton,* China] (1865) **:** a soft thick dress crepe made in plain weave with fine crosswise ribs
Can·ton·ese \ˌkant-ᵊn-ˈēz, -ˈēs\ *n, pl* **Cantonese** (1857) **1 :** a native or inhabitant of Canton, China **2 :** the dialect of Chinese spoken in and around Canton — **Cantonese** *adj*
can·ton flannel \ˌkan-ˌtän-\ *n, often cap C* [*Canton,* China] (ca. 1879) **:** FLANNEL 1c
can·ton·ment \kan-ˈtōn-mənt, -ˈtän-\ *n* (1756) **1 :** usu. temporary quarters for troops **2 :** a permanent military station in India
Can·ton ware \ˈkan-ˌtän-\ *n* (ca. 1902) **:** ceramic ware exported from China esp. during the 18th and 19th centuries by way of Canton and including blue-and-white and enameled porcelain and various ornamented stonewares
can·tor \ˈkant-ər\ *n* [L, singer, fr. *cantus,* pp. of *canere* to sing] (1538) **1 :** a choir leader **:** PRECENTOR **2 :** a synagogue official who sings or chants liturgical music and leads the congregation in prayer — **can·to·ri·al** \kan-ˈtōr-ē-əl, -ˈtȯr-\ *adj*
can·trip \ˈkan-trəp\ *n* [prob. alter. of *caltrop*] (1719) **1** *chiefly Scot* **:** a witch's trick **:** SPELL **2** *chiefly Brit* **:** HOCUS-POCUS 2
can·tus \ˈkant-əs\ *n, pl* **can·tus** \ˈkant-əs, ˈkan-ˌtüs\ [ML] (1590) **1 :** CANTUS FIRMUS **2 :** the principal melody or voice
can·tus fir·mus \ˌkant-əs-ˈfi(ə)r-məs, -ˈfər-\ *n* [ML, lit., fixed song] (1847) **1 :** the plainsong or simple Gregorian melody orig. sung in unison and prescribed as to form and use by ecclesiastical tradition **2 :** a melodic theme or subject; *esp* **:** one for contrapuntal treatment
canty \ˈkant-ē\ *adj* [[1]*cant*] *dial Brit* (1720) **:** CHEERFUL, SPRIGHTLY
Ca·nuck \kə-ˈnək\ *n* [prob. alter. of *Canadian*] (1835) **:** a Canadian and esp. a French Canadian
[1]**can·vas** *also* **can·vass** \ˈkan-vəs\ *n* [ME *canevas,* fr. ONF, fr. (assumed) VL *cannabaceus* hempen, fr. L *cannabis* hemp — more at CANNABIS] (13c) **1 :** a firm closely woven cloth usu. of linen, hemp, or cotton used for clothing and formerly much used for tents and sails **2 :** a set of sails **:** SAIL **3 :** a piece of canvas used for a particular purpose **4 :** TENT; *also* **:** a group of tents **5 a :** a piece of cloth backed or framed as a surface for a painting; *also* **:** the painting on such a surface **b :** the background, setting, or scope of an historical or fictional account or narrative ⟨the crowded ~ of history⟩ **6 :** a coarse cloth so woven as to form regular meshes for working with the needle **7 :** the canvas-covered floor of a boxing or wrestling ring — **can·vas·like** \-və-ˌslīk\ *adj*
[2]**canvas** *vt* **-vased** *or* **-vassed; -vas·ing** *or* **-vass·ing** (1556) **:** to cover, line, or furnish with canvas
can·vas·back \ˈkan-vəs-ˌbak\ *n* (1782) **:** a No. American wild duck (*Aythya valisineria*) characterized esp. by the elongate sloping profile of the bill and head
[1]**can·vass** *also* **can·vas** \ˈkan-vəs\ *vt* (1508) **1** *obs* **:** to toss in a canvas sheet in sport or punishment **2 a :** to examine in detail; *specif* **:** to examine (votes) officially for authenticity **b :** DISCUSS, DEBATE **3 :** to go through (a district) or go to (persons) in order to solicit orders or political support or to determine opinions or sentiments ~ *vi* **:** to seek orders or votes **:** SOLICIT — **can·vass·er** *also* **can·vas·er** *n*
[2]**canvass** *also* **canvas** *n* (ca. 1608) **:** the act or an instance of canvassing; *esp* **:** a personal solicitation of votes or survey of public opinion
can·yon \ˈkan-yən\ *n* [AmerSp *cañón,* prob. alter. of obs. Sp *callón,* aug. of *calle* street, fr. L *callis* footpath] (1837) **:** a deep narrow valley with steep sides and often with a stream flowing through it
can·zo·ne \kan-ˈzō-nē, känt-ˈsō-(ˌ)nā\ *n, pl* **-nes** \-nēz, -(ˌ)nāz\ *or* **-ni** \-nē\ [It, fr. L *cantion-, cantio* song, fr. *cantus,* pp. of *canere* to sing — more at CHANT] (1589) **1 :** a medieval Italian or Provençal lyric poem **2 :** the musical setting of a canzone
can·zo·net \ˌkan-zə-ˈnet\ *n* [It *canzonetta,* dim. of *canzone*] (1588) **1 :** a light usu. strophic song **2 :** a part-song resembling but less elaborate than a madrigal
caou·tchouc \ˈkaů-ˌchůk, -ˌchük, -ˌchü\ *n* [F, fr. obs. Sp *cauchuc* (now *caucho*), fr. Quechua] (1775) **:** [1]RUBBER 2a
[1]**cap** \ˈkap\ *n, often attrib* [ME *cappe,* fr. OE *cæppe,* fr. LL *cappa* head covering, cloak] (bef. 12c) **1 a :** a head covering esp. with a visor and no brim **b :** a distinctive head covering emblematic of a position or office: as (1) **:** a cardinal's biretta (2) **:** MORTARBOARD **2 :** a natural cover or top: as **a :** an overlying rock layer that is usu. hard to penetrate **b** (1) **:** PILEUS (2) **:** CALYPTRA **c :** the top of a bird's head or a patch of distinctively colored feathers in this area **3 a :** something that serves as a cover or protection esp. for a tip, knob, or end ⟨a bottle ~⟩ **b :** a fitting for closing the end of a tube (as a water pipe or electric conduit) **c :** a layer of new rubber fused onto the worn surface of a pneumatic tire **4 :** an overlaying or covering structure ⟨the galleried ~ of the old water tower is open to visitors⟩ **5 :** a paper or metal container holding an explosive charge (as for a toy pistol) **6 :** an upper limit (as on expenditures) **:** CEILING **7 :** the symbol ∩ indicating the intersection of two sets — compare CUP 9 — **cap in hand :** in a respectful, humble, or sometimes fearful manner
[2]**cap** *vt* **capped; cap·ping** (15c) **1 a :** to provide or protect with a cap **b :** to give a cap to as a symbol of honor, rank, or achievement **2 :** to form a cap over **:** CROWN ⟨the mountains were *capped* with mist —John Buchan⟩ **3 a :** to follow with something more noticeable or more significant **:** OUTDO **b :** CLIMAX
ca·pa·bil·i·ty \ˌkā-pə-ˈbil-ət-ē\ *n, pl* **-ties** (1587) **1 :** the quality or state of being capable; *also* **:** ABILITY **2 :** a feature or faculty capable of development **:** POTENTIALITY **3 :** the facility or potential for an indicated use or deployment ⟨the ~ of a metal to be fused⟩ ⟨nuclear ~⟩
ca·pa·ble \ˈkā-pə-bəl, ˈkāp-bəl\ *adj* [MF or LL; MF *capable,* fr. LL *capabilis,* irreg. fr. L *capere* to take — more at HEAVE] (1579) **1 :** SUSCEPTIBLE ⟨a remark ~ of being misunderstood⟩ **2** *obs* **:** COMPREHENSIVE **3 :** having attributes (as physical or mental power) required for performance or accomplishment ⟨is ~ of intense concentration⟩ **4 :** having traits conducive to or features permitting ⟨this woman is ~ of murder by violence —Robert Graves⟩ ⟨an outer coat of light color ~ of reflecting solar heat —*Current Biog.*⟩ **5 :** having general efficiency and ability **6** *obs* **:** having legal right to own, enjoy, or perform — **ca·pa·ble·ness** \ˈkā-pə-bəl-nəs\ *n* — **ca·pa·bly** \-pə-blē\ *adv*
ca·pa·cious \kə-ˈpā-shəs\ *adj* [L *capac-, capax* capacious, capable, fr. L *capere*] (1614) **:** containing or capable of containing a great deal *syn* see SPACIOUS — **ca·pa·cious·ly** *adv* — **ca·pa·cious·ness** *n*
ca·pac·i·tance \kə-ˈpas-ət-ən(t)s\ *n* [*capacity*] (1909) **1 a :** the property of an electric nonconductor that permits the storage of energy as a result of electric displacement when opposite surfaces of the nonconductor are maintained at a difference of potential **b :** the measure of this property that is equal to the ratio of the charge on either surface to the potential difference between the surfaces **2 :** a part of a circuit or network that possesses capacitance — **ca·pac·i·tive** \-ˈpas-ət-iv\ *adj* — **ca·pac·i·tive·ly** *adv*
ca·pac·i·tate \kə-ˈpas-ə-ˌtāt\ *vt* **-tat·ed; -tat·ing** (1657) **1** *archaic* **:** to make capable **:** QUALIFY **2 :** to cause (sperm) to undergo capacitation
ca·pac·i·ta·tion \kə-ˌpas-ə-ˈtā-shən\ *n* (1951) **:** the change undergone by sperm in the female reproductive tract that enables them to penetrate and fertilize an egg
ca·pac·i·tor \kə-ˈpas-ət-ər\ *n* (1925) **:** a device giving capacitance and usu. consisting of conducting plates or foils separated by thin layers of dielectric (as air or mica) with the plates on opposite sides of the dielectric layers oppositely charged by a source of voltage and the electrical energy of the charged system stored in the polarized dielectric
[1]**ca·pac·i·ty** \kə-ˈpas-ət-ē, -ˈpas-tē\ *n, pl* **-ties** [ME *capacite,* fr. MF *capacité,* fr. L *capacitat-, capacitas,* fr. *capac-, capax*] (15c) **1 :** legal competency or fitness **2 a :** the potential or suitability for holding, storing, or accommodating **b :** the maximum amount or number that can be contained or accommodated ⟨a jug with a one-gallon ~⟩ ⟨the auditorium was filled to ~⟩ — see METRIC SYSTEM table, WEIGHT table **3 a :** an individual's mental or physical ability **:** APTITUDE, SKILL **b :** the faculty or potential for treating, experiencing, or appreciating ⟨~ for love⟩ **4 :** DUTY, POSITION, ROLE ⟨will be happy to serve in any ~⟩ **5 :** the facility or power to produce, perform, or deploy **:** CAPABILITY ⟨a plan to double the factory's ~⟩ ⟨stockpile of intercontinental missiles . . . of a sophistication that would insure a second strike ~ —Pierre Salinger⟩; *also* **:** maximum output ⟨industries running at three-quarter ~⟩ **6 a :** CAPACITANCE **b :** the quantity of electricity that a battery can deliver under specified conditions
[2]**capacity** *adj* (1897) **:** equaling maximum capacity ⟨a ~ crowd⟩
cap–a–pie *or* **cap–à–pie** \ˌkap-ə-ˈpē, -ˈpā\ *adv* [MF (*de*) *cap a pé* from head to foot] (1523) **:** from head to foot ⟨armed ~ for battle⟩
ca·par·i·son \kə-ˈpar-ə-sən\ *n* [MF *caparaçon,* fr. OSp *caparazón*] (1579) **1 a :** an ornamental covering for a horse **b :** decorative trappings and harness **2 :** rich clothing **:** ADORNMENT — **caparison** *vt*
[1]**cape** \ˈkāp\ *n, often attrib* [ME *cap,* fr. MF, fr. OProv, fr. L *caput* head — more at HEAD] (14c) **:** a point or extension of land jutting out into water as a peninsula or as a projecting point
[2]**cape** *n* [prob. fr. Sp *capa* cloak, fr. LL *cappa* head covering, cloak] (1565) **1 :** a sleeveless outer garment or part of a garment that fits closely at the neck and hangs loosely over the shoulders **2 :** the short feathers covering the shoulders of a fowl — see COCK illustration; see DUCK illustration
Cape buffalo \ˈkāp-\ *n* [*Cape* of Good Hope, Africa] (ca. 1890) **:** a large dangerous and often savage buffalo (*Synceros caffer*) of southern Africa
Cape Cod cottage \(ˌ)kāp-ˌkäd-\ *n* [*Cape Cod,* Mass.] (1916) **:** a compact rectangular dwelling of one or one-and-a-half stories usu. with a central chimney and steep gable roof
Cape Horn·er \kāp-ˈhȯr-nər\ *n* (1840) **:** a ship that voyages around Cape Horn
cape·let \ˈkāp-lət\ *n* (1912) **:** a small cape usu. covering the shoulders
cap·e·lin \ˈkap-(ə-)lən\ *n* [CanF *capelan,* fr. F, codfish, fr. OProv, chaplain, codfish, fr. ML *cappellanus* chaplain — more at CHAPLAIN] (1620) **:** a small northern sea fish (*Mallotus villosus*) related to the smelts
Ca·pel·la \kə-ˈpel-ə\ *n* [L, lit., she-goat, fr. *caper* he-goat — more at CAPRIOLE] **:** a star of the first magnitude in Auriga

\ə\ abut \ᵊ\ kitten, F table \ər\ further \a\ ash \ā\ ace \ä\ cot, cart
\aů\ out \ch\ chin \e\ bet \ē\ easy \g\ go \i\ hit \ī\ ice \j\ job
\ŋ\ sing \ō\ go \ȯ\ law \ȯi\ boy \th\ thin \t͟h\ the \ü\ loot \ů\ foot
\y\ yet \zh\ vision \à, k̲, ⁿ, œ, œ̄, ue, ue̅, ʸ\ *see* Guide to Pronunciation

1ca·per \ˈkā-pər\ *n* [back-formation fr. earlier *capers* (taken as a plural), fr. ME *caperis,* fr. L *capparis,* fr. Gk *kapparis*] (14c) **1 :** any of a genus (*Capparis* of the family Capparidaceae, the caper family) of low prickly shrubs of the Mediterranean region; *esp* **:** one (*C. spinosa*) cultivated for its buds **2 :** one of the greenish flower buds or young berries of the caper pickled and used as a seasoning or garnish

2caper *vi* **ca·pered; ca·per·ing** \-p(ə-)riŋ\ [prob. by shortening & alter. fr. *capriole*] (1588) **:** to leap or prance about in a playful manner **:** FROLIC

3caper *n* (1592) **1 :** a frolicsome leap **2 :** a capricious escapade **:** PRANK **3 :** an illegal or questionable act; *esp* **:** THEFT

cap·er·cail·lie \ˌkap-ər-ˈkāl-(y)ē\ *or* **cap·er·cail·zie** \-ˈkāl-zē\ *n* [ScGael *capalcoille,* lit., horse of the woods] (1536) **:** the largest Old World grouse (*Tetrao urogallus*)

cape·skin \ˈkāp-ˌskin\ *n* [*Cape* of Good Hope, Africa] (1919) **:** a light flexible leather made from sheepskins with the natural grain retained and used esp. for gloves and garments

Ca·pe·tian \kə-ˈpē-shən\ *adj* [Hugh *Capet*] (1836) **:** of or relating to the French royal house that ruled from 987 to 1328 — **Capetian** *n*

cape·work \ˈkāp-ˌwərk\ *n* (1926) **:** the art of the bullfighter in working a bull with the cape

cap·ful \ˈkap-ˌfu̇l\ *n* (1719) **:** as much as a cap will hold ⟨a ~ of detergent⟩

capful of wind (1719) **:** a sudden light breeze

ca·pi·as \ˈkā-pē-əs\ *n* [ME, fr. L, lit., you should seize, fr. *capere* to take — more at HEAVE] (15c) **:** an arrest warrant

cap·il·lar·i·ty \ˌkap-ə-ˈlar-ət-ē\ *n, pl* **-ties** (1830) **1 :** the property or state of being capillary **2 :** the action by which the surface of a liquid where it is in contact with a solid (as in a capillary tube) is elevated or depressed depending on the relative attraction of the molecules of the liquid for each other and for those of the solid

1cap·il·lary \ˈkap-ə-ˌler-ē, *Brit usu* kə-ˈpil-ə-rē\ *adj* [F or L; F *capillaire,* fr. L *capillaris,* fr. *capillus* hair] (15c) **1 a :** resembling a hair esp. in slender elongated form ⟨~ leaves⟩ **b :** having a very small bore ⟨a ~ tube⟩ **2 :** involving, held by, or resulting from surface tension ⟨~ water in the soil⟩ **3 :** of or relating to capillaries or capillarity

2capillary *n, pl* **-lar·ies** (1667) **:** a capillary tube; *esp* **:** any of the smallest blood vessels connecting arterioles with venules and forming networks throughout the body

capillary attraction *n* (1830) **:** the force of adhesion between a solid and a liquid in capillarity

1cap·i·tal \ˈkap-ət-ᵊl, ˈkap-tᵊl\ *n* [ME *capitale,* modif. of ONF *capitel,* fr. LL *capitellum* small head, top of column, dim. of L *capit-, caput*] (13c) **:** the uppermost member of a column or pilaster crowning the shaft and taking the weight of the entablature — see COLUMN illustration

2capital *adj* [ME, fr. L *capitalis,* fr. *capit-, caput* head — more at HEAD] (14c) **1** *of a letter* **:** of or conforming to the series A, B, C, etc. rather than a, b, c, etc. **2 a :** punishable by death ⟨a ~ crime⟩ **b :** involving execution ⟨~ punishment⟩ **c :** most serious ⟨ a ~ error⟩ **3 a :** chief in importance or influence ⟨the ~ importance of criticism in the work of creation itself —T. S. Eliot⟩ **b :** being the seat of government **4 :** of or relating to capital; *esp* **:** relating to or being assets that add to the long-term net worth of a corporation ⟨~ improvements⟩ **5 :** EXCELLENT ⟨a ~ book⟩

3capital *n* [F or It; F, fr. It *capitale,* fr. *capitale,* adj., chief, principal, fr. L *capitalis*] (1611) **1 a** (1) **:** a stock of accumulated goods esp. at a specified time and in contrast to income received during a specified period; *also* **:** the value of these accumulated goods (2) **:** accumulated goods devoted to the production of other goods (3) **:** accumulated possessions calculated to bring in income **b** (1) **:** net worth (2) **:** CAPITAL STOCK **c :** persons holding capital **d :** ADVANTAGE, GAIN ⟨make ~ of the situation⟩ **2** [2*capital*] **a :** a capital letter; *esp* **:** an initial capital letter **b :** a letter belonging to a style of alphabet modeled on the style customarily used in inscriptions **3** [2*capital*] **a :** a city serving as a seat of government **b :** a city preeminent in some special activity ⟨the fashion ~⟩

capital gain *n* (ca. 1921) **:** the increase in value of an asset (as stock or real estate) between the time it is bought and the time it is sold

capital goods *n pl* (1896) **:** 3CAPITAL 1a(1), 1a(2)

capital–intensive *adj* (1959) **:** having a high capital cost per unit of output; *esp* **:** requiring greater expenditure in the form of capital than of labor

cap·i·tal·ism \ˈkap-ət-ᵊl-ˌiz-əm, ˈkap-tᵊl-, *Brit also* kə-ˈpit-ᵊl-\ *n* (1854) **:** an economic system characterized by private or corporate ownership of capital goods, by investments that are determined by private decision rather than by state control, and by prices, production, and the distribution of goods that are determined mainly by competition in a free market

1cap·i·tal·ist \-əst\ *n* (1792) **1 :** a person who has capital esp. invested in business; *broadly* **:** a person of wealth **:** PLUTOCRAT **2 :** a person who favors capitalism

2capitalist *or* **cap·i·tal·is·tic** \ˌkap-ət-ᵊl-ˈis-tik, ˌkap-tᵊl- *Brit also* kə-ˌpit-ᵊl-\ *adj* (1845) **1 :** owning capital ⟨the ~ class⟩ **2 a :** practicing or advocating capitalism ⟨~ nations⟩ **b :** marked by capitalism ⟨~ period of history⟩ — **cap·i·tal·is·ti·cal·ly** \-ti-k(ə-)lē\ *adv*

cap·i·tal·iza·tion \ˌkap-ət-ᵊl-ə-ˈzā-shən, ˌkap-tᵊl-, *Brit also* kə-ˌpit-ᵊl-\ *n* (1860) **1 a :** the act or process of capitalizing **b :** a sum resulting from a process of capitalizing **c :** the total liabilities of a business including both ownership capital and borrowed capital **d :** the total par value or the stated value of no-par issues of authorized capital stock **2 :** the use of a capital letter in writing or printing

cap·i·tal·ize \ˈkap-ət-ᵊl-ˌiz, ˈkap-tᵊl-, *Brit also* kə-ˈpit-ᵊl-\ *vb* **-ized; -iz·ing** *vt* (1850) **1 :** to write or print with an initial capital or in capitals **2 a :** to convert into capital ⟨~ the company's reserve fund⟩ **b :** to treat as capital rather than as an expense **3 a :** to compute the present value of (an income extended over a period of time) **b :** to convert (a periodic payment) into an equivalent capital sum ⟨*capitalized* annuities⟩ **4 :** to supply capital for ~ *vi* **:** to gain by turning something to advantage **:** PROFIT ⟨~ on an opponent's mistake⟩

cap·i·tal·ly \ˈkap-ət-ᵊl-ē, ˈkap-tᵊl-\ *adv* (1619) **1 :** in a manner involving capital punishment **2 :** in a capital manner **:** EXCELLENTLY

capital sin *n* (ca. 1934) **:** DEADLY SIN

capital stock *n* (1709) **1 :** the outstanding shares of a joint-stock company considered as an aggregate **2 :** CAPITALIZATION 1d **3 :** the ownership element of a corporation divided into shares and represented by certificates

cap·i·tate \ˈkap-ə-ˌtāt\ *adj* [L *capitatus* headed, fr. *capit-, caput* head] (1661) **1 :** forming a head **2 :** abruptly enlarged and globose

cap·i·ta·tion \ˌkap-ə-ˈtā-shən\ *n* [LL *capitation-, capitatio* poll tax, fr. L *capit-, caput*] (1641) **1 :** a direct uniform tax imposed on each head or person **:** POLL TAX **2 :** a uniform per capita payment or fee

cap·i·tol \ˈkap-ət-ᵊl, ˈkap-tᵊl\ *n* [L *Capitolium,* temple of Jupiter at Rome on the Capitoline hill] (1699) **1 a :** a building in which a state legislative body meets **b :** a group of buildings in which the functions of state government are carried out **2** *cap* **:** the building in which the U.S. Congress meets at Washington

Capitol Hill *n* [*Capitol Hill,* Washington, site of the U.S. Capitol] (1943) **:** the legislative branch of the U.S. government

Cap·i·to·line \ˈkap-ət-ᵊl-ˌīn, *Brit usu* kə-ˈpit-ə-ˌlīn\ *adj* [L *capitolinus,* fr. *Capitolium*] (1618) **:** of or relating to the smallest of the seven hills of ancient Rome, the temple on it, or the gods worshiped there

ca·pit·u·lar \kə-ˈpich-ə-lər\ *adj* [ML *capitularis,* fr. *capitulum*] (1525) **:** of or relating to an ecclesiastical chapter

ca·pit·u·lary \-ˌler-ē\ *n, pl* **-lar·ies** [ML *capitulare,* lit., document divided into sections, fr. LL *capitulum* section, chapter — more at CHAPTER] (1650) **:** a civil or ecclesiastical ordinance; *also* **:** a collection of ordinances

ca·pit·u·late \kə-ˈpich-ə-ˌlāt\ *vi* **-lat·ed; -lat·ing** [ML *capitulatus,* pp. of *capitulare* to distinguish by heads or chapters, fr. LL *capitulum*] (1596) **1** *archaic* **:** PARLEY, NEGOTIATE **2 a :** to surrender often after negotiation of terms **b :** to cease resisting **:** ACQUIESCE ***syn*** see YIELD

ca·pit·u·la·tion \kə-ˌpich-ə-ˈlā-shən\ *n* (1535) **1 :** a set of terms or articles constituting an agreement between governments **2 a :** the act of surrendering or of yielding (as to a dominant influence) **b :** the terms of surrender

ca·pit·u·lum \kə-ˈpich-ə-ləm\ *n, pl* **-la** \-lə\ [NL, fr. L, small head — more at CHAPTER] (1755) **1 :** a rounded protuberance of an anatomical part (as a bone) **2 :** a racemose inflorescence (as of the buttonbush) with the axis shortened and dilated to form a rounded or flattened cluster of sessile flowers — see INFLORESCENCE illustration

1ca·po \ˈkā-(ˌ)pō\ *n, pl* **capos** [short for *capotasto,* fr. It, lit., head of fingerboard] (1926) **:** a movable bar attached to the fingerboard of a fretted instrument to uniformly raise the pitch of all the strings

2ca·po \ˈkäp-(ˌ)ō, ˈkap-\ *n, pl* **capos** [It, head, chief, fr. L *caput*] (ca. 1963) **:** the head of a branch of a crime syndicate

ca·pon \ˈkā-ˌpän, -pən\ *n* [ME, fr. OE *capūn,* prob. fr. ONF *capon,* fr. L *capon-, capo;* akin to Gk *koptein* to cut] (bef. 12c) **:** a castrated male chicken

ca·po·na·ta \ˌkäp-ə-ˈnät-ə\ *n* [It (Sicilian dial.)] (1951) **:** a relish of chopped eggplant and assorted vegetables

ca·pote \kə-ˈpōt\ *n* [F, fr. *cape* cloak, fr. LL *cappa*] (1799) **:** a usu. long and hooded cloak or overcoat

cap·pel·let·ti \ˌkap-ə-ˈlet-ē\ *n pl but sing or pl in constr* [It, pl. of *cappelletto,* dim. of *cappello* hat, fr. ML *cappellus* cap, dim. of LL *cappa* head covering — more at CAP] (1945) **:** pasta in the form of little peaked hats filled with a savory mixture

cap·per \ˈkap-ər\ *n* (1587) **1 :** one that caps: as **a :** a device that fits caps on bottles **b :** FINALE, CLIMAX, CLINCHER **2 :** a lure or decoy esp. in an illicit or questionable activity **:** SHILL

cap·ping \ˈkap-iŋ\ *n* (15c) **:** something that caps

cap·puc·ci·no \ˌkap-(y)ə-ˈchē-(ˌ)nō, ˌkäp-\ *n* [It, lit., Capuchin; fr. the likeness of its color to that of a Capuchin's habit] (1948) **:** espresso coffee mixed with frothed hot milk or cream and often flavored with cinnamon

cap·ric acid \ˌkap-rik-\ *n* [ISV, fr. L *capr-, caper* goat; fr. its odor — more at CAPRIOLE] (1836) **:** a fatty acid $C_{10}H_{20}O_2$ found in fats and oils and used in flavors and perfumes

ca·pric·cio \kə-ˈprē-ch(ē-ˌ)ō\ *n, pl* **-cios** [It] (1601) **1 :** FANCY, WHIMSY **2 :** CAPER, PRANK **3 :** an instrumental piece in free form usu. lively in tempo and brilliant in style

ca·price \kə-ˈprēs\ *n* [F, fr. It *capriccio,* lit., head with hair standing on end, shudder, fr. *capo* head (fr. L *caput*) + *riccio* hedgehog, fr. L *ericius* — more at HEAD, URCHIN] (1667) **1 a :** a sudden, impulsive, and seemingly unmotivated notion or action **b :** a sudden usu. unpredictable condition, change, or series of changes ⟨the ~s of the weather⟩ **2 :** a disposition to do things impulsively **3 :** CAPRICCIO 3

syn CAPRICE, WHIM, VAGARY, CROTCHET mean an irrational or unpredictable idea or desire. CAPRICE stresses lack of apparent motivation and suggests willfulness; WHIM implies a fantastic, capricious turn of mind or inclination; VAGARY stresses the erratic, irresponsible character of the notion or desire; CROTCHET implies an eccentric opinion or preference.

ca·pri·cious \kə-ˈprish-əs, -ˈprē-shəs\ *adj* (1601) **:** governed or characterized by caprice **:** IMPULSIVE UNPREDICTABLE ***syn*** see INCONSTANT — **ca·pri·cious·ly** *adv* — **ca·pri·cious·ness** *n*

Cap·ri·corn \ˈkap-ri-ˌkȯ(ə)rn\ *n* [ME *Capricorne,* fr. L *Capricornus* (gen. *Capricorni*), fr. *caper* goat + *cornu* horn — more at HORN] **1 :** a southern zodiacal constellation between Sagittarius and Aquarius **2 a :** the 10th sign of the zodiac in astrology — see ZODIAC table **b :** one born under this sign

cap·ri·fi·ca·tion \ˌkap-rə-fə-ˈkā-shən\ *n* [L *caprification-, caprificatio,* fr. *caprificatus,* pp. of *caprificare* to pollinate by caprification, fr. *caprificus*] (1601) **:** artificial pollination of figs that usu. bear only pistillate flowers by hanging male flowering branches of the caprifig in the trees to facilitate pollen transfer by a wasp to the edible figs

cap·ri·fig \ˈkap-rə-ˌfig\ *n* [ME *caprifige,* part trans. of L *caprificus,* fr. *capr-, caper* goat + *ficus* fig — more at FIG] (15c) **:** a wild fig (*Ficus carica sylvestris*) of southern Europe and Asia Minor used for caprification of the edible fig; *also* **:** its fruit

cap·rine \ˈkap-ˌrīn\ *adj* [L *caprinus,* fr. *capr-, caper*] (15c) **:** of, relating to, or being a goat

cap·ri·ole \ˈkap-rē-ˌōl\ *n* [MF or OIt; MF *capriole,* fr. OIt *capriola,* fr. *capriolo* roebuck, fr. L *capreolus* goat, roebuck, fr. *capr-, caper* he-goat; akin to OE *hæfer* goat, Gk *kapros* wild boar] (1594) **1 :** a playful leap **:** CAPER **2** *of a trained horse* **:** a vertical leap with a backward kick of the hind legs at the height of the leap — **capriole** *vi*

ca·pri pants \kə-ˌprē-\ *n pl, often cap C* [*Capri,* Italy] (1956) **:** close-fitting women's pants that end above the ankle — called also *capris*

cap·rock \ˈkap-ˌräk\ *n* (1867) **:** CAP 2a
ca·pro·ic acid \kə-ˌprō-ik-\ *n* [ISV, fr. L *capr-, caper*] (1839) **:** a liquid fatty acid $C_6H_{12}O_2$ that is found as a glyceral ester in fats and oils or made synthetically and used in pharmaceuticals and flavors
cap·ro·lac·tam \ˌkap-rō-ˈlak-ˌtam\ *n* [*capro-* (fr. L *capr-, caper*) + *lactone* + *amide*] (1944) **:** a white crystalline cyclic amide $C_6H_{11}NO$ used esp. in making one type of nylon
ca·pryl·ic acid \kə-ˌpril-ik-\ *n* [ISV *capryl*, a radical contained in it] (ca. 1845) **:** a fatty acid $C_8H_{16}O_2$ of rancid odor occurring in fats and oils and used in perfumes
cap·sa·icin \kap-ˈsā-ə-sən\ *n* [irreg. fr. NL *Capsicum*] (ca. 1890) **:** a colorless irritant phenolic amide $C_{18}H_{27}NO_3$ obtained from various capsicums
Cap·si·an \ˈkap-sē-ən\ *adj* [F *capsien*, fr. L *Capsa* Gafsa, Tunisia] (1915) **:** of or relating to a Paleolithic culture of northern Africa and southern Europe
cap·si·cum \ˈkap-si-kəm\ *n* [NL, perh. fr. L *capsa*] (1664) **1 :** any of a genus (*Capsicum*) of tropical herbs and shrubs of the nightshade family widely cultivated for their many-seeded usu. fleshy-walled berries — called also *pepper* **2 :** the dried ripe fruit of some capsicums (as *C. frutescens*) used as a gastric and intestinal stimulant
cap·sid \ˈkap-səd\ *n* [L *capsa* case + E [2]*-id* — more at CASE] (1961) **:** the outer protein shell of a virus particle
cap·size \ˈkap-ˌsīz, kap-ˈ\ *vb* **cap·sized; cap·siz·ing** [origin unknown] *vt* (1788) **:** to cause to overturn ⟨~ a canoe⟩ ~ *vi* **:** to turn over **:** become upset or overturned ⟨the canoe *capsized*⟩
cap sleeve *n* (1926) **:** a very short sleeve (as on a dress) that hangs over the edge of the shoulder without extending along the underside of the arm
cap·stan \ˈkap-stən, -ˌstan\ *n* [ME] (14c) **1 :** a machine for moving or raising heavy weights that consists of a vertical drum which can be rotated and around which cable is turned **2 :** a rotating shaft that drives tape at a constant speed in a recorder
cap·stone \ˈkap-ˌstōn\ *n* [[1]*cap*] (14c) **1 :** a coping stone **:** COPING **2 :** the high point **:** crowning achievement
cap·su·lar \ˈkap-sə-lər\ *adj* (ca. 1730) **1 :** of, relating to, or resembling a capsule **2 :** CAPSULATED
cap·su·lat·ed \-ˌlāt-əd\ *adj* (1668) **:** enclosed in a capsule
[1]**cap·sule** \ˈkap-səl, -(ˌ)sül\ *n* [F, fr. L *capsula*, dim. of *capsa* box — more at CASE] (1693) **1 a :** a membrane or sac enclosing a body part **b :** either of two layers of white matter in the cerebrum **2 :** a closed receptacle containing spores or seeds: as **a :** a dry dehiscent usu. many-seeded fruit composed of two or more carpels **b :** the spore case of a moss **3 :** a shell usu. of gelatin for packaging something (as a drug or vitamins); *also* **:** a usu. medicinal or nutritional preparation for oral use consisting of the shell and its contents **4 :** an often polysaccharide envelope surrounding a microorganism **5 :** an extremely brief condensation **:** OUTLINE, SURVEY **6 a :** a compact often sealed and detachable container or compartment **b :** a small pressurized compartment for an aviator or astronaut for flight or emergency escape; *specif* **:** SPACECRAFT

capstan 1

[2]**capsule** *vt* **cap·suled; cap·sul·ing** (1859) **1 :** to equip with or enclose in a capsule **2 :** to condense into or devise in a compact form
[3]**capsule** *adj* (1938) **1 :** extremely brief **2 :** small and very compact
cap·sul·ize \ˈkap-sə-ˌlīz\ *vt* **-ized; -iz·ing** (1945) **:** CAPSULE
[1]**cap·tain** \ˈkap-tən *also* ˈkap-ᵊn\ *n* [ME *capitane*, fr. MF *capitain*, fr. LL *capitaneus*, adj. & n., chief, fr. L *capit-, caput* head — more at HEAD] (14c) **1 a** (1) **:** a military leader **:** the commander of a unit or a body of troops (2) **:** a subordinate officer commanding under a sovereign or general (3) **:** a commissioned officer in the army, air force, or marine corps ranking above a first lieutenant and below a major **b :** a naval officer who is master or commander of a ship; *esp* **:** a commissioned officer in the navy ranking above a commander and below a commodore and in the coast guard ranking above a commander and below a rear admiral **c :** a senior pilot who commands the crew of an airplane **d :** an officer in a police department or fire department in charge of a unit (as a precinct or company) and usu. ranking above a lieutenant and below a chief **2 :** one who leads or supervises: as **a :** a leader of a sports team or side **b :** HEADWAITER **c :** a person in charge of hotel bellhops — called also *bell captain* **3 :** a person of importance or influence in a field ⟨~s of industry⟩ — **cap·tain·cy** \-sē\ *n* — **cap·tain·ship** \-ˌship\ *n*
[2]**captain** *vt* (1598) **:** to be captain of **:** LEAD ⟨~*ed* the football team⟩
captain's chair *n* (1946) **:** an armchair with a saddle seat and a low curved back with vertical spindles
captain's mast *n* (1941) **:** MAST 3
cap·tan \ˈkap-ˌtan\ *n* [origin unknown] (ca. 1952) **:** a fungicide $C_9H_8Cl_3NO_2S$ used on agricultural crops
[1]**cap·tion** \ˈkap-shən\ *n* [ME *capcioun*, fr. L *caption-, captio* act of taking, fr. *captus*, pp. of *capere* to take — more at HEAVE] (1670) **1 :** the part of a legal document that shows where, when, and by what authority it was taken, found, or executed **2 a :** the heading esp. of an article or document **:** TITLE **b :** the explanatory comment or designation accompanying a pictorial illustration **c :** a motion-picture subtitle — **caption·less** \-ləs\ *adj*
[2]**caption** *vt* **cap·tioned; cap·tion·ing** \-sh(ə-)niŋ\ (1901) **:** to furnish with a caption
cap·tious \ˈkap-shəs\ *adj* [ME *capcious*, fr. MF or L; MF *captieux* fr. L *captiosus*, fr. *captio*] (14c) **1 :** marked by an often ill-natured inclination to stress faults and raise objections **2 :** calculated to confuse, entrap, or entangle in argument ***syn*** see CRITICAL — **cap·tious·ly** *adv* — **cap·tious·ness** *n*
cap·ti·vate \ˈkap-tə-ˌvāt\ *vt* **-vat·ed; -vat·ing** (1555) **1** *archaic* **:** SEIZE, CAPTURE **2 :** to influence and dominate by some special charm, art, or trait and with an irresistible appeal ***syn*** see ATTRACT — **cap·ti·va·tion** \ˌkap-tə-ˈvā-shən\ *n* — **cap·ti·va·tor** \ˈkap-tə-ˌvāt-ər\ *n*
cap·tive \ˈkap-tiv\ *adj* [ME, fr. L *captivus*, fr. *captus*, pp. of *capere*] (14c) **1 a :** taken and held as or as if a prisoner of war **b :** kept within bounds **:** CONFINED **2 :** held under control of another but having the appearance of independence; *esp* **:** owned or controlled by another concern and operated for its needs rather than for an open market ⟨a ~ mine⟩ **3 :** being such involuntarily because of a situation that makes free choice or departure difficult ⟨the airline passengers were a ~ audience⟩ — **captive** *n*
cap·tiv·i·ty \kap-ˈtiv-ət-ē\ *n* (14c) **1 :** the state of being captive ⟨some birds thrive in ~⟩ **2** *obs* **:** a group of captives
cap·tor \ˈkap-tər, -ˌtȯ(ə)r\ *n* [LL, fr. L *captus*] (1688) **:** one that has captured a person or thing
[1]**cap·ture** \ˈkap-chər, -shər\ *n* [MF, fr. L *captura*, fr. *captus*] (1541) **1 :** the act of catching, winning, or gaining control by force, stratagem, or guile **2 :** one that has been taken; *esp* **:** a prize ship **3 :** a move in various board games (as checkers or chess) that gains an opponent's man **4 :** the coalescence of an atomic nucleus with a subatomic particle that may result in an emission from or fission of the nucleus **5 :** the act of recording in a permanent file ⟨data ~⟩
[2]**capture** *vt* **cap·tured; cap·tur·ing** \ˈkap-chə-riŋ, ˈkap-shriŋ\ (1795) **1 a :** to take captive; *also* **:** to gain control of esp. by force ⟨~ a city⟩ **b :** to gain or win esp. through effort ⟨*captured* 60% of the vote⟩ **2 :** to emphasize, represent, or preserve (as a scene, mood, or quality) in a more or less permanent form ⟨at any such moment as a photograph might ~ —C. E. Montague⟩ **3 :** to captivate and hold the interest of **4 :** to take according to the rules of a game **5 :** to bring about the capture of (an elementary particle) ***syn*** see CATCH
capture the flag *n* (ca. 1925) **:** a game in which players on each of two teams seek to capture the other team's flag and return it to their side without being captured and imprisoned
ca·puche \kə-ˈpüch, -ˈpüsh\ *n* [It *cappuccio*, fr. *cappa* cloak, fr. LL] (1600) **:** HOOD; *esp* **:** the cowl of a Capuchin friar
ca·pu·chin \ˈkap-(y)ə-shən, *esp for 3 also* kə-ˈp(y)ü-\ *n* [MF, fr. OIt *cappuccino*, fr. *cappuccio*; fr. his cowl] (1596) **1** *cap* **:** a member of the Order of Friars Minor Capuchin forming since 1529 an austere branch of the first order of St. Francis of Assisi engaged in missionary work and preaching **2 :** a hooded cloak for women **3 :** any of a genus (*Cebus*) of So. American monkeys; *esp* **:** one (*C. capucinus*) with the hair on its crown resembling a monk's cowl
Cap·u·let \ˈkap-yə-lət\ *n* **:** the family of Juliet in Shakespeare's *Romeo and Juliet*
cap·y·bara \ˌkap-i-ˈbar-ə, -ˈbär-\ *n* [Pg *capibara*, fr. Tupi] (1774) **:** a tailless largely aquatic So. American rodent (*Hydrochoerus capybara*) often exceeding four feet in length
car \ˈkär\ *n* [ME *carre*, fr. AF, fr. L *carra*, pl. of *carrum*, alter. of *carrus*, of Celt origin; akin to OIr & MW *carr* vehicle; akin to L *currere* to run] (14c) **1 :** a vehicle moving on wheels: **a** *archaic* **:** CARRIAGE, CART, CHARIOT **b :** a vehicle adapted to the rails of a railroad or street railway **c :** AUTOMOBILE **2 :** the passenger compartment of an elevator **3 :** the part of an airship or balloon that carries the power plant, personnel, and cargo
ca·ra·bao \ˌkar-ə-ˈbaů, ˌkär-\ *n, pl* **-bao** *or* **-baos** [PhilSp, fr. Eastern Bisayan *karabáw*] (1900) **:** WATER BUFFALO
ca·ra·bid \ˈkar-ə-bəd, kə-ˈrab-əd\ *n* [deriv. of Gk *karabos* horned beetle; akin to Gk *keras* horn — more at HORN] (1835) **:** any of a large family (Carabidae) of usu. carnivorous and often shining black or metallic beetles — **carabid** *adj*
car·a·bi·neer *or* **car·a·bi·nier** \ˌkar-ə-bə-ˈni(ə)r\ *n* [F *carabinier*, fr. *carabine* carbine] (1672) **1 :** a cavalry soldier armed with a carbine; *specif* **:** a member of the British 6th Dragoon Guards **2 :** CARABINERO
car·a·bi·ner \ˌkar-ə-ˈbē-nər\ *n* [G *karabiner*] (1920) **:** an oblong metal ring that snaps into the hole in a piton to hold a freely running rope
ca·ra·bi·ne·ro \ˌkar-ə-bə-ˈne(ə)r-(ˌ)ō, ˌkär-\ *n, pl* **-ros** [Sp, fr. *carabina* carbine, fr. F *carabine*] (1845) **1 :** a member of a Spanish national police force serving esp. as frontier guards **2 :** a customs or coast guard officer in the Philippines
ca·ra·bi·nie·re \ˌkar-ə-bən-ˈye(ə)r-(ˌ)ā, ˌkär-\ *n, pl* **-nie·ri** \-ˈye(ə)r-ē\ [It, fr. F *carabinier*] (1847) **:** a member of the Italian national police force
car·a·cal \ˈkar-ə-ˌkal\ *n* [F, fr. Sp, fr. Turk *karakulak*, lit., black-ear, fr. *kara* black + *kulak* ear] (1760) **:** a long-legged reddish brown nocturnal cat (*Felis caracal* or *Lynx caracal*) of savannas in Africa and parts of Asia that has long pointed ears with a tuft of black hairs at the tip
ca·ra·ca·ra \ˌkar-ə-ˈkar-ə, -ə-kə-ˈrä\ *n* [Sp *caracara* & Pg *caracará*, fr. Tupi *caracará*, of imit. origin] (1838) **:** any of various large long-legged mostly So. American hawks resembling vultures in habits
car·a·cole \ˈkar-ə-ˌkōl\ *n* [F, fr. Sp *caracol* snail, spiral stair, caracole] (1614) **:** a half turn to right or left executed by a mounted horse — **caracole** *vb*
ca·rafe \kə-ˈraf, -ˈräf\ *n* [F, fr. It *caraffa*, fr. Ar *gharrāfah*] (1786) **:** a bottle with a flaring lip used to hold beverages and esp. wine
car·a·mel \ˈkär-məl; ˈkar-ə-məl, -ˌmel\ *n* [F, fr. Sp *caramelo*, fr. Pg, icicle, caramel, fr. LL *calamellus* small reed — more at SHAWM] (1725) **1 :** an amorphous brittle brown and somewhat bitter substance obtained by heating sugar and used as a coloring and flavoring agent **2 :** a firm chewy usu. caramel-flavored candy
car·a·mel·ize \-mə-ˌlīz\ *vb* **-ized; -iz·ing** *vt* (1727) **:** to change (sugar or the sugar content of a food) into caramel ~ *vi* **:** to change to caramel
ca·ran·gid \kə-ˈran-jəd, -ˈraŋ-gəd\ *adj* [deriv. of F *carangue* shad, horse mackerel, fr. Sp *caranga*] (1931) **:** of or relating to a large family (Carangidae) of marine spiny-finned fishes including important food fishes — **carangid** *n*
car·a·pace \ˈkar-ə-ˌpās\ *n* [F, fr. Sp *carapacho*] (1836) **1 :** a bony or chitinous case or shield covering the back or part of the back of an animal (as a turtle or crab) **2 :** a protective, decorative, or disguising shell ⟨the ~ of reserve he built around himself — M.M. Mintz⟩
[1]**carat** *var of* KARAT
[2]**car·at** \ˈkar-ət\ *n* [prob. fr. ML *carratus*, fr. Ar *qīrāt* bean pod, a small weight, fr. Gk *keration* carob bean, a small weight, fr. dim. of *kerat-, keras* horn — more at HORN] (15c) **:** a unit of weight for precious stones equal to 200 milligrams
[1]**car·a·van** \ˈkar-ə-ˌvan\ *n* [It *caravana*, fr. Per *kārwān*] (1588) **1 a :** a company of travelers on a journey through desert or hostile regions;

\ə\ abut \ᵊ\ kitten, F table \ər\ further \a\ ash \ā\ ace \ä\ cot, cart \aů\ out \ch\ chin \e\ bet \ē\ easy \g\ go \i\ hit \ī\ ice \j\ job \ŋ\ sing \ō\ go \ȯ\ law \ȯi\ boy \th\ thin \t͟h\ the \ü\ loot \ů\ foot \y\ yet \zh\ vision \á, k̲, ⁿ, œ, œ̄, ue, ue̅, ʸ\ *see* Guide to Pronunciation

also : a train of pack animals **b** : a group of vehicles traveling together in a file **2 a** : a covered wagon or motor vehicle equipped as traveling living quarters **b** *Brit* : TRAILER 3b
[2]**caravan** *vi* **-vanned** *or* **-vaned** \-ˌvānd\; **-van·ning** *or* **-van·ing** (1885) : to travel in a caravan
car·a·van·ner \-ˌvan-ər\ *n* (1909) **1** *or* **car·a·van·er** \-ˌvan-\ : one that travels in a caravan **2** *Brit* : one that goes camping with a trailer
car·a·van·sa·ry \ˌkar-ə-ˈvan(t)-sə-rē\ *or* **car·a·van·se·rai** \-sə-ˌrī\ *n, pl* **-ries** *or* **-rais** *or* **-rai** [Per *kārwānsarāī*, fr. *kārwān* caravan + *sarāī* palace, inn] (1599) **1** : an inn surrounding a court in eastern countries where caravans rest at night **2** : HOTEL, INN
car·a·vel \ˈkar-ə-ˌvel, -vəl\ *n* [MF *caravelle*, fr. OPg *caravela*] (1527) : any of several sailing ships; *specif* : a small 15th and 16th century ship that has broad bows, high narrow poop, and usu. three masts with lateen or both square and lateen sails
car·a·way \ˈkar-ə-ˌwā\ *n* [ME, prob. fr. ML *carvi*, fr. Ar *karawyā*, fr. Gk *karon*] (13c) **1** : a biennial usu. white-flowered aromatic herb (*Carum carvi*) of the carrot family **2** : the pungent fruit of the caraway used in seasoning and medicine — called also *caraway seed*
carb \ˈkärb\ *n, slang* (1952) : CARBURETOR
carb- *or* **carbo-** *comb form* [F, fr. *carbone*] : carbon : carbonic : carbonyl : carboxyl ⟨*carb*ide⟩ ⟨*carbo*hydrate⟩
car·ba·chol \ˈkär-bə-ˌkȯl, -ˌkōl\ *n* [*carba*mic acid + *chol*ine] (ca. 1940) : a synthetic parasympathomimetic drug $C_6H_{15}ClN_2O_2$ that is used in veterinary medicine and topically in glaucoma
car·ba·mate \ˈkär-bə-ˌmāt, kär-ˈbam-ˌāt\ *n* (1888) : a salt or ester of carbamic acid; *esp* : one that is a synthetic organic insecticide
car·bam·ic acid \(ˌ)kär-ˌbam-ik-\ *n* [ISV *carbam*ide + *-ic*] (1869) : an acid CH_3NO_2 known in the form of salts and esters that is a half amide of carbonic acid
carb·amide \ˈkär-bə-ˌmīd, kär-ˈbam-əd\ *n* [ISV *carb-* + *amide*] (1865) : UREA
carb·ami·no \ˌkär-bə-ˈmē-(ˌ)nō\ *adj* (1925) : relating to any carbamic acid derivative formed by reaction of carbon dioxide with an amino acid or a protein (as hemoglobin)
carb·an·ion \kär-ˈban-ˌī-ən, -ˌī-ˌän\ *n* (1933) : an organic ion carrying a negative charge at a carbon position — compare CARBONIUM ION
car·barn \ˈkär-ˌbärn\ *n* (1880) : a building that houses the cars of a street railway or the buses of a bus system
car·ba·ryl \ˈkär-bə-ˌril\ *n* [*car*bamate + *ar*omatic + *-yl*] (ca. 1963) : a carbamate insecticide $C_{12}H_{11}NO_2$ effective against numerous crop, forage, and forest pests — compare SEVIN
car·ba·zole \ˈkär-bə-ˌzōl\ *n* [ISV] (1887) : a crystalline slightly basic cyclic compound $C_{12}H_9N$ found in anthracene and used in making dyes
car bed *n* (1953) : a portable bed for an infant
car·bide \ˈkär-ˌbīd\ *n* [ISV] (1865) **1** : a binary compound of carbon with a more electropositive element; *esp* : CALCIUM CARBIDE **2** : a very hard material made of carbon and one or more heavy metals
car·bine \ˈkär-ˌbēn, -ˌbīn\ *n* [F *carabine*, fr. MF *carabin* carabineer] (1605) **1** : a short-barreled lightweight firearm orig. used by cavalry **2** : a modern repeating rifle that is shorter and lighter than the standard, fires lighter ammunition, and is used as a supplementary military arm or for hunting in dense brush
car·bi·nol \ˈkär-bə-ˌnȯl, -ˌnōl\ *n* [ISV, fr. obs. G *karbin* methyl, fr. G *karb-* carb-] (ca. 1890) : METHANOL; *also* : an alcohol derived from it
car·bo·cy·clic \ˌkär-bō-ˈsī-klik, -ˈsik-lik\ *adj* [ISV] (1899) : being or having an organic ring composed of carbon atoms
car·bo·hy·drase \ˌkär-bō-ˈhī-ˌdrās, -bə-, -ˌdrāz\ *n* [ISV *carbohydr*ate + *-ase*] (1910) : any of a group of enzymes (as amylase) that promote hydrolysis or synthesis of a carbohydrate (as a disaccharide)
car·bo·hy·drate \-ˌdrāt, -drət\ *n* (1869) : any of various neutral compounds of carbon, hydrogen, and oxygen (as sugars, starches, and celluloses) most of which are formed by green plants and which constitute a major class of animal foods
car·bol·ic \kär-ˈbäl-ik\ *n* (1884) : PHENOL 1
carbolic acid *n* [ISV *carb-* + L *oleum* oil — more at OIL] (ca. 1864) : PHENOL 1
car·bon \ˈkär-bən\ *n, often attrib* [F *carbone*, fr. L *carbon-, carbo* ember, charcoal] (1789) **1** : a nonmetallic chiefly tetravalent element found native (as in the diamond and graphite) or as a constituent of coal, petroleum, and asphalt, of limestone and other carbonates, and of organic compounds or obtained artificially in varying degrees of purity esp. as carbon black, lampblack, activated carbon, charcoal, and coke — see ELEMENT table **2 a** : a sheet of carbon paper **b** : CARBON COPY **3 a** : a carbon rod used in an arc lamp **b** : a piece of carbon used as an element in a voltaic cell — **car·bon·less** \-ləs\ *adj*
car·bo·na·ceous \ˌkär-bə-ˈnā-shəs\ *adj* (1791) **1** : rich in carbon **2** : relating to, containing, or composed of carbon **3** : CARBONOUS 2
[1]**car·bo·na·do** \ˌkär-bə-ˈnäd-(ˌ)ō, -ˈnäd-\ *n, pl* **-dos** *or* **-does** [Sp *carbonada*] *archaic* (1586) : a piece of meat scored before grilling
[2]**carbonado** *vt* (1611) **1** *archaic* : to make a carbonado of **2** *archaic* : CUT
[3]**carbonado** *n, pl* **-dos** [Pg, lit., carbonated] (1852) : an impure opaque dark-colored fine-grained aggregate of diamond particles valuable for its superior toughness
car·bo·nara \ˌkär-bə-ˈnär-ə\ *n* [It, fr. *alla carbonara* from the charcoal grill] (1963) : a pasta dish made with a white cheese sauce that incorporates bits of bacon and ham ⟨spaghetti ~⟩
[1]**car·bon·ate** \ˈkär-bə-ˌnāt, -nət\ *n* (1794) : a salt or ester of carbonic acid
[2]**car·bon·ate** \-ˌnāt\ *vt* **-at·ed; -at·ing** (1805) **1** : to convert into a carbonate **2** : to impregnate with carbon dioxide ⟨*carbonated* beverage⟩ — **car·bon·ation** \ˌkär-bə-ˈnā-shən\ *n*
carbon black *n* (1889) : any of various colloidal black substances consisting wholly or principally of carbon obtained usu. as soot and used esp. as pigments
carbon copy *n* (1895) **1** : a copy made by carbon paper **2** : DUPLICATE
carbon cycle *n* (1912) **1** : the cycle of carbon in living beings in which carbon dioxide is fixed by photosynthesis to form organic nutrients and is ultimately restored to the inorganic state by respiration and protoplasmic decay **2** : a cycle of thermonuclear reactions in which four hydrogen atoms synthesize into a helium atom with the release of nuclear energy and which is held to be the source of most of the energy radiated by the sun and stars
carbon dating *n* (1951) : the determination of the age of old material (as an archaeological or paleontological specimen) by means of the content of carbon 14 — **carbon–date** \ˌkär-bən-ˈdāt\ *vt*
carbon dioxide *n* (1869) : a heavy colorless gas CO_2 that does not support combustion, dissolves in water to form carbonic acid, is formed esp. in animal respiration and in the decay or combustion of animal and vegetable matter, is absorbed from the air by plants in photosynthesis, and is used in the carbonation of beverages
carbon disulfide *n* (1869) : a colorless flammable poisonous liquid CS_2 used as a solvent for rubber and as an insect fumigant — called also *carbon bisulfide*
carbon 14 \-(ˈ)fȯr(t)-ˈtēn, -(ˈ)fȯr(t)-\ *n* (1936) : a heavy radioactive isotope of carbon of mass number 14 used esp. in tracer studies and in dating archaeological and geological materials
car·bon·ic \kär-ˈbän-ik\ *adj* (1791) : of, relating to, or derived from carbon, carbonic acid, or carbon dioxide
carbonic acid *n* (1791) : a weak dibasic acid H_2CO_3 known only in solution that reacts with bases to form carbonates
carbonic acid gas *n* (ca. 1880) : CARBON DIOXIDE
carbonic an·hy·drase \-an-ˈhī-ˌdrās, -ˌdrāz\ *n* [*carbonic* + *anhydr*ous + *-ase*; fr. its promotion of dehydration] (1841) : a zinc-containing enzyme that occurs in living tissues (as red blood cells) and aids carbon-dioxide transport from the tissues and its release from the blood in the lungs by catalyzing the reversible hydration of carbon dioxide to carbonic acid
car·bon·if·er·ous \ˌkär-bə-ˈnif-(ə-)rəs\ *adj* (1799) **1** : producing or containing carbon or coal **2** *cap* : of, relating to, or being the period of the Paleozoic era between the Devonian and the Permian or the corresponding system of rocks that includes coal beds — **Carboniferous** *n*
car·bo·ni·um ion \kär-ˌbō-nē-əm-\ *n* [*carb-* + *-onium*] (1902) : an organic ion carrying a positive charge at a carbon position — compare CARBANION
car·bon·iza·tion \ˌkär-bə-nə-ˈzā-shən\ *n* (1804) : the process of carbonizing; *esp* : DESTRUCTIVE DISTILLATION
car·bon·ize \ˈkär-bə-ˌnīz\ *vb* **-ized; -iz·ing** *vt* (1806) **1** : to convert into carbon or a carbonic residue **2** : CARBURIZE 1 ~ *vi* : to become carbonized : CHAR
carbon monoxide *n* (1873) : a colorless odorless very toxic gas CO that burns to carbon dioxide with a blue flame and is formed as a product of the incomplete combustion of carbon
car·bon·nade *also* **car·bo·nade** \ˌkär-bə-ˈnäd\ *n* [Fr, lit., grilled meat, fr. It *carbonata* charcoal grilled] (1877) : a beef stew cooked in beer
car·bon·ous \ˈkär-bə-nəs\ *adj* (1794) **1** : derived from, containing, or resembling carbon **2** : brittle and dark in color
carbon paper *n* (1878) **1** : gelatin-coated paper used in the carbon process **2** : a thin paper faced with a waxy pigmented coating so that when placed between two sheets of paper the pressure of writing or typing on the top sheet causes transfer of pigment to the bottom sheet
carbon process *n* (1879) : a photographic printing process utilizing a sheet of paper coated with bichromated gelatin mixed with a pigment
carbon tetrachloride *n* (ca. 1903) : a colorless nonflammable toxic liquid CCl_4 that has an odor resembling that of chloroform and is used as a solvent and a refrigerant
carbon 12 \-ˈtwelv\ *n* (1946) : an isotope of carbon of mass number 12 that is the most abundant carbon isotope
car·bon·yl \ˈkär-bə-ˌnil, -ˌnēl\ *n* (1869) **1** : a bivalent radical CO occurring in aldehydes, ketones, carboxylic acids, esters, acid halides, and amides **2** : a compound of the carbonyl radical with a metal — **car·bon·yl·ic** \ˌkär-bə-ˈnil-ik\ *adj*
Car·bo·run·dum \ˌkär-bə-ˈrən-dəm\ *trademark* — used for various abrasives
carboxy- *or* **carbox-** *comb form* : carboxyl
car·box·yl \kär-ˈbäk-səl\ *n* [ISV] (1869) : a univalent radical COOH typical of organic acids — called also *carboxyl group* — **car·box·yl·ic** \ˌkär-(ˌ)bäk-ˈsil-ik\ *adj*
car·box·yl·ase \kär-ˈbäk-sə-ˌlās, -ˌlāz\ *n* [ISV] (1911) : an enzyme that catalyzes decarboxylation or carboxylation
[1]**car·box·yl·ate** \-ˌlāt\ *vt* **-at·ed; -at·ing** (1927) : to introduce carboxyl or carbon dioxide into (a compound) with formation of a carboxylic acid — **car·box·yl·ation** \(ˌ)kär-ˌbäk-sə-ˈlā-shən\ *n*
[2]**car·box·yl·ate** \-ˌlāt, -lət\ *n* (ca. 1928) : a salt or ester of a carboxylic acid
carboxylic acid *n* (1902) : an organic acid (as acetic acid) containing one or more carboxyl groups
car·boxy·meth·yl·cel·lu·lose \kär-ˌbäk-sē-ˌmeth-əl-ˈsel-yə-ˌlōs, -ˌlōz\ *n* (1947) : an acid ether derivative of cellulose that in the form of its sodium salt is used as a thickening, emulsifying, and stabilizing agent and as a bulk laxative and antacid in medicine
car·boxy·pep·ti·dase \-ˈpep-tə-ˌdās, -ˌdāz\ *n* (1930) : an enzyme that hydrolyzes peptides and esp. polypeptides by splitting off sequentially the amino acids at the end of the peptide chain which contain free carboxyl groups
car·boy \ˈkär-ˌbȯi\ *n* [Per *qarāba*, fr. Ar *qarrābah* demijohn] (1753) : a bottle or rectangular container of about 5 to 15 gallons capacity for liquids that is made of glass, plastic, or metal and is often cushioned in a special container

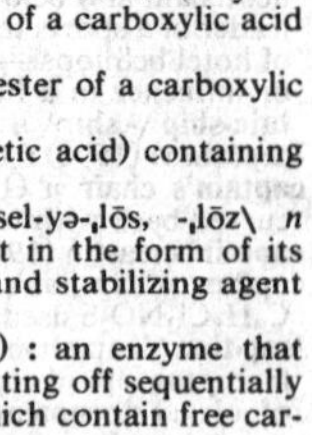
carboy

car·bun·cle \ˈkär-ˌbəŋ-kəl\ *n* [ME, fr. OF, fr. L *carbunculus* small coal, carbuncle, dim. of *carbon-, carbo* charcoal, ember — more at CARBON] (13c) **1 a** *obs* : any of several red precious stones **b** : the garnet cut cabochon **2** : a painful local purulent inflammation of the skin and deeper tissues with multiple openings for the discharge of pus and usu. necrosis and sloughing of dead tissue — **car·bun·cled** \-kəld\ *adj* — **car·bun·cu·lar** \kär-ˈbəŋ-kyə-lər\ *adj*
car·bu·ret \ˈkär-b(y)ə-ˌrāt, *esp by chemists* -ˌret\ *vt* **-ret·ed** *also* **-ret·ted; -ret·ing** *also* **-ret·ting** [obs. *carburet* (carbide)] (1869) **1** : to combine chemically with carbon **2** : to enrich (as gas) by mixing with volatile

carbon compounds (as hydrocarbons) — **car·bu·re·tion** \ˌkär-b(y)ə-ˈrā-shən\ *n*

car·bu·re·tor \ˈkär-b(y)ə-ˌrāt-ər\ *n* (1864) : an apparatus for supplying an internal-combustion engine with vaporized fuel mixed with air in an explosive mixture

car·bu·ret·ter *or* **car·bu·ret·tor** \ˌkär-byə-ˈret-ər, ˈkär-byə-ˌ\ *chiefly Brit var of* CARBURETOR

car·bu·rize \ˈkär-b(y)ə-ˌrīz\ *vt* **-rized; -riz·ing** [obs. *carburet* (carbide)] (ca. 1889) **1** : to combine or impregnate (as metal) with carbon **2** : CARBURET 2 — **car·bu·ri·za·tion** \ˌkär-b(y)ə-rə-ˈzā-shən\ *n*

car·ca·net \ˈkär-kə-nət\ *n* [MF *carcan*] *archaic* (1530) : an ornamental necklace or headband

car·case \ˈkär-kəs\ *Brit var of* CARCASS

car·cass \ˈkär-kəs\ *n* [ME *carcays,* fr. MF *carcasse,* fr. OF *carcois*] (14c) **1** : a dead body : CORPSE; *esp* : the dressed body of a meat animal **2** : the living, material, or physical body **3** : the decaying or worthless remains of a structure ⟨the ~ of an abandoned automobile⟩ **4** : the foundation structure of something (as a tire)

carcin- *or* **carcino-** *comb form* [Gk *karkin-, karkino-,* fr. *karkinos* — more at CANCER] **1** : crab ⟨*carcinology*⟩ **2** : tumor : cancer ⟨*carcinogenic*⟩

car·cin·o·gen \kär-ˈsin-ə-jən, ˈkärs-ᵊn-ə-ˌjen\ *n* (1936) : a substance or agent producing or inciting cancer — **car·ci·no·gen·e·sis** \ˌkärs-ᵊn-ō-ˈjen-ə-səs\ *n* — **car·ci·no·gen·ic** \-ˈjen-ik\ *adj* — **car·ci·no·ge·nic·i·ty** \-jə-ˈnis-ət-ē\ *n*

car·ci·noid \ˈkärs-ᵊn-ˌȯid\ *n* (1926) : a benign or malignant tumor arising esp. from the mucosa of the gastrointestinal tract

car·ci·no·ma \ˌkärs-ᵊn-ˈō-mə\ *n, pl* **-mas** *or* **-ma·ta** \-mət-ə\ [L, fr. Gk *karkinōma* cancer, fr. *karkinos*] (1721) : a malignant tumor of epithelial origin — **car·ci·no·ma·tous** \-ˈō-mət-əs\ *adj*

car·ci·no·ma·to·sis \-ˌō-mə-ˈtō-səs\ *n* [NL, fr. L *carcinomat-, carcinoma*] (1903) : a condition in which multiple carcinomas develop simultaneously usu. after dissemination from a primary source

car·ci·no·sar·co·ma \ˈkärs-ᵊn-ō-(ˌ)sär-ˈkō-mə\ *n, pl* **-mas** *or* **-ma·ta** \-mət-ə\ (ca. 1927) : a malignant tumor combining elements of carcinoma and sarcoma

car coat *n* (1958) : a three-quarter-length overcoat

[1]card \ˈkärd\ *vt* (14c) : to cleanse, disentangle, and collect together (as fibers) by the use of a card preparatory to spinning — **card·er** *n*

[2]card *n* [ME *carde,* fr. MF, fr. LL *cardus* thistle, fr. L *carduus* — more at CHARD] (15c) **1** : an instrument or machine for carding fibers that consists usu. of bent wire teeth set closely in rows in a thick piece of leather fastened to a back **2** : an implement for raising a nap on cloth

[3]card *n* [ME *carde,* modif. of MF *carte,* prob. fr. OIt *carta,* lit., leaf of paper, fr. L *charta* leaf of papyrus, fr. Gk *chartēs*] (15c) **1** : PLAYING CARD **2** *pl but sing or pl in constr* **a** : a game played with cards **b** : card playing **3** : something compared to a valuable playing card in one's hand **4** : a usu. clownishly amusing person : WAG **5** : COMPASS CARD **6 a** : a flat stiff usu. small and rectangular piece of material (as paper or plastic): as **(1)** : POSTCARD **(2)** : VISITING CARD **(3)** : CREDIT CARD **(4)** : one on which computer information is stored (as in the form of punched holes or magnetic encoding) **(5)** : one bearing electronic circuit components for insertion into a larger electronic device (as a computer) **b** : PROGRAM; *esp* : a sports program **c (1)** : a wine list **(2)** : MENU **d** : GREETING CARD — **in the cards** *also* **on the cards** : INEVITABLE

[4]card *vt* (1844) **1** : to place or fasten on or by means of a card **2** : to provide with a card **3** : to list or record on a card **4** : SCORE **5** : to ask for identification (as in a bar)

car·da·mom \ˈkärd-ə-məm, -ˌmäm\ *n* [L *cardamomum,* fr. Gk *kardamōmon,* blend of *kardamon* peppergrass & *amōmon,* an Indian spice plant] (14c) : the aromatic capsular fruit of an East Indian herb (*Elettaria cardamomum*) of the ginger family with seeds used as a condiment and in medicine; *also* : this plant

[1]card·board \ˈkärd-ˌbō(ə)rd, -ˌbȯ(ə)rd\ *n* (1848) : PAPERBOARD

[2]cardboard *adj* (1901) **1 a** : made of or as if of cardboard **b** : FLAT, TWO-DIMENSIONAL **2** : UNREAL, STEREOTYPED ⟨a play with ~ characters⟩

card–car·ry·ing \ˈkärd-ˌkar-ē-iŋ\ *adj* [fr. the assumption that such a person carries a card identifying him as a member] (1948) **1** : being a full-fledged member esp. of a Communist party **2** : being strongly identified with a group (as of people with a common interest) ⟨~ members of the ecology movement —Richard Neuhaus⟩

card catalog *n* (1854) : a catalog (as of books) in which the entries are arranged systematically on cards

card·hold·er \ˈkärd-ˌhōl-dər\ *n* (1909) : one who possesses a card and esp. a credit card

cardi- *or* **cardio-** *comb form* [Gk *kardi-, kardio-,* fr. *kardia* — more at HEART] : heart : cardiac and ⟨*cardiogram*⟩ ⟨*cardiovascular*⟩

car·dia \ˈkärd-ē-ə\ *n, pl* **-di·ae** \-ē-ˌē\ *or* **-dias** [NL, fr. Gk *kardia* heart, upper orifice of the stomach] (1782) : the opening of the esophagus into the stomach; *also* : the part of the stomach adjoining this opening

-car·dia \ˈkärd-ē-ə\ *n comb form* [NL, fr. Gk *kardia*] : heart action or location (of a specified type) ⟨dextro*cardia*⟩ ⟨tachy*cardia*⟩

[1]car·di·ac \ˈkärd-ē-ˌak\ *adj* [L *cardiacus,* fr. Gk *kardiakos,* fr. *kardia*] (1601) **1 a** : of, relating to, situated near, or acting on the heart **b** : of or relating to the cardia of the stomach **2** : of, relating to, or affected with heart disease

[2]cardiac *n* (ca. 1929) : a person with heart disease

cardiac muscle *n* (ca. 1903) : the principal muscle tissue of the vertebrate heart made up of striated fibers that appear to be separated from each other under the electron microscope but that function in long-term rhythmic contraction as if in protoplasmic continuity

car·di·al·gia \ˌkärd-ē-ˈal-j(ē-)ə\ *n* [NL, fr. Gk *kardialgia,* fr. *kardia* + *-algia*] (1655) **1** : HEARTBURN **2** : pain in the heart

car·di·gan \ˈkärd-i-gən\ *n* [James Thomas Brudenell, 7th Earl of *Cardigan* †1868 Eng. soldier] (1868) : a usu. collarless sweater or jacket that opens the full length of the center front

Cardigan Welsh corgi *n* [*Cardigan* county, Wales] (1935) : a Welsh corgi with rounded ears, slightly bowed forelegs, and long tail — called also *Cardigan;* see WELSH CORGI illustration

[1]car·di·nal \ˈkärd-nəl, -ᵊn-əl\ *n* [ME, fr. ML *cardinalis,* fr. LL *cardinalis* adj., principal, fr. L, of a hinge, fr. *cardin-, cardo* hinge; akin to OE *hratian* to rush, Gk *skairein* to dance] (12c) **1** : a high ecclesiastical official of the Roman Catholic Church who ranks next below the pope and is appointed by him to assist him as a member of the college of cardinals **2** : CARDINAL NUMBER — usu. used in pl. **3** : a woman's short hooded cloak orig. of scarlet cloth **4** [fr. its color, resembling that of the cardinal's robes] : a crested finch (*Richmondena cardinalis,* syn. *Cardinalis cardinalis*) of the eastern U.S. and adjacent Canada, the southwestern U.S., and Mexico to Belize which has a black face and heavy red bill in both sexes and is nearly completely red in the male — **car·di·nal·ship** \-ˌship\ *n*

[2]cardinal *adj* (14c) : of basic importance : MAIN, CHIEF, PRIMARY ⟨~ point of speech⟩ ***syn*** see ESSENTIAL — **car·di·nal·ly** \-ē\ *adv*

car·di·nal·ate \-ət, -ˌāt\ *n* (1645) : the office, rank, or dignity of a cardinal

cardinal flower *n* (1698) : a No. American lobelia (*Lobelia cardinalis*) that bears a spike of brilliant red flowers

car·di·nal·i·ty \ˌkärd-ᵊn-ˈal-ət-ē\ *n, pl* **-ties** [[1]*cardinal* + *-ity*] (1935) : the number of elements in a given mathematical set

cardinal number *n* (1591) **1** : a number (as 1, 5, 15) that is used in simple counting and that indicates how many elements there are in an assemblage — see NUMBER table **2** : the property that a mathematical set has in common with all sets that can be put in one-to-one correspondence with it

cardinal point *n* (1755) : one of the four principal compass points north, south, east, and west

cardinal virtue *n* (14c) **1** : one of the four classically defined natural virtues prudence, justice, temperance, or fortitude **2** : a quality designated as a major virtue

car·dio·gen·ic \ˈkärd-ē-ō-ˈjen-ik\ *adj* (ca. 1923) : originating in the heart : caused by a cardiac condition ⟨~ shock⟩

car·dio·gram \ˈkärd-ē-ə-ˌgram\ *n* [ISV] (1876) : the curve or tracing made by a cardiograph

car·dio·graph \-ˌgraf\ *n* [ISV] (1870) : an instrument that registers graphically movements of the heart — **car·dio·graph·ic** \ˌkärd-ē-ə-ˈgraf-ik\ *adj* — **car·di·og·ra·phy** \ˌkärd-ē-ˈäg-rə-fē\ *n*

car·di·oid \ˈkärd-ē-ˌȯid\ *n* (1753) : a heart-shaped curve that is traced by a point on the circumference of a circle rolling completely around an equal fixed circle and has the general equation $\rho = a(1 + \cos\theta)$ in polar coordinates

car·di·ol·o·gy \ˌkärd-ē-ˈäl-ə-jē\ *n* [ISV] (1847) : the study of the heart and its action and diseases — **car·di·o·log·i·cal** \-ē-ə-ˈläj-i-kəl\ *adj* — **car·di·ol·o·gist** \-ē-ˈäl-ə-jəst\ *n*

car·dio·my·op·a·thy \ˈkärd-ē-ō-(ˌ)mī-ˈäp-ə-thē\ *n, pl* **-thies** [*cardi-* + *my-* + *-pathy*] (ca. 1965) : a typically chronic disorder of heart muscle that may involve hypertrophy and obstructive damage to the heart

car·di·op·a·thy \ˌkärd-ē-ˈäp-ə-thē\ *n, pl* **-thies** (1885) : any disease of the heart

car·dio·pul·mo·nary \ˈkärd-ē-ō-ˈpu̇l-mə-ˌner-ē, -ˈpəl-\ *adj* (ca. 1881) : of or relating to the heart and lungs

cardiopulmonary resuscitation *n* (1972) : a procedure designed to restore normal breathing after cardiac arrest that includes the clearance of air passages to the lungs, heart massage by the exertion of pressure on the chest, and the use of drugs

car·dio·re·spi·ra·to·ry \ˈkärd-ē-ō-ˈres-p(ə-)rə-ˌtōr-ē, -ri-ˈspī-rə-, -ˌtȯr-\ *adj* (1892) : of or relating to the heart and the respiratory system : CARDIOPULMONARY ⟨~ ailments⟩

car·dio·ton·ic \ˌkärd-ē-ō-ˈtän-ik\ *adj* (1927) : tending to increase the tonus of heart muscle — **cardiotonic** *n*

car·dio·vas·cu·lar \-ˈvas-kyə-lər\ *adj* [ISV] (1879) : of, relating to, or involving the heart and blood vessels

-car·di·um \ˈkärd-ē-əm\ *n comb form, pl* **-car·dia** \-ē-ə\ [NL, fr. Gk *kardia*] : heart ⟨epi*cardium*⟩

car·doon \kär-ˈdün\ *n* [F *cardon,* fr. LL *cardon-, cardo* thistle, fr. *cardus,* fr. L *carduus* thistle, artichoke — more at CHARD] (1611) : a large perennial plant (*Cynara cardunculus*) related to the artichoke and cultivated for its edible root and leafstalks

card·play·er \ˈkärd-ˌplā-ər\ *n* (1589) : one that plays cards

card·sharp·er \-ˌshär-pər\ *or* **card·sharp** \-ˌshärp\ *n* (1859) : one who habitually cheats at cards

[1]care \ˈke(ə)r, ˈka(ə)r\ *n* [ME, fr. OE *caru;* akin to OHG *kara* lament, L *garrire* to chatter] (bef. 12c) **1** : suffering of mind : GRIEF **2 a** : a disquieted state of blended uncertainty, apprehension, and responsibility **b** : a cause for such anxiety **3 a** : painstaking or watchful attention **b** : MAINTENANCE ⟨floor-*care* products⟩ **4** : regard coming from desire or esteem **5** : CHARGE, SUPERVISION ⟨under a doctor's ~⟩ **6** : a person or thing that is an object of attention, anxiety, or solicitude ⟨the flower garden was her special ~⟩

syn CARE, CONCERN, SOLICITUDE, ANXIETY, WORRY mean a troubled or engrossed state of mind or the thing that causes this. CARE implies oppression of the mind weighed down by responsibility or disquieted by apprehension; CONCERN implies a troubled state of mind because of personal interest, relation, or affection; SOLICITUDE implies great concern and connotes either thoughtful or hovering attentiveness toward another; ANXIETY stresses anguished uncertainty or fear of misfortune or failure; WORRY suggests fretting over matters that may or may not be real cause for anxiety.

[2]care *vb* **cared; car·ing** *vi* (bef. 12c) **1 a** : to feel trouble or anxiety **b** : to feel interest or concern ⟨~ about freedom⟩ **2** : to give care ⟨~ for the sick⟩ **3 a** : to have a liking, fondness, or taste ⟨don't ~ for her⟩ **b** : to have an inclination ⟨would you ~ for some pie⟩ ~ *vt* **1** : to be concerned about or to the extent of **2** : WISH ⟨if you ~ to go⟩ — **car·er** *n* — **care less** : not to care — used positively and negatively with the same meaning ⟨I could *care less* what happens⟩ ⟨I couldn't *care less* about her⟩

[1]ca·reen \kə-ˈrēn\ *n* [MF *carène* keel, fr. OIt *carena,* fr. L *carina* keel, lit., nutshell; akin to Gk *karyon* nut] *archaic* (1591) : the act or process of careening : the state of being careened

2careen *vt* (1600) **1 a :** to cause (a boat) to lean over on one side **b :** to clean, caulk, or repair (a boat) in this position **2 :** to cause to heel over ~ *vi* **1 a :** to careen a boat **b :** to undergo this process **2 :** to heel over **3 :** to sway from side to side : LURCH ⟨a ~*ing* carriage being pulled wildly along a street by a team of runaway horses —J. P. Getty⟩ **4 :** CAREER

1ca·reer \kə-ˈri(ə)r\ *n* [MF *carrière*, fr. OProv *carriera* street, fr. ML *carraria* road for vehicles, fr. L *carrus* car] (1580) **1 a :** COURSE, PASSAGE **b :** speed in a course ⟨ran at full ~⟩ **2 :** ENCOUNTER, CHARGE **3 :** a field for or pursuit of consecutive progressive achievement esp. in public, professional, or business life ⟨Washington's ~ as a soldier⟩ **4 :** a profession for which one trains and which is undertaken as a permanent calling ⟨a ~ diplomat⟩

2career *vi* (1647) **:** to go at top speed esp. in a headlong manner ⟨a car ~*ed* off the road⟩

ca·reer·ism \-ˌiz-əm\ *n* (1933) **:** the policy or practice of advancing one's career often at the cost of one's integrity — **ca·reer·ist** \-əst\ *n*

care·free \ˈke(ə)r-ˌfrē, ˈka(ə)r-\ *adj* (1795) **:** free from care: as **a :** having no worries or troubles **b :** IRRESPONSIBLE ⟨is ~ with his money⟩

care·ful \-fəl\ *adj* **care·ful·ler; care·ful·lest** (bef. 12c) **1** *archaic* **a :** SOLICITOUS, ANXIOUS **b :** filling with care or solicitude **2 :** exercising or taking care **3 a :** marked by attentive concern and solicitude **b :** marked by wary caution or prudence ⟨be very ~ with knives⟩ **c :** marked by painstaking effort to avoid errors or omissions — often used with *of* or an infinitive ⟨~ of money⟩ ⟨~ to adjust the machine⟩ — **care·ful·ly** \-f(ə-)lē\ *adv* — **care·ful·ness** \-fəl-nəs\ *n*

syn CAREFUL, METICULOUS, SCRUPULOUS, PUNCTILIOUS mean showing close attention to detail. CAREFUL implies attentiveness and cautiousness in avoiding mistakes ⟨a *careful* worker⟩ METICULOUS may imply either commendable extreme carefulness or a hampering finicky caution over small points ⟨*meticulous* scholarship⟩ SCRUPULOUS applies to what is proper or fitting or ethical ⟨*scrupulous* honesty⟩ PUNCTILIOUS implies minute, even excessive attention to fine points ⟨*punctilious* observance of ritual⟩

care·less \-ləs\ *adj* (bef. 12c) **1 a :** free from care : UNTROUBLED ⟨~ days⟩ **b :** INDIFFERENT, UNCONCERNED ⟨~ of the consequences⟩ **2 :** not taking care **3 :** not showing or receiving care: **a :** NEGLIGENT, SLOVENLY ⟨writing that is ~ and full of errors⟩ **b :** UNSTUDIED, SPONTANEOUS ⟨~ grace⟩ **c** *obs* **:** UNVALUED, DISREGARDED — **care·less·ly** *adv* — **care·less·ness** *n*

1ca·ress \kə-ˈres\ *n* [F *caresse*, fr. It *carezza*, fr. *caro* dear, fr. L *carus* — more at CHARITY] (1611) **1 :** an act or expression of kindness or affection : ENDEARMENT **2 a :** a light stroking, rubbing, or patting **b :** KISS — **ca·res·sive** \-ˈres-iv\ *adj* — **ca·res·sive·ly** *adv*

2caress *vt* (1658) **1 :** to treat with tokens of fondness, affection, or kindness : CHERISH **2 a :** to touch or stroke lightly in a loving or endearing manner **b :** to touch or affect as if with a caress ⟨echoes that ~ the ear⟩ — **ca·ress·er** *n* — **ca·ress·ing·ly** \-iŋ-lē\ *adv*

car·et \ˈkar-ət\ *n* [L, there is lacking, fr. *carēre* to lack, be without — more at CASTE] (1681) **:** a wedge-shaped mark made on written or printed matter to indicate the place where something is to be inserted

care·tak·er \ˈke(ə)r-ˌtā-kər, ˈka(ə)r-\ *n* (1858) **1 :** one that takes care of the house or land of an owner who may be absent **2 :** one temporarily fulfilling the function of office ⟨a ~ government⟩ **3 :** one that gives physical or emotional care and support ⟨served as ~ to the younger children⟩ — **care·take** \-ˌtāk\ *vb* — **care·tak·ing** *n*

care·worn \-ˌwō(ə)rn, -ˌwȯ(ə)rn\ *adj* (1828) **:** showing the effect of grief or anxiety ⟨a ~ face⟩

car·ex \ˈka(ə)r-ˌeks\ *n, pl* **car·i·ces** \ˈkar-ə-ˌsēz\ [NL, genus name, fr. L, sedge] (14c) **:** any of a genus (*Carex*) of perennial sedges that have seedlike achenes enclosed in a sac in the axil of a bract

car·fare \ˈkär-ˌfa(ə)r, -ˌfe(ə)r\ *n* (1870) **:** passenger fare (as on a bus)

car·ful \ˈkär-ˌfu̇l\ *n* (1832) **:** as much or as many as a car will hold

car·go \ˈkär-(ˌ)gō\ *n, pl* **cargoes** *or* **cargos** [Sp, load, charge, fr. *cargar* to load, fr. LL *carricare* — more at CHARGE] (1657) **:** the goods or merchandise conveyed in a ship, airplane, or vehicle : FREIGHT

cargo cult *n* (1949) **:** a Melanesian religious movement characterized by attempts to obtain goods of industrial societies by magical means

cargo pocket *n* (1974) **:** a large pocket usu. with a flap and a pleat

car·hop \ˈkär-ˌhäp\ *n* [*car* + *-hop* (as in *bellhop*)] (1937) **:** one who serves customers at a drive-in restaurant

Car·ib \ˈkar-əb\ *n* [NL *Caribes* (pl.), fr. Sp *Caribe*, fr. Arawakan *Carib* — more at CANNIBAL] (1555) **1 :** a member of an Indian people of northern So. America and the Lesser Antilles **2 :** the language of the Caribs

Ca·ri·ban \ˈkar-ə-bən, kə-ˈrē-bən\ *n* (1901) **1 :** a member of a group of Indian peoples of northern So. America, the Lesser Antilles, and the Caribbean coast of Honduras, Guatemala, and British Honduras **2 :** the language family comprising the languages of the Cariban peoples

Ca·rib·be·an \ˌkar-ə-ˈbē-ən, kə-ˈrib-ē-\ *adj* [NL *Caribbaeus*, fr. *Caribes*] (1777) **:** of or relating to the Caribs, the eastern and southern West Indies, or the Caribbean sea

ca·ri·be \kə-ˈrē-bē\ *n* [AmerSp, fr. Sp, Carib, cannibal] (1868) **:** PIRANHA

car·i·bou \ˈkar-ə-ˌbü\ *n, pl* **caribou** *or* **caribous** [CanF, of Algonquian origin] (1665) **:** any of several large deer (subspecies of *Rangifer tarandus*) of northern No. America and Siberia that have palmate antlers in both sexes and are grouped with the reindeer in one species

1car·i·ca·ture \ˈkar-i-kə-ˌchu̇(ə)r, -ˌt(y)u̇(ə)r\ *n* [It *caricatura*, lit., act of loading, fr. *caricare* to load, fr. LL *carricare*] (1712) **1 :** exaggeration by means of often ludicrous distortion of parts or characteristics **2 :** a representation esp. in literature or art that has the qualities of caricature **3 :** a distortion so gross as to seem like caricature — **car·i·ca·tur·al** \ˌkar-i-kə-ˈchu̇r-əl, -ˈt(y)u̇r-\ *adj* — **car·i·ca·tur·ist** \ˈkar-i-kə-ˌchu̇r-əst, -ˌt(y)u̇r-\ *n*

syn CARICATURE, BURLESQUE, PARODY, TRAVESTY mean a comic or grotesque imitation. CARICATURE implies ludicrous exaggeration of the characteristic features of a subject; BURLESQUE implies mockery either through treating a trivial subject in a mock-heroic style or through giving a serious or lofty subject a frivolous treatment; PARODY applies esp. to treatment of a trivial or ludicrous subject in the exactly imitated style of a well-known author or work; TRAVESTY implies that the subject remains unchanged but that the style is extravagant or absurd.

2caricature *vt* **-tured; -tur·ing** (1762) **:** to make or draw a caricature of : represent in caricature ⟨the portrait *caricatured* its subject⟩

car·ies \ˈka(ə)r-ēz, ˈke(ə)r-\ *n, pl* **caries** [L, decay; akin to Gk *kēr* death] (1634) **:** a progressive destruction of bone or tooth; *esp* **:** tooth decay

car·il·lon \ˈkar-ə-ˌlän, -lən\ *n* [F, alter. of OF *quarregnon*, fr. LL *quaternion-*, *quaternio* set of four — more at QUATERNION] (1775) **1 a :** a set of fixed chromatically tuned bells sounded by hammers controlled from a keyboard **b :** an electronic instrument imitating a carillon **2 :** a composition for the carillon

car·il·lon·neur \ˌkar-ə-lə-ˈnər, ˌkar-ē-ə-ˈnər\ *n* [F, fr. *carillon*] (1772) **:** a carillon player

ca·ri·na \kə-ˈrī-nə, -ˈrē-\ *n, pl* **-ri·nas** *or* **-ri·nae** \-ˈrī-ˌnē, -ˈrē-ˌnī\ [NL, fr. L, keel — more at CAREEN] (1704) **1 :** a keel-shaped anatomical part, ridge, or process; *esp* **:** the part of a papilionaceous flower that encloses the stamens and pistil **2** *cap* **:** a constellation in the southern hemisphere lying near the Southern Cross

car·i·nate \ˈkar-ə-ˌnāt, -nət\ *or* **car·i·nat·ed** \-ˌnāt-əd\ *adj* (1781) **:** having or shaped like a keel or carina

ca·ri·o·ca \ˌkar-ē-ˈō-kə\ *n* [Pg, fr. Tupi] (1830) **1** *cap* **:** a native or resident of Rio de Janeiro **2 a :** a variation of the samba **b :** the music for this dance

car·i·ous \ˈkar-ē-əs, ˈker-\ *adj* [L *cariosus*, fr. *caries*] (1676) **:** affected with caries

cark·ing \ˈkär-kiŋ\ *adj* [ME, fr. *carken*, lit., to load, burden, fr. ONF *carquier*, fr. LL *carricare*] (1565) **:** BURDENSOME, ANNOYING

carl *or* **carle** \ˈkar(-ə)l\ *n* [ME, fr. OE *-carl*, fr. ON *karl* man, carl; akin to OE *ceorl* churl — more at CHURL] (bef. 12c) **1 :** a man of the common people **2** *chiefly dial* **:** CHURL, BOOR

car·line *or* **car·lin** \ˈkär-lən\ *n* [ME *kerling*, fr. ON, fr. *karl* man] *chiefly Scot* (14c) **:** WOMAN; *esp* **:** an old woman

car·ling \ˈkär-liŋ, -lən\ *n* [F *carlingue*, fr. ONF *calingue*, fr. ON *kerling*, lit., old woman] (1611) **:** a fore-and-aft member supporting a deck of a ship or framing a deck opening

Car·list \ˈkär-ləst\ *n* [Sp *carlista*, fr. Don *Carlos*] (1830) **:** a supporter of Don Carlos or his successors as having rightful title to the Spanish throne — **Carlist** *adj*

car·load \ˈkär-ˈlōd, -ˌlōd\ *n* (1854) **1 :** a load that fills a car **2 :** the minimum number of tons required for shipping at carload rates

carload rate *n* (1906) **:** a rate for large shipments lower than that quoted for less-than-carload lots of the same class

Car·lo·vin·gian \ˌkär-lə-ˈvin-j(ē-)ən\ *adj* [F *carlovingien*, prob. fr. ML *Car*lus Charles + F *-ovingien* (as in *mérovingien* Merovingian)] (1781) **:** CAROLINGIAN

car·ma·gnole \ˈkär-mən-ˌyōl\ *n* [F] (1793) **1 :** a lively song popular at the time of the first French Revolution **2 :** a street dance in a meandering course to the tune of the carmagnole

car·mak·er \ˈkär-ˌmā-kər\ *n* (1954) **:** an automobile manufacturer

Car·mel·ite \ˈkär-mə-ˌlīt\ *n* [ME, fr. ML *carmelita*, fr. *Carmel* Mount Carmel, Palestine] (15c) **:** a member of the Roman Catholic mendicant Order of Our Lady of Mount Carmel founded in the 12th century — **Carmelite** *adj*

car·mi·na·tive \kär-ˈmin-ət-iv, ˈkär-mə-ˌnāt-\ *adj* [F *carminatif*, fr. L *carminatus*, pp. of *carminare* to card, fr. *carmin-*, *carmen* card, fr. *carrere* to card — more at CHARD] (15c) **:** expelling gas from the alimentary canal so as to relieve colic or griping — **carminative** *n*

car·mine \ˈkär-mən, -ˌmīn\ *n* [F *carmin*, fr. ML *carminium*, irreg. fr. Ar *qirmiz* kermes + L *minium* — more at MINIUM] (1712) **1 :** a rich crimson or scarlet lake made from cochineal **2 :** a vivid red

car·nage \ˈkär-nij\ *n* [F, fr. ML *carnaticum* tribute consisting of animals or meat, fr. L *carn-*, *caro*] (1656) **1 :** the flesh of slain animals or men **2 :** great and bloody slaughter (as in battle)

car·nal \ˈkärn-ᵊl\ *adj* [ME, fr. ONF or LL; ONF, fr. LL *carnalis*, fr. L *carn-*, *caro* flesh; akin to Gk *keirein* to cut — more at SHEAR] (14c) **1 :** BODILY, CORPOREAL **2 a :** marked by sexuality **b :** relating to or given to crude bodily pleasures and appetites **3 a :** TEMPORAL **b :** WORLDLY — **car·nal·i·ty** \kär-ˈnal-ət-ē\ *n* — **car·nal·ly** \ˈkärn-ᵊl-ē\ *adv*

syn CARNAL, FLESHLY, SENSUAL, ANIMAL mean having a relation to the body. CARNAL may mean only this but more often connotes derogatorily an action or manifestation of man's lower nature; FLESHLY is somewhat less derogatory than CARNAL; SENSUAL may apply to any gratification of a bodily desire or pleasure but commonly implies sexual appetite with absence of the spiritual or intellectual; ANIMAL stresses a relation to man's physical as distinguished from his rational nature.

car·nall·ite \ˈkärn-ᵊl-ˌīt\ *n* [G *carnallit*, fr. Rudolf von *Carnall* †1874 Ger. mining engineer] (1876) **:** a mineral $KMgCl_3 \cdot 6H_2O$ consisting of hydrous potassium-magnesium chloride important as a source of potassium

car·nas·si·al \kär-ˈnas-ē-əl\ *adj* [F *carnassier* carnivorous, deriv. of L *carn-*, *caro*] (ca. 1849) **:** of, relating to, or being teeth of a carnivore often larger and longer than adjacent teeth and adapted for cutting rather than tearing — **carnassial** *n*

car·na·tion \kär-ˈnā-shən\ *n* [MF, fr. OIt *carnagione*, fr. *carne* flesh, fr. L *carn-*, *caro*] (1535) **1 a** (1) **:** the variable color of human flesh (2) **:** a pale to grayish yellow **b :** a moderate red **2 :** a plant of any of numerous often cultivated and usu. double-flowered varieties or subspecies of an Old World pink (*Dianthus caryophyllus*) orig. flesh-colored but now found in many color variations

car·nau·ba \kär-ˈnȯ-bə, -ˈnau̇-; ˌkär-nə-ˈü-bə\ *n* [Pg] (1866) **:** a fan-leaved palm (*Copernicia cerifera*) of Brazil that has an edible root and yields a useful leaf fiber and carnauba wax

carnauba wax *n* (1854) **:** a hard brittle high-melting wax from the leaves of the carnauba palm used chiefly in polishes

car·ne·lian \kär-ˈnēl-yən\ *n* [alter. of *cornelian*, fr. ME *corneline*, fr. MF, perh. fr. *cornelle* cornel] (1695) **:** a hard tough chalcedony that has a reddish color and is used in jewelry

car·ni·tine \ˈkär-nə-ˌtēn\ *n* [ISV, deriv. of L *carn-*, *caro* meat, flesh] (ca. 1922) **:** a white betaine that is an essential vitamin for some insect larvae (as a mealworm) and that occurs in vertebrate muscle

car·ni·val \ˈkär-nə-vəl\ *n* [It *carnevale*, alter. of earlier *carnelevare*, lit., removal of meat, fr. *carne* flesh (fr. L *carn-*, *caro*) + *levare* to remove, fr. L, to raise] (1549) **1 :** a season or festival of merrymaking before Lent **2 :** an instance of merrymaking, feasting, or masquerading **3**

a : a traveling enterprise offering amusements b : an organized program of entertainment or exhibition : FESTIVAL ⟨a winter ~⟩
car·niv·o·ra \kär-ˈniv-ə-rə\ *n pl* [L, neut. pl of *carnivorus*] (1865) : carnivorous mammals
car·ni·vore \ˈkär-nə-ˌvō(ə)r, -ˌvȯ(ə)r\ *n* [deriv. of L *carnivorus*] (1840) **1** : a flesh-eating animal; *esp* : any of an order (Carnivora) of flesh-eating mammals **2** : an insectivorous plant
car·niv·o·rous \kär-ˈniv-(ə-)rəs\ *adj* [L *carnivorus,* fr. *carn-, caro* flesh + *-vorus* -vorous — more at CARNAL] (1646) **1** : subsisting or feeding on animal tissues **2** *of a plant* : subsisting on nutrients obtained from the breakdown of animal protoplasm **3** : of or relating to the carnivores **4** : RAPACIOUS — **car·niv·o·rous·ly** *adv* — **car·niv·o·rous·ness** *n*
car·no·tite \ˈkär-nə-ˌtīt\ *n* [F, fr. M. A. *Carnot* †1920 Fr. inspector general of mines] (1899) : a mineral $K_2(UO_2)_2(VO_4)_2{\cdot}3H_2O$ consisting of a hydrous radioactive vanadate of uranium and potassium that is a source of radium and uranium
car·ny *or* **car·ney** *or* **car·nie** \ˈkär-nē\ *n, pl* **carnies** *or* **carneys** (1933) **1** : CARNIVAL 3a **2** : one who works with a carnival — **carny** *adj*
car·ob \ˈkar-əb\ *n* [MF *carobe,* fr. ML *carrubium,* fr. Ar *kharrūbah*] (1548) **1** : a Mediterranean evergreen leguminous tree (*Ceratonia siliqua*) with racemose red flowers **2** : a carob pod; *also* : its sweet pulp
ca·roche \kə-ˈrōch, -ˈrōsh\ *n* [MF *carroche,* fr. OIt *carroccio,* aug. of *carro* car, fr. L *carrus*] (1591) : a luxurious or stately horse-drawn carriage
[1]**car·ol** \ˈkar-əl\ *n* [ME *carole,* fr. MF, modif. of LL *choraula* choral song, fr. L, choral accompanist, fr. Gk *choraulēs,* fr. *choros* chorus + *aulein* to play a reed instrument, fr. *aulos,* a reed instrument — more at ALVEOLUS] (14c) **1** : an old round dance with singing **2** : a song of joy or mirth ⟨the ~ of a bird —Lord Byron⟩ **3** : a popular song or ballad of religious joy
[2]**carol** *vb* **-oled** *or* **-olled; -ol·ing** *or* **-ol·ling** *vi* (14c) **1** : to sing esp. in a joyful manner **2** : to sing carols; *specif* : to go about outdoors in a group singing Christmas carols ~ *vt* **1** : to praise in or as if in song **2** : to sing esp. in a cheerful manner : WARBLE — **car·ol·er** *or* **car·ol·ler** \-ə-lər\ *n*
Car·o·line \ˈkar-ə-ˌlīn, -lən\ *or* **Car·o·le·an** \ˌkar-ə-ˈlē-ən\ *adj* [NL *carolinus,* fr. ML *Carolus* Charles] (1562) : of or relating to Charles — used esp. with reference to Charles I and Charles II of England
Car·o·lin·gian \ˌkar-ə-ˈlin-j(ē-)ən\ *adj* [F *carolingien,* fr. ML *karolingi* French people, prob. fr. (assumed) OHG *karling* Frenchman, fr. *Karl* Charles] (1881) : of or relating to a Frankish dynasty dating from about A.D. 613 and including among its members the rulers of France from 751 to 987, of Germany from 752 to 911, and of Italy from 774 to 961 — **Carolingian** *n*
[1]**car·om** \ˈkar-əm\ *n* [by shortening & alter. fr. obs. *carambole,* fr. Sp *carambola*] (1779) **1 a** : a shot in billiards in which the cue ball strikes each of two object balls **b** : a shot in pool in which an object ball strikes another ball before falling into a pocket — compare COMBINATION SHOT **2** : a rebounding esp. at an angle
[2]**carom** *vi* (1860) **1** : to strike and rebound : GLANCE ⟨the car ~*ed* off several trees⟩ **2** : to make a carom
car·o·tene \ˈkar-ə-ˌtēn\ *n* [ISV, fr. LL *carota* carrot] (1861) : any of several orange or red crystalline hydrocarbon pigments (as $C_{40}H_{56}$) that occur in the chromoplasts of plants and in the fatty tissues of plant-eating animals and are convertible to vitamin A
ca·rot·enoid *also* **ca·rot·i·noid** \kə-ˈrät-ᵊn-ˌȯid\ *n* (1911) : any of various usu. yellow to red pigments (as carotenes) found widely in plants and animals and characterized chemically by a long aliphatic polyene chain composed of isoprene units — **carotenoid** *adj*
ca·rot·id \kə-ˈrät-əd\ *adj* [F or Gk; F *carotide,* fr. Gk *karōtides* carotid arteries, fr. *karoun* to stupefy; akin to Gk *kara* head — more at CEREBRAL] (1667) : of, relating to, or being the chief artery or pair of arteries that pass up the neck and supply the head — **carotid** *n*
carotid body *n* (1940) : a small body of vascular tissue that adjoins the carotid sinus, functions as a chemoreceptor sensitive to change in the oxygen content of blood, and mediates reflex changes in respiratory activity
carotid sinus *n* (1944) : a small but richly innervated arterial enlargement that is located near the point in the neck where either carotid artery divides to form its main branches and that functions in the regulation of heart rate and blood pressure
ca·rous·al \kə-ˈrau̇-zəl\ *n* (1765) : CAROUSE 2
[1]**ca·rouse** \kə-ˈrau̇z\ *n* [MF *carrousse,* fr. *carous,* adv., all out (in *boire carous* to empty the cup), fr. G *gar aus*] (1559) **1** *archaic* : a large draft of liquor : TOAST **2** : a drunken revel
[2]**carouse** *vb* **ca·roused; ca·rous·ing** *vi* (1567) **1** : to drink liquor deeply or freely **2** : to take part in a carouse ~ *vt, obs* : to drink up : QUAFF — **ca·rous·er** *n*
car·ou·sel \ˌkar-ə-ˈsel *also* -ˈzel; ˈkar-ə-ˌ\ *n* [F *carrousel,* fr. It *carosello*] (1650) **1** : a tournament or exhibition in which horsemen execute evolutions **2 a** : MERRY-GO-ROUND **b** : a circular conveyer on which objects are placed ⟨the luggage ~ at the airport⟩
[1]**carp** \ˈkärp\ *vi* [ME *carpen,* of Scand origin; akin to Icel *karpa* to dispute] (14c) : to find fault or complain querulously — **carp·er** *n*
[2]**carp** *n* (1904) : COMPLAINT
[3]**carp** *n, pl* **carp** *or* **carps** [ME *carpe,* fr. MF, fr. LL *carpa,* prob. of Gmc origin; akin to OHG *karpfo* carp] (15c) **1** : a large variable Old World soft-finned freshwater fish (*Cyprinus carpio*) of sluggish waters often raised for food; *also* : any of various related cyprinid fishes **2** : a fish (as the European sea bream) resembling a carp
carp- *or* **carpo-** *comb form* [F & NL, fr. Gk *karp-, karpo-,* fr. *karpos* — more at HARVEST] : fruit ⟨*carpology*⟩
-carp \ˌkärp\ *n comb form* [NL *-carpium,* fr. Gk *-karpion,* fr. *karpos*] : part of a fruit ⟨meso*carp*⟩ : fruit ⟨schizo*carp*⟩
car·pac·cio \kär-ˈpäch(-ē)-ō\ *n* [Vittore *Carpaccio;* fr. the prominent use of red in his painting] (1969) : slices of raw beef served with a sauce
[1]**car·pal** \ˈkär-pəl\ *adj* [NL *carpalis,* fr. *carpus*] (1743) : relating to the carpus
[2]**carpal** *n* (1855) : a carpal element or bone
car park *n, chiefly Brit* (1926) : PARKING LOT
car·pe di·em \ˌkär-pe-ˈdē-ˌem, -ˈdī-, -əm\ *n* [L, lit., pluck the day] (1817) : the enjoyment of the pleasures of the moment without concern for the future ⟨the *carpe diem* theme in poetry⟩
car·pel \ˈkär-pəl\ *n* [NL *carpellum,* fr. Gk *karpos* fruit] (1835) : one of the structures in a seed plant comprising the innermost whorl of a flower, functioning as megasporophylls, and collectively constituting the gynoecium — **car·pel·lary** \-pə-ˌler-ē\ *adj* — **car·pel·late** \-ˌlāt, -lət\ *adj*

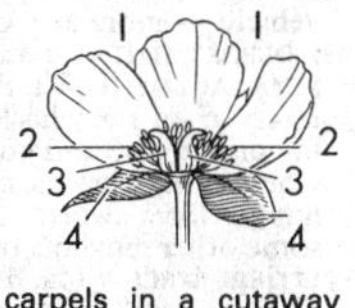

carpels in a cutaway flower: *1* petals, *2* stamens, *3* carpels, *4* sepals

[1]**car·pen·ter** \ˈkär-pən-tər, ˈkärp-ᵊm-tər\ *n* [ME, fr. ONF *carpentier,* fr. L *carpentarius* carriage maker, fr. *carpentum* carriage, of Celt origin; akin to OIr *carr* vehicle — more at CAR] (14c) : a workman who builds or repairs wooden structures or their structural parts
[2]**carpenter** *vb* **-tered; -ter·ing** \-t(ə-)riŋ\ *vi* (1815) : to follow the trade of a carpenter ⟨~*ed* when he was young⟩ ~ *vt* **1** : to make by or as if by carpentry **2** : to put together often in a mechanical manner ⟨~*ed* many television scripts⟩
carpenter ant *n* (1883) : an ant (esp. genus *Campanotus*) that gnaws galleries in dead or decayed wood
carpenter bee *n* (1838) : any of various solitary bees (*Xylocopa* and related genera) that gnaw galleries in sound timber
car·pen·try \-trē\ *n* (14c) **1** : the art or trade of a carpenter; *specif* : the art of shaping and assembling structural woodwork **2** : timberwork constructed by a carpenter **3** : the form or manner of putting together the parts (as of a literary or musical composition) : STRUCTURE, ARRANGEMENT
car·pet \ˈkär-pət\ *n* [ME, fr. MF *carpite,* fr. OIt *carpita,* fr. *carpire* to pluck, modif. of L *carpere* to pluck — more at HARVEST] (15c) **1** : a heavy woven or felted fabric used as a floor covering; *also* : a floor covering made of this fabric **2** : a surface resembling or suggesting a carpet — **carpet** *vt* — **on the carpet** : before an authority for censure or reproof
[1]**car·pet·bag** \-ˌbag\ *n* (1830) : a traveling bag made of carpet and widely used in the U.S. in the 19th century
[2]**carpetbag** *adj* (1870) : of, relating to, or characteristic of carpetbaggers ⟨a ~ government⟩
car·pet·bag·ger \-ˌbag-ər\ *n* [fr. their carrying all their belongings in carpetbags] (1864) **1** : a Northerner in the South after the American Civil War usu. seeking private gain under the reconstruction governments **2** : OUTSIDER; *esp* : a nonresident who meddles in politics — **car·pet·bag·gery** \-ˌbag-(ə-)rē\ *n*
car·pet·bag·ging \-ˌbag-iŋ\ *adj* (1870) : [2]CARPETBAG
carpetbag steak *n* (1958) : a thick piece of steak in which a pocket is cut and stuffed with oysters
carpet beetle *n* (1889) : any of several small dermestid beetles (esp. *Anthrenus scrophulariae* and *Attagenus megatoma*) whose larvae damage woolen goods
carpet bombing *n* (1944) : the dropping of large numbers of bombs so as to cause uniform devastation over a given area — **carpet bomb** *vb*
car·pet·ing \ˈkär-pət-iŋ\ *n* (1758) : material for carpets; *also* : CARPETS
car·pet·weed \ˈkär-pət-ˌwēd\ *n* (1784) : a No. American mat-forming weed (*Mollugo verticillata* of the family Aizoaceae, the carpetweed family)
-car·pic \ˈkär-pik\ *adj comb form* [prob. fr. NL *-carpicus,* fr. Gk *karpos* fruit] : -CARPOUS ⟨poly*carpic*⟩
carp·ing \ˈkär-piŋ\ *adj* (1581) : marked by or inclined to querulous and often perverse criticism ***syn*** see CRITICAL — **carp·ing·ly** \-piŋ-lē\ *adv*
car·po·go·ni·um \ˌkär-pə-ˈgō-nē-əm\ *n, pl* **-nia** \-nē-ə\ [NL] (1882) : the flask-shaped egg-bearing portion of the female reproductive branch in some thallophytes — **car·po·go·ni·al** \-nē-əl\ *adj*
car·pool \ˈkär-ˌpül\ *vi* (1967) : to participate in a car pool — **car·pool·er** *n*
car pool *n* (ca. 1943) : a joint arrangement by a group of private automobile owners in which each in turn drives his own car and carries the other passengers; *also* : the group entering into such an agreement
car·po·phore \ˈkär-pə-ˌfō(ə)r, -ˌfȯ(ə)r\ *n* [prob. fr. NL *carpophorum,* fr. *carp-* + *-phorum* -phore] (ca. 1864) **1** : the stalk of a fungal fruiting body; *also* : the entire fruiting body **2** : a slender prolongation of a floral axis from which the carpels are suspended
car·port \ˈkär-ˌpō(ə)rt, -ˌpȯ(ə)rt\ *n* (1939) : an open-sided automobile shelter sometimes formed by extension of a roof from the side of a building
car·po·spore \ˈkär-pə-ˌspō(ə)r, -ˌspȯ(ə)r\ *n* (1881) : a diploid spore of a red alga
-car·pous \ˈkär-pəs\ *adj comb form* [NL *-carpus,* fr. Gk *-karpos,* fr. *karpos* fruit — more at HARVEST] : having (such) fruit or (so many) fruits ⟨poly*carpous*⟩ — **-car·py** \ˌkär-pē\ *n comb form*
car·pus \ˈkär-pəs\ *n, pl* **car·pi** \-ˌpī, -(ˌ)pē\ [NL, fr. Gk *karpos* — more at WHARF] (1679) **1** : WRIST 1 **2** : the bones of the wrist
car·rack \ˈkar-ək, -ik\ *n* [ME *carrake,* fr. MF *caraque,* fr. OSp *carraca,* fr. Ar *qarāqir,* pl. of *qurqūr* merchant ship] (14c) : a beamy sailing ship of the 14th and 15th centuries
car·ra·geen *also* **car·ra·gheen** \ˈkar-ə-ˌgēn\ *n* [*Carragheen,* near Waterford, Ireland] (1834) **1** : IRISH MOSS 2 **2** : CARRAGEENAN
car·ra·geen·an *or* **car·ra·geen·in** \ˌkar-ə-ˈgē-nən\ *n* [*carrageen* + [3]*-an* or *-in*] (ca. 1889) : a colloid extracted from various red algae and esp. Irish moss and used esp. as a suspending agent (as in foods) and as a clarifying agent (as for beverages) and in controlling crystal growth in frozen confections
car·re·four \ˌkar-ə-ˈfu̇(ə)r\ *n* [MF, fr. LL *quadrifurcum,* neut. of *quadrifurcus* having four forks, fr. L *quadri-* + *furca* fork] (15c) **1** : CROSSROADS **2** : SQUARE, PLAZA ⟨the farmers . . . preferred the open ~ for their transactions —Thomas Hardy⟩
car·rel \ˈkar-əl\ *n* [alter. of ME *carole* round dance, ring — more at CAROL] (1593) : a table that is often partitioned or enclosed and is used for individual study esp. in a library

car·riage \ˈkar-ij\ *n* [ME *cariage,* fr. ONF, fr. *carier* to transport in a vehicle — more at CARRY] (14c) **1 :** the act of carrying **2 a** *archaic* **:** DEPORTMENT **b :** manner of bearing the body **:** POSTURE **3** *archaic* **:** MANAGEMENT **4 :** the price or expense of carrying **5** *obs* **:** BURDEN, LOAD **6 a :** a wheeled vehicle; *esp* **:** a horse-drawn vehicle designed for private use and comfort **b** *Brit* **:** a railway passenger coach **7 :** a wheeled support carrying a burden **8** *obs* **:** IMPORT, SENSE **9** *obs* **:** a hanger for a sword **10 :** a movable part of a machine for supporting some other movable object or part ⟨a typewriter ~⟩ ***syn*** see BEARING

carriage trade *n* (ca. 1909) **:** trade from well-to-do or upper-class people; *also* **:** well-to-do people

car·riage·way \ˈkar-ij-ˌwā\ *n, Brit* (1800) **:** a road used by vehicular traffic **:** HIGHWAY; *specif* **:** LANE 2b

car·rick bend \ˌkar-ik-\ *n* [prob. fr. obs. E *carrick* carrack, fr. ME *carrake, carryk*] (1819) **:** a knot used to join the ends of two large ropes — see KNOT illustration

car·ri·er \ˈkar-ē-ər\ *n* (14c) **1 :** one that carries **:** BEARER, MESSENGER **2 a :** an individual or organization engaged in transporting passengers or goods for hire **b :** a transportation line carrying mail between post offices **c :** a postal employee who delivers or collects mail **d :** one that delivers newspapers **e :** an entity (as a hole or an electron) capable of carrying an electric charge **3 a :** a container for carrying **b :** a device or machine that carries **:** CONVEYER **4 :** AIRCRAFT CARRIER **5 a :** a bearer and transmitter of a causative agent of an infectious disease; *esp* **:** one who carries in his system the causative agent of a disease (as typhoid fever) to which he is immune **b :** an individual (as one heterozygous for a recessive) having a specified gene that is not expressed or only weakly expressed in its phenotype **6 a :** a usu. inactive accessory substance **:** VEHICLE ⟨a ~ for a drug or an insecticide⟩ **b :** a substance (as a catalyst) by whose agency some element or group is transferred from one compound to another **7 a :** an electric wave or alternating current whose modulations are used as signals in radio, telephonic, or telegraphic transmission **b :** a telecommunication company **8 :** an organization acting as an insurer

carrier pigeon *n* (1647) **1 :** a pigeon used to carry messages; *esp* **:** HOMING PIGEON **2 :** any of a breed of large long-bodied show pigeons

car·ri·on \ˈkar-ē-ən\ *n* [ME *caroine,* fr. AF, fr. (assumed) VL *caronia,* irreg. fr. L *carn-, caro* flesh — more at CARNAL] (13c) **:** dead and putrefying flesh; *also* **:** flesh unfit for food

carrion crow *n* (1528) **:** a uniformly black crow (*Corvus corone corone*) occurring in much of western Europe

car·ron·ade \ˌkar-ə-ˈnād\ *n* [*Carron,* Scotland] (1779) **:** an obsolete short light iron cannon

car·rot \ˈkar-ət\ *n* [MF *carotte,* fr. LL *carota,* fr. Gk *karōton*] (1533) **1 :** a biennial herb (*Daucus carota* of the family Umbelliferae, the carrot family) with a usu. orange spindle-shaped edible root; *also* **:** its root **2 :** a promised often illusory reward or advantage

car·rot–and–stick \ˌkar-ət-ᵊn-ˈstik\ *adj* [fr. the traditional alternatives of driving a donkey on by either holding out a carrot or whipping it with a stick] (1951) **:** characterized by use of alternating reward and punishment ⟨~ foreign policy⟩

car·roty \-ət-ē\ *adj* (1696) **1 :** resembling carrots in color **2 :** having hair the color of carrots

car·rou·sel *var of* CAROUSEL

[1]**car·ry** \ˈkar-ē\ *vb* **car·ried; car·ry·ing** [ME *carien,* fr. ONF *carier* to transport in a vehicle, fr. *car* vehicle, fr. L *carrus* — more at CAR] *vt* (14c) **1 :** to move while supporting (as a package) **:** TRANSPORT ⟨her legs refused to ~ her further —Ellen Glasgow⟩ **2 :** to convey by direct communication ⟨~ tales about a friend⟩ **3** *chiefly dial* **:** CONDUCT, ESCORT **4 :** to influence by mental or emotional appeal **:** SWAY **5 :** to get possession or control of **:** CAPTURE ⟨*carried* off the prize⟩ **6 :** to transfer from one place (as a column) to another ⟨~ a number in adding⟩ **7 :** to contain and direct the course of ⟨the drain *carries* sewage⟩ **8 a :** to wear or have on one's person **b :** to bear upon or within one ⟨is *~ing* an unborn child⟩ **9 a :** to have as a mark, attribute, or property ⟨~ a scar⟩ **b :** IMPLY, INVOLVE ⟨the crime *carried* a heavy penalty⟩ **10 :** to hold or comport (as one's person) in a specified manner **11 :** to sustain the weight or burden of ⟨pillars ~ an arch⟩ **12 :** to bear as a crop **13 :** to sing with reasonable correctness of pitch ⟨~ a tune⟩ **14 a :** to keep in stock for sale **b :** to provide sustenance for ⟨land *~ing* 10 head of cattle⟩ **c :** to have or maintain on a list or record ⟨~ a person on a payroll⟩ **15 :** to maintain and cause to continue through financial support or personal effort ⟨he *carried* the magazine single-handedly⟩ **16 :** to prolong in space, time, or degree ⟨~ a principle too far⟩ **17 a :** to gain victory for; *esp* **:** to secure the adoption or passage of **b :** to win a majority of votes in (as a legislative body or a state) **18 :** to present (as a news story or a television program) for public consumption ⟨newspapers ~ weather reports⟩ **19 a :** to bear the charges of holding or having (as stocks or merchandise) from one time to another **b :** to keep on one's books as a debtor ⟨a merchant *carries* a customer⟩ **20 :** to hold to and follow after (as a scent) **21 :** to hoist and maintain (a sail) in use **22 :** to cover (a distance) or pass (an object) at a single stroke in golf **23 :** to allow (an opponent) to make a good showing by lessening one's opposition ~ *vi* **1 :** to act as a bearer **2 a :** to reach or penetrate to a distance ⟨voices ~ well⟩ **b :** to convey itself to a reader or audience **3 :** to undergo or admit of carriage in a specified way **4** *of a hunting dog* **:** to keep and follow the scent **5 :** to win adoption ⟨the motion *carried* by a vote of 71-25⟩ — **carry a torch** *or* **carry the torch 1 :** CRUSADE **2 :** to be in love esp. without reciprocation **:** cherish a longing or devotion ⟨she still *carries a torch* for him even though their engagement is broken⟩ — **carry the ball :** to perform or assume the chief role **:** bear the major portion of work or responsibility — **carry the day :** WIN, PREVAIL

[2]**carry** *n* (1618) **1 a :** the act or method of carrying ⟨fireman's ~⟩ **b :** PORTAGE **c :** the act of rushing with the ball in football ⟨averaged four yards per ~⟩ **2 :** carrying power; *esp* **:** the range of a gun or projectile or of a struck or thrown ball **3 :** the position assumed by a color-bearer with the flag or guidon held in position for marching **4 :** a quantity that is transferred in addition from one number place to the adjacent one of higher place value

car·ry·all \ˈkar-ē-ˌȯl\ *n* (1714) **1** [by folk etymology fr. F *carriole,* fr. OProv *carriola,* deriv. of L *carrus* car] **a :** a light covered carriage for four or more persons **b :** a passenger automobile used as a small bus **2** [[1]*carry* + *all*] **:** a capacious bag or carrying case **3 :** a self-loading carrier esp. for hauling earth and crushed rock

carry away *vt* (1537) **1 :** CARRY OFF **2 :** to arouse to a high and often excessive degree of emotion or enthusiasm

car·ry·back \ˈkar-ē-ˌbak\ *n* (1942) **:** a loss sustained or a portion of a credit not used in a given period that may be deducted from taxable income of a prior period

car·ry·for·ward \ˈkar-ē-ˌfȯr-wərd, *Southern also* -ˌfär-\ *n* (1898) **:** CARRYOVER

carrying capacity *n* (1883) **:** the population (as of deer) that an area will support without undergoing deterioration

carrying charge *n* (1894) **1 :** expense incident to ownership or use of property **2 :** a charge added to the price of merchandise sold on the installment plan

car·ry·ing–on \ˌkar-ē-iŋ-ˈȯn, -ˈän\ *n, pl* **carryings–on** (1663) **:** foolish, excited, or improper behavior; *also* **:** an instance of such behavior

carry off *vt* (1680) **1 :** to cause the death of ⟨the plague *carried off* thousands⟩ **2 :** to perform easily or successfully **:** BRING OFF ⟨the actress *carried off* her part brilliantly in spite of only a few rehearsals⟩

car·ry·on \ˈkar-ē-ˌȯn, -ˌän\ *n* (1955) **:** a piece of luggage suitable for being carried aboard an airplane by a passenger — **car·ry–on** \ˈkar-ē-ˌȯn, -ˌän\ *adj*

carry on *vt* (1644) **:** to maintain in operation ⟨*carried on* the business⟩ ~ *vi* **1 :** to behave in a foolish, excited, or improper manner ⟨embarrassed by the way he *carries on*⟩ **2 :** to continue one's course or activity in spite of hindrance or discouragement

car·ry·out \ˈkar-ē-ˌau̇t\ *n* (1966) **:** a food item packaged to be carried out and consumed away from its place of sale — **carryout** *adj*

carry out \ˌkar-ē-ˈau̇t\ *vt* (1605) **1 :** to put into execution ⟨*carry out* a plan⟩ **2 :** to bring to a successful issue **:** COMPLETE, ACCOMPLISH ⟨you will be paid when you have *carried out* the assignment⟩ **3 :** to continue to an end or stopping point

car·ry·over \ˈkar-ē-ˌō-vər\ *n* (1894) **1 :** the act or process of carrying over **2 :** something carried over

carry over \ˌkar-ē-ˈō-vər\ *vt* (1745) **1 a :** to hold over (as goods) for another season **b :** to transfer (an amount) to the next column, page, or book relating to the same account **2 :** to deduct (a loss or an unused credit) for taxable income of a later period ~ *vi* **:** to persist from one stage or sphere of activity to another

carry through *vt* (1605) **:** CARRY OUT ~ *vi* **:** PERSIST, SURVIVE ⟨feelings that *carry through* to the present⟩

car·sick \ˈkär-ˌsik\ *adj* (1908) **:** affected with motion sickness esp. in an automobile — **car sickness** *n*

[1]**cart** \ˈkärt\ *n* [ME, prob. fr. ON *kartr;* akin to OE *crǣt* cart, OE *cradol* cradle] (13c) **1 :** a heavy usu. horse-drawn 2-wheeled vehicle used for farming or transporting freight **2 :** a lightweight 2-wheeled vehicle drawn by a horse, pony, or dog **3 :** a small wheeled vehicle

[2]**cart** *vt* (15c) **1 :** to carry or convey in or as if in a cart ⟨buses to ~ the kids to and from school —L. S. Gannett⟩ **2 :** to take or drag away without ceremony or by force — usu. used with *off* ⟨they *~ed* him off to jail⟩ — **cart·er** *n*

cart·age \ˈkärt-ij\ *n* (15c) **:** the act of or rate charged for carting

carte blanche \ˈkärt-ˈbläⁿsh, -ˈblänch\ *n, pl* **cartes blanches** \ˈkärt-ˈbläⁿsh(-əz), -ˈblänch(-əz)\ [F, lit., blank document] (1754) **:** full discretionary power ⟨was given *carte blanche* to build, landscape, and furnish the house⟩

carte du jour \ˌkärt-də-ˈzhu̇(ə)r\ *n, pl* **cartes du jour** \ˌkärt(s)-\ [F, lit., card of the day] (1936) **:** MENU

car·tel \kär-ˈtel\ *n* [F, letter of defiance, fr. OIt *cartello,* lit., placard, fr. *carta* leaf of paper — more at CARD] (1692) **1 :** a written agreement between belligerent nations **2 :** a combination of independent commercial or industrial enterprises designed to limit competition or fix prices **3 :** a combination of political groups for common action

Car·te·sian \kär-ˈtē-zhən\ *adj* [NL *cartesianus,* fr. *Cartesius* Descartes] (1656) **:** of or relating to René Descartes or his philosophy — **Cartesian** *n* — **Car·te·sian·ism** \-zhə-ˌniz-əm\ *n*

Cartesian coordinate *n* (ca. 1889) **1 :** either of two coordinates that locate a point on a plane and measure its distance from either of two intersecting straight-line axes along a line parallel to the other axis **2 :** any of three coordinates that locate a point in space and measure its distance from any of three intersecting coordinate planes measured parallel to that one of three straight-line axes that is the intersection of the other two planes

Cartesian plane *n* (1960) **:** a plane whose points are labeled with Cartesian coordinates

Cartesian product *n* (1958) **:** a set that is constructed from two given sets and comprises all pairs of elements such that one element of the pair is from the first set and the other element is from the second set

Car·thu·sian \kär-ˈth(y)ü-zhən\ *n* [ML *cartusiensis,* irreg. fr. OF *Chartrouse,* motherhouse of the Carthusian order, near Grenoble, France] (14c) **:** a member of an austere contemplative religious order founded by St. Bruno in 1084 — **Carthusian** *adj*

car·ti·lage \ˈkärt-ᵊl-ij, ˈkärt-lij\ *n* [L *cartilagin-, cartilago;* prob. akin to L *cratis* wickerwork — more at HURDLE] (15c) **1 :** a translucent elastic tissue that composes most of the skeleton of embryonic and very young vertebrates and becomes for the most part converted into bone in the higher vertebrates **2 :** a part or structure composed of cartilage

car·ti·lag·i·nous \ˌkärt-ᵊl-ˈaj-ə-nəs\ *adj* (15c) **:** composed of, relating to, or resembling cartilage

cartilaginous fish *n* (1695) **:** any of the fishes (esp. class Chondrichthyes) having the skeleton wholly or largely composed of cartilage; *also* **:** CYCLOSTOME

cart·load \ˈkärt-ˈlōd, -ˌlōd\ *n* (14c) **1 :** as much as a cart will hold **2 :** one third of a cubic yard (as of dirt)

car·tog·ra·pher \kär-ˈtäg-rə-fər\ *n* (ca. 1847) **:** one that makes maps

car·tog·ra·phy \-fē\ *n* [F *cartographie,* fr. *carte* card, map + *-graphie* -graphy — more at CARD] (ca. 1847) **:** the science or art of making maps — **car·to·graph·ic** \ˌkärt-ə-ˈgraf-ik\ *also* **car·to·graph·i·cal** \-i-kəl\ *adj* — **car·to·graph·i·cal·ly** \-i-k(ə-)lē\ *adv*

[1]**car·ton** \ˈkärt-ᵊn\ *n* [F, fr. It *cartone* pasteboard] (ca. 1864) **:** a usu. cardboard box or container

[2]**carton** *vt* (1921) **:** to pack or enclose in a carton ~ *vi* **:** to shape cartons from cardboard sheets

car·toon \kär-ˈtün\ *n* [It *cartone* pasteboard, cartoon, aug. of *carta* leaf of paper — more at CARD] (1671) **1 :** a preparatory design, drawing, or painting (as for a fresco) **2 a :** a drawing intended as satire, caricature, or humor ⟨a political ~⟩ **b :** COMIC STRIP **3 :** ANIMATED CARTOON **4 :** CARICATURE 2 — **cartoon** *vb* — **car·toon·ing** *n* — **car·toon·ish** \-ˈtü-nish\ *adj* — **car·toon·ist** \-ˈtü-nəst\ *n*

car·top \ˈkär-ˌtäp\ *adj* (1946) **:** suitable in size and weight for carrying on top of an automobile ⟨a ~ fishing boat⟩ — **car·top·per** \-ˌtäp-ər\ *n*

car·touche *also* **car·touch** \kär-ˈtüsh\ *n* [F *cartouche,* fr. It *cartoccio,* fr. *carta*] (1611) **1 :** a gun cartridge with a paper case **2 :** an ornate or ornamental frame **3 :** an oval or oblong figure (as on ancient Egyptian monuments) enclosing a sovereign's name

car·tridge \ˈkär-trij, *dial* ˈka-trij\ *n* [alter. of earlier *cartage,* modif. of MF *cartouche*] (1579) **:** a case or container that holds a substance, device, or material which is difficult, troublesome, or awkward to handle and that usu. can be easily changed: as **a :** a tube of metal, paper, or both containing a complete charge for a firearm and usu. an initiating device (as a primer) **b :** a case containing an explosive charge for blasting **c :** an often cylindrical container for insertion into a larger mechanism or apparatus **d :** CASSETTE 2 **e :** a small case in a phonograph pickup containing the needle and the mechanism for translating stylus motion into electrical voltage **f :** a case containing a reel of magnetic tape arranged for insertion into a recorder or player **g :** a removable case containing a magnetic tape or one or more disks and used as a computer storage medium **h :** a case for holding printed circuit chips containing a computer program ⟨a video-game ~⟩

cartridge belt *n* (1874) **1 :** a belt having a series of loops for holding cartridges **2 :** a belt worn around the waist and designed for carrying various attachable equipment (as a cartridge case, canteen, or compass)

car·tu·lary \ˈkär-chə-ˌler-ē\ *n, pl* **-lar·ies** [ML *chartularium,* fr. *chartula* charter — more at CHARTER] (1541) **:** a collection of charters; *esp* **:** a book holding copies of the charters and title deeds of an estate

1**cart·wheel** \ˈkärt-ˌ(h)wēl\ *n* (1855) **1 :** a large coin (as a silver dollar) **2 :** a lateral handspring with arms and legs extended

2**cartwheel** *vi* (1917) **:** to move like a turning wheel; *specif* **:** to perform cartwheels — **cart·wheel·er** *n*

ca·run·cle \ˈkar-ˌəŋ-kəl, kə-ˈrəŋ-\ *n* [obs. F *caruncule,* fr. L *caruncula* little piece of flesh, dim. of *caro* flesh — more at CARNAL] (1615) **1 :** a naked fleshy outgrowth (as a bird's wattle) **2 :** an outgrowth on a seed adjacent to the micropyle

car·va·crol \ˈkär-və-ˌkrȯl, -ˌkrōl\ *n* [ISV, fr. NL *carvi* (specific epithet of *Carum carvi* caraway) + L *acr-, acer* sharp — more at CARAWAY, EDGE] (1854) **:** a liquid phenol $C_{10}H_{14}O$ found in essential oils of various mints (as thyme) and used as a fungicide and disinfectant

carve \ˈkärv\ *vb* **carved; carv·ing** [ME *kerven,* fr. OE *ceorfan;* akin to OHG *kerban* to notch, Gk *graphein* to scratch, write] *vt* (bef. 12c) **1 :** to cut with care or precision ⟨*carved* fretwork⟩ **2 :** to make or get by or as if by cutting — often used with *out* ⟨~ out a career⟩ **3 :** to cut into pieces or slices ⟨*carved* the turkey⟩ ~ *vi* **1 :** to cut up and serve meat **2 :** to work as a sculptor or engraver — **carv·er** *n*

car·vel \ˈkär-vəl, -ˌvel\ *n* [ME *carvile,* fr. MF *carvelle*] (15c) **:** CARAVEL

car·vel–built \-ˌbilt\ *adj* [prob. fr. D *karveel-,* fr. *karveel* caravel, fr. MF *carvelle*] (1798) **:** built with the planks meeting flush at the seams

carv·en \ˈkär-vən\ *adj* (14c) **:** wrought or ornamented by carving

carv·ing \ˈkär-viŋ\ *n* (13c) **1 :** the act or art of one who carves **2 :** a carved object, design, or figure

car wash *n* (1956) **:** an area or structure equipped with facilities for washing automobiles

cary- *or* **caryo-** — see KARY-

cary·at·id \ˌkar-ē-ˈat-əd, ˈkar-ē-ə-ˌtid\ *n, pl* **-ids** *or* **-i·des** \ˌkar-ē-ˈat-ə-ˌdēz\ [L *caryatides,* pl., fr. Gk *karyatides* priestesses of Artemis at Caryae, caryatids, fr. *Karyai* Caryae in Laconia] (1563) **:** a draped female figure supporting an entablature

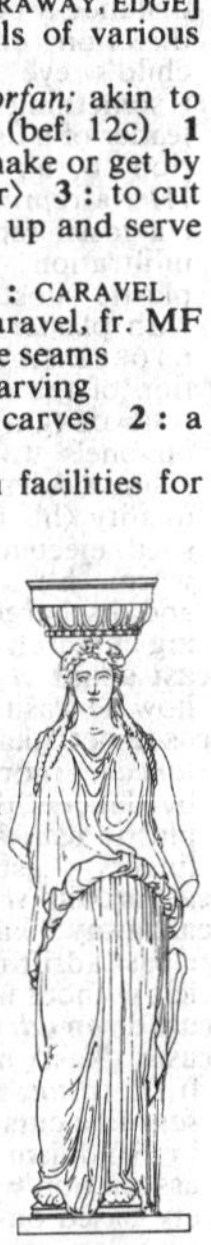

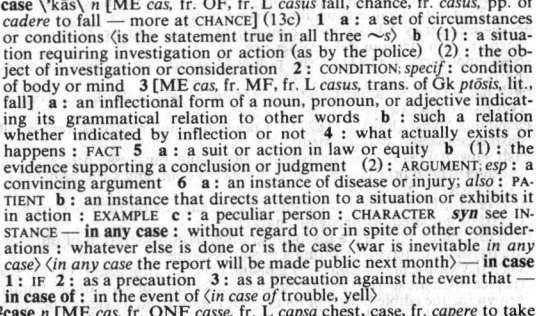

caryatid

cary·op·sis \ˌkar-ē-ˈäp-səs\ *n, pl* **-op·ses** \-ˌsēz\ *also* **-si·des** \-sə-ˌdēz\ [NL] (1830) **:** a small one-seeded dry indehiscent fruit (as of Indian corn or wheat) in which the fruit and seed fuse in a single grain

ca·sa \ˈkäs-ə\ *n* [Sp & It, fr. L, cabin] *Southwest* (1844) **:** DWELLING

ca·sa·ba \kə-ˈsäb-ə\ *n* [*Kasaba* (now Turgutlu), Turkey] (1889) **:** any of several winter melons with yellow rind and sweet flesh

Ca·sa·no·va \ˌkaz-ə-ˈnō-və, ˌkas-\ *n* [Giacomo Girolamo *Casanova*] (1888) **:** LOVER; *esp* **:** a man who is a promiscuous and unscrupulous lover

Cas·bah \ˈkaz-ˌbä, ˈkäz-\ *n* [F, fr. Ar dial. *qaṣbah*] (1944) **1 :** a No. African castle or fortress **2 :** the native section of a No. African city

cas·ca·bel \ˈkas-kə-ˌbel\ *n* [Sp, lit., small bell like a sleigh bell] (1639) **1 :** a projection behind the breech of a muzzle-loading cannon **2 :** a small hollow perforated spherical bell enclosing a loose pellet

1**cas·cade** \(ˈ)kas-ˈkād\ *n* [F, fr. It *cascata,* fr. *cascare* to fall, fr. (assumed) VL *casicare,* fr. L *casus,* pp. of *cadere* to fall] (1641) **1 :** a steep usu. small fall of water; *esp* **:** one of a series **2 a :** something arranged in a series or in a succession of stages so that each stage derives from or acts upon the product of the preceding **b :** a fall of material (as lace) that hangs in a zigzag line **3 :** something falling or rushing forth in quantity ⟨a ~ of sound⟩ ⟨a ~ of coins⟩

2**cascade** *vb* **cas·cad·ed; cas·cad·ing** *vi* (1702) **:** to fall or pour in or as if in a cascade ~ *vt* **1 :** to cause to fall like a cascade **2 :** to connect in a cascade arrangement

cas·cara \ka-ˈskar-ə\ *n* [Sp *cáscara* bark, fr. *cascar* to crack, break, fr. (assumed) VL *quassicare* to shake, break, fr. L *quassare* — more at QUASH] (1879) **1 :** CASCARA BUCKTHORN **2 :** CASCARA SAGRADA

cascara buckthorn *n* (ca. 1900) **:** a buckthorn (*Rhamnus purshiana*) of the Pacific coast of the U.S. yielding cascara sagrada

cascara sa·gra·da \-sə-ˈgräd-ə\ *n* [AmerSp *cáscara sagrada,* lit., sacred bark] (1885) **:** the dried bark of cascara buckthorn used as a laxative

cas·ca·ril·la \ˌkas-kə-ˈril-ə, -ˈrē-(y)ə\ *n* [Sp, dim. of *cáscara*] (1686) **:** the aromatic bark of a West Indian shrub (*Croton eluteria*) of the spurge family used for making incense and as a tonic; *also* **:** this shrub

1**case** \ˈkās\ *n* [ME *cas,* fr. OF, fr. L *casus* fall, chance, fr. *casus,* pp. of *cadere* to fall — more at CHANCE] (13c) **1 a :** a set of circumstances or conditions ⟨is the statement true in all three ~*s*⟩ **b** (1) **:** a situation requiring investigation or action (as by the police) (2) **:** the object of investigation or consideration **2 :** CONDITION; *specif* **:** condition of body or mind **3** [ME *cas,* fr. MF, fr. L *casus,* trans. of Gk *ptōsis,* lit., fall] **a :** an inflectional form of a noun, pronoun, or adjective indicating its grammatical relation to other words **b :** such a relation whether indicated by inflection or not **4 :** what actually exists or happens **:** FACT **5 a :** a suit or action in law or equity **b** (1) **:** the evidence supporting a conclusion or judgment (2) **:** ARGUMENT; *esp* **:** a convincing argument **6 a :** an instance of disease or injury; *also* **:** PATIENT **b :** an instance that directs attention to a situation or exhibits it in action **:** EXAMPLE **c :** a peculiar person **:** CHARACTER ***syn*** see INSTANCE — **in any case :** without regard to or in spite of other considerations **:** whatever else is done or is the case ⟨war is inevitable *in any case*⟩ ⟨*in any case* the report will be made public next month⟩ — **in case 1 :** IF **2 :** as a precaution **3 :** as a precaution against the event that — **in case of :** in the event of ⟨*in case of* trouble, yell⟩

2**case** *n* [ME *cas,* fr. ONF *casse,* fr. L *capsa* chest, case, fr. *capere* to take — more at HEAVE] (14c) **1 a :** a box or receptacle for holding something **b :** a box together with its contents **c :** SET; *specif* **:** PAIR **2 :** an outer covering or housing **3 :** a divided tray for holding printing type **4 :** the frame of a door or window **:** CASING

3**case** *vt* **cased; cas·ing** (1575) **1 :** to enclose in or cover with or as if with a case **:** ENCASE **2 :** to line (as a well) with supporting material (as metal pipe) **3 :** to inspect or study esp. with intent to rob

ca·se·ation \ˌkā-sē-ˈā-shən\ *n* [L *caseus* cheese — more at CHEESE] (1866) **:** necrosis with conversion of damaged tissue into a soft cheesy substance — **ca·se·ate** \ˈkā-sē-ˌāt\ *vi*

case·bear·er \ˈkās-ˌbar-ər, -ˌber-\ *n* (1895) **:** an insect larva that forms a protective case (as of silk)

case·book \-ˌbu̇k\ *n* (1762) **1 :** a book containing records of illustrative cases that is used for reference and instruction (as in law or medicine) **2 :** a compilation of primary and secondary documents relating to a central topic together with scholarly comment, exercises, and study aids that is designed to serve as a sourcebook for short papers (as in a course in composition) or as a point of departure for a research paper

cased glass \ˈkāst-\ *n* (1849) **:** glass consisting of two or more fused layers of different colors often decorated by cutting so that the inner layers show through — called also *case glass*

case goods *n pl* (1922) **1 :** furniture (as bureaus or bookcases) that provides interior storage space; *also* **:** dining-room and bedroom furniture sold as sets **2 :** products (as liquor or canned milk) often sold by the case

case hard·en \ˈkās-ˌhärd-ᵊn\ *vt* (1677) **1 :** to harden (a ferrous alloy) so that the surface layer is harder than the interior **2 :** to make callous or insensible — **case–hard·ened** *adj*

case history *n* (1894) **:** a record of history, environment, and relevant details (as of individual behavior or condition) esp. for use in analysis or illustration

ca·sein \kā-ˈsēn, ˈkā-sē-ən\ *n* [prob. fr. F *caséine,* fr. L *caseus*] (1841) **:** a phosphoprotein of milk: as **a :** one that is precipitated from milk by heating with an acid or by the action of lactic acid in souring and is used in making paints and adhesives **b :** one that is produced when milk is curdled by rennet, is the chief constituent of cheese, and is used in making plastics

ca·sein·ate \kā-ˈsē-ˌnāt, ˈkā-sē-ə-ˌnāt\ *n* (1904) **:** a compound of casein with a metal (as calcium or sodium)

case in point (1965) **:** an illustrative, relevant, or pertinent case **:** EXAMPLE

case knife *n* (1704) **1 :** SHEATH KNIFE **2 :** a table knife

case law *n* (1861) **:** law established by judicial decision in cases

case·load \ˈkā-ˌslōd\ *n* (1938) **:** the number of cases handled (as by a court or clinic) usu. in a particular period

case·mate \ˈkā-ˌsmāt\ *n* [MF, fr. OIt *casamatta*] (1575) **:** a fortified position or chamber or an armored enclosure on a warship from which guns are fired through embrasures

case·ment \ˈkā-smənt\ *n* [ME, hollow molding, prob. fr. ONF *encassement* frame, fr. *encasser* to enchase, frame, fr. *en-* + *casse*] (15c) **:** a window sash that opens on hinges at the side; *also* **:** a window with such a sash

ca·se·ous \ˈkā-sē-əs\ *adj* [L *caseus* cheese] (1661) **:** marked by caseation; *also* **:** CHEESY

ca·sern *or* **ca·serne** \kə-ˈzərn\ *n* [F *caserne*] (1696) **:** a military barracks in a garrison town

case shot *n* (1675) **:** an artillery projectile consisting of a number of balls or metal fragments enclosed in a case

case study *n* (1875) **1 :** an intensive analysis of an individual unit (as a person or community) stressing developmental factors in relation to environment **2 :** CASE HISTORY

case system *n* (ca. 1889) **:** a system of teaching law in which instruction is chiefly on the basis of leading or selected cases as primary authorities instead of from textbooks

case·work \ˈkā-ˌswərk\ *n* (1886) **:** social work involving direct consideration of the problems, needs, and adjustments of the individual case (as a person or family) — **case·work·er** \-ˌswər-kər\ *n*

1**cash** \ˈkash\ *n* [MF or OIt; MF *casse* money box, fr. OIt *cassa,* fr. L *capsa* chest — more at CASE] (1596) **1 :** ready money **2 :** money or its equivalent paid promptly after purchasing — **cash·less** \-ləs\ *adj*

2**cash** *vt* (1811) **1 :** to pay or obtain cash for ⟨~ a check⟩ **2 :** to lead and win a bridge trick with (a card that is the highest remaining card of its suit) — **cash·able** \-ə-bəl\ *adj*

3**cash** *n, pl* **cash** [Pg *caixa,* fr. Tamil *kācu,* a small copper coin, fr. Skt *karṣa,* a weight of gold or silver; akin to OPer *karsha-,* a weight] (1598) **1 :** any of various coins of small value in China and southern India; *esp*

: a Chinese coin usu. of copper alloy that has a square hole in the center 2 : a unit of value equivalent to one cash

[1]**cash-and-car·ry** \ˌkash-ən-ˈkar-ē\ *adj* (1917) : sold or provided for cash and usu. without delivery service

[2]**cash-and-carry** *n* (1921) : the policy of selling on a cash-and-carry basis

cash bar *n* (1972) : a bar (as at a reception) at which drinks are sold — compare OPEN BAR

cash·book \ˈkash-ˌbu̇k\ *n* (1622) : a book in which record is kept of all cash receipts and disbursements

cash cow *n* (1979) : a consistently profitable business, property, or product whose profits are used to finance a company's investments in other areas

cash crop *n* (1868) : a readily salable crop (as cotton or tobacco) produced or gathered primarily for market

cash discount *n* (1917) : a discount granted in consideration of immediate payment or payment within a prescribed time

ca·shew \ˈkash-(ˌ)ü, kə-ˈshü\ *n* [Pg *acajú, cajú,* fr. Tupi *acajú*] (1598) : a tropical American tree (*Anacardium occidentale*) of the sumac family grown for the edible kernel of its nut, for a gum from its stem, and for a phenolic oil located between the two shells of the nut; *also* : CASHEW NUT

cashew nut *n* (ca. 1755) : the kidney-shaped kernel of the fruit of the cashew that is edible when roasted

cash flow *n* (1954) : a measure of an organization's liquidity that usu. consists of net income after taxes plus noncash charges (as depreciation) against income

[1]**ca·shier** \ka-ˈshi(ə)r, kə-\ *vt* [D *casseren,* fr. MF *casser* to discharge, annul — more at QUASH] (1592) 1 : to dismiss from service; *esp* : to dismiss dishonorably 2 : REJECT, DISCARD

[2]**cash·ier** \ka-ˈshi(ə)r\ *n* [D or MF; D *kassier,* fr. MF *cassier,* fr. *casse* money box] (1596) : one that has charge of money: as **a** : a high officer in a bank or trust company responsible for moneys received and expended **b** : one who collects and records payments

cashier's check *n* (1867) : a check drawn by a bank on its own funds and signed by the cashier

cash in *vt* (1888) : to obtain cash for ⟨*cashed in* all his bonds⟩ ~ *vi* 1 **a** : to retire from a gambling game **b** : to settle accounts and withdraw from an involvement (as a business deal) 2 : to obtain advantage or financial profit ⟨wheeler-dealers trying to *cash in*⟩ — often used with *on* ⟨a chance of *cashing in* on a best-seller⟩

cash·mere \ˈkazh-ˌmi(ə)r, ˈkash-\ *n* [*Cashmere* (Kashmir)] (1684) 1 : fine wool from the undercoat of the cashmere goat; *also* : a yarn of this wool 2 : a soft twilled fabric made orig. from cashmere

cashmere goat *n* (ca. 1909) : an Indian goat raised esp. for its undercoat of fine soft wool that constitutes the cashmere wool of commerce

cash register *n* (1879) : a business machine that usu. has a money drawer, indicates the amount of each sale, and records the amount of money received and often automatically makes change

cas·ing \ˈkā-siŋ\ *n* (1791) 1 : something that encases : material for encasing: as **a** : an enclosing frame esp. around a door or window opening **b** : a metal pipe used to case a well **c** : TIRE 2b **d** : a membranous case for processed meat 2 : a space formed between two parallel lines of stitching through at least two layers of cloth into which something (as a rod or string) may be inserted

ca·si·no \kə-ˈsē-(ˌ)nō\ *n, pl* **-nos** [It, fr. *casa* house, fr. L, cabin] (1744) 1 : a building or room used for social amusements; *specif* : one used for gambling 2 : SUMMERHOUSE 3 *also* **cas·si·no** : a card game in which each player wins cards by matching or combining cards in his hand with those exposed on the table

ca·si·ta \kə-ˈsēt-ə\ *n* [Sp, dim. of *casa*] (1923) : a small house

cask \ˈkask\ *n* [MF *casque* helmet, fr. Sp *casco* potsherd, skull, helmet] (15c) 1 : a barrel-shaped vessel of staves, headings, and hoops usu. for liquids 2 : a cask and its contents; *also* : the quantity contained in a cask

cas·ket \ˈkas-kət\ *n* [ME, perh. modif. of MF *cassette*] (15c) 1 : a small chest or box (as for jewels) 2 : a usu. fancy coffin — **casket** *vt*

casque \ˈkask\ *n* [MF — more at CASK] (1580) 1 : a piece of armor for the head : HELMET 2 : an anatomic structure suggestive of a helmet

Cas·san·dra \kə-ˈsan-drə\ *n* [L, fr. Gk *Kassandra*] 1 : a daughter of Priam endowed with the gift of prophecy but fated never to be believed 2 : one that predicts misfortune or disaster

cas·sa·va \kə-ˈsäv-ə\ *n* [Sp *cazabe* cassava bread, fr. Taino *caçábi*] (1555) : any of several plants (genus *Manihot*) of the spurge family grown in the tropics for their fleshy edible rootstocks which yield a nutritious starch; *also* : the rootstock

cas·se·role \ˈkas-ə-ˌrōl *also* ˈkaz-\ *n* [F, saucepan, fr. MF, irreg. fr. *casse* ladle, dripping pan, deriv. of Gk *kyathos* ladle] (1708) 1 : a deep round usu. porcelain dish with a handle used for heating substances in the laboratory 2 : a dish in which food may be baked and served 3 : the food cooked and served in a casserole

cas·sette *also* **ca·sette** \kə-ˈset, ka-\ *n* [F, fr. MF, dim. of ONF *casse* case] (1793) 1 : CASKET 1 2 : a usu. flat case or container that holds a substance, device, or material which is difficult, troublesome, or awkward to handle and that can be easily changed: as **a** : a lightproof magazine for holding film or plates for use in a camera; *esp* : one in which film passes from reel to reel **b** : a plastic cartridge containing magnetic tape with the tape on one reel passing to the other

cas·sia \ˈkash-ə\ *n* [ME, fr. OE, fr. L, fr. Gk *kassia,* of Sem origin; akin to Heb *qĕṣī'āh* cassia] (bef. 12c) 1 : a coarse cinnamon bark (as from *Cinnamomum cassia*) 2 : any of a genus (*Cassia*) of leguminous herbs, shrubs, and trees of warm regions

cas·si·mere \ˈkaz-ə-ˌmi(ə)r, ˈkas-\ *n* [obs. *Cassimere* (Kashmir)] (1784) : a smooth twilled usu. wool fabric

Cas·si·ni division \kə-ˈsē-nē-\ *n* [Gian Domenico *Cassini* †1712 Ital. astronomer] (ca. 1909) : the dark region between the two brightest rings of Saturn

Cas·si·o·pe·ia \ˌkas-ē-ə-ˈpē-(y)ə\ *n* [L, fr. Gk *Kassiopeia*] 1 : the wife of the Ethiopian King Cepheus who became mother of Andromeda by him and was later changed into a constellation 2 [L (gen. *Cassiopeiae*), fr. Gk *Kassiopeia*] : a northern constellation between Andromeda and Cepheus

Cassiopeia's Chair *n* : a group of stars in the constellation Cassiopeia resembling a chair

cas·sit·er·ite \kə-ˈsit-ə-ˌrīt\ *n* [F *cassitérite,* fr. Gk *kassiteros* tin] (1858) : a brown or black mineral that consists of tin dioxide SnO_2 and is the chief source of metallic tin

cas·sock \ˈkas-ək\ *n* [MF *casaque,* fr. Per *kazhāghand* padded jacket, fr. *kazh* raw silk + *āghand* stuffed] (1631) : an ankle-length garment with close-fitting sleeves worn esp. in Roman Catholic and Anglican churches by the clergy and by laymen assisting in services

cas·sou·let \ˌkas-ə-ˈlā\ *n* [F, fr. F dial, lit., stone dish, dim. of *cassolo* bowl, dim. of *casso* ladle] (ca. 1929) : a casserole of beans baked with herbs and meat (as pork sausage, goose, and lamb)

cas·so·wary \ˈkas-ə-ˌwer-ē\ *n, pl* **-war·ies** [Malay *kĕsuari*] (1611) : any of several large ratite birds (genus *Casuarius*) esp. of New Guinea and Australia closely related to the emu

[1]**cast** \ˈkast\ *vb* **cast; cast·ing** [ME *casten,* fr. ON *kasta;* perh. akin to ON *kös* heap] *vt* (13c) 1 **a** : to cause to move by throwing ⟨~ a fishing lure⟩ **b** : DIRECT ⟨~ a glance⟩ **c** (1) : to put forth ⟨the fire ~s a warm glow⟩ (2) : to place as if by throwing ⟨~ doubt on their reliability⟩ **d** : to deposit (a ballot) formally **e** (1) : to throw off or away ⟨the horse ~ a shoe⟩ (2) : to get rid of : DISCARD ⟨~ off all restraint⟩ (3) : SHED, MOLT (4) : to bring forth; *esp* : to give birth to prematurely **f** : to throw to the ground esp. in wrestling **g** : to build by throwing up earth 2 **a** (1) : to perform arithmetical operations on : ADD (2) : to calculate by means of astrology **b** *archaic* : DECIDE, INTEND 3 **a** : to dispose or arrange into parts or into a suitable form or order **b** (1) : to assign the parts of (a dramatic production) to actors (2) : to assign (as an actor) to a role or part 4 **a** : to give a shape to (a substance) by pouring in liquid or plastic form into a mold and letting harden without pressure ⟨~ steel⟩ **b** : to form by this process 5 : TURN ⟨~ the scale slightly⟩ 6 : to make (a knot or stitch) by looping or catching up 7 : TWIST, WARP ⟨a beam ~ by age⟩ ~ *vi* 1 : to throw something; *specif* : to throw out a lure with a fishing rod 2 *dial Brit* : VOMIT 3 *dial Eng* : to bear fruit : YIELD 4 **a** : to perform addition **b** *obs* : ESTIMATE, CONJECTURE 5 : WARP 6 : to range over land in search of a trail — used of hunting dogs or trackers 7 **a** : VEER **b** : to wear ship 8 : to take form in a mold ***syn*** see THROW — **cast lots** : to draw lots to determine a matter by chance

[2]**cast** *n* (14c) 1 **a** : an act of casting **b** : something that happens as a result of chance **c** : a throw of dice **d** : a throw of a line (as a fishing line) or net 2 **a** : the form in which a thing is constructed **b** (1) : the set of actors in a dramatic production (2) : a set (as in a narrative) of characters or persons **c** : the arrangement of draperies in a painting 3 : the distance to which a thing can be thrown; *specif* : the distance a bow can shoot 4 **a** : a turning of the eye in a particular direction; *also* : EXPRESSION ⟨this freakish, elfish ~ came into the child's eye —Nathaniel Hawthorne⟩ **b** : a slight strabismus 5 : something that is thrown or the quantity thrown: as **a** *Brit* : the leader of a fishing line **b** : the quantity of metal cast at a single operation 6 **a** : something that is formed by casting in a mold or form: as (1) : a reproduction (as of a statue) in metal or plaster : CASTING (2) : a fossil reproduction of the details of a natural object by mineral infiltration **b** : an impression taken from an object with a liquid or plastic substance : MOLD **c** : a rigid dressing of gauze impregnated with plaster of paris for immobilizing a diseased or broken part 7 : FORECAST, CONJECTURE 8 **a** : an overspread of a color or modification of the appearance of a substance by a trace of some added hue : SHADE ⟨gray with a greenish ~⟩ **b** : TINGE, SUGGESTION 9 **a** : a ride on one's way in a vehicle : LIFT **b** *Scot* : HELP, ASSISTANCE 10 **a** : SHAPE, APPEARANCE ⟨the delicate ~ of her features⟩ **b** : characteristic quality ⟨his father's conservative ~ of mind⟩ 11 : something that is shed, ejected, or thrown out or off: as **a** : the excrement of an earthworm **b** : a mass of soft matter formed in cavities of diseased organs and discharged from the body **c** : the skin of an insect 12 : the ranging in search of a trail by a dog, hunting pack, or tracker

cast about *vt* (1575) : to lay plans concerning : CONTRIVE ⟨*cast about* how he was to go⟩ ~ *vi* : to look around : SEEK ⟨*cast about* for a seat⟩

cas·ta·net \ˌkas-tə-ˈnet\ *n* [Sp *castañeta,* fr. *castaña* chestnut, fr. L *castanea* — more at CHESTNUT] (1647) : a percussion instrument used esp. by dancers that consists of two small shells of hard wood, ivory, or plastic usu. fastened to the thumb and clicked together by the other fingers — usu. used in pl.

cast around *vi* (1946) : CAST ABOUT

cast·away \ˈkas-tə-ˌwā\ *adj* (1542) 1 : thrown away : REJECTED 2 **a** : cast adrift or ashore as a survivor of a shipwreck **b** : thrown out or left without friends or resources — **castaway** *n*

cast down *adj* (14c) : DOWNCAST

caste \ˈkast\ *n* [Pg *casta,* lit., race, lineage, fr. fem. of *casto* pure, chaste, fr. L *castus;* akin to L *carēre* to be without, Gk *keazein* to split, Skt *śasati* he cuts to pieces] (1613) 1 : one of the hereditary social classes in Hinduism that restrict the occupation of their members and their association with the members of other castes 2 **a** : a division of society based on differences of wealth, inherited rank or privilege, profession, or occupation **b** : the position conferred by caste standing : PRESTIGE 3 : a system of rigid social stratification characterized by hereditary status, endogamy, and social barriers sanctioned by custom, law, or religion 4 : a specialized form (as the soldier or worker of an ant) of a polymorphic social insect that carries out a particular function in the colony — **caste·ism** \ˈkas-ˌtiz-əm\ *n*

cas·tel·lan \ˈkas-tə-lən\ *n* [ME *castelleyn,* fr. ONF *castelain,* fr. L *castellanus* occupant of a castle, fr. *castellanus* of a castle, fr. *castellum* castle] (14c) : a governor or warden of a castle or fort

cas·tel·lat·ed \ˈkas-tə-ˌlāt-əd\ *adj* [ML *castellatus,* pp. of *castellare* to fortify, fr. L *castellum*] (1679) 1 : having battlements like a castle 2 : having or supporting a castle

cast·er \ˈkas-tər\ *n* (14c) 1 : one that casts; *esp* : a machine that casts type 2 *or* **cas·tor** \-tər\ **a** : a usu. silver table vessel with a perforated top for sprinkling a seasoning (as sugar or spice) **b** : a usu. revolving metal stand bearing condiment containers (as cruets, mustard pot, and often shakers) for table use : a cruet stand 3 : a wheel or set of wheels mounted in a swivel frame and used for supporting furniture, trucks, and portable machines 4 : the slight usu. backward tilt of the upper end of the kingbolt of an automobile for giving directional stability to the front wheels

cas·ti·gate \ˈkas-tə-ˌgāt\ *vt* **-gat·ed; -gat·ing** [L *castigatus,* pp. of *castigare* — more at CHASTEN] (1607) : to subject to severe punishment, reproof, or criticism ***syn*** see PUNISH — **cas·ti·ga·tion** \ˌkas-tə-ˈgā-shən\ *n* — **cas·ti·ga·tor** \ˈkas-tə-ˌgāt-ər\ *n*

cas·tile soap \(ˌ)kas-ˌtēl-\ *n, often cap C* [*Castile,* region of Spain] (15c) **:** a fine hard bland soap made from olive oil and sodium hydroxide; *also* **:** any of various similar soaps

Cas·til·ian \ka-ˈstil-yən\ *n* (1796) **1 :** a native or inhabitant of Castile; *broadly* **:** SPANIARD **2 a :** the dialect of Castile **b :** the official and literary language of Spain based on this dialect — **Castilian** *adj*

cast·ing *n* (14c) **1 :** something (as excrement) that is cast out or off **2 :** the act of one that casts: as **a :** the throwing of a fishing line by means of a rod and reel **b :** the assignment of parts and duties to actors or performers **3 :** something cast in a mold

casting vote *n* (1678) **:** a deciding vote cast by a presiding officer to break a tie

cast–iron *adj* (1692) **1 :** made of cast iron **2 :** resembling cast iron: as **a :** capable of withstanding great strain ⟨a ~ stomach⟩ **b :** not admitting change, adaptation, or exception **:** RIGID ⟨a ~ will⟩

cast iron *n* (1664) **:** a commercial alloy of iron, carbon, and silicon that is cast in a mold and is hard, brittle, nonmalleable, and incapable of being hammer-welded but more easily fusible than steel

[1]**cas·tle** \ˈkas-əl\ *n* [ME *castel,* fr. OE, fr. ONF, fr. L *castellum* fortress, castle, dim. of *castrum* fortified place; akin to L *castrare* to castrate] (bef. 12c) **1 a :** a large fortified building or set of buildings **b :** a massive or imposing house **2 :** a retreat safe against intrusion or invasion **3 :** [3]ROOK

[2]**castle** *vb* **cas·tled; cas·tling** \ˈkas-(ə-)liŋ\ *vt* (1587) **1 :** to establish in a castle **2 :** to move (the chess king) in castling ~ *vi* **:** to move a chess king two squares toward a rook and in the same move the rook to the square next past the king

cas·tled \ˈkas-əld\ *adj* (1789) **:** CASTELLATED

castle in the air (1580) **:** an impracticable project **:** DAYDREAM — called also *castle in Spain*

cast–off \ˈkas-ˌtȯf\ *adj* (1746) **:** thrown away or aside — **cast·off** *n*

cast off \(ˈ)kas-ˈtȯf\ *vt* (1602) **1 :** LOOSE ⟨*cast off* a hunting dog⟩ **2 :** UNFASTEN ⟨*cast off* a boat⟩ **3 :** to remove (a stitch) from a knitting needle in such a way as to prevent unraveling ~ *vi* **1 :** to unfasten or untie a boat or a line **2 :** to turn one's partner in a square dance and pass around the outside of the set and back **3 :** to finish a knitted fabric by casting off all stitches

cast on *vt* (1840) **:** to place (stitches) on a knitting needle for beginning or enlarging knitted work

cas·tor \ˈkas-tər\ *n* [ME, fr. L, fr. Gk *kastōr,* fr. *Kastōr* Castor] (14c) **1 :** BEAVER 1a **2 :** CASTOREUM **3 :** a beaver hat

Cas·tor \ˈkas-tər\ *n* [L, fr. Gk *Kastōr*] **1 :** one of the Dioscuri **2 :** the more northern of the two bright stars in Gemini

castor bean *n* (1819) **:** the very poisonous seed of the castor-oil plant; *also* **:** CASTOR-OIL PLANT

cas·to·re·um \ka-ˈstōr-ē-əm, -ˈstȯr-\ *n* [ME *castorium,* fr. L *castoreum,* fr. *castor*] (14c) **:** a bitter strong-smelling creamy orange-brown substance that consists of the dried perineal glands of the beaver and their secretion and is used esp. by perfumers — called also *castor*

castor oil *n* [prob. fr. its former use as a substitute for castor in medicine] (1746) **:** a pale viscous fatty oil from castor beans used esp. as a cathartic or lubricant

castor–oil plant *n* (1836) **:** a tropical Old World herb (*Ricinus communis*) widely grown as an ornamental or for its oil-rich castor beans

castor sugar *or* **caster sugar** *n* [*caster*] *chiefly Brit* (1855) **:** finely granulated white sugar

cast out *vt* (13c) **:** to drive out **:** EXPEL

cas·trate \ˈkas-ˌtrāt\ *vt* **cas·trat·ed; cas·trat·ing** [L *castratus,* pp. of *castrare;* akin to Skt *śasati* he cuts to pieces — more at CASTE] (1613) **1 a :** to deprive of the testes **:** GELD **b :** to deprive of the ovaries **:** SPAY **2 :** to render impotent or deprive of vitality esp. by psychological means — **castrate** *n* — **cas·trat·er** *or* **cas·tra·tor** \-ˌtrāt-ər\ *n* — **cas·tra·tion** \ka-ˈstrā-shən\ *n* — **cas·tra·to·ry** \ˈkas-trə-ˌtōr-ē, -ˌtȯr-\ *adj*

cas·tra·to \ka-ˈsträt-(ˌ)ō, kə-\ *n, pl* **-ti** \-ē\ [It, fr. pp. of *castrare* to castrate, fr. L] (1763) **:** a singer castrated before puberty to preserve the soprano or contralto range of his voice

Cas·tro·ism \ˈkas-(ˌ)trō-ˌiz-əm\ *n* (1960) **:** the political, economic, and social principles and policies of Fidel Castro — **Cas·tro·ite** \-ˌīt\ *n*

[1]**ca·su·al** \ˈkazh-(ə-)wəl, ˈkazh-əl\ *adj* [ME, fr. MF & LL; MF *casuel,* fr. LL *casualis,* fr. L *casus* fall, chance — more at CASE] (14c) **1 :** subject to, resulting from, or occurring by chance **2 a :** occurring without regularity **:** OCCASIONAL **b :** employed for irregular periods **3 a :** feeling or showing little concern **:** NONCHALANT **b** (1) **:** INFORMAL, NATURAL (2) **:** designed for informal use ***syn*** see ACCIDENTAL, RANDOM — **ca·su·al·ly** \-ē\ *adv* — **ca·su·al·ness** *n*

[2]**casual** *n* (1852) **1 :** a casual or migratory worker **2 :** an officer or enlisted man awaiting assignment or transportation to his unit

ca·su·al·ty \ˈkazh-əl-tē, ˈkazh-(ə-)wəl-\ *n, pl* **-ties** (15c) **1 :** serious or fatal accident **:** DISASTER **2 a :** a military person lost through death, wounds, injury, sickness, internment, or capture or through being missing in action **b :** a person or thing injured, lost, or destroyed ⟨the ex-senator was a ~ of the last election⟩

casual water *n* (1899) **:** a temporary accumulation of water not forming a regular hazard of a golf course

ca·su·a·ri·na \ˌkazh-ə-(wə-)ˈrē-nə\ *n* [NL, genus name, fr. Malay (*pohon*) *kĕsuari,* lit., cassowary tree; fr. the resemblance of its twigs to cassowary feathers] (1806) **:** any of a genus (*Casuarina* of the family Casuarinaceae) of dicotyledonous chiefly Australian trees which have whorls of scalelike leaves and jointed stems resembling horsetails and some of which yield a heavy hard wood

ca·su·ist \ˈkazh-(ə-)wəst\ *n* [prob. fr. Sp *casuista,* fr. L *casus* fall, chance — more at CASE] (1609) **:** one skilled in or given to casuistry — **ca·su·is·tic** \ˌkazh-ə-ˈwis-tik\ *or* **ca·su·is·ti·cal** \-ti-kəl\ *adj*

ca·su·ist·ry \ˈkazh-(ə-)wə-strē\ *n, pl* **-ries** (1725) **1 :** a resolving of specific cases of conscience, duty, or conduct through interpretation of ethical principles or religious doctrine **2 :** specious argument **:** RATIONALIZATION ⟨no ~ will convince us that this serious loss is really a victory⟩

ca·sus bel·li \ˌkäs-əs-ˈbel-ˌē, ˌkā-səs-ˈbel-ˌī\ *n, pl* **ca·sus belli** \ˌkäs-ˌüs-, ˌkā-ˌsüs-\ [NL, occasion of war] (1849) **:** an event or action that justifies or allegedly justifies war or conflict

[1]**cat** \ˈkat\ *n, often attrib* [ME, fr. OE *catt,* prob. fr. LL *cattus, catta* cat] (bef. 12c) **1 a :** a carnivorous mammal (*Felis catus*) long domesticated and kept by man as a pet or for catching rats and mice **b :** any of a family (Felidae) including the domestic cat, lion, tiger, leopard, jaguar, cougar, wildcat, lynx, and cheetah **c :** the fur or pelt of the domestic cat **2 :** a malicious woman **3 :** a strong tackle used to hoist an anchor to the cathead of a ship **4 a :** CATBOAT **b :** CATAMARAN **5 :** CAT-O'-NINE-TAILS **6 :** CATFISH **7** *slang* **:** GUY

[2]**cat** *vb* **cat·ted; cat·ting** *vt* (1769) **:** to bring (an anchor) up to the cathead ~ *vi* **:** to search for a sexual mate — often used with *around*

Cat \ˈkat\ *trademark* — used for a Caterpillar tractor

cata- *or* **cat-** *or* **cath-** *prefix* [Gk *kata-, kat-, kath-,* fr. *kata* down, in accordance with, by; akin to L *com-* with — more at CO-] **:** down ⟨*cataclinal*⟩

cat·a·bol·ic \ˌkat-ə-ˈbäl-ik\ *adj* (1876) **:** of or relating to catabolism — **cat·a·bol·i·cal·ly** \-i-k(ə-)lē\ *adv*

ca·tab·o·lism \kə-ˈtab-ə-ˌliz-əm\ *n* [Gk *katabolē* throwing down, fr. *kataballein* to throw down, fr. *kata-* + *ballein* to throw — more at DEVIL] (1876) **:** destructive metabolism involving the release of energy and resulting in the breakdown of complex materials within the organism

ca·tab·o·lite \-ˌlīt\ *n* (ca. 1909) **:** a product of catabolism

ca·tab·o·lize \-ˌlīz\ *vb* **-lized; -liz·ing** *vt* (ca. 1926) **:** to subject to catabolism ~ *vi* **:** to undergo catabolism

cat·a·chre·sis \ˌkat-ə-ˈkrē-səs\ *n, pl* **-chre·ses** \-ˌsēz\ [L, fr. Gk *katachrēsis* misuse, fr. *katachrēsthai* to use up, misuse, fr. *kata-* + *chrēsthai* to use] (1553) **1 :** use of the wrong word for the context **2 :** use of a forced and esp. paradoxical figure of speech (as *blind mouths*) — **cat·a·chres·tic** \-ˈkres-tik\ *or* **cat·a·chres·ti·cal** \-ti-kəl\ *adj* — **cat·a·chres·ti·cal·ly** \-ti-k(ə-)lē\ *adv*

cat·a·clysm \ˈkat-ə-ˌkliz-əm\ *n* [F *cataclysme,* fr. L *cataclysmos,* fr. Gk *kataklysmos,* fr. *kataklyzein* to inundate, fr. *kata-* + *klyzein* to wash — more at CLYSTER] (1637) **1 :** FLOOD, DELUGE **2 :** a violent geologic change of the earth's surface **3 :** a momentous and violent event marked by overwhelming upheaval and demolition ***syn*** see DISASTER — **cat·a·clys·mal** \ˌkat-ə-ˈkliz-məl\ *or* **cat·a·clys·mic** \-mik\ *adj* — **cat·a·clys·mi·cal·ly** \-mi-k(ə-)lē\ *adv*

cat·a·comb \ˈkat-ə-ˌkōm\ *n* [MF *catacombe,* prob. fr. OIt *catacomba,* fr. LL *catacumbae,* pl.] (15c) **1 :** a subterranean cemetery of galleries with recesses for tombs — usu. used in pl. **2 :** something resembling a catacomb: as **a :** an underground passageway or group of passageways **b :** a complex set of interrelated things ⟨the endless ~s of formal education —Kingman Brewster, Jr.⟩ — **cat·a·comb·ic** \ˌkat-ə-ˈkō-mik\ *adj*

cata·di·op·tric \ˌkat-ə-dī-ˈäp-trik\ *adj* [*cata-* + *dioptric*] (1723) **:** belonging to, produced by, or involving both the reflection and the refraction of light

ca·tad·ro·mous \kə-ˈtad-rə-məs\ *adj* [prob. fr. NL *catadromus,* fr. *cata-* + *-dromus* -dromous] (1880) **:** living in fresh water and going to the sea to spawn ⟨~ eels⟩

cat·a·falque \ˈkat-ə-ˌfȯ(l)k, -ˌfalk\ *n* [It *catafalco,* fr. (assumed) VL *catafalicum* scaffold, fr. *cata-* + L *fala* siege tower] (1641) **1 :** an ornamental structure sometimes used in funerals for the lying in state of the body **2 :** a pall-covered coffin-shaped structure used at requiem masses celebrated after burial

Cat·a·lan \ˈkat-ᵊl-ən, -ˌan\ *n* [Sp *Catalán*] (15c) **1 :** a native or inhabitant of Catalonia **2 :** the Romance language of Catalonia, Valencia, Andorra, and the Balearic islands — **Catalan** *adj*

cat·a·lase \ˈkat-ᵊl-ˌās, -ˌāz\ *n* [*catalysis*] (1901) **:** a red crystalline enzyme that consists of a protein complex with hematin groups and catalyzes the decomposition of hydrogen peroxide into water and oxygen — **cat·a·lat·ic** \ˌkat-ᵊl-ˈat-ik\ *adj*

cat·a·lec·tic \ˌkat-ᵊl-ˈek-tik\ *adj* [LL *catalecticus,* fr. Gk *katalēktikos,* fr. *katalēgein* to leave off, fr. *kata-* + *lēgein* to stop — more at SLACK] (1589) **:** lacking a syllable at the end or ending in an incomplete foot — **catalectic** *n*

cat·a·lep·sy \ˈkat-ᵊl-ˌep-sē\ *n, pl* **-sies** [ME *catalempsi,* fr. ML *catalepsia,* fr. LL *catalepsis,* fr. Gk *katalēpsis,* lit., act of seizing, fr. *katalambanein* to seize, fr. *kata-* + *lambanein* to take — more at LATCH] (14c) **:** a condition of suspended animation and loss of voluntary motion in which the limbs remain in whatever position they are placed — **cat·a·lep·tic** \ˌkat-ᵊl-ˈep-tik\ *adj or n* — **cat·a·lep·ti·cal·ly** \-ti-k(ə-)lē\ *adv*

cat·a·lex·is \ˌkat-ᵊl-ˈek-səs\ *n, pl* **-lex·es** \-ˌsēz\ [NL, fr. Gk *katalēxis* close, cadence, fr. *katalēgein*] (1830) **:** omission or incompleteness usu. in the last foot of a line in metrical verse

[1]**cat·a·log** *or* **cat·a·logue** \ˈkat-ᵊl-ˌȯg, -ˌäg\ *n* [ME *cateloge,* fr. MF *catalogue,* fr. LL *catalogus,* fr. Gk *katalogos,* fr. *katalegein* to list, enumerate, fr. *kata-* + *legein* to gather, speak — more at LEGEND] (15c) **1 :** LIST, REGISTER **2 a :** a complete enumeration of items arranged systematically with descriptive details **b :** a pamphlet or book that contains such a list **c :** material in such a list

[2]**catalog** *or* **catalogue** *vb* **-loged** *or* **-logued; -log·ing** *or* **-logu·ing** *vt* (1598) **1 :** to make a catalog of **2 :** to enter in a catalog; *esp* **:** to classify (books or information) descriptively ~ *vi* **1 :** to make or work on a catalog **2 :** to become listed in a catalog at a specified price ⟨this stamp ~s at $2⟩ — **cat·a·log·er** *or* **cat·a·logu·er** *n*

cat·a·logue rai·son·né \-ˌrāz-ᵊn-ˈā\ *n, pl* **cat·a·logues rai·son·nés** \-ˌȯg(z)-ˌrāz-ᵊn-ˈā\ [F, lit., reasoned catalog] (1784) **:** a systematic annotated catalog; *esp* **:** a critical bibliography

ca·tal·pa \kə-ˈtal-pə, -ˈtȯl-\ *n* [Creek *kutuhlpa,* lit., head with wings] (1730) **:** any of a small genus (*Catalpa*) of American and Asian trees of the trumpet-creeper family with cordate leaves and pale showy flowers in terminal racemes

ca·tal·y·sis \kə-ˈtal-ə-səs\ *n, pl* **-y·ses** \-ˌsēz\ [Gk *katalysis* dissolution, fr. *katalyein* to dissolve, fr. *kata-* cata- + *lyein* to dissolve, release — more at LOSE] (1836) **1 :** a modification and esp. increase in the rate of a chemical reaction induced by material unchanged chemically at the end

\ə\ abut \ᵊ\ kitten, F table \ər\ further \a\ ash \ā\ ace \ä\ cot, cart \au̇\ out \ch\ chin \e\ bet \ē\ easy \g\ go \i\ hit \ī\ ice \j\ job \ŋ\ sing \ō\ go \ȯ\ law \ȯi\ boy \th\ thin \t͟h\ the \ü\ loot \u̇\ foot \y\ yet \zh\ vision \à, k̟, ⁿ, œ, œ̄, ue, ue̅, ʸ\ see Guide to Pronunciation

of the reaction   **2 :** an action or reaction between two or more persons or forces precipitated by a separate agent and esp. by one that is essentially unaltered by the reaction ⟨a representative list of questions . . . valuable for the ∼ of class discussions —B. S. Meyer & D. B. Anderson⟩

cat·a·lyst \'kat-ᵊl-əst\ n (1902)   **1 :** a substance (as an enzyme) that initiates a chemical reaction and enables it to proceed under different conditions (as at a lower temperature) than otherwise possible   **2 :** an agent that induces catalysis; *broadly* : one that provokes significant change ⟨his book was the ∼ of the peace movement⟩

cat·a·lyt·ic \,kat-ᵊl-'it-ik\ adj (1836)   **:** causing, involving, or relating to catalysis ⟨a ∼ reaction⟩ ⟨a ∼ personality⟩ — **cat·a·lyt·i·cal·ly** \-'it-i-k(ə-)lē\ adv

catalytic converter n (1964)   **:** a device containing a catalyst for converting automobile exhaust into mostly harmless products

catalytic cracker n (1947)   **:** the unit in a petroleum refinery in which cracking is carried out in the presence of a catalyst

cat·a·lyze \'kat-ᵊl-,īz\ vt **-lyzed; -lyz·ing** (1902)   **1 :** to bring about the catalysis of (a chemical reaction)   **2 :** to bring about : INSPIRE   **3 :** to alter significantly by catalysis ⟨innovations in basic chemical theory that have *catalyzed* the field and its technology —*Newsweek*⟩ — **cat·a·lyz·er** n

cat·a·ma·ran \,kat-ə-mə-'ran, 'kat-ə-mə-,ran\ n [Tamil *kaṭṭumaram*, fr. *kaṭṭu* to tie + *maram* tree] (1673)   **1 :** a raft consisting of logs or pieces of wood lashed together and propelled by paddles or sails   **2 :** a boat with twin hulls or planing surfaces side by side

cata·me·nia \,kat-ə-'mē-nē-ə\ n pl [NL, fr. Gk *katamēnia*, fr. neut. pl. of *katamēnios* monthly, fr. *kata* by + *mēn* month — more at CATA-, MOON] (1750) : MENSES — **cata·me·ni·al** \-nē-əl\ adj

cat·a·mite \'kat-ə-,mīt\ n [L *catamitus*, fr. *Catamitus* Ganymede, fr. Etruscan *Catmite*, fr. Gk *Ganymēdēs*] (1593) : a boy kept by a pederast

cat·a·mount \'kat-ə-,maunt\ n [short for *cat-a-mountain*] (1664) : any of various wild cats: as   **a :** COUGAR   **b :** LYNX

cat–a–moun·tain \,kat-ə-'maunt-ᵊn\ n [ME *cat of the mountaine*] (15c) : any of various wild cats

cat and mouse n (ca. 1923) : behavior like that of a cat with a mouse; esp : the act of toying with something before tormenting or destroying it — **cat–and–mouse** \,kat-ᵊn-'maus\ adj

cat·a·pho·re·sis \,kat-ə-fə-'rē-səs\ n, pl **-re·ses** \-,sēz\ [NL] (1898) : ELECTROPHORESIS — **cat·a·pho·ret·ic** \-'ret-ik\ adj — **cat·a·pho·ret·i·cal·ly** \-i-k(ə-)lē\ adv

cat·a·plasm \'kat-ə-,plaz-əm\ n [MF *cataplasme*, fr. L *cataplasma*, fr. Gk *kataplasma*, fr. *kataplassein* to plaster over, fr. *kata-* + *plassein* to mold — more at PLASTER] (1541) : POULTICE

cat·a·plexy \'kat-ə-,plek-sē\ n, pl **-plex·ies** \-,sēz\ [G *kataplexie*, fr. Gk *kataplēxis*, fr. *kataplēssein* to strike down, terrify, fr. *kata-* + *plēssein* to strike — more at PLAINT] (1883) : sudden loss of muscle power following a strong emotional stimulus

¹cat·a·pult \'kat-ə-,pəlt, -,pult\ n [MF or L; MF *catapulte*, fr. L *cata-*

pulta, fr. Gk *katapaltēs*, fr. *kata-* + *pallein* to hurl — more at POLEMIC] (1577)   **1 :** an ancient military device for hurling missiles   **2 :** a device for launching an airplane at flying speed (as from an aircraft carrier)

²catapult vt (1848) : to throw or launch by or as if by a catapult ∼ vi : to become catapulted

cat·a·ract \'kat-ə-,rakt\ n [L *cataracta* waterfall, portcullis, fr. Gk *kataraktēs*, fr. *katarassein* to dash down, fr. *kata-* cata- + *arassein* to strike, dash] (15c)   **1** [MF or ML; MF *cataracte*, fr. ML *cataracta*, fr. L, portcullis] **:** a clouding of the lens of the eye or of its surrounding transparent membrane that obstructs the passage of light   **2   a** *obs* : WATERSPOUT   **b :** WATERFALL; *esp* : a large one over a precipice   **c :** steep rapids in a river   **d :** DOWNPOUR, FLOOD — **cat·a·rac·tous** \,kat-ə-'rak-təs\ adj

ca·tarrh \kə-'tär\ n [MF or LL; MF *catarrhe*, fr. LL *catarrhus*, fr. Gk *katarrhous*, fr. *katarrhein* to flow down, fr. *kata-* + *rhein* to flow — more at STREAM] (14c) **:** inflammation of a mucous membrane; esp : one chronically affecting the human nose and air passages — **ca·tarrh·al** \-əl\ adj — **ca·tarrh·al·ly** \-ə-lē\ adv

cat·ar·rhine \'kat-ə-,rīn\ adj [NL *Catarrhina*, fr. Gk *katarrhina*, neut. pl. of *katarrhin* hook-nosed, fr. *kata-* + *rhin-, rhis* nose] (1863) : of, relating to, or being any of a division (Catarrhina) of primates comprising the Old World monkeys, higher apes, and man that have the nostrils close together and directed downward, 32 teeth, and the tail when present never prehensile — **catarrhine** n

ca·tas·tro·phe \kə-'tas-trə-(,)fē\ n [Gk *katastrophē*, fr. *katastrephein* to overturn, fr. *kata-* + *strephein* to turn — more at STROPHE] (1540)   **1 :** the final event of the dramatic action esp. of a tragedy   **2 :** a momentous tragic event ranging from extreme misfortune to utter overthrow or ruin   **3 :** a violent and sudden change in a feature of the earth   **4 :** utter failure : FIASCO   *syn* see DISASTER — **cat·a·stroph·ic** \,kat-ə-'sträf-ik\ adj — **cat·a·stroph·i·cal·ly** \-i-k(ə-)lē\ adv

cata·to·nia \,kat-ə-'tō-nē-ə\ n [NL, fr. G *katatonie*, fr. *kata-* cata- + NL *tonus*] (ca. 1891) **:** catatonic schizophrenia

cata·ton·ic \-'tän-ik\ adj (1904) **:** of, relating to, being, resembling, or affected by schizophrenia characterized esp. by a marked psychomotor disturbance that may involve stupor or mutism, negativism, rigidity, purposeless excitement, and inappropriate or bizarre posturing — **catatonic** n — **cata·ton·i·cal·ly** \-i-k(ə-)lē\ adv

Ca·taw·ba \kə-'tö-bə\ n (1716)   **1** pl **Catawba** or **Catawbas** : a member of an American Indian people of No. Carolina and So. Carolina   **2 :** the language of the Catawba people   **3 :** any of various wines produced from a pale red native American grape

cat·bird \'kat-,bərd\ n (1709) : an American songbird (*Dumetella carolinensis*) dark gray in color with black cap and reddish coverts under the tail

catbird seat n (1942) : a position of great prominence or advantage

cat·boat \'kat-,bōt\ n (1878) : a sailboat having a cat rig and usu. a centerboard and being of light draft and broad beam

cat 1a: *1* Abyssinian, *2* Burmese, *3* Himalayan, *4* Manx, *5* Maine coon, *6* Persian with tabby markings, *7* rex, *8* Siamese

cat·bri·er \-ˌbrī(-ə)r\ *n* (1839) **:** any of several prickly climbers (genus *Smilax*) of the lily family

cat burglar *n* (1925) **:** a burglar who is esp. adept at entering and leaving the place he burglarizes without attracting notice

cat·call \-ˌkȯl\ *n* (1749) **:** a loud or raucous cry made to express disapproval (as at a sports event) — **catcall** *vb*

[1]**catch** \ˈkach, ˈkech\ *vb* **caught** \ˈkȯt\; **catch·ing** [ME *cacchen,* fr. ONF *cachier* to hunt, fr. (assumed) VL *captiare,* alter. of L *captare* to chase, fr. *captus,* pp. of *capere* to take — more at HEAVE] *vt* (13c) **1 a :** to capture or seize esp. after pursuit **b :** to take or entangle in or as if in a snare **c :** DECEIVE **d :** to discover unexpectedly **:** FIND ⟨*caught* in the act⟩ **e :** to check suddenly or momentarily **f :** to become suddenly aware of **2 a :** to take hold of **:** SEIZE **b :** to affect suddenly **c :** INTERCEPT **d :** to avail oneself of **:** TAKE **e :** to obtain through effort **:** GET **f :** to get entangled ⟨~ a sleeve on a nail⟩ **3 :** to become affected by: as **a :** CONTRACT ⟨~ a cold⟩ **b :** to respond sympathetically to the point of being imbued with ⟨~ the spirit of an occasion⟩ **c :** to be struck by **d :** to suffer from **:** RECEIVE ⟨~ hell⟩ **4 a :** to seize and hold firmly **b :** FASTEN **5 :** to take or get usu. momentarily or quickly ⟨~ a glimpse of a friend⟩ **6 a :** OVERTAKE **b :** to get aboard in time ⟨~ the bus⟩ **7 :** ATTRACT, ARREST **8 :** to make contact with **:** STRIKE **9 a :** to grasp by the senses or the mind **:** APPREHEND **b :** to apprehend and fix by artistic means **10 a :** SEE, WATCH **b :** to listen to ~ *vi* **1 :** to grasp hastily or try to grasp **2 :** to become caught **3** *of a crop* **:** to come up and become established **4 :** to play the position of catcher on a baseball team — **catch·able** \ˈkach-ə-bəl, ˈkech-\ *adj*

syn CATCH, CAPTURE, TRAP, SNARE, ENTRAP, ENSNARE, BAG mean to come to possess or control by or as if by seizing. CATCH implies the seizing of something in motion or in flight or in hiding; CAPTURE suggests taking by overcoming resistance or difficulty; TRAP, SNARE, ENTRAP, ENSNARE imply seizing by some device that holds the one caught at the mercy of his captor; TRAP and SNARE apply more commonly to physical seizing, ENTRAP and ENSNARE more often to figurative; BAG implies shooting down a fleeing or distant prey.

— **catch fire 1 :** to become ignited **2 :** to become fired with enthusiasm ⟨the poet *caught fire* from the philosopher's talk⟩ **3 :** to increase greatly in scope, interest, or effectiveness ⟨this stock has not *caught fire* — yet —*Forbes*⟩ — **catch it :** to incur blame, reprimand, or punishment — **catch one's breath :** to rest long enough to restore normal breathing

[2]**catch** *n* (15c) **1 :** something caught; *esp* **:** the total quantity caught at one time ⟨a large ~ of fish⟩ **2 a :** the act, action, or fact of catching **b :** a game in which a ball is thrown and caught **3 :** something that checks or holds immovable ⟨the safety ~ of her pin broke⟩ **4 :** one worth catching esp. as a spouse **5 :** a round for three or more unaccompanied usu. male voices often with suggestive or obscene lyrics **6 :** FRAGMENT, SNATCH **7 :** a concealed difficulty or complication ⟨there must be a ~ to it somewhere⟩ **8 :** the germination of a field crop to such an extent that replanting is unnecessary

catch·all \ˈkach-ˌȯl, ˈkech-\ *n* (1838) **:** something to hold or include odds and ends or a wide variety of things — **catchall** *adj*

catch–as–catch–can \ˌkach-əz-ˌkach-ˈkan, ˌkech-əz-ˌkech-\ *adj* (1764) **:** using any available means or method **:** UNPLANNED ⟨a ~ existence begging and running errands —*Time*⟩

catch·er \ˈkach-ər, ˈkech-\ *n* (15c) **:** one that catches; *specif* **:** a baseball player stationed behind home plate

catch·fly \-ˌflī\ *n* (1597) **:** any of various plants (as of the genera *Lychnis* and *Silene*) with viscid stems to which small insects adhere

catch·ing *adj* (1590) **1 :** INFECTIOUS, CONTAGIOUS **2 :** CATCHY, ALLURING

catch·ment \ˈkach-mənt, ˈkech-\ *n* (1847) **1 :** the action of catching water **2 :** something that catches water; *also* **:** the amount of water caught

catchment area *n* (1940) **:** the geographical area served by an institution

catch on *vi* (1883) **1 :** UNDERSTAND, LEARN ⟨the police *caught on* to what he was doing⟩ **2 :** to become popular ⟨this movement has already *caught on* in other states — Bernard Smith⟩

catch out *vt* (1816) **:** to detect in error or wrongdoing **:** ENTRAP ⟨the Court . . . is now *caught out* by history — Ed Yoder⟩

catch·pen·ny \ˈkach-ˌpen-ē, ˈkech-\ *adj* (1757) **:** designed esp. to appeal to the ignorant or unwary through sensationalism or cheapness ⟨a ~ newspaper with many lurid photographs⟩

catch·phrase \-ˌfrāz\ *n* (1850) **:** an expression that is used repeatedly and conveniently to characterize or represent a person, group, idea, or point of view **:** SLOGAN

catch·pole *or* **catch·poll** \-ˌpōl\ *n* [ME *cacchepol,* fr. OE *cæcepol,* fr. (assumed) ONF *cachepol,* lit., chicken chaser, fr. ONF *cachier* + *pol* chicken, fr. L *pullus* — more at CATCH, PULLET] (bef. 12c) **:** a sheriff's deputy; *esp* **:** one who makes arrests for debt

catch–22 \ˌkach-ˌtwent-ē-ˈtü, ˌkech-\ *n, pl* **catch–22's** *or* **catch–22s** *often cap C* [fr. *Catch-22,* paradoxical rule found in the novel *Catch-22* (1961) by Joseph Heller] (1963) **1 :** a problematic situation for which the only solution is denied by a circumstance inherent in the problem or by a rule ⟨the show-business ~ — no work unless you have an agent, no agent unless you've worked — Mary Murphy⟩; *also* **:** the circumstance or rule that denies a solution **2 a :** an illogical, unreasonable, or senseless situation **b :** a measure or policy whose effect is the opposite of what was intended **c :** a situation presenting two equally undesirable alternatives **3 :** a hidden difficulty or means of entrapment **:** CATCH

catch·up \ˈkech-əp, ˈkach-; ˈkat-səp\ *var of* CATSUP

[1]**catch–up** \ˈkach-ˌəp, ˈkech-\ *adj* (1945) **:** intended to catch up to a theoretical norm or a competitor's accomplishments

[2]**catch–up** *n* (1948) **:** the act or fact of catching up or trying to catch up (as with a norm or competitor); *also* **:** an increase intended to achieve catch-up

catch up \(ˈ)kach-ˈəp, (ˈ)kech-\ *vt* (14c) **1 a :** to pick up often abruptly ⟨the thief *caught* the purse *up* and ran⟩ **b :** ENSNARE, ENTANGLE ⟨education has been *caught up* in a stultifying mythology, largely of its own devising — N. M. Pusey⟩ **c :** ENTHRALL ⟨the . . . public was *caught up* in the car's magic — D. A. Jedlicka⟩ **2 :** to provide with the latest information ⟨*catch* me *up* on the news⟩ ~ *vi* **1 :** to travel fast enough to overtake an advance party ⟨*catch up* with the group ahead⟩ **2 :** to bring about arrest for illicit activities ⟨the police *caught up* with the thieves⟩ **3 a :** to bring something to completion ⟨*catch up* on the bookkeeping⟩ **b :** to acquire belated information ⟨*catch up* on the news⟩

catch·word \ˈkach-ˌwərd, ˈkech-\ *n* (1730) **1 a :** a word under the right-hand side of the last line on a book page that repeats the first word on the following page **b :** GUIDE WORD **2 :** a word or expression repeated until it becomes representative of a party, school, or point of view

catchy \ˈkach-ē, ˈkech-\ *adj* **catch·i·er; -est** (1831) **1 :** tending to catch the interest or attention ⟨a ~ title⟩ **2 :** FITFUL, IRREGULAR ⟨~ breathing⟩ **3 :** TRICKY ⟨a ~ question⟩

cat distemper *n* (ca. 1950) **:** PANLEUKOPENIA

cate \ˈkāt\ *n* [ME, article of purchased food, short for *acate,* fr. ONF *acat* purchase, fr. *acater* to buy, fr. (assumed) VL *accaptare,* fr. L *acceptare* to accept] *archaic* (15c) **:** a dainty or choice food

cat·e·che·sis \ˌkat-ə-ˈkē-səs\ *n, pl* **-che·ses** \-ˌsēz\ [LL, fr. Gk *katēchēsis,* fr. *katēchein* to teach] (1753) **:** oral instruction of catechumens — **cat·e·chet·i·cal** \-ˈket-i-kəl\ *adj*

cat·e·chin \ˈkat-ə-ˌkin\ *n* [ISV *catechu* + *-in*] (1853) **:** a crystalline compound $C_{15}H_{14}O_6$ that is related chemically to the flavones, is found in catechu, and is used in dyeing and tanning

cat·e·chism \ˈkat-ə-ˌkiz-əm\ *n* (1502) **1 :** oral instruction **2 :** a manual for catechizing; *specif* **:** a summary of religious doctrine often in the form of questions and answers **3 a :** a set of formal questions put as a test **b :** something resembling a catechism esp. in being a rote response or formulaic statement — **cat·e·chis·mal** \ˌkat-ə-ˈkiz-məl\ *adj* — **cat·e·chis·tic** \-ˈkis-tik\ *adj*

cat·e·chist \ˈkat-ə-ˌkist, ˈkat-i-kəst\ *n* (1563) **:** one that catechizes: as **a :** a teacher of catechumens **b :** a native in a missionary district who does Christian teaching — **cat·e·chis·tic** \ˌkat-ə-ˈkis-tik\ *adj*

cat·e·chize \ˈkat-ə-ˌkīz\ *vt* **-chized; -chiz·ing** [LL *catechizare,* fr. Gk *katēchein* to teach, lit., to din into, fr. *kata-* cata- + *ēchein* to resound, fr. *ēchē* sound — more at ECHO] (15c) **1 :** to instruct systematically esp. by questions, answers, and explanations and corrections; *specif* **:** to give religious instruction in such a manner **2 :** to question systematically or searchingly — **cat·e·chi·za·tion** \ˌkat-i-kə-ˈzā-shən\ *n* — **cat·e·chiz·er** \ˈkat-ə-ˌkī-zər\ *n*

cat·e·chol \ˈkat-ə-ˌkȯl, -ˌkōl\ *n* (1880) **1 :** CATECHIN **2 :** PYROCATECHOL

cat·e·chol·amine \ˌkat-ə-ˈkō-lə-ˌmēn, -ˈkȯ-\ *n* (1954) **:** any of various amines (as epinephrine, norepinephrine, and dopamine) that function as hormones or neurotransmitters or both

cat·e·chol·amin·er·gic \-ˌkō-lə-mē-ˈnər-jik, -ˌkȯ-\ *adj* [*catecholamine* + *-ergic*] (1970) **:** involving, liberating, or mediated by catecholamine

cat·e·chu \ˈkat-ə-ˌchü, -ˌshü\ *n* [prob. fr. Malay *kachu,* of Dravidian origin; akin to Tamil & Kannada *kācu* catechu] (1683) **:** any of several dry, earthy, or resinous astringent substances obtained from tropical plants of Asia: as **a :** an extract of the heartwood of an East Indian acacia (*Acacia catechu*) **b :** GAMBIER

cat·e·chu·men \ˌkat-ə-ˈkyü-mən\ *n* [ME *cathecumyn,* fr. MF *cathecumine,* fr. LL *catechumenus,* fr. Gk *katēchoumenos,* pres. pass. part. of *katēchein*] (15c) **1 :** a convert to Christianity receiving training in doctrine and discipline before baptism **2 :** one receiving instruction in the basic doctrines of Christianity before admission to communicant membership in a church

cat·e·gor·i·cal \ˌkat-ə-ˈgȯr-i-kəl, -ˈgär-\ *also* **cat·e·gor·ic** \-ik\ *adj* [LL *categoricus,* fr. Gk *katēgorikos,* fr. *katēgoria*] (1598) **1 :** ABSOLUTE, UNQUALIFIED ⟨a ~ denial⟩ **2 a :** of, relating to, or constituting a category **b :** involving, according with, or considered with respect to specific categories — **cat·e·gor·i·cal·ly** \-i-k(ə-)lē\ *adv*

categorical imperative *n* (1827) **:** a moral obligation or command that is unconditionally and universally binding

cat·e·go·rize \ˈkat-i-gə-ˌrīz\ *vt* **-rized; -riz·ing** (1705) **:** to put into a category **:** CLASSIFY — **cat·e·go·ri·za·tion** \ˌkat-i-gə-rə-ˈzā-shən\ *n*

cat·e·go·ry \ˈkat-ə-ˌgōr-ē, -ˌgȯr-\ *n, pl* **-ries** [LL *categoria,* fr. Gk *katēgoria* predication, category, fr. *katēgorein* to accuse, affirm, predicate, fr. *kata-* + *agora* public assembly — more at GREGARIOUS] (1588) **1 :** any of several fundamental and distinct classes to which entities or concepts belong **2 :** a division within a system of classification

ca·te·na \kə-ˈtē-nə\ *n, pl* **-nae** \-(ˌ)nē\ *or* **-nas** [ML, fr. L, chain — more at CHAIN] (1641) **:** a connected series of related things

cat·e·nary \ˈkat-ə-ˌner-ē, *esp Brit* kə-ˈtē-nə-rē\ *n, pl* **-nar·ies** [NL *catenaria,* fr. L, fem. of *catenarius* of a chain, fr. *catena*] (1788) **1 :** the curve assumed by a cord of uniform density and cross section that is perfectly flexible but not capable of being stretched and that hangs freely from two fixed points **2 :** something in the form of a catenary — **catenary** *adj*

cat·e·nate \ˈkat-ə-ˌnāt\ *vt* **-nat·ed; -nat·ing** [L *catenatus,* pp. of *catenare,* fr. *catena*] (1623) **:** to connect in a series **:** LINK — **cat·e·na·tion** \ˌkat-ə-ˈnā-shən\ *n*

ca·ter \ˈkāt-ər\ *vb* [obs. *cater* (buyer of provisions), fr. ME *catour,* short for *acatour,* fr. AF, fr. ONF *acater* to buy — more at CATE] *vi* (1600) **1 :** to provide a supply of food **2 :** to supply what is required or desired ⟨~*ed* to her whims all day long⟩ ~ *vt* **:** to provide food and service for ⟨~*ed* the banquet⟩ — **ca·ter·er** \-ər-ər\ *n* — **ca·ter·ess** \ˈkāt-ə-rəs\ *n*

cat·er·an \ˈkat-ə-rən\ *n* [ME *ketharan,* prob. fr. ScGael *ceathairneach* freebooter, robber] (14c) **:** a former military irregular or brigand of the Scottish Highlands

cat·er·cor·ner \ˌkat-ē-ˈkȯ(r)-nər, ˌkat-ə-, ˌkit-ē-; ˈkat-ē-ˌ, ˈkat-ə-ˌ, ˈkit-ē-ˌ\ *or* **cat·er–cor·nered** \-nərd\ *adv or adj* [obs. *cater* (four-spot) + E *corner*] (1843) **:** in a diagonal or oblique position **:** on a diagonal or oblique line ⟨the house stood ~ across the square⟩

ca·ter–cous·in \ˈkāt-ər-ˌkəz-ᵊn\ *n* [perh. fr. obs. *cater* (buyer of provisions)] (1547) **:** an intimate friend

cat·er·pil·lar \ˈkat-ə(r)-ˌpil-ər\ *n, often attrib* [ME *catyrpel,* fr. ONF *catepelose,* lit., hairy cat] (15c) **:** the elongated wormlike larva of a butterfly or moth; *also* **:** any of various similar larvae

Caterpillar *trademark* — used for a tractor made for use on rough or soft ground and moved on two endless metal belts

cat·er·waul \ˈkat-ər-ˌwȯl\ *vi* [ME *caterwawen*] (14c) **1 :** to make a harsh cry **2 :** to quarrel noisily — **caterwaul** *n*

cat·fac·ing \ˈkat-ˌfā-siŋ\ *n* (1940) **:** a disfigurement or malformation of fruit suggesting a cat's face in appearance

cat·fish \-ˌfish\ *n* (1612) **:** any of numerous usu. stout-bodied large-headed fishes (order Ostariophysi) with long tactile barbels

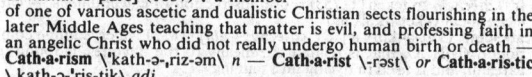

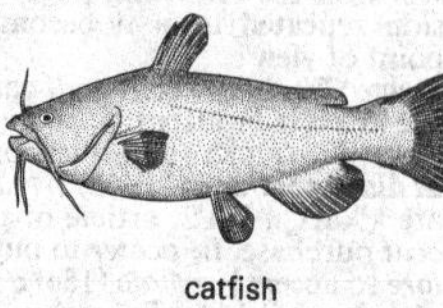
catfish

cat·gut \-ˌgət\ *n* (1599) **:** a tough cord made usu. from sheep intestines

cath- — see CATA-

Cath·ar \ˈkath-ˌär\ *n, pl* **Cath·a·ri** \ˈkath-ə-ˌrī, -ˌrē\ *or* **Cathars** [LL *cathari* (pl.), fr. LGk *katharoi,* fr. Gk, pl. of *katharos* pure] (1637) **:** a member of one of various ascetic and dualistic Christian sects flourishing in the later Middle Ages teaching that matter is evil, and professing faith in an angelic Christ who did not really undergo human birth or death — **Cath·a·rism** \ˈkath-ə-ˌriz-əm\ *n* — **Cath·a·rist** \-rəst\ *or* **Cath·a·ris·tic** \ˌkath-ə-ˈris-tik\ *adj*

ca·thar·sis \kə-ˈthär-səs\ *n, pl* **ca·thar·ses** \-ˌsēz\ [NL, fr. Gk *katharsis,* fr. *kathairein* to cleanse, purge, fr. *katharos*] (1803) **1 :** PURGATION **2 a :** purification or purgation of the emotions (as pity and fear) primarily through art **b :** a purification or purgation that brings about spiritual renewal or release from tension **3 :** elimination of a complex by bringing it to consciousness and affording it expression

[1]**ca·thar·tic** \kə-ˈthärt-ik\ *adj* [LL or Gk; LL *catharticus,* fr. Gk *kathartikos,* fr. *kathairein*] (1612) **:** of, relating to, or producing catharsis

[2]**cathartic** *n* (1651) **:** a cathartic medicine **:** PURGATIVE

cat·head \ˈkat-ˌhed\ *n* (1626) **:** a projecting piece of timber or iron near the bow of a ship to which the anchor is hoisted and secured

ca·thect \kə-ˈthekt, ka-\ *vt* [NL *cathexis*] (1925) **:** to invest with mental or emotional energy

ca·thec·tic \kə-ˈthek-tik, ka-\ *adj* [NL *cathexis*] (1927) **:** of, relating to, or invested with mental or emotional energy

ca·the·dra \kə-ˈthē-drə\ *n* [L, chair — more at CHAIR] (15c) **:** a bishop's official throne

[1]**ca·the·dral** \kə-ˈthē-drəl\ *adj* (13c) **1 :** of, relating to, or containing a cathedra **2 :** emanating from a chair of authority **3 :** suggestive of a cathedral

[2]**cathedral** *n* (1587) **1 :** a church that is the official seat of a diocesan bishop **2 :** something that resembles or suggests a cathedral ⟨higher education has been . . . the secular ~ of our time — David Riesman⟩

ca·thep·sin \kə-ˈthep-sən\ *n* [Gk *kathepsein* to digest (fr. *kata-* cata- + *hepsein* to boil) + E *-in*] (1929) **:** any of several intracellular proteinases of animal tissue that aid in autolysis in some diseased conditions and after death

cath·er·ine wheel \ˌkath-(ə-)rən-\ *n, often cap C* [St. *Catherine* of Alexandria †*ab*307 Christian martyr] (15c) **1 :** a wheel with spikes projecting from the rim **2 :** PINWHEEL 1 **3 :** CARTWHEEL 2

cath·e·ter \ˈkath-ət-ər, ˈkath-tər\ *n* [LL, fr. Gk *kathetēr,* fr. *kathienai* to send down, fr. *kata-* cata- + *hienai* to send — more at JET] (1601) **:** a tubular medical device for insertion into canals, vessels, passageways, or body cavities usu. to permit injection or withdrawal of fluids or to keep a passage open

cath·e·ter·iza·tion \ˌkath-ət-ə-rə-ˈzā-shən, ˌkath-tə-rə-\ *n* (1849) **:** the use of or introduction of a catheter (as in or into the bladder, trachea, or heart) — **cath·e·ter·ize** \ˌkath-ət-ə-ˌrīz, ˌkath-tə-\ *vt*

ca·thex·is \kə-ˈthek-səs, ka-\ *n, pl* **ca·thex·es** \-ˌsēz\ [NL (intended as trans. of G *besetzung*), fr. Gk *kathexis* holding, fr. *katechein* to hold fast, occupy, fr. *kata-* + *echein* to have, hold — more at SCHEME] (1922) **:** investment of mental or emotional energy in a person, object, or idea

cath·ode \ˈkath-ˌōd\ *n* [Gk *kathodos* way down, fr. *kata-* + *hodos* way — more at CEDE] (1834) **1 :** the negative terminal of an electrolytic cell — compare ANODE **2 :** the positive terminal of a primary cell or of a storage battery that is delivering current **3 :** the electron-emitting electrode of an electron tube — **ca·thod·ic** \ka-ˈthäd-ik\ *or* **cath·od·al** \ˈkath-ˌōd-ᵊl\ *adj* — **ca·thod·i·cal·ly** \-i-k(ə-)lē\ *or* **cath·od·al·ly** \-ē\ *adv*

cathode ray *n* (1880) **1 :** one of the high-speed electrons projected in a stream from the heated cathode of a vacuum tube under the propulsion of a strong electric field **2 :** a stream of cathode-ray electrons

cathode–ray tube *n* (1905) **:** a vacuum tube in which cathode rays usu. in the form of a slender beam are projected on a fluorescent screen and produce a luminous spot

cath·o·lic \ˈkath-(ə-)lik\ *adj* [MF & LL; MF *catholique,* fr. LL *catholicus,* fr. Gk *katholikos* universal, general, fr. *katholou* in general, fr. *kata* by + *holos* whole — more at CATA-, SAFE] (14c) **1 :** COMPREHENSIVE, UNIVERSAL; *esp* **:** broad in sympathies, tastes, or interests **2** *cap* **a :** of, relating to, or forming the church universal **b :** of, relating to, or forming the ancient undivided Christian church or a church claiming historical continuity from it; *specif* **:** ROMAN CATHOLIC — **ca·thol·i·cal·ly** \kə-ˈthäl-i-k(ə-)lē\ *adv* — **ca·thol·i·cize** \kə-ˈthäl-ə-ˌsīz\ *vb*

Cath·o·lic \ˈkath-(ə-)lik\ *n* (15c) **1 :** a person who belongs to the universal Christian church **2 :** a member of a Catholic church; *specif* **:** ROMAN CATHOLIC

Catholic Apostolic *adj* (1837) **:** of or relating to a Christian sect founded in 19th century England in anticipation of Christ's second coming

ca·thol·i·cate \kə-ˈthäl-ə-ˌkāt, -ˈthäl-i-kət\ *n* (ca. 1847) **:** the jurisdiction of a catholicos

Catholic Epistles *n pl* (1582) **:** the five New Testament letters including James, I and II Peter, I John, and Jude addressed to the early Christian churches at large

Ca·thol·i·cism \kə-ˈthäl-ə-ˌsiz-əm\ *n* (1613) **1 :** the faith, practice, or system of Catholic Christianity **2 :** ROMAN CATHOLICISM

cath·o·lic·i·ty \ˌkath(-ə)-ˈlis-ət-ē\ *n, pl* **-ties** (1704) **1** *cap* **:** the character of being in conformity with a Catholic church **2 a :** liberality of sentiments or views ⟨~ of viewpoint — W. V. O'Connor⟩ **b :** UNIVERSALITY **c :** comprehensive range ⟨the ~ of subjects represented by the press's trade list — *Current Biog.*⟩

ca·thol·i·con \kə-ˈthäl-ə-ˌkän\ *n* [F or ML; F, fr. ML, fr. Gk *katholikon,* neut. of *katholikos*] (15c) **:** CURE-ALL, PANACEA

ca·thol·i·cos \kə-ˈthäl-i-kəs\ *n, pl* **-i·cos·es** \-kə-səz\ *or* **-i·coi** \-ˈthäl-ə-ˌkȯi\ *often cap* [LGk *katholikos,* fr. Gk, general] (1625) **:** a primate of certain Eastern churches and esp. of the Armenian or of the Nestorian church

cat·house \ˈkat-ˌhau̇s\ *n* (1931) **:** a house of prostitution

cat·ion \ˈkat-ˌī-ən\ *n* [Gk *kation,* neut. of *katiōn,* prp. of *katienai* to go down, fr. *kata-* cata- + *ienai* to go — more at ISSUE] (1834) **:** the ion in an electrolyzed solution that migrates to the cathode; *broadly* **:** a positively charged ion

cat·ion·ic \ˌkat-(ˌ)ī-ˈän-ik\ *adj* (ca. 1920) **1 :** of or relating to cations **2 :** characterized by an active and esp. surface-active cation ⟨a ~ dye⟩ — **cat·ion·i·cal·ly** \-i-k(ə-)lē\ *adv*

cat·kin \ˈkat-kən\ *n* [fr. its resemblance to a cat's tail] (1578) **:** a usu. long ament densely crowded with bracts

cat·like \ˈkat-ˌlīk\ *adj* (1600) **:** resembling a cat; *esp* **:** STEALTHY ⟨with ~ tread, upon our prey we steal —W. S. Gilbert⟩

cat·mint \-ˌmint\ *n* (13c) **:** CATNIP

cat·nap \-ˌnap\ *n* (1823) **:** a very short light nap — **catnap** *vi*

cat·nap·per *or* **cat·nap·er** \ˈkat-ˌnap-ər\ *n* [[1]*cat* + *-napper* (as in *kidnapper*)] (1942) **:** one that steals cats usu. to sell them for research

cat·nip \-ˌnip\ *n* [[1]*cat* + obs. *nep* (catnip), fr. ME, fr. OE *nepte,* fr. L *nepeta*] (1712) **1 :** a strong-scented mint (*Nepeta cataria*) that has whorls of small pale flowers in terminal spikes and contains a substance attractive to cats **2 :** something very attractive

cat–o'–nine–tails \ˌkat-ə-ˈnīn-ˌtālz\ *n, pl* **cat–o'–nine–tails** [fr. the resemblance of its scars to the scratches of a cat] (1665) **:** a whip made of usu. nine knotted lines or cords fastened to a handle

ca·top·tric \kə-ˈtäp-trik\ *adj* [Gk *katoptrikos,* fr. *katoptron* mirror, fr. *katopsesthai* to be going to observe, fr. *kata-* cata- + *opsesthai* to be going to see — more at OPTIC] (1774) **:** of or relating to a mirror or reflected light; *also* **:** produced by reflection — **ca·top·tri·cal·ly** \-tri-k(ə-)lē\ *adv*

cat rig *n* (1867) **:** a rig consisting of a single mast far forward carrying a single large sail extended by a boom — **cat–rigged** \ˈkat-ˈrigd\ *adj*

CAT scan \ˈkat-, ˌsē-ˌā-ˈtē-\ *n* [computerized axial tomography] (1975) **:** an image made by computerized axial tomography

CAT scanner *n* (1975) **:** a medical instrument consisting of integrated X-ray and computing equipment and used for computerized axial tomography

cat's cradle *n* (1768) **1 :** a game in which a string looped in a pattern like a cradle on the fingers of one person's hands is transferred to the hands of another so as to form a different figure **2 :** INTRICACY ⟨the socioreligious *cat's cradle* of small Greek communities — *Times Lit. Supp.*⟩

cat's–eye \ˈkat-ˌsī\ *n, pl* **cat's–eyes** (1599) **1 :** any of various gems (as a chrysoberyl or a chalcedony) exhibiting opalescent reflections from within **2 :** a marble with eyelike concentric circles

cat's–paw \ˈkat-ˌspȯ\ *n, pl* **cat's–paws** (1769) **1 :** a light air that ruffles the surface of the water in irregular patches during a calm **2** [fr. the fable of the monkey that used a cat's paw to draw chestnuts from the fire] **:** one used by another as a tool **:** DUPE **3 :** a hitch in the bight of a rope so made as to form two eyes into which a tackle may be hooked — see KNOT illustration

cat·sup \ˈkech-əp, ˈkach-; ˈkat-səp\ *n* [Malay *kĕchap* spiced fish sauce] (1690) **:** a seasoned tomato puree

cat·tail \ˈkat-ˌtāl\ *n* (1548) **:** any of a genus (*Typha* of the family Typhaceae, the cattail family) of tall reedy marsh plants with brown furry fruiting spikes; *esp* **:** a plant (*Typha latifolia*) with long flat leaves used for making mats and chair seats

cat·tery \ˈkat-ə-rē\ *n, pl* **-ter·ies** (1834) **:** an establishment for the breeding and boarding of cats

cat·tle \ˈkat-ᵊl\ *n pl* [ME *catel,* fr. ONF, personal property, fr. ML *capitale,* fr. L, neut. of *capitalis* of the head — more at CAPITAL] (13c) **1 :** domesticated quadrupeds held as property or raised for use; *specif* **:** bovine animals on a farm or ranch **2 :** human beings esp. en masse

cattle call *n* (1952) **:** a mass audition (as of actors)

cattle egret *n* (ca. 1899) **:** a small white egret (*Bubulcus ibis*) with a yellow bill and in the breeding season buff on the crown, breast, and back that has been introduced into the eastern U.S. from the Old World

cattle grub *n* (1926) **:** any of several heel flies esp. in the larval stage; *esp* **:** COMMON CATTLE GRUB

cat·tle·man \-mən, -ˌman\ *n* (1864) **:** a man who tends or raises cattle

cattle tick *n* (1869) **:** a tick (*Boophilus annulatus*) that infests cattle in the southern U.S. and tropical America and transmits the causative agent of Texas fever

cat·tleya \ˈkat-lē-ə; kat-ˈlā-ə, -ˈlē-\ *n* [NL, fr. Wm. *Cattley* †1832 Eng. patron of botany] (1828) **:** any of a genus (*Cattleya*) of tropical American epiphytic orchids with showy hooded flowers

[1]**cat·ty** \ˈkat-ē\ *n, pl* **catties** [Malay *kati*] (1598) **:** any of various units of weight of China and southeast Asia varying around $1^1/_3$ pounds; *also* **:** a standard Chinese unit equal to 1.1023 pounds

[2]**catty** *adj* **cat·ti·er; -est** (1903) **1 :** resembling a cat; *esp* **:** slyly spiteful **:** MALICIOUS **2 :** of or relating to a cat — **cat·ti·ly** \ˈkat-ᵊl-ē\ *adv* — **cat·ti·ness** \ˈkat-ē-nəs\ *n*

cat·ty–cor·ner *or* **cat·ty–cor·nered** *var of* CATERCORNER

cat·walk \ˈkat-ˌwȯk\ *n* (1885) **:** a narrow walkway (as along a bridge)

Cau·ca·sian \kȯ-ˈkā-zhən, -ˈkazh-ən\ *adj* (1807) **1 :** of or relating to the Caucasus or its inhabitants **2 a :** of or relating to the white race of mankind as classified according to physical features **b :** of or relating to the white race as defined by law specif. as composed of persons of European, No. African, or southwest Asian ancestry — **Caucasian** *n* — **Cau·ca·soid** \ˈkȯ-kə-ˌsȯid\ *adj or n*

Cau·chy sequence \kō-ˌshē-\ *n* [Augustin-Louis *Cauchy* †1857 Fr. mathematician] (1955) **:** a sequence of elements in a metric space such that for any positive number no matter how small there exists a term in the sequence for which the distance between any two consecutive or nonconsecutive terms beyond this term is less than an arbitrarily small number

[1]**cau·cus** \ˈkȯ-kəs\ *n* [prob. of Algonquian origin] (1763) **:** a closed meeting of a group of persons belonging to the same political party or faction usu. to select candidates or to decide on policy; *also* **:** a group of people united to promote an agreed-upon cause

[2]**caucus** *vi* (1788) **:** to hold or meet in a caucus

cau·dad \ˈkȯ-ˌdad\ *adv* [L *cauda*] (1889) **:** toward the tail or posterior end

cau·dal \ˈkȯd-ᵊl\ *adj* [NL *caudalis,* fr. L *cauda* tail — more at COWARD] (1661) **1 :** of, relating to, or being a tail **2 :** situated in or directed toward the hind part of the body — **cau·dal·ly** \-ᵊl-ē\ *adv*

cau·date \ˈkȯ-ˌdāt\ *adj* (1600) **:** having a tail or a taillike appendage **:** TAILED

caudate nucleus *n* (ca. 1903) **:** the most medial of the four basal ganglia in each cerebral hemisphere — called also *caudate*

cau·dex \ˈkȯ-ˌdeks\ *n, pl* **cau·di·ces** \ˈkȯd-ə-ˌsēz\ *or* **cau·dex·es** [L, tree trunk or stem — more at CODE] (1797) **1 :** the stem of a palm or tree fern **2 :** the woody base of a perennial plant

cau·di·llis·mo \ˌkau̇-t͟hē-ˈ(y)ēz-(ˌ)mō, -t͟hēl-ˈyēz-\ *n* [Sp, fr. *caudillo* + *-ismo* -ism] (1927) **:** the doctrine or practice of a caudillo **:** DICTATORSHIP

cau·di·llo \kau̇-ˈt͟hē-(ˌ)(y)ō, -ˈt͟hēl-(ˌ)yō\ *n, pl* **-llos** [Sp, fr. LL *capitellum* small head — more at CADET] (1852) **:** a Spanish or Latin-American military dictator

cau·dle \ˈkȯd-ᵊl\ *n* [ME *caudel,* fr. ONF, fr. *caut* warm, fr. L *calidus* — more at CALDRON] (14c) **:** a drink (as for invalids) usu. of warm ale or wine mixed with bread or gruel, eggs, sugar, and spices

¹**caught** \ˈkȯt\ *past and past part of* CATCH

²**caught** *adj* (1858) **:** PREGNANT — often used in the phrase *get caught*

caul \ˈkȯl\ *n* [ME *calle,* fr. MF *cale*] (14c) **1 :** the large fatty omentum covering the intestines **2 :** the inner fetal membrane of higher vertebrates esp. when covering the head at birth

cauldron *var of* CALDRON

cau·li·flow·er \ˈkȯ-li-ˌflau̇(-ə)r, ˈkäl-i-\ *n, often attrib* [It *cavolfiore,* fr. *cavolo* cabbage (fr. LL *caulus,* fr. L *caulis* stem, cabbage) + *fiore* flower, fr. L *flor-, flos* — more at HOLE, BLOW] (1597) **:** a garden plant (*Brassica oleracea botrytis*) related to the cabbage and grown for its compact edible head of usu. white undeveloped flowers; *also* **:** its flower cluster

cauliflower ear *n* (1909) **:** an ear deformed from injury and excessive growth of reparative tissue

cau·li·flow·er·et \ˌkȯ-li-ˌflau̇(-ə)-ˈret, ˌkäl-i-\ *n* (1946) **:** a bite-size piece of cauliflower

cau·line \ˈkȯ-ˌlīn\ *adj* [prob. fr. NL *caulinus,* fr. L *caulis*] (1756) **:** of, relating to, or growing on a stem; *specif* **:** growing on the upper part of a stem

¹**caulk** \ˈkȯk\ *vt* [ME *caulken,* fr. ONF *cauquer* to trample, fr. L *calcare,* fr. *calc-, calx* heel — more at CALK] (15c) **1 :** to stop up and make watertight the seams of (as a boat) by filling with a waterproofing compound or material **2 :** to stop up and make tight against leakage (as the seams of a boat, the cracks in a window frame, or the joints of a pipe) — **caulk·er** *n*

²**caulk** *also* **caulk·ing** \ˈkȯ-kiŋ\ *n* (1954) **:** material used to caulk

³**caulk** *var of* CALK

caus·al \ˈkȯ-zəl\ *adj* (1530) **1 :** expressing or indicating cause **:** CAUSATIVE ⟨a ~ clause introduced by *since*⟩ **2 :** of, relating to, or constituting a cause ⟨the ~ agent of a disease⟩ **3 :** involving causation or a cause ⟨the relationship . . . was not one of ~ antecedence so much as one of analogous growth — H. O. Taylor⟩ **4 :** arising from a cause ⟨a ~ development⟩ — **caus·al·ly** \-zə-lē\ *adv*

cau·sal·gia \kȯ-ˈzal-j(ē-)ə, -ˈsal-\ *n* [NL, fr. Gk *kausos* fever + NL *-algia;* akin to Gk *kaiein* to burn — more at CAUSTIC] (1872) **:** a constant usu. burning pain resulting from injury to a peripheral nerve — **cau·sal·gic** \-jik\ *adj*

cau·sal·i·ty \kȯ-ˈzal-ət-ē\ *n, pl* **-ties** (1603) **1 :** a causal quality or agency **2 :** the relation between a cause and its effect or between regularly correlated events or phenomena

cau·sa·tion \kȯ-ˈzā-shən\ *n* (1646) **1 a :** the act or process of causing **b :** the act or agency which produces an effect **2 :** CAUSALITY

caus·ative \ˈkȯ-zət-iv\ *adj* (15c) **1 :** effective or operating as a cause or agent ⟨cholera . . . is spread through food and water that are contaminated with the ~ bacteria —L.K. Altman⟩ **2 :** expressing causation — **causative** *n* — **caus·ative·ly** *adv*

¹**cause** \ˈkȯz\ *n* [ME, fr. OF, fr. L *causa*] (13c) **1 a :** a reason for an action or condition **:** MOTIVE **b :** something that brings about an effect or a result **c :** a person or thing that is the occasion of an action or state; *esp* **:** an agent that brings something about **2 a :** a ground of legal action **b :** CASE **3 :** a matter or question to be decided **4 :** a principle or movement militantly defended or supported — **cause·less** \-ləs\ *adj*

syn CAUSE, DETERMINANT, ANTECEDENT, REASON, OCCASION mean something that produces an effect. CAUSE applies to any event, circumstance, or condition that brings about or helps bring about a result; DETERMINANT applies to a cause that fixes the nature of what results; ANTECEDENT applies to that which has preceded and may therefore be in some degree responsible for what follows; REASON applies to a traceable or explainable cause of a known effect; OCCASION applies to a particular time or situation at which underlying causes become effective.

²**cause** *vt* **caused; caus·ing** (14c) **1 :** to serve as a cause or occasion of **2 :** to effect by command, authority, or force — **caus·er** *n*

'cause \(ˈ)kȯz, (ˈ)kəz\ *conj* (14c) **:** BECAUSE

cause cé·lè·bre \ˌkōz-sə-ˈleb(-rə), ˌkȯz-, -ˈlebrᵊ\ *n, pl* **causes cé·lè·bres** *same*\ [F, lit., celebrated case] (1763) **1 :** a legal case that excites widespread interest **2 :** a notorious incident or episode

cau·se·rie \ˌkōz-(ə-)ˈrē\ *n* [F, fr. *causer* to chat, fr. L *causari* to plead, discuss, fr. *causa*] (1827) **1 :** an informal conversation **:** CHAT **2 :** a short informal composition

cause·way \ˈkȯz-ˌwā\ *n* [ME *cauciwey,* fr. *cauci* + *wey* way] (15c) **1 :** a raised way across wet ground or water **2 :** HIGHWAY; *esp* **:** one of ancient Roman construction in Britain — **causeway** *vt*

cau·sey \ˈkȯ-zē\ *n, pl* **causeys** [ME *cauci,* fr. ONF *caucie,* fr. ML *calciata* paved highway, prob. deriv. of L *calc-, calx* limestone] (14c) **1 :** CAUSEWAY 1 **2** *obs* **:** CAUSEWAY 2

¹**caus·tic** \ˈkȯ-stik\ *adj* [L *causticus,* fr. Gk *kaustikos,* fr. *kaiein* to burn; akin to Lith *kulė* smut of plants] (15c) **1 :** capable of destroying or eating away by chemical action **:** CORROSIVE **2 :** INCISIVE, BITING ⟨~ wit⟩ **3 :** relating to or being the surface or curve of a caustic — **caus·ti·cal·ly** \-sti-k(ə-)lē\ *adv* — **caus·tic·i·ty** \kȯ-ˈstis-ət-ē\ *n*

syn CAUSTIC, MORDANT, ACRID, SCATHING mean stingingly incisive. CAUSTIC suggests a biting wit; MORDANT suggests a wit that is used with deadly effectiveness; ACRID implies bitterness and often malevolence; SCATHING implies indignant attacks delivered with fierce severity.

²**caustic** *n* (15c) **1 :** a caustic agent: as **a :** a substance that burns or destroys organic tissue by chemical action **b :** SODIUM HYDROXIDE **2 :** the envelope of rays emanating from a point and reflected or refracted by a curved surface

caustic lime *n* (1813) **:** ¹LIME 2a

caustic potash *n* (1869) **:** POTASSIUM HYDROXIDE

caustic soda *n* (1876) **:** SODIUM HYDROXIDE

cau·ter·ize \ˈkȯt-ə-ˌrīz\ *vt* **-ized; -iz·ing** (15c) **1 :** to sear with a cautery or caustic **2 :** to make insensible **:** DEADEN — **cau·ter·iza·tion** \ˌkȯt-ə-rə-ˈzā-shən\ *n*

cau·tery \ˈkȯt-ə-rē\ *n, pl* **-ter·ies** [L *cauterium,* fr. Gk *kautērion* branding iron, fr. *kaiein*] (15c) **1 :** the act or effect of cauterizing **:** CAUTERIZATION **2 :** an agent (as a hot iron or caustic) used to burn, sear, or destroy tissue

¹**cau·tion** \ˈkȯ-shən\ *n* [L *caution-, cautio* precaution, fr. *cautus,* pp. of *cavēre* to be on one's guard — more at HEAR] (1600) **1 :** WARNING, ADMONISHMENT **2 :** PRECAUTION **3 :** prudent forethought to minimize risk **4 :** one that arouses astonishment or commands attention ⟨some shoes you see . . . these days are a ~ — *Esquire*⟩

²**caution** *vt* **cau·tioned; cau·tion·ing** \ˈkȯ-sh(ə-)niŋ\ (1683) **:** to advise caution to

cau·tion·ary \ˈkȯ-shə-ˌner-ē\ *adj* (1638) **:** having the characteristics of, serving as, or offering a caution ⟨a ~ tale⟩

cau·tious \ˈkȯ-shəs\ *adj* (1640) **:** marked by or given to caution — **cau·tious·ly** *adv* — **cau·tious·ness** *n*

syn CAUTIOUS, CIRCUMSPECT, WARY, CHARY mean prudently watchful and discreet in the face of danger or risk. CAUTIOUS implies the exercise of forethought usu. prompted by fear of danger; CIRCUMSPECT suggests less fear and stresses the surveying of all possible consequences before acting or deciding; WARY emphasizes suspiciousness and alertness in watching for danger and cunning in escaping it; CHARY implies a cautious reluctance to give, act, or speak freely.

cav·al·cade \ˌkav-əl-ˈkād, ˈkav-əl-ˌ\ *n* [F, ride on horseback, fr. OIt *cavalcata,* fr. *cavalcare* to go on horseback, fr. LL *caballicare,* fr. L *caballus* horse; akin to Gk dial. *kaballeion* horse-drawn vehicle] (1644) **1 a :** a procession of riders or carriages **b :** a procession of vehicles or ships **2 :** a dramatic sequence or procession **:** SERIES

¹**cav·a·lier** \ˌkav-ə-ˈli(ə)r\ *n* [MF, fr. OIt *cavaliere,* fr. OProv *cavalier,* fr. LL *caballarius* horseman, fr. L *caballus*] (1589) **1 :** a gentleman trained in arms and horsemanship **2 :** a mounted soldier **:** KNIGHT **3** *cap* **:** an adherent of Charles I of England **4 :** GALLANT

²**cavalier** *adj* (1641) **1 :** DEBONAIR **2 :** marked by or given to offhand dismissal of important matters **:** DISDAINFUL **3 a** *cap* **:** of or relating to the party of Charles I of England in his struggles with the Puritans and Parliament **b :** ARISTOCRATIC **c** *cap* **:** of or relating to the English Cavalier poets of the mid-17th century — **ca·va·lier·ism** \-ˌiz-əm\ *n* — **cav·a·lier·ly** *adv*

ca·val·la \kə-ˈval-ə\ *n, pl* **-la** *or* **-las** [Sp *caballa,* a fish, fr. LL, mare, fem. of L *caballus*] (1624) **1** *also* **ca·val·ly** \-ˈval-ē\ **:** any of various carangid fishes (esp. genus *Caranx*) **2 :** CERO

cav·al·let·ti *also* **cav·a·let·ti** \ˌkav-ə-ˈlet-ē\ *n pl but sing or pl in constr* [It, pl. of *cavalletto* trestle, dim. of *cavallo* horse, fr. L *caballus*] (1950) **:** a series of timber jumps that are adjustable in height for schooling horses

cav·al·ry \ˈkav-əl-rē\ *n, pl* **-ries** [It *cavalleria* cavalry, chivalry, fr. *cavaliere*] (1546) **1 :** an army component mounted on horseback or moving in motor vehicles or helicopters and assigned to combat missions that require great mobility **2 :** HORSEMEN ⟨a thousand ~ in flight⟩

cav·al·ry·man \-rē-mən, -ˌman\ *n* (1860) **:** a cavalry soldier

cav·a·ti·na \ˌkav-ə-ˈtē-nə, ˌkäv-\ *n* [It, fr. *cavata* production of sound from an instrument, extraction, fr. *cavare* to dig out, fr. L, to make hollow, fr. *cavus*] (1813) **1 :** an operatic solo simpler and briefer than an aria **2 :** a songlike instrumental piece or movement

¹**cave** \ˈkāv\ *n* [ME, fr. OF, fr. L *cava,* fr. *cavus* hollow; akin to ON *hūnn* cub, Gk *kyein* to be pregnant, *koilos* hollow, Skt *śvayati* he swells] (13c) **1 :** a natural underground chamber or series of chambers open to the surface **2 :** a usu. underground chamber for storage ⟨a wine~⟩; *also* **:** the articles stored there

²**cave** *vt* **caved; cav·ing** (15c) **:** to form a cave in or under **:** HOLLOW, UNDERMINE

³**cave** \ˈkāv\ *vb* **caved; cav·ing** [prob. alter. of *calve*] *vi* (1513) **1 :** to fall in or down esp. from being undermined **2 :** to cease to resist **:** SUBMIT — usu. used with *in* ~ *vt* **:** to cause to fall or collapse — usu. used with *in*

ca·ve·at \ˈkav-ē-ˌät, -ˌat; ˈkäv-ē-ˌät\ *n* [L, let him beware, fr. *cavēre* — more at HEAR] (1549) **1 a :** a warning enjoining one from certain acts or practices **b :** an explanation to prevent misinterpretation **2 :** a legal warning to a judicial officer to suspend a proceeding until the opposition has a hearing

caveat emp·tor \-ˈem(p)-tər, -ˌtȯ(ə)r\ *n* [NL, let the buyer beware] (1523) **:** a principle in commerce: without a warranty the buyer takes the risk of quality upon himself

cave dweller *n* (1865) **1 :** one (as a prehistoric man) that dwells in a cave **2 :** one that lives in a city apartment building

cave–in \ˈkā-ˌvin\ *n* (1860) **1 :** the action of caving in **2 :** a place where earth has caved in

cave·man \ˈkāv-ˌman\ *n* (1865) **1 :** a cave dweller esp. of the Stone Age **2 :** one who acts in a rough primitive manner esp. toward women

cav·er \ˈkā-vər\ *n* (1932) **:** one that studies or explores caves

¹**cav·ern** \ˈkav-ərn\ *n* [ME *caverne,* fr. MF, fr. L *caverna,* fr. *cavus*] (14c) **:** an underground chamber often of large or indefinite extent **:** CAVE

²**cavern** *vt* (1630) **1 :** to place in or as if in a cavern **2 :** to form a cavern of **:** HOLLOW — used with *out*

\ə\ abut \ᵊ\ kitten, F table \ər\ further \a\ ash \ā\ ace \ä\ cot, cart \au̇\ out \ch\ chin \e\ bet \ē\ easy \g\ go \i\ hit \ī\ ice \j\ job \ŋ\ sing \ō\ go \ȯ\ law \ȯi\ boy \th\ thin \t͟h\ the \ü\ loot \u̇\ foot \y\ yet \zh\ vision \à, k̲, ⁿ, œ, œ̄, ue, ue̅, ʸ\ *see* Guide to Pronunciation

cav·er·nic·o·lous \ˌkav-ər-ˈnik-ə-ləs\ *adj* (1889) : inhabiting caves

cav·ern·ous \ˈkav-ər-nəs\ *adj* (15c) **1** : having caverns or cavities **2** : constituting or suggesting a cavern **3** *of animal tissue* : composed largely of vascular sinuses and capable of dilating with blood to bring about the erection of a body part — **cav·ern·ous·ly** *adv*

ca·vet·to \kə-ˈvet-(ˌ)ō, kä-\ *n, pl* **-ti** \-ē\ [It, fr. *cavo* hollow, fr. L *cavus*] (1664) : a concave molding having a curve that roughly approximates a quarter circle — see MOLDING illustration

cav·i·ar *or* **cav·i·are** \ˈkav-ē-ˌär *also* ˈkäv-\ *n* [earlier *cavery, caviarie,* fr. obs. It *caviari,* pl. of *caviaro,* fr. Turk *havyar*] (1560) **1** : processed salted roe of large fish (as sturgeon) **2** : something considered too delicate or lofty for mass appreciation ⟨the play, I remember, pleased not the million; 'twas ~ to the general — Shak.⟩

cav·il \ˈkav-əl\ *vb* **-iled** *or* **-illed; -il·ing** *or* **-il·ling** \-(ə-)liŋ\ [L *cavillari* to jest, cavil, fr. *cavilla* raillery; akin to L *calvi* to deceive — more at CALUMNY] *vi* (1542) : to raise trivial and frivolous objection ~ *vt* : to raise trivial objections to — **cavil** *n* — **cav·il·er** *or* **cav·il·ler** \-(ə-)lər\ *n*

cav·ing \ˈkā-viŋ\ *n* (1932) : the sport of exploring caves : SPELUNKING

cav·i·tary \ˈkav-ə-ˌter-ē\ *adj* (1835) : of, relating to, or characterized by bodily cavitation ⟨~ tuberculosis⟩ ⟨~ lesions⟩

cav·i·tate \ˈkav-ə-ˌtāt\ *vb* **-tat·ed; -tat·ing** *vi* (1909) : to form cavities or bubbles ~ *vt* : to cavitate in

cav·i·ta·tion \ˌkav-ə-ˈtā-shən\ *n* [*cavity* + *-ation*] (1895) : the process of cavitating: as **a** : the formation of partial vacuums in a liquid by a swiftly moving solid body (as a propeller) or by high-frequency sound waves; *also* : the pitting and wearing away of solid surfaces (as of metal or concrete) as a result of the collapse of these vacuums in surrounding liquid **b** : the formation of cavities in an organ or tissue esp. in disease

cav·i·ty \ˈkav-ət-ē\ *n, pl* **-ties** [MF *cavité,* fr. LL *cavitas,* fr. L *cavus*] (1541) **1** : an unfilled space within a mass; *esp* : a hollowed-out space **2** : an area of decay in a tooth : CARIES

ca·vort \kə-ˈvȯ(ə)rt\ *vi* [perh. alter. of *curvet*] (1793) **1** : PRANCE **2** : to engage in extravagant behavior

ca·vy \ˈkā-vē\ *n, pl* **cavies** [NL *Cavia,* genus name, fr. obs. Pg *çavia* (now *savia*), fr. Tupi *sawiya* rat] (1796) **1** : any of several short-tailed rough-haired So. American rodents (family Caviidae); *esp* : GUINEA PIG **2** : any of several rodents related to the cavies

caw \ˈkȯ\ *vi* [imit.] (1590) : to utter the harsh raucous natural call of the crow or a similar cry — **caw** *n*

cay \ˈkē, ˈkā\ *n* [Sp *cayo* — more at KEY] (1707) : a low island or reef of sand or coral

cay·enne pepper \(ˌ)kī-ˌen-, (ˌ)kā-\ *n* [by folk etymology fr. earlier *cayan,* modif. of Tupi *kyinha*] (1756) **1** : a pungent condiment consisting of the ground dried fruits or seeds of hot peppers **2** : HOT PEPPER 2; *esp* : a cultivated pepper with very long twisted pungent red fruits **3** : the fruit of a cayenne pepper

cay·man *var of* CAIMAN

Ca·yu·ga \kā-ˈ(y)ü-gə, ki-, kī-; ˈkyü-\ *n, pl* **Cayuga** *or* **Cayugas** (1744) **1 a** : an American Indian people of New York **b** : a member of this people **2** : the language of the Cayuga people

Cay·use \ˈkī-ˌ(y)üs, kī-ˈ\ *n, pl* **Cayuse** *or* **Cayuses** (1825) **1** : a member of an American Indian people of Oregon and Washington **2** *pl cayuses, not cap, West* : a native range horse

CB \ˌsē-ˈbē\ *n* (1965) : CITIZENS BAND

CBer \(ˌ)sē-ˈbē-ər, -ˈbi(ə)r\ *n* (1965) : one that operates a CB radio

CCD \ˌsē-(ˌ)sē-ˈdē\ *n* (1973) : CHARGE-COUPLED DEVICE

C clef *n* (1596) : a movable clef indicating middle C by its placement on one of the lines of the staff

CD \ˌsē-ˈdē\ *n* (1979) : COMPACT DISC

CD–ROM \ˌsē-ˌdē-ˈräm\ *n* [compact *d*isc *r*ead-*o*nly *m*emory] (1983) : a compact disc containing data that can be read by a computer

[1]**cease** \ˈsēs\ *vb* **ceased; ceas·ing** [ME *cesen,* fr. MF *cesser,* fr. L *cessare* to delay, fr. *cessus,* pp. of *cedere*] *vt* (14c) : to cause to come to an end esp. gradually : no longer continue ⟨the dying man soon *ceased* to breathe⟩ ~ *vi* **1 a** : to come to an end ⟨when will this quarreling ~⟩ **b** : to bring an activity or action to an end : DISCONTINUE ⟨cried for hours without *ceasing*⟩ **2** *obs* : to die out : become extinct ***syn*** see STOP

[2]**cease** *n* (14c) : CESSATION — usu. used with *without*

cease and desist order *n* (1926) : an order from an administrative agency to refrain from a method of competition or a labor practice found by the agency to be unfair

cease–fire \ˈsēs-ˈfī(ə)r\ *n* (1859) **1** : a military order to cease firing **2** : a suspension of active hostilities

cease·less \ˈsē-sləs\ *adj* (1586) : continuing without cease : CONSTANT — **cease·less·ly** *adv* — **cease·less·ness** *n*

ce·cro·pia moth \si-ˌkrō-pē-ə-\ *n* [NL *cecropia,* fr. L, fem. of *Cecropius* Athenian, fr. Gk *Kekropios,* fr. *Kekrops* Cecrops, legendary king of Athens] (1868) : a large silkworm moth (*Samia cecropia*) of the eastern U.S.

ce·cum \ˈsē-kəm\ *n, pl* **ce·ca** \-kə\ [NL, fr. L *intestinum caecum,* lit., blind intestine] (ca. 1721) : a cavity open at one end (as the blind end of a duct); *esp* : the blind pouch in which the large intestine begins and into which the ileum opens from one side — **ce·cal** \-kəl\ *adj* — **ce·cal·ly** \-kə-lē\ *adv*

ce·dar \ˈsēd-ər\ *n* [ME *cedre,* fr. OF, fr. L *cedrus,* fr. Gk *kedros*] (12c) **1 a** : any of a genus (*Cedrus*) of usu. tall coniferous trees (as the cedar of Lebanon or the deodar) of the pine family noted for their fragrant durable wood **b** : any of numerous coniferous trees (as of the genera *Juniperus, Chamaecyparis,* or *Thuja*) that resemble the true cedars esp. in the fragrance and durability of their wood **2** : the wood of a cedar

ce·dar–ap·ple rust \ˌsēd-ə-ˌrap-əl-\ *n* (1946) : a destructive fungous disease esp. of the apple caused by a rust fungus (*Gymnosporangium juniperi-virginianae*) that completes part of its life cycle esp. on the leaves and fruit of the apple and the rest esp. on the common red cedar (*Juniperus virginiana*)

ce·dar·bird \-ˌbərd\ *n* (1883) : CEDAR WAXWING

ce·darn \ˈsēd-ərn\ *adj, archaic* (1634) : made or suggestive of cedar

cedar of Leb·a·non \-ˈleb-(ə-)nən\ (13c) : a long-lived evergreen tree (*Cedrus libani*) with short fascicled leaves and erect cones that is native to Asia Minor

cedar waxwing *n* (1844) : a long-crested brown waxwing (*Bombycilla cedrorum*) of temperate No. America with a yellow band on the tip of the tail

ce·dar·wood \ˈsēd-ər-ˌwu̇d\ *n* (15c) : the wood of a cedar that is esp. repellent to insects

cede \ˈsēd\ *vt* **ced·ed; ced·ing** [F or L; F *céder,* fr. L *cedere* to go, withdraw, yield; prob. akin to L *cis* on this side and to Gk *hodos* road, way, L *sedēre* to sit — more at HE, SIT] (1754) **1** : to yield or grant typically by treaty **2** : ASSIGN, TRANSFER — **ced·er** *n*

ce·di \ˈsād-ē\ *n* [Akan *sedie* cowry] (1965) — see MONEY table

ce·dil·la \si-ˈdil-ə\ *n* [Sp, the obs. letter *ç* (actually a medieval form of the letter *z*), cedilla, fr. dim. of *ceda, zeda* the letter *z,* fr. LL *zeta* — more at ZED] (1599) : the diacritical mark ¸ placed under a letter (as *ç* in French) to indicate an alteration or modification of its usual phonetic value (as in the French word *façade*)

cee \ˈsē\ *n* (1542) : the letter *c*

cei·ba \ˈsā-bə\ *n* [Sp] (1797) **1** : a massive tropical tree (*Ceiba pentandra*) of the silk-cotton family with large pods filled with seeds invested with a silky floss that yields the fiber kapok **2** : KAPOK

ceil \ˈsē(ə)l\ *vt* [ME *celen,* prob. fr. (assumed) MF *celer,* fr. L *caelare* to carve, fr. *caelum* chisel; akin to L *caedere* to cut — more at CONCISE] (15c) **1** : to furnish (as a wooden ship) with a lining **2** : to furnish with a ceiling

ceil·ing \ˈsē-liŋ\ *n* [ME *celing,* fr. *celen*] (14c) **1 a** : the overhead inside lining of a room **b** : material used to ceil a wall or roof of a room **2** : something thought of as an overhanging shelter or a lofty canopy ⟨a ~ of stars⟩ **3 a** : the height above the ground from which prominent objects on the ground can be seen and identified **b** : the height above the ground of the base of the lowest layer of clouds when over half of the sky is obscured **4 a** : ABSOLUTE CEILING **b** : SERVICE CEILING **5** : an upper usu. prescribed limit ⟨a ~ on prices, rents, and wages⟩ — **ceil·inged** \-liŋd\ *adj*

ceil·om·e·ter \sē-ˈläm-ət-ər\ *n* [*ceil*ing + *-o-* + *-meter*] (1943) : a photoelectric instrument for determining by triangulation the height of the cloud ceiling above the earth

cein·ture \saⁿ(n)-ˈt(y)u̇(ə)r, ˈsan-chər\ *n* [MF, fr. L *cinctura* — more at CINCTURE] (15c) : a belt or sash for the waist

cel·a·don \ˈsel-ə-ˌdän, -əd-ᵊn\ *n* [F *céladon*] (1768) **1** : a grayish yellow green **2** : a ceramic glaze originated in China that is greenish in color and is used esp. on various stonewares and porcelains; *also* : an article with a celadon glaze

cel·an·dine \ˈsel-ən-ˌdīn, -ˌdēn\ *n* [ME *celidoine,* fr. MF, fr. L *chelidonia,* fr. fem. of *chelidonius* of the swallow, fr. Gk *chelidonios,* fr. *chelidon-, chelidōn* swallow] (12c) **1 a** : a yellow-flowered biennial herb (*Chelidonium majus*) of the poppy family **2** : a European perennial herb (*Ranunculus ficaria*) of the buttercup family that has been introduced locally into the U.S. — called also *lesser celandine*

-cele \ˌsēl\ *n comb form* [MF, fr. L, fr. Gk *kēlē;* akin to OE *hēala* hernia] : tumor : hernia ⟨varicocele⟩

ce·leb \sə-ˈleb\ *n* (1912) : CELEBRITY 2

cel·e·brant \ˈsel-ə-brənt\ *n* (1839) : one who celebrates; *specif* : the priest officiating at the Eucharist

cel·e·brate \ˈsel-ə-ˌbrāt\ *vb* **-brat·ed; -brat·ing** [L *celebratus,* pp. of *celebrare* to frequent, celebrate, fr. *celebr-, celeber* much frequented, famous; akin to L *celer*] *vt* (15c) **1** : to perform (a sacrament or solemn ceremony) publicly and with appropriate rites ⟨~ the mass⟩ **2 a** : to honor (as a holiday) by solemn ceremonies or by refraining from ordinary business **b** : to demonstrate satisfaction in (as an anniversary) by festivities or other deviation from routine **3** : to hold up or play up for public notice ⟨his poetry ~*s* the glory of nature⟩ ~ *vi* **1** : to observe a holiday, perform a religious ceremony, or take part in a festival **2** : to observe a notable occasion with festivities ***syn*** see KEEP — **cel·e·bra·tion** \ˌsel-ə-ˈbrā-shən\ *n* — **cel·e·bra·tor** \ˈsel-ə-ˌbrāt-ər\ *n* — **cel·e·bra·to·ry** \-brə-ˌtōr-ē, -ˌtȯr-\ *adj*

cel·e·brat·ed *adj* (1665) : widely known and often referred to ***syn*** see FAMOUS — **cel·e·brat·ed·ness** *n*

ce·leb·ri·ty \sə-ˈleb-rət-ē\ *n, pl* **-ties** (15c) **1** : the state of being celebrated **2** : a celebrated person

ce·le·ri·ac \sə-ˈler-ē-ˌak, -ˈlir-\ *n* [irreg. fr. *celery*] (1743) : a celery grown for its knobby edible root

ce·ler·i·ty \sə-ˈler-ət-ē\ *n* [ME *celerite,* fr. MF *célérité,* fr. L *celeritat-, celeritas,* fr. *celer* swift — more at HOLD] (15c) : rapidity of motion or action

syn CELERITY, ALACRITY mean quickness in movement or action. CELERITY implies speed in accomplishing work; ALACRITY stresses promptness in response to suggestion or command.

cel·ery \ˈsel-(ə-)rē\ *n, pl* **-er·ies** [prob. fr. It dial. *seleri,* pl. of *selero,* modif. of LL *selinon,* fr. Gk] (1664) : a European herb (*Apium graveolens*) of the carrot family; *specif* : one of a cultivated variety (*A. graveolens dulce*) with leafstalks eaten raw or cooked

celery cabbage *n* (1930) : a Chinese cabbage (*Brassica pekinensis*) that forms elongate cylindrical heads and has pale green or cream-colored leaves

ce·les·ta \sə-ˈles-tə\ *or* **ce·leste** \sə-ˈlest\ *n* [F *célesta,* alter. of *céleste,* lit., heavenly, fr. L *caelestis*] (1899) : a keyboard instrument with hammers that strike steel plates producing a tone similar to that of a glockenspiel

[1]**ce·les·tial** \sə-ˈles(h)-chəl\ *adj* [ME, fr. MF, fr. L *caelestis* celestial, fr. *caelum* sky; akin to OE *hādor* brightness] (14c) **1** : of, relating to, or suggesting heaven or divinity **2** : of or relating to the sky or visible heavens ⟨the sun, moon, and stars are ~ bodies⟩ **3 a** : ETHEREAL, OTHERWORLDLY **b** : OLYMPIAN, SUPREME **4** [*Celestial* Empire, old name for China] *cap* : of or relating to China or the Chinese — **ce·les·tial·ly** \-chə-lē\ *adv*

[2]**celestial** *n* (1573) **1** : a heavenly or mythical being **2** *cap* : CHINESE 1a

celestial equator *n* (1875) : the great circle on the celestial sphere midway between the celestial poles

celestial globe *n* (1762) : a globe depicting the celestial bodies

celestial hierarchy *n* (1883) : a traditional hierarchy of angels ranked from lowest to highest into the following nine orders: angels, archangels, principalities, powers, virtues, dominions, thrones, cherubim, and seraphim

celestial horizon *n* (ca. 1899) : HORIZON 1b(2)

celestial marriage *n* (1924) : a special order of Mormon marriage solemnized in a Mormon temple and held to be binding for a future life as well as the present one

celestial navigation *n* (ca. 1939) : navigation by observation of the positions of celestial bodies

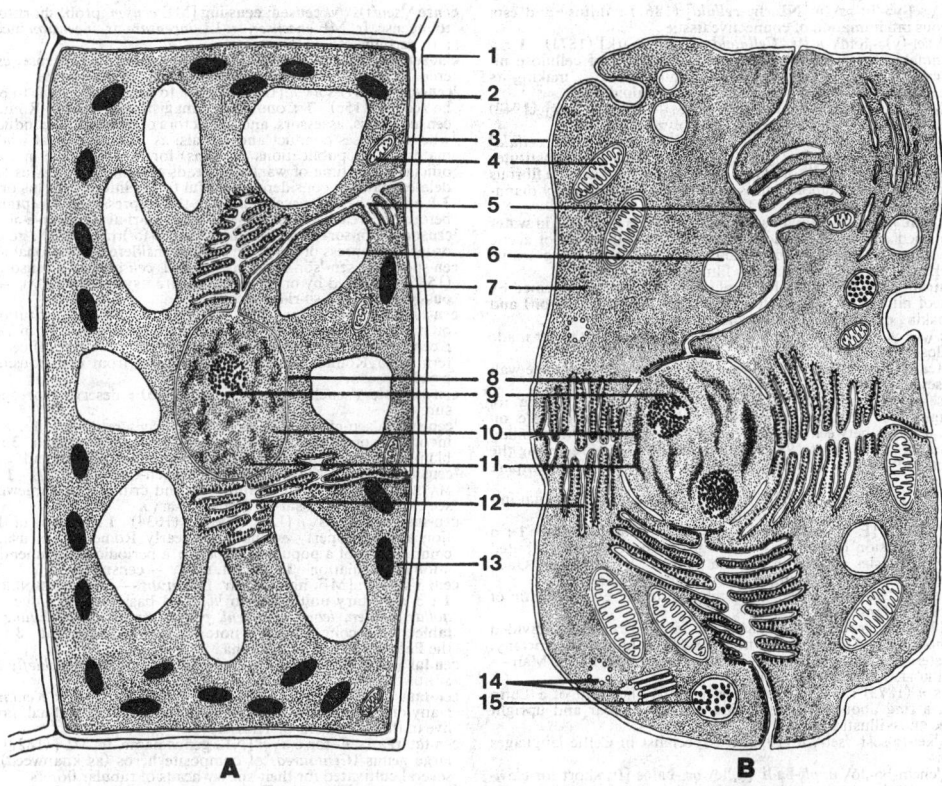

cell 4 (schematic): *A* plant, *B* animal: *1* cell wall, *2* middle lamella, *3* plasma membrane, *4* mitochondrion, *5* Golgi apparatus, *6* vacuole, *7* cytoplasm, *8* nuclear membrane, *9* nucleolus, *10* nucleus, *11* chromatin, *12* endoplasmic reticulum with associated ribosomes, *13* chloroplast, *14* centriole, *15* lysosome

celestial pole *n* (ca. 1902) : one of the two points on the celestial sphere around which the diurnal rotation of the stars appears to take place
celestial sphere *n* (1879) : an imaginary sphere of infinite radius against which the celestial bodies appear to be projected and of which the apparent dome of the visible sky forms half
ce·les·tite \'sel-ə-ˌstit, sə-'les-ˌtit\ *n* [G *zölestin*, fr. L *caelestis*] (1854) : a usu. white mineral SrSO₄ consisting of the sulfate of strontium
ce·li·ac \'sē-lē-ˌak\ *adj* [L *coeliacus*, fr. Gk *koiliakos*, fr. *koilia* cavity, fr. *koilos* hollow — more at CAVE] (1662) : of or relating to the abdominal cavity
celiac disease *n* (1936) : a chronic nutritional disturbance in young children characterized by defective digestion and utilization of fats and by abdominal distention, diarrhea, and fatty stools
cel·i·ba·cy \'sel-ə-bə-sē\ *n* (1663) **1** : the state of not being married **2 a** : abstention from sexual intercourse **b** : abstention by vow from marriage
cel·i·bate \'sel-ə-bət\ *n* [L *caelibatus*, fr. *caelib-, caelebs* unmarried; akin to Skt *kevala* alone and to OE *libban* to live] (ca. 1847) : one who lives in celibacy — **celibate** *adj*
cell \'sel\ *n* [ME, fr. OE, religious house and OF *celle* hermit's cell, fr. L *cella* small room; akin to L *celare* to conceal — more at HELL] (bef. 12c) **1** : a small religious house dependent on a monastery or convent **2 a** : a one-room dwelling occupied by a solitary person (as a hermit) **b** : a single room (as in a convent or prison) usu. for one person **3 a** : a small compartment, cavity, or bounded space: as **a** : one of the compartments of a honeycomb **b** : a membranous area bounded by veins in the wing of an insect **4** : a small usu. microscopic mass of protoplasm bounded externally by a semipermeable membrane, usu. including one or more nuclei and various nonliving products, capable alone or interacting with other cells of performing all the fundamental functions of life, and forming the least structural unit of living matter capable of functioning independently **5 a** (1) : a receptacle (as a cup or jar) containing electrodes and an electrolyte either for generating electricity by chemical action or for use in electrolysis (2) : FUEL CELL **b** : a single unit in a device for converting radiant energy into electrical energy or for varying the intensity of an electrical current in accordance with radiation **6** : a unit in a statistical array comprising a group of individuals and formed by the intersection of a column and a row **7** : the basic and usu. smallest unit of an organization or movement; *esp* : the primary unit of a Communist organization **8** : a portion of the atmosphere that behaves as a unit
cel·lar \'sel-ər\ *n* [ME *celer*, fr. AF, fr. L *cellarium* storeroom, fr. *cella*] (13c) **1 a** : BASEMENT; *also* : a covered excavation **b** : the lowest grade or rank; *esp* : the lowest place in the standings (as of an athletic league) **2** : a stock of wines
cel·lar·age \'sel-ə-rij\ *n* (1602) : cellar space esp. for storage
cel·lar·er \'sel-ər-ər\ *n* [ME *celerer*, fr. OF, fr. LL *cellariarius*, fr. L *cellarium*] (13c) : an official (as in a monastery) in charge of provisions
cel·lar·ette *or* **cel·lar·et** \ˌsel-ə-'ret\ *n* (ca. 1806) : a case or sideboard for holding bottles of wine or liquor

cell body *n* (1878) : the nucleus-containing central part of a neuron exclusive of its axons and dendrites
cell cycle *n* (1974) : the complete series of events from one cell division to the next — compare G₁ PHASE, G₂ PHASE, M PHASE, S PHASE
cell division *n* (1882) : the process by which cells multiply involving both nuclear and cytoplasmic division — compare MEIOSIS, MITOSIS
-celled \'seld\ *adj comb form* : having (such or so many) cells ⟨single=celled organisms⟩
cell membrane *n* (1870) **1** : PLASMA MEMBRANE **2** : CELL WALL
cel·lo \'chel-(ˌ)ō\ *n, pl* **cellos** [short for *violoncello*] (1876) : the bass member of the violin family tuned an octave below the viola — **cel·list** \'chel-əst\ *n*
cel·lo·bi·ose \ˌsel-ə-'bi-ˌōs, -ˌōz\ *n* [ISV *cellulose + -o- + biose* (disaccharide), fr. ¹*bi- + -ose*] (1902) : a faintly sweet disaccharide C₁₂H₂₂O₁₁ obtained by partial hydrolysis of cellulose
cel·loi·din \se-'lȯid-ᵊn\ *n* [*cellulose + -oid + -in*] (1883) : a purified pyroxylin used chiefly in microscopy
cel·lo·phane \'sel-ə-ˌfān\ *n* [F, fr. *cellulose + -phane* (as in *diaphane* diaphanous, fr. ML *diaphanus*)] (1912) : regenerated cellulose in thin transparent sheets used esp. for packaging
cell plate *n* (1882) : a disk formed in the phragmoplast of a dividing plant cell that eventually forms the middle lamella of the wall between the daughter cells
cell sap *n* (ca. 1889) **1** : the liquid contents of a plant cell vacuole **2** : HYALOPLASM
cell theory *n* (ca. 1890) : a theory in biology that includes one or both of the statements that the cell is the fundamental structural and functional unit of living matter and that the organism is composed of autonomous cells with its properties being the sum of those of its cells
cel·lu·lar \'sel-yə-lər\ *adj* [NL *cellularis*, fr. *cellula* living cell, fr. L, dim. of *cella* small room] (ca. 1739) **1** : of, relating to, or consisting of cells **2** : containing cavities : having a porous texture ⟨~ rocks⟩ **3** : of, relating to, or being a radiotelephone system in which a geographical area (as a city) is divided into small sections each served by a transmitter of limited range so that any available radio channel can be used in different parts of the area simultaneously — **cel·lu·lar·i·ty** \ˌsel-yə-'lar-ət-ē\ *n*
cel·lu·lase \'sel-yə-ˌlās, -ˌlāz\ *n* [ISV *cellul*ose + *-ase*] (1903) : an enzyme that hydrolyzes cellulose
cel·lule \'sel-(ˌ)yü(ə)l\ *n* [L *cellula*] (1830) : a small cell
cel·lu·lite \'sel-yə-ˌlit, -ˌlēt\ *n* [F, fr. *cellule* cell + *-ite* ¹-ite] (1974) : lumpy fat found in the thighs, hips, and buttocks of some women

cel·lu·li·tis \ˌsel-yə-ˈlīt-əs\ *n* [NL, fr. *cellula*] (1861) **:** diffuse and esp. subcutaneous inflammation of connective tissue

cel·lu·loid \ˈsel-(y)ə-ˌlȯid\ *n* [fr. *Celluloid,* a trademark] (1871) **1 :** a tough flammable thermoplastic composed essentially of cellulose nitrate and camphor **2 :** a motion-picture film ⟨a work . . . making its third appearance on ~ — John McCarten⟩ — **celluloid** *adj*

cel·lu·lo·lyt·ic \ˌsel-yə-lō-ˈlit-ik\ *adj* [*cellulose* + *-o-* + *-lytic*] (1943) **:** hydrolyzing or having the capacity to hydrolyze cellulose

cel·lu·lose \ˈsel-yə-ˌlōs, -ˌlōz\ *n* [F, fr. *cellule* living cell, fr. NL *cellula*] (1835) **:** a polysaccharide $(C_6H_{10}O_5)_x$ of glucose units that constitutes the chief part of the cell walls of plants, occurs naturally in such fibrous products as cotton and kapok, and is the raw material of many manufactured goods (as paper, rayon, and cellophane)

cellulose acetate *n* (1895) **:** any of several compounds insoluble in water that are formed esp. by the action of acetic acid, anhydride of acetic acid, and sulfuric acid on cellulose and are used for making textile fibers, packaging sheets, photographic films, and varnishes

cellulose nitrate *n* (1880) **:** any of several esters of nitric acid formed by the action of nitric acid on cellulose (as paper, linen, or cotton) and used for making explosives, plastics, and varnishes

cel·lu·los·ic \ˌsel-yə-ˈlō-sik, -zik\ *adj* (ca. 1881) **:** of, relating to, or made from cellulose

cell wall *n* (ca. 1847) **:** the firm nonliving and usu. chiefly cellulose wall that encloses and supports most plant cells — see CELL illustration

Cel·sius \ˈsel-sē-əs, -shəs\ *adj* [Anders *Celsius*] (1850) **:** relating to, conforming to, or having the international thermometric scale on which the interval between the triple point of water and the boiling point of water is divided into 99.99 degrees with 0.01° representing the triple point and 100° the boiling point ⟨10° ~ ⟩ — abbr. *C;* compare CENTIGRADE

celt \ˈselt\ *n* [LL *celtis* chisel] (1715) **:** a prehistoric stone or metal implement shaped like a chisel or ax head

Celt \ˈkelt, ˈselt\ *n* [F *Celte,* sing. of *Celtes,* fr. L *Celtae*] (1607) **1 :** a member of a division of the early Indo-European peoples distributed from the British Isles and Spain to Asia Minor **2 :** a modern Gael, Highland Scot, Irishman, Welshman, Cornishman, or Breton

[1]**Celt·ic** \ˈkel-tik, ˈsel-\ *adj* (1656) **:** of, relating to, or characteristic of the Celts or their languages

[2]**Celtic** *n* (1739) **:** a group of Indo-European languages usu. subdivided into Brythonic and Goidelic and now largely confined to Brittany, Wales, western Ireland, the Scottish Highlands, and the Isle of Man — see INDO-EUROPEAN LANGUAGES table

Celtic cross *n* (1873) **:** a cross having essentially the form of a Latin cross with a ring about the intersection of the crossbar and upright shaft — see CROSS illustration

Celt·i·cist \ˈkel-tə-səst, ˈsel-\ *n* (1912) **:** a specialist in Celtic languages or cultures

cem·ba·lo \ˈchem-bə-ˌlō\ *n, pl* **-ba·li** \-(ˌ)lē\ *or* **-balos** [It, short for *clavicembalo*] (ca. 1801) **:** HARPSICHORD

[1]**ce·ment** \si-ˈment\ *n* [ME *sement,* fr. MF *ciment,* fr. L *caementum* stone chips used in making mortar, fr. *caedere* to cut — more at CONCISE] (14c) **1 :** a powder of alumina, silica, lime, iron oxide, and magnesia burned together in a kiln and finely pulverized and used as an ingredient of mortar and concrete; *also* **:** CONCRETE **2 :** a binding element or agency: as **a :** a substance to make objects adhere to each other **b :** something serving to unite firmly ⟨justice is the ~ that holds a political community together —R. M. Hutchins⟩ **3 :** CEMENTUM **4 :** a plastic composition usu. made of zinc, copper, or silica for filling dental cavities **5 :** the fine-grained groundmass or glass of a porphyry

[2]**cement** *vt* (15c) **1 :** to unite or make firm by or as if by cement **2 :** to overlay with concrete ~ *vi* **:** to become cemented — **ce·ment·er** *n*

ce·men·ta·tion \ˌsē-ˌmen-ˈtā-shən\ *n* (1594) **1 :** a process of surrounding a solid with a powder and heating the whole so that the solid is changed by chemical combination with the powder **2 :** the act or process of cementing **:** the state of being cemented

ce·ment·ite \si-ˈment-ˌīt\ *n* [[1]*cement*] (1888) **:** a hard brittle iron carbide Fe_3C that occurs in steel, cast iron, and iron-carbon alloys

ce·men·ti·tious \ˌsē-ˌmen-ˈtish-əs\ *adj* (ca. 1828) **:** having the properties of cement

ce·men·tum \si-ˈment-əm\ *n* [NL, fr. L *caementum*] (1842) **:** a specialized external bony layer of the part of a tooth normally within the gum — see TOOTH illustration

cem·e·tery \ˈsem-ə-ˌter-ē\ *n, pl* **-ter·ies** [ME *cimitery,* fr. MF *cimitere,* fr. LL *coemeterium,* fr. Gk *koimētērion* sleeping chamber, burial place, fr. *koiman* to put to sleep; akin to L *cunae* cradle] (15c) **:** a burial ground

cen- *or* **ceno-** *or* **caen-** *or* **caeno-** *comb form* [Gk *kain-, kaino-,* fr. *kainos* — more at RECENT] **:** new **:** recent ⟨*Cenozoic*⟩

cen·a·cle \ˈsen-i-kəl\ *n* [LL *cenaculum* the room where Christ and his disciples had the Last Supper, fr. L, dining room, fr. *cena* dinner] (1889) **:** a retreat house; *esp* **:** one for Roman Catholic women directed by nuns of the Society of Our Lady of the Cenacle

-cene \ˌsēn\ *adj comb form* [Gk *kainos*] **:** recent — in names of geologic periods ⟨*Eocene*⟩

cen·o·bite \ˈsen-ə-ˌbīt, *esp Brit* ˈsēn-\ *n* [LL *coenobita,* fr. *coenobium* monastery, fr. LGk *koinobion,* deriv. of Gk *koin-* coen- + *bios* life — more at QUICK] (1500) **:** a member of a religious group living together in a monastic community — **cen·o·bit·ic** \ˌsen-ə-ˈbit-ik, ˌsēn-\ *adj*

ce·no·spe·cies \ˈsē-nə-ˌspē-(ˌ)shēz, ˈsen-ə-, -(ˌ)sēz\ *n* [*coen-* + *species*] (1922) **:** a group of related biological taxonomic units capable by reason of closely related genotypes of essentially free gene interchange

ceno·taph \ˈsen-ə-ˌtaf\ *n* [F *cénotaphe,* fr. L *cenotaphium,* fr. Gk *kenotaphion,* fr. *kenos* empty + *taphos* tomb] (1603) **:** a tomb or a monument erected in honor of a person or group of persons whose remains are elsewhere

ce·no·te \si-ˈnōt-ē\ *n* [Sp, fr. Maya *tzonot*] (1841) **:** a deep sinkhole in limestone with a pool at the bottom that is found esp. in Yucatán

Ce·no·zo·ic \ˌsē-nə-ˈzō-ik, ˌsen-ə-\ *adj* (1854) **:** of, relating to, or being an era of geological history that extends from the beginning of the Tertiary period to the present time and is marked by a rapid evolution of mammals and birds and of grasses, shrubs, and higher flowering plants and by little change in the invertebrates; *also* **:** relating to the system of rocks formed in this era — see GEOLOGIC TIME table — **Cenozoic** *n*

cense \ˈsen(t)s\ *vt* **censed; cens·ing** [ME *censen,* prob. short for *encensen* to incense, fr. MF *encenser,* fr. LL *incensare,* fr. *incensum* incense] (14c) **:** to perfume esp. with a censer

cen·ser \ˈsen(t)-sər\ *n* (13c) **:** a vessel for burning incense; *esp* **:** a covered incense burner swung on chains in a religious ritual

[1]**cen·sor** \ˈsen(t)-sər\ *n* [L, fr. *censēre* to assess, tax; akin to Skt *śaṁsati* he recites] (15c) **1 :** one of two magistrates of early Rome acting as census takers, assessors, and inspectors of morals and conduct **2 :** one who supervises conduct and morals: as **a :** an official who examines materials (as publications or films) for objectionable matter **b :** an official (as in time of war) who reads communications (as letters) and deletes material considered harmful to the interests of his organization **3 :** a hypothetical psychic agency that represses unacceptable notions before they reach consciousness — **cen·so·ri·al** \sen-ˈsōr-ē-əl, -ˈsȯr-\ *adj*

[2]**censor** *vt* **cen·sored; cen·sor·ing** \ˈsen(t)s-(ə-)riŋ\ (1882) **:** to examine in order to suppress or delete anything considered objectionable

cen·so·ri·ous \sen-ˈsōr-ē-əs, -ˈsȯr-\ *adj* [L *censorius* of a censor, fr. *censor*] (1536) **:** marked by or given to censure ***syn*** see CRITICAL — **cen·so·ri·ous·ly** *adv* — **cen·so·ri·ous·ness** *n*

cen·sor·ship \ˈsen(t)-sər-ˌship\ *n* (1591) **1 a :** the institution, system, or practice of censoring **b :** the actions or practices of censors; *esp* **:** censorial control exercised repressively **2 :** the office, power, or term of a Roman censor **3 :** exclusion from consciousness by the psychic censor

cen·sur·able \ˈsench-(ə-)rə-bəl\ *adj* (1635) **:** deserving or open to censure

[1]**cen·sure** \ˈsen-chər\ *n* [L *censura,* fr. *censēre*] (14c) **1 :** a judgment involving condemnation **2** *archaic* **:** OPINION, JUDGMENT **3 :** the act of blaming or condemning sternly **4 :** an official reprimand

[2]**censure** *vt* **cen·sured; cen·sur·ing** \ˈsench-(ə-)riŋ\ (1587) **1** *obs* **:** ESTIMATE, JUDGE **2 :** to find fault with and criticize as blameworthy ***syn*** see CRITICIZE — **cen·sur·er** \ˈsen-chər-ər\ *n*

cen·sus \ˈsen(t)-səs\ *n* [L, fr. *censēre*] (1634) **1 :** a count of the population and a property evaluation in early Rome **2 :** a usu. complete enumeration of a population; *specif* **:** a periodic governmental enumeration of population **3 :** COUNT, TALLY — **census** *vt*

cent \ˈsent\ *n* [MF, hundred, fr. L *centum* — more at HUNDRED] (1782) **1 :** a monetary unit equal to 1/100 of a basic unit of value — see *birr, dollar, gulden, leone, lilangeni, pound, rand, rupee, shilling* at MONEY table **2 :** a coin, token, or note representing one cent **3 :** the fen of the People's Republic of China

cen·tal \ˈsent-ᵊl\ *n* [L *centum* + E *-al* (as in *quintal*)] *chiefly Brit* (1870) **:** HUNDREDWEIGHT 1

cen·taur \ˈsen-ˌtȯ(ə)r\ *n* [ME, fr. L *Centaurus,* fr. Gk *Kentauros*] (14c) **:** any of a race of creatures fabled to be half man and half horse and to live in the mountains of Thessaly

cen·tau·rea \sen-ˈtȯr-ē-ə\ *n* [NL, genus name, fr. ML] (1829) **:** any of a large genus (*Centaurea*) of composite herbs (as knapweed) including several cultivated for their showy heads of tubular florets

Cen·tau·rus \-ˈtȯr-əs\ *n* [L (gen. *Centauri*)] **:** a southern constellation between the Southern Cross and Hydra

cen·tau·ry \ˈsen-ˌtȯr-ē\ *n, pl* **-ries** [ME *centaure,* fr. MF *centaurée,* fr. ML *centaurea,* fr. L *centaureum,* fr. Gk *kentaureion,* fr. *Kentauros*] (14c) **1 :** any of a genus (*Centaurium*) of low herbs of the gentian family; *esp* **:** an Old World herb (*C. umbellatum*) formerly used as a tonic **2 :** an American plant (*Sabatia angularis*) closely related to centaury

[1]**cen·ta·vo** \sen-ˈtäv-(ˌ)ō\ *n, pl* **-vos** [Sp, lit., hundredth, fr. L *centum* hundred] (1883) — see *boliviano, colon, cordoba, lempira, peso, quetzal, sucre* at MONEY table

[2]**cen·ta·vo** \-ˈtäv-(ˌ)ü, -(ˌ)ō\ *n, pl* **-vos** [Pg, fr. Sp] (1883) — see *escudo, metical* at MONEY table

cen·te·nar·i·an \ˌsent-ᵊn-ˈer-ē-ən\ *n* (ca. 1841) **:** one that is 100 years old or older — **centenarian** *adj*

cen·te·na·ry \sen-ˈten-ə-rē, ˈsent-ᵊn-ˌer-ē, *esp Brit* sen-ˈtē-nə-rē\ *n, pl* **-ries** [LL *centenarium,* fr. L *centenarius* of a hundred, fr. *centeni* one hundred each, fr. *centum* hundred — more at HUNDRED] (1607) **:** CENTENNIAL — **centenary** *adj*

cen·ten·ni·al \sen-ˈten-ē-əl\ *n* [L *centum* + E *-ennial* (as in *biennial*)] (1876) **:** a 100th anniversary or its celebration — **centennial** *adj* — **cen·ten·ni·al·ly** \-ə-lē\ *adv*

[1]**cen·ter** \ˈsent-ər\ *n* [ME *centre,* fr. MF, fr. L *centrum,* fr. Gk *kentron* sharp point, center of a circle, fr. *kentein* to prick; akin to OHG *hantag* pointed] (14c) **1 a :** the point around which a circle or sphere is described; *broadly* **:** a point that is related to a geometrical figure in such a way that for any point on the figure there is another point on the figure such that a straight line joining the two points is bisected by the original point — called also *center of symmetry* **b :** the center of the circle inscribed in a regular polygon **2 a :** a point, area, person, or thing that is most important or pivotal in relation to an indicated activity, interest, or condition ⟨a railroad ~⟩ ⟨the ~ of the controversy⟩ **b :** a source from which something originates ⟨a propaganda ~⟩ **c :** a group of nerve cells having a common function ⟨respiratory ~⟩ **d :** a region of concentrated population ⟨an urban ~⟩ **3 a :** the middle part (as of the forehead or a stage) **b** *often cap* (1) **:** a grouping of political figures holding moderate views esp. between those of conservatives and liberals (2) **:** the views of such politicians (3) **:** the adherents of such views **4 :** a player occupying a middle position on a team: as **a :** the football player in the middle of a line who passes the ball between his legs to a back to start a down **b :** the usu. tallest player on a basketball team who usu. plays near the basket **5 a :** one of two tapered rods which support work in a lathe or grinding machine and about or with which the work revolves **b :** a conical recess in the end of work (as a shaft) for receiving such a center

[2]**center** *vb* **cen·tered; cen·ter·ing** \ˈsent-ə-riŋ, ˈsen-triŋ\ *vt* (1610) **1 :** to place or fix at or around a center or central area or position ⟨~ the picture on the wall⟩ **2 :** to gather to a center **:** CONCENTRATE ⟨~*s* her hopes on her son⟩ **3 :** to adjust (as lenses) so that the axes coincide **4 a :** to pass (a ball or puck) from either side toward the middle of the playing area **b :** to hand or pass (a football) backward between one's legs to a back to start a down ~ *vi* **:** to have a center **:** FOCUS

usage The intransitive verb *center* is most commonly used with the prepositions *in, on, at,* and *around. At* appears to be favored in mathematical contexts; the others are found in a broad range of contexts.

Center around, a standard idiom, is often objected to as illogical. Since it is an idiom, its criticism on the grounds of logic is irrelevant. But if you want to avoid criticism, you can choose *center on* (most common in edited prose) or *center in* or substitute *revolve around* for *center around.*

cen·ter·board \'sent-ər-,bō(ə)rd, -,bȯ(ə)rd\ *n* (1867) **:** a retractable keel used esp. in sailboats

cen·tered \'sent-ərd\ *adj* (ca. 1889) **1 :** having a center — often used in combination ⟨a dark-*centered* coneflower⟩ **2 :** having a center of curvature — often used in combination ⟨a 3-*centered* arch⟩

center field *n* (1857) **1 :** the position of the player for defending center field **2 :** the part of the baseball outfield between right and left field — **center fielder** *n*

cen·ter·fold \'sent-ər-,fōld\ *n* (1952) **1 :** a foldout that is the center spread of a magazine **2 :** a picture (as of a nude) on a centerfold

cen·ter·line \,sent-ər-'līn\ *n* (1807) **:** a real or imaginary line that is equidistant from the surface or sides of something (as a machine part or a roadway)

center of curvature (1866) **:** the center of the circle whose center lies on the concave side of a curve on the normal to a given point of the curve and whose radius is equal to the radius of curvature at that point

center of gravity (1659) **1 :** CENTER OF MASS **2 :** the point at which the entire weight of a body may be considered as concentrated so that if supported at this point the body would remain in equilibrium in any position **3 :** CENTER 2a

center of mass (1879) **:** the point in a body or system of bodies at which the whole mass may be considered as concentrated

cen·ter·piece \'sent-ər-,pēs\ *n* (1803) **1 :** an object occupying a central position; *esp* **:** an adornment in the center of a table **2 :** one (as an event, concept, or policy) that is of central importance or interest

center punch *n* (1879) **:** a hand punch consisting of a short steel bar with a hardened conical point at one end used for marking the centers of holes to be drilled

cen·tes·i·mal \sen-'tes-ə-məl\ *adj* [L *centesimus* hundredth, fr. *centum*] (1829) **:** marked by or relating to division into hundredths

1**cen·tes·i·mo** \chen-'tez-ə-,mō\ *n, pl* **-mi** \-(,)mē\ [It] (1851) — see *lira* at MONEY table

2**cen·tes·i·mo** \sen-'tes-ə-,mō\ *n, pl* **-mos** [Sp *centésimo*] (ca. 1883) — see *balboa, peso* at MONEY table

centi- *comb form* [F&L; F, hundredth, fr. L, hundred, fr. *centum* — more at HUNDRED] **1 :** hundred ⟨*centi*pede⟩ **2 :** hundredth part ⟨*centi*second⟩

cen·ti·grade \'sent-ə-,grād, 'sänt-\ *adj* [F, fr. L *centi-* hundred + F *grade*] (1801) **:** relating to, conforming to, or having a thermometric scale on which the interval between the freezing point of water and the boiling point of water is divided into 100 degrees with 0° representing the freezing point and 100° the boiling point ⟨10° ~⟩ — abbr. *C;* compare CELSIUS

cen·ti·gram \-,gram\ *n* (1801) — see METRIC SYSTEM table

cen·ti·li·ter \'sent-i-,lēt-ər, 'sänt-\ *n* (1801) — see METRIC SYSTEM table

cen·til·lion \sen-'til-yən\ *n, often attrib* [L *centum* + E *-illion* (as in *million*)] (ca. 1889) — see NUMBER table

cen·time \'sän-,tēm, 'sen-\ *n* [F, fr. *cent* hundred, fr. L *centum*] (1801) — see *dinar, dirham, franc, gourde* at MONEY table

cen·ti·me·ter \'sent-ə-,mēt-ər, 'sänt-\ *n* (1801) — see METRIC SYSTEM table

centimeter–gram–second *adj* (1875) **:** of, relating to, or being a system of units based on the centimeter as the unit of length, the gram as the unit of mass, and the solar second as the unit of time — abbr. *cgs*

cen·ti·mo \'sent-ə-,mō\ *n, pl* **-mos** [Sp *céntimo*] (1899) — see *bolivar, colon, dobra, guarani, peseta* at MONEY table

cen·ti·pede \'sent-ə-,pēd\ *n* [L *centipeda,* fr. *centi-* + *ped-, pes* foot — more at FOOT] (1601) **:** any of a class (Chilopoda) of long flattened many-segmented predaceous arthropods with each segment bearing one pair of legs of which the foremost pair is modified into poison fangs

cent·ner \'sent-nər\ *n* [prob. fr. LG] (1683) **:** a unit of weight used in Germany and Scandinavia usu. equal to 110.23 pounds; *also* **:** a unit used in the U.S.S.R. equal to 220.46 pounds

cen·to \'sen-(,)tō\ *n, pl* **cen·to·nes** \sen-'tō-(,)nēz\ [LL, fr. L, patchwork garment; akin to OHG *hadara* rag, Skt *kanthā* patched garment] (1605) **:** a literary work made up of parts from other works

centr- *or* **centri-** *or* **centro-** *comb form* [Gk *kentr-, kentro-,* fr. *kentron* center — more at CENTER] **:** center ⟨*centri*fugal⟩ ⟨*centr*oid⟩

centra *pl of* CENTRUM

1**cen·tral** \'sen-trəl\ *adj* [L *centralis,* fr. *centrum* center — more at CENTER] (1647) **1 :** containing or constituting a center **2 :** of cardinal importance **:** ESSENTIAL, PRINCIPAL ⟨the ~ character of the novel⟩ **3 a :** situated at, in, or near the center **b :** easily accessible from outlying districts ⟨a ~ location for the new theater⟩ **4 a :** centrally placed and superseding separate scattered units ⟨~ heating⟩ **b :** controlling or directing local or branch activities ⟨the ~ committee⟩ **5 :** holding to a middle between extremes **:** MODERATE **6 :** of, relating to, or comprising the brain and spinal cord; *also* **:** originating within the central nervous system ⟨~ deafness⟩ — **cen·tral·ly** \-trə-lē\ *adv*

2**central** *n* (1889) **1 :** a telephone exchange or operator **2 :** a central office or bureau usu. controlling others ⟨weather ~⟩

central angle *n* (ca. 1904) **:** an angle formed by two radii of a circle

central bank *n* (1922) **:** a national bank that operates to establish monetary and fiscal policy and to control the money supply and interest rate

central city *n* (1950) **:** a city that constitutes the densely populated center of a metropolitan area and is characterized by a concentration of cultural and commercial facilities serving the area and by a population disproportionately high in disadvantaged persons

cen·tral·ism \'sen-trə-,liz-əm\ *n* (1831) **:** the concentration of power and control in the central authority of an organization (as a political or educational system) — compare FEDERALISM — **cen·tral·ist** \-ləst\ *n or adj* — **cen·tral·is·tic** \,sen-trə-'lis-tik\ *adj*

cen·tral·i·ty \sen-'tral-ət-ē\ *n, pl* **-ties** (1647) **1 :** the quality or state of being central **2 :** central situation **3 :** tendency to remain in or at the center

cen·tral·ize \'sen-trə-,līz\ *vb* **-ized; -iz·ing** *vi* (1800) **:** to form a center **:** cluster around a center ~ *vt* **1 :** to bring to a center **:** CONSOLIDATE ⟨~ all the data in one file⟩ **2 :** to concentrate by placing power and authority in a center or central organization — **cen·tral·iza·tion** \,sen-trə-lə-'zā-shən\ *n* — **cen·tral·iz·er** \'sen-trə-,lī-zər\ *n*

central limit theorem *n* (1951) **:** any of several fundamental theorems of probability and statistics that state the conditions under which the distribution of a sum of independent random variables is approximated by the normal distribution; *esp* **:** a special case of the central limit theorem which is much applied in sampling and which states that the distribution of a mean of a sample from a population with finite variance is approximated by the normal distribution as the number in the sample becomes large

central nervous system *n* (1895) **:** the part of the nervous system which in vertebrates consists of the brain and spinal cord, to which sensory impulses are transmitted and from which motor impulses pass out, and which supervises and coordinates the activity of the entire nervous system — compare AUTONOMIC NERVOUS SYSTEM

central processing unit *n* (ca. 1969) **:** PROCESSOR 2a(2)

central tendency *n* (ca. 1928) **:** the degree of clustering of the values of a statistical distribution that is usu. measured by the arithmetic mean, mode, or median

central time *n, often cap C* (1883) **:** the time of the 6th time zone west of Greenwich that includes the central U.S. — see TIME ZONE illustration

cen·tre *chiefly Brit var of* CENTER

cen·tric \'sen-trik\ *adj* [Gk *kentrikos* of the center, fr. *kentron*] (1590) **1 :** located in or at a center **:** CENTRAL ⟨a ~ point⟩ **2 :** concentrated about or directed to a center ⟨a ~ activity⟩ **3 :** of, relating to, or having a centromere **4 :** of, relating to, or resembling an order (Centrales) of diatoms having the surface markings centrally arranged — **cen·tri·cal·ly** \-tri-k(ə-)lē\ *adv* — **cen·tric·i·ty** \sen-'tris-ət-ē\ *n*

-cen·tric \'sen-trik\ *adj comb form* [ML *-centricus,* fr. L *centrum* center] **:** having (such) a center or (such or so many) centers ⟨poly*centric*⟩ **:** having (something specified) as its center ⟨helio*centric*⟩

1**cen·trif·u·gal** \sen-'trif-yə-gəl, -'trif-i-gəl\ *adj* [NL *centrifugus,* fr. *centr-* + L *fugere* to flee — more at FUGITIVE] (1721) **1 :** proceeding or acting in a direction away from a center or axis **2 :** using or acting by centrifugal force ⟨a ~ pump⟩ **3 :** EFFERENT **4 :** tending away from centralization **:** SEPARATIST ⟨~ tendencies in modern society⟩ — **centrif·u·gal·ly** \-gə-lē\ *adv*

2**centrifugal** *n* (1866) **:** a centrifugal machine or a drum in such a machine

centrifugal force *n* (1721) **1 :** the force that tends to impel a thing or parts of a thing outward from a center of rotation **2 :** the force that an object moving along a circular path exerts on the body constraining the object and that acts outwardly away from the center of rotation ⟨a stone whirled on a string exerts *centrifugal force* on the string⟩

cen·trif·u·ga·tion \,sen-trə-fyů-'gā-shən, -f(y)ə-\ *n* (1903) **:** the process of centrifuging

1**cen·tri·fuge** \'sen-trə-,fyüj\ *n* [F, fr. *centrifuge* centrifugal, fr. NL *centrifugus*] (1887) **:** a machine using centrifugal force for separating substances of different densities, for removing moisture, or for simulating gravitational effects

2**centrifuge** *vt* **-fuged; -fug·ing** (1895) **:** to subject to centrifugal action esp. in a centrifuge

cen·tri·ole \'sen-trē-,ōl\ *n* [G *zentriol,* fr. *zentrum* center] (1896) **:** one of a pair of cellular organelles that are adjacent to the nucleus, function in the formation of the mitotic apparatus, and consist of a cylinder with nine microtubules arranged peripherally in a circle — see CELL illustration

cen·trip·e·tal \sen-'trip-ət-ᵊl\ *adj* [NL *centripetus,* fr. *centr-* + L *petere* to go to, seek — more at FEATHER] (1709) **1 :** proceeding or acting in a direction toward a center or axis **2 :** AFFERENT **3 :** tending toward centralization **:** UNIFYING — **cen·trip·e·tal·ly** \-ᵊl-ē\ *adv*

centripetal force *n* (1709) **:** the force that is necessary to keep an object moving in a circular path and that is directed inward toward the center of rotation ⟨a string on the end of which a stone is whirled about exerts *centripetal force* on the stone⟩

cen·trist \'sen-trəst\ *n* (1872) **1** *often cap* **:** a member of a center party **2 :** one who holds moderate views — **cen·trism** \-,triz-əm\ *n*

cen·troid \'sen-,trȯid\ *n* (1882) **1 :** CENTER OF MASS **2 :** a point whose coordinates are the averages of the corresponding coordinates of a given set and which for a given planar or three-dimensional figure (as a triangle or sphere) corresponds to the center of mass of a thin plate of uniform thickness and consistency or a body of uniform consistency having the same boundary

cen·tro·mere \'sen-trə-,mi(ə)r\ *n* [ISV] (1936) **:** the point on a chromosome by which it appears to attach to the spindle in mitosis — **cen·tro·mer·ic** \,sen-trə-'mi(ə)r-ik, -'mer-\ *adj*

cen·tro·some \'sen-trə-,sōm\ *n* [G *zentrosom,* fr. *zentr-* centr- + *-som* -some] (1897) **1 :** CENTRIOLE **2 :** the centriole-containing region of clear cytoplasm adjacent to the cell nucleus

cen·tro·sym·met·ric \,sen-trə-sə-'me-trik\ *adj* (ca. 1909) **:** symmetric with respect to a central point ⟨~ molecules⟩ ⟨a ~ curve⟩

cen·trum \'sen-trəm\ *n, pl* **centrums** *or* **cen·tra** \-trə\ [L — more at CENTER] (1854) **1 :** CENTER **2 :** the body of a vertebra — see VERTEBRA illustration

cen·tum \'kent-əm, 'ken-,tům\ *adj* [L, hundred; fr. the fact that its initial sound (a velar stop) is the representative of an IE palatal stop — more at HUNDRED] (1901) **:** of, relating to, or constituting an Indo-European language group characterized by the retention of the Proto-Indo-European stops *k, g,* and *gh* in certain environments — compare SATEM

cen·tu·ri·on \sen-'t(y)ůr-ē-ən\ *n* [ME, fr. MF & L; MF, fr. L *centurion-, centurio,* fr. *centuria*] (13c) **:** an officer commanding a Roman century

cen·tu·ry \'sench-(ə-)rē\ *n, pl* **-ries** [L *centuria,* irreg. fr. *centum* hundred] (1533) **1 :** a subdivision of the Roman legion **2 :** a group, sequence, or series of 100 like things **3 :** a period of 100 years esp. of the Christian era or of the preceding period of human history **4 :** a race over a hundred units (as yards or miles)

century plant *n* (1764) **:** a Mexican agave (*Agave americana*) maturing and flowering only once in many years and then dying

\ə\ abut \ᵊ\ kitten, F table \ər\ further \a\ ash \ā\ ace \ä\ cot, cart \aů\ out \ch\ chin \e\ bet \ē\ easy \g\ go \i\ hit \ī\ ice \j\ job \ŋ\ sing \ō\ go \ȯ\ law \ȯi\ boy \th\ thin \t͟h\ the \ü\ loot \ů\ foot \y\ yet \zh\ vision \à, k̲, ⁿ, œ, œ̄, ue, ue̅, ʸ\ *see* Guide to Pronunciation

ceorl \'chā-,ȯr(ə)l\ *n* [OE — more at CHURL] (bef. 12c) : a freeman of the lowest rank in Anglo-Saxon England

cèpe *or* **cepe** \'sēp, sep\ *also* **cep** \'sep\ *n* [F, fr. F dial. *cep* tree trunk, mushroom, fr. L *cippus* stake, post] (1865) : a wild edible mushroom of the genus *Boletus* (esp. *B. edulis*)

cephal- *or* **cephalo-** *comb form* [L, fr. Gk *kephal-, kephalo-,* fr. *kephalē*] : head ⟨*cephal*ad⟩ ⟨*Cephalo*poda⟩

ceph·a·lad \'sef-ə-,lad\ *adv* (1887) : toward the head or anterior end of the body

ceph·a·lex·in \,sef-ə-'lek-sən\ *n* [*cephalo*sporin + *-ex-* (arbitrary infix) + *-in*] (1967) : a semisynthetic cephalosporin with a spectrum of antibiotic activity similar to the penicillins

ce·phal·ic \sə-'fal-ik\ *adj* [MF *céphalique,* fr. L *cephalicus,* fr. Gk *kephalikos,* fr. *kephalē* head; akin to OHG *gebal* skull, ON *gafl* gable] (1599) **1** : of or relating to the head **2** : directed toward or situated on or in or near the head — **ce·phal·i·cal·ly** \-i-k(ə-)lē\ *adv*

cephalic index *n* (1866) : the ratio multiplied by 100 of the maximum breadth from side to side of the head to its maximum length from top to bottom

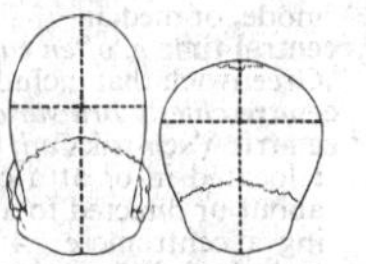

cephalic index: dotted lines on the brachycephalic (right) and dolichocephalic (left) skulls above indicate measurements taken

ceph·a·lin \'kef-ə-lən, 'sef-\ *n* [ISV] (ca. 1899) : PHOSPHATIDYLETHANOLAMINE

ceph·a·li·za·tion \,sef-ə-lə-'zā-shən\ *n* (1864) : an evolutionary tendency to specialization of the body with concentration of sensory and neural organs in an anterior head

ceph·a·lom·e·try \,sef-ə-'läm-ə-trē\ *n* [ISV] (ca. 1900) : the science of measuring the head — **ceph·a·lo·met·ric** \-lō-'me-trik\ *adj*

ceph·a·lo·pod \'sef-ə-lə-,päd\ *n* [deriv. of *cephal-* + Gk *pod-, pous* foot — more at FOOT] (1826) : any of a class (Cephalopoda) of mollusks including the squids, cuttlefishes, and octopuses that have a tubular siphon under the head, a group of muscular arms around the front of the head which are usu. furnished with suckers, highly developed eyes, and usu. a bag of inky fluid which can be ejected for defense or concealment — **cephalopod** *adj*

ceph·a·lor·i·dine \,sef-ə-'lȯr-ə-,dēn, -'lär-\ *n* [prob. fr. *cephalo*sporin + *-idine*] (1965) : a broad-spectrum antibiotic $C_{19}H_{17}N_3O_4S_2$ derived from cephalosporin

ceph·a·lo·spo·rin \,sef-ə-lə-'spōr-ən, -'spȯr-\ *n* [*Cephalosporium,* genus of fungi + *-in*] (1951) : any of several antibiotics produced by an imperfect fungus (genus *Cephalosporium*)

ceph·alo·thin \'sef-ə-lə-thən, -,thin\ *n* [*cephalo*sporin + *thi-* + *-in*] (1962) : a semisynthetic broad-spectrum antibiotic $C_{16}H_{15}N_2NaO_6S_2$ that is an analogue of a cephalosporin

ceph·a·lo·tho·rax \,sef-ə-lə-'thō(ə)r-,aks, -,thȯ(ə)r-\ *n* [ISV] (1835) : the united head and thorax of an arachnid or higher crustacean

Ce·phe·id \'sef-(ē-)id, 'sēf-\ *n* [ISV, fr. *Cepheus*] (ca. 1903) : one of a class of pulsating stars whose intrinsic light variations are very regular

Ce·pheus \'sē-,fyüs; 'sē-fē-əs, 'sef-ē-\ *n* [L (gen. *Cephei*), fr. Gk *Kēpheus*] : a constellation between Cygnus and the north pole

ce·ra·ceous \sə-'rā-shəs\ *adj* [L *cera* wax — more at CERUMEN] (1768) : resembling wax

ce·ra·mal \sə-'ram-əl, 'ser-ə-,mal\ *n* [*ceramic* + *alloy*] (ca. 1948) : CERMET

¹ce·ram·ic \sə-'ram-ik, *esp Brit* kə-\ *adj* [Gk *keramikos,* fr. *keramos* potter's clay, pottery] (1850) : of or relating to the manufacture of any product (as earthenware, porcelain, or brick) made essentially from a nonmetallic mineral (as clay) by firing at a high temperature; *also* : of or relating to such a product

²ceramic *n* (1859) **1** *pl but sing in constr* : the art or process of making ceramic articles **2** : a product of ceramic manufacture

ce·ra·mist \sə-'ram-əst, 'ser-ə-məst\ *or* **ce·ram·i·cist** \sə-'ram-ə-səst\ *n* (1855) : one who engages in ceramics

ce·ras·tes \sə-'ras-(,)tēz\ *n* [ME, fr. L, fr. Gk *kerastēs,* lit., horned, fr. *keras*] (14c) : a venomous viper (*Cerastes cornutus*) of the Near East having a horny process over each eye — called also *horned viper*

ce·rate \'si(ə)r-,āt\ *n* [L *ceratum* wax salve, fr. *cera* wax — more at CERUMEN] (15c) : an unctuous preparation for external use consisting of wax or resin or spermaceti mixed with oil, lard, and medicinal ingredients

Cer·ber·us \'sər-b(ə-)rəs\ *n* [L, fr. Gk *Kerberos*] : a 3-headed dog that in Greek myth guards the entrance to Hades — **Cer·ber·e·an** \,sər-bə-'rē-ən\ *adj*

-cer·cal \'sər-kəl\ *adj comb form* [F *-cerque,* fr. Gk *kerkos* tail] : -tailed ⟨homo*cercal*⟩

cer·car·ia \(,)sər-'kar-ē-ə, -'ker-\ *n, pl* **-i·ae** \-ē-,ē\ [NL, fr. Gk *kerkos*] (ca. 1841) : a usu. tadpole-shaped larval trematode worm produced in a molluscan host by a redia — **cer·car·i·al** \-ē-əl\ *adj*

cer·cis \'sər-səs\ *n* [NL, genus name, fr. Gk *kerkis* Judas tree] (1797) : any of a small genus (*Cercis*) of leguminous shrubs or low trees (as a redbud)

cer·cus \'sər-kəs\ *n, pl* **cer·ci** \'sər-,sī, -,kī\ [NL, fr. Gk *kerkos*] (1826) : either of a pair of simple or segmented appendages at the posterior end of various arthropods

¹cere \'si(ə)r\ *vt* **cered; cer·ing** [ME *ceren* to wax, fr. MF *cirer,* fr. L *cerare,* fr. *cera*] (15c) : to wrap in or as if in a cerecloth

²cere *n* [ME *sere,* fr. MF *cire,* fr. ML *cera,* fr. L, wax] (15c) : a usu. waxy protuberance or tumid area at the base of the bill of a bird

¹ce·re·al \'sir-ē-əl\ *adj* [F or L; F *céréale,* fr. L *cerealis* of Ceres, of grain, fr. *Ceres*] (1818) : relating to grain or to the plants that produce it; *also* : made of grain

²cereal *n* (1832) **1** : a plant (as a grass) yielding farinaceous grain suitable for food; *also* : its grain **2** : a prepared foodstuff of grain

cereal leaf beetle *n* (1962) : a small reddish brown black-headed Old World chrysomelid beetle (*Oulema melanopus*) that feeds on cereal grasses and is a serious threat to U.S. grain crops

cer·e·bel·lum \,ser-ə-'bel-əm\ *n, pl* **-bellums** *or* **-bel·la** \-'bel-ə\ [ML, fr. L, dim. of *cerebrum*] (1565) : a large dorsally projecting part of the brain concerned esp. with the coordination of muscles and the maintenance of bodily equilibrium, situated between the brain stem and the back of the cerebrum, and formed in man of two lateral lobes and a median lobe — see BRAIN illustration — **cer·e·bel·lar** \-'bel-ər\ *adj*

cerebr- *or* **cerebro-** *comb form* [*cerebrum*] **1** : brain : cerebrum ⟨*cere*bration⟩ **2** : cerebral and ⟨*cerebro*spinal⟩

ce·re·bral \sə-'rē-brəl, 'ser-ə-\ *adj* [F *cérébral,* fr. L *cerebrum* brain; akin to Gk *kara* head, *keras* horn — more at HORN] (1816) **1 a** : of or relating to the brain or the intellect **b** : of, relating to, or being the cerebrum **2 a** : appealing to intellectual appreciation ⟨~ drama⟩ **b** : primarily intellectual in nature ⟨a ~ society⟩ — **ce·re·bral·ly** \-brə-lē\ *adv*

cerebral accident *n* (1947) : an occurrence of sudden damage (as by hemorrhage) to the cerebral vascular system — compare STROKE 5

cerebral cortex *n* (1926) : the surface layer of gray matter of the cerebrum that functions chiefly in coordination of higher nervous activity

cerebral hemisphere *n* (1816) : either of the two hollow convoluted lateral halves of the cerebrum — see BRAIN illustration

cerebral palsy *n* (1922) : a disability resulting from damage to the brain before or during birth and outwardly manifested by muscular incoordination and speech disturbances — compare SPASTIC PARALYSIS — **cerebral–palsied** *adj*

cer·e·brate \'ser-ə-,brāt\ *vi* **-brat·ed; -brat·ing** [back-formation fr. *cerebration,* fr. *cerebrum*] (1915) : to use the mind : THINK — **cer·e·bra·tion** \,ser-ə-'brā-shən\ *n*

ce·re·bro·side \'ser-ə-brə-,sīd, sə-'rē-\ *n* [*cerebrose* (galactose)] (1883) : any of various lipids found esp. in nerve tissue

ce·re·bro·spi·nal \sə-,rē-brō-'spīn-ᵊl, ,ser-ə-brō-\ *adj* (1826) : of or relating to the brain and spinal cord or to these together with the cranial and spinal nerves that innervate voluntary muscles

cerebrospinal fluid *n* (ca. 1889) : a liquid that is comparable to serum and is secreted from the blood into the lateral ventricles of the brain

cerebrospinal meningitis *n* (1889) : inflammation of the meninges of both brain and spinal cord; *specif* : an infectious epidemic and often fatal meningitis caused by the meningococcus

ce·re·bro·vas·cu·lar \sə-,rē-brō-'vas-kyə-lər, ,ser-ə-brō-\ *adj* (1935) : of or involving the cerebrum and the blood vessels supplying it

ce·re·brum \sə-'rē-brəm, 'ser-ə-brəm\ *n, pl* **-brums** *or* **-bra** \-brə\ [L] (1615) **1** : BRAIN 1a **2** : an enlarged anterior or upper part of the brain: *esp* : the expanded anterior portion of the brain that in higher mammals overlies the rest of the brain, consists of cerebral hemispheres and connecting structures, and is considered to be the seat of conscious mental processes : TELENCEPHALON

cere·cloth \'si(ə)r-,klȯth\ *n* [alter. of earlier *cered cloth* (waxed cloth)] (1553) : cloth treated with melted wax or gummy matter and formerly used esp. for wrapping a dead body

cere·ment \'ser-ə-mənt, 'si(ə)r-mənt\ *n* (1602) : a shroud for the dead; *esp* : CERECLOTH — usu. used in pl.

¹cer·e·mo·ni·al \,ser-ə-'mō-nē-əl\ *adj* (14c) : marked by, involved in, or belonging to ceremony : stressing careful attention to form and detail — **cer·e·mo·ni·al·ism** \-ə-,liz-əm\ *n* — **cer·e·mo·ni·al·ist** \-ə-ləst\ *n* — **cer·e·mo·ni·al·ly** \-ə-lē\ *adv*

syn CEREMONIAL, CEREMONIOUS, FORMAL, CONVENTIONAL mean marked by attention to or adhering strictly to prescribed forms. CEREMONIAL and CEREMONIOUS both imply strict attention to what is prescribed by custom or by ritual, but CEREMONIAL applies to things that are associated with ceremonies ⟨a *ceremonial* offering⟩, CEREMONIOUS to persons addicted to ceremony or to acts attended by ceremony ⟨a *ceremonious* old man⟩ FORMAL applies both to things prescribed by and to persons obedient to custom and may suggest stiff, restrained, or old-fashioned behavior ⟨a *formal* report⟩ ⟨a *formal* manner⟩ CONVENTIONAL implies accord with general custom and usage and may suggest a stodgy lack of originality or independence ⟨*conventional* courtesy⟩ ⟨they are not moral; they are only *conventional* — G. B. Shaw⟩

²ceremonial *n* (14c) : a ceremonial act, action, or system

cer·e·mo·ni·ous \,ser-ə-'mō-nē-əs\ *adj* (1553) **1** : devoted to forms and ceremony : PUNCTILIOUS **2** : of, relating to, or constituting a ceremony **3** : according to formal usage or prescribed procedures **4** : marked by ceremony — **cer·e·mo·ni·ous·ly** *adv* — **cer·e·mo·ni·ous·ness** *n*

cer·e·mo·ny \'ser-ə-,mō-nē\ *n, pl* **-nies** [ME *ceremonie,* fr. MF *cérémonie,* fr. L *caerimonia*] (14c) **1** : a formal act or series of acts prescribed by ritual, protocol, or convention ⟨the marriage ~⟩ **2 a** : a conventional act of politeness or etiquette ⟨the ~ of introduction⟩ **b** : an action performed only formally with no deep significance **c** : a routine action performed with elaborate pomp **3 a** : prescribed procedures : USAGES ⟨the ~ attending an inauguration⟩ **b** : observance of an established code of civility or politeness ⟨the door opened without ~ and the man strode in⟩

Ce·ren·kov radiation \chər-'(y)eŋ-kəf-\ *n* [P. A. *Cherenkov*] (1939) : light produced by charged particles (as electrons) traversing a transparent medium at a speed greater than that of light in the same medium — called also *Cerenkov light*

Ce·res \'si(ə)r-(,)ēz\ *n* [L] **1** : the Roman goddess of agriculture — compare DEMETER **2** : the largest asteroid and the one first discovered

ce·re·us \'sir-ē-əs\ *n* [NL, genus name, fr. L, wax candle, fr. *cera* wax — more at CERUMEN] (1730) : any of various cacti (as of the genus *Cereus*) of the western U.S. and tropical America

ce·ric \'si(ə)r-ik, 'ser-\ *adj* (1838) : of, relating to, or containing cerium esp. with a valence of four

ce·rise \sə-'rēs, -'rēz\ *n* [F, lit., cherry, fr. LL *ceresia* — more at CHERRY] (1844) : a moderate red

ce·ri·um \'sir-ē-əm\ *n* [NL, fr. *Ceres*] (1804) : a malleable ductile metallic element that is the most abundant of the rare-earth group — see ELEMENT table

cer·met \'sər-,met\ *n* [*ceramic* + *metal*] (1948) : a strong alloy of a heat-resistant compound (as titanium carbide) and a metal (as nickel) used esp. for turbine blades — called also *ceramal*

cero \'se(ə)r-(,)ō\ *n, pl* **cero** *or* **ceros** [modif. of Sp *sierra* saw, cero] (1884) : either of two large food and sport fishes (*Scomberomorus cavalla* and *S. regalis*) of the warmer parts of the western Atlantic ocean

ce·rous \'sir-əs\ *adj* (ca. 1863) : of, relating to, or containing cerium esp. with a valence of three

¹cer·tain \'sərt-ᵊn\ *adj* [ME, fr. OF, fr. (assumed) VL *certanus,* fr. L *certus,* fr. pp. of *cernere* to sift, discern, decide; akin to Gk *krinein* to separate, decide, judge, *keirein* to cut — more at SHEAR] (13c) **1 a** : FIXED, SETTLED ⟨guaranteed a ~ percentage of the profit⟩ **b** : proved to be true **2** : of a specific but unspecified character, quantity, or degree : PARTICULAR ⟨the house has a ~ charm⟩ ⟨everyone has a ~

amount of success⟩ 3 a : DEPENDABLE, RELIABLE ⟨a ~ remedy for the disease⟩ b : INDISPUTABLE ⟨it is ~ that we exist⟩ 4 a : INEVITABLE ⟨the ~ advance of age and decay⟩ b : incapable of failing : DESTINED — used with a following infinitive ⟨she is ~ to do well⟩ 5 : assured in mind or action *syn* see SURE — **cer·tain·ly** *adv* — **for certain** : as a certainty : ASSUREDLY

²**certain** *pron, pl in constr* (15c) : certain ones

cer·tain·ty \'sərt-ᵊn-tē\ *n, pl* **-ties** (14c) 1 : something that is certain 2 : the quality or state of being certain esp. on the basis of objective evidence

syn CERTAINTY, CERTITUDE, ASSURANCE, CONVICTION mean a state of being free from doubt. CERTAINTY and CERTITUDE are very close, but CERTAINTY may stress the existence of objective proof, CERTITUDE may emphasize a faith in something not needing or not capable of proof; ASSURANCE implies confidence rather than intellectual certainty; CONVICTION applies esp. to belief strongly held by an individual.

cer·tes \'sərt-ēz, 'sərts\ *adv* [ME, fr. OF, fr. *cert* certain, fr. L *certus*] *archaic* (13c) : in truth : CERTAINLY

¹**cer·tif·i·cate** \(ˌ)sər-'tif-i-kət\ *n* [ME *certificat,* fr. MF, fr. ML *certificatum,* fr. LL, neut. of *certificatus,* pp. of *certificare* to certify] (15c) 1 : a document containing a certified statement esp. as to the truth of something; *specif* : a document certifying that one has fulfilled the requirements of and may practice in a field 2 : something serving the same end as a certificate 3 : a document evidencing ownership or debt ⟨a ~ of deposit⟩

²**cer·tif·i·cate** \-'tif-ə-ˌkāt\ *vt* **-cat·ed; -cat·ing** (1884) : to testify to or authorize by a certificate — **cer·tif·i·ca·to·ry** \-'tif-i-kə-ˌtōr-ē, -ˌtȯr-\ *adj*

cer·ti·fi·ca·tion \ˌsərt-ə-fə-'kā-shən\ *n* (15c) 1 : the act of certifying : the state of being certified 2 : a certified statement

certified mail *n* (1955) : first class mail for which proof of delivery is secured but no indemnity value is claimed

certified milk *n* (1899) : milk produced in dairies that operate under the rules and regulations of an authorized medical milk commission

certified public accountant *n* (ca. 1922) : an accountant who has met the requirements of a state law and has been granted a state certificate

cer·ti·fy \'sərt-ə-ˌfī\ *vt* **-fied; -fy·ing** [ME *certifien,* fr. MF *certifier,* fr. LL *certificare,* fr. L *certus* certain — more at CERTAIN] (14c) 1 : to attest authoritatively: as a : CONFIRM b : to present in formal communication c : to attest as being true or as represented or as meeting a standard d : to attest officially to the insanity of 2 : to inform with certainty : ASSURE 3 : to guarantee (a personal check) as to signature and amount by so indicating on the face 4 : CERTIFICATE, LICENSE — **cer·ti·fi·able** \-ˌfī-ə-bəl\ *adj* — **cer·ti·fi·ably** \-blē\ *adv* — **cer·ti·fi·er** \-ˌfī(-ə)r\ *n*

syn CERTIFY, ATTEST, WITNESS, VOUCH mean to testify to the truth or genuineness of something. CERTIFY usu. applies to a written statement, esp. one carrying a signature or seal; ATTEST applies to oral or written testimony usu. from experts or witnesses; WITNESS applies to the subscribing of one's own name to a document as evidence of its genuineness; VOUCH applies to one who testifies as a competent authority or a reliable person and who will defend his affirmation. *syn* see in addition APPROVE

cer·tio·ra·ri \ˌsər-sh(ē-)ə-'ra(ə)r-ē, -'rär-ē\ *n* [ME, fr. L, lit., to be informed; fr. the use of the word in the writ] (15c) : a writ of a superior court to call up the records of an inferior court or a body acting in a quasi-judicial capacity

cer·ti·tude \'sərt-ə-ˌt(y)üd\ *n* [ME, fr. LL *certitudo,* fr. L *certus*] (15c) 1 : the state of being or feeling certain 2 : certainty of act or event *syn* see CERTAINTY

ce·ru·le·an \sə-'rü-lē-ən\ *adj* [L *caeruleus* dark blue] (1667) : resembling the blue of the sky

ce·ru·lo·plas·min \sə-ˌrü-lō-'plaz-mən\ *n* [ISV *cerulo* (fr. L *caeruleus*) + *plasma* + *-in*] (ca. 1952) : an alpha globulin active in the biological storage and transport of copper

ce·ru·men \sə-'rü-mən\ *n* [NL, irreg. fr. L *cera* wax, prob. fr. Gk *kēros*] (1741) : the yellow waxy secretion from the glands of the external ear — called also *earwax* — **ce·ru·mi·nous** \-mə-nəs\ *adj*

ce·ruse \sə-'rüs, 'si(ə)r-ˌüs\ *n* [ME, fr. MF *céruse,* fr. L *cerussa*] (14c) 1 : white lead as a pigment 2 : a cosmetic containing white lead

ce·rus·site \sə-'rəs-ˌīt\ *n* [G *zerussit,* fr. L *cerussa*] (1850) : a mineral $PbCO_3$ consisting of lead carbonate occurring in colorless transparent crystals and also in massive form

cer·ve·lat \'sər-və-ˌlat, -ˌlä\ *n* [obs. F (now *cervelas*)] (1613) : smoked sausage made from a combination of pork and beef

cervic- *or* **cervici-** *or* **cervico-** *comb form* [L *cervic-, cervix* neck] : neck : cervix of an organ ⟨*cervic*itis⟩ : cervical and ⟨*cervico*thoracic⟩

cer·vi·cal \'sər-vi-kəl\ *adj* (1681) : of or relating to a neck or cervix

cer·vi·ci·tis \ˌsər-və-'sīt-əs\ *n* (1889) : inflammation of the uterine cervix

cer·vine \'sər-ˌvīn\ *adj* [L *cervinus* of a deer, fr. *cervus* stag, deer — more at HART] (ca. 1828) : of, relating to, or resembling deer

cer·vix \'sər-viks\ *n, pl* **cer·vi·ces** \'sər-və-ˌsēz, (ˌ)sər-'vī-(ˌ)sēz\ *or* **cer·vix·es** [L *cervic-, cervix*] (15c) 1 : NECK; *esp* : the back part of the neck 2 : a constricted portion of an organ or part; *esp* : the narrow outer end of the uterus

ce·sar·e·an *also* **ce·sar·i·an** \si-'zar-ē-ən, -'zer-\ *n* [fr. the belief that Julius Caesar was born this way] (ca. 1903) : CESAREAN SECTION — **cesarean** *also* **cesarian** *adj*

cesarean section *also* **cesarian section** *n* (1615) : surgical incision of the walls of the abdomen and uterus for delivery of offspring

ce·si·um \'sē-zē-əm\ *n* [NL, fr. L *caesius* bluish gray] (1861) : a silver-white soft ductile element of the alkali metal group that is the most electropositive element known and that is used esp. in photoelectric cells — see ELEMENT table

cess \'ses\ *n* [prob. short for *success*] *chiefly Irish* (1830) : LUCK — usu. used in the phrase *bad cess to you*

ces·sa·tion \se-'sā-shən\ *n* [ME *cessacioun,* fr. MF *cessation,* fr. L *cessation-, cessatio* delay, idleness, fr. *cessatus,* pp. of *cessare* to delay, be idle — more at CEASE] (15c) : a temporary or final ceasing (as of action) : STOP

ces·sion \'sesh-ən\ *n* [ME, fr. MF, fr. L *cession-, cessio,* fr. *cessus,* pp. of *cedere* to withdraw — more at CEDE] (15c) : a yielding to another : CONCESSION

cess·pit \'ses-ˌpit\ *n* [*cesspool* + *pit*] (1777) : a pit for the disposal of refuse (as sewage)

cess·pool \-ˌpül\ *n* [by folk etymology fr. ME *suspiral* vent, cesspool, fr. MF *souspirail* ventilator, fr. *souspirer, soupirer* to sigh, fr. L *suspirare,* lit., to draw a long breath — more at SUSPIRE] (1782) : an underground reservoir for liquid waste (as household sewage)

ces·ta \'ses-tə\ *n* [Sp, lit., basket, fr. L *cista* box, basket] (ca. 1902) : a narrow curved wicker basket used to catch and propel the ball in jai alai

ces·tode \'ses-ˌtōd\ *n* [deriv. of Gk *kestos* girdle] (ca. 1879) : any of a subclass (Cestoda) of internally parasitic flatworms comprising the tapeworms — **cestode** *adj*

¹**ces·tus** \'ses-təs\ *n, pl* **ces·ti** \-ˌtī\ [L, girdle, belt, fr. Gk *kestos,* fr. *kestos* stitched; akin to Gk *kentron* sharp point — more at CENTER] (1557) : a woman's belt; *esp* : a symbolic one worn by a bride

²**cestus** *n* [L *caestus,* fr. *caedere* to strike — more at CONCISE] (1734) : a hand covering of leather bands often loaded with lead or iron and used by boxers in ancient Rome

ce·su·ra *var of* CAESURA

ce·ta·cean \si-'tā-shən\ *n* [deriv. of L *cetus* whale, fr. Gk *kētos*] (1836) : any of an order (Cetacea) of aquatic mostly marine mammals including the whales, dolphins, porpoises, and related forms with large head, fishlike nearly hairless body, and paddle-shaped forelimbs — **cetacean** *adj* — **ce·ta·ceous** \-shəs\ *adj*

ce·tane \'sē-ˌtān\ *n* [fr. *cetyl* (the radical $C_{16}H_{33}$)] (1871) : a colorless oily hydrocarbon $C_{16}H_{34}$ found in petroleum

cetane number *n* (1935) : a measure of the ignition value of a diesel fuel that represents the percentage by volume of cetane in a mixture of liquid methylnaphthalene that gives the same ignition lag as the oil being tested — called also *cetane rating* — compare OCTANE NUMBER

ce·te·ris pa·ri·bus \ˌkāt-ə-rə-'spar-ə-bəs\ *adv* [NL, other things being equal] (1601) : if all other relevant things, factors, or elements remain unaltered

ce·tol·o·gy \sē-'täl-ə-jē\ *n* [ISV, fr. Gk *kētos* + E *-logy*] (ca. 1828) : a branch of zoology dealing with the whales — **ce·tol·o·gist** \-jəst\ *n*

Ce·tus \'sēt-əs\ *n* [L (gen. *Ceti*), lit., whale] : an equatorial constellation south of Pisces and Aries

ce·tyl alcohol \'sēt-ᵊl-\ *n* [ISV *cet-* (fr. L *cetus* whale) + *-yl*; fr. its occurrence in spermaceti] (1873) : a waxy crystalline alcohol $C_{16}H_{34}O$ found in the form of its ester in spermaceti and used in pharmaceutical and cosmetic preparations and in making detergents

ce·vi·che \sə-'vē-(ˌ)chā, -chē\ *var of* SEVICHE

Cha·blis \sha-'blē, shə-, shä-; 'shab-(ˌ)lē\ *n, pl* **Cha·blis** \-'blēz, -(ˌ)lēz\ [F, fr. *Chablis,* France] (1668) 1 : a dry sharp white Burgundy wine 2 : a semidry soft white California wine that is a blend of several grapes

cha–cha \'chä-(ˌ)chä\ *n* [AmerSp *cha-cha-cha*] (ca. 1954) : a fast rhythmic ballroom dance of Latin-American origin with a basic pattern of three steps and a shuffle

chac·ma baboon \ˌchäk-mə-\ *n* [Hottentot] (1835) : a large dusky baboon (*Papio ursinus*) of southern African savannas — called also *chacma*

cha·conne \shä-'kȯn, sha-, -'kän, -'kən\ *n* [F&Sp; F *chaconne,* fr. Sp *chacona*] (1685) 1 : an old Spanish dance tune of Latin American origin 2 : a musical composition in moderate triple time typically consisting of variations on a repeated succession of chords

chad \'chad\ *n* [perh. fr. Sc, gravel] (1947) : small pieces of paper or cardboard produced in punching paper tape or data cards; *also* : a piece of chad — **chad·less** \-ləs\ *adj*

Chad \'chad\ *n* (ca. 1949) : a subfamily of the Afro-Asiatic language family comprising numerous languages of northern Nigeria and Cameroons

chae·ta \'kēt-ə\ *n, pl* **chae·tae** \'kē-ˌtē\ [NL, fr. Gk *chaitē* long flowing hair] (1864) : BRISTLE, SETA — **chae·tal** \kēt-ᵊl\ *adj*

chae·to·gnath \'kēt-ˌäg-ˌnath, -ə(g)-\ *n* [deriv. of Gk *chaitē* + *gnathos* jaw — more at GNATH-] (1889) : any of a class or phylum (Chaetognatha) of small free-swimming marine worms with movable curved chaetae on either side of the mouth — **chaetognath** *adj*

¹**chafe** \'chāf\ *vb* **chafed; chaf·ing** [ME *chaufen* to warm, fr. MF *chaufer,* fr. (assumed) VL *calfare,* alter. of L *calefacere,* fr. *calēre* to be warm + *facere* to make — more at LEE, DO] *vt* (14c) 1 : IRRITATE, VEX 2 : to warm by rubbing esp. with the hands 3 a : to rub so as to wear away : ABRADE ⟨the boat *chafed* her sides against the dock⟩ b : to make sore by or as if by rubbing ~ *vi* 1 : to feel irritation or discontent : FRET ⟨~s at his restrictive desk job⟩ 2 : to rub and thereby cause wear or irritation

²**chafe** *n* (1551) 1 : a state of vexation : RAGE 2 : injury or wear caused by friction; *also* : FRICTION, RUBBING

cha·fer \'chā-fər\ *n* [ME *cheaffer,* fr. OE *ceafor;* akin to OE *ceafl* jowl — more at JOWL] (bef. 12c) : any of various large beetles (esp. family Scarabaeidae)

¹**chaff** \'chaf\ *n* [ME *chaf,* fr. OE *ceaf;* akin to OHG *cheva* husk] (bef. 12c) 1 : the seed coverings and other debris separated from the seed in threshing grain 2 : something comparatively worthless 3 : the scales borne on the receptacle among the florets in the heads of many composite plants 4 : material (as strips of foil or clusters of fine wires) ejected into the air for reflecting radar waves (as for confusing an enemy's radar detection or for tracking a descending spacecraft) — **chaffy** \-ē\ *adj*

²**chaff** *n* [prob. fr. ¹*chaff*] (1648) : light jesting talk : BANTER

³**chaff** *vt* (1850) : to tease good-naturedly ~ *vi* : JEST, BANTER

¹**chaf·fer** \'chaf-ər\ *n* [ME *chaffare,* fr. *chep* trade + *fare* journey — more at CHEAP, FARE] *archaic* (13c) : a haggling about price

²**chaffer** *vb* **chaf·fered; chaf·fer·ing** \'chaf-(ə-)riŋ\ *vi* (14c) 1 : HAGGLE 2 *Brit* : to exchange small talk : CHATTER ~ *vt* 1 : EXCHANGE, BARTER 2 : to bargain for — **chaf·fer·er** \-ər-ər\ *n*

chaf·finch \'chaf-(ˌ)inch\ *n* [ME, fr. OE *ceaffinc,* fr. *ceaf* + *finc* finch — more at FINCH] (bef. 12c) : a European finch (*Fringilla coelebs*) of which the male has a reddish breast plumage and a cheerful song

chaf·ing dish \ˈchā-fiŋ-\ *n* [ME *chafing,* prp. of *chaufen, chafen* to warm] (15c) **:** a utensil for cooking or keeping food warm esp. at the table

Cha·gas' disease \ˈshäg-əs-(əz-)\ *n* [Carlos *Chagas* †1934 Braz. physician] (1912) **:** a tropical American disease that is caused by a trypanosome (*Trypanosoma cruzi*) and is marked by prolonged high fever, edema, and enlargement of the spleen, liver, and lymph nodes

[1]**cha·grin** \shə-ˈgrin\ *n* [F, fr. *chagrin* sad] (1681) **:** disquietude or distress of mind caused by humiliation, disappointment, or failure

[2]**chagrin** *vt* **cha·grined** \-ˈgrind\; **cha·grin·ing** \-ˈgrin-iŋ\ (1733) **:** to vex acutely by disappointing or humiliating

Chai·ma \ˈchī-mə\ *n* [Sp *Chaima,* of AmerInd origin] (1901) **1 :** a member of a Cariban people of the coast of Venezuela **2 :** the language of the Chaima people

[1]**chain** \ˈchān\ *n, often attrib* [ME *cheyne,* fr. MF *chaeine,* fr. L *catena;* akin to L *cassis* net] (14c) **1 a :** a series of usu. metal links or rings connected to or fitted into one another and used for various purposes (as support, restraint, transmission of mechanical power, or measurement) **b :** a series of links used or worn as an ornament or insignia **c** (1) **:** a measuring instrument of 100 links used in surveying (2) **:** a unit of length equal to 66 feet **2 :** something that confines, restrains, or secures **3 a :** a series of things linked, connected, or associated together ⟨a ~ of events⟩ **b :** a number of atoms or chemical groups united like links in a chain

[2]**chain** *vt* (14c) **1 :** to obstruct or protect by a chain **2 :** to fasten, bind, or connect with or as if with a chain; *also* **:** FETTER

chaî·né \sha-ˈnā\ *n* [F, fr. pp. of *chaîner* to chain] (1897) **:** a series of short usu. fast turns by which a ballet dancer moves across the stage

chain gang *n* (1834) **:** a gang of convicts chained together esp. as an outside working party

chain letter *n* (1905) **:** a letter sent to several persons with a request that each send copies of the letter to an equal number of persons

chain mail *n* (1822) **:** flexible armor of interlinked metal rings

chain of command (1898) **:** a series of executive positions in order of authority ⟨a military *chain of command*⟩

chain·omat·ic \ˌchā-nə-ˈmat-ik\ *adj* [fr. *Chainomatic,* a trademark] *of a balance or scale* (1916) **:** having suspended from the beam an adjustable fine chain whose length is measured to determine minute weights

chain pickerel *n* [fr. the markings resembling chains on the sides] (1905) **:** a large greenish black pickerel (*Esox niger*) with dark markings along the sides that is common in quiet waters of eastern No. America

chain printer *n* (1966) **:** a line printer in which the printing element is type carried on a continuous chain

chain–re·act·ing pile \ˌchān-rē-ˌak-tiŋ-\ *n* (1946) **:** REACTOR 3b

chain reaction *n* (ca. 1902) **1 :** a series of events so related to each other that each one initiates the next **2 :** a self-sustaining chemical or nuclear reaction yielding energy or products that cause further reactions of the same kind — **chain–re·act** \ˌchān-rē-ˈakt\ *vi*

chain rule *n* (ca. 1864) **:** a mathematical rule concerning the differentiation of a function of a function (as $f[u(x)]$) by which under suitable conditions of continuity and differentiability one function is differentiated with respect to the second considered as an independent variable and then the second function is differentiated with respect to the independent variable ⟨if $v = u^2$ and $u = 3x^2 + 2$ the derivative of v by the *chain rule* is $2u(6x)$ or $12x(3x^2 + 2)$⟩

chain saw *n* (1944) **:** a portable power saw that has teeth linked together to form an endless chain

chain–smoke \ˈchān-ˈsmōk\ *vi* (1930) **:** to smoke esp. cigarettes continually often by lighting each from the previous one ~ *vt* **:** to smoke (as cigarettes) almost without interruption — **chain–smok·er** \-ˈsmō-kər\ *n*

chain stitch *n* (1859) **1 :** an ornamental stitch like chain links **2 :** a machine stitch forming a chain on the underside of the work

chain store *n* (1910) **:** one of numerous usu. retail stores having the same ownership and selling the same lines of goods

chain·wheel \ˈchān-ˌ(h)wēl\ *n* (1845) **:** SPROCKET WHEEL

[1]**chair** \ˈche(ə)r, ˈcha(ə)r\ *n* [ME *chaiere,* fr. OF, fr. L *cathedra,* fr. Gk *kathedra,* fr. *kata-* cata- + *hedra* seat — more at SIT] (13c) **1 a :** a seat typically having four legs and a back for one person **b :** ELECTRIC CHAIR **2 a :** an official seat or a seat of authority, state, or dignity **b :** an office or position of authority or dignity ⟨holds a university ~⟩ **c :** CHAIRMAN 1 **3 :** a sedan chair **4 :** a position of employment usu. of one occupying a chair or desk; *specif* **:** the position of a player in an orchestra or band **5 :** any of various devices that hold up or support

[2]**chair** *vt* (1552) **1 :** to install in office **2** *chiefly Brit* **:** to carry on the shoulders in acclaim ⟨we ~*ed* you through the market place —A. E. Housman⟩ **3 :** to preside as chairman of

chair car *n* (1880) **1 :** a railroad car having pairs of chairs with individually adjustable backs on each side of the aisle **2 :** PARLOR CAR

chair lift *n* (1940) **:** a motor-driven conveyor consisting of a series of seats suspended from an overhead moving cable and used for transporting skiers or sightseers up or down a long slope or mountainside

[1]**chair·man** \ˈche(ə)r-mən, ˈcha(ə)r-\ *n* (1654) **1 a :** the presiding officer of a meeting or an organization or committee **b :** the administrative officer of a department of instruction (as in a college) **2 :** a carrier of a sedan chair — **chair·man·ship** \-ˌship\ *n*

[2]**chairman** *vt* **-maned** *or* **-manned; -man·ing** *or* **-man·ning** (1888) **:** CHAIR 3

chair·per·son \-ˌpərs-ᵊn\ *n* (1971) **:** CHAIRMAN 1

chair·wom·an \-ˌwu̇m-ən\ *n* (1685) **:** a woman who acts as chairman

chaise \ˈshāz\ *n* [F, chair, chaise, alter. of OF *chaiere*] (1701) **1 a :** a two-wheeled carriage for one or two persons with a calash top and the body hung on leather straps and usu. drawn by one horse **b :** a similar four-wheeled pleasure carriage **c :** POST CHAISE **2 :** a light carriage or pleasure cart **3 :** CHAISE LONGUE

chaise longue \ˈshāz-ˈlȯŋ\ *n, pl* **chaise longues** *also* **chaises longues** \ˈshāz-ˈlȯŋ(z)\ [F *chaise longue,* lit., long chair] (1800) **:** a long reclining chair

chaise lounge \ˈshāz-ˈlau̇nj, ˈchās-\ *n* [by folk etymology fr. F *chaise longue*] (1921) **:** CHAISE LONGUE

cha·la·za \kə-ˈlā-zə, -ˈlaz-ə\ *n, pl* **-zae** \-ˌzē\ *or* **-zas** [NL, fr. Gk, hailstone] (1704) **1 :** either of a pair of spiral bands in the white of a bird's egg that extend from the yolk and attach to opposite ends of the lining membrane — see EGG illustration **2 :** the point at the base of a plant ovule where the seed stalk is attached — **cha·la·zal** \-ˈlā-zəl, -ˈlaz-əl\ *adj*

Chal·ce·do·ni·an \ˌkal-sə-ˈdō-nē-ən\ *adj* (1788) **:** of or relating to Chalcedon or the ecumenical council held there in A.D. 451 declaring Monophysitism heretical — **Chalcedonian** *n*

chal·ce·do·ny \kal-ˈsed-ᵊn-ē, chal-; ˈkal-sə-ˌdō-nē, ˈchal-, -ˌdän-ē\ *n, pl* **-nies** [ME *calcedonie,* a precious stone, fr. LL *chalcedonius,* fr. Gk *Chalkēdōn* Chalcedon] (13c) **:** a translucent quartz that is commonly pale blue or gray with nearly waxlike luster — **chal·ce·don·ic** \ˌkal-sə-ˈdän-ik\ *adj*

chal·cid \ˈkal-səd\ *n* [deriv. of Gk *chalkos* copper, bronze] (ca. 1882) **:** any of a large superfamily (Chalcidoidea) of mostly minute hymenopterous insects parasitic in the larval state on the larvae or pupae of other insects — **chalcid** *adj*

chal·co·gen \ˈkal-kə-jən\ *n* [prob. fr. G *chalkogen,* fr. *chalk-* bronze, ore (fr. Gk *chalkos*) + *-gen;* fr. the occurrence of oxygen and sulfur in many ores] (ca. 1961) **:** any of the elements oxygen, sulfur, selenium, and tellurium

chal·co·gen·ide \-jə-ˌnīd\ *n* (1945) **:** a binary compound of a chalcogen with a more electropositive element or radical

chal·co·py·rite \ˌkal-kə-ˈpī-ˌrīt\ *n* [NL *chalcopyrites,* fr. Gk *chalkos* + L *pyrites*] (1835) **:** a yellow mineral $CuFeS_2$ consisting of copper-iron sulfide and constituting an important ore of copper

Chal·da·ic \kal-ˈdā-ik\ *adj or n* (1662) **:** CHALDEAN

Chal·de·an \kal-ˈdē-ən\ *n* [L *Chaldaeus* Chaldean, astrologer, fr. Gk *Chaldaios,* fr. *Chaldaia* Chaldea, region of ancient Babylonia] (1581) **1 a :** a member of an ancient Semitic people that became dominant in Babylonia **b :** the Semitic language of the Chaldeans **2 :** a person versed in the occult arts — **Chaldean** *adj*

Chal·dee \ˈkal-ˌdē\ *n* [ME *Caldey,* prob. fr. MF *chaldée,* fr. L *Chaldaeus*] (14c) **1 :** the Aramaic vernacular that was the original language of some parts of the Bible **2 :** CHALDEAN 1a

chal·dron \ˈchȯl-drən\ *n* [MF *chauderon,* fr. *chaudere* pot, fr. LL *caldaria* — more at CALDRON] (1615) **:** any of various old units of measure varying from 32 to 72 imperial bushels

cha·let \sha-ˈlā, ˈshal-(ˌ)ā\ *n* [F] (1782) **1 :** a remote herdsman's hut in the Alps **2 a :** a Swiss dwelling with unconcealed structural members and a wide overhang at the front and sides **b :** a cottage or house in chalet style

chalet 2a

chal·ice \ˈchal-əs\ *n* [ME, fr. AF, fr. L *calic-, calix;* akin to Gk *kalyx* calyx] (12c) **1 :** a drinking cup **:** GOBLET; *esp* **:** the eucharistic cup **2 :** the cup-shaped interior of a flower

[1]**chalk** \ˈchȯk\ *n* [ME, fr. OE *cealc,* fr. L *calc-, calx* lime, fr. Gk *chalix* pebble; akin to Gk *skallein* to hoe — more at SHELL] (bef. 12c) **1 a :** a soft white, gray, or buff limestone composed chiefly of the shells of foraminifers **b :** chalk or a chalky material esp. when used in the form of a crayon **2 a :** a mark made with chalk **b** *Brit* **:** a point scored in a game — **chalky** \ˈchȯ-kē\ *adj*

[2]**chalk** *vt* (1580) **1 :** to rub or mark with chalk **2 :** to write or draw with chalk **3 a :** to delineate roughly **:** SKETCH ⟨~ out a plan of attack⟩ **b :** to set down or add up with or as if with chalk **:** TOT — usu. used with *up* ⟨~ up the casualties on the bulletin board⟩ ~ *vi* **:** to become chalky

chalk·board \ˈchȯk-ˌbō(ə)rd, -ˌbȯ(ə)rd\ *n* (1936) **:** BLACKBOARD

chalk up *vt* (1826) **1 :** ASCRIBE, CREDIT **2 :** ATTAIN, ACHIEVE ⟨*chalk up* a record score for the season⟩

chal·lah *also* **chal·la** \ˈkäl-ə, ˈhäl-ə\ *n* [Heb] (1927) **:** egg-rich yeast-leavened white bread that is usu. braided or twisted before baking and is traditionally eaten by Jews on the Sabbath and holidays

[1]**chal·lenge** \ˈchal-ənj\ *vb* **chal·lenged; chal·leng·ing** [ME *chalengen* to accuse, fr. OF *chalengier,* fr. L *calumniari* to accuse falsely, fr. *calumnia* calumny] *vt* (13c) **1 :** to demand as due or deserved **:** REQUIRE ⟨an event that ~*s* explanation⟩ **2 :** to order to halt and prove identity ⟨the sentry *challenged* the stranger⟩ **3 :** to dispute esp. as being unjust, invalid, or outmoded **:** IMPUGN ⟨new data that ~*s* old assumptions⟩ **4 :** to question formally the legality or legal qualifications of **5 a :** to confront or defy boldly **:** DARE **b :** to call out to duel or combat **c :** to invite into competition **6 :** to arouse or stimulate esp. by presenting with difficulties **7 :** to administer a physiological and esp. an immunologic challenge to (an organism or cell) ~ *vi* **1 :** to make or present a challenge **2 :** to take legal exception — **chal·leng·er** *n*

[2]**challenge** *n* (14c) **1 a :** a summons that is often threatening, provocative, stimulating, or inciting; *specif* **:** a summons to a duel to answer an affront **b :** an invitation to compete in a sport **2 a :** a calling to account or into question **:** PROTEST **b :** an exception taken to a juror before he is sworn **c :** a sentry's command to halt and prove identity **d :** a questioning of the right or validity of a vote or voter **3 :** a stimulating or interesting task or problem ⟨looking for new ~*s*⟩ **4 :** the process of provoking or testing physiological activity by exposure to a specific substance; *esp* **:** a test of immunity by exposure to virulent infective material after specific immunization

chal·leng·ing \-ən-jiŋ\ *adj* (1842) **1 :** arousing competitive interest, thought, or action ⟨the curriculum should have ~ intellectual content⟩ **2 :** invitingly provocative **:** FASCINATING ⟨a ~ personality⟩ — **chal·leng·ing·ly** \-jiŋ-lē\ *adv*

chal·lis \ˈshal-ē\ *n, pl* **chal·lises** \ˈshal-ēz\ [prob. fr. the name *Challis*] (ca. 1837) **:** a lightweight soft clothing fabric made of cotton, wool, or synthetic yarns

cha·lone \ˈkā-ˌlōn, ˈkal-ˌōn\ *n* [Gk *chalōn,* prp. of *chalan* to slacken] (1914) **:** an internal secretion that is held to inhibit mitosis in a specific tissue — compare HORMONE

[1]**cha·ly·be·ate** \kə-ˈlē-bē-ət, -ˈlib-ē-\ *adj* [prob. fr. NL *chalybeatus,* irreg. fr. L *chalybs* steel, fr. Gk *chalyb-, chalyps,* fr. *Chalybes,* ancient people in Asia Minor] (1634) **:** impregnated with salts of iron; *also* **:** having a taste due to iron ⟨~ springs⟩

[2]**chalybeate** *n* (1667) **:** a chalybeate liquid or medicine

cham \ˈkam\ *var of* KHAN

cham·ae·phyte \ˈkam-i-ˌfīt\ *n* [Gk *chamai* on the ground + E *-phyte* — more at HUMBLE] (1913) **:** a perennial plant that bears its overwintering buds just above the surface of the soil

[1]**cham·ber** \'chām-bər\ *n* [ME *chambre,* fr. OF, fr. LL *camera,* fr. L, arched roof, fr. Gk *kamara* vault; akin to L *camur* curved] (13c) **1** : ROOM; *esp* : BEDROOM **2** : a natural or artificial enclosed space or cavity **3 a** : a hall for the meetings of a deliberative, legislative, or judicial body ⟨the senate ~⟩ **b** : a room where a judge transacts business — usu. used in pl. **c** : the reception room of a person of rank or authority **4 a** : a legislative or judicial body; *esp* : either of the houses of a bicameral legislature **b** : a voluntary board or council **5 a** : the part of the bore of a gun that holds the charge **b** : a compartment in the cartridge cylinder of a revolver — **cham·bered** \-bərd\ *adj*

[2]**chamber** *vt* **cham·bered; cham·ber·ing** \-b(ə-)riŋ\ (1575) **1** : to place in or as if in a chamber : HOUSE **2** : to serve as a chamber for; *esp* : to accommodate in the chamber of a firearm

[3]**chamber** *adj* (1706) : being, relating to, or performing chamber music

chambered nautilus *n* (1858) : NAUTILUS 1

cham·ber·lain \'chām-bər-lən\ *n* [ME, fr. OF *chamberlayn,* of Gmc origin; akin to OHG *chamarling* chamberlain, fr. *chamara* chamber, fr. LL *camera*] (13c) **1** : an attendant on a sovereign or lord in his bedchamber **2 a** : a chief officer in the household of a king or nobleman **b** : TREASURER **3** : an often honorary papal attendant; *specif* : a priest having a rank of honor below domestic prelate

cham·ber·maid \-,mād\ *n* (1587) : a maid who makes beds and does general cleaning of bedrooms (as in a hotel)

chamber music *n* (1789) : music and esp. instrumental ensemble music intended for performance in a private room or small auditorium and usu. having one performer for each part

chamber of commerce (1788) : an association of businessmen to promote commercial and industrial interests in the community

chamber of horrors (1849) : a place in which macabre or horrible objects are exhibited; *also* : a collection of such exhibits

chamber orchestra *n* (1926) : a small orchestra usu. with one player for each part

chamber pot *n* (1570) : a bedroom vessel for urination and defecation

cham·bray \'sham-,brā, -brē\ *n* [irreg. fr. *Cambrai,* France] (1814) : a lightweight clothing fabric with colored warp and white filling yarns

cha·me·leon \kə-'mēl-yən\ *n* [ME *camelion,* fr. MF, fr. L *chamaeleon,* fr. Gk *chamaileōn,* fr. *chamai* on the ground + *leōn* lion — more at HUMBLE] (14c) **1** : any of a group (Rhiptoglossa) of Old World lizards with granular skin, prehensile tail, independently movable eyeballs, and unusual ability to change the color of the skin **2** : a fickle or changeable person or thing **3** : any of various American lizards (as of the genus *Anolis*) capable of changing their color; *esp* : AMERICAN CHAMELEON — **cha·me·le·on·ic** \-,mē-lē-'än-ik\ *adj*

[1]**cham·fer** \'cham(p)-fər, 'cham-pər\ *vt* **cham·fered; cham·fer·ing** \-f(ə-)riŋ, -p(ə-)riŋ\ (1565) **1** : to cut a furrow in (as a column) : GROOVE **2** : to make a chamfer on : BEVEL

[2]**chamfer** *n* [MF *chanfreint,* fr. pp. of *chanfraindre* to bevel, fr. *chant* edge (fr. L *canthus* iron tire) + *fraindre* to break, fr. L *frangere* — more at CANT, BREAK] (ca. 1842) : a beveled edge

cham·fron \'sham-frən, 'cham-\ *n* [ME *shamfron,* fr. MF *chanfrein*] (15c) : the headpiece of a horse's bard

cham·ois \'sham-ē, *sense 1 also* sham-'wä\ *n, pl* **cham·ois** *also* **cham·oix** *sense 1* 'sham-ē(z) *or* sham-'wä(z), *senses 2 & 3* 'sham-ēz\ [MF, fr. LL *camox*] (1560) **1** : a small goatlike antelope (*Rupicapra rupicapra*) of Europe and the Caucasus **2** *also* **cham·my** *or* **sham·my** \'sham-ē\ : a soft pliant leather prepared from the skin of the chamois or from sheepskin **3** : a cotton fabric made in imitation of chamois leather

cham·o·mile \'kam-ə-,mīl, -,mēl\ *n* [ME *camemille,* fr. ML *camomilla,* modif. of L *chamaemelon,* fr. Gk *chamaimēlon,* fr. *chamai* + *mēlon* apple] (12c) : any of a genus (*Anthemis,* esp. the common European *A. nobilis*) of composite herbs with strong-scented foliage and flower heads that contain a bitter medicinal principle; *also* : a similar plant of a related genus (*Matricaria,* esp. *M. chamomilla*)

[1]**champ** \'champ, 'chämp, 'chȯmp\ *vb* [perh. imit.] *vt* (14c) **1** : CHOMP **2** : MASH, TRAMPLE ~ *vi* **1** : to make biting or gnashing movements **2** : to show impatience of delay or restraint — usu. used in the phrase *champing at the bit* ⟨he was ~*ing* at the bit to begin⟩

[2]**champ** \'champ\ *n* (1868) : CHAMPION

cham·pac *or* **cham·pak** \'cham-,pak, 'chəm-(,)pək\ *n* [Hindi & Skt; Hindi *campak,* fr. Skt *campaka*] (1770) : an East Indian tree (*Michelia champaca*) of the magnolia family with yellow flowers

cham·pagne \sham-'pān\ *n* [F, fr. *Champagne,* France] (1664) **1** : a white sparkling wine made in the old province of Champagne, France; *also* : a similar wine made elsewhere **2** : a pale orange yellow to light grayish yellowish brown

cham·paign \sham-'pān\ *n* [ME *champaine,* fr. MF *champagne,* fr. LL *campania* — more at CAMPAIGN] (15c) **1** : an expanse of level open country : PLAIN **2** *archaic* : BATTLEFIELD — **champaign** *adj*

cham·pers \'sham-pərz\ *n pl but sing in constr, slang Brit* (1955) : CHAMPAGNE 1

cham·per·ty \'cham-pərt-ē\ *n* [ME *champartie,* fr. MF *champart* field rent, fr. *champ* field (fr. L *campus*) + *part* portion — more at CAMP, PART] (15c) : a proceeding by which a person not a party in a suit bargains to aid in or carry on its prosecution or defense in consideration of a share of the matter in suit — **cham·per·tous** \-pərt-əs\ *adj*

cham·pi·gnon \sham-'pin-yən, cham-\ *n* [MF, fr. *champagne*] (1578) : an edible fungus; *esp* : the common meadow mushroom (*Agaricus campestris*)

[1]**cham·pi·on** \'cham-pē-ən\ *n* [ME, fr. OF, fr. ML *campion-, campio,* of WGmc origin; akin to OE *cempa* warrior] (13c) **1** : WARRIOR, FIGHTER **2** : a militant advocate or defender ⟨a ~ of civil rights⟩ **3** : one that does battle for another's rights or honor ⟨God will raise me up a ~ —Sir Walter Scott⟩ **4** : a winner of first prize or first place in competition; *also* : one who shows marked superiority ⟨a ~ at selling⟩

[2]**champion** *vt* (1605) **1** *archaic* : CHALLENGE, DEFY **2** : to protect or fight for as a champion **3** : to act as militant supporter of : UPHOLD ⟨always ~*s* the cause of the underdog⟩ ***syn*** see SUPPORT

cham·pi·on·ship \-,ship\ *n* (1825) **1** : designation as champion **2** : the act of championing : DEFENSE ⟨his ~ of freedom of speech⟩ **3** : a contest held to determine a champion

champ·le·vé \,shäⁿl-ə-'vā\ *adj* [F] (1856) : of, relating to, or being a style of enamel decoration in which the enamel is applied and fired in cells depressed (as by incising) into a metal background — compare CLOISONNÉ — **champlevé** *n*

[1]**chance** \'chan(t)s\ *n* [ME, fr. OF, fr. (assumed) VL *cadentia* fall, fr. L *cadent-, cadens,* prp. of *cadere* to fall; akin to Skt *śad* to fall] (14c) **1 a** : something that happens unpredictably without discernible human intention or observable cause **b** : the assumed impersonal purposeless determiner of unaccountable happenings : LUCK **c** : the fortuitous or incalculable element in existence : CONTINGENCY **2** : a situation favoring some purpose : OPPORTUNITY ⟨needed a ~ to relax⟩ **3** : a fielding opportunity in baseball **4 a** : the possibility of an indicated or a favorable outcome in an uncertain situation; *also* : the degree of likelihood of such an outcome ⟨a small ~ of success⟩ **b** *pl* : the more likely indications ⟨~*s* are he's already gone⟩ **5 a** : RISK ⟨not taking any ~*s*⟩ **b** : a raffle ticket — **chance** *adj* — **by chance** : in the haphazard course of events ⟨they met *by chance* but parted by design⟩

[2]**chance** *vb* **chanced; chanc·ing** *vi* (14c) **1 a** : to take place or come about by chance : HAPPEN **b** : to be found by chance **c** : to have the good or bad luck ⟨we *chanced* to meet⟩ **2** : to come or light by chance ~ *vt* **1** : to leave the outcome of to chance **2** : to accept the hazard of : RISK

chance·ful \'chan(t)s-fəl\ *adj* (1594) **1** *archaic* : CASUAL **2** : EVENTFUL

chan·cel \'chan(t)-səl\ *n* [ME, fr. MF, fr. LL *cancellus* lattice, fr. L *cancelli;* fr. the latticework enclosing it — more at CANCEL] (14c) : the part of a church containing the altar and seats for the clergy and choir

chan·cel·lery *or* **chan·cel·lory** \'chan(t)-s(ə-)lə-rē, -səl-rē\ *n, pl* **-ler·ies** *or* **-lor·ies** (14c) **1 a** : the position, court, or department of a chancellor **b** : the building or room where a chancellor has his office **2** : the office of secretary of the court of a person high in authority **3** : the office or staff of an embassy or consulate

chan·cel·lor \'chan(t)-s(ə-)lər\ *n* [ME *chanceler,* fr. OF *chancelier,* fr. LL *cancellarius* doorkeeper, secretary, fr. *cancellus*] (12c) **1 a** : the secretary of a nobleman, prince, or king **b** : the lord chancellor of Great Britain **c** *Brit* : the chief secretary of an embassy **d** : a Roman Catholic priest heading the office in which diocesan business is transacted and recorded **2 a** : the titular head of a British university **b** (1) : a university president (2) : the chief executive officer in some state systems of higher education **3 a** : a lay legal officer or adviser of an Anglican diocese **b** : a judge in a court of chancery or equity in various states of the U.S. **4** : the chief minister of state in some European countries — **chan·cel·lor·ship** \-,ship\ *n*

chancellor of the exchequer *often cap C&E* (14c) : a member of the British cabinet in charge of the public income and expenditure

chance–med·ley \'chan(t)-'smed-lē\ *n* [AF *chance medlée* mingled chance] (15c) **1** : accidental homicide not entirely without fault of the killer but without evil intent **2** : haphazard action : CONFUSION

chance music *n* (1964) : music in which significant elements are determined randomly or left to the discretion of the performer

chan·cery \'chan(t)s-(ə-)rē\ *n, pl* **-cer·ies** [ME *chancerie,* alter. of *chancellerie* chancellery, fr. OF, fr. *chancelier*] (14c) **1 a** *cap* : a high court of equity in England and Wales with common-law functions and jurisdiction over causes in equity **b** : a court of equity in the American judicial system **c** : the principles and practice of judicial equity **2** : a record office for public archives or those of ecclesiastical, legal, or diplomatic proceedings **3 a** : a chancellor's court or office or the building in which he has his office **b** : the office in which the business of a Roman Catholic diocese is transacted and recorded **c** : the office of an embassy : CHANCELLERY 3 — **in chancery 1** : in litigation in a court of chancery; *also* : under the superintendence of the lord chancellor ⟨a ward *in chancery*⟩ **2** : in a hopeless predicament

chan·cre \'shaŋ-kər\ *n* [F, fr. L *cancer*] (1605) : a primary sore or ulcer at the site of entry of a pathogen (as in tularemia); *esp* : the initial lesion of syphilis — **chan·crous** \-k(ə-)rəs\ *adj*

chan·croid \'shaŋ-,krȯid\ *n* (1861) : a venereal disease caused by a hemophilic bacterium (*Hemophilus ducreyi*) and characterized by chancres that differ from those of syphilis in lacking firm indurated margins — called also *soft chancre* — **chan·croi·dal** \shaŋ-'krȯid-ᵊl\ *adj*

chancy \'chan(t)-sē\ *adj* **chanc·i·er; -est** (1513) **1** *Scot* : bringing good luck : AUSPICIOUS **2** : uncertain in outcome or prospect : RISKY **3** : occurring by chance : HAPHAZARD — **chanc·i·ness** *n*

chan·de·lier \,shan-də-'li(ə)r\ *n* [F, lit., candlestick, modif. of L *candelabrum*] (1736) : a branched often ornate lighting fixture suspended from a ceiling — **chan·de·liered** \-'li(ə)rd\ *adj*

chan·delle \shan-'del, shäⁿ-\ *n* [F, lit., candle] (1918) : an abrupt climbing turn of an airplane in which the momentum of the plane is used to attain a higher rate of climb — **chandelle** *vi*

chan·dler \'chan-(d)lər\ *n* [ME *chandeler,* fr. MF *chandelier,* fr. OF, fr. *chandelle* candle, fr. L *candela*] (14c) **1** : a maker or seller of tallow or wax candles and usu. soap **2** : a retail dealer in provisions and supplies or equipment of a specified kind ⟨a yacht ~⟩

chan·dlery \-(d)lə-rē\ *n, pl* **-dler·ies** (15c) **1** : a place where candles are kept **2** : the business of a chandler **3** : the commodities sold by a chandler

[1]**change** \'chānj\ *vb* **changed; chang·ing** [ME *changen,* fr. OF *changier,* fr. L *cambiare* to exchange, of Celt origin; akin to OIr *camm* crooked; akin to Gk *skambos* crooked — more at HOOP] *vt* (13c) **1 a** : to make different in some particular ⟨never bothered to ~ his will⟩ **b** : to make radically different : TRANSFORM ⟨can't ~ human nature⟩ **c** : to give a different position, course, or direction to **2 a** : to replace with another ⟨let's ~ the subject⟩ **b** : to make a shift from one to another : SWITCH ⟨always ~*s* sides in an argument⟩ **c** : to exchange for an equivalent sum or comparable item **d** : to undergo a modification of ⟨foliage *changing* color⟩ **e** : to put fresh clothes or covering on ⟨~ a bed⟩ ~ *vi* **1** : to become different ⟨her mood ~*s* every hour⟩ **2** *of the moon* : to pass from one phase to another **3** : to shift one's means of conveyance : TRANSFER ⟨on the bus trip he had to ~ twice⟩ **4** *of the voice* : to shift to lower register : BREAK **5** : to undergo transformation, transition, or substitution ⟨winter *changed* to spring⟩ **6** : to put

on different clothes **7 :** EXCHANGE, SWITCH ⟨neither liked his seat so they *changed* with each other⟩ — **chang·er** *n*

syn CHANGE, ALTER, VARY, MODIFY mean to make or become different. CHANGE implies making either an essential difference often amounting to a loss of original identity or a substitution of one thing for another; ALTER implies a difference in some particular respect without suggesting loss of identity; VARY stresses a breaking away from sameness, duplication, or exact repetition; MODIFY suggests a difference that limits, restricts, or adapts to a new purpose.

— **change hands :** to pass from the possession of one owner to that of another ⟨money *changes hands* many times⟩

[2]change *n* (13c) **1 :** the act, process, or result of changing: as **a :** ALTERATION ⟨a ~ in the weather⟩ **b :** TRANSFORMATION ⟨a time of vast social ~⟩ ⟨going through ~*s*⟩ **c :** SUBSTITUTION ⟨a ~ of scenery⟩ **d :** the passage of the moon from one monthly revolution to another; *also* **:** the passage of the moon from one phase to another **2 :** a fresh set of clothes **3** *Brit* **:** EXCHANGE 5a **4 a :** money in small denominations received in exchange for an equivalent sum in larger denominations **b :** money returned when a payment exceeds the amount due **c :** coins of low denominations ⟨a pocketful of ~⟩ **5 :** an order in which a set of bells is struck in change ringing

change·able \'chān-jə-bəl\ *adj* (13c) **:** capable of change: as **a :** able or apt to vary ⟨~ weather⟩ **b :** subject to change **:** ALTERABLE **c :** FICKLE **d :** IRIDESCENT — **change·abil·i·ty** \,chān-jə-'bil-ət-ē\ *n* — **change·able·ness** \'chān-jə-bəl-nəs\ *n* — **change·ably** \-blē\ *adv*

change·ful \'chānj-fəl\ *adj* (1606) **:** notably variable **:** UNCERTAIN — **change·ful·ly** \-fə-lē\ *adv* — **change·ful·ness** *n*

change·less \'chānj-ləs\ *adj* (1580) **:** marked by the absence of change **:** CONSTANT — **change·less·ly** *adv* — **change·less·ness** *n*

change·ling \'chānj-liŋ\ *n* (1555) **1** *archaic* **:** TURNCOAT **2 :** a child secretly exchanged for another in infancy **3** *archaic* **:** IMBECILE — **changeling** *adj*

change off *vi* (1873) **1 :** to alternate with another at doing an act **2 :** to alternate between two different acts or instruments or between an action and a rest period

change of heart (1828) **:** a reversal in position or attitude

change of life (1834) **:** [2]CLIMACTERIC 2

change of pace (1912) **1 :** CHANGE-UP **2 :** an interruption of continuity by a shift to a different activity

change·over \'chān-,jō-vər\ *n* (1907) **:** CONVERSION, TRANSITION

change ringing *n* (1872) **:** the art or practice of ringing a set of tuned bells (as in the bell tower of a church) in continually varying order

change–up \'chān-,jəp\ *n* (1949) **:** a slow pitch in baseball thrown for deception with the same motion as a fastball

[1]chan·nel \'chan-ᵊl\ *n* [ME *chanel,* fr. MF, fr. L *canalis* channel — more at CANAL] (14c) **1 a :** the bed where a natural stream of water runs **b :** the deeper part of a river, harbor, or strait **c :** a strait or narrow sea between two close landmasses **d :** a means of communication or expression: as **(1) :** a path along which data passes or along which data may be stored serially (as in a computer) **(2)** *pl* **:** a fixed or official course of communication ⟨went through established military ~*s* with his grievances⟩ **e :** a way, course, or direction of thought or action ⟨new ~*s* of exploration⟩ **f :** a band of frequencies of sufficient width for a single radio or television communication **2 :** a usu. tubular enclosed passage **:** CONDUIT **3 :** a long gutter, groove, or furrow **4 :** a metal bar of flattened U-shaped section

[2]channel *vt* **-neled** *or* **-nelled; -nel·ing** *or* **-nel·ling** (15c) **1 a :** to form, cut, or wear a channel in **b :** to make a groove in ⟨~ a chair leg⟩ **2 :** to convey or direct into or through a channel ⟨~ his energy into constructive activities⟩

[3]channel *n* [alter. of *chainwale,* fr. *chain* + *wale*] (1769) **:** one of the flat ledges of heavy plank or metal bolted edgewise to the outside of a ship to increase the spread of the shrouds

channel bass *n* (1889) **:** a large coppery drum (*Sciaenops ocellatus*) with a black spot at the base of the tail that is an important game and food fish of the Atlantic coast of No. and So. America — called also *red drum, redfish*

channel catfish *n* (1836) **:** a large black-spotted catfish (*Ictalurus punctatus*) that is an important freshwater food fish of the U.S. and Canada — called also *channel cat*

chan·nel·ize \'chan-ᵊl-,īz\ *vt* **-ized; -iz·ing** (1609) **1 :** CHANNEL **2 :** to straighten by means of a channel ⟨~ a stream⟩ — **chan·nel·iza·tion** \,chan-ᵊl-ə-'zā-shən\ *n*

chan·son \shä^{n}-sō^{n}\ *n, pl* **chan·sons** \-sō^{n}(z)\ [F, fr. L *cantion-, cantio,* fr. *cantus,* pp.] (1602) **:** SONG; *specif* **:** a music-hall or cabaret song

chan·son de geste \-sō^{n}-də-zhest\ *n, pl* **chansons de geste** *same*\ [F, lit., song of heroic deeds] (1868) **:** any of several Old French epic poems of the 11th to the 13th centuries

chan·son·nier \,shä^{n}-sō-'nyā\ *n* [F, fr. *chanson*] (1887) **:** a writer or singer of chansons; *esp* **:** a cabaret singer

[1]chant \'chant\ *vb* [ME *chaunten,* fr. MF *chanter,* fr. L *cantare,* fr. *cantus,* pp. of *canere;* akin to OE *hana* rooster, Gk *kanachē* ringing sound] *vi* (14c) **1 :** to make melodic sounds with the voice; *esp* **:** to sing a chant **2 :** to recite in a monotonous repetitive tone ~ *vt* **1 :** to utter as in chanting **2 :** to celebrate or praise in song or chant

[2]chant *n* (1671) **1 :** SONG **2 a :** PLAINSONG **b :** a rhythmic monotonous utterance or song ⟨the ~ of an auctioneer⟩ **c :** a composition for chanting

chant·er \'chant-ər\ *n* (14c) **1 :** one that chants: **a :** CHORISTER **b :** CANTOR **2 :** the chief singer in a chantry **3 :** the reed pipe of a bagpipe with finger holes on which the melody is played

chan·te·relle \,shant-ə-'rel, ,shänt-\ *n* [F] (1775) **:** an edible mushroom (*Cantharellus cibarius*) of rich yellow color and pleasant aroma

chan·teuse \shä^{n}-'tə(r)z, shan-'tüz\ *n, pl* **chan·teuses** \-'tə(r)z(-əz), -'tüz(-əz)\ [F, fem. of *chanteur* singer, fr. *chanter*] (1888) **:** a female concert or nightclub singer

chan·tey *or* **chan·ty** \'shant-ē, 'chant-\ *n, pl* **chanteys** *or* **chanties** [modif. of F *chanter*] (1856) **:** a song sung by sailors in rhythm with their work

chan·ti·cleer \,chant-ə-'kli(ə)r, ,shant-\ *n* [ME *Chantecleer,* rooster in verse narratives, fr. OF *Chantecler,* rooster in the *Roman de Renart*] (14c) **:** ROOSTER

Chan·til·ly lace \shan-,til-ē-\ *n* [trans. of F *dentelle de Chantilly,* fr. *Chantilly,* France] (1848) **:** a delicate silk, linen, or synthetic lace having a six-sided mesh ground and a floral or scrolled design — called also *Chantilly*

chan·try \'chan-trē\ *n, pl* **chantries** [ME *chanterie,* fr. MF, singing, fr. *chanter*] (14c) **1 :** an endowment for the chanting of masses commonly for the founder **2 :** a chapel endowed by a chantry

Cha·nu·kah \'kän-ə-kə, 'hän-\ *var of* HANUKKAH

cha·os \'kā-,äs\ *n* [L, fr. Gk — more at GUM] (15c) **1** *obs* **:** CHASM, ABYSS **2 a** *often cap* **:** a state of things in which chance is supreme; *esp* **:** the confused unorganized state of primordial matter before the creation of distinct forms — compare COSMOS **b :** a state of utter confusion ⟨the citywide blackout caused ~⟩ **c :** a confused mass or mixture ⟨a ~ of television antennas⟩ — **cha·ot·ic** \kā-'ät-ik\ *adj* — **cha·ot·i·cal·ly** \-i-k(ə-)lē\ *adv*

[1]chap \'chap\ *n* (14c) **:** a crack in or a sore roughening of the skin caused by exposure to wind or cold

[2]chap *vb* **chapped; chap·ping** [ME *chappen;* akin to MD *cappen* to cut down] *vi* (15c) **:** to open in slits or chinks **:** CRACK ⟨hands often ~ in winter⟩ ~ *vt* **:** to cause to open in slits or cracks ⟨*chapped* lips⟩

[3]chap \'chäp, 'chap\ *n* [origin unknown] (1555) **1 a :** the fleshy covering of a jaw; *also* **:** JAW — usu. used in pl. ⟨a wolf's ~*s*⟩ **2 :** the forepart of the face — usu. used in pl.

[4]chap *n* [short for *chapman*] (1716) **1 :** FELLOW 4c **2** *Southern & Midland* **:** BABY, CHILD

chap·a·ra·jos *or* **chap·a·re·jos** \,shap-ə-'rā-(,)ōs, -əs\ *n pl* [MexSp *chaparreras*] (1861) **:** CHAPS

chap·ar·ral \,shap-ə-'ral, -'rel\ *n* [Sp, fr. *chaparro* dwarf evergreen oak, fr. Basque *txapar*] (1850) **1 :** a thicket of dwarf evergreen oaks; *broadly* **:** a dense impenetrable thicket of shrubs or dwarf trees **2 :** an ecological community occurring widely in southern California and comprised of shrubby plants esp. adapted to dry summers and moist winters

chaparral cock *n* (1853) **:** ROADRUNNER — called also *chaparral bird*

chap·book \'chap-,bu̇k\ *n* [*chap*man + *book*] (1798) **:** a small book containing ballads, poems, tales, or tracts

chape \'chāp, 'chap\ *n* [ME, scabbard, fr. MF, cape, fr. LL *cappa*] (14c) **:** the metal mounting or trimming of a scabbard or sheath

cha·peau \sha-'pō, shə-\ *n, pl* **cha·peaus** \-'pōz\ *or* **cha·peaux** \-'pō(z)\ [MF, fr. OF *chapel* — more at CHAPLET] (1523) **:** HAT

chap·el \'chap-əl\ *n* [ME, fr. OF *chapele,* fr. ML *cappella,* fr. dim. of LL *cappa* cloak; fr. the cloak of St. Martin of Tours preserved as a sacred relic in a chapel built for that purpose] (13c) **1 :** a subordinate or private place of worship: as **a :** a place of worship serving a residence or institution **b :** a small house of worship usu. associated with a main church **c :** a room or recess in a church for meditation and prayer or small religious services **2 :** a choir of singers belonging to a chapel (as of a prince) **3 :** a chapel service or assembly at a school or college **4 :** an association of the employees in a printing office **5 :** a place of worship used by a Christian group other than an established church ⟨a nonconformist ~⟩ **6 a :** FUNERAL HOME **b :** a room for funeral services in a funeral home

chapel of ease (1538) **:** a chapel or dependent church built to accommodate an expanding parish

[1]chap·er·on *or* **chap·er·one** \'shap-ə-,rōn\ *n* [F *chaperon,* lit., hood, fr. MF, head covering, fr. *chape*] (1720) **1 :** a person (as a matron) who for propriety accompanies one or more young unmarried women in public or in mixed company **2 :** an older person who accompanies young people at a social gathering to ensure proper behavior; *broadly* **:** one delegated to ensure proper behavior

[2]chaperon *or* **chaperone** *vb* **-oned; -on·ing** *vt* (1796) **1 :** ESCORT **2 :** to act as chaperon to or for ~ *vi* **:** to act as a chaperon — **chap·er·on·age** \-,rō-nij\ *n*

chap·fall·en \'chap-,fȯ-lən, 'chäp-\ *adj* (1598) **1 :** having the lower jaw hanging loosely **2 :** cast down in spirit **:** DEPRESSED

chap·i·ter \'chap-ət-ər\ *n* [ME *chapitre,* fr. MF, alter. of OF *chapitle,* fr. L *capitulum,* lit., little head] (15c) **:** the capital of a column

chap·lain \'chap-lən\ *n* [ME *chapelain,* fr. OF, fr. ML *cappellanus,* fr. *cappella*] (12c) **1 :** a clergyman in charge of a chapel **2 :** a clergyman officially attached to a branch of the military, to an institution, or to a family or court **3 :** a person chosen to conduct religious exercises (as at a meeting of a club or society) **4 :** a clergyman appointed to assist a bishop (as at a liturgical function) — **chap·lain·cy** \-sē\ *n* — **chap·lain·ship** \-,ship\ *n*

chap·let \'chap-lət\ *n* [ME *chapelet,* fr. MF, fr. OF, dim. of *chapel* hat, garland, fr. ML *cappellus* head covering, fr. LL *cappa*] (14c) **1 :** a wreath to be worn on the head **2 a :** a string of beads **b :** a part of a rosary comprising five decades **3 :** a small molding carved with small decorative forms — **chap·let·ed** \-lət-əd\ *adj*

chap·man \'chap-mən\ *n* [ME, fr. OE *cēapman,* fr. *cēap* trade + *man* — more at CHEAP] (bef. 12c) **1** *archaic* **:** MERCHANT, TRADER **2** *Brit* **:** PEDDLER

chaps \'shaps, 'chaps\ *n pl* [modif. of MexSp *chaparreras*] (1884) **:** leather leggings joined together by a belt or lacing, often having flared outer flaps, and worn over the trousers esp. by western ranch hands

chap·ter \'chap-tər\ *n* [ME *chapitre* division of a book, meeting of canons, fr. OF, fr. LL *capitulum* division of a book & ML, meeting place of canons, fr. L, dim. of *capit-, caput* head — more at HEAD] (13c) **1 a :** a main division of a book **b :** something resembling a chapter in being a significant specified unit ⟨with his death a ~ was closed in the history of the industry⟩ **2 a :** a regular meeting of the canons of a cathedral or collegiate church or of the members of a religious house **b :** the body of canons of a cathedral or collegiate church **3 :** a local branch of a society or fraternity

chapter house *n* (12c) **1 :** the building or rooms where a chapter meets **2 :** the residence of a local chapter of a fraternity or sorority

[1]char \'chär\ *n, pl* **char** *or* **chars** [origin unknown] (1662) **:** any of a genus (*Salvelinus*) of small-scaled trouts

[2]char *vb* **charred; char·ring** [back-formation fr. *charcoal*] *vt* (1679) **1 :** to convert to charcoal or carbon usu. by heat **:** BURN **2 :** to burn slightly or partly **:** SCORCH ⟨the fire *charred* the beams⟩ ~ *vi* **:** to become charred **:** BURN

[3]char *n* (1879) **:** a charred substance **:** CHARCOAL; *specif* **:** a combustible residue remaining after the destructive distillation of coal

[4]**char** *vi* **charred; char·ring** [back-formation fr. *charwoman*] (1732) : to work as a cleaning woman

[5]**char** *n* [short for *charwoman*] *Brit* (1906) : CHARWOMAN

char·a·banc \ˈshar-ə-ˌbaŋ\ *n* [F *char à bancs*, lit., wagon with benches] *Brit* (1914) : a sightseeing motor coach

char·a·cin \ˈkar-ə-sən\ *n* [deriv. of Gk *charak-*, *charax* pointed stake, a fish] (1882) : any of a family (Characidae) of usu. small brightly colored tropical freshwater fishes — **characin** *adj*

[1]**char·ac·ter** \ˈkar-ik-tər\ *n* [ME *caracter*, fr. MF *caractère*, fr. L *character* mark, distinctive quality, fr. Gk *charaktēr*, fr. *charassein* to scratch, engrave] (14c) **1 a :** a conventionalized graphic device placed on an object as an indication of ownership, origin, or relationship **b :** a graphic symbol (as a hieroglyph or alphabet letter) used in writing or printing **c :** a magical or astrological emblem **d :** ALPHABET **e** (1) : WRITING, PRINTING (2) : style of writing or printing (3) : CIPHER **f :** a symbol (as a letter or number) that represents information; *also* : a representation of such a character that may be accepted by a computer **2 a :** one of the attributes or features that make up and distinguish the individual **b** (1) : a feature used to separate distinguishable things into categories; *also* : a group or kind so separated ⟨people of this ∼⟩ ⟨advertising of a very primitive ∼⟩ (2) : the detectable expression of the action of a gene or group of genes (3) : the aggregate of distinctive qualities characteristic of a breed, strain, or type ⟨a wine of great ∼⟩ **c :** the complex of mental and ethical traits marking and often individualizing a person, group, or nation ⟨assess a person's ∼ by studying his handwriting⟩ **d :** main or essential nature esp. as strongly marked and serving to distinguish ⟨excess sewage gradually changed the ∼ of the lake⟩ **3 :** POSITION, CAPACITY ⟨his ∼ as a town official⟩ **4 :** a short literary sketch of the qualities of a social type **5 :** REFERENCE 4b **6 a :** a person marked by notable or conspicuous traits : PERSONAGE ⟨a notorious campus ∼⟩ **b :** one of the persons of a drama or novel **c :** the personality or part which an actor recreates **d :** characterization esp. in drama or fiction **e :** PERSON, INDIVIDUAL ⟨some ∼ just stole her purse⟩ **7 :** REPUTATION **8 :** moral excellence and firmness ⟨a man of sound ∼⟩ ***syn*** see DISPOSITION, QUALITY, TYPE — **char·ac·ter·less** \-ləs\ *adj* — **in character :** in accord with a person's usual qualities or traits — **out of character :** not in accord with a person's usual qualities or traits

[2]**character** *vt* (1591) **1** *archaic* : ENGRAVE, INSCRIBE **2 a** *archaic* : REPRESENT, PORTRAY **b :** CHARACTERIZE

[3]**character** *adj* (1893) **1 :** capable of portraying an unusual or eccentric personality often markedly different (as in age) from the player ⟨a ∼ actor⟩ **2 :** requiring the qualities of a character actor ⟨a ∼ role⟩

character assassination *n* (1949) : the slandering of a person usu. with the intention of destroying public confidence in him

char·ac·ter·ful \ˈkar-ik-tər-fəl\ *adj* (1901) **1 :** markedly expressive of character ⟨a ∼ face⟩ **2 :** marked by character ⟨a ∼ decision⟩

[1]**char·ac·ter·is·tic** \ˌkar-ik-tə-ˈris-tik\ *n* (1664) **1 :** a distinguishing trait, quality, or property **2 :** the integral part of a common logarithm **3 :** the smallest positive integer *n* which for an operation in a ring or field yields 0 when any element is used *n* times with the operation

[2]**characteristic** *adj* (1665) : revealing, distinguishing, or typical of the individual character — **char·ac·ter·is·ti·cal·ly** \-ti-k(ə-)lē\ *adv*

syn CHARACTERISTIC, INDIVIDUAL, PECULIAR, DISTINCTIVE mean indicating a special quality or identity. CHARACTERISTIC applies to something that distinguishes or identifies a person or thing or class; INDIVIDUAL stresses qualities that distinguish one from all other members of the same kind or class; PECULIAR applies to qualities possessed only by a particular individual or class or kind and stresses rarity or uniqueness; DISTINCTIVE indicates qualities distinguishing and uncommon and often superior or praiseworthy.

characteristic equation *n* (ca. 1925) : an equation in which the characteristic polynomial of a matrix is set equal to 0

characteristic polynomial *n* (ca. 1957) : the determinant of a square matrix in which an arbitrary variable (as *x*) is subtracted from each of the elements along the principal diagonal

characteristic root *n* (ca. 1957) : EIGENVALUE

characteristic value *n* (1956) : EIGENVALUE

characteristic vector *n* (ca. 1957) : EIGENVECTOR

char·ac·ter·iza·tion \ˌkar-ik-t(ə-)rə-ˈzā-shən\ *n* (1814) : the act of characterizing; *esp* : the artistic representation (as in fiction or drama) of human character or motives

char·ac·ter·ize \ˈkar-ik-tə-ˌrīz\ *vt* **-ized; -iz·ing** (1633) **1 :** to describe the character or quality of ⟨∼*s* him as ambitious⟩ **2 :** to be a characteristic of : DISTINGUISH ⟨a personality *characterized* by good humor⟩

char·ac·ter·olog·i·cal \ˌkar-ik-t(ə-)rə-ˈläj-i-kəl\ *adj* [*characterology* (study of character)] (1916) : of, relating to, or based on character or the study of character including its development and its differences in different individuals — **char·ac·ter·olog·i·cal·ly** \-ˈläj-i-k(ə-)lē\ *adv*

character witness *n* (1952) : one that gives evidence concerning the reputation, conduct, and moral nature of a party to a legal action

char·ac·tery \ˈkar-ik-t(ə-)rē, kə-ˈrak-\ *n, pl* **-ter·ies** (1598) : a system of written letters or symbols used in the expression of thought

cha·rade \shə-ˈrād\ *n* [F] (1776) **1 :** a word represented in riddling verse or by picture, tableau, or dramatic action **2** *pl* : a game in which each syllable of a word or phrase is acted out by some of the persons playing the game while the others try to guess the word or phrase **3 :** an empty or deceptive act or pretense ⟨his concern was a ∼⟩

cha·ras \ˈchär-əs\ *n* [Hindi *caras*] (1839) : HASHISH

char·broil \ˈchär-ˌbrȯi(ə)l\ *vt* (1968) : to broil on a rack over hot charcoal — **char·broil·er** \-ˌbrȯi-lər\ *n*

[1]**char·coal** \ˈchär-ˌkōl\ *n* [ME *charcole*] (14c) **1 :** a dark or black porous carbon prepared from vegetable or animal substances (as from wood by charring in a kiln from which air is excluded) **2 a :** a piece or pencil of fine charcoal used in drawing **b :** a charcoal drawing

[2]**charcoal** *vt* (1965) : CHARBROIL

char·cu·te·rie \(ˌ)shär-ˌküt-ə-ˈrē\ *n* [F, lit., pork-butcher's shop, fr. MF *chaircuiterie*, fr. *chaircutier* pork butcher, fr. *chair cuite* cooked meat, fr. OF *char* (fr. L *carn-*, *caro*) flesh + *cuite*, fem. of *cuit*, pp. of *cuire* to cook, fr. L *coquere* — more at COOK, CARNAL] (1901) : a delicatessen specializing in dressed meats and meat dishes; *also* : the products sold in such a shop

chard \ˈchärd\ *n* [F *carde*, fr. OProv *cardo* edible cardoon, fr. L *carduus* thistle, artichoke; akin to MLG *harst* rake, L *carrere* to card] (1658) : a beet (*Beta vulgaris cicla*) whose large leaves and succulent stalks are often cooked as a vegetable — called also *Swiss chard*

char·don·nay \ˌshärd-ᵊn-ˈā\ *n, often cap* [F] (ca. 1941) : a dry white table wine of Chablis type

chare \ˈcha(ə)r, ˈche(ə)r\ *or* **char** \ˈchär\ *n* [ME *char* turn, piece of work, fr. OE *cierr*; akin to OE *cierran* to turn] (bef. 12c) : CHORE

[1]**charge** \ˈchärj\ *vb* **charged; charg·ing** [ME *chargen*, fr. OF *chargier*, fr. LL *carricare*, fr. L *carrus* wheeled vehicle — more at CAR] *vt* (13c) **1 a** *archaic* : to lay or put a load on or in : LOAD **b** (1) : to place a charge (as of powder) in (2) : to load or fill to capacity **c** (1) : to restore the active materials in (a storage battery) by the passage of a direct current through in the opposite direction to that of discharge (2) : to give an electric charge to **d** (1) : to assume as a heraldic bearing (2) : to place a heraldic bearing on **e :** to fill or furnish fully ⟨the music is *charged* with excitement⟩ **2 a :** to impose a task or responsibility on ⟨∼ him with the job of finding a new meeting place⟩ **b :** to command, instruct, or exhort with right or authority ⟨I ∼ you not to go⟩ **c** *of a judge* : to give a charge to (a jury) **3 a :** BLAME ⟨∼*s* him as the instigator⟩ **b :** to make an assertion against esp. by ascribing guilt for an offense : ACCUSE ⟨∼*s* him with armed robbery⟩ ⟨∼*s* them with hypocrisy⟩ **c :** to place the guilt or blame for ⟨∼ her failure to negligence⟩ **d :** to assert as an accusation ⟨∼*s* that he distorted the data⟩ **4 a :** to bring (a weapon) into position for attack : LEVEL ⟨∼ a lance⟩ **b :** to rush against or bear down upon : ATTACK; *also* : to rush into (an opponent) usu. illegally in various sports **5 a** (1) : to impose a pecuniary burden on ⟨∼ his estate with debts incurred⟩ (2) : to impose or record as pecuniary obligation ⟨∼ debts to an estate⟩ **b** (1) : to fix or ask as fee or payment ⟨∼*s* $50 for an office visit⟩ (2) : to ask payment of (a person) ⟨∼ a client for expenses⟩ **c :** to record (an item) as an expense, debt, obligation, or liability ⟨∼ a purchase to a customer⟩ ∼ *vi* **1 :** to rush forward in or as if in assault : ATTACK; *also* : to charge an opponent in sports **2 :** to ask or set a price **3 :** to charge an item to an account ⟨∼ now, pay later⟩ ***syn*** see COMMAND

[2]**charge** *n* (13c) **1 a** *obs* : a material load or weight **b :** a figure borne on a heraldic field **2 a :** the quantity that an apparatus is intended to receive and fitted to hold **b :** a store or accumulation of impelling force ⟨the deeply emotional ∼ of the drama⟩ **c :** a definite quantity of electricity; *esp* : an excess or deficiency of electrons in a body **d :** THRILL, KICK ⟨got a ∼ out of the game⟩ **3 a :** OBLIGATION, REQUIREMENT **b :** MANAGEMENT, SUPERVISION ⟨has ∼ of the home office⟩ **c :** the ecclesiastical jurisdiction (as a parish) committed to a clergyman **d :** a person or thing committed to the care of another **4 a :** INSTRUCTION, COMMAND **b :** instruction in points of law given by a court to a jury **5 a :** EXPENSE, COST ⟨gave the banquet at his own ∼⟩ **b :** the price demanded for something ⟨no admission ∼⟩ **c :** a debit to an account ⟨the purchase was a ∼⟩ **d :** the record of a loan (as of a book from a library) **6 a :** ACCUSATION, INDICTMENT ⟨a ∼ of assault with intent to kill⟩ **b :** a statement of complaint or hostile criticism ⟨denied the ∼*s* of nepotism that were leveled against him⟩ **7 :** a violent rush forward (as to attack) — **in charge :** having control or custody of something ⟨he is *in charge* of the training program⟩

charge·able \ˈchär-jə-bəl\ *adj* (15c) **1** *archaic* : financially burdensome : EXPENSIVE **2 :** liable to be charged: as **a :** liable to be accused or held responsible **b :** suitable to be charged to a particular account **c :** qualified to be made a charge on the county or parish

charge account *n* (1903) : a customer's account with a creditor (as a merchant) to which the purchase of goods is charged

charge–coupled device *n* (1973) : a semiconductor device that is used esp. as an optical sensor and that stores charge and transfers it sequentially to an amplifier and detector — called also *CCD*

charged \ˈchärjd\ *adj* (14c) **1 :** possessing strong emotion or vigorous purpose ⟨attacked the author in a highly ∼ review⟩ **2 :** capable of arousing strong emotion ⟨a politically ∼ subject⟩

char·gé d'af·faires \(ˌ)shär-ˌzhād-ə-ˈfa(ə)r, -ˈfe(ə)r\ *n, pl* **chargés d'affaires** \-ˌzhād-ə-, -ˌzhāz-də-\ [F, lit., one charged with affairs] (1767) **1 :** a subordinate diplomat who substitutes for an absent ambassador or minister **2 :** a diplomat inferior in rank to an ambassador or minister and accredited by one government to the foreign minister of another

charge of quarters (1918) : an enlisted man designated to handle administrative matters in his unit esp. after duty hours

[1]**char·ger** \ˈchär-jər\ *n* [ME *chargeour*; akin to ME *chargen* to charge] (14c) : a large flat dish or platter

[2]**charg·er** *n* (1711) **1 :** one that charges: as **a :** an appliance for holding or inserting a charge of powder or shot in a gun **b :** a cartridge clip **2 :** a horse for battle or parade

char·i·ness \ˈchar-ē-nəs, ˈcher-\ *n* (1571) **1 :** the quality or state of being chary : CAUTION **2 :** carefully preserved state : INTEGRITY

[1]**char·i·ot** \ˈchar-ē-ət\ *n* [ME, fr. MF, fr. OF, fr. *char* wheeled vehicle, fr. L *carrus* — more at CAR] (14c) **1 :** a light four-wheeled pleasure or state carriage **2 :** a two-wheeled horse-drawn battle car of ancient times used also in processions and races

[2]**chariot** *vi* (1627) : to drive or ride in or as if in a chariot ∼ *vt* : to carry in or as if in a chariot

char·i·o·teer \ˌchar-ē-ə-ˈti(ə)r\ *n* (14c) **1 :** one who drives a chariot **2** *cap* : the constellation Auriga

cha·ris·ma \kə-ˈriz-mə\ *also* **char·ism** \ˈka(ə)r-ˌiz-əm\ *n, pl* **cha·ris·ma·ta** \kə-ˈriz-mət-ə\ *also* **charisms** [Gk *charisma* favor, gift, fr. *charizesthai* to favor, fr. *charis* grace; akin to Gk *chairein* to rejoice — more at YEARN] (1641) **1 :** an extraordinary power (as of healing) given a Christian by the Holy Spirit for the good of the church **2 a :** a personal magic of leadership arousing special popular loyalty or enthusiasm for a public figure (as a political leader or military commander) **b :** a special magnetic charm or appeal ⟨the ∼ of a popular actor⟩

[1]**char·is·mat·ic** \ˌkar-əz-ˈmat-ik\ *adj* [*charisma*] (ca. 1868) **1 :** of, relating to, or constituting charisma **2 :** having, exhibiting, or based on charisma ⟨∼ sects⟩ ⟨∼ leader⟩

[2]charismatic *n* (1935) : a member of a charismatic religious group or movement

char·i·ta·ble \'char-ət-ə-bəl\ *adj* (14c) **1** : full of love for and goodwill toward others : BENEVOLENT **2 a** : liberal in benefactions to the needy : GENEROUS **b** : of or relating to charity ⟨~ institutions⟩ **3** : merciful or kind in judging others : LENIENT — **char·i·ta·ble·ness** *n* — **char·i·ta·bly** \-blē\ *adv*

char·i·ty \'char-ət-ē\ *n, pl* **-ties** [ME *charite,* fr. OF *charité,* fr. LL *caritat-, caritas* Christian love, fr. L, dearness, fr. *carus* dear; akin to OE *hōre* whore, Skt *kāma* love] (12c) **1** : benevolent goodwill toward or love of humanity **2 a** : generosity and helpfulness esp. toward the needy or suffering; *also* : aid given to those in need **b** : an institution engaged in relief of the poor **c** : public provision for the relief of the needy **3 a** : a gift for public benevolent purposes **b** : an institution (as a hospital) founded by such a gift **4** : lenient judgment of others *syn* see MERCY

cha·ri·va·ri \ˌshiv-ə-'rē, 'shiv-ə-ˌ\ *n* [F, fr. LL *caribaria* headache, fr. Gk *karēbaria,* fr. *kara, karē* head + *barys* heavy — more at CEREBRAL, GRIEVE] (1681) : SHIVAREE

char·ka *or* **char·kha** \'chər-kə, 'chär-\ *n* [Hindi *carkha;* akin to Skt *cakra* — more at WHEEL] (1880) : a domestic spinning wheel used in India chiefly for spinning cotton

char·la·tan \'shär-lə-tən, -lət-ᵊn\ *n* [It *ciarlatano,* prob. alter. of *cerretano,* lit., inhabitant of Cerreto, fr. *Cerreto,* Italy] (1611) **1** : QUACK 2 ⟨~*s* killing their patients with empirical procedures⟩ **2** : one making usu. showy pretenses to knowledge or ability : FRAUD, FAKER — **char·la·tan·ism** \-ˌiz-əm\ *n* — **char·la·tan·ry** \-rē\ *n*

Charles's Wain \ˌchärl-zəz-'wān, 'chärlz-'wān\ *n* [*Charlemagne*] : DIPPER 3a

Charles·ton \'chärl-stən\ *n* [*Charleston,* S. C.] (1923) : a lively ballroom dance in which the knees are twisted in and out and the heels are swung sharply outward on each step

char·ley horse \'chär-lē-ˌhȯrs\ *n* [fr. *Charley,* nickname for *Charles*] (1888) : a muscular strain or bruise esp. of the quadriceps that is characterized by pain and stiffness

char·lie *also* **char·ley** \'chär-lē\ *n, often cap* [prob. fr. *Charlie,* name of a clown] *Brit* (1946) : FOOL

Char·lie \'chär-lē\ [fr. the name *Charlie*] (1946) — a communications code word for the letter *c*

char·lock \'chär-ˌläk, -lək\ *n* [ME *cherlok,* fr. OE *cerlic*] (bef. 12c) : a mustard (*Brassica kaber*) that is often troublesome in grainfields — called also *wild mustard*

char·lotte \'shär-lət\ *n* [F] (1796) : a dessert consisting of a filling (as of fruit, whipped cream, or custard) layered with or placed in a mold lined with strips of bread, ladyfingers, or biscuits

char·lotte russe \ˌshär-lət-'rüs\ *n* [F, lit., Russian charlotte] (1845) : a charlotte made with sponge cake or ladyfingers and a whipped-cream or custard-gelatin filling

[1]charm \'chärm\ *n* [ME *charme,* fr. MF, fr. L *carmen* song, fr. *canere* to sing — more at CHANT] (14c) **1 a** : the chanting or reciting of a magic spell : INCANTATION **b** : an act or expression believed to have magic power **2** : something worn about the person to ward off evil or ensure good fortune : AMULET **3 a** : a trait that fascinates, allures, or delights **b** : a physical grace or attraction — used in pl. **c** : compelling attractiveness ⟨the island possessed great ~⟩ **4** : a small ornament worn on a bracelet or chain **5** : a quantum characteristic of a quark or fundamental particle that accounts for the unexpectedly long lifetime of the J particle, explains difficulties in the theory of weak interactions, and has a value of zero for most known particles — **charm·less** \-ləs\ *adj*

[2]charm *vt* (14c) **1 a** : to affect by or as if by magic : COMPEL **b** : to please, soothe, or delight by compelling attraction ⟨~*s* customers with his suave manner⟩ **2** : to endow with supernatural powers by means of charms; *also* : to protect by spells, charms, or supernatural influences **3** : to control (an animal) typically by charms (as the playing of music) ⟨~ a snake⟩ ~ *vi* **1** : to practice magic and enchantment **2** : to have the effect of a charm : FASCINATE *syn* see ATTRACT

charmed \'chärmd\ *adj* (1974) : having charm ⟨a ~ antiquark⟩

charmed circle *n* (1900) : a group marked by exclusiveness

charm·er \'chär-mər\ *n* (14c) **1** : ENCHANTER, MAGICIAN **2** : one that pleases or fascinates

charm·ing \'chär-miŋ\ *adj* (1663) : extremely pleasing or delightful : ENTRANCING — **charm·ing·ly** \-miŋ-lē\ *adv*

char·nel \'chärn-ᵊl\ *n* [ME, fr. MF, fr. ML *carnale,* fr. LL, neut. of *carnalis* of the flesh — more at CARNAL] (14c) : a building or chamber in which bodies or bones are deposited — called also *charnel house* — **charnel** *adj*

Cha·ro·lais \ˌshar-ə-'lā\ *n* [*Charolais,* district in eastern France] (1893) : any of a French breed of large white cattle used primarily for beef and crossbreeding

Char·on \'kar-ən, 'ker-\ *n* [L, fr. Gk *Charōn*] **1** : a son of Erebus who in Greek myth ferries the souls of the dead over the Styx **2** : the moon of Pluto

char·poy \'chär-ˌpȯi\ *n, pl* **charpoys** [Hindi *cārpāī*] (1845) : a bed consisting of a frame strung with tapes or light rope that is used esp. in India

char·qui \'chär-kē, 'shär-\ *n* [Sp, fr. Quechua *ch'arki* dried meat] (1604) : jerked beef

charr \'chär\ *var of* CHAR

[1]chart \'chärt\ *n* [MF *charte,* fr. L *charta* piece of papyrus, document — more at CARD] (1571) **1** : MAP: as **a** : an outline map exhibiting something (as climatic or magnetic variations) in its geographical aspects **b** : a map for the use of navigators **2 a** : a sheet giving information in tabular form **b** : GRAPH **c** : DIAGRAM **d** : a sheet of paper ruled and graduated for use in a recording instrument **e** : a listing according to sales or popularity — usu. used in pl. ⟨number one on the ~*s* —Tim Cahill⟩

[2]chart *vt* (1842) **1** : to make a map or chart of **2** : to lay out a plan for

[1]char·ter \'chärt-ər\ *n* [ME *chartre,* fr. OF, fr. ML *chartula,* fr. L, dim. of *charta*] (13c) **1** : a written instrument or contract (as a deed) executed in due form **2 a** : a grant or guarantee of rights, franchises, or privileges from the sovereign power of a state or country **b** : a written instrument that creates and defines the franchises of a city, educational institution, or corporation **c** : CONSTITUTION **3** : a written instrument from the authorities of a society creating a lodge or branch **4** : a special privilege, immunity, or exemption **5** : a mercantile lease of a ship or some principal part of it **6** : a charter travel arrangement

[2]charter *vt* (15c) **1 a** : to establish, enable, or convey by charter **b** *Brit* : CERTIFY ⟨a ~*ed* mechanical engineer⟩ **2** : to hire, rent, or lease for usu. exclusive and temporary use ⟨~*ed* a boat for deep-sea fishing⟩ *syn* see HIRE — **char·ter·er** \-ər-ər\ *n*

[3]charter *adj* (1905) : of, relating to, or being a travel arrangement in which transportation (as a bus or plane) is hired by and for one specific group of people ⟨a ~ flight⟩

chartered accountant *n, Brit* (1855) : a member of a chartered institute of accountants

charter member *n* (ca. 1909) : an original member of a group (as a society or corporation) — **charter membership** *n*

Char·tism \'chärt-ˌiz-əm\ *n* [ML *charta* charter, fr. L, document] (1839) : the principles and practices of a body of 19th century English political reformers advocating better social and industrial conditions for the working classes — **Char·tist** \'chärt-əst\ *n or adj*

chart·ist \'chärt-əst\ *n* (ca. 1961) **1** : CARTOGRAPHER **2** : an analyst of market action whose predictions of market courses are based on study of graphic presentations of past market performance

char·treuse \shär-'trüz, -'trüs\ *n* [*Chartreuse*] (1884) : a variable color averaging a brilliant yellow green

Chartreuse *trademark* —used for a usu. green or yellow liqueur

char·tu·lary \'kär-chə-ˌler-ē\ *n, pl* **-lar·ies** [ML *chartularium*] (1571) : CARTULARY

char·wom·an \'chär-ˌwu̇m-ən\ *n* [*chare* + *woman*] (1596) : a cleaning woman esp. in a large building

chary \'cha(ə)r-ē, 'che(ə)r-\ *adj* **chari·er; -est** [ME, sorrowful, dear, fr. OE *cearig* sorrowful, fr. *caru* sorrow — more at CARE] (bef. 12c) **1** *archaic* : DEAR, TREASURED **2** : discreetly cautious: as **a** : hesitant and vigilant about dangers and risks **b** : slow to grant, accept, or expend ⟨a person very ~ of compliments⟩ *syn* see CAUTIOUS —**chari·ly** \'char-ə-lē, 'cher-\ *adv*

Cha·ryb·dis \kə-'rib-dəs *also* shə- *or* chə-\ *n* [L, fr. Gk] : a whirlpool off the coast of Sicily personified in Greek myth as a female monster — compare SCYLLA

[1]chase \'chās\ *n* (13c) **1 a** : the hunting of wild animals — used with *the* **b** : the act of chasing : PURSUIT **c** : an earnest or frenzied seeking after something desired **2** : something pursued : QUARRY **3** : a tract of unenclosed land used as a game preserve **4** : a sequence (as in a movie) in which the characters pursue one another

[2]chase *vb* **chased; chas·ing** [ME *chasen,* fr. MF *chasser,* fr. (assumed) VL *captiare* — more at CATCH] *vt* (14c) **1 a** : to follow rapidly : PURSUE **b** : HUNT **c** : to follow regularly or persistently with the intention of attracting or alluring **2** *obs* : HARASS **3** : to seek out — often used with *down* ⟨detectives *chasing* down clues⟩ **4** : to cause to depart or flee : DRIVE ⟨~ the dog out of the garden⟩ **5** : to cause the removal of (a baseball pitcher) by a batting rally ~ *vi* **1** : to chase an animal, person, or thing ⟨~ after material possessions⟩ **2** : RUSH, HASTEN ⟨*chased* all over town looking for a place to stay⟩

syn CHASE, PURSUE, FOLLOW, TRAIL mean to go after or on the track of something or someone. CHASE implies going swiftly after and trying to overtake something fleeing or running; PURSUE suggests a continuing effort to overtake, reach, attain; FOLLOW puts less emphasis upon speed or intent to overtake; TRAIL may stress a following of tracks or traces rather than a visible object.

[3]chase *vt* **chased; chas·ing** [ME *chassen,* modif. of MF *enchasser* to set] (15c) **1 a** : to ornament (metal) by indenting with a hammer and tools without a cutting edge **b** : to make by such indentation **c** : to set with gems **2 a** : GROOVE, INDENT **b** : to cut (a thread) with a chaser

[4]chase *n* [F *chas* eye of a needle, fr. LL *capsus* enclosed space, fr. L, pen, alter. of *capsa* box — more at CASE] (1611) **1** : GROOVE, FURROW **2** : the bore of a cannon **3 a** : TRENCH **b** : a channel (as in a wall) for something to lie in or pass through

[5]chase *n* [prob. fr. F *châsse* frame, fr. L *capsa*] (1612) : a rectangular steel or iron frame in which letterpress matter is locked (as for printing)

[1]chas·er \'chā-sər\ *n* (14c) **1** : one that chases **2** : a mild drink (as beer) taken after hard liquor

[2]chaser *n* (1707) : a skilled worker who produces ornamental chasing

[3]chaser *n* (ca. 1864) : a tool for cutting screw threads

Cha·sid \'has-əd, 'käs-\ *n, pl* **Cha·si·dim** \'has-əd-əm, kä-'sēd-\ *var of* HASID

chasm \'kaz-əm\ *n* [L *chasma,* fr. Gk; akin to L *hiare* to yawn — more at YAWN] (1596) **1** : a deep cleft in the earth : GORGE **2** : a marked division, separation, or difference ⟨a political ~ between the two countries⟩

[1]chas·sé \sha-'sā\ *vi* **chas·séd; chas·sé·ing** [F, n., fr. pp. of *chasser* to chase] (1803) **1** : to make a chassé **2** : SASHAY

[2]chassé *n* (1828) : a sliding dance step resembling the galop

chasse·pot \'shas-(ə-)ˌpō\ *n* [F, fr. Antoine A. *Chassepot* †1905 Fr. inventor] (1869) : a bolt-action rifle firing a paper cartridge

chas·seur \sha-'sər\ *n* [F, fr. MF *chasser*] (1796) **1** : HUNTER, HUNTSMAN **2** : one of a body of light cavalry or infantry trained for rapid maneuvering **3** : a liveried attendant : FOOTMAN

chas·sis \'chas-ē, 'shas-ē *also* 'chas-əs\ *n, pl* **chas·sis** \-ēz\ [F *châssis,* fr. (assumed) VL *capsicum,* fr. L *capsa* box — more at CASE] (ca. 1864) **1** : the frame upon which is mounted the body (as of an automobile or airplane), the working parts (as of a radio), the recoiling parts (of a cannon), or the roof, walls, floors, and facing (as of a building) **2** : the frame and working parts as opposed to the body (as of an automobile) or cabinet (as of a radio or television set)

chaste \'chāst\ *adj* **chast·er; chast·est** [ME, fr. OF, fr. L *castus* pure — more at CASTE] (13c) **1** : innocent of unlawful sexual intercourse **2** : CELIBATE **3** : pure in thought and act : MODEST **4 a** : severely simple in design or execution : AUSTERE ⟨the ~ hospital corridor⟩ ⟨~ poetry⟩ **b** : CLEAN, SPOTLESS — **chaste·ly** *adv* — **chaste·ness** \'chās(t)-nəs\ *n*

syn CHASTE, PURE, MODEST, DECENT mean free from all taint of what is lewd or salacious. CHASTE primarily implies a refraining from acts or even thoughts or desires that are not virginal or not sanctioned by marriage vows; PURE differs from CHASTE in implying innocence and absence of temptation rather than control of one's impulses and actions; MODEST and DECENT apply esp. to deportment and dress as outward signs of inward chastity or purity.

chas·ten \'chās-ᵊn\ *vt* **chas·tened; chas·ten·ing** \'chās-niŋ, -ᵊn-iŋ\ [alter. of obs. E *chaste* to chasten, fr. ME *chasten,* fr. OF *chastier,* fr. L *castigare,* fr. *castus* + *-igare* (fr. *agere* to drive) — more at ACT] (13c) **1** : to correct by punishment or suffering : DISCIPLINE; *also* : PURIFY **2 a** : to prune (as a work or style of art) of excess, pretense, or falsity : REFINE **b** : to cause to be more humble or restrained : SUBDUE ***syn*** see PUNISH — **chas·ten·er** \'chās-nər, -ᵊn-ər\ *n*

chas·tise \(')chas-'tīz\ *vt* **chas·tised; chas·tis·ing** [ME *chastisen,* alter. of *chasten*] (14c) **1** : to inflict punishment on (as by whipping) **2** : to censure severely : CASTIGATE **3** *archaic* : CHASTEN 2 ***syn*** see PUNISH — **chas·tise·ment** \(')chas-'tīz-mənt *also* 'chas-təz-\ *n* — **chas·tis·er** \(')chas-'tī-zər\ *n*

chas·ti·ty \'chas-tət-ē\ *n* (13c) **1** : the quality or state of being chaste: as **a** : abstention from unlawful sexual intercourse **b** : abstention from all sexual intercourse **c** : purity in conduct and intention **d** : restraint and simplicity in design or expression **2** : personal integrity

chastity belt *n* (1931) : a belt device (as of medieval times) designed to prevent sexual intercourse on the part of the woman wearing it

cha·su·ble \'chaz(h)-ə-bəl, 'chas-ə-\ *n* [MF, fr. LL *casubla* hooded garment] (14c) : a sleeveless outer vestment worn by the officiating priest at mass

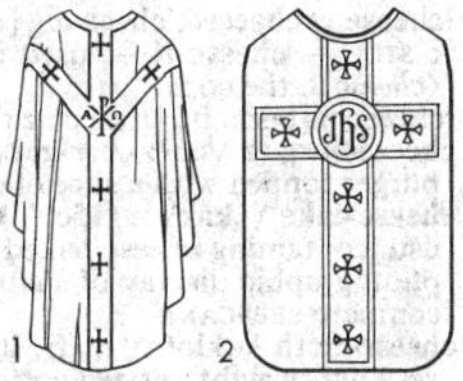

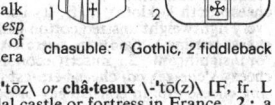

chasuble: *1* Gothic, *2* fiddleback

1chat \'chat\ *vb* **chat·ted; chat·ting** [ME *chatten,* short for *chatteren*] *vi* (15c) **1** : CHATTER, PRATTLE **2** : to talk in an informal or familiar manner ~ *vt, chiefly Brit* : to talk to; *esp* : to talk lightly or glibly with — often used with *up*

2chat *n* (1530) **1** : idle small talk : CHATTER **2** : light familiar talk; *esp* : CONVERSATION **3** [imit.] : any of several songbirds (as of the genera *Saxicola* or *Icteria*)

châ·teau \sha-'tō\ *n, pl* **châ·teaus** \-'tōz\ *or* **châ·teaux** \-'tō(z)\ [F, fr. L *castellum* castle] (1739) **1** : a feudal castle or fortress in France **2** : a large country house : MANSION **3** : a French vineyard estate

cha·teau·bri·and \(,)sha-,tō-brē-'ä^{n}\ *n, often cap* [François René de *Chateaubriand*] (1877) : a large tenderloin steak usu. grilled or broiled and served with a sauce (as béarnaise)

chat·e·lain \'shat-ᵊl-,ān\ *n* [MF *châtelain,* fr. L *castellanus* occupant of a castle] (15c) : CASTELLAN

chat·e·laine \'shat-ᵊl-,ān\ *n* [F *châtelaine,* fem. of *châtelain*] (1845) **1 a** : the wife of a castellan : the mistress of a château **b** : the mistress of a household or of a large establishment **2** : a clasp or hook for a watch, purse, or bunch of keys

cha·toy·ance \shə-'tȯi-ən(t)s\ *n* (ca. 1909) : CHATOYANCY

cha·toy·an·cy \-ən-sē\ *n* (1894) : the quality or state of being chatoyant

1cha·toy·ant \shə-'tȯi-ənt\ *adj* [F, fr. prp. of *chatoyer* to shine like a cat's eyes] (1816) : having a changeable luster or color with an undulating narrow band of white light ⟨a ~ gem⟩

2chatoyant *n* (ca. 1828) : a chatoyant gem

chat show *n, Brit* (1971) : TALK SHOW

chat·tel \'chat-ᵊl\ *n* [ME *chatel* property, fr. MF, fr. ML *capitale* — more at CATTLE] (14c) **1** : an item of tangible movable or immovable property except real estate, freehold, and things (as buildings) connected with real property **2** : SLAVE, BONDSMAN

1chat·ter \'chat-ər\ *vb* [ME *chatteren,* of imit. origin] *vi* (13c) **1** : to utter rapidly succeeding sounds suggestive of language but inarticulate and indistinct ⟨squirrels *~ed* angrily⟩ ⟨a *~ing* stream⟩ **2** : to talk idly, incessantly, or fast : JABBER **3 a** : to click repeatedly or uncontrollably ⟨teeth *~ing* with cold⟩ ⟨machine guns *~ing*⟩ **b** *of a tool* : to vibrate rapidly in cutting **c** : to operate with an irregularity that causes rapid intermittent noise or vibration ⟨*~ing* brakes⟩ ~ *vt* **1** : to utter rapidly, idly, or indistinctly **2** : to cut unevenly with a chattering tool — **chat·ter·er** *n*

2chatter *n* (13c) **1** : the action or sound of chattering **2** : idle talk : PRATTLE

chat·ter·box \'chat-ər-,bäks\ *n* (1774) : one who engages in much idle talk

chatter mark *n* (1888) **1** : a fine undulation formed on the surface of work by a chattering tool **2** : one of a series of short curved cracks on a glaciated rock surface transverse to the glacial striae

chat·ty \'chat-ē\ *adj* **chat·ti·er; -est** (1762) **1** : fond of chatting : TALKATIVE ⟨a ~ neighbor⟩ **2** : having the style and manner of light familiar conversation ⟨a ~ letter⟩ — **chat·ti·ly** \'chat-ᵊl-ē\ *adv* — **chat·ti·ness** \'chat-ē-nəs\ *n*

1chauf·feur \'shō-fər, shō-'\ *n* [F, lit., stoker, fr. *chauffer* to heat, fr. MF *chaufer* — more at CHAFE] (1899) **1** : a person employed to drive a motor vehicle **2** : one that transports others by operating a motor vehicle

2chauffeur *vb* **chauf·feured; chauf·feur·ing** \'shō-f(ə-)riŋ, shō-'fər-iŋ\ *vi* (1917) : to do the work of a chauffeur ~ *vt* **1** : to transport in the manner of a chauffeur ⟨*~s* the children to school⟩ **2** : to operate (as an automobile) as chauffeur

chaul·moo·gra \chȯl-'mü-grə\ *n* [Beng *cāulmugrā*] (1815) : any of several East Indian trees (family Flacourtiaceae) that yield an acrid oil used esp. formerly in treating leprosy and skin diseases

chaunt \'chȯnt, 'chänt\, **chaunter** *var of* CHANT, CHANTER

chaus·sure \shō-'sür\ *n, pl* **chaussures** *same*\ [ME *chaucer,* fr. MF *chaussure*] (14c) **1** : FOOTGEAR **2** *pl* : SHOES

chau·tau·qua \shə-'tȯ-kwə\ *n, often cap* [*Chautauqua,* lake in western N.Y.] (1873) : an institution that flourished in the late 19th and early 20th centuries providing popular education combined with entertainment in the form of lectures, concerts, and plays often presented outdoors or in a tent

chau·vin·ism \'shō-və-,niz-əm\ *n* [F *chauvinisme,* fr. Nicolas *Chauvin,* character noted for his excessive patriotism and devotion to Napoleon in Théodore and Hippolyte Cogniard's play *La cocarde tricolore* (1831)] (1870) **1** : excessive or blind patriotism — compare JINGOISM **2** : undue partiality or attachment to a group or place to which one belongs or has belonged **3** : an attitude of superiority toward members of the opposite sex; *also* : behavior expressive of such an attitude — **chau·vin·ist** \-və-nəst\ *n or adj* — **chau·vin·is·tic** \,shō-və-'nis-tik\ *adj* — **chau·vin·is·ti·cal·ly** \-ti-k(ə-)lē\ *adv*

1chaw \'chȯ\ *vb* [by alter.] *vt, dial* (1530) : to grind (as tobacco) with the teeth ~ *vi, dial* : CHEW

2chaw *n, dial* (1709) : a chew esp. of tobacco

chaw·ba·con \'chȯ-,bā-kən\ *n* ['*chaw* + *bacon*] (ca. 1811) : BUMPKIN, HICK

cha·yo·te \chä-'yōt-ē, chī-'ōt-\ *n* [Sp, fr. Nahuatl *chayotli*] (1887) : the pear-shaped fruit of a West Indian annual vine (*Sechium edule*) of the gourd family that is widely cultivated as a vegetable; *also* : the plant — called also *mirliton*

1cheap \'chēp\ *n* [ME *chep,* fr. OE *cēap* trade; akin to OHG *kouf* trade; both fr. L *caupo* tradesman] *obs* (bef. 12c) : BARGAIN — **on the cheap** : at minimum expense : CHEAPLY ⟨schools that are run *on the cheap*⟩

2cheap *adj* (1509) **1 a** : purchasable below the going price or the real value **b** : charging or obtainable at a low price **c** : depreciated in value (as by currency inflation) ⟨~ dollars⟩ **2** : gained with little effort ⟨a ~ victory⟩ **3 a** : of inferior quality or worth : TAWDRY, SLEAZY **b** : contemptible because of lack of any fine, lofty, or redeeming qualities **c** : STINGY **4 a** : yielding small satisfaction **b** : paying or able to pay less than going prices **5** *of money* : obtainable at a low rate of interest **6** *Brit* : specially reduced in price — **cheap** *adv* — **cheap·ish** \'chē-pish\ *adj* — **cheap·ish·ly** *adv* — **cheap·ly** \'chēp-lē\ *adv* — **cheap·ness** *n*

cheap·en \'chē-pən\ *vb* **cheap·ened; cheap·en·ing** \'chēp-(ə-)niŋ\ *vt* (1574) **1** [obs. E *cheap* (to price, bid for)] *archaic* **a** : to ask the price of **b** : to bid or bargain for **2 a** : to make cheap in price or value **b** : to lower in general esteem **c** : to make tawdry, vulgar, or inferior ~ *vi* : to become cheap

cheap·ie \'chē-pē\ *n* (ca. 1945) : one that is cheap; *esp* : an inexpensively produced motion picture — **cheapie** *adj*

1cheap·jack \'chēp-,jak\ *n* [*cheap* + the name *Jack*] (1851) **1** : a haggling huckster **2** : a dealer in cheap merchandise

2cheap·jack *adj* (1865) **1** : being inferior, cheap, or worthless ⟨~ movie companies⟩ **2** : unscrupulously opportunistic ⟨~ speculators⟩

cheapo \'chē-(,)pō\ *adj* (1972) : CHEAP

cheap shot *n* (1971) **1** : an act of deliberate roughness against a defenseless opponent esp. in a contact sport **2** : an unfair statement that takes advantage of a known weakness of the target

cheap·skate \'chēp-,skāt\ *n* (1896) : a miserly or stingy person; *esp* : one who tries to avoid his share of costs or expenses

1cheat \'chēt\ *vt* (1590) **1** : to deprive of something valuable by the use of deceit or fraud **2** : to influence or lead by deceit, trick, or artifice **3** : to defeat the purpose or blunt the effects of ⟨~ winter of its dreariness — Washington Irving⟩ ~ *vi* **1 a** : to practice fraud or trickery **b** : to violate rules dishonestly (as at cards or on an examination) **2** : to be sexually unfaithful — often used with *on* — **cheat·er** *n*

syn CHEAT, COZEN, DEFRAUD, SWINDLE mean to get something by dishonesty or deception. CHEAT suggests using trickery that escapes observation; COZEN implies artful persuading or flattering to attain a thing or a purpose; DEFRAUD stresses depriving one of his rights and usu. connotes deliberate perversion of the truth; SWINDLE implies large-scale cheating by misrepresentation or abuse of confidence.

2cheat *n* [earlier *cheat* forfeited property, fr. ME *chet* escheat, short for *eschete* — more at ESCHEAT] (1641) **1** : the act or an instance of fraudulently deceiving : DECEPTION, FRAUD **2** : one that cheats : PRETENDER, DECEIVER **3** : any of several grasses; *esp* : the common chess (*Bromus secalinus*) **4** : the obtaining of property from another by an intentional active distortion of the truth

1check \'chek\ *n* [ME *chek,* fr. MF *eschec,* fr. Ar *shāh,* fr. Per, lit., king; akin to Gk *ktasthai* to acquire, Skt *kṣatra* dominion] (14c) **1** : exposure of a chess king to an attack from which he must be protected or moved to safety **2 a** : a sudden stoppage of a forward course or progress : ARREST **b** : a checking of an opposing player (as in ice hockey) **3** : a sudden pause or break in a progression **4** *archaic* : REPRIMAND, REBUKE **5** : one that arrests, limits, or restrains : RESTRAINT ⟨against all *~s,* rebukes, and manners, I must advance — Shak.⟩ **6 a** : a standard for testing and evaluation : CRITERION **b** : EXAMINATION **c** : INSPECTION, INVESTIGATION ⟨a loyalty ~ on government employees⟩ **d** : the act of testing or verifying; *also* : the sample or unit used for testing or verifying **7** : a written order directing a bank to pay money as instructed : DRAFT **8 a** : a ticket or token showing ownership or identity or indicating payment made ⟨a baggage ~⟩ **b** : a counter in various games **c** : a slip indicating the amount due : BILL **9** [ME *chek,* short for *cheker* checker] **a** : a pattern in squares that resembles a checkerboard **b** : a fabric woven or printed with such a design **10** : a mark typically ✓ placed beside an item to show it has been noted, examined, or verified **11** : CRACK, BREAK **12** : a rabbet-shaped cutting : RABBET — **check·less** \-ləs\ *adj* — **in check** : under restraint or control ⟨held the enemy *in check*⟩

2check *vt* (14c) **1** : to put (a chess king) in check **2** *chiefly dial* : REBUKE, REPRIMAND **3 a** : to slow or bring to a stop : BRAKE ⟨hastily *~ed* the impulse⟩ **b** : to block the progress of (as a hockey player) **4 a** : to restrain or diminish the action or force of : CONTROL **b** : to slack or ease off and then belay again (as a rope) **5 a** : to compare with a source, original, or authority : VERIFY **b** : to inspect for satisfactory condition, accuracy, safety, or performance — usu. used with *out* **c** : to mark with a check as examined, verified, or satisfactory — often used with *off* ⟨*~ed* off each item⟩ **6 a** : to consign (as luggage) to a common carrier from which one has purchased a passenger ticket ⟨*~ed* his bags before boarding⟩ **b** : to ship or accept for shipment under such a consignment **7** : to mark into squares : CHECKER **8** : to leave or accept for safekeeping in a checkroom **9** : to make checks or chinks

\ə\ abut \ᵊ\ kitten, F table \ər\ further \a\ ash \ā\ ace \ä\ cot, cart \au̇\ out \ch\ chin \e\ bet \ē\ easy \g\ go \i\ hit \ī\ ice \j\ job \ŋ\ sing \ō\ go \ȯ\ law \ȯi\ boy \th\ thin \t͟h\ the \ü\ loot \u̇\ foot \y\ yet \zh\ vision \à, k̲, ^{n}, œ, œ̄, ue, ue̅, ^{y}\ *see* Guide to Pronunciation

in : cause to crack ⟨the sun ~*s* timber⟩ ~ *vi* **1 a** *of a dog* : to stop in a chase esp. when scent is lost **b** : to halt through caution, uncertainty, or fear : STOP **2 a** : to investigate conditions ⟨~*ed* on the passengers' safety⟩ **b** : to correspond point for point : TALLY ⟨the description ~*s* with the photograph⟩ — often used with *out* ⟨his story ~*ed* out⟩ **3** : to draw a check on a bank **4** : to waive the right to initiate the betting in a round of poker **5** : CRACK, SPLIT *syn* see RESTRAIN — **check·able** \'chek-ə-bəl\ *adj* — **check into 1** : to check in at ⟨*check into* a hotel⟩ **2** : INVESTIGATE — **check up on** : INVESTIGATE

check·book \'chek-,bu̇k\ *n* (ca. 1847) : a book containing blank checks to be drawn on a bank

1**check·er** \'chek-ər\ *n* [ME *cheker,* fr. MF *eschequier,* fr. *eschec*] (14c) **1** *archaic* : CHESSBOARD **2** : a square or spot resembling the markings of a checkerboard **3** [back-formation fr. *checkers*] : a man in checkers

2**checker** *vt* **check·ered; check·er·ing** \'chek-(ə-)riŋ\ (15c) **1 a** : to variegate with different colors or shades **b** : to vary with contrasting elements or situations ⟨had a ~*ed* career⟩ **2** : to mark into squares

3**checker** *n* (1535) **1** : one that checks **2** : an employee who checks out purchases in a self-service store (as a supermarket)

check·er·ber·ry \'chek-ə(r)-,ber-ē\ *n* [*checker* (wild service tree) + *berry*] (1776) **1** : any of several reddish berries; *esp* : the spicy red berrylike fruit of an American wintergreen (*Gaultheria procumbens*) **2** : a plant producing checkerberries

check·er·bloom \-ər-,blüm\ *n* [prob. fr. 1*checker* + *bloom*] (1923) : a mallow (*Sidalcea malvaeflora*) of the western U.S. with pink to reddish purple flowers

check·er·board \-ə(r)-,bō(ə)rd, -,bȯ(ə)rd\ *n* (1775) **1** : a board used in various games (as checkers) with usu. 64 squares in 2 alternating colors **2** : something that has a pattern or arrangement like a checkerboard

check·ers \'chek-ərz\ *n pl but sing in constr* (1712) : a checkerboard game for 2 players each with 12 men

check in *vi* (1918) **1** : to register at a hotel **2** : to report one's presence or arrival by supplying requisite information ⟨*check in* at a convention⟩ ~ *vt* : to satisfy all requirements in returning ⟨*check in* the equipment after using⟩

checking account *n* (ca. 1909) : a bank account against which the depositor can draw checks

check·list \'chek-,list\ *n* (1853) : INVENTORY; *esp* : a complete list

check mark *n* (1917) : CHECK 10 — **check·mark** *vt*

1**check·mate** \'chek-,māt\ *vt* [ME *chekmaten,* fr. *chekmate,* interj. used to announce checkmate, fr. MF *eschec mat,* fr. Ar *shāh māt,* fr. Per, lit., the king is left unable to escape] (14c) **1** : to arrest, thwart, or counter completely **2** : to check (a chess opponent's king) so that escape is impossible

2**checkmate** *n* (15c) **1 a** : the act of checkmating **b** : the situation of a checkmated king **2** : a complete check

check·off \'chek-,ȯf\ *n* (1911) **1** : the deduction of union dues from a worker's paycheck by the employer **2** : AUTOMATIC 2

check off \-'ȯf\ *vt* (1839) **1** : to eliminate from further consideration **2** : to deduct (union dues) from a worker's paycheck ~ *vi* : to change a play at the line of scrimmage in football by calling an automatic

check·out \'chek-,au̇t\ *n* (1933) **1** : the action or an instance of checking out **2** : the time at which a lodger must vacate his room (as in a hotel) or be charged for retaining it **3** : a counter at which checking out is done **4 a** : the action of examining and testing something for performance, suitability, or readiness **b** : the action of familiarizing oneself with the operation of a mechanical thing (as an airplane)

check out \-'au̇t\ *vi* (1921) : to vacate and pay for one's lodging (as at a hotel) ~ *vt* **1** : to satisfy all requirements in taking away ⟨*checked out* a library book⟩ **2 a** : to itemize and reckon up the total cost of and receive payment for (outgoing merchandise) esp. in a self-service store **b** : to have the cost totaled and pay for (purchases) at a checkout

check over *vt* (1945) : EXAMINE, INVESTIGATE

check·point \'chek-,pȯint\ *n* (1926) : a point at which a check is performed ⟨vehicles were inspected at various ~*s*⟩

check·rein \-,rān\ *n* (1809) **1** : a short rein looped over a hook on the saddle of a harness to prevent a horse from lowering his head **2** : a branch rein connecting the driving rein of one horse of a pair with the bit of the other

check·room \-,rüm, -,ru̇m\ *n* (1900) : a room at which baggage, parcels, or clothing is checked

check·up \-,əp\ *n* (1921) : EXAMINATION; *esp* : a general physical examination

ched·dar \'ched-ər\ *n, often cap* [*Cheddar,* England] (1661) : a hard white or yellow smooth-textured cheese with a flavor that ranges from mild to strong as the cheese matures

che·der \'kād-ər, 'ked-\ *var of* HEDER

chee·cha·ko \chi-'chäk-(,)ō, -'chȯk-\ *n, pl* **-kos** [Chinook Jargon *chee chahco,* fr. Chinook *t'shi* new + Nootka *chako* to come] *chiefly Northwest* (1897) : TENDERFOOT 1

1**cheek** \'chēk\ *n* [ME *cheke,* fr. OE *cēace;* akin to MLG *kāke* jawbone] (bef. 12c) **1** : the fleshy side of the face below the eye and above and to the side of the mouth; *broadly* : the lateral aspect of the head **2** : something suggestive of the human cheek in position or form; *esp* : one of two laterally paired parts **3** : insolent boldness and flaunted self-assurance **4** : BUTTOCK 1 *syn* see TEMERITY — **cheek·ful** \-,fu̇l\ *n* — **cheek by jowl** : in close proximity

2**cheek** *vt* (1840) : to speak rudely or impudently to

cheek·bone \'chēk-'bōn, -,bōn\ *n* (ca. 1755) : the prominence below the eye that is formed by the zygomatic bone; *also* : ZYGOMATIC BONE

-cheeked \'chēkt\ *adj comb form* : having cheeks of a specified nature ⟨rosy-*cheeked*⟩

cheeky \'chē-kē\ *adj* **cheek·i·er; -est** (1859) : having or showing cheek : IMPUDENT — **cheek·i·ly** \-kə-lē\ *adv* — **cheek·i·ness** \-kē-nəs\ *n*

cheep \'chēp\ *vi* [imit.] (1513) **1** : to utter faint shrill sounds : PEEP **2** : to utter a single word or sound — **cheep** *n*

1**cheer** \'chi(ə)r\ *n* [ME *chere* face, cheer, fr. OF, face] (13c) **1 a** *obs* : FACE **b** *archaic* : facial expression **2** : state of mind or heart : SPIRIT ⟨be of good ~ — Mt 9:2(AV)⟩ **3** : lightness of mind and feeling : ANIMATION, GAIETY **4** : hospitable entertainment : WELCOME **5** : food and drink for a feast : FARE **6** : something that gladdens ⟨words of ~⟩ **7** : a shout of applause or encouragement

2**cheer** *vt* (14c) **1 a** : to instill with hope or courage : COMFORT — usu. used with *up* **b** : to make glad or happy — usu. used with *up* **2** : to urge on or encourage esp. by shouts ⟨~*ed* the team on⟩ **3** : to applaud with shouts ~ *vi* **1** *obs* : to be mentally or emotionally disposed **2** : to grow or be cheerful : REJOICE — usu. used with *up* **3** : to utter a shout of applause or triumph — **cheer·er** *n*

cheer·ful \'chir-fəl\ *adj* (15c) **1 a** : full of good spirits : MERRY **b** : UNGRUDGING ⟨~ obedience⟩ **2** : conducive to cheer : likely to dispel gloom or worry ⟨sunny ~ room⟩ — **cheer·ful·ly** \-f(ə-)lē\ *adv* — **cheer·ful·ness** \-fəl-nəs\ *n*

cheer·io \,chi(ə)r-ē-'ō\ *interj* [*cheery* + *-o*] *chiefly Brit* (1910) — usu. used as a farewell and sometimes as a greeting or toast

cheer·lead·er \'chi(ə)r-,lēd-ər\ *n* (1903) : one that calls for and directs organized cheering (as at a football game) — **cheer·lead** \-,lēd\ *vt*

cheer·less \'chi(ə)r-ləs\ *adj* (1579) : lacking qualities that cheer : BLEAK, JOYLESS ⟨a ~ room⟩ — **cheer·less·ly** *adv* — **cheer·less·ness** *n*

cheers \'chi(ə)rz\ *interj* (1919) — used as a toast

cheery \'chi(ə)r-ē\ *adj* **cheer·i·er; -est** (15c) **1** : marked by cheerfulness or good spirits **2** : causing or suggesting cheerfulness — **cheer·i·ly** \'chir-ə-lē\ *adv* — **cheer·i·ness** \'chir-ē-nəs\ *n*

1**cheese** \'chēz\ *n, often attrib* [ME *chese,* fr. OE *cēse,* fr. L *caseus* cheese; akin to OE *hwatherian* to foam, Skt *kvathati* it boils] (bef. 12c) **1 a** : a food consisting of the coagulated, compressed, and usu. ripened curd of milk separated from the whey **b** : an often cylindrical cake of this food **2** : something resembling cheese in shape or consistency

2**cheese** *vt* **cheesed; chees·ing** [origin unknown] (1812) : to put an end to : STOP — **cheese it** — used in the imperative as a warning of danger ⟨*cheese it,* the cops⟩

3**cheese** *n* [perh. fr. Urdu *chīz* thing] *slang* (1910) : someone important

cheese·burg·er \'chēz-,bər-gər\ *n* [*cheese* + *hamburger*] (1938) : a hamburger topped with a slice of cheese

cheese·cake \-,kāk\ *n* (15c) **1** : a dessert consisting of a creamy filling usu. containing cheese baked in a pastry or pressed-crumb shell **2** : a photographic display of shapely and scantily clothed female figures — compare BEEFCAKE

cheese·cloth \-,klȯth\ *n* [fr. its use in the making of cheese] (14c) : a very lightweight unsized cotton gauze

cheese·par·ing \-,pa(ə)r-iŋ, -,pe(ə)r-\ *n* (1597) **1** : something worthless or insignificant **2** : miserly economizing — **cheeseparing** *adj*

cheesy \'chē-zē\ *adj* **chees·i·er; -est** (14c) **1 a** : resembling or suggesting cheese esp. in consistency or odor **b** : containing cheese **2** *slang* : SHABBY, CHEAP — **chees·i·ness** *n*

chee·tah \'chēt-ə\ *n* [Hindi *cītā,* fr. Skt *citrakāya* tiger, fr. *citra* bright + *kāya* body] (1610) : a long-legged spotted swift-moving African and formerly Asian cat (*Acinonyx jubatus*) about the size of a small leopard that has blunt nonretractile claws and is often trained to run down game

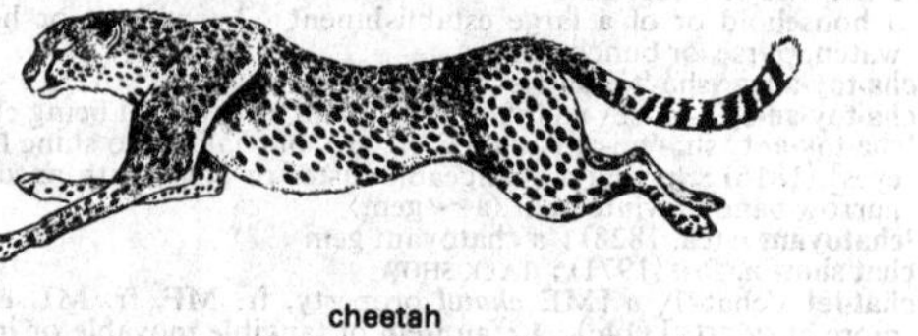

cheetah

chef \'shef\ *n* [F, short for *chef de cuisine* head of the kitchen] (1826) **1** : a skilled cook who manages the kitchen (as of a restaurant) **2** : COOK — **chef** *vi* — **chef·dom** \-dəm\ *n*

chef d'oeu·vre \shā-dœvrᵊ, (')shā-'də(r)v\ *n, pl* **chefs d'oeuvre** \-dœvrᵊ, -'də(r)v(z)\ [F *chef-d'oeuvre,* lit., leading work] (1619) : a masterpiece esp. in art or literature

Che·ha·lis \chə-'hā-ləs\ *n, pl* **Chehalis** *or* **Che·ha·lis·es** [fr. *Chehalis,* one of their villages on Grays Harbor, Wash., fr. *Chehalis,* lit., sand] (1844) **1 a** : a Salishan people of Washington **b** : a member of such people **2** : the language of the Chehalis people

che·la \'kē-lə\ *n, pl* **che·lae** \-(,)lē\ [NL, fr. Gk *chēlē* claw] (1646) : a pincerlike organ or claw borne by a limb of a crustacean or arachnid

1**che·late** \'kē-,lāt\ *adj* (1826) **1** : resembling or having chelae **2** : of, relating to, or having a ring structure that usu. contains a metal ion held by coordination bonds — **chelate** *n*

2**chelate** *vb* **che·lat·ed; che·lat·ing** *vt* (1922) : to combine with (a metal) so as to form a chelate ring ~ *vi* : to react so as to form a chelate ring — **che·lat·able** \-,lāt-ə-bəl\ *adj* — **che·la·tion** \kē-'lā-shən\ *n* — **che·la·tor** \-,lāt-ər\ *n*

che·lic·era \ki-'lis-ə-rə\ *n, pl* **-er·ae** \-,rē\ [NL, fr. F *chélicère,* fr. Gk *chēlē* + *keras* horn — more at HORN] (1835) : one of the anterior pair of appendages of an arachnid often specialized as fangs — **che·lic·er·al** \-ə-rəl\ *adj*

che·li·ped \'kē-lə-,ped\ *n* [Gk *chēlē* claw + L *ped-, pes* foot] (1869) : one of the pair of legs that bears the large chelae in decapod crustaceans

Chel·le·an *or* **Chel·li·an** \'shel-ē-ən\ *adj* [F *chelléen,* fr. *Chelles,* France] (ca. 1893) : ABBEVILLIAN

che·lo·ni·an \ki-'lō-nē-ən\ *n* [Gk *chelōnē* tortoise] (1826) : TURTLE — **chelonian** *adj*

chem- *or* **chemo-** *also* **chemi-** *comb form* [NL, fr. LGk *chēmeia* alchemy — more at ALCHEMY] **1** : chemical : chemistry ⟨*chemosmosis*⟩ ⟨*chemotaxis*⟩ **2** : chemically ⟨*chemisorb*⟩

Chem·a·ku·an \,chem-ə-'kü-ən\ *n* (ca. 1930) : a language stock of the Mosan phylum in the state of Washington

chem·ic \'kem-ik\ *adj* [NL *chimicus* alchemist, fr. ML *alchimicus,* fr. *alchymia* alchemy] (1576) **1** *archaic* : ALCHEMIC **2** : CHEMICAL

1**chem·i·cal** \'kem-i-kəl\ *adj* (1576) **1** : of, relating to, used in, or produced by chemistry **2 a** : acting or operated or produced by chemicals **b** : detectable by chemical means — **chem·i·cal·ly** \-i-k(ə-)lē\ *adv*

2**chemical** *n* (1747) : a substance (as an element or chemical compound) obtained by a chemical process or used for producing a chemical effect

chemical engineering *n* (1888) : engineering dealing with the industrial application of chemistry

chemical warfare *n* (1917) : tactical warfare using incendiary mixtures, smokes, or irritant, burning, poisonous, or asphyxiating gases

che·mi·lu·mi·nes·cence \ˌkem-i-ˌlü-mə-'nes-ᵊn(t)s, ˌkē-mi-\ *n* [ISV] (1905) : luminescence (as bioluminescence) due to chemical reaction usu. at low temperatures — **che·mi·lu·mi·nes·cent** \-'nes-ᵊnt\ *adj*

che·min de fer \shə-ˌman-də-'fe(ə)r\ *n, pl* **che·mins de fer** \-ˌman-də-\ [F, lit., railroad] (1891) : a card game in which two hands are dealt, any number of players may bet against the dealer, and the winning hand is the one that comes closer to but does not exceed a count of nine on two or three cards

chemi·os·mot·ic \ˌkem-ē-äz-'mät-ik\ *adj* (1967) : relating to or being a hypothesis that seeks to explain the mechanism of ATP formation in oxidative phosphorylation by mitochondria and chloroplasts without recourse to the formation of high-energy intermediates by postulating the formation of an energy gradient of hydrogen ions across the organelle membranes that results in the reversible movement of hydrogen ions to the outside and is generated by electron transport or the activity of electron carriers

che·mise \shə-'mēz, -'mēs\ *n* [ME, fr. OF, shirt, fr. LL *camisia*] (13c) **1** : a woman's one-piece undergarment **2** : a loose straight-hanging dress

chem·i·sette \ˌshem-i-'zet\ *n* [F, dim. of *chemise*] (1807) : a woman's garment; *esp* : one (as of lace) to fill the open front of a dress

che·mism \'kem-ˌiz-əm, 'kē-ˌmiz-\ *n* (1851) **1** : chemical activity or affinity **2** : operation in obedience to chemical laws

che·mi·sorb \'kem-i-ˌsȯ(ə)rb, 'kē-mi-, -ˌzȯ(ə)rb\ *vt* [*chem-* + *-sorb* (as in *adsorb*)] (1935) : to take up and hold usu. irreversibly by chemical forces — **che·mi·sorp·tion** \ˌkem-i-'sȯrp-shən, ˌkē-mi-, -'zȯrp-\ *n*

chem·ist \'kem-əst\ *n* [NL *chimista*, short for ML *alchimista*] (1562) **1** *a obs* : ALCHEMIST **b** : one trained in chemistry **2** *Brit* : PHARMACIST

chem·is·try \'kem-ə-strē\ *n, pl* **-tries** (1646) **1** : a science that deals with the composition, structure, and properties of substances and with the transformations that they undergo **2 a** : the composition and chemical properties of a substance ⟨the ~ of iron⟩ **b** : chemical processes and phenomena (as of an organism) ⟨blood ~⟩ **3** : a strong mutual attraction, attachment, or sympathy ⟨matching personalities or some other special ~ or vibes to make the relationship click —Roy Rowan⟩

che·mo·au·to·tro·phic \ˌkē-mō-ˌȯt-ə-'trō-fik *also* ˌkem-ō-\ *adj* (1945) : being autotrophic and oxidizing some inorganic compound as a source of energy ⟨~ bacteria⟩ — **che·mo·au·tot·ro·phy** \-ȯ-'tä-trə-fē\ *n*

che·mo·pro·phy·lax·is \-ˌprō-fə-'lak-səs *also* -ˌpräf-ə-\ *n* (1936) : the prevention of infectious disease by the use of chemical agents — **che·mo·pro·phy·lac·tic** \-'lak-tik\ *adj*

che·mo·re·cep·tion \-ri-'sep-shən\ *n* [ISV] (1919) : the physiological reception of chemical stimuli — **che·mo·re·cep·tive** \-'sep-tiv\ *adj*

che·mo·re·cep·tor \-ri-'sep-tər\ *n* [ISV] (1906) : a sense organ (as a taste bud) responding to chemical stimuli

che·mo·sphere \'kē-mə-ˌsfi(ə)r, 'kem-ə-\ *n* (1950) : a stratum of the upper atmosphere in which photochemical reactions are prevalent and which begins about 20 miles (30 kilometers) above the earth's surface

che·mo·sur·gery \ˌkē-mō-'sərj-(ə-)rē *also* ˌkem-ō-\ *n* (1945) : chemical removal of diseased or unwanted tissue — **che·mo·sur·gi·cal** \-'sər-ji-kəl\ *adj*

che·mo·syn·the·sis \-'sin(t)-thə-səs\ *n* [ISV] (1901) : synthesis of organic compounds (as in living cells) by energy derived from chemical reactions — **che·mo·syn·thet·ic** \-sin-'thet-ik\ *adj*

che·mo·tac·tic \-'tak-tik\ *adj* (1887) : involving, inducing, or exhibiting chemotaxis — **che·mo·tac·ti·cal·ly** \-ti-k(ə-)lē\ *adv*

che·mo·tax·is \-'tak-səs\ *n* [NL] (ca. 1887) : orientation or movement of an organism or cell in relation to chemical agents

che·mo·tax·on·o·my \-(ˌ)tak-'sän-ə-mē\ *n* (1963) : the classification of plants and animals based on similarities and differences in biochemical composition — **che·mo·tax·o·nom·ic** \-ˌtak-sə-'näm-ik\ *adj* — **che·mo·tax·on·o·mist** \-(ˌ)tak-'sän-ə-məst\ *n*

che·mo·ther·a·peu·tic \-ˌther-ə-'pyüt-ik\ *adj* (1907) : of, relating to, or used in chemotherapy — **chemotherapeutic** *or* **che·mo·ther·a·peu·ti·cal** \-i-kəl\ *n* — **che·mo·ther·a·peu·ti·cal·ly** \-i-k(ə-)lē\ *adv*

che·mo·ther·a·py \-'ther-ə-pē\ *n* [ISV] (1910) : the use of chemical agents in the treatment or control of disease or mental illness — **che·mo·ther·a·pist** \-pəst\ *n*

che·mot·ro·pism \ki-'mä-trə-ˌpiz-əm, ke-\ *n* [ISV] (1897) : orientation of cells or organisms in relation to chemical stimuli

chem·ur·gy \'kem-(ˌ)ər-jē, kə-'mər-\ *n* (1934) : a branch of applied chemistry that deals with industrial utilization of organic raw materials esp. from farm products — **chem·ur·gic** \kə-'mər-jik, ke-\ *adj* — **chem·ur·gi·cal·ly** \-ji-k(ə-)lē\ *adv*

che·nille \shə-'nē(ə)l\ *n* [F, lit., caterpillar, fr. L *canicula*, dim. of *canis* dog; fr. its hairy appearance — more at HOUND] (1738) **1** : a wool, cotton, silk, or rayon yarn with protruding pile; *also* : a pile-face fabric with a filling of this yarn **2** : an imitation of chenille yarn or fabric

che·no·pod \'kē-nə-ˌpäd, 'ken-ə-\ *n* [deriv. of Gk *chēn* goose + *podion*, dim. of *pod-, pous* foot — more at FOOT] (1555) : any plant of the goosefoot family

cheong·sam \'chȯŋ-ˌsäm\ *n* [Chin (Cant) *ch'eùng shaam*, lit., long gown] (1952) : a dress with a slit skirt and a mandarin collar worn esp. by oriental women

cheque \'chek\ *chiefly Brit var of* [1]CHECK 7

che·quer \'chek-ər\ *chiefly Brit var of* CHECKER

cher·i·moya \ˌcher-ə-'mȯi-(y)ə, ˌchir-\ *n* [Sp *chirimoya*] (1736) : a round, oblong, or heart-shaped fruit with a pitted rind that is borne by a widely cultivated tropical American tree (*Annona cherimola*) of the custard-apple family; *also* : this tree

cher·ish \'cher-ish\ *vt* [ME *cherisshen*, fr. MF *cheriss-*, stem of *cherir* to cherish, fr. OF, fr. *chier* dear, fr. L *carus* — more at CHARITY] (14c) **1 a** : to hold dear : feel or show affection for **b** : to keep or cultivate with care and affection : NURTURE **2** : to entertain or harbor in the mind deeply and resolutely ⟨still ~*es* that memory⟩ ***syn*** see APPRECIATE

cher·no·zem \ˌcher-nə-'zyȯm, -'zem\ *n* [Russ, lit., black earth] (1841) : any of a group of dark-colored zonal soils with a deep rich humus horizon found in regions (as the grasslands of central No. America) of temperate to cool climate — **cher·no·zem·ic** \-'zhȯm-ik, -'zem-\ *adj*

Cher·o·kee \'cher-ə-(ˌ)kē\ *n, pl* **Cherokee** *or* **Cherokees** [prob. fr. Creek *tciloki* people of a different speech] (1674) **1** : a member of an American Indian people orig. of Tennessee and No. Carolina **2** : the language of the Cherokee people

Cherokee rose *n* (1823) : a Chinese climbing rose (*Rosa laevigata*) with a fragrant white blossom

che·root \shə-'rüt, chə-\ *n* [Tamil *curuṭṭu*, lit., roll] (1669) : a cigar cut square at both ends

cher·ry \'cher-ē\ *n, pl* **cherries** [ME *chery*, fr. ONF *cherise* (taken as a plural), fr. LL *ceresia*, fr. L *cerasus* cherry tree, fr. Gk *kerasos* — more at CORNEL] (14c) **1 a** : any of numerous trees and shrubs (genus *Prunus*) of the rose family that bear pale yellow to deep red or blackish smooth-skinned drupes enclosing a smooth seed and that belong to any of several varieties including some cultivated for their fruits or ornamental flowers **b** : the fruit of a cherry **c** : the wood of a cherry **2** : a variable color averaging a moderate red **3 a** : HYMEN **b** : VIRGINITY — **cher·ry·like** \-ē-ˌlīk\ *adj*

cherry bomb *n* (1953) : a powerful globular red firecracker

cherry picker *n* (1934) : a traveling crane equipped for holding a passenger at the end of the boom

cher·ry·stone \'cher-ē-ˌstōn\ *n* (1880) : a small quahog

chert \'chərt, 'chat\ *n* [origin unknown] (1679) : a rock resembling flint and consisting essentially of a large amount of fibrous chalcedony with smaller amounts of cryptocrystalline quartz and amorphous silica — **cherty** \-ē\ *adj*

cher·ub \'cher-əb\ *n, pl* **cher·u·bim** \'cher-(y)ə-ˌbim, 'ker-\ [L, fr. Gk *cheroub*, fr. Heb *kĕrūbh*] (13c) **1** *pl* : an order of angels — see CELESTIAL HIERARCHY **2** *pl* **cherubs a** : a beautiful usu. winged child in painting and sculpture **b** : an innocent-looking usu. chubby and rosy person — **che·ru·bic** \chə-'rü-bik\ *adj* — **che·ru·bi·cal·ly** \-bi-k(ə-)lē\ *adv* — **cher·ub·like** \'cher-əb-ˌlīk\ *adj*

cher·vil \'chər-vəl\ *n* [ME *cherville*, fr. OE *cerfille*; akin to OHG *kervila*] (bef. 12c) : an aromatic herb (*Anthriscus cerefolium*) of the carrot family with divided leaves that are often used in soups and salads; *also* : any of several related plants

Ches·a·peake Bay retriever \ˌches-(ə-)ˌpēk-ˌbā-\ *n* (ca. 1909) : a large brown sporting dog developed in Maryland and having a dense oily water-shedding coat

Chesh·ire cat \ˌchesh-ər-\ *n* [*Cheshire*, England] (1866) : a broadly grinning cat in Lewis Carroll's *Alice's Adventures in Wonderland*

Cheshire cheese *n* (1597) : a cheese similar to cheddar made chiefly in Cheshire, England

[1]**chess** \'ches\ *n* [ME *ches*, fr. MF *esches*, acc. pl. of *eschec* check at chess — more at CHECK] (14c) : a game for 2 players each of whom moves his 16 pieces according to fixed rules across a checkerboard and tries to checkmate his opponent's king — **chess·board** \-ˌbō(ə)rd, -ˌbȯ(ə)rd\ *n* — **chess·man** \-ˌman, -mən\ *n*

[2]**chess** *n* [origin unknown] (1736) : a weedy annual bromegrass (*Bromus secalinus*) widely distributed as a weed esp. in grain; *broadly* : any of several weedy bromegrasses

chest \'chest\ *n* [ME, fr. OE *cest, cist* chest, box, fr. L *cista*, fr. Gk *kistē* basket, hamper; perh. akin to OIr *cess, ciss* basket] (bef. 12c) **1 a** : a container for storage or shipping; *esp* : a box with a lid used esp. for the safekeeping of belongings **b** : a cupboard used esp. for the storing of medicines or first-aid supplies **2** : the place where money of a public institution is kept : TREASURY; *also* : the fund so kept **3** : the part of the body enclosed by the ribs and sternum — **chest·ful** \-ˌfu̇l\ *n*

-chest·ed \'ches-təd\ *adj comb form* : having (such) a chest ⟨flat-*chested*⟩

ches·ter·field \'ches-tər-ˌfēld\ *n* [fr. a 19th cent. Earl of *Chesterfield*] (1852) **1** : a single-breasted or double-breasted semifitted overcoat with velvet collar **2** : a davenport usu. with upright armrests

Ches·ter White \ˌches-tər-\ *n* [*Chester* County, Pa.] (1856) : any of a breed of large white swine

[1]**chest·nut** \'ches-(ˌ)nət\ *n* [ME *chasteine, chesten* chestnut tree, fr. MF *chastaigne*, fr. L *castanea*, fr. Gk *kastanea*] (14c) **1 a** : any of a genus (*Castanea*) of trees or shrubs of the beech family; *esp* : an American tree (*C. dentata*) that was formerly a dominant or codominant member of many deciduous forests of the eastern U.S. but has now been largely eliminated by the chestnut blight and seldom grows beyond the shrub or sapling stage **b** : the edible nut of a chestnut **c** : the wood of a chestnut **2** : a grayish to reddish brown **3** : HORSE CHESTNUT **4** : a chestnut-colored animal; *specif* : a horse having a body color of any shade of pure or reddish brown with mane, tail, and points of the same or a lighter shade — compare [2]BAY 1, [1]SORREL 1 **5** : a callosity on the inner side of the leg of the horse **6 a** : an old joke or story **b** : something (as a musical piece) repeated to the point of staleness

[2]**chestnut** *adj* (1555) **1** : of the color chestnut **2** : of, relating to, or resembling a chestnut

chestnut blight *n* (ca. 1909) : a destructive disease of the American chestnut marked by cankers of the bark and cambium and caused by an imported fungus (*Endothia parasitica* syn. *Cryphonectria parasitica*)

chestnut oak *n* (1703) : any of several oaks having oblong to lanceolate leaves with crenate or serrate edges: as **a** : CHINQUAPIN OAK **b** : a medium-sized oak (*Quercus prinus*) of eastern No. America with large acorns and leaves that are shiny yellow-green above and paler below

chest of drawers (1649) : a piece of furniture designed to contain a set of drawers (as for holding clothing)

chesty \'ches-tē\ *adj* **chest·i·er; -est** (1899) **1** : proudly or arrogantly self-assertive **2** : marked by a large or well-developed chest

chet·rum \'chē-trəm, 'che-\ *n, pl* **chetrums** *or* **chetrum** [native name in Bhutan] (1973) — see *ngultrum* at MONEY table

che·val–de–frise \shə-ˌval-də-'frēz\ *n, pl* **che·vaux–de–frise** \shə-ˌvōd-ə-\ [F, lit., horse from Friesland] (1668) **1** : a defense consisting of a timber or an iron barrel covered with projecting spikes and often strung with barbed wire **2** : a protecting line (as of spikes) on top of a wall — usu. used in pl.

\ə\ abut \ᵊ\ kitten, F table \ər\ further \a\ ash \ā\ ace \ä\ cot, cart \au̇\ out \ch\ chin \e\ bet \ē\ easy \g\ go \i\ hit \ī\ ice \j\ job \ŋ\ sing \ō\ go \ȯ\ law \ȯi\ boy \th\ thin \t͟h\ the \ü\ loot \u̇\ foot \y\ yet \zh\ vision \á, k̲, ⁿ, œ, œ̄, ue, ue̅, ʸ\ see Guide to Pronunciation

che·val glass \shə-ˈval-\ *n* [F *cheval* horse, support] (1828) **:** a full-length mirror in a frame in which it may be tilted

che·va·lier \ˌshev-ə-ˈli(ə)r, *esp for 1b & 2 also* shə-ˈval-ˌyā\ *n* [ME, fr. MF, fr. LL *caballarius* horseman — more at CAVALIER] (14c) **1 a :** CAVALIER 2 **b :** a member of any of various orders of knighthood or of merit (as the Legion of Honor) **2 a :** a member of the lowest rank of French nobility **b :** a cadet of the French nobility **3 :** a chivalrous man

che·ve·lure \shəv-ˈlu̇r\ *n* [F, fr. L *capillatura,* fr. *capillatus* having hair, fr. *capillus* hair] (15c) **:** a head of hair

chev·i·ot \ˈshev-ē-ət, *esp Brit* ˈchev-\ *n, often cap* (1815) **1 :** any of a breed of hardy hornless medium-wooled sheep that are a source of quality mutton and have their origin in the Cheviot hills **2 a :** a fabric of cheviot wool **b :** a heavy rough napped plain or twill fabric of coarse wool or worsted **c :** a sturdy soft-finished plain or twill cotton shirting

chev·ron \ˈshev-rən\ *n* [ME, fr. MF, rafter, chevron, fr. (assumed) VL *caprion-, caprio* rafter; akin to L *caper* goat] (14c) **:** a figure, pattern, or object having the shape of a V or an inverted V: as **a** *or* **chev·er·on** \-(ə-)rən\ **:** a heraldic charge consisting of two diagonal stripes meeting at an angle usu. with the point up **b :** a sleeve badge that usu. consists of one or more chevron-shaped stripes that indicates the wearer's rank and service (as in the armed forces)

[1]**chew** \ˈchü\ *vb* [ME *chewen,* fr. OE *cēowan;* akin to OHG *kiuwan* to chew, OSlav *žĭvati*] *vt* (bef. 12c) **:** to crush, grind, or gnaw (as food) with or as if with the teeth **:** MASTICATE ~ *vi* **:** to chew something; *specif* **:** to chew tobacco — **chew·able** \-ə-bəl\ *adj* — **chew·er** *n* — **chewy** \ˈchü-ē\ *adj* — **chew the rag** *or* **chew the fat** *slang* **:** to make friendly familiar conversation **:** CHAT

[2]**chew** *n* (13c) **1 :** the act of chewing **2 :** something for chewing

chewing gum *n* (1850) **:** a sweetened and flavored insoluble plastic material (as a preparation of chicle) used for chewing

che·wink \chi-ˈwiŋk\ *n* [imit.] (1794) **:** TOWHEE 1

chew out *vt* (1943) **:** REPRIMAND, BAWL OUT

chew over *vt* (1939) **:** to meditate on **:** think about reflectively

Chey·enne \shī-ˈan, -ˈen\ *n, pl* **Cheyenne** *or* **Cheyennes** [CanF, fr. Dakota *Shaiyena,* fr. *shaia* to speak unintelligibly] (1778) **1 :** a member of an American Indian people of the western plains of the U.S. **2 :** the Algonquian language of the Cheyenne people

chez \ˌshā\ *prep* [F, fr. L *casae* at home, locative of *casa* house] (1740) **:** at or in the home or business place of

chi \ˈkī\ *n* [Gk *chei, chi*] (15c) **:** the 22d letter of the Greek alphabet — see ALPHABET table

Chi·an·ti \kē-ˈänt-ē, -ˈant-\ *n* [It, fr. the *Chianti* mt. range, Italy] (1833) **:** a dry usu. red wine from the Tuscany region of Italy; *also* **:** a similar wine made elsewhere

Chi·an turpentine \ˈkī-ən-\ *n* [*Chios,* Greece] (ca. 1890) **:** TURPENTINE 1a

chiao \ˈjau̇\ *n, pl* **chiao** [Chin (Pek) *chiao*^{3}] (ca. 1916) **:** a monetary unit of the People's Republic of China equal to $^1/_{10}$ yuan

chiar·oscu·rist \kē-ˌär-ə-ˈsk(y)u̇r-əst, kē-ˌar-\ *n* (1784) **:** an artist who specializes in chiaroscuro

chiar·oscu·ro \-ˈsk(y)u̇(ə)r-(ˌ)ō\ *n, pl* **-ros** [It, fr. *chiaro* clear, light + *oscuro* obscure, dark] (1686) **1 :** pictorial representation in terms of light and shade without regard to color **2 :** the arrangement or treatment of light and dark parts in a pictorial work of art **3 :** a 16th century woodcut technique involving the use of several blocks to print different tones of the same color; *also* **:** a print made by this technique

chi·asm \ˈkī-ˌaz-əm\ *n* [NL *chiasma*] (1870) **:** CHIASMA 1

chi·as·ma \kī-ˈaz-mə\ *n, pl* **-ma·ta** \-mət-ə\ [NL, X-shaped configuration, fr. Gk, crosspiece, fr. *chiazein* to mark with a chi, fr. *chi* (x)] (1839) **1 :** an anatomical intersection or decussation — compare OPTIC CHIASMA **2 :** a cross-shaped configuration of paired chromatids visible in the diplotene of meiotic prophase and considered the cytological equivalent of genetic crossing-over — **chi·as·mat·ic** \ˌkī-əz-ˈmat-ik\ *adj*

chi·as·mus \kī-ˈaz-məs\ *n* [NL, fr. Gk *chiasmos,* fr. *chiazein* to mark with a chi] (1871) **:** an inverted relationship between the syntactic elements of parallel phrases (as in Goldsmith's *to stop too fearful, and too faint to go*)

chiaus \ˈchau̇s(h)\ *n* [Turk *çavuş,* fr. *çav* voice, news] (1599) **:** a Turkish messenger or sergeant

Chib·cha \ˈchib-(ˌ)chä\ *n, pl* **Chibcha** *or* **Chibchas** [Sp, of AmerInd origin] (1814) **1 :** a member of an Indian people of central Colombia **2 :** the extinct language of the Chibcha people

Chib·chan \-chən\ *adj* (1902) **:** of, relating to, or constituting a language stock of Colombia and Central America

chi·bouk *or* **chi·bouque** \chə-ˈbük, shə-\ *n* [F *chibouque,* fr. Turk *çubuk*] (1813) **:** a long-stemmed Turkish tobacco pipe with a clay bowl

[1]**chic** \ˈshēk\ *n* [F] (1856) **1 :** smart elegance and sophistication esp. of dress or manner **:** STYLE ⟨wears her clothes with superb ~⟩ **2 :** a stylish mode of dress or manner associated with a currently fashionable life-style or ideology

[2]**chic** *adj* (1865) **1 :** cleverly stylish **:** SMART ⟨the woman who is ~ adapts fashion to her own personality —Elizabeth L. Post⟩ **2 :** currently fashionable ⟨a ~ restaurant⟩ — **chic·ly** *adv* — **chic·ness** *n*

Chi·ca·na \chi-ˈkän-ə, shi-\ *n* [modif. of Sp *mejicana,* fem. of *mejicano*] (1967) **:** a female Chicano — **Chicana** *adj*

[1]**chi·cane** \shik-ˈān, chik-\ *vb* **chi·caned; chi·can·ing** [F *chicaner,* fr. MF, to quibble, prevent justice] *vi* (1672) **:** to use chicanery ⟨a wretch he had taught to lie and ~ —George Meredith⟩ ~ *vt* **:** TRICK, CHEAT

[2]**chicane** *n* (1686) **1 :** CHICANERY **2 a :** an obstacle on a racecourse **b :** a series of tight turns in opposite directions in an otherwise straight stretch of a road-racing course **3 :** the absence of trumps in a hand of cards

chi·ca·nery \-ˈān-(ə-)rē\ *n, pl* **-ner·ies** (1609) **1 :** deception by artful subterfuge or sophistry **:** TRICKERY **2 :** a piece of sharp practice (as at law) **:** TRICK

Chi·ca·no \chi-ˈkän-(ˌ)ō, shi-\ *n, pl* **-nos** [MexSp, alter. of *mejicano* Mexican] (ca. 1954) **:** an American of Mexican descent — **Chicano** *adj*

[1]**chi·chi** \ˈshē-(ˌ)shē, ˈchē-(ˌ)chē\ *n* [F] (1908) **1 :** frilly or elaborate ornamentation **2 :** AFFECTATION, PRECIOSITY **3 :** CHIC

[2]**chichi** *adj* (1926) **1 :** elaborately ornamented **:** SHOWY, FRILLY ⟨a ~ dress⟩ **2 :** ARTY, PRECIOUS ⟨~ poetry⟩ **3 :** CHIC, FASHIONABLE ⟨a ~ nightclub⟩

chick \ˈchik\ *n* (15c) **1 a :** CHICKEN; *esp* **:** one newly hatched **b :** the young of any bird **2 :** CHILD **3 :** a young woman

chick·a·dee \ˈchik-ə-(ˌ)dē\ *n* [imit.] (1838) **:** any of several crestless American titmice (genus *Penthestes* or *Parus*) usu. with the crown of the head sharply demarked and darker than the body

chick·a·ree \ˈchik-ə-ˌrē\ *n* [imit.] (1829) **:** an American red squirrel (*Sciurus hudsonicus*); *also* **:** a related squirrel

Chick·a·saw \ˈchik-ə-ˌsȯ\ *n, pl* **Chickasaw** *or* **Chickasaws** (1674) **1 :** a member of an American Indian people of Mississippi and Alabama **2 :** a dialect of Choctaw spoken by the Chickasaw

[1]**chick·en** \ˈchik-ən\ *n* [ME *chiken,* fr. OE *cicen* young chicken] (bef. 12c) **1 a :** the common domestic fowl (*Gallus gallus*) esp. when young; *also* **:** its flesh used as food — compare JUNGLE FOWL **b :** any of various birds or their young **2 :** a young woman **3 a :** COWARD **b :** any of various contests in which the participants risk personal safety in order to see which one will give up first **4** *slang* [prob. short for *chickenshit* petty details] **:** the petty details of duty or discipline **5 :** a young male homosexual

[2]**chicken** *adj* (1941) **1** *slang* **a :** SCARED **b :** TIMID, COWARDLY **2** *slang* **a :** insistent on petty details of duty or discipline **b :** PETTY, UNIMPORTANT

[3]**chicken** *vi* **chick·ened; chick·en·ing** \ˈchik-(ə-)niŋ\ (1943) **:** to lose one's nerve — usu. used with *out* ⟨seemed to exhibit courage, manliness, and conviction when others ~*ed* out —J. R. Seeley⟩

chicken colonel *n* [fr. the eagle serving as insignia of the rank] *slang* (1947) **:** COLONEL 1a

chicken feed *n, slang* (1836) **:** a paltry sum (as in profits or wages)

chicken hawk *n* (1827) **:** a hawk that preys or is believed to prey on chickens

chick·en·heart·ed \ˌchik-ən-ˈhärt-əd\ *adj* (1681) **:** TIMID, COWARDLY

chick·en–liv·ered \-ˈliv-ərd\ *adj* (1872) **:** FAINTHEARTED, COWARDLY

chicken pox *n* (1727) **:** an acute contagious virus disease esp. of children that is marked by low-grade fever and formation of vesicles

chicken snake *n* (1709) **:** RAT SNAKE

chicken wire *n* [fr. its use for making enclosures for chickens] (ca. 1904) **:** a light galvanized wire netting of hexagonal mesh

chick–pea \ˈchik-ˌpē\ *n* [by folk etymology, fr. ME *chiche,* fr. MF, fr. L *cicer*] (1548) **:** an Asian leguminous herb (*Cicer arietinum*) cultivated for its short pods with one or two seeds; *also* **:** its seed

chick·weed \ˈchik-ˌwēd\ *n* (14c) **:** any of various low-growing small-leaved weedy plants of the pink family (esp. genera *Arenaria, Cerastium,* and *Stellaria*); *esp* **:** a cosmopolitan weed (*Stelleria media*) naturalized in the U.S. from Eurasia

chi·cle \ˈchik-əl, -lē\ *n* [Sp, fr. Nahautl *chictli*] (1889) **:** a gum from the latex of the sapodilla used as the chief ingredient of chewing gum

chic·o·ry *also* **chick·o·ry** \ˈchik-(ə-)rē\ *n, pl* **-ries** [ME *cicoree,* fr. MF *cichorée, chicorée,* fr. L *cichoreum,* fr. Gk *kichoreia*] (14c) **1 :** a thick-rooted usu. blue-flowered European perennial composite herb (*Cichorium intybus*) widely grown for its roots and as a salad plant — compare ENDIVE 2 **2 :** the dried ground roasted root of chicory used to flavor or adulterate coffee

chide \ˈchīd\ *vb* **chid** \ˈchid\ *or* **chid·ed** \ˈchīd-əd\; **chid** *or* **chid·den** \ˈchid-ᵊn\ *or* **chided; chid·ing** \ˈchīd-iŋ\ [ME *chiden,* fr. OE *cīdan* to quarrel, chide, fr. *cīd* strife] *vi* (bef. 12c) **:** to speak out in angry or displeased rebuke ~ *vt* **:** to voice disapproval to **:** reproach in a usu. mild and constructive manner **:** SCOLD ***syn*** see REPROVE

[1]**chief** \ˈchēf\ *adj* (13c) **1 :** accorded highest rank or office ⟨~ librarian⟩ **2 :** of greatest importance, significance, or influence ⟨the ~ reasons⟩

[2]**chief** *adv, archaic* (14c) **:** CHIEFLY

[3]**chief** *n* [ME, fr. MF, head, chief, fr. L *caput* head — more at HEAD] (15c) **1 :** the upper part of a heraldic field **2 :** the head of a body of persons or an organization **:** LEADER ⟨~ of police⟩ **3 :** the principal or most valuable part — **chief·dom** \-dəm\ *n* — **chief·ship** \-ˌship\ *n* — **in chief :** in the chief position or place — often used in titles ⟨commander *in chief*⟩

chief executive *n* (1833) **:** a principal executive officer: as **a :** the president of a republic **b :** the governor of a state

chief justice *n* (1692) **:** the presiding or principal judge of a court of justice

[1]**chief·ly** \ˈchē-flē\ *adv* (14c) **1 :** most importantly **:** PRINCIPALLY, ESPECIALLY **2 :** for the most part **:** MOSTLY, MAINLY

[2]**chiefly** *adj* (1870) **:** of or relating to a chief ⟨~ duties⟩

chief master sergeant *n* (1959) **:** a noncommissioned officer in the air force ranking above a senior master sergeant

chief master sergeant of the air force (ca. 1961) **:** the ranking noncommissioned officer in the air force serving as adviser to the chief of staff

chief of naval operations (1915) **:** the commanding officer of the navy and a member of the Joint Chiefs of Staff

chief of staff (ca. 1881) **1 :** the ranking officer of a staff in the armed forces serving as principal adviser to a commander **2 :** the commanding officer of the army or air force and a member of the Joint Chiefs of Staff

chief of state (1950) **:** the formal head of a national state as distinguished from the head of the government

chief petty officer *n* (ca. 1887) **:** an enlisted man in the navy or coast guard ranking above a petty officer first class and below a senior chief petty officer

chief·tain \ˈchēf-tən\ *n* [ME *chieftaine,* fr. MF *chevetain,* fr. LL *capitaneus* chief — more at CAPTAIN] (14c) **:** a chief esp. of a band, tribe, or clan — **chief·tain·ship** \-ˌship\ *n*

chief·tain·cy \-sē\ *n, pl* **-cies** (1788) **1 :** the rank, dignity, office, or rule of a chieftain **2 :** a region or a people ruled by a chief **:** CHIEFDOM

chief warrant officer *n* (ca. 1917) **:** a warrant officer of senior rank in the armed forces; *also* **:** a commissioned officer in the navy or coast guard ranking below an ensign

chiel \ˈchē(ə)l\ *or* **chield** \ˈchē(ə)ld\ *n* [ME (Sc) *cheld,* alter. of ME *child* child] *chiefly Scot* (1728) **:** FELLOW, LAD

chiff·chaff \ˈchif-ˌchaf\ *n* [imit.] (1780) **:** a small grayish European warbler (*Phylloscopus collybita*)

[1]**chif·fon** \shif-ˈän, ˈshif-ˌ\ *n* [F, lit., rag, fr. *chiffe* old rag, alter. of MF *chipe,* fr. ME *chip* chip] (1765) **1 :** an ornamental addition (as a knot of ribbons) to a woman's dress **2 :** a sheer fabric esp. of silk

[2]**chiffon** *adj* (1903) **1 :** resembling chiffon in sheerness or softness **2 :** having a light delicate texture achieved usu. by adding whipped egg whites or whipped gelatin ⟨lemon ~ pie⟩

chif·fo·nier \ˌshif-ə-ˈni(ə)r\ *n* [F *chiffonnier,* fr. *chiffon*] (1765) **:** a high narrow chest of drawers

chif·fo·robe \ˈshif-ə-ˌrōb\ *n* [*chiffo*nier + ward*robe*] (1908) **:** a combination of wardrobe and chest of drawers

chig·ger \ˈchig-ər, ˈjig-\ *n* (1769) **1 :** CHIGOE 1 **2** [of African origin; akin to Wolof *jiga* insect] **:** a 6-legged mite larva (family Trombiculidae) that sucks the blood of vertebrates and causes intense irritation

chi·gnon \ˈshēn-ˌyän\ *n* [F, fr. MF *chaignon* chain, collar, nape] (1783) **:** a knot of hair that is worn at the back of the head and esp. at the nape of the neck

chi·goe \ˈchig-(ˌ)ō, ˈchē-(ˌ)gō\ *n* [of Cariban origin; akin to Galibi *chico* chigoe] (1691) **1 :** a tropical flea (*Tunga penetrans*) of which the fertile female causes great discomfort by burrowing under the skin— called also *chigger* **2 :** CHIGGER 2

Chi·hua·hua \chə-ˈwä-(ˌ)wä, shə-, -wə\ *n* [MexSp, fr. *Chihuahua,* Mexico] (1858) **:** any of a breed of very small roundheaded dogs that occur in short-coated and long-coated varieties

Chihuahua

chil·blain \ˈchil-ˌblān\ *n* [[1]*chill*] (1547) **:** an inflammatory swelling or sore caused by exposure (as of the feet or hands) to cold

child \ˈchī(ə)ld\ *n, pl* **chil·dren** \ˈchil-drən, -dərn\ *often attrib* [ME, fr. OE *cild;* akin to Goth *kilthei* womb, Skt *jathara* belly] (bef. 12c) **1 a :** an unborn or recently born person **b** *dial* **:** a female infant **2 a :** a young person esp. between infancy and youth **b :** a childlike or childish person **c :** a person not yet of age **3** *usu* **childe** \ˈchī(ə)ld\ *archaic* **:** a youth of noble birth **4 a :** a son or daughter of human parents **b :** DESCENDANT **5 :** one strongly influenced by another or by a place or state of affairs **6 :** PRODUCT, RESULT ⟨barbed wire . . . is truly a ~ of the plains — W. P. Webb⟩ — **child·less** \ˈchī(ə)l-(d)ləs\ *adj* — **child·less·ness** *n* — **with child :** PREGNANT

child·bear·ing \ˈchīl(d)-ˌbar-iŋ, -ˌber-\ *adj* (14c) **:** of or relating to the process of conceiving, being pregnant with, and giving birth to children ⟨women of ~ age⟩ — **childbearing** *n*

child·bed \-ˌbed\ *n* (13c) **:** the condition of a woman in childbirth

childbed fever *n* (1928) **:** PUERPERAL FEVER

child·birth \ˈchīl(d)-ˌbərth\ *n* (15c) **:** PARTURITION

child·hood \ˈchīld-ˌhu̇d\ *n* (bef. 12c) **1 :** the state or period of being a child **2 :** the early period in the development of something

child·ish \ˈchīl-dish\ *adj* (bef. 12c) **1 :** of, relating to, or befitting a child or childhood **2 a :** marked by or suggestive of immaturity and lack of poise ⟨a ~ spiteful remark⟩ **b :** lacking complexity **:** SIMPLE ⟨it's a ~ device, but it works⟩ **c :** deteriorated with age esp. in mind **:** SENILE — **child·ish·ly** *adv* — **child·ish·ness** *n*

child·like \ˈchī(ə)l-ˌ(d)līk\ *adj* (1586) **:** of, relating to, or resembling a child or childhood; *esp* **:** marked by innocence, trust, and ingenuousness — **child·like·ness** *n*

child·ly \ˈchī(ə)l-(d)lē\ *adj* (bef. 12c) **:** CHILDLIKE

child·proof \ˈchīl(d)-ˌprüf\ *adj* (1956) **:** designed to prevent tampering by children ⟨~ pill bottles⟩

child's play *n* (14c) **1 :** an extremely simple task or act **2 :** something that is insignificant ⟨his injury was *child's play* compared with the damage he inflicted⟩

Chile saltpeter \ˈchil-ē-\ *n* [*Chile,* So. America] (ca. 1909) **:** sodium nitrate esp. occurring naturally (as in caliche) — called also *Chile niter*

chili *or* **chile** *or* **chil·li** \ˈchil-ē\ *n, pl* **chil·ies** *or* **chil·es** *or* **chil·lies** [Sp *chile,* fr. Nahuatl *chīlli*] (1604) **1 a :** HOT PEPPER **b** *usu chilli, chiefly Brit* **:** a pepper whether hot or sweet **2 a :** a thick sauce of meat and chilies **b :** CHILI CON CARNE

chil·i·ad \ˈkil-ē-ˌad, -əd\ *n* [LL *chiliad-, chilias,* fr. Gk, fr. *chilioi* thousand] (1598) **1 :** a group of 1000 **2 :** MILLENNIUM 2a

chil·i·asm \ˈkil-ē-ˌaz-əm\ *n* [NL *chiliasmus,* fr. LL *chiliastes* one that believes in chiliasm, fr. *chilias*] (1610) **:** MILLENARIANISM — **chil·i·ast** \-ē-ˌast, -ē-əst\ *n* — **chil·i·as·tic** \ˌkil-ē-ˈas-tik\ *adj*

chili con car·ne \ˌchil-ē-ˌkän-ˈkär-nē, -kən-\ *n* [AmerSp *chile con carne* chili with meat] (1857) **:** a spiced stew of ground beef and minced chilies or chili powder usu. with beans

chili powder *n* (1938) **:** a condiment made with chilies ground to a powder

chili sauce *n* (1880) **:** a spiced tomato sauce usu. made with red and green peppers

[1]**chill** \ˈchil\ *n* [ME *chile* chill, frost, fr. OE *ciele;* akin to OE *ceald* cold] (bef. 12c) **1 a :** a sensation of cold accompanied by shivering **b :** a disagreeable sensation of coldness **2 :** a moderate but disagreeable degree of cold **3 :** a check to enthusiasm or warmth of feeling ⟨felt the ~ of his opponent's stare⟩

[2]**chill** *adj* (14c) **1 a :** moderately cold **b :** COLD, RAW **2 :** affected by cold ⟨~ travelers⟩ **3 :** DISTANT, FORMAL ⟨a ~ reception⟩ **4 :** DEPRESSING, DISPIRITING ⟨~ penury — Thomas Gray⟩ — **chill·ness** *n*

[3]**chill** *vi* (14c) **1 a :** to become cold **b :** to shiver or quake with or as if with cold **2 :** to become taken with a chill **3** *of a metal* **:** to become surface-hardened by sudden cooling ~ *vt* **1 a :** to make cold or chilly **b :** to make cool esp. without freezing **2 :** to affect as if with cold **:** DISPIRIT, DISCOURAGE, DETER ⟨were ~*ed* by the drab austerity and the police-state atmosphere — William Attwood⟩ **3 :** to harden the surface of (metal) by sudden cooling — **chill·ing·ly** \-iŋ-lē\ *adv*

chill·er \ˈchil-ər\ *n* (1798) **1 :** one that chills **2 :** an eerie or frightening story of murder, violence, or the supernatural

chill factor *n* (1965) **:** WINDCHILL

chil·lum \ˈchil-əm\ *n* [Hindi *cilam,* fr. Per *chilam*] (1781) **1 :** the part of a water pipe that contains the substance (as tobacco or hashish) which is smoked; *also* **:** a quantity of a substance thus smoked **2 :** a funnel-shaped clay pipe for smoking

chilly \ˈchil-ē\ *adj* **chill·i·er; -est** (1570) **1 :** noticeably cold **:** CHILLING **2 :** unpleasantly affected by cold **3 :** lacking warmth of feeling **4 :** tending to arouse fear or apprehension ⟨~ suspicions⟩ — **chill·i·ly** \ˈchil-ə-lē\ *adv* — **chill·i·ness** \ˈchil-ē-nəs\ *n*

chi·mae·ra \kī-ˈmir-ə, kə-\ *n* [NL, genus name, fr. L, chimera] (1804) **:** any of a family (Chimaeridae) of marine elasmobranch fishes with a tapering or threadlike tail and usu. no anal fin

chimaeric, chimaerism *Brit var of* CHIMERIC, CHIMERISM

[1]**chime** \ˈchīm\ *n* [ME *chimbe,* fr. OE *cimb-;* akin to OE *camb* comb] (bef. 12c) **:** the edge or rim of a cask

[2]**chime** *n* [ME, cymbal, fr. MF *chimbe,* fr. OF, fr. L *cymbalum* cymbal] (14c) **1 :** an apparatus for chiming a bell or set of bells **2 a :** a musically tuned set of bells **b :** one of a set of objects giving a bell-like sound when struck **3 a :** the sound of a set of bells — usu. used in pl. **b :** a musical sound suggesting that of bells **4 :** ACCORD, HARMONY ⟨such happy ~ of fact and theory —Henry Maudsley⟩

[3]**chime** *vb* **chimed; chim·ing** *vi* (14c) **1 a :** to make a musical and esp. a harmonious sound **b :** to make the sounds of a chime **2 :** to be or act in accord ⟨the music and the mood *chimed* well together⟩ ~ *vt* **1 :** to cause to sound musically by striking **2 :** to produce by chiming **3 :** to call or indicate by chiming ⟨the clock *chimed* midnight⟩ **4 :** to utter repetitively **:** DIN 2 — **chim·er** *n*

chime in *vi* (1681) **1 :** to break into a conversation or discussion esp. to express an opinion **2 :** to combine harmoniously ⟨the artist's illustrations *chime in* perfectly with the text —*Book Production*⟩ ~ *vt* **:** to remark while chiming in

chi·me·ra *or* **chi·mae·ra** \kī-ˈmir-ə, kə-\ *n* [L *chimaera,* fr. Gk *chimaira* she-goat, chimera; akin to Gk *cheimōn* winter — more at HIBERNATE] **1 a** *cap* **:** a fire-breathing she-monster in Greek mythology having a lion's head, a goat's body, and a serpent's tail **b :** an imaginary monster compounded of incongruous parts **2 :** an illusion or fabrication of the mind; *esp* **:** an unrealizable dream ⟨a fancy, a ~ in my brain, troubles me in my prayer —John Donne⟩ **3 :** an individual, organ, or part consisting of tissues of diverse genetic constitution and occurring esp. in plants at a graft union

chi·mere \shə-ˈmi(ə)r, chə-\ *n* [ME *chimmer, chemeyr*] (14c) **:** a loose sleeveless robe worn by Anglican bishops over the rochet

chi·me·ric \kī-ˈmir-ik, kə-, -ˈmer-\ *adj* (1973) **:** relating to or being a genetic chimera

chi·me·ri·cal \kī-ˈmer-i-kəl, kə-, -ˈmir-\ *also* **chi·me·ric** \-ik\ *adj* [*chimera*] (1638) **1 :** existing only as the product of unchecked imagination **:** fantastically visionary or improbable **2 :** given to fantastic schemes ***syn*** see IMAGINARY — **chi·me·ri·cal·ly** \-i-k(ə-)lē\ *adv*

chi·me·rism \kī-ˈmi(ə)r-ˌiz-əm, kə-; ˈkī-mə-ˌriz-\ *n* (1961) **:** the state of being a genetic chimera

chi·mi·chan·ga \ˌchim-ē-ˈchäŋ-gə\ *n* [MexSp, lit., trinket] (1982) **:** a tortilla wrapped around a filling (as of meat) and deep-fried

chim·ney \ˈchim-nē\ *n, pl* **chimneys** [ME, fr. MF *cheminée,* fr. LL *caminata,* fr. L *caminus* furnace, fireplace, fr. Gk *kaminos;* akin to Gk *kamara* vault — more at CHAMBER] (14c) **1** *dial* **:** FIREPLACE, HEARTH **2 :** a vertical structure incorporated into a building and enclosing a flue or flues that carry off smoke; *esp* **:** the part of such a structure extending above a roof **3 :** SMOKESTACK **4 :** a tube usu. of glass placed around a flame (as of a lamp) **5 :** something (as a narrow cleft in rock) resembling a chimney

chim·ney·piece \ˈchim-nē-ˌpēs\ *n* (1680) **:** an ornamental construction over and around a fireplace that includes the mantel

chimney pot *n* (1830) **:** a usu. earthenware pipe placed at the top of a chimney

chimney sweep *n* (1727) **:** one whose occupation is cleaning soot from chimney flues — called also *chimney sweeper*

chimney swift *n* (1849) **:** a small sooty-gray bird (*Chaetura pelagica*) with long narrow wings that often builds its nest inside an unused chimney — called also *chimney swallow*

chimp \ˈchimp, ˈshimp\ *n* (1877) **:** CHIMPANZEE

chim·pan·zee \ˌchim-ˌpan-ˈzē, ˌshim-, -pən-; chim-ˈpan-zē, shim-\ *n* [Kongo dial. *chimpenzi*] (1738) **:** an anthropoid ape (*Pan troglodytes*) of equatorial Africa that is smaller and more arboreal than the gorilla

[1]**chin** \ˈchin\ *n* [ME, fr. OE *cinn;* akin to OHG *kinni* chin, L *gena* cheek, Gk *genys* jaw, cheek] (bef. 12c) **1 :** the lower portion of the face lying below the lower lip and including the prominence of the lower jaw **2 :** the surface beneath or between the branches of the lower jaw — **chin·less** \-ləs\ *adj*

[2]**chin** *vb* **chinned; chin·ning** *vt* (1869) **1 :** to bring to or hold with the chin ⟨*chinned* his violin⟩ **2 :** to raise (oneself) while hanging by the hands until the chin is level with the support ~ *vi, slang* **:** to talk idly

chi·na \ˈchī-nə\ *n* [Per *chīnī* Chinese porcelain] (1579) **1 :** PORCELAIN; *also* **:** vitreous porcelain wares (as dishes, vases, or ornaments) for domestic use **2 :** earthenware or porcelain tableware

China aster *n* (1794) **:** a common annual garden aster (*Callistephus chinensis*) native to northern China that occurs in many showy forms

chi·na·ber·ry \ˈchī-nə-ˌber-ē, *Southern also* ˈchā-nē-ˌber-ē\ *n* (1890) **:** a small Asian tree (*Melia azedarach*) of the mahogany family naturalized in the southern U.S. where it is widely planted for shade or ornament

china clay *n* (1840) **:** KAOLIN

china closet *n* (1771) **:** a cabinet or cupboard for the storage or display of household china

Chi·na·man \ˈchī-nə-mən\ *n* (1849) **:** a native of China **:** CHINESE — often taken to be offensive

China rose *n* (1731) **:** any of numerous garden roses derived from a shrubby Chinese rose (*Rosa chinensis*)

Chi·na·town \ˈchī-nə-ˌtau̇n\ *n* (1857) **:** the Chinese quarter of a city

China tree *n* (1819) **:** CHINABERRY

chi·na·ware \ˈchī-nə-ˌwa(ə)r, -ˌwe(ə)r\ *n* (1634) **:** tableware made of china

chin·bone \ˈchin-ˈbōn, -ˌbōn\ *n* (bef. 12c) **:** MANDIBLE; *esp* **:** the median anterior part of the human mandible

\ə\ abut \ᵊ\ kitten, F table \ər\ further \a\ ash \ā\ ace \ä\ cot, cart \au̇\ out \ch\ chin \e\ bet \ē\ easy \g\ go \i\ hit \ī\ ice \j\ job \ŋ\ sing \ō\ go \ȯ\ law \ȯi\ boy \th\ thin \t͟h\ the \ü\ loot \u̇\ foot \y\ yet \zh\ vision \à, k̲, ⁿ, œ, œ̄, ue, ue̅, ʸ\ *see* Guide to Pronunciation

chinch \'chinch\ *n* [Sp *chinche,* fr. L *cimic-, cimex*] (1616) : BEDBUG

chinch bug *n* (1785) : a small black-and-white bug (*Blissus leucopterus*) very destructive to cereal grasses

chin·che·rin·chee \ˌchin-chə-ri(n)-'chē, ˌchiŋ-kə-\ *n, pl* **chincherinchee** *or* **chincherinchees** [origin unknown] (1904) : a southern African perennial bulbous herb (*Ornithogalum thyrsoides*) with long-lasting spikes of starry white to golden-yellow blossoms

chin·chil·la \chin-'chil-ə\ *n* [Sp] (1604) **1** : a small rodent (*Chinchilla laniger*) that is the size of a large squirrel, has very soft fur of a pearly gray color, is native to the mountains of Peru and Chile, and is extensively bred in captivity; *also* : its fur **2** : a heavy twilled woolen coating

¹chine \'chīn\ *n* [ME, fr. MF *eschine,* of Gmc origin; akin to OHG *scina* shinbone, needle — more at SHIN] (14c) **1** : BACKBONE, SPINE; *also* : a cut of meat including all or part of the backbone **2** : RIDGE, CREST **3** : the intersection of the bottom and the sides of a flat or V-bottomed boat

²chine *vt* **chined; chin·ing** (ca. 1611) : to cut through the backbone of (as in butchering)

Chi·nese \chī-'nēz, -'nēs\ *n, pl* **Chinese** (1606) **1 a** : a native or inhabitant of China **b** : a person of Chinese descent **2** : a group of related languages used by the people of China that are often mutually unintelligible in their spoken form but share a single system of writing and that constitute a branch of the Sino-Tibetan language family; *specif* : MANDARIN — **Chinese** *adj*

Chinese boxes *n pl* (1829) : a set of boxes graduated in size so that each fits into the next larger one

Chinese cabbage *n* (1842) : either of two Asian brassicas now grown in the U.S. and widely used as greens: **a** : BOK CHOY **b** : CELERY CABBAGE

Chinese checkers *n pl but sing or pl in constr* (1938) : a game in which each player seeks to be the first to transfer a set of marbles from a home point to the opposite point of a pitted 6-pointed star by single moves or jumps

Chinese chestnut *n* (ca. 1909) : an Asian chestnut (*Castanea mollissima*) that is resistant to chestnut blight

Chinese copy *n* (1920) : an exact imitation or duplicate that includes defects as well as desired qualities

Chinese gooseberry *n* (1925) : a subtropical vine (*Actinidia chinensis*) that bears kiwi fruit; *also* : KIWI FRUIT

Chinese lacquer *n* (1900) : LACQUER 1b

Chinese lantern *n* (1825) : a collapsible translucent covering for a light

Chinese parsley *n* (ca. 1953) : CILANTRO

Chinese puzzle *n* (1815) **1** : an intricate or ingenious puzzle **2** : something intricate and obscure

Chinese wall *n* [*Chinese Wall,* a defensive wall built in the 3d cent. B.C. between China and Mongolia] (1900) : a strong barrier; *esp* : a serious obstacle to understanding

Ching *or* **Ch'ing** \'chiŋ\ *n* [Chin (Pek) *ch'ing¹*] : a Manchu dynasty in China dated 1644–1912 and the last imperial dynasty

¹chink \'chiŋk\ *n* [prob. alter. of ME *chin* crack, fissure, fr. OE *cine;* akin to OE *cīnan* to gape, OHG *chīnan* to split open] (1552) **1** : a means of evasion or escape : LOOPHOLE ⟨a ~ in the law⟩ **2** : a small cleft, slit, or fissure ⟨a ~ in the curtain⟩ **3** : a narrow beam of light shining through a chink

²chink *vt* (1748) : to fill the chinks of (as by caulking) ⟨~ a log cabin⟩

³chink *n* [imit.] (1573) **1** *archaic* : COIN, MONEY **2** : a short sharp sound

⁴chink *vi* (1589) : to make a slight sharp metallic sound ~ *vt* : to cause to make a chink

chi·no \'chē-(ˌ)nō, 'shē-\ *n, pl* **chinos** [AmerSp] (1943) **1** : a usu. khaki cotton twill of the type used for military uniforms **2** *pl* : an article of clothing made of chino

Chi·no- \ˌchī-(ˌ)nō\ *comb form* : Chinese and ⟨*Chino*-Japanese⟩

chi·noi·se·rie \shēn-'wäz-(ə-)rē, ˌshēn-ˌwäz-(ə-)'rē\ *n* [F, fr. *chinois* Chinese, fr. *Chine* China] (1883) : a style in art (as in decoration) reflecting Chinese qualities or motifs; *also* : an object or decoration in this style

Chi·nook \shə-'nu̇k, chə-, -'nük\ *n, pl* **Chinook** *or* **Chinooks** [Chehalis *Tsinúk*] (1805) **1** : a member of an American Indian people of Oregon **2** : a Chinookan language of the Chinook and other nearby peoples **3** *not cap* **a** : a warm moist southwest wind of the coast from Oregon northward **b** : a warm dry wind that descends the eastern slopes of the Rocky mountains

Chi·nook·an \-ən\ *n* (ca. 1890) : a language family of Washington and Oregon — **Chinookan** *adj*

Chinook Jargon *n* (1840) : a pidgin language based on Chinook and other Indian languages, French, and English and formerly used as a lingua franca in the northwestern U.S. and on the Pacific coast of Canada and Alaska

chinook salmon *n* (1851) : a large commercially important salmon (*Oncorhynchus tshawytscha*) that occurs in the northern Pacific ocean and usu. has red flesh

chin·qua·pin \'chiŋ-ki-ˌpin\ *n* [alter. of earlier *chincomen,* of Algonquian origin] (1612) **1** : the edible nut of a chinquapin **2** : any of several trees (genera *Castanea* or *Castanopsis*); *esp* : a dwarf chestnut (*Castanea pumila*) of the U.S.

chinquapin oak *n* (1785) : either of two chestnut oaks (*Quercus muhlenbergii* and *Q. prinoides*) of the eastern U.S.

chintz \'chin(t)s\ *n* [earlier *chints,* pl. of *chint,* fr. Hindi *chīṭ*] (1614) **1** : a printed calico from India **2** : a usu. glazed printed cotton fabric

chintzy \'chin(t)-sē\ *adj* **chintz·i·er; -est** (1851) **1** : decorated with or as if with chintz **2 a** : GAUDY, CHEAP ⟨~ toys⟩ **b** : STINGY

chin–up \'chin-ˌəp\ *n* (1954) : the act or an instance of chinning oneself performed esp. as a conditioning exercise

chin–wag \-ˌwag\ *n, slang* (1879) : CONVERSATION, CHAT

¹chip \'chip\ *n* [ME] (14c) **1 a** : a small usu. thin and flat piece (as of wood or stone) cut, struck, or flaked off **b** (1) : a small thin slice of food; *esp* : POTATO CHIP (2) : FRENCH FRY **2** : something small, worthless, or trivial **3 a** : one of the counters used as a token for money in poker and other games **b** *pl* : MONEY — used esp. in the phrase *in the chips* **4** : a piece of dried dung — usu. used in combination ⟨cow ~⟩ **5** : a flaw left after a chip is removed **6** : INTEGRATED CIRCUIT **7** : CHIP SHOT — **chip off the old block** : a child that resembles his parent — **chip on one's shoulder** : a challenging or belligerent attitude

²chip *vb* **chipped; chip·ping** *vt* (1606) **1 a** : to cut or hew with an edged tool **b** (1) : to cut or break (a small piece) from something (2) : to cut or break a fragment from (3) : to cut into chips ⟨~ a tree stump⟩ **2** *Brit* : CHAFF, BANTER ~ *vi* **1** : to break off in small pieces **2** : to play a chip shot

chip·board \'chip-ˌbō(ə)rd, -ˌbȯ(ə)rd\ *n* (1919) : a paperboard made from wastepaper

chip in *vb* (1861) : CONTRIBUTE ⟨everyone *chipped in* for the gift⟩

chip·munk \'chip-ˌməŋk\ *n* [alter. of earlier *chitmunk,* of Algonquian origin; akin to Ojibwa *atchitamō* squirrel] (1832) : any of numerous small striped semiterrestrial American squirrels (genera *Tamias* and *Eutamias*)

chipped beef \'chip(t)-\ *n* (1859) : smoked dried beef sliced thin

Chip·pen·dale \'chip-ən-ˌdāl\ *adj* [Thomas *Chippendale*] (1876) : of or relating to an 18th century English furniture style characterized by graceful outline and often ornate rococo ornamentation

¹chip·per \'chip-ər\ *n* (1513) : one that chips

²chipper *adj* [perh. alter. of E dial. *kipper* (lively)] (1837) : GAY, SPRIGHTLY

Chip·pe·wa \'chip-ə-ˌwȯ, -ˌwä, -ˌwā, -wə\ *n, pl* **Chippewa** *or* **Chippewas** (1671) : OJIBWA

chip shot *n* (1909) : a short usu. low approach shot in golf that lofts the ball to the green and allows it to roll

chir- *or* **chiro-** *comb form* [L, fr. Gk *cheir-, cheiro-,* fr. *cheir;* akin to Hitt *kesar* hand] : hand ⟨*chiro*practic⟩

Chi–Rho \'kī-'rō, 'kē-\ *n, pl* **Chi–Rhos** [*chi* + *rho*] (1868) : a Christian monogram and symbol formed from the first two letters X and P of the Greek word for *Christ* — called also *Christogram*

Chir·i·ca·hua \ˌchir-ə-'kä-wə\ *n, pl* **Chiricahua** *or* **Chiricahuas** (1885) : a member of an Apache people of Arizona

chirimoya *var of* CHERIMOYA

chirk \'chərk\ *vb* [ME *charken, chirken* to creak, chirp, fr. OE *cearcian* to creak; akin to OE *cracian* to crack] (bef. 12c) : CHEER ⟨play with her and ~ her up a little —Harriet B. Stowe⟩

chi·rog·ra·phy \kī-'räg-rə-fē\ *n* (1654) **1** : HANDWRITING, PENMANSHIP **2** : CALLIGRAPHY 1 — **chi·rog·ra·pher** \-fər\ *n* — **chi·ro·graph·ic** \ˌkī-rə-'graf-ik\ *or* **chi·ro·graph·i·cal** \-i-kəl\ *adj*

chi·ro·man·cy \'kī-rə-ˌman(t)-sē\ *n* [prob. fr. MF *chiromancie,* fr. ML *chiromantia,* fr. Gk *cheir-* chir- + *-manteia* -mancy — more at -MANCY] (1528) : PALMISTRY — **chi·ro·man·cer** \-ˌman(t)-sər\ *n*

chi·ron·o·mid \kī-'rän-ə-məd\ *n* [deriv. of Gk *cheironomos* one who gestures with his hands] (1915) : any of a family (Chironomidae) of midges that lack piercing mouthparts — **chironomid** *adj*

chi·rop·o·dy \kə-'räp-əd-ē, shə- *also* kī-\ *n* [*chir-* + *pod-,* fr. its original concern with both hands and feet] (1886) : PODIATRY — **chi·rop·o·dist** \-əd-əst\ *n*

chi·ro·prac·tic \'kī-rə-ˌprak-tik\ *n* [*chir-* + Gk *praktikos* practical, operative — more at PRACTICAL] (1898) : a system of therapy which holds that disease results from a lack of normal nerve function and which employs manipulation and specific adjustment of body structures (as the spinal column) — **chi·ro·prac·tor** \-tər\ *n*

chi·rop·ter·an \kī-'räp-tə-rən\ *n* [deriv. of Gk *cheir* hand + *pteron* wing — more at FEATHER] (1835) : ³BAT

chirp \'chərp\ *n* [imit.] (ca. 1755) : the characteristic short sharp sound esp. of a small bird or insect — **chirp** *vi*

chirpy \'chər-pē\ *adj* **chirp·i·er; -est** (1837) **1 a** : making chirps **b** : suggestive of chirping ⟨a ~ voice⟩ **2** : cheerfully lively ⟨a ~ manner⟩ — **chirp·i·ly** \-pə-lē\ *adv*

chirr \'chər\ *n* [imit.] (1600) : the short vibrant or trilled sound characteristic of an insect (as a grasshopper or cicada) — **chirr** *vi*

chir·rup \'chər-əp, 'chir-\ *n* [imit.] (1788) : CHIRP — **chirrup** *vi*

chir·rupy \'chər-ə-pē, 'chir-\ *adj* (1874) : CHIRPY

chi·rur·geon \kī-'rər-jən\ *n* [ME *cirurgian,* fr. OF *cirurgien,* fr. *cirurgie* surgery] *archaic* (13c) : SURGEON

¹chis·el \'chiz-əl\ *n* [ME, fr. ONF, prob. alter. of *chisoir* goldsmith's chisel, fr. (assumed) VL *caesorium* cutting instrument, fr. L *caesus,* pp. of *caedere* to cut — more at CONCISE] (14c) : a metal tool with a cutting edge at the end of a blade used in dressing, shaping, or working a solid material (as wood, stone, or metal)

²chisel *vb* **-eled** *or* **-elled; -el·ing** *or* **-el·ling** \'chiz-(ə-)liŋ\ *vt* (1509) **1** : to cut or work with or as if with a chisel **2** : to employ shrewd or unfair practices on in order to obtain one's end; *also* : to obtain by such practices ⟨~ a job⟩ ~ *vi* **1** : to work with or as if with a chisel **2 a** : to employ shrewd or unfair practices **b** : to thrust oneself : INTRUDE ⟨~ in on a racket⟩ — **chis·el·er** *or* **chis·el·ler** \-(ə-)lər\ *n*

chis·eled *or* **chis·elled** \'chiz-əld\ *adj* (1821) : formed or crafted as if with a chisel ⟨~ good looks⟩ ⟨a ~ essay⟩

chi–square \'kī-'skwa(ə)r, -'skwe(ə)r\ *n, often attrib* (ca. 1934) : a statistic that is a sum of terms each of which is a quotient obtained by dividing the square of the difference between the observed and theoretical values of a quantity by the theoretical value

chi–square distribution *n* (ca. 1956) : a probability density function that gives the distribution of the sum of the squares of a number of independent random variables each with a normal distribution with zero mean and unit variance, that has the property that the sum of two or more random variables with such a distribution also has one, and that is widely used in testing statistical hypotheses esp. about the theoretical and observed values of a quantity and about population variances and standard deviations

¹chit \'chit\ *n* [ME *chitte* kitten, cub] (1624) **1** : CHILD **2** : a pert young woman

²chit *n* [Hindi *ciṭṭhī*] (1757) **1** : a short letter or note; *esp* : a signed voucher of a small debt (as for food) **2** : a small slip of paper with writing on it

chit·chat \'chit-ˌchat\ *n* [redupl. of *chat*] (1710) : SMALL TALK, GOSSIP — **chitchat** *vi*

chi·tin \'kīt-ᵊn\ *n* [F *chitine,* fr. Gk *chitōn*] (1836) : a horny polysaccharide that forms part of the hard outer integument esp. of insects and crustaceans — **chi·tin·ous** \'kīt-ᵊn-əs, 'kīt-nəs\ *adj*

chi·ton \'kīt-ᵊn, 'kī-ˌtän\ *n* [NL, genus name, fr. Gk *chitōn* tunic; of Sem origin; akin to Heb *kuttōneth* tunic] (1816) **1** : any of an order (Polyplacophora) of elongated bilaterally symmetrical marine mollusks with a dorsal shell of calcareous plates **2** [Gk *chitōn*] : the basic garment of ancient Greece worn usu. knee-length by men and full-length by women

chit·ter \'chit-ər\ *vi* [ME *chiteren,* prob. of imit. origin] (13c) : TWITTER, CHIRP; *also* : CHATTER

chit·ter·lings *or* **chit·lins** \'chit-lənz\ *n pl* [ME *chiterling*] (13c) : the intestines of hogs esp. when prepared as food

chi·val·ric \shə-'val-rik\ *adj* (1797) : relating to chivalry : CHIVALROUS

chiv·al·rous \'shiv-əl-rəs\ *adj* (14c) **1** : VALIANT **2** : of, relating to, or characteristic of chivalry and knight-errantry **3 a** : marked by honor, generosity, and courtesy **b** : marked by gracious courtesy and high-minded consideration esp. to women ***syn*** see CIVIL — **chiv·al·rous·ly** *adv* — **chiv·al·rous·ness** *n*

chiv·al·ry \'shiv-əl-rē\ *n, pl* **-ries** [ME *chivalrie,* fr. MF *chevalerie,* fr. *chevalier*] (14c) **1** : mounted men-at-arms **2** *archaic* **a** : martial valor **b** : knightly skill **3** : gallant or distinguished gentlemen **4** : the system, spirit, or customs of medieval knighthood **5** : the qualities of the ideal knight : chivalrous conduct

chive \'chīv\ *n* [ME, fr. ONF, fr. L *cepa* onion] (14c) : a perennial plant (*Allium schoenoprasum*) related to the onion

chivy *or* **chiv·vy** \'chiv-ē\ *vt* **chiv·ied** *or* **chiv·vied; chivy·ing** *or* **chiv·vy·ing** [*chivy,* n. (chase, hunt), prob. fr. E dial. *Chevy Chase* chase, confusion, fr. the name of a ballad describing the battle of Otterburn (1388)] (ca. 1840) **1** : to tease or annoy with persistent petty attacks **2** : to move or obtain by small maneuvers

chla·myd·ia \klə-'mid-ē-ə\ *n, pl* **-i·ae** \-ē-,ē\ [NL, fr. Gk *chlamyd-, chlamys*] (ca. 1931) **1** : any of a genus (*Chlamydia,* family Chlamydiaceae) of coccoid to spherical gram-negative intracellular rickettsial parasites including one (*C. trachomatis*) that causes or is associated with various diseases of the eye and urogenital tract including trachoma, lymphogranuloma venereum, and some forms of urethritis **2** : a disease or infection caused by chlamydiae — **chla·myd·i·al** \-ē-əl\ *adj*

chla·mydo·spore \klə-'mid-ə-,spō(ə)r, -,spȯ(ə)r\ *n* [L *chlamyd-* + *-o-* + ISV *spore*] (1884) : a thick-walled usu. resting spore

chla·mys \'klam-əs, 'klām-əs\ *n, pl* **chla·mys·es** *or* **chla·my·des** \-ə-,dēz\ [L *chlamyd-, chlamys,* fr. Gk] (1699) : a short oblong mantle worn by young men of ancient Greece

chlamys

Chloe \'klō-ē\ *n* [L, fr. Gk *Chloē*] : a lover of Daphnis in a Greek pastoral romance

chlor- *or* **chloro-** *comb form* [NL, fr. Gk, fr. *chlōros* greenish yellow — more at YELLOW] **1** : green ⟨*chlorine*⟩ ⟨*chlorosis*⟩ **2** : chlorine : containing chlorine ⟨*chloric*⟩ ⟨*chloroprene*⟩

chlor·ac·ne \klōr-'ak-nē, klȯr-\ *n* (ca. 1928) : an eruption on the skin resembling acne and resulting from exposure to chlorine or its compounds

chlo·ral \'klōr-əl, 'klȯr-\ *n* [F, fr. *chlor-* + *al*cool alcohol] (1838) **1** : a pungent colorless oily aldehyde CCl_3CHO used in making DDT and chloral hydrate **2** : CHLORAL HYDRATE

chloral hydrate *n* (ca. 1889) : a bitter white crystalline drug $C_2H_3Cl_3O_2$ used as a hypnotic and sedative or in knockout drops

chlo·ral·ose \'klōr-ə-,lōs, 'klȯr-, -,lōz\ *n* (1893) : a bitter crystalline compound $C_8H_{11}Cl_3O_6$ used esp. to anesthetize animals — **chlo·ral·osed** \-,lōst, -,lōzd\ *adj*

chlo·ra·mine \'klōr-ə-,mēn, 'klȯr-\ *n* [ISV] (1893) : any of various compounds containing nitrogen and chlorine

chlor·am·phen·i·col \,klōr-,am-'fen-i-,kȯl, ,klȯr-, -,kōl\ *n* [*chlor-* + *amid-* + *phen-* + *nitr-* + *glycol*] (ca. 1949) : a broad-spectrum antibiotic $C_{11}H_{12}Cl_2N_2O_5$ isolated from cultures of a soil microorganism (*Streptomyces venezuelae*) or prepared synthetically

chlo·rate \'klō(ə)r-,āt, 'klȯ(ə)r-\ *n* (1823) : a salt containing the group ClO_3 ⟨~ of potassium⟩

chlor·dane \'klō(ə)r-,dān\ *also* **chlor·dan** \-,dan\ *n* [*chlor-* + *indane, indan* (C_9H_{10})] (ca. 1947) : a highly chlorinated viscous volatile liquid insecticide $C_{10}H_6Cl_8$

chlor·di·az·epox·ide \,klōr-dī-,az-ə-'päk-,sīd, ,klȯr-\ *n* [*chlor-* + *di-* + *az-* + *epoxide*] (1962) : a benzodiazepine $C_{16}H_{14}ClN_3O$ related to diazepam and used in the form of its hydrochloride esp. as a tranquilizer and in the treatment of alcoholism — compare LIBRIUM

chlo·rel·la \klə-'rel-ə\ *n* [NL, genus name, fr. Gk *chlōros*] (1904) : any of a genus (*Chlorella*) of unicellular green algae

chlor·en·chy·ma \klōr-'eŋ-kə-mə, klȯr-\ *n* (1894) : chlorophyll-containing parenchyma of plants

chlo·ride \'klō(ə)r-,īd, 'klȯ(ə)r-\ *n* [G *chlorid,* fr. *chlor-* + *-id* -ide] (1812) : a compound of chlorine with another element or group; *esp* : a salt or ester of hydrochloric acid

chloride of lime (1826) : BLEACHING POWDER

chlo·ri·nate \'klōr-ə-,nāt, 'klȯr-\ *vt* **-nat·ed; -nat·ing** (1856) : to treat or cause to combine with chlorine or a chlorine compound — **chlo·ri·na·tion** \,klōr-ə-'nā-shən, ,klȯr-\ *n* — **chlo·ri·na·tor** \'klōr-ə-,nāt-ər, 'klȯr-\ *n*

chlorinated lime *n* (1876) : BLEACHING POWDER

chlo·rine \'klō(ə)r-,ēn, 'klȯ(ə)r-, -ən\ *n* (1810) : a halogen element that is isolated as a heavy greenish yellow gas of pungent odor and is used esp. as a bleach, oxidizing agent, and disinfectant in water purification — see ELEMENT table

chlo·rin·i·ty \klōr-'in-ət-ē, klȯr-\ *n* [*chlorine* + *-ity*] (ca. 1931) : a measure of the concentration of halides in one kilogram of seawater

[1]**chlo·rite** \'klō(ə)r-,īt, 'klȯ(ə)r-\ *n* [G *chlorit,* fr. L *chloritis,* a green stone, fr. Gk *chlōritis,* fr. *chlōros*] (1794) : any of a group of monoclinic usu. green minerals associated with and resembling the micas — **chlo·rit·ic** \klōr-'it-ik, klȯr-\ *adj*

[2]**chlorite** *n* [prob. fr. F, fr. *chlor-*] (1853) : a salt containing the group ClO_2 ⟨~ of sodium⟩

chloro- — see CHLOR-

chlo·ro·ben·zene \,klōr-ō-'ben-,zēn, ,klȯr-, -ben-'\ *n* [ISV] (ca. 1889) : a colorless flammable volatile toxic liquid C_6H_5Cl used in organic synthesis (as of DDT) and as a solvent

chlo·ro·flu·o·ro·car·bon \,klōr-ō-,flu̇(-ə)r-ō-'kär-bən, ,klȯr-\ *n* (1949) : any of a group of compounds that contain carbon, chlorine, fluorine, and sometimes hydrogen and are used as refrigerants, cleaning solvents, and aerosol propellants and in the manufacture of plastic foams

chlo·ro·flu·o·ro·meth·ane \-'meth-,ān, *Brit usu* -'mē-,thān\ *n* (1965) : any of a group of gaseous chlorofluorocarbons that contain one carbon atom and four chlorine and fluorine atoms and that are used esp. as aerosol propellants and refrigerants

[1]**chlo·ro·form** \'klōr-ə-,fȯrm, 'klȯr-\ *n* [F *chloroforme,* fr. *chlor-* + *formyle* formyl; fr. its having been regarded as a trichloride of this group] (1838) : a colorless volatile heavy toxic liquid $CHCl_3$ with an ether odor used esp. as a solvent or as a veterinary anesthetic

[2]**chloroform** *vt* (1848) : to treat with or as if with chloroform esp. so as to produce anesthesia, insensibility, or death

chlo·ro·gen·ic acid \,klōr-ə-,jen-ik-, ,klȯr-\ *n* (ca. 1889) : a crystalline acid $C_{16}H_{18}O_9$ occurring in various plant parts (as coffee beans)

chlo·ro·hy·drin \,klōr-ə-'hī-drən, ,klȯr-\ *n* [ISV, fr. *chlor-* + *hydr-*] (ca. 1890) : any of various organic compounds derived from glycols or polyhydroxy alcohols by substitution of chlorine for part of the hydroxyl groups

Chlo·ro·my·ce·tin \,klōr-ō-mī-'sēt-ᵊn, ,klȯr-\ *trademark* — used for chloramphenicol

chlo·ro·phyll \'klōr-ə-,fil, 'klȯr-, -fəl\ *n* [F *chlorophylle,* fr. *chlor-* + Gk *phyllon* leaf — more at BLADE] (1819) **1** : the green photosynthetic coloring matter of plants found in chloroplasts and made up chiefly of a blue-black ester $C_{55}H_{72}MgN_4O_5$ and a dark green ester $C_{55}H_{70}MgN_4O_6$ — called also respectively *chlorophyll a, chlorophyll b* **2** : a waxy green chlorophyll-containing substance extracted from green plants and used as a coloring agent or deodorant — **chlo·ro·phyl·lous** \,klōr-ə-'fil-əs, ,klȯr-\ *also* **chlo·ro·phyl·lose** \-'fil-,ōs, -(,)fil-'\ *adj*

chlo·ro·pic·rin \,klōr-ə-'pik-rən, ,klȯr-\ *n* [G *chlorpikrin,* fr. *chlor-* + Gk *pikros* sharp — more at PAINT] (ca. 1889) : a colorless liquid CCl_3NO_2 that causes tears and vomiting and is used esp. as a soil fumigant

chlo·ro·plast \'klōr-ə-,plast, 'klȯr-\ *n* [ISV] (1887) : a plastid that contains chlorophyll and is the site of photosynthesis and starch formation — see CELL illustration — **chlo·ro·plas·tic** \,klōr-ə-'plas-tik, ,klȯr-\ *adj*

chlo·ro·prene \-,prēn\ *n* [*chlor-* + iso*prene*] (1931) : a colorless liquid C_4H_5Cl used esp. in making neoprene by polymerization

chlo·ro·quine \'klōr-ə-,kwēn, 'klȯr-\ *n* [*chlor-* + *quinoline*] (1946) : an antimalarial drug $C_{18}H_{26}ClN_3$ administered as the bitter crystalline diphosphate

chlo·ro·sis \klə-'rō-səs\ *n* (1678) **1** : an iron-deficiency anemia in young girls characterized by a greenish color of the skin — called also *greensickness* **2** : a diseased condition in green plants marked by yellowing or blanching — **chlo·rot·ic** \-'rät-ik\ *adj* — **chlo·rot·i·cal·ly** \-i-k(ə-)lē\ *adv*

chlo·ro·thi·a·zide \,klōr-ə-'thī-ə-,zīd, ,klȯr-, -zəd\ *n* (ca. 1931) : a thiazide diuretic $C_7H_6ClN_3O_4S_2$ used esp. to treat edema and to increase the effectiveness of antihypertensive drugs

chlo·rous \'klōr-əs, 'klȯr-\ *adj* (1845) : relating to or obtained from chlorine esp. with a valence of three

chlor·prom·a·zine \klōr-'präm-ə-,zēn, klȯr-\ *n* [*chlor-* + *propyl* + *methyl* + *phenothiazine*] (1952) : a phenothiazine derivative $C_{17}H_{19}ClN_2S$ used as a tranquilizer esp. in the form of its hydrochloride to suppress the more flagrant symptoms of disturbed behavior (as in schizophrenia)

chlor·prop·amide \-'präp-ə-,mīd, -'prōp-\ *n* [*chlor-* + *propane* + *amide*] (1960) : a sulfonyl urea drug $C_{10}H_{13}ClN_2O_3S$ used orally to reduce blood sugar in the treatment of mild diabetes

chlor·tet·ra·cy·cline \,klōr-,te-trə-'sī-,klēn, ,klȯr-\ *n* (1953) : a yellow crystalline antibiotic $C_{22}H_{23}ClN_2O_8$ produced by a soil actinomycete (*Streptomyces aureofaciens*), used in the treatment of diseases, and added to animal feeds for stimulating growth

cho·ano·cyte \kō-'an-ə-,sīt\ *n* [ISV *choan-* funnel-shaped (fr. Gk *choanē* funnel) + *-cyte*] (1888) : COLLAR CELL

[1]**chock** \'chäk\ *n* [origin unknown] (1769) **1** : a wedge or block for steadying a body (as a cask) and holding it motionless, for filling in an unwanted space, or for blocking the movement of a wheel **2** : a heavy metal casting (as on the bow or stern of a ship) with two short horn-shaped arms curving inward between which ropes or hawsers may pass for mooring or towing

[2]**chock** *adv* (1834) : as closely or as completely as possible

[3]**chock** *vt* (1840) : to stop or make fast with or as if with chocks

[1]**chock·a·block** \'chäk-ə-,bläk\ *adv* (1840) : CHOCK ⟨~ full⟩

[2]**chockablock** *adj* (ca. 1890) **1** : brought close together **2** : very full

chock–full *or* **chock·ful** \'chək-'fu̇l, 'chäk-\ *adj* [ME *chokkefull,* prob. fr. *choken* to choke + *full*] (15c) : full to the limit : CRAMMED

choc·o·hol·ic \,chäk-ə-'hȯl-ik, ,chȯk-, -'häl-\ *n* [*chocolate* + *-holic* (as in *alcoholic*)] (1968) : a person who craves or compulsively consumes chocolate

choc·o·late \'chäk-(ə-)lət, 'chȯk-\ *n* [Sp, fr. Nahuatl *xocoatl*] (1604) **1** : a beverage made by mixing chocolate with water or milk **2** : a food prepared from ground roasted cacao beans **3** : a small candy with a center (as a fondant) and a chocolate coating **4** : a variable color averaging a brownish gray — **chocolate** *adj*

chocolate–box *adj* [fr. the pictures formerly commonly seen on boxes of chocolates] (1901) : superficially pretty or sentimental

choc·o·laty *or* **choc·o·lat·ey** \'chäk-(ə-)lət-ē, 'chȯk-\ *adj* (1926) : made of or like chocolate; *also* : having a rich chocolate flavor

Choc·taw \'chäk-(,)tȯ\ *n, pl* **Choctaw** *or* **Choctaws** [Choctaw *Chahta*] (1722) **1** : a member of an American Indian people of Mississippi, Alabama, and Louisiana **2** : the language of the Choctaw and Chickasaw people

[1]**choice** \'chȯis\ *n* [ME *chois,* fr. OF, fr. *choisir* to choose, of Gmc origin; akin to OHG *kiosan* to choose — more at CHOOSE] (13c) **1** : the act of choosing : SELECTION **2** : power of choosing : OPTION **3 a** : the best part : CREAM **b** : a person or thing chosen **4** : a sufficient number

and variety to choose among **5 :** care in selecting **6 :** a grade of meat between prime and good — **of choice :** to be preferred
syn CHOICE, OPTION, ALTERNATIVE, PREFERENCE, SELECTION, ELECTION mean the act or opportunity of choosing or the thing chosen. CHOICE suggests the opportunity or privilege of choosing freely; OPTION implies a power to choose that is specifically granted or guaranteed; ALTERNATIVE implies a necessity to choose one and reject another possibility; PREFERENCE suggests the guidance of choice by one's judgment or predilections; SELECTION implies a wide range of choice; ELECTION implies an end or purpose which requires exercise of judgment.

[2]**choice** *adj* **choic·er; choic·est** (14c) **1 :** worthy of being chosen **:** SELECT **2 :** selected with care **3 a :** of high quality **b :** of a grade between prime and good ⟨~ meat⟩ — **choice·ly** *adv* — **choice·ness** *n*
syn CHOICE, EXQUISITE, ELEGANT, RARE, DAINTY, DELICATE mean having qualities that appeal to a cultivated taste. CHOICE stresses preeminence in quality or kind; EXQUISITE implies a perfection in workmanship or design that appeals only to very sensitive taste; ELEGANT applies to what is rich and luxurious but restrained by good taste; RARE suggests an uncommon excellence; DAINTY and DELICATE both imply exquisiteness, subtlety, fragility, but DAINTY sometimes carries an additional suggestion of smallness and of appeal to the eye or palate.

[1]**choir** \ˈkwī(-ə)r\ *n* [ME *quer,* fr. MF *cuer,* fr. ML *chorus,* fr. L, chorus — more at CHORUS] (14c) **1 :** an organized company of singers esp. in church service **2 :** a group of instruments of the same class ⟨a brass ~⟩ **3 :** an organized group of persons or things **4 :** a division of angels **5 :** the part of a church occupied by the singers or by the clergy; *also* **:** the part of a church where the services are performed **6 :** a group organized for ensemble speaking

[2]**choir** *vi* (1596) **:** to sing or sound in chorus or concert

choir·boy \ˈkwī(-ə)r-ˌbȯi\ *n* (1837) **:** a boy member of a choir

choir loft *n* (1929) **:** a gallery occupied by a church choir

choir·mas·ter \-ˌmas-tər\ *n* (1860) **:** the director of a choir (as in a church)

[1]**choke** \ˈchōk\ *vb* **choked; chok·ing** [ME *choken,* alter. of *achoken,* fr. OE *acēocian*] *vt* (14c) **1 :** to check normal breathing of by compressing or obstructing the windpipe or by poisoning or adulterating available air **2 a :** to check the growth, development, or activity of ⟨the flowers were *choked* by the weeds⟩ **b :** to obstruct by filling up or clogging ⟨leaves *choked* the drain⟩ **c :** to fill completely **:** JAM ⟨dandelions *choked* the strips of lawn dividing the auto lanes —Herman Wouk⟩ **3 :** to enrich the fuel mixture of (a motor) by partially shutting off the air intake of the carburetor **4 :** to grip (as a baseball bat) some distance from the end of the handle **~** *vi* **1 :** to become choked in breathing **2 a :** to become obstructed or checked **b :** to become or feel constricted in the throat (as from strong emotion) — usu. used with *up* ⟨*choked* up and couldn't finish the speech⟩ **3 :** to shorten one's grip esp. on the handle of a bat — usu. used with *up* **4 :** to lose one's composure and fail to perform effectively in a critical situation

[2]**choke** *n* (1786) **1 :** something that obstructs passage or flow: as **a :** a valve for choking a gasoline engine **b :** a constriction in an outlet (as of an oil well) that restricts flow **c :** REACTOR 2 **d :** a narrowing toward the muzzle in the bore of a shotgun to constrict the shot pattern **e :** an attachment that allows variation of muzzle constriction of a shotgun **2 :** the act of choking **3 :** the filamentous center of an artichoke head

choke·ber·ry \-ˌber-ē\ *n* (1778) **:** a small berrylike astringent fruit; *also* **:** a shrub (genus *Aronia*) of the rose family bearing chokeberries

choke chain *n* (1948) **:** a collar that may be tightened as a noose and that is used esp. in training and controlling powerful or stubborn dogs — called also *choke collar*

choke·cher·ry \ˈchōk-ˌcher-ē, -ˈcher-\ *n* (1784) **:** any of several American wild cherries (esp. *Prunus virginiana*) with bitter or astringent fruit; *also* **:** this fruit

choke coil *n* (ca. 1896) **:** REACTOR 2

choke·damp \ˈchōk-ˌdamp\ *n* (1741) **:** BLACKDAMP

choke off *vt* (1818) **:** to bring to a stop or to an end as if by choking

chok·er \ˈchō-kər\ *n* (1552) **1 :** one that chokes **2 :** something (as a collar or necklace) worn closely about the throat or neck

chok·ing \ˈchō-kiŋ\ *adj* (1562) **1 :** producing the feeling of strangulation ⟨a ~ cloud of smog⟩ **2 :** indistinct in utterance — used esp. of a person's voice ⟨a low ~ laugh⟩ — **chok·ing·ly** \-kiŋ-lē\ *adv*

choky \ˈchō-kē\ *adj* (1579) **:** tending to cause choking or to become choked

chol- *or* **chole-** *or* **cholo-** *comb form* [Gk *chol-, cholē-, cholo-,* fr. *cholē, cholos* — more at GALL] **:** bile **:** gall ⟨*chol*ate⟩ ⟨*chole*lith⟩

chol·an·gi·og·ra·phy \kə-ˌlan-jē-ˈäg-rə-fē, (ˌ)kō-\ *n* (1936) **:** roentgenographic visualization of the bile ducts after ingestion or injection of a radiopaque substance — **chol·an·gio·graph·ic** \-jē-ə-ˈgraf-ik\ *adj*

cho·late \ˈkō-ˌlāt\ *n* (1845) **:** a salt or ester of cholic acid

cho·le·cal·cif·er·ol \ˌkō-lə-(ˌ)kal-ˈsif-ə-ˌrōl, -ˌrȯl\ *n* [ISV, fr. *chol-* + *calciferol*] (ca. 1931) **:** an alcohol $C_{27}H_{43}OH$ that is the predominating form of vitamin D in most fish-liver oils and is formed in the skin on exposure to sunlight or ultraviolet rays — called also *vitamin* D_3

cho·le·cys·tec·to·my \-(ˌ)sis-ˈtek-tə-mē\ *n, pl* **-mies** [NL *cholecystis* gallbladder (fr. *chol-* + Gk *kystis* bladder) + ISV *-ectomy* — more at CYST] (1885) **:** surgical excision of the gallbladder — **cho·le·cys·tec·to·mized** \-ˌmīzd\ *adj*

cho·le·cys·ti·tis \-ˈtīt-əs\ *n* [NL, fr. *cholecystis*] (1866) **:** inflammation of the gallbladder

cho·le·cys·to·ki·nin \-ˌsis-tə-ˈkī-nən\ *n* [NL *cholecystis* + E *-o-* + *kinin*] (ca. 1929) **:** a hormone secreted by the duodenal mucosa that regulates the emptying of the gallbladder and secretion of enzymes by the pancreas — called also *cholecystokinin-pancreozymin, pancreozymin*

cho·le·li·thi·a·sis \ˌkō-li-lith-ˈī-ə-səs\ *n* [NL *chol-* + *lithiasis*] (ca. 1860) **:** production of gallstones; *also* **:** the resulting abnormal condition

cho·ler \ˈkäl-ər, ˈkō-lər\ *n* [ME *coler,* fr. MF *colere,* fr. L *cholera* bilious disease, fr. Gk, fr. *cholē*] (14c) **1 a** *archaic* **:** YELLOW BILE **b** *obs* **:** BILE 1a **2** *obs* **:** the quality or state of being bilious **3 :** the quality or state of being irascible

chol·era \ˈkäl-ə-rə\ *n* [ME *colera* bile, fr. L *cholera*] (14c) **:** any of several diseases of man and domestic animals usu. marked by severe gastrointestinal symptoms; *esp* **:** an acute diarrheal disease caused by an enterotoxin produced by a comma-shaped gram-negative bacillus (*Vibrio cholerae*) when it is present in large numbers in the proximal part of the human small intestine — compare ASIATIC CHOLERA

chol·era mor·bus \ˌkäl-ə-rə-ˈmȯr-bəs\ *n* [NL, lit., the disease cholera] (1673) **:** a gastrointestinal disturbance characterized by griping, diarrhea, and sometimes vomiting — not used technically

cho·ler·ic \ˈkäl-ə-rik, kə-ˈler-ik\ *adj* (1583) **1 :** easily moved to often unreasonable or excessive anger **:** hot-tempered **2 :** ANGRY, IRATE — **cho·ler·i·cal·ly** \-ri-k(ə-)lē, -i-k(ə-)lē\ *adv*

cho·le·sta·sis \ˌkō-lə-ˈstā-səs\ *n, pl* **-sta·ses** \-ˌsēz\ [NL *chol-* + *stasis*] (ca. 1931) **:** a checking or failure of bile flow — **cho·le·stat·ic** \-ˈstat-ik\ *adj*

cho·le·ster·ic \-ˈster-ik, kə-ˈles-tə-rik\ *adj* [*cholesteric* relating to cholesterol, fr. F *cholesterique*] (1942) **:** of, relating to, or being the phase of a liquid crystal characterized by arrangement of molecules in layers with the long molecular axes parallel to one another in the plane of each layer and incrementally displaced in successive layers to give helical stacking — compare NEMATIC, SMECTIC

cho·les·ter·ol \kə-ˈles-tə-ˌrōl, -ˌrȯl\ *n* [ISV, fr. *chol-* + Gk *stereos* solid] (1894) **:** a steroid alcohol $C_{27}H_{45}OH$ present in animal cells and body fluids, important in physiological processes, and implicated experimentally as a factor in arteriosclerosis

cho·le·styr·amine \(ˌ)kō-ˌles-tə-ˈram-ˌēn, kə-; ˌkō-lə-ˈstir-ə-ˌmēn\ *n* [perh. *chol-* + *styr-* (alter. of *sterol*) + *amine*] (ca. 1962) **:** a basic resin that forms insoluble complexes with bile acids and has been used to lower cholesterol levels in hypercholesterolemic patients

cho·lic acid \ˌkō-lik-\ *n* [Gk *cholikos* bilious, fr. *cholē*] (1846) **:** a crystalline bile acid $C_{24}H_{40}O_5$

cho·line \ˈkō-ˌlēn\ *n* [ISV] (1869) **:** a base $C_5H_{15}NO_2$ that occurs in many animal and plant products and is a vitamin of the B complex essential to the liver function

cho·lin·er·gic \ˌkō-lə-ˈnər-jik\ *adj* [ISV acetyl*choline* + *-ergic*] (1934) **1** *of autonomic nerve fibers* **:** liberating or activated by acetylcholine **2 :** resembling acetylcholine esp. in physiologic action — **cho·lin·er·gi·cal·ly** \-ji-k(ə-)lē\ *adv*

cho·lin·es·ter·ase \ˌkō-lə-ˈnes-tə-ˌrās, -ˌrāz\ *n* (1932) **1 :** ACETYLCHOLINESTERASE **2 :** an enzyme that hydrolyzes choline esters and that is found esp. in blood plasma — called also *pseudocholinesterase*

cho·li·no·lyt·ic \ˌkō-lə-nō-ˈlit-ik\ *adj* [*choline* + *-o-* + *-lytic*] (1960) **:** interfering with the action of acetylcholine or cholinergic agents — **cholinolytic** *n*

chol·la \ˈchȯi-(y)ə\ *n* [MexSp, fr. Sp, head] (1846) **:** any of several arborescent very spiny cacti (genus *Opuntia*) of the southwestern U.S. and Mexico

chomp \ˈchämp, ˈchȯmp\ *vb* [alter. of *champ*] *vi* (ca. 1847) **:** to chew or bite on something **~** *vt* **:** to chew or bite on

chon \ˈchän\ *n, pl* **chon** [Korean] — see *won* at MONEY table

chondr- *or* **chondri-** *or* **chondro-** *comb form* [NL, fr. Gk *chondr-, chondro-,* fr. *chondros* grain, cartilage] **:** cartilage ⟨*chondro*cranium⟩

chon·drio·some \ˈkän-drē-ə-ˌsōm\ *n* [Gk *chondrion,* dim. of *chondros* + ISV *-some*] (1910) **:** MITOCHONDRION

chon·drite \ˈkän-ˌdrīt\ *n* [ISV, fr. Gk *chondros* grain] (1883) **:** a meteoric stone characterized by the presence of chondrules — **chon·drit·ic** \kän-ˈdrit-ik\ *adj*

chon·dro·cra·ni·um \ˌkän-drō-ˈkrā-nē-əm\ *n* (1875) **:** the embryonic cartilaginous cranium; *also* **:** the part of the adult skull derived therefrom

chon·droi·tin \kän-ˈdrȯit-ᵊn, -ˈdrō-ət-ᵊn\ *n* [ISV *chondroit*ic acid (an acid found in cartilage) + *-in*] (ca. 1900) **:** a mucopolysaccharide occurring in sulfated form in various animal tissues (as cartilage and tendons)

chon·drule \ˈkän-(ˌ)drül\ *n* [Gk *chondros* grain] (1889) **:** a rounded granule of cosmic origin often found embedded in meteoric stones and sometimes free in marine sediments

choose \ˈchüz\ *vb* **chose** \ˈchōz\; **cho·sen** \ˈchōz-ᵊn\; **choos·ing** \ˈchü-ziŋ\ [ME *chosen,* fr. OE *cēosan;* akin to OHG *kiosan* to choose, L *gustare* to taste] *vt* (bef. 12c) **1 a :** to select freely and after consideration ⟨~ a career⟩ **b :** to decide on esp. by vote **:** ELECT ⟨*chose* her president⟩ **2 a :** to have a preference for ⟨~ one bank over another⟩ **b :** DECIDE ⟨*chose* to go by train⟩ **~** *vi* **1 :** to make a selection **2 :** to take an alternative — used after *cannot* and usu. followed by *but* ⟨when earth is so kind, men cannot ~ but be happy —J. A. Froude⟩ — **choos·er** \ˈchü-zər\ *n*

choose up *vt* (ca. 1925) **:** to form (sides) esp. for a game by having opposing captains choose their players **~** *vi* **:** to form sides for a game ⟨let's *choose up* and play ball⟩

choosy *or* **choos·ey** \ˈchü-zē\ *adj* **choos·i·er; -est** (1862) **:** fastidiously selective **:** PARTICULAR

[1]**chop** \ˈchäp\ *vb* **chopped; chop·ping** [ME *chappen, choppen* — more at CHAP] *vt* (14c) **1 a :** to cut into or sever usu. by repeated blows of a sharp instrument **b :** to cut into pieces — often used with *up* **c :** to weed and thin out (young cotton) **d :** to cut as if by chopping ⟨~ prices⟩ **2 :** to strike (as a ball) with a short quick downward stroke **3 :** to subject to the action of a chopper ⟨~ a beam of light⟩ **~** *vi* **1 :** to make a quick stroke or repeated strokes with or as if with a sharp instrument (as an ax) **2** *archaic* **:** to move or act suddenly or violently

[2]**chop** *n* (14c) **1 a :** a forceful usu. slanting blow with or as if with an ax or cleaver **b :** a sharp downward blow or stroke **2 :** a small cut of meat often including part of a rib — see LAMB illustration **3 :** a mark made by or as if by chopping **4 :** material that has been chopped up **5 a :** a short abrupt motion (as of a wave) **b :** a stretch of choppy sea **6 :** CHOPPER 5

[3]**chop** *n* [Hindi *chāp* stamp] (1614) **1 a :** a seal or official stamp or its impression **b :** a license validated by a seal **2 a :** a mark on goods or coins to indicate nature or quality **b :** a kind, brand, or lot of goods bearing the same chop **c :** QUALITY, GRADE ⟨a chef of the first ~⟩

[4]**chop** *vi* **chopped; chop·ping** [ME *chappen, choppen* to barter, fr. OE *cēapian*] (1642) **1 :** to change direction **2 :** to veer with or as if with wind — **chop logic :** to argue with sophistical reasoning and minute distinctions

chop–chop \ˈchäp-ˌchäp\ *adv* [Pidgin E, redupl. of *chop* fast — more at CHOPSTICK] (1834) **:** without delay **:** QUICKLY

chop·fall·en \ˈchäp-ˌfȯ-lən\ *var of* CHAPFALLEN

chop·house \ˈchäp-ˌhau̇s\ *n* (1690) **:** RESTAURANT

cho·pine \shä-'pēn, chä-\ *n* [MF *chapin,* fr. OSp] (1577) **:** a woman's shoe of the 16th and 17th centuries with a very high sole designed to increase stature and protect the feet from mud and dirt

chop·log·ic \'chäp-,läj-ik\ *n* [obs. *chop* (to exchange, trade), fr. ME *choppen* to barter] (1533) **:** involved and often specious argumentation — **choplogic** *adj*

chop mark *n* (1949) **:** an indentation made on a coin to attest weight, silver content, or legality — **chop–marked** \'chäp-,märkt\ *adj*

[1]**chop·per** \'chäp-ər\ *n* (1552) **1 :** one that chops **2** *pl, slang* **:** TEETH **3 :** a device that interrupts an electric current or a beam of radiation (as light) at short regular intervals **4 :** HELICOPTER **5 :** a high-bouncing batted baseball **6 :** a customized motorcycle

[2]**chopper** *vb* (1955) **:** HELICOPTER

chop·pi·ness \'chäp-ē-nəs\ *n* (1881) **:** the quality or state of being choppy

chopping block *n* (1703) **:** a wooden block on which material (as meat, wood, or vegetables) is cut, split, or diced

[1]**chop·py** \'chäp-ē\ *adj* **chop·pi·er; -est** [[2]*chop*] (1605) **:** being roughened **:** CHAPPED

[2]**choppy** *adj* **chop·pi·er; -est** [[4]*chop*] (1865) **:** CHANGEABLE, VARIABLE ⟨a ~ wind⟩

[3]**choppy** *adj* **choppier; -est** [[1]*chop*] (1867) **1 :** rough with small waves **2 :** JERKY, DISCONNECTED ⟨a ~ style of writing⟩ — **chop·pi·ly** \'chäp-ə-lē\ *adv*

chops \'chäps\ *n pl* [alter. of [4]*chap*] (1589) **1 :** JAW **2 a :** MOUTH **b :** the fleshy covering of the jaws ⟨a dog licking its ~⟩ **3** *slang* **:** EMBOUCHURE; *broadly* **:** the technical facility of a musical performer

chop·stick \'chäp-,stik\ *n* [Pidgin E, fr. *chop* fast (of Chinese origin; akin to Cant *kap*) + E *stick*] (1699) **:** one of a pair of slender sticks held between thumb and fingers and used chiefly in oriental countries to lift food to the mouth

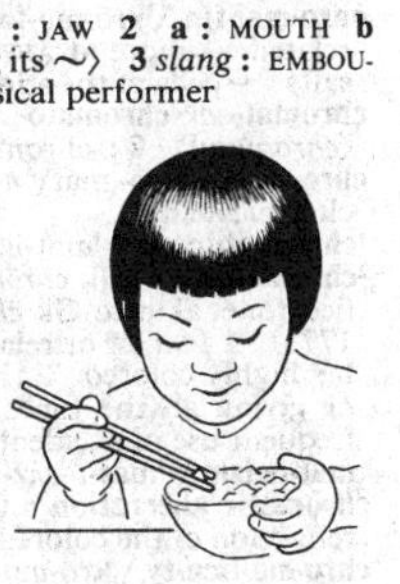

chopsticks

chop su·ey \chäp-'sü-ē\ *n, pl* **chop sueys** [Chin (Cant) *shap sui* odds and ends, fr. *shap* miscellaneous + *sui* bits] (1888) **:** a dish prepared chiefly from bean sprouts, bamboo shoots, water chestnuts, onions, mushrooms, and meat or fish and served with rice and soy sauce

cho·ra·gus \kə-'rā-gəs\ *or* **cho·re·gus** \-'rē-, -'rā-\ *n* [L & Gk; L *choragus,* fr. Gk *choragos, chorēgos,* fr. *choros* chorus + *agein* to lead — more at AGENT] (1625) **1 :** the leader of a chorus or choir; *broadly* **:** the leader of any group or movement **2 :** a leader of a dramatic chorus in ancient Greece — **cho·rag·ic** \-'raj-ik\ *adj*

cho·ral \'kōr-əl, 'kȯr-\ *adj* [F or ML; F *choral,* fr. ML *choralis,* fr. L *chorus*] (1587) **1 :** of or relating to a chorus or choir ⟨a ~ group⟩ **2 :** sung or designed for singing by a choir ⟨a ~ arrangement⟩ — **cho·ral·ly** \-ə-lē\ *adv*

cho·rale *also* **cho·ral** \kə-'ral, -'räl\ *n* [G *choral,* short for *choralgesang* choral song] (1841) **1 :** a hymn or psalm sung to a traditional or composed melody in church; *also* **:** a harmonization of a chorale melody ⟨a Bach ~⟩ **2 :** CHORUS, CHOIR

chorale prelude *n* (ca. 1924) **:** a composition usu. for organ based on a chorale

[1]**chord** \'kȯ(ə)rd\ *n* [alter. of ME *cord,* short for *accord*] (14c) **:** three or more musical tones sounded simultaneously

[2]**chord** *vi* (14c) **1 :** ACCORD **2 :** to play chords esp. on a stringed instrument ~ *vt* **1 :** to make chords on **2 :** HARMONIZE

[3]**chord** *n* [alter. of [1]*cord*] (15c) **1 :** CORD 3a **2 :** a straight line joining two points on a curve; *specif* **:** the segment of a secant between its intersections with a curve **3 :** an individual emotion or disposition ⟨struck a responsive ~⟩ **4 :** either of the two outside members of a truss connected and braced by the web members **5 :** the straight line joining the leading and trailing edges of an airfoil

chord·al \'kȯrd-ᵊl\ *adj* (1848) **1 :** of, relating to, or suggesting a chord **2 :** relating to music characterized more by harmony than by counterpoint

chor·da·meso·derm \,kȯrd-ə-'mez-ə-,dərm *also* -'mes-\ *n* [NL *chorda* cord + E *mesoderm*] (1939) **:** the portion of the embryonic mesoderm that forms notochord and related structures and induces the formation of neural structures — **chor·da·meso·der·mal** \-,mez-ə-'dər-məl, -,mes-\ *adj*

chor·date \'kȯrd-ət, 'kȯ(ə)r-,dāt\ *n* [deriv. of L *chorda* cord] (1897) **:** any of a phylum or subkingdom (Chordata) of animals having at least at some stage of development a notochord, dorsally situated central nervous system, and gill clefts and including the vertebrates, lancelets, and tunicates — **chordate** *adj*

chord organ *n* (1953) **:** an electronic organ with buttons to produce simple chords

chore \'chō(ə)r, 'chȯ(ə)r\ *n* [alter. of *chare*] (1751) **1** *pl* **:** the regular or daily light work of a household or farm **2 :** a routine task or job **3 :** a difficult or disagreeable task ***syn*** see TASK

-chore \,kō(ə)r, ,kȯ(ə)r\ *n comb form* [Gk *chōrein* to withdraw, go; akin to Gk *chēros* bereaved — more at HEIR] **:** plant distributed by (such) an agency ⟨zoochore⟩ — **-cho·rous** \'kōr-əs, 'kȯr-\ *adj comb form* — **-cho·ry** \,kōr-ē, ,kȯr-\ *n comb form*

cho·rea \kə-'rē-ə\ *n* [NL, fr. L, dance, fr. Gk *choreia,* fr. *choros* chorus] (1804) **:** a nervous disorder (as of man or dogs) marked by spasmodic movements of limbs and facial muscles and by incoordination — **cho·re·ic** \-'rē-ik\ *adj*

cho·re·i·form \kə-'rē-ə-,fȯ(ə)rm\ *adj* [ISV] (ca. 1909) **:** resembling chorea ⟨~ convulsions⟩

cho·reo·graph \'kōr-ē-ə-,graf, 'kȯr-\ *vt* (1943) **1 :** to compose the choreography of **2 :** to arrange or direct the movements, progress, or details of ~ *vi* **:** to engage in choreography — **cho·re·og·ra·pher** \,kōr-ē-'äg-rə-fər, ,kȯr-\ *n*

cho·re·og·ra·phy \,kōr-ē-'äg-rə-fē, ,kȯr-\ *n, pl* **-phies** [F *chorégraphie,* fr. Gk *choreia* + F *-graphie* -graphy] (1789) **1 :** the art of symbolically representing dancing **2 a :** the composition and arrangement of dances esp. for ballet **b :** a composition created by this art **3 :** something resembling choreography ⟨a snail-paced ~ of delicate high diplomacy —Wolfgang Saxon⟩ — **cho·reo·graph·ic** \,kōr-ē-ə-'graf-ik, ,kȯr-\ *adj* — **cho·reo·graph·i·cal·ly** \-i-k(ə-)lē\ *adv*

cho·ric \'kōr-ik, 'kȯr-, 'kär-\ *adj* (1830) **:** of, relating to, or being in the style of a chorus and esp. a Greek chorus

cho·rine \'kō(ə)r-,ēn, 'kȯ(ə)r-\ *n* [*chorus* + *-ine*] (1922) **:** CHORUS GIRL

cho·rio·al·lan·to·is \,kōr-ē-(,)ō-ə-'lant-ə-wəs, ,kȯr-\ *n* [NL, fr. Gk *chorion* + NL *allantois*] (1933) **:** a vascular fetal membrane composed of the fused chorion and adjacent wall of the allantois that in the hen's egg is used as a living culture medium for viruses and for tissues — **cho·rio·al·lan·to·ic** \-,al-ən-'tō-ik\ *adj*

cho·rio·car·ci·no·ma \-,kärs-ᵊn-'ō-mə\ *n* [NL, fr. *chorion* + *carcinoma*] (ca. 1901) **:** a malignant tumor developing in the uterus from trophoblast and rarely in the testes from a neoplasm

cho·ri·on \'kōr-ē-,än, 'kȯr-\ *n* [NL, fr. Gk] (1545) **:** the highly vascular outer embryonic membrane of higher vertebrates that in placental mammals is associated with the allantois in the formation of the placenta

cho·ri·on·ic \,kōr-ē-'än-ik, ,kȯr-\ *adj* (1892) **1 :** of, relating to, or being part of the chorion ⟨~ villi⟩ **2 :** secreted or produced by chorionic or a related tissue (as in the placenta or a choriocarcinoma) ⟨human ~ gonadotropin⟩

cho·ris·ter \'kōr-ə-stər, 'kȯr-, 'kär-\ *n* [ME *querister,* fr. AF *cueristre,* fr. ML *chorista,* fr. L *chorus*] (14c) **1 :** a singer in a choir; *specif* **:** CHOIRBOY **2 :** the leader of a church choir

cho·ri·zo \chə-'rē-(,)zō, -(,)sō\ *n, pl* **-zos** [Sp] (1846) **:** pork sausage highly seasoned esp. with chili powder and garlic

C–horizon *n* (1935) **:** the layer of a soil profile lying beneath the B-horizon and consisting essentially of more or less weathered parent rock

cho·rog·ra·phy \kə-'räg-rə-fē\ *n* [L *chorographia,* fr. Gk *chōrographia,* fr. *chōros* place + *-graphia* -graphy] (1559) **1 :** the art of describing or mapping a region or district **2 :** a description or map of a region; *also* **:** the physical conformation and features of such a region — **cho·rog·ra·pher** \-rə-fər\ *n* — **cho·ro·graph·ic** \,kȯr-ə-'graf-ik, ,kär-\ *adj*

cho·roid \'kō(ə)r-,ȯid, 'kȯ(ə)r-\ *also* **cho·ri·oid** \'kōr-ē-,ȯid, 'kȯr-\ *n* [NL *choroides* resembling the chorion, fr. Gk *chorioeidēs,* fr. *chorion* chorion] (1683) **:** a vascular membrane containing large branched pigment cells that lies between the retina and the sclera of the vertebrate eye — called also *choroid coat* — see EYE illustration — **choroid** *or* **cho·roi·dal** \kə-'rȯid-ᵊl\ *adj*

chor·tle \'chȯrt-ᵊl\ *vb* **chor·tled; chor·tling** \'chȯrt-liŋ, -ᵊl-iŋ\ [blend of *chuckle* and *snort*] *vi* (1872) **1 :** to sing or chant exultantly ⟨he *chortled* in his joy —Lewis Carroll⟩ **2 :** to laugh or chuckle esp. in satisfaction or exultation ~ *vt* **:** to say or sing with a chortling intonation — **chortle** *n* — **chor·tler** \'chȯrt-lər, -ᵊl-ər\ *n*

[1]**cho·rus** \'kōr-əs, 'kȯr-\ *n* [L, ring dance, chorus, fr. Gk *choros*] (1606) **1 a :** a company of singers and dancers in Athenian drama participating in or commenting on the action; *also* **:** a similar company in later plays **b :** a character in Elizabethan drama who speaks the prologue and epilogue and comments on the action **c :** an organized company of singers who sing in concert **:** CHOIR; *specif* **:** a body of singers who sing the choral parts of a work (as in opera) **d :** a group of dancers and singers supporting the featured players in a musical comedy or revue **2 a :** a part of a song or hymn recurring at intervals **b :** the part of a drama sung or spoken by the chorus **c :** a composition to be sung by a number of voices in concert **d :** the main part of a popular song; *also* **:** a jazz variation on a melodic theme **3 a :** something performed, sung, or uttered simultaneously by a number of persons or animals ⟨a ~ of boos⟩ ⟨that eternal ~ of "Are we there yet?" from the back seat —Sheila More⟩ **b :** sounds so uttered ⟨visitors are taken to the woods by car to hear the mournful ~*es* of howling wolves —Bob Gaines⟩ — **in chorus :** in unison

[2]**chorus** *vt* (1826) **:** to sing or utter in chorus

chorus boy *n* (1943) **:** a young man who sings or dances in the chorus of a theatrical production (as a musical or revue)

chorus girl *n* (1894) **:** a young woman who sings or dances in the chorus of a theatrical production (as a musical or revue)

[1]**chose** *past of* CHOOSE

[2]**chose** \'shōz\ *n* [F, fr. L *causa* cause, reason] (1670) **:** a piece of personal property **:** THING

[1]**cho·sen** \'chōz-ᵊn\ *n, pl* **chosen** (13c) **:** one who is the object of choice or of divine favor **:** an elect person

[2]**chosen** *adj* [ME, fr. pp. of *chosen* to choose] (14c) **1 :** selected or marked for favor or special privilege ⟨a ~ few⟩ **2 :** ELECT

chott \'shät\ *n* [F *chott,* fr. Ar *shaṭṭ*] (1877) **:** a shallow saline lake of northern Africa; *also* **:** the dried bed of such a lake

Chou \'jō\ *n* [Chin (Pek) *Chou*[1]] **:** a Chinese dynasty traditionally dated 1122 to about 256 B.C. and marked by the development of the philosophical schools of Confucius, Mencius, Lao-tzu, and Mo Ti

chough \'chəf\ *n* [ME] (13c) **:** either of two Old World birds (*Pyrrhocorax pyrrhocorax* and *P. graculus*) that are related to the crows and have red legs and glossy black plumage

[1]**chouse** \'chau̇s\ *vt* **choused; chous·ing** [Turk *çavuş* doorkeeper, messenger] (1708) **:** CHEAT, TRICK

[2]**chouse** *vt* **choused; chous·ing** [origin unknown] *West* (1920) **:** to drive or herd roughly

[1]**chow** \'chau̇\ *n* [perh. fr. Chin (Pek) *chiao*[3] dough filled with meat] (1856) **:** FOOD, VICTUALS

[2]**chow** *vi* (1917) **:** EAT — often used with *down*

[3]**chow** *n* [by shortening] (1889) **:** CHOW CHOW

chow·chow \'chau̇-,chau̇\ *n* [Pidgin E] (1850) **1 :** a Chinese preserve of ginger, fruits, and peels in heavy syrup **2 :** a relish of chopped mixed pickles in mustard sauce

chow chow \'chau̇-,chau̇\ *n, often cap both Cs* [fr. a Chin dial. word akin to Cant *kaú* dog] (ca. 1886) **:** a heavy-coated blocky dog with a broad

\ə\ abut \ᵊ\ kitten, F table \ər\ further \a\ ash \ā\ ace \ä\ cot, cart \au̇\ out \ch\ chin \e\ bet \ē\ easy \g\ go \i\ hit \ī\ ice \j\ job \ŋ\ sing \ō\ go \ȯ\ law \ȯi\ boy \th\ thin \t͟h\ the \ü\ loot \u̇\ foot \y\ yet \zh\ vision \á, k̲, ⁿ, œ, œ̄, ue, ue̅, ʸ\ *see* Guide to Pronunciation

head and muzzle, a very full ruff of long hair, and a distinctive blue-black tongue and black-lined mouth — called also *chow*

chow chow

[1]**chow·der** \'chau̇d-ər\ *vt* (1732) : to make chowder of

[2]**chowder** *n* [F *chaudière* kettle, contents of a kettle, fr. LL *caldaria* — more at CALDRON] (1751) : a soup or stew of seafood (as clams or mussels) usu. made with milk or tomatoes, salt pork, onions, and other vegetables (as potatoes); *also* : a soup resembling chowder ⟨corn ~⟩

chow·der·head \-,hed\ *n* (1833) : DOLT, BLOCKHEAD — **chow·der·head·ed** \,chau̇d-ər-'hed-əd\ *adj*

chow·hound \'chau̇-,hau̇nd\ *n* (1942) : one fond of eating

chow line *n* (1919) : a line of people waiting to be served food

chow mein \'chau̇-'mān\ *n* [Chin (Pek) *ch'ao*^{3} *mien*^{4}, fr. *ch'ao*^{3} to fry + *mien*^{4} dough] (1903) : a seasoned stew of shredded or diced meat, mushrooms, and vegetables that is usu. served with fried noodles

chres·tom·a·thy \kre-'stäm-ə-thē\ *n, pl* **-thies** [NL *chrestomathia*, fr. Gk *chrēstomatheia*, fr. *chrēstos* useful + *manthanein* to learn — more at MATHEMATICAL] (1832) **1 :** a selection of passages compiled as an aid to learning a language **2 :** a volume of selected passages or stories of an author

chrism \'kriz-əm\ *n* [ME *crisme*, fr. OE *crisma*, fr. LL *chrisma*, fr. Gk, ointment, fr. *chriein* to anoint] (bef. 12c) : consecrated oil used in Greek and Latin churches esp. in baptism, confirmation, and ordination

chris·mon \'kriz-,män\ *n, pl* **chris·ma** \-mə\ *or* **chrismons** [ML, fr. L *Christus* Christ + LL *monogramma* monogram] (1872) : CHI-RHO

chris·om \'kriz-əm\ *n* [ME *crisom*, short for *crisom cloth*, fr. *crisom* chrism + *cloth*] (13c) : a white cloth or robe put on a person at baptism as a symbol of innocence

chrisom child *n* (1542) : a child that dies in its first month

Christ \'krīst\ *n* [ME *Crist*, fr. OE, fr. L *Christus*, fr. Gk *Christos*, lit., anointed, fr. *chriein*] (bef. 12c) **1 :** MESSIAH **2 :** JESUS **3 :** an ideal type of humanity **4** *Christian Science* : the ideal truth that comes as a divine manifestation of God to destroy incarnate error — **Christ·like** \-,līk\ *adj* — **Christ·ly** \-lē\ *adj*

chris·ten \'kris-ᵊn\ *vt* **chris·tened; chris·ten·ing** \'kris-niŋ, -ᵊn-iŋ\ [ME *cristnen*, fr. OE *cristnian*, fr. *cristen* Christian, fr. L *christianus*] (bef. 12c) **1 a :** BAPTIZE **b :** to name at baptism **2 :** to name or dedicate (as a ship) by a ceremony suggestive of baptism **3 :** NAME **4 :** to use for the first time

Chris·ten·dom \'kris-ᵊn-dəm\ *n* [ME *cristendom*, fr. OE *cristendōm*, fr. *cristen* + *-dom* -dom] (bef. 12c) **1 :** CHRISTIANITY 1 **2 :** the part of the world in which Christianity prevails

chris·ten·ing *n* (14c) : the ceremony of baptizing and naming a child

[1]**Chris·tian** \'kris(h)-chən\ *n* [L *christianus*, adj. & n., fr. Gk *christianos*, fr. *Christos*] (1526) **1 a :** one who professes belief in the teachings of Jesus Christ **b** (1) : DISCIPLE 2 (2) : a member of one of the Churches of Christ separating from the Disciples of Christ in 1906 (3) : a member of the Christian denomination having part in the union of the United Church of Christ concluded in 1961 **2 :** the hero in Bunyan's *Pilgrim's Progress*

[2]**Christian** *adj* (1553) **1 a :** of or relating to Christianity ⟨~ scriptures⟩ **b :** based on or conforming with Christianity ⟨~ ethics⟩ **2 a :** of or relating to a Christian ⟨~ responsibilities⟩ **b :** professing Christianity ⟨a ~ affirmation⟩ **3 :** commendably decent or generous ⟨has a very ~ concern for others⟩ — **Chris·tian·ly** *adj or adv*

Christian Brother *n* (1819) : a member of the Roman Catholic institute of Brothers of the Christian Schools founded by St. John Baptist de la Salle in France in 1684 and dedicated to education

Christian era *n* (1657) : the period dating from the birth of Christ

chris·ti·ania \,kris(h)-chē-'an-ē-ə, ,kris-tē-, -'än-\ *n* [*Christiania*, former name of Oslo, Norway] (1905) : CHRISTIE

Chris·tian·i·ty \,kris(h)-chē-'an-ət-ē, ,kris-tē-'an-, kris(h)-'chan-\ *n* (14c) **1 :** the religion derived from Jesus Christ, based on the Bible as sacred scripture, and professed by Eastern, Roman Catholic, and Protestant bodies **2 :** conformity to the Christian religion **3 :** CHRISTENDOM 2

Chris·tian·ize \'kris(h)-chə-,nīz\ *vt* **-ized; -iz·ing** (1593) : to make Christian — **Chris·tian·iza·tion** \,kris(h)-chə-nə-'zā-shən\ *n* — **Chris·tian·iz·er** \'kris(h)-chə-,nī-zər\ *n*

Christian name *n* (1549) : GIVEN NAME

Christian Science *n* (1867) : a religion founded by Mary Baker Eddy in 1866 that was organized under the official name of the Church of Christ, Scientist, that derives its teachings from the Scriptures as understood by its adherents, and that includes a practice of spiritual healing based on the teaching that cause and effect are mental and that sin, sickness, and death will be destroyed by a full understanding of the divine principle of Jesus's teaching and healing — **Christian Scientist** *n*

chris·tie *or* **chris·ty** \'kris-tē\ *n, pl* **christies** [by shortening & alter. fr. *christiania*] (1920) : a skiing turn used for altering the direction of hill descent or for stopping and executed usu. at high speed by shifting the body weight forward and skidding into a turn with parallel skis

Christ·mas \'kris-məs\ *n, often attrib* [ME *Christemasse*, fr. OE *Cristes mæsse*, lit., Christ's mass] (bef. 12c) **1 :** a Christian feast on December 25 or among the Eastern Orthodox on January 7 that commemorates the birth of Christ and is usu. observed as a legal holiday **2 :** CHRISTMASTIDE — **Christ·mas·sy** *or* **Christ·masy** \-mə-sē\ *adj*

Christmas cactus *n* [fr. its annual blooming around Christmastime] (ca. 1900) : a branching So. American cactus (*Zygocactus truncatus*) with flat stems, short joints, and showy red zygomorphic flowers — called also *crab cactus*

Christmas card *n* (1883) : a greeting card sent at Christmas

Christmas club *n* (ca. 1910) : a savings account in which regular deposits are made throughout the year to provide money for Christmas shopping

Christmas fern *n* (1878) : a No. American evergreen fern (*Polystichum acrostichoides*) used for decoration in winter

Christmas rose *n* (1688) : a European herb (*Helleborus niger*) of the buttercup family that has white or purplish flowers produced in winter

Christ·mas·tide \'kris-mə-,stīd\ *n* (1626) : the festival season from Christmas Eve till after New Year's Day or esp. in England till Epiphany

Christ·mas·time \-mə-,stīm\ *n* (1837) : the Christmas season

Christmas tree *n* (1835) **1 :** a usu. evergreen tree decorated at Christmas **2 :** an oil-well control device consisting of an assembly of fittings placed at the top of the well

Chris·to·cen·tric \,kris-tə-'sen-trik, ,krīs-\ *adj* [Gk *Christos* Christ + E *-centric*] (1873) : centering theologically on Christ

Chris·to·gram \'kris-tə-,gram, 'krīs-\ *n* [Gk *Christos* + E *-gram*] (1900) : a graphic symbol of Christ; *esp* : CHI-RHO

Chris·tol·o·gy \kris-'täl-ə-jē, krīs-\ *n* [Gk *Christos* + E *-logy*] (1673) : theological interpretation of the person and work of Christ — **Chris·to·log·i·cal** \,kris-tə-'läj-i-kəl, 'krīs-\ *adj*

Christ's–thorn \'krīs(ts)-'thȯ(ə)rn\ *or* **Christ–thorn** \'krīs(t)-\ *n* (1562) : any of several prickly or thorny shrubs of Palestine (esp. the shrub *Paliurus spina-christi* or the jujube *Ziziphus jujuba*)

chrom- *or* **chromo-** *comb form* [ISV, fr. Gk *chrōma* color] **1 :** chromium ⟨*chromize*⟩ **2 a :** color : colored ⟨*chromosphere*⟩ **b :** pigment ⟨*chromogen*⟩ **c :** color (sense 15)

chro·ma \'krō-mə\ *n* [Gk *chrōma*] (1889) **1 :** SATURATION 4a **2 :** a quality of color combining hue and saturation

chro·maf·fin \'krō-mə-fən\ *adj* [ISV *chrom-* + L *affinis* bordering on, related — more at AFFINITY] (1903) : staining deeply with chromium salts ⟨~ cells of the adrenal medulla⟩

chromat- *or* **chromato-** *comb form* [Gk *chrōmat-*, *chrōma*] **1 :** color ⟨*chromatid*⟩ **2 :** chromatin ⟨*chromatolysis*⟩

chro·mate \'krō-,māt\ *n* [F, fr. Gk *chrōma*] (1819) : a salt or ester of chromic acid

[1]**chro·mat·ic** \krō-'mat-ik\ *n* (1708) : ACCIDENTAL 2

[2]**chromatic** *adj* [Gk *chrōmatikos*, fr. *chrōmat-*, *chrōma* skin, color, modified tone; akin to Gk *chrōs* color, OE *grēot* sand — more at GRIT] (ca. 1775) **1 a :** of or relating to color or color phenomena or sensations **b :** highly colored **2 :** of or relating to chroma **3 a :** of, relating to, or giving all the tones of the chromatic scale **b :** characterized by frequent use of accidentals — **chro·mat·i·cal·ly** \-i-k(ə-)lē\ *adv* — **chro·mat·i·cism** \-'mat-ə-,siz-əm\ *n*

chromatic aberration *n* (1831) : aberration caused by the differences in refraction of the colored rays of the spectrum

chro·ma·tic·i·ty \,krō-mə-'tis-ət-ē\ *n* (1921) : the quality of color characterized by its dominant or complementary wavelength and purity taken together

chro·mat·ics \krō-'mat-iks\ *n pl but sing in constr* (1790) : the branch of colorimetry that deals with hue and saturation

chromatic scale *n* (1789) : a musical scale consisting entirely of half steps

chro·ma·tid \'krō-mə-təd\ *n* (1900) : one of the usu. paired and parallel strands of a duplicated chromosome joined by a single centromere — compare CHROMONEMA

chro·ma·tin \'krō-mət-ən\ *n* (1882) : the part of a cell nucleus that stains intensely with basic dyes; *specif* : a complex of a nucleic acid with basic proteins of protamine or histone type that is present in chromosomes and carries the genes — see CELL illustration — **chro·ma·tin·ic** \,krō-mə-'tin-ik\ *adj*

chro·mato·gram \krō-'mat-ə-,gram, krə-\ *n* (1922) : the pattern formed on the adsorbent medium by the layers of components separated by chromatography

chro·mato·graph \krō-'mat-ə-,graf, krə-\ *n* (1946) : an instrument for producing chromatograms — **chromatograph** *vb* — **chro·ma·tog·ra·pher** \,krō-mə-'täg-rə-fər\ *n*

chro·ma·tog·ra·phy \,krō-mə-'täg-rə-fē\ *n* (1937) : a process in which a chemical mixture carried by a liquid or gas is separated into components as a result of differential distribution of the solutes as they flow around or over a stationary liquid or solid phase — **chro·mato·graph·ic** \krō-,mat-ə-'graf-ik, krə-\ *adj* — **chro·mato·graph·i·cal·ly** \-i-k(ə-)lē\ *adv*

chro·ma·tol·y·sis \,krō-mə-'täl-ə-səs\ *n* [NL] (1901) : the dissolution and breaking up of chromophil material (as chromatin) of a cell — **chro·mato·lyt·ic** \krō-,mat-ᵊl-'it-ik, krə-\ *adj*

chro·mato·phore \krō-'mat-ə-,fō(ə)r, krə-, -,fȯ(ə)r\ *n* [ISV] (ca. 1859) **1 :** a pigment-bearing cell; *esp* : one of the cells of an animal integument capable of causing skin color changes by expanding or contracting **2 :** the organelle of photosynthesis in blue-green algae and photosynthetic bacteria; *broadly* : CHROMOPLAST, CHLOROPLAST

[1]**chrome** \'krōm\ *n* [F, fr. Gk *chrōma*] (1800) **1 a :** CHROMIUM **b :** a chromium pigment **2 :** something plated with an alloy of chromium

[2]**chrome** *vt* **chromed; chrom·ing** (1876) **1 :** to treat with a compound of chromium (as in dyeing) **2 :** CHROMIZE

-chrome \,krōm\ *n comb form or adj comb form* [ML *-chromat-*, *-chroma* colored thing, fr. Gk *chrōmat-*, *chrōma*] **1 :** colored thing ⟨helio*chrome*⟩ : colored ⟨hetero*chrome*⟩ **2 :** coloring matter ⟨uro*chrome*⟩

chrome alum *n* (ca. 1889) : an alum with trivalent chromium; *esp* : a dark violet salt $KCr(SO_4)_2{\cdot}12H_2O$ used in tanning, in photography, and as a mordant in dyeing

chrome green *n* (ca. 1859) : any of various brilliant green pigments containing or consisting of chromium compounds

chrome red *n* (ca. 1859) : a red pigment consisting of basic lead chromate $PbCrO_4{\cdot}PbO$

chrome yellow *n* (1819) : a yellow pigment consisting essentially of neutral lead chromate $PbCrO_4$

chro·mic \'krō-mik\ *adj* (1800) : of, relating to, or derived from chromium esp. with a valence of three

chromic acid *n* (1800) : an acid H_2CrO_4 analogous to sulfuric acid but known only in solution and esp. in the form of its salts

chro·mi·nance \'krō-mə-nən(t)s\ *n* [*chrom-* + *luminance*] (1952) : the difference between a color and a chosen reference color of the same luminous intensity in color television

chro·mite \'krō-,mīt\ *n* [G *chromit*, fr. *chrom-*] (1840) **1 :** a mineral $FeCr_2O_4$ that consists of an oxide of iron and chromium **2 :** an oxide of bivalent chromium

chro·mi·um \ˈkrō-mē-əm\ *n* [NL, fr. F *chrome*] (1807) : a blue-white metallic element found naturally only in combination and used esp. in alloys and in electroplating — see ELEMENT table
chro·mize \ˈkrō-ˌmīz\ *vt* **chro·mized; chro·miz·ing** (1939) : to treat (metal) with chromium in order to form a protective surface alloy
chro·mo \ˈkrō(ˌ)mō\ *n, pl* **chromos** (1868) : CHROMOLITHOGRAPH
chro·mo·cen·ter \ˈkrō-mə-ˌsent-ər\ *n* (ca. 1926) : a densely staining nuclear body associated with the chromatin of some cells
chro·mo·dy·nam·ics \ˌkrō-mə-dī-ˈnam-iks\ *n pl but sing in constr* (1976) : a theory that describes the strong interactions that bind quarks together to form hadrons
chro·mo·gen \ˈkrō-mə-jən\ *n* [ISV] (1858) **1 a :** a precursor of a biochemical pigment **b :** a compound not itself a dye but containing a chromophore and so capable of becoming one **2 :** a pigment-producing microorganism — **chro·mo·gen·ic** \ˌkrō-mə-ˈjen-ik\ *adj*
chro·mo·litho·graph \ˌkrō-mə-ˈlith-ə-ˌgraf\ *n* (1860) : a picture printed in colors from a series of lithographic stones or plates — **chro·mo·litho·graph·ic** \-ˌlith-ə-ˈgraf-ik\ *adj* — **chro·mo·li·thog·ra·phy** \-lith-ˈäg-rə-fē\ *n*
chro·mo·mere \ˈkrō-mə-ˌmi(ə)r\ *n* [ISV] (1891) : one of the small bead-shaped and heavily staining concentrations of chromatin that are linearly arranged along the chromosome — **chro·mo·mer·ic** \ˌkrō-mə-ˈmer-ik, -ˈmi(ə)r-\ *adj*
chro·mo·ne·ma \ˌkrō-mə-ˈnē-mə\ *n, pl* **-ne·ma·ta** \-ˈnē-mət-ə\ [NL, fr. *chrom-* + Gk *nēmat-, nēma* thread — more at NEMAT-] (1925) : the coiled filamentous core of a chromatid — **chro·mo·ne·mat·ic** \-ni-ˈmat-ik\ *adj*
chro·mo·phil \ˈkrō-mə-ˌfil\ *adj* [ISV] (1899) : staining readily with dyes
chro·mo·phobe \-ˌfōb\ *adj* (ca. 1909) : resisting staining with dyes ⟨~ cells⟩
chro·mo·phore \ˈkrō-mə-ˌfō(ə)r, -ˌfȯ(ə)r\ *n* [ISV] (1879) : a chemical group that gives rise to color in a molecule — **chro·mo·phor·ic** \ˌkrō-mə-ˈfȯr-ik, -ˈfär-\ *adj*
chro·mo·plast \ˈkrō-mə-ˌplast\ *n* [ISV] (1885) : a colored plastid usu. containing red or yellow pigment (as carotene)
chro·mo·pro·tein \ˌkrō-mə-ˈprō-ˌtēn, -ˈprōt-ē-ən\ *n* (1924) : a compound (as hemoglobin) of a protein with a metal-containing pigment (as heme) or a carotenoid
chro·mo·some \ˈkrō-mə-ˌsōm, -ˌzōm\ *n* [ISV] (1889) : one of the linear or sometimes circular basophilic bodies of viruses, bacteria, blue-green algae, and the cell nucleus of all other unicellular or multicellular organisms that contain most or all of the DNA or RNA comprising the genes of the individual — **chro·mo·som·al** \ˌkrō-mə-ˈsō-məl, -ˈzō-\ *adj* — **chro·mo·som·al·ly** \-mə-lē\ *adv*
chromosome number *n* (1910) : the usu. constant number of chromosomes characteristic of a particular kind of animal or plant
chro·mo·sphere \ˈkrō-mə-ˌsfi(ə)r\ *n* (1868) : the lower part of the atmosphere of the sun that is thousands of miles thick and is composed chiefly of hydrogen gas; *also* : a similar part of the atmosphere of any star — **chro·mo·spher·ic** \ˌkrō-mə-ˈsfi(ə)r-ik, -ˈsfer-\ *adj*
chro·mous \ˈkrō-məs\ *adj* (1840) : of, relating to, or derived from chromium esp. with a valence of two
chron- *or* **chrono-** *comb form* [Gk, fr. *chronos*] : time ⟨*chronogram*⟩
chron·ax·ie *also* **chron·axy** \ˈkrōn-ˌak-sē, ˈkrän-\ *n* [F *chronaxie*, fr. *chron-* + Gk *axia* value, fr. *axios* worthy] (1917) : the minimum time required for excitation of a structure (as a nerve cell) by a constant electric current of twice the threshold voltage
chron·ic \ˈkrän-ik\ *adj* [F *chronique*, fr. Gk *chronikos* of time, fr. *chronos*] (1601) **1 a :** marked by long duration or frequent recurrence : not acute ⟨~ indigestion⟩ ⟨~ experiments⟩ **b :** suffering from a chronic disease ⟨the special needs of ~ patients⟩ **2 a :** always present or encountered; *esp* : constantly vexing, weakening, or troubling ⟨~ petty warfare⟩ **b :** being such habitually ⟨a ~ grumbler⟩ — **chronic** *n* — **chron·i·cal·ly** \-i-k(ə-)lē\ *adv* — **chro·nic·i·ty** \krä-ˈnis-ət-ē, krō-\ *n*
1**chron·i·cle** \ˈkrän-i-kəl\ *n* [ME *cronicle*, fr. AF, alter. of OF *chronique*, fr. L *chronica*, fr. Gk *chronika*, fr. neut. pl. of *chronikos*] (14c) **1 :** a usu. continuous and detailed historical account of events arranged in order of time without analysis or interpretation **2 :** NARRATIVE
2**chronicle** *vt* **-cled; -cling** \-k(ə-)liŋ\ (15c) **1 :** to record in or as if in a chronicle **2 :** LIST, DESCRIBE — **chron·i·cler** \-k(ə-)lər\ *n*
chronicle play *n* (1902) : a play with a theme from history consisting usu. of rather loosely connected episodes chronologically arranged
Chron·i·cles \ˈkrän-i-kəlz\ *n pl but sing in constr* : either of two historical books of canonical Jewish and Christian Scripture — see BIBLE table
chro·no·gram \ˈkrän-ə-ˌgram, ˈkrō-nə-\ *n* (1621) : an inscription, sentence, or phrase in which certain letters express a date or epoch
chro·no·graph \ˈkrän-ə-ˌgraf, ˈkrō-nə-\ *n* (ca. 1864) : an instrument for measuring and recording time intervals: as **a :** an instrument having a revolving drum on which a stylus makes marks **b :** a watch for indicating intervals of elapsed time (as with a sweep-second hand or a digital display) **c :** an instrument for measuring the time of flight of projectiles — **chro·no·graph·ic** \ˌkrän-ə-ˈgraf-ik, ˌkrō-nə-\ *adj* — **chro·nog·ra·phy** \krə-ˈnäg-rə-fē\ *n*
chro·nol·o·ger \krə-ˈnäl-ə-jər\ *n* (1572) : CHRONOLOGIST
chro·no·log·i·cal \ˌkrän-ᵊl-ˈäj-i-kəl, ˌkrōn-\ *also* **chro·no·log·ic** \-ik\ *adj* (1614) : of, relating to, or arranged in or according to the order of time ⟨~ tables of American history⟩; *also* : reckoned in units of time ⟨~ age⟩ — **chro·no·log·i·cal·ly** \-i-k(ə-)lē\ *adv*
chro·nol·o·gist \krə-ˈnäl-ə-jəst\ *n* (1611) : an expert in chronology
chro·nol·o·gy \-jē\ *n, pl* **-gies** [NL *chronologia*, fr. *chron-* + *-logia* -logy] (1593) **1 :** the science that deals with measuring time by regular divisions and that assigns to events their proper dates **2 :** a chronological table or list **3 :** an arrangement in order of occurrence
chro·nom·e·ter \krə-ˈnäm-ət-ər\ *n* (1735) : an instrument for measuring time : TIMEPIECE; *esp* : one designed to keep time with great accuracy
chro·no·met·ric \ˌkrän-ə-ˈme-trik, ˌkrō-nə-\ *or* **chro·no·met·ri·cal** \-tri-kəl\ *adj* (1830) : of or relating to a chronometer or chronometry — **chro·no·met·ri·cal·ly** \-tri-k(ə-)lē\ *adv*
chro·nom·e·try \krə-ˈnäm-ə-trē\ *n* (1833) **1 :** the science of measuring time **2 :** the measuring of time by periods or divisions
chro·no·scope \ˈkrän-ə-ˌskōp, ˈkrō-nə-\ *n* (1846) : an instrument for precise measurement of small time intervals
chrys- *or* **chryso-** *comb form* [Gk, fr. *chrysos*] : gold : yellow ⟨*chrysarobin*⟩
chrys·a·lid \ˈkris-ə-ləd\ *n* (1777) : CHRYSALIS — **chrysalid** *adj*
chrys·a·lis \ˈkris-ə-ləs\ *n, pl* **chry·sal·i·des** \kris-ˈal-ə-ˌdēz\ *or* **chrys·a·lis·es** [L *chrysallid-, chrysallis* gold-colored pupa of butterflies, fr. Gk, fr. *chrysos* gold, of Sem origin] (1601) **1 :** a pupa of a butterfly; *broadly* : an insect pupa **2 :** a protecting covering : a sheltered state or stage of being or growth ⟨a budding writer could not emerge from his ~ too soon —William Du Bois⟩
chry·san·the·mum \kris-ˈan(t)-thə-məm *also* kriz-\ *n* [L, fr. Gk *chrysanthemon*, fr. *chrys-* + *anthemon* flower; akin to Gk *anthos* flower] (1551) **1 :** any of various composite plants (genus *Chrysanthemum*) including weeds, ornamentals grown for their brightly colored often double flower heads, and others important as sources of medicinals and insecticides **2 :** a flower head of an ornamental chrysanthemum

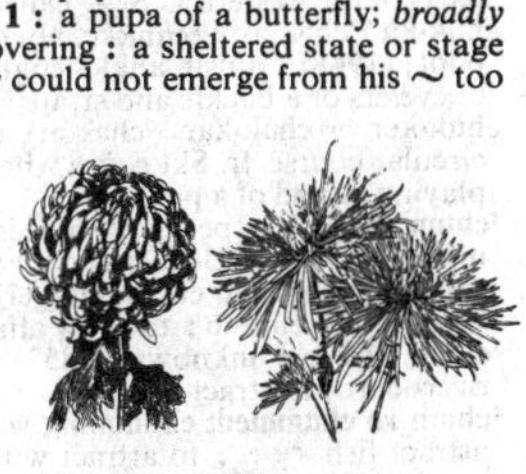

chrysanthemum 2

chrys·a·ro·bin \ˌkris-ə-ˈrō-bən\ *n* [*chrys-* + *araroba* + *-in*] (1887) : a powder obtained from Goa powder and used to treat skin diseases
Chry·se·is \krī-ˈsē-əs\ *n* [L, fr. Gk *Chryseïs*] : a daughter of a priest of Apollo in the *Iliad* narrative taken at Troy by Agamemnon but later restored to her father
chryso·ber·yl \ˈkris-ə-ˌber-əl\ *n* [L *chrysoberyllus*, fr. Gk *chrysobēryllos*, fr. *chrys-* + *bēryllos* beryl] (14c) **1** *obs* : a yellowish beryl **2 :** a usu. yellow or pale green mineral $BeAl_2O_4$ consisting of beryllium aluminum oxide with a little iron and sometimes used as a gem
chrys·o·lite \ˈkris-ə-ˌlīt\ *n* [ME *crisolite*, fr. MF, fr. L *chrysolithos*, fr. Gk, fr. *chrys-* + *-lithos* -lite] (14c) : OLIVINE
chrys·o·me·lid \ˌkris-ə-ˈmel-əd, -ˈmēl-\ *n* [deriv. of Gk *chrysomēlolonthē* golden cockchafer] (ca. 1924) : any of a large family (Chrysomelidae) of small, usu. oval and smooth, shining, and brightly colored beetles (as the Colorado potato beetle) — **chrysomelid** *adj*
chryso·phyte \ˈkris-ə-ˌfīt\ *n* [deriv. of Gk *chrysos* + *phyton* plant — more at PHYT-] (1959) : GOLDEN-BROWN ALGA
chrys·o·prase \ˈkris-ə-ˌprāz\ *n* [ME *crisopace*, fr. OF, fr. L *chrysoprasus*, fr. Gk *chrysoprasos*, fr. *chrys-* + *prason* leek; akin to L *porrum* leek] (13c) : an apple-green chalcedony valued as a gem
chrys·o·tile \-ˌtīl\ *n* [G *chrysotil*, fr. *chrys-* + *-til* fiber, fr. Gk *tillein* to pluck] (1850) : a mineral consisting of a fibrous silky serpentine and constituting a kind of asbestos
chthon·ic \ˈthän-ik\ *also* **chtho·ni·an** \ˈthō-nē-ən\ *adj* [Gk *chthon-, chthōn* earth — more at HUMBLE] (1882) : INFERNAL ⟨~ deities⟩
chub \ˈchəb\ *n, pl* **chub** *or* **chubs** [ME *chubbe*] (15c) **1 :** any of various freshwater cyprinid fishes (esp. of the genera *Gila, Hybopsis,* and *Nocomis*) **2 :** any of several marine or freshwater fishes that are not cyprinids
chub·bi·ly \ˈchəb-ə-lē\ *adv* (1909) : in the manner of one that is chubby
chub·by \ˈchəb-ē\ *adj* **chub·bi·er; -est** [*chub*] (1722) : PLUMP ⟨a ~ boy⟩ — **chub·bi·ness** \ˈchəb-ē-nəs\ *n*
1**chuck** \ˈchək\ *vb* [ME *chukken*] (14c) : CLUCK
2**chuck** *n* (1588) — used as a term of endearment
3**chuck** *vt* [origin unknown] (1583) **1 :** PAT, TAP **2 a :** TOSS **b :** DISCARD ⟨~*ed* his old shirt⟩ **c :** DISMISS, OUST — used esp. with *out* ⟨was ~*ed* out of office⟩ **3 :** to have done with ⟨~*ed* his job⟩ — **chuck it** : QUIT, YIELD
4**chuck** *n* (1611) **1 :** a pat or nudge under the chin **2 :** TOSS, JERK
5**chuck** *n* [E dial. *chuck* (lump)] (1723) **1 :** a cut of beef that includes most of the neck, the parts about the shoulder blade, and those about the first three ribs — see BEEF illustration **2** *chiefly West* : FOOD **3 :** an attachment for holding a workpiece or tool in a machine (as a drill press or lathe)
chuck·hole \ˈchək-ˌhōl, ˈchəg-\ *n* [3*chuck* + *hole*] (1836) : a hole or rut in a road
chuck·le \ˈchək-əl\ *vi* **chuck·led; chuck·ling** \-(ə-)liŋ\ [prob. freq. of 1*chuck*] (1803) **1 :** to laugh inwardly or quietly **2 :** to make a continuous gentle sound resembling suppressed mirth ⟨the clear bright water *chuckled* over gravel—B. A. Williams⟩ — **chuckle** *n* — **chuck·le·some** \-əl-səm\ *adj* — **chuck·ling·ly** \-(ə-)liŋ-lē\ *adv*
chuck·le·head \ˈchək-əl-ˌhed\ *n* [*chuckle* (lumpish) + *head*] (1731) : BLOCKHEAD — **chuck·le·head·ed** \ˌchək-əl-ˈhed-əd\ *adj*
chuck wagon *n* [5*chuck*] (1890) : a wagon carrying supplies and provisions for cooking (as on a ranch)
chuck·wal·la \ˈchək-ˌwäl-ə\ *or* **chuck·a·wal·la** \ˈchək-ə-ˌwäl-ə\ *n* [MexSp *chacahuala*] (1893) : a large edible herbivorous lizard (*Sauromalus obesus* of the family Iguanidae) of desert regions of the southwestern U.S.
chuck–will's–wid·ow \ˌchək-ˌwilz-ˈwid-(ˌ)ō, -ˈwid-ə(-w)\ *n* [imit.] (1791) : a goatsucker (*Caprimulgus carolinensis*) of the southern U.S.
1**chuff** \ˈchəf\ *n* [ME *chuffe*] (15c) : BOOR, CHURL
2**chuff** *vi* [imit.] (1914) : to produce noisy exhaust or exhalations : proceed or operate with chuffs ⟨the ~*ing* and snorting of switch engines — Paul Gallico⟩
3**chuff** *n* (1915) : the sound of noisy exhaust or exhalations
chuffed \ˈchəft\ *adj, Brit* (1957) : PROUD, SATISFIED
chuf·fy \ˈchəf-ē\ *adj* **chuf·fi·er; -est** [perh. fr. E dial. *chuff* chubby] (1611) : FAT, CHUBBY
1**chug** \ˈchəg\ *n* [imit.] (1866) : a dull explosive sound made by or as if by a laboring engine
2**chug** *vi* **chugged; chug·ging** (1896) : to move or go with or as if with chugs ⟨a locomotive *chugging* along⟩ — **chug·ger** *n*
3**chug** *vt* **chugged; chug·ging** (ca. 1968) : CHUGALUG

chug·a·lug \'chəg-ə-,ləg\ *vb* **-lugged; -lug·ging** [imit.] *vi* (1956) **:** to drink a container (as of beer) without pause ~ *vt* **:** to drink a container of (as beer) without pause; *also* **:** GUZZLE

chu·kar partridge \chə-'kär-\ *n* [Hindi *cakor*] (1814) **:** a largely gray and black Indian partridge (*Alectoris graeca chukar*) introduced into dry parts of the western U.S. — called also *chukar*

chuk·ka \'chək-ə\ *n* [*chukka*, alter. of *chukker*; fr. a similar polo player's boot] (1948) **:** a usu. ankle-length leather boot with two or three pairs of eyelets or a buckle and strap

chuk·ker *or* **chuk·kar** \'chək-ər\ *or* **chuk·ka** \'chək-ə\ *n* [Hindi *cakkar* circular course, fr. Skt *cakra* wheel, circle — more at WHEEL] (1898) **:** a playing period of a polo game

[1]**chum** \'chəm\ *n* [perh. by shortening & alter. fr. *chamber fellow* (roommate)] (1684) **:** a close friend **:** PAL — **chum·ship** \-,ship\ *n*

[2]**chum** *vi* **chummed; chum·ming** (1730) **1 :** to room together **2 a :** to be a close friend **b :** to show affable friendliness

[3]**chum** *n* [origin unknown] (1857) **:** chopped fish or other matter thrown overboard to attract fish

[4]**chum** *vb* **chummed; chumming** *vi* (1857) **:** to throw chum overboard to attract fish ~ *vt* **:** to attract with chum ⟨*chumming* the fish with cut-up shrimp⟩

[5]**chum** *n* [perh. fr. Chinook Jargon *tsum, tzum* spots, writing] (ca. 1903) **:** CHUM SALMON

chum·my \'chəm-ē\ *adj* **chum·mi·er; -est** (1884) **:** INTIMATE, SOCIABLE — **chum·mi·ly** \'chəm-ə-lē\ *adv* — **chum·mi·ness** \'chəm-ē-nəs\ *n*

chump \'chəmp\ *n* [perh. blend of *chunk* and *lump*] (1883) **:** FOOL, DUPE

chum salmon *n* [[5]*chum*] (1923) **:** a salmon (*Oncorhynchus keta*) of the northern Pacific — called also *chum*

[1]**chunk** \'chəŋk\ *n* [perh. alter. of *chuck* (short piece of wood)] (1691) **1 :** a short thick piece or lump (as of wood or coal) **2 :** a large noteworthy quantity ⟨bet a sizable ~ of money on the race⟩ **3 :** a strong thickset horse usu. smaller than a draft horse

[2]**chunk** *vi* [imit.] (1890) **:** to make a dull plunging or explosive sound ⟨the rhythmic ~*ing* of thrown quoits —John Updike⟩

chunky \'chəŋ-kē\ *adj* **chunk·i·er; -est** (1751) **1 :** short and thick or broad; *esp* **:** STOCKY **2 :** filled with chunks ⟨~ peanut butter⟩ — **chunk·i·ly** \-kə-lē\ *adv*

chun·ter \'chənt-ər\ *vi* [prob. of imit. origin] *Brit* (1599) **:** to talk in a low inarticulate way **:** MUTTER

[1]**church** \'chərch\ *n* [ME *chirche*, fr. OE *cirice*; akin to OHG *kirihha* church; both fr. a prehistoric WGmc word derived fr. LGk *kyriakon*, fr. Gk, neut. of *kyriakos* of the lord, fr. *kyrios* lord, master, fr. *kyros* power; akin to L *cavus* hollow — more at CAVE] (bef. 12c) **1 :** a building for public and esp. Christian worship **2 :** the clergy or officialdom of a religious body **3 :** a body or organization of religious believers: as **a :** the whole body of Christians **b :** DENOMINATION **c :** CONGREGATION **4 :** a public divine worship ⟨goes to ~ every Sunday⟩ **5 :** the clerical profession ⟨considered the ~ as a possible career⟩

[2]**church** *adj* (bef. 12c) **1 :** of or relating to a church ⟨~ government⟩ **2** *chiefly Brit* **:** of or relating to the established church

[3]**church** *vt* (14c) **:** to bring to church to receive one of its rites

churched \'chərcht\ *adj* (14c) **:** affiliated with a church

church father *n* (1856) **:** FATHER 4

church·go·er \'chərch-,gō(-ə)r\ *n* (1687) **:** one who habitually attends church — **church·go·ing** \-,gō-iŋ, -,gȯ(-)iŋ\ *adj or n*

church·ian·i·ty \,chər-chē-'an-ət-ē\ *n* [*church* + *-ianity* (as in *Christianity*)] (1837) **:** the usu. excessive or sectarian attachment to the practices and interests of a particular church

church·ing *n* (15c) **:** the administration or reception of a rite of the church; *specif* **:** a ceremony in some churches by which women after childbirth are received in the church with prayers, blessings, and thanksgiving

church key *n* (1953) **:** an implement with a triangular pointed head for piercing the tops of cans (as of beer)

church·less \'chərch-ləs\ *adj* (1641) **:** not affiliated with a church

church·ly \'chərch-lē\ *adj* (bef. 12c) **1 :** of or relating to a church **2 :** suitable to or suggestive of a church **3 :** adhering to a church **4 :** CHURCHY 2 — **church·li·ness** *n*

church·man \'chərch-mən\ *n* (14c) **1 :** CLERGYMAN **2 :** a member of a church

church·man·ship \-mən-,ship\ *n* (1680) **:** the attitude, belief, or practice of a churchman

church mode *n* (ca. 1864) **:** one of eight scales prevalent in medieval music each utilizing a different pattern of intervals and beginning on a different tone

Church of England (1534) **:** the established episcopal church of England

church register *n* (1846) **:** a parish register of baptisms, marriages, and deaths

church school *n* (1862) **1 :** a school providing a general education but supported by a particular church in contrast to a public school or a nondenominational private school **2 :** an organization of officers, teachers, and pupils for purposes of moral and religious education under the supervision of a local church

Church Slavonic *n* (1850) **:** OLD CHURCH SLAVONIC

church·war·den \'chərch-,wȯrd-ᵊn\ *n* (15c) **1 :** one of two lay parish officers in Anglican churches with responsibility esp. for parish property and alms **2 :** a long-stemmed clay pipe

church·wom·an \-,wu̇m-ən\ *n* (1722) **:** a woman who is a member of a church

churchy \'chər-chē\ *adj* (1843) **1 :** marked by strict conformity or zealous adherence to the forms or beliefs of a church **2 :** of or suggestive of a church

church·yard \'chərch-,yärd\ *n* (12c) **:** a yard that belongs to a church and is often used as a burial ground

churl \'chər(-ə)l\ *n* [ME, fr. OE *ceorl* man, ceorl; akin to Gk *gēras* old age — more at CORN] (bef. 12c) **1 :** CEORL **2 :** a medieval peasant **3 :** RUSTIC, COUNTRYMAN **4 a :** a rude ill-bred person **b :** a stingy morose person

churl·ish \'chər-lish\ *adj* (bef. 12c) **1 :** of, resembling, or characteristic of a churl **:** VULGAR **2 :** ILL-NATURED, PEEVISH **3 :** difficult to work with or deal with **:** INTRACTABLE ⟨~ soil⟩ ***syn*** see BOORISH — **churl·ish·ly** *adv* — **churl·ish·ness** *n*

[1]**churn** \'chərn\ *n* [ME *chyrne*, fr. OE *cyrin*; akin to OE *corn* grain; fr. the granular appearance of cream as it is churned — more at CORN] (bef. 12c) **:** a vessel for making butter in which milk or cream is agitated in order to separate the oily globules from the watery medium

[2]**churn** *vt* (15c) **1 :** to agitate (milk or cream) in a churn in order to make butter **2 a :** to stir or agitate violently ⟨an old stern-wheeler ~*ing* the muddy river⟩ **b :** to make (as foam) by so doing **3 :** to make (the account of a client) excessively active by frequent purchases and sales primarily in order to generate commissions ~ *vi* **1 :** to work a churn **2 a :** to produce or be in violent motion **b :** to proceed by means of rotating members (as wheels)

churn out *vt* (1912) **:** to produce mechanically or copiously **:** GRIND OUT ⟨the usual pap which has been *churned out* about this superstar —William Murphy⟩

churr \'chər\ *vi* [imit.] (1555) **:** to make a vibrant or whirring noise like that made by some insects (as the cockchafer) or by some birds (as the partridge) — **churr** *n*

chur·ri·gue·resque \,chu̇r-i-gə-'resk\ *adj, often cap* [Sp *churrigueresco*, fr. José *Churriguera* †1725 Span. architect] (1845) **:** of or relating to a Spanish baroque architectural style characterized by elaborate surface decoration or its Latin-American adaptation

[1]**chute** \'shüt\ *n* [F, fr. OF, fr. *cheoir* to fall, fr. L *cadere* — more at CHANCE] (1613) **1 a :** FALL 6b **b :** a quick descent (as in a river) **:** RAPID **2 :** an inclined plane, sloping channel, or passage down or through which things may pass **:** SLIDE **3 :** PARACHUTE

[2]**chute** *vb* **chut·ed; chut·ing** *vt* (1884) **:** to convey by a chute ~ *vi* **1 :** to go in or as if in a chute **2 :** to utilize a chute (as by passing ore down it)

chut·ist \'shüt-əst\ *n* (1920) **:** PARACHUTIST

chut·ney \'chət-nē\ *n, pl* **chutneys** [Hindi *caṭnī*] (1813) **:** a thick sauce of Indian origin that contains fruits, vinegar, sugar, and spices and is used as a condiment

chutz·pah *also* **chutz·pa** \'hu̇t-spə, 'ku̇t-, -(,)spä\ *n* [Yiddish, fr. LHeb *ḥuṣpāh*] (1892) **:** supreme self-confidence **:** NERVE, GALL ***syn*** see TEMERITY

chyle \'kī(ə)l\ *n* [LL *chylus*, fr. Gk *chylos* juice, chyle, fr. *chein* to pour — more at FOUND] (1541) **:** lymph that is milky from emulsified fats, characteristically present in the lacteals, and most apparent during intestinal absorption of fats — **chy·lous** \'kī-ləs\ *adj*

chy·lo·mi·cron \,kī-lō-'mī-,krän\ *n* [Gk *chylos* + *mikron*, neut. of *mikros* small — more at MICRO-] (1921) **:** a microscopic lipid particle common in the blood during fat digestion and assimilation

chyme \'kīm\ *n* [NL *chymus*, fr. LL, chyle, fr. Gk *chymos* juice, fr. *chein*] (1607) **:** the semifluid mass of partly digested food expelled by the stomach into the duodenum

chy·mo·tryp·sin \,kī-mō-'trip-sən\ *n* [*chyme* + *-o-* + *trypsin*] (1933) **:** a pancreatic proteinase that acts on proteins by breaking internal peptide bonds — **chy·mo·tryp·tic** \-tik\ *adj*

chy·mo·tryp·sin·o·gen \-,trip-'sin-ə-jən\ *n* (1933) **:** a zymogen that is converted by trypsin to chymotrypsin

ciao \'chau̇\ *interj* [It, fr. It dial., alter. of *schiavo* (I am your) slave, fr. ML *sclavus* — more at SLAVE] (1964) — used conventionally as an utterance at meeting or parting

ci·bo·ri·um \sə-'bōr-ē-əm, -'bȯr-\ *n, pl* **-ria** \-ē-ə\ [ML, fr. L, cup, fr. Gk *kibōrion*] (1651) **1 :** a goblet-shaped vessel for holding eucharistic bread **2 :** BALDACHIN; *specif* **:** a freestanding vaulted canopy supported by four columns over a high altar

ci·ca·da \sə-'kād-ə, -'käd-; sī-'kād-\ *n, pl* **-das** *also* **-dae** \-'kād-(,)ē, -'käd-\ [NL, genus name, fr. L, cicada] (14c) **:** any of a family (Cicadidae) of homopterous insects with a stout body, wide blunt head, and large transparent wings

ci·ca·la \sə-'käl-ə\ *n* [It, fr. ML, alter. of L *cicada*] (1820) **:** CICADA

cic·a·tri·cial \,sik-ə-'trish-əl\ *adj* (1881) **:** of or relating to a cicatrix

ci·ca·trix \'sik-ə-,triks, sə-'kā-triks\ *n, pl* **ci·ca·tri·ces** \,sik-ə-'trī-(,)sēz, sə-'kā-trə-,sēz\ [L *cicatric-, cicatrix*] (15c) **1 :** a scar resulting from formation and contraction of fibrous tissue in a flesh wound **2 :** a mark resembling a scar esp. when caused by the previous attachment of a part or organ: as **a :** a mark left on a stem after the fall of a leaf or bract **b :** HILUM 1a

cic·a·tri·za·tion \,sik-ə-trə-'zā-shən\ *n* (15c) **:** scar formation at the site of a healing wound — **cic·a·trize** \'sik-ə-,trīz\ *vt*

ci·ce·ro·ne \,sis-ə-'rō-nē, ,chē-chə-\ *n, pl* **-ni** \-(,)nē\ [It, fr. *Cicerone* Cicero] (1726) **:** a guide who conducts sightseers

cich·lid \'sik-ləd\ *n* [deriv. of Gk *kichlē* thrush, a kind of wrasse; akin to Gk *chelidōn* swallow — more at CELANDINE] (1884) **:** any of a family (Cichlidae) of mostly tropical spiny-finned freshwater fishes including several kept in tropical aquariums — **cichlid** *adj*

ci·cis·beo \,chē-chəz-'bā-(,)ō\ *n, pl* **-bei** \-'bā-,ē\ [It] (1718) **:** LOVER, GALLANT — **ci·cis·be·ism** \-'bā-,iz-əm\ *n*

-cid·al \'sīd-ᵊl\ *adj comb form* [LL *-cidalis*, fr. L *-cida*] **:** killing **:** having power to kill ⟨filaricidal⟩

-cide \,sīd\ *n comb form* [MF, fr. L *-cida*, fr. *caedere* to cut, kill — more at CONCISE] **1 :** killer ⟨insecticide⟩ **2** [MF, fr. L *-cidium*, fr. *caedere*] **:** killing ⟨suicide⟩

ci·der \'sīd-ər\ *n* [ME *sidre*, fr. MF, fr. LL *sicera* strong drink, fr. Gk *sikera*, fr. Heb *shēkhār*] (14c) **1 :** the expressed juice of fruit (as apples) used as a beverage or for making other products (as applejack) **2** *Brit* **:** fermented apple juice often made sparkling by carbonation or fermentation in a sealed container

cider vinegar *n* (1851) **:** vinegar made from fermented cider

ci–de·vant \,sēd-ə-'väⁿ\ *adj* [F, lit., formerly] (1726) **:** FORMER

ci·gar \sig-'är\ *n* [Sp *cigarro*] (1730) **:** a small roll of tobacco leaf for smoking

cig·a·rette *also* **cig·a·ret** \,sig-ə-'ret, 'sig-ə-,\ *n* [F *cigarette*, dim. of *cigare* cigar, fr. Sp *cigarro*] (1835) **:** a slender roll of cut tobacco enclosed in paper and meant to be smoked; *also* **:** a similar roll of another substance (as marijuana)

cig·a·ril·lo \,sig-ə-'ril-(,)ō, -'rē-(,)(y)ō\ *n, pl* **-los** [Sp *cigarrillo* cigarette, dim. of *cigarro* cigar] (1832) **1 :** a very small cigar **2 :** a cigarette wrapped in tobacco rather than paper

ci·lan·tro \si-'län-(,)trō, -'lan-\ *n* [Sp, coriander, fr. LL *coliandrum*, alter. of L *coriandrum* — more at CORIANDER] (1903) **:** leaves of coriander used as a flavoring or garnish

cil·i·ary \'sil-ē-ˌer-ē\ *adj* (1691) **1 :** of or relating to cilia **2 :** of, relating to, or being the annular suspension of the lens of the eye

cil·i·ate \'sil-ē-ət, -ē-ˌāt\ *n* (ca. 1910) **:** any of a subphylum (Ciliophora) of ciliated protozoans

cil·i·at·ed \'sil-ē-ˌāt-əd\ *or* **cil·i·ate** \-ē-ət, -ē-ˌāt\ *adj* (1753) **:** provided with cilia ⟨*ciliated* epithelium⟩ ⟨leaves with *ciliate* petioles⟩ — **cil·i·a·tion** \ˌsil-ē-'ā-shən\ *n*

cil·i·um \'sil-ē-əm\ *n, pl* **cil·ia** \-ē-ə\ [NL, fr. L, eyelid; akin to L *celare* to conceal — more at HELL] (1794) **1 :** a minute short hairlike process often forming part of a fringe; *esp* **:** one of a cell that is capable of lashing movement and serves esp. in free unicellular organisms to produce locomotion or in higher forms a current of fluid **2 :** EYELASH

ci·met·i·dine \sī-'met-ə-ˌdēn\ *n* [*ci-* (alter. of *cyan-*) + *methyl* + *-idine*] (1976) **:** a histamine analogue $C_{10}H_{16}N_6S$ that has been used esp. in the short-term treatment of duodenal ulcers

[1]**Cim·me·ri·an** \sə-'mir-ē-ən\ *adj* (1580) **:** very dark or gloomy **:** STYGIAN ⟨there under ebon shades . . . in dark ~ desert ever dwell —John Milton⟩

[2]**Cimmerian** *n* [L *Cimmerii*, a mythical people, fr. Gk *Kimmerioi*] (1588) **:** any of a mythical people described by Homer as dwelling in a remote realm of mist and gloom

[1]**cinch** \'sinch\ *n* [Sp *cincha*, fr. L *cingula* girdle, girth, fr. *cingere*] (1859) **1 :** a girth for a pack or saddle **2 :** a tight grip **3 a :** a thing done with ease **b :** a certainty to happen

[2]**cinch** *vt* (1866) **1 :** to put a cinch on **2 :** to make certain **:** ASSURE ~ *vi* **:** to perform the act of cinching **:** tighten the cinch — often used with *up*

cin·cho·na \siŋ-'kō-nə, sin-'chō-\ *n* [NL, genus name, fr. the countess of *Chinchón* †1641 wife of the Peruvian viceroy] (1800) **1 :** any of a genus (*Cinchona*) of So. American trees and shrubs of the madder family **2 :** the dried bark of a cinchona (as *C. ledgeriana*) containing alkaloids (as quinine) and used as a specific in malaria

cin·cho·nine \'siŋ-kə-ˌnēn, 'sin-chə-\ *n* (1825) **:** a bitter white crystalline alkaloid $C_{19}H_{22}N_2O$ found esp. in cinchona bark and used like quinine

cin·cho·nism \'siŋ-kə-ˌniz-əm, 'sin-chə-\ *n* (1857) **:** a disorder due to excessive or prolonged use of cinchona or its alkaloids and marked by temporary deafness, ringing in the ears, headache, dizziness, and rash

cinc·ture \'siŋ(k)-chər\ *n* [L *cinctura* girdle, fr. *cinctus*, pp. of *cingere* to gird] (1600) **1 :** the act of encircling **2 a :** an encircling area **b :** GIRDLE, BELT; *esp* **:** a cord or sash of cloth worn around an ecclesiastical vestment (as an alb) or the habit of a religious

cin·der \'sin-dər\ *n* [ME *sinder*, fr. OE; akin to OHG *sintar* dross, slag] (bef. 12c) **1 :** the slag from a metal furnace **:** DROSS **2 a** *pl* **:** ASHES **b :** a fragment of ash **3 a :** a partly burned combustible in which fire is extinct **b :** a hot coal without flame **c :** a partly burned coal capable of further burning without flame **4 :** a fragment of lava from an erupting volcano — **cinder** *vt* — **cin·dery** \-d(ə-)rē\ *adj*

cinder block *n* (1926) **:** a hollow rectangular building block made of cement and coal cinders

Cin·der·el·la \ˌsin-də-'rel-ə\ *n* [after *Cinderella*, fairy-tale heroine who is used as a drudge by her stepmother but ends up happily married to a prince] (1840) **:** one resembling the fairy-tale Cinderella: as **a :** one suffering undeserved neglect **b :** one suddenly lifted from obscurity to honor or significance

cine \'sin-ē\ *n* [short for *cinema*] (1908) **:** MOTION PICTURE

cine- *comb form* [*cinema*] **:** motion picture ⟨*cine*camera⟩ ⟨*cine*film⟩ ⟨*cine*-X ray⟩

cine·ast \'sin-ē-ˌast, -ē-əst\ *or* **cine·aste** \-ˌast\ *or* **ciné·aste** \'sin-ē-ˌast\ *n* [F *cinéaste*, fr. *ciné* cine + *-aste* (as in *enthousiaste* enthusiast)] (1926) **:** a devotee of motion pictures

cin·e·ma \'sin-ə-mə, *Brit also* -ˌmä\ *n* [short for *cinematograph*] (1909) **1 a :** MOTION PICTURE — usu. used attributively **b :** a motion-picture theater **2 a :** MOVIES; *esp* **:** the motion-picture industry **b :** the art or technique of making motion pictures

cin·e·ma·go·er \-ˌgō(-ə)r\ *n* (1920) **:** MOVIEGOER

cin·e·ma·theque \ˌsin-ə-mə-'tek\ *n* [F *cinémathèque* film library, fr. *cinéma* cinema + *-thèque* (as in *bibliothèque* library)] (1966) **:** a small movie house specializing in avant-garde films

cin·e·mat·ic \ˌsin-ə-'mat-ik\ *adj* (1916) **1 :** of, relating to, suggestive of, or suitable for motion pictures or the filming of motion pictures ⟨~ principles and techniques⟩ **2 :** filmed and presented as a motion picture ⟨~ fantasies⟩ — **cin·e·mat·i·cal·ly** \-'mat-i-k(ə-)lē\ *adv*

cin·e·ma·tize \'sin-ə-mə-ˌtīz\ *vt* **-tized; -tiz·ing** (1916) **:** to make a motion picture of (as a novel) **:** adapt for motion pictures

cin·e·mat·o·graph \ˌsin-ə-'mat-ə-ˌgraf\ *n* [F *cinématographe*, fr. Gk *kinēmat-, kinēma* movement (fr. *kinein* to move) + F *-o-* + *-graphe* -graph — more at HIGHT] (1896) **1** *chiefly Brit* **:** a motion-picture camera, projector, theater, or show **2** *chiefly Brit* **:** CINEMA 2b

cin·e·ma·tog·ra·pher \ˌsin-ə-mə-'täg-rə-fər\ *n* (1897) **1 :** a motion-picture cameraman **2 :** a motion-picture projectionist

cin·e·ma·tog·ra·phy \ˌsin-ə-mə-'täg-rə-fē\ *n* (1897) **:** the art or science of motion-picture photography — **cin·e·mat·o·graph·ic** \-ˌmat-ə-'graf-ik\ *adj* — **cin·e·mat·o·graph·i·cal·ly** \-i-k(ə-)lē\ *adv*

ci·né·ma vé·ri·té \'sin-ə-mə-ˌver-ə-'tā\ *n* [F *cinéma-vérité*, lit., truth cinema] (1963) **:** the art or technique of filming a motion picture so as to convey candid realism

cin·e·ole \'sin-ē-ˌōl\ *n* [ISV, by transposition fr. NL *oleum cinae* wormseed oil] (1885) **:** a liquid $C_{10}H_{18}O$ with a camphor odor contained in many essential oils (as of eucalyptus) and used esp. as an expectorant

cin·er·ar·ia \ˌsin-ə-'rer-ē-ə, -'rar-\ *n* [NL, fr. L, fem. of *cinerarius* of ashes, fr. *ciner-, cinis* ashes; akin to Gk *konis* dust, ashes] (1597) **:** any of several pot plants deriving from a perennial composite herb (*Senecio cruentus*) of the Canary islands and having heart-shaped leaves and clusters of bright flower heads

cin·er·ar·i·um \-ē-əm\ *n, pl* **-ia** \-ē-ə\ [L, fr. *ciner-, cinis*] (1880) **:** a place to receive the ashes of the cremated dead — **cin·er·ary** \'sin-ə-ˌrer-ē\ *adj*

ci·ne·re·ous \sə-'nir-ē-əs\ *adj* [L *cinereus*, fr. *ciner-, cinis*] (1661) **1 :** gray tinged with black **2 :** resembling or consisting of ashes

cin·er·in \'sin-ə-rən\ *n* [L *ciner-, cinis*] (1948) **:** either of two compounds $C_{20}H_{28}O_3$ and $C_{21}H_{28}O_5$ of high insecticidal properties

cin·gu·lum \'siŋ-gyə-ləm\ *n, pl* **-la** \-lə\ [NL, fr. L, girdle, fr. *cingere* to gird — more at CINCTURE] (1845) **:** an anatomical band or encircling ridge — **cin·gu·late** \-lət\ *adj*

cin·na·bar \'sin-ə-ˌbär\ *n* [ME *cynabare*, fr. MF & L; MF *cenobre*, fr. L *cinnabaris*, fr. Gk *kinnabari*, of non-IE origin; akin to Ar *zinjafr* cinnabar] (15c) **1 :** artificial red mercuric sulfide used esp. as a pigment **2 :** native red mercuric sulfide HgS that is the only important ore of mercury — **cin·na·bar·ine** \-ˌbär-ˌīn, ˌsin-ə-'bär-ən\ *adj*

cinnabar moth *n* (ca. 1889) **:** a European moth (*Tyria jacobeae*) with grayish black forewings marked with red and clear reddish pink hind wings that has been introduced into the U.S. in attempts to control ragwort on the leaves of which its larvae feed — called also *cinnabar*

cin·nam·ic acid \sə-ˌnam-ik-\ *n* [F *cinnamique* of cinnamon, fr. *cinname* cinnamon, fr. L *cinnamonum*] (ca. 1864) **:** a white crystalline odorless acid $C_9H_8O_2$ found esp. in cinnamon oil and storax

cin·na·mon \'sin-ə-mən\ *n, often attrib* [ME *cynamone*, fr. L *cinnamomum, cinnamon*, fr. Gk *kinnamōmon, kinnamon*, of non-IE origin; akin to Heb *qinnāmōn* cinnamon] (14c) **1 a :** a tree that yields cinnamon **b :** the highly aromatic bark of any of several trees (genus *Cinnamomum*) of the laurel family used as a spice **2 :** a light yellowish brown

cinnamon fern *n* (1818) **:** a large No. American fern (*Osmunda cinnamomea*) with cinnamon-colored spore-bearing fronds shorter than and separate from the green foliage fronds

cinnamon stone *n* (1805) **:** ESSONITE

cin·quain \'siŋ-ˌkān, 'saŋ-\ *n* [F, fr. *cinq* five, fr. L *quinque* — more at FIVE] (1882) **:** a 5-line stanza

cin·que·cen·tist \ˌchiŋ-kwi-'chent-əst\ *n* (1871) **:** an Italian of the cinquecento; *esp* **:** a poet or artist of this period

cin·que·cen·to \ˌchiŋ-kwi-'chen-(ˌ)tō\ *n* [It, lit., five hundred, fr. *cinque* five (fr. L *quinque*) + *cento* hundred, fr. L *centum* — more at HUNDRED] (1760) **:** the 16th century esp. in Italian art and literature

cinque·foil \'siŋk-ˌfȯil, 'saŋk-\ *n* [ME *sink foil*, fr. MF *cincfoille*, fr. L *quinquefolium*, fr. *quinque* five + *folium* leaf — more at BLADE] (14c) **1 :** any of a genus (*Potentilla*) of plants of the rose family with 5-lobed leaves **2 :** a design enclosed by five joined foils

ci·on *var of* SCION

ciop·pi·no \chə-'pē-(ˌ)nō\ *n* [It] (1936) **:** a dish of fish and shellfish cooked usu. with tomatoes, wine, spices, and herbs

[1]**ci·pher** \'sī-fər\ *n, often attrib* [ME, fr. MF *cifre*, fr. ML *cifra*, fr. Ar *ṣifr* empty, cipher, zero] (14c) **1 a :** ZERO 1a **b :** one that has no weight, worth, or influence **:** NONENTITY **2 a :** a method of transforming a text in order to conceal its meaning — compare CODE 3b **b :** a message in code **3 :** ARABIC NUMERAL **4 :** a combination of symbolic letters; *esp* **:** the interwoven initials of a name

[2]**cipher** *vb* **ci·phered; ci·pher·ing** \-f(ə-)riŋ\ *vi* (1530) **:** to use figures in a mathematical process ~ *vt* **1 :** ENCIPHER **2 :** to compute arithmetically

cipher alphabet *n* (1935) **:** a set of one-to-one equivalences between a sequence of plaintext letters and the sequence of their cipher substitutes used in cryptography

ci·pher·text \'sī-fər-ˌtekst\ *n* (1939) **:** the enciphered form of a text or of its elements — compare PLAINTEXT

ci·pho·ny \'sī-fə-nē\ *n* [*cipher* + tele*phony*] (1956) **:** the electronic scrambling of voice transmissions

cir·ca \'sər-kə, 'ki(ə)r-(ˌ)kä\ *prep* [L, fr. *circum* around — more at CIRCUM-] (1861) **:** at, in, or of approximately — used esp. with dates ⟨born ~ 1600⟩

cir·ca·di·an \sər-'kād-ē-ən; 'sər-kə-'dē-ən, -'dī-\ *adj* [L *circa* about + *dies* day + E *-an* — more at DEITY] (1954) **:** being, having, characterized by, or occurring in approximately 24-hour periods or cycles (as of biological activity or function) ⟨~ oscillations⟩ ⟨~ periodicity⟩ ⟨~ rhythms in activity⟩ ⟨~ leaf movements⟩

Cir·cas·sian \(ˌ)sər-'kash-ən\ *n* [*Circassia*, Russia] (1555) **1 :** a member of a group of peoples of the Caucasus of Caucasian race but not of Indo-European speech **2 :** the language of the Circassian peoples — **Circassian** *adj*

Circassian walnut *n* (1914) **:** the light brown irregularly black-veined wood of the English walnut much used for veneer and cabinetwork

Cir·ce \'sər-(ˌ)sē\ *n* [L, fr. Gk *Kirkē*] **:** a sorceress who changes Odysseus' men into swine but is forced by Odysseus to change them back

cir·ci·nate \'sərs-ᵊn-ˌāt\ *adj* [L *circinatus*, pp. of *circinare* to round, fr. *circinus* pair of compasses, fr. *circus*] (1830) **:** ROUNDED, COILED; *esp* **:** rolled in the form of a flat coil with the apex as a center ⟨~ fern fronds unfolding⟩ — **cir·ci·nate·ly** *adv*

[1]**cir·cle** \'sər-kəl\ *n, often attrib* [ME *cercle*, fr. OF, fr. L *circulus*, dim. of *circus* circle, circus, fr. or akin to Gk *krikos, kirkos* ring; akin to OE *hring* ring — more at RING] (12c) **1 a :** RING, HALO **b :** a closed plane curve every point of which is equidistant from a fixed point within the curve **c :** the plane surface bounded by such a curve **2 :** the orbit or period of revolution of a celestial body **3 :** something in the form of a circle or section of a circle: as **a :** DIADEM **b :** an instrument of astronomical observation the graduated limb of which consists of an entire circle **c :** a balcony or tier of seats in a theater **d :** a circle formed on the surface of a sphere by the intersection of a plane that passes through it ⟨~ of latitude⟩ **e :** ROTARY 2 **4 :** an area of action or influence **:** REALM **5 a :** CYCLE, ROUND ⟨the wheel has come full ~⟩ **b :** fallacious reasoning in which something to be demonstrated is covertly assumed **6 :** a group of persons sharing a common interest or revolving about a common center ⟨the sewing ~ of her church⟩ ⟨the gossip of court ~*s*⟩ **7 :** a territorial or administrative division or district **8 :** a curving side street

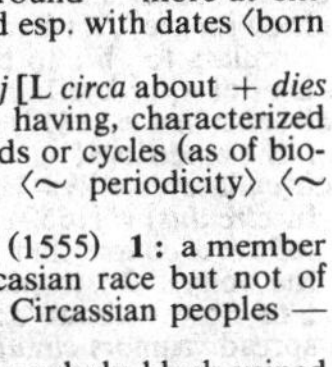

circle 1b: *AB* diameter; *C* center; *CD, CA, CB* radii; *EKF* arc on chord *EF*; *EFKL* (area) segment on chord *EF*; *ACD* (area) sector; *GH* secant; *TPM* tangent at point *P*; *EKFBPDA* circumference

[2]**circle** *vb* **cir·cled; cir·cling** \-k(ə-)liŋ\ *vt* (14c) **1 :** to enclose in or as if in a circle **2 :** to move or revolve around ~ *vi* **1 a :** to move in or as if in a circle **b :** CIRCULATE **2 :** to describe or extend in a circle — **cir·cler** \-k(ə-)lər\ *n*

circle graph *n* (1928) **:** a circular chart cut by radii into segments illustrating relative magnitudes or frequencies — called also *pie chart*

cir·clet \'sər-klət\ *n* (15c) **:** a little circle; *esp* **:** a circular ornament

[1]**cir·cuit** \'sər-kət\ *n, often attrib* [ME, fr. MF *circuite,* fr. L *circuitus,* fr. pp. of *circumire, circuire* to go around, fr. *circum-* + *ire* to go — more at ISSUE] (14c) **1 a :** a usu. circular line encompassing an area **b :** the space enclosed within such a line **2 a :** a course around a periphery **b :** a circuitous or indirect route **3 a :** a regular tour (as by a traveling judge or preacher) around an assigned district or territory **b :** the route traveled **c :** a group of church congregations ministered to by one pastor **4 a :** the complete path of an electric current including usu. the source of electric energy **b :** an assemblage of electronic elements **:** HOOKUP **c :** a two-way communication path between points (as in a computer) **5 a :** an association of similar groups **:** LEAGUE **b :** a number or series of public outlets (as theaters, radio shows, or arenas) offering the same kind of presentation **c :** a number of similar social gatherings ⟨cocktail ~⟩ — **cir·cuit·al** \-kət-ᵊl\ *adj*

[2]**circuit** *vt* (15c) **:** to make a circuit about ~ *vi* **:** to make a circuit

circuit breaker *n* (1872) **:** a switch that automatically interrupts an electric circuit under an infrequent abnormal condition

circuit court *n* (1708) **:** a court that sits at two or more places within one judicial district

circuit judge *n* (1801) **:** a judge who holds a circuit court

cir·cu·itous \(,)sər-'kyü-ət-əs\ *adj* (1664) **1 :** not being forthright or direct in language or action **2 :** having a circular or winding course ⟨a ~ route⟩ — **cir·cu·itous·ly** *adv* — **cir·cu·itous·ness** *n*

circuit rider *n* (1837) **:** a clergyman assigned to a circuit esp. in a rural area

cir·cuit·ry \'sər-kə-trē\ *n, pl* **-ries** (1946) **1 :** the detailed plan of an electric circuit **2 :** the components of an electric circuit

cir·cu·ity \(,)sər-'kyü-ət-ē\ *n, pl* **-ities** [irreg. fr. *circuit*] (1626) **:** lack of straightforwardness **:** INDIRECTION ⟨mired so deeply in its own complicated ~ of words —C. O. Gregory⟩

[1]**cir·cu·lar** \'sər-kyə-lər\ *adj* [ME *circuler,* fr. MF, fr. LL *circularis,* fr. L *circulus* circle] (15c) **1 a :** having the form of a circle **:** ROUND **b :** moving in or describing a circle or spiral **2 a :** of or relating to a circle or its mathematical properties ⟨a ~ arc⟩ **b :** having a circular base or bases ⟨a ~ cylinder⟩ **3 :** CIRCUITOUS, INDIRECT ⟨a ~ explanation⟩ **4 :** being or involving reasoning that uses in the argument or proof a conclusion to be proved or one of its unproved consequences **5 :** marked by or moving in a cycle **6 :** intended for circulation — **cir·cu·lar·i·ty** \,sər-kyə-'lar-ət-ē\ *n* — **cir·cu·lar·ly** \'sər-kyə-lər-lē\ *adv* — **cir·cu·lar·ness** *n*

[2]**circular** *n* (1789) **:** a paper (as a leaflet) intended for wide distribution

circular dichroism *n* (ca. 1961) **1 :** the property (as of an optically active medium) of unequal absorption of right and left plane-polarized light so that the emergent light is elliptically polarized **2 :** a spectroscopic technique that makes use of circular dichroism

circular file *n* (1967) **:** WASTEBASKET

circular function *n* (1884) **:** TRIGONOMETRIC FUNCTION

cir·cu·lar·ize \'sər-kyə-lə-,rīz\ *vt* **-ized; -iz·ing** (1848) **1 a :** to send circulars to **b :** to poll by questionnaire **2 :** PUBLICIZE — **cir·cu·lar·iza·tion** \,sər-kyə-lə-rə-'zā-shən\ *n*

circular saw *n* (1817) **:** a power saw with a circular cutting blade; *also* **:** the blade itself

cir·cu·late \'sər-kyə-,lāt\ *vb* **-lat·ed; -lat·ing** [L *circulatus,* pp. of *circulare,* fr. *circulus*] *vi* (1650) **1 :** to move in a circle, circuit, or orbit; *esp* **:** to follow a course that returns to the starting point ⟨blood ~s through the body⟩ **2 :** to pass from person to person or place to place: as **a :** to flow without obstruction **b :** to become well-known or widespread ⟨rumors *circulated* through the town⟩ **c :** to go from group to group at a social gathering **d :** to come into the hands of readers; *specif* **:** to become sold or distributed ~ *vt* **:** to cause to circulate — **cir·cu·lat·able** \-,lāt-ə-bəl\ *adj* — **cir·cu·la·tive** \-,lāt-iv\ *adj* — **cir·cu·la·tor** \-,lāt-ər\ *n*

circulating decimal *n* (1768) **:** REPEATING DECIMAL

cir·cu·la·tion \,sər-kyə-'lā-shən\ *n* (1654) **1 :** orderly movement through a circuit; *esp* **:** the movement of blood through the vessels of the body induced by the pumping action of the heart **2 :** FLOW **3 a :** passage or transmission from person to person or place to place; *esp* **:** the interchange of currency ⟨coins in ~⟩ **b :** the extent of dissemination: as (1) **:** the average number of copies of a publication sold over a given period (2) **:** the total number of items borrowed from a library

cir·cu·la·to·ry \'sər-kyə-lə-,tōr-ē, -,tȯr-\ *adj* (1605) **:** of or relating to circulation or the circulatory system ⟨~ failure⟩

circulatory system *n* (1862) **:** the system of blood, blood vessels, lymphatics, and heart concerned with the circulation of the blood and lymph

circum- *prefix* [OF or L; OF, fr. L, fr. *circum,* fr. *circus* circle — more at CIRCLE] **:** around **:** about ⟨*circum*polar⟩

cir·cum·am·bi·ent \,sər-kə-'mam-bē-ənt\ *adj* [LL *circumambient-, circumambiens,* prp. of *circumambire* to surround in a circle, fr. L *circum-* + *ambire* to go around — more at AMBIENT] (1633) **:** being on all sides **:** ENCOMPASSING — **cir·cum·am·bi·ent·ly** *adv*

cir·cum·am·bu·late \-byə-,lāt\ *vt* **-lat·ed; -lat·ing** [LL *circumambulatus,* pp. of *circumambulare,* fr. L *circum-* + *ambulare* to walk] (ca. 1656) **:** to circle on foot esp. ritualistically — **cir·cum·am·bu·la·tion** \-,mam-byə-'lā-shən\ *n*

cir·cum·cen·ter \'sər-kəm-,sent-ər\ *n* (ca. 1889) **:** the point at which the perpendicular bisectors of the sides of a triangle intersect and which is equidistant from the three vertices

cir·cum·cir·cle \-,sər-kəl\ *n* (1885) **:** a circle which passes through all the vertices of a polygon (as a triangle)

cir·cum·cise \'sər-kəm-,sīz\ *vt* **-cised; -cis·ing** [ME *circumcisen,* fr. L *circumcisus,* pp. of *circumcidere,* fr. *circum-* + *caedere* to cut — more at CONCISE] (13c) **:** to cut off the prepuce of (a male) or the clitoris of (a female) — **cir·cum·cis·er** *n*

cir·cum·ci·sion \,sər-kəm-'sizh-ən, 'sər-kəm-,\ *n* (12c) **1 a :** the act of circumcising; *specif* **:** a Jewish rite performed on male infants as a sign of inclusion in the Jewish religious community **b :** the condition of being circumcised **2** *cap* **:** January 1 observed as a church festival in commemoration of the circumcision of Jesus

cir·cum·fer·ence \sə(r)-'kəm(p)-fərn(t)s, -f(ə-)rən(t)s\ *n* [ME, fr. MF, fr. L *circumferentia,* fr. *circumferre* to carry around, fr. *circum-* + *ferre* to carry — more at BEAR] (14c) **1 :** the perimeter of a circle **2 :** the external boundary or surface of a figure or object **:** PERIPHERY — **cir·cum·fer·en·tial** \-,kəm(p)-fə-'ren-chəl\ *adj*

[1]**cir·cum·flex** \'sər-kəm-,fleks\ *adj* [L *circumflexus,* pp. of *circumflectere* to bend around, mark with a circumflex, fr. *circum-* + *flectere* to bend] (1577) **1 :** characterized by the pitch, quantity, or quality indicated by a circumflex **2 :** marked with a circumflex

[2]**circumflex** *n* (1609) **:** a mark ˆ, ˜, or ¯ orig. used in Greek over long vowels to indicate a rising-falling tone and in other languages to mark length, contraction, or a particular vowel quality

cir·cum·flu·ent \(,)sər-'kəm-flə-wənt, ,sər-kəm-'flü-ənt\ *adj* [fr. L *circumfluent-, circumfluens,* prp. of *circumfluere* to flow around, fr. *circum-* + *fluere* to flow] (1577) **:** flowing round or surrounding in the manner of a fluid — **cir·cum·flu·ous** \(,)sər-'kəm-flə-wəs\ *adj*

cir·cum·fuse \,sər-kəm-'fyüz\ *vt* **-fused; -fus·ing** [L *circumfusus,* pp. of *circumfundere* to pour around, fr. *circum-* + *fundere* to pour — more at FOUND] (1605) **:** SURROUND, ENVELOP — **cir·cum·fu·sion** \-'fyü-zhən\ *n*

cir·cum·ja·cent \,sər-kəm-'jās-ᵊnt\ *adj* [L *circumjacent-, circumjacens,* prp. of *circumjacēre* to lie around, fr. *circum-* + *jacēre* to lie — more at ADJACENT] (15c) **:** lying adjacent on all sides **:** SURROUNDING

cir·cum·lo·cu·tion \,sər-kəm-lō-'kyü-shən\ *n* [L *circumlocution-, circumlocutio,* fr. *circum-* + *locutio* speech, fr. *locutus,* pp. of *loqui* to speak] (15c) **1 :** the use of an unnecessarily large number of words to express an idea **2 :** evasion in speech — **cir·cum·loc·u·to·ry** \-'läk-yə-,tōr-ē, -,tȯr-\ *adj*

cir·cum·lu·nar \,sər-kəm-'lü-nər\ *adj* (ca. 1909) **:** revolving about or surrounding the moon

cir·cum·nav·i·gate \-'nav-ə-,gāt\ *vt* [L *circumnavigatus,* pp. of *circumnavigare* to sail around, fr. *circum-* + *navigare* to navigate] (1634) **:** to go completely around (as the earth) esp. by water; *also* **:** to go around instead of through **:** BYPASS ⟨~ a congested area⟩ — **cir·cum·nav·i·ga·tion** \-,nav-ə-'gā-shən\ *n* — **cir·cum·nav·i·ga·tor** \-'nav-ə-,gāt-ər\ *n*

cir·cum·po·lar \,sər-kəm-'pō-lər\ *adj* (1686) **1 :** continually visible above the horizon ⟨a ~ star⟩ **2 :** surrounding or found in the vicinity of a terrestrial pole

cir·cum·scis·sile \-'sis-əl, -,īl\ *adj* [L *circumscissus,* pp. of *circumscindere* to tear around, fr. *circum-* + *scindere* to cut, split — more at SHED] (1835) **:** dehiscing by fissure around the capsule of the fruit

cir·cum·scribe \'sər-kəm-,skrīb\ *vt* [L *circumscribere,* fr. *circum-* + *scribere* to write, draw — more at SCRIBE] (1835) **1 a :** to constrict the range or activity of definitely and clearly **b :** to define or mark off carefully **2 a :** to draw a line around **b :** to surround by a boundary **3 :** to construct or be constructed around (a geometrical figure) so as to touch as many points as possible ***syn*** see LIMIT

cir·cum·scrip·tion \,sər-kəm-'skrip-shən\ *n* [L *circumscription-, circumscriptio,* fr. *circumscriptus,* pp. of *circumscribere*] (1531) **1 :** the act of circumscribing **:** the state of being circumscribed: as **a :** DEFINITION, DELIMITATION **b :** LIMITATION **2 :** something that circumscribes: as **a :** LIMIT, BOUNDARY **b :** RESTRICTION **3 :** a circumscribed area or district

cir·cum·spect \'sər-kəm-,spekt\ *adj* [ME, fr. MF or L; MF *circonspect,* fr. L *circumspectus,* fr. pp. of *circumspicere* to look around, be cautious, fr. *circum-* + *specere* to look — more at SPY] (15c) **:** careful to consider all circumstances and possible consequences **:** PRUDENT ***syn*** see CAUTIOUS — **cir·cum·spec·tion** \,sər-kəm-'spek-shən\ *n* — **cir·cum·spect·ly** \'sər-kəm-,spek-tlē\ *adv*

cir·cum·stance \'sər-kəm-,stan(t)s, -stən(t)s\ *n* [ME, fr. OF, fr. L *circumstantia,* fr. *circumstant-, circumstans,* prp. of *circumstare* to stand around, fr. *circum-* + *stare* to stand — more at STAND] (13c) **1 a :** a condition, fact, or event accompanying, conditioning, or determining another **:** an essential or inevitable concomitant ⟨the weather is a ~ to be taken into consideration⟩ **b :** a subordinate or accessory fact or detail ⟨cost is a minor ~ in this case⟩ **c :** a piece of evidence that indicates the probability or improbability of an event (as a crime) ⟨the ~ of the missing weapon told against him⟩ ⟨the ~s suggest murder⟩ **2 a :** the sum of essential and environmental factors (as of an event or situation) ⟨constant and rapid change in economic ~ —G. M. Trevelyan⟩ **b :** state of affairs **:** EVENTUALITY ⟨open rebellion was a rare ~⟩ — often used in pl. ⟨a victim of ~s⟩ **c** *pl* **:** situation with regard to wealth ⟨he was in easy ~s⟩ **3 :** attendant formalities and ceremonial ⟨pride, pomp, and ~ of glorious war —Shak.⟩ **4 :** an event that constitutes a detail (as of a narrative or course of events) ⟨considering each ~ in turn⟩ ***syn*** see OCCURRENCE

cir·cum·stanced \-,stan(t)st, -stən(t)st\ *adj* (1611) **:** placed in particular circumstances esp. in regard to property or income

cir·cum·stan·tial \,sər-kəm-'stan-chəl\ *adj* (1600) **1 :** belonging to, consisting in, or dependent on circumstances **2 :** pertinent but not essential **:** INCIDENTAL **3 :** marked by careful attention to detail **:** abounding in factual details ⟨a ~ account of the fight⟩ **4 :** CEREMONIAL — **cir·cum·stan·ti·al·i·ty** \-,stan-chē-'al-ət-ē\ *n* — **cir·cum·stan·tial·ly** \-'stanch-(ə-)lē\ *adv*

syn CIRCUMSTANTIAL, MINUTE, PARTICULAR, DETAILED mean dealing with a matter fully and usu. point by point. CIRCUMSTANTIAL implies fullness of detail that fixes something described in time and space ⟨a *circumstantial* account of our visit⟩ MINUTE implies close and searching attention to the smallest details ⟨a *minute* examination of a fossil⟩ PARTICULAR implies a precise attention to every detail ⟨a *particular* description of the scene of the crime⟩ DETAILED stresses abundance or completeness of detail ⟨a *detailed* analysis of the event⟩

circumstantial evidence *n* (1736) **:** evidence that tends to prove a fact by proving other events or circumstances which afford a basis for a reasonable inference of the occurrence of the fact at issue

cir·cum·stan·ti·ate \,sər-kəm-'stan-chē-,āt\ *vt* **-at·ed; -at·ing** (ca. 1652) **:** to supply with circumstantial evidence or support

cir·cum·stel·lar \,sər-kəm-'stel-ər\ *adj* (1951) **:** surrounding or occurring in the vicinity of a star

1cir·cum·val·late \-ˈval-ˌāt\ *vt* **-lat·ed; -lat·ing** [L *circumvallatus,* pp. of *circumvallare,* fr. *circum-* + *vallum* rampart — more at WALL] (ca. 1755) **:** to surround by or as if by a rampart — **cir·cum·val·la·tion** \-ˌval-ˈā-shən\ *n*

2cir·cum·val·late \-ˈval-ˌāt, -ˈval-ət\ *adj* (1849) **:** being any of approximately 12 large papillae near the back of the tongue each of which is surrounded with a marginal sulcus and supplied with taste buds responsive to bitter flavors

cir·cum·vent \ˌsər-kəm-ˈvent\ *vt* [L *circumventus,* pp. of *circumvenire,* fr. *circum-* + *venire* to come — more at COME] (1553) **1 a :** to hem in **b :** to make a circuit around **2 :** to manage to get around esp. by ingenuity or stratagem ⟨the setup ~*ed* the red tape of immigration — Lynne McTaggart⟩ ***syn*** see FRUSTRATE — **cir·cum·ven·tion** \-ˈven-chən\ *n*

cir·cum·vo·lu·tion \(ˌ)sər-ˌkəm-və-ˈlü-shən, ˌsər-kəm-vō-\ *n* [ME *circumvolucioun,* fr. ML *circumvolution-, circumvolutio,* fr. L *circumvolutus,* pp. of *circumvolvere* to revolve, fr. *circum-* + *volvere* to roll — more at VOLUBLE] (15c) **:** an act or instance of turning around an axis

cir·cus \ˈsər-kəs\ *n, often attrib* [L, circle, circus — more at CIRCLE] (14c) **1 a :** a large arena enclosed by tiers of seats on three or all four sides and used esp. for sports or spectacles (as athletic contests, exhibitions of horsemanship, or in ancient times chariot racing) **b :** a public spectacle **2 a :** an arena often covered by a tent and used for variety shows usu. including feats of physical skill, wild animal acts, and performances by clowns **b :** a circus performance **c :** the physical plant, livestock, and personnel of such a circus **d :** something suggestive of a circus (as in frenzied activity or noisy confusion) ⟨huge political clambakes, outsize chowder parties and other eating ~*es* —Thomas Mario⟩ **3 a** *obs* **:** CIRCLE, RING **b** *Brit* **:** a usu. circular area at an intersection of streets — **cir·cusy** \-kə-sē\ *adj*

ci·ré *also* **ci·re** \sə-ˈrā\ *n* [F, fr. pp. of *cirer* to wax, fr. *cire* wax, fr. L *cera* — more at CERUMEN] (1921) **1 :** a highly glazed finish for fabrics usu. achieved by applying wax to the fabric **2 :** a fabric or garment with a ciré finish

cirque \ˈsərk\ *n* [F, fr. L *circus*] (1601) **1** *archaic* **:** CIRCUS **2 :** CIRCLE, CIRCLET **3 :** a deep steep-walled basin on a mountain shaped like half a bowl

cirr- *or* **cirri-** *or* **cirro-** *comb form* [NL *cirrus*] **:** cirrus ⟨*cirri*ped⟩ ⟨*cirr*ose⟩ ⟨*cirro*stratus⟩

cir·rho·sis \sə-ˈrō-səs\ *n, pl* **-rho·ses** \-ˌsēz\ [NL, fr. Gk *kirrhos* orange-colored; akin to OE *hār* gray — more at HOAR] (1839) **:** fibrosis esp. of the liver with hardening caused by excessive formation of connective tissue followed by contraction — **cir·rhot·ic** \-ˈrät-ik\ *adj or n*

cir·ro·cu·mu·lus \ˌsir-ō-ˈkyü-myə-ləs\ *n* [NL] (ca. 1803) **:** a cloud form of small white rounded masses at a high altitude usu. in regular groupings forming a mackerel sky — see CLOUD illustration

cir·ro·stra·tus \ˌsir-ō-ˈstrāt-əs, -ˈstrat-\ *n* [NL] (ca. 1803) **:** a fairly uniform layer of high stratus darker than cirrus — see CLOUD illustration

cir·rous \ˈsir-əs\ *adj* (1815) **:** resembling cirrus clouds

cir·rus \ˈsir-əs\ *n, pl* **cir·ri** \ˈsi(ə)r-ˌī\ [NL, fr. L, curl] (1708) **1 :** TENDRIL **2 :** a slender usu. flexible animal appendage: as **a :** an arm of a barnacle — see BARNACLE illustration **b :** a filament of a crinoid **c :** a fused group of cilia functioning like a limb on some protozoans **d :** the male copulatory organ of various invertebrate animals **3 :** a wispy white cloud usu. of minute ice crystals formed at altitudes of 20,000 to 40,000 feet (6,000 to 12,000 meters) — see CLOUD illustration

cis \ˈsis\ *adj* [L, lit., on this side] (1888) **:** having or characterized by certain atoms or groups on the same side of the molecule

cis- *prefix* [L, fr. *cis* — more at HE] **1 :** on this side ⟨*cis*-border⟩ ⟨*cis*atlantic⟩ **2** *usu ital* **:** cis ⟨*cis*-dichloroethylene⟩ — compare TRANS- 2b

cis·al·pine \(ˈ)sis-ˈal-ˌpīn\ *adj* (1542) **:** situated on the south side of the Alps ⟨*Cisalpine* Gaul⟩ — compare TRANSALPINE

cis·co \ˈsis-(ˌ)kō\ *n, pl* **ciscoes** [short for CanF *ciscoette*] (1848) **:** any of various whitefishes (genus *Coregonus*) including important food fishes (esp. *C. artedii*) of the Great Lakes region

cis·lu·nar \(ˈ)sis-ˈlü-nər\ *adj* (1867) **:** lying between the earth and the moon or the moon's orbit ⟨~ space⟩

cissy *Brit var of* SISSY

cist \ˈsist, ˈkist\ *n* [W, chest, fr. L *cista*] (1804) **:** a neolithic or Bronze Age burial chamber typically lined with stone

Cis·ter·cian \sis-ˈtər-shən\ *n* [ML *Cistercium* Cîteaux] (14c) **:** a member of a monastic order founded by St. Robert of Molesme in 1098 at Cîteaux, France, under an austere Benedictine rule — **Cistercian** *adj*

cis·tern \ˈsis-tərn\ *n* [ME, fr. OF *cisterne,* fr. L *cisterna,* fr. *cista* box, chest — more at CHEST] (13c) **1 :** an artificial reservoir for storing liquids and esp. water; *specif* **:** an often underground tank for storing rainwater **2 :** a large usu. silver vessel formerly used (as in cooling wine) at the dining table **3 :** a fluid-containing sac or cavity in an organism

cis·ter·na \sis-ˈtər-nə\ *n, pl* **-nae** \-ˌnē\ [NL, fr. L, reservoir] (ca. 1860) **:** CISTERN 3: as **a :** one of the large spaces under the arachnoid membrane **b :** one of the interconnected flattened vesicles or tubules comprising the endoplasmic reticulum — **cis·ter·nal** \-nəl\ *adj*

cis·tron \ˈsis-ˌträn\ *n* [*cis-* + *trans-* + 2*-on*] (1957) **:** a segment of DNA which specifies a single functional unit (as a protein or enzyme) and within which two heterozygous and closely linked recessive mutations are expressed in the phenotype when on different chromosomes but not when on the same chromosome — **cis·tron·ic** \sis-ˈträn-ik\ *adj*

cit·a·del \ˈsit-əd-ᵊl, -ə-ˌdel\ *n* [MF *citadelle,* fr. OIt *cittadella,* dim. of *cittade* city, fr. ML *civitat-, civitas* — more at CITY] (1562) **1 :** a fortress that commands a city **2 :** STRONGHOLD

ci·ta·tion \sī-ˈtā-shən\ *n* (13c) **1 :** an official summons to appear (as before a court) **2 a :** an act of quoting; *esp* **:** the citing of a previously settled case at law **b :** EXCERPT, QUOTE **3 :** MENTION: as **a :** a formal statement of the achievements of a person receiving an academic honor **b :** specific reference in a military dispatch to meritorious performance of duty ***syn*** see ENCOMIUM — **ci·ta·tion·al** \-shnəl, -shən-ᵊl\ *adj*

cite \ˈsīt\ *vt* **cit·ed; cit·ing** [MF *citer* to cite, summon, fr. L *citare* to put in motion, rouse, summon, fr. *citus,* pp. of *ciēre* to stir, move — more at HIGHT] (15c) **1 :** to call upon officially or authoritatively to appear (as before a court) **2 :** to quote by way of example, authority, or proof **3 a :** to refer to; *esp* **:** to mention formally in commendation or praise **b :** to name in a citation **4 :** to bring forward or call to another's attention esp. as an example, proof, or precedent ***syn*** see SUMMON — **citable** \ˈsīt-ə-bəl\ *adj*

cith·a·ra \ˈsith-ə-rə, ˈkith-\ *var of* KITHARA

cith·er \ˈsith-ər, ˈsith-\ *n* [F *cithare,* fr. L *cithara* kithara, fr. Gk *kithara*] (1606) **:** CITTERN

cit·ied \ˈsit-ēd\ *adj* (1612) **:** occupied by cities

citi·fied \ˈsit-i-ˌfīd\ *adj* (1828) **:** of, relating to, or characteristic of a sophisticated urban style of living — often used disparagingly

citi·fy \-ˌfī\ *vt* **-fied; -fy·ing** (1825) **:** URBANIZE

cit·i·zen \ˈsit-ə-zən *also* -sən\ *n* [ME *citizein,* fr. AF *citezein,* alter. of OF *citeien,* fr. *cité* city] (14c) **1 :** an inhabitant of a city or town; *esp* **:** one entitled to the rights and privileges of a freeman **2 a :** a member of a state **b :** a native or naturalized person who owes allegiance to a government and is entitled to protection from it **3 :** a civilian as distinguished from a specialized servant of the state — **cit·i·zen·ly** \-zən-lē *also* -sən-\ *adj*

syn CITIZEN, SUBJECT, NATIONAL mean a person owing allegiance to and entitled to the protection of a sovereign state. CITIZEN is preferred for one owing allegiance to a state in which sovereign power is retained by the people and sharing in the political rights of those people; SUBJECT implies allegiance to a personal sovereign such as a monarch; NATIONAL designates one who may claim the protection of a state and applies esp. to one living or traveling outside that state.

cit·i·zen·ess \-zə-nəs *also* -sə-\ *n* (1796) **:** a female citizen

cit·i·zen·ry \-zən-rē *also* -sən-\ *n, pl* **-ries** (1819) **:** a whole body of citizens

citizen's arrest *n* (1952) **:** an arrest made not by a law officer but by a citizen who derives his authority from the fact that he is a citizen

citizens band *n* (1965) **:** a range of radio-wave frequencies that in the U.S. is allocated officially for private radio communications

cit·i·zen·ship \ˈsit-ə-zən-ˌship\ *n* (1611) **1 :** the status of being a citizen **2 a :** membership in a community (as a college) **b :** the quality of an individual's response to membership in a community

citr- *or* **citri-** *or* **citro-** *comb form* [NL, fr. *Citrus,* genus name] **1 :** citrus ⟨*citri*culture⟩ **2 :** citric acid ⟨*citr*ate⟩

cit·ral \ˈsi-ˌtral\ *n* [ISV] (1891) **:** an unsaturated liquid isomeric aldehyde $C_{10}H_{16}O$ of many essential oils that has a strong lemon and verbena odor and is used esp. in perfumery and as a flavoring

ci·trate \ˈsi-ˌtrāt\ *n* [ISV] (1794) **:** a salt or ester of citric acid

cit·ric acid \ˌsi-trik-\ *n* [ISV] (1813) **:** a tricarboxylic acid $C_6H_8O_7$ occurring in cellular metabolism, obtained esp. from lemon and lime juices or by fermentation of sugars, and used as a flavoring

citric acid cycle *n* (1942) **:** KREBS CYCLE

cit·ri·cul·ture \ˈsi-trə-ˌkəl-chər\ *n* (1916) **:** the cultivation of citrus fruits — **cit·ri·cul·tur·ist** \ˌsi-trə-ˈkəlch-(ə-)rəst\ *n*

1cit·rine \ˈsi-ˌtrīn\ *adj* [ME, fr. MF *citrin,* fr. ML *citrinus,* fr. L *citrus* citron tree] (14c) **:** resembling a citron or lemon esp. in color

2ci·trine \si-ˈtrēn\ *n* (1748) **:** a black quartz changed in color by heating into a semiprecious yellow stone resembling topaz

ci·tri·nin \si-ˈtrī-nən\ *n* [NL *citrinum* (specific epithet of *Penicillium citrinum* + E 1*-in*] (ca. 1931) **:** a toxic antibiotic $C_{13}H_{14}O_5$ that is produced esp. by a penicillium (*Penicillium citrinum*) and an aspergillus (*Aspergillus niveus*) and is bactericidal for some gram-positive bacteria

cit·ron \ˈsi-trən\ *n* [ME, fr. MF, fr. OProv, modif. of L *citrus*] (15c) **1 a :** a fruit like the lemon in appearance and structure but larger **b :** a small shrubby citrus tree (*Citrus medica*) that produces citrons **c :** the preserved rind of the citron used esp. in cakes and puddings **2 :** a small hard-fleshed watermelon used esp. in pickles and preserves

cit·ro·nel·la \ˌsi-trə-ˈnel-ə\ *n* [NL, fr. F *citronnelle* lemon balm, fr. *citron*] (1858) **:** a fragrant grass (*Cymbopogon nardus*) of southern Asia that yields an oil used in perfumery and as an insect repellent; *also* **:** its oil

cit·ro·nel·lal \-ˈnel-ˌal\ *n* [ISV, fr. NL *citronella*] (1893) **:** a lemon-odored aldehyde $C_{10}H_{18}O$ found in many essential oils and used in perfumery

cit·ro·nel·lol \-ˈnel-ˌȯl, -ˌōl\ *n* [ISV *citronell-* (fr. NL *citronella*) + *-ol*] (1872) **:** an unsaturated liquid alcohol $C_{10}H_{20}O$ with a roselike odor that is found in two optically active forms in many essential oils (as rose oil) and is used in perfumery and soaps

ci·trov·o·rum factor \sə-ˈträv-ə-rəm-\ *n* [NL *citrovorum* (specific epithet of *Leuconostoc citrovorum*), fr. *citr-* + *-vorum,* neut. of L *-vorus* -vorous] (1948) **:** a metabolically active form of folic acid that has been used in cancer therapy to protect normal cells against methotrexate

cit·rul·line \ˈsi-trə-ˌlēn\ *n* [ISV, fr. NL *Citrullus,* genus name of the watermelon] (1930) **:** a crystalline amino acid $C_6H_{13}N_3O_3$ formed esp. as an intermediate in the conversion of ornithine to arginine in the living system

cit·rus \ˈsi-trəs\ *n, pl* **citrus** *or* **cit·rus·es** *often attrib* [NL, genus name, fr. L] (1825) **:** any of a group of often thorny trees and shrubs (*Citrus* and related genera) of the rue family grown in warm regions for their edible fruit (as the orange) with firm usu. thick rind and pulpy flesh

citrus red mite *n* (1935) **:** a comparatively large mite (*Panonychus citri*) that is a destructive pest on the foliage of citrus — called also *citrus red spider*

cit·tern \ˈsit-ərn\ *or* **cith·ern** \ˈsith-ərn, ˈsith-\ *or* **cith·ren** \ˈsith-rən\ *n* [blend of *cither* and *gittern*] (1566) **:** a Renaissance stringed instrument like a guitar with a flat pear-shaped body

city \ˈsit-ē\ *n, pl* **cit·ies** *often attrib* [ME *citie* large or small town, fr. OF *cité,* fr. ML *civitat-, civitas,* fr. L, citizenship, state, city of Rome, fr. *civis* citizen — more at HOME] (13c) **1 a :** an inhabited place of greater size, population, or importance than a town or village **b :** an incorporated British town usu. of major size or importance having the status of an episcopal see **c :** the financial district of London **d :** a usu. large or important municipality in the U.S. governed under a charter granted by the state **e :** an incorporated municipal unit of the highest class in Canada **2 :** CITY-STATE **3 :** the people of a city

city clerk *n* (1919) : a public officer charged with recording the official proceedings and vital statistics of a city
city council *n* (1789) : the legislative body of a city
city editor *n* (1834) : a newspaper editor usu. in charge of local news and staff assignments
city father *n* (1845) : a member (as an alderman or councilman) of the governing body of a city
city hall *n* (1675) **1 :** the chief administrative building of a city **2 a :** a municipal government **b :** city officialdom or bureaucracy ⟨you can't fight *city hall*⟩
city manager *n* (1913) : an official employed by an elected council to direct the administration of a city government
city planning *n* (1912) : the drawing up of an organized arrangement (as of streets, parks, and business and residential areas) of a city — **city planner** *n*
city room *n* (1919) : the department where local news is handled in a newspaper editorial office
city·scape \'sit-ē-,skāp\ *n* (1856) **1 :** a city viewed as a scene ⟨the skyscrapers which now bedizen the American ~ —*Amer. Mercury*⟩ **2 :** an artistic representation of a city
city slicker *n* (1924) : SLICKER 2b
city–state \'sit-ē-'stāt, -,stāt\ *n* (1893) : an autonomous state consisting of a city and surrounding territory
city·wide \'sit-ē-,wīd\ *adj* (1961) : including all parts of a city
civ·et \'siv-ət\ *n* [MF *civette*, fr. OIt *zibetto*, fr. Ar *zabād* civet perfume] (1532) **1 :** CIVET CAT **2 :** a thick yellowish musky-odored substance found in a pouch near the sexual organs of the civet cat and used in perfume
civet cat *n* (1607) **1 a :** any of several carnivorous mammals (family Viverridae); *esp* **:** a long-bodied short-legged African animal (*Civettictis civetta*) that produces most of the civet of commerce **b :** CACOMISTLE **c :** any of the small spotted skunks (genus *Spilogale*) of western No. America **2 :** the fur of a civet cat

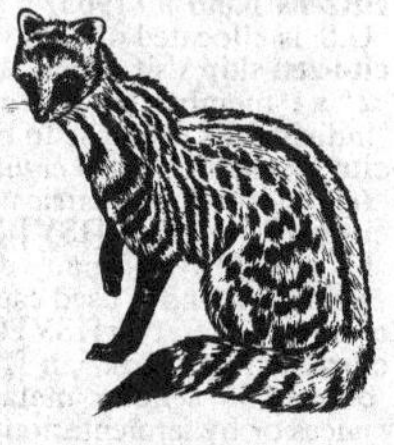
civet cat 1a

civ·ic \'siv-ik\ *adj* [L *civicus*, fr. *civis* citizen] (1542) : of or relating to a citizen, a city, citizenship, or civil affairs — **civ·i·cal·ly** \'siv-i-k(ə-)lē\ *adv*
civ·ic–mind·ed \,siv-ik-'mīn-dəd\ *adj* (1947) : disposed to look after civic needs and interests — **civ·ic–mind·ed·ness** *n*
civ·ics \'siv-iks\ *n pl but sing or pl in constr* (1886) : a social science dealing with the rights and duties of citizens
civ·il \'siv-əl\ *adj* [ME, fr. MF, fr. L *civilis*, fr. *civis*] (14c) **1 a :** of or relating to citizens ⟨~ liberties⟩ **b :** of or relating to the state or its citizenry **2 a :** CIVILIZED ⟨~ society⟩ **b :** adequate in courtesy and politeness : MANNERLY **3 a :** of, relating to, or based on civil law **b :** relating to private rights and to remedies sought by action or suit distinct from criminal proceedings **c :** established by law **4** *of time* **:** based on the mean sun and legally recognized for use in ordinary affairs **5 :** of, relating to, or involving the general public, their activities, needs, or ways, or civic affairs as distinguished from special (as military or religious) affairs
syn CIVIL, POLITE, COURTEOUS, GALLANT, CHIVALROUS mean observant of the forms required by good breeding. CIVIL often suggests little more than the avoidance of overt rudeness ⟨a *civil* reply that showed a lack of real enthusiasm⟩ POLITE commonly implies polish of speech and manners and sometimes suggests an absence of cordiality ⟨the minister's conversation was as *polite* as it was condescending⟩ COURTEOUS implies more actively considerate or dignified politeness ⟨clerks who were unfailingly *courteous* to customers⟩ GALLANT and CHIVALROUS imply courteous attentiveness esp. to women; GALLANT suggests spirited and dashing behavior and ornate expressions of courtesy ⟨a *gallant* suitor of the old school⟩ CHIVALROUS suggests high-minded and self-sacrificing behavior ⟨a *chivalrous* display of duty⟩
civil death *n* (1767) : the status of a living person equivalent in its legal consequences to natural death; *specif* : deprivation of civil rights
civil defense *n* (1939) : the complex of protective measures and emergency relief activities conducted by civilians in case of hostile attack, sabotage, or natural disaster
civil disobedience *n* (1849) : refusal to obey governmental demands or commands esp. as a nonviolent and usu. collective means of forcing concessions from the government
civil engineer *n* (1792) : an engineer whose training or occupation is in the designing and construction of public works (as roads or harbors) and of various private works — **civil engineering** *n*
ci·vil·ian \sə-'vil-yən *also* -'vi-yən\ *n* (14c) **1 :** a specialist in Roman or modern civil law **2 a :** one not on active duty in a military, police, or fire-fighting force **b :** OUTSIDER 1 — **civilian** *adj*
ci·vil·ian·ize \-yə-,nīz\ *vt* **-ized; -iz·ing** (1870) : to convert from military to civilian status or control — **ci·vil·ian·iza·tion** \-,vil-yə-nə-'zā-shən\ *n*
civ·i·li·sa·tion, civ·i·lise *chiefly Brit var of* CIVILIZATION, CIVILIZE
ci·vil·i·ty \sə-'vil-ət-ē\ *n, pl* **-ties** (1533) **1** *archaic* **:** training in the humanities **2 a :** COURTESY, POLITENESS **b :** a polite act or expression
civ·i·li·za·tion \,siv-ə-lə-'zā-shən\ *n* (1772) **1 a :** a relatively high level of cultural and technological development; *specif* : the stage of cultural development at which writing and the keeping of written records is attained **b :** the culture characteristic of a particular time or place **2 :** the process of becoming civilized **3 a :** refinement of thought, manners, or taste **b :** a situation of urban comfort
civ·i·lize \'siv-ə-,līz\ *vb* **-lized; -liz·ing** *vt* (1601) **1 :** to cause to develop out of a primitive state; *specif* : to bring to a technically advanced and rationally ordered stage of cultural development **2 a :** EDUCATE, REFINE **b :** SOCIALIZE 1 ~ *vi* **:** to acquire the customs and amenities of a civil community — **civ·i·liz·er** *n*
civ·i·lized *adj* (1611) : characteristic of a state of civilization
civil law *n, often cap C&L* (14c) **1 :** Roman law esp. as set forth in the Justinian code **2 :** the body of private law developed from Roman law and used in Louisiana and in many countries outside the English-speaking world **3 :** the law established by a nation or state for its own jurisdiction **4 :** the law of civil or private rights
civil liberty *n* (1644) : freedom from arbitrary governmental interference (as with the right of free speech) specif. by denial of governmental power and in the U.S. esp. as guaranteed by the Bill of Rights — usu. used in pl. — **civil lib·er·tar·i·an** \-,lib-ər-'ter-ē-ən\ *n or adj*
civ·il·ly \'siv-ə(l)-lē\ *adv* (15c) **1 :** in terms of civil rights, law, or matters ⟨~ dead⟩ **2 :** in a civil manner : POLITELY
civil marriage *n* (ca. 1891) : a marriage performed by a magistrate
civil rights *n pl, often attrib* (1721) : the nonpolitical rights of a citizen; *esp* **:** the rights of personal liberty guaranteed to U.S. citizens by the 13th and 14th amendments to the Constitution and by acts of Congress
civil servant *n* (1800) **1 :** a member of a civil service **2 :** a member of the administrative staff of an international agency (as the United Nations)
civil service *n* (1785) : the administrative service of a government or international agency exclusive of the armed forces; *esp* : one in which appointments are determined by competitive examination
civil war *n* (15c) : a war between opposing groups of citizens of the same country
Civ·i·tan \'siv-ə-,tan\ *n* [*Civitan (club)*] (1926) : a member of a major national and international service club
civ·vy *also* **civ·ie** \'siv-ē\ *n, pl* **civvies** *also* **civies** (1889) **1** *pl* **:** civilian clothes as distinguished from a particular uniform (as of the military) **2 :** CIVILIAN
¹clab·ber \'klab-ər\ *n* [short for *bonnyclabber*] *chiefly dial* (1634) : sour milk that has thickened or curdled
²clabber *vi, chiefly dial* (ca. 1879) : CURDLE
clach·an \'klak-ən\ *n* [ME, fr. ScGael] *Scot & Irish* (15c) : HAMLET
¹clack \'klak\ *vb* [ME *clacken*, of imit. origin] *vi* (13c) **1 :** CHATTER, PRATTLE **2 :** to make an abrupt striking sound or series of sounds **3** *of fowl* **:** CACKLE, CLUCK ~ *vt* **1 :** to cause to make a clatter **2 :** to produce with a chattering sound; *specif* : BLAB — **clack·er** *n*
²clack *n* (15c) **1 a :** rapid continuous talk : CHATTER **b :** TONGUE **2** *archaic* **:** an object (as a clack valve) that produces clapping or rattling noises usu. in regular rapid sequence **3 :** a sound of clacking ⟨the ~ of a typewriter⟩
clack valve *n* (1726) : a valve usu. hinged at one edge that permits flow of fluid in one direction only and that closes with a clacking sound
Clac·to·ni·an \klak-'tō-nē-ən\ *adj* [*Clacton*-on-Sea, England] (1932) : of or relating to a Lower Paleolithic culture usu. characterized by stone flakes with a half cone at the point of striking
¹clad \'klad\ *adj* [pp. of *clothe*] (bef. 12c) **1 :** being covered or clothed ⟨ivy-*clad* buildings⟩ **2** *of a coin* **:** consisting of outer layers of one metal bonded to a core of a different metal
²clad *vt* **clad; clad·ding** (1939) : SHEATHE, FACE; *specif* : to cover (a metal) with another metal by bonding
³clad *n* (1941) **1 :** a composite material formed by cladding; *specif* : a clad coin **2 :** CLADDING; *specif* : the outer layer of a clad coin
clad- *or* **clado-** *comb form* [NL, fr. Gk *klad-, klado-*, fr. *klados* branch, shoot of a tree; akin to OE *holt* woods — more at HOLT] : slip : sprout ⟨*clado*phyll⟩
clad·ding \'klad-iŋ\ *n* (1936) : something that covers or overlays ⟨stone ~ on a building wall⟩; *specif* : metal coating bonded to a metal core
cla·dis·tic \klə-'dis-tik, kla-\ *adj* (ca. 1960) : based on phylogenetic relationships ⟨a ~ system of classification⟩ — **cla·dis·ti·cal·ly** \-ti-k(ə-)lē\ *adv*
cla·dis·tics \-tiks\ *n pl but sing in constr* (1966) : biological systematics based on phylogenetic relationships
cla·doc·er·an \klə-'däs-ə-rən\ *n* [NL *Cladocera*, fr. *clad-* + Gk *keras* horn — more at HORN] (ca. 1909) : any of an order (Cladocera) of minute chiefly freshwater branchiopod crustaceans that includes the water fleas
clad·ode \'klad-,ōd\ *n* [NL *cladodium*, fr. Gk *klados*] (1870) : CLADOPHYLL — **cla·do·di·al** \kla-'dōd-ē-əl\ *adj*
clado·gen·e·sis \,klad-ə-'jen-ə-səs\ *n* (1953) : evolutionary change characterized by treelike branching of taxa — compare ANAGENESIS — **cla·do·ge·net·ic** \,klad-ō-jə-'net-ik\ *adj* — **clado·ge·net·i·cal·ly** \-i-k(ə-)lē\ *adv*
clado·gram \'klad-ə-,gram\ *n* (1966) : a branching diagrammatic tree used in biological classification to illustrate phylogenetic relationships
clado·phyll \'klad-ə-,fil\ *n* (1879) : a branch assuming the form of and closely resembling an ordinary foliage leaf and often bearing leaves or flowers on its margins
¹claim \'klām\ *vt* [ME *claimen*, fr. MF *clamer*, fr. L *clamare* to cry out, shout; akin to L *calare* to call — more at LOW] (14c) **1 a :** to ask for esp. as a right ⟨~*ed* the inheritance⟩ **b :** to call for : REQUIRE ⟨this matter ~*s* our attention⟩ **c :** TAKE 16b ⟨the accident ~*ed* his life⟩ **2 :** to take as the rightful owner ⟨went to ~ his bags at the station⟩ **3 a :** to assert in the face of possible contradiction : MAINTAIN ⟨~*ed* that he'd been cheated⟩ **b :** to claim to have ⟨organization . . . which ~*s* 11,000 . . . members —Rolling Stone⟩ ***syn*** see DEMAND — **claim·able** \'klā-mə-bəl\ *adj* — **claim·er** *n*
²claim *n* (14c) **1 :** a demand for something due or believed to be due ⟨insurance ~⟩ **2 a :** a right to something; *specif* : a title to a debt, privilege, or other thing in the possession of another **b :** an assertion open to challenge ⟨a ~ of authenticity⟩ **3 :** something that is claimed; *esp* : a tract of land staked out
claim·ant \'klā-mənt\ *n* (15c) : one that asserts a right or title ⟨a ~ to an estate⟩
claiming race *n* (1935) : a horse race in which each entry is offered for sale for a specified price that must be deposited before the race
clair·au·di·ence \kla(ə)r-'ȯd-ē-ən(t)s, kle(ə)r-, -'äd-\ *n* [*clair-* (as in *clairvoyance*) + *audience* (act of hearing)] (1864) : the power or faculty of hearing something not present to the ear but regarded as having objective reality — **clair·au·di·ent** \-ənt\ *adj* — **clair·au·di·ent·ly** *adv*
clair·voy·ance \kla(ə)r-'vȯi-ən(t)s, kle(ə)r-\ *n* (1847) **1 :** the power or faculty of discerning objects not present to the senses **2 :** ability to perceive matters beyond the range of ordinary perception : PENETRATION
¹clair·voy·ant \-ənt\ *adj* [F, fr. *clair* clear (fr. L *clarus*) + *voyant*, prp. of *voir* to see, fr. L *vidēre* — more at WIT] (1671) **1 :** unusually perceptive : DISCERNING **2 :** of or relating to clairvoyance — **clair·voy·ant·ly** *adv*
²clairvoyant *n* (1851) : one having the power of clairvoyance

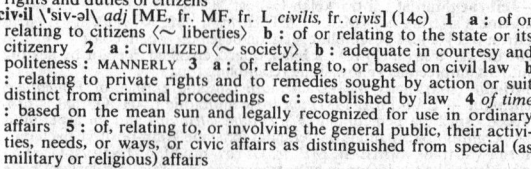

[1]**clam** \'klam\ *n* [ME, fr. OE *clamm* bond, fetter; akin to OHG *klamma* constriction, L *glomus* ball] (bef. 12c) **:** CLAMP, CLASP

[2]**clam** *n, often attrib* [[1]*clam;* fr. the clamping action of the shells] (1520) **1 a :** any of numerous edible marine bivalve mollusks living in sand or mud **b :** a freshwater mussel **2 :** a stolid or closemouthed person **3 :** CLAMSHELL **4 :** DOLLAR 3

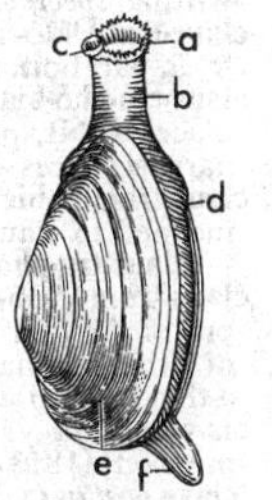

clam 1a: *a* incurrent orifice, *b* siphon, *c* excurrent orifice, *d* mantle, *e* shell, *f* foot

[3]**clam** *vi* **clammed; clam·ming** (1636) **:** to gather clams esp. by digging — **clam·mer** \-ər\ *n*

cla·mant \'klā-mənt, 'klam-ənt\ *adj* [L *clamant-, clamans,* prp. of *clamare* to cry out] (1639) **1 :** CLAMOROUS, BLATANT **2 :** demanding attention **:** URGENT — **cla·mant·ly** *adv*

clam·bake \'klam-,bāk\ *n* (1835) **1 a :** an outdoor party; *esp* **:** a seashore outing where food is usu. cooked on heated rocks covered by seaweed **b :** the food served at a clambake **2 :** a gathering characterized by noisy sociability; *esp* **:** a political rally

clam·ber \'klam-(b)ər\ *vi* **clam·bered; clam·ber·ing** \'klam-b(ə-)riŋ, 'klam-(ə-)riŋ\ [ME *clambren;* akin to OE *climban* to climb] (14c) **:** to climb awkwardly (as by scrambling) ⟨~*ed* over the rocks⟩ — **clam·ber·er** \-(b)ər-ər\ *n*

clam·my \'klam-ē\ *adj* **clam·mi·er; -est** [ME, prob. fr. *clammen* to smear, stick, fr. OE *clǣman;* akin to OE *clǣg* clay] (14c) **1 :** being damp, soft, sticky, and usu. cool ⟨a ~ and intensely cold mist —Charles Dickens⟩ **2 a :** lacking normal human warmth ⟨the ~ atmosphere of an institution⟩ **b :** ALOOF, REPELLENT — **clam·mi·ly** \'klam-ə-lē\ *adv* — **clam·mi·ness** \'klam-ē-nəs\ *n*

[1]**clam·or** \'klam-ər\ *n* [ME, fr. MF *clamour,* fr. L *clamor,* fr. *clamare* to cry out — more at CLAIM] (14c) **1 a :** noisy shouting **b :** a loud continuous noise **2 :** insistent public expression (as of support or protest) ⟨a ~ against increased taxes⟩

[2]**clamor** *vb* **clam·ored; clam·or·ing** \'klam-(ə-)riŋ\ *vi* (14c) **1 :** to make a din **2 :** to become loudly insistent ⟨~*ed* for his impeachment⟩ ~ *vt* **1 :** to utter or proclaim insistently and noisily **2 :** to influence by means of clamor

[3]**clamor** *vt* [origin unknown] *obs* (1611) **:** SILENCE

clam·or·ous \'klam-(ə-)rəs\ *adj* (15c) **1 :** marked by confused din or outcry **:** TUMULTUOUS ⟨the busy ~ market⟩ **2 :** noisily insistent ***syn*** see VOCIFEROUS — **clam·or·ous·ly** *adv* — **clam·or·ous·ness** *n*

clam·our \'klam-ər\ *chiefly Brit var of* CLAMOR

[1]**clamp** \'klamp\ *n* [ME, prob. fr. (assumed) MD *klampe;* akin to OE *clamm* bond, fetter — more at CLAM] (14c) **1 :** a device designed to bind or constrict or to press two or more parts together so as to hold them firmly **2 :** any of various instruments or appliances having parts brought together for holding or compressing something

[2]**clamp** *vt* (1677) **1 :** to fasten with or as if with a clamp **2 a :** to place by decree **:** IMPOSE — often used with *on* ⟨~*ed* on a curfew after the riots⟩ **b :** to hold tightly

clamp·down \'klamp-,daůn\ *n* (1940) **:** the act or action of making regulations and restrictions more stringent **:** CRACKDOWN ⟨a ~ on charge accounts, bank loans, and other inflationary influences —*Time*⟩

clamp down \(')klamp-'daůn\ *vi* (1937) **:** to impose restrictions **:** become repressive ⟨the police are *clamping down* on speeders⟩

clams casino *n pl but sing or pl in constr, often cap 2d C* (1952) **:** clams on the half shell usu. topped with green pepper and baked or broiled

clam·shell \'klam-,shel\ *n* (1877) **1 :** the shell of a clam **2 a :** a bucket or grapple (as on a dredge) having two hinged jaws **b :** an excavating machine having a clamshell **c :** either of a pair of doors (as in an airplane tail) that open out and away from each other

clam up *vi* (1916) **:** to become silent ⟨he *clammed up* when asked for details⟩

clam worm *n* (ca. 1885) **:** any of several large burrowing polychaete worms (as a nereis) often used as bait

clan \'klan\ *n* [ME, fr. ScGael *clann* offspring, clan, fr. OIr *cland* plant, offspring, fr. L *planta* plant] (15c) **1 a :** a Celtic group esp. in the Scottish Highlands comprising a number of households whose heads claim descent from a common ancestor **b :** SIB 3 **2 :** a group united by a common interest or common characteristics

clan·des·tine \klan-'des-tən *also* -,tīn *or* -,tēn *or* 'klan-dəs-\ *adj* [MF or L; MF *clandestin,* fr. L *clandestinus,* irreg. fr. *clam* secretly; akin to L *celare* to hide — more at HELL] (1566) **:** held in or conducted with secrecy **:** SURREPTITIOUS ***syn*** see SECRET — **clan·des·tine·ly** *adv* — **clan·des·tine·ness** *n* — **clan·des·tin·i·ty** \,klan-də-'stin-ət-ē, -des-'tin-\ *n*

[1]**clang** \'klaŋ\ *vb* [L *clangere;* akin to Gk *klazein* to scream, bark, OE *hliehhan* to laugh] *vi* (1576) **1 a :** to make a loud metallic ringing sound ⟨anvils ~*ed*⟩ **b :** to go with a clang **2 :** to utter the characteristic harsh cry of a bird ~ *vt* **:** to cause to clang ⟨~ a bell⟩

[2]**clang** *n* (1596) **1 :** a loud ringing metallic sound ⟨the ~ of a fire alarm⟩ **2 :** a harsh cry of a bird (as a crane or goose)

[1]**clan·gor** \'klaŋ-ər *also* -gər\ *n* [L *clangor,* fr. *clangere*] (1593) **:** a resounding clang or medley of clangs ⟨the ~ of hammers⟩ — **clan·gor·ous** \-(g)ə-rəs\ *adj* — **clan·gor·ous·ly** *adv*

[2]**clangor** *vi* (1837) **:** to make a clangor

clan·gour \'klaŋ-ər, -gər\ *chiefly Brit var of* CLANGOR

[1]**clank** \'klaŋk\ *vb* [prob. imit.] *vi* (1656) **1 :** to make a clank or series of clanks ⟨the radiator hissed and ~*ed*⟩ **2 :** to go with or as if with a clank ⟨tanks ~*ing* through the streets⟩ ~ *vt* **:** to cause to clank — **clank·ing·ly** \'klaŋ-kiŋ-lē\ *adv*

[2]**clank** *n* (1656) **:** a sharp brief metallic ringing sound

clan·nish \'klan-ish\ *adj* (1776) **1 :** of or relating to a clan **2 :** tending to associate only with a select group of similar background or status ⟨~ immigrants⟩ — **clan·nish·ly** *adv* — **clan·nish·ness** *n*

clans·man \'klanz-mən\ *n* (1810) **:** a member of a clan

[1]**clap** \'klap\ *vb* **clapped** *also* **clapt; clap·ping** [ME *clappen,* fr. OE *clæppan;* akin to OHG *klaphōn* to beat, L *glēba* clod — more at CLIP] *vt* (bef. 12c) **1 :** to strike (as two flat hard surfaces) together so as to produce a sharp percussive noise **2 a :** to strike (the hands) together repeatedly usu. in applause **b :** APPLAUD **3 :** to strike with the flat of the hand in a friendly way ⟨*clapped* his friend on the shoulder⟩ **4 :** to place, put, or set esp. energetically ⟨~ him into jail⟩ **5 :** to improvise hastily ~ *vi* **1 :** to produce a percussive sound; *esp* **:** SLAM **2 :** to go abruptly or briskly **3 :** APPLAUD

[2]**clap** *n* (13c) **1 :** a device that makes a clapping noise **2** *obs* **:** a sudden stroke of fortune and esp. ill fortune **3 :** a loud percussive noise; *specif* **:** a sudden crash of thunder **4 a :** a sudden blow **b :** a friendly slap ⟨a ~ on the shoulder⟩ **5 :** the sound of clapping hands; *esp* **:** APPLAUSE

[3]**clap** *n* [MF *clapoir* bubo] (1587) **:** GONORRHEA — often used with *the*

clap·board \'klab-ərd; 'kla(p)-,bō(ə)rd, -,bȯ(ə)rd\ *n* [part trans. of D *klaphout* stave wood] (1598) **1** *archaic* **:** a size of board for making staves and wainscoting **2 :** a narrow board usu. thicker at one edge than the other used for siding — **clapboard** *vt*

clapped–out \(')klap-'daůt, (')klapt-'aůt\ *adj, Brit* (1946) **:** WORN-OUT; *also* **:** TIRED

clap·per \'klap-ər\ *n* (14c) **:** one that claps: as **a :** the tongue of a bell **b :** a mechanical device that makes noise esp. by the banging of one part against another **c :** a person who applauds

clap·per·claw \'klap-ər-,klȯ\ *vt* [perh. fr. *clapper* + *claw* (v.)] (1590) **1** *dial Eng* **:** to claw with the nails **2** *dial Eng* **:** SCOLD, REVILE

[1]**clap·trap** \'klap-,trap\ *n* [[2]*clap;* fr. its attempt to win applause] (1799) **:** pretentious nonsense **:** TRASH

[2]**claptrap** *adj* (1815) **:** characterized by or suggestive of claptrap; *esp* **:** of a cheap showy nature ⟨~ sentiment⟩

claque \'klak\ *n* [F, fr. *claquer* to clap, of imit. origin] (1864) **1 :** a group hired to applaud at a performance **2 :** a group of sycophants

cla·queur \kla-'kər\ *n* [F, fr. *claquer* to clap] (1837) **:** a member of a claque

clar·ence \'klar-ən(t)s\ *n* [duke of *Clarence,* later William IV of England] (1837) **:** a closed four-wheeled four-passenger carriage

clar·et \'klar-ət\ *n* [ME, fr. MF (*vin*) *claret* clear wine, fr. *claret* clear, fr. *cler* clear] (14c) **1 :** a red Bordeaux wine; *also* **:** a similar wine produced elsewhere **2 :** a dark purplish red — **claret** *adj*

clar·i·fy \'klar-ə-,fī\ *vb* **-fied; -fy·ing** [ME *clarifien,* fr. MF *clarifier,* fr. LL *clarificare,* fr. L *clarus* clear — more at CLEAR] *vt* (14c) **1 :** to make (as a liquid) clear or pure usu. by freeing from suspended matter **2 :** to free of confusion **3 :** to make understandable ~ *vi* **:** to become clear — **clar·i·fi·ca·tion** \,klar-ə-fə-'kā-shən\ *n* — **clar·i·fi·er** \'klar-ə-,fī(-ə)r\ *n*

clar·i·net \,klar-ə-'net, 'klar-ə-nət\ *n* [F *clarinette,* prob. deriv. of ML *clarion-, clario*] (1796) **:** a single-reed woodwind instrument having a cylindrical tube with a moderately flared bell and a usual range from D below middle C upward for 3½ octaves — **clar·i·net·ist** *or* **clar·i·net·tist** \,klar-ə-'net-əst\ *n*

[1]**clar·i·on** \'klar-ē-ən\ *n* [ME, fr. MF & ML; MF *clairon,* fr. ML *clarion-, clario,* fr. L *clarus*] (14c) **1 :** a medieval trumpet with clear shrill tones **2 :** the sound of or as if of a clarion

[2]**clarion** *adj* (1841) **:** brilliantly clear; *esp* **:** STENTORIAN ⟨a ~ call to action⟩

clar·i·ty \'klar-ət-ē\ *n* [ME *clarite,* fr. L *claritat-, claritas,* fr. *clarus*] (14c) **:** the quality or state of being clear **:** LUCIDITY ⟨the ~ of her voice⟩

clark·ia \'klär-kē-ə\ *n* [NL, fr. William *Clark*] (1827) **:** a showy annual herb (genus *Clarkia*) of the evening-primrose family of the Pacific slope of No. America

cla·ro \'klär-(,)ō\ *n, pl* **claros** [Sp, fr. *claro* light, fr. L *clarus*] (1891) **:** a light-colored generally mild cigar

clary \'kla(ə)r-ē, 'kle(ə)r-\ *n, pl* **clar·ies** [ME *clarie,* fr. MF *sclaree,* fr. ML *sclareia*] (14c) **:** an aromatic mint (*Salvia sclarea*) of southern Europe used as an adulterant in wines, as a condiment, and medicinally

[1]**clash** \'klash\ *vb* [imit] *vi* (1500) **1 :** to make a clash ⟨cymbals ~*ed*⟩ **2 :** to come into conflict ⟨where ignorant armies ~ by night —Matthew Arnold⟩ ~ *vt* **:** to cause to clash — **clash·er** *n*

[2]**clash** *n* (1513) **1 :** a noisy usu. metallic sound of collision **2 a :** a hostile encounter **:** SKIRMISH ⟨a ~ between the two armies⟩ **b :** a sharp conflict ⟨a ~ of opinions⟩

[1]**clasp** \'klasp\ *n* [ME *claspe*] (14c) **1 a :** a device (as a hook) for holding objects or parts together **b :** a device (as a bar) attached to a military medal to indicate an additional award of the medal or the action or service for which it was awarded **2 :** a holding or enveloping with or as if with the hands or arms

[2]**clasp** *vt* (14c) **1 :** to fasten with or as if with a clasp ⟨a robe ~*ed* with a brooch⟩ **2 :** to enclose and hold with the arms; *specif* **:** EMBRACE **3 :** to seize with or as if with the hand **:** GRASP

clasp·er \'klas-pər\ *n* (1839) **:** a male copulatory structure: **a :** one of a pair of external anal processes of an insect **b :** one of a pair of organs on the pelvic fins of elasmobranch fishes

clasp knife *n* (ca. 1755) **:** POCKETKNIFE; *esp* **:** a large one-bladed folding knife having a catch to hold the blade open

[1]**class** \'klas\ *n, often attrib* [F *classe,* fr. L *classis* group called to arms, class of citizens; akin to L *calare* to call — more at LOW] (1602) **1 a :** a body of students meeting regularly to study the same subject **b :** the period during which such a body meets **c :** a course of instruction **d :** a body of students or alumni whose year of graduation is the same **2 a :** a group sharing the same economic or social status ⟨the working ~⟩ **b :** social rank; *esp* **:** high social rank **c :** high quality **:** ELEGANCE **3 :** a group, set, or kind sharing common attributes: as **a :** a major category in biological taxonomy ranking above the order and below the phylum or division **b :** a collection of adjacent and discrete or continuous values of a random variable **c :** SET 21 **4 :** a division or rating based on grade or quality

[2]**class** *vt* (1705) **:** CLASSIFY

class act *n* (1976) **:** something of outstanding quality or prestige

class action *n* (1952) **:** a legal action undertaken by one or more plaintiffs on behalf of themselves and all other persons having an identical interest in the alleged wrong

class–con·scious *adj* (1903) **1 :** actively aware of one's common status with others in a particular economic or social level of society **2 :** believing in and actively aware of class struggle — **class consciousness** *n*

[1]**clas·sic** \ˈklas-ik\ *adj* [F or L; F *classique,* fr. L *classicus* of the highest class of Roman citizens, of the first rank, fr. *classis*] (1613) **1 a :** of recognized value : serving as a standard of excellence **b :** TRADITIONAL, ENDURING **c :** characterized by simple tailored lines in fashion year after year ⟨a ~ suit⟩ **2 :** of or relating to the ancient Greeks and Romans or their culture : CLASSICAL **3 a :** historically memorable **b :** noted because of special literary or historical associations ⟨Paris is the ~ refuge of expatriates⟩ **4 a :** AUTHENTIC, AUTHORITATIVE **b :** TYPICAL ⟨a ~ example of guilt by association⟩

[2]**classic** *n* (1711) **1 :** a literary work of ancient Greece or Rome **2 a :** a work of enduring excellence; *also* **:** its author **b :** an authoritative source **3 :** a typical or perfect example **4 :** a traditional event ⟨a football ~⟩

clas·si·cal \ˈklas-i-kəl\ *adj* [L *classicus*] (1599) **1 :** STANDARD, CLASSIC **2 a :** of or relating to the ancient Greek and Roman world and esp. to its literature, art, architecture, or ideals **b :** versed in the classics **3 a :** of or relating to music of the late 18th and early 19th centuries characterized by an emphasis on balance, clarity, and moderation; *also* **:** of or relating to a composer of this music **b :** of, relating to, or being music in the educated European tradition that includes such forms as art song, chamber music, opera, and symphony as distinguished from folk or popular music or jazz **4 a :** AUTHORITATIVE, TRADITIONAL **b** (1) **:** of or relating to a form or system considered of first significance in earlier times ⟨~ Mendelian genetics versus modern molecular genetics⟩ (2) **:** not involving relativity, wave mechanics, or quantum theory ⟨~ physics⟩ **c :** conforming to a pattern of usage sanctioned by a body of literature rather than by everyday speech **5 :** concerned with or giving instruction in the humanities, the fine arts, and the broad aspects of science ⟨a ~ curriculum⟩

classical conditioning *n* (1949) **:** conditioning in which the conditioned stimulus (as the sound of a bell) is paired with and precedes the unconditioned stimulus (as the sight of food) until the conditioned stimulus alone is sufficient to elicit the response (as salivation in a dog) — compare OPERANT CONDITIONING

clas·si·cal·i·ty \ˌklas-ə-ˈkal-ət-ē\ *n* (1819) **1 :** the quality or state of being classic **2 :** classical scholarship

clas·si·cal·ly \ˈklas-i-k(ə-)lē\ *adv* (1772) **:** in a classic or classical manner

clas·si·cism \ˈklas-ə-ˌsiz-əm\ *n* (1830) **1 a :** the principles or style embodied in the literature, art, or architecture of ancient Greece and Rome **b :** classical scholarship **c :** a classical idiom or expression **2 :** adherence to traditional standards (as of simplicity, restraint, and proportion) that are universally and enduringly valid

clas·si·cist \-səst\ *n* (1830) **1 :** an advocate or follower of classicism **2 :** a classical scholar — **clas·si·cis·tic** \ˌklas-ə-ˈsis-tik\ *adj*

clas·si·cize \ˈklas-ə-ˌsīz\ *vb* **-cized; -ciz·ing** *vt* (1854) **:** to make classic or classical ~ *vi* **:** to follow classic style

clas·si·co \ˈklas-i-(ˌ)kō\ *adj* [It, fr. L *classicus*] (1968) **:** produced in a delimited area of Italy known for its standards of quality — used of chianti

clas·si·fi·ca·tion \ˌklas-(ə-)fə-ˈkā-shən\ *n* (1790) **1 :** the act or process of classifying **2 a :** systematic arrangement in groups or categories according to established criteria; *specif* **:** TAXONOMY **b :** CLASS, CATEGORY — **clas·si·fi·ca·to·ri·ly** \ˌklas-(ə-)fə-kə-ˈtōr-ə-lē, kla-ˌsif-ə-, -ˈtȯr-\ *adv* — **clas·si·fi·ca·to·ry** \ˈklas-(ə-)fə-kə-ˌtōr-ē, kla-ˈsif-ə-, -ˌtȯr-; ˈklas-(ə-)fə-ˌkāt-ə-rē\ *adj*

clas·si·fied \ˈklas-ə-ˌfīd\ *adj* (1889) **1 :** divided into classes or placed in a class ⟨~ ads⟩ **2 :** withheld from general circulation for reasons of national security ⟨~ information⟩

clas·si·fi·er \ˈklas-ə-ˌfī(-ə)r\ *n* (1819) **1 :** one that classifies; *specif* **:** a machine for sorting out the constituents of a substance (as ore) **2 :** a word or morpheme used with numerals or with nouns designating countable or measurable objects

clas·si·fy \ˈklas-ə-ˌfī\ *vt* **-fied; -fy·ing** (1799) **1 :** to arrange in classes ⟨~*ing* books according to subject matter⟩ **2 :** to assign (as a document) to a category — **clas·si·fi·able** \-ˌfī-ə-bəl\ *adj*

class interval *n* (1929) **:** CLASS 3b; *also* **:** its numerical width

clas·sis \ˈklas-əs\ *n, pl* **clas·ses** \ˈklas-ˌēz\ [NL, fr. L, class] (1593) **1 :** a governing body in some Reformed churches (as in the former Reformed Church in the U.S.) corresponding to a presbytery **2 :** the district governed by a classis

class·ism \ˈklas-ˌiz-əm\ *n* (1842) **:** prejudice or discrimination based on class — **class·ist** \ˈklas-əst\ *adj*

class·less \ˈklas-ləs\ *adj* (1878) **1 :** belonging to no particular social class **2 :** free from distinctions of social class ⟨a ~ society⟩ — **class·less·ness** *n*

class·mate \-ˌmāt\ *n* (1713) **:** a member of the same class in a school or college

class·room \-ˌrüm, -ˌru̇m\ *n* (1870) **:** a place where classes meet

classy \ˈklas-ē\ *adj* **class·i·er; -est** (1891) **:** ELEGANT, STYLISH — **class·i·ness** *n*

clast \ˈklast\ *n* [Gk *klastos* broken, fr. *klan* to break — more at HALT] (1952) **:** a fragment of rock

clas·tic \ˈklas-tik\ *adj* [ISV] (1877) **:** made up of fragments of preexisting rocks ⟨a ~ sediment⟩ — **clastic** *n*

clath·rate \ˈklath-ˌrāt\ *adj* [L *clathratus,* furnished with a lattice, fr. *clathri* (pl.) lattice, fr. Gk *klēithron* bar, fr. *kleiein* to close — more at CLOSE] (1906) **:** relating to or being a compound formed by the inclusion of molecules of one kind in cavities of the crystal lattice of another — **clathrate** *n*

[1]**clat·ter** \ˈklat-ər\ *vb* [ME *clatren,* fr. (assumed) OE *clatrian;* of imit. origin] *vi* (13c) **1 :** to talk noisily or rapidly **2 :** to make a rattling sound ⟨the dishes ~*ed* on the shelf⟩ **3 :** to move or go with a clatter ⟨~*ed* down the stairs⟩ ~ *vt* **:** to cause to clatter — **clat·ter·er** \-ər-ər\ *n* — **clat·ter·ing·ly** \ˈklat-ə-riŋ-lē\ *adv*

[2]**clatter** *n* (14c) **1 :** a rattling sound (as of hard bodies striking together) ⟨the ~ of pots and pans⟩ **2 :** COMMOTION ⟨the midday ~ of the business district⟩ **3 :** noisy chatter — **clat·tery** \ˈklat-ə-rē\ *adj*

clau·di·ca·tion \ˌklȯd-ə-ˈkā-shən\ *n* [L *claudication-, claudicatio,* fr. *claudicatus,* pp. of *claudicare* to limp, fr. *claudus* lame; akin to L *claudere* to close — more at CLOSE] (15c) **:** the quality or state of being lame : LIMPING

claus·al \ˈklȯ-zəl\ *adj* (1904) **:** relating to or of the nature of a clause

clause \ˈklȯz\ *n* [ME, fr. OF, fr. ML *clausa* close of a rhetorical period, fr. L, fem. of *clausus,* pp. of *claudere*] (13c) **1 :** a group of words containing a subject and predicate and functioning as a member of a complex or compound sentence **2 :** a separate section of a discourse or writing; *specif* **:** a distinct article in a formal document

claus·tral \ˈklȯ-strəl\ *adj* [ME, fr. ML *claustralis,* fr. *claustrum* cloister, fr. L, bar, bolt, fr. *claudere* to close — more at CLOSE] (15c) **:** CLOISTRAL

claus·tro·pho·bia \ˌklȯ-strə-ˈfō-bē-ə\ *n* [NL, fr. L *claustrum* confined place + NL *phobia*] (1879) **:** abnormal dread of being in closed or narrow spaces — **claus·tro·phobe** \ˈklȯ-strə-ˌfōb\ *n*

claus·tro·pho·bic \ˌklȯ-strə-ˈfō-bik\ *adj* (1889) **1 :** suffering from or inclined to claustrophobia **2 :** inducing or suggesting claustrophobia — **claus·tro·pho·bi·cal·ly** \-bi-k(ə-)lē\ *adv*

claus·trum \ˈklȯ-strəm, ˈklau̇-\ *n, pl* **claus·tra** \-strə\ [L] (ca. 1848) **:** the one of the four basal ganglia in each cerebral hemisphere that consists of a thin lamina of gray matter separated from the lenticular nucleus by a thin layer of white matter

cla·vate \ˈklā-ˌvāt\ *adj* [NL *clavatus,* fr. L *clava* club, fr. *clavus* nail, knot in wood] (1813) **:** gradually thickening near the distal end : CLAVIFORM

[1]**clave** *past of* CLEAVE

[2]**clave** \ˈklä-(ˌ)vā, ˈklāv\ *n* [AmerSp, fr. Sp, keystone, clef, fr. L *clavis*] (1928) **:** one of a pair of cylindrical hardwood sticks that are used as a percussion instrument

cla·ver \ˈklā-vər\ *vi* [prob. of Celt origin; akin to ScGael *clabaire* babbler] *chiefly Scot* (1605) **:** PRATE, GOSSIP — **claver** *n, chiefly Scot*

clav·i·chord \ˈklav-ə-ˌkȯ(ə)rd\ *n* [ML *clavichordium,* fr. L *clavis* key + *chorda* string — more at CORD] (15c) **:** an early keyboard instrument having strings struck by tangents attached directly to the key ends — **clav·i·chord·ist** \-əst\ *n*

clav·i·cle \ˈklav-i-kəl\ *n* [F *clavicule,* fr. NL *clavicula,* fr. L, dim. of L *clavis;* akin to Gk *kleid-, kleis* key, L *claudere* to close — more at CLOSE] (1615) **:** a bone of the vertebrate pectoral girdle typically serving to link the scapula and sternum — called also *collarbone* — **cla·vic·u·lar** \kla-ˈvik-yə-lər, klə-\ *adj*

cla·vier \klə-ˈvi(ə)r; ˈklāv-ē-ər, ˈklav-\ *n* [F, fr. OF, key bearer, fr. L *clavis*] (1708) **1 :** the keyboard of a musical instrument **2** [G *klavier,* fr. F *clavier*] **:** an early keyboard instrument — **cla·vier·ist** \klə-ˈvir-əst; ˈklāv-ē-ə-rəst, ˈklav-\ *n* — **cla·vier·is·tic** \klə-ˌvi(ə)r-ˈis-tik; ˌklāv-ē-ə-ˈris-tik, ˌklav-\ *adj*

clav·i·form \ˈklav-ə-ˌfȯrm\ *adj* [L *clava* club] (1817) **:** shaped like a club

[1]**claw** \ˈklȯ\ *n, often attrib* [ME *clawe,* fr. OE *clawu* hoof, claw; akin to ON *klō* claw, OE *cliewen* ball — more at CLEW] (bef. 12c) **1 :** a sharp usu. slender and curved nail on the toe of an animal **2 :** any of various similar sharp curved processes esp. if at the end of a limb (as of an insect); *also* **:** a limb ending in such a process **3 :** one of the pincerlike organs terminating some limbs of various arthropods (as a lobster or scorpion) **4 :** something that resembles a claw; *specif* **:** the forked end of a tool (as a hammer) **5 :** a wound from or as if from a claw — **clawed** \ˈklȯd\ *adj*

[2]**claw** *vt* (bef. 12c) **:** to rake, seize, dig, or progress with or as if with claws ~ *vi* **:** to scrape, scratch, dig, or pull with or as if with claws

claw·ham·mer \ˈklȯ-ˌham-ər\ *adj* (1964) **:** of or relating to a style of banjo playing using the thumb and one or more fingers picking or strumming in a downward direction

claw hammer *n* (1769) **1 :** a hammer with one end of the head forked for pulling out nails **2 :** TAILCOAT

[1]**clay** \ˈklā\ *n, often attrib* [ME, fr. OE *clǣg;* akin to OHG *klīwa* bran, LL *glut-, glus* glue, MGk *glia*] (bef. 12c) **1 a :** an earthy material that is plastic when moist but hard when fired, that is composed mainly of fine particles of hydrous aluminum silicates and other minerals, and that is used for brick, tile, and pottery; *specif* **:** soil composed chiefly of this material having particles less than a specified size **b :** EARTH, MUD **2 a :** a substance that resembles clay in plasticity and is used for modeling **b :** the human body as distinguished from the spirit **3 :** CLAY COURT — **clay·ey** \ˈklā-ē\ *adj* — **clay·ish** \ˈklā-ish\ *adj*

[2]**clay** *vt* (1523) **:** to treat or cover with clay; *also* **:** to filter through clay

clay·bank \ˈklā-ˌbaŋk\ *n* (1853) **:** a horse of yellowish color

clay court *n* (1916) **:** a tennis court with a clay surface or a synthetic surface that resembles clay

clay loam *n* (ca. 1891) **:** a loam containing from 20 to 30 percent clay

clay mineral *n* (1947) **:** any of a group of hydrous silicates of aluminum and sometimes other metals formed chiefly in weathering processes and occurring esp. in clay and shale

clay·more \ˈklā-ˌmō(ə)r, -ˌmȯ(ə)r\ *n* [ScGael *claidheamh mōr,* lit., great sword] (1772) **:** a large 2-edged sword formerly used by Scottish Highlanders; *also* **:** their basket-hilted broadsword

clay·pan \-ˌpan\ *n* (1837) **:** hardpan consisting mainly of clay

clay pigeon *n* (1888) **:** a saucer-shaped target usu. made of baked clay and pitch and thrown from a trap in skeet and trapshooting

clay·ware \ˈklā-ˌwa(ə)r, -ˌwe(ə)r\ *n* (1890) **:** articles made of fired clay

[1]**clean** \ˈklēn\ *adj* [ME *clene,* fr. OE *clǣne;* akin to OHG *kleini* delicate, dainty, Gk *glainoi* ornaments] (bef. 12c) **1 a :** free from dirt or pollution ⟨changed to ~ clothes⟩ ⟨ship with a ~ bottom⟩ **b :** free from contamination or disease **c :** relatively free from radioactive fallout ⟨a ~ atomic explosion⟩ **2 a :** UNADULTERATED, PURE ⟨the ~ thrill of one's first flight⟩ **b** *of a precious stone* **:** having no interior flaws visible **c :** free from growth that hinders tillage **3 a :** free from moral corruption or sinister connections of any kind ⟨a candidate with a ~ record⟩ **b :** free from offensive treatment of sexual subjects and from the use of obscenity ⟨a ~ joke⟩ **c :** observing the rules : FAIR ⟨a ~ fight⟩ **4 :** ceremonially or spiritually pure ⟨and all who are ~ may eat flesh — Lev 7:19 (RSV)⟩ **5 a :** THOROUGH, COMPLETE ⟨a ~ break with the past⟩ **b :** deftly executed : SKILLFUL ⟨~ ballet technique⟩ **6 a :** relatively free from error or blemish : CLEAR; *specif* **:** LEGIBLE ⟨~ copy⟩ **b :** UNENCUMBERED ⟨~ bill of sale⟩ **7 a :** characterized by clarity and precision : TRIM ⟨a ~ prose style⟩ ⟨architecture with ~ almost austere lines⟩ **b :** EVEN, SMOOTH ⟨a ~ edge⟩ ⟨a sharp blow causing a ~ break⟩ **8 a :** EMPTY ⟨the whaling ship returned with a ~ hold⟩ **b** *slang* **:** having no contraband (as weapons or drugs) in one's possession **9 :** habitually neat — **clean·ness** \ˈklēn-nəs\ *n*

[2]**clean** *adv* (bef. 12c) **1 a :** so as to clean ⟨a new broom sweeps ~⟩ **b :** in a clean manner ⟨play the game ~⟩ **2 :** all the way : COMPLETELY ⟨the bullet went ~ through his arm⟩

[3]clean *vt* (15c) **1 a :** to rid of dirt, impurities, or extraneous matter **b :** REMOVE, ERADICATE — usu. used with *up* or *off* ⟨~ up that mess⟩ **2 a :** STRIP, EMPTY ⟨the tree was ~*ed* of fruit by hurricane winds⟩ ⟨the hungry men quickly ~*ed* the platter⟩ **b :** to deprive of money or possessions — often used with *out* ⟨they ~*ed* him out completely⟩ ~ *vi* **:** to undergo or perform a process of cleaning ⟨~ up before dinner⟩ — **clean·able** \ˈklē-nə-bəl\ *adj* — **clean house 1 :** to clean a house and its furniture **2 :** to eradicate whatever is obstructive, thwarting, or degrading — **clean one's clock :** to beat one in a fight or competition — **clean up one's act :** to behave in a more acceptable manner

[4]clean *n* (1872) **:** an act of cleaning dirt esp. from the surface of something

clean and jerk *n* (1939) **:** a lift in weight lifting in which the weight is raised to shoulder height, held momentarily, and then quickly thrust overhead usu. with a lunge or a spring from the legs — compare PRESS, SNATCH

clean–cut \ˈklēn-ˈkət\ *adj* (1843) **1 :** cut so that the surface or edge is smooth and even **2 :** sharply defined **3 :** of wholesome appearance

clean·er \ˈklē-nər\ *n* (1792) **1 :** one whose work is cleaning **2 :** a preparation for cleaning **3 :** an implement or machine for cleaning — **to the cleaners** *slang* **:** to or through the experience of being deprived of all one's money

clean·hand·ed \ˈklēn-ˈhan-dəd\ *adj* (1728) **:** innocent of wrongdoing

clean–limbed \ˈklēn-ˈlimd\ *adj* (15c) **:** well proportioned **:** TRIM ⟨~ youths⟩

[1]clean·ly \ˈklēn-lē\ *adv* (bef. 12c) **:** in a clean manner

[2]clean·ly \ˈklen-lē\ *adj* **clean·li·er; -est** (1500) **1 :** careful to keep clean **:** FASTIDIOUS **2 :** habitually kept clean — **clean·li·ness** *n*

clean room \ˈklēn-ˌ\ *n* (1963) **:** a room for the manufacture or assembly of objects (as precision parts) that is maintained at a high level of cleanliness by special means

cleanse \ˈklenz\ *vb* **cleansed; cleans·ing** [ME *clensen,* fr. OE *clǣnsian* to purify, fr. *clǣne* clean] (bef. 12c) **:** CLEAN

cleans·er \ˈklen-zər\ *n* (bef. 12c) **1 :** one that cleanses **2 :** a preparation (as a scouring powder or a skin cream) used for cleaning

[1]clean·up \ˈklē-ˌnəp\ *n* (1872) **1 :** an act or instance of cleaning **2 :** an exceptionally large profit **:** KILLING

[2]cleanup *adj* (1937) **:** being in the fourth position in the batting order of a baseball team

clean up \(ˈ)klē-ˈnəp\ *vi* (1920) **:** to make a spectacular profit in a business enterprise or a killing in speculation or gambling

[1]clear \ˈkli(ə)r\ *adj* [ME *clere,* fr. OF *cler,* fr. L *clarus* clear, bright; akin to L *calare* to call — more at LOW] (13c) **1 a :** BRIGHT, LUMINOUS **b :** CLOUDLESS; *specif* **:** less than one-tenth covered ⟨a ~ sky⟩ **c :** free from mist, haze, or dust ⟨a ~ day⟩ **d :** UNTROUBLED, SERENE ⟨a ~ gaze⟩ **2 :** CLEAN, PURE: as **a :** free from blemishes **b :** easily seen through **:** TRANSPARENT **c :** free from abnormal sounds on auscultation **3 a :** easily heard **b :** easily visible **:** PLAIN **c :** free from obscurity or ambiguity **:** easily understood **:** UNMISTAKABLE **4 a :** capable of sharp discernment **:** KEEN **b :** free from doubt **:** SURE **5 :** free from guile or guilt **:** INNOCENT **6 :** unhampered by restriction or limitation: as **a :** unencumbered by debts or charges **b :** NET ⟨a ~ profit⟩ **c :** UNQUALIFIED, ABSOLUTE **d :** free from obstruction **e :** emptied of contents or cargo **f :** free from entanglement **g :** BARE, DENUDED — **clear·ly** *adv* — **clear·ness** *n*

syn CLEAR, TRANSPARENT, TRANSLUCENT, LIMPID mean capable of being seen through. CLEAR implies absence of cloudiness, haziness, or muddiness ⟨*clear* water⟩ TRANSPARENT implies being so clear that objects can be seen distinctly ⟨a *transparent* sheet of film⟩ TRANSLUCENT implies the passage of light but not a clear view of what lies beyond ⟨*translucent* frosted glass⟩ LIMPID suggests the soft clearness of pure water ⟨pale *limpid* blue eyes⟩

syn CLEAR, PERSPICUOUS, LUCID mean quickly and easily understood. CLEAR implies freedom from obscurity, ambiguity, or undue complexity; PERSPICUOUS applies to a style that is simple and elegant as well as clear; LUCID suggests a clear logical coherence and evident order of arrangement. ***syn*** see in addition EVIDENT

[2]clear *adv* (14c) **1 :** in a clear manner ⟨to cry loud and ~⟩ **2 :** all the way ⟨can see ~ to the mountains on a day like this⟩

[3]clear *vt* (14c) **1 a :** to make clear or translucent **b :** to free from pollution or cloudiness **2 a :** to free from accusation or blame **:** EXONERATE, VINDICATE ⟨the opportunity to ~ himself⟩ **b :** to certify as trustworthy ⟨~ a person for top secret military work⟩ **3 a :** to give insight to **:** ENLIGHTEN **b :** to make intelligible **:** EXPLAIN ⟨~ up the mystery⟩ **4 a :** to free from obstructing, unneeded, or accumulated material or things: as **(1) :** OPEN **(2) :** to remove unwanted growth or items from ⟨~ the land of timber⟩ **(3) :** to rid or make a rasping noise as if ridding (the throat) of phlegm **(4) :** to erase stored or displayed data from (as a computer or calculator) **b :** DISENTANGLE ⟨~ a fishing line⟩ **c :** to remove from an area or place ⟨~ the dishes from the table⟩ **d :** TRANSMIT, DISPATCH **5 a :** to submit for approval **b :** AUTHORIZE ⟨the chairman ~*ed* the article for publication⟩ **6 a :** to free from obligation or encumbrance **b :** SETTLE, DISCHARGE ⟨~ an account⟩ **c (1) :** to free (a ship or shipment) by payment of duties or harbor fees **(2) :** to pass through (customs) **d :** to gain without deduction **:** NET ⟨~ a profit⟩ **e :** to put through a clearinghouse **7 a :** to go over, under, or by without touching **b :** PASS ⟨the bill ~*ed* the legislature⟩ ~ *vi* **1 a :** to become clear ⟨it ~*ed* up quickly after the rain⟩ **b :** to go away **:** VANISH ⟨the symptoms ~*ed* gradually⟩ **c :** SELL **2 a :** to obtain permission to discharge cargo **b :** to conform to regulations or pay requisite fees prior to leaving port **3 :** to pass through a clearinghouse **4 :** to go to an authority (as for approval) before becoming effective — **clear·able** \ˈklir-ə-bəl\ *adj* — **clear·er** \ˈklir-ər\ *n* — **clear the air** *also* **clear the atmosphere :** to remove elements of hostility, tension, confusion, or uncertainty from the mood or temper of the time

[4]clear *n* (1715) **1 :** a clear space or part **2 :** a high arcing shot over an opponent's head in badminton — **in the clear 1 :** in inside measurement **2 :** free from guilt or suspicion **3 :** in plaintext **:** not in code or cipher ⟨a message sent *in the clear*⟩

clear–air turbulence *n* (1955) **:** sudden severe turbulence occurring in cloudless regions that causes violent jarring or buffeting of aircraft

clear·ance \ˈklir-ən(t)s\ *n* (1563) **1 :** an act or process of clearing: as **a :** the removal of buildings from an area (as a city slum) **b :** the act of clearing a ship at the customhouse; *also* **:** the papers showing that a ship has cleared **c :** the offsetting of checks and other claims among banks through a clearinghouse **d :** certification as clear of objection **:** AUTHORIZATION **e :** a sale to clear out stock **2 :** the distance by which one object clears another or the clear space between them **3 :** the volume of blood or plasma that could be freed of a specified constituent in a specified time (usu. one minute) by its excretion into the urine through the kidneys — called also *renal clearance*

clear–cut \ˈkli(ə)r-ˈkət\ *adj* (1855) **1 :** sharply outlined **:** DISTINCT **2 :** free from ambiguity or uncertainty **:** UNAMBIGUOUS

clear–cut·ting \-ˌkət-iŋ\ *also* **clear–cut** \-ˈkət\ *n* (1922) **:** removal of all the trees in a stand of timber; *also* **:** the area so treated — **clear–cut** *vt*

clear–eyed \ˈkli(ə)r-ˈīd\ *adj* (1530) **:** CLEAR-SIGHTED

clear·head·ed \-ˈhed-əd\ *adj* (1709) **:** having a clear understanding **:** PERCEPTIVE — **clear·head·ed·ly** *adv* — **clear·head·ed·ness** *n*

clear·ing \ˈkli(ə)r-iŋ\ *n* (14c) **1 :** the act or process of making or becoming clear **2 :** a tract of land cleared of wood and brush **3 a :** a method of exchanging and offsetting commercial papers or accounts with cash settlement only of the balances due after the clearing **b** *pl* **:** the gross amount of balances so adjusted

clear·ing·house \-ˌhau̇s\ *n* (1832) **1 :** an establishment maintained by banks for settling mutual claims and accounts **2 :** a central agency for the collection, classification, and distribution esp. of information

clear out *vi* (1742) **:** DEPART ~ *vt* **:** to drive out or away usu. forcibly

clear–sight·ed \ˈkli(ə)r-ˈsīt-əd\ *adj* (1586) **1 :** having clear vision **2 :** DISCERNING — **clear–sight·ed·ly** *adv* — **clear–sight·ed·ness** *n*

clearstory *var of* CLERESTORY

clear·wing \-ˌwiŋ\ *n* (1868) **:** a moth (as of the families Aegeriidae or Sphingidae) having the wings largely transparent and devoid of scales

[1]cleat \ˈklēt\ *n* [ME *clete* wedge, fr. (assumed) OE *clēat;* akin to MHG *klōz* lump — more at CLOUT] (15c) **1 a :** a wedge-shaped piece fastened to or projecting from something and serving as a support or check **b :** a wooden or metal fitting usu. with two projecting horns around which a rope may be made fast **2 a :** a strip fastened across something to give strength or hold in position **b (1) :** a projecting piece (as on the bottom of a shoe) that furnishes a grip **(2)** *pl* **:** shoes equipped with cleats

[2]cleat *vt* (1794) **1 :** to secure to or by a cleat **2 :** to provide with a cleat

cleav·able \ˈklē-və-bəl\ *adj* (ca. 1864) **:** capable of being split

cleav·age \ˈklē-vij\ *n* (1816) **1 a :** the quality of a crystallized substance or rock of splitting along definite planes **b :** a fragment (as of a diamond) obtained by splitting **2 :** the action of cleaving **:** the state of being cleft **3 :** the series of synchronized mitotic cell divisions of the fertilized egg that results in the formation of the blastomeres and changes the single-celled zygote into a multicellular embryo; *also* **:** one of these cell divisions **4 :** the splitting of a molecule into simpler molecules **5 :** the depression between a woman's breasts esp. when made visible by the wearing of a low-cut dress

[1]cleave \ˈklēv\ *vi* **cleaved** \ˈklēvd\ *or* **clove** \ˈklōv\ *also* **clave** \ˈklāv\; **cleaved; cleav·ing** [ME *clevien,* fr. OE *clifian;* akin to OHG *kleben* to stick, OE *clǣg* clay — more at CLAY] (bef. 12c) **:** to adhere firmly and closely or loyally and unwaveringly ***syn*** see STICK

[2]cleave *vb* **cleaved** \ˈklēvd\ *also* **cleft** \ˈkleft\ *or* **clove** \ˈklōv\; **cleaved** *also* **cleft** *or* **clo·ven** \ˈklō-vən\; **cleav·ing** [ME *cleven,* fr. OE *clēofan;* akin to ON *kljūfa* to split, L *glubere* to peel, Gk *glyphein* to carve] *vt* (bef. 12c) **1 :** to divide by or as if by a cutting blow **:** SPLIT **2 :** to separate into distinct parts and esp. into groups having divergent views ~ *vi* **1 :** to split esp. along the grain **2 :** to penetrate or pass through something by or as if by cutting ***syn*** see TEAR

cleav·er \ˈklē-vər\ *n* (14c) **1 :** one that cleaves; *esp* **:** a butcher's implement for cutting animal carcasses into joints or pieces **2 :** a rock ridge protruding from a glacier or snowfield

cleav·ers \ˈklē-vərz\ *n pl but sing or pl in constr* [ME *clivre,* alter. of OE *clife* burdock, cleavers; akin to OE *clifian* to cleave, adhere] (bef. 12c) **:** an annual bedstraw (*Galium aparine*) that has numerous stalked white flowers, stems covered with curved prickles, and whorls of bristle-tipped leaves; *also* **:** a related plant

cleek \ˈklēk\ *n* [ME (northern) *cleke,* fr. *cleken* to clutch] *chiefly Scot* (15c) **:** a large hook (as for a pot over a fire)

clef \ˈklef\ *n* [F, lit., key, fr. L *clavis* — more at CLAVICLE] (1577) **:** a sign placed at the beginning of a musical staff to determine the pitch of the notes

[1]cleft \ˈkleft\ *n* [ME *clift,* fr. OE *geclyft;* akin to OE *clēofan* to cleave] (bef. 12c) **1 :** a space or opening made by splitting **:** FISSURE **2 :** a usu. V-shaped indented formation **:** a hollow between ridges or protuberances ⟨the anal ~ of the human body⟩

[2]cleft *adj* [ME, fr. pp. of *cleven*] (14c) **:** partially split or divided; *specif* **:** divided about halfway to the midrib ⟨a ~ leaf⟩

cleft palate *n* (1841) **:** congenital fissure of the roof of the mouth

clei·do·ic \klī-ˈdō-ik\ *adj* [Gk *kleidoun* to fasten, lock in (fr. *kleid-, kleis* key) + E *-ic* — more at CLAVICLE] *of an egg* (ca. 1931) **:** enclosed in a relatively impervious shell which reduces free exchange with the environment ⟨the eggs of birds are ~⟩

cleis·tog·a·mous \klī-ˈstäg-ə-məs\ *also* **cleis·to·gam·ic** \ˌklī-stə-ˈgam-ik\ *adj* [Gk *kleistos* closed (fr. *kleiein* to close) + ISV *-gamous* — more at CLOSE] (1874) **:** characterized by or being small inconspicuous closed self-pollinating flowers additional to and often more fruitful than showier ones on the same plant ⟨violets are ~⟩ — **cleis·tog·a·mous·ly** \klī-ˈstäg-ə-məs-lē\ *adv* — **cleis·tog·a·my** \-ˈstäg-ə-mē\ *n*

cle·ma·tis \ˈklem-ət-əs; kli-ˈmat-əs, -ˈmāt-, -ˈmät-\ *n* [NL, genus name, fr. L, fr. Gk *klēmatis* brushwood, clematis, fr. *klēmat-, klēma* twig, fr. Gk *klan* to break — more at HALT] (1578) **:** a vine or herb (genera *Clematis, Atragene,* or *Viorna*) of the buttercup family having three leaflets on each leaf and usu. white, red, pink, or purple flowers

clem·en·cy \ˈklem-ən-sē\ *n, pl* **-cies** (15c) **1 a :** disposition to be merciful and esp. to moderate the severity of punishment due **b :** an act or instance of leniency **2 :** pleasant mildness of weather ***syn*** see MERCY

clem·ent \ˈklem-ənt\ *adj* [ME, fr. L *clement-, clemens;* akin to L *clinare* to lean — more at LEAN] (15c) **1 :** inclined to be merciful : LENIENT ⟨a ~ judge⟩ **2 :** MILD ⟨~ weather for November⟩ — **clem·ent·ly** *adv*

[1]clench \ˈklench\ *vt* [ME *clenchen,* fr. OE *-clencan;* akin to OE *clingan* to cling] (13c) **1 :** CLINCH 2 **2 :** to hold fast : CLUTCH ⟨~*ed* the arms of the chair⟩ **3 :** to set or close tightly ⟨~ one's teeth⟩ ⟨~ one's fists⟩

[2]clench *n* (15c) **1 :** the end of a nail that is turned back in clinching it **2 :** an act or instance of clenching

clepe \ˈklēp\ *vt* **cleped** \ˈklēpt, ˈklept\; **yclept** \i-ˈklept\ *also* **cleped** *or* **ycleped** \i-ˈklēpt, -ˈklept\; **clep·ing** \ˈklē-piŋ\ [ME *clepen,* fr. OE *clipian* to speak, call; akin to OFris *kleppa* to ring, knock] *archaic* (bef. 12c) **:** NAME, CALL

clep·sy·dra \ˈklep-sə-drə\ *n, pl* **-dras** *or* **-drae** \-ˌdrē, -ˌdrī\ [L, fr. Gk *klepsydra,* fr. *kleptein* to steal + *hydōr* water — more at KLEPT-, WATER] (1646) **:** WATER CLOCK

clere·sto·ry \ˈkli(ə)r-ˌstōr-ē, -ˌstȯr-\ *n* [ME, fr. *clere* clear + *story*] (15c) **1 :** an outside wall of a room or building that rises above an adjoining roof and contains windows **2 :** GALLERY

cler·gy \ˈklər-jē\ *n, pl* **clergies** [ME *clergie,* fr. OF, knowledge, learning, fr. *clerc* clergyman] (13c) **1 :** a group ordained to perform pastoral or sacerdotal functions in a Christian church **2 :** the official or sacerdotal class of a non-Christian religion

cler·gy·man \-ji-mən\ *n* (1577) **:** a member of the clergy

cler·gy·wom·an \-ji-ˌwu̇m-ən\ *n* (1673) **:** a woman who is a member of the clergy

cler·ic \ˈkler-ik\ *n* [LL *clericus*] (1621) **:** a member of the clergy

[1]cler·i·cal \ˈkler-i-kəl\ *adj* (1592) **1 :** of, relating to, or characteristic of the clergy **2 :** of or relating to a clerk — **cler·i·cal·ly** \-i-k(ə-)lē\ *adv*

[2]clerical *n* (1837) **1 :** a member of the clergy **2 :** CLERICALIST **3 :** CLERK **4** *pl* **:** clerical garments

clerical collar *n* (1948) **:** a narrow stiffly upright white collar worn buttoned at the back of the neck by members of the clergy

cler·i·cal·ism \ˈkler-i-kə-ˌliz-əm\ *n* (1864) **:** a policy of maintaining or increasing the power of a religious hierarchy

cler·i·cal·ist \-ləst\ *n* (1881) **:** one that favors maintained or increased ecclesiastical power and influence

cler·i·hew \ˈkler-i-ˌhyü\ *n* [Edmund *Clerihew* Bentley †1956 Eng. writer] (1928) **:** a light verse quatrain rhyming *aabb* and usu. dealing with a person named in the initial rhyme

cler·i·sy \ˈkler-ə-sē\ *n* [G *klerisei* clergy, fr. ML *clericia,* fr. LL *clericus* cleric] (1818) **:** INTELLIGENTSIA

[1]clerk \ˈklərk, *Brit usu* ˈklärk\ *n* [ME, fr. OF *clerc* & OE *cleric, clerc,* both fr. LL *clericus,* fr. LGk *klērikos,* fr. Gk *klēros* lot, inheritance (in allusion to Deut 18:2), stick of wood; akin to Gk *klan* to break — more at HALT] (bef. 12c) **1 :** CLERIC **2** *archaic* **:** SCHOLAR **3 a :** an official responsible (as to a government agency) for correspondence, records, and accounts and vested with specified powers or authority (as to issue writs or other processes as ordered by a court) ⟨city ~⟩ **b :** one employed to keep records or accounts or to perform general office work **c :** one who works at a sales or service counter — **clerk·ship** \-ˌship\ *n*

[2]clerk *vi* (1551) **:** to act or work as a clerk

clerk·ly \ˈklər-klē, *Brit usu* ˈklär-\ *adj* (15c) **1 :** of, relating to, or characteristic of a clerk **2** *archaic* **:** SCHOLARLY — **clerkly** *adv*

clev·er \ˈklev-ər\ *adj* [ME *cliver,* prob. of Scand origin] (13c) **1 a :** skillful or adroit in using the hands or body **:** NIMBLE **b :** mentally quick and resourceful but often lacking in depth and soundness **2 :** marked by wit or ingenuity **3** *dial* **a :** GOOD **b :** easy to use or handle — **clev·er·ish** \-(ə-)rish\ *adj* — **clev·er·ly** \-ər-lē\ *adv* — **clev·er·ness** \-ər-nəs\ *n*

syn CLEVER, ADROIT, CUNNING, INGENIOUS mean having or showing practical wit or skill in contriving. CLEVER stresses physical or mental quickness, deftness, or great aptitude; ADROIT often implies a skillful use of expedients to achieve one's purpose in spite of difficulties; CUNNING implies great skill in constructing or creating; INGENIOUS suggests the power of inventing or discovering a new way of accomplishing something. ***syn*** see in addition INTELLIGENT

clev·is \ˈklev-əs\ *n* [earlier *clevi,* prob. of Scand origin] (1592) **:** SHACKLE 3

[1]clew *or* **clue** \ˈklü\ *n* [ME *clewe,* fr. OE *cliewen;* akin to OHG *kliuwa* ball, Skt *glau* lump] (bef. 12c) **1 :** a ball of thread, yarn, or cord **2** *usu clue* **:** something that guides through an intricate procedure or maze of difficulties; *specif* **:** a piece of evidence that leads one toward the solution of a problem **3 a :** a lower corner or only the after corner of a sail **b :** a metal loop attached to the lower corner of a sail **c** *pl* **:** a combination of lines by which a hammock is suspended

[2]clew *or* **clue** *vt* **clewed** *or* **clued; clew·ing** *or* **clue·ing** *or* **clu·ing** (15c) **1 :** to roll into a ball **2** *usu clue* **a :** to provide with a clue **b :** to give reliable information to ⟨~ me in on how it happened⟩ **3 :** to haul (a sail) up or down by ropes through the clews

cli·ché *also* **cli·che** \klē-ˈshā, ˈklē-ˌ, kli-ˈ\ *n* [F, lit., stereotype, fr. pp. of *clicher* to stereotype, of imit. origin] (1892) **1 :** a trite phrase or expression; *also* **:** the idea expressed by it **2 :** a hackneyed theme or situation **3 :** something (as a menu item) that has become overly familiar or commonplace — **cliché** *adj*

cli·chéd \-ˈshād\ *adj* (1928) **1 :** marked by or abounding in clichés **2 :** HACKNEYED

[1]click \ˈklik\ *vt* (1581) **:** to strike, move, or produce with a click ⟨~*ed* his heels together⟩ ~ *vi* **1 :** to make a click **2 a :** to fit or agree exactly **b :** to fit together **:** hit it off ⟨they did not ~ as friends⟩ **c :** to function smoothly **d :** SUCCEED ⟨a movie that ~*s*⟩

[2]click *n* [prob. imit.] (1611) **1 a :** a slight sharp noise **b :** a speech sound in some languages made by enclosing air between two stop articulations of the tongue, enlarging the enclosure to rarefy the air, and suddenly opening the enclosure **2 :** DETENT

click beetle *n* (1861) **:** any of a family (Elateridae) of beetles able to right themselves with a click when inverted

click stop *n* (1950) **:** a turnable control device (as for a camera diaphragm opening) that engages with a definite click at specific setting positions

cli·ent \ˈklī-ənt\ *n* [ME, fr. MF & L; MF *client,* fr. L *client-, cliens;* akin to L *clinare* to lean — more at LEAN] (14c) **1 :** one that is under the protection of another **:** DEPENDENT **2 a :** a person who engages the professional advice or services of another ⟨a lawyer's ~*s*⟩ **b :** CUSTOMER ⟨hotel ~*s*⟩ **c :** a person served by or utilizing the services of a social agency ⟨a welfare ~⟩ **3 :** CLIENT STATE — **cli·ent·age** \-ən-tij\ *n* — **cli·en·tal** \klī-ˈent-ᵊl, ˈklī-ənt-\ *adj* — **client·less** \ˌklī-ənt-ləs\ *adj*

cli·en·tele \ˌklī-ən-ˈtel, ˌklē-ən- *also* ˌklē-ˌän-\ *n* [F *clientèle,* fr. L *clientela,* fr. *client-, cliens*] (1563) **:** a body of clients ⟨a shop that caters to an exclusive ~⟩

client state *n* (1918) **:** a country that is economically, politically, or militarily dependent on another country

cliff \ˈklif\ *n* [ME *clif,* fr. OE; akin to OE *clifian* to adhere to] (bef. 12c) **:** a very steep, vertical, or overhanging face of rock, earth, or ice **:** PRECIPICE — **cliffy** \ˈklif-ē\ *adj*

cliff dweller *n* (1881) **1** *often cap C&D* **a :** a member of a prehistoric American Indian people of the southwestern U.S. who built their homes on rock ledges or in the natural recesses of canyon walls and cliffs **b :** a member of any cliff-dwelling people **2 :** a resident of a large usu. metropolitan apartment building — **cliff dwelling** *n*

cliff–hang \ˈklif-ˌhaŋ\ *vi* [back-formation fr. *cliff-hanger*] (1946) **:** to await the outcome of a suspenseful situation

cliff–hang·er \-ˌhaŋ-ər\ *n* (1937) **1 :** an adventure serial or melodrama; *esp* **:** one presented in installments each ending in suspense **2 :** a contest whose outcome is in doubt up to the very end; *broadly* **:** a suspenseful situation — **cliff–hang·ing** \-iŋ\ *adj*

[1]cli·mac·ter·ic \klī-ˈmak-t(ə-)rik; ˌklī-ˌmak-ˈter-ik, -ˈtir-\ *adj* [L *climactericus,* fr. Gk *klimaktērikos,* fr. *klimaktēr* critical point, lit., rung of a ladder, fr. *klimak-, klimax* ladder] (1582) **1 :** constituting or relating to a climacteric **2 :** CRITICAL, CRUCIAL

[2]climacteric *n* (1630) **1 :** a major turning point or critical stage **2 :** MENOPAUSE; *also* **:** a corresponding period in the male during which sexual activity and competence are reduced **3 :** the marked and sudden rise in the respiratory rate of fruit just prior to full ripening

cli·mac·tic \klī-ˈmak-tik, klə-\ *adj* (1872) **:** of, relating to, or constituting a climax — **cli·mac·ti·cal·ly** \-ti-k(ə-)lē\ *adv*

cli·mate \ˈklī-mət\ *n* [ME *climat,* fr. MF, fr. LL *climat-, clima,* fr. Gk *klimat-, klima* inclination, latitude, climate, fr. *klinein* to lean — more at LEAN] (14c) **1 :** a region of the earth having specified climatic conditions **2 a :** the average course or condition of the weather at a place over a period of years as exhibited by temperature, wind velocity, and precipitation **b :** the prevailing set of conditions (as of temperature and humidity) indoors ⟨a *climate*-controlled office⟩ **3 :** the prevailing influence or environmental conditions characterizing a group or period **:** ATMOSPHERE ⟨a ~ of fear⟩

cli·ma·tic \klī-ˈmat-ik, klə-\ *adj* (ca. 1828) **1 :** of or relating to climate **2 :** resulting from or influenced by the climate rather than the soil ⟨forests that had reverted to the ~ type⟩ — compare EDAPHIC 2 — **cli·mat·i·cal·ly** \-i-k(ə-)lē\ *adv*

climatic climax *n* (ca. 1928) **:** the one of the ecological climaxes possible in a particular climatic area whose stability is directly due to the influence of climate — compare EDAPHIC CLIMAX

cli·ma·tol·o·gy \ˌklī-mə-ˈtäl-ə-jē\ *n* (1843) **:** the science that deals with climates and their phenomena — **cli·ma·to·log·i·cal** \ˌklī-mət-ᵊl-ˈäj-i-kəl\ *adj* — **cli·ma·to·log·i·cal·ly** \-k(ə-)lē\ *adv* — **cli·ma·tol·o·gist** \-mə-ˈtäl-ə-jəst\ *n*

[1]cli·max \ˈklī-ˌmaks\ *n* [L, fr. Gk *klimax* ladder, fr. *klinein* to lean] (1589) **1 :** a figure of speech in which a series of phrases or sentences is arranged in ascending order of rhetorical forcefulness **2 a :** the highest point **:** CULMINATION **b :** the point of highest dramatic tension or a major turning point in the action (as of a play) **c :** ORGASM **d :** MENOPAUSE **3 :** a relatively stable stage or community esp. of plants that is achieved through successful adjustment to an environment; *esp* **:** the final stage in ecological succession ***syn*** see SUMMIT — **cli·max·less** *adj*

[2]climax *vt* (1835) **:** to bring to a climax ⟨~*ed* his boxing career with a knockout⟩ ~ *vi* **:** to come to a climax ⟨a riot ~*ing* in the destruction of several houses⟩

[1]climb \ˈklīm\ *vb* [ME *climben,* fr. OE *climban;* akin to OE *clifian* bond, fetter — more at CLEAVE] *vi* (bef. 12c) **1 a :** to go upward with gradual or continuous progress **:** RISE, ASCEND **b :** to increase gradually **c :** to slope upward **2 a :** to go upward or raise oneself esp. by grasping or clutching with the hands ⟨~*ed* upon her father's knee⟩ **b** *of a plant* **:** to ascend in growth (as by twining) **3 :** to go about or down usu. by grasping or holding with the hands ⟨~ down the ladder⟩ **4 :** to get into or out of clothing usu. with some haste or effort ⟨the firemen ~*ed* into their clothes⟩ ~ *vt* **1 :** to go upward on or along, to the top of, or over ⟨~ a hill⟩ **2 :** to draw or pull oneself up, over, or to the top of by using hands and feet ⟨children ~*ing* the tree⟩ **3 :** to grow up or over — **climb·able** \ˈklī-mə-bəl\ *adj*

[2]climb *n* (1577) **1 :** a place where climbing is necessary to progress **2 :** the act or an instance of climbing **:** RISE, ASCENT

climb·er \ˈklī-mər\ *n* (15c) **1 :** one that climbs or helps in climbing **2 :** one who attempts to gain a superior social or business position

climbing iron *n* (1857) **:** a steel framework with spikes attached that may be affixed to one's boots for climbing

clime \ˈklīm\ *n* [LL *clima*] (14c) **:** CLIMATE ⟨traveled to warmer ~*s*⟩

clin- *or* **clino-** *comb form* [NL, fr. Gk *klinein* to lean — more at LEAN] **:** lean **:** slant ⟨*clino*meter⟩

-cli·nal \ˈklīn-ᵊl\ *adj comb form* [ISV, fr. Gk *klinein*] **:** sloping ⟨mono*clinal*⟩

[1]clinch \ˈklinch\ *vb* [prob. alter. of [1]*clench*] *vt* (1542) **1 :** CLENCH 3 **2 a :** to turn over or flatten the protruding pointed end of (a driven nail); *also* **:** to treat (a screw, bolt, or rivet) in a similar way **b :** to fasten in this way **3 a :** to make final or irrefutable **:** SETTLE ⟨that ~*ed* the argument⟩ **b :** WIN ~ *vi* **1 :** to hold an opponent (as in boxing) at close quarters with one or both arms **2 :** to hold fast or firmly — **clinch·ing·ly** \ˈklin-chiŋ-lē\ *adv*

[2]clinch *n* (1659) **1 :** a fastening by means of a clinched nail, rivet, or bolt; *also* **:** the clinched part of a nail, rivet, or bolt **2** *archaic* **:** PUN **3 :** an act or instance of clinching in boxing **4 :** EMBRACE

clinch·er \ˈklin-chər\ *n* (1737) **:** one that clinches: as **a :** a decisive fact, argument, act, or remark ⟨the expense was the ~ that persuaded us to give up the enterprise〉 **b :** a tire with flanged beads fitting into the wheel rim

cline \ˈklīn\ *n* [Gk *klinein*] (1938) **:** a gradient of morphological or physiological change exhibited by a group of related organisms usu. along a line of environmental or geographic transition — **clin·al** \ˈklī-nᵊl\ *adj* — **clin·al·ly** \-ᵊl-ē\ *adv*

-cline \ˌklīn\ *n comb form* [back-formation fr. *-clinal*] **:** slope 〈mono*cline*〉

1**cling** \ˈkliŋ\ *vi* **clung** \ˈkləŋ\; **cling·ing** [ME *clingen*, fr. OE *clingan*; akin to OHG *klunga* tangled ball of thread] (bef. 12c) **1 a :** to hold together **b :** to adhere as if glued firmly **c :** to hold or hold on tightly or tenaciously **2 a :** to have a strong emotional attachment or dependence **b :** to remain or linger as if resisting complete dissipation or dispersal 〈the odor *clung* to the room for hours〉 ***syn*** see STICK — **cling·er** \ˈkliŋ-ər\ *n* — **clingy** \ˈkliŋ-ē\ *adj*

2**cling** *n* (1641) **:** an act or instance of clinging **:** ADHERENCE

cling·stone \ˈkliŋ-ˌstōn\ *n* (1705) **:** any of various fruit (as some peaches or plums) with flesh that adheres strongly to the pit

clin·ic \ˈklin-ik\ *n* [F *clinique*, fr. Gk *klinikē* medical practice at the sickbed, fr. fem. of *klinikos* of a bed, fr. *klinē* bed, fr. *klinein* — more at LEAN] (1843) **1 :** a class of medical instruction in which patients are examined and discussed **2 :** a group meeting devoted to the analysis and solution of concrete problems or to the acquiring of specific skills or knowledge in a particular field 〈writing ~*s*〉 〈golf ~*s*〉 **3 a :** a facility (as of a hospital) for diagnosis and treatment of outpatients **b :** a group practice in which several physicians work cooperatively

-clin·ic \ˈklin-ik\ *adj comb form* [ISV, fr. Gk *klinein*] **1 :** inclining **:** dipping 〈iso*clinic*〉 **2 :** having (so many) oblique intersections of the axes 〈mono*clinic*〉 〈tri*clinic*〉

clin·i·cal \ˈklin-i-kəl\ *adj* (ca. 1755) **1 :** of, relating to, or conducted in or as if in a clinic: as **a :** involving direct observation of the patient **b :** diagnosable by or based on clinical observation **2 :** analytical, detached, or coolly dispassionate 〈a ~ attitude〉 — **clin·i·cal·ly** \-k(ə-)lē\ *adv*

clinical thermometer *n* (1878) **:** a thermometer for measuring body temperature that has a constriction in the tube where the column of liquid breaks and continues to indicate the maximum temperature to which the thermometer was exposed until reset by shaking

cli·ni·cian \klin-ˈish-ən\ *n* (1875) **1 :** one qualified in the clinical practice of medicine, psychiatry, or psychology as distinguished from one specializing in laboratory or research techniques or in theory **2 :** one who conducts a clinic

clinico- *comb form* **:** clinical and 〈*clinico*pathological〉 〈*clinico*statistical〉

clin·i·co·path·o·log·ic \ˈklin-i-(ˌ)kō-ˌpath-ə-ˈläj-ik\ *or* **clin·i·co·path·o·log·i·cal** \-ˈläj-i-kəl\ *adj* (1898) **:** relating to or concerned both with the signs and symptoms directly observable by the physician and with the results of laboratory examination — **clin·i·co·path·o·log·i·cal·ly** \-i-k(ə-)lē\ *adv*

1**clink** \ˈkliŋk\ *vb* [ME *clinken*, of imit. origin] *vi* (14c) **:** to give out a slight sharp short metallic sound ~ *vt* **:** to cause to clink

2**clink** *n* (15c) **:** a clinking sound

3**clink** *n* [prob. fr. *Clink*, a prison in Southwark, London, England] (1575) **1** *slang* **:** a prison cell **2** *slang* **:** JAIL, PRISON

1**clin·ker** \ˈkliŋ-kər\ *n* [alter. of earlier *klincard* (a hard yellowish Dutch brick)] (1641) **1 :** a brick that has been burned too much in the kiln **2 :** stony matter fused together **:** SLAG

2**clinker** *vb* **clin·kered; clin·ker·ing** \ˈkliŋ-k(ə-)riŋ\ *vt* (1866) **1 :** to cause to form clinker **2 :** to clear out the clinkers from ~ *vi* **:** to turn to clinker under heat

3**clink·er** \ˈkliŋ-kər\ *n* [1*clink*] (1836) **1** *Brit* **:** something first-rate **2 a :** a wrong note **b :** a serious mistake or error **:** BONER **c :** an utter failure **:** FLOP 〈the play turned out to be a ~〉 **d :** something of poor quality

clink·er–built \-ˌbilt\ *adj* [*clinker*, n. (clinch)] (1769) **:** having the external planks or plates overlapping like the clapboards on a house 〈a ~ boat〉

clink·ety–clank \ˌkliŋ-kət-ē-ˈklaŋk\ *n* [imit.] (1901) **:** a repeated usu. rhythmic clanking sound 〈the ~ of a loose tire chain〉

cli·nom·e·ter \klī-ˈnäm-ət-ər\ *n* (1811) **:** any of various instruments for measuring angles of elevation or inclination — **cli·no·met·ric** \ˌklī-nə-ˈme-trik\ *adj* — **cli·nom·e·try** \klī-ˈnäm-ə-trē\ *n*

-cli·nous \ˈklī-nəs\ *adj comb form* [prob. fr. NL *-clinus*, fr. Gk *klinē* bed — more at CLINIC]**:** having the androecium and gynoecium in a (single or different) flower or (two separate) flowers 〈di*clinous*〉

1**clin·quant** \ˈkliŋ-kənt, klaⁿ-käⁿ\ *adj* [MF, fr. prp. of *clinquer* to glitter, lit., to clink, of imit. origin] (1591) **:** glittering with gold or tinsel

2**clinquant** *n* [F, fr. *clinquant*, adj.] (1682) **:** imitation gold leaf **:** TINSEL

clin·to·nia \klin-ˈtō-nē-ə\ *n* [NL, genus name, fr. DeWitt *Clinton*] (1843) **:** any of a genus (*Clintonia*) of herbs of the lily family with yellow or white flowers

Clio \ˈklī-(ˌ)ō, ˈklē-\ *n* [L, fr. Gk *Kleiō*] **1 :** the Greek Muse of history **2** *pl* **Cli·os :** a statuette awarded annually by a professional organization for notable achievement in radio and television commercials

clio·met·rics \klī-ə-ˈme-triks\ *n pl but sing in constr* (ca. 1966) **:** the application of methods developed in other fields (as economics, statistics, and data processing) to the study of history — **clio·met·ric** \-trik\ *adj* — **clio·met·ri·cian** \-me-ˈtrish-ən\ *n*

1**clip** \ˈklip\ *vt* **clipped; clip·ping** [ME *clippen*, fr. OE *clyppan*; akin to OHG *klāftra* fathom, L *gleba* clod, *globus* globe] (bef. 12c) **1 :** ENCOMPASS **2 a :** to hold in a tight grip **:** CLUTCH **b :** to clasp or fasten with a clip

2**clip** *n* (15c) **1 :** any of various devices that grip, clasp, or hook **2 :** a device to hold cartridges for charging the magazines of some rifles; *also* **:** a magazine from which ammunition is fed into the chamber of a firearm **3 :** a piece of jewelry held in position by a spring clip

3**clip** *vb* **clipped; clip·ping** [ME *clippen*, fr. ON *klippa*] *vt* (13c) **1 a :** to cut or cut off with or as if with shears 〈~ a dog's hair〉 〈~ an hour off traveling time〉 **b :** to cut off the distal or outer part of **c** (1) **:** 3EXCISE (2) **:** to cut items out of (as a newspaper) **2 a :** CURTAIL, DIMINISH 〈tried to ~ his influence〉 **b :** to abbreviate in speech or writing **3 :** HIT, PUNCH **4 :** to illegally block (an opposing player) in football **5 :** to take money from unfairly or dishonestly esp. by overcharging 〈the nightclub *clipped* the tourist for $200〉 ~ *vi* **1 :** to clip something **2 :** to travel or pass rapidly **3 :** to clip an opposing player in football

4**clip** *n* (15c) **1 a** *pl, Scot* **:** SHEARS **b :** a 2-bladed instrument for cutting esp. the nails **2 :** something that is clipped: as **a :** the product of a single shearing (as of sheep) **b :** a crop of wool of a sheep, a flock, or a region **c :** a section of filmed or videotaped material **d :** a clipping esp. from a newspaper **3 :** an act of clipping **4 :** a sharp blow **5 :** RATE 4a 〈continues at a brisk ~〉 **6 :** a single instance or occasion **:** TIME 〈he charged $10 a ~〉 — often used in the phrase *at a clip* 〈trained 1000 workers at a ~〉

clip·board \ˈklip-ˌbō(ə)rd, -ˌbȯ(ə)rd\ *n* (1896) **:** a small writing board with a spring clip at the top for holding papers

clip–clop \ˈklip-ˈkläp\ *n* [imit.] (1884) **:** the sound made by or as if by a horse walking on a hard surface — **clip–clop** *vi*

clip joint *n* (1933) **1** *slang* **:** a place of public entertainment (as a nightclub) that makes a practice of defrauding patrons (as by overcharging) **2** *slang* **:** a business that makes a practice of overcharging

clip–on \ˌklip-ˌȯn, -ˌän\ *adj* (1909) **:** of or relating to something that clips on 〈a ~ tie〉 〈~ earrings〉

clip on \(ˈ)klip-ˈȯn, -ˈän\ *vi* (1961) **:** to be capable of being fastened by an attached clip 〈the medal *clips on* to the coat lapel〉

clip·per \ˈklip-ər\ *n* (14c) **1 :** one that clips something **2 :** an implement for clipping esp. hair, fingernails, or toenails — usu. used in pl. **3 a :** one that moves swiftly **b :** a fast sailing ship; *esp* **:** one with long slender lines, an overhanging bow, tall raking masts, and a large sail area

clip·ping \ˈklip-iŋ\ *n* (15c) **:** something that is clipped off or out of something; *esp* **:** an item clipped from a publication

clip·sheet \ˈklip-ˌshēt\ *n* (1926) **:** a sheet of newspaper material issued by an organization for clipping and reprinting

clique \ˈklēk, ˈklik\ *n* [F] (1711) **:** a narrow exclusive circle or group of persons; *esp* **:** one held together by common interests, views, or purposes — **cliqu·ey** *or* **cliquy** \ˈklē-kē, ˈklik-\ *adj* — **cliqu·ish** \-ish\ *adj* — **cliqu·ish·ly** *adv* — **cliqu·ish·ness** *n*

cli·tel·lum \klī-ˈtel-əm\ *n, pl* **-la** \-ə\ [NL, modif. of L *clitellae* packsaddle] (1839) **:** a thickened glandular section of the body wall of some annelids that secretes a viscid sac in which the eggs are deposited

cli·to·ris \ˈklit-ə-rəs, kli-ˈtȯr-əs\ *n, pl* **cli·to·ri·des** \kli-ˈtȯr-ə-ˌdēz\ [NL, fr. Gk *kleitoris*] (1615) **:** a small organ at the anterior or ventral part of the vulva homologous to the penis — **cli·to·ral** \ˈklit-ə-rəl\ *or* **cli·tor·ic** \kli-ˈtȯr-ik, -ˈtär-\ *adj*

clo·aca \klō-ˈā-kə\ *n, pl* **-acae** \-ˌkē, -ˌsē\ [L; akin to Gk *klyzein* to wash — more at CLYSTER] (1656) **1 :** 3SEWER **2** [NL, fr. L] **:** the common chamber into which the intestinal, urinary, and generative canals discharge in birds, reptiles, amphibians, and many fishes; *also* **:** a comparable chamber of an invertebrate — **clo·acal** \-ˈā-kəl\ *adj*

1**cloak** \ˈklōk\ *n* [ME *cloke*, fr. ONF *cloque* bell, cloak, fr. ML *clocca* bell; fr. its shape] (13c) **1 :** a loose outer garment **2 :** something that conceals **:** PRETENSE, DISGUISE

2**cloak** *vt* (1509) **:** to cover or hide with or as if with a cloak ***syn*** see DISGUISE

cloak–and–dag·ger *adj* (1860) **:** dealing in or suggestive of melodramatic intrigue and action usu. involving secret agents and espionage

cloak·room \ˈklō-ˌkrüm, -ˌkru̇m\ *n* (1852) **1 a :** a room in which outdoor clothing may be placed during one's stay **b :** a room or cubicle where garments, parcels, and luggage may be checked for temporary safekeeping **2 :** an anteroom of a legislative chamber where members may relax and confer privately with colleagues

1**clob·ber** \ˈkläb-ər\ *n* [origin unknown] *slang Brit* (1879) **:** wearing apparel

2**clobber** *vt* **clob·bered; clob·ber·ing** \-(ə-)riŋ\ [origin unknown] (1943) **1 :** to pound mercilessly; *also* **:** to hit with force **:** SMASH **2 :** to defeat overwhelmingly

clo·chard \ˈklō-shərd, klō-ˈshär\ *n* [F, fr. *clocher* to limp, fr. (assumed) VL *cloppicare*, fr. LL *cloppus* lame] (1937) **:** TRAMP, VAGRANT

cloche \ˈklōsh\ *n* [F, lit., bell, fr. ML *clocca*] (1882) **1** *Brit* **:** a transparent plant cover used outdoors esp. for protection against cold **2 :** a woman's small close-fitting hat usu. with deep rounded crown and very narrow brim

1**clock** \ˈkläk\ *n, often attrib* [ME *clok*, fr. MD *clocke* bell, clock, fr. ONF or ML; ONF *cloque* bell, fr. ML *clocca*, of Celt origin; akin to MIr *clocc* bell] (14c) **1 :** a device other than a watch for indicating or measuring time commonly by means of hands moving on a dial **2 :** a registering device with a dial and indicator attached to a mechanism to measure or gauge its functioning or to record its output; *specif* **:** SPEEDOMETER **3 :** TIME CLOCK **4 :** a synchronizing device (as in a computer) that produces pulses at regular intervals — **around the clock 1 :** continuously for 24 hours **:** day and night without cessation **2 :** without relaxation and heedless of time — **kill the clock** *or* **run out the clock :** to use up as much as possible of the playing time remaining in a game (as football) while retaining possession of the ball or puck esp. to protect a lead

2**clock** *vt* (1883) **1 :** to time with a stopwatch or by an electric timing device **2 :** to register on a mechanical recording device 〈wind velocities were ~*ed* at 80 miles per hour〉 ~ *vi* **:** to register on a time sheet or time clock **:** PUNCH — used with *in, out, on, off* 〈he ~*ed* in late〉 — **clock·er** *n*

3**clock** *n* [perh. fr. 1*clock*] (1530) **:** an ornamental figure on the ankle or side of a stocking or sock

clock·like \ˈkläk-ˌlīk\ *adj* (1741) **:** unusually regular, undeviating, and precise 〈does his job with ~ efficiency〉

clock radio *n* (1965) **:** a combination clock and radio device in which the clock can be set to turn on the radio at a designated time

clock–watcher \-ˌwäch-ər\ *n* (1911) **:** a person (as a worker or student) who keeps close watch on the passage of time — **clock–watch·ing** \-iŋ\ *n*

clock·wise \ˈkläk-ˌwīz\ *adv* (1888) **:** in the direction in which the hands of a clock rotate as viewed from in front — **clockwise** *adj*

\ə\ **abut** \ᵊ\ **kitten, F table** \ər\ **further** \a\ **ash** \ā\ **ace** \ä\ **cot, cart** \au̇\ **out** \ch\ **chin** \e\ **bet** \ē\ **easy** \g\ **go** \i\ **hit** \ī\ **ice** \j\ **job** \ŋ\ **sing** \ō\ **go** \ȯ\ **law** \ȯi\ **boy** \th\ **thin** \t͟h\ **the** \ü\ **loot** \u̇\ **foot** \y\ **yet** \zh\ **vision** \á, k̲, ⁿ, œ, œ̄, ue, ue̅, ʸ\ *see* Guide to Pronunciation

clock·work \\ˈ-ˌwərk\\ *n* (1662) **1 :** machinery containing a train of wheels of small size (as in a mechanical toy or a bomb-actuating device) **2 :** something that seems to perform in response to clockwork or to be controlled by clockwork

clod \\ˈkläd\\ *n* [ME, alter. of *clot*] (15c) **1 a :** a lump or mass esp. of earth or clay **b :** SOIL, EARTH **2 :** OAF, DOLT — **clod·dish** \\ˈkläd-ish\\ *adj* — **clod·dish·ness** *n* — **clod·dy** \\ˈkläd-ē\\ *adj*

clod·hop·per \\ˈkläd-ˌhäp-ər\\ *n* (ca. 1690) **1 :** a clumsy and uncouth rustic **2 :** a large heavy shoe

clod·hop·ping \\-ˌhäp-iŋ\\ *adj* (1843) **:** BOORISH, RUDE

clod·poll *or* **clod·pole** \\ˈkläd-ˌpōl\\ *n* (1601) **:** BLOCKHEAD

clo·fi·brate \\klō-ˈfīb-ˌrāt, -ˈfib-\\ *n* [perh. fr. *chlor-* + *fibr-* + *propionate*] (1964) **:** a compound $C_{12}H_{15}ClO_3$ used esp. to lower abnormally high concentrations of fats and cholesterol in the blood

[1]clog \\ˈkläg, ˈklȯg\\ *n* [ME *clogge* short thick piece of wood] (14c) **1 a :** a weight attached esp. to an animal to hinder motion **b :** something that shackles or impedes **:** ENCUMBRANCE 1 **2 :** a shoe, sandal, or overshoe having a thick typically wooden sole

[2]clog *vb* **clogged; clog·ging** *vt* (1526) **1 a :** to impede with a clog **:** HINDER **b :** to halt or retard the progress, operation, or growth of **:** ENCUMBER ⟨restraints that have been *clogging* the market —T. W. Arnold⟩ **2 :** to fill beyond capacity **:** OVERLOAD ⟨cars *clogged* the main street for hours⟩ **~** *vi* **1 :** to become filled with extraneous matter ⟨the heater *clogged* with dust⟩ **2 :** to unite in a mass **:** CLOT **3 :** to dance a clog dance ***syn*** see HAMPER

clog dance *n* (1869) **:** a dance in which the performer wears clogs and beats out a clattering rhythm on the floor — **clog dancer** *n* — **clog dancing** *n*

cloi·son·né \\ˌklȯiz-ᵊn-ˈā, klə-ˌwäz-\\ *adj* [F, fr. pp. of *cloisonner* to partition] (1863) **:** of, relating to, or being a style of enamel decoration in which the enamel is applied and fired in raised cells (as of soldered wires) on a usu. metal background — compare CHAMPLEVÉ — **cloisonné** *n*

[1]clois·ter \\ˈklȯi-stər\\ *n* [ME *cloistre*, fr. OF, fr. ML *claustrum*, fr. L, bar, bolt, fr. *claudere* to close — more at CLOSE] (13c) **1 a :** an area within a monastery or convent to which the religious are normally restricted **b :** a monastic establishment **c :** monastic life **2 :** a covered passage on the side of a court usu. having one side walled and the other an open arcade or colonnade

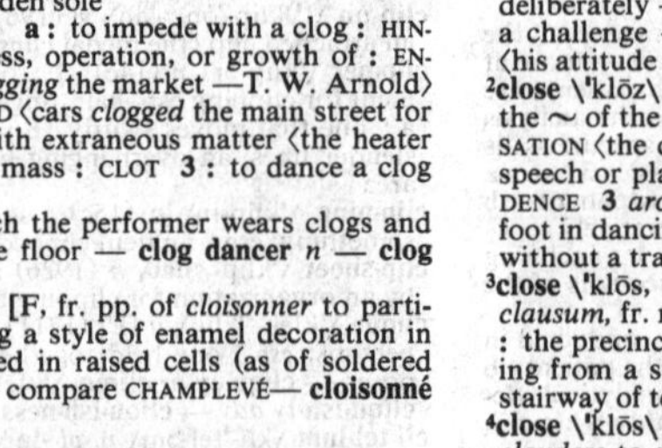

cloister 2

[2]cloister *vt* **clois·tered; clois·ter·ing** \\-st(ə-)riŋ\\ (1581) **1 :** to seclude from the world in or as if in a cloister ⟨a scientist who **~***s* himself in a laboratory⟩ **2 :** to surround with a cloister ⟨**~***ed* gardens⟩

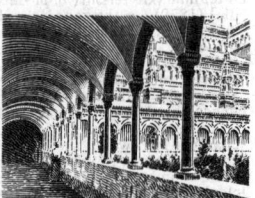

clois·tral \\ˈklȯi-strəl\\ *adj* (1605) **:** of, relating to, or suggestive of a cloister

clois·tress \\ˈklȯi-strəs\\ *n, obs* (1601) **:** NUN

clo·mi·phene \\ˈklō-mə-ˌfēn\\ *n* [*chlor-* + *amine* + *-phene* (fr. *phenyl*)] (1963) **:** an ovulation-inducing synthetic drug $C_{26}H_{28}ClNO$

clomp \\ˈklämp, ˈklȯmp, ˈkləmp\\ *vi* (1850) **:** [2]CLUMP 1

[1]clone \\ˈklōn\\ *n* [Gk *klōn* twig, slip; akin to Gk *klan* to break — more at HALT] (1903) **1 a :** the aggregate of the asexually produced progeny of an individual **b :** an individual grown from a single somatic cell of its parent and genetically identical to it **2 :** one that appears to be a copy of an original form — **clon·al** \\ˈklōn-ᵊl\\ *adj* — **clon·al·ly** \\-ᵊl-ē\\ *adv*

[2]clone *vb* **cloned; clon·ing** *vt* (1947) **1 :** to propagate a clone from **2 :** to make a copy of **~** *vi* **:** to produce a clone

clo·ni·dine \\ˈklän-ə-ˌdēn, ˈklōn-, -ˌdīn\\ *n* [*chlor-* + *aniline* + *imide* + [2]*-ine*] (ca. 1970) **:** an antihypertensive drug $C_9H_9Cl_2N_3$ used to treat essential hypertension and to prevent migraine headache

[1]clonk \\ˈkläŋk, ˈklȯŋk\\ *vi* [imit.] (1930) **:** to make a dull hollow thumping sound **~** *vt* **:** to cause to clonk

[2]clonk *n* (1952) **:** a clonking sound

clo·nus \\ˈklō-nəs\\ *n* [NL, fr. Gk *klonos* agitation — more at HOLD] (1817) **:** a rapid succession of alternating contractions and partial relaxations of a muscle occurring in some nervous diseases — **clon·ic** \\ˈklän-ik\\ *adj* — **clo·nic·i·ty** \\klō-ˈnis-ət-ē, klä-\\ *n*

cloot \\ˈklüt\\ *n* [prob. of Scand origin; akin to ON *klō* claw] (1725) **1** *Scot* **:** a cloven hoof **2** *pl, cap, Scot* **:** CLOOTIE

Cloot·ie \\ˈklüt-ē\\ *n* [dim. of *cloot*] *chiefly Scot* — used as a name of the devil

clop \\ˈkläp\\ *n* [imit.] (1899) **:** a sound made by or as if by a hoof or wooden shoe against the pavement — **clop** *vi*

clop–clop \\ˈkläp-ˌkläp\\ *n* (1901) **:** a sound of rhythmically repeated clops — **clop–clop** *vi*

clo·que *also* **clo·qué** \\klō-ˈkā, ˈklō-ˌ\\ *n* [F *cloqué*, fr. pp. of *cloquer* to become blistered, fr. F dial. (Picard) *cloque* bell, bubble, fr. ML *clocca* bell — more at CLOCK] (1936) **1 :** a fabric with an embossed design **2 :** a fabric esp. of piqué with small woven figures

[1]close \\ˈklōz\\ *vb* **closed; clos·ing** [ME *closen*, fr. OF *clos-*, stem of *clore*, fr. L *claudere*] *vt* (13c) **1 a :** to move so as to bar passage through something ⟨**~** the gate⟩ **b :** to block against entry or passage ⟨**~** a street⟩ **c :** to deny access to ⟨because of drought the governor *closed* the woodlands⟩ **d :** SCREEN, EXCLUDE ⟨**~** a view⟩ **e :** to suspend or stop the operations of ⟨**~** school⟩ — often used with *down* **2** *archaic* **:** ENCLOSE, CONTAIN **3 a :** to bring to an end or period ⟨**~** a charge account⟩ **b :** to conclude discussion or negotiation about ⟨the question is *closed*⟩; *also* **:** to consummate by performing something previously agreed ⟨**~** a transfer of real estate title⟩ **4 a :** to bring or bind together the parts or edges of ⟨a *closed* fist⟩ **b :** to fill up (as an opening) **c :** to make complete by circling or enveloping or by making continuous ⟨**~** a circuit⟩ **~** *vi* **1 a :** to contract, fold, swing, or slide so as to leave no opening ⟨the door *closed* quietly⟩ **b :** to cease operation ⟨the factory *closed* down⟩ ⟨the stores **~** at 9 p.m.⟩ **2 a :** to draw near ⟨the ship was *closing* with the island⟩ **b :** to engage in a struggle at close quarters **:** GRAPPLE ⟨**~** with the enemy⟩ **3 a :** to come together **:** MEET **b :** to draw the free foot up to the supporting foot in dancing **4 :** to enter into or complete an agreement **5 :** to come to an end or period — **clos·able** *or* **close·able** \\ˈklō-zə-bəl\\ *adj* — **clos·er** *n*

syn CLOSE, END, CONCLUDE, FINISH, COMPLETE, TERMINATE mean to bring or come to a stopping point or limit. CLOSE usu. implies that something has been in some way open as well as unfinished ⟨*close* a debate⟩ END conveys a strong sense of finality ⟨the harvest is past, the summer is *ended*, and we are not saved — Jer 8:20 (AV)⟩ CONCLUDE may imply a formal closing (as of a meeting) ⟨the service *concluded* with a blessing⟩ FINISH may stress completion of a final step in a process ⟨after it is painted, the house will be *finished*⟩ COMPLETE implies the removal of all deficiencies or a successful finishing of what has been undertaken ⟨[his] education was ended, if not *completed* —J. T. Farrell⟩ TERMINATE implies the setting of a limit in time or space ⟨your employment *terminates* after three months⟩

— **close one's doors 1 :** to refuse admission ⟨the nation *closed its doors* to immigrants⟩ **2 :** to go out of business ⟨after nearly 40 years he had to *close his doors* for lack of trade⟩ — **close one's eyes to :** to ignore deliberately — **close ranks :** to unite in a concerted stand esp. to meet a challenge — **close the door :** to be uncompromisingly obstructive ⟨his attitude *closed the door* to further negotiation⟩

[2]close \\ˈklōz\\ *n* (14c) **1 a :** a coming or bringing to a conclusion ⟨at the **~** of the party⟩ **b :** a conclusion or end in time or existence **:** CESSATION ⟨the decade drew to a **~**⟩ **c :** the concluding passage (as of a speech or play) **2 :** the conclusion of a musical strain or period **:** CADENCE **3** *archaic* **:** a hostile encounter **4 :** the movement of the free foot in dancing toward or into contact with the supporting foot with or without a transfer of weight

[3]close \\ˈklōs, *U.S. also* ˈklōz\\ *n* [ME *clos*, lit., enclosure, fr. OF *clos*, fr. L *clausum*, fr. neut. of *clausus*, pp.] (13c) **1 a :** an enclosed area **b** *Brit* **:** the precinct of a cathedral **2** *chiefly Brit* **a :** a narrow passage leading from a street to a court and the houses within or to the common stairway of tenements **b :** a road closed at one end

[4]close \\ˈklōs\\ *adj* **clos·er; clos·est** [ME *clos*, fr. MF, fr. L *clausus*, pp. of *claudere* to shut, close; akin to Gk *kleiein* to close, OHG *sliozan*, OE *hlot* lot] (14c) **1 :** having no openings **:** CLOSED **2 a :** confined or carefully guarded ⟨five days of **~** arrest⟩ **b** (1) *of a vowel* **:** HIGH 11 (2) **:** formed with the tongue in a higher position than for the other vowel of a pair **3 :** restricted to a privileged class **4 a :** SECLUDED, SECRET **b :** SECRETIVE ⟨she could tell us something if she would . . . but she was as **~** as wax —A. Conan Doyle⟩ **5 :** STRICT, RIGOROUS ⟨keep **~** watch⟩ **6 :** hot and stuffy **7 :** reluctant to part with money or possessions **:** cautious and often stingy in expenditure **8 :** having little space between items or units **9 a :** fitting tightly or exactly **b :** very short or near to the surface ⟨the barber gave him a **~** shave⟩ **c :** matching or blending without gap **10 :** being near in time, space, effect, or degree **11 :** INTIMATE, FAMILIAR **12 a :** ACCURATE, PRECISE ⟨a **~** study⟩ **b :** marked by fidelity to an original ⟨a **~** copy of an old master⟩ **c :** TERSE, COMPACT **13 :** decided or won by a narrow margin ⟨a **~** baseball game⟩ **14 :** difficult to obtain ⟨money is **~**⟩ **15** *of punctuation* **:** characterized by liberal use esp. of commas ***syn*** see STINGY — **close·ly** *adv* — **close·ness** *n* — **close to home :** within one's personal interests so that one is strongly affected ⟨the audience felt that the speaker's remarks hit pretty *close to home*⟩

[5]close \\ˈklōs\\ *adv* (15c) **:** in a close position or manner

close call \\ˈklōs-\\ *n* (1881) **:** a narrow escape

close corporation \\ˈklōs-\\ *n* (1920) **:** a corporation whose stock is not publicly traded but held by a few persons who are often those active in the management

close–cropped \\ˈklō-ˌskräpt\\ *adj* (ca. 1891) **1 :** clipped short **2 :** having the hair clipped short

closed \\ˈklōzd\\ *adj* (13c) **1 a :** not open **b :** ENCLOSED **c :** composed entirely of closed tubes or vessels ⟨a **~** circulatory system⟩ **2 a :** forming a self-contained unit allowing no additions ⟨**~** association⟩ **b** (1) **:** traced by a moving point that returns to an arbitrary starting point ⟨**~** curve⟩; *also* **:** so formed that every plane section is a closed curve ⟨**~** surface⟩ (2) **:** characterized by mathematical elements that when subjected to an operation produce only elements of the same set ⟨the set of whole numbers is **~** under addition and multiplication⟩ (3) **:** containing all the limit points of every possible subset ⟨a **~** interval contains its endpoints⟩ **c :** characterized by continuous return and reuse of the working substance ⟨a **~** cooling system⟩ **d** *of a racecourse* **:** having the same starting and finishing point **3 a :** confined to a few ⟨**~** membership⟩ **b :** excluding participation of outsiders or witnesses **:** conducted in strict secrecy **c :** rigidly excluding outside influence ⟨a **~** mind⟩ **4 :** ending in a consonant ⟨**~** syllable⟩

closed book *n* (1913) **:** something beyond comprehension **:** ENIGMA

closed–cap·tioned \\(ˌ)klōz(d)-ˈkap-shənd\\ *adj, of a television program* (1980) **:** broadcast so that captions appear only on the screen of a receiver equipped with a decoder

closed chain *n* (1904) **:** RING 10

closed circuit *n* (1949) **:** a television installation in which the signal is transmitted by wire to a limited number of receivers

closed corporation *n* (1924) **:** CLOSE CORPORATION

closed couplet *n* (1910) **:** a rhymed couplet in which the sense is complete

closed–door \\ˌklōz-ˌdō(ə)r, -ˌdȯ(ə)r\\ *adj* (ca. 1928) **:** barring public and press ⟨a **~** session of the investigating committee⟩

closed–end \\ˌklōz-ˌdend\\ *adj* (1938) **:** having a fixed capitalization of shares that are traded on the market at prices determined by the operation of the law of supply and demand ⟨a **~** investment company⟩ — compare OPEN-END

closed loop *n* (1951) **:** an automatic control system for an operation or process in which feedback in a closed path or group of paths acts to maintain output at a desired level

close·down \\ˈklōz-ˌdau̇n\\ *n* (1889) **:** an instance of suspending or stopping operations

closed shop *n* (1904) **:** an establishment in which the employer by agreement hires only union members in good standing

closed stance *n* (ca. 1934) **:** a preparatory position (as in baseball batting or golf) in which the forward foot (as the left foot of a right-handed person) is closer to the line of play than the back foot — compare OPEN STANCE

close·fist·ed \\ˈklōs-ˈfis-təd\\ *adj* (1608) **:** STINGY, TIGHTFISTED

close–grained \-ˈgrānd\ *adj* (1754) **:** having a closely compacted smooth texture; *esp* **:** having narrow annual rings or small wood elements

close–hauled \-ˈhȯld\ *adj* (1769) **:** having the sails set for sailing as nearly against the wind as the ship will go

close in \(ˈ)klō-ˈzin\ *vi* (14c) **1 :** to gather in close all around with an oppressing or isolating effect ⟨despair *closed in* on her⟩ **2 :** to approach to close quarters esp. for an attack, raid, or arrest ⟨intelligence agents *closed in* on him⟩ **3 :** to grow dark ⟨the short November day was already *closing in* —Ellen Glasgow⟩ **~** *vt* **1 :** to encircle closely and isolate **2 :** to enshroud to such an extent as to preclude entrance or exit ⟨the airport is *closed in*⟩

close–knit \ˈklō-ˈsnit\ *adj* (1926) **:** bound together by intimate social or cultural ties or by close economic or political ties ⟨~ families⟩

close·mouthed \ˈklō-ˈsmau̇thd, -ˈsmau̇tht\ *adj* (1881) **:** cautious in speaking **:** UNCOMMUNICATIVE; *also* **:** SECRETIVE

close order *n* (1796) **:** an arrangement of troops for formations, drill, or marching according to an exact scheme prescribing fixed distances and intervals

close·out \ˈklō-ˌzau̇t\ *n* (1925) **1 :** a clearing out by a sale usu. at reduced prices of the whole remaining stock (as of a business) **2 :** an article offered or bought at a closeout

close out \(ˈ)klō-ˈzau̇t\ *vt* (14c) **1 a :** EXCLUDE **b :** PRECLUDE ⟨*close out* his chances⟩ **2 a :** to dispose of a whole stock of by sale **b :** to dispose of (a business) **c :** SELL ⟨*closed out* his share of the business⟩ **d :** to put (an account) in order for disposal or transfer **3 a :** TERMINATE **b :** to discontinue operation **~** *vi* **1 :** to sell out a business **2 :** to buy or sell securities or commodities in order to terminate an account (as when margin is exhausted)

close quarters \ˈklōs-\ *n pl* (1809) **:** immediate contact or close range ⟨fought at *close quarters*⟩

close shave \ˈklōs(h)-\ *n* (1834) **:** a narrow escape

close·stool \ˈklōs-ˌstül\ *n* (15c) **:** a stool holding a chamber pot

¹clos·et \ˈkläz-ət, ˈklȯz-\ *n* [ME, fr. MF, dim. of *clos* enclosure] (14c) **1 a :** an apartment or small room for privacy **b :** a monarch's or official's private chamber for counsel or devotions **2 :** a cabinet or recess for china, household utensils, or clothing **:** CUPBOARD **3 :** a place of retreat or privacy **4 :** WATER CLOSET **5 :** a state or condition of secrecy, privacy, or obscurity — **clo·set·ful** \-ˌfu̇l\ *n*

²closet *vt* (1595) **1 :** to shut up in or as if in a closet **2 :** to take into a closet for a secret interview

³closet *adj* (1612) **1 :** closely private **2 :** working in or suited to the closet as the place of seclusion or study **:** THEORETICAL **3 :** being so in private ⟨a ~ racist⟩

closet drama *n* (1922) **:** drama suited primarily for reading rather than production

closet queen *n* (1967) **:** one who secretly engages in homosexual activities while leading an ostensibly heterosexual life — often used derogatorily

close–up \ˈklō-ˌsəp *also* -ˌzəp\ *n* (1913) **1 :** a photograph or movie shot taken at close range **2 :** an intimate view or examination of something

close up \(ˈ)klō-ˈsəp\ *adv* (1926) **:** at close range

clos·ing \ˈklō-ziŋ\ *n* (1596) **1 :** a concluding part (as of a speech) **2 :** a closable gap (as in an article of wear) **3 :** a meeting of parties to a real-estate deal for formally transferring title

clos·trid·i·um \klä-ˈstrid-ē-əm\ *n, pl* **-ia** \-ē-ə\ [NL, genus name, fr. Gk *klōstēr* spindle, fr. *klōthein* to spin] (1884) **:** any of various spore-forming mostly anaerobic soil or intestinal bacteria (esp. genus *Clostridium*) — compare BOTULINUM — **clos·trid·i·al** \-ē-əl\ *adj*

clo·sure \ˈklō-zhər\ *n* [ME, fr. MF, fr. L *clausura,* fr. *clausus,* pp. of *claudere* to close — more at CLOSE] (14c) **1** *archaic* **:** means of enclosing **:** ENCLOSURE **2 :** an act of closing **:** the condition of being closed ⟨~ of the eyelids⟩ **3 :** something that closes ⟨pocket with zipper ~⟩ **4** [trans. of F *clôture*] **:** CLOTURE **5 :** the property that a number system or a set has when it is mathematically closed under an operation **6 :** a set that contains a given set together with all the limit points of the given set

¹clot \ˈklät\ *n* [ME, fr. OE *clott;* akin to MHG *klōz* lump, ball — more at CLOUT] (bef. 12c) **1 :** a portion of a substance cleaving together in a thick nondescript mass (as of clay or gum) **2 a :** a roundish viscous lump formed by coagulation of a portion of liquid or by melting **b :** a coagulated mass produced by clotting of blood **3** *Brit* **:** BLOCKHEAD **4 :** CLUSTER, GROUP

²clot *vb* **clot·ted; clot·ting** *vi* (bef. 12c) **1 :** to become a clot **:** form clots **2 :** to undergo a sequence of complex chemical and physical reactions that results in conversion of fluid blood into a coagulated mass **:** COAGULATE **~** *vt* **1 :** to cause to clot **2 :** to fill with clots

cloth \ˈklȯth\ *n, pl* **cloths** \ˈklȯthz, ˈklȯths\ *often attrib* [ME, fr. OE *clāth* cloth, garment; akin to OE *clīthan* to adhere to, LL *glut-, glus* glue] (bef. 12c) **1 a :** a pliable material made usu. by weaving, felting, or knitting natural or synthetic fibers and filaments **b :** a similar material (as of glass) **2 :** a piece of cloth adapted for a particular purpose; *esp* **:** TABLECLOTH **3 a :** a distinctive dress of a profession or calling **b :** the dress of the clergy; *also* **:** CLERGY

clothe \ˈklōth\ *vt* **clothed** *or* **clad** \ˈklad\; **cloth·ing** [ME *clothen,* fr. OE *clāthian,* fr. *clāth*] (bef. 12c) **1 a :** to cover with or as if with cloth or clothing **:** DRESS **b :** to provide with clothes **2 :** to express or enhance by suitably significant language **:** COUCH ⟨treaties *clothed* in stately phraseology⟩ **3 :** to endow esp. with power or a quality

clothes \ˈklō(th)z\ *n pl, often attrib* [ME, fr. OE *clāthas,* pl. of *clāth*] (bef. 12c) **1 :** CLOTHING **2 :** BEDCLOTHES **3 :** all the cloth articles of personal and household use that can be washed

clothes·horse \-ˌhȯ(ə)rs\ *n* (1775) **1 :** a frame on which to hang clothes **2 :** a conspicuously dressy person

¹clothes·line \-ˌlīn\ *n* (1830) **:** a line (as of cord) on which clothes may be hung to dry

²clothesline *vt* (1964) **:** to knock down (a football player) by catching him by the neck with an outstretched arm

clothes moth *n* (1753) **:** any of several small yellowish or buff-colored moths (esp. genera *Tinea* and *Tineola* of the family Tineidae) whose larvae eat wool, fur, or feathers

clothes peg *n, Brit* (1825) **:** CLOTHESPIN

clothes·pin \ˈklō(th)z-ˌpin\ *n* (1846) **:** a forked piece of wood or plastic or a small spring clamp used for fastening clothes on a clothesline

clothes·press \-ˌpres\ *n* (1713) **:** a receptacle for clothes

clothes tree *n* (1929) **:** an upright post-shaped stand with hooks or pegs around the top on which to hang clothes

cloth·ier \ˈklōth-yər, ˈklō-thē-ər\ *n* [ME, alter. of *clother,* fr. *cloth*] (14c) **:** one who makes or sells clothing

cloth·ing \ˈklō-thiŋ\ *n* (13c) **:** garments in general; *also* **:** COVERING

cloth yard *n* (15c) **:** a yard esp. for measuring cloth; *specif* **:** a unit of 37 inches equal to the Scotch ell and used also as a length for arrows

clotted cream *n* (1878) **:** a thick cream made chiefly in England by slowly heating whole milk on which the cream has been allowed to rise and then skimming the cooled cream from the top — called also *Cornish cream, Devonshire cream*

clo·ture \ˈklō-chər\ *n* [F *clôture,* lit., closure, alter. of MF *closure*] (1871) **:** the closing or limitation of debate in a legislative body esp. by calling for a vote — **cloture** *vt*

¹cloud \ˈklau̇d\ *n, often attrib* [ME, rock, cloud, fr. OE *clūd;* akin to Gk *gloutos* buttock] (bef. 12c) **1 a :** a visible mass of particles of water or ice in the form of fog, mist, or haze suspended usu. at a considerable height in the air **b :** a light filmy, puffy, or billowy mass seeming to float in the air; *also* **:** something suggesting such a mass ⟨a ~ of memories⟩ **2 a :** a usu. visible mass of minute particles suspended in the air or in a gas; *also* **:** one of the masses of obscuring matter in interstellar space **b :** an aggregate of charged particles (as electrons) **3 :** a great crowd or multitude **:** SWARM ⟨~*s* of mosquitoes⟩ **4 :** something that has a dark, lowering, or threatening aspect ⟨~*s* of war⟩ ⟨a ~ of suspicion⟩ **5 :** something that obscures or blemishes ⟨a ~ of ambiguity⟩ **6 :** a dark or opaque vein or spot (as in marble)

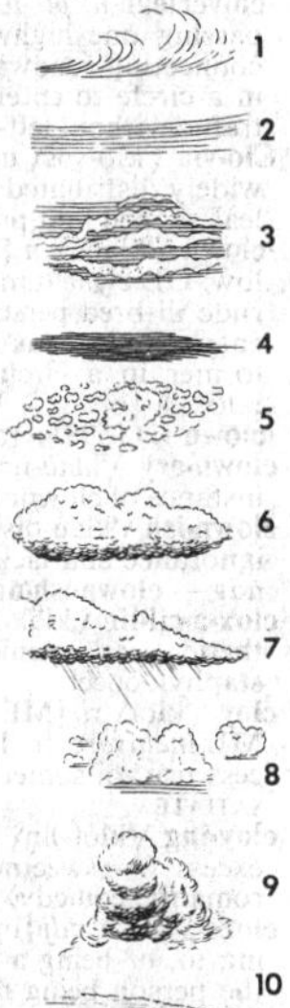

cloud 1a: *1* cirrus, *2* cirrostratus, *3* cirrocumulus, *4* altostratus, *5* altocumulus, *6* stratocumulus, *7* nimbostratus, *8* cumulus, *9* cumulonimbus, *10* stratus

²cloud *vi* (1562) **1 :** to grow cloudy — usu. used with *over* or *up* ⟨~*ed* over before the storm⟩ **2 a** *of facial features* **:** to become troubled, apprehensive, or distressed in appearance **b :** to become blurry, dubious, or ominous — often used with *over* **3 :** to billow up in the form of a cloud **~** *vt* **1 a :** to envelop or hide with or as if with a cloud ⟨smog ~*ed* our view⟩ **b :** to make opaque esp. by condensation of moisture **c :** to make murky esp. with smoke or mist **2 :** to make unclear or confused ⟨~ the issue⟩ **3 :** TAINT, SULLY ⟨a ~*ed* reputation⟩ **4 :** to cast gloom over

cloud·ber·ry \ˈklau̇d-ˌber-ē\ *n* (1597) **:** a creeping herbaceous raspberry (*Rubus chamaemorus*) of north temperate regions; *also* **:** its pale amber-colored edible fruit

cloud·burst \-ˌbərst\ *n* (1869) **1 :** a sudden copious rainfall **2 :** DELUGE 2

cloud chamber *n* (1897) **:** a vessel containing air saturated with water vapor whose sudden expansion reveals the passage of an ionizing particle by a trail of visible droplets

cloud–cuck·oo–land \(ˈ)klau̇d-ˈkük-(ˌ)ü-ˌland, -ˈku̇k-\ *n* [trans. of Gk *nephelokokkygia*] (1899) **:** a realm of fantasy or of whimsical or foolish behavior

cloud·land \ˈklau̇d-ˌland\ *n* (1817) **1 :** the region of the clouds **2 :** the realm of visionary speculation or poetic imagination

cloud·less \-ləs\ *adj* (14c) **:** free from clouds **:** CLEAR — **cloud·less·ly** *adv* — **cloud·less·ness** *n*

cloud·let \ˈklau̇d-lət\ *n* (1788) **:** a small cloud

cloud nine *n* [perh. fr. the ninth and highest heaven of Dante's Paradise, whose inhabitants are most blissful because nearest to God] (1959) **:** a feeling of well-being or elation— usu. used with *on*

cloudy \ˈklau̇d-ē\ *adj* **cloud·i·er; -est** (14c) **1 :** of, relating to, or resembling cloud **2 :** darkened by gloom or anxiety **3 a :** overcast with clouds; *specif* **:** six tenths to nine tenths covered with clouds **b :** having a cloudy sky **4 :** obscure in meaning ⟨~ issues⟩; *also* **:** uncertain as to fact or outcome ⟨a ~ future⟩ **5 :** dimmed or dulled as if by clouds ⟨a ~ mirror⟩ **6 :** uneven in color or texture **7 :** having visible material in suspension **:** MURKY — **cloud·i·ly** \ˈklau̇d-ᵊl-ē\ *adv* — **cloud·i·ness** \ˈklau̇d-ē-nəs\ *n*

¹clout \ˈklau̇t\ *n* [ME, fr. OE *clūt;* akin to MHG *klōz* lump, Russ *gluda*] (bef. 12c) **1 a** *dial chiefly Brit* **:** a piece of cloth or leather **:** RAG **b :** a household cloth **c :** an article of clothing (as for infants) **2 :** a blow esp. with the hand; *also* **:** a hit in baseball **3 :** a white cloth on a stake or frame used as a target in archery **4 :** PULL, INFLUENCE ⟨political ~⟩

²clout *vt* (14c) **1 :** to cover or patch with a clout **2 :** to hit forcefully

¹clove \ˈklōv\ *n* [ME, fr. OE *clufu;* akin to OE *clēofan* to cleave] (bef. 12c) **:** one of the small bulbs (as in garlic) developed in the axils of the scales of a large bulb

²clove *past of* CLEAVE

³clove \ˈklōv\ *n* [alter. of ME *clowe,* fr. OF *clou (de girofle),* lit., nail of clove, fr. L *clavus* nail; akin to L *claudere* to shut — more at CLOSE] (13c) **:** the dried flower bud of a tropical tree (*Eugenia aromatica*) of the myrtle family that is used as a spice and is the source of an oil; *also* **:** this tree

clove hitch \ˈklōv-\ *n* [ME *cloven, clove* divided, fr. pp. of *clevien* to cleave] (1769) **:** a knot securing a rope temporarily to an object (as a post or spar) and consisting of a turn around the object, over the standing part, around the object again, and under the last turn — see KNOT illustration

clo·ven \ˈklō-vən\ *past part of* CLEAVE

cloven foot *n* (13c) **1 :** a foot (as of a sheep) divided into two parts at its distal extremity **2** [fr. the traditional representation of Satan as cloven-footed] **:** the sign of devilish character — **clo·ven–foot·ed** \ˌklō-vən-ˈfu̇t-əd\ *adj*
cloven hoof *n* (1870) **:** CLOVEN FOOT — **clo·ven–hoofed** \ˌklō-vən-ˈhu̇ft, -ˈhüft, -ˈhu̇vd, -ˈhüvd\ *adj*
clove pink *n* (ca. 1855) **:** CARNATION 2
clo·ver \ˈklō-vər\ *n* [ME, fr. OE *clāfre;* akin to OHG *klēo* clover] (bef. 12c) **:** any of a genus (*Trifolium*) of low leguminous herbs having trifoliolate leaves and flowers in dense heads and including many that are valuable for forage and attractive to bees; *also* **:** any of various other leguminous plants (as of the genera *Melilotus, Lespedeza,* or *Medicago*) — **in clover** *or* **in the clover :** in prosperity or in pleasant circumstances
¹clo·ver·leaf \-ˌlēf\ *adj* (1917) **:** resembling a clover leaf in shape
²cloverleaf *n, pl* **-leafs** \-ˌlēfs\ *or* **-leaves** \-ˌlēvz\ (1931) **:** a road plan passing one highway over another and routing turning traffic onto connecting roadways which branch only to the right and lead around in a circle to enter the other highway from the right and thus merge traffic without left-hand turns or direct crossings
Clo·vis \ˈklō-vəs\ *adj* [*Clovis,* New Mexico] (1956) **:** of or relating to a widely distributed prehistoric culture of No. America characterized by leaf-shaped flint projectile points having fluted sides
¹clown \ˈklau̇n\ *n* [prob. of LG origin; akin to Fris *klönne* clumsy fellow, OE *clyne* lump of metal] (1563) **1 :** FARMER, COUNTRYMAN **2 :** a rude ill-bred person **:** BOOR **3 a :** a fool, jester, or comedian in an entertainment (as a play); *specif* **:** a grotesquely dressed comedy performer in a circus **b :** one who habitually plays the buffoon **c :** JOKER 1b
²clown *vi* (1599) **:** to act as or like a clown
clown·ery \ˈklau̇-nə-rē\ *n, pl* **-er·ies** (1589) **:** clownish behavior or an instance of clownishness **:** BUFFOONERY
clown·ish \ˈklau̇-nish\ *adj* (1570) **:** resembling or befitting a clown (as in ignorance and lack of sophistication) ***syn*** see BOORISH — **clown·ish·ly** *adv* — **clown·ish·ness** *n*
clox·a·cil·lin \ˌkläk-sə-ˈsil-ən\ *n* [*chlor-* + *oxacillin*] (1963) **:** a semisynthetic oral penicillin $C_{19}H_{17}ClN_3NaO_5S$ effective esp. against staphylococci
cloy \ˈklȯi\ *vb* [ME *acloien* to lame, fr. MF *encloer* to drive in a nail, fr. ML *inclavare,* fr. L *in* + *clavus* nail] *vt* (1530) **:** to surfeit with an excess usu. of something orig. pleasing ~ *vi* **:** to cause surfeit ***syn*** see SATIATE
cloy·ing \ˈklȯ(-)iŋ\ *adj* (1752) **:** disgusting or distasteful by reason of excess ⟨~ sweetness⟩; *also* **:** excessively sweet or sentimental ⟨a ~ romantic comedy⟩ — **cloy·ing·ly** *adv*
cloze \ˈklōz\ *adj* [by shortening and alter. fr. *closure*] (1954) **:** of, relating to, or being a test of reading comprehension that involves having the person being tested supply words which have been systematically deleted from a text
¹club \ˈkləb\ *n, often attrib* [ME *clubbe,* fr. ON *klubba;* akin to OHG *kolbo* club, OE *clamm* bond] (13c) **1 a :** a heavy usu. tapering staff esp. of wood wielded as a weapon **b :** a stick or bat used to hit a ball in any of various games **c :** something resembling a club **2 a :** a figure that resembles a stylized clover leaf on each playing card of one of the four suits; *also* **:** a card marked with this figure **b** *pl but sing or pl in constr* **:** the suit comprising cards marked with a club **3 a :** an association of persons for some common object usu. jointly supported and meeting periodically; *also* **:** a group identified by some common characteristic ⟨nations in the nuclear ~⟩ **b :** the meeting place of a club **c :** an association of persons participating in a plan by which they agree to make regular payments or purchases in order to secure some advantage **d :** NIGHTCLUB **e :** an athletic association or team
²club *vb* **clubbed; club·bing** *vt* (1593) **1 a :** to beat or strike with or as if with a club **b :** to gather into a club-shaped mass ⟨*clubbed* her hair⟩ **2 a :** to unite or combine for a common cause **b :** to contribute to a common fund ~ *vi* **1 :** to form a club **:** COMBINE **2 :** to pay a share of a common expense
club·ba·ble *or* **club·able** \ˈkləb-ə-bəl\ *adj* (1783) **:** SOCIABLE
club bag *n* (1926) **:** a rectangular and usu. leather traveling bag that tapers to a purselike opening at the top and that is often zippered
clubbed \ˈkləbd\ *adj* (14c) **:** shaped like a club ⟨~ antennae⟩
club·ber \ˈkləb-ər\ *n* (1633) **:** a member of a club
club·by \ˈkləb-ē\ *adj* **club·bi·er; -est** (1859) **:** characteristic of a club or club members: as **a :** SOCIABLE **b :** open only to qualified or approved persons **:** SELECT — **club·bi·ness** *n*
club car *n* (1895) **:** LOUNGE CAR
club chair *n* (1919) **:** a deep low thickly upholstered easy chair often with rather low back and heavy sides and arms
club cheese *n* (1916) **:** a process cheese made by grinding cheddar and other cheeses usu. with added condiments and seasoning
club coupe *n* (1947) **:** an automobile resembling a coupe in having only two doors but with a full-width rear seat accessible by tilting the front-seat backs forward
club·foot \ˈkləb-ˈfu̇t\ *n* (1538) **:** a misshapen foot twisted out of position from birth; *also* **:** this deformity — **club·foot·ed** \-ˈfu̇t-əd\ *adj*
club fungus *n* (1899) **:** any of a family (Clavariaceae) of basidiomycetes with a simple or branched often club-shaped sporophore
club·house \ˈkləb-ˌhau̇s\ *n* (1818) **1 :** a house occupied by a club or used for club activities **2 :** locker rooms used by an athletic team
club moss *n* (1597) **:** any of an order (Lycopodiales) of primitive vascular plants (as ground pine) often with the sporangia borne in club-shaped strobili
club·root \ˈkləb-ˌrüt, -ˌru̇t\ *n* (1846) **:** a disease of cabbages and related plants caused by a slime mold (*Plasmodiophora brassicae*) producing swellings or distortions of the root
club sandwich *n* (1903) **:** a sandwich of three slices of bread with two layers of various meats (as chicken or turkey) and lettuce, tomato, and mayonnaise
club soda *n* (1942) **:** SODA WATER 2a
club steak *n* (1915) **:** a small steak cut from the end of the short loin — see BEEF illustration
¹cluck \ˈklək\ *vb* [imit.] *vi* (15c) **1 :** to make a cluck **2 :** to make a clicking sound with the tongue **3 :** to express interest or concern ⟨critics ~*ed* over the new developments⟩ ~ *vt* **1 :** to call with a cluck **2 :** to express with interest or concern
²cluck *n* (1703) **1 :** the characteristic sound made by a hen esp. in calling her chicks **2 :** a stupid or naive person
clue *var of* CLEW
clum·ber spaniel \ˌkləm-bər-\ *n, often cap C&S* [*Clumber,* estate in Nottinghamshire, England] (1883) **:** a large massive heavyset spaniel with a dense silky largely white coat
¹clump \ˈkləmp\ *n* [prob. fr. LG *klump;* akin to OE *clamm*] (1586) **1 :** a group of things clustered together ⟨a ~ of bushes⟩ **2 :** a compact mass **3 :** a heavy tramping sound — **clumpy** \ˈkləm-pē\ *adj*
²clump *vi* (1665) **1 :** to walk or move clumsily and noisily **2 :** to form clumps ~ *vt* **:** to arrange in or cause to form clumps ⟨the serum ~*s* the bacteria⟩
clum·sy \ˈkləm-zē\ *adj* **clum·si·er; -est** [prob. fr. obs. E *clumse* (benumbed with cold)] (1597) **1 a :** lacking dexterity, nimbleness, or grace ⟨~ fingers⟩ **b :** lacking tact or subtlety ⟨a ~ joke⟩ **2 :** awkward or inefficient in use or construction **:** UNWIELDY ***syn*** see AWKWARD — **clum·si·ly** \-zə-lē\ *adv* — **clum·si·ness** \-zē-nəs\ *n*
clung *past and past part of* CLING
¹clunk \ˈkləŋk\ *vb* [imit.] *vi* (1796) **1 :** to make a clunk **2 :** to hit something with a clunk ~ *vt* **:** to strike or hit with a clunk
²clunk *n* (1823) **1 :** a blow or the sound of a blow **:** THUMP **2 :** a dull or stupid person
clunk·er \ˈkləŋ-kər\ *n* (1943) **1 :** an old or badly working piece of machinery; *esp* **:** JALOPY **2 :** someone or something notably unsuccessful
clunky \ˈkləŋ-kē\ *adj* **clunk·i·er; -est** (1968) **:** clumsy in style, form, or execution ⟨a ~ thriller⟩ ⟨~ earrings⟩
clu·pe·id \ˈklü-pē-əd\ *n* [deriv. of L *clupea,* a small river fish] (1880) **:** any of a large family (Clupeidae) of soft-finned teleost fishes (as herrings) having a laterally compressed body and a forked tail — **clupeid** *adj*
¹clus·ter \ˈkləs-tər\ *n* [ME, fr. OE *clyster;* akin to OE *clott* clot] (bef. 12c) **1 :** a number of similar things growing together or of things or persons collected or grouped closely together **:** BUNCH **2 :** two or more consecutive consonants or vowels in a segment of speech **3 :** a group of buildings and esp. houses built close together on a sizable tract in order to preserve open spaces larger than the individual yard for common recreation **4 :** an aggregation of stars, galaxies, or supergalaxies that appear close together in the sky and seem to have common properties (as distance) ***syn*** see GROUP — **clus·tery** \-t(ə-)rē\ *adj*
²cluster *vb* **clus·tered; clus·ter·ing** \-t(ə-)riŋ\ *vt* (14c) **1 :** to collect into a cluster ⟨~ the tents together⟩ **2 :** to furnish with clusters ~ *vi* **:** to grow or assemble in a cluster
cluster headache *n* (1953) **:** a headache that is characterized by severe pain in the eye or temple and tends to recur in a series of attacks
¹clutch \ˈkləch\ *vb* [ME *clucchen,* fr. OE *clyccan;* akin to MIr *glacc* hand] *vt* (bef. 12c) **1 :** to grasp or hold with or as if with the hand or claws usu. strongly, tightly, or suddenly **2** *obs* **:** CLENCH ~ *vi* **1 :** to seek to grasp and hold **2 :** to operate an automobile clutch ***syn*** see TAKE
²clutch *n* (13c) **1 a :** the claws or a hand in the act of grasping or seizing firmly **b :** an often cruel or unrelenting control, power, or possession ⟨the fell ~ of circumstance —W. E. Henley⟩ **c :** the act of grasping, holding, or restraining **2 :** a device for gripping an object (as at the end of a chain or tackle) **3 a :** a coupling used to connect and disconnect a driving and a driven part of a mechanism **b :** a lever operating such a clutch **4 :** a tight or critical situation **:** PINCH ⟨come through in the ~⟩ **5 :** CLUTCH BAG
³clutch *adj* (1944) **1 :** made or done in a crucial situation ⟨a ~ hit drove in the winning run⟩ **2 :** successful in a crucial situation ⟨a ~ pitcher⟩
⁴clutch *n* [alter. of dial. E *cletch* (hatching, brood)] (1721) **1 :** a nest of eggs or a brood of chicks **2 :** GROUP, BUNCH
clutch bag *n* (1949) **:** a woman's small usu. strapless handbag
¹clut·ter \ˈklət-ər\ *vb* [ME *clotteren* to clot, fr. *clot*] *vi, chiefly dial* (1649) **:** to run in disorder ~ *vt* **:** to fill or cover with scattered or disordered things that impede movement or reduce effectiveness — often used with *up*
²clutter *n* (1649) **1 a :** a crowded or confused mass or collection **b :** things that clutter a place **2 :** interfering echoes visible on a radar screen caused by reflection from objects other than the target **3** *chiefly dial* **:** DISTURBANCE, HUBBUB
Clydes·dale \ˈklīdz-ˌdāl\ *n* (1786) **:** a heavy draft horse with feathering on the legs of a breed orig. from Clydesdale, Scotland
clyp·e·us \ˈklip-ē-əs\ *n, pl* **clyp·ei** \-ē-ˌī, -ē-ˌē\ [NL, fr. L, round shield] (1834) **:** a plate on the anterior median aspect of an insect's head
clys·ter \ˈklis-tər\ *n* [ME, fr. MF or L; MF *clistere,* fr. L *clyster,* fr. Gk *klystēr,* fr. *klyzein* to wash out; akin to L *cloaca* sewer, OE *hlūtor* clean] (14c) **:** ENEMA
Cly·tem·nes·tra \ˌklīt-əm-ˈnes-trə\ *n* [L, fr. Gk *Klytaimnēstra*] **:** the wife and murderess of Agamemnon
c–mitosis \ˌsē-\ *n* [colchicine + *mitosis*] (1944) **:** an artificially induced abortive nuclear division in which the chromosome number is doubled — **c–mitotic** *adj*
cni·do·blast \ˈnīd-ə-ˌblast\ *n* [NL *cnida* nematocyst, fr. Gk *knidē* nettle] (1884) **:** a cell that develops a nematocyst or develops into a nematocyst
co- *prefix* [ME, fr. L, fr. *com-;* akin to OE *ge-,* perfective and collective prefix, Gk *koinos* common] **1 :** with **:** together **:** joint **:** jointly ⟨coexist⟩ ⟨coheir⟩ **2 :** in or to the same degree ⟨coextensive⟩ **3 a :** one that is associated in an action with another **:** fellow **:** partner ⟨coauthor⟩ ⟨coworker⟩ **b :** having a usu. lesser share in duty or responsibility **:** alternate **:** deputy ⟨copilot⟩ **4 :** of, relating to, or constituting the complement of an angle ⟨cosine⟩ ⟨codeclination⟩

co·ac·tor	**co·cham·pi·on**	**co·cul·ti·va·tion**
co·ad·min·is·tra·tion	**co·com·pos·er**	**co·cul·ture**
co·ag·gre·gate	**co·con·spir·a·tor**	**co·cu·ra·tor**
co·ar·rang·er	**co·con·trib·u·tor**	**co·de·fen·dant**
co·au·thor	**co·coun·sel**	**co·de·sign**
co·au·thor·ship	**co·cre·ate**	**co·de·vel·op**
co·cap·tain	**co·cre·ator**	**co·de·vel·op·er**
co·cat·a·lyst	**co·cul·ti·vate**	**co·di·rect**

co·di·rec·tor
co·dis·cov·er·er
co·drive
co·driv·er
co·eter·nal
co·eter·nal·ly
co·eter·ni·ty
co·ex·ec·u·tor
co·fa·vor·ite
co·fea·ture
co·fi·nance
co·found
co·found·er
co·head
co·head·lin·er
co·heir
co·heir·ess
co·hold·er
co·host
co·host·ess
co·iden·ti·ty
co·in·vent
co·in·ven·tor
co·in·ves·ti·ga·tor
co·join
co·lead
co·lead·er
co·man·age
co·man·age·ment
co·man·ag·er
co–oc·cur
co–oc·cur·rence
co–oc·cur·rent
co–of·fi·cial
co–of·fi·ci·ate
co–op·er·ant
co–or·ga·niz·er
co–own
co–own·er
co·part·ner
co·part·ner·ship
co·pay·ment
co·pre·sent
co·pres·i·dent
co·prince
co·prin·ci·pal
co·pris·on·er
co·pro·cess·ing
co·pro·duce
co·pro·duc·er
co·pro·duc·tion
co·pro·mot·er
co·pro·pri·etor
co·pros·per·i·ty
co·pub·lish
co·pub·lish·er
co·pu·ri·fy
co·re·cip·i·ent
co·res·i·dence
co·res·i·dent
co·res·i·dent·tial
co·script
co·script·writ·er
co·spon·sor
co·spon·sor·ship
co·star
co·sur·fac·tant
co·trans·duce
co·trans·duc·tion
co·trans·fer
co·trans·port
co·trust·ee
co·win·ner
co·work·er
co·write

co·ac·er·vate \kō-'as-ər-ˌvāt\ *n* [L *coacervatus,* pp. of *coacervare* to heap up, fr. *co-* + *acervus* heap] (1929) : an aggregate of colloidal droplets held together by electrostatic attractive forces — **co·acer·vate** \ˌkō-ə-'sər-vət\ *adj* — **co·ac·er·va·tion** \(ˌ)kō-ˌas-ər-'vā-shən\ *n*

[1]**coach** \'kōch\ *n, often attrib* [ME *coche,* fr. MF, fr. G *kutsche,* fr. Hung *kocsi* (*szekér*), lit., wagon, fr. *Kocs,* Hungary] (1556) **1 a :** a large usu. closed four-wheeled carriage having doors in the sides and an elevated seat in front for the driver **b :** a railroad passenger car intended primarily for day travel **c :** BUS 1a **d :** TRAILER 3b **e :** an enclosed automobile with permanent top and two doors **f :** a class of passenger air transportation at a lower fare than first class **2** [fr. the concept that the tutor conveys the student through his examinations] **a :** a private tutor **b :** one who instructs or trains a performer or a team of performers; *specif* **:** one who instructs players in the fundamentals of a competitive sport and directs team strategy ⟨football ~⟩

[2]**coach** *vt* (1849) **1 :** to train intensively (as by instruction and demonstration) ⟨~ pupils⟩ **2 :** to act as coach of ⟨~ tennis⟩ ⟨~ a team⟩ ~ *vi* **1 :** to go in a coach **2 :** to instruct, direct, or prompt as a coach — **coach·able** \'kō-chə-bəl\ *adj* — **coach·er** *n*

coach dog *n* (1840) **:** DALMATIAN

coach·man \'kōch-mən\ *n* (1579) **:** a man whose business is to drive a coach or carriage

co·act \kō-'akt\ *vi* (1606) **:** to act or work together — **co·ac·tive** \-'ak-tiv\ *adj*

co·ac·tion \-'ak-shən\ *n* (1625) **1 :** joint action **2 :** the interaction between individuals or kinds (as species) in an ecological community

co·adapt·ed \ˌkō-ə-'dap-təd\ *adj* (1836) **:** mutually adapted esp. by natural selection ⟨~ gene complexes⟩ — **co·ad·ap·ta·tion** \ˌkō-ˌad-ˌap-'tā-shən, -əp-\ *n*

co·ad·ju·tor \ˌkō-ə-'jüt-ər, kō-'aj-ət-ər\ *n* [ME *coadjutour,* fr. MF *coadjuteur,* fr. L *coadjutor,* fr. *co-* + *adjutor* aid, fr. *adjutus,* pp. of *adjuvare* to help — more at AID] (15c) **1 :** one who works together with another **:** ASSISTANT **2 :** a bishop assisting a diocesan bishop and often having the right of succession — **coadjutor** *adj*

co·ad·ju·trix \ˌkō-ə-'jü-triks, kō-'aj-ə-(ˌ)triks\ *n, pl* **co·ad·ju·tri·ces** \ˌkō-ə-'jü-trə-ˌsēz, (ˌ)kō-ˌaj-ə-'trī-(ˌ)sēz\ [NL, fem. of *coadjutor*] (1646) **:** a female coadjutor

co·ag·u·lant \kō-'ag-yə-lənt\ *n* (1770) **:** something that produces coagulation

co·ag·u·lase \kō-'ag-yə-ˌlās, -ˌlāz\ *n* (1914) **:** any of several enzymes that cause coagulation (as of blood)

[1]**co·ag·u·late** \-lət, -ˌlāt\ *adj, archaic* (14c) **:** being clotted or congealed

[2]**co·ag·u·late** \kō-'ag-yə-ˌlāt\ *vb* **-lat·ed; -lat·ing** [L *coagulatus,* pp. of *coagulare* to curdle, fr. *coagulum* curdling agent, fr. *cogere* to drive together — more at COGENT] *vt* (15c) **1 :** to cause to become viscous or thickened into a coherent mass **:** CURDLE, CLOT **2 :** to gather together or form into a mass or group ~ *vi* **:** to become coagulated — **co·ag·u·la·bil·i·ty** \kō-ˌag-yə-lə-'bil-ət-ē\ *n* — **co·ag·u·la·ble** \-'ag-yə-lə-bəl\ *adj* — **co·ag·u·la·tion** \-'lā-shən\ *n*

co·ag·u·lum \kō-'ag-yə-ləm\ *n, pl* **-u·la** \-lə\ *or* **-ulums** [L] (1658) **:** a coagulated mass or substance **:** CLOT

[1]**coal** \'kōl\ *n, often attrib* [ME *col,* fr. OE; akin to OHG & ON *kol* burning ember, OIr *gual* coal] (bef. 12c) **1 :** a piece of glowing carbon or charred wood **:** EMBER **2 :** CHARCOAL 1 **3 a :** a black or brownish black solid combustible substance formed by the partial decomposition of vegetable matter without free access of air and under the influence of moisture and often increased pressure and temperature that is widely used as a natural fuel **b** *pl, Brit* **:** pieces or a quantity of the fuel broken up for burning

[2]**coal** *vt* (1602) **1 :** to burn to charcoal **:** CHAR **2 :** to supply with coal ~ *vi* **:** to take in coal

co·alesce \ˌkō-ə-'les\ *vi* **co·alesced; co·alesc·ing** [L *coalescere,* fr. *co-* + *alescere* to grow — more at OLD] (ca. 1656) **1 :** to grow together **2 a :** to unite into a whole **:** FUSE ⟨separate townships have *coalesced* into a single, sprawling colony —Donald Gould⟩ **b :** to unite for a common end **:** join forces ⟨people with different points of view ~ into opposing factions —I. L. Horowitz⟩ **3 :** to arise from the combination of distinct elements ⟨an organized and a popular resistance immediately *coalesced* —C. C. Menges⟩ ***syn*** see MIX — **co·ales·cence** \-'les-ᵊn(t)s\ *n* — **co·ales·cent** \-ᵊnt\ *adj*

coal·field \'kōl-ˌfēld\ *n* (1813) **:** a region in which deposits of coal occur

coal·fish \-ˌfish\ *n* (1603) **:** any of several blackish or dark-backed fishes (as a pollack or sablefish)

coal gas *n* (1809) **:** gas made from coal: as **a :** the mixture of gases thrown off by burning coal **b :** gas made by carbonizing bituminous coal in retorts and used for heating and lighting

coal·hole \'kōl-ˌhōl\ *n* (1661) **1** *Brit* **:** a compartment for storing coal **2 :** a hole for coal (as an opening in a sidewalk leading to a coal bin)

coal·ifi·ca·tion \ˌkō-lə-fə-'kā-shən\ *n* (1911) **:** a process in which vegetable matter becomes converted into coal of increasingly higher rank with anthracite as the final product — **coal·ify** \'kō-lə-ˌfī\ *vt*

coaling station *n* (1853) **:** a port at which ships may coal

co·ali·tion \ˌkō-ə-'lish-ən\ *n* [F, fr. L *coalitus,* pp. of *coalescere*] (1612) **1 a :** the act of coalescing **:** UNION **b :** a body formed by the coalescing of orig. distinct elements **:** COMBINATION **2 :** a temporary alliance of distinct parties, persons, or states for joint action — **co·ali·tion·ist** \-'lish-(ə-)nəst\ *n*

coal measures *n pl* (1665) **:** beds of coal with the associated rocks

coal oil *n* (1858) **1 :** petroleum or a refined oil prepared from it **2 :** KEROSENE

Coal·sack \'kōl-ˌsak\ *n* (1870) **:** either of two dark nebulae in the Milky Way located one near the Northern Cross and the other near the Southern Cross

coal seam *n* (1849) **:** a bed of coal usu. thick enough to be mined with profit

coal tar *n* (1785) **:** tar obtained by distillation of bituminous coal and used esp. in making dyes and drugs

coam·ing \'kō-miŋ\ *n* [prob. irreg. fr. *comb*] (1611) **:** a raised frame (as around a hatchway in the deck of a ship) to keep out water

co–an·chor \(ˈ)kō-'aŋ-kər\ *n* (1973) **:** a newscaster who shares the duties of anchoring a news broadcast — **co–anchor** *vt*

co·apt \kō-'apt\ *vt* [LL *coaptare,* fr. L *co-* + *aptus* fastened, fit — more at APT] (1570) **:** to fit together and make fast — **co·ap·ta·tion** \(ˌ)kō-ˌap-'tā-shən\ *n*

co·arc·tate \kō-'ärk-ˌtāt\ *adj* [L *coarctatus,* pp. of *coarctare, coartare* to press together, fr. *co-* + *artus* narrow, confined; akin to L *artus* joint — more at ARTICLE] (15c) **:** enclosed in a rigid case ⟨~ insect pupae⟩

co·arc·ta·tion \(ˌ)kō-ˌärk-'tā-shən\ *n* (1545) **:** a stricture or narrowing esp. of a canal or vessel (as the aorta)

coarse \'kō(ə)rs, 'kȯ(ə)rs\ *adj* **coars·er; coars·est** [ME *cors,* fr. *course,* n.] (14c) **1 :** of ordinary or inferior quality or value **:** COMMON **2 a** (1) **:** composed of relatively large parts or particles ⟨~ sand⟩ (2) **:** loose or rough in texture ⟨~ cloth⟩ **b :** adjusted or designed for heavy, fast, or less delicate work ⟨a ~ saw with large teeth⟩ **c :** not precise or detailed with respect to adjustment or discrimination **3 :** crude or unrefined in taste, manners, or language **4 :** harsh, raucous, or rough in tone — **coarse·ly** *adv* — **coarse·ness** *n*

syn COARSE, VULGAR, GROSS, OBSCENE, RIBALD mean offensive to good taste or morals. COARSE implies roughness, rudeness, or crudeness of spirit, behavior, or language; VULGAR often implies boorishness or ill-breeding; GROSS implies extreme coarseness and insensitiveness; OBSCENE applies to anything strongly repulsive to the sense of decency and propriety esp. in sexual matters; RIBALD applies to what is amusingly or picturesquely vulgar or irreverent or mildly indecent.

coarse–grained \'kō(ə)rs-'grānd, 'kȯ(ə)rs-\ *adj* (1768) **1 :** having a coarse grain **2 :** CRUDE

coars·en \'kōrs-ᵊn, 'kȯrs-\ *vb* **coars·ened; coars·en·ing** \'kōrs-niŋ, 'kȯrs-, -ᵊn-iŋ\ *vt* (1805) **:** to make coarse ~ *vi* **:** to become coarse

[1]**coast** \'kōst\ *n* [ME *cost,* fr. MF *coste,* fr. L *costa* rib, side; akin to OSlav *kostĭ* bone] (14c) **1 :** the land near a shore **:** SEASHORE **2** *obs* **:** BORDER, FRONTIER **3 a :** a hill or slope suited to coasting **b :** a slide down a slope (as on a sled) **4** *often cap* **:** the Pacific coast of the U.S. — **coast·al** \'kōs-tᵊl\ *adj* — **coast·wise** \'kōs-ˌtwīz\ *adv or adj* — **from coast to coast :** across an entire nation or continent

[2]**coast** *vt* (14c) **1** *obs* **:** to move along or past the side of **:** SKIRT **2 :** to sail along the shore of ~ *vi* **1 a** *archaic* **:** to travel on land along a coast or along or past the side of something **b :** to sail along the shore **2 a :** to slide, run, or glide downhill by the force of gravity **b :** to move along without or as if without further application of propulsive power (as by momentum or gravity) **c :** to proceed easily without special application of effort or concern

coast·er \'kō-stər\ *n* (1574) **1 :** one that coasts: as **a :** a person engaged in coastal traffic or commerce **b :** a ship sailing along a coast or engaged in trade between ports of the same country **2 :** a resident of a seacoast **3 a :** a tray or decanter stand usu. of silver and sometimes on wheels **b :** a shallow container or a plate or mat to protect a surface **4 a :** a small vehicle (as a sled or wagon) used in coasting **b :** ROLLER COASTER

coaster brake *n* (1899) **:** a brake in the hub of the rear wheel of a bicycle operated by reverse pressure on the pedals

coaster wagon *n* (1911) **:** a child's toy wagon often used for coasting

coast guard *n* (1833) **1 :** a military or naval force employed in guarding a coast or responsible for the safety, order, and operation of maritime traffic in neighboring waters **2** *usu* **coast·guard** *chiefly Brit* **:** COASTGUARDSMAN

coast·guards·man \'kōs(t)-ˌgärdz-mən\ *or* **coast·guard·man** \-ˌgärd-mən\ *n* (1841) **:** a member of a coast guard

coast·land \-ˌland\ *n* (1852) **:** land bordering the sea

coast·line \'kōst-ˌlīn\ *n* (1860) **1 :** a line that forms the boundary between the land and the ocean or a lake **2 :** the outline or shape of a coast

coast redwood *n* (ca. 1898) **:** REDWOOD 3

coast–to–coast \'kōs-tə-'kōst\ *adj* (1911) **:** extending or airing across an entire nation or continent

coast·ward \'kōs-twərd\ *or* **coast·wards** \-twərdz\ *adv* (1853) **:** toward the coast — **coastward** *adj*

[1]**coat** \'kōt\ *n, often attrib* [ME *cote,* fr. MF, of Gmc origin; akin to OHG *kozza* coarse wool mantle] (14c) **1 a :** an outer garment varying in length and style according to fashion and use **b :** something resembling a coat **2 :** the external growth on an animal **3 :** a layer of one substance covering another ⟨a ~ of paint⟩ — **coat·ed** \-əd\ *adj* — **coat·less** *adj*

[2]**coat** *vt* (14c) **1 :** to cover with a coat **2 :** to cover or spread with a finishing, protecting, or enclosing layer — **coat·er** *n*

coat·dress \'kōt-,dres\ *n* (1854) : a dress styled like a coat usu. with a front buttoning from neckline to hemline
coat hanger *n* (1895) : a slender arched device (as of wood, metal, or plastic) which is shaped typically somewhat like a person's shoulders and over which garments may be hung
co·ati \kə-'wät-ē, kwä-'tē\ *n* [Pg *coatí*, fr. Tupi] (1676) : a tropical American mammal (genus *Nasua*) related to the raccoon but with a longer body and tail and a long flexible snout

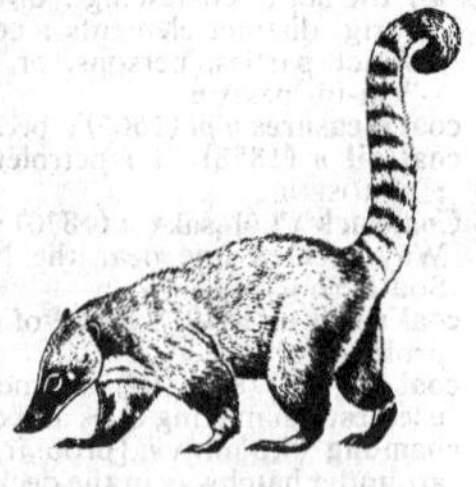
coati

co·ati·mun·di \kə-,wät-i-'mən-dē, ,kwät-, -'mu̇n-\ *n* [Tupi] (1676) : COATI
coat·ing \'kōt-iŋ\ *n* (1768) **1** : cloth for coats **2** : COAT, COVERING
coat of arms [trans. of F *cotte d'armes*] (14c) **1** : a tabard or surcoat embroidered with armorial bearings **2 a** : the particular heraldic bearings (as of a person) usu. depicted on an escutcheon often with accompanying adjuncts (as a crest, motto, and supporters) **b** : a similar symbolic emblem
coat of mail (15c) : a garment of metal scales or chain mail worn as armor
coat·rack \'kōt-,rak\ *n* (1915) : a stand or rack fitted with pegs, hooks, or hangers and used for the temporary storage of garments
coat·room \-,rüm, -,ru̇m\ *n* (1870) : CLOAKROOM
coat·tail \'kōt-,tāl\ *n* (1600) **1** : the rear flap of a man's coat **2** *pl* : the skirts of a dress coat, cutaway, or frock coat — **on one's coattails** : with the help of another; *esp* : with the benefit of another's political prestige ⟨congressmen riding into office *on the president's coattails*⟩
coat tree *n* (1944) : CLOTHES TREE
[1]**coax** \'kōks\ *vt* [earlier *cokes*, fr. *cokes*, n. (simpleton)] (1589) **1** *obs* : FONDLE, PET **2** : to influence or gently urge by caressing or flattering : WHEEDLE **3** : to draw, gain, or persuade by means of gentle urging or flattery **4** : to manipulate with great perseverance and usu. with considerable effort toward a desired state or activity ⟨~ a fire to burn⟩
[2]**co·ax** \'kō-,aks\ *n* (1949) : COAXIAL CABLE — called also *coax cable*
co·ax·i·al \(')kō-'ak-sē-əl\ *adj* (1881) **1** : having coincident axes **2** : mounted on concentric shafts — **co·ax·i·al·ly** \-sē-ə-lē\ *adv*
coaxial cable *n* (1936) : a transmission line that consists of a tube of electrically conducting material surrounding a central conductor held in place by insulators and that is used to transmit telegraph, telephone, and television signals of high frequency — called also *coaxial line*
[1]**cob** \'käb\ *n* [ME *cobbe* leader] (15c) **1** : a male swan **2** *dial Eng* : a rounded mass, lump, or heap **3** : a crudely struck old Spanish coin of irregular shape **4** : CORNCOB 1 **5** : a stocky short-legged riding horse — **cob·by** \'käb-ē\ *adj*
[2]**cob** *n* [prob. fr. [1]*cob*] (1602) : a mixture that consists of unburned clay usu. with straw as a binder and that is used for constructing walls of small buildings
co·bal·a·min \kō-'bal-ə-mən\ *also* **co·bal·a·mine** \-,mēn\ *n* [*cobalt* + *vitamin*] (1956) : a member of the vitamin B_{12} group; *broadly* : the vitamin B_{12} group
co·balt \'kō-,bȯlt\ *n* [G *kobalt*, alter. of *kobold*, lit., goblin, fr. MHG *kobolt*; fr. its occurrence in silver ore, believed to be due to goblins] (1683) : a tough lustrous silver-white magnetic metallic element that is related to and occurs with iron and nickel and is used esp. in alloys — see ELEMENT table
cobalt blue *n* (1835) : a greenish blue pigment consisting essentially of cobalt oxide and alumina
cobalt chloride *n* (1885) : a chloride of cobalt; *esp* : the dichloride $CoCl_2$ that is blue when dehydrated, turns red in the presence of moisture, and is used to indicate humidity
co·bal·tic \kō-'bȯl-tik\ *adj* (1782) : of, relating to, or containing cobalt esp. with a valence of three
co·balt·ite \'kō-,bȯl-,tīt, kō-'\ *or* **co·balt·ine** \-,tēn\ *n* [*cobaltite*, alter. of *cobaltine*, fr. F, fr. *cobalt*] (1868) : a mineral consisting of a grayish to silver-white cobalt sulfur arsenide CoAsS used in making smalt
co·bal·tous \kō-'bȯl-təs\ *adj* (1863) : of, relating to, or containing cobalt esp. with a valence of two
cobalt 60 *n* (1946) : a heavy radioactive isotope of cobalt of the mass number 60 produced in nuclear reactors and used as a source of gamma rays (as for radiotherapy)
cob·ber \'käb-ər\ *n* [origin unknown] *Austral* (1895) : BUDDY
[1]**cob·ble** \'käb-əl\ *vt* **cob·bled**; **cob·bling** \-(ə-)liŋ\ [ME *coblen*, perh. back-formation fr. *cobelere* cobbler] (15c) **1** *chiefly Brit* : to mend or patch coarsely **2** : REPAIR, MAKE ⟨~ shoes⟩ **3** : to make or put together roughly or hastily — often used with *together* or *up*
[2]**cobble** *n* [back-formation fr. *cobblestone*] (1600) **1** : a naturally rounded stone larger than a pebble and smaller than a boulder; *esp* : such a stone used in paving a street or in construction **2** *pl, chiefly Brit* : lump coal about the size of small cobblestones
cob·bled *adj* (1888) : paved with cobblestones
cob·bler \'käb-lər\ *n* [ME *cobelere*] (13c) **1** : a mender or maker of shoes and often of other leather goods **2** *archaic* : a clumsy workman **3** : a tall iced drink consisting usu. of wine, rum, or whiskey, and sugar garnished with mint or a slice of lemon or orange **4** : a deep-dish fruit pie with a thick top crust
cob·ble·stone \'käb-əl-,stōn\ *n* [ME, fr. *cobble-* (prob. fr. *cob*) + *stone*] (15c) : [2]COBBLE 1 — **cob·ble·stoned** \-,stōnd\ *adj*
co·bel·lig·er·ent \,kō-bə-'lij-(ə-)rənt\ *n* (1813) : a country fighting with another power against a common enemy — **cobelligerent** *adj*
co·bia \'kō-bē-ə\ *n* [origin unknown] (1873) : a large percoid fish (*Rachycentron canadum*) of warm seas that is a food and sport fish
co·ble \'kō-bəl\ *n* [ME] (14c) **1** *Scot* : a short flat-bottomed rowboat **2** : a flat-floored fishing boat with a rudder extending below the keel and a lugsail on a raking mast
cob·nut \'käb-,nət\ *n* (1580) : the fruit of a European hazel (*Corylus avellana grandis*); *also* : the plant bearing this fruit
CO·BOL *or* **Co·bol** \'kō-,bȯl\ *n* [*common business oriented language*] (1960) : a standardized business language for programming a computer
co·bra \'kō-brə\ *n* [Pg *cobra (de capello)*, lit., hooded snake, fr. L *colubra* snake; akin to L *scelus* crime — more at CYLINDER] (1802) : any of several venomous Asian and African elapid snakes (genus *Naja*) that when excited expand the skin of the neck into a hood by movement of the anterior ribs; *also* : any of several related African snakes
cob·web \'käb-,web\ *n* [ME *coppeweb*, fr. *coppe* spider (fr. OE ātorcoppe) + *web*; akin to MD *coppe* spider] (14c) **1** : the network spread by a spider **2** : a single thread spun by a spider or insect larva **3** : something resembling a spider web ⟨filled with the ~s of bigotry, suspicion and restraint —Robert Smylie⟩ — **cob·webbed** \-,webd\ *adj* — **cob·web·by** \-,web-ē\ *adj*
co·ca \'kō-kə\ *n* [Sp, fr. Quechua *kúka*] (1577) **1** : any of several So. American shrubs (genus *Erythroxylon*, family Erythroxylaceae); *esp* : one (*E. coca*) with leaves resembling tea **2** : dried leaves of a coca (as *E. coca*) containing alkaloids including cocaine
co·caine \kō-'kān, 'kō-,\ *n* (1874) : a bitter crystalline alkaloid $C_{17}H_{21}NO_4$ that is obtained from coca leaves, is used as a local anesthetic, can result in psychological dependence, and in large doses produces intoxication like that from hemp
co·cain·ize \kō-'kā-,nīz\ *vt* **-ized; -iz·ing** (1887) : to treat or anesthetize with cocaine — **co·cain·iza·tion** \-,kā-nə-'zā-shən\ *n*
co·car·box·yl·ase \,kō-kär-'bäk-sə-,lās, -,lāz\ *n* [*co-* + *carboxylase*] (1932) : a coenzyme $C_{12}H_{19}ClN_4O_7P_2S{\cdot}H_2O$ that is a pyrophosphate of thiamine and is important in metabolic reactions (as decarboxylation in the Krebs cycle)
co·car·cin·o·gen \,kō-kär-'sin-ə-jən, kō-'kärs-ᵊn-ə-,jen\ *n* (ca. 1931) : an agent that aggravates the carcinogenic effects of another substance — **co·car·cin·o·gen·ic** \,kō-,kärs-ᵊn-ō-'jen-ik\ *adj*
coc·cid \'käk-səd\ *n* [NL *Coccus*, genus of scales, fr. Gk *kokkos* grain, kermes] (1892) : SCALE INSECT, MEALYBUG
coc·cid·i·oi·do·my·co·sis \(,)käk-,sid-ē-,ȯid-ō-(,)mī-'kō-səs\ *n* [NL, fr. *Coccidioides*, genus of fungi (fr. *coccidium*) + *mycosis*] (1937) : a disease of man and lower animals caused by a fungus (*Coccidioides immitis*) and marked esp. by fever and localized pulmonary symptoms
coc·cid·i·o·sis \(,)käk-,sid-ē-'ō-səs\ *n, pl* **-o·ses** \-,sēz\ (1892) : infestation with or disease caused by coccidia
coc·cid·i·um \käk-'sid-ē-əm\ *n, pl* **-ia** \-ē-ə\ [NL, dim. of *coccus*] (1879) : any of an order (Coccidia) of protozoans usu. parasitic in the digestive epithelium of vertebrates
coc·coid \'käk-,ȯid\ *adj* (1893) : related to or resembling a coccus : GLOBOSE — **coccoid** *n*
coc·cus \'käk-əs\ *n, pl* **coc·ci** \'käk-,(s)ī, 'käk-(,)(s)ē\ [NL, fr. Gk *kokkos*] (1800) : a spherical bacterium — **coc·cal** \'käk-əl\ *adj*
-coccus *n comb form, pl* **-cocci** [NL, fr. Gk *kokkos*] : berry-shaped organism ⟨Micro*coccus*⟩
coc·cy·geal \käk-'sij-(ē-)əl\ *adj* [ML *coccygeus* of the coccyx, fr. Gk *kokkyk-*, *kokkyx*] (1836) : of or relating to the coccyx
coc·cyx \'käk-siks\ *n, pl* **coc·cy·ges** \'käk-sə-,jēz\ *also* **coc·cyx·es** \'käk-sik-səz\ [NL, fr. Gk *kokkyx* cuckoo, coccyx; fr. its resemblance to a cuckoo's beak] (1615) : the end of the spinal column beyond the sacrum in man and tailless apes
co·chair \(')kō-'che(ə)r, -'cha(ə)r\ *vt* (1964) : to serve as cochairman of
co·chair·man \(')kō-'che(ə)r-mən, -'cha(ə)r-\ *n* (1932) : a joint chairman, vice-chairman, or assistant chairman
Co·chin Chi·na \,kō-chən-'chī-nə\ *n* [*Cochin China*, Vietnam] (1850) : any of an Asian breed of large domestic fowl with thick plumage, small wings and tail, and densely feathered legs and feet — called also *Cochin*
co·chi·neal \'käch-ə-,nēl, 'kō-chə-\ *n* [MF & Sp; MF *cochenille*, fr. OSp *cochinilla* wood louse, cochineal] (1582) : a red dye consisting of the dried bodies of female cochineal insects used esp. as a biological stain and as an indicator
cochineal insect *n* (1801) : a small bright red cactus-feeding scale insect (*Dactylopius coccus*) the females of which are the source of cochineal
co·chlea \'kō-klē-ə, 'käk-lē-\ *n, pl* **co·chle·as** *or* **co·chle·ae** \-(k)lē-,ē, -,ī\ [NL, fr. L, snail, snail shell, fr. Gk *kochlias*, fr. *kochlos* land snail; akin to Gk *konchē* mussel] (1688) : a division of the labyrinth of the ear of higher vertebrates that is usu. coiled like a snail shell and is the seat of the hearing organ — see EAR illustration — **co·chle·ar** \'kō-klē-ər, 'käk-lē-\ *adj*
[1]**cock** \'käk\ *n* [ME *cok*, fr. OE *cocc*, of imit. origin] (bef. 12c) **1 a** : the adult male of the domestic fowl (*Gallus gallus*) **b** : the male of birds other than the domestic fowl **c** : WOODCOCK **d** *archaic* : the crowing of a cock; *also* : COCKCROW **e** : WEATHERCOCK **2** : a device (as a faucet or valve) for regulating the flow of a liquid **3 a** : a chief person : LEADER **b** : a person of spirit and often of a certain swagger or arrogance **4 a** : the hammer in the lock of a firearm **b** : the cocked position of the hammer **5** : PENIS — usu. considered vulgar — **cock of the walk** : one that dominates a group or situation esp. overbearingly

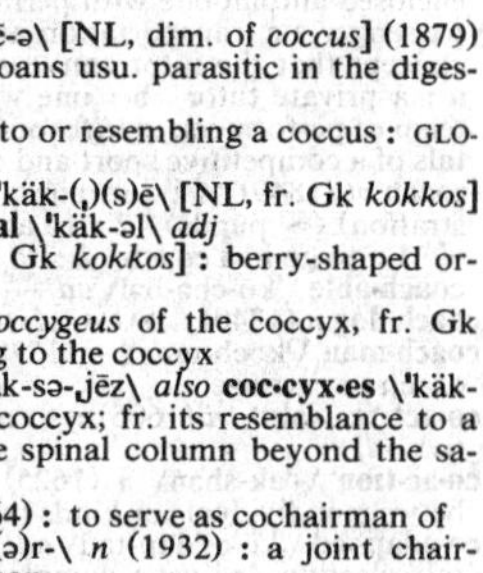

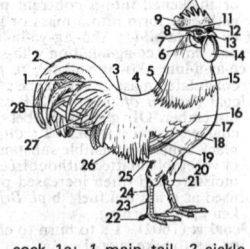

cock 1a: *1* main tail, *2* sickle feathers, *3* saddle, *4* back, *5* cape, *6* ear lobe, *7* ear, *8* eye, *9* blade, *10* points, *11* base, *12* comb, *13* beak, *14* wattles, *15* hackle, *16* wing bow, *17* breast, *18* wing bar, *19* secondaries, *20* primaries, *21* hock, *22* claw, *23* spur, *24* shank, *25* down, *26* saddle feathers, *27* tail coverts, *28* lesser sickle feathers

[2]**cock** *vi* (1575) **1** : STRUT, SWAGGER **2** : to turn, tip, or stick up **3** : to position the hammer of a firearm for firing ~ *vt* **1 a** : to draw the hammer of (a firearm) back and set for firing; *also* : to set (the trigger) for firing **b** : to draw or bend back in preparation for throwing or hitting **c** : to set a mechanism (as a camera shutter) for tripping **2 a** : to set erect **b** : to turn, tip, or tilt usu. to one side **3** : to turn up (as a hat brim) — **cock a snook** *or* **cock snooks** \-'snu̇k(s), -'snüks\ : to thumb the nose
[3]**cock** *n* (1717) : TILT, SLANT ⟨~ of the head⟩
[4]**cock** *n* [ME *cok*, of Scand origin] (14c) : a small pile (as of hay)
[5]**cock** *vt* (14c) : to put (as hay) into cocks

cock·ade \kä-ˈkād\ *n* [modif. of F *cocarde,* fr. fem. of *cocard* vain, fr. *coq* cock, fr. OF *coc,* of imit. origin] (1709) : an ornament (as a rosette) worn on the hat as a badge — **cock·ad·ed** \-ˈkād-əd\ *adj*

cock–a–hoop \ˌkäk-ə-ˈhüp, -ˈhu̇p\ *adj* [fr. the phrase *to set cock a hoop* to be festive] (1663) **1** : triumphantly boastful : EXULTING **2** : AWRY

Cock·aigne \kä-ˈkān\ *n* [ME *cokaygne,* fr. MF *(pais de) cocaigne* land of plenty] (14c) : an imaginary land of great luxury and ease

cock–a–leek·ie \ˌkäk-i-ˈlē-kē\ *n* [alter. of *cockie* (dim. of 1*cock*) + *leekie,* dim. of *leek*] (1737) : a soup made of chicken and leeks

cock·a·lo·rum \ˌkäk-ə-ˈlōr-əm, -ˈlȯr-\ *n, pl* **-rums** [prob. modif. of obs. Flem *kockeloeren* to crow, of imit. origin] (1715) **1** : a self-important little man **2** : LEAPFROG **3** : boastful talk

cock·a·ma·my *or* **cock·a·ma·mie** \ˌkäk-ə-ˈmā-mē\ *adj* [E dial. *cockamamy* decal, alter. of E *decalcomania*] (1960) : RIDICULOUS, INCREDIBLE ⟨of all the ~ excuses I ever heard —Leo Rosten⟩

cock–and–bull story \ˌkäk-ən-ˈbu̇l-\ *n* (1795) : an incredible story told as true

cock·a·tiel \ˌkäk-ə-ˈtē(ə)l\ *n* [D *kaketielje,* deriv. of Malay *kakatua*] (1880) : a small crested gray Australian parrot (*Nymphicus hollandicus*) with a yellow head

cock·a·too \ˈkäk-ə-ˌtü\ *n, pl* **-toos** [D *kaketoe,* fr. Malay *kakatua,* fr. *kakak* elder sibling + *tua* old] (1634) : any of numerous large noisy usu. showy and crested chiefly Australasian parrots (esp. genus *Kakatoe*)

cock·a·trice \ˈkäk-ə-trəs, -ˌtrīs\ *n* [ME *cocatrice,* fr. MF *cocatris* ichneumon, cockatrice, fr. ML *cocatric-, cocatrix* ichneumon] (14c) : a legendary serpent that is hatched by a reptile from a cock's egg and that has a deadly glance

cock·boat \ˈkäk-ˌbōt\ *n* (15c) : a small boat; *esp* : one used as a tender to a larger boat

cock·cha·fer \ˈkäk-ˌchā-fər\ *n* [1*cock* + *chafer*] (1712) : a large European beetle (*Melolontha melolontha*) destructive to vegetation as an adult and to roots as a larva; *also* : any of various related beetles

cock·crow \ˈkäk-ˌkrō\ *n* (13c) : DAWN

cocked hat \ˈkäkt-\ *n* (1673) **1** : a hat with brim turned up to give a 3-cornered appearance **2** : a hat with brim turned up on two sides and worn either front to back or sideways

1**cock·er** \ˈkäk-ər\ *vt* [ME *cokeren*] (15c) : INDULGE, PAMPER

2**cocker** *n* (1689) : a keeper or handler of fighting cocks

cock·er·el \ˈkäk-(ə-)rəl\ *n* [ME *cokerelle,* fr. MF dial. *kokerel,* dim. of OF *coc*] (15c) : a young male domestic fowl

cock·er spaniel \ˌkäk-ər-\ *n* [*cocking* (woodcock hunting)] (1885) : any of a breed of small spaniels with long ears, square muzzle, and silky coat

cock·eye \ˈkäk-ˈī, -ˌī\ *n* (1825) : a squinting eye

cock·eyed \ˈkäk-ˈīd\ *adj* (1821) **1** : having a cockeye **2 a** : ASKEW, AWRY **b** : slightly crazy : TOPSY-TURVY ⟨a ~ scheme⟩ **c** : DRUNK — **cock·eyed·ly** \(ˈ)käk-ˈī(-ə)d-lē\ *adv* — **cock·eyed·ness** \-ˈīd-nəs\ *n*

cock·fight \ˈkäk-ˌfīt\ *n* (1565) : a contest of gamecocks usu. fitted with metal spurs — **cock·fight·ing** \-ˌfīt-iŋ\ *adj or n*

cock·horse \ˈkäk-ˌhȯ(ə)rs\ *n* [perh. fr. *cock,* adj., (male) + *horse*] (1540) : ROCKING HORSE

1**cock·le** \ˈkäk-əl\ *n* [ME, fr. OE *coccel*] (bef. 12c) : any of several weedy plants of the pink family; *esp* : CORN COCKLE

2**cockle** *n* [ME *cokille,* fr. MF *coquille* shell, modif. of L *conchylia,* pl. of *conchylium,* fr. Gk *konchylion,* fr. *konchē* conch] (14c) **1** : a bivalve mollusk (family Cardiidae) having a shell with convex radially ribbed valves; *esp* : a common edible European bivalve (*Cardium edule*) **2** : COCKLESHELL

3**cockle** *n* [MF *coquille*] (15c) : PUCKER, WRINKLE — **cockle** *vb*

cock·le·bur \ˈkäk-əl-ˌbər, ˈkək-\ *n* (1804) : any of a genus (*Xanthium*) of prickly-fruited composite plants; *also* : one of its stiff-spined fruits

cock·le·shell \ˈkäk-əl-ˌshel\ *n* (15c) **1 a** : the shell or one of the shell valves of a cockle **b** : a shell (as a scallop shell) suggesting a cockleshell **2** : a light flimsy boat

cock·les of the heart \ˌkäk-əlz-\ [perh. fr. 2*cockle*] (1671) : the core of one's being — usu. used in the phrase *to warm the cockles of the heart*

cock·loft \ˈkäk-ˌlȯft\ *n* [prob. fr. 1*cock*] (1589) : a small garret

cock·ney \ˈkäk-nē\ *n, pl* **cockneys** [ME *cokeney,* lit., cocks' egg, fr. *coken* (gen. pl. of *cok* cock) + *ey* egg, fr. OE *ǣg*] (14c) **1** *obs* **a** : a spoiled child **b** : a squeamish woman **2 a** : a native of London and esp. of the East End of London **b** : the dialect of London or of the East End of London — **cockney** *adj* — **cock·ney·fy** \ˈkäk-ni-ˌfī\ *vt* — **cock·ney·ish** \-ish\ *adj* — **cock·ney·ism** \-ˌiz-əm\ *n*

cock·pit \ˈkäk-ˌpit\ *n* (1587) **1 a** : a pit or enclosure for cockfights **b** : a place noted for esp. bloody, violent, or long-continued conflict **2** *obs* : the pit of a theater **3 a** : an apartment of an old sailing warship used as quarters for junior officers and for treatment of the wounded in an engagement **b** : an open space aft of a decked area from which a small ship is steered **c** : a space in the fuselage of an airplane for the pilot or the pilot and passengers or in large passenger planes the pilot and crew — see AIRPLANE illustration **d** : CAPSULE 6b **e** : the driver's compartment in an automobile (as a racing car)

cock·roach \ˈkäk-ˌrōch\ *n* [by folk etymology fr. Sp *cucaracha* cockroach, irreg. fr. *cuca* caterpillar] (1623) : any of an order (Blattaria) of chiefly nocturnal insects including some that are domestic pests

cocks·comb \ˈkäk-ˌskōm\ *n* (1542) **1** : COXCOMB **2** : a garden plant (genus *Celosia*) of the amaranth family grown for its flowers

cocks·foot \-ˌfu̇t\ *n* (1697) : a tall hay and pasture grass (*Dactylis glomerata*) that grows in tufts with loose open panicles

cock·shut \ˈkäk-ˌshət\ *n* [fr. the time poultry are shut in to rest] *dial Eng* (1598) : evening twilight

cock·shy \-ˌshī\ *n, pl* **cockshies** [1*cock* + *shy,* n.] (1836) **1 a** : a throw at an object set up as a mark **b** : a mark or target so set up **2** : an object or person taken as a butt (as of criticism)

cock·suck·er \-ˌsək-ər\ *n* (ca. 1891) : one who performs fellatio — usu. considered obscene; often used as a generalized term of abuse

cock·sure \ˈkäk-ˈshu̇(ə)r\ *adj* [prob. fr. 1*cock* + *sure*] (1603) **1** : feeling perfect assurance sometimes on inadequate grounds **2** : marked by overconfidence or presumptuousness : COCKY ***syn*** see SURE — **cock·sure·ly** *adv* — **cock·sure·ness** *n*

1**cock·tail** \ˈkäk-ˌtāl\ *n* [prob. fr. 1*cock* + *tail*] (1806) **1 a** : an iced drink of wine or distilled liquor mixed with flavoring ingredients **b** : something resembling or suggesting such a drink **2** : an appetizer served as a first course at a meal

2**cocktail** *adj* (1865) **1** : of, relating to, or set aside for cocktails ⟨a ~ hour⟩ **2** : designed for semiformal wear ⟨~ dress⟩

3**cocktail** *n* [1*cock* + *tail*] (1808) : a horse with its tail docked

cocktail glass *n* (1907) : a bell-shaped drinking glass usu. having a foot and stem and holding about three ounces

cocktail lounge *n* (1939) : a public room (as in a hotel, club, or restaurant) where cocktails and other drinks are served

cocktail party *n* (1928) : an informal or semiformal party or gathering at which cocktails are served

cocktail table *n* (1946) : COFFEE TABLE

cock–up \ˈkäk-ˌəp\ *n, Brit* (ca. 1948) : MESS 3b

cocky \ˈkäk-ē\ *adj* **cock·i·er; -est** (1768) **1** : boldly or brashly self-confident **2** : JAUNTY — **cock·i·ly** \ˈkäk-ə-lē\ *adv* — **cock·i·ness** \ˈkäk-ē-nəs\ *n*

co·co \ˈkō-(ˌ)kō\ *n, pl* **cocos** [Sp & Pg; Sp, fr. Pg *côco,* lit., bogeyman] (1555) : the coconut palm; *also* : its fruit

co·coa \ˈkō-(ˌ)kō\ *n* [modif. of Sp *cacao*] (1577) **1** : CACAO 1 **2 a** : powdered ground roasted cacao beans from which a portion of the fat has been removed **b** : a beverage prepared by heating cocoa with water or milk

cocoa bean *n* (1855) : CACAO 2

cocoa butter *n* (1899) : a pale vegetable fat with a low melting point obtained from cacao beans

co·co·nut \ˈkō-kə-(ˌ)nət\ *n* (1593) **1** : the drupaceous fruit of the coconut palm whose outer fibrous husk yields coir and whose nut contains thick edible meat and coconut milk **2** : the edible meat of the coconut

coconut crab *n* (ca. 1899) : a large edible coconut-eating burrowing land crab (*Birgus latro*) widely distributed about islands of the tropical Indian and Pacific oceans

coconut oil *n* (1838) : a nearly colorless fatty oil or white semisolid fat extracted from fresh coconuts and used esp. in making soaps and food products

coconut palm *n* (1852) : a tall pinnate-leaved tropical palm (*Cocos nucifera*) prob. of American origin

1**co·coon** \kə-ˈkün\ *n* [F *cocon,* fr. Prov *coucoun,* fr. *coco* shell, fr. L *coccum* excrescence on a tree, fr. Gk *kokkos* grain, seed, kermes] (1699) **1 a** : an envelope often largely of silk which an insect larva forms about itself and in which it passes the pupa stage **b** : any of various other protective coverings produced by animals **2 a** : a covering suggesting a cocoon **b** : a protective covering placed or sprayed over military or naval equipment in storage

2**cocoon** *vt* (1881) : to wrap or envelop esp. tightly in or as if in a cocoon

co·cotte \kō-ˈkȯt\ *n, pl* **cocottes** \-ˈkȯt(s)\ [F] (1867) : PROSTITUTE

co·cur·ric·u·lar \ˌkō-kə-ˈrik-yə-lər\ *adj* (1949) : being outside of but usu. complementing the regular curriculum

cod \ˈkäd\ *n, pl* **cod** *also* **cods** [ME] (14c) **1 a** : a soft-finned fish (*Gadus morrhua*) of the colder parts of the No. Atlantic that is a major food fish **b** : a fish of the cod family (Gadidae); *esp* : a Pacific fish (*Gadus macrocephalus*) closely related to the Atlantic cod **2** : any of various spiny-finned fishes resembling the true cods

co·da \ˈkōd-ə\ *n* [It, lit., tail, fr. L *cauda*] (ca. 1753) **1 a** : a concluding musical section that is formally distinct from the main structure **b** : a concluding part of a literary or dramatic work **2** : something that serves to round out, conclude, or summarize and that has an interest of its own

cod·dle \ˈkäd-ᵊl\ *vt* **cod·dled; cod·dling** \ˈkäd-liŋ, -ᵊl-iŋ\ [perh. fr. *caudle*] (1598) **1** : to cook (as eggs) in liquid slowly and gently just below the boiling point **2** : to treat with extreme care : PAMPER — **cod·dler** \ˈkäd-lər, -ᵊl-ər\ *n*

1**code** \ˈkōd\ *n* [ME, fr. MF, fr. L *caudex, codex* trunk of a tree, tablet of wood covered with wax for writing on, book; akin to L *cudere* to beat — more at HEW] (14c) **1** : a systematic statement of a body of law; *esp* : one given statutory force **2** : a system of principles or rules ⟨moral ~⟩ **3 a** : a system of signals or symbols for communication **b** : a system of symbols (as letters, numbers, or words) used to represent assigned and often secret meanings **4** : GENETIC CODE — **code·less** \-ləs\ *adj*

2**code** *vb* **cod·ed; cod·ing** *vt* (1815) : to put in or into the form or symbols of a code ~ *vi* : to specify the genetic code ⟨a gene that ~s for a protein⟩ — **cod·able** \ˈkōd-ə-bəl\ *adj* — **cod·er** *n*

code·book *n* (1884) : a book containing an alphabetical list of words or expressions with their code group equivalents

co·dec·li·na·tion \(ˌ)kō-ˌdek-lə-ˈnā-shən\ *n* (1812) : the complement of the declination

code group *n* (1931) : one of the constituent groups of letters or numbers in an encoded text

co·deine \ˈkō-ˌdēn, ˈkōd-ē-ən\ *n* [F *codéine,* fr. Gk *kōdeia* poppyhead, fr. *kōos* cavity; akin to Gk *koilos* hollow] (1838) : a morphine derivative $C_{18}H_{21}NO_3 \cdot H_2O$ that is found in opium, is weaker in action than morphine, and is used esp. in cough remedies

code name *n* (1919) : a word made to serve as a code designation — **code–name** \(ˈ)kōd-ˈnām\ *vt*

co·de·ter·mi·na·tion \ˌkō-di-ˌtər-mə-ˈnā-shən\ *n* (1949) : the participation of labor with management in the determination of business policy

code word *n* (1884) **1** : CODE NAME **2** : CODE GROUP **3** : EUPHEMISM

co·dex \ˈkō-ˌdeks\ *n, pl* **co·di·ces** \ˈkōd-ə-ˌsēz, ˈkäd-\ [L] (1670) : a manuscript book esp. of Scripture, classics, or ancient annals

cod·fish \ˈkäd-ˌfish\ *n* (14c) : COD; *also* : its flesh used as food

cod·ger \ˈkäj-ər\ *n* [prob. alter. of *cadger*] (1756) : a mildly eccentric or disreputable fellow ⟨old ~⟩

cod·i·cil \ˈkäd-ə-səl, -ˌsil\ *n* [MF *codicille,* fr. L *codicillus,* dim. of *codic-, codex* book] (15c) **1** : a legal instrument made subsequently to a will and modifying it **2** : APPENDIX, SUPPLEMENT — **cod·i·cil·la·ry** \ˌkäd-ə-ˈsil-ə-rē\ *adj*

\ə\ abut \ᵊ\ kitten, F table \ər\ further \a\ ash \ā\ ace \ä\ cot, cart \au̇\ out \ch\ chin \e\ bet \ē\ easy \g\ go \i\ hit \ī\ ice \j\ job \ŋ\ sing \ō\ go \ȯ\ law \ȯi\ boy \th\ thin \t͟h\ the \ü\ loot \u̇\ foot \y\ yet \zh\ vision \ȧ, k̲, ⁿ, œ, œ̄, ue, ue̅, ʸ\ see Guide to Pronunciation

co·di·col·o·gy \\ˌkōd-ə-ˈkäl-ə-jē, ˌkäd-\\ *n* [L *codic-, codex* + *-o-* + E *-logy*] (1953) : the study of manuscripts as cultural artifacts for historical purposes — **co·di·co·log·i·cal** \\-kə-ˈläj-i-kəl\\ *adj*

cod·i·fy \\ˈkäd-ə-ˌfī, ˈkōd-\\ *vt* **-fied; -fy·ing** (1800) **1 :** to reduce to a code **2 a :** SYSTEMATIZE **b :** CLASSIFY — **cod·i·fi·abil·i·ty** \\ˌkäd-ə-ˌfī-ə-ˈbil-ət-ē, ˌkōd-\\ *n* — **cod·i·fi·ca·tion** \\-fə-ˈkā-shən\\ *n*

1**cod·ling** \\ˈkäd-liŋ\\ *n* (13c) **1 :** a young cod **2 :** any of several hakes (esp. genus *Urophycis*)

2**cod·ling** \\ˈkäd-liŋ\\ *or* **cod·lin** \\-lən\\ *n* [alter. of ME *querdlyng*] (15c) : a small immature apple; *also* : any of several elongated greenish English cooking apples

codling moth *n* (1861) : a small moth (*Laspeyresia pomonella*) whose larva lives in apples, pears, quinces, and English walnuts

cod–liver oil *n* (1783) : an oil obtained from the liver of the cod and closely related fishes and used as a source of vitamins A and D

co·dom·i·nant \\(ˈ)kō-ˈdäm-ə-nənt\\ *adj* (ca. 1900) **1 a :** forming part of the main canopy of a forest ⟨~ trees⟩ **b :** sharing in the controlling influence of a biotic community **2 :** being fully expressed in the heterozygous condition ⟨two ~ alleles⟩ — **codominant** *n*

co·don \\ˈkō-ˌdän\\ *n* [1*code* + 2*-on*] (1963) : a specific sequence of three consecutive nucleotides that is part of the genetic code and that specifies a particular amino acid in a protein or starts or stops protein synthesis

cod·piece \\ˈkäd-ˌpēs\\ *n* [ME *codpese,* fr. *cod* bag, scrotum (fr. OE *codd*) + *pese* piece] (15c) : a flap or bag concealing an opening in the front of men's breeches esp. in the 15th and 16th centuries

cods·wal·lop \\ˈkädz-ˌwäl-əp\\ *n* [origin unknown] *Brit* (1963) : NONSENSE

1**co·ed** \\ˈkō-ˌed\\ *adj* (1889) **1 :** of or relating to a coed **2 :** COEDUCATIONAL **3 :** open to or used by both men and women

2**coed** *n* [short for *coeducational student*] (1893) : a student and esp. a female student in a coeducational institution

co–edi·tion \\ˌkō-ə-ˈdish-ən\\ *n* (1964) : an edition of a book published simultaneously by more than one publisher usu. in different countries and in different languages

co·ed·i·tor \\(ˈ)kō-ˈed-ət-ər\\ *n* (1873) : one who collaborates with another in editing a newspaper, magazine, or book — **co·ed·it** \\-ˈed-ət\\ *vt*

co·ed·u·ca·tion \\(ˌ)kō-ˌej-ə-ˈkā-shən\\ *n* (1852) : the education of students of both sexes at the same institution

co·ed·u·ca·tion·al \\-shnəl, -shən-ᵊl\\ *adj* (1881) : of or relating to coeducation — **co·ed·u·ca·tion·al·ly** \\-ē\\ *adv*

co·ef·fi·cient \\ˌkō-ə-ˈfish-ənt\\ *n* [NL *coefficient-, coefficiens,* fr. L *co-* + *efficient-, efficiens* efficient] (ca. 1708) **1 :** any of the factors of a product considered in relation to a specific factor; *esp* : a constant factor of a term as distinguished from a variable **2 a :** a number that serves as a measure of some property or characteristic (as of a substance, device, or process) ⟨~ of expansion of a metal⟩ **b :** MEASURE

coefficient of correlation (ca. 1909) : CORRELATION COEFFICIENT

coefficient of viscosity (1922) : VISCOSITY 3

coel·acanth \\ˈsē-lə-ˌkan(t)th\\ *n* [deriv. of Gk *koilos* hollow + *akantha* spine — more at CAVE, ACANTHUS] (1857) : any of a family (Coelacanthidae) of mostly extinct fishes (as latimeria) — **coelacanth** *adj* — **coel·acan·thine** \\ˌsē-lə-ˈkan-ˌthīn, -ˈkan(t)-thən\\ *adj*

-coele *or* **-coel** \\ˌsēl\\ *n comb form* [prob. fr. NL *-coela,* fr. neut. pl. of *-coelus* hollow, concave, fr. Gk *-koilos,* fr. *koilos*] : cavity : chamber : ventricle ⟨blasto*coel*⟩ ⟨entero*coele*⟩

coel·en·ter·ate \\si-ˈlent-ə-ˌrāt, -rət\\ *n* [deriv. of Gk *koilos* + *enteron* intestine — more at INTER-] (1888) : any of a phylum (Coelenterata) of basically radially symmetrical invertebrate animals including the corals, sea anemones, jellyfishes, and hydroids — **coelenterate** *adj*

coel·en·ter·on \\-ˌrän, -rən\\ *n, pl* **-tera** \\-rə\\ [NL, fr. Gk *koilos* + *enteron*] (1893) : the internal cavity of a coelenterate

coe·li·ac \\ˈsē-lē-ˌak\\ *var of* CELIAC

coe·lom \\ˈsē-ləm\\ *n, pl* **coeloms** *or* **coe·lo·ma·ta** \\si-ˈlō-mət-ə\\ [G, fr. Gk *koilōma* cavity, fr. *koilos*] (1878) : the usu. epithelium-lined space between the body wall and the digestive tract of metazoans above the lower worms — **coe·lo·mate** \\ˈsē-lə-ˌmāt\\ *adj or n* — **coe·lo·mic** \\si-ˈläm-ik, -ˈlō-mik\\ *adj*

coen- *or* **coeno-** *comb form* [NL, fr. Gk *koin-, koino-,* fr. *koinos* — more at CO-] : common : general ⟨*coeno*cyte⟩

coe·no·bite \\ˈsē-nə-ˌbīt\\ *var of* CENOBITE

coe·no·cyte \\ˈsē-nə-ˌsīt\\ *n* [ISV] (1897) **1 a :** a multinucleate mass of protoplasm resulting from repeated nuclear division unaccompanied by cell fission **b :** an organism consisting of such a structure **2 :** SYNCYTIUM 1 — **coe·no·cyt·ic** \\ˌsē-nə-ˈsit-ik\\ *adj*

coe·nu·rus \\si-ˈn(y)u̇r-əs\\ *n, pl* **-nu·ri** \\-ˈn(y)u̇(ə)r-ˌī\\ [NL, fr. *coen-* + Gk *oura* tail] (1876) : a complex tapeworm larva consisting of a sac from the inner wall of which numerous scolices develop

co·en·zyme \\(ˈ)kō-ˈen-ˌzīm\\ *n* (1908) : a thermostable nonprotein compound that forms the active portion of an enzyme system after combination with an apoenzyme — **co·en·zy·mat·ic** \\(ˌ)kō-ˌen-zə-ˈmat-ik, -(ˌ)zī-\\ *adj* — **co·en·zy·mat·i·cal·ly** \\-i-k(ə-)lē\\ *adv*

coenzyme A *n* (1949) : a coenzyme $C_{21}H_{36}N_7O_{16}P_3S$ that occurs in all living cells and is essential to the metabolism of carbohydrates, fats, and some amino acids — compare ACETYL COENZYME A

coenzyme Q *n* (1958) : UBIQUINONE

co·equal \\(ˈ)kō-ˈē-kwəl\\ *adj* (14c) : equal with one another — **coequal** *n* — **co·equal·i·ty** \\ˌkō-ē-ˈkwäl-ət-ē\\ *n* — **co·equal·ly** \\(ˈ)kō-ˈē-kwə-lē\\ *adv*

co·erce \\kō-ˈərs\\ *vt* **co·erced; co·erc·ing** [L *coercēre,* fr. *co-* + *arcēre* to shut up, enclose — more at ARK] (15c) **1 :** to restrain or dominate by force ⟨religion in the past has tried to ~ the irreligious —W.R. Inge⟩ **2 :** to compel to an act or choice **3 :** to enforce or bring about by force or threat ⟨~ the compliance of the rest of the community —Scott Buchanan⟩ — **co·erc·ible** \\-ˈər-sə-bəl\\ *adj*

co·er·cion \\-ˈər-zhən, -shən\\ *n* (15c) : the act, process, or power of coercing

co·er·cive \\-ˈər-siv\\ *adj* (1600) : serving or intended to coerce — **co·er·cive·ly** *adv* — **co·er·cive·ness** *n*

coercive force *n* (1827) : the opposing magnetic intensity that must be applied to a magnetized material to remove the residual magnetism

co·er·civ·i·ty \\ˌkō-ˌər-ˈsiv-ət-ē\\ *n* (1898) : the property of a material determined by the value of the coercive force when the material has been magnetized to saturation

co·eta·ne·ous \\ˌkō-ə-ˈtā-nē-əs\\ *adj* [L *coaetaneus,* fr. *co-* + *aetas* age — more at AGE] (1608) : COEVAL

co·eter·nal \\ˌkō-i-ˈtərn-ᵊl\\ *adj* (14c) : equally or jointly eternal — **co·eter·nal·ly** \\-ᵊl-ē\\ *adv* — **co·eter·ni·ty** \\-ˈtər-nət-ē\\ *n*

co·eval \\kō-ˈē-vəl\\ *adj* [L *coaevus,* fr. *co-* + *aevum* age, lifetime — more at AGE] (1622) : of the same or equal age, antiquity, or duration ***syn*** see CONTEMPORARY — **coeval** *n* — **co·eval·i·ty** \\ˌkō-(ˌ)ē-ˈval-ət-ē\\ *n*

co·evo·lu·tion \\ˌkō-ˌev-ə-ˈlü-shən *also* -ˌē-və-\\ *n* (1965) : evolution involving successive changes in two or more ecologically interdependent species (as of a plant and its pollinators) that affect their interactions — **co·evo·lu·tion·ary** \\-shə-ˌner-ē\\ *adj* — **co·evolve** \\ˌkō-i-ˈvälv, -ˈvȯlv\\ *vi*

co·ex·ist \\ˌkō-ig-ˈzist\\ *vi* (1667) **1 :** to exist together or at the same time **2 :** to live in peace with each other esp. as a matter of policy — **co·ex·is·tence** \\-ˈzis-tən(t)s\\ *n* — **co·ex·is·tent** \\-tənt\\ *adj*

co·ex·ten·sive \\ˌkō-ik-ˈsten(t)-siv\\ *adj* (1771) : having the same spatial or temporal scope or boundaries — **co·ex·ten·sive·ly** *adv*

co·fac·tor \\ˈkō-ˌfak-tər\\ *n* (ca. 1909) **1 :** the signed minor of an element of a square matrix or of a determinant with the sign positive if the sum of the column number and row number of the element is even and with the sign negative if it is odd **2 :** a substance that acts with another substance to bring about certain effects; *esp* : COENZYME

cof·fee \\ˈkȯ-fē, ˈkäf-ē\\ *n, often attrib* [It & Turk; It *caffè,* fr. Turk *kahve,* fr. Ar *qahwa*] (1598) **1 a :** a beverage made by percolation, infusion, or decoction from the roasted and ground or pounded seeds of a coffee tree; *also* : these seeds either green or roasted **b :** COFFEE TREE 1 **2 :** a cup of coffee ⟨two ~s⟩ **3 :** COFFEE HOUR

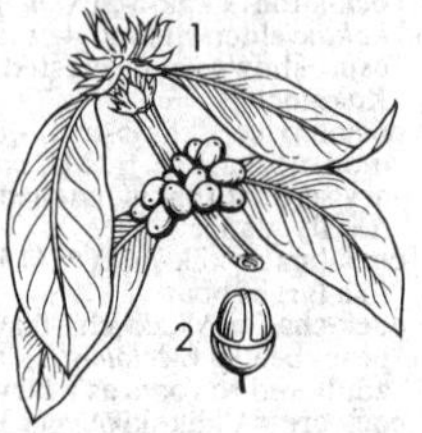

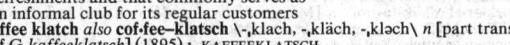

coffee: *1* flowering and fruiting branch with leaves, *2* fruit with pericarp partly removed to show seeds

coffee break *n* (1951) : a short period for rest and refreshments

coffee cake *n* (1879) : a sweet rich bread often with added fruit, nuts, and spices that is sometimes glazed after baking

coffee hour *n* (1952) **1 :** a usu. fixed occasion of informal meeting and chatting at which refreshments are served **2 :** COFFEE BREAK

cof·fee·house \\-ˌhau̇s\\ *n* (1612) : an establishment that sells coffee and usu. other refreshments and that commonly serves as an informal club for its regular customers

coffee klatch *also* **cof·fee–klatsch** \\-ˌklach, -ˌkläch, -ˌkləch\\ *n* [part trans. of G *kaffeeklatsch*] (1895) : KAFFEEKLATSCH

cof·fee·mak·er \\-ˌmā-kər\\ *n* (1930) : a utensil in which coffee is brewed

coffee mill *n* (1691) : a mill for grinding coffee beans

cof·fee·pot \\-ˌpät\\ *n* (1704) : a pot for brewing and serving coffee

coffee ring *n* (ca. 1924) : coffee cake in the shape of a ring

coffee roll *n* (1945) : a sweet roll

coffee room *n* (1712) : a room where refreshments are served

coffee royal *n* (1921) : a drink of black coffee and a liquor

coffee shop *n* (1836) : a small restaurant

coffee table *n* (1877) : a low table customarily placed in front of a sofa — called also *cocktail table*

coffee–table book *n* (1962) : an expensive, lavishly illustrated, and oversize book suitable for display on a coffee table

coffee tree *n* (1741) **1 a :** a large evergreen shrub or small tree (*Coffea arabica*) of the madder family that is native to Africa but is now widely cultivated in warm regions for its seeds which form most of the coffee of commerce **b :** a tree (genus *Coffea*) related to the coffee tree **2 :** KENTUCKY COFFEE TREE

1**cof·fer** \\ˈkȯ-fər, ˈkäf-ər\\ *n* [ME *coffre,* fr. OF, fr. L *cophinus* basket, fr. Gk *kophinos*] (13c) **1 :** CHEST, BOX; *esp* : STRONGBOX **2 :** TREASURY — usu. used in pl. **3 :** the chamber of a canal lock **4 :** a recessed panel in a vault, ceiling, or soffit

2**coffer** *vt* (14c) **1 :** to store or hoard up in a coffer **2 :** to form (as a ceiling) with recessed panels

cof·fer·dam \\-ˌdam\\ *n* (1736) **1 :** a watertight enclosure from which water is pumped to expose the bottom of a body of water and permit construction (as of a pier) **2 :** a watertight structure for making repairs below the waterline of a ship

1**cof·fin** \\ˈkȯ-fən\\ *n* [ME, basket, receptacle, fr. MF *cofin,* fr. L *cophinus*] (14c) **1 :** a box or chest for burying a corpse **2 :** the horny body forming the hoof of a horse's foot

2**coffin** *vt* (1564) : to enclose in or as if in a coffin

coffin bone *n* (1720) : the bone enclosed within the hoof of the horse — called also *pedal bone*

coffin corner *n* (1940) : one of the corners formed by a goal line and a sideline on a football field into which a punt is often aimed so that it may go out of bounds close to the defender's goal line

coffin nail *n, slang* (1888) : CIGARETTE

cof·fle \\ˈkȯ-fəl, ˈkäf-əl\\ *n* [Ar *qāfila* caravan] (1799) : a train of slaves or animals fastened together

co·func·tion \\(ˈ)kō-ˈfəŋ(k)-shən\\ *n* (1909) : a trigonometric function whose value for the complement of an angle is equal to the value of a given trigonometric function of the angle itself ⟨the sine is the ~ of the cosine⟩

1**cog** \\ˈkäg\\ *n* [ME *cogge,* of Scand origin; akin to Norw *kug* cog; akin to OE *cycgel* cudgel] (13c) **1 :** a tooth on the rim of a wheel or gear **2 :** a subordinate but vital person or part — **cogged** \\ˈkägd\\ *adj*

2**cog** *vb* **cogged; cog·ging** [obs. *cog* (a trick)] *vi* (1532) **1** *obs* : to cheat in throwing dice **2** *obs* : DECEIVE **3** *obs* : to use venal flattery ~ *vt* **1 :** to direct the fall of (dice) fraudulently **2** *obs* : WHEEDLE

3**cog** *vt* **cogged; cog·ging** [prob. alter. of *cock* (cog)] (1823) : to connect (as timbers or joists) by means of mortises and tenons

4**cog** *n* (1856) : a tenon on a beam or timber

co·gen·cy \\ˈkō-jən-sē\\ *n* (1667) : the quality or state of being cogent

co·gen·e·ra·tion \\ˌkō-ˌjen-ə-ˈrā-shən\\ *n* (1978) : the use of waste heat (as in steam) from an industrial process to produce electricity or the use of steam from electric power generation as a heating source

co·gent \\ˈkō-jənt\\ *adj* [L *cogent-, cogens,* prp. of *cogere* to drive together, collect, fr. *co-* + *agere* to drive — more at AGENT] (1659) **1 a :** appealing forcibly to the mind or reason : CONVINCING ⟨~ evidence⟩ **b :** PERTINENT, RELEVANT ⟨a ~ analysis of a problem⟩ **2 :** having power to compel or constrain ⟨~ forces⟩ ***syn*** see VALID — **co·gent·ly** *adv*

cog·i·ta·ble \'käj-ət-ə-bəl\ *adj* (15c) : CONCEIVABLE, THINKABLE

cog·i·tate \'käj-ə-ˌtāt\ *vb* **-tat·ed; -tat·ing** [L *cogitatus,* pp. of *cogitare* to think, think about, fr. *co-* + *agitare* to drive, agitate] *vt* (1563) : to ponder or meditate on usu. intently ~ *vi* : MEDITATE, PONDER ***syn*** see THINK

cog·i·ta·tion \ˌkäj-ə-'tā-shən\ *n* (13c) **1 a :** the act of cogitating : MEDITATION **b :** the capacity to think or reflect **2 :** a single thought

cog·i·ta·tive \'käj-ə-ˌtāt-iv\ *adj* (15c) **1 :** of or relating to cogitation **2 :** capable of or given to cogitation

co·gi·to \'käg-i-ˌtō, 'käj-, 'kōg-\ *n* [NL *cogito, ergo sum,* lit., I think, therefore I am, principle stated by René Descartes] (1838) **1 :** the philosophic principle that one's existence is demonstrated by the fact that one thinks **2 :** the intellectual processes of the self or ego

co·gnac \'kōn-ˌyak *also* 'kòn- *or* 'kän-\ *n* [F, fr. *Cognac,* France] (1775) : a brandy from the departments of Charente and Charente-Maritime distilled from white wine

[1]**cog·nate** \'käg-ˌnāt\ *adj* [L *cognatus,* fr. *co-* + *gnatus, natus,* pp. of *nasci* to be born; akin to L *gignere* to beget — more at KIN] (1645) **1 :** of the same or similar nature : generically alike **2 :** related by blood; *also* : related on the mother's side **3 a :** related by descent from the same ancestral language **b** *of a word or morpheme* : related by derivation, borrowing, or descent **c** *of a substantive* : related to a verb usu. by derivation and serving as its object to reinforce the meaning — **cog·nate·ly** *adv*

[2]**cognate** *n* (1754) : one that is cognate with another

cog·na·tion \käg-'nā-shən\ *n* (14c) : cognate relationship

cog·ni·tion \käg-'nish-ən\ *n* [ME *cognicioun,* fr. L *cognition-, cognitio,* fr. *cognitus,* pp. of *cognoscere* to become acquainted with, know, fr. *co-* + *gnoscere* to come to know — more at KNOW] (15c) : the act or process of knowing including both awareness and judgment; *also* : a product of this act — **cog·ni·tion·al** \-'nish-nəl, -'nish-ən-ᵊl\ *adj*

cog·ni·tive \'käg-nət-iv\ *adj* (1586) **1 :** of, relating to, or involving cognition ⟨the ~ elements of perception —C. H. Hamburg⟩ **2 :** based on or capable of being reduced to empirical factual knowledge — **cog·ni·tive·ly** *adv* — **cog·ni·tiv·i·ty** \ˌkäg-nə-'tiv-ət-ē\ *n*

cognitive dissonance *n* (1957) : psychological conflict resulting from incongruous beliefs and attitudes held simultaneously

cog·ni·za·ble \'käg-nə-zə-bəl, käg-'nī-\ *adj* (1678) **1 :** capable of being known **2 :** capable of being judicially heard and determined — **cog·ni·za·bly** \-blē\ *adv*

cog·ni·zance \'käg-nə-zən(t)s\ *n* [ME *conisaunce,* fr. MF *conoissance,* fr. *conoistre* to know, fr. L *cognoscere*] (14c) **1 :** a distinguishing mark or emblem (as a heraldic bearing) **2 a :** KNOWLEDGE, AWARENESS ⟨had no ~ of the situation⟩ **b :** NOTICE, ACKNOWLEDGMENT ⟨take ~ of their achievement⟩ **3 :** JURISDICTION, RESPONSIBILITY

cog·ni·zant \-zənt\ *adj* (1820) : knowledgeable of something esp. through personal experience; *also* : MINDFUL ***syn*** see AWARE

cog·nize \käg-'nīz\ *vt* **cog·nized; cog·niz·ing** [back-formation fr. *cognizance*] (1836) : KNOW, UNDERSTAND — **cog·niz·er** *n*

cog·no·men \käg-'nō-mən, 'käg-nə-\ *n, pl* **cognomens** *or* **cog·no·mi·na** \käg-'näm-ə-nə, -'nō-mə-\ [L, irreg. fr. *co-* + *nomen* name — more at NAME] (1809) **1 :** SURNAME; *esp* : the third of usu. three names of a person among the ancient Romans **2 :** NAME; *esp* : a distinguishing nickname or epithet — **cog·nom·i·nal** \käg-'näm-ən-ᵊl\ *adj*

co·gno·scen·te \ˌkän-(y)ə-'shent-ē, ˌkäg-nə-\ *n, pl* **-scen·ti** \-ē\ [obs. It (now *conoscente*), fr. *cognoscente,* adj., wise, fr. L *cognoscent-, cognoscens,* prp. of *cognoscere*] (1776) : a person who is esp. knowledgeable in a subject (as fine arts or fashion) : CONNOISSEUR

cog·nos·ci·ble \käg-'näs-ə-bəl\ *adj* [LL *cognoscibilis,* fr. L *cognoscere*] (1644) : COGNIZABLE, KNOWABLE

co·gon \kō-'gōn\ *n* [Sp *cogón,* fr. Tag, Bisayan *kugon*] (1898) : any of several coarse tall grasses (genus *Imperata*) used esp. in the Philippines for thatching

cog railway *n* (1896) : a steep mountain railroad that has a rail with cogs which engages a cogwheel on the locomotive to ensure traction

cog·wheel \'käg-ˌ(h)wēl\ *n* (14c) : a wheel with cogs or teeth

co·hab·it \kō-'hab-ət\ *vi* [LL *cohabitare,* fr. L *co-* + *habitare* to inhabit, fr. *habitus,* pp. of *habēre* to have] (1530) **1 :** to live together as or as if husband and wife **2 a :** to live together or in company ⟨buffaloes *~ing* with crossbred cows —*Biol. Abstracts*⟩ **b :** to exist together ⟨two strains in his philosophy . . . ~ in each of his major works —Justus Buchler⟩ — **co·hab·i·tant** \-ət-ənt\ *n* — **co·hab·i·ta·tion** \(ˌ)kō-ˌhab-ə-'tā-shən\ *n*

co·heir \(')kō-'a(ə)r, -'e(ə)r\ *n* (15c) : a joint heir

co·heir·ess \-əs\ *n* (1630) : a joint heiress

co·here \kō-'hi(ə)r\ *vb* **co·hered; co·her·ing** [L *cohaerēre,* fr. *co-* + *haerēre* to stick — more at HESITATE] *vi* (1598) **1 a :** to hold together firmly as parts of the same mass; *broadly* : STICK, ADHERE **b :** to display cohesion of plant parts **2 :** to hold together as a mass of parts that cohere **3 a :** to become united in principles, relationships, or interests **b :** to be logically or aesthetically consistent ~ *vt* : to cause (parts or components) to cohere ***syn*** see STICK

co·her·ence \kō-'hir-ən(t)s, -'her-\ *n* (1580) **1 :** the quality or state of cohering: as **a :** systematic or logical connection or consistency **b :** integration of diverse elements, relationships, or values **2 :** the property of being coherent

co·her·en·cy \kō-'hir-ən-sē, -'her-\ *n, pl* **-cies** (1630) : COHERENCE

co·her·ent \-ənt\ *adj* [MF or L; MF *cohérent,* fr. L *cohaerent-, cohaerens,* prp. of *cohaerēre*] (1578) **1 :** having the quality of cohering; *esp* : COHESIVE, COORDINATED ⟨a ~ plan for action⟩ **2 :** logically or aesthetically ordered or integrated : CONSISTENT ⟨~ style⟩ ⟨a ~ argument⟩ **3 :** relating to electromagnetic waves that have a definite relationship to each other: as **a :** composed of two wave trains with a constant difference in phase **b :** producing coherent light ⟨a ~ source⟩ — **co·her·ent·ly** *adv*

co·her·er \kō-'hir-ər\ *n* (1894) : a radio detector in which an imperfectly conducting contact between pieces of conductive material loosely resting against each other is materially improved in conductance by the passage of high-frequency current

co·he·sion \kō-'hē-zhən\ *n* [L *cohaesus,* pp. of *cohaerēre*] (1660) **1 :** the act or state of sticking together tightly; *esp* : UNITY ⟨the lack of ~ in the Party —*Times Lit. Supp.*⟩ **2 :** union between similar plant parts or organs **3 :** molecular attraction by which the particles of a body are united throughout the mass — **co·he·sion·less** \-ləs\ *adj*

co·he·sive \kō-'hē-siv, -ziv\ *adj* (ca. 1721) : exhibiting or producing cohesion or coherence ⟨a ~ social unit⟩ ⟨~ soils⟩ — **co·he·sive·ly** *adv* — **co·he·sive·ness** *n*

co·ho \'kō-(ˌ)hō\ *n, pl* **cohos** *or* **coho** [origin unknown] (1869) : a rather small salmon (*Oncorhynchus kisutch*) with light-colored flesh that is native to both coasts of the No. Pacific and is stocked in the Great Lakes

co·hort \'kō-ˌhò(ə)rt\ *n* [MF & L; MF *cohorte,* fr. L *cohort-, cohors* — more at COURT] (15c) **1 a :** one of 10 divisions of an ancient Roman legion **b :** a group of warriors or soldiers **c :** BAND, GROUP **d :** a group of individuals having a statistical factor (as age or class membership) in common in a demographic study ⟨a ~ of premedical students⟩ **2 :** COMPANION, COLLEAGUE ⟨a silk hat materialized in the air beside me . . . and my special, only technically unassigned ~ grinned up at me —J. D. Salinger⟩

co·hosh \'kō-ˌhäsh\ *n* [of Algonquian origin; akin to Natick *kôshki* it is rough] (1796) : any of several American medicinal or poisonous plants: **a :** BLACK COHOSH **b :** BLUE COHOSH **c :** BANEBERRY

co·iden·ti·ty \ˌkō-ī-'den(t)-ət-ē, ˌkō-ə-'den(t)-\ *n* (1927) : identity between two or more things

[1]**coif** \'kòif, *in sense 2 usu* 'kwäf\ *n* [ME *coife,* fr. MF, fr. LL *cofea*] (14c) **1 :** a close-fitting cap: as **a :** a hoodlike cap worn under a veil by nuns **b :** a protective usu. metal skullcap formerly worn under a hood of mail **c :** a white cap formerly worn by English lawyers and esp. by serjeants-at-law; *also* : the order or rank of a serjeant-at-law **2 :** COIFFURE

[2]**coif** \'kòif, 'kwäf\ *vt* **coiffed** *or* **coifed; coif·fing** *or* **coif·ing** (15c) **1 :** to cover or dress with or as if with a coif **2 :** to arrange (hair) by brushing, combing, or curling

coif·feur \kwä-'fər\ *n* [F, fr. *coiffer*] (1847) : a male hairdresser

coif·feuse \kwä-'fə(r)z, -'f(y)üz\ *n* [F, fem. of *coiffeur*] (1870) : a female hairdresser

coif·fure \kwä-'fyu̇(ə)r\ *n* [F, fr. *coiffer* to cover with a coif, arrange (hair), fr. *coife*] (1631) : a style or manner of arranging the hair

coif·fured *adj* (1907) **1 :** being dressed ⟨beautifully ~ hair⟩ **2 :** having the hair brushed, combed, and curled ⟨stylishly ~ women⟩

coign of van·tage \ˌkòi-nə-'vant-ij\ [*coign,* earlier spelling of [1]*coin* (corner)] (1605) : an advantageous position

[1]**coil** \'kòi(ə)l\ *n* [origin unknown] (1567) **1 :** TURMOIL **2 :** TROUBLE; *also* : everyday cares and worries ⟨when we have shuffled off this mortal ~ —Shak.⟩

[2]**coil** *vb* [F *coillir, cuillir* to gather — more at CULL] *vt* (1611) **1 :** to wind into rings or spirals **2 :** to roll or twist into a shape resembling a coil ~ *vi* **1 :** to move in a circular or spiral course **2 :** to form or lie in a coil — **coil·abil·i·ty** \ˌkòi-lə-'bil-ət-ē\ *n*

[3]**coil** *n* (1661) **1 a (1) :** a series of loops **(2) :** SPIRAL **b :** a single loop of such a coil **2 a :** a number of turns of wire wound around a core (as of iron) to create a magnetic field for an electromagnet or an induction coil **b :** INDUCTION COIL **3 :** a series of connected pipes in rows, layers, or windings **4 :** a roll of postage stamps; *also* : a stamp from such a roll

[1]**coin** \'kòin\ *n* [ME, fr. MF, wedge, corner, fr. L *cuneus* wedge] (14c) **1** *archaic* **a :** CORNER, CORNERSTONE, QUOIN **b :** WEDGE **2 a :** a usu. flat piece of metal issued by governmental authority as money **b :** metal money **c :** something resembling a coin esp. in shape **3 :** a standard or valid mode of expression ⟨perhaps wisecracks . . . are respectable literary ~ in the U.S. —*Times Lit. Supp.*⟩ **4 :** something having two different and usu. opposing sides — usu. used in the phrase *the other side of the coin* **5 :** MONEY ⟨I'm in it for the ~ —Sinclair Lewis⟩

[2]**coin** *vt* (14c) **1 a :** to make (a coin) esp. by stamping : MINT **b :** to convert (metal) into coins **c :** to shape (a piece of metal) in a mold or die **2 :** CREATE, INVENT ⟨~ a phrase⟩ — **coin·er** *n* — **coin money :** to get rich quickly

[3]**coin** *adj* (1559) **1 :** of or relating to coins **2 :** operated by coins

coin·age \'kòi-nij\ *n* (14c) **1 :** the act or process of coining **2 a :** COINS **b :** something (as a word) made up or invented

co·in·cide \ˌkō-ən-'sīd, 'kō-ən-ˌ\ *vi* **-cid·ed; -cid·ing** [ML *coincidere,* fr. L *co-* + *incidere* to fall on, fr. *in-* + *cadere* to fall — more at CHANCE] (1719) **1 a :** to occupy the same place in space or time **b :** to occupy exactly corresponding or equivalent positions on a scale or in a series **2 :** to correspond in nature, character, or function **3 :** to be in accord or agreement : CONCUR ***syn*** see AGREE

co·in·ci·dence \kō-'in(t)-səd-ən(t)s, -sə-ˌden(t)s\ *n* (1605) **1 :** the act or condition of coinciding : CORRESPONDENCE **2 :** the occurrence of events that happen at the same time by accident but seem to have some connection; *also* : any of these occurrences

co·in·ci·dent \-səd-ənt, -sə-ˌdent\ *adj* [F *coincident,* fr. ML *coincident-, coincidens,* prp. of *coincidere*] (1563) **1 :** of similar nature : HARMONIOUS ⟨a theory ~ with the facts⟩ **2 :** occupying the same space or time ⟨~ events⟩ ***syn*** see CONTEMPORARY — **co·in·ci·dent·ly** *adv*

co·in·ci·den·tal \(ˌ)kō-ˌin(t)-sə-'dent-ᵊl\ *adj* (1800) **1 :** resulting from a coincidence **2 :** occurring or existing at the same time — **co·in·ci·den·tal·ly** \-'dent-lē, -ᵊl-ē\ *adv*

coin lock *n* (1926) : a lock released by the insertion of a coin

coin machine *n* (1920) : SLOT MACHINE

coin–op \'kòi-ˌnäp\ *n* (1961) : a self-service laundry where the machines are operated by coins

co·in·sur·ance \ˌkō-ən-'shu̇r-ən(t)s, *chiefly Southern* (')kō-'in-ˌ\ *n* (1889) **1 :** joint assumption of risk (as by two underwriters) with another **2 :** insurance (as fire insurance) in which the insured is obligated to maintain coverage on a risk at a stipulated percentage of its total value or in the event of loss suffer a penalty in proportion to the deficiency

co·in·sure \ˌkō-ən-'shu̇(ə)r\ *vt* (1899) : to insure jointly — **co·in·sur·er** *n*

coir \'kòi(-ə)r\ *n* [Tamil *kayiṟu* rope] (1582) : a stiff coarse fiber from the outer husk of a coconut

cois·trel \'kȯi-strəl\ *n* [MF *coustillier* soldier carrying a short sword, fr. *coustille* short sword, fr. L *cultellus* knife — more at CUTLASS] *archaic* (1581) : a mean fellow : VARLET

co·ition \kō-'ish-ən\ *n* [LL, fr. L *coition-, coitio* a coming together, fr. *coitus*, pp. of *coire* to come together, fr. *co-* + *ire* to go — more at ISSUE] (1615) : COITUS — **co·ition·al** \-'ish-nəl, -ən-ᵊl\ *adj*

co·itus \'kō-ət-əs, kō-'ēt-\ *n* [L, fr. *coitus*, pp.] (1855) : physical union of male and female genitalia accompanied by rhythmic movements usu. leading to the ejaculation of semen from the penis into the female reproductive tract; *also* : INTERCOURSE 3 — compare ORGASM — **co·ital** \-ət-ᵊl, -'ēt-\ *adj* — **co·ital·ly** \-ᵊl-ē\ *adv*

coitus in·ter·rup·tus \-,int-ə-'rəp-təs\ *n* [NL, interrupted coitus] (1900) : coitus which is purposely interrupted in order to prevent ejaculation of sperm into the vagina

coitus re·ser·va·tus \-,rez-ər-'vät-əs, -'vāt-\ *n* [NL, reserved coitus] (1903) : COITUS INTERRUPTUS

1**coke** \'kōk\ *n* [ME; akin to Sw *kälk* pith, Gk *gelgis* bulb of garlic] (1669) : the residue of coal left after destructive distillation and used as fuel; *also* : a similar residue left by other materials (as petroleum) distilled to dryness

2**coke** *vb* **coked; cok·ing** *vt* (1763) : to change into coke ~ *vi* : to become coke or like coke

3**coke** *n* [by shortening & alter.] (ca. 1903) : COCAINE

Coke \'kōk\ *trademark* — used for a cola drink

col \'käl\ *n* [F, fr. MF, neck, fr. L *collum*] (1855) **1** : a saddle-shaped depression in the crest of a ridge **2** : a pass in a mountain range

1**col-** — see COM-

2**col-** *or* **coli-** *or* **colo-** *comb form* [NL, fr. L *colon*] **1** : colon ⟨*colitis*⟩ ⟨*colostomy*⟩ **2** : colon bacillus ⟨*coliform*⟩

1**cola** *pl of* COLON

2**co·la** \'kō-lə\ *n* [fr. *Coca-Cola*, a trademark] (1922) : a carbonated soft drink containing sugar, caffeine, phosphoric acid or citric acid, caramel, and flavoring from extracts usu. of kola nuts and sometimes of coca leaves

col·an·der \'kəl-ən-dər, 'käl-\ *n* [ME *colyndore*, prob. modif. of OProv *colador*, fr. ML *colatorium*, fr. L *colatus*, pp. of *colare* to sieve, fr. *colum* sieve] (14c) : a perforated utensil for washing or draining food

co·lat·i·tude \(')kō-'lat-ə-,t(y)üd\ *n* (1790) : the complement of the latitude

Col·by \'kōl-bē\ *n* [prob. fr. the name *Colby*] (ca. 1942) : a moist mild cheese similar to cheddar

col·can·non \käl-'kan-ən\ *n* [IrGael *cāl ceannan*, lit., white-headed cabbage] (1774) : potatoes and cabbage boiled and mashed together with butter and seasoning

col·chi·cine \'käl-chə-,sēn, 'käl-kə-\ *n* (ca. 1847) : a poisonous alkaloid $C_{22}H_{25}NO_6$ extracted from the corms or seeds of the meadow saffron (*Colchicum autumnale*) and used on mitotic cells to induce polyploidy and in the treatment of gout

col·chi·cum \'käl-chi-kəm, 'käl-ki-\ *n* [NL, genus name, fr. L, a kind of plant with a poisonous root, fr. Gk *kolchikon*, lit., product of Colchis] (1597) **1** : any of a genus (*Colchicum*) of Old World corm-producing herbs of the lily family with flowers that resemble crocuses **2** : the dried corm or dried ripe seeds of autumn crocus containing colchicine, possessing emetic, diuretic, and cathartic action, and used for gout and rheumatism

col·co·thar \'käl-kə-,thär\ *n* [ML, fr. MF or OSp; MF *colcotar*, fr. OSp *cólcotar*, fr. Ar dial. *qulquṭār*] (1605) : a reddish brown oxide of iron left as a residue when ferrous sulfate is heated and used as glass polish and as a pigment

1**cold** \'kōld\ *adj* [ME, fr. OE *ceald, cald*; akin to OHG *kalt* cold, L *gelu* frost, *gelare* to freeze] (bef. 12c) **1 a** : having or being a temperature that is noticeably lower than body temperature and esp. that is uncomfortable for humans ⟨it is ~ outside today⟩ ⟨a ~ drafty attic⟩ **b** : having a relatively low temperature or one lower than normal or expected ⟨the bath water has gotten ~⟩ ⟨trying to heat it with a ~ flame⟩ **c** : not heated: as (1) *of food* : served without heating esp. after initial cooking or processing ⟨~ cereal⟩ ⟨~ roast beef⟩ (2) : served chilled or with ice ⟨a ~ drink⟩ (3) : involving processing without the use of heat ⟨~ working of steel⟩ **2 a** : marked by a lack of the warmth of normal human emotion, friendliness, or compassion ⟨a ~ stare⟩ ⟨got a ~ reception⟩; *also* : not moved to enthusiasm ⟨the movie leaves me ~⟩ **b** : not colored or affected by personal feeling or bias : DETACHED, INDIFFERENT ⟨~ chronicles recorded by an outsider —Andrew Sarris⟩; *also* : IMPERSONAL, OBJECTIVE ⟨~ facts⟩ ⟨~ reality⟩ **c** : marked by sure familiarity : PAT ⟨had the routine down ~⟩ **3** : conveying the impression of being cold: as **a** : DEPRESSING, GLOOMY ⟨~ gray skies⟩ **b** : COOL 6a **4 a** : marked by the loss of normal body heat ⟨~ hands⟩; *esp* : DEAD **b** : giving the appearance of being dead : UNCONSCIOUS ⟨passed out ~⟩ **5 a** : having lost freshness or vividness : STALE ⟨dogs trying to pick up a ~ scent⟩ ⟨had to transcribe ~ notes⟩ **b** : far off the mark : not close to finding or solving — used esp. in children's games **c** : marked by poor or unlucky performance ⟨the team's shooting turned ~ in the second half⟩ **d** : not prepared or suitably warmed up — **cold·ish** *adj* — **cold·ly** \'kōl-(d)lē\ *adv* — **cold·ness** \'kōl(d)-nəs\ *n* — **in cold blood** : with premeditation : DELIBERATELY

2**cold** *n* (bef. 12c) **1** : a condition of low temperature ⟨extremes of heat and ~⟩; *esp* : cold weather **2** : bodily sensation produced by loss or lack of heat ⟨they died of the ~⟩ **3** : a bodily disorder popularly associated with chilling; *specif* : COMMON COLD — **out in the cold** : deprived of benefits given others : NEGLECTED ⟨the plan benefits management but leaves labor *out in the cold*⟩

3**cold** *adv* (1889) **1** : with utter finality : ABSOLUTELY, COMPLETELY ⟨turned down ~⟩; *also* : ABRUPTLY ⟨stopped them ~⟩ **2 a** : without introduction or advance notice ⟨walked in ~ for an appointment⟩ **b** : without preparation or warm-up ⟨was asked to perform the solo ~⟩

cold–blood·ed \'kōl(d)-'bləd-əd\ *adj* (1595) **1 a** : done or acting without consideration, compunction, or clemency ⟨~ murder⟩ **b** : MATTER-OF-FACT, EMOTIONLESS ⟨a ~ assessment⟩ **2** : having cold blood; *specif* : having a body temperature not internally regulated but approximating that of the environment **3** *or* **cold·blood** \-'bləd\ : of mixed or inferior breeding **4** : noticeably sensitive to cold — **cold–blood·ed·ly** *adv* — **cold–blood·ed·ness** *n*

cold cash *n* (1925) : money in hand

cold chisel *n* (1699) : a chisel made of tool steel of a strength, shape, and temper suitable for chipping or cutting cold metal

cold·cock \(')kōl(d)-'käk\ *vt* [origin unknown] (ca. 1927) : to knock unconscious

cold comfort *n* (1906) : quite limited sympathy, consolation, or encouragement

cold cream *n* (1709) : a soothing and cleansing cosmetic

cold cuts *n pl* (1945) : sliced assorted cold cooked meats

cold duck *n* [trans. of G *kalte ente*, a drink made of a mixture of fine wines] (1969) : a beverage that consists of a blend of sparkling burgundy and champagne

cold–eyed \'kōl-'dīd\ *adj* (1950) : COLD, COLD-BLOODED, DISPASSIONATE

cold feet *n pl* (1893) : apprehension or doubt strong enough to prevent a planned course of action

cold fish *n* (1924) : a cold aloof person

cold frame *n* (1851) : a usu. glass-covered frame without artificial heat used to protect plants and seedlings

cold front *n* (1921) : an advancing edge of a cold air mass

cold·heart·ed \'kōld-'härt-əd\ *adj* (1606) : marked by lack of sympathy, interest, or sensitivity — **cold·heart·ed·ly** *adv* — **cold·heart·ed·ness** *n*

cold rubber *n* (1948) : a wear-resistant synthetic rubber made at a low temperature (as 41° F or 5° C) and used esp. for tire treads

cold shoulder *n* (1816) : intentionally cold or unsympathetic treatment — **cold–shoul·der** *vt*

cold sore *n* (ca. 1909) : the group of blisters appearing about or within the mouth in herpes simplex

cold storage *n* (1895) **1** : storage (as of food) in a cold place for preservation **2** : a condition of being held or continued without being acted on : ABEYANCE

cold store *n* (1895) : a building for cold storage

cold sweat *n* (1706) : concurrent perspiration and chill usu. associated with fear, pain, or shock

cold turkey *n* (1916) **1** : unrelieved blunt language or procedure **2** : abrupt complete cessation of the use of an addictive drug; *also* : the symptoms experienced by one undergoing withdrawal from a drug **3** : a cold aloof person — **cold turkey** *adv or adj or vt*

cold type *n* (1949) : composition or typesetting (as photocomposition) done without the casting of metal; *specif* : such composition produced directly on paper by a typewriter mechanism

cold war *n* (1945) **1** *often cap C&W* : a conflict over ideological differences (as of the U.S. and the U.S.S.R.) carried on by methods short of sustained overt military action and usu. without breaking off diplomatic relations — compare HOT WAR **2** : a condition of rivalry, mistrust, and often open hostility short of violence esp. between power groups (as labor and management)

cold warrior *n* (1949) : one that supports or is engaged in a cold war

cold–water *adj* (1830) : rented usu. with only running water but not heat or utility service provided ⟨a ~ flat⟩

cold water *n* (1808) : depreciation of something as being ill-advised, unwarranted, or worthless ⟨threw *cold water* on our hopes⟩

cold wave *n* (1872) **1** : a period of unusually cold weather **2** : a permanent wave set by a chemical preparation without the use of heat

cole \'kōl\ *n* [ME, fr. OE *cāl*, fr. L *caulis* stem, cabbage — more at HOLE] (bef. 12c) : any of a genus (*Brassica*) of herbaceous plants (as broccoli, Brussels sprouts, cabbage, cauliflower, kohlrabi, and rape)

cole·man·ite \'kōl-mə-,nīt\ *n* [William T. *Coleman* †1893 Am. businessman and mine owner] (1884) : a mineral $Ca_2B_6O_{11}\cdot 5H_2O$ consisting of a hydrous calcium borate occurring in brilliant colorless or white massive monoclinic crystals

co·le·op·tera \,kō-lē-'äp-tə-rə\ *n pl* [NL, deriv. of Gk *koleon* sheath + *pteron* wing — more at FEATHER] (1873) : insects that are beetles — **co·le·op·ter·ist** \-tə-rəst\ *n* — **co·le·op·ter·ous** \-tə-rəs\ *adj*

co·le·op·ter·an \-tə-rən\ *n* (1847) : 1BEETLE 1 — **coleopteran** *adj*

co·le·op·tile \-'äp-tᵊl\ *n* [NL *coleoptilum*, fr. Gk *koleon* + *ptilon* down; akin to Gk *pteron*] (ca. 1866) : the first leaf of a monocotyledon forming a protective sheath about the plumule

co·leo·rhi·za \,kō-lē-ə-'rī-zə\ *n, pl* **-zae** \-(,)zē\ [NL, fr. Gk *koleon* + NL *-rhiza*] (ca. 1866) : the sheath investing the hypocotyl in some plants through which the roots burst

cole·slaw \'kōl-,slȯ\ *n* [D *koolsla*, fr. *kool* cabbage + *sla* salad] (1794) : a salad made of raw sliced or chopped cabbage

co·le·us \'kō-lē-əs\ *n* [NL, genus name, fr. Gk *koleos, koleon* sheath] (1885) : any of a large genus (*Coleus*) of herbs of the mint family

cole·wort \'kōl-,wərt, -,wȯ(ə)rt\ *n* (14c) : COLE; *esp* : one (as kale) that forms no head

coli- — see COL-

1**col·ic** \'käl-ik\ *n* [ME, fr. MF *colique*, fr. L *colicus* colicky, fr. Gk *kōlikos*, fr. *kōlon*, alter. of *kolon* colon] (15c) : a paroxysm of acute abdominal pain localized in a hollow organ and caused by spasm, obstruction, or twisting

2**colic** *adj* (15c) : of or relating to colic : COLICKY ⟨~ crying⟩

3**co·lic** \'kō-lik, 'käl-ik\ *adj* (1615) : of or relating to the colon ⟨~ lymph nodes⟩

co·li·cin \'kō-lə-sən\ *also* **co·li·cine** \-,sēn\ *n* [3*colic* + *-in* or *-ine*] (1947) : any of various antibacterial substances that are produced by some strains of intestinal bacteria and inhibit macromolecular synthesis (as of DNA or proteins)

col·icky \'käl-i-kē\ *adj* (1742) **1** : relating to or associated with colic ⟨~ pain⟩ **2** : suffering from colic ⟨~ babies⟩

col·ic·root \'käl-ik-,rüt, -,rut\ *n* (1840) : any of several plants having roots used in folk medicine to treat colic; *esp* : either of two bitter herbs (*Aletris farinosa* and *A. aurea*) of the lily family

co·li·form \'kō-lə-,fȯrm, 'käl-ə-\ *adj* [NL *Escherichia coli* colon bacillus + E *-form*] (1906) : relating to, resembling, or being the colon bacillus — **coliform** *n*

co·lin·ear \(')kō-'lin-ē-ər\ *adj* (1927) **1** : COLLINEAR **2** : having corresponding parts arranged in the same linear order ⟨a gene and the protein it determines are ~⟩ — **co·lin·ear·i·ty** \(,)kō-,lin-ē-'ar-ət-ē\ *n*

co·li·phage \'kō-lə-,fāj, -,fäzh\ *n* [NL *Escherichia coli* colon bacillus + E *-phage*] (1944) : any bacteriophage active against the colon bacillus

col·i·se·um \,käl-ə-'sē-əm\ *n* [ML *Colosseum, Colisseum*] (1708) **1** *cap* : COLOSSEUM 1 **2** : a large sports stadium or building designed like the Colosseum for public entertainments

co·lis·tin \kə-ˈlis-tən, kō-\ *n* [NL *colistinus,* specific epithet of the bacterium producing it] (ca. 1951) **:** a polymyxin produced by a bacterium (*Bacillus polymyxa* var. *colistinus*) from Japanese soil

co·li·tis \kō-ˈlīt-əs, kə-\ *n* (1860) **:** inflammation of the colon

coll- *or* **collo-** *comb form* [NL, fr. Gk *koll-, kollo-,* fr. *kolla* — more at PROTOCOL] **1 :** glue ⟨*coll*enchyma⟩ **2 :** colloid ⟨*collo*type⟩

col·lab·o·rate \kə-ˈlab-ə-ˌrāt\ *vi* **-rat·ed; -rat·ing** [LL *collaboratus,* pp. of *collaborare* to labor together, fr. L *com-* + *laborare* to labor] (1871) **1 :** to work jointly with others or together esp. in an intellectual endeavor **2 :** to cooperate with or willingly assist an enemy of one's country and esp. an occupying force **3 :** to cooperate with an agency or instrumentality with which one is not immediately connected — **col·lab·o·ra·tion** \-ˌlab-ə-ˈrā-shən\ *n* — **col·lab·o·ra·tive** \-ˈlab-ə-ˌrāt-iv, -(ə-)rət-\ *adj or n* — **col·lab·o·ra·tor** \-ˈlab-ə-ˌrāt-ər\ *n*

col·lab·o·ra·tion·ism \kə-ˌlab-ə-ˈrā-shə-ˌniz-əm\ *n* (1923) **:** the advocacy or practice of collaboration with an enemy — **col·lab·o·ra·tion·ist** \-sh(ə-)nəst\ *adj or n*

col·lage \kə-ˈläzh, kȯ-, kō-\ *n* [F, gluing, fr. *coller* to glue, fr. *colle* glue, fr. (assumed) VL *colla,* fr. Gk *kolla*] (1919) **1 :** an artistic composition made of various materials (as paper, cloth, or wood) glued on a picture surface **2 :** the art of making collages **3 :** an assembly of diverse fragments ⟨a ~ of ideas⟩ **4 :** a work (as a film) having disparate scenes in rapid succession without transitions — **collage** *vt* — **col·lag·ist** \-ˈläzh-əst\ *n*

col·la·gen \ˈkäl-ə-jən\ *n* [Gk *kolla* + ISV *-gen*] (1865) **:** an insoluble fibrous protein that occurs in vertebrates as the chief constituent of connective tissue fibrils and in bones and yields gelatin and glue on prolonged heating with water — **col·lag·e·nous** \kə-ˈlaj-ə-nəs\ *adj*

col·la·ge·nase \kə-ˈlaj-ə-ˌnās, ˈkäl-ə-jə-, -ˌnāz\ *n* (ca. 1926) **:** any of a group of proteolytic enzymes that decompose collagen and gelatin

1**col·lapse** \kə-ˈlaps\ *vb* **col·lapsed; col·laps·ing** [L *collapsus,* pp. of *collabi,* fr. *com-* + *labi* to fall, slide — more at SLEEP] *vi* (1732) **1 :** to fall or shrink together abruptly and completely **:** fall into a jumbled or flattened mass through the force of external pressure ⟨a blood vessel that *collapsed*⟩ **2 :** to break down completely **:** DISINTEGRATE ⟨his case had *collapsed* in a mass of legal wreckage —Erle Stanley Gardner⟩ **3 :** to cave or fall in or give way **4 :** to suddenly lose force, significance, effectiveness, or worth **5 :** to break down in vital energy, stamina, or self-control through exhaustion or disease; *esp* **:** to fall helpless or unconscious **6 :** to fold down into a more compact shape ⟨a chair that ~*s*⟩ ~ *vt* **:** to cause to collapse — **col·laps·ibil·i·ty** \-ˌlap-sə-ˈbil-ət-ē\ *n* — **col·laps·ible** \-ˈlap-sə-bəl\ *adj*

2**collapse** *n* (1801) **1 a :** a breakdown in vital energy, strength, or stamina **b :** a state of extreme prostration and physical depression (as from circulatory failure or great loss of body fluids) **c :** an airless state of all or part of a lung originating spontaneously or induced surgically **2 :** the act or action of collapsing ⟨the cutting of many tent ropes, the ~ of the canvas —Rudyard Kipling⟩ **3 :** a sudden failure **:** BREAKDOWN, RUIN ⟨the tragedy inherent in the ~ of a society⟩ **4 :** a sudden loss of force, value, or effect ⟨the ~ of respect for ancient law and custom —L. S. B. Leakey⟩

1**col·lar** \ˈkäl-ər\ *n* [ME *coler,* fr. OF, fr. L *collare,* fr. *collum* neck; akin to OE *heals* neck, *hwēol* wheel — more at WHEEL] (13c) **1 :** a band, strip, or chain worn around the neck: as **a :** a band that serves to finish or decorate the neckline of a garment **b :** a short necklace **c :** a band about the neck of an animal **d :** a part of the harness of draft animals fitted over the shoulders and taking strain when a load is drawn **e :** an indication of control **:** a token of subservience **f :** a protective or supportive device (as a brace or cast) worn around the neck **2 :** something resembling a collar in shape or use (as a ring or round flange to restrain motion or hold something in place) **3 :** any of various animal structures or markings similar to a collar **4 :** an act of collaring **:** ARREST, CAPTURE — **col·lared** \-ərd\ *adj* — **col·lar·less** \-ər-ləs\ *adj*

2**collar** *vt* (1613) **1 a :** to seize by the collar or neck **b :** APPREHEND, GRAB **c :** to get control of **:** PREEMPT ⟨we can ~ nearly the whole of this market —Roald Dahl⟩ **d :** to stop and detain in unwilling conversation **2 :** to put a collar on

col·lar·bone \ˈkäl-ər-ˌbōn, ˌkäl-ər-ˈ\ *n* (1500) **:** CLAVICLE

collar cell *n* (ca. 1889) **:** a flagellated endodermal cell that lines the cavity of a sponge and has a contractile protoplasmic cup surrounding the flagellum — called also *choanocyte*

col·lard \ˈkäl-ərd\ *n* [alter. of *colewort*] (1755) **:** a stalked smooth-leaved kale — usu. used in pl.

col·late \kə-ˈlāt, kä-, kō-; ˈkäl-ˌāt, ˈkōl-ˌ\ *vt* **col·lat·ed; col·lat·ing** [back-formation fr. *collation*] (1612) **1 a :** to compare critically **b :** to collect, compare carefully in order to verify, and often to integrate or arrange in order **2** [L *collatus,* pp.] **:** to institute (a cleric) to a benefice **3 a :** to verify the order of (printed sheets) **b :** to assemble in proper order; *esp* **:** to assemble (as printed sheets) in order for binding ***syn*** see COMPARE — **col·la·tor** \-ˈlāt-ər, -ˌāt-\ *n*

1**col·lat·er·al** \kə-ˈlat-ə-rəl, -ˈla-trəl\ *adj* [ME, prob. fr. MF, fr. ML *collateralis,* fr. L *com-* + *lateralis* lateral] (14c) **1 a :** accompanying as secondary or subordinate **:** CONCOMITANT ⟨digress into ~ matters⟩ **b :** INDIRECT **c :** serving to support or reinforce **:** ANCILLARY **2 :** belonging to the same ancestral stock but not in a direct line of descent **3 :** parallel, coordinate, or corresponding in position, order, time, or significance ⟨~ states like Athens and Sparta⟩ **4 a :** of, relating to, or being collateral used as security (as for payment of a debt or performance of a contract) **b :** secured by collateral — **col·lat·er·al·i·ty** \-ˌlat-ə-ˈral-ət-ē\ *n* — **col·lat·er·al·ly** \-ˈlat-ə-rə-lē, -ˈla-trə-\ *adv*

2**collateral** *n* (1691) **1 :** a collateral relative **2 :** property (as securities) pledged by a borrower to protect the interests of the lender **3 :** a branch of a bodily part (as a vein)

col·lat·er·al·ize \kə-ˈlat-ə-rə-ˌlīz, -ˈla-trə-\ *vt* **-ized; -iz·ing** (1941) **1 :** to make (a loan) secure with collateral **2 :** to use (as securities) for collateral

col·la·tion \kə-ˈlā-shən, kä-, kō-\ *n* (14c) **1** [ME, fr. ML *collation-, collatio,* fr. LL, conference, fr. L, bringing together, comparison, fr. *collatus* (pp. of *conferre* to bring together, bestow upon), fr. *com-* + *latus,* pp. of *ferre* to carry — more at BEAR] **a :** a light meal allowed on fast days in place of lunch or supper **b :** a light meal **2** [ME, fr. L *collation-, collatio*] **:** the act, process, or result of collating

col·league \ˈkäl-ˌēg *also* -ig\ *n* [MF *collegue,* fr. L *collega,* fr. *com-* + *legare* to appoint, depute — more at LEGATE] (1533) **:** an associate in a profession or in a civil or ecclesiastical office — **col·league·ship** \-ˌship\ *n*

1**col·lect** \ˈkäl-ikt *also* -ˌekt\ *n* [ME *collecte,* fr. OF, fr. ML *collecta,* short for *oratio ad collectam* prayer upon assembly] (13c) **1 :** a short prayer comprising an invocation, petition, and conclusion; *specif, often cap* **:** one preceding the eucharistic Epistle and varying with the day **2 :** COLLECTION

2**col·lect** \kə-ˈlekt\ *vb* [L *collectus,* pp. of *colligere* to collect, fr. *com-* + *legere* to gather — more at LEGEND] *vt* (1573) **1 a :** to bring together into one body or place **b :** to gather or exact from a number of persons or sources ⟨~ taxes⟩ **2 :** INFER, DEDUCE **3 :** to gain or regain control of ⟨~ his thoughts⟩ **4 :** to claim as due and receive payment for **5 :** to call for **:** PICK UP ⟨~ his girl and bring her in to the cinema —F. T. B. Macartney⟩ ~ *vi* **1 :** to come together in a band, group, or mass **:** GATHER **2 a :** to collect objects **b :** to receive payment ⟨~*ing* on the insurance⟩ ***syn*** see GATHER — **col·lect·ible** *or* **col·lect·able** \-ˈlek-tə-bəl\ *adj*

3**col·lect** \kə-ˈlekt\ *adv or adj* (1893) **:** to be paid for by the receiver

col·lec·ta·nea \ˌkäl-ˌek-ˈtā-nē-ə\ *n pl* [L, neut. pl. of *collectaneus* collected, fr. *collectus,* pp.] (1791) **:** collected writings; *also* **:** literary items forming a collection

col·lect·ed \kə-ˈlek-təd\ *adj* (1610) **1 :** possessed of calmness and composure often through concentrated effort **2 :** gathered together ⟨the ~ works of Scott⟩ ***syn*** see COOL — **col·lect·ed·ly** *adv* — **col·lect·ed·ness** *n*

col·lect·ible *or* **col·lect·able** \kə-ˈlek-tə-bəl\ *n* (1953) **:** an object that is collected by fanciers; *esp* **:** one other than such traditionally collectible items as art, stamps, coins, and antiques

col·lec·tion \kə-ˈlek-shən\ *n* (14c) **1 :** the act or process of collecting **2 a :** something collected; *esp* **:** an accumulation of objects gathered for study, comparison, or exhibition **b :** GROUP, AGGREGATE **c :** a set of apparel designed for sale usu. in a particular season

1**col·lec·tive** \kə-ˈlek-tiv\ *adj* (15c) **1 :** denoting a number of persons or things considered as one group or whole ⟨*flock* is a ~ word⟩ **2 a :** formed by collecting **:** AGGREGATED **b** *of a fruit* **:** MULTIPLE **3 a :** of, relating to, or being a group of individuals **b :** involving all members of a group as distinct from its individuals **4 :** marked by similarity among or with the members of a group **5 :** collectivized or characterized by collectivism **6 :** shared or assumed by all members of the group — **col·lec·tive·ly** *adv*

2**collective** *n* (1655) **1 :** a collective body **:** GROUP **2 :** a cooperative unit or organization; *specif* **:** COLLECTIVE FARM

collective bargaining *n* (1891) **:** negotiation between an employer and labor union representatives usu. on wages, hours, and working conditions

collective farm *n* (1919) **:** a farm esp. in a communist country formed from many small holdings collected into a single unit for joint operation under governmental supervision

collective mark *n* (1938) **:** a trademark or a service mark of a group (as a cooperative association)

collective security *n* (1934) **:** the maintenance by common action of the security of all members of an association of nations

collective unconscious *n* (ca. 1917) **:** the genetically determined part of the unconscious that esp. in the psychoanalytic theory of C. G. Jung occurs in all the members of a people or race

col·lec·tiv·isa·tion, col·lec·tiv·ise *chiefly Brit var of* COLLECTIVIZATION, COLLECTIVIZE

col·lec·tiv·ism \kə-ˈlek-ti-ˌviz-əm\ *n* (1857) **:** a political or economic theory advocating collective control esp. over production and distribution or a system marked by such control — **col·lec·tiv·ist** \-vəst\ *adj or n* — **col·lec·tiv·is·tic** \-ˌlek-ti-ˈvis-tik\ *adj* — **col·lec·tiv·is·ti·cal·ly** \-ti-k(ə-)lē\ *adv*

col·lec·tiv·i·ty \kə-ˌlek-ˈtiv-ət-ē, ˌkäl-ˌek-\ *n, pl* **-ties** (1862) **1 :** the quality or state of being collective **2 :** a collective whole; *esp* **:** the people as a body

col·lec·tiv·ize \kə-ˈlek-ti-ˌvīz\ *vt* **-ized; -iz·ing** (1893) **:** to organize under collective control — **col·lec·tiv·iza·tion** \kə-ˌlek-ti-və-ˈzā-shən\ *n*

col·lec·tor \kə-ˈlek-tər\ *n* (14c) **1 :** an official who collects funds or moneys **2 :** one that makes a collection ⟨stamp ~⟩ **3 :** an object or device that collects ⟨the statuette was a dust ~⟩ — **col·lec·tor·ship** \-ˌship\ *n*

collector's item *n* (1932) **:** an item whose rarity or excellence makes it esp. worth collecting; *broadly* **:** COLLECTIBLE

col·leen \kä-ˈlēn, ˈkäl-ˌēn\ *n* [IrGael *cailīn*] (1828) **:** an Irish girl

col·lege \ˈkäl-ij\ *n, often attrib* [ME, fr. MF, fr. L *collegium* society, fr. *collega* colleague — more at COLLEAGUE] (14c) **1 :** a body of clergy living together and supported by a foundation **2 :** a building used for an educational or religious purpose **3 a :** a self-governing constituent body of a university offering living quarters and instruction but not granting degrees ⟨Balliol and Magdalen *Colleges* at Oxford⟩ **b :** a preparatory or high school **c :** an independent institution of higher learning offering a course of general studies leading to a bachelor's degree **d :** a part of a university offering a specialized group of courses **e :** an institution offering instruction usu. in a professional, vocational, or technical field ⟨war ~⟩ ⟨business ~⟩ **4 :** COMPANY, GROUP; *specif* **:** an organized body of persons engaged in a common pursuit or having common interests or duties **5 a :** a group of persons considered by law to be a unit **b :** a body of electors — compare ELECTORAL COLLEGE **6 :** the faculty, students, or administration of a college

College Board *service mark* — used for administration of tests of aptitude and achievement considered by some colleges in determining admission and placement of students

college try *n* [fr. the phrase "give it the old *college try*"] (1952) **:** a zealous all-out effort

\ə\ abut \ᵊ\ kitten, F table \ər\ further \a\ ash \ā\ ace \ä\ cot, cart \au̇\ out \ch\ chin \e\ bet \ē\ easy \g\ go \i\ hit \ī\ ice \j\ job \ŋ\ sing \ō\ go \ȯ\ law \ȯi\ boy \th\ thin \t͟h\ the \ü\ loot \u̇\ foot \y\ yet \zh\ vision \à, k̲, ⁿ, œ, œ̄, ue, ue̅, ʸ\ *see* Guide to Pronunciation

col·le·gial \kə-ˈlē-j(ē-)əl, *esp for 2a also* -ˈlē-gē-əl\ *adj* (14c) **1 :** COLLEGIATE **2 a :** marked by power or authority vested equally in each of a number of colleagues **b :** characterized by equal sharing of authority esp. by Roman Catholic bishops — **col·le·gial·ly** \-ē\ *adv*

col·le·gi·al·i·ty \-ˌlē-jē-ˈal-ət-ē, -ˌlē-gē-\ *n* (1887) **:** the relationship of colleagues; *specif* **:** the participation of bishops in the government of the Roman Catholic Church in collaboration with the pope

col·le·gian \kə-ˈlē-j(ē-)ən\ *n* (14c) **:** a student or recent graduate of a college

col·le·giate \kə-ˈlē-jət, -jē-ət\ *adj* [ML *collegiatus,* fr. L *collegium*] (15c) **1 :** of or relating to a collegiate church **2 :** of, relating to, or comprising a college **3 :** COLLEGIAL 2 **4 :** designed for or characteristic of college students — **col·le·giate·ly** *adv*

collegiate church *n* (15c) **1 :** a church other than a cathedral that has a chapter of canons **2 :** a church or corporate group of churches under the joint pastorate of two or more ministers

col·le·gi·um \kə-ˈleg-ē-əm, -ˈlāg-\ *n, pl* **-gia** \-ē-ə\ *or* **-gi·ums** [modif. of Russ *kollegya,* fr. L *collegium*] (1917) **:** a group in which each member has approximately equal power and authority

col·lem·bo·lan \kə-ˈlem-bə-lən\ *n* [deriv. of *coll-* + Gk *embolos* wedge, stopper — more at EMBOLUS] (1873) **:** any of an order (Collembola) of small primitive wingless arthropods related to or classed among the insects — called also *springtail* — **collembolan** *or* **col·lem·bo·lous** \-ləs\ *adj*

col·len·chy·ma \kə-ˈleŋ-kə-mə, kä-\ *n* [NL] (1857) **:** a plant tissue of living usu. elongated cells with walls variously thickened esp. at the angles but capable of further growth — compare SCLERENCHYMA — **col·len·chy·ma·tous** \ˌkäl-ən-ˈkim-ət-əs, -ˈkī-mət-\ *adj*

col·let \ˈkäl-ət\ *n* [MF, dim. of *col* collar, fr. L *collum* neck — more at COLLAR] (1528) **:** a metal band, collar, ferrule, or flange: as **a :** a small collar pierced to receive the inner end of a balance spring on a timepiece **b :** a circle or flange in which a gem is set

col·le·te·ri·al gland \ˌkäl-ə-ˌtir-ē-əl-, -ˌter-\ *n* (1870) **:** a gland in female insects that secretes a cement by which the eggs are glued together or attached to an external object

col·lide \kə-ˈlīd\ *vi* **col·lid·ed; col·lid·ing** [L *collidere,* fr. *com-* + *laedere* to injure by striking — more at LESION] (1700) **1 :** to come together with solid or direct impact **2 :** CLASH

col·lid·er \kə-ˈlīd-ər\ *n* (1980) **:** a particle accelerator in which two beams of particles moving in opposite directions are made to collide

col·lie \ˈkäl-ē\ *n* [prob. fr. E dial. *colly* (black)] (1651) **:** any of a breed of large dogs developed in Scotland that occur in rough-coated and smooth-coated varieties

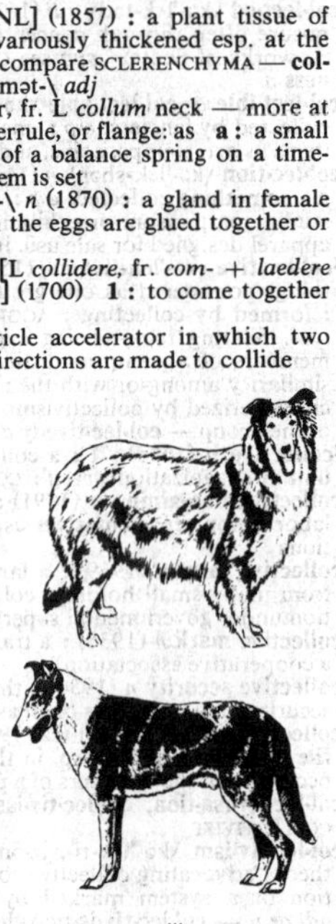

collie

col·lier \ˈkäl-yər\ *n* [ME *colier,* fr. *col* coal] (13c) **1 :** one that produces charcoal **2 :** a coal miner **3 :** a ship for transporting coal

col·liery \ˈkäl-yə-rē\ *n, pl* **-lier·ies** (1635) **:** a coal mine and its connected buildings

col·lie·shang·ie \ˈkäl-ē-ˌshaŋ-ē, ˈkəl-\ *n* [perh. fr. *collie* + *shang* (kind of meal)] *Scot* (1737) **:** SQUABBLE, BRAWL

col·li·gate \ˈkäl-ə-ˌgāt\ *vb* **-gat·ed; -gat·ing** [L *colligatus,* pp. of *colligare,* fr. *com-* + *ligare* to tie — more at LIGATURE] *vt* (1545) **1 :** to bind, unite, or group together **2 :** to subsume (isolated facts) under a general concept ~ *vi* **:** to be or become a member of a group or unit — **col·li·ga·tion** \ˌkäl-ə-ˈgā-shən\ *n*

col·li·ga·tive \ˈkäl-ə-ˌgāt-iv\ *adj* (1901) **:** depending on the number of particles (as molecules) and not on the nature of the particles ⟨pressure is a ~ property⟩

col·li·mate \ˈkäl-ə-ˌmāt\ *vt* **-mat·ed; -mat·ing** [L *collimatus,* pp. of *collimare,* MS var. of *collineare* to make straight, fr. *com-* + *linea* line] (1837) **1 :** to adjust the line of sight of (a transit or level) **2 :** to make (as rays of light) parallel — **col·li·ma·tion** \ˌkäl-ə-ˈmā-shən\ *n*

col·li·ma·tor \ˈkäl-ə-ˌmāt-ər\ *n* (1865) **1 :** a device for producing a beam of parallel rays (as of light) or for forming an infinitely distant virtual image that can be viewed without parallax **2 :** a device for obtaining a beam of molecules, atoms, nuclear particles, or X rays of limited cross section

col·lin·ear \kə-ˈlin-ē-ər, kä-\ *adj* [ISV] (1863) **1 :** lying on or passing through the same straight line **2 :** having axes lying end to end in a straight line ⟨~ antenna elements⟩ — **col·lin·ear·i·ty** \-ˌlin-ē-ˈar-ət-ē\ *n*

col·lins \ˈkäl-ənz\ *n* [prob. fr. the name *Collins*] (1939) **:** a tall iced drink consisting of soda water, sugar, lemon or lime juice, and liquor (as gin)

col·lin·sia \kə-ˈlin-zē-ə, kä-\ *n* [NL, genus name, fr. Zaccheus *Collins* †1831 Am. botanist] (1821) **:** any of a genus (*Collinsia*) of U.S. biennial or annual herbs of the figwort family

col·li·sion \kə-ˈlizh-ən\ *n* [ME, fr. L *collision-, collisio,* fr. *collisus,* pp. of *collidere*] (15c) **1 :** an act or instance of colliding **:** CLASH **2 :** an encounter between particles (as atoms or molecules) resulting in exchange or transformation of energy — **col·li·sion·al** \-ˈlizh-nəl, -ən-ᵊl\ *adj*

collision course *n* (1944) **:** a course (as of moving bodies or antithetical philosophies) that will result in collision or conflict if continued unaltered

collo- — see COLL-

col·lo·cate \ˈkäl-ə-ˌkāt\ *vb* **-cat·ed; -cat·ing** [L *collocatus,* pp. of *collocare,* fr. *com-* + *locare* to place, fr. *locus* place — more at STALL] *vt* (1513) **:** to set or arrange in a place or position; *esp* **:** to set side by side ~ *vi* **:** to occur in conjunction with something

col·lo·ca·tion \ˌkäl-ə-ˈkā-shən\ *n* (1605) **:** the act or result of placing or arranging together; *specif* **:** a noticeable arrangement or conjoining of linguistic elements (as words) — **col·lo·ca·tion·al** \-shnəl, -shən-ᵊl\ *adj*

col·lo·di·on \kə-ˈlōd-ē-ən\ *n* [modif. of NL *collodium,* fr. Gk *kollōdēs* glutinous, fr. *kolla* glue] (1851) **:** a viscous solution of pyroxylin used esp. as a coating for wounds or for photographic films

col·logue \kə-ˈlōg\ *vi* **col·logued; col·logu·ing** [origin unknown] (1646) **1** *dial* **:** INTRIGUE, CONSPIRE **2 :** to talk privately **:** CONFER

col·loid \ˈkäl-ˌȯid\ *n* [ISV *coll-* + *-oid*] (1849) **1 :** a gelatinous or mucinous substance found in tissues in disease (as in the thyroid) or normally **2 a :** a substance that is in a state of division preventing passage through a semipermeable membrane, consists of particles too small for resolution with an ordinary light microscope, and in suspension or solution fails to settle out and diffracts a beam of light **b :** a system consisting of a colloid together with the gaseous, liquid, or solid medium in which it is dispersed — **col·loi·dal** \kə-ˈlȯid-ᵊl, kä-\ *adj* — **col·loi·dal·ly** \-ᵊl-ē\ *adv*

col·lop \ˈkäl-əp\ *n* [ME] (14c) **1 :** a small piece or slice esp. of meat **2 :** a fold of fat flesh

col·lo·qui·al \kə-ˈlō-kwē-əl\ *adj* (1751) **1 :** of or relating to conversation **:** CONVERSATIONAL **2 a :** used in or characteristic of familiar and informal conversation **b :** using conversational style — **colloquial** *n* — **col·lo·qui·al·i·ty** \-ˌlō-kwē-ˈal-ət-ē\ *n* — **col·lo·qui·al·ly** \-ˈlō-kwē-ə-lē\ *adv*

col·lo·qui·al·ism \-ˈlō-kwē-ə-ˌliz-əm\ *n* (1810) **1 a :** a colloquial expression **b :** a local or regional dialect expression **2 :** colloquial style

col·lo·quist \ˈkäl-ə-kwəst\ *n* (1792) **:** SPEAKER

col·lo·qui·um \kə-ˈlō-kwē-əm\ *n, pl* **-qui·ums** *or* **-quia** \-kwē-ə\ [L, colloquy] (1844) **:** a usu. academic meeting at which specialists deliver addresses on a topic or on related topics and then answer questions relating to them

col·lo·quy \ˈkäl-ə-kwē\ *n, pl* **-quies** [L *colloquium,* fr. *colloqui* to converse, fr. *com-* + *loqui* to speak] (15c) **1 :** a high-level serious discussion **:** CONFERENCE **2 :** CONVERSATION, DIALOGUE

col·lo·type \ˈkäl-ə-ˌtīp\ *n* [ISV] (1883) **1 :** a photomechanical process for making prints directly from a hardened film of gelatin or other colloid that has ink-receptive and ink-repellent parts **2 :** a print made by collotype

col·lude \kə-ˈlüd\ *vi* **col·lud·ed; col·lud·ing** [L *colludere,* fr. *com-* + *ludere* to play, fr. *ludus* game — more at LUDICROUS] (1535) **:** CONSPIRE, PLOT

col·lu·sion \kə-ˈlü-zhən\ *n* [ME, fr. MF, fr. L *collusion-, collusio,* fr. *collusus,* pp. of *colludere*] (14c) **:** secret agreement or cooperation esp. for an illegal or deceitful purpose — **col·lu·sive** \-ˈlü-siv, -ziv\ *adj* — **col·lu·sive·ly** *adv*

col·lu·vi·um \kə-ˈlü-vē-əm\ *n, pl* **-via** \-vē-ə\ *or* **-vi·ums** [NL, fr. ML, offscourings, alter. of L *colluvies,* fr. *colluere* to wash, fr. *com-* + *lavere* to wash — more at LYE] (ca. 1936) **:** rock detritus and soil accumulated at the foot of a slope — **col·lu·vi·al** \-vē-əl\ *adj*

col·ly \ˈkäl-ē\ *vt* **col·lied; col·ly·ing** [alter. of ME *colwen,* fr. (assumed) OE *colgian,* fr. OE *col* coal] *dial chiefly Brit* (15c) **:** to blacken with or as if with soot

col·lyr·i·um \kə-ˈlir-ē-əm\ *n, pl* **-ia** \-ē-ə\ *or* **-i·ums** [L, fr. Gk *kollyrion* pessary, eye salve, fr. dim. of *kollyra* roll of bread] (14c) **:** EYEWASH 1

col·ly·wob·bles \ˈkäl-ē-ˌwäb-əlz\ *n pl but sing or pl in constr* [prob. by folk etymology, fr. NL *cholera morbus,* lit., the disease cholera] (1823) **:** BELLYACHE

colo- — see COL-

col·o·bus monkey \ˈkäl-ə-bəs-\ *n* [NL *colobus,* fr. Gk *kolobos* docked, mutilated, fr. *kolos* docked; akin to L *clades* destruction — more at HALT] (1889) **:** any of a genus (*Colobus*) of long-tailed African monkeys — called also *colobus*

col·o·cynth \ˈkäl-ə-ˌsin(t)th\ *n* [L *colocynthis,* fr. Gk *kolokynthis*] (1565) **:** a Mediterranean and African herbaceous vine (*Citrullus colocynthis*) related to the watermelon; *also* **:** its spongy fruit from which a powerful cathartic is prepared

co·log·a·rithm \(ˈ)kō-ˈlȯg-ə-ˌrith-əm, -ˈläg-\ *n* (1881) **:** the logarithm of the reciprocal of a number

co·logne \kə-ˈlōn\ *n* [*Cologne,* Germany] (1814) **1 :** a perfumed liquid composed of alcohol and fragrant oils **2 :** a cream or paste of cologne sometimes formed into a semisolid stick — **co·logned** \-ˈlōnd\ *adj*

[1]**co·lon** \ˈkō-lən\ *n, pl* **colons** *or* **co·la** \-lə\ [L, fr. Gk *kolon*] (14c) **:** the part of the large intestine that extends from the cecum to the rectum — **co·lon·ic** \kō-ˈlän-ik\ *adj*

[2]**colon** *n, pl* **colons** *or* **co·la** \-lə\ [L, part of a poem, fr. Gk *kōlon* limb, part of a strophe — more at CALK] (ca. 1550) **1** *pl* **cola :** a rhythmical unit of an utterance; *specif, in Greek or Latin verse* **:** a system or series of from two to not more than six feet having a principal accent and forming part of a line **2** *pl* **colons a :** a punctuation mark : used chiefly to direct attention to matter (as a list, explanation, or quotation) that follows **b :** the sign : used between the parts of a numerical expression of time in hours and minutes (as in 1:15) or in hours, minutes, and seconds (as in 8:25:30), in a bibliographical reference (as in *Nation* 130:20), in a ratio where it is usu. read as "to" (as in 4:1 read "four to one"), or in a proportion where it is usu. read as "is to" or when doubled as "as" (as in 2:1::8:4 read "two is to one as eight is to four")

[3]**co·lon** \kō-lōⁿ, kə-ˈlōn\ *n* [F, fr. L *colonus*] (1888) **:** a colonial farmer or plantation owner

co·lón *also* **co·lone** \kə-ˈlōn\ *n, pl* **co·lo·nes** \-ˈlō-ˌnās\ [Sp *colón*] (1892) — see MONEY table

colon bacillus *n* (ca. 1909) **:** any of various bacilli (esp. genera *Escherichia* and *Aerobacter*) that are normally commensal in vertebrate intestines; *esp* **:** one (*E. coli*) used extensively in genetic research

col·o·nel \ˈkərn-ᵊl\ *n* [alter. of *coronel,* fr. MF, modif. of OIt *colonnello* column of soldiers, colonel, dim. of *colonna* column, fr. L *columna*] (1548) **1 a :** a commissioned officer in the army, air force, or marine corps ranking above a lieutenant colonel and below a brigadier general **b :** LIEUTENANT COLONEL **2 :** a minor titular official of a state esp. in southern or midland U.S. — used as an honorific title — **col·o·nel·cy** \-ᵊl-sē\ *n*

Colonel Blimp \ˌkərn-ᵊl-ˈblimp\ *n* [*Colonel Blimp,* cartoon character created by David Low] (1937) **:** a pompous person with out-of-date or ultraconservative views; *broadly* **:** REACTIONARY — **Colonel Blimp·ism** \-ˈblim-ˌpiz-əm\ *n*

[1]**co·lo·nial** \kə-ˈlō-nē-əl, -nyəl\ *adj* (1776) **1 :** of, relating to, or characteristic of a colony **2** *often cap* **:** of or relating to the original 13 colonies forming the United States: as **a :** made or prevailing in America during the colonial period ⟨~ architecture was a modification of English Georgian⟩ **b :** adapted from or reminiscent of an American

colonial mode of design ⟨~ furniture⟩ **3 :** possessing or composed of colonies ⟨a ~ empire⟩ — **co·lo·nial·ize** \-ˌīz\ *vt* — **co·lo·nial·ly** \-ē\ *adv* — **co·lo·nial·ness** *n*

[2]colonial *n* (ca. 1864) **1 :** a member or inhabitant of a colony **2 a :** a product made for use in a colony **b :** a product exhibiting colonial style

co·lo·nial·ism \kə-ˈlō-nē-ə-ˌliz-əm, -nyə-ˌliz-\ *n* (1853) **1 :** the quality or state of being colonial **2 :** something characteristic of a colony **3 a :** control by one power over a dependent area or people **b :** a policy advocating or based on such control — **co·lo·nial·ist** \-ləst\ *n or adj* — **co·lo·nial·is·tic** \-ˌlō-nē-ə-ˈlis-tik, -nyə-ˈlis-\ *adj*

[1]co·lon·ic \kō-ˈlän-ik, kə-\ *adj* (ca. 1885) **:** of or relating to the colon of the intestine

[2]colonic *n* (1939) **:** irrigation of the colon **:** ENEMA

col·o·nist \ˈkäl-ə-nəst\ *n* (1701) **1 :** a member or inhabitant of a colony **2 :** one that colonizes or settles in a new country

col·o·ni·za·tion \ˌkäl-ə-nə-ˈzā-shən\ *n* (1770) **:** an act or instance of colonizing — **col·o·ni·za·tion·ist** \-sh(ə-)nəst\ *n*

col·o·nize \ˈkäl-ə-ˌnīz\ *vb* **-nized; -niz·ing** *vt* (1622) **1 a :** to establish a colony in or on or of **b :** to establish in a colony **2 :** to send illegal or irregularly qualified voters into ⟨*colonizing* doubtful districts⟩ **3 :** to infiltrate with usu. subversive militants for propaganda and strategy reasons ⟨~ industries⟩ ~ *vi* **:** to make or establish a colony **:** SETTLE — **col·o·niz·er** *n*

col·on·nade \ˌkäl-ə-ˈnād\ *n* [F, fr. It *colonnato,* fr. *colonna* column] (1718) **:** a series of columns set at regular intervals and usu. supporting the base of a roof structure — **col·on·nad·ed** \-ˈnād-əd\ *adj*

co·lo·nus \kə-ˈlō-nəs\ *n, pl* **-ni** \-ˌnī, -(ˌ)nē\ [L, lit., farmer] (1888) **:** a free-born serf in the later Roman Empire who could sometimes own property but who was bound to the land and obliged to pay a rent usu. in produce

col·o·ny \ˈkäl-ə-nē\ *n, pl* **-nies** [ME *colonie,* fr. MF & L; MF, fr. L *colonia,* fr. *colonus* farmer, colonist, fr. *colere* to cultivate — more at WHEEL] (14c) **1 a :** a body of people living in a new territory but retaining ties with the parent state **b :** the territory inhabited by such a body **2 :** a distinguishable localized population within a species ⟨~ of termites⟩ **3 a :** a circumscribed mass of microorganisms usu. growing in or on a solid medium **b :** the aggregation of zooids of a compound animal **4 a :** a group of individuals or things with common characteristics or interests situated in close association ⟨an artist ~⟩ **b :** the section occupied by such a group **5 :** a group of persons institutionalized away from others ⟨a leper ~⟩ ⟨a penal ~⟩; *also* **:** the land or buildings occupied by such a group

col·o·phon \ˈkäl-ə-fən, -ˌfän\ *n* [L, fr. Gk *kolophōn* summit, finishing touch; akin to L *culmen* top — more at HILL] (1621) **1 :** an inscription placed at the end of a book or manuscript usu. with facts relative to its production **2 :** an identifying device used by a printer or a publisher

co·lo·pho·ny \kə-ˈläf-ə-nē, ˈkäl-ə-ˌfō-\ *n, pl* **-nies** [ME *colophonie,* deriv. of Gk *Kolophōn* Colophon, an Ionian city] (14c) **:** ROSIN

[1]col·or \ˈkəl-ər\ *n, often attrib* [ME *colour,* fr. OF, fr. L *color;* akin to L *celare* to conceal — more at HELL] (13c) **1 a :** a phenomenon of light (as red, brown, pink, or gray) or visual perception that enables one to differentiate otherwise identical objects **b :** the aspect of objects and light sources that may be described in terms of hue, lightness, and saturation for objects and hue, brightness, and saturation for light sources — used in this sense as the psychological basis for definitions of color in this dictionary **c :** a hue as contrasted with black, white, or gray **2 a :** an outward often deceptive show **:** APPEARANCE ⟨his story has the ~ of truth⟩ **b :** a legal claim to or appearance of a right, authority, or office **c :** a pretense offered as justification **:** PRETEXT ⟨she could have drawn from the Versailles treaty the ~ of legality for any action she chose —*Yale Rev.*⟩ **d :** an appearance of authenticity **:** PLAUSIBILITY ⟨lending ~ to this notion⟩ **3 :** complexion tint: **a :** the tint characteristic of good health **b :** BLUSH **4 a :** vividness or variety of effects of language **b :** LOCAL COLOR **5 a :** an identifying badge, pennant, or flag — usu. used in pl. ⟨a ship sailing under Swedish ~*s*⟩ **b :** colored clothing distinguishing one as a member of a particular group or representative of a particular person or thing — usu. used in pl. ⟨a jockey wearing the ~*s* of his stable⟩ **6 a** *pl* **:** position as to a question or course of action **:** STAND ⟨the USSR changed neither its ~*s* nor its stripes during all of this —Norman Mailer⟩ **b :** CHARACTER, NATURE — usu. used in pl. ⟨showed himself in his true ~*s*⟩ **7 a :** the use or combination of colors **b :** two or more hues employed in a medium of presentation ⟨movies in ~⟩ ⟨~ television⟩ **8** *pl* **a :** a naval or nautical salute to a flag being hoisted or lowered **b :** ARMED FORCES **9 :** VITALITY, INTEREST ⟨the play had a good deal of ~ to it⟩ **10 :** something used to give color **:** PIGMENT **11 :** tonal quality in music ⟨the ~ and richness of the cello⟩ **12 :** skin pigmentation esp. other than white characteristic of race **13 :** a small particle of gold in a gold miner's pan after washing **14 :** analysis of game action or strategy, statistics and background information on participants, and often anecdotes provided by a sportscaster to give variety and interest to the broadcast of a game or contest **15 :** a hypothetical property of quarks that differentiates each type into three forms having a distinct role in binding quarks together — **col·or·ism** \-ə-ˌriz-əm\ *n*

[2]color *vb* **col·ored; col·or·ing** \ˈkəl-(ə-)riŋ\ *vt* (14c) **1 a :** to give color to **b :** to change the color of (as by dyeing, staining, or painting) **2 :** to change as if by dyeing or painting: as **a :** MISREPRESENT, DISTORT **b :** GLOSS, EXCUSE ⟨~ a lie⟩ **c :** INFLUENCE ⟨the lives of most of us have been ~*ed* by politics —Christine Weston⟩ **3 :** CHARACTERIZE, LABEL ⟨call it progress; ~ it inevitable with shades of job security —C. E. Price⟩ ~ *vi* **:** to take on color; *specif* **:** BLUSH — **col·or·er** \ˈkəl-ər-ər\ *n*

col·or·able \ˈkəl-(ə-)rə-bəl\ *adj* (14c) **1 :** seemingly valid or genuine **2 :** intended to deceive **:** COUNTERFEIT ⟨~ piety⟩ — **col·or·ably** \-blē\ *adv*

Col·o·ra·do potato beetle \ˌkäl-ə-ˈrad-ō-, -ˈräd-\ *n* [*Colorado,* state of U.S.] (1918) **:** a black-and-yellow striped beetle (*Leptinotarsa decimlineata*) that feeds on the leaves of the potato — called also *potato beetle, potato bug*

col·or·ation \ˌkəl-ə-ˈrā-shən\ *n* (1626) **1 a :** the state of being colored ⟨the dark ~ of his skin⟩ **b :** use or choice of colors (as by an artist) **c :** arrangement of colors ⟨the brilliant ~ of a butterfly's wing⟩ **2 a :** characteristic quality ⟨the newspapers . . . took on the former ~ of the magazine —L. B. Seltzer⟩ **b :** aspect suggesting an attitude **:** PERSUASION ⟨the chameleon talent for taking on the intellectual ~ of whatever idea he happened to fasten onto —Budd Schulberg⟩ **3 :** subtle variation of intensity or quality of tone ⟨a wide range of ~ from the orchestra⟩

col·or·a·tu·ra \ˌkəl-ə-rə-ˈt(y)u̇r-ə\ *n* [obs. It, lit., coloring, fr. LL, fr. L *coloratus,* pp. of *colorare* to color, fr. *color*] (1740) **1 :** elaborate embellishment in vocal music; *broadly* **:** music with ornate figuration **2 :** a soprano with a light agile voice specializing in coloratura

color bar *n* (1913) **:** a barrier preventing colored persons from participating with whites in various activities — called also *color line*

col·or–bear·er \ˈkəl-ər-ˌbar-ər, -ˌber-\ *n* (ca. 1891) **:** one that carries a color or standard esp. in a military parade or drill

col·or–blind \-ˌblīnd\ *adj* (1854) **1 :** affected with partial or total inability to distinguish one or more chromatic colors **2 :** INSENSITIVE, OBLIVIOUS **3 :** not recognizing differences of race ⟨tried to get the welfare establishment . . . to abandon its ~ policy —D. P. Moynihan⟩; *esp* **:** free from racial prejudice ⟨a white man with an invisible black skin in a ~ community —James Farmer⟩ — **color blindness** *n*

col·or·bred \-ˌbred\ *adj* (1948) **:** selectively bred for the development of particular colors ⟨pure ~ dogs⟩

col·or·cast \-ˌkast\ *n* [*color* + tele*cast*] (1949) **:** a television broadcast in color — **colorcast** *vb*

[1]col·ored \ˈkəl-ərd\ *adj* (14c) **1 :** having color **2 a :** COLORFUL **b :** marked by exaggeration or bias **3 a :** of a race other than the white; *esp* **:** NEGRO **b :** of mixed race **4 :** of or relating to colored persons

[2]colored *n, pl* **colored** *or* **coloreds** *often cap* (1938) **:** a colored person

col·or·fast \ˈkəl-ər-ˌfast\ *adj* (1926) **:** having color that retains its original hue without fading or running — **col·or·fast·ness** \-ˌfas(t)-nəs\ *n*

col·or–field \-ˌfē(ə)ld\ *adj* (1964) **:** of, relating to, or being abstract painting in which color is emphasized and form and surface are correspondingly de-emphasized

color filter *n* (1900) **:** FILTER 3b

col·or·ful \ˈkəl-ər-fəl\ *adj* (1889) **1 :** having striking colors **2 :** full of variety or interest — **col·or·ful·ly** \-f(ə-)lē\ *adv* — **col·or·ful·ness** \-fəl-nəs\ *n*

color guard *n* (1823) **:** an honor guard for the colors of an organization

col·or·if·ic \ˌkəl-ə-ˈrif-ik\ *adj* (1676) **:** capable of communicating color

col·or·im·e·ter \ˌkəl-ə-ˈrim-ət-ər\ *n* [ISV] (ca. 1863) **:** an instrument or device for determining and specifying colors; *specif* **:** one used for chemical analysis by comparison of a liquid's color with standard colors — **col·or·i·met·ric** \ˌkəl-ə-rə-ˈme-trik\ *adj* — **col·or·i·met·ri·cal·ly** \-tri-k(ə-)lē\ *adv* — **col·or·im·e·try** \ˌkəl-ə-ˈrim-ə-trē\ *n*

col·or·ing \ˈkəl-(ə-)riŋ\ *n* (14c) **1 a :** the act of applying colors **b :** something that produces color or color effects **c** (1) **:** the effect produced by applying or combining colors (2) **:** natural color (3) **:** COMPLEXION, COLORATION **d :** change of appearance (as by adding color) **2 :** INFLUENCE, BIAS **3 :** COLOR 4 **4 :** TIMBRE, QUALITY

col·or·ist \ˈkəl-ə-rəst\ *n* (1686) **:** one that colors or deals with color — **col·or·is·tic** \ˌkəl-ə-ˈris-tik\ *adj* — **col·or·is·ti·cal·ly** \-ti-k(ə-)lē\ *adv*

col·or·ize \ˈkəl-ə-ˌrīz\ *vt* **-ized; -iz·ing** (1979) **:** to add color to (a black-and-white film) by means of a computer — **col·or·iza·tion** \ˌkəl-ə-rə-ˈzā-shən\ *n*

col·or·less \ˈkəl-ər-ləs\ *adj* (14c) **:** lacking color: as **a :** PALLID, BLANCHED **b :** DULL, UNINTERESTING — **col·or·less·ly** *adv* — **col·or·less·ness** *n*

color phase *n* (1927) **1 :** a seasonally variant pelage color **2 a :** a genetic variant manifested by the occurrence of a skin or pelage color unlike the wild type of the animal group in which it appears **b :** an individual marked by such a variant

color photography *n* (1902) **:** photographic reproduction of images in nearly natural colors

colorpoint shorthair *n* (1974) **:** any of a breed of domestic cats of Siamese type and coat pattern but occurring in different colors — called also *colorpoint*

color temperature *n* (1916) **:** the temperature at which a blackbody emits radiant energy competent to evoke a color the same as that evoked by radiant energy from a given source (as a lamp)

co·los·sal \kə-ˈläs-əl\ *adj* (1712) **1 :** of, relating to, or resembling a colossus **2 :** of a bulk, extent, power, or effect approaching or suggesting the stupendous or incredible **3 :** of an exceptional or astonishing degree *syn* see ENORMOUS — **co·los·sal·ly** \-ə-lē\ *adv*

col·os·se·um \ˌkäl-ə-ˈsē-əm\ *n* [ML, fr. L, neut. of *colosseus* colossal, fr. *colossus*] (1708) **1** *cap* **:** an amphitheater built in Rome in the first century A.D. **2 :** COLISEUM 2

Co·los·sians \kə-ˈläsh-ənz *also* -ˈläs(h)-ē-ənz\ *n pl but sing in constr* **:** a letter written by St. Paul to the Christians of Colossae and included as a book in the New Testament — see BIBLE table

co·los·sus \kə-ˈläs-əs\ *n, pl* **co·los·si** \-ˈläs-ˌī\ [L, fr. Gk *kolossos*] (14c) **1 :** a statue of gigantic size and proportions **2 :** one that resembles a colossus in size or scope

co·los·to·my \kə-ˈläs-tə-mē\ *n, pl* **-mies** [ISV [2]*col-* + *-stomy*] (1888) **:** surgical formation of an artificial anus

co·los·trum \kə-ˈläs-trəm\ *n* [L, beestings] (1577) **:** milk secreted for a few days after parturition and characterized by high protein and antibody content — **co·los·tral** \-trəl\ *adj*

col·our \ˈkəl-ər\ *chiefly Brit var of* COLOR

-c·o·lous \k-ə-ləs\ *adj comb form* [L *-cola* inhabitant; akin to L *colere* to inhabit — more at WHEEL] **:** living or growing in or on ⟨areni*colous*⟩

col·por·tage \ˈkäl-ˌpōrt-ij, -ˌpȯrt-; ˌkäl-pōr-ˈtäzh, -pȯr-\ *n* (ca. 1846) **:** a colporteur's work

col·por·teur \ˈkäl-ˌpōrt-ər, -ˌpȯrt-; ˌkäl-pōr-ˈtər, -pȯr-\ *n* [F, alter. of MF *comporteur,* fr. *comporter* to bear, peddle] (1796) **:** a peddler of religious books

colt \ˈkōlt\ *n* [ME, fr. OE; akin to OE *cild* child] (bef. 12c) **1 a :** FOAL **b :** a young male horse that is either sexually immature or has not attained an arbitrarily designated age **2 :** a young untried person

colt·ish \ˈkōl-tish\ *adj* (14c) **1 a :** not subjected to discipline **b :** FRISKY, PLAYFUL **2 :** of, relating to, or resembling a colt — **colt·ish·ly** *adv* — **colt·ish·ness** *n*

colts·foot \ˈkōlts-ˌfu̇t\ *n, pl* **coltsfoots** (14c) **:** any of various plants with large rounded leaves resembling the foot of a colt; *esp* **:** a perennial composite herb (*Tussilago farfara*) with yellow flower heads appearing before the leaves

col·u·brid \ˈkäl-(y)ə-brəd\ *n* [deriv. of L *colubra* snake; akin to L *scelus* crime — more at CYLINDER] (1887) **:** any of a large cosmopolitan family (Colubridae) of nonvenomous snakes — **colubrid** *adj*

col·u·brine \-ˌbrīn\ *adj* (1528) **1 :** of, relating to, or resembling a snake **2 :** COLUBRID

co·lu·go \kə-ˈlü-(ˌ)gō\ *n, pl* **-gos** [prob. native name in Malaya] (ca. 1890) **:** FLYING LEMUR

col·um·bar·i·um \ˌkäl-əm-ˈbar-ē-əm, -ˈber-\ *n, pl* **-ia** \-ē-ə\ [L, lit., dovecote, fr. *columba* dove] (1846) **1 :** a structure of vaults lined with recesses for cinerary urns **2 :** a recess in a columbarium

Co·lum·bia \kə-ˈləm-bē-ə\ *n* [NL, fr. Christopher *Columbus*] (1775) **:** the United States

Co·lum·bi·an \-bē-ən\ *adj* (1757) **:** of or relating to the United States or to Christopher Columbus

col·um·bine \ˈkäl-əm-ˌbīn\ *n* [ME, fr. ML *columbina*, fr. L, fem. of *columbinus* like a dove, fr. *columba* dove; akin to OHG *holuntar* elder tree, Gk *kolymbos* a bird, *kelainos* black] (14c) **:** any of a genus (*Aquilegia*) of plants of the buttercup family with irregular showy spurred flowers: as **a :** a red-flowered plant (*A. canadensis*) of eastern No. America **b :** a blue-flowered plant (*A. coerulea*) of the Rocky mountains

Col·um·bine \-ˌbīn, -ˌbēn\ *n* [It *Colombina*] **:** the saucy sweetheart of Harlequin in comedy and pantomime

co·lum·bite \kə-ˈləm-ˌbīt, ˈkäl-əm-\ *n* [NL *columbium*] (1805) **:** a black mineral $(Fe,Mn)(Nb,Ta)_2O_6$ consisting essentially of iron and niobium

co·lum·bi·um \kə-ˈləm-bē-əm\ *n* [NL, fr. *Columbia*] (1801) **:** NIOBIUM

Co·lum·bus Day \kə-ˈləm-bəs-\ *n* (1893) **1 :** October 12 formerly observed as a legal holiday in many states of the U.S. in commemoration of the landing of Columbus in the Bahamas in 1492 **2 :** the second Monday in October observed as a legal holiday in many states of the U.S.

col·u·mel·la \ˌkäl-(y)ə-ˈmel-ə\ *n, pl* **-mel·lae** \-ˈmel-(ˌ)ē, -ˌī\ [NL, fr. L, dim. of *columna*] (1848) **1 a :** the bony or partly cartilaginous rod connecting the tympanic membrane with the internal ear in birds and in many reptiles and amphibians **b :** the bony central axis of the cochlea **2 :** the central column or axis of a spiral univalve shell **3 :** the axis of the capsule in mosses and in some liverworts **4 :** the central sterile portion of the sporangium in various fungi (*Mucor* and related genera) — **col·u·mel·lar** \-ˈmel-ər\ *adj*

col·umn \ˈkäl-əm\ *n* [ME *columne*, fr. MF *colomne*, fr. L *columna*, fr. *columen* top; akin to L *collis* hill — more at HILL] (15c) **1 a :** a vertical arrangement of items printed or written on a page **b :** one of two or more vertical sections of a printed page separated by a rule or blank space **c :** an accumulation arranged vertically **:** STACK **d :** one in a usu. regular series of newspaper or magazine articles ⟨gossip ~⟩ **2 :** a supporting pillar; *esp* **:** one consisting of a usu. round shaft, a capital, and a base **3 :** something resembling a column in form, position, or function ⟨a ~ of water⟩ **4 :** a long row (as of soldiers) **5 :** one of the vertical lines of elements of a determinant or matrix — **col·umned** \-əmd\ *adj*

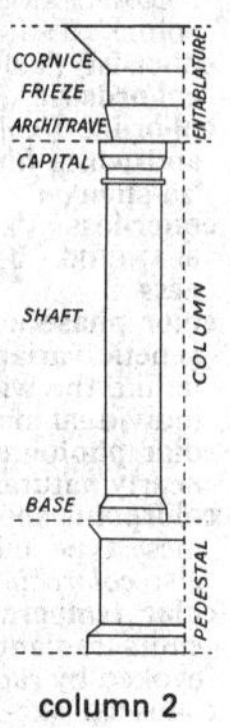
CORNICE
FRIEZE
ARCHITRAVE
CAPITAL
ENTABLATURE
SHAFT
COLUMN
BASE
PEDESTAL
column 2

co·lum·nar \kə-ˈləm-nər\ *adj* (1728) **1 :** of, relating to, or characterized by columns **2 :** of, relating to, being, or composed of tall narrow somewhat cylindrical or prismatic epithelial cells

co·lum·ni·a·tion \kə-ˌləm-nē-ˈā-shən\ *n* [modif. of L *columnation-*, *columnatio*, fr. *columna*] (1592) **:** the employment or the arrangement of columns in a structure

col·um·nist \ˈkäl-əm-(n)əst *also* ˈkäl-yəm-\ *n* (1920) **:** one who writes a newspaper or magazine column — **col·um·nis·tic** \ˌkäl-əm-ˈnis-tik *also* -yəm-\ *adj*

col·za \ˈkäl-zə, ˈkōl-\ *n* [F, fr. D *koolzaad*, fr. MD *coolsaet*, fr. *coole* cabbage + *saet* seed] (1712) **1 :** any of several coles; *esp* **:** one (as rape) producing seed used as a source of oil **2 :** RAPESEED

com- *or* **col-** *or* **con-** *prefix* [ME, fr. OF, fr. L, with, together, thoroughly — more at CO-] **:** with **:** together **:** jointly — usu. *com-* before *b*, *p*, or *m* ⟨commingle⟩, *col-* before *l* ⟨collinear⟩, and *con-* before other sounds ⟨concentrate⟩

¹co·ma \ˈkō-mə\ *n* [NL, fr. Gk *kōma* deep sleep] (1646) **1 :** a state of profound unconsciousness caused by disease, injury, or poison **2 :** a state of mental or physical sluggishness **:** TORPOR

²coma *n, pl* **co·mae** \-ˌmē, -ˌmī\ [L, hair, fr. Gk *komē*] (1669) **1 :** a tufted bunch (as of branches, bracts, or seed hairs) **2 :** the head of a comet usu. containing a nucleus **3 :** an optical aberration in which the image of a point source is a comet-shaped blur — **co·mat·ic** \kō-ˈmat-ik\ *adj*

Co·ma Ber·e·ni·ces \ˈkō-mə-ˌber-ə-ˈnī-(ˌ)sēz\ *n* [L (gen. *Comae Berenices*), lit., Berenice's hair] **:** a constellation north of Virgo and between Boötes and Leo

co·mak·er \(ˈ)kō-ˈmā-kər\ *n* (ca. 1934) **:** one that participates in an agreement; *specif* **:** one who stands to meet a financial obligation in the event of the maker's default

Co·man·che \kə-ˈman-chē\ *n, pl* **Comanche** *or* **Comanches** [Sp, of Shoshonean origin; perh. akin to Hopi *kománči* scalp lock] (1806) **:** a member of an American Indian people ranging from Wyoming and Nebraska south into New Mexico and northwestern Texas

Co·man·che·an \-chē-ən\ *adj* [*Comanche*, Texas] (1903) **:** of, relating to, or being the period of the Mesozoic era between the Jurassic and the Cretaceous or the corresponding system of rocks — **Comanchean** *n*

co·mate \(ˈ)kō-ˈmāt, ˈkō-ˌ\ *n* (1576) **:** COMPANION

co·ma·tose \ˈkō-mə-ˌtōs, ˈkäm-ə-\ *adj* [F *comateux*, fr. Gk *kōmat-*, *kōma*] (1755) **1 :** of, resembling, or affected with coma **2 :** characterized by lethargic inertness **:** TORPID ⟨a ~ economy⟩

co·mat·u·lid \kō-ˈmach-ə-ləd\ *n* [deriv. of LL *comatulus* having hair neatly curled, fr. L *comatus* hairy, fr. *coma*] (1884) **:** any of an order (Comatulida) of free-swimming stalkless crinoids — called also *feather star*

¹comb \ˈkōm\ *n* [ME, fr. OE *camb*; akin to OHG *kamb* comb, Gk *gomphos* tooth] (bef. 12c) **1 a :** a toothed instrument used esp. for adjusting, cleaning, or confining hair **b :** a structure resembling such a comb; *esp* **:** any of several toothed devices used in handling or ordering textile fibers **c :** CURRYCOMB **2 a :** a fleshy crest on the head of the domestic fowl and other gallinaceous birds — see COCK illustration **b :** something (as the ridge of a roof) resembling the comb of a cock **3 :** HONEYCOMB — **combed** \ˈkōmd\ *adj* — **comb·like** \ˈkōm-ˌlīk\ *adj*

²comb *vt* (14c) **1 :** to draw a comb through for the purpose of arranging or cleaning **2 :** to pass across with a scraping or raking action **3 a :** to eliminate (as with a comb) by a thorough going-over **b :** to search or examine systematically **4 :** to use in a combing action **~** *vi* **:** to roll over or break into foam ⟨waves ~⟩

¹com·bat \kəm-ˈbat, ˈkäm-ˌ\ *vb* **-bat·ed** *or* **-bat·ted; -bat·ing** *or* **-bat·ting** [MF *combattre*, fr. (assumed) VL *combattere*, fr. L *com-* + *battuere* to beat — more at BATTLE] *vi* (1543) **:** to engage in combat **:** FIGHT **~** *vt* **1 :** to fight with **:** BATTLE **2 :** to struggle against; *esp* **:** to strive to reduce or eliminate ***syn*** see OPPOSE

²com·bat \ˈkäm-ˌbat\ *n* (1546) **1 :** a fight or contest between individuals or groups **2 :** CONFLICT, CONTROVERSY **3 :** active fighting in a war **:** ACTION ⟨casualties suffered in ~⟩

³com·bat \ˈkäm-ˌbat\ *adj* (1939) **1 :** relating to combat ⟨~ missions⟩ **2 :** designed or destined for combat ⟨~ troops⟩

com·bat·ant \kəm-ˈbat-ᵊnt *also* ˈkäm-bət-ənt\ *n* (15c) **:** one that is engaged in or ready to engage in combat — **combatant** *adj*

combat fatigue *n* (1943) **:** a traumatic psychoneurotic reaction or an acute psychotic reaction occurring under conditions (as wartime combat) that cause intense stress — called also *battle fatigue*

com·bat·ive \kəm-ˈbat-iv\ *adj* (1834) **:** marked by eagerness to fight or contend — **com·bat·ive·ly** *adv* — **com·bat·ive·ness** *n*

combe \ˈküm, ˈkōm\ *n* [ME *coumbe*, *cumbe*, fr. OE *cumb*, of Celt origin; akin to W *cwm* valley] (bef. 12c) **1** *Brit* **:** a deep narrow valley **2** *Brit* **:** a valley or basin on the flank of a hill

comb·er \ˈkō-mər\ *n* (1646) **1 :** one that combs **2 :** a long curling wave of the sea

com·bi·na·tion \ˌkäm-bə-ˈnā-shən\ *n, often attrib* (14c) **1 a :** a result or product of combining; *esp* **:** an alliance of individuals, corporations, or states united to achieve a social, political, or economic end **b :** two or more persons working as a team **2 :** an ordered sequence: as **a :** a sequence of letters or numbers chosen in setting a lock; *also* **:** the mechanism operating or moved by the sequence **b :** any subset of a set considered without regard to order within the subset **3 :** any of various one-piece undergarments for the upper and lower parts of the body **4 :** an instrument designed to perform two or more tasks **5 a :** the act or process of combining; *esp* **:** that of uniting to form a chemical compound **b :** the quality or state of being combined — **com·bi·na·tion·al** \-shnəl, -shən-ᵊl\ *adj*

combination shot *n* (ca. 1909) **:** a shot in pool in which a ball is pocketed by an object ball

com·bi·na·tive \ˈkäm-bə-ˌnāt-iv, kəm-ˈbī-nət-\ *adj* (1855) **1 :** tending or able to combine **2 :** resulting from combination

com·bi·na·to·ri·al \ˌkäm-bə-nə-ˈtōr-ē-əl, kəm-ˌbī-nə-, -ˈtȯr-\ *adj* (1818) **1 :** of, relating to, or involving combinations **2 :** of or relating to the arrangement of, operation on, and selection of discrete mathematical elements belonging to finite sets or making up geometric configurations — **com·bi·na·to·ri·al·ly** \-ē-ə-lē\ *adv*

com·bi·na·tor·ics \-ˈtȯr-iks, -ˈtär-\ *n pl but sing in constr* (1961) **:** combinatorial mathematics

com·bi·na·to·ry \kəm-ˈbī-nə-ˌtōr-ē, -ˌtȯr-\ *adj* (1647) **:** COMBINATIVE

¹com·bine \kəm-ˈbīn\ *vb* **com·bined; com·bin·ing** [ME *combinen*, fr. MF *combiner*, fr. LL *combinare*, fr. L *com-* + *bini* two by two — more at BIN-] *vt* (15c) **1 a :** to bring into such close relationship as to obscure individual characters **:** MERGE **b :** to cause to unite into a chemical compound **c :** to unite into a single number or expression ⟨~ fractions and simplify⟩ **2 :** INTERMIX, BLEND **3 :** to possess in combination **~** *vi* **1 a :** to become one **b :** to unite to form a chemical compound **2 :** to act together ***syn*** see JOIN — **com·bin·er** *n*

²com·bine \ˈkäm-ˌbīn\ *n* (1886) **1 :** a combination esp. of business or political interests **2 :** a harvesting machine that heads, threshes, and cleans grain while moving over a field

³com·bine \ˈkäm-ˌbīn\ *vt* **com·bined; com·bin·ing** (1926) **:** to harvest with a combine

comb·ing \ˈkō-miŋ\ *var of* COAMING

comb·ings \ˈkō-miŋz\ *n pl* (1656) **:** loose hair removed by a comb

combing wool *n* (1757) **:** long-staple strong-fibered wool found suitable for combing and used esp. in the manufacture of worsteds

com·bin·ing form \kəm-ˌbī-niŋ-\ *n* (1884) **:** a linguistic form that occurs only in compounds or derivatives and can be distinguished descriptively from an affix by its ability to occur as one immediate constituent of a form whose only other immediate constituent is an affix (as *cephal-* in *cephalic*) or by its being an allomorph of a morpheme having another allomorph that may occur alone or can be distinguished historically from an affix by the fact that it is borrowed from another language in which it is descriptively a word or a combining form

comb jelly *n* (1889) **:** CTENOPHORE

com·bo \ˈkäm-(ˌ)bō\ *n, pl* **combos** [by shortening & alter.] (1929) **1 :** COMBINATION **2 :** a usu. small jazz or dance band

com·bust \kəm-ˈbəst\ *vb* [L *combustus*, pp. of *comburere* to burn up, irreg. fr. *com-* + *urere* to burn — more at EMBER] (15c) **:** BURN

com·bus·ti·ble \kəm-ˈbəs-tə-bəl\ *adj* (1529) **1 :** capable of combustion **2 :** easily excited — **com·bus·ti·bil·i·ty** \-ˌbəs-tə-ˈbil-ət-ē\ *n* — **combustible** *n* — **com·bus·ti·bly** \-ˈbəs-tə-blē\ *adv*

com·bus·tion \kəm-ˈbəs-chən\ *n* (15c) **1 :** an act or instance of burning **2 a :** a chemical process (as an oxidation) accompanied by the evolution of light and heat **b :** a slower oxidation **3 :** violent agitation **:** TUMULT — **com·bus·tive** \-ˈbəs-tiv\ *adj*

com·bus·tor \-ˈbəs-tər\ *n* (1945) **:** a chamber (as in a gas turbine or a jet engine) in which combustion occurs

come \ˈkəm, *sometimes without stress when a stress follows*\ *vb* **came** \ˈkām\; **come; com·ing** \ˈkəm-iŋ\ [ME *comen,* fr. OE *cuman;* akin to OHG *queman* to come, L *venire,* Gk *bainein* to walk, go] *vi* (bef. 12c) **1 a :** to move toward something : APPROACH ⟨~ here⟩ **b :** to move or journey to a vicinity with a specified purpose ⟨~ see us⟩ ⟨~ and see what's going on⟩ **c** (1) **:** to reach a particular station in a series ⟨now we ~ to the section on health⟩ (2) **:** to arrive in due course ⟨the time has ~⟩ **d** (1) **:** to approach in kind or quality ⟨this ~*s* near perfection⟩ (2) **:** to reach a condition ⟨*came* to regard him as a friend⟩ **e** (1) **:** to advance toward accomplishment ⟨learning new ways doesn't ~ easy⟩ ⟨the job is *coming* nicely⟩ (2) **:** to advance in a particular manner ⟨~ running when I call⟩ (3) **:** to advance, rise, or improve in rank or condition ⟨has ~ a long way⟩ **f :** to get along : FARE — often used with *along* **g :** EXTEND ⟨her dress *came* to her ankles⟩ **2 a** (1) **:** to arrive at a particular place, end, result, or conclusion ⟨*came* to his senses⟩ ⟨~ untied⟩ (2) **:** AMOUNT ⟨taxes ~ to more than it's worth⟩ **b** (1) **:** to appear to the mind ⟨the answer *came* to him⟩ (2) **:** to appear on a scene : make an appearance ⟨children ~ equipped to learn any language⟩ **c :** HAPPEN, OCCUR ⟨no harm will ~ to you⟩ **d :** ORIGINATE, ARISE ⟨wine ~*s* from grapes⟩ ⟨~ of sturdy stock⟩ **e :** to enter or assume a condition ⟨artillery *came* into action⟩ **f :** to fall within a field of view or a range of application ⟨this ~*s* within the terms of the treaty⟩ **g :** to issue forth ⟨a sob *came* from her throat⟩ **h :** to take form ⟨churn till the butter ~*s*⟩ **i :** to be available ⟨this model ~*s* in several sizes⟩ ⟨as good as they ~⟩ **j :** to experience orgasm **3 :** to fall to a person in a division or inheritance of property **4** *obs* **:** to become moved favorably : RELENT **5 :** to turn out to be ⟨good clothes ~ high⟩ **6 :** BECOME ⟨a dream that *came* true⟩ ~ *vt* **1 :** to approach or be near (an age) ⟨a child *coming* eight years old⟩ **2 :** to take on the aspect of ⟨~ the stern parent⟩ — **come a cropper :** to fail completely — **come at :** to accomplish an understanding or mastery of : ATTAIN ⟨art is not something to *come at* by dint of study —Clive Bell⟩ — **come by :** to get possession of : ACQUIRE ⟨a good job can be hard to *come by*⟩ — **come into :** to acquire as a possession or achievement ⟨*come into* a fortune⟩ — **come into one's own :** to achieve one's potential; *also* **:** to gain recognition — **come off it :** to cease foolish or pretentious talk or behavior — **come over :** to seize suddenly and strangely ⟨what's *come over* you⟩ — **come to :** to be a question of ⟨when it *comes to* pitching horseshoes, he's the champ⟩ — **come to oneself :** to get hold of oneself : regain self-control — **come to pass :** HAPPEN

come about *vi* (14c) **1 :** HAPPEN **2 :** to change direction ⟨the wind has *come about* into the north⟩ **3 :** to shift to a new tack

come across *vi* (1910) **1 :** to give over or furnish something demanded; *esp* **:** to pay over money **2 :** to produce an impression ⟨*comes across* as a good speaker⟩ **3 :** COME THROUGH 2

come along *vi* (1694) **1 :** to accompany someone who leads the way ⟨asked me to *come along* on the trip⟩ **2 :** to make progress ⟨work is *coming along* well⟩ **3 :** to make an appearance ⟨won't just marry the first man that *comes along*⟩

come around *vi* (1934) **1 :** COME ROUND **2 :** MENSTRUATE

come·back \ˈkəm-ˌbak\ *n* (1889) **1 a :** a sharp or witty reply : RETORT **b :** a cause for complaint **2 :** RECOVERY

come back \(ˌ)kəm-ˈbak\ *vi* (1850) **1 :** to return to life or vitality **2 :** to return to memory ⟨it's all *coming back* to me now⟩ **3 :** REPLY, RETORT **4 :** to regain a former favorable condition or position

come by *vi* (1863) **:** to make a visit

co·me·di·an \kə-ˈmē-dē-ən\ *n* (1581) **1** *archaic* **a :** a writer of comedies **b :** an actor who plays comic roles **2 :** a comical individual; *specif* **:** a professional entertainer who uses any of various physical or verbal means to be amusing

co·me·dic \-ˈmēd-ik, -ˈmed-\ *adj* (1639) **1 :** of or relating to comedy **2 :** COMICAL 2

co·me·di·enne \-ˌmē-dē-ˈen\ *n* [F *comédienne,* fem. of *comédien* comedian, fr. *comédie*] (1860) **:** a female comedian

com·e·do \ˈkäm-ə-ˌdō\ *n, pl* **com·e·do·nes** \ˌkäm-ə-ˈdō-(ˌ)nēz\ [NL, fr. L, glutton, fr. *comedere* to eat — more at COMESTIBLE] (1866) **:** BLACKHEAD 1

come·down \ˈkəm-ˌdau̇n\ *n* (1840) **:** a descent in rank or dignity

come down \(ˌ)kəm-ˈdau̇n\ *vi* (1611) **1 a :** to pass by tradition ⟨a story that has *come down* from medieval times⟩ **b :** to pass from a usu. high source ⟨word *came down* that the strike was over⟩ **2 a :** to reduce itself : AMOUNT ⟨it *comes down* to this⟩ **b :** to deal directly with ⟨when you *come down* to it, we all depend on others⟩ **3 :** to lose or fall in estate or condition ⟨ has *come down* in the world⟩ **4 :** to place oneself in opposition ⟨*came down* hard on gambling⟩ **5 :** to become ill ⟨*came down* with measles⟩ **6 :** COME OUT 2

com·e·dy \ˈkäm-əd-ē\ *n, pl* **-dies** [ME, fr. MF *comedie,* fr. L *comoedia,* fr. Gk *kōmōidia,* fr. *kōmos* revel + *aeidein* to sing — more at ODE] (14c) **1 a :** a drama of light and amusing character and typically with a happy ending **b :** the genre of dramatic literature dealing with the comic or with the serious in a light or satirical manner — compare TRAGEDY **2 a :** a medieval narrative that ends happily ⟨Dante's *Divine Comedy*⟩ **b :** a literary work written in a comic style or treating a comic theme **3 :** a ludicrous or farcical event or series of events **4 a :** the comic element ⟨the ~ of many life situations⟩ **b :** humorous entertainment ⟨nightclub ~⟩

comedy drama *n* (1885) **:** serious drama that is interspersed with comedy

comedy of manners (1822) **:** comedy that satirically portrays the manners and fashions of a particular class or set

come–hith·er \(ˌ)kəm-ˈhith-ər, (ˌ)kə-ˈmith-\ *adj* (1900) **:** sexually provocative ⟨that ~ look in your eyes⟩

come in *vi* (14c) **1 a :** to arrive on a scene ⟨new models *coming in*⟩ **b :** to become available ⟨data began *coming in*⟩ **2 :** to place among those finishing ⟨*came in* last⟩ **3 a :** to function in an indicated manner ⟨*come in* handy⟩ **b :** to make reply to a signal or call ⟨*came in* loud and clear⟩ **4 :** to assume a role or function ⟨that's where you *come in*⟩ **5 :** to attain maturity, fruitfulness, or production — **come in for :** to become subject to ⟨*coming in for* increasing criticism⟩

come·ly \ˈkəm-lē *also* ˈkōm- *or* ˈkäm-\ *adj* **come·li·er, -est** [ME *comly,* alter. of OE *cȳmlic* glorious, fr. *cȳme* lively, fine; akin to OHG *kūmig* weak, Gk *goan* to lament] (bef. 12c) **1 :** having a pleasing appearance : not homely or plain **2 :** pleasurably conforming to notions of good appearance, fitness, or proportion ***syn*** see BEAUTIFUL — **come·li·ness** *n*

come off *vi* (1596) **1 a :** to acquit oneself : FARE ⟨*came off* well in the contest⟩ **b :** APPEAR, SEEM **2 :** SUCCEED ⟨a television series that never *came off* —*TV Guide*⟩ **3 :** HAPPEN, OCCUR

come–on \ˈkəm-ˌȯn, -ˌän\ *n* (1902) **1 :** an attraction used esp. in sales promotion **2 :** an often sexual advance

come on \(ˌ)kəm-ˈȯn, -ˈän\ *vi* (15c) **1 a :** to advance by degrees ⟨darkness *came on*⟩ **b :** to begin by degrees ⟨rain *came on* toward noon⟩ **2 :** PLEASE — used in cajoling or pleading **3 :** to project an indicated personal image ⟨*comes on* as a liberal⟩ **4 :** to show sexual interest in someone; *also* **:** to make sexual advances ⟨tried to *come on* to her⟩

come out *vi* (13c) **1 a :** to come into public view : make a public appearance ⟨a new magazine has *come out*⟩ **b :** to become evident ⟨his pride *came out* in his refusal to accept help⟩ **2 :** to declare oneself esp. in public utterance ⟨*came out* in favor of the popular candidate⟩ **3 :** to turn out in an outcome : end up ⟨everything will *come out* all right⟩ **4 :** to make a debut **5 :** to openly declare one's homosexuality — **coming–out** \ˌkəm-iŋ-ˈau̇t\ *adj* — **come out with 1 :** to give expression to ⟨*came out with* an interesting proposal⟩ **2 :** PUBLISH

come–out·er \(ˌ)kə-ˈmau̇t-ər\ *n* (1840) **1 :** one who withdraws from something established (as a religious body) **2 :** one who advocates political reform

come over *vi* (1576) **1 a :** to change from one side (as of a controversy) to the other **b :** to visit casually : drop in ⟨*come over* whenever you like⟩ **2** *Brit* **:** BECOME

com·er \ˈkəm-ər\ *n* (14c) **1 :** one that comes or arrives ⟨all ~*s*⟩ **2 :** one making rapid progress or showing promise

come round *vi* (1818) **1 :** to change direction **2 :** to return to a former condition; *esp* **:** to come to **3 :** to accede to a particular opinion or course of action ⟨knew you'd *come round* to our side eventually⟩

[1]**co·mes·ti·ble** \kə-ˈmes-tə-bəl\ *adj* [MF, fr. ML *comestibilis,* fr. L *comestus,* pp. of *comedere* to eat, fr. *com-* + *edere* to eat — more at EAT] (15c) **:** EDIBLE

[2]**comestible** *n* (1837) **:** FOOD — usu. used in pl.

com·et \ˈkäm-ət\ *n* [ME *comete,* fr. OE *cometa,* fr. L, fr. Gk *komētēs,* lit., long-haired, fr. *koman* to wear long hair, fr. *komē* hair] (bef. 12c) **:** a celestial body that consists of a fuzzy head usu. surrounding a bright nucleus, that often when in the part of its orbit near the sun develops a long tail which points away from the sun, and that has an orbit varying in eccentricity between nearly round and parabolic — **com·e·tary** \-ə-ˌter-ē\ *adj* — **co·met·ic** \kə-ˈmet-ik, kä-\ *adj*

come through *vi* (1914) **1 :** to do what is needed or expected ⟨*came through* in the clutch⟩ **2 :** to become communicated

come to *vi* (1572) **1 :** to recover consciousness **2 a :** to bring a ship's head nearer the wind : LUFF **b :** to come to anchor or to a stop

come up *vi* (14c) **1 :** RISE 6 **2 :** to come near : make an approach ⟨*came up* and introduced himself⟩ **3 :** to rise in rank or status ⟨an officer who *came up* from the ranks⟩ **4 a :** to come to attention or consideration ⟨the question never *came up*⟩ **b :** to occur in the course of time ⟨any problem that may *come up*⟩ **5 :** to turn out to be ⟨the coin *came up* tails⟩ — **come up with :** to produce esp. in dealing with a problem or challenge ⟨*came up with* a solution⟩

come·up·pance \(ˌ)kə-ˈməp-ən(t)s\ *n* [*come up* + *-ance*] (1859) **:** a deserved rebuke or penalty : DESERTS

com·fit \ˈkəm(p)-fət, ˈkäm(p)-\ *n* [ME *confit,* fr. MF, fr. pp. of *confire* to prepare, fr. L *conficere,* fr. *com-* + *facere* to make — more at DO] (13c) **:** a candy consisting of a piece of fruit, a root (as licorice), a nut, or a seed coated and preserved with sugar

[1]**com·fort** \ˈkəm(p)-fərt\ *n* (13c) **1 :** strengthening aid: **a :** ASSISTANCE, SUPPORT ⟨accused of giving aid and *comfort* to the enemy⟩ **b :** consolation in time of trouble or worry : SOLACE **2 a :** a feeling of relief or encouragement **b :** contented well-being **3 :** a satisfying or enjoyable experience ⟨the ~ of a good meal after hard work⟩ **4 :** one that gives or brings comfort ⟨the ~*s* of civilization⟩ — **com·fort·less** \-ləs\ *adj*

[2]**comfort** *vt* [ME *comforten,* fr. OF *conforter,* fr. LL *confortare* to strengthen greatly, fr. L *com-* + *fortis* strong — more at FORT] (13c) **1 :** to give strength and hope to : CHEER **2 :** to ease the grief or trouble of : CONSOLE — **com·fort·ing·ly** \-iŋ-lē\ *adv*

com·fort·able \ˈkəm(p)(f)-tə(r)-bəl, ˈkəm(p)-fə(r)t-ə-bəl, ˈkəm-fə(r)-bəl\ *adj* (14c) **1 a :** affording or enjoying contentment and security ⟨a ~ income⟩ **b :** affording or enjoying physical comfort ⟨a ~ chair⟩ ⟨was too ~ to move⟩ **2 a :** free from vexation or doubt ⟨~ assumptions⟩ **b :** free from stress or tension ⟨a ~ routine⟩ — **com·fort·able·ness** *n* — **com·fort·ably** \-blē\ *adv*

syn COMFORTABLE, COZY, SNUG, EASY, RESTFUL mean enjoying or providing a position of contentment and security. COMFORTABLE applies to anything that encourages serenity, well-being, or complacency as well as physical ease; COZY suggests warmth, shelter, assured ease, and friendliness; SNUG suggests having just enough space for comfort and safety but no more; EASY implies relief from or absence of anything likely to cause physical or mental discomfort or constraint; RESTFUL applies to whatever induces or contributes to rest or relaxation.

com·fort·er \ˈkəm(p)-fə(r)t-ər\ *n* (14c) **1 a** *cap* **:** HOLY SPIRIT **b :** one that gives comfort **2 a :** a long narrow usu. knitted neck scarf **b :** a warm bed covering : QUILT

comfort station *n* (ca. 1913) **:** REST ROOM

com·frey \ˈkəm(p)-frē\ *n, pl* **comfreys** [ME *cumfirie,* fr. OF, fr. L *conferva*] (13c) **:** any of a genus (*Symphytum*) of plants of the borage family with coarse hairy entire leaves and flowers in one-sided racemes

com·fy \ˈkəm(p)-fē\ *adj* [by shortening & alter.] (1829) **:** COMFORTABLE

[1]**com·ic** \ˈkäm-ik\ *adj* [L *comicus,* fr. Gk *kōmikos,* fr. *kōmos* revel] (14c) **1 :** of, relating to, or marked by comedy **2 :** causing laughter or amusement : FUNNY **3 :** of or relating to comic strips ***syn*** see LAUGHABLE

[2]**comic** *n* (1581) **1 :** COMEDIAN **2 :** the comic element **3 a :** COMIC STRIP **b** (1) **:** COMIC BOOK (2) *pl* **:** the part of a newspaper devoted to comic strips

\ə\ abut \ᵊ\ kitten, F table \ər\ further \a\ ash \ā\ ace \ä\ cot, cart
\au̇\ out \ch\ chin \e\ bet \ē\ easy \g\ go \i\ hit \ī\ ice \j\ job
\ŋ\ sing \ō\ go \ȯ\ law \ȯi\ boy \th\ thin \th\ the \ü\ loot \u̇\ foot
\y\ yet \zh\ vision \à, k, ⁿ, œ, œ̄, ue, ue̅, ʸ\ *see* Guide to Pronunciation

com·i·cal \'käm-i-kəl\ *adj* (15c) **1** *obs* **:** of or relating to comedy **2** **:** causing laughter esp. because of a startlingly or unexpectedly humorous impact ***syn*** see LAUGHABLE — **com·i·cal·i·ty** \,käm-i-'kal-ət-ē\ *n* — **com·i·cal·ly** \'käm-i-k(ə-)lē\ *adv*

comic book *n* (1941) **:** a magazine containing sequences of comic strips

comic–opera *adj* (1906) **:** not to be taken seriously ⟨a ~ regime⟩

comic opera *n* (1762) **:** opera characterized by spoken dialogue, humorous episodes, and a usu. sentimental plot ending happily

comic relief *n* (1875) **:** a relief from the emotional tension of a drama that is provided by the interposition of a comic episode or element

comic strip *n* (1920) **:** a group of cartoons in narrative sequence

1**com·ing** \'kəm-iŋ\ *n* (13c) **:** an act or instance of arriving

2**coming** *adj* (15c) **1 :** immediately due in sequence or development ⟨in the ~ year⟩ **2 :** gaining importance

co·min·gle \kə-'miŋ-gəl\ *vt* (1602) **:** COMMINGLE

coming-of-age *n* (1916) **:** the attainment of prominence, respectability, or recognition

Com·in·tern \'käm-ən-,tərn\ *n* [Russ *Komintern*, fr. *Kommunisticheskiĭ Intern*atsional Communist International] (1923) **:** the Communist International established in 1919 in an attempt to supersede the Second International of Socialist organizations and dissolved in 1943

co·mi·tia \kə-'mish-(ē-)ə\ *n, pl* **comitia** [L, pl. of *comitium*, fr. *com-* + *itus*, pp. of *ire* to go — more at ISSUE] (1734) **:** any of several public assemblies of the people in ancient Rome for legislative, judicial, and electoral purposes — **co·mi·tial** \-'mish-əl\ *adj*

co·mi·ty \'käm-ət-ē, 'kō-mət-\ *n, pl* **-ties** [L *comitat-, comitas*, fr. *comis* courteous, fr. OL *cosmis*, fr. *com-* + *-smis* (akin to Skt *smayate* he smiles) — more at SMILE] (15c) **1 a :** friendly social atmosphere **:** social harmony ⟨group activities promoting ~⟩ **b :** a loose widespread community based on common social institutions ⟨the ~ of civilization⟩ **c :** COMITY OF NATIONS **d :** the informal and voluntary recognition by courts of one jurisdiction of the laws and judicial decisions of another **2 :** avoidance of proselytizing members of another religious denomination

comity of nations (1862) **1 :** the courtesy and friendship of nations marked esp. by mutual recognition of executive, legislative, and judicial acts **2 :** the group of nations practicing international comity

com·ma \'käm-ə\ *n* [LL, fr. L, part of a sentence, fr. Gk *komma* segment, clause, fr. *koptein* to cut — more at CAPON] (1554) **1 :** a punctuation mark , used esp. as a mark of separation within the sentence **2 :** PAUSE, INTERVAL **3 :** any of several nymphalid butterflies (genus *Polygonia*) with a silvery comma-shaped mark on the underside of the hind wings

comma fault *n* (ca. 1934) **:** the careless or unjustified use of a comma between coordinate main clauses not connected by a conjunction

1**com·mand** \kə-'mand\ *vb* [ME *comanden*, fr. MF *comander*, fr. (assumed) VL *commandare*, alter. of L *commendare* to commit to one's charge — more at COMMEND] *vt* (14c) **1 :** to direct authoritatively **:** ORDER **2 :** to exercise a dominating influence over: as **a :** to have at one's immediate disposal **b :** to demand or receive as one's due ⟨~*s* a high fee⟩ **c :** to overlook or dominate from a strategic position **d :** to have military command of as senior officer **3** *obs* **:** to order or request to be given ~ *vi* **1 :** to have or exercise direct authority **:** GOVERN **2 :** to give orders **3 :** to be commander **4 :** to dominate as if from an elevated place — **com·mand·able** \-'man-də-bəl\ *adj*

syn COMMAND, ORDER, BID, ENJOIN, DIRECT, INSTRUCT, CHARGE mean to issue orders. COMMAND and ORDER imply authority and usu. some degree of formality and impersonality; COMMAND stresses official exercise of authority, ORDER may suggest peremptory or arbitrary exercise; BID suggests giving orders peremptorily (as to children or servants); ENJOIN implies giving an order or direction authoritatively and urgently and often with admonition or solicitude; DIRECT and INSTRUCT both connote expectation of obedience and usu. concern specific points of procedure or method, INSTRUCT sometimes implying greater explicitness or formality; CHARGE adds to ENJOIN an implication of imposing as a duty or responsibility.

2**command** *n* (15c) **1 :** the act of commanding **2 a :** the ability to control **:** MASTERY **b :** the authority or right to command ⟨the officer in ~⟩ **c (1) :** the power to dominate **(2) :** scope of vision **d :** facility in use ⟨a good ~ of French⟩ **3 a :** an order given **b :** an electrical signal that actuates a device (as a control mechanism in a spacecraft or one step in a computer); *also* **:** the activation of a device by means of such a signal **4 :** the personnel, area, or organization under a commander; *specif* **:** a unit of the U.S. Air Force higher than an air force **5 :** a position of highest usu. military authority ***syn*** see POWER

3**command** *adj* (1826) **:** done on command or request ⟨a ~ performance⟩

com·man·dant \'käm-ən-,dant, -,dänt\ *n* (1687) **:** COMMANDING OFFICER

command car *n* (1941) **:** an open armored car designed esp. for military reconnaissance and capable of traveling over rough terrain

com·man·deer \,käm-ən-'di(ə)r\ *vt* [Afrik *kommandeer*, fr. F *commander* to command, fr. OF *comander*] (1881) **1 a :** to compel to perform military service **b :** to seize for military purposes **2 :** to take arbitrary or forcible possession of

com·mand·er \kə-'man-dər\ *n* (14c) **1 :** one in an official position of command or control: as **a :** COMMANDING OFFICER **b :** the presiding officer of a society or organization **2 :** a commissioned officer in the navy or coast guard ranking above a lieutenant commander and below a captain — **com·mand·er·ship** \-,ship\ *n*

commander in chief (1564) **:** one who holds the supreme command of an armed force

com·mand·ery \kə-'man-d(ə-)rē\ *n, pl* **-er·ies** (15c) **1 :** a district under the control of a commander of an order of knights **2 :** an assembly or lodge in a secret order

com·mand·ing \kə-'man-diŋ\ *adj* (1591) **1 :** drawing attention or priority ⟨a ~ presence⟩ **2 :** difficult to overcome ⟨a ~ lead⟩ — **com·mand·ing·ly** \-diŋ-lē\ *adv*

commanding officer *n* (1720) **:** an officer in command; *esp* **:** an officer in the armed forces in command of an organization or installation

com·mand·ment \kə-'man(d)-mənt\ *n* (13c) **1 :** the act or power of commanding **2 :** something that is commanded; *specif* **:** one of the biblical Ten Commandments

command module *n* (1962) **:** a space vehicle module designed to carry the crew, the chief communication equipment, and the equipment for reentry

com·man·do \kə-'man-(')dō\ *n, pl* **-dos** *or* **-does** [Afrik *kommando*, fr. D *commando* command, fr. Sp *comando*, fr. *comandar* to command, fr. LL *commandare*] (1834) **1** *So Afr* **a :** a military unit or command of the Boers **b :** a raiding expedition **2 a :** a military unit trained and organized as shock troops esp. for hit-and-run raids into enemy territory **b :** a member of such a unit

command post *n* (ca. 1918) **:** a post at which the commander of a unit in the field receives orders and exercises command

command sergeant major *n* (1967) **:** a noncommissioned officer in the army ranking above a first sergeant

comma splice *n* (1924) **:** COMMA FAULT

com·me·dia del·l'ar·te \kə-mād-ē-ə-(,)del-'ärt-ē, -,med-\ *n* [It, lit., comedy of art] (1877) **:** Italian comedy of the 16th to 18th centuries improvised from standardized situations and stock characters

comme il faut \,kəm-ē(l)-'fō\ *adj* [F, lit., as it should be] (1756) **:** conforming to accepted standards **:** PROPER

com·mem·o·rate \kə-'mem-ə-,rāt\ *vt* **-rat·ed; -rat·ing** [L *commemoratus*, pp. of *commemorare*, fr. *com-* + *memorare* to remind of, fr. *memor* mindful — more at MEMORY] (1638) **1 :** to call to remembrance **2 :** to mark by some ceremony or observation **:** OBSERVE **3 :** to serve as a memorial of ⟨a plaque that ~*s* the battle⟩ ***syn*** see KEEP — **com·mem·o·ra·tor** \-,rāt-ər\ *n*

com·mem·o·ra·tion \kə-,mem-ə-'rā-shən\ *n* (14c) **1 :** the act of commemorating **2 :** something that commemorates

com·mem·o·ra·tive \kə-'mem-(ə-)rət-iv, -'mem-ə-,rāt-iv\ *adj* (1612) **:** intended as a commemoration **:** COMMEMORATING — **commemorative** *n* — **com·mem·o·ra·tive·ly** *adv*

com·mence \kə-'men(t)s\ *vb* **com·menced; com·menc·ing** [ME *comencen*, fr. MF *comencer*, fr. (assumed) VL *cominitiare*, fr. L *com-* + LL *initiare* to begin, fr. L, to initiate] *vt* (14c) **:** to enter upon **:** BEGIN ⟨~ proceedings⟩ ~ *vi* **1 :** to have or make a beginning **:** START **2** *chiefly Brit* **:** to begin to be or to act as **3** *chiefly Brit* **:** to take a degree at a university ***syn*** see BEGIN — **com·menc·er** *n*

com·mence·ment \kəm-'men(t)-smənt\ *n* (13c) **1 :** an act, instance, or time of commencing **2 a :** the ceremonies or the day for conferring degrees or diplomas **b :** the period of activities at this time

com·mend \kə-'mend\ *vb* [ME *commenden*, fr. L *commendare*, fr. *com-* + *mandare* to entrust — more at MANDATE] *vt* (14c) **1 :** to entrust for care or preservation **2 :** to recommend as worthy of confidence or notice **3 :** to mention with approbation **:** PRAISE ~ *vi* **:** to commend or serve as a commendation of something — **com·mend·able** \-'men-də-bəl\ *adj* — **com·mend·ably** \-blē\ *adv* — **com·mend·er** *n*

com·men·da·tion \,käm-ən-'dā-shən, -,en-\ *n* (14c) **1 a :** an act of commending **b :** something (as a formal citation) that commends **2** *archaic* **:** COMPLIMENT

com·men·da·to·ry \kə-'men-də-,tōr-ē, -,tȯr-\ *adj* (1555) **:** serving to commend

com·men·sal \kə-'men(t)-səl\ *adj* [ME, fr. ML *commensalis*, fr. L *com-* + LL *mensalis* of the table, fr. L *mensa* table] (1877) **:** of, relating to, or living in a state of commensalism — **commensal** *n* — **com·men·sal·ly** \-sə-lē\ *adv*

com·men·sal·ism \-sə-,liz-əm\ *n* (1870) **:** a relation between two kinds of organisms in which one obtains food or other benefits from the other without damaging or benefiting it

com·men·su·ra·ble \kə-'men(t)s(-ə)-rə-bəl, -'mench(-ə)-\ *adj* (1557) **1 :** having a common measure; *specif* **:** divisible by a common unit an integral number of times **2 :** COMMENSURATE 2 — **com·men·su·ra·bil·i·ty** \-,men(t)s(-ə)-rə-'bil-ət-ē, -,mench(-ə)-\ *n* — **com·men·su·ra·bly** \-'men(t)s(-ə)-rə-blē, -'mench(-ə)-\ *adv*

com·men·su·rate \kə-'men(t)s(-ə)-rət, -'mench(-ə)-\ *adj* [LL *commensuratus*, fr. L *com-* + LL *mensuratus*, pp. of *mensurare* to measure, fr. L *mensura* measure — more at MEASURE] (1641) **1 :** equal in measure or extent **:** COEXTENSIVE ⟨lived a life ~ with the early years of the republic⟩ **2 :** corresponding in size, extent, amount, or degree **:** PROPORTIONATE ⟨was given a job ~ with his abilities⟩ **3 :** COMMENSURABLE 1 — **com·men·su·rate·ly** *adv* — **com·men·su·ra·tion** \-,men(t)-sə-'rā-shən, -,men-chə-\ *n*

1**com·ment** \'käm-,ent\ *n* [ME, fr. LL *commentum*, fr. L, invention, fr. neut. of *commentus*, pp. of *comminisci* to invent, fr. *com-* + *-minisci* (akin to *ment-*, *mens* mind) — more at MIND] (14c) **1 :** COMMENTARY **2 :** a note explaining, illustrating, or criticizing the meaning of a writing **3 a :** an observation or remark expressing an opinion or attitude **b :** a judgment expressed indirectly ⟨this film is a ~ on current moral standards⟩

2**comment** *vt* (15c) **:** to make a comment on ⟨the discovery . . . is hardly ~*ed* by the press —*Nation*⟩ ~ *vi* **:** to explain or interpret something by comment ⟨~*ing* on recent developments⟩

com·men·tary \'käm-ən-,ter-ē\ *n, pl* **-tar·ies** (15c) **1 a :** an explanatory treatise — usu. used in pl. **b :** a record of events usu. written by a participant — usu. used in pl. **2 a :** a systematic series of explanations or interpretations (as of a writing) **b :** COMMENT 2 **3 a :** something that serves for illustration or explanation ⟨the dark, airless apartments and sunless factories . . . are a sad ~ upon our civilization —H. A. Overstreet⟩ **b :** an expression of opinion

com·men·tate \'käm-ən-,tāt\ *vb* **-tat·ed; -tat·ing** [back-formation fr. *commentator*] *vt* (1794) **:** to give a commentary on ~ *vi* **:** to comment in a usu. expository or interpretive manner; *also* **:** to act as a commentator

com·men·ta·tor \-,tāt-ər\ *n* (14c) **:** one who gives a commentary; *esp* **:** one who reports and discusses news on radio or television

1**com·merce** \'käm-(,)ərs\ *n* [MF, fr. L *commercium*, fr. *com-* + *merc-, merx* merchandise] (1537) **1 :** social intercourse **:** interchange of ideas, opinions, or sentiments **2 :** the exchange or buying and selling of commodities on a large scale involving transportation from place to place **3 :** SEXUAL INTERCOURSE ***syn*** see BUSINESS

2**com·merce** \'käm-(,)ərs, kə-'mərs\ *vi* **com·merced; com·merc·ing** *archaic* (1596) **:** COMMUNE

1**com·mer·cial** \kə-'mər-shəl\ *adj* (1598) **1 a (1) :** occupied with or engaged in commerce or work intended for commerce ⟨a ~ artist⟩ **(2) :** of or relating to commerce ⟨~ regulations⟩ **(3) :** characteristic of commerce ⟨~ weights⟩ **(4) :** suitable, adequate, or prepared for commerce ⟨found oil in ~ quantities⟩ **b (1) :** being of an average or inferior quality ⟨~ oxalic acid⟩ **(2) :** producing artistic work of low standards for quick market success **2 a :** viewed with regard to profit ⟨a

~ success⟩ **b :** designed for a large market **3 :** emphasizing skills and subjects useful in business **4 :** supported by advertisers ⟨~ TV⟩ — **com·mer·ci·al·i·ty** \kə-ˌmərsh(-ē)-ˈal-ət-ē\ *n* — **com·mer·cial·ly** \-ˈmərsh-(ə-)lē\ *adv*

²**commercial** *n* (1935) **:** an advertisement broadcast on radio or television

commercial bank *n* (1910) **:** a bank organized chiefly to handle the everyday financial transactions of businesses (as through demand deposit accounts and short-term commercial loans)

com·mer·cial·ism \kə-ˈmər-shə-ˌliz-əm\ *n* (1849) **1 :** commercial spirit, institutions, or methods **2 :** excessive emphasis on profit — **com·mer·cial·ist** \-ˈmərsh-(ə-)ləst\ *n* — **com·mer·cial·is·tic** \-ˌmər-shə-ˈlis-tik\ *adj*

com·mer·cial·ize \kə-ˈmər-shə-ˌlīz\ *vt* **-ized; -iz·ing** (1830) **1 a :** to manage on a business basis for profit **b :** to develop commerce in **2 :** to exploit for profit ⟨~ Christmas⟩ **3 :** to debase in quality for more profit — **com·mer·cial·iza·tion** \-ˌmərsh-(ə-)lə-ˈzā-shən\ *n*

commercial paper *n* (1836) **:** short-term unsecured discounted paper usu. sold by one company to another for immediate cash needs

commercial traveler *n* (1855) **:** TRAVELING SALESMAN

com·mie \ˈkäm-ē\ *n, often cap* [by shortening & alter.] (1940) **:** COMMUNIST

com·mi·na·tion \ˌkäm-ə-ˈnā-shən\ *n* [ME, fr. MF or L; MF, fr. L *commination-, comminatio,* fr. *comminatus,* pp. of *comminari* to threaten, fr. *com-* + *minari* to threaten] (15c) **:** DENUNCIATION — **com·mi·na·to·ry** \ˈkäm-ə-nə-ˌtōr-ē, -ˌtȯr-; kə-ˈmin-ə-, -ˈmīn-\ *adj*

com·min·gle \kə-ˈmiŋ-gəl, kä-\ *vt* (1626) **1 :** to blend thoroughly into a harmonious whole **2 :** to combine (funds or properties) into a common fund or stock ⟨~ accounts⟩ ~ *vi* **:** to become commingled ***syn*** see MIX

com·mi·nute \ˈkäm-ə-ˌn(y)üt\ *vt* **-nut·ed; -nut·ing** [L *comminutus,* pp. of *comminuere,* fr. *com-* + *minuere* to lessen — more at MINOR] (1626) **:** to reduce to minute particles **:** PULVERIZE — **com·mi·nu·tion** \ˌkäm-ə-ˈn(y)ü-shən\ *n*

com·mis·er·ate \kə-ˈmiz-ə-ˌrāt\ *vb* **-at·ed; -at·ing** [L *commiseratus,* pp. of *commiserari,* fr. *com-* + *miserari* to pity, fr. *miser* wretched] *vt* (1605) **:** to feel or express sorrow or compassion for ~ *vi* **:** to feel or express sympathy **:** CONDOLE ⟨~*s* with them on their loss⟩ — **com·mis·er·at·ing·ly** *adv* — **com·mis·er·a·tive** \-ˈmiz-ə-ˌrāt-iv\ *adj*

com·mis·er·a·tion \-ˌmiz-ə-ˈrā-shən\ *n* (1585) **:** the act of commiserating

com·mis·sar \ˈkäm-ə-ˌsär\ *n* [Russ *komissar,* fr. G *kommissar,* fr. ML *commissarius*] (1918) **1 a :** a Communist party official assigned to a military unit to teach party principles and policies and to ensure party loyalty **b :** one that attempts to control public opinion or its expression **2 :** the head of a government department in the U.S.S.R. until 1946 — **com·mis·sar·i·al** \ˌkäm-ə-ˈsär-ē-əl, -ˈser-\ *adj*

com·mis·sar·i·at \ˌkäm-ə-ˈser-ē-ət, -ˈsar-, *esp for 3* -ˈsär-\ *n* [NL *commissariatus,* fr. ML *commissarius*] (1779) **1 :** a system for supplying an army with food **2 :** food supplies **3** [Russ *komissariat,* fr. G *kommissariat,* fr. NL *commissariatus*] **:** a government department in the U.S.S.R. until 1946

com·mis·sary \ˈkäm-ə-ˌser-ē\ *n, pl* **-sar·ies** [ME *commissarie,* fr. ML *commissarius,* fr. L *commissus,* pp.] (14c) **1 :** one delegated by a superior to execute a duty or an office **2 a :** a store for equipment and provisions; *esp* **:** a supermarket operated for military personnel **b :** food supplies **c :** a lunchroom esp. in a motion-picture studio

¹**com·mis·sion** \kə-ˈmish-ən\ *n* [ME, fr. MF, fr. L *commission-, commissio* act of bringing together, fr. *commissus,* pp. of *committere*] (14c) **1 a :** a formal written warrant granting the power to perform various acts or duties **b :** a certificate conferring military rank and authority; *also* **:** the rank and authority so conferred **2 :** an authorization or command to act in a prescribed manner or to perform prescribed acts **:** CHARGE **3 a :** authority to act for, in behalf of, or in place of another **b :** a task or matter entrusted to one as an agent for another **4 a :** a group of persons directed to perform some duty **b :** a government agency having administrative, legislative, or judicial powers **c :** a city council having legislative and executive functions **5 :** an act of committing something **6 :** a fee paid to an agent or employee for transacting a piece of business or performing a service; *esp* **:** a percentage of the money received from a total paid to the agent responsible for the business **7 :** an act of entrusting or giving authority — **in commission** *or* **into commission 1 :** under the authority of commissioners **2** *of a ship* **:** ready for active service **3 :** in use or in condition for use — **on commission :** with commission serving as partial or full pay for work done — **out of commission 1 :** out of active service or use **2 :** out of working order

²**commission** *vt* **com·mis·sioned; com·mis·sion·ing** \-ˈmish-(ə-)niŋ\ (15c) **1 :** to furnish with a commission: as **a :** to confer a formal commission on ⟨was ~*ed* lieutenant⟩ **b :** to appoint or assign to a task or function ⟨the writer who was ~*ed* to do the biography⟩ **2 :** to order to be made ⟨wealthy persons who ~*ed* portraits of themselves⟩ **3 :** to put (a ship) in commission

com·mis·sion·aire \kə-ˌmish-ə-ˈna(ə)r, -ˈne(ə)r\ *n* [F *commissionnaire,* fr. *commission*] *chiefly Brit* (1765) **:** a uniformed attendant

commissioned officer *n* (15c) **:** an officer of the armed forces holding by a commission a rank of second lieutenant or ensign or above

com·mis·sion·er \kə-ˈmish-(ə-)nər\ *n* (15c) **:** a person with a commission: as **a :** a member of a commission **b :** the representative of the governmental authority in a district, province, or other unit often having both judicial and administrative powers **c :** the officer in charge of a department or bureau of the public service **d :** the administrative head of a professional sport — **com·mis·sion·er·ship** \-ˌship\ *n*

commission merchant *n* (1796) **:** BROKER 1b

commission plan *n* (1919) **:** a method of municipal government under which a small elective commission exercises both executive and legislative powers and each commissioner directly administers one or more municipal departments

com·mis·sure \ˈkäm-ə-ˌshu̇(ə)r\ *n* [ME, fr. MF or L; MF, fr. L *commissura* a joining, fr. *commissus,* pp.] (15c) **1 :** a point or line of union or junction esp. between two anatomical parts (as adjacent heart valves) **2 :** a connecting band of nerve tissue in the brain or spinal cord — **com·mis·sur·al** \ˌkäm-ə-ˈshu̇r-əl\ *adj*

com·mit \kə-ˈmit\ *vb* **com·mit·ted; com·mit·ting** [ME *committen,* fr. L *committere* to connect, entrust, fr. *com-* + *mittere* to send] *vt* (14c) **1 a :** to put into charge or trust **:** ENTRUST **b :** to place in a prison or mental institution **c :** to consign or record for preservation ⟨~ it to memory⟩ **d :** to put into a place for disposal or safekeeping **e :** to refer (as a legislative bill) to a committee for consideration and report **2 :** to carry into action deliberately **:** PERPETRATE ⟨~ a crime⟩ **3 a :** OBLIGATE, BIND **b :** to pledge or assign to some particular course or use ⟨all available troops were *committed* to the attack⟩ **c :** to reveal the views of ⟨refused to ~ himself on the issue⟩ ~ *vi* **1** *obs* **:** to perpetrate an offense **2 :** to obligate or pledge oneself — **com·mit·ta·ble** \-ˈmit-ə-bəl\ *adj*

syn COMMIT, ENTRUST, CONFIDE, CONSIGN, RELEGATE mean to assign to a person or place esp. for safekeeping. COMMIT may express the general idea of delivering into another's charge or the special sense of transferring to a superior power or to a special place of custody; ENTRUST implies committing with trust and confidence; CONFIDE implies entrusting with assurance or reliance; CONSIGN suggests transferring to remove from one's control with formality or finality; RELEGATE implies a consigning to a particular class or sphere often with a suggestion of getting rid of.

com·mit·ment \kə-ˈmit-mənt\ *n* (1621) **1 a :** an act of committing to a charge or trust: as **(1) :** a consignment to a penal or mental institution **(2) :** an act of referring a matter to a legislative committee **b :** MITTIMUS **2 a :** an agreement or pledge to do something in the future; *esp* **:** an engagement to assume a financial obligation at a future date **b :** something pledged **c :** the state of being obligated or emotionally impelled ⟨a ~ to a cause⟩

com·mit·tal \kə-ˈmit-ᵊl\ *n* (1818) **:** COMMITMENT, CONSIGNMENT

com·mit·tee \kə-ˈmit-ē, *sense 1 also* ˌkäm-ə-ˈtē\ *n* (15c) **1** *archaic* **:** a person to whom a charge or trust is committed **2 a :** a body of persons delegated to consider, investigate, take action on, or report on some matter; *esp* **:** a group of fellow legislators chosen by a legislative body to give consideration to legislative matters **b :** a self-constituted organization for the promotion of a common object

com·mit·tee·man \kə-ˈmit-ē-mən, -ˌman\ *n* (1654) **1 :** a member of a committee **2 :** a party leader of a ward or precinct

committee of the whole (1753) **:** the whole membership of a legislative house sitting as a committee and operating under informal rules

com·mit·tee·wom·an \-ˌwu̇m-ən\ *n* (1847) **1 :** a female member of a committee **2 :** a female party leader of a ward or precinct

com·mix \kə-ˈmiks, kä-\ *vb* [back-formation fr. ME *comixt* blended, fr. L *commixtus,* pp. of *commiscēre* to mix together, fr. *com-* + *miscēre* to mix — more at MIX] *vt* (15c) **:** MINGLE, BLEND ~ *vi* **:** to become mingled or blended

com·mix·ture \-chər\ *n* [L *commixtura,* fr. *commixtus*] (1592) **1 :** the act or process of mixing **:** the state of being mixed **2 :** COMPOUND, MIXTURE

com·mode \kə-ˈmōd\ *n* [F, fr. *commode,* adj., suitable, convenient, fr. L *commodus,* fr. *com-* + *modus* measure — more at METE] (1688) **1 :** a woman's ornate cap popular in the late 17th and early 18th centuries **2 a :** a low chest of drawers **b :** a movable washstand with a cupboard underneath **c :** a boxlike structure holding a chamber pot under an open seat; *also* **:** CHAMBER POT **d :** TOILET 3b

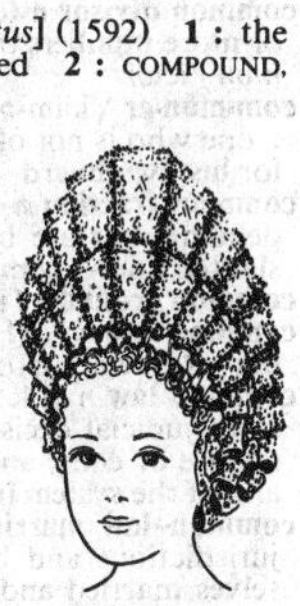

commode 1

com·mo·di·ous \kə-ˈmōd-ē-əs\ *adj* [ME, useful, fr. MF *commodieux,* fr. ML *commodiosus,* irreg. fr. L *commodum* convenience, fr. neut. of *commodus*] (15c) **1 :** comfortably or conveniently spacious **:** ROOMY ⟨a ~ closet⟩ **2** *archaic* **:** HANDY, SERVICEABLE ***syn*** see SPACIOUS — **com·mo·di·ous·ly** *adv* — **com·mo·di·ous·ness** *n*

com·mod·i·ty \kə-ˈmäd-ət-ē\ *n, pl* **-ties** [ME *commoditee,* fr. MF *commodité,* fr. L *commoditat-, commoditas,* fr. *commodus*] (15c) **1 :** an economic good: as **a :** a product of agriculture or mining **b :** an article of commerce esp. when delivered for shipment ⟨*commodities* futures⟩ **2 a :** something useful or valuable **b :** CONVENIENCE, ADVANTAGE **3** *obs* **:** QUANTITY, LOT

com·mo·dore \ˈkäm-ə-ˌdō(ə)r, -ˌdȯ(ə)r\ *n* [prob. modif. of D *commandeur* commander, fr. F, fr. OF *comandeor,* fr. *comander* to command] (1695) **1 a :** a former captain in the navy in command of a squadron **b :** a commissioned officer in the navy ranking above captain and below rear admiral and having an insignia of one star **2 :** the ranking officer commanding a body of merchant ships **3 :** the chief officer of a yacht club or boating association

¹**com·mon** \ˈkäm-ən\ *adj* [ME *commun,* fr. OF, fr. L *communis* — more at MEAN] (13c) **1 a :** of or relating to a community at large **:** PUBLIC ⟨work for the ~ good⟩ **b :** known to the community ⟨~ nuisances⟩ **2 a :** belonging to or shared by two or more individuals or by all members of a group ⟨buried in a ~ grave⟩ **b :** belonging equally to two or more mathematical entities ⟨triangles with a ~ base⟩ **c :** having two or more branches ⟨~ carotid artery⟩ **3 a :** occurring or appearing frequently **:** FAMILIAR ⟨a ~ sight⟩ **b :** of the best known kind **c :** VERNACULAR 2 ⟨~ names⟩ **4 a :** WIDESPREAD, GENERAL ⟨~ knowledge⟩ **b :** characterized by a lack of privilege or special status ⟨~ people⟩ **c :** just satisfying accustomed criteria **:** ELEMENTARY ⟨~ decency⟩ **5 a :** falling below ordinary standards **:** SECOND-RATE **b :** lacking refinement **:** COARSE ⟨~ manners⟩ **6 a :** either masculine or feminine in gender **b :** denoting relations by a single case form that in a more highly inflected language might be denoted by two or more different case forms **7 :** of, relating to, or being common stock — **com·mon·ly** *adv* — **com·mon·ness** \-ən-nəs\ *n*

syn COMMON, ORDINARY, PLAIN, FAMILIAR, POPULAR, VULGAR mean generally met with and not in any way special, strange, or unusual. COMMON implies usual everyday quality or frequency of occurrence ⟨a *common* error⟩ ⟨lacked *common* honesty⟩ and may additionally suggest inferiority or coarseness ⟨O hard is the bed . . . and *common* the blanket and cheap —A. E. Housman⟩ ORDINARY stresses conformance in quality or kind with the regular order of things ⟨an *ordinary* pleasant summer day⟩ ⟨a very *ordinary* sort of man⟩ PLAIN is likely to suggest homely simplicity ⟨the *plain* people everywhere . . . wish to live in peace — F. D. Roosevelt⟩ FAMILIAR stresses the fact of being generally known and easily recognized ⟨a *familiar* melody⟩ POPULAR applies to what is accepted by or prevalent among people in general sometimes in contrast to upper classes or special groups ⟨a *popular* tune⟩ VULGAR, otherwise similar to POPULAR, is likely to carry derogatory connotations (as of inferiority or coarseness) ⟨goods designed to appeal to the *vulgar* taste⟩

²**common** *n* (14c) **1** *pl* **:** the common people **2** *pl but sing in constr* **:** a dining hall **3** *pl but sing or pl in constr, often cap* **a :** the political group or estate comprising the commoners **b :** the parliamentary representatives of the commoners **c :** HOUSE OF COMMONS **4 :** the legal right of taking a profit in another's land in common with the owner **5 :** a piece of land subject to common use: as **a :** undivided land used esp. for pasture **b :** a public open area in a municipality **6 a :** a religious service suitable for any of various festivals **b :** the ordinary of the Mass **7 :** COMMON STOCK — **in common :** shared together

com·mon·age \'käm-ə-nij\ *n* (1649) **1 :** community land **2 :** COMMONALTY 1a(2)

com·mon·al·i·ty \ˌkäm-ə-'nal-ət-ē\ *n, pl* **-ties** [ME *communalitie,* alter. of *communalte*] (14c) **1 :** the common people **2 a :** possession of common features or attributes **:** COMMONNESS **b :** a common feature or attribute

com·mon·al·ty \'käm-ən-ᵊl-tē\ *n, pl* **-ties** [ME *communalte,* fr. MF *comunalté,* fr. *comunal* communal] (14c) **1 a** (1) **:** the common people (2) **:** the political estate formed by the common people **b :** a usage or practice common to members of a group **2 :** a general group or body

common carrier *n* (15c) **:** an individual or corporation undertaking to transport for compensation persons, goods, or messages

common cattle grub *n* (1942) **:** a cattle grub (*Hypoderma lineatum*) which is found throughout the U.S. and whose larva is particularly destructive to cattle

common chord *n* (1864) **:** TRIAD 2

common cold *n* (1786) **:** an acute virus disease of the upper respiratory tract marked by inflammation of mucous membranes

common denominator *n* (1594) **1 :** a common multiple of the denominators of a number of fractions **2 :** a common trait or theme

common difference *n* (ca. 1891) **:** the difference between two consecutive terms of an arithmetic progression

common divisor *n* (ca. 1847) **:** a number or expression that divides two or more numbers or expressions without remainder — called also *common factor*

com·mon·er \'käm-ə-nər\ *n* (14c) **1 a :** one of the common people **b :** one who is not of noble rank **2 :** a student (as at Oxford) who pays for his own board

common fraction *n* (ca. 1891) **:** a fraction in which the numerator and denominator are both integers and are separated by a horizontal or slanted line — compare DECIMAL FRACTION

common ground *n* (1926) **:** a basis of mutual interest or understanding

common–law *adj* (1848) **1 :** of, relating to, or based on the common law **2 :** relating to or based on a common-law marriage

common law *n* (14c) **:** the body of law developed in England primarily from judicial decisions based on custom and precedent, unwritten in statute or code, and constituting the basis of the English legal system and of the system in all of the U.S. except Louisiana

common–law marriage *n* (1900) **1 :** a marriage recognized in some jurisdictions and based on the parties' agreement to consider themselves married and sometimes also on their cohabitation **2 :** the cohabitation of a couple even when it does not constitute a legal marriage

common logarithm *n* (ca. 1891) **:** a logarithm whose base is 10

common market *n* (1952) **:** an economic unit formed to remove trade barriers among its members

common measure *n* (1718) **:** a meter consisting chiefly of iambic lines of 7 accents each arranged in rhymed pairs usu. printed in 4-line stanzas — called also *common meter*

common multiple *n* (ca. 1890) **:** a multiple of each of two or more numbers or expressions

common noun *n* (ca. 1864) **:** a noun that may occur with limiting modifiers (as *a* or *an, some, every,* and *my*) and that designates any one of a class of beings or things

¹**com·mon·place** \'käm-ən-ˌplās\ *n* [trans. of L *locus communis* widely applicable argument, trans. of Gk *koinos topos*] (1561) **1** *archaic* **:** a striking passage entered in a commonplace book **2 a :** an obvious or trite observation **b :** something commonly found

²**commonplace** *adj* (1609) **:** commonly found **:** ORDINARY, UNREMARKABLE — **com·mon·place·ness** *n*

commonplace book *n* (1578) **:** a book of memorabilia

common pleas *n pl* (15c) **1 a :** actions over which the English crown did not claim exclusive jurisdiction **b :** civil actions between English subjects **2** *sing in constr* **:** COURT OF COMMON PLEAS

common ratio *n* (1875) **:** the ratio of each term of a geometric progression to the term preceding it

common room *n* (1683) **1 :** a lounge available to all members of a residential community **2 :** a room in a college for the use of the faculty

common salt *n* (1676) **:** SALT 1a

common school *n* (1656) **:** a free public school

common sense *n* (1535) **1 :** the unreflective opinions of ordinary men **2 :** sound and prudent but often unsophisticated judgment ***syn*** see SENSE — **com·mon·sense** \ˌkäm-ən-ˌsen(t)s\ *adj* — **com·mon·sen·si·ble** \-'sen(t)-sə-bəl\ *adj* — **com·mon·sen·si·bly** \-blē\ *adv* — **com·mon·sen·si·cal** \- 'sen(t)-si-kəl\ *adj*

common situs picketing *n* (1965) **:** the picketing of an entire construction site by a trade union having a grievance with only a single subcontractor working there

common stock *n* (1888) **:** capital stock other than preferred stock

common time *n* (1674) **:** a musical tempo marked by four beats per measure with the quarter note receiving a single beat

common touch *n* (1944) **:** the gift of appealing to or arousing the sympathetic interest of the common people

com·mon·weal \'käm-ən-ˌwēl\ *n* (14c) **1** *archaic* **:** COMMONWEALTH **2 :** the general welfare

com·mon·wealth \-ˌwelth *also* -ˌweltth\ *n* (15c) **1** *archaic* **:** COMMONWEAL 2 **2 :** a nation, state, or other political unit: as **a :** one founded on law and united by compact or tacit agreement of the people for the common good **b :** one in which supreme authority is vested in the people **c :** REPUBLIC **3** *cap* **a :** the English state from the death of Charles I in 1649 to the Restoration in 1660 **b :** PROTECTORATE 1b **4 :** a state of the U.S. — used officially of Kentucky, Massachusetts, Pennsylvania, and Virginia **5** *cap* **:** a federal union of constituent states — used officially of Australia **6** *often cap* **:** an association of self-governing autonomous states more or less loosely associated in a common allegiance (as to the British crown) **7** *often cap* **:** a political unit having local autonomy but voluntarily united with the U.S. — used officially of Puerto Rico and of the Northern Mariana islands

Commonwealth Day *n* (1958) **:** May 24 observed in parts of the British Commonwealth as the anniversary of Queen Victoria's birthday

common year *n* (ca. 1909) **:** a calendar year containing no intercalary period

com·mo·tion \kə-'mō-shən\ *n* [ME, fr. MF, fr. L *commotion-, commotio,* fr. *commotus,* pp. of *commovēre*] (15c) **1 :** a condition of civil unrest or insurrection **2 :** steady or recurrent motion **3 :** mental excitement or confusion **4 a :** an agitated disturbance **:** TO-DO **b :** noisy confusion **:** AGITATION

com·move \kə-'müv, kä-\ *vt* **com·moved; com·mov·ing** [ME *commoeven,* fr. MF *commuev-,* pres. stem of *commovoir,* fr. L *commovēre,* fr. *com-* + *movēre* to move] (14c) **1 :** to move violently **:** AGITATE **2 :** to rouse intense feeling in **:** excite to passion

com·mu·nal \kə-'myün-ᵊl, 'käm-yən-ᵊl\ *adj* [F, fr. LL *communalis,* fr. L *communis*] (1811) **1 :** of or relating to one or more communes **2 :** of or relating to a community **3 a :** characterized by collective ownership and use of property **b :** participated in, shared, or used in common by members of a group or community **4 :** of, relating to, or based on racial or cultural groups — **com·mu·nal·ly** \-ē\ *adv*

com·mu·nal·ism \-ᵊl-ˌiz-əm\ *n* (1871) **1 :** social organization on a communal basis **2 :** loyalty to a sociopolitical grouping based on religious or ethnic affiliation — **com·mu·nal·ist** \-ᵊl-əst\ *n or adj*

com·mu·nal·i·ty \ˌkäm-yu̇-'nal-ət-ē\ *n, pl* **-ties** (1901) **1 :** communal state or character **2 :** a feeling of group solidarity

com·mu·nal·ize \kə-'myün-ᵊl-ˌīz, 'käm-yən-\ *vt* **-ized; -iz·ing** (1881) **:** to make communal

com·mu·nard \ˌkäm-yu̇-'När(d)\ *n* [F] (1874) **1** *cap* **:** one who supported or participated in the Commune of Paris in 1871 **2 :** a person who lives in a commune

¹**com·mune** \kə-'myün\ *vb* **com·muned; com·mun·ing** [ME *communen* to converse, administer Communion, fr. MF *comunier* to converse, administer or receive Communion, fr. LL *communicare,* fr. L] *vt, obs* (15c) **:** to talk over **:** DISCUSS ⟨have more to ~ — Shak.⟩ ~ *vi* **1 :** to receive Communion **2 :** to communicate intimately ⟨~ with nature⟩

²**com·mune** \'käm-ˌyün; kə-'myün, kä-\ *n* [F, alter. of MF *comugne,* fr. ML *communia,* fr. L, neut. pl. of *communis*] (1673) **1 :** the smallest administrative district of many countries esp. in Europe **2 :** COMMONALTY 1a **3 :** COMMUNITY: as **a :** a medieval usu. municipal corporation **b** (1)**:** MIR (2)**:** an often rural community organized on a communal basis

com·mu·ni·ca·ble \kə-'myü-ni-kə-bəl\ *adj* (14c) **1 :** capable of being communicated **:** TRANSMITTABLE ⟨~ disease⟩ **2 :** COMMUNICATIVE — **com·mu·ni·ca·bil·i·ty** \-ˌmyü-ni-kə-'bil-ət-ē\ *n* — **com·mu·ni·ca·ble·ness** \-'myü-ni-kə-bəl-nəs\ *n* — **com·mu·ni·ca·bly** \-blē\ *adv*

com·mu·ni·cant \-'myü-ni-kənt\ *n* (1552) **1 :** a church member entitled to receive Communion; *broadly* **:** a member of a fellowship **2 :** one that communicates; *specif* **:** INFORMANT — **communicant** *adj*

com·mu·ni·cate \kə-'myü-nə-ˌkāt\ *vb* **-cat·ed; -cat·ing** [L *communicatus,* pp. of *communicare* to impart, participate, fr. *communis* common — more at MEAN] *vt* (1526) **1** *archaic* **:** SHARE **2 a :** to convey knowledge of or information about **:** make known ⟨~ a story⟩ **b :** to reveal by clear signs ⟨his fear *communicated* itself to his friends⟩ **3 :** to cause to pass from one to another ⟨some diseases are easily *communicated*⟩ ~ *vi* **1 :** to receive Communion **2 :** to transmit information, thought, or feeling so that it is satisfactorily received or understood **3 :** to open into each other **:** CONNECT ⟨the rooms ~⟩ — **com·mu·ni·ca·tee** \-ˌmyü-ni-kə-'tē\ *n* — **communicator** \-'myü-nə-ˌkāt-ər\ *n*

com·mu·ni·ca·tion \kə-ˌmyü-nə-'kā-shən\ *n* (14c) **1 :** an act or instance of transmitting **2 a :** information communicated **b :** a verbal or written message **3 a :** a process by which information is exchanged between individuals through a common system of symbols, signs, or behavior ⟨the function of pheromones in insect ~⟩; *also* **:** exchange of information **b :** personal rapport ⟨a lack of ~ between old and young persons⟩ **4** *pl* **a :** a system (as of telephones) for communicating **b :** a system of routes for moving troops, supplies, and vehicles **c :** personnel engaged in communicating **5** *pl but sing or pl in constr* **a :** a technique for expressing ideas effectively (as in speech) **b :** the technology of the transmission of information (as by the printed word or telecommunication) — **com·mu·ni·ca·tion·al** \-shnəl, -shən-ᵊl\ *adj*

com·mu·ni·ca·tive \kə-'myü-nə-ˌkāt-iv, -ni-kət-iv\ *adj* (1654) **1 :** tending to communicate **:** TALKATIVE **2 :** of or relating to communication — **com·mu·ni·ca·tive·ly** *adv* — **com·mu·ni·ca·tive·ness** *n*

com·mu·ni·ca·to·ry \kə-'myü-ni-kə-ˌtōr-ē, -ˌtȯr-\ *adj* (1646) **1 :** designed to communicate information ⟨~ letters⟩ **2 :** COMMUNICATIVE 2

com·mu·nion \kə-'myü-nyən\ *n* [ME, fr. L *communion-, communio* mutual participation, fr. *communis*] (14c) **1 :** an act or instance of sharing **2 a** *cap* **:** a Christian sacrament in which bread and wine are partaken of as a commemoration of the death of Christ **b :** the act of receiving the sacrament **c** *cap* **:** the part of the Mass in which the sacrament is received **d** *cap* **:** a variable verse of Scripture traditionally said or sung at mass during the people's communion — called also *Communion Verse* **3 :** intimate fellowship or rapport **:** COMMUNICATION **4 :** a body of Christians having a common faith and discipline ⟨the Anglican ~⟩

Communion Sunday *n* (1878) **:** a Sunday (as the first Sunday of the month) on which a Protestant church regularly holds a Communion service

com·mu·ni·qué \kə-'myü-nə-ˌkā, -ˌmyü-nə-'\ *n* [F, fr. pp. of *communiquer* to communicate, fr. L *communicare*] (1852) **:** BULLETIN 1

com·mu·nism \ˈkäm-yə-ˌniz-əm\ *n* [F *communisme,* fr. *commun* common] (1840) **1 a :** a theory advocating elimination of private property **b :** a system in which goods are owned in common and are available to all as needed **2** *cap* **a :** a doctrine based on revolutionary Marxian socialism and Marxism-Leninism that is the official ideology of the U.S.S.R. **b :** a totalitarian system of government in which a single authoritarian party controls state-owned means of production with the professed aim of establishing a stateless society **c :** a final stage of society in Marxist theory in which the state has withered away and economic goods are distributed equitably

com·mu·nist \ˈkäm-yə-nəst\ *n* (1840) **1 :** an adherent or advocate of communism **2** *cap* **:** COMMUNARD **3 a** *cap* **:** a member of a Communist party or movement **b** *often cap* **:** an adherent or advocate of a Communist government, party, or movement **4** *often cap* **:** one held to engage in left-wing, subversive, or revolutionary activities — **communist** *adj, often cap* — **com·mu·nis·tic** \ˌkäm-yə-ˈnis-tik\ *adj, often cap* — **com·mu·nis·ti·cal·ly** \-ti-k(ə-)lē\ *adv*

com·mu·ni·tar·i·an \kə-ˌmyü-nə-ˈter-ē-ən\ *adj* (ca. 1909) **:** of or relating to social organization in small cooperative partially collectivist communities — **communitarian** *n* — **com·mu·ni·tar·i·an·ism** \-ē-ə-ˌniz-əm\ *n*

com·mu·ni·ty \kə-ˈmyü-nət-ē\ *n, pl* **-ties** [ME *comunete,* fr. MF *comuneté,* fr. L *communitat-, communitas,* fr. *communis*] (14c) **1 :** a unified body of individuals: as **a :** STATE, COMMONWEALTH **b :** the people with common interests living in a particular area; *broadly* **:** the area itself ⟨the problems of a large ~⟩ **c :** an interacting population of various kinds of individuals (as species) in a common location **d :** a group of people with a common characteristic or interest living together within a larger society ⟨a ~ of retired persons⟩ **e :** a group linked by a common policy **f :** a body of persons or nations having a common history or common social, economic, and political interests ⟨the international ~⟩ **g :** a body of persons of common and esp. professional interests scattered through a larger society ⟨the academic ~⟩ **2 :** society at large **3 a :** joint ownership or participation ⟨~ of goods⟩ **b :** common character **:** LIKENESS ⟨~ of interests⟩ **c :** social activity **:** FELLOWSHIP **d :** a social state or condition

community antenna television *n* (1953) **:** CABLE TELEVISION

community center *n* (1915) **:** a building or group of buildings for a community's educational and recreational activities

community chest *n* (1919) **:** a general fund accumulated from individual subscriptions to defray demands on a community for charity and social welfare

community college *n* (1948) **:** a nonresidential 2-year college that is usu. government-supported

community property *n* (ca. 1925) **:** property held jointly by husband and wife

com·mu·nize \ˈkäm-yə-ˌnīz\ *vt* **-nized; -niz·ing** [back-formation fr. *communization*] (1888) **1 a :** to make common **b :** to make into state-owned property **2 :** to subject to Communist principles of organization — **com·mu·ni·za·tion** \ˌkäm-yə-nə-ˈzā-shən\ *n*

com·mu·tate \ˈkäm-yə-ˌtāt\ *vt* **-tat·ed; -tat·ing** [back-formation fr. *commutation*] (1890) **:** to reverse every other half cycle of (an alternating current) so as to form a unidirectional current

com·mu·ta·tion \ˌkäm-yə-ˈtā-shən\ *n* [ME, fr. MF, fr. L *commutation-, commutatio,* fr. *commutatus,* pp. of *commutare*] (15c) **1 :** EXCHANGE, TRADE **2 :** REPLACEMENT; *specif* **:** a substitution of one form of payment or charge for another **3 :** a change of a legal penalty or punishment to a lesser one **4 :** an act or process of commuting **5 :** the action of commutating

commutation ticket *n* (1848) **:** a transportation ticket sold for a fixed number of trips over the same route during a limited period

com·mu·ta·tive \ˈkäm-yə-ˌtāt-iv, kə-ˈmyüt-ət-\ *adj* (ca. 1755) **1 :** of, relating to, or showing commutation **2 :** of, relating to, or characterized by the combination of elements of a given set under a specified operation in such a manner that the result is independent of the order in which the elements are taken ⟨a ~ group⟩ ⟨addition of the positive integers is ~⟩

com·mu·ta·tiv·i·ty \kə-ˌmyüt-ə-ˈtiv-ət-ē, ˌkäm-yə-tə-\ *n* (1929) **:** the property of being commutative ⟨the ~ of a mathematical operation⟩

com·mu·ta·tor \ˈkäm-yə-ˌtāt-ər\ *n* (1839) **1 :** a switch for reversing the direction of an electric current **2 :** a series of bars or segments so connected to armature coils of a dynamo that rotation of the armature will in conjunction with fixed brushes result in unidirectional current output in the case of a generator and in the reversal of the current into the coils in the case of a motor **3 :** an element of a mathematical group that when multiplied by the product of two given elements yields the product of the elements in reverse order

[1]**com·mute** \kə-ˈmyüt\ *vb* **com·mut·ed; com·mut·ing** [L *commutare* to change, exchange, fr. *com-* + *mutare* to change — more at MISS] *vt* (15c) **1 a :** CHANGE, ALTER **b :** to give in exchange for another **:** EXCHANGE **2 :** to convert (as a payment) into another form **3 :** to exchange (a penalty) for another less severe **4 :** COMMUTATE ~ *vi* **1 :** to make up **:** COMPENSATE **2 :** to pay in gross **3 :** to travel back and forth regularly (as between a suburb and a city) **4 :** to yield the same mathematical result regardless of order — used of two elements undergoing an operation or of two operations on elements — **com·mut·able** \-ˈmyüt-ə-bəl\ *adj*

[2]**commute** *n* (1954) **:** a trip made in commuting

com·mut·er \kə-ˈmyüt-ər\ *n* (ca. 1864) **1 :** a person who commutes (as between a suburb and a city) **2 :** a small airline that carries passengers relatively short distances on a regular schedule

co·mo·no·mer \(ˌ)kō-ˈmän-ə-mər, -ˈmō-nə-\ *n* [*co-* + *monomer*] (1945) **:** one of the constituents of a copolymer

[1]**comp** \ˈkämp\ *n* [short for *complimentary*] (1887) **:** a complimentary ticket; *broadly* **:** something provided free of charge

[2]**comp** \ˈkämp, ˈkəmp\ *vi* [short for *accompany*] (1949) **:** to punctuate and support a jazz solo with irregularly spaced chords

[1]**com·pact** \kəm-ˈpakt, käm-ˈ, ˈkäm-ˌ\ *adj* [ME, firmly put together, fr. L *compactus,* fr. pp. of *compingere* to put together, fr. *com-* + *pangere* to fasten — more at PACT] (14c) **1 :** predominantly formed or filled **:** COMPOSED, MADE **2 a :** having parts or units closely packed or joined ⟨a ~ woolen⟩ **b :** not diffuse or verbose ⟨a ~ statement⟩ **c :** occupying a small volume by reason of efficient use of space ⟨a ~ camera⟩ ⟨a ~ formation of troops⟩ **d :** short-bodied, solid, and without excess flesh **3 :** being a metric space with the property that for any collection of open sets which contains it there is a subset of the collection with a finite number of elements which also contains it — **com·pact·ly** *adv* — **com·pact·ness** *n*

[2]**compact** *vt* (15c) **1 :** to make up by connecting or combining **:** COMPOSE **2 a :** to knit or draw together **:** COMBINE **b :** to press together **:** COMPRESS ~ *vi* **:** to become compacted — **com·pact·ible** \-ˈpak-tə-bəl, -ˌpak-\ *adj* — **com·pac·tor** *also* **com·pact·er** \-ˈpak-tər, -ˌpak-\ *n*

[3]**com·pact** \ˈkäm-ˌpakt\ *n* (1601) **:** something that is compact or compacted: **a :** a small cosmetic case (as for compressed powder) **b :** an automobile smaller than an intermediate but larger than a subcompact

[4]**com·pact** \ˈkäm-ˌpakt\ *n* [L *compactum,* fr. neut. of *compactus,* pp. of *compacisci* to make an agreement, fr. *com-* + *pacisci* to contract — more at PACT] (1591) **:** an agreement or covenant between two or more parties

compact disc *n* (1980) **:** a small plastic optical disc usu. containing recorded music

com·pac·tion \kəm-ˈpak-shən, käm-\ *n* (14c) **:** the act or process of compacting **:** the state of being compacted

[1]**com·pan·ion** \kəm-ˈpan-yən\ *n* [ME *compainoun,* fr. OF *compagnon,* fr. LL *companion-, companio,* fr. L *com-* + *panis* bread, food — more at FOOD] (13c) **1 :** one that accompanies another **:** COMRADE, ASSOCIATE **2** *obs* **:** RASCAL **3 a :** one that is closely connected with something similar **b :** one employed to live with and serve another

[2]**companion** *vt* (1622) **:** ACCOMPANY ~ *vi* **:** to keep company

[3]**companion** *n* [by folk etymology fr. D *kampanje* poop deck] (1762) **1 :** a hood covering at the top of a companionway **2 :** COMPANIONWAY

com·pan·ion·able \kəm-ˈpan-yə-nə-bəl\ *adj* (14c) **:** marked by, conducive to, or suggestive of companionship **:** SOCIABLE — **com·pan·ion·able·ness** *n* — **com·pan·ion·ably** \-blē\ *adv*

com·pan·ion·ate \kəm-ˈpan-yə-nət\ *adj* (1926) **:** relating to or having the manner of companions; *specif* **:** harmoniously or suitably accompanying

companionate marriage *n* (1927) **:** a proposed form of marriage in which legalized birth control would be practiced, the divorce of childless couples by mutual consent permitted, and neither party would have any financial or economic claim on the other

companion cell *n* (1887) **:** a living nucleated cell that is closely associated in origin, position, and probably function with a cell making up part of a sieve tube of a vascular plant

companion piece *n* (1844) **:** a work (as of literature) that is associated with and complements another

com·pan·ion·ship \kəm-ˈpan-yən-ˌship\ *n* (1548) **:** the fellowship existing among companions

com·pan·ion·way \-yən-ˌwā\ *n* [[3]*companion*] (1840) **:** a ship's stairway from one deck to another

[1]**com·pa·ny** \ˈkəmp-(ə-)nē\ *n, pl* **-nies** *often attrib* [ME *companie,* fr. OF *compagnie,* fr. *compain* companion, fr. LL *companio*] (13c) **1 a :** association with another **:** FELLOWSHIP ⟨enjoy a person's ~⟩ **b :** COMPANIONS, ASSOCIATES ⟨know a person by the ~ he keeps⟩ **c :** VISITORS, GUESTS ⟨having ~ for dinner⟩ **2 a :** a group of persons or things ⟨a ~ of horsemen⟩ **b :** a body of soldiers; *specif* **:** a unit (as of infantry) consisting usu. of a headquarters and two or more platoons **c :** an organization of performing artists **d :** the officers and men of a ship **e :** a fire-fighting unit **3 a :** a chartered commercial organization or medieval trade guild **b :** an association of persons for carrying on a commercial or industrial enterprise **c :** those members of a partnership firm whose names do not appear in the firm name ⟨John Doe and *Company*⟩

[2]**company** *vt* **-nied; -ny·ing** (14c) **:** ACCOMPANY ⟨may . . . fair winds ~ your safe return —John Masefield⟩ ~ *vi* **:** ASSOCIATE

company officer *n* (1844) **:** a commissioned officer in the army, air force, or marine corps of the rank of captain, first lieutenant, or second lieutenant — called also *company grade officer;* compare FIELD OFFICER, GENERAL OFFICER

company town *n* (1927) **:** a community that is dependent on one firm for all or most of the necessary services or functions of town life (as employment, housing, and stores)

company union *n* (1917) **:** an unaffiliated labor union of the employees of a single firm; *esp* **:** one dominated by the employer

com·pa·ra·bil·i·ty \ˌkäm-p(ə-)rə-ˈbil-ət-ē, ÷kəm-ˌpar-ə-\ *n* (1843) **:** the quality or state of being comparable

com·pa·ra·ble \ˈkäm-p(ə-)rə-bəl, ÷kəm-ˈpar-ə-bəl\ *adj* (15c) **1 :** capable of or suitable for comparison **2 :** EQUIVALENT, SIMILAR ⟨fabrics of ~ quality⟩ — **com·pa·ra·ble·ness** *n* — **com·pa·ra·bly** \-blē\ *adv*

com·par·a·tist \kəm-ˈpar-ət-əst\ *n* [*comparative* + *-ist*] (1933) **:** one that uses a comparative method (as in the study of literature)

[1]**com·par·a·tive** \kəm-ˈpar-ət-iv\ *adj* (15c) **1 :** of, relating to, or constituting the degree of comparison in a language that denotes increase in the quality, quantity, or relation expressed by an adjective or adverb **2 :** considered as if in comparison to something else as a standard not quite attained **:** RELATIVE ⟨a ~ stranger⟩ **3 :** characterized by systematic comparison esp. of likenesses and dissimilarities ⟨~ anatomy⟩ — **com·par·a·tive·ly** *adv* — **com·par·a·tive·ness** *n*

[2]**comparative** *n* (15c) **1 a :** one that compares with another esp. on equal footing **:** RIVAL **b :** one that makes witty or mocking comparisons **2 :** the comparative degree or form in a language

com·par·a·tiv·ist \kəm-ˈpar-ət-i-vəst\ *n* (1887) **:** COMPARATIST

com·par·a·tor \kəm-ˈpar-ət-ər\ *n* (1883) **:** a device for comparing something with a similar thing or with a standard measure

[1]**com·pare** \kəm-ˈpa(ə)r, -ˈpe(ə)r\ *vb* **com·pared; com·par·ing** [ME *comparen,* fr. MF *comparer,* fr. L *comparare* to couple, compare, fr. *compar* like, fr. *com-* + *par* equal] *vt* (14c) **1 :** to represent as similar **:** LIKEN **2 :** to examine the character or qualities of esp. in order to discover resemblances or differences **3 :** to inflect or modify (an adjective or

adverb) according to the degrees of comparison ~ *vi* **1** : to bear being compared **2** : to make comparisons **3** : to be equal or alike
syn COMPARE, CONTRAST, COLLATE mean to set side by side in order to show differences and likenesses. COMPARE implies an aim of showing relative values or excellences by bringing out characteristic qualities whether similar or divergent; CONTRAST implies an emphasis on differences; COLLATE implies minute and critical inspection in order to note points of agreement or divergence.

[2]**compare** *n* (1589) : the possibility of comparing ⟨beauty beyond ~⟩

com·par·i·son \kəm-ˈpar-ə-sən\ *n* [ME, fr. MF *comparaison*, fr. L *comparation-, comparatio*, fr. *comparatus*, pp. of *comparare*] (14c) **1** : the act or process of comparing: **a** : the representing of one thing or person as similar to or like another ⟨a ~ of man to monkey⟩ **b** : an examination of two or more items to establish similarities and dissimilarities **2** : identity of features : SIMILARITY ⟨several points of ~ between two authors⟩ **3** : the modification of an adjective or adverb to denote different levels of quality, quantity, or relation

comparison shop *vi* (1970) : to compare prices (as of competing brands) in order to find the best value

com·part \kəm-ˈpärt\ *vt* [It *compartire*, fr. LL *compartiri* to share out, fr. L *com-* + *partiri* to share, fr. *part-, pars* part, share] (1624) : to mark out into parts; *specif* : to lay out in parts according to a plan

[1]**com·part·ment** \kəm-ˈpärt-mənt\ *n* [MF *compartiment*, fr. It *compartimento*, fr. *compartire*] (1564) **1** : a separate division or section **2** : one of the parts into which an enclosed space is divided — **com·part·men·tal** \kəm-ˌpärt-ˈment-ᵊl, ˌkäm-\ *adj*

[2]**com·part·ment** \-ˌment, -mənt\ *vt* (1918) : COMPARTMENTALIZE

com·part·men·tal·ize \kəm-ˌpärt-ˈment-ᵊl-ˌīz, ˌkäm-\ *vt* **-ized; -iz·ing** (1925) : to separate into isolated compartments or categories — **com·part·men·tal·iza·tion** \-ˌment-ᵊl-ə-ˈzā-shən\ *n*

com·part·men·ta·tion \kəm-ˌpärt-mən-ˈtā-shən, -ˌmen-\ *n* (1926) : division into separate sections or units

[1]**com·pass** \ˈkəm-pəs *also* ˈkäm-\ *vt* [ME *compassen*, fr. OF *compasser* to measure, fr. (assumed) VL *compassare* to pace off, fr. L *com-* + *passus* pace] (13c) **1** : to devise or contrive often with craft or skill **2 a** : ENCOMPASS **b** : to travel entirely around ⟨~ the earth⟩ **3 a** : BRING ABOUT, ACHIEVE **b** : to get into one's possession or power : OBTAIN **4** : COMPREHEND — **com·pass·able** \-pə-sə-bəl\ *adj*

[2]**compass** *n* (14c) **1 a** : BOUNDARY, CIRCUMFERENCE ⟨within the ~ of the city walls⟩ **b** : a circumscribed space ⟨within the narrow ~ of 21 pages —V. L. Parrington⟩ **c** : RANGE, SCOPE ⟨the ~ of a voice⟩ **2** : a curved or roundabout course ⟨a ~ of seven days' journey — 2 Kings 3:9 (AV)⟩ **3 a** : a device for determining directions by means of a magnetic needle or group of needles turning freely on a pivot and pointing to the magnetic north **b** : any of various nonmagnetic devices that serve the same purpose as the magnetic compass **c** : an instrument for describing circles or transferring measurements that consists of two pointed branches joined at the top by a pivot — usu. used in pl.; called also *pair of compasses* ***syn*** see RANGE

[3]**compass** *adj* (14c) **1** : forming a curve ⟨a ~ timber⟩ **2** : semicircular in plan — used of a bow window

compass card *n* (1874) : the circular card attached to the needles of a mariner's compass on which are marked the 32 points of the compass and the 360° of the circle

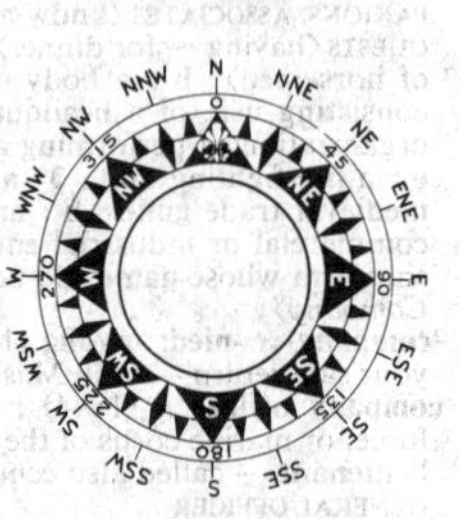

compass card

com·pas·sion \kəm-ˈpash-ən\ *n* [ME, fr. MF or LL; MF, fr. LL *compassion-, compassio*, fr. *compassus*, pp. of *compati* to sympathize, fr. L *com-* + *pati* to bear, suffer — more at PATIENT] (14c) : sympathetic consciousness of others' distress together with a desire to alleviate it — **com·pas·sion·less** \-ləs\ *adj*

[1]**com·pas·sion·ate** \kəm-ˈpash-(ə-)nət\ *adj* (1587) **1** : having or showing compassion : SYMPATHETIC **2** : granted because of unusual distressing circumstances affecting an individual — used of some military privileges (as leaves) — **com·pas·sion·ate·ly** *adv* — **com·pas·sion·ate·ness** *n*

[2]**com·pas·sion·ate** \-ˈpash-ə-ˌnāt\ *vt* **-at·ed; -at·ing** (1592) : PITY

compass plant *n* (1848) : a coarse yellow-flowered composite plant (*Silphium laciniatum*) with large pinnatifid leaves—called also *rosinweed*

com·pat·i·ble \kəm-ˈpat-ə-bəl\ *adj* [MF, fr. ML *compatibilis*, lit., sympathetic, fr. LL *compati*] (15c) **1** : capable of existing or operating together in harmony ⟨~ theories⟩ ⟨~ devices⟩ **2** : capable of cross-fertilizing freely or uniting vegetatively **3** : being or relating to a system in which color television broadcasts may be received in black and white on receivers without special modification **4** : capable of forming a homogeneous mixture that neither separates nor is altered by chemical interaction — **com·pat·i·bil·i·ty** \-ˌpat-ə-ˈbil-ət-ē\ *n* — **com·pat·i·ble·ness** \-ˈpat-ə-bəl-nəs\ *n* — **com·pat·i·bly** \-blē\ *adv*

com·pa·tri·ot \kəm-ˈpā-trē-ət, käm-, -trē-ˌät, *chiefly Brit* -ˈpa-\ *n* [F *compatriote*, fr. LL *compatriota*, fr. L *com-* + LL *patriota* fellow countryman — more at PATRIOT] (1611) **1** : a fellow countryman **2** : COMPEER, COLLEAGUE — **com·pa·tri·ot·ic** \kəm-ˌpā-trē-ˈät-ik, ˌkäm-, *chiefly Brit* -ˌpa-\ *adj*

[1]**com·peer** \ˈkäm-ˌpi(ə)r, käm-ˈ, kəm-ˈ\ *n* [ME, fr. OF *compere*, lit., godfather, fr. ML *compater*, fr. L *com-* + *pater* father — more at FATHER] (13c) : COMPANION

[2]**compeer** *n* [modif. of L *compar*, fr. *compar*, adj., like — more at COMPARE] (15c) : EQUAL, PEER — **compeer** *vt, obs*

com·pel \kəm-ˈpel\ *vt* **com·pelled; com·pel·ling** [ME *compellen*, fr. MF *compellir*, fr. L *compellere*, fr. *com-* + *pellere* to drive — more at FELT] (14c) **1** : to drive or urge forcefully or irresistibly **2** : to cause to do or occur by overwhelming pressure **3** *archaic* : to drive together — **com·pel·la·ble** \-ˈpel-ə-bəl\ *adj* — **com·pel·ler** *n*

com·pel·la·tion \ˌkäm-pə-ˈlā-shən, -ˌpel-ˈā-\ *n* [L *compellation-, compellatio*, fr. *compellatus*, pp. of *compellare* to address, fr. *com-* + *-pellare* (as in *appellare* to accost, appeal to)] (1603) **1** : an act or action of addressing someone **2** : APPELLATION 1

com·pel·ling \kəm-ˈpel-iŋ\ *adj* (1606) **1** : FORCEFUL **2** : demanding attention — **com·pel·ling·ly** *adv*

com·pend \ˈkäm-ˌpend\ *n* [ML *compendium*] (1596) : COMPENDIUM

com·pen·di·ous \kəm-ˈpen-dē-əs\ *adj* (14c) : marked by brief expression of a comprehensive matter ***syn*** see CONCISE — **com·pen·di·ous·ly** *adv* — **com·pen·di·ous·ness** *n*

com·pen·di·um \kəm-ˈpen-dē-əm\ *n, pl* **-di·ums** *or* **-dia** \-dē-ə\ [ML, fr. L, saving, shortcut, fr. *compendere* to weigh together, fr. *com-* + *pendere* to weigh — more at PENDANT] (1589) **1** : a brief summary of a larger work or of a field of knowledge : ABSTRACT **2 a** : a list of a number of items **b** : COLLECTION

com·pen·sa·ble \kəm-ˈpen(t)-sə-bəl\ *adj* (1661) : that is to be or can be compensated — **com·pen·sa·bil·i·ty** \kəm-ˌpen(t)-sə-ˈbil-ət-ē, ˌkäm-\ *n*

com·pen·sate \ˈkäm-pən-ˌsāt, -ˌpen-\ *vb* **-sat·ed; -sat·ing** [L *compensatus*, pp. of *compensare*, fr. *compensus*, pp. of *compendere*] *vt* (1646) **1** : to be equivalent to : COUNTERBALANCE **2** : to make an appropriate and usu. counterbalancing payment to **3 a** : to provide with means of counteracting variation **b** : to neutralize the effect of (variations) ~ *vi* **1** : to supply an equivalent — used with *for* **2** : to offset an error, defect, or undesired effect ***syn*** see PAY — **com·pen·sa·tive** \ˈkäm-pən-ˌsāt-iv, -ˌpen-; kəm-ˈpen(t)-sət-\ *adj* — **com·pen·sa·tor** \ˈkäm-pən-ˌsāt-ər, -ˌpen-\ *n* — **com·pen·sa·to·ry** \kəm-ˈpen(t)-sə-ˌtōr-ē, -ˌtȯr-\ *adj*

com·pen·sa·tion \ˌkäm-pən-ˈsā-shən, -ˌpen-\ *n* (14c) **1 a** : something that constitutes an equivalent or recompense ⟨age has its ~s⟩; *specif* : payment to an unemployed or injured worker or his dependents **b** : PAYMENT, REMUNERATION **2 a (1)** : correction of an organic defect or loss by hypertrophy or by increased functioning of another organ or unimpaired parts of the same organ **(2)** : a psychological mechanism by which feelings of inferiority, frustration, or failure in one field are counterbalanced by achievement in another **b** : adjustment of the phase retardation of one light ray with respect to that of another — **com·pen·sa·tion·al** \-shnəl, -shən-ᵊl\ *adj*

compensatory education *n* (1965) : educational programs intended to make up for experiences (as cultural) lacked by disadvantaged children

[1]**com·pere** *or* **com·père** \ˈkäm-ˌpe(ə)r\ *n* [F *compère*, lit., godfather — more at COMPEER] *Brit* (1914) : the master of ceremonies of an entertainment (as a television program)

[2]**compere** *or* **compère** *vb* **com·pered** *or* **com·pèred; com·per·ing** *or* **com·pèr·ing** *vt, Brit* (1933) : to act as compere for ~ *vi, Brit* : to act as a compere

com·pete \kəm-ˈpēt\ *vi* **com·pet·ed; com·pet·ing** [LL *competere* to seek together, fr. L, to come together, agree, be suitable, fr. *com-* + *petere* to go to, seek — more at FEATHER] (1620) : to strive consciously or unconsciously for an objective (as position, profit, or a prize) : be in a state of rivalry

com·pe·tence \ˈkäm-pət-ən(t)s\ *n* (1632) **1** : a sufficiency of means for the necessities and conveniences of life ⟨provided his family with a comfortable ~ —Rex Ingamells⟩ **2** : the quality or state of being competent: as **a** : the properties of an embryonic field that enable it to respond in a characteristic manner to an organizer **b** : readiness of bacteria to undergo genetic transformation **3** : the knowledge that enables a person to speak and understand a language — compare PERFORMANCE

com·pe·ten·cy \-pət-ən-sē\ *n, pl* **-cies** (1596) : COMPETENCE

com·pe·tent \ˈkäm-pət-ənt\ *adj* [ME, suitable, fr. MF & L; MF, fr. L *competent-, competens*, fr. prp. of *competere*] (14c) **1** : having requisite or adequate ability or qualities : FIT ⟨a ~ workman⟩ ⟨a ~ piece of work⟩ **2** : proper or rightly pertinent **3** : legally qualified or adequate ⟨a ~ witness⟩ **4** : having the capacity to function or develop in a particular way; *specif* : having the capacity to respond (as by producing an antibody) to an antigenic determinant ⟨immunologically ~ cells⟩ ***syn*** see SUFFICIENT — **com·pe·tent·ly** *adv*

com·pe·ti·tion \ˌkäm-pə-ˈtish-ən\ *n* [LL *competition-, competitio*, fr. L *competitus*, pp. of *competere*] (1605) **1** : the act or process of competing : RIVALRY **2** : a contest between rivals; *also* : one's competitors ⟨faced tough ~⟩ **3** : the effort of two or more parties acting independently to secure the business of a third party by offering the most favorable terms **4** : active demand by two or more organisms or kinds of organisms for some environmental resource in short supply

com·pet·i·tive \kəm-ˈpet-ət-iv\ *adj* (1829) **1** : relating to, characterized by, or based on competition ⟨~ sports⟩ **2** : inclined, desiring, or suited to compete ⟨a ~ breed of men —Ken Purdy⟩ ⟨salary benefits must be ~ —M. S. Eisenhower⟩ **3** : depending for effectiveness on the relative concentration of two or more substances ⟨~ inhibition of an enzyme⟩ — **com·pet·i·tive·ly** *adv* — **com·pet·i·tive·ness** *n*

com·pet·i·tor \kəm-ˈpet-ət-ər\ *n* (1534) : one that competes: as **a** : RIVAL **b** : one selling or buying goods or services in the same market as another **c** : an organism that lives in competition with another

com·pi·la·tion \ˌkäm-pə-ˈlā-shən *also* -ˌpī-\ *n* (15c) **1** : the act or process of compiling **2** : something compiled

com·pile \kəm-ˈpī(ə)l\ *vt* **com·piled; com·pil·ing** [ME *compilen*, fr. MF *compiler*, fr. L *compilare* to plunder] (14c) **1** : to collect and edit into a volume **2** : to compose out of materials from other documents **3** : to run (as a program) through a compiler **4** : to build up gradually ⟨*compiled* a record of four wins and two losses⟩

com·pil·er \kəm-ˈpī-lər\ *n* (14c) **1** : one that compiles **2** : a computer program that translates an entire set of instructions written in a higher-level symbolic language (as COBOL) into machine language before the instructions can be executed

com·pla·cence \kəm-ˈplās-ᵊn(t)s\ *n* (15c) **1** : calm or secure satisfaction with one's self or lot : SELF-SATISFACTION **2** *obs* : COMPLAISANCE **3** : UNCONCERN

com·pla·cen·cy \-ᵊn-sē\ *n, pl* **-cies** (1650) **1** : COMPLACENCE; *esp* : self-satisfaction accompanied by unawareness of actual dangers or deficiencies **2** : an instance of complacency

com·pla·cent \kəm-ˈplās-ᵊnt\ *adj* [L *complacent-, complacens*, prp. of *complacēre* to please greatly, fr. *com-* + *placēre* to please — more at PLEASE] (ca. 1755) **1** : COMPLAISANT 1 **2** : SELF-SATISFIED ⟨a ~ smile⟩ **3** : UNCONCERNED — **com·pla·cent·ly** *adv*

com·plain \kəm-ˈplān\ *vi* [ME *compleynen*, fr. MF *complaindre*, fr. (assumed) VL *complangere*, fr. L *com-* + *plangere* to lament — more at PLAINT] (14c) **1** : to express grief, pain, or discontent **2** : to make a formal accusation or charge — **com·plain·er** *n* — **com·plain·ing·ly** \-ˈplā-niŋ-lē\ *adv*

com·plain·ant \kəm-ˈplā-nənt\ *n* (15c) **:** the party who makes the complaint in a legal action or proceeding
com·plaint \kəm-ˈplānt\ *n* [ME *compleynte,* fr. MF *complainte,* fr. OF, fr. *complaindre*] (14c) **1 :** expression of grief, pain, or dissatisfaction **2 a :** something that is the cause or subject of protest or outcry **b :** a bodily ailment or disease **3 :** a formal allegation against a party
com·plai·sance \kəm-ˈplās-ᵊn(t)s, -ˈplāz-; ˌkäm-plā-ˈzan(t)s, -plə-, -ˈzän(t)s\ *n* (1651) **:** disposition to please or comply **:** AFFABILITY
com·plai·sant \-ᵊnt, -ˈzant, -ˈzänt\ *adj* [F, fr. MF, fr. prp. of *complaire* to gratify, acquiesce, fr. L *complacēre*] (1647) **1 :** marked by an inclination to please or oblige **2 :** tending to consent to others' wishes ***syn*** see AMIABLE — **com·plai·sant·ly** *adv*
com·pleat \kəm-ˈplēt\ *adj* [archaic variant of *complete* in *The Compleat Angler* (1653) by Izaak Walton] (1526) **:** COMPLETE 3
com·plect·ed \kəm-ˈplek-təd\ *adj* [irreg. fr. *complexion*] (1806) **:** having a specified facial complexion ⟨a tall, thin man, fairly dark ~ —E. J. Kahn⟩
usage Not an error, nor a dialectal term, nor nonstandard — all of which it has been labeled — *complected* still manages to raise hackles. It is an Americanism, apparently nonexistent in British English. Its currency in American English is attested as early as 1806 (by Meriwether Lewis) and it appears in the works of such notable American writers as Mark Twain, O. Henry, James Whitcomb Riley, and William Faulkner. Recent evidence shows that neither *complected* nor *complexioned,* recommended by handbooks as a substitute, is much used in print. Apparently many writers simply avoid using either.
1**com·ple·ment** \ˈkäm-plə-mənt\ *n* [ME, fr. L *complementum,* fr. *complēre* to fill up, complete, fr. *com-* + *plēre* to fill — more at FULL] (14c) **1 a :** something that fills up, completes, or makes perfect **b :** the quantity or number required to make a thing complete ⟨the usual ~ of eyes and ears —Francis Parkman⟩; *esp* **:** the whole force or personnel of a ship **c :** one of two mutually completing parts **:** COUNTERPART **2 a :** an angle or arc that when added to a given angle or arc equals a right angle in measure **b :** the set of all elements that do not belong to a given set and are contained in a particular mathematical set containing the given set **c :** a number that when added to another number of the same sign yields zero if the significant digit farthest to the left is discarded **3 :** the interval in music required with a given interval to complete the octave **4 :** an added word or expression by which a predication is made complete ⟨*president* and *beautiful* in "they elected him president" and "he thought her beautiful" are ~*s*⟩ **5 :** the thermolabile substance in normal blood serum and plasma that in combination with antibodies causes the destruction esp. of particulate antigens (as bacteria and foreign blood corpuscles)

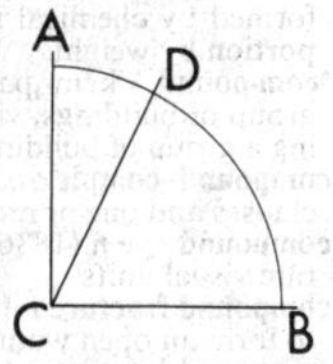

complement 2a: *ACB* right angle, *ACD* complement of *DCB* (and vice versa), *AD* complement of *DB* (and vice versa)

2**com·ple·ment** \-ˌment\ *vi, obs* (1602) **:** to exchange formal courtesies ~ *vt* **1 :** to be complementary to **2** *obs* **:** COMPLIMENT
com·ple·men·tal \ˌkäm-plə-ˈment-ᵊl\ *adj* (1602) **1 :** relating to or being a complement **2** *obs* **:** CEREMONIOUS, COMPLIMENTARY
com·ple·men·tar·i·ty \ˌkäm-plə-(ˌ)men-ˈtar-ət-ē, -mən-\ *n* (1911) **:** the quality or state of being complementary
com·ple·men·ta·ry \ˌkäm-plə-ˈment-ə-rē, -ˈmen-trē\ *adj* (1829) **1 :** relating to or constituting one of a pair of contrasting colors that produce a neutral color when combined in suitable proportions **2 :** serving to fill out or complete **3 :** mutually supplying each other's lack **4 :** being complements of each other ⟨~ acute angles⟩ **5 :** characterized by the capacity for precise pairing of purine and pyrimidine bases between strands of DNA and sometimes RNA such that the structure of one strand determines the other — **com·ple·men·ta·ri·ly** \-ˈmen-trə-lē, -(ˌ)men-ˈter-ə-lē, -ˈment-ə-rə-lē\ *adv* — **com·ple·men·ta·ri·ness** \-ˈment-ə-rē-nəs, -ˈmen-trē-\ *n* — **complementary** *n*
com·ple·men·ta·tion \ˌkäm-plə-(ˌ)men-ˈtā-shən, -mən-\ *n* (1942) **1 :** the operation of determining the complement of a mathematical set **2 :** production of normal phenotype in an individual heterozygous for two closely related mutations with one on each homologous chromosome and at a slightly different position
complement fixation *n* (1906) **:** the process of binding serum complement to the product formed by the union of an antibody and the antigen for which it is specific that occurs when complement is added to a suitable mixture of such an antibody and antigen
complement–fixation test *n* (1911) **:** a diagnostic test for the presence of a particular antibody in the serum of a patient that involves inactivation of the complement in the serum, addition of measured amounts of the antigen for which the antibody is specific and of foreign complement, and detection of the presence or absence of complement fixation by the addition of a suitable indicator system — compare WASSERMAN TEST
1**com·plete** \kəm-ˈplēt\ *adj* **com·plet·er; -est** [ME *complet,* fr. MF, fr. L *completus,* fr. pp. of *complēre*] (14c) **1 a :** having all necessary parts, elements, or steps ⟨~ diet⟩ **b :** having all four sets of floral organs **:** MONOCLINOUS **c** *of a subject or predicate* **:** including modifiers, complements, or objects **2 :** brought to an end **:** CONCLUDED ⟨a ~ period of time⟩ **3 :** highly proficient ⟨a ~ artist⟩ **4 a :** fully carried out **:** THOROUGH ⟨a ~ renovation⟩ **b :** TOTAL, ABSOLUTE ⟨~ silence⟩ **5** *of insect metamorphosis* **:** characterized by the occurrence of a pupal stage between the motile immature stages and the adult — compare INCOMPLETE b **6** *of a metric space* **:** having the property that every Cauchy sequence of elements converges to a limit in the space ***syn*** see FULL — **com·plete·ly** *adv* — **com·plete·ness** *n* — **com·ple·tive** \-ˈplēt-iv\ *adj*
2**complete** *vt* **com·plet·ed; com·plet·ing** (15c) **1 :** to bring to an end and esp. into a perfected state ⟨~ a painting⟩ **2 a :** to make whole or perfect ⟨its song ~*s* the charm of this bird⟩ **b :** to mark the end of ⟨a rousing chorus ~*s* the show⟩ **c :** EXECUTE, FULFILL ⟨~ a contract⟩ **3 :** to carry out (a forward pass) successfully ***syn*** see CLOSE
complete fertilizer *n* (1900) **:** a fertilizer that contains the three chief plant nutrients nitrogen, phosphoric acid, and potash
com·ple·tion \kəm-ˈplē-shən\ *n* (1657) **1 :** the act or process of completing **2 :** the quality or state of being complete

1**com·plex** \ˈkäm-ˌpleks\ *n* (1643) **1 :** a whole made up of complicated or interrelated parts ⟨a ~ of university buildings⟩ ⟨a ~ of welfare programs⟩ ⟨the military-industrial ~⟩ **2 a :** a group of culture traits relating to a single activity (as hunting), process (as use of flint), or culture unit **b (1) :** a group of repressed desires and memories that exerts a dominating influence upon the personality **(2) :** an exaggerated reaction to a subject or situation **c :** a group of obviously related units of which the degree and nature of the relationship is imperfectly known **3 :** a complex substance (as a coordination complex) in which the constituents are more intimately associated than in a simple mixture
2**com·plex** \käm-ˈpleks, kəm-ˈ, ˈkäm-ˌ\ *adj* [L *complexus,* pp. of *complecti* to embrace, comprise (a multitude of objects), fr. *com-* + *plectere* to braid — more at PLY] (1652) **1 a :** composed of two or more parts **:** COMPOSITE **b (1)** *of a word* **:** having a bound form as one or more of its immediate constituents ⟨*unmanly* is a ~ word⟩ **(2)** *of a sentence* **:** consisting of a main clause and one or more subordinate clauses **2 :** hard to separate, analyze, or solve **3 :** of, concerned with, being, or containing complex numbers ⟨a ~ root⟩ ⟨~ analysis⟩ — **com·plex·ly** *adv* — **com·plex·ness** *n*
syn COMPLEX, COMPLICATED, INTRICATE, INVOLVED, KNOTTY mean having confusingly interrelated parts. COMPLEX suggests the unavoidable result of a necessary combining and does not imply a fault or failure; COMPLICATED applies to what offers great difficulty in understanding, solving, or explaining; INTRICATE suggests such interlacing of parts as to make it nearly impossible to follow or grasp them separately; INVOLVED implies extreme complication and often disorder; KNOTTY suggests complication and entanglement that make solution or understanding improbable.
3**com·plex** *like* 2\ *vt* (1658) **1 :** to make complex or into a complex **2 :** CHELATE — **com·plex·ation** \ˌkäm-ˌplek-ˈsā-shən, kəm-\ *n*
complex fraction *n* (1827) **:** a fraction with a fraction or mixed number in the numerator or denominator or both — compare SIMPLE FRACTION
com·plex·i·fy \käm-ˈplek-sə-ˌfī, kəm-\ *vb* **-fied; -fy·ing** *vt* (1830) **:** to make complex ~ *vi* **:** to become complex
com·plex·ion \kəm-ˈplek-shən\ *n* [ME, fr. MF, fr. ML *complexion-, complexio,* fr. L, combination, fr. *complexus*] (14c) **1 :** the combination of the hot, cold, moist, and dry qualities held in medieval physiology to determine the quality of a body **2 a :** an individual complex of ways of thinking or feeling **b :** a complex of attitudes and inclinations **3 :** the hue or appearance of the skin and esp. of the face ⟨a dark ~⟩ **4 :** overall aspect or character ⟨by changing the ~ of the legislative branch —Trevor Armbrister⟩ — **com·plex·ion·al** \-shnəl, -shən-ᵊl\ *adj* — **com·plex·ioned** \-shənd\ *adj*
com·plex·i·ty \kəm-ˈplek-sət-ē, käm-\ *n, pl* **-ties** (1685) **1 :** the quality or state of being complex **2 :** something complex
complex number *n* (1860) **:** a number of the form $a + b\sqrt{-1}$ where *a* and *b* are real numbers
complex plane *n* (ca. 1909) **:** a plane whose points are identified by means of complex numbers
com·pli·ance \kəm-ˈplī-ən(t)s\ *n* (1647) **1 a :** the act or process of complying to a desire, demand, or proposal or to coercion **b :** conformity in fulfilling official requirements **2 :** a disposition to yield to others **3 :** the ability of an object to yield elastically when a force is applied **:** FLEXIBILITY
com·pli·an·cy \-ən-sē\ *n* (1643) **:** COMPLIANCE
com·pli·ant \-ənt\ *adj* (1642) **:** ready or disposed to comply **:** SUBMISSIVE — **com·pli·ant·ly** *adv*
com·pli·ca·cy \ˈkäm-pli-kə-sē\ *n, pl* **-cies** [2*complicate*] (ca. 1828) **1 :** the quality or state of being complicated **2 :** something that is complicated
1**com·pli·cate** \ˈkäm-plə-ˌkāt\ *vb* **-cat·ed; -cat·ing** *vt* (1621) **1 :** to combine esp. in an involved or inextricable manner **2 :** to make complex or difficult **3 :** INVOLVE; *esp* **:** to cause to be more complex or severe ⟨a virus disease *complicated* by bacterial infection⟩
2**com·pli·cate** \-pli-kət\ *adj* [L *complicatus,* pp. of *complicare* to fold together, fr. *com-* + *plicare* to fold — more at PLY] (1628) **1 :** COMPLEX, INTRICATE **2 :** CONDUPLICATE
com·pli·cat·ed \ˈkäm-plə-ˌkāt-əd\ *adj* (1656) **1 :** consisting of parts intricately combined **2 :** difficult to analyze, understand, or explain ***syn*** see COMPLEX — **com·pli·cat·ed·ly** *adv* — **com·pli·cat·ed·ness** *n*
com·pli·ca·tion \ˌkäm-plə-ˈkā-shən\ *n* (15c) **1 a :** COMPLEXITY, INTRICACY; *esp* **:** a situation or a detail of character complicating the main thread of a plot **b :** a making difficult, involved, or intricate **c :** a complex or intricate feature or element **d :** a difficult factor or issue often appearing unexpectedly and changing existing plans, methods, or attitudes **2 :** a secondary disease or condition developing in the course of a primary disease or condition
com·plice \ˈkäm-pləs, ˈkəm-\ *n* [ME, fr. MF, fr. LL *complic-, complex,* fr. L, closely connected, fr. *complicare*] *archaic* (15c) **:** ASSOCIATE
com·plic·it \kəm-ˈplis-ət\ *adj* (1973) **:** having complicity
com·plic·it·ous \-ət-əs\ *adj* (1860) **:** COMPLICIT
com·plic·i·ty \kəm-ˈplis-ət-ē, -ˈplis-tē\ *n, pl* **-ties** (ca. 1656) **1 :** association or participation in or as if in a wrongful act **2 :** an instance of complicity
com·pli·er \-ˈplī(-ə)r\ *n* (1644) **:** one that complies
1**com·pli·ment** \ˈkäm-plə-mənt\ *n* [F, fr. It *complimento,* fr. Sp *cumplimiento,* fr. *cumplir* to be courteous — more at COMPLY] (1578) **1 a :** an expression of esteem, respect, affection, or admiration; *esp* **:** an admiring remark **b :** formal and respectful recognition **:** HONOR **2** *pl* **:** best wishes **:** REGARDS ⟨accept my ~*s*⟩ ⟨~*s* of the season⟩
2**com·pli·ment** \-ˌment\ *vt* (1649) **1 :** to pay a compliment to **2 :** to present with a token of esteem
com·pli·men·ta·ry \ˌkäm-plə-ˈment-ə-rē, -ˈmen-trē\ *adj* (1628) **1 a :** expressing or containing a compliment **b :** FAVORABLE ⟨the novel received ~ reviews⟩ **2 :** given free as a courtesy or favor ⟨~ tickets⟩

\ə\ abut \ᵊ\ kitten, F table \ər\ further \a\ ash \ā\ ace \ä\ cot, cart \au̇\ out \ch\ chin \e\ bet \ē\ easy \g\ go \i\ hit \ī\ ice \j\ job \ŋ\ sing \ō\ go \ȯ\ law \ȯi\ boy \th\ thin \th\ the \ü\ loot \u̇\ foot \y\ yet \zh\ vision \à, k̟, ⁿ, œ, œ̄, ue, ue̅, ʸ\ *see* Guide to Pronunciation

— **com·pli·men·ta·ri·ly** \-ˈmen-trə-lē, -(ˌ)men-ˈter-ə-lē, -ˈment-ə-rə-lē\ *adv*
complimentary close *n* (1919) : the words (as *sincerely yours*) that conventionally come immediately before the signature of a letter and express the sender's regard for the receiver — called also *complimentary closing*
com·pline \ˈkäm-plən, -ˌplīn\ *n, often cap* [ME *compline, complie,* fr. OF *complie,* modif. of LL *completa,* fr. L, fem. of *completus* complete] (13c) : the seventh and last of the canonical hours
¹com·plot \ˈkäm-ˌplät\ *n* [MF *complot* crowd, plot] *archaic* (1577) : PLOT, CONSPIRACY
²com·plot \kəm-ˈplät, käm-\ *vb, archaic* (1579) : PLOT
com·ply \kəm-ˈplī\ *vi* **com·plied; com·ply·ing** [It *complire,* fr. Sp *cumplir* to complete, perform what is due, be courteous, fr. L *complēre* to complete] (1602) **1** *obs* : to be ceremoniously courteous **2** : to conform or adapt one's actions to another's wishes, to a rule, or to necessity
com·po \ˈkäm-(ˌ)pō\ *n, pl* **compos** [short for *composition*] (1823) : any of various composition materials
¹com·po·nent \kəm-ˈpō-nənt, ˈkäm-ˌ, käm-ˈ\ *n* [L *component-, componens,* prp. of *componere* to put together — more at COMPOUND] (1645) **1** : a constituent part : INGREDIENT **2 a** : any one of the vector terms added to form a vector sum or resultant **b** : a coordinate of a vector; *also* : either member of an ordered pair of numbers ***syn*** see ELEMENT — **com·po·nen·tial** \ˌkäm-pə-ˈnen-chəl\ *adj*
²component *adj* (1664) : serving or helping to constitute : CONSTITUENT
¹com·port \kəm-ˈpō(ə)rt, -ˈpȯ(ə)rt\ *vb* [MF *comporter* to bear, conduct, fr. L *comportare* to bring together, fr. *com-* + *portare* to carry — more at PORT] *vi* (1589) : to be fitting : ACCORD ⟨acts that ~ with ideals⟩ ~ *vt* : BEHAVE; *esp* : to behave in a manner conformable to what is right, proper, or expected ⟨~*ed* himself well in the emergency⟩ ***syn*** see BEHAVE
²com·port \ˈkäm-ˌpō(ə)rt, -ˌpȯ(ə)rt\ *n* (1771) : COMPOTE 2
com·port·ment \kəm-ˈpōrt-mənt, -ˈpȯrt-\ *n* (1599) : BEARING, DEMEANOR
com·pose \kəm-ˈpōz\ *vb* **com·posed; com·pos·ing** [MF *composer,* fr. L *componere* (perf. indic. *composui*) — more at COMPOUND] *vt* (15c) **1 a** : to form by putting together : FASHION ⟨a committee *composed* of three representatives—*Current Biog.*⟩ **b** : to form the substance of : CONSTITUTE ⟨*composed* of many ingredients⟩ **c** : to produce (as columns or pages of type) by composition **2 a** : to create by mental or artistic labor : PRODUCE ⟨~ a sonnet sequence⟩ **b** (1) : to formulate and write (a piece of music) (2) : to compose music for **3** : to deal with or act on so as to reduce to a minimum ⟨~ their differences⟩ **4** : to arrange in proper or orderly form ⟨~ her clothing⟩ **5** : to free from agitation : CALM, SETTLE ⟨~ a patient⟩ ~ *vi* : to practice composition
com·posed \-ˈpōzd\ *adj* (1607) : free from agitation : CALM; *esp* : SELF-POSSESSED ***syn*** see COOL — **com·pos·ed·ly** \-ˈpō-zəd-lē\ *adv* — **com·pos·ed·ness** \-ˈpō-zəd-nəs\ *n*
com·pos·er \kəm-ˈpō-zər\ *n* (1597) : one that composes; *esp* : a person who writes music
composing room *n* (1737) : the department in a printing office where typesetting and related operations are performed
composing stick *n* (1679) : a tray with an adjustable slide that a compositor holds in one hand and sets type into with the other
¹com·pos·ite \käm-ˈpäz-ət, kəm-ˈ, *esp Brit* ˈkäm-pə-zit\ *adj* [L *compositus,* pp. of *componere*] (15c) **1** : made up of distinct parts: as **a** *cap* : relating to or being a modification of the Corinthian order combining angular Ionic volutes with the acanthus-circled bell of the Corinthian **b** : of or relating to a very large family (Compositae) of dicotyledonous herbs, shrubs, and trees often considered to be the most highly evolved plants and characterized by florets arranged in dense heads that resemble single flowers **c** : factorable into two or more prime factors other than 1 and itself ⟨8 is a positive ~ integer⟩ **2** : combining the typical or essential characteristics of individuals making up a group ⟨the ~ man called the Poet—Richard Poirier⟩ **3** *of a statistical hypothesis* : specifying a range of values for one or more statistical parameters — compare SIMPLE 10 — **com·pos·ite·ly** *adv*
²composite *n* (15c) **1** : something composite : COMPOUND **2** : a composite plant **3** : COMPOSITE FUNCTION
³composite *vt* **-it·ed; -it·ing** (1923) : to make composite or into something composite ⟨*composited* four soil samples⟩
composite function *n* (1965) : a function whose values are found from two given functions by applying one function to an independent variable and then applying the second function to the result and whose domain consists of those values of the independent variable for which the result yielded by the first function lies in the domain of the second
com·po·si·tion \ˌkäm-pə-ˈzish-ən\ *n* [ME *composicioun,* fr. MF *composition,* fr. L *composition-, compositio,* fr. *compositus*] (14c) **1 a** : the act or process of composing; *specif* : arrangement into proper proportion or relation and esp. into artistic form **b** (1) : the arrangement of type for printing ⟨hand ~⟩ (2) : the production of type or typographic characters (as in photocomposition) arranged for printing **2 a** : the manner in which something is composed **b** : general makeup ⟨the changing ethnic ~ of the city —Leonard Buder⟩ **c** : the qualitative and quantitative makeup of a chemical compound **3** : mutual settlement or agreement **4** : a product of mixing or combining various elements or ingredients **5** : an intellectual creation: as **a** : a piece of writing; *esp* : a school exercise in the form of a brief essay **b** : a written piece of music esp. of considerable size and complexity **6** : the quality or state of being compound **7** : the operation of forming a composite function; *also* : COMPOSITE FUNCTION — **com·po·si·tion·al** \-ˈzish-nəl, -ən-ᵊl\ *adj* — **com·po·si·tion·al·ly** \-ē\ *adv*
com·pos·i·tor \kəm-ˈpäz-ət-ər\ *n* (1533) : one who sets type
com·pos men·tis \ˌkäm-pə-ˈsment-əs\ *adj* [L, lit., having mastery of one's mind] (1616) : of sound mind, memory, and understanding
¹com·post \ˈkäm-ˌpōst, *esp Brit* -ˌpäst\ *n* [MF, fr. ML *compostum,* fr. L, neut. of *compositus, compostus,* pp. of *componere*] (1587) **1** : a mixture that consists largely of decayed organic matter and is used for fertilizing and conditioning land **2** : MIXTURE, COMPOUND
²compost *vt* (ca. 1778) : to convert (as plant debris) to compost
com·po·sure \kəm-ˈpō-zhər\ *n* (1647) : a calmness or repose esp. of mind, bearing, or appearance : SELF-POSSESSION
com·pote \ˈkäm-ˌpōt\ *n* [F, fr. OF *composte,* fr. L *composta,* fem. of *compostus,* pp.] (1693) **1** : a dessert of fruit cooked in syrup **2** : a bowl of glass, porcelain, or metal usu. with a base and stem from which compotes, fruits, nuts, or sweets are served
¹com·pound \käm-ˈpau̇nd, kəm-ˈ, ˈkäm-ˌ\ *vb* [ME *compounen,* fr. MF *compondre,* fr. L *componere,* fr. *com-* + *ponere* to put — more at POSITION] *vt* (14c) **1** : to put together (parts) so as to form a whole : COMBINE ⟨~ ingredients⟩ **2** : to form by combining parts ⟨~ a medicine⟩ **3** : to settle amicably : adjust by agreement ⟨~ a debt⟩ **4 a** : to pay (interest) on both the accrued interest and the principal **b** : to add to : AUGMENT ⟨we ~*ed* our error in later policy—Robert Lekachman⟩ **5** : to agree for a consideration not to prosecute (an offense) ⟨~ a felony⟩ ~ *vi* **1** : to become joined in a compound **2** : to come to terms of agreement — **com·pound·able** \-ə-bəl\ *adj* — **com·pound·er** *n*
²com·pound \ˈkäm-ˌpau̇nd, käm-ˈ, kəm-ˈ\ *adj* [ME *compouned,* pp. of *compounen*] (14c) **1** : composed of or resulting from union of separate elements, ingredients, or parts: as **a** : composed of united similar elements esp. of a kind usu. independent ⟨a ~ plant ovary⟩ **b** : having the blade divided to the midrib and forming two or more leaflets on a common axis ⟨a ~ leaf⟩ **2** : involving or used in a combination **3 a** *of a word* : constituting a compound **b** *of a sentence* : having two or more main clauses
³com·pound \ˈkäm-ˌpau̇nd\ *n* (1530) **1 a** : a word consisting of components that are words (as *rowboat, high school, devil-may-care*) **b** : a word consisting of any of various combinations of words, combining forms, or affixes (as *anthropology, kilocycle, builder*) **2** : something formed by a union of elements or parts; *specif* : a distinct substance formed by chemical union of two or more ingredients in definite proportion by weight
⁴com·pound \ˈkäm-ˌpau̇nd\ *n* [by folk etymology fr. Malay *kampong* group of buildings, village] (1679) : a fenced or walled-in area containing a group of buildings and esp. residences
compound–complex *adj, of a sentence* (1923) : having two or more main clauses and one or more subordinate clauses
compound eye *n* (1836) : an eye (as of an insect) made up of many separate visual units
compound fracture *n* (1543) : a bone fracture produced in such a way as to form an open wound through which bone fragments usu. protrude
compound interest *n* (1660) : interest computed on the sum of an original principal and accrued interest
compound microscope *n* (ca. 1864) : a microscope consisting of an objective and an eyepiece mounted in a drawtube
compound number *n* (1557) : a number (as 2 ft. 5 in.) involving different denominations or more than one unit
com·pra·dor \ˌkäm-prə-ˈdō(ə)r\ *or* **com·pra·dore** \-ˈdō(ə)r, -ˈdȯ(ə)r\ *n* [Pg *comprador,* lit., buyer] (1840) **1** : a Chinese agent engaged by a foreign establishment in China to have charge of its Chinese employees and to act as an intermediary in business affairs **2** : INTERMEDIARY
com·pre·hend \ˌkäm-pri-ˈhend\ *vt* [ME *comprehenden,* fr. L *comprehendere,* fr. *com-* + *prehendere* to grasp — more at PREHENSILE] (14c) **1** : to grasp the nature, significance, or meaning of **2** : to include as an integral part ⟨philosophy's scope ~s the truth of everything which man may understand —H. O. Taylor⟩ **3** : to include by construction or implication : COMPRISE ***syn*** see UNDERSTAND, INCLUDE — **com·pre·hend·ible** \-ˈhen-də-bəl\ *adj*
com·pre·hen·si·ble \-ˈhen(t)-sə-bəl\ *adj* (1598) : capable of being comprehended : INTELLIGIBLE — **com·pre·hen·si·bil·i·ty** \-ˌhen(t)-sə-ˈbil-ət-ē\ *n* — **com·pre·hen·si·ble·ness** \-ˈhen(t)-sə-bəl-nəs\ *n* — **com·pre·hen·si·bly** \-blē\ *adv*
com·pre·hen·sion \ˌkäm-pri-ˈhen-chən\ *n* [MF & L; MF, fr. L *comprehension-, comprehensio,* fr. *comprehensus,* pp. of *comprehendere* to understand, comprise] (15c) **1 a** : the act or action of grasping with the intellect : UNDERSTANDING **b** : knowledge gained by comprehending **c** : the capacity for understanding fully **2 a** : the act or process of comprising **b** : the faculty or capability of including : COMPREHENSIVENESS **3** : CONNOTATION 3
com·pre·hen·sive \-ˈhen(t)-siv\ *adj* (1614) **1** : covering completely or broadly : INCLUSIVE ⟨~ examinations⟩ ⟨~ insurance⟩ **2** : having or exhibiting wide mental grasp ⟨~ knowledge⟩ — **com·pre·hen·sive·ly** *adv* — **com·pre·hen·sive·ness** *n*
¹com·press \kəm-ˈpres\ *vb* [ME *compressen,* fr. LL *compressare* to press hard, fr. L *compressus,* pp. of *comprimere* to compress, fr. *com-* + *premere* to press — more at PRESS] *vt* (14c) **1** : to press or squeeze together **2** : to reduce in size or volume as if by squeezing ~ *vi* : to undergo compression ***syn*** see CONTRACT
²com·press \ˈkäm-ˌpres\ *n* [MF *compresse,* fr. *compresser* to compress, fr. LL *compressare*] (1599) **1** : a folded cloth or pad applied so as to press upon a body part **2** : a machine for compressing
com·pressed \kəm-ˈprest *also* ˈkäm-ˌ\ *adj* (14c) **1** : pressed together : reduced in size or volume (as by pressure) **2** : flattened as though subjected to compression: **a** : flattened laterally ⟨petioles ~⟩ **b** : narrow from side to side and deep in a dorsoventral direction — **compressed·ly** \kəm-ˈprest-lē, -ˈpres-əd-lē\ *adv*
compressed air *n* (1669) : air under pressure greater than that of the atmosphere
com·press·ible \kəm-ˈpres-ə-bəl\ *adj* (1691) : capable of being compressed — **com·press·ibil·i·ty** \-ˌpres-ə-ˈbil-ət-ē\ *n*
com·pres·sion \kəm-ˈpresh-ən\ *n* (15c) **1 a** : the act, process, or result of compressing **b** : the state of being compressed **2** : the process of compressing the fuel mixture in a cylinder of an internal-combustion engine (as in an automobile) **3** : a much compressed fossil plant — **com·pres·sion·al** \-ˈpresh-nəl, -ən-ᵊl\ *adj*
compressional wave *n* (1887) : a longitudinal wave (as a sound wave) propagated by the elastic compression of the medium — called also *compression wave*
com·pres·sive \kəm-ˈpres-iv\ *adj* (1572) **1** : of or relating to compression **2** : tending to compress — **com·pres·sive·ly** *adv*
com·pres·sor \-ˈpres-ər\ *n* (1839) : one that compresses: as **a** : a muscle that compresses a part **b** : a machine that compresses gases
com·prise \kəm-ˈprīz\ *vt* **com·prised; com·pris·ing** [ME *comprisen,* fr. MF *compris,* pp. of *comprendre,* fr. L *comprehendere*] (15c) **1** : to include esp. within a particular scope ⟨civilization as Lenin used the term would then certainly have *comprised* the changes that are now

associated in our minds with "developed" rather than "developing" states —*Times Lit. Supp.*⟩ **2 :** to be made up of ⟨a committee *comprising* three faculty members and three public members⟩ **3 :** COMPOSE, CONSTITUTE ⟨a misconception as to what ~*s* a literary generation —William Styron⟩ ⟨about 8 percent of our military forces are *comprised* of women —Jimmy Carter⟩

usage Although it has been in use since the late 18th century, sense 3 is still attacked as wrong. Why it has been singled out is not clear, but until comparatively recent times it was found chiefly in scientific or technical writing rather than belles lettres. Our current evidence shows a slight shift in usage: sense 3 is somewhat more frequent in recent literary use than the earlier senses. You should be aware, however, that if you use sense 3 you may be subject to criticism for doing so, and you may want to choose a safer synonym such as *compose* or *make up.*

1**com·pro·mise** \ˈkäm-prə-ˌmīz\ *n* [ME, mutual promise to abide by an arbiter's decision, fr. MF *compromis,* fr. L *compromissum,* fr. neut. of *compromissus,* pp. of *compromittere* to promise mutually, fr. *com-* + *promittere* to promise — more at PROMISE] (15c) **1 a :** settlement of differences by arbitration or by consent reached by mutual concessions **b :** something blending qualities of two different things **2 :** a concession to something derogatory or prejudicial ⟨a ~ of principles⟩

2**compromise** *vb* **-mised; -mis·ing** *vt* (1598) **1** *obs* **:** to bind by mutual agreement **2 :** to adjust or settle by mutual concessions **3 :** to expose to discredit or mischief ~ *vi* **1 :** to come to agreement by mutual concession **2 :** to make a shameful or disreputable concession — **com·pro·mis·er** *n*

compt \ˈkau̇nt, ˈkäm(p)t\ *archaic var of* COUNT

comp·trol·ler \kən-ˈtrō-lər, ˈkäm(p)-ˌ, ˌkäm(p)-ˈ\ *n* [ME, alter. of *conterroller* controller] (15c) **1 :** a royal-household official who examines and supervises expenditures **2 :** a public official who audits government accounts and sometimes certifies expenditures **3 :** CONTROLLER 1c — **comp·trol·ler·ship** \-ˌship\ *n*

com·pul·sion \kəm-ˈpəl-shən\ *n* [ME, fr. MF or LL; MF, fr. LL *compulsion-, compulsio,* fr. L *compulsus,* pp. of *compellere* to compel] (15c) **1 a :** an act of compelling **:** the state of being compelled **b :** a force that compels **2 :** an irresistible impulse to perform an irrational act

com·pul·sive \-ˈpəl-siv\ *adj* (1588) **1 :** having power to compel **2 :** of, relating to, caused by, or suggestive of psychological compulsion or obsession ⟨~ actions⟩ — **com·pul·sive·ly** *adv* — **com·pul·sive·ness** *n* — **com·pul·siv·i·ty** \kəm-ˌpəl-ˈsiv-ət-ē, ˌkäm-\ *n*

com·pul·so·ry \kəm-ˈpəls-(ə-)rē\ *adj* (1581) **1 :** MANDATORY, ENFORCED **2 :** COERCIVE, COMPELLING — **com·pul·so·ri·ly** \-(ə-)rə-lē\ *adv*

com·punc·tion \kəm-ˈpəŋ(k)-shən\ *n* [ME *compunccioun,* fr. MF *componction,* fr. LL *compunction-, compunctio,* fr. L *compunctus,* pp. of *compungere* to prick hard, sting, fr. *com-* + *pungere* to prick — more at PUNGENT] (14c) **1 a :** anxiety arising from awareness of guilt ⟨~*s* of conscience⟩ **b :** distress of mind over an anticipated action or result ⟨he showed no ~ in planning devilish engines of . . . destruction —Havelock Ellis⟩ **2 :** a twinge of misgiving **:** SCRUPLE ⟨cheated without ~⟩ ***syn*** see PENITENCE, QUALM — **com·punc·tious** \-shəs\ *adj*

com·pur·ga·tion \ˌkäm-(ˌ)pər-ˈgā-shən\ *n* [LL *compurgation-, compurgatio,* fr. L *compurgatus,* pp. of *compurgare* to clear completely, fr. *com-* + *purgare* to purge] (1658) **:** the clearing of an accused person by oaths of persons who swear to his veracity or innocence

com·pur·ga·tor \ˈkäm-(ˌ)pər-ˌgāt-ər\ *n* (1533) **:** one that under oath vouches for the character or conduct of an accused person

com·put·able \kəm-ˈpyüt-ə-bəl\ *adj* (1646) **:** capable of being computed — **com·put·abil·i·ty** \-ˌpyüt-ə-ˈbil-ət-ē\ *n*

com·pu·ta·tion \ˌkäm-pyu̇-ˈtā-shən\ *n* (15c) **1 a :** the act or action of computing **:** CALCULATION **b :** the use or operation of a computer **2 :** a system of reckoning **3 :** an amount computed — **com·pu·ta·tion·al** \-shnəl, -shən-ᵊl\ *adj*

1**com·pute** \kəm-ˈpyüt\ *n* (1588) **:** COMPUTATION

2**compute** *vb* **com·put·ed; com·put·ing** [L *computare* — more at COUNT] *vt* (1616) **:** to determine esp. by mathematical means ⟨~ your income tax⟩; *also* **:** to determine or calculate by means of a computer ~ *vi* **1 :** to make calculation **:** RECKON **2 :** to use a computer

computed tomography *n* (ca. 1977) **:** radiography in which a three-dimensional image of a body structure is constructed by computer from a series of plane cross-sectional images made along an axis — called also *computed axial tomography, computerized axial tomography, computerized tomography*

com·put·er \kəm-ˈpyüt-ər\ *n, often attrib* (1646) **:** one that computes; *specif* **:** a programmable electronic device that can store, retrieve, and process data — **com·put·er·like** \-ˌlīk\ *adj*

com·put·er·ese \-ˌpyüt-ə-ˈrēz, -ˈrēs\ *n* (ca. 1960) **:** jargon used by computer technologists

com·put·er·ise *chiefly Brit var of* COMPUTERIZE

com·put·er·ist \kəm-ˈpyüt-ə-rəst\ *n* (1973) **:** a person who uses or operates a computer

com·put·er·ize \kəm-ˈpyüt-ə-ˌrīz\ *vt* **-ized; -iz·ing** (1957) **1 :** to carry out, control, or produce by means of a computer **2 :** to equip with computers **3 a :** to store in a computer **b :** to put in a form that a computer can use — **com·put·er·iz·able** \-ˌrī-zə-bəl\ *adj* — **com·put·er·iza·tion** \-ˌpyüt-ə-rə-ˈzā-shən\ *n*

com·put·er·nik \kəm-ˈpyüt-ər-ˌnik\ *n* [*computer* + *-nik*] (1968) **:** COMPUTERIST

com·rade \ˈkäm-ˌrad, -rəd, *esp Brit* -ˌräd\ *n* [MF *camarade* group sleeping in one room, roommate, companion, fr. OSp *camarada,* fr. *cámara* room, fr. LL *camera, camara* — more at CHAMBER] (1544) **1 a :** an intimate friend or associate **:** COMPANION **b :** a fellow soldier **2** [fr. its use as a form of address by communists] **:** COMMUNIST — **com·rade·li·ness** \-lē-nəs\ *n* — **com·rade·ly** *adj* — **com·rade·ship** \-ˌship\ *n*

com·rad·ery \ˈkäm-ˌrad-(ə-)rē, -rəd-rē, -ˌräd-(ə-)rē\ *n* (1879) **:** CAMARADERIE

Comsat \ˈkäm-ˌsat\ *service mark* — used for communications services involving an artificial satellite

Com·stock·ery \ˈkäm-ˌstäk-ə-rē *also* ˈkəm-\ *n* [Anthony *Comstock* + E *-ery*] (1905) **1 :** strict censorship of materials considered obscene **2 :** censorious opposition to alleged immorality (as in literature)

Com·stock·ian \käm-ˈstäk-ē-ən *also* ˌkəm-\ *adj* (1921) **:** of or relating to Comstockery

com·symp \ˈkäm-ˌsimp\ *n* [*communist* + *sympathizer*] (ca. 1961) **:** a person sympathetic to communist causes — usu. used disparagingly

Comt·ian *or* **Comt·ean** \ˈkäm(p)-tē-ən, ˈkōⁿ(n)t-ē-\ *adj* (1846) **:** of or relating to Auguste Comte or his doctrines — **Comt·ism** \ˈkäm(p)-ˌtiz-əm, ˈkōⁿ(n)t-ˌiz-\ *n* — **Comt·ist** \ˈkäm(p)-təst, ˈkōⁿ(n)t-əst\ *adj or n*

1**con** \ˈkän\ *vt* **conned; con·ning** [ME *connen* to know, learn, study, alter. of *cunnen* to know, infin. of *can* — more at CAN] (13c) **1 :** to commit to memory **2 :** to study or examine closely **:** PERUSE

2**con** *var of* CONN

3**con** *adv* [ME, short for *contra*] (15c) **:** on the negative side **:** in opposition ⟨so much has been written pro and ~⟩

4**con** *n* (1589) **1 :** an argument or evidence in opposition **2 :** the negative position or one holding it ⟨an appraisal of the pros and ~*s*⟩

5**con** *adj* [by shortening] (1889) **:** CONFIDENCE

6**con** *vt* **conned; con·ning** (1896) **1 :** SWINDLE **2 :** PERSUADE, CAJOLE

7**con** *n* [by shortening] (1893) **:** CONVICT

8**con** *n* [short for *consumption*] *slang* (1915) **:** a destructive disease of the lungs; *esp* **:** TUBERCULOSIS

con- — see COM-

con amo·re \ˌkän-ə-ˈmōr-ē, ˌkō-nə-ˈmōr-(ˌ)ā, -ˈmȯr-\ *adv* [It] (1739) **1 :** with love, devotion, or zest **2 :** in a tender manner — used as a direction in music

con ani·ma \kä-ˈnan-ə-ˌmä, kō-ˈnän-i-\ *adv* [It, lit., with spirit] (1906) **:** in a spirited manner — used as a direction in music

co·na·tion \kō-ˈnā-shən\ *n* [L *conation-, conatio* act of attempting, fr. *conatus,* pp. of *conari* to attempt — more at DEACON] (1836) **:** an inclination (as an instinct, a drive, a wish, or a craving) to act purposefully **:** IMPULSE 3 — **co·na·tive** \ˈkō-nət-iv, -ˌnāt-; ˈkän-ət-\ *adj*

con brio \kän-ˈbrē-(ˌ)ō, kōn-\ *adv* [It, lit., with vigor] (ca. 1891) **:** in a vigorous or brisk manner — used as a direction in music

con·ca·nav·a·lin \ˌkän-kə-ˈnav-ə-lən\ *n* [*com-* + *canavalin* (a noncrystalline globulin found in the jack bean), fr. NL *Canavalia,* genus name of the jack bean] (1919) **:** either of two crystalline globulins occurring in the jack bean; *esp* **:** one that is a potent hemagglutinin

1**con·cat·e·nate** \kän-ˈkat-ə-nət, kən-\ *adj* [ME, fr. LL *concatenatus,* pp. of *concatenare* to link together, fr. L *com-* + *catena* chain — more at CHAIN] (15c) **:** linked together

2**concatenate** \-ˌnāt\ *vt* **-nat·ed; -nat·ing** (1598) **:** to link together in a series or chain — **con·cat·e·na·tion** \(ˌ)kän-ˌkat-ə-ˈnā-shən, kən-\ *n*

1**con·cave** \kän-ˈkāv, ˈkän-ˌ\ *adj* [MF, fr. L *concavus,* fr. *com-* + *cavus* hollow — more at CAVE] (15c) **1 :** hollowed or rounded inward like the inside of a bowl **2 :** arched in **:** curving in — used of the side of a curve or surface on which neighboring normals to the curve or surface converge and on which lies the chord joining two neighboring points of the curve or surface

2**con·cave** \ˈkän-ˌkāv\ *n* (1552) **:** a concave line or surface

con·cav·i·ty \kän-ˈkav-ət-ē\ *n, pl* **-ties** (15c) **1 :** a concave line, surface, or space **:** HOLLOW **2 :** the quality or state of being concave

con·ca·vo–convex \kän-ˌkā-vō-\ *adj* (1676) **1 :** concave on one side and convex on the other **2 :** having the concave side curved more than the convex

con·ceal \kən-ˈsē(ə)l\ *vt* [ME *concelen,* fr. MF *conceler,* fr. L *concelare,* fr. *com-* + *celare* to hide — more at HELL] (14c) **1 :** to prevent disclosure or recognition of **2 :** to place out of sight ***syn*** see HIDE — **con·ceal·able** \-ˈsē-lə-bəl\ *adj* — **con·ceal·er** \-ˈsē-lər\ *n* — **con·ceal·ing·ly** \-ˈsē-liŋ-lē\ *adv* — **con·ceal·ment** \-ˈsē(ə)l-mənt\ *n*

con·cede \kən-ˈsēd\ *vb* **con·ced·ed; con·ced·ing** [F or L; F *concéder,* fr. L *concedere,* fr. *com-* + *cedere* to yield — more at CEDE] *vt* (1632) **1 :** to grant as a right or privilege **2 a :** to accept as true, valid, or accurate ⟨the right of the state to tax is generally *conceded*⟩ **b :** to acknowledge grudgingly or hesitantly ~ *vi* **:** to make concession **:** YIELD ***syn*** see GRANT — **con·ced·ed·ly** \-ˈsēd-əd-lē\ *adv* — **con·ced·er** *n*

1**con·ceit** \kən-ˈsēt\ *n* [ME, fr. *conceiven*] (14c) **1 a** (1) **:** a result of mental activity **:** THOUGHT (2) **:** individual opinion **b :** favorable opinion; *esp* **:** excessive appreciation of one's own worth or virtue **2 :** a fancy article **3 a :** a fanciful idea **b :** an elaborate or strained metaphor **c :** use or presence of such conceits in poetry

2**conceit** *vt* (1557) **1** *obs* **:** CONCEIVE, UNDERSTAND **2** *dial* **:** IMAGINE **3** *dial Brit* **:** to take a fancy to

con·ceit·ed \-ˈsēt-əd\ *adj* [1*conceit*] (1593) **1 :** ingeniously contrived **:** FANCIFUL **2 :** having an excessively high opinion of oneself — **con·ceit·ed·ly** *adv* — **con·ceit·ed·ness** *n*

con·ceiv·able \kən-ˈsē-və-bəl\ *adj* (15c) **:** capable of being conceived **:** IMAGINABLE — **con·ceiv·abil·i·ty** \kən-ˌsē-və-ˈbil-ət-ē\ *n* — **con·ceiv·able·ness** \-ˈsē-və-bəl-nəs\ *n* — **con·ceiv·ably** \-blē\ *adv*

con·ceive \kən-ˈsēv\ *vb* **con·ceived; con·ceiv·ing** [ME *conceiven,* fr. MF *conceivre,* fr. L *concipere* to take in, conceive, fr. *com-* + *capere* to take — more at HEAVE] *vt* (14c) **1 a :** to become pregnant with (young) **b :** to cause to begin **:** ORIGINATE **2 a :** to take into one's mind ⟨~ a prejudice⟩ **b :** to form a conception of **:** IMAGINE, IMAGE **3 :** to apprehend by reason or imagination **:** UNDERSTAND **4 :** to be of the opinion ~ *vi* **1 :** to become pregnant **2 :** to have a conception — usu. used with *of* ⟨~*s* of death as emptiness⟩ ***syn*** see THINK — **con·ceiv·er** *n*

con·cel·e·brant \kən-ˈsel-ə-brənt, kän-\ *n* (ca. 1931) **:** one that concelebrates a Eucharist or Mass

con·cel·e·brate \kən-ˈsel-ə-ˌbrāt, kän-\ *vb* [L *concelebratus,* pp. of *concelebrare* to celebrate in great numbers, fr. *com-* + *celebrare* to celebrate] *vt* (1879) **:** to participate in (a Eucharist) as a joint celebrant who recites the canon in unison with other celebrants ~ *vi* **:** to participate as a celebrant in a concelebrated Eucharist — **con·cel·e·bra·tion** \(ˌ)kän-ˌsel-ə-ˈbrā-shən, kən-\ *n*

con·cent \kən-ˈsent\ *n* [L *concentus,* fr. *concentus,* pp. of *concinere* to sing together, fr. *com-* + *canere* to sing — more at CHANT] *archaic* (1585) **:** HARMONY

con·cen·ter \kən-ˈsent-ər, kän-\ *vb* [F *concentrer,* fr. *com-* + *centre* center] *vt* (1630) **:** to draw or direct to a common center **:** CONCENTRATE ~ *vi* **:** to come to a common center

\ə\ abut \ᵊ\ kitten, F table \ər\ further \a\ ash \ā\ ace \ä\ cot, cart \au̇\ out \ch\ chin \e\ bet \ē\ easy \g\ go \i\ hit \ī\ ice \j\ job \ŋ\ sing \ō\ go \ȯ\ law \ȯi\ boy \th\ thin \t͟h\ the \ü\ loot \u̇\ foot \y\ yet \zh\ vision \à, k̲, ⁿ, œ, œ̄, ue, ue̅, ʸ\ *see* Guide to Pronunciation

[1]**con·cen·trate** \ˈkän(t)-sən-ˌtrāt, -ˌsen-\ *vb* **-trat·ed; -trat·ing** [*com-* + L *centrum* center] *vt* (1646) **1 a :** to bring or direct toward a common center or objective : FOCUS **b :** to gather into one body, mass, or force ⟨power was *concentrated* in a few able hands⟩ **2 a :** to make less dilute ⟨~ syrup⟩ **b :** to separate a valuable material from ⟨~ an ore⟩ **c :** to express or exhibit in condensed form **~** *vi* **1 :** to draw toward or meet in a common center **2 :** GATHER, COLLECT **3 :** to concentrate one's powers, efforts, or attention ⟨~ on a problem⟩ — **con·cen·tra·tive** \-ˌtrāt-iv\ *adj* — **con·cen·tra·tor** \-ˌtrāt-ər\ *n*

[2]**concentrate** *n* (1883) **1 :** something concentrated; *esp* **:** a food reduced in bulk by elimination of fluid ⟨orange juice ~⟩ **2 :** a feedstuff (as grains) relatively rich in digestible nutrients — compare ROUGHAGE

con·cen·tra·tion \ˌkän(t)-sən-ˈtrā-shən, -ˌsen-\ *n* (1634) **1 :** the act or process of concentrating **:** the state of being concentrated; *esp* **:** direction of attention to a single object **2 :** a concentrated mass or thing **3 :** the relative content of a component : STRENGTH

concentration camp *n* (1901) **:** a camp where persons (as prisoners of war, political prisoners, or refugees) are detained or confined

con·cen·tric \kən-ˈsen-trik, (ˈ)kän-\ *adj* [ML *concentricus,* fr. L *com-* + *centrum* center] (14c) **1 :** having a common center ⟨~ circles⟩ **2 :** having a common axis : COAXIAL — **con·cen·tri·cal·ly** \-tri-k(ə-)lē\ *adv* — **con·cen·tric·i·ty** \ˌkän-ˌsen-ˈtris-ət-ē\ *n*

con·cept \ˈkän-ˌsept\ *n* [L *conceptum,* neut. of *conceptus,* pp. of *concipere* to conceive] (1835) **1 :** something conceived in the mind : THOUGHT, NOTION **2 :** an abstract or generic idea generalized from particular instances ***syn*** see IDEA

con·cep·ta·cle \kən-ˈsep-ti-kəl\ *n* [NL *conceptaculum,* fr. L, receptacle, fr. *conceptus,* pp. of *concipere* to take in] (1835) **:** an external cavity containing reproductive cells in algae (as of the genus *Fucus*)

con·cep·tion \kən-ˈsep-shən\ *n* [ME *concepcioun,* fr. OF *conception,* fr. L *conception-, conceptio,* fr. *conceptus*] (14c) **1 a (1) :** the act of becoming pregnant **:** the state of being conceived **(2) :** EMBRYO, FETUS **b** *archaic* **:** BEGINNING ⟨joy had the like ~ in our eyes —Shak.⟩ **2 a :** the capacity, function, or process of forming or understanding ideas or abstractions or their symbols **b :** a general idea : CONCEPT **c :** a complex product of abstract or reflective thinking **d :** the sum of a person's ideas and beliefs concerning something **3 :** the originating of something in the mind ***syn*** see IDEA — **con·cep·tion·al** \-shnəl, -shən-ᵊl\ *adj* — **con·cep·tive** \-ˈsep-tiv\ *adj*

con·cep·tu·al \kən-ˈsep-chə(-wə)l, kän-, -ˈsepsh-wəl\ *adj* [ML *conceptualis* of thought, fr. LL *conceptus* act of conceiving, thought, fr. L *conceptus,* pp.] (1834) **:** of, relating to, or consisting of concepts — **con·cep·tu·al·i·ty** \-ˌsep-chə-ˈwal-ət-ē, -shə-\ *n* — **con·cep·tu·al·ly** *adv*

conceptual art *n* (ca. 1969) **:** art in which the artist's intent is to convey a concept rather than to create an art object — **conceptual artist** *n*

con·cep·tu·al·ism \-ˈsep-chə(-wə)-ˌliz-əm, -ˈsepsh-wə-\ *n* (1837) **:** a theory in philosophy intermediate between realism and nominalism that universals exist in the mind as concepts of discourse or as predicates which may be properly affirmed of reality — **con·cep·tu·al·is·tic** \-ˌsep-chə(-wə)-lis-tik, -ˌsepsh-wə-\ *adj* — **con·cep·tu·al·is·ti·cal·ly** \-ti-k(ə-)lē\ *adv*

con·cep·tu·al·ist \-ˈsep-chə(-wə)-ləst, -ˈsepsh-wə-\ *n* (ca. 1785) **:** an adherent to the tenets of conceptualism or of conceptual art

con·cep·tu·al·ize \-ˈsep-chə(-wə)-ˌlīz, -ˈsepsh-wə-\ *vt* **-ized; -iz·ing** (1909) **:** to form a concept of; *esp* **:** to interpret conceptually — **con·cep·tu·al·iza·tion** \-ˌsep-chə(-wə)-lə-ˈzā-shən, -ˌsepsh-wə-\ *n* — **con·cep·tu·al·iz·er** \-ˈsep-chə(-wə)-ˌlī-zər, -ˈsepsh-wə-\ *n*

con·cep·tus \kən-ˈsep-təs\ *n* [L, one conceived, fr. pp. of *concipere* to conceive] (1940) **:** FETUS

[1]**con·cern** \kən-ˈsərn\ *vb* [ME *concernen,* fr. MF & ML; MF *concerner,* fr. ML *concernere,* fr. LL, to sift together, mingle, fr. L *com-* + *cernere* to sift — more at CERTAIN] *vt* (15c) **1 a :** to relate to **:** be about ⟨the novel ~*s* three soldiers⟩ **b :** to bear on **2 :** to have an influence on **:** INVOLVE; *also* **:** to be the business or affair of ⟨the problem ~*s* us all⟩ **3 :** to be a care, trouble, or distress to ⟨her ill health ~*s* me⟩ **4 :** ENGAGE, OCCUPY ⟨he ~*s* himself with trivia⟩ **~** *vi, obs* **:** to be of importance : MATTER

[2]**concern** *n* (1655) **1 a :** marked interest or regard usu. arising through a personal tie or relationship **b :** an uneasy state of blended interest, uncertainty, and apprehension **2 :** something that relates or belongs to one : AFFAIR **3 :** matter for consideration **4 :** an organization or establishment for business or manufacture **5 :** CONTRIVANCE, GADGET ***syn*** see CARE

con·cerned *adj* (1656) **1 :** ANXIOUS, WORRIED ⟨~ for her safety⟩ **2 a :** interestedly engaged ⟨~ with books and music⟩ **b :** culpably involved : IMPLICATED ⟨arrested all ~⟩

con·cern·ing *prep* (15c) **:** relating to : REGARDING

con·cern·ment \kən-ˈsərn-mənt\ *n* (1621) **1 :** something in which one is concerned **2 :** IMPORTANCE, CONSEQUENCE **3** *archaic* **:** INVOLVEMENT, PARTICIPATION **4 :** SOLICITUDE, ANXIETY

[1]**con·cert** \ˈkän(t)-sərt, ˈkän-ˌsərt\ *n* [F, fr. It *concerto,* fr. *concertare*] (1586) **1** *obs* **:** musical harmony : CONCORD **2 a :** agreement in design or plan **:** union formed by mutual communication of opinion and views **b :** a concerted action ⟨the sacrifice was hailed with a ~ of praise⟩ **3 :** a public performance of music or dancing — **concert** *adj* — **in concert :** TOGETHER

[2]**con·cert** \kən-ˈsərt\ *vb* [F *concerter,* fr. OIt *concertare,* fr. LL, fr. L, to contend, fr. *com-* + *certare* to strive, fr. *certus* decided, determined — more at CERTAIN] *vt* (1694) **1 :** to make a plan for ⟨~ measures for aiding the poor⟩ **2 :** to settle or adjust by conferring and reaching an agreement ⟨got together to ~ their differences⟩ **~** *vi* **:** to act in harmony or conjunction

con·cert·ed \kən-ˈsərt-əd\ *adj* (1716) **1 a :** mutually contrived or agreed on ⟨a ~ effort⟩ **b :** performed in unison ⟨~ artillery fire⟩ **2 :** arranged in parts for several voices or instruments — **con·cert·ed·ly** *adv* — **con·cert·ed·ness** *n*

con·cert·go·er \ˈkän(t)-sərt-ˌgō(-ə)r, ˈkän-ˌsərt-\ *n* (1855) **:** one who frequently attends concerts — **con·cert·go·ing** \-ˌgō-iŋ, -ˌgȯ(-)iŋ\ *n or adj*

con·cert grand \ˌkän(t)-sərt-, ˌkän-ˌsərt-\ *n* (ca. 1891) **:** a grand piano of the largest size adapted in volume, timbre, and brilliance of tone to concert use

con·cer·ti·na \ˌkän(t)-sər-ˈtē-nə\ *n* (1837) **1 :** a musical instrument of the accordion family **2 :** a coiled barbed wire for use as an obstacle — called also *concertina wire*

con·cer·ti·no \ˌkän-chər-ˈtē-(ˌ)nō\ *n, pl* **-nos** [It, dim. of *concerto*] (1801) **1 :** the solo instruments in a concerto grosso **2 :** a short concerto

con·cert·ize \ˈkän(t)-sər-ˌtīz\ *vi* **-ized; -iz·ing** (1883) **:** to perform professionally in concerts

con·cert·mas·ter \ˈkän(t)-sərt-ˌmas-tər\ *or* **con·cert·meis·ter** \-ˌmī-stər\ *n* [G *konzertmeister,* fr. *konzert* concert + *meister* master] (1876) **:** the leader of the first violins of an orchestra and by custom usu. the assistant to the conductor

con·cer·to \kən-ˈchert-(ˌ)ō *also* -ˈchərt-\ *n, pl* **-ti** \-(ˌ)ē\ *or* **-tos** [It, fr. *concerto* concert] (1730) **:** a piece for one or more soloists and orchestra with three contrasting movements

concerto gros·so \-ˈgrō-(ˌ)sō, -ˈgrȯ-\ *n, pl* **concerti gros·si** \-(ˌ)sē\ [It, lit., big concerto] (1724) **:** a baroque orchestral composition featuring a small group of solo instruments contrasting with the full orchestra

concert pitch *n* (1767) **1 :** INTERNATIONAL PITCH **2 :** a high state of fitness, tension, or readiness

con·ces·sion \kən-ˈsesh-ən\ *n* [F or L; F, fr. L *concession-, concessio,* fr. *concessus,* pp. of *concedere* to concede] (15c) **1 a :** the act or an instance of conceding **b :** the admitting of a point claimed in argument **2 :** something conceded: **a :** ACKNOWLEDGMENT, ADMISSION **b :** GRANT **c (1) :** a grant of land or property esp. by a government in return for services or for a particular use **(2) :** a right to undertake and profit by a specified activity **(3) :** a lease of a portion of premises for a particular purpose; *also* **:** the portion leased or the activities carried on — **con·ces·sion·al** \-ˈsesh-nəl, -ən-ᵊl\ *adj* — **con·ces·sion·ary** \-ˈsesh-ə-ˌner-ē\ *adj*

con·ces·sion·aire \kən-ˌsesh-ə-ˈna(ə)r, -ˈne(ə)r\ *n* [F *concessionnaire,* fr. *concession*] (1862) **:** the owner or operator of a concession; *esp* **:** one that operates a refreshment stand at a recreational center

con·ces·sion·er \kən-ˈsesh-(ə-)nər\ *n* (ca. 1891) **:** CONCESSIONAIRE

con·ces·sive \kən-ˈses-iv\ *adj* (1711) **1 :** denoting concession ⟨a ~ clause⟩ **2 :** making for or being a concession — **con·ces·sive·ly** *adv*

conch \ˈkäŋk, ˈkänch, ˈkȯŋk\ *n, pl* **conchs** \ˈkäŋks, ˈkȯŋks\ *or* **conch·es** \ˈkän-chəz\ [L *concha* mussel, mussel shell, fr. Gk *konchē;* akin to Skt *śaṅkha* conch shell] (14c) **1 :** any of various large spiral-shelled marine gastropod mollusks (as of the genera *Strombus* and *Cassis*); *also* **:** its shell used esp. for cameos **2** *often cap* **:** a native or resident of the Florida keys **3 :** CONCHA 2

conch- *or* **concho-** *comb form* [Gk *konch-, koncho-,* fr. *konchē*] **:** shell ⟨*conch*ology⟩ ⟨*conch*iolin⟩

con·cha \ˈkäŋ-kə\ *n, pl* **con·chae** \-ˌkē, -ˌkī\ [It & L; It *conca* semidome, apse, fr. LL *concha,* fr. L, shell] (1598) **1 a :** the plain semidome of an apse **b :** APSE **2 :** something shaped like a shell; *esp* **:** the largest and deepest concavity of the external ear — **con·chal** \-kəl\ *adj*

con·choi·dal \käŋ-ˈkȯid-ᵊl, kän-\ *adj* [Gk *konchoeidēs* like a mussel, fr. *konchē*] (1666) **:** having elevations or depressions shaped like the inside surface of a bivalve shell — **con·choi·dal·ly** \-ᵊl-ē\ *adv*

con·chol·o·gy \käŋ-ˈkäl-ə-jē\ *n* (1776) **1 :** a branch of zoology that deals with shells **2 :** a treatise on shells — **con·chol·o·gist** \-jəst\ *n*

con·cierge \kōⁿ-ˈsyerzh\ *n, pl* **con·cierges** \-ˈsyerzh(-əz)\ [F, modif. of L *conservus* fellow slave, fr. *com-* + *servus* slave] (1647) **1 :** a resident in an apartment building esp. in France who serves as doorkeeper, landlord's representative, and janitor **2 :** a usu. multilingual hotel staff member esp. in Europe who handles luggage and mail, makes reservations, and arranges tours for the guests

con·cil·i·ar \kən-ˈsil-ē-ər\ *adj* [L *concilium* council] (1677) **:** of, relating to, or issued by a council — **con·cil·i·ar·ly** *adv*

con·cil·i·ate \kən-ˈsil-ē-ˌāt\ *vb* **-at·ed; -at·ing** [L *conciliatus,* pp. of *conciliare* to assemble, unite, win over, fr. *concilium* assembly, council — more at COUNCIL] *vt* (1545) **1 :** to gain (as goodwill) by pleasing acts **2 :** to make compatible : RECONCILE **3 :** APPEASE **~** *vi* **:** to become friendly or agreeable ***syn*** see PACIFY — **con·cil·i·a·tion** \-ˌsil-ē-ˈā-shən\ *n* — **con·cil·i·a·tive** \-ˈsil-ē-ˌāt-iv\ *adj* — **con·cil·i·a·tor** \-ˌāt-ər\ *n* — **con·cil·ia·to·ry** \-ˈsil-yə-ˌtōr-ē, -ˈsil-ē-ə-, -ˌtȯr-\ *adj*

con·cin·ni·ty \kən-ˈsin-ət-ē\ *n, pl* **-ties** [L *concinnitas,* fr. *concinnus* skillfully put together] (1531) **:** harmony or elegance of design esp. of literary style in adaptation of parts to a whole or to each other

con·cise \kən-ˈsīs\ *adj* [L *concisus,* fr. pp. of *concidere* to cut up, fr. *com-* + *caedere* to cut, strike; akin to MHG *heie* mallet, Arm *xait'* to prick] (1590) **1 :** marked by brevity of expression or statement : free from all elaboration and superfluous detail **2 :** cut short : BRIEF — **con·cise·ly** *adv* — **con·cise·ness** *n*

syn CONCISE, TERSE, SUCCINCT, LACONIC, SUMMARY, PITHY, COMPENDIOUS mean very brief in statement or expression. CONCISE suggests the removal of all that is superfluous or elaborative; TERSE implies pointed conciseness; SUCCINCT implies the greatest possible compression; LACONIC implies brevity to the point of seeming rude, indifferent, or mysterious; SUMMARY suggests the statement of main points with no elaboration or explanation; PITHY adds to SUCCINCT or TERSE the implication of richness of meaning or substance; COMPENDIOUS applies to a treatment at once full in scope and brief and concise in treatment.

con·ci·sion \kən-ˈsizh-ən\ *n* [ME, fr. L *concision-, concisio,* fr. *concisus,* pp.] (14c) **1** *archaic* **:** a cutting up or off **2 :** the quality or state of being concise

con·clave \ˈkän-ˌklāv\ *n* [ME, fr. MF or ML; MF, fr. ML, fr. L, room that can be locked up, fr. *com-* + *clavis* key — more at CLAVICLE] (15c) **1 :** a private meeting or secret assembly; *esp* **:** a meeting of Roman Catholic cardinals secluded continuously while choosing a pope **2 :** a gathering of a group or association

con·clude \kən-ˈklüd\ *vb* **con·clud·ed; con·clud·ing** [ME *concluden,* fr. L *concludere* to shut up, end, infer, fr. *com-* + *claudere* to shut — more at CLOSE] *vt* (14c) **1** *obs* **:** to shut up : ENCLOSE **2 :** to bring to an end esp. in a particular way or with a particular action ⟨~ a meeting with a prayer⟩ **3 a :** to reach as a logically necessary end by reasoning **:** infer on the basis of evidence ⟨*concluded* that her argument was sound⟩ **b :** to make a decision about : DECIDE ⟨*concluded* he would wait a little longer⟩ **c :** to come to an agreement on : EFFECT ⟨~ a sale⟩ **4 :** to bring about as a result : COMPLETE **~** *vi* **1 :** END **2 a :** to form a final judgment **b :** to reach a decision or agreement ***syn*** see CLOSE, INFER — **con·clud·er** *n*

con·clu·sion \kən-ˈklü-zhən\ *n* [ME, fr. MF, fr. L *conclusion-, conclusio,* fr. *conclusus,* pp. of *concludere*] (14c) **1 a :** a reasoned judgment **:** INFERENCE **b :** the necessary consequence of two or more propositions taken as premises; *esp* **:** the inferred proposition of a syllogism **2 :** the last part of something: as **a :** RESULT, OUTCOME **b** *pl* **:** trial of strength or skill — used in the phrase *try conclusions* **c :** a final summation **d :** the final decision in a law case **e :** the final part of a pleading in law **3 :** an act or instance of concluding

con·clu·sive \-ˈklü-siv, -ziv\ *adj* (1612) **1 :** of or relating to a conclusion **2 :** putting an end to debate or question esp. by reason of irrefutability — **con·clu·sive·ly** *adv* — **con·clu·sive·ness** *n*

syn CONCLUSIVE, DECISIVE, DETERMINATIVE, DEFINITIVE mean bringing to an end. CONCLUSIVE applies to reasoning or logical proof that puts an end to debate or questioning; DECISIVE may apply to something that ends a controversy, a contest, or any uncertainty; DETERMINATIVE adds an implication of giving a fixed course or direction; DEFINITIVE applies to what is put forth as final and permanent.

con·coct \kən-ˈkäkt, kän-\ *vt* [L *concoctus,* pp. of *concoquere* to cook together, fr. *com-* + *coquere* to cook — more at COOK] (1675) **1 :** to prepare by combining crude materials **2 :** DEVISE, FABRICATE — **con·coct·er** *n* — **con·coc·tion** \-ˈkäk-shən\ *n* — **con·coc·tive** \-ˈkäk-tiv\ *adj*

con·com·i·tance \kən-ˈkäm-ət-ən(t)s, kän-\ *n* (1535) **:** ACCOMPANIMENT; *esp* **:** a conjunction that is regular and is marked by correlative variation of accompanying elements

1**con·com·i·tant** \-ət-ənt\ *adj* [L *concomitant-, concomitans,* prp. of *concomitari* to accompany, fr. *com-* + *comitari* to accompany, fr. *comit-, comes* companion — more at COUNT] (1607) **:** accompanying esp. in a subordinate or incidental way — **con·com·i·tant·ly** *adv*

2**concomitant** *n* (1621) **:** something that accompanies or is collaterally connected with something else **:** ACCOMPANIMENT

con·cord \ˈkän-ˌkȯ(ə)rd, ˈkäŋ-\ *n* [ME, fr. MF *concorde,* fr. L *concordia,* fr. *concord-, concors* agreeing, fr. *com-* + *cord-, cor* heart — more at HEART] (14c) **1 a :** a state of agreement **:** HARMONY **b :** a simultaneous occurrence of two or more musical tones that produces an impression of agreeableness or resolution on a listener — compare DISCORD **2 :** agreement by stipulation, compact, or covenant **3 :** grammatical agreement

con·cor·dance \kən-ˈkȯrd-ᵊn(t)s, kän-\ *n* [ME, fr. MF, fr. ML *concordantia,* fr. L *concordant-, concordans,* prp. of *concordare* to agree, fr. *concord-, concors*] (14c) **1 :** an alphabetical index of the principal words in a book or the works of an author with their immediate contexts **2 :** CONCORD, AGREEMENT

con·cor·dant \-ᵊnt\ *adj* [ME, fr. MF, fr. L *concordant-, concordans*] (15c) **:** CONSONANT, AGREEING — **con·cor·dant·ly** *adv*

con·cor·dat \kən-ˈkȯr-ˌdat\ *n* [F, fr. ML *concordatum,* fr. L, neut. of *concordatus,* pp. of *concordare*] (1616) **:** COMPACT, COVENANT; *specif* **:** an agreement between a pope and a sovereign or government for the regulation of ecclesiastical matters

con·cours d'e·le·gance \(ˌ)kōⁿ-ˌkü(ə)r-ˌdā-lā-ˈgäⁿs\ *n* [F *concours d'élégance,* lit., competition of elegance] (1950) **:** a show or contest of vehicles and accessories in which the entries are judged chiefly on excellence of appearance and turnout

con·course \ˈkän-ˌkō(ə)rs, ˈkäŋ-, -ˌkȯ(ə)rs\ *n* [ME, fr. MF & L; MF *concours,* fr. L *concursus,* fr. *concursus,* pp. of *concurrere* to run together — more at CONCUR] (14c) **1 :** an act or process of coming together and merging **2 :** a meeting produced by voluntary or spontaneous coming together **3 a :** an open space where roads or paths meet **b :** an open space or hall (as in a railroad terminal) where crowds gather

con·cres·cence \kən-ˈkres-ᵊn(t)s, kän-\ *n* [L *concrescentia,* fr. *concrescent-, concrescens,* prp. of *concrescere* to grow together, fr. *com-* + *crescere* to grow — more at CRESCENT] (1614) **1 :** increase by the addition of particles **2 :** a growing together **:** COALESCENCE; *esp* **:** convergence and fusion of the lateral lips of the blastopore to form the primordium of an embryo — **con·cres·cent** \-ᵊnt\ *adj*

1**con·crete** \(ˈ)kän-ˈkrēt, ˈkän-ˌ, kən-ˈ\ *adj* [ME, fr. L *concretus,* fr. pp. of *concrescere*] (14c) **1 :** naming a real thing or class of things ⟨the word *poem* is ~, *poetry* is abstract⟩ **2 :** formed by coalition of particles into one solid mass **3 a :** characterized by or belonging to immediate experience of actual things or events **b :** SPECIFIC, PARTICULAR **c :** REAL, TANGIBLE **4 :** relating to or made of concrete — **con·crete·ly** *adv* — **con·crete·ness** *n*

2**con·crete** \ˈkän-ˌkrēt, kän-ˈ\ *vb* **con·cret·ed; con·cret·ing** *vt* (1635) **1 a :** to form into a solid mass **:** SOLIDIFY **b :** COMBINE, BLEND **2 :** to make actual or real **:** cause to take on the qualities of reality **3 :** to cover with, form of, or set in concrete ~ *vi* **:** to become concreted

3**con·crete** \ˈkän-ˌkrēt, (ˈ)kän-ˈ\ *n* (1656) **1 :** a mass formed by concretion or coalescence of separate particles of matter in one body **2 :** a hard strong building material made by mixing a cementing material (as portland cement) and a mineral aggregate (as sand and gravel) with sufficient water to cause the cement to set and bind the entire mass **3 :** a waxy essence of flowers prepared by extraction and evaporation and used in perfumery

concrete music *n* (1950) **:** MUSIQUE CONCRÈTE

concrete poetry *n* (1958) **:** poetry in which the poet's intent is conveyed by the graphic patterns of letters, words, or symbols rather than by the conventional arrangement of words

con·cre·tion \kän-ˈkrē-shən, kən-\ *n* (1514) **1 :** something concreted: as **a :** a hard usu. inorganic mass (as a bezoar or tophus) formed in a living body **b :** a mass of mineral matter found generally in rock of a composition different from its own and produced by deposition from aqueous solution in the rock **2 :** the act or process of concreting **:** the state of being concreted ⟨~ of ideas in an hypothesis⟩ — **con·cre·tion·ary** \-shə-ˌner-ē\ *adj*

con·cret·ism \kän-ˈkrēt-ˌiz-əm, ˈkän-ˌ\ *n* (1865) **:** representation of abstract things as concrete; *esp* **:** the theory or practice of concrete poetry — **con·cret·ist** \-ˈkrēt-əst, -ˌkrēt-\ *n*

con·cret·ize \-ˌīz\ *vb* **-ized; -iz·ing** *vt* (1884) **:** to make concrete, specific, or definite ⟨tried to ~ his ideas⟩ ~ *vi* **:** to become concrete — **con·cret·i·za·tion** \(ˌ)kän-ˌkrēt-ə-ˈzā-shən\ *n*

con·cu·bi·nage \kän-ˈkyü-bə-nij, kən-\ *n* (14c) **1 :** cohabitation of persons not legally married **2 :** the state of being a concubine

con·cu·bine \ˈkäŋ-kyu̇-ˌbīn, ˈkän-\ *n* [ME, fr. MF, fr. L *concubina,* fr. *com-* + *cubare* to lie — more at HIP] (14c) **1 :** a woman living in a socially recognized state of concubinage **2 :** MISTRESS

con·cu·pis·cence \kän-ˈkyü-pə-sən(t)s, kən-\ *n* [ME, fr. MF, fr. LL *concupiscentia,* fr. L *concupiscent-, concupiscens,* prp. of *concupiscere* to desire ardently, fr. *com-* + *cupere* to desire — more at COVET] (14c) **:** strong desire; *esp* **:** sexual desire — **con·cu·pis·cent** \-sənt\ *adj*

con·cu·pis·ci·ble \-ˈkyü-pə-sə-bəl\ *adj* [ME, fr. MF or LL; MF, fr. LL *concupiscibilis,* fr. L *concupiscere*] (14c) **:** LUSTFUL, DESIROUS

con·cur \kən-ˈkər, kän-\ *vi* **con·curred; con·cur·ring** [ME *concurren,* fr. L *concurrere,* fr. *com-* + *currere* to run — more at CAR] (15c) **1 :** to act together to a common end or single effect **2 a :** APPROVE ⟨~ in a statement⟩ **b :** to express agreement ⟨~ with an opinion⟩ **3** *obs* **:** to come together **:** MEET **4 :** to happen together **:** COINCIDE ***syn*** see AGREE

con·cur·rence \-ˈkər-ən(t)s, -ˈkə-rən(t)s\ *n* (15c) **1 a :** agreement or union in action **:** COOPERATION **b (1) :** agreement in opinion or design **(2) :** CONSENT **2 :** a coming together **:** CONJUNCTION **3 :** a coincidence of equal powers in law

con·cur·rent \-ˈkər-ənt, -ˈkə-rənt\ *adj* [ME, fr. MF & L; MF, fr. L *concurrent-, concurrens,* prp. of *concurrere*] (14c) **1 :** operating or occurring at the same time **2 a :** CONVERGENT; *specif* **:** meeting or intersecting in a point **b :** running parallel **3 :** acting in conjunction **4 :** exercised over the same matter or area by two different authorities ⟨~ jurisdiction⟩ — **concurrent** *n* — **con·cur·rent·ly** *adv*

concurrent resolution *n* (1802) **:** a resolution passed by both houses of a legislative body that lacks the force of law

con·cuss \kən-ˈkəs\ *vt* [L *concussus,* pp.] (1597) **:** to affect with or as if with concussion

con·cus·sion \kən-ˈkəsh-ən\ *n* [MF or L; MF, fr. L *concussion-, concussio,* fr. *concussus,* pp. of *concutere* to shake violently, fr. *com-* + *quatere* to shake] (15c) **1 :** AGITATION, SHAKING **2 a :** a hard blow or collision **b :** a stunning, damaging, or shattering effect from a hard blow; *esp* **:** a jarring injury of the brain resulting in disturbance of cerebral function — **con·cus·sive** \-ˈkəs-iv\ *adj*

con·demn \kən-ˈdem\ *vt* [ME *condemnen,* fr. MF *condemner,* fr. L *condemnare,* fr. *com-* + *damnare* to condemn — more at DAMN] (14c) **1 :** to declare to be reprehensible, wrong, or evil usu. after weighing evidence and without reservation **2 a :** to pronounce guilty **:** CONVICT **b :** SENTENCE, DOOM **3 :** to adjudge unfit for use or consumption **4 :** to declare convertible to public use under the right of eminent domain ***syn*** see CRITICIZE — **con·dem·nable** \-ˈdem-(n)ə-bəl\ *adj* — **con·dem·na·to·ry** \-nə-ˌtōr-ē, -ˌtȯr-\ *adj* — **con·demn·er** \-ˈdem-ər\ *or* **con·dem·nor** \kən-ˈdem-ər; kən-ˌdem-ˈnȯ(ə)r, ˌkän-\ *n*

con·dem·na·tion \ˌkän-ˌdem-ˈnā-shən, -dəm-\ *n* (14c) **1 :** CENSURE, BLAME **2 :** the act of judicially condemning **3 :** the state of being condemned **4 :** a reason for condemning

con·den·sate \ˈkän-dən-ˌsāt, -ˌden-; kən-ˈden-\ *n* (ca. 1885) **:** a product of condensation; *esp* **:** a liquid obtained by condensation of a gas or vapor ⟨steam ~⟩

con·den·sa·tion \ˌkän-ˌden-ˈsā-shən, -dən-\ *n* (1603) **1 :** the act or process of condensing: as **a :** a chemical reaction involving union between molecules often with elimination of a simple molecule (as water) to form a new more complex compound of often greater molecular weight **b :** a reduction to a denser form (as from steam to water) **c :** compression of a written or spoken work into more concise form **2 :** the quality or state of being condensed **3 :** a product of condensing; *esp* **:** an abridgment of a literary work — **con·den·sa·tion·al** \-shnəl, -shən-ᵊl\ *adj*

con·dense \kən-ˈden(t)s\ *vb* **con·densed; con·dens·ing** [ME *condensen,* fr. MF *condenser,* fr. L *condensare,* fr. *com-* + *densare* to make dense, fr. *densus* dense] *vt* (15c) **:** to make denser or more compact; *esp* **:** to subject to condensation ~ *vi* **:** to undergo condensation ***syn*** see CONTRACT — **con·dens·able** *also* **con·dens·ible** \-ˈden(t)-sə-bəl\ *adj*

con·densed *adj* (15c) **:** reduced to a more compact form; *esp* **:** having a face that is narrower than that of a typeface not so characterized

condensed milk *n* (1863) **:** evaporated milk with sugar added

con·dens·er \kən-ˈden(t)-sər\ *n* (1686) **1 :** one that condenses: as **a :** a lens or mirror used to concentrate light on an object **b :** an apparatus in which gas or vapor is condensed **2 :** CAPACITOR

con·de·scend \ˌkän-di-ˈsend\ *vi* [ME *condescenden,* fr. MF *condescendre,* fr. LL *condescendere,* fr. L *com-* + *descendere* to descend] (14c) **1 a :** to descend to a less formal or dignified level **:** UNBEND **b :** to waive the privileges of rank **2 :** to assume an air of superiority

con·de·scen·dence \-ˈsen-dən(t)s\ *n* (1638) **:** CONDESCENSION

con·de·scend·ing *adj* (1707) **:** showing or characterized by condescension **:** PATRONIZING — **con·de·scend·ing·ly** \-ˈsen-diŋ-lē\ *adv*

con·de·scen·sion \ˌkän-di-ˈsen-chən\ *n* [LL *condescension-, condescensio,* fr. *condescensus,* pp. of *condescendere*] (1647) **1 :** voluntary descent from one's rank or dignity in relations with an inferior **2 :** patronizing attitude or behavior

con·dign \kən-ˈdīn, ˈkän-ˌ\ *adj* [ME *condigne,* fr. MF, fr. L *condignus* very worthy, fr. *com-* + *dignus* worthy — more at DECENT] (15c) **:** DESERVED, APPROPRIATE ⟨~ punishment⟩ — **con·dign·ly** *adv*

con·di·ment \ˈkän-də-mənt\ *n* [ME, fr. MF, fr. L *condimentum,* fr. *condire* to pickle, fr. *condere* to build, store up, fr. *com-* + *-dere* to put — more at DO] (15c) **:** something used to enhance the flavor of food; *esp* **:** a pungent seasoning — **con·di·men·tal** \ˌkän-də-ˈment-ᵊl\ *adj*

1**con·di·tion** \kən-ˈdish-ən\ *n* [ME *condicion,* fr. MF, fr. L *condicion-, condicio* terms of agreement, condition, fr. *condicere* to agree, fr. *com-* + *dicere* to say, determine — more at DICTION] (14c) **1 a :** a premise upon which the fulfillment of an agreement depends **:** STIPULATION **b** *obs* **:** COVENANT **c :** a provision making the effect of a legal instrument contingent upon an uncertain event; *also* **:** the event itself **2 :** something essential to the appearance or occurrence of something else **:** PREREQUISITE: as **a :** an environmental requirement ⟨available oxygen is an essential ~ for animal life⟩ **b :** the subordinate clause of a conditional sentence **3 a :** a restricting or modifying factor **:** QUALIFICATION **b :** an unsatisfactory academic grade that may be raised by

\ə\ abut \ᵊ\ kitten, F table \ər\ further \a\ ash \ā\ ace \ä\ cot, cart \au̇\ out \ch\ chin \e\ bet \ē\ easy \g\ go \i\ hit \ī\ ice \j\ job \ŋ\ sing \ō\ go \ȯ\ law \ȯi\ boy \th\ thin \t͟h\ the \ü\ loot \u̇\ foot \y\ yet \zh\ vision \á, k̲, ⁿ, œ, œ̄, ue, ue̅, ʸ\ see Guide to Pronunciation

doing additional work **4 a :** a state of being **b :** social status : RANK **c :** a usu. defective state of health ⟨a serious heart ~⟩ **d :** a state of physical fitness or readiness for use ⟨the car was in good ~⟩ ⟨exercising to get into ~⟩ **e** *pl* **:** attendant circumstances **5 a** *obs* **:** temper of mind **b** *obs* **:** TRAIT **c** *pl, archaic* **:** MANNERS, WAYS

²condition *vb* **con·di·tioned; con·di·tion·ing** \-'dish-(ə-)niŋ\ *vi, archaic* (15c) **:** to make stipulations ~ *vt* **1 :** to agree by stipulating **2 :** to make conditional **3 a :** to put into a proper state for work or use **b :** AIR-CONDITION **4 :** to give a grade of condition to **5 a :** to adapt, modify, or mold so as to conform to an environing culture **b :** to modify so that an act or response previously associated with one stimulus becomes associated with another — **con·di·tion·able** \-(ə-)nə-bəl\ *adj* — **con·di·tion·er** \-(ə-)nər\ *n*

con·di·tion·al \kən-'dish-nəl, -ən-ᵊl\ *adj* (14c) **1 :** subject to, implying, or dependent upon a condition ⟨a ~ promise⟩ **2 :** expressing, containing, or implying a supposition ⟨the ~ clause *if he speaks*⟩ **3 a :** true only for certain values of the variables or symbols involved ⟨~ equations⟩ **b :** stating the case when one or more random variables are fixed or one or more events are known ⟨~ frequency distribution⟩ **4 a :** CONDITIONED 3 ⟨~ reflex⟩ ⟨~ response⟩ **b :** established by conditioning as the stimulus eliciting a conditional response — **conditional** *n* — **con·di·tion·al·i·ty** \-,dish-ə-'nal-ət-ē\ *n* — **con·di·tion·al·ly** \-'dish-nə-lē, -ən-ᵊl-ē\ *adv*

conditional probability *n* (1961) **:** the probability that a given event will occur if it is certain that another event has taken place or will take place

con·di·tioned *adj* (1656) **1 :** CONDITIONAL **2 :** brought or put into a specified state **3 :** determined or established by conditioning

con·do \'kän-(,)dō\ *n* [by shortening] (1972) **:** CONDOMINIUM 3

con·dole \kən-'dōl\ *vb* **con·doled; con·dol·ing** [LL *condolēre*, fr. L *com-* + *dolēre* to feel pain; akin to Gk *daidalos* ingeniously formed] *vi* (1590) **1** *obs* **:** GRIEVE **2 :** to express sympathetic sorrow ⟨we ~ with you in your misfortune⟩ ~ *vt, archaic* **:** LAMENT, GRIEVE — **con·do·la·to·ry** \-'dō-lə-,tōr-ē, -,tór-\ *adj*

con·do·lence \kən-'dō-lən(t)s, 'kän-də-\ *n* (1603) **1 :** sympathy with another in sorrow **2 :** an expression of sympathy

con·dom \'kän-dəm, 'kən-\ *n* [origin unknown] (ca. 1706) **:** a sheath commonly of rubber worn over the penis (as to prevent conception or venereal infection during coitus)

con·do·min·i·um \,kän-də-'min-ē-əm\ *n, pl* **-ums** [NL, fr. L *com-* + *dominium* domain] (1705) **1 a :** joint dominion; *esp* **:** joint sovereignty by two or more nations **b :** a government operating under joint rule **2 :** a politically dependent territory under condominium **3 a :** individual ownership of a unit in a multiunit structure (as an apartment building) or on land owned in common (as a town house complex); *also* **:** a unit so owned **b :** a building containing condominiums

con·do·na·tion \,kän-də-'nā-shən, -dō-\ *n* (1625) **:** implied pardon of an offense by treating the offender as if it had not been committed

con·done \kən-'dōn\ *vt* **con·doned; con·don·ing** [L *condonare* to forgive, fr. *com-* + *donare* to give — more at DONATION] (1857) **:** to pardon or overlook voluntarily; *esp* **:** to treat as if trivial, harmless, or of no importance ⟨~ corruption in politics⟩ ***syn*** see EXCUSE — **con·don·able** \-'dō-nə-bəl\ *adj* — **con·don·er** *n*

con·dor \'kän-dər, -,dó(ə)r\ *n* [Sp *cóndor*, fr. Quechua *kúntur*] (1604) **1 :** a very large American vulture (*Vultur gryphus*) of the high Andes having the head and neck bare and the plumage dull black with a downy white neck ruff and white patches on the wings — compare CALIFORNIA CONDOR **2** *pl* **condors** *or* **con·do·res** \kən-'dōr-,ās, -'dór-\ **:** a coin (as the centesimo of Chile) bearing the picture of a condor

con·dot·tie·re \,kän-də-'tye(ə)r-ē, ,kän-,dät-ē-'e(ə)r-\ *n, pl* **-tie·ri** \-ē\ [It] (1794) **1 :** a leader of a band of mercenaries common in Europe between the 14th and 16th centuries; *also* **:** a member of such a band **2 :** a mercenary soldier

con·duce \kən-'d(y)üs\ *vi* **con·duced; con·duc·ing** [ME *conducen* to conduct, fr. L *conducere* to conduct, conduce, fr. *com-* + *ducere* to lead — more at TOW] (1586) **:** to lead or tend to a particular and usu. desirable result **:** CONTRIBUTE

con·du·cive \-'d(y)ü-siv\ *adj* (1646) **:** tending to promote or assist ⟨an atmosphere ~ to education⟩ — **con·du·cive·ness** *n*

¹con·duct \'kän-(,)dəkt\ *n* [alter. of ME *conduit*, fr. MF, act of leading, escort, fr. ML *conductus*, fr. L *conductus*, pp. of *conducere*] (15c) **1** *obs* **:** ESCORT, GUIDE **2 :** the act, manner, or process of carrying on **:** MANAGEMENT **3 :** a mode or standard of personal behavior esp. as based on moral principles

²con·duct \kən-'dəkt *also* 'kän-,dəkt\ *vt* (15c) **1 :** to bring by or as if by leading **:** GUIDE ⟨~ tourists through a museum⟩ **2 a :** to lead from a position of command ⟨~ a siege⟩ ⟨~ a class⟩ **b :** to direct or take part in the operation or management of ⟨~ an experiment⟩ ⟨~ a business⟩ ⟨~ an investigation⟩ **c :** to direct the performance of ⟨~ an orchestra⟩ ⟨~ an opera⟩ **3 a :** to convey in a channel **b :** to act as a medium for conveying **4 :** to cause (oneself) to act or behave in a particular and esp. in a controlled manner ~ *vi* **1** *of a road or passage* **:** to show the way **:** LEAD **2 a :** to act as leader or director **b :** to have the quality of transmitting light, heat, sound, or electricity — **con·duct·ibil·i·ty** \kən-,dək-tə-'bil-ət-ē\ *n* — **con·duct·ible** \-'dək-tə-bəl\ *adj*

syn CONDUCT, MANAGE, CONTROL, DIRECT mean to use one's powers to lead, guide, or dominate. CONDUCT implies taking responsibility for the acts and achievements of a group; MANAGE implies direct handling and manipulating or maneuvering toward a desired result; CONTROL implies a regulating or restraining in order to keep within bounds or on a course; DIRECT implies constant guiding and regulating so as to achieve smooth operation. ***syn*** see in addition BEHAVE

con·duc·tance \kən-'dək-tən(t)s\ *n* (1885) **1 :** conducting power **2 :** the readiness with which a conductor transmits an electric current **:** the reciprocal of electrical resistance

con·duc·tion \kən-'dək-shən\ *n* (1541) **1 :** the act of conducting or conveying **2 :** transmission through or by means of a conductor; *also* **:** CONDUCTIVITY **3 :** the transmission of excitation through living tissue and esp. nervous tissue

con·duc·tive \kən-'dək-tiv\ *adj* (1528) **:** having conductivity **:** relating to conduction (as of electricity)

con·duc·tiv·i·ty \,kän-,dək-'tiv-ət-ē, kən-\ *n, pl* **-ties** (1837) **:** the quality or power of conducting or transmitting: as **a :** the reciprocal of electrical resistivity **b :** the quality of living matter responsible for the transmission of and progressive reaction to stimuli

con·duc·to·met·ric *or* **con·duc·ti·met·ric** \kən-,dək-tə-'me-trik\ *adj* (ca. 1926) **1 :** of or relating to the measurement of conductivity **2 :** being or relating to titration based on determination of changes in the electrical conductivity of the solution

con·duc·tor \kən-'dək-tər\ *n* (15c) **:** one that conducts: as **a :** GUIDE **b :** a collector of fares in a public conveyance **c :** the leader of a musical ensemble **d :** a substance or body capable of transmitting electricity, heat, or sound — **con·duc·to·ri·al** \,kän-,dək-'tōr-ē-əl, kən-, -'tór-\ *adj*

con·duc·tress \kən-'dək-trəs\ *n* (1885) **:** a female conductor

con·duit \'kän-,d(y)ü-ət *also* -d(w)ət\ *n* [ME — more at CONDUCT] (14c) **1 :** a natural or artificial channel through which something (as a fluid) is conveyed **2** *archaic* **:** FOUNTAIN **3 :** a pipe, tube, or tile for protecting electric wires or cables **4 :** a means of transmitting or distributing ⟨a ~ for illicit payments⟩ ⟨a ~ of information⟩

con·du·pli·cate \(')kän-'d(y)ü-pli-kət\ *adj* [L *conduplicatus*, pp. of *conduplicare* to double, fr. *com-* + *duplic-, duplex* double — more at DUPLEX] (1777) **:** folded lengthwise — used of leaves or petals in the bud — **con·du·pli·ca·tion** \,kän-,d(y)ü-pli-'kā-shən\ *n*

con·dy·lar \'kän-də-lər\ *adj* (1876) **:** of or relating to a condyle

con·dyle \'kän-,dīl *also* -dᵊl\ *n* [F & L; F, fr. L *condylus* knuckle, fr. Gk *kondylos*] (1634) **:** an articular prominence of a bone; *esp* **:** either of a pair that resembles knuckles — **con·dy·loid** \-də-,lóid\ *adj*

con·dy·lo·ma \,kän-də-'lō-mə\ *n* [NL, fr. Gk *kondylōma*, fr. *kondylos*] (ca. 1656) **:** a warty growth on the skin or adjoining mucous membrane usu. near the anus and genital organs — **con·dy·lo·ma·tous** \-mət-əs\ *adj*

¹cone \'kōn\ *n* [MF or L; MF, fr. L *conus*, fr. Gk *kōnos* — more at HONE] (1562) **1 a :** a mass of ovule-bearing or pollen-bearing scales or bracts in trees of the pine family or in cycads that are arranged usu. on a somewhat elongated axis **b :** any of several flower or fruit clusters suggesting a cone **2 a :** a solid generated by rotating a right triangle about one of its legs — called also *right circular cone* **b :** a solid bounded by a circular or other closed plane base and the surface formed by line segments joining every point of the boundary of the base to a common vertex — see VOLUME table **c :** a surface traced by a moving straight line passing through a fixed vertex **3 :** something that resembles a cone in shape: as **a :** one of the short sensory end organs of the vertebrate retina that function in color vision **b :** any of numerous somewhat conical tropical gastropod mollusks (family Conidae) **c :** the apex of a volcano **d :** a crisp cone-shaped wafer for holding ice cream

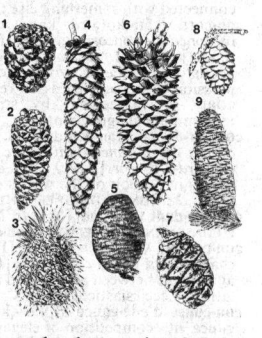

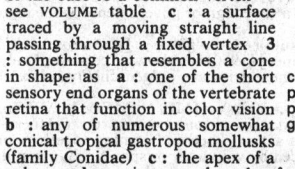

cone 1a: *1* stone pine, *2* cluster pine, *3* Santa Lucia fir, *4* sugar pine, *5* deodar, *6* big-cone pine, *7* giant sequoia, *8* red spruce, *9* Nordmann's fir

²cone *vt* **coned; con·ing** (ca. 1859) **1 :** to make cone-shaped **2 :** to bevel like the slanting surface of a cone ⟨~ a tire⟩

cone·flow·er \'kōn-,flaù(-ə)r\ *n* (1817) **:** any of several composite plants having cone-shaped flower disks; *esp* **:** RUDBECKIA

cone·nose \'kōn-,nōz\ *n* (ca. 1891) **:** any of various large bloodsucking bugs (esp. genus *Triatoma*) including some capable of inflicting painful bites — called also *assassin bug, kissing bug*

con es·pres·sio·ne \,kän-,es-(,)pres-ē-'ō-nē, ,kōn-, -'ō-(,)nā\ *adv* [It, lit., with expression] (ca. 1891) **:** with feeling — used as a direction in music

Con·es·to·ga \,kän-ə-'stō-gə\ *n* [*Conestoga*, Pa.] (1750) **:** a broad-wheeled covered wagon drawn usu. by six horses and used esp. for transporting freight across the prairies

co·ney \'kō-nē\ *n, pl* **coneys** [ME *conies*, pl., fr. OF *conis*, pl. of *conil*, fr. L *cuniculus*] (13c) **1 a** (1) **:** RABBIT; *esp* **:** the European rabbit (*Oryctolagus cuniculus*) (2) **:** PIKA **b :** HYRAX **c :** rabbit fur **2** *archaic* **:** DUPE **3 :** any of several fishes; *esp* **:** a dusky black-spotted reddish-finned grouper (*Cephalopholis fulvus*) of the tropical Atlantic

con·fab \kən-'fab, 'kän-,\ *vi* **con·fabbed; con·fab·bing** (1741) **:** CONFABULATE — **con·fab** \'kän-,fab, kən-'\ *n*

con·fab·u·late \kən-'fab-yə-,lāt\ *vi* **-lat·ed; -lat·ing** [L *confabulatus*, pp. of *confabulari*, fr. *com-* + *fabulari* to talk, fr. *fabula* story — more at FABLE] (1613) **1 :** CHAT **2 :** to hold a discussion **:** CONFER — **con·fab·u·la·tion** \kən-,fab-yə-'lā-shən, ,kän-\ *n* — **con·fab·u·la·tor** \kən-'fab-yə-,lāt-ər\ *n* — **con·fab·u·la·to·ry** \-lə-,tōr-ē, -,tór-\ *adj*

con·fect \kən-'fekt\ *vt* [L *confectus*, pp. of *conficere* to prepare — more at COMFIT] (14c) **1 :** to put together from varied material ⟨writers ~*ing* best sellers⟩ **2 a :** PREPARE **b :** PRESERVE — **con·fect** \'kän-,\ *n*

con·fec·tion \kən-'fek-shən\ *n* (15c) **1 :** the act or process of confecting **2 :** something confected: as **a :** a fancy dish or sweetmeat; *also* **:** a sweet food **b :** a medicinal preparation usu. made with sugar, syrup, or honey **c :** a piece of fine craftsmanship

con·fec·tion·ary \-shə-,ner-ē\ *n, pl* **-ar·ies** (1605) **1** *archaic* **:** CONFECTIONER **2 :** CONFECTIONERY 3 **3 :** SWEETS — **confectionary** *adj*

con·fec·tion·er \-sh(ə-)nər\ *n* (1591) **:** a manufacturer of or dealer in confections

confectioners' sugar *n* (ca. 1891) **:** a refined finely powdered sugar

con·fec·tion·ery \-shə-,ner-ē\ *n, pl* **-er·ies** (1545) **1 :** sweet foods (as candy or pastry) **2 :** the confectioner's art or business **3 :** a confectioner's shop

con·fed·er·a·cy \kən-'fed-(ə-)rə-sē\ *n, pl* **-cies** (14c) **1 :** a league or compact for mutual support or common action **:** ALLIANCE **2 :** a combination of persons for unlawful purposes **:** CONSPIRACY **3 :** the body formed by persons, states, or nations united by a league; *specif, cap* **:** the 11 southern states seceding from the U.S. in 1860 and 1861 — **con·fed·er·al** \-(ə-)rəl\ *adj* — **con·fed·er·al·ist** \-əst\ *n*

1**con·fed·er·ate** \kən-ˈfed-(ə-)rət\ *adj* [ME *confederat,* fr. LL *confoederatus,* pp. of *confoederare* to unite by a league, fr. L *com-* + *foeder-, foedus* compact — more at FEDERAL] (14c) **1 :** united in a league **:** ALLIED **2** *cap* **:** of or relating to the Confederate States of America

2**confederate** *n* (15c) **1 :** ALLY, ACCOMPLICE **2** *cap* **:** an adherent of the Confederate States of America or their cause

3**con·fed·er·ate** \-ˈfed-ə-ˌrāt\ *vb* **-at·ed; -at·ing** *vt* (1531) **:** to unite in a confederacy ~ *vi* **:** to band together — **con·fed·er·a·tive** \-ˈfed-(ə-)rət-iv, -ə-ˌrāt-\ *adj*

Confederate Memorial Day *n* (1899) **:** any of several days appointed for the commemoration of servicemen of the Confederacy

confederate rose *n, often cap C* (1930) **:** a Chinese mallow (*Hibiscus mutabilis*) with white or pink flowers that become deep red at night

con·fed·er·a·tion \kən-ˌfed-ə-ˈrā-shən\ *n* (15c) **1 :** an act of confederating **:** a state of being confederated **:** ALLIANCE **2 :** LEAGUE

con·fer \kən-ˈfər\ *vb* **con·ferred; con·fer·ring** [L *conferre* to bring together, fr. *com-* + *ferre* to carry — more at BEAR] *vt* (1542) **1 :** to bestow from or as if from a position of superiority ⟨*conferred* an honorary degree on her⟩ ⟨knowing how to read was a gift *conferred* with manhood —Murray Kempton⟩ **2 :** to give (as a property or characteristic) to someone or something ⟨a reputation for power will ~ power —John Spanier⟩ ~ *vi* **:** to compare views or take counsel **:** CONSULT **syn** see GIVE — **con·fer·ment** \-ˈfər-mənt\ *n* — **con·fer·ra·ble** \-ˈfər-ə-bəl\ *adj* — **con·fer·ral** \-ˈfər-əl\ *n* — **con·fer·rer** \-ˈfər-ər\ *n*

con·fer·ee \ˌkän-fə-ˈrē\ *n* (1771) **:** one who confers with others

con·fer·ence \ˈkän-f(ə-)rən(t)s, -fərn(t)s, *for 2 usu* kən-ˈfər-ən(t)s\ *n* (1527) **1 a :** a meeting of two or more persons for discussing matters of common concern **b :** a usu. formal interchange of views **:** CONSULTATION **c :** a meeting of members of the two branches of a legislature to adjust differences **d :** CAUCUS **2** *also* **con·fer·rence** \kən-ˈfər-ən(t)s\ **:** BESTOWAL, CONFERMENT **3 a :** a representative assembly or administrative organization of a denomination **b :** a territorial division of a denomination **4 :** an association of athletic teams — **con·fer·en·tial** \ˌkän-fə-ˈren-chəl\ *adj*

conference call *n* (1941) **:** a telephone call by which a caller can speak with several people at the same time

con·fess \kən-ˈfes\ *vb* [ME *confessen,* fr. MF *confesser,* fr. OF, fr. *confes* having confessed, fr. L *confessus,* pp. of *confitēri* to confess, fr. *com-* + *fatēri* to confess; akin to L *fari* to speak — more at BAN] *vt* (14c) **1 :** to tell or make known (as something wrong or damaging to oneself) **:** ADMIT **2 a :** to acknowledge (sin) to God or to a priest **b :** to receive the confession of (a penitent) **3 :** to declare faith in or adherence to **:** PROFESS **4 :** to give evidence of ~ *vi* **1 a :** to disclose one's faults; *specif* **:** to unburden one's sins or the state of one's conscience to God or to a priest **b :** to hear a confession **2 :** ADMIT, OWN **syn** see ACKNOWLEDGE — **con·fess·able** \-ə-bəl\ *adj*

con·fessed·ly \-ˈfes-əd-lē, -ˈfest-lē\ *adv* (1640) **:** by confession

con·fes·sion \kən-ˈfesh-ən\ *n* (14c) **1 :** an act of confessing; *specif* **:** a disclosure of one's sins in the sacrament of penance **2 :** a statement of what is confessed: as **a :** a written acknowledgment of guilt by a party accused of an offense **b :** a formal statement of religious beliefs **:** CREED **3 :** an organized religious body having a common creed — **con·fes·sion·al** \-ˈfesh-nəl, -ən-ᵊl\ *adj* — **con·fes·sion·al·ism** \-ˌiz-əm\ *n* — **con·fes·sion·al·ist** \-əst\ *n* — **con·fes·sion·al·ly** \-ē\ *adv*

confessional *n* (1727) **1 :** a place where a priest hears confessions **2 :** the practice of confessing to a priest

con·fes·sor \kən-ˈfes-ər, *1 & 3 also* ˈkän-ˌfes-ər, *3 also* ˈkän-fə-ˌsȯ(ə)r\ *n* (12c) **1 :** one who gives heroic evidence of faith but does not suffer martyrdom **2 :** one that confesses **3 a :** a priest who hears confessions **b :** a priest who is one's regular spiritual guide

con·fet·ti \kən-ˈfet-ē\ *n* [It, pl. of *confetto* sweetmeat, fr. ML *confectum,* fr. L, neut. of *confectus,* pp. of *conficere* to prepare — more COMFIT] (1815) **:** small bits or streamers of brightly colored paper made for throwing (as at weddings)

con·fi·dant \ˈkän-fə-ˌdant, -ˌdänt; ˈkän-fəd-ənt\ *n* [F *confident,* fr. It *confidente,* fr. *confidente* confident, trustworthy, fr. L *confident-, confidens*] (1646) **:** one to whom secrets are entrusted; *esp* **:** INTIMATE

con·fi·dante *like* CONFIDANT\ *n* [F *confidente,* fem. of *confident*] (1696) **:** CONFIDANT; *esp* **:** one who is a woman

con·fide \kən-ˈfīd\ *vb* **con·fid·ed; con·fid·ing** [ME *confiden,* fr. MF or L; MF *confider,* fr. L *confidere,* fr. *com-* + *fidere* to trust — more at BIDE] *vi* (15c) **1 :** to have confidence **:** TRUST **2 :** to show confidence by imparting secrets ~ *vt* **1 :** to tell confidentially **2 :** ENTRUST **syn** see COMMIT — **con·fid·er** *n*

1**con·fi·dence** \ˈkän-fəd-ən(t)s, -fə-ˌden(t)s\ *n* (15c) **1 a :** faith or belief that one will act in a right, proper, or effective way ⟨have ~ in a leader⟩ **b :** a feeling or consciousness of one's powers or of reliance on one's circumstances ⟨he had perfect ~ in his ability to succeed⟩ ⟨met the risk with brash ~⟩ **2 :** the quality or state of being certain **:** CERTITUDE ⟨they had every ~ of success⟩ **3 a :** a relation of trust or intimacy ⟨took his friend into his ~⟩ **b :** reliance on another's discretion ⟨their story was told in strictest ~⟩ **c :** support esp. in a legislative body ⟨vote of ~⟩ **4 :** a communication made in confidence **:** SECRET

syn CONFIDENCE, ASSURANCE, SELF-POSSESSION, APLOMB mean a state of mind or a manner marked by easy coolness and freedom from uncertainty, diffidence, or embarrassment. CONFIDENCE stresses faith in oneself and one's powers without any suggestion of conceit or arrogance ⟨had the *confidence* that comes only from long experience⟩ ASSURANCE carries a stronger implication of certainty and may suggest arrogance or lack of objectivity in assessing one's own powers ⟨had a conceited *assurance* of his own worth⟩ SELF-POSSESSION implies an ease or coolness under stress that reflects perfect self-control and command of one's powers ⟨he answered the insolent question with complete *self-possession*⟩ APLOMB applies to the bearing or behavior under difficulties of a person with marked assurance or self-possession but usu. carries none of the unpleasant connotations often felt in ASSURANCE ⟨meet a challenge with *aplomb*⟩

2**confidence** *adj* (1849) **:** of or relating to swindling by false promises ⟨a ~ game⟩

confidence interval *n* (1934) **:** a group of continuous or discrete adjacent values that is used to estimate a statistical parameter (as a mean or variance) and that tends to include the true value of the parameter a predetermined proportion of the time if the process of finding the group of values is repeated a number of times

confidence limits *n pl* (1939) **:** the end points of a confidence interval

con·fi·dent \ˈkän-fəd-ənt, -fə-ˌdent\ *adj* [L *confident-, confidens,* fr. prp. of *confidere*] (1576) **1 :** characterized by assurance; *esp* **:** SELF-RELIANT **2** *obs* **:** TRUSTFUL, CONFIDING **3 a :** full of conviction **:** CERTAIN **b :** COCKSURE — **con·fi·dent·ly** *adv*

con·fi·den·tial \ˌkän-fə-ˈden-chəl\ *adj* (1759) **1 :** marked by intimacy or willingness to confide ⟨a ~ tone⟩ **2 :** PRIVATE, SECRET ⟨~ information⟩ **3 :** entrusted with confidences ⟨~ clerk⟩ **4 :** containing information whose unauthorized disclosure could be prejudicial to the national interest — compare SECRET, TOP SECRET — **con·fi·den·ti·al·i·ty** \-ˌden-chē-ˈal-ət-ē\ *n* — **con·fi·den·tial·ly** \-ˈdench-(ə-)lē\ *adv* — **con·fi·den·tial·ness** \-ˈden-chəl-nəs\ *n*

con·fid·ing \kən-ˈfīd-iŋ\ *adj* (1829) **:** tending to confide **:** TRUSTFUL — **con·fid·ing·ly** \-iŋ-lē\ *adv* — **con·fid·ing·ness** *n*

con·fig·u·rat·ed \kən-ˈfig-(y)ə-ˌrāt-əd\ *adj* (ca. 1752) **:** having a patterned surface — used of glass or metal

con·fig·u·ra·tion \kən-ˌfig-(y)ə-ˈrā-shən, ˌkän-\ *n* [LL *configuration-, configuratio* similar formation, fr. L *configuratus,* pp. of *configurare* to form from or after, fr. *com-* + *figurare* to form, fr. *figura* figure] (1646) **1 a :** relative arrangement of parts or elements: as (1) **:** SHAPE ⟨fish of nondescript ~ —Cassandra Tate⟩ (2) **:** contour of land ⟨~ of the mountains⟩ (3) **:** functional arrangement ⟨a small business computer system in its simplest ~⟩ **b :** something (as a figure, contour, pattern, or apparatus) produced by such arrangement **c :** the stable structural makeup of a chemical compound esp. with reference to the space relations of the constituent atoms **2 :** GESTALT ⟨personality ~⟩ **syn** see FORM — **con·fig·u·ra·tion·al** \-shnəl, -shən-ᵊl\ *adj* — **con·fig·u·ra·tion·al·ly** \-ē\ *adv* — **con·fig·u·ra·tive** \-ˈfig-(y)ə-rət-iv\ *adj*

con·fig·ure \kən-ˈfig-yər, *esp Brit* -ˈfig-ər\ *vt* **-ured; -ur·ing** (14c) **:** to set up for operation esp. in a particular way ⟨a fighter plane *configured* for the Malaysian air force⟩

1**con·fine** \ˈkän-ˌfīn *also* kən-ˈ\ *n* [MF or L; MF *confines,* pl., fr. L *confine* border, fr. neut. of *confinis* adjacent, fr. *com-* + *finis* end] (15c) **1** *pl* **a :** something (as borders or walls) that encloses ⟨in the ~s of the big city slums —J. B. Conant⟩ ⟨outside the ~s of the office or hospital —W.A. Nolen⟩; *also* **:** something that restrains ⟨escape from the ~s of soot and clutter —E.S. Muskie⟩ **b :** SCOPE 3 ⟨work within the ~s of a small group —Frank Newman⟩ ⟨beyond all the known ~s of history —Alfred Kazin⟩ **2 a** *archaic* **:** RESTRICTION **b** *obs* **:** PRISON

2**con·fine** \kən-ˈfīn\ *vb* **con·fined; con·fin·ing** *vi, archaic* (1523) **:** BORDER ~ *vt* **1 a :** to hold within a location **b :** IMPRISON **2 :** to keep within limits ⟨will ~ my remarks to one subject⟩ **syn** see LIMIT — **con·fin·er** *n*

con·fined \kən-ˈfīnd\ *adj* (1772) **:** undergoing childbirth

con·fine·ment \kən-ˈfīn-mənt\ *n* (1646) **:** an act of confining **:** the state of being confined ⟨solitary ~⟩; *esp* **:** LYING-IN

con·firm \kən-ˈfərm\ *vt* [ME *confirmen,* fr. OF *confirmer,* fr. L *confirmare,* fr. *com-* + *firmare* to make firm, fr. *firmus* firm] (13c) **1 :** to make firm or firmer **:** STRENGTHEN **2 :** to give approval to **:** RATIFY **3 :** to administer the rite of confirmation to **4 :** to give new assurance of the validity of **:** remove doubt about by authoritative act or indisputable fact — **con·firm·abil·i·ty** \-ˌfər-mə-ˈbil-ət-ē\ *n* — **con·firm·able** \-ˈfər-mə-bəl\ *adj*

syn CONFIRM, CORROBORATE, SUBSTANTIATE, VERIFY, AUTHENTICATE, VALIDATE mean to attest to the truth or validity of something. CONFIRM implies the removing of doubts by an authoritative statement or indisputable fact; CORROBORATE suggests the strengthening of what is already partly established; SUBSTANTIATE implies the offering of evidence that sustains the contention; VERIFY implies the establishing of correspondence of actual facts or details with those proposed or guessed at; AUTHENTICATE implies establishing genuineness by adducing legal or official documents or expert opinion; VALIDATE implies establishing validity by authoritative affirmation or by factual proof.

con·fir·ma·tion \ˌkän-fər-ˈmā-shən\ *n* (14c) **1 :** an act or process of confirming: as **a** (1) **:** a Christian rite conferring the gift of the Holy Spirit and among Protestants full church membership (2) **:** a ceremony confirming Jewish youths in their ancestral faith **b :** the ratification of an executive act by a legislative body **2 a :** confirming proof **:** CORROBORATION **b :** the process of supporting a statement by evidence — **con·fir·ma·tion·al** \-shnəl, -shən-ᵊl\ *adj*

con·fir·ma·to·ry \kən-ˈfər-mə-ˌtōr-ē, -ˌtȯr-\ *adj* (1636) **:** serving to confirm **:** CORROBORATIVE

con·firmed \kən-ˈfərmd\ *adj* (14c) **1 a :** marked by long continuance and likely to persist ⟨a ~ habit⟩ **b :** fixed in habit and unlikely to change ⟨a ~ bachelor⟩ **2 :** having received the rite of confirmation — **con·firm·ed·ly** \-ˈfər-məd-lē\ *adv* — **con·firmed·ness** \-ˈfər-məd-nəs, -ˈfərm(d)-nəs\ *n*

con·fis·ca·ble \kən-ˈfis-kə-bəl\ *adj* (ca. 1730) **:** liable to confiscation

con·fis·cat·able \ˈkän-fə-ˌskāt-ə-bəl\ *adj* (1863) **:** CONFISCABLE

1**con·fis·cate** \ˈkän-fə-ˌskāt, kən-ˈfis-kət\ *adj* [L *confiscatus,* pp. of *confiscare* to confiscate, fr. *com-* + *fiscus* treasury — more at FISCAL] (1533) **1 :** appropriated by the government **:** FORFEITED **2 :** deprived of property by confiscation

2**con·fis·cate** \ˈkän-fə-ˌskāt\ *vt* **-cat·ed; -cat·ing** (1552) **1 :** to seize as forfeited to the public treasury **2 :** to seize by or as if by authority — **con·fis·ca·tion** \ˌkän-fə-ˈskā-shən\ *n* — **con·fis·ca·tor** \ˈkän-fə-ˌskāt-ər\ *n* — **con·fis·ca·to·ry** \kən-ˈfis-kə-ˌtōr-ē, -ˌtȯr-\ *adj*

con·fi·te·or \kən-ˈfēt-ē-ˌȯ(ə)r, -ē-ər\ *n* [ME, fr. L, lit., I confess, fr. the opening words — more at CONFESS] (13c) **:** a liturgical form in which sinfulness is acknowledged and intercession for God's mercy requested

con·fi·ture \ˈkän-fə-ˌchu̇(ə)r, -ˌt(y)u̇(ə)r\ *n* [F, fr. MF, fr. *confit* comfit] (1802) **:** preserved or candied fruit **:** JAM

con·fla·grant \kən-ˈflā-grənt\ *adj* [L *conflagrant-, conflagrans,* prp. of *conflagrare* to burn, fr. *com-* + *flagrare* to burn — more at BLACK] (1656) **:** BURNING, BLAZING

con·fla·gra·tion \ˌkän-flə-ˈgrā-shən\ *n* [L *conflagration-, conflagratio,* fr. *conflagratus,* pp. of *conflagrare*] (1656) **1 :** FIRE; *esp* **:** a large disastrous fire **2 :** CONFLICT

con·flate \kən-ˈflāt\ *vt* **con·flat·ed; con·flat·ing** [L *conflatus,* pp. of *conflare* to blow together, fuse, fr. *com-* + *flare* to blow — more at BLOW] (1610) **1 a :** to bring together **:** FUSE **b :** CONFUSE **2 :** to combine (as two readings of a text) into a composite whole

con·fla·tion \-ˈflā-shən\ *n* (15c) **:** BLEND, FUSION; *esp* **:** a composite reading or text

¹con·flict \ˈkän-ˌflikt\ *n* [ME, fr. L *conflictus* act of striking together, fr. *conflictus,* pp. of *confligere* to strike together, fr. *com-* + *fligere* to strike — more at PROFLIGATE] (15c) **1 :** FIGHT, BATTLE, WAR **2 a :** competitive or opposing action of incompatibles **:** antagonistic state or action (as of divergent ideas, interests, or persons) **b :** mental struggle resulting from incompatible or opposing needs, drives, wishes, or external or internal demands **3 :** the opposition of persons or forces that gives rise to the dramatic action in a drama or fiction ***syn*** see DISCORD — **con·flict·ful** \ˈkän-ˌflikt-fəl\ *adj* — **con·flic·tu·al** \kän-ˈflik-ch(ə-w)əl, kən-\ *adj*

²con·flict \kən-ˈflikt, ˈkän-ˌ\ *vi* (15c) **1** *archaic* **:** to contend in warfare **2 :** to show antagonism or irreconcilability — **con·flic·tion** \kən-ˈflik-shən, kän-\ *n* — **con·flic·tive** \kən-ˈflik-tiv, ˈkän-ˌ\ *adj*

con·flict·ing *adj* (1607) **:** being in conflict, collision, or opposition **:** INCOMPATIBLE — **con·flict·ing·ly** \-ˈflik-tiŋ-lē, -ˌflik-\ *adv*

conflict of interest (1951) **:** a conflict between the private interests and the official responsibilities of a person in a position of trust (as a government or corporate official)

con·flu·ence \ˈkän-ˌflü-ən(t)s, kən-ˈ\ *n* (15c) **1 :** a coming or flowing together, meeting, or gathering at one point ⟨a happy ~ of weather and scenery⟩ **2 a :** the flowing together of two or more streams **b :** the place of meeting of two streams **c :** the combined stream formed by conjunction

¹con·flu·ent \-ənt\ *adj* [L *confluent-, confluens,* prp. of *confluere* to flow together, fr. *com-* + *fluere* to flow — more at FLUID] (15c) **1 :** flowing or coming together; *also* **:** run together ⟨~ pustules⟩ **2 :** characterized by confluent lesions ⟨~ smallpox⟩

²confluent *n* (1850) **:** a confluent stream; *broadly* **:** TRIBUTARY

con·flux \ˈkän-ˌfləks\ *n* [ML *confluxus,* fr. L *confluxus,* pp. of *confluere*] (1606) **:** CONFLUENCE

con·fo·cal \(ˈ)kän-ˈfō-kəl\ *adj* (1867) **:** having the same foci ⟨~ ellipses⟩ ⟨~ lenses⟩ — **con·fo·cal·ly** \-kə-lē\ *adv*

con·form \kən-ˈfȯ(ə)rm\ *vb* [ME *conformen,* fr. MF *conformer,* fr. L *conformare,* fr. *com-* + *formare* to form, fr. *forma* form] *vt* (14c) **:** to give the same shape, outline, or contour to **:** bring into harmony or accord ⟨~ furrows to the slope of the land⟩ ~ *vi* **1 :** to be similar or identical; *also* **:** to be in agreement or harmony — used with *to* or *with* **2 a :** to be obedient or compliant — usu. used with *to* **b :** to act in accordance with prevailing standards or customs ***syn*** see ADAPT — **con·form·er** *n* — **con·form·ism** \-ˈfȯr-ˌmiz-əm\ *n* — **con·form·ist** \-məst\ *n or adj*

con·form·able \kən-ˈfȯr-mə-bəl\ *adj* (15c) **1 :** corresponding in form or character **:** SIMILAR — usu. used with *to* **2 :** SUBMISSIVE, COMPLIANT **3 :** following in unbroken sequence — used of geologic strata formed under uniform conditions — **con·form·ably** \-blē\ *adv*

con·for·mal \kən-ˈfȯr-məl, (ˈ)kän-\ *adj* [LL *conformalis* having the same shape, fr. L *com-* + *formalis* formal, fr. *forma*] (1893) **1 :** leaving the size of the angle between corresponding curves unchanged ⟨~ transformation⟩ **2** *of a map* **:** representing small areas in their true shape

con·for·mance \kən-ˈfȯr-mən(t)s\ *n* (1606) **:** CONFORMITY

con·for·ma·tion \ˌkän-(ˌ)fȯr-ˈmā-shən, -fər-\ *n* (1511) **1 :** the act of conforming or producing conformity **:** ADAPTATION **2 :** formation of something by appropriate arrangement of parts or elements **:** an assembling into a whole ⟨the gradual ~ of the embryo⟩ **3 a :** correspondence esp. to a model or plan **b :** STRUCTURE **c :** the shape or proportionate dimensions esp. of an animal **d :** any of the spatial arrangements of a molecule that can be obtained by rotation of the atoms about a single bond ***syn*** see FORM — **con·for·ma·tion·al** \-shnəl, -shən-ᵊl\ *adj*

con·for·mi·ty \kən-ˈfȯr-mət-ē\ *n, pl* **-ties** (15c) **1 :** correspondence in form, manner, or character **:** AGREEMENT ⟨behaved in ~ with his beliefs⟩ **2 :** an act or instance of conforming **3 :** action in accordance with some specified standard or authority **:** OBEDIENCE ⟨~ to social custom⟩

con·found \kən-ˈfau̇nd, kän-\ *vt* [ME *confounden,* fr. MF *confondre,* fr. L *confundere* to pour together, confuse, fr. *com-* + *fundere* to pour — more at FOUND] (14c) **1 a** *archaic* **:** to bring to ruin **:** DESTROY **b :** BAFFLE, FRUSTRATE ⟨conferences . . . are not for accomplishment but to ~ knavish tricks —J.K. Galbraith⟩ **2** *obs* **:** CONSUME, WASTE **3 a :** to put to shame **:** DISCOMFIT ⟨a performance that ~*ed* his critics⟩ **b :** REFUTE ⟨sought to ~ his arguments⟩ **4 :** DAMN **5 :** to throw (a person) into confusion or perplexity **6 a :** to fail to discern differences between **:** mix up **b :** to increase the confusion of ***syn*** see PUZZLE — **con·found·er** *n*

con·found·ed \kən-ˈfau̇n-dəd, (ˈ)kän-ˈ, ˈkän-ˌ\ *adj* (14c) **1 :** CONFUSED, PERPLEXED **2 :** DAMNED — **con·found·ed·ly** *adv*

con·fra·ter·ni·ty \ˌkän-frə-ˈtər-nət-ē\ *n* [ME *confraternite,* fr. MF *confraternité,* fr. ML *confraternitat-, confraternitas,* fr. *confrater* fellow, brother, fr. L *com-* + *frater* brother — more at BROTHER] (15c) **1 :** a society devoted to a religious or charitable cause **2 :** fraternal union

con·frere \ˈkän-ˌfre(ə)r, kōⁿ-ˌ, kän-ˈ, kōⁿ-ˈ, kən-ˈ\ *n* [ME, fr. MF, trans. of ML *confrater*] (15c) **:** COLLEAGUE, COMRADE

con·front \kən-ˈfrənt\ *vt* [MF *confronter* to border on, confront, fr. ML *confrontare* to bound, fr. L *com-* + *front-, frons* forehead, front — more at BRINK] (1568) **1 :** to face esp. in challenge **:** OPPOSE ⟨scholars must ~ society, often in conflict —Paul Goodman⟩ **2 a :** to cause to meet **:** bring face-to-face ⟨~ a reader with statistics⟩ **b :** to meet face-to-face **:** ENCOUNTER ⟨~*ed* the possibility of failure⟩ — **con·front·al** \-ˈfrənt-ᵊl\ *n* — **con·front·er** *n*

con·fron·ta·tion \ˌkän-(ˌ)frən-ˈtā-shən\ *n* (1632) **:** the act of confronting **:** the state of being confronted: as **a :** a face-to-face meeting **b :** the clashing of forces or ideas **:** CONFLICT **c :** COMPARISON ⟨the flashbacks bring into meaningful ~ present and past, near and far —R. J. Clements⟩ — **con·fron·ta·tion·al** \-shnəl, -shən-ᵊl\ *adj* — **con·fron·ta·tion·ist** \-sh(ə-)nəst\ *n or adj*

Con·fu·cian \kən-ˈfyü-shən\ *adj* (1837) **:** of or relating to the Chinese philosopher Confucius or his teachings or followers — **Confucian** *n* — **Con·fu·cian·ism** \-shə-ˌniz-əm\ *n*

con·fuse \kən-ˈfyüz\ *vt* **con·fused; con·fus·ing** [back-formation fr. ME *confused* perplexed, fr. MF *confus,* fr. L *confusus,* pp. of *confundere*] (14c) **1** *archaic* **:** to bring to ruin **2 a :** to make embarrassed **:** ABASH **b :** to disturb in mind or purpose **:** THROW OFF ⟨interrogators who do their best to frighten, ~ and bewilder him —Aldous Huxley⟩ **3 a :** to make indistinct **:** BLUR ⟨stop *confusing* the issue⟩ **b :** to mix indiscriminately **:** JUMBLE **c :** to fail to differentiate from an often similar or related other ⟨~ money with comfort⟩ — **con·fus·ing·ly** \-ˈfyü-ziŋ-lē\ *adv*

con·fused \-ˈfyüzd\ *adj* (14c) **1 :** being perplexed or disconcerted ⟨the ~ students⟩ **2 :** INDISTINGUISHABLE ⟨a zigzag, crisscross, ~ trail —Harry Hervey⟩ **3 :** being disordered or mixed up ⟨a contradictory and often ~ philosophy⟩ — **con·fused·ly** \-ˈfyüz(-ə)d-lē\ *adv* — **con·fused·ness** \-ˈfyü-zəd-nəs, -ˈfyüz(d)-\ *n*

con·fu·sion \kən-ˈfyü-zhən\ *n* (14c) **1 :** an act or instance of confusing **2 :** the quality or state of being confused — **con·fu·sion·al** \-ˈfyüzh-nəl, -ˈfyü-zhən-ᵊl\ *adj*

con·fu·ta·tion \ˌkän-fyü-ˈtā-shən\ *n* (15c) **1 :** the act or process of confuting **:** REFUTATION **2 :** something (as an argument or statement) that confutes — **con·fu·ta·tive** \kən-ˈfyüt-ət-iv\ *adj*

con·fute \kən-ˈfyüt\ *vt* **con·fut·ed; con·fut·ing** [L *confutare,* fr. *com-* + *-futare* to beat — more at BEAT] (1529) **1 :** to overwhelm in argument **:** refute conclusively ⟨Elijah . . . *confuted* the prophets of Baal . . . with . . . bitter mockery —G. B. Shaw⟩ **2** *obs* **:** CONFOUND — **con·fut·er** *n*

con·ga \ˈkäŋ-gə\ *n* [AmerSp, fr. Sp, fem. of *congo* of the Congo, fr. *Congo,* region in Africa] (1935) **1 :** a Cuban dance of African origin involving three steps followed by a kick and performed by a group usu. in single file **2 :** a tall barrel-shaped or tapering drum of Afro-Cuban origin that is played with the hands

conga line *n* (1947) **:** SNAKE DANCE 2

con·gé \kōⁿ-ˈzhā, ˈkän-ˌjā\ *n* [F, fr. L *commeatus* going back and forth, leave, fr. *commeatus,* pp. of *commeare* to go back and forth, fr. *com-* + *meare* to go — more at PERMEATE] (1702) **1 a :** a formal permission to depart **b :** DISMISSAL **2 :** a ceremonious bow **3 :** FAREWELL **4 :** an architectural molding of concave profile — see MOLDING illustration

con·geal \kən-ˈjē(ə)l\ *vb* [ME *congelen,* fr. MF *congeler,* fr. L *congelare,* fr. *com-* + *gelare* to freeze — more at COLD] *vt* (14c) **1 :** to change from a fluid to a solid state by or as if by cold **2 :** to make viscid or curdled **:** COAGULATE **3 :** to make rigid, fixed, or immobile ~ *vi* **:** to become congealed **:** SOLIDIFY — **con·geal·ment** \-mənt\ *n*

con·gee \ˈkän-(ˌ)jē\ *n* (14c) **:** CONGÉ

con·ge·la·tion \ˌkän-jə-ˈlā-shən\ *n* (14c) **:** the process or result of congealing

con·ge·ner \ˈkän-jə-nər, kən-ˈjē-\ *n* [L, of the same kind, fr. *com-* + *gener-, genus* kind — more at KIN] (1730) **1 :** a member of the same taxonomic genus as another plant or animal **2 :** a person or thing resembling another in nature or action ⟨the New England private schools and their ~*s* west of the Alleghenies —Oliver La Farge⟩ — **con·ge·ner·ic** \ˌkän-jə-ˈner-ik\ *adj* — **con·ge·ner·ous** \kən-ˈjē-nə-rəs, -ˈjen-ə-, (ˈ)kän-\ *adj*

con·ge·nial \kən-ˈjēn-yəl\ *adj* [*com-* + *genius*] (1625) **1 :** having the same nature, disposition, or tastes **:** KINDRED **2 a :** existing or associated together harmoniously **b :** PLEASANT; *esp* **:** agreeably suited to one's nature, tastes, or outlook **c :** SOCIABLE, GENIAL — **con·ge·nial·i·ty** \-ˌjē-nē-ˈal-ət-ē, -ˌjēn-ˈyal-\ *n* — **con·ge·nial·ly** \-ˈjēn-yə-lē\ *adv*

con·gen·i·tal \kän-ˈjen-ə-tᵊl\ *adj* [L *congenitus,* fr. *com-* + *genitus,* pp. of *gignere* to bring forth — more at KIN] (1796) **1 a :** existing at or dating from birth ⟨~ idiocy⟩ **b :** constituting an essential characteristic **:** INHERENT ⟨~ fear of snakes⟩ **c :** acquired during development in the uterus and not through heredity ⟨~ syphilis⟩ **2 :** being such by nature ⟨~ liar⟩ — **con·gen·i·tal·ly** \-tᵊl-ē\ *adv*

con·ger eel \ˌkäŋ-gər-\ *n* [ME *congre,* fr. OF, fr. L *congr-, conger,* fr. Gk *gongros;* akin to ON *kǫkkr* ball, L *gingiva* gum] (1602) **:** a large strictly marine scaleless eel (*Conger oceanicus*) important as a food fish; *broadly* **:** any of various related eels (family Congridae)

con·ge·ries \ˈkän-jə-(ˌ)rēz\ *n, pl* **congeries** *same*\ [L, fr. *congerere*] (1619) **:** AGGREGATION, COLLECTION

con·gest \kən-ˈjest\ *vb* [L *congestus,* pp. of *congerere* to bring together, fr. *com-* + *gerere* to bear — more at CAST] *vt* (1856) **1 :** to cause an excessive fullness of the blood vessels of (as an organ) **2 :** CLOG ⟨traffic ~*ed* the highways⟩ **3 :** to concentrate in a small or narrow space ~ *vi* **:** to become congested — **con·ges·tion** \-ˈjes(h)-chən\ *n* — **con·ges·tive** \-ˈjes-tiv\ *adj*

congestive heart failure *n* (ca. 1935) **:** heart failure in which the heart is unable to maintain an adequate circulation of blood in the bodily tissues or to pump out the venous blood returned to it by the veins

con·glo·bate \kän-ˈglō-ˌbāt, kən-\ *vt* **-bat·ed; -bat·ing** [L *conglobatus,* pp. of *conglobare,* fr. *com-* + *globus* globe] (1635) **:** to form into a round compact mass — **con·glo·bate** \-bət, -ˌbāt\ *adj* — **con·glo·ba·tion** \ˌkän-(ˌ)glō-ˈbā-shən\ *n*

con·globe \kän-ˈglōb, kən-\ *vt* **con·globed; con·glob·ing** (1535) **:** CONGLOBATE

¹con·glom·er·ate \kən-ˈgläm-(ə-)rət\ *adj* [L *conglomeratus,* pp. of *conglomerare* to roll together, fr. *com-* + *glomerare* to wind into a ball, fr. *glomer-, glomus* ball — more at CLAM] (1572) **:** made up of parts from various sources or of various kinds ⟨an ethnically ~ culture⟩

²con·glom·er·ate \-ə-ˌrāt\ *vb* **-at·ed; -at·ing** *vi* (1642) **:** to gather into a mass or coherent whole ⟨numbers of dull people *conglomerated* round her —Virginia Woolf⟩ ~ *vt* **:** ACCUMULATE — **con·glom·er·a·tive** \-ˈgläm-(ə-)rət-iv, -ə-ˌrāt-\ *adj* — **con·glom·er·a·tor** \-ˈgläm-ə-ˌrāt-ər\ *n*

³con·glom·er·ate \-(ə-)rət\ *n* (1818) **1 :** a composite mass or mixture; *specif* **:** rock composed of rounded fragments varying from small pebbles to large boulders in a cement (as of hardened clay) **2 :** a widely diversified corporation — **con·glom·er·at·ic** \kən-ˌgläm-ə-ˈrat-ik, ˌkän-\ *adj*

con·glom·er·a·tion \kən-ˌgläm-ə-ˈrā-shən, ˌkän-\ *n* (1626) **1 :** the act of conglomerating **:** the state of being conglomerated **2 :** something conglomerated **:** a mixed coherent mass

con·glu·ti·nate \kən-ˈglüt-ᵊn-ˌāt, kän-\ *vb* **-nat·ed; -nat·ing** [L *conglutinatus,* pp. of *conglutinare* to glue together, fr. *com-* + *glutin-, gluten* glue] *vt* (15c) **:** to unite by or as if by a glutinous substance ~ *vi* **:** to become conglutinated ⟨blood platelets ~ in blood clotting⟩ — **con·glu·ti·na·tion** \kən-ˌglüt-ᵊn-ˈā-shən, kän-\ *n*

Congo red *n* [*Congo,* territory in Africa] (1885) **:** an azo dye $C_{32}H_{22}N_6Na_2O_6S_2$ that is red in alkaline and blue in acid solution and that is used esp. as an indicator and as a biological stain

con·gou \ˈkäŋ-(ˌ)gō, -(ˌ)gü\ *n* [prob. fr. Chin (Amoy) *kong-hu* pains taken] (1725) **:** a black tea from China

con·grat·u·late \kən-ˈgrach-ə-ˌlāt, -ˈgraj-\ *vt* **-lat·ed; -lat·ing** [L *congratulatus,* pp. of *congratulari* to wish joy, fr. *com-* + *gratulari* to wish joy, fr. *gratus* pleasing — more at GRACE] (1539) **1** *archaic* **:** to express sympathetic pleasure at (an event) **2 :** to express vicarious pleasure to (a person) on the occasion of success or good fortune **3** *obs* **:** SALUTE, GREET — **con·grat·u·la·tor** \-ə-ˌlāt-ər\ *n* — **con·grat·u·la·to·ry** \-(ə-)lə-ˌtōr-ē, -ˌtȯr-\ *adj*

con·grat·u·la·tion \kən-ˌgrach-ə-ˈlā-shən, -ˌgraj-\ *n* (15c) **1 :** the act of congratulating **2 :** a congratulatory expression — usu. used in pl.

con·gre·gant \ˈkäŋ-gri-gənt\ *n* (1886) **:** one that congregates; *specif* **:** a member of a congregation

con·gre·gate \-ˌgāt\ *vb* **-gat·ed; -gat·ing** [ME *congregaten,* fr. L *congregatus,* pp. of *congregare,* fr. *com-* + *greg-, grex* flock — more at GREGARIOUS] *vt* (15c) **:** to collect into a group or crowd **:** ASSEMBLE ~ *vi* **:** to come together into a group, crowd, or assembly ***syn*** see GATHER — **con·gre·ga·tor** \-ˌgāt-ər\ *n*

con·gre·ga·tion \ˌkäŋ-gri-ˈgā-shən\ *n* (14c) **1 a :** an assembly of persons **:** GATHERING; *esp* **:** an assembly of persons met for worship and religious instruction **b :** a religious community: as (1) **:** an organized body of believers in a particular locality (2) **:** a Roman Catholic religious institute with only simple vows (3) **:** a group of monasteries forming an independent subdivision of an order **2 :** the act or an instance of congregating or bringing together **:** the state of being congregated **3 :** a body of cardinals and officials forming an administrative division of the papal curia

con·gre·ga·tion·al \-shnəl, -shən-ᵊl\ *adj* (1639) **1 :** of or relating to a congregation **2** *cap* **:** of or relating to a body of Protestant churches deriving from the English Independents of the 17th century and affirming the essential importance and the autonomy of the local congregation **3 :** of or relating to church government placing final authority in the assembly of the local congregation — **con·gre·ga·tion·al·ism** \-shnə-ˌliz-əm, -shən-ᵊl-ˌiz-\ *n, often cap* — **con·gre·ga·tion·al·ist** \-shnə-ləst, -shən-ᵊl-əst\ *n or adj, often cap*

con·gress \ˈkäŋ-grəs *also* -rəs, *Brit usu* ˈkäŋ-ˌgres\ *n* [L *congressus,* fr. *congressus,* pp. of *congredi* to come together, fr. *com-* + *gradi* to go — more at GRADE] (1528) **1 a :** the act or action of coming together and meeting **b :** COITUS **2 :** a formal meeting of delegates for discussion and usu. action on some question **3 :** the supreme legislative body of a nation and esp. of a republic **4 :** an association usu. made up of delegates from constituent organizations **5 :** a single meeting or session of a group — **con·gres·sio·nal** \kən-ˈgresh-nəl, kän-, -ən-ᵊl\ *adj* — **con·gres·sio·nal·ly** \-ē\ *adv*

congress gaiter *n, often cap C* [fr. its former popularity with U.S. congressmen] (1852) **:** an ankle-high shoe with elastic gussets in the sides

congressional district *n* (1812) **:** a territorial division of a state from which a member of the U.S. House of Representatives is elected

Congressional Medal *n* (1900) **:** MEDAL OF HONOR

con·gress·man \ˈkäŋ-(g)rə-smən\ *n* (1780) **:** a member of a congress; *esp* **:** a member of the U.S. House of Representatives

con·gress·peo·ple \-(g)rə-ˌspē-pəl\ *n pl* (1973) **:** congressmen or congresswomen

con·gress·per·son \-(g)rə-ˌspər-sən\ *n* (1972) **:** a congressman or congresswoman

con·gress·wom·an \-(g)rə-ˌswu̇m-ən\ *n* (1917) **:** a female member of a congress; *esp* **:** a female member of the U.S. House of Representatives

con·gru·ence \kən-ˈgrü-ən(t)s, ˈkäŋ-grə-wən(t)s\ *n* (1533) **1 :** the quality or state of agreeing, coinciding, or being congruent **2 :** a statement that two numbers or geometric figures are congruent

con·gru·en·cy \-ən-sē, -wən-\ *n, pl* **-cies** (15c) **:** CONGRUENCE

con·gru·ent \kən-ˈgrü-ənt, ˈkäŋ-grə-wənt\ *adj* [L *congruent-, congruens,* prp. of *congruere*] (15c) **1 :** CONGRUOUS **2 :** superposable so as to be coincident throughout **3 :** having the difference divisible by a given modulus ⟨12 is ~ to 2 (modulo 5) since 12−2=2·5⟩ **4 :** relating to the melting point at which there coexist for a compound both liquid and solid phases having the same composition — **con·gru·ent·ly** *adv*

con·gru·ity \kən-ˈgrü-ət-ē, kän-\ *n, pl* **-ities** (14c) **1 :** the quality or state of being congruent or congruous **2 :** a point of agreement

con·gru·ous \ˈkäŋ-grə-wəs\ *adj* [L *congruus,* fr. *congruere* to come together, agree, fr. *com-* + *-gruere* (akin to Gk *zachreēs* attacking violently)] (1599) **1 a :** being in agreement, harmony, or correspondence **b :** conforming to the circumstances or requirements of a situation **:** APPROPRIATE ⟨a ~ room to work in —G. B. Shaw⟩ **2 :** marked or enhanced by harmonious agreement among constituent elements ⟨a ~ theme in music⟩ — **con·gru·ous·ly** *adv* — **con·gru·ous·ness** *n*

¹con·ic \ˈkän-ik\ *adj* (1570) **1 :** of or relating to a cone **2 :** CONICAL — **co·nic·i·ty** \kō-ˈnis-ət-ē\ *n*

²conic *n* (1879) **:** CONIC SECTION

con·i·cal \ˈkän-i-kəl\ *adj* (1570) **:** resembling a cone esp. in shape — **con·i·cal·ly** \-k(ə-)lē\ *adv*

conic section *n* (1664) **1 :** a plane curve, line, or point that is the intersection of or bounds the intersection of a plane and a cone with two nappes **2 :** a curve generated by a point which always moves so that the ratio of its distance from a fixed point to its distance from a fixed line is constant

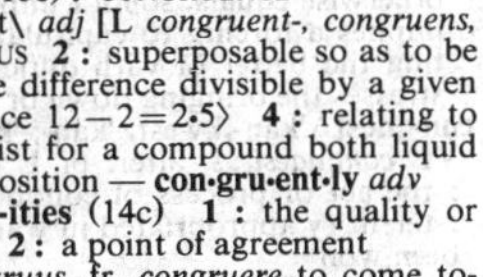

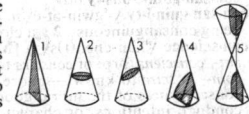

conic section 1: *1* straight lines, *2* circle, *3* ellipse, *4* parabola, *5* hyperbola

co·nid·io·phore \kə-ˈnid-ē-ə-ˌfō(ə)r, -ˌfȯ(ə)r\ *n* [NL *conidium* + ISV *-phore*] (1874) **:** a structure that bears conidia; *specif* **:** a specialized hyphal branch that produces conidia usu. by the successive cutting off of parts of the sporophore through the growth of septa

co·nid·i·um \kə-ˈnid-ē-əm\ *n, pl* **-ia** \-ē-ə\ [NL, fr. Gk *konis* dust — more at INCINERATE] (1856) **:** an asexual spore produced on a conidiophore — **co·nid·i·al** \-ē-əl\ *adj*

co·ni·fer \ˈkän-ə-fər *also* ˈkō-nə-\ *n* [deriv. of L *conifer* cone-bearing, fr. *conus* cone + *-fer*] (14c) **:** any of an order (Coniferales) of mostly evergreen trees and shrubs including forms (as pines) with true cones and others (as yews) with an arillate fruit — **co·nif·er·ous** \kō-ˈnif-(ə-)rəs, kə-\ *adj*

co·ni·ine \ˈkō-nē-ˌēn\ *n* [G *koniin,* fr. LL *conium* hemlock, fr. Gk *kōneion*] (1831) **:** a poisonous alkaloid $C_8H_{17}N$ found in poison hemlock (*Conium maculatum*)

con·jec·tur·al \kən-ˈjek-chə-rəl, -ˈjeksh-rəl\ *adj* (1553) **1 :** of the nature of or involving or based on conjecture **2 :** given to conjectures — **con·jec·tur·al·ly** \-ē\ *adv*

¹con·jec·ture \kən-ˈjek-chər\ *n* [ME, fr. MF or L; MF, fr. L *conjectura,* fr. *conjectus,* pp. of *conicere,* lit., to throw together, fr. *com-* + *jacere* to throw — more at JET] (14c) **1** *obs* **a :** interpretation of omens **b :** SUPPOSITION **2 a :** inference from defective or presumptive evidence **b :** a conclusion deduced by surmise or guesswork

²conjecture *vb* **-tured; -tur·ing** \-ˈjek-chə-riŋ, -ˈjek-shriŋ\ *vt* (15c) **1 :** to arrive at by conjecture **2 :** to make conjectures as to ~ *vi* **:** to form conjectures — **con·jec·tur·er** \-ˈjek-chər-ər\ *n*

con·join \kən-ˈjȯin, kän-\ *vb* [ME *conjoinen,* fr. MF *conjoindre,* fr. L *conjungere,* fr. *com-* + *jungere* to join — more at YOKE] *vt* (14c) **:** to join together (as separate entities) for a common purpose ~ *vi* **:** to join together for a common purpose

con·joined \-ˈjȯind\ *adj* (1570) **:** being, coming, or brought together so as to meet, touch, or overlap ⟨~ heads on a coin⟩

con·joint \-ˈjȯint\ *adj* [ME, fr. MF, pp. of *conjoindre*] (14c) **1 :** UNITED, CONJOINED **2 :** related to, made up of, or carried on by two or more in combination **:** JOINT — **con·joint·ly** *adv*

con·ju·gal \ˈkän-ji-gəl, kən-ˈjü-\ *adj* [MF or L; MF, fr. L *conjugalis,* fr. *conjug-, conjux* husband, wife, fr. *conjungere* to join, unite in marriage] (1545) **:** of or relating to the married state or to married persons and their relations **:** CONNUBIAL — **con·ju·gal·i·ty** \ˌkän-ji-ˈgal-ət-ē, -jü-\ *n* — **con·ju·gal·ly** \ˈkän-ji-gə-lē, kən-ˈjü-\ *adv*

conjugal rights *n pl* (ca. 1891) **:** the sexual rights or privileges implied by and involved in the marriage relationship **:** the right of sexual intercourse between husband and wife

con·ju·gant \ˈkän-ji-gənt\ *n* (1910) **:** either of a pair of conjugating gametes or organisms

¹con·ju·gate \ˈkän-ji-gət, -jə-ˌgāt\ *adj* [ME *conjugat,* fr. L *conjugatus,* pp. of *conjugare* to unite, fr. *com-* + *jugare* to join, fr. *jugum* yoke — more at YOKE] (15c) **1 a :** joined together esp. in pairs **:** COUPLED **b :** acting or operating as if joined **2 a :** having features in common but opposite or inverse in some particular **b :** relating to or being conjugate complex numbers ⟨complex roots occurring in ~ pairs⟩ **3** *of an acid or base* **:** related by the difference of a proton ⟨the acid NH_4 and the base NH_3 are ~ to each other⟩ **4 :** having the same derivation and therefore usu. some likeness in meaning ⟨~ words⟩ **5** *of two leaves of a book* **:** forming a single piece — **con·ju·gate·ly** *adv* — **con·ju·gate·ness** *n*

²con·ju·gate \-jə-ˌgāt\ *vb* **-gat·ed; -gat·ing** *vt* (1530) **1 :** to give in prescribed order the various inflectional forms of — used esp. of a verb **2 :** to join together ~ *vi* **1 :** to become joined together **2 a :** to pair and fuse in conjugation **b :** to pair in synapsis

³conjugate *like* ¹\ *n* (1586) **1 :** something conjugate **:** a product of conjugating **2 :** CONJUGATE COMPLEX NUMBER **3 :** an element of a mathematical group that is equal to a given element of the group multiplied on the right by another element and on the left by the inverse of the latter element

conjugate complex number *n* (ca. 1909) **:** one of two complex numbers (as *a* + *bi* and *a* − *bi*) differing only in the sign of the imaginary part

con·ju·gat·ed *adj* (1882) **1 :** formed by the union of two compounds or united with another compound ⟨~ bile acids⟩ **2 :** relating to or containing a system of two double bonds separated by a single bond ⟨~ fatty acids⟩

conjugated protein *n* (1921) **:** a compound of a protein with a nonprotein ⟨hemoglobin is a *conjugated protein* of heme and globin⟩ — compare SIMPLE PROTEIN

con·ju·ga·tion \ˌkän-jə-ˈgā-shən\ *n* (15c) **1 a :** a schematic arrangement of the inflectional forms of a verb **b :** verb inflection **c :** a class of verbs having the same type of inflectional forms ⟨the weak ~⟩ **d :** a set of the simple or derivative inflectional forms of a verb esp. in Sanskrit or the Semitic languages ⟨the causative ~⟩ **2 :** the act of conjugating **:** the state of being conjugated **3 a :** fusion of usu. similar gametes with ultimate union of their nuclei that among lower thallophytes replaces the typical fertilization of higher forms **b :** temporary cytoplasmic union with exchange of nuclear material that is the usual sexual process in ciliated protozoans **c :** the one-way transfer of DNA between bacteria in cellular contact — **con·ju·ga·tion·al** \-shnəl, -shən-ᵊl\ *adj* — **con·ju·ga·tion·al·ly** \-ē\ *adv*

¹con·junct \kən-ˈjəŋ(k)t, kän-\ *adj* [ME, fr. L *conjunctus,* pp. of *conjungere*] (15c) **1 :** UNITED, JOINED **2 :** JOINT **3 :** relating to melodic progression by intervals of no more than a major second — compare DISJUNCT

²con·junct \ˈkän-ˌjəŋ(k)t\ *n* (1667) **:** something joined or associated with another; *specif* **:** one of the components of a conjunction

con·junc·tion \kən-ˈjəŋ(k)-shən\ *n* (14c) **1 :** the act or an instance of conjoining **:** the state of being conjoined **:** COMBINATION **2 :** occurrence together in time or space **:** CONCURRENCE **3 a :** the apparent meeting or passing of two or more celestial bodies in the same degree of the zodiac **b :** a configuration in which two celestial bodies have their least apparent separation **4 :** an uninflected linguistic form that joins together sentences, clauses, phrases, or words **:** CONNECTIVE **5 :** a complex sentence in logic true if and only if each of its components is

\ə\ abut \ᵊ\ kitten, F table \ər\ further \a\ ash \ā\ ace \ä\ cot, cart \au̇\ out \ch\ chin \e\ bet \ē\ easy \g\ go \i\ hit \ī\ ice \j\ job \ŋ\ sing \ō\ go \ȯ\ law \ȯi\ boy \th\ thin \t͟h\ the \ü\ loot \u̇\ foot \y\ yet \zh\ vision \á, k̲, ⁿ, œ, œ̄, ue, u̅e, ʸ\ see Guide to Pronunciation true — **con·junc·tion·al** \-shnəl, -shən-ᵊl\ *adj* — **con·junc·tion·al·ly** \-ē\ *adv*

con·junc·ti·va \ˌkän-ˌjəŋ(k)-ˈtī-və, kən-\ *n, pl* **-vas** *or* **-vae** \-(ˌ)vē\ [NL, fr. LL, fem. of *conjunctivus* conjoining, fr. L *conjunctus*] (14c) **:** the mucous membrane that lines the inner surface of the eyelids and is continued over the forepart of the eyeball — see EYE illustration — **con·junc·ti·val** \-vəl\ *adj*

con·junc·tive \kən-ˈjəŋ(k)-tiv\ *adj* (1581) **1 :** CONNECTIVE **2 :** CONJUNCT, CONJOINED **3 :** being or functioning like a conjunction **4 :** COPULATIVE 1a — **conjunctive** *n* — **con·junc·tive·ly** *adv*

con·junc·ti·vi·tis \kən-ˌjəŋ(k)-ti-ˈvīt-əs\ *n* (1835) **:** inflammation of the conjunctiva

con·junc·ture \kən-ˈjəŋ(k)-chər\ *n* (1605) **1 :** CONJUNCTION, UNION **2 :** a combination of circumstances or events usu. producing a crisis **:** JUNCTURE

con·ju·ra·tion \ˌkän-jü-ˈrā-shən, ˌkən-\ *n* (14c) **1 :** the act or process of conjuring **:** INCANTATION **2 :** an expression or trick used in conjuring **3 :** a solemn appeal **:** ADJURATION

con·jure *vt 2 & vi senses* ˈkän-jər *also* ˈkən-; *vt 1* kən-ˈju̇(ə)r\ *vb* **con·jured; con·jur·ing** \ˈkänj-(ə-)riŋ, ˈkənj-; kən-ˈju̇(ə)r-iŋ\ [ME *conjuren,* fr. OF *conjurer,* fr. L *conjurare* to swear together, fr. *com-* + *jurare* to swear — more at JURY] *vt* (13c) **1 :** to charge or entreat earnestly or solemnly **2 a :** to summon by invocation or incantation **b (1) :** to affect or effect by or as if by magic **(2) :** IMAGINE, CONTRIVE — often used with *up* ⟨we ~ up our own metaphors for our own needs —R. J. Kaufmann⟩ ~ *vi* **1 a :** to summon a devil or spirit by invocation or incantation **b :** to practice magical arts **2 :** to use a conjurer's tricks **:** JUGGLE

con·jur·er *or* **con·ju·ror** \ˈkän-jər-ər, ˈkən-\ *n* (14c) **1 :** one that practices magic arts **:** WIZARD **2 :** one that performs feats of sleight of hand and illusion **:** MAGICIAN, JUGGLER

[1]**conk** \ˈkäŋk, ˈkȯŋk\ *vt* [slang *conk* (head); prob. alter. of *conch*] (1821) **:** to hit esp. on the head **:** KNOCK OUT

[2]**conk** *n* [prob. alter. of *conch*] (1847) **:** the visible fruiting body of a tree fungus; *also* **:** decay caused by such a fungus — **conky** \-ē\ *adj*

[3]**conk** *vi* [prob. imit.] (1918) **1 :** BREAK DOWN; *esp* **:** STALL — usu. used with *out* ⟨the motor suddenly ~*ed* out⟩ **2 a :** FAINT **b :** to go to sleep — usu. used with *off* or *out* ⟨~*ed* out for a while after lunch⟩ **c :** DIE ⟨I caught pneumonia. I almost ~*ed* —Truman Capote⟩

[4]**conk** *vt* [prob. by shortening & alter. fr. *congolene* (a hydrocarbon produced from Congo copal and used for straightening hair)] (1950) **:** to straighten out (hair) usu. by the use of chemicals

[5]**conk** *n* (1964) **:** a hairstyle in which the hair is straightened out and flattened down or lightly waved — called also *process*

conk·er \ˈkäŋ-kər\ *n* [*conch* + *-er;* fr. the original use of a snail shell on a string in the game] (1877) **1** *pl* **:** a game popular in England in which each player swings a horse chestnut on a string to try to break one held by his opponent **2 :** a horse chestnut esp. when used in conkers

con mo·to \kän-ˈmō-(ˌ)tō, kōn-\ *adv* [It] (ca. 1891) **:** with movement **:** in a spirited manner — used as a direction in music

[1]**conn** \ˈkän\ *vt* [alter. of ME *condien* to conduct, fr. MF *conduire,* fr. L *conducere*] (1626) **:** to conduct or direct the steering of (as a ship)

[2]**conn** *n* (1810) **:** the control exercised by one who conns a ship

con·nate \kä-ˈnāt, ˈkän-ˌāt\ *adj* [LL *connatus,* pp. of *connasci* to be born together, fr. L *com-* + *nasci* to be born — more at NATION] (1641) **1 :** AKIN, CONGENIAL **2 :** INNATE, INBORN **3 :** congenitally or firmly united ⟨~ leaves⟩ **4 :** born or originated together **5 :** entrapped in sediments at the time of their deposition ⟨~ water⟩ — **con·nate·ly** *adv*

con·nat·u·ral \kä-ˈnach-(ə-)rəl, kə-\ *adj* [ML *connaturalis,* fr. L *com-* + *naturalis* natural] (1592) **1 :** connected by nature **:** INBORN **2 :** of the same nature — **con·nat·u·ral·i·ty** \-ˌnach-ə-ˈral-ət-ē\ *n* — **con·nat·u·ral·ly** \-ˈnach-(ə-)rə-lē\ *adv*

con·nect \kə-ˈnekt\ *vb* [ME *connecten,* fr. L *conectere, connectere,* fr. *com-* + *nectere* to bind; akin to L *nodus* knot — more at NET] *vi* (15c) **1 :** to become joined ⟨the two rooms ~ by a hallway⟩ ⟨ideas that ~ easily to form a theory⟩ **2 :** to make a successful hit, shot, or throw ⟨~*ed* for a home run⟩ ⟨~*ed* on 60 percent of his shots —*N.Y. Times*⟩ **3 :** to have or establish a rapport ⟨tried to ~ with the younger generation⟩ ~ *vt* **1 :** to join or fasten together usu. by something intervening **2 :** to place or establish in relationship ***syn*** see JOIN — **con·nect·able** *also* **con·nect·ible** \-ˈnek-tə-bəl\ *adj* — **con·nec·tor** *also* **con·nect·er** \-ˈnek-tər\ *n*

con·nect·ed *adj* (1712) **1 :** joined or linked together **2 :** having the parts or elements logically linked together ⟨presented a thoroughly ~ view of the problem⟩ **3 :** related by blood or marriage **4 :** having a social, professional, or commercial relationship **5** *of a set* **:** having the property that any two of its points can be joined by a line completely contained in the set; *also* **:** incapable of being separated into two or more closed disjoint subsets — **con·nect·ed·ly** *adv* — **con·nect·ed·ness** *n*

connecting rod *n* (1839) **:** a rod that transmits power from one rotating part of a machine to another in reciprocating motion

con·nec·tion \kə-ˈnek-shən\ *n* [L *connexion-, connexio,* fr. *conexus,* pp. of *conectere*] (14c) **1 :** the act of connecting **:** the state of being connected: as **a :** causal or logical relation or sequence ⟨the ~ between two ideas⟩ **b :** contextual relations or associations ⟨in this ~ the word has a different meaning⟩ **c :** a relation of personal intimacy (as of family ties) **d :** COHERENCE, CONTINUITY **2 a :** something that connects **:** LINK ⟨a loose ~ in the wiring⟩ **b :** a means of communication or transport **3 :** a person connected with others esp. by marriage, kinship, or common interest ⟨has powerful ~*s* in high places⟩ **4 :** a social, professional, or commercial relationship: as **a :** POSITION, JOB **b :** an arrangement to execute orders or advance interests of another ⟨a firm's foreign ~*s*⟩ **c :** a source of contraband (as illegal drugs) **5 :** a set of persons associated together: as **a :** DENOMINATION **b :** CLAN — **con·nec·tion·al** \-shnəl, -shən-ᵊl\ *adj*

[1]**con·nec·tive** \kə-ˈnek-tiv\ *adj* (1655) **:** serving to connect — **con·nec·tive·ly** *adv*

[2]**connective** *n* (1751) **:** something that connects: as **a :** a linguistic form that connects words or word groups **b :** the tissue connecting the pollen sacs of an anther **c :** a logical term (as *or, if-then, and, not*) or a symbol for it that relates propositions in such a way that the truth or falsity of the resulting statement is determined by the truth or falsity of the components

connective tissue *n* (1846) **:** a tissue of mesodermal origin rich in intercellular substance or interlacing processes with little tendency for the cells to come together in sheets or masses; *specif* **:** connective tissue of stellate or spindle-shaped cells with interlacing processes that pervades, supports, and binds together other tissues and forms ligaments, tendons, and aponeuroses

con·nec·tiv·i·ty \(ˌ)kä-ˌnek-ˈtiv-ət-ē, kə-\ *n, pl* **-ties** (1893) **:** the quality or state of being connective or connected ⟨~ of a surface⟩

con·nex·ion \kə-ˈnek-shən\ *chiefly Brit var of* CONNECTION

conning tower *n* (1870) **1 :** an armored pilothouse (as on a battleship) **2 :** a raised cylindrical structure on the deck of an early submarine used esp. for navigation and attack direction

con·nip·tion \kə-ˈnip-shən\ *n* [origin unknown] (1833) **:** a fit of rage, hysteria, or alarm

con·niv·ance \kə-ˈnī-vən(t)s\ *n* (1611) **:** the act of conniving; *esp* **:** knowledge of and active or passive consent to wrongdoing

con·nive \kə-ˈnīv\ *vi* **con·nived; con·niv·ing** [F or L; F *conniver,* fr. L *conivēre, connivēre* to close the eyes, connive, fr. *com-* + *-nivēre* (akin to *nictare* to wink); akin to OE & OHG *hnīgan* to bow, L *nicere* to beckon] (1602) **1 :** to pretend ignorance of or fail to take action against something one ought to oppose **2 a :** to be indulgent or in secret sympathy **:** WINK **b :** to cooperate secretly or have a secret understanding **3 :** CONSPIRE, INTRIGUE — **con·niv·er** *n*

con·ni·vent \-ˈnī-vənt\ *adj* [L *conivent-, conivens,* prp. of *conivēre*] (1757) **:** converging but not fused ⟨~ stamens⟩

con·nois·seur \ˌkän-ə-ˈsər *also* -ˈsu̇(ə)r\ *n* [obs. F (now *connaisseur*), fr. OF *connoisseor,* fr. *connoistre* to know, fr. L *cognoscere* — more at COGNITION] (1714) **1 :** EXPERT; *esp* **:** one who understands the details, technique, or principles of an art and is competent to act as a critical judge **2 :** one who enjoys with discrimination and appreciation of subtleties ⟨a ~ of fine wines⟩ — **con·nois·seur·ship** \-ˌship\ *n*

con·no·ta·tion \ˌkän-ə-ˈtā-shən\ *n* (1532) **1 a :** something suggested by a word or thing **:** IMPLICATION ⟨the ~*s* of comfort that surrounded that old chair⟩ **b :** the suggesting of a meaning by a word apart from the thing it explicitly names or describes **2 :** the signification of something ⟨that abuse of logic which consists in moving counters about as if they were known entities with a fixed ~ —W. R. Inge⟩ **3 :** an essential property or group of properties of a thing named by a term in logic — compare DENOTATION — **con·no·ta·tion·al** \-shnəl, -shən-ᵊl\ *adj*

con·no·ta·tive \ˈkän-ə-ˌtāt-iv, kə-ˈnōt-ət-iv\ *adj* (1614) **1 :** connoting or tending to connote **2 :** relating to connotation — **con·no·ta·tive·ly** *adv*

con·note \kə-ˈnōt, kä-\ *vt* **con·not·ed; con·not·ing** [ML *connotare,* fr. L *com-* + *notare* to note] (1665) **1 :** to be associated with or inseparable from as a consequence or concomitant ⟨the remorse so often *connoted* by guilt⟩ **2 a :** to convey in addition to exact explicit meaning ⟨all the misery that poverty ~*s*⟩ **b :** to imply as a logical connotation

con·nu·bi·al \kə-ˈn(y)ü-bē-əl\ *adj* [L *conubialis,* fr. *conubium, connubium* marriage, fr. *com-* + *nubere* to marry — more at NUPTIAL] (ca. 1656) **:** of or relating to the married state **:** CONJUGAL — **con·nu·bi·al·ism** \-bē-ə-ˌliz-əm\ *n* — **con·nu·bi·al·i·ty** \-ˌn(y)ü-bē-ˈal-ət-ē\ *n* — **con·nu·bi·al·ly** \-ˈn(y)ü-bē-ə-lē\ *adv*

co·no·dont \ˈkō-nə-ˌdänt\ *n* [ISV *con-* (fr. Gk *kōnos* cone) + *-odont*] (1859) **:** a Paleozoic fossil that may consist of the teeth of an extinct cyclostome or more probably the remains of an invertebrate

co·noid \ˈkō-ˌnȯid\ *or* **co·noi·dal** \kō-ˈnȯid-ᵊl\ *adj* (1668) **:** shaped like or nearly like a cone ⟨~ shells⟩ ⟨~ pottery⟩ — **conoid** *n*

con·quer \ˈkäŋ-kər\ *vb* **con·quered; con·quer·ing** \-k(ə-)riŋ\ [ME *conqueren* to acquire, conquer, fr. OF *conquerre,* fr. (assumed) VL *conquaerere,* fr. L *conquirere* to search for, collect, fr. *com-* + *quaerere* to ask, search] *vt* (13c) **1 :** to gain or acquire by force of arms **:** SUBJUGATE **2 :** to overcome by force of arms **:** VANQUISH **3 :** to gain mastery over or win by overcoming obstacles or opposition ⟨~*ed* the mountain⟩ **4 :** to overcome by mental or moral power **:** SURMOUNT ⟨~*ed* her fear⟩ ~ *vi* **:** to be victorious — **con·quer·or** \-kər-ər\ *n*

syn CONQUER, VANQUISH, DEFEAT, SUBDUE, REDUCE, OVERCOME, OVERTHROW mean to get the better of by force or strategy. CONQUER implies gaining mastery of; VANQUISH implies a complete overpowering; DEFEAT does not imply the finality or completeness of VANQUISH which it otherwise equals; SUBDUE implies a defeating and suppression; REDUCE implies a forcing to capitulate or surrender; OVERCOME suggests getting the better of with difficulty or after hard struggle; OVERTHROW stresses the bringing down or destruction of enemy power.

con·quest \ˈkän-ˌkwest, ˈkäŋ-; ˈkäŋ-kwəst\ *n* [ME, fr. MF, fr. (assumed) VL *conquaesitus,* alter. of L *conquisitus,* pp. of *conquirere*] (14c) **1 :** the act or process of conquering **2 a :** something conquered; *esp* **:** territory appropriated in war **b :** a person whose favor or hand has been won

con·qui·an \ˈkäŋ-kē-ən\ *n* [MexSp *conquián* — more at COONCAN] (1889) **:** a card game for two played with 40 cards from which all games of rummy developed

con·quis·ta·dor \kȯŋ-ˈkēs-tə-ˌdȯ(ə)r, kän-ˈk(w)is-, kən-\ *n, pl* **con·quis·ta·do·res** \(ˌ)kȯŋ-ˌkēs-tə-ˈdȯr-ēz, -ˈdȯr-ˌās, -ˈdȯr-, (ˌ)kän-ˌk(w)is-, kən-\ *or* **con·quis·ta·dors** [Sp, deriv. of L *conquirere*] (1830) **:** one that conquers; *specif* **:** a leader in the Spanish conquest of America and esp. of Mexico and Peru in the 16th century

con·san·guine \kän-ˈsaŋ-gwən, kən-\ *adj* (1610) **:** CONSANGUINEOUS

con·san·guin·e·ous \ˌkän-ˌsan-ˈgwin-ē-əs, -ˌsaŋ-\ *adj* [L *consanguineus,* fr. *com-* + *sanguin-, sanguis* blood — more at SANGUINE] (1601) **:** of the same blood or origin; *specif* **:** descended from the same ancestor — **con·san·guin·e·ous·ly** *adv*

con·san·guin·i·ty \-ˈgwin-ət-ē\ *n, pl* **-ties** (14c) **1 :** the quality or state of being consanguineous **2 :** a close relation or connection

con·science \ˈkän-chən(t)s\ *n* [ME, fr. OF, fr. L *conscientia,* fr. *conscient-, consciens,* prp. of *conscire* to be conscious, be conscious of guilt, fr. *com-* + *scire* to know — more at SCIENCE] (13c) **1 a :** the sense or consciousness of the moral goodness or blameworthiness of one's own conduct, intentions, or character together with a feeling of obligation to do right or be good **b :** a faculty, power, or principle enjoining good acts **c :** the part of the superego in psychoanalysis that transmits commands and admonitions to the ego **2** *archaic* **:** CONSCIOUSNESS **3 :** conformity to the dictates of conscience **:** CONSCIENTIOUSNESS **4 :** sensitive regard for fairness or justice **:** SCRUPLE — **con·science·less** \-ləs\ *adj* — **in all conscience** *or* **in conscience :** in all fairness

conscience money *n* (1848) : money paid usu. anonymously to relieve the conscience by restoring what has been wrongfully acquired

con·sci·en·tious \ˌkän-chē-ˈen-chəs\ *adj* (1611) **1** : governed by or conforming to the dictates of conscience : SCRUPULOUS ⟨a ~ public servant⟩ **2** : METICULOUS, CAREFUL ⟨a ~ listener⟩ ***syn*** see UPRIGHT — **con·sci·en·tious·ly** *adv* — **con·sci·en·tious·ness** *n*

conscientious objection *n* (1916) : objection on moral or religious grounds (as to service in the armed forces or to bearing arms)

conscientious objector *n* (1899) : one who refuses to serve in the armed forces or bear arms on the grounds of moral or religious principles

con·scio·na·ble \ˈkänch-(ə-)nə-bəl\ *adj* [irreg. fr. *conscience*] (1549) : CONSCIENTIOUS

[1]**con·scious** \ˈkän-chəs\ *adj* [L *conscius*, fr. *com-* + *scire* to know] (1601) **1** *archaic* : sharing another's knowledge or awareness of an inward state or outward fact **2** : perceiving, apprehending, or noticing with a degree of controlled thought or observation **3** : personally felt ⟨~ guilt⟩ **4** : capable of or marked by thought, will, design, or perception **5** : SELF-CONSCIOUS **6** : having mental faculties undulled by sleep, faintness, or stupor : AWAKE ⟨became ~ after the anesthesia wore off⟩ **7** : done or acting with critical awareness ⟨made a ~ effort to avoid the same mistakes⟩ **8 a** : likely to notice, consider, or appraise ⟨a bargain-*conscious* shopper⟩ **b** : being concerned or interested ⟨a budget-*conscious* businessman⟩ **c** : marked by strong feelings or notions ⟨a race-*conscious* society⟩ ***syn*** see AWARE — **con·scious·ly** *adv*

[2]**conscious** *n* (1919) : CONSCIOUSNESS 5

con·scious·ness \ˈkän-chə-snəs\ *n* (1632) **1 a** : the quality or state of being aware esp. of something within oneself **b** : the state or fact of being conscious of an external object, state, or fact **c** : AWARENESS; *esp* : concern for some social or political cause **2** : the state of being characterized by sensation, emotion, volition, and thought : MIND **3** : the totality of conscious states of an individual **4** : the normal state of conscious life **5** : the upper level of mental life of which the person is aware as contrasted with unconscious processes

consciousness–raising *n* (1971) : an increasing of concerned awareness esp. of some social or political issue

con·scribe \kən-ˈskrīb\ *vt* **con·scribed; con·scrib·ing** [L *conscribere*] (1613) **1** : LIMIT, CIRCUMSCRIBE ⟨ill-health . . . *conscribed* the force of his intentions —*Times Lit. Supp.*⟩ **2** : to enlist forcibly : CONSCRIPT

[1]**con·script** \ˈkän-ˌskript\ *adj* [MF, fr. L *conscriptus*, pp. of *conscribere* to enroll, fr. *com-* + *scribere* to write — more at SCRIBE] (15c) **1** : enrolled into service by compulsion : DRAFTED **2** : made up of conscripted persons

[2]**conscript** *n* (1800) : a conscripted person (as a military recruit)

[3]**con·script** \kən-ˈskript\ *vt* (1813) : to enroll into service by compulsion : DRAFT ⟨was ~*ed* into the army⟩

con·scrip·tion \kən-ˈskrip-shən\ *n* (1528) : compulsory enrollment of persons esp. for military service : DRAFT

[1]**con·se·crate** \ˈkän(t)-sə-ˌkrāt\ *adj* (14c) : dedicated to a sacred purpose

[2]**consecrate** *vt* **-crat·ed; -crat·ing** [ME *consecraten*, fr. L *consecratus*, pp. of *consecrare*, fr. *com-* + *sacrare* to consecrate — more at SACRED] (14c) **1** : to induct (a person) into a permanent office with a religious rite; *esp* : to ordain to the office of bishop **2 a** : to make or declare sacred; *esp* : to devote irrevocably to the worship of God by a solemn ceremony **b** : to effect the liturgical transubstantiation of (eucharistic bread and wine) **c** : to devote to a purpose with or as if with deep solemnity or dedication **3** : to make inviolable or venerable ⟨principles *consecrated* by the weight of history⟩ ***syn*** see DEVOTE — **con·se·cra·tive** \-ˌkrāt-iv\ *adj* — **con·se·cra·tor** \-ˌkrāt-ər\ *n* — **con·se·cra·to·ry** \ˈkän(t)-si-krə-ˌtōr-ē, -ˌtȯr-\ *adj*

con·se·cra·tion \ˌkän(t)-sə-ˈkrā-shən\ *n* (14c) **1** : the act or ceremony of consecrating **2** : the state of being consecrated **3** *cap* : the part of a Communion rite in which the bread and wine are consecrated

con·se·cu·tion \ˌkän(t)-si-ˈkyü-shən\ *n* [L *consecution-*, *consecutio*, fr. *consecutus*, pp. of *consequi* to follow along — more at CONSEQUENT] (1532) : SEQUENCE

con·sec·u·tive \kən-ˈsek-(y)ət-iv\ *adj* (1611) : following one after the other in order : SUCCESSIVE — **con·sec·u·tive·ly** *adv* — **con·sec·u·tive·ness** *n*

con·sen·su·al \kən-ˈsench-(ə-)wəl, -ˈsen-chəl\ *adj* [L *consensus* + E *-al*] (1754) **1 a** : existing or made by mutual consent without an act of writing ⟨a ~ contract⟩ **b** : involving or based on mutual consent ⟨~ acts⟩ **2** : relating to or being the constrictive pupillary response of an eye that is covered when the other eye is exposed to light — **con·sen·su·al·ly** \-ē\ *adv*

con·sen·sus \kən-ˈsen(t)-səs\ *n*, *often attrib* [L, fr. *consensus*, pp. of *consentire*] (1858) **1 a** : general agreement : UNANIMITY ⟨the ~ of their opinion, based on reports that had drifted back from the border —John Hersey⟩ **b** : the judgment arrived at by most of those concerned ⟨the ~ was to abandon the project⟩ **2** : group solidarity in sentiment and belief

usage The phrase *consensus of opinion*, which is not actually redundant (see sense 1a; the sense that takes the phrase is slightly older), has been so often claimed as a redundancy that it has become relatively rare in edited prose. Sense 1a has not become extinct but sense 1b has far outstripped it in frequency of use. Sense 1b is also growing in attributive use esp. in the phrase *consensus politics*.

[1]**con·sent** \kən-ˈsent\ *vi* [ME *consenten*, fr. L *consentire*, fr. *com-* + *sentire* to feel — more at SENSE] (13c) **1** : to give assent or approval : AGREE **2** *archaic* : to be in concord in opinion or sentiment ***syn*** see ASSENT — **con·sent·ing·ly** \-iŋ-lē\ *adv*

[2]**consent** *n* (14c) **1** : compliance in or approval of what is done or proposed by another : ACQUIESCENCE ⟨he shall have power, by and with the advice and ~ of the Senate, to make treaties —*U.S. Constitution*⟩ **2** : agreement as to action or opinion; *specif* : voluntary agreement by a people to organize a civil society and give authority to the government — **con·sent·er** *n*

con·sen·ta·ne·ous \ˌkän(t)-sən-ˈtā-nē-əs, ˌkän-ˌsen-\ *adj* [L *consentaneus*, fr. *consentire* to agree] (1625) **1** : expressing agreement : SUITED **2** : done or made by the consent of all — **con·sen·ta·ne·ous·ly** *adv*

consent decree *n* (1925) : a judicial decree that sanctions a voluntary agreement between parties in dispute

con·se·quence \ˈkän(t)-sə-ˌkwen(t)s, -si-kwən(t)s\ *n* (14c) **1** : a conclusion derived through logic : INFERENCE **2** : something produced by a cause or necessarily following from a set of conditions **3 a** : importance with respect to power to produce an effect : MOMENT **b** : social importance **4** : the appearance of importance; *esp* : SELF-IMPORTANCE ***syn*** see EFFECT, IMPORTANCE — **in consequence** : as a result : CONSEQUENTLY

[1]**con·se·quent** \-kwənt, -ˌkwent\ *n* (14c) **1 a** : DEDUCTION 2b **b** : the conclusion of a conditional sentence **2** : the second term of a ratio

[2]**consequent** *adj* [MF, fr. L *consequent-*, *consequens*, prp. of *consequi* to follow along, fr. *com-* + *sequi* to follow — more at SUE] (15c) **1** : following as a result or effect ⟨removal of the trees and ~ exposure to sun, rain and wind . . . may cause serious degradation of the soil —C. J. Taylor⟩ **2** : observing logical sequence : RATIONAL

con·se·quen·tial \ˌkän(t)-sə-ˈkwen-chəl\ *adj* (1626) **1** : of the nature of a secondary result : INDIRECT **2** : CONSEQUENT **3** : having significant consequences : IMPORTANT ⟨a grave and ~ event⟩ **4** : SELF-IMPORTANT — **con·se·quen·ti·al·i·ty** \-ˌkwen-chē-ˈal-ət-ē\ *n* — **con·se·quen·tial·ly** \-ˈkwench-(ə-)lē\ *adv* — **con·se·quen·tial·ness** \-ˈkwen-chəl-nəs\ *n*

con·se·quent·ly \ˈkän(t)-sə-ˌkwent-lē, -si-kwənt-\ *adv* (15c) : as a result : in view of the foregoing : ACCORDINGLY

con·ser·van·cy \kən-ˈsər-vən-sē\ *n*, *pl* **-cies** [alter. of obs. *conservacy* conservation, fr. AF *conservacie*, fr. ML *conservatia*, fr. L *conservatus*, pp.] (1755) **1** *Brit* : a board regulating fisheries and navigation in a river or port **2 a** : CONSERVATION **b** : an organization or area designated to conserve and protect natural resources

con·ser·va·tion \ˌkän(t)-sər-ˈvā-shən\ *n* [ME, fr. MF, fr. L *conservation-*, *conservatio*, fr. *conservatus*, pp. of *conservare*] (14c) **1** : a careful preservation and protection of something; *esp* : planned management of a natural resource to prevent exploitation, destruction, or neglect **2** : the preservation of a physical quantity during transformations or reactions — **con·ser·va·tion·al** \-shnəl, -shən-ᵊl\ *adj*

con·ser·va·tion·ist \-sh(ə-)nəst\ *n* (1870) : one who advocates conservation esp. of natural resources

conservation of charge (ca. 1949) : a principle in physics: the total electric charge of an isolated system remains constant irrespective of whatever internal changes may take place

conservation of energy (1853) : a principle in physics: the total energy of an isolated system remains constant irrespective of whatever internal changes may take place with energy disappearing in one form reappearing in another

conservation of mass (1884) : a principle in classical physics: the total mass of any material system is neither increased nor diminished by reactions between the parts — called also *conservation of matter*

con·ser·va·tism \kən-ˈsər-və-ˌtiz-əm\ *n* (1835) **1** *cap* **a** : the principles and policies of a Conservative party **b** : the Conservative party **2 a** : disposition in politics to preserve what is established **b** : a political philosophy based on tradition and social stability, stressing established institutions, and preferring gradual development to abrupt change **3** : the tendency to prefer an existing or traditional situation to change

[1]**con·ser·va·tive** \kən-ˈsər-vət-iv\ *adj* (14c) **1** : PRESERVATIVE **2 a** : of or relating to a philosophy of conservatism **b** *cap* : of or constituting a political party professing the principles of conservatism: as (1) : of or constituting a party of the United Kingdom advocating support of established institutions (2) : PROGRESSIVE CONSERVATIVE **3 a** : tending or disposed to maintain existing views, conditions, or institutions : TRADITIONAL **b** : marked by moderation or caution ⟨a ~ estimate⟩ **c** : marked by or relating to traditional norms of taste, elegance, style, or manners ⟨a ~ suit⟩ **4** : of or relating to Conservative Judaism — **con·ser·va·tive·ly** *adv* — **con·ser·va·tive·ness** *n*

[2]**conservative** *n* (1831) **1 a** : an adherent or advocate of political conservatism **b** *cap* : a member or supporter of a conservative political party **2 a** : one who adheres to traditional methods or views **b** : a cautious or discreet person

Conservative Judaism *n* (1946) : Judaism as practiced esp. among some U.S. Jews with adherence to the Torah and Talmud but with allowance for some departures in keeping with differing times and circumstances — compare ORTHODOX JUDAISM

con·ser·va·tize \-ˌtīz\ *vb* **-tized; -tiz·ing** *vi* (1849) : to grow conservative ~ *vt* : to make conservative ⟨unions are being *conservatized* —Theodore Levitt⟩

con·ser·va·toire \kən-ˈsər-və-ˌtwär\ *n* [F, fr. It *conservatorio*] (1845) : CONSERVATORY 2

con·ser·va·tor \kən-ˈsər-vət-ər, -və-ˌtȯ(ə)r; ˈkän(t)-sər-ˌvāt-ər\ *n* (15c) **1 a** : one that preserves from injury or violation : PROTECTOR **b** : one that is responsible for the care, restoration, and repair of museum articles **2** : a person, official, or institution designated to take over and protect the interests of an incompetent **3** : an official charged with the protection of something affecting public welfare and interests — **con·ser·va·to·ri·al** \kən-ˌsər-və-ˈtōr-ē-əl, (ˌ)kän-, -ˈtȯr-\ *adj*

con·ser·va·to·ry \kən-ˈsər-və-ˌtōr-ē, -ˌtȯr-\ *n*, *pl* **-ries** (1664) **1** : a greenhouse for growing or displaying plants **2** [It *conservatorio* home for foundlings, music school, fr. L *conservatus*, pp.] : a school specializing in one of the fine arts ⟨a music ~⟩

[1]**con·serve** \kən-ˈsərv\ *vt* **con·served; con·serv·ing** [ME *conserven*, fr. MF *conserver*, fr. L *conservare*, fr. *com-* + *servare* to keep, guard, observe] (14c) **1** : to keep in a safe or sound state ⟨he *conserved* and enlarged the estate he inherited⟩; *esp* : to avoid wasteful or destructive use of ⟨~ natural resources⟩ **2** : to preserve with sugar **3** : to maintain (a quantity) constant during a process of chemical, physical, or evolutionary change — **con·serv·er** *n*

[2]**con·serve** \ˈkän-ˌsərv\ *n* (15c) **1** : SWEETMEAT; *esp* : a candied fruit **2** : PRESERVE; *specif* : one prepared from a mixture of fruits

con·sid·er \kən-ˈsid-ər\ *vb* **con·sid·ered; con·sid·er·ing** \-(ə-)riŋ\ [ME *consideren*, fr. MF *considerer*, fr. L *considerare*, lit., to observe the stars, fr. *com-* + *sider-*, *sidus* star — more at SIDEREAL] *vt* (14c) **1** : to think about carefully: as **a** : to think of esp. with regard to taking some action ⟨is ~*ing* you for the job⟩ ⟨~*ed* moving to the city⟩ ⟨~ a sugges-

\ə\ abut \ᵊ\ kitten, F table \ər\ further \a\ ash \ā\ ace \ä\ cot, cart \au̇\ out \ch\ chin \e\ bet \ē\ easy \g\ go \i\ hit \ī\ ice \j\ job \ŋ\ sing \ō\ go \ȯ\ law \ȯi\ boy \th\ thin \th\ the \ü\ loot \u̇\ foot \y\ yet \zh\ vision \à, k, ⁿ, œ, œ̄, ue, ue̅, ʸ\ see Guide to Pronunciation

tion⟩ **b :** to take into account ⟨defendant's youth must be ~*ed*⟩ **2 :** to regard or treat in an attentive or kindly way ⟨he ~*ed* her every wish⟩ **3 :** to gaze on steadily or reflectively **4 :** to come to judge or classify ⟨~ thrift essential⟩ **5 :** REGARD ⟨his works are well ~*ed* abroad⟩ **6 :** SUPPOSE **~** *vi* **:** REFLECT, DELIBERATE ⟨paused a moment to ~⟩

syn CONSIDER, STUDY, CONTEMPLATE, WEIGH mean to think about in order to arrive at a judgment or decision. CONSIDER may suggest giving thought to in order to reach a suitable conclusion, opinion, or decision; STUDY implies sustained purposeful concentration and attention to details and minutiae; CONTEMPLATE stresses focusing one's thoughts on something but does not imply coming to a conclusion or decision; WEIGH implies attempting to reach the truth or arrive at a decision by balancing conflicting claims or evidence.

[1]**con·sid·er·able** \-ˈsid-ər(-ə)-bəl, -ˈsid-rə-bəl\ *adj* (1619) **1 :** worth consideration **:** SIGNIFICANT **2 :** large in extent or degree ⟨a ~ number⟩ — **con·sid·er·ably** \-blē\ *adv*

[2]**considerable** *n* (1685) **:** a considerable amount, degree, or extent

con·sid·er·ate \kən-ˈsid-(ə-)rət\ *adj* (1572) **1 :** marked by or given to careful consideration **:** CIRCUMSPECT **2 :** thoughtful of the rights and feelings of others — **con·sid·er·ate·ly** *adv* — **con·sid·er·ate·ness** *n*

con·sid·er·ation \kən-ˌsid-ə-ˈrā-shən\ *n* (14c) **1 :** continuous and careful thought ⟨after long ~ he agreed to their requests⟩ **2 a :** a matter weighed or taken into account when formulating an opinion or plan ⟨economic ~*s* forced her to leave college⟩ **b :** a taking into account **3 :** thoughtful and sympathetic regard **4 :** an opinion obtained by reflection **5 :** ESTEEM, REGARD ⟨the family built themselves a large, ugly villa . . . and became people of ~ —V. S. Pritchett⟩ **6 a :** RECOMPENSE, PAYMENT **b :** the inducement to a contract or other legal transaction; *specif* **:** an act or forbearance or the promise thereof done or given by one party in return for the act or promise of another — **in consideration of :** as payment or recompense for ⟨a small fee *in consideration of* many kind services⟩

con·sid·ered \kən-ˈsid-ərd\ *adj* (1627) **1 :** matured by extended deliberative thought ⟨his ~ opinion⟩ **2 :** regarded with respect or esteem

[1]**con·sid·er·ing** \-(ə-)riŋ\ *prep* (14c) **:** in view of **:** taking into account ⟨he did well ~ his limitations⟩

[2]**considering** *conj* (15c) **:** INASMUCH AS ⟨~ he was new at the job, he did quite well⟩

con·sign \kən-ˈsīn\ *vb* [MF *consigner,* fr. L *consignare,* fr. *com-* + *signum* sign, mark, seal] *vt* (1528) **1 :** to give over to another's care **2 :** to give, transfer, or deliver into the hands or control of another; *also* **:** to commit esp. to a final destination or fate ⟨~*ed* his books to the devil⟩ **3 :** to send or address to an agent to be cared for or sold **~** *vi, obs* **:** AGREE, SUBMIT ***syn*** see COMMIT — **con·sign·able** \-ˈsī-nə-bəl\ *adj* — **con·sig·na·tion** \ˌkän-ˌsī-ˈnā-shən, ˌkän(t)-sig-\ *n* — **con·sign·or** \ˌkän(t)-sə-ˈnȯ(ə)r, ˌkän-ˌsī-, kən-ˌsī-\ *n*

con·sign·ee \ˌkän(t)-sə-ˈnē, ˌkän-ˌsī-, kən-ˌsī-\ *n* (1789) **:** one to whom something is consigned or shipped

[1]**con·sign·ment** \kən-ˈsīn-mənt\ *n* (1668) **1 :** the act or process of consigning **2 :** something consigned esp. in a single shipment — **on consignment :** shipped to a dealer who pays only for what he sells and who may return what is unsold ⟨goods shipped *on consignment*⟩

[2]**consignment** *adj* (1913) **:** of, relating to, or received as goods on consignment ⟨a ~ sale⟩

[1]**con·sist** \kən-ˈsist\ *vi* [MF & L; MF *consister,* fr. L *consistere,* lit., to stand together, fr. *com-* + *sistere* to take a stand; akin to L *stare* to stand — more at STAND] (1523) **1 :** LIE, RESIDE — used with *in* ⟨liberty ~*s* in the absence of obstructions —A. E. Housman⟩ **2** *archaic* **a :** EXIST, BE **b :** to be capable of existing **3 :** to be composed or made up — used with *of* ⟨breakfast ~*ed* of cereal, milk, and fruit⟩ **4 :** to be consistent ⟨it ~*s* with the facts⟩

[2]**con·sist** \ˈkän-ˌsist\ *n* (1898) **:** makeup or composition (as of coal sizes or a railroad train) by classes, types, or grades and arrangement

con·sis·tence \kən-ˈsis-tən(t)s\ *n* (1626) **:** CONSISTENCY

con·sis·ten·cy \kən-ˈsis-tən-sē\ *n, pl* **-cies** (1594) **1 a** *archaic* **:** condition of adhering together **:** firmness of material substance **b :** firmness of constitution or character **:** PERSISTENCY **2 :** degree of firmness, density, viscosity, or resistance to movement or separation of constituent particles ⟨boil the juice to the ~ of a thick syrup⟩ **3 a :** agreement or harmony of parts or features to one another or a whole **:** CORRESPONDENCE; *specif* **:** ability to be asserted together without contradiction **b :** harmony of conduct or practice with profession ⟨followed his own advice with ~⟩

con·sis·tent \kən-ˈsis-tənt\ *adj* [L *consistent-, consistens,* prp. of *consistere*] (1647) **1** *archaic* **:** possessing firmness or coherence **2 a :** marked by harmony, regularity, or steady continuity **:** free from variation or contradiction ⟨a ~ style in painting⟩ **b :** COMPATIBLE — usu. used with *with* **c :** showing steady conformity to character, profession, belief, or custom ⟨a ~ supporter of women's rights⟩ **3 :** tending to be arbitrarily close to the true value of the parameter estimated as the sample becomes large ⟨a ~ statistical estimator⟩

con·sis·tent·ly \-lē\ *adv* (1706) **1 :** in a consistent manner **2 :** OFTEN

con·sis·to·ri·al \ˌkän-ˌsis-ˈtōr-ē-əl, -ˈtȯr-, kən-\ *adj* (15c) **:** of or relating to a consistory

con·sis·to·ry \kən-ˈsis-t(ə-)rē\ *n, pl* **-ries** [ME *consistorie,* fr. MF, fr. ML & LL; ML *consistorium* church tribunal, fr. LL, imperial council, fr. L *consistere*] (14c) **1 :** a solemn assembly **:** COUNCIL **2 :** a church tribunal or governing body: as **a :** a solemn meeting of Roman Catholic cardinals convoked and presided over by the pope **b :** a church session in some Reformed churches **3 :** the organization that confers the degrees of the Ancient and Accepted Scottish Rite of Freemasonry usu. from the 19th to the 32d inclusive; *also* **:** a meeting of such an organization

con·so·ci·ate \kən-ˈsō-s(h)ē-ˌāt\ *vb* **-at·ed; -at·ing** [L *consociatus,* pp. of *consociare,* fr. *com-* + *socius* companion — more at SOCIAL] *vt* (1566) **:** to bring into association **~** *vi* **:** to associate esp. in fellowship or partnership

con·so·ci·a·tion \-ˌsō-sē-ˈā-shən, -shē-\ *n* (1593) **1 :** association in fellowship or alliance **2 :** an association of churches or religious societies **3 :** an ecological community with a single dominant — **con·so·ci·a·tion·al** \-shnəl, -shən-ᵊl\ *adj*

con·so·la·tion \ˌkän(t)-sə-ˈlā-shən\ *n* (14c) **1 :** the act or an instance of consoling **:** the state of being consoled **:** COMFORT **2 :** something that consoles; *specif* **:** a contest held for those who have lost early in a tournament ⟨the losers met in a ~ game⟩ — **con·so·la·to·ry** \kən-ˈsō-lə-ˌtōr-ē, -ˈsäl-ə-, -ˌtȯr-\ *adj*

consolation prize *n* (1886) **:** a prize given to a runner-up or a loser in a contest

[1]**con·sole** \ˈkän-ˌsōl\ *n* [F] (1664) **1 :** an architectural member projecting from a wall to form a bracket or from a keystone for ornament **2 :** CONSOLE TABLE **3 a :** an upright case which houses the keyboards and controlling mechanisms of an organ and from which the organ is played **b :** a panel or cabinet on which are mounted dials, switches, and other apparatus used in centrally monitoring and controlling electrical or mechanical devices **4 a :** a cabinet (as for a radio or television set) designed to rest directly on the floor **b :** a small storage cabinet between bucket seats in an automobile

[2]**con·sole** \kən-ˈsōl\ *vt* **con·soled; con·sol·ing** [F *consoler,* fr. L *consolari,* fr. *com-* + *solari* to console — more at SILLY] (1693) **:** to alleviate the grief, sense of loss, or trouble of ⟨~ a widow⟩ — **con·sol·ing·ly** \-ˈsō-liŋ-lē\ *adv*

console table *n* (1813) **:** a table fixed to a wall with its top supported by consoles or front legs; *broadly* **:** a table designed to fit against a wall

con·so·lette \ˌkän(t)-sə-ˈlet\ *n* [[1]*console* + *-ette*] (1941) **:** a small cabinet containing a radio, television, or record player

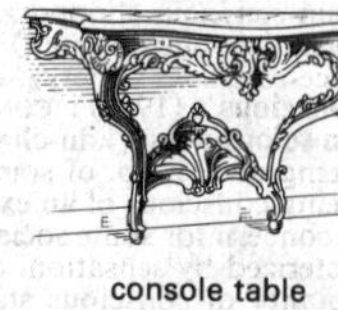
console table

con·sol·i·date \kən-ˈsäl-ə-ˌdāt\ *vb* **-dat·ed; -dat·ing** [L *consolidatus,* pp. of *consolidare* to make solid, fr. *com-* + *solidus* solid] *vt* (1511) **1 :** to join together into one whole **:** UNITE ⟨~ several small school districts⟩ **2 :** to make firm or secure **:** STRENGTHEN ⟨~ their hold on first place⟩ **3 :** to form into a compact mass **~** *vi* **:** to become consolidated; *specif* **:** MERGE ⟨the two companies *consolidated*⟩ — **con·sol·i·da·tor** \-ˌdāt-ər\ *n*

consolidated school *n* (1911) **:** a public school formed by merging other schools

con·sol·i·da·tion \kən-ˌsäl-ə-ˈdā-shən\ *n* (15c) **1 :** the act or process of consolidating **:** the state of being consolidated **2 :** the process of uniting **:** the quality or state of being united; *specif* **:** the unification of two or more corporations by dissolution of existing ones and creation of a single new corporation — compare MERGER **3 :** pathological alteration of lung tissue from an aerated condition to one of solid consistency

con·som·mé \ˌkän(t)-sə-ˈmā\ *n* [F, fr. pp. of *consommer* to complete, boil down, fr. L *consummare* to complete — more at CONSUMMATE] (1815) **:** a clear soup made from well-seasoned stock

con·so·nance \ˈkän(t)-s(ə-)nən(t)s\ *n* (15c) **1 :** harmony or agreement among components **2 a :** correspondence or recurrence of sounds esp. in words; *specif* **:** recurrence or repetition of consonants esp. at the end of stressed syllables without the similar correspondence of vowels ⟨the final sounds of "stroke" and "luck" exhibit ~⟩ **b :** CONCORD 1b **c :** SYMPATHETIC VIBRATION, RESONANCE

con·so·nan·cy \-s(ə-)nən-sē\ *n, pl* **-cies** (14c) **:** CONSONANCE 1

[1]**con·so·nant** \ˈkän(t)-s(ə-)nənt\ *adj* [MF, fr. L *consonant-, consonans,* prp. of *consonare* to sound together, agree, fr. *com-* + *sonare* to sound — more at SOUND] (15c) **1 :** being in agreement or harmony **:** free from elements making for discord **2 :** marked by musical consonances **3 :** having similar sounds ⟨~ words⟩ **4 :** relating to or exhibiting consonance **:** RESONANT — **con·so·nant·ly** *adv*

[2]**consonant** *n* [ME, fr. L *consonant-, consonans,* fr. prp. of *consonare*] (1603) **1 :** one of a class of speech sounds (as \p\, \g\, \n\, \l\, \s\, \r\) characterized by constriction or closure at one or more points in the breath channel **2 :** a letter representing a consonant — usu. used in English of any letter except *a, e, i, o,* and *u*

con·so·nan·tal \ˌkän(t)-sə-ˈnant-ᵊl\ *adj* (1795) **:** relating to, being, or marked by a consonant or group of consonants

consonant shift *n* (1888) **:** a set of regular changes in consonant articulation in the history of a language or dialect: **a :** such a set affecting the Indo-European stops and distinguishing the Germanic languages from the other Indo-European languages — called also *first consonant shift;* compare GRIMM'S LAW **b :** such a set affecting the Germanic stops and distinguishing High German from the other Germanic languages — called also *second consonant shift*

[1]**con·sort** \ˈkän-ˌsȯ(ə)rt\ *n* [ME, fr. MF, fr. L *consort-, consors,* lit., one who shares a common lot, fr. *com-* + *sort-, sors* lot, share — more at SERIES] (15c) **1 :** ASSOCIATE **2 :** a ship accompanying another **3 :** SPOUSE — compare PRINCE CONSORT

[2]**consort** *n* [MF *consorte,* fr. *consort*] (1584) **1 :** GROUP, ASSEMBLY ⟨a ~ of specialists⟩ **2 :** CONJUNCTION, ASSOCIATION ⟨he ruled in ~ with his father⟩ **3 a :** a group of singers or instrumentalists performing together **b :** a set of musical instruments of the same family

[3]**con·sort** \kən-ˈsȯ(ə)rt, kän-ˈ, ˈkän-ˌ\ *vt* (1588) **1 :** UNITE, ASSOCIATE **2** *obs* **:** ESCORT **~** *vi* **1 :** to keep company ⟨~*ing* with criminals⟩ **2** *obs* **:** to make harmony **:** PLAY **3 :** ACCORD, HARMONIZE ⟨the illustrations ~ admirably with the text — *Times Lit. Supp.*⟩

con·sor·tium \kən-ˈsȯrt-ē-əm, -ˈsȯr-sh(ē-)əm\ *n, pl* **-sor·tia** \-ˈsȯrt-ē-ə, -ˈsȯr-sh(ē-)ə\ *also* **-sortiums** [L, fellowship, fr. *consort-, consors*] (1829) **1 :** an agreement, combination, or group (as of companies) formed to undertake an enterprise beyond the resources of any one member **2 :** ASSOCIATION, SOCIETY **3 :** the legal right of one spouse to the company, affection, and service of the other

con·spe·cif·ic \ˌkän(t)-spi-ˈsif-ik\ *adj* (1859) **:** of the same species — **conspecific** *n*

con·spec·tus \kən-ˈspek-təs\ *n* [L, fr. *conspectus,* pp. of *conspicere*] (1839) **1 :** a usu. brief survey or summary often providing an overall view **2 :** OUTLINE, SYNOPSIS

con·spi·cu·ity \ˌkän(t)-spə-ˈkyü-ət-ē\ *n* (1601) **:** CONSPICUOUSNESS

con·spic·u·ous \kən-ˈspik-yə-wəs\ *adj* [L *conspicuus,* fr. *conspicere* to get sight of, fr. *com-* + *specere* to look — more at SPY] (1545) **1 :** obvious to the eye or mind **2 :** attracting attention **:** STRIKING **3 :** marked by a noticeable violation of good taste ***syn*** see NOTICEABLE — **con·spic·u·ous·ly** *adv*

conspicuous consumption *n* (1899) : lavish or wasteful spending thought to enhance social prestige

con·spic·u·ous·ness *n* (1661) : the quality or state of being conspicuous

con·spir·a·cy \kən-ˈspir-ə-sē\ *n, pl* **-cies** [ME *conspiracie,* fr. L *conspiratus,* pp. of *conspirare*] (14c) **1** : the act of conspiring together **2 a** : an agreement among conspirators **b** : a group of conspirators ***syn*** see PLOT

conspiracy of silence (1865) : a secret agreement to keep silent about an occurrence, situation, or subject esp. in order to promote or protect selfish interests

con·spi·ra·tion \ˌkän(t)-spə-ˈrā-shən, -(ˌ)spir-ˈā-\ *n* (14c) **1** : the act or action of plotting or secretly combining **2** : a joint effort toward a particular end — **con·spi·ra·tion·al** \-shnəl, -shən-ᵊl\ *adj*

con·spir·a·tor \kən-ˈspir-ət-ər\ *n* (15c) : one that conspires : PLOTTER

con·spir·a·to·ri·al \kən-ˌspir-ə-ˈtōr-ē-əl, -ˈtȯr-\ *adj* (1855) : of, relating to, or suggestive of a conspiracy — **con·spir·a·to·ri·al·ly** \-ē-ə-lē\ *adv*

con·spire \kən-ˈspī(ə)r\ *vb* **con·spired; con·spir·ing** [ME *conspiren,* fr. MF *conspirer,* fr. L *conspirare* to breathe together, agree, conspire, fr. *com-* + *spirare* to breathe — more at SPIRIT] *vt* (14c) : PLOT, CONTRIVE ~ *vi* **1 a** : to join in a secret agreement to do an unlawful or wrongful act or to use such means to accomplish a lawful end **b** : SCHEME **2** : to act in harmony toward a common end ⟨circumstances *conspired* to defeat his efforts⟩

con spi·ri·to \kän-ˈspir-ə-ˌtō, kōn-\ *adv* [It] (ca. 1891) : with spirit or animation — used as a direction in music

con·sta·ble \ˈkän(t)-stə-bəl, ˈkən(t)-\ *n* [ME *conestable,* fr. OF, fr. LL *comes stabuli,* lit., officer of the stable] (13c) **1** : a high officer of a medieval royal or noble household **2** : the warden or governor of a royal castle or a fortified town **3 a** : a public officer usually of a town or township responsible for keeping the peace and for minor judicial duties **b** *Brit* : POLICEMAN; *esp* : one ranking below sergeant

[1]**con·stab·u·lary** \kən-ˈstab-yə-ˌler-ē\ *adj* (1824) : of or relating to a constable or constabulary

[2]**constabulary** *n, pl* **-lar·ies** (1837) **1** : the organized body of constables of a particular district or country **2** : an armed police force organized on military lines but distinct from the regular army

con·stan·cy \ˈkän(t)-stən-sē\ *n, pl* **-cies** (1526) **1 a** : steadfastness of mind under duress : FORTITUDE **b** : FIDELITY, LOYALTY **2** : freedom from change

[1]**con·stant** \ˈkän(t)-stənt\ *adj* [ME, fr. MF, fr. L *constant-, constans,* fr. prp. of *constare* to stand firm, be consistent, fr. *com-* + *stare* to stand — more at STAND] (14c) **1** : marked by firm steadfast resolution or faithfulness : exhibiting constancy of mind or attachment **2** : INVARIABLE, UNIFORM **3** : continually occurring or recurring : REGULAR ***syn*** see FAITHFUL, CONTINUAL — **con·stant·ly** *adv*

[2]**constant** *n* (1832) : something invariable or unchanging: as **a** : a number that has a fixed value in a given situation or universally or that is characteristic of some substance or instrument **b** : a number that is assumed not to change value in a given mathematical discussion **c** : a term in logic with a fixed designation

con·stan·tan \ˈkän(t)-stən-ˌtan\ *n* [fr. the fact that its resistance remains constant under change of temperature] (1903) : an alloy of copper and nickel used for electrical resistors and in thermocouples

con·stel·late \ˈkän(t)-stə-ˌlāt\ *vb* **-lat·ed; -lat·ing** *vt* (1643) **1** : to unite in a cluster **2** : to set or adorn with or as if with constellations ~ *vi* : CLUSTER

con·stel·la·tion \ˌkän(t)-stə-ˈlā-shən\ *n* [ME *constellacioun,* fr. MF *constellation,* fr. LL *constellation-, constellatio,* fr. *constellatus* studded with stars, fr. L *com-* + *stella* star — more at STAR] (14c) **1** : the configuration of stars esp. at one's birth **2** : any of 88 arbitrary configurations of stars or an area of the celestial sphere covering one of these configurations **3** : an assemblage, collection, or gathering of usu. related persons, qualities, or things ⟨a ~ of . . . relatives, friends, and hangers-on —Brendan Gill⟩ **4** : PATTERN, ARRANGEMENT ⟨taking advantage of the shifting ~ of power throughout the known world —H. D. Lasswell⟩ — **con·stel·la·to·ry** \kən-ˈstel-ə-ˌtōr-ē, -ˌtȯr-\ *adj*

con·ster·nate \ˈkän(t)-stər-ˌnāt\ *vt* **-nat·ed; -nat·ing** (1651) : to fill with consternation

con·ster·na·tion \ˌkän(t)-stər-ˈnā-shən\ *n* [F or L; F, fr. L *consternation-, consternatio,* fr. *consternatus,* pp. of *consternare* to bewilder, alarm, fr. *com-* + *-sternare* (akin to OE *starian* to stare) — more at STARE] (ca. 1611) : amazement or dismay that hinders or throws into confusion ⟨the two . . . stared at each other in ~, and neither knew what to do —Pearl Buck⟩

con·sti·pate \ˈkän(t)-stə-ˌpāt\ *vt* **-pat·ed; -pat·ing** [ML *constipatus,* pp. of *constipare,* fr. L, to crowd together, fr. *com-* + *stipare* to press together — more at STIFF] (1533) **1** : to make costive : cause constipation in **2** : to make immobile, inactive, or dull : STULTIFY ⟨so much clutter . . . will tend to ~ the novel's working order —*Times Lit. Supp.*⟩

con·sti·pat·ed *adj* (ca. 1899) : stilted or stodgy in appearance, expression, or action

con·sti·pa·tion \ˌkän(t)-stə-ˈpā-shən\ *n* (15c) **1** : abnormally delayed or infrequent passage of dry hardened feces **2** : STULTIFICATION

con·stit·u·en·cy \kən-ˈstich-(ə-)wən-sē\ *n, pl* **-cies** (1831) **1 a** : a body of citizens entitled to elect a representative (as to a legislative or executive position) **b** : the residents in an electoral district **c** : an electoral district **2 a** : a group or body that patronizes, supports, or offers representation ⟨there was no ~ of millionaires to back him⟩ **b** : the people involved in or served by an organization (as a business or institution) ⟨the big dailies and urban TV stations are not in touch with the special problems of their own *constituencies* —J. P. Lyford⟩

[1]**con·stit·u·ent** \kən-ˈstich-(ə-)wənt\ *n* [F *constituant,* fr. MF, fr. prp. of *constituer* to constitute, fr. L *constituere*] (1622) **1** : one who authorizes another to act for him : PRINCIPAL **2 a** : one of a group who elects another to represent him in public office **b** : a resident in a constituency **3** : an essential part : COMPONENT, ELEMENT **4** : one of two or more linguistic forms that enter into a construction or a compound and are either immediate (as *he* and *writes reviews* in the construction "he writes reviews") or ultimate (as *he, write, -s, review,* and *-s* in the same construction) ***syn*** see ELEMENT

[2]**constituent** *adj* [L *constituent-, constituens,* prp. of *constituere*] (1660) **1** : serving to form, compose, or make up a unit or whole : COMPONENT **2** : having the power to create a government or frame or amend a constitution ⟨a ~ assembly⟩ — **con·stit·u·ent·ly** *adv*

con·sti·tute \ˈkän(t)-stə-ˌt(y)üt\ *vt* **-tut·ed; -tut·ing** [L *constitutus,* pp. of *constituere* to set up, constitute, fr. *com-* + *statuere* to set — more at STATUTE] (15c) **1** : to appoint to an office, function, or dignity **2** : SET UP, ESTABLISH: as **a** : ENACT **b** : FOUND **c** (1) : to give due or lawful form to (2) : to legally process **3** : MAKE UP, FORM, COMPOSE ⟨12 months ~ a year⟩ ⟨high school dropouts who ~ a major problem in large city slums —J. B. Conant⟩

con·sti·tu·tion \ˌkän(t)-stə-ˈt(y)ü-shən\ *n* (14c) **1** : an established law or custom : ORDINANCE **2** : the act of establishing, making, or setting up **3 a** : the physical makeup of the individual comprising inherited qualities modified by environment **b** : the structure, composition, physical makeup, or nature of something **4** : the mode in which a state or society is organized; *esp* : the manner in which sovereign power is distributed **5 a** : the basic principles and laws of a nation, state, or social group that determine the powers and duties of the government and guarantee certain rights to the people in it **b** : a written instrument embodying the rules of a political or social organization — **con·sti·tu·tion·less** \-ləs\ *adj*

[1]**con·sti·tu·tion·al** \-shnəl, -shən-ᵊl\ *adj* (1682) **1** : relating to, inherent in, or affecting the constitution of body or mind **2** : of, relating to, or entering into the fundamental makeup of something : ESSENTIAL **3** : being in accordance with or authorized by the constitution of a state or society ⟨a ~ government⟩ **4** : regulated by or ruling according to a constitution ⟨a ~ monarchy⟩ **5** : of or relating to a constitution **6** : loyal to or supporting an established constitution or form of government

[2]**constitutional** *n* (1829) : a walk taken for one's health

con·sti·tu·tion·al·ism \-ˌiz-əm\ *n* (1832) : adherence to or government according to constitutional principles; *also* : a constitutional system of government — **con·sti·tu·tion·al·ist** \-əst\ *n*

con·sti·tu·tion·al·i·ty \-ˌt(y)ü-shə-ˈnal-ət-ē\ *n* (1787) : the quality or state of being constitutional; *esp* : accordance with the provisions of a constitution ⟨questioned the ~ of the law⟩

con·sti·tu·tion·al·ize \-ˈt(y)ü-shnəl-ˌīz, -shən-ᵊl-\ *vt* **-ized; -iz·ing** (1831) : to provide with a constitution : organize along constitutional principles — **con·sti·tu·tion·al·iza·tion** \-ˌt(y)ü-shnəl-ə-ˈzā-shən, -shən-ᵊl-\ *n*

con·sti·tu·tion·al·ly \-ˈt(y)ü-shnə-lē, -shən-ᵊl-ē\ *adv* (1742) **1 a** : in accordance with one's constitution ⟨~ unable to grasp subtleties⟩ **b** : in structure, composition, or constitution ⟨despite repeated heatings the material remained ~ the same⟩ **2** : in accordance with a political constitution ⟨was not ~ eligible to fill the office⟩

con·sti·tu·tive \ˈkän(t)-stə-ˌt(y)üt-iv, kən-ˈstich-ət-iv\ *adj* (1592) **1** : having the power to enact or establish : CONSTRUCTIVE **2** : CONSTITUENT, ESSENTIAL **3** : relating to or dependent on constitution ⟨a ~ property of all electrolytes⟩ — **con·sti·tu·tive·ly** *adv*

con·strain \kən-ˈstrān\ *vt* [ME *constrainen,* fr. MF *constraindre,* fr. L *constringere* to constrict, constrain, fr. *com-* + *stringere* to draw tight — more at STRAIN] (14c) **1 a** : to force by imposed stricture, restriction, or limitation **b** : to restrict the motion of (a mechanical body) to a particular mode **2** : to force or produce in an unnatural or strained manner ⟨a ~*ed* smile⟩ **3** : to secure by or as if by bonds : CONFINE **4** : to bring into narrow compass; *also* : to clasp tightly **5** : to hold back by or as if by force ⟨~*ing* my mind not to wander from the task —Charles Dickens⟩ — **con·strained·ly** \-ˈstrā-nəd-lē, -ˈstrān-dlē\ *adv*

con·straint \kən-ˈstrānt\ *n* [ME, fr. MF *constrainte,* fr. *constraindre*] (15c) **1 a** : the act of constraining **b** : the state of being checked, restricted, or compelled to avoid or perform some action ⟨the ~ and monotony of a monastic life —Matthew Arnold⟩ **c** : a constraining condition, agency, or force : CHECK ⟨put legal ~*s* on the board's activities⟩ **2 a** : repression of one's own feelings, behavior, or actions **b** : a sense of being constrained : EMBARRASSMENT

con·strict \kən-ˈstrikt\ *vb* [L *constrictus,* pp. of *constringere*] *vt* (1732) **1 a** : to make narrow or draw together **b** : COMPRESS, SQUEEZE ⟨~ a nerve⟩ **2** : to stultify, stop, or cause to falter : INHIBIT ~ *vi* : to become constricted ***syn*** see CONTRACT — **con·stric·tive** \-ˈstrik-tiv\ *adj*

con·stric·tion \-ˈstrik-shən\ *n* (15c) **1** : an act or product of constricting **2** : the quality or state of being constricted **3** : something that constricts

con·stric·tor \-ˈstrik-tər\ *n* (1735) **1** : one that constricts **2** : a muscle that contracts a cavity or orifice or compresses an organ **3** : a snake (as a boa constrictor) that kills prey by compression in its coils

con·stringe \kən-ˈstrinj\ *vt* **con·stringed; con·string·ing** [L *constringere*] (1604) **1** : to cause to shrink ⟨cold ~*s* the pores⟩ **2** : CONSTRICT — **con·strin·gent** \-ˈstrin-jənt\ *adj*

[1]**con·struct** \kən-ˈstrəkt\ *vt* [L *constructus,* pp. of *construere,* fr. *com-* + *struere* to build — more at STRUCTURE] (1663) **1** : to make or form by combining or arranging parts or elements : BUILD; *also* : CONTRIVE, DEVISE **2** : to set in logical order **3** : to draw (a geometrical figure) with suitable instruments and under specified conditions — **con·struct·ible** \-ˈstrək-tə-bəl\ *adj* — **con·struc·tor** \-tər\ *n*

[2]**con·struct** \ˈkän-ˌstrəkt\ *n* (1871) : something constructed esp. by mental synthesis ⟨form a ~ of a physical object by mentally assembling and integrating sense-data⟩

con·struc·tion \kən-ˈstrək-shən\ *n* (14c) **1** : the act or result of construing, interpreting, or explaining **2 a** : the process, art, or manner of constructing something; *also* : a thing constructed **b** : the construction industry ⟨working in ~⟩ **3** : the arrangement and connection of words or groups of words in a sentence : syntactical arrangement **4** : a sculpture that is put together out of separate pieces of often disparate materials — **con·struc·tion·al** \-shnəl, -shən-ᵊl\ *adj* — **con·struc·tion·al·ly** \-ē\ *adv*

con·struc·tion·ist \-sh(ə-)nəst\ *n* (1838) : one who construes a legal document (as the U.S. Constitution) in a specific way ⟨a strict ~⟩

construction paper *n* (ca. 1924) : a thick groundwood paper available in many colors and used esp. for school artwork

con·struc·tive \kən-ˈstrək-tiv\ *adj* (1680) **1** : declared such by judicial construction or interpretation ⟨~ fraud⟩ **2** : of or relating to construction or creation **3** : promoting improvement or development ⟨~ criticism⟩ — **con·struc·tive·ly** *adv* — **con·struc·tive·ness** *n*

con·struc·tiv·ism \kən-ˈstrək-ti-ˌviz-əm\ *n, often cap* (1923) : a nonobjective art movement originating in Russia and concerned with formal organization of planes and expression of volume in terms of modern industrial materials (as glass and plastic) — **con·struc·tiv·ist** \-ti-vəst\ *adj or n, often cap*

¹con·strue \kən-ˈstrü\ *vb* **con·strued; con·stru·ing** [ME *construen*, fr. LL *construere*, fr. L, to construct] *vt* (14c) **1** : to analyze the arrangement and connection of words in (a sentence or sentence part) **2** : to understand or explain the sense or intention of usu. in a particular way or with respect to a given set of circumstances ⟨*construed* my actions as hostile⟩ ~ *vi* : to construe a sentence or sentence part esp. in connection with translating — **con·stru·able** \-ˈstrü-ə-bəl\ *adj*

²con·strue \ˈkän-ˌstrü\ *n* (1844) : an act of construing esp. by piecemeal translation; *also* : the translated version resulting from such an act

con·sub·stan·tial \ˌkän(t)-səb-ˈstan-chəl\ *adj* [LL *consubstantialis*, fr. L *com-* + *substantia* substance] (14c) : of the same substance

con·sub·stan·ti·a·tion \ˌkän(t)-səb-ˌstan-chē-ˈā-shən\ *n* (1597) : the actual substantial presence and combination of the body of Christ with the eucharistic bread and wine according to a teaching associated with Martin Luther — compare TRANSUBSTANTIATION

con·sue·tude \ˈkän(t)-swi-ˌt(y)üd, kən-ˈsü-ə-\ *n* [ME, fr. L *consuetudo* — more at CUSTOM] (14c) : social usage : CUSTOM — **con·sue·tu·di·nary** \ˌkän(t)-swi-ˈt(y)üd-ᵊn-ˌer-ē, kən-ˌsü-ə-\ *adj*

con·sul \ˈkän(t)-səl\ *n* [ME, fr. L; akin to L *consulere* to consult] (14c) **1 a** : either of two annually elected chief magistrates of the Roman republic **b** : one of three chief magistrates of the French republic from 1799 to 1804 **2** : an official appointed by a government to reside in a foreign country to represent the commercial interests of citizens of the appointing country — **con·sul·ar** \-s(ə-)lər\ *adj* — **con·sul·ship** \-səl-ˌship\ *n*

con·sul·ate \-s(ə-)lət\ *n* (14c) **1** : a government by consuls **2** : the office, term of office, or jurisdiction of a consul **3** : the residence or official premises of a consul

consulate general *n, pl* **consulates general** (1883) : the residence, office, or jurisdiction of a consul general

consul general *n, pl* **consuls general** (1812) : a consul of the first rank stationed in an important place or having jurisdiction in several places or over several consuls

¹con·sult \kən-ˈsəlt\ *vb* [MF or L; MF *consulter*, fr. L *consultare*, fr. *consultus*, pp. of *consulere* to deliberate, counsel, consult] *vt* (1527) **1** : to have regard to : CONSIDER **2 a** : to ask the advice or opinion of ⟨~ a doctor⟩ **b** : to refer to ⟨~ a dictionary⟩ ~ *vi* **1** : to consult an individual **2** : to deliberate together : CONFER **3** : to serve as a consultant — **con·sult·er** *n*

²con·sult \kən-ˈsəlt, ˈkän-ˌ\ *n* (1560) : CONSULTATION

con·sul·tan·cy \kən-ˈsəlt-ᵊn-sē\ *n, pl* **-cies** (1955) **1** : CONSULTATION **2** : an agency that provides consulting services **3** : the position of a consultant

con·sul·tant \kən-ˈsəlt-ᵊnt\ *n* (1697) **1** : one who consults another **2** : one who gives professional advice or services : EXPERT — **con·sul·tant·ship** \-ˌship\ *n*

con·sul·ta·tion \ˌkän(t)-səl-ˈtā-shən\ *n* (15c) **1** : COUNCIL, CONFERENCE; *specif* : a deliberation between physicians on a case or its treatment **2** : the act of consulting or conferring

con·sul·ta·tive \kən-ˈsəl-tət-iv, ˈkän(t)-səl-ˌtāt-iv\ *adj* (1583) : of, relating to, or intended for consultation : ADVISORY ⟨~ committee⟩

con·sult·ing \kən-ˈsəl-tiŋ\ *adj* (1801) **1** : providing professional or expert advice ⟨a ~ architect⟩ **2** : of or relating to consultation or a consultant ⟨the ~ room of a psychiatrist⟩

con·sul·tive \kən-ˈsəl-tiv\ *adj* (1616) : CONSULTATIVE

con·sul·tor \kən-ˈsəl-tər\ *n* (ca. 1611) : one that consults or advises; *esp* : an adviser to a Roman Catholic bishop, provincial, or sacred congregation

¹con·sum·able \kən-ˈsü-mə-bəl\ *adj* (1641) : capable of being consumed

²consumable *n* (1802) : something (as food or fuel) that is consumable — usu. used in pl.

con·sume \kən-ˈsüm\ *vb* **con·sumed; con·sum·ing** [ME *consumen*, fr. MF or L; MF *consumer*, fr. L *consumere*, fr. *com-* + *sumere* to take up, take, fr. *sub-* up + *emere* to take — more at SUB-, REDEEM] *vt* (14c) **1** : to do away with completely : DESTROY ⟨fire *consumed* several buildings⟩ **2 a** : to spend wastefully : SQUANDER **b** : USE UP ⟨writing *consumed* much of his time⟩ **3** : to eat or drink esp. in great quantity ⟨*consumed* several kegs of beer⟩ **4** : to engage fully : ENGROSS ⟨*consumed* with curiosity⟩ ~ *vi* **1** : to waste or burn away : PERISH **2** : to utilize economic goods

con·sum·ed·ly \-ˈsü-məd-lē\ *adv* (1707) : as if consumed : EXCESSIVELY

con·sum·er \kən-ˈsü-mər\ *n, often attrib* (15c) : one that consumes: as **a** : one that utilizes economic goods **b** : an organism requiring complex organic compounds for food which it obtains by preying on other organisms or by eating particles of organic matter — compare PRODUCER 4 — **con·sum·er·ship** \-ˌship\ *n*

consumer credit *n* (1927) : credit granted to an individual esp. to finance the purchase of consumer goods or to defray personal or family expenses

consumer goods *n pl* (1890) : goods that directly satisfy human wants

con·sum·er·ism \kən-ˈsü-mə-ˌriz-əm\ *n* (1944) **1** : the promotion of the consumer's interests **2** : the theory that an increasing consumption of goods is economically desirable; *also* : a preoccupation with and an inclination toward the buying of consumer goods — **con·sum·er·ist** \-rəst\ *n*

consumer price index *n* (ca. 1948) : an index measuring the change in the cost of typical wage-earner purchases of goods and services expressed as a percentage of the cost of these same goods and services in some base period — called also *cost-of-living index*

con·sum·ing \kən-ˈsü-miŋ\ *adj* (1920) : deeply felt : ARDENT ⟨a ~ interest⟩; *also* : ENGROSSING

¹con·sum·mate \kən-ˈsəm-ət, ˈkän(t)-sə-mət\ *adj* [ME, fr. L *consummatus*, pp. of *consummare* to sum up, finish, fr. *com-* + *summa* sum] (15c) **1** : complete in every detail : PERFECT **2** : extremely skilled and accomplished ⟨a ~ liar⟩ **3** : of the highest degree ⟨~ skill⟩ ⟨~ cruelty⟩ — **con·sum·mate·ly** *adv*

²con·sum·mate \ˈkän(t)-sə-ˌmāt\ *vb* **-mat·ed; -mat·ing** *vt* (1530) **1 a** : FINISH, COMPLETE ⟨~ a business deal⟩ **b** : to make perfect **c** : ACHIEVE **2** : to make (marital union) complete by sexual intercourse ⟨~ a marriage⟩ ~ *vi* : to become perfected — **con·sum·ma·tive** \ˈkän(t)-sə-ˌmāt-iv, kən-ˈsəm-ət-iv\ *adj* — **con·sum·ma·tor** \ˈkän(t)-sə-ˌmāt-ər\ *n*

con·sum·ma·tion \ˌkän-sə-ˈmā-shən\ *n* (14c) **1** : the act of consummating ⟨the ~ of a contract by mutual signature⟩; *specif* : the consummating of a marriage **2** : the ultimate end : FINISH

con·sum·ma·to·ry \kən-ˈsəm-ə-ˌtōr-ē, -ˌtȯr-\ *adj* (1648) **1** : of or relating to consummation : CONCLUDING **2** : of, relating to, or being a response or act (as eating or copulating) that terminates a period of usu. goal-directed behavior

con·sump·tion \kən-ˈsəm(p)-shən\ *n* [ME *consumpcioun*, fr. L *consumption-*, *consumptio*, fr. *consumptus*, pp. of *consumere*] (14c) **1 a** : a progressive wasting away of the body esp. from pulmonary tuberculosis **b** : TUBERCULOSIS **2** : the act or process of consuming **3** : the utilization of economic goods in the satisfaction of wants or in the process of production resulting chiefly in their destruction, deterioration, or transformation

¹con·sump·tive \-ˈsəm(p)-tiv\ *adj* (1647) **1** : tending to consume **2** : of, relating to, or affected with consumption — **con·sump·tive·ly** *adv*

²consumptive *n* (1666) : a person affected with consumption

¹con·tact \ˈkän-ˌtakt\ *n* [F or L; F, fr. L *contactus*, fr. *contactus*, pp. of *contingere* to have contact with — more at CONTINGENT] (1626) **1 a** : union or junction of surfaces **b** : the apparent touching or mutual tangency of the limbs of two celestial bodies or of the disk of one body with the shadow of another during an eclipse, transit, or occultation **c** (1) : the junction of two electrical conductors through which a current passes (2) : a special part made for such a junction **2 a** : ASSOCIATION, RELATIONSHIP **b** : CONNECTION, COMMUNICATION **c** : direct visual observation of the earth's surface made from an airplane esp. as an aid to navigation **d** : an establishing of communication with someone or an observing or receiving of a significant signal from a person or object ⟨radar ~ with Mars⟩ **3** : one serving as a carrier or source **4** : CONTACT LENS

²con·tact \ˈkän-ˌtakt, kən-ˈ\ *vi* (1834) : to make contact ~ *vt* **1** : to bring into contact **2 a** : to enter or be in contact with : JOIN **b** : to get in communication with ⟨~ your local dealer⟩

usage A few stalwart defenders of the language still object to the use of *contact* as a verb, esp. in sense 2b. But most commentators concede that it has become established as standard.

³con·tact \ˈkän-ˌtakt\ *adj* (1859) : maintaining, involving, or activated or caused by contact ⟨~ poisons⟩ ⟨~ sports⟩

contact flying \ˈkän-ˌtak(t)-\ *n* (1938) : navigation of an airplane by means of direct observation of landmarks

contact inhibition \ˈkän-ˌtakt-\ *n* (1965) : cessation of cellular undulating movements upon contact with other cells with accompanying cessation of cell growth and division

contact lens \ˌkän-ˌtak(t)-\ *n* (1888) : a thin lens designed to fit over the cornea

contact print \ˌkän-ˌtak(t)-\ *n* (1890) : a photographic print made with the negative in contact with the sensitized paper, plate, or film

con·ta·gion \kən-ˈtā-jən\ *n* [ME, fr. MF & L; MF, fr. L *contagion-*, *contagio*, fr. *contingere* to have contact with, pollute] (14c) **1 a** : the transmission of a disease by direct or indirect contact **b** : a contagious disease **c** : a disease-producing agent (as a virus) **2 a** : POISON **b** : contagious influence, quality, or nature **c** : corrupting influence or contact **3 a** : rapid communication of an influence (as a doctrine or emotional state) **b** : an influence that spreads rapidly

con·ta·gious \-jəs\ *adj* (15c) **1** : communicable by contact : CATCHING ⟨~ diseases⟩ **2** : bearing contagion **3** : used for contagious diseases ⟨a ~ ward⟩ **4** : exciting similar emotions or conduct in others ⟨~ enthusiasm⟩ — **con·ta·gious·ly** *adv* — **con·ta·gious·ness** *n*

contagious abortion *n* (1910) : a contagious or infectious disease (as a brucellosis) of domestic animals characterized by abortion

con·ta·gium \kən-ˈtā-j(ē-)əm\ *n, pl* **-gia** \-j(ē-)ə\ [L, contagion, fr. *contingere*] (1870) : a virus or living organism capable of causing a communicable disease

con·tain \kən-ˈtān\ *vb* [ME *conteinen*, fr. OF *contenir*, fr. L *continēre* to hold together, hold in, contain, fr. *com-* + *tenēre* to hold — more at THIN] *vt* (13c) **1** : to keep within limits: as **a** : RESTRAIN, CONTROL **b** : CHECK, HALT **c** : to follow successfully a policy of containment toward **d** : to prevent (as an enemy or opponent) from advancing or from making a successful attack **2 a** : to have within : HOLD **b** : COMPRISE, INCLUDE **3 a** : to be divisible by usu. without a remainder **b** : ENCLOSE, BOUND ~ *vi* : to restrain oneself — **con·tain·able** \-ˈtā-nə-bəl\ *adj*

syn CONTAIN, HOLD, ACCOMMODATE mean to have or be capable of having within. CONTAIN implies the actual presence of a specified substance or quantity within something; HOLD implies the capacity of containing or the usual or permanent function of containing or keeping; ACCOMMODATE stresses holding without crowding or inconvenience.

contained *adj* (1653) : RESTRAINED; *also* : CALM

con·tain·er \kən-ˈtā-nər\ *n* (15c) : one that contains; *esp* : a receptacle or a flexible covering for the shipment of goods

con·tain·er·board \-ˌbō(ə)rd, -ˌbȯ(ə)rd\ *n* (ca. 1924) : corrugated or solid paperboard used for making containers

con·tain·er·iza·tion \kən-ˌtā-nə-rə-ˈzā-shən\ *n* (1956) : a shipping method in which a large amount of material (as merchandise) is packaged together in one large container

con·tain·er·ize \kən-ˈtā-nə-ˌrīz\ *vt* **-ized; -iz·ing** (1956) **1** : to ship by containerization **2** : to pack in containers

con·tain·er·port \-nər-ˌpō(ə)rt, -ˌpȯ(ə)rt\ *n* (1970) : a shipping port specially equipped to handle containerized cargo

con·tain·er·ship \-nər-ˌship\ *n* (1966) : a ship esp. designed or equipped for carrying containerized cargo

con·tain·ment \kən-ˈtān-mənt\ *n* (1655) **1** : the act, process, or means of containing **2** : the policy, process, or result of preventing the expansion of a hostile power or ideology

con·tam·i·nant \kən-ˈtam-ə-nənt\ *n* (ca. 1922) **:** something that contaminates

con·tam·i·nate \kən-ˈtam-ə-ˌnāt\ *vt* **-nat·ed; -nat·ing** [L *contaminatus,* pp. of *contaminare;* akin to L *contagio* contagion] (15c) **1 a :** to soil, stain, corrupt, or infect by contact or association ⟨bacteria *contaminated* the wound⟩ **b :** to make inferior or impure by admixture ⟨iron *contaminated* with phosphorus⟩ **2 :** to make unfit for use by the introduction of unwholesome or undesirable elements — **con·tam·i·na·tive** \-ˌnāt-iv\ *adj* — **con·tam·i·na·tor** \-ˌnāt-ər\ *n*

syn CONTAMINATE, TAINT, POLLUTE, DEFILE mean to make impure or unclean. CONTAMINATE implies intrusion of or contact with dirt or foulness from an outside source ⟨water *contaminated* by industrial wastes⟩ ⟨the bigotry of elders that may *contaminate* young minds⟩ TAINT stresses the loss of purity or cleanliness that follows contamination ⟨*tainted* meat⟩ ⟨his unkindness may defeat my life, but never *taint* my love —Shak.⟩ POLLUTE, sometimes interchangeable with *contaminate,* distinctively may imply that the process which begins with contamination is complete and that what was pure or clean has been made foul, poisoned, or filthy ⟨the *polluted* waters of the lake, in parts no better than an open cesspool⟩ DEFILE implies befouling of what could or should have been kept clean and pure or held sacred and commonly suggests violation or desecration ⟨*defile* a hero's memory with slanderous innuendo⟩

con·tam·i·na·tion \kən-ˌtam-ə-ˈnā-shən\ *n* (15c) **1 :** a process of contaminating **:** a state of being contaminated **2 :** CONTAMINANT

conte \kō^{n}t\ *n* [F] (1787) **:** a usu. short tale of adventure

con·temn \kən-ˈtem\ *vt* [ME *contempnen,* fr. MF *contempner,* fr. L *contemnere,* fr. *com-* + *temnere* to despise — more at STAMP] (15c) **:** to view or treat with contempt **:** SCORN ***syn*** see DESPISE — **con·tem·ner** *also* **con·tem·nor** \-ˈtem-(n)ər\ *n*

con·tem·plate \ˈkänt-əm-ˌplāt, ˈkän-ˌtem-\ *vb* **-plat·ed; -plat·ing** [L *contemplatus,* pp. of *contemplari,* fr. *com-* + *templum* space marked out for observation of auguries — more at TEMPLE] *vi* (1592) **:** PONDER, MEDITATE ~ *vt* **1 :** to view or consider with continued attention **:** meditate on **2 :** to have in view as contingent or probable or as an end or intention ***syn*** see CONSIDER — **con·tem·pla·tor** \-ˌplāt-ər\ *n*

con·tem·pla·tion \ˌkänt-əm-ˈplā-shən, ˌkän-ˌtem-\ *n* (13c) **1 a :** concentration on spiritual things as a form of private devotion **b :** a state of mystical awareness of God's being **2 :** an act of considering with attention **:** STUDY **3 :** the act of regarding steadily **4 :** INTENTION, EXPECTATION

¹con·tem·pla·tive \kən-ˈtem-plət-iv; ˈkänt-əm-ˌplāt-, ˈkän-ˌtem-\ *adj* (14c) **:** marked by or given to contemplation; *specif* **:** of or relating to a religious order devoted to prayer and penance — **con·tem·pla·tive·ly** *adv* — **con·tem·pla·tive·ness** *n*

²contemplative *n* (14c) **:** one who practices contemplation

con·tem·po·ra·ne·ity \kən-ˌtem-p(ə-)rə-ˈnē-ət-ē, -ˈnā-\ *n* (1772) **:** the quality or state of being contemporaneous or contemporary

con·tem·po·ra·ne·ous \kən-ˌtem-pə-ˈrā-nē-əs\ *adj* [L *contemporaneus,* fr. *com-* + *tempor-, tempus* time — more at TEMPORAL] (1656) **:** existing, occurring, or originating during the same time ***syn*** see CONTEMPORARY — **con·tem·po·ra·ne·ous·ly** *adv* — **con·tem·po·ra·ne·ous·ness** *n*

¹con·tem·po·rary \kən-ˈtem-pə-ˌrer-ē\ *adj* [*com-* + L *tempor-, tempus*] (1631) **1 :** happening, existing, living, or coming into being during the same period of time **2 a :** SIMULTANEOUS **b :** marked by characteristics of the present period **:** MODERN, CURRENT — **con·tem·po·rar·i·ly** \-ˌtem-pə-ˈrer-ə-lē\ *adv*

syn CONTEMPORARY, CONTEMPORANEOUS, COEVAL, SYNCHRONOUS, SIMULTANEOUS, COINCIDENT mean existing or occurring at the same time. CONTEMPORARY is likely to apply to people and what relates to them, CONTEMPORANEOUS to events; both suggest time measured in years; COEVAL refers usu. to periods, ages, eras, eons; SYNCHRONOUS implies exact correspondence in time and esp. in periodic intervals; SIMULTANEOUS implies correspondence in a moment of time; COINCIDENT is applied to events and may be used in order to avoid implication of causal relationship.

²contemporary *n, pl* **-rar·ies** (1646) **1 :** one that is contemporary with another **2 :** one of the same or nearly the same age as another

con·tempt \kən-ˈtem(p)t\ *n* [ME, fr. L *contemptus,* fr. *contemptus,* pp. of *contemnere*] (14c) **1 a :** the act of despising **:** the state of mind of one who despises **:** DISDAIN **b :** lack of respect or reverence for something **2 :** the state of being despised **3 :** willful disobedience to or open disrespect of a court, judge, or legislative body ⟨~ of court⟩

con·tempt·ible \kən-ˈtem(p)-tə-bəl\ *adj* (14c) **1 :** worthy of contempt **2** *obs* **:** SCORNFUL, CONTEMPTUOUS — **con·tempt·i·bil·ity** \-ˌtem(p)-tə-ˈbil-ət-ē\ *n* — **con·tempt·ible·ness** *n* — **con·tempt·ibly** \-ˈtem(p)-tə-blē\ *adv*

syn CONTEMPTIBLE, DESPICABLE, PITIABLE, SORRY, SCURVY mean arousing or deserving scorn. CONTEMPTIBLE may imply any quality provoking scorn or a low standing in any scale of values; DESPICABLE may imply utter worthlessness and usu. suggests arousing an attitude of moral indignation; PITIABLE applies to what inspires mixed contempt and pity; SORRY may stress pitiable inadequacy or may suggest wretchedness or sordidness; SCURVY adds to DESPICABLE an implication of arousing disgust.

con·temp·tu·ous \-ˈtem(p)-chə(-wə)s, -ˈtem(p)sh-wəs\ *adj* [L *contemptus*] (1595) **:** manifesting, feeling, or expressing contempt — **con·temp·tu·ous·ly** *adv* — **con·temp·tu·ous·ness** *n*

con·tend \kən-ˈtend\ *vb* [MF or L; MF *contendre,* fr. L *contendere,* fr. *com-* + *tendere* to stretch — more at THIN] *vi* (15c) **1 :** to strive or vie in contest or rivalry or against difficulties **:** STRUGGLE **2 :** to strive in debate **:** ARGUE ~ *vt* **1 :** MAINTAIN, ASSERT ⟨~*ed* that he was right⟩ **2 :** to struggle for **:** CONTEST — **con·tend·er** *n*

¹con·tent \kən-ˈtent\ *adj* [ME, fr. MF, fr. L *contentus,* fr. pp. of *continēre* to hold in, contain — more at CONTAIN] (15c) **:** CONTENTED, SATISFIED

²content *vt* (15c) **1 :** to appease the desires of **2 :** to limit (oneself) in requirements, desires, or actions

³content *n* (1579) **:** CONTENTMENT ⟨ate to his heart's ~⟩

⁴con·tent \ˈkän-ˌtent\ *n* [ME, fr. L *contentus,* pp. of *continēre* to contain] (15c) **1 a :** something contained — usu. used in pl. ⟨the jar's ~*s*⟩ ⟨the drawer's ~*s* ⟩ **b :** the topics or matter treated in a written work ⟨table of ~*s*⟩ **2 a :** SUBSTANCE, GIST **b :** MEANING, SIGNIFICANCE **c :** the events, physical detail, and information in a work of art — compare FORM 10c **3 a :** the matter dealt with in a field of study **b :** a part, element, or complex of parts **4 :** the amount of specified material contained **:** PROPORTION

content analysis *n* (1945) **:** analysis of the manifest and latent content of a body of communicated material (as a book or film) through a classification, tabulation, and evaluation of its key symbols and themes in order to ascertain its meaning and probable effect

con·tent·ed \kən-ˈtent-əd\ *adj* (1526) **:** feeling or manifesting satisfaction with one's possessions, status, or situation ⟨a ~ smile⟩ — **con·tent·ed·ly** *adv* — **con·tent·ed·ness** *n*

con·ten·tion \kən-ˈten-chən\ *n* [ME *contencioun,* fr. MF, fr. L *contention-, contentio,* fr. *contentus,* pp. of *contendere*] (14c) **1 :** an act or instance of contending **2 :** a point advanced or maintained in a debate or argument **3 :** RIVALRY, COMPETITION ***syn*** see DISCORD

con·ten·tious \kən-ˈten-chəs\ *adj* (15c) **1 :** likely to cause contention ⟨a ~ argument⟩ **2 :** exhibiting an often perverse and wearisome tendency to quarrels and disputes ⟨a man of a most ~ nature⟩ ***syn*** see BELLIGERENT — **con·ten·tious·ly** *adv* — **con·ten·tious·ness** *n*

con·tent·ment \kən-ˈtent-mənt\ *n* (15c) **1 :** the quality or state of being contented **2 :** something that contents

con·tent word \ˈkän-ˌtent-\ *n* (1940) **:** a word that primarily expresses lexical meaning — compare FUNCTION WORD

con·ter·mi·nous \kən-ˈtər-mə-nəs, kän-\ *adj* [L *conterminus,* fr. *com-* + *terminus* boundary — more at TERM] (1631) **1 :** having a common boundary **2 :** COTERMINOUS **3 :** enclosed within one common boundary ⟨the 48 ~ states of the United States⟩ — **con·ter·mi·nous·ly** *adv*

¹con·test \kən-ˈtest, ˈkän-\ *vb* [MF *contester,* fr. L *contestari* (*litem*) to bring an action at law, fr. *contestari* to call to witness, fr. *com-* + *testis* witness — more at TESTAMENT] *vi* (1603) **:** STRIVE, VIE ~ *vt* **:** to make the subject of dispute, contention, or litigation; *esp* **:** DISPUTE, CHALLENGE — **con·test·able** \-ə-bəl\ *adj* — **con·test·er** *n*

²con·test \ˈkän-ˌtest\ *n* (1647) **1 :** a struggle for superiority or victory **:** COMPETITION **2 :** a competition in which each contestant performs without direct contact with or interference from his competitors

con·tes·tant \kən-ˈtes-tənt, *also* ˈkän-ˌ\ *n* (1665) **1 :** one that participates in a contest **2 :** one that contests an award or decision

con·tes·ta·tion \ˌkän-ˌtes-ˈtā-shən\ *n* (1580) **:** CONTROVERSY

con·text \ˈkän-ˌtekst\ *n* [ME, weaving together of words, fr. L *contextus* connection of words, coherence, fr. *contextus,* pp. of *contexere* to weave together, fr. *com-* + *texere* to weave — more at TECHNICAL] (1568) **1 :** the parts of a discourse that surround a word or passage and can throw light on its meaning **2 :** the interrelated conditions in which something exists or occurs **:** ENVIRONMENT, SETTING — **con·text·less** \-ˌteks-tləs\ *adj* — **con·tex·tu·al** \kän-ˈteks-chə(-wə)l, kən-\ *adj* — **con·tex·tu·al·ly** \-ē\ *adv*

con·tex·ture \kən-ˈteks-chər, ˈkän-ˌ, kän-ˈ\ *n* [F, fr. L *contextus,* pp.] (1603) **1 :** the act, process, or manner of weaving parts into a whole; *also* **:** a structure so formed ⟨a ~ of lies⟩ **2 :** CONTEXT

con·ti·gu·ity \ˌkänt-ə-ˈgyü-ət-ē\ *n, pl* **-ities** (1641) **:** the quality or state of being contiguous **:** PROXIMITY

con·tig·u·ous \kən-ˈtig-yə-wəs\ *adj* [L *contiguus,* fr. *contingere* to have contact with — more at CONTINGENT] (1611) **1 :** being in actual contact **:** touching along a boundary or at a point **2** *of angles* **:** ADJACENT 2 **3 :** next or near in time or sequence **4 :** touching or connected throughout in an unbroken sequence ⟨~ row houses⟩ ⟨the ~ 48 states⟩ ***syn*** see ADJACENT — **con·tig·u·ous·ly** *adv* — **con·tig·u·ous·ness** *n*

con·ti·nence \ˈkänt-^{ə}n-ən(t)s\ *n* (14c) **1 :** SELF-RESTRAINT; *esp* **:** a refraining from sexual intercourse **2 :** the ability to retain a bodily discharge voluntarily ⟨fecal ~⟩

¹con·ti·nent \ˈkänt-^{ə}n-ənt\ *adj* [ME, fr. MF, fr. L *continent-, continens,* fr. prp. of *continēre* to hold in — more at CONTAIN] (14c) **1 :** exercising continence **2** *obs* **:** RESTRICTIVE — **con·ti·nent·ly** *adv*

²con·ti·nent \ˈkänt-^{ə}n-ənt, ˈkänt-nənt\ *n* [in senses 1 & 2, fr. L *continent-, continens,* prp. of *continēre,* to hold together, contain; in senses 3 & 4, fr. L *continent-, continens* continuous mass of land, mainland, fr. *continent-, continens,* prp.] (1541) **1** *archaic* **:** CONTAINER, CONFINES **2** *archaic* **:** EPITOME **3 :** MAINLAND **4 a :** one of the six or seven great divisions of land on the globe **b** *cap* **:** the continent of Europe — used with *the*

¹con·ti·nen·tal \ˌkänt-^{ə}n-ˈent-^{ə}l\ *adj* (1760) **1 :** of, relating to, or characteristic of a continent ⟨~ waters⟩; *specif, often cap* **:** of or relating to the continent of Europe as distinguished from the British Isles **2** *often cap* **:** of or relating to the colonies later forming the U.S. ⟨*Continental* Congress⟩ — **con·ti·nen·tal·ly** \-^{ə}l-ē\ *adv*

²continental *n* (1777) **1 a** *often cap* **:** an American soldier of the Revolution in the Continental army **b** (1) **:** a piece of Continental paper currency (2) **:** the least bit ⟨not worth a ~⟩ **2 :** an inhabitant of a continent and esp. the continent of Europe

continental breakfast *n, often cap C* (1911) **:** a light breakfast (as of rolls or toast and coffee)

continental code *n* (1922) **:** the international Morse code

continental drift *n* (1926) **:** a hypothetical slow movement of the continents on a deep-seated viscous zone within the earth

continental shelf *n* (1892) **:** a shallow submarine plain of varying width forming a border to a continent and typically ending in a steep slope to the oceanic abyss

continental slope *n* (1900) **:** the usu. steep slope from a continental shelf to the ocean floor

con·tin·gence \kən-ˈtin-jən(t)s\ *n* (1530) **1 :** CONTINGENCY **2 :** TANGENCY

con·tin·gen·cy \kən-ˈtin-jən-sē\ *n, pl* **-cies** (1561) **1 :** the quality or state of being contingent **2 :** a contingent event or condition: as **a :** an event (as an emergency) that is of possible but uncertain occurrence ⟨trying to provide for every ~⟩ **b :** something liable to happen as an adjunct to something else ***syn*** see JUNCTURE

contingency table *n* (ca. 1947) **:** a table of data in which the row entries tabulate the data according to one variable and the column entries

\ə\ abut \$^ə$\ kitten, F table \ər\ further \a\ ash \ā\ ace \ä\ cot, cart \au̇\ out \ch\ chin \e\ bet \ē\ easy \g\ go \i\ hit \ī\ ice \j\ job \ŋ\ sing \ō\ go \ȯ\ law \ȯi\ boy \th\ thin \t͟h\ the \ü\ loot \u̇\ foot \y\ yet \zh\ vision \à, k̲, ^{n}, œ, œ̄, ue, u̅e̅, ^{y}\ *see* Guide to Pronunciation

tabulate it according to another variable and which is used esp. in the study of the correlation between variables

[1]con·tin·gent \kən-'tin-jənt\ *adj* [ME, fr. MF, fr. L *contingent-, contingens,* prp. of *contingere* to have contact with, befall, fr. *com-* + *tangere* to touch — more at TANGENT] (14c) **1 :** likely but not certain to happen **:** POSSIBLE **2 :** not logically necessary; *esp* **:** EMPIRICAL **3 a :** happening by chance or unforeseen causes **b :** subject to chance or unseen effects **:** UNPREDICTABLE **c :** intended for use in circumstances not completely foreseen **4 :** dependent on or conditioned by something else **5 :** not necessitated **:** determined by free choice ***syn*** see ACCIDENTAL — **con·tin·gent·ly** *adv*

[2]contingent *n* (1548) **1 :** something contingent **:** CONTINGENCY **2 :** a representative group **:** DELEGATION, DETACHMENT

con·tin·u·al \kən-'tin-yə(-wə)l\ *adj* [ME, fr. MF, fr. L *continuus* continuous] (14c) **1 :** continuing indefinitely in time without interruption ⟨~ fear⟩ **2 :** recurring in steady rapid succession **3 :** forming a continuous series — **con·tin·u·al·ly** \-ē\ *adv*

syn CONTINUAL, CONTINUOUS, CONSTANT, INCESSANT, PERPETUAL, PERENNIAL mean characterized by continued occurrence or recurrence. CONTINUAL implies a close prolonged succession or recurrence; CONTINUOUS usu. implies an uninterrupted flow or spatial extension; CONSTANT implies uniform or persistent occurrence or recurrence; INCESSANT implies ceaseless or uninterrupted activity; PERPETUAL suggests unfailing repetition or lasting duration; PERENNIAL implies enduring existence often through constant renewal.

con·tin·u·ance \kən-'tin-yə-wən(t)s\ *n* (14c) **1 :** CONTINUATION **2 :** the extent of continuing **:** DURATION **3 :** the quality of enduring **:** PERMANENCE **4 :** an adjournment of court proceedings to a future day

con·tin·u·ant \-yə-wənt\ *n* (1861) **:** something that continues or serves as a continuation (as a consonant that may be prolonged without alteration during one emission of breath) — **continuant** *adj*

continuate *adj, obs* (1555) **:** CONTINUOUS, UNINTERRUPTED

con·tin·u·a·tion \kən-ˌtin-yə-'wā-shən\ *n* (14c) **1 :** the act or fact of continuing in or the prolongation of a state or activity **2 :** resumption after an interruption **3 :** something that continues, increases, or adds

con·tin·u·a·tive \kən-'tin-yə-ˌwāt-iv, -wət-iv\ *adj* (1684) **:** expressing continuity or continuation (as of an idea or action)

con·tin·u·a·tor \-ˌwāt-ər\ *n* (1646) **:** one that continues

con·tin·ue \kən-'tin-(ˌ)yü, -yə(-w)\ *vb* **-tin·ued; -tinu·ing** [ME *continuen,* fr. MF *continuer,* fr. L *continuare,* fr. *continuus*] *vi* (14c) **1 :** to maintain without interruption a condition, course, or action **2 :** to remain in existence **:** ENDURE **3 :** to remain in a place or condition **:** STAY **4 :** to resume an activity after interruption ~ *vt* **1 a :** KEEP UP, MAINTAIN ⟨~*s* walking⟩ **b :** to keep going or add to **:** PROLONG; *also* **:** to resume after intermission **2 :** to cause to continue **3 :** to allow to remain in a place or condition **:** RETAIN **4 :** to postpone (a legal proceeding) by a continuance — **con·tinu·er** \-yə-wər\ *n*

syn CONTINUE, LAST, ENDURE, ABIDE, PERSIST mean to exist over a period of time or indefinitely. CONTINUE applies to a process going on without ending; LAST, esp. when unqualified, may stress existing beyond what is normal or expected; ENDURE adds an implication of resisting destructive forces or agencies; ABIDE implies stable and constant existing esp. as opposed to mutability; PERSIST suggests outlasting the normal or appointed time and often connotes obstinacy or doggedness.

con·tin·ued *adj* (15c) **1 :** lasting or extending without interruption ⟨~ success⟩ **2 :** resumed after interruption ⟨a ~ story⟩

continued fraction *n* (ca. 1864) **:** a fraction whose numerator is an integer and whose denominator is an integer plus a fraction whose numerator is an integer and whose denominator is an integer plus a fraction and so on

con·tinu·ing \kən-'tin-yə-wiŋ\ *adj* (14c) **1 :** CONTINUOUS, CONSTANT ⟨~ poverty⟩ **2 :** needing no renewal **:** ENDURING ⟨~ fame⟩ — **con·tinu·ing·ly** *adv*

continuing education *n* (1954) **:** formal courses of study for part-time students **:** ADULT EDUCATION

con·ti·nu·ity \ˌkänt-ᵊn-'(y)ü-ət-ē\ *n, pl* **-ities** (15c) **1 a :** uninterrupted connection, succession, or union **b :** uninterrupted duration or continuation without essential change **2 :** something that has, exhibits, or provides continuity: as **a :** a script or scenario in the performing arts **b :** transitional spoken or musical matter esp. for a radio or television program **c :** the story and dialogue of a comic strip **3 :** the property characteristic of a continuous function

con·tin·uo \kən-'tin-(y)ə-ˌwō\ *n, pl* **-u·os** [It, fr. *continuo* continuous, fr. L *continuus*] (1724) **:** a bass part (as for a keyboard or stringed instrument) used esp. in baroque ensemble music and consisting of a succession of bass notes with figures that indicate the required chords — called also *figured bass, thoroughbass*

con·tin·u·ous \kən-'tin-yə-wəs\ *adj* [L *continuus,* fr. *continēre* to hold together — more at CONTAIN] (1673) **1 :** marked by uninterrupted extension in space, time, or sequence **2** *of a function* **:** having the property that the absolute value of the numerical difference between the value at a given point and the value at any point in a neighborhood of the given point can be made as close to zero as desired by choosing the neighborhood small enough ***syn*** see CONTINUAL — **con·tin·u·ous·ly** *adv* — **con·tin·u·ous·ness** *n*

con·tin·u·um \kən-'tin-yə-wəm\ *n, pl* **-ua** \-yə-wə\ *also* **-u·ums** [L, neut. of *continuus*] (1646) **1 :** a coherent whole characterized as a collection, sequence, or progression of values or elements varying by minute degrees ⟨"good" and "bad" . . . stand at opposite ends of a ~ instead of describing the two halves of a line —Wayne Shumaker⟩ ⟨"air" and "space" form an indivisible operational medium, a ~ best described as aerospace —Martin Caidin⟩ **2 :** the set of real numbers including both the rationals and the irrationals; *broadly* **:** a compact set which cannot be separated into two sets neither of which contains a limit point of the other

con·tort \kən-'tó(ə)rt\ *vb* [L *contortus,* pp. of *contorquēre,* fr. *com-* + *torquēre* to twist — more at TORTURE] *vt* (15c) **:** to twist in a violent manner ⟨features ~*ed* with fury⟩ ~ *vi* **:** to twist into a strained shape or expression ***syn*** see DEFORM — **con·tor·tion** \-'tór-shən\ *n* — **con·tor·tive** \-'tórt-iv\ *adj*

con·tor·tion·ist \kən-'tór-sh(ə-)nəst\ *n* (1859) **:** one who contorts; *specif* **:** an acrobat able to twist the body into unusual postures — **con·tor·tion·is·tic** \-ˌtór-shə-'nis-tik\ *adj*

[1]con·tour \'kän-ˌtú(ə)r\ *n* [F, fr. It *contorno,* fr. *contornare* to round off, fr. ML, to turn around — more at TURN] (1662) **1 :** an outline esp. of a curving or irregular figure **:** SHAPE; *also* **:** the line representing this outline **2 :** the general form or structure of something **:** CHARACTERISTIC — often used in pl. ⟨~*s* of a melody⟩ ⟨to delineate the tortured psychological ~*s* of the tribal past —B. J. Phillips⟩ ***syn*** see OUTLINE

[2]contour *adj* (1844) **1 :** following contour lines or forming furrows or ridges along them ⟨~ flooding⟩ ⟨~ farming⟩ **2 :** made to fit the contour of something ⟨a ~ couch⟩ ⟨~ sheets⟩

[3]contour *vt* (1871) **1 a :** to shape the contour of **b :** to shape so as to fit contours **2 :** to construct (as a road) in conformity to a contour

contour feather *n* (1867) **:** one of the medium-sized feathers that form the general covering of a bird and determine the external contour

contour line *n* (1844) **:** a line (as on a map) connecting the points on a land surface that have the same elevation

contour map *n* (1862) **:** a map having contour lines

con·tra \'kän-trə\ *prep* [L] (15c) **1 :** AGAINST — used chiefly in the phrase *pro and contra* **2 :** in opposition or contrast to — used before a proper name

contra- *prefix* [ME, fr. L, fr. *contra* against, opposite — more at COUNTER] **1 :** against **:** contrary **:** contrasting ⟨*contra*distinction⟩ **2 :** pitched below normal bass ⟨*contra*octave⟩

con·tra·band \'kän-trə-ˌband\ *n* [It *contrabbando,* fr. ML *contrabannum,* fr. *contra-* + *bannus, bannum* decree, of Gmc origin; akin to OHG *bannan* to command — more at BAN] (1529) **1 :** illegal or prohibited traffic in goods **:** SMUGGLING **2 :** goods or merchandise whose importation, exportation, or possession is forbidden; *also* **:** smuggled goods **3 :** a Negro slave who during the Civil War escaped to or was brought within the Union lines — **contraband** *adj*

con·tra·band·ist \-ˌban-dəst\ *n* (ca. 1818) **:** SMUGGLER

con·tra·bass \'kän-trə-ˌbās\ *n* [It *contrabbasso,* fr. *contra-* + *basso* bass] (1598) **:** DOUBLE BASS — **con·tra·bass·ist** \-ˌbā-səst\ *n*

con·tra·bas·soon \ˌkän-trə-bə-'sün, -ba-\ *n* (1891) **:** a double-reed woodwind instrument having a range an octave lower than that of the bassoon

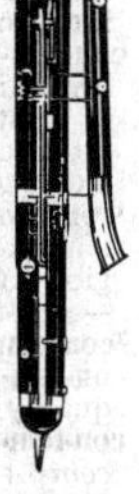
contrabassoon

con·tra·cep·tion \ˌkän-trə-'sep-shən\ *n* [*contra-* + *conception*] (1886) **:** deliberate prevention of conception or impregnation — **con·tra·cep·tive** \-'sep-tiv\ *adj or n*

[1]con·tract \'kän-ˌtrakt\ *n* [ME, fr. L *contractus,* fr. *contractus,* pp. of *contrahere* to draw together, make a contract, reduce in size, fr. *com-* + *trahere* to draw — more at DRAW] (14c) **1 a :** a binding agreement between two or more persons or parties; *esp* **:** one legally enforceable **b :** a business arrangement for the supply of certain goods or services at a fixed price ⟨make machine parts on ~⟩ **c :** the act of marriage or an agreement to marry **2 :** a document describing the terms of a contract **3 :** the final bid to win a specified number of tricks in bridge **4 :** an order or arrangement for a hired assassin to kill someone

[2]con·tract *vt 2a & vi 1 usu* 'kän-ˌtrakt, *others usu* kən-'\ *vb* [ME *contracten,* fr. MF or L; MF *contracter* to agree upon, fr. L *contractus*] *vt* (14c) **1 a :** to bring on oneself esp. inadvertently **:** INCUR ⟨~*ing* debts⟩ **b :** to become affected with ⟨~ pneumonia⟩ **2 a :** to establish or undertake by contract **b :** BETROTH; *also* **:** to establish (a marriage) formally **c (1) :** to hire by contract **(2) :** to purchase (as goods or services) on a contract basis — often used with *out* **3 a :** LIMIT, RESTRICT **b :** KNIT, WRINKLE ⟨frown ~*ed* his brow⟩ **c :** to draw together **:** CONCENTRATE **4 :** to reduce to smaller size by or as if by squeezing or forcing together **5 :** to shorten (as a word) by omitting one or more sounds or letters ~ *vi* **1 :** to make a contract **2 :** to draw together so as to become diminished in size ⟨metal ~*s* on cooling⟩; *also* **:** to become less in compass, duration, or length ⟨muscle ~*s* in tetanus⟩ — **con·tract·ibil·i·ty** \kən-ˌtrak-tə-'bil-ət-ē, ˌkän-\ *n* — **con·tract·ible** \kən-'trak-tə-bəl, 'kän-ˌ\ *adj*

syn CONTRACT, SHRINK, CONDENSE, COMPRESS, CONSTRICT, DEFLATE mean to decrease in bulk or volume. CONTRACT applies to a drawing together of surfaces or particles or a reduction of area or length; SHRINK implies a contracting or a loss of material and stresses a falling short of original dimensions; CONDENSE implies a reducing of something homogeneous to greater compactness without significant loss of content; COMPRESS implies a pressing into a small compass and definite shape usu. against resistance; CONSTRICT implies a tightening that reduces diameter; DEFLATE implies a contracting by reducing the internal pressure of contained air or gas.

contract bridge \ˌkän-ˌtrakt-\ *n* (1924) **:** a bridge game distinguished by the fact that overtricks do not count toward game or slam bonuses

con·trac·tile \kən-'trak-tᵊl, -ˌtīl\ *adj* (1706) **:** having or concerned with the power or property of contracting ⟨~ proteins of muscle fibrils⟩ — **con·trac·til·i·ty** \ˌkän-ˌtrak-'til-ət-ē\ *n*

contractile vacuole *n* (1877) **:** a vacuole in a unicellular organism that contracts regularly to discharge fluid from the body

con·trac·tion \kən-'trak-shən\ *n* (15c) **1 a :** the action or process of contracting **:** the state of being contracted **b :** the shortening and thickening of a functioning muscle or muscle fiber **c :** a reduction in business activity **2 :** a shortening of a word, syllable, or word group by omission of a sound or letter; *also* **:** a form produced by such shortening — **con·trac·tion·al** \-shnəl, -shən-ᵊl\ *adj* — **con·trac·tive** \kən-'trak-tiv, 'kän-ˌ\ *adj*

con·trac·tor \'kän-ˌtrak-tər (*usual for 1*), kən-'\ *n* (1548) **1 :** one that contracts or is party to a contract: as **a :** one that contracts to perform work or provide supplies on a large scale **b :** one that contracts to erect buildings **2 :** something (as a muscle) that contracts or shortens

con·trac·tu·al \kən-'trak-chə(-wə)l, kän-, -'traksh-wəl\ *adj* (1861) **:** of, relating to, or constituting a contract — **con·trac·tu·al·ly** \-ē\ *adv*

con·trac·ture \kən-'trak-chər\ *n* (1658) **:** a permanent shortening (as of muscle, tendon, or scar tissue) producing deformity or distortion

con·tra·dict \ˌkän-trə-'dikt\ *vt* [L *contradictus,* pp. of *contradicere,* fr. *contra-* + *dicere* to say, speak — more at DICTION] (1570) **1 :** to assert the contrary of **:** take issue with **2 :** to imply the opposite or a denial of ⟨your actions ~ your words⟩ ***syn*** see DENY — **con·tra·dict·able** \-'dik-tə-bəl\ *adj* — **con·tra·dic·tor** \-'dik-tər\ *n*

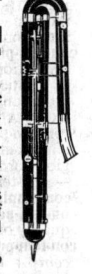

con·tra·dic·tion \ˌkän-trə-ˈdik-shən\ *n* (14c) **1 :** the act of contradicting **2 :** a proposition, statement, or phrase that asserts or implies both the truth and falsity of something **3 a :** logical incongruity **b :** a situation in which inherent factors, actions, or propositions are inconsistent or contrary to one another

con·tra·dic·tious \-shəs\ *adj* (1604) **1 :** CONTRADICTORY, OPPOSITE **2 :** given to or marked by contradiction **:** CONTRARY

[1]**con·tra·dic·to·ry** \ˌkän-trə-ˈdik-t(ə-)rē\ *n, pl* **-ries** (14c) **:** a proposition so related to another that if either of the two is true the other is false and if either is false the other must be true

[2]**contradictory** *adj* (1534) **:** involving, causing, or constituting a contradiction ⟨ill-planned and often ~ proposals⟩ ***syn*** see OPPOSITE — **con·tra·dic·to·ri·ly** \-t(ə-)rə-lē\ *adv* — **con·tra·dic·to·ri·ness** \-t(ə-)rē-nəs\ *n*

con·tra·dis·tinc·tion \ˌkän-trə-dis-ˈtiŋ(k)-shən\ *n* (1647) **:** distinction of markedly different or contrasting concepts ⟨painting in ~ to sculpture⟩ — **con·tra·dis·tinc·tive** \-ˈtiŋ(k)-tiv\ *adj* — **con·tra·dis·tinc·tive·ly** *adv*

con·tra·dis·tin·guish \-ˈtiŋ-gwish\ *vt* (1622) **:** to distinguish by contrasting qualities

con·trail \ˈkän-ˌtrāl\ *n* [*con*densation *trail*] (1943) **:** streaks of condensed water vapor created in the air by an airplane or rocket at high altitudes

con·tra·in·di·cate \ˌkän-trə-ˈin-də-ˌkāt\ *vt* (1666) **:** to make (a treatment or procedure) inadvisable

con·tra·in·di·ca·tion \-ˌin-də-ˈkā-shən\ *n* (ca. 1623) **:** something (as a symptom or condition) that makes a particular treatment or procedure inadvisable

con·tra·lat·er·al \-ˈlat-ə-rəl, -ˈla-trəl\ *adj* [ISV] (1882) **:** occurring on or acting in conjunction with similar parts on an opposite side

con·tral·to \kən-ˈtral-(ˌ)tō\ *n, pl* **-tos** [It, fr. *contra-* + *alto*] (1730) **1 a :** a singing voice having a range between tenor and mezzo-soprano **b :** a person having this voice **2 :** the part sung by a contralto

con·tra·oc·tave \ˌkän-trə-ˈäk-tiv, -təv, -ˌtāv\ *n* (ca. 1891) **:** the musical octave that begins on the third C below middle C — see PITCH illustration

con·tra·po·si·tion \-pə-ˈzish-ən\ *n* [LL *contraposition-, contrapositio,* fr. L *contrapositus,* pp. of *contraponere* to place opposite, fr. *contra-* + *ponere* to place — more at POSITION] (1551) **:** the relationship between two propositions when the subject and predicate of one are respectively the negation of the predicate and the negation of the subject of the other

con·tra·pos·i·tive \-ˈpäz-ət-iv, -ˈpäz-tiv\ *n* (1870) **:** a proposition resulting from an operation of immediate inference in which the terms of a given proposition are permuted and negated ⟨"all not-*P* is not-*S*" is the ~ of "all *S* is *P*"⟩

con·trap·tion \kən-ˈtrap-shən\ *n* [perh. blend of *contrivance, trap,* and *invention*] (ca. 1825) **:** DEVICE, GADGET

con·tra·pun·tal \ˌkän-trə-ˈpənt-^{ə}l\ *adj* [It *contrappunto* counterpoint, fr. ML *contrapunctus* — more at COUNTERPOINT] (1845) **1 :** POLYPHONIC **2 :** of, relating to, or marked by counterpoint — **con·tra·pun·tal·ly** \-^{ə}l-ē\ *adv*

con·tra·pun·tist \-ˈpənt-əst\ *n* (1776) **:** one who writes counterpoint

con·tra·ri·ety \ˌkän-trə-ˈrī-ət-ē\ *n, pl* **-eties** [ME *contrariete,* fr. MF *contrarieté,* fr. LL *contrarietat-, contrarietas,* fr. L *contrarius* contrary] (14c) **1 :** the quality or state of being contrary **2 :** something contrary

con·trar·i·ous \kən-ˈtrer-ē-əs, kän-\ *adj* (13c) **:** PERVERSE, ANTAGONISTIC

con·trari·wise \ˈkän-ˌtrer-ē-ˌwīz, kən-ˈ\ *adv* (14c) **1 :** on the contrary **2 :** VICE VERSA **3 :** in a contrary manner

[1]**con·trary** \ˈkän-ˌtrer-ē\ *n, pl* **-trar·ies** (13c) **1 :** a fact or condition incompatible with another **:** OPPOSITE — usu. used with *the* **2 :** one of a pair of opposites **3 a :** a proposition so related to another that though both may be false they cannot both be true — compare SUBCONTRARY **b :** either of two terms (as black and white) that cannot both be affirmed of the same subject — **by contraries** *obs* **:** in a manner opposite to what is logical or expected — **on the contrary :** just the opposite — **to the contrary 1 :** on the contrary **2 :** NOTWITHSTANDING

[2]**con·trary** \ˈkän-ˌtrer-ē, *4 often* kən-ˈtre(ə)r-ē\ *adj* [ME *contrarie,* fr. MF *contraire,* fr. L *contrarius,* fr. *contra* opposite] (14c) **1 :** being so different as to be at opposite extremes **:** OPPOSITE ⟨come to the ~ conclusion⟩ ⟨went off in ~ directions⟩; *also* **:** being opposite to or in conflict with each other ⟨~ viewpoints⟩ ⟨~ propositions⟩ **2 :** being not in conformity with what is usual or expected ⟨actions ~ to company policy⟩ ⟨the result was ~ to our plan⟩ ⟨~ evidence⟩ **3 :** UNFAVORABLE — used of wind or weather **4 :** temperamentally unwilling to accept control or advice ⟨a ~ child⟩ — **con·trari·ly** \-ˌtrer-ə-lē, -ˈtrer-\ *adv* — **con·trari·ness** \-ˌtrer-ē-nəs, -ˈtrer-\ *n*

syn CONTRARY, PERVERSE, RESTIVE, BALKY, WAYWARD mean inclined to resist authority or control. CONTRARY implies a temperamental unwillingness to accept orders or advice; PERVERSE may imply wrongheaded, determined, or cranky opposition to what is reasonable or normal; RESTIVE suggests unwillingness or inability to submit to discipline or follow orders; BALKY suggests a refusing to proceed in a desired direction or course of action; WAYWARD suggests strong-willed capriciousness and irregularity in behavior. ***syn*** see in addition OPPOSITE

[3]**con·trary** *\like* [2]*\ adv* (15c) **:** CONTRARIWISE, CONTRARILY

contrary to *prep* (14c) **:** in conflict with **:** DESPITE ⟨*contrary to* orders, he set out alone⟩

[1]**con·trast** \kən-ˈtrast, ˈkän-ˌ\ *vb* [F *contraster,* fr. MF, to oppose, resist, alter. of *contrester,* fr. (assumed) VL *contrastare,* fr. L *contra-* + *stare* to stand — more at STAND] *vt* (1695) **:** to set off in contrast **:** compare or appraise in respect to differences ⟨~ European and American manners⟩ — often used with *to* or *with* ⟨~*ing* her with other women — Victoria Sackville-West⟩ ~ *vi* **:** to form a contrast ***syn*** see COMPARE — **con·trast·able** \-ə-bəl\ *adj*

[2]**con·trast** \ˈkän-ˌtrast\ *n* (1711) **1 a :** juxtaposition of dissimilar elements (as color, tone, or emotion) in a work of art **b :** degree of difference between the lightest and darkest parts of a picture **2 a :** the difference or degree of difference between things having similar or comparable natures ⟨the ~ between the two forms of government⟩ **b :** comparison of similar objects to set off their dissimilar qualities **:** the state of being so compared ⟨the book is brilliant by ~ with earlier efforts⟩ ⟨the enforced simplicity in this diary . . . is in ~ to the intensity of his former life —*Times Lit. Supp.*⟩ **3 :** a person or thing that exhibits differences when compared with another

con·tras·tive \kən-ˈtras-tiv, ˈkän-ˌ\ *adj* (1841) **:** forming or consisting of a contrast — **con·tras·tive·ly** *adv*

con·trasty \ˈkän-ˌtras-tē\ *adj* (1891) **:** having or producing in photography great contrast between highlights and shadows

con·tra·vene \ˌkän-trə-ˈvēn\ *vt* **-vened; -ven·ing** [MF or LL; MF *contrevenir,* fr. LL *contravenire,* fr. L *contra-* + *venire* to come — more at COME] (1567) **1 :** to go or act contrary to **:** VIOLATE ⟨~ a law⟩ **2 :** to oppose in argument **:** CONTRADICT ⟨~ a proposition⟩ ***syn*** see DENY — **con·tra·ven·er** *n*

con·tra·ven·tion \ˌkän-trə-ˈven-chən\ *n* [MF, fr. LL *contraventus,* pp. of *contravenire*] (1579) **:** the act of contravening **:** VIOLATION

con·tre·danse \ˈkän-trə-ˌdan(t)s, kō^{n}-trə-dä^{n}s\ *or* **con·tra dance** \ˈkän-trə-ˌdan(t)s\ *n* [F *contredanse,* by folk etymology fr. E *country-dance*] (1803) **1 :** a folk dance in which couples face each other in two lines or in a square **2 :** a piece of music for a contredanse

con·tre·temps \ˈkän-trə-ˌtä^{n}, kō^{n}-trə-tä^{n}\ *n, pl* **con·tre·temps** \-(ˌ)tä^{n}(z)\ [F, fr. *contre-* counter- + *temps* time, fr. L *tempus* — more at TEMPORAL] (1769) **:** an inopportune and embarrassing occurrence or situation

con·trib·ute \kən-ˈtrib-yət, -(ˌ)yüt *also (esp before -ed or -ing)*-ˈtrib-ət; *chiefly Brit also* ˈkän-trə-ˌbyüt\ *vb* **-ut·ed; -ut·ing** [L *contributus,* pp. of *contribuere,* fr. *com-* + *tribuere* to grant — more at TRIBUTE] *vt* (1530) **1 :** to give or supply in common with others **2 :** to supply (as an article) for a publication ~ *vi* **1 a :** to give a part to a common fund or store **b :** to play a significant part in bringing about an end or result **2 :** to submit articles to a publication — **con·trib·u·tor** \-(y)ət-ər\ *n*

con·tri·bu·tion \ˌkän-trə-ˈbyü-shən\ *n* (14c) **1 :** a payment (as a levy or tax) imposed by military, civil, or ecclesiastical authorities usu. for a special or extraordinary purpose **2 :** the act of contributing; *also* **:** the thing contributed — **con·trib·u·tive** \kən-ˈtrib-yət-iv\ *adj* — **con·trib·u·tive·ly** *adv*

con·trib·u·to·ry \kən-ˈtrib-yə-ˌtōr-ē, -ˌtȯr-\ *adj* (15c) **1 a :** subject to a levy of supplies, money, or men **b :** contributing to a common fund or enterprise **2 :** of, relating to, or forming a contribution

con·trite \ˈkän-ˌtrīt, kən-ˈ\ *adj* [ME *contrit,* fr. MF, fr. ML *contritus,* fr. L, pp. of *conterere* to grind, bruise, fr. *com-* + *terere* to rub — more at THROW] (14c) **1 :** grieving and penitent for sin or shortcoming **2 :** proceeding from contrition ⟨~ sighs⟩ — **con·trite·ly** *adv* — **con·trite·ness** *n*

con·tri·tion \kən-ˈtrish-ən\ *n* (14c) **:** the state of being contrite **:** REPENTANCE ***syn*** see PENITENCE

con·triv·ance \kən-ˈtrī-vən(t)s\ *n* (1627) **1 a :** a thing contrived; *esp* **:** a mechanical device **b :** an artificial arrangement or development **2 :** the act or faculty of contriving **:** the state of being contrived

con·trive \kən-ˈtrīv\ *vb* **con·trived; con·triv·ing** [ME *controven, contreven,* fr. MF *controver,* fr. (assumed) LL *contropare* to compare] *vt* (14c) **1 a :** DEVISE, PLAN ⟨~ ways of handling the situation⟩ **b :** to form or create in an artistic or ingenious manner ⟨*contrived* household utensils from stone⟩ **2 :** to bring about by stratagem or with difficulty **:** MANAGE ~ *vi* **:** to make schemes — **con·triv·er** *n*

con·trived *adj* (15c) **:** ARTIFICIAL, LABORED

[1]**con·trol** \kən-ˈtrōl\ *vt* **con·trolled; con·trol·ling** [ME *controllen,* fr. MF *contreroller,* fr. *contrerolle* copy of an account, audit, fr. ML *contrarotulus,* fr. L *contra-* + *rotulus,* little wheel — more at ROLL] (15c) **1 :** to check, test, or verify by evidence or experiments **2 a :** to exercise restraining or directing influence over **:** REGULATE **b :** to have power over **:** RULE **c :** to reduce the incidence or severity of esp. to innocuous levels ⟨~ an insect population⟩ ⟨~ a disease⟩ ***syn*** see CONDUCT — **con·trol·la·bil·i·ty** \-ˌtrō-lə-ˈbil-ət-ē\ *n* — **con·trol·la·ble** \-ˈtrō-lə-bəl\ *adj* — **con·trol·ment** \-ˈtrōl-mənt\ *n*

[2]**control** *n, often attrib* (1590) **1 a :** an act or instance of controlling; *also* **:** power or authority to guide or manage **b :** skill in the use of a tool, instrument, technique, or artistic medium **c :** the regulation of economic activity esp. by government directive — usu. used in pl. ⟨price ~s⟩ **2 :** RESTRAINT, RESERVE **3 :** one that controls: as **a** (1) **:** an experiment in which the subjects are treated as in a parallel experiment except for omission of the procedure or agent under test and which is used as a standard of comparison in judging experimental effects — called also *control experiment* (2) **:** one (as an organism, culture, or group) that is part of a control **b :** a mechanism used to regulate or guide the operation of a machine, apparatus, or system **c :** an organization that directs a spaceflight ⟨mission ~⟩ **d :** a personality or spirit believed to actuate the utterances or performances of a spiritualist medium ***syn*** see POWER

con·trolled \kən-ˈtrōld\ *adj* (1586) **1 :** RESTRAINED **2 :** having the capacity to affect behavior and regulated by law with regard to possession and use ⟨~ drugs⟩

con·trol·ler \kən-ˈtrō-lər, ˈkän-ˌ\ *n* [ME *conterroller,* fr. MF *contrerolleur,* fr. *contrerolle*] (15c) **1 a :** COMPTROLLER 1 **b :** COMPTROLLER 2 **c :** the chief accounting officer of a business enterprise or an institution (as a college) **2 :** one that controls or has power or authority to control — **con·trol·ler·ship** \-ˌship\ *n*

controlling interest *n* (ca. 1924) **:** sufficient stock ownership in a corporation to exert control over policy

control surface *n* (1917) **:** a movable airfoil designed to change the attitude of an aircraft

con·tro·ver·sial \ˌkän-trə-ˈvər-shəl, -ˈvər-sē-əl\ *adj* (1583) **1 :** of, relating to, or arousing controversy ⟨a ~ public figure⟩ **2 :** given to controversy **:** DISPUTATIOUS — **con·tro·ver·sial·ism** \-ˌiz-əm\ *n* — **con·tro·ver·sial·ist** \-əst\ *n* — **con·tro·ver·sial·ly** \-ē\ *adv*

con·tro·ver·sy \ˈkän-trə-ˌvər-sē, *Brit also* kən-ˈträv-ər-sē\ *n, pl* **-sies** [ME *controversie,* fr. L *controversia,* fr. *controversus* disputable, lit., turned opposite, fr. *contro-* (akin to *contra-*) + *versus,* pp. of *vertere* to turn — more at WORTH] (14c) **1 :** a discussion marked esp. by the expression of opposing views **:** DISPUTE **2 :** QUARREL, STRIFE

con·tro·vert \ˈkän-trə-ˌvərt, ˌkän-trə-ˈ\ *vb* [*controversy*] *vt* (1609) **:** to dispute or oppose by reasoning ⟨~ a point in a discussion⟩ ~ *vi* **:** to engage in controversy — **con·tro·vert·er** \-ər\ *n* — **con·tro·vert·ible** \-ə-bəl\ *adj*

\ə\ abut \$^{ə}$\ kitten, F table \ər\ further \a\ ash \ā\ ace \ä\ cot, cart \au̇\ out \ch\ chin \e\ bet \ē\ easy \g\ go \i\ hit \ī\ ice \j\ job \ŋ\ sing \ō\ go \ȯ\ law \ȯi\ boy \th\ thin \th\ the \ü\ loot \u̇\ foot \y\ yet \zh\ vision \à, k, ^{n}, œ, ǣ, ue, ue̅, ^{y}\ *see* Guide to Pronunciation

con·tu·ma·cious \ˌkän-t(y)ə-ˈmā-shəs, ˌkän-chə-\ *adj* (1600) : stubbornly disobedient : REBELLIOUS — **con·tu·ma·cious·ly** *adv*

con·tu·ma·cy \kən-ˈt(y)ü-mə-sē; ˈkän-t(y)ə-, ˈkän-chə-\ *n* [ME *contumacie,* fr. L *contumacia,* fr. *contumac-, contumax* insubordinate, fr. *com-* + *tumēre* to swell, be proud — more at THUMB] (13c) : stubborn resistance to authority; *specif* : willful contempt of court

con·tu·me·li·ous \ˌkän-t(y)ə-ˈmē-lē-əs, ˌkän-chə-\ *adj* (15c) : insolently abusive and humiliating — **con·tu·me·li·ous·ly** *adv*

con·tume·ly \kän-ˈt(y)ü-mə-lē, kən-; ˈkän-t(y)ə-ˌmē-lē, ˈkän-chə-; *in "Hamlet"* ˈkän-(ˌ)tyüm-lē *or* ˈkän-chəm-\ *n, pl* **-lies** [ME *contumelie,* fr. MF, fr. L *contumelia;* perh. akin to L *contumacia*] (14c) : rude language or treatment arising from haughtiness and contempt; *also* : an instance of such language or treatment

con·tu·sion \kən-ˈt(y)ü-zhən\ *n* [ME *conteschown,* fr. MF *contusion,* fr. L *contusion-, contusio,* fr. *contusus,* pp. of *contundere* to beat, bruise, fr. *com-* + *tundere* to beat — more at STINT] (15c) : injury to tissue usu. without laceration : BRUISE 1a — **con·tuse** \-ˈt(y)üz\ *vt*

co·nun·drum \kə-ˈnən-drəm\ *n* [origin unknown] (1645) **1** : a riddle whose answer is or involves a pun **2 a** : a question or problem having only a conjectural answer **b** : an intricate and difficult problem ***syn*** see MYSTERY

con·ur·ba·tion \ˌkän-(ˌ)ər-ˈbā-shən\ *n* [*com-* + L *urb-, urbs* city] (1915) : an aggregation or continuous network of urban communities

co·nus ar·te·ri·o·sus \ˈkō-nə-sär-ˌtir-ē-ˈō-səs\ *n, pl* **co·ni ar·te·ri·o·si** \-ˌnī-är-ˌtir-ē-ˈō-ˌsī\ [NL, lit., arterial cone] (ca. 1860) **1** : a conical prolongation of the right ventricle in mammals from which the pulmonary arteries emerge — called also *conus* **2** : a prolongation of the ventricle of amphibians and some fishes that has a spiral valve separating venous blood going to the respiratory arteries from blood going to the aorta and systemic arteries

con·va·lesce \ˌkän-və-ˈles\ *vi* **-lesced; -lesc·ing** [L *convalescere,* fr. *com-* + *valescere* to grow strong, fr. *valēre* to be strong, be well — more at WIELD] (15c) : to recover health and strength gradually after sickness or weakness — **con·va·les·cence** \-ˈles-ᵊn(t)s\ *n* — **con·va·les·cent** \-ᵊnt\ *adj or n*

con·vect \kən-ˈvekt\ *vb* [back-formation fr. *convection*] *vi* (1881) : to transfer heat by convection ~ *vt* : to circulate (warm air) by convection

con·vec·tion \kən-ˈvek-shən\ *n* [LL *convection-, convectio,* fr. L *convectus,* pp. of *convehere* to bring together, fr. *com-* + *vehere* to carry — more at WAY] (ca. 1623) **1** : the action or process of conveying **2 a** : the circulatory motion that occurs in a fluid at a nonuniform temperature owing to the variation of its density and the action of gravity **b** : the transfer of heat by this automatic circulation of a fluid — **con·vec·tion·al** \-shnəl, -shən-ᵊl\ *adj* — **con·vec·tive** \-ˈvek-tiv\ *adj*

convection oven *n* (1973) : an oven having a fan that circulates hot air uniformly and continuously around food

con·vec·tor \-ˈvek-tər\ *n* (1907) : a heating unit in which air heated by contact with a heating device (as a radiator or a tube with fins) in a casing circulates by convection

con·vene \kən-ˈvēn\ *vb* **con·vened; con·ven·ing** [ME *convenen,* fr. MF *convenir* to come together, fr. L *convenire*] *vi* (15c) : to come together in a body ~ *vt* **1** : to summon before a tribunal **2** : to cause to assemble ***syn*** see SUMMON — **con·ven·er** *or* **con·ve·nor** \-ˈvē-nər\ *n*

1con·ve·nience \kən-ˈvēn-yən(t)s\ *n* (14c) **1** : fitness or suitability for performing an action or fulfilling a requirement **2 a** : something (as an appliance, device, or service) conducive to comfort or ease **b** : TOILET 3 **3** : a suitable time : OPPORTUNITY **4** : freedom from discomfort : EASE

2convenience *adj* (1917) : designed for quick and easy preparation or use

convenience store *n* (1965) : a small often franchised market that is open long hours

con·ve·nien·cy \-yən-sē\ *n, archaic* (1601) : CONVENIENCE

con·ve·nient \kən-ˈvēn-yənt\ *adj* [ME, fr. L *convenient-, conveniens,* fr. prp. of *convenire* to come together, be suitable, fr. *com-* + *venire* to come — more at COME] (14c) **1** *obs* : SUITABLE, PROPER **2 a** : suited to personal comfort or to easy performance **b** : suited to a particular situation **c** : affording accommodation or advantage **3** : being near at hand : HANDY — **con·ve·nient·ly** *adv*

1con·vent \ˈkän-vənt, -ˌvent\ *n* [ME *covent,* fr. OF, fr. ML *conventus,* fr. L, assembly, fr. *conventus,* pp. of *convenire*] (13c) : a local community or house of a religious order or congregation; *esp* : an establishment of nuns

2con·vent \kən-ˈvent\ *vb* [L *conventus,* pp.] *obs* (1514) : CONVENE

con·ven·ti·cle \kən-ˈvent-i-kəl\ *n* [ME, fr. L *conventiculum,* dim. of *conventus* assembly] (14c) **1** : ASSEMBLY, MEETING **2** : an assembly of an irregular or unlawful character **3** : an assembly for religious worship; *esp* : a secret meeting for worship not sanctioned by law **4** : MEETINGHOUSE — **con·ven·ti·cler** \-k(ə-)lər\ *n*

con·ven·tion \kən-ˈven-chən\ *n* [ME, fr. MF or L; MF, fr. L *convention-, conventio,* fr. *conventus,* pp.] (15c) **1 a** : AGREEMENT, CONTRACT **b** : an agreement between states for regulation of matters affecting all of them **c** : a compact between opposing commanders esp. concerning prisoner exchange or armistice **d** : a general agreement about basic principles or procedures; *also* : a principle or procedure accepted as true or correct by convention **2 a** : the summoning or convening of an assembly **b** : an assembly of persons met for a common purpose; *esp* : a meeting of the delegates of a political party for the purpose of formulating a platform and selecting candidates for office **c** : the usu. state or national organization of a religious denomination **3 a** : usage or custom esp. in social matters **b** : a rule of conduct or behavior **c** : a practice in bidding or playing that conveys information between partners in a card game (as bridge) **d** : an established technique, practice, or device (as in literature or the theater)

con·ven·tion·al \kən-ˈvench-nəl, -ˈven-chən-ᵊl\ *adj* (15c) **1** : formed by agreement or compact **2 a** : according with, sanctioned by, or based on convention **b** (1) : lacking originality or individuality : TRITE (2) : ORDINARY, COMMONPLACE **3 a** : according with a mode of artistic representation that simplifies or provides symbols or substitutes for natural forms **b** : of traditional design **4** : of, resembling, or relating to a convention, assembly, or public meeting **5** : not making use of nuclear weapons ⟨~ warfare⟩ ***syn*** see CEREMONIAL — **con·ven·tion·al·ism** \-ˌiz-əm\ *n* — **con·ven·tion·al·ist** \-əst\ *n* — **con·ven·tion·al·iza·tion** \-ˌvench-nə-lə-ˈzā-shən, -ˌven-chən-ᵊl-ə-ˈzā-\ *n* — **con·ven·tion·al·ize** \-ˈvench-nə-ˌlīz, -ˈven-chən-ᵊl-ˌīz\ *vt* — **con·ven·tion·al·ly** \-ē\ *adv*

con·ven·tion·al·i·ty \-ˌven-chə-ˈnal-ət-ē\ *n, pl* **-ties** (1834) **1** : a conventional usage, practice, or thing **2** : the quality or state of being conventional; *specif* : adherence to conventions

con·ven·tion·eer \kən-ˌven-chə-ˈni(ə)r\ *n* (1926) : a person attending a convention

1con·ven·tu·al \kən-ˈvench-(ə-)wəl, kän-\ *adj* [ME, fr. MF or ML; MF, fr. ML *conventualis,* fr. *conventus* convent] (15c) **1** : of, relating to, or befitting a convent or monastic life : MONASTIC **2** *cap* : of or relating to the Conventuals — **con·ven·tu·al·ly** \-ē\ *adv*

2conventual *n* (1533) **1** *cap* : a member of the Order of Friars Minor Conventual forming a branch of the first order of St. Francis of Assisi under a mitigated rule **2** : a member of a conventual community

con·verge \kən-ˈvərj\ *vb* **con·verged; con·verg·ing** [ML *convergere,* fr. L *com-* + *vergere* to bend, incline — more at WRENCH] *vi* (1691) **1** : to tend or move toward one point or one another : come together : MEET **2** : to come together and unite in a common interest or focus **3** : to approach a limit as the number of terms increases without limit ~ *vt* : to cause to converge

con·ver·gence \kən-ˈvər-jən(t)s\ *n* (1713) **1** : the act of converging and esp. moving toward union or uniformity; *esp* : coordinated movement of the two eyes so that the image of a single point is formed on corresponding retinal areas **2** : the state or property of being convergent **3** : independent development of similar characters (as of bodily structure or cultural traits) often associated with similarity of habits or environment

con·ver·gen·cy \-jən-sē\ *n* (1709) : CONVERGENCE

con·ver·gent \-jənt\ *adj* (1727) **1** : tending to move toward one point or to approach each other : CONVERGING ⟨~ lines⟩ **2** : exhibiting convergence in form, function, or development ⟨~ evolution⟩ **3 a** *of an improper integral* : having a value that is a real number **b** : characterized by having the *n*th term or the sum of the first *n* terms approach a finite limit ⟨a ~ sequence⟩ ⟨a ~ series⟩

con·vers·able \kən-ˈvər-sə-bəl\ *adj* (1631) **1** *archaic* : relating to or suitable for social interaction **2** : pleasant and easy to converse with

con·ver·sance \kən-ˈvərs-ᵊn(t)s *also* ˈkän-vər-sən(t)s\ *n* (1609) : the quality or state of being conversant

con·ver·san·cy \-ᵊn-sē, -sən-sē\ *n* (1798) : CONVERSANCE

con·ver·sant \kən-ˈvərs-ᵊnt *also* ˈkän-vər-sənt\ *adj* (14c) **1** *archaic* : CONCERNED, OCCUPIED **2** *archaic* : having frequent or familiar association **3** : having knowledge or experience — used with *with*

con·ver·sa·tion \ˌkän-vər-ˈsā-shən\ *n* [ME *conversacioun,* fr. MF *conversation,* fr. L *conversation-, conversatio,* fr. *conversatus,* pp. of *conversari* to live, keep company with, fr. *conversus,* pp. of *convertere* to turn around] (14c) **1** *obs* : CONDUCT, BEHAVIOR **2 a** (1) : oral exchange of sentiments, observations, opinions, or ideas (2) : an instance of such exchange : TALK **b** : an informal discussion of an issue by representatives of governments, institutions, or groups **c** : an exchange similar to conversation; *esp* : real-time interaction with a computer esp. through a keyboard — **con·ver·sa·tion·al** \-shnəl, -shən-ᵊl\ *adj* — **con·ver·sa·tion·al·ly** \-ē\ *adv*

con·ver·sa·tion·al·ist \-shnə-ləst, -shən-ᵊl-əst\ *n* (1836) : one who converses a great deal or who excels in conversation

conversation piece *n* (1712) **1** : a painting of a group of persons in their customary surroundings **2** : something (as a novel or unusual object) that stimulates conversation

con·ver·sa·zi·o·ne \ˌkän-vər-ˌsät-sē-ˈō-nē, ˌkōn-\ *n, pl* **-ones** *or* **-o·ni** \-ˈō-(ˌ)nē\ [It, lit. conversation, fr. L *conversation-, conversatio*] (1739) : a meeting for conversation esp. about art, literature, or science

1con·verse \ˈkän-ˌvərs\ *n* (1500) **1** *obs* : social interaction **2** : CONVERSATION

2con·verse \kən-ˈvərs\ *vi* **con·versed; con·vers·ing** [ME *conversen,* fr. MF *converser,* fr. L *conversari*] (1586) **1** *archaic* **a** : to become occupied or engaged **b** : to have acquaintance or familiarity **2 a** : to exchange thoughts and opinions in speech : TALK **b** : to carry on an exchange similar to a conversation; *esp* : to interact with a computer — **con·vers·er** \-ˈvər-sər\ *n*

3con·verse \ˈkän-ˌvərs\ *n* [L *conversus,* pp.] (1570) : something reversed in order, relation, or action: as **a** : a theorem formed by interchanging the hypothesis and conclusion of a given theorem **b** : a proposition obtained by interchange of the subject and predicate of a given proposition ⟨"no *P* is *S*" is the ~ of "no *S* is *P*"⟩

4con·verse \kən-ˈvərs, ˈkän-ˌ\ *adj* (1794) **1** : reversed in order, relation, or action **2** : being a logical or mathematical converse ⟨the ~ theorem⟩ — **con·verse·ly** *adv*

con·ver·sion \kən-ˈvər-zhən, -shən\ *n* [ME, fr. MF, fr. L *conversion-, conversio,* fr. *conversus*] (14c) **1** : the act of converting : the process of being converted — compare GENE CONVERSION **2** : an experience associated with a definite and decisive adoption of religion **3 a** : the operation of finding a converse in logic or mathematics **b** : reduction of a mathematical expression by clearing of fractions **4** : a successful try for point or free throw **5** : something converted from one use to another — **con·ver·sion·al** \-ˈvərzh-nəl, -ˈvərsh-, -ən-ᵊl\ *adj*

conversion reaction *n* (1912) : a psychoneurosis in which bodily symptoms (as paralysis of the limbs) appear without physical basis — called also *conversion hysteria*

1con·vert \kən-ˈvərt\ *vb* [ME *converten,* fr. MF *convertir,* fr. L *convertere,* to turn around, transform, convert, fr. *com-* + *vertere* to turn — more at WORTH] *vt* (14c) **1 a** : to bring over from one belief, view, or party to another **b** : to bring about a religious conversion in **2 a** : to alter the physical or chemical nature or properties of esp. in manufacturing **b** (1) : to change from one form or function to another (2) : to alter for more effective utilization (3) : to appropriate without right **c** : to exchange for an equivalent **3** *obs* : TURN **4** : to subject to logical conversion **5 a** : to make a goal after receiving (a pass) from a teammate **b** : to make (a spare) in bowling ~ *vi* **1** : to undergo conversion **2** : to make good on a try for point after touchdown or on a free throw ***syn*** see TRANSFORM

2con·vert \ˈkän-ˌvərt\ *n* (1561) : one that is converted

con·vert·er \kən-ˈvərt-ər\ *n* (1533) : one that converts: as **a** : the furnace used in the Bessemer process **b** *or* **con·ver·tor** \-ˈvərt-ər\ : a device employing mechanical rotation for changing electrical energy from one form to another; *also* : a radio device for converting one frequency to another **c** : a device for adapting a television or radio receiver to receive channels for which it was not orig. designed **d** : a device that accepts data in one form and converts it to another ⟨analog-digital ~⟩ **e** : CATALYTIC CONVERTER

¹con·vert·ible \kən-ˈvərt-ə-bəl\ *adj* (14c) **1** : capable of being converted **2** : having a top that may be lowered or removed ⟨~ coupe⟩ **3** : capable of being exchanged for a specified equivalent (as another currency or security) ⟨a bond ~ to 12 shares of common stock⟩ — **con·vert·ibil·i·ty** \-ˌvərt-ə-ˈbil-ət-ē\ *n* — **con·vert·ible·ness** \-ˈvərt-ə-bəl-nəs\ *n* — **con·vert·ibly** \-blē\ *adv*

²convertible *n* (1615) : something convertible; *esp* : a convertible automobile

con·verti·plane *or* **con·verta·plane** \kən-ˈvərt-ə-ˌplān\ *n* (1949) : an aircraft that takes off and lands like a helicopter and is convertible to a fixed-wing configuration for forward flight

con·vex \kän-ˈveks; ˈkän-ˌ, kən-ˈ\ *adj* [MF or L; MF *convexe*, fr. L *convexus* vaulted, concave, convex, fr. *com-* + *-vexus*; prob. akin to L *vehere* to carry — more at WAY] (1571) **1 a** : curved or rounded like the exterior of a sphere or circle **b** : being a continuous function or part of a continuous function with the property that a line joining any two points on its graph lies on or above the graph **2 a** *of a set of points* : containing all points in a line joining any two constituent points **b** *of a geometric figure* : comprising a convex set when combined with its interior ⟨a ~ polygon⟩

con·vex·i·ty \kən-ˈvek-sət-ē, kän-\ *n, pl* **-ties** (1599) **1** : the quality or state of being convex **2** : a convex surface or part

con·vexo–con·cave \-ˌvek-(ˌ)sō-\ *adj* (1693) **1** : CONCAVO-CONVEX **2** : having the convex side of greater curvature than the concave

con·vey \kən-ˈvā\ *vt* **con·veyed; con·vey·ing** [ME *conveyen*, fr. MF *conveier* to accompany, escort, fr. (assumed) VL *conviare*, fr. L *com-* + *via* way — more at VIA] (14c) **1** *obs* : LEAD, CONDUCT **2 a** : to bear from one place to another; *esp* : to move in a continuous stream or mass **b** : to impart or communicate by statement, suggestion, gesture, or appearance **c** (1) *archaic* : STEAL (2) *obs* : to carry away secretly **d** : to transfer or deliver to another; *specif* : to transfer by a sealed writing **e** : to cause to pass from one place or person to another : TRANSMIT

con·vey·ance \kən-ˈvā-ən(t)s\ *n* (15c) **1** : the action of conveying **2** : a means or way of conveying: as **a** : an instrument by which title to property is conveyed **b** : a means of transport : VEHICLE

con·vey·anc·er \-ən-sər\ *n* (1650) : one whose business is conveyancing

con·vey·anc·ing \-ən-siŋ\ *n* (1714) : the act or business of drawing deeds, leases, or other writings for transferring the title to property

con·vey·er *or* **con·vey·or** \kən-ˈvā-ər\ *n* (1513) : one that conveys: as **a** : a person who transfers property **b** *usu conveyor* : a mechanical apparatus for carrying packages or bulk material from place to place (as by an endless moving belt or a chain of receptacles)

con·vey·or·ize \-ə-ˌrīz\ *vt* **-ized; -iz·ing** (1941) : to equip with a conveyor — **con·vey·or·iza·tion** \-ˌvā-ə-rə-ˈzā-shən\ *n*

¹con·vict \kən-ˈvikt\ *adj, archaic* (14c) : having been convicted

²con·vict \kən-ˈvikt\ *vt* [ME *convicten*, fr. L *convictus*, pp. of *convincere* to refute, convict] (14c) **1** : to find or prove to be guilty **2** : to convince of error or sinfulness

³con·vict \ˈkän-ˌvikt\ *n* (15c) **1** : a person convicted of and under sentence for a crime **2** : a person serving a usu. long prison sentence

con·vic·tion \kən-ˈvik-shən\ *n* (15c) **1** : the act or process of convicting of a crime esp. in a court of law **2 a** : the act of convincing a person of error or of compelling the admission of a truth **b** : the state of being convinced of error or compelled to admit the truth **3 a** : a strong persuasion or belief **b** : the state of being convinced ***syn*** see CERTAINTY, OPINION

con·vince \kən-ˈvin(t)s\ *vt* **con·vinced; con·vinc·ing** [L *convincere* to refute, convict, prove, fr. *com-* + *vincere* to conquer — more at VICTOR] (1530) **1** *obs* **a** : to overcome by argument **b** : OVERPOWER, OVERCOME **2** *obs* : DEMONSTRATE, PROVE **3** : to bring by argument to belief, consent, or a course of action : PERSUADE ⟨*convinced* them to leave the country⟩ ⟨they were *convinced* that he had drowned⟩ — **con·vinc·er** *n*

con·vinc·ing \kən-ˈvin(t)-siŋ\ *adj* (1624) **1** : satisfying or assuring by argument or proof ⟨a ~ test of a new product⟩ **2** : having power to convince of the truth, rightness, or reality of something : PLAUSIBLE ⟨told a ~ story⟩ ***syn*** see VALID — **con·vinc·ing·ly** \-siŋ-lē\ *adv* — **con·vinc·ing·ness** *n*

con·viv·ial \kən-ˈviv-yəl, -ˈviv-ē-əl\ *adj* [LL *convivialis*, fr. L *convivium* banquet, fr. *com-* + *vivere* to live — more at QUICK] (1668) : relating to, occupied with, or fond of feasting, drinking, and good company — **con·viv·i·al·i·ty** \-ˌviv-ē-ˈal-ət-ē\ *n* — **con·viv·ial·ly** \-ˈviv-yə-lē, -ˈviv-ē-ə-lē\ *adv*

con·vo·ca·tion \ˌkän-və-ˈkā-shən\ *n* [ME, fr. MF, fr. L *convocation-, convocatio*, fr. *convocatus*, pp. of *convocare*] (14c) **1 a** : an assembly of persons convoked **b** (1) : an assembly of bishops and representative clergy of the Church of England (2) : a consultative assembly of clergy and lay delegates from one part of an Episcopal diocese; *also* : a territorial division of an Episcopal diocese **c** : a ceremonial assembly of members of a college or university **2** : the act or process of convoking — **con·vo·ca·tion·al** \-shnəl, -shən-ᵊl\ *adj*

con·voke \kən-ˈvōk\ *vt* **con·voked; con·vok·ing** [MF *convoquer*, fr. L *convocare*, fr. *com-* + *vocare* to call — more at VOICE] (1598) : to call together to a meeting ***syn*** see SUMMON

con·vo·lute \ˈkän-və-ˌlüt\ *vb* **-lut·ed; -lut·ing** [L *convolutus*, pp. of *convolvere*] (1702) : TWIST, COIL

con·vo·lut·ed *adj* (ca. 1755) **1** : having convolutions **2** : INVOLVED, INTRICATE

convoluted tubule *n* (1950) **1** : PROXIMAL CONVOLUTED TUBULE **2** : DISTAL CONVOLUTED TUBULE

con·vo·lu·tion \ˌkän-və-ˈlü-shən\ *n* (1545) **1** : a form or shape that is folded in curved or tortuous windings **2** : one of the irregular ridges on the surface of the brain and esp. of the cerebrum of higher mammals

con·volve \kən-ˈvälv, -ˈvölv *also* -ˈväv *or* -ˈvöv\ *vb* **con·volved; con·volv·ing** [L *convolvere*, fr. *com-* + *volvere* to roll — more at VOLUBLE] *vt* (1650) : to roll together : WRITHE ~ *vi* : to roll together or circulate involvedly

con·vol·vu·lus \kən-ˈväl-vyə-ləs, -ˈvöl- *also* -ˈväv-yə- *or* -ˈvöv-yə-\ *n, pl* **-lus·es** *or* **-li** \-ˌlī, -ˌlē\ [NL, fr. L *convolvere*] (1548) : any of a genus (*Convolvulus*) of erect, trailing, or twining herbs and shrubs of the morning-glory family

¹con·voy \ˈkän-ˌvȯi, kən-ˈ\ *vt* [ME *convoyen*, fr. MF *conveier, convoier* — more at CONVEY] (14c) : ACCOMPANY; *esp* : to escort for protection

²con·voy \ˈkän-ˌvȯi\ *n* (1523) **1** : one that convoys; *esp* : a protective escort (as for ships) **2** : the act of convoying **3** : a group convoyed or organized for convenience or protection in moving

con·vul·sant \kən-ˈvəl-sənt\ *adj* (1825) : causing convulsions : CONVULSIVE 1 — **convulsant** *n*

con·vulse \kən-ˈvəls\ *vt* **con·vulsed; con·vuls·ing** [L *convulsus*, pp. of *convellere* to pluck up, convulse, fr. *com-* + *vellere* to pluck — more at VULNERABLE] (1643) : to shake or agitate violently; *esp* : to shake with or as if with irregular spasms ***syn*** see SHAKE

con·vul·sion \kən-ˈvəl-shən\ *n* (1585) **1** : an abnormal violent and involuntary contraction or series of contractions of the muscles **2 a** : a violent disturbance **b** : an uncontrolled fit : PAROXYSM — **con·vul·sion·ary** \-shə-ˌner-ē\ *adj*

con·vul·sive \kən-ˈvəl-siv\ *adj* (1615) **1** : constituting or producing a convulsion **2** : attended or affected with convulsions ***syn*** see FITFUL — **con·vul·sive·ly** *adv* — **con·vul·sive·ness** *n*

cony *var of* CONEY

coo \ˈkü\ *vi* [imit.] (1670) **1** : to make the low soft cry of a dove or pigeon or a similar sound **2** : to talk fondly, amorously, or appreciatively ⟨an album that will be ~*ed* over by condescending classical music critics —Ellen Sander⟩ — **coo** *n*

¹cook \ˈku̇k\ *n* [ME, fr. OE *cōc*, fr. L *coquus*, fr. *coquere* to cook; akin to OE *āfigen* fried, Gk *pessein* to cook] (bef. 12c) **1** : one who prepares food for eating **2** : a technical or industrial process comparable to cooking food; *also* : a substance so processed

²cook *vi* (14c) **1** : to prepare food for eating by means of heat **2** : to undergo the action of being cooked ⟨the rice is ~*ing* now⟩ **3** : OCCUR, HAPPEN ⟨find out what was ~*ing* in the committee⟩ **4** : to perform, do, or proceed well ⟨the jazz quartet was ~*ing* along⟩ ⟨the party ~*ed* right through the night⟩ ~ *vt* **1** : CONCOCT, IMPROVISE — usu. used with *up* ⟨~*ed* up a scheme⟩ **2** : to prepare for eating by a heating process **3** : FALSIFY, DOCTOR ⟨an old hand at company manipulation, he prepares to ~ the books —*Punch*⟩ **4** : to subject to the action of heat or fire — **cook one's goose** : to ruin one irretrievably

cook·book \-ˌbu̇k\ *n* (1809) : a book of cooking directions and recipes; *broadly* : a book of detailed instructions

cook cheese *n* (1941) : an unripened cheese made from curd that has been cooked to a soft consistency

cooked cheese \ˈku̇k-ˈchēz\ *n* (ca. 1953) : COOK CHEESE

cook·er \ˈku̇k-ər\ *n* (1869) : one that cooks: as **a** : a utensil, device, or apparatus for cooking **b** : one who tends a cooking process : COOK **c** *Brit* : STOVE

cook·ery \ˈku̇k-(ə-)rē\ *n, pl* **-er·ies** (14c) **1** : the art or practice of cooking **2** : an establishment for cooking

cook·ie *or* **cooky** \ˈku̇k-ē\ *n, pl* **cook·ies** [D *koekje*, dim. of *koek* cake] (1703) **1** : a small flat or slightly raised cake **2 a** : an attractive woman ⟨a buxom French ~ who haunts the . . . colony's one night spot —*Newsweek*⟩ **b** : PERSON, GUY ⟨a very tough ~ indeed, who can break a man's wrist without a quiver of distaste —John Crosby⟩

cookie sheet *n* (1926) : a flat rectangle of metal with at least one rolled edge used esp. for the baking of cookies or biscuits

cook·ing *adj* (1813) : suitable for or used in cooking ⟨~ apples⟩

cooking top *n* (1962) : a built-in cabinet-top cooking apparatus consisting usu. of four heating units for gas or electricity

cook off *vi, of a cartridge* (1945) : to fire as a result of overheating

cook·out \ˈku̇k-ˌau̇t\ *n* (1947) : an outing at which a meal is cooked and served in the open; *also* : the meal cooked

cook·shack \-ˌshak\ *n* (1909) : a shack used for cooking

cook·shop \-ˌshäp\ *n* (1552) : a shop supplying or serving cooked food

Cook's tour \ˈku̇ks-\ *n* [Thomas Cook & Son, Eng. travel agency] (1906) : a quick tour in which attractions are viewed cursorily

cook·stove \ˈku̇k-ˌstōv\ *n* (1824) : a stove for cooking

cook·ware \ˈku̇k-ˌwa(ə)r, -ˌwe(ə)r\ *n* (1953) : utensils used in cooking

¹cool \ˈkül\ *adj* [ME *col*, fr. OE *cōl*; akin to OHG *kuoli* cool, OE *ceald* cold] (bef. 12c) **1** : moderately cold : lacking in warmth **2 a** : marked by steady dispassionate calmness and self-control ⟨a ~ and calculating administrator —*Current Biog.*⟩ **b** : lacking ardor or friendliness ⟨a ~ impersonal manner⟩ **c** *of jazz* : marked by restrained emotion and the frequent use of counterpoint **d** : free from tensions or violence ⟨meeting with minority groups in an attempt to keep the city ~⟩ **3** — used as an intensive ⟨a ~ million dollars⟩ **4** : marked by deliberate effrontery or lack of due respect or discretion ⟨a ~ reply⟩ **5** : facilitating or suggesting relief from heat ⟨a ~ dress⟩ **6 a** *of a color* : producing an impression of being cool; *specif* : of a hue in the range violet through blue to green **b** *of a musical tone* : relatively lacking in timbre or resonance **7** *slang* : very good : EXCELLENT **8** : employing understatement and a minimum of detail to convey information and usu. requiring the listener, viewer, or reader to complete the message ⟨another indication of the very ~ . . . character of this medium —H. M. McLuhan⟩ — compare HOT 10 — **cool·ish** \ˈkü-lish\ *adj* — **cool·ly** *also* **cooly** \-ˈkül-(l)ē\ *adv* — **cool·ness** \ˈkül-nəs\ *n*

syn COOL, COMPOSED, COLLECTED, UNRUFFLED, IMPERTURBABLE, NONCHALANT mean free from agitation or excitement. COOL may imply calmness, deliberateness, or dispassionateness; COMPOSED implies freedom from agitation as a result of self-discipline or a sedate disposition; COLLECTED implies a concentration of mind that eliminates distractions esp. in moments of crisis; UNRUFFLED suggests apparent serenity and poise in the face of setbacks or in the midst of excitement; IMPERTURBABLE implies coolness or assurance even under severe provocation; NONCHALANT stresses an easy coolness of manner or casualness that suggests indifference or unconcern.

\ə\ abut \ᵊ\ kitten, F table \ər\ further \a\ ash \ā\ ace \ä\ cot, cart \au̇\ out \ch\ chin \e\ bet \ē\ easy \g\ go \i\ hit \ī\ ice \j\ job \ŋ\ sing \ō\ go \ȯ\ law \ȯi\ boy \th\ thin \th̲\ the \ü\ loot \u̇\ foot \y\ yet \zh\ vision \à, k̲, ⁿ, œ, ǣ, ue, ue̅, ʸ\ see Guide to Pronunciation

2cool *vi* (bef. 12c) **1 :** to become cool : lose heat or warmth ⟨placed the pie in the window to ∼⟩ — sometimes used with *off* or *down* **2 :** to lose ardor or passion ⟨his anger ∼*ed*⟩ ∼ *vt* **1 :** to make cool : impart a feeling of coolness to ⟨∼*ed* the room with a fan⟩ — often used with *off* or *down* ⟨a swim ∼*ed* us off a little⟩ **2 a :** to moderate the heat, excitement, or force of : CALM ⟨∼*ed* her growing anger⟩ **b :** to slow or lessen the growth or activity of — usu. used with *off* or *down* ⟨wants to ∼ off the economy without freezing it —*Newsweek*⟩ — **cool it :** to calm down : go easy ⟨the word went out to the young to *cool it* —W. M. Young⟩ — **cool one's heels :** to wait or be kept waiting for a long time esp. from or as if from disdain or discourtesy

3cool *n* (15c) **1 :** a cool time, place, or situation ⟨the ∼ of the evening⟩ **2 a :** a lack of excitement or enthusiasm : INDIFFERENCE ⟨wears her ∼ like perfume, without a . . . single expression to disturb her aristocratic unconcern —Hubert Saal⟩ **b :** SELF-CONFIDENCE, SOPHISTICATION ⟨girls, from 9 to 12, who are only beginning to awaken to the world around and have not yet developed any ∼ about themselves —J. K. Sale & Ben Apfelbaum⟩ **3 :** POISE, COMPOSURE ⟨press questions . . . seemed to rattle him and he lost his ∼ —*New Republic*⟩

4cool *adv* (1951) **:** in a casual and nonchalant manner ⟨they learn to play it ∼, not really involve themselves —Marilyn B. Noble⟩

cool·ant \ˈkü-lənt\ *n* (1926) **:** a usu. fluid cooling agent

cool·er \ˈkü-lər\ *n* (1575) **1 :** one that cools: as **a :** a container for cooling liquids **b :** REFRIGERATOR **2 :** LOCKUP, JAIL; *esp* **:** a cell for violent or unmanageable prisoners **3 :** a tall iced drink usu. with an alcoholic beverage as a base

Coo·ley's anemia \ˌkü-lēz-\ *n* [Thomas B. *Cooley* †1945 Am. pediatrician] (ca. 1935) **:** a familial hypochromic anemia that is characterized by the presence of microcytes, by splenomegaly, and by changes in the bones and skin and that occurs esp. in children of Mediterranean parents — called also *thalassemia*

cool·head·ed \ˈkül-ˈhed-əd\ *adj* (1777) **:** not easily excited

coo·lie \ˈkü-lē\ *n* [Hindi *kulī*] (1638) **:** an unskilled laborer or porter usu. in or from the Far East hired for low or subsistence wages

coolie hat *n* (1924) **:** a conical-shaped usu. straw hat worn esp. to protect the head from the heat of the sun

cool·ing–off \ˌkü-liŋ-ˈȯf\ *adj* (1926) **:** designed to allow passions to cool or to permit negotiation between parties ⟨a ∼ period⟩

coombe *or* **coomb** \ˈküm\ *var of* COMBE

coon \ˈkün\ *n* (1742) **1 :** RACCOON **2 :** NEGRO — usu. taken to be offensive

coon·can \ˈkün-ˌkan\ *n* [by folk etymology fr. MexSp *conquián* conquian, fr. Sp *¿con quién?* with whom?] (1889) **:** a game of rummy played with two packs including two jokers

coon cat *n* (1901) **:** MAINE COON

coon cheese \ˈkün-\ *n* [prob. fr. *coon* (Negro); fr. the color of the coating] (1953) **:** a sharp cheddar cheese that has been cured at higher than usual temperature and humidity and that is usu. coated with black wax

coon·hound \ˈkün-ˌhau̇nd\ *n* (1920) **:** a sporting dog trained to hunt raccoons; *esp* **:** BLACK-AND-TAN COONHOUND

coon's age *n* (1844) **:** a long while ⟨best fried chicken I've tasted for a *coon's age* —Sinclair Lewis⟩

coon·skin \ˈkün-ˌskin\ *n* (1818) **1 :** the skin or pelt of the raccoon **2 :** an article (as a cap or coat) made of coonskin

coon·tie \ˈkünt-ē\ *n* [Seminole *kunti* coontie flour] (1791) **:** any of several tropical American woody plants (genus *Zamia*) of the cycad family whose roots and stems yield a starchy foodstuff — called also *arrowroot*

1coop \ˈküp, ˈku̇p\ *n* [ME *cupe;* akin to OE *cȳpe* basket, *cot* cot] (14c) **1 :** a cage or small enclosure (as for poultry); *also* **:** a small building for housing poultry **2 a :** a confined area **b :** JAIL

2coop *vt* (1563) **1 :** to confine in a restricted and often crowded area — usu. used with *up* **2 :** to place or keep in a coop : PEN — often used with *up*

co–op \ˈkō-ˌäp, kō-ˈ; ˈküp\ *n* (1869) **:** COOPERATIVE

1coo·per \ˈkü-pər, ˈku̇p-ər\ *n* [ME *couper, cowper,* fr. MD *cūper* (fr. *cūpe* cask) or MLG *kūper,* fr. *kūpe* cask; MD *cūpe* & MLG *kūpe,* fr. L *cupa;* akin to Gk *kypellon* cup — more at HIVE] (14c) **:** one that makes or repairs wooden casks or tubs

2cooper *vb* **coo·pered; coo·per·ing** \ˈkü-p(ə-)riŋ, ˈku̇p-(ə-)riŋ\ *vt* (1742) **:** to work as a cooper on ∼ *vi* **:** to work at or do coopering

coo·per·age \ˈkü-p(ə-)rij, ˈku̇p-(ə-)\ *n* (1705) **1 :** a cooper's work or products **2 :** a cooper's place of business

co·op·er·ate \kō-ˈäp-(ə-)ˌrāt\ *vi* [LL *cooperatus,* pp. of *cooperari,* fr. L *co-* + *operari* to work — more at OPERATE] (1616) **1 :** to act or work with another or others : act together **2 :** to associate with another or others for mutual benefit — **co·op·er·a·tor** \-ˌrāt-ər\ *n*

co·op·er·a·tion \(ˌ)kō-ˌäp-ə-ˈrā-shən\ *n* (14c) **1 :** the action of cooperating : common effort **2 :** association of persons for common benefit — **co·op·er·a·tion·ist** \-sh(ə-)nəst\ *n*

1co·op·er·a·tive \kō-ˈäp-(ə-)rət-iv, -ˈäp-ə-ˌrāt-\ *adj* (1603) **1 a :** marked by cooperation ⟨∼ efforts⟩ **b :** marked by a willingness and ability to work with others ⟨∼ neighbors⟩ **2 :** of, relating to, or organized as a cooperative **3 :** relating to or comprising a program of combined liberal arts and technical studies at different schools — **co·op·er·a·tive·ly** *adv* — **co·op·er·a·tive·ness** *n*

2cooperative *n* (1883) **:** an enterprise or organization owned by and operated for the benefit of those using its services

Coo·per's hawk \ˈkü-pərz-, ˈku̇p-ərz-\ *n* [William *Cooper* †1864 Am. naturalist] (1828) **:** an American hawk (*Accipiter cooperii*) that is larger than the similarly colored sharp-shinned hawk and has a more rounded tail

co–opt \kō-ˈäpt\ *vt* [L *cooptare,* fr. *co-* + *optare* to choose — more at OPTION] (1651) **1 a :** to choose or elect as a member **b :** to appoint as a colleague or assistant **2 a :** to take into a group (as a faction, movement, or culture) **:** ABSORB, ASSIMILATE ⟨the students are ∼*ed* by a system they serve even in their struggle against it —A. C. Danto⟩ **b :** TAKE OVER, APPROPRIATE — **co–op·ta·tion** \ˌkō-ˌäp-ˈtā-shən\ *n* — **co–op·ta·tive** \kō-ˈäp-tət-iv\ *adj* — **co–op·tion** \-ˈäp-shən\ *n* — **co–op·tive** \-ˈäp-tiv\ *adj*

1co·or·di·nate \kō-ˈȯrd-nət, -ᵊn-ət, -ᵊn-ˌāt\ *adj* [prob. fr. *co-* + *-ordinate* (as in *subordinate*)] (1641) **1 a :** equal in rank, quality, or significance **b :** being of equal rank in a sentence ⟨∼ clauses⟩ **2 :** relating to or marked by coordination **3 a :** being a university that awards degrees to men and women taught usu. by the same faculty but attending separate classes often on separate campuses **b :** being one of the colleges and esp. the women's branch of a coordinate university **4 :** of, relating to, or being a system of indexing by two or more terms so that documents may be retrieved through the intersection of index terms — **co·or·di·nate·ly** *adv* — **co·or·di·nate·ness** *n*

2co·or·di·nate \kō-ˈȯrd-ᵊn-ˌāt\ *vb* **-nat·ed; -nat·ing** *vt* (1665) **1 :** to put in the same order or rank **2 :** to bring into a common action, movement, or condition : HARMONIZE **3 :** to attach so as to form a coordination complex ∼ *vi* **1 :** to be or become coordinate esp. so as to act together in a smooth concerted way **2 :** to combine by means of a coordinate bond — **co·or·di·na·tive** \kō-ˈȯrd-nət-iv, -ᵊn-ət-, -ᵊn-ˌāt-\ *adj* — **co·or·di·na·tor** \-ᵊn-ˌāt-ər\ *n*

3co·or·di·nate \-ˈȯrd-nət, -ᵊn-ət, -ᵊn-ˌāt\ *n* (1823) **1 a :** any of a set of numbers used in specifying the location of a point on a line, on a surface, or in space **b :** any one of a set of variables used in specifying the state of a substance or the motion of a particle or momentum **2 :** one who is of equal rank, authority, or importance with another **3** *pl* **:** articles (as of clothing) designed to be used together and to attain their effect through pleasing contrast (as of color, material, or texture)

coordinate bond *n* (1938) **:** a covalent bond held to consist of a pair of electrons supplied by only one of the two atoms it joins

co·or·di·nat·ed \-ᵊn-ˌāt-əd\ *adj* (1939) **:** able to use more than one set of muscle movements to a single end ⟨a well-*coordinated* athlete⟩

coordinate geometry *n* (ca. 1909) **:** ANALYTIC GEOMETRY

coordinating conjunction *n* (1911) **:** a conjunction that joins together words or word groups of equal grammatical rank

co·or·di·na·tion \(ˌ)kō-ˌȯrd-ᵊn-ˈā-shən\ *n* [F or LL; F, fr. LL *coordination-, coordinatio,* fr. L *co-* + *ordination-, ordinatio* arrangement, fr. *ordinatus,* pp. of *ordinare* to arrange — more at ORDAIN] (1643) **1 :** the act or action of coordinating **2 :** the harmonious functioning of parts for most effective results

coordination complex *n* (1951) **:** a compound or ion with a central usu. metallic atom or ion combined by coordinate bonds with a definite number of surrounding ions, groups, or molecules

coot \ˈküt\ *n* [ME *coote;* akin to D *koet* coot] (14c) **1 :** any of various sluggish slow-flying slaty-black birds (genus *Fulica*) of the rail family that somewhat resemble ducks and have lobed toes and the upper mandible prolonged on the forehead as a horny frontal shield **2 :** any of several No. American scoters **3 :** a harmless simple person; *broadly* **:** FELLOW 4c

coo·tie \ˈküt-ē\ *n* [perh. modif. of Malay *kutu*] (1917) **:** BODY LOUSE

1cop \ˈkäp\ *n* [ME, fr. OE *copp*] (bef. 12c) **1** *dial chiefly Eng* **:** TOP, CREST **2 :** a cylindrical or conical mass of thread, yarn, or roving wound on a quill or tube; *also* **:** a quill or tube upon which it is wound

2cop *vt* **copped; cop·ping** [perh. fr. D *kapen* to steal, fr. Fris *kāpia* to take away; akin to OHG *kouf* trade — more at CHEAP] (1704) **1** *slang* **:** to get hold of : CATCH, CAPTURE; *also* **:** PURCHASE **2** *slang* **:** STEAL, SWIPE — **cop a plea :** to plead guilty to a lesser charge in order to avoid standing trial for a more serious one; *broadly* **:** to admit fault and plead for mercy

3cop *n* [short for *3copper*] (1859) **:** POLICEMAN

co·pa·cet·ic *or* **co·pe·set·ic** *also* **co·pa·set·ic** \ˌkō-pə-ˈset-ik\ *adj* [origin unknown] (1919) **:** very satisfactory

co·pai·ba \kō-ˈpī-bə, -ˈpā-; ˌkō-pə-ˈē-bə\ *n* [Sp & Pg; Sp, fr. Pg *copaíba,* of Tupian origin; akin to Guarani *cupaiba* copaiba] (1712) **:** a stimulant oleoresin obtained from several pinnate-leaved So. American leguminous trees (genus *Copaifera*); *also* **:** one of these trees

co·pal \ˈkō-pəl, -ˌpal; kō-ˈpal\ *n* [Sp, fr. Nahuatl *copalli* resin] (1577) **:** a recent or fossil resin from various tropical trees

co·par·ce·nary \kō-ˈpärs-ᵊn-ˌer-ē\ *n, pl* **-nar·ies** (1503) **1 :** joint heirship **2 :** joint ownership

co·par·ce·ner \-ˈpärs-nər, -ᵊn-ər\ *n* (15c) **:** a joint heir

1cope \ˈkōp\ *n* [ME, fr. OE *-cāp,* fr. LL *cappa* head covering] (bef. 12c) **1 :** a long enveloping ecclesiastical vestment **2 a :** something resembling a cope (as by concealing or covering) ⟨the dark sky's starry ∼ —P. B. Shelley⟩ **b :** COPING

2cope *vt* **coped; cop·ing** (14c) **:** to cover or furnish with a cope or coping

3cope *vb* **coped; cop·ing** [ME *copen, coupen,* fr. MF *couper* to strike, cut, fr. OF, fr. *coup* blow, fr. LL *colpus,* alter. of L *colaphus,* fr. Gk *kolaphos* buffet] *vi* (14c) **1** *obs* **:** STRIKE, FIGHT **2 a :** to maintain a contest or combat usu. on even terms or with success — used with *with* **b :** to deal with and attempt to overcome problems and difficulties — often used with *with* **3** *archaic* **:** MEET, ENCOUNTER ∼ *vt* **1** *obs* **:** to meet in combat **2** *obs* **:** to come in contact with **3** *obs* **:** MATCH

4cope *vt* **coped; cop·ing** [prob. fr. F *couper* to cut] (ca. 1909) **1 :** NOTCH **2 :** to shape (a structural member) to fit a coping or conform to the shape of another member

copeck *var of* KOPECK

co·pe·pod \ˈkō-pə-ˌpäd\ *n* [deriv. of Gk *kōpē* oar + *pod-, pous* foot; akin to OE *hæft* handle — more at HAFT] (1836) **:** any of a large subclass (Copepoda) of usu. minute freshwater and marine crustaceans — **copepod** *adj*

cop·er \ˈkō-pər\ *n* [E dial. *cope* (to trade)] *Brit* (1825) **:** a horse dealer; *esp* **:** a dishonest one

Co·per·ni·can \kō-ˈpər-ni-kən, kə-\ *adj* [Nicolaus *Copernicus*] (1667) **1 :** of or relating to Copernicus or the belief that the earth rotates daily on its axis and the planets revolve in orbits around the sun **2 :** of radical or major importance or degree ⟨effected a ∼ revolution in philosophy —*Times Lit. Supp.*⟩ — **Copernican** *n* — **Co·per·ni·can·ism** \-kə-ˌniz-əm\ *n*

cope·stone \ˈkōp-ˌstōn\ *n* (1567) **1 :** a stone forming a coping **2 :** a finishing touch : CROWN

copi·er \ˈkäp-ē-ər\ *n* (1597) **:** one that copies; *specif* **:** a machine for making copies of graphic matter (as printing, drawings, or pictures)

co·pi·hue \kō-ˈpē-(ˌ)wā\ *n* [AmerSp, fr. Araucanian *copiu*] (1929) **:** a showy climbing vine (*Lapageria rosea*) with deep rosy red trumpet-shaped flowers and oval edible yellowish fruits that is the national flower of Chile

co·pi·lot \ˈkō-ˌpī-lət\ *n* (1927) **:** a qualified pilot who assists or relieves the pilot but is not in command

cop·ing \'kō-piŋ\ *n* (1601) **:** the covering course of a wall usu. with a sloping top

cop·ing saw \'kō-piŋ-\ *n* [fr. prp. of [4]*cope*] (1931) **:** a handsaw with a very narrow blade held under tension in a U-shaped frame and used esp. for cutting curves in wood

cop·ing·stone \'kō-piŋ-,stōn\ *n, chiefly Brit* (1778) **:** COPESTONE

co·pi·ous \'kō-pē-əs\ *adj* [ME, fr. L *copiosus*, fr. *copia* abundance, fr. *co-* + *ops* wealth — more at OPULENT] (14c) **1 a :** yielding something abundantly ⟨a ~ harvest⟩ ⟨~ springs⟩ **b :** plentiful in number ⟨~ references to other writers⟩ **2 a :** full of thought, information, or matter **b :** profuse or exuberant in words, expression, or style ⟨a ~ talker⟩ **3 :** present in large quantity **:** taking place on a large scale ⟨~ weeping⟩ ⟨~ food and drink⟩ ***syn*** see PLENTIFUL — **co·pi·ous·ly** *adv* — **co·pi·ous·ness** *n*

co·pla·nar \(')kō-'plā-nər, -,när\ *adj* (1862) **:** lying or acting in the same plane — **co·pla·nar·i·ty** \,kō-plā-'nar-ət-ē\ *n*

co·pol·y·mer \(')kō-'päl-ə-mər\ *n* (1936) **:** a product of copolymerization — **co·pol·y·mer·ic** \,kō-,päl-ə-'mer-ik\ *adj*

co·po·ly·mer·iza·tion \,kō-pə-,lim-ə-rə-'zā-shən, ,kō-,päl-ə-mə-\ *n* (1936) **:** the polymerization of two substances (as two different monomers) together — **co·po·ly·mer·ize** \,kō-pə-'lim-ə-,rīz, ,kō-'päl-ə-mə-\ *vb*

cop–out \'käp-,au̇t\ *n* (ca. 1963) **1 :** an excuse for copping out **:** PRETEXT **2 :** the means for copping out **3 :** one who cops out **4 :** the act or an instance of copping out

cop out \(')käp-'au̇t\ *vi* (1964) **:** to back out (as of an unwanted responsibility) — often used with *on* or *of*

[1]**cop·per** \'käp-ər\ *n, often attrib* [ME *coper*, fr. OE, fr. LL *cuprum* copper, fr. L (*aes*) *Cyprium*, lit., Cyprian metal] (bef. 12c) **1 :** a common reddish metallic element that is ductile and malleable and one of the best conductors of heat and electricity — see ELEMENT table **2 :** a coin or token made of copper or bronze **3** *chiefly Brit* **:** a large boiler (as for cooking) **4 :** any of various small butterflies (family Lycaenidae) with usu. copper-colored wings — **cop·pery** \'käp-(ə-)rē\ *adj*

[2]**copper** *vt* **cop·pered; cop·per·ing** \'käp-(ə-)riŋ\ (1530) **:** to coat or sheathe with or as if with copper

[3]**copper** *n* [[2]*cop*] (1846) **:** POLICEMAN 1

cop·per·as \'käp-(ə-)rəs\ *n* [ME *coperas*, fr. OF *couperose*, fr. ML *cuprosa*, prob. fr. *aqua cuprosa* copper water, fr. LL *cuprum*] (14c) **:** a green hydrated ferrous sulfate $FeSO_4 \cdot 7H_2O$ used esp. in making inks and pigments

cop·per·head \'käp-ər-,hed\ *n* (1775) **1 :** a common pit viper (*Agkistrodon contortrix*) of the eastern and central U.S. usu. having a copper-colored head and often a reddish brown hourglass pattern on the body **2 :** a person in the northern states who sympathized with the South during the Civil War

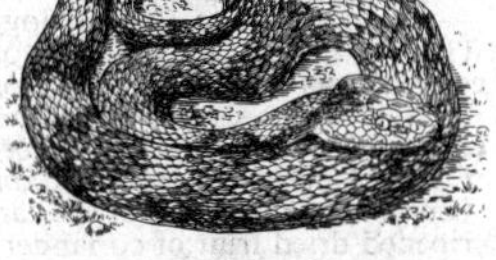

copperhead 1

cop·per·plate \'käp-ər-,plāt\ *n* (1663) **1 :** an engraved or etched copper printing plate; *also* **:** a print made from such a plate **2 :** a neat script handwriting based on engraved models

copper pyrites *n* (1776) **:** CHALCOPYRITE

cop·per·smith \'käp-ər-,smith\ *n* (14c) **:** a worker in copper

copper sulfate *n* (ca. 1893) **:** a sulfate of copper; *esp* **:** the normal sulfate that is white in the anhydrous form but blue in the crystalline hydrous form $CuSO_4 \cdot 5H_2O$ and that is often used as an algicide and fungicide

cop·pice \'käp-əs\ *n* [MF *copeiz*, fr. *couper* to cut — more at COPE] (1538) **1 :** a thicket, grove, or growth of small trees **2 :** forest originating mainly from shoots or root suckers rather than seed — **coppice** *vb*

copr- *or* **copro-** *comb form* [NL, fr. Gk *kopr-*, *kopro-*, fr. *kopros* akin to Skt *śakṛt* dung] **:** dung **:** feces ⟨*copro*lite⟩

co·pra \'kō-prə *also* 'käp-rə\ *n* [Pg, fr. Malayalam *koppara*] (1584) **:** dried coconut meat yielding coconut oil

co·prod·uct \(')kō-'präd-(,)əkt\ *n* (1942) **:** BY-PRODUCT 1

cop·ro·lite \'käp-rə-,līt\ *n* (1829) **:** fossil excrement — **cop·ro·lit·ic** \,käp-rə-'lit-ik\ *adj*

co·proph·a·gous \kä-'präf-ə-gəs\ *adj* [Gk *koprophagos*, fr. *kopr-* + *-phagos* -phagous] (1826) **:** feeding on dung — **co·proph·a·gy** \-ə-jē\ *n*

cop·ro·phil·ia \,käp-rə-'fil-ē-ə\ *n* [NL] (1923) **:** marked interest in excrement; *esp* **:** the use of feces or filth for sexual excitement — **cop·ro·phil·i·ac** \-ē-,ak\ *n*

co·proph·i·lous \kä-'präf-ə-ləs\ *adj* (ca. 1900) **:** growing or living on dung ⟨~ fungi⟩

copse \'käps\ *n* [by alter.] (1578) **:** COPPICE 1

Copt \'käpt\ *n* [Ar *qubṭ* Copts, fr. Coptic *gyptios* Egyptian, fr. Gk *aigyptios*] (1615) **1 :** a member of the traditional Monophysite Christian church originating and centering in Egypt **2 :** a member of a people descended from the ancient Egyptians

cop·ter \'käp-tər\ *n* (1943) **:** HELICOPTER

[1]**Cop·tic** \'käp-tik\ *adj* (1678) **:** of or relating to the Copts, their liturgical language, or their church

[2]**Coptic** *n* (1711) **:** an Afro-Asiatic language descended from ancient Egyptian and used as the liturgical language of the Coptic church

cop·u·la \'käp-yə-lə\ *n* [L, bond — more at COUPLE] (1619) **:** something that connects: as **a :** the connecting link between subject and predicate of a proposition **b :** LINKING VERB

cop·u·late \'käp-yə-,lāt\ *vi* **-lat·ed; -lat·ing** [L *copulatus*, pp. of *copulare* to join, fr. *copula*] (1632) **1 :** to engage in sexual intercourse **2** *of gametes* **:** to fuse permanently — **cop·u·la·tion** \,käp-yə-'lā-shən\ *n* — **cop·u·la·to·ry** \'käp-yə-lə-,tōr-ē, -,tȯr-\ *adj*

[1]**cop·u·la·tive** \'käp-yə-lət-iv, -,lāt-\ *adj* (14c) **1 a :** joining together coordinate words or word groups and expressing addition of their meanings ⟨a ~ conjunction⟩ **b :** functioning as a copula **2 :** relating to or serving for copulation **3 :** of or relating to coupling of chemical compounds or groups

[2]**copulative** *n* (1530) **:** a copulative word

[1]**copy** \'käp-ē\ *n, pl* **cop·ies** [ME *copie*, fr. MF, fr. ML *copia*, fr. L, abundance — more at COPIOUS] (14c) **1 :** an imitation, transcript, or reproduction of an original work (as a letter, a painting, a piece of furniture, or a dress) **2 :** one of a series of esp. mechanical reproductions of an original impression; *also* **:** an individual example of such a reproduction ⟨a presentation ~⟩ **3** *archaic* **:** something to be imitated **:** MODEL **4 a :** matter to be set esp. for printing **b :** something considered printable or newsworthy — used in the singular and without an article ⟨remarks that make good ~ — Norman Cousins⟩ **c :** text esp. of an advertisement ***syn*** see REPRODUCTION

[2]**copy** *vb* **cop·ied; copy·ing** *vt* (14c) **1 :** to make a copy of **2 :** to model oneself on ~ *vi* **1 :** to make a copy **2 :** to undergo copying ⟨the document did not ~ well⟩

syn COPY, IMITATE, MIMIC, APE, MOCK mean to make something so that it resembles an existing thing. COPY suggests duplicating an original as nearly as possible ⟨*copied* the painting and sold the fake as an original⟩ IMITATE suggests following a model or a pattern but may allow for some variation ⟨*imitate* a poet's style⟩ MIMIC implies a close copying (as of voice or mannerism) often for fun, ridicule, or lifelike imitation ⟨pupils *mimicking* their teacher⟩ APE may suggest presumptuous, slavish, or inept imitating of a superior original ⟨American fashion designers *aped* their European colleagues⟩ MOCK usu. implies imitation with derision ⟨*mocking* a vain man's pompous manner⟩

copy·book \'käp-ē-,bu̇k\ *n* (1588) **:** a book formerly used in teaching penmanship and containing models for imitation

copy·boy \-,bȯi\ *n* (1888) **:** one who carries copy and runs errands

[1]**copy·cat** \-,kat\ *n* (1896) **:** one who slavishly imitates or adopts the behavior or practices of another

[2]**copycat** *vb* **copy·cat·ted; copy·cat·ting** *vi* (1926) **:** to act as a copycat ~ *vt* **:** IMITATE

copy·desk \-,desk\ *n* (1921) **:** the desk at which newspaper copy is edited

copy editor *n* (1899) **:** an editor who prepares copy for the printer; *also* **:** one who edits and headlines newspaper copy — **copy–ed·it** \'käp-ē-,ed-ət\ *vt*

copy·hold \'käp-ē-,hōld\ *n* (15c) **1 :** a former tenure of land in England and Ireland by right of being recorded in the court of the manor **2 :** an estate held by copyhold

copy·hold·er \-,hōl-dər\ *n* (1874) **1 :** a device for holding copy esp. for a typesetter **2 :** one who reads copy for a proofreader

copy·ist \'käp-ē-əst\ *n* (1699) **1 :** one who makes copies **2 :** IMITATOR

copy·read·er \-,rēd-ər\ *n* (1892) **:** COPY EDITOR — **copy·read** \-,rēd\ *vt*

[1]**copy·right** \-,rīt\ *n* (1735) **:** the exclusive legal right to reproduce, publish, and sell the matter and form of a literary, musical, or artistic work — **copyright** *adj*

[2]**copyright** *vt* (1806) **:** to secure a copyright on — **copy·right·able** \-ə-bəl\ *adj*

copy·writ·er \'käp-ē-,rīt-ər\ *n* (1911) **:** a writer of advertising or publicity copy

coq au vin \,kō-kō-'vaⁿ, ,käk-ō-\ *n* [F, cock with wine] (1938) **:** chicken cooked in usu. red wine

[1]**co·quet** *n* [F, dim. of *coq* cock] (1691) **1** \kō-'ket, -'kā\ **:** a man who indulges in coquetry **2** \-'ket\ **:** COQUETTE

[2]**co·quet** \kō-'ket\ *adj* (1697) **:** COQUETTISH

[3]**co·quet** *or* **co·quette** \-'ket\ *vi* **co·quet·ted; co·quet·ting** (1701) **1 :** to play the coquette **:** FLIRT **2 :** to deal with something playfully rather than seriously ***syn*** see TRIFLE

co·que·try \'kō-kə-trē, kō-'ke-trē\ *n, pl* **-tries** (1656) **:** a flirtatious act or attitude

co·quette \kō-'ket\ *n* [F, fem. of *coquet*] (ca. 1611) **:** a woman who endeavors without sincere affection to gain the attention and admiration of men — **co·quett·ish** \-ish\ *adj* — **co·quett·ish·ly** *adv* — **co·quett·ish·ness** *n*

co·qui·na \kō-'kē-nə\ *n* [Sp, prob. irreg. dim. of *concha* shell] (1837) **1 :** a soft whitish limestone formed of broken shells and corals cemented together and used for building **2 :** a small marine clam (genus *Donax*) used for broth or chowder

cor·a·cle \'kȯr-ə-kəl, 'kär-\ *n* [W *corwgl*] (ca. 1547) **1 :** a small boat made by covering a wicker frame with hide or leather and used by the ancient Britons **2 :** a boat made of broad hoops covered with horsehide or tarpaulin and used in parts of the British Isles

cor·a·coid \'kȯr-ə-,kȯid, 'kär-\ *adj* [NL *coracoides*, fr. Gk *korakoeidēs*, lit., like a raven, fr. *korak-*, *korax* raven — more at RAVEN] (1836) **:** of, relating to, or being a process of the scapula in most mammals or a well-developed cartilage bone of many lower vertebrates that extends from the scapula to or toward the sternum — **coracoid** *n*

cor·al \'kȯr-əl, 'kär-\ *n* [ME, fr. MF, fr. L *corallium*, fr. Gk *korallion*] (14c) **1 a :** the calcareous or horny skeletal deposit produced by anthozoan or rarely hydrozoan polyps; *esp* **:** a richly red precious coral secreted by a gorgonian (*Corallium nobile*) **b :** a polyp or polyp colony together with its membranes and skeleton **2 :** a piece of coral and esp. of red coral **3 a :** a bright reddish ovary (as of a lobster or scallop) **b :** a variable color averaging a deep pink — **coral** *adj* — **cor·al·loid** \-ə-,lȯid\ *adj*

cor·al·bells \'kȯr-əl-,belz, 'kär-\ *n pl but sing or pl in constr* (1900) **:** a perennial alumroot (*Heuchera sanguinea*) widely cultivated for its feathery spikes of tiny coral flowers

cor·al·ber·ry \-,ber-ē\ *n* (1859) **:** an American dwarf shrub (*Symphoricarpos orbiculatus*) that bears clusters of small flowers succeeded by red berries

[1]**cor·al·line** \'kȯr-ə-,līn, 'kär-\ *n* (1543) **1 :** any of a family (Corallinaceae) of calcareous red algae **2 :** a bryozoan or hydroid that resembles a coral

[2]**coralline** *adj* [MF, fr. fem. of *corallin* coral-like, fr. LL *corallinus*, fr. L *corallium*] (1660) **:** of, relating to, or resembling coral or a coralline

coral snake *n* (1760) **1 :** any of several venomous chiefly tropical New World elapid snakes (genus *Micrurus*) brilliantly banded in red, black, and yellow or white that include two (*M. fulvius* and *M. euryxanthus*)

\ə\ abut \ᵊ\ kitten, F table \ər\ further \a\ ash \ā\ ace \ä\ cot, cart
\au̇\ out \ch\ chin \e\ bet \ē\ easy \g\ go \i\ hit \ī\ ice \j\ job
\ŋ\ sing \ō\ go \ȯ\ law \ȯi\ boy \th\ thin \t͟h\ the \ü\ loot \u̇\ foot
\y\ yet \zh\ vision \à, k̲, ⁿ, œ, œ̄, ue, ue̅, ʸ\ *see* Guide to Pronunciation

ranging northward into the southern U.S. **2 :** any of several harmless snakes resembling the coral snakes

co·ran·to \kə-ˈrant-(ˌ)ō\ *n, pl* **-tos** *or* **-toes** [modif. of F *courante*] (1564) **:** COURANTE

cor·ban \ˈkȯ(ə)r-ˌban\ *n* [Heb *qorbān* offering] (14c) **:** a sacrifice or offering to God among the ancient Hebrews

cor·beil *or* **cor·beille** \ˈkȯr-bəl, kȯr-ˈbā\ *n* [F *corbeille,* lit., basket, fr. LL *corbicula*] (1800) **:** a sculptured basket of flowers or fruit as an architectural decoration

[1]**cor·bel** \ˈkȯr-bəl\ *n* [ME, fr. MF, fr. dim. of *corp* raven, fr. L *corvus* — more at RAVEN] (15c) **:** an architectural member that projects from within a wall and supports a weight; *esp* **:** one that is stepped upward and outward from a vertical surface

[2]**corbel** *vt* **-beled** *or* **-belled; -bel·ing** *or* **-bel·ling** (1843) **:** to furnish with or make into a corbel

corbeling *n* (1548) **1 :** corbel work **2 :** the construction of a corbel

cor·bic·u·la \kȯr-ˈbik-yə-lə\ *n, pl* **-lae** \-(ˌ)lē, -ˌlī\ [LL, dim. of L *corbis* basket] (1816) **:** POLLEN BASKET

cor·bie \ˈkȯr-bē\ *n* [ME, modif. of MF *corbin,* fr. L *corvinus* of a raven] *chiefly Scot* (15c) **:** a carrion crow; *also* **:** RAVEN

corbie gable *n* (1853) **:** a gable having corbiesteps

cor·bie·step \ˈkȯr-bē-ˌstep\ *n* (1808) **:** one of a series of steps terminating the upper part of a gable wall

cor·bi·na \kȯr-ˈbē-nə\ *n* [MexSp, fr. Sp *corvina,* an acanthopterygian fish, fr. fem. of *corvino* of a raven, fr. L *corvinus*] (1901) **:** any of several American marine fishes; *esp* **:** a spotted whiting (*Menticirrhus undulatus*) favored by surf casters along the California coast

[1]**cord** \ˈkȯ(ə)rd\ *n* [ME, fr. MF *corde,* fr. L *chorda* string, fr. Gk *chordē* — more at YARN] (14c) **1 a :** a long slender flexible material usu. consisting of several strands (as of thread or yarn) woven or twisted together **b :** the hangman's rope **2 :** a moral, spiritual, or emotional bond **3 a :** an anatomical structure (as a nerve or the umbilical cord) resembling a cord **b :** a small flexible insulated electrical cable having a plug at one or both ends used to connect a lamp or other appliance with a receptacle **4 :** a unit of wood cut for fuel equal to a stack 4x4x8 feet or 128 cubic feet **5 a :** a rib like a cord on a textile **b** (1) **:** a fabric made with such ribs or a garment made of such a fabric (2) *pl* **:** trousers made of such a fabric

[2]**cord** *vt* (15c) **1 :** to furnish, bind, or connect with a cord **2 :** to pile up (wood) in cords — **cord·er** *n*

cord·age \ˈkȯrd-ij\ *n* (1598) **1 :** ropes or cords; *esp* **:** the ropes in the rigging of a ship **2 :** the number of cords (as of wood) on a given area

cor·date \ˈkȯ(ə)r-ˌdāt\ *adj* [NL *cordatus,* fr. L *cord-, cor*] (1769) **:** shaped like a heart ⟨a ~ leaf⟩ — **cor·date·ly** *adv*

cord·ed \ˈkȯrd-əd\ *adj* (14c) **1 a :** made of or provided with cords or ridges; *specif* **:** muscled in ridges **b** *of a muscle* **:** TENSE, TAUT **2 :** bound, fastened, or wound about with cords **3 :** striped or ribbed with or as if with cord **:** TWILLED

[1]**cor·dial** \ˈkȯr-jəl\ *n* (14c) **1 :** a stimulating medicine or drink **2 :** LIQUEUR

[2]**cordial** *adj* [ME, fr. ML *cordialis,* fr. L *cord-, cor* heart — more at HEART] (15c) **1** *obs* **:** of or relating to the heart **:** VITAL **2 :** tending to revive, cheer, or invigorate **3 a :** sincerely or deeply felt ⟨a ~ dislike for each other⟩ **b :** warmly and genially affable ⟨~ relations⟩ ***syn*** see GRACIOUS — **cor·dial·ly** \ˈkȯrj-(ə-)lē\ *adv* — **cor·dial·ness** \ˈkȯr-jəl-nəs\ *n*

cor·dial·i·ty \ˌkȯr-jē-ˈal-ət-ē, kȯr-ˈjal- *also* kȯrd-ˈyal-\ *n* (1611) **:** sincere affection and kindness **:** cordial regard

cordia pulmonalia *pl of* COR PULMONALE

cor·di·er·ite \ˈkȯrd-ē-ə-ˌrīt\ *n* [F, fr. Pierre L. A. *Cordier* †1861 Fr. geologist] (ca. 1814) **:** a blue mineral $(Mg,Fe)_2Al_4Si_5O_{18}$ with vitreous luster and strong dichroism consisting of a silicate of aluminum, iron, and magnesium

cor·di·form \ˈkȯrd-ə-ˌfȯrm\ *adj* [F *cordiforme,* fr. L *cord-, cor* + F *-iforme* -iform] (1828) **:** shaped like a heart ⟨a ~ sea-urchin test⟩

cor·dil·le·ra \ˌkȯrd-ᵊl-ˈ(y)er-ə *also* kȯr-ˈdil-ə-rə\ *n* [Sp] (1704) **:** a system of mountain ranges often consisting of a number of more or less parallel chains — **cor·dil·le·ran** \-ˈ(y)er-ən, -ə-rən\ *adj*

cord·ite \ˈkȯ(ə)r-ˌdīt\ *n* (1889) **:** a smokeless powder composed of nitroglycerin, guncotton, and a petroleum substance usu. gelatinized by addition of acetone and pressed into cords resembling brown twine

cord·less \ˈkȯrd-ləs\ *adj* (1906) **:** having no cord; *esp* **:** powered by a battery ⟨~ tools⟩

cor·do·ba \ˈkȯrd-ə-bə, -ə-və\ *n* [Sp *córdoba,* fr. Francisco Fernández de *Córdoba* †1526 Span. explorer] (1913) — see MONEY table

[1]**cor·don** \ˈkȯrd-ᵊn, ˈkȯ(ə)r-ˌdän\ *n* [F, dim. of *corde* cord] (15c) **1 a :** an ornamental cord or ribbon **b :** STRINGCOURSE **2 a :** a line of troops or of military posts enclosing an area to prevent passage **b :** a line of persons or objects around a person or place ⟨a ~ of police⟩

[2]**cordon** *vt* (1561) **:** to form a protective or restrictive cordon around — usu. used with *off*

[1]**cor·do·van** \ˈkȯrd-ə-vən\ *adj* [OSp *cordovano,* fr. *Córdova* (now *Córdoba*), Spain] (1591) **1** *cap* **:** of or relating to Córdoba and esp. Córdoba, Spain **2 :** made of cordovan leather

[2]**cordovan** *n* (1625) **1 :** a soft fine-grained colored leather **2 :** dense nonporous leather tanned from the inner layer of horsehide

[1]**cor·du·roy** \ˈkȯrd-ə-ˌrȯi\ *n, pl* **-roys** [origin unknown] (ca. 1787) **1 a** *pl* **:** trousers of corduroy fabric **b :** a durable usu. cotton pile fabric with vertical ribs or wales **2 :** a road built of logs laid side by side transversely

[2]**corduroy** *vt* **-royed; -roy·ing** (1854) **:** to build (a road) of logs laid side by side transversely; *also* **:** to build a corduroy road across

cord·wain \ˈkȯ(ə)r-ˌdwān\ *n* [ME *cordwane,* fr. MF *cordoan,* fr. OSp *cordovano, cordován*] *archaic* (14c) **:** cordovan leather

cord·wain·er \-ˌdwā-nər\ *n* (14c) **1** *archaic* **:** a worker in cordovan leather **2 :** SHOEMAKER — **cord·wain·ery** \-ˌdwā-nə-rē\ *n*

cord·wood \ˈkȯ(ə)r-ˌdwu̇d\ *n* (1638) **:** wood piled or sold in cords

[1]**core** \ˈkō(ə)r, ˈkȯ(ə)r\ *n, often attrib* [ME] (14c) **1 :** a central and often foundational part usu. distinct from the enveloping part by a difference in nature ⟨~ of the city⟩: as **a :** the usu. inedible central part of some fruits (as a pineapple); *esp* **:** the papery or leathery carpels composing the ripened ovary in a pome fruit **b :** the portion of a foundry mold that shapes the interior of a hollow casting **c :** a part removed from the interior of a mass esp. to determine the interior composition or a hidden condition **d** (1) **:** the central strand around which other strands twist in some ropes (2) **:** a vertical space (as for elevator shafts, stairways, or plumbing apparatus) in a multistory building **e** (1) **:** a mass of iron serving to concentrate and intensify the magnetic field resulting from a current in a surrounding coil (2) **:** a tiny doughnut-shaped piece of magnetic material (as ferrite) used in computer memories (3) **:** a computer memory consisting of an array of cores strung on fine wires; *broadly* **:** the internal memory of a computer **f :** the central part of the earth having a radius of about 2100 miles (3400 kilometers) and physical properties different from those of the surrounding parts; *also* **:** the central part of a celestial body **g :** a nodule of stone (as flint or obsidian) from which flakes have been struck for making implements **h :** the conducting wire with its insulation in an electric cable **i :** a layer of wood on which veneers are glued (as in making plywood) **j :** an arrangement of a course of studies that combines under basic topics material from subjects conventionally separated and aims to provide a common background for all students ⟨~ curriculum⟩ **k :** the place in a nuclear reactor where fission occurs **2 a :** a basic, essential, or enduring part (as of an individual, a class, or an entity) **b :** the essential meaning **:** GIST ⟨the ~ of the argument⟩ **c :** the inmost or most intimate part ⟨honest to the ~⟩

[2]**core** *vt* **cored; cor·ing** (15c) **:** to remove a core from — **cor·er** *n*

[3]**core** *n* [perh. alter. of ME *chore* chorus, company, perh. fr. L *chorus*] *chiefly Scot* (1622) **:** a group of people

core city *n* (1965) **:** INNER CITY

co·re·li·gion·ist \ˌkō-ri-ˈlij-(ə-)nəst\ *n* (1842) **:** one of the same religion

co·re·mi·um \kə-ˈrē-mē-əm\ *n, pl* **-mia** \-mē-ə\ [NL, fr. Gk *korēma* broom, fr. *korein* to sweep] (1929) **:** a fruiting body characteristic of certain imperfect fungi (as the Stilbellaceae) that consists of a sterile stalk of parallel or fascicled hyphae and a terminal head of fertile or spore-bearing branches

co·re·op·sis \ˌkōr-ē-ˈäp-səs, ˌkȯr-\ *n, pl* **coreopsis** [NL, genus name, fr. Gk *koris* bedbug + NL *-opsis;* akin to Gk *keirein* to cut — more at SHEAR] (1753) **:** any of a genus (*Coreopsis*) of composite herbs widely grown for their showy flower heads

co·re·pres·sor \ˌkō-ri-ˈpres-ər\ *n* (1962) **:** a substance that activates or inactivates a particular genetic repressor by combining with it

co·req·ui·site \kō-ˈrek-wə-zət\ *n* (1947) **:** a formal course of study required to be taken simultaneously with another

co·re·spon·dent \ˌkō-ri-ˈspän-dənt\ *n* (1857) **:** a person named as guilty of adultery with the defendant in a divorce suit

corf \ˈkȯ(ə)rf\ *n, pl* **corves** \ˈkȯ(ə)rvz\ [ME, basket, fr. MD *corf* or MLG *korf,* fr. L *corbis* basket] *Brit* (1653) **:** a basket, tub, or truck used in a mine

cor·gi \ˈkȯr-gē\ *n, pl* **corgis** [W, fr. *cor* dwarf (akin to Gk *keirein* to cut) + *ci* dog; akin to OIr *cū* dog, OE *hund* — more at HOUND, SHEAR] (1926) **1 :** CARDIGAN WELSH CORGI **2 :** PEMBROKE WELSH CORGI

co·ri·a·ceous \ˌkōr-ē-ˈā-shəs, ˌkȯr-\ *adj* [LL *coriaceus* — more at CUIRASS] (1674) **:** resembling leather ⟨~ sporangia⟩

co·ri·an·der \ˈkōr-ē-ˌan-dər, ˌkōr-ē-ˈ, ˈkȯr-, ˌkȯr-\ *n* [ME *coriandre,* fr. OF, fr. L *coriandrum,* fr. Gk *koriandron*] (13c) **1 :** an Old World herb (*Coriandrum sativum*) of the carrot family with aromatic fruits **2 :** the ripened dried fruit of coriander used as a flavoring — called also *coriander seed*

[1]**Co·rin·thi·an** \kə-ˈrin(t)-thē-ən\ *n* (14c) **1 :** a native or resident of Corinth, Greece **2 :** a merry profligate man

[2]**Corinthian** *adj* (1594) **1 :** of, relating to, or characteristic of Corinth or Corinthians **2 :** of or relating to the lightest and most ornate of the three Greek orders of architecture characterized esp. by its bell-shaped capital enveloped with acanthuses

Co·rin·thi·ans \-thē-ənz\ *n pl but sing in constr* **:** either of two letters written by St. Paul to the Christians of Corinth and included as books in the New Testament — see BIBLE table

Co·ri·o·lis force \ˌkōr-ē-ˈō-ləs-, ˌkȯr-\ *n* [Gaspard G. *Coriolis* †1843 Fr. civil engineer] (1923) **:** an apparent force that as a result of the earth's rotation deflects moving objects (as projectiles or air currents) to the right in the northern hemisphere and to the left in the southern hemisphere

co·ri·um \ˈkōr-ē-əm, ˈkȯr-\ *n, pl* **co·ria** \-ē-ə\ [NL, fr. L, leather — more at CUIRASS] (1836) **:** DERMIS

[1]**cork** \ˈkȯ(ə)rk\ *n* [ME, cork, bark, prob. fr. Ar *qurq,* fr. L *cortic-, cortex*] (15c) **1 a :** the elastic tough outer tissue of the cork oak that is used esp. for stoppers and insulation **b :** PHELLEM **2 :** a usu. cork stopper for a bottle or jug **3 :** a fishing float

[2]**cork** *vt* (1580) **1 :** to furnish or fit with cork or a cork **2 :** to stop up with a cork **3 :** to blacken with burnt cork

cork·age \ˈkȯr-kij\ *n* (1838) **:** a charge (as by a restaurant) for opening a bottle of wine bought elsewhere

cork·board \ˈkȯ(ə)rk-ˌbō(ə)rd, -ˌbȯ(ə)rd\ *n* (ca. 1893) **:** a heat-insulating material made of compressed granulated cork; *also* **:** a bulletin board made with this material

cork cambium *n* (1878) **:** PHELLOGEN

corked \ˈkȯ(ə)rkt\ *adj* (1830) **:** CORKY 2

cork·er \ˈkȯr-kər\ *n* (1881) **1 :** one that corks containers (as bottles) **2 :** one that is excellent or remarkable

cork·ing \ˈkȯr-kiŋ\ *adj or adv* (1895) **:** extremely fine — often used as an intensive esp. before *good* ⟨had a ~ good time⟩

cork oak *n* (1873) **:** an oak (*Quercus suber*) of southern Europe and northern Africa that is the source of the cork of commerce

[1]**cork·screw** \ˈkȯrk-ˌskrü\ *n* (1720) **:** a pointed spiral piece of metal with a handle used for pulling corks from bottles

[2]**corkscrew** *adj* (1815) **:** resembling a corkscrew **:** SPIRAL

[3]**corkscrew** *vt* (1837) **1 :** WIND **2 :** to draw out with difficulty **3 :** to twist into a spiral ~ *vi* **:** to move in a winding course

cork·wood \ˈkȯr-ˌkwu̇d\ *n* (1756) **:** any of several trees having light or corky wood; *esp* **:** a small or shrubby tree (*Leitneria floridana*) of the southeastern U.S. that has extremely light soft wood

corky \ˈkȯr-kē\ *adj* **cork·i·er; -est** (ca. 1755) **1 :** resembling cork **2 :** having an unpleasant odor and taste (as from a tainted cork) ⟨~ wine⟩ — **cork·i·ness** \-kē-nəs\ *n*

corm \ˈkȯ(ə)rm\ *n* [NL *cormus,* fr. Gk *kormos* tree trunk, fr. *keirein* to cut — more at SHEAR] (1830) **:** a rounded thick modified underground stem base bearing membranous or scaly leaves and buds and acting as a vegetative reproductive structure — compare BULB, TUBER

corm·el \ˈkȯr-məl, kȯr-ˈmel\ *n* [dim. of *corm*] (ca. 1900) : a small or secondary corm produced by a larger corm
cor·mo·rant \ˈkȯrm-(ə-)rənt, ˈkȯr-mə-ˌrant\ *n* [ME *cormeraunt*, fr. MF *cormorant*, fr. OF *cormareng*, fr. *corp* raven + *marenc* of the sea, fr. L *marinus* — more at CORBEL, MARINE] (14c) **1** : any of various dark-colored web-footed seabirds (family Phalacrocoracidae) that have a long neck, wedge-shaped tail, hooked bill, and a patch of bare often brightly colored distensible skin under the mouth and are used in eastern Asia for catching fish **2** : a gluttonous, greedy, or rapacious person
[1]**corn** \ˈkȯ(ə)rn\ *n, often attrib* [ME, fr. OE; akin to OHG & ON *korn* grain, L *granum*] (bef. 12c) **1** *chiefly dial* : a small hard particle : GRAIN **2** : a small hard seed **3 a** : the seeds of a cereal grass and esp. of the important cereal crop of a particular region (as wheat in Britain, oats in Scotland and Ireland, and Indian corn in the New World and Australia) **b** : the kernels of sweet corn served as a vegetable while still soft and milky **4** : a plant that produces corn **5** : CORN WHISKEY **6** : something (as writing, music, or acting) that is corny
[2]**corn** *vt* (1560) **1** : to form into grains : GRANULATE **2 a** : to preserve or season with salt in grains **b** : to cure or preserve in brine containing preservatives and often seasonings ⟨~*ed* beef⟩ **3** : to feed with corn ⟨~ the horses⟩
[3]**corn** *n* [ME *corne*, fr. MF, horn, corner, fr. L *cornu* horn, point — more at HORN] (15c) : a local hardening and thickening of epidermis (as on a toe)
[1]**corn·ball** \ˈkȯ(ə)rn-ˌbȯl\ *n* [*corn ball* (ball of popcorn and molasses); influenced in meaning by [1]*corn* 6] (1949) : an unsophisticated person; *also* : something corny
[2]**cornball** *adj* (1951) : CORNY
corn borer *n* (1919) : any of several insects that bore in maize: as **a** : EUROPEAN CORN BORER **b** : SOUTHWESTERN CORN BORER
corn bread *n* (1750) : bread made with cornmeal
corn chip *n* (1950) : a piece of a dry crisp snack food prepared from a seasoned cornmeal batter
corn·cob \ˈkȯ(ə)rn-ˌkäb\ *n* (1793) **1** : the axis on which the kernels of Indian corn are arranged **2** : an ear of Indian corn
corncob pipe *n* (1832) : a tobacco pipe with a bowl made from a corncob
corn cockle *n* (1713) : an annual hairy weed (*Agrostemma githago*) of the pink family with purplish red flowers that is found in grainfields
corn·crake \ˈkȯ(ə)rn-ˌkrāk\ *n* (15c) : a common Eurasian short-billed rail (*Crex crex*) that frequents grainfields — called also *land rail*
corn·crib \-ˌkrib\ *n* (1681) : a crib for storing ears of Indian corn
corn dodger *n, chiefly Southern & Midland* (1834) : a cake of corn bread that is fried, baked, or boiled as a dumpling
cor·nea \ˈkȯr-nē-ə\ *n* [ML, fr. L, fem. of *corneus* horny, fr. *cornu*] (14c) : the transparent part of the coat of the eyeball that covers the iris and pupil and admits light to the interior — see EYE illustration — **cor·ne·al** \-əl\ *adj*
corn earworm *n* (1889) : a noctuid moth (*Heliothis zea*) whose large striped yellow-headed larva is esp. destructive to Indian corn, tomatoes, and cotton bolls
cor·nel \ˈkȯrn-ᵊl, ˈkȯr-ˌnel\ *n* [deriv. of L *cornus* cornel cherry tree; akin to Gk *kerasos* cherry tree] (1551) : any of various shrubs or trees (*Cornus* and related genera) with very hard wood and perfect flowers; *specif* : DOGWOOD
cor·ne·lian \kȯr-ˈnēl-yən\ *n* (15c) : CARNELIAN
cor·ne·ous \ˈkȯr-nē-əs\ *adj* [L *corneus*] (1646) : HORNY
[1]**cor·ner** \ˈkȯ(r)-nər\ *n* [ME, fr. OF *cornere*, fr. *corne* horn, corner] (13c) **1 a** : the point where converging lines, edges, or sides meet : ANGLE **b** : the place of intersection of two streets or roads **c** : a piece designed to form, mark, or protect a corner **2** : the angular part or space between meeting lines, edges, or borders near the vertex of the angle ⟨the southwest ~ of the state⟩ ⟨the ~s of the tablecloth⟩: as **a** : the area of a playing field or court near the intersection of the sideline and the goal line or baseline **b (1)** : either of the four angles of a boxing ring; *esp* : the angle in which a boxer rests or is worked on by his seconds during periods between rounds **(2)** : a group of supporters, well-wishers, or adherents associated esp. with a contestant **c** : the side of home plate nearest to or farthest from a batter ⟨a fast ball over the outside ~⟩ **d** : CORNER KICK **e** : the outside of a football formation **3 a** : a private, secret, or remote place ⟨a quiet ~ of New England⟩ ⟨to every ~ of the earth⟩ ⟨dark ~s of the mind⟩ **b** : a difficult or embarrassing situation : a position from which escape or retreat is difficult or impossible ⟨was backed into a ~⟩ **4** : control or ownership of enough of the available supply of a commodity or security esp. to permit manipulation of the price **5** : a point at which significant change occurs — often used in the phrase *turn a corner* — **cor·nered** \-nərd\ *adj* — **around the corner** : at hand : IMMINENT ⟨good times are just *around the corner*⟩
[2]**corner** *adj* (13c) **1** : situated at a corner ⟨the ~ drugstore⟩ **2** : used or fitted for use in or on a corner ⟨a ~ table⟩
[3]**corner** *vb* **cor·nered; cor·ner·ing** \ˈkȯ(r)n-(ə-)riŋ\ *vt* (1824) **1 a** : to drive into a corner ⟨the animal is dangerous when ~*ed*⟩ **b** : to catch and hold the attention of esp. so as to force an interview **2** : to get a corner on ⟨~ the wheat market⟩ ~ *vi* **1** : to meet or converge at a corner or angle **2** : to turn a corner ⟨a car that ~s well⟩
cor·ner·back \ˈkȯ(r)-nər-ˌbak\ *n* (1970) : a defensive halfback in football who defends the flank
corner kick *n* (1882) : a free kick in soccer from close to the point of intersection of the goal line and touchline
cor·ner·man \ˈkȯ(r)-nər-ˌman\ *n* (1957) : one who plays in or near the corner: as **a** : CORNERBACK **b** : a basketball forward
cor·ner·stone \ˈkȯ(r)-nər-ˌstōn\ *n* (13c) **1** : a stone forming a part of a corner or angle in a wall; *specif* : such a stone laid at a formal ceremony **2** : a basic element : FOUNDATION ⟨a ~ of foreign policy⟩
cor·ner·ways \-ˌwāz\ *adv* (1922) : DIAGONALLY
cor·ner·wise \-ˌwīz\ *adv* (15c) : DIAGONALLY
cor·net \kȯr-ˈnet, *Brit usu* ˈkȯr-nit\ *n* [ME, fr. MF, fr. dim. of *corn* horn, fr. L *cornu*] (14c) **1** : a valved brass instrument resembling a trumpet in design and range but having a shorter partly conical tube and less brilliant tone **2** : something shaped like a cone: as **a** : a piece of paper twisted for use as a container **b** : a cone-shaped pastry shell that is often filled with whipped cream **c** *Brit* : an ice-cream cone — **cor·net·ist** *or* **cor·net·tist** \-ˈnet-əst, -ni-tist\ *n*
corn-fed \ˈkȯ(ə)rn-ˌfed\ *adj* (15c) **1** : fed or fattened on grain (as corn) ⟨~ hogs⟩ **2** : looking well-fed : PLUMP **3** : CORNY
corn·field \-ˌfēld\ *n* (14c) : a field in which corn is grown
corn·flakes \-ˌflāks\ *n pl* (1907) : toasted flakes made from the coarse meal of hulled corn for use as a breakfast cereal
corn flour *n, Brit* (1791) : CORNSTARCH
corn·flow·er \ˈkȯ(ə)rn-ˌflau̇(-ə)r\ *n* (1527) **1** : CORN COCKLE **2** : BACHELOR'S BUTTON
cornflower blue *n* (1907) : a moderate purplish blue
Corn·husk·er \ˈkȯ(ə)rn-ˌhəs-kər\ *n* (ca. 1948) : a native or resident of Nebraska — used as a nickname
corn·husk·ing \ˈkȯ(ə)rn-ˌhəs-kiŋ\ *n* (1786) : a social gathering esp. of farm families to husk corn
[1]**cor·nice** \ˈkȯr-nəs, -nish\ *n* [MF, fr. It] (1563) **1 a** : the molded and projecting horizontal member that crowns an architectural composition **b** : a top course that crowns a wall **2** : a decorative band of metal or wood used to conceal curtain fixtures **3** : an overhanging mass of snow, ice, or rock usu. on a ridge

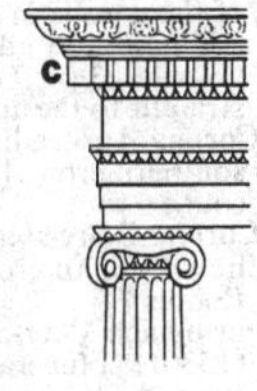

cornice 1a

[2]**cornice** *vt* **cor·niced; cor·nic·ing** (1744) : to furnish or crown with a cornice
cor·niche \kȯr-ˈnēsh\ *n* [F *cornice, corniche*, lit., cornice] (1837) : a road built along a coast and esp. along the face of a cliff
cor·nic·u·late cartilage \kȯr-ˌnik-yə-lət-\ *n* [L *corniculatus* horned, fr. *corniculum*, dim. of *cornu* horn] (ca. 1909) : a small nodule of yellow elastic cartilage articulating with the apex of the arytenoid
cor·ni·fi·ca·tion \ˌkȯr-nə-fə-ˈkā-shən\ *n* [L *cornu* horn + E *-i-* + *-fication*] (1843) **1** : conversion into horn or a horny substance or tissue **2** : the conversion of the vaginal epithelium from the columnar to the squamous type
[1]**Cor·nish** \ˈkȯr-nish\ *adj* [*Corn*wall, England + E *-ish*] (14c) : of, relating to, or characteristic of Cornwall, Cornishmen, or Cornish
[2]**Cornish** *n* (1547) **1** : a Celtic language of Cornwall extinct since the late 18th century **2** : any of an English breed of domestic fowls much used in crossbreeding for meat production
Cornish cream *n* (1905) : CLOTTED CREAM
Cor·nish·man \-mən\ *n* (15c) : a native or resident of Cornwall, England
Corn Law *n* (1766) : one of a series of laws in force in Great Britain before 1846 prohibiting or discouraging the importation of grain
corn leaf aphid *n* (1939) : a dusky greenish or brownish aphid (*Rhopalosiphum maidis*) that feeds on the flowers and foliage of various commercially important grasses (as Indian corn)
corn·meal \ˈkȯ(ə)rn-ˈmē(ə)l, -ˌmēl\ *n* (1749) : meal ground from corn
corn oil *n* (1900) : a yellow fatty oil obtained from the germ of Indian corn kernels and used chiefly in salad oil, in soft soap, and in margarine
corn pone *n, Southern & Midland* (1859) : corn bread often made without milk or eggs and baked or fried
corn poppy *n* (ca. 1859) : an annual red-flowered poppy (*Papaver rhoeas*) common in European grainfields and cultivated in several varieties
corn rootworm *n* (1892) : any of several beetles (genus *Diabrotica* of the family Galerucidae) whose root-eating larvae are pests esp. of corn
corn·row \ˈkȯ(ə)rn-ˌrō\ *vt* [fr. the fancied resemblance of the braids to rows of corn] (1971) : to style (hair) by dividing into sections that are braided usu. flat to the scalp in rows — **cornrow** *n*
corn silk *n* (1861) : the silky styles on an ear of Indian corn
corn snow *n* (1935) : granular snow formed by alternate thawing and freezing
corn·stalk \ˈkȯ(ə)rn-ˌstȯk\ *n* (1645) : a stalk of Indian corn
corn·starch \-ˌstärch\ *n* (1853) : starch made from corn and used in foods as a thickening agent, in making corn syrup and sugars, and in the manufacture of adhesives and sizes for paper and textiles
corn sugar *n* (1850) : DEXTROSE; *esp* : dextrose made by hydrolysis of cornstarch
corn syrup *n* (1903) : a syrup containing dextrins, maltose, and dextrose that is obtained by partial hydrolysis of cornstarch
cor·nu \ˈkȯr-(ˌ)n(y)ü\ *n, pl* **cor·nua** \-n(y)ə-wə\ [L] (1691) : HORN; *esp* : a horn-shaped anatomical structure — **cor·nu·al** \-n(y)ə-wəl\ *adj*
cor·nu·co·pia \ˌkȯr-n(y)ə-ˈkō-pē-ə\ *n* [LL, fr. L *cornu copiae* horn of plenty] (1508) **1** : a curved goat's horn overflowing with fruit and ears of grain that is used as a decorative motif emblematic of abundance **2** : an inexhaustible store : ABUNDANCE **3** : a receptacle shaped like a horn or cone — **cor·nu·co·pi·an** \-pē-ən\ *adj*
cor·nu·to \kȯr-ˈn(y)üt-(ˌ)ō\ *n, pl* **-tos** [It, fr. L *cornutus* having horns, fr. *cornu*] (15c) : CUCKOLD
corn whiskey *n* (1780) : whiskey distilled from a mash made up of not less than 80 percent corn — compare BOURBON
[1]**corny** \ˈkȯr-nē\ *adj* **corn·i·er; -est** (14c) **1** *archaic* : tasting strongly of malt **2** : of or relating to corn **3** : mawkishly old-fashioned : tiresomely simple and sentimental : TRITE — **corn·i·ly** \ˈkȯrn-ᵊl-ē\ *adv* — **corn·i·ness** \ˈkȯr-nē-nəs\ *n*
[2]**corny** *adj* **corn·i·er; -est** (1707) : relating to or having corns on the feet
cor·o·dy \ˈkȯr-əd-ē, ˈkär-\ *n, pl* **-dies** [ME *corodie*, fr. ML *corrodium*] (15c) : an allowance of provisions for maintenance dispensed as a charity
co·rol·la \kə-ˈräl-ə, -ˈrōl-\ *n* [NL, fr. L, dim. of *corona*] (1753) : the petals of a flower constituting the inner floral envelope surrounding the sporophylls — **co·rol·late** \kə-ˈräl-ət; ˈkȯr-ə-ˌlāt, ˈkär-\ *adj*
cor·ol·lary \ˈkȯr-ə-ˌler-ē, ˈkär-, *Brit* kə-ˈräl-ə-rē\ *n, pl* **-lar·ies** [ME *corolarie*, fr. LL *corollarium*, fr. L, money paid for a garland, gratuity, fr. *corolla*] (14c) **1** : a proposition inferred immediately from a proved

proposition with little or no additional proof **2 a :** something that naturally follows : RESULT **b :** something that incidentally or naturally accompanies or parallels — **corollary** *adj*

cor·o·man·del \ˌkȯr-ə-ˈman-dᵊl, ˌkär-\ *n* [*Coromandel* coast region, India] (1845) **:** an East Indian timber tree (*Diospyros melanoxylon*) with a hard dark-colored wood — called also *coromandel ebony*

co·ro·na \kə-ˈrō-nə\ *n* [L, garland, crown, cornice — more at CROWN] (1563) **1 :** the projecting part of a classic cornice **2 a :** a usu. colored circle often seen around and close to a luminous body (as the sun or moon) caused by diffraction produced by suspended droplets or occas. particles of dust **b :** the tenuous outermost part of the atmosphere of the sun appearing as a halo around the moon's black disk during a total eclipse of the sun; *also* **:** a similar portion of the atmosphere of a star **c :** a circle of light made by the apparent convergence of the streamers of the aurora borealis **d :** the upper portion of a bodily part (as a tooth or the skull) **e :** an appendage on the inner side of the corolla in some flowers (as the daffodil, jonquil, or milkweed) **f :** a faint glow adjacent to the surface of an electrical conductor at high voltage **3** [fr. *La Corona,* a trademark] **:** a long cigar having the sides straight to the unsealed end and being roundly blunt at the sealed end

Corona Aus·tra·lis \-ȯ-ˈstrā-ləs, -ä-\ *n* [NL (gen. *Coronae Australis*), lit., southern crown] **:** a southern constellation adjoining Sagittarius on the south

Corona Bo·re·al·is \-ˌbōr-ē-ˈal-əs, -ˌbȯr-\ *n* [NL (gen. *Coronae Borealis*), lit., northern crown] **:** a northern constellation between Hercules and Boötes

cor·o·nach \ˈkȯr-ə-nək, ˈkär-\ *n* [ScGael *corranach* & IrGael *corānach*] (1530) **:** a funeral dirge sung or played on the bagpipes in Scotland and Ireland

co·ro·na·graph *also* **co·ro·no·graph** \kə-ˈrō-nə-ˌgraf\ *n* (1885) **:** a telescope for observation of the sun's corona

[1]**cor·o·nal** *also* **cor·o·nel** \ˈkȯr-ən-ᵊl, ˈkär-\ *n* [ME *coronal,* fr. AF, fr. L *coronalis* of a crown, fr. *corona*] (14c) **:** a circlet for the head usu. implying rank or dignity

[2]**co·ro·nal** \ˈkȯr-ən-ᵊl, ˈkär-; kə-ˈrōn-\ *adj* (15c) **1 :** of or relating to a corona or crown **2 a :** lying in the direction of the coronal suture **b :** of or relating to the frontal plane that passes through the long axis of the body

coronal suture *n* (1615) **:** a suture extending across the skull between the parietal and frontal bones

co·ro·na ra·di·a·ta \kə-ˈrō-nə-ˌrād-ē-ˈät-ə, -ˈāt-\ *n, pl* **co·ro·nae ra·di·a·tae** \-(ˌ)nē-ˌrād-ē-ˈāt-(ˌ)ē, -ˈät-\ [NL, lit., crown with rays] (1892) **:** the zone of small follicular cells immediately surrounding the ovum in the graafian follicle and accompanying the ovum on its discharge from the follicle

[1]**cor·o·nary** \ˈkȯr-ə-ˌner-ē, ˈkär-\ *adj* (1646) **1 :** of, relating to, resembling, or being a crown or coronal **2 :** of, relating to, or being the coronary arteries or veins of the heart; *broadly* **:** of or relating to the heart

[2]**coronary** *n, pl* **-nar·ies** (1893) **1 a :** CORONARY ARTERY **b :** CORONARY VEIN **2 :** CORONARY THROMBOSIS

coronary artery *n* (1741) **:** either of two arteries, one on the right and one on the left, that arise from the aorta immediately above the semilunar valves and supply the tissues of the heart itself

coronary occlusion *n* (1946) **:** the partial or complete blocking (as by a thrombus, by spasm, or by sclerosis) of a coronary artery

coronary sinus *n* (1831) **:** a venous channel that is derived from the sinus venosus, is continuous with the largest of the cardiac veins, receives most of the blood from the walls of the heart, and empties into the right atrium

coronary thrombosis *n* (1926) **:** the blocking of a coronary artery of the heart by a thrombus

coronary vein *n* (ca. 1828) **:** any of several veins that drain the tissues of the heart and empty into the coronary sinus

cor·o·na·tion \ˌkȯr-ə-ˈnā-shən, ˌkär-\ *n* [ME *coronacion,* fr. MF *coronation,* fr. *coroner* to crown] (14c) **:** the act or occasion of crowning; *also* **:** accession to the highest office

cor·o·ner \ˈkȯr-ə-nər, ˈkär-\ *n* [ME, an officer of the crown, fr. AF, fr. OF *corone* crown, fr. L *corona*] (14c) **:** a public officer whose principal duty is to inquire by an inquest into the cause of any death which there is reason to suppose is not due to natural causes

cor·o·net \ˌkȯr-ə-ˈnet, ˌkär-\ *n* [MF *coronette,* fr. OF *coronete,* fr. *corone*] (15c) **1 :** a small or lesser crown usu. signifying a rank below that of a sovereign **2 :** an ornamental wreath or band for the head usu. for wear by women on formal occasions **3 :** the lower part of a horse's pastern where the horn terminates in skin — see HORSE illustration

co·ro·tate \(ˈ)kō-ˈrō-ˌtāt\ *vi* (1962) **:** to rotate in conjunction with or at the same rate as another rotating body — **co·ro·ta·tion** \ˌkō-rō-ˈtā-shən\ *n*

corpora *pl of* CORPUS

[1]**cor·po·ral** \ˈkȯr-p(ə-)rəl\ *n* [ME, fr. MF, fr. ML *corporale,* fr. L, neut. of *corporalis;* fr. the doctrine that the bread of the Eucharist becomes or represents the body of Christ] (14c) **:** a linen cloth on which the eucharistic elements are placed

[2]**corporal** *adj* [ME, fr. MF, fr. L *corporalis,* fr. *corpor-, corpus* body — more at MIDRIFF] (14c) **1 :** of, relating to, or affecting the body ⟨~ punishment⟩ **2** *obs* **:** CORPOREAL, PHYSICAL — **cor·po·ral·ly** \-p(ə-)rə-lē\ *adv*

[3]**corporal** *n* [MF, lowest noncommissioned officer, alter. of *caporal,* fr. OIt *caporale,* fr. *capo* head, fr. L *caput* — more at HEAD] (1579) **:** a noncommissioned officer ranking in the army above a private first class and below a sergeant and in the marine corps above a lance corporal and below a sergeant

cor·po·ral·i·ty \ˌkȯr-pə-ˈral-ət-ē\ *n, pl* **-ties** (14c) **:** the quality or state of being or having a body or a material or physical existence

corporal's guard *n* (1844) **1 :** the small detachment commanded by a corporal **2 :** a small group

cor·po·rate \ˈkȯr-p(ə-)rət\ *adj* [L *corporatus,* pp. of *corporare* to make into a body, fr. *corpor-, corpus*] (1512) **1 a :** formed into an association and endowed by law with the rights and liabilities of an individual **:** INCORPORATED **b :** of or relating to a corporation ⟨a plan to reorganize the ~ structure⟩ **2 :** of, relating to, or formed into a unified body of individuals ⟨human law arises by the ~ action of a people —G. H. Sabine⟩ ⟨a ~ society⟩ **3 :** CORPORATIVE 2 — **cor·po·rate·ly** *adv*

cor·po·ra·tion \ˌkȯr-pə-ˈrā-shən\ *n* (15c) **1 a** *obs* **:** a group of merchants or traders united in a trade guild **b :** the municipal authorities of a town or city **2 :** a body formed and authorized by law to act as a single person although constituted by one or more persons and legally endowed with various rights and duties including the capacity of succession **3 :** an association of employers and employees in a basic industry or of members of a profession organized as an organ of political representation in a corporative state **4 :** POTBELLY 1

cor·po·rat·ism \ˈkȯr-p(ə-)rət-ˌiz-əm\ *n* (1890) **:** the organization of a society into industrial and professional corporations serving as organs of political representation and exercising some control over persons and activities within their jurisdiction — **cor·po·rat·ist** \-p(ə-)rət-əst\ *adj*

cor·po·ra·tive \ˈkȯr-pə-ˌrāt-iv, -p(ə-)rət-\ *adj* (1833) **1 :** of or relating to a corporation **2 :** of or relating to corporatism ⟨a ~ state⟩

cor·po·ra·tiv·ism \ˈkȯr-pə-ˌrāt-i-ˌviz-əm, -p(ə-)rət-\ *n* (1930) **:** CORPORATISM

cor·po·ra·tor \ˈkȯr-pə-ˌrāt-ər\ *n* (1784) **:** a corporation organizer, member, or stockholder

cor·po·re·al \kȯr-ˈpōr-ē-əl, -ˈpȯr-\ *adj* [L *corporeus* of the body, fr. *corpor-, corpus*] (15c) **1 :** having, consisting of, or relating to a physical material body: as **a :** not spiritual **b :** not immaterial or intangible **:** SUBSTANTIAL **2** *archaic* **:** CORPORAL ***syn*** see MATERIAL — **cor·po·re·al·ly** \-ē-ə-lē\ *adv* — **cor·po·re·al·ness** *n*

cor·po·re·al·i·ty \(ˌ)kȯr-ˌpōr-ē-ˈal-ət-ē, -ˌpȯr-\ *n, pl* **-ties** (1651) **:** corporeal existence

cor·po·re·ity \ˌkȯr-pə-ˈrē-ət-ē, -ˈrā-\ *n, pl* **-ities** (1621) **:** the quality or state of having or being a body **:** MATERIALITY

cor·po·sant \ˈkȯr-pə-ˌsant, -ˌzant\ *n* [Pg *corpo-santo,* lit., holy body] (1655) **:** SAINT ELMO'S FIRE

corps \ˈkō(ə)r\, ˈkȯ(ə)r\ *n, pl* **corps** \ˈkō(ə)rz, ˈkȯ(ə)rz\ [F, fr. L *corpus* body] (1711) **1 a :** an organized subdivision of the military establishment ⟨Marine *Corps*⟩ ⟨Signal *Corps*⟩ **b :** a tactical unit usu. consisting of two or more divisions and auxiliary arms and services **2 :** a group of persons associated together or acting under common direction; *esp* **:** a body of persons having a common activity or occupation ⟨the press ~⟩ **3 :** CORPS DE BALLET

corps de bal·let \ˌkōrd-ə-(ˌ)ba-ˈlā, ˌkȯrd-\ *n, pl* **corps de ballet** *same, or* ˌkōrz-də-, ˌkȯrz-\ [F] (1826) **:** the ensemble of a ballet company

corps d'elite \ˌkōr-dā-ˈlēt, ˌkȯr-\ *n, pl* **corps d'elite** *same, or* ˌkōrz-dā-, ˌkȯrz-\ [F *corps d'élite*] (1884) **1 :** a body of picked troops **2 :** a group of the best people in a category

corpse \ˈkȯ(ə)rps\ *n* [ME *corps,* fr. MF, fr. L *corpus*] (13c) **1** *obs* **:** a human or animal body whether living or dead **2 a :** a dead body esp. of a human being **b :** something discarded or defunct ⟨the ~ of a city . . . that once had been so beautiful —*Nat'l Geographic*⟩

corps·man \ˈkō(ə)r(z)-mən, ˈkȯ(ə)r(z)-\ *n* (1926) **1 :** an enlisted man trained to give first aid and minor medical treatment **2 :** a member of a government-sponsored service corps

cor·pu·lence \ˈkȯr-pyə-lən(t)s\ *n* (1581) **:** the state of being excessively fat

cor·pu·len·cy \-lən-sē\ *n, pl* **-cies** (1646) **:** CORPULENCE

cor·pu·lent \-lənt\ *adj* [ME, fr. L *corpulentus,* fr. *corpus*] (14c) **:** having a large bulky body **:** OBESE — **cor·pu·lent·ly** *adv*

cor pul·mo·na·le \ˌkȯr-ˌpu̇l-mə-ˈnäl-ē, -ˌpəl-, -ˈnal-\ *n, pl* **cor·dia pul·mo·na·lia** \ˈkȯrd-ē-ə- . . . -ˈnäl-ē-ə, -ˈnal-\ [NL, lit., pulmonary heart] (1857) **:** disease of the heart characterized by hypertrophy and dilatation of the right ventricle and secondary to disease of the lungs or their blood vessels

cor·pus \ˈkȯr-pəs\ *n, pl* **cor·po·ra** \-p(ə-)rə\ [ME, fr. L] (15c) **1 :** the body of a man or animal esp. when dead **2 a :** the main part or body of a bodily structure or organ ⟨the ~ of the uterus⟩ **b :** the main body or corporeal substance of a thing; *specif* **:** the principal of a fund or estate as distinct from income or interest **3 a :** all the writings or works of a particular kind or on a particular subject; *esp* **:** the complete works of an author **b :** a collection or body of knowledge or evidence; *esp* **:** a collection of recorded utterances used as a basis for the descriptive analysis of a language

corpus al·la·tum \-ə-ˈlāt-əm, -ˈlät-\ *n, pl* **corpora al·la·ta** \-ˈlāt-ə, -ˈlät-ə\ [NL, lit., applied body] (1947) **:** one of a pair of separate or fused bodies in many insects that are sometimes closely associated with the corpora cardiaca and that secrete hormones (as juvenile hormone)

corpus cal·lo·sum \-ka-ˈlō-səm\ *n, pl* **corpora cal·lo·sa** \-sə\ [NL, lit., callous body] (1706) **:** the great band of commissural fibers uniting the cerebral hemispheres in man and in the higher mammals — see BRAIN illustration

corpus car·di·a·cum \-kär-ˈdī-ə-kəm\ *n, pl* **corpora car·di·a·ca** \-ə-kə\ [NL, lit., cardiac body] (1960) **:** one of a pair of separate or fused bodies of nervous tissue in many insects that lie posterior to the brain and dorsal to the esophagus and that function in the storage and secretion of brain hormone

Cor·pus Chris·ti \ˌkȯr-pə-ˈskris-tē\ *n* [ME, fr. ML, lit., body of Christ] (14c) **:** the Thursday after Trinity observed as a Roman Catholic festival in honor of the Eucharist

cor·pus·cle \ˈkȯr-(ˌ)pəs-əl\ *n* [L *corpusculum,* dim. of *corpus*] (1660) **1 :** a minute particle **2 a :** a living cell; *esp* **:** one (as a red or white blood cell or a cell in cartilage or bone) not aggregated into continuous tissues **b :** any of various small circumscribed multicellular bodies — **cor·pus·cu·lar** \kȯr-ˈpəs-kyə-lər\ *adj*

cor·pus de·lic·ti \-di-ˈlik-ˌtī, -(ˌ)tē\ *n, pl* **corpora delicti** [NL, lit., body of the crime] (1832) **1 :** the substantial and fundamental fact necessary to prove the commission of a crime **2 :** the material substance (as the body of the victim of a murder) upon which a crime has been committed

corpus lu·te·um \-ˈlüt-ē-əm\ *n, pl* **corpora lu·tea** \-ē-ə\ [NL, lit., yellowish body] (1788) **:** a reddish yellow mass of progesterone-secreting endocrine tissue that forms from a ruptured graafian follicle in the mammalian ovary

cor·rade \kə-ˈrād\ *vb* **cor·rad·ed; cor·rad·ing** [L *corradere* to scrape together, fr. *com-* + *radere* to scrape — more at RAT] *vt* (1646) **:** to wear away by abrasion ~ *vi* **:** to crumble away through abrasion — **cor·ra·sion** \-ˈrā-zhən\ *n* — **cor·ra·sive** \-ˈrā-siv, -ziv\ *adj*

1cor·ral \kə-'ral, -'rel\ *n* [Sp, fr. (assumed) VL *currale* enclosure for vehicles, fr. L *currus* cart, fr. *currere* to run — more at CURRENT] (1582) **1 :** a pen or enclosure for confining or capturing livestock **2 :** an enclosure made with wagons for defense of an encampment

2corral *vt* **cor·ralled; cor·ral·ling** (1847) **1 :** to enclose in a corral **2 :** to arrange (wagons) so as to form a corral **3 :** COLLECT, GATHER ⟨*corralling* votes for the upcoming election⟩

1cor·rect \kə-'rekt\ *vt* [ME *correcten,* fr. L *correctus,* pp. of *corrigere,* fr. *com-* + *regere* to lead straight — more at RIGHT] (14c) **1 a :** to make or set right **:** AMEND **b :** COUNTERACT, NEUTRALIZE **c :** to alter or adjust so as to bring to some standard or required condition ⟨~ a lens for spherical aberration⟩ **2 a :** to punish (as a child) with a view to reforming or improving **b :** to point out usu. for amendment the errors or faults of ⟨spent the day ~*ing* tests⟩ — **cor·rect·able** \-'rek-tə-bəl\ *adj* — **cor·rec·tor** \-'rek-tər\ *n*

syn CORRECT, RECTIFY, EMEND, REMEDY, REDRESS, AMEND, REFORM, REVISE mean to make right what is wrong. CORRECT implies taking action to remove errors, faults, deviations, defects; RECTIFY implies a more essential changing to make something right, just, or properly controlled or directed; EMEND specif. implies correction of a text or manuscript; REMEDY implies removing or making harmless a cause of trouble, harm, or evil; REDRESS implies making compensation or reparation for an unfairness, injustice, or imbalance; AMEND, REFORM, REVISE imply an improving by making corrective changes, AMEND usu. suggesting slight changes, REFORM implying drastic change, and REVISE suggesting a careful examination of something and the making of necessary changes. ***syn*** see in addition PUNISH

2correct *adj* [ME, corrected, fr. L *correctus,* fr. pp. of *corrigere*] (1676) **1 :** conforming to an approved or conventional standard ⟨relations . . . were ~ but not very friendly —W. L. Shirer⟩ **2 :** conforming to or agreeing with fact, logic, or known truth **3 :** conforming to a set figure ⟨enclosed the ~ return postage⟩ — **cor·rect·ly** \kə-'rek-(t)lē\ *adv* — **cor·rect·ness** \-'rek(t)-nəs\ *n*

syn CORRECT, ACCURATE, EXACT, PRECISE, NICE, RIGHT mean conforming to fact, standard, or truth. CORRECT usu. implies freedom from fault or error; ACCURATE implies fidelity to fact or truth attained by exercise of care; EXACT stresses a very strict agreement with fact, standard, or truth; PRECISE adds to EXACT an emphasis on sharpness of definition or delimitation; NICE stresses great precision and delicacy of adjustment or discrimination; RIGHT is close to CORRECT but has a stronger positive emphasis on conformity to fact or truth rather than mere absence of error or fault.

corrected time *n* (1891) **:** a boat's elapsed time less her time allowance in yacht racing

cor·rec·tion \kə-'rek-shən\ *n* (14c) **1 :** the action or an instance of correcting: as **a :** AMENDMENT, RECTIFICATION **b :** REBUKE, PUNISHMENT **c :** a bringing into conformity with a standard **d :** NEUTRALIZATION, COUNTERACTION ⟨~ of acidity⟩ **2 :** a decline in market price or business activity following and counteracting a rise **3 a :** something substituted in place of what is wrong ⟨marking ~*s* on the students' papers⟩ **b :** a quantity applied by way of correcting (as for adjustment or inaccuracy of an instrument) **4 :** the treatment and rehabilitation of offenders through a program involving penal custody, parole, and probation; *also* **:** the administration of such treatment as a matter of public policy — usu. used in pl. — **cor·rec·tion·al** \-shnəl, -shən-ᵊl\ *adj*

cor·rec·ti·tude \kə-'rek-tə-,t(y)üd\ *n* [blend of *correct* and *rectitude*] (1893) **:** correctness or propriety of conduct

cor·rec·tive \kə-'rek-tiv\ *adj* (1531) **:** tending to correct ⟨~ lenses⟩ ⟨~ punishment⟩ — **corrective** *n* — **cor·rec·tive·ly** *adv*

1cor·re·late \'kȯr-ə-lət, 'kär-, -,lāt\ *n* [back-formation fr. *correlation*] (1643) **1 :** either of two things so related that one directly implies or is complementary to the other (as husband and wife) **2 :** a phenomenon (as brain activity) that accompanies another phenomenon (as behavior), is usu. parallel to it (as in form, type, development, or distribution), and is related in some way to it — **correlate** *adj*

2cor·re·late \-,lāt\ *vb* **-lat·ed; -lat·ing** *vi* (1742) **:** to bear reciprocal or mutual relations **:** CORRESPOND ~ *vt* **1 a :** to establish a mutual or reciprocal relation between ⟨~ activities in the lab and the field⟩ **b :** to show correlation or a causal relationship between **2 :** to present or set forth so as to show relationship ⟨he ~*s* the findings of the scientists, the psychologists, and the mystics —Eugene Exman⟩ — **cor·re·lat·able** \-,lāt-ə-bəl\ *adj* — **cor·re·lat·or** \-,lāt-ər\ *n*

cor·re·la·tion \,kȯr-ə-'lā-shən, ,kär-\ *n* [ML *correlation-, correlatio,* fr. L *com-* + *relation-, relatio* relation] (1561) **1 :** the act of correlating **2 :** the state or relation of being correlated; *specif* **:** a relation existing between phenomena or things or between mathematical or statistical variables which tend to vary, be associated, or occur together in a way not expected on the basis of chance alone ⟨the obviously high positive ~ between scholastic aptitude and college entrance —J. B. Conant⟩ — **cor·re·la·tion·al** \-shnəl, -shən-ᵊl\ *adj*

correlation coefficient *n* (ca. 1909) **:** a number or function that indicates the degree of correlation between two sets of data or between two random variables and that is equal to their covariance divided by the product of their standard deviations

cor·rel·a·tive \kə-'rel-ət-iv\ *adj* (1530) **1 :** naturally related **:** CORRESPONDING **2 :** reciprocally related **3 :** regularly used together but typically not adjacent ⟨the ~ conjunctions *either . . . or*⟩ — **correlative** *n* — **cor·rel·a·tive·ly** *adv*

cor·re·spond \,kȯr-ə-'spänd, ,kär-\ *vi* [MF or ML; MF *correspondre,* fr. ML *correspondēre,* fr. L *com-* + *respondēre* to respond] (1529) **1 a :** to be in conformity or agreement **:** SUIT ⟨fulfillment seldom ~*s* to anticipation⟩ **b :** to compare closely **:** MATCH — usu. used with *to* or *with* **c :** to be equivalent or parallel **2 :** to communicate with a person by exchange of letters ⟨frequently ~*s* with his cousin⟩

cor·re·spon·dence \-'spän-dən(t)s\ *n* (15c) **1 a :** the agreement of things with one another **b :** a particular similarity **c :** a relation between sets in which each member of one set is associated with one or more members of the other — compare FUNCTION 5a **2 a :** communication by letters; *also* **:** the letters exchanged **b :** the news, information, or opinion contributed by a correspondent to a newspaper or periodical

correspondence course *n* (1902) **:** a course offered by a correspondence school

correspondence school *n* (1889) **:** a school that teaches nonresident students by mailing them lessons and exercises which upon completion are returned to the school for grading

cor·re·spon·den·cy \,kȯr-ə-'spän-dən-sē, ,kär-\ *n, pl* **-cies** (1589) **:** CORRESPONDENCE

1cor·re·spon·dent \,kȯr-ə-'spän-dənt, ,kär-\ *adj* [ME, fr. MF or ML; MF, fr. ML *correspondent-, correspondens,* prp. of *correspondēre*] (15c) **1 :** CORRESPONDING **2 :** FITTING, CONFORMING — used with *with* or *to* ⟨the outcome was entirely ~ with my wishes⟩

2correspondent *n* (1630) **1 :** something that corresponds **2 a :** one who communicates with another by letter **b :** one who has regular commercial relations with another **c :** one who contributes news or commentary to a publication (as a newspaper) or a radio or television network often from a distant place ⟨a war ~⟩

cor·re·spond·ing *adj* (1579) **1 a :** having or participating in the same relationship (as kind, degree, position, correspondence, or function) esp. with regard to the same or like wholes (as geometric figures or sets) ⟨~ parts of similar triangles⟩ **b :** RELATED, ACCOMPANYING ⟨all rights carry with them ~ responsibilites —W. P. Paepcke⟩ **2 a :** charged with the duty of writing letters ⟨~ secretary⟩ **b :** participating or serving at a distance and by mail ⟨a ~ member of the society⟩ — **cor·re·spond·ing·ly** \-'spän-diŋ-lē\ *adv*

corresponding angles *n pl* (1797) **:** any pair of angles each of which is on the same side of one of two lines cut by a transversal and on the same side of the transversal

cor·re·spon·sive \,kȯr-ə-'spän(t)-siv, ,kär-\ *adj* (1606) **:** mutually responsive

cor·ri·da \kō-'rē-thə\ *n* [Sp, lit., act of running] (1896) **:** BULLFIGHT

cor·ri·dor \'kȯr-əd-ər, 'kär-, -ə-,dȯ(ə)r\ *n* [MF, fr. OIt *corridore,* fr. *correre* to run, fr. L *currere* — more at CURRENT] (1814) **1 :** a passageway (as in a hotel) into which compartments or rooms open **2 :** a usu. narrow passageway or route: as **a :** a narrow strip of land through foreign-held territory **b (1) :** a restricted lane for air traffic **(2) :** a restricted path a spacecraft must follow to accomplish its mission **:** WINDOW 9 **3 :** a densely populated strip of land including two or more major cities ⟨the Northeast ~ stretching from Washington into New England —S. D. Browne⟩

cor·rie \'kȯr-ē, 'kär-ē\ *n* [ScGael *coire,* lit., kettle] (1795) **:** CIRQUE 3

Cor·rie·dale \-,dāl\ *n* [*Corriedale,* ranch in New Zealand] (1902) **:** any of a dual-purpose breed of rather large usu. hornless sheep developed in New Zealand

cor·ri·gen·dum \,kȯr-ə-'jen-dəm, ,kär-\ *n, pl* **-da** \-də\ [L, neut. of *corrigendus,* gerundive of *corrigere* to correct] (1850) **:** an error in a printed work discovered after printing and shown with its correction on a separate sheet

cor·ri·gi·ble \'kȯr-ə-jə-bəl, 'kär-\ *adj* [ME, fr. MF, fr. ML *corrigibilis,* fr. L *corrigere*] (15c) **:** capable of being set right **:** REPARABLE ⟨a ~ defect⟩ — **cor·ri·gi·bil·i·ty** \,kȯr-ə-jə-'bil-ət-ē, ,kär-\ *n*

cor·ri·val \kə-'rī-vəl, kō-, kō-\ *n* [MF, fr. L *corrivalis,* fr. *com-* + *rivalis* rival] (1579) **:** RIVAL, COMPETITOR — **corrival** *adj*

cor·rob·o·rant \kə-'räb-ə-rənt\ *adj, archaic* (1626) **:** having an invigorating effect — used of a medicine

cor·rob·o·rate \kə-'räb-ə-,rāt\ *vt* **-rat·ed; -rat·ing** [L *corroboratus,* pp. of *corroborare,* fr. *com-* + *robor-, robur* strength] (1543) **:** to support with evidence or authority **:** make more certain ***syn*** see CONFIRM — **cor·rob·o·ra·tion** \-,räb-ə-'rā-shən\ *n* — **cor·rob·o·ra·tive** \-'räb-ə-,rāt-iv, -'räb-(ə-)rət-\ *adj* — **cor·rob·o·ra·tor** \-'räb-ə-,rāt-ər\ *n* — **cor·rob·o·ra·to·ry** \-'räb-(ə-)rə-,tōr-ē, -,tȯr-\ *adj*

cor·rob·o·ree \kə-'räb-ə-rē\ *n* [native name in New South Wales, Australia] (1793) **1 :** a nocturnal festivity with songs and symbolic dances by which the Australian aborigines celebrate events of importance **2** *Austral* **a :** a noisy festivity **b :** TUMULT

cor·rode \kə-'rōd\ *vb* **cor·rod·ed; cor·rod·ing** [ME *corroden,* fr. L *corrodere* to gnaw to pieces, fr. *com-* + *rodere* to gnaw — more at RAT] *vt* (15c) **1 :** to eat away by degrees as if by gnawing; *esp* **:** to wear away gradually usu. by chemical action ⟨the metal was *corroded* beyond repair⟩ **2 :** to weaken or destroy gradually **:** UNDERMINE ⟨manners and miserliness that ~ the human spirit —Bernard DeVoto⟩ ~ *vi* **:** to undergo corrosion — **cor·rod·ible** \-'rōd-ə-bəl\ *adj*

cor·ro·dy *var of* CORODY

cor·ro·sion \kə-'rō-zhən\ *n* [ME, fr. LL *corrosion-, corrosio* act of gnawing, fr. L *corrosus,* pp. of *corrodere*] (15c) **1 :** the action, process, or effect of corroding **2 :** a product of corroding

cor·ro·sive \-'rō-siv, -ziv\ *adj* (14c) **1 :** tending or having the power to corrode ⟨~ acids⟩ ⟨~ action⟩ ⟨the ~ effects of alcoholism⟩ **2 :** bitingly sarcastic ⟨~ satire⟩ — **corrosive** *n* — **cor·ro·sive·ly** *adv* — **cor·ro·sive·ness** *n*

corrosive sublimate *n* (1706) **:** MERCURIC CHLORIDE

cor·ru·gate \'kȯr-ə-,gāt, 'kär-\ *vb* **-gat·ed; -gat·ing** [L *corrugatus,* pp. of *corrugare,* fr. *com-* + *ruga* wrinkle — more at ROUGH] *vt* (1620) **:** to form or shape into wrinkles or folds or into alternating ridges and grooves **:** FURROW ~ *vi* **:** to become corrugated

cor·ru·gat·ed *adj* (ca. 1623) **:** having corrugations ⟨~ paper⟩; *also* **:** made of corrugated material (as paperboard) ⟨~ boxes⟩

corrugated iron *n* (1856) **:** usu. galvanized sheet iron or sheet steel shaped into straight parallel regular and equally curved ridges and hollows

cor·ru·ga·tion \,kȯr-ə-'gā-shən, ,kär-\ *n* (1528) **1 :** the act of corrugating **2 :** a ridge or groove of a surface that has been corrugated

1cor·rupt \kə-'rəpt\ *vb* [ME *corrupten,* fr. L *corruptus,* pp. of *corrumpere,* fr. *com-* + *rumpere* to break — more at REAVE] *vt* (14c) **1 a :** to change from good to bad in morals, manners, or actions; *also* **:** BRIBE **b :** to degrade with unsound principles or moral values **2 :** ROT, SPOIL **3 :** to subject (a person) to corruption of blood **4 :** to alter from the original or correct form or version ~ *vi* **1 a :** to become tainted or rotten **b :** to become morally debased **2 :** to cause disintegration or ruin *syn* see DEBASE — **cor·rupt·er** *or* **cor·rup·tor** \-ˈrəp-tər\ *n* — **cor·rupt·ibil·i·ty** \-ˌrəp-tə-ˈbil-ət-ē\ *n* — **cor·rupt·ible** \-ˈrəp-tə-bəl\ *adj* — **cor·rupt·ibly** \-blē\ *adv*

2corrupt *adj* [ME, fr. MF or L; MF, fr. L *corruptus*, fr. pp. of *corrumpere*] (14c) **1 a :** morally degenerate and perverted **:** DEPRAVED **b :** characterized by improper conduct (as bribery or the selling of favors) ⟨~ judges⟩ **2** *archaic* **:** PUTRID, TAINTED *syn* see VICIOUS — **cor·rupt·ly** \-ˈrəp-(t)lē\ *adv* — **cor·rupt·ness** \-ˈrəp(t)-nəs\ *n*

cor·rup·tion \kə-ˈrəp-shən\ *n* (14c) **1 a :** impairment of integrity, virtue, or moral principle **:** DEPRAVITY **b :** DECAY, DECOMPOSITION **c :** inducement to wrong by improper or unlawful means (as bribery) **d :** a departure from the original or from what is pure or correct **2** *archaic* **:** an agency or influence that corrupts **3** *chiefly dial* **:** PUS

cor·rup·tion·ist \-sh(ə-)nəst\ *n* (1810) **:** one who practices or defends corruption esp. in politics

corruption of blood (1563) **:** the effect of an attainder upon a person which bars him from inheriting, retaining, or transmitting any estate, rank, or title

cor·rup·tive \kə-ˈrəp-tiv\ *adj* (15c) **:** producing or tending to produce corruption — **cor·rup·tive·ly** *adv*

cor·sage \kȯr-ˈsäzh, -ˈsäj, ˈkȯr-ˌ\ *n* [F, bust, bodice, fr. OF, bust, fr. *cors* body, fr. L *corpus*] (1843) **1 :** the waist or bodice of a dress **2 :** an arrangement of flowers to be worn as a fashion accessory

cor·sair \ˈkȯr-ˌsa(ə)r, -ˌse(ə)r\ *n* [MF & OIt; MF *corsaire* pirate, fr. OProv *corsari*, fr. OIt *corsaro*, fr. ML *cursarius*, fr. L *cursus* course — more at COURSE] (1549) **:** PIRATE; *esp* **:** a privateer of the Barbary coast

corse \ˈkȯ(ə)rs\ *n* [ME *cors*, fr. MF] *archaic* (14c) **:** CORPSE

corse·let *for 1* ˈkȯr-slət, *for 2* ˌkȯr-sə-ˈlet\ *n* (1500) **1** *or* **cors·let** [MF, dim. of *cors* body, bodice] **a :** a piece of armor covering the trunk but usu. not the arms or legs **b :** a pikeman's armor including helmet **2** *or* **cor·se·lette** [fr. *Corselette*, a trademark] **:** an undergarment combining girdle and brassiere

1cor·set \ˈkȯr-sət\ *n* [ME, fr. OF, dim. of *cors*] (13c) **1 :** a usu. close-fitting and often laced medieval jacket **2 :** a woman's close-fitting boned supporting undergarment that is often hooked and laced and that extends from above or beneath the bust or from the waist to below the hips and has garters attached

2corset *vt* (ca. 1847) **1 :** to dress in or fit with a corset **2 :** to restrict closely **:** control rigidly

cor·se·tiere \ˌkȯr-sə-ˈti(ə)r, -ˈtye(ə)r\ *n* [F *corsetière*, fem. of *corsetier*, fr. *corset*] (1848) **:** one who makes, fits, or sells corsets, girdles, or brassieres

cor·tege *also* **cor·tège** \kȯr-ˈtezh, ˈkȯr-ˌ\ *n* [F *cortège*, fr. It *corteggio*, fr. *corteggiare* to court, fr. *corte* court, fr. L *cohort-*, *cohors* throng — more at COURT] (1648) **1 :** a train of attendants **:** RETINUE **2 :** PROCESSION; *esp* **:** a funeral procession

cor·tex \ˈkȯr-ˌteks\ *n, pl* **cor·ti·ces** \ˈkȯrt-ə-ˌsēz\ *or* **cor·tex·es** [L *cortic-*, *cortex* bark — more at CUIRASS] (1677) **1 a :** the outer or superficial part of an organ or body structure (as the kidney, adrenal gland, or a hair); *esp* **:** the outer layer of gray matter of the cerebrum and cerebellum **b :** the outer part of some organisms (as paramecia) **2 :** a plant bark or rind (as cinchona) used medicinally **3 a :** the typically parenchymatous layer of tissue external to the vascular tissue and internal to the corky or epidermal tissues of a green plant; *broadly* **:** all tissues external to the xylem **b :** an outer or investing layer of various algae, lichens, or fungi

cor·ti·cal \ˈkȯrt-i-kəl\ *adj* (1671) **1 :** of, relating to, or consisting of cortex **2 :** involving or resulting from the action or condition of the cerebral cortex — **cor·ti·cal·ly** \-k(ə-)lē\ *adv*

cortico- *comb form* **1 :** cortex ⟨*cortico*adrenal⟩ **2 :** cortical and ⟨*cortico*spinal⟩

cor·ti·coid \ˈkȯrt-i-ˌkȯid\ *n* (1941) **:** CORTICOSTEROID — **corticoid** *adj*

cor·ti·co·ste·roid \ˌkȯrt-i-kō-ˈsti(ə)r-ˌȯid *also* -ˈste(ə)r-\ *n* (1944) **:** any of various adrenal-cortex steroids (as corticosterone, cortisone, and aldosterone)

cor·ti·co·ste·rone \ˌkȯrt-ə-ˈkäs-tə-ˌrōn, -i-kō-stə-ˈ; ˌkȯrt-i-kō-ˈsti(ə)r-ˌōn, -ˈste(ə)r-\ *n* (1937) **:** a colorless crystalline steroid hormone $C_{21}H_{30}O_4$ of the adrenal cortex that is important in protein and carbohydrate metabolism

cor·ti·co·tro·pin \ˌkȯrt-i-kō-ˈtrō-pən\ *or* **cor·ti·co·tro·phin** \-fən\ *n* [*cortico-* + *-tropic* + *-in*] (1946) **:** ACTH; *also* **:** a preparation of ACTH that is used esp. in the treatment of rheumatoid arthritis and rheumatic fever

cor·tin \ˈkȯrt-ᵊn\ *n* (1928) **:** the active principle of the adrenal cortex

cor·ti·sol \ˈkȯrt-ə-ˌsȯl, -ˌzȯl, -ˌsōl, -ˌzōl\ *n* [*cortis*one + *-ol*] (1951) **:** HYDROCORTISONE

cor·ti·sone \-ˌsōn, -ˌzōn\ *n* [alter. of *corticosterone*] (1949) **:** a glucocorticoid $C_{21}H_{28}O_5$ of the adrenal cortex used esp. in the treatment of rheumatoid arthritis

co·run·dum \kə-ˈrən-dəm\ *n* [Tamil *kuruntam*, fr. Skt *kuruvinda* ruby] (1728) **:** a very hard mineral Al_2O_3 that consists of aluminum oxide occurring in massive form and as variously colored crystals which include the ruby and sapphire, that can be synthesized, and that is used as an abrasive (hardness 9, sp. gr. 3.95–4.10)

co·rus·cant \kə-ˈrəs-kənt\ *adj* (15c) **:** SHINING, GLITTERING

cor·us·cate \ˈkȯr-ə-ˌskāt, ˈkär-\ *vi* **-cat·ed; -cat·ing** [L *coruscatus*, pp. of *coruscare* to flash] (1705) **1 :** to give off or reflect light in bright beams or flashes **:** SPARKLE **2 :** to be brilliant or showy in technique or style

cor·us·ca·tion \ˌkȯr-ə-ˈskā-shən, ˌkär-\ *n* (15c) **1 :** GLITTER, SPARKLE **2 :** a flash of wit

cor·vée \ˈkȯr-ˌvā, kȯr-ˈ\ *n* [ME *corvee*, fr. MF, fr. ML *corrogata*, fr. L, fem. of *corrogatus*, pp. of *corrogare* to collect, requisition, fr. *com-* + *rogare* to ask — more at RIGHT] (14c) **1 :** unpaid labor (as on roads) due from a feudal vassal to his lord **2 :** labor exacted in lieu of taxes by public authorities esp. for highway construction or repair

corves *pl of* CORF

cor·vette \kȯr-ˈvet\ *n* [F] (1636) **1 :** a warship ranking in the old sailing navies next below a frigate **2 :** a highly maneuverable armed escort ship that is smaller than a destroyer

cor·vi·na \kȯr-ˈvē-nə\ *var of* CORBINA

cor·vine \ˈkȯr-ˌvīn\ *adj* [L *corvinus*, fr. *corvus* raven — more at RAVEN] (ca. 1656) **:** of or relating to the crows **:** resembling a crow

Cor·vus \ˈkȯr-vəs\ *n* [L (gen. *Corvi*), lit., raven] **:** a small constellation adjoining Virgo on the south

Cor·y·bant \ˈkȯr-ə-ˌbant, ˈkär-\ *n, pl* **Cor·y·bants** \-ˌban(t)s\ *or* **Cor·y·ban·tes** \ˌkȯr-ə-ˈbant-ēz, ˌkär-\ [MF *Corybante*, fr. L *Corybas*, fr. Gk *Korybas*] (14c) **:** one of the attendants or priests of Cybele noted for orgiastic processions and rites — **cor·y·ban·tic** \ˌkȯr-ə-ˈbant-ik, ˌkär-\ *adj*

co·ryd·a·lis \kə-ˈrid-ᵊl-əs\ *n* [NL, genus name, fr. Gk *korydallis* crested lark; akin to L *cornu* horn — more at HORN] (1818) **:** any of a large genus (*Corydalis*) of herbs of the fumitory family with racemose irregular flowers

cor·ymb \ˈkȯr-ˌim(b), ˈkär-, -əm(b)\ *n, pl* **corymbs** \-ˌimz, -əmz\ [F *corymbe*, fr. L *corymbus* cluster of fruit or flowers, fr. Gk *korymbos*] (1776) **:** a flat-topped inflorescence; *specif* **:** one in which the flower stalks arise at different levels on the main axis and reach about the same height and in which the outer flowers open first and the inflorescence is indeterminate — **cor·ymbed** \-ˌimd, -əmd\ *adj* — **cor·ym·bose** \-əm-ˌbōs\ *adj* — **cor·ym·bose·ly** *adv*

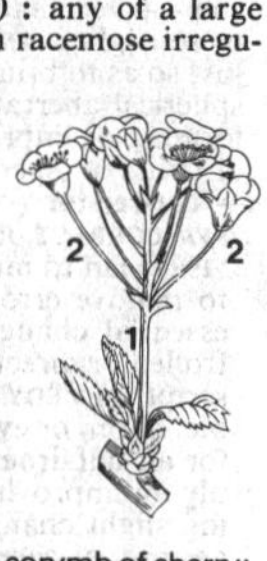

corymb of cherry: *1* peduncle, *2* pedicels

co·ry·ne·bac·te·ri·um \ˌkȯr-ə-(ˌ)nē-bak-ˈtir-ē-əm, kə-ˌrin-ə-\ *n* [NL, genus name, fr. Gk *korynē* club; akin to L *cornu* horn] (1973) **:** any of a large genus (*Corynebacterium*) of usu. gram-positive nonmotile bacteria that occur as irregular or branching rods and include numerous important parasites of man, lower animals, and plants — **co·ry·ne·bac·te·ri·al** \-ē-əl\ *adj*

co·ryne·form \kə-ˈrin-ə-ˌfȯrm\ *adj* (1952) **:** being or resembling corynebacteria

cor·y·phae·us \ˌkȯr-ə-ˈfē-əs, ˌkär-\ *n, pl* **-phaei** \-ˈfē-ˌī\ [L, leader, fr. Gk *koryphaios*, fr. *koryphē* summit; akin to L *cornu*] (1611) **1 :** the leader of a chorus **2 :** the leader of a party or school of thought

co·ry·phée \ˌkȯr-i-ˈfā\ *n* [F, fr. L *coryphaeus*] (1828) **:** a ballet dancer who dances in a small group instead of in the corps de ballet or as a soloist

co·ry·za \kə-ˈrī-zə\ *n* [LL, fr. Gk *koryza* nasal mucus; akin to OHG *hroz* nasal mucus, Skt *kardama* mud] (1634) **:** an acute inflammatory contagious disease involving the upper respiratory tract; *esp* **:** COMMON COLD — **co·ry·zal** \-zəl\ *adj*

co·se·cant \(ˈ)kō-ˈsē-ˌkant, -kənt\ *n* [NL *cosecant-*, *cosecans*, fr. *co-* + *secant-*, *secans* secant] (ca. 1706) **:** the trigonometric function that for an acute angle is the ratio between the hypotenuse of a right triangle of which the angle is considered part and the leg opposite the angle

co·set \ˈkō-ˌset\ *n* (1928) **:** a subset of a mathematical group that consists of all the products obtained by multiplying either on the right or the left a fixed element of the group by each of the elements of a given subgroup

1cosh \ˈkäsh\ *n* [perh. fr. Romany *kosh* stick] *chiefly Brit* (1869) **:** a weighted weapon similar to a blackjack

2cosh *vt, chiefly Brit* (1896) **:** to strike or assault with or as if with a cosh

co·sig·na·to·ry \(ˈ)kō-ˈsig-nə-ˌtōr-ē, -ˌtȯr-\ *n* (1865) **:** a joint signer

co·sign·er \ˈkō-ˌsī-nər\ *n* (1903) **:** COSIGNATORY; *esp* **:** a joint signer of a promissory note

co·sine \ˈkō-ˌsīn\ *n* [NL *cosinus*, fr. *co-* + ML *sinus* sine] (1635) **:** the trigonometric function that for an acute angle is the ratio between the leg adjacent to the angle when it is considered part of a right triangle and the hypotenuse

cos lettuce \ˈkäs-, ˈkōs-\ *n* [*Kos*, *Cos*, Gk island] (1699) **:** ROMAINE

1cos·met·ic \käz-ˈmet-ik\ *n* (1650) **:** something that is cosmetic; *specif* **:** a cosmetic preparation for external use

2cosmetic *adj* [Gk *kosmētikos* skilled in adornment, fr. *kosmein* to arrange, adorn, fr. *kosmos* order] (1650) **1 :** of, relating to, or making for beauty esp. of the complexion **:** BEAUTIFYING ⟨~ salves⟩ **2 :** done or made for the sake of appearance: as **a :** correcting defects esp. of the face ⟨~ surgery⟩ **b :** DECORATIVE, ORNAMENTAL **c :** not substantive **:** SUPERFICIAL ⟨~ changes⟩ — **cos·met·i·cal·ly** \-i-k(ə-)lē\ *adv*

cosmetic case *n* (1948) **:** a small piece of luggage esp. for cosmetics

cos·me·ti·cian \ˌkäz-mə-ˈtish-ən\ *n* (1919) **:** one who is professionally trained in the use of cosmetics

cos·met·i·cize \käz-ˈmet-ə-ˌsīz\ *vt* **-cized; -ciz·ing** (1824) **:** to make (something unpleasant or ugly) superficially attractive

cos·me·tol·o·gist \ˌkäz-mə-ˈtäl-ə-jəst\ *n* (1926) **:** one who gives beauty treatments (as to skin and hair) — called also *beautician*

cos·me·tol·o·gy \-jē\ *n* [F *cosmétologie*, fr. *cosmétique* cosmetic (fr. E *cosmetic*) + *-logie* -logy] (1847) **:** the cosmetic treatment of the skin, hair, and nails

cos·mic \ˈkäz-mik\ *also* **cos·mi·cal** \-mi-kəl\ *adj* [Gk *kosmikos*, fr. *kosmos* order, universe] (1838) **1 :** of or relating to the cosmos, the extraterrestrial vastness, or the universe in contrast to the earth alone **2 :** characterized by greatness esp. in extent, intensity, or comprehensiveness — **cos·mi·cal·ly** \-mi-k(ə-)lē\ *adv*

cosmic dust *n* (1881) **:** very fine particles of solid matter found in any part of the universe

cosmic noise *n* (1947) **:** unidentified celestial radio-frequency radiation; *esp* **:** such radiation originating from outside the Milky Way

cosmic ray *n* (1925) **:** a stream of atomic nuclei of heterogeneous extremely penetrating character that enter the earth's atmosphere from outer space at speeds approaching that of light and bombard atmospheric atoms to produce secondary particles (as mesons) possessing some of the original energy

cos·mo·chem·is·try \ˌkäz-mō-ˈkem-ə-strē\ *n* [Gk *kosmos* universe] (1940) **:** a branch of chemistry that deals with the chemical composition and changes in the universe — **cos·mo·chem·i·cal** \-ˈkem-i-kəl\ *adj*

cos·mo·gen·ic \ˌkäz-mə-ˈjen-ik\ *adj* [*cosmic* ray + *-o-* + *-genic*] (1883) **:** produced by the action of cosmic rays ⟨~ carbon 14⟩

cos·mog·o·ny \käz-ˈmäg-ə-nē\ *n, pl* **-nies** [NL *cosmogonia*, fr. Gk *kosmogonia*, fr. *kosmos* + *gonos* offspring; akin to Gk *genos* race — more at KIN] (1766) **1 :** the creation or origin of the world or universe **2 :** a theory of the origin of the universe — **cos·mo·gon·ic** \ˌkäz-mə-ˈgän-ik\ *or* **cos·mo·gon·i·cal** \-i-kəl\ *adj* — **cos·mog·o·nist** \käz-ˈmäg-ə-nəst\ *n*

cos·mog·ra·phy \käz-ˈmäg-rə-fē\ *n, pl* **-phies** [ME *cosmographie*, fr. LL *cosmographia*, fr. Gk *kosmographia*, fr. *kosmos* + *-graphia*

-graphy] (14c) **1 :** a general description of the world or of the universe **2 :** the science that deals with the constitution of the whole order of nature — **cos·mog·ra·pher** \-fər\ *n* — **cos·mo·graph·ic** \ˌkäz-mə-ˈgraf-ik\ *or* **cos·mo·graph·i·cal** \-i-kəl\ *adj* — **cos·mo·graph·i·cal·ly** \-i-k(ə-)lē\ *adv*

Cos·mo·line \ˈkäz-mə-ˌlēn\ *trademark* — used for petrolatum

cos·mol·o·gy \käz-ˈmäl-ə-jē\ *n, pl* **-gies** [NL *cosmologia,* fr. Gk *kosmos* + NL *-logia* -logy] (1656) **1 :** a branch of metaphysics that deals with the nature of the universe **2 :** a branch of astronomy that deals with the origin, structure, and space-time relationships of the universe; *also* **:** a theory dealing with these matters — **cos·mo·log·i·cal** \ˌkäz-mə-ˈläj-i-kəl\ *adj* — **cos·mo·log·i·cal·ly** \-i-k(ə-)lē\ *adv* — **cos·mol·o·gist** \käz-ˈmäl-ə-jəst\ *n*

cos·mo·naut \ˈkäz-mə-ˌnȯt, -ˌnät\ *n* [part trans. of Russ *kosmonavt,* fr. Gk *kosmos* + Russ *-navt* (as in *aeronavt* aeronaut)] (1959) **:** a Soviet traveler beyond the earth's atmosphere **:** ASTRONAUT

cos·mop·o·lis \käz-ˈmäp-ə-ləs\ *n* [NL, back-formation fr. *cosmopolites*] (1892) **:** a cosmopolitan city

[1]**cos·mo·pol·i·tan** \ˌkäz-mə-ˈpäl-ət-ᵊn\ *n* (1645) **:** COSMOPOLITE

[2]**cosmopolitan** *adj* (1844) **1 :** having worldwide rather than limited or provincial scope or bearing **2 :** having wide international sophistication **:** WORLDLY **3 :** composed of persons, constituents, or elements from all or many parts of the world **4 :** found in most parts of the world and under varied ecological conditions ⟨a ~ herb⟩ — **cos·mo·pol·i·tan·ism** \-ᵊn-ˌiz-əm\ *n*

cos·mop·o·lite \käz-ˈmäp-ə-ˌlīt\ *n* [NL *cosmopolites,* fr. Gk *kosmopolitēs,* fr. *kosmos* + *politēs* citizen] (1595) **:** a cosmopolitan person or organism — **cos·mo·po·li·tism** \käz-ˈmäp-ə-ˌlīt-ˌiz-əm, -lə-ˌtiz-; ˌkäz-mə-ˈpäl-ə-ˌtiz-\ *n*

cos·mos \ˈkäz-məs, *1 & 2 also* -ˌmōs, -ˌmäs\ *n* [Gk *kosmos*] (13c) **1 a :** an orderly harmonious systematic universe — compare CHAOS **b :** ORDER, HARMONY **2 :** a complex orderly self-inclusive system **3** *pl* **cosmos** \-məs, -məz\ *also* **cos·mos·es** \-mə-səz\ [NL, genus name, fr. Gk *kosmos*] **:** any of a genus (*Cosmos*) of tropical American composite herbs; *esp* **:** a widely cultivated tall fall-blooming annual (*C. bipinnatus*) with yellow or red disks and showy ray flowers

cos·sack \ˈkäs-ˌak, -ək\ *n* [Russ *kazak* & Ukrainian *kozak,* fr. Turk *kazak* free person] (1589) **:** a member of a group of frontiersmen of southern Russia organized as cavalry in the czarist army

[1]**cos·set** \ˈkäs-ət\ *n* [origin unknown] (1579) **:** a pet lamb; *broadly* **:** PET

[2]**cosset** *vt* (1659) **:** to treat as a pet **:** PAMPER

[1]**cost** \ˈkȯst\ *n* (13c) **1 a :** the amount or equivalent paid or charged for something **:** PRICE **b :** the outlay or expenditure (as of effort or sacrifice) made to achieve an object **2 :** loss or penalty incurred in gaining something **3** *pl* **:** expenses incurred in litigation; *esp* **:** those given by the law or the court to the prevailing party against the losing party — **cost·less** \-ləs\ *adj* — **cost·less·ly** *adv*

[2]**cost** *vb* **cost; cost·ing** [ME *costen,* fr. MF *coster,* fr. (assumed) VL *costare,* fr. L *constare* to stand firm, to cost — more at CONSTANT] *vi* (14c) **1 :** to require expenditure or payment ⟨the best goods ~ more⟩ **2 :** to require effort, suffering, or loss ~ *vt* **1 :** to have a price of **2 :** to cause (someone) to pay, suffer, or lose something ⟨frequent absences ~ him his job⟩ **3** *past* **cost·ed :** to estimate or set the cost of

cos·ta \ˈkäs-tə\ *n, pl* **cos·tae** \-(ˌ)tē, -ˌtī\ [L — more at COAST] (ca. 1860) **1 :** [1]RIB 1a **2 :** a part (as the midrib of a leaf or the anterior vein of an insect wing) that resembles a rib — **cos·tal** \-tᵊl\ *adj*

cost accountant *n* (1918) **:** a specialist in cost accounting

cost accounting *n* (1913) **:** the systematic recording and analysis of the costs of material, labor, and overhead incident to production

cos·tard \ˈkäs-tərd\ *n* [ME] (13c) **1 :** any of several large English cooking apples **2** *archaic* **:** NODDLE, PATE

cost–ben·e·fit \(ˈ)kȯs(t)-ˈben-ə-ˌfit\ *adj* (1963) **:** of, relating to, or being economic analysis that assigns a numerical value to the cost-effectiveness of usu. industrial operations or procedures

cost–ef·fec·tive \ˌkȯs-tə-ˈfek-tiv\ *adj* (1967) **:** economical in terms of tangible benefits produced by money spent ⟨~ measures to combat poverty⟩ — **cost–ef·fec·tive·ness** *n*

cos·ter \ˈkäs-tər\ *n, Brit* (1851) **:** COSTERMONGER

cos·ter·mon·ger \-ˌməŋ-gər, -ˌmäŋ-\ *n* [*costard* + *monger*] *Brit* (1514) **:** a hawker of fruit or vegetables

cos·tive \ˈkäs-tiv, ˈkȯs-\ *adj* [ME, fr. MF *costivé,* pp. of *costiver* to constipate, fr. L *constipare*] (15c) **1 a :** affected with constipation **b :** causing constipation **2 :** slow in action or expression **3 :** NIGGARDLY — **cos·tive·ly** *adv* — **cos·tive·ness** *n*

cost·ly \ˈkȯs(t)-lē\ *adj* **cost·li·er; -est** (14c) **1 a :** commanding a high price esp. because of intrinsic worth ⟨~ gems⟩ **b :** RICH, SPLENDID **2 :** made or done at heavy expense or sacrifice ⟨a ~ mistake⟩ — **cost·li·ness** *n*

cost·mary \ˈkȯst-ˌmer-ē, ˈkäst-\ *n, pl* **-mar·ies** [ME *costmarie,* fr. *coste* costmary (fr. OE *cost,* fr. L *costum,* fr. Gk *kostos,* a fragrant root) + *Marie* the Virgin Mary] (14c) **:** a tansy-scented composite herb (*Chrysanthemum majus*) used as a potherb and in flavoring

cost of living (1896) **:** the cost of purchasing those goods and services which are included in an accepted standard level of consumption

cost–of–living index *n* (1913) **:** CONSUMER PRICE INDEX

cost–plus \ˈkȯs(t)-ˈpləs\ *adj* (1918) **1 :** paid on the basis of a fixed fee or a percentage added to actual cost ⟨a ~ contract⟩ **2 :** of or relating to a cost-plus contract

cost–push \ˈkȯs(t)-ˌpu̇sh\ *n* (1951) **:** an increase or upward trend in production costs (as wages) that tends to result in increased consumer prices irrespective of the level of demand — compare DEMAND-PULL — **cost–push** *adj*

cos·trel \ˈkäs-trəl\ *n* [ME, fr. MF *costerel,* fr. *costier* at the side, fr. *coste* rib, side — more at COAST] (14c) **:** a flat usu. earthenware container for liquids with loops through which a belt or cord may be passed for easy carrying — called also *pilgrim bottle*

[1]**cos·tume** \ˈkäs-ˌt(y)üm *also* -təm *or* -ˌchüm\ *n* [F, fr. It, custom, dress, fr. L *consuetudin-, consuetudo* custom — more at CUSTOM] (1715) **1 :** the prevailing fashion in coiffure, jewelry, and apparel of a period, country, or class **2 :** an outfit worn to create the appearance characteristic of a particular period, person, place, or thing ⟨Halloween ~s⟩ **3 :** a person's ensemble of outer garments; *esp* **:** a woman's ensemble of dress with coat or jacket — **cos·tum·ey** *adj*

[2]**cos·tume** \käs-ˈt(y)üm *also* -ˈchüm; *or like* [1]\ *vt* **cos·tumed; cos·tum·ing** (1823) **1 :** to provide with a costume **2 :** to design costumes for ⟨~ a play⟩

[3]**costume** *like* [1]\ *adj* (1884) **1 :** characterized by the use of costumes ⟨a ~ ball⟩ ⟨a ~ drama⟩ **2 :** suitable for or enhancing the effect of a particular costume ⟨a ~ handbag⟩

costume jewelry *n* (1933) **:** inexpensive jewelry designed for wear with current fashions

cos·tum·er \ˈkäs-ˌt(y)ü-mər *also* -ˌchü-; käs-ˈ\ *n* (ca. 1864) **1 :** one that deals in or makes costumes **2 :** CLOTHES TREE

cos·tum·ery \-mə-rē\ *n* (1838) **1 :** articles of costume **2 :** the art of costuming

cos·tu·mi·er \käs-ˈt(y)ü-mē-ˌā, -mē-ər\ *n* [F] *chiefly Brit* (1831) **:** COSTUMER 1

co·sy \ˈkō-zē\ *var of* COZY

[1]**cot** \ˈkät\ *n* [ME, fr. OE; akin to ON *kot* small hut, L *guttur* throat] (bef. 12c) **1 :** a small house **2 :** COVER, SHEATH; *esp* **:** STALL 4

[2]**cot** *n* [Hindi *khāṭ* bedstead, fr. Skt *khaṭvā,* of Dravidian origin; akin to Tamil *kaṭṭil* bedstead] (1634) **:** a small usu. collapsible bed often of fabric stretched on a frame

co·tan·gent \(ˈ)kō-ˈtan-jənt\ *n* [NL *cotangent-, cotangens,* fr. *co-* + *tangent-, tangens* tangent] (1635) **:** the trigonometric function that for an acute angle is the ratio between the leg adjacent to the angle when it is considered part of a right triangle and the leg opposite

[1]**cote** \ˈkōt, ˈkät\ *n* [ME, fr. OE] (bef. 12c) **1** *dial Eng* **:** [1]COT 1 **2 :** a shed or coop for small domestic animals and esp. pigeons

[2]**cote** \ˈkōt\ *vt* [prob. fr. MF *cotoyer*] *obs* (1555) **:** to pass by

co·te·rie \ˈkōt-ə-(ˌ)rē, ˌkōt-ə-ˈ\ *n* [F, fr. MF, tenants, fr. OF *cotier* cotter, of Gmc origin; akin to OE *cot* hut] (1738) **:** an intimate and often exclusive group of persons with a unifying common interest or purpose; *broadly* **:** SET 18

co·ter·mi·nous \(ˈ)kō-ˈtər-mə-nəs\ *adj* [alter. of *conterminous*] (1799) **1 :** having the same or coincident boundaries ⟨~ states⟩ **2 :** coextensive in scope or duration ⟨~ interests⟩ — **co·ter·mi·nous·ly** *adv*

co·thur·nus \kō-ˈthər-nəs\ *n, pl* **-ni** \-ˌnī, -(ˌ)nē\ [L, fr. Gk *kothornos*] (1606) **1 :** a high thick-soled laced boot worn by actors in Greek and Roman tragic drama — called also *co·thurn* \ˈkō-ˌthərn, kō-ˈ\ **2 :** the dignified somewhat stilted style of ancient tragedy

co·tid·al \(ˈ)kō-ˈtīd-ᵊl\ *adj* (1833) **:** indicating equality in the tides or a coincidence in the time of high or low tide

co·til·lion \kō-ˈtil-yən\ *also* **co·til·lon** \kō-ˈtil-yən, kō-tē-(y)ōⁿ\ *n* [F *cotillon,* lit., petticoat, fr. OF, fr. *cote* coat] (1766) **1 :** a ballroom dance for couples that resembles the quadrille **2 :** an elaborate dance with frequent changing of partners carried out under the leadership of one couple at formal balls **3 :** a formal ball

co·to·neas·ter \kə-ˈtō-nē-ˌas-tər, ˈkät-ᵊn-ˌēs-\ *n* [NL, genus name, fr. L *cydonia, cotoneum* quince + NL *-aster*] (1882) **:** any of a genus (*Cotoneaster*) of Old World flowering shrubs of the rose family

cot·quean \ˈkät-ˌkwēn\ *n* (1592) **1** *archaic* **:** a coarse masculine woman **2** *archaic* **:** a man who busies himself with women's work or affairs

Cots·wold \ˈkät-ˌswōld\ *n* [*Cotswold* hills, England] (ca. 1658) **:** a sheep of an English breed of large long-wooled sheep

cot·ta \ˈkät-ə\ *n* [ML, of Gmc origin; akin to OHG *kozza* coarse mantle — more at COAT] (1848) **:** a waist-length surplice

cot·tage \ˈkät-ij\ *n* [ME *cotage,* fr. (assumed) AF, fr. ME *cot* — more at COT] (14c) **1 :** the dwelling of a farm laborer or small farmer **2 :** a small usu. frame one-family house **3 :** a small detached dwelling unit at an institution **4 :** a small house for vacation use — **cot·tag·ey** \-ij-ē\ *adj*

cottage cheese *n* (1848) **:** a bland soft white cheese made from the curds of skim milk — called also *Dutch cheese, pot cheese, smearcase*

cottage curtains *n pl* (1943) **:** a double set of upper and lower straight-hanging window curtains

cottage industry *n* (1921) **1 :** an industry whose labor force consists of family units working at home with their own equipment **2 :** a small and often informally organized industry

cottage pudding *n* (1909) **:** plain cake covered with a hot sweet sauce

cot·tag·er \ˈkät-ij-ər\ *n* (1550) **:** one who lives in a cottage

cottage tulip *n* (1928) **:** any of various tall-growing tulips that flower in the middle of the tulip-flowering season

[1]**cot·ter** *or* **cot·tar** \ˈkät-ər\ *n* [ME *cottar,* fr. ML *cotarius,* fr. ME *cot*] (14c) **:** a peasant or farm laborer who occupies a cottage and sometimes a small holding of land usu. in return for services

[2]**cotter** *n* [origin unknown] (14c) **1 :** a wedge-shaped or tapered piece used to fasten together parts of a structure **2 :** COTTER PIN

cotter pin *n* (1881) **:** a half-round metal strip bent into a pin whose ends can be flared after insertion through a slot or hole

[1]**cot·ton** \ˈkät-ᵊn\ *n, often attrib* [ME *coton,* fr. MF, fr. Ar *quṭn*] (14c) **1 a :** a soft usu. white fibrous substance composed of the hairs surrounding the seeds of various erect freely branching tropical plants (genus *Gossypium*) of the mallow family **b :** a plant producing cotton; *esp* **:** one grown for its cotton **c :** a crop of cotton **2 a :** fabric made of cotton **b :** yarn spun from cotton **3 :** a downy cottony substance produced by various plants (as the cottonwood)

[2]**cotton** *vi* **cot·toned; cot·ton·ing** \ˈkät-niŋ, -ᵊn-iŋ\ (1605) **1 :** to take a liking ⟨~s to people easily⟩ **2 :** to come to understand — used with *to* or *on to* ⟨~*ed* on to the fact that our children work furiously —H. M. McLuhan⟩

cotton candy *n* (1926) **:** a candy made of spun sugar

cotton gin *n* (1796) **:** a machine that separates the seeds, hulls, and foreign material from cotton

cotton grass *n* (1597) **:** any of a genus (*Eriophorum*) of sedges with tufted spikes

cot·ton·mouth \ˈkät-ᵊn-ˌmau̇th\ *n* [so called fr. the white interior of its mouth] (1832) **:** WATER MOCCASIN

cottonmouth moccasin *n* (1879) **:** WATER MOCCASIN

cot·ton–pick·ing \ˌkät-ᵊn-ˌpik-iŋ, -ˌpik-ən\ *adj* (1952) **1 :** DAMNED — used as a generalized expression of disapproval ⟨a ~ hypocrite⟩ **2 :** DAMNED — used as an intensive ⟨out of his ~ mind —Irving Kristol⟩
cot·ton·seed \ˈkät-ᵊn-ˌsēd\ *n* (1774) **:** the seed of the cotton plant
cottonseed oil *n* (1833) **:** a pale yellow semidrying fatty oil that is obtained from the cottonseed and is used chiefly in salad and cooking oils and after hydrogenation in shortenings and margarine
cotton stainer *n* (1856) **:** any of several red and black or dark brown bugs (genus *Dysdercus*) that damage and stain the lint of developing cotton; *specif* **:** a red and brown bug (*D. suturellus*) that attacks cotton in the southern U.S.
cot·ton·tail \ˈkät-ᵊn-ˌtāl\ *n* (1869) **:** any of several rather small No. American rabbits (genus *Sylvilagus*) sandy brown in color with a white-tufted underside of the tail
cot·ton·weed \-ˌwēd\ *n* (1562) **:** any of various weedy plants (as cudweed) with hoary pubescence or cottony seeds
cot·ton·wood \-ˌwu̇d\ *n* (1802) **:** a poplar with a tuft of cottony hairs on the seed; *esp* **:** one (*Populus deltoides*) of the eastern and central U.S. often cultivated for its rapid growth and luxuriant foliage
cotton wool *n* (14c) **:** raw cotton; *esp* **:** cotton batting
cot·tony \ˈkät-nē, -ᵊn-ē\ *adj* (1578) **:** resembling cotton in appearance or character: as **a :** covered with hairs or pubescence **b :** SOFT
cot·tony–cush·ion scale \-ˈku̇sh-ən-\ *n* (1886) **:** a scale insect (*Icerya purchasi*) introduced into the U.S. from Australia that infests citrus and other plants
cotyl- *or* **cotyli-** *or* **cotylo-** *comb form* [Gk *kotyl-, kotylo-,* fr. *kotylē* cup; akin to L *catinus* bowl — more at KETTLE] **:** cup **:** organ or part like a cup ⟨*cotyl*oid⟩ ⟨*cotyli*form⟩
-cot·yl \ˌkät-ᵊl\ *n comb form* [*cotyledon*] **:** cotyledon ⟨di*cotyl*⟩
cot·y·le·don \ˌkät-ᵊl-ˈēd-ᵊn\ *n* [NL, fr. Gk *kotylēdōn* cup-shaped hollow, fr. *kotylē*] (1540) **1 :** a lobule of the mammalian placenta **2 :** the first leaf or one of the first pair or whorl of leaves developed by the embryo of a seed plant or of some lower plants (as ferns) — **cot·y·le·don·ary** \-ˈēd-ᵊn-ˌer-ē\ *adj*
co·ty·lo·saur \ˈkät-ᵊl-ō-ˌsȯ(ə)r, kə-ˈtil-ə-\ *n* [NL *Cotylosauria,* group name, deriv. of Gk *kotylē* & *sauros* lizard] (1902) **:** any of an order (Cotylosauria) of extinct ancient primitive reptiles with short legs and massive bodies that were prob. the earliest truly terrestrial vertebrate animals
co·type \ˈkō-ˌtīp\ *n* (1893) **:** any of several secondary taxonomic types
[1]**couch** \ˈkau̇ch\ *vb* [ME *couchen,* fr. MF *coucher,* fr. L *collocare* to set in place — more at COLLOCATE] *vt* (14c) **1 :** to lay (oneself) down for rest or sleep **2 :** to embroider (a design) by laying down a thread and fastening it with small stitches at regular intervals **3 :** to place or hold level and pointed forward ready for use **4 :** to phrase or express in a specified manner ⟨the memorandum was ~*ed* in strong language —W. L. Shirer⟩ **5 :** to treat (a cataract) by displacing the lens of the eye into the vitreous humor ~ *vi* **1 :** to lie down or recline for sleep or rest **2 :** to lie in ambush
[2]**couch** *n* (14c) **1 a :** an article of furniture (as a bed or sofa) for sitting or reclining **b :** a couch on which a patient reclines when undergoing psychoanalysis **2 :** the den of an animal (as an otter) — **on the couch :** receiving psychiatric treatment
couch·ant \ˈkau̇-chənt\ *adj* [ME, fr. MF, fr. prp. of *coucher*] (15c) **:** lying down esp. with the head up ⟨a heraldic lion ~⟩
couch grass \ˈkau̇ch-, ˈküch-\ *n* [alter. of *quitch* (grass)] (1790) **1 :** QUACK GRASS **2 :** any of several grasses that resemble quack grass in spreading by creeping rhizomes
couch potato *n* (1983) **:** a person who spends a great deal of time watching television
cou·dé \kü-ˈdā\ *adj* [F *coudé* bent like an elbow, fr. *coude* elbow, fr. L *cubitum* — more at HIP] (1888) **1** *of a telescope* **:** constructed so that the light is reflected along the polar axis to come to a focus at a fixed place where the holder for a photographic plate or a spectrograph may be mounted **2 :** of or relating to a coudé telescope
cou·gar \ˈkü-gər *also* -ˌgär\ *n, pl* **cougars** *also* **cougar** [F *couguar,* fr. NL *cuguacuarana,* modif. of Tupi *suasuarana,* lit., false deer, fr. *suasú* deer + *rana* false] (1774) **:** a large powerful tawny brown cat (*Felis concolor*) formerly widespread in the Americas but now extinct in many areas — called also *catamount, mountain lion, panther, puma*

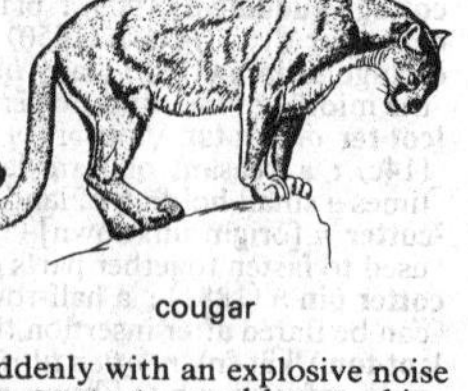
cougar

[1]**cough** \ˈkȯf\ *vb* [ME *coughen,* fr. (assumed) OE *cohhian;* akin to MHG *küchen* to breathe heavily] *vi* (14c) **1 :** to expel air from the lungs suddenly with an explosive noise **2 :** to make a noise like that of coughing ~ *vt* **:** to expel by coughing — often used with *up* ⟨~ up mucus⟩
[2]**cough** *n* (14c) **1 :** a condition marked by repeated or frequent coughing **2 :** an act or sound of coughing
cough drop *n* (1831) **:** a lozenge or troche used to relieve coughing
cough syrup *n* (1877) **:** any of various sweet usu. medicated liquids used to relieve coughing
cough up *vt* (1894) **:** HAND OVER, DELIVER ⟨*cough up* the money⟩
could \kəd, (ˈ)ku̇d\ [ME *couthe, coude,* fr. OE *cūthe;* akin to OHG *konda* could] (bef. 12c) *past of* CAN — used in auxiliary function in the past ⟨we found we ~ go⟩, in the past conditional ⟨we said we would go if we ~⟩, and as an alternative to *can* suggesting less force or certainty or as a polite form in the present ⟨~ you do this for me⟩ ⟨if you ~ come we would be pleased⟩
could·est \ˈku̇d-əst\ *archaic past 2d sing of* CAN
couldn't \ˈku̇d-ᵊnt, -ᵊn, *dial also* ˈku̇t-ᵊn(t) *or* (ˈ)ku̇nt\ **:** could not
couldst \kədst, (ˈ)ku̇dst, kətst, (ˈ)ku̇tst\ *archaic past 2d sing of* CAN
cou·lee \ˈkü-lē\ *n* [CanF *coulée,* fr. F, flowing, flow of lava, fr. *couler* to flow, fr. L *colare* to strain, fr. *colum* sieve] (1807) **1 a :** a small stream **b :** a dry streambed **c :** a usu. small or shallow ravine **:** GULLY **2 :** a thick sheet or stream of lava
cou·lisse \kü-ˈlēs, -ˈlis\ *n* [F] (1819) **1 a :** a side scene of a stage; *also* **:** the space between the side scenes **b :** a backstage area **c :** HALLWAY **2 :** a piece of timber having a groove in which something glides
cou·loir \kül-ˈwär\ *n* [F, lit., strainer, fr. LL *colatorium,* fr. L *colatus,* pp. of *colare*] (1822) **:** a mountainside gorge esp. in the Swiss Alps
[1]**cou·lomb** \ˈkü-ˌläm, -ˌlōm, kü-ˈ\ *n* [Charles A. de *Coulomb*] (ca. 1881) **:** the practical meter-kilogram-second unit of electric charge equal to the quantity of electricity transferred by a current of one ampere in one second
[2]**coulomb** *or* **cou·lom·bic** \kü-ˈläm-(b)ik, -ˈlōm-\ *adj* (ca. 1889) **:** of, relating to, or being the electrostatic force of attraction or repulsion between charged particles
cou·lo·me·ter \ˈkü-lə(m)-ˌmēt-ər, kü-ˈläm-ət-ər\ *n* [alter. of *coulombmeter,* fr. *coulomb* + *-meter*] (ca. 1889) **:** an instrument of chemical analysis that determines the amount of a substance released in electrolysis by measurement of the quantity of electricity used — **cou·lo·met·ric** \ˌkü-lə-ˈme-trik\ *adj* — **cou·lo·met·ri·cal·ly** \-tri-k(ə-)lē\ *adv* — **cou·lom·e·try** \kü-ˈläm-ə-trē\ *n*
coul·ter \ˈkōl-tər\ *n* [ME *colter,* fr. OE *culter* & OF *coltre,* both fr. L *culter* plowshare; akin to Gk *skallein* to hoe — more at SHELL] (bef. 12c) **:** a cutting tool (as a knife or sharp disc) that is attached to the beam of a plow, makes a vertical cut in the surface, and permits clean separation and effective covering of the soil and materials being turned under
cou·ma·rin \ˈkü-mə-rən\ *n* [F *coumarine,* fr. *coumarou* tonka bean tree, fr. Sp or Pg; Sp *coumarú,* fr. Pg, fr. Tupi] (1830) **:** a toxic white crystalline lactone $C_9H_6O_2$ with an odor of new-mown hay found in plants or made synthetically and used esp. in perfumery
cou·ma·rone \-ˌrōn\ *n* [ISV *coumarin* + *-one*] (1883) **:** a compound C_8H_6O found in coal tar and polymerized with indene to form thermoplastic resins used esp. in adhesives and printing inks — called also *benzofuran*
[1]**coun·cil** \ˈkau̇n(t)-səl\ *n* [ME *counceil,* fr. OF *concile,* fr. L *concilium,* fr. *com-* + *calare* to call — more at LOW] (12c) **1 :** an assembly or meeting for consultation, advice, or discussion **2 :** a group elected or appointed as an advisory or legislative body **3 a :** a usu. administrative body **b :** an executive body whose members are equal in power and authority **c :** a governing body of delegates from local units of a federation **4 :** deliberation in a council **5 a :** a federation of or a central body uniting a group of organizations **b :** a local chapter of an organization **c :** CLUB, SOCIETY
[2]**council** *adj* (14c) **1** *Brit* **:** built, maintained, or operated by a local governing agency ⟨~ housing⟩ ⟨~ flats⟩ **2 :** used for councils esp. by or with No. American Indians ⟨a ~ ground⟩
coun·cil·lor *or* **coun·cil·or** \ˈkau̇n(t)-s(ə-)lər\ *n* (13c) **:** a member of a council — **coun·cil·lor·ship** \-ˌship\ *n*
coun·cil·man \ˈkau̇n(t)-səl-mən\ *n* (1659) **:** a member of a council (as of a town or city) — **coun·cil·man·ic** \ˌkau̇n(t)-səl-ˈman-ik\ *adj*
council of ministers *often cap C&M* (ca. 1909) **:** CABINET 3b
coun·cil·wom·an \ˈkau̇n(t)-səl-ˌwu̇m-ən\ *n* (1928) **:** a female member of a council
[1]**coun·sel** \ˈkau̇n(t)-səl\ *n* [ME *conseil,* fr. OF, fr. L *consilium,* fr. *consulere* to consult; akin to Gk *helein* to take — more at SELL] (13c) **1 a :** advice given esp. as a result of consultation **b :** a policy or plan of action or behavior **2 :** DELIBERATION, CONSULTATION **3 a** *archaic* **:** PURPOSE **b :** guarded thoughts or intentions **4 a** *pl* **counsel** (1) **:** a lawyer engaged in the trial or management of a case in court (2) **:** a lawyer appointed to advise and represent in legal matters an individual client or a corporate and esp. a public body **b :** CONSULTANT 2 *syn* see ADVICE
[2]**counsel** *vb* **-seled** *or* **-selled; -sel·ing** *or* **-sel·ling** \-s(ə-)liŋ\ *vt* (14c) **:** ADVISE ⟨~*ed* them to avoid rash actions —George Orwell⟩ ~ *vi* **:** CONSULT ⟨~*ed* with her husband⟩
coun·sel·ee \ˌkau̇n(t)-sə-ˈlē\ *n* (1923) **:** one who is being counseled
coun·sel·ing *n* (1915) **:** professional guidance of the individual by utilizing psychological methods esp. in collecting case history data, using various techniques of the personal interview, and testing interests and aptitudes
coun·sel·or *or* **coun·sel·lor** \ˈkau̇n(t)-s(ə-)lər\ *n* (13c) **1 :** ADVISER **2 :** LAWYER; *specif* **:** one that gives advice in law and manages cases for clients in court **3 :** one who has supervisory duties at a summer camp — **coun·sel·or·ship** \-ˌship\ *n*
counselor–at–law *n, pl* **counselors–at–law** (1654) **:** COUNSELOR 2
[1]**count** \ˈkau̇nt\ *vb* [ME *counten,* fr. MF *conter, compter,* fr. L *computare,* fr. *com-* + *putare* to consider — more at PAVE] *vt* (14c) **1 a :** to indicate or name by units or groups so as to find the total number of units involved **:** NUMBER **b :** to name the numbers in order up to and including ⟨~ ten⟩ **c :** to include in a tallying and reckoning ⟨about 100 present, ~*ing* children⟩ **d :** to call aloud (beats or time units) ⟨~ cadence⟩ ⟨~ eighth notes⟩ **2 a :** CONSIDER, ACCOUNT ⟨~ oneself lucky⟩ **b :** to record as of an opinion or persuasion ⟨~ me as uncommitted⟩ **3 :** to include or exclude by or as if by counting ⟨~ me in⟩ ~ *vi* **1 a :** to recite or indicate the numbers in order by units or groups ⟨~ by fives⟩ **b :** to count the units in a group **2 :** to rely or depend on someone or something ⟨~*ed* on his parents to help with the expenses⟩ **3 :** ADD, TOTAL ⟨it ~*s* up to a sizable amount⟩ **4 :** to have value or significance ⟨these are the people who really ~⟩ — **count heads** *or* **count noses :** to count the number present — **count on :** to look forward to as certain **:** ANTICIPATE ⟨*counted on* winning⟩
[2]**count** *n* (14c) **1 a :** the action or process of counting **b :** a total obtained by counting **:** TALLY **2** *archaic* **a :** RECKONING, ACCOUNT **b :** CONSIDERATION, ESTIMATION **3 a :** ALLEGATION, CHARGE; *specif* **:** one separately stating the cause of action or prosecution in a legal declaration or indictment ⟨guilty on all ~*s*⟩ **b :** a specific point under consideration **:** ISSUE **4 :** the total number of individual things in a given unit or sample obtained by counting all or a subsample of them ⟨bacteria ~⟩ **5 a :** the calling off of the seconds from one to ten when a boxer has been knocked down **b :** the number of balls and strikes charged to a baseball batter during one turn ⟨the ~ stood at 3 and 2⟩ **c :** SCORE ⟨tied the ~ with a minute to play⟩
[3]**count** *n* [MF *comte,* fr. LL *comit-, comes,* fr. L, companion, one of the imperial court, fr. *com-* + *ire* to go — more at ISSUE] (15c) **:** a European nobleman whose rank corresponds to that of a British earl
count·able \ˈkau̇nt-ə-bəl\ *adj* (15c) **:** capable of being counted; *esp* **:** DENUMERABLE ⟨a ~ set⟩ — **count·abil·i·ty** \ˌkau̇nt-ə-ˈbil-ət-ē\ *n* — **count·ably** \ˈkau̇nt-ə-blē\ *adv*

count·down \ˈkau̇nt-ˌdau̇n\ *n* (1952) **:** an audible backward counting in fixed units (as seconds) from an arbitrary starting number to mark the time remaining before an event; *also* **:** preparations carried on during such a count — **count down** \-ˈdau̇n\ *vi*

[1]**coun·te·nance** \ˈkau̇nt-ᵊn-ən(t)s, ˈkau̇nt-nən(t)s\ *n* [ME *contenance,* fr. MF, fr. ML *continentia,* fr. L, restraint, fr. *continent-, continens,* prp. of *continēre* to hold together — more at CONTAIN] (13c) **1** *obs* **:** BEARING, DEMEANOR **2 a :** calm expression **b :** mental composure **c :** LOOK, EXPRESSION **3** *archaic* **a :** ASPECT, SEMBLANCE **b :** PRETENSE **4 :** FACE, VISAGE; *esp* **:** the face as an indication of mood, emotion, or character **5 :** bearing or expression that offers approval or sanction **:** moral support

[2]**countenance** *vt* **-nanced; -nanc·ing** (1568) **:** to extend approval or toleration to **:** SANCTION ⟨never *countenanced* violence⟩ — **coun·te·nanc·er** *n*

[1]**count·er** \ˈkau̇nt-ər\ *n* [ME *countour,* fr. MF *comptouer,* fr. ML *computatorium* computing place, fr. L *computatus,* pp. of *computare*] (14c) **1 :** a piece (as of metal or ivory) used in reckoning or in games **2 :** something of value in bargaining **:** ASSET **3 :** a level surface (as a table, shelf or display case) over which transactions are conducted or food is served or on which goods are displayed or work is conducted ⟨jewelry ~⟩ ⟨a lunch ~⟩ — **over the counter 1 :** in or through a broker's office rather than through a stock exchange ⟨stock bought *over the counter*⟩ **2 :** without a prescription ⟨drugs available *over the counter*⟩ — **under the counter :** by surreptitious means **:** in an illicit and private manner

[2]**coun·ter** \ˈkau̇nt-ər\ *vb* [ME *countren,* fr. MF *contre*] *vt* (14c) **1 a :** to act in opposition to **:** OPPOSE **b :** OFFSET, NULLIFY ⟨tried to ~ the trend toward depersonalization⟩ **2 :** to adduce in answer ⟨we ~*ed* that our warnings had been ignored⟩ ~ *vi* **:** to meet attacks or arguments with defensive or retaliatory steps

[3]**count·er** *n* [ME, fr. MF *conteor,* fr. *compter* to count] (15c) **:** one that counts; *esp* **:** a device for indicating a number or amount

[4]**coun·ter** *adv* [ME *contre,* fr. MF, fr. L *contra* against, opposite; akin to L *com-* with, together — more at CO-] (15c) **1 :** in an opposite or wrong direction **2 :** to or toward a different or opposite direction, result, or effect ⟨values that run ~ to those of society⟩

[5]**coun·ter** *n* (15c) **1 :** CONTRARY, OPPOSITE **2 :** the after portion of a boat from the waterline to the extreme outward swell or stern overhang **3 a :** the act of making an attack while parrying one (as in boxing or fencing); *also* **:** a blow thus given in boxing **b :** an agency or force that offsets **:** CHECK **4 :** a stiffener to give permanent form to a boot or shoe upper around the heel **5 :** an area within the face of a letter wholly or partly enclosed by strokes **6 :** a football play in which the ballcarrier goes in a direction opposite to the movement of the play

[6]**coun·ter** *adj* (1596) **1 :** marked by or tending toward or in an opposite direction or effect **2 :** given to or marked by opposition, hostility, or antipathy **3 :** situated or lying opposite ⟨the ~ side⟩ **4 :** recalling or ordering back by a superseding contrary order **:** COUNTERMANDING ⟨~ orders from the colonel⟩

coun·ter- *prefix* [ME *contre-,* fr. MF, fr. *contre*] **1 a :** contrary **:** opposite ⟨*counter*clockwise⟩ ⟨*counter*march⟩ **b :** opposing **:** retaliatory ⟨*counter*force⟩ ⟨*counter*offensive⟩ **2 :** complementary **:** corresponding ⟨*counter*weight⟩ ⟨*counter*part⟩ **3 :** duplicate **:** substitute ⟨*counter*foil⟩

coun·ter·ac·cu·sa·tion
coun·ter·ad
coun·ter·ad·ap·ta·tion
coun·ter·ad·ver·tis·ing
coun·ter·agent
coun·ter·ag·gres·sion
coun·ter·ar·gue
coun·ter·ar·gu·ment
coun·ter·as·sas·si·na·tion
coun·ter·as·sault
coun·ter·bid
coun·ter·blast
coun·ter·block·ade
coun·ter·blow
coun·ter·cam·paign
coun·ter·charge
coun·ter·com·mer·cial
coun·ter·com·plaint
coun·ter·con·ven·tion
coun·ter·coup
coun·ter·crit·i·cism
coun·ter·cry
coun·ter·de·mand
coun·ter·dem·on·strate
coun·ter·dem·on·stra·tion
coun·ter·dem·on·stra·tor
coun·ter·de·ploy·ment
coun·ter·ed·u·ca·tion·al
coun·ter·ef·fort
coun·ter·ev·i·dence
coun·ter·fire
coun·ter·force
coun·ter·gov·ern·ment
coun·ter·hy·poth·e·sis
coun·ter·im·age
coun·ter·in·cen·tive
coun·ter·in·fla·tion·ary
coun·ter·in·flu·ence
coun·ter·in·stance
coun·ter·in·sti·tu·tion
coun·ter·mag·net
coun·ter·mea·sure
coun·ter·memo
coun·ter·mo·bi·li·za·tion
coun·ter·move
coun·ter·move·ment
coun·ter·myth
coun·ter·or·der
coun·ter·pe·ti·tion
coun·ter·pick·et
coun·ter·play
coun·ter·play·er
coun·ter·ploy
coun·ter·pow·er
coun·ter·pres·sure
coun·ter·pro·ject
coun·ter·pro·pa·gan·da
coun·ter·pro·test
coun·ter·ques·tion
coun·ter·raid
coun·ter·ral·ly
coun·ter·re·ac·tion
coun·ter·re·form·er
coun·ter·re·sponse
coun·ter·re·tal·i·a·tion
coun·ter·ri·ot·er
coun·ter·sci·en·tif·ic
coun·ter·shot
coun·ter·snip·er
coun·ter·spell
coun·ter·state
coun·ter·state·ment
coun·ter·step
coun·ter·strat·e·gist
coun·ter·strat·e·gy
coun·ter·stroke
coun·ter·style
coun·ter·sub·ver·sive
coun·ter·sue
coun·ter·sug·ges·tion
coun·ter·suit
coun·ter·sur·veil·lance
coun·ter·tac·tics
coun·ter·ten·den·cy
coun·ter·ter·ror
coun·ter·ter·ror·ism
coun·ter·ter·ror·ist
coun·ter·threat
coun·ter·thrust
coun·ter·tra·di·tion
coun·ter·trans·port
coun·ter·trend
coun·ter·uni·ver·si·ty
coun·ter·vi·o·lence
coun·ter·world

coun·ter·act \ˌkau̇nt-ə-ˈrakt\ *vt* (1678) **:** to make ineffective or restrain or neutralize the usu. ill effects of by an opposite force — **coun·ter·ac·tion** \-ˈrak-shən\ *n* — **coun·ter·ac·tive** \-ˈrak-tiv\ *adj*

[1]**coun·ter·at·tack** \ˈkau̇nt-ə-rə-ˌtak\ *n* (1893) **:** an attack made to counter another attack

[2]**counterattack** *vi* (1916) **:** to make a counterattack ~ *vt* **:** to make a counterattack against — **coun·ter·at·tack·er** *n*

[1]**coun·ter·bal·ance** \ˈkau̇nt-ər-ˌbal-ən(t)s, ˌkau̇nt-ər-ˈ\ *n* (ca. 1611) **1 :** a weight that balances another **2 :** a force or influence that offsets or checks an opposing force

[2]**counterbalance** \ˌkau̇nt-ər-ˈ, ˈkau̇nt-ər-ˌ\ *vt* (ca. 1611) **1 :** to oppose or balance with an equal weight or force **2 :** to equip with counterbalances

coun·ter·change \ˈkau̇nt-ər-ˌchānj\ *vt* (1613) **1 :** INTERCHANGE, TRANSPOSE **2 :** CHECKER 1a

[1]**coun·ter·check** \-ˌchek\ *n* (1559) **:** a check or restraint often operating against something that is itself a check

[2]**countercheck** *vt* (1587) **1 :** CHECK, COUNTERACT **2 :** to check a second time for verification

counter check *n* (1856) **:** a check obtainable at a bank usu. to be cashed only at the bank by the drawer

[1]**coun·ter·claim** \ˈkau̇nt-ər-ˌklām\ *n* (1784) **:** an opposing claim esp. in law

[2]**counterclaim** *vi* (1881) **:** to enter or plead a counterclaim ~ *vt* **:** to ask in a counterclaim

coun·ter·clock·wise \ˌkau̇nt-ər-ˈkläk-ˌwīz\ *adv* (1888) **:** in a direction opposite to that in which the hands of a clock rotate as viewed from in front — **counterclockwise** *adj*

coun·ter·con·di·tion·ing \-kən-ˈdish-(ə-)niŋ\ *n* (1962) **:** conditioning in order to replace an undesirable response (as fear) to a stimulus (as an engagement in public speaking) by a favorable one

coun·ter·cul·ture \ˈkau̇nt-ər-ˌkəl-chər\ *n* (1968) **:** a culture with values and mores that run counter to those of established society — **coun·ter·cul·tur·al** \ˌkau̇nt-ər-ˈkəlch-(ə-)rəl\ *adj* — **coun·ter·cul·tur·ist** \-(ə-)rəst\ *n*

[1]**coun·ter·cur·rent** \ˈkau̇nt-ər-ˌkər-ənt, -ˌkə-rənt\ *n* (1684) **:** a current flowing in a direction opposite that of another current

[2]**countercurrent** \ˌkau̇nt-ər-ˈ\ *adj* (1799) **1 :** flowing in an opposite direction **2 :** involving flow of materials in opposite directions ⟨~ dialysis⟩ — **coun·ter·cur·rent·ly** *adv*

coun·ter·cy·cli·cal \-ˈsī-kli-kəl, -ˈsik-li-\ *adj* (1944) **:** calculated to check excessive developments in a business cycle **:** COMPENSATORY ⟨~ budget policies⟩

coun·ter·es·pi·o·nage \ˌkau̇nt-ə-ˈres-pē-ə-ˌnäzh, -ˌnäj, -nij, *Canad also* -ˌnazh; -ˌres-pē-ə-ˈnäzh; -rə-ˈspē-ə-nij\ *n* (1899) **:** espionage directed toward detecting and thwarting enemy espionage

coun·ter·ex·am·ple \ˈkau̇nt-ə-rig-ˌzam-pəl\ *n* (1957) **:** an example that disproves a proposition or theory

[1]**coun·ter·feit** \ˈkau̇nt-ər-ˌfit\ *vt* (14c) **:** to imitate or feign esp. with intent to deceive ⟨~*ed* interest that they did not feel⟩; *also* **:** to make a fraudulent replica of ⟨~*ing* $20 bills⟩ ~ *vi* **1 :** to try to deceive by pretense or dissembling **2 :** to engage in counterfeiting something of value *syn* see ASSUME — **coun·ter·feit·er** *n*

[2]**counterfeit** *adj* [ME *countrefet,* fr. MF *contrefait,* fr. pp. of *contrefaire* to imitate, fr. *contre-* + *faire* to make, fr. L *facere* — more at DO] (14c) **1 :** made in imitation of something else with intent to deceive **:** FORGED ⟨~ money⟩ **2 a :** INSINCERE, FEIGNED ⟨~ sympathy⟩ **b :** marked by false pretense **:** SHAM, PRETENDED

[3]**counterfeit** *n* (15c) **1 :** something counterfeit **:** FORGERY **2 :** something likely to be mistaken for something of higher value ⟨pity was a ~ of love —Harry Hervey⟩ *syn* see IMPOSTURE

coun·ter·flow \ˈkau̇nt-ər-ˌflō\ *n* (1870) **:** the flow of a fluid in opposite directions (as in an apparatus)

coun·ter·foil \-ˌfȯil\ *n* (1706) **:** a detachable stub (as on a check or ticket) usu. serving as a record or receipt

coun·ter·guer·ril·la *also* **coun·ter·gue·ril·la** \ˌkau̇nt-ər-gə-ˈril-ə, -g(y)i-, -ge-\ *n* (1901) **:** a guerrilla who is trained to thwart enemy guerrilla operations

coun·ter·in·sur·gen·cy \ˌkau̇nt-ə-rin-ˈsər-jən-sē\ *n* (1962) **:** organized military activity designed to counter insurgency — **coun·ter·in·sur·gent** \-jənt\ *n*

coun·ter·in·tel·li·gence \ˌkau̇nt-ə-rin-ˈtel-ə-jən(t)s\ *n* (1940) **:** organized activity of an intelligence service designed to block an enemy's sources of information, to deceive the enemy, to prevent sabotage, and to gather political and military information

coun·ter·in·tu·itive \-rin-ˈt(y)ü-ət-iv\ *adj* (1964) **:** contrary to intuition ⟨the results were surprising and ~⟩

coun·ter·ir·ri·tant \-ˈrir-ə-tənt\ *n* (1854) **1 :** an agent applied locally to produce superficial inflammation with the object of reducing inflammation in deeper adjacent structures **2 :** an irritation or discomfort that diverts attention from another — **counterirritant** *adj*

count·er·man \ˈkau̇nt-ər-ˌman, -mən\ *n* (1853) **:** one who tends a counter

[1]**coun·ter·mand** \ˈkau̇nt-ər-ˌmand, ˌkau̇nt-ər-ˈ\ *vt* [ME *countermaunden,* fr. MF *contremander,* fr. *contre-* counter- + *mander* to command, fr. L *mandare* — more at MANDATE] (15c) **1 :** to revoke (a command) by a contrary order **2 :** to recall or order back by a superseding contrary order ⟨~ reinforcements⟩

[2]**coun·ter·mand** \ˈkau̇nt-ər-ˌmand\ *n* (1548) **1 :** a contrary order **2 :** the revocation of an order or command

coun·ter·march \ˈkau̇nt-ər-ˌmärch\ *n* (1598) **1 :** a marching back; *specif* **:** a movement in marching by which a unit of troops reverses direction while marching but keeps the same order **2 :** a march (as of political demonstrators) designed to counter the effect of another march — **countermarch** *vi*

coun·ter·mel·o·dy \-ˌmel-əd-ē\ *n* (1926) **:** a secondary melody that is sounded simultaneously with the principal one

[1]**coun·ter·mine** \-ˌmīn\ *n* (1548) **1 :** a tunnel for intercepting an enemy mine **2 :** a stratagem for defeating an attack **:** COUNTERPLOT

[2]**countermine** *vt* (1580) **1 :** to thwart by secret measures **2 :** to oppose or intercept with a countermine ~ *vi* **:** to make or lay down countermines

coun·ter·of·fen·sive \ˈkau̇nt-ə-rə-ˌfen(t)-siv\ *n* (1918) **:** a large-scale military offensive undertaken by a force previously on the defensive

coun·ter·of·fer \-ˌrȯf-ər, -ˌräf-\ *n* (1788) **:** a return offer made by one who has rejected an offer

coun·ter·pane \ˈkau̇nt-ər-ˌpān\ *n* [alter. of ME *countrepointe,* modif. of MF *coute pointe,* lit., embroidered quilt] (15c) **:** BEDSPREAD

coun·ter·part \-ˌpärt\ *n* (15c) **1 :** one of two corresponding copies of a legal instrument **:** DUPLICATE **2 a :** a thing that fits another perfectly

\ə\ abut \ᵊ\ kitten, F table \ər\ further \a\ ash \ā\ ace \ä\ cot, cart \au̇\ out \ch\ chin \e\ bet \ē\ easy \g\ go \i\ hit \ī\ ice \j\ job \ŋ\ sing \ō\ go \ȯ\ law \ȯi\ boy \th\ thin \th\ the \ü\ loot \u̇\ foot \y\ yet \zh\ vision \à, k, ⁿ, œ, œ̄, ue, ue̅, ʸ\ see Guide to Pronunciation

b : something that completes : COMPLEMENT **3 a** : one remarkably similar to another **b** : one having the same function or characteristics as another : EQUIVALENT ⟨college presidents and their ∼s in business⟩
coun·ter·plan \'kaůnt-ər-,plan\ n (1788) **1** : a plan designed to counter another plan **2** : an alternate or substitute plan
coun·ter·plea \-,plē\ n (1565) : a replication to a legal plea
¹coun·ter·plot \-,plät\ n (1611) : a plot designed to thwart an opponent's plot
²counterplot vt (1662) : to intrigue against : foil with a plot
¹coun·ter·point \'kaůnt-ər-,pôint\ n [MF contrepoint, fr. ML contrapunctus, fr. L contra- counter- + ML punctus musical note, melody, fr. L, act of pricking, fr. punctus, pp. of pungere to prick — more at POINT] (15c) **1 a** : one or more independent melodies added above or below a given melody **b** : the combination of two or more independent melodies into a single harmonic texture in which each retains its linear character : POLYPHONY **2 a** : a complementing or contrasting item : OPPOSITE **b** : use of contrast or interplay of elements in a work of art (as a drama)
²counterpoint vt (1875) **1** : to compose or arrange in counterpoint **2** : to set off or emphasize by juxtaposition : set in contrast ⟨∼s opposing themes ... hope and apathy —Curt Leviant⟩
¹coun·ter·poise \-,pôiz\ vt [ME counterpesen, fr. MF contrepeser, fr. contre- + peser to weigh — more at POISE] (14c) : COUNTERBALANCE
²counterpoise n (15c) **1** : COUNTERBALANCE **2** : an equivalent power or force acting in opposition **3** : a state of balance
coun·ter·pose \'kaůnt-ər-'pōz\ vt [counter- + -pose (as in compose)] (1594) : to place in opposition, contrast, or equilibrium ⟨counterposed an alternative solution to the problem⟩
coun·ter·pro·duc·tive \-prə-'dək-tiv\ adj (1962) : tending to hinder the attainment of a desired goal ⟨violence as a means to achieve an end is ∼ —W. E. Brock b1930⟩
coun·ter·pro·gram·ming \,kaůnt-ər-'prō-,gram-iη, -grəm-\ n (1966) : the scheduling of programs by television networks so as to attract audiences away from simultaneously telecast programs of competitors
coun·ter·pro·pos·al \'kaůnt-ər-prə-,pō-zəl\ n (1885) : a return proposal made by one who has rejected a proposal
coun·ter·punch \'kaůnt-ər-,pənch\ n (1942) : a counter in boxing; also : a countering blow or attack — **counterpunch** vi — **coun·ter·punch·er** \-,pən-chər\ n
coun·ter·ref·or·ma·tion \,kaůnt-ə(r),ref-ər-'mā-shən\ n (1840) **1** usu Counter-Reformation : the reform movement in the Roman Catholic Church following the Reformation **2** : a reformation designed to counter the effects of a previous reformation
coun·ter·rev·o·lu·tion \-,rev-ə-'lü-shən\ n (1793) **1** : a revolution directed toward overthrowing a government or social system established by a previous revolution **2** : a movement to counteract revolutionary trends — **coun·ter·rev·o·lu·tion·ary** \-sha-,ner-ē\ adj or n
coun·ter·shad·ing \'kaůnt-ər-,shād-iη\ n (1896) : coloration (as of an animal) with parts normally in shadow being light or parts normally illuminated being dark
coun·ter·shaft \-,shaft\ n (ca. 1864) : a shaft that receives motion from a main shaft and transmits it to a working part
coun·ter·sign \-,sīn\ n (1591) **1** : a signature attesting the authenticity of a document already signed by another **2** : a sign given in reply to another; specif : a military secret signal that must be given by one wishing to pass a guard — **countersign** vt — **coun·ter·sig·na·ture** \,kaůnt-ər-'sig-nə-,chů(ə)r, -chər, -,t(y)ů(ə)r\ n
¹coun·ter·sink \'kaůnt-ər-,siηk\ vt -sunk \-,səηk\; -sink·ing (1816) **1** : to make a countersink on **2** : to set the head of (as a screw) at or below the surface
²countersink n (1816) **1** : a bit or drill for making a countersink **2** : a funnel-shaped enlargement at the outer end of a drilled hole
coun·ter·spy \'kaůnt-ər-,spī\ n (1939) : a spy engaged in counterespionage
coun·ter·stain \-,stān\ vt (1895) : to stain (as a microscopy specimen) so as to color parts (as the cytoplasm of cells) not colored by another stain (as a nuclear stain) — **counterstain** n
coun·ter·ten·or \-,ten-ər\ n [ME countretenour, fr. MF contretenour, fr. contre- + teneur tenor] (15c) : an adult male who is able to sing in an alto range
coun·ter·top \-,täp\ n [¹counter + top] (1897) : the flat working surface on top of waist-level kitchen cabinets
coun·ter·vail \,kaůnt-ər-'vā(ə)l\ vb [ME countrevailen, fr. MF contrevaloir, fr. contre- counter- + valoir to be worth, fr. L valēre — more at WIELD] vt (14c) **1** : to compensate for **2** archaic : EQUAL, MATCH **3** : to exert force against : COUNTERACT ∼ vi : to exert force against an opposing and often bad or harmful force or influence
coun·ter·view \'kaůnt-ər-,vyü\ n (1590) **1** archaic : CONFRONTATION **2** : an opposite point of view
coun·ter·weight \-,wāt\ n (1693) : an equivalent weight or force : COUNTERBALANCE — **counterweight** vt
count·ess \'kaůnt-əs\ n (12c) **1** : the wife or widow of an earl or count **2** : a woman who holds in her own right the rank of earl or count
coun·ti·an \'kaůnt-ē-ən\ n (15c) : a native or resident of a usu. specified county
count·ing·house \'kaůnt-iη-,haůs\ n (15c) : a building, room, or office used for keeping books and transacting business
counting number n (ca. 1965) : NATURAL NUMBER
counting room n (1712) : COUNTINGHOUSE
counting tube n (1937) : an ionization chamber designed to respond to passage through it of fast-moving ionizing particles and usu. connected to some device for counting the particles — called also counter tube
count·less \'kaůnt-ləs\ adj (1588) : too numerous to be counted : MYRIAD — **count·less·ly** adv
count noun n (1952) : a noun (as bean or sheet) that forms a plural and is used with a numeral, with words such as many or few, or with the indefinite article a or an — compare MASS NOUN
count palatine n (1596) **1 a** : a high judicial official in the Holy Roman Empire **b** : a count of the Holy Roman Empire having imperial powers in his own domain **2** : the proprietor of a county palatine in England or Ireland
coun·tri·fied also **coun·try·fied** \'kən-tri-,fīd\ adj [country + -fied (as in glorified)] (1653) **1** : RURAL, RUSTIC **2** : UNSOPHISTICATED **3** : played or sung in the manner of country music ⟨∼ rock⟩

¹coun·try \'kən-trē\ n, pl countries [ME contree, fr. OF contrée, fr. ML contrata, fr. L contra against, on the opposite side] (13c) **1** : an indefinite usu. extended expanse of land : REGION **2 a** : the land of a person's birth, residence, or citizenship **b** : a political state or nation or its territory **3 a** : the people of a state or district : POPULACE **b** : JURY **c** : ELECTORATE **2 4** : rural as distinguished from urban areas **5** : COUNTRY MUSIC — **coun·try·ish** \-trē-ish\ adj
²country adj (14c) **1** : of, relating to, or characteristic of the country **2** : prepared or processed with farm supplies and procedures **3** : of or relating to country music ⟨∼ singers⟩
country and western n (1960) : COUNTRY MUSIC
country club n (1867) : a suburban club for social life and recreation; esp : one having a golf course
coun·try-dance \'kən-trē-,dan(t)s\ n (1579) : any of various native English dances in which partners face each other esp. in rows
country gentleman n (1632) **1** : a well-to-do country resident : an owner of a country estate **2** : one of the English landed gentry
country house n (14c) : a house in the country; specif : COUNTRYSEAT
coun·try·man \'kən-trē-mən, 3 often -,man\ n (14c) **1** : an inhabitant or native of a specified country **2** : COMPATRIOT **3** : one living in the country or marked by country ways : RUSTIC
country mile n (1950) : a long distance
country music n (1952) : music derived from or imitating the folk style of the Southern U.S. or of the Western cowboy
country rock n (1968) : ROCKABILLY
coun·try·seat \,kən-trē-'sēt\ n (1583) : a mansion or estate in the country
coun·try·side \'kən-trē-,sīd\ n (1727) **1** : a rural area **2** : the inhabitants of a countryside
country singer n (1955) : one who sings country music or in the style of country music
coun·try·wom·an \'kən-trē-,wům-ən\ n (15c) **1** : a woman compatriot **2** : a woman resident of the country
¹coun·ty \'kaůnt-ē\ n, pl counties [ME counte, fr. MF conté, fr. ML comitatus, fr. LL, office of a count, fr. comit-, comes count — more at COUNT] (14c) **1** : the domain of a count **2 a** : one of the territorial divisions of Great Britain and Ireland constituting the chief units for administrative, judicial, and political purposes **b** (1) : the people of a county (2) Brit : the gentry of a county **3** : the largest territorial division for local government within a state of the U.S. **4** : the largest local administrative unit in various countries — **county** adj
²county n, pl counties [modif. of MF comte] obs (15c) : ³COUNT
county agent n (1705) : a consultant employed jointly by federal and state governments to provide information about agriculture and home economics
county court n (1535) : a court in some states that has a designated jurisdiction usu. both civil and criminal within the limits of a county
county fair n (1856) : a fair usu. held annually at a set location in a county esp. to exhibit local agricultural products and livestock
county palatine n (15c) : the territory of a count palatine
county seat n (1803) : a town that is the seat of county administration
county town n, chiefly Brit (1670) : COUNTY SEAT
¹coup \'küp\ n [ME coupen to strike, fr. MF couper — more at COPE] chiefly Scot (1572) : OVERTURN, UPSET
²coup \'kü\ n, pl coups \'küz\ [F, blow, stroke — more at COPE] (1791) **1** : a brilliant, sudden, and usu. highly successful stroke or act **2** : COUP D'ÉTAT
coup de grace \,küd-ə-'gräs\ n, pl coups de grace \,küd-ə-\ [F coup de grâce, lit., stroke of mercy] (1699) **1** : a death blow or shot administered to end the suffering of one mortally wounded **2** : a decisive finishing blow, act, or event
coup de main \-'maⁿ\ n, pl coups de main \,küd-ə-\ [F, lit., hand stroke] (1758) : a sudden attack in force
coup d'état \,küd-ā-'tä, küd-(,)ā-, -ə-\ n, pl coups d'état \-'tä(z), -,tä(z)\ [F, lit., stroke of state] (1646) : a sudden decisive exercise of force in politics; esp : the violent overthrow or alteration of an existing government by a small group
coup de the·atre \,küd-ə-tā-'ätr°\ n, pl coups de theatre \,küd-ə-\ [F coup de théâtre, lit., stroke of theater] (1747) **1** : a sudden sensational turn in a play; also : a sudden dramatic effect or turn of events **2** : a theatrical success
coup d'oeil \kü-'də(r), -'dəi\ n, pl coups d'oeil \same\ [F, lit., stroke of the eye] (1739) : a brief survey : GLANCE
cou·pé or **coupe** \kü-'pā, 2 often 'küp\ n [F coupé, fr. pp. of couper to cut] (1834) **1** : a four-wheeled closed horse-drawn carriage for two persons inside with an outside seat for the driver in front **2** usu coupe **a** : a closed 2-door automobile for usu. two persons **b** : a usu. closed 2-door automobile with a full-width rear seat
¹cou·ple \'kəp-əl\ vb cou·pled; cou·pling \-(ə-)liη\ vt (13c) **1 a** : to connect for consideration together **b** : to join for combined effect **2 a** : to fasten together : LINK **b** : to bring (two electric circuits) into such close proximity as to permit mutual influence **3** : to join in marriage or sexual union ∼ vi **1** : to unite in sexual union **2** : JOIN **3** : to unite chemically usu. with elimination of a simple molecule
²cou·ple \'kəp-əl; "couple of" is often ,kəp-lə(v)\ n [ME, pair, bond, fr. OF cople, fr. L copula bond, fr. co- + apere to fasten — more at APT] (13c) **1 a** : a man and woman married, engaged, or otherwise paired **b** : two persons paired together **2** : PAIR, BRACE **3** : something that joins or links two things together: as **a** : two equal and opposite forces that act along parallel lines **b** : GALVANIC COUPLE **4** : an indefinite small number : FEW ⟨a ∼ of days ago⟩
usage In the second half of the 19th century the propriety of the phrase a couple of came under attack. Even though the attack was completely baseless, the phrase has been in both literary and oral use since at least the 15th century — its repercussions can still be detected in some handbooks. It should cause no concern. It has been standard for 500 years.
³couple adj (1924) : TWO; also : FEW — used with a ⟨a ∼ drinks⟩
usage The adjective use of a couple, without of, has been called nonstandard, but it is not. It is a 20th century Americanism, more common in speech than in writing. It is most frequently used with periods of time ⟨a couple weeks⟩ and numbers ⟨a couple hundred⟩ ⟨a couple dozen⟩ It is not used in formal prose.

cou·ple·ment \'kəp-əl-mənt\ *n* [MF, fr. *coupler* to join, fr. L *copulare*, fr. *copula*] (1548) *archaic* : the act or result of coupling
cou·pler \'kəp-(ə-)lər\ *n* (1552) **1** : one that couples **2** : a contrivance on a keyboard instrument by which keyboards or keys are connected to play together
cou·plet \'kəp-lət\ *n* [MF, dim. of *cople*] (1580) **1** : two successive lines of verse forming a unit marked usu. by rhythmic correspondence, rhyme, or the inclusion of a self-contained utterance : DISTICH **2** : COUPLE **3** : one of the musical episodes alternating with the main theme (as in a rondo)
cou·pling \'kəp-liŋ (*usual for 2*), -ə-liŋ\ *n* (14c) **1** : the act of bringing or coming together : PAIRING; *specif* : sexual union **2** : a device that serves to connect the ends of adjacent parts or objects **3** : the joining of or the part of the body that joins the hindquarters to the forequarters of a quadruped **4** : means of electric connection of two electric circuits by having a part common to both
cou·pon \'k(y)ü-ˌpän\ *n* [F, fr. OF, piece, fr. *couper* to cut — more at COPE] (1822) **1** : a statement of due interest to be cut from a bearer bond when payable and presented for payment **2** : a form surrendered in order to obtain an article, service, or accommodation: as **a** : one of a series of attached tickets or certificates often to be detached and presented as needed **b** : a ticket or form authorizing purchases of rationed commodities **c** : a certificate or similar evidence of a purchase redeemable in premiums **d** : a part of a printed advertisement to be cut off to use as an order blank or inquiry form or to obtain a discount on merchandise
cou·pon·ing \'k(y)ü-ˌpän-iŋ\ *n* (1954) : the distribution or redemption of coupons
cour·age \'kər-ij, 'kə-rij\ *n* [ME *corage*, fr. OF, fr. *cuer* heart, fr. L *cor* — more at HEART] (14c) : mental or moral strength to venture, persevere, and withstand danger, fear, or difficulty
syn COURAGE, METTLE, SPIRIT, RESOLUTION, TENACITY mean mental or moral strength to resist opposition, danger, or hardship. COURAGE implies firmness of mind and will in the face of danger or extreme difficulty; METTLE suggests an ingrained capacity for meeting strain or difficulty with fortitude and resilience; SPIRIT also suggests a quality of temperament enabling one to hold one's own or keep up one's morale when opposed or threatened; RESOLUTION stresses firm determination to achieve one's ends; TENACITY adds to RESOLUTION implications of stubborn persistence and unwillingness to admit defeat.
cou·ra·geous \kə-'rā-jəs\ *adj* (13c) : having or characterized by courage : BRAVE — **cou·ra·geous·ly** *adv* — **cou·ra·geous·ness** *n*
cou·rante \kü-'ränt, -'rant\ *n* [MF, fr. *courir* to run, fr. L *currere* — more at CAR] (1586) **1** : a dance of Italian origin marked by quick running steps **2** : music in quick triple time or in a mixture of 3/2 and 6/4 time
cou·reur de bois \kü-ˌrərd-əb-'wä\ *n, pl* **coureurs de bois** *same*\ [CanF, lit., woods runner] (1672) : a French or half-breed trapper of No. America and esp. of Canada
cour·gette \kür-'zhet\ *n* [F dial., dim. of *courge* gourd, fr. L *cucurbita*] *chiefly Brit* (1931) : ZUCCHINI
cou·ri·er \'kür-ē-ər, 'kər-ē-, 'kə-rē-\ *n* [MF *courrier*, fr. OIt *corriere*, fr. *correre* to run, fr. L *currere*] (14c) **1** : MESSENGER; as **a** : a member of a diplomatic service entrusted with bearing messages **b** (1) : an espionage agent transferring secret information (2) : a runner of contraband **c** : a member of the armed services whose duties include carrying mail, information, or supplies **2** : a traveler's paid attendant; *esp* : a tourists' guide employed by a travel agency
[1]**course** \'kō(ə)rs, 'kȯ(ə)rs\ *n* [ME, fr OF, fr. L *cursus*, fr. *cursus*, pp. of *currere* to run — more at CAR] (13c) **1** : the act or action of moving in a path from point to point **2** : the path over which something moves or extends: as **a** : RACECOURSE **b** (1) : the direction of flight of an airplane usu. measured as a clockwise angle from north; *also* : the projected path of a flight (2) : a point of the compass **c** : WATERCOURSE **d** : GOLF COURSE **3** **a** : accustomed procedure or normal action ⟨the law taking its ~⟩ **b** : a chosen manner of conducting oneself : way of acting ⟨our wisest ~ is to retreat⟩ **c** : progression through a development or period or a series of acts or events; *esp* : LIFE HISTORY, CAREER **4** : an ordered process or succession: as **a** : a number of lectures or other matter dealing with a subject; *also* : a series of such courses constituting a curriculum **b** : a series of doses or medicaments administered over a designated period **5** **a** : a part of a meal served at one time **b** : LAYER; *esp* : a continuous level range of brick or masonry throughout a wall **c** : the lowest sail on a square-rigged mast — **in due course** : after a normal passage of time : in the expected or allotted time — **of course** **1** : following the ordinary way or procedure **2** : as might be expected
[2]**course** *vb* **coursed; cours·ing** *vt* (15c) **1** : to follow close upon : PURSUE **2** **a** : to hunt or pursue (game) with hounds **b** : to cause (dogs) to run (as after game) **3** : to run or move swiftly through or over : TRAVERSE ⟨jets *coursed* the area daily⟩ ~ *vi* : to run or pass rapidly along or as if along an indicated path ⟨blood *coursing* through his veins⟩
course of study (1821) **1** : CURRICULUM **2** : COURSE 4a
[1]**cours·er** \'kōr-sər, 'kȯr-\ *n* [ME, fr. MF *coursier*, fr. OF *course*] (14c) : a swift or spirited horse : CHARGER
[2]**courser** *n* (1600) **1** : a dog for coursing **2** : one that courses : HUNTSMAN **3** : any of various birds (subfamily Cursoriinae of the family Glareolidae) of Africa and southern Asia related to the plovers and noted for their speed in running
cours·ing *n* (1538) **1** : the pursuit of running game with dogs that follow by sight instead of by scent **2** : the act of one that courses
[1]**court** \'kō(ə)rt, 'kȯ(ə)rt\ *n, often attrib* [ME, fr. OF, fr. L *cohort-, cohors* enclosure, throng, cohort, fr. *co-* + *-hort-, -hors* (akin to *hortus* garden) — more at YARD] (12c) **1** **a** : the residence or establishment of a sovereign or similar dignitary **b** : a sovereign's formal assembly of his councillors and officers **c** : the sovereign and his officers and advisers who are the governing power **d** : the family and retinue of a sovereign **e** : a reception held by a sovereign **2** **a** (1) : a manor house or large building surrounded by usu. enclosed grounds (2) : MOTEL **b** : an open space enclosed wholly or partly by buildings or circumscribed by a single building **c** : a quadrangular space walled or marked off for playing one of various games with a ball (as lawn tennis, handball, or basketball) or a division of such a court **d** : a wide alley with only one opening onto a street **3** **a** : an official assembly for the transaction of judicial business **b** : a session of such a court ⟨~ is now adjourned⟩ **c** : a place (as a chamber) for the administration of justice **d** : a judge or judges in session; *also* : a faculty or agency of judgment or evaluation ⟨rest our case in the ~ of world opinion —L. H. Marks⟩ **4** **a** : an assembly or board with legislative or administrative powers **b** : PARLIAMENT, LEGISLATURE **5** : conduct or attention intended to win favor or dispel hostility : HOMAGE ⟨pay ~ to the king⟩
[2]**court** *vt* (1571) **1** **a** : to seek to gain or achieve **b** (1) : ALLURE, TEMPT (2) : to act so as to invite or provoke ⟨~s disaster⟩ **2** **a** : to seek the affections of; *esp* : to seek to win a pledge of marriage from **b** *of an animal* : to perform actions in order to attract for mating **3** **a** : to seek to attract by attentions or flattery **b** : to seek an alliance with ~ *vi* **1** : to engage in social activities leading to engagement and marriage **2** *of an animal* : to engage in activity leading to mating
court bouillon \(ˈ)kü(ə)r-, (ˈ)kō(ə)r-, (ˈ)kȯ(ə)r-\ *n* [F *court-bouillon*, fr. *court* short (fr. L *curtus* shortened) + *bouillon* — more at SHEAR] (1723) : a liquid made usu. with water, white wine, vegetables, and seasonings and used to poach fish
cour·te·ous \'kərt-ē-əs, *esp Brit* 'kȯrt-\ *adj* [ME *corteis*, fr. OF, fr. *court*] (13c) **1** : marked by polished manners, gallantry, or ceremonial usage of a court **2** : marked by respect for and consideration of others ***syn*** see CIVIL — **cour·te·ous·ly** *adv* — **cour·te·ous·ness** *n*
cour·te·san \'kōrt-ə-zən, 'kȯrt-, -ˌzan *also* 'kərt-\ *n* [MF *courtisane*, fr. OIt *cortigiana* woman courtier, fem. of *cortigiano* courtier, fr. *corte* court, fr. L *cohort-, cohors*] (1549) : a prostitute with a courtly, wealthy, or upper-class clientele
[1]**cour·te·sy** \'kərt-ə-sē, *esp Brit* 'kȯrt-\ *n, pl* **-sies** [ME *corteisie*, fr. OF, fr. *corteis*] (13c) **1** **a** : courteous behavior **b** : a courteous act or expression **2** **a** : general allowance despite facts : INDULGENCE ⟨hills called mountains by ~ only⟩ **b** (1) : consideration, cooperation, and generosity in providing (as a gift or privilege) — used chiefly in the phrases *through the courtesy of* or *by courtesy of* or sometimes simply *courtesy of* (2) : AGENCY, MEANS
[2]**courtesy** *adj* (1613) : granted, provided, or performed as a courtesy or by way of courtesy ⟨made a ~ call on the ambassador⟩
courtesy card *n* (1934) : a card entitling its holder to some special privilege
courtesy title *n* (1865) **1** : a title (as "Lord" added to the Christian name of a peer's younger son) used in addressing certain lineal relatives of British peers **2** : a title (as "Professor" for any teacher) taken by the user and commonly accepted without consideration of official right
court·house \'kō(ə)rt-ˌhau̇s, 'kȯ(ə)rt-\ *n* (15c) **1** **a** : a building in which courts of law are regularly held **b** : the principal building in which county offices are housed **2** : COUNTY SEAT
court·ier \'kōrt-ē-ər, 'kōrt-yər, 'kȯrt-; 'kōr-chər, 'kȯr-\ *n* (14c) **1** : one in attendance at a royal court **2** : one who practices flattery
[1]**court·ly** \'kō(ə)rt-lē, 'kȯ(ə)rt-\ *adj* **court·li·er; -est** (15c) **1** **a** : of a quality befitting the court : ELEGANT **b** : insincerely flattering **2** : favoring the policy or party of the court — **court·li·ness** *n*
[2]**courtly** *adv* (1592) : in a courtly manner : POLITELY
courtly love *n* (1896) : a late medieval conventionalized code prescribing conduct and emotions of ladies and their lovers
[1]**court-mar·tial** \'kōrt-ˌmär-shəl, 'kȯrt-, -'mär-\ *n, pl* **courts-martial** *also* **court-martials** (15c) **1** : a court consisting of commissioned officers and in some instances enlisted personnel for the trial of members of the armed forces or others within its jurisdiction **2** : a trial by court-martial
[2]**court-martial** *vt* **-mar·tialed** *also* **-mar·tialled; -mar·tial·ing** *also* **-mar·tial·ling** \-ˌmärsh-(ə-)liŋ, -'märsh-\ (1859) : to subject to trial by court-martial
court of appeals *often cap C&A* (1777) : a court hearing appeals from the decisions of lower courts — called also *court of appeal*
court of claims (1691) : a court that has jurisdiction over claims (as against a government)
court of common pleas (1687) **1** : a former English superior court having civil jurisdiction **2** : an intermediate court in some American states that usu. has civil and criminal jurisdiction
court of domestic relations (1926) : a court that has jurisdiction and often special advisory powers over family disputes involving the rights and duties of husband, wife, parent, or child esp. in matters affecting the support, custody, and welfare of children
court of honor (1687) : a tribunal (as a military court) for investigating questions of personal honor
court of inquiry (1757) : a military court that inquires into and reports on some military matter (as an officer's questionable conduct)
court of law (14c) : a court that hears cases and decides them on the basis of statutes or the common law
court of record (15c) : a court whose acts and proceedings are kept on permanent record
Court of St. James's \-sənt-'jāmz(-əz), -sānt-\ [fr. *St. James's* Palace, London, former seat of the British court] (1848) : the British court
court of sessions (1705) : any of various state criminal courts of record
court order *n* (1650) : an order issuing from a competent court that requires a party to do or abstain from doing a specified act
court plaster *n* [fr. its use for beauty spots by ladies at royal courts] (1772) : an adhesive plaster esp. of silk coated with isinglass and glycerin
court reporter *n* (1894) : a stenographer who records and transcribes a verbatim report of all proceedings in a court of law
court·room \'kō(ə)rt-ˌrüm, 'kȯ(ə)rt-, -ˌru̇m\ *n* (1677) : a room in which a court of law is held
court·ship \-ˌship\ *n* (1596) : the act, process, or period of courting
court·side \-ˌsīd\ *n* (1969) : the area at the edge of a court (as for tennis or basketball)
court tennis *n* (ca. 1890) : a game played with a ball and racket in an enclosed court divided by a net

court·yard \ˈkō(ə)rt-ˌyärd, ˈkȯ(ə)rt-\ *n* (1552) **:** a court or enclosure adjacent to a building (as a house or palace)
cous·cous \ˈkü-ˌsküs\ *n* [F *couscous, couscoussou,* fr. Ar *kuskus,* fr. *kaskasa* to pound, pulverize] (1600) **:** a No. African dish consisting of steamed semolina served with meat and vegetables
cous·in \ˈkəz-ᵊn\ *n* [ME *cosin,* fr. OF, fr. L *consobrinus,* fr. *com-* + *sobrinus* cousin on the mother's side, fr. *soror* sister — more at SISTER] (13c) **1 a :** a child of one's uncle or aunt **b :** a relative descended from one's grandparent or more remote ancestor in a different line **c :** KINSMAN, RELATIVE ⟨a distant ~⟩ **2 :** one associated with or related to another **:** COUNTERPART **3 —** used as a title by a sovereign in addressing a nobleman **4 :** a person of a race or people ethnically or culturally related ⟨our English ~*s*⟩ **— cous·in·hood** \-ˌhu̇d\ *n* **— cous·in·ly** *adj* **— cous·in·ship** \-ˌship\ *n*
cous·in·age \ˈkəz-ᵊn-ij\ *n* (14c) **1 :** relationship of cousins **:** KINSHIP **2 :** a collection of cousins **:** KINFOLK
cous·in–ger·man \ˌkəz-ᵊn-ˈjər-mən\ *n, pl* **cous·ins–ger·man** \-ᵊnz-\ [ME *cosin germain,* fr. MF, fr. OF, fr. *cosin* + *germain* german] (14c) **:** COUSIN 1a
Cousin Jack \ˌkəz-ᵊn-ˈjak\ *n* (1880) **:** CORNISHMAN; *esp* **:** a Cornish miner
1couth \ˈküth\ *adj* [back-formation fr. *uncouth*] (1896) **:** SOPHISTICATED, POLISHED
2couth *n* (1956) **:** POLISH, REFINEMENT ⟨I expected kindness and gentility . . . but there is such a thing as too much ~ —S.J. Perelman⟩
couth·ie \ˈkü-thē\ *adj* [ME *couth*] (1719) *chiefly Scot* **:** PLEASANT, KINDLY
cou·ture \kü-ˈtu̇(ə)r, -ˈtu̅e̅r\ *n* [F, fr. OF *cousture* sewing, fr. (assumed) VL *consutura,* fr. L *consutus,* pp. of *consuere* to sew together, fr. *com-* + *suere* to sew — more at SEW] (1908) **1 :** the business of designing, making, and selling fashionable custom-made women's clothing **2 :** the designers and establishments engaged in couture **3 :** the clothes created by couture
cou·tu·ri·er \kü-ˈtu̇r-ē-ər, -ē-ˌā\ *n* [F, dressmaker, fr. OF *cousturier* tailor's assistant, fr. *cousture*] (1899) **:** an establishment engaged in couture; *also* **:** the proprietor of or designer for such an establishment
cou·tu·ri·ere \kü-ˈtu̇r-ē-ər, -ē-ˌe(ə)r\ *n* [F *couturière,* fr. OF *cousturiere,* fem. of *cousturier*] (1818) **:** a woman who is a couturier
cou·vade \kü-ˈväd\ *n* [F, fr. MF, cowardly inactivity, fr. *cover* to sit on, brood over — more at COVEY] (1865) **:** a custom in some cultures in accordance with which when a child is born the father takes to bed as if bearing the child and submits himself to fasting, purification, or taboos
co·va·lence \(ˈ)kō-ˈvā-lən(t)s\ *n* (1919) **:** valence characterized by the sharing of electrons; *also* **:** the number of pairs of electrons an atom can share with its neighbors — compare ELECTROVALENCE **— co·va·lent** \-lənt\ *adj* **— co·va·lent·ly** *adv*
co·va·len·cy \-lən-sē\ *n* (1919) **:** COVALENCE
covalent bond *n* (1939) **:** a nonionic chemical bond formed by shared electrons
co·vari·ance \(ˈ)kō-ˈver-ē-ən(t)s, -ˈvar-\ *n* (1931) **1 :** the expected value of the product of the deviations of two random variables from their respective means **2 :** the arithmetic mean of the products of the deviations of corresponding values of two quantitative variables from their respective means
co·var·i·ant \-ənt\ *adj* [ISV] (1905) **:** varying with something else so as to preserve certain mathematical interrelations
1cove \ˈkōv\ *n* [ME, den, fr. OE *cofa;* akin to OE *cot*] (bef. 12c) **1 :** a recessed place **:** CONCAVITY: as **a :** an architectural member with a concave cross section **b :** a trough for concealed lighting at the upper part of a wall **2 :** a small sheltered inlet or bay **3 a :** a deep recess or small valley in the side of a mountain **b :** a level area sheltered by hills or mountains
2cove *vt* **coved; cov·ing** (1756) **:** to make in a hollow concave form
3cove *n* [Romany *kova* thing, person] *Brit* (1567) **:** MAN, FELLOW
co·ven \ˈkəv-ən, ˈkō-vən\ *n* [ME *covin* band, fr. MF, fr. ML *convenium* agreement, fr. L *convenire* to agree — more at CONVENTION] (1500) **1 :** an assembly or band of usu. 13 witches **2 :** a collection of individuals with similar interests or activities ⟨a ~ of intellectuals⟩
1cov·e·nant \ˈkəv-(ə-)nənt\ *n* [ME, fr. MF, fr. prp. of *covenir* to agree, fr. L *convenire*] (14c) **1 :** a usu. formal, solemn, and binding agreement **:** COMPACT **2 a :** a written agreement or promise usu. under seal between two or more parties esp. for the performance of some action **b :** the common-law action to recover damages for breach of such a contract **— cov·e·nan·tal** \ˌkəv-ə-ˈnant-ᵊl\ *adj*
2cov·e·nant \ˈkəv-(ə-)nənt, -ə-ˌnant\ *vt* (14c) **:** to promise by a covenant **:** PLEDGE **~** *vi* **:** to enter into a covenant **:** CONTRACT
cov·e·nan·tee \ˌkəv-ə-ˌnan-ˈtē, -nən-\ *n* (1649) **:** the person to whom a promise in the form of a covenant is made
cov·e·nant·er \ˈkəv-ə-ˌnant-ər, *1 also* ˌkəv-ə-ˈ\ *n* (1638) **1** *cap* **:** a signer or adherent of the Scottish National Covenant of 1638 **2 :** one that makes a covenant
cov·e·nan·tor \ˈkəv-ə-ˌnant-ər; ˌkəv-ə-ˌnan-ˈtȯ(ə)r, -nən-\ *n* (1649) **:** a party bound by a covenant
Cov·en·try \ˈkəv-ən-trē, ˈkäv-\ *n* [*Coventry,* England] (1765) **:** a state of ostracism or exclusion ⟨sent to ~⟩
1cov·er \ˈkəv-ər\ *vb* **cov·ered; cov·er·ing** \ˈkəv-(ə-)riŋ\ [ME *coveren,* fr. OF *covrir,* fr. L *cooperire,* fr. *co-* + *operire* to close, cover; akin to OE *werian* to guard] *vt* (13c) **1 a :** to guard from attack **b (1) :** to have within the range of one's guns **:** COMMAND **(2) :** to hold within range of an aimed firearm **c (1) :** to afford protection or security to **:** INSURE **(2) :** to afford protection against or compensation for **d (1) :** to guard (an opponent) in order to obstruct a play **(2) :** to be in position to receive a throw to (a base in baseball) **e (1) :** to make provision for (a demand or charge) by means of a reserve or deposit ⟨his balance was insufficient to ~ his check⟩ **(2) :** to maintain a check on esp. by patrolling **(3) :** to protect by contrivance or expedient **2 a :** to hide from sight or knowledge **:** CONCEAL ⟨~ up a scandal⟩ **b :** to lie over **:** ENVELOP **3 :** to lay or spread something over **:** OVERLAY **4 a :** to spread over **b :** to appear here and there on the surface of **5 :** to place or set a cover or covering over **6 a :** to copulate with (a female animal) ⟨a horse ~*s* a mare⟩ **b :** to sit on and incubate (eggs) **7 :** to invest with a large or excessive amount of something ⟨~*s* himself with glory⟩ **8 :** to play a higher-ranking card on (a previously played card) **9 :** to have sufficient scope to include or take into account **:** COMPRISE **10 :** to deal with **:** TREAT **11 a :** to have as one's territory or field of activity ⟨one salesman ~*s* the whole state⟩ **b :** to report news about **12 :** to pass over **:** TRAVERSE **13 :** to place one's stake in equal jeopardy with in a bet **14 :** to buy securities or commodities for delivery against (an earlier short sale) **~** *vi* **1 :** to conceal something illicit, blameworthy, or embarrassing from notice ⟨~ up for a friend⟩ **2 :** to act as a substitute or replacement during an absence **— cov·er·able** \ˈkəv-(ə-)rə-bəl\ *adj* **— cov·er·er** \-ər-ər\ *n* **— cover one's tracks :** to conceal traces in order to elude pursuers **— cover the ground** *or* **cover ground :** to deal with a subject or assignment in a particular manner ⟨the new book of science *covers* a lot of *ground*⟩
2cover *n, often attrib* (14c) **1 :** something that protects, shelters, or guards: as **a :** natural shelter for an animal; *also* **:** the factors that provide such shelter **b (1) :** a position or situation affording protection from enemy fire **(2) :** the protection offered by airplanes in tactical support of a military operation **2 :** something that is placed over or about another thing: **a :** LID, TOP **b :** a binding or case for a book or the analogous part of a magazine; *also* **:** the front or back of such a binding **c :** an overlay or outer layer esp. for protection ⟨a mattress ~⟩ **d :** a tablecloth and the other table accessories **e :** COVER CHARGE **f :** ROOF **g :** a cloth used on a bed **h :** something (as vegetation or snow) that covers the ground **i :** the extent to which clouds obscure the sky **3 a :** something that conceals or obscures ⟨under ~ of darkness⟩ **b :** a masking device **:** PRETEXT ⟨the project was a ~ for intelligence operations⟩ **4 :** an envelope or wrapper for mail **5 :** one who substitutes for another during an absence **— cov·er·less** \-ər-ləs\ *adj* **— under cover 1 :** in an envelope or wrapper **2 :** under concealment **:** in secret
cov·er·age \ˈkəv-(ə-)rij\ *n* (1912) **1 :** the act or fact of covering **2 :** something that covers: as **a :** inclusion within the scope of an insurance policy or protective plan **:** INSURANCE **b :** the amount available to meet liabilities **c :** inclusion within the scope of discussion or reporting ⟨the news ~ of the trial⟩ **3 :** the total group covered **:** SCOPE: as **a :** all the risks covered by the terms of an insurance contract **b :** the number or percentage of persons reached by a communications medium
cov·er·all \ˈkəv-ə-ˌrȯl\ *n* (1824) **:** a one-piece outer garment worn to protect other garments — usu. used in pl. **— cov·er·alled** \-ˌrȯld\ *adj*
cov·er–all \ˈkəv-ə-ˌrȯl\ *adj* (1895) **:** COMPREHENSIVE ⟨~ provisions⟩
cover charge *n* (1921) **:** a charge made by a restaurant or nightclub in addition to the charge for food and drink
cover crop *n* (1899) **:** a crop planted to prevent soil erosion and to provide humus
covered bridge *n* (1809) **:** a bridge that has its roadway protected by a roof and enclosing sides
covered smut *n* (1900) **:** a smut disease of grains in which the spore masses are held together by the persistent grain membrane and glumes
covered wagon *n* (1745) **:** a wagon with a canvas top supported by bowed strips of wood or metal
cover girl *n* (1915) **:** an attractive young woman whose picture appears on a magazine cover
cover glass *n* (1881) **1 :** a piece of very thin glass used to cover material on a glass microscope slide **2 :** a sheet of plain glass applied to a transparency for protection
1cov·er·ing \ˈkəv-(ə-)riŋ\ *n* (14c) **:** something that covers or conceals
2covering *adj* (1887) **:** containing explanation of or additional information about an accompanying communication ⟨a ~ letter⟩
cov·er·let \ˈkəv-ər-lət, -(ˌ)lid\ *n* [ME, alter. of *coverlite,* fr. AF *coverelyth,* fr. OF *covrir* + *lit* bed, fr. L *lectus* — more at LIE] (14c) **:** BEDSPREAD
cover shot *n* (1946) **:** a wide-angle photographic shot that includes a whole scene
cov·er·slip \ˈkəv-ər-ˌslip\ *n* (1875) **:** COVER GLASS 1
cover story *n* (1948) **:** a story accompanying a magazine-cover illustration
1co·vert \ˈkō-(ˌ)vərt, kō-ˈ; ˈkəv-ərt\ *adj* [ME, fr. MF, pp. of *covrir* to cover] (14c) **1 :** not openly shown, engaged in, or avowed **:** VEILED ⟨a ~ alliance⟩ **2 :** covered over **:** SHELTERED **3 :** being married and under the authority or protection of one's husband ***syn*** see SECRET **— co·vert·ly** *adv* **— co·vert·ness** *n*
2co·vert \ˈkəv-ər(t), ˈkō-vərt\ *n* (14c) **1 a :** hiding place **:** SHELTER **b :** a thicket affording cover for game **c :** a masking or concealing device **2 :** a feather covering the bases of the quills of the wings and tail of a bird — see BIRD illustration **3 :** a firm durable twilled sometimes waterproofed cloth usu. of mixed-color yarns
cov·er·ture \ˈkəv-ər-ˌchu̇(ə)r, -chər, -ˌt(y)u̇(ə)r\ *n* (13c) **1 a :** COVERING **b :** SHELTER **2 :** the status a woman acquires upon marriage under common law
cov·er–up \ˈkəv-ə-ˌrəp\ *n* (1927) **1 :** a device or stratagem for masking or concealing ⟨his garrulousness is a ~ for insecurity⟩; *also* **:** a usu. concerted effort to keep an illegal or unethical act or situation from being made public **2 :** a loose outer garment
cov·et \ˈkəv-ət\ *vb* [ME *coveiten,* fr. OF *coveitier,* fr. *coveitié* desire, modif. of L *cupiditat-, cupiditas,* fr. *cupidus* desirous, fr. *cupere* to desire; akin to Gk *kapnos* smoke] *vt* (13c) **1 :** to wish for enviously **2 :** to desire (what belongs to another) inordinately or culpably **~** *vi* **:** to feel inordinate desire for what belongs to another ***syn*** see DESIRE **— cov·et·able** \-ə-bəl\ *adj* **— cov·et·er** \-ər\ *n* **— cov·et·ing·ly** \-iŋ-lē\ *adv*
cov·et·ous \-əs\ *adj* (13c) **1 :** marked by inordinate desire for wealth or possessions or for another's possessions **2 :** having a craving for possession ⟨~ of power⟩ **— cov·et·ous·ly** *adv* **— cov·et·ous·ness** *n*
syn COVETOUS, GREEDY, ACQUISITIVE, GRASPING, AVARICIOUS mean having or showing a strong desire for material possessions. COVETOUS implies inordinate desire often for another's possessions; GREEDY stresses lack of restraint and often of discrimination in desire; ACQUISITIVE implies both eagerness to possess and ability to acquire and keep; GRASPING adds to COVETOUS and GREEDY an implication of selfishness and often suggests unfair or ruthless means; AVARICIOUS implies obsessive acquisitiveness esp. of money and strongly suggests stinginess.
cov·ey \ˈkəv-ē\ *n, pl* **coveys** [ME, fr. MF *covee,* fr. OF, fr. *cover* to sit on, brood over, fr. L *cubare* to lie — more at HIP] (14c) **1 :** a mature bird or pair of birds with a brood of young; *also* **:** a small flock **2 :** COMPANY, GROUP

¹cow \'kaù\ *n* [ME *cou*, fr. OE *cū*; akin to OHG *kuo* cow, L *bos* head of cattle, Gk *bous*, Skt *go*] (bef. 12c) **1** : the mature female of cattle (genus *Bos*) or of any animal the male of which is called *bull* (as the moose) **2** : a domestic bovine animal regardless of sex or age — **cowy** \-ē\ *adj*

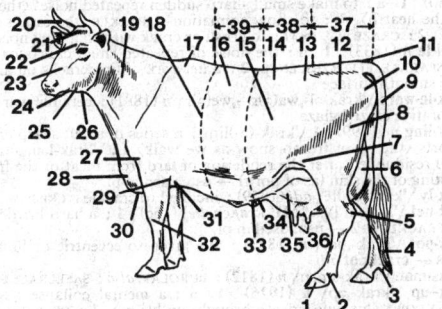

cow 1: *1* hoof, *2* pastern, *3* dewclaw, *4* switch, *5* hock, *6* rear udder, *7* flank, *8* thigh, *9* tail, *10* pinbone, *11* tail head, *12* thurl, *13* hip, *14* barrel, *15* ribs, *16* crops, *17* withers, *18* heart girth, *19* neck, *20* horn, *21* poll, *22* forehead, *23* bridge of nose, *24* muzzle, *25* jaw, *26* throat, *27* point of shoulder, *28* dewlap, *29* point of elbow, *30* brisket, *31* chest floor, *32* knee, *33* milk well, *34* milk vein, *35* fore udder, *36* teats, *37* rump, *38* loin, *39* chine

²cow *vt* [prob. of Scand origin; akin to Dan *kue* to subdue] (1605) : to intimidate with threats or show of strength : DAUNT — **cowed·ly** \'kaù(-ə)d-lē\ *adv*

cow·ard \'kaù(-ə)rd\ *n* [ME, fr. OF *coart*, fr. *coe* tail, fr. L *cauda*] (13c) : one who shows disgraceful fear or timidity — **coward** *adj*

cow·ard·ice \-əs\ *n* [ME *cowardise*, fr. MF *coardise*, fr. *coart*] (14c) : lack of courage or resolution

¹cow·ard·ly \-lē\ *adv* (14c) : in a cowardly manner

²cowardly *adj* (15c) : being, resembling, or befitting a coward ⟨a ~ retreat⟩ — **cow·ard·li·ness** *n*

syn COWARDLY, PUSILLANIMOUS, CRAVEN, DASTARDLY mean having or showing a lack of courage. COWARDLY implies a weak or ignoble lack of courage; PUSILLANIMOUS suggests a contemptible lack of courage; CRAVEN suggests extreme defeatism and complete lack of resistance; DASTARDLY implies behavior that is both cowardly and treacherous or skulking or outrageous.

cow·bane \'kaù-,bān\ *n* (1776) : any of several poisonous plants (as a water hemlock) of the carrot family

cow·bell \-,bel\ *n* (1652) : a bell hung around the neck of a cow to make a sound by which the cow can be located

cow·ber·ry \-,ber-ē\ *n* (1800) : any of several pasture shrubs (as mountain cranberry); *also* : the fruit of a cowberry

cow·bird \-,bərd\ *n* (1810) : a small No. American blackbird (*Molothrus ater*) that lays its eggs in the nests of other birds

cow·boy \-,bòi\ *n* (1623) : one who tends cattle or horses; *esp* : a usu. mounted cattle-ranch hand

cowboy boot *n* (1895) : a boot made with a high arch, a high Cuban heel, and usu. fancy stitching

cowboy hat *n* (1895) : a wide-brimmed hat with a large soft crown — called also *ten-gallon hat*

cow·catch·er \'kaù-,kach-ər, -,kech-\ *n* (1838) : an inclined frame on the front of a railroad locomotive for throwing obstacles off the track

cow college *n* (1913) **1** : a college that specializes in agriculture **2** : a provincial college or university that lacks culture, sophistication, and tradition

cow·er \'kaù(-ə)r\ *vi* [ME *couren*, of Scand origin; akin to ON *kura* to cower; akin to Gk *gyros* circle, OE *cot*] (14c) : to shrink away or crouch quivering (as in abject fear or grave distress) from something that menaces, domineers, or dismays **syn** see FAWN

cow·fish \'kaù-,fish\ *n* (1634) : any of various small bright-colored fishes (family Ostraciidae) with projections resembling horns over the eyes

cow·girl \-,gər(-ə)l\ *n* (1884) : a girl or woman who tends cattle or horses

cow·hage *also* **cow·age** \'kaù-ij\ *n* [Hindi *kavāc*] (1640) : a tropical leguminous woody vine (*Mucuna pruritum*) with crooked pods covered with barbed hairs that cause severe itching; *also* : these hairs sometimes used as a vermifuge

cow·hand \-,hand\ *n* (1886) : COWBOY

cow·herd \-,hərd\ *n* (bef. 12c) : one who tends cows

¹cow·hide \-,hīd\ *n* (1640) **1** : the hide of a cow; *also* : leather made from this hide **2** : a coarse whip of rawhide or braided leather

²cowhide *vt* **cow·hid·ed; cow·hid·ing** (1794) : to flog with a cowhide whip

cow town *n* (1853) : COW PONY

¹cowl \'kaù(ə)l\ *n* [ME *cowle*, fr. OE *cugele*, fr. LL *cuculla* monk's hood, fr. L *cucullus* hood] (bef. 12c) **1 a** : a hood or long hooded cloak esp. of a monk **b** : a draped neckline on a woman's garment **2 a** : a chimney covering designed to improve the draft **b** : the top portion of the front part of an automobile body forward of the two front doors to which are attached the windshield and instrument board **c** : COWLING

²cowl *vt* (1536) : to cover with or as if with a cowl

cow·lick \'kaù-,lik\ *n* (1598) : a lock or tuft of hair growing in a different direction from the rest of the hair

cowl·ing \'kaù-liŋ\ *n* (1917) : a removable metal covering that houses the engine and sometimes a part of the fuselage or nacelle of an airplane; *also* : a metal cover for an engine

cowl·staff \'kōl-,staf, 'kaù(ə)l-\ *n* [ME *cuvelstaff*, fr. *cuvel* vessel (fr. OE *cȳfel*, fr. ONF *cuvele* small vat) + *staff*] *archaic* (13c) : a staff from which a vessel is suspended and carried between two persons

cow·man \'kaù-mən, -,man\ *n* (1824) **1** : COWHERD, COWBOY **2** : a cattle owner or rancher

cow parsnip *n* (1548) : a tall perennial No. American plant (*Heracleum lanatum*) of the carrot family with large compound leaves and broad umbels of white or purplish flowers; *also* : a related plant (*H. sphondylium*) naturalized in the U.S. from the Old World

cow·pat \'kaù-,pat\ *n* (1937) : a dropping of cow dung

cow·pea \'kaù-,pē\ *n* (1776) : a sprawling leguminous herb (*Vigna sinensis*) related to the bean and widely cultivated in the southern U.S. esp. for forage and green manure; *also* : its edible seed — called also *black=eyed pea*

Cow·per's gland \,kaù-pərz-, ,kü-pərz-, ,kaù-pərz-\ *n* [William *Cowper* †1709 Eng. surgeon] (1738) : either of two small glands discharging into the male urethra — compare BARTHOLIN'S GLAND

cow·poke \'kaù-,pōk\ *n* (1881) : COWBOY

cow pony *n* (1874) : a strong and agile saddle horse trained for herding cattle

cow·pox \'kaù-,päks\ *n* (1798) : a mild eruptive disease of the cow that when communicated to man protects against smallpox

cow·punch·er \-,pən-chər\ *n* (1878) : COWBOY

cow·rie *or* **cow·ry** \'kaù(ə)r-ē\ *n, pl* **cowries** [Hindi *kaurī*] (1662) : any of numerous marine gastropods (family Cypraeidae) that are widely distributed in warm seas and have glossy and often brightly colored shells

cow·slip \'kaù-,slip\ *n* [ME *cowslyppe*, fr. OE *cūslyppe*, lit., cow dung, fr. *cū* cow + *slypa, slyppe* paste] (bef. 12c) **1 a** : a common British primrose (*Primula veris*) with fragrant yellow or purplish flowers **2** : MARSH MARIGOLD

cow town *n* (1885) **1** : a town or city that serves as a market center or shipping point for cattle **2** : a small unsophisticated town within a cattle-raising area

¹cox \'käks\ *n* (1869) : COXSWAIN

²cox *vb* (1920) : COXSWAIN

coxa \'käk-sə\ *n, pl* **cox·ae** \-,sē, -,sī\ [L, hip; akin to OHG *hāhsina* hock, Skt *kakṣa* armpit] (1826) : the basal segment of a limb of various arthropods (as an insect) — **cox·al** \-səl\ *adj*

cox·comb \'käk-,skōm\ *n* [ME *cokkes comb*, lit., cock's comb] (1573) **1 a** *obs* : a jester's cap adorned with a strip of red **b** *archaic* : PATE, HEAD **2 a** *obs* : FOOL **b** : a conceited foolish person : FOP — **cox·comb·i·cal** \,käk-'skō-mi-kəl, -'skäm-i-\ *adj*

cox·comb·ry \'käk-,skəm-rē, -,skōm-\ *n, pl* **-ries** (1608) : behavior that is characteristic of a coxcomb : FOPPERY

Cox·sack·ie virus \,(,)käk-,sak-ē-\ *n* [*Coxsackie*, N.Y.] (1949) : any of several viruses related to that of poliomyelitis and associated with human diseases

¹cox·swain \'käk-sən, -,swān\ *n* [ME *cokswayne*, fr. *cok* cockboat + *swain* servant] (15c) **1** : a sailor who has charge of a ship's boat and its crew and who usu. steers **2** : a steersman of a racing shell who usu. directs the crew

²coxswain *vt* (1928) : to direct as coxswain ~ *vi* : to act as coxswain

¹coy \'kòi\ *adj* [ME, quiet, shy, fr. MF *coi* calm, fr. L *quietus* quiet] (14c) **1 a** : shrinking from contact or familiarity **b** : marked by cute, coquettish, or artful playfulness **2** : showing reluctance to make a definite commitment ⟨ ~ about it⟩ **syn** see SHY — **coy·ly** *adv* — **coy·ness** *n*

²coy *vt, obs* (14c) : CARESS ~ *vi, archaic* : to act coyly

coy·dog \'kòi-,dòg\ *n* [*coyote* + *dog*] (1950) : a hybrid between a coyote and a feral dog

coy·ote \'kī-,ōt, kī-'ōt-ē\ *n, pl* **coyotes** *or* **coyote** [MexSp, fr. Nahuatl *coyotl*] (1759) : a small canid (*Canis latrans*) native to western No. America that is closely related to the American wolf

coy·o·til·lo \,kī-ə-'til-(,)ō, ,kòi-ə-, -'tē-(,)yō\ *n* [MexSp, dim. of *coyote*] (1896) : a low poisonous shrub (*Karwinskia humboldtiana*) of the buckthorn family of the southwestern U.S. and Mexico

coy·pu \'kòi-(,)pü, kòi-'\ *n* [AmerSp *coipú*, fr. Araucanian *coypu*] (1793) : NUTRIA

coz \'kəz\ *n* [by shortening & alter.] (1559) : COUSIN

coyote

coz·en \'kəz-ᵊn\ *vt* **coz·ened; coz·en·ing** \'kəz-niŋ, -ᵊn-iŋ\ [obs. It *cozzonare*, fr. It *cozzone* horse trader, fr. L *cocion-, cocio* trader] (1573) **1** : to deceive, win over, or induce to do something by artful coaxing and wheedling or shrewd trickery **2** : to gain by cozening someone ⟨~ed his supper out of the old woman⟩ **syn** see CHEAT — **coz·en·er** \-ᵊn-ər\ *n*

coz·en·age \'kəz-nij, -ᵊn-ij\ *n* (1583) **1** : the art or practice of cozening : FRAUD **2** : an act or an instance of cozening

¹co·zy \'kō-zē\ *adj* **co·zi·er; -est** [prob. of Scand origin; akin to Norw *koselig* cozy] (1709) **1** : enjoying or affording warmth and ease : SNUG **2 a** : marked by the intimacy of the family or a close group **b** : suggesting close association or connivance ⟨a ~ agreement⟩ **3** : marked by a discreet and cautious attitude or procedure **syn** see COMFORTABLE — **co·zi·ly** \-zə-lē\ *adv* — **co·zi·ness** \-zē-nəs\ *n*

²cozy *n, pl* **cozies** (1863) : a padded covering esp. for a teapot to keep the contents hot

³cozy *adv* (1946) : in a cautious manner ⟨play it ~ and wait for the other team to make a mistake —Bobby Dodd⟩

cozy up *vi* (1937) : to attain or try to attain familiarity, friendship, or intimacy : ingratiate oneself ⟨*cozying up* to the boss⟩

CQ \'sē-'kyü\ [abbr. for *call to quarters*] (1924) — communication code letters used at the beginning of radiograms of general information or safety notices or by shortwave amateurs as an invitation to talk to other shortwave amateurs

¹crab \'krab\ *n, often attrib* [ME *crabbe*, fr. OE *crabba*; akin to OHG *krebiz* crab, OE *ceorfan* to carve] (bef. 12c) **1** : any of numerous chiefly marine broadly built crustaceans: **a :** any of a tribe (Brachyura) with a short broad usu. flattened carapace, a small abdomen that curls forward beneath the body, short antennae, and the anterior pair of limbs modified as grasping pincers **b :** any of various crustaceans (tribe Anomura) resembling true crabs in the more or less reduced condition of the abdomen **2** *cap* **:** CANCER 1 **3 :** any of various machines for raising or hauling heavy weights **4 :** failure to raise an oar clear of the water on recovery of a stroke or missing the water altogether when attempting a stroke — used in the phrase *catch a crab* **5** *pl* **:** infestation with crab lice **6 :** apparent sideways motion of an airplane headed into a crosswind

2**crab** *vb* **crabbed; crab·bing** *vt* (1918) **1 :** to cause to move sideways or in an indirect or diagonal manner; *specif* **:** to head (an airplane) by means of the rudder into a crosswind to counteract drift **2 :** to subject to crabbing ~ *vi* **1 a** (1) **:** to move sideways indirectly or diagonally (2) **:** to crab an airplane **b :** to scuttle or scurry sideways **2 :** to fish for crabs — **crab·ber** *n*

3**crab** *n* [ME *crabbe,* perh. fr. *crabbe* 1crab] (14c) **:** CRAB APPLE

4**crab** *n* (1580) **:** an ill-tempered person **:** CROSSPATCH

5**crab** *vb* **crabbed; crab·bing** [ME *crabben,* prob. back-formation fr. *crabbed*] *vt* (1662) **1 :** to make sullen **:** SOUR ⟨old age has *crabbed* his nature⟩ **2 :** to complain about peevishly **3 :** SPOIL, RUIN ~ *vi* **:** CARP, GROUSE ⟨always ~*s* about the weather⟩ — **crab·ber** *n*

crab apple *n* [ME *crabbe,* perh. fr. *crabbe* 1crab] (1712) **1 a :** a small wild sour apple **b :** an often highly colored sour apple of any of several cultivated varieties **2 :** a tree that produces crab apples

crab·bed \ˈkrab-əd\ *adj* [ME, partly fr. *crabbe* 1crab, partly fr. *crabbe* crab apple] (14c) **1 :** MOROSE, PEEVISH **2 :** difficult to read or understand ⟨~ handwriting⟩ ***syn*** see SULLEN — **crab·bed·ness** *n*

crab·by \ˈkrab-ē\ *adj* **crab·bi·er; -est** [4crab] (1776) **:** CROSS, ILL-NATURED

crab cactus *n* (1900) **:** CHRISTMAS CACTUS

crab·grass \ˈkrab-ˌgras\ *n* (1743) **:** a grass (esp. *Digitaria sanguinalis*) that has creeping or decumbent stems which root freely at the nodes and that is often a pest in turf or cultivated lands

crab louse *n* (1547) **:** a sucking louse (*Phthirus pubis*) infesting the pubic region of the human body

crab·meat \ˈkrab-ˌmēt\ *n* (1876) **:** the edible part of a crab

crab·stick \ˈkrab-ˌstik\ *n* (1703) **1 :** a stick, cane, or cudgel of crab apple tree wood **2 :** a crabbed ill-natured person

crab·wise \-ˌwīz\ *adv* (1898) **1 :** SIDEWAYS **2 :** in a sidling or cautiously indirect manner

1**crack** \ˈkrak\ *vb* [ME *crakken,* fr. OE *cracian;* akin to Skt *jarate* it crackles — more at CRANE] *vi* (bef. 12c) **1 :** to make a very sharp explosive sound ⟨the whip ~*s* through the air⟩ **2 :** to break, split, or snap apart **3 :** FAIL: as **a :** to lose control or effectiveness under pressure — often used with *up* **b :** to fail in tone ⟨his voice ~*ed*⟩ **4 :** to go or travel at good speed — usu. used with *on* ⟨the steamboat ~*ed* on⟩ **5 :** to break up into simpler chemical compounds usu. as a result of heating ~ *vt* **1 a :** to break so that fissures appear on the surface ⟨~ a mirror⟩ **b :** to break with a sudden sharp sound ⟨~ nuts⟩ **2 :** to tell esp. suddenly or strikingly ⟨~ a joke⟩ **3 :** to strike with a sharp noise **:** RAP ⟨then ~*s* him over the head⟩ ⟨~*ed* a two-run homer in the fifth —*N. Y. Times*⟩ **4 a** (1) **:** to open (as a bottle) for drinking (2) **:** to open (a book) for studying **b :** to puzzle out and expose, solve, or reveal the mystery of ⟨~ a code⟩ **c :** to break into ⟨~ a safe⟩ **d :** to open slightly ⟨~ the throttle⟩ **e :** to break through (as a barrier) so as to gain acceptance or recognition **5 a :** to impair seriously or irreparably **:** WRECK ⟨~ a car up⟩ **b :** to destroy the tone of (a voice) **c :** DISORDER, CRAZE **d :** to interrupt sharply or abruptly ⟨the criticism ~*ed* our complacency⟩ **6 :** to cause to make a sharp noise ⟨~ one's knuckles⟩ **7 a** (1) **:** to subject (hydrocarbons) to cracking (2) **:** to produce by cracking ⟨~*ed* gasoline⟩ **b :** to break up (chemical compounds) into simpler compounds by means of heat

2**crack** *n* (14c) **1 a :** a loud roll or peal ⟨a ~ of thunder⟩ **b :** a sudden sharp noise ⟨the ~ of rifle fire⟩ **2 :** a sharp witty remark **:** QUIP **3 a :** a narrow break **:** FISSURE ⟨a ~ in the ice⟩ **b :** a narrow opening ⟨leave the door open a ~⟩ **4 a :** a weakness or flaw caused by decay, age, or deficiency **:** UNSOUNDNESS **b :** a broken tone of the voice **c :** CRACKPOT **5 :** MOMENT, INSTANT ⟨the ~ of dawn⟩ **6 :** HOUSEBREAKING, BURGLARY **7 :** a sharp resounding blow ⟨gave him a ~ on the head⟩ **8 :** ATTEMPT, TRY ⟨her first ~ at writing a novel⟩ **9 :** highly purified cocaine in the form of small chips used for smoking

3**crack** *adj* (1793) **:** of superior excellence or ability ⟨a ~ marksman⟩

crack·back \ˈkrak-ˌbak\ *n* (1967) **:** a blind-side block on a defensive back in football by a pass receiver who starts downfield and then cuts back to the middle of the line

crack·brain \-ˌbrān\ *n* (1570) **:** an erratic person **:** CRACKPOT — **crack-brained** \-ˈbrānd\ *adj*

crack·down \-ˌdau̇n\ *n* (1935) **:** an act or instance of cracking down

crack down \-ˈdau̇n\ *vi* (1933) **:** to take positive regulatory or disciplinary action

cracked \ˈkrakt\ *adj* (15c) **1 a :** broken (as by a sharp blow) so that the surface is fissured ⟨~ china⟩ **b :** broken into coarse particles ⟨~ wheat⟩ **c :** marked by harshness, dissonance, or failure to sustain a tone ⟨a ~ voice⟩ **2 :** mentally disturbed **:** CRAZY

crack·er \ˈkrak-ər\ *n* (15c) **1** *chiefly dial* **:** a bragging liar **:** BOASTER **2 :** something that makes a cracking or snapping noise: as **a :** FIRECRACKER **b :** the snapping end of a whiplash **:** SNAPPER **c :** a paper holder for a party favor that pops when the ends are pulled sharply **3** *pl* **:** NUTCRACKER **4 :** a dry thin crispy baked bread product that may be leavened or unleavened **5 a :** a poor usu. Southern white — usu. used disparagingly **b** *cap* **:** a native or resident of Florida or Georgia — used as a nickname **6 :** the equipment in which cracking (as of petroleum) is carried out

crack·er–bar·rel \-ˌbar-əl\ *adj* [fr. the former use of the country store cracker barrel as a locus for lounging and informal conversation] (1916) **:** suggestive of the friendly homespun character of a country store ⟨a ~ philosopher⟩

crack·er·jack \ˈkrak-ər-ˌjak\ *also* **crack·a·jack** \-ə-ˌjak\ *n* [prob. alter. of 3crack + jack (man)] (1894) **:** a person or thing of marked excellence — **crackerjack** *adj*

Cracker Jack *trademark* — used for a candied popcorn confection

crack·ers \ˈkrak-ərz\ *adj* [prob. alter. of *cracked*] *chiefly Brit* (1938) **:** CRAZY

1**crack·ing** \ˈkrak-iŋ\ *adj* (1830) **:** very impressive or effective **:** GREAT

2**cracking** *adv* (1903) **:** VERY, EXTREMELY ⟨a ~ good book⟩

3**cracking** *n* (1895) **:** a process in which relatively heavy hydrocarbons are broken up by heat into lighter products (as gasoline)

1**crack·le** \ˈkrak-əl\ *vb* **crack·led; crack·ling** \-(ə-)liŋ\ [freq. of 1*crack*] *vi* (1560) **1 a :** to make small sharp sudden repeated noises ⟨the fire ~*s* on the hearth⟩ **b :** to show animation **:** SPARKLE ⟨the essays ~ with wit⟩ **2 :** CRAZE *vi* 3 ~ *vt* **:** to crush or crack with snapping noises

2**crackle** *n* (1833) **1 a :** the noise of repeated small cracks or reports **b :** SPARKLE, EFFERVESCENCE **2 :** a network of fine cracks on an otherwise smooth surface

crack·le·ware \ˈkrak-əl-ˌwa(ə)r, -ˌwe(ə)r\ *n* (1881) **:** ceramic ware with a decorative crazed glaze

crack·ling *n* (1599) **1** \ˈkrak-(ə-)liŋ\ **:** a series of small sharp cracks or reports ⟨the ~ of frozen snow as we walk⟩ **2** \ˈkrak-lən, -liŋ\ **:** the crisp residue left after the rendering of lard from meat or the frying or roasting of the skin (as of pork) — usu. used in pl.

crack·ly \ˈkrak-(ə-)lē\ *adj* (1859) **:** inclined to crackle **:** CRISP

crack·nel \ˈkrak-nᵊl\ *n* [ME *krakenelle*] (15c) **1 :** a hard brittle biscuit **2 :** CRACKLING 2 — usu. used in pl.

crack·pot \ˈkrak-ˌpät\ *n* (1883) **:** one given to eccentric or lunatic notions — **crackpot** *adj*

cracks·man \ˈkrak-smən\ *n* (1812) **:** BURGLAR; *also* **:** SAFECRACKER

crack–up \ˈkrak-ˌəp\ *n* (1926) **1 a :** a mental collapse **:** NERVOUS BREAKDOWN ⟨his wife's death brought on his ~⟩ **b :** COLLAPSE, BREAKDOWN **2 :** CRASH, WRECK ⟨an automobile ~⟩

crack up \-ˈəp\ *vi* (1829) **1 :** to smash up a vehicle (as by losing control) ⟨*cracked up* on a curve⟩ **2 :** to laugh out loud ~ *vt* **1 :** PRAISE, 3TOUT ⟨wasn't all that it was *cracked up* to be⟩ **2 :** to cause to laugh out loud ⟨that joke really *cracks* him *up*⟩

-c·ra·cy \k-rə-sē\ *n comb form* [MF & LL; MF *-cratie,* fr. LL *-cratia,* fr. Gk *-kratia,* fr. *kratos* strength, power — more at HARD] **1 :** form of government; *also* **:** state having such a form ⟨mono*cracy*⟩ **2 :** social or political class (as of powerful persons) ⟨mobo*cracy*⟩ **3 :** theory of social organization ⟨techno*cracy*⟩

1**cra·dle** \ˈkrād-ᵊl\ *n* [ME *cradel,* fr. OE *cradol;* akin to OHG *kratto* basket, Skt *grantha* knot] (bef. 12c) **1 a :** a bed or cot for a baby usu. on rockers or pivots **b :** a framework or support suggestive of a baby's cradle: as (1) **:** a framework of bars and rods (2) **:** the support for a telephone receiver or handset **c** (1) **:** an implement with rods like fingers attached to a scythe and used formerly for harvesting grain (2) **:** a low frame on casters on which mechanics lie while working under an automobile **d :** a frame to keep the bedclothes from contact with an injured part of the body **2 a :** the earliest period of life **:** INFANCY ⟨from the ~ to the grave⟩ **b :** a place of origin ⟨the ~ of civilization⟩ **3 :** a rocking device used in panning for gold

2**cradle** *vb* **cra·dled; cra·dling** \ˈkrād-liŋ, -ᵊl-iŋ\ *vt* (15c) **1 a :** to place or keep in or as if in a cradle **b :** SHELTER, REAR **c :** to support protectively or intimately ⟨*cradling* the injured man's head in her arms⟩ **2 :** to cut (grain) with a cradle scythe **3 :** to place, raise, support, or transport on a cradle **4 :** to wash in a miner's cradle ~ *vi, obs* **:** to rest in or as if in a cradle

cra·dle·song \ˈkrād-ᵊl-ˌsȯŋ\ *n* (14c) **:** LULLABY

1**craft** \ˈkraft\ *n* [ME, strength, skill, fr. OE *cræft;* akin to OHG *kraft* strength] (bef. 12c) **1 :** skill in planning, making, or executing **:** DEXTERITY **2 :** an occupation or trade requiring manual dexterity or artistic skill ⟨the carpenter's ~⟩ ⟨the ~ of writing plays⟩ ⟨~*s* such as pottery, carpentry, and sewing⟩ **3 :** skill in deceiving to gain an end ⟨used ~ and guile to close the deal⟩ **4 :** the members of a trade or trade association **5** *pl usu* **craft a :** a boat esp. of small size **b :** AIRCRAFT **c :** SPACECRAFT ***syn*** see ART

2**craft** *vt* (15c) **:** to make or produce with care, skill, or ingenuity ⟨is ~*ing* a new sculpture⟩ ⟨a carefully ~*ed* story⟩

crafts·man \ˈkraf(t)-smən\ *n* (13c) **1 :** a workman who practices a trade or handicraft **:** ARTISAN **2 :** one who creates or performs with skill or dexterity esp. in the manual arts ⟨jewelry made by European *craftsmen*⟩ — **crafts·man·like** \-ˌlīk\ *adj* — **crafts·man·ship** \-ˌship\ *n*

crafts·wom·an \ˈkraf(t)-ˌswu̇m-ən\ *n* (13c) **1 :** a woman artisan **2 :** a woman who is skilled in a craft

craft union *n* (1922) **:** a labor union with membership limited to workmen of the same craft — compare INDUSTRIAL UNION

crafty \ˈkraf-tē\ *adj* **craft·i·er; -est** (bef. 12c) **1** *dial chiefly Brit* **:** SKILLFUL, CLEVER **2 a :** adept in the use of subtlety and cunning **b :** marked by subtlety and guile ⟨a ~ scheme⟩ ***syn*** see SLY — **craft·i·ly** \ˈkraf-tə-lē\ *adv* — **craft·i·ness** \-tē-nəs\ *n*

1**crag** \ˈkrag\ *n* [ME, of Celt origin; akin to OIr *crec* crag] (14c) **1 :** a steep rugged rock or cliff **2** *archaic* **:** a sharp detached fragment of rock — **crag·ged** \ˈkrag-əd\ *adj*

2**crag** *n* [ME, fr. MD *crāghe;* akin to OE *crǣga* throat — more at CRAW] *chiefly Scot* (14c) **:** NECK, THROAT

crag·gy \ˈkrag-ē\ *adj* **crag·gi·er; -est** (15c) **1 :** full of crags ⟨~ slopes⟩ **2 :** ROUGH, RUGGED ⟨a ~ face⟩ — **crag·gi·ly** \ˈkrag-ə-lē\ *adv* — **crag·gi·ness** \ˈkrag-ē-nəs\ *n*

crags·man \ˈkragz-mən\ *n* (1816) **:** one that is expert in climbing crags or cliffs

crake \ˈkrāk\ *n* [ME, prob. fr. ON *krāka* crow or *krākr* raven; akin to OE *crāwan* to crow] (14c) **1 :** any of various rails; *esp* **:** a short-billed rail (as the corncrake) **2 :** the corncrake's cry

1**cram** \ˈkram\ *vb* **crammed; cram·ming** [ME *crammen,* fr. OE *crammian;* akin to Gk *ageirein* to collect — more at GREGARIOUS] *vt* (bef. 12c) **1 :** to pack tight **:** JAM ⟨~ a suitcase with clothes⟩ **2 a :** to fill with food to satiety **:** STUFF **b :** to eat voraciously **:** BOLT ⟨the child ~*s* his food⟩ **3 :** to thrust in or as if in a rough or forceful manner ⟨*crammed* the letters into his pocket⟩ **4 :** to prepare hastily for an examination ⟨~ the students for the test⟩ ~ *vi* **1 :** to eat greedily or to satiety **:** STUFF **2 :** to study hastily for an imminent examination — **cram·mer** *n*

2**cram** *n* (1810) **1 :** a compressed multitude or crowd **:** CRUSH **2 :** last-minute study for an examination

cram·be \ˈkram-(ˌ)bē\ *n* [NL, genus name, fr. L, cabbage, fr. Gk *krambē;* akin to Gk *karphos* dry stalk — more at HARP] (1962) **:** an annual Mediterranean crucifer (*Crambe abyssinica*) cultivated as an oilseed crop

cram·bo \ˈkram-(ˌ)bō\ *n, pl* **cramboes** [alter. of earlier *crambe,* fr. L, cabbage] (1660) **:** a game in which one player gives a word or line of verse to be matched in rhyme by other players

cram·oi·sie *or* **cram·oi·sy** \ˈkram-ˌȯi-zē, ˈkram-ə-zē\ *n, pl* **-sies** [ME *crammassy,* fr. MF *cramoisi,* fr. *cramoisi* crimson] (15c) **:** crimson cloth

[1]**cramp** \ˈkramp\ *n* [ME *crampe,* fr. MF, of Gmc origin; akin to LG *krampe* hook] (14c) **1 :** a painful involuntary spasmodic contraction of a muscle **2 :** a temporary paralysis of muscles from overuse — compare WRITER'S CRAMP **3 :** sharp abdominal pain — usu. used in pl.

[2]**cramp** *n* [LG or obs. D *krampe* hook; akin to OE *cradol* cradle] (15c) **1 a :** a usu. iron device bent at the ends and used to hold timbers or blocks of stone together **b :** [1]CLAMP **2 a :** something that confines **:** SHACKLE **b :** the state of being confined — **cramp** *adj*

[3]**cramp** *vt* (15c) **1 :** to affect with or as if with a cramp or cramps **2 a :** CONFINE, RESTRAIN ⟨was ~*ed* in the tiny apartment⟩ **b :** to restrain from free expression — used esp. in the phrase *cramp one's style* **3 :** to turn (the front wheels of a vehicle) to right or left **4 :** to fasten or hold with a cramp ~ *vi* **:** to suffer from cramps

cram·pon \ˈkram-ˌpän\ *n* [MF *crampon,* of Gmc origin; akin to LG *krampe*] (15c) **1 :** a hooked clutch or dog for raising heavy objects — usu. used in pl. **2 :** CLIMBING IRON — usu. used in pl.

cran·ber·ry \ˈkran-ˌber-ē, -b(ə-)rē\ *n* [part trans. of LG *kraanbere,* fr. *kraan* crane + *bere* berry] (1647) **1 :** the red acid berry produced by some plants (as *Vaccinium oxycoccos* and *V. macrocarpon*) of the heath family; *also* **:** a plant producing these **2 :** any of various plants with a fruit that resembles a cranberry

cranberry bush *n* (1778) **:** a shrubby or arborescent viburnum (*Viburnum trilobum*) of No. America and Europe with prominently 3-lobed leaves and red fruit

cranch \ˈkränch\ *var of* CRAUNCH

[1]**crane** \ˈkrān\ *n* [ME *cran,* fr. OE; akin to OHG *krano* crane, Gk *geranos,* L *grus,* Skt *jaratē* it crackles] (bef. 12c) **1 :** any of a family (Gruidae of the order Gruiformes) of tall wading birds superficially resembling the herons but structurally more nearly related to the rails **2 :** any of several herons **3 :** an often horizontal projection swinging about a vertical axis: as **a :** a machine for raising, shifting, and lowering heavy weights by means of a projecting swinging arm or with the hoisting apparatus supported on an overhead track **b :** an iron arm in a fireplace for supporting kettles **c :** a boom for holding a motion-picture or television camera

[2]**crane** *vb* **craned; cran·ing** *vt* (1570) **1 :** to raise or lift by or as if by a crane **2 :** to stretch (as the neck) toward an object of attention ⟨*craning* her neck to get a better view⟩ ~ *vi* **1 :** to stretch one's neck toward an object of attention ⟨I *craned* out of the window of my compartment —Webb Waldron⟩ **2 :** HESITATE

crane fly *n* (1658) **:** any of numerous long-legged slender two-winged flies (family Tipulidae) that resemble large mosquitoes but do not bite

cranes·bill \ˈkrānz-ˌbil\ *n* (1548) **:** GERANIUM 1

crani- *or* **cranio-** *comb form* [ML *cranium*] **:** cranium ⟨*crani*ate⟩ **:** cranial and ⟨*cranio*sacral⟩

cra·ni·al \ˈkrā-nē-əl\ *adj* (1800) **1 :** of or relating to the skull or cranium **2 :** CEPHALIC — **cra·ni·al·ly** \-ə-lē\ *adv*

cranial index *n* (1868) **:** the ratio multiplied by 100 of the maximum breadth of the skull to its maximum length

cranial nerve *n* (1840) **:** any of the nerves that arise in pairs from the lower surface of the brain one on each side and pass through openings in the skull to the periphery of the body and that comprise 12 pairs in reptiles, birds, and mammals and usu. 10 in fishes and amphibians

cra·ni·ate \ˈkrā-nē-ət, -ˌāt\ *adj* (ca. 1879) **:** having a cranium — **craniate** *n*

cra·nio·ce·re·bral \ˌkrā-nē-ō-sə-ˈrē-brəl, -ˈser-ə-\ *adj* (ca. 1903) **:** involving both cranium and brain ⟨~ injury⟩

cra·nio·fa·cial \-ˈfā-shəl\ *adj* (1852) **:** of, relating to, or involving both the cranium and the face

cra·ni·ol·o·gy \ˌkrā-nē-ˈäl-ə-jē\ *n* [prob. fr. G *kraniologie,* fr. *kranio-* crani- + *-logie* -logy] (1851) **:** a science dealing with variations in size, shape, and proportions of skulls among the races of men

cra·ni·om·e·try \-ˈäm-ə-trē\ *n* [ISV] (ca. 1828) **:** a science dealing with cranial measurement

cra·nio·sa·cral \ˈkrā-nē-ō-ˈsak-rəl, -ˈsā-krəl\ *adj* (ca. 1923) **:** PARASYMPATHETIC

cra·ni·ot·o·my \ˌkrā-nē-ˈät-ə-mē\ *n* [ISV] (1855) **:** surgical opening of the skull

cra·ni·um \ˈkrā-nē-əm\ *n, pl* **-ni·ums** *or* **-nia** \-nē-ə\ [ML, fr. Gk *kranion;* akin to Gk *kara* head — more at CEREBRAL] (15c) **:** SKULL; *specif* **:** the part that encloses the brain **:** BRAINCASE

[1]**crank** \ˈkraŋk\ *n* [ME *cranke,* fr. OE *cranc-* (as in *crancstæf,* a weaving instrument); akin to OE *cradol* cradle] (bef. 12c) **1 :** a bent part of an axle or shaft or an arm keyed at right angles to the end of a shaft by which circular motion is imparted to or received from the shaft or by which reciprocating motion is changed into circular motion or vice versa **2 a** *archaic* **:** BEND **b :** a twist or turn of speech **:** CONCEIT — used esp. in the phrase *quips and cranks* **c** (1) **:** CAPRICE, CROTCHET (2) **:** an eccentric person; *also* **:** one that is overly enthusiastic about a particular subject or activity **d :** a bad-tempered person **:** GROUCH

[2]**crank** *vi* (1592) **1 :** to move with a winding course **:** ZIGZAG **2 a :** to turn a crank (as in starting an automobile engine) **b :** to come into being or get started by or as if by the turning of a crank ⟨as the political season ~*s* up, with barbecues . . . in the offing —*Newsweek*⟩ ~ *vt* **1 :** to bend into the shape of a crank **2 :** to furnish or fasten with a crank **3 a :** to move or operate by or as if by a crank ⟨~ the window down⟩ **b :** to start by use of a crank — often used with *up*

[3]**crank** *adj* [ME *cranke,* of unknown origin] (15c) **1** *chiefly dial* **:** MERRY, HIGH-SPIRITED **2** *chiefly dial* **:** COCKY, CONFIDENT

[4]**crank** *adj* [short for *crank-sided* (easily tipped)] *of a boat* (ca. 1696) **:** easily tipped by an external force

[5]**crank** *adj* [Sc, bent, distorted, prob. fr. [1]*crank*] (1649) **:** out of kilter **:** LOOSE ⟨~ machinery⟩

crank·case \ˈkraŋk-ˌkās\ *n* (ca. 1878) **:** the housing of a crankshaft

[1]**cran·kle** \ˈkraŋ-kəl\ *vb* **cran·kled; cran·kling** \-k(ə-)liŋ\ [freq. of [2]*crank*] *vt, obs* (1594) **:** to break into turns, bends, or angles **:** CRINKLE ~ *vi, archaic* **:** WIND, ZIGZAG

[2]**crankle** *n* (1598) **:** BEND, CRINKLE

crank out *vt* (1956) **:** to produce esp. in a mechanical manner

crank·pin \ˈkraŋk-ˌpin\ *n* (1839) **:** the cylindrical piece which forms the handle of a crank or to which the connecting rod is attached

crank·shaft \ˈkraŋk-ˌshaft\ *n* (1854) **:** a shaft driven by or driving a crank

[1]**cranky** \ˈkraŋ-kē\ *adj* **crank·i·er; -est** [[1]*crank* & [3]*crank*] (1821) **1 a :** marked by eccentricity **b :** given to fretful fussiness **:** readily angered when opposed **:** CROTCHETY **2 :** full of twists and turns **:** TORTUOUS ⟨a ~ road⟩ **3 :** working erratically **:** UNPREDICTABLE ⟨a ~ old tractor⟩ **4** *dial* **:** CRAZY, IMBECILE — **crank·i·ly** \-kə-lē\ *adv* — **crank·i·ness** \-kē-nəs\ *n*

[2]**cranky** *adj* [[5]*crank*] *of a boat* (1841) **:** liable to heel or tip

cran·nog \ˈkran-ˌȯg, kra-ˈnōg\ *n* [ScGael *crannag* & IrGael *crannōg*] (1608) **:** an artificial fortified island constructed in a lake or marsh orig. in prehistoric Ireland and Scotland

cran·ny \ˈkran-ē\ *n, pl* **crannies** [ME *crany,* fr. MF *cren, cran* notch] (15c) **1 :** a small break or slit **:** CREVICE **2 :** an obscure nook or corner — **cran·nied** \-ēd\ *adj*

cran·reuch \ˈkran-ˌrük\ *n* [prob. modif. of ScGael *crannreotha*] (1682) *Scot* **:** HOARFROST, RIME

[1]**crap** \ˈkrap\ *vi* **crapped; crap·ping** (ca. 1897) **:** DEFECATE — usu. considered vulgar

[2]**crap** *n* [ME *crappe* chaff, residue from rendered fat, perh. fr. OF *crappe* chaff, residue, fr. ML *crappa*] (1898) **1 a :** EXCREMENT — usu. considered vulgar **b :** the act of defecating — usu. considered vulgar **2 :** NONSENSE, RUBBISH — sometimes considered vulgar

[3]**crap** *n* [back-formation fr. *craps*] (1885) **1** — used as an attributive form of *craps* ⟨~ game⟩ ⟨~ table⟩ **2 :** a throw of 2, 3, or 12 in the game of craps losing the shooter his bet unless he has a point — called also *craps;* compare NATURAL

[4]**crap** *vi* **crapped; crap·ping** (1930) **1 :** to throw a crap **2 :** to throw a seven while trying to make a point — usu. used with *out*

[1]**crape** \ˈkrāp\ *n* [alter. of F *crêpe,* fr. MF *crespe* curly, fr. L *crispus* — more at CRISP] (1633) **1 :** CREPE **2 :** a band of crepe worn on a hat or sleeve as a sign of mourning

[2]**crape** *vt* **craped; crap·ing** (1815) **:** to cover or shroud with or as if with crape

[3]**crape** *vt* **craped; crap·ing** [F *crêper,* fr. L *crispare,* fr. *crispus*] (1774) **:** to make (the hair) curly

crape myrtle *n* (1850) **:** an East Indian shrub (*Lagerstroemia indica*) of the loosestrife family widely grown in warm regions for its flowers

crap·per \ˈkrap-ər\ *n* [[1]*crap*] (ca. 1932) **:** TOILET — usu. considered vulgar

crap·pie \ˈkräp-ē\ *n* [CanF *crapet*] (1856) **1 :** BLACK CRAPPIE **2 :** WHITE CRAPPIE

crap·py \ˈkrap-ē\ *adj* **crap·pi·er; -est** *slang* (1846) **:** markedly inferior in quality **:** LOUSY

craps \ˈkraps\ *n pl but sing or pl in constr* [LaF, fr. F *crabs, craps,* fr. E *crabs* lowest throw at hazard, fr. pl. of [1]*crab*] (1843) **1 :** a gambling game played with two dice **2 :** [3]CRAP 2

crap·shoot \ˈkrap-ˌshüt\ *n* (1971) **:** a risky business venture

crap·shoot·er \ˈkrap-ˌshüt-ər\ *n* (1895) **:** one who plays craps

crap·u·lous \ˈkrap-yə-ləs\ *adj* [LL *crapulosus,* fr. L *crapula* intoxication, fr. Gk *kraipalē*] (1536) **1 :** marked by intemperance esp. in eating or drinking **2 :** sick from excessive indulgence in liquor

[1]**crash** \ˈkrash\ *vb* [ME *crasschen*] *vt* (15c) **1 a :** to break violently and noisily **:** SMASH **b :** to damage (an airplane) in landing **2 a :** to cause to make a loud noise ⟨~ the cymbals together⟩ **b :** to force (as one's way) through with loud crashing noises **3 :** to enter or attend without invitation or without paying ⟨~ the party⟩ ~ *vi* **1 a :** to break or go to pieces with or as if with violence and noise; *esp* **:** to undergo a financial crash **b :** to crash an airplane **2 :** to make a smashing noise ⟨thunder ~*ing* overhead⟩ **3 :** to move or force one's way with or as if with a crash ⟨~*es* into the room⟩ **4** *slang* **:** to experience the aftereffects (as dysphoria or depression) of drug intoxication **5** *slang* **:** to spend the night in a particular place **:** SLEEP — **crasher** *n*

[2]**crash** *n* (1580) **1 :** a loud sound (as of things smashing) ⟨a ~ of thunder⟩ **2 :** a breaking to pieces by or as if by collision; *also* **:** an instance of crashing ⟨a plane ~⟩ **3 :** a sudden decline (as of a population) or failure (as of a business) ⟨a stockmarket ~⟩ **4** *slang* **:** the process of crashing after drug intoxication

[3]**crash** *adj* (1952) **:** marked by a concerted effort and effected in the shortest possible time ⟨a ~ program to teach dropouts how to read⟩

[4]**crash** *n* [prob. fr. Russ *krashenina* colored linen] (1812) **:** a coarse fabric used for draperies, toweling, and clothing and for strengthening joints of cased-in books

crash dive *n* (1918) **:** a dive made by a submarine in the least possible time — **crash–dive** *vi*

crash helmet *n* (ca. 1918) **:** a usu. plastic or leather helmet that is worn (as by motorcyclists) as protection for the head in the event of an accident

crash·ing \ˈkrash-iŋ\ *adj* (1924) **1 :** UTTER, ABSOLUTE ⟨a ~ bore⟩ **2 :** SUPERLATIVE ⟨a ~ effect⟩

crash–land \ˈkrash-ˈland\ *vt* (1941) **:** to land (an airplane or spacecraft) under emergency conditions usu. with damage to the craft ~ *vi* **:** to crash-land an airplane or spacecraft — **crash landing** *n*

crash pad *n* (1939) **1 :** protective padding (as on the inside of an automobile or a military tank) **2 :** a place where free temporary lodging is available ⟨a hippie *crash pad*⟩

crash·wor·thy \ˈkrash-ˌwər-t͟hē\ *adj* (1966) **:** resistant to the effects of collision ⟨~ cars⟩ — **crash·wor·thi·ness** *n*

crass \ˈkras\ *adj* [L *crassus* thick, gross; akin to L *cratis* wickerwork — more at HURDLE] (1660) **:** having or indicating such grossness of mind as precludes delicacy and discrimination ***syn*** see STUPID — **crass·ly** *adv* — **crass·ness** *n*

cras·si·tude \ˈkras-ə-ˌt(y)üd\ *n* (1679) **:** the quality or state of being crass **:** GROSSNESS; *also* **:** an instance of grossness

-crat \ˌkrat\ *n comb form* [F *-crate,* back-formation fr. *-cratie* -cracy] **1** : advocate or partisan of a (specified) theory of government ⟨theo*crat*⟩ **2** : member of a (specified) dominant class ⟨pluto*crat*⟩ — **-crat·ic** \ˈkrat-ik\ *adj comb form*

cratch \ˈkrach\ *n* [ME *cracche,* fr. OF *creche* manger — more at CRÈCHE] (14c) **1** : a crib or rack esp. for fodder; *also* : FRAME **2** *archaic* : MANGER

[1]crate \ˈkrāt\ *n* [L *cratis*] (15c) **1** : an open box of wooden slats or a usu. wooden protective case or framework for shipping **2** : JALOPY

[2]crate *vt* **crat·ed; crat·ing** (1871) : to pack in a crate

[1]cra·ter \ˈkrāt-ər\ *n* [L, mixing bowl, crater, fr. Gk *kratēr,* fr. *kerannynai* to mix; akin to OE *hrēran* to stir — more at RARE] (1613) **1** \ˈkrāt-ər\ **a** : the bowl-shaped depression around the orifice of a volcano **b** : a depression formed by the impact of a meteorite **c** : a hole in the ground made by the explosion of a bomb or shell **d** : an eroded lesion **e** : a dimple in a painted surface **2** \ˈkrāt-ər, krä-ˈte(ə)r\ : KRATER

[2]crater *vi* (1884) : to exhibit or form craters ~ *vt* : to form craters in

cra·ter·let \ˈkrāt-ər-lət\ *n* (1881) : a small crater

C ration *n* (1942) : a canned field ration of the U. S. Army

cra·ton \ˈkrā-ˌtän, ˈkra-\ *n* [G *kraton,* modif. of Gk *kratos* strength — more at HARD] (1944) : a stable relatively immobile area of the earth's crust that forms the nuclear mass of a continent or the central basin of an ocean — **cra·ton·ic** \krə-ˈtän-ik, krā-, kra-\ *adj*

craunch \ˈkrȯnch, ˈkränch\ *vb* [prob. imit.] (1631) : CRUNCH — **craunch** *n*

cra·vat \krə-ˈvat\ *n* [F *cravate,* fr. *Cravate* Croatian] (1658) **1** : a band or scarf worn around the neck **2** : NECKTIE

crave \ˈkrāv\ *vb* **craved; crav·ing** [ME *craven,* fr. OE *crafian;* akin to ON *krefja* to crave, demand] *vt* (bef. 12c) **1** : to ask for earnestly : BEG, DEMAND ⟨~ a pardon for neglect⟩ **2 a** : to want greatly : NEED ⟨~*s* drugs⟩ **b** : to yearn for ⟨~ a vanished youth⟩ ~ *vi* : to have a strong or inward desire ⟨~*s* after affection⟩ ***syn*** see DESIRE — **crav·er** *n*

cra·ven \ˈkrā-vən\ *adj* [ME *cravant*] (13c) **1** *archaic* : DEFEATED, VANQUISHED **2** : lacking any courage : contemptibly fainthearted ***syn*** see COWARDLY — **craven** *n* — **cra·ven·ly** *adv* — **cra·ven·ness** \-vən-nəs\ *n*

crav·ing \ˈkrā-viŋ\ *n* (1633) : a great desire or longing; *esp* : an abnormal desire (as for a habit-forming drug)

craw \ˈkrȯ\ *n* [ME *crawe,* fr. (assumed) OE *cræga;* akin to Gk *bronchos* trachea, throat, L *vorare* to devour — more at VORACIOUS] (bef. 12c) **1** : the crop of a bird or insect **2** : the stomach esp. of a lower animal

craw·dad \ˈkrȯ-ˌdad\ *n* [alter. of *crawfish*] *chiefly Midland* (ca. 1905) : CRAYFISH 1

[1]craw·fish \ˈkrȯ-ˌfish\ *n* [by folk etymology fr. ME *crevis, kraveys*] (1624) **1** : CRAYFISH 1 **2** : SPINY LOBSTER

[2]crawfish *vi* (1842) : to retreat from a position : back out

[1]crawl \ˈkrȯl\ *vb* [ME *crawlen,* fr. ON *krafla;* akin to OE *crabba* crab] *vi* (14c) **1** : to move slowly in a prone position without or as if without the use of limbs ⟨the snake ~*ed* into its hole⟩ **2** : to move or progress slowly or laboriously ⟨traffic ~*s* along at 10 miles an hour⟩ **3** : to advance by guile or servility ⟨~*ing* into favor by toadying to his boss⟩ **4** : to spread by extending stems or tendrils **5 a** : to be alive or swarming with or as if with creeping things ⟨a kitchen ~*ing* with ants⟩ **b** : to have the sensation of insects creeping over one ⟨the story made her flesh ~⟩ **6** : to fail to stay evenly spread — used of paint, varnish, or glaze ~ *vt* **1** : to move upon in or as if in a creeping manner **2** : to reprove harshly ⟨they got no good right to ~ me for what I wrote —Marjorie K. Rawlings⟩

[2]crawl *n* (1818) **1 a** : the act or action of crawling **b** : slow or laborious progress **c** *chiefly Brit* : a going from one pub to another **2** : a prone speed swimming stroke consisting of alternating overarm strokes and a flutter kick **3** : lettering that moves vertically or horizontally across a television or motion-picture screen and gives information (as performer credits or news bulletins)

[3]crawl *n* [Afrik *kraal* pen —more at KRAAL] (1769) : an enclosure in shallow waters (as for confining lobsters)

crawl·er *n* (1649) **1** : one that crawls **2 a** : a Caterpillar tractor **b** : a vehicle (as a crane) that travels on endless chain belts

crawl space *n* (1946) : a shallow unfinished space beneath the first floor or under the roof of a building esp. for access to plumbing or wiring

crawl·way \ˈkrȯl-ˌwā\ *n* (1909) : a low passageway (as in a cave) that can be traversed only by crawling

crawly \ˈkrȯ-lē\ *adj* (1860) : CREEPY 1

cray·fish \ˈkrā-ˌfish\ *n* [by folk etymology fr. ME *crevis,* fr. MF *crevice,* of Gmc origin; akin to OHG *krebiz* crab — more at CRAB] (14c) **1** : any of numerous freshwater crustaceans (tribe Astacura) resembling the lobster but usu. much smaller **2** : SPINY LOBSTER

[1]cray·on \ˈkrā-ˌän, -ən; ˈkran\ *n* [F, crayon, pencil, fr. dim. of *craie* chalk, fr. L *creta*] (1644) **1** : a stick of white or colored chalk or of colored wax used for writing or drawing **2** : a crayon drawing

[2]crayon *vt* (1662) : to draw with a crayon — **cray·on·ist** \ˈkrā-ə-nəst\ *n*

[1]craze \ˈkrāz\ *vb* **crazed; craz·ing** [ME *crasen* to crush, craze, of Scand origin; akin to OSw *krasa* to crush] *vt* (14c) **1** *obs* : BREAK, SHATTER **2** : to produce minute cracks on the surface or glaze of **3** : to make insane or as if insane ⟨*crazed* by pain and fear⟩ ~ *vi* **1** *archaic* : SHATTER, BREAK **2** : to become insane **3** : to develop a mesh of fine cracks

[2]craze *n* (1534) **1** : an exaggerated and often transient enthusiasm : MANIA **2** : a crack in a surface or coating (as of glaze or enamel) ***syn*** see FASHION

[1]cra·zy \ˈkrā-zē\ *adj* **cra·zi·er; -est** (1583) **1 a** : full of cracks or flaws : UNSOUND **b** : CROOKED, ASKEW **2 a** : MAD, INSANE **b** (1) : IMPRACTICAL (2) : ERRATIC **c** : being out of the ordinary : UNUSUAL ⟨a taste for ~ hats⟩ **3 a** : distracted with desire or excitement ⟨a thrill-*crazy* mob⟩ **b** : absurdly fond : INFATUATED ⟨he's ~ about the girl⟩ **c** : passionately preoccupied : OBSESSED ⟨~ about boats⟩ — **cra·zi·ly** \-zə-lē\ *adv* — **cra·zi·ness** \-zē-nəs\ *n* — **like crazy** : to an extreme degree ⟨everyone dancing *like crazy*⟩

[2]crazy *n, pl* **cra·zies** (1867) : one who is or acts crazy; *esp* : such a one associated with a radical or extremist political cause

crazy bone *n* (1876) : FUNNY BONE

crazy quilt *n* (1886) **1** : a patchwork quilt without a design **2** : JUMBLE, HODGEPODGE

cra·zy·weed \ˈkrā-zē-ˌwēd\ *n* (1889) : LOCOWEED

C–re·ac·tive protein \ˌsē-rē-ˌak-tiv-\ *n* [*C-polysaccharide* (a polysaccharide found in the cell wall of pneumococci and precipitated by this protein), fr. *carbohydrate*] (ca. 1956) : a protein present in blood serum in various abnormal states (as inflammation or neoplasia)

[1]creak \ˈkrēk\ *vi* [ME *creken* to croak, of imit. origin] (1583) : to make a prolonged grating or squeaking sound often as a result of being worn out; *also* : to proceed slowly with or as if with creaking wheels ⟨the story ~*s* along to a dull conclusion⟩

[2]creak *n* (1605) : a rasping or grating noise

creaky \ˈkrē-kē\ *adj* **creak·i·er; -est** (1834) **1** : marked by creaking : SQUEAKY ⟨~ shoes⟩ **2** : DILAPIDATED, DECREPIT ⟨a ~ old house⟩ — **creak·i·ly** \-kə-lē\ *adv*

[1]cream \ˈkrēm\ *n, often attrib* [ME *creime, creme,* fr. MF *craime, cresme,* fr. LL *cramum,* of Celt origin; akin to W *cramen* scab] (14c) **1** : the yellowish part of milk containing from 18 to about 40 percent butterfat **2 a** : a food prepared with cream **b** : something having the consistency of cream; *esp* : a usu. emulsified medicinal or cosmetic preparation **3** : the choicest part : BEST ⟨the ~ of the crop⟩ **4** : CREAMER 2 **5 a** : a pale yellow **b** : a cream-colored animal — **cream·i·ly** \ˈkrē-mə-lē\ *adv* — **cream·i·ness** \-mē-nəs\ *n* — **creamy** \-mē\ *adj*

[2]cream *vi* (1596) **1** : to form cream or a surface layer like the cream on standing milk **2** : to break into or cause something to break into a creamy froth; *also* : to move like froth ~ *vt* **1 a** : SKIM 1c **b** : to remove (something choice) from an aggregate ⟨she has ~*ed* off her favorite stories from her earlier books —*Times Lit. Supp.*⟩ **2** : to furnish, prepare, or treat with cream; *also* : to dress with a cream sauce **3 a** : to beat into a creamy froth **b** : to work or blend to the consistency of cream ⟨~ butter and sugar together⟩ **c** (1) : to defeat decisively ⟨was ~*ed* in the first round⟩ (2) : WRECK ⟨~*ed* the car on the turnpike⟩ **4** : to cause to form a surface layer of or like cream

cream cheese *n* (1583) : a mild soft unripened cheese made from whole sweet milk enriched with cream

cream·cups \ˈkrēm-ˌkəps\ *n pl but sing or pl in constr* (1888) : any of several California annuals (esp. *Platystemon californicus*) of the poppy family

cream·er \ˈkrē-mər\ *n* (1858) **1** : a device for separating cream from milk **2** : a small vessel for serving cream **3** : a nondairy product used as a substitute for cream (as in coffee)

cream·ery \ˈkrēm-(ə-)rē\ *n, pl* **-er·ies** (1872) : an establishment where butter and cheese are made or where milk and cream are prepared or sold

cream of tartar (1662) : a white crystalline salt $C_4H_5KO_6$ used esp. in baking powder and in certain treatments of metals

cream puff *n* (1880) **1** : a round shell of light pastry filled with whipped cream or a cream filling **2** : an ineffectual person **3** : something trifling or inconsiderable

cream soda *n* (1854) : a carbonated soft drink flavored with vanilla and sweetened with sugar

[1]crease \ˈkrēs\ *n* [prob. alter. of earlier *creaste,* fr. ME *creste* crest] (1578) **1** : a line, mark, or ridge made by or as if by folding a pliable substance **2** : a specially marked area in various sports; *esp* : an area surrounding or in front of a goal (as in lacrosse or hockey) — **creaseless** \-ləs\ *adj*

[2]crease *vb* **creased; creas·ing** *vt* (1588) **1** : to make a crease in or on : WRINKLE ⟨old age had *creased* her face⟩ **2** : to wound slightly esp. by grazing ~ *vi* : to become creased — **creas·er** *n*

[1]cre·ate \krē-ˈāt, ˈkrē-ˌ\ *vb* **cre·at·ed; cre·at·ing** [ME *createn,* fr. L *creatus,* pp. of *creare* — more at CRESCENT] *vt* (14c) **1** : to bring into existence ⟨God *created* the heaven and the earth —Gen 1:1 (AV)⟩ **2 a** : to invest with a new form, office, or rank ⟨was *created* a lieutenant⟩ **b** : to produce or bring about by a course of action or behavior ⟨her arrival *created* a terrible fuss⟩ ⟨~ new jobs for the unemployed⟩ **3** : CAUSE, OCCASION ⟨famine ~*s* high food prices⟩ **4 a** : to produce through imaginative skill ⟨~ a painting⟩ **b** : DESIGN ⟨~*s* dresses⟩ ~ *vi* : to make or bring into existence something new ***syn*** see INVENT

[2]create *adj, archaic* (15c) : CREATED

cre·atine \ˈkrē-ə-ˌtēn, -ət-ᵊn\ *n* [ISV, fr. Gk *kreat-, kreas* flesh — more at RAW] (1840) : a white crystalline nitrogenous substance $C_4H_9N_3O_2$ found esp. in the muscles of vertebrates either free or as phosphocreatine

creatine phosphate *n* (ca. 1947) : PHOSPHOCREATINE

cre·at·i·nine \krē-ˈat-ᵊn-ˌēn, -ᵊn-ən\ *n* [G *kreatinin,* fr. *kreatin* creatine] (1851) : a white crystalline strongly basic compound $C_4H_7N_3O$ formed from creatine and found esp. in muscle, blood, and urine

cre·ation \krē-ˈā-shən\ *n* [ME *creacioun,* fr. MF or L: MF *creation,* fr. L *creation-, creatio,* fr. *creatus*] (14c) **1** : the act of creating; *esp* : the act of bringing the world into ordered existence **2** : the act of making, inventing, or producing: as **a** : the act of investing with a new rank or office **b** : the first representation of a dramatic role **3** : something that is created: as **a** : WORLD **b** : creatures singly or in aggregate **c** : an original work of art **d** : a new usu. striking article of clothing

cre·ation·ism \-shə-ˌniz-əm\ *n* (1880) : a doctrine or theory holding that matter, the various forms of life, and the world were created by God out of nothing — compare EVOLUTION 5b — **cre·ation·ist** \-shə-nəst\ *n or adj*

cre·ative \krē-ˈāt-iv\ *adj* (1678) **1** : marked by the ability or power to create : given to creating ⟨the ~ impulse⟩ ⟨nature is a ~ agent⟩ **2** : having the quality of something created rather than imitated : IMAGINATIVE ⟨the ~ arts⟩ — **cre·ative·ly** *adv* — **cre·ative·ness** *n*

creative evolution *n* [trans. of F *évolution créatrice*] (1909) : evolution that is a creative product of a vital force rather than a spontaneous process explicable in terms of scientific laws — compare EMERGENT EVOLUTION

cre·ativ·i·ty \ˌkrē-(ˌ)ā-ˈtiv-ət-ē, ˌkrē-ə-\ *n* (1875) **1** : the quality of being creative **2** : the ability to create

cre·ator \krē-ˈāt-ər\ *n* (13c) : one that creates usu. by bringing something new or original into being; *esp, cap* : GOD 1

crea·ture \ˈkrē-chər\ *n* [ME, fr. OF, fr. LL *creatura,* fr. L *creatus,* pp.] (14c) **1** : something created either animate or inanimate: as **a** : a lower animal; *esp* : a farm animal **b** : a human being : PERSON **c** : a being of anomalous or uncertain aspect or nature ⟨~*s* of fantasy⟩ **2** : one that is the servile dependent or tool of another : INSTRUMENT — **crea·tur·al** \ˈkrēch-(ə-)rəl\ *adj* — **crea·ture·hood** \ˈkrē-chər-ˌhu̇d\ *n* — **crea·ture·li·ness** \-chər-lē-nəs\ *n* — **crea·ture·ly** \-chər-lē\ *adj*

creature comfort *n* (1659) : something (as food, warmth, or special accommodations) that gives bodily comfort

crèche \ˈkresh, ˈkrāsh\ *n* [F, fr. OF *creche* manger, crib, of Gmc origin; akin to OHG *krippa* manger — more at CRIB] (1854) **1** : DAY NURSERY **2** : a foundling hospital **3** : a representation of the Nativity scene

cre·dence \ˈkrēd-ᵊn(t)s\ *n* [ME, fr. MF or ML; MF, fr. ML *credentia,* fr. L *credent-, credens,* prp. of *credere* to believe, trust — more at CREED] (14c) **1** : mental acceptance as true or real ⟨give ~ to gossip⟩ **2** : CREDENTIALS — used in the phrase *letters of credence* **3** [MF, fr. OIt *credenza*] : a Renaissance sideboard used chiefly for valuable plate **4** : a small table where the bread and wine rest before consecration ***syn*** see BELIEF

cre·dent \ˈkrēd-ᵊnt\ *adj* [L *credent-, credens,* prp.] (1602) **1** *archaic* : giving credence : CONFIDING **2** *obs* : CREDIBLE

[1]**cre·den·tial** \kri-ˈden-chəl\ *adj* (15c) : warranting credit or confidence — used chiefly in the phrase *credential letters*

[2]**credential** *n* (1674) **1** : something that gives a title to credit or confidence **2** *pl* : testimonials showing that a person is entitled to credit or has a right to exercise official power **3** : CERTIFICATE, DIPLOMA

[3]**credential** *vt* **-tialed** *also* **-tialled; -tial·ing** *also* **-tial·ling** (1888) : to furnish with credentials ⟨to ~ adequate academic performance —K. P. Cross⟩

cre·den·tial·ism \-chə-ˌliz-əm\ *n* (1967) : undue emphasis on credentials (as college degrees) as prerequisites to employment

cre·den·za \kri-ˈden-zə\ *n* [It, lit., belief, confidence, fr. ML *credentia*] (1880) **1** : CREDENCE 3 **2** : a sideboard, buffet, or bookcase patterned after a Renaissance credence; *esp* : one without legs

cred·i·bil·i·ty \ˌkred-ə-ˈbil-ət-ē\ *n* (1594) **1** : the quality or power of inspiring belief ⟨an account lacking in ~⟩ **2** : capacity for belief ⟨strains her reader's ~ —*Times Lit. Supp.*⟩

credibility gap *n* (1966) **1 a** : lack of trust ⟨a special *credibility gap* is likely to open between the generations —Kenneth Keniston⟩ **b** : lack of believability ⟨a *credibility gap* created by contradictory official statements —Samuel Ellenport⟩ **2** : DISCREPANCY ⟨the *credibility gap* between the professed ideals . . . and their actual practices —Jeanne L. Noble⟩

cred·i·ble \ˈkred-ə-bəl\ *adj* [ME, fr. L *credibilis,* fr. *credere*] (14c) **1** : offering reasonable grounds for being believed ⟨a ~ account of an accident⟩ ⟨~ witnesses⟩ **2** : of sufficient capability to be militarily effective ⟨a ~ deterrent⟩ ⟨~ forces⟩ — **cred·i·bly** \ˈkred-ə-blē\ *adv*

[1]**cred·it** \ˈkred-ət\ *vt* [partly fr. [2]*credit;* partly fr. L *creditus,* pp.] (1541) **1** : to supply goods on credit to **2** : to trust in the truth of : BELIEVE **3** *archaic* : to bring credit or honor upon **4** : to enter upon the credit side of an account **5 a** : to consider usu. favorably as the source, agent, or performer of an action or the possessor of a trait ⟨~*s* him with an excellent sense of humor⟩ **b** : to attribute to some person ⟨they ~ the invention to him⟩ ***syn*** see ASCRIBE

[2]**credit** *n* [MF, fr. OIt *credito,* fr. L *creditum* something entrusted to another, loan, fr. neut. of *creditus,* pp. of *credere* to believe, entrust — more at CREED] (1542) **1 a** : the balance in a person's favor in an account **b** : an amount or sum placed at a person's disposal by a bank **c** : time given for payment for goods or services sold on trust ⟨long-term ~⟩ **d (1)** : an entry on the right-hand side of an account constituting an addition to a revenue, net worth, or liability account **(2)** : a deduction from an expense or asset account **e** : any one of or the sum of the items entered on the right-hand side of an account **f** : a deduction from an amount otherwise due **2** : reliance on the truth or reality of something ⟨give ~ to idle rumors⟩ **3 a** : influence or power derived from enjoying the confidence of another or others **b** : good name : ESTEEM; *also* : financial or commercial trustworthiness **4** *archaic* : CREDIBILITY **5** : a source of honor ⟨a ~ to the school⟩ **6 a** : something that gains or adds to reputation or esteem : HONOR ⟨took no ~ for his kindly act⟩ **b** : RECOGNITION, ACKNOWLEDGMENT ⟨quite willing to accept undeserved ~⟩ **7** : recognition by name of a person contributing to a performance (as a film or telecast) **8 a** : recognition by a school or college that a student has fulfilled a requirement leading to a degree **b** : CREDIT HOUR ***syn*** see BELIEF, INFLUENCE

cred·it·able \ˈkred-ət-ə-bəl\ *adj* (1526) **1** : worthy of belief **2** : sufficiently good to bring esteem or praise **3** : worthy of commercial credit **4** : capable of being assigned — **cred·it·abil·i·ty** \ˌkred-ət-ə-ˈbil-ət-ē\ *n* — **cred·it·able·ness** \ˈkred-ət-ə-bəl-nəs\ *n* — **cred·it·ably** \-blē\ *adv*

credit card *n* (1888) : a card authorizing purchases on credit

credit hour *n* (1927) : the unit of measuring educational credit based on a given number of classroom periods per week throughout a term

credit line *n* (1926) **1** : a line, note, or name that acknowledges the source of an item (as a news dispatch or television program) **2** : LINE OF CREDIT

cred·i·tor \ˈkred-ət-ər\ *n* (15c) : one to whom a debt is owed; *esp* : a person to whom money or goods are due

credit union *n* (1921) : a cooperative association that makes small loans to its members at low interest rates

cred·it·wor·thy \ˈkred-ət-ˌwər-t͟hē\ *adj* (1924) : being financially sound enough to justify the extension of credit — **cred·it·wor·thi·ness** *n*

cre·do \ˈkrēd-(ˌ)ō, ˈkrād-\ *n, pl* **credos** [ME, fr. L, I believe] (12c) : CREED

cre·du·li·ty \kri-ˈd(y)ü-lət-ē\ *n* (15c) : undue readiness of belief

cred·u·lous \ˈkrej-ə-ləs\ *adj* [L *credulus,* fr. *credere*] (1576) **1** : ready to believe esp. on slight or uncertain evidence **2** : proceeding from credulity — **cred·u·lous·ly** *adv* — **cred·u·lous·ness** *n*

Cree \ˈkrē\ *n, pl* **Cree** *or* **Crees** [short for earlier *Christeno,* fr. CanF *Christino,* prob. modif. of Ojibwa *Kenistenoag*] (1744) **1** : a member of an Indian people of Manitoba and Saskatchewan **2** : the Algonquian language of the Cree Indians

creed \ˈkrēd\ *n* [ME *crede,* fr. OE *crēda,* fr. L *credo* (first word of the Apostles' and Nicene Creeds), fr. *credere* to believe, trust, entrust; akin to OIr *cretim* I believe, Skt *śrad-dadhāti* he believes] (bef. 12c) **1** : a brief authoritative formula of religious belief **2** : a set of fundamental beliefs; *also* : a guiding principle — **creed·al** *or* **cre·dal** \ˈkrēd-ᵊl\ *adj*

creek \ˈkrēk, ˈkrik\ *n* [ME *crike, creke,* fr. ON *-kriki* bend; akin to ON *krōkr* hook — more at CROOK] (13c) **1** *chiefly Brit* : a small inlet or bay narrower and extending farther inland than a cove **2** : a natural stream of water normally smaller than and often tributary to a river **3** *archaic* : a narrow or winding passage — **up the creek** : in a difficult or perplexing situation

Creek \ˈkrēk\ *n* (1725) **1** : an American Indian confederacy of peoples chiefly of Muskogean stock of Alabama, Georgia, and Florida **2** : a member of any of the Creek peoples **3** : the Muskogean language of the Creek Indians

[1]**creel** \ˈkrē(ə)l\ *n* [ME *creille, crele,* prob. fr. (assumed) MF *creille* grill, fr. L *craticula* — more at GRILL] (14c) **1** : a wicker basket (as for carrying newly caught fish) **2** : a bar with skewers for holding bobbins in a spinning machine

[2]**creel** *vt* (1844) : to put (caught fish) in a creel

[1]**creep** \ˈkrēp\ *vi* **crept** \ˈkrept\; **creep·ing** [ME *crepen,* fr. OE *crēopan;* akin to Gk *grypos* curved, bent] (bef. 12c) **1 a** : to move along with the body prone and close to the ground **b** : to move slowly on hands and knees **2 a** : to go very slowly ⟨the hours *crept* by⟩ **b** : to go timidly or cautiously so as to escape notice ⟨she *crept* away from the festive scene⟩ **c** : to enter or advance gradually so as to be almost unnoticed ⟨age ~*s* upon us⟩ ⟨a note of irritation *crept* into her voice⟩ **3** : to have the sensation of being covered with creeping things ⟨the thought made his flesh ~⟩ **4** *of a plant* : to spread or grow over a surface rooting at intervals or clinging with tendrils, stems, or aerial roots **5 a** : to slip or gradually shift position **b** : to change shape permanently from prolonged stress or exposure to high temperatures

[2]**creep** *n* (1818) **1** : a movement of or like creeping ⟨traffic moving at a ~⟩ **2** : a distressing sensation like that caused by the creeping of insects over one's flesh; *esp* : a feeling of apprehension or horror — usu. used in pl. with *the* ⟨that gives me the *creeps*⟩ **3** : a feed trough or enclosure that young animals can enter while adults are excluded **4** : the slow change of dimensions of an object from prolonged exposure to high temperature or stress **5** : an unpleasant or obnoxious person

creep·age \ˈkrē-pij\ *n* (1903) : gradual movement : CREEP

creep·er \ˈkrē-pər\ *n* (bef. 12c) **1** : one that creeps: as **a** : a creeping plant **b** : a bird (as of the family Certhiidae) that creeps about on trees or bushes searching for insects **c** : a creeping insect or reptile **2** : GRAPNEL **3** : any of various devices used for creeping: as **a** : a fixture with iron points worn on the shoe to prevent slipping **b** : a low wheeled platform for supporting the body when working under an automobile **4** : a device for supplying or moving material in a steady flow **5** : a usu. one-piece garment for a child at the crawling age

creep·ing \ˈkrē-piŋ\ *adj* (14c) : developing or advancing by slow imperceptible degrees ⟨a period of ~ inflation⟩

creeping eruption *n* (1926) : a skin disorder marked by a spreading red line of eruption and caused esp. by larvae (as of hookworms not normally parasitic in man) burrowing beneath the human skin

creepy \ˈkrē-pē\ *adj* **creep·i·er; -est** (1831) **1** : producing a nervous shivery apprehension ⟨~ things were crawling over us⟩ ⟨a ~ horror story⟩ **2** : of, relating to, or being a creep : annoyingly unpleasant — **creep·i·ly** \-pə-lē\ *adv* — **creep·i·ness** \-pē-nəs\ *n*

creese *var of* KRIS

cre·mains \kri-ˈmānz\ *n pl* [blend of *cremated* and *remains*] (1947) : the ashes of a cremated human body

cre·mate \ˈkrē-ˌmāt, kri-ˈ\ *vt* **cre·mat·ed; cre·mat·ing** [L *crematus,* pp. of *cremare* to burn up, cremate] (1874) : to reduce (as a dead body) to ashes by burning — **cre·ma·tion** \kri-ˈmā-shən\ *n*

cre·ma·to·ri·um \ˌkrē-mə-ˈtōr-ē-əm, ˌkrem-ə-, -ˈtȯr-\ *n, pl* **-ri·ums** *or* **-ria** \-ē-ə\ (1880) : CREMATORY

cre·ma·to·ry \ˈkrē-mə-ˌtōr-ē, ˈkrem-ə-, -ˌtȯr-\ *n, pl* **-ries** (1876) : a furnace for cremating; *also* : an establishment containing such a furnace — **crematory** *adj*

crème *or* **creme** \ˈkrem, ˈkrēm\ *n, pl* **crèmes** *or* **cremes** \ˈkrem(z), ˈkrēmz\ [F, fr. OF *cresme* — more at CREAM] (1845) **1** : cream or a preparation made with or resembling cream used in cooking **2** : a sweet liqueur **3** : CREAM 2b

crème de ca·cao \ˌkrēm-də-ˈkō-(ˌ)kō; ˌkrem-də-kə-ˈkau̇, -kə-ˈkā-(ˌ)ō\ *n* [F, lit., cream of cacao] (1904) : a sweet brown or white liqueur flavored with cacao beans and vanilla

crème de la crème \ˌkrem-də-lä-ˈkrem, -lə-\ *n* [F, lit., cream of the cream] (1848) : the very best

crème de menthe \ˌkrem-də-ˈmen(t)th, ˌkrēm-, -ˈmint, ˌkrem-də-ˈmänt\ *n* [F, lit., cream of mint] (1901) : a sweet green or white mint-flavored liqueur

cre·nate \ˈkrē-ˌnāt\ *or* **cre·nat·ed** \-ˌnāt-əd\ *adj* [NL *crenatus,* fr. ML *crena* notch] (1794) : having the margin or surface cut into rounded scallops ⟨a ~ leaf⟩

cre·na·tion \kri-ˈnā-shən\ *n* (1846) **1 a** : a crenate formation; *esp* : one of the rounded projections on an edge (as of a coin) **b** : the quality or state of being crenate **2** : shrinkage of red blood cells in hypertonic solution resulting in crenate margins

cren·el \ˈkren-ᵊl\ *or* **cre·nelle** \krə-ˈnel\ *n* [MF *crenel,* fr. OF, dim. of *cren* notch, fr. *crener* to notch; akin to ML *crena* notch] (15c) : one of the embrasures alternating with merlons in a battlement — see BATTLEMENT illustration

cren·el·late *or* **cren·el·ate** \ˈkren-ᵊl-ˌāt\ *vt* **-lat·ed** *or* **-at·ed; -lat·ing** *or* **-at·ing** (1851) : to furnish with battlements — **cren·el·late** \-ˌāt, -ət\ *adj* — **cren·el·la·tion** \ˌkren-ᵊl-ˈā-shən\ *n*

cren·el·lat·ed \ˈkren-ᵊl-ˌāt-əd\ *adj* (ca. 1823) : having battlements

cren·u·late \ˈkren-yə-lət, -ˌlāt\ *or* **cren·u·lat·ed** \-ˌlāt-əd\ *adj* [NL *crenulatus,* fr. *crenula,* dim. of ML *crena*] (1794) : having an irregularly wavy or serrate outline ⟨a ~ shoreline⟩ — **cren·u·la·tion** \ˌkren-yə-ˈlā-shən\ *n*

cre·ole \ˈkrē-ˌōl\ *adj* (1748) **1** *often cap* : of or relating to Creoles or their language **2** : relating to or being highly seasoned food typically prepared with rice, okra, tomatoes, and peppers ⟨shrimp~⟩

Cre·ole \ˈkrē-ˌōl\ *n* [F *créole,* fr. Sp *criollo,* fr. Pg *crioulo* white person born in the colonies] (1604) **1** : a person of European descent born esp. in the West Indies or Spanish America **2** : a white person de-

\ə\ abut \ᵊ\ kitten, F table \ər\ further \a\ ash \ā\ ace \ä\ cot, cart \au̇\ out \ch\ chin \e\ bet \ē\ easy \g\ go \i\ hit \ī\ ice \j\ job \ŋ\ sing \ō\ go \ȯ\ law \ȯi\ boy \th\ thin \t͟h\ the \ü\ loot \u̇\ foot \y\ yet \zh\ vision \à, k̲, ⁿ, œ, œ̄, ue, ue̅, ʸ\ *see* Guide to Pronunciation

scended from early French or Spanish settlers of the U.S. Gulf states and preserving their speech and culture **3** : a person of mixed French or Spanish and Negro descent speaking a dialect of French or Spanish **4 a** : the French dialect spoken by many Negroes in southern Louisiana **b** : HAITIAN **c** *not cap* : a language based on two or more languages that serves as the native language of its speakers

¹cre·o·sote \ˈkrē-ə-ˌsōt\ *n* [G *kreosot,* fr. Gk *kreas* flesh + *sōtēr* preserver, fr. *sōzein* to preserve, fr. *sōs* safe; fr. its antiseptic properties — more at RAW, THUMB] (1835) **1** : a clear or yellowish flammable oily liquid mixture of phenolic compounds obtained by the distillation of wood tar esp. from beech wood **2** : a brownish oily liquid consisting chiefly of aromatic hydrocarbons obtained by distillation of coal tar and used esp. as a wood preservative

²creosote *vt* **-sot·ed; -sot·ing** (1846) : to treat with creosote

creosote bush *n* (1846) : a resinous desert shrub (*Larrea divaricata* of the family Zygophyllaceae) found in the southwestern U.S. and Mexico

crepe *or* **crêpe** \ˈkrāp\ *n* [F *crêpe*] (1797) **1** : a light crinkled fabric woven of any of various fibers **2** : CRAPE 2 **3** : a small very thin pancake — **crepe** *adj* — **crep·ey** *or* **crepy** \ˈkrā-pē\ *adj*

crepe de chine \ˌkrāp-də-ˈshēn\ *n, often cap 2d C* [F *crêpe de Chine,* lit., China crepe] (1872) : a soft fine or sheer clothing crepe esp. of silk

crepe myrtle *or* **crêpe myrtle** *n* (1916) : CRAPE MYRTLE

crepe paper *n* (1897) : paper with a crinkled or puckered texture

crepe rubber *n* (1907) : crude rubber in the form of nearly white to brown crinkled sheets used esp. for shoe soles

crepe su·zette \ˌkrāp-sü-ˈzet\ *n, pl* **crepes suzette** \ˌkrāp(s)-sü-ˈzet\ *or* **crepe suzettes** \ˌkrāp-sü-ˈzets\ [F *crêpe Suzette,* fr. *crêpe* pancake + *Suzette* Susy] (1922) : a thin folded or rolled pancake in a hot orange-butter sauce that is sprinkled with a liqueur (as cognac or curaçao) and set ablaze for serving

crep·i·tant \ˈkrep-ət-ənt\ *adj* (1855) : having or making a crackling sound

crep·i·tate \ˈkrep-ə-ˌtāt\ *vi* **-tat·ed; -tat·ing** [L *crepitatus,* pp. of *crepitare* to crackle, fr. *crepitus,* pp. of *crepare* to rattle, crack — more at RAVEN] (ca. 1828) : to make a crackling sound : CRACKLE — **crep·i·ta·tion** \ˌkrep-ə-ˈtā-shən\ *n*

cre·pon \ˈkrā-ˌpän\ *n* [F, fr. *crêpe*] (ca. 1864) : a heavy crepe fabric with lengthwise crinkles

crept *past and past part of* CREEP

cre·pus·cu·lar \kri-ˈpəs-kyə-lər\ *adj* (1668) **1** : of, relating to, or resembling twilight : DIM **2** : active in the twilight ⟨~ insects⟩

cre·pus·cule \kri-ˈpəs-(ˌ)kyü(ə)l\ *or* **cre·pus·cle** \-ˈpəs-əl\ *n* [L *crepusculum,* fr. *creper* dusky] (1665) : TWILIGHT

¹cre·scen·do \krə-ˈshen-(ˌ)dō\ *n, pl* **-dos** *or* **-does** [It, fr. *crescendo,* adj., increasing, gerund of *crescere* to grow, increase, fr. L] (1776) **1 a** : a gradual increase; *specif* : a gradual increase in volume of a musical passage **b** : the peak of a gradual increase : CLIMAX ⟨complaints about stifling smog conditions reach a ~ —*Down Beat*⟩ **2** : a crescendo musical passage — **crescendo** *vi*

mark indicating crescendo 2

²crescendo *adv or adj* (1789) : with an increase in volume — used as a direction in music

¹cres·cent \ˈkres-ᵊnt\ *n* [ME *cressant,* fr. MF *creissant,* fr. prp. of *creistre* to grow, increase, fr. L *crescere;* akin to OHG *hirsi* millet, L *creare* to create, Gk *koros* surfeit] (14c) **1 a** : the moon at any stage between new moon and first quarter and between last quarter and the succeeding new moon when less than half of the illuminated hemisphere is visible **b** : the figure of the moon at such a stage defined by a convex and a concave edge **2** : something shaped like a crescent — **cres·cen·tic** \kre-ˈsent-ik, krə-\ *adj*

²crescent *adj* [L *crescent-, crescens,* prp. of *crescere*] (1574) : marked by an increase

cres·cive \ˈkres-iv\ *adj* [L *crescere* to grow] (1566) : marked by gradual spontaneous development — **cres·cive·ly** *adv*

cre·sol \ˈkrē-ˌsȯl, -ˌsōl\ *n* [ISV, irreg. fr. *creosote*] (ca. 1869) : any of three poisonous colorless crystalline or liquid isomeric phenols C_7H_8O

cress \ˈkres\ *n* [ME *cresse,* fr. OE *cærse, cressa;* akin to OHG *kressa* cress] (bef. 12c) : any of numerous crucifers (esp. genera *Lepidium* and *Nasturtium*) with moderately pungent leaves used in salads and garnishes

cres·set \ˈkres-ət\ *n* [ME, fr. MF, fr. OF *craisset,* fr. *craisse* grease — more at GREASE] (14c) : an iron vessel or basket used for holding an illuminant (as burning oil) and mounted as a torch or suspended as a lantern

Cres·si·da \ˈkres-əd-ə\ *n* : a Trojan woman of medieval legend who pledges herself to Troilus but while a captive of the Greeks gives herself to Diomedes

¹crest \ˈkrest\ *n* [ME *creste,* fr. MF, fr. L *crista;* akin to OE *hrisian* to shake, L *curvus* curved — more at CROWN] (14c) **1 a** : a showy tuft or process on the head of an animal and esp. a bird — see BIRD illustration **b** : the plume or identifying emblem worn on a knight's helmet; *also* : the top of a helmet **c** (1) : a heraldic representation of the crest (2) : a heraldic device depicted above the escutcheon but not upon a helmet (3) : COAT OF ARMS 2a **d** : a ridge or prominence on a part of an animal body **2** : something suggesting a crest esp. in being an upper prominence, edge, or limit: as **a** : PEAK; *esp* : the top line of a mountain or hill **b** : the ridge of a roof or top of a wave **3 a** : a high point of an action or process and esp. of one that is rhythmic **b** : CLIMAX, CULMINATION ⟨at the ~ of his fame⟩ — **crest·al** \ˈkres-tᵊl\ *adj* — **crest·less** \-ləs\ *adj*

²crest *vt* (15c) **1** : to furnish with a crest; *also* : CROWN **2** : to reach the crest of ⟨~*ed* the hill and looked around⟩ ~ *vi* : to rise to a crest ⟨waves ~*ing* in the storm⟩

crest·ed \ˈkres-təd\ *adj* (14c) : having a crest ⟨a ~ bird⟩

crested wheatgrass *n* (1923) : either of two grasses (*Agropyron cristatum* or *A. desertorum*) that were introduced from Russia and are grown in the U.S. for forage and for erosion control

crest·fall·en \ˈkrest-ˌfȯ-lən\ *adj* (1589) **1** : having a drooping crest or hanging head **2** : feeling shame or humiliation : DEJECTED — **crest·fall·en·ly** *adv* — **crest·fall·en·ness** \-lən-nəs\ *n*

crest·ing \ˈkres-tiŋ\ *n* (1869) : a decorative edging or railing (as on pottery or furniture)

cre·syl \ˈkres-əl, ˈkrē-ˌsil\ *n* [ISV *cres*ol + *-yl*] (ca. 1893) : TOLYL

cre·syl·ic \kri-ˈsil-ik\ *adj* [ISV *cresyl* + *-ic*] (1863) : of or relating to cresol or creosote

cre·ta·ceous \kri-ˈtā-shəs\ *adj* [L *cretaceus,* fr. *creta* chalk] (1675) **1** : having the characteristics of or abounding in chalk **2** *cap* : of, relating to, or being the last period of the Mesozoic era or the corresponding system of rocks — **Cretaceous** *n*

cre·tin \ˈkrēt-ᵊn\ *n* [F *crétin,* fr. F dial. *cretin* Christian, human being, kind of idiot found in the Alps, fr. L *christianus* Christian] (1779) **1** : one afflicted with cretinism **2** : a stupid, vulgar, or insensitive person : CLOD, LOUT — **cre·tin·ous** \-ᵊn-əs\ *adj*

cre·tin·ism \-ᵊn-ˌiz-əm\ *n* (1801) : a usu. congenital abnormal condition marked by physical stunting and mental deficiency and caused by severe thyroid deficiency

cre·tonne \ˈkrē-ˌtän, kri-ˈ\ *n* [F, fr *Creton,* Normandy] (1870) : a strong cotton or linen cloth used esp. for curtains and upholstery

Creutz·feldt–Ja·kob disease *also* **Creutz·feld–Ja·cob disease** \ˌkrȯits-ˌfelt-ˌyä-(ˌ)kōb-\ *n* [Hans G. *Creutzfeldt* †1964 Ger. psychiatrist and Alfons M. *Jakob* †1931 Ger. psychiatrist] (ca. 1966) : a rare progressive fatal encephalopathy caused by a slow virus and marked by premature dementia in middle age and gradual loss of muscular coordination

cre·val·le \kri-ˈval-ē\ *n* [by alter.] (1897) : CAVALLA 1; *esp* : JACK CREVALLE

cre·vasse \kri-ˈvas\ *n* [F, fr. OF *crevace*] (1813) **1** : a deep crevice or fissure (as in a glacier or the earth) **2** : a breach in a levee

crev·ice \ˈkrev-əs\ *n* [ME, fr. MF *crevace,* fr. OF, fr. *crever* to break, fr. L *crepare* to crack — more at RAVEN] (14c) : a narrow opening resulting from a split or crack (as in a cliff) : FISSURE

¹crew \ˈkrü\ *chiefly Brit past of* CROW

²crew \ˈkrü\ *n* [ME *crue,* lit., reinforcement, fr. MF *creue* increase, fr. *creistre* to grow — more at CRESCENT] (15c) **1** *archaic* : a band or force of armed men **2** : a group of people associated together in a common activity or by common traits or interests **3 a** : a company of people working on one job or under one foreman or operating a machine **b** : the whole company belonging to a ship sometimes including the officers and master; *also* : one who assists the skipper of a sailboat **c** : the persons who have duties on an aircraft in flight **d** : the rowers and coxswain of a racing shell; *also* : ROWING — **crew·less** \-ləs\ *adj*

³crew *vi* (1935) : to act as a member of a crew ~ *vt* : to serve as a crew member on (as a ship or aircraft)

crew cut *n* (1942) : a very short haircut in which the hair resembles the bristle surface of a brush

crew·el \ˈkrü-əl\ *n* [ME *crule*] (15c) **1** : slackly twisted worsted yarn used for embroidery **2** : CREWELWORK

crew·el·work \-ˌwərk\ *n* (1863) : embroidery worked with crewel

crew·man \ˈkrü-mən\ *n* (1932) : a member of a crew

crew neck *n* [fr. the wearing of such style by oarsmen] (1940) **1** : a round collarless neckline **2** *usu* **crew·neck** \ˈkrü-ˌnek\ : a sweater with a crew neck

crew sock *n* (1948) : a short bulky usu. ribbed sock

¹crib \ˈkrib\ *n* [ME, fr. OE *cribb;* akin to OHG *krippa* manger, Gk *griphos* reed basket, OE *cradol* cradle] (bef. 12c) **1** : a manger for feeding animals **2** : an enclosure esp. of framework: as **a** : a stall for a stabled animal **b** : a small child's bedstead with high enclosing usu. slatted sides **c** : any of various devices resembling a crate or framework in structure **d** : a building for storage : BIN **3** : a small narrow room or dwelling : HUT, SHACK **4** : the cards discarded in cribbage for the dealer to use in scoring **5 a** : a small theft **b** : PLAGIARISM **c** : a literal translation; *esp* : PONY 3 **d** : a summary and key to understanding a literary work **e** : something used for cheating in an examination **6** : CRÈCHE 3

²crib *vb* **cribbed; crib·bing** *vt* (1605) **1** : CONFINE, CRAMP **2** : to provide with or put into a crib; *esp* : to line or support with a framework of timber **3** : PILFER, STEAL; *esp* : PLAGIARIZE ~ *vi* **1 a** : STEAL, PLAGIARIZE **b** : to use a crib : CHEAT **2** : to have the vice of crib biting — **crib·ber** *n*

crib·bage \ˈkrib-ij\ *n* [ˈ*crib*] (1630) : a card game for two players in which each player tries to form various counting combinations of cards

crib·bing \ˈkrib-iŋ\ *n* (1841) : material for use in making a crib

crib biting *n* (1831) : a vice of horses in which they gnaw (as at the manger) while slobbering and salivating

crib death *n* (ca. 1966) : SUDDEN INFANT DEATH SYNDROME

crib·ri·form \ˈkrib-rə-ˌfȯrm\ *adj* [L *cribrum* sieve; akin to L *cernere* to sift — more at CERTAIN] (1741) : pierced with small holes

cri·ce·tid \krī-ˈsēt-əd, -ˈset-\ *n* [deriv. of NL *Cricetus,* genus name, of Slav origin; akin to Czech *křeček* hamster] (1960) : any of a family (Cricetidae) of small rodents including the hamsters — **cricetid** *adj*

¹crick \ˈkrik\ *n* [ME *cryk*] (15c) : a painful spasmodic condition of muscles (as of the neck or back)

²crick *vt* (1861) **1** : to cause a crick in (as the neck) **2** : to turn or twist (as the head) esp. into a strained position

¹crick·et \ˈkrik-ət\ *n* [ME *criket,* fr. MF *criquet,* of imit. origin] (14c) **1** : a leaping orthopteran insect (family Gryllidae) noted for the chirping notes produced by the male by rubbing together specially modified parts of the forewings **2** : a low wooden footstool **3** : a small metal toy or signaling device that makes a sharp click or snap when pressed

²cricket *n* [MF *criquet* goal stake in a bowling game] (1598) **1** : a game played with a ball and bat by two sides of usu. 11 players each on a large field centering upon two wickets each defended by a batsman **2** : fair and honorable behavior

³cricket *vi* (1809) : to play the game of cricket — **crick·et·er** *n*

cri·coid \ˈkrī-ˌkȯid\ *adj* [NL *cricoides,* fr. Gk *krikoeidēs* ring-shaped, fr. *krikos* ring — more at CIRCLE] (1727) : of, relating to, or being a cartilage of the larynx with which arytenoid cartilages articulate

cri de coeur \ˌkrēd-ə-ˈkər\ *n, pl* **cris de coeur** *same*\ [F, lit., cry from the heart] (1904) : a passionate outcry (as of appeal or protest)

cri·er \ˈkrī(-ə)r\ *n* (14c) : one that cries: **a** : an officer who proclaims the orders of a court **b** : TOWN CRIER

cri·key *or* **crick·ey** \ˈkrī-kē\ *interj* [euphemism for *Christ*] (1838) — used as a mild oath

crime \ˈkrīm\ *n* [ME, fr. MF, fr. L *crimen* accusation, fault, crime] (14c) **1 :** an act or the commission of an act that is forbidden or the omission of a duty that is commanded by a public law and that makes the offender liable to punishment by that law; *esp* **:** a gross violation of law **2 :** a grave offense esp. against morality **3 :** criminal activity ⟨efforts to fight ~⟩ **4 :** something reprehensible, foolish, or disgraceful ⟨it's a ~ to waste good food⟩ ***syn*** see OFFENSE

crime against humanity (1945) **:** atrocity (as extermination or enslavement) that is directed esp. against an entire population or part of a population on specious grounds and without regard to individual guilt or responsibility even on such grounds

crime against nature (1828) **:** SODOMY

1**crim·i·nal** \ˈkrim-ən-ᵊl, ˈkrim-nəl\ *adj* [ME, fr. MF or LL; MF *criminel,* fr. LL *criminalis,* fr. L *crimin-* *crimen* crime] (15c) **1 :** relating to, involving, or being a crime ⟨~ neglect⟩ **2 :** relating to crime or to the prosecution of suspects in a crime ⟨~ statistics⟩ ⟨brought ~ action⟩ **3 :** guilty of crime; *also* **:** of or befitting a criminal ⟨a ~ mind⟩ **4 :** DISGRACEFUL — **crim·i·nal·ly** \-ē\ *adv*

2**criminal** *n* (1626) **1 :** one who has committed a crime **2 :** a person who has been convicted of a crime

criminal conversation *n* (1768) **:** adultery considered as a tort

criminal court *n* (1678) **:** a court that has jurisdiction to try and punish offenders against criminal law

crim·i·nal·is·tics \ˌkrim-ən-ᵊl-ˈis-tiks, ˌkrim-nə-ˈlis-\ *n pl but sing in constr* (ca. 1943) **:** application of scientific techniques in collecting and analyzing physical evidence in criminal cases

crim·i·nal·i·ty \ˌkrim-ə-ˈnal-ət-ē\ *n* (ca. 1611) **1 :** the quality or state of being criminal **2 :** criminal activity ⟨urban ~⟩

crim·i·nal·ize \ˈkrim-ən-ᵊl-ˌīz, ˈkrim-nə-ˌlīz\ *vt* **-ized; -iz·ing** (ca. 1956) **:** to make illegal **:** OUTLAW; *also* **:** to turn into or treat as a criminal — **crim·i·nal·iza·tion** \ˌkrim-ən-ᵊl-ə-ˈzā-shən, ˌkrim-nə-lə-ˈzā-\ *n*

criminal law *n* (1590) **:** the law of crimes and their punishments

criminal lawyer *n* (1869) **:** a lawyer who specializes in criminal law; *esp* **:** a lawyer who represents defendants in criminal cases

crim·i·nate \ˈkrim-ə-ˌnāt\ *vt* **-nat·ed; -nat·ing** [L *criminatus,* pp. of *criminari,* fr. *crimin-, crimen* accusation] (1645) **:** INCRIMINATE — **crim·i·na·tion** \ˌkrim-ə-ˈnā-shən\ *n*

crim·i·nol·o·gy \ˌkrim-ə-ˈnäl-ə-jē\ *n* [It *criminologia,* fr. L *crimin-, crimen* + It *-o-* + *-logia* -logy] (1890) **:** the scientific study of crime as a social phenomenon, of criminals, and of penal treatment — **crim·i·no·log·i·cal** \-ən-ᵊl-ˈäj-i-kəl\ *adj* — **crim·i·no·log·i·cal·ly** \-k(ə-)lē\ *adv* — **crim·i·nol·o·gist** \ˌkrim-ə-ˈnäl-ə-jəst\ *n*

crim·i·nous \ˈkrim-ə-nəs\ *adj* (15c) **:** CRIMINAL

1**crimp** \ˈkrimp\ *vt* [D or LG *krimpen* to shrivel; akin to LG *krampe* hook — more at CRAMP] (14c) **1 :** to cause to become wavy, bent, or pinched: as **a :** to form (leather) into a desired shape **b :** to give (synthetic fibers) a curl or wave like that of natural fibers **c :** to draw or pinch in or together in glass manufacturing ⟨~ the neck of a vase⟩ **d :** to pinch or press together (as the margins of a pie crust) in order to seal **2 :** to be an inhibiting or restraining influence on **:** CRAMP ⟨dealers whose sales had been ~*ed* by credit controls —*Time*⟩

2**crimp** *n* (1863) **1 :** something produced by or as if by crimping: as **a :** a section of hair artificially waved or curled **b :** a succession of waves (as in wool fiber) **c :** a bend or crease formed in something **2 :** something that cramps or inhibits **:** RESTRAINT, CURB

3**crimp** *n* [perh. fr. 1*crimp*] (1758) **:** a person who entraps or forces men into shipping as sailors or into enlisting in an army or navy

4**crimp** *vt* (1812) **:** to trap into military or sea service **:** IMPRESS

crimpy \ˈkrim-pē\ *adj* **crimp·i·er; -est** (1888) **:** having a crimped appearance **:** FRIZZY

1**crim·son** \ˈkrim-zən\ *n* [ME *crimisin,* fr. OSp *cremesín,* fr. Ar *qirmizī,* fr. *qirmiz* kermes] (15c) **:** any of several deep purplish reds

2**crimson** *adj* (15c) **:** of the color crimson

3**crimson** *vt* (1601) **:** to make crimson ~ *vi* **:** to become crimson; *esp* **:** BLUSH

1**cringe** \ˈkrinj\ *vi* **cringed; cring·ing** [ME *crengen;* akin to OE *cringan* to yield, *cradol* cradle] (13c) **1 :** to draw in or contract one's muscles involuntarily (as from cold or pain) **2 :** to shrink in fear or servility **3 :** to behave in an excessively humble or servile way ***syn*** see FAWN — **cring·er** *n*

2**cringe** *n* (1597) **:** a cringing act; *specif* **:** a servile bow

crin·gle \ˈkriŋ-gəl\ *n* [LG *kringel,* dim. of *kring* ring; akin to OE *cradol* cradle] (1627) **:** a loop or grommet at the corner of a sail to which a line is attached

1**crin·kle** \ˈkriŋ-kəl\ *vb* **crin·kled; crin·kling** \-k(ə-)liŋ\ [ME *crynkelen;* akin to OE *cringan* to yield] *vi* (14c) **1 a :** to form many short bends or ripples **b :** WRINKLE **2 :** to give forth a thin crackling sound **:** RUSTLE ⟨*crinkling* silks⟩ ~ *vt* **:** to cause to crinkle **:** make crinkles in

2**crinkle** *n* (1596) **1 :** WRINKLE, CORRUGATION, PUCKER **2 :** any of several plant diseases marked by crinkling of leaves — **crin·kly** \-k(ə-)lē\ *adj*

cri·noid \ˈkrī-ˌnȯid\ *n* [deriv. of Gk *krinon* lily] (1847) **:** any of a large class (Crinoidea) of echinoderms usu. having a somewhat cup-shaped body with five or more feathery arms — **crinoid** *adj*

crin·o·line \ˈkrin-ᵊl-ən\ *n* [F, fr. It *crinolino,* fr. *crino* horsehair (fr. L *crinis* hair; akin to L *crista* crest) + *lino* flax, linen, fr. L *linum* — more at CREST] (1830) **1 :** an open-weave fabric of horsehair or cotton that is usu. stiffened and used esp. for interlinings and millinery **2 :** a full stiff skirt or underskirt made of crinoline; *also* **:** HOOPSKIRT — **crinoline** *or* **crin·o·lined** \-ənd\ *adj*

cri·ol·lo \krē-ˈō(l)-(ˌ)yō\ *n, pl* **-llos** [Sp] (1604) **1 a :** a person of pure Spanish descent born in Spanish America **b :** a person born and usu. raised in a Spanish-American country **2 :** a domestic animal of a breed or strain developed in Latin America; *esp, usu cap* **:** a hardy muscular pony of a breed orig. developed in Argentina — **criollo** *adj*

1**crip·ple** \ˈkrip-əl\ *n* [ME *cripel,* fr. OE *crypel;* akin to OE *crēopan* to creep — more at CREEP] (bef. 12c) **1 :** a lame or partly disabled person or animal **2 :** something flawed or imperfect

2**cripple** *adj* (13c) **:** being a cripple **:** LAME

3**cripple** *vt* **crip·pled; crip·pling** \-(ə-)liŋ\ (1607) **1 :** to deprive of the use of a limb and esp. a leg **2 :** to deprive of strength, efficiency, wholeness, or capability for service ***syn*** see MAIM, WEAKEN — **crip·pler** \-(ə-)lər\ *n*

cri·sis \ˈkrī-səs\ *n, pl* **cri·ses** \ˈkrī-ˌsēz\ [L, fr. Gk *krisis,* lit., decision, fr. *krinein* to decide — more at CERTAIN] (15c) **1 a :** the turning point for better or worse in an acute disease or fever **b :** a paroxysmal attack of pain, distress, or disordered function **c :** an emotionally significant event or radical change of status in a person's life **2 :** the decisive moment (as in a literary plot) **3 a :** an unstable or crucial time or state of affairs in which a decisive change is impending; *esp* **:** one with the distinct possibility of a highly undesirable outcome ⟨a financial ~⟩ **b :** a situation that has reached a critical phase ⟨the energy ~⟩ ⟨the environmental ~⟩ ***syn*** see JUNCTURE

1**crisp** \ˈkrisp\ *adj* [ME, fr. OE, fr. L *crispus;* akin to L *curvus* curved — more at CROWN] (bef. 12c) **1 :** CURLY, WAVY; *also* **:** having close stiff or wiry curls or waves **2 a :** easily crumbled **:** BRITTLE **b :** being desirably firm and fresh ⟨~ lettuce⟩ **3 a :** being sharp, clean-cut, and clear ⟨a ~ illustration⟩; *also* **:** concise and to the point ⟨a ~ reply⟩ **b :** noticeably neat ⟨~ new clothes⟩ **c :** BRISK, LIVELY ⟨a ~ tale of intrigue⟩ ⟨~ musical tempi⟩ **d :** FROSTY, SNAPPY ⟨~ winter weather⟩; *also* **:** FRESH, INVIGORATING ⟨~ autumn air⟩ ⟨a ~ white wine⟩ ***syn*** see FRAGILE — **crisp·ly** *adv* — **crisp·ness** *n*

2**crisp** *vt* (14c) **1 :** CURL, CRIMP **2 :** to cause to ripple **:** WRINKLE **3 :** to make or keep crisp ~ *vi* **1 :** CURL **2 :** RIPPLE **3 :** to become crisp — **crisp·er** *n*

3**crisp** *n* (14c) **1 a :** something crisp or brittle ⟨burned to a ~⟩ **b** *chiefly Brit* **:** POTATO CHIP **2 :** a baked dessert of fruit with crumb topping ⟨apple ~⟩

crisp·en \ˈkris-pən\ *vt* (1943) **:** to make crisp ~ *vi* **:** to become crisp

crispy \ˈkris-pē\ *adj* **crisp·i·er; -est** (14c) **:** CRISP — **crisp·i·ness** *n*

1**criss·cross** \ˈkris-ˌkrȯs\ *vt* (1818) **1 :** to mark with intersecting lines **2 :** to pass back and forth through or over ~ *vi* **:** to go or pass back and forth

2**crisscross** *adj* (1846) **:** marked or characterized by crisscrossing — **crisscross** *adv*

3**crisscross** *n* [obs. *christcross, crisscross* (mark of a cross)] (1876) **1 :** a crisscross pattern **:** NETWORK **2 :** the state of being at cross-purposes

cris·ta \ˈkris-tə\ *n, pl* **cris·tae** \-ˌtē, -ˌtī\ [NL, fr. L, crest] (1960) **:** any of the inwardly projecting folds of the inner membrane of a mitochondrion

cri·te·ri·on \krī-ˈtir-ē-ən *also* krə-\ *n, pl* **-ria** \-ē-ə\ [Gk *kritērion,* fr. *krinein* to judge, decide — more at CERTAIN] (1631) **1 :** a characterizing mark or trait **2 :** a standard on which a judgment or decision may be based ***syn*** see STANDARD

usage The plural *criteria* has often been mistaken for a singular ⟨let me now return to the third *criteria* —R. M. Nixon⟩ ⟨that really is the *criteria* —Burt Lance⟩ Many of our examples, like the two foregoing, are taken from speech. We note, however, that use as a singular appears to be increasing in edited prose, and it may be that in time *criteria* will establish itself as a singular as *agenda* and *candelabra* have.

1**crit·ic** \ˈkrit-ik\ *n* [L *criticus,* fr. Gk *kritikos* able to discern or judge, fr. *krinein*] (1588) **1 a :** one who expresses a reasoned opinion on any matter esp. involving a judgment of its value, truth, righteousness, beauty, or technique **b :** one who engages often professionally in the analysis, evaluation, or appreciation of works of art or artistic performances **2 :** one given to harsh or captious judgment

2**critic** *n* [Gk *kritikē* art of the critic, fr. fem. of *kritikos*] (1656) **1** *archaic* **:** CRITICISM **2** *archaic* **:** CRITIQUE

crit·i·cal \ˈkrit-i-kəl\ *adj* (1547) **1 a :** of, relating to, or being a turning point or specially important juncture ⟨~ phase⟩: (1) **:** relating to or being the stage of a disease at which an abrupt change for better or worse may be expected; *also* **:** being or relating to an illness or condition involving danger of death ⟨~ care⟩ (2) **:** relating to or being a state in which or a measurement or point at which some quality, property, or phenomenon suffers a definite change ⟨~ temperature⟩ **b :** CRUCIAL, DECISIVE ⟨~ test⟩ **c :** INDISPENSABLE, VITAL ⟨a component ~ to the operation of a machine⟩ ⟨provides ~ services⟩ **d :** being in or approaching a state of crisis ⟨a ~ shortage of doctors⟩ ⟨a ~ situation⟩ **2 a :** inclined to criticize severely and unfavorably **b :** consisting of or involving criticism ⟨~ writings⟩; *also* **:** of or relating to the judgment of critics ⟨the play was a ~ success⟩ **c :** exercising or involving careful judgment or judicious evaluation **d :** including variant readings and scholarly emendations ⟨a ~ edition⟩ **3 :** characterized by risk or uncertainty **4 a :** of sufficient size to sustain a chain reaction — used of a mass of fissionable material **b :** sustaining a chain reaction — used of a nuclear reactor — **crit·i·cal·i·ty** \ˌkrit-ə-ˈkal-ət-ē\ *n* — **crit·i·cal·ly** \ˈkrit-i-k(ə-)lē\ *adv* — **crit·i·cal·ness** \-kəl-nəs\ *n*

syn CRITICAL, HYPERCRITICAL, FAULTFINDING, CAPTIOUS, CARPING, CENSORIOUS mean inclined to look for and point out faults and defects. CRITICAL may also imply an effort to see a thing clearly and truly in order to judge it fairly; often it implies harshness in judging; HYPERCRITICAL suggests a tendency to judge by unreasonably strict standards; FAULTFINDING implies a querulous or exacting temperament; CAPTIOUS suggests a readiness to detect trivial faults or raise objections on trivial grounds; CARPING implies an ill-natured or perverse picking of flaws; CENSORIOUS implies a disposition to be severely critical and condemnatory. ***syn*** see in addition ACUTE

critical angle *n* (1873) **1 :** the least angle of incidence at which total reflection takes place **2 :** the angle of attack at which the flow about an airfoil changes abruptly with corresponding abrupt changes in the lift and drag

critical point *n* (1876) **:** a point on the graph of a function where the derivative is zero or infinite

critical region *n* (1951) **:** the set of outcomes of a statistical test for which the null hypothesis is to be rejected

critical value *n* (ca. 1909) **:** the value of an independent variable corresponding to a critical point of a function

crit·ic·as·ter \ˈkrit-i-ˌkas-tər\ *n* (1684) **:** an inferior or petty critic

criticise *Brit var of* CRITICIZE

crit·i·cism \'krit-ə-,siz-əm\ *n* (1607) **1 a :** the act of criticizing usu. unfavorably **b :** a critical observation or remark **c :** CRITIQUE **2 :** the art of evaluating or analyzing works of art or literature **3 :** the scientific investigation of literary documents (as the Bible) in regard to such matters as origin, text, composition, or history

crit·i·cize \'krit-ə-,sīz\ *vb* **-cized; -ciz·ing** *vi* (1649) **:** to act as a critic ~ *vt* **1 :** to consider the merits and demerits of and judge accordingly **:** EVALUATE **2 :** to find fault with **:** point out the faults of — **crit·i·ciz·able** \-,sī-zə-bəl\ *adj* — **crit·i·ciz·er** *n*

syn CRITICIZE, REPREHEND, BLAME, CENSURE, REPROBATE, CONDEMN, DENOUNCE mean to find fault with openly. CRITICIZE implies finding fault esp. with methods or policies or intentions; REPREHEND implies both criticism and severe rebuking; BLAME may imply simply the opposite of *praise* but more often suggests the placing of responsibility for something bad or unfortunate; CENSURE carries a stronger suggestion of authority and of reprimanding than BLAME; REPROBATE implies strong disapproval or firm refusal to sanction; CONDEMN usu. suggests an unqualified and final unfavorable judgment; DENOUNCE adds to CONDEMN the implication of a public declaration.

1**cri·tique** \krə-'tēk, kri-\ *n* [alter. of 2*critic*] (1702) **:** an act of criticizing; *esp* **:** a critical estimate or discussion

2**critique** *vt* **cri·tiqued; cri·tiqu·ing** (1751) **:** CRITICIZE, REVIEW

crit·ter \'krit-ər\ *n* [by alter.] (1815) **:** CREATURE

1**croak** \'krōk\ *vb* [ME *croken,* of imit. origin] *vi* (15c) **1 a :** to make a deep harsh sound **b :** to speak in a hoarse throaty voice **2 :** GRUMBLE 1 **3** *slang* **:** DIE ~ *vt* **1 :** to utter in a hoarse raucous voice **2** *slang* **:** KILL

2**croak** *n* (1561) **:** a hoarse harsh cry or sound — **croaky** \'krō-kē\ *adj*

croak·er \'krō-kər\ *n* (1637) **1 :** an animal that croaks **2 :** any of various fishes (esp. family Sciaenidae) that produce croaking or grunting noises **3** *slang* **:** DOCTOR

Croat \'krō-,at, 'krō(-ə)t\ *n* [NL *Croata,* fr. Serbo-Croatian *Hrvat*] (ca. 1702) **:** CROATIAN

Cro·atian \krō-'ā-shən\ *n* (1555) **1 :** a native or inhabitant of Croatia **2 :** a south Slavic language spoken by the Croatian people and distinct from Serbian chiefly in its use of the Latin alphabet — **Croatian** *adj*

croc \'kräk\ *n* [by shortening] (1884) **:** CROCODILE

1**cro·chet** \krō-'shā\ *n* [F, hook, crochet, fr. MF, dim. of *croche* hook, of Scand origin; akin to ON *krōkr* hook — more at CROOK] (1848) **:** needlework consisting of the interlocking of looped stitches formed with a single thread and a hooked needle

2**crochet** *vt* (1858) **:** to make of crochet ⟨~*ed* a doily⟩ ~ *vi* **:** to work with crochet — **cro·chet·er** \-'shā-ər\ *n*

cro·cid·o·lite \krō-'sid-ᵊl-,īt\ *n* [G *krokydolith,* fr. Gk *krokyd-, krokys* nap on cloth (akin to Gk *krekein* to weave) + G *-lith* -lite — more at REEL] (1835) **:** a lavender-blue or leek-green mineral of the amphibole group that occurs in silky fibers and massively — compare TIGEREYE

1**crock** \'kräk\ *n* [ME, fr. OE *crocc;* akin to MHG *krūche* crock] (bef. 12c) **1 :** a thick earthenware pot or jar **2** [fr. its formation on cooking pots] *dial* **:** SOOT, SMUT **3 :** coloring matter that rubs off from cloth or dyed leather **4 :** BUNKUM — usu. used with *a*

2**crock** *vt* (1642) **1 :** to put or preserve in a crock **2** *dial* **:** to soil with crock **:** SMUDGE ~ *vi* **:** to transfer color (as when rubbed or washed) ⟨a suede that will not ~⟩

3**crock** *n* [ME *crok,* prob. of Scand origin; akin to Norw dial. *krokje* crock; prob. akin to OE *crycc* crutch] (1528) **1 :** one that is broken-down, disabled, or impaired **2 :** a complaining medical patient whose illness is largely imaginary or psychosomatic

4**crock** *vt* (1896) **:** to cause to become disabled ~ *vi* **:** BREAK DOWN

crocked \'kräkt\ *adj* (ca. 1927) **:** DRUNK

crock·ery \'kräk-(ə-)rē\ *n* (1755) **:** EARTHENWARE

crock·et \'kräk-ət\ *n* [ME *croket,* fr. ONF *croquet* crook, dim. of *croc* hook, of Scand origin; akin to ON *krōkr* hook] (1673) **:** an ornament usu. in the form of curved and bent foliage used on the edge of a gable or spire — **crock·et·ed** \-ət-əd\ *adj*

Crock–pot \'kräk-,pät\ *trademark* — used for an electric cooking pot

croc·o·dile \'kräk-ə-,dīl\ *n* [ME & L; ME *cocodrille,* fr. MF, fr. ML *cocodrillus,* alter. of L *crocodilus,* fr. Gk *krokodilos* lizard, crocodile, fr. *krokē* shingle, pebble + *drilos* worm; akin to Skt *śarkara* pebble — more at SUGAR] (14c) **1 a :** any of several large voracious thick-skinned long-bodied aquatic reptiles (as of the genus *Crocodylus*) of tropical and subtropical waters; *broadly* **:** CROCODILIAN **b :** the skin or hide of a crocodile **2** *chiefly Brit* **:** a number of persons (as schoolchildren) moving in a long file

crocodile 1a

crocodile bird *n* (1868) **:** an African plover (*Pluvianus aegyptius*) that lights on the crocodile and eats its insect parasites

crocodile tears *n pl* (1563) **:** false or affected tears **:** hypocritical sorrow

croc·o·dil·ian \,kräk-ə-'dil-ē-ən, -'dil-yən\ *n* (1837) **:** any of an order (Loricata) of reptiles including the crocodiles, alligators, and related extinct forms — **crocodilian** *adj*

croco·ite \'kräk-ə-,wīt\ *or* **croc·oi·site** \'kräk-wə-,zīt\ *n* [modif. of F *crocoise,* fr. Gk *krokoeis* saffron-colored, fr. *krokos* saffron, of Sem origin] (ca. 1844) **:** a mineral $PbCrO_4$ consisting of lead chromate

cro·cus \'krō-kəs\ *n, pl* **cro·cus·es** [NL, genus name, fr. L, saffron, fr. Gk *krokos*] (14c) **1** *pl also* **crocus** *or* **cro·ci** \-,kē, -,kī, -,sī\ **:** any of a large genus (*Crocus*) of herbs of the iris family having solitary long-tubed flowers and slender linear leaves **2 a :** a dark red ferric oxide used for polishing metals **b :** SAFFRON 1

Croe·sus \'krē-səs\ *n* [*Croesus,* fr. L, fr. Gk *Kroisos*] (1650) **:** a very rich man

croft \'krȯft\ *n* [ME, fr. OE; akin to OE *crēopan* to creep — more at CREEP] (bef. 12c) **1** *chiefly Brit* **:** a small enclosed field usu. adjoining a house **2** *chiefly Brit* **:** a small farm worked by a tenant — **croft·er** \'krȯf-tər\ *n, chiefly Brit*

crois·sant \k(rə-,)wä-'sä^n\ *n, pl* **croissants** \-'sä^n(z)\ [F, lit., crescent, fr. MF *creissant*] (1899) **:** a flaky rich crescent-shaped roll

Croix de Guerre \k(rə-,)wäd-i-'ge(ə)r\ *n* [F, lit., war cross] (1915) **:** a French military decoration awarded for gallant action in war

Cro–Ma·gnon \krō-'mag-nən, -'man-yən\ *n* [*Cro-Magnon,* a cave near Les Eyzies, France] (1869) **:** a tall erect race of men known from skeletal remains found chiefly in southern France and classified as the same species (*Homo sapiens*) as recent man

crom·lech \'kräm-,lek\ *n* [W, lit., bent stone] (1695) **1 :** DOLMEN **2 :** a circle of monoliths usu. enclosing a dolmen or mound

crone \'krōn\ *n* [ME, fr. ONF *carogne,* lit., carrion, fr. (assumed) VL *caronia* — more at CARRION] (14c) **:** a withered old woman

Cro·nus \'krō-nəs, 'krän-əs\ *n* [L, fr. Gk *Kronos*] **:** a Titan dethroned by his son Zeus

cro·ny \'krō-nē\ *n, pl* **cronies** [perh. fr. Gk *chronios* long-lasting, fr. *chronos* time] (1665) **:** a close friend esp. of long standing **:** PAL

cro·ny·ism \-nē-,iz-əm\ *n* (1840) **:** partiality to cronies esp. as evidenced in the appointment of political hangers-on to office without regard to their qualifications

1**crook** \'krůk\ *vt* (12c) **:** BEND ~ *vi* **:** CURVE, WIND

2**crook** *n* [ME *crok,* fr. ON *krōkr* hook; akin to OE *cradol* cradle] (13c) **1 :** an implement having a bent or hooked form: as **a :** POTHOOK **b** (1) **:** a shepherd's staff (2) **:** CROSIER 1 **2 :** a person who engages in fraudulent or criminal practices **3 :** BEND, CURVE **4 :** a part of something that is hook-shaped, curved, or bent ⟨the ~ of an umbrella handle⟩

3**crook** *adj, Austral & NewZeal* (1898) **:** not right: **a :** UNSATISFACTORY **b :** DISHONEST, CROOKED **c :** IRRITABLE, ANGRY — used esp. in the phrase *go crook* **d :** ILL, UNWELL

crook·back \'krůk-,bak\ *n* (1508) **1** *obs* **:** a crooked back **2** *obs* **:** HUNCHBACK — **crook·backed** \-'bakt\ *adj*

crook·ed \'krůk-əd\ *adj* (13c) **1 :** not straight ⟨a ~ road⟩ ⟨your tie is ~⟩ **2 :** DISHONEST ⟨a ~ election⟩ ⟨~ politicians⟩ — **crook·ed·ly** *adv* — **crook·ed·ness** *n*

crook·ery \'krůk-ə-rē\ *n* (1927) **:** crooked dealings or practices

Crookes tube \'krůks-\ *n* [Sir William *Crookes*] (ca. 1889) **:** a vacuum tube evacuated to a high degree for demonstrating the properties of cathode rays

crook·neck \'krůk-,nek\ *n* (1784) **:** a squash with a long recurved neck

croon \'krün\ *vb* [ME *croynen,* fr. MD *cronen;* akin to OE *cran* crane] *vi* (15c) **1** *chiefly Scot* **:** BELLOW, BOOM **2 :** to sing in a gentle murmuring manner; *esp* **:** to sing in a soft intimate manner adapted to amplifying systems ~ *vt* **:** to sing (as a popular song or a lullaby) in a crooning manner — **croon** *n*

croon·er \'krü-nər\ *n* (1930) **:** one that croons; *esp* **:** a singer of popular songs

1**crop** \'kräp\ *n* [ME, craw, head of a plant, yield of a field, fr. OE *cropp* craw, head of a plant; akin to OHG *kropf* goiter, craw, OE *crēopan* to creep — more at CREEP] (bef. 12c) **1 :** the stock or handle of a whip; *also* **:** a riding whip with a short straight stock and a loop **2 :** a pouched enlargement of the gullet of many birds that serves as a receptacle for food and for its preliminary maceration; *also* **:** an enlargement of the gullet of another animal (as an insect) **3** [2*crop*] **a :** the part of the chine of a quadruped (as a domestic cow) lying immediately behind the withers — usu. used in pl.; see COW illustration **b :** an earmark on an animal; *esp* **:** one made by a straight cut squarely removing the upper part of the ear **c :** a close cut of the hair **4 a :** a plant or animal or plant or animal product that can be grown and harvested extensively for profit or subsistence ⟨an apple ~⟩ ⟨a ~ of wool⟩ **b :** the product or yield of something formed together ⟨the ice ~⟩ **c :** a batch or lot of something produced during a particular cycle ⟨a new ~ of candidates⟩ ⟨the current ~ of films⟩ **d :** COLLECTION ⟨a ~ of lies⟩ **5 :** the total yearly production from a specified area

2**crop** *vb* **cropped; crop·ping** *vt* (13c) **1 a :** to remove the upper or outer parts of ⟨~ a hedge⟩ ⟨~ a dog's ears⟩ **b :** HARVEST ⟨~ trout⟩ **c :** to cut off short **:** TRIM ⟨~ a photograph⟩ **2 :** to cause (land) to bear a crop ⟨planned to ~ another 40 acres⟩; *also* **:** to grow as a crop ~ *vi* **1 :** to feed by cropping something **2 :** to yield or make a crop **3 :** to appear unexpectedly or casually ⟨problems ~ up daily⟩

crop duster *n* (1939) **:** one who sprays crops with fungicidal or insecticidal dusts from an airplane

crop–eared \'kräp-'i(ə)rd\ *adj* (1530) **:** having the ears cropped

crop·land \-,land\ *n* (1846) **:** land that is suited to or used for crops

1**crop·per** \'kräp-ər\ *n* (15c) **1 :** one that crops **2 :** one that raises crops; *specif* **:** SHARECROPPER

2**cropper** *n* [prob. fr. E dial. *crop* neck, fr. 1*crop*] (1858) **1 :** a severe fall **2 :** a sudden or violent failure or collapse

crop rotation *n* (1909) **:** the practice of growing different crops in succession on the same land chiefly to preserve the productive capacity of the soil

cro·quet \krō-'kā\ *n* [F dial., hockey stick, fr. ONF, crook — more at CROCKET] (1858) **1 :** a game in which players using mallets drive wooden balls through a series of wickets set out on a lawn **2 :** the act of driving away an opponent's croquet ball by striking one's own ball placed against it — **croquet** *vt*

cro·quette \krō-'ket\ *n* [F, fr. *croquer* to crunch, eat greedily] (1706) **:** a small often rounded mass consisting usu. of minced meat, fish, or vegetable coated with egg and bread crumbs and fried in deep fat

cro·qui·gnole \'krō-kən-,(y)ōl\ *n* [F, flip, fr. *croquer*] (1932) **:** a method used in waving the hair by winding it on curlers from the ends of the hair toward the scalp

cro·quis \krō-'kē\ *n, pl* **cro·quis** \-'kē(z)\ [F, fr. *croquer* to crunch, sketch] (1805) **:** a rough draft **:** SKETCH

crore \'krō(ə)r, 'krȯ(ə)r\ *n, pl* **crores** *also* **crore** [Hindi *karoṛ*] (1609) **:** a unit of value equal to ten million rupees or 100 lakhs

cro·sier \'krō-zhər\ *n* [ME *croser* crosier bearer, fr. MF *crossier,* fr. *crosse* crosier, of Gmc origin; akin to OE *crycc* crutch — more at CRUTCH] (14c) **1 :** a staff resembling a shepherd's crook carried by bishops and abbots as a symbol of office — see VESTMENT illustration **2 :** a plant structure with a coiled end

1**cross** \'krȯs\ *n* [ME, fr. OE, fr. ON or OIr; ON *kross,* fr. (assumed) OIr *cross,* fr. L *cruc-, crux* — more at RIDGE] (bef. 12c) **1 a :** a structure consisting of an upright with a transverse beam used esp. by the ancient Romans for execution **b** *often cap* **:** the cross on which Jesus was crucified **2 a :** CRUCIFIXION **b :** an affliction that tries one's virtue, steadfastness, or patience **3 :** a cruciform sign made to invoke the blessing of Christ esp. by touching the forehead, breast, and shoulders **4 a :** a device composed of an upright bar traversed by a horizontal one; *specif* **:** one used as a Christian symbol **b** *cap* **:** the Christian religion **5 :** a structure (as a monument) shaped like or surmounted by a

cross **6** : a figure or mark formed by two intersecting lines crossing at their midpoints; *specif* : such a mark used as a signature **7** : a cruciform badge, emblem, or decoration **8** : the intersection of two ways or lines : CROSSING **9** : ANNOYANCE, THWARTING ⟨a ∼ in love⟩ **10 a** : an act of crossing dissimilar individuals **b** : a crossbred individual or kind **c** : one that combines characteristics of two different types or individuals **11 a** : a fraudulent or dishonest contest **b** : dishonest or illegal practices — used esp. in the phrase *on the cross* **12** : a movement from one part of a theater stage to another **13** : a hook thrown over the opponent's lead in boxing **14** *cap* **a** : NORTHERN CROSS **b** : SOUTHERN CROSS **15** : a security transaction in which a broker acts for both buyer and seller (as in the placing of a large lot of common stock) — called also *cross-trade*

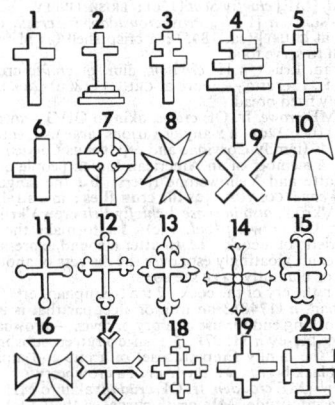

cross 4a: *1* Latin, *2* Calvary, *3* patriarchal, *4* papal, *5* Lorraine, *6* Greek, *7* Celtic, *8* Maltese, *9* Saint Andrew's, *10* tau, *11* pommée, *12* botonée, *13* fleury, *14* avellan, *15* moline, *16* formée, *17* fourchée, *18* crosslet, *19* quadrate, *20* potent

²**cross** *vt* (14c) **1 a** : to lie or be situated across **b** : INTERSECT **2** : to make the sign of the cross upon or over **3** : to cancel by marking a cross on or drawing a line through : strike out ⟨∼ names off a list⟩ **4** : to place or fold crosswise one over the other ⟨∼ the arms⟩ **5 a** (1) : to run counter to : OPPOSE (2) : to deny the validity of : CONTRADICT **b** : to confront in a troublesome manner : OBSTRUCT **c** (1) : to spoil completely : DISRUPT — used with *up* ⟨his failure to appear ∼ed up the whole program⟩ (2) : to turn against : BETRAY ⟨∼ed me up on the deal⟩ **6 a** : to extend across : TRAVERSE ⟨a highway ∼ing the entire state⟩ **b** : REACH, ATTAIN ⟨only two ∼ed the finish line⟩ **c** : to go from one side of to the other ⟨∼ a street⟩ **7 a** : to draw a line across **b** : to mark or figure with lines : STREAK **8** : to cause (an animal or plant) to interbreed with one of a different kind : HYBRIDIZE **9** : to meet and pass on the way ⟨our letters must have ∼ed each other⟩ **10** : to occur to ⟨it never ∼ed my mind⟩ **11** : to carry or take across something ⟨∼ed the children at the intersection⟩ ∼ *vi* **1 a** : to move, pass, or extend across something ⟨∼ed through France⟩ **b** : to move or pass from one character, condition, or allegiance to another — used with *over* **2** : to lie or be athwart each other **3** : to meet in passing esp. from opposite directions **4** : INTERBREED, HYBRIDIZE — **cross·er** *n* — **cross swords** : to engage in a dispute

³**cross** *adj* (15c) **1 a** : lying across or athwart **b** : moving across ⟨∼ traffic⟩ **2 a** : running counter : OPPOSITE **b** : mutually opposed ⟨∼ purposes⟩ **3** : involving mutual interchange : RECIPROCAL **4** : marked by typically transitory bad temper : GRUMPY **5** : extending over or treating several groups or classes ⟨a ∼ sample from 25 colleges⟩ **6** : CROSSBRED, HYBRID — **cross·ly** *adv* — **cross·ness** *n*

⁴**cross** *prep* (1551) : ACROSS

⁵**cross** *adv* (1577) : not parallel : CRISSCROSS, CROSSWISE

cross·abil·i·ty \ˌkrò-sə-'bil-ət-ē\ *n* (1916) : the ability of different species or varieties to cross with each other

cross·able \'krò-sə-bəl\ *adj* (1865) : capable of being crossed

cross action *n* (ca. 1859) : a legal action brought by a defendant in a suit against the person who has sued him and on the same subject matter

cross·bar \'krós-ˌbär\ *n* (1562) : a transverse bar or stripe

cross·bear·er \'krós-ˌbar-ər, -ˌber-\ *n* (1568) : CRUCIFER 1

cross·bill \-ˌbil\ *n* (1672) : any of a genus (*Loxia*) of finches with strongly curved mandibles that cross each other

cross·bones \-ˌbōnz\ *n pl* (1798) : two leg or arm bones placed or depicted crosswise — compare SKULL AND CROSSBONES

cross·bow \-ˌbō\ *n* (15c) : a weapon for discharging quarrels and stones that consists chiefly of a short bow mounted crosswise near the end of a wooden stock

cross·bow·man \-mən\ *n* (1500) : one (as a soldier or a hunter) whose weapon is a crossbow

cross·bred \'krós-'bred\ *adj* (1856) : HYBRID; *specif* : produced by interbreeding two pure but different breeds, strains, or varieties — **cross·bred** \-ˌbred\ *n*

crossbow

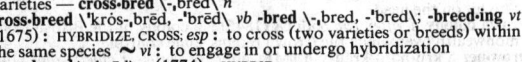

¹**cross·breed** \'krós-ˌbrēd, -'brēd\ *vb* -**bred** \-ˌbred, -'bred\; -**breed·ing** *vt* (1675) : HYBRIDIZE, CROSS; esp : to produce (two varieties or breeds) within the same species ∼ *vi* : to engage in or undergo hybridization

²**cross·breed** \-ˌbrēd\ *n* (1774) : HYBRID

¹**cross·check** \-'chek\ *vt* (ca. 1929) **1** : to obstruct in ice hockey or lacrosse by thrusting one's stick held in both hands across an oppo-

nent's face or body **2** : to check (as data or reports) from various angles or sources to determine validity or accuracy

²**cross-check** *n* (1937) : an act or instance of cross-checking

¹**cross-coun·try** \'krò-'skən-trē\ *adj* (1767) **1** : extending or moving across a country ⟨a ∼ concert tour⟩ **2** : proceeding over countryside (as across fields and through woods) and not by roads **3** : of or relating to racing or skiing over the countryside instead of over a track or run — **cross-country** *adv*

²**cross-country** *n* (1925) : cross-country racing or skiing

cross-court \'krò-'skō(ə)rt, -'skò(ə)rt\ *adv or adj* (1915) : to or toward the opposite side of a court (as in tennis or basketball)

cross-cul·tur·al \'krò-'skəlch-(ə-)rəl\ *adj* (1942) : dealing with or offering comparison between two or more different cultures or cultural areas — **cross-cul·tur·al·ly** \-(ə-)rə-lē\ *adv*

cross-cur·rent \'krò-'skər-ənt, -'skə-rənt\ *n* (1598) **1** : a current running counter to the general forward direction **2** : a conflicting tendency — usu. used in pl. ⟨political ∼s⟩

¹**cross·cut** \'krò-ˌskət, -'skət\ *vt* (1590) **1** : to cut, go, or move across or through **2** : to cut with a crosscut saw **3** : to subject (as movie scenes) to crosscutting

²**crosscut** *adj* (1645) **1** : made or used for cutting transversely ⟨a saw with ∼ teeth⟩ **2** : cut across or transversely ⟨a ∼ incision⟩

³**cross·cut** \'krò-ˌskət\ *n* (1789) **1** : something that cuts across or through; *specif* : a mine working driven horizontally and at right angles to an adit, drift, or level **2** : CROSS SECTION **3** : CROSSCUT SAW **4** : an instance of crosscutting (in a movie)

crosscut saw *n* (1645) : a saw designed chiefly to cut across the grain of wood — compare RIPSAW

cross·cut·ting \'krò-ˌskət-iŋ\ *n* (1930) : a technique esp. in filmmaking of interweaving bits of two or more separate scenes

cross-dress·ing \'krós-'dres-iŋ\ *n* (1911) : the wearing of clothes designed for the opposite sex — **cross-dress** *vi* — **cross-dress·er** *n*

crosse \'krós\ *n* [F, lit., crosier — more at CROSIER] (1867) : the stick used in lacrosse

cross-ex·am·ine \ˌkrò-sig-'zam-ən\ *vt* (1664) : to examine by a series of questions designed to check or discredit the answers to previous questions — **cross-ex·am·i·na·tion** \-ˌzam-ə-'nā-shən\ *n* — **cross-ex·am·in·er** \-'zam-ə-)nər\ *n*

cross-eye \'krò-ˌsī\ *n* (1826) **1** : strabismus in which the eye turns inward toward the nose **2** *pl* \-'sīz\ : eyes affected with cross-eye — **cross-eyed** \-'sīd\ *adj*

cross-fer·tile \'krós-'fərt-ᵊl\ *adj* (1929) : fertile in a cross or capable of cross-fertilization

cross-fer·til·iza·tion \-ˌfərt-ᵊl-ə-'zā-shən\ *n* (1876) **1 a** : fertilization in which the gametes are produced by separate individuals or sometimes by individuals of different kinds **b** : CROSS-POLLINATION **2** : interchange or interaction (as between different ideas, cultures, or categories) esp. of a broadening or productive nature

cross-fer·til·ize \-'fərt-ᵊl-ˌīz\ *vt* (1876) : to accomplish cross-fertilization of ∼ *vi* : to undergo cross-fertilization

cross-file \-'fī(ə)l\ *vi* (1949) : to register as a candidate in the primary elections of more than one political party ∼ *vt* : to register (a person) as a candidate from more than one party

cross fire *n* (ca.1859) **1** : firing (as in combat) from two or more points so that the lines of fire cross; *also* : a situation wherein the forces of opposing factions meet or cross **2** : rapid or heated interchange

cross-grained \'krós-'grānd\ *adj* (1647) **1** : difficult to deal with **2** : having the grain or fibers running diagonally, transversely, or irregularly

cross hair *n* (1884) : one of the fine wires or threads in the focus of the eyepiece of an optical instrument used as a reference line in the field or for marking the instrumental axis

cross·hatch \'krós-ˌhach\ *vt* (1822) : to mark with two series of parallel lines that intersect — **crosshatch** *n* — **cross-hatch·ing** *n*

cross·head \-ˌhed\ *n* (1827) : a metal block to which one end of a piston rod is secured, which slides on parallel guides, and which has a pin for attachment of the connecting rod

cross-in·dex \'krò-'sin-ˌdeks\ *vt* (1892) **1** : to index (an item) under a second or more than one heading **2** : to supply (as a book) with a cross-referenced index — **cross-index** *n*

cross·ing \'krò-siŋ\ *n* (1575) **1** : the act or action of crossing: as **a** : a traversing or traveling across **b** : an opposing, blocking, or thwarting esp. in an unfair or dishonest manner **2 a** : a place or structure (as on a street or over a river) where pedestrians or vehicles cross; *esp* : CROSSWALK **b** : a place where a railroad track crosses a street

cross·ing-over \ˌkrò-siŋ-'ō-vər\ *n* (1912) : an interchange of genes or segments between homologous chromosomes

cross-legged \'krò-'sleg(-ə)d, -'släg(-ə)d\ *adv or adj* (1530) **1** : with legs crossed and knees spread wide apart **2** : with one leg placed over and across the other

cross·let \'krò-slət\ *n* (15c) : a small cross; *esp* : one used as a heraldic bearing — see CROSS illustration

cross-link \'krò-ˌsliŋk\ *n* (1936) : a crosswise connecting part (as an atom or group) that connects parallel chains in a complex chemical molecule (as a polymer) — **cross-link** *vb*

cross-link·age \'krò-ˌsliŋ-kij\ *n* (1937) : the process of forming cross-links; *also* : CROSS-LINK

cross multiply *vi* (1951) : to find the two products obtained by multiplying the numerator of each of two fractions by the denominator of the other — **cross multiplication** *n*

cross-na·tion·al \'krò-'snash-nəl, -ən-ᵊl\ *adj* (1965) : of or relating to two or more nations

cross of Lor·raine \-ə-'rän, -lò-\ [*Lorraine*, France] (ca. 1892) : a cross with two crossbars the lower one of which is longer than the upper one — see CROSS illustration

---

\ə\ abut \ᵊ\ kitten, F table \ər\ further \a\ ash \ā\ ace \ä\ cot, cart \aù\ out \ch\ chin \e\ bet \ē\ easy \g\ go \i\ hit \ī\ ice \j\ job \ŋ\ sing \ō\ go \ò\ law \òi\ boy \th\ thin \th̲\ the \ü\ loot \ù\ foot \y\ yet \zh\ vision \à, k̲, ⁿ, œ, œ̄, ɥ, ᵜ̄, ᵞ\ *see* Guide to Pronunciation

cros·sop·ter·yg·ian \ˌkrä-ˌsäp-tə-ˈrij(-ē)-ən\ *n* [NL *Crossopterygii* (order name), fr. *cross* + Gk *pteryg-, pteryx* wing, fin; akin to Gk *pteron* wing — more at FEATHER] (ca. 1889) **:** any of a large group (Crossopterygii) of fishes (as latimeria) that have paired fins suggesting limbs, that may be ancestral to the terrestrial vertebrates, and that are mostly extinct — called also *lobe-fin* — **crossopterygian** *adj*

cross·over \ˈkrȯ-ˌsō-vər\ *n* (1884) **1 :** CROSSING 2a **2 :** an instance or product of genetic crossing-over **3 :** a voter registered as a member of one political party who votes in the primary of the other party **4 :** a broadening of popular musical appeal that is often the result of a change of musical style; *also* **:** a musician who has achieved a crossover

cross·patch \ˈkrȯ-ˌspach\ *n* [[3]*cross* + *patch* (fool)] (ca. 1700) **:** GROUCH 2

cross·piece \ˈkrȯ-ˌspēs\ *n* (1607) **:** a horizontal member (as of a structure)

cross–pol·li·nate \ˈkrȯ-ˈspäl-ə-ˌnāt\ *vt* (ca. 1900) **:** to subject to cross-pollination

cross–pol·li·na·tion \ˌkrȯ-ˌspäl-ə-ˈnā-shən\ *n* (1882) **:** the transfer of pollen from one flower to the stigma of another

cross–pol·li·nize \ˈkrȯ-ˈspäl-ə-ˌnīz\ *vt* (1902) **:** CROSS-POLLINATE

cross product *n* (1929) **:** VECTOR PRODUCT

cross–pur·pose \ˈkrȯ-ˈspər-pəs\ *n* (1681) **:** a purpose usu. unintentionally contrary to another purpose of oneself or of someone else ⟨the two were always working at ~*s*⟩

cross–ques·tion \ˈkrȯ-ˈskwes(h)-chən\ *n* (1760) **:** a question asked in cross-examination — **cross–question** *vt*

cross–re·ac·tion \ˌkrȯs-rē-ˈak-shən\ *n* (1946) **:** reaction of one antigen with antibodies developed against another antigen — **cross–re·act** \-rē-ˈakt\ *vi* — **cross–re·ac·tiv·i·ty** \-(ˌ)rē-ˌak-ˈtiv-ət-ē\ *n*

cross–re·fer \ˌkrȯs-ri-ˈfər\ *vt* (ca. 1909) **:** to refer (a reader) by a notation or direction from one place to another (as in a book, list, or catalog) ~ *vi* **:** to make a cross-reference

[1]cross–ref·er·ence \ˈkrȯs-ˈref-ərn(t)s, -ˈref-(ə-)rən(t)s\ *n* (1834) **:** a notation or direction at one place (as in a book or filing system) to pertinent information at another place

[2]cross–reference *vt* (1902) **:** to supply with cross-references

cross–re·sis·tance \ˌkrȯs-ri-ˈzis-tən(t)s\ *n* (1946) **:** tolerance (as of an insect population) to a normally toxic substance (as an insecticide) that is acquired not as a result of direct exposure but by exposure to a related substance

cross·road \ˈkrȯs-ˌrōd, -ˈrōd\ *n* (1719) **1 :** a road that crosses a main road or runs cross-country between main roads **2** *usu pl but sing or pl in constr* **a :** the place of intersection of two or more roads **b** (1) **:** a small community located at such a crossroads (2) **:** a central meeting place **c :** a crucial point esp. where a decision must be made

cross·ruff \ˈkrȯs-ˌrəf, -ˈrəf\ *n* (1862) **:** a series of plays in a card game in which partners alternately trump different suits and lead to each other for that purpose — **crossruff** *vb*

cross section *n* (1884) **1 a :** a cutting or piece of something cut off at right angles to an axis; *also* **:** a representation of such a cutting **b :** SECTION 3b **2 :** a measure of the probability of an encounter between particles such as will result in a specified effect (as ionization or capture) **3 :** a composite representation typifying the constituents of a thing in their relations — **cross–section** *vt* — **cross–sec·tion·al** *adj*

cross–ster·ile \ˈkrȯs-ˈ(s)ter-əl\ *adj* (1947) **:** mutually sterile — **cross–ste·ril·i·ty** \ˌkrȯs-(s)tə-ˈril-ət-ē\ *n*

cross–stitch \ˈkrȯs-ˌ(s)tich\ *n* (1710) **1 :** a needlework stitch that forms an X **2 :** work having cross-stitch — **cross–stitch** *vb*

cross talk *n* (1887) **:** unwanted signals in a communication channel (as in a telephone, radio, or computer) caused by transference of energy from another circuit (as by leakage or coupling)

cross–tol·er·ance \ˈkrȯ-ˈstäl(-ə)-rən(t)s\ *n* (ca. 1923) **:** tolerance or resistance to a drug that develops through continued use of another drug with similar pharmacological action

cross·town \ˈkrȯ-ˈstau̇n\ *adj* (1886) **1 :** situated at opposite points of a town **2 :** extending or running across a town ⟨a ~ street⟩ ⟨a ~ bus⟩

cross–trade \ˈkrȯ-ˌsträd\ *n* (ca. 1923) **:** CROSS 15

cross·trees \ˈkrȯ-(ˌ)strēz\ *n* (1626) **:** two horizontal crosspieces of timber or metal supported by trestletrees at a masthead that spread the upper shrouds in order to support the mast

cross vault *n* (1850) **:** a vault formed by the intersection of two or more simple vaults — called also *cross vaulting*

cross·walk \ˈkrȯ-ˌswȯk\ *n* (1744) **:** a specially paved or marked path for pedestrians crossing a street or road

cross·way \ˈkrȯ-ˌswā\ *n* (14c) **:** CROSSROAD — often used in pl.

cross·ways \-ˌswāz\ *adv* (1564) **:** CROSSWISE, DIAGONALLY

cross·wind \ˈkrȯ-ˌswind\ *n* (ca. 1920) **:** a wind blowing in a direction not parallel to a course (as of an airplane)

[1]cross·wise \ˈkrȯ-ˌswīz\ *adv* (14c) **1** *archaic* **:** in the form of a cross **2 :** so as to cross something **:** ACROSS ⟨logs laid ~⟩

[2]crosswise *adj* (1903) **:** TRANSVERSE, CROSSING

cross·word \ˌkrȯ-ˌswərd\ *n* (1914) **:** a puzzle in which words are filled into a pattern of numbered squares in answer to correspondingly numbered clues and in such a way that the words read across and down

crotch \ˈkräch\ *n* [prob. alter. of [1]*crutch*] (1573) **1 :** a pole with a forked end used esp. as a prop **2 :** an angle formed by the parting of two legs, branches, or members — **crotched** \ˈkräch t\ *adj*

crotch·et \ˈkräch-ət\ *n* [ME *crochet*, fr. MF — more at CROCHET] (14c) **1** *obs* **a :** a small hook or hooked instrument **b :** BROOCH **2 a :** a highly individual and usu. eccentric opinion or preference **b :** a peculiar trick or device **3 :** QUARTER NOTE ***syn*** see CAPRICE

crotch·ety \ˈkräch-ət-ē\ *adj* (1825) **1 :** given to crotchets **:** subject to whims, crankiness, or ill temper ⟨a ~ old man⟩ **2 :** full of or arising from crotchets — **crotch·et·i·ness** \-ē-nəs\ *n*

cro·ton \ˈkrōt-ᵊn\ *n* [NL, genus name, fr. Gk *krotōn* castor-oil plant] (1751) **1 :** any of a genus (*Croton*) of herbs and shrubs of the spurge family: as **a :** one (*C. eluteria*) of the Bahamas yielding cascarilla bark **b :** an East Indian plant (*C. tiglium*) yielding croton oil **2 :** any of a genus (*Codiaeum*) of shrubs related to the crotons

Cro·ton bug \ˈkrōt-ᵊn-\ *n* [*Croton* river, N.Y., used as a water supply for New York City] (1877) **:** GERMAN COCKROACH

croton oil *n* (ca. 1831) **:** a viscid acrid fixed oil from an East Indian croton (*Croton tiglium*) formerly used as a drastic cathartic but now used esp. in pharmacological experiments as an irritant

crouch \ˈkrau̇ch\ *vb* [ME *crouchen*] *vi* (14c) **1 a :** to lower the body stance esp. by bending the legs ⟨a sprinter ~*ed* and waited for the gun⟩ **b :** to lie close to the ground with the legs bent ⟨a pair of cats, ~*ing* on the brink of a fight —Aldous Huxley⟩ **2 :** to bend or bow servilely **:** CRINGE ~ *vt* **:** to bow esp. in humility or fear **:** BEND — **crouch** *n*

[1]croup \ˈkrüp\ *n* [ME *croupe*, fr. OF, of Gmc origin; akin to OHG *kropf* craw — more at CROP] (14c) **:** the rump of a quadruped

[2]croup *n* [E dial. *croup* to cry hoarsely, cough, prob. of imit. origin] (1765) **:** a spasmodic laryngitis esp. of infants marked by episodes of difficult breathing and hoarse metallic cough — **croup·ous** \ˈkrü-pəs\ *adj* — **croupy** \-pē\ *adj*

crou·pi·er \ˈkrü-pē-ər, -pē-ˌā\ *n* [F, lit., rider on the croup of a horse, fr. *croupe* croup] (1731) **:** an employee of a gambling casino who collects and pays bets and assists at the gaming tables

crouse \ˈkrüs\ *adj* [ME] *chiefly Scot* (15c) **:** BRISK, LIVELY

crous·tade \krü-ˈstäd\ *n* [F, fr. Prov *croustado*, fr. *crosta* crust, fr. L *crusta* — more at CRUST] (ca. 1845) **:** a crisp shell (as of toast or puff pastry) in which to serve food

crou·ton \ˈkrü-ˌtän, krü-ˈ\ *n* [F *croûton*, dim. of *croûte* crust, fr. MF *crouste*, fr. OF, fr. L *crusta* — more at CRUST] (1806) **:** a small cube of toasted or crisply fried bread

[1]crow \ˈkrō\ *n* [ME *crowe*, fr. OE *crāwe*; akin to OHG *krāwa* crow, OE *crāwan* to crow] (bef. 12c) **1 :** any of various large usu. entirely glossy black oscine birds (family Corvidae and esp. genus *Corvus*) **2 :** CROWBAR **3** *cap* **a :** a member of an American Indian people of the region between the Platte and Yellowstone rivers **b :** the language of the Crow people **4** *cap* **:** CORVUS — **as the crow flies :** in a straight line

[2]crow *vi* **crowed** \ˈkrōd\ *also in sense 1 chiefly Brit* **crew** \ˈkrü\; **crow·ing** [ME *crowen*, fr. OE *crāwan*] (bef. 12c) **1 :** to make the loud shrill sound characteristic of a cock **2 :** to utter a sound expressive of pleasure **3 a :** to exult gloatingly esp. over the distress of another **b :** to brag exultantly or blatantly ***syn*** see BOAST

[3]crow *n* (13c) **1 :** the cry of the cock **2 :** a triumphant cry

crow·bar \ˈkrō-ˌbär\ *n* (1748) **:** an iron or steel bar that is usu. wedge-shaped at the working end for use as a pry or lever — **crowbar** *vt*

crow·ber·ry \ˈkrō-ˌber-ē\ *n* (1597) **1 :** an evergreen subshrub (*Empetrum nigrum* of the family Empetraceae) of arctic and alpine regions with an insipid black berry **2 :** the fruit of a crowberry

[1]crowd \ˈkrau̇d\ *vb* [ME *crouden*, fr. OE *crūdan*; akin to MHG *kroten* to crowd, OE *crod* multitude, MIr *gruth* curds] *vi* (bef. 12c) **1 a :** to press on **:** HURRY **b :** to press close **2 :** to collect in numbers ~ *vt* **1 a :** to fill by pressing or thronging together **b :** to press, force, or thrust into a small space **2 :** PUSH, FORCE ⟨~*ed* us off the sidewalk⟩ **3 a :** to urge on **b :** to put on (sail) in excess of the usual for greater speed **4 :** to put pressure on ⟨don't ~ me, I'll pay⟩ **5 :** THRONG, JOSTLE **6 :** to press or stand close to

[2]crowd *n* (1567) **1 :** a large number of persons esp. when collected into a somewhat compact body without order **:** THRONG **2 :** the great body of the people **:** POPULACE **3 :** a large number of things close together **4 :** a group of people having something (as a habit, interest, or occupation) in common ⟨in with the wrong ~⟩

syn CROWD, THRONG, CRUSH, MOB, HORDE mean an assembled multitude usu. of people. CROWD implies a close gathering and pressing together; THRONG strongly suggests movement and pushing; CRUSH emphasizes the compactness of the group, the difficulty of individual movement, and the attendant discomfort; MOB implies a disorderly crowd with the potential for violence; HORDE suggests a rushing or tumultuous crowd.

[3]crowd \ˈkrau̇d, ˈkrüd\ *n* [ME *crowde*, fr. MW *crwth*] (14c) **1 :** an ancient Celtic stringed instrument that is plucked or bowed — called also *crwth* **2** *dial Eng* **:** VIOLIN

crowd·ed·ness \ˈkrau̇d-əd-nəs\ *n* (1823) **:** the quality or state of being crowded

crow·die \ˈkrau̇-dē\ *n* [Sc, alter. of ME *crud* curds — more at CURD] (1820) **:** a soft white Scottish cheese made from curds

crow·foot \ˈkrō-ˌfu̇t\ *n, pl* **crow·feet** \-ˌfēt\ (15c) **1** *pl usu* **crowfoots :** any of numerous plants having leaves with cleft lobes; *esp* **:** any of a genus (*Ranunculus*) of plants of the buttercup family that are mostly yellow-flowered herbs **2 :** CROW'S-FOOT 1 — usu. used in pl. **3 :** a number of small lines of a boat rove through a long block

crow·keep·er \ˈkrō-ˌkē-pər\ *n, dial Eng* (1562) **:** a person employed to scare off crows

[1]crown \ˈkrau̇n\ *n, often attrib* [ME *coroune, crowne*, fr. OF *corone*, fr. L *corona* wreath, crown, fr. Gk *korōnē*; akin to Gk *korōnos* curved, L *curvus*, MIr *cruind* round] (12c) **1 :** a reward of victory or mark of honor; *esp* **:** the title representing the championship in a sport **2 :** a royal or imperial headdress or cap of sovereignty **:** DIADEM **3 :** the highest part: as **a :** the topmost part of the skull or head **b :** the summit of a mountain **c :** the head of foliage of a tree or shrub **d :** the part of a hat or other headgear covering the crown of the head **e :** the part of a tooth external to the gum or an artificial substitute for this — see TOOTH illustration **4 :** a wreath, band, or circular ornament for the head **5 :** something resembling a wreath or crown **6** *often cap* **a** (1) **:** imperial or regal power **:** SOVEREIGNTY (2) **:** the government under a constitutional monarchy **b :** MONARCH **7 :** something that imparts splendor, honor, or finish **:** CULMINATION **8 a :** any of several old gold coins with a crown as part of the device **b :** a former usu. silver British coin worth five shillings **9 a :** KORUNA **b :** KRONA **c :** KRONE **10 a :** the region of a seed plant at which stem and root merge **b :** the thick arching end of the shank of an anchor where the arms join it — **crowned** \ˈkrau̇nd\ *adj*

[2]crown *vt* [ME *corounen*, fr. OF *coroner*, fr. L *coronare*, fr. *corona*] (12c) **1 a :** to place a crown or wreath on the head of; *specif* **:** to invest with regal dignity and power **b :** to recognize officially as ⟨they ~*ed* her athlete of the year⟩ **2 :** to bestow something on as a mark of honor or recompense **:** ADORN **3 :** SURMOUNT, TOP; *esp* **:** to top (a checker) with a checker to make a king **4 :** to bring to a successful conclusion **:** CLIMAX **5 :** to provide with something like a crown: as **a :** to fill so that the surface forms a crown **b :** to put an artifical crown on (a tooth) **6 :** to hit on the head

crown colony *n, often cap both Cs* (1845) **:** a colony of the British Commonwealth over which the Crown retains some control

crow·ner \ˈkrü-nər, ˈkrau̇-\ *n* [ME, alter. of *coroner*] *chiefly dial* (14c) **:** CORONER

crown·et \ˈkrau̇-nət\ *n, archaic* (15c) **:** CORONET

crown gall *n* (ca. 1900) **:** a disease that affects many species of plants and is caused by a bacterium (*Agrobacterium tumefaciens*) which forms tumorous enlargements just below the ground on the stem

crown glass *n* (1706) **1 :** a glass blown and whirled into the form of a disk with a center lump left by the worker's rod **2 :** alkali-lime silicate optical glass having relatively low index of refraction and low dispersion value

crown jewels *n pl* (1649) **:** the jewels (as crown and scepter) belonging to a sovereign's regalia

crown land *n* (1625) **1 :** land belonging to the crown and yielding revenues that the reigning sovereign is entitled to **2 :** public land in some British dominions or colonies

crown lens *n* (1834) **:** the crown glass component of an achromatic lens

crown of thorns (1964) **:** a starfish (*Acanthaster planci*) of the Pacific region that is covered with long spines and is destructive to the coral of coral reefs — called also *crown-of-thorns starfish*

crown prince *n* (1791) **:** a male heir apparent to a crown or throne

crown princess *n* (1863) **1 :** the wife of a crown prince **2 :** a female heir apparent or heir presumptive to a crown or throne

crown roast *n* (ca. 1909) **:** a fancy roast of lamb, veal, or pork made from the rib portions of two loins skewered together at the ends to form a circle

crown rust *n* (1899) **:** a leaf rust of oats and other grasses that is caused by a fungus (*Puccinia coronata*) and is characterized by rounded light-orange uredinia and buried telia

crown saw *n* (ca. 1864) **:** a saw having teeth at the edge of a hollow cylinder

crown vetch *n* (ca. 1900) **:** a European herb (*Coronilla varia*) that is naturalized in the eastern U.S. and has umbels of pink-and-white flowers and sharp-angled pods

crow's-foot \ˈkrōz-ˌfu̇t\ *n, pl* **crow's-feet** \-ˌfēt\ (14c) **1 :** any of the wrinkles around the outer corners of the eyes — usu. used in pl. **2 :** CROWFOOT 1

crow's nest *n* (1818) **:** a partly enclosed platform high on a ship's mast for use as a lookout; *also* **:** a similar lookout (as for traffic control)

crow·step \ˈkrō-ˌstep\ *n* (1822) **:** CORBIESTEP

cro·zier *var of* CROSIER

cruces *pl of* CRUX

cru·cial \ˈkrü-shəl\ *adj* [F, fr. L *cruc-, crux* cross — more at RIDGE] (1706) **1** *archaic* **:** CRUCIFORM **2 a :** important or essential as resolving a crisis **:** DECISIVE ⟨a ~ step⟩ **b :** marked by final determination of a doubtful issue ⟨the ~ game of a series⟩ **c :** IMPORTANT, SIGNIFICANT ⟨what use we make of them will be the ~ question —Stanley Kubrick⟩ ***syn*** see ACUTE — **cru·cial·ly** \ˈkrüsh-(ə-)lē\ *adv*

cru·cian carp \ˌkrü-shən-\ *n* [modif. of LG *karuse,* fr. MHG *karusse,* fr. Lith *karušis*] (1836) **:** a European carp (*Carassius carassius*) — called also *crucian*

cru·ci·ate \ˈkrü-shē-ˌāt\ *adj* [NL *cruciatus,* fr. L *cruc-, crux*] (1826) **:** cross-shaped **:** CRUCIFORM

cru·ci·ble \ˈkrü-sə-bəl\ *n* [ME *corusible,* fr. ML *crucibulum*] (15c) **1 :** a vessel of a very refractory material (as porcelain) used for melting and calcining a substance that requires a high degree of heat **2 :** a severe test **3 :** a place or situation in which concentrated forces interact to cause or influence change or development ⟨conditioned by having grown up within the ~ of Chinatown —Tom Wolfe⟩

crucible steel *n* (1879) **:** hard cast steel made in pots that are lifted from the furnace before the metal is poured into molds

cru·ci·fer \ˈkrü-sə-fər\ *n* [deriv. of L *cruc-, crux* + *-fer*] (1574) **1 :** one who carries a cross esp. at the head of an ecclesiastical procession **2 :** any of a family (Cruciferae) of plants including the cabbage and mustard — **cru·cif·er·ous** \krü-ˈsif-(ə-)rəs\ *adj*

cru·ci·fix \ˈkrü-sə-ˌfiks\ *n* [ME, fr. LL *crucifixus* the crucified Christ, fr. *crucifixus,* pp. of *crucifigere* to crucify, fr. L *cruc-, crux* + *figere* to fasten — more at DIKE] (13c) **:** a representation of Christ on the cross

cru·ci·fix·ion \ˌkrü-sə-ˈfik-shən\ *n* (15c) **1 a :** the act of crucifying **b** *cap* **:** the crucifying of Christ **2 :** extreme and painful punishment, affliction, or suffering

cru·ci·form \ˈkrü-sə-ˌfȯrm\ *adj* [L *cruc-, crux* + E *-form*] (1661) **:** forming or arranged in a cross — **cruciform** *n*

cru·ci·fy \ˈkrü-sə-ˌfī\ *vt* **-fied; -fy·ing** [ME *crucifien,* fr. OF *crucifier,* fr. LL *crucifigere*] (14c) **1 :** to put to death by nailing or binding the hands and feet to a cross **2 :** to destroy the power of **:** MORTIFY ⟨~ the flesh⟩ **3 :** to treat cruelly **:** TORTURE, PERSECUTE

cruck \ˈkrək\ *n* [ME *crokke,* prob. var. of *crok* crook] (1888) **:** one of a pair of curved timbers forming a principal support of a roof in primitive English house construction

[1]crud \ˈkrəd\ *n* [ME *curd, crudd*] (14c) **1** *dial* **:** [1]CURD **2 a :** a deposit or incrustation of filth, grease, or refuse **b** *slang* **:** something disagreeable or disgusting **:** RUBBISH **c** *slang* **:** a despicable person **3 :** a usu. ill-defined or imperfectly identified bodily disorder — **crud·dy** \ˈkrəd-ē\ *adj*

[2]crud *vb* **crud·ded; crud·ding** *dial* (14c) **:** [2]CURD

[1]crude \ˈkrüd\ *adj* **crud·er; crud·est** [ME, fr. L *crudus* raw — more at RAW] (14c) **1 :** existing in a natural state and unaltered by cooking or processing ⟨~ oil⟩ **2** *archaic* **:** UNRIPE, IMMATURE **3 :** marked by the primitive, gross, or elemental or by uncultivated simplicity or vulgarity ⟨a ~ stereotype⟩ **4 :** rough or inexpert in plan or execution ⟨a ~ shelter⟩ **5 :** lacking a covering, glossing, or concealing element **:** OBVIOUS ⟨~ facts⟩ **6 :** tabulated without being broken down into classes ⟨~ death rate⟩ ***syn*** see RUDE — **crude·ly** *adv* — **crude·ness** *n*

[2]crude *n* (1904) **:** a substance in its natural unprocessed state; *esp* **:** unrefined petroleum

cru·di·tés \krüe-dē-tā, ˌkrüd-i-ˈtā\ *n pl* [F, pl. of *crudité* raw food, fr. MF, indigestibility, fr. L *cruditas* indigestion, fr. *crudus* raw — more at RAW] (ca. 1966) **:** pieces of raw vegetables (as celery and carrot sticks) served as an hors d'oeuvre often with a dip

cru·di·ty \ˈkrüd-ət-ē\ *n, pl* **-ties** (1547) **1 :** the quality or state of being crude **2 :** something that is crude

cru·el \ˈkrü-əl\ *adj* **cru·el·er** *or* **cru·el·ler; cru·el·est** *or* **cru·el·lest** [ME, fr. OF, fr. L *crudelis,* irreg. fr. *crudus*] (13c) **1 :** disposed to inflict pain or suffering **:** devoid of humane feelings **2 a :** causing or conducive to injury, grief, or pain ⟨a ~ joke⟩ **b :** unrelieved by leniency ***syn*** see FIERCE — **cru·el·ly** \ˈkrü-ə-lē\ *adv* — **cru·el·ness** *n*

cru·el·ty \ˈkrü-əl-tē\ *n, pl* **-ties** [ME *cruelte,* fr. OF *cruelté,* fr. L *crudelitat-, crudelitas,* fr. *crudelis*] (13c) **1 :** the quality or state of being cruel **2 a :** a cruel action **b :** inhuman treatment **3 :** marital conduct held (as in a divorce action) to endanger life or health or to cause mental suffering or fear

cru·et \ˈkrü-ət\ *n* [ME, fr. AF, dim. of OF *crue,* of Gmc origin; akin to OE *crocc* crock] (13c) **1 :** a vessel to hold wine or water for the Eucharist **2 :** a usu. glass bottle used to hold a condiment (as oil or vinegar) for use at the table

[1]cruise \ˈkrüz\ *vb* **cruised; cruis·ing** [D *kruisen* to make a cross, cruise, fr. MD *crucen,* fr. *crūce* cross, fr. L *cruc-, crux* — more at RIDGE] *vi* (1651) **1 :** to sail about touching at a series of ports **2 :** to be on one's way **:** GO ⟨I'll ~ over to her house to see if she's home⟩ **3 :** to travel for the sake of traveling **4 a :** to go about the streets at random but on the lookout for possible developments ⟨the cabdriver *cruised* for an hour before being hailed⟩ **b :** to search (as in public places) for a sexual partner **5 a** *of an airplane* **:** to fly at the most efficient operating speed **b** *of an automobile* **:** to travel at a speed suitable for being maintained for a long distance ~ *vt* **1 :** to cruise over or about **2 :** to inspect (as land) with reference to possible lumber yield **3 a :** to search in (a public place) for a sexual partner **b :** to approach and suggest sexual relations to

[2]cruise *n* (ca. 1706) **:** an act or an instance of cruising; *esp* **:** a tour by ship

cruise control *n* (1974) **:** an electronic device in an automobile that controls the throttle so as to maintain a constant speed

cruise missile *n* (ca. 1960) **:** a guided missile that has a terrain-following radar system and that flies at moderate speed and low altitude

cruis·er \ˈkrü-zər\ *n* (1679) **1 :** a boat or vehicle that cruises; *specif* **:** SQUAD CAR **2 :** a large fast moderately armored and gunned warship usu. of 6000 to 15,000 tons displacement **3 :** a motorboat with cabin, plumbing, and other arrangements necessary for living aboard — called also *cabin cruiser* **4 :** a person who cruises

crul·ler \ˈkrəl-ər\ *n* [D *krulle,* a twisted cake, fr. *krul* curly, fr. MD *crul* — more at CURL] (1818) **1 :** a small sweet cake in the form of a twisted strip fried in deep fat **2** *Northern & Midland* **:** an unraised doughnut

[1]crumb \ˈkrəm\ *n* [ME *crumme,* fr. OE *cruma;* akin to MHG *krume* crumb] (bef. 12c) **1 a :** a small fragment esp. of something baked (as bread) **b :** a porous aggregate of soil particles **2 :** BIT ⟨a ~ of good news⟩ **3 :** the soft part of bread **4** *slang* **:** a worthless person

[2]crumb *vt* (15c) **1 :** to break into crumbs **2 :** to cover or thicken with crumbs **3 :** to remove crumbs from ⟨~ a table⟩

crum·ble \ˈkrəm-bəl\ *vb* **crum·bled; crum·bling** \-b(ə-)liŋ\ [alter. of ME *kremelen,* freq. of OE *gecrymian* to crumble, fr. *cruma*] *vt* (15c) **:** to break into small pieces ~ *vi* **1 :** to fall into small pieces **:** DISINTEGRATE **2 :** to fall into ruin **:** COLLAPSE ⟨marriages ~⟩ — **crumble** *n*

crum·blings \ˈkrəm-b(ə-)liŋz\ *n pl* (1660) **:** crumbled particles **:** CRUMBS

crum·bly \-b(ə-)lē\ *adj* **crum·bli·er; -est** (1523) **:** easily crumbled **:** FRIABLE ⟨~ soil⟩ — **crum·bli·ness** *n*

crumb structure *n* [trans. of G *krümelstruktur*] (ca. 1906) **:** a soil condition suitable for farming in which the soil particles are aggregated into crumbs

crumhorn *var of* KRUMMHORN

crum·mie *or* **crum·my** \ˈkrəm-ē\ *n, pl* **crummies** [Sc *crumb* crooked, fr. ME, fr. OE] *chiefly Scot* (1724) **:** COW; *esp* **:** one with crumpled horns

crum·my *or* **crumby** \ˈkrəm-ē\ *adj* **crum·mi·er** *or* **crumb·i·er; -est** [ME *crumme*] (1567) **1** *obs* **:** CRUMBLY **2 a :** MISERABLE, FILTHY **b :** CHEAP, WORTHLESS — **crum·mi·ness** *n*

[1]crump \ˈkrəmp\ *vi* [imit.] (1646) **1 :** CRUNCH **2 :** to explode heavily

[2]crump *n* (1787) **1 :** a crunching sound **2 :** SHELL, BOMB

[3]crump *adj* [perh. alter. of *crimp* (friable)] *chiefly Scot* (1787) **:** BRITTLE

crum·pet \ˈkrəm-pət\ *n* [perh. fr. ME *crompid* (*cake*) wafer, lit., curled-up cake, fr. *crumped,* pp. of *crumpen* to curl up, fr. *crump, crumb* crooked, fr. OE *crumb;* akin to OHG *krump* crooked] (1694) **:** a small round unsweetened bread cooked on a griddle and usu. split and toasted before serving

[1]crum·ple \ˈkrəm-pəl\ *vb* **crum·pled; crum·pling** \-p(ə-)liŋ\ [(assumed) ME *crumplen,* freq. of ME *crumpen*] *vt* (15c) **1 :** to press, bend, or crush out of shape **:** RUMPLE **2 :** to cause to collapse ~ *vi* **1 :** to become crumpled **2 :** COLLAPSE

[2]crumple *n* (15c) **:** a wrinkle or crease made by crumpling — **crum·ply** \ˈkrəm-p(ə-)lē\ *adj*

[1]crunch \ˈkrənch\ *vb* [alter. of *craunch*] *vi* (1814) **1 :** to chew or press with a crushing noise **2 :** to make one's way with a crushing noise ~ *vt* **:** to chew, press, or grind with a crunching sound — **crunch·able** \ˈkrən-chə-bəl\ *adj*

[2]crunch *n* (1836) **1 :** an act of crunching **2 :** a sound made by crunching **3 :** a tight or critical situation: as **a :** a critical point in the buildup of pressure between opposing elements **:** SHOWDOWN **b :** a severe economic squeeze (as on credit) **c :** SHORTAGE ⟨an energy ~⟩

crunch·er \ˈkrən-chər\ *n* (1946) **1 :** one that crunches **2 :** a finishing blow

crunchy \ˈkrən-chē\ *adj* **crunch·i·er; -est** (1913) **:** making a crunching sound — **crunch·i·ly** \-chə-lē\ *adv* — **crunch·i·ness** \-chē-nəs\ *n*

crup·per \ˈkrəp-ər, ˈkru̇p-\ *n* [ME *cruper,* fr. OF *crupiere,* fr. *croupe* hindquarters] (14c) **1 :** a leather loop passing under a horse's tail and buckled to the saddle **2 :** [1]CROUP; *broadly* **:** BUTTOCKS

cru·ral \ˈkru̇(ə)r-əl\ *adj* [L *crur-, crus* leg] (1599) **:** of or relating to the thigh or leg; *specif* **:** FEMORAL ⟨~ artery⟩

crus \ˈkrüs, ˈkrəs\ *n, pl* **cru·ra** \ˈkru̇(ə)r-ə\ [L *crur-, crus;* akin to Arm *srunk* shinbones] (ca. 1727) **1 :** the part of the hind limb between the femur or thigh and the tarsus or ankle **:** SHANK **2 :** any of various anatomical parts that resemble a leg or a pair of legs

[1]cru·sade \krü-ˈsād\ *n* [blend of MF *croisade* & Sp *cruzada;* both derivs. of L *cruc-, crux* cross] (1577) **1** *cap* **:** any of the military expeditions undertaken by Christian powers in the 11th, 12th, and 13th centuries to win the Holy Land from the Muslims **2 :** a remedial enterprise undertaken with zeal and enthusiasm

2**crusade** *vi* **cru·sad·ed; cru·sad·ing** (1732) **:** to engage in a crusade — **cru·sad·er** *n*

cru·sa·do \krü-'sä-(,)dō\ *also* **cru·za·do** \-'zä-(,)dō, -(,)ü\ *n, pl* **-does** *or* **-dos** [Pg *cruzado,* lit., marked with a cross] (1544) **:** an old gold or silver coin of Portugal having a cross on the reverse

cruse \'krüz, 'krüs\ *n* [ME; akin to OE *crūse* pitcher] (13c) **:** a small vessel (as a jar or pot) for holding a liquid (as water or oil)

1**crush** \'krəsh\ *vb* [ME *crusshen,* fr. MF *cruisir,* of Gmc origin; akin to MLG *krossen* to crush] *vt* (15c) **1 a :** to squeeze or force by pressure so as to alter or destroy structure **b :** to squeeze together into a mass **2 :** HUG, EMBRACE **3 :** to reduce to particles by pounding or grinding **4 a :** to suppress or overwhelm as if by pressure or weight **b :** to oppress or burden grievously **c :** to subdue completely **5 :** CROWD, PUSH **6** *archaic* **:** DRINK ~ *vi* **1** *obs* **:** CRASH **2 :** to become crushed **3 :** to advance with or as if with crushing — **crush·able** \-ə-bəl\ *adj* — **crush·er** *n* — **crush·ing·ly** *adv*

2**crush** *n* (1599) **1 :** an act of crushing **2 :** the quantity of material crushed **3 :** a crowding together esp. of many people **4 :** an intense and usu. passing infatuation ⟨have a ~ on someone⟩; *also* **:** the object of infatuation ***syn*** see CROWD — **crush·proof** \-,prüf\ *adj*

crust \'krəst\ *n* [ME, fr. L *crusta;* akin to OE *hrūse* earth, Gk *kryos* icy cold, *krystallos* ice, crystal, L *crudus* raw — more at RAW] (14c) **1 a :** the hardened exterior or surface part of bread **b :** a piece of this or of bread grown dry or hard **2 :** the pastry cover of a pie **3 :** a hard or brittle external coat or covering: as **a :** a hard surface layer (as of soil or snow) **b :** the outer part of a planet, moon, or asteroid composed essentially of crystalline rocks **c :** a deposit built up on the interior surface of a wine bottle during long aging **d :** an encrusting deposit of dried secretions or exudate; *esp* **:** SCAB **4 :** GALL, NERVE — **crust** *vb* — **crust·al** \'krəs-tᵊl\ *adj* — **crust·less** \'krəs(t)-ləs\ *adj*

crus·ta·cea \,krəs-'tā-sh(ē-)ə\ *n pl* [NL, group name, fr. neut. pl. of *crustaceus*] (1814) **:** arthropods that are crustaceans

crus·ta·cean \,krəs-'tā-shən\ *n* (1835) **:** any of a large class (Crustacea) of mostly aquatic arthropods that have a chitinous or calcareous and chitinous exoskeleton, a pair of often much modified appendages on each segment, and two pairs of antennae and that include the lobsters, shrimps, crabs, wood lice, water fleas, and barnacles — **crustacean** *adj*

crus·ta·ceous \-shəs\ *adj* [NL *crustaceus,* fr. L *crusta* crust, shell] (1656) **:** of, relating to, having, or forming a crust or shell; *esp* **:** CRUSTOSE

crust·ifi·ca·tion \,krəs-tə-fə-'kā-shən\ *n* (1893) **:** INCRUSTATION

crus·tose \'krəs-,tōs\ *adj* [L *crustosus* crusted, fr. *crusta*] (1879) **:** having a thin thallus adhering closely to the substratum of rock, bark, or soil ⟨~ lichens⟩ — compare FOLIOSE, FRUTICOSE

crusty \'krəs-tē\ *adj* **crust·i·er; -est** (15c) **1 :** having or being a crust **2 :** giving an effect of surly incivility in address or disposition ***syn*** see BLUFF — **crust·i·ly** \-tə-lē\ *adv* — **crust·i·ness** \-tē-nəs\ *n*

1**crutch** \'krəch\ *n* [ME *crucche,* fr. OE *crycc;* akin to OHG *krucka* crutch, OE *cradol* cradle] (bef. 12c) **1 a :** a support typically fitting under the armpit for use by the disabled in walking **b :** PROP, STAY **2 :** a forked leg rest constituting the pommel of a sidesaddle **3 :** the crotch of a human being or an animal **4 :** a forked support

2**crutch** *vt* (1681) **:** to support on crutches **:** prop up

crux \'krəks, 'krüks\ *n, pl* **crux·es** *also* **cru·ces** \'krü-,sēz\ [L *cruc-, crux* cross, torture — more at RIDGE] (1718) **1 :** a puzzling or difficult problem **:** an unsolved question **2 :** an essential point requiring resolution or resolving an outcome ⟨the ~ of the problem⟩ **3 :** a main or central feature (as of an argument)

cru·za·do \krü-'zäd-(,)ō, -(,)ü\ *n, pl* **-dos** [Pg] (1986) — see MONEY table

Cru·zan \krü-'zan\ *n* [(assumed) AmerSp *cruzano,* fr. *Santa Cruz* St. Croix] (1958) **:** a native or inhabitant of St. Croix — **Cruzan** *adj*

cru·zei·ro \krü-'ze(ə)r-(,)ō, -(,)ü\ *n, pl* **-ros** [Pg] (1927) **:** the former basic monetary unit of Brazil replaced in 1986 by the cruzado

crwth \'krüth\ *n* [W] (14c) **:** 3CROWD 1

1**cry** \'krī\ *vb* **cried; cry·ing** [ME *crien,* fr. OF *crier,* fr. L *quiritare* to cry out for help (from a citizen), to scream, fr. *Quirit-, Quiris,* name for the Roman citizen] *vt* (13c) **1 :** to utter loudly **:** SHOUT **2** *archaic* **:** BEG, BESEECH **3 :** to proclaim publicly **:** ADVERTISE ⟨~ their wares⟩ ~ *vi* **1 :** to call loudly **:** SHOUT **2 :** to shed tears often noisily **:** WEEP, SOB **3 :** to utter a characteristic sound or call **4 :** to require or suggest strongly a remedy or disposition ⟨a hundred things which ~ out for planning —Roger Burlingame⟩ — **cry havoc :** to sound an alarm — **cry over spilled milk :** to express vain regrets for what cannot be recovered or undone — **cry wolf :** to give alarm unnecessarily

2**cry** *n, pl* **cries** (13c) **1 :** an instance of crying: as **a :** an inarticulate utterance of distress, rage, or pain **b** *obs* **:** OUTCRY, CLAMOR **2 a** *obs* **:** PROCLAMATION **b** *pl, Scot* **:** BANNS **3 :** ENTREATY, APPEAL **4 :** a loud shout **5 :** WATCHWORD, SLOGAN **6 a :** common report **b :** a general opinion **7 :** the public voice raised in protest or approval **8 :** a fit of weeping **9 :** the characteristic sound or call of an animal **10 a :** a pack of hounds **b :** PURSUIT — used in the phrase *in full cry* **11 :** DISTANCE — usu. used in the phrase *a far cry*

cry- *or* **cryo-** *comb form* [G *kryo-,* fr. Gk, fr. *kryos* — more at CRUST] **:** cold **:** freezing ⟨*cry*anesthesia⟩ ⟨*cryo*gen⟩

cry·ba·by \'krī-,bā-bē\ *n* (1852) **:** one who cries or complains easily or often

cry down *vt* (1598) **:** DISPARAGE, DEPRECIATE

cry·ing \'krī-iŋ\ *adj* (1607) **1 :** calling for notice ⟨a ~ need⟩ **2 :** NOTORIOUS, HEINOUS ⟨a ~ shame⟩

cryo·bi·ol·o·gy \,krī-ō-bī-'äl-ə-jē\ *n* (1960) **:** the study of the effects of extremely low temperature on biological systems — **cryo·bi·o·log·i·cal** \-,bī-ə-'läj-i-kəl\ *adj* — **cryo·bi·ol·o·gist** \-bī-'äl-ə-jəst\ *n*

cry off *vt* (1928) **:** to call off (as a bargain) ~ *vi, chiefly Brit* **:** to beg off

cryo·gen \'krī-ə-jən\ *n* (1875) **:** a substance for obtaining low temperatures **:** REFRIGERANT — called also *cryogenic*

cryo·gen·ic \,krī-ə-'jen-ik\ *adj* (1896) **1 a :** of or relating to the production of very low temperatures **b :** being or relating to very low temperatures **2 a :** requiring or involving the use of a cryogenic temperature **b :** requiring cryogenic storage **c :** suitable for storage of a cryogenic substance — **cryo·gen·i·cal·ly** \-i-k(ə-)lē\ *adv*

cryo·gen·ics \-iks\ *n pl but sing in constr* (ca. 1934) **:** a branch of physics that deals with the production and effects of very low temperatures

cry·og·e·ny \krī-'äj-ə-nē\ *n* (1913) **:** CRYOGENICS

cryo·lite \'krī-ə-,līt\ *n* [ISV] (1801) **:** a mineral Na_3AlF_6 consisting of sodium-aluminum fluoride found in Greenland usu. in white cleavable masses and used in making soda and aluminum

cry·on·ics \krī-'än-iks\ *n pl but usu sing in constr* [*cry-* + *-onics* (as in *electronics*)] (1967) **:** the practice of freezing a dead diseased human in hopes of bringing him back to life at some future time when a cure for his disease has been developed — **cry·on·ic** \-ik\ *adj*

cryo·phil·ic \,krī-ə-'fil-ik\ *adj* (1942) **:** thriving at low temperatures

cryo·probe \'krī-ə-,prōb\ *n* (1965) **:** a blunt chilled instrument used to freeze tissues in cryosurgery

cryo·pro·tec·tive \,krī-ō-prə-'tek-tiv\ *adj* (1967) **:** serving to protect from freezing ⟨an extracellular ~ agent⟩ — **cryo·pro·tec·tant** \-'tek-tənt\ *n or adj*

cryo·scope \'krī-ə-,skōp\ *n* (1920) **:** an instrument for determining freezing points

cry·os·co·py \krī-'äs-kə-pē\ *n* [ISV] (ca. 1900) **:** the determination of the lowered freezing points produced in liquid by dissolved substances to determine molecular weights of solutes and various properties of solutions — **cryo·scop·ic** \,krī-ə-'skäp-ik\ *adj*

cryo·stat \'krī-ə-,stat\ *n* [ISV] (1913) **:** an apparatus for maintaining a constant low temperature esp. below 0°C — **cryo·stat·ic** \,krī-ə-'stat-ik\ *adj*

cryo·sur·gery \,krī-ō-'sərj-(ə-)rē\ *n* (1962) **:** surgery in which the tissue to be dissected is frozen (as by the use of liquid nitrogen) — **cryo·sur·geon** \-'sər-jən\ *n* — **cryo·sur·gi·cal** \-ji-kəl\ *adj*

cryo·ther·a·py \-'ther-ə-pē\ *n* (1926) **:** the therapeutic use of cold

cryo·tron \'krī-ə-,trän\ *n* [*cry-* + *-tron*] (1956) **:** a device performing some of the functions of an electron tube and utilizing the fact that a changing magnetic field can cause a superconductive element to oscillate between a state of low and high resistance

crypt \'kript\ *n* [L *crypta,* fr. Gk *kryptē,* fr. fem. of *kryptos* hidden, fr. *kryptein* to hide; akin to ON *hreysi* heap of stones, Lith *krauti* to pile up] (1789) **1 a :** a chamber (as a vault) wholly or partly underground; *esp* **:** a vault under the main floor of a church **b :** a chamber in a mausoleum **2 a :** an anatomical pit or depression **b :** a simple tubular gland

crypt- *or* **crypto-** *comb form* [NL, fr. Gk *kryptos*] **1 :** hidden **:** covered ⟨*crypto*genic⟩ **2 :** unavowed ⟨*crypto*fascist⟩ **3 :** CRYPTOGRAPHIC ⟨*crypto*system⟩ ⟨*crypto*security⟩

crypt·anal·y·sis \,krip-tə-'nal-ə-səs\ *n* [*crypt*ogram + *analysis*] (1923) **1 :** the solving of cryptograms or cryptographic systems **2 :** the theory of solving cryptograms or cryptographic systems **:** the art of devising methods for this — called also *cryptanalytics* — **crypt·an·a·lyt·ic** \,krip-,tan-ᵊl-'it-ik\ *adj* — **crypt·an·a·lyze** \krip-'tan-ᵊl-,īz\ *vt*

crypt·an·a·lyst \krip-'tan-ᵊl-əst\ *n* (1921) **:** a specialist in cryptanalysis

cryp·ta·rithm \'krip-tə-,rith-əm\ *n* [*crypt-* + *-arithm* (as in *logarithm*)] (1943) **:** an arithmetic problem in which letters have been substituted for numbers and which is solved by finding all possible pairings of digits with letters that produce a numerically correct answer

cryp·tic \'krip-tik\ *adj* [LL *crypticus,* fr. Gk *kryptikos,* fr. *kryptos*] (1638) **1 :** SECRET, OCCULT **2 :** intended to be obscure or mysterious ⟨a ~ policy⟩ **3 :** serving to conceal ⟨~ coloration in animals⟩; *also* **:** exhibiting cryptic coloration ⟨~ animals⟩ **4 :** UNRECOGNIZED ⟨a ~ infection⟩ **5 :** employing cipher or code ***syn*** see OBSCURE — **cryp·ti·cal·ly** \-ti-k(ə-)lē\ *adv*

1**cryp·to** \'krip-(,)tō\ *n, pl* **cryptos** [*crypt-*] (1946) **:** one who adheres or belongs secretly to a party, sect, or other group

2**crypto** *adj* (1952) **:** CRYPTOGRAPHIC

cryp·to·coc·co·sis \,krip-tə-(,)kä-'kō-səs\ *n, pl* **-co·ses** \-(,)sēz\ (1938) **:** an infectious disease that is caused by a fungus (*Cryptococcus neoformans*) and is characterized by the production of nodular lesions or abscesses in the lungs, subcutaneous tissues, joints, and esp. the brain and meninges

cryp·to·coc·cus \-'käk-əs\ *n, pl* **-coc·ci** \-'käk-,(s)ī, -(,)(s)ē\ [NL, genus name, fr. *crypt-* + *-coccus*] (ca. 1902) **:** any of a genus (*Cryptococcus*) of budding imperfect fungi that resemble yeasts and include a number of saprophytes and a few serious pathogens — **cryp·to·coc·cal** \-'käk-əl\ *adj*

cryp·to·crys·tal·line \,krip-tō-'kris-tə-lən\ *adj* [ISV] (1862) **:** having a crystalline structure so fine that no distinct particles are recognizable under the microscope

cryp·to·gam \'krip-tə-,gam\ *n* [deriv. of Gk *kryptos* + *-gamia* -gamy] (1847) **:** a plant (as a fern, moss, alga, or fungus) reproducing by spores and not producing flowers or seed — **cryp·to·gam·ic** \,krip-tə-'gam-ik\ *or* **cryp·tog·a·mous** \krip-'täg-ə-məs\ *adj*

cryp·to·gen·ic \,krip-tə-'jen-ik\ *adj* (1908) **:** of obscure or unknown origin ⟨a ~ disease⟩

cryp·to·gram \'krip-tə-,gram\ *n* [F *cryptogramme,* fr. *crypt-* + *-gramme* -gram] (1880) **1 :** a communication in cipher or code **2 :** a figure or representation having a hidden significance — **cryp·to·gram·mic** \,krip-tə-'gram-ik\ *adj*

1**cryp·to·graph** \'krip-tə-,graf\ *n* (1849) **1 :** CRYPTOGRAM **2 :** a device for enciphering and deciphering

2**cryptograph** *vt* (ca. 1923) **:** ENCRYPT

cryp·tog·ra·pher \krip-'täg-rə-fər\ *n* (1641) **:** a specialist in cryptography: as **a :** a clerk who enciphers and deciphers messages **b :** one who devises cryptographic methods or systems **c :** CRYPTANALYST

cryp·to·graph·ic \,krip-tə-'graf-ik\ *adj* (1824) **:** of, relating to, or using cryptography — **cryp·to·graph·i·cal·ly** \-i-k(ə-)lē\ *adv*

cryp·tog·ra·phy \krip-'täg-rə-fē\ *n* [NL *cryptographia,* fr. *crypt-* + *-graphia* -graphy] (1658) **1 :** secret writing **2 :** the enciphering and deciphering of messages in secret code or cipher **3 :** CRYPTANALYSIS

cryp·tol·o·gy \krip-'täl-ə-jē\ *n* (1645) **:** the scientific study of cryptography and cryptanalysis — **cryp·to·log·ic** \,krip-tə-'läj-ik\ *or* **cryp·to·log·i·cal** \-i-kəl\ *adj* — **cryp·tol·o·gist** \krip-'täl-ə-jəst\ *n*

cryp·to·me·ria \,krip-tə-'mir-ē-ə\ *n* [NL, genus name, fr. *crypt-* + Gk *meros* part — more at MERIT] (1841) **:** an evergreen tree (*Cryptomeria japonica*) of the pine family that is a valuable timber tree of Japan

crypt·or·chid \krip-'tór-kəd\ *n* [NL *cryptorchid-, cryptorchis,* fr. *crypt-* + *orchid-, orchis* testicle, fr. Gk *orchis* — more at ORCHIS] (1874) **:** one affected with cryptorchidism — **cryptorchid** *adj*

crypt·or·chi·dism \-kə-,diz-əm\ *or* **crypt·or·chism** \-,kiz-əm\ *n* (ca. 1882) **:** a condition in which one or both testes fail to descend normally

cryp·to·zo·ite \ˌkrip-tə-ˈzō-ˌīt\ *n* [*crypt-* + *-zoite* (as in *sporozoite*)] (1946) **:** a malaria parasite that develops in tissue cells and gives rise to the forms that invade blood cells

1crys·tal \ˈkris-tᵊl\ *n* [ME *cristal,* fr. OF, fr. L *crystallum,* fr. Gk *krystallos* — more at CRUST] (13c) **1 :** quartz that is transparent or nearly so and that is either colorless or only slightly tinged **2 :** something resembling crystal in transparency and colorlessness **3 :** a body that is formed by the solidification of a chemical element, a compound, or a mixture and has a regularly repeating internal arrangement of its atoms and often external plane faces **4 :** a clear colorless glass of superior quality; *also* **:** objects or ware of such glass **5 :** the glass or transparent plastic cover over a watch or clock dial **6 :** a crystalline material used in electronics as a frequency-determining element or for rectification **7 :** powdered methamphetamine

2crystal *adj* (14c) **1 :** consisting of or resembling crystal **:** CLEAR, LUCID **2 :** relating to or using a crystal ⟨a ~ radio receiver⟩

crystal ball *n* (1855) **1 :** a sphere esp. of quartz crystal traditionally used by fortune-tellers **2 :** a means or method of predicting future events

crystal detector *n* (1905) **:** a detector that depends for its operation on the rectifying action of the surface of contact between various crystals (as of galena) and a metallic electrode

crystal gazing *n* (1889) **1 :** the art or practice of concentrating on a glass or crystal globe with the aim of inducing a psychic state in which divination can be performed **2 :** the attempt to predict future events or make difficult judgments esp. without adequate data — **crystal gazer** *n*

crystall- *or* **crystallo-** *comb form* [Gk *krystallos*] **:** crystal

crys·tal·line \ˈkris-tə-lən *also* -ˌlīn, -ˌlēn\ *adj* [ME *cristallin,* fr. MF & L; MF, fr. L *crystallinus,* fr. Gk *krystallinos,* fr. *krystallos*] (15c) **1 :** made of crystal **:** composed of crystals **2 :** resembling crystal: as **a :** TRANSPARENT **b :** CLEAR-CUT **3 :** constituting or relating to a crystal — **crys·tal·lin·i·ty** \ˌkris-tə-ˈlin-ət-ē\ *n*

crystalline lens *n* (1794) **:** the lens of the eye in vertebrates

crys·tal·lite \ˈkris-tə-ˌlīt\ *n* [G *kristallit,* fr. Gk *krystallos*] (1805) **1 a :** a minute mineral form like those common in glassy volcanic rocks usu. not referable to any mineral species but marking the first step in crystallization **b :** a single grain in a polycrystalline substance **2 :** MICELLE — **crys·tal·lit·ic** \ˌkris-tə-ˈlit-ik\ *adj*

crys·tal·li·za·tion \ˌkris-tə-lə-ˈzā-shən\ *n* (1665) **:** the process of crystallizing; *also* **:** a form resulting from this

crys·tal·lize *also* **crys·tal·ize** \ˈkris-tə-ˌlīz\ *vb* **-lized; -liz·ing** *vt* (1598) **1 :** to cause to form crystals or assume crystalline form **2 :** to cause to take a definite form ⟨tried to ~ his thoughts⟩ **3 :** to coat with crystals esp. of sugar ⟨~ grapes⟩ ~ *vi* **:** to become crystallized — **crys·tal·liz·able** \-ˌlī-zə-bəl\ *adj* — **crys·tal·liz·er** *n*

crys·tal·lized *adj* (1667) **1 :** formed into crystals **2 :** coated with crystals esp. of sugar **:** CANDIED **3 :** definite in form

crys·tal·log·ra·phy \ˌkris-tə-ˈläg-rə-fē\ *n* (1802) **:** the science dealing with the system of forms among crystals, their structure, and their forms of aggregation — **crys·tal·log·ra·pher** \-fər\ *n* — **crys·tal·lo·graph·ic** \-lə-ˈgraf-ik\ *or* **crys·tal·lo·graph·i·cal** \-i-kəl\ *adj* — **crys·tal·lo·graph·i·cal·ly** \-i-k(ə-)lē\ *adv*

crys·tal·loid \ˈkris-tə-ˌlȯid\ *n* (1861) **:** a substance that forms a true solution and is capable of being crystallized — **crystalloid** *or* **crys·tal·loi·dal** \ˌkris-tə-ˈlȯid-ᵊl\ *adj*

crystal pleat *n* (1976) **:** any of a series of narrow sharply pressed pleats all turned in one direction — **crystal pleated** *adj*

crystal violet *n* (ca. 1893) **:** a triphenylmethane dye found in gentian violet

cry up *vt* (1593) **:** to enhance in value or repute by public praise

cte·noid \ˈtē-ˌnȯid, ˈte-ˌnȯid\ *adj* [ISV, fr. Gk *ktenoeidēs,* fr. *kten-, kteis* comb — more at PECTINATE] (1872) **:** having the margin toothed ⟨~ scale⟩; *also* **:** having or consisting of ctenoid scales ⟨~ fishes⟩

cteno·phore \ˈten-ə-ˌfō(ə)r, -ˌfȯ(ə)r\ *n* [deriv. of Gk *kten-, kteis* + *pherein* to carry — more at BEAR] (1884) **:** any of a phylum (Ctenophora) of marine animals superficially resembling jellyfishes but having decided biradial symmetry and swimming by means of eight meridional bands of transverse ciliated plates — called also *comb jelly* — **cte·noph·o·ran** \tə-ˈnäf-ə-rən\ *n or adj*

C–type \ˈsē-ˌtīp\ *adj* (1969) **:** relating to or being any of the oncornaviruses in which the structure containing the nucleic acid is spherical and centrally located ⟨~ virus particles⟩

cua·dri·lla \kwä-ˈdrē(l)-yə\ *n* [Sp, dim. of *cuadra* square, fr. L *quadra*] (1893) **:** the team assisting the matador in the bullring

cub \ˈkəb\ *n* [origin unknown] (1530) **1 a :** a young carnivorous mammal (as a bear or lion) **b :** a young shark **2 :** a young person **3 :** APPRENTICE; *esp* **:** an inexperienced newspaper reporter

cub·age \ˈkyü-bij\ *n* (1840) **:** cubic content, volume, or displacement

Cu·ban heel \ˌkyü-bən-\ *n* [*Cuba,* West Indies] (1908) **:** a broad medium-high heel with a moderately curved back

cu·ba·ture \ˈkyü-bə-ˌchü(ə)r, -ˌchər, -ˌt(y)u̇(ə)r\ *n* [*cube* + *-ature* (as in *quadrature*)] (1679) **1 :** determination of cubic contents **2 :** cubic content

cub·by \ˈkəb-ē\ *n, pl* **cubbies** [obs. E *cub* pen, fr. D *kub* thatched roof; akin to OE *cofa* den — more at COVE] (1868) **:** a snug place **:** a cramped space

cub·by·hole \ˈkəb-ē-ˌhōl\ *n* (ca. 1842) **1 :** CUBBY **2 :** PIGEONHOLE 2

1cube \ˈkyüb\ *n* [ME, fr. L *cubus,* fr. Gk *kybos* cube, vertebra — more at HIP] (14c) **1 :** the regular solid of six equal square sides — see VOLUME table **2 :** the product got by taking a number three times as a factor **3** *pl* **:** cubic inches — used of the displacement of an automobile engine

2cube *adj* (1570) **:** raised to the third power

3cube *vt* **cubed; cub·ing** (1588) **1 :** to raise to the third power **2 :** to form into a cube **3 :** to cut partly through (a steak) in a checkered pattern to increase tenderness by breaking the fibers — **cub·er** *n*

4cu·be *or* **cu·bé** \ˈkyü-ˌbā, kyü-ˈ\ *n* [AmerSp *cubé*] (1924) **:** any of several tropical American plants (genus *Lonchocarpus*) furnishing rotenone

cu·beb \ˈkyü-ˌbeb\ *n* [MF *cubebe,* fr. OF, fr. ML *cubeba,* fr. Ar *kubābah*] (14c) **:** the dried unripe berry of a tropical shrub (*Piper cubeba*) of the pepper family that is crushed and smoked in cigarettes for catarrh

cube root *n* (ca. 1696) **:** a number whose cube is a given number

cube steak *n* (1930) **:** a thin slice of beef that has been cubed

1cu·bic \ˈkyü-bik\ *adj* (1500) **1 :** having the form of a cube **:** CUBICAL **2 a :** relating to the cube considered as a crystal form **b :** ISOMETRIC 1b **3 a :** THREE-DIMENSIONAL **b :** being the volume of a cube whose edge is a specified unit ⟨~ inch⟩ **4 :** of third degree, order, or power ⟨a ~ polynomial⟩

2cubic *n* (1799) **:** a cubic curve, equation, or polynomial

cu·bi·cal \ˈkyü-bi-kəl\ *adj* (1500) **1 :** CUBIC; *esp* **:** shaped like a cube **2 :** relating to volume — **cu·bi·cal·ly** \-k(ə-)lē\ *adv*

cubic equation *n* (ca. 1727) **:** a polynomial equation in which the highest sum of exponents of variables in any term is three

cu·bi·cle \ˈkyü-bi-kəl\ *n* [L *cubiculum,* fr. *cubare* to lie, recline — more at HIP] (15c) **1 :** a sleeping compartment partitioned off from a large room **2 :** a small partitioned space; *esp* **:** CARREL

cubic measure *n* (1660) **:** a unit (as cubic inch or cubic centimeter) for measuring volume — see METRIC SYSTEM table, WEIGHT table

cub·ism \ˈkyü-ˌbiz-əm\ *n* (1911) **:** a style of art that stresses abstract structure at the expense of other pictorial elements esp. by displaying several aspects of the same object simultaneously and by fragmenting the form of depicted objects — **cub·ist** \-bəst\ *n* — **cubist** *or* **cu·bis·tic** \kyü-ˈbis-tik\ *adj*

cu·bit \ˈkyü-bət\ *n* [ME, fr. L *cubitum* elbow, cubit — more at HIP] (14c) **:** any of various ancient units of length based on the length of the forearm from the elbow to the tip of the middle finger and usu. equal to about 18 inches but sometimes to 21 or more

1cu·boid \ˈkyü-ˌbȯid\ *adj* (ca. 1828) **1 :** approximately cubical in shape **2 :** relating to or being the cuboid

2cuboid *n* (1839) **:** the outermost bone in the distal row of tarsal bones of many higher vertebrates

cu·boi·dal \kyü-ˈbȯid-ᵊl\ *adj* (1803) **1 :** somewhat cubical **2 :** composed of nearly cubical elements ⟨~ epithelium⟩

Cub Scout *n* (ca. 1935) **:** a member of the scouting program of the Boy Scouts of America for boys of the age range 8 to 10

cuck·ing stool \ˈkək-iŋ-\ *n* [ME *cucking stol,* lit., defecating chair] (12c) **:** a chair formerly used for punishing offenders (as dishonest tradesmen) by public exposure or ducking in water

cuck·old \ˈkək-əld, -(ˌ)ōld\ *n* [ME *cokewold*] (13c) **:** a man whose wife is unfaithful — **cuckold** *vt*

cuck·old·ry \-əl-drē\ *n* (1529) **1 :** the practice of making cuckolds **2 :** the state of being a cuckold

1cuck·oo \ˈkük-(ˌ)ü, ˈku̇k-\ *n, pl* **cuckoos** [ME *cuccu,* of imit. origin] (13c) **1 :** a largely grayish brown European bird (*Cuculus canorus*) that is a parasite given to laying its eggs in the nests of other birds which hatch them and rear the offspring; *broadly* **:** any of a large family (Cuculidae of the order Cuculiformes) to which this bird belongs **2 :** the call of the cuckoo **3 :** a silly or slightly crackbrained person

cuckoo 1

2cuckoo *vt* (1620) **:** to repeat monotonously as a cuckoo does its call

3cuckoo *adj* (1627) **1 :** of, relating to, or resembling the cuckoo **2 :** deficient in sense or intelligence **:** SILLY

cuckoo clock *n* (1789) **:** a wall or shelf clock that announces the hours by sounds resembling a cuckoo's call

cuck·oo·flow·er \ˈkük-(ˌ)ü-ˌflau̇(-ə)r, ˈku̇k-\ *n* (1578) **1 :** a bitter cress (*Cardamine pratensis*) of Europe and America **2 :** RAGGED ROBIN

cuck·oo·pint \-ˌpint\ *n* [ME *cuccupintel,* fr. *cuccu* + *pintel* pintle] (15c) **:** a European arum (*Arum maculatum*) with erect spathe and short purple spadix

cuckoo spit *n* (1592) **1 :** a frothy secretion exuded on plants by the nymphs of spittle insects **2 :** SPITTLE INSECT

cu·cul·late \ˈkyü-kə-ˌlāt, kyü-ˈkəl-ət\ *adj* [ML *cucullatus,* fr. L *cucullus* hood] (1794) **:** having the shape of a hood **:** HOODED ⟨a ~ leaf⟩

cu·cum·ber \ˈkyü-(ˌ)kəm-bər\ *n* [ME, fr. MF *cocombre,* fr. L *cucumer-, cucumis*] (14c) **:** the fruit of a vine (*Cucumis sativus*) of the gourd family cultivated as a garden vegetable; *also* **:** this vine

cucumber mosaic *n* (1916) **:** a virus disease esp. of cucumbers that is transmitted by an aphid and produces mottled foliage and often pale warty fruits

cucumber tree *n* (1781) **:** any of several American magnolias (esp. *Magnolia acuminata*) having fruit resembling a small cucumber

cu·cur·bit \kyü-ˈkər-bət\ *n* [ME *cucurbite,* fr. MF, fr. L *cucurbita* gourd] (14c) **1 :** a vessel or flask for distillation used with or forming part of an alembic **2 :** a plant of the gourd family

cud \ˈkəd, ˈku̇d\ *n* [ME *cudde,* fr. OE *cwudu;* akin to OHG *kuti* glue, Skt *jatu* gum] (bef. 12c) **1 :** food brought up into the mouth by a ruminating animal from its first stomach to be chewed again **2 :** 2QUID

cud·bear \ˈkəd-ˌba(ə)r, -ˌbe(ə)r\ *n* [irreg. fr. Dr. *Cuthbert* Gordon, 18th cent. Scot. chemist] (1771) **:** a reddish coloring matter from lichens

1cud·dle \ˈkəd-ᵊl\ *vb* **cud·dled; cud·dling** \ˈkəd-liŋ, -ᵊl-iŋ\ [origin unknown] *vt* (1520) **:** to hold close for warmth or comfort or in affection ~ *vi* **:** to lie close or snug **:** NESTLE, SNUGGLE

2cuddle *n* (1825) **:** a close embrace

cud·dle·some \ˈkəd-ᵊl-səm\ *adj* (1876) **:** CUDDLY

cud·dly \ˈkəd-lē, -ᵊl-ē\ *adj* **cud·dli·er; -est** (1915) **:** fit for or inviting cuddling

1cud·dy \ˈkəd-ē\ *n, pl* **cuddies** [origin unknown] (1660) **1 a :** a small cabin formerly under the poop deck **b :** the galley or pantry of a small ship **2 :** a small room or cupboard

2cud·dy *or* **cud·die** \ˈku̇d-ē, ˈkəd-\ *n, pl* **cuddies** [perh. fr. *Cuddy,* nickname for *Cuthbert*] (1714) **1** *dial Brit* **:** DONKEY **2** *dial Brit* **:** BLOCKHEAD

1cud·gel \ˈkəj-əl\ *n* [ME *kuggel,* fr. OE *cycgel;* akin to MHG *kugele* ball] (bef. 12c) **:** a short heavy club

\ə\ abut \ᵊ\ kitten, F table \ər\ further \a\ ash \ā\ ace \ä\ cot, cart \au̇\ out \ch\ chin \e\ bet \ē\ easy \g\ go \i\ hit \ī\ ice \j\ job \ŋ\ sing \ō\ go \ȯ\ law \ȯi\ boy \th\ thin \t͟h\ the \ü\ loot \u̇\ foot \y\ yet \zh\ vision \à, k̲, ⁿ, œ, œ̄, ue, ue̅, ʸ\ see Guide to Pronunciation

[2]**cudgel** *vt* **-geled** *or* **-gelled; -gel·ing** *or* **-gel·ling** \-(ə-)liŋ\ (1596) **:** to beat with or as if with a cudgel — **cudgel one's brains :** to think hard (as for a solution to a problem)

cud·weed \ˈkəd-ˌwēd, ˈku̇d-\ *n* (1548) **:** any of several composite plants (as of the genus *Gnaphalium*) with silky or woolly foliage

[1]**cue** \ˈkyü\ *n* [ME *cu*] (15c) **:** the letter *q*

[2]**cue** *n* [prob. fr. *qu*, abbr. (used as a direction in actors' copies of plays) of L *quando* when] (1553) **1 a :** a signal (as a word, phrase, or bit of stage business) to a performer to begin a specific speech or action **b :** something serving a comparable purpose **:** HINT **2 :** a feature indicating the nature of something perceived **3** *archaic* **:** the part one has to perform in or as if in a play **4** *archaic* **:** MOOD, HUMOR

[3]**cue** *vt* **cued; cu·ing** *or* **cue·ing** (1922) **1 :** to give a cue to **:** PROMPT **2 :** to insert into a continuous performance ⟨~ in sound effects⟩

[4]**cue** *n* [F *queue*, lit., tail, fr. L *cauda*] (1749) **1 a :** a leather-tipped tapering rod for striking the cue ball (as in billiards and pool) **b :** a long-handled instrument with a concave head for shoving disks in shuffleboard **2 :** QUEUE 2

[5]**cue** *vb* **cued; cu·ing** *or* **cue·ing** *vt* (1772) **1 :** QUEUE **2 :** to strike with a cue ~ *vi* **1 :** QUEUE **2 :** to use a cue

cue ball *n* (1881) **:** the ball a player strikes with his cue in billiards and pool

cues·ta \ˈkwes-tə\ *n* [Sp, fr. L *costa* side, rib — more at COAST] (1818) **:** a hill or ridge with a steep face on one side and a gentle slope on the other

[1]**cuff** \ˈkəf\ *n* [ME] (14c) **1 :** something (as a part of a sleeve or glove) encircling the wrist **2 :** the turned-back hem of a trouser leg **3 :** HANDCUFF — usu. used in pl. **4 :** an inflatable band that is wrapped around an extremity to control the flow of blood through the part when recording blood pressure with a sphygmomanometer — **cuff·less** \-ləs\ *adj* — **off the cuff :** without preparation **:** AD LIB — **on the cuff :** on credit

[2]**cuff** *vt* (1693) **1 :** to furnish with a cuff **2 :** HANDCUFF

[3]**cuff** *vb* [perh. fr. obs. E, glove, fr. ME] *vt* (1530) **:** to strike esp. with or as if with the palm of the hand **:** BUFFET ~ *vi* **:** FIGHT, SCUFFLE

[4]**cuff** *n* (1570) **:** a blow with the hand esp. when open **:** SLAP

cuff link *n* (1897) **:** a usu. ornamental device consisting of two parts joined by a shank, chain, or bar for passing through buttonholes to fasten shirt cuffs — usu. used in pl.

cui bo·no \(ˈ)kwē-ˈbō-(ˌ)nō\ *n* [L, to whose advantage?] (1604) **1 :** a principle that probable responsibility for an act or event lies with one having something to gain **2 :** usefulness or utility as a principle in estimating the value of an act or policy

[1]**cui·rass** \kwi-ˈras, kyu̇-\ *n* [ME *curas*, fr. MF *curasse*, fr. LL *coreacea*, fem. of *coreaceus* leathern, fr. L *corium* skin, leather; akin to OE *heortha* deerskin, L *cortex* bark, Gk *keirein* to cut — more at SHEAR] (15c) **1 :** a piece of armor covering the body from neck to waist; *also* **:** the breastplate of such a piece **2 :** something (as bony plates covering an animal) resembling a cuirass

[2]**cuirass** *vt* (1863) **:** to cover or armor with a cuirass

cui·ras·sier \ˌkwir-ə-ˈsi(ə)r, ˌkyu̇r-\ *n* (1625) **:** a mounted soldier wearing a cuirass

Cui·se·naire rod \ˌkwē-zə-ˈna(ə)r-, -ˈne(ə)r-\ *n* [fr. *Cuisenaire*, a trademark] (1954) **:** any of a set of colored rods usu. of 1 centimeter cross section and of 10 lengths from 1 to 10 centimeters and that are used for teaching number concepts and the basic operations of arithmetic

cui·sine \kwi-ˈzēn, kwē-\ *n* [F, lit., kitchen, fr. LL *coquina* — more at KITCHEN] (1786) **:** manner of preparing food **:** style of cooking; *also* **:** the food prepared

cuisse \ˈkwis\ *also* **cuish** \ˈkwish\ *n* [ME *cusseis*, pl., fr. MF *cuissaux*, pl. of *cuissel*, fr. *cuisse* thigh, fr. L *coxa* hip — more at COXA] (14c) **:** a piece of plate armor for the front of the thigh — see ARMOR illustration

cuit·tle \ˈküt-ᵊl, ˈkət-\ *vt* **cuit·tled; cuit·tling** \ˈküt-liŋ, ˈkət-, -ᵊl-iŋ\ [origin unknown] *Scot* (1565) **:** COAX, WHEEDLE

cuke \ˈkyük\ *n* (1903) **:** CUCUMBER

cul–de–sac \ˈkəl-di-ˌsak, ˈku̇l-; ˌkəl-di-ˈ, ˌku̇l-\ *n, pl* **culs–de–sac** \ˈkəl(z)-, ˈku̇l(z)-, ˌkəl(z)-, ˌku̇l(z)-\ *also* **cul–de–sacs** \-ˌsaks, -ˈsaks\ [F, lit., bottom of the bag] (1738) **1 :** a blind diverticulum or pouch **2 :** a street closed at one end

cu·let \ˈkyü-lət, ˈkəl-ət\ *n* [F, fr. dim. of *cul* backside, fr. L *culus*; akin to L *cutis* skin — more at HIDE] (1678) **1 :** the small flat facet at the bottom of a brilliant parallel to the table — see BRILLIANT illustration **2 :** plate armor covering the buttocks

cu·lex \ˈkyü-ˌleks\ *n* [NL, fr. L, gnat; akin to OIr *cuil* gnat] (15c) **:** any of a large cosmopolitan genus (*Culex*) of mosquitoes that includes the common house mosquito (*C. pipiens*) of Europe and No. America — **cu·li·cine** \ˈkyü-lə-ˌsīn\ *adj or n*

cu·li·nary \ˈkəl-ə-ˌner-ē, ˈkyü-lə-\ *adj* [L *culinarius*, fr. *culina* kitchen — more at KILN] (1638) **:** of or relating to the kitchen or cookery

[1]**cull** \ˈkəl\ *vt* [ME *cullen*, fr. MF *cuillir*, fr. L *colligere* to bind together — more at COLLECT] (13c) **1 :** to select from a group **:** CHOOSE ⟨~*ed* the best passages from the poet's work⟩ **2 :** to identify and remove the culls from — **cull·er** *n*

[2]**cull** *n* (1829) **:** something rejected esp. as being inferior or worthless ⟨how to separate good-looking pecans from ~*s* —*Washington Post*⟩

cul·len·der \ˈkəl-ən-dər\ *var of* COLANDER

cul·let \ˈkəl-ət\ *n* [perh. fr. F *cueillette* act of gathering, fr. L *collecta*, fr. fem. of *collectus*, pp. of *colligere*] (1817) **:** broken or refuse glass usu. added to new material to facilitate melting in making glass

cul·lion \ˈkəl-yən\ *n* [ME *coillon* testicle, fr. MF, fr. (assumed) VL *coleon-*, *coleo*, fr. L *coleus* scrotum] *archaic* (16c) **:** a mean or base fellow

[1]**cul·ly** \ˈkəl-ē\ *n, pl* **cullies** [perh. alter. of *cullion*] (1664) **:** one easily tricked or imposed on **:** DUPE

[2]**cully** *vt* **cul·lied; cul·ly·ing** *archaic* (1676) **:** CHEAT, DECEIVE

[1]**culm** \ˈkəlm\ *n* [ME] (14c) **1 :** refuse coal screenings **:** SLACK **2 :** a Mississippian formation in which marine fossil-bearing beds alternate with those containing plant remains

[2]**culm** *n* [L *culmus* stalk — more at HAULM] (ca. 1657) **:** a monocotyledonous stem

cul·mi·nant \ˈkəl-mə-nənt\ *adj* (1605) **1 :** being at greatest altitude or on the meridian **2 :** fully developed

cul·mi·nate \ˈkəl-mə-ˌnāt\ *vb* **-nat·ed; -nat·ing** [ML *culminatus*, pp. of *culminare*, fr. LL, to crown, fr. L *culmin-*, *culmen* top — more at HILL] *vi* (1647) **1** *of a celestial body* **:** to reach its highest altitude; *also* **:** to be directly overhead **2 a :** to rise to or form a summit **b :** to reach the highest or a climactic or decisive point ~ *vt* **:** to bring to a head or to the highest point

cul·mi·na·tion \ˌkəl-mə-ˈnā-shən\ *n* (1633) **1 :** the action of culminating **2 :** culminating position **:** CLIMAX ***syn*** see SUMMIT

cu·lotte \ˈkü-ˌlät, ˈkyü-; k(y)ü-ˈlät\ *n* [F, breeches, fr. dim. of *cul* backside — more at CULET] (1911) **:** a divided skirt; *also* **:** a garment having a divided skirt — often used in pl.

cul·pa·ble \ˈkəl-pə-bəl\ *adj* [ME *coupable*, fr. MF, fr. L *culpabilis*, fr. *culpare* to blame, fr. *culpa* guilt] (14c) **1** *archaic* **:** GUILTY, CRIMINAL **2 :** meriting condemnation or blame esp. as wrong or harmful ⟨~ negligence⟩ ***syn*** see BLAMEWORTHY — **cul·pa·bil·i·ty** \ˌkəl-pə-ˈbil-ət-ē\ *n* — **cul·pa·ble·ness** \ˈkəl-pə-bəl-nəs\ *n* — **cul·pa·bly** \-blē\ *adv*

cul·prit \ˈkəl-prət, -ˌprit\ *n* [AF *cul.* (abbr. of *culpable* guilty) + *prest*, *prit* ready (i.e., to prove it), fr. L *praestus* — more at PRESTO] (1678) **1 :** one accused of or charged with a crime **2 :** one guilty of a crime or a fault

cult \ˈkəlt\ *n* [F & L; F *culte*, fr. L *cultus* care, adoration, fr. *cultus*, pp. of *colere* to cultivate — more at WHEEL] (1679) **1 :** formal religious veneration **:** WORSHIP **2 :** a system of religious beliefs and ritual; *also* **:** its body of adherents **3 :** a religion regarded as unorthodox or spurious; *also* **:** its body of adherents **4 :** a system for the cure of disease based on dogma set forth by its promulgator **5 a :** great devotion to a person, idea, or thing; *esp* **:** such devotion regarded as a literary or intellectual fad **b :** a usu. small circle of persons united by devotion or allegiance to an artistic or intellectual movement or figure — **cul·tic** \ˈkəl-tik\ *adj* — **cult·ism** \ˈkəl-ˌtiz-əm\ *n* — **cult·ist** \ˈkəl-təst\ *n*

cultch *also* **culch** \ˈkəlch\ *n* [perh. fr. a F dial. form of F *couche* couch] (1667) **1 :** material (as oyster shells) laid down on oyster grounds to furnish points of attachment for the spat **2** *chiefly NewEng* **:** CLUTTER, TRASH

cul·ti·gen \ˈkəl-tə-jən\ *n* [*culti*vated + *-gen*] (1924) **1 :** a cultivated organism (as Indian corn) of a variety or species for which a wild ancestor is unknown **2 :** CULTIVAR

cul·ti·va·ble \ˈkəl-tə-və-bəl\ *adj* (1682) **:** capable of being cultivated — **cul·ti·va·bil·i·ty** \ˌkəl-tə-və-ˈbil-ət-ē\ *n*

cul·ti·var \ˈkəl-tə-ˌvär, -ˌve(ə)r, -ˌva(ə)r\ *n* [*culti*vated + *var*iety] (1923) **:** an organism of a kind originating and persistent under cultivation

cul·ti·vate \ˈkəl-tə-ˌvāt\ *vt* **-vat·ed; -vat·ing** [ML *cultivatus*, pp. of *cultivare*, fr. *cultivus* cultivable, fr. L *cultus*, pp.] (1620) **1 :** to prepare or prepare and use for the raising of crops; *also* **:** to loosen or break up the soil about (growing plants) **2 a :** to foster the growth of ⟨~ vegetables⟩ **b :** CULTURE 2a **c :** to improve by labor, care, or study **:** REFINE ⟨~ the mind⟩ **3 :** FURTHER, ENCOURAGE ⟨~ the arts⟩ **4 :** to seek the society of **:** make friends with — **cul·ti·vat·able** \-ˌvāt-ə-bəl\ *adj*

cul·ti·vat·ed *adj* (1665) **:** REFINED, EDUCATED ⟨~ speech⟩ ⟨~ tastes⟩

cul·ti·va·tion \ˌkəl-tə-ˈvā-shən\ *n* (1719) **1 :** the act or art of cultivating or tilling **2 :** CULTURE, REFINEMENT

cul·ti·va·tor \ˈkəl-tə-ˌvāt-ər\ *n* (1665) **:** one that cultivates; *esp* **:** an implement for loosening the soil while crops are growing

cul·tur·al \ˈkəlch(-ə)-rəl\ *adj* (ca. 1864) **1 :** of or relating to culture or culturing **2 :** concerned with the fostering of plant or animal growth — **cul·tur·al·ly** \-rə-lē\ *adv*

cultural anthropology *n* (1933) **:** anthropology that deals with human culture esp. with respect to social structure, language, law, politics, religion, magic, art, and technology — compare PHYSICAL ANTHROPOLOGY — **cultural anthropologist** *n*

[1]**cul·ture** \ˈkəl-chər\ *n* [ME, fr. MF, fr. L *cultura*, fr. *cultus*, pp.] (15c) **1 :** CULTIVATION, TILLAGE **2 :** the act of developing the intellectual and moral faculties esp. by education **3 :** expert care and training ⟨beauty ~⟩ **4 a :** enlightenment and excellence of taste acquired by intellectual and aesthetic training **b :** acquaintance with and taste in fine arts, humanities, and broad aspects of science as distinguished from vocational and technical skills **5 a :** the integrated pattern of human knowledge, belief, and behavior that depends upon man's capacity for learning and transmitting knowledge to succeeding generations **b :** the customary beliefs, social forms, and material traits of a racial, religious, or social group **6 :** cultivation of living material in prepared nutrient media; *also* **:** a product of such cultivation

[2]**culture** *vt* **cul·tured; cul·tur·ing** \ˈkəlch-(ə-)riŋ\ (1510) **1 :** CULTIVATE **2 a :** to grow in a prepared medium **b :** to start a culture from

cul·tured \ˈkəl-chərd\ *adj* (1743) **1 :** CULTIVATED **2 :** produced under artificial conditions ⟨~ viruses⟩ ⟨~ pearls⟩

culture shock *n* (ca. 1960) **:** a sense of confusion and uncertainty sometimes with feelings of anxiety that may affect people exposed to an alien culture without adequate preparation

cul·tus \ˈkəl-təs\ *n* [L, adoration] (1640) **:** CULT

cul·ver \ˈkəl-vər, ˈku̇l-\ *n* [ME, fr. OE *culfer*, fr. (assumed) VL *columbra*, fr. L *columbula*, dim. of L *columba* dove — more at COLUMBINE] (bef. 12c) **:** PIGEON

cul·ver·in \ˈkəl-və-rən\ *n* [ME, fr. MF *couleuvrine*, fr. *couleuvre* snake, fr. L *colubra*] (15c) **:** an early firearm: **a :** a rude musket **b :** a long cannon (as an 18-pounder) of the 16th and 17th centuries

cul·vert \ˈkəl-vərt\ *n* [origin unknown] (1773) **1 :** a transverse drain **2 :** a conduit for a culvert **3 :** a bridge over a culvert

cum \(ˌ)ku̇m, (ˌ)kəm\ *prep* [L; akin to L *com-* — more at CO-] (1871) **:** WITH **:** combined with **:** along with

Cu·ma·na·go·to \(ˌ)kü-ˌmän-ə-ˈgōt-(ˌ)ō\ *n, pl* **Cumanagoto** *or* **Cumanagotos** [Sp, of AmerInd origin] (ca. 1895) **1 :** a member of a Cariban people of Venezuela **2 :** the language of the Cumanagoto people

[1]**cum·ber** \ˈkəm-bər\ *vt* **cum·bered; cum·ber·ing** \-b(ə-)riŋ\ [ME *cumbren*] (14c) **1** *archaic* **:** TROUBLE, HARASS **2 a :** to hinder by being in the way ⟨~*ed* with heavy clothing⟩ **b :** to clutter up ⟨rocks ~*ing* the yard⟩ **c :** to burden needlessly ⟨~ the memory with trival facts⟩

[2]**cumber** *n* (14c) **:** something that cumbers; *esp* **:** HINDRANCE

cum·ber·some \ˈkəm-bər-səm\ *adj* (1535) **1** *dial* **:** BURDENSOME, TROUBLESOME **2 :** unwieldy because of heaviness and bulk **3 :** slow-moving **:** PONDEROUS ***syn*** see HEAVY — **cum·ber·some·ly** *adv* — **cum·ber·some·ness** *n*

cum·brous \ˈkəm-b(ə-)rəs\ *adj* (15c) **:** CUMBERSOME ***syn*** see HEAVY — **cum·brous·ly** *adv* — **cum·brous·ness** *n*

cum·in \'kəm-ən\ *n* [ME, fr. OE *cymen*, fr. L *cuminum*, fr. Gk *kyminon*, of Sem origin] (bef. 12c) : a low plant (*Cuminum cyminum*) of the carrot family long cultivated for its aromatic seeds; *also* : the fruit or seed of cumin used as a spice

cum lau·de \kům-'lau̇d-ə, -ē; ˌkəm-'lȯd-ē\ *adv or adj* [NL, with praise] (1893) : with distinction ⟨graduated *cum laude*⟩ — compare MAGNA CUM LAUDE, SUMMA CUM LAUDE

cum·mer·bund \'kəm-ər-ˌbənd\ *n* [Hindi *kamarband*, fr. Per, fr. *kamar* waist + *band* band] (1616) : a broad waistband usu. worn in place of a vest with men's dress clothes and adapted in various styles of women's clothes

cum·shaw \'kəm-ˌshȯ\ *n* [Chin (Amoy) *kam sia* grateful thanks (a phrase used by beggars)] (1839) : PRESENT, GRATUITY

cumul- *or* **cumuli-** *or* **cumulo-** *comb form* [NL, fr. L *cumulus*] : cumulus and ⟨*cumulo*cirrus⟩

cu·mu·late \'kyü-myə-ˌlāt\ *vb* **-lat·ed; -lat·ing** [L *cumulatus*, pp. of *cumulare*, fr. *cumulus* mass] *vt* (1534) **1** : to gather or pile in a heap **2** : to combine into one **3** : to build up by addition of new material ~ *vi* : to become massed — **cu·mu·late** \-lət, -ˌlāt\ *adj* — **cu·mu·la·tion** \ˌkyü-myə-'lā-shən\ *n*

cu·mu·la·tive \'kyü-myə-lət-iv, -ˌlāt-\ *adj* (1605) **1 a** : made up of accumulated parts **b** : increasing by successive additions **2 a** : tending to prove the same point ⟨~ evidence⟩ **b** : additional rather than repeated ⟨~ legacy⟩ **3 a** : taking effect upon completion of another sentence ⟨~ sentence⟩ **b** : increasing in severity with repetition of the offense ⟨~ penalty⟩ **4** : formed by the addition of new material of the same kind ⟨~ book index⟩ **5** : summing or integrating overall data or values of a random variable less than or less than or equal to a specified value ⟨~ normal distribution⟩ ⟨~ frequency distribution⟩ — **cu·mu·la·tive·ly** *adv* — **cu·mu·la·tive·ness** *n*

cumulative distribution function *n* (ca. 1965) : DISTRIBUTION FUNCTION

cu·mu·li·form \'kyü-myə-lə-ˌfȯrm\ *adj* (1885) : of the form of a cumulus

cu·mu·lo·cir·rus \ˌkyü-myə-lō-'sir-əs\ *n* [NL] (ca. 1907) : a small cumulus cloud at a high altitude having the white delicacy of the cirrus

cu·mu·lo·nim·bus \-'nim-bəs\ *n* [NL] (1887) : cumulus cloud often spread out in the shape of an anvil extending to great heights — see CLOUD illustration

cu·mu·lo·stra·tus \-'strāt-əs, -'strat-\ *n* [NL] (ca. 1803) : a cumulus whose base extends horizontally as a stratus cloud

cu·mu·lous \'kyü-myə-ləs\ *adj* (1815) : resembling cumulus

cu·mu·lus \-ləs\ *n, pl* **-li** \-ˌlī, -ˌlē\ [L] (1659) **1** : HEAP, ACCUMULATION **2** [NL, fr. L] : a massy cloud form having a flat base and rounded outlines often piled up like a mountain — see CLOUD illustration

cunc·ta·tion \ˌkəŋ(k)-'tā-shən\ *n* [L *cunctation-*, *cunctatio*, fr. *cunctatus*, pp. of *cunctari* to hesitate; akin to Skt *śaṅkate* he wavers, OE *hangian* to hang] (1585) : DELAY — **cunc·ta·tive** \'keŋ(k)-ˌtāt-iv, -tət-\ *adj*

cu·ne·ate \'kyü-nē-ˌāt, -ət\ *adj* [L *cuneatus*, fr. *cuneus* wedge; akin to Skt *śūla* spear] (1810) : narrowly triangular with the acute angle toward the base ⟨a ~ leaf⟩

¹cu·ne·i·form \kyü-'nē-ə-ˌfȯrm, 'kyü-n(ē-)ə-\ *adj* [prob. fr. F *cunéiforme*, fr. MF, fr. L *cuneus* + MF *-iforme* -iform] (1677) **1** : having the shape of a wedge **2** : composed of or written in wedge-shaped characters ⟨~ alphabet⟩

²cuneiform *n* (1808) **1** : a cuneiform part; *specif* : a cuneiform bone or cartilage **2** : cuneiform writing

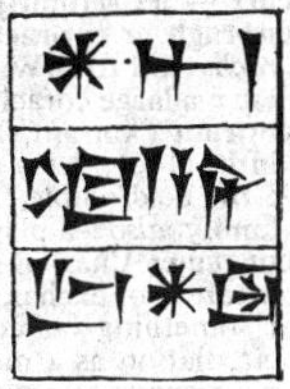

cuneiform 2

cun·ner \'kən-ər\ *n* [origin unknown] (1602) : either of two wrasses: **a** : an English wrasse (*Crenilabrus melops*) **b** : a wrasse (*Tautogolabrus adspersus*) abundant on the New England shore

cun·ni·lin·gus \ˌkən-i-'liŋ-gəs\ *also* **cun·ni·linc·tus** \-'liŋ(k)-təs\ *n* [*cunnilingus*, NL, fr. L, one who licks the vulva, fr. *cunnus* vulva (akin to L *cutis* skin) + *lingere* to lick; *cunnilinctus*, NL, fr. L *cunnus* + *linctus*, act of licking, fr. *linctus*, pp. of *lingere* — more at LICK, HIDE] (1887) : oral stimulation of the vulva or clitoris

¹cun·ning \'kən-iŋ\ *adj* [ME, fr. prp. of *can* know] (14c) **1** : dexterous or crafty in the use of special resources (as skill or knowledge) or in attaining an end ⟨a ~ plotter⟩ **2** : characterized by wiliness and trickery ⟨~ schemes⟩ **3** : prettily appealing : CUTE ***syn*** see CLEVER, SLY — **cun·ning·ly** \-iŋ-lē\ *adv* — **cun·ning·ness** *n*

²cunning *n* (14c) **1** *obs* **a** : KNOWLEDGE, LEARNING **b** : magic art **2** : dexterous skill and subtlety (as in inventing, devising, or executing) ⟨high-ribbed vault . . . with perfect ~ framed — William Wordsworth⟩ **3** : CRAFT, SLYNESS ***syn*** see ART

cunt \'kənt\ *n* [ME *cunte*; akin to MLG *kunte* female pudenda, MHG *kotze* prostitute; akin to OE *cot* den] (14c) : the female pudenda; *also* : coitus with a woman — usu. considered obscene

¹cup \'kəp\ *n* [ME *cuppe*, fr. OE, fr. LL *cuppa* cup, alter. of L *cupa* tub; akin to OE *hȳf* hive — more at HIVE] (bef. 12c) **1** : an open bowl-shaped drinking vessel **2 a** : a drinking vessel and its contents **b** : the consecrated wine of the Communion **3** : something that falls to one's lot **4** : an ornamental cup offered as a prize (as in a championship) **5 a** : something resembling a cup **b** : a cup-shaped plant organ **c** : an athletic supporter reinforced usu. with plastic to provide extra protection to the wearer **d** : either of two parts of a brassiere that are shaped like and fit over the breasts **e** : the metal case inside a hole in golf; *also* : the hole itself **6** : a usu. iced beverage resembling punch but served from a pitcher rather than a bowl **7** : a half pint : eight ounces **8** : a food served in a cup-shaped usu. footed vessel ⟨fruit ~⟩ **9** : the symbol ∪ indicating the union of two sets — compare CAP 7 — **cup·like** \-ˌlīk\ *adj* — **in one's cups** : DRUNK

²cup *vt* **cupped; cup·ping** (14c) **1** : to treat by cupping **2 a** : to curve into the shape of a cup ⟨*cupped* his hands around his mouth⟩ **b** : to place in or as if in a cup

cup·bear·er \'kəp-ˌbar-ər, -ˌber-\ *n* (15c) : one who has the duty of filling and handing around the cups in which wine is served

cup·board \'kəb-ərd\ *n* (1530) : a closet with shelves where dishes, utensils, or food is kept; *also* : a small closet

cup·cake \'kəp-ˌkāk\ *n* (1828) : a small cake baked in a cuplike mold

¹cu·pel \kyü-'pel, 'kyü-pəl\ *n* [F *coupelle*, dim. of *coupe* cup, fr. LL *cuppa*] (1605) : a small shallow porous cup esp. of bone ash used in assaying to separate precious metals from lead

²cupel *vt* **-pelled** *or* **-peled; -pel·ling** *or* **-pel·ing** (1644) : to refine by means of a cupel — **cu·pel·ler** *n*

cu·pel·la·tion \ˌkyü-pə-'lā-shən, -ˌpe-\ *n* (1691) : refinement (as of gold or silver) in a cupel by exposure to high temperature in a blast of air by which the lead, copper, tin, and other unwanted metals are oxidized and partly sink into the porous cupel

cup·ful \'kəp-ˌfu̇l\ *n, pl* **cup·fuls** \-ˌfu̇lz\ *also* **cups·ful** \'kəps-ˌfu̇l\ (12c) **1** : as much as a cup will hold **2** : CUP 7

cup fungus *n* (ca. 1905) : any of an order (Pezizales) of epigeal mostly saprophytic fungi with a fleshy or horny apothecium that is often colored and is typically shaped like a cup, saucer, or disk

Cu·pid \'kyü-pəd\ *n* [L *Cupido*] **1** : the Roman god of erotic love — compare EROS **2** *not cap* : a figure that represents Cupid as a naked usu. winged boy often holding a bow and arrow

cu·pid·i·ty \kyu̇-'pid-ət-ē\ *n, pl* **-ties** [ME *cupidite*, fr. MF *cupidité*, fr. L *cupiditat-*, *cupiditas* — more at COVET] (15c) **1** : inordinate desire for wealth : AVARICE, GREED **2** : strong desire : LUST

Cupid's bow *n* (1858) : a bow that consists of two convex curves usu. with recurved ends

cup of tea (1932) **1** : something one likes or excels in ⟨I see already that storytelling isn't my *cup of tea* — John Barth⟩ **2** : a thing to be reckoned with : MATTER ⟨poltergeists are a different *cup of tea* —D. B. W. Lewis⟩

cu·po·la \'kyü-pə-lə, ⸗⸗ˌlō\ *n* [It, fr. L *cupula*, dim. of *cupa* tub] (1549) **1 a** : a rounded vault resting on a circular or other base and forming a roof or a ceiling **b** : a small structure built on top of a roof **2** : a vertical cylindrical furnace for melting iron in the foundry that has tuyeres and tapping spouts near the bottom — **cu·po·laed** \-ləd, ⸗⸗ˌlōd\ *adj*

cup·pa \'kəp-ə\ *n* [short for *cuppa tea*, pronunciation spelling of *cup of tea*] *chiefly Brit* (1934) : a cup of tea

cup·ping *n* (14c) : an operation of drawing blood to the surface of the body by use of a glass vessel evacuated by heat

cup·py \'kəp-ē\ *adj* **cup·pi·er; -est** (1882) **1** : resembling a cup **2** : full of small depressions ⟨a ~ racetrack⟩

cupr- *or* **cupri-** *or* **cupro-** *comb form* [LL *cuprum* — more at COPPER] **1** : copper ⟨*cupri*ferous⟩ **2** : copper and ⟨*cupro*nickel⟩

cu·pric \'k(y)ü-prik\ *adj* (1799) : of, relating to, or containing copper with a valence of two

cu·prif·er·ous \k(y)ü-'prif-(ə-)rəs\ *adj* (1784) : containing copper

cu·prite \'k(y)ü-ˌprīt\ *n* [G *kuprit*, fr. LL *cuprum*] (ca. 1850) : a mineral Cu_2O consisting of copper oxide and constituting an ore of copper

cu·pro·nick·el \ˌk(y)ü-prō-'nik-əl\ *n* (1900) : an alloy of copper and nickel; *esp* : one containing about 70 percent copper and 30 percent nickel

cu·prous \'k(y)ü-prəs\ *adj* (1669) : of, relating to, or containing copper with a valence of one

cu·pu·late \'kyü-pyə-ˌlāt, -lət\ *adj* (1835) : shaped like, having, or bearing a cupule

cu·pule \'kyü-(ˌ)pyü(ə)l\ *n* [NL *cupula*, fr. LL, dim. of L *cupa* tub — more at CUP] (1826) : a cup-shaped anatomical structure: as **a** : an involucre characteristic of the oak in which the bracts are indurated and coherent **b** : an outer integument partially enclosing the seed of some seed ferns

cur \'kər\ *n* [ME, short for *curdogge*, fr. (assumed) ME *curren* to growl + ME *dogge* dog; prob. akin to OE *cran* crane] (13c) **1** : a mongrel or inferior dog **2** : a surly or cowardly fellow

cur·able \'kyu̇r-ə-bəl\ *adj* (14c) : capable of being cured — **cur·abil·i·ty** \ˌkyu̇r-ə-'bil-ət-ē\ *n* — **cur·able·ness** \'kyu̇r-ə-bəl-nəs\ *n* — **cur·ably** \-blē\ *adv*

cu·ra·çao \'k(y)u̇r-ə-ˌsō, -ˌsau̇, ˌk(y)u̇r-ə-'\ *also* **cu·ra·çoa** *same, or* ˌk(y)u̇r-ə-'sō-ə\ *n* [D *curaçao*, fr. *Curaçao*, Netherlands Antilles] (1813) : a liqueur flavored with the dried peel of the sour orange

cu·ra·cy \'kyu̇r-ə-sē\ *n, pl* **-cies** (1682) : the office or term of office of a curate

cu·ra·re *also* **cu·ra·ri** \k(y)u̇-'rär-ē\ *n* [Pg & Sp *curare*, fr. Carib *kurari*] (1777) : a dried aqueous extract esp. of a vine (as *Strychnos toxifera* of the family Loganiaceae or *Chondodendron tomentosum* of the family Menispermaceae) used in arrow poisons by So. American Indians and in medicine to produce muscular relaxation

cu·ra·rine \-'rär-ən, -ˌēn\ *n* (1863) : any of several alkaloids from curare

cu·ra·rize \-'rär-ˌīz\ *vt* **-rized; -riz·ing** (1875) : to treat with curare — **cu·ra·ri·za·tion** \-ˌrär-ə-'zā-shən\ *n*

cu·ras·sow \'k(y)u̇r-ə-ˌsō\ *n* [alter. of *Curaçao*] (1685) : any of several large arboreal game birds (esp. genus *Crax*) of So. and Central America related to the domestic fowls

cu·rate \'kyu̇r-ət *also* 'kyu̇(ə)r-ˌāt\ *n* [ME, fr. ML *curatus*, fr. *cura* cure of souls, fr. L, care] (14c) **1** : a clergyman in charge of a parish **2** : a clergyman serving as assistant (as to a rector) in a parish

cu·ra·tive \'kyu̇r-ət-iv\ *adj* (15c) : relating to or used in the cure of diseases — **curative** *n* — **cu·ra·tive·ly** *adv*

cu·ra·tor \'kyu̇(ə)r-ˌāt-ər, kyu̇-'rāt-, 'kyu̇r-ət-\ *n* [L, fr. *curatus*, pp. of *curare* to care, fr. *cura* care] (1632) : one that has the care and superintendence of something; *esp* : one in charge of a museum, zoo, or other place of exhibit — **cu·ra·to·ri·al** \ˌkyu̇r-ə-'tōr-ē-əl, -'tȯr-\ *adj* — **cu·ra·tor·ship** \'kyu̇(ə)r-ˌāt-ər-ˌship, kyu̇-'rāt-, 'kyu̇r-ət-\ *n*

¹curb \'kərb\ *n* [MF *courbe* curve, curved piece of wood or iron, fr. *courbe* curved, fr. L *curvus*] (15c) **1** : a bit that exerts severe pressure on a horse's jaws; *also* : the chain or strap attached to it **2** : an enclosing frame, border, or edging **3** : CHECK, RESTRAINT ⟨a price ~⟩ **4** : a raised edge or margin to strengthen or confine **5** : an edging (as of concrete) built along a street to form part of a gutter **6** [fr. the fact that it orig. transacted its business on the street] : a market for trading in securities not listed on a stock exchange

\ə\ abut \ᵊ\ kitten, F table \ər\ further \a\ ash \ā\ ace \ä\ cot, cart \au̇\ out \ch\ chin \e\ bet \ē\ easy \g\ go \i\ hit \ī\ ice \j\ job \ŋ\ sing \ō\ go \ȯ\ law \ȯi\ boy \th\ thin \t͟h\ the \ü\ loot \u̇\ foot \y\ yet \zh\ vision \à, ḵ, ⁿ, œ, œ̄, ue, ue̅, ʸ\ *see* Guide to Pronunciation

[2]curb *vt* (1530) **1 :** to furnish with a curb **2 :** to check or control with or as if with a curb ⟨trying to ~ her curiosity⟩ **3 :** to lead (a dog) to a suitable place (as a gutter) for defecation ***syn*** see RESTRAIN

curb·ing \'kər-biŋ\ *n* (1838) **1 :** the material for a curb **2 :** CURB

curb roof *n* (1733) **:** a roof with a ridge at the center and a double slope on each of its two sides

curb service *n* (1931) **:** service extended (as by a restaurant) to persons sitting in parked automobiles

curb·side \'kərb-,sīd\ *n* (1946) **1 :** the side of a pavement bordered by a curb **2 :** SIDEWALK

[1]curb·stone \-,stōn\ *n* (1791) **:** a stone or edging of concrete forming a curb

[2]curbstone *adj* (1848) **1 :** operating on the street without maintaining an office ⟨a ~ broker⟩ **2 :** not having the benefit of training or experience ⟨a ~ critic⟩

curb weight *n* (1949) **:** the weight of an automobile with standard equipment and fuel, oil, and coolant

curch \'kərch\ *n* [ME] *Scot* (14c) **:** KERCHIEF 1

cur·cu·lio \(,)kər-'kyü-lē-,ō\ *n, pl* **-li·os** [L, grain weevil] (1756) **:** any of various weevils; *esp* **:** one that injures fruit

cur·cu·ma \'kər-kyə-mə\ *n* [NL, genus name, fr. Ar *kurkum* saffron] (1617) **:** TURMERIC 1

[1]curd \'kərd\ *n* [ME *crud;* prob. akin to OE *crūdan* to press — more at CROWD] (14c) **1 :** the thick casein-rich part of coagulated milk **2 :** something suggesting the curd of milk — **curdy** \-ē\ *adj*

[2]curd *vb* (14c) **:** COAGULATE, CURDLE

cur·dle \'kərd-ᵊl\ *vb* **cur·dled; cur·dling** \'kərd-liŋ, -ᵊl-iŋ\ [freq. of [2]*curd*] *vt* (1590) **1 :** to cause curds to form in **2 :** SPOIL, SOUR ~ *vi* **1 :** to form curds; *also* **:** to congeal as if by forming curds ⟨a scream *curdled* in her throat⟩ **2 :** to go bad or wrong **:** SPOIL

[1]cure \'kyu̇(ə)r\ *n* [ME, fr. OF, fr. ML & L; ML *cura,* cure of souls, fr. L, care] (14c) **1 a :** spiritual charge **:** CARE **b :** pastoral charge of a parish **2 a :** recovery or relief from a disease **b :** something (as a drug or treatment) that cures a disease **c :** a course or period of treatment ⟨take the ~ for alcoholism⟩ **d :** SPA **3 :** something that corrects, heals, or permanently alleviates a harmful or troublesome situation ⟨more money is not a certain ~ for the problem⟩ **4 :** a process or method of curing — **cure·less** \-ləs\ *adj*

[2]cure *vb* **cured; cur·ing** *vt* (14c) **1 a :** to restore to health, soundness, or normality **b :** to bring about recovery from **2 a :** to deal with in a way that eliminates or rectifies ⟨nothing would ~ the unpleasant odor⟩ **b :** to free from something objectionable or harmful **3 :** to prepare by chemical or physical processing for keeping or use ~ *vi* **1 a :** to undergo a curing process **b :** SET 11 **2 :** to effect a cure — **cur·er** *n*

syn CURE, HEAL, REMEDY mean to rectify an unhealthy or undesirable condition. CURE implies restoration to health after disease; HEAL may also apply to this but commonly suggests restoring to soundness after a wound or sore; REMEDY suggests correction or relief of a morbid or evil condition.

cu·ré \kyu̇-'rā, 'kyu̇(ə)r-,ā\ *n* [F, fr. OF, fr. ML *curatus* — more at CURATE] (1655) **:** a parish priest

cure–all \'kyu̇(ə)r-,ȯl\ *n* (1821) **:** a remedy for all ills **:** PANACEA

cu·ret·tage \,kyu̇r-ə-'täzh\ *n* (1897) **:** a surgical scraping or cleaning by means of a curette

[1]cu·rette *also* **cu·ret** \kyu̇-'ret\ *n* [F *curette,* fr. *curer* to cure, fr. L *curare,* fr. *cura*] (1753) **:** a scoop, loop, or ring used in performing curettage

[2]curette *also* **curet** *vt* **cu·rett·ed; cu·rett·ing** (1888) **:** to perform curettage on — **cu·rette·ment** \kyu̇-'ret-mənt\ *n*

cur·few \'kər-(,)fyü\ *n* [ME, fr. MF *covrefeu,* signal given to bank the hearth fire, curfew, fr. *covrir* to cover + *feu* fire, fr. L *focus* hearth] (14c) **1 :** a regulation enjoining the withdrawal of usu. specified persons (as juveniles or military personnel) from the streets or the closing of business establishments or places of assembly at a stated hour **2 a :** the sounding of a bell or other signal to announce the beginning of a time of curfew **b :** the signal used **3 a :** the hour at which a curfew becomes effective **b :** the period during which a curfew is in effect

cu·ria \'k(y)u̇r-ē-ə\ *n, pl* **cu·ri·ae** \'kyu̇r-ē-,ē, 'ku̇r-ē-,ī\ [L, *co-* + *vir* man — more at VIRILE] (1600) **1 a :** a division of the ancient Roman people comprising several gentes of a tribe **b :** the place of assembly of one of these divisions **2 a :** the court of a medieval king **b :** a court of justice **3** *often cap* **:** the body of congregations, tribunals, and offices through which the pope governs the Roman Catholic Church — **cu·ri·al** \'kyu̇r-ē-əl\ *adj*

cu·rie \'kyu̇(ə)r-(,)ē, kyu̇-'rē\ *n* [Marie & Pierre *Curie*] (1910) **1 :** a unit quantity of any radioactive nuclide in which 3.7×10^{10} disintegrations occur per second **2 :** a unit of radioactivity equal to 3.7×10^{10} disintegrations per second

Curie point *n* (ca. 1913) **1 :** the temperature at which there is a transition between the ferromagnetic and paramagnetic phases **2 :** a temperature at which the anomalies that characterize a ferroelectric substance disappear — called also *Curie temperature*

cu·rio \'kyu̇r-ē-,ō\ *n, pl* **cu·ri·os** [short for *curiosity*] (1851) **:** something considered novel, rare, or bizarre **:** CURIOSITY

cu·ri·o·sa \,kyu̇r-ē-'ō-sə, -'ō-zə\ *n pl* [NL, fr. L, neut. pl. of *curiosus*] (1883) **:** CURIOSITIES, RARITIES; *esp* **:** unusual or erotic books

cu·ri·os·i·ty \,kyu̇r-ē-'äs-ət-ē, -'äs-tē\ *n, pl* **-ties** (14c) **1 :** desire to know: **a :** inquisitive interest in others' concerns **:** NOSINESS **b :** interest leading to inquiry ⟨intellectual ~⟩ **2** *archaic* **:** undue nicety or fastidiousness **3 a :** one that arouses interest esp. for uncommon or exotic characteristics **b :** an unusual knickknack **:** CURIO **c :** a curious trait or aspect

cu·ri·ous \'kyu̇r-ē-əs\ *adj* [ME, fr. MF *curios,* fr. L *curiosus* careful, inquisitive, fr. *cura* cure] (14c) **1 a** *archaic* **:** made carefully **b** *obs* **:** ABSTRUSE **c** *archaic* **:** precisely accurate **2 a :** marked by desire to investigate and learn **b :** marked by inquisitive interest in others' concerns **:** NOSY **3 :** exciting attention as strange, novel, or unexpected **:** ODD — **cu·ri·ous·ly** *adv* — **cu·ri·ous·ness** *n*

syn CURIOUS, INQUISITIVE, PRYING mean interested in what is not one's personal or proper concern. CURIOUS, a neutral term, basically connotes an active desire to learn or to know ⟨children are *curious* about everything⟩ INQUISITIVE suggests impertinent and habitual curiosity and persistent quizzing ⟨dreaded the visits of their *inquisitive* relatives⟩ PRYING implies busy meddling and officiousness ⟨*prying* neighbors who refuse to mind their own business⟩

cu·rite \'kyu̇(ə)r-,īt\ *n* [F, fr. Pierre *Curie*] (1922) **:** a radioactive mineral $2PbO\cdot 5UO_3\cdot 4H_2O$ found in orange acicular crystals

cu·ri·um \'kyu̇r-ē-əm\ *n* [NL, fr. Marie & Pierre *Curie*] (1946) **:** a metallic radioactive trivalent element artificially produced — see ELEMENT table

[1]curl \'kər(-ə)l\ *vb* [ME *curlen,* fr. *crul* curly, prob. fr. MD; akin to OHG *krol* curly, OE *cradol* cradle] *vt* (14c) **1 :** to form (as the hair) into coils or ringlets **2 :** to form into a curved shape **:** TWIST ⟨~*ed* his lip in a sneer⟩ **3 :** to furnish with curls ~ *vi* **1 a :** to grow in coils or spirals **b :** to form ripples or crinkles ⟨bacon ~*ing* in a pan⟩ **2 :** to move or progress in curves or spirals **:** WIND ⟨the path ~*ed* along the mountainside⟩ **3 :** TWIST, CONTORT **4 :** to play the game of curling

[2]curl *n* (1602) **1 :** a lock of hair that coils **:** RINGLET **2 :** something having a spiral or winding form **:** COIL **3 :** the action of curling **:** the state of being curled **4 :** an abnormal rolling or curling of leaves **5 :** a curved or spiral marking in the grain of wood **6 :** TENDRIL **7 :** a hollow arch of water formed when the crest of a breaking wave spills forward

curl·er \'kər-lər\ *n* (1748) **1 :** one that curls; *esp* **:** a device on which hair is wound for curling **2 :** a player of curling

cur·lew \'kərl-(,)(y)ü\ *n, pl* **curlews** *or* **curlew** [ME, fr. MF *corlieu,* of imit. origin] (14c) **:** any of various largely brownish chiefly migratory birds (esp. genus *Numenius*) related to the woodcocks but distinguished by long legs and a long slender down-curved bill

[1]curli·cue *also* **curly·cue** \'kər-li-,kyü\ *n* [*curly* + *cue* (a braid of hair)] (1843) **:** a fancifully curved or spiral figure **:** FLOURISH

[2]curlicue *vb* **-cued; -cu·ing** *vi* (1844) **:** to form curlicues ~ *vt* **:** to embellish with curlicues

curl·ing \'kər-liŋ\ *n* (1620) **:** a game in which two teams of four men each slide curling stones over a stretch of ice toward a target circle

curling iron *n* (ca. 1632) **:** a rod-shaped usu. metal instrument which is heated and around which a lock of hair to be curled or waved is wound

curling stone *n* (1620) **:** an ellipsoid stone or occas. piece of iron with a gooseneck handle used in the game of curling

curl·pa·per \'kər(-ə)l-,pā-pər\ *n* (1817) **:** a strip or piece of paper around which a lock of hair is wound for curling

curl up *vi* (1861) **:** to arrange oneself in or as if in a ball or curl ⟨*curl up* by the fire⟩ ⟨*curl up* with a good book⟩

curly \'kər-lē\ *adj* **curl·i·er; -est** (1772) **1 :** tending to curl; *also* **:** having curls **2 :** having the grain composed of fibers that undulate without crossing and that often form alternating light and dark lines ⟨~ maple⟩ — **curl·i·ness** *n*

curly–coat·ed retriever \,kər-lē-,kōt-əd-\ *n* (1885) **:** any of a breed of sporting dogs with a short curly coat

curly top *n* (1901) **:** a destructive virus disease esp. of beets that kills young plants and causes curling and puckering of the leaves in older plants

cur·mud·geon \(,)kər-'məj-ən\ *n* [origin unknown] (1577) **1** *archaic* **:** MISER **2 :** a crusty, ill-tempered, and usu. old man — **cur·mud·geon·ly** *adj*

curn \'kərn\ *or* **cur·ran** \'kə-rən\ *n* [ME *curn;* akin to ME *corn*] (14c) **1** *Scot* **:** GRAIN **2** *Scot* **:** a small number **:** FEW

curr \'kər\ *vi* [imit.] (1677) **:** to make a murmuring sound (as of doves)

cur·ragh *or* **cur·rach** \'kə-rə(k)\ *n* [ME *currok,* fr. IrGael *currach, curach;* akin to MW *corwg* coracle — more at CORACLE] (15c) **:** CORACLE; *esp* **:** a large coracle with a keel

cur·rant \'kər-ənt, 'kə-rənt\ *n* [ME *raison of Coraunte,* lit., raisin of Corinth] (14c) **1 :** a small seedless raisin grown chiefly in the Levant **2 :** the acid edible fruit of several shrubs (genus *Ribes*) of the saxifrage family; *also* **:** a plant bearing currants

cur·ren·cy \'kər-ən-sē, 'kə-rən-\ *n, pl* **-cies** (1699) **1 a :** circulation as a medium of exchange **b :** general use, acceptance, or prevalence **2 a :** something (as coins, government notes, and bank notes) that is in circulation as a medium of exchange **b :** paper money in circulation **c :** a common article for bartering **d :** a medium of verbal or intellectual expression

[1]cur·rent \'kər-ənt, 'kə-rənt\ *adj* [ME *curraunt,* fr. OF *curant,* prp. of *courre* to run, fr. L *currere* — more at CAR] (14c) **1 a** *archaic* **:** RUNNING, FLOWING **b (1) :** presently elapsing **(2) :** occurring in or existing at the present time **(3) :** most recent ⟨the ~ issue⟩ **2 :** used as a medium of exchange **3 :** generally accepted, used, practiced, or prevalent at the moment — **cur·rent·ly** *adv* — **cur·rent·ness** *n*

[2]current *n* (14c) **1 a :** the part of a fluid body (as air or water) moving continuously in a certain direction **b :** the swiftest part of a stream **c :** a tidal or nontidal movement of lake or ocean water **d :** flow marked by force or strength **2 a :** a tendency or course of events that is usu. the result of an interplay of forces ⟨~*s* of public opinion⟩ **b :** a prevailing mood **:** STRAIN **3 :** a flow of electric charge; *also* **:** the rate of such flow ***syn*** see TENDENCY

current assets *n pl* (ca. 1909) **:** assets of a short-term nature that are readily convertible to cash

cur·ri·cle \'kər-i-kəl, 'kə-ri-\ *n* [L *curriculum* running, chariot] (1756) **:** a 2-wheeled chaise usu. drawn by two horses

cur·ric·u·lar \kə-'rik-yə-lər\ *adj* (ca. 1909) **:** of or relating to a curriculum

cur·ric·u·lum \-ləm\ *n, pl* **-la** \-lə\ *also* **-lums** [NL, fr. L, running, fr. *currere*] (1633) **1 :** the courses offered by an educational institution **2 :** a set of courses constituting an area of specialization

cur·ric·u·lum vi·tae \kə-,rik-ə-ləm-'wē-,tī, -yə-ləm-'vīt-ē\ *n, pl* **cur·ric·u·la vitae** \-lə-\ [L, course of (one's) life] (1902) **:** a short account of one's career and qualifications prepared typically by an applicant for a position

cur·ri·ery \'kər-ē-ə-rē, 'kə-rē-\ *n, pl* **-er·ies** (ca. 1889) **1 :** the trade of a currier of leather **2 :** a place where currying is done

cur·rish \'kər-ish\ *adj* (1565) **1 :** resembling a cur **:** MONGREL **2 :** IGNOBLE — **cur·rish·ly** *adv*

[1]cur·ry \'kər-ē, 'kə-rē\ *vt* **cur·ried; cur·ry·ing** [ME *currayen,* fr. OF *correer* to prepare, curry, fr. (assumed) VL *conredare,* fr. L *com-* + a base of Gmc origin; akin to Goth *garaiths* arrayed — more at READY] (13c) **1 :** to clean the coat of (as a horse) with a currycomb **2 :** to treat (tanned leather) esp. by incorporating oil or grease **3 :** BEAT, THRASH

— **cur·ri·er** *n* — **curry fa·vor** \-ˈfā-vər\ [ME *currayen favel* to curry a chestnut horse] : to seek to gain favor by flattery or attention

²**cur·ry** *also* **cur·rie** \ˈkər-ē, ˈkə-rē\ *n, pl* **curries** [Tamil-Malayalam *kari*] (1598) **1** : a food or dish seasoned with curry powder ⟨shrimp ~⟩ **2** : CURRY POWDER

³**curry** *vt* **cur·ried; cur·ry·ing** (1839) : to flavor or cook with curry powder or a curry sauce

cur·ry·comb \-ˌkōm\ *n* (1573) : a comb made of rows of metallic teeth or serrated ridges and used esp. to curry horses — **currycomb** *vt*

curry powder *n* (1810) : a condiment consisting of several pungent ground spices (as cayenne pepper, fenugreek, and turmeric)

¹**curse** \ˈkərs\ *n* [ME *curs,* fr. OE] (bef. 12c) **1** : a prayer or invocation for harm or injury to come upon one : IMPRECATION **2** : something that is cursed or accursed **3** : evil or misfortune that comes as if in response to imprecation or as retribution **4** : a cause of great harm or misfortune : TORMENT **5** : MENSTRUATION — used with *the*

²**curse** *vb* **cursed; curs·ing** *vt* (12c) **1** **a** : to call upon divine or supernatural power to send injury upon **b** : to execrate in fervent and often profane terms **2** : to use profanely insolent language against : BLASPHEME **3** : to bring great evil upon : AFFLICT ~ *vi* : to utter imprecations : SWEAR ***syn*** see EXECRATE

cursed \ˈkər-səd, ˈkərst\ *also* **curst** \ˈkərst\ *adj* (13c) : being under or deserving a curse — **cursed·ly** *adv* — **cursed·ness** *n*

¹**cur·sive** \ˈkər-siv\ *adj* [F or ML; F *cursif,* fr. ML *cursivus,* lit., running, fr. L *cursus,* pp. of *currere* to run] (1784) : RUNNING, COURSING: as **a** *of writing* : flowing often with the strokes of successive characters joined and the angles rounded **b** : having a flowing, easy, impromptu character — **cur·sive·ly** *adv* — **cur·sive·ness** *n*

²**cursive** *n* (1861) **1** : a manuscript written in cursive writing **2** : a style of printed letter resembling handwriting

cur·sor \ˈkər-sər, -ˌsȯ(ə)r\ *n* [L, runner, fr. *cursus,* pp.] (1594) **1** : a part (as a transparent slide with a line) moved back and forth over a surface (as of a mathematical instrument) to enable accurate readings to be made **2** : a usu. manually controllable bright figure (as a pointer) on a computer display to indicate a character to be revised or a position where data is to be entered

cur·so·ri·al \ˌkər-ˈsōr-ē-əl, -ˈsȯr-\ *adj* (1836) : adapted to or involving running

cur·so·ry \ˈkərs-(ə-)rē\ *adj* [LL *cursorius* of running, fr. L *cursus* running, fr. *cursus,* pp.] (1601) : rapidly and often superficially performed or produced : HASTY ⟨a ~ glance⟩ ***syn*** see SUPERFICIAL **cur·so·ri·ly** \-rə-lē\ *adv* — **cur·so·ri·ness** \-rē-nəs\ *n*

curt \ˈkərt\ *adj* [L *curtus* shortened — more at SHEAR] (1630) **1** **a** : sparing of words : TERSE **b** : marked by rude or peremptory shortness : BRUSQUE **2** : shortened in linear dimension ***syn*** see BLUFF — **curt·ly** *adv* — **curt·ness** *n*

cur·tail \(ˌ)kər-ˈtā(ə)l\ *vt* [by folk etymology fr. earlier *curtal* to dock an animal's tail, fr. *curtal,* n., docked-tailed animal, fr. MF *courtault* — more at CURTAL] (1580) : to make less by or as if by cutting off or away some part ⟨~ the power of the executive branch⟩ ⟨~ inflation⟩ ***syn*** see SHORTEN — **cur·tail·er** \-ˈtā-lər\ *n*

cur·tail·ment \-ˈtā(ə)l-mənt\ *n* (1794) : the act of curtailing : the state of being curtailed

¹**cur·tain** \ˈkərt-ᵊn\ *n* [ME *curtine,* fr. OF, fr. LL *cortina* (trans. of Gk *aulaia,* fr. *aulē* court), fr. L *cohort-, cohors* enclosure, court — more at COURT] (14c) **1** : a hanging screen usu. capable of being drawn back or up; *esp* : window drapery **2** : a device or agency that conceals or acts as a barrier — compare IRON CURTAIN **3** **a** : the part of a bastioned front that connects two neighboring bastions **b** (1) : a similar stretch of plain wall (2) : a nonbearing exterior wall **4** **a** : the movable screen separating the stage from the auditorium of a theater **b** : the ascent or opening (as at the beginning of a play) of a stage curtain; *also* : its descent or closing (as at the end of an act) **c** : the final situation, line, or scene of an act or play **d** : the time at which a theatrical performance begins **e** *pl* : END; *esp* : DEATH ⟨it will be ~*s* for us if we're caught⟩

²**curtain** *vt* **cur·tained; cur·tain·ing** \ˈkərt-niŋ, -ᵊn-iŋ\ (14c) **1** : to furnish with or as if with curtains **2** : to veil or shut off with or as if with a curtain

curtain call *n* (1884) : an appearance by a performer (as after the final curtain of a play) in response to the applause of the audience

curtain lecture *n* [fr. its orig. being given behind the curtains of a bed] (1633) : a private lecture by a wife to her husband

curtain raiser *n* (1886) **1** : a short play usu. of one scene that is presented before the main full-length drama **2** : a usu. short preliminary to a main event

curtain wall *n* (1853) : a nonbearing exterior wall between columns or piers

cur·tal \ˈkərt-ᵊl\ *adj* [MF *courtault,* fr. *court* short, fr. L *curtus*] (1576) **1** *obs* : having a docked tail **2** *obs* : BRIEF, CURTAILED **3** *archaic* : wearing a short frock

cur·tal ax *or* **cur·tle ax** \ˈkərt-ᵊl-\ *n* [modif. of MF *coutelas*] (1579) : CUTLASS

cur·te·sy \ˈkərt-ə-sē\ *n, pl* **-sies** [ME *corteisie* courtesy] (1523) : the future potential interest that a husband has in the real property of his wife arising upon the birth to them of a child alive and capable for at least an instant of inheriting from her — compare DOWER

cur·ti·lage \ˈkərt-ᵊl-ij\ *n* [ME, fr. MF *cortillage,* fr. *cortil* courtyard, fr. *cort* court] (14c) : a piece of ground (as a yard or courtyard) within the fence surrounding a house

¹**curt·sy** *or* **curt·sey** \ˈkərt-sē\ *vi* **curt·sied** *or* **curt·seyed; curt·sy·ing** *or* **curt·sey·ing** [alter. of *courtesy*] (1553) : to make a curtsy

²**curtsy** *or* **curtsey** *n, pl* **curtsies** *or* **curtseys** (1575) : an act of civility, respect, or reverence made mainly by women and consisting of a slight lowering of the body with bending of the knees

cu·rule \ˈkyü(ə)r-ˌül\ *adj* [L *curulis,* alter. of *currulis* of a chariot, fr. *currus* chariot, fr. *currere* to run] (1600) **1** : of or relating to a seat reserved in ancient Rome for the use of the highest dignitaries **2** : privileged to sit in a curule chair

cur·va·ceous *also* **cur·va·cious** \ˌkər-ˈvā-shəs\ *adj* (ca. 1935) : having curves suggestive of a well-proportioned feminine figure

cur·va·ture \ˈkər-və-ˌchu̇(ə)r, -chər, -ˌt(y)u̇(ə)r\ *n* (1603) **1** : the act of curving : the state of being curved **2** : a measure or amount of curving; *specif* : the rate of change of the angle through which the tangent to a curve turns in moving along the curve and which for a circle is equal to the reciprocal of the radius **3** **a** : an abnormal curving (as of the spine) **b** : a curved surface of an organ

¹**curve** \ˈkərv\ *adj* [L *curvus* curved] *archaic* (15c) : bent or formed into a curve

²**curve** *vb* **curved; curv·ing** [L *curvare,* fr. *curvus*] *vi* (1594) : to have or take a turn, change, or deviation from a straight line or plane surface without sharp breaks or angularity ~ *vt* **1** : to cause to curve **2** : to throw a curveball to (a batter) **3** : to grade (as an examination) on a curve

³**curve** *n* (1696) **1** **a** : a line esp. when curved: as (1) : the path of a moving point (2) : a line defined by an equation so that the coordinates of its points are functions of a single independent variable or parameter **b** : the graph of a variable **2** : something curved: as **a** : a curving line of the human body **b** *pl* : PARENTHESIS **3** **a** : CURVEBALL **b** : TRICK, DECEPTION **4** : a distribution indicating the relative performance of individuals measured against each other that is used esp. in assigning good, medium, or poor grades to usu. predetermined proportions of students rather than in assigning grades based on predetermined standards of achievement — **curvy** \ˈkər-vē\ *adj*

curve·ball \ˈkərv-ˌbȯl\ *n* (1936) : a baseball pitch thrown so that it swerves from a normal or expected course; *esp* : one that curves to the left when thrown from the right hand or to the right when thrown from the left hand — **curveball** *vb*

curve fitting *n* (ca. 1924) : the empirical determination of a curve or function that approximates a set of data

¹**cur·vet** \(ˌ)kər-ˈvet\ *n* [It *corvetta,* fr. MF *courbette,* fr. *courber* to curve, fr. L *curvare*] (1575) : a prancing leap of a horse in which the hind legs are raised just before the forelegs touch the ground

²**curvet** *vi* **-vet·ted** *or* **-vet·ed; -vet·ting** *or* **-vet·ing** (1592) : to make a curvet; *also* : PRANCE, CAPER

cur·vi·lin·ear \ˌkər-və-ˈlin-ē-ər\ *adj* [L *curvus* + *linea* line] (1710) **1** : consisting of or bounded by curved lines : represented by a curved line **2** : marked by flowing tracery ⟨~ Gothic⟩ — **cur·vi·lin·ear·i·ty** \-ˌlin-ē-ˈar-ət-ē\ *n*

cu·sec \ˈkyü-ˌsek\ *n* [*cu*bic foot per *sec*ond] (1903) : a volumetric unit of flow equal to a cubic foot per second

cush·at \ˈkəsh-ət\ *n* [ME *cowschote,* fr. OE *cūscote*] *chiefly Scot* (bef. 12c) : RINGDOVE 1

cu·shaw \ku̇-ˈshȯ, ˈkü-ˌ\ *n* [perh. of Algonquian origin; akin to *escushaw* it is green (in some Algonquian language of Virginia)] (1588) : WINTER CROOKNECK

Cush·ing's disease \ˈku̇sh-iŋz-\ *n* [Harvey *Cushing*] (ca. 1935) : Cushing's syndrome esp. when caused by excessive production of ACTH by the pituitary gland

Cushing's syndrome *n* (1937) : an abnormal bodily condition characterized by obesity and muscular weakness associated with the excessive production of hydrocortisone due to adrenal or pituitary dysfunction

¹**cush·ion** \ˈku̇sh-ən\ *n* [ME *cusshin,* fr. MF *coissin,* fr. (assumed) VL *coxinus,* fr. L *coxa* hip — more at COXA] (14c) **1** : a soft pillow or pad usu. used for sitting, reclining, or kneeling **2** : a bodily part resembling a pad **3** : something resembling a cushion: as **a** : PILLOW 3 **b** : RAT 3 **c** : a pad of springy rubber along the inside of the rim of a billiard table **d** : the head of a drill brace **e** : a padded insert in a shoe **f** : an artificial pool provided to absorb the kinetic energy of falling water and so prevent erosion **g** : an elastic body for reducing shock **h** : a mat laid under a large rug to ease the effect of wear **4** : something (as an economic factor or a medical procedure) serving to mitigate the effects of disturbances or disorders — **cush·ion·less** \-ləs\ *adj* — **cush·iony** \-ə-nē\ *adj*

²**cushion** *vt* **cush·ioned; cush·ion·ing** \-(ə-)niŋ\ (1735) **1** : to seat or place on a cushion **2** : to suppress by ignoring **3** : to furnish with a cushion **4** **a** : to mitigate the effects of **b** : to protect against force or shock **5** : to check gradually so as to minimize shock of moving parts

Cush·it·ic \ˌkəsh-ˈit-ik, ku̇sh-\ *n* [*Cush* (Kush), Africa] (1899) : a subfamily of the Afro-Asiatic language family comprising various languages spoken in East Africa and esp. in Ethiopia and Somaliland — **Cushitic** *adj*

cushy \ˈku̇sh-ē\ *adj* **cushi·er; cushi·est** [Hindi *khush* pleasant, fr. Per *khūsh*] (1915) : entailing little hardship or difficulty : EASY ⟨a ~ job with a high salary⟩ — **cushi·ly** \ˈku̇sh-ə-lē\ *adv*

cusk \ˈkəsk\ *n, pl* **cusk** *or* **cusks** [prob. alter. of *tusk* (a kind of codfish)] (1616) **1** : a large edible marine fish (*Brosme brosme*) related to the cod **2** : BURBOT

cusp \ˈkəsp\ *n* [L *cuspis* point] (1585) : POINT, APEX: as **a** : either horn of a crescent moon **b** : a fixed point on a mathematical curve at which a point tracing the curve would exactly reverse its direction of motion **c** : an ornamental pointed projection formed by or arising from the intersection of two arcs or foils **d** (1) : a point on the grinding surface of a tooth (2) : a fold or flap of a cardiac valve **e** : a point of transition (as from one astrological sign to another or one historical period to the next) : TURNING POINT — **cus·pate** \ˈkəs-ˌpāt, -pət\ *adj* — **cusped** \ˈkəspt\ *adj*

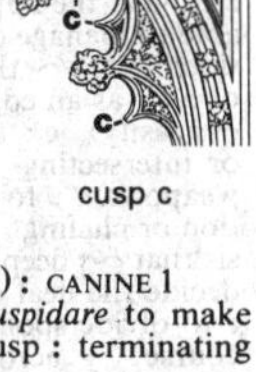

cusp c

cus·pid \ˈkəs-pəd\ *n* [back-formation fr. *bicuspid*] (1878) : CANINE 1

cus·pi·date \ˈkəs-pə-ˌdāt\ *adj* [L *cuspidatus,* pp. of *cuspidare* to make pointed, fr. *cuspid-, cuspis* point] (1692) : having a cusp : terminating in a point ⟨a ~ leaf⟩ ⟨~ molars⟩

cus·pi·da·tion \ˌkəs-pə-ˈdā-shən\ *n* (1848) : decoration with cusps

cus·pi·dor \ˈkəs-pə-ˌdȯ(ə)r, -ˌdō(ə)r\ *n* [Pg *cuspidouro* place for spitting, fr. *cuspir* to spit, fr. L *conspuere,* fr. *com-* + *spuere* to spit — more at SPEW] (1735) : SPITTOON

¹**cuss** \ˈkəs\ *n* [alter. of *curse*] (1775) **1** : CURSE **2** : FELLOW 4c

[2]**cuss** *vb* (1815) : CURSE — **cuss·er** *n*
cuss·ed \ˈkəs-əd\ *adj* (1840) **1** : CURSED **2** : OBSTINATE, CANTANKEROUS — **cuss·ed·ly** *adv*
cuss·ed·ness *n* (1857) : disposition to willful perversity : OBSTINACY
cuss·word \ˈkəs-ˌwərd\ *n* (1872) **1** : SWEARWORD **2** : a term of abuse : a derogatory term
cus·tard \ˈkəs-tərd\ *n* [ME, a kind of pie, prob. fr. Prov *croustado* pie shell — more at CROUSTADE] (1628) : a pudding-like usu. sweetened mixture made of eggs and milk
custard apple *n* (1657) **1 a** : any of several chiefly tropical American soft-fleshed edible fruits **b** : any of a genus (*Annona* of the family Annonaceae, the custard-apple family) of trees or shrubs bearing this fruit; *esp* : a small West Indian tree (*A. reticulata*) **2** : PAPAW 2
cus·to·di·al \ˌkəs-ˈtōd-ē-əl\ *adj* (1772) : relating to guardianship; *specif* : marked by or given to watching and protecting rather than seeking to cure ⟨~ care⟩
cus·to·di·an \ˌkəs-ˈtōd-ē-ən\ *n* (1781) : one that guards and protects or maintains; *esp* : one entrusted with guarding and keeping property or records or with custody or guardianship of prisoners or inmates — **cus·to·di·an·ship** \-ˌship\ *n*
cus·to·dy \ˈkəs-təd-ē\ *n, pl* **-dies** [ME *custodie,* fr. L *custodia* guarding, fr. *custod-, custos* guardian] (15c) : immediate charge and control (as over a ward or a suspect) exercised by a person or an authority : SAFEKEEPING
[1]**cus·tom** \ˈkəs-təm\ *n* [ME *custume,* fr. OF, fr. L *consuetudin-, consuetudo,* fr. *consuetus,* pp. of *consuescere* to accustom, fr. *com-* + *suescere* to accustom; akin to *suus* one's own — more at SUICIDE] (13c) **1 a** : a usage or practice common to many or to a particular place or class or habitual with an individual **b** : long-established practice considered as unwritten law **c** : repeated practice **d** : the whole body of usages, practices, or conventions that regulate social life **2** *pl* **a** : duties, tolls, or imposts imposed by the sovereign law of a country on imports or exports **b** *usu sing in constr* : the agency, establishment, or procedure for collecting such customs **3 a** : business patronage **b** : usu. habitual patrons : CUSTOMERS ***syn*** see HABIT
[2]**custom** *adj* (1830) **1** : made or performed according to personal order **2** : specializing in custom work or operation ⟨a ~ tailor⟩
cus·tom·ary \ˈkəs-tə-ˌmer-ē\ *adj* (1600) **1** : based on or established by custom **2** : commonly practiced, used, or observed ***syn*** see USUAL — **cus·tom·ari·ly** \ˌkəs-tə-ˈmer-ə-lē\ *adv* — **cus·tom·ari·ness** \ˈkəs-tə-ˌmer-ē-nəs\ *n*
cus·tom–built \ˌkəs-təm-ˈbilt\ *adj* (1925) : built to individual specifications
cus·tom·er \ˈkəs-tə-mər\ *n* [ME *custumer,* fr. *custume*] (15c) **1** : one that purchases a commodity or service **2** : an individual usu. having some specified distinctive trait ⟨a real tough ~⟩
cus·tom·house \ˈkəs-təm-ˌhau̇s\ *also* **cus·toms·house** \-təmz-\ *n* (15c) : a building where customs and duties are paid or collected and where vessels are entered and cleared
cus·tom·ize \ˈkəs-tə-ˌmīz\ *vt* **-ized; -iz·ing** (1926) : to build, fit, or alter according to individual specifications — **cus·tom·iz·er** *n*
cus·tom–made \ˌkəs-təm-ˈ(m)ād\ *adj* (1855) : made to individual specifications
cus·tom–tai·lor \-ˈtā-lər\ *vt* (1895) : to alter, plan, or build according to individual specifications or needs
[1]**cut** \ˈkət\ *vb* **cut; cut·ting** [ME *cutten*] *vt* (13c) **1 a** : to penetrate with or as if with an edged instrument **b** : to hurt the feelings of **c** : to strike sharply with a cutting effect **d** : to strike (a ball) with a glancing blow that imparts a reverse spin **e** : to experience the growth of (a tooth) through the gum **2 a** : TRIM, PARE ⟨~ one's nails⟩ **b** : to shorten by omissions **c** : DISSOLVE, DILUTE, ADULTERATE **d** : to reduce in amount ⟨~ costs⟩ **3 a** : MOW, REAP **b** (1) : to divide into parts with an edged tool ⟨~ bread⟩ (2) : FELL, HEW **c** (1) : to separate or discharge from an organization : DETACH (2) : to single out and isolate ⟨~ a calf out from the herd⟩ **d** : to change the direction of sharply **e** : to go or pass around or about **4 a** : to divide into segments **b** : INTERSECT, CROSS **c** : BREAK, INTERRUPT ⟨~ our supply lines⟩ **d** (1) : to divide (a deck of cards) into two portions (2) : to draw (a card) from the deck **e** : to divide into shares : SPLIT **5 a** : STOP, CEASE ⟨~ the nonsense⟩ **b** : to refuse to recognize (an acquaintance) : OSTRACIZE **c** : to absent oneself from (as a class) **d** : to stop (a motor) by opening a switch **e** : to stop the filming of (a motion-picture scene) **6 a** : to make by or as if by cutting: as (1) : CARVE ⟨~ stone⟩ (2) : to shape by grinding ⟨~ a diamond⟩ (3) : ENGRAVE (4) : to shear or hollow out **b** : to record sounds (as speech or music) on (a phonograph record) **c** : to type on a stencil **7 a** : to engage in (a frolicsome or mischievous action) ⟨on summer nights strange capers are ~ under the thin guise of a Christian festival —D. C. Peattie⟩ ⟨in his sixty-seventh year with a heart that ~ didoes —H. R. Warfel⟩ **b** : to give the appearance or impression of ⟨~ a fine figure⟩ **8** : to be able to manage or handle a situation — usu. used in negative constructions ⟨can't ~ that kind of work anymore⟩ ~ *vi* **1 a** : to function as or as if as an edged tool **b** : to undergo incision or severance ⟨cheese ~*s* easily⟩ **c** : to perform the operation of dividing, severing, incising, or intersecting **d** : to make a stroke with a whip, sword, or other weapon **e** : to wound feelings or sensibilities **f** : to cause constriction or chafing **g** : to be of effect, influence, or significance ⟨an analysis that ~*s* deep⟩ **2 a** (1) : to divide a pack of cards esp. in order to decide the deal or settle a bet (2) : to draw a card from the pack **b** : to divide spoils : SPLIT **3 a** : to proceed obliquely from a straight course ⟨~ across the yard⟩ **b** : to move swiftly ⟨a yacht *cutting* through the water⟩ **c** : to describe an oblique or diagonal line **d** : to change sharply in direction : SWERVE **e** : to make an abrupt transition from one sound or image to another in motion pictures, radio, or television **4** : to stop photographing motion pictures — **cut corners** : to perform some action in the quickest, easiest, or cheapest way — **cut ice** : to be of importance — usu. used in negative constructions — **cut it** : to cut the mustard — **cut the mustard** : to achieve the standard of performance necessary for success
[2]**cut** *n* (14c) **1** : something that is cut or cut off: as **a** : a length of cloth varying from 40 to 100 yards **b** : the yield of products cut esp. during one harvest **c** : a segment or section of a meat carcass or a part of one **d** : a group of animals selected from a herd **e** : SHARE ⟨took his ~ of the profits⟩ **2** : a product of cutting: as **a** : a creek, channel, or inlet made by excavation or worn by natural action **b** (1) : an opening made with an edged instrument (2) : a wound made by something sharp : GASH **c** : a surface or outline left by cutting **d** : a passage cut as a roadway **e** : a grade or step esp. in a social scale ⟨a ~ above the ordinary⟩ **f** : a subset of a set such that when it is subtracted from the set the remainder is not connected **g** : a pictorial illustration **h** : [1]BAND 7 **3** : the act or an instance of cutting: as **a** : a gesture or expression that hurts the feelings ⟨made an unkind ~⟩ **b** : a straight passage or course **c** : a stroke or blow with the edge of a knife or other edged tool **d** : a lash with or as if with a whip **e** : the act of reducing or removing a part ⟨a ~ in pay⟩ **f** : an act or turn of cutting cards; *also* : the result of cutting **4** : a voluntary absence from a class **5 a** : a stroke that cuts a ball; *also* : the spin imparted by such a stroke **b** : a swing by a batter at a pitched baseball **c** : an exchange of captures in checkers **6** : an abrupt transition from one sound or image to another in motion pictures, radio, or television **7 a** : the shape and style in which a thing is cut, formed, or made ⟨clothes of the latest ~⟩ **b** : PATTERN, TYPE **c** : HAIRCUT — **cut of one's jib** : APPEARANCE, STYLE
cut·abil·i·ty \ˌkət-ə-ˈbil-ət-ē\ *n* (1965) : the proportion of lean salable meat yielded by a carcass
cut–and–dried \ˌkət-ᵊn-ˈdrīd\ *also* **cut–and–dry** \-ˈdrī\ *adj* (1710) : being or done according to a plan, set procedure, or formula : ROUTINE
cut–and–try \-ᵊn-ˈtrī\ *adj* (1903) : marked by experimental procedure : EMPIRICAL
cu·ta·ne·ous \kyu̇-ˈtā-nē-əs\ *adj* [NL *cutaneus,* fr. L *cutis* skin — more at HIDE] (1578) : of, relating to, or affecting the skin — **cu·ta·ne·ous·ly** *adv*
[1]**cut·away** \ˈkət-ə-ˌwā\ *adj* (1841) : having or showing parts cut away
[2]**cutaway** *n* (1849) **1** : a coat with skirts tapering from the front waistline to form tails at the back **2 a** : a cutaway picture or representation **b** : a shot that interrupts the main action of a film or television program to take up a related subject or to depict action supposed to be going on at the same time as the main action **3** : a back dive in which the head is lowered toward the board after the takeoff
cut·back \ˈkət-ˌbak\ *n* (1897) **1** : something cut back **2** : REDUCTION
cut back \ˌkət-ˈbak\ *vt* (1871) : to shorten by cutting : PRUNE ~ *vi* : to interrupt the sequence of a plot (as of a movie) by introducing events prior to those last presented
cutch \ˈkəch\ *n* [modif. of Malay *kachu*] (1617) : CATECHU a
cut down *vt* (1821) **1 a** : to remodel by removing extras or unwanted furnishings and fittings **b** : to remake in a smaller size **2 a** : to strike down and kill or incapacitate **b** : KNOCK DOWN ~ *vi* : to reduce or curtail volume or activity ⟨*cut down* on his smoking⟩ — **cut down to size** : to reduce from an inflated or exaggerated importance to true or suitable stature
cute \ˈkyüt\ *adj* **cut·er; cut·est** [short for *acute*] (1731) **1** : CLEVER, SHREWD **2** : attractive or pretty esp. in a dainty or delicate way **3** : obviously straining for effect — **cute·ly** *adv* — **cute·ness** *n*
cute·sy \ˈkyüt-sē\ *adj* **cute·si·er; -est** [*cute* + *-sy* (as in *folksy*)] (1914) : self-consciously cute : MANNERED
cut glass *n* (1800) : glass ornamented with patterns cut into its surface by an abrasive wheel and polished
cut–grass \ˈkət-ˌgras\ *n* (1840) : a grass (esp. genus *Leersia*) with minute hooked bristles along the edges of the leaf blade
cu·ti·cle \ˈkyüt-i-kəl\ *n* [L *cuticula,* dim. of *cutis* skin — more at HIDE] (1615) **1** : SKIN, PELLICLE: as **a** : an external investment secreted usu. by epidermal cells **b** : the outermost layer of animal integument (as in man) when composed of epidermis **c** : a thin continuous fatty film on the external surface of many higher plants **2** : dead or horny epidermis — **cu·tic·u·lar** \kyu̇-ˈtik-yə-lər\ *adj*
cut·ie *or* **cut·ey** \ˈkyüt-ē\ *n, pl* **cuties** *or* **cuteys** [*cute* + *-ie*] (1768) : an attractive person; *esp* : a pretty girl
cu·tin \ˈkyüt-ᵊn\ *n* [ISV, fr. L *cutis*] (ca. 1863) : an insoluble mixture containing waxes, fatty acids, soaps, and resinous material that forms a continuous layer on the outer epidermal wall of a plant
cut–in \ˈkət-ˌin\ *n* (1883) : something cut in — **cut–in** *adj*
cut in \ˌkət-ˈin\ *vi* (1612) **1** : to thrust oneself into a position between others or belonging to another **2** : to join in something suddenly ⟨*cut in* on the conversation⟩ **3** : to interrupt a dancing couple and take one as one's partner **4** : to become automatically connected or started in operation ~ *vt* **1** : to mix with cutting motions ⟨after sifting the flour into a mixing bowl, *cut* the lard *in*⟩ **2** : to introduce into a number, group, or sequence **3** : to connect into an electrical circuit to a mechanical apparatus so as to permit operation **4** : to include esp. among those benefiting or favored ⟨*cut* them *in* on the profits⟩
cu·tin·ized \ˈkyüt-ᵊn-ˌīzd\ *adj* (1901) : infiltrated with cutin ⟨~ epidermal cells⟩
cu·tis \ˈkyüt-əs\ *n, pl* **cu·tes** \ˈkyü-ˌtēz\ *or* **cu·tis·es** [L] (1603) : DERMIS
cut·lass *also* **cut·las** \ˈkət-ləs\ *n* [MF *coutelas,* aug. of *coutel* knife, fr. L *cultellus,* dim. of *culter* knife, plowshare] (1594) **1** : a short curving sword formerly used by sailors on warships **2** : MACHETE
cut·ler \ˈkət-lər\ *n* [ME, fr. MF *coutelier,* fr. LL *cultellarius,* fr. L *cultellus*] (15c) : one who makes, deals in, or repairs cutlery
cut·lery \ˈkət-lə-rē\ *n* (15c) **1** : the business of a cutler **2** : edged or cutting tools; *specif* : implements for cutting and eating food
cut·let \ˈkət-lət\ *n* [F *côtelette,* fr. OF *costelette,* dim. of *coste* rib, side, fr. L *costa* — more at COAST] (ca. 1706) **1** : a small slice of meat for broiling or frying ⟨a veal ~⟩ **2** : a flat croquette of chopped meat or fish
cut·line \ˈkət-ˌlīn\ *n* (1943) : CAPTION, LEGEND
cut·off \ˈkət-ˌȯf\ *n* (1741) **1** : the act or action of cutting off **2 a** : the new and relatively short channel formed when a stream cuts through the neck of an oxbow **b** : SHORTCUT 1 **c** : a channel made to straighten a stream **3** : a device for cutting off **4 a** : something cut off **b** *pl* : shorts orig. made from jeans with the legs cut off at the knees or higher **5** : the point, date, or period for a cutoff — **cutoff** *adj*
cut off \ˌkət-ˈȯf\ *vt* (14c) **1** : to bring to an untimely end **2** : to stop the passage of **3** : SHUT OFF, BAR **4** : DISCONTINUE, TERMINATE **5** : SEPARATE, ISOLATE **6** : DISINHERIT **7 a** : to stop the operation of : TURN OFF **b** : to stop or interrupt while in communication ⟨the operator *cut* me *off*⟩ ~ *vi* : to cease operating
cut·out \ˈkət-ˌau̇t\ *n* (1851) **1** : something cut out or off from something else **2** : one that cuts out — **cutout** *adj*

1cut out \ˌkət-ˈau̇t\ *vt* (15c) **1 :** to form by erosion **2 :** to determine or assign through necessity ⟨you've got your work *cut out* for you⟩ **3 :** to take the place of : SUPPLANT **4 :** to put an end to : desist from ⟨wasteful expenditures that must be *cut out*⟩ **5 :** DEPRIVE, DEFRAUD **6 a :** to remove from a series or circuit : DISCONNECT **b :** to make inoperative ~ *vi* **1 :** to depart in haste **2 :** to cease operating **3 :** to swerve out of a traffic line

2cut out *adj* (1926) : naturally fitted or suited ⟨not *cut out* to be a lawyer⟩

cut·over \ˌkət-ˌō-vər\ *adj* (1899) : having most of the salable timber cut

cut·purse \ˈkət-ˌpərs\ *n* (14c) : PICKPOCKET

cut–rate \ˈkət-ˈrāt\ *adj* (1903) **1 :** marked by, offering, or making use of a reduced rate or price ⟨~ stores⟩ **2 :** SECOND-RATE, CHEAP

cut·ta·ble \ˈkət-ə-bəl\ *adj* (15c) : capable of being cut : ready for cutting

cut·ter \ˈkət-ər\ *n* (15c) **1 :** one that cuts: **a :** one whose work is cutting or involves cutting **b** (1) : an instrument, machine, machine part, or tool that cuts (2) : a device for vibrating a cutting stylus in disc recording (3) : the cutting stylus or its point **2 a :** a ship's boat for carrying stores or passengers **b :** a fore-and-aft rigged sailing boat with a jib, forestaysail, mainsail, and single mast **c :** a small armed boat in government service **3 :** a light sleigh

1cut·throat \ˈkət-ˌthrōt\ *n* (1535) **1 :** one likely to cut throats **2 :** a cruel unprincipled person

2cutthroat *adj* (1567) **1 :** MURDEROUS, CRUEL **2 :** marked by unprincipled practices : RUTHLESS ⟨~ competition⟩ **3 :** characterized by each player playing for himself rather than having a permanent partner — used esp. of partnership games adapted for three players ⟨~ bridge⟩

cutthroat contract *n* (ca. 1944) : contract bridge in which partnerships are determined by the bidding

cutthroat trout *n* (ca. 1891) : a large trout (*Salmo clarki*) native to cold lakes and rivers from northern California to southern Alaska — called also *cutthroat*

cut time *n* (1951) : duple or quadruple time with the beat represented by a half note

1cut·ting \ˈkət-iŋ\ *n* (14c) **1 :** something cut or cut off, out, or over: as **a :** a plant section originating from stem, leaf, or root and capable of developing into a new plant **b :** HARVEST **2 :** something made by cutting; *esp* : RECORDING

2cutting *adj* (15c) **1 :** given to or designed for cutting; *esp* : SHARP, EDGED **2 :** marked by sharp piercing cold **3 :** inclined or likely to wound the feelings of others esp. because of a ruthless incisiveness ⟨a ~ remark⟩ **4 :** INTENSE, PIERCING ⟨a ~ pain⟩ — **cut·ting·ly** \-iŋ-lē\ *adv*

cutting board *n* (1825) : a board on which something (as food or cloth) is placed for cutting

cutting edge *n* (1951) **1 :** the foremost part or place : FOREFRONT **2 :** a sharp effect or quality

cutting horse *n* (1881) : an agile saddle horse trained to separate individual animals from a cattle herd

cut·tle·bone \ˈkət-ᵊl-ˌbōn\ *n* [ME *cotul* cuttlefish (fr. OE *cudele*) + E *bone*] (1547) : the shell of cuttlefishes used for polishing powder or for supplying cage birds with lime and salts

cut·tle·fish \-ˌfish\ *n* [ME *cotul* + E *fish*] (15c) : any of a family (Sepiidae) of 10-armed marine cephalopod mollusks differing from the related squid in having a calcified internal shell

cut·ty sark \ˈkət-ē-ˌsärk\ *n* [E dial. *cutty* (short) + *sark*] (1779) **1** *chiefly Scot* : a short garment; *esp* : a woman's short undergarment **2** *chiefly Scot* : WOMAN, HUSSY

cutty stool *n* (1820) **1** *chiefly Scot* : a low stool **2 :** a seat in a Scottish church where offenders formerly sat for public rebuke

cut·up \ˈkət-ˌəp\ *n* (1843) : one who clowns or acts boisterously

cut up \ˌkət-ˈəp\ *vt* (1580) **1 a :** to cut into parts or pieces **b :** to injure or damage by or as if by cutting : GASH, SLASH **2 :** to subject to hostile criticism : CENSURE ~ *vi* **1 :** to undergo being cut up **2 :** to behave in a comic, boisterous, or unruly manner : CLOWN

cut·wa·ter \ˈkət-ˌwȯt-ər, -ˌwät-\ *n* (1644) : the forepart of a ship's stem

cut·work \-ˌwərk\ *n* (15c) : embroidery usu. on linen in which a design is outlined in buttonhole stitch and the intervening material then cut away

cut·worm \-ˌwərm\ *n* (ca. 1808) : any of various smooth-bodied noctuid moth caterpillars which are chiefly nocturnal and many of which feed on plant stems near ground level

cu·vette \kyü-ˈvet\ *n* [F, dim. of *cuve* tub, fr. L *cupa* — more at CUP] (ca. 1909) : a small often transparent laboratory vessel (as a tube)

cwm \ˈküm\ *n* [W, valley] (1853) : CIRQUE 3

-cy \sē\ *n suffix* [ME *-cie*, fr. OF, fr. L *-tia*, partly fr. *-t-* (final stem consonant) + *-ia* -y, partly fr. Gk *-tia*, *-teia*, fr. *-t-* (final stem consonant) + *-ia*, *-eia* -y] **1 :** action : practice ⟨mendican*cy*⟩ **2 :** rank : office ⟨baronet*cy*⟩ ⟨chaplain*cy*⟩ **3 :** body : class ⟨magistra*cy*⟩ **4 :** state : quality ⟨accura*cy*⟩ ⟨bankrupt*cy*⟩ ⟨normal*cy*⟩ — often replacing a final *-t* or *-te* of the base word

cy·an \ˈsī-ˌan, -ən\ *n* [Gk *kyanos*] (ca. 1889) : a greenish blue color — used in photography and color printing of one of the primary colors

cyan- *or* **cyano-** *comb form* [G, fr. Gk *kyan-*, *kyano-*, fr. *kyanos* dark blue enamel] **1 :** dark blue : blue ⟨*cyano*type⟩ **2 :** cyanogen ⟨*cyan*ide⟩ **3 :** cyanide ⟨*cyano*genetic⟩

cy·an·a·mide \sī-ˈan-ə-məd\ *n* [ISV] (1838) **1 :** a caustic acidic compound CH_2N_2 **2 :** CALCIUM CYANAMIDE

cy·a·nate \ˈsī-ə-ˌnāt, -nət\ *n* [ISV] (1845) : a salt (as ammonium cyanate) or ester of cyanic acid

cy·an·ic \sī-ˈan-ik\ *adj* [ISV] (1832) **1 :** relating to or containing cyanogen **2 :** of a blue or bluish color

cyanic acid *n* (1838) : a strong acid HOCN used to prepare cyanates

1cy·a·nide \ˈsī-ə-ˌnīd, -nəd\ *n* [ISV] (1826) : a compound (as potassium cyanide) of cyanogen usu. with a more electropositive element or group

2cy·a·nide \-ˌnīd\ *vt* **-nid·ed; -nid·ing** (1894) : to treat with a cyanide; *specif* : to treat (iron or steel) with molten cyanide to produce a hard surface

cyanide process *n* (1890) : a method of extracting gold and silver from ores by treatment with a sodium cyanide or calcium cyanide solution

cy·a·nine \ˈsī-ə-ˌnēn, -nən\ *n* [ISV] (ca. 1872) : any of various dyes that sensitize photographic film to light from the green, yellow, red, and infrared regions of the spectrum

cy·a·nite \ˈsī-ə-ˌnīt\ *var of* KYANITE

cy·a·no \ˈsī-ə-(ˌ)nō, sī-ˈan-(ˌ)ō\ *adj* [*cyan-*] (ca. 1961) : relating to or containing the cyanogen group

cy·a·no·ac·ry·late \ˌsī-ə-nō-ˈak-rə-ˌlāt, sī-ˌan-ō-\ *n* (1963) : any of several liquid acrylate monomers that readily polymerize anionically and are used as adhesives in industry and in closing wounds in surgery

cy·a·no·co·bal·a·min \-kō-ˈbal-ə-mən\ *also* **cy·a·no·co·bal·a·mine** \-ˌmēn\ *n* [*cyan-* + *cobalt* + *vitamin*] (1950) : VITAMIN B_{12}

cy·a·no·eth·yl·ate \-ˈeth-ə-ˌlāt\ *vt* (1942) : to introduce a cyano-ethyl group CNC_2H_4 into (a compound) usu. by means of acrylonitrile ⟨~ cotton⟩ — **cy·a·no·eth·yl·ation** \-ˌeth-ə-ˈlā-shən\ *n*

cy·ano·gen \sī-ˈan-ə-jən\ *n* [F *cyanogène*, fr. *cyan-* + *gène* -gen] (1826) **1 :** a univalent group CN present in simple and complex cyanides **2 :** a colorless flammable poisonous gas $(CN)_2$

cy·a·no·gen·et·ic \ˌsī-ə-nō-jə-ˈnet-ik, sī-ˌan-ō-\ *or* **cy·a·no·gen·ic** \-ˈjen-ik\ *adj* (ca. 1902) : capable of producing cyanide (as hydrogen cyanide) ⟨a ~ plant⟩ ⟨a ~ glucoside⟩ — **cy·a·no·gen·e·sis** \-ˈjen-ə-səs\ *n*

cy·a·no·hy·drin \-ˈhī-drən\ *n* [ISV, fr. *cyan-* + *hydr-* + *-in*] (ca. 1925) : any of various compounds containing both cyano and hydroxyl groups

cy·a·no·sis \ˌsī-ə-ˈnō-səs\ *n* [NL, fr. Gk *kyanōsis* dark blue color, fr. *kyan-* cyan-] (1834) : a bluish or purplish discoloration (as of skin) due to deficient oxygenation of the blood — **cy·a·not·ic** \-ˈnät-ik\ *adj*

cy·an·urate \ˌsī-ə-ˈn(y)u̇(ə)r-ˌāt, -ˈn(y)u̇r-ət\ *n* (ca. 1890) : a salt or ester of cyanuric acid

cy·an·uric acid \ˌsī-ə-ˌn(y)u̇r-ik-\ *n* [*cyan-* + *urea*] (1838) : a crystalline weak acid $C_3N_3(OH)_3$ yielding cyanic acid when heated

Cyb·e·le \ˈsib-ə-(ˌ)lē\ *n* [L, fr. Gk *Kybelē*] : a nature goddess of the ancient peoples of Asia Minor

cy·ber·nat·ed \ˈsī-bər-ˌnāt-əd\ *adj* (1962) : characterized by or involving cybernation ⟨a ~ bakery⟩ ⟨a ~ society⟩

cy·ber·na·tion \ˌsī-bər-ˈnā-shən\ *n* [*cyber*netics + *-ation*] (1962) : the automatic control of a process or operation (as in manufacturing) by means of computers

cy·ber·ne·ti·cian \ˌsī-(ˌ)bər-nə-ˈtish-ən\ *n* (1951) : a specialist in cybernetics

cy·ber·net·i·cist \ˌsī-bər-ˈnet-ə-səst\ *n* (1948) : CYBERNETICIAN

cy·ber·net·ics \ˌsī-bər-ˈnet-iks\ *n pl but sing in constr* [Gk *kybernētēs* pilot, governor (fr. *kybernan* to steer, govern) + E *-ics*] (1948) : the science of communication and control theory that is concerned esp. with the comparative study of automatic control systems (as the nervous system and brain and mechanical-electrical communication systems) — **cy·ber·net·ic** \-ik\ *also* **cy·ber·net·i·cal** \-i-kəl\ *adj* — **cy·ber·net·i·cal·ly** \-i-k(ə-)lē\ *adv*

cy·borg \ˈsī-ˌbȯ(ə)rg\ *n* [*cyb*ernetic + *org*anism] (ca. 1962) : a human being who is linked (as for temporary adaptation to a hostile space environment) to one or more mechanical devices upon which some of his vital physiological functions depend

cy·cad \ˈsī-kəd\ *n* [NL *Cycad-*, *Cycas*] (1845) : any of an order (Cycadales) of gymnosperms that are represented by a single surviving family (Cycadaceae) of tropical plants resembling palms but reproducing by means of spermatozoids

cy·cad·e·oid \sī-ˈkad-ē-ˌȯid\ *n* [NL *Cycadeoidales*, group name, deriv. of *Cycad-*, *Cycas*] (1928) : any of an extinct order (Cycadeoidales or Bennettitales) of cycadophytes that differ from the cycads chiefly in having the reproductive organs on the trunk embedded in a thick external covering of persistent leaf bases

cy·cado·phyte \sī-ˈkad-ə-ˌfīt\ *n* [NL *Cycadophytae*, group name, irreg. fr. *Cycad-*, *Cycas* + *phyton* plant — more at -PHYTE] (ca. 1911) : any of a subclass (Cycadophytae) of unbranched gymnosperms with pinnate leaves, large pith, little xylem, and a thick cortex that includes the cycads, cycadeoids, and seed ferns

cy·ca·sin \ˈsī-kə-sən\ *n* [*cycas* + *-in*] (ca. 1965) : a glucoside $C_8H_{16}N_2O_7$ that occurs in cycads and results in toxic and carcinogenic effects when introduced into mammals

cycl- *or* **cyclo-** *comb form* [NL, fr. Gk *kykl-*, *kyklo-*, fr. *kyklos*] **1 :** circle ⟨*cyclo*meter⟩ **2 :** cyclic ⟨*cyclo*hexane⟩

cy·cla·mate \ˈsī-klə-ˌmāt, -mət\ *n* [*cyclo*hexyl-sulf*amate*] (1951) : an artificially prepared salt of sodium or calcium used esp. formerly as a sweetener but now largely discontinued because of the possibly harmful effects of its metabolic breakdown product cyclohexylamine

cy·cla·men \ˈsī-klə-mən, ˈsik-lə-\ *n* [NL, genus name, fr. Gk *kyklaminos*] (1550) : any of a genus (*Cyclamen*) of plants of the primrose family having showy nodding flowers

cy·clase \ˈsī-ˌklās, -ˌklāz\ *n* [*cycl-* + *-ase*] (1946) : an enzyme (as adenylate cyclase) that catalyzes cyclization of a compound

cy·claz·o·cine \sī-ˈklaz-ə-ˌsēn, -sən\ *n* [*cycl-* + *azocine* (C_7H_7N), of unknown origin] (1966) : an analgesic drug $C_{18}H_{25}NO$ that inhibits the effect of morphine and related addictive drugs and is used in the treatment of drug addiction

1cy·cle \ˈsī-kəl, *6 is also* ˈsik-əl\ *n* [F or LL; F, fr. LL *cyclus*, fr. Gk *kyklos* circle, wheel, cycle — more at WHEEL] (14c) **1 :** an interval of time during which a sequence of a recurring succession of events or phenomena is completed **2 a :** a course or series of events or operations that recur regularly and usu. lead back to the starting point **b :** one complete performance of a vibration, electric oscillation, current alternation, or other periodic process **c :** a permutation of a set of ordered elements in which each element takes the place of the next and the last becomes first **3 :** a circular or spiral arrangement: as **a :** an imaginary circle or orbit in the heavens **b :** WHORL **c :** RING 10 **4 :** a long period of time : AGE **5 a :** a group of poems, plays, novels, or songs treating the same theme **b :** a series of narratives dealing typically with the exploits of a legendary hero **6 a :** BICYCLE **b :** TRICYCLE **c :** MOTORCYCLE **7 :** the series of a single, double, triple, and home run hit in any order by one player during one baseball game

2cy·cle \ˈsī-kəl, *2 is also* ˈsik-əl\ *vb* **cy·cled; cy·cling** \ˈsī-k(ə-)liŋ, ˈsik(-ə)-\ *vi* (1842) **1 a :** to pass through a cycle **b :** to recur in cycles **2 :** to ride a cycle; *specif* : BICYCLE ~ *vt* : to cause to go through a cycle — **cy·cler** \'sī-k(ə-)lər, 'sik-(ə-)\ *n*

cy·clic \'sī-klik *also* 'sik-lik\ *or* **cy·cli·cal** \'sī-kli-kəl, 'sik-li-\ *adj* (1794) **1 a** : of, relating to, or being a cycle **b** : moving in cycles ⟨~ time⟩ **2** *cyclic* : being a mathematical group that has an element such that every element of the group can be expressed as one of its powers — **cy·cli·cal·ly** \-k(ə-)lē\ *also* **cy·clic·ly** \'sī-kli-klē, 'sik-li-\ *adv*

cyclic AMP *n* (ca. 1966) : a cyclic mononucleotide of adenosine that has been implicated in control mechanisms regulating metabolism and function in the nervous system — called also *adenosine 3′,5′-monophosphate*

cyclic GMP \-ˌjē-(ˌ)em-'pē\ *n* [guanosine + *mon-* + phosphate] (1972) : a cyclic mononucleotide of guanosine that has been implicated with cyclic AMP as a second messenger in addition to hormones in the control of cellular processes

cy·clic·i·ty \sī-'klis-ət-ē, sik-'lis-\ *n* (1944) : the quality or state of being cyclic ⟨estrous ~⟩

cy·clist \'sī-k(ə-)ləst, 'sik(-ə-)\ *n* (1882) : one who rides a cycle

cy·cli·tol \'sī-klə-ˌtȯl, 'sik-lə-ˌtōl\ *n* [*cycl-* + *-itol* (as in *inositol*)] (ca. 1943) : an alicyclic polyhydroxy compound (as inositol)

cy·cli·za·tion \ˌsī-k(ə-)lə-'zā-shən, ˌsik-\ *n* (1909) : formation of one or more rings in a chemical compound — **cy·clize** \'sī-k(ə-)ˌlīz, 'sik-\ *vb*

cy·clo \'sē-(ˌ)klō, 'sik-(ˌ)lō\ *n, pl* **cyclos** [prob. fr. F, short for (assumed) *cyclotaxi*, fr. moto*cyclette* motorcycle + *-o-* + *taxi*] (1964) : a 3-wheeled motor-driven taxi

cy·clo·ad·di·tion \ˌsī-(ˌ)klō-ə-'dish-ən\ *n* (1963) : a chemical reaction leading to ring formation in a compound

cy·clo·al·i·phat·ic \ˌsī-klō-ˌal-ə-'fat-ik\ *adj* (1936) : ALICYCLIC

cy·clo·di·ene \-'dī-ˌēn, -dī-'\ *n* [*cycl-* + *diene*] (1942) : an organic insecticide (as aldrin, dieldrin, chlordane, or endosulfan) with a chlorinated methylene group forming a bridge across a 6-membered carbon ring

cy·clo·gen·e·sis \-'jen-ə-səs\ *n* [*cyclone* + *genesis*] (ca. 1938) : the development or intensification of a cyclone

cy·clo·hex·ane \ˌsī-klō-'hek-ˌsān\ *n* [ISV] (ca. 1909) : a pungent saturated cyclic hydrocarbon C_6H_{12} found in petroleum or made synthetically and used chiefly as a solvent and in organic synthesis

cy·clo·hex·a·none \-'hek-sə-ˌnōn\ *n* [*cyclohexane* + *-one*] (ca. 1909) : a liquid ketone $C_6H_{10}O$ used esp. as a solvent and in organic synthesis

cy·clo·hex·i·mide \-'hek-sə-ˌmīd, -məd\ *n* [*cyclohexane* + *imide*] (ca. 1950) : an agricultural fungicide $C_{15}H_{23}NO_4$ that inhibits protein synthesis and is obtained from a soil bacterium (*Streptomyces griseus*)

cy·clo·hex·yl·amine \-hek-'sil-ə-ˌmēn\ *n* [*cyclohexane* + *-yl* + *amine*] (1943) : an amine ($C_6H_{11}NH_2$) of cyclohexane that is a prob. harmful metabolic breakdown product of cyclamate

[1]**cy·cloid** \'sī-ˌklȯid\ *n* [F *cycloïde*, fr. Gk *kykloeidēs* circular, fr. *kyklos*] (1661) **1** : a curve that is generated by a point on the circumference of a circle as it rolls along a straight line **2** : something having a curved or circular form ⟨a cloud ~⟩ — **cy·cloi·dal** \sī-'klȯid-ᵊl\ *adj*

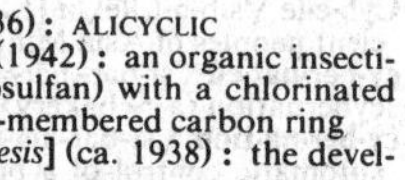

cycloid 1

[2]**cycloid** *adj* (1851) **1** : smooth with concentric lines of growth ⟨~ scales⟩; *also* : having or consisting of cycloid scales **2** : relating to or being a personality characterized by alternating high and low moods — compare CYCLOTHYMIC

cy·clom·e·ter \sī-'kläm-ət-ər\ *n* (1880) : a device made for recording the revolutions of a wheel and often used for registering distance traversed by a wheeled vehicle

cy·clone \'sī-ˌklōn\ *n* [modif. of Gk *kyklōma* wheel, coil, fr. *kykloun* to go around, fr. *kyklos* circle] (1848) **1 a** : a storm or system of winds that rotates about a center of low atmospheric pressure clockwise in the southern hemisphere and counterclockwise in the northern, advances at a speed of 20 to 30 miles an hour, and often brings abundant rain **b** : TORNADO **c** : LOW 1b **2** : any of various centrifugal devices for separating materials (as solid particles from gases or liquids) — **cy·clon·ic** \sī-'klän-ik\ *adj* — **cy·clon·i·cal·ly** \-i-k(ə-)lē\ *adv*

cyclone cellar *n* (1887) : a cellar or covered excavation designed for protection from dangerous windstorms (as tornadoes)

cy·clo·ole·fin \ˌsī-klō-'ō-lə-fən\ *n* [ISV] (ca. 1923) : a hydrocarbon (as of the formula C_nH_{2n-2}) containing an unsaturated ring — **cy·clo·ole·fin·ic** \-ˌō-lə-'fin-ik\ *adj*

cy·clo·par·af·fin \-'par-ə-fən\ *n* (1900) : a saturated cyclic hydrocarbon of the formula C_nH_{2n}

cy·clo·pe·an \ˌsī-klə-'pē-ən, sī-'klō-pē-\ *adj* (1641) **1** *often cap* : of, relating to, or characteristic of a Cyclops **2** : HUGE, MASSIVE **3** : of or relating to a style of stone construction marked typically by the use of large irregular blocks without mortar

cy·clo·pe·dia *also* **cy·clo·pae·dia** \ˌsī-klə-'pēd-ē-ə\ *n* (1728) : ENCYCLOPEDIA — **cy·clo·pe·dic** \-'pēd-ik\ *adj*

cy·clo·phos·pha·mide \ˌsī-klō-'fäs-fə-ˌmīd\ *n* (1960) : an immunosuppressive and antineoplastic agent $C_7H_{15}Cl_2N_2O_2P$ used esp. against lymphomas and some leukemias

cy·clo·pro·pane \ˌsī-klə-'prō-ˌpān\ *n* [ISV] (1894) : a saturated cyclic gaseous hydrocarbon C_3H_6 used esp. as a general anesthetic

cy·clops \'sī-ˌkläps\ *n* [L, fr. Gk *Kyklōps*, fr. *kykl-* cycl- + *ōps* eye] (1513) **1** *pl* **cy·clo·pes** \sī-'klō-(ˌ)pēz\ *cap* : any of a race of giants in Greek mythology with a single eye in the middle of the forehead **2** *pl* **cyclops** [NL, genus name, fr. L] : any of a genus (*Cyclops*) of freshwater copepod water fleas

cy·clo·ra·ma \ˌsī-klə-'ram-ə, -'räm-\ *n* [*cycl-* + *-orama* (as in *panorama*)] (1840) **1** : a large pictorial representation encircling the spectator and often having real objects as a foreground **2** : a curved curtain or wall used as a background of a stage set to suggest unlimited space — **cy·clo·ram·ic** \-'ram-ik\ *adj*

cy·clo·ser·ine \ˌsī-klō-'se(ə)r-ˌēn\ *n* (1952) : an amino antibiotic $C_3H_6N_2O_2$ produced by an actinomycete (*Streptomyces orchidaceus*)

cy·clo·sis \sī-'klō-səs\ *n* [NL, fr. Gk *kyklōsis* encirclement, fr. *kykloun* to go around] (1835) : the streaming of protoplasm within a cell

cy·clo·stome \'sī-klə-ˌstōm\ *n* [deriv. of Gk *kykl-* + *stoma* mouth — more at STOMACH] (1835) : any of a class (Cyclostomi or Cyclostomata) of lowly craniate vertebrates having a large sucking mouth with no jaws and comprising the hagfishes and lampreys

cy·clo·style \-ˌstīl\ *n* [fr. *Cyclostyle*, a trademark] (1883) : a machine for making multiple copies that utilizes a stencil cut by a graver whose tip is a small rowel — **cyclostyle** *vt*

cy·clo·thy·mic \ˌsī-klə-'thī-mik\ *adj* [NL *cyclothymia* (fr. G *zyklothymie*, fr. *zykl-* cycl- + *-thymie* -thymia) + E *-ic*] (1923) : relating to or being an affective disorder characterized by the alternation of depressed moods with elevated, expansive, or irritable moods without psychotic features — compare CYCLOID 2 — **cy·clo·thy·mia** \-'thī-mē-ə\ *n*

cy·clo·tom·ic \-'täm-ik\ *adj* [*cyclotomy* (mathematical theory of the division of the circle into equal parts), fr. *cycl-* + *-tomy*] (1879) : relating to, being, or containing a polynomial of the form $x^{p-1} + x^{p-2} + \ldots + x + 1$ where p is a prime number

cy·clo·tron \'sī-klə-ˌträn\ *n* [*cycl-* + *-tron*; fr. the circular movement of the particles] (1935) : an accelerator in which charged particles (as protons, deuterons, or ions) are propelled by an alternating electric field in a constant magnetic field

cy·der *Brit var of* CIDER

cyg·net \'sig-nət\ *n* [ME *sygnett*, fr. MF *cygne* swan, fr. L *cycnus*, *cygnus*, fr. Gk *kyknos*] (15c) : a young swan

Cyg·nus \'sig-nəs\ *n* [L (gen. *Cygni*), lit., swan] : a northern constellation between Lyra and Pegasus in the Milky Way

cyl·in·der \'sil-ən-dər\ *n* [MF or L; MF *cylindre*, fr. L *cylindrus*, fr. Gk *kylindros*, fr. *kylindein* to roll; akin to OE *sceol* squinting, L *scelus* crime, Gk *skelos* leg, *skolios* crooked] (1570) **1 a** : the surface traced by a straight line moving parallel to a fixed straight line and intersecting a fixed planar closed curve **b** : the space bounded by a cylinder and two parallel planes cutting all its elements — see VOLUME table **2** : a cylindrical body: as **a** : the turning chambered breech of a revolver **b** (1) : the piston chamber in an engine (2) : a chamber in a pump from which the piston expels the fluid **c** : any of various rotating members in a press (as a printing press); *esp* : one that impresses paper on an inked form **d** : a cylindrical clay object inscribed with cuneiform inscriptions — **cyl·in·dered** \-dərd\ *adj*

cylinder seal *n* (1887) : a cylinder (as of stone) engraved in intaglio and used esp. in ancient Mesopotamia to roll an impression on wet clay

cy·lin·dri·cal \sə-'lin-dri-kəl\ *also* **cy·lin·dric** \-drik\ *adj* (1646) : relating to or having the form or properties of a cylinder — **cy·lin·dri·cal·ly** \-dri-k(ə-)lē\ *adv*

cylindrical coordinate *n* (ca. 1934) : any of the coordinates in space obtained by constructing in a plane a polar coordinate system and on a line perpendicular to the plane a linear coordinate system

cy·ma \'sī-mə\ *n* [Gk *kyma*, lit., wave] (1563) **1** : a projecting molding whose profile is a double curve **2** : a double curve formed by the union of a concave line and a convex line

cy·ma·tium \sī-'mā-sh(ē-)əm\ *n, pl* **-tia** \-sh(ē-)ə\ [L, fr. Gk *kymation*, dim. of *kymat-*, *kyma*] (1563) : a crowning molding in classic architecture; *esp* : CYMA

cym·bal \'sim-bəl\ *n* [ME, fr. OE *cymbal* & MF *cymbale*, fr. L *cymbalum*, fr. Gk *kymbalon*, fr. *kymbē* bowl, boat — more at HUMP] (bef. 12c) : a concave brass plate that produces a brilliant clashing tone and that is struck with a drumstick or is used in pairs struck glancingly together — **cym·bal·ist** \-bə-ləst\ *n*

cym·bid·i·um \sim-'bid-ē-əm\ *n* [NL, genus name, fr. L *cymba* boat, fr. Gk *kymbē*] (1815) : any of a genus (*Cymbidium*) of tropical Old World orchids with showy boat-shaped flowers

cyme \'sīm\ *n* [NL *cyma*, fr. L, cabbage sprout, fr. Gk *kyma* swell, wave, cabbage sprout, fr. *kyein* to be pregnant — more at CAVE] (1794) : an inflorescence in which all floral axes terminate in a single flower; *esp* : a determinate inflorescence of this type containing several flowers with the first-opening central flower terminating the main axis and subsequent flowers developing from lateral buds see INFLORESCENCE illustrated

cy·mene \'sī-ˌmēn\ *n* [F *cymène*, fr. Gk *kyminon* cumin + F *-ène* -ene — more at CUMIN] (ca. 1863) : any of three liquid isomeric hydrocarbons $C_{10}H_{14}$; *esp* : a colorless liquid of pleasant odor from essential oils

cym·ling \'sim-lən, -liŋ\ *n* [prob. alter. of *simnel*] (1779) : a summer squash having a scalloped edge

cy·mo·phane \'sī-mə-ˌfān\ *n* [F, fr. Gk *kyma* wave + F *-phane* -phane] (1804) : CHRYSOBERYL; *esp* : an opalescent chrysoberyl

cy·mose \'sī-ˌmōs\ *adj* (1807) : of, relating to, being, or bearing a cyme

[1]**Cym·ric** \'kəm-rik, 'kim-\ *adj* (1839) : of, relating to, or characteristic of the non-Gaelic Celtic people of Britain or their language; *specif* : WELSH

[2]**Cymric** *n* (ca. 1890) : BRYTHONIC; *specif* : the Welsh language

Cym·ry \-rē\ *n pl* [W] (1688) : the Brythonic Celts; *specif* : WELSH

cyn·ic \'sin-ik\ *n* [MF or L, MF *cynique*, fr. L *cynicus*, fr. Gk *kynikos*, lit., like a dog, fr. *kyn-*, *kyōn* dog — more at HOUND] (1547) **1** *cap* : an adherent of an ancient Greek school of philosophers who held the view that virtue is the only good and that its essence lies in self-control and independence **2** : a faultfinding captious critic; *esp* : one who believes that human conduct is motivated wholly by self-interest — **cynic** *adj*

cyn·i·cal \'sin-i-kəl\ *adj* (1588) **1** : CAPTIOUS, PEEVISH **2** : having or showing the attitude or temper of a cynic; *esp* : contemptuously distrustful of human nature and motives ⟨those ~ men who say that democracy cannot be honest and efficient—F.D. Roosevelt⟩ — **cyn·i·cal·ly** \-k(ə-)lē\ *adv*

syn CYNICAL, MISANTHROPIC, PESSIMISTIC, MISOGYNISTIC mean deeply distrustful. CYNICAL implies having a sneering disbelief in sincerity or integrity; MISANTHROPIC suggests a rooted distrust and dislike of human beings and their society; PESSIMISTIC implies having a gloomy, distrustful view of life; MISOGYNISTIC applies to a man having a deep-seated distrust of and aversion to women.

cyn·i·cism \'sin-ə-ˌsiz-əm\ *n* (1672) **1** *cap* : the doctrine of the Cynics **2 a** : cynical character, attitude, or quality **b** : an expression of such quality

cy·no·mol·gus monkey \ˌsī-nə-ˌmäl-gəs-\ *n* [NL, alter. of *cynamolgus*, fr. L, member of an ancient tribe in Africa, fr. Gk *Kynamolgoi*, lit., dog milkers] (1936) : a macaque (*Macaca irus* syn. *M. cynomolgus*) of southeastern Asia, Borneo, and the Philippines that is used esp. in medical research

cy·no·sure \'sī-nə-ˌshu̇(ə)r, 'sin-ə-\ *n* [MF & L; MF, Ursa Minor, guide, fr. L *cynosura* Ursa Minor, fr. Gk *kynosoura*, fr. *kynos oura*, lit., dog's tail] **1** *cap* : the northern constellation Ursa Minor; *also* : NORTH STAR

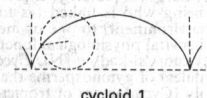

2 : one that serves to direct or guide 3 : a center of attraction or attention

Cyn·thia \'sin(t)-thē-ə\ *n* [L, fr. fem. of *Cynthius* of Cynthus, fr. *Cynthus,* mountain on Delos where she was born, fr. Gk *Kynthos*] 1 : ARTEMIS 2 : MOON

cy·pher *chiefly Brit var of* CIPHER

1cy pres \(')sī-'prā, (')sē-\ *n* [AF, so near, as near (as may be)] (1802) : a rule providing for the interpretation of instruments in equity as nearly as possible in conformity to the intention of the testator when literal construction is illegal, impracticable, or impossible — called also *cy pres doctrine*

2cy pres *adv* (1885) : in accordance with the rule of cy pres

1cy·press \'sī-prəs\ *n* [ME, fr. MF *ciprès,* fr. L *cyparissus,* fr. Gk *kyparissos*] (14c) 1 a (1) : any of a genus (*Cupressus*) of symmetrical mostly evergreen trees of the pine family with overlapping leaves resembling scales (2) : any of several coniferous trees other than the cypresses; *esp* : BALD CYPRESS 1 b : the wood of a cypress tree 2 : branches of cypress used as a symbol of mourning

2cypress *n* [ME *ciprus, cipres,* fr. *Cyprus,* Mediterranean island] (15c) : a silk or cotton usu. black gauze formerly used for mourning

cypress vine *n* (1819) : a tropical American vine (*Quamoclit pennata*) of the morning-glory family with red or white tubular flowers and finely dissected leaves

cyp·ri·an \'sip-rē-ən\ *n, often cap* [L *cyprius* of Cyprus, fr. Gk *kyprios,* fr. *Kypros* Cyprus, birthplace of Aphrodite] (1829) : PROSTITUTE

cyp·ri·nid \'sip-rə-nəd\ *n* [deriv. of L *cyprinus* carp, fr. Gk *kyprinos*] (ca. 1893) : any of a family (Cyprinidae) of soft-finned freshwater fishes including the carps and minnows — **cyprinid** *adj*

cy·prin·odont \sə-'prin-ə-,dänt\ *n* [deriv. of L *cyprinus* + Gk *odont-, odous* tooth — more at TOOTH] (1857) : any of an order (Microcyprini) of soft-finned fishes including the topminnows and killifishes — **cyprinodont** *adj*

cyp·ri·pe·di·um \,sip-rə-'pēd-ē-əm\ *n* [NL, genus name, fr. LL *Cypris,* a name for Venus + Gk *pedilon* sandal] (1813) : any of a genus (*Cypripedium* or *Paphiopedalum*) of leafy-stemmed terrestrial orchids having large usu. showy drooping flowers with the lip inflated or pouched — compare LADY'S SLIPPER

cy·pro·hep·ta·dine \,sī-prō-'hep-tə-,dēn\ *n* [*cyclic* + *propyl* + *hepta-* + *piperidine*] (1971) : a drug $C_{21}H_{21}N$ that acts antagonistically to histamine and serotonin and is used esp. in the treatment of asthma

cy·prot·er·one \sī-'prät-ə-,rōn\ *n* [prob. fr. *cycl-* + *progesterone*] (1966) : a synthetic steroid that inhibits androgenic secretions (as testosterone)

Cy·re·na·ic \,sir-ə-'nā-ik, ,sī-rə-\ *n* [L *cyrenaicus,* fr. Gk *kyrēnaikos,* fr. *Kyrēnē* Cyrene, Africa, home of Aristippus, author of the doctrine] (1586) : an adherent or advocate of the doctrine that pleasure is the chief end of life — **Cyrenaic** *adj* — **Cy·re·na·icism** \-'nā-ə-,siz-əm\ *n*

Cy·ril·lic \sə-'ril-ik\ *adj* [St. *Cyril,* reputed inventor of the Cyrillic alphabet] (1842) : of, relating to, or constituting an alphabet used for writing Old Church Slavonic and for Russian and various other Slavic languages

cyst \'sist\ *n* [NL *cystis,* fr. Gk *kystis* bladder, pouch] (1720) 1 : a closed sac having a distinct membrane and developing abnormally in a cavity or structure of the body 2 : a body resembling a cyst: as a : a resting spore of many algae b : an air vesicle (as of a rockweed) c : a capsule formed about a minute organism going into a resting or spore stage; *also* : this capsule with its contents d : a resistant cover about a parasite produced by the parasite or the host

cyst- *or* **cysti-** *or* **cysto-** *comb form* [F, fr. Gk *kyst-, kysto-,* fr. *kystis*] : bladder ⟨*cyst*itis⟩ : sac ⟨*cysto*carp⟩

-cyst \,sist\ *n comb form* [NL *-cystis,* fr. Gk *kystis*] : bladder : sac ⟨blasto*cyst*⟩

cys·te·amine \sis-'tē-ə-mən\ *n* [*cysteine* + *amine*] (1943) : a cysteine derivative C_2H_7NS that has been used in the prevention of radiation sickness (as of cancer patients)

cys·te·ine \'sis-tə-,ēn\ *n* [ISV, fr. *cystine* + *-ein*] (1884) : a crystalline sulfur-containing amino acid $C_3H_7NO_2S$ readily oxidizable to cystine

cys·tic \'sis-tik\ *adj* (1713) 1 : relating to, composed of, or containing cysts 2 : of or relating to the urinary bladder or the gallbladder 3 : enclosed in a cyst

cys·ti·cer·coid \,sis-tə-'sər-,kȯid\ *n* (1858) : a tapeworm larva having an invaginated scolex and solid tailpiece

cys·ti·cer·co·sis \,sis-tə-(,)sər-'kō-səs\ *n, pl* **-co·ses** \-'kō-,sēz\ [NL] (1905) : infestation with or disease caused by cysticerci

cys·ti·cer·cus \-'sər-kəs\ *n, pl* **-cer·ci** \-'sər-,sī, -,kī\ [NL, fr. *cyst-* + Gk *kerkos* tail] (1841) : a tapeworm larva that consists of a fluid-filled sac containing an invaginated scolex and is situated in the tissues of an intermediate host

cystic fibrosis *n* (1954) : a common hereditary disease esp. in Caucasian populations that appears usu. in early childhood, involves generalized disorder of exocrine glands, and is marked esp. by faulty digestion due to a deficiency of pancreatic enzymes, by difficulty in breathing, and by excessive loss of salt in the sweat

cys·tine \'sis-,tēn\ *n* [fr. its discovery in bladder stones] (1843) : a crystalline amino acid $C_6H_{12}N_2O_4S_2$ that is widespread in proteins (as keratins) and is a major metabolic sulfur source

cys·tin·uria \,sis-tə-'n(y)u̇r-ē-ə\ *n* [NL] (1853) : a familial metabolic defect characterized by excretion of excessive amounts of cystine in the urine

cys·ti·tis \sis-'tīt-əs\ *n* [NL] (ca. 1864) : inflammation of the urinary bladder

cys·to·carp \'sis-tə-,kärp\ *n* [ISV] (1875) : the fruiting structure produced in the red algae after fertilization

cys·to·lith \'sis-tə-,lith\ *n* [G *zystolith,* fr. *zyst-* cyst- + *-lith*] (1857) : a calcium carbonate concretion arising from the cellulose wall of cells of higher plants

cys·to·scope \'sis-tə-,skōp\ *n* [ISV] (1889) : an instrument for the visual examination of the bladder and for the passage of instruments under visual control — **cys·to·scop·ic** \,sis-tə-'skäp-ik\ *adj*

cyt- *or* **cyto-** *comb form* [G *zyt-, zyto-,* fr. Gk *kytos* hollow vessel — more at HIDE] 1 : cell ⟨*cyto*logy⟩ 2 : cytoplasm ⟨*cyto*kinesis⟩

-cyte \,sīt\ *n comb form* [NL *-cyta,* fr. Gk *kytos* hollow vessel] : cell ⟨leuko*cyte*⟩

Cyth·er·ea \,sith-ə-'rē-ə\ *n* [L, fr. Gk *Kythereia,* fr. *Kythēra* Cythera, island associated with Aphrodite] : APHRODITE

Cyth·er·e·an \-'rē-ən\ *adj* (1885) : of or relating to the planet Venus

cy·ti·dine \'sit-ə-,dēn, 'sīt-\ *n* [*cytosine* + *-idine*] (1911) : a nucleoside containing cytosine

cy·ti·dyl·ic acid \,sit-ə-,dil-ik-, ,sīt-\ *n* [*cytidine* + *-yl* + *-ic*] (1936) : a nucleotide containing cytosine

cy·to·cha·la·sin \,sīt-ō-kə-'lā-sən\ *n* [*cyt-* + Gk *chalasis* slackening + E *-in*] (1967) : any of a group of metabolites isolated from fungi (esp. *Helminthosporium dematioideum*) that inhibit various cell processes

cy·to·chem·is·try \-'kem-ə-strē\ *n* (ca. 1905) 1 : microscopical biochemistry 2 : the chemistry of cells — **cy·to·chem·i·cal** \-'kem-i-kəl\ *adj*

cy·to·chrome \'sīt-ə-,krōm\ *n* (1925) : any of several intracellular hemoprotein respiratory pigments that are enzymes functioning as transporters of electrons to molecular oxygen by undergoing alternate oxidation and reduction

cytochrome c *n, often ital 2d c* (1940) : the most abundant and stable of the cytochromes

cytochrome oxidase *n* (1942) : an iron-porphyrin enzyme important in cell respiration because of its ability to catalyze the oxidation of reduced cytochrome c in the presence of oxygen

cy·to·dif·fer·en·ti·a·tion \'sīt-ō-,dif-ə-,ren-chē-'ā-shən\ *n* (1959) : the development of specialized cells (as muscle, blood, or nerve cells) from undifferentiated precursors

cy·to·ge·net·ics \,sīt-ō-jə-'net-iks\ *n pl but sing or pl in constr* [ISV] (1942) : a branch of biology that deals with the study of heredity and variation by the methods of both cytology and genetics — **cy·to·ge·net·ic** \-jə-'net-ik\ *or* **cy·to·ge·net·i·cal** \-i-kəl\ *adj* — **cy·to·ge·net·i·cal·ly** \-i-k(ə-)lē\ *adv* — **cy·to·ge·net·i·cist** \-'net-ə-səst\ *n*

cy·to·ki·ne·sis \,sīt-ō-kə-'nē-səs, -kī-\ *n* [NL] (1919) 1 : the cytoplasmic changes accompanying mitosis 2 : cleavage of the cytoplasm into daughter cells following nuclear division — **cy·to·ki·net·ic** \-'net-ik\ *adj*

cy·to·ki·nin \,sīt-ə-'kī-nən\ *n* [*cyt-* + *kinin*] (1965) : any of various plant growth substances that are usu. derivatives of adenine

cy·tol·o·gy \sī-'täl-ə-jē\ *n* [ISV] (1889) 1 : a branch of biology dealing with the structure, function, multiplication, pathology, and life history of cells 2 : the cytological aspects of a process or structure — **cy·to·log·i·cal** \,sīt-ᵊl-'äj-i-kəl\ *or* **cy·to·log·ic** \-'äj-ik\ *adj* — **cy·to·log·i·cal·ly** \-i-k(ə-)lē\ *adv* — **cy·tol·o·gist** \sī-'täl-ə-jəst\ *n*

cy·to·ly·sin \,sīt-ᵊl-'īs-ᵊn\ *n* [ISV] (ca. 1903) : a substance (as an antibody that lyses bacteria) producing cytolysis

cy·tol·y·sis \sī-'täl-ə-səs\ *n* [NL] (1907) : the usu. pathologic dissolution or disintegration of cells — **cy·to·lyt·ic** \,sīt-ᵊl-'it-ik\ *adj*

cy·to·me·gal·ic \,sīt-ō-mi-'gal-ik\ *adj* [NL *cytomegalia* condition of having enlarged cells (fr. *cyt-* + *megal-* + *-ia*) + E *-ic*] (1952) : characterized by or causing the formation of enlarged cells

cy·to·meg·a·lo·vi·rus \,sīt-ə-,meg-ə-lō-'vī-rəs\ *n* [NL, fr. *cytomegalia* + *-o-* + *virus*] (1963) : any of several viruses that cause cellular enlargement and formation of eosinophilic inclusion bodies esp. in the nucleus and include the causative agent of a severe disease esp. of newborns that usu. affects the salivary glands, brain, kidneys, liver, and lungs

cy·to·mem·brane \,sīt-ō-'mem-,brān\ *n* (1962) : one of the cellular membranes including those of the plasmalemma, endoplasmic reticulum, nuclear envelope, and Golgi apparatus; *specif* : UNIT MEMBRANE

cy·to·path·ic \,sīt-ə-'path-ik\ *adj* (1952) : of, relating to, characterized by, or producing pathological changes in cells

cy·to·patho·gen·ic \-,path-ə-'jen-ik\ *adj* [*cyt-* + *pathogenic*] (1952) : pathologic for or destructive to cells — **cy·to·patho·ge·nic·i·ty** \-jə-'nis-ət-ē\ *n*

cy·to·phil·ic \,sīt-ə-'fil-ik\ *adj* (ca. 1909) : having an affinity for cells ⟨~ antibodies⟩

cy·to·pho·tom·e·try \-fō-'täm-ə-trē\ *n* (1955) : photometry applied to the study of the cell or its constituents — **cy·to·pho·to·met·ric** \-,fōt-ə-'me-trik\ *adj*

cy·to·plasm \'sīt-ə-,plaz-əm\ *n* [ISV] (1874) : the protoplasm of a cell external to the nuclear membrane — see CELL illustration — **cy·to·plas·mic** \,sīt-ə-'plaz-mik\ *adj* — **cy·to·plas·mi·cal·ly** \-mi-k(ə-)lē\ *adv*

cy·to·sine \'sīt-ə-,sēn\ *n* [ISV *cyt-* + *-ose* + *-ine*] (1894) : a pyrimidine base $C_4H_5N_3O$ that codes genetic information in the polynucleotide chain of DNA or RNA — compare ADENINE, GUANINE, THYMINE, URACIL

cy·to·sol \'sīt-ə-,säl, -,sȯl\ *n* (1970) : the fluid portion of the cytoplasm exclusive of organelles and membranes that is usu. obtained as the supernatant fraction from high-speed centrifugation of a tissue homogenate — **cy·to·sol·ic** \,sīt-ə-'säl-ik, -'sȯl-\ *adj*

cy·to·stat·ic \,sīt-ə-'stat-ik\ *adj* (1949) : tending to retard cellular activity and multiplication ⟨~ treatment of tumor cells⟩ — **cytostatic** *n* — **cy·to·stat·i·cal·ly** \-i-k(ə-)lē\ *adv*

cy·to·tax·on·o·my \,sīt-ō-(,)tak-'sän-ə-mē\ *n* (ca. 1930) 1 : study of the relationships and classification of organisms using both classical systematic techniques and comparative studies of chromosomes 2 : the nuclear cytologic makeup of a kind of organism — **cy·to·tax·o·nom·ic** \-,tak-sə-'näm-ik\ *adj* — **cy·to·tax·o·nom·i·cal·ly** \-i-k(ə-)lē\ *adv*

cy·to·tech·nol·o·gist \,sīt-ə-tek-'näl-ə-jəst\ *n* (1961) : a medical technician trained in the identification of cells and cellular abnormalities (as in cancer) — **cy·to·tech·nol·o·gy** \-ə-jē\ *n*

cy·to·tox·ic \,sīt-ə-'täk-sik\ *adj* (1904) 1 : of or relating to a cytotoxin 2 : toxic to cells ⟨~ properties of platinum⟩ — **cy·to·tox·ic·i·ty** \-(,)täk-'sis-ət-ē\ *n*

cy·to·tox·in \-'täk-sən\ *n* (1902) : a substance (as a toxin or antibody) having a toxic effect on cells

czar \'zär, '(t)sär\ *n* [NL *czar,* fr. Russ *tsar',* prob. fr. Goth *kaisar,* fr. Gk or L; Gk, fr. L *Caesar* — more at CAESAR] (1555) 1 : EMPEROR; *specif* : the ruler of Russia until the 1917 revolution 2 : one having great power or authority ⟨a banking ~⟩ — **czar·dom** \'zärd-əm, '(t)särd-\ *n*

czar·das \'chär-ˌdash, -ˌdäsh\ *n, pl* **czardas** [Hung *csárdás*] (1860) : a Hungarian dance to music in duple time in which the dancers start slowly and finish with a rapid whirl

czar·e·vitch \'zär-ə-ˌvich, '(t)sär-\ *n* [Russ *tsarevich*, fr. *tsar'* + *-evich*, patronymic suffix] (1710) : an heir apparent of a Russian czar

cza·ri·na \zä-'rē-nə, (t)sä-\ *n* [prob. modif. of G *zarin*, fr. *zar* czar, fr. Russ *tsar'*] (1717) : the wife of a czar

czar·ism \'zär-ˌiz-əm, '(t)sär-\ *n* (1855) **1** : the government of Russia under the czars **2** : autocratic rule — **czar·ist** \'zär-əst, '(t)sär-\ *n or adj*

cza·ri·tza \zä-'rit-sə, (t)sä-, -'rēt-\ *n* [Russ *tsaritsa*, fem. of *tsar'*] (1698) : CZARINA

Czech \'chek\ *n* [Czech *Čech*] (1841) **1** : a native or inhabitant of Czechoslovakia; *esp* : a native or inhabitant of Bohemia, Moravia, or Silesia provinces **2** : the Slavic language of the Czechs — **Czech** *adj* — **Czech·ish** \-ish\ *adj*

d \'dē\ *n, pl* **d's** *or* **ds** \'dēz\ *often cap, often attrib* **1 a** : the 4th letter of the English alphabet **b** : a graphic representation of this letter **c** : a speech counterpart of orthographic *d* **2** : 500 — see NUMBER table **3** : the 2d tone of a C-major scale **4** : a graphic device for reproducing the letter *d* **5** : one designated *d* esp. as the 4th in order or class **6 a** : a grade rating a student's work as poor in quality **b** : one graded or rated with a D **7** : something shaped like the letter D; *specif* : a semicircle on a pool table about 23 inches in diameter for use esp. in snooker

d- \ˌdē, 'dē\ *prefix* [ISV, fr. *dextr-*] **1** : dextrorotatory ⟨*d*-tartaric acid⟩ **2** : having a similar configuration at a selected carbon atom to the configuration of dextrorotatory glyceraldehyde — usu. printed as a small capital ⟨D-fructose⟩

-d *symbol* — used after the figure 2 or 3 to indicate the ordinal number second or third ⟨2d⟩ ⟨53d⟩

'd \d, əd\ *vb* **1** : HAD **2** : WOULD **3** : DID

DA \ˌdē-'ā\ *n* [*duck's ass*; fr. its resemblance to the tail of a duck] (1951) : DUCKTAIL

¹dab \'dab\ *n* [ME *dabbe*] (14c) **1** : a sudden blow or thrust : POKE **2** : a gentle touch or stroke : PAT

²dab *vb* **dabbed; dab·bing** *vt* (1562) **1** : to strike or touch lightly : PAT **2** : to apply lightly or irregularly : DAUB ~ *vi* : to make a dab — **dab·ber** *n*

³dab *n* (1729) **1** : a small amount **2** : DAUB

⁴dab *n* [AF *dabbe*] (15c) : FLATFISH; *esp* : any of several flounders (genus *Limanda*)

⁵dab *n* [perh. alter. of *adept*] *chiefly Brit* (1691) : a skillful person

dab·ble \'dab-əl\ *vb* **dab·bled; dab·bling** \-(ə-)liŋ\ [perh. freq. of *dab*] *vt* (1557) : to wet by splashing or by little dips or strokes : SPATTER ~ *vi* **1 a** : to paddle, splash, or play in or as if in water **b** : to reach with the bill to the bottom of shallow water in order to obtain food **2** : to work or concern oneself superficially ⟨~s in art⟩

dab·bler \-(ə-)lər\ *n* (1611) : one that dabbles: as **a** : one not deeply engaged in or concerned with something **b** : a duck (as a mallard or shoveler) that feeds by dabbling — called also *dabbling duck, puddle duck, river duck, surface feeder* **syn** see AMATEUR

dab·bling \-(ə-)liŋ\ *n* (ca. 1847) : a superficial or intermittent interest, investigation, or experiment ⟨his ~s in philosophy and art⟩

dab·chick \'dab-ˌchik\ *n* [prob. irreg. fr. obs. E *dop* (to dive) + E *chick*] (1575) : any of several small grebes

dab hand *n* [*dab*] *chiefly Brit* (ca. 1828) : EXPERT

da ca·po \dä-'käp-(ˌ)ō, də-\ *adv or adj* [It] (ca. 1724) : from the beginning — used as a direction in music to repeat

dace \'dās\ *n, pl* **dace** [ME *dace, darce*, fr. MF *dars*, fr. ML *darsus*] (15c) **1** : a small freshwater European cyprinid fish (*Leuciscus leuciscus*) **2** : any of various small No. American freshwater cyprinid fishes

da·cha \'däch-ə\ *n* [Russ, lit., gift; akin to L *datus* given — more at DATE] (1896) : a Russian country cottage used esp. in the summer

dachs·hund \'däks-ˌhúnt, -ˌhúnd; 'däk-sənt; 'dash-ˌhaúnd, -ənd\ *n* [G, fr. *dachs* badger + *hund* dog] (1881) : any of a German breed of long-bodied, short-legged dogs that occur in short-haired, long-haired, and wirehaired varieties

Da·cron \'dā-ˌkrän, 'dak-ˌrän\ *trademark* — used for a synthetic polyester textile fiber

dac·tyl \'dak-t²l\ *n* [ME *dactile*, fr. L *dactylus*, fr. Gk *daktylos*, lit., finger; fr. the fact that the first of three syllables is the longest, like the joints of the finger] (14c) : a metrical foot consisting of one long and two short syllables or of one stressed and two unstressed syllables (as in *tenderly*) — **dac·tyl·ic** \dak-'til-ik\ *adj or n*

dactyl- *or* **dactylo-** *comb form* [Gk *daktyl-, daktylo-*, fr. *daktylos*] : finger : toe : digit ⟨*dactyl*itis⟩

dac·ty·lol·o·gy \ˌdak-tə-'läl-ə-jē\ *n* (ca. 1656) : the art of communicating ideas by signs made with the fingers

-dac·ty·lous \'dak-tə-ləs\ *adj comb form* [Gk *-daktylos*, fr. *daktylos*] : having (such or so many) fingers or toes ⟨di*dactylous*⟩

dad \'dad\ *n* [prob. baby talk] (15c) : FATHER

Da·da \'däd-(ˌ)ä\ *n* [F] (1919) : a movement in art and literature based on deliberate irrationality and negation of traditional artistic values; *also* : the art and literature produced by this movement — **da·da·ism** \-ˌiz-əm\ *n, often cap* (1919) : DADA — **da·da·ist** \-ˌist\ *n or adj, often cap* — **da·da·is·tic** \ˌdäd-ä-'is-tik\ *adj, often cap*

dad·dy \'dad-ē\ *n, pl* **daddies** (15c) : FATHER

dad·dy long·legs \ˌdad-ē-'lȯŋ-ˌlegz, -ˌlägz\ *n, pl* **daddy longlegs** (1814) : any of various animals with long slender legs: as **a** : CRANE FLY **b** : HARVESTMAN

¹da·do \'dād-(ˌ)ō\ *n, pl* **dadoes** [It, die, plinth] (1664) **1 a** : the part of a pedestal of a column between the base and the surbase **b** : the lower part of an interior wall when specially decorated or faced; *also* : the decoration adorning this part of a wall **2** : a groove made by dadoing **3** : a tool (as a plane) for dadoing

²dado *vt* **da·doed; da·do·ing** (1890) **1** : to provide with a dado **2 a** : to set into a groove **b** : to cut a rectangular groove in (as a plank)

dado 1a: 1 surbase, 2 dado, 3 base

dae·dal \'dēd-²l\ *adj* [L *daedalus*, fr. Gk *daidalos* — more at CONDOLE] (1590) **1 a** : SKILLFUL, ARTISTIC **b** : INTRICATE ⟨the computer's ~ circuitry⟩ **2** : adorned with many things ⟨visions of cloud and light and ~ earth are the airman's daily scene —Laurence Binyon⟩

Dae·da·lus \'ded-²l-əs, 'dēd-\ *n* [L, fr. Gk *Daidalos*] : the legendary builder of the Cretan labyrinth who makes wings to enable himself and his son Icarus to escape imprisonment — **Dae·da·lian** \di-'dāl-yən\ *or* **Dae·da·lean** \di-'dāl-yən; ˌded-²l-'ē-ən, ˌdēd-\ *adj*

dae·mon *var of* DEMON

daff \'daf\ *vt* [alter. of *doff*] (1596) **1** *archaic* : to thrust aside **2** *obs* : to put off (as with an excuse)

daf·fo·dil \'daf-ə-ˌdil\ *n* [prob. fr. D *de affodil* the asphodel, fr. *de* the (fr. MD) + *affodil* asphodel, fr. MF *afrodille*, fr. L *asphodelus*; akin to OHG *thaz* the — more at THAT, ASPHODEL] (1548) : any of various bulbous herbs (genus *Narcissus*); *esp* : a plant whose flowers have a large corona elongated into a trumpet — compare JONQUIL

daf·fy \'daf-ē\ *adj* **daf·fi·er; -est** [obs. E *daff*, n. (fool)] (1884) : CRAZY, FOOLISH — **daf·fi·ly** \'daf-ə-lē\ *adv*

daft \'daft\ *adj* [ME *dafte* gentle, stupid; akin to OE *gedæfte* mild, gentle, ME *defte* deft, L *faber* smith] (14c) **1 a** : SILLY, FOOLISH **b** : MAD, INSANE **2** *Scot* : frivolously gay — **daft·ly** *adv* — **daft·ness** \'daf(t)-nəs\ *n*

dag \'dag\ *n* [ME *dagge*] (14c) **1** : a hanging end or shred **2** : matted or manure-coated wool

dag·ger \'dag ər\ *n* [ME] (14c) **1** : a sharp pointed knife for stabbing **2** : something that resembles a dagger **b** : a character † used as a reference mark or to indicate a death date

da·go \'dā-(ˌ)gō\ *n, pl* **dagos** *or* **dagoes** [alter. of earlier *diego*, fr. *Diego*, a common Sp given name] (1832) : a person of Italian or Spanish birth or descent — usu. used disparagingly

da·guerre·o·type \də-'ger-(ē-)ə-ˌtīp\ *n* [F *daguerréotype*, fr. L. J. M. *Daguerre* + F *-o- + type*] (1839) : an early photograph produced on a silver or a silver-covered copper plate; *also* : the process of producing such photographs — **daguerreotype** *vt* — **da·guerre·o·ty·py** \-ˌtī-pē\ *n*

dah \'dä\ *n* [imit.] (1940) : a dash in radio or telegraphic code

dahl·ia \'dal-yə, 'däl-, *U.S. also & Brit usu* 'dāl-\ *n* [NL, genus name, fr. Anders *Dahl* †1789 Swed. botanist] (1840) : any of a genus (*Dahlia*) of American tuberous-rooted composite herbs having opposite pinnate leaves and rayed flower heads and including many that are cultivated as ornamentals

dai·kon \'dīk-ən\ *n* [Jp, fr. *dai* big + *kon* root] (1876) : a radish (*Raphanus sativus longipinnatus*) of Japan with long hard durable roots that are eaten cooked or raw

¹dai·ly \'dā-lē\ *adj* (15c) **1 a** : occurring, made, or acted upon every day **b** : issued every day or every weekday **c** : of or providing for every day **2 a** : reckoned by the day ⟨average ~ wage⟩ **b** : covering the period of or based on a day ⟨~ statistics⟩ — **dai·li·ness** *n*

²daily *adv* (15c) **1** : every day **2** : every weekday

³daily *n, pl* **dailies** (1823) **1** : a newspaper published every weekday **2** *Brit* : a servant who works on a daily basis **3** *pl* : RUSH 6

daily double *n* (1942) : a system of betting (as on horse races) in which the bettor must pick the winners of two stipulated races in order to win

daily dozen *n* (1919) **1** : a series of physical exercises to be performed daily : WORKOUT **2** : a set of routine duties or tasks

dai·mon \'dī-ˌmōn\ *n, pl* **dai·mo·nes** \'dī-mə-ˌnēz\ *or* **daimons** [Gk *daimōn*] (1852) : DEMON 2, 3 — **dai·mon·ic** \dī-'män-ik\ *adj*

dai·myo *or* **dai·mio** \'dī-mē-ˌō, (')dī-'myō\ *n, pl* **-myos** *or* **-mios** [Jp *daimyō*] (1727) : a Japanese feudal baron

¹dain·ty \'dänt-ē\ *n, pl* **dainties** [ME *deinte*, fr. OF *deintié*, fr. L *dignitat-, dignitas* dignity, worth] (14c) **1 a** : something delicious to the taste **b** : something choice or pleasing **2** *obs* : FASTIDIOUSNESS

²dainty *adj* **dain·ti·er; -est** (14c) **1 a** : tasting good : TASTY **b** : attractively prepared and served **2** : marked by delicate or diminutive beauty, form, or grace **3** *obs* : CHARY, RELUCTANT **4 a** : marked by fastidious discrimination or finical taste **b** : showing avoidance of anything rough **syn** see CHOICE — **dain·ti·ly** \'dänt-²l-ē\ *adv* — **dain·ti·ness** \'dänt-ē-nəs\ *n*

dai·qui·ri \ˈdī-kə-rē, ˈdak-ə-\ *n* [*Daiquirí*, Cuba] (1921) **:** a cocktail made of rum, lime juice, and sugar

dairy \ˈde(ə)r-ē, ˈda(ə)r-\ *n, pl* **dair·ies** [ME *deyerie*, fr. *deye* dairymaid, fr. OE *dǣge* kneader of bread; akin to OE *dāg* dough — more at DOUGH] (13c) **1 :** a room, building, or establishment where milk is kept and butter or cheese is made **2 a :** the department of farming or of a farm that is concerned with the production of milk, butter, and cheese **b :** a farm devoted to such production **3 :** an establishment for the sale or distribution chiefly of milk and milk products

dairy breed *n* (1858) **:** a cattle breed developed chiefly for milk production

dairy cattle *n pl* (1895) **:** cattle of one of the dairy breeds

dairy·ing \ˈder-ē-iŋ\ *n* (1649) **:** the business of operating a dairy

dairy·maid \-ē-ˌmād\ *n* (1599) **:** a woman employed in a dairy

dairy·man \-ē-mən, -ˌman\ *n* (1784) **:** one who operates a dairy farm or works in a dairy

da·is \ˈdā-əs, ˈdī-\ *n* [ME *deis*, fr. OF, fr. LL *discus* high table, fr. L, dish, quoit — more at DISH] (13c) **:** a raised platform in a hall or large room

dai·shi·ki \dī-ˈshē-kē\ *var of* DASHIKI

dai·sy \ˈdā-zē\ *n, pl* **daisies** [ME *dayeseye*, fr. OE *dægeseāge*, fr. *dæg* day + *ēage* eye] (bef. 12c) **1 :** a composite plant (as of the genera *Bellis* or *Chrysanthemum*) having a flower head with well-developed ray flowers usu. arranged in one or a few whorls: as **a :** a low European herb (*Bellis perennis*) with white or pink ray flowers — called also *English daisy* **b :** a leafy-stemmed perennial herb (*Chrysanthemum leucanthemum*) that has long white ray flowers and a yellow disk and is often a troublesome weed in parts of the U.S. — called also *oxeye daisy* **2 :** the flower head of a daisy **3 :** a first-rate person or thing

daisy ham *n* (ca. 1938) **:** a boned and smoked piece of pork from the shoulder

daisy wheel *n* [fr. its resemblance to the flower] (ca. 1978) **:** a printing element of an electric typewriter or printer that consists of a disk with spokes bearing type

Da·ko·ta \də-ˈkōt-ə\ *n, pl* **Dakotas** *also* **Dakota** (1804) **1 :** a member of an American Indian people of the northern Mississippi valley **2 :** the language of the Dakota people

Da·lai La·ma \ˌdäl-ˌī-ˈläm-ə, ˌdäl-ˌā-, ˌdal-\ *n* [Mongolian *dalai* ocean] (1698) **:** the spiritual head of Lamaism

dal·a·pon \ˈdal-ə-ˌpän\ *n* [perh. fr. *di-* + *alpha* + *propionic* acid] (1953) **:** an herbicide $C_3H_4Cl_2O_2$ that kills monocotyledonous plants selectively and is used esp. on unwanted grasses

da·la·si \dä-ˈläs-ē\ *n, pl* **dalasi** *or* **dalasis** [native name in Gambia] (1971) — see MONEY table

dale \ˈdā(ə)l\ *n* [ME, fr. OE *dæl*; akin to OHG *tal* valley, Gk *tholos* rotunda] (bef. 12c) **:** VALLEY, VALE ⟨went riding over hill and ∼⟩

dales·man \ˈdā(ə)lz-mən\ *n, Brit* (1769) **:** one living or born in a dale

da·leth \ˈdäl-ˌeth, -ˌet\ *n* [Heb *dāleth*, fr. *deleth* door] (1823) **:** the 4th letter of the Hebrew alphabet — see ALPHABET table

dal·li·ance \ˈdal-ē-ən(t)s\ *n* (14c) **:** an act of dallying: as **a :** PLAY; *esp* **:** amorous play **b :** frivolous action **:** TRIFLING

Dal·lis grass \ˈdal-əs-\ *n* [perh. alter. of *Dallas*, Texas] (ca. 1922) **:** a tall tufted tropical perennial grass (*Paspalum dilatatum*) introduced as a pasture and forage grass in the southern U.S.

Dall sheep \ˈdȯl-\ *or* **Dall's sheep** \ˈdȯlz-\ *n* [William H. *Dall* †1927 Am. naturalist] (ca. 1910) **:** a large white wild sheep (*Ovis montana dalli* or *O. dalli*) of northwestern No. America

dal·ly \ˈdal-ē\ *vi* **dal·lied; dal·ly·ing** [ME *dalyen*, fr. AF *dalier*] (15c) **1 a :** to act playfully; *esp* **:** to play amorously **b :** to deal lightly **:** TOY ⟨accused him of ∼*ing* with a serious problem⟩ **2 a :** to waste time **b :** LINGER, DAWDLE ***syn*** see TRIFLE, DELAY — **dal·li·er** *n*

dal·ma·tian \dal-ˈmā-shən\ *n, often cap* [fr. the supposed origin of the breed in Dalmatia] (1810) **:** any of a breed of medium-sized dogs having a white short-haired coat with black or brown spots

dal·mat·ic \dal-ˈmat-ik\ *n* [ME *dalmatyk*, fr. OE *dalmatice*, fr. LL *dalmatica*, fr. L, fem. of *dalmaticus* Dalmatian, fr. *Dalmatia*] (bef. 12c) **1 :** a wide-sleeved overgarment with slit sides worn by a deacon or prelate — see VESTMENT illustration **2 :** a robe worn by a British sovereign at his or her coronation

dal se·gno \däl-ˈsān-(ˌ)yō\ *adv* [It, from the sign] (ca. 1854) — used as a direction in music to return to the sign that marks the beginning of a repeat

[1]**dam** \ˈdam\ *n* [ME *dam*, *dame* lady, dam — more at DAME] (13c) **:** a female parent — used esp. of a domestic animal

[2]**dam** *n* [ME] (14c) **1 :** a body of water confined by a barrier **2 a :** a barrier preventing the flow of water or of loose solid materials (as soil or snow); *esp* **:** a barrier built across a watercourse for impounding water **b :** a barrier to check the flow of liquid, gas, or air

[3]**dam** *vt* **dammed; dam·ming** (15c) **1 :** to provide or restrain with a dam **2 :** to stop up **:** BLOCK

[1]**dam·age** \ˈdam-ij\ *n* [ME, fr. MF, fr. *dam* damage, fr. L *damnum*] (14c) **1 :** loss or harm resulting from injury to person, property, or reputation **2** *pl* **:** compensation in money imposed by law for loss or injury **3 :** EXPENSE, COST ⟨"What's the ∼?" he asked the waiter⟩

[2]**damage** *vt* **dam·aged; dam·ag·ing** (14c) **:** to cause damage to ***syn*** see INJURE — **dam·age·abil·i·ty** \ˌdam-ij-ə-ˈbil-ət-ē\ *n* — **dam·ag·er** *n*

dam·ag·ing *adj* (ca. 1828) **:** causing or able to cause damage **:** INJURIOUS ⟨has a ∼ effect on wildlife⟩ — **dam·ag·ing·ly** \ˈdam-ij-iŋ-lē\ *adv*

[1]**dam·a·scene** \ˈdam-ə-ˌsēn, ˌdam-ə-ˈ\ *n* (14c) **1** *cap* **:** a native or inhabitant of Damascus **2 :** DAMASK 2b

[2]**damascene** *adj* (14c) **1** *cap* **:** of, relating to, or characteristic of Damascus or the Damascenes **2 :** of or relating to damask or the art of damascening

[3]**damascene** *vt* **-scened; -scen·ing** [MF *damasquiner*, fr. *damasquin* of Damascus] (1585) **:** to ornament (as iron or steel) with wavy patterns like those of watered silk or with inlaid work of precious metals

Da·mas·cus steel \də-ˌmas-kə(s)-\ *n* (ca. 1727) **:** hard elastic steel ornamented with wavy patterns and used esp. for sword blades

[1]**dam·ask** \ˈdam-əsk\ *n* [ME *damaske*, fr. ML *damascus*, fr. *Damascus*] (14c) **1 :** a firm lustrous fabric (as of linen, cotton, silk, or rayon) made with flat patterns in a satin weave on a plain-woven ground on jacquard looms **2 a :** DAMASCUS STEEL **b :** the characteristic markings of this steel **3 :** a grayish red

[2]**damask** *adj* (15c) **1 :** made of or resembling damask **2 :** of the color damask

damask rose *n* [obs. *Damask* of Damascus, fr. obs. *Damask* Damascus] (1540) **:** a large hardy fragrant pink rose (*Rosa damascena*) that is cultivated in Asia Minor as a source of attar of roses and is a parent of many hybrid perpetual roses

dame \ˈdām\ *n* [ME, fr. OF, fr. L *domina*, fem. of *dominus* master; akin to L *domus* house — more at TIMBER] (13c) **1 :** a woman of rank, station, or authority: as **a** *archaic* **:** the mistress of a household **b :** the wife or daughter of a lord **c :** a female member of an order of knighthood — used as a title prefixed to the given name **2 a :** an elderly woman **b :** WOMAN

dame school *n* (1817) **:** a school in which the rudiments of reading and writing were taught by a woman in her own home

dame's violet *n* (1578) **:** a Eurasian perennial plant (*Hesperis matronalis*) widely cultivated for its spikes of showy, single or double, and fragrant white or purple flowers — called also *dame's rocket, rocket*

dam·mar *or* **dam·ar** \ˈdam-ər\ *n* [Malay *damar*] (15c) **1 :** any of various hard resins derived esp. from evergreen trees (genus *Agathis*) of the pine family **2 :** a clear to yellow resin obtained in Malaya from several timber trees (family Dipterocarpaceae) and used in varnishes and inks

[1]**damn** \ˈdam\ *vb* **damned; damn·ing** \ˈdam-iŋ\ [ME *dampnen*, fr. OF *dampner*, fr. L *damnare*, fr. *damnum* damage, loss, fine] *vt* (13c) **1 :** to condemn to a punishment or fate; *esp* **:** to condemn to hell **2 a :** to condemn vigorously and often irascibly for some real or fancied fault or defect ⟨∼*ed* the storm for their delay⟩ **b :** to condemn as a failure by public criticism **3 :** to bring ruin on **4 :** to swear at **:** CURSE ∼ *vi* **:** CURSE, SWEAR ***syn*** see EXECRATE

[2]**damn** *n* (1619) **1 :** the utterance of the word *damn* as a curse **2 :** a minimum amount or degree (as of care or consideration) **:** the least bit ⟨don't give a ∼⟩

[3]**damn** *adj or adv* (1775) **:** DAMNED ⟨a ∼ nuisance⟩ ⟨ran ∼ fast⟩ — **damn well :** beyond doubt or question **:** CERTAINLY ⟨knew *damn well* what would happen⟩

dam·na·ble \ˈdam-nə-bəl\ *adj* (14c) **1 :** liable to or deserving condemnation **2 :** very bad **:** DETESTABLE ⟨∼ weather⟩ — **dam·na·ble·ness** *n* — **dam·na·bly** \-blē\ *adv*

dam·na·tion \dam-ˈnā-shən\ *n* (14c) **:** the act of damning **:** the state of being damned

dam·na·to·ry \ˈdam-nə-ˌtōr-ē, -ˌtȯr-\ *adj* (1682) **:** expressing, imposing, or causing condemnation **:** CONDEMNATORY

[1]**damned** \ˈdam(d)\ *adj* **damned·er** \ˈdam-dər\; **damned·est** *or* **damnd·est** \-dəst\ (1563) **1 :** DAMNABLE ⟨hoping to get away from this ∼ smog⟩ **2 :** COMPLETE, UTTER — often used as an intensive **3 :** EXTRAORDINARY — used in the superlative ⟨the ∼*est* contraption he ever saw⟩

[2]**damned** \ˈdam(d)\ *adv* (1757) **:** EXTREMELY, VERY ⟨a ∼ good job⟩

damned·est *or* **damnd·est** \ˈdam-dəst\ *n* (1830) **:** UTMOST, BEST — used chiefly in the phrase *do one's damnedest* ⟨doing his ∼ to win⟩

dam·ni·fy \ˈdam-nə-ˌfī\ *vt* **-fied; -fy·ing** [MF *damnifier*, fr. OF, fr. LL *damnificare*, fr. L *damnificus* injurious, fr. *damnum* damage] (1512) **:** to cause loss or damage to ⟨intimidation — the freedom to ∼ another person with impunity —Henry Hazlitt⟩

damn·ing \ˈdam-iŋ\ *adj* (1599) **1 :** bringing damnation ⟨a ∼ sin⟩ **2 :** causing or leading to condemnation or ruin ⟨presented some ∼ testimony⟩ — **damn·ing·ly** \-iŋ-lē\ *adv*

Dam·o·cles \ˈdam-ə-ˌklēz\ *n* [L, fr. Gk *Damoklēs*] **:** a courtier of ancient Syracuse held to have been seated at a banquet beneath a sword hung by a single hair — **Dam·o·cle·an** \ˌdam-ə-ˈklē-ən\ *adj*

Da·mon \ˈdā-mən\ *n* [L, fr. Gk *Damōn*] **:** a legendary Sicilian who pledges his life for his condemned friend Pythias

[1]**damp** \ˈdamp\ *n* [MD or MLG, vapor; akin to OHG *damph* vapor, OE *dimm* dim] (14c) **1 :** a noxious gas esp. in a coal mine **2 :** MOISTURE: **a :** HUMIDITY, DAMPNESS **b** *archaic* **:** FOG, MIST **3 a :** DISCOURAGEMENT, CHECK **b** *archaic* **:** DEPRESSION, DEJECTION

[2]**damp** *vt* (14c) **1 a :** to affect with or as if with a noxious gas **:** CHOKE **b :** to diminish the activity or intensity of — often used with *down* ⟨∼*ing* down the causes of inflation⟩ **c :** to check the vibration or oscillation of (as a string or voltage) **2 :** DAMPEN ∼ *vi* **:** to diminish progressively in vibration or oscillation

[3]**damp** *adj* (1590) **1 a** *archaic* **:** being confused, bewildered, or shocked **:** STUPEFIED **b :** DEPRESSED, DULL **2 :** slightly or moderately wet **:** MOIST; *also* **:** HUMID ***syn*** see WET — **damp·ish** \ˈdam-pish\ *adj* — **damp·ly** *adv* — **damp·ness** *n*

damp·en \ˈdam-pən\ *vb* **damp·ened; damp·en·ing** \ˈdamp-(ə-)niŋ\ *vt* (1630) **1 :** to check or diminish the activity or vigor of **:** DEADEN ⟨the heat ∼*ed* our spirits⟩ **2 :** to make damp ⟨the shower barely ∼*ed* the ground⟩ **3 :** DAMP 1c ∼ *vi* **1 :** to become damp **2 :** to become deadened or depressed — **damp·en·er** \ˈdamp-(ə-)nər\ *n*

damp·er \ˈdam-pər\ *n* (1748) **1 :** a dulling or deadening influence ⟨put a ∼ on the celebration⟩ **2 :** a device that damps: as **a :** a valve or plate (as in the flue of a furnace) for regulating the draft **b :** a small felted block to stop the vibration of a piano string **c :** a device designed to bring a mechanism to rest with minimum oscillation **d :** SHOCK ABSORBER

damp·ing–off \ˌdam-piŋ-ˈȯf\ *n* (1890) **:** a diseased condition of seedlings or cuttings caused by fungi and marked by wilting or rotting

dam·sel \ˈdam-zəl\ *also* **dam·o·sel** *or* **dam·o·zel** \ˈdam-ə-ˌzel\ *n* [ME *damesel*, fr. OF *dameisele*, fr. (assumed) VL *domnicella* young noblewoman, dim. of L *domina* lady] (13c) **:** a young woman: **a** *archaic* **:** a young unmarried woman of noble birth **b :** GIRL

dam·sel·fish \ˈdam-zəl-ˌfish\ *n* (1904) **:** any of numerous often brilliantly colored marine fishes (family Pomacentridae) living esp. along coral reefs — called also *demoiselle*

dam·sel·fly \-ˌflī\ *n* (1815) **:** any of numerous odonate insects (suborder Zygoptera) distinguished from dragonflies by laterally projecting eyes and petiolate wings folded above the body when at rest

dam·son \ˈdam-zən\ *n* [ME, fr. L *prunum damascenum*, lit., plum of Damascus] (14c) **:** an Asian plum (*Prunus insititia* or *P. domestica insititia*) cultivated for its small acid purple fruit; *also* **:** its fruit

\ə\ abut \ᵊ\ kitten, F table \ər\ further \a\ ash \ā\ ace \ä\ cot, cart \au̇\ out \ch\ chin \e\ bet \ē\ easy \g\ go \i\ hit \ī\ ice \j\ job \ŋ\ sing \ō\ go \ȯ\ law \ȯi\ boy \th\ thin \t͟h\ the \ü\ loot \u̇\ foot \y\ yet \zh\ vision \à, k̲, ⁿ, œ, œ̄, ue, ue̅, ʸ\ *see* Guide to Pronunciation

[1]**Dan** \'dan\ *n* [Heb *Dān*] : a son of Jacob and the traditional eponymous ancestor of one of the tribes of Israel

[2]**Dan** \(')dan\ *n* [ME, title of members of religious orders, fr. MF, fr. ML *domnus,* fr. L *dominus* master] *archaic* (13c) : MASTER, SIR

Dan·aë \'dan-ə-,ē\ *n* [L, fr. Gk *Danaē*] : a princess of Argos visited by Zeus in the form of a shower of gold and by him the mother of Perseus

[1]**dance** \'dan(t)s\ *vb* **danced; danc·ing** [ME *dauncen,* fr. OF *dancier*] *vi* (14c) **1** : to engage in or perform a dance **2** : to move or seem to move up and down or about in a quick or lively manner ~ *vt* **1** : to perform or take part in as a dancer **2** : to cause to dance **3** : to bring into a specified condition by dancing — **dance·able** \'dan(t)-sə-bəl\ *adj* — **danc·er** *n*

[2]**dance** *n, often attrib* (14c) **1** : an act or instance of dancing **2** : a series of rhythmic and patterned bodily movements usu. performed to music **3** : a social gathering for dancing **4** : a piece of music by which dancing may be guided **5** : the art of dancing

dan·de·li·on \'dan-dᵊl-,ī-ən\ *n* [MF *dent de lion,* lit., lion's tooth] (14c) : any of a genus (*Taraxacum*) of yellow-flowered composite plants; *esp* : an herb (*T. officinale*) sometimes grown as a potherb and nearly cosmopolitan as a weed

dan·der \'dan-dər\ *n* [alter. of *dandruff*] (1591) **1** : minute scales from hair, feathers, or skin that may be allergenic **2** : ANGER, TEMPER ⟨now don't get your ~ up⟩

dan·di·a·cal \dan-'dī-ə-kəl\ *adj* [[1]*dandy* + *-acal* (as in *demoniacal*)] (1831) : of, relating to, or suggestive of a dandy

Dan·die Din·mont terrier \,dan-dē-'din-,mänt-\ *n* [*Dandie Dinmont,* character owning six such dogs in the novel *Guy Mannering* by Sir Walter Scott] (1875) : any of a breed of terriers characterized by short legs, a long body, pendulous ears, a rough coat, and a full silky topknot

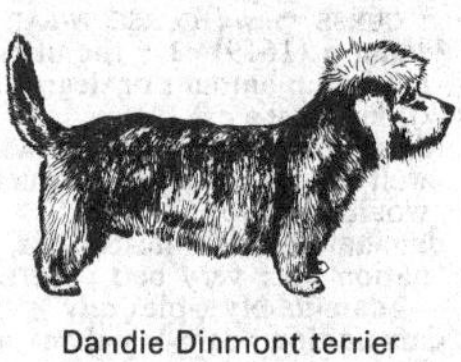
Dandie Dinmont terrier

dan·di·fy \'dan-di-,fī\ *vt* **-fied; -fy·ing** (1823) : to cause to resemble a dandy — **dan·di·fi·ca·tion** \,dan-di-fə-'kā-shən\ *n*

dan·dle \'dan-dᵊl\ *vt* **dan·dled; dan·dling** \-(d)liŋ, -dᵊl-iŋ\ [origin unknown] (1530) **1** : to move (as a baby) up and down in one's arms or on one's knee in affectionate play **2** : PAMPER, PET

dan·druff \'dan-drəf\ *n* [prob. fr. *dand-* (origin unknown) + *-ruff,* of Scand origin; akin to ON *hrūfa* scab; akin to OHG *hruf* scurf, Lith *kraupus* rough] (1545) : a scurf that forms on the scalp and comes off in small white or grayish scales — **dan·druffy** \-ē\ *adj*

[1]**dan·dy** \'dan-dē\ *n, pl* **dandies** [prob. short for *jack-a-dandy,* fr. [1]*jack* + *a* (of) + *dandy* (origin unknown)] (1780) **1** : a man who gives exaggerated attention to dress **2** : something excellent in its class **3** : a small 2-masted sailboat with a modified ketch rig — **dan·dy·ish** \-dē-ish\ *adj* — **dan·dy·ish·ly** *adv*

[2]**dandy** *adj* **dan·di·er; -est** (1792) **1** : of, relating to, or suggestive of a dandy : FOPPISH **2** : very good : FIRST-RATE ⟨a ~ place to stay⟩

dan·dy·ism \'dan-dē-,iz-əm\ *n* (1819) **1** : the style or conduct of a dandy **2** : a literary and artistic style of the latter part of the 19th century marked by artificiality and excessive refinement

Dane \'dān\ *n* [ME *Dan,* fr. ON *Danr*] (bef. 12c) **1** : a native or inhabitant of Denmark **2** : a person of Danish descent

dane·geld \'dān-,geld\ *n, often cap* [ME, fr. (assumed) *Danegeld, Denegeld,* fr. *Dane, Dene* Danes + *-geld* (as in *wergeld*)] (bef. 12c) : an annual tax believed to have been imposed orig. to buy off Danish invaders in England or to have maintain forces to oppose them but continued as a land tax

Dane·law \'dān-,lȯ\ *n* (bef. 12c) **1** : the law in force in the part of England held by the Danes before the Norman Conquest **2** : the part of England under the Danelaw

dang \'daŋ\ *adj or adv* [euphemism] (1914) : DAMN

[1]**dan·ger** \'dān-jər\ *n* [ME *daunger,* fr. OF *dangier,* alter. of *dongier,* fr. (assumed) VL *dominiarium,* fr. L *dominium* ownership] (13c) **1 a** *archaic* : JURISDICTION **b** *obs* : REACH, RANGE **2** *obs* : HARM, DAMAGE **3** : exposure or liability to injury, pain, harm, or loss ⟨a place where children could play without ~⟩ **4** : a case or cause of danger ⟨the ~s of mining⟩

[2]**danger** *vt, archaic* (14c) : ENDANGER

dan·ger·ous \'dānj-(ə-)rəs\ *adj* (15c) **1** : exposing to or involving danger **2** : able or likely to inflict injury — **dan·ger·ous·ly** *adv* — **dan·ger·ous·ness** *n*

syn DANGEROUS, HAZARDOUS, PRECARIOUS, PERILOUS, RISKY mean bringing or involving the chance of loss or injury. DANGEROUS applies to something that may cause harm or loss unless dealt with carefully; HAZARDOUS implies great and continuous risk of harm or failure and small chance of successfully avoiding disaster; PRECARIOUS suggests both insecurity and uncertainty; PERILOUS strongly implies the immediacy of danger; RISKY often applies to a known and accepted danger.

[1]**dan·gle** \'daŋ-gəl\ *vb* **dan·gled; dan·gling** \-g(ə-)liŋ\ [prob. of Scand origin; akin to Dan *dangle* to dangle] *vi* (1590) **1** : to hang loosely and usu. so as to be able to swing freely **2** : to be a hanger-on or a dependent **3** : to occur in a sentence without having a normally expected syntactic relation to the rest of the sentence ⟨the word *climbing* in "Climbing the mountain the cabin came into view" is *dangling*⟩ ~ *vt* **1** : to cause to dangle : SWING **2** : to keep hanging uncertainly — **dan·gler** \-g(ə-)lər\ *n*

[2]**dangle** *n* (1756) **1** : the action of dangling **2** : something that dangles

Dan·iel \'dan-yəl *also* 'dan-ᵊl\ *n* [Heb *Dānī'ēl*] **1** : the Jewish hero of the Book of Daniel who as an exile in Babylon interprets dreams, gives accounts of apocalyptic visions, and is divinely delivered from a den of lions **2** : a book of narratives, visions, and prophecies in canonical Jewish and Christian Scripture — see BIBLE table

da·nio \'dā-nē-,ō\ *n, pl* **da·ni·os** [NL, genus name] (ca. 1885) : any of several small brightly colored Asian cyprinid fishes

[1]**Dan·ish** \'dā-nish\ *adj* (bef. 12c) : of, relating to, or characteristic of Denmark, the Danes, or the Danish language

[2]**Danish** *n* (15c) **1** : the Germanic language of the Danes **2** *pl* **Danish** : a piece of Danish pastry

Danish pastry *n* (1928) : a pastry made of a rich raised dough

dank \'daŋk\ *adj* [ME *danke*] (1573) : unpleasantly moist or wet *syn* see WET — **dank·ly** *adv* — **dank·ness** *n*

dan·seur \dän-'sər, dän-\ *n* [F, fr. *danser* to dance] (1828) : a male ballet dancer

dan·seuse \dän-'sə(r)z, dän-'süz\ *n* [F, fem. of *danseur*] (1828) : a female ballet dancer

Dan·te·an \'dant-ē-ən\ *n* (1850) : a student or admirer of Dante

daph·ne \'daf-nē\ *n* [NL, genus name, fr. L, laurel, fr. Gk *daphnē*] (ca. 1864) : any of a genus (*Daphne*) of Eurasian shrubs of the mezereon family with apetalous flowers whose colored calyx resembles a corolla

Daph·ne \'daf-nē\ *n* [L, fr. Gk *Daphnē*] : a nymph who is transformed into a laurel tree to escape the pursuing Apollo

daph·nia \'daf-nē-ə\ *n* [NL, genus name] (1935) : any of a genus (*Daphnia*) of minute freshwater branchiopod crustaceans with biramous antennae used as locomotor organs — compare WATER FLEA

Daph·nis \'daf-nəs\ *n* [L, fr. Gk] : a Sicilian shepherd renowned in Greek myth as the inventor of pastoral poetry

dap·per \'dap-ər\ *adj* [ME *dapyr,* fr. MD *dapper* quick, strong; akin to OHG *tapfar* heavy, OSlav *debelŭ* thick] (15c) **1 a** : neat and trim in appearance **b** : excessively spruce and stylish **2** : alert and lively in movement and manners — **dap·per·ly** *adv* — **dap·per·ness** *n*

[1]**dap·ple** \'dap-əl\ *n* [ME *dappel-gray,* adj., gray variegated with spots of a different color] (1580) **1** : any of numerous usu. cloudy and rounded spots or patches of a color or shade different from their background **2** : the quality or state of being dappled **3** : a dappled animal

[2]**dapple** *vb* **dap·pled; dap·pling** \-(ə-)liŋ\ *vt* (1599) : to mark with dapples ~ *vi* : to become marked with dapples

dap·pled *also* **dap·ple** *adj* (15c) : marked with small spots or patches contrasting with the background ⟨a ~ fawn⟩

darb \'därb\ *n* [perh. alter. of [5]*dab*] (ca. 1915) : one that is extremely attractive or desirable

Dar·by and Joan \,där-bē-ən-'jō(-ə)n, -jō-'an\ *n* [prob. fr. *Darby & Joan,* couple in an 18th cent. song] (1857) : a happily married usu. elderly couple

Dard \'därd\ *n* (ca. 1885) : a complex of Indic languages spoken in the upper valley of the Indus — see INDO-EUROPEAN LANGUAGES table

Dar·dan \'därd-ᵊn\ *adj or n* [L *Dardanus,* fr. Gk *Dardanos*] *archaic* (1606) : TROJAN

Dar·da·ni·an \där-'dā-nē-ən\ *adj* (1596) : TROJAN

Dar·dic \'därd-ik\ *n* (1910) : DARD

[1]**dare** \'da(ə)r, 'de(ə)r\ *vb* **dared; dar·ing** [ME *dar* (1st & 3d sing. pres. indic.), fr. OE *dear;* akin to OHG *gitar* (1st & 3d sing. pres. indic.) dare, L *infestus* hostile] *verbal auxiliary* (bef. 12c) : to be sufficiently courageous to ⟨no one *dared* say a word⟩ ~ *vi* : to have sufficient courage ⟨try it if you ~⟩ ~ *vt* **1 a** : to challenge to perform an action esp. as a proof of courage ⟨*dared* him to jump⟩ **b** : to confront boldly : DEFY ⟨*dared* the anger of his family⟩ **2** : to have the courage to contend against, venture, or try ⟨the actress *dared* a new interpretation of this classic role⟩ — **dar·er** \'dar-ər, 'der-\ *n*

[2]**dare** *n* (1594) **1** : an act or instance of daring : CHALLENGE ⟨foolishly took a ~⟩ **2** : imaginative or vivacious boldness : DARING

[1]**dare·dev·il** \'da(ə)r-,dev-əl, 'de(ə)r-\ *n* (1794) : a recklessly bold person — **dare·dev·il·ry** \-əl-rē\ *n* — **dare·dev·il·try** \-əl-trē\ *n*

[2]**daredevil** *adj* (1832) : recklessly and often ostentatiously daring *syn* see ADVENTUROUS

dareful *adj, obs* (1605) : DARING

daren't \'da(ə)r-ənt, 'de(ə)r-\ : dare not

dare·say \(')da(ə)r-'sā, (')de(ə)r-\ *vt* (14c) : venture to say : think probable — used in pres. 1st sing. ~ *vi* : AGREE, SUPPOSE — used in pres. 1st sing.

[1]**dar·ing** *adj* (1582) : venturesomely bold in action or thought *syn* see ADVENTUROUS — **dar·ing·ly** \-iŋ-lē\ *adv* — **dar·ing·ness** *n*

[2]**daring** *n* (1611) : venturesome boldness

Dar·jee·ling \där-'jē-liŋ\ *n* [*Darjeeling,* India] (1882) : a tea of high quality grown esp. in the mountainous districts of northern India

[1]**dark** \'därk\ *adj* [ME *derk,* fr. OE *deorc;* akin to OHG *tarchannen* to hide, Gk *thrassein* to trouble] (bef. 12c) **1 a** : devoid or partially devoid of light : not receiving, reflecting, transmitting, or radiating light **b** : transmitting only a portion of light **2 a** : wholly or partially black **b** *of a color* : of low or very low lightness **3 a** : arising from or showing evil traits or desires : EVIL ⟨the ~ powers that lead to war⟩ **b** : DISMAL, GLOOMY ⟨had a ~ view of the future⟩ **c** : lacking knowledge or culture **4** : not clear to the understanding **5** : not fair in complexion : SWARTHY **6** : SECRET ⟨kept his plans ~⟩ **7** : possessing depth and richness ⟨a ~ voice⟩ **8** : closed to the public ⟨the theater is ~ in the summer⟩ *syn* see OBSCURE — **dark·ish** \'där-kish\ *adj* — **dark·ly** *adv* — **dark·ness** *n*

[2]**dark** *n* (13c) **1 a** : a place or time of little or no light : NIGHT, NIGHTFALL **b** : absence of light : DARKNESS **2** : a dark or deep color — **in the dark 1** : in secrecy ⟨most of his dealings were done *in the dark*⟩ **2** : in ignorance ⟨kept the public *in the dark* about the agreement⟩

[3]**dark** *vi, obs* (14c) : to grow dark ~ *vt* : to make dark

dark adaptation *n* (1909) : the phenomena including dilation of the pupil, increase in retinal sensitivity, shift of the region of maximum luminosity toward the blue, and regeneration of visual purple by which the eye adapts to conditions of reduced illumination — **dark–adapt·ed** \,där-kə-'dap-təd\ *adj*

Dark Ages *n pl* (1730) : the period from about A.D. 476 to about 1000; *broadly* : MIDDLE AGES

dark·en \'där-kən\ *vb* **dark·ened; dark·en·ing** \'därk-(ə-)niŋ\ *vi* (14c) : to grow dark : become obscured ~ *vt* **1** : to make dark **2** : to make less clear : OBSCURE ⟨the financial crisis ~*ed* the future of the company⟩ **3** : TAINT, TARNISH **4** : to cast a gloom over **5** : to make of darker color — **dark·en·er** \'därk-(ə-)nər\ *n*

dark field *n* (1927) : the dark area that serves as the background for objects viewed in an ultramicroscope

dark–field microscope *n* (1926) : ULTRAMICROSCOPE

dark horse *n* (1831) **1** : a usu. little known contestant (as a racehorse) that makes an unexpectedly good showing **2** : a political candidate unexpectedly nominated usu. as a compromise between factions

dark lantern *n* (1650) : a lantern that can be closed to conceal the light

dar·kle \ˈdär-kəl\ *vi* **dar·kled; dar·kling** \-k(ə-)liŋ\ [back-formation fr. *darkling*] (1800) **1 a :** to grow dark **b :** to become clouded or gloomy **2 :** to become concealed in the dark

[1]dark·ling \ˈdär-kliŋ\ *adv* [ME *derkelyng,* fr. *derk* dark + *-lyng* -ling] (15c) **:** in the dark

[2]dark·ling *adj* (1739) **1 :** DARK **2 :** done or taking place in the dark

darkling beetle *n* (1816) **:** a usu. hard-bodied black sluggish terrestrial plant-eating beetle (family Tenebrionidae)

dark reaction *n* (1927) **:** the synthetic phase of photosynthesis that does not require the presence of light and that involves the reduction of carbon dioxide to form carbohydrate

dark·room \ˈdär-ˌkrüm, -ˌkru̇m\ *n* (1841) **:** a room with no light or with a safelight for handling and processing light-sensitive photographic materials

dark·some \ˈdärk-səm\ *adj* (ca. 1530) **:** gloomily somber **:** DARK

darky *also* **dark·ie** \ˈdär-kē\ *n, pl* **darkies** (1775) **:** NEGRO — often taken to be offensive

[1]dar·ling \ˈdär-liŋ\ *n* [ME *derling,* fr. OE *dēorling,* fr. *dēore* dear] (bef. 12c) **1 :** a dearly loved person **2 :** FAVORITE

[2]darling *adj* (1509) **1 :** dearly loved **:** FAVORITE **2 :** very pleasing **:** CHARMING — **dar·ling·ly** \-liŋ-lē\ *adv* — **dar·ling·ness** *n*

[1]darn \ˈdärn\ *vb* [prob. fr. F dial. *darner*] *vt* (1600) **1 :** to mend with interlacing stitches **2 :** to embroider by filling in with long running or interlacing stitches ~ *vi* **:** to do darning — **darn·er** *n*

[2]darn *n* (1720) **:** a place that has been darned ⟨a sweater full of ~*s*⟩

[3]darn *adj or adv* [euphemism] (1781) **:** DAMNED

[4]darn *vb* (1787) **:** DAMN — **darned** \ˈdärn(d)\ *adj or adv*

[5]darn *n* (1840) **:** DAMN

dar·nel \ˈdärn-ᵊl\ *n* [ME] (14c) **:** any of several usu. weedy grasses (genus *Lolium*)

darning needle *n* (1761) **1 :** a long needle with a large eye for use in darning **2 :** DRAGONFLY, DAMSELFLY

[1]dart \ˈdärt\ *n* [ME, fr. MF, of Gmc origin; akin to OHG *tart* dart, OE *daroth*] (14c) **1 a** *archaic* **:** a light spear **b (1) :** a small missile usu. with a pointed shaft at one end and feathers at the other **(2)** *pl but sing in constr* **:** a game in which darts are thrown at a target **2 a :** something projected with sudden speed; *esp* **:** a sharp glance **b :** something causing sudden pain or distress ⟨~*s* of sarcasm⟩ **3 :** something with a slender pointed shaft or outline; *specif* **:** a stitched tapering fold in a garment **4 :** a quick movement ⟨made a ~ for the door⟩

[2]dart *vt* (1580) **1 :** to throw with a sudden movement **2 :** to thrust or move with sudden speed ~ *vi* **:** to move suddenly or rapidly ⟨~*ed* across the street⟩

dart board *n* (1901) **:** a usu. circular board (as of compressed bristles) used as a target in the game of darts

dart·er \ˈdärt-ər\ *n* (1813) **1 :** ANHINGA **2 :** any of numerous small American freshwater percoid fishes (esp. genera *Ammocrypta, Etheostoma,* and *Percina* of the family Percidae)

Dar·win·i·an \där-ˈwin-ē-ən\ *adj* (1860) **:** of or relating to Charles Darwin, his theories, or his followers — **Darwinian** *n*

Dar·win·ism \ˈdär-wə-ˌniz-əm\ *n* (1864) **:** a theory of the origin and perpetuation of new species of animals and plants that offspring of a given organism vary, that natural selection favors the survival of some of these variations over others, that new species have arisen and may continue to arise by these processes, and that widely divergent groups of plants and animals have arisen from the same ancestors; *broadly* **:** biological evolutionism — **Dar·win·ist** \-wə-nəst\ *n or adj*

Dar·win's finches \ˌdär-wənz-\ *n pl* [Charles *Darwin*] (1947) **:** finches of a subfamily (Geospizinae) having great variation in bill shape and confined mostly to the Galapagos islands

Dar·win tulip \ˌdär-wən-\ *n* (1889) **:** a tall late-flowering tulip with the flowers single and of one color

[1]dash \ˈdash\ *vb* [ME *dasshen*] *vt* (14c) **1 :** to knock, hurl, or thrust violently **2 :** to break by striking or knocking **3 :** SPLASH, SPATTER **4 a :** RUIN, DESTROY ⟨the news ~*ed* his hopes⟩ **b :** DEPRESS, SADDEN **c :** to make ashamed **5 :** to affect by mixing in something different ⟨milk ~*ed* with brandy⟩ ⟨his delight was ~*ed* with bitterness over the delay⟩ **6 :** to complete, execute, or finish off hastily — used with *down* or *off* ⟨~*ed* down a drink⟩ ⟨~ off a letter⟩ **7** [euphemism]**:** [1]DAMN 4 ~ *vi* **1 :** to move with sudden speed ⟨~*ed* through the rain⟩ **2 :** SMASH

[2]dash *n* (14c) **1 a** *archaic* **:** BLOW **b (1) :** a sudden burst or splash **(2) :** the sound produced by such a burst **2 a :** a stroke of a pen **b :** a punctuation mark — used esp. to indicate a break in the thought or structure of a sentence **3 :** a small usu. distinctive addition ⟨a ~ of salt⟩ ⟨a ~ of humor⟩ **4 :** flashy display **5 :** animation in style and action **6 a :** a sudden onset, rush, or attempt **b :** a short fast race **7 :** a long click or buzz forming a letter or part of a letter (as in Morse code) **8 :** DASHBOARD 2

dash·board \ˈdash-ˌbō(ə)rd, -ˌbȯ(ə)rd\ *n* (1846) **1 :** a screen on the front of a usu. horse-drawn vehicle to intercept water, mud, or snow **2 :** a panel extending across an automobile, airplane, or motorboat below the windshield and usu. containing dials and controls

dashed \ˈdasht\ *adj* (ca. 1889) **:** made up of a series of dashes ⟨a ~ line⟩

da·sheen \da-ˈshēn, də-\ *n* [origin unknown] (ca. 1899) **:** TARO

dash·er \ˈdash-ər\ *n* (1790) **1 :** a dashing person **2 :** one that dashes; *specif* **:** a device having blades for agitating a liquid or semisolid

dashi \ˈdäsh-(ˌ)ē\ *n* [Jp, lit., broth] (ca. 1961) **:** a fish broth made from dried bonito

da·shi·ki \də-ˈshē-kē\ *n* [modif. of Yoruba *danshiki*] (ca. 1968) **:** a usu. brightly colored loose-fitting pullover garment

dash·ing *adj* (1796) **1 :** marked by vigorous action **:** SPIRITED ⟨a ~ young horse⟩ **2 :** marked by smartness esp. in dress and manners — **dash·ing·ly** \-iŋ-lē\ *adv*

dash·pot \ˈdash-ˌpät\ *n* (1861) **:** a device for cushioning or damping a movement (as of a mechanical part) to avoid shock

das·sie \ˈdäs-ē\ *n* [Afrik] (1786) **:** HYRAX

das·tard \ˈdas-tərd\ *n* [ME] (15c) **:** COWARD; *esp* **:** one who commits malicious acts

das·tard·ly \-lē\ *adj* (1576) **:** despicably mean or cowardly ***syn*** see COWARDLY — **das·tard·li·ness** *n*

da·ta \ˈdāt-ə, ˈdat- *also* ˈdät-\ *n pl but sing or pl in constr, often attrib* [L, pl. of *datum*] (1646) **:** factual information (as measurements or statistics) used as a basis for reasoning, discussion, or calculation ⟨the ~ is plentiful and easily available —H. A. Gleason, Jr.⟩ ⟨comprehensive ~ on economic growth have been published —N. H. Jacoby⟩

usage Although still occas. marked with a disapproving [sic], *data* is well established both as a singular and as a plural noun. The singular *data* is regularly used as a mass noun denoting a collection of material; it is almost never used as a count noun equivalent to *datum.* Our evidence shows plural use to be considerably more common than singular use.

data bank *n* (ca. 1966) **:** DATA BASE

data base *n* (1967) **:** a collection of data organized esp. for rapid search and retrieval (as by a computer)

data processing *n* (1954) **:** the converting of raw data to machine-readable form and its subsequent processing (as storing, updating, combining, rearranging, or printing out) by a computer — **data processor** *n*

[1]date \ˈdāt\ *n* [ME, fr. OF, deriv. of L *dactylus* — more at DACTYL] (13c) **1 :** the oblong edible fruit of a palm (*Phoenix dactylifera*) **2 :** the tall palm with pinnate leaves that yields the date

[2]date *n* [ME, fr. MF, fr. LL *data,* fr. *data* (as in *data Romae* given at Rome), fem. of L *datus,* pp. of *dare* to give; akin to L *dos* gift, dowry, Gk *didonai* to give] (14c) **1 a :** the time at which an event occurs ⟨the ~ of his birth⟩ **b :** a statement of the time of execution or making ⟨the ~ on the letter⟩ **2 :** DURATION **3 :** the period of time to which something belongs **4 a :** an appointment for a specified time; *esp* **:** a social engagement between two persons of opposite sex **b :** a person of the opposite sex with whom one has a social engagement **5 :** an engagement for a professional performance (as of a dance band) — **to date :** up to the present moment

[3]date *vb* **dat·ed; dat·ing** *vt* (15c) **1 :** to determine the date of ⟨~ an antique⟩ **2 :** to record the date of **:** mark with the date **3 a :** to mark with characteristics typical of a particular period **b :** to show up plainly the age of **4 :** to make or have a date with ~ *vi* **1 :** to reckon chronologically **2 :** ORIGINATE ⟨a friendship *dating* from college days⟩ **3 :** to become dated — **dat·able** *or* **date·able** \ˈdāt-ə-bəl\ *adj* — **dat·er** \ˈdāt-ər\ *n*

dat·ed *adj* (1731) **1 :** provided with a date ⟨a ~ document⟩ **2 :** OUTMODED, OLD-FASHIONED ⟨~ formalities⟩ — **dat·ed·ly** *adv* — **dat·ed·ness** *n*

date·less \ˈdāt-ləs\ *adj* (1593) **1 :** ENDLESS **2 :** having no date **3 :** too ancient to be dated **4 :** TIMELESS ⟨the play's ~ theme⟩

date·line \ˈdāt-ˌlīn\ *n* (1888) **1 :** a line in a written document or a printed publication giving the date and place of composition or issue **2** *usu* **date line :** a hypothetical line approximately along the 180th meridian designated as the place where each calendar day begins — **dateline** *vt*

dating bar *n* (1967) **:** a bar that caters esp. to young unmarried men and women

[1]da·tive \ˈdāt-iv\ *adj* [ME *datif,* fr. L *dativus,* lit., relating to giving, fr. *datus*] (15c) **:** of, relating to, or being the grammatical case that marks typically the indirect object of a verb, the object of some prepositions, or a possessor

[2]dative *n* (15c) **:** a dative case or form

dative bond *n* [fr. the donation of electrons by one of the atoms] (ca. 1929) **:** COORDINATE BOND

da·tum \ˈdāt-əm, ˈdat-, ˈdät-\ *n* [L, fr. neut. of *datus*] (1646) **1** *pl* **da·ta** \-ə\ **:** something given or admitted esp. as a basis for reasoning or inference **2** *pl* **datums :** something used as a basis for calculating or measuring ***usage*** see DATA

da·tu·ra \də-ˈt(y)u̇r-ə\ *n* [NL, genus name, fr. Hindi *dhatūrā* jimsonweed] (1598) **:** any of a genus (*Datura*) of widely distributed strong-scented herbs, shrubs, or trees of the nightshade family including some used as sources of medicinal alkaloids (as stramonium) or in folk rites or illicitly for their poisonous, narcotic, or hallucinogenic properties — compare JIMSONWEED

[1]daub \ˈdȯb, ˈdäb\ *vb* [ME *dauben,* fr. MF *dauber*] *vt* (14c) **1 :** to cover or coat with soft adhesive matter **:** PLASTER **2 :** to coat with a dirty substance **3 a :** to apply coloring material crudely to **b :** to apply (as paint) crudely ~ *vi* **1** *archaic* **:** to put on a false exterior **2 :** to apply colors crudely — **daub·er** *n*

[2]daub *n* (15c) **1 :** material used to daub walls **2 :** an act or instance of daubing **3 :** something daubed on **:** SMEAR **4 :** a crude picture

daube \ˈdōb\ *n* [F, prob. fr. obs. It *dobba*] (1723) **:** a stew of braised meat, vegetables, herbs, and spices

[1]daugh·ter \ˈdȯt-ər\ *n* [ME *doughter,* fr. OE *dohtor;* akin to OHG *tohter* daughter, Gk *thygatēr*] (bef. 12c) **1 a (1) :** a human female having the relation of child to parent **(2) :** a female offspring of a lower animal **b :** a human female having a specified ancestor or belonging to a group of common ancestry **2 :** something considered as a daughter ⟨the United States is a ~ of Great Britain⟩ **3 :** an atomic species that is the product of the radioactive decay of a given element — **daugh·ter·less** \-ləs\ *adj*

[2]daughter *adj* (1614) **1 :** having the characteristics or relationship of a daughter **2 :** belonging to the first generation of offspring, organelles, or molecules produced by reproduction, division, or replication ⟨~ cell⟩ ⟨~ DNA molecules⟩

daugh·ter–in–law \ˈdȯt-ə-rən-ˌlȯ, -ərn-ˌlȯ\ *n, pl* **daugh·ters–in–law** \-ər-zən-\ (14c) **:** the wife of one's son

dau·no·my·cin \ˌdȯ-nə-ˈmīs-ᵊn, ˌdau̇-\ *n* [(assumed) It *daunomicina,* fr. *Daunia,* ancient region of Apulia, Italy + It *-o-* + *-micina* -mycin] (1964) **:** an antibiotic $C_{27}H_{29}NO_{10}$ that is a nitrogenous glycoside and is used as an antineoplastic agent

dau·no·ru·bi·cin \-ˈrü-bə-sən\ *n* [*dauno-* (as in *daunomycin*) + L *ruber* red + *-mycin* — more at RED] (ca. 1968) **:** DAUNOMYCIN

daunt \ˈdȯnt, ˈdänt\ *vt* [ME *daunten,* fr. MF *danter,* alter. of *donter,* fr. L *domitare* to tame, fr. *domitus,* pp. of *domare* — more at TAME] (14c) **:** to lessen the courage of **:** COW, SUBDUE ***syn*** see DISMAY — **daunt·ing·ly** \-iŋ-lē\ *adv*

daunt·less \'lәs\ *adj* (1593) : FEARLESS, UNDAUNTED ⟨a ~ hero⟩ — **daunt·less·ly** *adv* — **daunt·less·ness** *n*
dau·phin \'dō-fәn\ *n, often cap* [MF *dalfin,* fr. OF, title of lords of the Dauphiné, fr. *Dalfin,* a surname] (15c) : the eldest son of a king of France
dau·phine \dō-'fēn\ *n, often cap* [F] (ca. 1864) : the wife of the dauphin
da·ven \'däv-әn\ *vi* [Yiddish *davnen*] (ca. 1930) : to recite the prescribed prayers in a Jewish liturgy
dav·en·port \'dav-әn-,pō(ә)rt, 'dav-ᵊm-, -,pȯ(ә)rt\ *n* [prob. fr. the name *Davenport*] (1853) **1** : a small compact writing desk **2** : a large upholstered sofa often convertible into a bed
Da·vid \'dā-vәd\ *n* [Heb *Dāwīdh*] : a Hebrew shepherd who became the second king of Israel in succession to Saul according to biblical accounts — **Da·vid·ic** \dә-'vid-ik, dā-\ *adj*
da·vit \'dā-vәt, 'dav-әt\ *n* [prob. fr. the name *David*] (15c) : a crane that projects over the side of a ship or a hatchway and is used esp. for boats, anchors, or cargo

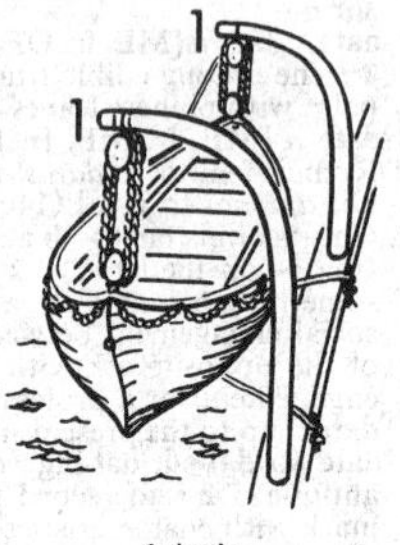

1 davit

Da·vy Jones \,dā-vē-'jōnz\ *n* (1751) : the bottom of the sea personified
Da·vy Jones's locker \,dā-vē-,jōnz(-әz)-\ *n* (ca. 1774) : the bottom of the ocean
[1]**daw** \'dȯ, 'dä\ *vi* [ME *dawen,* fr. OE *dagian;* akin to OHG *tagēn* to dawn, OE *dæg* day] *chiefly Scot* (bef. 12c) : DAWN
[2]**daw** \'dȯ\ *n* [ME *dawe;* akin to OHG *taha* jackdaw] (15c) : JACKDAW
daw·dle \'dȯd-ᵊl\ *vb* **daw·dled; daw·dling** \'dȯd-liŋ, -ᵊl-iŋ\ [origin unknown] *vi* (1656) **1** : to spend time idly **2** : to move lackadaisically ⟨*dawdled* up the hill⟩ ~ *vt* : to spend fruitlessly or lackadaisically ⟨*dawdled* the day away⟩ ***syn*** see DELAY — **daw·dler** \'dȯd-lәr, -ᵊl-әr\ *n*
[1]**dawn** \'dȯn, 'dän\ *vi* [ME *dawnen,* prob. back-formation fr. *dawning* daybreak, alter. of *dawing,* fr. OE *dagung,* fr. *dagian*] (15c) **1** : to begin to grow light as the sun rises **2** : to begin to appear or develop **3** : to begin to be perceived or understood ⟨the truth finally ~*ed* on us⟩
[2]**dawn** *n* (1559) **1** : the first appearance of light in the morning followed by sunrise **2** : BEGINNING ⟨the ~ of the space age⟩
daw·son·ite \'dȯ-sә-,nīt\ *n* [Sir John W. *Dawson* + E *-ite*] (1874) : a mineral $NaAL(CO_3)(OH)_2$ consisting of a basic aluminum sodium carbonate
day \'dā\ *n* [ME, fr. OE *dæg;* akin to OHG *tag* day] (bef. 12c) **1** **a** : the time of light between one night and the next **b** : DAYLIGHT 1, 2 **2** **a** : the period of the earth's rotation on its axis **b** : the time required by a celestial body to turn once on its axis **3** : the mean solar day of 24 hours beginning at mean midnight **4** : a specified day or date **5** : a specified time or period : AGE ⟨in grandfather's ~⟩ **6** : the conflict or contention of the day ⟨played hard and won the ~⟩ **7** : the time established by usage or law for work, school, or business **8** : a period of existence or prominence of a person or thing — **day after day** : for an indefinite or seemingly endless number of days — **day in, day out** : for an indefinite number of successive days
Day·ak \'dī-,ak\ *n* [Malay, up-country] (1836) **1** : a member of any of several Indonesian peoples of the interior of Borneo **2** : the language of the Dayak peoples
day·bed \'dā-,bed\ *n* (1818) **1** : a chaise longue of a type made 1680–1780 **2** : a couch that can be converted into a bed
day·book \-,bu̇k\ *n* (1580) : DIARY, JOURNAL
day·break \-,brāk\ *n* (1530) : DAWN
day–care \'dā-,ke(ә)r, -,ka(ә)r\ *adj* (1947) : of, relating to, or providing supervision and facilities for preschool children during the day ⟨~ centers⟩
[1]**day·dream** \'dā-,drēm\ *n* (1685) : a pleasant visionary usu. wishful creation of the imagination — **day·dream·like** \-,līk\ *adj*
[2]**daydream** *vi* (1820) : to have a daydream — **day·dream·er** *n*
day·flower \'dā-,flau̇(-ә)r\ *n* (ca. 1688) : any of a genus (*Commelina*) of herbs of the spiderwort family having one petal smaller than the other two; *esp* : a blue-flowered weed (*C. communis*) with the smaller petal white
Day–Glo \'dā-,glō\ *trademark* — used for fluorescent materials
day·glow \'dā-,glō\ *n* (ca. 1960) : airglow seen during the day
day laborer *n* (1548) : one who works for daily wages esp. as an unskilled laborer
day letter *n* (ca. 1913) : a telegram sent during the day that has a lower priority than a regular telegram
[1]**day·light** \'dā-,līt\ *n* (13c) **1** : the light of day **2** : DAYTIME **3** : DAWN **4** **a** : knowledge or understanding of something that has been obscure ⟨began to see ~ on the problem⟩ **b** : the quality or state of being open : OPENNESS **5** *pl* **a** : CONSCIOUSNESS **b** : mental soundness or stability : WITS ⟨scared the ~*s* out of him⟩
[2]**daylight** *vt* (1885) **1** : to provide with daylight **2** : to remove obstructions (as trees and brush) from in order to provide greater visibility ⟨~ an intersection⟩ ~ *vi* : to supply daylight
daylight saving time *n* (1919) : time usu. one hour ahead of standard time — called also *daylight time*
day·lily \'dā-,lil-ē\ *n* (1597) : any of various Eurasian plants (genus *Hemerocallis*) of the lily family that have short-lived flowers resembling lilies and are widespread in cultivation and as escapes
day·long \,dā-,lȯŋ\ *adj* (1855) : lasting all day ⟨a ~ tour⟩
day·mare \'dā-,ma(ә)r, -,me(ә)r\ *n* [*day* + *-mare* (as in *nightmare*)] (1737) : a nightmarish fantasy experienced while awake
day–neutral *adj* (1941) : developing and maturing regardless of relative length of alternating exposures to light and dark periods — compare LONG-DAY, SHORT-DAY
day nursery *n* (1850) : a public center for the care and training of young children; *specif* : NURSERY SCHOOL
Day of Atonement (1611) : YOM KIPPUR
day one *n, often cap D&O* (1971) : the first day or very beginning of something
day·room \'dā-,rüm, -,ru̇m\ *n* (1823) : a room (as in a hospital) equipped for reading, writing, and recreation
days \'dāz\ *adv* (bef. 12c) : in the daytime repeatedly : on any day
day school *n* (1838) : an elementary or secondary school held on weekdays; *specif* : a private school without boarding facilities
day·side \'dā-,sīd\ *n* (1965) : the side of a planet in sunlight
days of grace (1726) : the days allowed for payment of a note or an insurance premium after it becomes due
day·star \'dā-,stär\ *n* (bef. 12c) **1** : MORNING STAR **2** : SUN 1a
day student *n* (1883) : a student who attends regular classes at a college or preparatory school but does not live at the institution
[1]**day·time** \'dā-,tīm\ *n* (1535) : the time during which there is daylight
[2]**daytime** *adj* (1900) : taking place, existing, or presented during the daytime ⟨~ flights⟩ ⟨~ soap operas⟩
day·times \'dā-,tīmz\ *adv* (1854) : during the day or during the workday repeatedly : DAYS ⟨has a housekeeper ~⟩
day–to–day \,dāt-ә-,dā\ *adj* (1883) **1** : taking place, made, or done in the course of successive days ⟨~ problems⟩ **2** : providing for a day at a time with little thought for the future ⟨lived an aimless ~ existence⟩
day–trip·per \'dā-,trip-әr\ *n* (1897) : one who takes a trip that does not last overnight
daze \'dāz\ *vt* **dazed; daz·ing** [ME *dasen,* fr. (assumed) ON *dasa;* akin to ON *dasask* to become exhausted] (14c) **1** : to stupefy esp. by a blow : STUN **2** : to dazzle with light — **daze** *n* — **dazed·ness** \'dā-zәd-nәs, 'dāz(d)-\ *n*
daz·zle \'daz-әl\ *vb* **daz·zled; daz·zling** \-(ә-)liŋ\ [freq. of *daze*] *vi* (15c) **1** : to lose clear vision esp. from looking at bright light **2** **a** : to shine brilliantly **b** : to arouse admiration by an impressive display ~ *vt* **1** : to overpower with light **2** : to impress deeply, overpower, or confound with brilliance ⟨*dazzled* the crowd with his oratory⟩ — **dazzle** *n* — **daz·zler** \-(ә-)lәr\ *n* — **daz·zling·ly** \-(ә-)liŋ-lē\ *adv*
D day *n* [*D,* abbr. for *day*] (1918) : a day set for launching an operation; *specif* : June 6, 1944, on which Allied forces began the invasion of France in World War II
DDD \,dēd-(,)ē-'dē\ *n* [*d*ichloro-*d*iphenyl-*d*ichloro-ethane] (1946) : an insecticide $(ClC_6H_4)_2CHCHCl_2$ closely related chemically and similar in properties to DDT
DDT \,dēd-(,)ē-'tē\ *n* [*d*ichloro-*d*iphenyl-*t*richloro-ethane] (1943) : a colorless odorless water-insoluble crystalline insecticide $C_{14}H_9Cl_5$ that tends to accumulate in ecosystems and has toxic effects on many vertebrates
DDVP \,dēd-(,)ē-,vē-'pē\ *n* [*d*imethyl + *d*ichlor- + *v*inyl + *p*hosphate] (1954) : DICHLORVOS
de- *prefix* [ME, fr. OF *de-, des-,* partly fr. L *de-* from, down, away (fr. *de,* prep.) and partly fr. L *dis-;* L *de* akin to OIr *di* from, OE *tō* to — more at TO, DIS-] **1** **a** : do the opposite of ⟨*de*vitalize⟩ ⟨*de*activate⟩ **b** : reverse of ⟨*de*-emphasis⟩ **2** **a** : remove (a specified thing) from ⟨*de*louse⟩ ⟨*de*hydrogenate⟩ **b** : remove from (a specified thing) ⟨*de*throne⟩ **3** : reduce ⟨*de*value⟩ **4** : something derived from (a specified thing) ⟨*de*compound⟩ : derived from something (of a specified nature) ⟨*de*nominative⟩ **5** : get off of (a specified thing) ⟨*de*train⟩ **6** : having a molecule characterized by the removal of one or more atoms (of a specified element) ⟨*de*oxy-⟩
de·acid·i·fy \,dē-ә-'sid-ә-,fī\ *vt* (1786) : to remove acid from : reduce the acidity of (as by neutralization) — **de·acid·i·fi·ca·tion** \-,sid-ә-fә-'kā-shәn\ *n*
dea·con \'dē-kәn\ *n* [ME *dekene,* fr. OE *dēacon,* fr. LL *diaconus,* fr. Gk *diakonos,* lit., servant, fr. *dia-* + *-konos* (akin to *enkonein* to be active); akin to L *conari* to attempt] (bef. 12c) : a subordinate officer in a Christian church: as **a** : a Roman Catholic cleric ranking below a priest and above a subdeacon **b** : one of the laymen elected by a church with congregational polity to serve in worship, in pastoral care, and on administrative committees **c** : a Mormon in the lowest grade of the Aaronic priesthood
dea·con·ess \'dē-kә-nәs\ *n* (15c) : a woman chosen to assist in the church ministry; *specif* : one in a Protestant order
deacon's bench *n* (1922) : a bench with usu. spindled arms and back
de·ac·ti·vate \(')dē-'ak-tә-,vāt\ *vt* (1927) : to make inactive or ineffective — **de·ac·ti·va·tion** \(,)dē-,ak-tә-'vā-shәn\ *n* — **de·ac·ti·va·tor** \(')dē-'ak-tә-,vāt-әr\ *n*
[1]**dead** \'ded\ *adj* [ME *deed,* fr. OE *dēad;* akin to ON *dauthr* dead, *deyja* to die, OHG *tōt* dead — more at DIE] (bef. 12c) **1** : deprived of life : having died **2** **a** (1) : having the appearance of death : DEATHLY ⟨in a ~ faint⟩ (2) : lacking power to move, feel, or respond : NUMB **b** : very tired **c** (1) : incapable of being stirred emotionally or intellectually : UNRESPONSIVE ⟨~ to pity⟩ (2) : grown cold : EXTINGUISHED ⟨~ coals⟩ **3** **a** : INANIMATE, INERT ⟨~ matter⟩ **b** : BARREN, INFERTILE ⟨~ soil⟩ **c** : no longer producing or functioning : EXHAUSTED ⟨a ~ battery⟩ **4** **a** (1) : lacking power or effect ⟨a ~ law⟩ (2) : no longer having interest, relevance, or significance ⟨a ~ issue⟩ **b** : no longer in use : OBSOLETE ⟨a ~ language⟩ **c** : no longer active : EXTINCT ⟨a ~ volcano⟩ **d** : lacking in gaiety or animation ⟨a ~ party⟩ **e** (1) : lacking in commercial activity : QUIET (2) : commercially idle or unproductive ⟨~ capital⟩ **f** : lacking elasticity ⟨a ~ tennis ball⟩ **g** : being out of action or out of use; *specif* : free from any connection to a source of voltage and free from electric charges **h** (1) : being out of play ⟨a ~ ball⟩ ⟨~ cards⟩ (2) : temporarily forbidden to play or to make a certain play in croquet **5** **a** : not running or circulating : STAGNANT ⟨~ water⟩ **b** : not turning ⟨a ~ lathe center⟩ **c** : not imparting motion or power although otherwise functioning ⟨a ~ rear axle⟩ **d** : lacking warmth, vigor, or taste **6** **a** : absolutely uniform ⟨a ~ level⟩ **b** (1) : UNERRING (2) : EXACT ⟨~ center of the target⟩ (3) : certain to be doomed ⟨a ~ duck⟩ (4) : IRREVOCABLE ⟨a ~ loss⟩ **c** : ABRUPT ⟨brought to a ~ stop⟩ **d** : COMPLETE, ABSOLUTE ⟨a ~ silence⟩ **7** : devoid of former occupants ⟨~ villages⟩ — **dead·ness** *n*
syn DEAD, DEFUNCT, DECEASED, DEPARTED, LATE mean devoid of life. DEAD applies literally to what is deprived of vital force but is used figuratively of anything that has lost any attribute (as energy, activity, radiance) suggesting life; DEFUNCT stresses cessation of active existence or operation; DECEASED, DEPARTED, and LATE apply to persons who have died recently, DECEASED occurring esp. in legal use, DEPARTED usu. as a euphemism, and LATE esp. with reference to a person in a specific relation or status.
[2]**dead** *n, pl* **dead** (bef. 12c) **1** : one that is dead — usu. used collectively **2** : the state of being dead ⟨raised him from the ~ —Col 2:12(RSV)⟩ **3** : the time of greatest quiet ⟨the ~ of night⟩

3dead *adv* (14c) **1 :** ABSOLUTELY, UTTERLY ⟨~ certain⟩ **2 :** suddenly and completely ⟨stopped ~⟩ **3 :** DIRECTLY ⟨~ ahead⟩

dead air *n* (ca. 1943) **:** a period of silence esp. during a radio or television broadcast

dead–air space *n* (1902) **:** a sealed or unventilated air space

1dead·beat \ˈded-ˌbēt\ *n* (ca. 1874) **1 :** one who persistently fails to pay his debts or his way **2 :** LOAFER

2deadbeat *adj* (ca. 1864) **:** having a pointer that gives a reading with little or no oscillation

dead bolt *n* (ca. 1902) **:** a lock bolt that is moved by turning the knob or key without action of a spring

dead center *n* (ca. 1864) **:** either of the two positions at the ends of a stroke in a crank and connecting rod when the crank and rod are in the same straight line — called also *dead point*

dead·en \ˈded-ᵊn\ *vb* **dead·ened; dead·en·ing** \ˈded-niŋ, -ᵊn-iŋ\ *vt* (1665) **1 :** to impair in vigor or sensation **:** BLUNT ⟨~*ed* his enthusiasm⟩ **2 a :** to deprive of brilliance **b :** to make vapid or spiritless **c :** to make (as a wall) impervious to sound **3 :** to deprive of life **:** KILL ~ *vi* **:** to become dead **:** lose life or vigor — **dead·en·er** \ˈded-nər, -ᵊn-ər\ *n* — **dead·en·ing·ly** \-niŋ-lē, -ᵊn-iŋ-\ *adv*

1dead–end \ˌded-ˌend\ *adj* (1919) **1 a :** lacking opportunities for advancement ⟨a ~ job⟩ **b :** lacking an exit ⟨a ~ street⟩ **2 :** TOUGH ⟨~ kids⟩ — **dead–end·ed·ness** \(ˈ)ded-ˈen-dəd-nəs\ *n*

2dead–end \ˈded-ˈend\ *vi* (1944) **:** to come to a dead end **:** TERMINATE

dead end \ˈded-ˈend\ *n* (1886) **1 :** an end (as of a street) without an exit **2 :** a position, situation, or course of action that leads to nothing further

dead·en·ing *n* (ca. 1874) **:** material used to soundproof walls or floors

dead·eye \ˈded-ˌī\ *n* (1748) **1 :** a rounded wood block that is encircled by a rope or an iron band and pierced with holes to receive the lanyard and that is used esp. to set up shrouds and stays **2 :** an unerring marksman

dead·fall \-ˌfȯl\ *n* (1611) **1 :** a trap so constructed that a weight (as a heavy log) falls on an animal and kills or disables it **2 :** a tangled mass of fallen trees and branches

dead hand *n* (14c) **1 :** MORTMAIN 2 **2 :** the oppressive influence of the past

1dead·head \ˈded-ˌhed\ *n* (1841) **1 :** one who has not paid for a ticket **2 :** a dull or stupid person

2deadhead *vi* (1911) **:** to make a return trip without a load ~ *vt* **:** to remove the faded flowers of (a plant) esp. to keep a neat appearance and to promote reblooming by preventing seed production

dead heat *n* (1840) **:** a tie with no single winner of a race

dead letter *n* (1663) **1 :** something that has lost its force or authority without being formally abolished **2 :** a letter that is undeliverable and unreturnable by the post office

dead·light \ˈded-ˌlīt\ *n* (1726) **1 a :** a metal cover or shutter fitted to a port to keep out light and water **b :** a heavy glass set in a ship's deck or hull to admit light **2 :** a skylight made so as not to open

dead·line \-ˌlīn\ *n* (1864) **1 :** a line drawn within or around a prison that a prisoner passes at the risk of being shot **2 :** a date or time before which something must be done; *specif* **:** the time after which copy is not accepted for a particular issue of a publication

dead load *n* (ca. 1888) **:** a constant load that in structures (as a bridge, building, or machine) is due to the weight of the members, the supported structure, and permanent attachments or accessories

dead·lock \ˈded-ˌläk\ *n* (1779) **1 :** a state of inaction or neutralization resulting from the opposition of equally powerful uncompromising persons or factions **:** STANDSTILL **2 :** a tie score — **deadlock** *vt*

1dead·ly \ˈded-lē\ *adj* **dead·li·er; -est** (bef. 12c) **1 :** likely to cause or capable of producing death ⟨a ~ disease⟩ ⟨a ~ instrument⟩ **2 a :** aiming to kill or destroy **:** IMPLACABLE ⟨a ~ enemy⟩ **b :** highly effective ⟨a ~ exposé⟩ **c :** UNERRING ⟨a ~ marksman⟩ **d :** marked by determination or extreme seriousness **3 a :** tending to deprive of force or vitality ⟨a ~ habit⟩ **b :** suggestive of death esp. in dullness or lack of animation ⟨~ bores⟩ ⟨a ~ conversation⟩ **4 :** very great **:** EXTREME — **dead·li·ness** *n*

syn DEADLY, MORTAL, FATAL, LETHAL mean causing or capable of causing death. DEADLY applies to an established or very likely cause of death ⟨a *deadly* disease⟩ MORTAL implies that death has occurred or is inevitable ⟨a *mortal* wound⟩ FATAL stresses the inevitability of what has in fact resulted in death or destruction ⟨*fatal* consequences⟩ LETHAL applies only to something that is bound to cause death or exists for the destruction of life ⟨*lethal* gas⟩

2deadly *adv* (bef. 12c) **1** *archaic* **:** in a manner to cause death **:** MORTALLY **2 :** suggesting death **3 :** EXTREMELY ⟨~ serious⟩

deadly nightshade *n* (1578) **:** BELLADONNA 1

deadly sin *n* (13c) **:** one of seven sins of pride, covetousness, lust, anger, gluttony, envy, and sloth held to be fatal to spiritual progress — called also *capital sin*

dead man's float *n* (ca. 1946) **:** a prone floating position with the arms extended forward

dead march *n* (1603) **:** a solemn march for a funeral

dead metaphor *n* (1922) **:** a word or phrase (as *time is running out*) that has lost its metaphoric force through common usage

dead–on \ˈded-ˈȯn, -ˈän\ *adj* (ca. 1897) **:** precisely correct **:** deadly accurate

1dead·pan \ˈded-ˌpan\ *adj* (ca. 1928) **:** marked by an impassive matter-of-fact manner, style, or expression ⟨a ~ comedy⟩

2deadpan *adv* (1933) **:** in a deadpan manner ⟨played the role ~⟩

3deadpan *vt* (1942) **:** to express in a deadpan manner — **dead·pan·ner** *n*

dead point *n* (1830) **:** DEAD CENTER

dead reckoning *n* (1613) **1 :** the determination without the aid of celestial observations of the position of a ship or aircraft from the record of the courses sailed or flown, the distance made, and the known or estimated drift **2 :** GUESSWORK — **dead reckon** *vb* — **dead reckoner** *n*

dead space *n* (ca. 1923) **:** the portion of the respiratory system which is external to the bronchioles and through which air must pass to reach the bronchioles and alveoli

dead·weight \ˈded-ˈwāt\ *n* (1660) **1 :** the unrelieved weight of an inert mass **2 :** DEAD LOAD **3 :** a ship's load including the total weight of cargo, fuel, stores, crew, and passengers

dead·wood \-ˌwu̇d\ *n* (15c) **1 :** wood dead on the tree **2 :** useless personnel or material **3 :** solid timbers built in at the extreme bow and stern of a ship when too narrow to permit framing **4 :** bowling pins that have been knocked down but remain on the alley

de·aer·ate \(ˈ)dē-ˈa(-ə)r-ˌāt, -ˈe(-ə)r-\ *vt* (1791) **:** to remove air or gas from — **de·aer·a·tion** \ˌdē-ˌa(-ə)r-ˈā-shən, -ˌe(-ə)r-\ *n*

deaf \ˈdef\ *adj* [ME *deef,* fr. OE *dēaf;* akin to Gk *typhlos* blind, *typhein* to smoke, L *fumus* smoke — more at FUME] (bef. 12c) **1 :** lacking or deficient in the sense of hearing **2 :** unwilling to hear or listen **:** not to be persuaded ⟨was overwrought and ~ to reason⟩ — **deaf·ish** \ˈdef-ish\ *adj* — **deaf·ly** *adv* — **deaf·ness** *n*

deaf·en \ˈdef-ən\ *vt* **deaf·ened; deaf·en·ing** \-(ə-)niŋ\ (1597) **1 :** to make deaf **2 :** to make (as a wall) soundproof

deaf·en·ing *adj* (1597) **1 :** that deafens **2 :** very loud **:** EARSPLITTING ⟨fell with a ~ clap⟩ — **deaf·en·ing·ly** *adv*

deaf–mute \ˈdef-ˌmyüt\ *n* (1837) **:** a deaf person who cannot speak — **deaf–mute** *adj*

1deal \ˈdē(ə)l\ *n* [ME *deel,* fr. OE *dǣl;* akin to OE *dāl* division, portion, OHG *teil* part] (bef. 12c) **1** *obs* **:** PART, PORTION **2 :** a usu. large or indefinite quantity or degree ⟨a great ~ of support⟩ ⟨a good ~ faster⟩ **3 a :** the act or right of distributing cards to players in a card game **b :** HAND 9b

2deal *vb* **dealt** \ˈdelt\; **deal·ing** \ˈdē-liŋ\ *vt* (bef. 12c) **1 a :** to give as one's portion **:** APPORTION ⟨tried to ~ justice to all men⟩ ⟨*dealt* out three sandwiches apiece⟩ **b :** to distribute (playing cards) to players in a game **2 :** ADMINISTER, DELIVER ⟨*dealt* him a blow⟩ **3 :** SELL ⟨~*s* marijuana⟩ ~ *vi* **1 :** to distribute the cards in a card game **2 :** to concern oneself or itself ⟨the book ~*s* with education⟩ **3 a :** to engage in bargaining **:** TRADE **b :** to sell or distribute something as a business ⟨~ in insurance⟩ **4 :** to take action with regard to someone or something ⟨~ with an offender⟩ ***syn*** see DISTRIBUTE — **deal·er** \ˈdē-lər\ *n*

3deal *n* (1588) **1 :** an act of dealing **:** TRANSACTION **2 :** PACKAGE DEAL **3 :** treatment received ⟨a dirty ~⟩ **4 :** an arrangement for mutual advantage

4deal *n* [MD or MLG *dele* plank; akin to OHG *dili* plank — more at THILL] (14c) **1 a** *Brit* **:** a board of fir or pine **b :** sawed yellow-pine lumber nine inches or wider and three, four, or five inches thick **2 :** pine or fir wood — **deal** *adj*

de·alat·ed \(ˈ)dē-ˈā-ˌlāt-əd\ *adj* (1904) **:** divested of the wings — used of postnuptial adults of insects (as ants) that drop their wings after a nuptial flight — **de·ala·tion** \ˌdē-(ˌ)ā-ˈlā-shən\ *n*

deal·er·ship \ˈdē-lər-ˌship\ *n* (1916) **:** an authorized sales agency ⟨an automobile ~⟩

deal·fish \ˈdē(ə)l-ˌfish\ *n* [*4deal*] (1845) **:** any of several long thin fishes (genus *Trachipterus* of the family Trachipteridae) inhabiting the deep sea

deal·ing *n* (15c) **1 :** method of business **:** manner of conduct **2** *pl* **:** friendly or business interactions

dealing box *n* (1929) **:** a case that holds a deck of playing cards so that they may be dealt one by one

de·am·i·nase \(ˈ)dē-ˈam-ə-ˌnās, -ˌnāz\ *n* [*de-* + *amino* + *-ase*] (1920) **:** an enzyme that hydrolyzes amino compounds (as amino acids) with removal of the amino group

de·am·i·nate \-ˌnāt\ *vt* **-nat·ed; -nat·ing** (1926) **:** to remove the amino group from (a compound) — **de·am·i·na·tion** \(ˌ)dē-ˌam-ə-ˈnā-shən\ *n*

de·am·i·nize \(ˈ)dē-ˈam-ə-ˌnīz\ *vt* **-nized; -niz·ing** (1923) **:** DEAMINATE

dean \ˈdēn\ *n* [ME *deen,* fr. MF *deien,* fr. LL *decanus,* lit., chief of ten, fr. L *decem* ten — more at TEN] (14c) **1 a :** the head of the chapter of a collegiate or cathedral church **b :** a Roman Catholic priest who supervises one district of a diocese **2 a :** the head of a division, faculty, college, or school of a university **b :** a college or secondary school administrator in charge of counseling and disciplining students ⟨~ of men⟩ **3 :** DOYEN 1 — **dean** *vi* — **dean·ship** \-ˌship\ *n*

dean·ery \ˈdēn-(ə-)rē\ *n, pl* **-er·ies** (15c) **:** the office, jurisdiction, or official residence of a clerical dean

dean's list *n* (ca. 1926) **:** a list of students receiving special recognition from the dean of a college because of superior scholarship

1dear \ˈdi(ə)r\ *adj* [ME *dere,* fr. OE *dēor*] (bef. 12c) **:** SEVERE, SORE ⟨in our ~ peril —Shak.⟩

2dear *adj* [ME *dere,* fr. OE *dēore;* akin to OHG *tiuri* distinguished, costly] (bef. 12c) **1** *obs* **:** NOBLE **2 :** highly valued **:** PRECIOUS ⟨a ~ friend⟩ **3 :** AFFECTIONATE, FOND **4 :** high or exorbitant in price **:** EXPENSIVE ⟨eggs are very ~ just now⟩ **5 :** HEARTFELT — **dear** *adv* — **dear·ly** *adv* — **dear·ness** *n*

3dear *n* (13c) **1 :** a loved one **:** SWEETHEART **2 :** a lovable person

Dear John \-ˈjän\ *n* (ca. 1945) **:** a letter (as to a soldier) in which a wife asks for a divorce or a girlfriend breaks off an engagement or a friendship

dearth \ˈdərth\ *n* [ME *derthe,* fr. (assumed) OE *dierth;* akin to OHG *tiurida* glory, costliness — more at -TH] (13c) **1 :** scarcity that makes dear; *specif* **:** FAMINE **2 :** an inadequate supply **:** LACK

dea·sil \ˈdē-zəl\ *adv* [ScGael *deiseil;* akin to L *dexter* right hand] (1771) **:** CLOCKWISE — compare WIDDERSHINS

death \ˈdeth\ *n* [ME *deeth,* fr. OE *dēath;* akin to ON *dauthi* death, *deyja* to die — more at DIE] (bef. 12c) **1 :** a permanent cessation of all vital functions **:** the end of life — compare BRAIN DEATH **2 :** the cause or occasion of loss of life ⟨drinking was the ~ of him⟩ **3** *cap* **:** the destroyer of life represented usu. as a skeleton with a scythe **4 :** the state of being dead **5 a :** the passing or destruction of something inanimate ⟨the ~ of vaudeville⟩ **b :** EXTINCTION **6 :** CIVIL DEATH **7 :** SLAUGHTER **8** *Christian Science* **:** the lie of life in matter **:** that which is unreal and untrue **:** ILLUSION — **to death :** beyond endurance **:** EXCESSIVELY ⟨bored *to death*⟩

death·bed \ˈdeth-ˈbed\ *n* (bef. 12c) **1 :** the bed in which a person dies **2 :** the last hours of life — **on one's deathbed :** near the point of death

death benefit *n* (1921) **:** money payable to the beneficiary of a deceased

death·blow \ˈdeth-ˈblō\ *n* (1795) **:** a destructive or killing stroke or event

\ə\ abut \ᵊ\ kitten, F table \ər\ further \a\ ash \ā\ ace \ä\ cot, cart \au̇\ out \ch\ chin \e\ bet \ē\ easy \g\ go \i\ hit \ī\ ice \j\ job \ŋ\ sing \ō\ go \ȯ\ law \ȯi\ boy \th\ thin \t͟h\ the \ü\ loot \u̇\ foot \y\ yet \zh\ vision \à, k̲, ⁿ, œ, œ̄, ue, ue̅, ʸ\ *see* Guide to Pronunciation

death camas *n* (1889) : any of several plants (genus *Zigadenus*) of the lily family that cause poisoning of livestock in the western U. S.
death camp *n* (1944) : a concentration camp in which large numbers of prisoners are systematically killed
death cap *n* (1925) : a destroying angel (*Amanita phalloides*) — called also *death cup*
death duty *n, chiefly Brit* (1881) : DEATH TAX
death instinct *n* (1922) : an innate and unconscious tendency toward self-destruction postulated in psychoanalytic theory to explain aggressive and destructive behavior not satisfactorily explained by the pleasure principle — called also *Thanatos*; compare EROS 2
death·less \'deth-ləs\ *adj* (1598) : IMMORTAL, IMPERISHABLE ⟨~ fame⟩ — **death·less·ly** *adv* — **death·less·ness** *n*
death·ly \'deth-lē\ *adj* (bef. 12c) **1** : FATAL **2** : of, relating to, or suggestive of death ⟨a ~ pallor⟩ — **deathly** *adv*
death mask *n* (1877) : a cast taken from the face of a dead person
death rattle *n* (1822) : a rattling or gurgling sound produced by air passing through mucus in the lungs and air passages of a dying person
death row *n* (1950) : a prison area housing inmates sentenced to death
death's–head \'deths-,hed\ *n* (1596) : a human skull emblematic of death
deaths·man \'deth-smən\ *n, archaic* (1589) : EXECUTIONER
death tax *n* (1937) : a tax arising on the transmission of property after the owner's death; *esp* : ESTATE TAX
death trap *n* (1835) : a structure or situation that is potentially very dangerous to life
death warrant *n* (1692) **1** : a warrant for the execution of a death sentence **2** : DEATHBLOW
[1]**death·watch** \'deth-,wäch\ *n* [*death* + *watch* (timepiece); fr. the superstition that its ticking presages death] (1646) : a small insect that makes a ticking sound: as **a** : DEATHWATCH BEETLE **b** : BOOK LOUSE
[2]**deathwatch** *n* [*death* + *watch* (vigil)] (ca. 1890) **1** : a vigil kept over the dead or dying **2** : the guard set over a criminal before his execution
deathwatch beetle *n* (1877) : any of various small beetles (family Anobiidae) that are common in old houses where they bore in woodwork and furniture
death wish *n* (1913) : the conscious or unconscious desire for the death of another or of oneself
deb \'deb\ *n* [by shortening] (1920) : DEBUTANTE
de·ba·cle \di-'bäk-əl, -'bak-; dā-'bäk(lə), 'dā-, ; *also* 'deb-i-kəl\ *n* [F *débâcle*, fr. *débâcler* to unbar, fr. MF *desbacler*, fr. *des-* de- + *bacler* to bar, fr. OProv *baclar*, fr. (assumed) VL *bacculare*, fr. L *baculum* staff — more at PEG] (1802) **1** : a tumultuous breakup of ice in a river **2** : a violent disruption (as of an army) : ROUT **3 a** : a great disaster **b** : a complete failure : FIASCO
de·bar \di-'bär\ *vt* [ME *debarren*, fr. MF *desbarrer* to unbar, fr. *des-* de- + *barrer* to bar] (15c) : to bar from having or doing something : PRECLUDE — **de·bar·ment** \-mənt\ *n*
[1]**de·bark** \di-'bärk\ *vb* [F *debarquer*, fr. *de-* + *barque* bark (ship)] (1654) : DISEMBARK — **de·bar·ka·tion** \,dē-,bär-'kā-shən\ *n*
[2]**de·bark** \(')dē-'bärk\ *vt* (1742) : to remove bark from
de·base \di-'bās\ *vt* (1565) **1** : to lower in status, esteem, quality, or character **2 a** : to reduce the intrinsic value of (a coin) by increasing the base-metal content **b** : to reduce the exchange value of (a monetary unit) — **de·base·ment** \-'bā-smənt\ *n* — **de·bas·er** \-'bā-sər\ *n*
syn DEBASE, VITIATE, DEPRAVE, CORRUPT, DEBAUCH, PERVERT mean to cause deterioration or lowering in quality or character. DEBASE implies a loss of position, worth, value, or dignity; VITIATE implies a destruction of purity, validity, or effectiveness by allowing entrance of a fault or defect; DEPRAVE implies moral deterioration by evil thoughts or influences; CORRUPT implies loss of soundness, purity, or integrity; DEBAUCH implies a debasing through sensual indulgence; PERVERT implies a twisting or distorting from what is natural or normal. ***syn*** see in addition ABASE
de·bat·able \di-'bāt-ə-bəl\ *adj* (1536) **1** : claimed by more than one country ⟨~ border territory⟩ **2 a** : open to dispute : QUESTIONABLE **b** : open to debate **3** : capable of being debated
[1]**de·bate** \di-'bāt\ *n* (14c) : a contention by words or arguments: as **a** : the formal discussion of a motion before a deliberative body according to the rules of parliamentary procedure **b** : a regulated discussion of a proposition between two matched sides
[2]**debate** *vb* **de·bat·ed**; **de·bat·ing** [ME *debaten*, fr. MF *debatre*, fr. OF, fr. *de-* + *batre* to beat, fr. L *battuere* — more at BATTLE] *vi* (14c) **1** *obs* : FIGHT, CONTEND **2 a** : to contend in words **b** : to discuss a question by considering opposed arguments **3** : to participate in a debate ~ *vt* **1 a** : to argue about **b** : to engage (an opponent) in debate **2** : to turn over in one's mind ***syn*** see DISCUSS — **de·bate·ment** \-'bāt-mənt\ *n* — **de·bat·er** *n*
[1]**de·bauch** \di-'bȯch, -'bäch\ *vt* [MF *debaucher*, fr. OF *desbauchier* to scatter, rough-hew (timber), fr. *des-* de- + *bauch* beam, of Gmc origin; akin to OHG *balko* beam — more at BALK] (1595) **1 a** *archaic* : to make disloyal **b** : to seduce from chastity **2 a** : to lead away from virtue or excellence **b** : to corrupt by intemperance or sensuality ***syn*** see DEBASE — **de·bauch·er** *n*
[2]**debauch** *n* (1603) **1** : an act or occasion of debauchery **2** : ORGY
de·bauch·ee \di-,bȯch-'ē, -,bäch-; ,deb-ə-'shē, -'shā\ *n* [F *débauché*, fr. pp. of *débaucher*] (1661) : one given to debauchery
de·bauch·ery \di-'bȯch-(ə-)rē, -'bäch-\ *n, pl* **-er·ies** (1642) **1 a** : extreme indulgence in sensuality **b** *pl* : ORGIES **2** *archaic* : seduction from virtue or duty
de·ben·ture \di-'ben-chər\ *n* [ME *debentur*, fr. L, they are due, 3d pl. pres. pass. of *debēre* to owe — more at DEBT] (15c) **1** *Brit* : a corporate security other than an equity security : BOND **2** : a bond backed by the general credit of the issuer rather than a specific lien on particular assets
de·bil·i·tate \di-'bil-ə-,tāt\ *vt* **-tat·ed**; **-tat·ing** [L *debilitatus*, pp. of *debilitare* to weaken, fr. *debilis* weak] (1533) : to impair the strength of : ENFEEBLE ***syn*** see WEAKEN — **de·bil·i·ta·tion** \-,bil-ə-'tā-shən\ *n*
de·bil·i·ty \di-'bil-ət-ē\ *n, pl* **-ties** [MF *debilité*, fr. L *debiltat-*, *debilitas*, fr. *debilis*] (15c) : WEAKNESS, INFIRMITY
[1]**deb·it** \'deb-ət\ *vt* (1682) : to enter upon the debit side of an account : charge with a debit
[2]**debit** *n* [L *debitum* debt] (1776) **1** : a record of an indebtedness; *specif* : an entry on the left-hand side of an account constituting an addition to an expense or asset account or a deduction from a revenue, net worth, or liability account **2** : the sum of the items so entered **3** : a charge against a bank deposit account **4** : DRAWBACK, SHORTCOMING
debit card *n* (1977) : a card like a credit card by which money may be withdrawn or the cost of purchases paid directly from the holder's bank account without the payment of interest
deb·o·nair \,deb-ə-'na(ə)r, -'ne(ə)r\ *adj* [ME *debonere*, fr. OF *debonaire*, fr. *de bon aire* of good family or nature] (13c) **1** *archaic* : GENTLE, COURTEOUS **2 a** : SUAVE, URBANE **b** : LIGHTHEARTED, NONCHALANT — **deb·o·nair·ly** *adv* — **deb·o·nair·ness** *n*
de·bone \(')dē-'bōn\ *vt* (1944) : BONE ⟨*deboned* the meat⟩ — **de·bon·er** *n*
Deb·o·rah \'deb-(ə-)rə\ *n* [Heb *Dĕbhōrāh*] : a Hebrew prophetess who rallied the Israelites in their struggles against the Canaanites
de·bouch \di-'bau̇ch, -'büsh\ *vb* [F *déboucher*, fr. *dé-* de- + *bouche* mouth, fr. L *bucca* cheek — more at POCK] *vt* (1745) : to cause to emerge ~ *vi* **1** : to march out into open ground **2** : EMERGE, ISSUE
de·bouch·ment \-mənt\ *n* (ca. 1823) **1** : the act or process of debouching **2** : a mouth or outlet esp. of a river
de·bou·chure \di-,bü-'shu̇(ə)r\ *n* (1832) : DEBOUCHMENT 2
de·bride·ment \di-'brēd-mənt, dā-, -,mänt, -,mä^{n}\ *n* [F *débridement*, fr. *débrider* to remove unhealthy tissue, lit., to unbridle, fr. MF *desbrider*, fr. *des-* de- + *bride* bridle, fr. MHG *brīdel* — more at BRIDLE] (ca. 1842) : the surgical removal of lacerated, devitalized, or contaminated tissue — **de·bride** \di-'brēd, dā-\ *vt*
de·brief \di-'brēf, 'dē-\ *vt* (1945) **1** : to interrogate (as a pilot) in order to obtain useful information **2** : to instruct not to reveal any classified information after release from a sensitive position
de·bris \də-'brē, dā-', 'dā-,, *Brit usu* 'deb-(,)rē\ *n, pl* **de·bris** \-'brēz, -,brēz, -(,)rēz\ [F *débris*, fr. MF, fr. *debriser* to break to pieces, fr. OF *debrisier*, fr. *de-* + *brisier* to break — more at BRISANCE] (1708) **1** : the remains of something broken down or destroyed : RUINS **2** : an accumulation of fragments of rock
debt \'det\ *n* [ME *dette*, *debte*, fr. OF *dette* something owed, fr. (assumed) VL *debita*, fr. L, pl. of *debitum* debt, fr. neut. of *debitus*, pp. of *debēre* to owe, fr. *de-* + *habēre* to have — more at GIVE] (13c) **1** : SIN, TRESPASS **2** : something owed : OBLIGATION **3** : a state of owing **4** : the common-law action for the recovery of money held to be due — **debt·less** \-ləs\ *adj*
debt·or \'det-ər\ *n* (13c) **1** : one guilty of neglect or violation of duty **2** : one who owes a debt
de·bug \(')dē-'bəg\ *vt* (1945) **1** : to eliminate errors in or malfunctions of **2** : to remove a concealed microphone or wiretapping device from
de·bunk \(')dē-'bəŋk\ *vt* (1923) : to expose the sham or falseness of ⟨~ a legend⟩ — **de·bunk·er** *n*
de·but \'dā-,byü, dā-'\ *n* [F *début*, fr. *débuter* to begin, fr. MF *desbuter* to play first, fr. *des-* de- + *but* starting point, goal — more at BUTT] (1751) **1** : a first appearance ⟨made her singing ~⟩ **2** : a formal entrance into society — **debut** *vi*
deb·u·tant \'deb-yu̇-,tänt\ *n* [F *débutant*, fr. prp. of *débuter*] (1821) : one making a debut
deb·u·tante \'deb-yu̇-,tänt\ *n* [F *débutante*, fem. of *débutant*] (1817) : a young woman making her formal entrance into society
deca- *or* **dec-** *or* **deka-** *or* **dek-** *comb form* [ME, fr. L, fr. Gk *deka-*, *dek-*, fr. *deka* — more at TEN] : ten ⟨*deca*merous⟩ ⟨*deka*volt⟩
de·cade \'dek-,ād, -əd; de-'kād; *3 is usually* 'dek-əd\ *n* [ME, fr. MF *décade*, fr. LL *decad-*, *decas*, fr. Gk *dekad-*, *dekas*, fr. *deka*] (15c) **1** : a group or set of 10 **2** : a period of 10 years **3** : a division of the rosary that consists primarily of 10 Hail Marys
dec·a·dence \'dek-əd-ən(t)s *also* di-'kād-ən(t)s\ *n* [MF, fr. ML *decadentia*, fr. LL *decadent-*, *decadens*, prp. of *decadere* to fall, sink — more at DECAY] (1549) **1** : the process of becoming decadent : the quality or state of being decadent **2** : a period of decline ***syn*** see DETERIORATION
dec·a·den·cy \-ən-sē, -ən-sē\ *n* (1632) : DECADENCE 1
[1]**dec·a·dent** \'dek-əd-ənt *also* di-'kād-ənt\ *adj* [back-formation fr. *decadence*] (1837) **1** : marked by decay or decline **2** : of, relating to, or having the characteristics of the decadents — **dec·a·dent·ly** *adv*
[2]**decadent** *n* (1886) **1** : one of a group of late 19th century French and English writers tending toward artificial and unconventional subjects and subtilized style **2** : one that is decadent
de·caf \'dē-,kaf\ *n* [short for *decaffeinated*] (1984) : decaffeinated coffee
de·caf·fein·at·ed \(')dē-'kaf-(ē-)ə-,nāt-əd\ *adj* (1921) : having the caffeine removed ⟨~ coffee⟩ ⟨~ tea⟩
deca·gon \'dek-ə-,gän\ *n* [NL *decagonum*, fr. Gk *dekagōnon*, fr. *deka-* deca- + *-gōnon* -gon] (1613) : a plane polygon of 10 angles and 10 sides

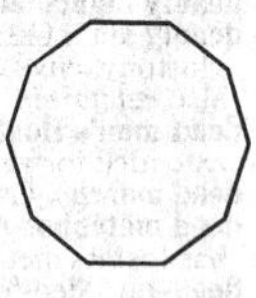

decagon

deca·gram \-,gram\ *n* [F *décagramme*, fr. *déca-* deca- + *gramme* gram] (1810) : DEKAGRAM
deca·he·dron \,dek-ə-'hē-drən\ *n* [ISV] (ca. 1828) : a polyhedron of 10 faces
de·cal \'dē-,kal, di-'kal\ *n* [short for *decalcomania*] (1937) : a picture, design, or label made to be transferred (as to glass) from specially prepared paper
de·cal·ci·fi·ca·tion \(,)dē-,kal-sə-fə-'kā-shən\ *n* (1859) : the removal or loss of calcium or calcium compounds (as from bones or soil)
de·cal·ci·fy \(')dē-'kal-sə-,fī\ *vt* [ISV] (1847) : to remove calcium or calcium compounds from
de·cal·co·ma·nia \di-,kal-kə-'mā-nē-ə\ *n* [F *décalcomanie*, fr. *décalquer* to copy by tracing (fr. *dé-* de- + *calquer* to trace, fr. It *calcare*, lit., to trample, fr. L) + *manie* mania, fr. LL *mania* — more at CAULK] (1865) **1** : the art or process of transferring pictures and designs from specially prepared paper (as to glass) **2** : DECAL
de·ca·les·cence \,dē-kə-'les-ən(t)s, ,dek-ə-\ *n* [ISV *de-* + *-calescence* (as in *recalescence*)] (ca. 1893) : a decrease in temperature that occurs while heating metal through a range in which change in structure occurs
deca·li·ter \'dek-ə-,lēt-ər\ *n* [F *décalitre*, fr. *déca-* + *litre* liter] (1810) : DEKALITER
deca·logue \'dek-ə-,lȯg, -,läg\ *n* [ME *decaloge*, fr. LL *decalogus*, fr. Gk *dekalogos*, fr. *deka-* + *logos* word — more at LEGEND] (14c) **1** *cap*

: TEN COMMANDMENTS **2** : a basic set of rules carrying binding authority

[1]**deca·me·ter** \'dek-ə-ˌmēt-ər\ *n* [F *décamètre,* fr. *déca-* + *mètre* meter] (1810) : DEKAMETER

[2]**de·cam·e·ter** \de-'kam-ət-ər, də-\ *n* [Gk *dekametron,* fr. *deka-* + *metron* measure, meter] (1821) : a line of verse consisting of 10 metrical feet

deca·me·tho·ni·um \ˌdek-ə-mə-'thō-nē-əm\ *n* [*decamethonium* (an ammonium ion), fr. *deca-* + *methylene* + *-onium*] (ca. 1949) : a synthetic ion used in the form of either its bromide or iodide salts ($C_{16}H_{38}Br_2N_2$ or $C_{16}H_{38}I_2N_2$) as a skeletal muscle relaxant; *also* : either of these salts

deca·met·ric \ˌdek-ə-'me-trik\ *adj* [*decameter* + *-ic;* fr. the wavelength range being between 1 and 10 dekameters] (1950) : of, relating to, or being a radio wave of high frequency

de·camp \di-'kamp\ *vi* [F *décamper,* fr. MF *descamper,* fr. *des-* de- + *camper* to camp] (1676) **1** : to break up a camp **2** : to depart suddenly : ABSCOND — **de·camp·ment** \-mənt\ *n*

dec·ane \'dek-ˌān\ *n* [ISV *deca-*] (ca. 1875) : any of several isomeric liquid hydrocarbons $C_{10}H_{22}$ of the methane series

dec·a·no·ic acid \ˌdek-ə-ˌnō-ik-\ *n* [ISV, fr. *decane*] (ca. 1929) : CAPRIC ACID

de·cant \di-'kant\ *vt* [NL *decantare,* fr. L *de-* + ML *cantus* side, fr. L, iron ring round a carriage wheel — more at CANT] (1633) **1** : to draw off without disturbing the sediment or the lower liquid layers **2** : to pour from one vessel into another — **de·can·ta·tion** \ˌdē-ˌkan-'tā-shən\ *n*

de·cant·er \di-'kant-ər\ *n* (1712) : a vessel used to decant or to receive decanted liquids; *esp* : an ornamental glass bottle used for serving wine

de·cap·i·tate \di-'kap-ə-ˌtāt\ *vt* **-tat·ed; -tat·ing** [LL *decapitatus,* pp. of *decapitare,* fr. L *de-* + *capit-, caput* head — more at HEAD] (ca. 1611) : to cut off the head of : BEHEAD — **de·cap·i·ta·tion** \-ˌkap-ə-'tā-shən\ *n* — **de·cap·i·ta·tor** \-'kap-ə-ˌtāt-ər\ *n*

deca·pod \'dek-ə-ˌpäd\ *n* [NL *Decapoda,* order name] (1882) **1** : any of an order (Decapoda) of highly organized crustaceans (as shrimps, lobsters, and crabs) with five pairs of thoracic appendages one or more of which are modified into pincers, with stalked eyes, and with the head and thorax fused into a cephalothorax and covered by a carapace **2** : any of an order (Decapoda) of cephalopod mollusks including the cuttlefishes, squids, and related forms that have 10 arms — **decapod** *adj* — **de·cap·o·dan** \di-'kap-əd-ən\ *adj or n* — **de·cap·o·dous** \-əd-əs\ *adj*

de·car·bon·ate \(ˈ)dē-'kär-bə-ˌnāt\ *vt* (1831) : to remove carbon dioxide or carbonic acid from — **de·car·bon·ation** \(ˌ)dē-ˌkär-bə-'nā-shən\ *n*

de·car·bon·ize \(ˈ)dē-'kär-bə-ˌnīz\ *vt* [ISV] (1825) : to remove carbon from — **de·car·bon·iz·er** *n*

de·car·box·yl·ase \ˌdē-kär-'bäk-sə-ˌlās, -ˌlāz\ *n* (1940) : any of a group of enzymes that accelerate decarboxylation esp. of amino acids

de·car·box·yl·ate \-sə-ˌlāt\ *vt* (1922) : to remove carboxyl from — **de·car·box·yl·ation** \-ˌbäk-sə-'lā-shən\ *n*

de·car·bu·rize \(ˈ)dē-'kär-b(y)ə-ˌrīz\ *vt* (1856) : DECARBONIZE — **de·car·bu·ri·za·tion** \(ˌ)dē-ˌkär-b(y)ə-rə-'zā-shən\ *n*

dec·are \'dek-ˌa(ə)r, -ˌe(ə)r, -ˌär\ *n* [F *décare,* fr. *déca-* deca- + *are*] (1810) : a metric unit of area equal to 10 ares or 0.2471 acre

de·ca·su·al·iza·tion \(ˌ)dē-ˌkazh-(ə-)wə-lə-'zā-shən, -ˌkazh-ə-lə-\ *n* (1892) : the process of eliminating the employment of casual workers in order to stabilize the work force

deca·syl·lab·ic \ˌdek-ə-sə-'lab-ik\ *adj* [prob. fr. F *décasyllabique,* fr. Gk *dekasyllabos,* fr. *deka-* deca- + *syllabē* syllable] (1771) : consisting of 10 syllables or composed of verses of 10 syllables — **decasyllabic** *n* — **deca·syl·la·ble** \'dek-ə-ˌsil-ə-bəl, ˌdek-ə-'\ *n*

de·cath·lete \di-'kath-ˌlēt\ *n* [blend of *decathlon* and *athlete*] (1968) : an athlete who competes in the decathlon

de·cath·lon \di-'kath-lən, -ˌlän\ *n* [F *décathlon,* fr. *déca-* deca- + Gk *athlon* contest — more at ATHLETE] (1912) : a 10-event composite athletic contest consisting of the 100-meter, 400-meter, and 1500-meter runs, the 110-meter high hurdles, the javelin and discus throws, shot put, pole vault, high jump, and long jump

[1]**de·cay** \di-'kā\ *vb* [ME *decayen,* fr. ONF *decaïr,* fr. LL *decadere* to fall, sink, fr. L *de-* + *cadere* to fall — more at CHANCE] *vi* (15c) **1** : to decline from a sound or prosperous condition **2** : to decrease gradually in quantity, activity, or force **3** : to fall into ruin **4** : to decline in health, strength, or vigor **5** : to undergo decomposition ~ *vt* **1** *obs* : to cause to decay : IMPAIR ⟨infirmity that ~s the wise —Shak.⟩ **2** : to destroy by decomposition — **de·cay·er** *n*

syn DECAY, DECOMPOSE, ROT, PUTREFY, SPOIL mean to undergo destructive dissolution. DECAY implies a slow change from a state of soundness or perfection; DECOMPOSE stresses a breaking down by chemical change and when applied to organic matter a corruption; ROT is a close synonym of DECOMPOSE and often connotes foulness; PUTREFY implies the rotting of animal matter and offensiveness to sight and smell; SPOIL applies chiefly to the decomposition of foods.

[2]**decay** *n* (15c) **1** : gradual decline in strength, soundness, or prosperity or in degree of excellence or perfection **2** : a wasting or wearing away : RUIN **3** *obs* : DESTRUCTION, DEATH **4 a** : ROT; *specif* : aerobic decomposition of proteins chiefly by bacteria **b** : the product of decay **5** : a decline in health or vigor **6** : decrease in quantity, activity, or force: as **a** : spontaneous decrease in the number of radioactive atoms in radioactive material **b** : spontaneous disintegration (as of an atom or a meson)

Dec·ca \'dek-ə\ *n* [*Decca* Co., British firm which developed it] (1946) : a system of long-range navigation utilizing the phase differences of continuous-wave signals from synchronized ground transmitters

de·cease \di-'sēs\ *n* [ME *deces,* fr. MF, fr. L *decessus* departure, death, fr. *decessus,* pp. of *decedere* to depart, die, fr. *de-* + *cedere* to go — more at CEDE] (14c) : departure from life : DEATH — **decease** *vi*

[1]**de·ceased** \-'sēst\ *adj* (15c) : no longer living; *esp* : recently dead — used of persons ***syn*** see DEAD

[2]**deceased** *n, pl* **deceased** (1625) : a dead person ⟨the will of the ~⟩

de·ce·dent \di-'sēd-ᵊnt\ *n* [L *decedent-, decedens,* prp. of *decedere*] (1650) : a deceased person — used chiefly in law

de·ceit \di-'sēt\ *n* [ME *deceite,* fr. MF, fr. L *decepta,* fem. of *deceptus,* pp. of *decipere*] (14c) **1** : the act or practice of deceiving : DECEPTION **2** : an attempt or device to deceive : TRICK **3** : the quality of being deceitful : DECEITFULNESS

de·ceit·ful \-fəl\ *adj* (15c) : having a tendency or disposition to deceive: **a** : not honest ⟨a ~ child⟩ **b** : DECEPTIVE, MISLEADING ***syn*** see DISHONEST — **de·ceit·ful·ly** \-fə-lē\ *adv* — **de·ceit·ful·ness** *n*

de·ceiv·able \di-'sē-və-bəl\ *adj* (14c) **1** *archaic* : DECEITFUL, DECEPTIVE **2** *archaic* : capable of being deceived

de·ceive \di-'sēv\ *vb* **de·ceived; de·ceiv·ing** [ME *deceiven,* fr. MF *deceivre,* fr. L *decipere,* fr. *de-* + *capere* to take — more at HEAVE] *vt* (14c) **1** *archaic* : ENSNARE **2 a** *obs* : to be false to **b** *archaic* : to fail to fulfill **3** *obs* : CHEAT **4** : to cause to accept as true or valid what is false or invalid **5** *archaic* : to while away ~ *vi* : to practice deceit; *also* : to give a false impression ⟨this response might appear to be narcissistic, but appearance ~s —G.G. Gallup, Jr.⟩ — **de·ceiv·er** *n* — **de·ceiv·ing·ly** \-'sē-viŋ-lē\ *adv*

syn DECEIVE, MISLEAD, DELUDE, BEGUILE mean to lead astray or frustrate usu. by underhandedness. DECEIVE implies imposing a false idea or belief that causes ignorance, bewilderment, or helplessness; MISLEAD implies a leading astray that may or may not be intentional; DELUDE implies deceiving so thoroughly as to obscure the truth; BEGUILE stresses the use of charm and persuasion in deceiving.

de·cel·er·ate \(ˈ)dē-'sel-ə-ˌrāt\ *vb* **-at·ed; -at·ing** [*de-* + accelerate] *vt* (1899) **1** : to reduce the speed of : slow down **2** : to decrease the rate of progress of ~ *vi* : to move at decreasing speed — **de·cel·er·a·tion** \(ˌ)dē-ˌsel-ə-'rā-shən\ *n* — **de·cel·er·a·tor** \(ˈ)dē-'sel-ə-ˌrāt-ər\ *n*

De·cem·ber \di-'sem-bər\ *n* [ME *Decembre,* fr. OE or OF, both fr. L *December* (tenth month), fr. *decem* ten — more at TEN] (bef. 12c) : the 12th month of the Gregorian calendar

De·cem·brist \-brəst\ *n* (1867) : one taking part in the unsuccessful uprising against the Russian emperor Nicholas I in December 1825

de·cem·vir \di-'sem-vər\ *n* [L, back-formation fr. *decemviri,* pl., fr. *decem* + *viri,* pl. of *vir* man — more at VIRILE] (1703) : one of a ruling body of 10; *specif* : one of a body of 10 magistrates in ancient Rome — **de·cem·vi·ral** \-və-rəl\ *adj* — **de·cem·vi·rate** \-rət\ *n*

de·cen·cy \'dēs-ᵊn-sē\ *n, pl* **-cies** (1567) **1** *archaic* **a** : FITNESS **b** : ORDERLINESS **2 a** : the quality or state of being decent : PROPRIETY **b** : conformity to standards of taste, propriety, or quality **3** : standard of propriety — usu. used in pl. **4** *pl* : conditions or services considered essential for a proper standard of living **5** : literary decorum

de·cen·ni·al \di-'sen-ē-əl\ *adj* (ca. 1656) **1** : consisting of or lasting for 10 years **2** : occurring or being done every 10 years ⟨the ~ census⟩ — **decennial** *n* — **de·cen·ni·al·ly** \-ē-ə-lē\ *adv*

de·cen·ni·um \-ē-əm\ *n, pl* **-ni·ums** *or* **-nia** \-ē-ə\ [L, fr. *decem* + *annus* year — more at ANNUAL] (1685) : a period of 10 years : DECADE

de·cent \'dēs-ᵊnt\ *adj* [MF or L; MF, fr. L *decent-, decens,* prp. of *decēre* to be fitting; akin to L *decus* honor, *dignus* worthy, Gk *dokein* to seem, seem good] (1539) **1** *archaic* **a** : APPROPRIATE **b** : well-formed : HANDSOME **2 a** : conforming to standards of propriety, good taste, or morality **b** : modestly clothed **3** : free from immodesty or obscenity **4** : fairly good but not excellent : ADEQUATE, SATISFACTORY ⟨~ wages⟩ ⟨a ~ meal⟩ **5** : morally praiseworthy ⟨hard-working and ~ folks⟩ ***syn*** see CHASTE — **de·cent·ly** *adv*

de·cen·tral·iza·tion \(ˌ)dē-ˌsen-trə-lə-'zā-shən\ *n* (1846) **1** : the dispersion or distribution of functions and powers from a central authority to regional and local authorities **2** : the redistribution of population and industry from urban centers to outlying areas — **de·cen·tral·iza·tion·ist** \(ˌ)dē-ˌsen-trə-lə-'zā-sh(ə-)nəst\ *n*

de·cen·tral·ize \(ˈ)dē-'sen-trə-ˌlīz\ *vt* (1859) : to bring about the decentralization of ~ *vi* : to undergo decentralization

de·cep·tion \di-'sep-shən\ *n* [ME *decepcioun,* fr. MF *deception,* fr. LL *deception-, deceptio,* fr. L *deceptus,* pp. of *decipere* to deceive] (15c) **1 a** : the act of deceiving **b** : the fact or condition of being deceived **2** : something that deceives : TRICK — **de·cep·tion·al** \-shnəl, -shən-ᵊl\ *adj*

syn DECEPTION, FRAUD, DOUBLE-DEALING, SUBTERFUGE, TRICKERY mean the acts or practices of one who deliberately deceives. DECEPTION may or may not imply blameworthiness, since it may suggest cheating or merely tactical resource; FRAUD always implies guilt and often criminality in act or practice; DOUBLE-DEALING suggests treachery or at least action contrary to a professed attitude; SUBTERFUGE suggests the adoption of a stratagem or the telling of a lie in order to escape guilt or to gain an end; TRICKERY implies ingenious acts intended to dupe or cheat.

de·cep·tive \di-'sep-tiv\ *adj* (ca. 1611) : tending or having power to deceive : MISLEADING — **de·cep·tive·ly** *adv* — **de·cep·tive·ness** *n*

[1]**de·cer·e·brate** \(ˈ)dē-'ser-ə-ˌbrāt\ *vt* (ca. 1900) : to remove the cerebrum from; *also* : to make incapable of cerebral activity — **de·cer·e·bra·tion** \(ˌ)dē-ˌser-ə-'brā-shən\ *n*

[2]**de·cer·e·brate** \(ˈ)dē-'ser-ə-brət, -ˌbrāt; ˌdē-sə-'rē-brət\ *adj* (1897) **1** : characteristic of decerebration ⟨~ rigidity⟩ **2** : having the cerebrum removed or made inactive

de·cer·ti·fy \(ˈ)dē-'sərt-ə-ˌfī\ *vt* (1918) : to withdraw or revoke the certification of — **de·cer·ti·fi·ca·tion** \(ˌ)dē-ˌsərt-ə-fə-'kā-shən\ *n*

de·chlo·ri·nate \(ˈ)dē-'klōr-ə-ˌnāt, -'klȯr-\ *vt* (1941) : to remove chlorine from ⟨~ water⟩ — **de·chlo·ri·na·tion** \(ˌ)dē-ˌklōr-ə-'nā-shən, -ˌklȯr-\ *n*

deci- *comb form* [F *déci-,* fr. L *decimus* tenth, fr. *decem* ten — more at TEN] : tenth part ⟨*deci*normal⟩

deci·are \'des-ē-ˌa(ə)r, -ˌe(ə)r, -ˌär\ *n* [F *déciare,* fr. *déci-* + *are*] (1810) : a metric unit of area equal to 10 square meters or 11.96 square yards

deci·bel \'des-ə-ˌbel, -bəl\ *n* [ISV *deci-* + *bel*] (1928) **1 a** : a unit for expressing the ratio of two amounts of electric or acoustic signal power equal to 10 times the common logarithm of this ratio **b** : a unit for expressing the ratio of the magnitudes of two electric voltages or currents or analogous acoustic quantities equal to 20 times the common logarithm of the voltage or current ratio **2** : a unit for expressing the relative intensity of sounds on a scale from zero for the average least perceptible sound to about 130 for the average pain level **3** : degree of loudness; *also* : extremely loud sound — usu. used in pl.

\ə\ abut \ᵊ\ kitten, F table \ər\ further \a\ ash \ā\ ace \ä\ cot, cart
\au̇\ out \ch\ chin \e\ bet \ē\ easy \g\ go \i\ hit \ī\ ice \j\ job
\ŋ\ sing \ō\ go \ȯ\ law \ȯi\ boy \th\ thin \t͟h\ the \ü\ loot \u̇\ foot
\y\ yet \zh\ vision \á, k̲, ⁿ, œ, œ̄, ue, ue̅, ʸ\ *see* Guide to Pronunciation

de·cide \di-ˈsīd\ *vb* **de·cid·ed; de·cid·ing** [ME *deciden,* fr. MF *decider,* fr. L *decidere,* lit., to cut off, fr. *de-* + *caedere* to cut — more at CONCISE] *vt* (14c) **1 :** to arrive at a solution that ends uncertainty or dispute about ⟨important . . . that we ~ borderline cases in favor of individual freedom —Milton Friedman⟩ **2 :** to bring to a definitive end ⟨one blow *decided* the fight⟩ **3 :** to induce to come to a choice ⟨her pleas *decided* him to help⟩ ~ *vi* **:** to make a choice or judgment — **de·cid·abil·i·ty** \-ˌsīd-ə-ˈbil-ət-ē\ *n* — **de·cid·able** \-ˈsīd-ə-bəl\ *adj* — **de·cid·er** *n*
syn DECIDE, DETERMINE, SETTLE, RULE, RESOLVE mean to come or cause to come to a conclusion. DECIDE implies previous consideration of a matter causing doubt, wavering, debate, or controversy; DETERMINE implies fixing the identity, character, scope, or direction of something; SETTLE implies a decision reached by someone with power to end all dispute or uncertainty; RULE implies a determination by judicial or administrative authority; RESOLVE implies an expressed or clear decision or determination to do or refrain from doing something.

de·cid·ed *adj* (1790) **1 :** UNQUESTIONABLE ⟨a ~ advantage⟩ **2 :** free from doubt or wavering — **de·cid·ed·ly** *adv* — **de·cid·ed·ness** *n*

de·cid·ing *adj* (1658) **:** that decides **:** DECISIVE ⟨drove in the ~ run⟩

de·cid·ua \di-ˈsij-ə-wə\ *n, pl* **-u·ae** \-ə-ˌwē\ [NL, fr. L, fem. of *deciduus*] (1785) **1 :** the part of the mucous membrane lining the uterus that in higher placental mammals undergoes special modifications in preparation for and during pregnancy and is cast off at parturition **2 :** the part of the mucous membrane of the uterus cast off in the process of menstruation — **de·cid·u·al** \-wəl\ *adj*

de·cid·u·ate \-wət\ *adj* (1868) **:** having the fetal and maternal tissues firmly interlocked so that a layer of maternal tissue is torn away at parturition and forms a part of the afterbirth

de·cid·u·ous \di-ˈsij-ə-wəs\ *adj* [L *deciduus,* fr. *decidere* to fall off, fr. *de-* + *cadere* to fall — more at CHANCE] (1688) **1 :** falling off or shed seasonally or at a certain stage of development in the life cycle ⟨~ leaves⟩ ⟨~ teeth⟩ **2 :** having deciduous parts ⟨~ trees⟩ **3 :** EPHEMERAL — **de·cid·u·ous·ness** *n*

deci·gram \ˈdes-ə-ˌgram\ *n* [F *décigramme,* fr. *déci-* + *gramme* gram] (1810) — see METRIC SYSTEM table

dec·ile \ˈdes-ˌīl, -əl\ *n* [L *decem* ten — more at TEN] (1882) **:** any one of nine numbers that divide a frequency distribution into 10 classes such that each contains the same number of individuals; *also* **:** any one of these 10 classes — **decile** *adj*

deci·li·ter \ˈdes-ə-ˌlēt-ər\ *n* [F *décilitre,* fr. *déci-* + *litre* liter] (1801) — see METRIC SYSTEM table

de·cil·lion \di-ˈsil-yən\ *n, often attrib* [L decem + E *-illion* (as in *million*)] (1847) — see NUMBER table

[1]**dec·i·mal** \ˈdes(-ə)-məl\ *adj* [(assumed) NL *decimalis,* fr. ML, of a tithe, fr. L *decima* tithe — more at DIME] (1608) **:** numbered or proceeding by tens: **a :** based on the number 10; *esp* **:** expressed in or utilizing decimal notation esp with the decimal point **b :** subdivided into 10th or 100th units ⟨~ coinage⟩ — **dec·i·mal·ly** \-mə-lē\ *adv*

[2]**decimal** *n* (1651) **:** any real number expressed in base 10; *esp* **:** DECIMAL FRACTION

decimal fraction *n* (1660) **:** a fraction (as .25 = 25/100 or .025 = 25/1000) or mixed number (as 3.025 = 3 25/1000) in which the denominator is a power of 10 usu. expressed by use of the decimal point

dec·i·mal·ize \ˈdes(-ə)-mə-ˌlīz\ *vt* **-ized; -iz·ing** (1856) **:** to convert to a decimal system ⟨~ currency⟩ — **dec·i·mal·iza·tion** \ˌdes(-ə)-mə-lə-ˈzā-shən\ *n*

decimal notation *n* (1841) **:** expression of a number in base 10 by using one of the first nine integers or 0 in each place and letting each place value be a power of 10

decimal point *n* (ca. 1864) **:** the dot at the left of a proper decimal fraction (as .678) or between the parts of a mixed number (as 3.678) expressed by a whole number and a decimal fraction

dec·i·mate \ˈdes-ə-ˌmāt\ *vt* **-mat·ed; -mat·ing** [L *decimatus,* pp. of *decimare,* fr. *decimus* tenth, fr. *decem* ten] (1660) **1 :** to select by lot and kill every tenth man of **2 :** to take a tenth from **:** TITHE **3 :** to destroy a large part of — **dec·i·ma·tion** \ˌdes-ə-ˈmā-shən\ *n*

deci·me·ter \ˈdes-ə-ˌmēt-ər\ *n* [F *décimètre,* fr. *déci-* deci- + *mètre* meter] (1809) — see METRIC SYSTEM table

de·ci·pher \di-ˈsī-fər\ *vt* (1545) **1 a :** to convert into intelligible form **b :** DECODE **2** *obs* **:** DEPICT **3 :** to make out the meaning of despite indistinctness or obscurity — **de·ci·pher·able** \-f(ə-)rə-bəl\ *adj* — **de·ci·pher·er** \-fər-ər\ *n* — **de·ci·pher·ment** \-fər-mənt\ *n*

de·ci·sion \di-ˈsizh-ən\ *n* [MF, fr. L *decision-, decisio,* fr. *decisus,* pp. of *decidere* to decide] (15c) **1 a :** the act or process of deciding **b :** a determination arrived at after consideration **:** CONCLUSION **2 :** a report of a conclusion **3 :** promptness and firmness in deciding **:** DETERMINATION — **de·ci·sion·al** \-ˈsizh-nəl, -ən-ᵊl\ *adj*

decision theory *n* (1961) **:** a branch of statistical theory that attempts to quantify the process of making choices between alternatives

de·ci·sive \di-ˈsī-siv\ *adj* (1611) **1 :** having the power or quality of deciding **2 :** RESOLUTE, DETERMINED **3 :** UNMISTAKABLE, UNQUESTIONABLE ⟨a ~ superiority⟩ ***syn*** see CONCLUSIVE — **de·ci·sive·ly** *adv* — **de·ci·sive·ness** *n*

[1]**deck** \ˈdek\ *n* [ME *dekke* covering of a ship, deck, fr. (assumed) MD *dec* covering, prob. fr. MLG *vordeck,* fr. *vordecken* to cover, fr. *vor-* for- + *decken* to cover; akin to OHG *decchen* to cover — more at THATCH] (15c) **1 :** a platform in a ship serving usu. as a structural element and forming the floor for its compartments **2 :** something resembling the deck of a ship: as **a :** a story or tier of a building **b :** the roadway of a bridge **c :** a flat floored roofless area adjoining a house **d :** the lid of the compartment at the rear of the body of an automobile; *also* **:** the compartment **e :** a layer of clouds **f :** TAPE DECK 1b **3 a :** a pack of playing cards **b :** a packet of narcotics **c :** a group of usu. punched data processing cards — **on deck 1 :** ready for duty **2 :** next in line **:** next in turn

[2]**deck** *vt* [D *dekken* to cover; akin to OHG *decchen*] (1513) **1** *obs* **:** COVER **2 a :** to clothe elegantly **:** ARRAY ⟨~*ed* out in furs⟩ **b :** DECORATE ⟨~ the halls with boughs of holly —*English carol*⟩ **3** [[1]*deck*] **:** to furnish with or as if with a deck **4** [[1]*deck*] **:** to knock down forcibly **:** FLOOR ⟨~*ed* him with one punch⟩ ***syn*** see ADORN

deck chair *n* (1884) **:** a folding chair often having an adjustable leg rest

deck·er \ˈdek-ər\ *n* (1790) **:** something having a deck or a specified number of levels, floors, or layers — usu. used in combination ⟨many of the city's buses are double-*deckers*⟩

deck·hand \ˈdek-ˌhand\ *n* (1844) **:** a seaman who performs manual duties

deck·house \-ˌhau̇s\ *n* (1856) **:** a superstructure on a ship's upper deck

deck·ing \ˈdek-iŋ\ *n* (1580) **:** DECK; *also* **:** material for a deck

deck·le \ˈdek-əl\ *n* [G *deckel,* lit., cover, fr. *decken* to cover, fr. OHG *decchen*] (1816) **:** a frame around the edges of a mold used in making paper by hand; *also* **:** either of the bands around the edge of the wire of a papermaking machine that determine the width of the web

deckle edge *n* (ca. 1874) **:** the rough untrimmed edge of paper left by a deckle or produced artificially — **deck·le–edged** \ˌdek-ə-ˈlejd\ *adj*

deck tennis *n* [fr. its being played chiefly on the decks of ocean liners] (1927) **:** a game in which players toss a ring or quoit back and forth over a net stretched across a small court

de·claim \di-ˈklām\ *vb* [ME *declamen,* fr. L *declamare,* fr. *de-* + *clamare* to cry out; akin to L *calare* to call — more at LOW] *vi* (14c) **1 :** to speak rhetorically; *specif* **:** to recite something as an exercise in elocution **2 :** to speak pompously or bombastically **:** HARANGUE ~ *vt* **:** to deliver rhetorically; *specif* **:** to recite in elocution — **de·claim·er** *n* — **dec·la·ma·tion** \ˌdek-lə-ˈmā-shən\ *n*

de·clam·a·to·ry \di-ˈklam-ə-ˌtōr-ē, -ˌtȯr-\ *adj* (1581) **:** of, relating to, or marked by declamation or rhetorical display

de·clar·ant \di-ˈklar-ənt, -ˈkler-\ *n* (1681) **:** one that makes a declaration; *specif* **:** an alien who has declared his intention of becoming a citizen of the U.S. by signing his first papers

dec·la·ra·tion \ˌdek-lə-ˈrā-shən\ *n* (15c) **1 :** the act of declaring **:** ANNOUNCEMENT **2 a :** the first pleading in a common-law action **b :** a statement made by a party to a legal transaction usu. not under oath **3 a :** something that is declared **b :** the document containing such a declaration

de·clar·a·tive \di-ˈklar-ət-iv, -ˈkler-\ *adj* (1628) **:** making a declaration **:** DECLARATORY ⟨a ~ sentence⟩ — **de·clar·a·tive·ly** *adv*

de·clar·a·to·ry \-ə-ˌtōr-ē, -ˌtȯr-\ *adj* (15c) **1 :** serving to declare, set forth, or explain **2 a :** declaring what is the existing law ⟨~ statute⟩ **b :** declaring a legal right or interpretation ⟨a ~ judgment⟩

de·clare \di-ˈkla(ə)r, -ˈkle(ə)r\ *vb* **de·clared; de·clar·ing** [ME *declaren,* fr. MF *declarer,* fr. L *declarare,* fr. *de-* + *clarare* to make clear, fr. *clarus* clear — more at CLEAR] *vt* (14c) **1** *obs* **:** to make clear **2 :** to make known formally or explicitly **3 :** to make evident **:** SHOW **4 :** to state emphatically **:** AFFIRM ⟨~*s* his innocence⟩ **5 :** to make a full statement of (one's taxable or dutiable property) **6 a :** to announce (as a trump suit) in a card game **b :** MELD **7 :** to make payable ~ *vi* **1 :** to make a declaration **2 :** to avow one's support ***syn*** see ASSERT — **de·clar·able** \-ˈklar-ə-bəl, -ˈkler-\ *adj*
syn DECLARE, ANNOUNCE, PUBLISH, PROCLAIM, PROMULGATE mean to make known publicly. DECLARE implies explicitness and usu. formality in making known; ANNOUNCE implies the declaration for the first time of something that is of interest or has created speculation; PUBLISH implies making public through print; PROCLAIM implies declaring clearly, forcefully, and authoritatively; PROMULGATE implies the proclaiming of a dogma, doctrine, or law.

de·clar·er \di-ˈklar-ər, -ˈkler-\ *n* (14c) **:** one that declares; *specif* **:** the bridge player who names the trump and plays both his own hand and that of the dummy

de·class \(ˈ)dē-ˈklas\ *vt* (1888) **:** to remove from a class; *esp* **:** to assign to a lower social status

dé·clas·sé \ˌdā-ˌklas-ˈā, -ˌkläs-\ *adj* [F, fr. pp. of *déclasser* to declass] (1903) **1 :** fallen or lowered in class, rank, or social position **2 :** of inferior status

de·clas·si·fy \(ˈ)dē-ˈklas-ə-ˌfī\ *vt* (1945) **:** to remove or reduce the security classification of ⟨~ a secret document⟩ — **de·clas·si·fi·ca·tion** \(ˌ)dē-ˌklas-ə-fə-ˈkā-shən\ *n*

de·clen·sion \di-ˈklen-chən\ *n* [prob. alter. of earlier *declenson,* modif. of MF *declinaison,* fr. LL *declination-, declinatio,* fr. L, grammatical inflection, turning aside, fr. *declinatus,* pp. of *declinare* to inflect, turn aside] (15c) **1 a :** noun, adjective, or pronoun inflection esp. in some prescribed order of the forms **b :** a class of nouns or adjectives having the same type of inflectional forms **2 :** a falling off or away **:** DETERIORATION **3 :** DESCENT, SLOPE — **de·clen·sion·al** \-ˈklench-nəl, -ˈklen-chən-ᵊl\ *adj*

dec·li·na·tion \ˌdek-lə-ˈnā-shən\ *n* [ME *declinacioun,* fr. MF *declination,* fr. L *declination-, declinatio* turning aside, altitude of the pole] (14c) **1 :** angular distance north or south from the celestial equator measured along a great circle passing through the celestial poles **2 :** a turning aside or swerving **3 :** DETERIORATION ⟨moral ~⟩ **4 :** a bending downward **:** INCLINATION **5 :** a formal refusal **6 :** the angle formed between a magnetic needle and the geographical meridian — **dec·li·na·tion·al** \-shnəl, -shən-ᵊl\ *adj*

[1]**de·cline** \di-ˈklīn\ *vb* **de·clined; de·clin·ing** [ME *declinen,* fr. MF *decliner,* fr. L *declinare* to turn aside, inflect, fr. *de-* + *clinare* to incline — more at LEAN] *vi* (14c) **1 :** to turn from a straight course **:** STRAY **2 a :** to slope downward **:** DESCEND **b :** to bend down **:** DROOP **c :** to stoop to what is unworthy **3 a** *of a celestial body* **:** to sink toward setting **b :** to draw toward a close **:** WANE **4 :** to withhold consent ~ *vt* **1 :** to give in prescribed order the grammatical forms of (a noun, pronoun, or adjective) **2** *obs* **a :** AVERT **b :** AVOID **3 :** to cause to bend or bow downward **4 a :** to refuse to undertake, engage in, or comply with **b :** to refuse courteously ⟨~ an invitation⟩ — **de·clin·able** \-ˈklī-nə-bəl\ *adj*
syn DECLINE, REFUSE, REJECT, REPUDIATE, SPURN mean to turn away by not accepting, receiving, or considering. DECLINE often implies courteous refusal esp. of offers or invitations; REFUSE suggests more positiveness or ungraciousness and often implies the denial of something asked for; REJECT implies a peremptory refusal by sending away or discarding; REPUDIATE implies a casting off or disowning as untrue, unauthorized, or unworthy of acceptance; SPURN stresses contempt or disdain in rejection or repudiation.

[2]**decline** *n* (14c) **1 :** the process of declining: **a :** a gradual physical or mental sinking and wasting away **b :** a change to a lower state or level **2 :** the period during which something is approaching its end **3 :** a downward slope **:** DECLIVITY **4 :** a wasting disease; *esp* **:** pulmonary tuberculosis ***syn*** see DETERIORATION

de·cliv·i·tous \di-ˈkliv-ət-əs\ *adj* (1799) **:** moderately steep

de·cliv·i·ty \-ət-ē\ *n, pl* **-ties** [L *declivitat-, declivitas,* fr. *declivis* sloping down, fr. *de-* + *clivus* slope, hill; akin to L *clinare*] (1612) **1 :** downward inclination **2 :** a descending slope

de·co \dā-ˈkō, ˈdā-,; ˈdek-(,)ō\ *n, often cap* (1974) **:** ART DECO

de·coct \di-ˈkäkt\ *vt* [L *decoctus,* pp. of *decoquere,* fr. *de-* + *coquere* to cook — more at COOK] (15c) **1 :** to extract the flavor of by boiling **2 :** BOIL DOWN, CONCENTRATE

de·coc·tion \di-ˈkäk-shən\ *n* (15c) **1 :** the act or process of decocting **2 :** an extract obtained by decocting

de·code \(ˈ)dē-ˈkōd\ *vt* (1896) **:** to convert (a coded message) into intelligible language

de·cod·er \-ˈkōd-ər\ *n* (1920) **:** one that decodes; *esp* **:** an electronic device for unscrambling a television transmission

de·col·late \di-ˈkäl-,āt\ *vt* **-lat·ed; -lat·ing** [L *decollatus,* pp. of *decollare,* fr. *de-* + *collum* neck — more at COLLAR] (1599) **:** BEHEAD — **de·col·la·tion** \,dē-,kä-ˈlā-shən\ *n*

dé·col·le·tage \(,)dā-,käl-ə-ˈtäzh, ,dek-(ə-)lə-\ *n* [F, action of cutting or wearing a low neckline, fr. *décolleter*] (1894) **1 :** the low-cut neckline of a dress **2 :** a décolleté dress

dé·col·le·té \-ˈtā\ *adj* [F, fr. pp. of *décolleter* to give a low neckline to, fr. *dé-* de- + *collet* collar, fr. OF *colet,* fr. *col* collar, neck, fr. L *collum* neck] (1831) **1 :** wearing a strapless or low-necked dress **2 :** having a low-cut neckline

de·col·o·nize \(ˈ)dē-ˈkäl-ə-,nīz\ *vt* (1963) **:** to free from colonial status — **de·col·o·ni·za·tion** \(,)dē-,käl-ə-nə-ˈzā-shən\ *n*

de·col·or·ize \(ˈ)dē-ˈkəl-ə-,rīz\ *vt* **-ized; -iz·ing** (1836) **:** to remove color from ⟨~ vinegar by adsorption of impurities on activated charcoal⟩ — **de·col·or·iza·tion** \(,)dē-,kəl-ə-rə-ˈzā-shən\ *n* — **de·col·or·iz·er** \(ˈ)dē-ˈkəl-ə-,rī-zər\ *n*

de·com·mis·sion \,dē-kə-ˈmish-ən\ *vt* (1926) **:** to remove (as a ship) from service

de·com·pen·sa·tion \(,)dē-,käm-pən-ˈsā-shən, -,pen-\ *n* [ISV] (ca. 1903) **:** loss of compensation; *esp* **:** inability of the heart to maintain adequate circulation — **de·com·pen·sate** \(ˈ)dē-ˈkäm-pən-,sāt, -,pen-\ *vb*

de·com·pose \,dē-kəm-ˈpōz\ *vb* [F *décomposer,* fr. *dé-* de + *composer* to compose] *vt* (1751) **1 :** to separate into constituent parts or elements or into simpler compounds ⟨~ water by electrolysis⟩ ⟨~ a mathematical group into subgroups⟩ **2 :** ROT ~ *vi* **:** to undergo chemical breakdown **:** DECAY, ROT ⟨fruit ~s⟩ ***syn*** see DECAY — **de·com·pos·abil·i·ty** \-,pō-zə-ˈbil-ət-ē\ *n* — **de·com·pos·able** \-ˈpō-zə-bəl\ *adj* — **de·com·po·si·tion** \(,)dē-,käm-pə-ˈzish-ən\ *n*

de·com·pos·er \,dē-kəm-ˈpō-zər\ *n* (1821) **:** any of various organisms (as many bacteria and fungi) that return constituents of organic substances to ecological cycles by feeding on and breaking down dead protoplasm

de·com·pound \ˈdē-ˈkäm-,paund; ,dē-,käm-ˈ, -kəm-ˈ\ *adj, of a leaf* (ca. 1793) **:** having divisions that are themselves compound

de·com·press \,dē-kəm-ˈpres\ *vt* (1905) **:** to release from pressure or compression ~ *vi* **:** to undergo release from pressure; *esp* **:** RELAX ⟨need a week off to ~⟩ — **de·com·pres·sion** \-ˈpresh-ən\ *n*

decompression sickness *n* (ca. 1941) **:** 3BEND 3, AEROEMBOLISM 2

de·con·cen·trate \(ˈ)dē-ˈkän(t)-sən-,trāt, -,sen-\ *vt* (ca. 1889) **:** DECENTRALIZE — **de·con·cen·tra·tion** \(,)dē-,kän(t)-sən-ˈtrā-shən, -,sen-\ *n*

de·con·di·tion \,dē-kən-ˈdish-ən\ *vt* (1945) **1 :** to cause extinction of (a conditioned response) **2 :** to cause to lose physical fitness

de·con·ges·tant \,dē-kən-ˈjes-tənt\ *n* (1947) **:** an agent that relieves congestion (as of mucous membranes) — **decongestant** *adj*

de·con·ges·tion \,dē-kən-ˈjes(h)-chən\ *n* (1908) **:** the process of relieving congestion — **de·con·gest** \-ˈjest\ *vt* — **de·con·ges·tive** \-ˈjes-tiv\ *adj*

de·con·se·crate \(ˈ)dē-ˈkän(t)-sə-,krāt\ *vt* (1876) **:** to remove the sacred character of ⟨~ a church⟩ — **de·con·se·cra·tion** \(,)dē-,kän(t)-sə-ˈkrā-shən\ *n*

de·con·tam·i·nate \,dē-kən-ˈtam-ə-,nāt\ *vt* (1935) **:** to rid of contamination (as radioactive material) — **de·con·tam·i·na·tion** \-,tam-ə-ˈnā-shən\ *n* — **de·con·tam·i·na·tor** \-ˈtam-ə-,nāt-ər\ *n*

de·con·trol \,dē-kən-ˈtrōl\ *vt* (1919) **:** to end control of — **decontrol** *n*

de·cor *or* **dé·cor** \dā-ˈkȯ(ə)r, di-ˈ; ˈdek-,ȯ(ə)r, ˈdāk-,\ *n* [F *décor,* fr. *décorer* to decorate, fr. L *decorare*] (1897) **1 :** a stage setting **2 a :** DECORATION **b :** the style and layout of interior furnishings

dec·o·rate \ˈdek-ə-,rāt\ *vt* **-rat·ed; -rat·ing** [L *decoratus,* pp. of *decorare,* fr. *decor-, decus* ornament, honor — more at DECENT] (1530) **1 :** to add honor to **2 :** to furnish with something ornamental **3 :** to award a mark of honor to ***syn*** see ADORN

dec·o·ra·tion \,dek-ə-ˈrā-shən\ *n* (1530) **1 :** the act or process of decorating **2 :** ORNAMENT **3 :** a badge of honor (as a U.S. military award)

Decoration Day *n* [fr. the custom of decorating graves on this day] (1871) **:** MEMORIAL DAY

dec·o·ra·tive \ˈdek-(ə-)rət-iv, ˈdek-ə-,rāt-\ *adj* (1791) **:** serving to decorate; *esp* **:** purely ornamental — **dec·o·ra·tive·ly** *adv* — **dec·o·ra·tive·ness** *n*

1dec·o·ra·tor \ˈdek-ə-,rāt-ər\ *n* (ca. 1755) **:** one that decorates; *esp* **:** one that designs or executes interiors and their furnishings

2decorator *adj* (1950) **:** suitable for interior decoration ⟨~ fabrics⟩

dec·o·rous \ˈdek-ə-rəs *also* di-ˈkōr-əs *or* -ˈkȯr-\ *adj* [L *decorus,* fr. *decor* beauty, grace; akin to L *decēre* to be fitting — more at DECENT] (1673) **:** marked by propriety and good taste **:** CORRECT ⟨~ conduct⟩ — **dec·o·rous·ly** *adv* — **dec·o·rous·ness** *n*

de·cor·ti·ca·tion \(,)dē-,kȯrt-ə-ˈkā-shən\ *n* [L *decortication-, decorticatio,* fr. *decorticatus,* pp. of *decorticare* remove the bark from, fr. *de-* + *cortic-, cortex* bark — more at CUIRASS] (ca. 1623) **1 :** the act or process of removing the outer coverings (as bark or husks) from something (as fiber or seed) **2 :** the surgical removal of the cortex of an organ (as the brain), an enveloping membrane, or a constrictive fibrinous covering — **de·cor·ti·cate** \(ˈ)dē-ˈkȯrt-ə-,kāt\ *vt* — **de·cor·ti·cat·or** \-,kāt-ər\ *n*

de·co·rum \di-ˈkōr-əm, -ˈkȯr-\ *n* [L, fr. neut. of *decorus*] (1568) **1 :** literary and dramatic propriety **:** FITNESS **2 :** propriety and good taste in conduct or appearance **3 :** ORDERLINESS **4** *pl* **:** the conventions of polite behavior

de·cou·page *or* **dé·cou·page** \,dā-(,)kü-ˈpäzh\ *n* [F *découpage,* lit., act of cutting out, fr. MF, fr. *decouper* to cut out, fr. *de-* + *couper* to cut — more at COPE] (1946) **1 :** the art of decorating surfaces by applying cutouts (as of paper) and then coating with usu. several layers of finish (as lacquer or varnish) **2 :** work produced by decoupage

1de·coy \ˈdē-,kȯi, di-ˈ\ *n* [prob. fr. D *de kooi,* lit., the cage, fr. *de,* masc. def. art. (akin to OE *thæt,* neut. def. art.) + *kooi* cage, fr. L *cavea* — more at THAT, CAGE] (1641) **1 :** a pond into which wildfowl are lured for capture **2 :** someone or something used to lure or lead another into a trap; *esp* **:** an artificial bird used to attract live birds within shot

2de·coy \di-ˈkȯi, ˈdē-,\ *vt* (1660) **:** to lure by or as if by a decoy **:** ENTICE ***syn*** see LURE

1de·crease \di-ˈkrēs, ˈdē-,\ *vb* **de·creased; de·creas·ing** [ME *decreessen,* fr. (assumed) AF *decreistre,* fr. L *decrescere,* fr. *de-* + *crescere* to grow — more at CRESCENT] *vi* (14c) **:** to grow progressively less (as in size, amount, number, or intensity) ~ *vt* **:** to cause to decrease — **de·creas·ing·ly** \di-ˈkrē-siŋ-lē\ *adv*

syn DECREASE, LESSEN, DIMINISH, REDUCE, ABATE, DWINDLE mean to grow or make less. DECREASE suggests a progressive decline in size, amount, numbers, or intensity; LESSEN suggests a decline in amount rather than in number; DIMINISH emphasizes a perceptible loss and implies its subtraction from a total; REDUCE implies a bringing down or lowering; ABATE implies a reducing of something excessive or oppressive in force or amount; DWINDLE implies progressive lessening and is applied to things growing visibly smaller.

2de·crease \ˈdē-,krēs, di-ˈ\ *n* (14c) **1 :** the process of decreasing **2 :** an amount of diminution **:** REDUCTION

1de·cree \di-ˈkrē\ *n* [ME, fr. MF *decré,* fr. L *decretum,* fr. neut. of *decretus,* pp. of *decernere* to decide, fr. *de-* + *cernere* to sift, decide — more at CERTAIN] (14c) **1 :** an order usu. having the force of law **2 a :** a religious ordinance enacted by council or titular head **b :** a foreordaining will **3 a :** a judicial decision of the Roman emperor **b :** a judicial decision esp. in an equity or probate court

2decree *vb* **de·creed; de·cree·ing** *vt* (14c) **1 :** to command or enjoin by or as if by decree ⟨~ an amnesty⟩ **2 :** to determine or order judicially ⟨~ a punishment⟩ ~ *vi* **:** ORDAIN — **de·cre·er** \-ˈkrē-ər\ *n*

de·cree–law \di-ˈkrē-,lȯ\ *n* (1926) **:** a decree of a ruler or ministry having the force of a law enacted by the legislature

dec·re·ment \ˈdek-rə-mənt\ *n* [L *decrementum,* fr. *decrescere*] (1610) **1 :** a gradual decrease in quality or quantity **2 a :** the quantity lost by diminution or waste **b :** the amount of decrease (as of a variable) — **dec·re·men·tal** \,dek-rə-ˈment-ᵊl\ *adj*

de·crep·it \di-ˈkrep-ət\ *adj* [ME, fr. MF, fr. L *decrepitus*] (15c) **1 :** wasted and weakened by or as if by the infirmities of old age **2 a :** impaired by use or wear **:** WORN-OUT **b :** fallen into ruin or disrepair **3 :** DILAPIDATED, RUN-DOWN ***syn*** see WEAK — **de·crep·it·ly** *adv*

de·crep·i·tate \di-ˈkrep-ə-,tāt\ *vb* [prob. fr. (assumed) NL *decrepitatus,* pp. of *decrepitare,* fr. L *de-* + *crepitare* to crackle — more at CREPITATE] *vt* (1646) **:** to roast or calcine (as salt) so as to cause crackling or until crackling stops ~ *vi* **:** to become decrepitated — **de·crep·i·ta·tion** \-,krep-ə-ˈtā-shən\ *n*

de·crep·i·tude \di-ˈkrep-ə-,t(y)üd\ *n* (1603) **:** the quality or state of being decrepit

1de·cre·scen·do \,dā-krə-ˈshen-(,)dō\ *adv or adj* [It, lit., decreasing, fr. L *decrescendum,* gerund of *decrescere*] (1806) **:** with a decrease in volume — used as a direction in music

2decrescendo *n, pl* **-dos** (ca. 1880) **1 :** a gradual decrease in volume of a musical passage **2 :** a decrescendo musical passage

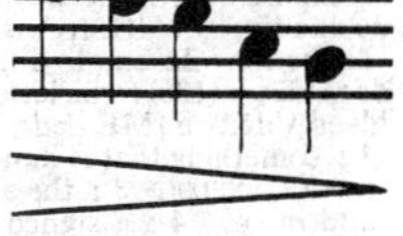

mark indicating decrescendo 2

de·cres·cent \di-ˈkres-ᵊnt\ *adj* [alter. of earlier *decressant,* prob. fr. AF, prp. of (assumed) AF *decreistre* to decrease] (1610) **:** becoming less by gradual diminution **:** DECREASING, WANING

de·cre·tal \di-ˈkrēt-ᵊl\ *n* [ME *decretale,* fr. MF, fr. LL *decretalis* of a decree, fr. L *decretum* decree] (14c) **:** DECREE; *esp* **:** a papal letter giving an authoritative decision on a point of canon law

de·cre·tive \-ˈkrēt-iv\ *adj* (1609) **:** having the force of a decree **:** DECRETORY

de·cre·to·ry \ˈdek-rə-,tōr-ē, -,tȯr-; di-ˈkrēt-ə-rē\ *adj* (1631) **:** relating to or fixed by a decree or decision

de·crim·i·nal·ize \(ˈ)dē-ˈkrim-ən-ᵊl-,īz, -ˈkrim-nəl-\ *vt* (1969) **:** to remove or reduce the criminal classification or status of; *esp* **:** to repeal a strict ban on while keeping under some form of regulation ⟨~ the possession of marijuana⟩ — **de·crim·i·nal·iza·tion** \(,)dē-,krim-ən-ᵊl-ə-ˈzā-shən, -,krim-nəl-\ *n*

de·cry \di-ˈkrī\ *vt* [F *décrier,* fr. OF *descrier,* fr. *des-* de- + *crier* to cry] (1617) **1 :** to depreciate (as a coin) officially or publicly **2 :** to express strong disapproval of ⟨~ the emphasis on sex⟩ — **de·cri·er** \-ˈkrī(-ə)r\ *n*

syn DECRY, DEPRECIATE, DISPARAGE, BELITTLE, MINIMIZE mean to express a low opinion of. DECRY implies open condemnation with intent to discredit; DEPRECIATE implies a representing as being of less value than commonly believed; DISPARAGE implies depreciation by indirect means such as slighting or invidious comparison; BELITTLE and MINIMIZE imply depreciation, BELITTLE suggesting usu. a contemptuous or envious attitude, MINIMIZE connoting less personal animus.

de·crypt \(ˈ)dē-ˈkript\ *vt* [ISV *de-* + *crypto*gram, *crypto*graph] (1935) **1 :** DECIPHER **2 :** DECODE — **de·cryp·tion** \-ˈkrip-shən\ *n*

de·cum·bent \di-ˈkəm-bənt\ *adj* [L *decumbent-, decumbens,* prp. of *decumbere* to lie down, fr. *de-* + *-cumbere* to lie down — more at HIP] (1656) **1 :** lying down **2** *of a plant* **:** reclining on the ground but with ascending apex or extremity

dec·u·ple \ˈdek-yə-pəl\ *adj* [F *décuple,* fr. MF, fr. LL *decuplus,* fr. L *decem* ten + *-plus* multiplied by — more at TEN, DOUBLE] (1613) **1 :** TENFOLD **2 :** taken in groups of 10

de·cu·ri·on \di-ˈkyu̇r-ē-ən\ *n* [ME *decurioun,* fr. L *decurion-, decurio,* fr. *decuria* division of ten, fr. *decem*] (14c) **1 :** a Roman cavalry officer in command of 10 men **2 :** a member of a Roman senate

\ə\ abut \ᵊ\ kitten, F table \ər\ further \a\ ash \ā\ ace \ä\ cot, cart \au̇\ out \ch\ chin \e\ bet \ē\ easy \g\ go \i\ hit \ī\ ice \j\ job \ŋ\ sing \ō\ go \ȯ\ law \ȯi\ boy \th\ thin \t͟h\ the \ü\ loot \u̇\ foot \y\ yet \zh\ vision \à, k̲, ⁿ, œ, œ̄, ue, ue̅, ʸ\ see Guide to Pronunciation

de·cur·rent \di-ˈkər-ənt, -ˈkə-rənt\ *adj* [L *decurrent-, decurrens,* prp. of *decurrere* to run down, fr. *de-* + *currere* to run — more at CAR] (ca. 1753) : running or extending downward along the stem ⟨~ leaves⟩

de·curved \(ˈ)dē-ˈkərvd\ *adj* [part trans. of LL *decurvatus,* fr. L *de-* + *curvatus* curved] (1835) : curved downward : bent down

[1]de·cus·sate \ˈdek-ə-ˌsāt, di-ˈkəs-ˌāt\ *vb* **-sat·ed; -sat·ing** [L *decussatus,* pp. of *decussare,* fr. *decussis* the number ten, numeral X, intersection, fr. *decem* + *ass-, as* unit — more at ACE] (1658) : INTERSECT, CROSS

[2]de·cus·sate \ˈdek-ə-ˌsāt, di-ˈkəs-ət\ *adj* (ca. 1823) : arranged in pairs each at right angles to the next pair above or below ⟨~ leaves⟩

de·cus·sa·tion \ˌdek-ə-ˈsā-shən, ˌdē-ˌkə-\ *n* (ca. 1656) **1 :** the action of crossing (as of nerve fibers) esp. in the form of an X **2 :** a crossed tract of nerve fibers passing between centers on opposite sides of the nervous system

[1]ded·i·cate \ˈded-i-kət\ *adj* [ME, fr. L *dedicatus,* pp. of *dedicare* to dedicate, fr. *de-* + *dicare* to proclaim, dedicate — more at DICTION] (14c) : DEDICATED

[2]ded·i·cate \ˈded-i-ˌkāt\ *vt* **-cat·ed; -cat·ing** (15c) **1 :** to devote to the worship of a divine being; *specif* **:** to set apart (a church) to sacred uses with solemn rites **2 a :** to set apart to a definite use ⟨money *dedicated* to their vacation fund⟩ **b :** to become committed to as a goal or way of life ⟨ready to ~ his life to public service⟩ **3 :** to inscribe or address by way of compliment ⟨~ a book to a friend⟩ **4 :** to open to public use ***syn*** see DEVOTE — **ded·i·ca·tor** \-ˌkāt-ər\ *n*

ded·i·cat·ed *adj* (1600) **1 :** devoted to a cause, ideal, or purpose : ZEALOUS ⟨a ~ scholar⟩ **2 :** given over to a particular purpose ⟨a ~ process control computer⟩ — **ded·i·cat·ed·ly** *adv*

ded·i·ca·tee \ˌded-i-kə-ˈtē\ *n* (1760) : one to whom a thing is dedicated

ded·i·ca·tion \ˌded-i-ˈkā-shən\ *n* (14c) **1 :** an act or rite of dedicating to a divine being or to a sacred use **2 :** a devoting or setting aside for a particular purpose **3 :** a name and often a message prefixed to a literary, musical, or artistic production in tribute to a person or cause **4 :** self-sacrificing devotion — **ded·i·ca·to·ry** \ˈded-i-kə-ˌtōr-ē, -ˌtȯr-\ *adj*

de·dif·fer·en·ti·a·tion \(ˌ)dē-ˌdif-ə-ˌren-chē-ˈā-shən\ *n* (1915) : reversion of specialized structures (as cells) to a more generalized or primitive condition often as a preliminary to major change — **de·dif·fer·en·ti·ate** \-ˈren-chē-ˌāt\ *vi*

de·duce \di-ˈd(y)üs\ *vt* **de·duced; de·duc·ing** [L *deducere,* lit., to lead away, fr. *de-* + *ducere* to lead — more at TOW] (15c) **1 :** to determine by deduction; *specif* **:** to infer from a general principle **2 :** to trace the course of ***syn*** see INFER — **de·duc·ible** \-ˈd(y)ü-sə-bəl\ *adj*

de·duct \di-ˈdəkt\ *vt* [L *deductus,* pp. of *deducere*] (15c) **1 :** to take away (an amount) from a total : SUBTRACT **2 :** DEDUCE, INFER

[1]de·duct·ible \di-ˈdək-tə-bəl\ *adj* (1856) : capable of being deducted — **de·duct·ibil·i·ty** \-ˌdək-tə-ˈbil-ət-ē\ *n*

[2]deductible *n* (1929) : a clause in an insurance policy that relieves the insurer of responsibility for an initial specified loss of the kind insured against

de·duc·tion \di-ˈdək-shən\ *n* (13c) **1 a :** an act of taking away ⟨~ of legitimate business expenses⟩ **b :** something that is or may be subtracted ⟨~*s* from his taxable income⟩ **2 a :** the deriving of a conclusion by reasoning; *specif* **:** inference in which the conclusion about particulars follows necessarily from general or universal premises — compare INDUCTION **b :** a conclusion reached by logical deduction

de·duc·tive \di-ˈdək-tiv\ *adj* (1665) **1 :** of, relating to, or provable by deduction **2 :** employing deduction in reasoning — **de·duc·tive·ly** *adv*

dee \ˈdē\ *n* (13c) : the letter *d*

[1]deed \ˈdēd\ *n* [ME *dede,* fr. OE *dǣd;* akin to OE *dōn* to do] (bef. 12c) **1 :** something that is done ⟨evil ~*s*⟩ **2 :** a usu. illustrious act or action : FEAT, EXPLOIT **3 :** the act of performing : ACTION ⟨righteous in word and in ~⟩ **4 :** a signed and usu. sealed instrument containing some legal transfer, bargain, or contract — **deed·less** \-ləs\ *adj*

[2]deed *vt* (1806) : to convey or transfer by deed

deed poll \-ˈpōl\ *n, pl* **deeds poll** [[1]*deed* + *poll,* adj. (having the edges cut even rather than indented), fr. [2]*poll*] *Brit* (1588) : a deed (as to change one's name) made and executed by only one party

deedy \ˈdēd-ē\ *adj* **deed·i·er; -est** *dial chiefly Eng* (1615) : INDUSTRIOUS

dee·jay \ˈdē-ˈjā\ *n* [*disc jockey*] (ca. 1949) : DISC JOCKEY

deem \ˈdēm\ *vb* [ME *demen,* fr. OE *dēman;* akin to OHG *tuomen* to judge, OE *dōm* doom] *vt* (bef. 12c) : to come to think or judge : HOLD ⟨~*ed* it wise to go slow⟩ ~ *vi* **:** to have an opinion : BELIEVE

de–em·pha·size \(ˈ)dē-ˈem(p)-fə-ˌsīz\ *vt* (1938) : to play down — **de–em·pha·sis** \-fə-səs\ *n*

[1]deep \ˈdēp\ *adj* [ME, fr. OE *dēop;* akin to OHG *tiof* deep, OE *dyppan* to dip — more at DIP] (bef. 12c) **1 :** extending far from some surface or area: as **a :** extending far downward ⟨a ~ well⟩ **b** (1) **:** extending well inward from an outer surface ⟨a ~ gash⟩ ⟨a *deep*-chested animal⟩ (2) **:** not located superficially within the body ⟨~ pressure receptors in muscles⟩ **c :** extending well back from a surface accepted as front ⟨a ~ closet⟩ **d :** extending far laterally from the center ⟨~ borders of lace⟩ **e :** occurring or located near the outer limits of the playing area ⟨hit to ~ right field⟩ **2 :** having a specified extension in an implied direction usu. downward or backward ⟨shelf 20 inches ~⟩ ⟨cars parked three-*deep*⟩ **3 a :** difficult to penetrate or comprehend : RECONDITE ⟨~ mathematical problems⟩ **b :** MYSTERIOUS, OBSCURE ⟨a ~ dark secret⟩ **c :** grave in nature or effect ⟨in ~*est* disgrace⟩ **d :** of penetrating intellect : WISE ⟨a ~ thinker⟩ **e :** INVOLVED, ENGROSSED ⟨~ in debt⟩ **f :** characterized by profundity of feeling or quality ⟨a ~ sleep⟩; *also* **:** DEEP-SEATED ⟨~ religious beliefs⟩ **4 a** *of color* **:** high in saturation and low in lightness **b :** having a low musical pitch or pitch range ⟨a ~ voice⟩ **5 a :** situated well within the boundaries ⟨a house ~ in the woods⟩ **b :** remote in time or space **c :** being below the level of the conscious ⟨~ neuroses⟩ **d :** covered, enclosed, or filled to a specified degree — usu. used in combination ⟨she was ankle-*deep* in mud⟩ **6 :** LARGE ⟨~ discounts⟩ ***syn*** see BROAD — **deep·ly** *adv* — **deep·ness** *n* — **in deep water :** in difficulty or distress

[2]deep *adv* (bef. 12c) **1 :** to a great depth : DEEPLY ⟨still waters run ~⟩ **2 :** far on : LATE ⟨danced ~ into the night⟩ **3 :** near the outer limits of the playing area ⟨the shortstop was playing ~⟩

[3]deep *n* (bef. 12c) **1 a :** a vast or immeasurable extent : ABYSS **b** (1) **:** the extent of surrounding space or time (2) **:** OCEAN **2 :** one of the deep portions of any body of water; *specif* **:** a generally long and narrow area in the ocean where the depth exceeds 3000 fathoms **3 :** the middle or most intense part ⟨the ~ of winter⟩ **4 :** any of the fathom points on a sounding line other than the marks

deep–dish pie *n* (1918) : a pie usu. with a fruit filling and no bottom crust that is baked in a deep dish

deep·en \ˈdē-pən, ˈdēp-ᵊm\ *vb* **deep·ened; deep·en·ing** \ˈdēp-(ə-)niŋ\ *vt* (1598) : to make deep or deeper ~ *vi* **:** to become deeper or more profound

deep fat *n* (1921) : hot fat or oil deep enough in a cooking utensil to cover the food to be fried

deep–freeze \ˈdēp-ˈfrēz\ *vt* **-froze** \-ˈfrōz\; **-fro·zen** \-ˈfrōz-ᵊn\ (1943) **1 :** QUICK-FREEZE **2 :** to store in a frozen state

deep freeze \ˈdēp-ˌfrēz\ *n* (1948) : COLD STORAGE 2 ⟨bill presently in *deep freeze* awaiting a new congress —*Newsweek*⟩

deep–fry \(ˈ)dēp-ˈfrī\ *vt* (1922) : to cook in deep fat

deep fryer *n* (1950) : a utensil suitable for deep-fat frying

deep–go·ing \ˈdēp-ˈgō-iŋ, -ˈgȯ(-)iŋ\ *adj* (1859) : FUNDAMENTAL ⟨a ~ theory⟩

deep pocket *n* (1976) **1 :** a person or an organization having substantial financial resources **2** *pl* **:** substantial financial resources

deep–root·ed \ˈdēp-ˈrüt-əd, -ˈrůt-\ *adj* (15c) : deeply implanted or established ⟨a ~ loyalty⟩

deep–sea \ˌdēp-ˌsē\ *adj* (1626) : of, relating to, or occurring in the deeper parts of the sea ⟨~ fishing⟩

deep–seat·ed \ˈdēp-ˈsēt-əd\ *adj* (1741) **1 :** situated far below the surface ⟨a ~ inflammation⟩ **2 :** firmly established ⟨a ~ tradition⟩

deep–six \ˈdēp-ˈsiks\ *vt* (1952) **1** *slang* **:** to throw away : DISCARD **2** *slang* **:** to throw overboard

deep six *n* [naval slang for "burial at sea"; perh. fr. the tradition of burying bodies six feet under ground] *slang* (1944) : a place of disposal or abandonment — used esp. in the phrase *give it the deep six*

deep space *n* (ca. 1952) : space well beyond the limits of the earth's atmosphere including space outside the solar system — called also *deep sky*

deep structure *n* (1964) : a formal representation of the underlying semantic content of a sentence; *also* **:** the structure which such a representation specifies

deer \ˈdi(ə)r\ *n, pl* **deer** *also* **deers** [ME, deer, animal, fr. OE *dēor* beast; akin to OHG *tior* wild animal, Skt *dhvaṁsati* he perishes] (bef. 12c) **1** *archaic* **:** ANIMAL; *esp* **:** a small mammal **2 :** a ruminant mammal (family Cervidae, the deer family) having two large and two small hooves on each foot and antlers borne by the males of nearly all and by the females of a few forms

deer·ber·ry \-ˌber-ē\ *n* (1814) **1 :** either of two shrubs (*Vaccinium stamineum* or *V. caesium*) of dry woods and scrub of the eastern U.S. **2 :** the edible fruit of a deerberry

deer·fly \ˈdi(ə)r-ˌflī\ *n* (1853) : any of numerous small horseflies (as of the genus *Chrysops*) that include important vectors of tularemia

deer·hound \-ˌhau̇nd\ *n* (1818) : SCOTTISH DEERHOUND

deer mouse *n* [fr. its agility] (1833) : WHITE-FOOTED MOUSE

deer·skin \ˈdi(ə)r-ˌskin\ *n* (14c) : leather made from the skin of a deer; *also* **:** a garment of this leather

deer·stalk·er \-ˌstȯ-kər\ *n* (1870) : a close-fitting hat with a visor at the front and the back and with earflaps that may be worn up or down — called also *deerstalker cap, deerstalker hat*

deer·yard \ˈdi(ə)r-ˌyärd\ *n* (1849) : a place where deer herd in winter

de–es·ca·late \(ˈ)dē-ˈes-kə-ˌlāt, ÷-kyə-\ *vi* (1964) : to decrease in extent, volume, or scope ~ *vt* **:** LIMIT 2b — **de–es·ca·la·tion** \(ˌ)dē-ˌes-kə-ˈlā-shən, ÷-kyə-\ *n* — **de–es·ca·la·to·ry** \(ˈ)dē-ˈes-kə-lə-ˌtōr-ē, -ˌtȯr-, ÷-kyə-\ *adj*

deet \ˈdēt\ *n* [prob. fr. *d. e. t.,* fr. *di-* + *ethyl* + *toluamide* (C_8H_9NO)] (1962) : a colorless oily liquid insect repellent $C_{12}H_{17}NO$

de·face \di-ˈfās\ *vt* [ME *defacen,* fr. MF *desfacier,* fr. OF, fr. *des-* de- + *face* front, face] (14c) **1 :** to mar the external appearance of : injure by effacing significant details ⟨~ an inscription⟩ **2 :** IMPAIR **3** *obs* **:** DESTROY — **de·face·ment** \-ˈfā-smənt\ *n* — **de·fac·er** *n*

[1]de fac·to \di-ˈfak-(ˌ)tō, dā-\ *adv* [NL] (1601) : in reality : ACTUALLY

[2]de facto *adj* (1696) **1 :** ACTUAL ⟨a *de facto* state of war⟩ **2 :** exercising power as if legally constituted ⟨a *de facto* government⟩ — compare DE JURE

de·fal·cate \di-ˈfal-ˌkāt, di-ˈfȯl-, ˈdef-əl-\ *vb* **-cat·ed; -cat·ing** [ML *defalcatus,* pp. of *defalcare,* fr. L *de-* + *falc-, falx* sickle] *vt, archaic* (1540) : DEDUCT, CURTAIL ~ *vi* **:** to engage in embezzlement — **de·fal·ca·tor** \-ˌkāt-ər\ *n*

de·fal·ca·tion \ˌdē-ˌfal-ˈkā-shən, ˌdē-ˌfȯl-, di-; ˌdef-əl-\ *n* (15c) **1** *archaic* **:** DEDUCTION **2 :** the act or an instance of embezzling **3 :** a failure to meet a promise or an expectation

def·a·ma·tion \ˌdef-ə-ˈmā-shən\ *n* (14c) : the act of defaming another : CALUMNY — **de·fam·a·to·ry** \di-ˈfam-ə-ˌtōr-ē, -ˌtȯr-\ *adj*

de·fame \di-ˈfām\ *vt* **de·famed; de·fam·ing** [ME *diffamen, defamen,* fr. MF & L; ME *diffamen* fr. MF *diffamer,* fr. L *diffamare,* fr. *dis-* + *fama* fame; ME *defamen* fr. MF *defamer,* fr. ML *defamare,* fr. L *de-* + *fama*] (14c) **1** *archaic* **:** DISGRACE **2 :** to harm the reputation of by libel or slander **3** *archaic* **:** ACCUSE ***syn*** see MALIGN — **de·fam·er** *n*

de·fang \(ˈ)dē-ˈfaŋ\ *vt* (1953) : to make harmless or less powerful

de·fat \(ˈ)dē-ˈfat\ *vt* (1919) : to remove fat from

[1]de·fault \di-ˈfȯlt\ *n* [ME *defaute, defaulte,* fr. OF *defaute,* fr. (assumed) VL *defallita,* fr. fem. of *defallitus,* pp. of *defallere* to be lacking, fail, fr. L *de-* + *fallere* to deceive — more at FAIL] (13c) **1 :** failure to do something required by duty or law : NEGLECT **2** *archaic* **:** FAULT **3 :** a failure to pay financial debts **4 a :** failure to appear at the required time in a legal proceeding **b :** failure to compete in or to finish an appointed contest — **in default of :** in the absence of

[2]default *vi* (15c) : to fail to fulfill a contract, agreement, or duty: as **a :** to fail to meet a financial obligation **b :** to fail to appear in court **c :** to fail to compete in or to finish an appointed contest; *also* **:** to forfeit a contest by such failure ~ *vt* **1 :** to fail to perform, pay, or make good **2 a :** FORFEIT **b :** to exclude (a player or a team) from a contest by default — **de·fault·er** *n*

de·fea·sance \di-ˈfēz-ᵊn(t)s\ *n* [ME *defesance,* fr. AF, fr. OF *deffesant,* prp. of *deffaire*] (15c) **1 a** (1) **:** the termination of a property interest in accordance with stipulated conditions (as in a deed) (2) **:** an instrument stating such conditions of limitation **b :** a rendering null or void **2 :** DEFEAT, OVERTHROW

de·fea·si·ble \di-ˈfē-zə-bəl\ *adj* (15c) **:** capable of being annulled or made void ⟨a ~ claim⟩ — **de·fea·si·bil·i·ty** \-ˌfē-zə-ˈbil-ət-ē\ *n*

1de·feat \di-ˈfēt\ *vt* [ME *deffeten,* fr. MF *deffait,* pp. of *deffaire* to destroy, fr. ML *disfacere,* fr. L *dis-* + *facere* to do — more at DO] (14c) **1** *obs* **:** DESTROY **2 a :** NULLIFY ⟨~ an estate⟩ **b :** FRUSTRATE ⟨~ a hope⟩ **3 :** to win victory over **:** BEAT ⟨~ the opposing team⟩ ***syn*** see CONQUER

2defeat *n* (1599) **1** *obs* **:** DESTRUCTION **2 :** frustration by nullification or by prevention of success ⟨the bill suffered ~ in the Senate⟩ **3 a :** an overthrow esp. of an army in battle **b :** the loss of a contest

de·feat·ism \-ˌiz-əm\ *n* (1918) **:** acceptance of or resignation to defeat — **de·feat·ist** \-əst\ *n or adj*

de·fea·ture \di-ˈfē-chər\ *n* [prob. fr. *de-* + *feature*] (1590) **1** *archaic* **:** DISFIGUREMENT **2 :** *archaic* **:** DEFEAT

def·e·cate \ˈdef-i-ˌkāt\ *vb* **-cat·ed; -cat·ing** [L *defaecatus,* pp. of *defaecare,* fr. *de-* + *faec-, faex* dregs, lees] *vt* (1575) **1 :** to free from impurity or corruption **:** REFINE **2 :** to discharge through the anus ~ *vi* **:** to discharge feces from the bowels — **def·e·ca·tion** \ˌdef-i-ˈkā-shən\ *n*

1de·fect \ˈdē-ˌfekt, di-ˈ\ *n* [ME, fr. MF, fr. L *defectus* lack, fr. *defectus,* pp. of *deficere* to desert, fail, fr. *de-* + *facere* to do — more at DO] (15c) **1 a :** an imperfection that impairs worth or utility **:** SHORTCOMING ⟨the grave ~*s* in our foreign policy⟩ **b :** an imperfection (as a vacancy or a foreign atom) in a crystal lattice **2** [L *defectus*] **:** a lack of something necessary for completeness, adequacy, or perfection **:** DEFICIENCY ⟨a hearing ~⟩ ***syn*** see BLEMISH

2de·fect \di-ˈfekt\ *vi* [L *defectus,* pp.] (1596) **1 :** to desert a cause or party often in order to espouse another **2 :** to leave one situation (as a job) often to go over to a rival ⟨the reporter ~*ed* to another network⟩ — **de·fec·tor** \-ˈfek-tər\ *n*

de·fec·tion \di-ˈfek-shən\ *n* (1552) **:** conscious abandonment of allegiance or duty (as to a person, cause, or doctrine) **:** DESERTION

1de·fec·tive \di-ˈfek-tiv\ *adj* (14c) **1 a :** lacking something essential **:** FAULTY ⟨a ~ pane of glass⟩ **b :** falling below the norm in structure or in mental or physical function ⟨~ eyesight⟩ **2 :** lacking one or more of the usual forms of grammatical inflection ⟨*must* is a ~ verb⟩ — **de·fec·tive·ly** *adv* — **de·fec·tive·ness** *n*

2defective *n* (1881) **:** a person who is subnormal physically or mentally

defective year *n* (ca. 1909) **:** a common year of 353 days or a leap year of 383 days in the Jewish calendar

de·fem·i·nize \(ˈ)dē-ˈfem-ə-ˌnīz\ *vt* (1907) **:** to divest of feminine qualities or characteristics **:** MASCULINIZE

de·fend \di-ˈfend\ *vb* [ME *defenden,* fr. OF *defendre,* fr. L *defendere,* fr. *de-* + *-fendere* to strike; akin to OE *gūth* battle, war, Gk *theinein* to strike] *vt* (14c) **1** *archaic* **:** PREVENT, FORBID **2 a :** to drive danger or attack away from **b :** to maintain in the face of argument or hostile criticism; *specif* **:** to prove valid (as a doctoral thesis) by answering questions in an oral exam **c :** to attempt to prevent an opponent from scoring at ⟨elects to ~ the south goal⟩ **3 :** to act as attorney for **4 :** to deny or oppose the right of a plaintiff in regard to (a suit or a wrong charged) **:** CONTEST **5 :** to seek to retain (as a title or position) against a challenge in a contest ~ *vi* **1 :** to take action against attack or challenge ⟨couldn't fight back, could only ~⟩ **2 :** to play or be on defense ⟨playing deep to ~ against a pass⟩ **3 :** to play against the high bidder in a card game

syn DEFEND, PROTECT, SHIELD, GUARD, SAFEGUARD mean to keep secure from danger or against attack. DEFEND denotes warding off actual or threatened attack; PROTECT implies the use of something (as a covering) as a bar to the admission or impact of what may attack or injure; SHIELD suggests protective intervention in imminent danger or actual attack; GUARD implies protecting with vigilance and force against expected danger; SAFEGUARD implies taking precautionary protective measures against merely possible danger. ***syn*** see in addition MAINTAIN

de·fend·able \di-ˈfen-də-bəl\ *adj* (1611) **:** DEFENSIBLE

1de·fen·dant \di-ˈfen-dənt\ *adj* (14c) **:** being on the defensive **:** DEFENDING

2defendant *n* (15c) **:** a person required to make answer in a legal action or suit — compare PLAINTIFF

de·fend·er \di-ˈfen-dər\ *n* (14c) **1 :** one that defends **2 :** a player in a sport (as football) assigned to a defensive position

de·fen·es·tra·tion \(ˌ)dē-ˌfen-ə-ˈstrā-shən\ *n* [*de-* + L *fenestra* window] (1620) **:** a throwing of a person or thing out of a window — **de·fen·es·trate** \(ˈ)dē-ˈfen-ə-ˌstrāt\ *vt*

1de·fense *or* **de·fence** \di-ˈfen(t)s; *as antonym of "offense," often* ˈdē-ˌ\ *n* [ME, fr. MF, fr. (assumed) VL *defensa,* fr. L, fem. of *defensus,* pp. of *defendere*] (14c) **1 a :** the act or action of defending ⟨the ~ of one's country⟩ ⟨to speak out in ~ of justice⟩ **b :** a defendant's denial, answer, or plea **2 :** capability of resisting attack **3 a :** means or method of defending or protecting oneself, one's team, or another; *also* **:** a defensive structure **b :** an argument in support or justification **c :** the collected facts and method adopted by a defendant to protect himself against a plaintiff's action **d :** a sequence of moves available in chess to the second player in the opening **4 a :** a defending party or group (as in a court of law) ⟨the ~ rested its case⟩ **b :** a defensive team **5 :** the military, governmental, and industrial aggregate esp. in its capacity of authorizing and supervising arms production ⟨appropriations for ~⟩ ⟨~ contract⟩ — **de·fense·less** \-ləs\ *adj* — **de·fense·less·ly** *adv* — **de·fense·less·ness** *n*

2defense *vt* **de·fensed; de·fens·ing** (1951) **:** to take specific defensive action against (an opposing team or player)

de·fense·man \-mən, -ˌman\ *n* (1895) **:** a player in a sport (as hockey) assigned to a defensive zone or position

defense mechanism *n* (1913) **1 :** an often unconscious mental process (as repression, projection, or sublimation) that makes possible compromise solutions to personal problems **2 :** a defensive reaction by an organism

de·fen·si·ble \di-ˈfen(t)-sə-bəl\ *adj* (14c) **:** capable of being defended — **de·fen·si·bil·i·ty** \di-ˌfen(t)-sə-ˈbil-ət-ē, ˌdē-\ *n* — **de·fen·si·bly** \-blē\ *adv*

1de·fen·sive \di-ˈfen(t)-siv, ˈdē-ˌ\ *adj* (15c) **1 :** serving to defend or protect **2 a :** devoted to resisting or preventing aggression or attack **b :** of or relating to the attempt to keep an opponent from scoring in a game or contest **3 a :** valuable in defensive play ⟨a ~ card in bridge⟩ **b :** designed to keep an opponent from being the highest bidder ⟨a ~ bid⟩ — **de·fen·sive·ly** *adv* — **de·fen·sive·ness** *n*

2defensive *n* (1601) **:** a defensive position — **on the defensive :** in the state or condition of being prepared for an expected aggression or attack

1de·fer \di-ˈfər\ *vt* **de·ferred; de·fer·ring** [ME *deferren, differren,* fr. MF *differer,* fr. L *differre* to postpone, be different — more at DIFFER] (14c) **1 :** PUT OFF, DELAY ⟨forced to ~ college because of financial problems⟩ **2 :** to postpone induction of (a person) into military service — **de·fer·rer** *n*

syn DEFER, POSTPONE, SUSPEND, STAY mean to delay an action or proceeding. DEFER implies a deliberate putting off to a later time; POSTPONE implies an intentional deferring usu. to a definite time; SUSPEND implies temporary stoppage with an added suggestion of waiting until some condition is satisfied; STAY suggests the stopping or checking by an intervening agency or authority. ***syn*** see in addition YIELD

2defer *vb* **deferred; deferring** [ME *deferren, differren,* fr. MF *deferer, defferer,* fr. LL *deferre,* fr. L, to bring down, bring, fr. *de-* + *ferre* to carry — more at BEAR] *vt* (15c) **:** to delegate to another ⟨he could ~ his job to no one —J. A. Michener⟩ ~ *vi* **:** to submit to another's wishes, opinion, or governance usu. through deference or respect ⟨a man who *deferred* only to God⟩

def·er·ence \ˈdef-(ə-)rən(t)s\ *n* (1660) **:** respect and esteem due a superior or an elder; *also* **:** affected or ingratiating regard for another's wishes ***syn*** see HONOR — **in deference to :** in consideration of

1def·er·ent \ˈdef-ə-rənt, -ˌer-ənt\ *adj* [L *deferent-, deferens,* prp. of *deferre*] (1626) **:** serving to carry down or out ⟨a ~ conduit⟩

2def·er·ent \ˈdef-(ə-)rənt\ *adj* [back-formation fr. *deference*] (1822) **:** DEFERENTIAL

def·er·en·tial \ˌdef-ə-ˈren-chəl\ *adj* (1822) **:** showing or expressing deference ⟨~ attention⟩ — **def·er·en·tial·ly** \-ˈrench-(ə-)lē\ *adv*

de·fer·ment \di-ˈfər-mənt\ *n* (1612) **:** the act of delaying or postponing; *specif* **:** official postponement of military service

de·fer·ra·ble \di-ˈfər-ə-bəl\ *adj* (1943) **:** capable of or suitable or eligible for being deferred — **deferrable** *n*

de·fer·ral \di-ˈfər-əl\ *n* (1895) **:** DEFERMENT

de·ferred *adj* (1651) **1 :** withheld for or until a stated time ⟨a ~ payment⟩ **2 :** charged in cases of delayed handling ⟨a ~ rate⟩

de·fer·ves·cence \ˌdē-(ˌ)fər-ˈves-ᵊn(t)s, ˌdef-ər-\ *n* [G *deferveszenz,* fr. L *defervescent-, defervescens,* prp. of *defervescere* to stop boiling, fr. *de-* + *fervescere* to begin to boil — more at EFFERVESCE] (1866) **:** the subsidence of a fever

de·fi·ance \di-ˈfī-ən(t)s\ *n* (14c) **1 :** the act or an instance of defying **:** CHALLENGE **2 :** disposition to resist **:** willingness to contend or fight — **in defiance of :** contrary to **:** DESPITE ⟨worked *in defiance of* doctor's orders⟩

de·fi·ant \-ənt\ *adj* [F *défiant,* fr. OF, prp. of *defier* to defy] (1837) **:** full of defiance **:** BOLD — **de·fi·ant·ly** *adv*

de·fi·bril·la·tion \(ˌ)dē-ˌfib-rə-ˈlā-shən, -ˌfīb-\ *n* (ca. 1890) **:** restoration of the rhythm of a fibrillating heart — **de·fi·bril·late** \(ˈ)dē-ˈfib-rə-ˌlāt, -ˈfīb-\ *vt* — **de·fi·bril·la·tor** \-ˌlāt-ər\ *n*

de·fi·brin·ate \(ˈ)dē-ˈfib-rə-ˌnāt, -ˈfīb-\ *vt* **-at·ed -at·ing** (1845) **:** to remove fibrin from (blood) — **de·fi·brin·ation** \(ˌ)dē-ˌfib-rə-ˈnā-shən, -ˌfīb-\ *n*

de·fi·cien·cy \di-ˈfish-ən-sē\ *n, pl* **-cies** (15c) **1 :** the quality or state of being deficient **:** INADEQUACY **2 a :** a shortage of substances necessary to health **b :** DELETION 1b(1)

deficiency disease *n* (1912) **:** a disease (as scurvy) caused by a lack of essential dietary elements and esp. a vitamin or mineral

1de·fi·cient \di-ˈfish-ənt\ *adj* [L *deficient-, deficiens,* prp. of *deficere* to be wanting — more at DEFECT] (1581) **1 :** lacking in some necessary quality or element ⟨~ in judgment⟩ **2 :** not up to a normal standard or complement **:** DEFECTIVE ⟨~ strength⟩ — **de·fi·cient·ly** *adv*

2deficient *n* (1640) **:** one that is deficient ⟨a mental ~⟩

def·i·cit \ˈdef-(ə-)sət, *Brit also* di-ˈfis-ət *or* ˈdē-fə-sət\ *n* [F *déficit,* fr. L *deficit* it is wanting, 3d sing. pres. indic. of *deficere*] (1782) **1 a (1) :** deficiency in amount or quality ⟨a ~ in rainfall⟩ **(2) :** a lack or impairment in a functional capacity ⟨cognitive ~*s*⟩ ⟨a hearing ~⟩ **b :** DISADVANTAGE ⟨a two-run homer in the sixth that overcame a 2-1 ~⟩ **2 a :** an excess of expenditure over revenue **b :** a loss in business operations

deficit spending *n* (1938) **:** the spending of public funds raised by borrowing rather than by taxation

de·fi·er \di-ˈfī(-ə)r\ *n* (1585) **:** one that defies

def·i·lade \ˈdef-ə-ˌlād, -ˌläd\ *vt* **-lad·ed; -lad·ing** [prob. fr. *de-* + *-filade* (as in *enfilade*)] (1828) **:** to arrange (fortifications) so as to protect the lines from frontal or enfilading fire and the interior from fire from above or behind — **defilade** *n*

1de·file \di-ˈfī(ə)l\ *vt* **de·filed; de·fil·ing** [ME *defilen,* alter. (influenced by OE *fȳlan* to defile) of *defoulen* to trample, defile, fr. OF *defouler* to trample, fr. *de-* + *fouler* to trample, lit., to full — more at FULL] (15c) **:** to make unclean or impure **:** BEFOUL, BESMIRCH: as **a :** to corrupt the purity or perfection of **:** DEBASE ⟨the countryside *defiled* by billboards⟩ **b :** to violate the chastity of **:** DEFLOWER **c :** to make physically unclean esp. with something unpleasant or contaminating ⟨boots *defiled* with blood⟩ **d :** to violate the sanctity of **:** DESECRATE ⟨~ a sanctuary⟩ **e :** SULLY, DISHONOR ***syn*** see CONTAMINATE — **de·file·ment** \-ˈfī(ə)l-mənt\ *n* — **de·fil·er** \-ˈfī-lər\ *n*

2de·file \di-ˈfī(ə)l, ˈdē-ˌfīl\ *n* [F *défilé,* fr. pp. of *défiler*] (1685) **:** a narrow passage or gorge

3de·file \di-ˈfī(ə)l, ˈdē-ˌfīl\ *vi* **de·filed; de·fil·ing** [F *défiler,* fr. *dé-* de- + *filer* to move in a column — more at FILE] (1707) **:** to march off in a line

de·fine \di-ˈfīn\ *vb* **de·fined; de·fin·ing** [ME *definen,* fr. MF & L; MF *definer,* fr. L *definire,* fr. *de-* + *finire* to limit, end, fr. *finis* boundary, end — more at FINAL] *vt* (14c) **1 a :** to determine or identify the essential qualities or meaning of ⟨~ a powerful position by salary and prestige⟩ ⟨whatever ~*s* us as human⟩ **b :** to discover and set forth the meaning of (as a word) **2 a :** to fix or mark the limits of **:** DEMAR-

\ə\ abut \ᵊ\ kitten, F table \ər\ further \a\ ash \ā\ ace \ä\ cot, cart
\au̇\ out \ch\ chin \e\ bet \ē\ easy \g\ go \i\ hit \ī\ ice \j\ job
\ŋ\ sing \ō\ go \ȯ\ law \ȯi\ boy \th\ thin \t͟h\ the \ü\ loot \u̇\ foot
\y\ yet \zh\ vision \á, k̲, ⁿ, œ, œ̄, ue, ue̅, ʸ\ see Guide to Pronunciation

CATE ⟨rigidly *defined* property lines⟩ **b :** to make distinct, clear, or detailed in outline ⟨the issues aren't too well *defined*⟩ **3 :** CHARACTERIZE, DISTINGUISH ⟨you ~ yourself by the choices you make —*Denison Univ. Bull.*⟩ ~ *vi* **:** to make a definition — **de·fin·able** \-'fī-nə-bəl\ *adj* — **de·fin·ably** \-blē\ *adv* — **de·fine·ment** \-'fīn-mənt \ *n* — **de·fin·er** \-'fī-nər\ *n*

de·fin·i·en·dum \di-,fin-ē-'en-dəm\ *n, pl* **-da** \-də\ [L, something to be defined, neut. of *definiendus,* gerundive of *definire*] (1871) **:** an expression that is being defined

de·fin·i·ens \di-'fin-ē-,enz\ *n, pl* **de·fin·i·en·tia** \di-,fin-ē-'en-ch(ē-)ə\ [L, prp. of *definire*] (1871) **:** an expression that defines **:** DEFINITION

def·i·nite \'def-(ə-)nət\ *adj* [L *definitus,* pp. of *definire*] (1553) **1 :** having distinct or certain limits ⟨set ~ standards for pupils to meet⟩ **2 a :** free of all ambiguity, uncertainty, or obscurity ⟨demanded a ~ answer⟩ **b :** UNQUESTIONABLE, DECIDED ⟨the quarterback was a ~ hero today⟩ **3 :** typically designating an identified or immediately identifiable person or thing ⟨the ~ article *the*⟩ **4 a :** being constant in number, usu. less than 20, and occurring in multiples of the petal number ⟨stamens ~⟩ **b :** CYMOSE ***syn*** see EXPLICIT — **def·i·nite·ly** *adv* — **def·i·nite·ness** *n*

definite integral *n* (1860) **:** a number that is the difference between the values of the indefinite integral of a given function for two values of the independent variable

def·i·ni·tion \,def-ə-'nish-ən\ *n* [ME *diffinicioun,* fr. MF *definition,* fr. L *definition-, definitio,* fr. *definitus,* pp.] (14c) **1 :** an act of determining; *specif* **:** the formal proclamation of a Roman Catholic dogma **2 a :** a statement expressing the essential nature of something (as by differentiation within a class) **b :** a statement of the meaning of a word or word group or a sign or symbol ⟨dictionary ~*s*⟩ **c :** a product of defining **3 :** the action or process of stating or formulating a definition **4 a :** the action or the power of describing, explaining, or making definite and clear ⟨the ~ of a telescope⟩ ⟨her comic genius is beyond ~⟩ **b** (1) **:** distinctness of outline or detail (as in a photograph) (2) **:** clarity esp. of musical sound in reproduction **c :** sharp demarcation of outlines or limits ⟨a jacket with definite waist ~⟩ — **def·i·ni·tion·al** \-'nish-nəl, -'nish-ən-ᵊl\ *adj*

¹de·fin·i·tive \di-'fin-ət-iv\ *adj* [ME *diffinityf,* fr. MF *definitif,* fr. L *definitivus,* fr. *definitus*] (14c) **1 :** serving to provide a final solution ⟨a ~ victory⟩ **2 :** authoritative and apparently exhaustive ⟨a ~ biography⟩ **3 :** serving to define or specify precisely ⟨~ laws⟩ **4 :** fully differentiated or developed **5** *of a postage stamp* **:** issued as a regular stamp for the country or territory in which it is to be used ***syn*** see CONCLUSIVE — **de·fin·i·tive·ly** *adv* — **de·fin·i·tive·ness** *n*

²definitive *n* (1951) **:** a definitive postage stamp — compare PROVISIONAL

definitive host *n* (1901) **:** the host in which the sexual reproduction of a parasite takes place

de·fi·ni·tize \'def-(ə-)nə-,tīz, di-'fin-ə-\ *vt* **-tized; -tiz·ing** (1876) **:** to make definite

de·fi·ni·tude \di-'fin-ə-,t(y)üd, -'fī-nə-\ *n* [irreg. fr. *definite*] (1836) **:** PRECISION, DEFINITENESS

def·la·grate \'def-lə-,grāt\ *vb* **-grat·ed; -grat·ing** [L *deflagratus,* pp. of *deflagrare* to burn down, fr. *de-* + *flagrare* to burn — more at BLACK] *vt* (1727) **:** to cause to deflagrate — compare DETONATE ~ *vi* **:** to burn rapidly with intense heat and sparks being given off — **def·la·gra·tion** \,def-lə-'grā-shən\ *n*

de·flate \di-'flāt, 'dē-\ *vb* **de·flat·ed; de·flat·ing** [*de-* + *-flate* (as in *inflate*)] *vt* (1891) **1 :** to release air or gas from **2 :** to reduce in size or importance ⟨~ his ego with cutting remarks⟩ **3 :** to reduce (a price level) or cause (a volume of credit) to contract ~ *vi* **:** to lose firmness through or as if through the escape of contained gas ***syn*** see CONTRACT — **de·fla·tor** \-'flāt-ər\ *n*

de·fla·tion \di-'flā-shən, 'dē-\ *n* (1891) **1 :** an act or instance of deflating **:** the state of being deflated **2 :** a contraction in the volume of available money or credit that results in a decline of the general price level **3 :** the erosion of soil by the wind — **de·fla·tion·ary** \-shə-,ner-ē\ *adj*

de·flect \di-'flekt\ *vb* [L *deflectere* to bend down, turn aside, fr. *de-* + *flectere* to bend] *vt* (1555) **:** to turn from a straight course or fixed direction **:** BEND ~ *vi* **:** to turn aside **:** DEVIATE — **de·flect·able** \-'flek-tə-bəl\ *adj* — **de·flec·tive** \-tiv\ *adj* — **de·flec·tor** \-tər\ *n*

de·flec·tion \di-'flek-shən\ *n* (1605) **1 :** a turning aside or off course **:** DEVIATION **2 :** the departure of an indicator or pointer from the zero reading on the scale of an instrument

de·flexed \'dē-,flekst, di-'\ *adj* [L *deflexus,* pp. of *deflectere*] (1826) **:** turned abruptly downward ⟨a ~ leaf⟩

de·flo·ra·tion \,def-lə-'rā-shən, ,dē-flə-\ *n* [ME *defloracioun,* fr. LL *defloration-, defloratio,* fr. *defloratus,* pp. of *deflorare*] (15c) **:** rupture of the hymen

de·flow·er \(')dē-'flau̇(-ə)r\ *vt* [ME *deflouren,* fr. MF or LL; MF *deflorer,* fr. LL *deflorare,* fr. L *de-* + *flor-, flos* flower — more at BLOW] (14c) **1 :** to deprive of virginity **:** RAVISH **2 :** to take away the prime beauty of — **de·flow·er·er** *n*

de·foam \(')dē-'fōm\ *vt* (1939) **:** to remove foam from **:** prevent the formation of foam in — **de·foam·er** *n*

de·fog \(')dē-'fóg, -'fäg\ *vt* (1904) **:** to remove fog or condensed moisture from — **de·fog·ger** *n*

de·fo·li·ant \(')dē-'fō-lē-ənt\ *n* (1943) **:** a chemical spray or dust applied to plants in order to cause the leaves to drop off prematurely

de·fo·li·ate \-lē-,āt\ *vt* [LL *defoliatus,* pp. of *defoliare,* fr. L *de-* + *folium* leaf — more at BLADE] (1791) **:** to deprive of leaves esp. prematurely — **de·fo·li·a·tion** \(,)dē-,fō-lē-'ā-shən\ *n* — **de·fo·li·a·tor** \(')dē-'fō-lē-,āt-ər\ *n*

de·force \(')dē-'fō(ə)rs, -'fó(ə)rs\ *vt* [ME *deforcen,* fr. MF *deforcier,* fr. *de-* + *forcier* to force] (15c) **1 :** to keep (as lands) by force from the rightful owner **2 :** to eject (a person) from possession by force — **de·force·ment** \-'fōr-smənt, -'fór-\ *n*

de·for·ciant \di-'fōr-shənt, -'fór-\ *n* [AF, fr. OF, prp. of *deforcier*] (15c) **:** one who deforces the rightful owner

de·for·es·ta·tion \(,)dē-,fór-ə-'stā-shən, -,fär-\ *n* (1874) **:** the action or process of clearing of forests; *also* **:** the state of having been cleared of forests — **de·for·est** \(')dē-'fór-əst, -'fär-\ *vt*

de·form \di-'fó(ə)rm, 'dē-\ *vb* [ME *deformen,* fr. MF or L; MF *deformer,* fr. L *deformare,* fr. *de-* + *formare* to form, fr. *forma* form] *vt* (15c) **1 :** to spoil the form of **2 a :** to spoil the looks of **:** DISFIGURE ⟨a face ~*ed* by bitterness⟩ **b :** to make hideous or monstrous **3 :** to alter the shape of by stress ~ *vi* **:** to become misshapen or changed in shape

syn DEFORM, DISTORT, CONTORT, WARP mean to mar or spoil by or as if by twisting. DEFORM may imply a change of shape through stress, injury, or some accident of growth; DISTORT and CONTORT both imply a wrenching from the natural, normal, or justly proportioned, but CONTORT suggests a more involved twisting and a more grotesque and painful result; WARP indicates physically an uneven shrinking that bends or twists out of a flat plane.

de·for·mal·ize \(')dē-'fór-mə-,līz\ *vt* (1880) **:** to make less formal

de·for·ma·tion \,dē-,fór-'mā-shən, ,def-ər-\ *n* (15c) **1 :** alteration of form or shape; *also* **:** the product of such alteration **2 :** the action of deforming **:** the state of being deformed **3 :** change for the worse — **de·for·ma·tion·al** \-shnəl, -shən-ᵊl\ *adj*

de·for·ma·tive \di-'fór-mət-iv\ *adj* (1641) **:** tending to deform

de·formed *adj* (15c) **:** distorted or unshapely in form **:** MISSHAPEN

de·for·mi·ty \di-'fór-mət-ē\ *n, pl* **-ties** [ME *deformite,* fr. MF *deformité,* fr. L *deformitat-, deformitas,* fr. *deformis* deformed, fr. *de-* + *forma*] (15c) **1 :** the state of being deformed **2 :** a physical blemish or distortion **:** DISFIGUREMENT **3 :** a moral or aesthetic flaw or defect

de·fraud \di-'fród\ *vt* [ME *defrauden,* fr. MF *defrauder,* fr. L *defraudare,* fr. *de-* + *fraudare* to cheat, fr. *fraud-, fraus* fraud] (14c) **:** to deprive of something by deception or fraud ***syn*** see CHEAT — **de·frau·da·tion** \,dē-,fró-'dā-shən\ *n* — **de·fraud·er** \di-'fród-ər\ *n*

de·fray \di-'frā\ *vt* [MF *deffrayer,* fr. *des-* de- + *frayer* to expend, fr. OF, fr. (assumed) OF *frai* expenditure, lit., damage by breaking, fr. L *fractum,* neut. of *fractus,* pp. of *frangere* to break — more at BREAK] (1543) **1 :** to provide for the payment of **:** PAY **2** *archaic* **:** to bear the expenses of — **de·fray·able** \-ə-bəl\ *adj* — **de·fray·al** \-'frā(-ə)l\ *n*

de·frock \(')dē-'fräk\ *vt* (1581) **:** UNFROCK

de·frost \di-'fróst, 'dē-\ *vt* (1895) **1 :** to release from a frozen state ⟨~ meat⟩ **2 :** to free from ice ⟨~ the refrigerator⟩ ~ *vi* **:** to thaw out esp. from a deep-frozen state — **de·frost·er** *n*

deft \'deft\ *adj* [ME *defte*] (15c) **:** marked by facility and skill ***syn*** see DEXTEROUS — **deft·ly** *adv* — **deft·ness** \'def(t)-nəs\ *n*

de·funct \di-'fəŋ(k)t\ *adj* [L *defunctus,* fr. pp. of *defungi* to finish, die, fr. *de-* + *fungi* to perform — more at FUNCTION] (1599) **:** having finished the course of life or existence ⟨her ~ aunt's will⟩ ⟨the committee is now ~⟩ ***syn*** see DEAD

de·fuse \(')dē-'fyüz\ *vt* (1943) **1 :** to remove the fuse from (as a mine or bomb) **2 :** to make less harmful, potent, or tense **:** CALM ⟨~ the crisis⟩

¹de·fy \di-'fī\ *vt* **de·fied; de·fy·ing** [ME *defyen* to renounce faith in, challenge, fr. MF *defier,* fr. *de-* + *fier* to entrust, fr. (assumed) VL *fidare,* alter. of L *fidere* to trust — more at BIDE] (14c) **1** *archaic* **:** to challenge to combat **2 :** to challenge to do something considered impossible **:** DARE **3 :** to confront with assured power of resistance **:** DISREGARD ⟨~ public opinion⟩ **4 :** to resist attempts at **:** WITHSTAND ⟨the paintings ~ classification⟩

²de·fy \di-'fī, 'dē-,\ *n, pl* **defies** (1580) **:** CHALLENGE, DEFIANCE

dé·ga·gé \,dā-,gä-'zhā\ *adj* [F, fr. pp. of *dégager* to redeem a pledge, free, fr. OF *desgagier,* fr. *des-* de- + *gage* pledge — more at GAGE] (1696) **1 :** free of constraint **:** NONCHALANT **2 :** being free and easy ⟨clothes with a ~ look⟩ **3 :** extended with toe pointed in preparation for a ballet step

de·gas \(')dē-'gas\ *vt* (1920) **:** to remove gas from ⟨~ an electron tube⟩

de Gaull·ism \di-'gō-,liz-əm, -'gó-\ *n* (1943) **:** GAULLISM — **de Gaull·ist** \-ləst\ *n*

de·gauss \(')dē-'gau̇s\ *vt* [*de-* + *gauss,* after Karl F. *Gauss*] (ca. 1940) **1 :** to make (a steel ship) effectively nonmagnetic by means of electrical coils carrying currents that neutralize the magnetism of the ship **2 :** DEMAGNETIZE — **de·gauss·er** *n*

de·gen·er·a·cy \di-'jen-(ə-)rə-sē\ *n, pl* **-cies** (1664) **1 :** the state of being degenerate **2 :** the process of becoming degenerate **3 :** sexual perversion **4 :** the coding of an amino acid by more than one codon of the genetic code

¹de·gen·er·ate \di-'jen-(ə-)rət\ *adj* [ME *degenerat,* fr. L *degeneratus,* pp. of *degenerare* to degenerate, fr. *de-* + *gener-, genus* race, kind — more at KIN] (15c) **1 a :** having declined (as in nature, character, structure, or function) from an ancestral or former state **b :** having sunk to a condition below that which is normal to a type; *esp* **:** having sunk to a lower and usu. peculiarly corrupt and vicious state **c :** DEGRADED **2 :** being mathematically simpler (as by having a factor or constant equal to zero) than the typical case ⟨the graph of a second degree equation yielding two intersecting lines is a ~ hyperbola⟩ **3 :** characterized by atoms stripped of their electrons and by very great density ⟨~ matter⟩; *also* **:** consisting of degenerate matter ⟨a ~ star⟩ **4 a :** having two or more states or subdivisions ⟨~ energy level⟩ **b** *of a semiconductor* **:** having a sufficient concentration of impurities to conduct electricity **5 :** having more than one codon representing an amino acid; *also* **:** being such a codon ***syn*** see VICIOUS — **de·gen·er·ate·ly** *adv* — **de·gen·er·ate·ness** *n*

²de·gen·er·ate \di-'jen-ə-,rāt\ *vi* (1545) **1 :** to pass from a higher to a lower type or condition **:** DETERIORATE **2 :** to sink into a low intellectual or moral state **3 :** to decline in quality ⟨his poetry gradually *degenerated* into jingles⟩ **4 :** to decline from a condition or from the standards of a species, race, or breed **5 :** to evolve or develop into a less autonomous or less functionally active form ⟨*degenerated* into dependent parasites⟩ ⟨the digestive system *degenerated*⟩ ~ *vt* **:** to cause to degenerate

³de·gen·er·ate \di-'jen-(ə-)rət\ *n* (1555) **:** one that is degenerate: as **a :** one degraded from the normal moral standard **b :** a sexual pervert **c :** one showing signs of reversion to an earlier culture stage

de·gen·er·a·tion \di-,jen-ə-'rā-shən, ,dē-\ *n* (15c) **1 :** degenerate condition **2 :** a lowering of effective power, vitality, or essential quality to an enfeebled and worsened kind or state **3 :** intellectual or moral decline **4 a :** progressive deterioration of physical characters from a level representing the norm of earlier generations or forms **b :** deterioration of a tissue or an organ in which its function is diminished or its structure is impaired **5 :** marked decline in excellence (as of workmanship or originality) ***syn*** see DETERIORATION

de·gen·er·a·tive \di-ˈjen-ə-ˌrāt-iv, -ˈjen-(ə-)rət-\ *adj* (ca. 1846) **:** of, relating to, or tending to cause degeneration ⟨a ~ disease⟩

de·glam·or·ize \(ˈ)dē-ˈglam-ə-ˌrīz\ *vt* (1938) **:** to remove the glamor from — **de·glam·or·iza·tion** \(ˌ)dē-ˌglam-ə-rə-ˈzā-shən\ *n*

de·glaze \(ˈ)dē-ˈglāz\ *vt* (ca. 1890) **1 :** to remove the glaze from **2 :** to dissolve the small particles of sautéed meat remaining in (a frying pan) by adding a liquid and heating

de·glu·ti·tion \ˌdē-glü-ˈtish-ən, ˌdeg-lü-\ *n* [F *déglutition,* fr. L *deglutitus,* pp. of *deglutire* to swallow down, fr. *de-* + *glutire, gluttire* to swallow — more at GLUTTON] (1650) **:** the act or process of swallowing

de·grad·able \di-ˈgrād-ə-bəl\ *adj* (ca. 1962) **:** capable of being chemically degraded ⟨~ detergents⟩ — compare BIODEGRADABLE

deg·ra·da·tion \ˌdeg-rə-ˈdā-shən\ *n* (1535) **1 :** the act or process of degrading **2 a :** decline to a low, destitute, or demoralized state **b :** moral or intellectual decadence **:** DEGENERATION — **deg·ra·da·tive** \ˈdeg-rə-ˌdāt-iv\ *adj*

de·grade \di-ˈgrād\ *vb* [ME *degraden,* fr. MF *degrader,* fr. LL *degradare,* fr. L *de-* + *gradus* step, grade — more at GRADE] *vt* (14c) **1 a :** to lower in grade, rank, or status **:** DEMOTE **b :** to strip of rank or honors **c :** to deprive of standing or true function **:** PERVERT **d :** to scale down in desirability or salability **2 a :** to bring to low esteem or into disrepute **b :** to drag down in moral or intellectual character **:** CORRUPT **3 :** to impair in respect to some physical property **4 :** to wear down by erosion **5 :** to reduce the complexity of (a chemical compound) **:** DECOMPOSE ~ *vi* **1 :** to pass from a higher grade or class to a lower **2** *of a chemical compound* **:** to become reduced in complexity **syn** see ABASE — **de·grad·er** *n* — **de·grad·ing·ly** \-ˈgrād-iŋ-lē\ *adv*

de·grad·ed *adj* (1643) **1 :** reduced far below ordinary standards of civilized life and conduct **2 :** characterized by degeneration of structure or function — **de·grad·ed·ly** *adv*

de·gran·u·la·tion \(ˌ)dē-ˌgran-yə-ˈlā-shən\ *n* (ca. 1941) **:** the process of losing granules ⟨~ of leukocytes⟩

de·grease \(ˈ)dē-ˈgrēs, -ˈgrēz\ *vt* (ca. 1889) **:** to remove grease from

de·gree \di-ˈgrē\ *n* [ME, fr. OF *degré,* fr. (assumed) VL *degradus,* fr. L *de-* + *gradus*] (13c) **1 :** a step or stage in a process, course, or order of classification ⟨advanced by ~*s*⟩ **2 a** *obs* **:** STEP, STAIR **b** *archaic* **:** a member of a series arranged in steps **3 :** a measure of damage to tissue caused esp. by disease — compare FIRST-DEGREE BURN, SECOND-DEGREE BURN, THIRD-DEGREE BURN **4 a :** the extent, measure, or scope of an action, condition, or relation ⟨the company's ~ of expansion was small⟩ **b :** relative intensity **c :** one of the forms or sets of forms used in the comparison of an adjective or adverb **d :** a legal measure of guilt or negligence ⟨found guilty of robbery in the first ~⟩ **5 a :** a rank or grade of official, ecclesiastical, or social position ⟨people of low ~⟩ **b** *archaic* **:** a particular standing esp. as to dignity or worth **c :** the civil condition or status of a person **6 :** a step in a direct line of descent or in the line of ascent to a common ancestor **7 a :** a grade of membership attained in a ritualistic order or society **b :** the formal ceremonies observed in the conferral of such a distinction **c :** a title conferred on students by a college, university, or professional school on completion of a program of study **d :** an academic title conferred to honor distinguished achievement or service **8** *archaic* **:** a position or space on the earth or in the heavens as measured by degrees of latitude **9 :** one of the divisions or intervals marked on a scale of a measuring instrument; *specif* **:** any of various units for measuring temperature **10 :** a unit of measure for angles and arcs that for angles is equal to an angle with its vertex at the center of a circle and its sides cutting off 1/360 of the circumference and that for an arc of a circle is equal to 1/360 of the circumference **11 a :** the sum of the exponents of the variable factors of a monomial **b :** the sum of the exponents of the variables in the term of highest degree in a polynomial, a polynomial function, or a polynomial equation **c :** the greatest power of the derivative of highest order in a differential equation after the equation has been rationalized and cleared of fractions with respect to the derivative **12 a :** a line or space of the musical staff **b :** a step, note, or tone of a musical scale — **de·greed** \-ˈgrēd\ *adj* — **to a degree 1 :** to a remarkable extent **2 :** in a small way

de·gree–day \di-ˈgrē-ˈdā\ *n* (1929) **:** a unit that represents one degree of declination from a given point (as 65°) in the mean daily outdoor temperature and that is used to measure heat requirements

degree of freedom (1867) **1 :** any of a limited number of ways in which a body may move or in which a dynamic system may change **2 :** one of the capabilities of a statistic for variation of which there are as many as the number of unrestricted and independent variables determining its value

de·gres·sive \di-ˈgres-iv, ˈdē-\ *adj* [*degression* (downward motion), (fr. ME, fr. ML *degression-, degressio,* fr. L *degressus,* pp. of *degredi* to step down, fr. *de-* + *gradi* to step) + *-ive* — more at GRADE] (1886) **:** tending to descend or decrease — **de·gres·sive·ly** *adv*

dé·grin·go·lade \ˌdā-ˌgra^{n}-(ŋ)gə-ˈläd\ *n* [F, fr. *dégringoler* to tumble down, fr. MF *desgringueler,* fr. *des-* de- + *gringueler* to tumble, fr. MLG *crinc* curve; akin to LG *kringel* loop — more at CRINGLE] (1883) **:** a rapid decline or deterioration (as in strength, position, or condition) **:** DOWNFALL

de·gum \(ˈ)dē-ˈgəm\ *vt* (1887) **:** to free from gum, a gummy substance, or sericin

de·gus·ta·tion \ˌdē-ˌgəs-ˈtā-shən, di-\ *n* [L *degustation-, degustatio,* fr. *degustus,* pp. of *degustare* to taste, fr. *de-* + *gustare* to taste — more at CHOOSE] (1656) **:** the action or an instance of tasting or savoring — **de·gust** \di-ˈgəst\ *vt*

de haut en bas \də-ō-tä^{n}-bä\ *adj or adv* [F, lit., from top to bottom] (1696) **:** of superiority **:** of or with condescension

de·hisce \di-ˈhis\ *vi* **de·hisced; de·hisc·ing** [L *dehiscere* to split open, fr. *de-* + *hiscere* to gape; akin to L *hiare* to yawn — more at YAWN] (1657) **:** to split along a natural line; *also* **:** to discharge contents by so splitting ⟨seedpods *dehiscing* at maturity⟩

de·his·cence \di-ˈhis-^{ə}n(t)s\ *n* [NL *dehiscentia,* fr. L *dehiscent-, dehiscens,* prp. of *dehiscere*] (ca. 1828) **:** an act or instance of dehiscing ⟨pollen freed by ~ of the anther⟩ — **de·his·cent** \-^{ə}nt\ *adj*

de·horn \(ˈ)dē-ˈhȯ(ə)rn\ *vt* (1888) **1 :** to deprive of horns **2 :** to prevent the growth of the horns of — **de·horn·er** *n*

de·hu·man·ize \(ˈ)dē-ˈhyü-mə-ˌnīz, (ˈ)dē-ˈyü-\ *vt* (1818) **:** to deprive of human qualities, personality, or spirit — **de·hu·man·iza·tion** \(ˌ)dē-ˌhyü-mə-nə-ˈzā-shən, (ˌ)dē-ˌyü-\ *n*

de·hu·mid·i·fy \ˌdē-hyü-ˈmid-ə-ˌfī, ˌdē-yü-\ *vt* (1927) **:** to remove moisture from (as air) — **de·hu·mid·i·fi·ca·tion** \-ˌmid-ə-fə-ˈkā-shən\ *n* — **de·hu·mid·i·fi·er** \-ˈmid-ə-ˌfī(-ə)r\ *n*

dehydr- *or* **dehydro-** *comb form* **1 :** dehydrated **2 :** dehydrogenated

de·hy·drate \(ˈ)dē-ˈhī-ˌdrāt\ *vt* (1876) **1 a :** to remove bound water or hydrogen and oxygen from (a chemical compound) in the proportion in which they form water **b :** to remove water from (as foods) **2 :** to deprive of vitality or savor ~ *vi* **:** to lose water or body fluids — **de·hy·dra·tor** \-ˌdrāt-ər\ *n*

de·hy·dra·tion \ˌdē-ˌhī-ˈdrā-shən\ *n* (1854) **:** the process of dehydrating; *esp* **:** an abnormal depletion of body fluids

de·hy·dro·chlo·ri·nase \(ˌ)dē-ˌhī-drə-ˈklōr-ə-ˌnās, -ˈklȯr-, -ˌnāz\ *n* (1956) **:** an enzyme that dehydrochlorinates a chlorinated hydrocarbon (as DDT) and is found esp. in some DDT resistant insects

de·hy·dro·chlo·ri·na·tion \-ˌklōr-ə-ˈnā-shən, -ˌklȯr-\ *n* [*de-* + *hydr-* + *chlorine* + *-ation*] (1936) **:** the process of removing hydrogen and chlorine or hydrogen chloride from a compound — **de·hy·dro·chlo·ri·nate** \-ˈklōr-ə-ˌnāt, -ˈklȯr-\ *vt*

de·hy·dro·ge·nase \ˌdē-(ˌ)hī-ˈdräj-ə-ˌnās, (ˈ)dē-ˈhī-drə-jə-, -ˌnāz\ *n* [ISV] (1923) **:** an enzyme that accelerates the removal of hydrogen from metabolites and its transfer to other substances ⟨succinic ~⟩

de·hy·dro·ge·nate \ˌdē-(ˌ)hī-ˈdräj-ə-ˌnāt, (ˈ)dē-ˈhī-drə-jə-\ *vt* (1850) **:** to remove hydrogen from — **de·hy·dro·ge·na·tion** \ˌdē-(ˌ)hī-ˌdräj-ə-ˈnā-shən, (ˌ)dē-ˌhī-drə-jə-\ *n*

de·ice \(ˈ)dē-ˈīs\ *vt* (ca. 1934) **:** to keep free or rid of ice — **de·ic·er** *n*

de·i·cide \ˈdē-ə-ˌsīd, ˈdā-ə-\ *n* [deriv. of L *deus* god + *-cidium, -cida* -cide — more at DEITY] (1611) **1 :** the act of killing a divine being or a symbolic substitute of such a being **2 :** the killer or destroyer of a god

deic·tic \ˈdīk-tik, ˈdāk-; dē-ˈik-\ *adj* [Gk *deiktikos,* fr. *deiktos,* verbal of *deiknynai* to show — more at DICTION] (1828) **:** showing or pointing out directly ⟨the words *this, that,* and *those* have a ~ function⟩

de·i·fi·ca·tion \ˌdē-ə-fə-ˈkā-shən, ˌdā-\ *n* (14c) **:** the act or an instance of deifying

de·i·fy \ˈdē-ə-ˌfī, ˈdā-\ *vt* **-fied; -fy·ing** [ME *deifyen,* fr. MF *deifier,* fr. LL *deificare,* fr. L *deus* god + *-ficare* -fy] (14c) **1 a :** to make a god of **b :** to take as an object of worship **2 :** to glorify as of supreme worth

deign \ˈdān\ *vb* [ME *deignen,* fr. OF *deignier,* fr. L *dignare, dignari,* fr. *dignus* worthy — more at DECENT] *vi* (14c) **:** to condescend reluctantly and with a strong sense of the affront to one's superiority that is involved ~ *vt* **:** to condescend to give or offer

deil \ˈdē(ə)l\ *n* [ME *devel, del*] *Scot* (12c) **:** DEVIL

de·in·sti·tu·tion·al·iza·tion \(ˌ)dē-ˌin(t)-stə-ˌt(y)üsh-nə-lə-ˈzā-shən, -ˌt(y)ü-shən-^{ə}l-ə-ˈzā-\ *n* (1969) **1 :** the release of institutionalized individuals (as mental patients) from institutional care to care in the community **2 :** the reform or modification of an institution to remove or disguise its institutional character — **de·in·sti·tu·tion·al·ize** \-ˈt(y)üsh-nə-ˌlīz, -ˈt(y)ü-shən-^{ə}l-ˌīz\ *vt*

de·ion·ize \(ˈ)dē-ˈī-ə-ˌnīz\ *vt* (1906) **:** to remove ions from ⟨~ water by ion exchange⟩ — **de·ion·iza·tion** \(ˌ)dē-ˌī-ə-nə-ˈzā-shən\ *n*

de·ism \ˈdē-ˌiz-əm, ˈdā-\ *n, often cap* (1682) **:** a movement or system of thought advocating natural religion, emphasizing morality, and in the 18th century denying the interference of the Creator with the laws of the universe — **de·ist** \ˈdē-əst, ˈdā-\ *n, often cap* — **de·is·tic** \dē-ˈis-tik, dā-\ *adj* — **de·is·ti·cal** \-ti-kəl\ *adj* — **de·is·ti·cal·ly** \-ti-k(ə-)lē\ *adv*

de·i·ty \ˈdē-ət-ē, ˈdā-\ *n, pl* **-ties** [ME *deitee,* fr. MF *deité,* fr. LL *deitat-, deitas,* fr. L *deus* god; akin to OE *Tīw,* god of war, L *divus* god, *dies* day, Gk *dios* heavenly, Skt *deva* heavenly, god] (14c) **1 a :** the rank or essential nature of a god **:** DIVINITY **b** *cap* **:** GOD 1, SUPREME BEING **2 :** a god or goddess ⟨the *deities* of ancient Greece⟩ **3 :** one exalted or revered as supremely good or powerful

dé·jà vu \ˌdā-ˌzhä-ˈv(y)ü, dā-zhä-vᵫ\ *n* [F *déjà vu,* adj., lit., already seen] (1903) **1 :** PARAMNESIA b **2 :** something overly or unpleasantly familiar ⟨the appointment seems like a case of *déjà vu* —E. B. Fiske⟩

[1]**de·ject** \di-ˈjekt\ *adj, archaic* (15c) **:** DEJECTED

[2]**deject** *vt* [ME *dejecten* to throw down, fr. L *dejectus,* pp. of *deicere,* fr. *de-* + *jacere* to throw — more at JET] (1603) **:** to make gloomy

de·jec·ta \di-ˈjek-tə\ *n pl* [NL, fr. L, neut. pl. of *dejectus*] (1887) **:** FECES, EXCREMENT

de·ject·ed \di-ˈjek-təd\ *adj* (1581) **1 :** cast down in spirits **:** DEPRESSED **2 a** *obs, of the eyes* **:** DOWNCAST **b** *archaic* **:** thrown down **3** *obs* **:** lowered in rank or condition — **de·ject·ed·ly** *adv* — **de·ject·ed·ness** *n*

de·jec·tion \di-ˈjek-shən\ *n* (15c) **:** lowness of spirits

de ju·re \(ˈ)dē-ˈju̇(ə)r-ē, (ˈ)dā-ˈyu̇(ə)r-\ *adv or adj* [NL] (1611) **:** by right **:** of right

deka- *or* **dek-** — see DECA-

deka·gram \ˈdek-ə-ˌgram\ *n* (ca. 1879) — see METRIC SYSTEM table

deka·li·ter \-ˌlēt-ər\ *n* (ca. 1879) — see METRIC SYSTEM table

deka·me·ter \-ˌmēt-ər\ *n* (ca. 1879) — see METRIC SYSTEM table

deka·met·ric \ˌdek-ə-ˈme-trik\ *adj* (1968) **:** DECAMETRIC

de·lam·i·na·tion \(ˌ)dē-ˌlam-ə-ˈnā-shən\ *n* (1877) **1 :** gastrula formation in which the endoderm is split off as a layer from the inner surface of the blastoderm and the archenteron is represented by the space between this endoderm and the yolk mass **2 :** separation into constituent layers — **de·lam·i·nate** \(ˈ)dē-ˈlam-ə-ˌnāt\ *vi*

de·late \di-ˈlāt\ *vt* **de·lat·ed; de·lat·ing** [L *delatus* (pp. of *deferre* to bring down, report, accuse), fr. *de-* + *latus,* pp. of *ferre* to bear — more at TOLERATE, BEAR] (15c) **1 :** ACCUSE, DENOUNCE **2 :** REPORT, RELATE — **de·la·tion** \-ˈlā-shən\ *n* — **de·la·tor** \-ˈlāt-ər\ *n*

Del·a·ware \ˈdel-ə-ˌwa(ə)r, -ˌwe(ə)r, -wər\ *n, pl* **Delaware** *or* **Delawares** [*Delaware* river] (1709) **1 :** a member of an American Indian people orig. of the Delaware valley **2 :** the Algonquian language of the Delaware

[1]**de·lay** \di-ˈlā\ *n* (13c) **1 a :** the act of delaying **:** the state of being delayed **b :** an instance of being delayed **2 :** the time during which something is delayed

[2]**delay** *vb* [ME *delayen,* fr. OF *delaier,* fr. *de-* + *laier* to leave, alter. of *laissier,* fr. L *laxare* to slacken, fr. *laxus* loose — more at SLACK] *vt* (14c)

\ə\ abut \$^{ə}$\ kitten, F table \ər\ further \a\ ash \ā\ ace \ä\ cot, cart \au̇\ out \ch\ chin \e\ bet \ē\ easy \g\ go \i\ hit \ī\ ice \j\ job \ŋ\ sing \ō\ go \ȯ\ law \ȯi\ boy \th\ thin \t͟h\ the \ü\ loot \u̇\ foot \y\ yet \zh\ vision \à, k̲, ^{n}, œ, œ̄, ue, ue̅, ^{y}\ *see* Guide to Pronunciation

1 : PUT OFF, POSTPONE 2 : to stop, detain, or hinder for a time ~ *vi* : to move or act slowly; *also* : to cause delay — **de·lay·er** *n* — **de·lay·ing** *adj*
syn DELAY, RETARD, SLOW, SLACKEN, DETAIN mean to cause to be late or behind in movement or progress. DELAY implies a holding back, usu. by interference, from completion or arrival; RETARD applies chiefly to motion and suggests reduction of speed without actual stopping; SLOW and SLACKEN both imply also a reduction of speed, SLOW often suggesting deliberate intention, SLACKEN an easing up or relaxing of power or effort; DETAIN implies a holding back beyond a reasonable or appointed time.
syn DELAY, PROCRASTINATE, LAG, LOITER, DAWDLE, DALLY mean to move or act slowly so as to fall behind. DELAY usu. implies a putting off (as a beginning or departure); PROCRASTINATE implies blameworthy delay esp. through laziness or apathy; LAG implies failure to maintain a speed set by others; LOITER and DAWDLE imply delay while in progress, esp. in walking, but DAWDLE more clearly suggests an aimless wasting of time; DALLY suggests delay through trifling or vacillation when promptness is necessary.

[1]**de·le** \ˈdē-(ˌ)lē\ *vt* **de·led; de·le·ing** [L, imper. sing. of *delēre*] (1705) : to delete esp. from typeset matter

[2]**dele** *n* (1821) : a mark indicating that something is to be deled

[1]**de·lec·ta·ble** \di-ˈlek-tə-bəl\ *adj* [ME, fr. MF, fr. L *delectabilis*, fr. *delectare* to delight — more at DELIGHT] (15c) 1 : highly pleasing : DELIGHTFUL 2 : DELICIOUS — **de·lec·ta·bil·i·ty** \-ˌlek-tə-ˈbil-ət-ē\ *n* — **de·lec·ta·bly** \-blē\ *adv*

[2]**delectable** *n* (1921) : something that is delectable

de·lec·ta·tion \ˌdē-ˌlek-ˈtā-shən, di-; ˌdel-ək-\ *n* (14c) 1 : DELIGHT 2 : ENJOYMENT

del·e·ga·ble \ˈdel-i-gə-bəl\ *adj* (1660) : capable of being delegated

del·e·ga·cy \-gə-sē\ *n, pl* **-cies** (15c) 1 **a** : the act of delegating **b** : appointment as delegate 2 : a body of delegates : BOARD

[1]**del·e·gate** \ˈdel-i-gət, -ˌgāt\ *n* [ME *delegat*, fr. ML *delegatus*, fr. L, pp. of *delegare* to delegate, fr. *de-* + *legare* to send — more at LEGATE] (14c) : a person acting for another: as **a** : a representative to a convention or conference **b** : a representative of a U.S. territory in the House of Representatives **c** : a member of the lower house of the legislature of Maryland, Virginia, or West Virginia

[2]**del·e·gate** \-ˌgāt\ *vb* **-gat·ed; -gat·ing** *vt* (ca. 1530) 1 : to entrust to another ⟨~ authority⟩ 2 : to appoint as one's representative ~ *vi* : to assign responsibility or authority — **del·e·ga·tee** \ˌdel-i-gə-ˈtē\ *n* — **del·e·ga·tor** \ˈdel-i-ˌgāt-ər\ *n*

del·e·ga·tion \ˌdel-i-ˈgā-shən\ *n* (1612) 1 : the act of empowering to act for another 2 : a group of persons chosen to represent others

de·le·git·i·ma·tion \ˌdē-lə-ˌjit-ə-ˈmā-shən\ *n* (1968) : a decline in or loss of prestige or authority

de·lete \di-ˈlēt\ *vt* **de·let·ed; de·let·ing** [L *deletus*, pp. of *delēre* to wipe out, destroy, fr. *de-* + *-lēre* (akin to L *linere* to smear) — more at LIME] (15c) : to eliminate esp. by blotting out, cutting out, or erasing

del·e·te·ri·ous \ˌdel-ə-ˈtir-ē-əs\ *adj* [Gk *dēlētērios*, fr. *dēleisthai* to hurt; akin to L *dolēre* to feel pain — more at CONDOLE] (1643) : harmful often in a subtle or unexpected way ⟨~ effects⟩ ⟨~ to health⟩ ***syn*** see PERNICIOUS — **del·e·te·ri·ous·ly** *adv* — **del·e·te·ri·ous·ness** *n*

de·le·tion \di-ˈlē-shən\ *n* [L *deletion-, deletio* destruction, fr. *deletus*] (1590) 1 **a** : something deleted **b** (1) : the absence of a section of genetic material from a chromosome (2) : the mutational process that results in a deletion 2 : the act of deleting

delft \ˈdelft\ *n* [*Delft*, Netherlands] (1723) 1 : tin-glazed Dutch earthenware with blue and white or polychrome decoration 2 : a ceramic ware resembling or imitative of Dutch delft

delft·ware \ˈdelf-ˌtwa(ə)r, -ˌtwe(ə)r\ *n* (1714) : DELFT

deli \ˈdel-ē\ *n, pl* **del·is** (1964) : DELICATESSEN

[1]**de·lib·er·ate** \di-ˈlib-ə-ˌrāt\ *vb* **-at·ed; -at·ing** *vi* (14c) : to think about or discuss issues and decisions carefully ~ *vt* : to think about deliberately and often with formal discussion before reaching a decision ***syn*** see THINK

[2]**de·lib·er·ate** \di-ˈlib-(ə-)rət\ *adj* [L *deliberatus*, pp. of *deliberare* to weigh in mind, ponder, irreg. fr. *de-* + *libra* scale, pound] (15c) 1 : characterized by or resulting from careful and thorough consideration ⟨a ~ decision⟩ 2 : characterized by awareness of the consequences ⟨~ falsehood⟩ 3 : slow, unhurried, and steady as though allowing time for decision on each individual action involved ⟨a ~ pace⟩ ***syn*** see VOLUNTARY — **de·lib·er·ate·ly** *adv* — **de·lib·er·ate·ness** *n*

de·lib·er·a·tion \di-ˌlib-ə-ˈrā-shən\ *n* (14c) 1 **a** : the act of deliberating **b** : a discussion and consideration by a group of persons of the reasons for and against a measure 2 : the quality or state of being deliberate — **de·lib·er·a·tive** \-ˈlib-ə-ˌrāt-iv, -ˈlib-(ə-)rət-\ *adj* — **de·lib·er·a·tive·ly** *adv* — **de·lib·er·a·tive·ness** *n*

del·i·ca·cy \ˈdel-i-kə-sē\ *n, pl* **-cies** (14c) 1 *obs* **a** : the quality or state of being luxurious **b** : INDULGENCE 2 : something pleasing to eat that is considered rare or luxurious ⟨considered caviar a ~⟩ 3 **a** : the quality or state of being dainty : FINENESS ⟨lace of great ~⟩ **b** : FRAILTY 1 4 : fineness or subtle expressiveness of touch (as in painting or music) 5 **a** : precise and refined perception and discrimination **b** : extreme sensitivity : PRECISION ⟨an electronic instrument of great ~⟩ 6 **a** : refined sensibility in feeling or conduct **b** : the quality or state of being squeamish 7 : the quality or state of requiring delicate handling

[1]**del·i·cate** \ˈdel-i-kət\ *adj* [ME *delicat*, fr. L *delicatus* delicate, addicted to pleasure; akin to L *delicere* to allure] (14c) 1 : pleasing to the senses: **a** : generally pleasant ⟨the climate's ~, the air most sweet —Shak.⟩ **b** : pleasing to the sense of taste or smell esp. in a mild or subtle way ⟨a ~ aroma⟩ ⟨a robust wine will dominate ~ dishes⟩ **c** : marked by daintiness or charm of color, lines, or proportions ⟨a ~ floral print⟩ ⟨an ample tear trilled down her ~ cheek —Shak.⟩ **d** : marked by fineness of structure, workmanship, or texture ⟨a ~ tracery⟩ ⟨~ fine hats —Shak.⟩ ⟨a ~ lace⟩ 2 **a** : marked by keen sensitivity or fine discrimination ⟨~ insights⟩ ⟨a more ~ syntactic analysis —R.H. Robins⟩ **b** : FASTIDIOUS, SQUEAMISH ⟨a person of ~ tastes⟩ 3 **a** : not robust in health or constitution : WEAK, SICKLY ⟨had been considered a ~ child⟩ **b** : easily torn or damaged : FRAGILE ⟨abused her ~ youth with drugs —Shak.⟩ ⟨the ~ chain of life⟩ 4 **a** : requiring careful handling: (1) : easily unsettled or upset ⟨a ~ balance⟩ ⟨the ~ relationships defined by the Constitution —*New Yorker*⟩ (2) : requiring skill or tact ⟨in a ~ position⟩ ⟨~ negotiations⟩ ⟨a ~ operation⟩ (3) : involving matters of a deeply personal nature : SENSITIVE ⟨this is a ~ matter. Could I possibly speak to you alone —Daphne Du Maurier⟩ ⟨moments of ~ feeling⟩ **b** : marked by care, skill, or tact ⟨~ handling of a difficult situation⟩ 5 : marked by great precision or sensitivity ⟨a ~ instrument⟩ ***syn*** see CHOICE — **del·i·cate·ly** *adv*

[2]**delicate** *n* (15c) : something delicate

del·i·ca·tes·sen \ˌdel-i-kə-ˈtes-ᵊn\ *n pl* [obs. G (now *delikatessen*), pl. of *delicatesse* delicacy, fr. F *délicatesse*, prob. fr. OIt *delicatezza*, fr. *delicato* delicate, fr. L *delicatus*] (1889) 1 : ready-to-eat food products (as cooked meats and prepared salads) 2 *sing, pl* **delicatessens** [*delicatessen (store)*] : a store where delicatessen are sold

de·li·cious \di-ˈlish-əs\ *adj* [ME, fr. MF, fr. LL *deliciosus*, fr. L *deliciae* delight, fr. *delicere* to allure] (14c) 1 : affording great pleasure : DELIGHTFUL 2 : appealing to one of the bodily senses esp. of taste or smell — **de·li·cious·ly** *adv* — **de·li·cious·ness** *n*

Delicious *n, pl* **De·li·cious·es** *or* **Delicious** (ca. 1903) : an important red or yellow market apple of American origin that has a crown of five rounded prominences at the blossom end

de·lict \di-ˈlikt\ *n* [L *delictum* fault, fr. neut. of *delictus*, pp. of *delinquere*] (1523) : an offense against the law

[1]**de·light** \di-ˈlīt\ *n* (13c) 1 : a high degree of gratification : JOY; *also* : extreme satisfaction 2 : something that gives great pleasure 3 *archaic* : the power of affording pleasure

[2]**delight** *vb* [ME *deliten*, fr. OF *delitier*, fr. L *delectare*, fr. *delectus*, pp. of *delicere* to allure, fr. *de-* + *lacere* to allure; akin to OE *lǣl* switch] *vi* (13c) 1 : to take great pleasure ⟨~*ed* in playing the guitar⟩ 2 : to give keen enjoyment ⟨a book certain to ~⟩ ~ *vt* : to give joy or satisfaction to — **de·light·er** *n*

de·light·ed *adj* (14c) 1 *obs* : DELIGHTFUL 2 : highly pleased — **de·light·ed·ly** *adv* — **de·light·ed·ness** *n*

de·light·ful \di-ˈlīt-fəl\ *adj* (1530) : highly pleasing — **de·light·ful·ly** \-fə-lē\ *adv* — **de·light·ful·ness** *n*

de·light·some \-ˈlīt-səm\ *adj* (1500) : very pleasing : DELIGHTFUL

De·li·lah \di-ˈlī-lə\ *n* [Heb *Dĕlīlāh*] : the mistress and betrayer of Samson in the book of Judges

de·lim·it \di-ˈlim-ət\ *vt* [F *délimiter*, fr. L *delimitare*, fr. *de-* + *limitare* to limit, fr. *limit-, limes* boundary, limit — more at LIMB] (1852) : to fix or define the limits of — **de·lim·i·ta·tion** \di-ˌlim-ə-ˈtā-shən, ˌdē-\ *n*

de·lim·it·er \di-ˈlim-ət-ər\ *n* (ca. 1962) : a character that marks the beginning or end of a unit of data (as on a magnetic tape)

de·lin·eate \di-ˈlin-ē-ˌāt\ *vt* **-eat·ed; -eat·ing** [L *delineatus*, pp. of *delineare*, fr. *de-* + *linea* line] (1559) 1 **a** : to indicate or represent by drawn or painted lines **b** : to mark the outline of ⟨lights *delineating* the narrow streets⟩ 2 : to describe, portray, or set forth with accuracy or in detail ⟨~ a character in the story⟩ ⟨~ the steps to be taken by the government⟩ — **de·lin·ea·tor** \-ē-ˌāt-ər\ *n*

de·lin·ea·tion \di-ˌlin-ē-ˈā-shən\ *n* (1570) 1 : the act of delineating 2 : something made by delineating — **de·lin·ea·tive** \-ˈlin-ē-ˌāt-iv\ *adj*

de·lin·quen·cy \di-ˈliŋ-kwən-sē, -ˈlin-\ *n, pl* **-cies** (1636) 1 **a** : a delinquent act **b** : conduct that is out of accord with accepted behavior or the law; *esp* : JUVENILE DELINQUENCY 2 : a debt on which payment is overdue

[1]**de·lin·quent** \-kwənt\ *n* (15c) : a delinquent person

[2]**delinquent** *adj* [L *delinquent-, delinquens*, prp. of *delinquere* to fail, offend, fr. *de-* + *linquere* to leave — more at LOAN] (1603) 1 : offending by neglect or violation of duty or of law 2 : being overdue in payment ⟨a ~ charge account⟩ 3 : of, relating to, or characteristic of delinquents : marked by delinquency — **de·lin·quent·ly** *adv*

del·i·quesce \ˌdel-i-ˈkwes\ *vi* **-quesced; -quesc·ing** [L *deliquescere*, fr. *de-* + *liquescere*, incho. of *liquēre* to be fluid — more at LIQUID] (1756) : to dissolve or melt away: **a** : to exhibit the behavior of a deliquescent substance **b** : to become soft or liquid with age — used of plant structures (as mushrooms)

del·i·ques·cent \-ˈkwes-ᵊnt\ *adj* [L *deliquescent-, deliquescens*, prp. of *deliquescere*] (1791) 1 : tending to melt or dissolve; *esp* : tending to undergo gradual dissolution and liquefaction by the attraction and absorption of moisture from the air 2 : having repeated division into branches ⟨elms are ~ trees⟩ — compare EXCURRENT 1a — **del·i·ques·cence** \-ᵊn(t)s\ *n*

de·lir·i·ous \di-ˈlir-ē-əs\ *adj* (1599) 1 : of, relating to, or characteristic of delirium 2 : affected with or marked by delirium — **de·lir·i·ous·ly** *adv* — **de·lir·i·ous·ness** *n*

de·lir·i·um \di-ˈlir-ē-əm\ *n* [L, fr. *delirare* to be crazy, fr. *de-* + *lira* furrow — more at LEARN] (ca. 1563) 1 : a mental disturbance characterized by confusion, disordered speech, and hallucinations 2 : frenzied excitement ⟨he would stride about his room in a ~ of joy —Thomas Wolfe⟩

delirium tre·mens \-ˈtrē-mənz, -ˈtrem-ənz\ *n* [NL, lit., trembling delirium] (1813) : a violent delirium with tremors that is induced by excessive and prolonged use of alcoholic liquors — called also *d.t.'s*

de·list \(ˈ)dē-ˈlist\ *vt* (1933) : to remove from a list; *esp* : to remove (a security) from the list of securities that may be dealt in on a particular exchange

de·liv·er \di-ˈliv-ər\ *vb* **de·liv·ered; de·liv·er·ing** \-(ə-)riŋ\ [ME *deliveren*, fr. OF *delivrer*, fr. LL *deliberare*, fr. L *de-* + *liberare* to liberate — more at LIBERAL] *vt* (13c) 1 : to set free ⟨and lead us not into temptation, but ~ us from evil —Mt 6:13 (AV)⟩ 2 **a** : to take and hand over to or leave for another : CONVEY ⟨~ a package⟩ **b** : HAND OVER, SURRENDER ⟨~*ed* the prisoners to the sheriff⟩ ⟨~*ed* themselves over to God⟩ 3 **a** : to assist in giving birth **b** : to aid in the birth of **c** : to cause (oneself) to produce as if by giving birth ⟨has ~*ed* himself of half an autobiography —H.C. Schonberg⟩ 4 : SPEAK, SING, UTTER ⟨~*ed* their lines with style⟩ ⟨~ a song⟩ ⟨~ a speech⟩ 5 : to send (something aimed or guided) to an intended target or destination ⟨ability to ~ nuclear warheads⟩ 6 **a** : to bring (as votes) to the support of a candidate or cause **b** : to come through with : PRODUCE ⟨can ~ the goods⟩ ⟨new car ~s high gas mileage⟩ ~ *vi* : to produce the promised, desired, or expected results : COME THROUGH ⟨can't ~ on all these promises⟩ ***syn*** see RESCUE — **de·liv·er·abil·i·ty** \-ˌliv-(ə-)rə-ˈbil-ət-ē\ *n* — **de·liv·er·able** \-ˈliv-(ə-)rə-bəl\ *adj* — **de·liv·er·er** \-ˈliv-ər-ər\ *n*

de·liv·er·ance \di-ˈliv-(ə-)rən(t)s\ *n* (13c) 1 : the act of delivering someone or something : the state of being delivered; *esp* : LIBERATION, RES-

CUE 2 : something delivered; *esp* : an opinion or decision (as the verdict of a jury) expressed publicly

de·liv·ery \di-'liv-(ə-)rē\ *n, pl* **-er·ies** (15c) : the act of delivering something; *also* : something delivered

delivery boy *n* (1920) : a person employed by a retail store to deliver small orders to customers on call

de·liv·ery·man \-(ə-)rē-mən, -ˌman\ *n* (1920) : a person who delivers wholesale or retail goods to customers usu. over a regular local route

dell \'del\ *n* [ME *delle;* akin to MHG *telle* ravine, OE *dæl* valley — more at DALE] (13c) : a secluded hollow or small valley usu. covered with trees or turf

delly *var of* DELI

de·lo·cal·ize \(ˈ)dē-'lō-kə-ˌlīz\ *vt* (1855) : to free from the limitations of locality; *specif* : to remove (electrons) from a particular position — **de·lo·cal·iza·tion** \(ˌ)dē-ˌlō-kə-lə-'zā-shən\ *n*

de·louse \(ˈ)dē-'lau̇s, -'lau̇z\ *vt* (1919) : to remove lice from

Del·phi·an \'del-fē-ən\ *adj* (1625) : DELPHIC

Del·phic \'del-fik\ *adj* (1599) **1** : of or relating to ancient Delphi or its oracle **2** : AMBIGUOUS, OBSCURE — **del·phi·cal·ly** \-fi-k(ə-)lē\ *adv*

del·phin·i·um \del-'fin-ē-əm\ *n* [NL, genus name, fr. Gk *delphinion* larkspur, dim. of *delphin-, delphis* dolphin; prob. fr. the shape of the nectary] (1664) : any of a large genus (*Delphinium*) of the buttercup family that comprises chiefly perennial erect branching herbs with palmately divided leaves and irregular flowers in showy spikes and includes several that are poisonous

Del·phi·nus \del-'fī-nəs, -'fē-\ *n* [L (gen. *Delphini*), lit., dolphin, fr. Gk *delphin-, delphis*] : a northern constellation nearly west of Pegasus

[1]**del·ta** \'del-tə\ *n* [ME *deltha,* fr. Gk *delta,* of Sem origin; akin to Heb *dāleth* daleth] (13c) **1** : the 4th letter of the Greek alphabet — see ALPHABET table **2** : something shaped like a capital Greek delta; *esp* : the alluvial deposit at the mouth of a river **3** : an increment of a variable — symbol Δ — **del·ta·ic** \del-'tā-ik\ *adj*

[2]**delta** *or* **δ-** *adj* (ca. 1937) : fourth in position in the structure of an organic molecule from a particular group or atom

Delta (1952) — a communications code word for the letter *d*

delta ray *n* (1908) : an electron ejected by an ionizing particle in its passage through matter

delta wave *n* (1936) : a high amplitude electrical rhythm of the brain with a frequency of less than 6 cycles per second that occurs esp. in deep sleep, in infancy, and in many diseased conditions of the brain — called also *delta, delta rhythm*

delta wing *n* [[1]*delta;* fr. its shape] (1946) : a triangular swept-back airplane wing with straight trailing edge

[1]**del·toid** \'del-ˌtȯid\ *n* [NL *deltoides,* fr. Gk *deltoeidēs* shaped like a delta, fr. *delta*] (ca. 1681) : a large triangular muscle that covers the shoulder joint and serves to raise the arm laterally

[2]**deltoid** *adj* (1753) **1** : having a triangular shape ⟨a ~ leaf⟩ **2** : relating to, associated with, or supplying the deltoid

del·toi·de·us \del-'tȯid-ē-əs\ *n, pl* **del·toi·dei** \-ē-ˌī\ [NL, alter. of *deltoides*] (ca. 1860) : DELTOID

de·lude \di-'lüd\ *vt* **de·lud·ed; de·lud·ing** [ME *deluden,* fr. L *deludere,* fr. *de-* + *ludere* to play — more at LUDICROUS] (15c) **1** : to mislead the mind or judgment of : impose on : DECEIVE, TRICK **2** *obs* **a** : FRUSTRATE, DISAPPOINT **b** : EVADE, ELUDE ***syn*** see DECEIVE — **de·lud·er** *n*

[1]**del·uge** \'del-ˌ(y)üj, -ˌ(y)üzh; də-'lüj, -'lüzh\ *n* [ME, fr. MF, fr. L *diluvium,* fr. *diluere* to wash away, fr. *dis-* + *lavere* to wash — more at LYE] (14c) **1 a** : an overflowing of the land by water **b** : a drenching rain **2** : an overwhelming amount or number

[2]**deluge** *vt* **del·uged; del·ug·ing** (1649) **1** : to overflow with water : INUNDATE **2** : OVERWHELM, SWAMP

de·lu·sion \di-'lü-zhən\ *n* [ME, fr. L *delusion-, delusio,* fr. *delusus,* pp. of *deludere*] (15c) **1 a** : the act of deluding : the state of being deluded **b** : an abnormal mental state characterized by the occurrence of delusions **2 a** : something that is falsely or delusively believed or propagated **b** : a persistent false psychotic belief regarding the self or persons or objects outside the self — **de·lu·sion·al** \-'lüzh-nəl, -'lü-zhən-ᵊl\ *adj* — **de·lu·sion·ary** \-zhə-ˌner-ē\ *adj*

de·lu·sive \-'lü-siv, -'lü-ziv\ *adj* (1605) **1** : likely to delude **2** : constituting a delusion — **de·lu·sive·ly** *adv* — **de·lu·sive·ness** *n*

de·lu·so·ry \-sə-rē, -zə-\ *adj* (15c) : DECEPTIVE, DELUSIVE

de·lus·ter \(ˈ)dē-'ləs-tər\ *vt* (1926) : to reduce the sheen of (as yarn or fabric)

de·luxe \di-'lu̇ks, -'ləks, -'lüks\ *adj* [F *de luxe,* lit., of luxury] (1819) : notably luxurious, elegant, or expensive ⟨a ~ edition⟩ ⟨~ hotels⟩

[1]**delve** \'delv\ *vb* **delved; delv·ing** [ME *delven,* fr. OE *delfan;* akin to OHG *telban* to dig] *vt, archaic* (bef. 12c) : EXCAVATE ~ *vi* **1** : to dig or labor with a spade **2** : to make a careful or detailed search for information ⟨*delved* into the past⟩ — **delv·er** *n*

[2]**delve** *n, archaic* (14c) : CAVE, HOLLOW

de·mag·ne·tize \(ˈ)dē-'mag-nə-ˌtīz\ *vt* (1842) : to deprive of magnetic properties — **de·mag·ne·ti·za·tion** \(ˌ)dē-ˌmag-nət-ə-'zā-shən\ *n* — **de·mag·ne·tiz·er** \(ˈ)dē-'mag-nə-ˌtī-zər\ *n*

dem·a·gog·ic \ˌdem-ə-'gäg-ik *also* -'gäj- *or* -'gōj-\ *adj* (1831) : of, relating to, or characteristic of a demagogue : employing demagoguery — **dem·a·gog·i·cal·ly** \-i-k(ə-)lē\ *adv*

dem·a·gogue *or* **dem·a·gog** \'dem-ə-ˌgäg\ *n* [Gk *dēmagōgos,* fr. *dēmos* people (akin to Gk *daiesthai* to divide) + *agōgos* leading, fr. *agein* to lead — more at TIDE, AGENT] (1651) **1** : a leader championing the cause of the common people in ancient times **2** : a leader who makes use of popular prejudices and false claims and promises in order to gain power — **demagogue** *vb* — **dem·a·gogu·ery** \-ˌgäg-(ə-)rē\ *n* — **dem·a·gogy** \-ˌgäg-ē, -ˌgäj-ē, -ˌgō-jē\ *n*

[1]**de·mand** \di-'mand\ *n* (13c) **1 a** : an act of demanding or asking esp. with authority **b** : something claimed as due **2** *archaic* : QUESTION **3 a** : willingness and ability to purchase a commodity or service **b** : the quantity of a commodity or service wanted at a specified price and time **4 a** : a seeking or state of being sought after ⟨in great ~ as an entertainer⟩ **b** : urgent need **5** : the requirement of work or of the expenditure of a resource ⟨equal to the ~*s* of the office⟩ ⟨oxygen ~ for waste oxidation⟩ — **on demand** : upon presentation and request for payment; *also* : when requested or needed

[2]**demand** *vb* [ME *demaunden,* fr. MF *demander,* fr. ML *demandare,* fr. L *de-* + *mandare* to enjoin — more at MANDATE] *vi* (14c) : to make a demand : ASK ~ *vt* **1** : to ask or call for with authority : claim as due or just ⟨~ payment of a debt⟩ **2** : to call for urgently, peremptorily, or insistently ⟨~*ed* that the rioters disperse⟩ **3 a** : to ask authoritatively or earnestly to be informed of **b** : to require to come : SUMMON **4** : to call for as useful or necessary — **de·mand·able** \-'man-də-bəl\ *adj* — **de·mand·er** *n*

syn DEMAND, CLAIM, REQUIRE, EXACT mean to ask or call for something as due or as necessary. DEMAND implies peremptoriness and insistence and often the right to make requests that are to be regarded as commands; CLAIM implies a demand for the delivery or concession of something due as one's own or one's right; REQUIRE suggests the imperativeness that arises from inner necessity, compulsion of law or regulation, or the exigencies of the situation; EXACT implies not only demanding but getting what one demands.

de·man·dant \di-'man-dənt\ *n* (15c) **1** *archaic* : the plaintiff in a real action **2** *archaic* : one who makes a demand or claim

demand deposit *n* (1923) : a bank deposit that can be withdrawn without advance notice

de·mand·ing *adj* (1926) : requiring much time, effort, or attention : EXACTING — **de·mand·ing·ly** \-'man-diŋ-lē\ *adv* — **de·mand·ing·ness** *n*

demand loan *n* (1913) : CALL LOAN

demand note *n* (1866) : a note payable on demand

de·mand–pull \di-'man(d)-ˌpu̇l\ *n* (1952) : an increase or upward trend in spendable money that tends to result in increased competition for available goods and services and a corresponding increase in consumer prices — compare COST-PUSH — **demand–pull** *adj*

dem·an·toid \'dem-ən-ˌtȯid\ *n* [G, fr. obs. G *demant* diamond, fr. MHG *diemant,* fr. OF *diamant* — more at DIAMOND] (ca. 1890) : a green andradite used as a gem

de·mar·cate \di-'mär-ˌkāt, 'dē-ˌ\ *vt* **-cat·ed; -cat·ing** [back-formation fr. *demarcation,* fr. Sp *demarcación,* fr. *demarcar* to delimit, fr. *de-* + *marcar* to mark, prob. fr. It *marcare,* of Gmc origin; akin to OHG *marha* boundary — more at MARK] (1816) **1** : DELIMIT **2** : to set apart : SEPARATE — **de·mar·ca·tion** \ˌdē-ˌmär-'kā-shən\ *n*

de·marche \dā-'märsh, di-', 'dā-ˌ\ *n* [F *démarche,* lit., gait, fr. MF, fr. *demarcher* to march, fr. OF *demarchier,* fr. *de-* + *marchier* to march] (1658) **1 a** : a course of action : MANEUVER **b** : a diplomatic move or maneuver **2** : a diplomatic representation

de·mark \di-'märk\ *vt* (1834) : DEMARCATE

de·ma·te·ri·al·ize \ˌdē-mə-'tir-ē-ə-ˌlīz\ *vt* (ca. 1864) : to cause to become or appear immaterial ~ *vi* : to lose or appear to lose materiality : become immaterial — **de·ma·te·ri·al·iza·tion** \-ˌtir-ē-əl-ə-'zā-shən\ *n*

deme \'dēm\ *n* [Gk *dēmos,* lit., people] (1833) **1** : a unit of local government in ancient Attica **2** : a local population of closely related organisms

[1]**de·mean** \di-'mēn\ *vt* **de·meaned; de·mean·ing** [ME *demenen,* fr. MF *demener* to conduct, fr. *de-* + *mener* to drive, fr. L *minare,* fr. *minari* to threaten — more at MOUNT] (14c) : to conduct or behave (oneself) usu. in a proper manner

[2]**demean** *vt* **de·meaned; de·mean·ing** [*de-* + [1]*mean*] (1601) : DEGRADE, DEBASE ***syn*** see ABASE

de·mean·or \di-'mē-nər\ *n* [[1]*demean*] (1509) : behavior toward others : outward manner ***syn*** see BEARING

demeanour *Brit var of* DEMEANOR

de·ment·ed \di-'ment-əd\ *adj* (1644) : MAD, INSANE — **de·ment·ed·ly** *adv* — **de·ment·ed·ness** *n*

de·men·tia \di-'men-chə\ *n* [L, fr. *dement-, demens* mad, fr. *de-* + *ment-, mens* mind — more at MENTAL] (1806) **1** : a condition of deteriorated mentality **2** : MADNESS, INSANITY — **de·men·tial** \-chəl\ *adj*

dementia prae·cox \-'prē-ˌkäks\ *n* [NL, lit., premature dementia] (1899) : SCHIZOPHRENIA

de·mer·it \di-'mer-ət\ *n* [ME, fr. MF *demerite,* fr. *de-* + *merite* merit] (15c) **1** *obs* : OFFENSE **2 a** : a quality that deserves blame or lacks merit : FAULT, DEFECT **b** : lack of merit **3** : a mark usu. entailing a loss of privilege given to an offender

De·mer·ol \'dem-ə-ˌrȯl, -ˌrōl\ *trademark* — used for meperidine

de·mer·sal \di-'mər-səl\ *adj* [L *demersus* (pp. of *demergere* to sink, fr. *de-* + *mergere* to dip, sink) + E *-al*—more at MERGE] (1889) : living near, deposited on, or sinking to the bottom of the sea ⟨~ fish⟩ ⟨~ fish eggs⟩

de·mesne \di-'mān, -'mēn\ *n* [ME, alter. of *demeyne,* fr. OF *demaine* — more at DOMAIN] (14c) **1** : legal possession of land as one's own **2** : REALM, DOMAIN **3** : manorial land actually possessed by the lord and not held by tenants **4 a** : the land attached to a mansion **b** : landed property : ESTATE **c** : REGION, TERRITORY

De·me·ter \di-'mēt-ər\ *n* [L, fr. Gk *Dēmētēr*] : the Greek goddess of agriculture — compare CERES

demi- *prefix* [ME, fr. *demi,* fr. MF, fr. VL *dimedius,* fr. *dis-* + *medius* mid—more at MID] **1** : half ⟨*demi*bastion⟩ **2** : one that partly belongs to (a specified type or class) ⟨*demi*god⟩

demi·god \'dem-i-ˌgäd\ *n* (1530) **1** : a mythological being with more power than a mortal but less than a god **2** : a person so outstanding that he seems to approach the divine

demi·john \'dem-i-ˌjän\ *n* [by folk etymology fr. F *dame-jeanne,* lit., Lady Jane] (1769) : a narrow-necked bottle of glass or stoneware enclosed in wickerwork and holding from 1 to 10 gallons

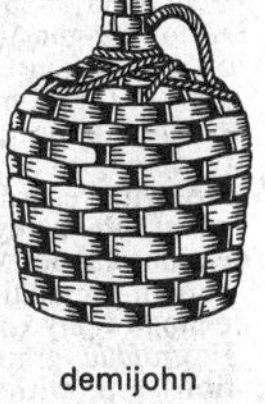

demijohn

de·mil·i·ta·rize \(ˈ)dē-'mil-ə-tə-ˌrīz, di-\ *vt* (1883) **1 a** : to do away with the military organization or potential of **b** : to prohibit (as a zone or frontier area) from being used for military purposes **2** : to rid of military characteristics or uses — **de·mil·i·tar·iza·tion** \(ˌ)dē-ˌmil-ə-t(ə-)rə-'zā-shən, di-\ *n*

demi·mon·daine \ˌdem-i-ˌmän-'dān, -'män-ˌ\ *n* [F *demi-mondaine,* fr. fem. of *demi-mondain,* fr. *demi-monde*] (1894) : a woman of the demimonde

demi·monde \'dem-i-ˌmänd\ *n* [F *demi-monde,* fr.

\ə\ abut \ᵊ\ kitten, F table \ər\ further \a\ ash \ā\ ace \ä\ cot, cart \au̇\ out \ch\ chin \e\ bet \ē\ easy \g\ go \i\ hit \ī\ ice \j\ job \ŋ\ sing \ō\ go \ȯ\ law \ȯi\ boy \th\ thin \t͟h\ the \ü\ loot \u̇\ foot \y\ yet \zh\ vision \à, k̲, ⁿ, œ, œ̄, ue, ue̅, ʸ\ *see* Guide to Pronunciation

demi- + *monde* world, fr. L *mundus* — more at MUNDANE] (1855) **1 a :** a class of women on the fringes of respectable society supported by wealthy lovers **b :** PROSTITUTES **2 :** DEMIMONDAINE **3 :** a group engaged in activity of doubtful legality or propriety

de·min·er·al·iza·tion \(ˌ)dē-ˌmin-(ə-)rə-lə-ˈzā-shən\ *n* (ca. 1903) **1 :** loss of minerals (as salts of calcium) from the body esp. in disease **2 :** the process of removing mineral matter or salts (as from water) — **de·min·er·al·ize** \(ˌ)dē-ˈmin-(ə-)rə-ˌlīz\ *vt* — **de·min·er·al·iz·er** \-ˌlī-zər\ *n*

demi·rep \ˈdem-i-ˌrep\ *n* [*demi-* + *rep* (reprobate)] (1749) **:** DEMIMONDAINE

1de·mise \di-ˈmīz\ *vb* **de·mised; de·mis·ing** *vt* (15c) **1 :** to convey (as an estate) by will or lease **2** *obs* **:** CONVEY, GIVE **3 :** to transmit by succession or inheritance ~ *vi* **1 :** DIE, DECEASE **2 :** to pass by descent or bequest ⟨the property *demised* to the king⟩

2demise *n* [MF, fem. of *demis,* pp. of *demettre* to dismiss, fr. L *demittere* to send down, fr. *de-* + *mittere* to send] (15c) **1 :** the conveyance of an estate **2 :** transfer of the sovereignty to a successor **3 a :** DEATH **b :** a cessation of existence or activity **c :** a loss of position or status

demi–sec \ˌdem-i-ˈsek\ *adj* [F] *of champagne* (1932) **:** moderately sweet

demi·semi·qua·ver \ˌdem-i-ˈsem-i-ˌkwā-vər\ *n* (ca. 1706) **:** THIRTY-SECOND NOTE

de·mis·sion \di-ˈmish-ən\ *n* [MF, fr. L *demission-, demissio* lowering, fr. *demissus,* pp. of *demittere*] (15c) **:** RESIGNATION, ABDICATION

de·mit \di-ˈmit\ *vb* **de·mit·ted; de·mit·ting** [MF *demettre*] *vt* (15c) **1** *archaic* **:** DISMISS **2 :** RESIGN ~ *vi* **:** to withdraw from office or membership

demi·tasse \ˈdem-i-ˌtas, -ˌtäs\ *n* [F *demi-tasse,* fr. *demi-* + *tasse* cup, fr. MF, fr. Ar *ṭass,* fr. Per *tast*] (1842) **:** a small cup of black coffee; *also* **:** the cup used to serve it

demi·urge \ˈdem-ē-ˌərj\ *n* [LL *demiurgus,* fr. Gk *dēmiourgos,* lit., one who works for the people, fr. *dēmios* of the people (fr. *dēmos* people) + *-ourgos* worker (fr. *ergon* work) — more at DEMAGOGUE, WORK] (1678) **1** *cap* **a :** a Platonic subordinate deity who fashions the sensible world in the light of eternal ideas **b :** a Gnostic subordinate deity who is the creator of the material world **2 :** one that is an autonomous creative force or decisive power — **demi·ur·gic** \-jik\ *or* **demi·ur·gi·cal** \-ji-kəl\ *adj*

demi·world \ˈdem-i-ˌwərld\ *n* [part trans. of F *demimonde*] (1862) **:** DEMIMONDE 3

demo \ˈdem-(ˌ)ō\ *n, pl* **dem·os** (1793) **1** *cap* **:** DEMOCRAT 2 **2 :** DEMONSTRATION **3 :** DEMONSTRATOR a

1de·mob \(ˈ)dē-ˈmäb, di-\ *vt, chiefly Brit* (1919) **:** DEMOBILIZE

2demob *n, chiefly Brit* (1945) **:** the act or process of demobilizing **:** DEMOBILIZATION

de·mo·bi·lize \di-ˈmō-bə-ˌlīz, (ˈ)dē-\ *vt* (1882) **1 :** DISBAND **2 :** to discharge from military service — **de·mo·bi·li·za·tion** \di-ˌmō-bə-lə-ˈzā-shən, (ˌ)dē-\ *n*

de·moc·ra·cy \di-ˈmäk-rə-sē\ *n, pl* **-cies** [MF *democratie,* fr. LL *democratia,* fr. Gk *dēmokratia,* fr. *dēmos* + *-kratia* -cracy] (1576) **1 a :** government by the people; *esp* **:** rule of the majority **b :** a government in which the supreme power is vested in the people and exercised by them directly or indirectly through a system of representation usu. involving periodically held free elections **2 :** a political unit that has a democratic government **3** *cap* **:** the principles and policies of the Democratic party in the U.S. **4 :** the common people esp. when constituting the source of political authority **5 :** the absence of hereditary or arbitrary class distinctions or privileges

dem·o·crat \ˈdem-ə-ˌkrat\ *n* (1740) **1 a :** an adherent of democracy **b :** one who practices social equality **2** *cap* **:** a member of the Democratic party of the U.S.

dem·o·crat·ic \ˌdem-ə-ˈkrat-ik\ *adj* (1602) **1 :** of, relating to, or favoring democracy **2** *often cap* **:** of or relating to one of the two major political parties in the U.S. evolving in the early 19th century from the anti-federalists and the Democratic-Republican party and associated in modern times with policies of broad social reform and internationalism **3 :** relating to, appealing to, or available to the broad masses of the people ⟨~ art⟩ **4 :** favoring social equality **:** not snobbish — **dem·o·crat·i·cal·ly** \-i-k(ə-)lē\ *adv*

democratic centralism *n* (1926) **:** a principle of Communist party organization in which party members participate in policy discussions and elections at all levels but are required to follow decisions made ultimately at higher levels

Democratic–Republican *adj* (1818) **:** of or relating to a major American political party of the early 19th century favoring a strict interpretation of the constitution to restrict the powers of the federal government and emphasizing states' rights

de·moc·ra·tize \di-ˈmäk-rə-ˌtīz\ *vt* **-tized; -tiz·ing** (1798) **:** to make democratic — **de·moc·ra·ti·za·tion** \-ˌmäk-rət-ə-ˈzā-shən\ *n* — **de·moc·ra·tiz·er** \-ˈmäk-rə-ˌtī-zər\ *n*

dé·mo·dé \ˌdā-mō-ˈdā\ *adj* [F, fr. *dé-* de- + *mode*] (1873) **:** no longer fashionable **:** OUT-OF-DATE

de·mod·ed \(ˈ)dē-ˈmōd-əd\ *adj* (1887) **:** DÉMODÉ

de·mod·u·late \(ˈ)dē-ˈmäj-ə-ˌlāt\ *vt* (1927) **:** to extract the intelligence from (a modulated radio, laser, or computer signal) — **de·mod·u·la·tion** \(ˌ)dē-ˌmäj-ə-ˈlā-shən\ *n* — **de·mod·u·la·tor** \(ˈ)dē-ˈmäj-ə-ˌlāt-ər\ *n*

De·mo·gor·gon \ˌdē-mə-ˈgȯr-gən, ˈdē-mə-ˌ\ *n* [LL] **:** a mysterious spirit or deity often explained as a primeval creator god who antedates the gods of Greek mythology

de·mo·graph·ic \ˌdē-mə-ˈgraf-ik, ˌdem-ə-\ *adj* (1882) **1 :** of or relating to demography **2 :** relating to the dynamic balance of a population esp. with regard to density and capacity for expansion or decline — **de·mo·graph·i·cal·ly** \-i-k(ə-)lē\ *adv*

de·mo·graph·ics \-iks\ *n pl* (ca. 1966) **:** the statistical characteristics of human populations (as age and income) used esp. to identify markets

de·mog·ra·phy \di-ˈmäg-rə-fē\ *n* [F *démographie,* fr. Gk *dēmos* people + F *-graphie* -graphy] (ca. 1880) **:** the statistical study of human populations esp. with reference to size and density, distribution, and vital statistics — **de·mog·ra·pher** \-fər\ *n*

dem·oi·selle \ˌdem-(w)ə-ˈzel\ *n* [F, fr. OF *dameisele* — more at DAMSEL] (1520) **1 :** a young lady **2 :** DAMSELFLY **3 :** DAMSELFISH

De·Moi·vre's theorem \di-ˈmȯi-vərz-, ˈmwäv(-rə)z-\ *n* [Abraham *De Moivre* †1754 Fr. mathematician] (ca. 1891) **:** a theorem of complex numbers: the *n*th power of a complex number has for its absolute value and its argument respectively the *n*th power of the absolute value and *n* times the argument of the complex number

de·mol·ish \di-ˈmäl-ish\ *vt* [MF *demoliss-,* stem of *demolir,* fr. L *demoliri,* fr. *de-* + *moliri* to construct, fr. *moles* mass — more at MOLE] (1570) **1 a :** TEAR DOWN, RAZE **b :** to break to pieces **:** SMASH **2 a :** to do away with **:** DESTROY **b :** to strip of any pretense of merit or credence **:** DISCREDIT — **de·mol·ish·er** *n* — **de·mol·ish·ment** \-ish-mənt\ *n*

de·mo·li·tion \ˌdem-ə-ˈlish-ən, ˌdē-mə-\ *n* (1549) **1 :** the act of demolishing; *esp* **:** destruction in war by means of explosives **2** *pl* **:** explosives for destruction in war — **de·mo·li·tion·ist** \-ˈlish-(ə-)nəst\ *n*

demolition derby *n* (ca. 1953) **:** a contest in which skilled drivers ram old cars into one another until only one car remains running

de·mon *or* **dae·mon** \ˈdē-mən\ *n* [ME *demon,* fr. LL & L; LL *daemon* evil spirit, fr. L, divinity, spirit, fr. Gk *daimōn*] (13c) **1 a :** an evil spirit **b :** an evil or undesirable emotion, trait, or state **2** *usu daemon* **:** an attendant power or spirit **:** GENIUS **3** *usu daemon* **:** a supernatural being of Greek mythology intermediate between gods and men **4 :** one that has unusual drive or effectiveness ⟨a ~ for work⟩ — **de·mo·ni·an** \di-ˈmō-nē-ən\ *adj* — **de·mon·iza·tion** \ˌdē-mə-nə-ˈzā-shən\ *n* — **de·mon·ize** \ˈdē-mə-ˌnīz\ *vt*

de·mon·e·tize \(ˈ)dē-ˈmän-ə-ˌtīz, -ˈmən-\ *vt* [F *démonétiser,* fr. *dé-* de- + L *moneta* coin — more at MINT] (1852) **1 :** to stop using (a metal) as a monetary standard **2 :** to deprive of value for official payment — **de·mon·e·ti·za·tion** \(ˌ)dē-ˌmän-ət-ə-ˈzā-shən, -ˌmən-\ *n*

1de·mo·ni·ac \di-ˈmō-nē-ˌak\ *also* **de·mo·ni·a·cal** \ˌdē-mə-ˈnī-ə-kəl\ *adj* [ME *demoniak,* fr. LL *daemoniacus,* fr. Gk *daimoniakos,* fr. *daimon-, daimōn*] (14c) **1 :** possessed or influenced by a demon **2 :** of, relating to, or suggestive of a demon **:** FIENDISH ⟨~ cruelty⟩ — **de·mo·ni·a·cal·ly** \ˌdē-mə-ˈnī-ə-k(ə-)lē\ *adv*

2demoniac *n* (14c) **:** one possessed by a demon

de·mon·ic \di-ˈmän-ik\ *also* **de·mon·i·cal** \-i-kəl\ *adj* (1662) **:** DEMONIAC 2 — **de·mon·i·cal·ly** \-i-k(ə-)lē\ *adv*

de·mon·ol·o·gy \ˌdē-mə-ˈnäl-ə-jē\ *n* (1597) **1 :** the study of demons or evil spirits **2 :** belief in demons **:** a doctrine of evil spirits **3 :** a catalog of enemies ⟨the liberal creed at that time put Big Business in a central place in its ~ —Carl Kaysen⟩ — **de·mon·o·log·i·cal** \ˌdē-mən-ᵊl-ˈäj-i-kəl\ *adj*

de·mon·stra·ble \di-ˈmän(t)-strə-bəl\ *adj* (15c) **1 :** capable of being demonstrated **2 :** APPARENT, EVIDENT — **de·mon·stra·bil·i·ty** \-ˌmän(t)-strə-ˈbil-ət-ē\ *n* — **de·mon·stra·bly** \-blē\ *adv*

dem·on·strate \ˈdem-ən-ˌstrāt\ *vb* **-strat·ed; -strat·ing** [L *demonstratus,* pp. of *demonstrare,* fr. *de-* + *monstrare* to show — more at MUSTER] *vt* (1552) **1 :** to show clearly **2 a :** to prove or make clear by reasoning or evidence **b :** to illustrate and explain esp. with many examples **3 :** to show or prove the value or efficiency of to a prospective buyer ~ *vi* **:** to make a demonstration ***syn*** see SHOW

dem·on·stra·tion \ˌdem-ən-ˈstrā-shən\ *n* (14c) **1 :** an act, process, or means of demonstrating to the intelligence: as **a (1) :** conclusive evidence **:** PROOF **(2) :** DERIVATION 5 **b :** a showing of the merits of a product or service to a prospective consumer **2 :** an outward expression or display **3 :** a show of armed force **4 :** a public display of group feelings toward a person or cause — **dem·on·stra·tion·al** \-shnəl, -shən-ᵊl\ *adj* — **dem·on·stra·tion·ist** \-sh(ə-)nəst\ *n*

1de·mon·stra·tive \di-ˈmän(t)-strət-iv\ *adj* (14c) **1 a :** demonstrating as real or true **b :** characterized or established by demonstration **2 :** pointing out the one referred to and distinguishing it from others of the same class ⟨~ pronouns⟩ **3 a :** marked by display of feeling **b :** inclined to display feelings openly — **de·mon·stra·tive·ly** *adv* — **de·mon·stra·tive·ness** *n*

2demonstrative *n* (15c) **:** a demonstrative word or morpheme

dem·on·stra·tor \ˈdem-ən-ˌstrāt-ər\ *n* (1611) **:** one that demonstrates: **a :** a product (as an automobile) used to demonstrate performance or merits to prospective buyers **b :** someone who engages in a public demonstration

de·mor·al·ize \di-ˈmȯr-ə-ˌlīz, ˈdē-, -ˈmär-\ *vt* (ca. 1793) **1 :** to corrupt the morals of **2 a :** to weaken the morale of **:** DISCOURAGE, DISPIRIT **b :** to upset or destroy the normal functioning of **c :** to throw into disorder — **de·mor·al·iza·tion** \di-ˌmȯr-ə-lə-ˈzā-shən, ˌdē-, -ˌmär-\ *n* — **de·mor·al·iz·er** \di-ˈmȯr-ə-ˌlī-zər, ˈdē-, -ˈmär-\ *n* — **de·mor·al·iz·ing·ly** \-ziŋ-lē\ *adv*

de·mos \ˈdē-ˌmäs\ *n* [Gk *dēmos* — more at DEMAGOGUE] (1831) **1 :** POPULACE **2 :** the common people of an ancient Greek state

de·mote \di-ˈmōt, ˈdē-\ *vt* **de·mot·ed; de·mot·ing** [*de-* + *-mote* (as in *promote*)] (ca. 1891) **1 :** to reduce to a lower grade or rank **2 :** to relegate to a less important position — **de·mo·tion** \-ˈmō-shən\ *n*

de·mot·ic \di-ˈmät-ik\ *adj* [Gk *dēmotikos,* fr. *dēmotēs* commoner, fr. *dēmos*] (1822) **1 :** of, relating to, or written in a simplified form of the ancient Egyptian hieratic writing **2 :** POPULAR, COMMON ⟨~ idiom⟩ **3 :** of or relating to the form of Modern Greek that is based on colloquial use

de·mount \(ˈ)dē-ˈmau̇nt\ *vt* (ca. 1930) **1 :** to remove from a mounted position **2 :** DISASSEMBLE — **de·mount·able** \-ə-bəl\ *adj*

1de·mul·cent \di-ˈməl-sənt\ *adj* [L *demulcent-, demulcens,* prp. of *demulcēre* to soothe, fr. *de-* + *mulcēre* to soothe] (1732) **:** SOOTHING

2demulcent *n* (1732) **:** a usu. mucilaginous or oily substance (as tragacanth) capable of soothing or protecting an abraded mucous membrane

1de·mur \di-ˈmər\ *vi* **de·murred; de·mur·ring** [ME *demeoren* to linger, fr. OF *demorer,* fr. L *demorari,* fr. *de-* + *morari* to linger, fr. *mora* delay — more at MEMORY] (13c) **1 :** to file a demurrer **2 :** to take exception **:** OBJECT — often used with *to* or *at* **3** *archaic* **:** DELAY, HESITATE

2demur *n* (13c) **1 :** hesitation (as in doing or accepting) usu. based on doubt of the acceptability of something offered or proposed **2 :** OBJECTION, PROTEST ***syn*** see QUALM

de·mure \di-ˈmyu̇(ə)r\ *adj* [ME] (14c) **1 :** RESERVED, MODEST **2 :** affectedly modest, reserved, or serious **:** COY — **de·mure·ly** *adv* — **de·mure·ness** *n*

de·mur·rage \di-ˈmər-ij, -ˈmə-rij\ *n* (1641) **1 :** the detention of a ship by the freighter beyond the time allowed for loading, unloading, or sailing **2 :** a charge for detaining a ship, freight car, or truck

de·mur·ral \di-ˈmər-əl, -ˈmə-rəl\ *n* (1810) **:** an act or instance of demurring

[1]**de·mur·rer** \di-ˈmər-ər, -ˈmə-rər\ *n* [MF *demorer,* v.] (1547) **1 :** a response in a court proceeding in which the defendant does not dispute the truth of the allegation but claims it is not sufficient grounds to justify legal action **2 :** OBJECTION

[2]**de·mur·rer** \-ˈmər-ər\ *n* [[1]*demur*] (1711) **:** one that demurs

de·my·e·lin·at·ing \(ˈ)dē-ˈmī-ə-lə-ˌnāt-iŋ\ *adj* (1940) **:** causing or characterized by the loss or destruction of myelin ⟨~ diseases⟩ ⟨a ~ agent⟩ — **de·my·e·lin·ation** \(ˌ)dē-ˌmī-ə-lə-ˈnā-shən\ *n*

de·mys·ti·fy \(ˈ)dē-ˈmis-tə-ˌfī\ *vt* (1963) **:** to remove the mystery from **:** EXPLICATE — **de·mys·ti·fi·ca·tion** \(ˌ)dē-ˌmis-tə-fə-ˈkā-shən\ *n*

de·my·thol·o·gize \ˌdē-mith-ˈäl-ə-ˌjīz\ *vt* (1950) **1 :** to divest of mythological forms in order to uncover the meaning underlying them ⟨~ the Gospels⟩ **2 :** to divest of mythical elements or associations — **de·my·thol·o·gi·za·tion** \-ˌäl-ə-jə-ˈzā-shən\ *n* — **de·my·thol·o·giz·er** \-ˈäl-ə-ˌjī-zər\ *n*

[1]**den** \ˈden\ *n* [ME, fr. OE *denn;* akin to OE *denu* valley, OHG *tenni* threshing floor, Gk *thenar* palm of the hand] (bef. 12c) **1 :** the lair of a wild usu. predatory animal **2 a** (1) **:** a hollow or cavern used esp. as a hideout (2) **:** a center of secret activity **b :** a small usu. squalid dwelling **3 :** a comfortable usu. secluded room **4 :** a subdivision of a Cub Scout pack made up of two or more boys

[2]**den** *vb* **denned; den·ning** *vi* (13c) **:** to live in or retire to a den ~ *vt* **:** to drive into a den

de·nar·i·us \di-ˈnar-ē-əs, -ˈner-\ *n, pl* **de·nar·ii** \-ē-ˌī, -ē-ˌē\ [ME, fr. L — more at DENIER] (15c) **1 :** a small silver coin of ancient Rome **2 :** a gold coin of the Roman Empire equivalent to 25 denarii

de·na·tion·al·ize \(ˈ)dē-ˈnash-nə-ˌlīz, -ˈnash-ən-ᵊl-ˌīz\ *vt* (1807) **1 :** to divest of national character or rights **2 :** to remove from ownership or control by the national government — **de·na·tion·al·iza·tion** \(ˌ)dē-ˌnash-nə-lə-ˈzā-shən, -ˌnash-ən-ᵊl-ə-ˈzā-\ *n*

de·nat·u·ral·ize \(ˈ)dē-ˈnach-(ə-)rə-ˌlīz\ *vt* (1800) **1 :** to make unnatural **2 :** to deprive of the rights and duties of a citizen — **de·nat·u·ral·iza·tion** \(ˌ)dē-ˌnach-(ə-)rə-lə-ˈzā-shən\ *n*

de·na·tur·ant \(ˈ)dē-ˈnāch-(ə-)rənt\ *n* (1905) **:** a denaturing agent

de·na·tur·ation \(ˌ)dē-ˌnā-chə-ˈrā-shən\ *n* (1882) **:** the process of denaturing

de·na·ture \(ˈ)dē-ˈnā-chər\ *vb* **de·na·tured; de·na·tur·ing** \-ˈnāch-(ə-)riŋ\ *vt* (1685) **1 :** DEHUMANIZE **2 :** to deprive of natural qualities: as **a :** to make (alcohol) unfit for drinking (as by adding an obnoxious substance) without impairing usefulness for other purposes **b :** to modify the molecular structure of (as a protein or DNA) esp. by heat, acid, alkali, or ultraviolet radiation so as to destroy or diminish some of the original properties and esp. the specific biological activity **c :** to add nonfissionable material to (fissionable material) so as to make unsuitable for use in an atom bomb ~ *vi* **:** to become denatured

de·na·zi·fy \(ˈ)dē-ˈnät-si-ˌfī, -ˈnat-\ *vt* **-fied; -fy·ing** (1940) **:** to rid of Nazism and its influence — **de·na·zi·fi·ca·tion** \(ˌ)dē-ˌnät-si-fə-ˈkā-shən, -ˌnat-\ *n*

dendr- *or* **dendro-** *comb form* [Gk, fr. *dendron;* akin to Gk *drys* tree — more at TREE] **:** tree ⟨*dendro*philous⟩ **:** resembling a tree ⟨*dendr*ite⟩

den·dri·form \ˈden-drə-ˌfȯrm\ *adj* (ca. 1847) **:** resembling a tree in structure

den·drite \ˈden-ˌdrīt\ *n* (1727) **1 :** a branching treelike figure produced on or in a mineral by a foreign mineral; *also* **:** the mineral so marked **2 :** a crystallized arborescent form **3 :** any of the usu. branching protoplasmic processes that conduct impulses toward the body of a nerve cell — **den·drit·ic** \den-ˈdrit-ik\ *adj*

den·dro·chro·nol·o·gy \ˌden-(ˌ)drō-krə-ˈnäl-ə-jē\ *n* (ca. 1928) **:** the science of dating events and variations in environment in former periods by comparative study of growth rings in trees and aged wood — **den·dro·chro·no·log·i·cal** \-ˌkrän-ᵊl-ˈäj-i-kəl, -ˌkrōn-\ *adj* — **den·dro·chro·no·log·i·cal·ly** \-i-k(ə-)lē\ *adv* — **den·dro·chro·nol·o·gist** \-krə-ˈnäl-ə-jəst\ *n*

den·dro·gram \ˈden-drə-ˌgram\ *n* (ca. 1953) **:** a branching diagram representing a hierarchy of categories based on degree of similarity or number of shared characteristics esp. in biological taxonomy — compare CLADOGRAM

den·droid \ˈden-ˌdrȯid\ *adj* [Gk *dendroeidēs,* fr. *dendron*] (ca. 1828) **:** resembling a tree in form **:** ARBORESCENT

den·drol·o·gy \den-ˈdräl-ə-jē\ *n* (ca. 1708) **:** the study of trees — **den·dro·log·ic** \ˌden-drə-ˈläj-ik\ *or* **den·dro·log·i·cal** \-i-kəl\ *adj* — **den·drol·o·gist** \den-ˈdräl-ə-jəst\ *n*

dene \ˈdēn\ *n* [ME, fr. OE *denu*] *Brit* (bef. 12c) **:** VALLEY

Dé·né \ˈden-ē\ *n, pl* **Déné** *or* **Dé·nés** \-ēz\ [F, fr. Déné] (1891) **1 :** a member of an Athapaskan people of the interior of Alaska and northwestern Canada **2 :** the language of the Déné people

Den·eb \ˈden-ˌeb, -əb\ *n* [Ar *dhanab al-dajāja,* lit., the tail of the hen] **:** a star of the first magnitude in Cygnus

den·e·ga·tion \ˌden-i-ˈgā-shən\ *n* [ME *denegacioun,* fr. MF or L; MF *denegation,* fr. L *denegation-, denegatio,* fr. *denegatus,* pp. of *denegare* to deny — more at DENY] (15c) **:** DENIAL

de·ner·vate \ˈdē-(ˌ)nər-ˌvāt\ *vt* **-vat·ed; -vat·ing** (1905) **:** to deprive of a nerve supply (as by cutting a nerve) — **de·ner·va·tion** \ˌdē-(ˌ)nər-ˈvā-shən\ *n*

den·gue \ˈdeŋ-gē, -ˌgā\ *n* [Sp] (1828) **:** an acute infectious disease caused by an arbovirus and characterized by headache, severe joint pain, and a rash — called also *breakbone fever, dengue fever*

de·ni·able \di-ˈnī-ə-bəl\ *adj* (1548) **:** capable of being denied — **de·ni·abil·i·ty** \-ˌnī-ə-ˈbil-ət-ē\ *n*

de·ni·al \di-ˈnī(-ə)l\ *n* (1528) **1 :** refusal to satisfy a request or desire **2 a** (1) **:** refusal to admit the truth or reality (as of a statement or charge) (2) **:** assertion that an allegation is false **b :** refusal to acknowledge a person or a thing **:** DISAVOWAL **3 :** the opposing by the defendant of an allegation of the opposite party in a lawsuit **4 :** SELF-DENIAL **5 :** negation in logic

[1]**de·ni·er** \di-ˈnī(-ə)r\ *n* (15c) **:** one that denies

[2]**de·nier** *n* [ME *denere,* fr. MF *denier,* fr. L *denarius,* coin worth ten asses, fr. *denarius* containing ten, fr. *deni* ten each, fr. *decem* ten — more at TEN] (15c) **1** \də-ˈni(ə)r, dən-ˈyā\ **:** a small orig. silver coin formerly used in western Europe **2** \ˈden-yər\ **:** a unit of fineness for silk, rayon, or nylon yarn equal to the fineness of a yarn weighing one gram for each 9000 meters ⟨100-*denier* yarn is finer than 150-*denier* yarn⟩

den·i·grate \ˈden-i-ˌgrāt\ *vt* **-grat·ed; -grat·ing** [L *denigratus,* pp. of *denigrare,* fr. *de-* + *nigrare* to blacken, fr. *nigr-, niger* black] (1526) **1 :** to cast aspersions on **:** DEFAME **2 :** to deny the importance or validity of **:** BELITTLE — **den·i·gra·tion** \ˌden-i-ˈgrā-shən\ *n* — **den·i·gra·tive** \ˈden-i-ˌgrāt-iv\ *adj* — **den·i·gra·tor** \-ˌgrāt-ər\ *n* — **den·i·gra·to·ry** \ˈden-i-grə-ˌtōr-ē, -ˌtȯr-\ *adj*

den·im \ˈden-əm\ *n* [F (*serge*) *de Nîmes* serge of Nîmes, France] (1695) **1 a :** a firm durable twilled usu. cotton fabric woven with colored warp and white filling threads **b :** a similar fabric woven in colored stripes **2** *pl* **:** overalls or trousers usu. of blue denim

de·ni·tri·fi·ca·tion \(ˌ)dē-ˌnī-trə-fə-ˈkā-shən\ *n* (1883) **:** an act or process of denitrifying; *specif* **:** reduction of nitrates or nitrites commonly by bacteria and usu. resulting in the escape of nitrogen into the air

de·ni·tri·fy \(ˈ)dē-ˈnī-trə-ˌfī\ *vt* (ca. 1890) **1 :** to remove nitrogen or its compound from **2 :** to convert (a nitrate or a nitrite) into a compound of a lower state of oxidation

den·i·zen \ˈden-ə-zən\ *n* [ME *denysen,* fr. MF *denzein,* fr. OF, inner, fr. *denz* within, fr. LL *deintus,* fr. L *de-* + *intus* within — more at ENT-] (15c) **1 :** INHABITANT **2 :** one admitted to residence in a foreign country; *esp* **:** an alien admitted to rights of citizenship **3 :** one that frequents a place

den mother *n* (1946) **:** a female adult leader of a Cub Scout den; *also* **:** a person seen in the role of leader or protector of a group

de·nom·i·nal \di-ˈnäm-ən-ᵊl\ *adj* (1951) **:** derived from a noun

de·nom·i·nate \di-ˈnäm-ə-ˌnāt\ *vt* [L *denominatus,* pp. of *denominare,* fr. *de-* + *nominare* to name — more at NOMINATE] (ca. 1552) **:** to give a name to **:** DESIGNATE

de·nom·i·nate number \di-ˌnäm-ə-nət-\ *n* [L *denominatus*] (1579) **:** a number (as 7 in 7 *feet*) that specifies a quantity in terms of a unit of measurement

de·nom·i·na·tion \di-ˌnäm-ə-ˈnā-shən\ *n* (14c) **1 :** an act of denominating **2 :** a value or size of a series of values or sizes (as of money) **3 :** NAME, DESIGNATION; *esp* **:** a general name for a category **4 :** a religious organization uniting in a single legal and administrative body a number of local congregations — **de·nom·i·na·tion·al** \-shnəl, -shən-ᵊl\ *adj*

de·nom·i·na·tion·al·ism \-shnəl-ˌiz-əm, -shən-ᵊl-\ *n* (1855) **1 :** devotion to denominational principles or interests **2 :** the emphasizing of denominational differences to the point of being narrowly exclusive **:** SECTARIANISM

de·nom·i·na·tive \di-ˈnäm-(ə-)nət-iv\ *adj* [L *de* from + *nomin-, nomen* name] (ca. 1783) **:** derived from a noun or adjective — **denominative** *n*

de·nom·i·na·tor \di-ˈnäm-ə-ˌnāt-ər\ *n* (ca. 1542) **1 :** the part of a fraction below the line signifying division that functions as the divisor of the numerator and in fractions with 1 as the numerator indicates into how many parts the unit is divided **2 a :** a common trait **b :** the average level (as of taste or opinion) **:** STANDARD

de·no·ta·tion \ˌdē-nō-ˈtā-shən\ *n* (1532) **1 :** an act or process of denoting **2 :** MEANING; *esp* **:** a direct specific meaning as distinct from an implied or associated idea **3 a :** a denoting term **:** NAME **b :** SIGN, INDICATION ⟨visible ~s of divine wrath⟩ **4 :** the totality of things to which a term is applicable esp. in logic — compare CONNOTATION

de·no·ta·tive \ˈdē-nō-ˌtāt-iv, di-ˈnōt-ət-iv\ *adj* (1611) **1 :** denoting or tending to denote **2 :** relating to denotation

de·note \di-ˈnōt\ *vt* [MF *denoter,* fr. L *denotare,* fr. *de-* + *notare* to note] (1592) **1 :** to serve as an indication of **:** BETOKEN ⟨the swollen bellies that ~ starvation⟩ **2 :** to serve as an arbitrary mark for ⟨red flares *denoting* danger⟩ **3 :** to make known **:** ANNOUNCE ⟨his crestfallen look *denoted* his distress⟩ **4 a :** to serve as a linguistic expression of the notion of **:** MEAN **b :** to stand for **:** DESIGNATE — **de·note·ment** \-ˈnōt-mənt\ *n*

de·noue·ment *also* **dé·noue·ment** \ˌdā-ˌnü-ˈmäⁿ, dā-ˈnü-ˌ\ *n* [F *dénouement,* lit., untying, fr. MF *desnouement,* fr. *desnouer* to untie, fr. OF *desnoer,* fr. *des-* de- + *noer* to tie, fr. L *nodare,* fr. *nodus* knot — more at NET] (1752) **1 :** the final outcome of the main dramatic complication in a literary work **2 :** the outcome of a complex sequence of events

de·nounce \di-ˈnau̇n(t)s\ *vt* **de·nounced; de·nounc·ing** [ME *denouncen,* fr. OF *denoncier* to proclaim, fr. L *denuntiare,* fr. *de-* + *nuntiare* to report — more at ANNOUNCE] (14c) **1 :** to pronounce esp. publicly to be blameworthy or evil **2** *archaic* **a :** PROCLAIM **b :** to announce threateningly **3 :** to inform against **:** ACCUSE **4** *obs* **:** PORTEND **5 :** to announce formally the termination of (as a treaty) ***syn*** see CRITICIZE — **de·nounce·ment** \-ˈnau̇n(t)-smənt\ *n* — **de·nounc·er** *n*

de no·vo \di-ˈnō-(ˌ)vō, dā-\ *adv* [L] (1627) **:** over again **:** ANEW

dense \ˈden(t)s\ *adj* **dens·er; dens·est** [L *densus;* akin to Gk *dasys* thick with hair or leaves] (15c) **1 :** marked by compactness or crowding together of parts **2 a :** marked by a stupid imperviousness to ideas or impressions **:** THICKHEADED **b :** EXTREME ⟨~ ignorance⟩ **3 :** having between any two elements at least one element ⟨the set of rational numbers is ~⟩ **4 :** demanding concentration to follow or comprehend ⟨~ prose⟩ **5 :** possessing relatively great retarding power upon light waves and consequently relatively high density ⟨a ~ glass⟩ **6 :** having high or relatively high opacity ⟨a ~ fog⟩ ⟨a ~ photographic negative⟩ ***syn*** see STUPID — **dense·ly** *adv* — **dense·ness** \ˈden(t)-snəs\ *n*

den·si·fy \ˈden(t)-sə-ˌfī\ *vt* **-fied; -fy·ing** (1820) **:** to make denser; *specif* **:** to increase the density of (wood) by pressure usu. with impregnation of a resin — **den·si·fi·ca·tion** \ˌden(t)-sə-fə-ˈkā-shən\ *n*

den·sim·e·ter \den-ˈsim-ət-ər\ *n* [L *densus* + ISV *-meter*] (1863) **:** an instrument for determining density or specific gravity — **den·si·met·ric** \ˌden(t)-sə-ˈme-trik\ *adj*

den·si·tom·e·ter \ˌden(t)-sə-ˈtäm-ət-ər\ *n* (1901) **:** an instrument for determining optical or photographic density — **den·si·to·met·ric** \ˌden(t)-sət-ə-ˈme-trik\ *adj* — **den·si·tom·e·try** \ˌden(t)-sə-ˈtäm-ə-trē\ *n*

den·si·ty \ˈden(t)-sət-ē, -stē\ *n, pl* **-ties** (1603) **1 :** the quality or state of being dense **2 :** the quantity per unit volume, unit area, or unit length:

as **a :** the mass of a substance per unit volume **b :** the distribution of a quantity (as mass, electricity, or energy) per unit usu. of space **c :** the average number of individuals or units per space unit ⟨a population ~ of 500 persons per square mile⟩ ⟨a housing ~ of 10 houses per acre⟩ **3 a :** the degree of opacity of a translucent medium **b :** the common logarithm of the opacity

density function *n* (ca. 1962) **:** PROBABILITY DENSITY FUNCTION

[1]**dent** \'dent\ *vt* (14c) **1 :** to make a dent in **2 :** to have a weakening effect on ~ *vi* **:** to form a dent by sinking inward **:** become dented

[2]**dent** *n* [ME, blow, alter. of *dint*] (1565) **1 :** a depression or hollow made by a blow or by pressure **2 a :** an impression or effect often made against resistance and usu. having a weakening effect **b :** initial progress **:** HEADWAY

[3]**dent** *n* [F, lit., tooth, fr. L *dent-, dens*] (1703) **:** TOOTH 3a

dent- *or* **denti-** *or* **dento-** *comb form* [ME *denti-*, fr. L, fr. *dent-, dens* tooth — more at TOOTH] **1 :** tooth **:** teeth ⟨*dent*algia⟩ ⟨*denti*form⟩ **2 :** dental and ⟨*dento*surgical⟩

[1]**den·tal** \'dent-ᵊl\ *adj* [L *dentalis*, fr. *dent-, dens*] (1594) **1 :** articulated with the tip or blade of the tongue against or near the upper front teeth **2 :** of or relating to the teeth or dentistry — **den·tal·ly** \-ē\ *adv*

[2]**dental** *n* (ca. 1755) **:** a dental consonant

dental floss *n* (1910) **:** a thread used to clean between the teeth

dental hygienist *n* (ca. 1922) **:** a licensed dental professional who cleans and examines teeth

den·ta·li·um \den-'tā-lē-əm\ *n, pl* **-lia** \-lē-ə\ [NL, genus name, fr. L *dentalis*] (1864) **:** any of a genus (*Dentalium*) of widely distributed tooth shells; *broadly* **:** TOOTH SHELL

dental technician *n* (1946) **:** one who makes dental appliances

den·tate \'den-,tāt\ *adj* [L *dentatus*, fr. *dent-, dens*] (1810) **:** having teeth or pointed conical projections ⟨a ~ margin of a leaf⟩

dent corn *n* (1872) **:** an Indian corn having kernels that contain both hard and soft starch and that become indented at maturity

den·ti·cle \'dent-i-kəl\ *n* [ME, fr. L *denticulus*, dim. of *dent-, dens*] (14c) **:** a conical pointed projection (as a small tooth)

den·tic·u·late \den-'tik-yə-lət\ *or* **den·tic·u·lat·ed** \-,lāt-əd\ *adj* (1661) **1 :** finely dentate or serrate ⟨a ~ shell⟩ ⟨a ~ margin of a leaf⟩ **2 :** cut into dentils — **den·tic·u·la·tion** \(,)den-,tik-yə-'lā-shən\ *n*

den·ti·form \'dent-ə-,fȯrm\ *adj* (1708) **:** shaped like a tooth

den·ti·frice \'dent-ə-frəs\ *n* [MF, fr. L *dentifricium*, fr. *denti-* + *fricare* to rub — more at FRICTION] (15c) **:** a powder, paste, or liquid for cleaning the teeth

den·til \'dent-ᵊl, 'den-,til\ *n* [obs. F *dentille*, fr. MF, dim. of *dent*] (1663) **:** one of a series of small projecting rectangular blocks forming a molding esp. under a cornice

den·tin \'dent-ᵊn\ *or* **den·tine** \'den-,tēn, den-'\ *n* (1840) **:** a calcareous material similar to but harder and denser than bone that composes the principal mass of a tooth — see TOOTH illustration — **den·tin·al** \den-'tēn-ᵊl, 'dent-ᵊn-əl\ *adj*

den·tist \'dent-əst\ *n* [F *dentiste*, fr. *dent*] (1752) **:** one who is skilled in and licensed to practice the prevention, diagnosis, and treatment of diseases, injuries, and malformations of the teeth, jaws, and mouth and who makes and inserts false teeth

den·tist·ry \'dent-ə-strē\ *n* (1838) **:** the art or profession of a dentist

den·ti·tion \den-'tish-ən\ *n* [L *dentition-, dentitio*, fr. *dentitus*, pp. of *dentire* to cut teeth, fr. *dent-, dens*] (1615) **1 :** the development and cutting of teeth **2 :** the character of a set of teeth esp. with regard to their number, kind, and arrangement — see TOOTH illustration **3 :** TEETH

den·tu·lous \'den-chə-ləs\ *adj* [back-formation fr. *edentulous*] (1926) **:** having teeth

den·ture \'den-chər\ *n* [F, fr. MF, *dent*] (1874) **1 :** a set of teeth **2 :** an artificial replacement for one or more teeth; *esp* **:** a set of false teeth

den·tur·ist \'den-chə-rəst\ *n* (1965) **:** a dental technician who makes, fits, and repairs dentures directly for the public

de·nu·cle·ar·ize \(')dē-'n(y)ü-klē-ə-,rīz, ÷-kyə-lə-,rīz\ *vt* **-ized; -iz·ing** (1958) **:** to remove nuclear arms from **:** prohibit the use of nuclear arms in — **de·nu·cle·ar·iza·tion** \(,)dē-,n(y)ü-klē-ə-rə-'zā-shən, ÷-kyə-lə-rə-\ *n*

de·nude \di-'n(y)üd\ *vt* **de·nud·ed; de·nud·ing** [L *denudare*, fr. *de-* + *nudus* bare — more at NAKED] (15c) **1 :** to deprive of something important **2 a :** to strip of all covering **b :** to lay bare by erosion **c :** to strip (land) of forests — **de·nu·da·tion** \,dē-(,)n(y)ü-'dā-shən, ,den-yù-\ *n* — **de·nu·da·tion·al** \-shnəl, -shən-ᵊl\ *adj* — **de·nude·ment** \di-'n(y)üd-mənt\ *n*

de·nu·mer·a·ble \di-'n(y)üm-(ə-)rə-bəl\ *adj* (1902) **:** capable of being put into one-to-one correspondence with the positive integers — **de·nu·mer·a·bil·i·ty** \-,n(y)üm-(ə-)rə-'bil-ət-ē\ *n* — **de·nu·mer·a·bly** \-'n(y)üm-(e-)rə-blē\ *adv*

de·nun·ci·a·tion \di-,nən(t)-sē-'ā-shən\ *n* (1842) **:** an act of denouncing; *esp* **:** a public condemnation — **de·nun·ci·a·tive** \-'nən(t)-sē-,āt-iv\ *adj* — **de·nun·ci·a·to·ry** \-sē-ə-,tōr-ē, -,tȯr-\ *adj*

de·ny \di-'nī\ *vt* **de·nied; de·ny·ing** [ME *denyen*, fr. MF *denier*, fr. L *denegare*, fr. *de-* + *negare* to deny — more at NEGATE] (14c) **1 :** to declare untrue **2 :** to disclaim connection with or responsibility for **:** DISAVOW **3 a :** to give a negative answer to **b :** to refuse to grant **c :** to restrain (oneself) from gratification of desires **4** *archaic* **:** DECLINE **5 :** to refuse to accept the existence, truth, or validity of — **de·ny·ing·ly** \-'nī-iŋ-lē\ *adv*

syn DENY, GAINSAY, CONTRADICT, CONTRAVENE mean to refuse to accept as true or valid. DENY implies a firm refusal to accept as true, to grant or concede, or to acknowledge the existence or claims of; GAINSAY implies disputing the truth of what another has said; CONTRADICT implies an open or flat denial; CONTRAVENE implies not so much an intentional opposition as some inherent incompatibility.

de·o·dar \'dē-ə-,där\ *also* **de·o·da·ra** \,dē-ə-'där-ə\ *n* [Hindi *deodār*, fr. Skt *devadāru*, lit., timber of the gods, fr. *deva* god + *dāru* wood — more at DEITY, TREE] (1804) **:** an East Indian cedar (*Cedrus deodara*)

de·odor·ant \dē-'ōd-ə-rənt\ *n* (1869) **:** a preparation that destroys or masks unpleasant odors — **deodorant** *adj*

de·odor·ize \dē-'ōd-ə-,rīz\ *vt* (1856) **1 :** to eliminate or prevent the offensive odor of **2 :** to make (something unpleasant or reprehensible) more acceptable ⟨the movie ~*s* his scandalous career⟩ — **de·odor·iza·tion** \-,ōd-ə-rə-'zā-shən\ *n* — **de·odor·iz·er** *n*

de·on·tol·o·gy \,dē-,än-'täl-ə-jē\ *n* [Gk *deont-, deon* that which is obligatory, fr. neut. of prp. of *dein* to lack, be needful — more at DEUTER-] (1826) **:** the theory or study of moral obligation — **de·on·to·log·i·cal** \,dē-,änt-ᵊl-'äj-i-kəl\ *adj* — **de·on·tol·o·gist** \,dē-,än-'täl-ə-jəst\ *n*

Deo vo·len·te \,dā-(,)ō-və-'lent-ē, ,dē-\ [L] (1767) **:** God being willing

de·ox·i·dize \(')dē-'äk-sə-,dīz\ *vt* (1794) **:** to remove oxygen from — **de·ox·i·da·tion** \(,)dē-,äk-sə-'dā-shən\ *n* — **de·ox·i·diz·er** \(')dē-'äk-sə-,dī-zər\ *n*

deoxy- *or* **desoxy-** *comb form* [ISV] **:** containing less oxygen in the molecule than the compound to which it is closely related ⟨*deoxy*ribonucleic acid⟩

de·ox·y·gen·ate \(')dē-'äk-si-jə-,nāt, ,dē-äk-'sij-ə-\ *vt* (1799) **:** to remove oxygen from — **de·ox·y·gen·ation** \(,)dē-,äk-si-jə-'nā-shən, ,dē-äk,sij-ə-\ *n*

de·ox·y·gen·at·ed *adj* (1799) **:** having the hemoglobin in the reduced state

de·oxy·ri·bo·nu·cle·ase \(')dē-'äk-si-,rī-bō-'n(y)ü-klē-,ās, -,āz\ *n* [*deoxyribonucleic* acid + *-ase*] (1946) **:** an enzyme that hydrolyzes DNA to nucleotides — called also *DNase*

de·oxy·ri·bo·nu·cle·ic acid \(')dē-'äk-si-,rī-bō-n(y)ù-,klē-ik-, -,klā-\ *n* [*deoxyribose* + *nucleic acid*] (1938) **:** DNA

de·oxy·ri·bo·nu·cle·o·tide \-'n(y)ü-klē-ə-,tīd\ *n* (1949) **:** a nucleotide that contains deoxyribose and is a constituent of DNA

de·oxy·ri·bose \(,)dē-,äk-si-'rī-,bōs, -,bōz\ *n* [ISV] (1931) **:** a pentose sugar $C_5H_{10}O_4$ that is a structural element of DNA

de·part \di-'pärt\ *vb* [ME *departen* to divide, go away, fr. OF *departir*, fr. *de-* + *partir* to divide, fr. L *partire*, fr. *part-, pars* part] *vi* (13c) **1 a :** to go away **:** LEAVE **b :** DIE **2 :** to turn aside **:** DEVIATE ~ *vt* **:** to go away from **:** LEAVE ***syn*** see SWERVE

de·part·ed *adj* (14c) **1 :** BYGONE **2 :** having died esp. recently ⟨mourning our ~ friend⟩ ***syn*** see DEAD

de·part·ment \di-'pärt-mənt\ *n* [F *département*, fr. MF, fr. *departir*] (1735) **1 :** a distinct sphere **:** PROVINCE **2 :** a functional or territorial division: as **a :** a major administrative division of a government **b :** a major territorial administrative subdivision **c :** a division of a college or school giving instruction in a particular subject **d :** a major division of a business **e :** a section of a department store handling a particular kind of merchandise **f :** a territorial subdivision made for the administration and training of military units — **de·part·men·tal** \di-,pärt-'ment-ᵊl, ,dē-\ *adj* — **de·part·men·tal·ly** \-ᵊl-ē\ *adv*

de·part·men·tal·ize \di-,pärt-'ment-ᵊl-,īz, ,dē-\ *vt* **-ized; -iz·ing** (ca. 1895) **:** to divide into departments — **de·part·men·tal·iza·tion** \-,ment-ᵊl-ə-'zā-shən\ *n*

department store *n* (1887) **:** a store selling a wide variety of goods and arranged in several departments

de·par·ture \di-'pär-chər\ *n* (15c) **1 a (1) :** the act or an instance of departing **(2)** *archaic* **:** DEATH **b :** a ship's position in latitude and longitude at the beginning of a voyage as a point from which to begin dead reckoning **c :** a setting out (as on a new course) **2 :** the distance due east or west made by a ship in its course **3 :** DIVERGENCE 2

de·pau·per·ate \di-'pȯ-pə-rət\ *adj* [ME *depauperat*, fr. ML *depauperatus*, pp. of *depauperare* to impoverish, fr. L *de-* + *pauperare* to impoverish, fr. *pauper* poor — more at POOR] (1670) **:** falling short of natural development or size — **de·pau·per·ation** \-,pȯ-pə-'rā-shən\ *n*

de·pend \di-'pend\ *vi* [ME *dependen*, fr. MF *dependre*, modif. of L *dependēre*, fr. *de-* + *pendēre* to hang — more at PENDANT] (15c) **1 a :** to be contingent **b :** to exist by virtue of a necessary relation **:** be conditioned or determined **2 :** to be pending or undecided **3 a :** to place reliance or trust **b :** to be dependent esp. for financial support **4 :** to hang down

de·pend·able \di-'pen-də-bəl\ *adj* (1735) **:** capable of being depended on **:** RELIABLE — **de·pend·abil·i·ty** \-,pen-də-'bil-ət-ē\ *n* — **de·pend·able·ness** *n* — **de·pend·ably** \-blē\ *adv*

de·pen·dence *also* **de·pen·dance** \di-'pen-dən(t)s\ *n* (15c) **1 :** the quality or state of being dependent; *esp* **:** the quality or state of being influenced or determined by or subject to another **2 :** RELIANCE, TRUST **3 :** one that is relied on ⟨he was her sole ~⟩ **4 a :** drug addiction **b :** HABITUATION 2b

de·pen·den·cy \-dən-sē\ *n, pl* **-cies** (1594) **1 :** DEPENDENCE 1 **2 :** something that is dependent on something else; *specif* **:** a territorial unit under the jurisdiction of a nation but not formally annexed by it

[1]**de·pen·dent** \di-'pen-dənt\ *adj* [ME *dependant*, fr. MF, prp. of *dependre*] (14c) **1 :** hanging down **2 a :** determined or conditioned by another **:** CONTINGENT **b (1) :** relying on another for support **(2) :** affected with a drug dependence **c :** subject to another's jurisdiction **d :** SUBORDINATE 3a **3 a :** not mathematically or statistically independent ⟨a ~ set of vectors⟩ ⟨~ events⟩ **b :** EQUIVALENT 6a ⟨~ equations⟩ — **de·pen·dent·ly** *adv*

[2]**dependent** *also* **de·pen·dant** \-dənt\ *n* (1523) **1** *archaic* **:** DEPENDENCY **2 :** one that is dependent; *esp* **:** a person who relies on another for support

dependent variable *n* (ca. 1852) **:** a mathematical variable whose value is determined by that of one or more other variables in a function ⟨in $z = x^2 + 3xy + y^2$, *z* is the *dependent variable*⟩

de·perm \(')dē-'pərm\ *vt* [*de-* + *perm*anent magnetism] (1944) **:** to reduce the magnetism of (a ship's steel hull) as a precaution against magnetically operated mines

de·per·son·al·iza·tion \(,)dē-,pər-snə-lə-'zā-shən, -,pərs-ᵊn-ə-lə-\ *n* (1906) **1 a :** an act or process of depersonalizing **b :** the quality or state of being depersonalized **2 :** a psychopathological syndrome characterized by loss of identity and feelings of unreality and strangeness about one's own behavior

de·per·son·al·ize \(')dē-'pər-snə-,līz, -'pərs-ᵊn-ə-\ *vt* (1866) **1 :** to deprive of the sense of personal identity ⟨schools that ~ students⟩ **2 :** to make impersonal

de·phos·phor·y·la·tion \(,)dē-,fäs-fȯr-ə-'lā-shən\ *n* [*de-* + *phosphoryl* + *-ation*] (1931) **:** the process of removing phosphate groups from an organic compound (as ATP) by hydrolysis; *also* **:** the resulting state — **de·phos·phor·y·late** \(')dē-fäs-'fȯr-ə-,lāt\ *vt*

de·pict \di-'pikt\ *vt* [L *depictus*, pp. of *depingere*, fr. *de-* + *pingere* to paint — more at PAINT] (15c) **1 :** to represent by a picture **2 :** DESCRIBE — **de·pic·ter** \-'pik-tər\ *n* — **de·pic·tion** \-'pik-shən\ *n*

de·pig·men·ta·tion \(,)dē-,pig-mən-'tā-shən, -,men-\ *n* (1889) **:** loss of normal pigmentation

dep·i·la·tion \,dep-ə-'lā-shən\ *n* [MF or ML; MF, fr. ML *depilation-, depilatio,* fr. L *depilatus,* pp. of *depilare,* fr. *de-* + *pilus* hair — more at PILE] (1547) : the removal of hair, wool, or bristles by chemical or mechanical methods — **dep·i·late** \'dep-ə-,lāt\ *vt*
de·pil·a·to·ry \di-'pil-ə-,tōr-ē, -,tȯr-\ *n, pl* **-ries** (1606) : an agent for removing hair, wool, or bristles — **depilatory** *adj*
de·plane \(')dē-'plān\ *vi* (1923) : to get out of an airplane
de·plete \di-'plēt\ *vt* **de·plet·ed; de·plet·ing** [L *depletus,* pp. of *deplēre,* fr. *de-* + *plēre* to fill — more at FULL] (1807) **1 :** to empty of a principal substance **2 :** to lessen markedly in quantity, content, power, or value — **de·plet·able** \-'plēt-ə-bəl\ *adj* — **de·ple·tion** \-'plē-shən\ *n* — **de·ple·tive** \-'plēt-iv\ *adj*
syn DEPLETE, DRAIN, EXHAUST, IMPOVERISH, BANKRUPT mean to deprive of something essential to existence or potency. DEPLETE implies a reduction in number or quantity so as to endanger the ability to function; DRAIN implies a gradual withdrawal and ultimate deprivation of what is necessary to a thing's existence; EXHAUST stresses a complete emptying or evacuation; IMPOVERISH suggests a deprivation of something essential to vigorous well-being; BANKRUPT suggests impoverishment to the point of imminent collapse.
de·plor·able \di-'plōr-ə-bəl, -'plȯr-\ *adj* (1612) **1 :** LAMENTABLE **2 :** BAD, WRETCHED — **de·plor·able·ness** *n* — **de·plor·ably** \-blē\ *adv*
de·plore \di-'plō(ə)r, -'plȯ(ə)r\ *vt* **de·plored; de·plor·ing** [MF or L; MF *deplorer,* fr. L *deplorare,* fr. *de-* + *plorare* to wail] (1567) **1 a :** to feel or express grief for **b :** to regret strongly **2 :** to consider unfortunate or deserving of deprecation — **de·plor·er** \-'plōr-ər\ *n* — **de·plor·ing·ly** \-iŋ-lē\ *adv*
syn DEPLORE, LAMENT, BEWAIL, BEMOAN mean to express grief or sorrow for something. DEPLORE implies regret for the loss or impairment of something of value; LAMENT implies a profound or demonstrative expression of sorrow; BEWAIL and BEMOAN imply sorrow, disappointment, or protest finding outlet in words or cries, BEWAIL commonly suggesting loudness, and BEMOAN lugubriousness, in uttering complaints or expressing regret.
de·ploy \di-'plȯi\ *vb* [F *déployer,* fr. L *displicare* to scatter — more at DISPLAY] *vt* (1786) **1 a :** to extend (a military unit) esp. in width **b :** to place in battle formation or appropriate positions **2 :** to spread out, utilize, or arrange esp. strategically ~ *vi* **:** to move in being deployed — **de·ploy·able** \-ə-bəl\ *adj* — **de·ploy·ment** \-mənt\ *n*
de·po·lar·ize \(')dē-'pō-lə-,rīz\ *vt* (1818) **1 :** to cause to become partially or wholly unpolarized **2 :** to prevent or remove polarization of (as a dry cell or cell membrane) **3 :** DEMAGNETIZE — **de·po·lar·iza·tion** \(,)dē-,pō-lə-rə-'zā-shən\ *n* — **de·po·lar·iz·er** \(')dē-'pō-lə-,rī-zər\ *n*
de·po·lit·i·cize \,dē-pə-'lit-ə-,sīz\ *vt* (1937) : to remove the political character of : take out of the realm of politics ⟨~ our foreign aid program⟩
de·po·ly·mer·ize \(')dē-pə-'lim-ə-,rīz, -'päl-ə-mə-\ *vt* (ca. 1909) : to decompose (macromolecules) into relatively simple compounds (as monomers) ~ *vi* **:** to undergo decomposition into simpler compounds — **de·po·ly·mer·iza·tion** \,dē-pə-'lim-ə-rə-'zā-shən, (,)dē-,päl-ə-mə-rə-\ *n*
de·pone \di-'pōn\ *vb* **de·poned; de·pon·ing** [ML *deponere,* fr. L, to put down, fr. *de-* + *ponere* to put — more at POSITION] (15c) : TESTIFY
[1]**de·po·nent** \di-'pō-nənt\ *adj* [LL *deponent-, deponens,* fr. L, prp. of *deponere*] (15c) : occurring with passive or middle voice forms but with active voice meaning ⟨the ~ verbs in Latin and Greek⟩
[2]**deponent** *n* (1530) **1 :** a deponent verb **2 :** one who gives evidence
de·pop·u·late \(')dē-'päp-yə-,lāt\ *vt* [L *depopulatus,* pp. of *depopulari,* fr. *de-* + *populari* to ravage] (1548) **1** *obs* **:** RAVAGE **2 :** to reduce greatly the population of — **de·pop·u·la·tion** \(,)dē-,päp-yə-'lā-shən\ *n*
de·port \di-'pō(ə)rt, -'pȯ(ə)rt\ *vt* [MF *deporter,* fr. L *deportare* to carry away, fr. *de-* + *portare* to carry — more at FARE] (1598) **1 :** to behave or comport (oneself) esp. in accord with a code **2** [L *deportare*] **a :** to carry away **b :** to send out of the country by legal deportation ***syn*** see BANISH, BEHAVE
de·port·able \di-'pōrt-ə-bəl, -'pȯrt-\ *adj* (1891) **1 :** punishable by deportation ⟨~ offenses⟩ **2 :** subject to deportation ⟨~ aliens⟩
de·por·ta·tion \,dē-,pōr-'tā-shən, -,pȯr-, -pər-\ *n* (1595) **1 :** an act or instance of deporting **2 :** the removal from a country of an alien whose presence is unlawful or prejudicial
de·por·tee \,dē-,pōr-'tē, di-, -,pȯr-\ *n* (1865) : one who has been deported or is under sentence of deportation
de·port·ment \di-'pōrt-mənt, -'pȯrt-\ *n* (1601) : the manner in which one conducts oneself : BEHAVIOR ***syn*** see BEARING
de·pos·al \di-'pō-zəl\ *n* (14c) : an act of deposing from office
de·pose \di-'pōz\ *vb* **de·posed; de·pos·ing** [ME *deposen,* fr. MF *deposer,* fr. OF, fr. LL *deponere* (perf. indic. *deposui*), fr. L, to put down] *vt* (14c) **1 :** to remove from a throne or other high position **2 :** to put down : DEPOSIT **3 a** [ME *deposen,* fr. ML *deponere,* fr. LL] **:** to testify to under oath or by affidavit **b :** AFFIRM, ASSERT ~ *vi* **:** to bear witness
[1]**de·pos·it** \di-'päz-ət\ *vb* **de·pos·it·ed** \-'päz-ət-əd, -'päz-təd\; **de·pos·it·ing** \-'päz-ət-iŋ, -'päz-tiŋ\ [L *depositus,* pp. of *deponere*] *vt* (1624) **1 :** to place esp. for safekeeping or as a pledge; *esp* **:** to put in a bank **2 a :** to lay down : PLACE **b :** to let fall (as sediment) ~ *vi* **:** to become deposited — **de·pos·i·tor** \-'päz-ət-ər, -'päz-tər\ *n*
[2]**deposit** *n* (1624) **1 :** the state of being deposited **2 :** something placed for safekeeping: as **a :** money deposited in a bank **b :** money given as a pledge or down payment **3 :** a place of deposit : DEPOSITORY **4 :** an act of depositing **5 a :** something laid down; *esp* **:** matter deposited by a natural process **b :** a natural accumulation (as of iron ore, coal, or gas)
de·pos·i·tary \di-'päz-ə-,ter-ē\ *n, pl* **-tar·ies** (1605) **1 :** a person to whom something is entrusted **2 :** DEPOSITORY 2
de·po·si·tion \,dep-ə-'zish-ən, ,dē-pə-\ *n* (14c) **1 :** an act of removing from a position of authority **2 a :** a testifying esp. before a court **b :** DECLARATION; *specif* **:** testimony taken down in writing under oath **3 :** an act or process of depositing **4 :** something deposited : DEPOSIT — **de·po·si·tion·al** \-'zish-nəl, -ən-ᵊl\ *adj*
de·pos·i·to·ry \di-'päz-ə-,tōr-ē, -,tȯr-\ *n, pl* **-ries** (1656) **1 :** DEPOSITARY 1 **2 :** a place where something is deposited esp. for safekeeping
depository library *n* (ca. 1930) : a library designated to receive U.S. government publications
deposit slip *n* (1903) : a slip listing and accompanying bank deposits
de·pot *1 & 2 are* 'dep-(,)ō *also* 'dēp-, *3 is* 'dēp- *sometimes* 'dep-\ *n* [F *dépôt,* fr. ML *depositum,* fr. L, neut. of *depositus*] (1795) **1 a :** a place for storing goods or motor vehicles **b :** STORE, CACHE **2 a :** a place for the storage of military supplies **b :** a place for the reception and forwarding of military replacements **3 :** a building for railroad or bus passengers or freight
de·prave \di-'prāv\ *vt* **de·praved; de·prav·ing** [ME *depraven,* fr. MF *depraver,* fr. L *depravare* to pervert, fr. *de-* + *pravus* crooked, bad — more at PRAIRIE] (14c) **1** *archaic* **:** to speak ill of : MALIGN **2 :** to make bad : CORRUPT; *esp* **:** to corrupt morally ***syn*** see DEBASE — **de·pra·va·tion** \,dep-rə-'vā-shən, ,dē-,prā-\ *n* — **de·prave·ment** \di-'prāv-mənt\ *n* — **de·prav·er** \di-'prā-vər\ *n*
de·praved \di-'prāvd\ *adj* (14c) : marked by corruption or evil; *esp* **:** PERVERTED — **de·praved·ly** \-'prā-vəd-lē, -'prāv-dlē\ *adv* — **de·praved·ness** \-'prā-vəd-nəs, -'prāv(d)-nəs\ *n*
de·prav·i·ty \di-'prav-ət-ē *also* -'prāv-\ *n, pl* **-ties** (1641) **1 :** the quality or state of being depraved **2 :** a corrupt act or practice
dep·re·cate \'dep-ri-,kāt\ *vt* **-cat·ed; -cat·ing** [L *deprecatus,* pp. of *deprecari* to avert by prayer, fr. *de-* + *precari* to pray — more at PRAY] (1641) **1 :** to express disapproval of **2 a :** to play down : make little of ⟨*deprecated* their own success⟩ **b :** BELITTLE, DISPARAGE — **dep·re·cat·ing·ly** \-,kāt-iŋ-lē\ *adv* — **dep·re·ca·tion** \,dep-ri-'kā-shən\ *n*
dep·re·ca·to·ry \'dep-ri-kə-,tōr-ē, -,tȯr-\ *adj* (1704) **1 :** seeking to avert disapproval : APOLOGETIC **2 :** serving to deprecate : DISAPPROVING — **dep·re·ca·to·ri·ly** \,dep-ri-kə-'tōr-ə-lē, -'tȯr-\ *adv*
de·pre·ci·ate \di-'prē-shē-,āt\ *vb* **-at·ed; -at·ing** [LL *depretiatus,* pp. of *depretiare,* fr. L *de-* + *pretium* price — more at PRICE] *vt* (15c) **1 :** to lower in estimation or esteem **2 :** to lower the price or estimated value of ~ *vi* **:** to fall in value ***syn*** see DECRY — **de·pre·cia·ble** \-shə-bəl\ *adj* — **de·pre·ci·at·ing·ly** \-shē-,āt-iŋ-lē\ *adv* — **de·pre·ci·a·tion** \-,prē-shē-'ā-shən\ *n* — **de·pre·ci·a·tive** \-'prē-shət-iv, -shē-,āt-iv\ *adj* — **de·pre·ci·a·tor** \-shē-,āt-ər\ *n* — **de·pre·cia·to·ry** \-shə-,tōr-ē, -,tȯr-\ *adj*
dep·re·date \'dep-rə-,dāt\ *vb* **-dat·ed; -dat·ing** [LL *depraedatus,* pp. of *depraedari,* fr. L *de-* + *praedari* to plunder — more at PREY] *vt* (1626) **:** to lay waste : PLUNDER, RAVAGE ~ *vi* **:** to engage in plunder — **dep·re·da·tion** \,dep-rə-'dā-shən\ *n* — **dep·re·da·tor** \'dep-rə-,dāt-ər, di-'pred-ət-\ *n* — **dep·re·da·to·ry** \,dep-ri-'dā-,tōr-ē, 'dep-ri-də-, -,tȯr-\ *adj*
de·press \di-'pres\ *vt* [ME *depressen,* fr. MF *depresser,* fr. L *depressus,* pp. of *deprimere* to press down, fr. *de-* + *premere* to press — more at PRESS] (14c) **1** *obs* **:** REPRESS, SUBJUGATE **2 a :** to press down ⟨~ a typewriter key⟩ **b :** to cause to sink to a lower position **3 :** to lessen the activity or strength of **4 :** SADDEN, DISCOURAGE **5 :** to decrease the market value or marketability of — **de·press·ible** \-ə-bəl\ *adj*
de·pres·sant \di-'pres-ᵊnt\ *n* (1876) : one that depresses; *specif* **:** an agent that reduces a bodily functional activity or an instinctive desire (as appetite) — **depressant** *adj*
de·pressed *adj* (1621) **1 :** low in spirits : SAD; *specif* **:** affected by psychological depression **2 a :** vertically flattened ⟨a ~ cactus⟩ **b :** having the central part lower than the margin **c :** lying flat or prostrate **d :** dorsoventrally flattened **3 :** suffering from economic depression; *esp* **:** UNDERPRIVILEGED **4 :** being below the standard
de·press·ing *adj* (1789) : that depresses; *esp* **:** causing emotional depression ⟨a ~ story⟩ — **de·press·ing·ly** \-iŋ-lē\ *adv*
de·pres·sion \di-'presh-ən\ *n* (14c) **1 a :** the angular distance of a celestial object below the horizon **b :** the size of an angle of depression **2 :** an act of depressing or a state of being depressed: as **a :** a pressing down : LOWERING **b** (1) **:** a state of feeling sad : DEJECTION (2) **:** a psychoneurotic or psychotic disorder marked esp. by sadness, inactivity, difficulty in thinking and concentration, a significant increase or decrease in appetite and time spent sleeping, feelings of dejection and hopelessness, and sometimes suicidal tendencies **c** (1) **:** a reduction in activity, amount, quality, or force (2) **:** a lowering of vitality or functional activity **3 :** a depressed place or part : HOLLOW **4 :** LOW 1b **5 :** a period of low general economic activity marked esp. by rising levels of unemployment
[1]**de·pres·sive** \di-'pres-iv\ *adj* (1620) **1 :** tending to depress **2 :** of, relating to, marked by, or affected by psychological depression — **de·pres·sive·ly** *adv*
[2]**depressive** *n* (1937) : one who is psychologically depressed
de·pres·sor \di-'pres-ər\ *n* [LL, fr. L *depressus*] (1611) : one that depresses: as **a :** a muscle that draws down a part — compare LEVATOR **b :** a device for pressing a part down or aside **c :** a nerve or nerve fiber that decreases the activity or the tone of the organ or part it innervates
de·pres·sur·ize \(')dē-'presh-ə-,rīz\ *vt* (1944) : to release pressure from
de·pri·va·tion \,dep-rə-'vā-shən, ,dē-,prī-\ *n* (15c) **1 :** the state of being deprived : PRIVATION; *specif* **:** removal from an office, dignity, or benefice **2 :** an act or instance of depriving : LOSS
de·prive \di-'prīv\ *vt* **de·prived; de·priv·ing** [ME *depriven,* fr. ML *deprivare,* fr. L *de-* + *privare* to deprive — more at PRIVATE] (14c) **1** *obs* **:** REMOVE **2 :** to take something away from ⟨a reorganization of the school . . . *deprived* him of his professorship —J. M. Phalen⟩ **3 :** to remove from office **4 :** to withhold something from ⟨a citizen *deprived* by accident of birth of one of his . . . rights —L. M. Chamberlain⟩
de·prived *adj* (15c) : marked by deprivation esp. of the necessities of life or of healthful environmental influences ⟨culturally ~ children⟩
depth \'depth\ *n, pl* **depths** \'dep(t)s, 'depths\ [ME, prob. fr. *dep* deep] (14c) **1 a** (1) **:** a deep place in a body of water (2) **:** a part that is far from the outside or surface ⟨the ~*s* of the woods⟩ (3) **:** ABYSS **b** (1) **:** a profound or intense state (as of thought or feeling) ⟨the ~*s* of reflection⟩; *also* **:** a reprehensibly low condition ⟨hadn't realized that standards had fallen to such ~*s*⟩ (2) **:** the middle of a time (as winter) (3) **:** an extreme state (as of misery) (4) **:** the worst part **2 a :** the perpendicular measurement downward from a surface **b :** the direct linear measurement from the point of viewing usu. from front to back

3 **:** the quality of being deep 4 **:** the degree of intensity ⟨~ of a color⟩; *also* **:** the quality of being profound (as in insight) or full (as of knowledge) 5 **:** the quality or state of being complete or thorough **:** THOROUGHNESS ⟨~ of indexing⟩ ⟨a study will be made in ~⟩ — **depth·less** \ˈdepth-ləs\ *adj*

depth charge *n* (1917) **:** an explosive device for use underwater esp. against submarines that is designed to detonate at a predetermined depth — called also *depth bomb*

depth perception *n* (ca. 1909) **:** the ability to judge the distance of objects and the spatial relationship of objects at different distances

depth psychology *n* (1924) **:** PSYCHOANALYSIS; *also* **:** psychology concerned esp. with the unconscious mind

dep·u·ta·tion \ˌdep-yə-ˈtā-shən\ *n* (14c) 1 **:** the act of appointing a deputy 2 **:** a group of people appointed to represent others

de·pute \di-ˈpyüt\ *vt* **de·put·ed; de·put·ing** [ME *deputen* to appoint, fr. MF *deputer,* fr. LL *deputare* to assign, fr. L, to consider (as), fr. *de-* + *putare* to consider] (14c) **:** DELEGATE

dep·u·tize \ˈdep-yə-ˌtīz\ *vb* **-tized; -tiz·ing** *vt* (ca. 1730) **:** to appoint as deputy ~ *vi* **:** to act as deputy — **dep·u·ti·za·tion** \ˌdep-yət-ə-ˈzā-shən\ *n*

dep·u·ty \ˈdep-yət-ē\ *n, pl* **-ties** [ME, fr. MF *deputé,* pp. of *deputer*] (15c) 1 **a :** a person appointed as a substitute with power to act **b :** a second-in-command or assistant who usu. takes charge when his superior is absent 2 **:** a member of the lower house of some legislative assemblies

de·rac·i·nate \(ˈ)dē-ˈras-ᵊn-ˌāt\ *vt* **-nat·ed; -nat·ing** [F *déraciner,* fr. MF *desraciner,* fr. *des-* de- + *racine* root, fr. LL *radicina,* fr. L *radic-, radix* — more at ROOT] (1599) **:** UPROOT — **de·rac·i·na·tion** \(ˌ)dē-ˌras-ᵊn-ˈā-shən\ *n*

de·rail \di-ˈrā(ə)l\ *vb* [F *dérailler* to throw off the track, fr. *dé-* de- + *rail,* fr. E] *vt* (1850) 1 **:** to cause to run off the rails 2 **:** to throw off course ~ *vi* **:** to leave the rails — **de·rail·ment** \-mənt\ *n*

de·rail·leur \di-ˈrā-lər\ *n* [F *dérailleur,* fr. *dérailler*] (ca. 1947) **:** a mechanism for shifting gears on a bicycle that operates by moving the chain from one set of exposed gears to another

de·range \di-ˈrānj\ *vt* **de·ranged; de·rang·ing** [F *déranger,* fr. MF *desrengier,* fr. *de-* + *reng* place — more at RANK] (1776) 1 **:** to disturb the operation or functions of 2 **:** DISARRANGE ⟨hatless, with tie *deranged* —G. W. Stonier⟩ 3 **:** to make insane — **de·range·ment** \-mənt\ *n*

der·by \ˈdər-bē, *esp Brit* ˈdär-\ *n, pl* **derbies** [Edward Stanley †1834, 12th earl of *Derby*] (1844) 1 **:** any of several horse races held annually and usu. restricted to three-year-olds 2 **:** a race or contest open to all comers or to a specified category of contestants ⟨bicycle ~⟩ 3 **:** a man's stiff felt hat with dome-shaped crown and narrow brim

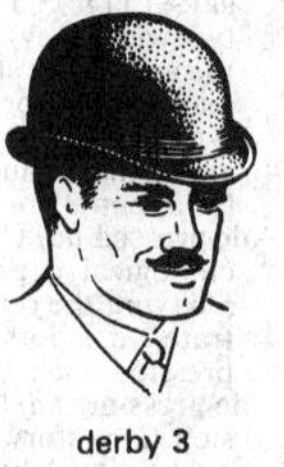
derby 3

de·re·al·iza·tion \(ˌ)dē-ˌrē-ə-lə-ˈzā-shən, -ˌri-ə-\ *n* (1942) **:** a feeling of altered reality that occurs often in schizophrenia and in some drug reactions

de·reg·u·la·tion \(ˌ)dē-ˌreg-yə-ˈlā-shən\ *n* (1965) **:** the act or process of removing restrictions and regulations — **de·reg·u·late** \(ˈ)dē-ˈreg-yə-ˌlāt\ *vt*

[1]**der·e·lict** \ˈder-ə-ˌlikt\ *adj* [L *derelictus,* pp. of *derelinquere* to abandon, fr. *de-* + *relinquere* to leave — more at RELINQUISH] (1649) 1 **:** abandoned esp. by the owner or occupant **:** RUN-DOWN 2 **:** lacking a sense of duty **:** NEGLIGENT

[2]**derelict** *n* (1670) 1 **a :** something voluntarily abandoned; *specif* **:** a ship abandoned on the high seas **b :** a tract of land left dry by receding water 2 **:** a destitute homeless social misfit **:** VAGRANT, BUM

der·e·lic·tion \ˌder-ə-ˈlik-shən\ *n* (1597) 1 **a :** an intentional abandonment **b :** the state of being abandoned 2 **:** a recession of water leaving permanently dry land 3 **a :** intentional or conscious neglect **:** DELINQUENCY ⟨~ of duty⟩ **b :** FAULT, SHORTCOMING

de·re·press \ˌdē-ri-ˈpres\ *vt* (1962) **:** to activate (a gene) by releasing from a blocked state — **de·re·pres·sion** \-ˈpresh-ən\ *n*

de·ride \di-ˈrīd\ *vt* **de·rid·ed; de·rid·ing** [L *deridēre,* fr. *de-* + *ridēre* to laugh — more at RIDICULOUS] (1530) 1 **:** to laugh at contemptuously 2 **:** to subject to usu. bitter or contemptuous ridicule ***syn*** see RIDICULE — **de·rid·er** *n* — **de·rid·ing·ly** \-ˈrīd-iŋ-lē\ *adv*

de ri·gueur \də-(ˌ)rē-ˈgər\ *adj* [F] (1833) **:** prescribed or required by fashion, etiquette, or custom **:** PROPER

de·ri·sion \di-ˈrizh-ən\ *n* [ME, fr. MF, fr. LL *derision-, derisio,* fr. L *derisus,* pp. of *deridēre*] (15c) 1 **a :** an act of deriding **b :** a state of being derided 2 **:** an object of ridicule or scorn **:** LAUGHINGSTOCK

de·ri·sive \di-ˈrī-siv, -ziv; -ˈriz-iv, -ˈris-\ *adj* (ca. 1662) **:** expressing or causing derision — **de·ri·sive·ly** *adv* — **de·ri·sive·ness** *n*

de·ri·so·ry \di-ˈrī-sə-rē, -zə-\ *adj* (1618) 1 **:** expressing derision **:** DERISIVE 2 **:** worthy of derision **:** RIDICULOUS

de·riv·able \di-ˈrī-və-bəl\ *adj* (1653) **:** capable of being derived

der·i·vate \ˈder-ə-ˌvāt\ *n* (1660) **:** DERIVATIVE

der·i·va·tion \ˌder-ə-ˈvā-shən\ *n* (15c) 1 **a** (1) **:** the formation of a word from another word or base (as by the addition of a usu. noninflectional affix) (2) **:** an act of ascertaining or stating the derivation of a word (3) **:** ETYMOLOGY 1 **b :** the relation of a word to its base 2 **a :** SOURCE, ORIGIN **b :** DESCENT, ORIGINATION 3 **:** something derived **:** DERIVATIVE 4 **:** an act or process of deriving 5 **:** a sequence of statements (as in logic or mathematics) showing that a result is a necessary consequence of previously accepted statements — **der·i·va·tion·al** \-shnəl, -shən-ᵊl\ *adj*

[1]**de·riv·a·tive** \di-ˈriv-ət-iv\ *n* (15c) 1 **:** a word formed by derivation 2 **:** something derived 3 **:** the limit of the ratio of the change in a function to the corresponding change in its independent variable as the latter change approaches zero 4 **a :** a chemical substance related structurally to another substance and theoretically derivable from it **b :** a substance that can be made from another substance in one or more steps

[2]**derivative** *adj* (ca. 1530) 1 **:** formed by derivation 2 **:** made up of or marked by derived elements — **de·riv·a·tive·ly** *adv* — **de·riv·a·tive·ness** *n*

de·rive \di-ˈrīv\ *vb* **de·rived; de·riv·ing** [ME *deriven,* fr. MF *deriver,* fr. L *derivare,* lit., to draw off water, fr. *de-* + *rivus* stream — more at RISE] *vt* (14c) 1 **a :** to take or receive esp. from a specified source **b :** to obtain from a specified source; *specif* **:** to obtain (a chemical substance) actually or theoretically from a parent substance 2 **:** INFER, DEDUCE 3 *archaic* **:** BRING 4 **:** to trace the derivation of ~ *vi* **:** to have or take origin **:** come as a derivative ***syn*** see SPRING — **de·riv·er** *n*

derm- *or* **derma-** *or* **dermo-** *comb form* [NL, fr. Gk *derm-, dermo-,* fr. *derma,* fr. *derein* to skin — more at TEAR] **:** skin ⟨*derm*al⟩ ⟨*dermo*tropic⟩

-derm \ˌdərm\ *n comb form* [prob. fr. F *-derme,* fr. Gk *derma*] **:** skin **:** covering ⟨ecto*derm*⟩

-der·ma \ˈdər-mə\ *n comb form, pl* **-dermas** *or* **-der·ma·ta** \-mət-ə\ [NL, fr. Gk *dermat-, derma* skin] **:** skin or skin ailment of a (specified) type ⟨sclero*derma*⟩

derm·abra·sion \ˌdər-mə-ˈbrā-zhən\ *n* (ca. 1954) **:** surgical removal of skin blemishes or imperfections (as scars or tattoos) by abrasion (as with sandpaper or wire brushes)

der·mal \ˈdər-məl\ *adj* (ca. 1803) 1 **:** of or relating to skin and esp. to the dermis **:** CUTANEOUS 2 **:** EPIDERMAL

der·map·ter·an \(ˌ)dər-ˈmap-tə-rən\ *n* [NL *Dermaptera,* order name, fr. *derm-* + Gk *pteron* wing — more at FEATHER] (ca. 1859) **:** any of an order (Dermaptera) of insects consisting of the earwigs and usu. a few related forms — **dermapteran** *adj* — **der·map·ter·ous** \-tə-rəs\ *adj*

dermat- *or* **dermato-** *comb form* [Gk, fr. *dermat-, derma*] **:** skin ⟨*dermat*itis⟩ ⟨*dermato*logy⟩

der·ma·ti·tis \ˌdər-mə-ˈtīt-əs\ *n* (1876) **:** inflammation of the skin

der·mat·o·gen \(ˌ)dər-ˈmat-ə-jən\ *n* [ISV] (1882) **:** the outer primary meristem of a plant or plant part

der·ma·to·glyph·ics \ˌdər-mət-ə-ˈglif-iks\ *n pl but sing or pl in constr* [*dermat-* + Gk *glyphein* to carve + E *-ics* — more at CLEAVE] (1926) 1 **:** skin patterns; *esp* **:** patterns of the specialized skin of the inferior surfaces of the hands and feet 2 **:** the science of the study of skin patterns — **der·ma·to·glyph·ic** \-ik\ *adj*

der·ma·tol·o·gy \ˌdər-mə-ˈtäl-ə-jē\ *n* (1819) **:** a branch of science dealing with the skin, its structure, functions, and diseases — **der·ma·to·log·ic** \-mət-ᵊl-ˈäj-ik\ *or* **der·ma·to·log·i·cal** \-i-kəl\ *adj* — **der·ma·tol·o·gist** \-mə-ˈtäl-ə-jəst\ *n*

der·ma·tome \ˈdər-mə-ˌtōm\ *n* [ISV *dermat-* + *-ome*] (1926) **:** the lateral wall of a somite from which the dermis is produced — **der·ma·to·mal** \ˌdər-mə-ˈtō-məl\ *adj*

der·ma·to·phyte \(ˌ)dər-ˈmat-ə-ˌfīt, ˈdər-mət-\ *n* [ISV] (1882) **:** a fungus parasitic on the skin or skin derivatives (as hair or nails) — **der·ma·to·phyt·ic** \(ˌ)dər-ˌmat-ə-ˈfit-ik, ˌdər-mət-\ *adj*

der·ma·to·sis \ˌdər-mə-ˈtō-səs\ *n, pl* **-to·ses** \-ˌsēz\ (1866) **:** a disease of the skin

-der·ma·tous \ˈdər-mət-əs\ *adj comb form* [Gk *dermat-, derma* skin] **:** having a (specified) type of skin ⟨sclero*dermatous*⟩

der·mes·tid \(ˌ)dər-ˈmes-təd\ *n* [deriv. of Gk *dermēstēs,* a leather-eating worm, lit., skin eater, fr. *derm-* + *edmenai* to eat — more at EAT] (ca. 1891) **:** any of a family (Dermestidae) of beetles with clubbed antennae that are very destructive to dried meat, fur, wool, and insect collections — **dermestid** *adj*

der·mis \ˈdər-məs\ *n* [NL, fr. LL *-dermis*] (ca. 1830) **:** the sensitive vascular inner mesodermic layer of the skin — called also *corium, cutis*

-der·mis \ˈdər-məs\ *n comb form* [LL, fr. Gk, fr. *derma*] **:** layer of skin or tissue ⟨endo*dermis*⟩

der·moid cyst \ˌdər-ˌmȯid-\ *n* (1872) **:** a cystic tumor often of the ovary that contains skin and skin derivatives (as hair or teeth) — called also *der·moid* \ˈdər-ˌmȯid\

der·mo·tro·pic \ˌdər-mə-ˈtrō-pik, -ˈträp-ik\ *adj* (1926) **:** attracted to, localizing in, or entering by way of the skin ⟨~ viruses⟩

der·nier cri \ˌdern-ˌyā-ˈkrē\ *n* [F, lit., last cry] (1896) **:** the newest fashion

der·o·gate \ˈder-ə-ˌgāt\ *vb* **-gat·ed; -gat·ing** [LL *derogatus,* pp. of *derogare,* fr. L, to annul (a law), detract, fr. *de-* + *rogare* to ask, propose (a law) — more at RIGHT] *vt* (15c) **:** to cause to seem inferior **:** DISPARAGE ~ *vi* 1 **:** to take away a part so as to impair **:** DETRACT 2 **:** to act beneath one's position or character — **der·o·ga·tion** \ˌder-ə-ˈgā-shən\ *n* — **de·ro·ga·tive** \di-ˈräg-ət-iv, ˈder-ə-ˌgāt-\ *adj*

de·rog·a·to·ry \di-ˈräg-ə-ˌtōr-ē, -ˌtȯr-\ *adj* (1502) 1 **:** detracting from the character or standing of something — often used with *to, of,* or *from* 2 **:** expressive of a low opinion **:** DISPARAGING ⟨~ remarks⟩ — **de·rog·a·to·ri·ly** \-ˌräg-ə-ˈtōr-ə-lē, -ˈtȯr-\ *adv*

der·rick \ˈder-ik\ *n* [obs. *derrick* hangman, gallows, fr. *Derick,* name of 17th cent. Eng. hangman] (1727) 1 **:** a hoisting apparatus employing a tackle rigged at the end of a beam 2 **:** a framework or tower over a deep drill hole (as of an oil well) for supporting boring tackle or for hoisting and lowering

der·ri·ere *or* **der·ri·ère** \ˌder-ē-ˈe(ə)r\ *n* [F *derrière,* fr. *derrière,* adj., hinder, fr. OF *deriere* adv., behind, fr. L *de retro,* fr. *de* from + *retro* back — more at DE-, RETRO-] (1774) **:** BUTTOCKS

der·ring–do \ˌder-iŋ-ˈdü\ *n* [ME *dorring don* daring to do, fr. *dorring* (gerund of *dorren* to dare) + *don* to do] (14c) **:** daring action **:** DARING ⟨deeds of ~⟩

der·rin·ger \ˈder-ən-jər\ *n* [Henry *Deringer* †1869 Am. inventor] (1853) **:** a short-barreled pocket pistol

der·ris \ˈder-əs\ *n* [NL, genus name, fr. Gk, skin, fr. *derein* to skin — more at TEAR] (1919) 1 **:** any of a large genus (*Derris*) of leguminous tropical Old World shrubs and woody vines including sources of poisons and esp. commercial sources of rotenone 2 **:** a preparation of derris roots and stems used as an insecticide

der·vish \ˈdər-vish\ *n* [Turk *derviş,* lit., beggar, fr. Per *darvēsh*] (1585) 1 **:** a member of a Muslim religious order noted for devotional exercises (as bodily movements leading to a trance) 2 **:** one that whirls or dances with or as if with the abandonment of a dervish

des- *prefix* [F *dés-,* fr. OF *des-* — more at DE-] **:** DE- 6 — esp. before vowels ⟨*des*oxy-⟩

de·sa·cral·ize \(ˈ)dē-ˈsā-krə-ˌlīz, -ˈsak-rə-\ *vt* **-ized; -iz·ing** (1911) **:** to divest ceremonially of supernatural qualities

de·sa·li·nate \(ˈ)dē-ˈsal-ə-ˌnāt *also* -ˈsā-lə-\ *vt* **-nat·ed; -nat·ing** (1949) **:** DESALT — **de·sa·li·na·tion** \(ˌ)dē-ˌsal-ə-ˈnā-shən *also* -ˌsā-lə-\ *n* — **de·sa·li·na·tor** \(ˈ)dē-ˈsal-ə-ˌnāt-ər *also* -ˈsā-lə-\ *n*

de·sa·li·nize \(ˈ)dē-ˈsal-ə-ˌnīz *also* -ˈsā-lə-\ *vt* **-nized; -niz·ing** (1963) **:** DESALT — **de·sa·li·ni·za·tion** \(ˌ)dē-ˌsal-ə-nə-ˈzā-shən *also* -ˌsā-lə-\ *n*

de·salt \(ˈ)dē-ˈsȯlt\ *vt* (1904) **:** to remove salt from — **de·salt·er** *n*

1des·cant \ˈdes-ˌkant\ *n* [ME *dyscant,* fr. ONF & ML; ONF *descant,* fr. ML *discantus,* fr. L *dis-* + *cantus* song — more at CHANT] (14c) **1 a** : a melody or counterpoint sung above the plainsong of the tenor **b** : the art of composing or improvising contrapuntal part music; *also* : the music so composed or improvised **c** : SOPRANO, TREBLE **d** : a superimposed counterpoint to a simple melody sung typically by some or all of the sopranos **2** : discourse or comment on a theme

2des·cant \ˈdes-ˌkant, des-ˈ, dis-ˈ\ *vi* (15c) **1** : to sing or play a descant; *broadly* : SING **2** : COMMENT, DISCOURSE

de·scend \di-ˈsend\ *vb* [ME *descenden,* fr. OF *descendre,* fr. L *descendere,* fr. *de-* + *scandere* to climb — more at SCAN] *vi* (14c) **1** : to pass from a higher place or level to a lower one ⟨~*ed* from the platform⟩ **2** : to pass in discussion from what is logically prior or more comprehensive **3 a** : to come down from a stock or source : DERIVE — usu. used in passive ⟨was ~*ed* from an ancient family⟩ **b** : to pass by inheritance ⟨an heirloom that has ~*ed* in the family⟩ **c** : to pass by transmission ⟨songs ~*ed* from early ballads⟩ **4** : to incline, lead, or extend downward ⟨the road ~*s* to the river⟩ **5** : to swoop or pounce down or make a sudden attack ⟨the plague ~*ed* upon them⟩ **6** : to proceed in a sequence or gradation from higher to lower or from more remote to nearer or more recent **7 a** : to lower oneself in status or dignity : STOOP **b** : to worsen and sink in condition or estimation ~ *vt* **1** : to pass, move, or climb down or down along **2** : to extend down along — **de·scend·ible** \-ˈsen-də-bəl\ *adj*

1de·scen·dant *or* **de·scen·dent** \di-ˈsen-dənt\ *adj* [MF & L; MF *descendant,* fr. L *descendent-, descendens,* prp. of *descendere*] (1572) **1** : moving or directed downward **2** : proceeding from an ancestor or source

2descendant *or* **descendent** *n* [F & L; F *descendant,* fr. LL *descendent-, descendens,* fr. L] (1600) **1** : one descended from another or from a common stock **2** : one deriving directly from a precursor or prototype

de·scend·er \di-ˈsen-dər, ˈdē-ˌ\ *n* (1802) : the part of a lowercase letter (as p) that descends below the main body of the letter; *also* : a letter that has such a part

de·scen·sion \di-ˈsen-chən\ *n, archaic* (14c) : DESCENT 2

de·scent \di-ˈsent\ *n* [ME, fr. MF *descente,* fr. OF *descendre*] (14c) **1 a** : derivation from an ancestor : BIRTH, LINEAGE ⟨of French ~⟩ **b** : transmission or devolution of an estate by inheritance usu. in the descending line **c** : the fact or process of originating from an ancestral stock **d** : the shaping or development in nature and character by transmission from a source : DERIVATION **2** : the act or process of descending **3** : a step downward in a scale of gradation; *specif* : one generation in an ancestral line or genealogical scale **4 a** : an inclination downward : SLOPE **b** : a descending way (as a downgrade or stairway) **c** *obs* : the lowest part **5 a** : ATTACK, INVASION **b** : a sudden disconcerting appearance (as for a visit) **6** : a downward step (as in station or value) : DECLINE ⟨~ of the family to actual poverty⟩

de·scribe \di-ˈskrīb\ *vt* **de·scribed; de·scrib·ing** [L *describere,* fr. *de-* + *scribere* to write — more at SCRIBE] (15c) **1** : to represent or give an account of in words ⟨~ a picture⟩ **2** : to represent by a figure, model, or picture : DELINEATE **3** *obs* : DISTRIBUTE **4** : to trace or traverse the outline of ⟨~ a circle⟩ **5** *archaic* : OBSERVE, PERCEIVE — **de·scrib·able** \-ˈskrī-bə-bəl\ *adj* — **de·scrib·er** *n*

de·scrip·tion \di-ˈskrip-shən\ *n* [ME *descripcioun,* fr. MF & L; MF *description,* fr. L *description-, descriptio,* fr. *descriptus,* pp. of *describere*] (14c) **1 a** : an act of describing; *specif* : discourse intended to give a mental image of something experienced (as a scene, person, or sensation) **b** : a descriptive statement or account ⟨a fascinating ~ of his adventures⟩ **2** : kind or character esp. as determined by salient features ⟨opposed to any tax of so radical a ~⟩ *syn* see TYPE

de·scrip·tive \di-ˈskrip-tiv\ *adj* (1751) **1** : serving to describe ⟨a ~ account⟩ **2** : referring to, constituting, or grounded in matters of observation or experience ⟨the ~ basis of science⟩ **3** *of a modifier* **a** : expressing the quality, kind, or condition of what is denoted by the modified term ⟨*hot* in "hot water" is a ~ adjective⟩ **b** : NONRESTRICTIVE **4** : of, relating to, or dealing with the structure of a language at a particular time usu. with exclusion of historical and comparative data ⟨~ linguistics⟩ — **de·scrip·tive·ly** *adv* — **de·scrip·tive·ness** *n*

de·scrip·tor \di-ˈskrip-tər\ *n* (1951) : something (as an index term) used to identify an item (as a subject or document) esp. in an information retrieval system

1de·scry \di-ˈskrī\ *vt* **de·scried; de·scry·ing** [ME *descrien,* fr. MF *descrier* to proclaim, decry] (14c) **1 a** : to catch sight of **b** : to find out : DISCOVER **2** *obs* : to make known : REVEAL

2descry *n, obs* (1605) : discovery or view from afar

Des·de·mo·na \ˌdez-də-ˈmō-nə\ *n* : the wife of Othello in Shakespeare's *Othello*

des·e·crate \ˈdes-i-ˌkrāt\ *vt* **-crat·ed; -crat·ing** [*de-* + *-secrate* (as in *consecrate*)] (1677) **1** : to violate the sanctity of : PROFANE **2** : to treat irreverently or contemptuously often in a way that provokes outrage on the part of others ⟨the kind of shore development . . . that has *desecrated* so many waterfronts — John Fischer⟩ — **des·e·crat·er** *or* **des·e·cra·tor** \-ˌkrāt-ər\ *n*

des·e·cra·tion \ˌdes-i-ˈkrā-shən\ *n* (1717) : an act or instance of desecrating : the state of being desecrated

de·seg·re·gate \(ˌ)dē-ˈseg-ri-ˌgāt\ *vt* (1952) : to eliminate segregation in; *specif* : to free of any law, provision, or practice requiring isolation of the members of a particular race in separate units ~ *vi* : to bring about desegregation

de·seg·re·ga·tion \(ˌ)dē-ˌseg-ri-ˈgā-shən\ *n* (1951) **1** : the act or process or an instance of desegregating **2** : the state of being desegregated

de·se·lect \ˌdē-sə-ˈlekt\ *vt* (1965) : to dismiss (a trainee) from a training program

de·sen·si·tize \(ˈ)dē-ˈsen(t)-sə-ˌtīz\ *vt* (1898) **1** : to make (a sensitized or hypersensitive individual) insensitive or nonreactive to a sensitizing agent **2** : to make (a photographic material) less sensitive or completely insensitive to radiation **3** : to make emotionally insensitive or callous; *specif* : to extinguish an emotional response (as of fear, anxiety, or guilt) to stimuli that formerly induced it — **de·sen·si·ti·za·tion** \(ˌ)dē-ˌsen-sət-ə-ˈzā-shən, -ˌsen-stə-ˈzā-\ *n* — **de·sen·si·tiz·er** \(ˈ)dē-ˈsen-sə-ˌtī-zər\ *n*

1des·ert \ˈdez-ərt\ *n* [ME, fr. OF, fr. LL *desertum,* fr. L, neut. of *desertus,* pp. of *deserere* to desert, fr. *de-* + *serere* to join together — more at SERIES] (13c) **1 a** : arid barren land; *esp* : a tract incapable of supporting any considerable population without an artificial water supply **b** : an area of water apparently devoid of life **2** *archaic* : a wild uninhabited and uncultivated tract **3** : a desolate or forbidding area ⟨lost in a ~ of doubt⟩ — **de·ser·tic** \de-ˈzərt-ik\ *adj*

2des·ert \ˈdez-ərt\ *adj* (13c) **1** : desolate and sparsely occupied or unoccupied ⟨a ~ island⟩ **2** : of or relating to a desert **3** *archaic* : FORSAKEN

3de·sert \di-ˈzərt\ *n* [ME *deserte,* fr. OF, fr. fem. of *desert,* pp. of *deservir* to deserve] (13c) **1** : the quality or fact of deserving reward or punishment **2** : deserved reward or punishment — usu. used in plural ⟨got his just ~*s*⟩ **3** : EXCELLENCE, WORTH

4de·sert \di-ˈzərt\ *vb* [F *déserter,* fr. LL *desertare,* fr. *desertus*] *vt* (1603) **1** : to withdraw from or leave usu. without intent to return **2 a** : to leave in the lurch ⟨~ a friend in trouble⟩ **b** : to abandon (military service) without leave ~ *vi* : to quit one's post, allegiance, or service without leave or justification; *esp* : to absent oneself from military duty without leave and without intent to return *syn* see ABANDON — **de·sert·er** *n*

de·sert·i·fi·ca·tion \di-ˌzərt-ə-fə-ˈkā-shən\ *n* [1*desert* + *-ification* (as in *saponification*)] (1974) : the process of becoming arid land or desert (as from land mismanagement or climate change)

de·ser·tion \di-ˈzər-shən\ *n* (1591) **1** : an act of deserting; *esp* : the abandonment without consent or legal justification of a person, post, or relationship and the associated duties and obligations ⟨sued for divorce on grounds of ~⟩ **2** : a state of being deserted or forsaken

desert locust *n* (1944) : a destructive migratory locust (*Schistocerca gregaria*) of southwestern Asia and parts of northern Africa

desert soil *n* (ca. 1938) : a soil that develops under sparse shrub vegetation in warm to cool arid climates with a light-colored surface soil usu. underlain by calcareous material and a hardpan layer

de·serve \di-ˈzərv\ *vb* **de·served; de·serv·ing** [ME *deserven,* fr. OF *deservir,* fr. L *deservire* to serve zealously, fr. *de-* + *servire* to serve] *vt* (13c) : to be worthy of : MERIT ⟨~*s* another chance⟩ ~ *vi* : to be worthy, fit, or suitable for some reward or requital ⟨have become recognized as they ~ —T. S. Eliot⟩ — **de·serv·er** *n*

de·served \-ˈzərvd\ *adj* (ca. 1552) : of, relating to, or being that which one deserves ⟨a ~ reputation⟩ — **de·served·ly** \-ˈzər-vəd-lē, -ˈzərv-dlē\ *adv* — **de·served·ness** \-ˈzər-vəd-nəs, -ˈzərv(d)-nəs\ *n*

1de·serv·ing \-ˈzər-viŋ\ *n* (14c) : DESERT, MERIT ⟨reward the proud according to their ~*s* —Charles Kingsley⟩

2deserving *adj* (1576) : MERITORIOUS, WORTHY; *specif* : meriting financial aid ⟨scholarships for ~ students⟩

de·sex \(ˈ)dē-ˈseks\ *vt* (1911) : CASTRATE, SPAY

de·sex·u·al·ize \(ˈ)dē-ˈseksh-(ə-)wə-ˌlīz, -ˈsek-shə-ˌlīz\ *vt* (1894) **1** : to deprive of sexual characters or power **2** : to divest of sexual quality — **de·sex·u·al·iza·tion** \(ˌ)dē-ˌseksh-(ə-)wə-lə-ˈzā-shən, -ˈsek-shə-lə-\ *n*

des·ha·bille \ˌdes-ə-ˈbē(ə)l, -ˈbil, -ˈbē\ *var of* DISHABILLE

des·ic·cant \ˈdes-i-kənt\ *n* (1676) : a drying agent (as calcium chloride)

des·ic·cate \ˈdes-i-ˌkāt\ *vb* **-cat·ed; -cat·ing** [L *desiccatus,* pp. of *desiccare* to dry up, fr. *de-* + *siccare* to dry, fr. *siccus* dry — more at SACK] *vt* (1575) **1** : to dry up **2** : to preserve (a food) by drying : DEHYDRATE **3** : to drain of emotional or intellectual vitality ~ *vi* : to become dried up — **des·ic·ca·tion** \ˌdes-i-ˈkā-shən\ *n* — **de·sic·ca·tive** \ˈdes-i-ˌkāt-iv, di-ˈsik-ət-\ *adj* — **des·ic·ca·tor** \ˈdes-i-ˌkāt-ər\ *n*

de·sid·er·ate \di-ˈsid-ə-ˌrāt, -ˈzid-\ *vt* **-at·ed; -at·ing** [L *desideratus,* pp. of *desiderare* to desire] (1645) : to entertain or express a wish to have or attain — **de·sid·er·a·tion** \-ˌsid-ə-ˈrā-shən, -ˌzid-\ *n* — **de·sid·er·a·tive** \-ˈsid-ə-ˌrāt-iv, -ˈsid-(ə-)rət-, -ˈzid-\ *adj*

de·sid·er·a·tum \-ˌsid-ə-ˈrät-əm, -ˌzid-, -ˈrāt-\ *n, pl* **-ta** \-ə\ [L, neut. of *desideratus*] (1652) : something desired as essential

1de·sign \di-ˈzīn\ *vb* [MF *designer,* fr. L *designare,* fr. *de-* + *signare* to mark, mark out — more at SIGN] *vt* (1548) **1 a** : to conceive and plan out in the mind ⟨he ~*ed* the perfect crime⟩ **b** : to have as a purpose : INTEND ⟨he ~*ed* to excel in his studies⟩ **c** : to devise for a specific function or end ⟨a book ~*ed* primarily as a college textbook⟩ **2** *archaic* : to indicate with a distinctive mark, sign, or name **3 a** : to make a drawing, pattern, or sketch of **b** : to draw the plans for **c** : to create, fashion, execute, or construct according to plan : DEVISE, CONTRIVE ~ *vi* **1** : to conceive or execute a plan **2** : to draw, lay out, or prepare a design — **de·sign·ed·ly** \-ˈzī-nəd-lē\ *adv*

2design *n* (1588) **1 a** : a particular purpose held in view by an individual or group ⟨he has ambitious ~*s* for his son⟩ **b** : deliberate purposive planning ⟨battle was joined . . . more by accident than ~ —John Buchan⟩ **2** : a mental project or scheme in which means to an end are laid down **3 a** : a deliberate undercover project or scheme : PLOT **b** *pl* : aggressive or evil intent — used with *on* or *against* ⟨he has ~*s* on the money⟩ **4** : a preliminary sketch or outline showing the main features of something to be executed : DELINEATION **5 a** : an underlying scheme that governs functioning, developing, or unfolding : PATTERN, MOTIF ⟨the general ~ of the epic⟩ **b** : a plan or protocol for carrying out or accomplishing something (esp. a scientific experiment); *also* : the process of preparing this **6** : the arrangement of elements or details in a product or work of art **7** : a decorative pattern **8** : the creative art of executing aesthetic or functional designs *syn* see INTENTION, PLAN

1des·ig·nate \ˈdez-ig-ˌnāt, -nət\ *adj* [L *designatus,* pp. of *designare*] (1646) : chosen for an office but not yet installed ⟨ambassador ~⟩

2des·ig·nate \-ˌnāt\ *vt* **-nat·ed; -nat·ing** (1791) **1** : to indicate and set apart for a specific purpose, office, or duty **2 a** : to point out the location of ⟨a marker *designating* the crest of the floodwaters⟩ **b** : INDICATE ⟨any task *designated* by the employer⟩ **c** : to distinguish as to class ⟨the area we ~ as that of spiritual values —J. B. Conant⟩ **d** : SPECIFY, STIPULATE **3** : DENOTE **4** : to call by a distinctive title, term, or expression — **des·ig·na·tive** \-ˌnāt-iv\ *adj* — **des·ig·na·tor** \-ˌnāt-ər\ *n* — **des·ig·na·to·ry** \-nə-ˌtōr-ē, -ˌtȯr-\ *adj*

designated hitter *n* (1973) **:** a baseball player designated at the start of the game to bat in place of the pitcher without causing the pitcher to be removed from the game

des·ig·na·tion \ˌdez-ig-ˈnā-shən\ *n* (14c) **1 :** the act of indicating or identifying **2 :** appointment to or selection for an office, post, or service **3 :** a distinguishing name, sign, or title **4 :** the relation between a sign and the thing signified

des·ig·nee \ˌdez-ig-ˈnē\ *n* (1925) **:** one who is designated

[1]de·sign·er \di-ˈzī-nər\ *n* (1662) **:** one that designs: as **a :** one who creates and often executes plans for a project or structure ⟨urban ~*s*⟩ ⟨a theater set ~⟩ **b :** one that creates and manufactures a new product style or design; *esp* **:** one who designs and manufactures high-fashion clothing ⟨the ~*'s* new fall line⟩

[2]designer *adj* (1966) **:** of, relating to, or produced by a designer ⟨~ wallpaper⟩ ⟨wearing a ~ original⟩; *also* **:** displaying the name, signature, or logo of a designer or manufacturer ⟨~ jeans⟩

de·sign·ing \di-ˈzī-niŋ\ *adj* (1653) **1 :** practicing forethought **2 :** CRAFTY, SCHEMING

de·sign·ment \di-ˈzīn-mənt\ *n, obs* (1583) **:** PLAN, PURPOSE

de·si·pra·mine \də-ˈzip-rə-ˌmēn, ˌdez-ə-ˈpram-ən\ *n* [*des*methyl (fr. *des-* + *methyl*) + *imipramine*] (1965) **:** a tricyclic antidepressant $C_{18}H_{22}N_2$

de·sir·abil·i·ty \di-ˌzī-rə-ˈbil-ət-ē\ *n, pl* **-ties** (1824) **1** *pl* **:** desirable conditions ⟨had understood and studied certain *desirabilities* —D. D. Eisenhower⟩ **2 :** the quality, fact, or degree of being desirable

[1]de·sir·able \di-ˈzī-rə-bəl\ *adj* (14c) **1 :** having pleasing qualities or properties **:** ATTRACTIVE ⟨a ~ woman⟩ **2 :** worth seeking or doing as advantageous, beneficial, or wise **:** ADVISABLE ⟨~ legislation⟩ — **de·sir·able·ness** *n* — **de·sir·ably** \-blē\ *adv*

[2]desirable *n* (1669) **:** one that is desirable

[1]de·sire \di-ˈzī(ə)r\ *vb* **de·sired; de·sir·ing** [ME *desiren,* fr. OF *desirer,* fr. L *desiderare,* perh. fr. *de-* + *sider-, sidus* star] *vt* (13c) **1 :** to long or hope for **2 a :** to express a wish for **:** REQUEST **b** *archaic* **:** to express a wish to **:** ASK **3** *obs* **:** INVITE **4** *archaic* **:** to feel the loss of ~ *vi* **:** to have or feel desire

syn DESIRE, WISH, WANT, CRAVE, COVET mean to have a longing for. DESIRE stresses the strength of feeling and often implies strong intention or aim; WISH sometimes implies a general or transient longing esp. for the unattainable; WANT specif. suggests a felt need or lack; CRAVE stresses the force of physical appetite or emotional need; COVET implies strong envious desire.

[2]desire *n* (14c) **1 :** conscious impulse toward something that promises enjoyment or satisfaction in its attainment **2 a :** LONGING, CRAVING **b :** sexual urge or appetite **3 :** a usu. formal request or petition for some action **4 :** something desired

de·sir·ous \di-ˈzī(ə)r-əs\ *adj* (14c) **:** impelled or governed by desire ⟨~ of fame⟩ — **de·sir·ous·ly** *adv* — **de·sir·ous·ness** *n*

de·sist \di-ˈzist, -ˈsist\ *vi* [MF *desister,* fr. L *desistere,* fr. *de-* + *sistere* to stand, stop; akin to L *stare* to stand — more at STAND] (15c) **:** to cease to proceed or act *syn* see STOP — **de·sis·tance** \-ˈzis-tən(t)s, -ˈsis-\ *n*

desk \ˈdesk\ *n* [ME *deske,* fr. ML *desca,* modif. of OIt *desco* table, fr. L *discus* dish, disc — more at DISH] (14c) **1 a :** a table, frame, or case with a sloping or horizontal surface esp. for writing and reading and often with drawers, compartments, and pigeonholes **b :** a reading table or lectern to support the book from which the liturgical service is read **c :** a table, counter, stand, or booth at which a person performs his duties **2 a :** a division of an organization specializing in a particular phase of activity ⟨the Russian ~ in the Department of State⟩ **b :** a seating position according to rank in an orchestra ⟨a first-*desk* violinist⟩

desk·man \ˈdesk-ˌman, -mən\ *n* (1913) **:** one that works at a desk; *specif* **:** a newspaperman who processes news and prepares copy

desk·top \-ˌtäp\ *adj* (1967) **:** of a size that can be conveniently used on a desk or table ⟨~ calculators⟩ — compare LAPTOP

desktop publishing *n* (1984) **:** the production of printed matter by means of a desktop computer having a layout program that integrates text and graphics

desm- *or* **desmo-** *comb form* [NL, fr. Gk, fr. *desmos,* fr. *dein* to bind — more at DIADEM] **:** bond **:** ligament ⟨*desmo*cyte⟩

des·man \ˈdez-mən\ *n, pl* **desmans** [short for Sw *desmansråtta,* fr. *desman* musk + *råtta* rat] (1774) **:** an aquatic insectivorous mammal (*Desmana moschata*) of Russia that resembles a mole

des·mid \ˈdez-məd\ *n* [deriv. of Gk *desmos*] (1862) **:** any of numerous unicellular or colonial green algae (order Zygnematales)

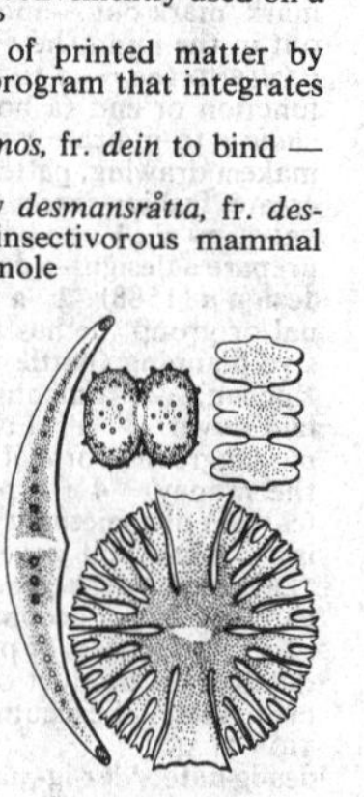

desmid

des·mo·some \ˈdez-mə-ˌsōm\ *n* (ca. 1932) **:** a specialized local thickening of the cell membrane of an epithelial cell that serves to anchor contiguous cells together

[1]des·o·late \ˈdes-ə-lət, ˈdez-\ *adj* [ME *desolat,* fr. L *desolatus,* pp. of *desolare* to abandon, fr. *de-* + *solus* alone] (14c) **1 :** devoid of inhabitants and visitors **:** DESERTED **2 :** joyless, disconsolate, and sorrowful through or as if through separation from a loved one **3 a :** showing the effects of abandonment and neglect **:** DILAPIDATED **b :** BARREN, LIFELESS ⟨a ~ landscape⟩ **c :** devoid of warmth, comfort, or hope **:** GLOOMY ⟨~ memories⟩ *syn* see ALONE — **des·o·late·ly** *adv* — **des·o·late·ness** *n*

[2]des·o·late \-ˌlāt\ *vt* **-lat·ed; -lat·ing** (14c) **:** to make desolate: **a :** to deprive of inhabitants **b :** to lay waste **c :** FORSAKE **d :** to make wretched — **des·o·lat·er** *or* **des·o·la·tor** \-ˌlāt-ər\ *n* — **des·o·lat·ing·ly** \-ˌlāt-iŋ-lē\ *adv*

des·o·la·tion \ˌdes-ə-ˈlā-shən, ˌdez-\ *n* (14c) **1 :** the action of desolating **2 a :** GRIEF, SADNESS **b :** LONELINESS **3 :** DEVASTATION, RUIN ⟨the flood left ~ in its wake⟩ **4 :** barren wasteland

de·sorb \(ˌ)dē-ˈsȯ(ə)rb, -ˈzȯ(ə)rb\ *vt* (1924) **:** to remove (a sorbed substance) by the reverse of adsorption or absorption

de·sorp·tion \-ˈsȯrp-shən, -ˈzȯrp-\ *n* (1924) **:** the process of desorbing

desoxy- — see DEOXY-

des·oxy·ri·bo·nu·cle·ic acid \de-ˌzäk-sē-ˈrī-bō-n(y)u̇-ˌklē-ik-, -ˌklā-\ *n* (1931) **:** DNA

[1]de·spair \di-ˈspa(ə)r, -ˈspe(ə)r\ *vb* [ME *despeiren,* fr. MF *desperer,* fr. L *desperare,* fr. *de-* + *sperare* to hope; akin to L *spes* hope — more at SPEED] *vi* (14c) **:** to lose all hope or confidence ⟨~ of winning⟩ ~ *vt, obs* **:** to lose hope for — **de·spair·er** *n*

[2]despair *n* (14c) **1 :** utter loss of hope **2 :** a cause of hopelessness ⟨an incorrigible child is the ~ of his parents⟩

de·spair·ing *adj* (15c) **:** given to, arising from, or marked by despair **:** devoid of hope *syn* see DESPONDENT — **de·spair·ing·ly** \-iŋ-lē\ *adv*

des·patch \dis-ˈpach\ *var of* DISPATCH

des·per·a·do \ˌdes-pə-ˈräd-(ˌ)ō, -ˈrād-\ *n, pl* **-does** *or* **-dos** [prob. alter. of obs. *desperate* desperado, fr. *desperate,* adj.] (1647) **:** a bold or violent criminal; *esp* **:** a bandit of the western U.S. in the 19th century

des·per·ate \ˈdes-p(ə-)rət, -pərt\ *adj* [L *desperatus,* pp. of *desperare*] (15c) **1 a :** having lost hope ⟨a ~ spirit crying for relief⟩ **b :** giving no ground for hope ⟨his situation was ~⟩ **2 a :** moved by despair ⟨men made ~ by abuse⟩ **b :** involving or employing extreme measures in an attempt to escape defeat or frustration ⟨made a ~ leap for the rope⟩ **3 :** suffering extreme need or anxiety ⟨~ for money⟩ **4 :** of extreme intensity **:** OVERPOWERING **5 :** SHOCKING, OUTRAGEOUS *syn* see DESPONDENT — **des·per·ate·ly** *adv* — **des·per·ate·ness** *n*

des·per·a·tion \ˌdes-pə-ˈrā-shən\ *n* (14c) **1 :** loss of hope and surrender to despair **2 :** a state of hopelessness leading to rashness

de·spi·ca·ble \di-ˈspik-ə-bəl, ˈdes-(ˌ)pik-\ *adj* [LL *despicabilis,* fr. L *despicari* to despise] (1553) **:** deserving to be despised **:** so worthless or obnoxious as to rouse moral indignation ⟨~ behavior⟩ *syn* see CONTEMPTIBLE — **de·spi·ca·ble·ness** *n* — **de·spi·ca·bly** \-blē\ *adv*

de·spir·i·tu·al·ize \(ˌ)dē-ˈspir-ich-(ə-)wə-ˌlīz, -ich-ə-ˌlīz\ *vt* (1868) **:** to deprive of spiritual character or influence

de·spise \di-ˈspīz\ *vt* **de·spised; de·spis·ing** [ME *despisen,* fr. OF *despis-,* stem of *despire,* fr. L *despicere,* fr. *de-* + *specere* to look — more at SPY] (13c) **1 :** to look down on with contempt or aversion ⟨*despised* the weak⟩ **2 :** to regard as negligible, worthless, or distasteful — **de·spise·ment** \-ˈspīz-mənt\ *n* — **de·spis·er** \-ˈspī-zər\ *n*

syn DESPISE, CONTEMN, SCORN, DISDAIN, SCOUT mean to regard as unworthy of one's notice or consideration. DESPISE may suggest an emotional response ranging from strong dislike to loathing; CONTEMN implies a vehement condemnation of a person or thing as low, vile, feeble, or ignominious; SCORN implies a ready or indignant contempt; DISDAIN implies an arrogant or supercilious aversion to what is regarded as unworthy; SCOUT suggests abrupt rejection or dismissal.

[1]de·spite \di-ˈspīt\ *n* [ME, fr. OF *despit,* fr. L *despectus,* fr. pp. of *despicere*] (13c) **1 :** the feeling or attitude of despising **:** CONTEMPT **2 :** MALICE, SPITE **3 a :** an act showing contempt or defiance **b :** DETRIMENT, DISADVANTAGE ⟨I know of no government which stands to its obligations, even in its own ~, more solidly —Sir Winston Churchill⟩ — **in despite of :** in spite of

[2]despite *vt* **de·spit·ed; de·spit·ing** (14c) **1** *archaic* **:** to treat with contempt **2** *obs* **:** to provoke to anger **:** VEX

[3]despite *prep* (15c) **:** in spite of ⟨ran ~ his injury⟩

de·spite·ful \di-ˈspīt-fəl\ *adj* (15c) **:** expressing malice or hate — **de·spite·ful·ly** \-fə-lē\ *adv* — **de·spite·ful·ness** *n*

de·spit·eous \dis-ˈpit-ē-əs\ *adj, archaic* (14c) **:** feeling or showing despite **:** MALICIOUS — **de·spit·eous·ly** *adv, archaic*

de·spoil \di-ˈspȯi(ə)l\ *vt* [ME *despoylen,* fr. MF *despoillier,* fr. L *despoliare,* fr. *de-* + *spoliare* to strip, rob — more at SPOIL] (14c) **:** to strip of belongings, possessions, or value **:** PILLAGE *syn* see RAVAGE — **de·spoil·er** *n* — **de·spoil·ment** \-ˈspȯi(ə)l-mənt\ *n*

de·spo·li·a·tion \di-ˌspō-lē-ˈā-shən\ *n* [LL *despoliation-, despoliatio,* fr. *despoliatus,* pp. of *despoliare*] (1657) **:** the condition of being despoiled **:** SPOLIATION

[1]de·spond \di-ˈspänd\ *vi* [L *despondēre,* fr. *de-* + *spondēre* to promise solemnly — more at SPOUSE] (1655) **:** to become discouraged or disheartened

[2]despond *n* (1678) **:** DESPONDENCY

de·spon·dence \di-ˈspän-dən(t)s\ *n* (1676) **:** DESPONDENCY

de·spon·den·cy \-dən-sē\ *n* (1653) **:** the state of being despondent **:** DEJECTION, HOPELESSNESS

de·spon·dent \-dənt\ *adj* [L *despondent-, despondens,* prp. of *despondēre*] (1699) **:** feeling extreme discouragement, dejection, or depression ⟨~ about his health⟩ — **de·spon·dent·ly** *adv*

syn DESPONDENT, DESPAIRING, DESPERATE, HOPELESS mean having lost all or nearly all hope. DESPONDENT implies a deep dejection arising from a conviction of the uselessness of further effort; DESPAIRING suggests the slipping away of all hope and often despondency; DESPERATE implies despair that prompts reckless action or violence in the face of defeat or frustration; HOPELESS suggests despair and the cessation of effort or resistance and often implies acceptance or resignation.

des·pot \ˈdes-pət, -ˌpät\ *n* [MF *despote,* fr. Gk *despotēs,* fr. *des-* (akin to *domos* house) + *-potēs* (akin to *posis* husband); akin to Skt *dampati* lord of the house — more at TIMBER, POTENT] (1562) **1 a :** a Byzantine emperor or prince **b :** a bishop or patriarch of the Eastern Orthodox Church **c :** an Italian hereditary prince or military leader during the Renaissance **2 a :** a ruler with absolute power and authority **:** AUTOCRAT **b :** a person exercising power abusively, oppressively, or tyrannically

des·pot·ic \des-ˈpät-ik, dis-\ *adj* (1650) **:** of, relating to, or characteristic of a despot — **des·pot·i·cal·ly** \-i-k(ə-)lē\ *adv*

des·po·tism \ˈdes-pə-ˌtiz-əm\ *n* (1727) **1 a :** rule by a despot **b :** despotic exercise of power **2 a :** a system of government in which the ruler has unlimited power **:** ABSOLUTISM **b :** a despotic state

des·qua·mate \ˈdes-kwə-ˌmāt\ *vi* **-mat·ed; -mat·ing** [L *desquamatus,* pp. of *desquamare,* fr. *de-* + *squama* scale — more at WHALE] (1828) **:** to peel off in scales — **des·qua·ma·tion** \ˌdes-kwə-ˈmā-shən\ *n*

des·sert \di-ˈzərt\ *n* [MF, fr. *desservir* to clear the table, fr. *des-* de- + *servir* to serve, fr. L *servire*] (1600) **1 :** a usu. sweet course or dish (as of pastry or ice cream) served at the end of a meal **2** *Brit* **:** a fresh fruit served after a sweet course

des·sert·spoon \-ˌspün\ *n* (1754) **:** a spoon intermediate in size between a teaspoon and a tablespoon for use in eating dessert

des·sert·spoon·ful \di-ˈzərt-ˌspün-ˌfu̇l, -ˈspün-\ *n* (1875) **1 :** as much as a dessertspoon will hold **2** *chiefly Brit* **:** a unit of measure equal to about 2½ fluidrams

dessert wine *n* (1773) **:** a usu. sweet wine typically served with dessert or afterward

de·sta·bi·lize \(ˈ)dē-ˈstā-bə-ˌlīz\ *vt* (1924) **1 :** to make unstable **2 :** to cause (as a government) to be incapable of functioning or surviving ⟨terrorists tried to ~ the new government⟩ — **de·sta·bi·li·za·tion** \(ˌ)dē-ˌstā-bə-lə-ˈzā-shən\ *n*

de·stain \(ˈ)dē-ˈstān\ *vt* (1927) **:** to selectively remove stain from (a specimen for microscopic study)

de–Sta·lin·iza·tion \(ˌ)dē-ˌstäl-ə-nə-ˈzā-shən, -ˌstal-\ *n* (1951) **:** the discrediting of Stalin and his policies

de Stijl \də-ˈstī(ə)l, -ˈstā(ə)l\ *n* [D *De Stijl,* lit., the style, magazine published by members of the school] (1934) **:** a school of art founded in Holland in 1917 typically using rectangular forms and the primary colors plus black and white and asymmetric balance

des·ti·na·tion \ˌdes-tə-ˈnā-shən\ *n* (15c) **1 :** the purpose for which something is destined **2 :** an act of appointing, setting aside for a purpose, or predetermining **3 :** a place to which one is journeying or to which something is sent ⟨kept their ~ secret⟩

des·tine \ˈdes-tən\ *vt* **des·tined; des·tin·ing** [ME *destinen,* fr. MF *destiner,* fr. L *destinare,* fr. *de-* + *-stinare* (akin to L *stare* to stand) — more at STAND] (14c) **1 :** to decree beforehand **:** PREDETERMINE **2 a :** to designate, assign, or dedicate in advance ⟨the younger son was *destined* for the ministry⟩ **b :** to direct, devise, or set apart for a specific purpose or place ⟨freight *destined* for English ports⟩

des·ti·ny \ˈdes-tə-nē\ *n, pl* **-nies** [ME *destinee,* fr. MF, fr. fem. of *destiné,* pp. of *destiner*] (14c) **1 :** something to which a person or thing is destined **:** FORTUNE **2 :** a predetermined course of events often held to be an irresistible power or agency ***syn*** see FATE

des·ti·tute \ˈdes-tə-ˌt(y)üt\ *adj* [ME, fr. L *destitutus,* pp. of *destituere* to abandon, deprive, fr. *de-* + *statuere* to set up — more at STATUTE] (15c) **1 :** lacking something needed or desirable ⟨a lake ~ of fish⟩ **2 :** lacking possessions and resources; *esp* **:** suffering extreme want ⟨a ~ old man⟩ — **des·ti·tute·ness** *n*

des·ti·tu·tion \ˌdes-tə-ˈt(y)ü-shən\ *n* (15c) **:** the state of being destitute; *esp* **:** such extreme want as threatens life unless relieved ***syn*** see POVERTY

des·trier \ˈdes-trē-ər, də-ˈstri(ə)r\ *n* [ME, fr. MF, fr. *destre* right hand, fr. L *dextra,* fr. fem. of *dexter*] *archaic* (14c) **:** WAR-HORSE; *also* **:** a charger used esp. in medieval tournaments

de·stroy \di-ˈstrȯi\ *vb* [ME *destroyen,* fr. OF *destruire,* fr. (assumed) VL *destrugere,* alter. of L *destruere,* fr. *de-* + *struere* to build — more at STRUCTURE] *vt* (13c) **1 :** to ruin the structure, organic existence, or condition of ⟨priceless art *~ed* by water⟩ **2 a :** to put out of existence **:** KILL **b :** NEUTRALIZE ⟨the moon *~s* the light of the stars⟩ **c :** ANNIHILATE, VANQUISH ⟨armies had been crippled but not *~ed* —W. L. Shirer⟩ ~ *vi* **:** to cause destruction

de·stroy·er \di-ˈstrȯi(-ə)r\ *n* (14c) **1 :** one that destroys **2 :** a small fast warship usu. armed with 5-inch guns, depth charges, torpedoes, mines, and sometimes guided missiles

destroyer escort *n* (1924) **:** a warship similar to but smaller than a destroyer

destroying angel *n* (ca. 1909) **:** a very poisonous mushroom (*Amanita phalloides*) varying in color from pure white to olive or yellow and having a prominent volva at the base; *also* **:** a related poisonous mushroom (*A. verna*)

1de·struct \di-ˈstrəkt\ *vt* [back-formation fr. *destruction*] (1957) **:** DESTROY

2de·struct \di-ˈstrəkt, ˈdē-ˌ\ *n* (1957) **:** the deliberate destruction of a rocket after launching esp. during a test; *also* **:** the deliberate destruction of a device or material (as to prevent its falling into enemy hands)

de·struc·ti·ble \di-ˈstrək-tə-bəl\ *adj* (ca. 1755) **:** capable of being destroyed — **de·struc·ti·bil·i·ty** \di-ˌstrək-tə-ˈbil-ət-ē\ *n*

de·struc·tion \di-ˈstrək-shən\ *n* [ME *destruccioun,* fr. MF *destruction,* fr. L *destruction-, destructio,* fr. *destructus,* pp. of *destruere*] (14c) **1 :** the state or fact of being destroyed **:** RUIN **2 :** the action or process of destroying something **3 :** a destroying agency

de·struc·tion·ist \-sh(ə-)nəst\ *n* (1833) **:** one who delights in or advocates destruction

de·struc·tive \di-ˈstrək-tiv\ *adj* (15c) **1 :** causing destruction **:** RUINOUS ⟨~ storm⟩ **2 :** designed or tending to destroy ⟨~ criticism⟩ — **de·struc·tive·ly** *adv* — **de·struc·tive·ness** *n*

destructive distillation *n* (ca. 1831) **:** decomposition of a substance (as wood, coal, or oil) by heat in a closed container and collection of the volatile products produced

de·struc·tiv·i·ty \di-ˌstrək-ˈtiv-ət-ē, ˌdē-\ *n* (1902) **:** capacity for destruction

de·struc·tor \di-ˈstrək-tər\ *n* (1881) **1 :** a furnace for burning refuse **:** INCINERATOR **2 :** a device for destroying a missile in flight

de·sue·tude \ˈdes-wi-ˌt(y)üd, di-ˈs(y)ü-ə-ˌt(y)üd\ *n* [F or L; F *désuétude,* fr. L *desuetudo,* fr. *desuetus,* pp. of *desuescere* to become unaccustomed, fr. *de-* + *suescere* to become accustomed; akin to L *sodalis* comrade — more at SIB] (15c) **:** discontinuance from use or exercise **:** DISUSE

de·sul·fur·ize \(ˈ)dē-ˈsəl-fə-ˌrīz\ *vt* (ca. 1859) **:** to remove sulfur or sulfur compounds from — **de·sul·fur·iza·tion** \(ˌ)dē-ˌsəl-fə-rə-ˈzā-shən\ *n*

des·ul·to·ry \ˈdes-əl-ˌtōr-ē, -ˌtȯr- *also* ˈdez-\ *adj* [L *desultorius,* fr. *desultus,* pp. of *desilire* to leap down, fr. *de-* + *salire* to leap — more at SALLY] (1581) **1 :** marked by lack of definite plan, regularity, or purpose ⟨a dragged-out ordeal of . . . ~ shopping —Herman Wouk⟩ **2 :** not connected with the main subject ***syn*** see RANDOM — **des·ul·to·ri·ly** \ˌdes-əl-ˈtōr-ə-lē, ˌdez-, -ˈtȯr-\ *adv* — **des·ul·to·ri·ness** \ˈdes-əl-ˌtōr-ē-nəs, ˈdez-, -ˌtȯr-\ *n*

de·tach \di-ˈtach\ *vt* [F *détacher,* fr. OF *destachier,* fr. *des-* de- + *-tachier* (as in *atachier* to attach)] (1686) **1 :** to separate esp. from a larger mass and usu. without violence or damage **2 :** DISENGAGE, WITHDRAW — **de·tach·abil·i·ty** \-ˌtach-ə-ˈbil-ət-ē\ *n* — **de·tach·able** \-ˈtach-ə-bəl\ *adj* — **de·tach·ably** \-blē\ *adv*

de·tached \di-ˈtacht\ *adj* (ca. 1706) **1 :** standing by itself **:** SEPARATE, UNCONNECTED; *specif* **:** not sharing any wall with another building ⟨~ house⟩ **2 :** exhibiting an aloof objectivity usu. free from prejudice or self-interest ⟨a ~ observer⟩ ***syn*** see INDIFFERENT — **de·tached·ly** \-ˈtach-əd-lē, -ˈtach-tlē\ *adv* — **de·tached·ness** \-ˈtach-əd-nəs, -ˈtach(t)-nəs\ *n*

detached service *n* (ca. 1918) **:** military service away from one's assigned organization

de·tach·ment \di-ˈtach-mənt\ *n* (1669) **1 :** the action or process of detaching **:** SEPARATION **2 a :** the dispatch of a body of troops or part of a fleet from the main body for a special mission or service **b :** the part so dispatched **c :** a permanently organized separate unit usu. smaller than a platoon and different in composition from normal units **3 a :** indifference to worldly concerns **:** ALOOFNESS **b :** freedom from bias or prejudice

1de·tail \di-ˈtā(ə)l, ˈdē-ˌtāl\ *n* [F *détail,* fr. OF *detail* slice, piece, fr. *detaillier* to cut in pieces, fr. *de-* + *taillier* to cut — more at TAILOR] (1603) **1 :** extended treatment of or attention to particular items **2 :** a part of a whole: as **a :** a small and subordinate part **:** PARTICULAR; *also* **:** a reproduction of such a part of a work of art **b :** a part considered or requiring to be considered separately from the whole **c :** the small elements that collectively constitute a work of art **d :** the small elements of a photographic image corresponding to those of the subject **3 a :** selection for a particular task (as in military service) of a person or a body of persons **b** (1) **:** the person or body selected (2) **:** the task to be performed ***syn*** see ITEM — **in detail :** with all the particulars

2detail *vt* (1637) **1 :** to report minutely and distinctly **:** SPECIFY ⟨*~ed* their grievances⟩ **2 :** to assign to a particular task **3 :** to furnish with the smaller elements of design and finish ⟨trimmings that ~ slips and petticoats⟩ ~ *vi* **:** to make detail drawings — **de·tail·er** *n*

de·tailed \di-ˈtā(ə)ld, ˈdē-ˌtāld\ *adj* (1740) **:** marked by abundant detail or by thoroughness in treating small items or parts ⟨the ~ study of history⟩ ***syn*** see CIRCUMSTANTIAL — **de·tailed·ly** \di-ˈtāl(-ə)d-lē, ˈdē-ˌ\ *adv* — **de·tailed·ness** \di-ˈtā-ləd-nəs, -ˈtāl(d)-, ˈdē-ˌ\ *n*

detail man *n* (1928) **:** a representative of a drug manufacturer who introduces new drugs to medical and pharmaceutical professionals (as pharmacists and physicians)

de·tain \di-ˈtān\ *vt* [ME *deteynen,* fr. MF *detenir,* fr. L *detinēre,* fr. *de-* + *tenēre* to hold — more at THIN] (15c) **1 :** to hold or keep in or as if in custody **2** *obs* **:** to keep back (as something due) **:** WITHHOLD **3 :** to restrain esp. from proceeding **:** STOP ***syn*** see KEEP, DELAY — **de·tain·ment** \-mənt\ *n*

de·tain·ee \di-ˌtā-ˈnē, ˌdē-\ *n* (ca. 1928) **:** a person held in custody esp. for political reasons

de·tain·er \di-ˈtā-nər\ *n* [AF *detener,* fr. *detener* to detain, fr. L *detinēre*] (1619) **1 :** the act of keeping something in one's possession; *specif* **:** the withholding from the rightful owner of something that has lawfully come into the possession of the holder **2 :** detention in custody **3 :** a writ authorizing the keeper of a prison to continue to hold a person in custody

de·tect \di-ˈtekt\ *vb* [ME *detecten,* fr. L *detectus,* pp. of *detegere* to uncover, detect, fr. *de-* + *tegere* to cover — more at THATCH] *vt* (1581) **1 :** to discover the true character of **2 :** to discover or determine the existence, presence, or fact of ⟨~ alcohol in the blood⟩ **3 :** DEMODULATE ~ *vi* **:** to work as a detective — **de·tect·abil·i·ty** \-ˌtek-tə-ˈbil-ət-ē\ *n* — **de·tect·able** \-ˈtek-tə-bəl\ *adj*

de·tect·a·phone \-ˈtek-tə-ˌfōn\ *n* (1927) **:** a telephonic apparatus with an attached microphone transmitter used esp. for secret listening

de·tec·tion \di-ˈtek-shən\ *n* (15c) **1 :** the act of detecting **:** the state or fact of being detected **2 :** the process of demodulating

1de·tec·tive \di-ˈtek-tiv\ *adj* (1843) **1 :** fitted for or used in detecting something ⟨a ~ device for coal gas⟩ **2 :** of or relating to detectives or their work ⟨a ~ novel⟩ — **de·tec·tive·like** \-ˌlīk\ *adj*

2detective *n* (1850) **:** one employed or engaged in detecting lawbreakers or in getting information that is not readily or publicly accessible

de·tec·tor \di-ˈtek-tər\ *n* (1541) **:** one that detects: as **a :** a device for detecting the presence of electric waves or of radioactivity **b :** a rectifier of high-frequency current used esp. for extracting the intelligence from a radio signal

de·tent \ˈdē-ˌtent, di-ˈ\ *n* [F *détente,* fr. MF *destente,* fr. *destendre* to slacken, fr. OF, fr. *des-* de- + *tendre* to stretch, fr. L *tendere* — more at THIN] (1688) **:** a device (as a catch, dog, or spring-operated ball) for positioning and holding one mechanical part in relation to another so that the device can be released by force applied to one of the parts

dé·tente \dā-tä^{n}(n)t\ *n* [F] (1908) **:** a relaxation of strained relations or tensions (as between nations)

de·ten·tion \di-ˈten-chən\ *n* [MF or LL; MF, fr. LL *detention-, detentio,* fr. L *detentus,* pp. of *detinēre* to detain] (15c) **1 :** the act or fact of detaining or holding back; *esp* **:** a holding in custody **2 :** the state of being detained; *esp* **:** a period of temporary custody prior to disposition by a court

detention home *n* (ca. 1930) **:** a house of detention for juvenile delinquents usu. under the supervision of a juvenile court

de·ter \di-ˈtər\ *vt* **de·terred; de·ter·ring** [L *deterrēre,* fr. *de-* + *terrēre* to frighten — more at TERROR] (1579) **1 :** to turn aside, discourage, or prevent from acting **2 :** INHIBIT — **de·ter·ment** \-ˈtər-mənt\ *n* — **de·ter·ra·bil·i·ty** \-ˌtər-ə-ˈbil-ət-ē\ *n* — **de·ter·ra·ble** \-ˈtər-ə-bəl\ *adj* — **de·ter·rer** \-ˈtər-ər\ *n*

de·terge \di-ˈtərj\ *vt* **de·terged; de·terg·ing** [F or L; F *déterger,* fr. L *detergēre,* fr. *de-* + *tergēre* to wipe — more at TERSE] (ca. 1623) **:** to wash off **:** CLEANSE — **de·terg·er** *n*

de·ter·gen·cy \di-ˈtər-jən-sē\ *n* (1710) **:** cleansing quality or power

1de·ter·gent \-jənt\ *adj* (1616) **:** that cleanses **:** CLEANSING

2detergent *n* (1676) **:** a cleansing agent: as **a :** SOAP **b :** any of numerous synthetic water-soluble or liquid organic preparations that are chemically different from soaps but are able to emulsify oils, hold dirt in suspension, and act as wetting agents **c :** an oil-soluble substance that holds insoluble foreign matter in suspension and is used in lubricating oils and dry-cleaning solvents

de·te·ri·o·rate \di-ˈtir-ē-ə-ˌrāt\ *vb* **-rat·ed; -rat·ing** [LL *deterioratus,* pp. of *deteriorare,* fr. L *deterior* worse, fr. *de-* + *-ter* (suffix as in L *uter* which of two) + *-ior* (compar. suffix) — more at WHETHER, -ER] *vt* (1572) **1 :** to make inferior in quality or value **:** IMPAIR **2 :** DISINTEGRATE ~ *vi*

: to become impaired in quality, functioning, or condition : DEGENERATE ⟨allowed a tradition of academic excellence to ~⟩ ⟨his health *deteriorated*⟩ — **de·te·ri·o·ra·tive** \-ˌrāt-iv\ *adj*

de·te·ri·o·ra·tion \di-ˌtir-ē-ə-ˈrā-shən\ *n* (ca. 1658) : the action or process of deteriorating : the state of having deteriorated

syn DETERIORATION, DEGENERATION, DECADENCE, DECLINE mean the falling from a higher to a lower level in quality, character, or vitality. DETERIORATION implies impairment of vigor, resilience, or usefulness; DEGENERATION stresses physical, intellectual, or esp. moral retrogression; DECADENCE presupposes a reaching and passing the peak of development and implies a turn downward with a consequent loss in vitality or energy; DECLINE differs from DECADENCE in suggesting a more markedly downward direction and greater momentum as well as more obvious evidence of deterioration.

de·ter·min·able \-ˈtərm-(ə-)nə-bəl\ *adj* (15c) **1** : capable of being determined, definitely ascertained, or decided upon **2** : liable to be terminated : TERMINABLE — **de·ter·min·able·ness** *n* — **de·ter·min·ably** \-blē\ *adv*

de·ter·mi·na·cy \di-ˈtər-mə-nə-sē\ *n, pl* **-cies** (1873) **1** : the quality or state of being determinate **2** **a** : the state of being definitely and unequivocally characterized : EXACTNESS **b** : the state of being determined or necessitated

de·ter·mi·nant \di-ˈtərm-(ə-)nənt\ *n* (1686) **1** : an element that identifies or determines the nature of something or that fixes or conditions an outcome **2** : a square array of numbers bordered on either side by a straight line with a value that is the algebraic sum of all the products that can be formed by taking as factors one element in succession from each row and column and giving to each product a positive or negative sign depending upon whether the number of permutations necessary to place the indices representing each factor's position in its row or column in the order of the natural numbers is odd or even **3** : GENE; *broadly* : a comparable subordinate agent (as a plasmagene) **4** : one of the chemical groupings that together determine the specific reactivity of an antigen or antibody ***syn*** see CAUSE — **de·ter·mi·nan·tal** \-ˌtər-mə-ˈnant-ᵊl\ *adj*

de·ter·mi·nate \di-ˈtərm-(ə-)nət\ *adj* [ME, fr. L *determinatus,* pp. of *determinare*] (14c) **1** : having defined limits **2** : definitely settled **3** : conclusively determined : DEFINITIVE **4** : CYMOSE **5** : relating to, being or undergoing egg cleavage in which each division irreversibly separates portions of the zygote with specific potencies for further development — **de·ter·mi·nate·ly** *adv* — **de·ter·mi·nate·ness** *n*

de·ter·mi·na·tion \di-ˌtər-mə-ˈnā-shən\ *n* (14c) **1** **a** : a judicial decision settling and ending a controversy **b** : the resolving of a question by argument or reasoning **2** *archaic* : TERMINATION **3** **a** : the act of deciding definitely and firmly; *also* : the result of such an act of decision **b** : the power or habit of deciding definitely and firmly **4** : a fixing or finding of the position, magnitude, value, or character of something: as **a** : the act, process, or result of an accurate measurement **b** : an identification of the taxonomic position of a plant or animal **5** **a** : the definition of a concept in logic by its essential constituents **b** : the addition of a differentia to a concept to limit its denotation **6** : direction or tendency to a certain end : IMPULSION **7** : the fixation of the destiny of undifferentiated embryonic tissue

de·ter·mi·na·tive \-ˈtər-mə-ˌnāt-iv, -ˈtərm-(ə-)nət-\ *adj* (1655) : having power or tendency to determine : tending to fix, settle, or define something ⟨regard experiments as ~ of the principles from which deductions could be made —S. F. Mason⟩ ***syn*** see CONCLUSIVE — **determinative** *n*

de·ter·mi·na·tor \di-ˈtər-mə-ˌnāt-ər\ *n* (1556) : DETERMINER

de·ter·mine \di-ˈtər-mən\ *vb* **de·ter·mined; de·ter·min·ing** \-ˈtərm-(ə-)niŋ\ [ME *determinen,* fr. MF *determiner,* fr. L *determinare,* fr. *de-* + *terminare* to limit, fr. *terminus* boundary, limit — more at TERM] *vt* (14c) **1** **a** : to fix conclusively or authoritatively **b** : to decide by judicial sentence **c** : to settle or decide by choice of alternatives or possibilities **d** : RESOLVE **2** **a** : to fix the form, position, or character of beforehand : ORDAIN ⟨two points ~ a straight line⟩ **b** : to bring about as a result : REGULATE ⟨demand ~s the price⟩ **3** **a** : to fix the boundaries of **b** : to limit in extent or scope **c** : to put or set an end to : TERMINATE ⟨~ an estate⟩ **4** **a** : to find out or come to a decision about by investigation, reasoning, or calculation ⟨~ the answer to the problem⟩ ⟨~ a position at sea⟩ **b** : to discover the taxonomic position or the generic and specific names of **5** : to bring about the determination of ⟨~ the fate of a cell⟩ ~ *vi* **1** : to come to a decision **2** : to come to an end or become void ***syn*** see DECIDE, DISCOVER

de·ter·mined \-ˈtər-mənd\ *adj* (1513) **1** : having reached a decision : firmly resolved ⟨~ to be a pilot⟩ **2** **a** : showing determination ⟨a ~ effort⟩ **b** : characterized by determination ⟨will deter all but the most ~ thief —*Security World*⟩ — **de·ter·mined·ly** \-mən-dlē, -mə-nəd-lē\ *adv* — **de·ter·mined·ness** \-mən(d)-nəs\ *n*

de·ter·min·er \-ˈtərm-(ə-)nər\ *n* (ca. 1530) : one that determines: as **a** : GENE, DETERMINANT 3 **b** : a word (as *his* in "his new car") belonging to a group of limiting noun modifiers characterized by occurrence before descriptive adjectives modifying the same noun

de·ter·min·ism \di-ˈtər-mə-ˌniz-əm\ *n* (1846) **1** **a** : a theory or doctrine that acts of the will, occurrences in nature, or social or psychological phenomena are causally determined by preceding events or natural laws ⟨explained behavior by the combination of an environmental and a genetic ~⟩ **b** : a belief in predestination **2** : the quality or state of being determined — **de·ter·min·ist** \-(ə-)nəst\ *n or adj* — **de·ter·min·is·tic** \-ˌtər-mə-ˈnis-tik\ *adj* — **de·ter·min·is·ti·cal·ly** \-ti-k(ə-)lē\ *adv*

de·ter·rence \di-ˈtər-ən(t)s, -ˈter-; -ˈtə-rən(t)s\ *n* (1861) **1** : the act or process of deterring ⟨the penalty for the crime of perjury is often no ~ to lying under oath —*New Republic*⟩ **2** : the maintaining of vast military power and weaponry in order to discourage war

de·ter·rent \-ənt, -rənt\ *adj* [L *deterrent-, deterrens,* prp. of *deterrēre* to deter] (1829) **1** : serving to deter **2** : relating to deterrence — **deterrent** *n* — **de·ter·rent·ly** *adv*

de·ter·sive \di-ˈtər-siv, -ziv\ *adj* [MF *detersif,* fr. L *detersus,* pp. of *detergēre* to deterge] (1586) : DETERGENT — **detersive** *n*

de·test \di-ˈtest\ *vt* [MF *detester* or L *detestari;* MF *detester,* fr. L *detestari,* lit., to curse while calling a deity to witness, fr. *de-* + *testari* to call to witness — more at TESTAMENT] (1533) **1** : to feel intense and often violent antipathy toward : LOATHE **2** *obs* : CURSE, DENOUNCE ***syn*** see HATE — **de·test·er** *n*

de·test·able \di-ˈtes-tə-bəl\ *adj* (15c) : arousing or meriting intense dislike : ABOMINABLE — **de·test·able·ness** *n* — **de·test·ably** \-blē\ *adv*

de·tes·ta·tion \ˌdē-ˌtes-ˈtā-shən, di-\ *n* (15c) **1** : extreme hatred or dislike : ABHORRENCE, LOATHING ⟨had a ~ of hypocrites⟩ **2** : an object of hatred or contempt

de·throne \di-ˈthrōn\ *vt* (1609) : to remove from a throne or place of power or prominence : DEPOSE — **de·throne·ment** \-mənt\ *n* — **de·thron·er** *n*

de·tick \(ˈ)dē-ˈtik\ *vt* (1925) : to remove ticks from ⟨dogs should be ~*ed* and sprayed⟩ — **de·tick·er** *n*

det·i·nue \ˈdet-ᵊn-ˌ(y)ü\ *n* [ME *detenewe,* fr. MF *detenue* detention, fr. fem. of *detenu,* pp. of *detenir* to detain] (15c) **1** : a common-law action for the recovery of a personal chattel wrongfully detained or of its value **2** : detention of something due; *esp* : the unlawful detention of a personal chattel from another

det·o·na·ble \ˈdet-ᵊn-ə-bəl, -ə-nə-\ *adj* (1884) : capable of being detonated — **det·o·na·bil·i·ty** \ˌdet-ᵊn-ə-ˈbil-ət-ē, ˌdet-ə-nə-\ *n*

det·o·nate \ˈdet-ᵊn-ˌāt, ˈdet-ə-ˌnāt\ *vb* **-nat·ed; -nat·ing** [L *detonatus,* pp. of *detonare* to thunder down, fr. *de-* + *tonare* to thunder — more at THUNDER] *vi* (1729) : to explode with sudden violence ~ *vt* **1** : to cause to detonate ⟨~ a bomb⟩ — compare DEFLAGRATE **2** : to set off in a burst of activity : SPARK ⟨programs that *detonated* controversies⟩ — **det·o·nat·able** \-ˌāt-ə-bəl, -ˌnāt-\ *adj* — **det·o·na·tive** \ˈdet-ᵊn-ˌāt-iv, ˈdet-ə-ˌnāt-\ *adj*

det·o·na·tion \ˌdet-ᵊn-ˈā-shən, ˌdet-ə-ˈnā-\ *n* (1686) **1** : the action or process of detonating **2** : rapid combustion in an internal-combustion engine that results in knocking — **det·o·na·tion·al** \-shnəl, -shən-ᵊl\ *adj*

det·o·na·tor \ˈdet-ᵊn-ˌāt-ər, -ə-ˌnāt-\ *n* (1822) : a device or small quantity of explosive used for detonating a high explosive

¹de·tour \ˈdē-ˌtu̇(ə)r *also* di-ˈ\ *n* [F *détour,* fr. OF *destor,* fr. *destorner* to divert, fr. *des-* de- + *torner* to turn — more at TURN] (1738) : a deviation from a direct course or the usual procedure; *specif* : a roundabout way temporarily replacing part of a route

²detour *vi* (1836) : to proceed by a detour ⟨~ around road construction⟩ ~ *vt* **1** : to send by a circuitous route **2** : to avoid by going around : BYPASS

de·tox·i·cate \(ˈ)dē-ˈtäk-sə-ˌkāt\ *vt* **-cat·ed; -cat·ing** [*de-* + L *toxicum* poison — more at TOXIC] (1867) : DETOXIFY — **de·tox·i·cant** \-si-kənt\ *n* — **de·tox·i·ca·tion** \(ˌ)dē-ˌtäk-sə-ˈkā-shən\ *n*

de·tox·i·fy \(ˈ)dē-ˈtäk-sə-ˌfī\ *vt* **-fied; -fy·ing** (ca. 1905) **1** : to remove a poison or toxin or the effect of such from **2** : to free (as a drug user or an alcoholic) from an intoxicating or an addictive substance in the body or from dependence on or addiction to such a substance — **de·tox·i·fi·ca·tion** \(ˌ)dē-ˌtäk-sə-fə-ˈkā-shən\ *n*

de·tract \di-ˈtrakt\ *vb* [ME *detracten,* fr. L *detractus,* pp. of *detrahere* to withdraw, disparage, fr. *de-* + *trahere* to draw — more at DRAW] *vt* (15c) **1** *archaic* : to speak ill of **2** *archaic* : to take away **3** : DIVERT ⟨~ attention⟩ ~ *vi* : to take away something ⟨an individual's image enhances or ~s from his power to persuade —Carll Tucker⟩ — **de·trac·tor** \-ˈtrak-tər\ *n*

de·trac·tion \di-ˈtrak-shən\ *n* (14c) **1** : a lessening of reputation or esteem esp. by envious, malicious, or petty criticism : BELITTLING, DISPARAGEMENT **2** : a taking away ⟨it is no ~ from its dignity or prestige —J. F. Golay⟩ — **de·trac·tive** \-ˈtrak-tiv\ *adj* — **de·trac·tive·ly** *adv*

de·train \(ˈ)dē-ˈtrān\ *vi* (1881) : to get off a railroad train ~ *vt* : to remove from a railroad train — **de·train·ment** \-mənt\ *n*

de·trib·al·ize \(ˈ)dē-ˈtrī-bə-ˌlīz\ *vt* **-ized; -iz·ing** (1920) : to cause to relinquish tribal identity : ACCULTURATE — **de·trib·al·iza·tion** \(ˌ)dē-ˌtrī-bə-lə-ˈzā-shən\ *n*

det·ri·ment \ˈde-trə-mənt\ *n* [ME, fr. MF or L; MF, fr. L *detrimentum,* fr. *deterere* to wear away, impair, fr. *de-* + *terere* to rub — more at THROW] (15c) **1** : INJURY, DAMAGE ⟨did hard work without ~ to his health⟩ **2** : a cause of injury or damage ⟨the long strike was a ~ to the industry⟩

¹det·ri·men·tal \ˌde-trə-ˈment-ᵊl\ *adj* (ca. 1656) : obviously harmful : DAMAGING ⟨the ~ effects of pollution⟩ ***syn*** see PERNICIOUS — **det·ri·men·tal·ly** \-ᵊl-ē\ *adv*

²detrimental *n* (1831) : an undesirable or harmful person or thing

de·tri·tion \di-ˈtrish-ən\ *n* (1674) : a wearing off or away

de·tri·tus \di-ˈtrīt-əs\ *n, pl* **de·tri·tus** \-ˈtrīt-əs, -ˈtrī-ˌtüs\ [F *détritus,* fr. L *detritus,* pp. of *deterere*] (1802) **1** : loose material (as rock fragments or organic particles) that results directly from disintegration **2** : a product of disintegration, destruction, or wearing away : DEBRIS — **de·tri·tal** \-ˈtrīt-ᵊl\ *adj*

de trop \də-ˈtrō\ *adj* [F] (1752) : too much or too many : SUPERFLUOUS ⟨the ridiculously complex plot was *de trop*⟩

de·tu·mes·cence \ˌde-t(y)ü-ˈmes-ᵊn(t)s\ *n* (1678) : subsidence or diminution of swelling or erection — **de·tu·mes·cent** \-ᵊnt\ *adj*

Deu·ca·lion \d(y)ü-ˈkāl-yən\ *n* [L, fr. Gk *Deukaliōn*] : a survivor with his wife Pyrrha of a great flood by which Zeus destroys the rest of the human race

¹deuce \ˈd(y)üs\ *n* [MF *deus* two, fr. L *duos,* acc. masc. of *duo* two — more at TWO] (15c) **1** **a** (1) : the face of a die that bears two spots (2) : a playing card bearing an index number two **b** : a throw of the dice yielding two points **2** : a tie in tennis after each side has scored 40 requiring two consecutive points by one side to win **3** [obs. E *deuce* bad luck] **a** : DEVIL, DICKENS — used chiefly as a mild oath ⟨what the ~ is he up to now⟩ **b** : something notable of its kind ⟨a ~ of a mess⟩

²deuce *vt* **deuced; deuc·ing** (1919) : to bring the score of (a tennis game or set) to deuce

deuc·ed \ˈd(y)ü-səd\ *adj* (1782) : DAMNED, CONFOUNDED ⟨in a ~ fix⟩ — **deuc·ed** *or* **deuc·ed·ly** *adv*

deuces wild *n* (1913) : a card game (as poker) in which each deuce may represent any card designated by its holder

de·us ex ma·chi·na \ˌdā-ə-ˌsek-ˈsmäk-i-nə, -ˌnä; -ˈsmak-ə-nə\ *n* [NL, a god from a machine, trans. of Gk *theos ek mēchanēs*] (1697) **1** : a god introduced by means of a crane in ancient Greek and Roman drama to decide the final outcome **2** : a person or thing (as in fiction or drama) that appears or is introduced suddenly and unexpectedly and provides a contrived solution to an apparently insoluble difficulty

deut- *or* **deuto-** *comb form* [ISV, fr. *deuter-*] : second : secondary ⟨*deuto*nymph⟩

[1]**deuter-** *or* **deutero-** *comb form* [alter. of ME *deutro-*, modif. of LL *deutero-*, fr. Gk *deuter-, deutero-*, fr. *deuteros;* prob. akin to L *dudum* formerly, Gk *dein* to lack] **:** second **:** secondary ⟨*deutero*genesis⟩
[2]**deuter-** *or* **deutero-** *comb form* [ISV] **:** deuterium **:** containing deuterium ⟨*deuter*ated⟩ ⟨*deutero*alkanes⟩
deu·ter·ag·o·nist \ˌd(y)üt-ə-ˈrag-ə-nəst\ *n* [Gk *deuteragōnistēs*, fr. *deuter-* + *agōnistēs* combatant, actor — more at PROTAGONIST] (1855) **1 :** the actor taking the part of second importance in a classical Greek drama **2 :** a person who serves as a foil to another
deu·ter·anom·a·lous \ˌd(y)üt-ə-rə-ˈnäm-ə-ləs\ *adj* [NL *deuteranomalia* (fr. [1]*deuter-* + L *anomalia* anomaly) abnormal trichromatism + E *-ous*] (ca. 1931) **:** exhibiting partial loss of green color vision so that an increased intensity of this color is required in a mixture of red and green to match a given yellow — **deu·ter·anom·a·ly** \-ˈnäm-ə-lē\ *n*
deu·ter·an·ope \ˈd(y)üt-ə-rə-ˌnōp\ *n* (1902) **:** an individual affected with deuteranopia
deu·ter·an·opia \ˌd(y)üt-ə-rə-ˈnō-pē-ə\ *n* [NL, fr. [1]*deuter-* + [2]*a-* + *-opia;* fr. the blindness to green, regarded as the second primary color] (ca. 1901) **:** color blindness marked by confusion of purplish red and green — **deu·ter·an·opic** \-ˈnō-pik, -ˈnäp-ik\ *adj*
deu·ter·ate \ˈdyüt-ə-ˌrāt\ *vt* **-at·ed; -at·ing** (1947) **:** to introduce deuterium into (a compound) — **deu·ter·a·tion** \ˌdyüt-ə-ˈrā-shən\ *n*
deu·te·ri·um \d(y)ü-ˈtir-ē-əm\ *n* [NL, fr. Gk *deuteros* second] (1933) **:** the hydrogen isotope that is of twice the mass of ordinary hydrogen and that occurs in water — called also *heavy hydrogen*
deuterium oxide *n* (1934) **:** heavy water D_2O composed of deuterium and oxygen
deu·tero·ca·non·i·cal \ˌd(y)üt-ə-rō-kə-ˈnän-i-kəl\ *adj* [NL *deuterocanonicus*, fr. [1]*deuter-* + LL *canonicus* canonical] (1684) **:** of, relating to, or constituting the books of Scripture contained in the Septuagint but not in the Hebrew canon
deu·ter·on \ˈd(y)üt-ə-ˌrän\ *n* [*deuterium*] (1933) **:** the nucleus of the deuterium atom consisting of one proton and one neutron
Deu·ter·o·nom·ic \ˌd(y)üt-ə-rə-ˈnäm-ik\ *adj* (1857) **1 :** of or relating to the book of Deuteronomy **2 :** marked by the literary style or theological content of Deuteronomy
Deu·ter·on·o·mist \ˌd(y)üt-ə-ˈrän-ə-məst\ *n* (1862) **:** one of the writers or editors of a Deuteronomic body of source material often distinguished in the earlier books of the Old Testament — **Deu·ter·on·o·mis·tic** \-ˌrän-ə-ˈmis-tik\ *adj*
Deu·ter·on·o·my \ˌd(y)üt-ə-ˈrän-ə-mē\ *n* [ME *Deutronomie*, fr. LL *Deuteronomium*, fr. Gk *Deuteronomion*, fr. *deuter-* + *nomos* law — more at NIMBLE] **:** the fifth book of canonical Jewish and Christian Scripture containing Mosaic laws and narrative material — see BIBLE table
deu·tero·stome \ˈd(y)üt-ə-rə-ˌstōm\ *n* [NL *Deuterostomia*, group name, fr. *deuter-* + Gk *stoma* mouth — more at STOMACH] (1950) **:** any of a major division (Deuterostomia) of the animal kingdom that includes the bilaterally symmetrical animals (as the chordates) with indeterminate cleavage and a mouth that does not arise from the blastopore
deu·to·plasm \ˈd(y)üt-ə-ˌplaz-əm\ *n* [ISV] (ca. 1884) **:** the nutritive inclusions of protoplasm; *esp* **:** the yolk reserves of an egg
deut·sche mark \ˌdȯich(-ə)-ˈmärk\ *n* [G, German mark] (1948) — see MONEY table
deut·zia \ˈd(y)üt-sē-ə\ *n* [NL, fr. Jean *Deutz* †1784? Du. patron of botanical research] (1837) **:** any of a genus (*Deutzia*) of the saxifrage family of ornamental shrubs with white or pink flowers
de·val·u·ate \(ˈ)dē-ˈval-yə-ˌwāt\ *vb* (1898) **:** DEVALUE
de·val·u·a·tion \(ˌ)dē-ˌval-yə-ˈwā-shən\ *n* (1914) **1 :** an official reduction in the exchange value of a currency by a lowering of its gold equivalency **2 :** a lessening esp. of status or stature **:** DECLINE
de·val·ue \(ˈ)dē-ˈval-(ˌ)yü, -yə(-w)\ *vt* (1918) **1 :** to institute the devaluation of (money) **2 :** to lessen the value of ~ *vi* **:** to institute devaluation
De·va·na·ga·ri \ˌdā-və-ˈnäg-ə-rē\ *n* [Skt *devanāgarī*, fr. *deva* divine + *nāgarī* script of the city — more at DEITY] (1781) **:** an alphabet usu. employed for Sanskrit and also used as a literary hand for various modern languages of India — see ALPHABET table
dev·as·tate \ˈdev-ə-ˌstāt\ *vt* **-tat·ed; -tat·ing** [L *devastatus*, pp. of *devastare*, fr. *de-* + *vastare* to lay waste — more at WASTE] (1634) **1 :** to bring to ruin or desolation by violent action **2 :** to reduce to chaos, disorder, or helplessness **:** OVERWHELM ⟨*devastated* by grief⟩ ⟨her wisecrack *devastated* the class⟩ ***syn*** see RAVAGE — **dev·as·tat·ing·ly** \-ˌstāt-iŋ-lē\ *adv* — **dev·as·ta·tion** \ˌdev-ə-ˈstā-shən\ *n* — **dev·as·tat·ive** \ˈdev-ə-ˌstāt-iv\ *adj* — **dev·as·ta·tor** \-ˌstāt-ər\ *n*
de·vel·op \di-ˈvel-əp\ *vb* [F *développer*, fr. MF *desveloper, desvoluper*, fr. *des-* de- + *-veloper, -voluper* (as in MF *enveloper* to enclose) — more at ENVELOP] *vt* (1750) **1 a :** to set forth or make clear by degrees or in detail **:** EXPOUND **b :** to make visible or manifest **c :** to treat (as in dyeing) with an agent to cause the appearance of color **d :** to subject (exposed photograph material) esp. to chemicals in order to produce a visible image; *also* **:** to make visible by such a method **e :** to elaborate (a musical idea) by the working out of rhythmic and harmonic changes in the theme **2 :** to work out the possibilities of **3 a (1) :** to make active **(2) :** to promote the growth of ⟨~*ed* his muscles⟩ **b :** to make available or usable ⟨~ its resources⟩ **c :** to move (a chess piece) from the original position to one providing more opportunity for effective use **4 a :** to cause to unfold gradually ⟨~*ed* his argument⟩ **b :** to expand by a process of growth ⟨~*ed* mature breasts in her early teens⟩ **c :** to cause to grow and differentiate along lines natural to its kind ⟨rain and sun ~ the grain⟩ **5 :** to acquire gradually ⟨~ an appreciation for ballet⟩ ~ *vi* **1 a :** to go through a process of natural growth, differentiation, or evolution by successive changes ⟨a blossom ~*s* from a bud⟩ **b :** to acquire secondary sex characters **2 a :** to become gradually manifest **b :** to become apparent **3 :** to develop one's pieces in chess — **de·vel·op·able** \-ˈvel-ə-pə-bəl\ *adj*
de·vel·op·er \-ə-pər\ *n* (1883) **:** one that develops: as **a :** a chemical used to develop exposed photographic materials **b :** a person who develops real estate; *esp* **:** one that improves and subdivides land and builds and sells houses thereon
de·vel·op·ing \-ə-piŋ\ *adj* (1964) **:** UNDERDEVELOPED 2 ⟨~ nations⟩
de·vel·op·ment \di-ˈvel-əp-mənt\ *n* (1756) **1 :** the act, process, or result of developing **2 :** the state of being developed **3 :** a developed tract of land; *esp* **:** one that has houses built thereon — **de·vel·op·men·tal** \-ˌvel-əp-ˈment-ᵊl\ *adj* — **de·vel·op·men·tal·ly** \-ᵊl-ē\ *adv*
de·verb·al \(ˈ)dē-ˈvər-bəl\ *adj* (1943) **:** DEVERBATIVE
de·verb·a·tive \(ˈ)dē-ˈvər-bət-iv\ *adj* (1930) **1 :** derived from a verb ⟨the ~ noun *developer* is derived from *develop*⟩ **2 :** used in derivation from a verb ⟨the ~ suffix *-er* in *developer*⟩ — **deverbative** *n*
de·vest \di-ˈvest\ *vt* [MF *desvestir*, fr. ML *disvestire*, fr. L *dis-* + *vestire* to clothe — more at VEST] (1563) **:** DIVEST
de·vi·ance \ˈdē-vē-ən(t)s\ *n* (1944) **:** deviant quality, state, or behavior
de·vi·an·cy \-ən-sē\ *n, pl* **-cies** (1947) **:** DEVIANCE
de·vi·ant \-ənt\ *adj* (15c) **:** deviating esp. from an accepted norm ⟨~ behavior⟩ — **deviant** *n*
[1]**de·vi·ate** \ˈdē-vē-ˌāt\ *vb* **-at·ed; -at·ing** [LL *deviatus*, pp. of *deviare*, fr. L *de-* + *via* way — more at VIA] *vi* (1633) **1 :** to stray esp. from a standard, principle, or topic **2 :** to depart from an established course or norm ~ *vt* **:** to cause to turn out of a previous course ***syn*** see SWERVE — **de·vi·a·tor** \-ˌāt-ər\ *n* — **de·vi·a·to·ry** \-ə-ˌtōr-ē, -ˌtȯr-\ *adj*
[2]**de·vi·ate** \-vē-ət, -vē-ˌāt\ *n* (1912) **1 :** one that deviates from a norm; *esp* **:** a person who differs markedly from a group norm **2 :** a statistical variable that gives the deviation of another variable from a fixed value (as the mean)
[3]**de·vi·ate** \-vē-ət, -vē-ˌāt\ *adj* (1929) **:** departing significantly from the behavioral norms of a particular society
de·vi·a·tion \ˌdē-vē-ˈā-shən\ *n* (15c) **:** an act or instance of deviating: as **a :** deflection of the needle of a compass caused by local magnetic influences (as in a ship) **b :** the difference between a value in a frequency distribution and a fixed number (as the mean) **c :** departure from an established ideology or party line **d :** noticeable or marked departure from accepted norms of behavior — **de·vi·a·tion·ism** \-shə-ˌniz-əm\ *n* — **de·vi·a·tion·ist** \-sh(ə-)nəst\ *n or adj*
de·vice \di-ˈvīs\ *n* [ME *devis, devise*, fr. MF, division, intention, fr. OF *deviser* to divide, regulate, tell — more at DEVISE] (14c) **1 :** something devised or contrived: as **a (1) :** PLAN, PROCEDURE, TECHNIQUE **(2) :** a scheme to deceive **:** STRATAGEM, TRICK **b :** something fanciful, elaborate, or intricate in design **c :** something (as a figure of speech) in a literary work designed to achieve a particular artistic effect **d** *archaic* **:** MASQUE, SPECTACLE **e :** a conventional stage practice or means (as a stage whisper) used to achieve a particular dramatic effect **f :** a piece of equipment or a mechanism designed to serve a special purpose or perform a special function **2 :** DESIRE, INCLINATION ⟨left to my own ~*s*⟩ **3 :** an emblematic design used esp. as a heraldic bearing
[1]**dev·il** \ˈdev-əl\ *n* [ME *devel*, fr. OE *dēofol*, fr. LL *diabolus*, fr. Gk *diabolos*, lit., slanderer, fr. *diaballein* to throw across, slander, fr. *dia-* + *ballein* to throw; akin to OHG *quellan* to well, gush] (bef. 12c) **1** *often cap* **:** the personal supreme spirit of evil often represented in Jewish and Christian belief as the tempter of mankind, the leader of all apostate angels, and the ruler of hell — usu. used with *the;* often used as an interjection, an intensive, or a generalized term of abuse ⟨what the ~ is this?⟩ ⟨the ~ you say!⟩ **2 :** an evil spirit **:** DEMON **3 a :** an extremely wicked person **:** FIEND **b** *archaic* **:** a great evil **4 :** a person of notable energy, recklessness, and dashing spirit; *also* **:** one who is mischievous ⟨those youngsters are little ~*s* today⟩ **5 :** FELLOW — usu. used in the phrases *poor devil, lucky devil* **6 a :** something very trying or provoking ⟨having a ~ of a time with this problem⟩ **b :** severe criticism or rebuke **:** HELL — used with *the* ⟨I'll probably catch the ~ for this⟩ **7** *Christian Science* **:** the opposite of Truth **:** a belief in sin, sickness, and death **:** EVIL, ERROR — **between the devil and the deep blue sea :** faced with two equally objectionable alternatives — **devil to pay :** severe consequences — used with *the*
[2]**devil** *vt* **-iled** *or* **-illed; -il·ing** *or* **-il·ling** \ˈdev-(ə-)liŋ\ (1800) **1 :** to season highly ⟨~*ed* eggs⟩ **2 :** TEASE, ANNOY
dev·il·fish \ˈdev-əl-ˌfish\ *n* (1709) **1 :** any of several extremely large rays (genera *Manta* and *Mobula*) widely distributed in warm seas **2 :** OCTOPUS; *broadly* **:** any large cephalopod

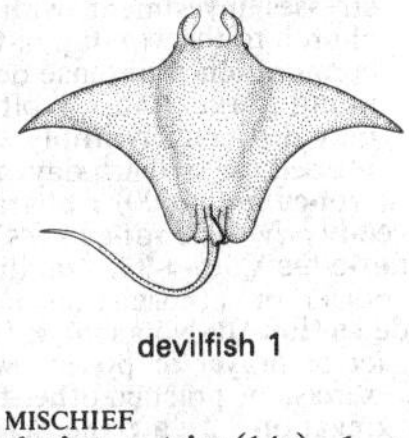
devilfish 1

dev·il·ish \ˈdev-(ə-)lish\ *adj* (15c) **1 :** resembling or befitting a devil: as **a :** EVIL, SINISTER **b :** MISCHIEVOUS, ROGUISH **2 :** EXTREME ⟨in a ~ hurry⟩ — **devilish** *adv* — **dev·il·ish·ly** *adv* — **dev·il·ish·ness** *n*
dev·il–may–care \ˌdev-əl-(ˌ)mā-ˈke(ə)r, -ˈka(ə)r\ *adj* (1837) **:** EASYGOING, CAREFREE
dev·il·ment \ˈdev-əl-mənt, -ˌment\ *n* (1771) **:** MISCHIEF
dev·il·ry \ˈdev-əl-rē\ *or* **dev·il·try** \-əl-trē\ *n, pl* **-ries** *or* **-tries** (14c) **1 a :** action performed with the help of the devil **:** WITCHCRAFT **b :** WICKEDNESS **c :** MISCHIEF **2 :** an act of devilry
devil's advocate *n* [trans. of NL *advocatus diaboli*] (1760) **1 :** a Roman Catholic official whose duty is to examine critically the evidence on which a demand for beatification or canonization rests **2 :** a person who champions the less accepted or approved cause for the sake of argument
devil's darning needle *n* (1809) **1 :** DRAGONFLY **2 :** DAMSELFLY
dev·il's food cake \ˈdev-əlz-ˌfüd-ˌkāk\ *n* (1905) **:** a rich chocolate cake
devil's paintbrush *n* (1900) **:** ORANGE HAWKWEED; *broadly* **:** any of various hawkweeds that are naturalized weeds in the eastern U.S.
devil theory *n* (1937) **:** a theory of history: political and social crises arise from the deliberate actions of evil or misguided leaders rather than as a natural result of conditions
dev·il·wood \ˈdev-əl-ˌwu̇d\ *n* (1818) **:** a small tree (*Osmanthus americanus*) of the southern U.S. that is related to the olive
de·vi·ous \ˈdē-vē-əs\ *adj* [L *devius*, fr. *de* from + *via* way — more at DEVIA] (1599) **1 :** OUT-OF-THE-WAY, REMOTE **2 a :** WANDERING, ROUNDABOUT ⟨a ~ path⟩ **b :** moving without a fixed course **:** ERRANT ⟨~ breezes⟩ **3 a :** deviating from a right, accepted, or common course

\ə\ abut \ᵊ\ kitten, F table \ər\ further \a\ ash \ā\ ace \ä\ cot, cart \au̇\ out \ch\ chin \e\ bet \ē\ easy \g\ go \i\ hit \ī\ ice \j\ job \ŋ\ sing \ō\ go \ȯ\ law \ȯi\ boy \th\ thin \t͟h\ the \ü\ loot \u̇\ foot \y\ yet \zh\ vision \á, k̲, ⁿ, œ, œ̄, ue, ue̅, ʸ\ see Guide to Pronunciation

b : not straightforward : CUNNING; *also* : DECEPTIVE — **de·vi·ous·ly** *adv* — **de·vi·ous·ness** *n*

[1]**de·vise** \di-ˈvīz\ *vt* **de·vised; de·vis·ing** [ME *devisen*, fr. OF *deviser* to divide, regulate, tell, modif. of (assumed) VL *divisare*, fr. L *divisus*, pp. of *dividere* to divide] (13c) **1 a :** to form in the mind by new combinations or applications of ideas or principles : INVENT **b** *archaic* : CONCEIVE, IMAGINE **c :** to plan to obtain or bring about : PLOT **2 :** to give (real estate) by will — compare BEQUEATH — **de·vis·able** \-ˈvī-zə-bəl\ *adj* — **de·vis·er** *n*

[2]**devise** *n* (15c) **1 :** the act of giving or disposing of real property by will **2 :** a will or clause of a will disposing of real property **3 :** property devised by will

de·vi·see \ˌdev-ə-ˈzē, di-ˌvī-ˈzē\ *n* (1542) **:** one to whom a devise of property is made

de·vi·sor \ˌdev-ə-ˈzȯ(ə)r; di-ˈvī-zər, -ˌvī-ˈzȯ(ə)r\ *n* (1542) **:** one who devises property in a will

de·vi·tal·ize \(ˈ)dē-ˈvīt-ᵊl-ˌīz\ *vt* (1849) **:** to deprive of life, vigor, or effectiveness

de·vit·ri·fy \(ˈ)dē-ˈvi-trə-ˌfī\ *vt* [F *dévitrifier*, fr. *dé-* de- + *vitrifier* to vitrify] (1832) **:** to deprive of glassy luster and transparency; *esp* **:** to change (as a glass) from a vitreous to a crystalline condition — **de·vit·ri·fi·able** \-ˌfī-ə-bəl\ *adj* — **de·vit·ri·fi·ca·tion** \(ˌ)dē-ˌvi-trə-fə-ˈkā-shən\ *n*

de·vo·cal·ize \(ˈ)dē-ˈvō-kə-ˌlīz\ *vt* (1877) **:** DEVOICE

de·voice \(ˈ)dē-ˈvȯis\ *vt* (1932) **:** to pronounce (as a sometimes or formerly voiced sound) without vibration of the vocal cords

de·void \di-ˈvȯid\ *adj* [ME, prob. short for *devoided*, pp. of *devoiden* to vacate, fr. MF *desvuidier* to empty, fr. OF, fr. *des-* dis- + *vuidier* to empty — more at VOID] (15c) **:** being without a usual, typical, or expected attribute or accompaniment ⟨a poem totally ~ of real quality⟩

de·voir \dəv-ˈwär, ˈdev-ˌ\ *n* [ME, alter. of *dever*, fr. MF *deveir*, fr. OF *devoir, deveir* to owe, be obliged, fr. L *debēre* — more at DEBT] (14c) **1 :** DUTY, RESPONSIBILITY **2 :** a formal act of civility or respect

de·vo·lu·tion \ˌdev-ə-ˈlü-shən *also* ˌdē-və-\ *n* [ML *devolution-, devolutio*, fr. L *devolutus*, pp. of *devolvere*] (1545) **1 :** transference (as of rights, powers, or responsibility) to another; *esp* **:** the surrender of powers to local authorities by a central government **2 :** retrograde evolution **:** DEGENERATION — **de·vo·lu·tion·ary** \-shə-ˌner-ē\ *adj* — **de·vo·lu·tion·ist** \-sh(ə-)nəst\ *n*

de·volve \di-ˈvälv, -ˈvȯlv *also* -ˈväv *or* -ˈvȯv\ *vb* **de·volved; de·volv·ing** [ME *devolven*, fr. L *devolvere*, fr. *de-* + *volvere* to roll — more at VOLUBLE] *vt* (15c) **:** to pass on (as rights or powers) from one person to another : HAND DOWN ~ *vi* **1 :** to pass by devolution **2 :** to degenerate through a gradual change or evolution

dev·on \ˈdev-ən\ *n, often cap* [*Devon*, England] (1834) **:** any of a breed of vigorous red dual-purpose cattle of English origin

De·vo·ni·an \di-ˈvō-nē-ən\ *adj* [*Devon*, England] (1612) **1 :** of or relating to Devonshire, England **2 :** of, relating to, or being the period of the Paleozoic era between the Silurian and the Mississippian or the corresponding system of rocks — **Devonian** *n*

Dev·on·shire cream \ˌdev-ən-ˌshi(ə)r-, -shər-\ *n* (ca. 1825) **:** CLOTTED CREAM

de·vote \di-ˈvōt\ *vt* **de·vot·ed; de·vot·ing** [L *devotus*, pp. of *devovēre*, fr. *de-* + *vovēre* to vow] (1586) **1 :** to commit by a solemn act ⟨*devoted* herself to serving God⟩ **2 :** to give over or direct (as time, money, or effort) to a cause, enterprise, or activity — **de·vote·ment** \-ˈvōt-mənt\ *n*

syn DEVOTE, DEDICATE, CONSECRATE, HALLOW mean to set apart for a special and often higher end. DEVOTE is likely to imply compelling motives and often attachment to an objective ⟨*devoted* his evenings to study⟩ ⟨*devote* money to charity⟩ DEDICATE implies solemn and exclusive devotion to a sacred or serious use or purpose ⟨we Americans are *dedicated* to improvement —Louis Kronenberger⟩ CONSECRATE stresses investment with a solemn or sacred quality ⟨*consecrate* a church to the worship of God⟩ and even in general use carries a strong connotation of intense devotion ⟨rules . . . *consecrated* by time —Edmund Burke⟩ HALLOW, often differing little from *dedicate* or *consecrate*, may distinctively imply an attribution of intrinsic sanctity ⟨the Lord blessed the sabbath day, and *hallowed* it —Exod 20:11 (AV)⟩

de·vot·ed *adj* (1600) **:** characterized by loyalty and devotion — **de·vot·ed·ly** *adv* — **de·vot·ed·ness** *n*

dev·o·tee \ˌdev-ə-ˈtē, -ˈtā; di-ˌvō-ˈtē\ *n* (1645) **:** an ardent follower, supporter, or enthusiast (as of a religion, art form, or sport)

de·vo·tion \di-ˈvō-shən\ *n* (13c) **1 a :** religious fervor : PIETY **b :** an act of prayer or private worship — usu. used in pl. **c :** a religious exercise or practice other than the regular corporate worship of a congregation **2 a :** the act of devoting **b :** the fact or state of being ardently dedicated and loyal (as to an idea or person) **3** *obs* **:** the object of one's devotion ***syn*** see FIDELITY

[1]**de·vo·tion·al** \-shnəl, -shən-ᵊl\ *adj* (1648) **:** of, relating to, or characterized by devotion — **de·vo·tion·al·ly** \-ē\ *adv*

[2]**devotional** *n* (1659) **:** a short worship service

de·vour \di-ˈvau̇(ə)r\ *vt* [ME *devouren*, fr. MF *devourer*, fr. L *devorare*, fr. *de-* + *vorare* to devour — more at VORACIOUS] (14c) **1 :** to eat up greedily or ravenously **2 :** to engulf or destroy as if by eating ⟨~*ed* by fire⟩ **3 :** to prey upon ⟨~*ed* by guilt⟩ **4 :** to enjoy avidly ⟨~*s* books⟩ — **de·vour·er** *n*

de·vout \di-ˈvau̇t\ *adj* [ME *devot*, fr. OF, fr. LL *devotus*, fr. L, pp. of *devovēre*] (13c) **1 :** devoted to religion or to religious duties or exercises **2 :** expressing devotion or piety ⟨a ~ attitude⟩ **3 :** EARNEST, SINCERE — **de·vout·ly** *adv* — **de·vout·ness** *n*

dew \ˈd(y)ü\ *n* [ME, fr. OE *dēaw*; akin to OHG *tou* dew, Gk *thein* to run] (bef. 12c) **1 :** moisture condensed upon the surfaces of cool bodies esp. at night **2 :** something resembling dew in purity, freshness, or power to refresh **3 :** moisture esp. when appearing in minute droplets: as **a :** TEARS **b :** SWEAT **c :** droplets of water produced by a plant in transpiration — **dew** *vt* — **dew·less** \-ləs\ *adj*

de·wan \di-ˈwän\ *n* [Hindi *dīwān*, fr. Per, account book] (1610) **:** an Indian official; *esp* **:** the prime minister of an Indian state

dew·ar \ˌd(y)ü-ər\ *n, often cap* [Sir James *Dewar*] (ca. 1909) **:** a glass or metal container that has an evacuated space between the walls, is often silvered on the innermost surface to prevent heat transfer, and is used esp. for storing liquefied gases — called also *Dewar flask;* compare VACUUM BOTTLE

de·wa·ter \(ˈ)dē-ˈwȯt-ər, -ˈwät-\ *vt* (ca. 1909) **:** to remove water from — **de·wa·ter·er** *n*

dew·ber·ry \ˈd(y)ü-ˌber-ē\ *n* (1578) **1 :** any of several sweet edible berries related to and resembling blackberries **2 :** a trailing or decumbent bramble (genus *Rubus*) that bears dewberries

dew·claw \ˈd(y)ü-ˌklȯ\ *n* (1576) **:** a vestigial digit not reaching to the ground on the foot of a mammal; *also* **:** a claw or hoof terminating such a digit — see COW illustration — **dew·clawed** \-ˌklȯd\ *adj*

dew·drop \ˈd(y)ü-ˌdräp\ *n* (13c) **:** a drop of dew

Dew·ey decimal classification \ˌd(y)ü-ē-\ *n* [Melvil *Dewey*] (1924) **:** a system of classifying books and other publications whereby main classes are designated by a three-digit number and subdivisions are shown by numbers after a decimal point — called also *Dewey decimal system*

dew·fall \ˈd(y)ü-ˌfȯl\ *n* (1622) **:** formation of dew; *also* **:** the time when dew begins to deposit

dew·lap \ˈd(y)ü-ˌlap\ *n* (14c) **:** loose skin hanging under the neck of various animals (as a bovine) — see COW illustration — **dew·lapped** \-ˌlapt\ *adj*

DEW line *also* **dew line** \ˈd(y)ü-\ *n* [*d*istant *e*arly *w*arning] (1953) **:** a line of radar stations across the top of North America to give advance warning of an enemy attack by aircraft or missiles from the north

de·worm \(ˈ)dē-ˈwərm\ *vt* (1926) **:** to rid (as a dog) of worms : WORM 1

dew point *n* (ca. 1833) **:** the temperature at which a vapor begins to condense

dew worm *n* (1599) **:** NIGHT CRAWLER

dewy \ˈd(y)ü-ē\ *adj* **dew·i·er; -est** (bef. 12c) **1 :** moist with, affected by, or suggestive of dew **2 :** INNOCENT, UNSOPHISTICATED ⟨from a ~ bride to an ill-mannered, murderous courtesan—Melvin Gussow⟩ — **dew·i·ly** \ˈd(y)ü-ə-lē\ *adv* — **dew·i·ness** \ˈd(y)ü-ē-nəs\ *n*

dewy–eyed \ˌd(y)ü-ē-ˈīd\ *adj* (1938) **:** naively credulous

dex \ˈdeks\ *n* (ca. 1961) **:** the sulfate of dextroamphetamine

dexa·meth·a·sone \ˌdek-sə-ˈmeth-ə-ˌsōn, -ˌzōn\ *n* [perh. fr. *Dexa*myl, a trademark + *meth*yl + *-sone* (as in *cortisone*)] (1958) **:** a synthetic adrenocortical steroid $C_{22}H_{29}FO_5$ used esp. as an anti-inflammatory agent

Dex·e·drine \ˈdek-sə-ˌdrēn, -drən\ *trademark* — used for a preparation of the sulfate of dextroamphetamine

dex·ies \ˈdek-sēz\ *n pl* [by shortening and alter. of *Dexedrine*] (1956) **:** tablets or capsules of the sulfate of dextroamphetamine

dex·ter \ˈdek-stər\ *adj* [L; akin to Gk *dexios* situated on the right, L *decēre* to be fitting — more at DECENT] (1562) **1 :** relating to or situated on the right **2 :** being or relating to the side of a heraldic shield at the right of the person bearing it — **dexter** *adv*

dex·ter·i·ty \dek-ˈster-ət-ē\ *n, pl* **-ties** [MF or L; MF *dexterité*, fr. L *dexteritat-, dexteritas*, fr. *dexter*] (1527) **1 :** mental skill or quickness : ADROITNESS **2 :** readiness and grace in physical activity; *esp* **:** skill and ease in using the hands

dex·ter·ous *or* **dex·trous** \ˈdek-st(ə-)rəs\ *adj* [L *dextr-*, *dexter* dextral, skillful] (1622) **1 :** mentally adroit and skillful : CLEVER **2 :** done with dexterity : ARTFUL **3 :** skillful and competent with the hands — **dex·ter·ous·ly** *adv* — **dex·ter·ous·ness** *n*

syn DEXTEROUS, ADROIT, DEFT mean ready and skilled in physical movement. DEXTEROUS implies expertness with consequent facility and quickness in manipulation; ADROIT implies dexterity but may also stress resourcefulness or artfulness or inventiveness; DEFT emphasizes lightness, neatness, and sureness of touch or handling.

dextr- *or* **dextro-** *comb form* [LL, fr. L *dextr-*, *dexter*] **1 :** right **:** on or toward the right ⟨*dextro*rotatory⟩ **2** *usu* **dextro-** **:** dextrorotatory ⟨*dextro*-tartaric acid⟩

dex·tral \ˈdek-strəl\ *adj* (1646) **:** of or relating to the right **:** inclined to the right: as **a :** RIGHT-HANDED 3 **b** *of a gastropod shell* **:** having the whorls coiling clockwise down the spire when viewed with the apex toward the observer and having the aperture situated on the right of the axis when held with the spire uppermost and with the aperture opening toward the observer

dex·tran \ˈdek-stran, -strən\ *n* [*dextr*ose + *-an*] (1879) **:** any of numerous polysaccharides $(C_6H_{10}O_5)_n$ that yield only glucose on hydrolysis: as **a :** any such compound of high molecular weight obtained by fermentation of sugar **b :** any such compound of reduced molecular weight obtained by acid hydrolysis of native dextran and used as a plasma substitute

dex·tran·ase \-strə-ˌnās, -ˌnāz\ *n* (ca. 1949) **:** a hydrolase that prevents tooth decay by breaking down dextran and eliminating dental plaque

dex·trin \ˈdek-strən\ *also* **dex·trine** \-ˌstrēn, -strən\ *n* [F *dextrine*, fr. *dextr-*] (1838) **:** any of various soluble gummy polysaccharides $(C_6H_{10}O_5)_n$ obtained from starch by the action of heat, acids, or enzymes and used as adhesives, as sizes for paper and textiles, and in syrups and beer

dex·tro \ˈdek-(ˌ)strō\ *adj* [*dextr-*] (ca. 1929) **:** DEXTROROTATORY

dex·tro·am·phet·amine \ˈdek-(ˌ)strō-am-ˈfet-ə-ˌmēn, -mən\ *n* (1943) **:** a compound consisting of the dextrorotatory form of amphetamine sulfate

dex·tro·ro·ta·tion \ˌdek-strə-rō-ˈtā-shən\ *n* (1882) **:** right-handed or clockwise rotation — used of the plane of polarization of light

dex·tro·ro·ta·to·ry \-ˈrōt-ə-ˌtȯr-ē, -ˌtȯr-\ *also* **dex·tro·ro·ta·ry** \-ˈrōt-ə-rē\ *adj* (1878) **:** turning clockwise or toward the right; *esp* **:** rotating the plane of polarization of light toward the right ⟨~ crystals⟩ — compare LEVOROTATORY

dex·trose \ˈdek-ˌstrōs, -ˌstrōz\ *n* (ca. 1869) **:** dextrorotatory glucose

dey \ˈdā\ *n* [F, fr. Turk *dayı*, lit., maternal uncle] (1659) **:** a ruling official of the Ottoman Empire in northern Africa

dhar·ma \ˈdər-mə, ˈdär-\ *n* [Skt; akin to L *firmus* firm] (1769) **1** *Hinduism* **:** an individual's duty fulfilled by observance of custom or law **2** *Hinduism & Buddhism* **a :** the basic principles of cosmic or individual existence : divine law **b :** conformity to one's duty and nature — **dhar·mic** \-mik\ *adj*

dhar·na \ˈdər-nə, ˈdär-\ *n* [Hindi *dharnā*, fr. Skt *dhāraṇa* support, prop; akin to L *firmus* firm] (1793) **:** a fast held at the door of an offender in India as an appeal for justice

dhole \ˈdōl\ *n* [perh. fr. Kanarese *tōla* wolf] (ca. 1827) **:** a fierce wild dog (*Cuon dukhunensis*) of India that hunts in packs

dho·ti \ˈdōt-ē\ *also* **dhoo·tie** \ˈdüt-ē\ *n* [Hindi *dhotī*] (1609) **:** a long loincloth worn by Hindu men

dhow \ˈdau̇\ *n* [Ar *dāwa*] (1802) **:** an Arab lateen-rigged boat usu. having a long overhang forward, a high poop, and a low waist
Dhu'l–Hij·ja \ˌdül-ˈhij-(ˌ)ä, ˌt͟hül-\ *n* [Ar *Dhū-l-ḥijjah,* lit., the one of the pilgrimage] (ca. 1769) **:** the 12th month of the Islamic year — see MONTH table
Dhu'l–Qa'·dah \-ˈkäd-(ˌ)ä\ *n* [Ar *Dhū-l-qa'dah,* lit., the one of the sitting] (ca. 1769) **:** the 11th month of the Islamic year — see MONTH table
dhur·rie \ˈdə-rē, ˈdər-ē\ *n* [Hindi *darī*] (1880) **:** a thick flat-woven cotton cloth or rug made in India
di- *comb form* [ME, fr. MF, fr. L, fr. Gk; akin to OE *twi-*] **1 :** twice **:** twofold **:** double ⟨*di*chromatic⟩ **2 :** containing two atoms, radicals, or groups ⟨*di*chloride⟩
dia- *also* **di-** *prefix* [ME, fr. OF, fr. L, fr. Gk, through, apart, fr. *dia;* akin to L *dis-*] **:** through ⟨*dia*positive⟩ **:** across ⟨*dia*dromous⟩
di·a·base \ˈdī-ə-ˌbās\ *n* [F, fr. Gk *diabasis* act of crossing over, fr. *diabainein* to cross over, fr. *dia-* + *bainein* to go — more at COME] (ca. 1816) **1** *archaic* **:** DIORITE **2** *chiefly Brit* **:** an altered basalt **3 :** a fine-grained rock of the composition of gabbro but with an ophitic texture — **di·a·ba·sic** \ˌdī-ə-ˈbā-sik\ *adj*
di·a·be·tes \ˌdī-ə-ˈbēt-ēz, -ˈbēt-əs\ *n* [L, fr. Gk *diabētēs,* lit., siphon, fr. *diabainein*] (15c) **:** any of various abnormal conditions characterized by the secretion and excretion of excessive amounts of urine; *esp* **:** DIABETES MELLITUS
diabetes in·sip·i·dus \-in-ˈsip-əd-əs\ *n* [NL, lit., insipid diabetes] (ca. 1860) **:** a disorder of the pituitary gland characterized by intense thirst and by the excretion of large amounts of urine
diabetes mel·li·tus \-ˈmel-ət-əs\ *n* [NL, lit., honey-sweet diabetes] (ca. 1860) **:** a familial constitutional disorder of carbohydrate metabolism characterized by inadequate secretion or utilization of insulin, by excessive urine production, by excessive amounts of sugar in the blood and urine, and by thirst, hunger, and loss of weight
1di·a·bet·ic \ˌdī-ə-ˈbet-ik\ *adj* (1799) **1 :** of, relating to, or occurring in diabetes or diabetics **2 :** affected with diabetes **3 :** suitable for diabetics ⟨~ food⟩
2diabetic *n* (1840) **:** a person affected with diabetes
dia·be·to·gen·ic \ˌdī-ə-ˌbet-ə-ˈjen-ik, -ˌbēt-\ *adj* (ca. 1903) **:** producing diabetes
di·a·ble·rie \dē-ˈäb-lə-(ˌ)rē, -ˈab-\ *n* [F, fr. OF, fr. *diable* devil, fr. LL *diabolus* — more at DEVIL] (1751) **1 :** black magic **:** SORCERY **2 a :** a representation in words or pictures of black magic or of dealings with the devil **b :** demon lore **3 :** mischievous conduct or manner
diabol- *or* **diabolo-** *comb form* [ME *deabol-,* fr. MF *diabol-,* fr. LL, fr. Gk, fr. *diabolos* — more at DEVIL] **:** devil ⟨*diabol*ism⟩
di·a·bol·ic \ˌdī-ə-ˈbäl-ik\ *or* **di·a·bol·i·cal** \-ˈbäl-i-kəl\ *adj* [ME *deabolik,* fr. MF *diabolique,* fr. LL *diabolicus,* fr. *diabolus*] (14c) **:** of, relating to, or characteristic of the devil **:** DEVILISH — **di·a·bol·i·cal·ly** \-i-k(ə-)lē\ *adv* — **di·a·bol·i·cal·ness** \-i-kəl-nəs\ *n*
di·ab·o·lism \dī-ˈab-ə-ˌliz-əm\ *n* (1614) **1 :** dealings with or possession by the devil **2 :** belief in or worship of devils **3 :** evil character or conduct — **di·ab·o·list** \-ləst\ *n*
di·ab·o·lize \-ˌlīz\ *vt* **-lized; -liz·ing** (1702) **:** to represent as or make diabolic
dia·chron·ic \ˌdī-ə-ˈkrän-ik\ *adj* (1857) **:** of, relating to, or dealing with phenomena esp. of language as they occur or change over a period of time — **dia·chron·i·cal·ly** \-ˈkrän-i-k(ə-)lē\ *adv* — **dia·chron·ic·ness** \-ik-nəs\ *n*
di·ach·ro·ny \dī-ˈak-rə-nē\ *n* [ISV *dia-* + *-chrony* (as in *synchrony*)] (ca. 1939) **1 :** diachronic analysis **2 :** change extending through time
1di·ac·id \(ˈ)dī-ˈas-əd\ *or* **di·acid·ic** \ˌdī-ə-ˈsid-ik\ *adj* (1866) **1 :** able to react with two molecules of a monobasic acid or one of a dibasic acid to form a salt or ester — used esp. of bases **2 :** containing two replaceable hydrogen atoms — used esp. of acid salts
2diacid *n* [ISV] (ca. 1923) **:** an acid with two acid hydrogen atoms
di·ac·o·nal \dī-ˈak-ən-ᵊl, dē-\ *adj* [LL *diaconalis,* fr. *diaconus* deacon — more at DEACON] (ca. 1611) **:** of or relating to a deacon or deaconess
di·ac·o·nate \-ˈak-ə-nət, -ˌnāt\ *n* (ca. 1727) **1 :** the office or period of office of a deacon or deaconess **2 :** an official body of deacons
di·a·crit·ic \ˌdī-ə-ˈkrit-ik\ *n* (1866) **:** an accent near or through an orthographic or phonetic character or combination of characters indicating a phonetic value different from that given the unmarked or otherwise marked element

DIACRITICS

´	(é)	acute accent	˘	(ŭ)	breve
`	(è)	grave accent	ˇ	(č)	haček
ˆ	(ô) *or* ˜ *or* ~	circumflex	¨	(oö)	diaeresis
˜	(ñ)	tilde	¸	(ç)	cedilla
¯	(ō)	macron			

di·a·crit·i·cal \ˌdī-ə-ˈkrit-i-kəl\ *also* **di·a·crit·ic** \-ˈkrit-ik\ *adj* [Gk *diakritikos* separative, fr. *diakrinein* to distinguish, fr. *dia-* + *krinein* to separate — more at CERTAIN] (1749) **1 :** serving as a diacritic **2 a :** DISTINCTIVE ⟨the ~ elements in culture — S. F. Nadel⟩ **b :** capable of distinguishing ⟨students of superior ~ powers⟩
di·adel·phous \ˌdī-ə-ˈdel-fəs\ *adj* [*di-* + *-adelphous*] (1807) **:** united by filaments into two fascicles — used of stamens
di·a·dem \ˈdī-ə-ˌdem, -əd-əm\ *n* [ME *diademe,* fr. OF, fr. L *diadema,* fr. Gk *diadēma,* fr. *diadein* to bind around, fr. *dia-* + *dein* to bind; akin to Skt *dāman* rope] (13c) **1 :** CROWN; *specif* **:** a royal headband **2 :** regal power or dignity
di·ad·ro·mous \dī-ˈad-rə-məs\ *adj, of a fish* (ca. 1949) **:** migratory between salt and fresh waters
di·aer·e·sis \dī-ˈer-ə-səs, *Brit also* -ˈir-\ *n, pl* **-e·ses** \-ˌsēz\ [LL *diaeresis,* fr. Gk *diairesis,* fr. *diairein* to divide, fr. *dia-* + *hairein* to take] (1611) **1 :** a mark ¨ placed over a vowel to indicate that the vowel is pronounced in a separate syllable (as in *naïve* or *Brontë*) **2 :** the break in a verse caused by the coincidence of the end of a foot with the end of a word — **di·ae·ret·ic** \ˌdī-ə-ˈret-ik\ *adj*
dia·gen·e·sis \ˌdī-ə-ˈjen-ə-səs\ *n* [NL] (ca. 1886) **1 :** recombination or rearrangement of constituents (as of a chemical or mineral) resulting in a new product **2 :** the conversion (as by compaction or chemical reaction) of sediment into rock — **dia·ge·net·ic** \ˌdī-ə-jə-ˈnet-ik\ *adj* — **dia·ge·net·i·cal·ly** \-ˈnet-i-k(ə-)lē\ *adv*
dia·geo·tro·pic \ˌdī-ə-ˌjē-ə-ˈtrō-pik, -ˈträp-ik\ *adj* (1880) **:** tending to grow at right angles to the line of gravity ⟨~ branches and roots⟩ — **dia·ge·ot·ro·pism** \-jē-ˈä-trə-ˌpiz-əm\ *n*
di·ag·nose \ˈdī-ig-ˌnōs, -ˌnōz, ˌdī-ig-ˈ, -əg-\ *vb* **-nosed; -nos·ing** [back-formation fr. *diagnosis*] *vt* (ca. 1859) **1 :** to recognize (as a disease) by signs and symptoms **2 :** to analyze the cause or nature of ⟨~ the problem⟩ ~ *vi* **:** to make a diagnosis — **di·ag·nos·able** *or* **di·ag·nose·able** \ˌdī-ig-ˈnō-sə-bəl, -əg-, -zə-\ *adj*
di·ag·no·sis \ˌdī-ig-ˈnō-səs, -əg-\ *n, pl* **-no·ses** \-ˌsēz\ [NL, fr. Gk *diagnōsis,* fr. *diagignōskein* to distinguish, fr. *dia-* + *gignōskein* to know — more at KNOW] (ca. 1681) **1 a :** the art or act of identifying a disease from its signs and symptoms **b :** the decision reached by diagnosis **2 :** a concise technical description of a taxon **3 a :** investigation or analysis of the cause or nature of a condition, situation, or problem ⟨~ of engine trouble⟩ **b :** a statement or conclusion from such an analysis
1di·ag·nos·tic \-ˈnäs-tik\ *also* **di·ag·nos·ti·cal** \-ti-kəl\ *adj* (1625) **1 :** of, relating to, or used in diagnosis **2 :** using the methods of or yielding a diagnosis ⟨a ~ service⟩ ⟨~ properties⟩ — **di·ag·nos·ti·cal·ly** \-ti-k(ə-)lē\ *adv*
2diagnostic *n* (1625) **1 :** the art or practice of diagnosis — often used in pl. **2 :** a distinguishing mark — **di·ag·nos·ti·cian** \-(ˌ)näs-ˈtish-ən\ *n*
1di·ag·o·nal \dī-ˈag-ən-ᵊl, -ˈag-nəl\ *adj* [L *diagonalis,* fr. Gk *diagōnios* from angle to angle, fr. *dia-* + *gōnia* angle; akin to Gk *gony* knee — more at KNEE] (1563) **1 a :** joining two vertices of a rectilinear figure that are nonadjacent or two vertices of a polyhedral figure that are not in the same face **b :** passing through two nonadjacent edges of a polyhedron ⟨a ~ plane⟩ **2 a :** inclined obliquely from a reference line (as the vertical) ⟨wood with a ~ grain⟩ **b :** having diagonal markings or parts ⟨a ~ weave⟩
2diagonal *n* (1571) **1 :** a diagonal straight line or plane **2 a (1) :** a diagonal direction **(2) :** a diagonal row, arrangement, or pattern **b :** something oriented in diagonal position **3 :** a mark / used typically to denote "or" (as in *and/or*), "and or" (as in *straggler/deserter*), or "per" (as in *feet/second*) — called also *solidus, virgule* — **on the diagonal :** in an oblique direction **:** DIAGONALLY
di·ag·o·nal·ize \-ˌīz\ *vt* **-ized; -iz·ing** (1942) **:** to put (a matrix) in a form with all the nonzero elements along the diagonal from upper left to lower right — **di·ag·o·nal·iz·able** \-ˌī-zə-bəl\ *adj* — **di·ag·o·nal·iza·tion** \-ˌag-ən-ᵊl-ə-ˈzā-shən, -ˌag-nə-lə-ˈzā-\ *n*
di·ag·o·nal·ly \dī-ˈag-ən-ᵊl-ē, -ˈag-nə-lē\ *adv* (1541) **:** in a diagonal manner
diagonal matrix *n* (ca. 1928) **:** a matrix that has all the nonzero elements located along the diagonal from upper left to lower right
1di·a·gram \ˈdī-ə-ˌgram\ *n* [Gk *diagramma,* fr. *diagraphein* to mark out by lines, fr. *dia-* + *graphein* to write — more at CARVE] (1619) **1 :** a graphic design that explains rather than represents; *esp* **:** a drawing that shows arrangement and relations (as of parts) **2 :** a line drawing made for mathematical or scientific purposes — **di·a·gram·ma·ble** \-ˌgram-ə-bəl\ *adj* — **di·a·gram·mat·ic** \ˌdī-ə-grə-ˈmat-ik\ *also* **di·a·gram·mat·i·cal** \-ˈmat-i-kəl\ *adj* — **di·a·gram·mat·i·cal·ly** \-i-k(ə-)lē\ *adv*
2diagram *vt* **-gramed** \-ˌgramd\ *or* **-grammed; -gram·ing** \-ˌgram-iŋ\ *or* **-gram·ming** (1840) **:** to represent by or put into the form of a diagram
dia·ki·ne·sis \ˌdī-ə-kə-ˈnē-səs, -(ˌ)kī-\ *n, pl* **-ne·ses** \-ˌsēz\ [NL, fr. *dia-* + Gk *kinēsis* motion, fr. *kinein* to move — more at HIGHT] (ca. 1902) **:** the final stage of the meiotic prophase marked by contraction of the bivalents
1di·al \ˈdī(-ə)l\ *n* [ME *dyal,* fr. (assumed) ML *dialis,* fr. L *dies* day — more at DEITY] (15c) **1 :** the face of a sundial **2** *obs* **:** TIMEPIECE **3 :** the graduated face of a timepiece **4 a :** a face upon which some measurement is registered usu. by means of graduations and a pointer ⟨the thermometer ~ reads 70°F⟩ **b :** a device (as a disk) that may be operated to make electrical connections or to regulate the operation of a machine and that usu. has guiding marks around its border ⟨a radio ~⟩ ⟨a telephone ~⟩
2dial *vb* **di·aled** *or* **di·alled; di·al·ing** *or* **di·al·ling** *vt* (1821) **1 :** to measure with a dial **2 :** to manipulate a device (as a dial) so as to operate, regulate, or select ⟨~ your favorite program⟩ ⟨~*ed* the wrong number⟩ ~ *vi* **1 :** to manipulate a dial **2 :** to make a telephone call or connection — **di·al·er** *n*
di·a·lect \ˈdī-ə-ˌlekt\ *n, often attrib* [MF *dialecte,* fr. L *dialectus,* fr. Gk *dialektos* conversation, dialect, fr. *dialegesthai* to converse — more at DIALOGUE] (1577) **1 a :** a regional variety of language distinguished by features of vocabulary, grammar, and pronunciation from other regional varieties and constituting together with them a single language of which no one variety is construed as standard ⟨the Doric ~ of ancient Greek⟩ **b :** one of two or more cognate languages ⟨French and Italian are Romance ~*s*⟩ **c :** a regional variety of a language usu. transmitted orally and differing distinctively from the standard language ⟨the Lancashire ~ of English⟩ **d :** a variety of a language used by the members of an occupational group ⟨the ~ of the atomic physicist⟩ **e :** a variety of language whose identity is fixed by a factor other than geography (as social class or educational level of its habitual users) ⟨spoke a rough peasant ~⟩ **2 :** manner or means of expressing oneself **:** PHRASEOLOGY — **di·a·lec·tal** \ˌdī-ə-ˈlek-tᵊl\ *adj* — **di·a·lec·tal·ly** \-tᵊl-ē\ *adv*
dialect atlas *n* (1932) **:** LINGUISTIC ATLAS
dialect geography *n* (1929) **:** LINGUISTIC GEOGRAPHY
di·a·lec·tic \ˌdī-ə-ˈlek-tik\ *n* [ME *dialetik,* fr. MF *dialetique,* fr. L *dialectica,* fr. Gk *dialektikē,* fr. fem. of *dialektikos* of conversation, fr. *dialektos*] (14c) **1 :** LOGIC 1a(1) **2 a :** discussion and reasoning by dialogue as a method of intellectual investigation; *specif* **:** the Socratic tech-

\ə\ abut \ᵊ\ kitten, F table \ər\ further \a\ ash \ā\ ace \ä\ cot, cart \au̇\ out \ch\ chin \e\ bet \ē\ easy \g\ go \i\ hit \ī\ ice \j\ job \ŋ\ sing \ō\ go \ȯ\ law \ȯi\ boy \th\ thin \t͟h\ the \ü\ loot \u̇\ foot \y\ yet \zh\ vision \á, k̲, ⁿ, œ, œ̄, ue, ue̅, ʸ\ *see* Guide to Pronunciation

niques of exposing false beliefs and eliciting truth **b :** the Platonic investigation of the eternal ideas **3 :** the logic of fallacy **4 a :** the Hegelian process of change in which a concept or its realization passes over into and is preserved and fulfilled by its opposite; *also* **:** the critical investigation of this process **b** (1) *usu pl but sing or pl in constr* **:** development through the stages of thesis, antithesis, and synthesis in accordance with the laws of dialectical materialism (2) **:** the investigation of this process (3) **:** the theoretical application of this process esp. in the social sciences **5** *usu pl but sing or pl in constr* **a :** any systematic reasoning, exposition, or argument that juxtaposes opposed or contradictory ideas and usu. seeks to resolve their conflict **b :** an intellectual exchange of ideas **6 :** the dialectical tension or opposition between two interacting forces or elements

di·a·lec·ti·cal \ˌdī-ə-ˈlek-ti-kəl\ *also* **di·a·lec·tic** \-tik\ *adj* (1548) **1 a :** of, relating to, or in accordance with dialectic ⟨~ method⟩ **b :** practicing, devoted to, or employing dialectic ⟨a ~ philosopher⟩ **2 :** of, relating to, or characteristic of a dialect — **di·a·lec·ti·cal·ly** \-ti-k(ə-)lē\ *adv*

dialectical materialism *n* (1927) **:** the Marxian theory that maintains the material basis of a reality constantly changing in a dialectical process and the priority of matter over mind — compare HISTORICAL MATERIALISM

di·a·lec·ti·cian \ˌdī-ə-ˌlek-ˈtish-ən\ *n* (1693) **1 :** one who is skilled in or practices dialectic **2 :** a student of dialects

di·a·lec·tol·o·gist \-ˈtäl-ə-jəst\ *n* (1883) **:** a specialist in dialectology

di·a·lec·tol·o·gy \-jē\ *n* [ISV] (ca. 1864) **1 :** the systematic study of dialect **2 :** the body of data available for study of a dialect — **di·a·lec·to·log·i·cal** \-ˌlek-tə-ˈläj-i-kəl\ *adj* — **di·a·lec·to·log·i·cal·ly** \-k(ə-)lē\ *adv*

di·al·lel \ˈdī-ə-ˌlel\ *adj* [Gk *allēlōn* reciprocating, confused] (ca. 1920) **:** relating to or being the crossing of each of several individuals with two or more others in order to determine the relative genetic contribution of each parent to specific characters in the offspring

di·a·log·ic \ˌdī-ə-ˈläj-ik\ *or* **di·a·log·i·cal** \-i-kəl\ *adj* (1833) **:** of, relating to, or characterized by dialogue ⟨~ writing⟩ — **di·a·log·i·cal·ly** \-i-k(ə-)lē\ *adv*

di·a·lo·gist \dī-ˈal-ə-jəst; ˈdī-ə-ˌlȯg-əst, -ˌläg-\ *n* (1660) **1 :** a writer of dialogues **2 :** one who participates in a dialogue — **di·a·lo·gis·tic** \(ˌ)dī-ˌal-ə-ˈjis-tik; ˌdī-ə-ˌlȯ-ˈgis-, -ˌlä-ˈgis-\ *adj*

1di·a·logue *also* **di·a·log** \ˈdī-ə-ˌlȯg, -ˌläg\ *n* [ME *dialoge*, fr. OF *dialogue*, fr. L *dialogus*, fr. Gk *dialogos*, fr. *dialegesthai* to converse, fr. *dia-* + *legein* to speak — more at LEGEND] (13c) **1 :** a written composition in which two or more characters are represented as conversing **2 a :** a conversation between two or more persons; *also* **:** a similar exchange between a person and something else (as a computer) **b :** an exchange of ideas and opinions **3 :** the conversational element of literary or dramatic composition **4 :** a musical composition for two or more parts suggestive of a conversation

2dialogue *vb* **-logued; -logu·ing** *vt* (1597) **:** to express in dialogue ~ *vi* **:** to take part in a dialogue

dial tone *n* (1923) **:** a tone emitted by a telephone as a signal that the system is ready for dialing

di·al·y·sate \dī-ˈal-ə-ˌzāt, -ˌsāt\ *or* **di·al·y·zate** \-ˌzāt\ *n* [*dialysis* or *dialyze* + *-ate*] (ca. 1867) **:** the material that passes through the membrane in dialysis; *also* **:** the liquid into which this material passes

di·al·y·sis \dī-ˈal-ə-səs\ *n, pl* **-y·ses** \-ˌsēz\ [NL, fr. Gk, separation, fr. *dialyein* to dissolve, fr. *dia-* + *lyein* to loosen — more at LOSE] (1861) **:** the separation of substances in solution by means of their unequal diffusion through semipermeable membranes; *esp* **:** such a separation of colloids from soluble substances — **di·a·lyt·ic** \ˌdī-ə-ˈlit-ik\ *adj*

di·a·lyze \ˈdī-ə-ˌlīz\ *vb* **-lyzed; -lyz·ing** *vt* (1861) **:** to subject to dialysis ~ *vi* **:** to undergo dialysis — **di·a·lyz·able** \-ˌlī-zə-bəl\ *adj* — **di·a·lyz·er** \-ˌlī-zər\ *n*

dia·mag·net \ˈdī-ə-ˌmag-nət\ *or* **dia·mag·net·ic** \ˌdī-ə-mag-ˈnet-ik\ *n* [*diamagnet* back-formation fr. *diamagnetic*, adj.] (ca. 1864) **:** a diamagnetic substance

diamagnetic *adj* (1846) **:** having a magnetic permeability less than that of a vacuum **:** slightly repelled by a magnet — **dia·mag·ne·tism** \-ˈmag-nə-ˌtiz-əm\ *n*

di·a·man·té \ˌdē-ə-ˌmän-ˈtā\ *n* [F, adj., like a diamond, fr. *diamant* diamond, fr. MF — more at DIAMOND] (1904) **:** a sparkling decoration (as of sequins) or material decorated with this ⟨a gown trimmed with ~⟩

di·am·e·ter \dī-ˈam-ət-ər\ *n* [ME *diametre*, fr. MF, fr. L *diametros*, fr. Gk, fr. *dia-* + *metron* measure — more at MEASURE] (14c) **1 :** a chord passing through the center of a figure or body **2 :** the length of a straight line through the center of an object **3 :** a unit of magnification of observations with a magnifying device equal to the number of times the linear dimensions of the object are increased ⟨a microscope magnifying 60 ~*s*⟩ — **di·am·e·tral** \-ˈam-ə-trəl\ *adj*

di·a·met·ric \ˌdī-ə-ˈme-trik\ *or* **di·a·met·ri·cal** \-tri-kəl\ *adj* (1553) **1 :** of, relating to, or constituting a diameter **:** located at the diameter **2 :** completely opposed **:** being at opposite extremes ⟨in ~ contradiction to his claims⟩ — **di·a·met·ri·cal·ly** \-tri-k(ə-)lē\ *adv*

di·amide \ˈdī-ə-ˌmīd, dī-ˈam-əd\ *n* (1866) **:** a compound containing two amido groups

di·amine \ˈdī-ə-ˌmēn, dī-ˈam-ən\ *n* [ISV] (1866) **:** a compound containing two amino groups

1di·a·mond \ˈdī-(ə-)mənd\ *n, often attrib* [ME *diamaunde*, fr. MF *diamant*, fr. OF, fr. LL *diamant-, diamas*, alter. of L *adamant-, adamas* hardest metal, diamond, fr. Gk] (14c) **1 a :** native crystalline carbon that is usu. nearly colorless, that when transparent and free from flaws is highly valued as a precious stone, and that is used industrially as an abrasive powder and in rock drills because of its great hardness; *also* **:** a piece of this substance **b :** crystallized carbon produced artificially **2 :** something that resembles a diamond (as in brilliance, value, or fine quality) **3 :** a square or rhombus-shaped figure usu. oriented with the long diagonal vertical **4 a :** a red diamond-shaped mark impressed on a playing card; *also* **:** a card so marked **b** *pl but sing or pl in constr* **:** the suit comprising cards so marked **5 :** a baseball infield; *also* **:** the entire playing field

2diamond *vt* (1751) **:** to adorn with or as if with diamonds

di·a·mond·back \ˈdī-(ə-)mən(d)-ˌbak\ *adj* (1891) **:** having marks like diamonds or lozenges on the back

diamondback rattlesnake *n* (1907) **:** a large and deadly rattlesnake (*Crotalus adamanteus*) of the southern U.S. — called also *diamondback, diamondback rattler*

diamondback terrapin *n* (1819) **:** any of several edible terrapins (genus *Malaclemys*) formerly widely distributed in salt marshes along the Atlantic and Gulf coasts but now much restricted

di·a·mond·if·er·ous \ˌdī-(ə-)mən-ˈdif-(ə-)rəs\ *adj* (1870) **:** yielding diamonds ⟨~ earth⟩

diamond in the rough (1853) **:** a person of exceptional qualities or potential but lacking refinement or polish

Di·ana \dī-ˈan-ə\ *n* [L] **:** an ancient Italian goddess of the forest and of childbirth who was identified with Artemis by the Romans

di·an·thus \dī-ˈan(t)-thəs\ *n* [NL, genus name, fr. Gk *dios* heavenly + *anthos* flower — more at DEITY, ANTHOLOGY] (1869) **:** 2PINK 1

di·a·pa·son \ˌdī-ə-ˈpāz-ᵊn, -ˈpās-\ *n* [ME, fr. L, fr. Gk (*hē*) *dia pasōn* (*chordōn symphōnia*), lit., the concord through all the notes, fr. *dia* through + *pasōn*, gen. fem. pl. of *pas* all — more at DIA-, PAN-] (1501) **1 a** (1) **:** a burst of harmonious sound (2) **:** a full deep outburst of sound **b :** the principal foundation stop in the organ extending through the complete range of the instrument **c** (1) **:** the entire compass of musical tones (2) **:** RANGE, SCOPE ⟨the vast ~ of his poetic talent⟩ **2 a :** TUNING FORK **b :** a standard of pitch

dia·pause \ˈdī-ə-ˌpȯz\ *n* [Gk *diapausis* pause, fr. *diapauein* to pause, fr. *dia-* + *pauein* to stop — more at PAUSE] (1893) **:** a period of physiologically enforced dormancy (as developmental arrest in an insect) between periods of activity

dia·paus·ing \-ˌpȯ-ziŋ\ *adj* (1944) **:** undergoing diapause

di·a·pe·de·sis \ˌdī-ə-pə-ˈdē-səs\ *n, pl* **-de·ses** \-ˌsēz\ [NL, fr. Gk *diapēdēsis* act of oozing through, fr. *diapēdan* to ooze through, fr. *dia-* + *pēdan* to leap] (1625) **:** the passage of blood cells through capillary walls into the tissues

1di·a·per \ˈdī(-ə)-pər\ *n* [ME *diapre*, fr. MF, fr. ML *diasprum*] (14c) **1 :** a fabric with a distinctive pattern: **a :** a rich silk fabric **b :** a soft usu. white linen or cotton fabric used for tablecloths or towels **2 :** an allover pattern consisting of one or more small repeated units of design (as geometric figures) connecting with one another or growing out of one another with continuously flowing or straight lines **3 :** a basic garment for infants consisting of a folded cloth or other absorbent material drawn up between the legs and fastened about the waist

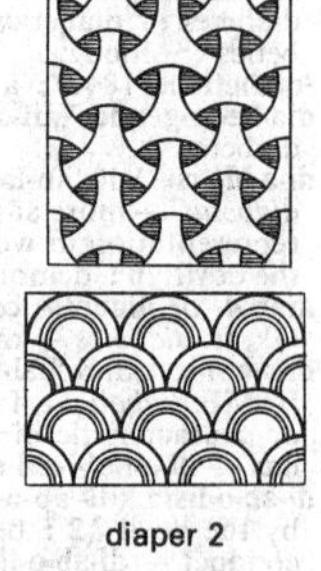
diaper 2

2diaper *vt* **di·a·pered; di·a·per·ing** \-p(ə-)riŋ\ (14c) **1 :** to ornament with diaper designs **2 :** to put on or change the diaper of (an infant)

di·a·pha·ne·ity \(ˌ)dī-ˌaf-ə-ˈnē-ət-ē, ˌdī-ə-fə-, -ˈnā-\ *n* (15c) **:** the quality or state of being diaphanous

di·aph·a·nous \dī-ˈaf-ə-nəs\ *adj* [ML *diaphanus*, fr. Gk *diaphanēs*, fr. *diaphainein* to show through, fr. *dia-* + *phainein* to show — more at FANCY] (1614) **1 :** characterized by such fineness of texture as to permit seeing through **2 :** characterized by extreme delicacy of form **:** ETHEREAL ⟨painted ~ landscapes⟩ **3 :** INSUBSTANTIAL, VAGUE ⟨had only a ~ hope of success⟩ — **di·aph·a·nous·ly** *adv* — **di·aph·a·nous·ness** *n*

dia·phone \ˈdī-ə-ˌfōn\ *n* (1906) **:** a fog signal similar to a siren but producing a blast of two tones

di·aph·o·rase \dī-ˈaf-ə-ˌrās, -ˌrāz\ *n* [Gk *diaphoros* different + E *-ase*] (1938) **:** a flavoprotein enzyme capable of oxidizing the reduced form of NAD

di·a·pho·re·sis \ˌdī-ə-fə-ˈrē-səs, (ˌ)dī-ˌaf-ə-\ *n, pl* **-re·ses** \-ˌsēz\ [LL, fr. Gk *diaphorēsis*, fr. *diaphorein* to dissipate by perspiration, fr. *dia-* + *pherein* to carry — more at BEAR] (ca. 1681) **:** PERSPIRATION; *esp* **:** profuse perspiration artificially induced

di·a·pho·ret·ic \-ˈret-ik\ *adj* (15c) **:** having the power to increase perspiration — **diaphoretic** *n*

1di·a·phragm \ˈdī-ə-ˌfram\ *n* [ME *diafragma*, fr. LL *diaphragma*, fr. Gk, fr. *diaphrassein* to barricade, fr. *dia-* + *phrassein* to enclose — more at FARCE] (14c) **1 :** a body partition of muscle and connective tissue; *specif* **:** the partition separating the chest and abdominal cavities in mammals **2 :** a dividing membrane or thin partition esp. in a tube **3 a :** a more or less rigid partition in the body or shell of an invertebrate **b :** a transverse septum in a plant stem **4 :** a device that limits the aperture of a lens or optical system — compare IRIS DIAPHRAGM **5 :** a thin flexible disk that vibrates (as in a microphone) **6 :** a molded cap usu. of thin rubber fitted over the uterine cervix to act as a mechanical contraceptive barrier — **di·a·phrag·mat·ic** \ˌdī-ə-frə(g)-ˈmat-ik, -ˌfrag-\ *adj* — **di·a·phrag·mat·i·cal·ly** \-ˈmat-i-k(ə-)lē\ *adv*

2diaphragm *vt* (1879) **1 :** to cut down the aperture of (as a lens) by a diaphragm **2 :** to equip with a diaphragm

di·aph·y·sis \dī-ˈaf-ə-səs\ *n, pl* **-y·ses** \-ˌsēz\ [NL, fr. Gk, spinous process of the tibia, fr. *diaphyesthai* to grow between, fr. *dia-* + *phyein* to bring forth — more at BE] (1831) **:** the shaft of a long bone — **di·aph·y·se·al** \(ˌ)dī-ˌaf-ə-ˈsē-əl\ *or* **di·a·phys·i·al** \ˌdī-ə-ˈfiz-ē-əl\ *adj*

di·a·pir \ˈdī-ə-ˌpi(ə)r\ *n* [Gk *diapeirein* to drive through, fr. *dia-* + *peirein* to pierce; akin to Gk *poros* passage — more at FARE] (ca. 1918) **:** an anticlinal fold in which a mobile core has broken through brittle overlying rocks — **di·a·pir·ic** \ˌdī-ə-ˈpir-ik\ *adj*

dia·pos·i·tive \ˌdī-ə-ˈpäz-ət-iv, -ˈpäz-tiv\ *n* (1893) **:** a transparent photographic positive (as a transparency)

di·ap·sid \dī-ˈap-səd\ *adj* [deriv. of Gk *di-* + *hapsid-, hapsis* arch — more at APSIS] (ca. 1909) **:** of, relating to, or including reptiles (as the crocodiles) with two pairs of temporal openings in the skull

di·ar·chy *var of* DYARCHY

di·a·rist \ˈdī-ə-rəst\ *n* (ca. 1818) **:** one who keeps a diary

di·ar·rhea *or* **di·ar·rhoea** \ˌdī-ə-ˈrē-ə\ *n* [ME *diaria*, fr. LL *diarrhoea*, fr. Gk *diarrhoia*, fr. *diarrhein* to flow through, fr. *dia-* + *rhein* to flow — more at STREAM] (14c) **:** abnormally frequent intestinal evacuations with more or less fluid stools — **di·ar·rhe·ic** \-ˈrē-ik\ *or* **di·ar·rhe·al** \-ˈrē-əl\ *also* **di·ar·rhet·ic** \-ˈret-ik\ *adj*

di·ar·thro·sis \ˌdī-är-ˈthrō-səs\ *n, pl* **-thro·ses** \-ˌsēz\ [NL, fr. Gk *diarthrōsis*, fr. *diarthroun* to joint, fr. *dia-* + *arthroun* to fasten by a joint, fr. *arthron* joint — more at ARTHR-] (1578) **1 :** articulation that permits free movement **2 :** a freely movable joint

di·a·ry \'dī-(ə-)rē\ *n, pl* **-ries** [L *diarium,* fr. *dies* day — more at DEITY] (1581) **1 :** a record of events, transactions, or observations kept daily or at frequent intervals : JOURNAL; *esp* : a daily record of personal activities, reflections, or feelings **2 :** a book intended or used for a diary

di·as·po·ra \dī-'as-p(ə-)rə\ *n* [Gk, dispersion, fr. *diaspeirein* to scatter, fr. *dia-* + *speirein* to sow — more at SPROUT] (1881) **1** *cap* **a :** the settling of scattered colonies of Jews outside Palestine after the Babylonian exile **b :** the area outside Palestine settled by Jews **c :** the Jews living outside Palestine or modern Israel **2 :** MIGRATION ⟨the great black ~ to the cities of the North and West in the 1940s and 1950s — *Newsweek*⟩ **3 :** people settled far from their ancestral homelands ⟨African ~⟩

di·a·spore \'dī-ə-,spō(ə)r, -,spȯ(ə)r\ *n* [F, fr. Gk *diaspora*] (1805) **:** a mineral consisting of aluminum hydrogen oxide $HAlO_2$

di·a·stase \'dī-ə-,stās, -,stāz\ *n* [F, fr. Gk *diastasis* separation, interval, fr. *diistanai* to separate, fr. *dia-* + *histanai* to cause to stand — more at STAND] (1838) **1 :** AMYLASE; *esp* : a mixture of amylases from malt **2 :** ENZYME

di·a·stat·ic \,dī-ə-'stat-ik\ *adj* (1881) **:** relating to or having the properties of diastase; *esp* : converting starch into sugar

di·a·ste·ma \,dī-ə-'stē-mə\ *n, pl* **-ma·ta** \-mət-ə\ [NL, fr. LL, interval, fr. Gk *diastēma,* fr. *diistanai*] (1854) **:** a space between teeth in a jaw

di·a·ste·reo·iso·mer \,dī-ə-,ster-ē-ō-'ī-sə-mər, -,stir-\ *or* **di·a·ste·reo·mer** \-'ster-ē-ō-(,)mər, -'stir-\ *n* (1936) **:** a stereoisomer that is not a mirror image of another stereoisomer of the same compound — compare ENANTIOMORPH — **di·a·ste·reo·iso·mer·ic** \-'ster-ē-ō-,ī-sə-'mer-ik, -'stir-\ *adj* — **di·a·ste·reo·isom·er·ism** \-ī-'säm-ə-,riz-əm\ *n*

di·as·to·le \dī-'as-tə-(,)lē\ *n* [Gk *diastolē* dilatation, fr. *diastellein* to expand, fr. *dia-* + *stellein* to send — more at STALL] (1578) **:** a rhythmically recurrent expansion; *esp* : the dilatation of the cavities of the heart during which they fill with blood — **di·a·stol·ic** \,dī-ə-'stäl-ik\ *adj*

di·as·tro·phism \dī-'as-trə-,fiz-əm\ *n* [Gk *diastrophē* twisting, fr. *diastrephein* to distort, fr. *dia-* + *strephein* to twist — more at STROPHE] (1890) **:** the process of deformation that produces in the earth's crust its continents and ocean basins, plateaus and mountains, folds of strata, and faults — **di·a·stroph·ic** \,dī-ə-'sträf-ik\ *adj* — **di·a·stroph·i·cal·ly** \-i-k(ə-)lē\ *adv*

di·a·tes·sa·ron \,dī-ə-'tes-ə-rən\ *n* [ME, fr. L, fr. Gk (*hē*) *dia tessarōn* (*chordōn symphōnia*), lit., the concord through four notes, fr. *dia* through + *tessarōn,* gen. of *tessares* four — more at DIA-, FOUR] (1803) **:** a harmony of the four Gospels edited and arranged into a single connected narrative

dia·ther·ma·nous \,dī-ə-'thər-mə-nəs\ *adj* [Gk *diatherman-,* stem of *diathermainein* to heat through, fr. *dia-* + *thermainein* to heat, fr. *thermos* warm, hot — more at WARM] (1834) **:** DIATHERMIC 1

dia·ther·mic \,dī-ə-'thər-mik\ *adj* (1840) **1 :** transmitting infrared radiation **2 :** of or relating to diathermy ⟨~ treatment⟩

dia·ther·my \'dī-ə-,thər-mē\ *n* [ISV] (1909) **:** the generation of heat in tissue by electric currents for medical or surgical purposes

di·ath·e·sis \dī-'ath-ə-səs\ *n, pl* **-e·ses** \-,sēz\ [NL, fr. Gk, lit., arrangement, fr. *diatithenai* to arrange, fr. *dia-* + *tithenai* to set — more at DO] (ca. 1681) **:** a constitutional predisposition toward a particular state or condition and esp. one that is abnormal or diseased — **di·a·thet·ic** \,dī-ə-'thet-ik\ *adj*

di·a·tom \'dī-ə-,täm\ *n* [deriv. of Gk *diatomos* cut in half, fr. *diatemnein* to cut through, fr. *dia-* + *temnein* to cut — more at TOME] (1845) **:** any of a class (Bacillariophyceae) of minute planktonic unicellular or colonial algae with silicified skeletons that form diatomite

di·a·to·ma·ceous \,dī-ət-ə-'mā-shəs, (,)dī-,at-\ *adj* (1847) **:** consisting of or abounding in diatoms or their siliceous remains ⟨~ silica⟩

diatomaceous earth *n* (1883) **:** DIATOMITE

di·atom·ic \,dī-ə-'täm-ik\ *adj* [ISV] (1869) **:** consisting of two atoms **:** having two atoms in the molecule

di·at·o·mite \dī-'at-ə-,mīt\ *n* (1887) **:** a light friable siliceous material derived chiefly from diatom remains and used esp. as a filter

dia·ton·ic \,dī-ə-'tän-ik\ *adj* [LL *diatonicus,* fr. Gk *diatonikos,* fr. *diatonos* stretching, fr. *diateinein* to stretch out, fr. *dia-* + *teinein* to stretch — more at THIN] (1694) **:** of or relating to a major or minor musical scale having five tones and two semitones — **dia·ton·i·cal·ly** \-'tän-i-k(ə-)lē\ *adv*

di·a·tribe \'dī-ə-,trīb\ *n* [L *diatriba,* fr. Gk *diatribē* pastime, discourse, fr. *diatribein* to spend (time), wear away, fr. *dia-* + *tribein* to rub — more at THROW] (1581) **1** *archaic* **:** a prolonged discourse **2 :** a bitter and abusive speech or writing **3 :** ironical or satirical criticism

di·az·e·pam \dī-'az-ə-,pam\ *n* [*di-* + *az-* + *epoxide* + *-am* (of unknown origin)] (1964) **:** a tranquilizer $C_{16}H_{13}ClN_2O$ used esp. to relieve anxiety and tension and as a muscle relaxant — compare VALIUM

di·azo \dī-'az-(,)ō, -'āz-\ *adj* [ISV *diaz-, diazo-,* fr. *di-* + *az-*] (1878) **1 :** relating to or containing the group N_2 composed of two nitrogen atoms united to a single carbon atom of an organic radical **2 :** relating to or containing diazonium **3 :** of or relating to a photograph or photocopy whose production involves the use of a coating of a diazo compound that is decomposed by exposure to light

di·a·zo·ni·um \,dī-ə-'zō-nē-əm\ *n* [ISV *di-* + *az-* + *-onium*] (1895) **:** the univalent cation N_2^+ that is composed of two nitrogen atoms united to carbon in an organic radical and that usu. exists in salts used in the manufacture of azo dyes

di·az·o·tize \dī-'az-ə-,tīz\ *vt* **-tized; -tiz·ing** [*di-* + *azote* + *-ize*] (ca. 1889) **:** to convert (a compound) into a diazo compound (as a diazonium salt) — **di·az·o·ti·za·tion** \-,az-ət-ə-'zā-shən\ *n*

di·ba·sic \(')dī-'bā-sik\ *adj* (1868) **1 :** having two replaceable hydrogen atoms — used of acids **2 :** containing two atoms of a univalent metal ⟨~ sodium phosphate Na_2HPO_4⟩ **3 :** having two hydroxyl groups — used of bases and basic salts

dib·ber \'dib-ər\ *n* (ca. 1736) **:** DIBBLE

[1]**dib·ble** \'dib-əl\ *n* [ME *debylle*] (15c) **:** a small hand implement used to make holes in the ground for plants, seeds, or bulbs

[2]**dibble** *vt* **dib·bled; dib·bling** \'dib-(ə-)liŋ\ (1583) **1 :** to plant with a dibble **2 :** to make holes in (soil) with or as if with a dibble

dibs \'dibz\ *n pl* [short for *dibstones* (jacks), fr. obs. *dib* (to dab)] (1812) **1** *slang* **:** money esp. in small amounts **2 :** CLAIM, RIGHTS ⟨I have ~ on that piece of cake⟩

di·bu·tyl phthal·ate \,dī-,byüt-ᵊl-'thal-,āt\ *n* [*di-* + *butyl* + *phthal*ic acid + *-ate*] (1925) **:** a colorless oily ester $C_{16}H_{22}O_4$ used chiefly as a solvent, plasticizer, pesticide, and repellent (as for chiggers and mites)

di·car·box·yl·ic \,dī-,kär-,bäk-'sil-ik\ *adj* (ca. 1890) **:** containing two carboxyl groups in the molecule

di·cast \'dī-,kast, 'dik-,ast\ *n* [Gk *dikastēs,* fr. *dikazein* to judge, fr. *dikē* judgment — more at DICTION] (ca. 1822) **:** an ancient Athenian performing the functions of both judge and juror at a trial

[1]**dice** \'dīs\ *n, pl* **dice** [ME *dyce,* fr. *dees, dyce,* pl. of *dee* die — more at DIE] (14c) **1 a :** DIE 1 **b :** a gambling game played with dice **2** *pl also* **dices :** a small cubical piece (as of food) **3 :** a close contest between two racing-car drivers for position during a race — **no dice :** of no avail **:** no use **:** FUTILE

[2]**dice** *vb* **diced; dic·ing** [ME *dycen,* fr. *dyce*] *vt* (14c) **1 a :** to cut into small cubes **b :** to ornament with square markings ⟨*diced* leather⟩ **2 a :** to bring by playing dice ⟨~ himself into debt⟩ **b :** to lose by dicing ⟨~ his money away⟩ ~ *vi* **1 :** to play games with dice ⟨~ for drinks in the bar —Malcolm Lowry⟩ **2 :** to take a chance ⟨the temptation to ~ with death —*Newsweek*⟩ — **dic·er** *n*

di·cen·tric \(')dī-'sen-trik\ *adj* (1937) **:** having two centromeres ⟨a ~ chromosome⟩ — **dicentric** *n*

dic·ey \'dī-sē\ *adj* **dic·i·er; -est** [[1]*dice* + *-y*] (1950) **:** RISKY, UNPREDICTABLE

dich- *or* **dicho-** *comb form* [LL, fr. Gk, fr. *dicha;* akin to Gk *di-*] **:** in two **:** apart ⟨*dicho*gamous⟩

di·cha·sium \dī-'kā-z(h)ē-əm, -zhəm\ *n, pl* **-sia** \-z(h)ē-ə, -zhə\ [NL, fr. Gk *dichasis* halving, fr. *dichazein* to halve, fr. *dicha*] (1875) **:** a cymose inflorescence that produces two main axes

dichlor- *or* **dichloro-** *comb form* **:** containing two atoms of chlorine ⟨*dichloro*ethylene⟩

di·chlo·ride \(')dī-'klō(ə)r-,īd, -'klȯ(ə)r-\ *n* (1823) **:** a binary compound containing two atoms of chlorine combined with an element or radical

di·chlo·ro·ben·zene \(,)dī-,klōr-ə-'ben-,zēn, -,klȯr-, -(,)ben-'\ *n* (1873) **:** any of three isomeric compounds $C_6H_4Cl_2$; *esp* : PARADICHLOROBENZENE

di·chlo·ro·di·flu·o·ro·meth·ane \-,dī-,flu̇r-ə-'meth-,ān\ *n* [*dichlor-* + *di-* + *fluor-* + *methane*] (1936) **:** a nontoxic nonflammable easily liquefiable gas CCl_2F_2 used as a refrigerant and as a propellant

di·chlor·vos \(')dī-'klō(ə)r-,väs, -'klȯ(ə)r-, -vəs\ *n* [*dichlor-* + *vinyl* + *phosphate*] (1957) **:** a nonpersistent organophosphorus pesticide $C_4H_7Cl_2O_4P$ that is used esp. against insects and is of low toxicity to humans — called also *DDVP*

di·chog·a·my \dī-'käg-ə-mē\ *n, pl* **-mies** [G *dichogamie,* fr. *dich-* + *-gamie* -gamy] (1862) **:** the production of male and female reproductive elements at different times by a hermaphroditic organism in order to ensure cross-fertilization — **di·chog·a·mous** \-ə-məs\ *adj*

di·chon·dra \dī-'kän-drə\ *n* [NL, genus name, fr. *di-* + Gk *chondros* grain — more at GRIND] (1947) **:** any of a genus (*Dichondra*) of chiefly tropical perennial herbs of the morning glory family that includes some (esp. *D. repens* or its varieties) used as a ground cover and a substitute for lawn grasses in warmer parts of the U.S.

dich·otic \(')dī-'kōt-ik\ *adj* [*dich-* + [2]*-otic*] (ca. 1909) **:** affecting or relating to the two ears differently in regard to a conscious aspect (as pitch or loudness) or a physical aspect (as frequency or energy) of sound — **dich·oti·cal·ly** \-i-k(ə-)lē\ *adv*

di·chot·o·mist \dī-'kät-ə-məst *also* də-\ *n* (ca. 1592) **:** one that dichotomizes

di·chot·o·mize \-,mīz\ *vb* **-mized; -miz·ing** [LL *dichotomos*] *vt* (1606) **:** to divide into two parts, classes, or groups ~ *vi* **:** to exhibit dichotomy — **di·chot·o·mi·za·tion** \-,kät-ə-mə-'zā-shən\ *n*

di·chot·o·mous \dī-'kät-ə-məs *also* də-\ *adj* [LL *dichotomos,* fr. Gk, fr. *dich-* + *temnein* to cut — more at TOME] (1752) **1 :** dividing into two parts **2 :** relating to, involving, or proceeding from dichotomy — **di·chot·o·mous·ly** *adv* — **di·chot·o·mous·ness** *n*

dichotomous key *n* (ca. 1891) **:** a key for the identification of organisms based on a series of choices between alternative characters

di·chot·o·my \dī-'kät-ə-mē *also* də-\ *n, pl* **-mies** [Gk *dichotomia,* fr. *dichotomos*] (1610) **1 :** a division or the process of dividing into two esp. mutually exclusive or contradictory groups **2 :** the phase of the moon or an inferior planet in which half its disk appears illuminated **3 a :** BIFURCATION; *esp* : repeated bifurcation (as of a plant's stem) **b :** a system of branching in which the main axis forks repeatedly into two branches **c :** branching of an ancestral line into two equal diverging branches

di·chro·ic \dī-'krō-ik\ *adj* [Gk *dichroos* two-colored, fr. *di-* + *chrōs* color — more at CHROMATIC] (ca. 1864) **1 :** having the property of dichroism ⟨a ~ crystal⟩ ⟨a ~ mirror⟩ **2 :** DICHROMATIC

di·chro·ism \'dī-(,)krō-,iz-əm\ *n* (1819) **:** the property of some crystals and solutions of absorbing one of two plane-polarized components of transmitted light more strongly than the other; *also* : the property of exhibiting different colors by reflected or transmitted light — compare CIRCULAR DICHROISM

di·chro·mat \'dī-krō-,mat, (')dī-'\ *n* [back-formation fr. *dichromatic*] (1902) **:** one affected with dichromatism

di·chro·mate \(')dī-'krō-,māt, 'dī-krō-\ *n* [ISV] (ca. 1864) **:** a usu. orange to red chromium salt containing the radical Cr_2O_7 ⟨~ of potassium⟩ — called also *bichromate*

di·chro·mat·ic \,dī-krō-'mat-ik\ *adj* (ca. 1847) **1 :** having or exhibiting two colors **2 :** having two color varieties or color phases independently of age or sex ⟨a ~ bird⟩ **3 :** of, relating to, or exhibiting dichromatism

di·chro·ma·tism \dī-'krō-mə-,tiz-əm\ *n* (1884) **1 :** the state or condition of being dichromatic **2 :** partial color blindness in which only two colors are perceptible

di·chro·scope \'dī-krə-,skōp\ *n* (1857) **:** an instrument for examining crystals for dichroism

dick \'dik\ *n* [*Dick,* nickname for *Richard*] (1553) **1** *chiefly Brit* : FELLOW, CHAP **2** : PENIS — usu. considered vulgar **3** [by shortening & alter.] : DETECTIVE

dick·cis·sel \dik-'sis-əl, 'dik-,\ *n* [imit.] (ca. 1886) : a common migratory black-throated finch (*Spiza americana*) of the central U.S.

dick·ens \'dik-ənz\ *n* [euphemism] (1598) : DEVIL, DEUCE

[1]dick·er \'dik-ər\ *n* [ME *dyker,* fr. L *decuria* quantity of ten, fr. *decem* ten — more at TEN] (13c) : the number or quantity of 10 esp. of hides or skins

[2]dicker *vi* **dick·ered; dick·er·ing** \'dik-(ə-)riŋ\ [origin unknown] (1802) : BARGAIN

[3]dicker *n* (1823) **1** : BARTER **2** : an act or session of haggling or bargaining

dick·ey *or* **dicky** *also* **dick·ie** \'dik-ē\ *n, pl* **dickeys** *or* **dick·ies** [*Dicky,* nickname for *Richard*] (1753) **1** : any of various articles of clothing: as **a** : a man's separate or detachable shirtfront **b** : a small fabric insert worn to fill in the neckline **2** *chiefly Brit* **a** : the driver's seat in a carriage **b** : a seat at the back of a carriage or automobile **3** : a small bird

Dick test \'dik-\ *n* [George F. *Dick* and Gladys H. *Dick*] (ca. 1925) : a test to determine susceptibility or immunity to scarlet fever by an injection of scarlet fever toxin

di·cli·nous \(')dī-'klī-nəs\ *adj* (1830) : having the stamens and pistils in separate flowers

di·cot \'dī-,kät\ *n* (1830) : DICOTYLEDON

di·cot·y·le·don \,dī-,kät-ᵊl-'ēd-ᵊn\ *n* [NL] (1877) : a plant with two seed leaves : a member of the one (Dicotyledones) of the two subclasses of angiospermous plants that comprises those with two cotyledons — **di·cot·y·le·don·ous** \-ᵊn-əs\ *adj*

di·cou·ma·rin \(')dī-'kü-mə-rən\ *n* (ca. 1727) : DICUMAROL

di·crot·ic \dī-'krät-ik\ *adj* [Gk *dikrotos,* fr. *di-* + *krotos* rattling noise, beat, fr. *krotein* to beat; akin to OE *hrindan* to push] (ca. 1811) **1** : *of the pulse* : having a double beat **2** : being or relating to the second part of the arterial pulse occurring during diastole of the heart or of an arterial pressure recording made during the same period — **di·cro·tism** \'dī-krə-,tiz-əm\ *n*

Dic·ta·phone \'dik-tə-,fōn\ *trademark* — used for a dictating machine

[1]dic·tate \'dik-,tāt, dik-'\ *vb* **dic·tat·ed; dic·tat·ing** [L *dictatus,* pp. of *dictare* to assert, dictate, fr. *dictus,* pp. of *dicere* to say — more at DICTION] *vi* (1592) **1** : to give dictation **2** : to speak or act domineeringly : PRESCRIBE ~ *vt* **1** : to speak or read for a person to transcribe or for a machine to record **2 a** : to issue as an order **b** : to impose, pronounce, or specify authoritatively

[2]dic·tate \'dik-,tāt\ *n* (1594) **1 a** : an authoritative rule, prescription, or injunction **b** : a ruling principle ⟨according to the ~*s* of his conscience⟩ **2** : a command by one in authority

dictating machine *n* (1939) : a machine used esp. for the recording of human speech for transcription

dic·ta·tion \dik-'tā-shən\ *n* (1656) **1 a** : PRESCRIPTION **b** : arbitrary command **2 a (1)** : the act or manner of uttering words to be transcribed **(2)** : material that is dictated or transcribed **b (1)** : the performing of music to be reproduced by a student **(2)** : music so reproduced

dic·ta·tor \'dik-,tāt-ər, dik-'\ *n* [L, fr. *dictatus*] (14c) **1 a** : a person granted absolute emergency power; *esp* : one appointed by the senate of ancient Rome **b** : one holding complete autocratic control **c** : one ruling absolutely and often oppressively **2** : one that dictates

dic·ta·to·ri·al \,dik-tə-'tōr-ē-əl, -'tȯr-\ *adj* (1701) **1 a** : of, relating to, or befitting a dictator ⟨~ power⟩ **b** : ruled by a dictator **2** : oppressive to or contemptuously overbearing toward others : arrogantly domineering — **dic·ta·to·ri·al·ly** \-ē-ə-lē\ *adv* — **dic·ta·to·ri·al·ness** *n*

syn DICTATORIAL, MAGISTERIAL, DOGMATIC, DOCTRINAIRE, ORACULAR mean imposing one's will or opinions on others. DICTATORIAL stresses autocratic, high-handed methods and a domineering manner; MAGISTERIAL stresses assumption or use of prerogatives appropriate to a magistrate or schoolmaster in forcing acceptance of one's opinions; DOGMATIC implies being unduly and offensively positive in laying down principles and expressing opinions; DOCTRINAIRE implies a disposition to follow abstract theories in framing laws or policies affecting people; ORACULAR implies the manner of one who delivers opinions in cryptic phrases or with pompous dogmatism.

dic·ta·tor·ship \dik-'tāt-ər-,ship, 'dik-,\ *n* (1542) **1** : the office of dictator **2** : autocratic rule, control, or leadership **3 a** : a form of government in which absolute power is concentrated in a dictator or a small clique **b** : a government organization or group in which absolute power is so concentrated **c** : a despotic state

dic·tion \'dik-shən\ *n* [L *diction-, dictio* speaking, style, fr. *dictus,* pp. of *dicere* to say; akin to OE *tēon* to accuse, L *dicare* to proclaim, dedicate, Gk *deiknynai* to show, *dikē* judgment, right] (1581) **1** *obs* : verbal description **2** : choice of words esp. with regard to correctness, clearness, or effectiveness **3 a** : vocal expression : ENUNCIATION **b** : pronunciation and enunciation of words in singing — **dic·tion·al** \-shnəl, -shən-ᵊl\ *adj* — **dic·tion·al·ly** \-ē\ *adv*

dic·tio·nary \'dik-shə-,ner-ē\ *n, pl* **-nar·ies** [ML *dictionarium,* fr. LL *diction-, dictio* word, fr. L, speaking] (1526) **1** : a reference book containing words usu. alphabetically arranged along with information about their forms, pronunciations, functions, etymologies, meanings, and syntactical and idiomatic uses **2** : a reference book listing alphabetically terms or names important to a particular subject or activity along with discussion of their meanings and applications **3** : a reference book giving for words of one language equivalents in another **4** : a list (as of phrases, synonyms, or hyphenation instructions) stored in machine-readable form (as on a disk) for reference by an automatic system (as for information retrieval or computerized typesetting)

dic·tum \'dik-təm\ *n, pl* **dic·ta** \-tə\ *also* **dictums** [L, fr. neut. of *dictus*] (ca. 1706) **1** : a formal authoritative pronouncement of a principle, proposition, or opinion **2** : a judicial opinion on a point other than the precise issue involved in determining a case

dicty- *or* **dictyo-** *comb form* [NL, fr. Gk *dikty-, diktyo-,* fr. *diktyon,* fr. *dikein* to throw] : net ⟨*dictyo*stele⟩ ⟨*dictyo*some⟩

dic·tyo·some \'dik-tē-ə-,sōm\ *n* (ca. 1930) : GOLGI BODY

dic·tyo·stele \'dik-tē-ə-,stēl, ,dik-tē-ə-'stē-lē\ *n* (ca. 1902) : a stele in which the vascular cylinder is broken up into a longitudinal series or network of vascular strands around a central pith (as in many ferns)

di·cu·ma·rol *also* **di·cou·ma·rol** \dī-'k(y)ü-mə-,rȯl, -,rōl\ *n* [*di-* + *coumarin* + *-ol*] (1943) : a crystalline compound $C_{19}H_{12}O_6$ orig. obtained from spoiled sweet clover hay and used to delay clotting of blood esp. in preventing and treating thromboembolic disease

di·cy·clic \(')dī-'sī-klik, -'sik-lik\ *adj* (ca. 1899) : BICYCLIC 2

did *past of* DO

di·dact \'dī-,dakt\ *n* [back-formation fr. *didactic*] (1954) : a didactic person

di·dac·tic \dī-'dak-tik, də-\ *adj* [Gk *didaktikos,* fr. *didaskein* to teach] (1658) **1 a** : designed or intended to teach **b** : intended to convey instruction and information as well as pleasure and entertainment **2** : making moral observations — **di·dac·ti·cal** \-ti-kəl\ *adj* — **di·dac·ti·cal·ly** \-ti-k(ə-)lē\ *adv* — **di·dac·ti·cism** \-tə-,siz-əm\ *n*

di·dac·tics \-tiks\ *n pl but sing or pl in constr* (ca. 1846) : systematic instruction : PEDAGOGY, TEACHINGS

di·dap·per \'dī-,dap-ər\ *n* [ME *dydoppar,* prob. alter. of OE *dūfedoppa* pelican, fr. *dūfan* to dive + *-doppa* (akin to OE *dyppan* to dip) dipper — more at DIVE, DIP] (14c) : a small grebe (as a dabchick)

did·dle \'did-ᵊl\ *vb* **did·dled; did·dling** \'did-liŋ, -ᵊl-iŋ\ [origin unknown] *vi* (1786) **1** : DAWDLE, FOOL **2** : FIDDLE, TOY — usu. used with *with* ⟨*diddled* with the machine until it broke⟩ ~ *vt* **1** *chiefly dial* : to move with short rapid motions **2** : to waste (as time) in trifling **3** : HOAX, SWINDLE — **did·dler** \'did-lər, -ᵊl-ər\ *n*

did·ger·i·doo \'dij-ə-rē-,dü, ,dij-ə-rē-'\ *n* [origin unknown] (1924) : a large bamboo or wooden trumpet of the Australian aborigines

didn't \'did-ᵊnt, -ᵊn, *dial also* 'dit-ᵊn(t) *or* (')dint\ : did not

di·do \'dīd-(,)ō\ *n, pl* **didoes** *or* **didos** [origin unknown] (1807) **1** : a mischievous or capricious act : PRANK, ANTIC — often used in the phrase *cut didoes* **2** : something that is frivolous or showy

Di·do \'dīd-(,)ō\ *n* [L, fr. Gk *Didō*] : a legendary queen of Carthage in Vergil's *Aeneid* who kills herself when Aeneas leaves her

didst \(')didst, (')ditst\ *archaic past 2d sing of* DO

di·dym·i·um \dī-'dim-ē-əm\ *n* [NL, fr. Gk *didymos* double, twin, testicle, fr. *dyo* two — more at TWO] (1842) : a mixture of rare-earth elements made up chiefly of neodymium and praseodymium and used esp. for coloring glass for optical filters

di·dyn·a·mous \(')dī-'din-ə-məs\ *adj* [deriv. of Gk *di-* + *dynamis* power — more at DYNAMIC] (1794) : having four stamens disposed in pairs of unequal length ⟨snapdragons are ~⟩

[1]die \'dī\ *vi* **died; dy·ing** \'dī-iŋ\ [ME *dien,* fr. or akin to ON *deyja* to die; akin to OHG *touwen* to die, OIr *duine* human being] (12c) **1** : to pass from physical life : EXPIRE **2** : to pass out of existence : CEASE ⟨their anger *died* at these words⟩ **3 a** : to suffer or face the pains of death **b** : SINK, LANGUISH ⟨*dying* from fatigue⟩ **c** : to long keenly or desperately ⟨*dying* to go⟩ **4 a** : to pass into an inferior state or situation ⟨they have developed competence which we . . . must utilize lest it wither and ~ —Ruth G. Strickland⟩ **b** : STOP ⟨the motor *died*⟩ **5** : to cease to be subject : become indifferent ⟨~ to worldly things⟩ — **die hard 1** : to be long in dying ⟨such rumors *die hard*⟩ **2** : to continue resistance against hopeless odds ⟨hard-shell conservatism *dies hard*⟩

[2]die \'dī\ *n, pl* **dice** \'dīs\ *or* **dies** \'dīz\ [ME *dee,* fr. MF *dé*] (14c) **1** *pl dice* : a small cube marked on each face with from one to six spots and used usu. in pairs in various games and in gambling by being shaken and thrown to come to rest at random on a flat surface **2** *pl usu dice* : something determined by or as if by a cast of dice : CHANCE **3** *pl dies* : DADO 1a **4** *pl dies* : any of various tools or devices for imparting a desired shape, form, or finish to a material or for impressing an object or material: as **a (1)** : the larger of a pair of cutting or shaping tools that when moved toward each other produce a desired form in or impress a desired device on an object by pressure or by a blow **(2)** : a device composed of a pair of such tools **b** : a hollow internally threaded screw-cutting tool used for forming screw threads **c** : a cutter to cut out blanks **d** : a mold into which molten metal or other material is forced **e** : a perforated block through which metal or plastic is drawn or extruded for shaping

[3]die *vt* **died; die·ing** (1703) : to cut or shape with a die

die·back \'dī-,bak\ *n* (ca. 1886) : a condition in woody plants in which peripheral parts are killed esp. by parasites

di·ecious *var of* DIOECIOUS

die down *vi* (1834) : DIMINISH, SUBSIDE ⟨the storm *died down*⟩

die·hard \'dī-,härd\ *n* (1912) : an irreconcilable opponent of change ⟨party ~*s* who allow no concession of any kind⟩

die–hard \'dī-,härd\ *adj* (1871) : strongly resisting change : completely and determinedly fixed ⟨a ~ conservative⟩ — **die–hard·ism** \-,iz-əm\ *n*

di·el \'dī-əl, -,el\ *adj* [irreg. fr. L *dies* day + E *-al*] (ca. 1935) : involving a 24-hour period that usu. includes a day and the adjoining night ⟨~ fluctuations in temperature⟩

diel·drin \'dē(ə)l-drən\ *n* [*Diels*-Alder reaction (an addition reaction forming a 6-membered ring), after Otto *Diels* & Kurt *Alder*] (ca. 1949) : a white crystalline persistent chlorinated hydrocarbon insecticide $C_{12}H_8Cl_6O$

di·elec·tric \,dī-ə-'lek-trik\ *n* [*dia-* + *electric*] (1837) : a nonconductor of direct electric current — **dielectric** *adj*

dielectric heating *n* (1944) : the rapid and uniform heating throughout a nonconducting material by means of a high-frequency electromagnetic field

di·en·ceph·a·lon \,dī-ən-'sef-ə-,län, ,dī-(,)en-, -lən\ *n* [NL, fr. *dia-* + *encephalon*] (ca. 1883) : the posterior subdivision of the forebrain — called also *betweenbrain* — **di·en·ce·phal·ic** \-sə-'fal-ik\ *adj*

di·ene \'dī-,ēn\ *n* [*di-* + *-ene*] (1917) : a compound containing two double bonds between carbon atoms; *esp* : DIOLEFIN

die–off \'dī-,ȯf\ *n* (1936) : a sudden sharp decline of a population (as of rabbits) that is not caused directly by human activity (as hunting)

die off \(')dī-'ȯf\ *vi* (1697) : to die sequentially either singly or in numbers so that the total number is greatly diminished

die out *vi* (1853) : to become extinct

di·er·e·sis *var of* DIAERESIS

die·sel \'dē-zəl, -səl\ *n* [Rudolf *Diesel*] (1894) **1** : DIESEL ENGINE **2** : a vehicle driven by a diesel engine

diesel–electric *adj* (1914) : of, relating to, or employing the combination of a diesel engine driving an electric generator ⟨a ~ locomotive⟩

diesel engine *n* (1894) : an internal-combustion engine in which air is compressed to a temperature sufficiently high to ignite fuel injected into the cylinder where the combustion and expansion actuate a piston

die·sel·ing \ˈdēz-(ə-)liŋ, ˈdēs-\ *n* (ca. 1955) **:** the continued operation of an internal-combustion engine after the ignition is turned off

die·sel·ize \ˈdē-zə-ˌlīz, ˈdē-sə-\ *vt* **-ized; -iz·ing** (1925) **:** to equip with a diesel engine or with electric locomotives having electric generators powered by diesel engines — **die·sel·iza·tion** \ˌdē-zə-lə-ˈzā-shən, ˌdē-sə-\ *n*

die·sink·er \ˈdī-ˌsiŋ-kər\ *n* (1815) **:** one that makes cutting and shaping dies — **die·sink·ing** *n*

Di·es Irae \ˌdē-(ˌ)ā-ˈsē-ˌrā\ *n* [ML, day of wrath; fr. the first words of the hymn] (ca. 1805) **:** a medieval Latin hymn on the Day of Judgment sung in requiem masses

di·esis \ˈdī-ə-səs\ *n, pl* **di·eses** \-ˌsēz\ [NL, sharp (in music), fr. L, quarter tone, small interval, fr. Gk, fr. *diïenai* to send through, fr. *dia-* + *hienai* to send — more at JET] (ca. 1706) **:** DOUBLE DAGGER

di·es·ter \ˈdī-ˌes-tər\ *n* (1935) **:** a compound containing two ester groupings

die·stock \ˈdī-ˌstäk\ *n* (1863) **:** a stock to hold dies used for cutting threads

di·es·trus \(ˈ)dī-ˈes-trəs\ *n* [NL, period of sexual quiescence, fr. *dia-* + *estrus*] (1942) **:** a period of sexual quiescence that intervenes between two periods of estrus — **di·es·trous** \-trəs\ *also* **di·es·tru·al** \-trə-wəl\ *adj*

[1]di·et \ˈdī-ət\ *n* [ME *diete,* fr. OF, fr. L *diaeta* prescribed diet, fr. Gk *diaita,* lit., manner of living, fr. *dia-* + *-aita* (akin to Gk *aisa* share)] (13c) **1 a :** food and drink regularly provided or consumed **b :** habitual nourishment **c :** the kind and amount of food prescribed for a person or animal for a special reason **2 :** something provided esp. habitually (as for use or enjoyment) ⟨a ~ of Broadway shows and nightclubs —Frederick Wyatt⟩

[2]diet *vt* (14c) **1 :** to cause to take food **:** FEED **2 :** to cause to eat and drink sparingly or according to prescribed rules ~ *vi* **:** to eat sparingly or according to prescribed rules — **di·et·er** *n*

[3]diet *n* [ML *dieta,* day's journey, assembly, fr. L *dies* day — more at DEITY] (15c) **1 :** a formal deliberative assembly of princes or estates **2 :** any of various national or provincial legislatures

[1]di·etary \ˈdī-ə-ˌter-ē\ *n, pl* **di·etar·ies** (15c) **:** the kinds and amounts of food available to or eaten by an individual, group, or population

[2]dietary *adj* (1614) **:** of or relating to a diet or to the rules of a diet — **di·etari·ly** \ˌdī-ə-ˈter-ə-lē\ *adv*

dietary law *n* (ca. 1930) **:** one of the laws observed by Orthodox Jews that permit or prohibit certain foods

di·etet·ic \ˌdī-ə-ˈtet-ik\ *adj* (1579) **1 :** of or relating to diet **2 :** adapted for use in special diets — **di·etet·i·cal·ly** \-i-k(ə-)lē\ *adv*

di·etet·ics \-ˈtet-iks\ *n pl but sing or pl in constr* (1541) **:** the science or art of applying the principles of nutrition to the diet

di·ether \(ˈ)dī-ˈē-thər\ *n* (1950) **:** a chemical containing two atoms of oxygen with ether linkages

di·eth·yl·car·bam·azine \ˌdī-ˌeth-əl-kär-ˈbam-ə-ˌzēn, -zən\ *n* [*di-* + *ethyl* + *carboxy-* + *amide* + *azine*] (1948) **:** an anthelmintic administered in the form of its crystalline citrate $C_{10}H_{21}N_3O \cdot C_6H_8O_7$ esp. to control filariasis in man and large roundworms in dogs and cats

di·eth·yl ether \(ˌ)dī-ˌeth-əl-\ *n* (ca. 1930) **:** ETHER 3a

di·eth·yl·stil·bes·trol \-stil-ˈbes-ˌtrȯl, -ˌtrōl\ *n* [ISV] (1938) **:** a colorless crystalline synthetic compound $C_{18}H_{20}O_2$ used as a potent estrogen — called also *stilbestrol*

di·eti·tian *or* **di·eti·cian** \ˌdī-ə-ˈtish-ən\ *n* [*dietitian* irreg. fr. [1]*diet*] (ca. 1846) **:** a specialist in dietetics

dif·fer \ˈdif-ər\ *vi* **dif·fered; dif·fer·ing** \-(ə-)riŋ\ [ME *differen,* fr. MF or L; MF *differer* to postpone, be different, fr. L *differre,* fr. *dis-* + *ferre* to carry — more at BEAR] (14c) **1 a :** to be unlike or distinct in nature, form, or characteristics ⟨the law of one state ~*s* from that of another⟩ **b :** to change from time to time or from one instance to another **:** VARY **2 :** to be of unlike or opposite opinion **:** DISAGREE ⟨they ~ on religious matters⟩

[1]dif·fer·ence \ˈdif-ərn(t)s, ˈdif-(ə-)rən(t)s\ *n* (14c) **1 a :** the quality or state of being different **b :** an instance of differing in nature, form, or quality **c** *archaic* **:** a characteristic that distinguishes one from another or from the average **d :** the element or factor that separates or distinguishes contrasting situations **2 :** distinction or discrimination in preference **3 a :** disagreement in opinion **:** DISSENSION **b :** an instance or cause of disagreement **4 :** the degree or amount by which things differ in quantity or measure; *specif* **:** REMAINDER 2b(1) **5 :** a significant change in or effect on a situation

[2]difference *vt* **-enced; -enc·ing** (15c) **:** DIFFERENTIATE, DISTINGUISH

dif·fer·ent \ˈdif-ərnt, ˈdif-(ə-)rənt\ *adj* [MF, fr. L *different-, differens,* prp. of *differre*] (14c) **1 :** partly or totally unlike in nature, form, or quality **:** DISSIMILAR ⟨could hardly be more ~⟩ — often followed by *from, than,* or chiefly Brit. *to* ⟨small, neat hand, very ~ from the captain's tottery characters —R. L. Stevenson⟩ ⟨vastly ~ in size than it was twenty-five years ago —N. M. Pusey⟩ ⟨a very ~ situation to the . . . one under which we live —Sir Winston Churchill⟩ **2 :** not the same: as **a :** DISTINCT ⟨~ age groups⟩ **b :** VARIOUS ⟨~ members of the class⟩ **c :** ANOTHER ⟨did not like the TV program so switched to a ~ channel⟩ **3 :** UNUSUAL, SPECIAL ⟨she was ~ and superior⟩ — **dif·fer·ent·ness** *n*

syn DIFFERENT, DIVERSE, DIVERGENT, DISPARATE, VARIOUS mean unlike in kind or character. DIFFERENT may imply little more than separateness but it may also imply contrast or contrariness ⟨*different* foods⟩ DIVERSE implies both distinctness and marked contrast ⟨such *diverse* interests as dancing and football⟩ DIVERGENT implies movement away from each other and unlikelihood of ultimate meeting or reconciliation ⟨went on to pursue two very *divergent* careers⟩ DISPARATE emphasizes incongruity or incompatibility ⟨*disparate* notions of freedom⟩ VARIOUS stresses the number of sorts or kinds ⟨*various* methods have been tried⟩

usage Numerous commentators have condemned *different than* in spite of its use since the 17th century by many of the best-known names in English literature. It is nevertheless standard and is even recommended in many of the handbooks when followed by a clause. *Different from,* the generally recommended safe choice, is more common and is even used in constructions where *than* would work more smoothly.

dif·fer·en·tia \ˌdif-ə-ˈren-ch(ē-)ə\ *n, pl* **-ti·ae** \-chē-ˌē, -chē-ˌī\ [L, difference, fr. *different-, differens*] (1690) **:** the element, feature, or factor that distinguishes one entity, state, or class from another; *esp* **:** a characteristic trait distinguishing a species from other species of the same genus

[1]dif·fer·en·tial \ˌdif-ə-ˈren-chəl\ *adj* (1647) **1 a :** of, relating to, or constituting a difference **:** DISTINGUISHING **b :** making a distinction between individuals or classes **c :** based on or resulting from a differential **d :** functioning or proceeding differently or at a different rate **2 :** being, relating to, or involving a differential or differentiation **3 a :** relating to quantitative differences **b :** producing effects by reason of quantitative differences — **dif·fer·en·tial·ly** \-ˈrench-(ə-)lē\ *adv*

[2]differential *n* (1704) **1 a :** the product of the derivative of a function of one variable by the increment of the independent variable **b :** a sum of products in which each product consists of a partial derivative of a given function of several variables multiplied by the corresponding increment and which contains as many products as there are independent variables in the function **2 :** a difference between comparable individuals or classes ⟨the price ~ between nationally advertised and private brands of staple food items⟩; *also* **:** the amount of such a difference ⟨the ~ between regular and high-test gasoline may exceed five cents a gallon⟩ **3 a :** DIFFERENTIAL GEAR **b :** a case covering a differential gear

differential calculus *n* (1702) **:** a branch of mathematics concerned chiefly with the study of the rate of change of functions with respect to their variables esp. through the use of derivatives and differentials

differential equation *n* (1763) **:** an equation containing differentials or derivatives of functions

differential gear *n* (ca. 1864) **:** an arrangement of gears forming an epicyclic train for connecting two shafts or axles in the same line, dividing the driving force equally between them, and permitting one shaft to revolve faster than the other — called also *differential gearing*

dif·fer·en·ti·ate \ˌdif-ə-ˈren-chē-ˌāt\ *vb* **-at·ed; -at·ing** *vt* (1816) **1 :** to obtain the mathematical derivative of **2 :** to mark or show a difference in **:** constitute a difference that distinguishes **3 :** to develop differential characteristics in **4 :** to cause differentiation of in the course of development **5 :** to express the specific distinguishing quality of **:** DISCRIMINATE ~ *vi* **1 :** to recognize or give expression to a difference **2 :** to become distinct or different in character **3 :** to undergo differentiation — **dif·fer·en·tia·bil·i·ty** \-ˌren-ch(ē-)ə-ˈbil-ət-ē\ *n* — **dif·fer·en·tia·ble** \-ˈren-ch(ē-)ə-bəl\ *adj*

dif·fer·en·ti·a·tion \-ˌren-chē-ˈā-shən\ *n* (1855) **1 :** the act or process of differentiating **2 :** development from the one to the many, the simple to the complex, or the homogeneous to the heterogeneous **3 a :** modification of body parts for performance of particular functions **b :** the sum of the processes whereby apparently indifferent cells, tissues, and structures attain their adult form and function **4 :** the processes by which various rock types are produced from a common magma

dif·fer·ent·ly \ˈdif-ərnt-lē, ˈdif-(ə-)rənt-\ *adv* (14c) **1 :** in a different manner **2 :** OTHERWISE

dif·fi·cile \ˌdē-fi-ˈsē(ə)l\ *adj* [F, lit., difficult] (1536) **:** STUBBORN, UNREASONABLE

dif·fi·cult \ˈdif-i-(ˌ)kəlt\ *adj* [back-formation fr. *difficulty*] (15c) **1 :** hard to do, make, or carry out **:** ARDUOUS ⟨a ~ climb⟩ **2 a :** hard to deal with, manage, or overcome ⟨a ~ child⟩ **b :** hard to understand **:** PUZZLING ⟨~ reading⟩ ***syn*** see HARD — **dif·fi·cult·ly** *adv*

dif·fi·cul·ty \-(ˌ)kəl-tē\ *n, pl* **-ties** [ME *difficulte,* fr. L *difficultas,* irreg. fr. *difficilis*] (14c) **1 :** the quality or state of being difficult **2 :** CONTROVERSY, DISAGREEMENT **3 :** OBJECTION **4 :** something difficult **:** IMPEDIMENT **5 :** EMBARRASSMENT, TROUBLE — usu. used in pl.

dif·fi·dence \ˈdif-əd-ən(t)s, -ə-ˌden(t)s\ *n* (15c) **:** the quality or state of being diffident

dif·fi·dent \-əd-ənt, -ə-ˌdent\ *adj* [L *diffident-, diffidens,* prp. of *diffidere* to distrust, fr. *dis-* + *fidere* to trust — more at BIDE] (15c) **1 :** hesitant in acting or speaking through lack of self-confidence **2** *archaic* **:** DISTRUSTFUL **3 :** RESERVED, UNASSERTIVE ***syn*** see SHY — **dif·fi·dent·ly** *adv*

dif·fract \dif-ˈrakt\ *vt* [back-formation fr. *diffraction*] (1803) **:** to cause to undergo diffraction

dif·frac·tion \dif-ˈrak-shən\ *n* [NL *diffraction-, diffractio,* fr. L *diffractus,* pp. of *diffringere* to break apart, fr. *dis-* + *frangere* to break — more at BREAK] (1673) **:** a modification which light undergoes in passing by the edges of opaque bodies or through narrow slits or in being reflected from ruled surfaces and in which the rays appear to be deflected and to produce fringes of parallel light and dark or colored bands; *also* **:** a similar modification of other waves (as sound waves)

diffraction grating *n* (1867) **:** GRATING 3

[1]dif·fuse \dif-ˈyüs\ *adj* [L *diffusus,* pp. of *diffundere* to spread out, fr. *dis-* + *fundere* to pour — more at FOUND] (15c) **1 :** being at once verbose and ill-organized **2 :** not concentrated or localized **:** SCATTERED ⟨~ sclerosis⟩ ***syn*** see WORDY — **dif·fuse·ly** *adv* — **dif·fuse·ness** *n*

[2]dif·fuse \dif-ˈyüz\ *vb* **dif·fused; dif·fus·ing** [MF or L; MF *diffuser,* fr. L *diffusus,* pp.] *vt* (15c) **1 a :** to pour out and permit or cause to spread freely **b :** EXTEND, SCATTER **c :** to spread thinly or wastefully **2 :** to subject to diffusion; *esp* **:** to break up and distribute (incident light) by reflection ~ *vi* **1 :** to spread out or become transmitted esp. by contact **2 :** to undergo diffusion

dif·fuse–po·rous \dif-ˌyüs-ˈpōr-əs, -ˈpȯr-\ *adj* [[1]*diffuse*] (ca. 1902) **:** having vessels more or less evenly distributed throughout an annual ring and not varying greatly in size — compare RING-POROUS

dif·fus·er \dif-ˈyü-zər\ *n* (1679) **1 :** one that diffuses: as **a :** a device (as a reflector) for distributing the light of a lamp evenly **b :** a screen (as of cloth or frosted glass) for softening lighting (as in photography) **c :** a device (as slats at different angles) for deflecting air from an outlet in various directions **2 :** a device for reducing the velocity and increasing the static pressure of a fluid passing through a system

dif·fus·ible \dif-ˈyü-zə-bəl\ *adj* (1782) **:** capable of diffusing or of being diffused

dif·fu·sion \dif-ˈyü-zhən\ *n* (14c) **1 :** the action of diffusing **:** the state of being diffused **2 :** PROLIXITY, DIFFUSENESS **3 a :** the process whereby particles of liquids, gases, or solids intermingle as the result of their spontaneous movement caused by thermal agitation and in dissolved substances move from a region of higher to one of lower concentration **b** (1) **:** reflection of light by a rough reflecting surface (2) **:** transmission of light through a translucent material **:** SCATTERING **4 :** the spread of cultural elements from one area or group of people to others by contact **5 :** the softening of sharp outlines in a photographic image — **dif·fu·sion·al** \-ˈyüzh-nəl, -ən-ᵊl\ *adj*

dif·fu·sion·ist \-ˈyüzh-(ə-)nəst\ *n* (1924) **:** an anthropologist who emphasizes the role of diffusion in the history of culture rather than independent invention or discovery — **dif·fu·sion·ism** \-ˈyü-zhə-ˌniz-əm\ *n*

dif·fu·sive \dif-ˈyü-siv, -ziv\ *adj* (1614) **:** tending to diffuse **:** characterized by diffusion ⟨~ motion of atoms⟩ — **dif·fu·sive·ly** *adv* — **dif·fu·sive·ness** *n* — **dif·fu·siv·i·ty** \dif-ˌyü-ˈsiv-ət-ē, -ˈziv-\ *n*

di·func·tion·al \(ˈ)dī-ˈfəŋ(k)-shnəl, -shən-ᵊl\ *adj* (1943) **:** of, relating to, or being a compound with two sites in the molecule that are highly reactive

[1]dig \ˈdig\ *vb* **dug** \ˈdəg\; **dig·ging** [ME *diggen*] *vt* (13c) **1 a :** to break up, turn, or loosen (earth) with an implement **b :** to prepare the soil of ⟨~ a garden⟩ **2 :** to bring to the surface by digging **:** UNEARTH **3 :** to hollow out or form by removing earth **:** EXCAVATE **4 :** to drive down so as to penetrate **:** THRUST **5 :** POKE, PROD **6 a :** to pay attention to **:** NOTICE ⟨~ that fancy hat⟩ **b :** UNDERSTAND, APPRECIATE ⟨if you . . . do something subtle . . . only one tenth of the audience will ~ it —Nat Hentoff⟩ **c :** LIKE, ADMIRE ⟨high school students ~ short poetry —David Burmester⟩ ~ *vi* **1 :** to turn up, loosen, or remove earth **:** DELVE **2 :** to work hard or laboriously **3 :** to advance by or as if by removing or pushing aside material

[2]dig *n* (1819) **1 a :** THRUST, POKE **b :** a cutting remark **2** *pl* **:** living accommodations **3 :** an archaeological excavation site; *also* **:** the excavation itself

dig·a·my \ˈdig-ə-mē\ *n, pl* **-mies** [LL *digamia*, fr. LGk, fr. Gk *digamos* married to two people, fr. *di-* + *-gamos* -gamous] (1635) **:** a second marriage after the termination of the first

di·gas·tric \(ˈ)dī-ˈgas-trik\ *adj* [NL *digastricus*, fr. *di-* + *gastricus* gastric] (ca. 1721) **:** of, relating to, or being a muscle with two bellies separated by a median tendon

di·ge·net·ic \ˌdī-jə-ˈnet-ik\ *adj* (1883) **:** of or relating to a subclass (Digenea) of trematode worms in which sexual reproduction as an internal parasite of a vertebrate alternates with asexual reproduction in a mollusk

[1]di·gest \ˈdī-ˌjest\ *n* [ME *Digest* compilation of Roman laws ordered by Justinian, fr. LL *Digesta*, pl., fr. L, collection of writings arranged under headings, fr. neut. pl. of *digestus*, pp. of *digerere* to arrange, distribute, digest, fr. *dis-* + *gerere* to carry — more at CAST] (14c) **1 :** a summation or condensation of a body of information: as **a :** a systematic compilation of legal rules, statutes, or decisions **b :** a periodical devoted to condensed versions of previously published articles **2 :** a product of digestion

[2]di·gest \dī-ˈjest, də-\ *vb* [ME *digesten*, fr. L *digestus*] *vt* (14c) **1 :** to distribute or arrange systematically **:** CLASSIFY **2 :** to convert (food) into absorbable form **3 :** to take into the mind or memory; *esp* **:** to assimilate mentally **4 a :** to soften, decompose, or break down by heat and moisture or chemicals **b :** to extract soluble ingredients from by warming with a liquid **5 :** to compress into a short summary ~ *vi* **1 :** to digest food **2 :** to become digested

di·gest·er \-ˈjes-tər\ *n* (15c) **1 :** one that digests or makes a digest **2 :** a vessel for digesting esp. plant or animal materials

di·gest·ibil·i·ty \-ˌjes-tə-ˈbil-ət-ē\ *n, pl* **-ties** (1740) **1 :** the fitness of something for digestion **2 :** the percentage of a foodstuff taken into the digestive tract that is absorbed into the body

di·gest·ible \-ˈjes-tə-bəl\ *adj* (14c) **:** capable of being digested

di·ges·tion \dī-ˈjes(h)-chən, də-\ *n* (14c) **:** the action, process, or power of digesting: as **a :** the process of making food absorbable by dissolving it and breaking it down into simpler chemical compounds that occurs in the living body chiefly through the action of enzymes secreted into the alimentary canal **b :** the process in sewage treatment by which organic matter in sludge is decomposed by anaerobic bacteria with the release of a burnable mixture of gases

[1]di·ges·tive \-ˈjes-tiv\ *n* (14c) **:** something that aids digestion esp. of food

[2]digestive *adj* (15c) **1 :** relating to or functioning in digestion ⟨the ~ system⟩ **2 :** having the power to cause or promote digestion ⟨~ enzymes⟩ — **di·ges·tive·ly** *adv*

digestive gland *n* (1940) **:** a gland secreting digestive enzymes

dig·ger \ˈdig-ər\ *n* (15c) **1 a :** one that digs **b :** a tool or machine for digging **2** *cap* **:** a No. American Indian (as a Paiute) who digs roots for food **3 :** an Australian or New Zealand soldier

digger wasp *n* (1880) **:** a burrowing wasp; *esp* **:** a usu. solitary wasp (superfamily Sphecoidea) that digs nest burrows in the soil and provisions them with insects or spiders paralyzed by stinging

dig·gings *n pl* (1538) **1 :** a place of excavating esp. for ore, metals, or precious stones **2 :** material dug out **3 a :** QUARTERS, PREMISES **b** *chiefly Brit* **:** lodgings for a student

dight \ˈdīt\ *vt* **dight·ed** *or* **dight; dight·ing** [ME *dighten*, fr. OE *dihtan* to arrange, compose, fr. L *dictare* to dictate, compose] *archaic* (13c) **:** DRESS, ADORN

dig in *vt* (1839) **:** to cover or incorporate by burying ⟨*dig in* compost⟩ ~ *vi* **1 :** to dig defensive trenches **2 a :** to go resolutely to work **b :** to begin eating **3 :** to hold stubbornly to a position **4 :** to make small depressions in the ground for better footing while batting (as in baseball)

dig·it \ˈdij-ət\ *n* [ME, fr. L *digitus* finger, toe — more at TOE] (14c) **1 a :** any of the Arabic numerals 1 to 9 and usu. the symbol 0 **b :** one of the elements that combine to form numbers in a system other than the decimal system **2 :** a unit of length based on the breadth of a finger and equal in English measure to $^3/_4$ inch **3 :** any of the divisions in which the limbs of amphibians and all higher vertebrates terminate, which are typically five in number but may be reduced (as in the horse), and which typically have a series of phalanges bearing a nail, claw, or hoof at the tip **:** FINGER, TOE

[1]dig·i·tal \ˈdij-ət-ᵊl\ *adj* [L *digitalis*] (ca. 1656) **1 :** of or relating to the fingers or toes **:** DIGITATE **2 :** done with a finger **3 :** of, relating to, or using calculation by numerical methods or by discrete units **4 :** of or relating to data in the form of numerical digits **5 :** providing a readout in numerical digits ⟨a ~ voltmeter⟩ **6 :** relating to a phonograph record made from a magnetic tape on which sound waves have been represented digitally so that in the record wow and flutter are eliminated and background noise is reduced — **dig·i·tal·ly** \-ᵊl-ē\ *adv*

[2]digital *n* (1878) **:** a part (as a key of an organ) that is depressed with a finger to produce a mechanical effect (as the moving of a lever or the closing of a circuit)

digital computer *n* (1947) **:** a computer that operates with numbers expressed directly as digits — compare ANALOG COMPUTER, HYBRID COMPUTER

dig·i·tal·in \ˌdij-ə-ˈtal-ən *also* -ˈtāl-\ *n* [NL *Digitalis*] (1837) **1 :** a white crystalline steroid glycoside $C_{36}H_{56}O_{14}$ obtained from seeds of the common foxglove **2 :** a mixture of the glycosides of digitalis leaves or seeds

dig·i·tal·is \-ˈtal-əs *also* -ˈtāl-\ *n* [NL, genus name, fr. L, of a finger, fr. *digitus*; fr. its finger-shaped corolla] (1664) **1 :** FOXGLOVE **2 :** the dried leaf of the common foxglove containing important glycosides and serving as a powerful cardiac stimulant and a diuretic

dig·i·ta·li·za·tion \ˌdij-ət-ᵊl-ə-ˈzā-shən\ *n* [*digitalis*] (1882) **:** the administration of digitalis until the desired physiological adjustment is attained; *also* **:** the bodily state so produced

[1]dig·i·ta·lize \ˈdij-ət-ᵊl-ˌīz\ *vt* **-lized; -liz·ing** [*digitalis*] (1927) **:** to subject to digitalization

[2]dig·i·tal·ize \ˈdij-ət-ᵊl-ˌīz\ *vt* **-ized; -iz·ing** [[1]*digital*] (1962) **:** DIGITIZE

dig·i·tate \ˈdij-ə-ˌtāt\ *adj* (1661) **1 :** having digits **2 :** resembling a finger; *specif* **:** having divisions arranged like the fingers of a hand ⟨~ leaves⟩ — **dig·i·tate·ly** *adv*

digiti- *comb form* [F, fr. L *digitus*] **:** digit **:** finger ⟨*digiti*form⟩

dig·i·ti·grade \ˈdij-ət-ə-ˌgrād\ *adj* [F, fr. *digiti-* + *-grade*] (ca. 1833) **:** walking on the digits with the posterior of the foot more or less raised

dig·i·tize \ˈdij-ə-ˌtīz\ *vt* **-tized; -tiz·ing** (1953) **:** to convert (as data or an image) to digital form — **dig·i·ti·za·tion** \ˌdij-ət-ə-ˈzā-shən\ *n* — **dig·i·tiz·er** \ˈdij-ə-ˌtī-zər\ *n*

dig·i·to·nin \ˌdij-ə-ˈtō-nən\ *n* [ISV *digit-* (fr. NL *Digitalis*) + *saponin*] (1875) **:** a steroid saponin $C_{56}H_{92}O_{29}$ occurring in the leaves and seeds of foxglove

digi·toxi·gen·in \ˌdij-ə-ˌtäk-sə-ˈjen-ən\ *n* [ISV, blend of *digitoxin* and *-gen*] (ca. 1909) **:** a steroid lactone $C_{23}H_{34}O_4$ obtained esp. by hydrolysis of digitoxin

digi·tox·in \ˌdij-ə-ˈtäk-sən\ *n* [ISV, blend of NL *Digitalis* and ISV *toxin*] (ca. 1883) **:** a poisonous glycoside $C_{41}H_{64}O_{13}$ that is the most active constituent of digitalis; *also* **:** a mixture of digitalis glycosides consisting chiefly of digitoxin

dig·ni·fied \ˈdig-nə-ˌfīd\ *adj* (1763) **:** showing or expressing dignity

dig·ni·fy \ˈdig-nə-ˌfī\ *vt* **-fied; -fy·ing** [MF *dignifier*, fr. LL *dignificare*, fr. L *dignus* worthy — more at DECENT] (15c) **1 :** to give distinction to **:** ENNOBLE **2 :** to confer dignity upon by changing name, appearance, or character

dig·ni·tary \ˈdig-nə-ˌter-ē\ *n, pl* **-tar·ies** (1672) **:** one who possesses exalted rank or holds a position of dignity or honor — **dignitary** *adj*

dig·ni·ty \ˈdig-nət-ē\ *n, pl* **-ties** [ME *dignete*, fr. OF *digneté*, fr. L *dignitat-, dignitas*, fr. *dignus*] (13c) **1 :** the quality or state of being worthy, honored, or esteemed **2 a :** high rank, office, or position **b :** a legal title of nobility or honor **3** *archaic* **:** DIGNITARY **4 :** formal reserve of manner or language

dig out *vt* (14c) **1 :** FIND, UNEARTH **2 :** to make hollow by digging

di·gox·in \dij-ˈäk-sən, dig-\ *n* [ISV *dig-* (fr. NL *Digitalis*) + *toxin*] (ca. 1930) **:** a poisonous cardiotonic steroid $C_{41}H_{64}O_{14}$ obtained from a foxglove (*Digitalis lanata*) and used similarly to digitalis

di·graph \ˈdī-ˌgraf\ *n* (1788) **1 :** a group of two successive letters whose phonetic value is a single sound (as *ea* in *bread* or *ng* in *sing*) or whose value is not the sum of a value borne by each in other occurrences (as *ch* in *chin* where the value is \t\ + \sh\ **2 :** a group of two successive letters **3 :** LIGATURE 4 — **di·graph·ic** \dī-ˈgraf-ik\ *adj* — **di·graph·i·cal·ly** \-i-k(ə-)lē\ *adv*

di·gress \dī-ˈgres, də-\ *vi* [L *digressus*, pp. of *digredi*, fr. *dis-* + *gradi* to step — more at GRADE] (1530) **:** to turn aside esp. from the main subject of attention or course of argument in writing or speaking ***syn*** see SWERVE

di·gres·sion \-ˈgresh-ən\ *n* (14c) **1 :** the act or an instance of digressing in a discourse or other usu. organized literary work **2** *archaic* **:** a going aside — **di·gres·sion·al** \-ˈgresh-nəl, -ən-ᵊl\ *adj* — **di·gres·sion·ary** \-ˈgresh-ə-ˌner-ē\ *adj*

di·gres·sive \-ˈgres-iv\ *adj* (1611) **:** characterized by digressions ⟨a ~ book⟩ — **di·gres·sive·ly** *adv* — **di·gres·sive·ness** *n*

dig up *vt* (14c) **:** FIND, UNEARTH

dihal- *or* **dihalo-** *comb form* **:** containing two atoms of a halogen

[1]di·he·dral \(ˈ)dī-ˈhē-drəl\ *adj* (ca. 1909) **1** *of airplane wing pairs* **:** inclined at a dihedral angle to each other **2** *of an airplane* **:** having wings that make with one another a dihedral angle esp. when the angle between the upper sides is less than 180°

[2]dihedral *n* (ca. 1909) **1 :** DIHEDRAL ANGLE **2 :** the angle between an aircraft supporting surface and a horizontal transverse line

dihedral angle *n* [*di-* + *-hedral*] (1826) **:** a figure formed by two intersecting planes

di·hy·brid \(ˌ)dī-ˈhī-brəd\ *adj* [ISV] (1907) **:** of, relating to, involving, or being an individual or strain that is heterozygous at two genetic loci — **dihybrid** *n*

dihydr- *or* **dihydro-** *comb form* **:** combined with two atoms of hydrogen

di·hy·dro·er·got·a·mine \(ˌ)dī-ˌhī-drō-ˌər-ˈgät-ə-ˌmēn\ *n* (1945) **:** a hydrogenated derivative $C_{33}H_{37}N_5O_5$ of ergotamine that is used in the treatment of migraine

di·hy·dro·strep·to·my·cin \-ˌstrep-tə-ˈmīs-ᵊn\ *n* (1946) **:** a toxic antibiotic $C_{21}H_{41}N_7O_{12}$ no longer used in medicine because of its tendency to impair hearing

dihydroxy- *comb form* **:** containing two hydroxyl groups

di·hy·droxy·ac·e·tone \ˌdī-hī-ˌdräk-sē-ˈas-ə-ˌtōn\ *n* (1895) **:** a glyceraldehyde isomer $C_3H_6O_3$ that is used esp. to stain the skin to resemble a tan

dik–dik \ˈdik-ˌdik\ *n* [native name in East Africa] (1883) **:** any of several small East African antelopes (genera *Madoqua, Rhynchotragus*)

[1]dike \ˈdīk\ *n* [ME, fr. OE *dīc* ditch, dike; akin to MHG *tīch* pond, dike, L *figere* to fasten, pierce] (bef. 12c) **1** : an artificial watercourse : DITCH **2 a** : a bank usu. of earth constructed to control or confine water : LEVEE **b** : a barrier preventing passage esp. of something undesirable **3 a** : a raised causeway **b** : a tabular body of igneous rock that has been injected while molten into a fissure

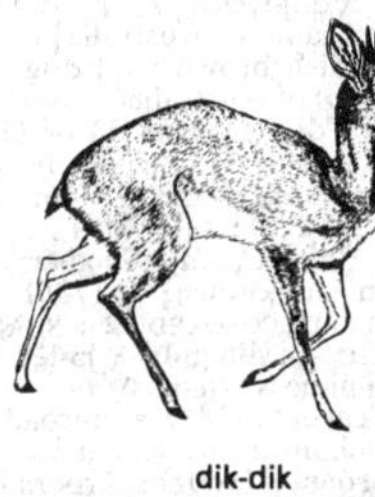

dik-dik

[2]dike *vt* **diked; dik·ing** (14c) **1** : to surround or protect with a dike **2** : to drain by a dike — **dik·er** *n*

[3]dike *var of* [2]DYKE

dik·tat \dik-ˈtät\ *n* [G, lit., something dictated, fr. NL *dictatum,* fr. L, neut. of *dictatus,* pp. of *dictare* to dictate] (1933) **1** : a harsh settlement unilaterally imposed (as on a defeated nation) **2** : DECREE, DICTATE

Di·lan·tin \dī-ˈlant-ᵊn, də-\ *trademark* — used for phenytoin

di·lap·i·date \də-ˈlap-ə-ˌdāt\ *vb* **-dat·ed; -dat·ing** [L *dilapidatus,* pp. of *dilapidare* to squander, destroy, fr. *dis-* + *lapidare* to throw stones, fr. *lapid-, lapis* stone — more at LAPIDARY] *vt* (ca. 1570) **1** : to bring into a condition of decay or partial ruin ⟨furniture is *dilapidated* by use — Janet Flanner⟩ **2** *archaic* : SQUANDER ~ *vi* : to become dilapidated — **di·lap·i·da·tion** \-ˌlap-ə-ˈdā-shən\ *n*

di·lap·i·dat·ed *adj* (1806) : decayed, deteriorated, or fallen into partial ruin esp. through neglect or misuse ⟨a ~ old house⟩

di·lat·an·cy \dī-ˈlāt-ᵊn-sē\ *n* (1885) : the property of being dilatant

di·lat·ant \-ᵊnt\ *adj* (1885) : increasing in viscosity and setting to a solid as a result of deformation by expansion, pressure, or agitation

di·la·ta·tion \ˌdil-ə-ˈtā-shən, ˌdī-lə-\ *n* (14c) **1** : amplification in writing or speech **2 a** : the condition of being stretched beyond normal dimensions esp. as a result of overwork or disease or of abnormal relaxation ⟨~ of the heart⟩ ⟨~ of the stomach⟩ **b** : DILATION 2 **3** : the action of expanding : the state of being expanded **4** : a dilated part or formation — **di·la·ta·tion·al** \-shnəl, -shən-ᵊl\ *adj*

di·late \dī-ˈlāt, ˈdī-ˌ\ *vb* **di·lat·ed; di·lat·ing** [ME *dilaten,* fr. MF *dilater,* fr. L *dilatare,* lit., to spread wide, fr. *dis-* + *latus* wide — more at LATITUDE] *vt* (14c) **1** *archaic* : to describe or set forth at length or in detail **2** : to enlarge or expand in bulk or extent : DISTEND ~ *vi* **1** : to comment at length : DISCOURSE ⟨~ on a topic⟩ **2** : to become wide : SWELL *syn* see EXPAND — **di·lat·abil·i·ty** \(ˌ)dī-ˌlāt-ə-ˈbil-ət-ē\ *n* — **di·lat·able** \dī-ˈlāt-ə-bəl, ˈdī-ˌ\ *adj* — **di·la·tor** \dī-ˈlāt-ər, ˈdī-ˌ\ *n*

di·lat·ed *adj* (15c) **1** : expanded laterally **2** *of an insect part* : having a broad expanded border **3** : expanded normally or abnormally in all dimensions

di·la·tion \dī-ˈlā-shən\ *n* (15c) **1** : the act or action of dilating : the state of being dilated : EXPANSION, DILATATION **2** : the action of stretching or enlarging an organ or part of the body

di·la·tive \dī-ˈlāt-iv, ˈdī-ˌ\ *adj* (15c) : causing dilation : tending to dilate

di·la·tom·e·ter \ˌdil-ə-ˈtäm-ət-ər, ˌdī-lə-\ *n* [ISV] (ca. 1883) : an instrument for measuring expansion — **di·la·to·met·ric** \-tō-ˈme-trik\ *adj* — **di·la·tom·e·try** \-ˈtäm-ə-trē\ *n*

dil·a·to·ry \ˈdil-ə-ˌtōr-ē, -ˌtȯr-\ *adj* [LL *dilatorius,* fr. L *dilatus* (pp. of *differre* to postpone, differ), fr. *dis-* + *latus,* pp. of *ferre* to carry — more at DIFFER, TOLERATE] (15c) **1** : tending or intended to cause delay ⟨~ tactics⟩ **2** : characterized by procrastination : TARDY ⟨~ in answering letters⟩ — **dil·a·to·ri·ly** \ˌdil-ə-ˈtōr-ə-lē, -ˈtȯr-\ *adv* — **dil·a·to·ri·ness** \ˈdil-ə-ˌtōr-ē-nəs, -ˌtȯr-\ *n*

dil·do \ˈdil-(ˌ)dō\ *n, pl* **dildos** [origin unknown] (1598) : an object serving as a penis substitute for vaginal insertion

di·lem·ma \də-ˈlem-ə *also* dī-\ *n* [LL, fr. LGk *dilēmmat-, dilēmma,* prob. back-formation fr. Gk *dilēmmatos* involving two assumptions, fr. *di-* + *lēmmat-, lēmma* assumption — more at LEMMA] (1523) **1** : an argument presenting two or more equally conclusive alternatives against an opponent **2 a** : a choice or a situation involving choice between equally unsatisfactory alternatives **b** : a difficult or persistent problem ⟨unemployment . . . the great central ~ of our advancing technology —August Heckscher⟩ — **dil·em·mat·ic** \ˌdil-ə-ˈmat-ik *also* ˌdī-lə-\ *adj*

dil·et·tante \ˈdil-ə-ˌtänt, -ˌtant; ˌdil-ə-ˈtänt(-ē), -ˈtant(-ē)\ *n, pl* **-tantes** *or* **-tan·ti** \-ˈtänt-ē, -ˈtant-ē\ [It, fr. prp. of *dilettare* to delight, fr. L *dilectare* — more at DELIGHT] (1748) **1** : an admirer or lover of the arts **2** : a person having a superficial interest in an art or a branch of knowledge : DABBLER *syn* see AMATEUR — **dilettante** *adj* — **dil·et·tant·ish** \-ˌtänt-ish, -ˌtant-, ˌdil-ə-ˈ\ *adj* — **dil·et·tan·tism** \-ˌtän-ˌtiz-əm, -ˌtan-, ˌdil-ə-ˈ\ *n*

[1]dil·i·gence \ˈdil-ə-jən(t)s\ *n* [ME, fr. MF, fr. L *diligentia,* fr. *diligent-, diligens*] (14c) **1 a** : persevering application : ASSIDUITY **b** *obs* : SPEED, HASTE **2** : the attention and care legally expected or required of a person (as a party to a contract)

[2]di·li·gence \ˈdil-ə-ˌzhäⁿs, ˈdil-ə-jən(t)s\ *n* [F, lit., haste, fr. MF, persevering application] (1742) : STAGECOACH

dil·i·gent \ˈdil-ə-jənt\ *adj* [ME, fr. MF, fr. L *diligent-, diligens,* fr. prp. of *diligere* to esteem, love, fr. *di-* (fr. *dis-* apart) + *legere* to select — more at LEGEND] (14c) : characterized by steady, earnest, and energetic application and effort : PAINSTAKING *syn* see BUSY — **dil·i·gent·ly** *adv*

dill \ˈdil\ *n* [ME *dile,* fr. OE; akin to OHG *tilli* dill] (bef. 12c) **1** : any of several plants of the carrot family; *esp* : a European herb (*Anethum graveolens*) with aromatic foliage and seeds both of which are used in flavoring foods and esp. pickles **2** : DILL PICKLE — **dilled** *adj*

dill pickle *n* (1904) : a pickle seasoned with fresh dill or dill juice

dil·ly \ˈdil-ē\ *n, pl* **dillies** [obs. slang *dilly,* adj. (delightful), irreg. fr. E *delightful*] (ca. 1935) : one that is remarkable or outstanding ⟨had a ~ of a storm⟩ ⟨for a practical joke, that was a ~⟩

dil·ly bag \ˈdil-ē-\ *n* [Australian *dhilla* hair] (1847) : an Australian mesh bag made of native fibers

dil·ly·dal·ly \ˈdil-ē-ˌdal-ē\ *vi* [redupl. of *dally*] (1741) : to waste time by loitering : DAWDLE

[1]dil·u·ent \ˈdil-yə-wənt\ *n* [L *diluent-, diluens,* prp. of *diluere*] (1721) : a diluting agent (as the vehicle in a medicinal preparation)

[2]diluent *adj* (1731) : making thinner or less concentrated by admixture : DILUTING

[1]di·lute \dī-ˈlüt, də-\ *vt* **di·lut·ed; di·lut·ing** [L *dilutus,* pp. of *diluere* to wash away, dilute, fr. *di-* + *lavere* to wash — more at LYE] (1555) **1** : ATTENUATE **2** : to make thinner or more liquid by admixture **3** : to diminish the strength, flavor, or brilliance of by admixture — **di·lut·er** *or* **di·lu·tor** \-ˈlüt-ər\ *n* — **di·lu·tive** \-ˈlüt-iv\ *adj*

[2]dilute *adj* (1605) : WEAK, DILUTED — **di·lute·ness** *n*

di·lu·tion \dī-ˈlü-shən, də-\ *n* (1646) **1** : the action of diluting : the state of being diluted **2** : something (as a solution) that is diluted **3** : a lessening of real value (as of equity) by a decrease in relative worth through attrition ⟨~ of savings by inflation⟩

di·lu·vi·al \də-ˈlü-vē-əl, dī-\ *or* **di·lu·vi·an** \-vē-ən\ *adj* [LL *diluvialis,* fr. L *diluvium* deluge — more at DELUGE] (ca. 1656) : of, relating to, or effected by a flood

[1]dim \ˈdim\ *adj* **dim·mer; dim·mest** [ME, fr. OE *dimm;* akin to OHG *timber* dark, Skt *dhamati* he blows — more at DAMP] (bef. 12c) **1 a** : emitting a limited or insufficient amount of light **b** : DULL, LUSTERLESS **c** : lacking pronounced, clear-cut, or vigorous quality or character **2 a** : seen indistinctly or without clear outlines or details **b** : perceived by the senses or mind indistinctly or weakly : FAINT ⟨had only a ~ notion of what was going on⟩ **c** : having little prospect of favorable result or outcome ⟨a ~ future⟩ **d** : characterized by an unfavorable, skeptical, or pessimistic attitude — usu. used in the phrase *take a dim view of* **3** : not perceiving clearly and distinctly ⟨~ eyes⟩ **4** : DIM-WITTED — **dim·ly** *adv* — **dim·ma·ble** \ˈdim-ə-bəl\ *adj* — **dim·ness** *n*

[2]dim *vb* **dimmed; dim·ming** *vt* (bef. 12c) **1** : to make dim or lusterless **2** : to reduce the light from (headlights) by switching to the low beam ~ *vi* : to become dim

[3]dim *n* (14c) **1** *archaic* : DUSK, DIMNESS **2 a** : a small light on an automobile for use in parking **b** : LOW BEAM

dime \ˈdīm\ *n* [ME, tenth part, tithe, fr. MF, fr. L *decima,* fr. fem. of *decimus* tenth, fr. *decem* ten — more at TEN] (1786) **1 a** : a coin of the U.S. worth $^1/_{10}$ dollar **b** : a petty sum of money **2** : a Canadian 10-cent piece — **a dime a dozen** : so plentiful or commonplace as to be of little esteem or slight value — **on a dime** : in a very small area ⟨these cars can turn *on a dime*⟩

di·men·hy·dri·nate \ˌdī-ˌmen-ˈhī-drə-ˌnāt\ *n* [*dime*thyl- + amine + *hydr-* + amine + *-ate*] (ca. 1950) : a crystalline compound $C_{24}H_{28}ClN_5O_3$ used esp. as an antihistaminic and to prevent nausea

dime novel *n* (1864) : a usu. paperback melodramatic novel

[1]di·men·sion \də-ˈmen-chən *also* dī-\ *n* [ME, fr. MF, fr. L *dimension-, dimensio,* fr. *dimensus,* pp. of *dimetiri* to measure out, fr. *dis-* + *metiri* to measure — more at MEASURE] (14c) **1 a** (1) : measure in one direction; *specif* : one of three coordinates determining a position in space or four coordinates determining a position in space and time (2) : one of a group of properties whose number is necessary and sufficient to determine uniquely each element of a system of usu. mathematical entities (as an aggregate of points in real or abstract space) ⟨the surface of a sphere has two ~*s*⟩; *also* : a parameter or coordinate variable assigned to such a property ⟨the three ~*s* of momentum⟩ (3) : the number of elements in a basis of a vector space **b** : the quality of spatial extension : MAGNITUDE, SIZE **c** : the range over which or the degree to which something extends : SCOPE — usu. used in pl. **d** : one of the elements or factors making up a complete personality or entity : ASPECT **2** *obs* : bodily form or proportions **3** : wood or stone cut to pieces of specified size — **di·men·sion·al** \-ˈmench-nəl, -ˈmen-chən-ᵊl\ *adj* — **di·men·sion·al·i·ty** \-ˌmen-chə-ˈnal-ət-ē\ *n* — **di·men·sion·al·ly** \-ˈmench-nə-lē, -ˈmen-chən-ᵊl-ē\ *adv* — **di·men·sion·less** \-ˈmen-chən-ləs\ *adj*

[2]dimension *vt* **di·men·sioned; di·men·sion·ing** \-ˈmench-(ə-)niŋ\ (1754) **1** : to form to the required dimensions **2** : to indicate the dimensions on (a drawing)

di·mer \ˈdī-mər\ *n* [ISV *di-* + *-mer* (as in *polymer*)] (ca. 1926) : a compound formed by the union of two radicals or two molecules of a simpler compound; *specif* : a polymer formed from two molecules of a monomer — **di·mer·ic** \(ˈ)dī-ˈmer-ik\ *adj* — **di·mer·iza·tion** \ˌdī-mə-rə-ˈzā-shən\ *n* — **di·mer·ize** \ˈdī-mə-ˌrīz\ *vt*

di·mer·cap·rol \ˌdī-mər-ˈkap-ˌrōl, -ˌrȯl\ *n* [*di-* + *mercaptan* + *propane* + *-ol*] (1947) : a compound $C_3H_8OS_2$ developed as an antidote against lewisite and used against other arsenicals and against mercurials — called also *BAL*

dim·er·ous \ˈdim-ə-rəs\ *adj* [NL *dimerus,* fr. L *di-* + NL *-merus* -merous] *of a flower* (1826) : having two members in each whorl

dime store *n* (ca. 1928) : FIVE-AND-TEN

dim·e·ter \ˈdim-ət-ər\ *n* [LL, fr. Gk *dimetros,* adj., being a dimeter, fr. *di-* + *metron* measure — more at MEASURE] (1589) : a line of verse consisting of two metrical feet or of two dipodies

di·meth·o·ate \dī-ˈmeth-ə-ˌwāt\ *n* [*dimethyl-* + *thio* acid + [1]*-ate*] (1960) : an insecticide $C_5H_{12}NO_3PS_2$ used on livestock and various crops

dimethyl- *comb form* : containing two methyl groups

di·meth·yl·hy·dra·zine \ˌdī-ˌmeth-əl-ˈhī-drə-ˌzēn\ *n* (1961) : either of two flammable corrosive isomeric liquids $C_2H_8N_2$ which are methylated derivatives of hydrazine and of which one is used in rocket fuels

di·meth·yl·ni·tros·amine \-nī-ˈtrō-sə-ˌmēn\ *n* (1965) : a carcinogenic nitrosamine $C_2H_6N_2O$ that occurs esp. in tobacco smoke

di·meth·yl sulfoxide \ˌdī-ˌmeth-əl-\ *n* (1964) : a compound $(CH_3)_2SO$ obtained as a by-product in wood-pulp manufacture and used as a solvent and in experimental medicine — called also *DMSO*

di·meth·yl·tryp·ta·mine \-ˈtrip-tə-ˌmēn\ *n* [*dimethyl-* + *tryp*tophan + *amine*] (1966) : an easily synthesized hallucinogenic drug $C_{12}H_{16}N_2$ that is chemically similar to but shorter acting than psilocybin — called also *DMT*

di·min·ish \də-ˈmin-ish\ *vb* [ME *deminishen,* alter. of *diminuen,* fr. MF *diminuer,* fr. LL *diminuere,* alter. of L *deminuere,* fr. *de-* + *minuere* to lessen — more at MINOR] *vt* (15c) **1** : to make less or cause to appear less **2** : to lessen the authority, dignity, or reputation of : BELITTLE **3**

: to cause to taper ~ *vi* **1** : to become gradually less (as in size or importance) : DWINDLE **2** : TAPER *syn* see DECREASE — **di·min·ish·able** \-ə-bəl\ *adj* — **di·min·ish·ment** \-mənt\ *n*
di·min·ished *adj, of a musical interval* (ca. 1727) : made one half step less than perfect or minor ⟨a ~ fifth⟩
diminishing returns *n pl* (1815) : a rate of yield that beyond a certain point fails to increase in proportion to additional investments of labor or capital
di·min·u·en·do \də-ˌmin-(y)ə-ˈwen-(ˌ)dō\ *adv or adj* [It, lit., diminishing, fr. LL *diminuendum,* gerund of *diminuere*] (1775) : DECRESCENDO — **diminuendo** *n*
dim·i·nu·tion \ˌdim-ə-ˈn(y)ü-shən\ *n* [ME *diminucioun,* fr. MF *diminution,* fr. ML *diminution-, diminutio,* alter. of L *deminution-, deminutio,* fr. *deminutus,* pp. of *deminuere*] (14c) : the act, process, or an instance of diminishing : DECREASE
1**di·min·u·tive** \də-ˈmin-yət-iv\ *n* [ME *diminutif,* fr. ML *diminutivum,* alter. of LL *deminutivum,* fr. neut. of *deminutivus,* adj., fr. *deminutus,* pp.] (14c) **1** : a diminutive word, affix, or name **2** : a diminutive individual
2**diminutive** *adj* (14c) **1** : indicating small size and sometimes the state or quality of being familiarly known, lovable, pitiable, or contemptible — used of affixes (as *-ette, -kin, -ling*) and of words formed with them (as *kitchenette, manikin, duckling*), of clipped forms (as *Jim*), and of altered forms (as *Peggy*); compare AUGMENTATIVE **2** : exceptionally or notably small : TINY *syn* see SMALL — **di·min·u·tive·ly** *adv* — **di·min·u·tive·ness** *n*
dim·i·ty \ˈdim-ət-ē\ *n, pl* **-ties** [alter. of ME *demyt,* prob. fr. MGk *dimitos* of double thread, fr. Gk *di-* + *mitos* warp thread] (15c) : a sheer usu. corded cotton fabric of plain weave in checks or stripes
dim·mer \ˈdim-ər\ *n* (ca. 1896) **1** : a device for regulating the intensity of an electric lighting unit **2** *pl* **a** : small lights on an automobile for use in parking **b** : LOW BEAM
di·mor·phic \(ˈ)dī-ˈmȯr-fik\ *adj* (1859) **1 a** : DIMORPHOUS 1 **b** : occurring in two distinct forms ⟨~ leaves of emergent plants⟩ ⟨a sexually ~ butterfly⟩ **2** : combining qualities of two kinds of individuals in one
di·mor·phism \-ˌfiz-əm\ *n* [ISV] (1832) : the condition or property of being dimorphic or dimorphous: as **a** (1) : the existence of two different forms (as of color or size) of a species esp. in the same population ⟨sexual ~⟩ (2) : the existence of an organ (as the leaves of a plant) in two different forms **b** : crystallization of a chemical compound in two different forms
di·mor·phous \(ˈ)dī-ˈmȯr-fəs\ *adj* [Gk *dimorphos* having two forms, fr. *di-* + *-morphos* -morphous] (1832) **1** : crystallizing in two different forms **2** : DIMORPHIC 1b
dim·out \ˈdim-ˌau̇t\ *n* (1942) : a restriction limiting the use or showing of lights at night esp. during the threat of an air raid; *also* : a condition of partial darkness produced by this restriction
1**dim·ple** \ˈdim-pəl\ *n* [ME *dympull;* akin to OHG *tumphilo* whirlpool, OE *dyppan* to dip — more at DIP] (15c) **1** : a slight natural indentation in the surface of some part of the human body **2** : a depression or indentation on a surface (as of a golf ball) — **dim·ply** \-p(ə-)lē\ *adj*
2**dimple** *vb* **dim·pled; dim·pling** \-p(ə-)liŋ\ *vt* (1602) : to mark with dimples ~ *vi* : to exhibit or form dimples
dim sum \ˈdim-ˈsəm\ *n* [Chin (Cant) *tím sam,* lit., small center] (1968) : traditional Chinese refreshments consisting chiefly of steamed or fried dumplings with a savory filling
dim·wit \ˈdim-ˌwit\ *n* (ca. 1922) : a stupid or mentally slow person
dim–wit·ted \-ˈwit-əd\ *adj* (1934) : not mentally bright : STUPID — **dim–wit·ted·ly** *adv* — **dim–wit·ted·ness** *n*
1**din** \ˈdin\ *n* [ME, fr. OE *dyne;* akin to ON *dynr* din, Skt *dhvanati* it roars] (bef. 12c) : a loud continued noise; *esp* : a welter of discordant sounds
2**din** *vb* **dinned; din·ning** *vi* (bef. 12c) : to make a loud noise ~ *vt* **1** : to assail with loud continued noise **2** : to impress by insistent repetition
di·nar \di-ˈnär, ˈdē-ˌ\ *n* [Ar *dīnār,* fr. LGk *dēnarion* denarius, fr. L *denarius* — more at DENIER] (1634) **1** : a gold coin formerly used in Muslim countries **2 a** —see MONEY table **b** —see *dirham, rial* at MONEY table
1**dine** \ˈdīn\ *vb* **dined; din·ing** [ME *dinen,* fr. OF *diner,* fr. (assumed) VL *disjejunare* to break one's fast, fr. L *dis-* + LL *jejunare* to fast, fr. L *jejunus* fasting] *vi* (13c) : to take dinner ~ *vt* : to give a dinner to
2**dine** *n, Scot* (15c) : DINNER
dine out *vi* (1816) : to eat a meal away from home
din·er \ˈdī-nər\ *n* (1815) **1** : one that dines **2 a** : DINING CAR **b** : a restaurant usu. resembling a dining car in shape
din·er–out \ˌdī-nə-ˈrau̇t\ *n, pl* **di·ners–out** \-nər-ˈzau̇t\ (1807) : one who dines out
di·nette \dī-ˈnet\ *n* (1925) : a small space usu. off a kitchen used for informal dining; *also* : furniture for such a space
1**ding** \ˈdiŋ\ *vb* [prob. imit.] *vt* (1582) : to dwell on with tiresome repetition ⟨keeps ~*ing* it into him that the less he smokes the better —Samuel Butler †1902⟩ ~ *vi* **1** : to make a ringing sound : CLANG **2** : to speak with tiresome reiteration
2**ding** *n* [*ding* (to strike), fr. ME *dingen*] (ca. 1945) : minor surface damage (as a dent)
ding–a–ling \ˈdiŋ-ə-ˌliŋ\ *n* [redupl. of 1*ding*] (ca. 1935) : NITWIT, KOOK
ding·bat \ˈdiŋ-ˌbat\ *n* [origin unknown] (1904) **1** : a typographical symbol or ornament (as ✱, ¶, or ✠) **2** : NITWIT, KOOK
1**ding·dong** \ˈdiŋ-ˌdȯŋ, -ˌdäŋ\ *n* [imit.] (1611) : the ringing sound produced by repeated strokes esp. on a bell
2**dingdong** *vi* (1659) **1** : to make a dingdong sound **2** : to repeat a sound or action tediously or insistently
3**dingdong** *adj* (1792) **1** : of, relating to, or resembling the ringing sound made by a bell **2** : marked by a rapid exchange or alternation
dinge \ˈdinj\ *n* [back-formation fr. *dingy*] (1846) : the condition of being dingy
din·ghy \ˈdiŋ-(k)ē, -gē\ *n, pl* **dinghies** [Bengali *ḍiṅgi* & Hindi *ḍiṅgī*] (1810) **1** : an East Indian rowboat or sailboat **2** : a small boat propelled by oars, sails, or motor that is often carried on a larger boat as a tender or a lifeboat **3** : a rubber life raft
din·gle \ˈdiŋ-gəl\ *n* [ME, abyss] (13c) : a small wooded valley : DELL
din·gle·ber·ry \ˈdiŋ-gəl-ˌber-ē\ *n* [origin unknown] (ca. 1923) : a shrub (*Vaccinium erythrocarpus*) of the southeastern U.S.; *also* : its globose dark red edible berry
din·go \ˈdiŋ-(ˌ)gō\ *n, pl* **dingoes** [native name in Australia] (1789) : a reddish brown wild dog (*Canis dingo*) of Australia

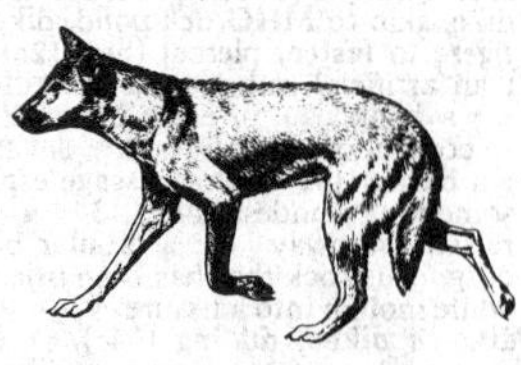
dingo

din·gus \ˈdiŋ-(g)əs\ *n* [D or G; D *dinges,* prob. fr. G *dings,* fr. gen. of *ding* thing, fr. OHG — more at THING] (1876) : DOODAD 1
din·gy \ˈdin-jē\ *adj* **din·gi·er; -est** [origin unknown] (1736) **1** : DIRTY, DISCOLORED **2** : SHABBY, SQUALID — **din·gi·ly** \-jə-lē\ *adv* — **din·gi·ness** \-jē-nəs\ *n*
dining car *n* (1838) : a railroad car in which meals are served
dining room *n* (1601) : a room used for the taking of meals
dinitro- *comb form* : containing two nitro groups
di·ni·tro·ben·zene \(ˌ)dī-ˌnī-trō-ˈben-ˌzēn, -(ˌ)ben-ˈ\ *n* [ISV] (1873) : any of three isomeric toxic compounds $C_6H_4(NO_2)_2$; *esp* : the yellow meta isomer used chiefly as a dye intermediate
di·ni·tro·phe·nol \-ˈfē-ˌnōl, -fi-ˈ\ *n* (ca. 1896) : any of six isomeric crystalline compounds $C_6H_4N_2O_5$ some of whose derivatives are pesticides
1**dink** \ˈdiŋk\ *n* [by shortening and alter.] (1903) : DINGHY
2**dink** *n* [*dink* (to hit with a drop shot), prob. of imit. origin] (1939) : DROP SHOT
din·key *or* **din·ky** \ˈdiŋ-kē\ *n, pl* **dinkeys** *or* **dinkies** [prob. fr. *dinky*] (1874) : a small locomotive used esp. for hauling freight, logging, and shunting
1**din·kum** \ˈdiŋ-kəm\ *adj* [prob. fr. E dial. *dinkum,* n., work] *Austral & NewZeal* (1894) : AUTHENTIC, GENUINE
2**dinkum** *adv, Austral & NewZeal* (ca. 1956) : TRULY, HONESTLY
din·ky \ˈdiŋ-kē\ *adj* **din·ki·er; -est** [Sc *dink* neat] (1880) : SMALL, INSIGNIFICANT
din·ner \ˈdin-ər\ *n, often attrib* [ME *diner,* fr. OF, fr. *diner* to dine] (14c) **1 a** : the principal meal of the day **b** : a formal feast or banquet **2** : TABLE D'HÔTE 2 **3** : the food prepared for a dinner ⟨eat your ~⟩ **4** : a packaged meal usu. for quick preparation ⟨warmed up a frozen Chinese ~⟩ — **din·ner·less** \-ləs\ *adj*
dinner jacket *n* (1891) : a jacket for formal evening wear
dinner theater *n* (1967) : a restaurant in which a play is presented after the meal is over
din·ner·time \ˈdin-ər-ˌtīm\ *n* (14c) : the time at which it is customary to eat dinner
din·ner·ware \-ˌwa(ə)r, -ˌwe(ə)r\ *n* (1895) : tableware other than flatware
di·no·fla·gel·late \ˌdī-nō-ˈflaj-ə-lət, -ˌlāt; -flə-ˈjel-ət\ *n* [deriv. of Gk *dinos* rotation, eddy + NL *flagellum*] (1889) : any of an order (Dinoflagellata) of chiefly marine planktonic usu. solitary phytoflagellates that include luminescent forms, forms important in marine food chains, and forms causing red tide
di·no·saur \ˈdī-nə-ˌsȯ(ə)r\ *n* [deriv. of Gk *deinos* terrible + *sauros* lizard — more at DIRE, SAURIAN] (1841) **1** : any of a group (Dinosauria) of extinct chiefly terrestrial carnivorous or herbivorous reptiles **2** : any of various large extinct reptiles other than the true dinosaurs **3** : one that is impractically large, out-of-date, or obsolete — **di·no·sau·ri·an** \ˌdī-nə-ˈsȯr-ē-ən\ *adj*
1**dint** \ˈdint\ *n* [ME, fr. OE *dynt;* akin to ON *dyntr* noise] (bef. 12c) **1** *archaic* : BLOW, STROKE **2** : FORCE, POWER **3** : 2DENT — **by dint of** : by force of : BECAUSE OF
2**dint** *vt* (1597) **1** : to make a dent in **2** : to impress or drive in with force
di·nu·cle·o·tide \(ˌ)dī-ˈn(y)ü-klē-ə-ˌtīd\ *n* (ca. 1927) : a nucleotide consisting of two units each composed of a phosphate, a pentose, and a nitrogen base
di·oc·e·san \dī-ˈäs-ə-sən *also* ˌdī-ə-ˈsēz-ᵊn\ *n* (15c) : a bishop having jurisdiction over a diocese
di·o·cese \ˈdī-ə-səs, -ˌsēz, -ˌsēs\ *n, pl* **-ces·es** \ˈdī-ə-ˌsēz, -ˌsē-zəz, -sə-səz, -sə-ˌsēz\ [ME *diocise,* fr. MF, fr. LL *diocesis,* alter. of *dioecesis,* fr. L, administrative division, fr. Gk *dioikēsis* administration, administrative division, fr. *dioikein* to keep house, govern, fr. *dia-* + *oikein* to dwell, manage, fr. *oikos* house — more at VICINITY] (14c) : the territorial jurisdiction of a bishop — **di·oc·e·san** \dī-ˈäs-ə-sən *also* ˌdī-ə-ˈsēz-ᵊn\ *adj*
di·ode \ˈdī-ˌōd\ *n* [ISV] (1919) **1** : a 2-electrode electron tube having a cathode and an anode **2** : a rectifier that consists of a semiconducting crystal with two terminals and that is analogous in use to an electron tube diode
di·oe·cious \(ˈ)dī-ˈē-shəs\ *adj* [deriv. of Gk *di-* + *oikos*] (1748) **1** : having male reproductive organs in one individual and female in another **2** : having staminate and pistillate flowers borne on different individuals — **di·oe·cism** \-ˈē-ˌsiz-əm\ *n*
di·ol \ˈdī-ˌōl, -ˌȯl\ *n* [ISV *di-* + 1*-ol*] (1923) : a compound (as glycol) containing two hydroxyl groups
di·ole·fin \dī-ˈō-lə-fən\ *n* [ISV] (ca. 1909) : any of a series of aliphatic hydrocarbons containing two double bonds — called also *diene*
Di·o·me·des \ˌdī-ə-ˈmēd-ēz\ *n* [L, fr. Gk *Diomēdēs*] : one of the Greek heroes of the Trojan War
Di·o·ny·sia \ˌdī-ə-ˈniz(h)-ē-ə, -ˈnis(h)-; -ˈnizh-ə, -ˈnish-; -ˈnī-sē-ə, -ˈnē-, -zē-\ *n pl* [L, fr. Gk, fr. neut. pl. of *dionysios* of Dionysus, fr. *Dionysos*] (ca. 1891) : ancient Greek festival observances held in seasonal cycles in honor of Dionysus; *esp* : such observances marked by dramatic performances
Di·o·ny·si·ac \-ˈniz(h)-ē-ˌak, -ˈnis(h)-; -ˈnī-zē-, -ˈnē-, -sē-\ *adj* [L *dionysiacus,* fr. Gk *dionysiakos,* fr. *Dionysos*] (1860) : DIONYSIAN 2 — **Dionysiac** *n*
Di·o·ny·sian \-ˈniz(h)-ē-ən, -ˈnis(h)-; -ˈnizh-ən, -ˈnish-; -ˈnī-sē-ən, -ˈnē-, -zē-\ *adj* (1607) **1 a** : of or relating to Dionysius **b** : of or related to the theological writings once mistakenly attributed to Dionysius the Areopagite **2 a** : devoted to the worship of Dionysus **b** : being of a frenzied or orgiastic character — compare APOLLONIAN
Di·o·ny·sus \ˌdī-ə-ˈnī-səs, -ˈnē-\ *n* [L, fr. Gk *Dionysos*] : BACCHUS
Di·o·phan·tine equation \ˌdī-ə-ˈfan-ˌtīn-, -ˈfant-ᵊn-\ *n* [*Diophantus,* 3d cent. A.D. Gk. mathematician] (ca. 1928) : an indeterminate polynomial equation with integral coefficients for which it is required to find all integral solutions

di·op·side \dī-ˈäp-ˌsīd\ *n* [F, fr. *di-* + Gk *opsis* appearance — more at OPTIC] (ca. 1808) : a green to white mineral that consists of pyroxene containing little or no aluminum — **di·op·sid·ic** \ˌdī-ˌäp-ˈsid-ik\ *adj*

di·op·ter \dī-ˈäp-tər\ *n* [*diopter* (an optical instrument), fr. MF *dioptre,* fr. L *dioptra,* fr. Gk, fr. *dia-* + *opsesthai* to be going to see — more at OPTIC] (ca. 1864) : a unit of measurement of the refractive power of lenses equal to the reciprocal of the focal length in meters

di·op·tric \dī-ˈäp-trik\ *adj* [Gk *dioptrikos* of a diopter (instrument), fr. *dioptra*] (1653) **1 :** relating to or functioning in refraction of a beam of light : REFRACTIVE; *specif* **:** assisting vision by refracting and focalizing light **2 :** produced by means of refraction

di·ora·ma \ˌdī-ə-ˈram-ə, -ˈräm-\ *n* [F, fr. *dia-* + *-orama* (as in *panorama,* fr. E)] (1823) **1 :** a scenic representation in which a partly translucent painting is seen from a distance through an opening **2 a :** a scenic representation in which sculptured figures and lifelike details are displayed usu. in miniature so as to blend indistinguishably with a realistic painted background **b :** a life-size exhibit of a wildlife specimen or scene with realistic natural surroundings and a painted background — **di·oram·ic** \-ˈram-ik\ *adj*

di·o·rite \ˈdī-ə-ˌrīt\ *n* [F, irreg. fr. Gk *diorizein* to distinguish, fr. *dia-* + *horizein* to define — more at HORIZON] (1826) : a granular crystalline igneous rock commonly of acid plagioclase and hornblende, pyroxene, or biotite — **di·o·rit·ic** \ˌdī-ə-ˈrit-ik\ *adj*

Di·os·cu·ri \ˌdī-əs-ˈkyu̇(ə)r-ˌī, dī-ˈäs-kyə-ˌrī\ *n pl* [NL, fr. Gk *Dioskouroi,* lit., sons of Zeus, fr. *Dios* (gen. of *Zeus;* akin to L *divus* divine) + *kouroi,* pl. of *koros, koaros* boy — more at DEITY, CRESCENT] : the twins Castor and Pollux reunited as stars in the sky by Zeus after Castor's death and regarded as patrons of athletes, soldiers, and mariners

di·ox·ane \dī-ˈäk-ˌsān\ *n* [ISV *di-* + *ox-* + *-ane*] (1912) : a flammable toxic liquid diether $C_4H_8O_2$ used esp. as a solvent

di·ox·ide \(ˈ)dī-ˈäk-ˌsīd\ *n* [ISV] (ca. 1847) : an oxide (as carbon dioxide) containing two atoms of oxygen in the molecule

di·ox·in \(ˈ)dī-ˈäk-sən\ *n* [[1]*di-* + *ox-* + *-in*] (1943) : any of several heterocyclic hydrocarbons that occur esp. as persistent toxic impurities in herbicides; *esp* **:** a teratogenic impurity $C_{12}H_4O_2Cl_4$ in 2,4,5-T

[1]**dip** \ˈdip\ *vb* **dipped; dip·ping** [ME *dippen,* fr. OE *dyppan;* akin to OHG *tupfen* to wash, Lith *dubus* deep] *vt* (bef. 12c) **1 a :** to plunge or immerse momentarily or partially under the surface (as of a liquid) so as to moisten, cool, or coat ⟨~ candles⟩ **b :** to thrust in a way to suggest immersion **c :** to immerse (as a sheep) in an antiseptic or parasiticidal solution **2 :** to lift a portion of by reaching below the surface with something shaped to hold liquid : LADLE **3 a** *archaic* **:** INVOLVE **b :** MORTGAGE **4 a :** to lower and then raise again ⟨~ a flag in salute⟩ **b** *chiefly Brit* **:** DIM 2 ~ *vi* **1 a :** to plunge into a liquid and quickly emerge **b :** to immerse something into a processing liquid or finishing material **2 a :** to suddenly drop down or out of sight **b** *of an airplane* **:** to drop suddenly before climbing **c :** to decline or decrease moderately and usu. temporarily ⟨prices *dipped*⟩ **3 a :** to reach down inside or below or as if inside or below a surface esp. to withdraw a part of the contents — used with *into* **b :** to make inroads for funds — used with *into* ⟨*dipped* into the family's savings⟩ **4 :** to examine something casually or tentatively; *specif* **:** to read superficially — used with *into* **5 :** to incline downward from the plane of the horizon — **dip·pa·ble** \ˈdip-ə-bəl\ *adj*

[2]**dip** *n* (1599) **1 :** an act of dipping; *esp* **:** a brief plunge into the water for sport or exercise **2 :** inclination downward: **a :** PITCH **b :** a sharp downward course : DROP **c :** the angle that a stratum or similar geological feature makes with a horizontal plane **3 :** the angle formed with the horizon by a magnetic needle free to rotate in the vertical plane **4 :** HOLLOW, DEPRESSION **5 :** something obtained by or used in dipping **6 a :** a sauce or soft mixture into which food may be dipped **b :** a liquid preparation into which an object may be dipped (as for cleansing or coloring) **7** *slang* **:** PICKPOCKET

di·pep·ti·dase \dī-ˈpep-tə-ˌdās, -ˌdāz\ *n* (1927) : any of various enzymes that hydrolyze dipeptides but not polypeptides

di·pep·tide \(ˈ)dī-ˈpep-ˌtīd\ *n* (ca. 1891) : a peptide that yields two molecules of amino acid on hydrolysis

di·pha·sic \(ˈ)dī-ˈfā-zik\ *adj* (1881) : having two phases

di·phe·nyl \(ˈ)dī-ˈfen-ᵊl, -ˈfēn-\ *n* (1873) : BIPHENYL

di·phe·nyl·amine \(ˌ)dī-ˌfen-ᵊl-ə-ˈmēn, -ˌfēn-, -ᵊl-ˈam-ən\ *n* [ISV] (1863) : a crystalline pleasant-smelling compound $(C_6H_5)_2NH$ used chiefly in the manufacture of dyes and in stabilizing explosives

di·phe·nyl·hy·dan·to·in \-hī-ˈdant-ə-wən\ *n* [*diphenyl* + *hydrogen* + *allantoin* (a chemical found in the allantoic liquid of cows)] (1937) : PHENYTOIN

di·phos·gene \(ˈ)dī-ˈfäz-ˌjēn\ *n* [ISV] (ca. 1922) : a liquid compound $C_2Cl_4O_2$ used as a poison gas in World War I

di·phos·phate \(ˈ)dī-ˈfäs-ˌfāt\ *n* (1826) : a phosphate containing two phosphate groups

di·phos·pho·gly·cer·ic acid \(ˈ)dī-ˈfäs-fō-glis-ˌer-ik-\ *n* (1959) : a diphosphate of glyceric acid that is an important intermediate in photosynthesis and in glycolysis and fermentation

di·phos·pho·pyr·i·dine nucleotide \-ˌpir-ə-ˌdēn-\ *n* [*di-* + *phosph-* + *pyridine*] (1938) : NAD

diph·the·ria \dif-ˈthir-ē-ə, ÷dip-\ *n* [NL, fr. F *diphthérie,* fr. Gk *diphthera* leather; fr. the toughness of the false membrane] (ca. 1851) : an acute febrile contagious disease marked by the formation of a false membrane esp. in the throat and caused by a bacterium that produces a toxin causing inflammation of the heart and nervous system — **diph·the·ri·al** \-ē-əl\ — **diph·the·rit·ic** \ˌdif-thə-ˈrit-ik, ˌdip-\ *adj*

[1]**diph·the·roid** \ˈdif-thə-ˌrȯid\ *adj* (1861) : resembling diphtheria

[2]**diphtheroid** *n* (1908) : a bacterium (esp. genus *Corynebacterium*) that resembles the bacterium of diphtheria but does not produce diphtheria toxin

diph·thong \ˈdif-ˌthȯŋ, ˈdip-\ *n* [ME *diptonge,* fr. MF *diptongue,* fr. LL *dipthongus,* fr. Gk *diphthongos,* fr. *di-* + *phthongos* voice, sound] (15c) **1 :** a gliding monosyllabic speech sound (as the vowel combination that forms the last part of *toy*) that starts at or near the articulatory position for one vowel and moves to or toward the position of another **2 :** DIGRAPH **3 :** the ligature æ or œ — **diph·thon·gal** \dif-ˈthȯŋ-(g)əl, dip-\ *adj*

diph·thong·iza·tion \(ˌ)dif-ˌthȯŋ-ə-ˈzā-shən, (ˌ)dip-\ *n* (1874) : the act of diphthongizing : the state of being diphthongized

diph·thong·ize \ˈdif-ˌthȯŋ-ˌīz, ˈdip-\ *vb* **-ized; -iz·ing** *vi, of a simple vowel* (1867) : to change into a diphthong ~ *vt* : to pronounce as a diphthong

diphy- *or* **diphyo-** *comb form* [NL, fr. Gk *diphy-,* fr. *diphyēs,* fr. *di-* + *phyein* to bring forth — more at BE] : double : bipartite ⟨*diphy*odont⟩

di·phy·let·ic \ˌdī-fī-ˈlet-ik\ *adj* (1902) : derived from two lines of evolutionary descent ⟨~ dinosaurs⟩

di·phy·odont \(ˈ)dī-ˈfī-ə-ˌdänt\ *adj* [ISV] (1854) : marked by the successive development of deciduous and permanent sets of teeth

dipl- *or* **diplo-** *comb form* [Gk, fr. *diploos* — more at DOUBLE] **1 :** double : twofold ⟨*diplo*pia⟩ **2 :** diploid ⟨*diplo*phase⟩

di·ple·gia \dī-ˈplē-j(ē-)ə\ *n* [NL] (ca. 1881) : paralysis of corresponding parts on both sides of the body

di·plex \ˈdī-ˌpleks\ *adj* [alter. of *duplex*] (ca. 1931) : relating to or being simultaneous transmission or reception of two radio signals using a common feature (as a single carrier or single antenna)

dip·lo·ba·cil·lus \ˌdip-lō-bə-ˈsil-əs\ *n* [NL] (1900) : any of various small aerobic gram-negative bacilli parasitic on mucous membranes

dip·lo·blas·tic \-ˈblas-tik\ *adj* (ca. 1884) : having two germ layers — used of an embryo or lower invertebrate that lacks a true mesoderm

dip·lo·coc·cus \-ˈkäk-əs\ *n* [NL, genus name] (ca. 1881) : any of a genus (*Diplococcus*) of gram-positive encapsulated bacteria that occur usu. in pairs, are parasitic, and include serious pathogens — **dip·lo·coc·cal** \-ˈkäk-əl\ *or* **dip·lo·coc·cic** \-ˈkäk-(s)ik\ *adj*

di·plod·o·cus \də-ˈpläd-ə-kəs, dī-\ *n* [NL, genus name, fr. *dipl-* + Gk *dokos* beam, fr. *dekesthai, dechesthai* to receive; akin to L *decēre* to be fitting — more at DECENT] (1928) : any of a genus (*Diplodocus*) of very large herbivorous dinosaurs from Colorado and Wyoming

dip·loe \ˈdip-lə-ˌwē\ *n* [NL, fr. Gk *diploē,* fr. *diploos* double] (ca. 1696) : cancellous bony tissue between the external and internal layers of the skull — **di·plo·ic** \də-ˈplō-ik, dī-\ *adj*

[1]**dip·loid** \ˈdip-ˌlȯid\ *adj* (1908) : having the basic chromosome number doubled — **dip·loi·dy** \-ˌlȯid-ē\ *n*

[2]**diploid** *n* (1908) : a single cell, individual, or generation characterized by the diploid chromosome number

di·plo·ma \də-ˈplō-mə\ *n, pl* **diplomas** [L, passport, diploma, fr. Gk *diplōma* folded paper, passport, fr. *diploun* to double, fr. *diploos*] (1622) **1** *pl also* **di·plo·ma·ta** \-mət-ə\ **:** an official or state document : CHARTER **2 :** a writing usu. under seal conferring some honor or privilege **3 :** a document bearing record of graduation from or of a degree conferred by an educational institution

di·plo·ma·cy \də-ˈplō-mə-sē\ *n* (1796) **1 :** the art and practice of conducting negotiations between nations **2 :** skill in handling affairs without arousing hostility : TACT

diploma mill *n* (1926) **1 :** an institution of higher education operating without supervision of a state or professional agency and granting diplomas without the usual required courses and attendance **2 :** an institution of higher education whose academic demands are minimal

dip·lo·mat \ˈdip-lə-ˌmat\ *n* [F *diplomate,* back-formation fr. *diplomatique*] (1813) : one employed or skilled in diplomacy

dip·lo·mate \ˈdip-lə-ˌmāt\ *n* [*diploma* + [1]*-ate*] (1879) : one who holds a diploma; *esp* **:** a physician qualified to practice in a medical specialty by advanced training and experience in the specialty followed by passing an intensive examination by a national board of senior specialists

dip·lo·mat·ic \ˌdip-lə-ˈmat-ik\ *adj* [in sense 1, fr. NL *diplomaticus,* fr. L *diplomat-, diploma;* in other senses, fr. F *diplomatique* connected with documents regulating international relations, fr. NL *diplomaticus*] (1711) **1 a :** PALEOGRAPHIC **b :** exactly reproducing the original ⟨a ~ edition⟩ **2 :** of, relating to, or concerned with diplomacy or diplomats ⟨~ relations⟩ **3 :** employing tact and conciliation esp. in situations of stress ***syn*** see SUAVE — **dip·lo·mat·i·cal·ly** \-i-k(ə-)lē\ *adv*

di·plo·ma·tist \də-ˈplō-mət-əst\ *n* (1815) : DIPLOMAT

dip·lont \ˈdip-ˌlänt\ *n* [ISV] (1925) : an organism with somatic cells having the diploid chromosome number — compare HAPLONT — **dip·lon·tic** \dip-ˈlänt-ik\ *adj*

dip·lo·phase \ˈdip-lə-ˌfāz\ *n* (ca. 1925) : a diploid phase in a life cycle

dip·lo·pia \dip-ˈlō-pē-ə\ *n* [NL] (ca. 1811) : a disorder of vision in which two images of a single object are seen because of unequal action of the eye muscles — called also *double vision* — **dip·lo·pic** \-ˈlō-pik, -ˈläp-ik\ *adj*

dip·lo·pod \ˈdip-lə-ˌpäd\ *n* [deriv. of Gk *dipl-* + *pod-, pous* foot — more at FOOT] (ca. 1864) : MILLIPEDE

dip·lo·tene \ˈdip-lə-ˌtēn\ *n* [ISV] (ca. 1925) : a stage of meiotic prophase which follows the pachytene and during which the paired homologous chromosomes begin to separate and chiasmata become visible — **diplotene** *adj*

dip net *n* (1820) : a small bag net with a handle that is used esp. to scoop small fish from the water

dip·no·an \ˈdip-nə-wən\ *adj* [deriv. of Gk *dipnoos,* fr. *di-* + *pnoē* breath, fr. *pnein* to breathe — more at SNEEZE] (1886) : of or relating to a group (Dipnoi) of fishes with pulmonary circulation, gills, and lungs — **dipnoan** *n*

dip·o·dy \ˈdip-əd-ē\ *n, pl* **-dies** [LL *dipodia,* fr. Gk, fr. *dipod-, dipous* having two feet, fr. *di-* + *pod-, pous*] (ca. 1844) : a prosodic unit or measure of two feet — **di·pod·ic** \dī-ˈpäd-ik\ *adj*

di·pole \ˈdī-ˌpōl\ *n* [ISV] (1912) **1 a :** a pair of equal and opposite electric charges or magnetic poles of opposite sign separated esp. by a small distance **b :** a body or system (as a molecule) having such charges **2 :** a radio antenna consisting of two horizontal rods in line with each other with their ends slightly separated — **di·po·lar** \ˈdī-ˌpō-lər, -ˈpō-\ *adj*

dip·per \ˈdip-ər\ *n* (14c) **1 :** any of a genus (*Cinclus* and esp. *C. cinclus* of the Old World and *C. mexicanus* of No. America) of birds that comprise an oscine family (Cinclidae) related to the thrushes and including individuals that are not web-footed but dive into swift mountain streams and walk on the bottom in search of food — called also *water ouzel* **2 :** one that dips: as **a :** a worker who dips articles **b**

: something (as a long-handled cup) used for dipping c *slang* : PICKPOCKET 3 *cap* a : the seven principal stars in the constellation of Ursa Major arranged in a form resembling a dipper — called also *Big Dipper* b : the seven principal stars in Ursa Minor similarly arranged with the North Star forming the outer end of the handle — called also *Little Dipper* — **dip·per·ful** \-ˌfu̇l\ *n*

dip·py \ˈdip-ē\ *adj* **dip·pi·er; -est** [origin unknown] (1903) : FOOLISH

dip·so \ˈdip-(ˌ)sō\ *n* [by shortening] (1880) : one affected with dipsomania

dip·so·ma·nia \ˌdip-sə-ˈmā-nē-ə, -nyə\ *n* [NL, fr. Gk *dipsa* thirst + LL *mania*] (ca. 1843) : an uncontrollable craving for alcoholic liquors — **dip·so·ma·ni·ac** \-nē-ˌak\ *n* — **dip·so·ma·ni·a·cal** \ˌdip-sō-mə-ˈnī-ə-kəl\ *adj*

dip·stick \ˈdip-ˌstik\ *n* (1927) : a graduated rod for indicating depth (as of oil in a crankcase)

dip·ter·an \ˈdip-tə-rən\ *adj* [deriv. of Gk *dipteros*] (ca. 1842) : of, relating to, or being a two-winged fly — **dipteran** *n*

dip·tero·carp \ˈdip-tə-rō-ˌkärp\ *n* [NL, deriv. of *dipterus* dipterous + *-carpus* -carpous] (ca. 1876) : any of a family (Dipterocarpaceae) of tall trees of tropical Asia, Indonesia, and the Philippines that have a 2-winged fruit and are the source of valuable timber, aromatic oils, and resins; *esp* : a member of the type genus (*Dipterocarpus*)

dip·ter·on \ˈdip-tə-ˌrän\ *n, pl* **-tera** \-rə\ [Gk, neut. of *dipteros*] (ca. 1891) : TWO-WINGED FLY

dip·ter·ous \ˈdip-tə-rəs\ *adj* [NL *dipterus*, fr. Gk *dipteros*, fr. *di-* + *pteron* wing — more at FEATHER] (1773) 1 : having two wings or winglike appendages 2 : of or relating to the two-winged flies

dip·tych \ˈdip-(ˌ)tik\ *n* [LL *diptycha*, pl., fr. Gk, fr. neut. pl. of *diptychos* folded in two, fr. *di-* + *ptychē* fold] (1622) 1 : a 2-leaved hinged tablet folding together to protect writing on its waxed surfaces 2 : a picture or series of pictures (as an altarpiece) painted or carved on two hinged tablets 3 : a work made up of two matching parts

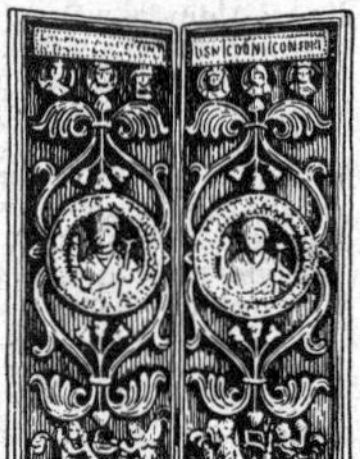

diptych 2

di·quat \ˈdī-ˌkwät\ *n* [*di-* + *quat*ernary] (1960) : a powerful nonpersistent herbicide $C_{12}H_{12}Br_2N_2$ that has been used to control water weeds (as the water hyacinth)

dir·dum \ˈdi(ə)rd-əm, ˈdərd-\ *n* [ME (northern dial.) *durdan*, fr. ScGael, grumbling, hum, dim. of *durd* hum] *Scot* (1709) : BLAME

dire \ˈdī(ə)r\ *adj* **dir·er; dir·est** [L *dirus*; akin to Gk *deinos* terrible, Skt *dvesti* he hates] (1567) 1 a : exciting horror ⟨~ suffering⟩ b : DISMAL, OPPRESSIVE ⟨~ days⟩ 2 : warning of disaster ⟨a ~ forecast⟩ 3 a : desperately urgent ⟨~ need⟩ b : EXTREME ⟨~ poverty⟩ — **dire·ly** *adv* — **dire·ness** *n*

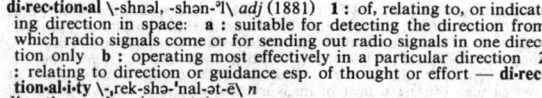

[1]**di·rect** \də-ˈrekt, dī-\ *vb* [ME *directen*, fr. L *directus* straight — more at DRESS] *vt* (14c) 1 a *obs* : to write (a letter) to a person b : to mark with the name and address of the intended recipient c : to impart orally d : to adapt in expression so as to have particular applicability ⟨a lawyer who ~*s* his appeals to intelligence and character⟩ 2 a : to regulate the activities or course of b : to carry out the organizing, energizing, and supervising of c : to dominate and determine the course of d : to train and lead performances of 3 : to cause to turn, move, or point undeviatingly or to follow a straight course ⟨X rays are ~*ed* through the body⟩ 4 : to point, extend, or project in a specified line or course 5 : to request or enjoin with authority 6 : to show or point out the way for ~ *vi* 1 : to point out, prescribe, or determine a course or procedure 2 : to act as director ***syn*** see COMMAND, CONDUCT

[2]**direct** *adj* [ME, fr. L *directus*] (14c) 1 *of a celestial body* : moving in the general planetary direction from west to east : not retrograde 2 a : stemming immediately from a source ⟨~ result⟩ b : being or passing in a straight line of descent from parent to offspring : LINEAL ⟨~ ancestor⟩ c : having no compromising or impairing element ⟨~ insult⟩ 3 a : proceeding from one point to another in time or space without deviation or interruption : STRAIGHT b : proceeding by the shortest way ⟨the ~ route⟩ 4 : NATURAL, STRAIGHTFORWARD ⟨~ manner⟩ 5 a : marked by absence of an intervening agency, instrumentality, or influence b : effected by the action of the people or the electorate and not by representatives c : consisting of or reproducing the exact words of a speaker or writer 6 : characterized by close logical, causal, or consequential relationship ⟨~ evidence⟩ 7 : capable of dyeing without the aid of a mordant : SUBSTANTIVE

[3]**direct** *adv* (14c) : in a direct way: as a : from point to point without deviation : by the shortest way ⟨suggesting I write to her ~ —John Willett⟩ b : from the source without interruption or diversion ⟨the writer must take his material ~ from life —Douglas Stewart⟩ c : without an intervening agency or step ⟨those who did go ~ to the people . . . rallied a considerable majority of the voters —H. S. Ashmore⟩

direct action *n* (1843) : action that seeks to achieve an end directly and by the most immediately effective means (as boycott or strike)

direct current *n* (ca. 1889) : an electric current flowing in one direction only and substantially constant in value — abbr. *DC*

di·rect·ed *adj* (1891) 1 : subject to supervision or regulation ⟨a ~ reading program for students⟩ 2 : having a positive or negative sense ⟨~ line segment⟩ — **di·rect·ed·ness** *n*

di·rec·tion \də-ˈrek-shən, dī-\ *n* (15c) 1 : guidance or supervision of action or conduct : MANAGEMENT 2 *archaic* : SUPERSCRIPTION 3 a : an explicit instruction : ORDER b : assistance in pointing out the proper route — usu. used in pl. ⟨received ~*s* to get to the beach⟩ 4 : the line or course on which something is moving or is aimed to move or along which something is pointing or facing 5 *archaic* : DIRECTORATE 1 6 a : a channel or direct course of thought or action b : TENDENCY, TREND c : a guiding, governing, or motivating purpose 7 a : the art and technique of directing an orchestra, band, or a show (as for stage or screen) b : a word, phrase, or sign indicating the appropriate tempo, mood, or intensity of a passage or movement in music — **di·rec·tion·less** \-ləs\ *adj*

di·rec·tion·al \-shnəl, -shən-ᵊl\ *adj* (1881) 1 : of, relating to, or indicating direction in space: a : suitable for detecting the direction from which radio signals come or for sending out radio signals in one direction only b : operating most effectively in a particular direction 2 : relating to direction or guidance esp. of thought or effort — **di·rec·tion·al·i·ty** \-ˌrek-shə-ˈnal-ət-ē\ *n*

direction angle *n* (ca. 1909) : an angle made by a given line with an axis of reference; *specif* : one of these angles made by a straight line with the three axes of a rectangular Cartesian coordinate system — usu. used in pl.

direction cosine *n* (ca. 1891) : one of the cosines of the three angles between a directed line in space and the positive direction of the axes of a rectangular Cartesian coordinate system — usu. used in pl.

direction finder *n* (1913) : a radio receiving device for determining the direction of incoming radio waves that typically consists of a coil antenna rotating freely on a vertical axis

[1]**di·rec·tive** \də-ˈrek-tiv, dī-\ *adj* (15c) 1 : serving or intended to guide, govern, or influence 2 : serving to point direction; *specif* : DIRECTIONAL 1b 3 : of or relating to psychotherapy or counseling in which the counselor introduces information, content, or attitudes not previously expressed by the client

[2]**directive** *n* (1899) : something that serves to direct, guide, and usu. impel toward an action or goal; *esp* : an authoritative instrument issued by a high-level body or official

di·rec·tiv·i·ty \də-ˌrek-ˈtiv-ət-ē, (ˌ)dī-\ *n* (1903) : the property of being directional

direct lighting *n* (1928) : lighting in which the greater part of the light goes directly from the source to the area lit

[1]**di·rect·ly** \də-ˈrek-(t)lē, dī-, *in sense 2* də-ˈrek-lē *or* ˈdrek-lē\ *adv* (15c) 1 : in a direct manner ⟨~ relevant⟩ ⟨the road runs ~ east and west⟩ 2 a : without delay : IMMEDIATELY b : in a little while : SHORTLY

[2]**di·rect·ly** \də-ˈrek-(t)lē, dī-; ˈdrek-lē\ *conj, chiefly Brit* (1795) : immediately after : AS SOON AS ⟨~ I received it I rang up the shipping company —F. W. Crofts⟩

direct mail *n* (1923) : printed matter (as circulars) prepared for soliciting business or contributions and mailed directly to individuals

di·rect·ness \də-ˈrek(t)-nəs, dī-\ *n* (1598) 1 : the character of being accurate in course or aim 2 : strict pertinence : STRAIGHTFORWARDNESS

direct object *n* (ca. 1904) : a grammatical object representing the primary goal or the result of the action of a verb ⟨*me* in "he hit me" and *house* in "we built a house" are *direct objects*⟩

di·rec·tor \də-ˈrek-tər, dī-\ *n* (15c) : one that directs: as a : the head of an organized group or administrative unit (as a bureau or school) b : one of a group of persons entrusted with the overall direction of a corporate enterprise c : one that supervises the production of a show (as for stage or screen) usu. with responsibility for action, lighting, music, and rehearsals d : CONDUCTOR c — **di·rec·tor·ship** \-ˌship\ *n*

di·rec·tor·ate \də-ˈrek-t(ə-)rət, dī-\ *n* (1837) 1 : the office of director 2 a : a board of directors (as of a corporation) b : membership on a board of directors 3 : an executive staff (as of a program, bureau, or department)

di·rec·to·ri·al \də-ˌrek-ˈtōr-ē-əl, (ˌ)dī-, -ˈtȯr-\ *adj* (1770) 1 : serving to direct 2 : of or relating to a director or to theatrical or motion-picture direction 3 : of, relating to, or administered by a directory

director's chair *n* [fr. its use by motion-picture directors on the set] (1953) : a lightweight folding armchair with a back and seat usu. of cotton duck

[1]**di·rec·to·ry** \də-ˈrek-t(ə-)rē, dī-\ *adj* (15c) : serving to direct; *specif* : providing advisory but not compulsory guidance

[2]**directory** *n, pl* **-ries** [ML *directorium*, fr. neut. of LL *directorius* directorial, fr. L *directus*, pp.] (15c) 1 a : a book or collection of directions, rules, or ordinances b : an alphabetical or classified list (as of names and addresses) 2 : a body of directors

direct primary *n* (1900) : a primary in which nominations of candidates for office are made by direct vote

direct product *n* (ca. 1925) : CARTESIAN PRODUCT; *esp* : a group that is the Cartesian product of two other groups

di·rec·tress \də-ˈrek-trəs, dī-\ *n* (1580) : a woman who is a director

di·rec·trice \də-ˌrek-ˈtrēs\ *n* [F, fr. ML *directric-, directrix*] (1631) : DIRECTRESS

di·rec·trix \-ˈrek-triks\ *n, pl* **-trix·es** \-trik-səz\ *also* **-tri·ces** \-trə-ˌsēz\ [ML, fem. of LL *director*, fr. L *directus*, pp.] (1622) 1 *archaic* : DIRECTRESS 2 : a fixed curve with which a generatrix maintains a given relationship in generating a geometric figure; *specif* : a straight line the distance to which from any point of a conic section is in fixed ratio to the distance from the same point to a focus

direct sum *n* (ca. 1928) : CARTESIAN PRODUCT — compare DIRECT PRODUCT

direct tax *n* (1776) : a tax exacted directly from the person on whom the ultimate burden of the tax is expected to fall

dire·ful \ˈdī(ə)r-fəl\ *adj* (1583) 1 : DREADFUL 2 : OMINOUS — **dire·ful·ly** \-fə-lē\ *adv*

dire wolf *n* (1925) : a large lupine mammal (*Canis dirus* or *Aenocyon dirus*) found in Pleistocene deposits of No. America

dirge \ˈdərj\ *n* [ME *dirige*, the Office of the Dead, fr. the first word of a LL antiphon, fr. L, imper. of *dirigere* to direct — more at DRESS] (13c) 1 : a song or hymn of grief or lamentation; *esp* : one intended to accompany funeral or memorial rites 2 : a slow, solemn, and mournful piece of music 3 : something (as a poem) that has the qualities of a dirge

dir·ham \də-ˈram\ *n* [Ar, fr. L *drachma* drachma] (1839) 1 — see MONEY table 2 — see *dinar, riyal* at MONEY table

[1]**di·ri·gi·ble** \ˈdir-ə-jə-bəl, də-ˈrij-ə-\ *adj* [L *dirigere*] (1581) : capable of being steered

[2]**dirigible** *n* [*dirigible (balloon)*] (1885) : AIRSHIP

[1]**dirk** \ˈdərk\ *n* [Sc *durk*] (1557) : a long straight-bladed dagger

[2]**dirk** *vt* (1599) : to stab with a dirk

dirl \ˈdir(ə)l, ˈdərl\ *vi* [prob. alter. of *thirl*] *Scot* (1715) : TREMBLE, QUIVER

dirndl \ˈdərn-dᵊl\ *n* [short for G *dirndlkleid*, fr. G dial. *dirndl* girl + G *kleid* dress, fr. MHG *kleit*; akin to OE *clāth* cloth] (1937) 1 : a dress style with tight bodice, short sleeves, low neck, and gathered skirt 2 : a full skirt with a tight waistband

dirt \'dərt\ *n* [ME *drit,* fr. ON; akin to OE *drītan* to defecate, L *foria* diarrhea] (14c) **1 a :** EXCREMENT **b :** a filthy or soiling substance ⟨as mud, dust, or grime⟩ **c** *archaic* **:** something worthless **d :** a contemptible person **2 a :** loose or packed soil or sand **:** EARTH **b** (1) **:** alluvial earth in placer mining (2) **:** slate and waste in coal mines **3 a :** an abject or filthy state **:** SQUALOR **b :** CORRUPTION, CHICANERY **c :** licentiousness of language or theme **d :** scandalous or malicious gossip **e :** embarrassing or incriminating information

dirt bike *n* (1972) **:** a usu. lightweight motorcycle designed for operation on unpaved surfaces

dirt farmer *n* (1920) **:** a farmer who earns his living by farming his own land; *esp* **:** one who farms without the help of hired hands or tenants

dirt–poor \'dərt-'pü(ə)r\ *adj* (1937) **:** lacking nearly all the essentials of life

[1]**dirty** \'dərt-ē\ *adj* **dirt·i·er; -est** (14c) **1 a :** not clean or pure ⟨~ clothes⟩ **b :** likely to befoul or defile with dirt ⟨~ jobs⟩ **c :** tedious, disagreeable, and unrecognized or thankless ⟨undertook the ~ tasks that no one else wanted to bother with⟩ **d :** contaminated with infecting organisms ⟨~ wounds⟩ **2 a :** morally unclean or corrupt: as (1) **:** INDECENT, VULGAR ⟨~ language⟩ (2) **:** DISHONORABLE, BASE ⟨~ deeds⟩; *also* **:** UNSPORTSMANLIKE ⟨~ players⟩ **b :** acquired by disreputable means **:** ILL-GOTTEN ⟨~ money⟩ **3 a :** ABOMINABLE, HATEFUL ⟨war is a ~ business⟩ **b :** highly regrettable **:** GRIEVOUS ⟨a ~ shame⟩ **4 :** FOGGY, STORMY **5 a** *of color* **:** not clear and bright **:** DULLISH ⟨drab *dirty*-pink walls⟩ **b :** characterized by a husky, rasping, or raw tonal quality — used esp. of jazz **6 :** conveying ill-natured resentment ⟨gave him a ~ look⟩ **7 :** having considerable fallout ⟨~ bombs⟩ — **dirt·i·ly** \'dərt-ᵊl-ē\ *adv* — **dirt·i·ness** \'dərt-ē-nəs\ *n*

syn DIRTY, FILTHY, FOUL, NASTY, SQUALID mean conspicuously unclean or impure. DIRTY emphasizes the presence of dirt more than an emotional reaction to it ⟨children *dirty* from play⟩ ⟨a *dirty* littered street⟩ FILTHY carries a strong suggestion of offensiveness and typically of gradually accumulated dirt that begrimes and besmears ⟨a stained greasy floor, utterly *filthy*⟩ FOUL implies extreme offensiveness and an accumulation of what is rotten or stinking ⟨the *foul* oil-and-garbage whiffs from the river —Herman Wouk⟩ NASTY applies to what is actually foul or is repugnant to one used to or expecting freshness, cleanliness, or sweetness ⟨it's a *nasty* job to clean up after a sick cat⟩ In practice, *nasty* is often weakened to the point of being no more than a synonym of *unpleasant* or *disagreeable* ⟨had a *nasty* fall⟩ ⟨his answer gave her a *nasty* shock⟩ SQUALID adds to the idea of dirtiness and filth that of slovenly neglect ⟨living in *squalid* poverty⟩ ⟨*squalid* slums⟩ All these terms are applicable to moral uncleanness or baseness or obscenity. DIRTY then stresses meanness or despicableness ⟨the creature's at his *dirty* work again —Alexander Pope⟩ while FILTHY and FOUL describe disgusting obscenity or loathsome behavior ⟨*filthy* language⟩ ⟨a *foul* story⟩ and NASTY implies a peculiarly offensive unpleasantness ⟨a cheap and *nasty* imitation of the real thing —Robert Wilkes⟩ Distinctively, SQUALID implies sordidness as well as baseness and dirtiness ⟨her life was a series of *squalid* affairs⟩

[2]**dirty** *adv* (ca. 1934) **:** in a dirty manner: as **a :** DECEPTIVELY, UNDERHANDEDLY ⟨fight ~⟩ **b :** INDECENTLY ⟨talk ~⟩

[3]**dirty** *vb* **dirt·ied; dirty·ing** *vt* (1591) **1 :** to make dirty **2 a :** to stain with dishonor **:** SULLY **b :** to debase by distorting the real nature of ~ *vi* **:** to become soiled

dirty linen *n* (1946) **:** private matters whose public exposure brings distress and embarrassment — called also *dirty laundry*

dirty old man *n* (1932) **:** a lecherous mature man

dirty pool *n* (1940) **:** underhanded or unsportsmanlike conduct

dirty word *n* (1842) **:** a word, expression, or idea that is inappropriate, opprobrious, or derogatory in a particular frame of reference ⟨commitment has become a *dirty word* in the mouths of those . . . reflecting the instant culture —J. R. Silber⟩

Dis \'dis\ *n* [L] **:** the Roman god of the underworld — compare PLUTO

dis- *prefix* [ME *dis-, des-,* fr. OF & L; OF *des-, dis-,* fr. L *dis-,* lit., apart; akin to OE *te-* apart, L *duo* two — more at TWO] **1 a :** do the opposite of ⟨*dis*establish⟩ **b :** deprive of (a specified quality, rank, or object) ⟨*dis*able⟩ ⟨*dis*prince⟩ ⟨*dis*frock⟩ **c :** exclude or expel from ⟨*dis*bar⟩ **2 :** opposite or absence of ⟨*dis*union⟩ ⟨*dis*affection⟩ **3 :** not ⟨*dis*agreeable⟩ **4 :** completely ⟨*dis*annul⟩ **5** [by folk etymology] **:** DYS- ⟨*dis*function⟩

dis·abil·i·ty \,dis-ə-'bil-ət-ē\ *n* (1581) **1 a :** the condition of being disabled **b :** inability to pursue an occupation because of physical or mental impairment **2 :** lack of legal qualification to do something **3 :** a disqualification, restriction, or disadvantage

dis·able \dis-'ā-bəl, diz-\ *vt* **dis·abled; dis·abling** \-b(ə-)liŋ\ (15c) **1 :** to deprive of legal right, qualification, or capacity **2 :** to make incapable or ineffective; *esp* **:** to deprive of physical, moral, or intellectual strength **:** CRIPPLE ***syn*** see WEAKEN — **dis·able·ment** \-bəl-mənt\ *n*

dis·abled *adj* (1633) **:** incapacitated by illness, injury, or wounds

dis·abuse \,dis-ə-'byüz\ *vt* [F *désabuser,* fr. *dés-* dis- + *abuser* to abuse] (1611) **:** to free from error or fallacy

di·sac·cha·ri·dase \(')dī-'sak-ə-rə-,dās, -,dāz\ *n* (1961) **:** an enzyme (as maltase or lactase) that hydrolyzes disaccharides

di·sac·cha·ride \(')dī-'sak-ə-,rīd\ *n* (1892) **:** any of a class of sugars (as sucrose) that yields on hydrolysis two monosaccharide molecules

dis·ac·cord \,dis-ə-'kȯ(ə)rd\ *vi* [ME *disacorden,* fr. MF *desacorder,* fr. *desacort* disagreement, fr. *des-* dis- + *acort* accord] (15c) **:** CLASH, DISAGREE — **disaccord** *n*

dis·ac·cus·tom \,dis-ə-'kəs-təm\ *vt* [MF *desaccoustumer,* fr. OF *desacostumer,* fr. *des-* + *acostumer* to accustom] (1530) **:** to free from a habit

[1]**dis·ad·van·tage** \,dis-əd-'vant-ij\ *n* [ME *disavauntage,* fr. MF *desavantage,* fr. OF, fr. *des-* + *avantage* advantage] (14c) **1 :** loss or damage esp. to reputation, credit, or finances **:** DETRIMENT **2 a :** an unfavorable, inferior, or prejudicial condition ⟨we were at a ~⟩ **b :** HANDICAP ⟨it put us under a serious ~⟩

[2]**disadvantage** *vt* (1534) **:** to place at a disadvantage **:** HARM

dis·ad·van·taged \-ijd\ *adj* (1879) **:** lacking in the basic resources or conditions (as standard housing, medical and educational facilities, and civil rights) believed to be necessary for an equal position in society — **dis·ad·van·taged·ness** \-ij(d)-nəs\ *n*

dis·ad·van·ta·geous \(,)dis-,ad-,van-'tā-jəs, -vən-\ *adj* (1603) **1 :** constituting a disadvantage **2 :** DEROGATORY, DISPARAGING — **dis·ad·van·ta·geous·ly** *adv* — **dis·ad·van·ta·geous·ness** *n*

dis·af·fect \,dis-ə-'fekt\ *vt* (1641) **:** to alienate the affection or loyalty of ***syn*** see ESTRANGE — **dis·af·fec·tion** \-'fek-shən\ *n*

dis·af·fect·ed *adj* (1632) **:** discontented and resentful esp. against authority **:** REBELLIOUS

dis·af·fil·i·ate \,dis-ə-'fil-ē-,āt\ *vt* (1870) **:** DISASSOCIATE ~ *vi* **:** to terminate an affiliation — **dis·af·fil·i·a·tion** \-,fil-ē-'ā-shən\ *n*

dis·af·firm \,dis-ə-'fərm\ *vt* (1531) **1 :** to refuse to confirm **:** ANNUL, REPUDIATE **2 :** CONTRADICT — **dis·af·fir·mance** \-'fər-mən(t)s\ *n*

dis·ag·gre·gate \(')dis-'ag-ri-,gāt\ *vt* (ca. 1828) **:** to separate into component parts ⟨~ sandstone⟩ ⟨~ demographic data⟩ ~ *vi* **:** to break up or apart ⟨the molecules of a gel ~ to form a sol⟩ — **dis·ag·gre·ga·tion** \(,)dis-,ag-ri-'gā-shən\ *n* — **dis·ag·gre·ga·tive** \(')dis-'ag-ri-,gāt-iv\ *adj*

dis·agree \,dis-ə-'grē\ *vi* [ME *disagreen,* fr. MF *desagreer,* fr. *des-* + *agreer* to agree] (15c) **1 :** to fail to agree ⟨the two accounts ~⟩ **2 :** to differ in opinion ⟨he *disagreed* with me on every topic⟩ **3 :** to cause discomfort or distress ⟨fried foods ~ with me⟩

dis·agree·able \-ə-bəl\ *adj* (15c) **1 :** causing discomfort **:** UNPLEASANT, OFFENSIVE **2 :** marked by ill temper **:** PEEVISH — **dis·agree·able·ness** *n* — **dis·agree·ably** \-blē\ *adv*

dis·agree·ment \,dis-ə-'grē-mənt\ *n* (15c) **1 :** the act of disagreeing **2 a :** the state of being at variance **:** DISPARITY **b :** QUARREL

dis·al·low \,dis-ə-'lau̇\ *vt* (14c) **1 :** to deny the force, truth, or validity of **2 :** to refuse to allow — **dis·al·low·ance** \-ən(t)s\ *n*

dis·am·big·u·ate \,dis-am-'big-yə-,wāt\ *vt* **-at·ed; -at·ing** (1963) **:** to establish a single semantic or grammatical interpretation for — **dis·am·big·u·a·tion** \-,big-yə-'wā-shən\ *n*

dis·an·nul \,dis-ə-'nəl\ *vt* (15c) **:** ANNUL, CANCEL

dis·ap·pear \,dis-ə-'pi(ə)r\ *vi* (15c) **1 :** to pass from view **2 a :** to cease to be **:** pass out of existence or notice — **dis·ap·pear·ance** \-'pir-ən(t)s\ *n*

dis·ap·point \,dis-ə-'pȯint\ *vb* [ME *disapoynten,* fr. MF *desapointier,* fr. *des-* dis- + *apointier* to arrange — more at APPOINT] *vt* (15c) **:** to fail to meet the expectation or hope of **:** FRUSTRATE ~ *vi* **:** to cause disappointment ⟨where the show ~s most is in the work of the younger generation —John Ashbery⟩

dis·ap·point·ed *adj* (1552) **1 :** defeated in expectation or hope **:** THWARTED **2** *obs* **:** not adequately equipped — **dis·ap·point·ed·ly** *adv*

dis·ap·point·ing *adj* (1530) **:** failing to meet expectations — **dis·ap·point·ing·ly** \-iŋ-lē\ *adv*

dis·ap·point·ment \,dis-ə-'pȯint-mənt\ *n* (1614) **1 :** the act or an instance of disappointing **:** the state or emotion of being disappointed **2 :** one that disappoints

dis·ap·pro·ba·tion \(,)dis-,ap-rə-'bā-shən\ *n* (1647) **:** the act or state of disapproving **:** the state of being disapproved **:** CONDEMNATION

dis·ap·prov·al \,dis-ə-'prü-vəl\ *n* (1662) **:** DISAPPROBATION, CENSURE

dis·ap·prove \-'prüv\ *vt* (15c) **1 :** to pass unfavorable judgment on **:** CONDEMN **2 :** to refuse approval to **:** REJECT ~ *vi* **:** to feel or express disapproval — **dis·ap·prov·er** *n* — **dis·ap·prov·ing·ly** \-'prü-viŋ-lē\ *adv*

dis·arm \(')dis-'ärm, diz-\ *vb* [ME *desarmen,* lit., to divest of arms, fr. MF *desarmer,* fr. OF, fr. *des-* + *armer* to arm] *vt* (14c) **1 a :** to deprive of means, reason, or disposition to be hostile **b :** to win over **2 a :** to divest of arms **b :** to deprive of a means of attack or defense **c :** to make harmless ~ *vi* **1 :** to lay aside arms **2 :** to give up or reduce armed forces — **dis·ar·ma·ment** \-'är-mə-mənt *also* -'ärm-ə-mənt\ *n* — **dis·arm·er** *n*

dis·arm·ing *adj* (ca. 1828) **:** allaying criticism or hostility **:** INGRATIATING — **dis·arm·ing·ly** \-'är-miŋ-lē\ *adv*

dis·ar·range \,dis-ə-'rānj\ *vt* (1744) **:** to disturb the arrangement or order of — **dis·ar·range·ment** \-mənt\ *n*

[1]**dis·ar·ray** \,dis-ə-'rā\ *n* (14c) **1 :** a lack of order or sequence **:** CONFUSION, DISORDER **2 :** disorderly dress **:** DISHABILLE

[2]**disarray** *vt* [ME *disarayen,* fr. MF *desarroyer,* fr. OF *desareer,* fr. *des-* + *areer* to array] (14c) **1 :** to throw into disorder **2 :** UNDRESS

dis·ar·tic·u·late \,dis-är-'tik-yə-,lāt\ *vi* (1830) **:** to become disjointed ~ *vt* **:** DISJOINT — **dis·ar·tic·u·la·tion** \-,tik-yə-'lā-shən\ *n*

dis·as·sem·ble \,dis-ə-'sem-bəl\ *vt* (1903) **:** to take apart ⟨~ a watch⟩ ~ *vi* **1 :** to come apart ⟨the frame ~s into sections⟩ **2 :** DISPERSE, SCATTER ⟨the crowd began to ~⟩ — **dis·as·sem·bly** \-blē\ *n*

dis·as·so·ci·ate \,dis-ə-'sō-s(h)ē-,āt\ *vt* (1603) **:** to detach from association **:** DISSOCIATE — **dis·as·so·ci·a·tion** \-,sō-sē-'ā-shən, -shē-\ *n*

di·sas·ter \diz-'as-tər, dis-\ *n* [MF & OIt; MF *desastre,* fr. OIt *disastro,* fr. *dis-* (fr. L) + *astro* star, fr. L *astrum* — more at ASTRAL] (1602) **1** *obs* **:** an unfavorable aspect of a planet or star **2 :** a sudden calamitous event bringing great damage, loss, or destruction; *broadly* **:** a sudden or great misfortune or failure

syn DISASTER, CATASTROPHE, CALAMITY, CATACLYSM mean an event or situation that is a terrible misfortune. DISASTER is an unforeseen, ruinous, and often sudden misfortune that happens either through lack of foresight or through some hostile external agency; CATASTROPHE implies a disastrous conclusion emphasizing finality; CALAMITY stresses personal reaction to a great public loss; CATACLYSM, orig. a deluge or geological convulsion, applies to an event or situation that produces an upheaval or complete reversal.

disaster area *n* (1960) **:** an area officially declared to be the scene of an emergency created by a disaster and therefore qualified to receive certain types of governmental aid (as emergency loans and relief supplies)

di·sas·trous \diz-'as-trəs *also* dis-\ *adj* (1603) **1 :** attended by or causing suffering or disaster **:** CALAMITOUS **2 :** TERRIBLE, HORRENDOUS ⟨a ~ score⟩ — **di·sas·trous·ly** *adv*

dis·avow \,dis-ə-'vau̇\ *vt* [ME *desavowen,* fr. MF *desavouer,* fr. OF, fr. *des-* dis- + *avouer* to avow] (14c) **1 :** to deny responsibility for **:** REPUDIATE **2 :** to refuse to acknowledge **:** DISCLAIM — **dis·avow·able** \-ə-bəl\ *adj* — **dis·avow·al** \-'vau̇(-ə)l\ *n*

dis·band \dis-'band\ *vb* [MF *desbander,* fr. *des-* + *bande* band] *vt* (1591) **:** to break up the organization of **:** DISSOLVE ~ *vi* **:** to break up as an organization **:** DISPERSE — **dis·band·ment** \-'ban(d)-mənt\ *n*

dis·bar \dis-'bär\ *vt* (1633) : to expel from the bar or the legal profession : deprive (an attorney) of legal status and privileges — **dis·bar·ment** \-mənt\ *n*
dis·be·lief \,dis-bə-'lēf\ *n* (1672) : the act of disbelieving : mental rejection of something as untrue
dis·be·lieve \-'lēv\ *vt* (ca. 1604) : to hold not to be true or real ~ *vi* : to withhold or reject belief — **dis·be·liev·er** *n*
dis·bud \(')dis-'bəd\ *vt* (1727) **1** : to thin out flower buds in order to improve the quality of bloom of **2** : to dehorn (cattle) by destroying the undeveloped horn bud
dis·bur·den \(')dis-'bərd-ᵊn\ *vt* (1531) **1 a** : to rid of a burden ⟨~ a pack animal⟩ **b** : UNBURDEN ⟨~ your conscience⟩ **2** : UNLOAD ⟨~*ed* their merchandise in the town square⟩ ~ *vi* : DISCHARGE ⟨the vessels ~*ed* at the dock⟩ — **dis·bur·den·ment** \-mənt\ *n*
dis·burse \dis-'bərs\ *vt* **dis·bursed; dis·burs·ing** [MF *desbourser*, fr. OF *desborser*, fr. *des-* + *borser* to get money, fr. *borse* burse] (1530) **1 a** : to pay out : expend esp. from a fund **b** : to make a payment in settlement of : DEFRAY **2** : DISTRIBUTE ⟨~ property by will⟩ — **dis·burs·er** *n*
dis·burse·ment \-'bər-smənt\ *n* (1596) : the act of disbursing; *also* : funds paid out
disc *var of* DISK
disc- *or* **disci-** *or* **disco-** *comb form* [L, fr. Gk *disk-, disko-*, fr. *diskos*] **1** : disk ⟨*disci*gerous⟩ **2** : phonograph record ⟨*disco*phile⟩
dis·calced \(')dis-'kalst\ *adj* [part trans. of L *discalceatus*, fr. *dis-* + *calceatus*, pp. of *calceare* to put on shoes, fr. *calceus* shoe, fr. *calc-, calx* heel — more at CALK] (1631) : UNSHOD, BAREFOOT ⟨~ friars⟩
dis·cant \'dis-,kant\ *var of* DESCANT
[1]**dis·card** \dis-'kärd, 'dis-,\ *vt* (1591) **1 a** : to remove (a playing card) from one's hand **b** : to play (any card except a trump) from a suit different from the one led **2** : to get rid of esp. as useless or unpleasant ~ *vi* : to discard a playing card — **dis·card·able** \-ə-bəl\ *adj* — **dis·card·er** *n*
syn DISCARD, CAST, SHED, SLOUGH, SCRAP, JUNK mean to get rid of. DISCARD implies the letting go or throwing away of something that has become useless or superfluous though often not intrinsically valueless; CAST, esp. when used with *off, away,* and *out,* implies a forceful rejection or repudiation; SHED and SLOUGH imply a throwing off of something both useless and encumbering and often suggest a consequent renewal of vitality or luster; SCRAP and JUNK imply throwing away or breaking up as worthless in existent form.
[2]**dis·card** \'dis-,kärd\ *n* (1744) **1 a** : the act of discarding in a card game **b** : a card discarded **2** : one that is cast off or rejected
dis·car·nate \dis-'kär-nət, -,nāt\ *adj* [*dis-* + *-carnate* (as in *incarnate*)] (1895) : having no physical body : INCORPOREAL
disc brake *n* (1904) : a brake that operates by the friction of a caliper pressing against the sides of a rotating disc

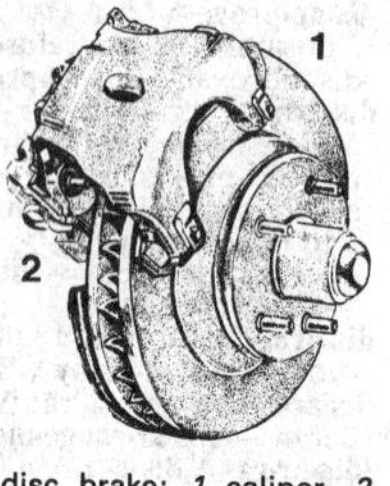

disc brake: *1* caliper, *2* disc

dis·cern \dis-'ərn, diz-\ *vb* [ME *discernen*, fr. MF *discerner*, fr. L *discernere* to separate, distinguish between, fr. *dis-* apart + *cernere* to sift — more at DIS-, CERTAIN] *vt* (14c) **1 a** : to detect with the eyes **b** : to detect with other senses than vision **2** : to recognize or identify as separate and distinct : DISCRIMINATE **3** : to come to know or recognize mentally ~ *vi* : to see or understand the difference — **dis·cern·er** *n* — **dis·cern·ible** *also* **dis·cern·able** \-'ər-nə-bəl\ *adj* — **dis·cern·ibly** \-blē\ *adv*
dis·cern·ing *adj* (ca. 1604) : revealing insight and understanding : DISCRIMINATING ⟨a ~ critic⟩ — **dis·cern·ing·ly** \-'ər-niŋ-lē\ *adv*
dis·cern·ment \dis-'ərn-mənt, diz-\ *n* (1586) **1** : the quality of being able to grasp and comprehend what is obscure : skill in discerning **2** : an act of discerning
syn DISCERNMENT, DISCRIMINATION, PERCEPTION, PENETRATION, INSIGHT, ACUMEN mean a power to see what is not evident to the average mind. DISCERNMENT stresses accuracy (as in reading character or motives or appreciating art); DISCRIMINATION stresses the power to distinguish and select what is true or appropriate or excellent; PERCEPTION implies quick and often sympathetic discernment (as of shades of feeling); PENETRATION implies a searching mind that goes beyond what is obvious or superficial; INSIGHT suggests depth of discernment coupled with understanding sympathy; ACUMEN implies characteristic penetration combined with keen practical judgment.
[1]**dis·charge** \dis(h)-'chärj, 'dis(h)-,\ *vb* [ME *dischargen*, fr. MF *descharger*, fr. LL *discarricare*, fr. L *dis-* + LL *carricare* to load — more at CHARGE] *vt* (14c) **1** : to relieve of a charge, load, or burden: **a** : UNLOAD **b** : to release from an obligation **2 a** : to let go : clear out ⟨the bus stopped to ~ passengers⟩ ⟨~ cargo⟩ **b** : SHOOT ⟨~ an arrow⟩ **c** : to release from confinement, custody, or care ⟨~ a prisoner⟩ **d** : to give outlet or vent to : EMIT **3 a** (1) : to dismiss from employment (2) : to release from service or duty ⟨~ a soldier⟩ **b** : to get rid of (as a debt or obligation) by performing an appropriate action (as payment) : FULFILL **c** : to set aside : ANNUL **d** : to order (a legislative committee) to end consideration of a bill in order to bring it before the house for action **4** : to bear and distribute (as the weight of a wall above an opening) **5** : to bleach out or remove (color or dye) in dyeing and printing textiles **6** : to cancel the record of the loan of (a library book) upon return ~ *vi* **1** : to throw off or deliver a load, charge, or burden **2 a** : GO OFF, FIRE — used of a gun **b** : RUN ⟨some dyes ~⟩ **c** : to pour forth fluid or other contents *syn* see PERFORM — **dis·charge·able** \-ə-bəl\ *adj* — **dis·charg·ee** \(,)dis(h)-,chär-'jē\ *n* — **dis·charg·er** \dis(h)-'chär-jər, 'dis(h)-,\ *n*
[2]**dis·charge** \'dis(h)-,chärj, dis(h)-'\ *n* (14c) **1 a** : the act of relieving of something that oppresses : RELEASE **b** : something that discharges or releases; *esp* : a certification of release or payment **2** : the state of being discharged or relieved **3** : the act of discharging or unloading **4** : legal release from confinement **5** : a firing off **6 a** : a flowing or issuing out ⟨a ~ of spores⟩; *also* : a rate of flow **b** : something that is emitted ⟨a purulent ~⟩ **7** : the act of removing an obligation or liability **8 a** : release or dismissal esp. from an office or employment **b** : complete separation from military service **9 a** : the equalization of a difference of electric potential between two points **b** : the conversion of the chemical energy of a battery into electrical energy
discharge lamp *n* (1936) : an electric lamp in which an enclosed gas or vapor glows or causes a phosphor coating on the lamp's inner surface to glow
discharge tube *n* (1898) : an electron tube which contains gas or vapor at low pressure and through which conduction takes place when a high voltage is applied
disci- — see DISC-
dis·ci·form \'dis-(k)ə-,fȯrm\ *adj* (1830) : round or oval in shape
dis·ci·ple \dis-'ī-pəl\ *n* [ME, fr. OE *discipul* & OF *desciple*, fr. LL and L; LL *discipulus* follower of Jesus Christ in his lifetime, fr. L, pupil] (bef. 12c) **1** : one who accepts and assists in spreading the doctrines of another: as **a** : one of the twelve in the inner circle of Christ's followers according to the Gospel accounts **b** : a convinced adherent of a school or individual **2** *cap* : a member of the Disciples of Christ founded in the U.S. in 1809 that holds the Bible alone to be the rule of faith and practice, usu. baptizes by immersion, and has a congregational polity *syn* see FOLLOWER — **dis·ci·ple·ship** \-,ship\ *n*
dis·ci·plin·able \,dis-ə-'plin-ə-bəl; 'dis-ə-plən-\ *adj* (15c) **1** : DOCILE, TEACHABLE **2** : subject to or deserving discipline ⟨a ~ offense⟩
dis·ci·pli·nar·i·an \,dis-ə-plə-'ner-ē-ən\ *n* (1639) : one who disciplines or enforces order — **disciplinarian** *adj*
dis·ci·plin·ary \'dis-ə-plə-,ner-ē, *esp Brit* ,dis-ə-'plin-ə-rē\ *adj* (1598) **1 a** : of or relating to discipline **b** : designed to correct or punish breaches of discipline ⟨took ~ action⟩ **2** : of or relating to a particular field of study — **dis·ci·plin·ar·i·ly** \,dis-ə-plə-'ner-ə-lē\ *adv* — **dis·ci·plin·ar·i·ty** \-'nar-ət-ē\ *n*
[1]**dis·ci·pline** \'dis-ə-plən\ *n* [ME, fr. OF & L; OF, fr. L *disciplina* teaching, learning, fr. *discipulus* pupil] (13c) **1** : PUNISHMENT **2** *obs* : INSTRUCTION **3** : a subject that is taught : a field of study **4** : training that corrects, molds, or perfects the mental faculties or moral character **5 a** : control gained by enforcing obedience or order **b** : orderly or prescribed conduct or pattern of behavior **c** : SELF-CONTROL **6** : a rule or system of rules governing conduct or activity — **dis·ci·plin·al** \-plən-ᵊl\ *adj*
[2]**discipline** *vt* **-plined; -plin·ing** (14c) **1** : to punish or penalize for the sake of discipline **2** : to train or develop by instruction and exercise esp. in self-control **3 a** : to bring (a group) under control ⟨~ troops⟩ **b** : to impose order upon ⟨the writer ~*s* and refines his style⟩ *syn* see PUNISH, TEACH — **dis·ci·plin·er** *n*
dis·ci·plined *adj* (14c) : marked by or possessing discipline ⟨a ~ mind⟩
disc jockey *n* (1941) : an announcer of a radio show of popular recorded music who often intersperses comments not related to the music
dis·claim \dis-'klām\ *vb* [ME *disclaimen*, fr. AF *disclaimer*, fr. *dis-* + *claimer* to claim, fr. OF *clamer*] *vi* (15c) **1** : to make a disclaimer **2 a** *obs* : to disavow all part or share **b** : to utter denial ~ *vt* **1** : to renounce a legal claim to **2** : DENY, DISAVOW ⟨~*ed* any knowledge of the contents of the letter⟩
dis·claim·er \-'klā-mər\ *n* (15c) **1 a** : a denial or disavowal of legal claim : relinquishment of or formal refusal to accept an interest or estate **b** : a writing that embodies a legal disclaimer **2 a** : DENIAL, DISAVOWAL **b** : REPUDIATION
dis·cla·ma·tion \,dis-klə-'mā-shən\ *n* (1592) : RENUNCIATION, DISAVOWAL
dis·cli·max \(')dis-'klī-,maks\ *n* (1935) : a relatively stable ecological community often including kinds of organisms foreign to the region and displacing the climax because of disturbance esp. by man
[1]**dis·close** \dis-'klōz\ *vt* [ME *disclosen*, fr. MF *desclos-*, stem of *desclore* to disclose, fr. ML *disclaudere* to open, fr. L *dis-* + *claudere* to close — more at CLOSE] (14c) **1** *obs* : to open up **2 a** : to expose to view **b** *archaic* : HATCH **c** : to make known or public ⟨demands that politicians ~ the sources of their income⟩ *syn* see REVEAL — **dis·clos·er** *n*
[2]**disclose** *n, obs* (1548) : DISCLOSURE
dis·clos·ing \-'klō-ziŋ\ *adj* (1965) : being or using an agent (as a tablet or liquid) that contains a usu. red dye that adheres to and stains dental plaque
dis·clo·sure \dis-'klō-zhər\ *n* (1598) **1** : the act or an instance of disclosing : EXPOSURE **2** : something disclosed : REVELATION
[1]**dis·co** \'dis-(,)kō\ *n, pl* **discos** [short for *discotheque*] (1964) **1** : a nightclub for dancing to live and recorded music often featuring flamboyant decor and special lighting **2** : popular dance music characterized by hypnotic rhythm, repetitive lyrics, and electronically produced sounds
[2]**disco** *vi* (1979) : to dance to disco music
disco- — see DISC-
dis·cog·ra·pher \dis-'käg-rə-fər\ *n* (1941) : one that compiles discographies
dis·cog·ra·phy \-fē\ *n, pl* **-phies** [F *discographie*, fr. *disc-* + *-graphie* -graphy] (1935) **1** : a descriptive list of phonograph records by category, composer, performer, or date of release **2** : the history of recorded music — **dis·co·graph·i·cal** \,dis-kə-'graf-i-kəl\ *also* **dis·co·graph·ic** \-ik\ *adj*
dis·coid \'dis-,kȯid\ *adj* [LL *discoides* quoit-shaped, fr. Gk *diskoeidēs*, fr. *diskos* disk] (1794) **1** : relating to or having a disk: as **a** *of a composite floret* : situated in the floral disk **b** *of a composite flower head* : having only tubular florets **2** : resembling a disk or discus : being flat and circular
dis·coi·dal \dis-'kȯid-ᵊl\ *adj* (ca. 1706) : of, resembling, or producing a disk
discoidal cleavage *n* (ca. 1909) : meroblastic cleavage in which a disk of cells is produced at the animal pole of the zygote (as in bird eggs)
dis·col·or \(')dis-'kəl-ər\ *vb* [ME *discolouren*, fr. MF *descolourer*, fr. LL *discolorari*, fr. L *discolor* of another color, fr. *dis-* + *color* color] *vt* (14c) : to alter or change the hue or color of ~ *vi* : to change color : STAIN, FADE
dis·col·or·ation \(,)dis-,kəl-ə-'rā-shən\ *n* (1642) **1** : the act of discoloring : the state of being discolored **2** : a discolored spot or formation : STAIN
dis·com·bob·u·late \,dis-kəm-'bäb-(y)ə-,lāt\ *vt* **-lat·ed; -lat·ing** [prob. alter. of *discompose*] (ca. 1916) : UPSET, CONFUSE ⟨the offensive had *discombobulated* all the German defensive arrangements —A. J. Liebling⟩ — **dis·com·bob·u·la·tion** \-,bäb-(y)ə-'lā-shən\ *n*

[1]**dis·com·fit** \dis-ˈkəm(p)-fət, *esp Southern* ˌdis-kəm-ˈfit\ *vt* [ME *discomfiten*, fr. OF *desconfit*, pp. of *desconfire*, fr. *des-* + *confire* to prepare — more at COMFIT] (13c) **1 a** *archaic* **:** to defeat in battle **b :** to frustrate the plans of **:** THWART **2 :** to put into a state of perplexity and embarrassment **:** DISCONCERT

[2]**discomfit** *n* (15c) **:** DISCOMFITURE

dis·com·fi·ture \dis-ˈkəm(p)-fə-ˌchu̇(ə)r, -chər, -ˌt(y)u̇(ə)r\ *n* (14c) **:** the act of discomfiting **:** the state of being discomfited

[1]**dis·com·fort** \dis-ˈkəm(p)-fərt\ *vt* [ME *discomforten*, fr. MF *desconforter*, fr. OF, fr. *des-* + *conforter* to comfort] (14c) **1** *archaic* **:** DISMAY **2 :** to make uncomfortable or uneasy — **dis·com·fort·able** \-ˈkəm(p)-fərt-ə-bəl, -ˈkəm(p)(f)-tə(r)-bəl\ *adj*

[2]**discomfort** *n* (14c) **1** *archaic* **:** DISTRESS, GRIEF **2 :** mental or physical uneasiness **:** ANNOYANCE ⟨he gave every sign of intense ~⟩

dis·com·mend \ˌdis-kə-ˈmend\ *vt* [ME *dyscommenden*] (15c) **1 :** DISAPPROVE, DISPARAGE **2 :** to cause to be viewed unfavorably

dis·com·mode \ˌdis-kə-ˈmōd\ *vt* **-mod·ed; -mod·ing** [MF *discommoder*, fr. *dis-* + *commode* convenient — more at COMMODE] (1721) **:** to cause inconvenience to **:** TROUBLE

dis·com·pose \ˌdis-kəm-ˈpōz\ *vt* (15c) **1 :** to destroy the composure or serenity of **2 :** to disturb the order of — **dis·com·po·sure** \-ˈpō-zhər\ *n*

syn DISCOMPOSE, DISQUIET, DISTURB, PERTURB, AGITATE, UPSET, FLUSTER mean to destroy capacity for collected thought or decisive action. DISCOMPOSE implies some degree of loss of self-control or self-confidence esp. through emotional stress; DISQUIET suggests loss of sense of security or peace of mind; DISTURB implies interference with one's mental processes caused by worry, perplexity, or interruption; PERTURB implies deep disturbance of mind and emotions; AGITATE suggests obvious external signs of nervous or emotional excitement; UPSET implies the disturbance of normal or habitual functioning by disappointment, distress, or grief; FLUSTER suggests bewildered agitation.

dis·con·cert \ˌdis-kən-ˈsərt\ *vt* [obs. F *disconcerter*, alter. of MF *desconcerter*, fr. *des-* + *concerter* to concert] (1687) **1 :** to throw into confusion **2 :** to disturb the composure of — **dis·con·cert·ing** *adj* — **dis·con·cert·ing·ly** \-iŋ-lē\ *adv*

dis·con·firm \ˌdis-kən-ˈfərm\ *vt* (1936) **:** to deny the validity of

dis·con·form·able \ˌdis-kən-ˈfȯr-mə-bəl\ *adj* (ca. 1905) **:** of or relating to a disconformity in rocks — **dis·con·form·ably** \-blē\ *adv*

dis·con·for·mi·ty \ˌdis-kən-ˈfȯr-mət-ē\ *n* (1587) **1 :** NONCONFORMITY **2 :** a break in a sequence of sedimentary rocks all of which have approximately the same dip

dis·con·nect \ˌdis-kə-ˈnekt\ *vt* (1709) **:** to sever the connection of or between ~ *vi* **1 :** to terminate a connection **2 :** to become detached or withdrawn ⟨he has periods when he ~*s* into silences —*Current Biog.*⟩ — **dis·con·nec·tion** \-ˈnek-shən\ *n*

dis·con·nect·ed *adj* (1789) **:** not connected **:** SEPARATE; *also* **:** INCOHERENT — **dis·con·nect·ed·ly** *adv* — **dis·con·nect·ed·ness** *n*

dis·con·so·late \dis-ˈkän(t)-s(ə-)lət\ *adj* [ME, fr. ML *disconsolatus*, fr. L *dis-* + *consolatus*, pp. of *consolari* to console] (14c) **1 :** CHEERLESS ⟨a clutch of ~ houses —D. H. Lawrence⟩ **2 :** DEJECTED, DOWNCAST ⟨the team returned ~ from three losses⟩ — **dis·con·so·late·ly** *adv* — **dis·con·so·late·ness** *n* — **dis·con·so·la·tion** \(ˌ)dis-ˌkän(t)-sə-ˈlā-shən\ *n*

[1]**dis·con·tent** \ˌdis-kən-ˈtent\ *adj* (15c) **:** DISCONTENTED

[2]**discontent** *vt* (1549) **:** to make discontented — **dis·con·tent·ment** \-mənt\ *n*

[3]**discontent** *n* (1591) **:** lack of contentment: **a :** a sense of grievance **:** DISSATISFACTION ⟨the winter of our ~ —Shak.⟩ **b :** restless aspiration for improvement

[4]**discontent** *n* (1596) **:** one who is discontented **:** MALCONTENT

dis·con·tent·ed *adj* (1525) **:** DISSATISFIED, MALCONTENT — **dis·con·tent·ed·ly** *adv* — **dis·con·tent·ed·ness** *n*

dis·con·tin·u·ance \ˌdis-kən-ˈtin-yə-wən(t)s\ *n* (14c) **1 :** the act or an instance of discontinuing **2 :** the interruption or termination of a legal action by failure to continue or by the plaintiff's entry of a discontinuing order

dis·con·tin·ue \ˌdis-kən-ˈtin-(ˌ)yü, -yə(-w)\ *vb* [ME *discontinuen*, fr. MF *discontinuer*, fr. ML *discontinuare*, fr. L *dis-* + *continuare* to continue] *vt* (14c) **1 :** to break the continuity of **:** cease to operate, administer, use, produce, or take **2 :** to abandon or terminate by a legal discontinuance ~ *vi* **:** to come to an end ***syn*** see STOP

dis·con·ti·nu·ity \(ˌ)dis-ˌkänt-ᵊn-ˈ(y)ü-ət-ē\ *n* (1570) **1 :** lack of continuity or cohesion **2 :** GAP 5 **3 a :** the property of being not mathematically continuous ⟨a point of ~⟩ **b :** an instance of being not mathematically continuous; *esp* **:** a value of an independent variable at which a function is not continuous

dis·con·tin·u·ous \ˌdis-kən-ˈtin-yə-wəs\ *adj* (1718) **1 a** (1) **:** not continuous ⟨a ~ series of events⟩ (2) **:** not continued **:** DISCRETE ⟨~ features of terrain⟩ **b :** lacking sequence or coherence **2 :** having one or more mathematical discontinuities — used of a variable or a function — **dis·con·tin·u·ous·ly** *adv*

dis·co·phile \ˈdis-kə-ˌfīl\ *n* (1940) **:** one who studies and collects phonograph records

[1]**dis·cord** \ˈdis-ˌkȯ(ə)rd\ *n* (13c) **1 a :** lack of agreement or harmony (as between persons, things, or ideas) **b :** active quarreling or conflict resulting from discord among persons or factions **:** STRIFE **2 a** (1) **:** a combination of musical sounds that strikes the ear harshly (2) **:** DISSONANCE **b :** a harsh or unpleasant sound

syn DISCORD, STRIFE, CONFLICT, CONTENTION, DISSENSION, VARIANCE mean a state or condition marked by a lack of agreement or harmony. DISCORD implies an intrinsic or essential lack of harmony producing quarreling, factiousness, or antagonism; STRIFE emphasizes a struggle for superiority rather than the incongruity or incompatibility of the persons or things involved; CONFLICT usu. stresses the action of forces in opposition but in static applications implies an irreconcilability as of duties or desires; CONTENTION applies to strife or competition that shows itself in quarreling, disputing, or controversy; DISSENSION implies strife or discord and stresses a division into factions; VARIANCE implies a clash between persons or things owing to a difference in nature, opinion, or interest.

[2]**dis·cord** \ˈdis-ˌkȯ(ə)rd, dis-ˈ\ *vi* [ME *discorden*, fr. OF *discorder*, fr. L *discordare*, fr. *discord-*, *discors* discordant, fr. *dis-* + *cord-*, *cor* heart — more at HEART] (14c) **:** DISAGREE, CLASH

dis·cor·dance \dis-ˈkȯrd-ᵊn(t)s\ *n* (14c) **1 :** the state or an instance of being discordant **2 :** DISSONANCE

dis·cor·dan·cy \-ᵊn-sē\ *n, pl* **-cies** (1607) **:** DISCORDANCE

dis·cor·dant \-ᵊnt\ *adj* (14c) **1 a :** being at variance **:** DISAGREEING **b :** QUARRELSOME **2 :** relating to a discord — **dis·cor·dant·ly** *adv*

dis·co·theque \ˈdis-kə-ˌtek, ˌdis-kə-ˈ\ *n* [F *discothèque*, fr. *disque* disk, record + *-o-* + *-thèque* (as in *bibliothèque* library)] (1954) **:** a usu. small intimate nightclub for dancing to live or recorded music; *also* **:** DISCO 1

[1]**dis·count** \ˈdis-ˌkau̇nt\ *n* (1622) **1 :** a reduction made from the gross amount or value of something: as **a** (1) **:** a reduction made from a regular or list price (2) **:** a proportionate deduction from a debt account usu. made for cash or prompt payment **b :** a deduction made for interest in advancing money upon or purchasing a bill or note not due **2 :** the act or practice of discounting **3 :** a deduction taken or allowance made

[2]**dis·count** \ˈdis-ˌkau̇nt, dis-ˈ\ *vb* [modif. of F *décompter*, fr. OF *desconter*, fr. ML *discomputare*, fr. L *dis-* + *computare* to count — more at COUNT] *vt* (1629) **1 a :** to make a deduction from usu. for cash or prompt payment **b :** to sell or offer for sale at a discount **2 :** to lend money on after deducting the discount **3 a :** to leave out of account **:** DISREGARD **b :** to underestimate the importance of **:** MINIMIZE **c** (1) **:** to make allowance for bias or exaggeration in (2) **:** to view with doubt **:** DISBELIEVE **d :** to take into account (as a future event) in present calculations ~ *vi* **:** to give or make discounts

dis·count·able \dis-ˈkau̇nt-ə-bəl, ˈdis-ˌ\ *adj* (1800) **1 :** set apart for discounting ⟨within the ~ period⟩ **2 :** subject to being discounted ⟨a ~ note⟩

[1]**dis·coun·te·nance** \dis-ˈkau̇nt-ᵊn-ən(t)s, -ˈkau̇nt-nən(t)s\ *vt* (1580) **1 :** ABASH, DISCONCERT **2 :** to look with disfavor on **:** discourage by evidence of disapproval

[2]**discountenance** *n* (1580) **:** DISAPPROBATION, DISFAVOR

dis·count·er \ˈdis-ˌkau̇nt-ər, dis-ˈ\ *n* (1732) **:** one that discounts; *specif* **:** DISCOUNT STORE

discount house *n* (1944) **:** DISCOUNT STORE

discount rate *n* (ca. 1927) **1 :** the interest on an annual basis deducted in advance on a loan **2 :** the charge levied by a central bank for advances and rediscounts

discount store *n* (1956) **:** a store where merchandise (as consumer durable goods) is sold at a discount from suggested list price

dis·cour·age \dis-ˈkər-ij, -ˈkə-rij\ *vt* **-aged; -ag·ing** [ME *discoragen*, fr. MF *descorager*, fr. OF *descoragier*, fr. *des-* dis- + *corage* courage] (15c) **1 :** to deprive of courage or confidence **:** DISHEARTEN **2 a :** to hinder by disfavoring **:** DETER **b :** to attempt to dissuade — **dis·cour·age·able** \-ə-bəl\ *adj* — **dis·cour·ag·er** *n* — **dis·cour·ag·ing·ly** \-iŋ-lē\ *adv*

dis·cour·age·ment \-mənt\ *n* (1561) **1 :** the act of discouraging **:** the state of being discouraged **2 :** something that discourages **:** DETERRENT

[1]**dis·course** \ˈdis-ˌkō(ə)rs, -ˌkȯ(ə)rs, dis-ˈ\ *n* [ME *discours*, fr. ML & LL *discursus*; ML, argument, fr. LL, conversation, fr. L, act of running about, fr. *discursus*, pp. of *discurrere* to run about, fr. *dis-* + *currere* to run — more at CAR] (14c) **1** *archaic* **:** the capacity of orderly thought or procedure **:** RATIONALITY **2 :** verbal interchange of ideas; *esp* **:** CONVERSATION **3 a :** formal and orderly and usu. extended expression of thought on a subject **b :** connected speech or writing **4** *obs* **:** social familiarity

[2]**dis·course** \dis-ˈkō(ə)rs, -ˈkȯ(ə)rs, ˈdis-ˌ\ *vb* **dis·coursed; dis·cours·ing** *vi* (1559) **1 :** to express oneself esp. in oral discourse **2 :** TALK, CONVERSE ~ *vt, archaic* **:** to give forth **:** UTTER — **dis·cours·er** *n*

dis·cour·te·ous \(ˈ)dis-ˈkərt-ē-əs\ *adj* (1578) **:** lacking courtesy **:** RUDE — **dis·cour·te·ous·ly** *adv* — **dis·cour·te·ous·ness** *n*

dis·cour·te·sy \-ˈkərt-ə-sē\ *n* (1555) **1 :** RUDENESS **2 :** a rude act

dis·cov·er \dis-ˈkəv-ər\ *vb* **dis·cov·ered; dis·cov·er·ing** \-ˈkəv-(ə-)riŋ\ [ME *discoveren*, fr. MF *descovrir*, fr. LL *discooperire*, fr. L *dis-* + *cooperire* to cover — more at COVER] *vt* (14c) **1 a :** to make known or visible **:** EXPOSE **b** *archaic* **:** DISPLAY **2 :** to obtain sight or knowledge of for the first time **:** FIND ⟨~ the solution of a puzzle⟩ ~ *vi* **:** to make a discovery — **dis·cov·er·able** \-ˈkəv-(ə-)rə-bəl\ *adj* — **dis·cov·er·er** \-ər-ər\ *n*

syn DISCOVER, ASCERTAIN, DETERMINE, UNEARTH, LEARN mean to find out what one did not previously know. DISCOVER may apply to something requiring exploration or investigation or to a chance encounter; ASCERTAIN implies effort to find the facts or the truth proceeding from awareness of ignorance or uncertainty; DETERMINE emphasizes the intent to establish the facts definitely or precisely; UNEARTH implies bringing to light something forgotten or hidden; LEARN may imply acquiring knowledge with little effort or conscious intention (as by simply being told) or it may imply study and practice. ***syn*** see in addition INVENT, REVEAL

dis·cov·ery \dis-ˈkəv-(ə-)rē\ *n, pl* **-er·ies** (1539) **1 a :** the act or process of discovering **b** (1) *archaic* **:** DISCLOSURE (2) *obs* **:** DISPLAY **c** *obs* **:** EXPLORATION **2 :** something discovered **3 :** the usu. pretrial disclosure of pertinent facts or documents by one or both parties to a civil action or proceeding

Discovery Day *n* (ca. 1913) **:** COLUMBUS DAY

[1]**dis·cred·it** \(ˈ)dis-ˈkred-ət\ *vt* (1559) **1 :** to refuse to accept as true or accurate **:** DISBELIEVE **2 :** to cause disbelief in the accuracy or authority of **3 :** to deprive of good repute **:** DISGRACE

[2]**discredit** *n* (1565) **1 :** loss of credit or reputation ⟨I knew stories to the ~ of England —W. B. Yeats⟩ **2 :** lack or loss of belief or confidence **:** DOUBT ⟨contradictions cast ~ on his testimony⟩

dis·cred·it·able \-ə-bəl\ *adj* (1640) **:** injurious to reputation — **dis·cred·it·ably** \-blē\ *adv*

dis·creet \dis-ˈkrēt\ *adj* [ME, fr. MF *discret*, fr. ML *discretus*, fr. L, pp. of *discernere* to separate, distinguish between — more at DISCERN] (14c) **1 :** having or showing discernment or good judgment in conduct and

\ə\ abut \ᵊ\ kitten, F table \ər\ further \a\ ash \ā\ ace \ä\ cot, cart \au̇\ out \ch\ chin \e\ bet \ē\ easy \g\ go \i\ hit \ī\ ice \j\ job \ŋ\ sing \ō\ go \ȯ\ law \ȯi\ boy \th\ thin \t͟h\ the \ü\ loot \u̇\ foot \y\ yet \zh\ vision \à, k̲, ⁿ, œ, œ̄, ue, uē, ʸ\ *see* Guide to Pronunciation

esp. in speech : PRUDENT; *esp* : capable of preserving prudent silence 2 : UNPRETENTIOUS, MODEST ⟨the warmth and ~ elegance of a civilized home —Joseph Wechsberg⟩ — **dis·creet·ly** *adv* — **dis·creet·ness** *n*

dis·crep·an·cy \dis-ˈkrep-ən-sē\ *n, pl* **-cies** (ca. 1623) **1** : the quality or state of being discrepant : DIFFERENCE **2** : an instance of being discrepant

dis·crep·ant \-ənt\ *adj* [L *discrepant-, discrepans,* prp. of *discrepare* to sound discordantly, fr. *dis-* + *crepare* to rattle, creak — more at RAVEN] (15c) : being at variance : DISAGREEING ⟨widely ~ conclusions⟩ — **dis·crep·ant·ly** *adv*

dis·crete \dis-ˈkrēt, ˈdis-ˌ\ *adj* [ME, fr. L *discretus*] (14c) **1** : constituting a separate entity : individually distinct **2 a** : consisting of distinct or unconnected elements : NONCONTINUOUS **b** : taking on or having a finite or countably infinite number of values : not mathematically continuous ⟨a ~ random variable⟩ ***syn*** see DISTINCT — **dis·crete·ly** *adv* — **dis·crete·ness** *n*

dis·cre·tion \dis-ˈkresh-ən\ *n* (14c) **1** : the quality of being discreet : CIRCUMSPECTION; *esp* : cautious reserve in speech **2** : ability to make responsible decisions **3 a** : individual choice or judgment ⟨left the decision to his ~⟩ **b** : power of free decision or latitude of choice within certain legal bounds ⟨reached the age of ~⟩ **4** : the result of separating or distinguishing ⟨breaking down every operation into discrete parts, and then making verbal the ~s that are made —Elinor Langer⟩

dis·cre·tion·ary \-ˈkresh-ə-ˌner-ē\ *adj* (1698) **1** : left to discretion : exercised at one's own discretion **2** : available for discretionary use ⟨~ purchasing power⟩

discretionary account *n* (ca. 1920) : a security or commodity market account in which an agent (as a broker) is given power of attorney allowing him to make independent decisions and buy and sell for the account of his principal

dis·crim·i·na·bil·i·ty \-ˌkrim-(ə-)nə-ˈbil-ət-ē\ *n, pl* **-ties** (ca. 1901) **1** : the quality of being discriminable ⟨the ~ of the various senses of a word⟩ **2** : the ability to discriminate

dis·crim·i·na·ble \dis-ˈkrim-(ə-)nə-bəl\ *adj* (1730) : capable of being discriminated — **dis·crim·i·na·bly** \-blē\ *adv*

dis·crim·i·nant \-ˈkrim-(ə-)nənt\ *n* (ca. 1948) : a mathematical expression providing a criterion for the behavior of another more complicated expression, relation, or set of relations

discriminant function *n* (ca. 1936) : a function of a set of variables (as measurements of taxonomic specimens) that is evaluated for samples of events or objects and used as an aid in discriminating between or classifying them

dis·crim·i·nate \dis-ˈkrim-ə-ˌnāt\ *vb* **-nat·ed; -nat·ing** [L *discriminatus,* pp. of *discriminare,* fr. *discrimin-, discrimen* distinction, fr. *discernere* to distinguish between — more at DISCERN] *vt* (1628) **1 a** : to mark or perceive the distinguishing or peculiar features of **b** : DISTINGUISH, DIFFERENTIATE ⟨~ hundreds of colors⟩ **2** : to distinguish by discerning or exposing differences; *esp* : to distinguish from another like object ~ *vi* **1 a** : to make a distinction ⟨~ among the methods which should be used⟩ **b** : to use good judgment **2** : to make a difference in treatment or favor on a basis other than individual merit ⟨~ in favor of your friends⟩ ⟨~ against a certain nationality⟩

dis·crim·i·nat·ing *adj* (1647) **1** : making a distinction : DISTINGUISHING **2** : marked by discrimination: **a** : DISCERNING, JUDICIOUS **b** : DISCRIMINATORY — **dis·crim·i·nat·ing·ly** \-ˌnāt-iŋ-lē\ *adv*

dis·crim·i·na·tion \dis-ˌkrim-ə-ˈnā-shən\ *n* (1648) **1 a** : the act of discriminating **b** : the process by which two stimuli differing in some aspect are responded to differently : DIFFERENTIATION **2** : the quality or power of finely distinguishing **3 a** : the act, practice, or an instance of discriminating categorically rather than individually **b** : prejudiced or prejudicial outlook, action, or treatment ⟨racial ~⟩ ***syn*** see DISCERNMENT — **dis·crim·i·na·tion·al** \-shnəl, -shən-ᵊl\ *adj*

dis·crim·i·na·tive \dis-ˈkrim-ə-ˌnāt-iv, -ˈkrim-(ə-)nət-\ *adj* (1677) **1** : making distinctions **2** : DISCRIMINATORY 2

dis·crim·i·na·tor \dis-ˈkrim-ə-ˌnāt-ər\ *n* (1828) : one that discriminates; *specif* : a circuit that can be adjusted to accept or reject signals of different characteristics (as amplitude or frequency)

dis·crim·i·na·to·ry \dis-ˈkrim-(ə-)nə-ˌtōr-ē, -ˌtȯr-\ *adj* (1828) **1** : DISCRIMINATIVE 1 **2** : applying or favoring discrimination in treatment — **dis·crim·i·na·to·ri·ly** \-ˌkrim-(ə-)nə-ˈtōr-ə-lē, -ˈtȯr-\ *adv*

dis·cur·sive \dis-ˈkər-siv\ *adj* [ML *discursivus,* fr. L *discursus,* pp. of *discurrere* to run about — more at DISCOURSE] (1598) **1 a** : moving from topic to topic without order : RAMBLING **b** : proceeding coherently from topic to topic **2** : marked by analytical reasoning — **dis·cur·sive·ly** *adv* — **dis·cur·sive·ness** *n*

dis·cus \ˈdis-kəs\ *n, pl* **dis·cus·es** [L — more at DISH] (1656) **1** : a disk (as of wood or plastic) that is thicker in the center than at the perimeter and that is hurled for distance as a track-and-field event; *also* : the event **2** : DISK 2, 3

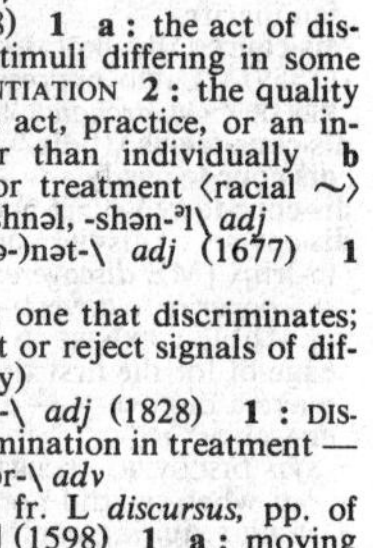

discus 1

dis·cuss \dis-ˈkəs\ *vt* [ME *discussen,* fr. L *discussus,* pp. of *discutere* to disperse, fr. *dis-* apart + *quatere* to shake — more at DIS-, QUASH] (14c) **1** *obs* : DISPEL **2 a** : to investigate by reasoning or argument **b** : to present in detail for examination or consideration ⟨~*ed* plans for the party⟩ **c** : to talk about **3** *obs* : DECLARE — **dis·cuss·able** *or* **dis·cuss·ible** \-ə-bəl\ *adj* — **dis·cuss·er** *n*

syn DISCUSS, ARGUE, DEBATE, DISPUTE mean to discourse about in order to reach conclusions or to convince. DISCUSS implies a sifting of possibilities esp. by presenting considerations pro and con; ARGUE implies the offering of reasons or evidence in support of convictions already held; DEBATE suggests formal or public argument between opposing parties; it may also apply to deliberation with oneself; DISPUTE implies contentious or heated argument.

dis·cus·sant \dis-ˈkəs-ᵊnt\ *n* (1926) : one who takes part in a formal discussion or symposium

dis·cus·sion \dis-ˈkəsh-ən\ *n* (14c) **1** : consideration of a question in open and usu. informal debate **2** : a formal treatment of a topic in speech or writing

[1]dis·dain \dis-ˈdān\ *n* [ME *desdeyne,* fr. OF *desdeign,* fr. *desdeignier*] (13c) : a feeling of contempt for what is beneath one : SCORN

[2]disdain *vt* [ME *desdeynen,* fr. MF *desdeignier,* fr. OF, fr. (assumed) VL *disdignare,* fr. L *dis-* + *dignare* to deign — more at DEIGN] (14c) **1** : to look with scorn on **2** : to refuse or abstain from because of disdain **3** : to treat disdainfully ***syn*** see DESPISE

dis·dain·ful \-fəl\ *adj* (1542) : full of or expressing disdain ***syn*** see PROUD — **dis·dain·ful·ly** \-fə-lē\ *adv* — **dis·dain·ful·ness** *n*

dis·ease \diz-ˈēz\ *n* [ME *disese,* fr. MF *desaise,* fr. *des-* dis- + *aise* ease] (14c) **1** *obs* : TROUBLE **2** : a condition of the living animal or plant body or of one of its parts that impairs the performance of a vital function : SICKNESS, MALADY **3** : a harmful development (as in a social institution) — **dis·eased** \-ˈēzd\ *adj*

dis·econ·o·my \ˌdis-i-ˈkän-ə-mē\ *n* (1937) **1** : a lack of economy **2** : a factor responsible for an increase in cost

dis·em·bark \ˌdis-əm-ˈbärk\ *vb* [MF *desembarquer,* fr. *des-* + *embarquer* to embark] *vt* (1582) : to remove to shore from a ship ~ *vi* **1** : to go ashore out of a ship **2** : to get out of a vehicle or craft — **dis·em·bar·ka·tion** \(ˌ)dis-ˌem-ˌbär-ˈkā-shən, -bər-\ *n*

dis·em·bar·rass \ˌdis-əm-ˈbar-əs\ *vt* (1726) : to free from something troublesome or superfluous ***syn*** see EXTRICATE

dis·em·body \ˌdis-əm-ˈbäd-ē\ *vt* (1714) : to divest of a body, of corporeal existence, or of reality

dis·em·bogue \ˌdis-əm-ˈbōg\ *vb* **-bogued; -bogu·ing** [modif. of Sp *desembocar,* fr. *des-* dis- (fr. L *dis-*) + *embocar* to put into the mouth, fr. *en* in (fr. L *in*) + *boca* mouth, fr. L *bucca* — more at POCK] *vi* (1595) : to flow or come forth from or as if from a channel ~ *vt* : to pour out : EMPTY

dis·em·bow·el \ˌdis-əm-ˈbau̇(-ə)l\ *vt* (1613) **1** : to take out the bowels of : EVISCERATE **2** : to remove the substance of — **dis·em·bow·el·ment** \-mənt\ *n*

dis·en·chant \ˌdis-ᵊn-ˈchant\ *vt* [MF *desenchanter,* fr. *des-* + *enchanter* to enchant] (1586) : to free from illusion — **dis·en·chant·er** *n* — **dis·en·chant·ing** *adj* — **dis·en·chant·ing·ly** \-iŋ-lē\ *adv* — **dis·en·chant·ment** \-mənt\ *n*

dis·en·cum·ber \ˌdis-ᵊn-ˈkəm-bər\ *vt* [MF *desencombrer,* fr. *des-* + *encombrer* to encumber] (1598) : to free from encumbrance : DISBURDEN ***syn*** see EXTRICATE

dis·en·dow \ˌdis-ᵊn-ˈdau̇\ *vt* (1861) : to strip of endowment — **dis·en·dow·er** \-ˈdau̇(-ə)r\ *n* — **dis·en·dow·ment** \-ˈdau̇-mənt\ *n*

dis·en·fran·chise \ˌdis-ᵊn-ˈfran-ˌchīz\ *vt* (1664) : DISFRANCHISE — **dis·en·fran·chise·ment** \-ˌchīz-mənt, -chəz-\ *n*

dis·en·gage \ˌdis-ᵊn-ˈgāj\ *vb* [F *désengager,* fr. MF, fr. *des-* + *engager* to engage] *vt* (1611) : to release from something that engages ~ *vi* : to release or detach oneself : WITHDRAW — **dis·en·gage·ment** \-mənt\ *n*

dis·en·tail \ˌdis-ᵊn-ˈtā(ə)l\ *vt* (1641) : to free from entail

dis·en·tan·gle \ˌdis-ᵊn-ˈtaŋ-gəl\ *vt* (1598) : to free from entanglement : UNRAVEL ~ *vi* : to become disentangled ***syn*** see EXTRICATE — **dis·en·tan·gle·ment** \-mənt\ *n*

dis·en·thrall *also* **dis·en·thral** \ˌdis-ᵊn-ˈthrȯl\ *vt* (1643) : to free from bondage : LIBERATE

dis·equil·i·brate \ˌdis-i-ˈkwil-ə-ˌbrāt\ *vt* (1891) : to put out of balance — **dis·equil·i·bra·tion** \-ˌkwil-ə-ˈbrā-shən\ *n*

dis·equi·lib·ri·um \(ˌ)dis-ˌē-kwə-ˈlib-rē-əm, -ˌek-wə-\ *n* (1840) : loss or lack of equilibrium

dis·es·tab·lish \ˌdis-ə-ˈstab-lish\ *vt* (1598) : to deprive of an established status; *esp* : to deprive of the status and privileges of an established church — **dis·es·tab·lish·ment** \-mənt\ *n*

dis·es·tab·lish·men·tar·i·an \-ˌstab-lish-ˌmen-ˈter-ē-ən, -mən-\ *n, often cap* [*disestablishment*] (1885) : one who opposes an established order — **disestablishmentarian** *adj, often cap*

[1]dis·es·teem \ˌdis-ə-ˈstēm\ *vt* (1594) : to regard with disfavor

[2]disesteem *n* (1603) : DISFAVOR, DISREPUTE

di·seuse \dē-ˈzə(r)z, -ˈzüz\ *n, pl* **di·seuses** \-ˈzə(r)z(-əz), -ˈzüz(-əz)\ [F, fem. of *diseur,* fr. OF, fr. *dire* to say, fr. L *dicere* — more at DICTION] (1895) : a skilled and usu. professional woman reciter

[1]dis·fa·vor \(ˈ)dis-ˈfā-vər\ *n* [prob. fr. MF *desfaveur,* fr. *des-* dis- + *faveur* favor, fr. OF *favor*] (1533) **1** : DISAPPROVAL, DISLIKE ⟨practices looked upon with ~⟩ **2** : the state or fact of being no longer favored ⟨fell into ~⟩ **3** : DISADVANTAGE

[2]disfavor *vt* (1570) : to withhold or withdraw favor from

dis·fea·ture \(ˈ)dis-ˈfē-chər\ *vt* (1659) : to mar the features of — **dis·fea·ture·ment** \-mənt\ *n*

dis·fig·ure \dis-ˈfig-yər, *esp Brit* -ˈfig-ər\ *vt* [ME *disfiguren,* fr. MF *desfigurer,* fr. *des-* + *figure* figure] (14c) **1** : to impair (as in beauty) by deep and persistent injuries ⟨a face *disfigured* by smallpox⟩ **2** *obs* : DISGUISE — **dis·fig·ure·ment** \-mənt\ *n*

dis·fran·chise \(ˈ)dis-ˈfran-ˌchīz\ *vt* (15c) : to deprive of a franchise, of a legal right, or of some privilege or immunity; *esp* : to deprive of the right to vote — **dis·fran·chise·ment** \-ˌchīz-mənt, -chəz-\ *n*

dis·frock \(ˈ)dis-ˈfräk\ *vt* (1837) : UNFROCK

dis·func·tion *var of* DYSFUNCTION

dis·fur·nish \(ˈ)dis-ˈfər-nish\ *vt* [MF *desfourniss-,* stem of *desfournir,* fr. *des-* + *fournir* to furnish] (1531) : to make destitute of possessions : DIVEST — **dis·fur·nish·ment** \-mənt\ *n*

dis·gorge \(ˈ)dis-ˈgȯ(ə)rj\ *vb* [ME, fr. MF *desgorger,* fr. *des-* + *gorge* to gouge] *vt* (15c) **1 a** : to discharge by the throat and mouth : VOMIT **b** : to discharge violently, confusedly, or as a result of force **c** : to give up on request or under pressure ⟨refused to ~ his ill-gotten gains⟩ **2** : to discharge the contents of (as the stomach) ~ *vi* : to discharge contents ⟨where the river ~*s* into the sea⟩

[1]dis·grace \dis-ˈgrās\ *vt* (1580) **1** *archaic* : to humiliate by a superior showing **2** : to be a source of shame to ⟨your actions *disgraced* the family⟩ **3** : to cause to lose favor or standing ⟨was *disgraced* by the hint of scandal⟩ — **dis·grac·er** *n*

[2]disgrace *n* [MF, fr. OIt *disgrazia,* fr. *dis-* (fr. L) + *grazia* grace, fr. L *gratia* — more at GRACE] (1586) **1 a** : the condition of one fallen from grace or honor **b** : loss of grace, favor, or honor **2** : something that disgraces ⟨your manners are a ~⟩

syn DISGRACE, DISHONOR, DISREPUTE, INFAMY, IGNOMINY mean the state or condition of suffering loss of esteem and of enduring reproach. DISGRACE often implies complete humiliation and sometimes ostracism; DISHONOR emphasizes the loss of honor that one has enjoyed or

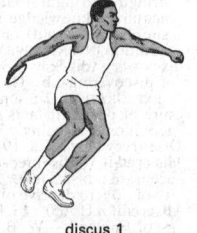

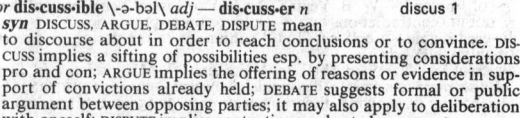

the loss of self-esteem; DISREPUTE stresses loss of one's good name or the acquiring of a bad reputation; INFAMY usu. implies notoriety as well as exceeding shame; IGNOMINY stresses the almost unendurable contemptibility or despicableness of the disgrace.

dis·grace·ful \dis-ˈgrās-fəl\ *adj* (1597) : bringing or involving disgrace — **dis·grace·ful·ly** \-fə-lē\ *adv* — **dis·grace·ful·ness** *n*

dis·grun·tle \dis-ˈgrənt-ᵊl\ *vt* **dis·grun·tled; dis·grun·tling** \-ˈgrənt-liŋ, -ᵊl-iŋ\ [*dis-* + *gruntle* (to grumble), fr. ME *gruntlen,* freq. of *grunten* to grunt] (1682) : to make ill-humored or discontented ⟨the workers are *disgruntled* with their wages⟩ — **dis·grun·tle·ment** \-ᵊl-mənt\ *n*

1dis·guise \dis-ˈgīz\ *vt* **dis·guised; dis·guis·ing** [ME *disgisen,* fr. MF *desguiser,* fr. OF, fr. *des-* + *guise* guise] (14c) **1 a :** to change the customary dress or appearance of **b :** to furnish with a false appearance or an assumed identity **2** *obs* : DISFIGURE **3 :** to obscure the existence or true state or character of : CONCEAL — **dis·guised·ly** \-ˈgīz(-ə)d-lē\ *adv* — **dis·guise·ment** \-ˈgīz-mənt\ *n* — **dis·guis·er** *n*

syn DISGUISE, CLOAK, MASK, DISSEMBLE mean to alter the dress or appearance so as to conceal the identity or true nature. DISGUISE implies a change in appearance or behavior that misleads by presenting a different apparent identity; CLOAK suggests a means of hiding a movement or an intention completely; MASK suggests some usu. obvious means of preventing recognition and need not imply deception or pretense; DISSEMBLE stresses simulation for the purpose of deceiving.

2disguise *n* (14c) **1 :** apparel assumed to conceal one's identity or counterfeit another's **2 :** the act of disguising **3 a :** form misrepresenting the true nature of something ⟨blessings in ~⟩ **b :** an artificial manner : PRETENSE ⟨threw off all ~⟩

1dis·gust \dis-ˈgəst\ *n* (1598) : marked aversion aroused by something highly distasteful : REPUGNANCE

2disgust *vb* [MF *desgouster,* fr. *des-* + *goust* taste, fr. L *gustus;* akin to L *gustare* to taste — more at CHOOSE] *vt* (1650) **1 :** to provoke to loathing, repugnance, or aversion : be offensive to **2 :** to cause (one) to lose an interest or intention ⟨his failures ~*ed* him to the point that he stopped trying⟩ ~ *vi* : to cause disgust — **dis·gust·ed** *adj* — **dis·gust·ed·ly** *adv*

dis·gust·ful \-ˈgəst-fəl\ *adj* (1616) **1 :** provoking disgust **2 :** full of or accompanied by disgust — **dis·gust·ful·ly** \-fə-lē\ *adv*

dis·gust·ing *adj* (1754) : exciting disgust — **dis·gust·ing·ly** \-ˈgəs-tiŋ-lē\ *adv*

1dish \ˈdish\ *n* [ME, fr. OE *disc* plate, fr. L *discus* quoit, disk, dish, fr. Gk *diskos,* fr. *dikein* to throw] (bef. 12c) **1 a :** a more or less concave vessel from which food is served **b :** the contents of a dish ⟨a ~ of strawberries⟩ **2 :** food prepared in a particular way **3 a (1) :** any of various shallow concave vessels; *broadly* : something shallowly concave **(2) :** a directional microwave antenna having a concave usu. parabolic reflector **b :** the state of being concave or the degree of concavity **4 a :** something that is favored ⟨entertainment that is just his ~⟩ **b :** an attractive woman

2dish *vt* (14c) **1 :** to put (as food for serving) into a dish — often used with *up* **2 :** PRESENT — usu. used with *up* **3 :** to make concave like a dish

dis·ha·bille \ˌdis-ə-ˈbē(ə)l, -ˈbil, -ˈbē\ *n* [F *déshabillé,* fr. pp. of *déshabiller* to undress, fr. *dés-* dis- + *habiller* to dress — more at HABILIMENT] (1673) **1 a** *archaic* : NEGLIGEE **b :** the state of being dressed in a casual or careless style **2 :** a deliberately careless or casual manner

dis·har·mon·ic \ˌdis-(ˌ)här-ˈmän-ik\ *adj* (1887) **1 :** having a combination of bodily characters that results in an unusual form or appearance **2 :** exhibiting or marked by allometry

dis·har·mo·ni·ous \-ˈmō-nē-əs\ *adj* (1659) **1 :** lacking in harmony **2** : DISHARMONIC

dis·har·mo·nize \(ˈ)dis-ˈhär-mə-ˌnīz\ *vt* (1801) : to make disharmonious

dis·har·mo·ny \-nē\ *n* (1602) : lack of harmony : DISCORD

dish·cloth \ˈdish-ˌklȯth\ *n* (ca. 1828) : a cloth for washing dishes

dish·clout \ˈdish-ˌklau̇t\ *n, Brit* (ca. 1530) : DISHCLOTH

dis·heart·en \(ˈ)dis-ˈhärt-ᵊn\ *vt* (1599) : to cause to lose spirit or morale — **dis·heart·en·ing·ly** \-ˈhärt-niŋ-lē, -ᵊn-iŋ-\ *adv* — **dis·heart·en·ment** \-ˈhärt-ᵊn-mənt\ *n*

dished \ˈdisht\ *adj* (1737) **1 :** CONCAVE **2** *of a pair of vehicle wheels* : nearer together at the bottom than at the top

di·shev·el \dish-ˈev-əl\ *vt* **di·shev·eled** *or* **di·shev·elled; di·shev·el·ing** *or* **di·shev·el·ling** \-ˈev-(ə-)liŋ\ [back-formation fr. *disheveled*] (1598) : to throw into disorder or disarray

di·shev·eled *or* **di·shev·elled** *adj* [ME *discheveled,* part trans. of MF *deschevelé,* fr. pp. of *descheveler* to disarrange the hair, fr. *des-* + *chevel* hair, fr. L *capillus*] (1583) : marked by disorder or disarray

dis·hon·est \(ˈ)dis-ˈän-əst\ *adj* [ME, fr. MF *deshoneste,* fr. *des-* + *honeste* honest] (14c) **1** *obs* : SHAMEFUL, UNCHASTE **2 :** characterized by lack of truth, honesty, or trustworthiness : UNFAIR, DECEPTIVE — **dis·hon·est·ly** *adv*

syn DISHONEST, DECEITFUL, MENDACIOUS, LYING, UNTRUTHFUL mean unworthy of trust or belief. DISHONEST implies a willful perversion of truth in order to deceive, cheat, or defraud; DECEITFUL usu. implies an intent to mislead and commonly suggests a false appearance or double-dealing; MENDACIOUS is less forthright than LYING, may suggest bland or even harmlessly mischievous deceit, and used of people often suggests a habit of telling untruths; LYING implies a specific act or instance rather than a habit or tendency; UNTRUTHFUL is a less brutal term than LYING and in application to accounts or description stresses a discrepancy between what is said and fact or reality rather than an intent to deceive.

dis·hon·es·ty \-ə-stē\ *n* (1599) **1 :** lack of honesty or integrity : disposition to defraud or deceive **2 :** a dishonest act : FRAUD

1dis·hon·or \(ˈ)dis-ˈän-ər\ *vt* (13c) **1 a :** to treat in a degrading manner **b :** to bring shame on **2 :** to refuse to accept or pay (as a draft, bill, check, or note)

2dishonor *n* [ME *dishonour,* fr. MF *deshonor,* fr. *des-* + *honor* honor] (14c) **1 :** lack or loss of honor or reputation **2 :** the state of one who has lost honor or prestige : SHAME **3 :** a cause of disgrace **4 :** the nonpayment or nonacceptance of commercial paper by the party on whom it is drawn ***syn*** see DISGRACE — **dis·hon·or·er** \-ˈän-ər-ər\ *n*

dis·hon·or·able \(ˈ)dis-ˈän-(ə-)rə-bəl, -ˈän-ər-bəl\ *adj* (1533) **1 :** lacking honor : SHAMEFUL ⟨~ conduct⟩ **2** *archaic* : not honored — **dis·hon·or·able·ness** *n* — **dis·hon·or·ably** \-blē\ *adv*

dish out *vt* (1641) : to give freely ⟨the blatant picturing of crime and disorder *dished out* by the cinema —R. T. Flewelling⟩

dish·pan \ˈdish-ˌpan\ *n* (1872) : a large flat-bottomed pan used for washing dishes

dishpan hands *n pl but sing or pl in constr* (1944) : a condition of dryness, redness, and scaling of the hands that results typically from repeated exposure to, sensitivity to, or overuse of cleaning materials (as detergents) used in housework

dish·rag \ˈdish-ˌrag\ *n* (1839) : DISHCLOTH

dish·ware \ˈdish-ˌwa(ə)r, -ˌwe(ə)r\ *n* (1946) : tableware (as of china) used in serving food

dish·wash·er \-ˌwȯsh-ər, -ˌwäsh-\ *n* (15c) **1 :** a worker employed to wash dishes **2 :** a machine for washing dishes

dish·wa·ter \-ˌwȯt-ər, -ˌwät-\ *n* (15c) : water in which dishes have been or are to be washed

dishy \ˈdish-ē\ *adj* **dish·i·er; -est** (1961) : ATTRACTIVE

1dis·il·lu·sion \ˌdis-ə-ˈlü-zhən\ *n* (1851) : the condition of being disenchanted

2disillusion *vt* **dis·il·lu·sioned; dis·il·lu·sion·ing** \-ˈlüzh-(ə-)niŋ\ (1855) : to leave without illusion — **dis·il·lu·sion·ment** \-ˈlü-zhən-mənt\ *n*

dis·in·cen·tive \ˌdis-ᵊn-ˈsent-iv\ *n* (1946) : DETERRENT

dis·in·cli·na·tion \(ˌ)dis-ˌin-klə-ˈnā-shən, -ˌiŋ-\ *n* (1647) : a preference for avoiding something : slight aversion

dis·in·cline \ˌdis-ᵊn-ˈklīn\ *vt* (1647) : to make unwilling

dis·in·clined *adj* (1647) : unwilling because of mild dislike or disapproval

syn DISINCLINED, HESITANT, RELUCTANT, LOATH, AVERSE mean lacking the will or desire to do something indicated. DISINCLINED implies lack of taste for or inclination toward and often active disapproval of the thing suggested; HESITANT implies a holding back through fear, uncertainty, or disinclination; RELUCTANT implies a holding back through unwillingness; LOATH implies hesitancy because of conflict with one's opinions, predilections, or liking; AVERSE implies a holding back from or avoiding because of distaste or repugnance.

dis·in·fect \ˌdis-ᵊn-ˈfekt\ *vt* [MF *desinfecter,* fr. *des-* + *infecter* to infect] (1598) : to free from infection esp. by destroying harmful microorganisms; *broadly* : CLEANSE — **dis·in·fec·tion** \-ˈfek-shən\ *n*

dis·in·fec·tant \-ˈfek-tənt\ *n* (1837) : an agent that frees from infection; *esp* : a chemical that destroys vegetative forms of harmful microorganisms esp. on inanimate objects but that may be less effective in destroying bacterial spores

dis·in·fest \ˌdis-ᵊn-ˈfest\ *vt* (ca. 1920) : to rid of small animal pests (as insects or rodents) — **dis·in·fes·ta·tion** \(ˌ)dis-ˌin-ˌfes-ˈtā-shən\ *n*

dis·in·fes·tant \ˌdis-ᵊn-ˈfes-tənt\ *n* (ca. 1943) : a disinfesting agent

dis·in·fla·tion \ˌdis-ᵊn-ˈflā-shən\ *n* (1880) : a reversal of inflationary pressures — **dis·in·fla·tion·ary** \-shə-ˌner-ē\ *adj*

dis·in·for·ma·tion \(ˈ)dis-ˌin-fər-ˈmā-shən\ *n* (1939) : false information deliberately and often covertly spread (as by the planting of rumors) in order to influence public opinion or obscure the truth

dis·in·gen·u·ous \ˌdis-ᵊn-ˈjen-yə-wəs\ *adj* (1655) : lacking in candor; *also* : giving a false appearance of simple frankness : CALCULATING — **dis·in·gen·u·ous·ly** *adv* — **dis·in·gen·u·ous·ness** *n*

dis·in·her·it \ˌdis-ᵊn-ˈher-ət\ *vt* [ME *disinheriten*] (15c) **1 :** to prevent deliberately from inheriting something (as by making a will) **2 :** to deprive of natural or human rights or of previously held special privileges — **dis·in·her·i·tance** \-ˈher-ət-ən(t)s\ *n*

dis·in·hi·bi·tion \(ˌ)dis-ˌin-(h)ə-ˈbish-ən\ *n* (ca. 1927) : loss of a conditioned reflex (as by the action of interfering stimuli)

dis·in·sec·tion \ˌdis-ᵊn-ˈsek-shən\ *n* (ca. 1927) : DISINSECTIZATION

dis·in·sect·iza·tion \-ˌsek-tə-ˈzā-shən\ *n* (1944) : removal of insects (as from an aircraft)

dis·in·te·grate \(ˈ)dis-ˈint-ə-ˌgrāt\ *vt* (1796) **1 :** to break or decompose into constituent elements, parts, or small particles **2 :** to destroy the unity or integrity of ~ *vi* **1 :** to break or separate into constituent elements or parts **2 :** to lose unity or integrity by or as if by breaking into parts **3 :** to undergo a change in composition ⟨an atomic nucleus that ~*s* because of radioactivity⟩ — **dis·in·te·gra·tion** \(ˌ)dis-ˌint-ə-ˈgrā-shən\ *n* — **dis·in·te·gra·tive** \(ˈ)dis-ˈint-ə-ˌgrāt-iv\ *adj* — **dis·in·te·gra·tor** \-ˌgrāt-ər\ *n*

dis·in·ter \ˌdis-ᵊn-ˈtər\ *vt* (1611) **1 :** to take out of the grave or tomb **2** : DISCLOSE, UNEARTH — **dis·in·ter·ment** \-mənt\ *n*

1dis·in·ter·est \(ˈ)dis-ˈin-trəst; -ˈint-ə-ˌrest, -ə-rəst, -ərst; -ˈin-ˌtrest\ *vt* (1612) : to divest of interest

2disinterest *n* (1658) **1 :** lack of self-interest : DISINTERESTEDNESS **2** : DISADVANTAGE **3 :** lack of interest : APATHY

dis·in·ter·est·ed *adj* (1612) **1 a :** not having the mind or feelings engaged : not interested ⟨telling them in a ~ voice —Tom Wicker⟩ ⟨Introverted. Unsocial ... *Disinterested* in women —J. A. Brussel⟩ **b** : no longer interested ⟨husband and wife become ~ in each other —T. I. Rubin⟩ **2 :** free from selfish motive or interest : UNBIASED ⟨a ~ decision⟩ ⟨~ intellectual curiosity is the lifeblood of real civilization —G. M. Trevelyan⟩ ***syn*** see INDIFFERENT — **dis·in·ter·est·ed·ly** *adv* — **dis·in·ter·est·ed·ness** *n*

usage *Disinterested* and *uninterested* have a tangled history. *Uninterested* orig. meant impartial, but this sense fell into disuse during the 18th century. About the same time the original sense of *disinterested* also disappeared, with *uninterested* developing a new sense — the present meaning — to take its place. The original sense of *uninterested* is still out of use, but the original sense of *disinterested* revived in the early 20th century. The revival has since been under frequent attack as an illiteracy and a blurring or loss of a useful distinction. Actual usage shows otherwise. Sense 2 of *disinterested* is still its most frequent sense, esp. in edited prose; it shows no sign of vanishing. A careful writer may choose sense 1a of *disinterested* in preference to *uninterested* for emphasis ⟨teaching the letters of the alphabet to her wiggling and supremely *disinterested* little daughter —C. L. Sulzberger⟩ Further, *disinterested* has developed a sense (1b), perhaps influenced by sense 1 of the prefix *dis-*, that contrasts with *uninterested* ⟨when I grow tired or *disinterested* in anything, I experience a disgust —Jack London, letter, 1914⟩ Still, use of senses 1a and 1b will incur the disapproval of some who may not fully appreciate the history of this word or the subtleties of its present use.

dis·in·ter·me·di·a·tion \ˌdis-ˌint-ər-ˌmēd-ē-ˈā-shən\ *n* (1967) **:** the diversion of savings from accounts with low fixed interest rates to direct investment in high-yielding instruments

dis·in·tox·i·cate \ˌdis-ᵊn-ˈtäk-sə-ˌkāt\ *vt* (1685) **:** DETOXIFY 2 — **dis·in·tox·i·ca·tion** \-ˌtäk-sə-ˈkā-shən\ *n*

dis·in·vest·ment \ˌdis-ᵊn-ˈves(t)-mənt\ *n* (1936) **:** consumption of capital

dis·join \(ˈ)dis-ˈjȯin\ *vb* [ME *disjoynen*, fr. MF *desjoindre*, fr. L *disjungere*, fr. *dis-* + *jungere* to join — more at YOKE] *vt* (15c) **:** to end the joining of ~ *vi* **:** to become detached

1dis·joint \-ˈjȯint\ *adj* [ME *disjoynt*, fr. MF *desjoint*, pp. of *desjoindre*] (15c) **1** *obs* **:** DISJOINTED 1a **2 :** having no elements in common ⟨~ mathematical sets⟩

2disjoint *vt* (15c) **1 :** to disturb the orderly structure or arrangement of **2 :** to take apart at the joints ~ *vi* **:** to come apart at the joints

dis·joint·ed *adj* (1586) **1 a :** being thrown out of orderly function ⟨a ~ society⟩ **b :** lacking coherence or orderly sequence ⟨an incomplete and ~ history⟩ **2 :** separated at or as if at the joint — **dis·joint·ed·ly** *adv* — **dis·joint·ed·ness** *n*

1dis·junct \dis-ˈjəŋ(k)t\ *adj* [ME, fr. L *disjunctus*, pp. of *disjungere* to disjoin] (15c) **:** marked by separation of or from usu. contiguous parts or individuals: as **a :** DISCONTINUOUS **b :** relating to melodic progression by intervals larger than a major second — compare CONJUNCT

2dis·junct \ˈdis-ˌjəŋ(k)t, dis-ˈ\ *n* (1921) **:** any of the alternatives that make up a logical disjunction

dis·junc·tion \dis-ˈjəŋ(k)-shən\ *n* (15c) **1 :** a sharp cleavage **:** DISUNION, SEPARATION ⟨the ~ between theory and practice⟩ **2 :** a compound sentence in logic formed by joining two simple statements by *or:* **a :** INCLUSIVE DISJUNCTION **b :** EXCLUSIVE DISJUNCTION

1disjunctive \-ˈjeŋ(k)-tiv\ *adj* (15c) **1 a :** relating to, being, or forming a logical disjunction **b :** expressing an alternative or opposition between the meanings of the words connected ⟨the ~ conjunction *or*⟩ **c :** expressed by mutually exclusive alternatives joined by *or* ⟨~ pleading⟩ **2 :** marked by breaks or disunity ⟨a ~ narrative sequence⟩ **3** *of a pronoun form* **:** stressed and not attached to the verb as an enclitic or proclitic — **dis·junc·tive·ly** *adv*

2disjunctive *n* (1530) **:** a disjunctive conjunction

dis·junc·ture \-ˈjəŋ(k)-chər\ *n* [ME, modif. (influenced by L *disjunctus*) of MF *desjointure*, fr. *desjoint* disjoint] (15c) **:** DISJUNCTION 1

1disk *or* **disc** \ˈdisk\ *n, often attrib* [L *discus* — more at DISH] (1664) **1 a** *archaic* **:** DISCUS 1 **b :** the seemingly flat figure of a celestial body ⟨the solar ~⟩ **2 :** any of various rounded and flattened animal anatomical structures (as an intervertebral disk) — compare SLIPPED DISK **3 :** the central part of the flower head of a typical composite made up of closely packed tubular flowers **4 a :** a thin circular object **b** *usu disc* **:** a phonograph record **c :** a round flat plate coated with a magnetic substance on which data for a computer is stored **d** *usu disc* **:** VIDEODISC **5** *usu disc* **:** one of the concave circular steel tools with sharpened edge making up the working part of a disc harrow or plow; *also* **:** an implement employing such tools — **disk·like** \-ˌlīk\ *adj*

2disk *or* **disc** *vt* (1884) **1 :** to cultivate with an implement (as a harrow or plow) that turns and loosens the soil with a series of disks **2** *usu disc* **:** to record on a phonograph disc

dis·kette \ˈdis-ˌket, ˌdis-ˈ\ *n* (1973) **:** FLOPPY DISK

disk flower *n* (1870) **:** one of the tubular flowers in the disk of a composite plant — called also *disk floret*

disk wheel *n* (ca. 1909) **:** a wheel presenting a solid surface from hub to rim

dis·lik·able *also* **dis·like·able** \(ˈ)dis-ˈlī-kə-bəl\ *adj* (1843) **:** easy to dislike

1dis·like \(ˈ)dis-ˈlīk\ *n* (1577) **1 :** a feeling of aversion or disapproval **2** *obs* **:** DISCORD

2dislike *vt* (1579) **1** *archaic* **:** DISPLEASE **2 :** to regard with dislike **:** DISAPPROVE **3** *obs* **:** to show aversion to — **dis·lik·er** *n*

dis·limn \(ˈ)dis-ˈlim\ *vb* (1606) **:** DIM

dis·lo·cate \ˈdis-lō-ˌkāt, -lə-; (ˈ)dis-ˈlō-\ *vt* [ML *dislocatus*, pp. of *dislocare*, fr. L *dis-* + *locare* to locate] (1605) **1 :** to put out of place; *specif* **:** to displace (a bone) from normal connections with another bone **2 :** DISRUPT

dis·lo·ca·tion \ˌdis-(ˌ)lō-ˈkā-shən, -lə-\ *n* [ME *dislocacioun*, fr. MF *dislocation*, fr. ML *dislocatus*, pp.] (15c) **:** the act of dislocating **:** the state of being dislocated: as **a :** displacement of one or more bones at a joint **:** LUXATION **b :** a discontinuity in the otherwise normal lattice structure of a crystal **c :** disruption of an established order

dis·lodge \(ˈ)dis-ˈläj\ *vb* [ME *disloggen*, fr. MF *desloger*, fr. *des-* + *loger* to lodge, fr. OF *loge* lodge] *vt* (15c) **1 :** to drive from a position of hiding, defense, or advantage **2 :** to force out of a secure or settled position ⟨*dislodged* the rock with a shovel⟩ ~ *vi* **:** to leave a lodging place — **dis·lodg·ment** *or* **dis·lodge·ment** *n*

dis·loy·al \(ˈ)dis-ˈlȯi(-ə)l\ *adj* [ME, fr. MF *desloial*, fr. OF, fr. *des-* + *loial* loyal] (15c) **:** lacking in loyalty **:** manifesting an absence of allegiance, devotion, obligation, faith, or support ⟨his ~ refusal to help his friend⟩ ***syn*** see FAITHLESS — **dis·loy·al·ly** \-ˈlȯi-ə-lē\ *adv*

dis·loy·al·ty \-ˈlȯi(-ə)l-tē\ *n* (15c) **:** lack of loyalty

dis·mal \ˈdiz-məl\ *adj* [ME, fr. *dismal*, n., days marked as unlucky in medieval calendars, fr. AF, fr. ML *dies mali*, lit., evil days] (15c) **1** *obs* **:** DISASTROUS, DREADFUL **2 :** showing or causing gloom or depression **3 :** lacking interest or merit — **dis·mal·ly** \-mə-lē\ *adv* — **dis·mal·ness** *n*

dis·man·tle \(ˈ)dis-ˈmant-ᵊl\ *vt* **dis·man·tled; dis·man·tling** \-ˈmant-liŋ, -ᵊl-iŋ\ [MF *desmanteler*, fr. *des-* + *mantel* mantle] (1602) **1 :** to take to pieces **2 :** to strip of dress or covering **:** DIVEST **3 :** to strip of furniture and equipment — **dis·man·tle·ment** \-ˈmant-ᵊl-mənt\ *n*

dis·mast \(ˈ)dis-ˈmast\ *vt* (1747) **:** to remove or break off the mast of

1dis·may \dis-ˈmā, diz-\ *vt* **dis·mayed; dis·may·ing** [ME *dismayen*, fr. (assumed) OF *desmaiier*, fr. OF *des-* + *-maiier* (as in *esmaiier* to dismay), fr. (assumed) VL *-magare*, of Gmc origin; akin to OHG *magan* to be able — more at MAY] (13c) **:** to deprive of courage, resolution, and initiative through the pressure of sudden fear or anxiety or great perplexity ⟨~*ed* at the size of his adversary⟩ — **dis·may·ing·ly** \-iŋ-lē\ *adv*

syn DISMAY, APPALL, HORRIFY, DAUNT mean to unnerve or deter by arousing fear, apprehension, or aversion. DISMAY implies that one is balked and perplexed or at a loss as to how to deal with something; APPALL implies that one is faced with that which perturbs, confounds, or shocks; HORRIFY stresses a reaction of horror or revulsion; DAUNT suggests a cowing, subduing, disheartening, or frightening in a venture requiring courage.

2dismay *n* (14c) **1 :** sudden loss of courage or resolution from alarm or fear **2 a :** sudden disappointment **b :** PERTURBATION

disme \ˈdīm\ *n* [obs. E, tenth, fr. obs. F, fr. MF *disme, dime* — more at DIME] (1792) **:** a U.S. 10-cent coin struck in 1792

dis·mem·ber \(ˈ)dis-ˈmem-bər\ *vt* **dis·mem·bered; dis·mem·ber·ing** \-b(ə-)riŋ\ [ME *dismembren*, fr. OF *desmembrer*, fr. *des-* + *membre* member] (13c) **1 :** to cut off or disjoin the limbs, members, or parts of **2 :** to break up or tear into pieces — **dis·mem·ber·ment** \-bər-mənt\ *n*

dis·miss \dis-ˈmis\ *vt* [modif. of L *dimissus*, pp. of *dimittere*, fr. *dis-* apart + *mittere* to send — more at DIS-, SMITE] (15c) **1 :** to permit or cause to leave ⟨~*ed* his visitor⟩ **2 :** to remove from position or service **:** DISCHARGE **3 a :** to bar from attention or serious consideration ⟨~*ed* the thought⟩ **b :** to put out of judicial consideration ⟨~*ed* all charges⟩ ***syn*** see EJECT — **dis·mis·sion** \-ˈmish-ən\ *n* — **dis·mis·sive** \-ˈmis-iv\ *adj*

dis·miss·al \-ˈmis-əl\ *n* (1818) **:** the act of dismissing **:** the fact or state of being dismissed

1dis·mount \(ˈ)dis-ˈmau̇nt\ *vb* [prob. modif. of MF *desmonter*, fr. *des-* + *monter* to mount] *vi* (1579) **1** *obs* **:** DESCEND **2 :** to alight from an elevated position (as on a horse) ~ *vt* **1 :** to throw down or remove from a mount or an elevated position; *esp* **:** UNHORSE **2 :** DISASSEMBLE

2dismount *n* (1654) **:** the act of dismounting

dis·obe·di·ence \ˌdis-ə-ˈbēd-ē-ən(t)s\ *n* (15c) **:** refusal or neglect to obey

dis·obe·di·ent \-ənt\ *adj* [ME, fr. MF *desobedient*, fr. OF, fr. *des-* + *obedient* obedient] (15c) **:** refusing or neglecting to obey — **dis·obe·di·ent·ly** *adv*

dis·obey \ˌdis-ə-ˈbā\ *vb* [ME *disobeyen*, fr. MF *desobeir*, fr. OF, fr. *des-* + *obeir* to obey] *vi* (14c) **:** to be disobedient ~ *vt* **:** to fail to obey — **dis·obey·er** *n*

dis·oblige \ˌdis-ə-ˈblīj\ *vt* [F *désobliger*, fr. MF, fr. *des-* + *obliger* to oblige] (1632) **1 :** to go counter to the wishes of **2 :** INCONVENIENCE

di·so·di·um phosphate \(ˌ)dī-ˌsōd-ē-əm-\ *n* (ca. 1928) **:** a sodium phosphate Na_2HPO_4

di·so·mic \(ˈ)dī-ˈsō-mik\ *adj* [*di-* + *-somic*] (1924) **:** having one or more chromosomes present in twice the normal number but not having the entire genome doubled

1dis·or·der \(ˈ)dis-ˈȯrd-ər, diz-\ *vt* (15c) **1 :** to disturb the order of **2 :** to disturb the regular or normal functions of

2disorder *n* (1530) **1 :** lack of order ⟨clothes in ~⟩ **2 :** breach of the peace or public order ⟨troubled times marked by social ~*s*⟩ **3 :** an abnormal physical or mental condition **:** AILMENT

dis·or·dered *adj* (1548) **1** *obs* **a :** morally reprehensible **b :** UNRULY **2 a :** marked by disorder **b :** not functioning in a normal orderly healthy way — **dis·or·dered·ly** *adv* — **dis·or·dered·ness** *n*

1dis·or·der·ly \-ˈȯrd-ər-lē\ *adv, archaic* (1564) **:** in a disorderly manner

2disorderly *adj* (1585) **1 :** engaged in conduct offensive to public order ⟨charged with being drunk and ~⟩ **2 :** characterized by disorder ⟨a ~ pile of clothes⟩ — **dis·or·der·li·ness** *n*

disorderly conduct *n* (1887) **:** a petty offense chiefly against public order and decency that falls short of an indictable misdemeanor

disorderly house *n* [euphemism] (ca. 1877) **:** BROTHEL

dis·or·ga·nize \(ˈ)dis-ˈȯr-gə-ˌnīz\ *vt* [F *désorganiser*, fr. *dés-* dis- + *organiser* to organize] (1793) **:** to destroy or interrupt the orderly structure or function of — **dis·or·ga·ni·za·tion** \(ˌ)dis-ˌȯrg-(ə-)nə-ˈzā-shən\ *n*

dis·or·ga·nized *adj* (1812) **:** lacking coherence, system, or central guiding agency ⟨~ work habits⟩

dis·ori·ent \(ˈ)dis-ˈȯr-ē-ˌent, -ˈȯr-\ *vt* [F *désorienter*, fr. *dés-* dis- + *orienter* to orient] (1655) **1 a :** to cause to lose bearings **:** displace from normal position or relationship **b :** to cause to lose the sense of time, place, or identity **2 :** CONFUSE

dis·ori·en·tate \-ē-ən-ˌtāt, -ē-ˌen-\ *vt* (ca. 1727) **:** DISORIENT — **dis·ori·en·ta·tion** \(ˌ)dis-ˌȯr-ē-ən-ˈtā-shən, -ˌȯr-, -ē-ˌen-\ *n*

dis·own \(ˈ)dis-ˈōn\ *vt* (1649) **1 :** to refuse to acknowledge as one's own **2 a :** to repudiate any connection or identification with **b :** to deny the validity or authority of — **dis·own·ment** \-mənt\ *n*

dis·par·age \dis-ˈpar-ij\ *vt* **-aged; -ag·ing** [ME *disparagen* to degrade by marriage below one's class, disparage, fr. MF *desparagier* to marry below one's class, fr. OF, fr. *des-* dis- + *parage* extraction, lineage, fr. *per* peer] (14c) **1 :** to lower in rank or reputation **:** DEGRADE **2 :** to depreciate by indirect means (as invidious comparison) **:** speak slightingly about ***syn*** see DECRY — **dis·par·age·ment** \-ij-mənt\ *n* — **dis·par·ag·er** *n* — **dis·par·ag·ing** *adj* — **dis·par·ag·ing·ly** \-ij-iŋ-lē\ *adv*

dis·pa·rate \dis-ˈpar-ət, ˈdis-p(ə-)rət\ *adj* [L *disparatus*, pp. of *disparare* to separate, fr. *dis-* + *parare* to prepare — more at PARE] (15c) **1 :** containing or made up of fundamentally different and often incongruous elements **2 :** markedly distinct in quality or character ***syn*** see DIFFERENT — **dis·pa·rate·ly** *adv* — **dis·pa·rate·ness** *n* — **dis·par·i·ty** \dis-ˈpar-ət-ē\ *n*

dis·part \(ˈ)dis-ˈpärt\ *vb* [It & L; It *dispartire*, fr. L, fr. *dis-* + *partire* to divide — more at PART] *archaic* (1590) **:** SEPARATE, DIVIDE

dis·pas·sion \(ˈ)dis-ˈpash-ən\ *n* (1692) **:** absence of passion **:** COOLNESS

dis·pas·sion·ate \-(ə-)nət\ *adj* (1594) **:** not influenced by strong feeling; *esp* **:** not affected by personal or emotional involvement ⟨a ~ critic⟩ ⟨a ~ approach to an issue⟩ ***syn*** see FAIR — **dis·pas·sion·ate·ly** *adv* — **dis·pas·sion·ate·ness** *n*

1dis·patch \dis-ˈpach\ *vb* [Sp *despachar* or It *dispacciare*, fr. Prov *despachar* to get rid of, fr. MF *despeechier* to set free, fr. OF, fr. *des-* + *-peechier* (as in *empeechier* to hinder) — more at IMPEACH] *vt* (1517) **1 :** to send off or away with promptness or speed esp. on official business **2 a :** to kill with quick efficiency **b** *obs* **:** DEPRIVE **3 :** to dispose of (as a task) rapidly or efficiently ~ *vi, archaic* **:** to make haste **:** HURRY ***syn*** see KILL — **dis·patch·er** *n*

2dispatch *n* (1571) **1 :** the act of dispatching: as **a** *obs* **:** DISMISSAL **b :** the act of killing **c** (1) **:** prompt settlement (as of an item of business) (2) : quick riddance d : a sending off : SHIPMENT 2 a : a message sent with speed; *esp* : an important official message sent by a diplomatic, military, or naval officer ⟨sent a ~ to the war department⟩ b : a news item filed by a correspondent 3 : promptness and efficiency in performance or transmission *syn* see HASTE

dispatch case *n* (ca. 1918) : a case for carrying papers

dis·pel \dis-ˈpel\ *vt* **dis·pelled; dis·pel·ling** [L *dispellere*, fr. *dis-* + *pellere* to drive, beat — more at FELT] (15c) : to drive away by or as if by scattering : DISSIPATE ⟨~ a misconception⟩ *syn* see SCATTER

dis·pens·able \dis-ˈpen(t)-sə-bəl\ *adj* (1649) : capable of being dispensed with : UNESSENTIAL — **dis·pens·abil·i·ty** \-ˌpen(t)-sə-ˈbil-ət-ē\ *n*

dis·pen·sa·ry \dis-ˈpen(t)s-(ə-)rē\ *n, pl* **-ries** (1699) : a place where medical or dental aid is dispensed

dis·pen·sa·tion \ˌdis-pən-ˈsā-shən, -ˌpen-\ *n* (14c) 1 a : a general state or ordering of things; *specif* : a system of revealed commands and promises regulating human affairs b : a particular arrangement or provision esp. of providence or nature 2 a : an exemption from a law or from an impediment, vow, or oath b : a formal authorization 3 a : the act of dispensing b : something dispensed or distributed — **dis·pen·sa·tion·al** \-shnəl, -shən-ᵊl\ *adj*

dis·pen·sa·to·ry \dis-ˈpen(t)-sə-ˌtōr-ē, -ˌtȯr-\ *n, pl* **-ries** (1566) : a medicinal formulary

dis·pense \dis-ˈpen(t)s\ *vb* **dis·pensed; dis·pens·ing** [ME *dispensen*, fr. ML & L; ML *dispensare* to grant dispensation, fr. L, to distribute, fr. *dispensus*, pp. of *dispendere* to weigh out, fr. *dis-* + *pendere* to weigh — more at SPIN] *vt* (14c) 1 a : to deal out in portions b : ADMINISTER ⟨~ justice⟩ 2 : to give dispensation to : EXEMPT 3 : to prepare and distribute (medication) ~ *vi, archaic* : to grant dispensation *syn* see DISTRIBUTE — **dispense with** 1 : to suspend the operation of ⟨a people that has *dispensed with* its monarchy⟩ 2 : to do without ⟨could *dispense with* his assistants⟩

dis·pens·er \-ˈpen(t)-sər\ *n* (14c) : one that dispenses: as a : a container that extrudes, sprays, or feeds out in convenient units b : a usu. mechanical device for vending merchandise

dis·peo·ple \(ˈ)dis-ˈpē-pəl\ *vt* (15c) : DEPOPULATE

dis·pers·al \dis-ˈpər-səl\ *n* (1821) : the act or result of dispersing; *esp* : the process or result of the spreading of organisms from one place to another

dis·per·sant \dis-ˈpər-sənt\ *n* (1941) : a dispersing agent; *esp* : a substance for promoting the formation and stabilization of a dispersion of one substance in another — **dispersant** *adj*

dis·perse \dis-ˈpərs\ *vb* **dis·persed; dis·pers·ing** [ME *dysparsen*, fr. MF *disperser*, fr. L *dispersus*, pp. of *dispergere* to scatter, fr. *dis-* + *spargere* to scatter — more at SPARK] *vt* (14c) 1 a : to cause to break up ⟨the meeting was *dispersed*⟩ b : to cause to become spread widely c : to cause to evaporate or vanish ⟨sunlight *dispersing* the vapor⟩ 2 : to spread or distribute from a fixed or constant source: as a *archaic* : DISSEMINATE b : to subject (as light) to dispersion c : to distribute (as fine particles) more or less evenly throughout a medium ~ *vi* 1 : to break up in random fashion ⟨the crowd *dispersed* at the police officer's request⟩ 2 a : to become dispersed b : DISSIPATE, VANISH ⟨the fog *dispersed* toward morning⟩ *syn* see SCATTER — **dis·persed·ly** \-ˈpər-səd-lē, -ˈpərst-lē\ *adv* — **dis·pers·er** *n* — **dis·pers·ible** \-ˈpər-sə-bəl\ *adj*

disperse system *n* (ca. 1915) : DISPERSION 5b

dis·per·sion \dis-ˈpər-zhən, -shən\ *n* (14c) 1 *cap* : DIASPORA 1a 2 : the act or process of dispersing : the state of being dispersed 3 : the scattering of the values of a frequency distribution from an average 4 : the separation of light into colors by refraction or diffraction with formation of a spectrum; *also* : the separation of nonhomogeneous radiation into components in accordance with some characteristic (as energy) 5 a : a dispersed substance b : a system consisting of a dispersed substance and the medium in which it is dispersed : COLLOID 2b

dis·per·sive \-ˈpər-siv, -ziv\ *adj* (1627) 1 : of or relating to dispersion ⟨a ~ medium⟩ ⟨the ~ power of a lens⟩ 2 : tending to disperse — **dis·per·sive·ly** *adv* — **dis·per·sive·ness** *n*

dis·per·soid \-ˈpər-ˌsȯid\ *n* (1911) : finely divided particles of one substance dispersed in another

dispir·it \(ˈ)dis-ˈpir-ət\ *vt* [*dis-* + *spirit*] (1647) : to deprive of morale or enthusiasm — **dispir·it·ed** *adj* — **dispir·it·ed·ly** *adv* — **dispir·it·ed·ness** *n*

dis·pit·eous \dis-ˈpit-ē-əs\ *adj* [alter. of *despiteous*] *archaic* (1803) : CRUEL

dis·place \(ˈ)dis-ˈplās\ *vt* [prob. fr. MF *desplacer*, fr. *des-* dis- + *place* place] (1553) 1 a : to remove from the usual or proper place; *specif* : to expel or force to flee from home or homeland b : to remove from an office, status, or job c *obs* : to drive out : BANISH 2 a : to remove physically out of position ⟨water *displaced* by a floating object⟩ b : to take the place of (as in a chemical reaction) : SUPPLANT *syn* see REPLACE — **dis·place·able** \-ˈplā-sə-bəl\ *adj*

dis·place·ment \dis-ˈplā-smənt\ *n* (1611) 1 : the act or process of displacing : the state of being displaced 2 a : the volume or weight of a fluid (as water) displaced by a floating body (as a ship) of equal weight b : the difference between the initial position of something (as a body or geometric figure) and any later position c : the volume displaced by a piston (as in a pump or an engine) in a single stroke; *also* : the total volume so displaced by all the pistons in an internal-combustion engine (as in an automobile) 3 a : the redirection of an emotion or impulse from its original object (as an idea or person) to something that is more acceptable b : the substitution of another form of behavior for what is usual or expected esp. when the usual response is nonadaptive

dis·plant \dis-ˈplant\ *vt* [MF *desplanter*, fr. *des-* + *planter* to plant, fr. LL *plantare*] (15c) 1 : DISPLACE, REMOVE 2 : SUPPLANT

1dis·play \dis-ˈplā\ *vb* [ME *displayen*, fr. AF *despleier*, fr. L *displicare* to scatter, fr. *dis-* + *plicare* to fold — more at PLY] *vt* (14c) 1 a : to put or spread before the view ⟨~ the flag⟩ b : to make evident ⟨~*ed* great skill⟩ c : to exhibit ostentatiously ⟨liked to ~ his erudition⟩ 2 *obs* : DESCRY ~ *vi* 1 *obs* : SHOW OFF 2 : to make a breeding display ⟨penguins ~*ed* and copulated⟩ *syn* see SHOW — **dis·play·able** \-ˈplā-ə-bəl\ *adj*

2display *n, often attrib* (1665) 1 a (1) : a setting or presentation of something in open view ⟨a fireworks ~⟩ (2) : a clear sign or evidence : EXHIBITION ⟨a ~ of courage⟩ b : ostentatious show c : type, composition, or printing designed to catch the eye d : an eye-catching arrangement by which something is exhibited e : an electronic device (as a cathode-ray tube in a computer or in a radar receiver or a liquid-crystal watch) that presents information in visual form; *also* : the visual information 2 : a pattern of behavior exhibited esp. by male birds in the breeding season

dis·please \(ˈ)dis-ˈplēz\ *vb* [ME *displesen*, fr. MF *desplaisir*, fr. (assumed) VL *displacēre*, fr. L *dis-* + *placēre* to please — more at PLEASE] *vt* (14c) 1 : to incur the disapproval or dislike of esp. by annoying ⟨could fire any employee who had ever *displeased* him⟩ 2 : to be offensive to ⟨abstract art ~*s* him⟩ ~ *vi* : to give displeasure ⟨signs of inattention calculated to ~⟩

dis·plea·sure \(ˈ)dis-ˈplezh-ər, -ˈplāzh-\ *n* (15c) 1 : the feeling of one that is displeased : DISFAVOR 2 : DISCOMFORT, UNHAPPINESS 3 *archaic* : OFFENSE, INJURY

dis·plode \dis-ˈplōd\ *vb* **dis·plod·ed; dis·plod·ing** [L *displodere*, fr. *dis-* + *plaudere* to clap, applaud] *archaic* (1667) : EXPLODE — **dis·plo·sion** \-ˈplō-zhən\ *n*

1dis·port \dis-ˈpō(ə)rt, -ˈpȯ(ə)rt\ *n, archaic* (14c) : SPORT, PASTIME

2disport *vb* [ME *disporten*, fr. MF *desporter*, fr. *des-* + *porter* to carry, fr. L *portare* — more at FARE] *vt* (14c) 1 : DIVERT, AMUSE 2 : DISPLAY ~ *vi* : to amuse oneself in light or lively fashion : FROLIC — **dis·port·ment** \-mənt\ *n*

1dis·pos·able \dis-ˈpō-zə-bəl\ *adj* (1643) 1 : subject to or available for disposal; *specif* : remaining to an individual after deduction of taxes ⟨~ income⟩ 2 : designed to be used once and then thrown away ⟨~ towels⟩ — **dis·pos·abil·i·ty** \-ˌpō-zə-ˈbil-ət-ē\ *n*

2disposable *n* (1963) : something (as a paper blanket) that is disposable

dis·pos·al \dis-ˈpō-zəl\ *n* (1630) 1 : the power or authority to dispose of ⟨the car was at my ~⟩ 2 : the act or process of disposing: as a : orderly placement or distribution b : REGULATION, ADMINISTRATION c : the act or action of presenting or bestowing something ⟨~ of favors⟩ d : systematic destruction; *esp* : destruction or transformation of garbage 3 [*garbage disposal unit*] : a device used to reduce waste matter (as by grinding)

1dis·pose \dis-ˈpōz\ *vb* **dis·posed; dis·pos·ing** [ME *disposen*, fr. MF *disposer*, fr. L *disponere* to arrange (perf. indic. *disposui*), fr. *dis-* + *ponere* to put — more at POSITION] *vt* (14c) 1 : to give a tendency to : INCLINE ⟨faulty diet ~*s* one to sickness⟩ 2 a : to put in place : set in readiness : ARRANGE ⟨*disposing* troops for withdrawal⟩ b *obs* : REGULATE c : BESTOW ~ *vi* 1 : to settle a matter finally 2 *obs* : to come to terms *syn* see INCLINE — **dis·pos·er** *n* — **dispose of** 1 : to place, distribute, or arrange esp. in an orderly way 2 a : to transfer to the control of another ⟨*disposing of* personal property to a total stranger⟩ b (1) : to get rid of ⟨waste that is hard to *dispose of*⟩ (2) : to deal with conclusively ⟨*disposed of* the matter efficiently⟩

2dispose *n* (1590) 1 *obs* : DISPOSAL 2 *obs* a : DISPOSITION b : DEMEANOR

dis·po·si·tion \ˌdis-pə-ˈzish-ən\ *n* [ME, fr. MF, fr. L *disposition-, dispositio*, fr. *dispositus*, pp. of *disponere*] (14c) 1 : the act or the power of disposing or the state of being disposed: as a : ADMINISTRATION, CONTROL b : final arrangement : SETTLEMENT ⟨the ~ of the case⟩ c (1) : transfer to the care or possession of another (2) : the power of such transferal d : orderly arrangement 2 a : prevailing tendency, mood, or inclination b : temperamental makeup c : the tendency of something to act in a certain manner under given circumstances — **dis·po·si·tion·al** \-ˈzish-nəl, -ˈzish-ən-ᵊl\ *adj*

syn DISPOSITION, TEMPERAMENT, TEMPER, CHARACTER, PERSONALITY mean the dominant quality or qualities distinguishing a person or group. DISPOSITION implies customary moods and attitude toward the life around one; TEMPERAMENT implies a pattern of innate characteristics associated with one's specific physical and nervous organization; TEMPER implies the qualities acquired through experience that determine how a person or group meets difficulties or handles situations; CHARACTER applies to the aggregate of moral qualities by which a person is judged apart from his intelligence, competence, or special talents; PERSONALITY applies to an aggregate of qualities that distinguish one as a person.

dis·pos·i·tive \dis-ˈpäz-ət-iv\ *adj* (1613) : directed toward or effecting disposition (as of a case) ⟨~ evidence⟩

dis·pos·sess \ˌdis-pə-ˈzes *also* -ˈses\ *vt* [MF *despossesser*, fr. *des-* dis- + *possesser* to possess] (1555) : to put out of possession or occupancy ⟨~*ed* the nobles of their wealth⟩ — **dis·pos·ses·sion** \-ˈzesh-ən *also* -ˈsesh-\ *n* — **dis·pos·ses·sor** \-ˈzes-ər *also* -ˈses-\ *n*

dis·pos·sessed *adj* (15c) : deprived of homes, possessions, and security

dis·po·sure \dis-ˈpō-zhər\ *n, archaic* (1569) : DISPOSAL, DISPOSITION

1dis·praise \(ˈ)dis-ˈprāz\ *vt* [ME *dispraisen*, fr. MF *despreisier*, fr. OF, fr. *des-* dis- + *preisier* to praise] (14c) : to comment on with disapproval or censure — **dis·prais·er** *n* — **dis·prais·ing·ly** \-ˈprā-ziŋ-lē\ *adv*

2dispraise *n* (15c) : an expression of disapproval : DISPARAGEMENT

dispread \dis-ˈpred\ *vt* (1590) : to spread abroad or out

dis·prize \(ˈ)dis-ˈprīz\ *vt* [MF *despriser*, fr. OF *despreisier*] *archaic* (15c) : UNDERVALUE, SCORN

dis·proof \(ˈ)dis-ˈprüf\ *n* (15c) 1 : the action of disproving 2 : evidence that disproves

1dis·pro·por·tion \ˌdis-prə-ˈpōr-shən, -ˈpȯr-\ *n* (1555) : lack of proportion, symmetry, or proper relation : DISPARITY; *also* : an instance of such disparity — **dis·pro·por·tion·al** \-shnəl, -shən-ᵊl\ *adj*

2disproportion *vt* (1593) : to make out of proportion : MISMATCH

dis·pro·por·tion·ate \-sh(ə-)nət\ *adj* (1555) : being out of proportion ⟨a ~ share⟩ — **dis·pro·por·tion·ate·ly** *adv*

dis·pro·por·tion·ation \-ˌpōr-shə-ˈnā-shən, -ˌpȯr-\ *n* (ca. 1929) : the transformation of a substance into two or more dissimilar substances usu. by simultaneous oxidation and reduction — **dis·pro·por·tion·ate** \-ˈpōr-shə-ˌnāt, -ˈpȯr-\ *vi*

dis·prove \(ˈ)dis-ˈprüv\ *vt* [ME *disproven,* fr. MF *desprover,* fr. *des-* + *prover* to prove] (14c) : to prove to be false or wrong : REFUTE — **dis·prov·able** \-ˈprü-və-bəl\ *adj*

dis·pu·tant \dis-ˈpyüt-ᵊnt, ˈdis-pyət-ənt\ *n* (1612) : one that is engaged in a dispute

dis·pu·ta·tion \ˌdis-pyə-ˈtā-shən\ *n* (14c) **1** : the act of disputing : DEBATE **2** : an academic exercise in oral defense of a thesis by formal logic

dis·pu·ta·tious \-shəs\ *adj* (1660) **1** : inclined to dispute **2** : provoking debate : CONTROVERSIAL — **dis·pu·ta·tious·ly** *adv* — **dis·pu·ta·tious·ness** *n*

1**dis·pute** \dis-ˈpyüt\ *vb* **dis·put·ed; dis·put·ing** [ME *disputen,* fr. OF *desputer,* fr. L *disputare* to discuss, fr. *dis-* + *putare* to think] *vi* (13c) : to engage in argument : DEBATE; *esp* : to argue irritably or with irritating persistence ~ *vt* **1 a** : to make the subject of disputation **b** : to call into question ⟨the honesty of his intent was never *disputed*⟩ **2 a** : to struggle against ⟨*disputed* the advance of the invaders⟩ **b** : to struggle over : CONTEST ⟨the defending troops *disputed* every inch of ground⟩ ***syn*** see DISCUSS — **dis·put·able** \dis-ˈpyüt-ə-bəl, ˈdis-pyət-\ *adj* — **dis·put·ably** \-blē\ *adv* — **dis·put·er** *n*

2**dispute** \dis-ˈpyüt, ˈdis-ˌ\ *n* (1608) **1 a** : verbal controversy : DEBATE **b** : QUARREL **2** *obs* : physical combat

dis·qual·i·fi·ca·tion \(ˌ)dis-ˌkwäl-ə-fə-ˈkā-shən\ *n* (1711) **1** : something that disqualifies or incapacitates **2** : the act of disqualifying : the state of being disqualified ⟨~ from office⟩

dis·qual·i·fy \(ˈ)dis-ˈkwäl-ə-ˌfī\ *vt* (1723) **1** : to deprive of the required qualities, properties, or conditions : make unfit **2** : to deprive of a power, right, or privilege **3** : to make ineligible for a prize or for further competition because of violations of the rules

dis·quan·ti·ty \(ˈ)dis-ˈkwän(t)-ət-ē\ *vt, obs* (1605) : DIMINISH, LESSEN

1**dis·qui·et** \(ˈ)dis-ˈkwī-ət\ *vt* (ca. 1530) : to take away the peace or tranquillity of : DISTURB, ALARM ***syn*** see DISCOMPOSE — **dis·qui·et·ing** *adj* — **dis·qui·et·ing·ly** \-iŋ-lē\ *adv*

2**disquiet** *n* (1581) : lack of peace or tranquillity : ANXIETY

3**disquiet** *adj, archaic* (1587) : UNEASY, DISQUIETED — **dis·qui·et·ly** *adv*

dis·qui·etude \(ˈ)dis-ˈkwī-ə-ˌt(y)üd\ *n* (1709) : ANXIETY, AGITATION

dis·qui·si·tion \ˌdis-kwə-ˈzish-ən\ *n* [L *disquisition-, disquisitio,* fr. *disquisitus,* pp. of *disquirere* to inquire diligently, fr. *dis-* + *quaerere* to seek] (1647) : a formal inquiry into or discussion of a subject : DISCOURSE

dis·rate \(ˈ)dis-ˈrāt\ *vt* (1811) : to reduce in rank : DEMOTE

1**dis·re·gard** \ˌdis-ri-ˈgärd\ *vt* (1641) : to pay no attention to : treat as unworthy of regard or notice ***syn*** see NEGLECT

2**disregard** *n* (1665) : the act of disregarding : the state of being disregarded : NEGLECT — **dis·re·gard·ful** \-fəl\ *adj*

dis·re·lat·ed \ˌdis-ri-ˈlāt-əd\ *adj* (1893) : not related

dis·re·la·tion \-ˈlā-shən\ *n* (1893) : lack of a fitting or proportionate connection or relationship

1**dis·rel·ish** \(ˈ)dis-ˈrel-ish\ *vt* (1604) : to find unpalatable or distasteful

2**disrelish** *n* (1625) : lack of relish : DISTASTE, DISLIKE

dis·re·mem·ber \ˌdis-ri-ˈmem-bər\ *vt* (1815) : FORGET

dis·re·pair \ˌdis-ri-ˈpa(ə)r, -ˈpe(ə)r\ *n* (1798) : the state of being in need of repair ⟨a building fallen into ~⟩

dis·rep·u·ta·ble \(ˈ)dis-ˈrep-yət-ə-bəl\ *adj* (1772) : not reputable — **dis·rep·u·ta·bil·i·ty** \(ˌ)dis-ˌrep-yət-ə-ˈbil-ət-ē\ *n* — **dis·rep·u·ta·ble·ness** \(ˈ)dis-ˈrep-yət-ə-bəl-nəs\ *n* — **dis·rep·u·ta·bly** \-blē\ *adv*

dis·re·pute \ˌdis-ri-ˈpyüt\ *n* (1653) : lack or decline of good reputation : a state of being held in low esteem ***syn*** see DISGRACE

1**dis·re·spect** \ˌdis-ri-ˈspekt\ *vt* (1614) : to have disrespect for

2**disrespect** *n* (1631) : lack of respect or reverence — **dis·re·spect·ful** \-fəl\ *adj* — **dis·re·spect·ful·ly** \-fə-lē\ *adv* — **dis·re·spect·ful·ness** *n*

dis·re·spect·able \ˌdis-ri-ˈspek-tə-bəl\ *adj* (1813) : not respectable — **dis·re·spect·abil·i·ty** \-ˌspek-tə-ˈbil-ət-ē\ *n*

dis·robe \(ˈ)dis-ˈrōb\ *vb* [MF *desrober,* fr. *des-* dis- + *robe* garment, fr. OF] *vt* (1581) : to strip of clothing or covering ~ *vi* : to take off one's clothing

dis·rupt \dis-ˈrəpt\ *vt* [L *disruptus,* pp. of *disrumpere,* fr. *dis-* + *rumpere* to break — more at REAVE] (15c) **1 a** : to break apart : RUPTURE **b** : to throw into disorder ⟨agitators trying to ~ the meeting⟩ **2** : to interrupt the normal course or unity of — **dis·rupt·er** *n* — **dis·rup·tion** \-ˈrəp-shən\ *n* — **dis·rup·tive** \-ˈrəp-tiv\ *adj* — **dis·rup·tive·ly** *adv* — **dis·rup·tive·ness** *n*

dis·sat·is·fac·tion \(ˌ)dis-ˌ(s)at-əs-ˈfak-shən\ *n* (1640) : the quality or state of being dissatisfied : DISCONTENT

dis·sat·is·fac·to·ry \-ˈfak-t(ə-)rē\ *adj* (ca. 1610) : causing dissatisfaction

dis·sat·is·fied \(ˈ)dis-ˈ(s)at-əs-ˌfīd\ *adj* (1675) : expressing or showing lack of satisfaction : not pleased or satisfied

dis·sat·is·fy \-ˌfī\ *vt* (1666) : to fail to satisfy : DISPLEASE

dis·save \(ˈ)dis-ˈ(s)āv\ *vi* (1936) : to use savings for current expenses

dis·seat \(ˈ)dis-ˈ(s)ēt\ *vt, archaic* (1612) : UNSEAT

dis·sect \dis-ˈekt; dī-ˈsekt, ˈdī-ˌ\ *vb* [L *dissectus,* pp. of *dissecare* to cut apart, fr. *dis-* + *secare* to cut — more at SAW] *vt* (1607) **1** : to separate into pieces : expose the several parts of (as an animal) for scientific examination **2** : to analyze and interpret minutely ~ *vi* : to make a dissection ***syn*** see ANALYZE — **dis·sec·tor** \-ər\ *n*

dis·sect·ed *adj* (1652) **1** : cut deeply into fine lobes ⟨a ~ leaf⟩ **2** : divided into hills and ridges (as by gorges) ⟨a ~ plateau⟩

dis·sec·tion \dis-ˈek-shən; dī-ˈsek-, ˈdī-ˌ\ *n* (1605) **1** : the act or process of dissecting : the state of being dissected **2** : an anatomical specimen prepared by dissecting

dis·seise *or* **dis·seize** \(ˈ)dis-ˈ(s)ēz\ *vt* **dis·seised** *or* **dis·seized; dis·seis·ing** *or* **dis·seiz·ing** [ME *disseisen,* fr. ML *disseisiare* & AF *disseisir,* fr. OF *dessaisir,* fr. *des-* + *saisir* to put in possession of — more at SEIZE] (14c) : to deprive esp. wrongfully of seisin : DISPOSSESS

dis·sei·sin *or* **dis·sei·zin** \-ˈ(s)ēz-ᵊn\ *n* [ME *dysseysyne,* fr. AF *disseisine,* fr. OF *dessaisine,* fr. *des-* dis- + *saisine* seisin] (14c) : the act of disseising : the state of being disseised

dis·sem·ble \dis-ˈem-bəl\ *vb* **dis·sem·bled; dis·sem·bling** \-b(ə-)liŋ\ [alter. of obs. *dissimule,* fr. ME *dissimulen,* fr. MF *dissimuler,* fr. L *dissimulare* — more at DISSIMULATE] *vt* (15c) **1** : to hide under a false appearance **2** : to put on the appearance of : SIMULATE ~ *vi* : to put on a false appearance : conceal facts, intentions, or feelings under some pretense ***syn*** see DISGUISE — **dis·sem·bler** \-b(ə-)lər\ *n*

dis·sem·i·nate \dis-ˈem-ə-ˌnāt\ *vt* **-nat·ed; -nat·ing** [L *disseminatus,* pp. of *disseminare,* fr. *dis-* + *seminare* to sow, fr. *semin-, semen* seed — more at SEMEN] (1603) **1** : to spread abroad as though sowing seed ⟨~ ideas⟩ **2** : to disperse throughout — **dis·sem·i·na·tion** \-ˌem-ə-ˈnā-shən\ *n* — **dis·sem·i·na·tor** \-ˈem-ə-ˌnāt-ər\ *n*

dis·sem·i·nat·ed *adj* (1876) : widely dispersed in a tissue, organ, or the entire body ⟨~ gonococcal disease⟩

dis·sem·i·nule \dis-ˈem-ə-ˌn(y)ü(ə)l\ *n* (1904) : a part or organ (as a seed or spore) of a plant that ensures propagation

dis·sen·sion *also* **dis·sen·tion** \dis-ˈen-chən\ *n* [ME, fr. MF, fr. L *dissension-, dissensio,* fr. *dissensus,* pp. of *dissentire*] (14c) : DISAGREEMENT; *esp* : partisan and contentious quarreling ***syn*** see DISCORD

1**dis·sent** \dis-ˈent\ *vi* [ME *dissenten,* fr. L *dissentire,* fr. *dis-* + *sentire* to feel — more at SENSE] (15c) **1** : to withhold assent **2** : to differ in opinion

2**dissent** *n* (1585) : difference of opinion: as **a** : religious nonconformity **b** : a justice's nonconcurrence with a decision of the majority — called also *dissenting opinion*

dis·sent·er \dis-ˈent-ər\ *n* (1639) **1** : one that dissents **2** *cap* : an English Nonconformist

dis·sen·tient \dis-ˈen-ch(ē-)ənt\ *adj* [L *dissentient-, dissentiens,* prp. of *dissentire*] (1651) : expressing dissent — **dissentient** *n*

dis·sent·ing \dis-ˈent-iŋ\ *adj, often cap* (1644) : belonging to the party of English Nonconformists

dis·sep·i·ment \dis-ˈep-ə-mənt\ *n* [L *dissaepimentum* partition, fr. *dissaepire* to divide, fr. *dis-* + *saepire* to fence in — more at SEPTUM] (ca. 1727) : a dividing tissue : SEPTUM; *esp* : a partition between cells of a compound plant ovary

dis·sert \dis-ˈərt\ *vi* [L *dissertus,* pp. of *disserere,* fr. *dis-* + *serere* to join, arrange — more at SERIES] (1657) : DISCOURSE

dis·ser·tate \ˈdis-ər-ˌtāt\ *vi* **-tat·ed; -tat·ing** [L *dissertatus,* pp. of *dissertare,* fr. *dissertus*] (1766) : DISCOURSE — **dis·ser·ta·tor** \-ˌtāt-ər\ *n*

dis·ser·ta·tion \ˌdis-ər-ˈtā-shən\ *n* (1651) : an extended usu. written treatment of a subject; *specif* : one submitted for a doctorate — **dis·ser·ta·tion·al** \-ˈtāsh-nəl, -ˈtā-shən-ᵊl\ *adj*

dis·serve \(ˈ)dis-ˈ(s)ərv\ *vt* (1618) : to serve badly or falsely : HARM

dis·ser·vice \(ˈ)dis-ˈ(s)ər-vəs\ *n* (1599) : ill service : INJURY

dis·sev·er \dis-ˈev-ər\ *vb* [ME *disseveren,* fr. OF *dessevrer,* fr. LL *disseparare,* fr. L *dis-* + *separare* to separate] *vt* (13c) : SEVER, SEPARATE ~ *vi* : to come apart : DISUNITE — **dis·sev·er·ance** \-ˈev-(ə-)rən(t)s\ *n* — **dis·sev·er·ment** \-ˈev-ər-mənt\ *n*

dis·si·dence \ˈdis-əd-ən(t)s\ *n* (ca. 1656) : DISSENT, DISAGREEMENT

dis·si·dent \-ənt\ *adj* [L *dissident-, dissidens,* prp. of *dissidēre* to sit apart, disagree, fr. *dis-* + *sedēre* to sit — more at SIT] (1534) : disagreeing with an opinion or a group : DISAFFECTED — **dissident** *n*

dis·sim·i·lar \(ˈ)dis-ˈ(s)im-(ə-)lər\ *adj* (1599) : UNLIKE — **dis·sim·i·lar·i·ty** \(ˌ)dis-ˌ(s)im-ə-ˈlar-ət-ē\ *n* — **dis·sim·i·lar·ly** \(ˈ)dis-ˈ(s)im-(ə-)lər-lē\ *adv*

dis·sim·i·late \(ˈ)dis-ˈim-ə-ˌlāt\ *vb* **-lat·ed; -lat·ing** [*dis-* + *-similate* (as in *assimilate*)] *vi* (1841) : to become dissimilar ~ *vt* : to make dissimilar — **dis·sim·i·la·to·ry** \-(ə-)lə-ˌtōr-ē, -ˌtȯr-\ *adj*

dis·sim·i·la·tion \(ˌ)dis-ˌim-ə-ˈlā-shən\ *n* (ca. 1874) : the change or omission of one of two identical or closely related sounds in a word

dis·si·mil·i·tude \ˌdis-(s)ə-ˈmil-ə-ˌt(y)üd\ *n* [L *dissimilitudo,* fr. *dissimilis* unlike, fr. *dis-* + *similis* like — more at SAME] (15c) : lack of resemblance

dis·sim·u·late \(ˈ)dis-ˈim-yə-ˌlāt\ *vb* **-lat·ed; -lat·ing** [L *dissimulatus,* pp. of *dissimulare,* fr. *dis-* + *simulare* to simulate] *vt* (15c) : to hide under a false appearance : DISSEMBLE ⟨refuse to ~ the facts of my life —Tennessee Williams⟩ ~ *vi* : to engage in dissembling — **dis·sim·u·la·tion** \(ˌ)dis-ˌim-yə-ˈlā-shən\ *n* — **dis·sim·u·la·tor** \(ˈ)dis-ˈim-yə-ˌlāt-ər\ *n*

dis·si·pate \ˈdis-ə-ˌpāt\ *vb* **-pat·ed; -pat·ing** [L *dissipatus,* pp. of *dissipare,* fr. *dis-* + *supare* to throw; akin to ON *svāf* spear, Skt *svapū* broom] *vt* (15c) **1 a** : to break up and drive off (as a crowd) **b** : to cause to spread out or spread thin to the point of vanishing : DISSOLVE ⟨a book whose argument is *dissipated* by its sweep —Jeff Greenfield⟩ **c** : to lose (as heat or electricity) irrecoverably : DISPEL **2 a** : to expend aimlessly or foolishly **b** : to use up esp. foolishly or heedlessly ⟨soon *dissipated* his estate⟩ ~ *vi* **1** : to separate into parts and scatter or vanish **2** : to be extravagant or dissolute in the pursuit of pleasure; *esp* : to drink to excess ***syn*** see SCATTER — **dis·si·pat·er** *n*

dis·si·pat·ed *adj* (1744) : given to or marked by dissipation : DISSOLUTE — **dis·si·pat·ed·ly** *adv* — **dis·si·pat·ed·ness** *n*

dis·si·pa·tion \ˌdis-ə-ˈpā-shən\ *n* (15c) **1** : the act or process of dissipating : the state of being dissipated: **a** : DISPERSION, DIFFUSION **b** *archaic* : DISSOLUTION, DISINTEGRATION **c** : wasteful expenditure **d** : intemperate living; *esp* : excessive drinking **2** : DIVERSION, AMUSEMENT

dis·si·pa·tive \ˈdis-ə-ˌpāt-iv\ *adj* (1684) : relating to dissipation esp. of heat

dis·so·cia·ble \(ˈ)dis-ˈō-sh(ē-)ə-bəl, -sē-ə-\ *adj* (1833) : SEPARABLE — **dis·so·cia·bil·i·ty** \(ˌ)dis-ˌō-sh(ē-)ə-ˈbil-ət-ē, -sē-ə-\ *n*

dis·so·cial \(ˈ)dis-ˈ(s)ō-shəl\ *adj* (1762) : UNSOCIAL, SELFISH

dis·so·ci·ate \(ˈ)dis-ˈō-s(h)ē-ˌāt\ *vb* **-at·ed; -at·ing** [L *dissociatus,* pp. of *dissociare,* fr. *dis-* + *sociare* to join, fr. *socius* companion — more at SOCIAL] *vt* (1623) **1** : to separate from association or union with another : DISCONNECT **2** : DISUNITE; *specif* : to subject to chemical dissociation ~ *vi* **1** : to undergo dissociation **2** : to mutate esp. reversibly

dis·so·ci·a·tion \(ˌ)dis-ˌō-sē-ˈā-shən, -shē-\ *n* (1611) **1** : the act or process of dissociating : the state of being dissociated: as **a** : the process by which a chemical combination breaks up into simpler constituents; *esp* : one that results from the action of energy (as heat) on a gas or of a solvent on a dissolved substance **b** : the separation of whole segments of the personality (as in multiple personality) or of discrete mental processes (as in the schizophrenias) from the mainstream of consciousness or of behavior **2** : the property inherent in some biological stocks (as of certain bacteria) of differentiating into two or more distinct and relatively permanent strains; *also* : such a strain — **dis·so·cia·tive** \(ˈ)dis-ˈō-s(h)ē-ˌāt-iv, -shət-iv\ *adj*

dis·sol·u·ble \dis-ˈäl-yə-bəl\ *adj* [L *dissolubilis,* fr. *dissolvere* to dissolve] (1534) : capable of being dissolved or disintegrated — **dis·sol·u·bil·i·ty** \-ˌäl-yə-ˈbil-ət-ē\ *n*

dis·so·lute \ˈdis-ə-ˌlüt, -lət\ *adj* [L *dissolutus,* fr. pp. of *dissolvere* to loosen, dissolve] (14c) : lacking restraint; *esp* : marked by indulgence in things (as drink or promiscuous sex) deemed vices — **dis·so·lute·ly** *adv* — **dis·so·lute·ness** *n*

dis·so·lu·tion \ˌdis-ə-ˈlü-shən\ *n* (14c) **1 :** the act or process of dissolving: as **a :** separation into component parts **b** (1) **:** DECAY, DISINTEGRATION (2) **:** DEATH ⟨grew convinced of his friend's approaching ~ —Elinor Wylie⟩ **c :** termination or destruction by breaking down, disrupting, or dispersing ⟨the ~ of the republic⟩ **d :** LIQUEFACTION **2** *obs* **:** PROFLIGACY

[1]**dis·solve** \diz-ˈälv, -ˈȯlv *also* -ˈäv *or* -ˈȯv\ *vb* [ME *dissolven,* fr. L *dissolvere,* fr. *dis-* + *solvere* to loosen — more at SOLVE] *vt* (14c) **1 a :** to cause to disperse or disappear **:** DESTROY **b :** to separate into component parts **:** DISINTEGRATE **c :** to bring to an end **:** TERMINATE ⟨~ parliament⟩ **2 a :** to cause to pass into solution ⟨~ sugar in water⟩ **b :** MELT, LIQUEFY **c :** to cause to be emotionally moved **d :** to cause to fade out in a dissolve **3** *archaic* **:** DETACH, LOOSEN **4 :** to clear up ⟨~ a problem⟩ ~ *vi* **1 a :** to become dissipated or decomposed **b :** BREAK UP, DISPERSE **c :** to fade away **2 a :** to become fluid **:** MELT **b :** to pass into solution **c :** to be overcome emotionally ⟨*dissolved* into tears⟩ ⟨*dissolved* in laughter⟩ **d :** to resolve itself as if by dissolution ⟨hate *dissolved* into fear⟩ **e :** to change by a dissolve ⟨the scene ~*s* to a Victorian parlor⟩ — **dis·solv·able** \-ˈäl-və-bəl, -ˈȯl-\ *adj* — **dis·solv·er** *n*

[2]**dissolve** *n* (1916) **:** a gradual superimposing of one motion-picture or television shot upon another on a screen

dis·so·nance \ˈdis-ə-nən(t)s\ *n* (15c) **1 :** lack of agreement; *esp* **:** inconsistency between the beliefs one holds or between one's actions and one's beliefs — compare COGNITIVE DISSONANCE **2 :** a mingling of discordant sounds; *specif* **:** a clashing or unresolved musical interval or chord

dis·so·nant \-nənt\ *adj* [MF or L; MF, fr. L *dissonant-, dissonans,* prp. of *dissonare* to be discordant, fr. *dis-* + *sonare* to sound — more at SOUND] (15c) **1 :** marked by dissonance **:** DISCORDANT **2 :** INCONGRUOUS **3 :** harmonically unresolved — **dis·so·nant·ly** *adv*

dis·suade \dis-ˈwād\ *vt* **dis·suad·ed; dis·suad·ing** [MF or L; MF *dissuader,* fr. L *dissuadēre,* fr. *dis-* + *suadēre* to urge — more at SWEET] (15c) **1 a :** to advise (a person) against something **b** *archaic* **:** to advise against (an action) **2 :** to turn from something by persuasion — **dis·suad·er** *n*

dis·sua·sion \dis-ˈwā-zhən\ *n* [MF or L; MF, fr. L *dissuasion-, dissuasio,* fr. *dissuasus,* pp. of *dissuadēre*] (15c) **:** the act of dissuading

dis·sua·sive \dis-ˈwā-siv, -ziv\ *adj* (1609) **:** tending to dissuade — **dis·sua·sive·ly** *adv* — **dis·sua·sive·ness** *n*

dis·syl·lab·ic \ˌdis-ə-ˈlab-ik, ˌdī-sə-\, **dis·syl·la·ble** \ˈdis-ˌil-ə-bəl, (ˈ)dis-ˈ(s)il-; ˈdī-ˌsil-, (ˈ)dī-ˈsil-\ *var of* DISYLLABIC, DISYLLABLE

dis·sym·me·try \(ˈ)dis-ˈ(s)im-ə-trē\ *n* (1845) **:** the absence of or the lack of symmetry — **dis·sym·met·ric** \ˌdis-(s)ə-ˈme-trik\ *adj*

[1]**dis·taff** \ˈdis-ˌtaf\ *n, pl* **distaffs** \-ˌtafs, -ˌtavz\ [ME *distaf,* fr. OE *distæf,* fr. *dis-* (akin to MLG *dise* bunch of flax) + *stæf* staff] (bef. 12c) **1 a :** a staff for holding the flax, tow, or wool in spinning **b :** woman's work or domain **2 :** the female branch or side of a family

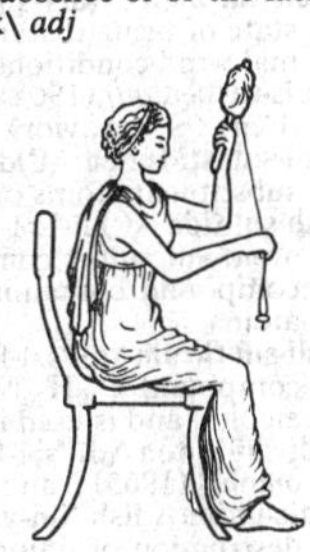
distaff 1a

[2]**distaff** *adj* (1633) **:** MATERNAL ⟨the ~ side of the family⟩ — compare SPEAR; *also* **:** FEMALE ⟨a ~ jockey⟩

dis·tain \dis-ˈtān\ *vt* [ME *disteynen,* fr. MF *desteindre* to take away the color of, fr. OF, fr. *des-* dis- + *teindre* to dye, fr. L *tingere* to wet, dye — more at TINGE] (14c) **1** *archaic* **:** STAIN **2** *archaic* **:** DISHONOR

dis·tal \ˈdis-tᵊl\ *adj* [*dist-* (as in *distant*) + *-al*] (1808) **1 :** far from the point of attachment or origin — compare PROXIMAL **2 :** of, relating to, or being the surface of a tooth that is next to the tooth behind it or that is farthest from the middle of the front of the jaw — compare MESIAL 2 — **dis·tal·ly** \-tᵊl-ē\ *adv*

distal convoluted tubule *n* (ca. 1961) **:** the convoluted portion of the vertebrate nephron that lies between the loop of Henle and the nonsecretory part of the nephron and that is concerned esp. with the concentration of urine

[1]**dis·tance** \ˈdis-tən(t)s\ *n* (13c) **1** *obs* **:** DISCORD **2 a :** separation in time **b :** the degree or amount of separation between two points, lines, surfaces, or objects measured along the shortest path joining them **c :** an extent of area or an advance along a route measured linearly **d :** an extent of advance away or along from a point considered primary or original **e :** EXPANSE **f :** length of a race or contest; *esp* **:** the full length ⟨go the ~⟩ **3 :** the quality or state of being distant: as **a :** spatial remoteness **b :** personal and esp. emotional separation; *also* **:** RESERVE, COLDNESS **c :** AESTHETIC DISTANCE **d :** DIFFERENCE, DISPARITY **4 :** a distant point or region

[2]**distance** *vt* **dis·tanced; dis·tanc·ing** (1578) **1 :** to place or keep at a distance **2 :** to leave far behind **:** OUTSTRIP

dis·tant \ˈdis-tənt\ *adj* [ME, fr. MF, fr. L *distant-, distans,* prp. of *distare* to stand apart, be distant, fr. *dis-* + *stare* to stand — more at STAND] (14c) **1 a :** separated in space **:** AWAY **b :** situated at a great distance **:** FAR-OFF **c :** separated by a great distance from each other **:** far apart **2 :** separated in a relationship other than spatial ⟨a ~ relative⟩ **3 :** different in kind **4 :** reserved or aloof in personal relationship **:** COLD ⟨~ politeness⟩ **5 a :** coming from or going to a distance ⟨~ voyages⟩ **b :** concerned with or directed toward things at a distance ⟨~ thoughts⟩ — **dis·tant·ly** *adv* — **dis·tant·ness** *n*

[1]**dis·taste** \(ˈ)dis-ˈtāst\ *vt* (1586) **1** *archaic* **:** to feel aversion to **2** *archaic* **:** OFFEND, DISPLEASE ~ *vi, obs* **:** to have an offensive taste

[2]**distaste** *n* (1598) **1 :** dislike of food or drink **b :** AVERSION, DISINCLINATION **2** *obs* **:** ANNOYANCE, DISCOMFORT

dis·taste·ful \(ˈ)dis-ˈtāst-fəl\ *adj* (1607) **1 :** objectionable because offensive to one's personal taste **:** DISAGREEABLE **2 :** unpleasant to the taste **:** LOATHSOME *syn* see REPUGNANT — **dis·taste·ful·ly** \-fə-lē\ *adv* — **dis·taste·ful·ness** *n*

[1]**dis·tem·per** \dis-ˈtem-pər\ *vt* [ME *distempren,* fr. LL *distemperare* to temper badly, fr. L *dis-* + *temperare* to temper] (14c) **1 :** to throw out of order **2** *archaic* **:** DERANGE, UNSETTLE

[2]**distemper** *n* (1555) **1 :** bad humor or temper **2 :** a disordered or abnormal bodily state esp. of quadruped mammals: as **a :** a highly contagious virus disease esp. of dogs marked by fever and by respiratory and sometimes nervous symptoms **b :** STRANGLES **c :** PANLEUKOPENIA **3 :** AILMENT, DISORDER ⟨political ~⟩ ⟨intellectual ~*s*⟩ — **dis·tem·per·ate** \-p(ə-)rət\ *adj*

[3]**distemper** *vt* [ME *distemperen,* fr. MF *destemprer,* fr. L *dis-* + *temperare*] (14c) **1** *obs* **:** to dilute with or soak, steep, or dissolve in a liquid **2 a :** to mix (ingredients) to produce distemper **b :** to paint in or with distemper

[4]**distemper** *n* (1632) **1 :** a process of painting in which the pigments are mixed with an emulsion of egg yolk, with size, or with white of egg as a vehicle and which is used for scene painting or mural decoration **2 a :** the paint or the prepared ground used in the distemper process **b :** a painting done in distemper

dis·tem·per·a·ture \dis-ˈtem-pə(r)-ˌchu̇(ə)r, -p(ə-)rə-, -chər, -ˌt(y)u̇(ə)r\ *n* (1531) **:** a disordered condition

dis·tend \dis-ˈtend\ *vb* [ME *distenden,* fr. L *distendere,* fr. *dis-* + *tendere* to stretch — more at THIN] *vt* (15c) **1 :** EXTEND **2 :** to enlarge from internal pressure **:** SWELL ~ *vi* **:** to become expanded *syn* see EXPAND

dis·ten·si·ble \-ˈten(t)-sə-bəl\ *adj* [*distens-* (fr. L *distensus,* pp. of *distendere*) + *-ible*] (ca. 1828) **:** capable of being distended — **dis·ten·si·bil·i·ty** \-ˌten(t)-sə-ˈbil-ət-ē\ *n*

dis·ten·sion *or* **dis·ten·tion** \dis-ˈten-chən\ *n* [L *distention-, distentio,* fr. *distentus,* pp. of *distendere*] (15c) **:** the act of distending or the state of being distended esp. unduly or abnormally

dis·tich \ˈdis-(ˌ)tik\ *n* [L *distichon,* fr. Gk, fr. neut. of *distichos* having two rows, fr. *di-* + *stichos* row, verse; akin to Gk *steichein* to go — more at STAIR] (1553) **:** a strophic unit of two lines

dis·ti·chous \ˈdis-ti-kəs\ *adj* [LL *distichus,* fr. Gk *distichos*] (ca. 1753) **:** disposed in two vertical rows ⟨~ leaves⟩

dis·till *also* **dis·til** \dis-ˈtil\ *vb* **dis·tilled; dis·till·ing** [ME *distillen,* fr. MF *distiller,* fr. LL *distillare,* alter. of L *destillare,* fr. *de-* + *stillare* to drip, fr. *stilla* drop; akin to OE *stān* stone — more at STONE] *vt* (14c) **1 :** to let fall, exude, or precipitate in drops or in a wet mist **2 a :** to subject to or transform by distillation **b :** to obtain by or as if by distillation **c :** to extract the essence of **:** CONCENTRATE ~ *vi* **1 a :** to fall or materialize in drops or in a fine moisture **:** DROP **b :** to appear slowly or in small quantities at a time **2 a :** to undergo distillation **b :** to perform distillation

dis·til·late \ˈdis-tə-ˌlāt, -lət; dis-ˈtil-ət\ *n* (ca. 1859) **1 :** a liquid product condensed from vapor during distillation **2 :** something resembling a distillate

dis·til·la·tion \ˌdis-tə-ˈlā-shən\ *n* (14c) **1 :** a process that consists of driving gas or vapor from liquids or solids by heating and condensing to liquid products and that is used esp. for purification, fractionation, or the formation of new substances **2 :** something distilled

dis·till·er \dis-ˈtil-ər\ *n* (1577) **:** one that distills esp. alcoholic liquors

dis·till·ery \dis-ˈtil-(ə-)rē\ *n, pl* **-er·ies** (1759) **:** the works where distilling (as of alcoholic liquors) is done

dis·tinct \dis-ˈtiŋ(k)t\ *adj* [ME, fr. MF, fr. L *distinctus,* fr. pp. of *distinguere*] (14c) **1 :** distinguishable to the eye or mind as discrete **:** SEPARATE ⟨a ~ cultural group⟩ ⟨teaching as ~ from research⟩ **2 :** presenting a clear unmistakable impression ⟨a neat ~ handwriting⟩ **3** *archaic* **:** notably decorated **4 a :** NOTABLE ⟨a ~ contribution to scholarship⟩ **b :** UNQUESTIONABLE ⟨a ~ possibility of snow⟩ ⟨a ~ British accent⟩ — **dis·tinct·ly** \-ˈtiŋ(k)-tlē, -ˈtiŋ-klē\ *adv* — **dis·tinct·ness** \-ˈtiŋt-nəs, -ˈtiŋk-nəs\ *n*

syn DISTINCT, SEPARATE, SEVERAL, DISCRETE mean not being each and every one the same. DISTINCT indicates that something is distinguished by the mind or eye as being apart or different from others; SEPARATE often stresses lack of connection or a difference in identity between two things; SEVERAL indicates distinctness, difference, or separation from similar items; DISCRETE strongly emphasizes individuality and lack of physical connection despite apparent similarity or seeming continuity. *syn* see in addition EVIDENT

dis·tinc·tion \dis-ˈtiŋ(k)-shən\ *n* (13c) **1 a** *archaic* **:** DIVISION **b :** CLASS **2 a :** the act of distinguishing a difference **:** DISCRIMINATION, DIFFERENTIATION **b :** the object or result of distinguishing **:** CONTRAST **3 :** a distinguishing mark **4 :** the quality or state of being distinguishable ⟨there is no appreciable ~ between the twins⟩ **5 a :** the quality or state of being distinguished or worthy ⟨a politician of some ~⟩ ⟨served with ~⟩ **b :** special honor or recognition ⟨took a law degree with ~⟩ ⟨won many ~*s*⟩

dis·tinc·tive \dis-ˈtiŋ(k)-tiv\ *adj* (15c) **1 a :** serving to distinguish **b :** having or giving style or distinction **2 :** capable of making a segment of utterance different in meaning as well as in sound from an otherwise identical utterance *syn* see CHARACTERISTIC — **dis·tinc·tive·ly** *adv* — **dis·tinc·tive·ness** *n*

dis·tin·gué \ˌdēs-ˌtaŋ-ˈgā, (ˌ)dis-; di-ˈstaŋ-ˌ\ *adj* [F, fr. pp. of *distinguer*] (1813) **:** distinguished esp. in manner or bearing

dis·tin·guish \dis-ˈtiŋ-(g)wish\ *vb* [MF *distinguer,* fr. L *distinguere,* lit., to separate by pricking, fr. *dis-* + *-stinguere* (akin to L *instigare* to urge on) — more at STICK] *vt* (1561) **1 :** to perceive a difference in **:** mentally separate ⟨so alike they could not be ~*ed*⟩ **2 a :** to mark as separate or different **b :** to separate into kinds, classes, or categories **c :** to set above or apart from others **d :** CHARACTERIZE **3 a :** DISCERN ⟨~*ed* a light in the distance⟩ **b :** to single out **:** take special notice of ⟨~ the sound of the piano in the orchestra⟩ ~ *vi* **:** to perceive a difference — **dis·tin·guish·abil·i·ty** \-ˌtiŋ-(g)wish-ə-ˈbil-ət-ē\ *n* — **dis·tin·guish·able** \-ˈtiŋ-(g)wish-ə-bəl\ *adj* — **dis·tin·guish·ably** \-blē\ *adv*

dis·tin·guished *adj* (1714) **1 :** marked by eminence, distinction, or excellence **2 :** befitting an eminent person *syn* see FAMOUS

Distinguished Conduct Medal *n* (1862) **:** a British military decoration awarded for distinguished conduct in the field

Distinguished Flying Cross *n* (1918) **1 :** a British military decoration awarded for acts of gallantry when flying in operations against an enemy **2 :** a U.S. military decoration awarded for heroism or extraordinary achievement while participating in an aerial flight

Distinguished Service Cross *n* (1914) **1 :** a British military decoration awarded for distinguished service against the enemy **2 :** a U.S. Army decoration awarded for extraordinary heroism during operations against an armed enemy

Distinguished Service Medal *n* (1914) **1 :** a U.S. military decoration awarded for exceptionally meritorious service to the government in a wartime duty of great responsibility **2 :** a British military decoration awarded for distinguished conduct in war

Distinguished Service Order *n* (1886) **:** a British military decoration awarded for special services in action

dis·tort \dis-ˈtȯ(ə)rt\ *vt* [L *distortus,* pp. of *distorquēre,* fr. *dis-* + *torquēre* to twist — more at TORTURE] (1586) **1 :** to twist out of the true meaning or proportion ‹~*ed* the facts› **2 :** to twist out of a natural, normal, or original shape or condition ‹a face ~*ed* by pain› **3 :** PERVERT ***syn*** see DEFORM — **dis·tort·er** *n*

dis·tor·tion \dis-ˈtȯr-shən\ *n* (1581) **1 :** the act of distorting **2 :** the quality or state of being distorted **:** a product of distortion: as **a :** a lack of proportionality in an image resulting from defects in the optical system **b :** falsified reproduction of an audio or video signal caused by change in the wave form of the original signal — **dis·tor·tion·al** \-shnəl, -shən-ᵊl\ *adj*

¹dis·tract \dis-ˈtrakt, ˈdis-ˌ\ *adj, archaic* (14c) **:** INSANE, MAD

²dis·tract \dis-ˈtrakt\ *vt* [ME *distracten,* fr. L *distractus,* pp. of *distrahere,* lit., to draw apart, fr. *dis-* + *trahere* to draw — more at DRAW] (14c) **1 a :** to turn aside **:** DIVERT **b :** to draw or direct (as one's attention) to a different object or in different directions at the same time **2 :** to stir up or confuse with conflicting emotions or motives **:** HARASS ***syn*** see PUZZLE — **dis·tract·i·bil·i·ty** \-ˌtrak-tə-ˈbil-ət-ē\ *n* — **dis·tract·ible** \-ˈtrak-tə-bəl\ *adj* — **dis·tract·ing·ly** \-tiŋ-lē\ *adv*

dis·tract·ed·ly *adv* (1597) **:** in the manner of one that is distracted

dis·trac·tion \dis-ˈtrak-shən\ *n* (15c) **1 :** the act of distracting or the state of being distracted; *esp* **:** mental confusion **2 :** something that distracts; *esp* **:** AMUSEMENT — **dis·trac·tive** \-ˈtrak-tiv\ *adj*

dis·train \dis-ˈtrān\ *vb* [ME *distreynen,* fr. OF *destreindre,* fr. ML *distringere,* fr. L, to draw apart, detain, fr. *dis-* + *stringere* to bind tight — more at STRAIN] *vt* (13c) **1 :** to force or compel to satisfy an obligation by means of a distress **2 :** to seize by distress ~ *vi* **:** to levy a distress — **dis·train·able** \-ˈtrā-nə-bəl\ *adj* — **dis·train·er** \-ˈtrā-nər\ *or* **dis·train·or** \-ˈtrā-nər, -ˌtrā-ˈnȯ(ə)r\ *n*

dis·traint \dis-ˈtrānt\ *n* [*distrain* + *-t* (as in *constraint*)] (1730) **:** the act or action of distraining

dis·trait \di-ˈstrā\ *adj* [F, fr. L *distractus*] (1711) **:** ABSENTMINDED; *esp* **:** inattentive or distracted because of anxiety or apprehension

dis·traught \dis-ˈtrȯt\ *adj* [ME, modif. of L *distractus*] (14c) **1 :** agitated with doubt or mental conflict **2 :** INSANE — **dis·traught·ly** *adv*

¹dis·tress \dis-ˈtres\ *n* [ME *destresse,* fr. OF, fr. (assumed) VL *districtia,* fr. L *districtus,* pp. of *distringere*] (13c) **1 a :** seizure and detention of the goods of another as pledge or to obtain satisfaction of a claim by the sale of the goods seized **b :** something that is distrained **2 a :** pain or suffering affecting the body, a bodily part, or the mind **:** TROUBLE ‹gastric ~› **b :** a painful situation **:** MISFORTUNE **3 :** a state of danger or desperate need ‹a ship in ~›

syn DISTRESS, SUFFERING, MISERY, AGONY mean the state of being in great trouble. DISTRESS implies an external and usu. temporary cause of great physical or mental strain and stress; SUFFERING implies conscious endurance of pain or distress; MISERY stresses the unhappiness attending esp. sickness, poverty, or loss; AGONY suggests pain too intense to be borne.

²distress *vt* (14c) **1 :** to subject to great strain or difficulties **2** *archaic* **:** to force or overcome by inflicting pain **3 :** to cause to worry or be troubled **:** UPSET **4 :** to mar (as wood or furniture) deliberately to give an effect of age — **dis·tress·ing·ly** \-iŋ-lē\ *adv*

³distress *adj* (1926) **1 :** offered for sale at a loss ‹~ merchandise› **2 :** involving distress goods ‹a ~ sale›

dis·tress·ful \dis-ˈtres-fəl\ *adj* (1591) **:** causing distress **:** full of distress — **dis·tress·ful·ly** \-fə-lē\ *adv* — **dis·tress·ful·ness** *n*

dis·trib·u·tary \dis-ˈtrib-yə-ˌter-ē\ *n, pl* **-tar·ies** (1863) **:** a river branch flowing away from the main stream

dis·trib·ute \dis-ˈtrib-yət, *Brit also* ˈdis-trib-ˌyüt\ *vb* **-ut·ed; -ut·ing** [ME *distributen,* fr. L *distributus,* pp. of *distribuere,* fr. *dis-* + *tribuere* to allot — more at TRIBUTE] *vt* (15c) **1 :** to divide among several or many **:** APPORTION ‹~ expenses› **2 a :** to spread out so as to cover something **:** SCATTER **b :** to give out or deliver esp. to members of a group ‹~ newspapers› ‹~ leaflets› ‹~ food to the needy› **c :** to place or position so as to be properly apportioned over or throughout an area ‹200 pounds neatly *distributed* on a 6-foot frame› **d :** to use (a term) so as to convey information about every member of the class named ‹the proposition "all men are mortal" ~*s* "man" but not "mortal"› **3 a :** to divide or separate esp. into kinds **b :** to return the units of (as typeset matter) to storage **4 :** to use in or as an operation so as to be mathematically distributive ‹addition is not *distributed* over multiplication› ~ *vi* **:** to be mathematically distributive ‹multiplication ~*s* over addition› — **dis·trib·u·tee** \dis-ˌtrib-yə-ˈtē\ *n*

syn DISTRIBUTE, DISPENSE, DIVIDE, DEAL, DOLE mean to give out, usu. in shares, to each member of a group. DISTRIBUTE implies an apportioning by separation of something into parts, units, or amounts; DISPENSE suggests the giving of a carefully weighed or measured portion to each of a group according to due or need; DIVIDE stresses the separation of a whole into parts and implies that the parts are equal; DEAL emphasizes the allotment of something piece by piece; DOLE implies a carefully measured portion that is often scant or niggardly.

dis·trib·ut·ed *adj* (1968) **:** characterized by a statistical distribution of a particular kind ‹a normally ~ random variable›

dis·tri·bu·tion \ˌdis-trə-ˈbyü-shən\ *n* (14c) **1 a :** the act or process of distributing **b :** the apportionment by a court of the personal property of an intestate **2 a :** the position, arrangement, or frequency of occurrence (as of the members of a group) over an area or throughout a space or unit of time **b :** the natural geographic range of an organism **3 a :** something distributed **b (1) :** FREQUENCY DISTRIBUTION **(2) :** PROBABILITY FUNCTION **(3) :** PROBABILITY DENSITY FUNCTION 2 **4 a :** a device by which something is distributed **b :** the pattern of branching and termination of a ramifying structure (as a nerve) **5 :** the marketing or merchandising of commodities — **dis·tri·bu·tion·al** \-shnəl, -shən-ᵊl\ *adj*

distribution function *n* (ca. 1909) **:** a function that gives the probability that a random variable is less than or equal to the independent variable of the function

dis·trib·u·tive \dis-ˈtrib-yət-iv\ *adj* (15c) **1 :** of or relating to distribution: as **a :** dealing a proper share to each of a group **b :** diffusing more or less evenly **2** *of a word* **:** referring singly and without exception to the members of a group ‹*each, either,* and *none* are ~› **3 a :** being an operation (as multiplication in $a(b + c) = ab + ac$) that produces the same result when operating on the whole mathematical expression as when operating on each part and collecting the results **b :** being or relating to a rule or property concerning a distributive operation ‹the ~ axiom for multiplication› — **dis·trib·u·tive·ly** *adv* — **dis·trib·u·tiv·i·ty** \-ˌtrib-yə-ˈtiv-ət-ē\ *n*

distributive education *n, often cap D&E* (1948) **:** a vocational program set up between schools and employers in which the student receives both classroom instruction and on-the-job training

dis·trib·u·tor \dis-ˈtrib-yət-ər\ *n* (1526) **1 :** one that distributes **2 :** one that markets a commodity; *esp* **:** WHOLESALER **3 :** an apparatus for directing the secondary current from the induction coil to the various spark plugs of an engine in their proper firing order

¹dis·trict \ˈdis-(ˌ)trikt\ *n, often attrib* [F, fr. ML *districtus* jurisdiction, district, fr. *districtus,* pp. of *distringere* to distrain — more at DISTRAIN] (1611) **1 :** a territorial division (as for administrative or electoral purposes) **2 :** an area, region, or section with a distinguishing character

²district *vt* (1792) **:** to divide or organize into districts

district attorney *n* (1789) **:** the prosecuting officer of a judicial district

district court *n* (1789) **:** a trial court that has jurisdiction over certain cases within a specific judicial district

district superintendent *n* (ca. 1909) **:** a church official supervising a district

¹dis·trust \(ˈ)dis-ˈtrəst\ *n* (1513) **:** the lack or absence of trust

²distrust *vt* (1548) **:** to have no trust or confidence in

dis·trust·ful \-ˈtrəst-fəl\ *adj* (1591) **:** having or showing distrust — **dis·trust·ful·ly** \-fə-lē\ *adv* — **dis·trust·ful·ness** *n*

dis·turb \dis-ˈtərb\ *vb* [ME *disturben, destourben,* fr. OF & L; OF *destourber,* fr. L *disturbare,* fr. *dis-* + *turbare* to throw into disorder — more at TURBID] *vt* (13c) **1 a :** to interfere with **:** INTERRUPT **b :** to alter the position or arrangement of **2 a :** to destroy the tranquillity or composure of **b :** to throw into disorder **c :** ALARM **d :** to put to inconvenience ~ *vi* **:** to cause disturbance ***syn*** see DISCOMPOSE — **dis·turb·er** *n* — **dis·turb·ing·ly** \-ˈtər-biŋ-lē\ *adv*

dis·tur·bance \dis-ˈtər-bən(t)s\ *n* (13c) **1 :** the act of disturbing **:** the state of being disturbed **2 :** a local variation from the average or normal wind conditions

dis·turbed *adj* (1904) **:** showing symptoms of emotional illness ‹~ children› ‹~ behavior›

di·sub·sti·tut·ed \(ˈ)dī-ˈsəb-stə-ˌt(y)üt-əd\ *adj* (ca. 1890) **:** having two substituent atoms or groups in a molecule

di·sul·fide \(ˈ)dī-ˈsəl-ˌfīd\ *n* (1863) **1 :** a compound containing two atoms of sulfur combined with an element or radical **2 :** an organic compound containing the bivalent group SS composed of two sulfur atoms

di·sul·fi·ram \dī-ˈsəl-fə-ˌram\ *n* [*disulf*ide + th*iourea* + *am*yl] (1952) **:** a compound $C_{10}H_{20}N_2S_4$ that causes a severe physiological reaction to alcohol and is used in the treatment of alcoholism

di·sul·fo·ton \dī-ˈsəl-fə-ˌtän\ *n* [*d*iethyl + *sulfo-* + *-ton* (prob. fr. *thionate*)] (1965) **:** an organophosphorus systemic insecticide $C_8H_{19}O_2PS_3$

dis·union \dish-ˈün-yən, (ˈ)dis(h)-ˈyün-\ *n* (15c) **1 :** the termination or destruction of union **:** SEPARATION **2 :** DISUNITY — **dis·union·ist** \-yə-nəst\ *n*

dis·unite \ˌdish-ü-ˈnīt, ˌdis(h)-yü-\ *vt* (1598) **:** DIVIDE, SEPARATE

dis·uni·ty \dish-ˈü-nət-ē, (ˈ)dis(h)-ˈyü-\ *n* (1632) **:** lack of unity; *esp* **:** DISSENSION

¹dis·use \dish-ˈüz, (ˈ)dis(h)-ˈyüz\ *vt* (15c) **:** to discontinue the use or practice of

²dis·use \-ˈüs, -ˈyüs\ *n* (15c) **:** cessation of use or practice

dis·util·i·ty \ˌdish-ü-ˈtil-ət-ē, ˌdis(h)-yü-\ *n* (1879) **:** the state or fact of being counterproductive

¹dis·val·ue \(ˈ)dis-ˈval-(ˌ)yü, -yə(-w)\ *vt* (1603) **1** *archaic* **:** UNDERVALUE, DEPRECIATE **2 :** to consider of little value

²disvalue *n* (1603) **1** *obs* **:** DISREGARD, DISESTEEM **2 :** a negative value

di·syl·la·ble \ˈdī-ˌsil-ə-bəl, (ˈ)dī-ˈsil-; ˈdis-ˌil-, (ˈ)dis-ˈ(s)il-\ *n* [part trans. of MF *dissilabe,* fr. L *disyllabus* having two syllables, fr. Gk *disyllabos,* fr. *di-* + *syllabē* syllable] (1589) **:** a linguistic form consisting of two syllables — **di·syl·lab·ic** \ˌdī-sə-ˈlab-ik, ˌdis-(s)ə-\ *adj*

dit \ˈdit\ *n* [imit.] (1940) **:** a dot in radio or telegraphic code

¹ditch \ˈdich\ *n* [ME *dich,* fr. OE *dīc* dike, ditch — more at DIKE] (bef. 12c) **:** a long narrow excavation dug in the earth (as for drainage)

²ditch *vt* (14c) **1 a :** to enclose with a ditch **b :** to dig a ditch in **2 a :** to cause (a train) to derail **b :** to make a forced landing of (an airplane) on water **3 :** to get rid of **:** DISCARD ~ *vi* **1 :** to dig a ditch **2 :** to crash-land at sea

ditch·dig·ger \-ˌdig-ər\ *n* (ca. 1897) **1 :** one that digs ditches **2 :** one employed at menial and usu. hard physical labor

dite \ˈdīt\ *n* [alter. of *doit*] *dial* (ca. 1877) **:** MITE, BIT

¹dith·er \ˈdith-ər\ *vi* **dith·ered; dith·er·ing** \-(ə-)riŋ\ [ME *didderen*] (15c) **1 :** SHIVER, TREMBLE **2 :** to act nervously or indecisively **:** VACILLATE — **dith·er·er** \-ər-ər\ *n*

²dither *n* (1819) **:** a highly nervous, excited, or agitated state **:** EXCITEMENT, CONFUSION — **dith·ery** \ˈdith-ə-rē\ *adj*

dithi- *or* **dithio-** *comb form* [ISV *di-* + *thi-*] **:** containing two atoms of sulfur usu. in place of two oxygen atoms

di·thio·car·ba·mate \ˌdī-ˌthī-ō-ˈkär-bə-ˌmāt\ *n* (1922) **:** any of several sulfur analogues of the carbamates including some used as fungicides

-di·thi·ol \(ˈ)dī-ˈthī-ˌȯl, -ˌōl\ *n comb form* [ISV] **:** containing two SH groups composed of sulfur and hydrogen

dith·y·ramb \ˈdith-i-ˌram(b)\ *n, pl* **-rambs** \-ˌramz\ [Gk *dithyrambos*] (1656) **1 :** a usu. short poem in an inspired wild irregular strain **2 :** a statement or writing in an exalted or enthusiastic vein — **dith·y·ram·bic** \ˌdith-i-ˈram-bik\ *adj* — **dith·y·ram·bi·cal·ly** \-bi-k(ə-)lē\ *adv*

dit·sy *also* **dit·zy** \ˈdit-sē\ *adj* **dits·i·er** *also* **ditz·i·er; -est** [origin unknown] (1973) **:** eccentrically silly, giddy, or inane **:** DIZZY

dit·ta·ny \'dit-ᵊn-ē\ *n, pl* **-nies** [ME *ditoyne*, fr. OF *ditayne*, fr. L *dictamnum*, fr. Gk *diktamnon*] (12c) **1 :** a pink-flowered herb (*Origanum dictamnus*) that is native to Crete **2 :** an American herb (*Conila origanoides*) of the mint family that has much-branched stems
[1]**dit·to** \'dit-(,)ō\ *n, pl* **dittos** [It dial., pp. of It *dire* to say, fr. L *dicere* — more at DICTION] (ca. 1678) **1 :** a thing mentioned previously or above — used to avoid repeating a word; often symbolized by inverted commas or apostrophes **2 :** a ditto mark
[2]**ditto** *adj* (1776) **:** having the same characteristics **:** SIMILAR
[3]**ditto** *vt* (1837) **1 :** to repeat the action or statement of **2** [fr. *Ditto*, a trademark] **:** to copy (as printed matter) on a duplicator
[4]**ditto** *adv* (ca. 1864) **:** as before or aforesaid **:** in the same manner
dit·ty \'dit-ē\ *n, pl* **ditties** [ME *ditee*, fr. MF *ditié* poem, fr. pp. of *ditier* to compose, fr. L *dictare* to dictate, compose] (14c) **:** an esp. simple and unaffected song
dit·ty bag \'dit-ē-\ *n* [origin unknown] (1852) **:** a bag used esp. by sailors to hold small articles of gear (as thread, needles, and tape)
ditty box *n* (ca. 1880) **:** a box used for the same purpose as a ditty bag
di·ure·sis \,dī-(y)ə-'rē-səs\ *n, pl* **-ure·ses** \-,sēz\ [NL] (ca. 1681) **:** an increased excretion of urine
di·uret·ic \,dī-(y)ə-'ret-ik\ *adj* [ME, fr. MF or LL; MF *diuretique*, fr. LL *diureticus*, fr. Gk *diourētikos*, fr. *diourein* to urinate, fr. *dia-* + *ourein* to urinate — more at URINE] (15c) **:** tending to increase the flow of urine — **diuretic** *n* — **di·uret·i·cal·ly** \-i-k(ə-)lē\ *adv*
[1]**di·ur·nal** \dī-'ərn-ᵊl\ *adj* [ME, fr. L *diurnalis* — more at JOURNAL] (14c) **1 a :** recurring every day ⟨~ task⟩ **b :** having a daily cycle ⟨~ tides⟩ **2 a :** of, relating to, or occurring in the daytime ⟨the city's ~ noises⟩ **b :** active chiefly in the daytime ⟨~ animals⟩ **c :** opening during the day and closing at night ⟨~ flowers⟩ — **di·ur·nal·ly** \-ᵊl-ē\ *adv*
[2]**diurnal** *n* (1600) **1** *archaic* **:** DIARY, DAYBOOK **2** *archaic* **:** JOURNAL
di·u·ron \'dī-(y)ə-,rän\ *n* [*di*chlor- + *ur*ea + [1]*-on*] (1957) **:** a persistent herbicide $C_9H_{10}Cl_2N_2O$ used esp. to control annual weeds
di·va \'dē-və\ *n, pl* **divas** *or* **di·ve** \-(,)vā\ [It, lit., goddess, fr. L, fem. of *divus* divine, god — more at DEITY] (1883) **:** PRIMA DONNA 1
di·va·gate \'dī-və-,gāt, 'div-ə-\ *vi* **-gat·ed; -gat·ing** [LL *divagatus*, pp. of *divagari*, fr. L *dis-* + *vagari* to wander — more at VAGARY] (1599) **:** to wander or stray from a course or subject **:** DIVERGE, DIGRESS — **di·va·ga·tion** \,dī-və-'gā-shən, ,div-ə-\ *n*
di·va·lent \(')dī-'vā-lənt\ *adj* (1869) **:** BIVALENT
di·van \di-'van, 'dī-,van, *esp in senses 1, 2, & 4 also* di-'vän, dī-'van\ *n* [Turk, fr. Per *dīwān* account book] (1586) **1 a :** the privy council of the Ottoman Empire **b :** COUNCIL **2 a :** a council chamber **b :** a smoking room **3 :** a large couch or sofa usu. without back or arms often designed for use as a bed **4 :** a collection of poems in Persian or Arabic usu. by one author
di·var·i·cate \dī-'var-ə-,kāt, də-\ *vi* **-cat·ed; -cat·ing** [L *divaricatus*, pp. of *divaricare*, fr. *dis-* + *varicare* to straddle — more at PREVARICATE] (1672) **:** to spread apart **:** branch off **:** DIVERGE
di·var·i·ca·tion \(,)dī-,var-ə-'kā-shən, də-\ *n* (1578) **1 :** the action, process, or fact of divaricating **2 :** a divergence of opinion
[1]**dive** \'dīv\ *vb* **dived** \'dīvd\ *or* **dove** \'dōv\; **dived; div·ing** [ME *diven*, *duven*, fr. OE *dȳfan* to dip & *dūfan* to dive; akin to OE *dyppan* to dip — more at DIP] *vi* (bef. 12c) **1 a :** to plunge into water headfirst; *specif* **:** to execute a dive **b :** SUBMERGE **2 a :** to descend or fall precipitously **b :** to plunge one's hand into something **c** *of an airplane* **:** to descend in a dive **3 a :** to plunge into some matter or activity **b :** LUNGE ~ *vt* **1 :** to thrust into something **2 :** to cause to descend
usage *Dive*, which was orig. a weak verb, developed a past tense *dove*, prob. by analogy with verbs like *drive, drove*. *Dove* exists in some British dialects and has become the standard past tense esp. in speech in the northern U.S. and some parts of Canada. It is also common in some parts of Pennsylvania and eastern So. Carolina and Georgia. Linguistic geographers indicate that its use in the U.S. is expanding. Although *dived* is somewhat more common in writing in the U.S. and is usual in British English, *dove* must be considered an acceptable variant.
[2]**dive** *n* (1700) **1 :** the act or an instance of diving: as **a** (1) **:** a plunge into water executed in a prescribed manner (2) **:** a submerging of a submarine (3) **:** a steep descent of an airplane at greater than the maximum horizontal speed **b :** a sharp decline **2 :** a disreputable entertainment establishment **3 :** a faked knockout — usu. used in the phrase *take a dive* **4 :** an offensive play in football in which the ball-carrier plunges into the line for short yardage
dive–bomb \'dīv-,bäm\ *vt* (1935) **:** to bomb from an airplane by making a steep dive toward the target before releasing the bomb — **dive–bomber** *n*
div·er \'dī-vər\ *n* (1506) **1 :** one that dives **2 a :** a person who stays underwater for long periods by having air supplied from the surface or by carrying a supply of compressed air **b :** any of various diving birds; *esp* **:** LOON
di·verge \də-'vərj, dī-\ *vb* **di·verged; di·verg·ing** [ML *divergere*, fr. L *dis-* + *vergere* to incline — more at WRENCH] *vi* (1665) **1 a :** to move or extend in different directions from a common point **:** draw apart ⟨*diverging* rays of light⟩ **b :** to become or be different in character or form **:** differ in opinion **2 :** to turn aside from a path or course **:** DEVIATE **3 :** to be mathematically divergent ~ *vt* **:** DEFLECT ***syn*** see SWERVE
di·ver·gence \-'vər-jən(t)s\ *n* (1656) **1 a :** a drawing apart (as of lines extending from a common center) **b :** DIFFERENCE, DISAGREEMENT **c :** the acquisition of dissimilar characters by related organisms in unlike environments **2 :** a deviation from a course or standard **3 :** the condition of being mathematically divergent
di·ver·gen·cy \-jən-sē\ *n, pl* **-cies** (1709) **:** DIVERGENCE
di·ver·gent \-jənt\ *adj* [L *divergent-, divergens*, prp. of *divergere*] (1696) **1 a :** diverging from each other **b :** differing from each other or from a standard **:** DEVIANT ⟨the ~ interests of capital and labor⟩ **2 :** relating to or being an infinite sequence that does not have a limit or an infinite series whose partial sums do not have a limit **3 :** causing divergence of rays ⟨a ~ lens⟩ ***syn*** see DIFFERENT — **di·ver·gent·ly** *adv*
di·vers \'dī-vərz\ *adj* [ME *divers, diverse*] (14c) **:** VARIOUS
di·verse \dī-'vərs, də-', 'dī-,\ *adj* [ME *divers, diverse*, fr. OF & L; OF *divers*, fr. L *diversus*, fr. pp. of *divertere*] (13c) **1 :** differing from one another **:** UNLIKE **2 :** composed of distinct elements or qualities ***syn*** see DIFFERENT — **di·verse·ly** *adv* — **di·verse·ness** *n*
di·ver·si·fy \də-'vər-sə-,fī, dī-\ *vb* **-fied; -fy·ing** *vt* (15c) **1 :** to make diverse **:** give variety to ⟨~ a course of study⟩ **2 :** to balance (as an investment portfolio) defensively by dividing funds among securities of different industries or of different classes **3 :** to increase the variety of the products of ~ *vi* **1 :** to produce variety **2 :** to engage in varied operations — **di·ver·si·fi·ca·tion** \-,vər-sə-fə-'kā-shən\ *n* — **di·ver·si·fi·er** \-'vər-sə-,fī(-ə)r\ *n*
di·ver·sion \də-'vər-zhən, dī-, -shən\ *n* (1626) **1 :** the act or an instance of diverting from a course, activity, or use **:** DEVIATION **2 :** something that diverts or amuses **:** PASTIME **3 :** an attack or feint that draws the attention and force of an enemy from the point of the principal operation
di·ver·sion·ary \də-'vər-zhə-,ner-ē, dī-, -shə-\ *adj* (1846) **:** tending to draw attention away from the principal concern **:** being a diversion
di·ver·sion·ist \-zhə-nəst, -shə-\ *n* (1937) **1 :** one engaged in diversionary activities **2 :** one characterized by political deviation
di·ver·si·ty \də-'vər-sət-ē, dī-\ *n, pl* **-ties** (14c) **1 :** the condition of being different **:** VARIETY **2 :** an instance or a point of difference
di·vert \də-'vərt, dī-\ *vb* [ME *diverten*, fr. MF & L; MF *divertir*, fr. L *divertere* to turn in opposite directions, fr. *dis-* + *vertere* to turn — more at WORTH] *vi* (15c) **:** to turn aside **:** DEVIATE ⟨was trained as a doctor but *~ed* to diplomacy⟩ ~ *vt* **1 a :** to turn from one course or use to another **:** DEFLECT **b :** DISTRACT **2 :** to give pleasure to esp. by distracting the attention from what burdens or distresses ***syn*** see AMUSE
di·ver·tic·u·li·tis \,dī-vər-,tik-yə-'līt-əs\ *n* (ca. 1900) **:** inflammation of a diverticulum
di·ver·tic·u·lo·sis \-'lō-səs\ *n* (1917) **:** an intestinal disorder characterized by the presence of many diverticula
di·ver·tic·u·lum \,dī-vər-'tik-yə-ləm\ *n, pl* **-la** \-lə\ [NL, fr. L, bypath, prob. alter. of *deverticulum*, fr. *devertere* to turn aside, fr. *de-* + *vertere*] (1647) **1 :** a pocket or closed branch opening off a main passage **2 :** an abnormal pouch or sac opening from a hollow organ (as the intestine or bladder)
di·ver·ti·men·to \di-,vərt-ə-'ment-(,)ō, -,vert-\ *n, pl* **-men·ti** \-'ment-(,)ē\ *or* **-mentos** [It, lit., diversion, fr. *divertire* to divert, amuse, fr. L *divertere*] (1823) **1 :** an instrumental chamber work in several movements usu. light in character **2 :** DIVERTISSEMENT 1
di·ver·tisse·ment \di-'vərt-əs-mənt, -əz-, *F* dē-ver-tē-smä^n\ *n, pl* **divertissements** \-mən(t)s, -smä^n(z)\ [F, lit., diversion, fr. *divertiss-* (stem of *divertir*)] (1728) **1 :** a ballet suite used as an interlude **2 :** DIVERTIMENTO 1 **3 :** DIVERSION, ENTERTAINMENT
Di·ves \'dī-(,)vēz\ *n* [ME, fr. L, rich, rich man; misunderstood as a proper name in Lk 16:19] (14c) **:** a rich man
di·vest \dī-'vest, də-\ *vt* [alter. of *devest*] (1583) **1 a :** to undress or strip esp. of clothing, ornament, or equipment **b :** to deprive or dispossess esp. of property, authority, or title **c :** RID, FREE **2 :** to take away from a person — **di·vest·ment** \-'ves(t)-mənt\ *n*
di·ves·ti·ture \dī-'ves-tə-,chu̇(ə)r, -chər, -t(y)u̇(ə)r, də-\ *n* [*divest* + *-iture* (as in *investiture*)] (1601) **1 :** the act of divesting **2 :** the compulsory transfer of title or disposal of interests (as stock in a corporation) upon government order
[1]**di·vide** \də-'vīd\ *vb* **di·vid·ed; di·vid·ing** [ME *dividen*, fr. L *dividere*, fr. *dis-* + *-videre* to separate — more at WIDOW] *vt* (14c) **1 a :** to separate into two or more parts, areas, or groups **b :** to separate into classes, categories, or divisions **c :** CLEAVE, PART **2 a :** to separate into portions and give out in shares **:** DISTRIBUTE **b :** to possess, enjoy, or make use of in common **c :** APPORTION **3 a :** to cause to be separate, distinct, or apart from one another **b :** to separate into opposing sides or parties **c :** to cause (a parliamentary body) to vote by division **4 a :** to mark divisions on **:** GRADUATE ⟨~ a sextant⟩ **b** (1) **:** to subject (a number or quantity) to the operation of finding how many times it contains another number or quantity ⟨~ 42 by 14⟩ (2) **:** to be used as a divisor with respect to (a dividend) ⟨4 *~s* 16 evenly⟩ (3) **:** to use as a divisor — used with *into* ⟨~ 14 into 42⟩ ~ *vi* **1 :** to perform mathematical division **2 a** (1) **:** to undergo replication, multiplication, fission, or separation into parts (2) **:** to branch out **b :** to become separated or disunited esp. in opinion or interest ***syn*** SEPARATE, DISTRIBUTE — **di·vid·able** \-'vīd-ə-bəl\ *adj*
[2]**divide** *n* (1642) **1 :** an act of dividing **2 a :** a dividing ridge between drainage areas **:** WATERSHED **b :** a point or line of division
di·vid·ed *adj* (14c) **1 a :** separated into parts or pieces **b** *of a leaf* **:** cut into distinct parts by incisions extending to the base or to the midrib **c :** having the opposing streams of traffic separated (as by a median strip) ⟨a ~ highway⟩ **2 a :** disagreeing with each other **:** DISUNITED **b :** directed or moved toward conflicting interests, states, or objects ⟨~ loyalties⟩ **3 :** separated by distance ⟨familiar objects from which she had never dreamed of being ~ —James Joyce⟩
div·i·dend \'div-ə-,dend, -əd-ənd\ *n* [ME *divident*, fr. L *dividendus*, gerundive of *dividere*] (15c) **1 :** an individual share of something distributed: as **a :** a share in a pro rata distribution (as of profits) to stockholders **b :** a share of surplus allocated to a policyholder in a participating insurance policy **2 a :** a resultant return or reward **b :** BONUS **3 a :** a number to be divided **b :** a sum or fund to be divided and distributed
di·vid·er \də-'vīd-ər\ *n* (1526) **1 :** one that divides **2** *pl* **:** an instrument for measuring or marking (as in dividing lines) **3 :** something serving as a partition between separate spaces within a larger area
di·vi–di·vi \,dē-vē-'dē-vē, ,div-ē-'div-ē\ *n* [Sp *dividivi*, of Cariban origin; akin to Cumanagoto *diwidiwi* divi-divi] (ca. 1837) **:** a small leguminous tree (*Caesalpinia coriaria*) of tropical America with twisted astringent pods that contain a large proportion of tannin
div·i·na·tion \,div-ə-'nā-shən\ *n* [ME *divinacioun*, fr. L *divination-*, *divinatio*, fr. *divinatus*, pp. of *divinare*] (14c) **1 :** the art or practice that seeks to foresee or foretell future events or discover hidden knowledge usu. by the interpretation of omens or by the aid of supernatural pow-

ers **2** : unusual insight : intuitive perception — **di·vi·na·to·ry** \də-ˈvin-ə-ˌtōr-ē, də-ˈvī-nə-, ˈdiv-ə-nə-, -ˌtȯr-\ *adj*

[1]di·vine \də-ˈvīn\ *adj* **di·vin·er; -est** [ME *divin,* fr. MF, fr. L *divinus,* fr. *divus* god — more at DEITY] (14c) **1 a :** of, relating to, or proceeding directly from God or a god ⟨the ~ right of kings⟩ **b :** being a deity ⟨the ~ Savior⟩ **c :** directed to a deity ⟨~ worship⟩ **2 a :** supremely good : SUPERB ⟨her pies were simply ~⟩ **b :** HEAVENLY, GODLIKE — **di·vine·ly** *adv*

[2]divine *n* [ME, fr. ML *divinus,* fr. L, soothsayer, fr. *divinus,* adj.] (14c) **1 :** CLERGYMAN **2 :** THEOLOGIAN

[3]divine *vb* **di·vined; di·vin·ing** [ME *divinen,* fr. MF & L; MF *diviner,* fr. L *divinare,* fr. *divinus,* n.] *vt* (14c) **1 :** to discover intuitively : INFER **2 :** to discover or locate (as water or minerals underground) usu. by means of a divining rod ~ *vi* **1 :** to practice divination : PROPHESY **2 :** to perceive intuitively *syn* see FORESEE

Divine Liturgy *n* (1870) : the eucharistic rite of Eastern churches

Divine Office *n* (14c) : the office for the canonical hours of prayer that priests and religious say daily

di·vin·er \də-ˈvī-nər\ *n* (14c) **1 :** one that practices divination : SOOTHSAYER **2 :** one that seeks to divine the location of water or minerals underground

divine right *n* (1600) : the right of a sovereign to rule as set forth by the theory of government that holds that a monarch receives the right to rule directly from God and not from the people

divine service *n* (14c) : a service of Christian worship; *specif* : such a service that is not sacramental in character

diving bell *n* (1661) : a diving apparatus consisting of a container open only at the bottom and supplied with compressed air by a hose

diving board *n* (1893) : SPRINGBOARD 1

diving duck *n* (1813) : any of various ducks (as a bufflehead) that frequent deep waters and obtain their food by diving

diving suit *n* (1908) : a waterproof suit with a removable helmet that is worn by a diver who is supplied with air pumped through a tube

divining rod *n* (1751) : a forked rod believed to indicate the presence of water or minerals esp. by dipping downward when held over a vein

di·vin·i·ty \də-ˈvin-ət-ē\ *n, pl* **-ties** (14c) **1 :** THEOLOGY **2 :** the quality or state of being divine **3** *often cap* : a divine being: as **a :** GOD 1 **b** (1) : GOD 2 (2) : GODDESS **4 :** fudge made of whipped egg whites, sugar, and nuts

divinity school *n* (1555) : a professional school having a religious curriculum esp. for ministerial candidates

di·vis·i·ble \də-ˈviz-ə-bəl\ *adj* (15c) : capable of being divided — **di·vis·i·bil·i·ty** \də-ˌviz-ə-ˈbil-ət-ē\ *n*

di·vi·sion \də-ˈvizh-ən\ *n* [ME, fr. MF, fr. L *division-, divisio,* fr. *divisus,* pp. of *dividere* to divide] (14c) **1 a :** the act or process of dividing : the state of being divided **b :** the act, process, or an instance of distributing among a number : DISTRIBUTION **c** *obs* : a method of arranging or disposing (as troops) **2 :** one of the parts or groupings into which a whole is divided or is divisible **3 :** the condition or an instance of being divided in opinion or interest : DISAGREEMENT, DISUNITY ⟨exploited the ~s between the two countries⟩ **4 a :** something that divides, separates, or marks off **b :** the act, process, or an instance of separating or keeping apart : SEPARATION **5 :** the mathematical operation of dividing something **6 a :** a self-contained major military unit capable of independent action **b :** a tactical military unit composed of headquarters and usu. three to five brigades **c** (1) : the basic naval administrative unit (2) : a tactical subdivision of a squadron of ships **d :** a unit of the U. S. Air Force higher than a wing and lower than an air force **7 a :** a portion of a territorial unit marked off for a particular purpose (as administrative or judicial functions) **b :** an administrative or operating unit of a governmental, business, or educational organization **8 :** the physical separation into different lobbies of the members of a parliamentary body voting for and against a question **9 :** plant propagation by dividing parts and planting segments capable of producing roots and shoots **10 :** a group of organisms forming part of a larger group; *specif* : a primary category of the plant kingdom **11 :** a competitive class or category (as in boxing or wrestling) *syn* see PART — **di·vi·sion·al** \-ˈvizh-nəl, -ən-ᵊl\ *adj*

di·vi·sion·ism \-ˈvizh-ə-ˌniz-əm\ *n, often cap* (1901) : POINTILLISM — **di·vi·sion·ist** \-ˈvizh-(ə-)nəst\ *n or adj*

division of labor (1776) : the breakdown of labor into its components and their distribution among different persons, groups, or machines to increase productive efficiency

division sign *n* (ca. 1934) **1 :** the symbol ÷ used to indicate division **2 :** the diagonal / used to indicate a fraction

di·vi·sive \də-ˈvī-siv *also* -ˈvis-iv *or* -ˈviz-iv *or* -ˈvī-ziv\ *adj* (1642) : creating disunity or dissension — **di·vi·sive·ly** *adv* — **di·vi·sive·ness** *n*

di·vi·sor \də-ˈvī-zər\ *n* (15c) : the number by which a dividend is divided

[1]di·vorce \də-ˈvō(ə)rs, -ˈvȯ(ə)rs *also* dī-\ *n* [ME *divorse,* fr. MF, fr. L *divortium,* fr. *divertere, divortere* to divert, to leave one's husband] (14c) **1 :** a legal dissolution of a marriage **2 :** SEPARATION, SEVERANCE

[2]divorce *vb* **di·vorced; di·vorc·ing** *vt* (15c) **1 a :** to end marriage with (one's spouse) by divorce **b :** to dissolve the marriage contract between **2 :** to terminate an existing relationship or union : SEPARATE ⟨~ church from state⟩ ~ *vi* : to obtain a divorce *syn* see SEPARATE — **di·vorce·ment** \-ˈvōr-smənt, -ˈvȯr-\ *n*

di·vor·cé \də-ˌvōr-ˈsā, -ˌvȯr-, -ˈsē, -ˈvōr-ˌ, -ˈvȯr-ˌ\ *n* (1877) : a divorced man

di·vor·cée \də-ˌvōr-ˈsā, -ˌvȯr-, -ˈsē, -ˈvōr-ˌ, -ˈvȯr-ˌ\ *n* [F, fr. fem. of *divorcé,* pp. of *divorcer* to divorce, fr. MF *divorse*] (1813) : a divorced woman

div·ot \ˈdiv-ət\ *n* [origin unknown] (15c) **1** *Scot* : a square of turf or sod **2 :** a piece of turf dug from a golf fairway in making a shot

di·vulge \də-ˈvəlj, dī-\ *vt* **di·vulged; di·vulg·ing** [ME *divulgen,* fr. L *divulgare,* fr. *dis-* + *vulgare* to make known, fr. *vulgus* mob — more at VULGAR] (15c) **1** *archaic* : to make public : PROCLAIM **2 :** to make known (as a confidence or secret) *syn* see REVEAL — **di·vul·gence** \-ˈvəl-jən(t)s\ *n*

div·vy \ˈdiv-ē\ *vt* **div·vied; div·vy·ing** [by shortening & alter. fr. *divide*] (1877) : DIVIDE, SHARE — often used with *up* ⟨*divvied* up the candy⟩

Dix·ie \ˈdik-sē\ *n* [name for the Southern states in the song *Dixie* (1859) by Daniel D. Emmett †1904 Am. songwriter] (1859) : the Southern states of the U.S.

Dix·ie·crat \-ˌkrat\ *n* (1948) : a dissident Southern Democrat; *specif* : a supporter of a 1948 presidential ticket opposing the civil rights stand of the Democrats — **Dix·ie·crat·ic** \ˌdik-sē-ˈkrat-ik\ *adj*

Dix·ie·land \-ˌland\ *n* [prob. fr. the *Original Dixieland Jazz Band*] (1927) : jazz music in duple time usu. played by a small band and characterized by ensemble and solo improvisation

di·zen \ˈdīz-ᵊn, ˈdiz-ᵊn\ *vt* [earlier *disen* to dress a distaff with flax, fr. MD] *archaic* (1619) : BEDIZEN

di·zy·got·ic \ˌdī-zī-ˈgät-ik\ *also* **di·zy·gous** \(ˈ)dī-ˈzī-gəs\ *adj* [*di-* + *zygotic, -zygous*] *of twins* (ca. 1916) : FRATERNAL

[1]diz·zy \ˈdiz-ē\ *adj* **diz·zi·er; -est** [ME *disy,* fr. OE *dysig* stupid; akin to OHG *tusig* stupid, L *furere* to rage — more at DUST] (bef. 12c) **1 :** FOOLISH, SILLY **2 a :** having a whirling sensation in the head with a tendency to fall **b :** mentally confused **3 a :** causing giddiness or mental confusion **b :** caused by or marked by giddiness **c :** extremely rapid — **diz·zi·ly** \ˈdiz-ə-lē\ *adv* — **diz·zi·ness** \-ē-nəs\ *n*

[2]dizzy *vt* **diz·zied; diz·zy·ing** (1501) **1 :** to make dizzy or giddy **2 :** BEWILDER ⟨prospects so brilliant as to ~ the mind⟩ — **diz·zy·ing·ly** \-ē-iŋ-lē\ *adv*

djel·la·ba *also* **djel·la·bah** \jə-ˈläb-ə\ *n* [F *djellaba,* fr. Ar *jallābīya*] (1919) : a long loose garment with full sleeves and a hood

djin·ni \jē-nē\ *or* **djinn** *or* **djin** \ˈjin\ *var of* JINNI

dl- \(ˈ)dē-ˈel, ˈdē-ˌ\ *prefix* **1** *also* **d,l-** : consisting of equal amounts of the dextro and levo forms of a specified compound ⟨*dl*-tartaric acid⟩ **2 :** consisting of equal amounts of the D- and L- forms of a specified compound ⟨DL-fructose⟩

D layer *n* (ca. 1934) : a layer that may exist within the D region of the ionosphere; *also* : D REGION

D–mark \ˌdȯich(-ə)-ˈmärk\ *n* (1948) : DEUTSCHE MARK

DMSO \ˌdē-ˌem-ˌes-ˈō\ *n* (1964) : DIMETHYL SULFOXIDE

DMT \ˌdē-(ˌ)em-ˈtē\ *n* (ca. 1966) : DIMETHYLTRYPTAMINE

DNA \ˌdē-ˌen-ˈā\ *n* [*d*eoxyribo*n*ucleic *a*cid] (1944) : any of various nucleic acids that are localized esp. in cell nuclei, are the molecular basis of heredity in many organisms, and are constructed of a double helix held together by hydrogen bonds between purine and pyrimidine bases which project inward from two chains containing alternate links of deoxyribose and phosphate — compare RECOMBINANT DNA

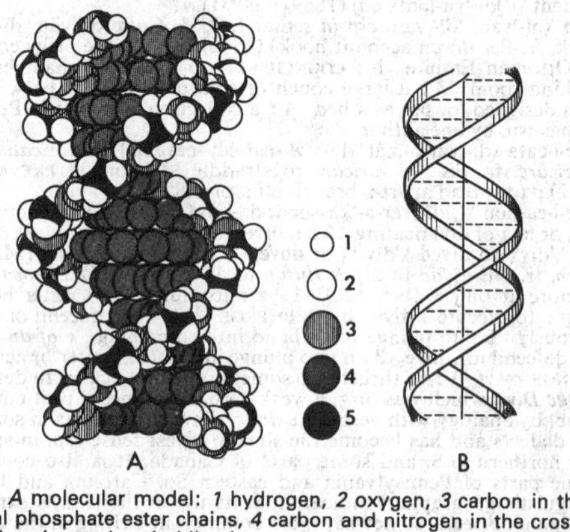

DNA: *A* molecular model: *1* hydrogen, *2* oxygen, *3* carbon in the helical phosphate ester chains, *4* carbon and nitrogen in the cross-linked purine and pyrimidine bases, *5* phosphorus; *B* double helix

DNA polymerase *n* (ca. 1962) : any of several polymerases that promote replication or repair of DNA usu. using single-stranded DNA as a template

DN·ase \(ˈ)dē-ˈen-ˌās, -ˌāz\ *also* **DNA·ase** \(ˌ)dē-ˌen-ˈā-ˌās, -ˌāz\ *n* (ca. 1956) : DEOXYRIBONUCLEASE

[1]do \(ˈ)dü, də(-w)\ *vb* **did** \(ˈ)did, dəd\; **done** \ˈdən\; **do·ing** \ˈdü-iŋ\; **does** \(ˈ)dəz\ [ME *don,* fr. OE *dōn;* akin to OHG *tuon* to do, L *-dere* to put, *facere* to make, do, Gk *tithenai* to place, set] *vt* (bef. 12c) **1 :** to bring to pass : CARRY OUT **2 :** PUT — used chiefly in *do to death* **3 a :** PERFORM, EXECUTE ⟨~ some work⟩ ⟨~ one's duty⟩ **b :** COMMIT ⟨crimes *done* deliberately⟩ **4 a :** BRING ABOUT, EFFECT ⟨sleep will ~ you good⟩ **b :** to give freely : PAY ⟨~ honor to his memory⟩ **5 :** to bring to an end : FINISH — used in the past participle ⟨the job is finally *done*⟩ **6 :** to put forth : EXERT ⟨*did* his best to win the race⟩ **7 :** to wear out esp. by physical exertion : EXHAUST ⟨at the end of the race they were pretty well *done*⟩ **8 :** to bring into existence : PRODUCE ⟨~ a biography on the general⟩ **9 a :** to play the role or character of **b :** MIMIC **c :** to act in or serve as producer of **10 :** to treat unfairly; *esp* : CHEAT ⟨*did* him out of his inheritance⟩ **11 :** to treat or deal with in any way typically with the sense of preparation or with that of care or attention: **a** (1) : to put in order : CLEAN ⟨was ~*ing* the kitchen when the phone rang⟩ (2) : to make ready for use : WASH ⟨*did* the dishes right after supper⟩ **b :** COOK ⟨like my steak *done* rare⟩ **c :** SET, ARRANGE ⟨had her hair *done*⟩ **d :** to apply cosmetics to ⟨wanted to ~ her face before the party⟩ **e :** DECORATE, FURNISH ⟨*did* the living room in Early American⟩ **12 a :** to work at esp. as a vocation ⟨what to ~ after college⟩ **b :** to prepare or work out esp. by studying ⟨~*ing* his homework⟩ **13 a :** to pass over (as distance) : TRAVERSE **b :** to travel at a speed of ⟨~*ing* 55 on the turnpike⟩ **14 :** TOUR ⟨~*ing* 12 countries in 30 days⟩ **15 :** to serve out (as a term) in prison **16 :** to serve the needs of : SUIT ⟨worms will ~ us for bait⟩ **17 :** to approve esp. by custom, opinion, or propriety ⟨you oughtn't to say a thing like that . . . it's not *done* —Dorothy Sayers⟩ **18** — used as a substitute verb to avoid repetition ⟨if you must make such a racket, ~ it somewhere else⟩ **19 :** USE *vt* 3 ⟨doesn't ~ drugs⟩ ~ *vi* **1 :** ACT, BEHAVE ⟨~ as I say⟩ **2 a :** GET ALONG, FARE ⟨~ well in school⟩ **b :** to carry on business or affairs : MANAGE ⟨we can ~ without your help⟩ **c :** to make good use ⟨~ with a cup of coffee⟩ **3** : to take place : HAPPEN ⟨what's ~*ing* across the street⟩ **4** : to come to or make an end : FINISH — used in the past participle **5** : to be active or busy ⟨let us then be up and ~*ing* —H. W. Longfellow⟩ **6** : to be adequate or sufficient : SERVE ⟨half of that will ~⟩ **7** : to be fitting : conform to custom or propriety ⟨won't ~ to be late⟩ **8** — used as a substitute verb to avoid repetition ⟨wanted to run and play as children ~⟩ **9** — used in the imperative after an imperative to add emphasis ⟨be quiet ~⟩ ~ *verbal auxiliary* **1 a** — used with the infinitive without *to* to form present and past tenses in legal and parliamentary language ⟨~ hereby bequeath⟩ and in poetry ⟨give what she *did* crave —Shak.⟩ **b** — used with the infinitive without *to* to form present and past tenses in declarative sentences with inverted word order ⟨fervently ~ we pray —Abraham Lincoln⟩, in interrogative sentences ⟨*did* you hear that⟩, and in negative sentences ⟨we *don't* know⟩ ⟨*don't* go⟩ **2** — used with the infinitive without *to* to form present and past tenses expressing emphasis ⟨I ~ say⟩ ⟨~ be careful⟩ — **do·able** \'dü-ə-bəl\ *adj* — **do a number on** : to defeat or confound thoroughly — **do away with 1** : to put an end to : ABOLISH **2** : to put to death : KILL — **do by** : to deal with : TREAT — **do for 1** : to attend to the wants and needs of : take care of ⟨*did for* her while she was sick⟩ **2** : to bring about the death or ruin of — **do one's thing** : to do what is personally satisfying — **do proud** : to give cause for pride or gratification — **to do** : necessary to be done ⟨ten thousand times I've done my best and all's *to do* again —A. E. Housman⟩

²**do** \'dü\ *n, pl* **dos** *or* **do's** \'düz\ (1599) **1** *chiefly dial* : FUSS, ADO **2** *archaic* : DEED, DUTY **3 a** : a festive get-together : AFFAIR, PARTY **b** *chiefly Brit* : BATTLE **4** : a command or entreaty to do something ⟨consider all the ~s and don'ts of the problem⟩ **5** *Brit* : CHEAT, SWINDLE

³**do** \'dō\ *n* [It] (ca. 1754) : the 1st tone of the diatonic scale in solmization

dob·bin \'däb-ən\ *n* [*Dobbin,* nickname for *Robert*] (1596) **1** : a farm horse **2** : a quiet plodding horse

dob·by \'däb-ē\ *n, pl* **dobbies** [perh. fr. Eng dial. *dobby* brownie, sprite, fr. *Dobby,* nickname for *Robert*] (1878) **1** : a loom attachment for weaving small figures **2** : a fabric or figured weave made with a dobby

Do·ber·man pin·scher \'dō-bər-mən-'pin-chər\ *n* [G *Dobermann-pinscher,* fr. Ludwig *Dobermann,* 19th cent. Ger. dog breeder + G *pinscher,* a breed of hunting dog] (1917) : a short-haired medium-sized dog of a breed of German origin — called also **Doberman**

do·bra \'dō-brə, 'dób-rə\ *n* [Pg, fr. fem. of *dobro* double, fr. L *duplus* — more at DOUBLE] (1977) — see MONEY table

Do·bro \'dō-(ˌ)brō\ *trademark* — used for an acoustic guitar having a metal resonator

dob·son \'däb-sən\ *n* [prob. fr. the name *Dobson*] (1884) : HELLGRAMMITE

dob·son·fly \-ˌflī\ *n* (ca. 1902) : a winged megalopterous insect (family Corydalidae) with very long slender mandibles in the male and a large carnivorous aquatic larva — compare HELLGRAMMITE

doc \'däk\ *n* (1850) : DOCTOR

do·cent \'dōs-ᵊnt, dō(t)-'sent\ *n* [obs. G (now *dozent*), fr. L *docent-, docens,* prp. of *docēre*] (1880) **1** : a college or university teacher or lecturer **2** : a person who conducts groups through a museum or art gallery

do·ce·tic \dō-'sēt-ik, -'set-\ *adj, often cap* [Gk *Dokētai* Docetists, fr. *dokein* to seem — more at DECENT] (1846) : of or relating to Docetism or the Docetists

Do·ce·tism \dō-'sēt-ˌiz-əm, 'dō-sə-ˌtiz-\ *n* (1846) : a belief opposed as heresy in early Christianity that Christ only seemed to have a human body and to suffer and die on the cross — **Do·ce·tist** \-'sēt-əst, -sət-əst\ *n*

doch-an-dor·rach \ˌdäk-ən-'dòr-ək\ *or* **doch-an-dor·ris** \-'dòr-əs\ *n* [ScGael & IrGael *deoch an doruis,* lit., drink of the door] *Scot & Irish* (1682) : a parting drink : STIRRUP CUP

doc·ile \'däs-əl *also* -ˌīl, *esp Brit* 'dō-ˌsīl\ *adj* [L *docilis,* fr. *docēre* to teach; akin to L *decēre* to be fitting — more at DECENT] (15c) **1** : easily taught **2** : easily led or managed : TRACTABLE **syn** see OBEDIENT — **doc·ile·ly** \'däs-ə(l)-lē\ *adv* — **do·cil·i·ty** \dä-'sil-ət-ē, dō-\ *n*

¹**dock** \'däk\ *n* [ME, fr. OE *docce;* akin to MD *docke* dock, ScGael *dogha* burdock] (bef. 12c) **1** : any of a genus (*Rumex*) of the buckwheat family of coarse weedy plants that have long taproots and are used as potherbs and in folk medicine **2** : any of several usu. broad-leaved weedy plants

²**dock** *n* [ME *dok,* perh. fr. OE *-docca* (as in *fingirdocca* finger muscle); akin to OHG *tocka* doll, ON *dokka* bundle] (14c) **1** : the solid part of an animal's tail as distinguished from the hair **2** : the part of an animal's tail left after it has been shortened

³**dock** *vt* (14c) **1 a** : to cut off the end of a body part of; *specif* : to remove part of the tail of **b** : to cut (as ears or a tail) short **2 a** : to take away a part of : ABRIDGE **b** : to subject (as wages) to a deduction **3** : to deprive of a benefit ordinarily due esp. as a penalty for a fault ⟨was ~*ed* for tardiness⟩

⁴**dock** *n* [prob. fr. MD *docke* dock, ditch, fr. L *duction-, ductio* act of leading — more at DOUCHE] (15c) **1** : a usu. artificial basin or enclosure for the reception of ships that is equipped with means for controlling the water height **2** : the waterway extending between two piers for the reception of ships **3** : a place (as a wharf or platform) for the loading or unloading of materials **4** : scaffolding for the inspection and repair of aircraft; *broadly* : HANGAR

⁵**dock** *vt* (1600) **1** : to haul or guide into a dock **2** : to join (as two spacecraft) mechanically while in space ~ *vi* **1** : to come into dock **2** : to become docked

⁶**dock** *n* [Flem *docke* cage] (1586) : the place in a criminal court where a prisoner stands or sits during trial — **in the dock** : on trial

dock·age \'däk-ij\ *n* (1648) **1** : a charge for the use of a dock **2** : the docking of ships **3** : docking facilities

¹**dock·er** \'däk-ər\ *n* (1810) : one that docks the tails of animals

²**docker** *n* (1887) : one connected with docks; *esp* : LONGSHOREMAN

¹**dock·et** \'däk-ət\ *n* [ME *doggette*] (15c) **1** : a brief written summary of a document : ABSTRACT **2 a** (1) : a formal abridged record of the proceedings in a legal action (2) : a register of such records **b** (1) : a list of legal causes to be tried (2) : a calendar of business matters to be acted on : AGENDA **3** : an identifying statement about a document placed on its outer surface or cover

²**docket** *vt* (1615) **1** : to place on the docket for legal action **2** : to make a brief abstract of (as a legal matter) and inscribe it in a list **3** : to inscribe (as a document) with an identifying statement

dock·hand \'däk-ˌhand\ *n* (1920) : LONGSHOREMAN

dock·land \-ˌland\ *n, Brit* (1904) : the part of a port occupied by docks; *also* : a residential section adjacent to docks

dock·side \-ˌsīd\ *n* (1887) : the shore or area adjacent to a dock

dock·work·er \-ˌwər-kər\ *n* (1921) : LONGSHOREMAN

dock·yard \-ˌyärd\ *n* (1704) **1** : SHIPYARD **2** *Brit* : NAVY YARD

¹**doc·tor** \'däk-tər\ *n* [ME *doctour* teacher, doctor, fr. MF & ML; MF, fr. ML *doctor,* fr. L, teacher, fr. *doctus,* pp. of *docēre* to teach — more at DOCILE] (14c) **1 a** : an eminent theologian declared a sound expounder of doctrine by the Roman Catholic Church — called also *doctor of the church* **b** : a learned or authoritative teacher **c** : a person who has earned one of the highest academic degrees (as a PhD) conferred by a university **d** : a person awarded an honorary doctorate (as an LLD or LittD) by a college or university **2 a** : one skilled or specializing in healing arts; *esp* : a physician, surgeon, dentist, or veterinarian licensed to practice his profession **b** : MEDICINE MAN **3 a** : material added (as to food) to produce a desired effect **b** : a blade (as of metal) for spreading a coating or scraping a surface **4** : a usu. makeshift and emergency mechanical contrivance or attachment for remedying a difficulty **5** : a person who restores or repairs things — **doc·tor·al** \-t(ə-)rəl\ *adj* — **doc·tor·less** \-tər-ləs\ *adj* — **doc·tor·ship** \-ˌship\ *n*

²**doctor** *vb* **doc·tored; doc·tor·ing** \-t(ə-)riŋ\ *vt* (1712) **1 a** : to give medical treatment to **b** : to restore to good condition : REPAIR ⟨~ an old clock⟩ **2 a** : to adapt or modify for a desired end by alteration or special treatment ⟨~*ed* the play to suit the audience⟩ ⟨the drink was ~*ed*⟩ **b** : to alter deceptively ⟨accused of ~*ing* the election returns⟩ ~ *vi* **1** : to practice medicine **2** *dial* : to take medicine

doc·tor·ate \'däk-t(ə-)rət\ *n* (1676) : the degree, title, or rank of a doctor

doctor book *n* (1902) : a book intended to supplement the knowledge of the individual in matters of home medication

¹**doc·tri·naire** \ˌdäk-trə-'na(ə)r, -'ne(ə)r\ *n* [F, fr. *doctrine*] (1831) : one who attempts to put into effect an abstract doctrine or theory with little or no regard for practical difficulties

²**doctrinaire** *adj* (1834) : of, relating to, or characteristic of a doctrinaire : DOGMATIC **syn** see DICTATORIAL — **doc·tri·nair·ism** \-'na(ə)r-ˌiz-əm, -'ne(ə)r-\ *n*

doc·trin·al \'däk-trən-ᵊl, *esp Brit* däk-'trīn-\ *adj* (15c) : of, relating to, or preoccupied with doctrine — **doc·trin·al·ly** \-ᵊl-ē\ *adv*

doc·trine \'däk-trən\ *n* [ME, fr. MF & L; MF, fr. L *doctrina,* fr. *doctor*] (14c) **1** *archaic* : TEACHING, INSTRUCTION **2 a** : something that is taught **b** : a principle or position or the body of principles in a branch of knowledge or system of belief : DOGMA **c** : a principle of law established through past decisions **d** : a statement of fundamental government policy esp. in international relations

docu·dra·ma \'däk-yə-ˌdräm-ə, -ˌdram-\ *n* [*documentary* + *drama*] (ca. 1961) : a television or motion-picture drama that deals with historical events

¹**doc·u·ment** \'däk-yə-mənt\ *n* [ME, fr. MF, fr. LL & L; LL *documentum* official paper, fr. L, lesson, proof, fr. *docēre* to teach — more at DOCILE] (15c) **1 a** *archaic* : PROOF, EVIDENCE **b** : an original or official paper relied on as the basis, proof, or support of something **c** : something (as a photograph or a recording) that serves as evidence or proof **2 a** : a writing conveying information **b** : a material substance (as a coin or stone) having on it a representation of the thoughts of men by means of some conventional mark or symbol **c** : DOCUMENTARY — **doc·u·men·tal** \ˌdäk-yə-'ment-ᵊl\ *adj*

²**doc·u·ment** \'däk-yə-ˌment\ *vt* (1711) **1** : to furnish documentary evidence of **2** : to furnish with documents **3 a** : to provide with factual or substantial support for statements made or a hypothesis proposed; *esp* : to equip with exact references to authoritative supporting information ⟨the thesis was well ~*ed* with footnotes on every page⟩ **b** : to construct or produce (as a movie or novel) with authentic situations or events ⟨his film ~*ed* the living conditions in the ghetto⟩ **4** : to furnish (a ship) with ship's papers — **doc·u·ment·able** \-ə-bəl, ˌdäk-yə-'\ *adj* — **doc·u·ment·er** \-ˌment-ər\ *n*

doc·u·men·tal·ist \ˌdäk-yə-'ment-ᵊl-əst\ *n* (1939) : a specialist in documentation

doc·u·men·tar·i·an \ˌdäk-yə-mən-'ter-ē-ən, -ˌmen-\ *n* [²*documentary*] (1943) : one who makes a documentary

doc·u·men·ta·rist \-'ment-ə-rəst\ *n* [²*documentary*] (1949) : DOCUMENTARIAN

¹**doc·u·men·ta·ry** \ˌdäk-yə-'ment-ə-rē, -'men-trē\ *adj* (1802) **1** : being or consisting of documents : contained or certified in writing ⟨~ evidence⟩ **2** : of, relating to, or employing documentation in literature or art; *broadly* : FACTUAL, OBJECTIVE ⟨a ~ film of the war⟩ — **doc·u·men·tar·i·ly** \-mən-'ter-ə-lē, -ˌmen-\ *adv*

²**documentary** *n, pl* **-ries** (1935) : a documentary presentation (as a film or novel)

doc·u·men·ta·tion \ˌdäk-yə-mən-'tā-shən, -ˌmen-\ *n* (1884) **1** : the act or an instance of furnishing or authenticating with documents **2 a** : the provision of documents in substantiation; *also* : documentary evidence **b** (1) : the use of historical documents (2) : conformity to historical or objective facts (3) : the provision of footnotes, appendices, or addenda referring to or containing documentary evidence **3** : INFORMATION SCIENCE **4** : the usu. printed instructions, comments, and information for using a particular piece or system of computer software or hardware — **doc·u·men·ta·tion·al** \-shnəl, -shən-ᵊl\ *adj*

¹**dod·der** \'däd-ər\ *n* [ME *doder*] (13c) : any of a genus (*Cuscuta*) of dicotyledonous leafless elongated wiry herbs that are deficient in chlorophyll and are parasitic on other plants

²**dodder** *vi* **dod·dered; dod·der·ing** \'däd-(ə-)riŋ\ [ME *dadiren*] (14c) **1** : to tremble or shake from weakness or age **2** : to progress feebly and unsteadily ⟨an old man ~*ing* down the walk⟩ — **dod·der·er** \-ər-ər\ *n*

\ə\ abut \ᵊ\ kitten, F table \ər\ further \a\ ash \ā\ ace \ä\ cot, cart \aú\ out \ch\ chin \e\ bet \ē\ easy \g\ go \i\ hit \ī\ ice \j\ job \ŋ\ sing \ō\ go \ò\ law \òi\ boy \th\ thin \t͟h\ the \ü\ loot \ù\ foot \y\ yet \zh\ vision \ä, ḵ, ⁿ, œ, œ̄, ᵫ, ᵮ, �\ see Guide to Pronunciation

dod·dered \'däd-ərd\ *adj* [prob. alter. of *dodded,* fr. pp. of E dial. *dod* to lop, fr. ME *dodden*] (1697) **1** : deprived of branches through age or decay ⟨a ~ oak⟩ **2** : INFIRM, ENFEEBLED

dod·der·ing \'däd-(ə-)riŋ\ *adj* (1898) : FEEBLE, SENILE ⟨a ~ old fogy⟩

dod·dery \-(ə-)rē\ *adj* (1866) **1** : DODDERED **2** : DODDERING

dodeca- *or* **dodec-** *comb form* [L, fr. Gk *dōdeka-, dōdek-,* fr. *dōdeka, dyōdeka,* fr. *dyō, dyo* two + *deka* ten] : twelve ⟨*dodecaphonic*⟩

do·deca·gon \dō-'dek-ə-ˌgän\ *n* [Gk *dōdekagōnon,* fr. *dōdeka-* + *-gōnon* -gon] (ca. 1658) : a polygon of 12 angles and 12 sides

do·deca·he·dron \ˌ(ˌ)dō-ˌdek-ə-'hē-drən\ *n, pl* **-drons** *or* **-dra** \-drə\ [Gk *dōdekaedron,* fr. *dōdeka-* + *-edron* -hedron] (ca. 1570) : a solid having 12 plane faces — **do·deca·he·dral** \-drəl\ *adj*

do·deca·phon·ic \ˌ(ˌ)dō-ˌdek-ə-'fän-ik\ *adj* [*dodeca-* + *phon-* + *-ic*] (1949) : TWELVE-TONE — **do·deca·phon·i·cal·ly** \-i-k(ə-)lē\ *adv* — **do·deca·pho·nist** \dō-'dek-ə-fə-nəst, -ˌfō-; ˌdōd-i-'kaf-ə-nəst\ *n* — **do·deca·pho·ny** \-nē\ *n*

¹dodge \'däj\ *vb* **dodged; dodg·ing** [origin unknown] *vi* (1568) **1** : to evade a responsibility or a duty esp. by trickery or deceit **2 a** : to move to and fro or from place to place usu. in an irregular course ⟨*dodged* through the crowd⟩ **b** : to make a sudden movement in a new direction ⟨as to evade a blow⟩ ⟨*dodged* behind the door⟩ ~ *vt* **1** : to evade ⟨as a duty⟩ usu. indirectly and by trickery ⟨*dodged* the draft by leaving the country⟩ **2 a** : to evade by a sudden or repeated shift of position **b** : to avoid an encounter with **3** : to reduce the intensity of ⟨a portion of a photograph⟩ by selectively shading during printing

²dodge *n* (1575) **1** : an act of evading by sudden bodily movement **2 a** : an artful device to evade, deceive, or trick **b** : EXPEDIENT

dodge·ball \'däj-ˌbȯl\ *n* (1922) : a game in which players stand in a circle and try to hit opponents within the circle with a large inflated ball

dodg·er \'däj-ər\ *n* (1568) **1** : one that dodges; *esp* : one who uses tricky devices **2** : a small leaflet : CIRCULAR **3** : CORN DODGER

dodg·ery \'däj-(ə-)rē\ *n, pl* **-er·ies** (1670) : EVASION, TRICKERY

dodgy \'däj-ē\ *adj* (1861) **1** *chiefly Brit* : EVASIVE, TRICKY **2** *Brit* : not sound, stable, or reliable **3** *Brit* : requiring skill or care in handling; *also* : CHANCY, RISKY

do·do \'dōd-(ˌ)ō\ *n, pl* **dodoes** *or* **dodos** [Pg *doudo,* fr. *doudo* silly, stupid] (1628) **1** : an extinct heavy flightless bird ⟨*Raphus cucullatus,* syn. *Didus ineptus*⟩ of the island of Mauritius that is related to the pigeon and larger than a turkey **b** : an extinct bird of the island of Réunion similar to and apparently closely related to the dodo **2 a** : one hopelessly behind the times **b** : a stupid person

doe \'dō\ *n, pl* **does** *or* **doe** [ME *do,* fr. OE *dā;* akin to G dial. *tē* doe] (bef. 12c) : the adult female fallow deer; *broadly* : the female esp. when adult of any of various mammals of which the male is called buck

do·er \'dü-ər\ *n* (14c) : one that takes an active part ⟨a thinker or a ~⟩

does *pres 3d sing of* DO, *pl of* DOE

doe·skin \'dō-ˌskin\ *n* (15c) **1** : the skin of does or leather made of it; *also* : soft leather from sheep- or lambskins **2** : a compact coating and sportswear fabric napped and felted for a smooth surface

doesn't \'dəz-ⁿt\ : does not

do·est \'dü-əst\ *archaic pres 2d sing of* DO

do·eth \'dü-əth\ *archaic pres 3d sing of* DO

doff \'däf, 'dȯf\ *vt* [ME *doffen,* fr. *don* to do + *of* off] (14c) **1 a** : to remove ⟨an article of wear⟩ from the body **b** : to take off ⟨the hat⟩ in greeting or as a sign of respect **2** : to rid oneself of : put aside ⟨among his intimate friends his studied reserve was ~ed —W. J. Ghent⟩

¹dog \'dȯg\ *n, often attrib* [ME, fr. OE *docga*] (bef. 12c) **1 a** : CANID: **a** : a highly variable domestic mammal ⟨*Canis familiaris*⟩ closely related to the common wolf ⟨*Canis lupus*⟩ **b** : a male dog **2 a** : a worthless person **b** : FELLOW, CHAP ⟨a lazy ~⟩ ⟨you lucky ~⟩ **3 a** : any of various usu. simple mechanical devices for holding, gripping, or fastening that consist of a spike, rod, or bar **b** : ANDIRON **4 a** : SUN DOG **b** : FOGBOW **5** : uncharacteristic or affected stylishness or dignity ⟨liked to put on the ~⟩ **6** *cap* : either of the constellations Canis Major or Canis Minor **7** *pl* : FEET **8** *pl* : RUIN ⟨go to the ~s⟩ **9** : one inferior of its kind: as **a** : an investment ⟨as a stock or bond⟩ not worth its price **b** : a slow-moving or undesirable piece of merchandise **10** : an unattractive girl or woman **11** : ¹HOT DOG — **dog·like** \'dȯ-ˌglīk\ *adj*

²dog *adj* (14c) **1** : CANINE **2** : SPURIOUS; *esp* : unlike that used by native speakers or writers ⟨~ Latin⟩ ⟨~ French⟩

³dog *vt* **dogged; dog·ging** (1519) **1 a** : to hunt or track like a hound **b** : to worry as if by pursuit with dogs : HOUND **2** : to fasten with a dog — **dog it** : to fail to do one's best : GOLDBRICK

⁴dog *adv* (ca. 1552) : EXTREMELY, UTTERLY ⟨*dog*-tired⟩

dog and pony show *n* (1970) : an often elaborate public relations or sales presentation

dog·bane \'dȯg-ˌbān\ *n* (1597) : any of a genus ⟨*Apocynum* of the family Apocynaceae, the dogbane family⟩ comprising chiefly tropical and often poisonous plants with milky juice and usu. showy flowers

dog biscuit *n* (ca. 1858) **1** : a hard dry cracker for dogs **2** : a hard coarse cracker ⟨as hardtack⟩ for human consumption

dog·cart \'dȯg-ˌkärt\ *n* (1668) **1** : a cart drawn by a dog **2** : a light two-wheeled carriage with two transverse seats set back to back

dog·catch·er \-ˌkach-ər, -ˌkech-\ *n* (1837) : a community official assigned to catch and dispose of stray dogs

dog collar *n* (1524) **1** : a collar for a dog **2** *slang* : CLERICAL COLLAR **3** : a wide flexible snug-fitting necklace

dog days *n pl* [fr. their being reckoned from the heliacal rising of the Dog Star ⟨Sirius⟩] (1538) **1** : the period between early July and early September when the hot sultry weather of summer usu. occurs in the northern hemisphere **2** : a period of stagnation or inactivity

dog·dom \'dȯg-dəm\ *n* (1854) : the world of dogs or of dog fanciers ⟨the elite of purebred ~ —W. R. Fletcher⟩

doge \'dōj\ *n* [It dial., fr. L *duc-, dux* leader — more at DUKE] (1549) : the chief magistrate in the republics of Venice and Genoa

dog-ear \'dȯ-ˌgi(ə)r\ *n* (1725) : the turned-down corner of a page esp. of a book — **dog-ear** *vt*

dog-eared \'dȯ-ˌgi(ə)rd\ *adj* (1784) **1** : having dog-ears ⟨a ~ book⟩ **2** : SHABBY, WORN

dog-eat–dog \ˌdȯ-ˌgēt-'dȯg\ *adj* (1834) : marked by ruthless self–interest ⟨~ competition⟩

dog·face \'dȯg-ˌfās\ *n* (1941) : SOLDIER; *esp* : INFANTRYMAN

dog fennel *n* (14c) **1** : a strong-scented European chamomile ⟨*Anthemis cotula*⟩ naturalized along roadsides in the U.S. **2** : an annual compos-

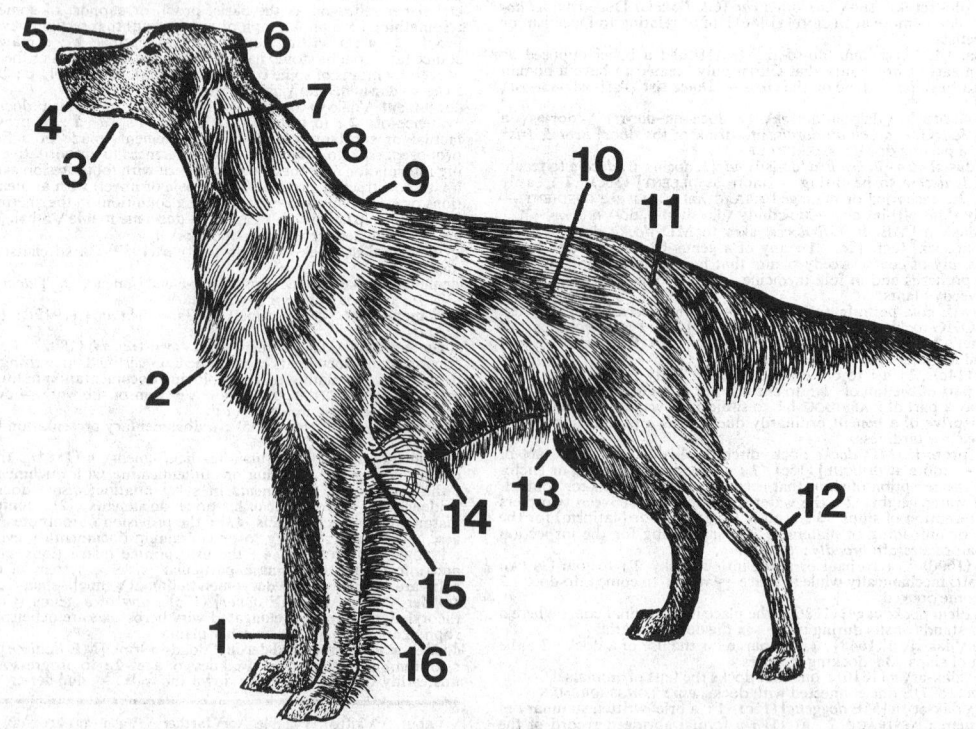

dog 1a: *1* pastern, *2* chest, *3* flews, *4* muzzle, *5* stop, *6* occiput, *7* leather, *8* crest, *9* withers, *10* loin, *11* point of rump, *12* hock or tarsus, *13* knee or stifle, *14* brisket, *15* elbow, *16* feathering

ite weed (*Eupatorium capillifolium*) with dissected leaves and a lax inflorescence

dog·fight \ˈdȯg-ˌfīt\ *n* (1656) **1 :** a fight between dogs; *broadly* **:** a fiercely disputed contest **2 :** a fight between two or more fighter planes usu. at close quarters — **dogfight** *vi*

dog·fish \-ˌfish\ *n* (15c) **:** any of various small sharks (as of the families Squalidae, Carcharhinidae, and Scyliorhinidae) that often appear in schools near shore, are destructive to fish, and have livers valued for oil and flesh often made into fertilizer

dog·ged \ˈdȯ-gəd\ *adj* (1653) **:** marked by stubborn determination ***syn*** see OBSTINATE — **dog·ged·ly** *adv* — **dog·ged·ness** *n*

1**dog·ger·el** \ˈdȯg-(ə-)rəl, ˈdäg-\ *adj* [ME *dogerel*] (14c) **:** loosely styled and irregular in measure esp. for burlesque or comic effect; *also* **:** marked by triviality or inferiority ⟨~ lines of verse⟩

2**doggerel** *n* (1630) **1 :** doggerel verse **2 :** an example of doggerel verse

dog·gery \ˈdȯ-gə-rē\ *n, pl* **-ger·ies** (1830) **:** a cheap saloon **:** DIVE

dog·gie bag *or* **doggy bag** \ˈdȯ-gē-\ *n* [1*doggy;* fr. the presumption that such leftovers are intended for a pet dog] (1963) **:** a bag used for carrying home leftover food and esp. meat from a meal eaten at a restaurant

dog·gish \ˈdȯ-gish\ *adj* (15c) **1 :** CANINE **2 :** stylish in a showy way — **dog·gish·ly** *adv* — **dog·gish·ness** *n*

dog·go \ˈdȯ-(ˌ)gō\ *adv* [prob. fr. 1*dog*] (1893) **:** in hiding — used chiefly in the phrase *to lie doggo*

1**dog·gone** \ˈdäg-ˈgän, ˈdȯg-ˈgȯn\ *vb* **dog·goned; dog·gon·ing** [euphemism for *God damn*] (1828) **:** DAMN

2**doggone** *n* (1928) **:** DAMN

dog·goned *or* **dog·gone** \ˌdäg-ˌgän(d), ˌdȯg-ˌgȯn(d)\ *adj or adv* (1851) **:** DAMNED

1**dog·gy** *or* **dog·gie** \ˈdȯ-gē\ *n, pl* **doggies** (1825) **:** a small dog

2**dog·gy** \ˈdȯ-gē\ *adj* **dog·gi·er; -est** (1859) **1 :** concerned with or fond of dogs ⟨a book for ~ experts⟩ **2 :** resembling or suggestive of a dog ⟨~ odor⟩ **3 :** STYLISH, SHOWY

dog·house \ˈdȯg-ˌhau̇s\ *n* (1611) **:** a shelter for a dog — **in the doghouse :** in a state of disfavor

do·gie \ˈdō-gē\ *n* [origin unknown] *chiefly West* (1888) **:** a motherless calf in a range herd

dog in the manger [fr. the fable of the dog who prevented an ox from eating hay which he did not want himself] (1573) **:** a person who selfishly withholds from others something useless to himself

1**dog·leg** \ˈdȯ-ˌgleg, -ˌglāg\ *adj* (1889) **:** crooked or bent like a dog's hind leg

2**dogleg** *n* (ca. 1909) **1 a :** something having an abrupt angle **b :** a sharp bend (as in a road) **2 :** a golf hole having an angled fairway

3**dogleg** *vi* (1947) **:** to proceed along a dogleg course ⟨the single narrow street that ~*s* through town —Russ Leadabrand⟩

dog·ma \ˈdȯg-mə, ˈdäg-\ *n, pl* **dogmas** *also* **dog·ma·ta** \-mət-ə\ [L *dogmat-, dogma,* fr. Gk, fr. *dokein* to seem — more at DECENT] (1638) **1 a :** something held as an established opinion; *esp* **:** a definite authoritative tenet **b :** a code of such tenets ⟨pedagogical ~⟩ **c :** a point of view or tenet put forth as authoritative without adequate grounds **2 :** a doctrine or body of doctrines concerning faith or morals formally stated and authoritatively proclaimed by a church

dog·mat·ic \dȯg-ˈmat-ik, däg-\ *adj* (ca. 1681) **1 :** characterized by or given to the use of dogmatism ⟨a ~ critic⟩ **2 :** of or relating to dogma ***syn*** see DICTATORIAL — **dog·mat·i·cal** \-i-kəl\ *adj* — **dog·mat·i·cal·ly** \-i-k(ə-)lē\ *adv* — **dog·mat·i·cal·ness** \-i-kəl-nəs\ *n*

dog·mat·ics \-iks\ *n pl but sing or pl in constr* (ca. 1855) **:** a branch of theology that seeks to interpret the dogmas of a religious faith

dogmatic theology *n* (1874) **:** DOGMATICS

dog·ma·tism \ˈdȯg-mə-ˌtiz-əm, ˈdäg-\ *n* (1603) **1 :** positiveness in assertion of opinion esp. when unwarranted or arrogant **2 :** a viewpoint or system of ideas based on insufficiently examined premises

dog·ma·tist \-mət-əst\ *n* (1541) **:** one who dogmatizes

dog·ma·tize \ˈdȯg-mə-ˌtīz, ˈdäg-\ *vb* **-tized; -tiz·ing** [F *dogmatiser,* fr. LL *dogmatizare,* fr. Gk *dogmatizein,* fr. *dogmat-, dogma*] *vi* (1611) **:** to speak or write dogmatically ~ *vt* **:** to state as a dogma or in a dogmatic manner — **dog·ma·ti·za·tion** \ˌdȯg-mət-ə-ˈzā-shən, ˌdäg-\ *n* — **dog·ma·tiz·er** *n*

dog·nap \ˈdȯg-ˌnap\ *vt* **-napped** *or* **-naped** \-ˌnapt\; **-nap·ping** *or* **-nap·ing** \-ˌnap-iŋ\ [1*dog* + *-nap* (as in *kidnap*)] (1947) **:** to steal (a dog) often for the purpose of selling to a scientific laboratory — **dog·nap·per** *or* **dog·nap·er** *n*

do–good \ˈdü-ˌgu̇d\ *adj* (1952) **:** designed sometimes impracticably and too zealously toward bettering the conditions under which others live — **do–good·ism** \-ˌiz-əm\ *n*

do–good·er \-ər\ *n* (1926) **:** an earnest usu. impractical and often naive and ineffectual humanitarian or reformer

do–good·ing \-iŋ\ *n* (1940) **:** the activities of a do-gooder — **do–gooding** *adj*

dog paddle *n* (1904) **:** an elementary form of swimming in which the arms paddle in the water and the legs maintain a kicking motion — **dog–pad·dle** *vi*

dog rose *n* [trans. of L *rosa canina,* trans. of Gk *kynorodon,* fr. *kyno-* (fr. *kyōn* dog) + *rhodon* rose — more at HOUND] (ca. 1597) **:** a common European wild rose (*Rosa canina*)

dogs·body \ˈdȯgz-ˌbäd-ē\ *n* [Brit naval slang *dogsbody* pudding made of peas, junior officer] *chiefly Brit* (1922) **:** DRUDGE

dog's chance *n* (1902) **:** a bare chance in one's favor

dog·sled \ˈdȯg-ˌsled\ *n* (1810) **:** a sled drawn by dogs

dog's life *n* (1542) **:** a miserable drab existence

Dog Star *n* **1 :** SIRIUS **2 :** PROCYON

dog tag *n* (1918) **1 :** a metal disk or plate on a dog collar bearing a license registration number **2 :** a military identification tag

dog·tooth \ˈdȯg-ˌtüth\ *n* (1552) **1 :** CANINE 1, EYETOOTH **2 :** an architectural ornament common in early English Gothic consisting usu. of four leaves radiating from a raised point at the center

dogtooth violet *n* (1629) **:** any of a genus (*Erythronium*) of small spring-flowering bulbous herbs of the lily family

1**dog·trot** \ˈdȯg-ˌträt\ *n* (15c) **1 :** a quick easy gait suggesting that of a dog **2** *Southern & Midland* **:** a roofed passage similar to a breezeway; *esp* **:** one connecting two parts of a cabin

2**dogtrot** *vi* (1900) **:** to move or progress at a dogtrot

dog·watch \ˈdȯ-ˌgwäch\ *n* (1700) **1 :** either of two watches of two hours on shipboard that extend from 4 to 6 and 6 to 8 p.m. **2 :** any of various night shifts; *esp* **:** the last shift

dog·wood \ˈdȯ-ˌgwu̇d\ *n* (1617) **:** any of a genus (*Cornus*) of trees and shrubs (family Cornaceae, the dogwood family) with heads of small flowers and often showy involucres

doi·ly \ˈdȯi-lē\ *n, pl* **doilies** [*Doily* or *Doyley fl* 1711 London draper] (1711) **1 :** a small napkin **2 :** a small often decorative mat

do in *vt* (1905) **1 a :** to bring about the defeat or destruction of **:** RUIN ⟨the financial loss *did* him *in*⟩ **b :** to bring about the death of **:** KILL ⟨tried to *do* him *in* with a club⟩ **c :** EXHAUST, WEAR OUT ⟨walking all day nearly *did* us *in*⟩ **2 :** CHEAT

do·ing \ˈdü-iŋ\ *n* (14c) **1 :** the act of performing or executing **:** ACTION ⟨that will take a great deal of ~⟩ **2** *pl* **a :** things that are done or that occur ⟨everyday ~*s*⟩ **b :** social activities

doit \ˈdȯit\ *n* [D *duit;* akin to ON *thveiti* small coin, *thveita* to hew] (1594) **1 :** an old Dutch coin equal to about 1/8 stiver **2 :** TRIFLE 1

do–it–your·self \ˌdü-ə-chər-ˈself\ *adj* (1952) **:** of, relating to, or designed for use by or as if by an amateur or hobbyist ⟨~ tools⟩ ⟨~ car model kit⟩ — **do–it–your·self·er** \-ˈsel-fər\ *n*

do·jo \ˈdō-(ˌ)jō\ *n, pl* **dojos** [Jp *dōjō,* fr. *dō* way, art + *-jō* ground] (1942) **:** a school for training in various arts of self-defense (as judo and karate)

Dol·by \ˈdȯl-bē, ˈdōl-\ *trademark* — used for an electronic device that eliminates noise from recorded sound or sound broadcast on FM radio

dol·ce \ˈdōl-(ˌ)chā\ *adj or adv* [It, lit., sweet, fr. L *dulcis* — more at DULCET] (ca. 1847) **:** SOFT, SMOOTH — used as a direction in music

dol·ce far nien·te \ˈdōl-chē-ˌfär-nē-ˈent-ē\ *n* [It, lit., sweet doing nothing] (1814) **:** pleasant relaxation in carefree idleness

dol·ce vi·ta \ˌdōl-chä-ˈvē-(ˌ)tä\ *n* [It, lit., sweet life] (1961) **:** a life of indolence and self-indulgence

dol·drums \ˈdōl-drəmz, ˈdäl-, ˈdȯl-\ *n pl* [prob. akin to OE *dol* foolish] (1811) **1 :** a spell of listlessness or despondency **:** BLUES **2 :** a part of the ocean near the equator abounding in calms, squalls, and light shifting winds **3 :** a state of inactivity, stagnation, or slump

1**dole** \ˈdōl\ *n* [ME, fr. OE *dāl* portion — more at DEAL] (bef. 12c) **1** *archaic* **:** one's allotted share, portion, or destiny **2 a (1) :** a giving or distribution of food, money, or clothing to the needy **(2) :** a grant of government funds to the unemployed **b :** something distributed at intervals to the needy **c :** something portioned out and distributed usu. grudgingly or bit by bit

2**dole** *vt* **doled; dol·ing** (15c) **1 :** to give or distribute as a charity **2 :** to give or deliver in small portions **:** PARCEL — used with *out* ***syn*** see DISTRIBUTE

3**dole** *n* [ME *dol,* fr. OF, fr. LL *dolus,* alter. of L *dolor*] *archaic* (13c) **:** GRIEF, SORROW

dole·ful \ˈdōl-fəl\ *adj* (13c) **1 :** causing grief or affliction ⟨a ~ loss⟩ **2 :** full of grief **:** CHEERLESS ⟨a ~ face⟩ **3 :** expressing grief **:** SAD ⟨a ~ melody⟩ — **dole·ful·ly** \-fə-lē\ *adv* — **dole·ful·ness** *n*

dol·er·ite \ˈdäl-ə-ˌrīt\ *n* [F *dolérite,* fr. Gk *doleros* deceitful, fr. *dolos* deceit; fr. its being easily mistaken for diorite — more at TALE] (1838) **1 :** any of various coarse basalts **2** *Brit* **:** DIABASE 3 **3 :** any of various dark igneous rocks whose constituents are not determinable megascopically — **dol·er·it·ic** \ˌdäl-ə-ˈrit-ik\ *adj*

dole·some \ˈdōl-səm\ *adj* (1533) **:** DOLEFUL

dolich- *or* **dolicho-** *comb form* [Gk, fr. *dolichos* — more at LONG] **:** long

dol·i·cho·ce·phal·ic \ˌdäl-i-kō-sə-ˈfal-ik\ *adj* (1849) **:** having a relatively long head with cephalic index of less than 75 — **dol·i·cho·ceph·a·ly** \-ˈsef-ə-lē\ *n*

doll \ˈdäl, ˈdȯl\ *n* [prob. fr. *Doll,* nickname for *Dorothy*] (1700) **1 :** a small-scale figure of a human being used esp. as a child's plaything **2 a (1) :** a pretty but often empty-headed young woman **(2) :** WOMAN **b :** DARLING, SWEETHEART **c :** an attractive person — **doll·ish** \-ish\ *adj* — **doll·ish·ly** *adv* — **doll·ish·ness** *n*

dol·lar \ˈdäl-ər\ *n, often attrib* [D or LG *daler,* fr. G *taler,* short for *joachimstaler,* fr. Sankt *Joachimsthal,* Bohemia, where talers were first made] (1553) **1 :** TALER **2 :** any of numerous coins patterned after the taler (as a Spanish peso) **3 a :** any of various basic monetary units (as in the U.S. and Canada) — see MONEY table **b :** a coin, note, or token representing one dollar

dollar averaging *n* (ca. 1926) **:** investment in a security at regular intervals of a uniform sum regardless of the price level in order to obtain an overall reduction in cost per unit — called also *dollar cost averaging*

dollar–a–year *adj* (1918) **:** compensated by a token salary usu. for government service ⟨a ~ man⟩

dollar day *n* (1949) **:** a day on which a merchant makes special offerings of goods and services for one dollar; *broadly* **:** a day on which bargain prices are offered

dollar diplomacy *n* (1910) **1 :** diplomacy used by a country to promote its financial or commercial interests abroad **2 :** diplomacy that seeks to strengthen the power of a country or effect its purposes in foreign relations by the use of its financial resources

dollar sign *n* (1881) **:** a mark $ placed before a number to indicate that it stands for dollars — called also *dollar mark*

doll·house \ˈdäl-ˌhau̇s, ˈdȯl-\ *n* (1783) **1 :** a child's small-scale toy house **2 :** a dwelling so small as to suggest resemblance to a house for dolls

1**dol·lop** \ˈdäl-əp\ *n* [origin unknown] (ca. 1825) **1 a :** a lump or blob of a usu. semiliquid substance ⟨a ~ of jelly⟩ **b :** a small usu. unmeasured amount of liquid **:** DASH ⟨coffee laced with a ~ of brandy⟩ **2 :** a small amount or admixture ⟨prose without one ~ of sentimentality —Ann Currah⟩

2**dollop** *vt* (ca. 1860) **:** to serve or dispense in dollops

doll up *vt* (1906) **1 :** to dress elegantly or extravagantly **2 :** to make more attractive (as by addition of decorative details)

\ə\ abut \ᵊ\ kitten, F table \ər\ further \a\ ash \ā\ ace \ä\ cot, cart
\au̇\ out \ch\ chin \e\ bet \ē\ easy \g\ go \i\ hit \ī\ ice \j\ job
\ŋ\ sing \ō\ go \ȯ\ law \ȯi\ boy \th\ thin \th\ the \ü\ loot \u̇\ foot
\y\ yet \zh\ vision \á, k, ⁿ, œ, œ̄, ue, ue̅, ʸ\ *see* Guide to Pronunciation

[1]**dol·ly** \'däl-ē, 'dȯ-lē\ *n, pl* **dollies** (1648) **1 :** DOLL **2 a :** a wooden-pronged instrument for beating and stirring clothes in the process of washing them in a tub **b :** a device turning on a vertical axis by a handle or winch for stirring ore to be washed **3 :** a heavy bar with a cupped head for holding against the head of a rivet while the other end is being headed **4 :** a compact narrow-gauge railroad locomotive for moving construction trains and for switching **5 a :** a platform on a roller or on wheels or casters for moving heavy objects **b :** a wheeled platform for a television or motion-picture camera

[2]**dolly** *vb* **dol·lied; dol·ly·ing** *vt* (1831) **1 :** to treat with a dolly **2 :** to move or convey on a dolly ~ *vi* **:** to move a motion-picture or television camera about on a dolly while shooting a scene

dol·ly·bird \'däl-ē-,bərd, 'dȯ-lē-\ *n, Brit* (1966) **:** a pretty young woman

Dol·ly Var·den trout \,däl-ē-'värd-ᵊn-\ *n* [after *Dolly Varden,* gaily dressed coquette in *Barnaby Rudge* (1841), novel by Charles Dickens] (ca. 1876) **:** a large char (*Salvelinus malma*) widespread in streams of western No. America and Japan as well as in coastal salt waters — called also *Dolly Varden*

dol·ma \'däl-mə, 'dȯl-, -(,)mä\ *n, pl* **dolmas** *or* **dol·ma·des** \däl-'mäd-(,)ēz, dȯl-\ [Turk, lit., something stuffed, fr. *dolma* stuffed] (ca. 1889) **:** a stuffed grape leaf or vegetable shell

dol·man \'dōl-mən, 'dȯl-, 'däl-\ *n, pl* **dolmans** [F *doliman,* fr. Turk *dolama,* a Turkish robe] (ca. 1872) **:** a woman's coat made with dolman sleeves

dolman sleeve *n* (1934) **:** a sleeve very wide at the armhole and tight at the wrist often cut in one piece with the bodice

dol·men \'dōl-mən, 'dȯl-, 'däl-\ *n* [F, fr. Bret *tolmen,* fr. *tol* table + *men* stone] (1859) **:** a prehistoric monument of two or more upright stones supporting a horizontal stone slab found esp. in Britain and France and thought to be a tomb

do·lo·mite \'dō-lə-,mīt, 'däl-ə-\ *n* [F, fr. Déodat de *Dolomieu* †1801 Fr. geologist] (1794) **1 :** a mineral $CaMg(CO_3)_2$ consisting of a calcium magnesium carbonate found in crystals and in extensive beds as a compact limestone **2 :** a limestone or marble rich in magnesium carbonate — **do·lo·mit·ic** \,dō-lə-'mit-ik, ,däl-ə-\ *adj*

do·lo·mi·tize \'dō-lə-mə-,tīz, 'däl-ə-\ *vt* **-tized; -tiz·ing** (1863) **:** to convert into dolomite — **do·lo·mi·ti·za·tion** \,dō-lə-mət-ə-'zā-shən, ,däl-ə-, -,mīt-\ *n*

do·lor \'dō-lər, 'däl-ər\ *n* [ME *dolour,* fr. MF, fr. L *dolor* pain, grief, fr. *dolēre* to feel pain, grieve — more at CONDOLE] (14c) **:** mental suffering or anguish **:** SORROW

do·lor·ous \'dō-lə-rəs, 'däl-ə-\ *adj* (15c) **:** causing, marked by, or expressive of misery or grief — **do·lor·ous·ly** *adv* — **do·lor·ous·ness** *n*

dolour *chiefly Brit var of* DOLOR

dol·phin \'däl-fən, 'dȯl-\ *n* [ME, fr. MF *dophin, daufin,* fr. OF *dalfin,* fr. OProv, fr. ML *dalfinus,* alter. of L *delphinus,* fr. Gk *delphin-, delphis;* akin to Gk *delphys* womb, Skt *garbha*] (14c) **1 a :** any of various small toothed whales (family Delphinidae) with the snout more or less elongated into a beak and the neck vertebrae partially fused **b :** PORPOISE 1 **2 :** either of two active pelagic percoid food fishes (genus *Coryphaena*) of tropical and temperate seas **3** *cap* **:** DELPHINUS **4 :** a spar or buoy for mooring boats; *also* **:** a cluster of closely driven piles used as a fender for a dock or as a mooring or guide for boats

dolphin 1a

dolphin striker *n* (ca. 1890) **:** a vertical spar under the end of the bowsprit of a sailboat to extend and support the martingale

dolt \'dōlt\ *n* [prob. akin to OE *dol* foolish] (1543) **:** a stupid person — **dolt·ish** \'dōl-tish\ *adj* — **dolt·ish·ly** *adv* — **dolt·ish·ness** *n*

Dom [L *dominus* master] (1716) **1** \(,)däm\ — used as a title for some monks and canons regular **2** \(,)dōⁿ\ — used as a title prefixed to the Christian name of a Portuguese or Brazilian man of rank

-dom \dəm\ *n suffix* [ME, fr. OE *-dōm;* akin to OHG *-tuom* -dom, OE *dōm* judgment — more at DOOM] **1 a :** dignity **:** office ⟨duke*dom*⟩ **b :** realm **:** jurisdiction ⟨king*dom*⟩ **2 :** state or fact of being ⟨free*dom*⟩ **3 :** those having a (specified) office, occupation, interest, or character ⟨official*dom*⟩

do·main \dō-'mān, də-\ *n* [ME *domayne,* fr. MF *domaine, demaine,* fr. L *dominium,* fr. *dominus*] (15c) **1 a :** complete and absolute ownership of land — compare EMINENT DOMAIN **b :** land so owned **2 :** a territory over which dominion is exercised **3 :** a region distinctively marked by some physical feature ⟨the ~ of rushing streams, tall trees, and lakes⟩ **4 :** a sphere of influence or activity ⟨the ~ of art⟩ **5 :** the set of elements to which a mathematical or logical variable is limited; *specif* **:** the set on which a function is defined **6 :** any of the small randomly oriented regions of uniform magnetization in a ferromagnetic substance **7 :** INTEGRAL DOMAIN

[1]**dome** \'dōm\ *n* [F, It, & L; F *dôme* dome, cathedral, fr. It *duomo* cathedral, fr. ML *domus* church, fr. L, house — more at TIMBER] (1513) **1** *archaic* **:** a stately building **:** MANSION **2 :** a large hemispherical roof or ceiling **3 :** a natural formation or structure that resembles the dome or cupola of a building **4 :** a form of crystal composed of planes parallel to a lateral axis that meet above in a horizontal edge like a roof **5 :** an upward fold in rock whose sides dip uniformly in all directions — **dom·al** \'dō-məl\ *adj*

[2]**dome** *vb* **domed; dom·ing** *vt* (1876) **1 :** to cover with a dome **2 :** to form into a dome ~ *vi* **:** to swell upward or outward like a dome

Domes·day Book \'dümz-,dā-, 'dōmz-\ *n* [ME, fr. *domesday* doomsday] (1591) **:** a record of a survey of English lands and landholdings made by order of William the Conqueror about 1086

[1]**do·mes·tic** \də-'mes-tik\ *adj* [MF *domestique,* fr. L *domesticus,* fr. *domus*] (15c) **1 a :** living near or about the habitations of humans **b :** TAME, DOMESTICATED **2 :** of, relating to, or carried on within a country and esp. one's own country ⟨~ politics⟩ ⟨~ wines⟩ **3 :** of or relating to the household or the family **4 :** devoted to home duties and pleasures **5 :** INDIGENOUS — **do·mes·ti·cal·ly** \-ti-k(ə-)lē\ *adv*

[2]**domestic** *n* (1613) **1 :** a household servant **2 :** an article of domestic manufacture — usu. used in pl.

domestic animal *n* (ca. 1855) **:** any of various animals (as the horse or sheep) domesticated by man so as to live and breed in a tame condition

[1]**do·mes·ti·cate** \də-'mes-ti-,kāt\ *vt* **-cat·ed; -cat·ing** (ca. 1639) **1 :** to bring into domestic use **:** ADOPT **2 :** to adapt (an animal or plant) to life in intimate association with and to the advantage of man **3 :** to fit for domestic life **4 :** to bring to the level of ordinary people **:** FAMILIARIZE — **do·mes·ti·ca·tion** \-,mes-ti-'kā-shən\ *n*

[2]**do·mes·ti·cate** \-kət, -,kāt\ *n* (1951) **:** a domesticated animal or plant

do·mes·tic·i·ty \,dō-,mes-'tis-ət-ē, -məs-; ,däm-əs-, -,es-; də-,mes-\ *n, pl* **-ties** (1721) **1 :** the quality or state of being domestic or domesticated **2 :** domestic activities or life **3** *pl* **:** domestic affairs

domestic prelate *n* (1929) **:** a priest having permanent honorary membership in the papal household

domestic relations court *n* (1939) **:** COURT OF DOMESTIC RELATIONS

domestic science *n* (1869) **:** instruction and training in domestic management and the household arts (as cooking and sewing)

dom·i·cal \'dō-mi-kəl, 'däm-i-\ *adj* (1846) **:** relating to, shaped like, or having a dome

[1]**do·mi·cile** \'däm-ə-,sīl, 'dō-mə-; 'däm-ə-səl\ *also* **dom·i·cil** \'däm-ə-səl\ *n* [MF, fr. L *domicilium,* fr. *domus*] (15c) **1 :** a dwelling place **:** place of residence **:** HOME **2 a :** a person's fixed, permanent, and principal home for legal purposes **b :** RESIDENCE 2b

[2]**domicile** *vt* **-ciled; -cil·ing** (1809) **:** to establish in or provide with a domicile

do·mi·cil·i·ary \,däm-ə-'sil-ē-,er-ē, ,dō-mə-\ *adj* (1790) **:** of, relating to, or constituting a domicile: as **a :** provided or taking place in the home ⟨~ meal service for elderly and housebound people⟩ **b :** providing care and living space for persons (as veterans) so disabled as to be unable to live independently ⟨the ~ section of the state hospital⟩

do·mi·cil·i·ate \,däm-ə-'sil-ē-,āt, ,dō-mə-\ *vb* **-at·ed; -at·ing** [L *domicilium*] *vt* (1778) **1 :** DOMICILE **2 :** DOMESTICATE 2, 4 ~ *vi* **:** RESIDE — **do·mi·cil·i·a·tion** \-,sil-ē-'ā-shən\ *n*

dom·i·nance \'däm(-ə)-nən(t)s\ *n* (1819) **:** the fact or state of being dominant: as **a :** dominant position in an order of forcefulness **:** ASCENDANCY; *specif* **:** the relative position of an individual in a social hierarchy **b :** the property of one of a pair of alleles or traits that suppresses expression of the other in the heterozygous condition **c :** the influence or control over ecological communities exerted by a dominant **d :** functional asymmetry between a pair of bodily structures (as the right and left hands)

[1]**dom·i·nant** \-nənt\ *adj* [MF or L; MF, fr. L *dominant-, dominans,* prp. of *dominari*] (15c) **1 :** commanding, controlling, or prevailing over all others **2 :** overlooking and commanding from a superior elevation **3 :** of, relating to, or exerting ecological dominance **4 :** being the one of a pair of bodily structures that is the more effective or predominant in action ⟨~ eye⟩ **5 :** of, relating to, or exerting genetic dominance — **dom·i·nant·ly** *adv*

syn DOMINANT, PREDOMINANT, PARAMOUNT, PREPONDERANT, SOVEREIGN mean superior to all others in power, influence, or importance. DOMINANT applies to something that is uppermost because ruling or controlling ⟨a *dominant* social class⟩ PREDOMINANT applies to something that exerts, often temporarily, the most marked influence ⟨a *predominant* emotion⟩ PARAMOUNT implies supremacy in importance, rank, or jurisdiction ⟨inflation was the *paramount* issue in the campaign⟩ PREPONDERANT applies to an element or factor that outweighs all others in influence or effect ⟨*preponderant* evidence in his favor⟩ SOVEREIGN indicates quality or rank to which everything else is clearly subordinate or inferior ⟨the *sovereign* power resides in the people⟩

[2]**dominant** *n* (1819) **1 :** the fifth note of a diatonic scale **2 a :** a dominant genetic character or factor **b :** any of one or more kinds of organism (as a species) in an ecological community that exerts a controlling influence on the environment and thereby largely determines what other kinds of organisms are present **c :** a dominant individual in a social hierarchy

dom·i·nate \'däm-ə-,nāt\ *vb* **-nat·ed; -nat·ing** [L *dominatus,* pp. of *dominari,* fr. *dominus* master — more at DAME] *vt* (1611) **1 :** RULE, CONTROL **2 :** to exert the supreme determining or guiding influence on **3 :** to overlook from a superior elevation or command because of superior height **4 :** to have a commanding or preeminent place or position in ⟨name brands ~ the market⟩ ~ *vi* **1 :** to have or exert mastery, control, or preeminence **2 :** to occupy a more elevated or superior position — **dom·i·na·tive** \-,nāt-iv\ *adj* — **dom·i·na·tor** \-,nāt-ər\ *n*

dom·i·na·tion \,däm-ə-'nā-shən\ *n* (14c) **1 :** supremacy or preeminence over another **2 :** exercise of mastery or preponderant influence **3** *pl* **:** DOMINION 3

dom·i·neer \,däm-ə-'ni(ə)r\ *vb* [D *domineren,* fr. F *dominer,* fr. L *dominari*] *vi* (1591) **:** to exercise arbitrary or overbearing control ~ *vt* **:** to tyrannize over

dom·i·neer·ing *adj* (1588) **:** inclined to domineer ***syn*** see MASTERFUL — **dom·i·neer·ing·ly** \-iŋ-lē\ *adv* — **dom·i·neer·ing·ness** *n*

do·min·i·cal \də-'min-i-kəl\ *adj* [LL *dominicalis,* fr. *dominicus* (*dies*) the Lord's day, fr. L *dominicus* of a lord, fr. *dominus* lord, master] (15c) **1 :** of or relating to Jesus Christ as Lord **2 :** of or relating to the Lord's day

Do·min·i·can \də-'min-i-kən\ *n* [St. *Dominic*] (1632) **:** a member of a mendicant order of friars founded by St. Dominic in 1215 and dedicated esp. to preaching — **Dominican** *adj*

dom·i·nick·er \'däm-ə-,nek-ər, -,nik-\ *also* **dom·i·nick** \-(,)nik, -nek\ *n, often cap* (1806) **:** DOMINIQUE

dom·i·nie *1 usu* 'däm-ə-nē, *2 usu* 'dō-mə-\ *n* [L *domine,* voc. of *dominus*] (1612) **1** *chiefly Scot* **:** SCHOOLMASTER **2 :** CLERGYMAN

do·min·ion \də-'min-yən\ *n* [ME *dominioun,* fr. MF *dominion,* modif. of L *dominium,* fr. *dominus*] (14c) **1 :** DOMAIN **2 :** supreme authority **:** SOVEREIGNTY **3** *pl* **:** an order of angels — see CELESTIAL HIERARCHY **4** *often cap* **:** a self-governing nation of the British Commonwealth other than the United Kingdom that acknowledges the British monarch as chief of state **5 :** absolute ownership ***syn*** see POWER

Dominion Day *n* (1867) **:** July 1 observed as a legal holiday in Canada in commemoration of the proclamation of dominion status in 1867

dom·i·nique \'däm-ə-(,)nik, -,nēk\ *n* [*Dominique* (Dominica), one of the Windward islands, West Indies] (1849) **:** any of an American breed of domestic fowl with a rose comb, yellow legs, and barred plumage; *broadly* **:** a barred fowl

dom·i·no \'däm-ə-ˌnō\ *n, pl* **-noes** *or* **-nos** [F, prob. fr. L (in the ritual formula *benedicamus Domino* let us bless the Lord)] (ca. 1694) **1 a** (1) : a long loose hooded cloak usu. worn with a half mask as a masquerade costume (2) : a half mask worn over the eyes with a masquerade costume **b** : a person wearing a domino **2** [F] **a** : a flat rectangular block (as of wood or plastic) whose face is divided into two equal parts that are blank or bear usu. from one to six dots arranged as on dice faces **b** *pl but usu sing in constr* : any of several games played with a set of usu. 28 dominoes **3** : a member of a group (as of nations) expected to behave in accordance with the domino theory

domino effect *n* (1966) : a cumulative effect produced when one event initiates a succession of similar events

domino theory *n* [fr. the fact that if dominoes are stood on end one slightly behind the other, a slight push on the first will topple the others] (1965) **1** : a theory that if one nation (as in Southeast Asia) becomes Communist-controlled the neighboring nations will also become Communist-controlled **2** : the theory that if one act or event is allowed to take place a series of similar acts or events will follow

1**don** \'dän\ *vt* **donned; don·ning** [*do* + *on*] (14c) **1** : to put on (an article of wear) **2** : to envelop oneself in : ASSUME

2**don** \'dän\ *n* [Sp, fr. L *dominus* master — more at DAME] (1523) **1** : a Spanish nobleman or gentleman — used as a title prefixed to the Christian name **2** *archaic* : a person of consequence : GRANDEE **3** : a head, tutor, or fellow in a college of Oxford or Cambridge University; *broadly* : a college or university professor **4** [It, title of respect, fr. *donno*, lit., lord, fr. L *dominus*] : a powerful Mafia leader

do·na \ˌdō-nə\ *n* [Pg, fr. L *domina* lady — more at DAME] (ca. 1897) : a Portuguese or Brazilian woman of rank — used as a title prefixed to the Christian name

do·ña \'dōn-yə\ *n* [Sp, fr. L *domina*] (1622) : a Spanish woman of rank — used as a title prefixed to the Christian name

do·nate \'dō-ˌnāt, dō-'\ *vb* **do·nat·ed; do·nat·ing** [back-formation fr. *donation*] *vt* (1785) **1** : to make a gift of; *esp* : to contribute to a public or charitable cause ⟨~ a site for a park⟩ **2** : to give off or transfer (as electrons) **~** *vi* : to make a donation ***syn*** see GIVE

do·na·tion \dō-'nā-shən\ *n* [ME *donatyowne*, fr. L *donation-, donatio*, fr. *donatus*, pp. of *donare* to present, fr. *donum* gift; akin to L *dare* to give — more at DATE] (15c) **1** : the action of making a gift esp. to a charity or public institution **2** : a free contribution : GIFT

Do·na·tism \'dō-nə-ˌtiz-əm, 'dän-ə-\ *n* [*Donatus*, 4th cent. bishop of Carthage] (1588) : the doctrines of a Christian sect arising in No. Africa in 311 and holding that sanctity is essential for the administration of sacraments and church membership — **Do·na·tist** \-təst\ *n*

1**do·na·tive** \'dō-nət-iv, 'dän-ət-\ *n* (15c) : a special gift or donation

2**do·na·tive** *same or* 'dō-ˌnāt-, dō-'\ *adj* [L *donativus*, fr. *donatus*] (1559) : characterized by, capable of, or subject to donation ⟨a ~ trust⟩

do·na·tor \'dō-ˌnāt-ər, dō-'\ *n* (15c) : DONOR

1**done** \'dən\ *past part of* DO

2**done** *adj* (14c) **1** : arrived at or brought to an end **2** : doomed to failure, defeat, or death **3** : gone by : OVER **4** : physically exhausted **5** : cooked sufficiently **6** : conformable to social convention

do·nee \dō-'nē\ *n* [*donor*] (1523) : a recipient of a gift

done for \'dən-ˌfȯ(ə)r\ *adj* (1803) **1** : sunk in defeat : BEATEN **2** : mortally stricken : DOOMED **3** : left with no capacity or opportunity for recovery : RUINED

done·ness \'dən-nəs\ *n* (1927) : the condition of being cooked to the desired degree

1**dong** \'dȯŋ, 'däŋ\ *n* [origin unknown] (ca. 1930) : PENIS — usu. considered vulgar

2**dong** *n, pl* **dong** [Annamese] (1948) — see MONEY table

don·jon \'dän-jən, 'dən-\ *n* [ME — more at DUNGEON] (14c) : a massive inner tower in a medieval castle

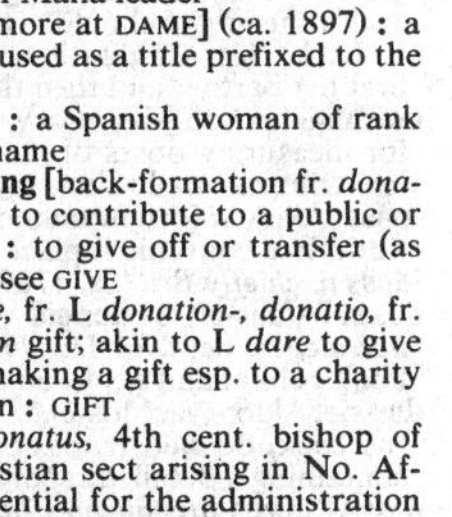

1 donjon

Don Juan \(ˌ)dän-'(h)wän, dän-'jü-ən\ *n* [Sp] **1** : a legendary Spaniard proverbial for his seduction of women **2** : a captivating man known as a great lover or seducer of women — **Don Juan·ism** \-'(h)wän-ˌiz-əm, -'jü-ə-ˌniz-\ *n*

don·key \'däŋ-kē, 'dəŋ-, 'dȯŋ-\ *n, pl* **don·keys** [origin unknown] (ca. 1785) **1** : the domestic ass (*Equus asinus*) **2** : a stupid or obstinate person

donkey engine *n* (1858) **1** : a small usu. portable auxiliary engine **2** : a small locomotive used in switching

donkey's years *n pl* (1916) : a very long time

don·key·work \'däŋ-kē-ˌwərk, 'dəŋ-, 'dȯŋ-\ *n* (1920) : monotonous and routine work : DRUDGERY

don·na \ˌdän-ə, ˌdȯn-\ *n, pl* **don·ne** \-(ˌ)ā\ [It, fr. L *domina*] (1740) : an Italian woman esp. of rank — used as a title prefixed to the Christian name

don·née \dȯ-'nā, (ˌ)də-\ *n, pl* **données** \-'nā(z)\ [F, fr. fem. of *donné*, pp. of *donner* to give, fr. L *donare* to donate — more at DONATION] (1876) : the set of assumptions on which a work of fiction or drama proceeds

don·nish \'dän-ish\ *adj* (1848) : of, relating to, or characteristic of a university don : PEDANTIC — **don·nish·ly** *adv* — **don·nish·ness** *n*

don·ny·brook \'dän-ē-ˌbrük\ *n, often cap* [*Donnybrook* Fair, annual Irish event known for its brawls] (1852) **1** : FREE-FOR-ALL **2** : a bitter quarrel carried on esp. publicly (as in politics)

do·nor \'dō-nər, -ˌnȯ(ə)r\ *n* [MF *doneur*, fr. L *donator*, fr. *donatus*] (15c) **1** : one that gives, donates, or presents something **2** : one used as a source of biological material (as blood or an organ) **3 a** : a compound capable of giving up a part (as an atom, chemical group, or subatomic particle) for combination with an acceptor **b** : an impurity that is added to a semiconductor to increase the number of mobile electrons

1**do–noth·ing** \'dü-ˌnəth-iŋ\ *n* (1579) : a shiftless or lazy person

2**do–nothing** *adj* (1832) : marked by inactivity; *specif* : marked by lack of initiative, disinclination to disturb the status quo, or failure to make positive progress — **do–noth·ing·ism** \-ˌiz-əm\ *n*

Don Qui·xote \ˌdän-kē-'(h)ōt-ē, ˌdäŋ-; dän-'kwik-sət\ *n* [Sp] : the idealistic and impractical hero of Cervantes' *Don Quixote*

don·sie *or* **don·sy** \'dän(t)-sē\ *adj* [perh. fr. ScGael *donas* evil, harm] (1786) **1** *dial Brit* : UNLUCKY **2** *Scot* **a** : RESTIVE **b** : SAUCY

1**don't** \(')dōnt\ **1** : do not **2** : does not

usage *Don't* is the earliest attested contraction of *does not* and until about 1900 was the standard form used in ordinary speech. Dialect surveys show that in the U.S. it is more common in educated speech in Midland and southern Atlantic seaboard regions than other areas but is widespread in all areas. Surveys of attitudes toward usage show it to be more widely disapproved than 40 years ago. It is considered nonstandard in writing.

2**don't** \'dōnt\ *n* (1894) : a command or entreaty not to do something

do·nut \'dō-(ˌ)nət\ *var of* DOUGHNUT

doo·dad \'dü-ˌdad\ *n* [origin unknown] (ca. 1905) **1** : a small article whose common name is unknown or forgotten : GADGET **2** : an ornamental attachment or decoration

1**doo·dle** \'düd-ᵊl\ *vb* **doo·dled; doo·dling** \'düd-liŋ, -ᵊl-iŋ\ [perh. fr. *doodle* (to ridicule)] *vi* (1937) **1** : to make a doodle **2** : DAWDLE, TRIFLE **~** *vt* : to produce by doodling — **doo·dler** \'düd-lər, -ᵊl-ər\ *n*

2**doodle** *n* (1937) : an aimless scribble, design, or sketch

doo·dle·bug \'düd-ᵊl-ˌbəg\ *n* [prob. fr. *doodle* (fool) + *bug*] (ca. 1866) **1** : the larva of an ant lion; *also* : any of several other insects **2** : a device (as a divining rod) used in attempting to locate underground gas, water, oil, or ores **3** : any of several small vehicles

doo·hick·ey \'dü-ˌhik-ē\ *n* [prob. fr. *doodad* + *hickey*] (1914) : DOODAD 1

1**doom** \'düm\ *n* [ME, fr. OE *dōm*; akin to OHG *tuom* condition, state, OE *dōn* to do] (bef. 12c) **1** : a law or ordinance esp. in Anglo-Saxon England **2 a** : JUDGMENT, DECISION; *esp* : a judicial condemnation or sentence **b** (1) : JUDGMENT 3a (2) : JUDGMENT DAY 1 **3 a** : DESTINY; *esp* : unhappy destiny **b** : DEATH, RUIN ***syn*** see FATE

2**doom** *vt* (15c) **1** : to give judgment against : CONDEMN **2 a** : to fix the fate of : DESTINE **b** : to make certain the failure or destruction of

doom·ful \'düm-fəl\ *adj* (1586) : presaging doom : OMINOUS — **doom·ful·ly** \-fə-lē\ *adv*

doom·say·er \'düm-ˌsā-ər\ *n* (1953) : one given to forebodings and predictions of impending calamity

dooms·day \'dümz-ˌdā\ *n* (bef. 12c) : JUDGMENT DAY

dooms·day·er \-ˌdā-ər, -ˌde(ə)r\ *n* (1972) : DOOMSAYER

doom·ster \'düm(p)-stər\ *n* (15c) **1** : JUDGE **2** : DOOMSAYER

door \'dō(ə)r, 'dȯ(ə)r\ *n, often attrib* [ME *dure, dor*, fr. OE *duru* door & *dor* gate; akin to OHG *turi* door, L *fores*, Gk *thyra*] (bef. 12c) **1** : a usu. swinging or sliding barrier by which an entry is closed and opened; *also* : a similar part of a piece of furniture **2** : DOORWAY **3** : a means of access ⟨~ to success⟩ — **door·less** \-ləs\ *adj* — **at one's door** : as a charge against one as being responsible ⟨laid the blame *at our door*⟩

door·bell \'dō(ə)r-ˌbel, 'dȯ(ə)r-\ *n* (1815) : a bell or set of chimes to be rung usu. by a push button at an outer door

do–or–die \'dü-ər-'dī, -ȯ(ə)r-\ *adj* (1879) **1** : doggedly determined to reach one's objective : INDOMITABLE **2** : presenting as the only alternatives complete success or complete ruin ⟨~ conflict⟩

door·jamb \'dō(ə)r-ˌjam, 'dȯ(ə)r-\ *n* (1837) : an upright piece forming the side of a door opening

door·keep·er \-ˌkē-pər\ *n* (1535) : one who tends a door

door·knob \-ˌnäb\ *n* (1846) : a knob that when turned releases a door latch

door·man \-ˌman, -mən\ *n* (ca. 1897) : one who tends the door of a building (as a hotel or theater) and assists people (as in calling taxis)

door·mat \-ˌmat\ *n* (1665) **1** : a mat placed before or inside a door for wiping dirt from the shoes **2** : one that submits without protest to abuse or indignities

door·nail \-ˌnāl, -'nā(ə)l\ *n* (14c) : a large-headed nail — used chiefly in the phrase *dead as a doornail*

door·plate \-ˌplāt\ *n* (1823) : a nameplate on a door

door·post \-ˌpōst\ *n* (1535) : DOORJAMB

door prize *n* (1951) : a prize awarded to the holder of a winning ticket passed out at the entrance to an entertainment or function

door·sill \'dō(ə)r-ˌsil, 'dȯ(ə)r-\ *n* (1563) : SILL 1b

door·step \-ˌstep\ *n* (1767) : a step before an outer door

door·stop \-ˌstäp\ *n* (1881) **1** : a device (as a wedge or weight) for holding a door open **2** : a projection attached to a wall or floor and usu. having a rubber-tipped end for preventing damaging contact between an opened door and the wall

door–to–door \ˌdōrt-ə-'dō(ə)r, ˌdȯrt-ə-'dȯ(ə)r\ *adj* (1902) **1** : being or making a usu. unsolicited call (as for selling or canvassing) at every residence in an area **2** : providing delivery to a specified address ⟨direct ~ service⟩ — **door–to–door** *adv*

door·way \'dō(ə)r-ˌwā, 'dȯ(ə)r-\ *n* (1799) **1** : the opening that a door closes; *esp* : an entrance into a building or room **2** : a means of gaining access ⟨exercise is a ~ to good health⟩

door·yard \-ˌyärd\ *n* (ca. 1764) : a yard next to the door of a house

doo–wop \'dü-ˌwäp\ *n* [fr. nonsense syllables typical of the style] (1969) : a vocal style of rock and roll that is characterized by the a cappella singing of usu. nonsense syllables in rhythmical support of the melody

doo·zer \'dü-zər\ *or* **doo·zy** \-zē\ *or* **doozie** *n, pl* **doozers** *or* **doozies** [perh. alter. of *daisy*] (ca. 1930) : an extraordinary one of its kind

do·pa \'dō-pə, -(ˌ)pä\ *n* [*d*ihydr*o*xy*p*henyl*a*lanine] (1917) : an amino acid $C_9H_{11}NO_4$ that in the levorotatory form is found in the broad bean and is used in the treatment of Parkinson's disease

do·pa·mine \'dō-pə-ˌmēn\ *n* [*dopa* + *amine*] (1959) : a decarboxylated form of dopa found esp. in the adrenal glands

do·pa·mi·ner·gic \ˌdō-pə-ˌmē-'nər-jik\ *adj* [*dopamine* + *-ergic*] (1972) : relating to, participating in, or activated by the neurotransmitter activity of dopamine or related substances

dop·ant \'dō-pənt\ *n* [2*dope*] (1962) : an impurity added usu. in minute amounts to a pure substance to alter its properties

\ə\ abut \ᵊ\ kitten, F table \ər\ further \a\ ash \ā\ ace \ä\ cot, cart \au̇\ out \ch\ chin \e\ bet \ē\ easy \g\ go \i\ hit \ī\ ice \j\ job \ŋ\ sing \ō\ go \ȯ\ law \ȯi\ boy \th\ thin \t͟h\ the \ü\ loot \u̇\ foot \y\ yet \zh\ vision \à, k̲, ⁿ, œ, œ̄, ue, ue̅, ʸ\ *see* Guide to Pronunciation

[1]**dope** \'dōp\ *n* [D *doop* sauce, fr. *dopen* to dip; akin to OE *dyppan* to dip] (1807) **1 a :** a thick liquid or pasty preparation **b :** a preparation for giving a desired quality to a substance or surface; *specif* : an antiknock added to gasoline **2 :** absorbent or adsorbent material used in various manufacturing processes (as the making of dynamite) **3 a** (1) : a preparation of an illicit, habit-forming, or narcotic drug (as opium, heroin, or marijuana) (2) : a preparation given to a racehorse to help or hinder its performance **b** *chiefly Southern* : a cola drink **c** (1) : a narcotic addict (2) : a stupid person **4 :** information esp. from a reliable source ⟨inside ~ on the scandal⟩

[2]**dope** *vb* **doped; dop·ing** *vt* (1868) **1 :** to treat or affect with dope; *specif* : to give a narcotic to **2 :** FIGURE OUT — usu. used with *out* **3 :** to treat with a dopant ⟨*doped* semiconductor⟩ ~ *vi* : to take dope — **dop·er** *n*

dope·ster \'dōp-stər\ *n* (1907) : a forecaster of the outcome of future events (as sports contests or elections)

dop·ey *also* **dopy** \'dō-pē\ *adj* **dop·i·er; -est** (1896) **1 a :** dulled by alcohol or a narcotic **b :** SLUGGISH, STUPEFIED **2 :** STUPID, FATUOUS — **dop·i·ness** *n*

dop·pel·gäng·er *or* **dop·pel·gang·er** \'dȯp-əl-ˌgeŋ-ər, ˌdəb-əl-'gaŋ-\ *n* [G *doppelgänger*, fr. *doppel-* double + *-gänger* goer] (1830) : a ghostly counterpart of a living person; *broadly* : DOUBLE 2

Dopp·ler \'däp-lər\ *adj* (1926) : of, relating to, or utilizing a shift in frequency in accordance with the Doppler effect; *also* : of or relating to Doppler radar

Doppler effect *n* [Christian J. *Doppler*] (1905) : a change in the frequency with which waves (as sound, light, or radio waves) from a given source reach an observer when the source and the observer are in rapid motion with respect to each other so that the frequency increases or decreases according to the speed at which the distance is decreasing or increasing

Doppler radar *n* (1954) : a radar system that utilizes the Doppler effect for measuring velocity

Dor·cas \'dȯr-kəs\ *n* [Gk *Dorkas*] : a Christian woman of New Testament times who made clothing for the poor

Do·ri·an \'dōr-ē-ən, 'dȯr-\ *n* [L *dorius* of Doris, fr. Gk *dōrios*, fr. *Dōris*, region of ancient Greece] (1662) : one of an ancient Hellenic race that completed the overthrow of Mycenaean civilization and settled esp. in the Peloponnisos and Crete — **Dorian** *adj*

[1]**Dor·ic** \'dȯr-ik, 'där-\ *adj* (1569) **1 :** of, relating to, or characteristic of the Dorians **2 :** belonging to the oldest and simplest Greek architectural order **3 :** of, relating to, or constituting Doric

[2]**Doric** *n* (1837) : a dialect of ancient Greek spoken esp. in the Peloponnisos, Crete, Sicily, and southern Italy

dorm \'dȯ(ə)rm\ *n* (1900) : DORMITORY

dor·man·cy \'dȯr-mən-sē\ *n* (1789) : the quality or state of being dormant

dor·mant \'dȯr-mənt\ *adj* [ME, fixed, stationary, fr. MF, fr. prp. of *dormir* to sleep, fr. L *dormire*; akin to Skt *drāti* he sleeps] (1500) **1 :** represented on a coat of arms in a lying position with the head on the forepaws **2 :** marked by a suspension of activity: as **a :** temporarily devoid of external activity ⟨a ~ volcano⟩ **b :** temporarily in abeyance yet capable of being activated or resumed ⟨a ~ judgment⟩ **3 a :** ASLEEP, INACTIVE **b :** having the faculties suspended : SLUGGISH **c :** having biological activity suspended: as (1) : being in a state of suspended animation (2) : not actively growing but protected (as by bud scales) from the environment — used of plant parts **4 :** associated with, carried out, or applied during a period of dormancy ⟨~ grafting⟩ *syn* see LATENT

dor·mer \'dȯr-mər\ *n* [MF *dormeor* dormitory, fr. L *dormitorium*] (1592) : a window set vertically in a structure projecting through a sloping roof; *also* : the roofed structure containing such a window

dor·mie *or* **dor·my** \'dȯr-mē\ *adj* [origin unknown] (1847) : being ahead by as many holes in golf as remain to be played

dor·mi·to·ry \'dȯr-mə-ˌtōr-ē, -ˌtȯr-\ *n, pl* **-ries** [L *dormitorium*, fr. *dormitus*, pp. of *dormire*] (15c) **1 :** a room for sleeping; *esp* : a large room containing numerous beds **2 :** a residence hall providing rooms for individuals or for groups usu. without private baths **3 :** a residential community inhabited chiefly by commuters

dor·mouse \'dȯ(ə)r-ˌmau̇s\ *n, pl* **dor·mice** \-ˌmīs\ [ME *dormowse*, perh. fr. MF *dormir* + ME *mous* mouse] (15c) : any of numerous small Old World rodents (family Gliridae) that resemble small squirrels

dor·nick \'dȯr-nik, 'dän-ik\ *n* [prob. fr. IrGael *dornōg*] (1840) : a small stone or chunk of rock

do·ron·i·cum \də-'rän-i-kəm\ *n* [NL, genus name, fr. Ar *darūnaj*, a plant of this genus] (1892) : any of a genus (*Doronicum*) of Eurasian perennial composite herbs including several cultivated for their showy yellow flower heads

dorp \'dȯ(ə)rp\ *n* [D, fr. MD; akin to OHG *dorf* village — more at THORP] (ca. 1570) : VILLAGE

dor·per \'dȯr-pər\ *n* [*Dor*set Horn + Blackhead *Per*sian (breeds of sheep)] (1949) : any of a breed of mutton-producing sheep with white body and black face developed in southern Africa

dors- *or* **dorsi-** *or* **dorso-** *comb form* [LL *dors-*, fr. L *dorsum*] **1 :** back ⟨*dors*ad⟩ **2 :** dorsal and ⟨*dorso*lateral⟩

dor·sad \'dȯ(ə)r-ˌsad\ *adv* (ca. 1803) : toward the back : DORSALLY

[1]**dorsal** *var of* DOSSAL

[2]**dor·sal** \'dȯr-səl\ *adj* [LL *dorsalis*, fr. L *dorsum* back] (1727) **1 :** relating to or situated near or on the back esp. of an animal or of one of its parts **2 :** ABAXIAL — **dor·sal·ly** \-sə-lē\ *adv*

[3]**dorsal** *n* (1834) : a dorsally located part; *esp* : a thoracic vertebra

dorsal lip *n* (1940) : the margin of the fold of blastula wall that delineates the dorsal limit of the blastopore, constitutes the primary organizer, and forms the point of origin of chordamesoderm

dorsal root *n* (ca. 1934) : the one of the two roots of a spinal nerve that passes dorsally to the spinal cord and consists of sensory fibers

dor·si·ven·tral \ˌdȯr-si-'ven-trəl\ *adj* (ca. 1882) **1 :** having distinct dorsal and ventral surfaces **2 :** DORSOVENTRAL 1 — **dor·si·ven·tral·i·ty** \-ven-'tral-ət-ē\ *n* — **dor·si·ven·tral·ly** \-'ven-trə-lē\ *adv*

dor·so·lat·er·al \ˌdȯr-sō-'lat-ə-rəl, -'la-trəl\ *adj* (1835) : of, relating to, or involving both the back and the sides

dor·so·ven·tral \-'ven-trəl\ *adj* [ISV] (1870) **1 :** relating to, involving, or extending along the axis joining the dorsal and ventral sides **2 :** DORSIVENTRAL 1 — **dor·so·ven·tral·i·ty** \-ven-'tral-ət-ē\ *n* — **dor·so·ven·tral·ly** \-trə-lē\ *adv*

dor·sum \'dȯr-səm\ *n, pl* **dor·sa** \-sə\ [L] (1840) **1 :** the upper surface of an appendage or part **2 :** BACK; *esp* : the entire dorsal surface of an animal

do·ry \'dōr-ē, 'dȯr-\ *n, pl* **dories** [Miskito *dóri* dugout] (1709) : a flat-bottomed boat with high flaring sides, sharp bow, and deep V-shaped transom

dos *or* **do's** *pl of* DO

dos·age \'dō-sij\ *n* (1867) **1 a :** the addition of an ingredient or the application of an agent in a measured dose **b :** the presence and relative representation or strength of a factor or agent **2 a :** DOSE 2 **b** (1) : the giving of a dose (2) : regulation or determination of doses **3 :** a dealing out of or an exposure to some experience in or as if in measured portions

[1]**dose** \'dōs\ *n* [F, fr. LL *dosis*, fr. Gk, lit., act of giving, fr. *didonai* to give — more at DATE] (15c) **1 a :** the measured quantity of a therapeutic agent to be taken at one time **b :** the quantity of radiation administered or absorbed **2 :** a portion of a substance added during a process **3 :** a part of an experience to which one is exposed ⟨a ~ of hard work⟩ **4 :** a gonorrheal infection

[2]**dose** *vt* **dosed; dos·ing** (1654) **1 :** to give a dose to; *esp* : to give medicine to **2 :** to divide (as a medicine) into doses **3 :** to treat with an application or agent

do–si–do \ˌdō-(ˌ)sē-'dō\ *n, pl* **do–si–dos** [F *dos-à-dos* back to back] (1926) : a square-dance figure: **a :** a figure in which the dancers pass each other right shoulder to right shoulder and circle each other back to back **b :** a figure in which the woman moves in a figure circling first her partner and then the man on her right

do·sim·e·ter \dō-'sim-ət-ər\ *n* [LL *dosis* + ISV *-meter*] (1938) : a device for measuring doses of radiations (as X rays) — **do·si·met·ric** \ˌdō-sə-'me-trik\ *adj* — **do·sim·e·try** \dō-'sim-ə-trē\ *n*

[1]**doss** \'däs\ *vi* [origin unknown] *chiefly Brit* (ca. 1785) : to sleep or bed down in a convenient place

[2]**doss** *n, chiefly Brit* (ca. 1789) : a crude or makeshift bed

dos·sal \'däs-əl\ *or* **dor·sal** \'dȯr-səl\ *or* **dos·sel** \'däs-əl\ *n* [ML *dossale*, *dorsale*, fr. neut. of LL *dorsalis* dorsal] (1851) : an ornamental cloth hung behind and above an altar

dos·sier \'dȯs-ˌyā, 'dȯs-ē-ˌā, 'däs-\ *n* [F, bundle of documents labeled on the back, dossier, fr. *dos* back, fr. L *dorsum*] (1880) : a file of papers containing a detailed report or detailed information

dost \(')dəst\ *archaic pres 2d sing of* DO

[1]**dot** \'dät\ *n* [(assumed) ME, fr. OE *dott* head of a boil; akin to OHG *tutta* nipple] (1674) **1 :** a small spot : SPECK **2 a** (1) : a small point made with a pointed instrument ⟨a ~ on the chart marked the ship's position⟩ (2) : a small round mark used in orthography or punctuation ⟨put a ~ over the *i*⟩ **b :** a centered point used as a multiplication sign (as in 6 • 5 = 30) **c** (1) : a point after a note or rest in music indicating augmentation of the time value by one half (2) : a point over or under a note indicating that it is to be played staccato **3 :** a precise point esp. in time ⟨arrived at six on the ~⟩ **4 :** a short click or buzz forming a letter or part of a letter (as in the Morse code)

[2]**dot** *vb* **dot·ted; dot·ting** *vt* (1740) **1 :** to mark with a dot **2 :** to intersperse with dots or objects scattered at random ⟨boats *dotting* the lake⟩ ~ *vi* : to make a dot — **dot·ter** *n*

[3]**dot** \'dät\ *n* [F, fr. L *dot-*, *dos* dowry] (1855) : DOWRY 2a

dot·age \'dōt-ij\ *n* (14c) : a state or period of senile decay marked by decline of mental poise and alertness — called also *second childhood*

do·tal \'dōt-ᵊl\ *adj* [L *dotalis*, fr. *dot-*, *dos*] (1513) : of or relating to a woman's marriage dowry

dot·ard \'dōt-ərd\ *n* (14c) : a person in his dotage

dote \'dōt\ *vi* **dot·ed; dot·ing** [ME *doten*; akin to MLG *dotten* to be foolish] (13c) **1 :** to exhibit mental decline of or like that of old age : be in one's dotage **2 :** to be lavish or excessive in one's attention, fondness, or affection — used esp. with *on* ⟨*doted* on her only grandchild⟩ — **dot·er** *n* — **dot·ing·ly** \'dōt-iŋ-lē\ *adv*

doth \(')dəth\ *archaic pres 3d sing of* DO

dot matrix *n* (1963) : a pattern of dots in a grid from which alphanumeric characters can be formed (as in printing)

dot product *n* [[1]*dot*; fr. its being commonly written *A* • *B*] (1901) : SCALAR PRODUCT

dotted swiss *n* (ca. 1924) : a sheer light muslin ornamented with evenly spaced raised dots

dot·ter·el \'dät-ə-rəl, 'dä-trəl\ *n* [ME *dotrelle*, irreg. fr. *doten* to dote] (15c) : a Eurasian plover (*Eudromias morinellus*) formerly common in England; *also* : any of various congeners chiefly of eastern Asia, Australia, and So. America

dot·tle \'dät-ᵊl\ *n* [ME *dottel* plug, fr. (assumed) ME *dot*] (ca. 1825) : unburned and partially burned tobacco caked in the bowl of a pipe

[1]**dot·ty** \'dät-ē\ *adj* **dot·ti·er; -est** [alter. of Sc *dottle* fool, fr. ME *dotel*, fr. *doten*] (15c) **1 a :** mentally unbalanced : CRAZY **b :** amiably eccentric ⟨an absentminded ~ old man⟩ **2 :** being obsessed or infatuated **3 :** amusingly absurd : RIDICULOUS ⟨some sublimely ~ exchanges of letters⟩ — **dot·ti·ly** \'dät-ᵊl-ē\ *adv* — **dot·ti·ness** \'dät-ē-nəs\ *n*

[2]**dotty** *adj* (1812) : composed of or marked by dots

Dou·ay Version \dü-'ā-\ *n* [*Douay*, France] (ca. 1931) : an English translation of the Vulgate used by Roman Catholics

[1]**dou·ble** \'dəb-əl\ *adj* [ME, fr. OF, fr. L *duplus* (akin to Gk *diploos*), fr. *duo* two + *-plus* multiplied by; akin to OE *-feald* -fold — more at TWO, -FOLD] (13c) **1 :** having a twofold relation or character : DUAL **2 :** consisting of two usu. combined members or parts ⟨an egg with a ~ yolk⟩ **3 a :** being twice as great or as many ⟨~ the number of expected applicants⟩ **b** *of a coin* : worth two of the specified amount ⟨~ eagle⟩ ⟨~ crown⟩ **4 :** marked by duplicity : DECEITFUL **5 :** folded in two **6 :** of extra size, strength, or value ⟨a ~ martini⟩ **7 :** having more than the normal number of floral leaves often at the expense of the sporophylls **8** *of rhyme* : involving correspondence of two syllables (as in *exciting* and *inviting*) **9 :** designed for the use of two persons ⟨~ room⟩ ⟨~ bed⟩ — **dou·ble·ness** *n*

[2]**double** *vb* **dou·bled; dou·bling** \'dəb-(ə-)liŋ\ *vt* (13c) **1 :** to make twice as great or as many: as **a :** to increase by adding an equal amount **b :** to amount to twice the number of **c :** to make a call in bridge that

increases the value of odd tricks or undertricks at (an opponent's bid) **2 a :** to make of two thicknesses **:** FOLD **b :** CLENCH ⟨*doubled* his fist⟩ **c :** to cause to stoop **3 :** to avoid by doubling **:** ELUDE **4 a :** to replace in a dramatic role **b :** to play (dramatic roles) by doubling **5 a** (1) **:** to advance or score (a base runner) by a double (2) **:** to bring about the scoring of (a run) by a double **b :** to put out (a base runner) in completing a double play **~** *vi* **1 a :** to become twice as much or as many **b :** to double a bid (as in bridge) **2 a :** to turn sharply and suddenly; *esp* **:** to turn back on one's course **b :** to follow a circuitous course **3 :** to become bent or folded usu. in the middle — usu. used with *up* ⟨he *doubled* up in pain⟩ **4 a :** to serve an additional purpose or perform an additional duty **b :** to play a dramatic role as a double **5 :** to make a double in baseball — **dou·bler** \-(ə-)lər\ *n*

[3]double *adv* (14c) **1 :** to twice the extent or amount **2 :** two together

[4]double *n* (14c) **1 :** something twice the usual size, strength, speed, quantity, or value: as **a :** a double amount **b :** a base hit in baseball that enables the batter to reach second base **2 :** one that is the counterpart of another **:** DUPLICATE: as **a :** a living person that closely resembles another living person **b :** WRAITH **c** (1) **:** UNDERSTUDY (2) **:** one who resembles an actor and takes his place in scenes calling for special skills (3) **:** an actor who plays more than one role in a production **3 a :** a sharp turn (as in running) **:** REVERSAL **b :** an evasive shift **4 :** something consisting of two paired members: as **a :** FOLD **b :** a combined bet placed on two different contests **c :** two consecutive strikes in bowling **5** *pl* **:** a game between two pairs of players **6 :** an act of doubling in a card game **7 :** a room (as in a hotel) for two guests — compare SINGLE 4

double agent *n* (1935) **:** a spy pretending to serve one government while actually serving another

double bar *n* (ca. 1674) **:** two adjacent vertical lines or a heavy single line separating principal sections of a musical composition

dou·ble–bar·rel \ˌdəb-əl-ˈbar-əl\ *n* (1811) **:** a double-barreled gun

dou·ble–bar·reled \-əld\ *adj* (1709) **1** *of a firearm* **:** having two barrels mounted side by side or one beneath the other **2 :** TWOFOLD; *esp* **:** having a double purpose ⟨asked a ~ question⟩

double bass *n* (1727) **:** the largest instrument in the violin family tuned a fifth below the cello — **double bass·ist** \-ˈbā-səst\ *n*

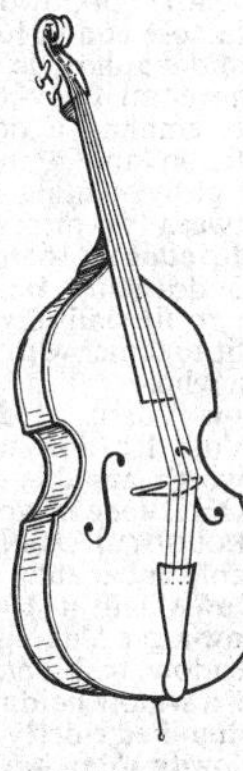

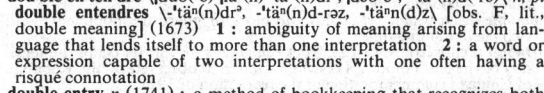

double bass

double bassoon *n* (ca. 1876) **:** CONTRABASSOON

double bill *n* (1917) **:** a bill (as at a theater) offering two principal features

double bind *n* (1956) **:** a psychological dilemma in which a usu. dependent person (as a child) receives conflicting interpersonal communications from a single source or faces disparagement no matter what his response to a situation; *broadly* **:** DILEMMA 2

dou·ble–blind \ˌdəb-əl-ˈblīnd\ *adj* (1950) **:** of, relating to, or being an experimental procedure in which neither the subjects nor the experimenters know the makeup of the test and control groups during the actual course of the experiments — compare SINGLE-BLIND

double boiler *n* (1879) **:** a cooking utensil consisting of two saucepans fitting together so that the contents of the upper can be cooked or heated by boiling water in the lower

double bond *n* (1889) **:** a chemical bond in which two pairs of electrons are shared by two atoms in a molecule

dou·ble–breast·ed \ˌdəb-əl-ˈbres-təd\ *adj* (1701) **1 :** having one half of the front lapped over the other and usu. a double row of buttons and a single row of buttonholes ⟨a ~ coat⟩ **2 :** having a double-breasted coat ⟨a ~ suit⟩

double–check \ˌdəb-əl-ˈchek, ˈdəb-əl-ˌ\ *vt* (1944) **:** to subject to a double check ⟨an article ~*ed* for accuracy⟩ **~** *vi* **:** to make a double check

double check *n* (1953) **:** a careful checking to determine accuracy, condition, or progress esp. of something already checked

dou·ble–cov·er \ˌdəb-əl-ˈkəv-ər\ *vt* (1966) **:** DOUBLE-TEAM

dou·ble–cross \ˌdəb-əl-ˈkrȯs\ *vt* (1903) **:** to deceive by double-dealing **:** BETRAY — **dou·ble–cross·er** *n*

double cross *n* (1834) **1 a :** an act of winning or trying to win a fight or match after agreeing to lose it **b :** an act of betraying or cheating an associate **2 :** a cross between first-generation hybrids of four separate inbred lines (as in the production of hybrid seed corn)

double dagger *n* (1706) **:** the character ‡ used as a reference mark — called also *diesis*

double date *n* (ca. 1931) **:** a date participated in by two couples — **double–date** *vi*

dou·ble–deal·er \ˌdəb-əl-ˈdē-lər\ *n* (1547) **:** one who practices double-dealing

[1]dou·ble–deal·ing \-ˈdē-liŋ\ *n* (1529) **:** action contradictory to a professed attitude **:** DUPLICITY ***syn*** see DECEPTION

[2]double–dealing *adj* (1587) **:** given to or marked by duplicity

dou·ble–deck \ˌdəb-əl-ˌdek\ *or* **dou·ble–decked** \-ˈdekt\ *adj* (1894) **:** having two decks, levels, or layers ⟨a ~ bus⟩ ⟨a ~ sandwich⟩

dou·ble–deck·er \-ˈdek-ər\ *n* (1835) **:** something that is double-deck

double decomposition *n* (1866) **:** METATHESIS b

dou·ble–dig·it \ˌdəb-əl-ˈdij-ət\ *adj* (1974) **:** amounting to 10 percent or more ⟨~ inflation⟩ ⟨~ price increases⟩

dou·ble–dip·per \-ˈdip-ər\ *n* (ca. 1974) **:** a government employee who draws a pension from one government department while working for another — **dou·ble–dip·ping** \-iŋ\ *n*

dou·ble–dome \ˈdəb-əl-ˌdōm\ *n* (1938) **:** INTELLECTUAL

double door *n* (1840) **:** an opening with two vertical doors that meet in the middle of the opening when closed — compare DUTCH DOOR

double dribble *n* (ca. 1949) **:** an illegal action in basketball made when a player dribbles the ball with two hands simultaneously or continues to dribble after allowing the ball to come to rest in one or both hands

dou·ble–edged \ˌdəb-ə-ˈlejd\ *adj* (15c) **1 :** having two cutting edges **2 a :** having a dual purpose or effect ⟨a spy with a ~ mission⟩ **b :** capable of being understood or interpreted in two ways ⟨a ~ remark⟩

dou·ble–end·ed \ˌdəb-ə-ˈlen-dəd\ *adj* (1874) **:** similar at both ends ⟨a ~ bolt⟩

dou·ble–end·er \-dər\ *n* (1864) **:** a ship with bow and stern of similar shape

dou·ble en·ten·dre \ˌdüb-(ə-)ˌlä^{n}(n)-ˈtä^{n}(n)drᵊ, ˌdəb-ə-, -ˈtä^{n}(n)d(-rə)\ *n, pl* **double entendres** \-ˈtä^{n}(n)drᵊ, -ˈtä^{n}(n)d-rəz, -ˈtä^{n}n(d)z\ [obs. F, lit., double meaning] (1673) **1 :** ambiguity of meaning arising from language that lends itself to more than one interpretation **2 :** a word or expression capable of two interpretations with one often having a risqué connotation

double entry *n* (1741) **:** a method of bookkeeping that recognizes both the receiving and the giving sides of a business transaction by debiting the amount of the transaction to one account and crediting it to another account so that the total debits equal the total credits

dou·ble–faced \ˌdəb-əl-ˈfāst\ *adj* (1575) **1 :** having two faces or sides designed for use ⟨a ~ bookshelf⟩ **2 :** HYPOCRITICAL, TWO-FACED

double fault *n* (ca. 1909) **:** two consecutive faults made while serving in tennis and resulting in the loss of a point — **dou·ble–fault** \ˌdəb-əl-ˈfȯlt\ *vi*

double feature *n* (1928) **:** a movie program consisting of two main films

double fertilization *n* (ca. 1909) **:** fertilization characteristic of seed plants in which one sperm nucleus fuses with the egg nucleus to form an embryo and another fuses with polar nuclei to form endosperm

Double Glouces·ter \-ˈgläs-tər, -ˌglȯs-\ *n* [*Gloucester,* England] (1816) **:** a firm mild orange-colored English cheese similar to cheddar

dou·ble·head·er \ˌdəb-əl-ˈhed-ər\ *n* (1878) **1 :** a train pulled by two locomotives **2 :** two games, contests, or events held consecutively on the same program

double helix *n* (1954) **:** a helix or spiral consisting of two strands in the surface of a cylinder that coil around its axis; *esp* **:** the structural arrangement of DNA in space that consists of paired polynucleotide strands stabilized by cross-links between purine and pyrimidine bases — compare ALPHA-HELIX, WATSON-CRICK MODEL — **dou·ble–he·li·cal** \-ˈhel-i-kəl, -ˈhē-li-\ *adj*

double hyphen *n* (1893) **:** a punctuation mark ⸗ used in place of a hyphen at the end of a line to indicate that the word so divided is normally hyphenated

double indemnity *n* (1924) **:** a provision in a life-insurance or accident policy whereby the company agrees to pay twice the face of the contract in case of accidental death

double jeopardy *n* (1910) **:** the putting of a person on trial for an offense for which he has previously been put on trial under a valid charge **:** two adjudications for one offense

dou·ble–joint·ed \ˌdəb-əl-ˈjȯint-əd\ *adj* (1831) **:** having a joint that permits an exceptional degree of freedom of motion of the parts joined

double knit *n* (ca. 1924) **:** a knitted fabric (as wool) made with a double set of needles to produce a double thickness of fabric with each thickness joined by interlocking stitches; *also* **:** an article of clothing made of such fabric

double negative *n* (1827) **:** a now substandard syntactic construction containing two negatives and having a negative meaning ⟨"I didn't hear nothing" is a *double negative*⟩

dou·ble–park \ˌdəb-əl-ˈpärk\ *vi* (ca. 1939) **:** to double-park a vehicle **~** *vt* **:** to park (a vehicle) beside a row of automobiles already parked parallel to the curb

double play *n* (1867) **:** a play in baseball by which two players are put out

dou·ble–quick \ˈdəb-əl-ˌkwik\ *n* (1834) **:** DOUBLE TIME — **double–quick** *vi*

double reed *n* (1879) **:** two reeds bound together with a slight separation between them so that air passing through them causes them to beat against one another and that are used as a sound-producing device in certain woodwind instruments (as members of the oboe family)

double refraction *n* (ca. 1828) **:** BIREFRINGENCE

dou·ble–ring \ˌdəb-əl-ˌriŋ\ *adj* (ca. 1959) **:** of or relating to a wedding ceremony in which each partner ceremonially gives the other a wedding ring while reciting vows

double salt *n* (ca. 1864) **1 :** a salt (as an alum) yielding on hydrolysis two different cations or anions **2 :** a salt regarded as a molecular combination of two distinct salts

dou·ble–space \ˌdəb-əl-ˈspās\ *vt* (ca. 1937) **:** to type (text) leaving alternate lines blank **~** *vi* **:** to type on every other line

dou·ble·speak \ˈdəb-əl-ˌspēk\ *n* (1952) **:** DOUBLE-TALK 2 — **dou·ble·speak·er** \-ˌspē-kər\ *n*

double standard *n* (1894) **1 :** BIMETALLISM **2 :** a set of principles that applies differently and usu. more rigorously to one group of people or circumstances than to another; *esp* **:** a code of morals that applies different and more severe standards of sexual behavior to women than to men

double star *n* (1781) **1 :** BINARY STAR **2 :** two stars in very nearly the same line of sight but seen as physically separate by means of a telescope

double sugar *n* (1956) **:** DISACCHARIDE

dou·blet \ˈdəb-lət\ *n* [ME, fr. MF, fr. *double*] (14c) **1 :** a man's close-fitting jacket worn in Europe esp. during the Renaissance **2 :** something consisting of two identical or similar parts: as **a :** a lens consisting of two components; *specif* **:** a small magnifying hand lens consisting of two single lenses in a metal cylinder **b :** a spectrum line having two close components **c :** a domino with the same number of spots on each end **3 :** a set of two identical or similar things: as **a :** two thrown dice with the same number of spots on the upper face **b :** one of nine pairs of microtubules found in cilia and flagella **4 :** one of a pair; *specif* **:** one of two or more words (as *guard* and *ward*) in the same language derived by different routes of transmission from the same source

dou·ble take \ˈdəb-əl-ˌtāk\ *n* (1930) **:** a delayed reaction to a surprising or significant situation after an initial failure to notice anything unusual — usu. used in the phrase *do a double take*

dou·ble–talk \-ˌtȯk\ *n* (1936) **1 :** language that appears to be earnest and meaningful but in fact is a mixture of sense and nonsense **2 :** inflated, involved, and often deliberately ambiguous language — **double–talk** *vi* — **dou·ble–talk·er** *n*
dou·ble–team \-ˌtēm\ *vt* (1860) **:** to block or guard (an opponent) with two players at one time
Double Ten *n* [trans. of Chin (Pek) *shuang*¹ *shih*²; fr. its being the tenth day of the tenth month] (1940) **:** October 10 observed by the Republic of China in commemoration of the revolution of 1911
dou·ble·think \ˈdəb-əl-ˌthiŋk\ *n* (1949) **:** a simultaneous belief in two contradictory ideas
dou·ble–time \ˈdəb-əl-ˌtīm\ *vi* (1943) **:** to move at double time
double time *n* (1853) **1 :** a marching cadence of 180 36-inch steps per minute **2 :** payment of a worker at twice the regular wage rate
dou·ble–tongue \ˌdəb-əl-ˈtəŋ\ *vi* (ca. 1900) **:** to cause the tongue to alternate rapidly between the positions for *t* and *k* so as to produce a fast succession of detached notes on a wind instrument
dou·ble–u *as at* W\ *n* (1840) **:** the letter *w*
double up *vi* (1789) **:** to share accommodations designed for one
double vision *n* (ca. 1860) **:** DIPLOPIA
dou·bloon \ˌdəb-ˈlün\ *n* [Sp *doblón,* aug. of *dobla,* an old Spanish coin, fr. L *dupla,* fem. of *duplus* double — more at DOUBLE] (1622) **:** an old gold coin of Spain and Spanish America
dou·bly \ˈdəb-(ə-)lē\ *adv* (14c) **1 :** in a twofold manner **2 :** to twice the degree
¹**doubt** \ˈdau̇t\ *vb* [ME *douten,* fr. OF *douter* to doubt, fr. L *dubitare;* akin to L *dubius* dubious] *vt* (13c) **1** *archaic* **:** FEAR **2 :** to be in doubt about ⟨he ∼s everyone's word⟩ **3 a :** to lack confidence in **:** DISTRUST ⟨find myself ∼*ing* him even when I know that he is honest —H. L. Mencken⟩ **b :** to consider unlikely ⟨I ∼ that it is authentic⟩ ∼ *vi* **:** to be uncertain — **doubt·able** \-ə-bəl\ *adj* — **doubt·er** *n* — **doubt·ing·ly** \-iŋ-lē\ *adv*
²**doubt** *n* (13c) **1 a :** uncertainty of belief or opinion that often interferes with decision-making **b :** a deliberate suspension of judgment **2 :** a state of affairs giving rise to uncertainty, hesitation, or suspense **3 a :** a lack of confidence **:** DISTRUST **b :** an inclination not to believe or accept ***syn*** see UNCERTAINTY — **no doubt :** ¹DOUBTLESS
doubt·ful \ˈdau̇t-fəl\ *adj* (14c) **1 :** giving rise to doubt **:** open to question ⟨it is ∼ that they ever knew what happened⟩ ⟨a ∼ proposition⟩ **2 a :** lacking a definite opinion, conviction, or determination ⟨they were ∼ about the advantages of the new system⟩ **b :** uncertain in outcome **:** UNDECIDED ⟨a ∼ progress⟩ ⟨the outcome of the election remains ∼⟩ **3 :** marked by qualities that raise doubts about worth, honesty, or validity — **doubt·ful·ly** \-fə-lē\ *adv* — **doubt·ful·ness** *n*
syn DOUBTFUL, DUBIOUS, PROBLEMATIC, QUESTIONABLE mean not affording assurance of the worth, soundness, or certainty of something. DOUBTFUL implies little more than a lack of conviction or certainty; DUBIOUS stresses suspicion, mistrust, or hesitation; PROBLEMATIC applies esp. to things whose existence, meaning, fulfillment, or realization is highly uncertain; QUESTIONABLE may imply no more than the existence of doubt but usu. suggests that the suspicions are well-grounded.
doubting Thom·as \-ˈtäm-əs\ *n* [St. *Thomas,* apostle who doubted Jesus' resurrection until he had proof of it (Jn 20:24–29)] (1883) **:** a habitually doubtful person
¹**doubt·less** \ˈdau̇t-ləs\ *adv* (14c) **1 :** without doubt **2 :** PROBABLY
²**doubtless** *adj* (14c) **:** free from doubt **:** CERTAIN — **doubt·less·ly** *adv* — **doubt·less·ness** *n*
douce \ˈdüs\ *adj* [ME, sweet, pleasant, fr. MF, fr. fem. of *douz,* fr. L *dulcis* sweet — more at DULCET] *chiefly Scot* (1721) **:** SOBER, SEDATE ⟨the ∼ faces of the mourners —L. J. A. Bell⟩ — **douce·ly** *adv, chiefly Scot*
dou·ceur \dü-ˈsər\ *n* [F, pleasantness, fr. LL *dulcor* sweetness, fr. L *dulcis*] (1763) **:** a conciliatory gift
douche \ˈdüsh\ *n* [F, fr. It *doccia,* fr. *docciare* to douche, fr. *doccia* water pipe, prob. back-formation fr. *doccione* conduit, fr. L *duction-, ductio* action of leading, fr. *ductus,* pp. of *ducere* to lead — more at TOW] (1766) **1 a :** a jet or current esp. of water directed against a part or into a cavity of the body **b :** an act of cleansing with a douche **2 :** a device for giving douches — **douche** *vb*
dough \ˈdō\ *n* [ME *dogh,* fr. OE *dāg;* akin to OHG *teic* dough, L *fingere* to shape, Gk *teichos* wall] (bef. 12c) **1 :** a mixture that consists essentially of flour or meal and a liquid (as milk or water) and is stiff enough to knead or roll **2 :** something resembling dough esp. in consistency **3 :** MONEY **4 :** DOUGHBOY — **dough·like** \-ˌlīk\ *adj*
dough box *n* (ca. 1944) **:** a rectangular wooden box mounted on legs that is used as a worktable and storage space
dough·boy \-ˌbȯi\ *n* (1865) **:** an American infantryman esp. in World War I
dough·face \-ˌfās\ *n* (1830) **:** a Northern congressman not opposed to slavery in the South before or during the Civil War; *also* **:** a Northerner sympathetic to the South during the same period — **dough–faced** \-ˈfāst\ *adj*
dough·foot \-ˌfu̇t\ *n, pl* **dough·feet** \-ˌfēt\ *or* **doughfoots** (1943) **:** INFANTRYMAN
dough·nut \-(ˌ)nət\ *n* (ca. 1809) **1 :** a small usu. ring-shaped cake fried in fat **2 :** something that resembles a doughnut esp. in shape; *specif* **:** TORUS 3
dough·ty \ˈdau̇t-ē\ *adj* **dough·ti·er; -est** [ME, fr. OE *dohtig;* akin to OHG *toug* is useful, Gk *teuchein* to make] (bef. 12c) **:** marked by fearless resolution **:** VALIANT — **dough·ti·ly** \ˈdau̇t-ᵊl-ē\ *adv* — **dough·ti·ness** \ˈdau̇t-ē-nəs\ *n*
doughy \ˈdō-ē\ *adj* **dough·i·er; -est** (1601) **:** resembling dough: as **a :** not thoroughly baked **b :** unhealthily pale **:** PASTY ⟨a ∼ complexion⟩
Doug·las fir \ˌdəg-ləs-\ *n* [David *Douglas* †1834 Scot. botanist] (1873) **:** a tall evergreen timber tree (*Pseudotsuga taxifolia*) of the western U.S. having thick bark, pitchy wood, and pendulous cones
Dou·kho·bor \ˈdü-kə-ˌbȯ(ə)r\ *n* [Russ *dukhoborets,* fr. *dukh* spirit + *borets* wrestler] (1876) **:** a member of a Christian sect of 18th century Russian origin emphasizing the duty of obeying the inner light and rejecting church or civil authority
do up *vt* (1666) **1 :** to prepare (as by cleaning or repairing) for wear or use ⟨*do up* a shirt⟩ ⟨*do up* old furniture⟩ **2 a :** to wrap up ⟨*do up* a package⟩ **b :** PUT UP, CAN **3 :** to deck out **:** CLOTHE
dour \ˈdu̇(ə)r, ˈdau̇(ə)r\ *adj* [ME, fr. L *durus* hard — more at DURING] (14c) **1 :** STERN, HARSH **2 :** OBSTINATE, UNYIELDING **3 :** GLOOMY, SULLEN — **dour·ly** *adv* — **dour·ness** *n*
dou·rou·cou·li \ˌdu̇r-ə-ˈkü-lē\ *n* [native name in So. America] (1842) **:** any of several small nocturnal monkeys (genus *Aotus*) of tropical America that have round heads, large eyes, and stocky bodies
¹**douse** \ˈdau̇s *also* ˈdau̇z\ *vb* **doused; dous·ing** [perh. fr. obs. E *douse* (to smite)] *vt* (1600) **1 :** to plunge into water **2 a :** to throw a liquid on **:** DRENCH **b :** SLOSH **3 :** EXTINGUISH ⟨∼ the lights⟩ ∼ *vi* **:** to fall or become plunged into water — **dous·er** *n*
²**douse** \ˈdau̇s *also* ˈdau̇z\ *n* (1881) **:** a heavy drenching
³**douse** \ˈdüs, ˈdau̇s\ *n, Brit* (1625) **:** BLOW, STROKE
⁴**douse** \ˈdau̇s\ *vt* **doused; dous·ing** (1627) **1 a :** FURL ⟨∼ a sail⟩ **b :** SLACKEN ⟨∼ a rope⟩ **2 :** DOFF ⟨*doused* my cap on entering the porch —W. M. Thackeray⟩
doux \ˈdü\ *adj* [F, lit., sweet, fr. OF *douz* — more at DOUCE] *of champagne* (ca. 1943) **:** very sweet
¹**dove** \ˈdəv\ *n* [ME, fr. (assumed) OE *dūfe;* akin to OHG *tūba* dove, and prob. to OE *dēaf* deaf] (13c) **1 :** any of numerous pigeons; *esp* **:** a small wild pigeon **2 :** a gentle woman or child **3 :** an individual who takes a conciliatory attitude (as in a dispute) and advocates negotiations and compromise; *esp* **:** an opponent of war — compare HAWK — **dov·ish** \ˈdəv-ish\ *adj* — **dov·ish·ness** *n*
²**dove** \ˈdōv\ *past of* DIVE
dove·cote \ˈdəv-ˌkōt, -ˌkät\ *also* **dove·cot** \-ˌkät\ *n* (15c) **1 :** a small compartmented raised house or box for domestic pigeons **2 :** a settled or harmonious group or organization ⟨theological ∼s throughout the world were set in an uproar —Cecil Roth⟩
dove·kie \ˈdəv-kē\ *n* [dim. of *dove*] (ca. 1859) **:** a small short-billed auk (*Alle alle*) breeding on arctic coasts and ranging south in winter
doven *var of* DAVEN
Dover sole *n* [prob. fr. *Dover,* England] (ca. 1911) **1 :** a common European sole (*Solea solea*) esteemed as a food fish **2 :** a brownish blotched flatfish (*Microstomus pacificus*) of the Pacific coast of No. America that is a market fish in California
Do·ver's powder \ˌdō-vərz-\ *n* [Thomas *Dover* †1742 Eng. physician] (1801) **:** a powder of ipecac and opium compounded in the U.S. with lactose and in England with potassium sulfate and used as an anodyne and diaphoretic
¹**dove·tail** \ˈdəv-ˌtāl\ *n* (1565) **:** something resembling a dove's tail; *esp* **:** a flaring tenon and a mortise into which it fits tightly making an interlocking joint between two pieces (as of wood)
²**dovetail** *vt* (1656) **1 a :** to join by means of dovetails **b :** to cut to a dovetail **2 a :** to fit skillfully to form a whole **b :** to fit together with ∼ *vi* **:** to fit together into a whole

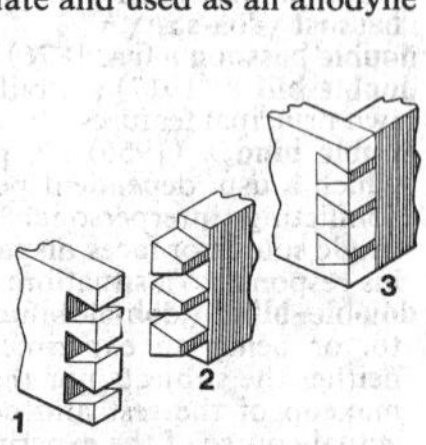

dovetail: *1* mortises, *2* tenons, *3* joint

dow \ˈdau̇\ *vi* **dought** \ˈdau̇t\ *or* **dowed** \ˈdau̇d\; **dow·ing** [ME *dow, deih* have worth, am able, fr. OE *dēah, dēag;* akin to OHG *toug* is worthy, is useful — more at DOUGHTY] *chiefly Scot* (bef. 12c) **:** to be able or capable
Dow \ˈdau̇\ *n* (1949) **:** DOW-JONES AVERAGE
dow·a·ger \ˈdau̇-i-jər\ *n* [MF *douagiere,* fr. *douage* dower, fr. *douer* to endow, fr. L *dotare,* fr. *dot-, dos* gift, dower — more at DATE] (1530) **1 :** a widow holding property or a title from her deceased husband **2 :** a dignified elderly woman
¹**dowdy** \ˈdau̇d-ē\ *n, pl* **dowd·ies** [dim. of *dowd* (dowdy), fr. ME *doude*] *archaic* (ca. 1581) **:** a dowdy woman
²**dowdy** *adj* **dowd·i·er; -est** (1676) **1 :** not neat or becoming in appearance **:** SHABBY **2 a :** lacking smartness or taste **b :** OLD-FASHIONED — **dowd·i·ly** \ˈdau̇d-ᵊl-ē\ *adv* — **dowd·i·ness** \ˈdau̇d-ē-nəs\ *n* — **dowdy·ish** \-ish\ *adj*
³**dowdy** *n* [origin unknown] (1936) **:** PANDOWDY
¹**dow·el** \ˈdau̇(-ə)l\ *n* [ME *dowle;* akin to OHG *tubili* plug, LGk *typhos* wedge] (13c) **1 :** a pin fitting into a hole in an abutting piece to prevent motion or slipping; *also* **:** a round rod or stick used esp. for cutting up into dowels **2 :** a piece of wood driven into a wall so that other pieces can be nailed to it
²**dowel** *vt* **-eled** *or* **-elled; -el·ing** *or* **-el·ling** (1713) **:** to fasten by or furnish with dowels
¹**dow·er** \ˈdau̇(-ə)r\ *n* [ME *dowere,* fr. MF *douaire,* modif. of ML *dotarium* — more at DOWRY] (14c) **1 :** the part of or interest in the real estate of a deceased husband given by law to his widow during her life — compare CURTESY **2 :** DOWRY
²**dower** *vt* (1605) **:** to supply with a dower or dowry **:** ENDOW
dow·itch·er \ˈdau̇-i-chər\ *n, pl* **dowitchers** *also* **dowitcher** [of Iroquoian origin; akin to Mohawk *tawis* dowitcher] (1841) **:** any of several long-billed wading birds (esp. *Limnodromus griseus* and *L. scolopaceus* of the family Scolopacidae) related to the sandpipers and breeding in arctic or subarctic Canada, Alaska, or Siberia
Dow–Jones average \ˌdau̇-ˌjōnz-\ *n* [Charles H. *Dow* †1902 & Edward D. *Jones* †1920 Am. financial statisticians] (1922) **:** an index of the relative price of securities based on the daily average price of selected lists of industrial, transportation, and utility common stocks
¹**down** \ˈdau̇n\ *n* [ME *doun* hill, fr. OE *dūn*] (bef. 12c) **1 :** an undulating usu. treeless upland with sparse soil — usu. used in pl. **2** *often cap* **:** a sheep of any breed originating in the downs of southern England
²**down** *adv* [ME *doun,* fr. OE *dūne,* short for *adūne, of dūne,* fr. *a-* (fr. *of*), *of* off, from + *dūne,* dat. of *dūn* hill] (bef. 12c) **1 a** (1) **:** toward or in a lower physical position (2) **:** to a lying or sitting position (3) **:** toward or to the ground, floor, or bottom **b :** as a down payment ⟨paid $10 ∼⟩ **c :** on paper ⟨put ∼ what he says⟩ **2 :** in a direction that is the opposite of up: as **a :** SOUTHWARD **b :** to or toward a point away from the speaker or the speaker's point of reference **3 :** to a lesser degree, level, or rate ⟨cool ∼ tensions⟩ ⟨slowed ∼ the car⟩ **4 :** to or toward a lower position in a series **5 :** to or in a lower or worse condition or status **6 :** from a past time **7 :** to or in a state of less activity or prominence **8 :** to a concentrated state ⟨got his report ∼ to three pages⟩ **9 :** into defeat ⟨voted the motion ∼⟩ — **down to the ground :** PERFECTLY, COMPLETELY ⟨that suits me *down to the ground*⟩

[3]down \(ˈ)dau̇n\ *prep* (14c) **:** down along, around, through, toward, in, into, or on ⟨fell ~ the stairs⟩
[4]down \ˈdau̇n\ *vt* (1562) **1 :** to cause to go or come down **2 :** to cause (a football) to be out of play **3 :** DEFEAT ~ *vi* **:** to go down
[5]down *adj* (1565) **1 a** (1) **:** occupying a low position; *specif* **:** lying on the ground ⟨~ timber⟩ (2) **:** directed or going downward ⟨attendance is ~⟩ **b :** lower in price **c :** not being in play in football because of wholly stopped progress or because the officials stop the play ⟨marked the ball ~ on the 15-yard line⟩ **d :** defeated or trailing an opponent (as in points scored) ⟨~ two tricks⟩ ⟨~ by two touchdowns⟩ **e** *in baseball* **:** OUT **2 a :** being in a state of reduced or low activity **b :** DEPRESSED, DEJECTED; *also* **:** DEPRESSING ⟨a ~ movie⟩ **c :** SICK ⟨~ with flu⟩ **3 :** DONE, FINISHED ⟨eight ~ and two to go⟩ **4 :** completely mastered **:** PAT ⟨had her lines ~⟩ — often used with *pat* ⟨had it ~ pat⟩ — **down on :** having a low opinion of or dislike for ⟨*down on* him⟩
[6]down *n* (1710) **1 :** DESCENT, DEPRESSION **2 :** an instance of putting down **3 a :** a complete play to advance the ball in football **b :** one of a series of four attempts to advance a football 10 yards **4 :** DISLIKE, GRUDGE **5 :** DOWNER
[7]down *n* [ME *doun,* fr. ON *dūnn*] (14c) **1 :** a covering of soft fluffy feathers; *also* **:** these feathers **2 :** something soft and fluffy like down
down–and–out \ˌdau̇-nən-ˈ(d)au̇t\ *adj* (1901) **1 :** DESTITUTE, IMPOVERISHED **2 :** physically weakened or incapacitated — **down–and–out** *or* **down–and–out·er** \-ˈ(d)au̇t-ər\ *n*
down–at–heel \ˌdau̇-nət-ˈhē(ə)l, -nat-\ *or* **down–at–heels** \-ˈhē(ə)lz\ *or* **down–at–the–heel** \-t͟hə-ˈhē(ə)l\ *or* **down–at–the–heels** \-ˈhē(ə)lz\ *adj* (1704) **:** SHABBY
[1]down·beat \ˈdau̇n-ˌbēt\ *n* (1876) **1 :** the downward stroke of a conductor indicating the principally accented note of a measure of music; *also* **:** the first beat of a measure **2 :** a decline in activity or prosperity
[2]downbeat *adj* (1950) **:** PESSIMISTIC, GLOOMY
down–bow \ˈdau̇n-ˌbō\ *n* (ca. 1891) **:** a stroke in playing a bowed instrument (as a violin) in which the bow is drawn across the strings from the heel to the tip
down·cast \ˈdau̇n-ˌkast\ *adj* (15c) **1 :** low in spirit **:** DEJECTED **2 :** directed downward ⟨with ~ eyes⟩
down·court \-ˈkō(ə)rt, -ˈkȯ(ə)rt\ *adv or adj* (1952) **:** in or into the opposite end of the court (as in basketball)
down·draft \-ˌdraft\ *n* (1849) **:** a downward current of gas (as air in a chimney or during a thunderstorm)
down east *adv or adj, often cap D&E* (1825) **:** in or into the northeast coastal section of the U.S. and parts of the Maritime Provinces of Canada; *specif* **:** in or into coastal Maine
down–east·er \dau̇-ˈnē-stər\ *n, often cap D&E* (1819) **:** one born or living down east
down·er \ˈdau̇-nər\ *n* (1967) **1 :** a depressant drug; *esp* **:** BARBITURATE **2 :** someone or something depressing
down·fall \ˈdau̇n-ˌfȯl\ *n* (14c) **1 a :** a sudden fall (as from high rank or power) **b :** a fall (as of snow or rain) esp. when sudden or heavy **2 :** something that causes a downfall (as of a person) ⟨drink was his ~⟩ — **down·fall·en** \-ˌfȯ-lən\ *adj*
down·field \-ˈfē(ə)ld\ *adv or adj* (1944) **:** in or into the part of the field toward which the offensive team is headed
[1]down·grade \ˈdau̇n-ˌgrād\ *n* (1858) **1 :** a downward grade (as of a road) **2 :** a descent toward an inferior state — used esp. in the phrase *on the downgrade*
[2]downgrade *vt* (1930) **1 :** MINIMIZE, DEPRECIATE **2 :** to lower in quality, value, status, or extent — **down·grad·ing** *n*
down·haul \ˈdau̇n-ˌhȯl\ *n* (1669) **:** a rope or line for hauling down or holding down a sail or spar
down·heart·ed \-ˈhärt-əd\ *adj* (1774) **:** DOWNCAST, DEJECTED — **down·heart·ed·ly** *adv* — **down·heart·ed·ness** *n*
[1]down·hill \ˈdau̇n-ˈhil\ *adv* (14c) **1 :** toward the bottom of a hill **2 :** toward a lower or inferior state or level — used esp. in the phrase *go downhill*
[2]down·hill \-ˌhil\ *n* (1591) **1 :** a descending gradient **2 :** a skiing race against time down a trail
[3]down·hill \-ˌhil\ *adj* (1727) **1 :** sloping downhill **2 :** of or relating to skiing downhill **3 :** being the lower one or part esp. of a set; *specif* **:** being nearer the bottom of an incline **4 :** not difficult **:** EASY ⟨had solved the biggest problems and the rest was ~⟩ **5 :** progressively worse ⟨the play was ~ after the first act⟩
down–home \ˌdau̇n-ˌhōm\ *adj* (1938) **:** of, relating to, or having qualities (as informality, simplicity, and earthiness) associated with the common people esp. of the Southern U.S. ⟨a restaurant with ~ cooking⟩
down·link \ˈdau̇n-ˌliŋk\ *n* (ca. 1969) **:** a communications channel for receiving transmissions from a spacecraft; *also* **:** such transmissions
down·load \ˈdau̇n-ˌlōd\ *vt* (1981) **:** to transfer (data) from a usu. large computer to the memory of another device (as a smaller computer)
down payment *n* (1926) **:** a part of the full price paid at the time of purchase or delivery with the balance to be paid later
down·play \ˈdau̇n-ˌplā\ *vt* (1954) **:** to play down **:** DE-EMPHASIZE
down·pour \-ˌpō(ə)r, -ˌpȯ(ə)r\ *n* (1811) **:** a pouring or streaming downward; *esp* **:** a heavy rain
down quark *n* (1976) **:** a quark having an electric charge of -1/3, zero charm, and zero strangeness
down·range \-ˈrānj\ *adv or adj* (1953) **:** away from a launching site and along the course of a test range ⟨a missile landing 5000 miles ~⟩
[1]down·right \-ˌrīt\ *adv* (13c) **1** *archaic* **:** straight down **2 :** OUTRIGHT, THOROUGHLY ⟨~ mean⟩ **3 :** FORTHRIGHT
[2]downright *adj* (ca. 1530) **1** *archaic* **:** directed vertically downward **2 :** OUTRIGHT, THOROUGH ⟨a ~ lie⟩ **3 :** PLAIN, BLUNT ⟨a ~ man⟩ — **down·right·ly** *adv* — **down·right·ness** *n*
down·riv·er \ˈdau̇n-ˈriv-ər\ *adv or adj* (1852) **:** toward or at a point nearer the mouth of a river
down·shift \-ˌshift\ *vi* (1955) **:** to shift an automotive vehicle into a lower gear — **downshift** *n*
down·side \ˈdau̇n-ˌsīd\ *n* (1946) **:** a downward trend
down·size \(ˈ)dau̇n-ˈsīz\ *vt* (1975) **:** to design or produce in smaller size
down·spout \ˈdau̇n-ˌspau̇t\ *n* (ca. 1896) **:** a vertical pipe for conducting rainwater from a roof
Down's syndrome \ˈdau̇n(z)-\ *or* **Down syndrome** *n* [J. L. H. *Down* †1896 Eng. physician] (ca. 1961) **:** a congenital condition which is characterized by moderate to severe mental deficiency, by slanting eyes, by a broad short skull, by broad hands with short fingers, and by trisomy of the chromosome numbered 21 in man — called also *mongolism*
[1]down·stage \ˈdau̇n-ˈstāj\ *adv or adj* (1898) **1 :** toward or at the front of a theatrical stage **2 :** toward a motion-picture or television camera
[2]down·stage \-ˌstāj\ *n* (1931) **:** the part of a stage that is nearest the audience or camera
[1]down·stairs \ˈdau̇n-ˈsta(ə)rz, -ˈste(ə)rz\ *adv* (1596) **:** down the stairs **:** on or to a lower floor
[2]down·stairs \ˌdau̇n-ˌsta(ə)rz, -ˌste(ə)rz\ *adj* (1819) **:** situated on the main, lower, or ground floor of a building
[3]down·stairs \ˈdau̇n-ˈ, ˈdau̇n-ˌ\ *n pl but sing or pl in constr* (1843) **:** the lower floor of a building
down·state \-ˌstāt\ *n* (1909) **:** the chiefly southerly sections of a state; *also* **:** the chiefly rural part of a state when the major metropolitan area is to the north — **down·state** \-ˈstāt\ *adj or adv* — **down·stat·er** \-ˈstāt-ər\ *n*
down·stream \ˈdau̇n-ˈstrēm\ *adv or adj* (1706) **1 :** in the direction of the flow of a stream **2 :** in or toward the latter stages of an industrial process (as oil refinement) ⟨investing money ~⟩
down·stroke \-ˌstrōk\ *n* (1852) **:** a downward stroke
down·swing \-ˌswiŋ\ *n* (1899) **1 :** a downward swing **2 :** DOWNTREND
down–the–line *adj* (1940) **:** COMPLETE ⟨a ~ union supporter⟩
down·time \ˈdau̇n-ˌtīm\ *n* (1928) **:** time during which production is stopped (as in a factory or on a machine) esp. during setup for an operation or when making repairs
down–to–earth \ˌdau̇n-tə-ˈ(w)ərth\ *adj* (1932) **:** PRACTICAL, REALISTIC ⟨a ~ appraisal of the situation⟩; *also* **:** STRAIGHTFORWARD
down·town \ˈdau̇n-ˈtau̇n\ *n* (1851) **:** the lower part of a town or city; *esp* **:** the main business district — **downtown** \ˌdau̇n-ˌtau̇n\ *adj or adv*
down·trend \-ˌtrend\ *n* (1926) **:** a downturn esp. in business and economic activity
down·trod·den \ˈdau̇n-ˈträd-ᵊn\ *adj* (1596) **:** suffering oppression
down·turn \-ˌtərn\ *n* (1926) **:** a downward turn esp. toward a decline in business activity
down under *adv* (1886) **:** into or in Australia or New Zealand
[1]down·ward \ˈdau̇n-wərd\ *or* **down·wards** \-wərdz\ *adv* (13c) **1 a :** from a higher to a lower place **b :** toward a direction that is the opposite of up **2 :** from a higher to a lower condition **3 a :** from an earlier time **b :** from an ancestor or predecessor
[2]downward *adj* (ca. 1552) **1 :** moving or extending downward **2 :** descending from a head, origin, or source — **down·ward·ly** *adv* — **down·ward·ness** *n*
down·wind \ˈdau̇n-ˈwind\ *adv or adj* (1855) **:** in the direction that the wind is blowing
downy \ˈdau̇-nē\ *adj* **down·i·er; -est** (1578) **1 :** resembling a bird's down **2 :** covered with down **3 :** made of down **4 :** SOFT, SOOTHING ⟨shake off this ~ sleep, death's counterfeit —Shak.⟩
downy mildew *n* (1886) **1 :** any of various parasitic lower fungi (family Peronosporaceae) that produce whitish masses of sporangiophores or conidiophores on the undersurface of the leaves of the host **2 :** a plant disease caused by a downy mildew
downy woodpecker *n* (1808) **:** a small black-and-white woodpecker (*Dendrocopos pubescens*) of No. America that has a white back and is smaller than the hairy woodpecker
dow·ry \ˈdau̇(ə)r-ē\ *n, pl* **dowries** [ME *dowarie,* fr. AF, irreg. fr. ML *dotarium,* fr. L *dot-, dos* gift, marriage portion — more at DATE] (14c) **1** *archaic* **:** DOWER 1 **2 a :** the money, goods, or estate that a woman brings to her husband in marriage **b :** a sum of money or its equivalent required of postulants by some orders of cloistered nuns **3 :** a gift of money or property by a man to or for his bride **4 :** a natural gift
dowsabel *n* [*Dowsabel,* fem. name] *obs* (1590) **:** SWEETHEART
[1]dowse *var of* DOUSE
[2]dowse \ˈdau̇z\ *vb* **dowsed; dows·ing** [origin unknown] *vi* (1894) **:** to use a divining rod ~ *vt* **:** to find (as water) by dowsing
dows·er \ˈdau̇-zər\ *n* (1838) **:** DIVINING ROD; *also* **:** a person who uses it
Dow theory *n* [Charles H. *Dow* †1902 Am. financial statistician] (1926) **:** a system of stock-market forecasting based on the observed swings of the market itself
dox·ol·o·gy \däk-ˈsäl-ə-jē\ *n, pl* **-gies** [ML *doxologia,* fr. LGk, fr. Gk *doxa* opinion, glory (fr. *dokein* to seem, seem good) + *-logia* -logy — more at DECENT] (1649) **:** a usu. liturgical expression of praise to God
doxo·ru·bi·cin \ˌdäk-sə-ˈrü-bə-sən\ *n* [*doxo-* (alter. of *deoxy-*) + L *rubus* red + *-cin* (as in *-mycin*)] (1977) **:** ADRIAMYCIN
doxy \ˈdäk-sē\ *n, pl* **dox·ies** [perh. modif. of obs. D *docke* doll, fr. MD] (1530) **1 :** FLOOZY, PROSTITUTE **2 :** MISTRESS 5a
doy·en \ˈdȯi-ən, -ˌ(y)en; ˈdwä-ˌyaⁿ(n)\ *n* [F, fr. LL *decanus* dean — more at DEAN] (1670) **1 a :** the senior member of a body or group **b :** a person uniquely skilled by long experience in some field of endeavor **2 :** the oldest example of a category
doy·enne \dȯi-ˈ(y)en, dwä-ˈyen\ *n* [F, fem. of *doyen*] (ca. 1897) **:** a woman who is a doyen
doy·ley *var of* DOILY
[1]doze \ˈdōz\ *vb* **dozed; doz·ing** [prob. of Scand origin; akin to ON *dūsa* to doze] *vt* (1693) **:** to pass (as time) drowsily ⟨*dozing* his life away⟩ ~ *vi* **1 a :** to sleep lightly **b :** to fall into a light sleep — usu. used with *off* **2 :** to be in a dull or stupefied condition — **doze** *n* — **doz·er** *n*
[2]doze *vt* **dozed; doz·ing** [prob. back-formation fr. *dozer* (bulldozer)] (1945) **:** BULLDOZE 2 — **doz·er** *n*
doz·en \ˈdəz-ᵊn\ *n, pl* **dozens** *or* **dozen** [ME *dozeine,* fr. MF *dozaine,* fr. *doze* twelve, fr. L *duodecim,* fr. *duo* two + *decem* ten — more at TWO, TEN] (14c) **1 :** a group of 12 **2 :** an indefinitely large number ⟨I've a ~ things to do⟩ — **dozen** *adj* — **doz·enth** \-ᵊn(t)th\ *adj*
dozy \ˈdō-zē\ *adj* **doz·i·er; -est** (1693) **:** DROWSY, SLEEPY — **doz·i·ness** *n*
DP \ˈdē-ˈpē\ *n, pl* **DP's** *or* **DPs** (ca. 1944) **:** a displaced person
D phase *n* (1945) **:** M PHASE
DPN \ˌdē-ˌpē-ˈen\ *n* [*d*iphosphopyridine *n*ucleotide] (1938) **:** NAD

[1]drab \'drab\ *n* [origin unknown] (ca. 1515) **1 :** SLATTERN **2 :** HARLOT

[2]drab *vi* **drabbed; drab·bing** (1594) **:** to associate with prostitutes

[3]drab *n* [MF *drap* cloth, fr. LL *drappus*] (1541) **1 :** any of various cloths of a dull brown or gray color; *esp* **:** a thick woolen coating or a heavy cotton **2 a :** a light olive brown **b :** a dull, lifeless, or faded appearance or quality

[4]drab *adj* **drab·ber; drab·best** (1686) **1 a :** of the dull brown color of drab **b :** of the color drab **2 :** characterized by dullness and monotony **:** CHEERLESS ⟨formal engagements are generally ~ and boring — Andrew Duncan⟩ — **drab·ly** *adv* — **drab·ness** *n*

[5]drab *n* [prob. alter. of *drib*] (1828) **:** a small amount — usu. used in the phrase *dribs and drabs*

drab·ble \'drab-əl\ *vb* **drab·bled; drab·bling** \-(ə-)liŋ\ [ME *drabelen*] *vt* (15c) **:** DRAGGLE ~ *vi* **:** to become wet and muddy

dra·cae·na \drə-'sē-nə\ *n* [NL, fr. LL, she-serpent, fr. Gk *drakaina,* fem. of *drakōn* serpent — more at DRAGON] (ca. 1823) **:** any of two genera (*Dracaena* and *Cordyline*) of Old World tropical shrubs or trees of the lily family with naked branches ending in tufts of sword-shaped leaves

drachm \'dram\ *n* [alter. of ME *dragme* — more at DRAM] (14c) **1 :** DRACHMA **2 :** DRAM

drach·ma \'drak-mə\ *n, pl* **drachmas** *or* **drach·mai** \-ˌmī\ *or* **drach·mae** \-(ˌ)mē, -ˌmī\ [L, fr. Gk *drachmē*— more at DRAM] (1525) **1 a :** any of various ancient Greek units of weight **b :** any of various modern units of weight; *esp* **:** DRAM 1 **2 a :** an ancient Greek silver coin equivalent to 6 obols **b** — see MONEY table

Dra·co \'drā-(ˌ)kō\ *n* [L (gen. *Draconis*), lit., dragon — more at DRAGON] **:** a northern circumpolar constellation within which is the north pole of the ecliptic

dra·co·ni·an \drā-'kō-nē-ən, drə-\ *adj, often cap* [L *Dracon-, Draco,* fr. Gk *Drakōn* Draco (Athenian lawgiver)] (1876) **1 :** of, relating to, or characteristic of Draco or the severe code of laws held to have been framed by him **2 :** HARSH, CRUEL

[1]dra·con·ic \drə-'kän-ik\ *adj* [L *dracon-, draco*] (1680) **:** of or relating to a dragon

[2]dra·con·ic \drā-'kän-ik, drə-\ *adj* (1708) **:** DRACONIAN

[1]draft \'draft, 'dräft\ *n* [ME *draght;* akin to OE *dragan* to draw — more at DRAW] (13c) **1 :** the act of drawing a net; *also* **:** the quantity of fish taken at one drawing **2 a :** the act or an instance of drinking or inhaling; *also* **:** the portion drunk or inhaled in one such act **b :** a portion poured out or mixed for drinking **:** DOSE **3 a :** the force required to pull an implement **b :** load or load-pulling capacity **4 a :** the act of moving loads by drawing or pulling **:** PULL **b :** a team of animals together with what they draw **5 a :** DELINEATION, REPRESENTATION; *specif* **:** a construction plan ⟨the ~ of a future building⟩ **b :** SCHEME, DESIGN **c :** a preliminary sketch, outline, or version ⟨the author's first ~⟩ **6 :** the act, result, or plan of drawing out or stretching **7 a :** the act of drawing (as from a cask) **b :** a portion of liquid so drawn ⟨a ~ of ale⟩ **c :** draft beer ⟨a glass of ~⟩ **8 :** the depth of water a ship draws esp. when loaded **9 a** (1) **:** a system or method for detaching or selecting individuals from a group (as for compulsory military service) (2) **:** an act or process of selecting an individual (as for political candidacy) without his expressed consent **b :** a group of individuals selected esp. by military draft **10 a :** an order for the payment of money drawn by one person or bank on another **b :** the act or an instance of drawing from or making demands upon something **:** DEMAND **11 a :** a current of air in a closed-in space **b :** a device for regulating the flow of air (as in a fireplace) **12 :** ANGLE, TAPER; *specif* **:** the taper given to a pattern or die so that the work can be easily withdrawn **13 :** a narrow border along the edge of a stone or across its face serving as a stonecutter's guide **14 :** a system whereby exclusive rights to selected new players are apportioned among professional teams — **on draft :** ready to be drawn from a receptacle ⟨beer *on draft*⟩

[2]draft *adj* (15c) **1 :** used or adapted for drawing loads ⟨~ animals⟩ **2 :** being or having been on draft ⟨drinking ~ beer⟩ **3 :** constituting a preliminary or tentative version, sketch, or outline ⟨a ~ treaty⟩

[3]draft *vt* (1714) **1 :** to detach or select for some purpose: as **a :** to conscript for military service **b :** to select (a professional athlete) by draft **2 a :** to draw the preliminary sketch, version, or plan of **b :** COMPOSE, PREPARE **3 :** to draw off or away ⟨water ~*ed* by pumps⟩ **4 :** to mark (as a stone) with a draft in masonry ~ *vi* **1 :** to practice draftsmanship **2 :** to drive close behind another car while racing so as to take advantage of the reduced air pressure created by the leading car — **draft·able** \'draf-tə-bəl, 'dräf-\ *adj* — **draft·ee** \draf-'tē, dräf-\ *n* — **draft·er** \'draf-tər, 'dräf-\ *n*

draft board *n* (1953) **:** a civilian board that registers, classifies, and selects men for compulsory military service

drafts·man \'draf(t)-smən, 'dräf(t)-\ *n* (1663) **1 :** one who draws plans and sketches (as of machinery or structures) **2 :** one who draws legal documents or other writings **3 :** an artist who excels in drawing — **drafts·man·ship** \-ˌship\ *n*

drafty \'draf-tē, 'dräf-\ *adj* **draft·i·er; -est** (1846) **:** of, relating to, or having a draft — **draft·i·ly** \-tə-lē\ *adv* — **draft·i·ness** \-tē-nəs\ *n*

[1]drag \'drag\ *n* (14c) **1 :** something used to drag with; *esp* **:** a device for dragging under water to detect or obtain objects **2 :** something that is dragged, pulled, or drawn along or over a surface: as **a :** HARROW **b :** a sledge for conveying heavy bodies **c :** CONVEYANCE **3 a :** the act or an instance of dragging or drawing: as (1) **:** a drawing along or over a surface with effort or pressure (2) **:** motion effected with slowness or difficulty; *also* **:** the condition of having or seeming to have such motion (3) **:** a draw on a pipe, cigarette, or cigar; *also* **:** a draft of liquid **b :** a movement, inclination, or retardation caused by or as if by dragging **c** *slang* **:** influence securing special favor **:** PULL **4 a :** something that retards motion or action **b** (1) **:** the retarding force acting on a body (as an airplane) moving through a fluid (as air) parallel and opposite to the direction of motion (2) **:** friction between engine parts; *also* **:** retardation due to friction **c :** BURDEN, ENCUMBRANCE ⟨the ~ of population growth on living standards⟩ **5 a :** an object drawn over the ground to leave a scented trail **b :** a clog fastened to a trap to prevent the escape of a trapped animal **6 :** STREET, ROAD ⟨the main ~⟩ **7** *slang* **:** a girl that one is escorting **8 :** clothing typical of one sex worn by a person of the opposite sex— often used in the phrase *in drag* **9 :** DRAG RACE **10 :** [5]BORE ⟨school is a ~ for some youngsters⟩ **11 :** COSTUME, OUTFIT, GETUP

[2]drag *vb* **dragged; drag·ging** [ME *draggen,* fr. ON *draga* — more at DRAW] *vt* (15c) **1 a** (1) **:** to draw slowly or heavily **:** HAUL (2) **:** to cause to move with painful or undue slowness or difficulty ⟨*dragging* the musical tempo⟩ (3) **:** to cause to trail along a surface ⟨wandered off *dragging* the leash⟩ **b :** to bring by force or compulsion ⟨had to ~ her husband to the opera⟩ **c** (1) **:** to pass (time) in lingering pain, tedium, or unhappiness (2) **:** PROTRACT ⟨~ a story out⟩ **2 a :** to explore with a drag **b :** to catch with a dragnet or trawl **3 :** to hit (a bunt) by trailing the bat while moving toward first base ~ *vi* **1 :** to hang or lag behind **2 :** to fish or search with a drag **3 :** to trail along on the ground **4 :** to move on or proceed laboriously or tediously ⟨the book ~*s*⟩ **5 :** DRAW 4a ⟨~ on a cigarette⟩ **6 :** to make a plucking or pulling movement **7 :** to participate in a drag race **syn** see PULL — **drag·ging·ly** \'drag-iŋ-lē\ *adv* — **drag one's feet** *or* **drag one's heels :** to act in a deliberately slow, dilatory, or ineffective manner

drag bunt *n* (ca. 1949) **:** a bunt in baseball made by a left-handed batter by trailing the bat while moving toward first base; *broadly* **:** a bunt made with the object of getting on base safely rather than sacrificing

dra·gée \dra-'zhā\ *n* [F, fr. MF *dragie* — more at DREDGE] (14c) **1 :** a sugar-coated medicated confection **2 a :** a sugar-coated nut **b :** a small silver-colored ball for decorating cakes

drag·ger \'drag-ər\ *n* (1500) **:** one that drags; *specif* **:** a fishing boat operating a trawl or dragnet

drag·gle \'drag-əl\ *vb* **drag·gled; drag·gling** \-(ə-)liŋ\ [freq. of *drag*] *vt* (1513) **:** to make wet and dirty by dragging ~ *vi* **1 :** to trail on the ground **2 :** STRAGGLE

drag·gle–tail \'drag-əl-ˌtāl\ *n* (1596) **:** SLATTERN

drag·gy \'drag-ē\ *adj* **drag·gi·er; -est** (15c) **:** SLUGGISH, DULL

drag·line \'drag-ˌlīn\ *n* (ca. 1911) **1 :** a line used in or for dragging **2 :** an excavating machine in which the bucket is attached by cables and operates by being drawn toward the machine

drag·net \'drag-ˌnet\ *n* (1541) **1 a :** a net drawn along the bottom of a body of water **:** TRAWL **b :** a net used on the ground (as to capture small game) **2 :** a network of measures for apprehension (as of criminals)

drag·o·man \'drag-ə-mən\ *n, pl* **-mans** *or* **men** \-mən\ [ME *drogman,* fr. MF, fr. OIt *dragomanno,* fr. MGk *dragomanos,* fr. Ar *tarjumān,* fr. Aram *tùrgĕmānā*] (14c) **:** an interpreter chiefly of Arabic, Turkish, or Persian employed esp. in the Near East

drag·on \'drag-ən\ *n* [ME, fr. OF, fr. L *dracon-, draco* serpent, dragon, fr. Gk *drakōn* serpent; akin to OE *torht* bright, Gk *derkesthai* to see, look at] (13c) **1** *archaic* **:** a huge serpent **2 :** a mythical animal usu. represented as a monstrous winged and scaly serpent or saurian with a crested head and enormous claws **3 :** a violent, combative, or very strict person **4 a :** a short musket formerly carried hooked to a soldier's belt; *also* **:** a soldier carrying such a musket **b :** an artillery tractor **5** *cap* **:** DRACO **6 :** something formidable or baneful — **drag·on·ish** \-ə-nish\ *adj*

drag·on·et \ˌdrag-ə-'net, 'drag-ə-nət\ *n* (14c) **1 :** a little dragon **2 :** any of various small often brightly colored scaleless marine fishes constituting a family (Callionymidae); *esp* **:** a European fish (*Callionymus lyra*) sometimes used as food

drag·on·fly \'drag-ən-ˌflī\ *n* (1626) **:** any of a suborder (Anisoptera) of odonate insects that are larger and stouter than damselflies, hold the wings horizontal in repose, and have rectal gills during the naiad stage; *broadly* **:** ODONATE

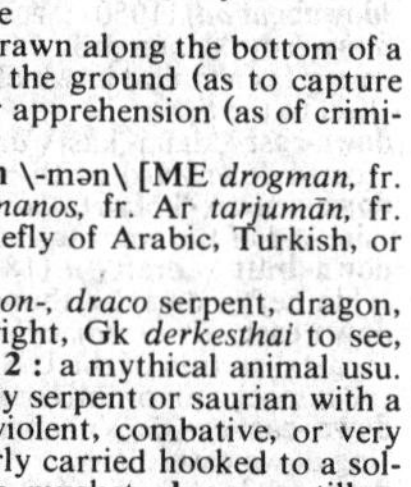

dragonfly

drag·on·head \-ˌhed\ *n* (1784) **:** any of several mints (genus *Dracocephalum*) often grown for their showy flower heads; *esp* **:** a No. American plant (*D. parviflorum*)

dragon lizard *n* (1927) **:** an Indonesian monitor lizard (*Varanus komodoensis*) that is the largest of all known lizards and reaches 11 feet in length

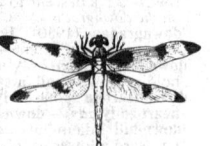

dragon's blood *n* (14c) **:** any of several resinous mostly dark-red plant products; *specif* **:** a resin from the fruit of a palm (genus *Daemonorops*) used for coloring varnish and in photoengraving

dragon's teeth *n pl* [fr. the dragon's teeth sown by Cadmus which sprang up as armed warriors who killed one another off] (1853) **1 :** seeds of strife **2 :** wedge-shaped concrete antitank barriers laid in multiple rows

[1]dra·goon \drə-'gün, dra-\ *n* [F *dragon* dragon, dragoon, fr. MF] (1622) **:** a member of a European military unit formerly composed of heavily armed mounted troops

[2]dragoon *vt* (1689) **1 :** to subjugate or persecute by harsh use of troops **2 :** to force or attempt to force into submission by violent measures **:** COERCE

drag queen *n* (ca. 1965) **:** a male homosexual who dresses as a woman

drag race *n* (1949) **:** an acceleration contest between vehicles (as automobiles) — **drag racing** *n*

drag·rope \'drag-ˌrōp\ *n* (1766) **:** a rope that drags or is used for dragging

drag·ster \'drag-stər\ *n* (ca. 1954) **1 :** a vehicle (as an automobile) built or modified for use in a drag race **2 :** one who participates in a drag race

drag strip *n* (1952) **:** the site of a drag race; *specif* **:** a strip of pavement with a racing area at least 1/4 mile long

drail \'drā(ə)l\ *n* [obs. E *drail* to drag, trail] (1634) **:** a heavy fishhook used in trolling

[1]drain \'drān\ *vb* [ME *draynen,* fr. OE *drēahnian* — more at DRY] *vt* (bef. 12c) **1** *obs* **:** FILTER **2 a :** to draw off (liquid) gradually or completely ⟨~*ed* all the water out⟩ **b :** to cause the gradual disappearance of **c :** to exhaust physically or emotionally **3 a :** to make gradually dry ⟨~ a swamp⟩ **b :** to carry away the surface water of ⟨the river that ~*s* the valley⟩ **c :** to deplete or empty by or as if by drawing off by degrees or in increments ⟨war that ~*s* a nation of youth and wealth⟩ **d :** to empty by drinking the contents of ⟨~ a glass of beer⟩ ~ *vi* **1 a :** to flow off gradually **b :** to disappear gradually **:** DWINDLE ⟨money ~*ing* away in expenses⟩ **2 :** to become emptied or freed of liquid by its flowing or dropping **3 :** to discharge surface or surplus water **syn** see DEPLETE — **drain·er** *n*

[2]**drain** *n* (1552) **1 :** a means (as a pipe) by which usu. liquid matter is drained **2 a :** the act of draining **b :** a gradual outflow or withdrawal : DEPLETION ⟨a ruinous dollar ~⟩ **3 :** something that causes depletion : BURDEN ⟨a ~ on the national resources⟩ — **down the drain :** to a state of being wasted or irretrievably lost ⟨years of work went *down the drain* in the fire⟩

drain·age \ˈdrā-nij\ *n* (1652) **1 :** the act, process, or mode of draining; *also* **:** something drained off **2 :** a device for draining : DRAIN; *also* **:** a system of drains **3 :** an area or district drained

drain·pipe \ˈdrān-ˌpīp\ *n* (1857) **:** a pipe for drainage

[1]**drake** \ˈdrāk\ *n* [ME; akin to OHG *antrahho* drake] (14c) **:** a male duck

[2]**drake** *n* [ME, dragon, fr. OE *draca,* fr. L *draco* — more at DRAGON] (1625) **1 :** a small piece of artillery of the 17th and 18th centuries **2 :** MAYFLY

dram \ˈdram\ *n* [ME *dragme,* fr. MF & LL; MF, dram, drachma, fr. LL *dragma,* fr. L *drachma,* fr. Gk *drachmē,* lit., handful, fr. *drassesthai* to grasp] (14c) **1 a —** see WEIGHT table **b :** FLUIDRAM **2 a :** a small portion of something to drink **b :** a small amount

dra·ma \ˈdräm-ə, ˈdram-\ *n* [LL *dramat-, drama,* fr. Gk, deed, drama, fr. *dran* to do, act] (1515) **1 :** a composition in verse or prose intended to portray life or character or to tell a story usu. involving conflicts and emotions through action and dialogue and typically designed for theatrical performance : PLAY — compare CLOSET DRAMA **2 :** dramatic art, literature, or affairs **3 a :** a state, situation, or series of events involving interesting or intense conflict of forces **b :** dramatic state, effect, or quality ⟨the ~ of the courtroom proceedings⟩

Dram·a·mine \ˈdram-ə-ˌmēn\ *trademark* — used for dimenhydrinate

dra·mat·ic \drə-ˈmat-ik\ *adj* (1589) **1 :** of or relating to the drama **2 a :** suitable to or characteristic of the drama : VIVID **b :** striking in appearance or effect **3** *of an opera singer* **:** having a powerful voice and a declamatory style — compare LYRIC — **dra·mat·i·cal·ly** \-i-k(ə-)lē\ *adv*

syn DRAMATIC, THEATRICAL, HISTRIONIC, MELODRAMATIC mean having a character or an effect like that of acted plays. DRAMATIC applies to situations in life and literature that stir the imagination and emotions deeply ⟨a *dramatic* meeting of leaders⟩ THEATRICAL implies a crude appeal through artificiality or exaggeration in gesture or vocal expression ⟨a *theatrical* oration⟩ HISTRIONIC applies to tones, gestures, and motions and suggests a deliberate affectation or staginess ⟨a *histrionic* show of grief⟩ MELODRAMATIC suggests an exaggerated emotionalism or an inappropriate theatricalism ⟨making a *melodramatic* scene in public⟩

dramatic irony *n* (ca. 1907) **:** IRONY 3b

dramatic monologue *n* (ca. 1935) **:** a literary work in which a character reveals himself in a monologue usu. addressed to a second person

dra·mat·ics \drə-ˈmat-iks\ *n pl but sing or pl in constr* (1796) **1 :** the study or practice of theatrical arts (as acting and stagecraft) **2 :** dramatic behavior or expression

dramatic unities *n pl* (ca. 1922) **:** the unities of time, place, and action that are observed in classical drama

dra·ma·tis per·so·nae \ˌdram-ət-ə-spər-ˈsō-(ˌ)nē, ˌdräm-, -ˌnī\ *n pl* [NL] (1730) **1 :** the characters or actors in a drama **2** *sing in constr* **:** a list of the characters or actors in a drama

dra·ma·tist \ˈdram-ət-əst, ˈdräm-\ *n* (1678) **:** PLAYWRIGHT

dra·ma·ti·za·tion \ˌdram-ət-ə-ˈzā-shən, ˌdräm-\ *n* (1796) **1 :** the act or process of dramatizing **2 :** a dramatized version (as of a novel)

dra·ma·tize \ˈdram-ə-ˌtīz, ˈdräm-\ *vb* **-tized; -tiz·ing** *vt* (1780) **1 :** to adapt (as a novel) for theatrical presentation **2 :** to present or represent in a dramatic manner ~ *vi* **1 :** to be suitable for dramatization **2 :** to behave dramatically : put on an act — **dra·ma·tiz·able** \-ˌtī-zə-bəl\ *adj*

dra·ma·turge *also* **dra·ma·turg** \ˈdram-ə-ˌtərj, ˈdräm-\ *n* (1870) **:** a specialist in dramaturgy

dra·ma·tur·gy \ˈdram-ə-ˌtər-jē, ˈdräm-\ *n* [G *dramaturgie,* fr. Gk *dramatourgia* dramatic composition, fr. *dramat-, drama* + *-ourgia* -urgy] (1801) **:** the art or technique of dramatic composition and theatrical representation — **dra·ma·tur·gic** \ˌdram-ə-ˈtər-jik, ˌdräm-\ *or* **dra·ma·tur·gi·cal** \-ji-kəl\ *adj* — **dra·ma·tur·gi·cal·ly** \-ji-k(ə-)lē\ *adv*

dram·mock \ˈdram-ək\ *n* [ScGael *dramag* foul mixture] *chiefly Scot* (1562) **:** raw oatmeal mixed with cold water

dram·shop \ˈdram-ˌshäp\ *n* (1723) **:** BARROOM

drank *past and past part of* DRINK

[1]**drape** \ˈdrāp\ *n* (1665) **1 a :** a drapery esp. for a window : CURTAIN **b :** a sterile covering used in an operating room — usu. used in pl. **2 :** arrangement in or of folds **3 :** the cut or hang of clothing — **drap·ey** \ˈdrā-pē\ *adj*

[2]**drape** *vb* **draped; drap·ing** [ME *drapen* to weave, fr. MF *draper,* fr. *drap* cloth — more at DRAB] *vt* (1847) **1 :** to cover or adorn with or as if with folds of cloth **2 :** to cause to hang or stretch out loosely or carelessly ⟨*draped* his legs over the chair⟩ **3 :** to arrange in flowing lines or folds ⟨a cleverly *draped* suit⟩ ~ *vi* **:** to become arranged in folds ⟨this silk ~s beautifully⟩ — **drap·able** *also* **drape·able** \ˈdrā-pə-bəl\ *adj* — **drap·abil·i·ty** *also* **drape·abil·i·ty** \ˌdrā-pə-ˈbil-ət-ē\ *n*

drap·er \ˈdrā-pər\ *n, chiefly Brit* (14c) **:** a dealer in cloth and sometimes also in clothing and dry goods

drap·ery \ˈdrā-p(ə-)rē\ *n, pl* **-er·ies** (14c) **1** *Brit* **:** DRY GOODS **2 a :** a decorative piece of material usu. hung in loose folds and arranged in a graceful design **b :** hangings of heavy fabric for use as a curtain **3 :** the draping or arranging of materials

dras·tic \ˈdras-tik\ *adj* [Gk *drastikos,* fr. *dran* to do] (1691) **1 :** acting rapidly or violently ⟨a ~ purgative⟩ **2 :** radical in effect or action : SEVERE ⟨~ measures⟩ — **dras·ti·cal·ly** \-ti-k(ə-)lē\ *adv*

drat \ˈdrat\ *vb* **drat·ted; drat·ting** [prob. euphemistic alter. of *God rot*] (1815) **:** DAMN — used as a mild oath

draught \ˈdraft\, **draughty** \ˈdraf-tē\ *chiefly Brit var of* DRAFT, DRAFTY

draughts \ˈdraf(t)s\ *n pl but sing or pl in constr* [ME *draghtes,* fr. pl. of *draght* draft, move in chess] *Brit* (15c) **:** CHECKERS

draughts·man *chiefly Brit var of* DRAFTSMAN

Dra·vid·i·an \drə-ˈvid-ē-ən\ *n* [Skt *Drāviḍa*] (1856) **1 :** a member of an ancient Australoid race of southern India **2 :** DRAVIDIAN LANGUAGES — **Dravidian** *adj*

Dravidian languages *n pl* (1871) **:** a language family of India, Ceylon, and Pakistan that includes Tamil, Telugu, Gondi, and Malayalam

[1]**draw** \ˈdrȯ\ *vb* **drew** \ˈdrü\; **drawn** \ˈdrȯn\; **draw·ing** [ME *drawen, dragen,* fr. OE *dragan;* akin to ON *draga* to draw, drag, L *trahere* to pull, draw] *vt* (bef. 12c) **1 :** to cause to move continuously toward or after a force applied in advance : HAUL, DRAG ⟨~ your chair up by the fire⟩: as **a :** to move (as a covering) over or to one side ⟨~ the drapes⟩ **b :** to pull up or out of a receptacle or place where seated or carried ⟨~ water from the well⟩ ⟨*drew* a gun⟩; *also* **:** to cause to come out of a container ⟨~ water for a bath⟩ **2 :** to cause to go in a certain direction (as by leading) ⟨*drew* him aside⟩ **3 a :** to bring by inducement or allure : ATTRACT ⟨honey ~s flies⟩ **b :** to bring in or gather from a specified group or area ⟨a college that ~s its students from many states⟩ **c :** BRING ON, PROVOKE ⟨*drew* enemy fire⟩ **d :** to bring out by way of response : ELICIT ⟨*drew* cheers from the audience⟩ **4 :** INHALE ⟨*drew* a deep breath⟩ **5 a :** to extract the essence from ⟨~ tea⟩ **b :** EVISCERATE ⟨plucking and ~*ing* a goose before cooking⟩ **c :** to derive to one's benefit ⟨*drew* inspiration from the old masters⟩ **6 :** to require (a specified depth) to float in ⟨a ship that ~s 12 feet of water⟩ **7 a :** ACCUMULATE, GAIN ⟨~*ing* interest⟩ **b :** to take (money) from a place of deposit **c :** to use in making a cash demand ⟨~*ing* a check against his account⟩ **d :** to receive regularly or in due course ⟨~ a salary⟩ **8 a :** to take (cards) from a stack or from the dealer **b :** to receive or take at random ⟨*drew* a winning number⟩ **9 :** to bend (a bow) by pulling back the string **10 :** to cause to shrink, contract, or tighten **11 :** to strike (a ball) so as to impart a backward spin **12 :** to leave (a contest) undecided : TIE **13 a (1) :** to produce a likeness or representation of by making lines on a surface ⟨~ a picture⟩ ⟨~ a graph with chalk⟩ **(2) :** to give a portrayal of : DELINEATE ⟨a writer who ~s his characters well⟩ **b :** to write out in due form ⟨~ a will⟩ **c :** to design or describe in detail : FORMULATE ⟨~ comparisons⟩ **14 :** to infer from evidence or premises ⟨~ a conclusion⟩ **15 :** to spread or elongate (metal) by hammering or by pulling through dies; *also* **:** to shape (plastic) by stretching or by pulling through dies ~ *vi* **1 :** to come or go steadily or gradually ⟨night ~s near⟩ **2 a :** to move something by pulling ⟨~*ing* at the well⟩ **b :** to exert an attractive force ⟨the play is ~*ing* well⟩ **3 a :** to pull back a bowstring **b :** to bring out a weapon ⟨*drew,* aimed, and fired⟩ **4 a :** to produce a draft ⟨the chimney ~s well⟩ ⟨~ on a cigar⟩ **b :** to swell out in a wind ⟨all sails ~*ing*⟩ **5 a :** to wrinkle or tighten up : SHRINK **b :** to change shape by pulling or stretching **6 a :** to cause blood or pus to localize at one point **b :** STEEP ⟨give the tea time to ~⟩ **7 :** to create a likeness or a picture in outlines : SKETCH **8 :** to come out even in a contest **9 a :** to make a written demand for payment of money on deposit **b :** to obtain resources (as of information) ⟨~*ing* from a common fund of knowledge⟩ ***syn*** see PULL — **draw·able** \-ə-bəl\ *adj* — **draw a bead on :** to take aim at — **draw a blank :** to fail to gain a desired object (as information sought); *also* **:** to be unable to think of something — **draw on** *or* **draw upon :** to use as a source of supply ⟨*drawing on* the whole community for support⟩ — **draw straws :** to decide or assign by lottery in which straws of unequal length are used — **draw the line** *or* **draw a line 1 :** to fix an arbitrary boundary between things that tend to intermingle ⟨*drawing a line* between art and pornography⟩ **2 :** to fix a boundary excluding what one will not tolerate or engage in

[2]**draw** *n* (1663) **1 :** the act or process of drawing: as **a :** a sucking pull on something held with the lips ⟨take a ~ on his pipe⟩ **b :** a removal of a handgun from its holster ⟨the sheriff was quicker on the ~⟩ **c :** backward spin given to a ball by striking it below center — compare FOLLOW **2 :** something that is drawn: as **a :** a card drawn to replace a discard in poker **b :** a lot or chance drawn at random **c :** the movable part of a drawbridge **3 :** a contest left undecided or deadlocked : TIE **4 :** something that draws attention or patronage **5 a :** the distance from the string to the back of a drawn bow **b :** the force required to draw a bow fully **6 :** a gully shallower than a ravine **7 :** the deal in draw poker to improve the players' hands after discarding **8 :** a football play in which the quarterback drops back as if to pass and then hands off to a back moving straight ahead — compare BOOTLEG 3

draw away *vi* (1670) **:** to move ahead (as of an opponent in a race)

draw·back \ˈdrȯ-ˌbak\ *n* (1697) **1 :** a refund of duties esp. on an imported product subsequently exported or used to produce a product for export **2 :** an objectionable feature : DISADVANTAGE

draw back \drȯ-ˈbak\ *vi* (14c) **:** to avoid an issue or commitment : RETREAT

draw·bar \ˈdrȯ-ˌbär\ *n* (1839) **1 :** a railroad coupler **2 :** a beam across the rear of a tractor to which implements are hitched

draw·bridge \-ˌbrij\ *n* (14c) **:** a bridge made to be raised up, let down, or drawn aside so as to permit or hinder passage

draw·down \-ˌdau̇n\ *n* (1918) **1 :** a lowering of a water level (as in a reservoir) **2 a :** the process of depleting **b :** REDUCTION

draw down \(ˌ)drȯ-ˈdau̇n\ *vt* (1949) **:** to deplete by using or spending ⟨an unfavorable trade balance *draws down* gold reserves⟩

draw·ee \drȯ-ˈē\ *n* (1766) **:** the person on whom an order or bill of exchange is drawn

draw·er \ˈdrȯ(-ə)r\ *n* (14c) **1 :** one that draws: as **a :** a person who draws liquor **b :** DRAFTSMAN **c :** one who draws a bill of exchange or order for payment or makes a promissory note **2** *pl* **:** an article of clothing (as underwear) for the lower body **3 :** a sliding box or receptacle opened by pulling out and closed by pushing in — **drawer·ful** \-ˌfu̇l\ *n*

draw in *vt* (1558) **1 :** to cause or entice to enter or participate ⟨heard the argument but would not be *drawn in*⟩ **2 :** to sketch roughly ⟨*drawing in* the first outlines⟩ ~ *vi* **1 a :** to draw to an end ⟨the day *drew in*⟩ **b :** to shorten seasonally ⟨the evenings are already *drawing in*⟩ **2 :** to become more cautious or economical

draw·ing \ˈdrȯ(-)iŋ\ *n* (14c) **1 :** an act or instance of drawing; *specif* **:** the process of deciding something by drawing lots **2 :** the art or technique of representing an object or outlining a figure, plan, or sketch by means of lines **3 :** something drawn or subject to drawing: as **a :** an amount drawn from a fund **b :** a representation formed by drawing : SKETCH

drawing account *n* (1924) **:** an account showing payments made to an employee (as a salesman) in advance of actual earnings or for traveling expenses

drawing board *n* (1725) **1 :** a board used as a base for drafting on paper **2 :** a planning stage ⟨a project still on the *drawing boards*⟩

drawing card *n* (1887) **:** one that attracts attention or patronage

drawing pin *n, Brit* (1859) **:** THUMBTACK

drawing room *n* [short for *withdrawing room*] (1642) **1 a :** a formal reception room **b :** a private room on a railroad passenger car with three berths and an enclosed toilet **2 :** a formal reception

drawing table *n* (1706) **:** a table with a surface adjustable for elevation and angle of incline

draw·knife \'drȯ-ˌnīf\ *n* (1703) **:** a woodworker's tool consisting of a blade with a handle at each end for use in shaving off surfaces — called also *drawshave*

1drawl \'drȯl\ *vb* [prob. freq. of *draw*] *vi* (1604) **:** to speak slowly with vowels greatly prolonged ~ *vt* **:** to utter in a slow lengthened tone — **drawl·er** *n* — **drawl·ing·ly** \'drȯ-liŋ-lē\ *adv*

2drawl *n* (1760) **:** a drawling manner of speaking — **drawly** \'drȯ-lē\ *adj*

drawn *past part of* DRAW

drawn butter *n* (1826) **:** melted butter often with seasoning

drawn·work \'drȯn-ˌwərk\ *n* (1595) **:** decoration on cloth made by drawing out threads according to a pattern

draw off *vt* (13c) **:** REMOVE, WITHDRAW ~ *vi* **:** to move apart **:** REGROUP ⟨the enemies' losses forced them to *draw off*⟩

draw on *vi* (15c) **:** APPROACH ⟨night *draws on*⟩ ~ *vt* **:** BRING ON, CAUSE

draw out *vt* (14c) **1 :** REMOVE, EXTRACT **2 :** to extend beyond a minimum in time **:** PROTRACT 2 **3 :** to cause to speak freely ⟨a reporter's ability to *draw* a person *out*⟩

draw·plate \'drȯ-ˌplāt\ *n* (1832) **:** a die with holes through which wires are drawn

draw play *n* (1952) **:** DRAW 8

draw poker *n* (1849) **:** poker in which each player is dealt five cards face down and after betting may get replacements for discards

draw·shave \'drȯ-ˌshāv\ *n* (1828) **:** DRAWKNIFE

draw shot *n* (1897) **:** a shot in billiards or pool made by striking the cue ball below its center to cause it to move back after striking the object ball

draw·string \'drȯ-ˌstriŋ\ *n* (1845) **:** a string, cord, or tape inserted into hems or casings or laced through eyelets for use in closing a bag or controlling fullness in garments or curtains

draw·tube \-'t(y)üb\ *n* (ca. 1891) **:** a telescoping tube (as for the eyepiece of a microscope)

draw up *vt* (1605) **1 :** to bring (as troops) into array **2 :** to prepare a draft or version of ⟨*draw up* plans⟩ **3 :** to straighten (oneself) to an erect posture esp. as an assertion of dignity or resentment **4 :** to bring to a halt ~ *vi* **:** to come to a halt

1dray \'drā\ *n* [ME *draye*, a wheelless vehicle, fr. OE *dræge* dragnet; akin to OE *dragan* to pull — more at DRAW] (14c) **:** a vehicle used to haul goods; *specif* **:** a strong low cart or wagon without sides

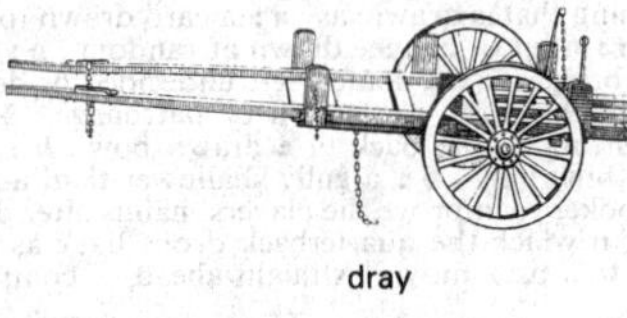

dray

2dray *vt* (1858) **:** to haul on a dray **:** CART

dray·age \'drā-ij\ *n* (1791) **:** the work or cost of hauling by dray

dray horse *n* (1709) **:** a horse adapted for drawing heavy loads

dray·man \'drā-mən\ *n* (1581) **:** one whose work is hauling by dray

1dread \'dred\ *vb* [ME *dreden*, fr. OE *drǣdan*] *vt* (bef. 12c) **1 a :** to fear greatly **b** *archaic* **:** to regard with awe **2 :** to feel extreme reluctance to meet or face ~ *vi* **:** to be apprehensive or fearful

2dread *n* (13c) **1 a :** great fear esp. in the face of impending evil **b :** extreme uneasiness in the face of a disagreeable prospect ⟨his ~ of paperwork⟩ **c** *archaic* **:** AWE **2 :** one causing fear or awe ***syn*** see FEAR

3dread *adj* (15c) **1 :** causing great fear or anxiety **2 :** inspiring awe

1dread·ful \'dred-fəl\ *adj* (13c) **1 a :** inspiring dread **:** causing great and oppressive fear **b :** inspiring awe or reverence **2 :** extremely bad, distasteful, unpleasant, or shocking **3 :** EXTREME ⟨~ disorder⟩ — **dread·ful·ly** \-f(ə-)lē\ *adv* — **dread·ful·ness** \-fəl-nəs\ *n*

2dreadful *n* (1873) **:** a cheap and sensational story or periodical

dread·locks \'dred-ˌläks\ *n pl* (1960) **:** long braids of hair worn by Rastafarians

dread·nought \'dred-ˌnȯt, -ˌnät\ *n* (1806) **1 :** a warm garment of thick cloth; *also* **:** the cloth **2** [*Dreadnought*, Brit. battleship] **:** a battleship whose main armament consists of big guns of the same caliber

1dream \'drēm\ *n, often attrib* [ME *dreem*, fr. OE *drēam* noise, joy, and ON *draumr* dream; akin to OHG *troum* dream] (13c) **1 :** a series of thoughts, images, or emotions occurring during sleep — compare REM SLEEP **2 :** an experience of waking life having the characteristics of a dream: as **a :** a visionary creation of the imagination **:** DAYDREAM **b :** a state of mind marked by abstraction or release from reality **:** REVERIE **c :** an object seen in a dreamlike state **:** VISION **3 :** something notable for its beauty, excellence, or enjoyable quality ⟨the new car is a ~ to operate⟩ **4 a :** a strongly desired goal or purpose ⟨a ~ of becoming president⟩ **b :** something that fully satisfies a wish **:** IDEAL ⟨a meal that was a gourmet's ~⟩ — **dream·ful** \-fəl\ *adj* — **dream·ful·ly** \-fə-lē\ *adv* — **dream·ful·ness** *n* — **dream·less** *adj* — **dream·less·ly** *adv* — **dream·less·ness** *n* — **dream·like** \'drēm-ˌlīk\ *adj*

2dream *vb* **dreamed** \'drem(p)t, 'drēmd\ *or* **dreamt** \'drem(p)t\; **dream·ing** \'drē-miŋ\ *vi* (13c) **1 :** to have a dream **2 :** to indulge in daydreams or fantasies ⟨~*ing* of a better future⟩ **3 :** to appear tranquil or dreamy ⟨houses ~ in leafy shadows —Gladys Taber⟩ ~ *vt* **1 :** to have a dream of **2 :** to consider as a possibility **:** IMAGINE **3 :** to pass (time) in reverie or inaction — usu. used with *away* ⟨~*ing* the hours away⟩ — **dream of :** to consider possible or fitting ⟨wouldn't *dream of* disturbing you⟩

dream·er \'drē-mər\ *n* (14c) **1 :** one that dreams **2 a :** one who lives in a world of fancy and imagination **b :** one who has ideas or conceives projects regarded as impractical **:** VISIONARY

dream·land \'drēm-ˌland\ *n* (1834) **:** an unreal delightful country existing only in imagination or in dreams **:** NEVER-NEVER LAND

dream up *vt* (1941) **:** to form in the mind **:** DEVISE, CONCOCT

dream vision *n* (1906) **:** a usu. medieval poem having a framework in which the poet pictures himself as falling asleep and envisioning in his dream a series of allegorical people and events

dream·world \'drēm-ˌwərld\ *n* (1817) **:** a world of illusion or fantasy

dreamy \'drē-mē\ *adj* **dream·i·er; -est** (1567) **1 a :** full of dreams ⟨a ~ night's sleep⟩ **b :** pleasantly abstracted from immediate reality **2 :** given to dreaming or fantasy ⟨a ~ child⟩ **3 a :** suggestive of a dream in vague or visionary quality ⟨a ~ recollection of the incident⟩ **b :** quiet and soothing **c :** DELIGHTFUL, PLEASING — **dream·i·ly** \-mə-lē\ *adv* — **dream·i·ness** \-mē-nəs\ *n*

drear \'dri(ə)r\ *adj* (1629) **:** DREARY — **drear** *n*

drea·ry \'dri(ə)r-ē\ *adj* **drea·ri·er; -est** [ME *drery*, fr. OE *drēorig* sad, bloody, fr. *drēor* gore; akin to OHG *trūrēn* to be sad, Goth *driusan* to fall, Gk *thrauein* to shatter, OE *dropa* drop] (bef. 12c) **1 :** SAD, DOLEFUL **2 :** causing feelings of cheerlessness **:** GLOOMY — **drea·ri·ly** \'drir-ə-lē\ *adv* — **drea·ri·ness** \'drir-ē-nəs\ *n*

dreck *also* **drek** \'drek\ *n* [Yiddish *drek* & G *dreck*, fr. MHG *drec;* akin to OE *threax* rubbish, L *stercus* excrement] (1922) **:** TRASH, RUBBISH

1dredge \'drej\ *vb* **dredged; dredg·ing** *vt* (1508) **1 a :** to dig, gather, or pull out with a dredge — often used with *up* **b :** to deepen (as a waterway) with a dredging machine **2 :** to bring to light by deep searching — often used with *up* ⟨*dredging* up memories⟩ ~ *vi* **1 :** to use a dredge **2 :** to search deeply — **dredg·er** *n*

2dredge *n* [prob. fr. Sc *dreg-* (in *dregbot* dredge boat)] (1602) **1 :** an apparatus usu. in the form of an oblong iron frame with an attached bag net used esp. for gathering fish and shellfish **2 :** a machine for removing earth usu. by buckets on an endless chain or a suction tube **3 :** a barge used in dredging

3dredge *vt* **dredged; dredg·ing** [obs. *dredge*, n., sweetmeat, fr. ME *drage, drege*, fr. MF *dragie*, modif. of L *tragemata* sweetmeats, fr. Gk *tragēmata*, pl. of *tragēma* sweetmeat, fr. *trōgein* to gnaw — more at TERSE] (1596) **:** to coat (food) by sprinkling (as with flour) — **dredg·er** *n*

dree \'drē\ *vt* **dreed; dree·ing** [ME *dreen*, fr. OE *drēogan* — more at DRUDGE] *chiefly Scot* (bef. 12c) **:** ENDURE, SUFFER

dreg \'dreg\ *n* [ME, fr. ON *dregg;* akin to L *fraces* dregs of oil, Gk *thrassein* to trouble — more at DARK] (14c) **1 :** sediment contained in a liquid or precipitated from it **:** LEES — usu. used in pl. **2 :** the most undesirable part — usu. used in pl. ⟨the ~s of society⟩ **3 :** the last remaining part **:** VESTIGE — **dreg·gy** \'dreg-ē\ *adj*

D region *n* (ca. 1930) **:** the lowest part of the ionosphere occurring approximately between 30 and 55 miles (50 and 90 kilometers) above the surface of the earth

dreich \'drēk̲\ *adj* [ME, of Scand origin; akin to ON *drjūgr* lasting] *chiefly Scot* (1813) **:** DREARY

drei·del *also* **dreidl** \'drād-ᵊl\ *n* [Yiddish *dreidl*, fr. *dreien* to turn, fr. MHG *drǣjen*, fr. OHG *drāen* — more at THROW] (1926) **1 :** a 4-sided toy marked with Hebrew letters and spun like a top in a game of chance **2 :** a children's game of chance played esp. at Hanukkah with a dreidel

1drench \'drench\ *n* (bef. 12c) **1 :** a poisonous or medicinal drink; *specif* **:** a large dose of medicine mixed with liquid and put down the throat of an animal **2 a :** something that drenches **b :** a quantity sufficient to drench or saturate

2drench *vt* [ME *drenchen*, fr. OE *drencan;* akin to OE *drincan* to drink] (bef. 12c) **1 a** *archaic* **:** to force to drink **b :** to administer a drench to (an animal) **2 :** to wet thoroughly (as by soaking or immersing in liquid) ⟨desserts ~*ed* with brandy⟩ **3 :** to soak or cover thoroughly with liquid that falls or is precipitated **4 :** to fill or cover completely as if by soaking or precipitation **:** SATURATE ⟨was ~*ed* in furs and diamonds —Richard Brautigan⟩ ***syn*** see SOAK — **drench·er** *n*

1dress \'dres\ *vb* [ME *dressen*, fr. MF *dresser*, fr. OF *drecier*, fr. (assumed) VL *directiare*, fr. L *directus* direct, pp. of *dirigere* to direct, fr. *dis-* + *regere* to lead straight — more at RIGHT] *vt* (14c) **1 a :** to make or set straight **b :** to arrange (as troops) in a straight line and at proper intervals **2 :** to prepare for use or service; *specif* **:** to prepare for cooking or for the table **3 :** to add decorative details or accessories to **:** EMBELLISH **4 a :** to put clothes on **b :** to provide with clothing **5** *archaic* **:** DRESS DOWN **6 a :** to apply dressings or medicaments to **b (1) :** to arrange (the hair) by combing, brushing, or curling **(2) :** to groom and curry (an animal) **c :** to kill and prepare for market or for consumption **d :** CULTIVATE, TEND; *esp* **:** to apply manure or fertilizer to **e :** to put through a finishing process; *specif* **:** to trim and smooth the surface of (as lumber or stone) ~ *vi* **1 a :** to put on clothing **b :** to put on or wear formal, elaborate, or fancy clothes ⟨guests were expected to ~ for dinner⟩ **2** *of a food animal* **:** to weigh after being dressed — often used with *out* **3 :** to align oneself with the next soldier in a line to make the line straight — **dress ship :** to ornament a ship for a celebration by hoisting national ensigns at the mastheads and running a line of signal flags and pennants from bow to stern

2dress *n* (1606) **1 :** APPAREL, CLOTHING **2 :** an outer garment (as for a woman or girl) usu. consisting of a one-piece bodice and skirt **3 :** covering, adornment, or appearance appropriate or peculiar to a particular time **4 :** a particular form of presentation **:** GUISE

3dress *adj* (1767) **1 :** relating to or used for a dress **2 :** suitable for a formal occasion **3 :** requiring or permitting formal dress ⟨a ~ affair⟩

dres·sage \drə-'säzh, dre-\ *n* (1936) **:** the execution by a trained horse of precision movements in response to barely perceptible signals from its rider

dress circle *n* (1825) **:** the first or lowest curved tier of seats above the main floor in a theater or opera house

dress down *vt* (ca. 1897) **:** to reprove severely ~ *vi* **:** to dress casually esp. for reasons of fashion

[1]**dress·er** \'dres-ər\ *n* (15c) **1** *obs* **:** a table or sideboard for preparing and serving food **2 :** a cupboard to hold dishes and cooking utensils **3 :** a chest of drawers or bureau with a mirror

[2]**dresser** *n* (1520) **:** one that dresses ⟨a fashionable ~⟩

dresser set *n* (ca. 1934) **:** a set of toilet articles including hairbrush, comb, and mirror for use at a dresser or dressing table

dress·ing *n* (15c) **1 a :** the act or process of one who dresses **b :** an instance of such act or process **2 a :** a sauce for adding to a dish (as a salad) **b :** a seasoned mixture usu. used as a stuffing (as for poultry) **3 a :** material (as ointment or gauze) applied to cover a lesion **b :** fertilizing material (as manure or compost)

dres·sing–down \'dres-iŋ-'dau̇n\ *n* (ca. 1890) **:** a severe reprimand

dressing glass *n* (1714) **:** a small mirror set to swing in a standing frame and used at a dresser or dressing table

dressing gown *n* (1777) **:** a robe (as of silk) worn esp. while dressing or resting

dressing room *n* (1675) **:** a room used chiefly for dressing; *esp* **:** a room in a theater for changing costumes and makeup

dressing table *n* (1692) **:** a table often fitted with drawers and a mirror in front of which one sits while dressing and grooming oneself

[1]**dress·mak·er** \'dres-ˌmā-kər\ *n* (1803) **:** one that makes dresses — **dress·mak·ing** \-ˌmā-kiŋ\ *n*

[2]**dressmaker** *adj, of women's clothes* (1904) **:** having softness, rounded lines, and intricate detailing ⟨a ~ suit⟩

dress rehearsal *n* (1828) **:** a full rehearsal of a play in costume and with stage properties shortly before the first performance

dress shield *n* (1884) **:** a pad worn inside a part of the clothing liable to be soiled by perspiration (as at the underarm)

dress shirt *n* (1892) **:** a man's shirt esp. for wear with evening dress; *broadly* **:** a shirt suitable for wear with a necktie

dress uniform *n* (ca. 1897) **:** a uniform for formal wear

dress up *vt* (1674) **1 a :** to attire in best or formal clothes **b :** to attire in clothes suited to a particular role **2 :** to present in a certain light (as by distortion or exaggeration) **:** EMBELLISH ⟨*dressed up* his story⟩ ~ *vi* **:** to get dressed up

dressy \'dres-ē\ *adj* **dress·i·er; -est** (1768) **1 :** showy in dress **2 :** STYLISH, SMART — **dress·i·ness** *n*

drew *past of* DRAW

Drey·fu·sard \ˌdri-f(y)ə-'sär(d), ˌdrā-, -'zär(d)\ *n* [F] (1898) **:** a defender or partisan of Alfred Dreyfus

drib \'drib\ *n* [prob. back-formation fr. *dribble* & *driblet*] (ca. 1730) **:** a small amount — usu. used in the phrase *dribs and drabs*

[1]**drib·ble** \'drib-əl\ *vb* **drib·bled; drib·bling** \-(ə-)liŋ\ [freq. of *drib* (to dribble)] *vi* (ca. 1589) **1 :** to fall or flow in drops or in a thin intermittent stream **:** TRICKLE **2 :** to let saliva trickle from a corner of the mouth **:** DROOL **3 :** to come or issue in piecemeal or desultory fashion **4 a :** to dribble a ball or puck **b** *of a ball* **:** to move with short bounces ~ *vt* **1 :** to let or cause to fall in drops little by little **2 :** to issue sporadically and in small bits **3 a :** to propel by successive slight taps or bounces with hand, foot, or stick **b :** to hit (as a baseball) so as to cause a slow bouncing — **drib·bler** \-(ə-)lər\ *n*

[2]**dribble** *n* (1680) **1 a :** a small trickling stream or flow **b :** a drizzling shower **2 :** a tiny or insignificant bit or quantity **3 :** an act, instance, or manner of dribbling a ball or puck — **drib·bly** \'drib-(ə)lē\ *adj*

drib·let \'drib-lət\ *n* (1678) **1 :** a trifling or small sum or part **2 :** a drop of liquid

dried–fruit beetle *n* (1916) **:** a small broad brown beetle (*Carpophilus hemipterus*) that is a cosmopolitan pest on stored products

dried–up \'drī-'dəp\ *adj* (1885) **:** being wizened and shriveled

[1]**drier** *comparative of* DRY

[2]**dri·er** *also* **dry·er** \'drī(-ə)r\ *n* (1528) **1 :** something that extracts or absorbs moisture **2 :** a substance that accelerates drying (as of oils, paints, and printing inks) **3** *usu dryer* **:** a device for drying

driest *superlative of* DRY

[1]**drift** \'drift\ *n* [ME; akin to OE *drīfan* to drive — more at DRIVE] (14c) **1 a :** the act of driving something along **b :** the flow or the velocity of the current of a river or ocean stream **2 :** something driven, propelled, or urged along or drawn together in a clump by or as if by a natural agency: as **a :** wind-driven snow, rain, cloud, dust, or smoke usu. at or near the ground surface **b (1) :** a mass of matter (as sand) deposited together by or as if by wind or water **(2) :** a helter-skelter accumulation **c :** DROVE, FLOCK **d :** something (as driftwood) washed ashore **e :** rock debris deposited by natural agents; *specif* **:** a deposit of clay, sand, gravel, and boulders transported by a glacier or by running water from a glacier **3 a :** a general underlying design or tendency **b :** the underlying meaning, import, or purport of what is spoken or written **4 :** something driven down upon or forced into a body: as **a :** a tool for ramming down or driving something **b :** a pin for stretching and aligning rivet holes **5 :** the motion or action of drifting esp. spatially and usu. under external influence: as **a :** a ship's deviation from its course caused by currents **b :** one of the slower movements of oceanic circulation **c :** the lateral motion of an airplane due to air currents **d :** an easy moderate more or less steady flow or sweep along a spatial course **e :** a gradual shift in attitude, opinion, or position **f :** an aimless course; *esp* **:** a foregoing of any attempt at direction or control **g :** a deviation from a true reproduction, representation, or reading **6 a :** a nearly horizontal mine passageway driven on or parallel to the course of a vein or rock stratum **b :** a small crosscut in a mine connecting two larger tunnels **7 a :** an assumed trend toward a general change in the structure of a language over a period of time **b :** GENETIC DRIFT **c :** a gradual change in the zero reading of an instrument or in any quantitive characteristic that is supposed to remain constant — **drifty** \'drif-tē\ *adj* ***syn*** see TENDENCY

[2]**drift** *vi* (1600) **1 a :** to become driven or carried along by a current of water, wind, or air **b :** to move or float smoothly and effortlessly **2 a :** to move along a line of least resistance **b :** to move in a random or casual way **c :** to become carried along subject to no guidance or control ⟨the conversation ~*ed* from one topic to another⟩ **3 a :** to accumulate in a mass or become piled up in heaps by wind or water **b :** to become covered with a drift **4 :** to vary or deviate from a set adjustment ~ *vt* **1 a :** to cause to be driven in a current **b** *West* **:** to drive (livestock) slowly esp. to allow grazing **2 a :** to pile in heaps **b :** to cover with drifts ⟨slopes that are heavily ~*ed* during the winter⟩ — **drift·ing·ly** \'drif-tiŋ-lē\ *adv*

drift·age \'drif-tij\ *n* (1768) **1 :** drifted material ⟨seaweed and other ~⟩ **2 :** a drifting of some object esp. through the action of wind or water **3 :** deviation from a set course due to drifting

drift·er \'drif-tər\ *n* (1864) **:** one that drifts; *esp* **:** one that travels or moves about aimlessly

drift fence *n* (1907) **:** a stretch of fence on rangeland esp. in the western U.S. for preventing cattle from drifting from their home range

drift·wood \'drif-ˌtwu̇d\ *n* (1633) **1 :** wood drifted or floated by water **2 :** FLOTSAM 2

[1]**drill** \'dril\ *n* (1611) **1 :** an instrument with an edged or pointed end for making holes in hard substances by revolving or by a succession of blows; *also* **:** a machine for operating such an instrument **2 :** the act or exercise of training soldiers in marching and the manual of arms **3 a :** a physical or mental exercise aimed at perfecting facility and skill esp. by regular practice **b :** a formal exercise by a team of marchers **c** *chiefly Brit* **:** the approved or correct procedure for accomplishing something efficiently **4 a :** a marine snail (*Urosalpinx cinerea*) destructive to oysters by boring through their shells and feeding on the soft parts **b :** any of several mollusks related to the drill **5 :** a drilling sound

[2]**drill** *vb* [D *drillen;* akin to OHG *drāen* to turn — more at THROW] *vt* (1622) **1 a :** to fix something in the mind or habit pattern of by repetitive instruction ⟨~ pupils in spelling⟩ **b :** to impart or communicate by repetition ⟨impossible to ~ the simplest idea into some people⟩ **c :** to train or exercise in military drill **2 a (1) :** to bore or drive a hole in **(2) :** to make by piercing action ⟨~*ed* holes an inch apart⟩ **b :** to hit with piercing effect ⟨~*ed* a single to right field⟩ ~ *vi* **1 :** to make a hole with a drill **2 :** to engage in an exercise **3 :** to act on with penetrating effect — **drill·abil·i·ty** \ˌdril-ə-'bil-ət-ē\ *n* — **drill·able** \-ə-bəl\ *adj* — **drill·er** \'dril-ər\ *n*

[3]**drill** *n* [prob. native name in West Africa] (1644) **:** a West African baboon (*Mandrillus leucophaeus*) closely related to the typical mandrills

[4]**drill** *n* [perh. fr. *drill* (rill)] (1727) **1 a :** a shallow furrow or trench into which seed is sown **b :** a row of seed sown in such a furrow **2 :** a planting implement that makes holes or furrows, drops in the seed and sometimes fertilizer, and covers them with earth

[5]**drill** *vt* (1740) **1 :** to sow (seeds) by dropping along a shallow furrow **2 a :** to sow with seed or set with seedlings inserted in drills **b :** to distribute seed or fertilizer in by means of a drill

[6]**drill** *n* [short for *drilling*] (1743) **:** a durable cotton fabric in twill weave

dril·ling \'dril-iŋ\ *n* [modif. of G *drillich,* fr. MHG *drilich* fabric woven with a threefold thread, fr. OHG *drilīh* made up of three threads, fr. L *trilic-, trilix,* fr. *tri-* + *licium* thread] (1640) **:** [6]DRILL

drill·mas·ter \'dril-ˌmas-tər\ *n* (1869) **1 :** an instructor in military drill **2 :** an instructor or director who maintains severe discipline and who often stresses the trivial and unimportant

drill press *n* (ca. 1864) **:** an upright drilling machine in which the drill is pressed to the work by a hand lever or by power

drill team *n* (1928) **:** an exhibition marching team that engages in precision drill

drily *var of* DRYLY

[1]**drink** \'driŋk\ *vb* **drank** \'draŋk\; **drunk** \'drəŋk\ *or* **drank; drink·ing** [ME *drinken,* fr. OE *drincan;* akin to OHG *trinkan* to drink] *vt* (bef. 12c) **1 a :** SWALLOW, IMBIBE **b :** to take in or suck up **:** ABSORB ⟨~*ing* air into his lungs⟩ **c :** to take in or receive avidly — usu. used with *in* ⟨*drank* in every word of the lecture⟩ **2 :** to join in a toast to ⟨I'll ~ your good health⟩ **3 :** to bring to a specified state by drinking alcoholic beverages ⟨*drank* himself into oblivion⟩ ⟨~*ing* his troubles away⟩ ~ *vi* **1 a :** to take liquid into the mouth for swallowing **b :** to receive into one's consciousness **2 :** to partake of alcoholic beverages **3 :** to make or join in a toast ⟨I'll ~ to that!⟩

[2]**drink** *n* (bef. 12c) **1 a :** liquid suitable for swallowing **b :** alcoholic liquor **2 :** a draft or portion of liquid **3 :** excessive consumption of alcoholic beverages **4 :** a sizable body of water — used with *the*

[1]**drink·able** \'driŋ-kə-bəl\ *adj* (1611) **:** suitable or safe for drinking — **drink·abil·i·ty** \ˌdriŋ-kə-'bil-ət-ē\ *n*

[2]**drinkable** *n* (1708) **:** a liquid suitable for drinking **:** BEVERAGE

drink·er \'driŋ-kər\ *n* (bef. 12c) **1 a :** one that drinks **b :** one that drinks alcoholic beverages esp. to a notable degree ⟨a heavy ~⟩ **2 :** WATERER b

drinking fountain *n* (1860) **:** a fixture with nozzle that delivers a stream of water for drinking

drinking song *n* (1597) **:** a song on a convivial theme appropriate for a group engaged in social drinking

[1]**drip** \'drip\ *vb* **dripped; drip·ping** [ME *drippen,* fr. OE *dryppan;* akin to OE *dropa* drop — more at DREARY] *vt* (bef. 12c) **1 :** to let fall in drops **2 :** to let out or seem to spill copiously ⟨her voice *dripping* sarcasm⟩ ~ *vi* **1 a :** to let fall drops of moisture or liquid **b :** to overflow with or as if with moisture ⟨a uniform *dripping* with gold braid⟩ ⟨a novel that ~*s* with sentimentality⟩ **2 :** to fall in or as if in drops **3 :** to waft or pass gently — **drip·per** *n*

[2]**drip** *n* (1669) **1 a :** a falling in drops **b :** liquid that falls, overflows, or is extruded in drops **2 :** the sound made by or as if by falling drops **3 :** a part of a cornice or other member that projects to throw off rainwater; *also* **:** an overlapping metal strip or an underneath groove for the same purpose **4 :** a device for the administration of a fluid at a slow rate esp. into a vein; *also* **:** a material so administered **5** *slang* **:** a dull or unattractive person

[3]**drip** *adj* (1895) **:** of, relating to, or being coffee made by letting boiling water drip slowly through finely ground coffee ⟨~ coffee⟩ ⟨a ~ pot⟩

[1]**drip–dry** \'drip-'drī\ *vi* (1953) **:** to dry with few or no wrinkles when hung wet ~ *vt* **:** to hang (as wet clothing) to drip-dry

\ə\ **abut** \ᵊ\ **kitten,** F **table** \ər\ **further** \a\ **ash** \ā\ **ace** \ä\ **cot, cart**
\au̇\ **out** \ch\ **chin** \e\ **bet** \ē\ **easy** \g\ **go** \i\ **hit** \ī\ **ice** \j\ **job**
\ŋ\ **sing** \ō\ **go** \ȯ\ **law** \ȯi\ **boy** \th\ **thin** \th\ **the** \ü\ **loot** \u̇\ **foot**
\y\ **yet** \zh\ **vision** \á, k̲, ⁿ, œ, œ̄, ue, ue̅, ʸ\ *see* Guide to Pronunciation

[2]**drip–dry** *adj* (1957) **:** made of a washable fabric that drip-dries
[3]**drip–dry** *n* (1959) **:** a drip-dry garment
drip·less \'drip-ləs\ *adj* (1887) **:** designed not to drip ⟨~ candles⟩
drip·ping \'drip-iŋ\ *n* (1530) **:** fat and juices drawn from meat during cooking — often used in pl.
drip·py \'drip-ē\ *adj* **drip·pi·er; -est** (1817) **1 :** characterized by dripping; *esp* **:** RAINY, DRIZZLY **2 :** MAWKISH 2
drip·stone \'drip-ˌstōn\ *n* (1812) **1 :** a stone drip (as over a window) **2 :** calcium carbonate in the form of stalactites or stalagmites
[1]**drive** \'drīv\ *vb* **drove** \'drōv\; **driv·en** \'driv-ən\; **driv·ing** \'drī-viŋ\ [ME *driven,* fr. OE *drīfan;* akin to OHG *trīban* to drive] *vt* (bef. 12c) **1 a :** to impart a forward motion to by physical force ⟨waves *drove* the boat against the shore⟩ **b :** to repulse, remove, or cause to go by force, authority, or influence ⟨~ the enemy back⟩ **c :** to set or keep in motion or operation ⟨~ machinery by electricity⟩ **2 a :** to direct the motions and course of (a draft animal) **b :** to operate the mechanism and controls and direct the course of (as a vehicle) **c :** to convey in a vehicle **d :** to float (logs) down a stream **3 :** to carry on or through energetically ⟨*driving* a hard bargain⟩ **4 a :** to exert inescapable or coercive pressure on **:** FORCE **b :** to compel to undergo or suffer a change (as in situation, awareness, or emotional state) ⟨*drove* him crazy⟩ **c :** to urge relentlessly to continuous exertion ⟨the sergeant *drove* his recruits⟩ **d :** to press or force into an activity, course, or direction ⟨the expensive drug habit that ~*s* addicts to steal⟩ **e :** to project, inject, or impress incisively ⟨*drove* his point home⟩ **5 a :** to frighten or prod (as game or cattle) into moving in a desired direction **b :** to go through (a district) driving game animals **6 :** to force (a passage) by pressing or digging **7 a :** to propel (an object of play) swiftly **b :** to hit (a golf ball) from the tee esp. with a driver **c :** to cause (a run or runner) to be scored in baseball — usu. used with *in* ~ *vi* **1 a :** to dash, plunge, or surge ahead rapidly or violently **b :** to progress with strong momentum ⟨the rain was *driving* hard⟩ **2 a :** to operate a vehicle; *also* **:** HANDLE ⟨an auto that ~*s* well⟩ **b :** to have oneself carried in a vehicle **3 :** to drive a golf ball ***syn*** see MOVE — **driv·able** *also* **drive·able** \'drī-və-bəl\ *adj* — **drive at :** to intend to express, convey, or accomplish ⟨did not understand what she was *driving at* —Eric Goldman⟩
[2]**drive** *n* (1785) **1 :** an act of driving: **a :** a trip in a carriage or automobile **b :** a collection and driving together of animals; *also* **:** the animals gathered **c :** a driving of cattle or sheep overland **d :** a hunt or shoot in which the game is driven within the hunter's range **e :** the guiding of logs downstream to a mill; *also* **:** the floating logs amassed in a drive **f** (1) **:** the act or an instance of driving an object of play (as a golf ball) (2) **:** the flight of a ball **2 a :** a private road **:** DRIVEWAY **b :** a public road for driving (as in a park) **3 :** the state of being hurried and under pressure **4 a :** a strong systematic group effort **:** CAMPAIGN **b :** a sustained offensive effort ⟨the ~ that ended in a touchdown⟩ **5 a :** the means for giving motion to a machine or machine part **b :** the means by which the propulsive power of an automobile is applied to the road ⟨front wheel ~⟩ **c :** the means by which the propulsion of an automotive vehicle is controlled and directed ⟨a left-hand ~⟩ **6 :** an offensive, aggressive, or expansionist move; *esp* **:** a strong military attack against enemy-held terrain **7 a :** an urgent, basic, or instinctual need **:** a motivating physiological condition of the organism ⟨a sexual ~⟩ **b :** an impelling culturally acquired concern, interest, or longing ⟨enslaved by a ~ for perfection⟩ **c :** dynamic quality **8 :** a device for reading and writing on magnetic media (as magnetic tape or disks) — **drive** *adj*
drive–in \'drī-ˌvin\ *n* (1937) **:** an establishment (as a theater or restaurant) so laid out that patrons can be accommodated while remaining in their automobiles — **drive-in** *adj*
[1]**driv·el** \'driv-əl\ *vb* **-eled** *or* **-elled; -el·ing** *or* **-el·ling** \-(ə-)liŋ\ [ME *drivelen,* fr. OE *dreflian;* akin to ON *draf* malt dregs, OE *deorc* dark] *vi* (bef. 12c) **1 :** to let saliva dribble from the mouth **:** SLAVER **2 :** to talk stupidly and carelessly ~ *vt* **1 :** to utter in an infantile or imbecilic way **2 :** to waste or fritter in a childish fashion — **driv·el·er** \-(ə-)lər\ *n*
[2]**drivel** *n* (14c) **1** *archaic* **:** DROOL 1 **2 :** NONSENSE
drive·line \'drīv-ˌlīn\ *n* (1949) **:** the parts including the universal joint and the drive shaft that connect the transmission with the driving axles of an automobile — called also *drivetrain*
driv·en *adj* (1887) **:** having a compulsive or urgent quality ⟨a ~ sense of obligation⟩ — **driv·en·ness** \'driv-ən-nəs\ *n*
driv·er \'drī-vər\ *n* (14c) **:** one that drives: as **a :** COACHMAN **b :** the operator of a motor vehicle **c :** an implement (as a hammer) for driving **d :** a mechanical piece for imparting motion to another piece **e :** a golf club with a wooden head and nearly straight face used in driving **f :** an electronic circuit that supplies input to another electronic circuit; *also* **:** LOUDSPEAKER — **driv·er·less** \-ləs\ *adj*
driver ant *n* (1859) **:** ARMY ANT; *specif* **:** any of various African and Asian ants (*Dorylus* or related genera) that move in vast armies
driver's license *n* (1944) **:** a license issued under governmental authority that permits the holder to operate a motor vehicle
driver's seat *n* (1923) **:** the position of top authority or dominance
drive shaft *n* (1895) **:** a shaft that transmits mechanical power
drive·train \'drīv-ˌtrān\ *n* (1954) **:** DRIVELINE
drive·way \-ˌwā\ *n* (1870) **:** a private road giving access from a public way to a building on abutting grounds
driv·ing *adj* (13c) **1 a :** communicating force ⟨a ~ wheel⟩ **b :** exerting pressure ⟨a ~ influence⟩ **2 a :** having great force ⟨a ~ rain⟩ **b :** acting with vigor **:** ENERGETIC ⟨a hard-*driving* worker⟩
driving range *n* (ca. 1949) **:** an area equipped with distance markers, clubs, balls, and tees for practicing golf drives
[1]**driz·zle** \'driz-əl\ *n* (1554) **:** a fine misty rain — **driz·zly** \'driz-(ə-)lē\ *adj*
[2]**drizzle** *vb* **driz·zled; driz·zling** \-(ə-)liŋ\ [perh. alter. of ME *drysnen* to fall, fr. OE *-drysnian* to disappear; akin to Goth *driusan* to fall — more at DREARY] *vt* (1584) **1 :** to shed or let fall in minute drops or particles **2 :** to make wet with minute drops ~ *vi* **:** to rain in very small drops or very lightly **:** SPRINKLE — **driz·zling·ly** \-(ə-)liŋ-lē\ *adv*
drogue \'drōg\ *n* [prob. alter. of [1]*drag*] (1875) **1 :** SEA ANCHOR **2 a :** a cylindrical or funnel-shaped device towed as a target by an airplane **b :** a small parachute for stabilizing or decelerating something (as an astronaut's capsule) or for pulling a larger parachute out of stowage **3 :** a funnel-shaped device which is attached to the end of a long flexible hose suspended from a tanker airplane in flight and into which the probe of another airplane in flight is fitted so as to receive fuel from the tanker airplane
droit \'drȯit, drə-'wä\ *n* [ME, fr. MF, fr. ML *directum,* fr. LL, neut. of *directus* just, fr. L, direct — more at DRESS] (15c) **:** a legal right ⟨~*s* of admiralty⟩
droit du sei·gneur \drwä-dūē-se-nʸœr\ *n* [F, right of the lord] (1825) **:** a supposed legal or customary right of a feudal lord to have sexual relations with a vassal's bride on her wedding night
[1]**droll** \'drōl\ *adj* [F *drôle,* fr. *drôle* scamp, fr. MF *drolle,* fr. MD, imp] (1623) **:** having a humorous, whimsical, or odd quality — **droll·ness** *n* — **drol·ly** \'drō(l)-lē\ *adv*
[2]**droll** *n* (1645) **:** one that amuses or diverts **:** JESTER, COMEDIAN
[3]**droll** *vi, archaic* (1654) **:** to make fun **:** JEST, SPORT
droll·ery \'drōl-(ə-)rē\ *n, pl* **-er·ies** (1597) **1 :** something that is droll: as **a :** a comic picture or drawing **b :** a usu. brief comic show or entertainment **c :** an amusing story **:** JEST **2 :** the act or an instance of jesting or burlesquing **3 :** whimsical humor
-drome \ˌdrōm\ *n comb form* [*hippodrome*] **1 :** racecourse ⟨motor*drome*⟩ **2 :** large specially prepared place ⟨aero*drome*⟩
drom·e·dary \'dräm-ə-ˌder-ē *also* 'drəm-\ *n, pl* **-dar·ies** [ME *dromedarie,* fr. OF *dromedaire,* fr. LL *dromedarius,* fr. L *dromad-, dromas,* fr. Gk, running; akin to Gk *dramein* to run, *dromos* racecourse, OE *treppan* to tread] (13c) **1 :** a camel of unusual speed bred and trained esp. for riding **2 :** CAMEL 1a
-d·ro·mous \d-rə-məs\ *adj comb form* [NL *-dromus,* fr. Gk *-dromos* (akin to Gk *dramein*)] **:** running ⟨cata*dromous*⟩
[1]**drone** \'drōn\ *n* [ME, fr. OE *drān;* akin to OHG *treno* drone, Gk *thrēnos* dirge] (bef. 12c) **1 :** the male of a bee (as the honeybee) that has no sting and gathers no honey — see HONEYBEE illustration **2 :** one that lives on the labors of others **:** PARASITE **3 :** a pilotless airplane, helicopter, or ship controlled by radio signals **4 :** DRUDGE
[2]**drone** *vb* **droned; dron·ing** *vi* (1500) **1 a :** to make a sustained deep murmuring, humming, or buzzing sound **b :** to talk in a persistently dull or monotonous tone **2 :** to pass, proceed, or act in a dull, drowsy, or indifferent manner ⟨the trial *droned* on for months⟩ ~ *vt* **1 :** to utter or pronounce with a drone **2 :** to pass or spend in dull or monotonous activity or in idleness ⟨*droned* away the precious years of youth⟩ — **dron·er** *n* — **dron·ing·ly** \'drō-niŋ-lē\ *adv*
[3]**drone** *n* (1500) **1 :** a deep sustained or monotonous sound **:** HUM **2 :** an instrument or part of an instrument (as one of the fixed-pitch pipes of a bagpipe) that sounds a continuous unvarying tone **3 :** PEDAL POINT
[1]**drool** \'drül\ *vb* [perh. alter. of *drivel*] *vi* (1802) **1 a :** to secrete saliva in anticipation of food **b :** DRIVEL 1 **2 :** to make an effusive show of pleasure **3 :** to talk nonsense ~ *vt* **:** to express sentimentally or effusively
[2]**drool** *n* (1869) **1 :** saliva trickling from the mouth **2 :** NONSENSE
[1]**droop** \'drüp\ *vb* [ME *drupen,* fr. ON *drūpa;* akin to OE *dropa* drop] *vi* (14c) **1 :** to hang or incline downward **2 :** to sink gradually **3 :** to become depressed or weakened **:** LANGUISH ~ *vt* **:** to let droop — **droop·ing·ly** \'drü-piŋ-lē\ *adv*
[2]**droop** *n* (1647) **:** the condition or appearance of drooping
droopy \'drü-pē\ *adj* **droop·i·er; -est** (13c) **1 :** drooping or tending to droop **2 :** GLOOMY
[1]**drop** \'dräp\ *n, often attrib* [ME, fr. OE *dropa* — more at DREARY] (bef. 12c) **1 a** (1) **:** the quantity of fluid that falls in one spherical mass (2) *pl* **:** a dose of medicine measured by drops; *specif* **:** a solution for dilating the pupil of the eye **b :** a minute quantity or degree of something nonmaterial or intangible **c :** a small quantity of drink **d :** the smallest practical unit of liquid measure **2 :** something that resembles a liquid drop: as **a :** a pendent ornament attached to a piece of jewelry; *also* **:** an earring with such a pendant **b :** a small globular cookie or candy **3** [[2]*drop*] **a :** the act or an instance of dropping **:** FALL **b :** a decline in quantity or quality **c :** a descent by parachute; *also* **:** the people or equipment dropped by parachute **d :** a central point or depository to which something (as mail) is brought for distribution or transmission **e :** a place used for the deposit and distribution of stolen or illegal goods **4 a :** the distance from a higher to a lower level or through which something drops **b :** a fall of electric potential **5 :** a slot into which something is to be dropped **6** [[2]*drop*] **:** something that drops, hangs, or falls: as **a :** a movable plate that covers the keyhole of a lock **b :** an unframed piece of cloth stage scenery; *also* **:** DROP CURTAIN **c :** a hinged platform on a gallows **d :** a fallen fruit **7 :** the advantage of having an opponent covered with a firearm; *broadly* **:** ADVANTAGE, SUPERIORITY — usu. used in the phrase *get the drop on* — **at the drop of a hat :** as soon as the slightest provocation is given **:** IMMEDIATELY — **drop in the bucket :** a part so small as to be negligible
[2]**drop** *vb* **dropped; drop·ping** *vi* (bef. 12c) **1 :** to fall in drops **2 a** (1) **:** to fall unexpectedly or suddenly (2) **:** to descend from one line or level to another **b :** to fall in a state of collapse or death **c** *of a card* **:** to become played by reason of the obligation to follow suit **d** *of a ball* **:** to roll into a hole or basket **3 :** to enter or pass as if without conscious effort of will into some state, condition, or activity ⟨*dropped* into sleep⟩ **4 a :** to cease to be of concern **:** LAPSE ⟨let the matter ~⟩ **b :** to become less ⟨production *dropped*⟩ — often used with *off* **5 :** to move with a favoring wind or current — usu. used with *down* ~ *vt* **1 :** to let fall **:** cause to fall **2 a :** to give up (as an idea) **b :** DISCONTINUE ⟨*dropped* what he was doing⟩ **c :** to break off an association or connection with **:** DISMISS ⟨~ a failing student⟩ **3 a :** to utter or mention in a casual way ⟨~ a suggestion⟩ ⟨~ names⟩ **b :** WRITE ⟨~ us a line soon⟩ **4 a :** to lower or cause to descend from one level or position to another **b :** to lower (wheels) in preparation for landing an airplane **c :** to cause to lessen or decrease **:** REDUCE ⟨*dropped* his speed⟩ **5** *of an animal* **:** to give birth to **6 a :** LOSE ⟨*dropped* three games⟩ ⟨*dropped* $50 in a poker game⟩ **b :** SPEND ⟨~ $20 for lunch⟩ **7 a :** to bring down with a shot or a blow **b :** to cause (a high card) to fall **c :** to toss or roll (a ball) into a hole or basket **8 a :** to set down from a ship or vehicle **:** DEPOSIT — usu. used with *off* **b :** AIR-DROP **9 :** to cause (the voice) to be less loud **10 a :** to leave (a letter representing a speech sound) unsounded ⟨~ the g in *running*⟩ **b :** to leave

out in writing **11** : to draw from an external point ⟨~ a perpendicular to the line⟩ **12** : to take (a drug) orally : SWALLOW ⟨~ acid⟩ — **drop behind** : to fail to keep up

drop back *vi* (1927) **1** : RETREAT **2** : to move straight back from the line of scrimmage — used of a back in football

drop by *vi* (ca. 1905) : to pay a brief casual visit

drop cloth *n* (ca. 1928) : a protective sheet (as of cloth or plastic) used esp. by painters to cover floors and furniture

drop curtain *n* (1832) : a stage curtain that can be lowered and raised

drop–dead *adj* (1970) : sensationally striking or attractive ⟨a ~ evening gown⟩

drop–forge \'dräp-'fō(ə)rj, -'fȯ(ə)rj\ *vt* (ca. 1899) : to forge between dies by means of a drop hammer or punch press — **drop forger** *n*

drop forging *n* (ca. 1884) : a forging made by the force of a dropped weight

drop front *n* (1927) : a hinged cover on the front of a desk that may be lowered to provide a surface for writing

drop hammer *n* (ca. 1864) : a power hammer raised and then released to drop (as on metal resting on an anvil or die)

drop·head \'dräp-,hed\ *n, Brit* (1932) : a convertible automobile

drop–in \'dräp-,in\ *n* (1941) **1** : one who drops in : a casual visitor **2** : an informal social gathering at which guests are invited to drop in

drop in *vi* (1600) : to pay an unexpected or casual visit

drop·kick \-'kik\ *n* (1857) : a kick made by dropping a ball to the ground and kicking it at the moment it starts to rebound

drop–kick \-'kik\ *vi* (ca. 1909) : to make a dropkick ~ *vt* : to score (a goal) with a dropkick — **drop·kick·er** *n*

drop leaf *n* (1882) : a hinged leaf on the side or end of a table that can be folded down

drop·let \'dräp-lət\ *n* (1607) : a tiny drop (as of a liquid)

droplet infection *n* (1907) : infection transmitted by airborne droplets of sputum containing infectious organisms

drop·light \'dräp-,līt\ *n* (1902) : an electric light suspended by a cord or on a portable extension

drop–off \'dräp-,ȯf\ *n* (1923) **1** : a very steep or perpendicular descent **2** : a marked dwindling or decline ⟨a ~ in attendance⟩

drop off \dräp-'ȯf\ *vi* (1820) : to fall asleep

drop·out \'dräp-,au̇t\ *n* (1930) **1 a** : one who drops out of school **b** : one who drops out of conventional society **c** : one who abandons an attempt or a chosen path ⟨a corporate ~⟩ **2** : a spot on a magnetic tape or disk from which data has disappeared

drop out \dräp-'au̇t\ *vi* (1883) : to withdraw from participation or membership : QUIT; *esp* : to withdraw from conventional society because of disenchantment with its values and mores

drop pass *n* (1949) : a pass in ice hockey in which the dribbler skates past the puck leaving it for a teammate following close behind

dropped egg *n* (1824) : a poached egg

drop·per \'dräp-ər\ *n* (ca. 1700) **1** : one that drops **2** : a short glass tube fitted with a rubber bulb and used to measure liquids by drops — called also *eyedropper, medicine dropper* — **drop·per·ful** \-,fu̇l\ *n*

drop·ping *n* (14c) **1** : something dropped **2** *pl* : DUNG

drop seat *n* (1926) **1** : a hinged seat (as in a taxi) that may be dropped down **2** : a seat (as in an undergarment) that falls down when unbuttoned

drop shot *n* (1908) : a delicately hit ball or shuttlecock (as in tennis, badminton, or rackets) that drops quickly after crossing the net or dies after hitting a wall

drop·si·cal \'dräp-si-kəl\ *adj* (1678) **1** : relating to or affected with dropsy **2** : TURGID, SWOLLEN

drop·sonde \'dräp-,sänd\ *n* [*drop* + *radiosonde*] (1946) : a radiosonde dropped by parachute from a high-flying airplane

drop·sy \'dräp-sē\ *n* [ME *dropesie*, short for *ydropesie*, fr. OF, fr. L *hydropisis*, modif. of Gk *hydrōps*, fr. *hydōr* water — more at WATER] (13c) : EDEMA

drop zone *n* (ca. 1943) : the area in which troops, supplies, or equipment are to be air-dropped; *also* : the target on which a skydiver lands

drosh·ky \'dräsh-kē\ *also* **dros·ky** \'dräs-kē\ *n, pl* **droshkies** *also* **droskies** [Russ *drozhki*, fr. *droga* pole of a wagon] (1808) : any of various 2- or 4-wheeled carriages used esp. in Russia

dro·soph·i·la \drō-'säf-ə-lə\ *n* [NL, genus name, fr. Gk *drosos* dew + NL *-phila*, fem. of *-philus* -phil] (ca. 1934) : any of a genus (*Drosophila*) of small two-winged flies used in genetic research

dross \'dräs, 'drȯs\ *n* [ME *dros*, fr. OE *drōs* dregs] (bef. 12c) **1** : the scum that forms on the surface of molten metal **2** : waste or foreign matter : IMPURITY **3** : something that is base, trivial, or inferior — **drossy** \-ē\ *adj*

drought *also* **drouth** \'drau̇t(h)\ *n* [ME, fr. OE *drūgath*, fr. *drūgian* to dry up; akin to OE *drȳge* dry — more at DRY] (bef. 12c) **1** : a period of dryness esp. when prolonged and causing extensive damage to crops or preventing their successful growth **2** : a prolonged or chronic shortage or lack of something — **drought·i·ness** *n* — **droughty** \-ē\ *adj*

[1]**drove** \'drōv\ *n* [ME, fr. OE *drāf*, fr. *drīfan* to drive — more at DRIVE] (bef. 12c) **1** : a group of animals driven or moving in a body **2 a** : a crowd of people moving or acting together **b** : a large group of similar things **3 a** : a chisel used to form a grooved or roughly shaped surface on stone **b** : the grooved surface so formed

[2]**drove** *past of* DRIVE

drov·er \'drō-vər\ *n* (14c) : one that drives cattle or sheep

drown \'drau̇n\ *vb* **drowned** \'drau̇nd\; **drown·ing** \'drau̇-niŋ\ [ME *drounen*] *vi* (14c) : to become drowned ~ *vt* **1 a** : to suffocate by submersion esp. in water **b** : to submerge esp. by a rise in the water level **c** : to soak, drench, or cover with a liquid ⟨~*ed* the french fries with catsup⟩ **2** : to engage (oneself) deeply and strenuously ⟨~*ed* himself in work⟩ **3** : to cause (a sound) not to be heard by making a loud noise — usu. used with *out* **4 a** : to drive out (as a sensation or an idea) ⟨~*ed* his sorrows in liquor⟩ **b** : OVERWHELM

drownd \'drau̇nd\, **drownd·ed** \'drau̇n-dəd\, **drownd·ing** \'drau̇n-diŋ\ *substand var of* DROWN, DROWNED, DROWNING

[1]**drowse** \'drau̇z\ *vb* **drowsed; drows·ing** [prob. akin to Goth *driusan* to fall — more at DREARY] *vi* (1573) **1** : to be inactive **2** : to fall into a light slumber ~ *vt* **1** : to make drowsy or inactive **2** : to pass (time) drowsily or in drowsing

[2]**drowse** *n* (1814) : the act or an instance of drowsing : DOZE

drowsy \'drau̇-zē\ *adj* **drows·i·er; -est** (1530) **1 a** : ready to fall asleep **b** : inducing or tending to induce sleep **c** : INDOLENT, LETHARGIC **2** : giving the appearance of peaceful inactivity — **drows·i·ly** \-zə-lē\ *adv* — **drows·i·ness** \-zē-nəs\ *n*

drub \'drəb\ *vb* **drubbed; drub·bing** [perh. fr. Ar *ḍaraba*] *vt* (1634) **1** : to beat severely (as with a cudgel) **2** : to abuse with words : BERATE ⟨the book was *drubbed* by every critic⟩ **3** : to defeat decisively ~ *vi* : DRUM, STAMP — **drub·ber** *n* — **drub·bing** *n*

[1]**drudge** \'drəj\ *vb* **drudged; drudg·ing** [ME *druggen*; prob. akin to OE *drēogan* to work, endure, L *firmus* firm] *vi* (14c) : to do hard, menial, or monotonous work ~ *vt* : to force to do hard, menial, or monotonous work — **drudg·er** *n*

[2]**drudge** *n* (15c) **1** : one who is obliged to do menial work **2** : one whose work is routine and boring

drudg·ery \'drəj-(ə-)rē\ *n, pl* **-er·ies** (1550) : dull, irksome, and fatiguing work : uninspiring or menial labor ***syn*** see WORK

drudg·ing \'drəj-iŋ\ *adj* (1548) : MONOTONOUS, TIRING — **drudg·ing·ly** \-iŋ-lē\ *adv*

[1]**drug** \'drəg\ *n* [ME *drogge*] (14c) **1 a** *obs* : a substance used in dyeing or chemical operations **b** : a substance used as a medication or in the preparation of medication **c** *according to the Food, Drug, and Cosmetic Act* (1) : a substance recognized in an official pharmacopoeia or formulary (2) : a substance intended for use in the diagnosis, cure, mitigation, treatment, or prevention of disease (3) : a substance other than food intended to affect the structure or function of the body (4) : a substance intended for use as a component of a medicine but not a device or a component, part, or accessory of a device **2** : a commodity that is not salable or for which there is no demand — used in the phrase *drug on the market* **3** : something that causes addiction or habituation — **drug·gy** \'drəg-ē\ *adj*

[2]**drug** *vb* **drugged; drug·ging** *vt* (1605) **1** : to affect with a drug; *esp* : to stupefy by a narcotic drug **2** : to administer a drug to **3** : to lull or stupefy as if with a drug ~ *vi* : to take drugs for narcotic effect

[3]**drug** *dial past of* DRAG

drug·get \'drəg-ət\ *n* [MF *droguet*, dim. of *drogue* trash, drug] (1580) **1** : a wool or partly wool fabric formerly used for clothing **2** : a coarse durable cloth used chiefly as a floor covering **3** : a rug having a cotton warp and a wool filling

drug·gie \'drəg-ē\ *n* (1967) : one who habitually uses drugs

drug·gist \'drəg-əst\ *n* (1611) : one who sells or dispenses drugs and medicines: as **a** : PHARMACIST **b** : one who owns or manages a drugstore

drug·mak·er \'drəg-,mā-kər\ *n* (1964) : one that manufactures pharmaceuticals

drug·store \-,stō(ə)r, -,stȯ(ə)r\ *n* (1810) : a retail store where medicines and miscellaneous articles (as food, cosmetics, and film) are sold : PHARMACY

drugstore cowboy *n* (1925) **1** : one who wears cowboy clothes but has had no experience as a cowboy **2** : one who loafs on street corners and in drugstores

dru·id \'drü-əd\ *n, often cap* [L *druides, druidae*, pl. fr. Gaulish *druides*; perh. akin to OE *trēow* tree] (1563) : one of an ancient Celtic priesthood appearing in Irish and Welsh sagas and Christian legends as magicians and wizards — **dru·id·ic** \drü-'id-ik\ *or* **dru·id·i·cal** \-i-kəl\ *adj, often cap*

dru·id·ism \'drü-ə-,diz-əm\ *n, often cap* (1715) : the system of religion, philosophy, and instruction of the druids

[1]**drum** \'drəm\ *n* [prob. fr. D *trom*; akin to MHG *trumme* drum] (1541) **1** : a percussion instrument consisting of a hollow shell or cylinder with a drumhead stretched over one or both ends that is beaten with the hands or with some implement (as a stick or wire brush) **2** : TYMPANIC MEMBRANE **3** : the sound of a drum; *also* : a sound similar to that of a drum **4** : something resembling a drum in shape: as **a** : a cylindrical machine or mechanical device or part **b** : a cylindrical container; *specif* : a usu. metal container for liquids having a capacity between 12 and 110 gallons **c** : a disk-shaped magazine for an automatic weapon **5** : any of various percoid fishes (family Sciaenidae) that make a drumming noise — **drum·like** \-,līk\ *adj*

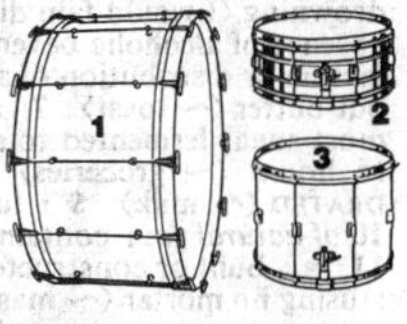

drum 1: *1* bass, *2* snare (orchestra), *3* snare (parade)

[2]**drum** *vb* **drummed; drum·ming** *vi* (1583) **1** : to make a succession of strokes or vibrations that produce sounds like drumbeats **2** : to beat a drum **3** : to throb or sound rhythmically **4** : to stir up interest : SOLICIT ~ *vt* **1** : to summon or enlist by or as if by beating a drum ⟨*drummed* into service⟩ **2** : to dismiss ignominiously : EXPEL — usu. used with *out* **3** : to drive or force by steady effort or reiteration ⟨*drummed* the speech into her head⟩ **4 a** : to strike or tap repeatedly **b** : to produce (rhythmic sounds) by such action

[3]**drum** *n* [ScGael *druim* back, ridge, fr. OIr *druimm*] (1725) **1** *chiefly Scot* : a long narrow hill or ridge **2** : DRUMLIN

drum·beat \'drəm-,bēt\ *n* (1855) **1** : a stroke on a drum or its sound **2** : vociferous advocacy of a cause — **drum·beat·er** \-ər\ *n* — **drum·beat·ing** \-iŋ\ *n*

drum·fire \'drəm-,fī(ə)r\ *n* (1916) **1** : artillery firing so continuous as to sound like a drumroll **2** : something suggestive of drumfire in intensity : BARRAGE ⟨a ~ of publicity⟩

drum·head \-,hed\ *n* (1622) **1** : the material (as skin or plastic) stretched over one or both ends of a drum **2** : the top of a capstan that is pierced with sockets for the levers used in turning it

drumhead court–martial *n* [fr. the use of a drumhead as a table] (1835) : a summary court-martial that tries offenses on the battlefield

drum·lin \'drəm-lən\ *n* [IrGael *druim* back, ridge (fr. OIr *druimm*) + E *-lin* (alter. of *-ling*)] (ca. 1833) : an elongate or oval hill of glacial drift

drum major *n* (1844) : the leader of a marching band
drum ma·jor·ette \ˌdrəm-ˌmā-jə-ˈret\ *n* (1938) **1** : a girl or woman who leads a marching band **2** : a baton twirler who accompanies a marching band
drum·mer \ˈdrəm-ər\ *n* (1573) **1** : one that plays a drum **2** : TRAVELING SALESMAN
drum printer *n* (1966) : a line printer in which the printing element is a revolving drum
drum·roll \ˈdrəm-ˌrōl\ *n* (1887) : a roll on a drum or its sound
drum·stick \-ˌstik\ *n* (1589) **1** : a stick for beating a drum **2** : the segment of a fowl's leg between the thigh and tarsus
drum up *vt* (1830) **1** : to bring about by persistent effort ⟨*drum up* some business⟩ **2** : INVENT, ORIGINATE ⟨*drum up* a new time-saving method⟩
¹drunk *past part of* DRINK
²drunk \ˈdrəŋk\ *adj* [ME *drunke,* alter. of *drunken*] (14c) **1** : having the faculties impaired by alcohol **2** : dominated by an intense feeling ⟨~ with power⟩ **3** : of, relating to, or caused by intoxication : DRUNKEN
³drunk *n* (1779) **1** : a period of drinking to intoxication or of being intoxicated ⟨a 2-day ~⟩ **2** : one who is drunk; *esp* : DRUNKARD
drunk·ard \ˈdrəŋ-kərd\ *n* (1530) : one who is habitually drunk
drunk·en \ˈdrəŋ-kən\ *adj* [ME, fr. OE *druncen,* fr. pp. of *drincan* to drink] (bef. 12c) **1** : DRUNK 1 ⟨a ~ driver⟩ **2** *obs* : saturated with liquid **3 a** : given to habitual excessive use of alcohol **b** : of, relating to, or characterized by intoxication ⟨they come from . . . broken homes, ~ homes —P. B. Gilliam⟩ **c** : resulting from or as if from intoxication ⟨a ~ brawl⟩ **4** : unsteady or lurching as if from alcoholic intoxication — **drunk·en·ly** *adv* — **drunk·en·ness** \-kən-nəs\ *n*
drunk·o·me·ter \ˌdrəŋ-ˈkäm-ət-ər, ˈdrəŋ-kə-ˌmēt-\ *n* (ca. 1934) : a device for measuring alcohol content of the blood by chemical analysis of the breath
dru·pa·ceous \drü-ˈpā-shəs\ *adj* (1822) **1** : of or relating to a drupe **2** : bearing drupes
drupe \ˈdrüp\ *n* [NL *drupa,* fr. L, overripe olive, fr. Gk *dryppa* olive] (ca. 1753) : a one-seeded indehiscent fruit having a hard bony endocarp, a fleshy mesocarp, and a thin exocarp that is flexible (as in the cherry) or dry and almost leathery (as in the almond)
drupe·let \ˈdrü-plət\ *n* (1880) : a small drupe; *specif* : one of the individual parts of an aggregate fruit (as the raspberry)
druth·ers \ˈdrəth-ərz\ *n pl* [*druther,* alter. of *would rather*] *dial* (1875) : free choice : PREFERENCE — used in the phrase *if one had one's druthers*
Druze *or* **Druse** \ˈdrüz\ *n* [Ar *Durūz,* pl., fr. Muḥammad ibn-Ismaʻīl al-*Darazīy* †1019 Muslim religious leader] (1786) : a member of a religious sect originating among Muslims and centered in the mountains of Lebanon and Syria
¹dry \ˈdrī\ *adj* **dri·er** \ˈdrī(-ə)r\; **dri·est** \ˈdrī-əst\ [ME, fr. OE *drȳge;* akin to OHG *truckan* dry, OE *drēahnian* to drain] (bef. 12c) **1 a** : free or relatively free from a liquid and esp. water **b** : not being in or under water ⟨~ land⟩ **c** : lacking precipitation or humidity ⟨~ climate⟩ **2 a** : characterized by exhaustion of a supply of liquid ⟨a ~ well⟩ ⟨the fountain pen ran ~⟩ **b** : devoid of running water ⟨a ~ ravine⟩ **c** : devoid of natural moisture ⟨my throat was ~ after the long hike⟩ **d** : no longer sticky or damp ⟨the paint is ~⟩ **e** : not giving milk ⟨a ~ cow⟩ **f** : lacking freshness : STALE **g** : ANHYDROUS **3 a** : marked by the absence or scantiness of secretions ⟨a ~ cough⟩ **b** : not shedding or accompanied by tears ⟨a ~ sob⟩ **4** *obs* : involving no bloodshed or drowning ⟨I would fain die a ~ death —Shak.⟩ **5 a** : marked by the absence of alcoholic beverages ⟨a ~ party⟩ **b** : prohibiting the manufacture or distribution of alcoholic beverages **6** : served or eaten without butter ⟨~ toast⟩ **7 a** : lacking sweetness : SEC **b** : having all or most sugar fermented to alcohol ⟨a ~ wine⟩ **8 a** : solid as opposed to liquid ⟨~ groceries⟩ **b** : reduced to powder or flakes : DEHYDRATED ⟨~ milk⟩ **9** : functioning without lubrication ⟨a ~ clutch⟩ **10** *of natural gas* : containing no recoverable hydrocarbon (as gasoline) **11 a** : built or constructed without a process that requires water; *also* : using no mortar ⟨~ masonry⟩ **b** : requiring no liquid in preparation or operation ⟨a ~ copy of the page⟩ **12 a** : not showing or communicating warmth, enthusiasm, or tender feeling : SEVERE ⟨a ~ style of painting⟩ **b** : WEARISOME, UNINTERESTING ⟨~ passages of description⟩ **c** : lacking embellishment : PLAIN ⟨the ~ facts⟩ **13 a** : not yielding what is expected or desired : UNPRODUCTIVE **b** : having no personal bias or emotional concern ⟨the ~ light of reason⟩ **c** : RESERVED, ALOOF **14** : marked by matter-of-fact, ironic, or terse manner of expression ⟨~ wit⟩ **15** : lacking smooth sound qualities ⟨a ~ rasping voice⟩ **16** : being a dry run ⟨a ~ rehearsal⟩ — **dry·ish** \ˈdrī-ish\ *adj* — **dry·ly** *adv* — **dry·ness** *n*
²dry *vb* **dried; dry·ing** *vt* (bef. 12c) : to make dry ~ *vi* : to become dry — **dry·able** \ˈdrī-ə-bəl\ *adj*
³dry *n, pl* **drys** (13c) **1** : the condition of being dry : DRYNESS **2** : something dry; *esp* : a dry place **3** : PROHIBITIONIST
dry·ad \ˈdrī-əd, -ˌad\ *n* [L *dryad-, dryas,* fr. Gk, fr. *drys* tree — more at TREE] (14c) : WOOD NYMPH
dry·as·dust \ˈdrī-əz-ˌdəst\ *adj* (1872) : BORING — **dryasdust** *n*
dry cell *n* (1893) : a voltaic cell whose contents are not spillable
dry–clean \ˈdrī-ˌklēn\ *vt* (1897) : to subject to dry cleaning ~ *vi* : to undergo dry cleaning — **dry–clean·able** \-ˈklē-nə-bəl\ *adj*
dry cleaner *n* (1897) : one whose business is dry cleaning
dry cleaning *n* (1817) **1** : the cleansing of fabrics with substantially nonaqueous organic solvents **2** : something that is dry-cleaned
dry–dock *vt* (1884) : to place in a dry dock
dry dock \ˈdrī-ˌdäk\ *n* (ca. 1627) : a dock that can be kept dry for use during the construction or repairing of ships
dry·er *var of* DRIER
dry–eyed \ˈdrī-ˈīd\ *adj* (1667) **1** : not moved to tears or to empathy **2** : marked by the absence of sentimentalism or romanticism ⟨an exercise in ~ nostalgia — Edith Oliver⟩
dry farming *n* (1878) : farming that is engaged in on nonirrigated land with little rainfall and that relies on moisture-conserving tillage and drought-resistant crops — **dry farm** *n* — **dry–farm** *vt* — **dry farmer** *n*
dry fly *n* (1846) : an artificial angling fly designed to float
dry goods \ˈdrī-ˌgu̇dz\ *n pl* (1657) : textiles, ready-to-wear clothing, and notions as distinguished esp. from hardware and groceries
dry hole *n* (1883) : a well (as for gas or oil) that proves unproductive
dry ice *n* (1925) : solidified carbon dioxide usu. in the form of blocks that at −78.5°C changes directly to a gas and that is used chiefly as a refrigerant
drying oil *n* (ca. 1865) : an oil (as linseed oil) that changes readily to a hard tough elastic substance when exposed in a thin film to air
dry kiln *n* (ca. 1909) : a heated chamber for drying and seasoning cut lumber
dry·land \ˈdrī-ˌland\ *adj* (1893) : of, relating to, or being a relatively arid region ⟨a ~ wheat state⟩; *also* : of, adapted to, practicing, or being agricultural methods (as dry farming) suited to such a region
dry·lot \ˈdrī-ˈlät\ *n* (1924) : an enclosure of limited size usu. bare of vegetation and used for fattening livestock
dry measure *n* (1688) : a series of units of capacity for dry commodities — see METRIC SYSTEM table, WEIGHT table
dry mop *n* (1933) : a long-handled mop for dusting floors — called also *dust mop*
dry–nurse *vt* (1581) **1** : to act as dry nurse to **2** : to give unnecessary supervision to
dry nurse *n* (1598) : a nurse who takes care of but does not breast-feed another woman's baby
dryo·pith·e·cine \ˌdrī-ō-ˈpith-ə-ˌsīn\ *n* [deriv. of Gk *drys* tree + *pithēkos* ape] (1948) : any of a subfamily (Dryopithecinae) of Miocene and Pliocene Old World anthropoid apes sometimes regarded as ancestors of both man and modern anthropoids — **dryopithecine** *adj*
dry out *vi* (1892) : to undergo an extended period of withdrawal from alcohol or drug use esp. at a special clinic
dry·point \ˈdrī-ˌpȯint\ *n* (1883) : an engraving made with a steel or jeweled point directly into the metal plate without the use of acid as in etching; *also* : a print made from such an engraving
dry–rot *vt* (1818) : to affect with dry rot ~ *vi* : to become affected with dry rot
dry rot *n* (1795) **1 a** : a decay of seasoned timber caused by fungi that consume the cellulose of wood leaving a soft skeleton which is readily reduced to powder **b** : a fungous rot of plant tissue in which the affected areas are dry and often firmer than normal or more or less mummified **2** : a fungus causing dry rot **3** : decay from within caused esp. by resistance to new forces ⟨art . . . infected by the *dry rot* of formalism —D. G. Mandelbaum⟩
dry run *n* (ca. 1942) **1** : a practice firing without ammunition **2** : a practice exercise : REHEARSAL, TRIAL
dry·salt·er \ˈdrī-ˌsȯl-tər\ *n, Brit* (1707) : a dealer in crude dry chemicals and dyes — **dry·salt·ery** \-tə-rē\ *n, Brit*
dry–shod \ˈdrī-ˈshäd\ *adj* (15c) : having dry shoes or feet
dry sink *n* (1951) : a wooden cabinet with a tray top for holding a wash basin
dry suit *n* (1955) : a close-fitting waterproof rubber suit used esp. by a skin diver
dry up *vt* (15c) : to end or close off the supply of ⟨*drying up* mortgage money⟩ ~ *vi* **1** : to disappear as if by evaporation, draining, or cutting off of a source of supply **2** : to wither or die through gradual loss of vitality **3** : to stop talking ⟨wished his buddy would *dry up*⟩
dry·wall \ˈdrī-ˌwȯl\ *n* (1952) : PLASTERBOARD
dry wash *n, West* (1872) : WASH 3d
dry well *n* (ca. 1942) : a hole in the ground filled with gravel or rubble to receive drainage water and allow it to percolate away
d.t.'s \(ˈ)dē-ˈtēz\ *n pl, often cap D&T* (1858) : DELIRIUM TREMENS
¹du·al \ˈd(y)ü-əl\ *adj* [L *dualis,* fr. *duo* two — more at TWO] (1607) **1** *of grammatical number* : denoting reference to two **2 a** : consisting of two parts or elements or having two like parts : DOUBLE **b** : having a double character or nature — **du·al·ly** \-ə(l)-lē\ *adv*
²dual *n* (1650) **1** : the dual number of a language **2** : a linguistic form in the dual
dual citizenship *n* (ca. 1924) : the status of an individual who is a citizen of two or more nations
du·al·ism \ˈd(y)ü-ə-ˌliz-əm\ *n* (1794) **1** : a theory that considers reality to consist of two irreducible elements or modes **2** : the quality or state of being dual or of having a dual nature **3 a** : a doctrine that the universe is under the dominion of two opposing principles one of which is good and the other evil **b** : a view of human beings as constituted of two irreducible elements (as matter and spirit) — **du·al·ist** \-ləst\ *n* — **du·al·is·tic** \ˌd(y)ü-ə-ˈlis-tik\ *adj* — **du·al·is·ti·cal·ly** \-ti-k(ə-)lē\ *adv*
du·al·i·ty \d(y)ü-ˈal-ət-ē\ *n, pl* **-ties** (15c) : DUALISM 2; *also* : DICHOTOMY
du·al·ize \ˈd(y)ü-ə-ˌlīz\ *vt* **-ized; -iz·ing** (1838) : to make dual
dual–purpose *adj* (1904) : having breed characteristics that serve two purposes ⟨~ cattle that supply milk and meat⟩
dual–purpose fund *n* (1967) : a closed-end investment company having two classes of shares with one entitled to all dividend income and the other to all gains from capital appreciation
¹dub \ˈdəb\ *vt* **dubbed; dub·bing** [ME *dubben,* fr. OE *dubbian;* akin to ON *dubba* to dub, OHG *tubili* plug] (bef. 12c) **1 a** : to confer knighthood on **b** : to call by a distinctive title, epithet, or nickname **2** : to trim or remove the comb and wattles of **3** : to execute poorly — **dub·ber** *n*
²dub *n* (1887) : one who is inept or clumsy
³dub *n* [ME (Sc dial.) *dubbe*] *chiefly Scot* (15c) : POOL, PUDDLE
⁴dub *vt* **dubbed; dub·bing** [by shortening & alter. fr. *double*] (1930) **1** : to add (sound effects or new dialogue) to a film or to a radio or television production — usu. used with *in* **2** : to provide (a motion-picture film) with a new sound track and esp. dialogue in a different language **3** : to make a new recording of (sound already recorded); *also* : to mix (recorded sound from different sources) into a single recording — **dub·ber** *n*
dub·bin \ˈdəb-ən\ *also* **dub·bing** \-ən, -iŋ\ *n* [*dubbing,* gerund of *dub* (to dress leather)] (1781) : a dressing of oil and tallow for leather
du·bi·ety \d(y)ü-ˈbī-ət-ē\ *n, pl* **-eties** [LL *dubietas,* fr. L *dubius*] (1750) **1** : a usu. hesitant uncertainty or doubt that tends to cause vacillation **2** : a matter of doubt *syn* see UNCERTAINTY
du·bi·ous \ˈd(y)ü-bē-əs\ *adj* [L *dubius,* fr. *dubare* to vacillate; akin to L *duo* two — more at TWO] (1548) **1** : giving rise to uncertainty: as **a** : of doubtful promise or outcome ⟨felt that our plan was a little ~⟩ **b** : questionable or suspect as to true nature of quality ⟨the practice is of

~ legality⟩ ⟨a person of ~ reliability⟩ ⟨the ~ honor of being the world's biggest polluter⟩ **2 :** unsettled in opinion : DOUBTFUL, SUSPICIOUS ⟨we were ~ about the whole affair⟩ ***syn*** see DOUBTFUL — **du·bi·ous·ly** *adv* — **du·bi·ous·ness** *n*

du·bi·ta·ble \'d(y)ü-bət-ə-bəl\ *adj* [L *dubitabilis,* fr. *dubitare* to doubt — more at DOUBT] (1624) : open to doubt or question

du·bi·ta·tion \ˌd(y)ü-bə-'tā-shən\ *n, archaic* (15c) : DOUBT

du·cal \'d(y)ü-kəl\ *adj* [ME, fr. MF, fr. LL *ducalis* of a leader, fr. L *duc-, dux* leader — more at DUKE] (15c) : of or relating to a duke or dukedom — **du·cal·ly** \-kə-lē\ *adv*

duc·at \'dək-ət\ *n* [ME, fr. MF, fr. OIt *ducato* coin with the doge's portrait on it, fr. *duca* doge, fr. LGk *douk-, doux* leader, fr. L *duc-, dux*] (14c) **1 :** a usu. gold coin formerly used in various European countries **2 :** TICKET

du·ce \'dü-(ˌ)chā\ *n* [It *(Il) Duce,* lit., the leader, title of Benito Mussolini, fr. L *duc-, dux*] (1923) : LEADER — used esp. for the leader of the Italian Fascist party

duch·ess \'dəch-əs\ *n* [ME *duchesse,* fr. MF, fr. *duc* duke] (14c) **1 :** the wife or widow of a duke **2 :** a woman who holds the rank of a duke in her own right

duchy \'dəch-ē\ *n, pl* **duch·ies** [ME *duche,* fr. MF *duché,* fr. *duc*] (14c) **1 :** the territory of a duke or duchess : DUKEDOM **2 :** special domain

[1]**duck** \'dək\ *n, pl* **ducks** *often attrib* [ME *doke,* fr. OE *dūce*] (bef. 12c) **1** *or pl* **duck a :** any of various swimming birds (family Anatidae, the duck family) in which the neck and legs are short, the body more or less depressed, the bill often broad and flat, and the sexes almost always different from each other in plumage **b :** the flesh of any of these birds used as food **2 :** a female duck — compare DRAKE **3** *chiefly Brit* : DARLING — often used in pl. but sing. in constr. **4 :** PERSON, CREATURE

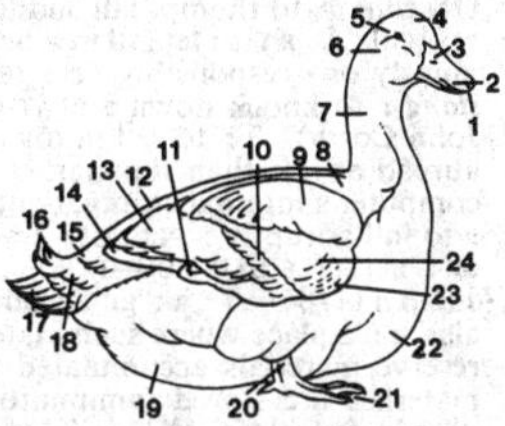

duck 1a: *1* bean, *2* bill, *3* nostril, *4* head, *5* eye, *6* auricular region, *7* neck, *8* cape, *9* shoulder, *10* coverts, *11* wing coverts, *12* saddle, *13* secondaries, *14* primaries, *15* rump, *16* drake feathers, *17* tail, *18* tail coverts, *19* down, *20* shank, *21* web, *22* breast, *23* wing front, *24* wing bow

[2]**duck** *vb* [ME *douken;* akin to OHG *tūhhan* to dive, OE *dūce* duck] *vt* (14c) **1 :** to thrust under water **2 :** to lower (as the head) quickly : BOW **3 :** AVOID, EVADE ⟨~ the issue⟩ ~ *vi* **1 a :** to plunge under the surface of water **b :** to descend suddenly : DIP **2 a :** to lower the head or body suddenly : DODGE **b :** BOW, BOB **3 a :** to move quickly **b :** to evade a duty, question, or responsibility : BACK OUT — **duck·er** *n*

[3]**duck** *n* (1554) : an instance of ducking

[4]**duck** *n* [D *doek* cloth; akin to OHG *tuoh* cloth, and perh. to Skt *dhvaja* flag] (1640) **1 :** a durable closely woven usu. cotton fabric **2** *pl* : light clothes made of duck

[5]**duck** *n* [*DUKW,* its code designation] (1943) : an amphibious truck

duck·bill \'dək-ˌbil\ *n* (1840) : PLATYPUS

duck·board \-ˌbō(ə)rd, -ˌbȯ(ə)rd\ *n* (ca. 1917) : a boardwalk or slatted flooring laid on a wet, muddy, or cold surface — usu. used in pl.

duck call *n* (1872) : a device for imitating the calls of ducks

duck–foot·ed \'dək-'fu̇t-əd\ *adv* (ca. 1891) : with feet pointed outward : FLAT-FOOTED

ducking stool *n* (1597) : a seat attached to a plank and formerly used to plunge culprits tied to it into water

duck·ling \'dək-liŋ\ *n* (15c) : a young duck

duck·pin \-ˌpin\ *n* (ca. 1910) **1 :** a small bowling pin shorter than a tenpin but proportionately wider at mid-diameter **2** *pl but sing in constr* : a bowling game using duckpins

ducks and drakes *or* **duck and drake** *n* (1583) : the pastime of skimming flat stones or shells along the surface of calm water — **play ducks and drakes with** *or* **make ducks and drakes of :** to use recklessly : SQUANDER ⟨*played ducks and drakes with* his money⟩

duck soup *n* (1912) : something easy to do

duck·tail \'dək-ˌtāl\ *n* [fr. its resemblance to the tail of a duck] (1947) : a hairstyle in which the hair on each side is slicked back to meet in a ridge at the back of the head

duck·weed \'dək-ˌwēd\ *n* (15c) : a small floating aquatic monocotyledonous plant (family Lemnaceae, the duckweed family)

ducky \'dək-ē\ *adj* **duck·i·er; -est** (1819) **1 :** SATISFACTORY, FINE ⟨everything is just ~⟩ **2 :** DARLING, CUTE ⟨a ~ little tearoom⟩

[1]**duct** \'dəkt\ *n* [NL *ductus,* fr. ML, aqueduct, fr. L, act of leading, fr. *ductus,* pp. of *ducere* to lead — more at TOW] (1667) **1 :** a bodily tube or vessel esp. when carrying the secretion of a gland **2 a :** a pipe, tube, or channel that conveys a substance **b :** a pipe or tubular runway for carrying an electric power line, telephone cables, or other conductors **3 a :** a continuous tube formed in plant tissue by a row of elongated cells that have lost their intervening end walls **b :** an elongated cavity (as a resin canal of a conifer) formed by disintegration or separation of cells **4 :** a layer (as in the atmosphere or the ocean) which occurs under usu. abnormal conditions and in which radio or sound waves are confined to a restricted path — **duc·tal** \'dək-tᵊl\ *adj* — **duct·less** \'dək-tləs\ *adj*

[2]**duct** *vt* (1936) **1 :** to convey (as a gas) through a duct; *also* : to propagate (as radio waves) through a duct **2 :** to enclose in a duct ⟨~*ed* fan⟩

duc·tile \'dək-tᵊl, -ˌtīl\ *adj* [MF & L; MF, fr. L *ductilis,* fr. *ductus,* pp.] (14c) **1 :** capable of being drawn out or hammered thin ⟨~ metal⟩ **2 :** easily led or influenced ⟨the ~ masses⟩ **3 :** capable of being fashioned into a new form ***syn*** see PLASTIC — **duc·til·i·ty** \ˌdək-'til-ət-ē\ *n*

duct·ing \'dək-tiŋ\ *n* (1945) : a system of ducts; *also* : the material composing a duct

ductless gland *n* (1849) : ENDOCRINE GLAND

duct·ule \'dək-(ˌ)t(y)ü(ə)l\ *n* (1883) : a small duct

duc·tus ar·te·ri·o·sus \'dək-təs-är-ˌtir-ē-'ō-səs\ *n* [NL, lit., arterial duct] (1811) : a short broad vessel in the fetus that connects the pulmonary artery with the aorta and conducts most of the blood directly from the right ventricle to the aorta bypassing the lungs

[1]**dud** \'dəd\ *n* [ME *dudde*] (1567) **1** *pl* **a :** CLOTHING **b :** personal belongings **2 a :** FAILURE ⟨the movie proved a box-office ~⟩ **b :** MISFIT **3 :** a bomb or missile that fails to explode

[2]**dud** *adj* (1903) : of little or no worth : VALUELESS ⟨~ checks⟩

dud·die *or* **dud·dy** \'dəd-ē\ *adj, Scot* (1718) : RAGGED, TATTERED

[1]**dude** \'d(y)üd\ *n* [origin unknown] (1883) **1 :** a man extremely fastidious in dress and manner : DANDY **2 :** a city man; *esp* : an Easterner in the West **3 :** FELLOW, GUY — **dud·ish** \'d(y)üd-ish\ *adj* — **dud·ish·ly** *adv*

[2]**dude** *vt* **dud·ed; dud·ing** (1899) : DRESS UP — usu. used with *up*

du·deen \dü-'dēn\ *n* [IrGael *dúidín,* dim. of *dúd* pipe] (1841) : a short tobacco pipe made of clay

dude ranch *n* (1921) : a vacation resort offering activities (as horseback riding) typical of western ranches

[1]**dud·geon** \'dəj-ən\ *n* [ME *dogeon,* fr. AF *digeon*] (15c) **1** *obs* : a wood used esp. for dagger hilts **2 a** *archaic* : a dagger with a handle of dudgeon **b** *obs* : a haft made of dudgeon

[2]**dudgeon** *n* [origin unknown] (1573) : a fit or state of indignation ⟨she stalked out in a ~ when her plan was rejected⟩ ***syn*** see OFFENSE

[1]**due** \'d(y)ü\ *adj* [ME, fr. MF *deu,* pp. of *devoir* to owe, fr. L *debēre* — more at DEBT] (14c) **1 :** owed or owing as a debt **2 a :** owed or owing as a natural or moral right ⟨everyone's right to dissent . . . is ~ the full protection of the Constitution —Nat Hentoff⟩ **b :** according to accepted notions or procedures : APPROPRIATE **3 a :** satisfying or capable of satisfying a need, obligation, or duty : ADEQUATE **b :** REGULAR, LAWFUL ⟨~ proof of loss⟩ **4 :** capable of being attributed : ASCRIBABLE — used with *to* ⟨this advance is partly ~ to a few men of genius —A. N. Whitehead⟩ **5 :** having reached the date at which payment is required : PAYABLE **6 :** required or expected in the prescribed, normal, or logical course of events : SCHEDULED — **due·ness** *n*

[2]**due** *n* (15c) : something due or owed: as **a :** something that rightfully belongs to one ⟨the artist has finally been accorded something of his ~⟩ **b :** a payment or obligation required by law or custom : DEBT **c** *pl* : FEES, CHARGES

[3]**due** *adv* (1597) **1** *obs* : DULY **2 :** DIRECTLY, EXACTLY ⟨~ north⟩

[1]**du·el** \'d(y)ü-əl\ *n* [ML *duellum,* fr. OL, war] (15c) **1 :** a combat between two persons; *specif* : a formal combat with weapons fought between two persons in the presence of witnesses **2 :** a conflict between antagonistic persons, ideas, or forces

[2]**duel** *vb* **du·eled** *or* **du·elled; du·el·ing** *or* **du·el·ling** *vi* (1645) : to fight a duel ~ *vt* : to encounter (an opponent) in a duel — **du·el·er** *or* **du·el·ler** *n* — **du·el·ist** *or* **du·el·list** \'d(y)ü-ə-ləst\ *n*

du·el·lo \d(y)ü-'el-(ˌ)ō\ *n, pl* **-los** [It, fr. ML *duellum*] (1588) **1 :** the rules or practice of dueling **2 :** DUEL

du·en·de \dü-'en-(ˌ)dā\ *n* [Sp dial., charm, fr. Sp, ghost, goblin, fr. *duen de casa,* prob. fr. *dueño de casa* owner of a house] (1964) : the power to attract through personal magnetism and charm

du·en·na \d(y)ü-'en-ə\ *n* [Sp *dueña,* fr. L *domina* mistress — more at DAME] (1623) **1 :** an elderly woman serving as governess and companion to the younger ladies in a Spanish or a Portuguese family **2 :** CHAPERON — **du·en·na·ship** \-ˌship\ *n*

due process *n* (ca. 1890) : a course of formal proceedings (as legal proceedings) carried out regularly and in accordance with established rules and principles

[1]**du·et** \d(y)ü-'et\ *n* [It *duetto,* dim. of *duo*] (ca. 1740) : a composition for two performers

[2]**duet** *vi* **du·et·ted; du·et·ting** (1822) : to perform a duet

due to *prep* (14c) : BECAUSE OF

usage When the *due* of *due to* is clearly an adjective ⟨deaths *due to* malaria⟩ ⟨success is *due to* hard work⟩ no one complains about the phrase. But when the phrase is clearly a preposition ⟨classes canceled *due to* snow⟩ many people object to it. Although its development parallels that of the synonymous *owing to* — to which no one objects — and it has been recognized as standard for decades, you will still run the risk of giving offense if you use it.

[1]**duff** \'dəf\ *n* [E dial., alter. of *dough*] (1838) **1 :** a boiled or steamed pudding often containing dried fruit **2 :** the partly decayed organic matter on the forest floor **3 :** fine coal : SLACK

[2]**duff** *n* [origin unknown] (ca. 1888) : BUTTOCKS ⟨get off your ~⟩

duf·fel *or* **duf·fle** \'dəf-əl\ *n* [D *duffel,* fr. *Duffel,* Belgium] (1677) **1 :** a coarse heavy woolen material with a thick nap **2 :** transportable personal belongings, equipment, and supplies **3 :** DUFFEL BAG

duffel bag *n* (1917) : a large cylindrical fabric bag for personal belongings

duf·fer \'dəf-ər\ *n* [origin unknown] (1756) **1 a :** a peddler esp. of cheap flashy articles **b :** something counterfeit or worthless **2 :** an incompetent, ineffectual, or clumsy person **3** *Austral* : a cattle rustler

duffle coat \'dəf-əl-\ *or* **duffel coat** *n* (1684) : a heavy usu. woolen medium-length coat with toggle fasteners and a hood — called also *duffle*

[1]**dug** *past and past part of* DIG

[2]**dug** \'dəg\ *n* [perh. of Scand origin; akin to OSw *dæggia* to suckle; akin to OE *delu* nipple — more at FEMININE] (ca. 1530) : UDDER; *also* : TEAT — usu. used of a suckling animal; usu. considered vulgar when used of a woman

du·gong \'dü-ˌgäŋ, -ˌgȯŋ\ *n* [NL, genus name, fr. Malay & Tag *duyong* sea cow] (1800) : an aquatic herbivorous mammal of a monotypic genus (*Dugong*) that has a bilobed tail and in the male upper incisors altered into tusks and that is related to the manatee — called also *sea cow*

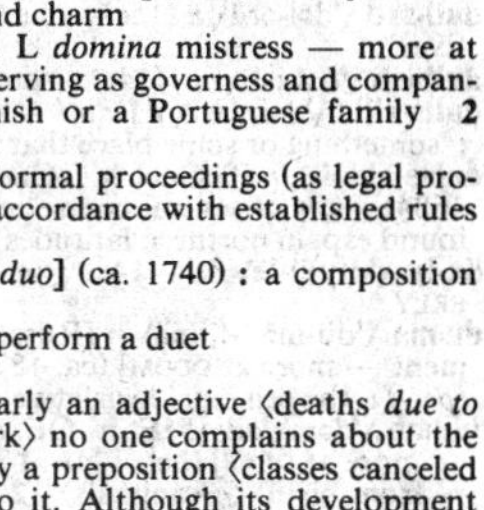
dugong

dug·out \'dəg-ˌau̇t\ *n* (1722) **1 :** a boat made by hollowing out a large

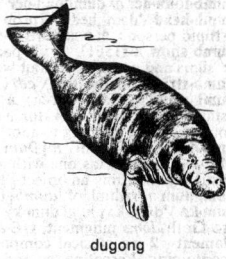

log 2 a : a shelter dug in a hillside; *also* : a shelter dug in the ground and roofed with sod b : an area in the side of a trench for quarters, storage, or protection 3 : either of two low shelters on either side of and facing a baseball diamond that contain the players' benches

dui·ker \'dī-kər\ *n* [Afrik, lit., diver, fr. *duik* to dive, fr. MD *dūken;* akin to OHG *tūhhan* to dive — more at DUCK] (1777) : any of several small African antelopes comprising two genera (*Cephalophus* and *Sylvicapra*)

duit *var of* DOIT

duke \'d(y)ük\ *n* [ME, fr. OF *duc,* fr. L *duc-, dux,* fr. *ducere* to lead — more at TOW] (12c) 1 : a sovereign ruler of a continental European duchy 2 : a nobleman of the highest hereditary rank; *esp* : a member of the highest grade of the British peerage 3 *slang* : FIST, HAND — usu. used in pl. 4 : any of several cultivated cherries between sweet cherries and sour cherries in character and prob. of hybrid origin — **duke·dom** \-dəm\ *n*

Du·kho·bor *var of* DOUKHOBOR

dul·cet \'dəl-sət\ *adj* [ME *doucet,* fr. MF, fr. *douz* sweet, fr. L *dulcis;* akin to Gk *glykys* sweet] (14c) 1 : sweet to the taste : LUSCIOUS 2 a : sweet to the ear : MELODIOUS b : AGREEABLE, SOOTHING ⟨could not . . . expect such ~ weather to last —Victoria Sackville-West⟩ — **dul·cet·ly** *adv*

dul·ci·fy \'dəl-sə-,fī\ *vt* **-fied; -fy·ing** [LL *dulcificare,* fr. L *dulcis*] (1599) 1 : to make sweet 2 : to make agreeable : MOLLIFY

dul·ci·mer \'dəl-sə-mər\ *n* [ME *dowcemere,* fr. MF *doulcemer,* fr. OIt *dolcimelo,* fr. *dolce* sweet, fr. L *dulcis*] (15c) 1 : a stringed instrument of trapezoidal shape played with light hammers held in the hands 2 *or* **dul·ci·more** \-,mō(ə)r, -,mȯ(ə)r\ : an American folk instrument with three or four strings stretched over an elongate fretted sound box held on the lap and played by plucking or strumming

dul·ci·nea \,dəl-sə-'nē-ə, -'sin-ē-ə\ *n* [Sp, fr. *Dulcinea* del Toboso, beloved of Don Quixote] (1748) : MISTRESS, SWEETHEART

1dull \'dəl\ *adj* [ME *dul;* akin to OE *dol* foolish and prob. to L *fumus* smoke — more at FUME] (13c) 1 : mentally slow : STUPID 2 a : slow in perception or sensibility : INSENSIBLE b : lacking zest or vivacity : LISTLESS 3 : slow in action : SLUGGISH 4 : lacking sharpness of edge or point 5 : lacking brilliance or luster 6 : lacking in force or intensity: as a : not clear : INDISTINCT ⟨the kerosene lamp gave a ~ light⟩ b : not resonant or ringing ⟨a ~ booming sound⟩ 7 *of a color* : low in saturation and low in lightness 8 : CLOUDY 9 : TEDIOUS, UNINTERESTING — **dull·ness** *or* **dul·ness** \'dəl-nəs\ *n* — **dul·ly** \'dəl-(l)ē\ *adv*

syn DULL, BLUNT, OBTUSE mean not sharp, keen, or acute. DULL suggests a lack or loss of keenness, zest, or pungency; BLUNT suggests an inherent lack of sharpness or quickness of feeling or perception; OBTUSE implies such bluntness as makes one insensitive in perception or imagination. *syn* see in addition STUPID

2dull *vt* (13c) : to make dull ⟨eyes and ears ~*ed* by age⟩ ~ *vi* : to become dull

dull·ard \'dəl-ərd\ *n* (15c) : one that is stupid, unimaginative, or insensitive

dull·ish \'dəl-ish\ *adj* (14c) : somewhat dull — **dull·ish·ly** *adv*

dulls·ville \'dəlz-,vil\ *n* [1*dull* + *-sville* (as in *Huntsville*)] *slang* (ca. 1965) : something or some place that is dull or boring; *also* : BOREDOM

dulse \'dəls\ *n* [ScGael & IrGael *duileasg;* akin to W *delysg* dulse] (ca. 1684) : any of several coarse red seaweeds (esp. *Rhodymenia palmata*) found esp. in northern latitudes and used as a food condiment

du·ly \'d(y)ü-lē\ *adv* (14c) : in a due manner, time, or degree : PROPERLY

du·ma \'dü-mə, -(,)mä\ *n* [Russ, of Gmc origin; akin to OE *dōm* judgment — more at DOOM] (ca. 1870) : a representative council in Russia; *specif* : the principal legislative assembly in czarist Russia

1dumb \'dəm\ *adj* [ME, fr. OE; akin to OHG *tumb* mute, OE *dēaf* deaf — more at DEAF] (bef. 12c) 1 : lacking the power of speech ⟨deaf and ~ from birth⟩ ⟨~ animals⟩ 2 : temporarily unable to speak (as from shock or astonishment) ⟨struck ~ with fear⟩ 3 : not expressed in uttered words ⟨~ grief⟩ 4 : SILENT; *also* : TACITURN 5 : lacking some usual attribute or accompaniment; *esp* : having no means of self-propulsion ⟨~ barge⟩ 6 a : markedly lacking in intelligence : STUPID b : showing a lack of intelligence ⟨the omission seems ~ and irresponsible —Eliot Fremont-Smith⟩ — sometimes used in the phrase *dumb luck* *syn* see STUPID — **dumb·ly** \'dəm-lē\ *adv* — **dumb·ness** *n*

usage There is some evidence that, when applied to persons who cannot speak, *dumb* may be considered offensive.

2dumb *vt* (1608) : to make silent : DEADEN ⟨would lie around, ~*ed* by the drugs —Norman Mailer⟩

dumb·bell \'dəm-,bel\ *n* (1785) 1 : a short bar with two identical spheres or with adjustable weighted disks attached to each end and used usu. in pairs for calisthenic exercise 2 : one that is dull and stupid

dumb·found *or* **dum·found** \,dəm-'faund\ *vt* [*dumb* + *-found* (as in *confound*)] (1653) : to confound briefly and usu. with astonishment *syn* see PUZZLE

dumb·found·er *or* **dum·foun·der** \-'faun-dər\ *vt* (1710) : DUMBFOUND

dumb·head \'dəm-,hed\ *n* [prob. trans. of G *dummkopf*] *slang* (1887) : a stupid person : BLOCKHEAD

dumb show *n* (1561) 1 : a part of a play presented in pantomime 2 : signs and gestures without words : PANTOMIME

dumb·struck \'dəm-,strək\ *adj* (1887) : made silent by astonishment

dumb·wait·er \'dəm-'wāt-ər\ *n* (1749) 1 : a portable serving table or stand 2 : a small elevator used for conveying food and dishes from one story of a building to another

dum·dum \'dəm-,dəm\ *n* [*Dum Dum,* arsenal near Calcutta, India] (ca. 1891) : a bullet (as one with a hollow point) that expands more than usual upon hitting an object

dum–dum *n* [redupl. of 1*dumb*] (1928) : a stupid person : DUMMY

dum·ka \'dům-kə\ *n, pl* **dum·ky** \-kē\ [Czech, elegy, of Gmc origin; akin to Goth *dōms* judgment, OE *dōm* doom] (1895) 1 : a Slavic song of lament 2 : a musical composition suggestive of a dumka but often containing alternating sad and gay passages

dumm·kopf \'dům-,kȯpf\ *n* [G, fr. *dumm* stupid + *kopf* head] (1809) : BLOCKHEAD

1dum·my \'dəm-ē\ *n, pl* **dummies** [1*dumb* + *-y*] (1598) 1 a : one who is incapable of speaking b : one who is habitually silent c : one who is stupid 2 a : the exposed hand in bridge played by the declarer in addition to his own hand b : a bridge player whose hand is a dummy 3 : an imitation, copy, or likeness of something used as a substitute: as a : MANNEQUIN b : a stuffed figure used by football players for tackling and blocking practice 4 : one seeming to act for itself but in reality acting for or at the direction of another ⟨a ~ corporation⟩ 5 : something usu. mechanically operated that serves to replace or aid a human being's work 6 a : a mock-up of a proposed publication (as a book or magazine) b : a set of pages (as for a newspaper or magazine) with the position of text and artwork indicated for the printer

2dummy *adj* (1846) 1 : having the appearance of being real : ARTIFICIAL ⟨~ foods in the display case⟩ 2 : existing in name only : FICTITIOUS ⟨bank accounts held in ~ names⟩

3dummy *vb* **dum·mied; dum·my·ing** *vt* (1928) : to make a dummy of (as a publication) — often used with *up* ⟨*dummied* up the front page⟩ ~ *vi, slang* : to refuse to talk — used with *up*

dummy variable *n* (1957) : an arbitrary mathematical symbol or variable that can be replaced by another without affecting the value of the expression in which it occurs

du·mor·ti·er·ite \d(y)ü-'mȯrt-ē-ə-,rīt\ *n* [F *dumortiérite,* fr. Eugène *Dumortier* †1876 Fr. paleontologist] (1881) : a bright blue or greenish blue mineral consisting of a silicate of aluminum and used esp. for jewelry

1dump \'dəmp\ *vb* [perh. fr. MD *dompen* to immerse, topple; akin to ON *dumpa* to thump, fall suddenly, OE *dyppan* to dip — more at DIP] *vt* (14c) 1 a : to let fall in a heap or mass b : to get rid of unceremoniously or irresponsibly c : JETTISON ⟨an airplane ~*ing* gasoline⟩ 2 *slang* : to knock down : BEAT ⟨the man rushed out and ~*ed* him —John Corry⟩ 3 : to sell in quantity at a very low price; *specif* : to sell abroad at less than the market price at home 4 : to copy (data in a computer's internal storage) onto an external storage medium ~ *vi* 1 : to fall abruptly : PLUNGE 2 : to dump refuse — **dump·er** *n* — **dump on** : BELITTLE, BAD-MOUTH

2dump *n* (1784) 1 a : an accumulation of refuse and discarded materials b : a place where such materials are dumped 2 a : a quantity of reserve materials accumulated at one place b : a place where such materials are stored ⟨ammunition ~⟩ 3 : a disorderly, slovenly, or dilapidated place 4 : an instance of dumping data stored in a computer

dump·ing *n* (1857) : the act of one that dumps; *esp* : the selling of goods in quantity at below market price

dump·ish \'dəm-pish\ *adj* [*dumps*] (1562) : SAD, MELANCHOLY

dump·ling \'dəm-pliŋ\ *n* [perh. alter. of *lump*] (1600) 1 a : a small mass of leavened dough cooked by boiling or steaming b : a usu. baked dessert of fruit wrapped in dough 2 : something soft and rounded like a dumpling; *esp* : a short fat person or animal

dumps \'dəm(p)s\ *n pl* [prob. fr. D *domp* haze, fr. MD *damp* — more at DAMP] (1529) : a gloomy state of mind : DESPONDENCY ⟨in the ~⟩

Dump·ster \'dəm(p)-stər\ *trademark* — used for a large trash receptacle

dump truck *n* (1930) : a truck for transporting and dumping loose materials

dumpy \'dəm-pē\ *adj* **dump·i·er; -est** [E dial. *dump* (lump)] (1750) 1 : being short and thick in build : SQUAT 2 : SHABBY, DINGY — **dump·i·ly** \-pə-lē\ *adv* — **dump·i·ness** \-pē-nəs\ *n*

dumpy level *n* (1838) : a surveyor's level with a short telescope rigidly fixed and rotating only in a horizontal plane

1dun \'dən\ *adj* [ME, fr. OE *dunn* — more at DUSK] (bef. 12c) 1 a : having the color dun b *of a horse* : having a grayish yellow coat with black mane and tail 2 : marked by dullness and drabness — **dun·ness** \'dən-nəs\ *n*

2dun *n* (14c) 1 : a dun horse 2 : a variable color averaging a nearly neutral slightly brownish dark gray 3 : a subadult mayfly; *also* : an artificial fly tied to imitate such an insect

3dun *vt* **dunned; dun·ning** [origin unknown] (1626) 1 : to make persistent demands upon for payment 2 : to plague or pester constantly

4dun *n* (1628) 1 : one who duns 2 : an urgent request; *esp* : a demand for payment

Dun·can Phyfe \,dəŋ-kən-'fīf\ *adj* (1926) : of, relating to, or constituting furniture designed and built by or in the style of Duncan Phyfe

dunce \'dən(t)s\ *n* [John *Duns* Scotus, whose once accepted writings were ridiculed in the 16th cent.] (1577) : one who is dull-witted or stupid

dunce cap *n* (1840) : a conical cap formerly used as a punishment for slow learners at school — called also *dunce's cap*

dun·der·head \'dən-dər-,hed\ *n* [perh. fr. D *donder* thunder + E *head;* akin to OHG *thonar* thunder — more at THUNDER] (1625) : DUNCE, BLOCKHEAD — **dun·der·head·ed** \,dən-dər-'hed-əd\ *adj*

dun·drea·ries \,dən-'dri(ə)r-ēz\ *n pl, often cap* [Lord *Dundreary,* character in the play *Our American Cousin* (1858), by Tom Taylor] (1922) : long flowing sideburns

dune \'d(y)ün\ *n* [F, fr. OF, fr. MD; akin to OE *dūn* down — more at DOWN] (1790) : a hill or ridge of sand piled up by the wind — **dune·like** \-,līk\ *adj*

dune buggy *n* (1956) : BEACH BUGGY

dune·land \'d(y)ün-,land\ *n* (1922) : an area having many dunes

1dung \'dəŋ\ *n* [ME, fr. OE; akin to ON *dyngja* manure pile, Lith *dengti* to cover] (bef. 12c) 1 : the excrement of an animal : MANURE 2 : something repulsive — **dungy** \'dəŋ-ē\ *adj*

2dung *vt* (bef. 12c) : to fertilize or dress with manure

dun·ga·ree \,dəŋ-gə-'rē, 'dəŋ-gə-,\ *n* [Hindi *dūgrī*] (1673) 1 : a heavy coarse durable cotton twill woven from colored yarns; *specif* : blue denim 2 *pl* : clothes made usu. of blue denim

dung beetle *n* (1634) : a beetle (as a tumblebug) that rolls balls of dung in which to lay eggs and on which the larvae feed

Dunge·ness crab \,dənj-(ə)-,nes-\ *n* [fr. *Dungeness,* village on Juan de Fuca strait, northwest Washington] (1925) : a large edible crab (*Cancer magister*) of the Pacific coast of No. America from Alaska to California

dun·geon \'dən-jən\ *n* [ME *donjon,* fr. MF, fr. (assumed) ML *dominion-, dominio,* fr. L *dominus* lord — more at DAME] (14c) 1 : DONJON 2 : a dark usu. underground prison or vault

dung·hill \'dəŋ-,hil\ *n* (14c) 1 : a heap of dung 2 : something (as a situation or condition) that is repulsive or degraded

du·nite \'dü-ˌnīt, 'dən-ˌīt\ *n* [Mt. *Dun,* New Zealand] (ca. 1868) : a granitoid igneous rock consisting chiefly of olivine — **du·nit·ic** \dü-'nit-ik, ˌdən-'it-\ *adj*

1dunk \'dəŋk\ *vb* [PaG *dunke,* fr. MHG *dunken,* fr. OHG *dunkōn* — *more at* TINGE] *vt* (1926) **1 :** to dip (as a piece of bread) into a beverage while eating **2 :** to dip or submerge temporarily in liquid ⟨~*ed* her in the swimming pool⟩ **3 :** to throw (a basketball) into the basket from above the rim ~ *vi* **1 :** to submerge oneself in water **2 :** to make a dunk shot in basketball

2dunk *n* (1944) **:** the act or action of dunking; *esp* **:** DUNK SHOT

Dun·ker \'dəŋ-kər\ *or* **Dun·kard** \-kərd\ *n* [PaG *Dunker,* fr. *dunke*] (1714) : a member of the Church of the Brethren or any of several other orig. German Baptist denominations practicing trine immersion and love feasts and refusing to take oaths or to perform military service

Dun·kirk \'dən-ˌkərk, ˌdən-'\ *n* [*Dunkirk* or *Dunkerque,* France, scene of the evacuation of Allied forces in 1940] (1941) **1 :** a retreat to avoid total defeat **2 :** a crisis situation that requires a desperate last effort to forestall certain failure ⟨the immediate effect would plainly be a ~ for U.S. foreign policy — *Time*⟩

dunk shot *n* (ca. 1961) **:** a shot in basketball made by jumping high into the air and throwing the ball down through the basket

dun·lin \'dən-lən\ *n, pl* **dunlins** *or* **dunlin** [1*dun* + *-lin* (alter. of *-ling*)] (ca. 1531) : a small widely distributed sandpiper (*Calidris alpina*) largely cinnamon to rusty brown above and white below

Dun·lop \'dən-ˌläp, ˌdən-'\ *n* [fr. *Dunlop,* Ayr co., Scotland] (ca. 1780) **:** a Scottish cheese similar to cheddar

dun·nage \'dən-ij\ *n* [origin unknown] (15c) **1 :** loose materials used to support and protect cargo in a ship's hold; *also* **:** padding in a shipping container **2 :** BAGGAGE

duo \'d(y)ü-(ˌ)ō\ *n, pl* **du·os** [It, fr. L, two — more at TWO] (1590) **1 :** DUET **2 :** PAIR

duo- *comb form* [L *duo*] **:** two

duo·de·cil·lion \ˌd(y)ü-ō-di-'sil-yən\ *n, often attrib* [L *duodecim* twelve + E *-illion* (as in *million*)] (1911) — see NUMBER table

duo·dec·i·mal \ˌd(y)ü-ə-'des-ə-məl\ *adj* [L *duodecim* — more at DOZEN] (1727) **:** of, relating to, or proceeding by twelve or the scale of twelves — **duodecimal** *n*

duo·dec·i·mo \-ˌmō\ *n, pl* **-mos** [L, abl. of *duodecimus* twelfth, fr. *duodecim*] (1658) **:** TWELVEMO

duoden- *or* **duodeno-** *comb form* [NL, fr. ML *duodenum*] **:** duodenum ⟨*duoden*itis⟩ ⟨*duodeno*gram⟩

du·o·de·num \ˌd(y)ü-ə-'dē-nəm, d(y)ü-'äd-ᵊn-əm\ *n, pl* **-de·na** \-'dē-nə, ᵊn-ə\ *or* **-denums** [ME, fr. ML, fr. L *duodeni* twelve each, fr. *duodecim* twelve; fr. its length, about 12 fingers' breadth] (14c) **:** the first part of the small intestine extending from the pylorus to the jejunum — **du·o·de·nal** \-'dēn-ᵊl, -ᵊn-əl\ *adj*

duo·logue \'d(y)ü-ə-ˌlȯg, -ˌläg\ *n* (1864) **:** a dialogue between two persons

duo·mo \'dwȯ-(ˌ)mō\ *n, pl* **duomos** [It — more at DOME] (1549) **:** CATHEDRAL

du·op·o·ly \d(y)ü-'äp-ə-lē\ *n, pl* **-lies** [*duo-* + *-poly* (as in *monopoly*)] (1920) **1 :** an oligopoly limited to two sellers **2 :** preponderant influence or control by two political powers — **du·op·o·lis·tic** \-ˌäp-ə-'lis-tik\ *adj*

dup \'dəp\ *vt* [contr. of *do up*] *archaic* (1547) **:** OPEN

1dupe \'d(y)üp\ *n* [F, fr. MF *duppe,* prob. alter. of *huppe* hoopoe] (1681) **:** one that is easily deceived or cheated **:** FOOL

2dupe *vt* **duped; dup·ing** (1704) **:** to make a dupe of — **dup·er** *n*

syn DUPE, GULL, TRICK, HOAX mean to deceive by underhanded means. DUPE suggests unwariness in the person deluded; GULL stresses credulousness or readiness to be imposed on (as through greed) on the part of the victim; TRICK implies an intent to delude by means of a ruse or fraud but does not always imply a vicious intent; HOAX implies the contriving of an elaborate or adroit imposture in order to deceive.

3dupe *n or vb* (ca. 1900) **:** DUPLICATE

dup·ery \'d(y)ü-p(ə-)rē\ *n, pl* **-er·ies** (1759) **1 :** the act or practice of duping **2 :** the condition of being duped

du·ple \'d(y)ü-pəl\ *adj* [L *duplus* double — more at DOUBLE] (15c) **1 :** having two elements **2 a :** marked by two or a multiple of two beats per measure of music ⟨~ time⟩ **b** *of rhythm* **:** consisting of a meter based on disyllabic feet

1du·plex \'d(y)ü-ˌpleks\ *adj* [L, fr. *duo* two + *-plex* -fold — more at TWO, -FOLD] (1567) **1 :** having two principal elements or parts **:** DOUBLE, TWOFOLD **2 :** allowing telecommunication in opposite directions simultaneously

2duplex *vt* (1833) **:** to make duplex

3duplex *n* (1922) **:** something duplex: as **a :** a 2-family house **b :** DUPLEX APARTMENT

duplex apartment *n* (ca. 1925) **:** an apartment having rooms on two floors

du·plex·er \'d(y)ü-ˌplek-sər\ *n* (ca. 1932) **:** a switching device that permits alternate transmission and reception with the same radio antenna

1du·pli·cate \'d(y)ü-pli-kət\ *adj* [ME, fr. L *duplicatus,* pp. of *duplicare* to double, fr. *duplic-, duplex*] (15c) **1 :** consisting of or existing in two corresponding or identical parts or examples ⟨~ invoices⟩ **2 :** being the same as another ⟨~ copies⟩

2du·pli·cate \'d(y)ü-pli-ˌkāt\ *vb* **-cat·ed; -cat·ing** *vt* (15c) **1 :** to make double or twofold ⟨the walls should be *duplicated* . . . in order to have a second line of defense —J. A. Steers⟩ **2 a :** to make an exact copy of ⟨~ the document⟩ **b :** to produce something equal to **:** REPEAT ⟨a feat that can never be *duplicated*⟩ ~ *vi* **:** to become duplicate **:** REPLICATE ⟨DNA in chromosomes ~*s*⟩ — **du·pli·ca·tive** \-ˌkāt-iv\ *adj*

3du·pli·cate \-kət\ *n* (1532) **1 :** either of two things exactly alike and usu. produced at the same time or by the same process **:** COPY **2 :** one that resembles or corresponds to another **:** COUNTERPART **3 :** two identical copies — used in the phrase *in duplicate* ***syn*** see REPRODUCTION

duplicate bridge *n* (1926) **:** a tournament form of contract bridge in which identical deals are played in order to compare individual scores

du·pli·ca·tion \ˌd(y)ü-pli-'kā-shən\ *n* (15c) **1 a :** the act or process of duplicating **b :** the quality or state of being duplicated **2 :** DUPLICATE, COUNTERPART **3 :** a part of a chromosome in which the genetic material is repeated; *also* **:** the process of forming a duplication

du·pli·ca·tor \'d(y)ü-pli-ˌkāt-ər\ *n* (1893) **:** one that duplicates; *specif* **:** a machine for making copies of typed, drawn, or printed matter

du·plic·i·tous \d(y)ü-'plis-ət-əs\ *adj* (1928) **:** marked by duplicity — **du·plic·i·tous·ly** *adv*

du·plic·i·ty \d(y)ü-'plis-ət-ē\ *n, pl* **-ties** (15c) **1 :** contradictory doubleness of thought, speech, or action; *esp* **:** the belying of one's true intentions by deceptive words or action **2 :** the quality or state of being double or twofold **3 :** the technically incorrect use of two or more distinct items (as claims, charges, or defenses) in a single legal action

du·ra·ble \'d(y)u̇r-ə-bəl\ *adj* [ME, fr. MF, fr. L *durabilis,* fr. *durare* to last — more at DURING] (14c) **:** able to exist for a long time without significant deterioration; *also* **:** designed to be durable ⟨~ goods⟩ ***syn*** see LASTING — **du·ra·bil·i·ty** \ˌd(y)u̇r-ə-'bil-ət-ē\ *n* — **du·ra·ble·ness** \'d(y)u̇r-ə-bəl-nəs\ *n* — **du·ra·bly** \-blē\ *adv*

durable press *n* (1966) **:** PERMANENT PRESS

du·ra·bles \'d(y)u̇r-ə-bəlz\ *n pl* (1941) **:** consumer goods (as vehicles and household appliances) that are typically used repeatedly over a period of years

du·ral·u·min \d(y)u̇-'ral-yə-mən\ *n* [fr. *Duralumin,* a trademark] (1910) **:** a light strong alloy of aluminum, copper, manganese, and magnesium

du·ra ma·ter \'d(y)u̇r-ə-ˌmāt-ər, -ˌmät-\ *n* [ME, fr. ML, lit., hard mother] (15c) **:** the tough fibrous membrane that envelops the brain and spinal cord external to the arachnoid and pia mater

du·rance \'d(y)u̇r-ən(t)s\ *n* [MF, fr. *durer* to endure, fr. L *durare*] (15c) **1** *archaic* **:** ENDURANCE **2 :** restraint by or as if by physical force — often used in the phrase *durance vile*

du·ra·tion \d(y)u̇-'rā-shən\ *n* (14c) **1 :** continuance in time **2 :** the time during which something exists or lasts

dur·bar \'dər-ˌbär, ˌdər-'\ *n* [Hindi *darbār,* fr. Per, fr. *dar* door + *bār* admission, audience] (1609) **1 :** court held by an Indian prince **2 :** a formal reception marked by pledges of fealty given to an Indian or African prince by his subjects or to the British monarch by native princes

du·ress \d(y)u̇-'res\ *n* [ME *duresse,* fr. MF *duresce* hardness, severity, fr. L *duritia,* fr. *durus*] (15c) **1 :** forcible restraint or restriction **2 :** compulsion by threat; *specif* **:** unlawful constraint

Dur·ham \'dər-əm, 'də-rəm, 'du̇r-əm\ *n* [County *Durham,* England] (1810) **:** SHORTHORN

Durham Rule *n* [Monte *Durham,* 20th cent. Am. litigant] (1955) **:** a legal hypothesis under which a person is not judged responsible for a criminal act that is attributed to a mental disease or defect

du·ri·an \'d(y)u̇r-ē-ən, -ē-ˌän\ *n* [Malay] (1588) **1 :** a large oval tasty but foul-smelling fruit with a prickly rind **2 :** an East Indian tree (*Durio zibethinus*) of the silk-cotton family that bears durians

dur·ing \ˌd(y)u̇r-iŋ\ *prep* [ME, fr. prp. of *duren* to last, fr. OF *durer,* fr. L *durare* to harden, endure, fr. *durus* hard; perh. akin to Skt *dāru* wood — more at TREE] (14c) **1 :** throughout the duration of ⟨swims every day ~ the summer⟩ **2 :** at a point in the course of **:** IN ⟨was offered a job ~ a visit to the capital⟩

dur·mast oak \ˌdər-ˌmast-\ *n* [perh. alter. of *dun mast,* fr. 1*dun* + *mast*] (1791) **:** a European oak (*Quercus sessiliflora* or *Q. petraea*) valued esp. for its dark heavy tough elastic wood and for its tannin-rich bark

durn \'dərn\, **durned** \'dərn(d)\ *var of* DARN, DARNED

du·ro \'du̇(ə)r-(ˌ)ō\ *n, pl* **duros** [Sp, short for *peso duro* hard peso] (ca. 1832) **:** a Spanish or Spanish American peso or silver dollar

du·roc \'d(y)u̇(ə)r-ˌäk\ *n* [*Duroc,* 19th cent. Am. stallion] *often cap* (1883) **:** any of a breed of large vigorous red American hogs

du·rom·e·ter \d(y)u̇-'räm-ət-ər\ *n* [L *durus* hard] (ca. 1890) **:** an instrument for measuring hardness

dur·ra *also* **du·ra** \'du̇r-ə\ *n* [Ar *dhurah*] (1798) **:** any of several grain sorghums widely grown in warm dry regions

durst \'dərst\ *archaic & dial past of* DARE

du·rum wheat \ˌd(y)u̇r-əm-, ˌdər-əm-, ˌdə-rəm-\ *n* [NL *durum,* fr. L, neut. of *durus* hard] (ca. 1903) **:** a wheat (*Triticum durum*) that yields a glutenous flour used esp. in macaroni and spaghetti — called also *durum*

1dusk \'dəsk\ *adj* [ME *dosk,* alter. of OE *dox;* akin to L *fuscus* dark brown, OE *dunn* dun, *dūst* dust] (bef. 12c) **:** DUSKY

2dusk *vi* (13c) **:** to become dark ~ *vt* **:** to make dark or gloomy

3dusk *n* (1622) **1 :** the darker part of twilight esp. at night **2 :** darkness or semidarkness caused by the shutting out of light

dusky \'dəs-kē\ *adj* **dusk·i·er; -est** (1558) **1 :** somewhat dark in color; *specif* **:** having dark skin **2 :** marked by slight or deficient light **:** SHADOWY — **dusk·i·ly** \-kə-lē\ *adv* — **dusk·i·ness** \-kē-nəs\ *n*

1dust \'dəst\ *n* [ME, fr. OE *dūst;* akin to OHG *tunst* storm, L *furere* to rage, Gk *thyein,* L *fumus* smoke — more at FUME] (bef. 12c) **1 :** fine dry particles of earth or pulverized matter **2 :** the particles into which something disintegrates **3 a :** something worthless **b :** a state of humiliation **4 a :** the earth esp. as a place of burial **b :** the surface of the ground **5 a :** a cloud of dust **b :** CONFUSION, DISTURBANCE **6** *archaic* **:** a single particle (as of earth) **7** *Brit* **:** refuse ready for collection — **dust·less** \-ləs\ *adj* — **dust·like** \-ˌlīk\ *adj*

2dust *vt* (1530) **1** *archaic* **:** to make dusty **2 :** to make free of dust **3 a :** to sprinkle with fine particles **b :** to sprinkle in the form of dust ~ *vi* **1** *of a bird* **:** to work dust into the feathers **2 :** to remove dust **3 :** to give off dust

dust·bin \'dəs(t)-ˌbin\ *n* (1848) **1** *Brit* **:** a can for trash or garbage **2 :** DUSTHEAP 2

dust bowl *n* (1936) **:** a region that suffers from prolonged droughts and dust storms

dust·cov·er \-ˌkəv-ər\ *n* (1899) **1 :** a cover (as of cloth or plastic) used to protect furniture or equipment from dust **2 :** DUST JACKET

dust devil *n* (1888) **:** a small whirlwind containing sand or dust

dust·er \'dəs-tər\ *n* (1576) **1 :** one that removes dust **2 a :** a lightweight overgarment to protect clothing from dust **b :** a dress-length housecoat **3 :** one that scatters fine particles; *specif* **:** a device for applying insecticidal or fungicidal dusts to crops **4 :** DUST STORM

\ə\ abut \ᵊ\ kitten, F table \ər\ further \a\ ash \ā\ ace \ä\ cot, cart
\au̇\ out \ch\ chin \e\ bet \ē\ easy \g\ go \i\ hit \ī\ ice \j\ job
\ŋ\ sing \ō\ go \ȯ\ law \ȯi\ boy \th\ thin \t͟h\ the \ü\ loot \u̇\ foot
\y\ yet \zh\ vision \à, k̲, ⁿ, œ, œ̄, ue, u̅e̅, ʸ\ see Guide to Pronunciation

dust·heap \'dəst-ˌ(h)ēp\ *n* (1654) **1 :** a pile of refuse **2 :** a category of forgotten items ⟨the ~ of history —*New Republic*⟩

dust jacket *n* (1926) **:** a paper cover for a book

dust·man \'dəs(t)-mən\ *n, Brit* (1707) **:** a collector of trash or garbage

dust mop *n* (1953) **:** DRY MOP

dust off *vt* (1940) **:** to bring out or back to use again

dust·pan \'dəs(t)-ˌpan\ *n* (1783) **:** a shovel-shaped pan for sweepings

dust storm *n* (1879) **1 :** a dust-laden whirlwind that moves across an arid region and is usu. associated with hot dry air and marked by high electrical tension **2 :** strong winds bearing clouds of dust

dust-up \'dəs-ˌtəp\ *n* (1897) **:** QUARREL, ROW

dust wrapper *n* (1932) **:** DUST JACKET

dusty \'dəs-tē\ *adj* **dust·i·er; -est** (13c) **1 :** covered or abounding with dust **2 :** consisting of dust **:** POWDERY **3 :** resembling dust **4 :** lacking vitality **:** DRY ⟨~ scholarship⟩ **5** *Brit* **:** UNSATISFACTORY — used esp. in the phrases *dusty answer* and *not so dusty* — **dust·i·ly** \'dəs-tə-lē\ *adv* — **dust·i·ness** \-tē-nəs\ *n*

dusty miller *n* (1825) **:** any of several plants having ashy-gray or white tomentose leaves; *esp* **:** an herbaceous artemisia (*Artemisia stelleriana*) with greyish foliage found along the eastern coast of the U.S.

dutch \'dəch\ *adv, often cap* (1914) **:** with each person paying his own way

[1]Dutch \'dəch\ *adj* [ME *Duch,* fr. MD *duutsch;* akin to OHG *diutisc* German, OE *thēod* nation, Goth *thiudisko* as a gentile, *thiuda* people, Oscan *touto* city] (14c) **1 a** *archaic* **:** of, relating to, or in any of the Germanic languages of Germany, Austria, Switzerland, and the Low Countries **b :** of, relating to, or in the Dutch of the Netherlands **2 a** *archaic* **:** of or relating to the Germanic peoples of Germany, Austria, Switzerland, and the Low Countries **b :** of or relating to the Netherlands or its inhabitants **c :** GERMAN **3 :** of or relating to the Pennsylvania Dutch or their language — **Dutch·ly** *adv*

[2]Dutch *n* (14c) **1 a** *archaic* (1) **:** any of the Germanic languages of Germany, Austria, Switzerland, and the Low Countries (2) **:** GERMAN 2 **b :** the Germanic language of the Netherlands **2 Dutch** *pl* **a** *archaic* **:** the Germanic peoples of Germany, Austria, Switzerland, and the Low Countries **b** *archaic* **:** people of Germanic descent **c :** the people of the Netherlands **3 :** PENNSYLVANIA DUTCH **4 :** DANDER ⟨his ~ is up⟩ **5 :** DISFAVOR, TROUBLE ⟨in ~ with the boss⟩

Dutch cheese *n* (1829) **:** COTTAGE CHEESE

Dutch clover *n* (1800) **:** WHITE CLOVER

Dutch Colonial *adj* (1922) **:** characterized by a gambrel roof with overhanging eaves

Dutch courage *n* (1812) **:** courage due to intoxicants

Dutch door *n* (ca. 1890) **:** a door divided horizontally so that the lower or upper part can be shut separately

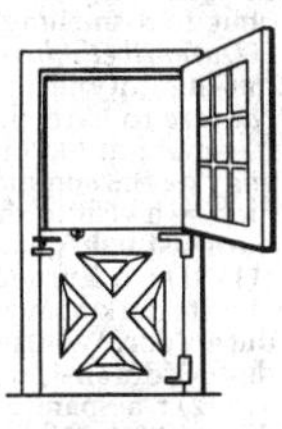

Dutch door

Dutch elm disease *n* (1927) **:** a disease of elms caused by an ascomycetous fungus (*Ceratostomella ulmi*) and characterized by yellowing of the foliage, defoliation, and death

Dutch hoe *n* (1744) **:** SCUFFLE HOE

dutch·man \'dəch-mən\ *n* (14c) **1** *cap* **a** *archaic* **:** a member of any of the Germanic peoples of Germany, Austria, Switzerland, and the Low Countries **b :** a native or inhabitant of the Netherlands **c :** a person of Dutch descent **d :** GERMAN 1a, 1b **2 :** a device for hiding or counteracting structural defects

Dutch·man's–breech·es \ˌdəch-mənz-'brich-əz\ *n pl but sing or pl in constr* (1837) **:** a delicate spring-flowering herb (*Dicentra cucullaria*) of the fumitory family occurring in the eastern U.S. and having finely divided leaves and cream-white double-spurred flowers

Dutchman's–pipe \-'pīp\ *n, pl* **Dutchman's–pipes** \-'pīps\ (1845) **:** a vine (*Aristolochia durior*) with large leaves and early summer flowers having the tube of the calyx curved like the bowl of a pipe

Dutch oven *n* (1769) **1 :** a metal shield for roasting before an open fire **2 :** a brick oven in which cooking is done by the preheated walls **3 a :** a cast-iron kettle with a tight cover that is used for baking in an open fire **b :** a heavy pot with a tight-fitting domed cover

dutch treat *adv* (1955) **:** on the basis of a Dutch treat

Dutch treat *n* (1887) **:** a meal or other entertainment for which each person pays his own way

Dutch uncle *n* (1837) **:** one who admonishes sternly and bluntly

du·te·ous \'d(y)üt-ē-əs\ *adj* [irreg. fr. *duty*] (1593) **:** DUTIFUL, OBEDIENT

du·ti·able \'d(y)üt-ē-ə-bəl\ *adj* (1774) **:** subject to a duty

du·ti·ful \'d(y)üt-i-fəl\ *adj* (ca. 1552) **1 :** filled with or motivated by a sense of duty **2 :** proceeding from or expressive of a sense of duty — **du·ti·ful·ly** \-f(ə-)lē\ *adv* — **du·ti·ful·ness** \-fəl-nəs\ *n*

du·ty \'d(y)üt-ē\ *n, pl* **duties** [ME *duete,* fr. AF *dueté,* fr. OF *deu* due] (13c) **1 :** conduct due to parents and superiors **:** RESPECT **2 a :** obligatory tasks, conduct, service, or functions that arise from one's position (as in life or in a group) **b :** assigned service or business; *esp* **:** active military service **3 a :** a moral or legal obligation **b :** the force of moral obligation **4 :** TAX; *esp* **:** a tax on imports **5 a** (1) **:** the work done by a machine under given conditions (2) **:** a measure of efficiency expressed in terms of the amount of work done in relation to the energy consumed **b** (1) **:** the service required (as of an electric machine) under specified conditions of load and rest (2) **:** functional application **:** USE; *esp* **:** use as a substitute ⟨making the word do ~ for the thing —Edward Sapir⟩ **6 :** the quantity of irrigation water required for the needs of a particular crop area ***syn*** see FUNCTION, TASK

du·um·vir \d(y)ü-'əm-vər\ *n* [L, fr. *duum* (gen. of *duo* two) + *vir* man] (1600) **1 :** one of two Roman officers or magistrates constituting a board or court **2 :** one of two people jointly holding power

du·um·vi·rate \-və-rət\ *n* (1656) **1 :** government or control by two people **2 :** two people associated in high office

du·vet \d(y)ü-'vā, 'd(y)ü-ˌ\ *n* [F] (1758) **:** COMFORTER 2b

duve·tyn \'d(y)ü-və-ˌtēn, 'dəv-ˌtēn\ *n* [F *duvetine,* fr. *duvet* down, fr. MF, alter. of (assumed) MF *dumet,* dim. of OF *dun, dum* down, fr. ON *dūnn* — more at DOWN] (1913) **:** a smooth lustrous velvety fabric

[1]dwarf \'dwȯ(ə)rf\ *n, pl* **dwarfs** \'dwȯ(ə)rfs\ *or* **dwarves** \'dwȯ(ə)rvz\ *often attrib* [ME *dwerg, dwerf,* fr. OE *dweorg, dweorh;* akin to OHG *twerg* dwarf] (bef. 12c) **1 :** a person of unusually small stature; *esp* **:** one whose bodily proportions are abnormal **2 :** an animal or plant much below normal size **3 :** a small legendary manlike being who is usu. misshapen and ugly and skilled as an artificer **4 :** a star (as the sun) of ordinary or low luminosity and relatively small mass and size — **dwarf·ish** \'dwȯr-fish\ *adj* — **dwarf·ish·ly** *adv* — **dwarf·ish·ness** *n* — **dwarf·like** \'dwȯr-ˌflīk\ *adj* — **dwarf·ness** \'dwȯrf-nəs\ *n*

[2]dwarf *vt* (1626) **1 :** to restrict the growth of **:** STUNT ⟨children ~*ed* by malnutrition⟩ **2 :** to cause to appear smaller ⟨the other buildings are ~*ed* by the skyscraper⟩ ~ *vi* **:** to become smaller

dwarf·ism \'dwȯr-ˌfiz-əm\ *n* (1865) **:** the condition of stunted growth

dwell \'dwel\ *vi* **dwelt** \'dwelt\ *or* **dwelled** \'dweld, 'dwelt\; **dwell·ing** [ME *dwellen,* fr. OE *dwellan* to go astray, hinder; akin to OHG *twellen* to tarry] (13c) **1 :** to remain for a time **2 a :** to live as a resident **b :** EXIST, LIE **3 a :** to keep the attention directed — used with *on* or *upon* ⟨tendency for man to ~ on his own mortality —Russell Baker⟩ **b :** to speak or write insistently — used with *on* or *upon* ⟨the discussion *dwelt* on police provocation⟩ — **dwell·er** *n*

dwell·ing *n* (14c) **:** a shelter (as a house or building) in which people live

dwin·dle \'dwin-dᵊl\ *vb* **dwin·dled; dwin·dling** \-(d)liŋ, -dᵊl-iŋ\ [prob. freq. of *dwine* to waste away, fr. ME, fr. OE *dwīnan;* akin to ON *dvīna* to pine away, *deyja* to die — more at DIE] *vi* (1596) **:** to become steadily less **:** SHRINK ~ *vt* **:** to make steadily less ***syn*** see DECREASE

DX \(ˈ)dē-'eks\ *n* (ca. 1924) **:** DISTANCE — used of long-distance radio transmission

dy- *or* **dyo-** *comb form* [LL, fr. Gk, fr. *dyo* — more at TWO] **:** two ⟨*dy*archy⟩

dy·ad \'dī-ˌad, -əd\ *n* [LL *dyad-, dyas,* fr. Gk, fr. *dyo*] (1675) **1 :** PAIR; *specif* **:** two individuals (as husband and wife) maintaining a sociologically significant relationship **2 :** a meiotic chromosome after separation of the two homologous members of a tetrad **3 :** a mathematical operator indicated by writing the symbols of two vectors without a dot or cross between (as AB) — **dy·ad·ic** \dī-'ad-ik\ *adj* — **dy·ad·i·cal·ly** \-i-k(ə-)lē\ *adv*

dy·ad·ic \dī-'ad-ik\ *n* (1884) **:** a mathematical expression formed by addition or subtraction of dyads

Dy·ak *var of* DAYAK

dy·ar·chy \'dī-ˌär-kē\ *n, pl* **-chies** (1640) **:** a government in which power is vested in two rulers or authorities

dyb·buk \'dib-ək\ *n, pl* **dyb·bu·kim** \ˌdib-ü-'kēm\ *also* **dybbuks** [LHeb *dibbūq*] (ca. 1903) **:** a wandering soul believed in Jewish folklore to enter and control a living body until exorcised by a religious rite

[1]dye \'dī\ *n* [ME *dehe,* fr. OE *dēah, dēag;* akin to L *fumus* smoke — more at FUME] (bef. 12c) **1 :** color from dyeing **2 :** a soluble or insoluble coloring matter

[2]dye *vb* **dyed; dye·ing** *vt* (bef. 12c) **1 :** to impart a new and often permanent color to esp. by impregnating with a dye **2 :** to impart (a color) by dyeing ⟨~*ing* blue on yellow⟩ ~ *vi* **:** to take up or impart color in dyeing — **dye·abil·i·ty** \ˌdī-ə-'bil-ət-ē\ *n* — **dye·able** \'dī-ə-bəl\ *adj* — **dy·er** \'dī(-ə)r\ *n*

dyed–in–the–wool \ˌdīd-ᵊn-t͟hə-'wu̇l\ *adj* (1579) **:** THOROUGHGOING, UNCOMPROMISING ⟨a ~ conservative⟩

dy·er's broom \'dī(-ə)rz-'brüm, -'bru̇m\ *n, pl* **dyer's brooms** (1817) **:** a low bushy yellow-flowered Eurasian leguminous shrub (*Genista tinctoria*) grown for ornament or formerly as the source of a yellow dye

dye·stuff \'dī-ˌstəf\ *n* (1837) **:** DYE 2

dye·wood \-ˌwu̇d\ *n* (1699) **:** a wood (as logwood or fustic) from which coloring matter is extracted for dyeing

dying *pres part of* DIE

[1]dyke *var of* DIKE

[2]dyke *n* [origin unknown] (ca. 1942) **:** LESBIAN — often used disparagingly

[1]dy·nam·ic \dī-'nam-ik\ *also* **dy·nam·i·cal** \-i-kəl\ *adj* [F *dynamique,* fr. Gk *dynamikos* powerful, fr. *dynamis* power, fr. *dynasthai* to be able] (1827) **1 a :** of or relating to physical force or energy **b :** of or relating to dynamics **:** ACTIVE **2 a :** marked by continuous usu. productive activity or change ⟨a ~ population⟩ **b :** marked by energy **:** FORCEFUL ⟨a ~ personality⟩ — **dy·nam·i·cal·ly** \-i-k(ə-)lē\ *adv*

[2]dynamic *n* (1879) **1 :** a dynamic force **2 :** DYNAMICS 2

dy·nam·ics \dī-'nam-iks\ *n pl but sing or pl in constr* (1788) **1 :** a branch of mechanics that deals with forces and their relation primarily to the motion but sometimes also to the equilibrium of bodies **2 :** the pattern of change or growth of an object or phenomenon ⟨population ~⟩ **3 :** variation and contrast in force or intensity (as in music)

dy·na·mism \'dī-nə-ˌmiz-əm\ *n* (ca. 1857) **1 a :** a theory that all phenomena (as matter or motion) can be explained as manifestations of force — compare MECHANISM **b :** DYNAMICS 2 **2 :** a dynamic or expansionist quality — **dy·na·mist** \-məst\ *n* — **dy·na·mis·tic** \ˌdī-nə-'mis-tik\ *adj*

[1]dy·na·mite \'dī-nə-ˌmīt\ *n* (1867) **1 :** a blasting explosive that is made of nitroglycerin absorbed in a porous material and that sometimes contains ammonium nitrate or cellulose nitrate; *also* **:** a blasting explosive that contains no nitroglycerin **2 :** one that has explosive force ⟨this letter is ~ —Erle Stanley Gardner⟩ — **dy·na·mit·ic** \ˌdī-nə-'mit-ik\ *adj*

[2]dynamite *vt* **-mit·ed; -mit·ing** (1881) **1 :** to blow up with dynamite **2 :** to cause the complete failure or destruction of — **dy·na·mit·er** *n*

dy·na·mo \'dī-nə-ˌmō\ *n, pl* **-mos** [short for *dynamoelectric machine*] (ca. 1882) **1 :** GENERATOR 3 **2 :** a forceful energetic individual

dy·na·mom·e·ter \ˌdī-nə-'mäm-ət-ər\ *n* [F *dynamomètre,* fr. Gk *dynamis* power + F *-mètre* -meter] (1810) **1 :** an instrument for measuring mechanical force **2 :** an apparatus for measuring mechanical power (as of an engine) — **dy·na·mo·met·ric** \-mō-'me-trik\ *adj* — **dy·na·mom·e·try** \-'mäm-ə-trē\ *n*

dy·na·mo·tor \'dī-nə-ˌmōt-ər\ *n* [*dynamo* + *motor*] (1899) **:** a motor generator combining the electric motor and generator

dy·nast \'dī-ˌnast, -nəst\ *n* [L *dynastes,* fr. Gk *dynastēs,* fr. *dynasthai* to be able, have power] (1631) **:** RULER

dy·nas·ty \'dī-nə-stē *also* -ˌnas-tē, *esp Brit* 'din-ə-stē\ *n, pl* **-ties** (14c) **1 :** a succession of rulers of the same line of descent **2 :** a powerful group or family that maintains its position for a considerable time — **dy·nas·tic** \dī-'nas-tik\ *adj* — **dy·nas·ti·cal·ly** \-ti-k(ə-)lē\ *adv*

dy·na·tron \'dī-nə-ˌträn\ *n* [Gk *dynamis* power] (1918) **:** a vacuum tube in which the secondary emission of electrons from the plate results in a decrease in the plate current as the plate voltage increases

dyne \'dīn\ *n* [F, fr. Gk *dynamis*] (1873) : the unit of force in the centimeter-gram-second system equal to the force that would give a free mass of one gram an acceleration of one centimeter per second per second

dy·node \'dī-,nōd\ *n* [Gk *dynamis*] (1939) : an electrode in an electron tube that functions to produce secondary emission of electrons

dys- *prefix* [ME *dis-* bad, difficult, fr. MF & L; MF *dis-*, fr. L *dys-*, fr. Gk; akin to OE *tō-, te-* apart, Skt *dus-* bad, difficult] 1 : abnormal ⟨*dys*hidrosis⟩ 2 : difficult ⟨*dys*phagia⟩ — compare EU- 3 : impaired ⟨*dys*function⟩ 4 : bad ⟨*dys*logistic⟩ — compare EU-

dys·ar·thria \dis-'är-thrē-ə\ *n* [NL, fr. *dys-* + *arthr-* + *-ia*] (1878) : difficulty in articulating words due to disease of the central nervous system

dys·cra·sia \dis-'krā-zh(ē-)ə\ *n* [NL, fr. ML, bad mixture of humors, fr. Gk *dyskrasia*, fr. *dys-* + *krasis* mixture, fr. *kerannynai* to mix — more at CRATER] (15c) : an abnormal condition of the body

dys·en·ter·ic \,dis-ᵊn-'ter-ik\ *adj* (1727) : of or relating to dysentery

dys·en·tery \'dis-ᵊn-,ter-ē\ *n, pl* **-ter·ies** [ME *dissenterie*, fr. L *dysenteria*, fr. Gk, fr. *dys-* + *enteron* intestine — more at INTER-] (14c) 1 : a disease characterized by severe diarrhea with passage of mucus and blood and usu. caused by infection 2 : DIARRHEA

dys·func·tion \(')dis-'fəŋ(k)-shən\ *n* (ca. 1916) : impaired or abnormal functioning — **dys·func·tion·al** \-shnəl, -shən-ᵊl\ *adj*

dys·gen·e·sis \(')dis-'jen-ə-səs\ *n* [NL] (ca. 1883) : defective development esp. of the gonads (as in Klinefelter's syndrome)

dys·gen·ic \(')dis-'jen-ik\ *adj* (1915) 1 : tending to promote survival of or reproduction by less well-adapted individuals (as the weak or diseased) esp. at the expense of well-adapted individuals (as the strong or healthy) ⟨the ~ effect of war⟩ 2 : biologically defective or deficient

dys·ki·ne·sia \,dis-kə-'nē-zh(ē-)ə, -,kī-\ *n* [NL, fr. Gk *dyskinesia* difficulty in moving, fr. *dys-* + *-kinesia*, fr. *kinesis* motion, fr. *kinein* to move — more at HIGHT] (ca. 1706) : impairment of voluntary movements resulting in fragmented or jerky motions (as in Parkinson's disease) — compare TARDIVE DYSKINESIA — **dys·ki·net·ic** \-'net-ik\ *adj*

dys·lex·ia \dis-'lek-sē-ə\ *n* [NL, fr. *dys-* + Gk *lexis* word, speech, fr. *legein* to say — more at LEGEND] (ca. 1886) : a disturbance of the ability to read — **dys·lex·ic** \-sik\ *adj or n*

dys·lo·gis·tic \,dis-lə-'jis-tik\ *adj* [*dys-* + *-logistic* (as in *eulogistic*)] (1802) : UNCOMPLIMENTARY — **dys·lo·gis·ti·cal·ly** \-ti-k(ə-)lē\ *adv*

dys·men·or·rhea \(,)dis-,men-ə-'rē-ə\ *n* [NL] (ca. 1810) : painful menstruation — **dys·men·or·rhe·ic** \-'rē-ik\ *adj*

dys·pep·sia \dis-'pep-shə, -sē-ə\ *n* [L, fr. Gk, fr. *dys-* + *pepsis* digestion, fr. *peptein, pessein* to cook, digest — more at COOK] (ca. 1706) : INDIGESTION

¹dys·pep·tic \-'pep-tik\ *adj* (1809) 1 : relating to or having dyspepsia 2 : showing a sour disposition — **dys·pep·ti·cal·ly** \-ti-k(ə-)lē\ *adv*

²dyspeptic *n* (1822) : a person having dyspepsia

dys·pha·gia \dis-'fā-j(ē-)ə\ *n* [NL] (1783) : difficulty in swallowing

dys·pha·sia \dis-'fā-zh(ē-)ə\ *n* [NL] (ca. 1883) : loss of or deficiency in the power to use or understand language as a result of injury to or disease of the brain — **dys·pha·sic** \-'fā-zik\ *n or adj*

dys·phe·mism \'dis-fə-,miz-əm\ *n* [*dys-* + *-phemism* (as in *euphemism*)] (1884) : the substitution of a disagreeable, offensive, or disparaging word or expression for an agreeable or inoffensive one; *also* : a word or expression so substituted — **dys·phe·mis·tic** \,dis-fə-'mis-tik\ *adj*

dys·pho·nia \dis-'fō-nē-ə\ *n* [NL] (ca. 1706) : defective use of the voice

dys·pho·ria \dis-'fōr-ē-ə, -'for-\ *n* [NL, fr. Gk, fr. *dysphoros* hard to bear, fr. *dys-* + *pherein* to bear — more at BEAR] (ca. 1842) : a state of feeling unwell or unhappy — **dys·phor·ic** \-'fór-ik, -'fär-\ *adj*

dys·pla·sia \dis-'plā-zh(ē-)ə\ *n* [NL] (ca. 1923) : abnormal growth or development (as of organs or cells); *broadly* : abnormal anatomic structure due to such growth — **dys·plas·tic** \-'plas-tik\ *adj*

dys·pnea \'dis(p)-nē-ə\ *n* [L *dyspnoea*, fr. Gk *dyspnoia*, fr. *dyspnoos* short of breath, fr. *dys-* + *pnein* to breathe — more at SNEEZE] (ca. 1681) : difficult or labored respiration — **dys·pne·ic** \-nē-ik\ *adj*

dyspnoea *chiefly Brit var of* DYSPNEA

dys·pro·si·um \dis-'prō-zē-əm, -zh(ē-)əm\ *n* [NL, fr. Gk *dysprositos* hard to get at, fr. *dys-* + *prositos* approachable, fr. *prosienai* to approach, fr. *pros-* + *ienai* to go — more at ISSUE] (1886) : an element of the rare-earth group that forms highly magnetic compounds — see ELEMENT table

dys·rhyth·mia \dis-'rith-mē-ə\ *n* [NL, fr. *dys-* + L *rhythmus* rhythm] (ca. 1909) : an abnormal rhythm; *esp* : a disordered rhythm exhibited in a record of electrical activity of the brain or heart — **dys·rhyth·mic** \-mik\ *adj*

dys·to·pia \(')dis-'tō-pē-ə\ *n* [NL, fr. *dys-* + *-topia* (as in *utopia*)] (ca. 1950) 1 : an imaginary place which is depressingly wretched and whose people lead a fearful existence 2 : ANTI-UTOPIA 2 — **dys·to·pi·an** \-pē-ən\ *adj*

dys·tro·phic \dis-'trō-fik\ *adj* (1893) 1 a : relating to or caused by faulty nutrition b : relating to or affected with a dystrophy ⟨a ~ patient⟩ 2 *of a lake* : brownish with much dissolved humic matter, a sparse bottom fauna, and a high oxygen consumption

dys·tro·phy \'dis-trə-fē\ *n, pl* **-phies** [NL *dystrophia*, fr. *dys-* + *-trophia* -trophy] (ca. 1901) 1 : a condition produced by faulty nutrition 2 : any myogenic atrophy; *esp* : MUSCULAR DYSTROPHY

dys·uria \dish-'(y)ùr-ē-ə, dis-'yùr-\ *n* [NL, fr. Gk *dysouria*, fr. *dys-* + *-ouria* -uria] (14c) : difficult or painful discharge of urine

e \'ē\ *n, pl* **e's** *or* **es** \'ēz\ *often cap, often attrib* 1 a : the 5th letter of the English alphabet b : a graphic representation of this letter c : a speech counterpart of orthographic *e* 2 : the 3d tone of a C-major scale 3 : a graphic device for reproducing the letter *e* 4 : one designated *e* esp. as the 5th in order or class; *specif* : the base of the system of natural logarithms having the approximate numerical value 2.71828 5 a : a grade rating a student's work as poor and usu. constituting a conditional pass b : a grade rating a student's work as failing c : one graded or rated with an E 6 : something shaped like the letter E

e- \(ᵊ)ē, i\ *prefix* [ME, fr. OF & L; OF, out, forth, away, fr. L, fr. *ex-*] 1 a : not ⟨*e*carinate⟩ b : missing : absent ⟨*e*dental⟩ 2 : out : on the outside ⟨*e*scribe⟩ 3 : thoroughly ⟨*e*vaporize⟩ 4 : forth ⟨*e*radiate⟩ 5 : away ⟨*e*luvium⟩

¹each \'ēch\ *adj* [ME *ech*, fr. OE *ǣlc*; akin to OHG *iogilih* each; both fr. a prehistoric WGmc compound whose first and second constituents respectively are represented by OE *ā* always and by OE *gelīc* alike] (bef. 12c) : being one of two or more distinct individuals having a similar relation and often constituting an aggregate

²each *pron* (bef. 12c) : each one

³each *adv* (bef. 12c) : to or for each : APIECE

each other *pron* (bef. 12c) : each of two or more in reciprocal action or relation ⟨looked at *each other* in surprise⟩

  usage Some handbooks and textbooks recommend that *each other* be restricted to reference to two and *one another* to reference to three or more. The distinction, while neat, is not observed in actual usage. *Each other* and *one another* are used interchangeably by good writers and have been since at least the sixteenth century.

ea·ger \'ē-gər\ *adj* [ME *egre*, fr. MF *aigre*, fr. L *acer* — more at EDGE] (14c) 1 a *archaic* : SHARP b *obs* : SOUR 2 : marked by keen, enthusiastic, or impatient desire or interest — **ea·ger·ly** *adv* — **ea·ger·ness** *n*

  syn EAGER, AVID, KEEN, ANXIOUS, ATHIRST mean moved by a strong and urgent desire or interest. EAGER implies ardor and enthusiasm and sometimes impatience at delay or restraint; AVID adds to EAGER the implication of insatiability or greed; KEEN suggests intensity of interest and quick responsiveness in action; ANXIOUS emphasizes fear of frustration or failure or disappointment; ATHIRST stresses yearning but not necessarily readiness for action.

eager beaver *n* (1943) : one who is extremely zealous in performing his assigned duties and in volunteering for more

ea·gle \'ē-gəl\ *n* [ME *egle*, fr. OF *aigle*, fr. L *aquila*] (13c) 1 : any of various large diurnal birds of prey of the accipiter family noted for their strength, size, gracefulness, keenness of vision, and powers of flight 2 : any of various esp. emblematic or symbolic figures or representations of an eagle: as a : the standard of the ancient Romans b : the seal or standard of a nation (as the U.S.) having an eagle as emblem c : one of a pair of silver insignia of rank worn by a military colonel or a navy captain 3 : a ten-dollar gold coin of the U.S. bearing an eagle on the reverse 4 : a golf score of two strokes less than par on a hole — compare BIRDIE 5 *cap* [Fraternal Order of *Eagles*] : a member of a major fraternal order

eagle eye *n* (1802) 1 : the ability to see or observe with exceptional keenness 2 : one that sees or observes keenly

eagle ray *n* (ca. 1856) : any of several widely distributed large active stingrays (family Myliobatidae) with broad pectoral fins like wings

ea·glet \'ē-glət\ *n* (1572) : a young eagle

eal·dor·man \'al-dər-mən\ *n* [OE — more at ALDERMAN] (bef. 12c) : the chief officer in a district (as a shire) in Anglo-Saxon England

Eames chair \'ēmz-\ *n* [Charles *Eames* †1978 Am. designer] (1950) : any of several chairs designed by Charles Eames to fit the contours of the body and to be made from modern materials (as molded plywood or fiberglass)

-ean — see -AN

¹ear \'i(ə)r\ *n* [ME *ere*, fr. OE *ēare*; akin to OHG *ōra* ear, L *auris*, Gk *ous*] (bef. 12c) 1 a : the characteristic vertebrate organ of hearing and equilibrium consisting in the typical mammal of a sound-collecting outer ear separated by the tympanic membrane from a sound-transmitting middle ear that in turn is separated from a sensory inner ear by membranous fenestrae b : any of various organs capable of detecting vibratory motion 2 a : the external ear of man and most mammals b : a human earlobe ⟨had her ~s pierced⟩ 3 a : the sense or act of hearing b : acuity of hearing c : sensitivity to musical tone and pitch; *also* : the ability to retain and reproduce music that has been heard d : sensitivity to nuances of language esp. as revealed in the command of verbal melody and rhythm or in the ability to render a spoken idiom accurately 4 : something resembling a mammalian ear

---

\ə\ abut \ᵊ\ kitten, F table \ər\ further \a\ ash \ā\ ace \ä\ cot, cart \aù\ out \ch\ chin \e\ bet \ē\ easy \g\ go \i\ hit \ī\ ice \j\ job \ŋ\ sing \ō\ go \ò\ law \òi\ boy \th\ thin \t͟h\ the \ü\ loot \ù\ foot \y\ yet \zh\ vision \ȧ, k̲, ⁿ, œ, œ̄, ᴜe, ᵫ, ʸ\ see Guide to Pronunciation

in shape or position: as **a :** a projecting part (as a lug or handle) **b :** either of a pair of tufts of lengthened feathers on the head of some birds **5 a :** sympathetic attention **b :** ATTENTION, AWARENESS **6 :** a space in the upper corner of the front page of a periodical (as a newspaper) usu. containing advertising for the periodical itself or a weather forecast — **by ear :** without reference to or memorization of written music : EXTEMPORANEOUSLY — **in one ear and out the other :** through one's mind without making an impression ⟨everything you say to him goes *in one ear and out the other*⟩ — **on one's ear :** in or into a state of irritation, shock, or discord ⟨his insults really put me *on my ear*⟩ ⟨he set the racing world *on its ear* by breaking 50 world records⟩ — **up to one's ears :** deeply involved : heavily implicated ⟨*up to his ears* in the conspiracy⟩

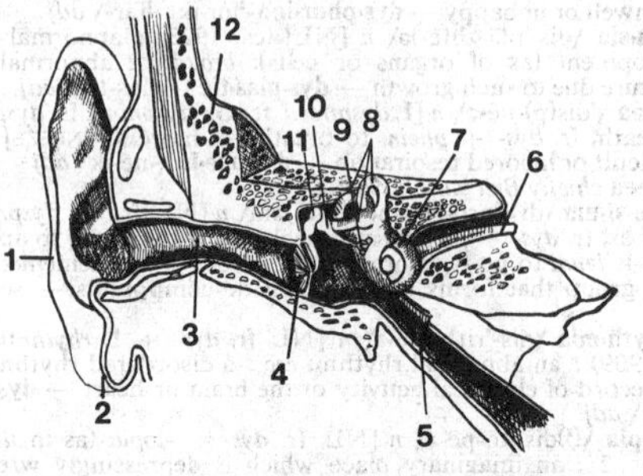

ear 1a: *1* pinna, *2* lobe, *3* auditory meatus, *4* tympanic membrane, *5* eustachian tube, *6* auditory nerve, *7* cochlea, *8* semicircular canals, *9* stapes, *10* incus, *11* malleus, *12* bones of skull

2**ear** *n* [ME *er*, fr. OE *ēar;* akin to OHG *ahir* ear, OE *ecg* edge — more at EDGE] (bef. 12c) **:** the fruiting spike of a cereal (as Indian corn) including both the seeds and protective structures

3**ear** *vi* (14c) **:** to form ears in the course of growing — often used with *up* ⟨the rye should be ~*ing* up⟩

ear·ache \ˈi(ə)r-ˌāk\ *n* (1789) **:** an ache or pain in the ear

ear·drop \-ˌdräp\ *n* (1720) **:** EARRING; *esp* **:** one with a pendant

ear·drum \-ˌdrəm\ *n* (1645) **:** TYMPANIC MEMBRANE

eared \ˈi(ə)rd\ *adj* (14c) **:** having ears esp. of a specified kind or number ⟨a big-*eared* man⟩ ⟨golden-*eared* corn⟩

eared seal *n* (1883) **:** any of a family (Otariidae) of seals including the sea lions and fur seals and having independent mobile hind limbs and small well-developed external ears — compare HAIR SEAL

ear·flap \ˈi(ə)r-ˌflap\ *n* (1907) **:** a warm covering for the ears; *esp* **:** an extension on the lower edge of a cap that may be folded up or down

ear·ful \ˈi(ə)r-ˌfu̇l\ *n* (1916) **1 :** an outpouring of news or gossip **2 :** a sharp reprimand

ear·ing \ˈi(ə)r-iŋ\ *n* [perh. fr. 1*ear*] (1626) **:** a line used to fasten a corner of a sail to the yard or gaff or to haul a reef cringle to the yard

earl \ˈər(-ə)l\ *n* [ME *erl*, fr. OE *eorl* warrior, nobleman; akin to ON *jarl* warrior, nobleman] (bef. 12c) **:** a member of the British peerage ranking below a marquess and above a viscount — **earl·dom** \-dəm\ *n*

earlier on *adv* (1934) **:** BEFORE ⟨discussed the matter *earlier on*⟩

earl marshal *n* (13c) **:** an officer of state in England serving chiefly as a royal attendant on ceremonial occasions, as marshal of state processions, and as head of the College of Arms

ear·lobe \ˈi(ə)r-ˌlōb\ *n* (1859) **:** the pendent part of the ear of man or some fowls

ear·lock \-ˌläk\ *n* (1775) **:** a curl of hair hanging in front of the ear

1**ear·ly** \ˈər-lē\ *adv* **ear·li·er; -est** [ME *erly*, fr. OE *ǣrlīce*, fr. *ǣr* early, soon — more at ERE] (bef. 12c) **1 a :** near the beginning of a period of time ⟨awoke ~ in the morning⟩ **b :** near the beginning of a course, process, or series ⟨~ in his senatorial career⟩ **2 a :** before the usual time **b** *archaic* **:** SOON **c :** sooner than related forms ⟨these apples bear ~⟩

2**early** *adj* **ear·li·er; -est** (13c) **1 a :** of, relating to, or occurring near the beginning of a period of time, a development, or a series **b** (1) **:** distant in past time (2) **:** PRIMITIVE **2 a :** occurring before the usual time **b :** occurring in the near future **c :** maturing or producing sooner than related forms ⟨an ~ peach⟩ — **ear·li·ness** *n*

Early American *n* (1895) **:** a style of furniture, architecture, or fabric originating in or characteristic of colonial America

early bird *n* [fr. the proverb, "the early bird catches the worm"] (ca. 1890) **1 :** an early riser **2 :** one that arrives early and esp. before possible competitors

early on *adv* (1928) **:** at or during an early point or stage ⟨the reasons were obvious *early on* in the experiment⟩

usage This adverb is sometimes objected to in American writing as an obtrusive Briticism. It is a relative newcomer to the language, having arisen in British English around 1928. It seems to have filled a need, however. It came into frequent use in American English in the late 1960s and is now well established on both sides of the Atlantic.

ear·ly·wood \ˈər-lē-ˌwu̇d\ *n* (ca. 1914) **:** SPRINGWOOD

1**ear·mark** \ˈi(ə)r-ˌmärk\ *n* (15c) **1 :** a mark of identification on the ear of an animal **2 :** a distinguishing mark ⟨all the ~*s* of poverty⟩

2**earmark** *vt* (1591) **1 a :** to mark (livestock) with an earmark **b :** to mark in a distinguishing manner ⟨dissipation ~*s* a man⟩ **2 :** to designate (as funds) for a specific use or owner

ear·muff \ˈi(ə)r-ˌməf\ *n* (1859) **:** one of a pair of ear coverings connected by a flexible band and worn as protection against cold or noises

1**earn** \ˈərn\ *vt* [ME *ernen*, fr. OE *earnian*] (bef. 12c) **1 a :** to receive as return for effort and esp. for work done or services rendered **b :** to bring in by way of return ⟨bonds ~*ing* 10% interest⟩ **2 a :** to come to be duly worthy of or entitled or suited to ⟨he had ~*ed* a promotion by his devotion to duty⟩ ⟨she ~*ed* her master's degree⟩ **b :** to make worthy of or obtain for ⟨his devotion to duty had ~*ed* him a promotion⟩ — **earn·er** *n*

2**earn** *vi* [prob. alter. of *yearn*] *obs* (1599) **:** GRIEVE

earned run *n* (1886) **:** a run in baseball that scores without benefit of an error before the fielding team has had a chance to make the third putout of the inning

earned run average *n* (1947) **:** the average number of earned runs per game scored against a pitcher in baseball determined by dividing the total of earned runs scored against him by the total number of innings pitched and multiplying by nine

1**ear·nest** \ˈər-nəst\ *n* [ME *ernest*, fr. OE *eornost;* akin to OHG *ernust* earnest] (bef. 12c) **:** a serious and intent mental state ⟨in ~⟩

2**earnest** *adj* (bef. 12c) **1 :** characterized by or proceeding from an intense and serious state of mind **2 :** GRAVE, IMPORTANT ***syn*** see SERIOUS — **ear·nest·ly** *adv* — **ear·nest·ness** \-nəs(t)-nəs\ *n*

3**earnest** *n* [ME *ernes*, *ernest*, fr. OF *erres*, pl. of *erre* earnest, fr. L *arra*, short for *arrabo*, fr. Gk *arrhabōn*, fr. Heb *'ērābhōn*] (13c) **1 :** something of value given by a buyer to a seller to bind a bargain **2 :** a token of what is to come **:** PLEDGE

earn·ings \ˈər-niŋz\ *n pl* (1675) **1 :** something (as wages) earned **2 :** the balance of revenue after deduction of costs and expenses

ear·phone \ˈi(ə)r-ˌfōn\ *n* (1924) **:** a device that converts electrical energy into sound waves and is worn over or inserted into the ear

ear pick *n* (14c) **:** a device often of precious metal for removing wax or foreign bodies from the ear

ear·piece \ˈi(ə)r-ˌpēs\ *n* (ca. 1843) **1 :** a part of an instrument (as a stethoscope or hearing aid) to which the ear is applied; *esp* **:** EARPHONE **2 :** one of the two sidepieces that support eyeglasses by passing over or behind the ears

ear·plug \-ˌpləg\ *n* (1904) **:** a device of pliable material for insertion into the outer opening of the ear (as to keep out water or deaden sound)

ear·ring \ˈi(ə)r-(ˌ)iŋ, -ˌriŋ\ *n* (bef. 12c) **:** an ornament for the earlobe

ear rot *n* (1926) **:** a condition of Indian corn that is characterized by molding and decay of the ears and that is caused by fungi (genera *Diplodia, Fusarium,* or *Gibberella*)

ear shell *n* (ca. 1859) **:** ABALONE

ear·shot \ˈi(ə)r-ˌshät\ *n* (1607) **:** the range within which the unaided voice may be heard

ear·split·ting \-ˌsplit-iŋ\ *adj* (1884) **:** distressingly loud or shrill ***syn*** see LOUD

1**earth** \ˈərth\ *n* [ME *erthe*, fr. OE *eorthe;* akin to OHG *erda* earth, Gk *era*] (bef. 12c) **1 :** the fragmental material composing part of the surface of the globe; *esp* **:** cultivable soil **2 :** the sphere of mortal life as distinguished from spheres of spirit life — compare HEAVEN, HELL **3 a :** areas of land as distinguished from sea and air **b :** the solid footing formed of soil **:** GROUND **4** *often cap* **:** the planet on which we live that is third in order from the sun — see PLANET table **5 a :** the people of the planet Earth **b :** the mortal body of man **c :** the pursuits, interests, and pleasures of earthly life as distinguished from spiritual concerns **6 :** the lair of a burrowing animal **7 :** a difficultly reducible metallic oxide (as alumina) formerly classed as an element — **earth·like** \-ˌlīk\ *adj* — **on earth :** among many possibilities — used as an intensive

2**earth** *vt* (1575) **1 :** to drive to hiding in the earth **2 :** to draw soil about (plants) **3** *chiefly Brit* **:** GROUND 3 ~ *vi, of a hunted animal* **:** to hide in the ground

earth·born \ˈərth-ˌbȯ(ə)rn\ *adj* (1667) **1 :** born on this earth **:** MORTAL **2 :** associated with earthly life ⟨~ cares⟩

earth·bound \-ˌbau̇nd\ *adj* (1605) **1 a :** fast in or to the soil ⟨~ roots⟩ **b :** restricted to land or to the surface of the earth **2 a :** bound by earthly interests **b :** PEDESTRIAN, UNIMAGINATIVE

earth·en \ˈər-thən, -t͟hən\ *adj* (13c) **1 :** made of earth **2 :** EARTHLY

earth·en·ware \-ˌwa(ə)r, -ˌwe(ə)r\ *n* (1673) **:** ceramic ware made of slightly porous opaque clay fired at low heat

earth·i·ly \ˈər-thə-lē, -t͟hə-\ *adv* (1953) **:** in an earthy manner

earth·light \ˈərth-ˌlīt\ *n* (1833) **:** EARTHSHINE

earth·ling \ˈərth-liŋ\ *n* (1593) **1 :** an inhabitant of the earth **2 :** WORLDLING

earth·ly \ˈərth-lē\ *adj* (bef. 12c) **1 a :** characteristic of or belonging to this earth **b :** relating to man's actual life on this earth **2 :** POSSIBLE ⟨there is no ~ reason for such behavior⟩ — **earth·li·ness** *n*

syn EARTHLY, MUNDANE, WORLDLY mean belonging to or characteristic of the earth. EARTHLY often implies a contrast with what is heavenly or spiritual ⟨*earthly* love⟩ WORLDLY and MUNDANE both imply a relation to the immediate concerns and activities of human beings, WORLDLY suggesting tangible personal gain or gratification ⟨*worldly* goods⟩ and MUNDANE suggesting reference to the immediate and practical ⟨a *mundane* discussion of finances⟩

earth mother *n, often cap E & M* (1902) **1 :** the earth viewed (as in primitive theology) as the divine source of terrestrial life **2 :** the female principle of fertility

earth·quake \ˈərth-ˌkwāk\ *n* (13c) **1 :** a shaking or trembling of the earth that is volcanic or tectonic in origin **2 :** UPHEAVAL 2

earth·rise \ˈərth-ˌrīz\ *n* (1968) **:** the rising of the earth above the horizon of the moon as seen from lunar orbit

earth science *n* (1939) **:** any of the sciences (as geology, meteorology, or oceanography) that deal with the earth or with one or more of its parts

earth·shak·er \ˈərth-ˌshā-kər\ *n* (1953) **:** one that is earthshaking

earth·shak·ing \-kiŋ\ *adj* (1948) **:** of fundamental importance — **earth·shak·ing·ly** \-kiŋ-lē\ *adv*

earth–shat·ter·ing \ˈərth-ˈshat-ə-riŋ\ *adj* (1970) **:** EARTHSHAKING

earth·shine \ˈərth-ˌshīn\ *n* (1876) **:** sunlight reflected by the earth that illuminates the dark part of the moon — called also *earthlight*

earth·star \-ˌstär\ *n* (1885) **:** a globose fungus (genus *Geastrum*) with a double wall whose outer layer splits into the shape of a star

earth tone *n* (1974) **:** any of various rich dark colors containing some brown

earth·ward \-wərd\ *or* **earth·wards** \-wərdz\ *adv* (14c) **:** toward the earth

earth·work \ˈərth-ˌwərk\ *n* (1633) **1 :** an embankment or other construction made of earth; *esp* **:** one used as a field fortification **2 :** the operations connected with excavations and embankments of earth **3 :** a work of art consisting of a portion of land (as a field or hill) that has been modified by the artist

earth·worm \-ˌwərm\ *n* (15c) : a terrestrial annelid worm (class Oligochaeta); *esp* : any of a family (Lumbricidae) of numerous widely distributed hermaphroditic worms that move through the soil by means of setae

earthy \'ər-thē, -t͟hē\ *adj* **earth·i·er; -est** (14c) **1** : consisting of, resembling, or suggesting earth ⟨an ~ flavor⟩ **2 a** *archaic* : EARTHLY, WORLDLY **b** : characteristic of or associated with mortal life on the earth ⟨an ~ vigorous person⟩ **3 a** : PRACTICAL, DOWN-TO-EARTH **b** : CRUDE, GROSS ⟨~ humor⟩ — **earth·i·ness** *n*

ear·wax \'i(ə)r-ˌwaks\ *n* (14c) : CERUMEN

[1]**ear·wig** \-ˌwig\ *n* [ME *erwigge,* fr. OE *ēarwicga,* fr. *ēare* ear + *wicga* insect — more at VETCH] (bef. 12c) : any of numerous insects (order Dermaptera) having slender many-jointed antennae and a pair of cerci resembling forceps at the end of the body

[2]**earwig** *vt* **ear·wigged; ear·wig·ging** (1837) : to annoy or attempt to influence by private talk

ear·wit·ness \'i(ə)r-'wit-nəs\ *n* (1594) : one who overhears something; *esp* : one who gives a report on what he has heard

ear·worm \-ˌwərm\ *n* (1802) : CORN EARWORM

[1]**ease** \'ēz\ *n* [ME *ese,* fr. OF *aise* convenience, comfort, fr. L *adjacent-, adjacens* neighboring — more at ADJACENT] (13c) **1** : the state of being comfortable: as **a** : freedom from pain or discomfort **b** : freedom from care **c** : freedom from labor or difficulty **d** : freedom from embarrassment or constraint : NATURALNESS **2** : relief from discomfort or obligation **3** : FACILITY, EFFORTLESSNESS **4** : an act of easing or a state of being eased; *esp* : a lowering trend in prices — **ease·ful** \-fəl\ *adj* — **ease·ful·ly** \-fə-lē\ *adv* — **at ease 1** : free from pain or discomfort **2 a** : free from restraint or formality **b** : standing silently (as in a military formation) with the feet apart, the right foot in place, and one or both hands behind the body — often used as a command

[2]**ease** *vb* **eased; eas·ing** *vt* (14c) **1** : to free from something that pains, disquiets, or burdens **2** : to make less painful : ALLEVIATE ⟨~ his suffering⟩ **3 a** : to lessen the pressure or tension of esp. by slackening, lifting, or shifting **b** : to maneuver gently or carefully **c** : to moderate or reduce esp. in amount or intensity **4** : to make less difficult ⟨~ credit⟩ **5 a** : to put the helm of (a ship) alee **b** : to let (a helm or rudder) come back a little after having been put hard over ~ *vi* **1** : to give freedom or relief **2** : to move or pass with freedom or with little resistance **3** : MODERATE, SLACKEN

ea·sel \'ē-zəl\ *n* [D *ezel,* lit., ass, fr. L *asinus* ass] (1634) : a frame for supporting something (as an artist's canvas)

ease·ment \'ēz-mənt\ *n* (14c) **1** : an act or means of easing or relieving (as from discomfort) **2** : an interest in land owned by another that entitles its holder to a specific limited use or enjoyment

eas·i·ly \'ēz-(ə-)lē\ *adv* (13c) **1** : in an easy manner **2** : by far **3** : WELL 10b ⟨it could ~ have been me⟩ **4** : at least ⟨cost $200 ~⟩

[1]**east** \'ēst\ *adv* [ME *est,* fr. OE *ēast;* akin to OHG *ōstar* to the east, L *aurora* dawn, Gk *ēōs, heōs*] (bef. 12c) : to, toward, or in the east

[2]**east** *adj* (bef. 12c) **1** : situated toward or at the east ⟨an ~ window⟩ **2** : coming from the east ⟨an ~ wind⟩

[3]**east** *n* (bef. 12c) **1 a** : the general direction of sunrise : the direction toward the right of one facing north **b** : the place on the horizon where the sun rises when it is near one of the equinoxes **c** : the compass point directly opposite to west **2** *cap* **a** : regions lying to the east of a specified or implied point of orientation **b** : regions having a culture derived from ancient non-European esp. Asian areas **3** : the altar end of a church **4** *often cap* **a** : the one of four positions at 90-degree intervals that lies to the east or at the right of a diagram **b** : a person (as a bridge player) occupying this position in the course of a specified activity

east·bound \'ēs(t)-ˌbau̇nd\ *adj* (1880) : traveling or heading east

east by north (1682) : a compass point that is one point north of due east : N78°45′E

east by south (1682) : a compass point that is one point south of due east : S78°45′E

Eas·ter \'ē-stər\ *n* [ME *estre,* fr. OE *ēastre;* akin to OHG *ōstarun* (pl.) Easter, OE *ēast* east] (bef. 12c) : a feast that commemorates Christ's resurrection and is observed with variations of date due to different calendars on the first Sunday after the paschal full moon

EASTER DATES

YEAR	ASH WEDNESDAY	EASTER	YEAR	ASH WEDNESDAY	EASTER
1983	Feb 16	Apr 3	1993	Feb 24	Apr 11
1984	Mar 7	Apr 22	1994	Feb 16	Apr 3
1985	Feb 20	Apr 7	1995	Mar 1	Apr 16
1986	Feb 12	Mar 30	1996	Feb 21	Apr 7
1987	Mar 4	Apr 19	1997	Feb 12	Mar 30
1988	Feb 17	Apr 3	1998	Feb 25	Apr 12
1989	Feb 8	Mar 26	1999	Feb 17	Apr 4
1990	Feb 28	Apr 15	2000	Mar 8	Apr 23
1991	Feb 13	Mar 31	2001	Feb 28	Apr 15
1992	Mar 4	Apr 19	2002	Feb 13	Mar 31

Easter egg *n* (1804) : an egg that is dyed bright colors and that is associated with the celebration of Easter

Easter lily *n* (1877) : any of several white cultivated lilies (esp. *Lilium longiflorum*) that bloom in early spring

[1]**east·er·ly** \'ē-stər-lē\ *adj or adv* [obs. *easter* (eastern)] (ca. 1548) **1** : situated toward or belonging to the east ⟨the ~ shore of the lake⟩ **2** : coming from the east ⟨an ~ storm⟩

[2]**easterly** *n, pl* **-lies** (1901) : a wind from the east

Easter Monday *n* (14c) : the Monday after Easter observed as a legal holiday in parts of the British Commonwealth and in No. Carolina

east·ern \'ē-stərn\ *adj* [ME *estern,* fr. OE *ēasterne;* akin to OHG *ōstrōni* eastern, OE *ēast* east] (bef. 12c) **1** *cap* : of, relating to, or characteristic of a region conventionally designated East **2** *cap* **a** : of, relating to, or being the Christian churches originating in the church of the Eastern Roman Empire **b** : EASTERN ORTHODOX **3 a** : lying toward the east **b** : coming from the east ⟨an ~ wind⟩ — **east·ern·most** \-ˌmōst\ *adj*

East·ern·er \'ē-stə(r)-nər\ *n* (1840) : a native or inhabitant of the East; *esp* : a native or resident of the eastern part of the U.S.

eastern hemisphere *n, often cap E&H* (1624) : the half of the earth to the east of the Atlantic ocean including Europe, Asia, and Africa

Eastern Orthodox *adj* (ca. 1900) : of or consisting of the Eastern churches that form a loose federation according primacy of honor to the patriarch of Constantinople and adhering to the decisions of the first seven ecumenical councils and to the Byzantine rite

eastern time *n, often cap E* (1883) : the time of the 5th time zone west of Greenwich that includes the eastern U.S. — see TIME ZONE illustration

eastern white pine *n* (1925) : WHITE PINE 1a

Eas·ter·tide \'ē-stər-ˌtīd\ *n* [ME *estertide,* fr. OE *ēastortīd,* fr. *ēastor* + *tīd* time — more at TIDE] (bef. 12c) : the period from Easter to Ascension Day, to Whitsunday, or to Trinity Sunday

East Germanic *n* (ca. 1901) : a subdivision of the Germanic languages that includes Gothic — see INDO-EUROPEAN LANGUAGES table

east·ing \'ē-stiŋ\ *n* (1628) **1** : easterly progress **2** : difference in longitude to the east from the last preceding point of reckoning

east–northeast *n* (14c) : a compass point that is two points north of due east : N67°30′E

east–southeast *n* (14c) : a compass point that is two points south of due east : S67°30′E

[1]**east·ward** \'ēs-twərd\ *adv or adj* (bef. 12c) : toward the east — **east·wards** \-twərdz\ *adv*

[2]**eastward** *n* (1695) : eastward direction or part ⟨sail to the ~⟩

[1]**easy** \'ē-zē\ *adj* **eas·i·er; -est** [ME *esy,* fr. OF *aaisié,* pp. of *aaisier* to ease, fr. *a-* ad- (fr. L *ad-*) + *aise* ease] (13c) **1 a** : causing or involving little difficulty or discomfort ⟨an ~ problem⟩ ⟨within ~ reach⟩ **b** : requiring or indicating little effort, thought, or reflection ⟨~ clichés⟩ ⟨~ mediocrity⟩ **2 a** : not severe : LENIENT **b** : not steep or abrupt ⟨~ slopes⟩ **c** : not difficult to endure or undergo ⟨an ~ penalty⟩ **d** : readily taken advantage of ⟨an ~ target for takeovers⟩ **e (1)** : readily available : easily come by ⟨~ pickings⟩ **(2)** : plentiful in supply at low or declining interest rates ⟨~ money⟩ **(3)** : less in demand and usu. lower in price ⟨bonds were *easier*⟩ **f** : PLEASANT ⟨~ listening⟩ ⟨~ on the eyes⟩ **3 a** : marked by peace and comfort ⟨the ~ life of a courtier⟩ **b** : not hurried or strenuous ⟨an ~ pace⟩ ⟨an ~ flick of the wrist⟩ **4 a** : free from pain, annoyance, or anxiety ⟨did all she could to make him *easier*⟩ **b** : marked by social ease ⟨an air of ~ assurance⟩ **c** : EASYGOING ⟨an ~ disposition⟩ **5 a** : giving ease, comfort, or relaxation ⟨~ chairs⟩ **b** : not burdensome or straitened ⟨bought on ~ terms⟩ ⟨living in ~ circumstances⟩ **c** : fitting comfortably : allowing freedom of movement ⟨~ jackets⟩ **d** : marked by ready facility ⟨an ~ flowing style⟩ **e** : felt or attained to readily, naturally, and spontaneously ⟨an ~ smile⟩ — **eas·i·ness** *n*

syn EASY, FACILE, SIMPLE, LIGHT, EFFORTLESS, SMOOTH mean not demanding effort or involving difficulty. EASY is applicable either to persons or things imposing tasks or to activity required by such tasks; FACILE often adds to EASY the connotation of undue haste or shallowness; SIMPLE stresses ease in understanding or dealing with because complication is absent; LIGHT stresses freedom from what is burdensome, and often suggests quickness of movement; EFFORTLESS stresses the appearance of ease and usu. implies the prior attainment of artistry or expertness; SMOOTH stresses the absence or removal of all difficulties, hardships, or obstacles. ***syn*** see in addition COMFORTABLE

[2]**easy** *adv* **eas·i·er; -est** (15c) **1** : EASILY 1 ⟨promises come ~⟩ **2 a** : without undue speed or excitement ⟨take it ~⟩ **b** : in or with moderation ⟨take it ~ on the gas pedal⟩ ⟨go ~ on the mustard⟩ **3 a** : without worry or care ⟨rest ~⟩ **b** : without a severe penalty ⟨got off ~⟩ **c** : without violent movement ⟨the boat rode ~⟩ **4** : EASILY 4 ⟨cost $500 ~⟩

easy·go·ing \ˌē-zē-'gō-iŋ, -'gȯ(-)iŋ\ *adj* (1674) **1** : taking life easy: as **a** : PLACID ⟨an ~ man⟩ **b** : indolent and careless ⟨his inertia, his laziness, his ~ ways —*Times Lit. Supp.*⟩ **c** : morally lax **2** : UNHURRIED, COMFORTABLE ⟨an ~ pace⟩ — **easy·go·ing·ness** *n*

easy mark *n* (ca. 1896) : one easily taken advantage of

easy street *n* (1900) : a situation with no worries

easy virtue *n* (ca. 1780) : sexually promiscuous behavior or habits ⟨ladies of *easy virtue*⟩

eat \'ēt\ *vb* **ate** \'āt, *chiefly Brit or substand* 'et\; **eat·en** \'ē-tᵊn\; **eat·ing** [ME *eten,* fr. OE *etan;* akin to OHG *ezzan* to eat, L *edere,* Gk *edmenai*] *vt* (bef. 12c) **1** : to take in through the mouth as food : ingest, chew, and swallow in turn **2** : to destroy, consume, or waste by or as if by eating : DEVOUR ⟨operating expenses *ate* up the profits⟩ **3 a** : to consume gradually : CORRODE **b** : to consume with vexation : BOTHER ⟨what's ~*ing* her now⟩ ~ *vi* **1** : to take food or a meal **2** : to affect something by gradual destruction or consumption — usu. used with *into, away,* or *at* — **eat·er** *n* — **eat crow** : to accept what one has fought against — **eat humble pie** : to apologize or retract under pressure — **eat one's heart out 1** : to grieve bitterly **2** : to be jealous — **eat one's words** : to retract what one has said — **eat out of one's hand** : to accept the domination of another

[1]**eat·able** \'ēt-ə-bəl\ *adj* (14c) : fit or able to be eaten

[2]**eatable** *n* (1672) **1** : something to eat **2** *pl* : FOOD

eat·ery \'ēt-ə-rē\ *n, pl* **-er·ies** (1901) : LUNCHEONETTE, RESTAURANT

eath \'ēth\ *adv or adj* [ME *ethe,* fr. OE *ēathe;* akin to OHG *ōdi* easy and perh. to L *avēre* to long for — more at AVID] *Scot* (bef. 12c) : EASY

eat·ing \'ēt-iŋ\ *adj* (15c) **1** : used for eating ⟨~ utensils⟩ **2** : suitable to eat ⟨the finest ~ fish⟩; *also* : suitable to eat raw ⟨an ~ apple⟩

eau de co·logne \ˌōd-ə-kə-'lōn\ *n, pl* **eaux de cologne** \ˌō(z)d-ə-\ [F, lit., Cologne water, fr. *Cologne,* Germany] (1802) : COLOGNE

eau–de–vie \ˌōd-ə-'vē\ *n, pl* **eaux–de–vie** \ˌō(z)d-ə-\ [F, lit., water of life, trans. of ML *aqua vitae*] (1748) : a clear brandy distilled from the fermented juice of fruit (as pears or raspberries)

\ə\ abut \ᵊ\ kitten, F table \ər\ further \a\ ash \ā\ ace \ä\ cot, cart \au̇\ out \ch\ chin \e\ bet \ē\ easy \g\ go \i\ hit \ī\ ice \j\ job \ŋ\ sing \ō\ go \ȯ\ law \ȯi\ boy \th\ thin \t͟h\ the \ü\ loot \u̇\ foot \y\ yet \zh\ vision \à, k̲, ⁿ, œ, œ̄, ue, ue̅, ʸ\ see Guide to Pronunciation

eaves \'ēvz\ *n pl* [ME *eves* (sing.), fr. OE *efes;* akin to OHG *obasa* portico, OE *ūp* up — more at UP] (bef. 12c) **1 :** the lower border of a roof that overhangs the wall **2 :** a projecting edge (as of a hill)
eaves·drop \'ēvz-,dräp\ *vi* [prob. back-formation fr. *eavesdropper,* lit., one standing under the drip from the eaves] (1606) : to listen secretly to what is said in private — **eaves·drop·per** *n*
eaves trough *n* (1878) : GUTTER 1a
[1]**ebb** \'eb\ *n* [ME *ebbe,* fr. OE *ebba;* akin to MD *ebbe* ebb, OE *of* from — more at OF] (bef. 12c) **1 :** the reflux of the tide toward the sea **2 :** a point or condition of decline ⟨faith had reached a low ∼⟩
[2]**ebb** *vi* (bef. 12c) **1 :** to recede from the flood **2 :** to fall from a higher to a lower level or from a better to a worse state ***syn*** see ABATE
ebb tide *n* (ca. 1828) **1 :** the tide while ebbing or at ebb **2 :** a period or state of decline
EBCDIC \'ep-sə-,dik, 'eb-\ *n* [extended binary coded decimal interchange code] (ca. 1966) : a code for representing alphanumeric information (as on magnetic tape)
eb·on \'eb-ən\ *adj* (15c) : EBONY
eb·o·nite \'eb-ə-,nīt\ *n* (1861) : hard rubber esp. when black
eb·o·nize \-,nīz\ *vt* **-nized; -niz·ing** (ca. 1828) : to stain black in imitation of ebony
[1]**eb·o·ny** \'eb-ə-nē\ *n, pl* **-nies** [prob. fr. LL *hebeninus* of ebony, fr. Gk *ebeninos,* fr. *ebenos* ebony, fr. Egypt *hbnj*] (14c) **1 :** a hard heavy wood yielded by various Old World tropical dicotyledonous trees (genus *Diospyros* of the family Ebonaceae, the ebony family) **2 a :** a tree yielding ebony **b :** any of several trees yielding wood resembling ebony
[2]**ebony** *adj* (1598) **1 :** made of or resembling ebony **2 :** BLACK, DARK
ebul·lience \i-'bu̇l-yən(t)s, -'bəl-\ *n* (1749) : the quality of lively or enthusiastic expression of thoughts or feelings : EXUBERANCE
ebul·lien·cy \-yən-sē\ *n* (1676) : EBULLIENCE
ebul·lient \-yənt\ *adj* [L *ebullient-, ebulliens,* prp. of *ebullire* to bubble out, fr. *e-* + *bullire* to bubble, boil — more at BOIL] (1599) **1 :** BOILING, AGITATED **2 :** characterized by ebullience — **ebul·lient·ly** *adv*
eb·ul·li·tion \,eb-ə-'lish-ən\ *n* (1534) **1 :** a sudden violent outburst or display **2 :** the act, process, or state of boiling or bubbling up
ec- *or* **eco-** *comb form* [LL *oeco-* household, fr. Gk *oik-, oiko-,* fr. *oikos* house — more at VICINITY] : habitat or environment ⟨*ecospecies*⟩
[1]**ec·cen·tric** \ik-'sen-trik, ek-\ *adj* [ML *eccentricus,* fr. Gk *ekkentros,* fr. *ex* out of + *kentron* center] (14c) **1 :** not having the same center ⟨∼ spheres⟩ **2 :** deviating from an established pattern or from accepted usage or conduct **3 a :** deviating from a circular path ⟨an ∼ orbit⟩ **b :** located elsewhere than at the geometrical center; *also* **:** having the axis or support so located ⟨an ∼ wheel⟩ ***syn*** see STRANGE — **ec·cen·tri·cal·ly** \-tri-k(ə-)lē\ *adv*
[2]**eccentric** *n* (1827) **1 :** a mechanical device consisting of a disk through which a shaft is keyed eccentrically and a circular strap which works freely round the rim of the disk for communicating its motion to one end of a rod whose other end is constrained to move in a straight line so as to produce reciprocating motion **2 :** an eccentric person
ec·cen·tric·i·ty \,ek-,sen-'tris-ət-ē\ *n, pl* **-ties** (1551) **1 a :** the quality or state of being eccentric **b :** deviation from an established pattern or norm; *esp* **:** odd or whimsical behavior **2 :** a mathematical constant that for a given conic section is the ratio of the distances from any point of the conic section to a focus and the corresponding directrix
ec·chy·mo·sis \,ek-i-'mō-səs\ *n, pl* **-mo·ses** \-,sēz\ [NL, fr. Gk *ekchymōsis,* fr. *ekchymousthai* to extravasate blood, fr. *ex-* + *chymos* juice — more at CHYME] (1541) : the escape of blood into the tissues from ruptured blood vessels — **ec·chy·mot·ic** \-'mät-ik\ *adj*
ecclesi- *or* **ecclesio-** *comb form* [ME *ecclesi-,* fr. LL *ecclesia,* fr. Gk *ekklēsia* assembly of citizens, church, fr. *ekkalein* to call forth, summon, fr. *ex-* + *kalein* to call — more at LOW] : church ⟨*ecclesiography*⟩
ec·cle·si·al \ik-'lē-zē-əl, e-'klē-\ *adj* (1649) : of or relating to a church
Ec·cle·si·as·tes \ik-,lē-zē-'as-(,)tēz, e-,klē-\ *n* [Gk *Ekklēsiastēs,* lit., preacher (trans. of Heb *Qōheleth*), fr. *ekklēsiastēs* member of an assembly, fr. *ekklēsia*] : a book of wisdom literature in canonical Jewish and Christian Scripture — see BIBLE table
[1]**ec·cle·si·as·tic** \-'as-tik\ *adj* (15c) : ECCLESIASTICAL
[2]**ecclesiastic** *n* (1651) : CLERGYMAN
ec·cle·si·as·ti·cal \-ti-kəl\ *adj* [ME, fr. LL *ecclesiasticus,* fr. LGk *ekklēsiastikos,* fr. Gk, of an assembly of citizens, fr. *ekklēsiastēs*] (15c) **1 :** of or relating to a church esp. as a formal and established institution ⟨∼ law⟩ **2 :** suitable for use in a church ⟨∼ vestments⟩ — **ec·cle·si·as·ti·cal·ly** \-ti-k(ə-)lē\ *adv*
ec·cle·si·as·ti·cism \-tə-,siz-əm\ *n* (1862) : excessive attachment to ecclesiastical forms and practices
Ec·cle·si·as·ti·cus \-ti-kəs\ *n* [LL, fr. *ecclesiasticus*] : a didactic book included in the Roman Catholic canon of the Old Testament and in the Protestant Apocrypha — see BIBLE table
ec·cle·si·ol·o·gy \ik-,lē-zē-'äl-ə-jē, e-,klē-\ *n, pl* **-gies** (ca. 1837) **1 :** the study of church architecture and adornment **2 :** theological doctrine relating to the church — **ec·cle·si·o·log·i·cal** \-zē-ə-'läj-i-kəl\ *adj*
ec·crine gland \'ek-rən-, -,rīn-, -,rēn-\ *n* [ISV *ec-* (fr. Gk *ex* out) + Gk *krinein* to separate — more at CERTAIN] (ca. 1927) : any of the rather small sweat glands that produce a fluid secretion without removing cytoplasm from the secreting cells and that are restricted to the human skin — called also *eccrine sweat gland*
ec·dys·i·ast \ek-'diz-ē-,ast, -ē-əst\ *n* [Gk *ekdysis*] (1940) : STRIPTEASER
ec·dy·sis \'ek-də-səs\ *n, pl* **ec·dy·ses** \-də-,sēz\ [NL, fr. Gk *ekdysis* act of getting out, fr. *ekdyein* to strip, fr. *ex-* + *dyein* to enter, don — more at ADYTUM] (ca. 1854) : the act of molting or shedding an outer cuticular layer (as in insects and crustaceans)
ec·dy·sone \'ek-də-,sōn\ *also* **ec·dy·son** \-,sän\ *n* [ISV *ecdysis* + hormone] (1956) : any of several arthropod hormones that in insects are produced by the prothoracic gland and that trigger molting and metamorphosis
ece·sis \i-'sē-səs, -'kē-\ *n* [NL, fr. Gk *oikēsis* inhabitation, fr. *oikein* to inhabit — more at ECUMENICAL] (ca. 1904) : the establishment of a plant or animal in a new habitat
[1]**ech·e·lon** \'esh-ə-,län\ *n* [F *échelon,* lit., rung of a ladder, fr. OF *eschelon,* fr. *eschele* ladder, fr. LL *scala* — more at SCALE] (1796) **1 a** (1) : an arrangement of a body of troops with its units each somewhat to the left or right of the one in the rear like a series of steps (2) : a formation of units or individuals resembling such an echelon (3) : a flight formation in which each airplane flies at a certain elevation above or below and at a certain distance behind and to the right or left of the airplane ahead **b :** any of several military units in echelon formation **2 a :** one of a series of levels or grades (as of leadership or responsibility) in an organization or field of activity **b :** a group of individuals at a particular level or grade in an organization
[2]**echelon** *vt* (1860) : to form or arrange in an echelon ∼ *vi* **:** to take position in an echelon
ech·e·ve·ria \,ech-ə-və-'rē-ə\ *n* [NL, genus name, fr. *Echeveria,* 19th cent. Mex. botanical illustrator] (1883) : any of a large genus (*Echeveria*) of tropical American succulent plants of the orpine family that have showy rosettes of often plushy basal leaves and axillary clusters of flowers with erect petals spreading only at the tips and that are often grown in warm regions as ornamentals
echid·na \i-'kid-nə\ *n* [NL, fr. L, viper, fr. Gk; akin to Gk *echis* viper, OHG *egala* leech] (1847) : an oviparous spiny-coated toothless burrowing nocturnal mammal (*Tachyglossus aculeatus*) of Australia, Tasmania, and New Guinea that has a long extensile tongue and long heavy claws and that feeds chiefly on ants — called also *spiny anteater*

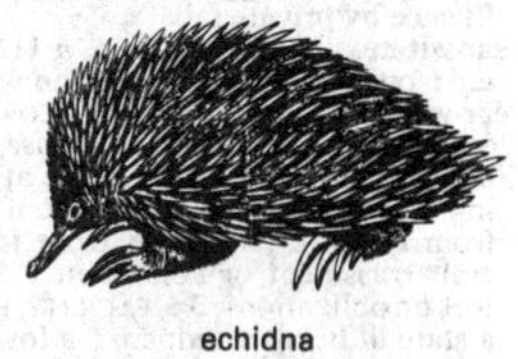
echidna

echin- *or* **echino-** *comb form* [L, fr. Gk, fr. *echinos* sea urchin] **1 :** prickle ⟨*Echinodermata*⟩ **2 :** sea urchin ⟨*echinite*⟩
echi·no·coc·co·sis \i-,kī-nə-kä-'kō-səs\ *n, pl* **-co·ses** \-,sēz\ [NL] (1900) : infestation with or disease caused by a small tapeworm (*Echinococcus granulosus*)
echi·no·coc·cus \i-,kī-nə-'käk-əs\ *n, pl* **-coc·ci** \-'käk-,(s)ī, -'käk-(,)(s)ē\ [NL, genus name] (ca. 1885) : any of a genus (*Echinococcus*) of tapeworms that alternate a minute adult living as a commensal in the intestine of carnivores with a hydatid larva invading tissues esp. of the liver of cattle, sheep, swine, and man and acting as a dangerous pathogen
echi·no·derm \i-'kī-nə-,dərm\ *n* [NL, fr. *echin-* + *-derm*] (1847) : any of a phylum (Echinodermata) of radially symmetrical coelomate marine animals including the starfishes, sea urchins, and related forms — **echi·no·der·ma·tous** \-,kī-nə-'dər-mət-əs\ *adj*
echi·noid \i-'kī-,nȯid, 'ek-ə-,nȯid\ *n* (1864) : SEA URCHIN
echi·nus \i-'kī-nəs\ *n, pl* **-ni** \-,nī\ [ME, fr. L, fr. Gk *echinos* hedgehog, sea urchin; akin to OE *igil* hedgehog, urchin] (14c) **1 :** SEA URCHIN **2 a :** the rounded molding forming the bell of the capital in the Greek Doric order **b :** a similar member in other orders
echi·uroid \,ek-i-'yu̇(ə)r-,ȯid\ *n* [NL, deriv. of Gk *echis* viper + *oura* tail — more at ASS] (ca. 1890) : any of a group (Echiuroidea) of marine worms of uncertain taxonomic affinities that have a sensitive but nonretractile proboscis above the mouth
[1]**echo** \'ek-(,)ō\ *n, pl* **ech·oes** [ME *ecco,* fr. MF & L; MF *echo,* fr. L, fr. Gk *ēchō;* akin to L *vagire* to wail, Gk *ēchē* sound] (14c) **1 a :** the repetition of a sound caused by reflection of sound waves **b :** the sound due to such reflection **2 a :** a repetition or imitation of another : REFLECTION **b :** REPERCUSSION, RESULT **c :** TRACE, VESTIGE **d :** RESPONSE **3 :** one who closely imitates or repeats another's words, ideas, or acts **4 :** a soft repetition of a musical phrase **5 a :** the repetition of a received radio signal due esp. to reflection of part of the wave from an ionized layer of the atmosphere **b** (1) : the reflection of transmitted radar signals by an object (2) : the visual indication of this reflection on a radarscope — **echo·ey** \'ek-,ō-ē\ *adj*
[2]**echo** *vb* **ech·oed; echo·ing** \'ek-(,)ō-iŋ, 'ek-ə-wiŋ\ *vi* (1596) **1 :** to resound with echoes **2 :** to produce an echo ∼ *vt* **1 :** REPEAT, IMITATE **2 :** to send back or repeat (a sound) by the reflection of sound waves
[1]**Echo** *n* [Gk *Ēchō*] : a nymph in Greek legend who pines away for love of Narcissus until nothing is left of her but her voice
[2]**Echo** (ca. 1956) — a communications code word for the letter *e*
echo·car·dio·gram \,ek-ō-'kärd-ē-ə-,gram\ *n* (1979) : a visual record made by echocardiography
echo·car·di·og·ra·phy \-,kärd-ē-'äg-rə-fē\ *n, pl* **-phies** (1979) : a noninvasive and painless diagnostic procedure for making a record of cardiac structure and functioning by means of high frequency sound waves reflected back from the heart — **echo·car·dio·graph·ic** \-ē-ə-'graf-ik\ *adj*
echo chamber *n* (1937) : a room with sound-reflecting walls used for producing hollow or echoing sound effects
echo·en·ceph·a·log·ra·phy \,ek-ō-in-,sef-ə-'läg-rə-fē\ *n* (ca. 1961) : the use of ultrasound in the examination and measurement of internal structures of the skull and in the diagnosis of abnormalities
echo·ic \i-'kō-ik, e-\ *adj* (1880) **1 :** formed in imitation of some natural sound : ONOMATOPOEIC **2 :** of or relating to an echo
echo·la·lia \,ek-ō-'lā-lē-ə\ *n* [NL] (ca. 1885) : the often pathological repetition of what is said by other people as if echoing them — **echo·lal·ic** \-'lal-ik\ *adj*
echo·lo·ca·tion \,ek-ō-lō-'kā-shən\ *n* (1944) : a process for locating distant or invisible objects (as prey) by means of sound waves reflected back to the emitter (as a bat or submarine) by the objects
echo sounder *n* (1927) : an instrument for determining the depth of a body of water or of an object below the surface by means of sound waves
echo·vi·rus \'ek-ō-,vī-rəs\ *n* [enteric cytopathogenic human orphan + *virus*] (1955) : any of a group of picornaviruses that are found in the gastrointestinal tract, that cause cytopathic changes in cells in tissue culture, and that are sometimes associated with respiratory ailments and meningitis
éclair \ā-'kla(ə)r, i-, -'kle(ə)r, 'ā-,, 'ē-,\ *n* [F, lit., lightning] (1861) : a usu. chocolate-frosted oblong light pastry with whipped cream or custard filling
éclair·cis·se·ment \ā-kler-sēs-(ə-)män\ *n, pl* **-ments** \-män(z)\ [F] (1667) : ENLIGHTENMENT, CLARIFICATION
eclamp·sia \i-'klam(p)-sē-ə\ *n* [NL, fr. Gk *eklampsis* sudden flashing, fr. *eklampein* to shine forth, fr. *ex* out + *lampein* to shine] (ca. 1860) : a convulsive state; *esp* **:** an attack of convulsions during pregnancy or parturition — **eclamp·tic** \-'klam(p)-tik\ *adj*

éclat \ā-'klä, 'ā-,\ *n* [F, splinter, burst, éclat] (1672) **1 :** ostentatious display : PUBLICITY **2 :** dazzling effect : BRILLIANCE **3 a :** brilliant or conspicuous success **b :** PRAISE, APPLAUSE

1**eclec·tic** \e-'klek-tik, i-\ *adj* [Gk *eklektikos,* fr. *eklegein* to select, fr. *ex* + *legein* to gather — more at LEGEND] (1683) **1 :** selecting what appears to be best in various doctrines, methods, or styles **2 :** composed of elements drawn from various sources — **eclec·ti·cal·ly** \-ti-k(ə-)lē\ *adv*

2**eclectic** *n* (1817) **:** one who uses an eclectic method or approach

eclec·ti·cism \-'klek-tə-,siz-əm\ *n* (1798) **:** the theory or practice of an eclectic method

1**eclipse** \i-'klips\ *n* [ME, fr. OF, fr. L *eclipsis,* fr. Gk *ekleipsis,* fr. *ekleipein* to omit, fail, suffer eclipse, fr. *ex* + *leipein* to leave — more at LOAN] (13c) **1 a :** the total or partial obscuring of one celestial body by another **b :** the passing into the shadow of a celestial body — compare OCCULTATION, TRANSIT **2 :** a falling into obscurity or decline; *also* **:** the state of being eclipsed **3 :** the state of being in eclipse plumage

2**eclipse** *vt* **eclipsed; eclips·ing** (13c) **:** to cause an eclipse of: as **a :** OBSCURE, DARKEN **b :** to reduce in importance or repute **c :** SURPASS

eclipse plumage *n* (1906) **:** comparatively dull plumage that is usu. of seasonal occurrence in birds exhibiting a distinct nuptial plumage

1**eclip·tic** \i-'klip-tik\ *adj* [ME *ecliptik,* fr. LL *ecliptica linea,* lit., line of eclipses] (14c) **:** of or relating to the ecliptic or an eclipse

2**ecliptic** *n* (15c) **1 :** the great circle of the celestial sphere that is the apparent path of the sun among the stars or of the earth as seen from the sun **:** the plane of the earth's orbit extended to meet the celestial sphere **2 :** a great circle drawn on a terrestrial globe making an angle of about 23° 27′ with the equator and used for illustrating and solving astronomical problems

ec·logue \'ek-,lȯg, -,läg\ *n* [ME *eclog,* fr. L *Eclogae,* title of Vergil's pastorals, lit., selections, pl. of *ecloga,* fr. Gk *eklogē,* fr. *eklegein* to select] (15c) **:** a poem in which shepherds converse

eclo·sion \i-'klō-zhən\ *n* [F *éclosion,* fr. *éclore* to hatch, fr. (assumed) VL *exclaudere,* alter. of L *excludere* to hatch out, exclude] *of an insect* (ca. 1889) **:** the act of emerging from the pupal case or hatching from the egg

eco- — see EC-

eco·ca·tas·tro·phe \,ē-(,)kō-kə-'tas-trə-fē, ,ek-(,)ō-\ *n* (1970) **:** a major destructive upset in the balance of nature esp. when caused by the intervention of man

eco·freak \'ē-(,)kō-,frēk, 'ek-(,)ō-\ *n* (1970) **:** a zealous environmentalist — usu. used disparagingly

ecol·o·gy \i-'käl-ə-jē, e-\ *n, pl* **-gies** [G *ökologie,* fr. *ök-* ec- + *-logie* -logy] (1858) **1 :** a branch of science concerned with the interrelationship of organisms and their environments **2 :** the totality or pattern of relations between organisms and their environment **3 :** HUMAN ECOLOGY — **eco·log·i·cal** \,ē-kə-'läj-i-kəl, ,ek-ə-\ *also* **eco·log·ic** \-ik\ *adj* — **eco·log·i·cal·ly** \-i-k(ə-)lē\ *adv* — **ecol·o·gist** \i-'käl-ə-jəst, e-\ *n*

econo·met·rics \i-,kän-ə-'me-triks\ *n pl but sing in constr* [blend of *economics* and *metric*] (1933) **:** the application of statistical methods to the study of economic data and problems — **econo·met·ric** \-trik\ *adj* — **econo·met·ri·cal·ly** \-tri-k(ə-)lē\ *adv* — **econo·me·tri·cian** \-mə-'trish-ən\ *n* — **econo·met·rist** \-'me-trəst\ *n*

eco·nom·ic \,ek-ə-'näm-ik, ,ē-kə-\ *adj* (1592) **1** *archaic* **:** of or relating to a household or its management **2 :** ECONOMICAL 2 **3 a :** of or relating to economics **b :** of, relating to, or based on the production, distribution, and consumption of goods and services **c :** of or relating to an economy **4 :** having practical or industrial significance or uses **:** affecting material resources **5 :** PROFITABLE

eco·nom·i·cal \-'näm-i-kəl\ *adj* (1579) **1** *archaic* **:** ECONOMIC 1 **2 :** marked by careful, efficient, and prudent use of resources **:** THRIFTY **3 :** operating with little waste or at a saving ***syn*** see SPARING — **eco·nom·i·cal·ly** \-i-k(ə-)lē\ *adv*

economic rent *n* (1889) **:** the return for the use of a factor in excess of the minimum required to bring forth its service

eco·nom·ics \,ek-ə-'näm-iks, ,ē-kə-\ *n pl but sing or pl in constr* (1792) **1 :** a social science concerned chiefly with description and analysis of the production, distribution, and consumption of goods and services **2 :** economic aspect or significance

econ·o·mist \i-'kän-ə-məst\ *n* (1586) **1** *archaic* **:** one who practices economy **2 :** a specialist in economics

econ·o·mize \-,mīz\ *vb* **-mized; -miz·ing** *vi* (1648) **:** to practice economy **:** be frugal ~ *vt* **:** to use more economically **:** SAVE — **econ·o·miz·er** *n*

1**econ·o·my** \i-'kän-ə-mē\ *n, pl* **-mies** [MF *yconomie,* fr. ML *oeconomia,* fr. Gk *oikonomia,* fr. *oikonomos* household manager, fr. *oikos* house + *nemein* to manage — more at VICINITY, NIMBLE] (1530) **1** *archaic* **:** the management of household or private affairs and esp. expenses **2 a :** thrifty and efficient use of material resources **:** frugality in expenditures; *also* **:** an instance or a means of economizing **:** SAVING **b :** efficient and concise use of nonmaterial resources (as effort, language, or motion) for the end proposed **3 :** the arrangement or mode of operation of something **:** ORGANIZATION **4 :** the structure of economic life in a country, area, or period; *specif* **:** an economic system

2**economy** *adj* (ca. 1906) **:** designed to save money ⟨~ cars⟩ ⟨~ measures⟩

eco·phys·i·ol·o·gy \,ē-kō-,fiz-ē-'äl-ə-jē, ,ek-ō-\ *n* (1962) **:** the science of the interrelationships between the physiology of organisms and their environment — **eco·phys·i·o·log·i·cal** \-ē-ə-'läj-i-kəl\ *adj*

eco·spe·cies \'ē-kō-,spē-(,)shēz, ,ek-ō-, -(,)sēz\ *n, pl* **ecospecies** (1922) **:** a subdivision of a cenospecies capable of free gene interchange between its members without impairment of fertility but less capable of fertile crosses with members of other subdivisions and typically more or less equivalent to the taxonomic species — **eco·spe·cif·ic** \,ē-kō-spi-'sif-ik, ,ek-ō-\ *adj*

eco·sphere \'ē-kō-,sfi(ə)r, 'ek-ō-\ *n* (1953) **:** the parts of the universe habitable by living organisms; *esp* **:** BIOSPHERE 1

eco·sys·tem \-,sis-təm\ *n* (1935) **:** the complex of a community and its environment functioning as an ecological unit in nature

eco·tone \'ē-kə-,tōn, 'ek-ə-\ *n* [*ec-* + Gk *tonos* tension — more at TONE] (1904) **:** a transition area between two adjacent ecological communities usu. exhibiting competition between organisms common to both

eco·type \-,tīp\ *n* (ca. 1922) **:** a subdivision of an ecospecies that comprises individuals interfertile with each other and with members of other ecotypes of the same ecospecies but surviving as a distinct group through environmental selection and isolation and that is comparable with a taxonomic subspecies — **eco·typ·ic** \,ē-kə-'tip-ik, ,ek-ə-\ *adj* — **eco·typ·i·cal·ly** \-i-k(ə-)lē\ *adv*

ecru \'ek-(,)rü, 'ā-(,)krü\ *n* [F *écru* unbleached, fr. OF *escru,* fr. *es-* completely (fr. L *ex-*) + *cru* raw, fr. L *crudus* — more at RAW] (1850) **:** BEIGE 2

ec·sta·sy \'ek-stə-sē\ *n, pl* **-sies** [ME *extasie,* fr. MF, fr. LL *ecstasis,* fr. Gk *ekstasis,* fr. *existanai* to derange, fr. *ex* out + *histanai* to cause to stand — more at EX-, STAND] (14c) **1 a :** a state of being beyond reason and self-control **b** *archaic* **:** SWOON **2 :** a state of overwhelming emotion; *esp* **:** rapturous delight **3 :** TRANCE; *esp* **:** a mystic or prophetic trance

syn ECSTASY, RAPTURE, TRANSPORT mean intense exaltation of mind and feelings. ECSTASY and RAPTURE both suggest a state of trance or near immobility produced by an overpowering emotion; ECSTASY may apply to any strong emotion (as joy, fear, rage, adoration); RAPTURE usu. implies intense bliss or beatitude; TRANSPORT applies to any powerful emotion that lifts one out of oneself and usu. provokes vehement expression or frenzied action.

1**ec·stat·ic** \ek-'stat-ik, ik-'stat-\ *adj* [ML *ecstaticus,* fr. Gk *ekstatikos,* fr. *existanai*] (1630) **:** of, relating to, or marked by ecstasy — **ec·stat·i·cal·ly** \-'stat-i-k(ə-)lē\ *adv*

2**ecstatic** *n* (1659) **:** one that is subject to ecstasies

ect- *or* **ecto-** *comb form* [NL, fr. Gk *ekto-,* fr. *ektos,* fr. *ex* out — more at EX-] **:** outside **:** external ⟨*ecto*mere⟩ — compare END-, EXO-

ec·to·com·men·sal \,ek-tō-kə-'men(t)-səl\ *adj* (1940) **:** living as a commensal on the body surface of another ⟨~ protozoans⟩

ec·to·derm \'ek-tə-,dərm\ *n* [ISV] (1861) **1 :** the outer cellular membrane of a diploblastic animal (as a jellyfish) **2 a :** the outermost of the three primary germ layers of an embryo **b :** a tissue (as neural tissue) derived from this germ layer — **ec·to·der·mal** \,ek-tə-'dər-məl\ *adj*

ec·to·morph \'ek-tə-,mȯrf\ *n* [*ecto*derm + *-morph*] (1940) **:** an ectomorphic individual

ec·to·mor·phic \,ek-tə-'mȯr-fik\ *adj* [*ecto*derm + *-morphic;* fr. the predominance in such types of structures developed from the ectoderm] (1940) **1 :** of or relating to the component in W. H. Sheldon's classification of body types that measures the body's degree of slenderness, angularity, and fragility **2 :** characterized by a light body build with slight muscular development

-ec·to·my \'ek-tə-mē\ *n comb form* [NL *-ectomia,* fr. Gk *ektemnein* to cut out, fr. *ex-* out + *temnein* to cut — more at TOME] **:** surgical removal ⟨gastr*ectomy*⟩

ec·to·par·a·site \,ek-tō-'par-ə-,sīt\ *n* [ISV] (1861) **:** a parasite that lives on the exterior of its host — **ec·to·par·a·sit·ic** \-,par-ə-'sit-ik\ *adj*

ec·top·ic \ek-'täp-ik\ *adj* [Gk *ektopos* out of place, fr. *ex-* + *topos* place — more at TOPIC] (1873) **:** occurring in an abnormal position or in an unusual manner or form ⟨~ lesions⟩ ⟨~ heartbeat⟩ — **ec·top·i·cal·ly** \-i-k(ə-)lē\ *adv*

ectopic pregnancy *n* (1929) **:** gestation elsewhere than in the uterus (as in a fallopian tube or in the peritoneal cavity)

ec·to·plasm \'ek-tə-,plaz-əm\ *n* (1883) **1 :** the outer relatively rigid granule-free layer of the cytoplasm usu. held to be a gel reversibly convertible to a sol **2 :** a substance held to produce spirit materialization and telekinesis — **ec·to·plas·mic** \,ek-tə-'plaz-mik\ *adj*

ec·to·therm \'ek-tə-,thərm\ *n* (1945) **:** a cold-blooded animal **:** POIKILOTHERM — **ec·to·ther·mic** \,ek-tə-'thər-mik\ *adj*

ec·to·tro·phic \,ek-tə-'trō-fik\ *adj, of a mycorrhiza* (1897) **:** growing in a close web on the surface of the associated root — compare ENDOTROPHIC

ecu \'ā-,kyü, ā-kᵫ\ *n, pl* **ecus** \-,kyüz, -kᵫ\ [MF, lit., shield, fr. OF *escu,* fr. L *scutum;* from the device of a shield on the coin — more at ESQUIRE] (1593) **:** any of various old French units of value; *also* **:** a coin representing this

ec·u·men·i·cal \,ek-yə-'men-i-kəl\ *adj* [LL *oecumenicus,* fr. LGk *oikoumenikos,* fr. Gk *oikoumenē* the inhabited world, fr. fem. of *oikoumenos,* pres. pass. part. of *oikein* to inhabit, fr. *oikos* house — more at VICINITY] (1563) **1 :** worldwide or general in extent, influence, or application **2 a :** of, relating to, or representing the whole of a body of churches **b :** promoting or tending toward worldwide Christian unity or cooperation — **ec·u·men·i·cal·ly** \-k(ə-)lē\ *adv*

ec·u·men·i·cal·ism \-'men-i-kə-,liz-əm\ *n* (1888) **:** ECUMENISM

ecumenical patriarch *n* (1862) **:** the patriarch of Constantinople as the dignitary given first honor in the Eastern Orthodox Church

ec·u·men·i·cism \,ek-yə-'men-ə-,siz-əm\ *n* (1961) **:** ECUMENISM — **ec·u·men·i·cist** \-səst\ *n*

ec·u·me·nic·i·ty \,ek-yə-mə-'nis-ət-ē, -me-\ *n* (1840) **:** the quality or state of being drawn close to others esp. through Christian ecumenical feeling or action

ec·u·men·ics \-'men-iks\ *n pl but sing in constr* (ca. 1937) **:** the study of the nature, mission, problems, and strategy of the Christian church from the perspective of its ecumenical character

ecu·me·nism \e-'kyü-mə-,niz-əm, i- *also* 'ek-yə-mə-,niz- *or* ,ek-yə-'men-,iz-\ *n* (1948) **:** ecumenical principles and practices esp. as shown among religious groups (as Christian denominations) — **ecu·me·nist** \e-'kyü-mə-nəst, i- *also* 'ek-yə-mə-nəst *or* ,ek-yə-'men-əst\ *n*

ec·ze·ma \ig-'zē-mə, 'eg-zə-mə, 'ek-sə-\ *n* [NL, fr. Gk *ekzema,* fr. *ekzein* to erupt, fr. *ex-* out + *zein* to boil — more at EX-, YEAST] (ca. 1753) **:** an inflammatory condition of the skin characterized by redness, itching, and oozing vesicular lesions which become scaly, crusted, or hardened — **ec·zem·a·tous** \ig-'zem-ət-əs\ *adj*

1**-ed** \d *after a vowel or* b, g, j, l, m, n, ŋ, r, t͟h, v, z, zh; əd, id *after* d, t; t *after other sounds; exceptions are pronounced at their entries*\ *vb suffix or*

\ə\ abut \ᵊ\ kitten, F table \ər\ further \a\ ash \ā\ ace \ä\ cot, cart \au̇\ out \ch\ chin \e\ bet \ē\ easy \g\ go \i\ hit \ī\ ice \j\ job \ŋ\ sing \ō\ go \ȯ\ law \ȯi\ boy \th\ thin \t͟h\ the \ü\ loot \u̇\ foot \y\ yet \zh\ vision \à, k̲, ⁿ, œ, œ̄, ue, ᵫ, ʸ\ *see* Guide to Pronunciation

adj suffix [ME, fr. OE *-ed, -od, -ad;* akin to OHG *-t,* pp. ending, L *-tus,* Gk *-tos,* suffix forming verbals] **1** — used to form the past participle of regular weak verbs ⟨end*ed*⟩ ⟨fad*ed*⟩ ⟨tri*ed*⟩ ⟨patt*ed*⟩ **2** — used to form adjectives of identical meaning from Latin-derived adjectives ending in *-ate* ⟨crenulat*ed*⟩ **3 a :** having : characterized by ⟨cultur*ed*⟩ ⟨two-legg*ed*⟩ **b :** having the characteristics of ⟨bigot*ed*⟩

²-ed *vb suffix* [ME *-ede, -de,* fr. OE *-de, -ede, -ode, -ade;* akin to OHG *-ta,* past ending (1st sing.) and prob. to OHG *-t,* pp. ending] — used to form the past tense of regular weak verbs ⟨judg*ed*⟩ ⟨deni*ed*⟩ ⟨dropp*ed*⟩

eda·cious \i-ˈdā-shəs\ *adj* [L *edac-, edax,* fr. *edere* to eat — more at EAT] (ca. 1798) **1** *archaic* **:** of or relating to eating **2 :** VORACIOUS — **edac·i·ty** \-ˈdas-ət-ē\ *n*

Edam \ˈēd-əm, ˈē-ˌdam\ *n* [*Edam,* Netherlands] (1836) **:** a yellow pressed cheese of Dutch origin usu. made in flattened balls and often coated with red wax

edaph·ic \i-ˈdaf-ik\ *adj* [Gk *edaphos* bottom, ground] (ca. 1900) **1 :** of or relating to the soil **2 :** resulting from or influenced by the soil rather than the climate — compare CLIMATIC 2 — **edaph·i·cal·ly** \-ˈdaf-i-k(ə-)lē\ *adv*

edaphic climax *n* (ca. 1934) **:** an ecological climax resulting from soil factors and commonly persisting through cycles of climatic and physiographic change — compare CLIMATIC CLIMAX

Ed·dic \ˈed-ik\ *adj* [ON *Edda,* a 13th cent. collection of mythological, heroic, and aphoristic poetry, prob. fr. *edda* great-grandmother] (1890) **:** of, relating to, or resembling the Old Norse *Edda*

¹ed·dy \ˈed-ē\ *n, pl* **eddies** [ME (Sc dial.) *ydy,* prob. fr. ON *itha*] (15c) **1 a :** a current of water or air running contrary to the main current; *esp* **:** a small whirlpool **b :** something moving similarly ⟨little *eddies* of people were dancing with each other in the streets —L. C. Stevens⟩ **2 :** a contrary or circular current (as of thought or policy)

²eddy *vb* **ed·died; ed·dy·ing** *vt* (1810) **:** to cause to move in an eddy **~** *vi* **:** to move in an eddy or in the manner of an eddy

eddy current *n* (1887) **:** an electric current induced by an alternating magnetic field

edel·weiss \ˈād-ᵊl-ˌwīs, -ˌvīs\ *n* [G, fr. *edel* noble (fr. OHG *adal*) + *weiss* white — more at ATHELING] (1862) **:** a small perennial composite herb (*Leontopodium alpinum*) having a dense woolly white pubescence and growing high in the Alps

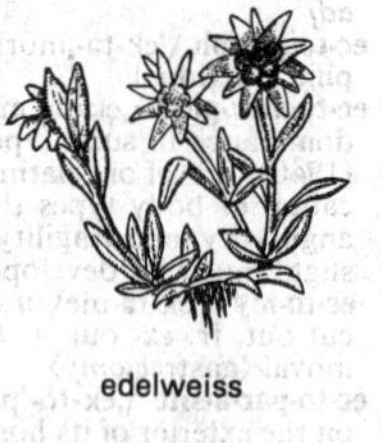

edelweiss

ede·ma \i-ˈdē-mə\ *n* [NL, fr. Gk *oidēma* swelling, fr. *oidein* to swell; akin to OE *ātor* poison, venom] (15c) **1 :** an abnormal excess accumulation of serous fluid in connective tissue or in a serous cavity — called also *dropsy* **2 a :** watery swelling of plant organs or parts **b :** any of various plant diseases characterized by such swellings — **edem·a·tous** \-ˈdem-ət-əs\ *adj*

Eden \ˈēd-ᵊn\ *n* [LL, fr. Heb *ʽĒdhen*] (13c) **1 :** PARADISE 2 **2 :** the garden where according to the account in Genesis Adam and Eve first lived — **Eden·ic** \i-ˈden-ik\ *adj*

¹eden·tate \(ˈ)ē-ˈden-ˌtāt\ *adj* [L *edentatus,* pp. of *edentare* to make toothless, fr. *e-* + *dent-, dens* tooth — more at TOOTH] (1828) **1 :** lacking teeth **2 :** being an edentate

²edentate *n* (1835) **:** any of an order (Edentata) of mammals having few or no teeth and including the sloths, armadillos, and New World anteaters and formerly also the pangolins and the aardvark

eden·tu·lous \(ˈ)ē-ˈden-chə-ləs\ *adj* [L *edentulus,* fr. *e-* + *dent-, dens*] (1782) **:** TOOTHLESS

Ed·gar \ˈed-gər\ *n* [*Edgar* Allan Poe, regarded as father of the detective story] (1947) **:** a statuette awarded annually by a professional organization for notable achievement in mystery-novel writing

¹edge \ˈej\ *n* [ME *egge,* fr. OE *ecg;* akin to L *acer* sharp, Gk *akmē* point] (bef. 12c) **1 a :** the cutting side of a blade **b :** the sharpness of a blade **c :** penetrating power **:** KEENNESS ⟨took the ~ off the proposal⟩ **d :** a noticeably harsh or sharp quality ⟨his voice had an ~ to it⟩ **2 a :** the line where an object or area begins or ends **:** BORDER ⟨the town stands on the ~ of a plain⟩ **b :** the narrow part adjacent to a border ⟨walk on the ~ of the deck⟩ **c :** a point near the beginning or the end; *esp* **:** BRINK, VERGE ⟨on the ~ of disaster⟩ **d :** a favorable margin **:** ADVANTAGE ⟨a competitive ~⟩ **3 :** a line or line segment that is the intersection of two plane faces (as of a pyramid) or of two planes — **edge·less** *adj* — **on edge :** ANXIOUS, NERVOUS

²edge *vb* **edged; edg·ing** *vt* (bef. 12c) **1 a :** to give an edge to **b :** to be on an edge of ⟨trees *edging* the lake⟩ **2 :** to move or force gradually ⟨*edged* him off the road⟩ **3 :** to incline (a ski) sideways so that one edge cuts into the snow **4 :** to defeat by a small margin — often used with *out* ⟨*edged* out her opponent by one point⟩ **~** *vi* **:** to advance by short moves ⟨the climbers *edged* along the cliff⟩

edged \ˈejd\ *adj* (14c) **1 :** having a specified kind of edge, boundary, or border or a specified number of edges ⟨rough-*edged*⟩ ⟨two-*edged*⟩ **2 :** SHARP, CUTTING ⟨an ~ knife⟩ ⟨an ~ remark⟩

edge effect *n* (1933) **:** the result of the presence of two adjoining plant communities (as in an ecotone) on the numbers and kinds of animals present in the immediate vicinity

edge–grain \ˌej-ˌgrān\ *or* **edge–grained** \ˈej-ˈgrānd\ *adj* (1906) **:** QUARTERSAWED

edge in *vt* (1683) **:** to work in **:** INTERPOLATE ⟨*edged in* a few remarks⟩

edg·er \ˈej-ər\ *n* (1591) **:** one that edges; *esp* **:** a tool used to trim the edge of a lawn along a sidewalk or curb

edge tool *n* (14c) **:** a tool with a sharp cutting edge

edge·ways \ˈej-ˌwāz\ *adv* (1566) **:** SIDEWAYS

edge·wise \-ˌwīz\ *adv* (1715) **:** EDGEWAYS

edg·ing *n* (1558) **:** something that forms an edge or border

edgy \ˈej-ē\ *adj* **edg·i·er; -est** (1775) **1 :** having an edge **:** SHARP ⟨displayed a perceptive, ~ wit —*New Yorker*⟩ **2 :** being on edge **:** TENSE, IRRITABLE — **edg·i·ly** \ˈej-ə-lē\ *adv* — **edg·i·ness** \ˈej-ē-nəs\ *n*

edh \ˈeth\ *n* [Icel *eth*] (ca. 1864) **:** the letter ð used in Old English and in Icelandic to represent either of the fricatives \th\ or \t͟h\ and in some phonetic alphabets to represent the fricative \t͟h\

ed·i·ble \ˈed-ə-bəl\ *adj* [LL *edibilis,* fr. L *edere* to eat — more at EAT] (1611) **:** fit to be eaten **:** EATABLE — **ed·i·bil·i·ty** \ˌed-ə-ˈbil-ət-ē\ *n* — **edible** *n* — **ed·i·ble·ness** \ˈed-ə-bəl-nəs\ *n*

edict \ˈē-ˌdikt\ *n* [L *edictum,* fr. neut. of *edictus,* pp. of *edicere* to decree, fr. *e-* + *dicere* to say — more at DICTION] (13c) **1 :** an official public proclamation having the force of law **2 :** ORDER, COMMAND ⟨we held firm to Grandmother's ~ —M. F. K. Fisher⟩ — **edic·tal** \i-ˈdik-tᵊl\ *adj*

ed·i·fi·ca·tion \ˌed-ə-fə-ˈkā-shən\ *n* (14c) **:** an act or process of edifying

edif·i·ca·to·ry \i-ˈdif-ə-kə-ˌtōr-ē, -ˌtȯr-\ *adj* (1649) **:** intended or suitable for edification

ed·i·fice \ˈed-ə-fəs\ *n* [ME, fr. MF, fr. L *aedificium,* fr. *aedificare*] (14c) **1 :** BUILDING; *esp* **:** a large or massive structure **2 :** a large abstract structure ⟨the keystone which holds together the social ~ —R. H. Tawney⟩

ed·i·fy \ˈed-ə-ˌfī\ *vt* **-fied; -fy·ing** [ME *edifien,* fr. MF *edifier,* fr. LL & L; LL *aedificare* to instruct or improve spiritually, fr. L, to erect a house, fr. *aedes* temple, house; akin to OE *ād* funeral pyre, L *aestas* summer] (14c) **1** *archaic* **a :** BUILD **b :** ESTABLISH **2 :** to instruct and improve esp. in moral and religious knowledge **:** ENLIGHTEN

¹ed·it \ˈed-ət\ *vt* (1791) **1 a :** to prepare (as literary material) for publication or public presentation ⟨~*ed* Poe's works⟩ **b :** to assemble (as a moving picture or tape recording) by cutting and rearranging **c :** to alter, adapt, or refine esp. to bring about conformity to a standard or to suit a particular purpose ⟨carefully ~*ed* his speech⟩ **2 :** to direct the publication of ⟨~*s* the daily newspaper⟩ **3 :** DELETE — usu. used with *out* — **ed·it·able** \-ə-bəl\ *adj*

²edit *n* (1955) **:** an instance of editing

edi·tion \i-ˈdish-ən\ *n* [MF, fr. L *edition-, editio* publication, edition, fr. *editus,* pp. of *edere* to bring forth, publish, fr. *e-* + *-dere* to put or *-dere* (fr. *dare* to give) — more at DO, DATE] (1555) **1 a :** the form or version in which a text is published ⟨a paperback ~⟩ ⟨the German ~⟩ **b** (1) **:** the whole number of copies published at one time (2) **:** a usu. special issue of a newspaper (as for a particular day or purpose) ⟨Sunday ~⟩ ⟨international ~⟩ (3) **:** one of the usu. several issues of a newspaper in a single day ⟨city ~⟩ ⟨late ~⟩ **2 a :** one of the forms in which something is presented ⟨this year's ~ of the annual charity ball⟩ **b :** the whole number of articles of one style put out at one time ⟨a limited ~ of collectors' pieces⟩ **3 :** COPY, VERSION

edi·tio prin·ceps \ā-ˌdit-ē-(ˌ)ō-ˈpriŋ-ˌkeps, i-ˌdish-ē-(ˌ)ō-ˈprin-ˌseps\ *n, pl* **edi·ti·o·nes prin·ci·pes** \ā-ˌdit-ē-ˈō-ˌnās-ˈpriŋ-kə-ˌpās, i-ˌdish-ē-ˈō-(ˌ)nēz-ˈprin(t)-sə-ˌpēz\ [NL, lit., first edition] (1802) **:** the first printed edition esp. of a work that circulated in manuscript before printing became common

ed·i·tor \ˈed-ət-ər\ *n* (1649) **1 :** one that edits esp. as an occupation **2 :** a device used in editing motion-picture film or magnetic tape **3 :** a computer program that permits the user to create or change a program in a computer system — **ed·i·tor·ship** \-ˌship\ *n*

¹ed·i·to·ri·al \ˌed-ə-ˈtōr-ē-əl, -ˈtȯr-\ *adj* (1744) **1 :** of or relating to an editor or editing ⟨an ~ office⟩ **2 :** being or resembling an editorial ⟨an ~ statement⟩ — **ed·i·to·ri·al·ly** \-ē-ə-lē\ *adv*

²editorial *n* (1830) **:** a newspaper or magazine article that gives the opinions of the editors or publishers; *also* **:** an expression of opinion that resembles such an article ⟨a television ~⟩

ed·i·to·ri·al·ist \-ē-ə-ləst\ *n* (1901) **:** a writer of editorials

ed·i·to·ri·al·ize \ˌed-ə-ˈtōr-ē-ə-ˌlīz, -ˈtȯr-\ *vi* **-ized; -iz·ing** (1856) **1 :** to express an opinion in the form of an editorial **2 :** to introduce opinion into the reporting of facts **3 :** to express an opinion (as on a controversial issue) — **ed·i·to·ri·al·iza·tion** \-ˌtōr-ē-ə-lə-ˈzā-shən, -ˌtȯr-\ *n* — **ed·i·to·ri·al·iz·er** *n*

editor in chief *n* (1873) **:** an editor who heads an editorial staff

Edom·ite \ˈēd-ə-ˌmīt\ *n* [*Edom* (Esau), ancestor of the Edomites] (14c) **:** a member of a Semitic people living south of the Dead sea in biblical times

EDTA \ˌē-ˌdē-ˌtē-ˈā\ *n* [*e*thylene*d*iamine*t*etra*a*cetic acid] (1954) **:** a white crystalline acid $C_{10}H_{16}N_2O_8$ used esp. as a chelating agent and in medicine as an anticoagulant and in the treatment of lead poisoning

ed·u·ca·ble \ˈej-ə-kə-bəl\ *adj* (1845) **:** capable of being educated; *specif* **:** capable of some degree of learning — **ed·u·ca·bil·i·ty** \ˌej-ə-kə-ˈbil-ət-ē\ *n*

ed·u·cate \ˈej-ə-ˌkāt\ *vb* **-cat·ed; -cat·ing** [ME *educaten* to rear, fr. L *educatus,* pp. of *educare* to rear, educate, fr. *educere* to lead forth — more at EDUCE] *vt* (15c) **1 a :** to provide schooling for **b :** to train by formal instruction and supervised practice esp. in a skill, trade, or profession **2 :** to develop mentally, morally, or aesthetically esp. by instruction **3 :** to persuade or condition to feel, believe, or act in a desired way or to accept something as desirable ⟨~ the public to support our position⟩ **~** *vi* **:** to educate a person or thing ***syn*** see TEACH

ed·u·cat·ed *adj* (1670) **1 :** having an education; *esp* **:** having an education beyond the average **2 a :** giving evidence of training or practice **:** SKILLED **b :** befitting one that is educated ⟨~ conversation⟩ **c :** based on some knowledge of fact ⟨an ~ guess⟩ — **ed·u·cat·ed·ness** *n*

ed·u·ca·tion \ˌej-ə-ˈkā-shən\ *n* (1531) **1 a :** the action or process of educating or of being educated; *also* **:** a stage of such a process **b :** the knowledge and development resulting from an educational process ⟨a man of little ~⟩ **2 :** the field of study that deals mainly with methods of teaching and learning in schools — **ed·u·ca·tion·al** \-shnəl, -shən-ᵊl\ *adj* — **ed·u·ca·tion·al·ly** \-ē\ *adv*

educational psychology *n* (1911) **:** psychology concerned with human maturation, school learning, teaching methods, guidance, and evaluation of aptitude and progress by standardized tests — **educational psychologist** *n*

educational television *n* (1951) **1 :** television that provides instruction esp. for students and sometimes by closed circuit **2 :** PUBLIC TELEVISION

ed·u·ca·tion·ese \ˌej-ə-ˌkā-shə-ˈnēz, -ˈnēs\ *n* (1954) **:** the jargonistic language used esp. by educational theorists

ed·u·ca·tion·ist \ˌej-ə-ˈkā-sh(ə-)nəst\ *also* **ed·u·ca·tion·al·ist** \-shnə-ləst, -shən-ᵊl-əst\ *n* (1829) **1** *chiefly Brit* **:** a professional educator **2 :** an educational theorist

ed·u·ca·tive \ˈej-ə-ˌkāt-iv\ *adj* (1856) **1 :** tending to educate **:** INSTRUCTIVE **2 :** of or relating to education

ed·u·ca·tor \ˈej-ə-ˌkāt-ər\ *n* (1673) **1 :** one skilled in teaching **:** TEACHER **2 a :** a student of the theory and practice of education **:** EDUCATIONIST 2 **b :** an administrator in education

educe \i-ˈd(y)üs\ *vt* **educed; educ·ing** [L *educere* to draw out, fr. *e-* + *ducere* to lead — more at TOW] (1603) **1 :** to bring out (as something latent) **2 :** DEDUCE — **educ·ible** \-ˈd(y)ü-sə-bəl\ *adj* — **educ·tion** \-ˈdək-shən\ *n*

syn EDUCE, EVOKE, ELICIT, EXTRACT, EXTORT mean to draw out something hidden, latent, or reserved. EDUCE implies the bringing out of something potential or latent; EVOKE implies a strong stimulus that arouses an emotion or an interest or recalls an image or memory; ELICIT usu. implies some effort or skill in drawing forth a response; EXTRACT implies the use of force or pressure in obtaining answers or information; EXTORT suggests a wringing or wresting from one who resists strongly.

educ·tor \i-ˈdək-tər\ *n* [LL, one that leads out, fr. L *eductus,* pp. of *educere*] (1794) **1 :** one that educes; *specif* **:** EJECTOR 2 **2 :** a device similar to an ejector for mixing two fluids

edul·co·rate \i-ˈdəl-kə-ˌrāt\ *vb* **-rat·ed; -rat·ing** [NL *edulcoratus,* pp. of *edulcorare,* fr. L *e-* + *dulcor* sweetness, fr. *dulcis* sweet — more at DULCET] *vt* (1660) **:** to free from harshness (as of attitude) **:** make pleasant

Ed·war·di·an \e-ˈdwär-dē-ən, -ˈdwȯrd-\ *adj* (1908) **:** of, relating to, or characteristic of Edward VII of England or his age: as **a :** characterized by opulence and a complacent sense of material security **b** *of clothing* **:** marked by the hourglass silhouette for women and long narrow fitted suits for men — **Edwardian** *n*

[1]-ee \ˈē, ˌē, ē\ *n suffix* [ME *-e,* fr. MF *-é,* fr. *-é,* pp. ending, fr. L *-atus*] **1 :** recipient or beneficiary of (a specified action) ⟨appoint*ee*⟩ ⟨grant*ee*⟩ **2 :** person furnished with (a specified thing) ⟨patent*ee*⟩ **3 :** person that performs (a specified action) ⟨escap*ee*⟩

[2]-ee *n suffix* [prob. alter. of *-y*] **1 :** one associated with ⟨barg*ee*⟩ **2 :** a particular esp. small kind of ⟨boot*ee*⟩ **3 :** one resembling or suggestive of ⟨goat*ee*⟩

eel \ˈē(ə)l\ *n* [ME *ele,* fr. OE *ǣl;* akin to OHG *āl* eel] (bef. 12c) **1 a :** any of numerous voracious elongate snakelike teleost fishes (order Apodes) that have a smooth slimy skin, lack pelvic fins, and have the median fins confluent around the tail **b :** any of numerous other elongate fishes (as of the order Symbranchii) **2 :** any of various nematodes — **eel·like** \ˈē(ə)l-ˌlīk\ *adj* — **eely** \ˈē-lē\ *adj*

eel·grass \ˈē(ə)l-ˌgras\ *n* (1790) **1 :** a submerged marine plant (*Zostera marina*) that has very long narrow leaves, is abundant along the No. Atlantic coast, and with related forms constitutes a monocotyledonous family (Zosteraceae, the eelgrass family) **2 :** TAPE GRASS

eel·pout \-ˌpau̇t\ *n* (bef. 12c) **1 :** any of various marine fishes resembling blennies (family Zoarcidae) **2 :** BURBOT

eel·worm \-ˌwərm\ *n* (1888) **:** a nematode worm; *esp* **:** any of various small free-living or plant-parasitic roundworms

-een \ˈēn\ *n suffix* [prob. fr. *ratteen*] **:** inferior fabric resembling (a specified fabric) **:** imitation ⟨velvet*een*⟩

e'en \(ˈ)ēn\ *adv* (13c) **:** EVEN

-eer \ˈi(ə)r\ *n suffix* [MF *-ier,* fr. L *-arius* — more at -ARY] **:** one that is concerned with professionally, conducts, or produces ⟨auction*eer*⟩ ⟨pamphlet*eer*⟩ — often in words with derogatory meaning ⟨profit*eer*⟩

e'er \(ˈ)e(ə)r, (ˈ)a(ə)r\ *adv* (1597) **:** EVER

ee·rie *also* **ee·ry** \ˈi(ə)r-ē\ *adj* **ee·ri·er; -est** [ME *eri,* fr. OE *earg* cowardly, wretched; akin to OHG *arg* cowardly, Gk *orcheisthai* to dance, shake, Skt *ṛghāyati* he shakes] (bef. 12c) **1** *chiefly Scot* **:** affected with fright **:** SCARED **2 a :** frightening because of strangeness or gloominess **b :** notably strange and mysterious **:** BAFFLING ⟨the *eeriest* mystery in modern court records — a persistent riddle —*Life*⟩ ***syn*** see WEIRD — **ee·ri·ly** \ˈir-ə-lē\ *adv* — **ee·ri·ness** \ˈir-ē-nəs\ *n*

ef \ˈef\ *n* (bef. 12c) **:** the letter *f*

ef·face \i-ˈfās, e-\ *vt* **ef·faced; ef·fac·ing** [ME, fr. MF *effacer,* fr. OF *esfacier,* fr. *e-* + *face* face] (15c) **1 :** to eliminate or make indistinct by or as if by wearing away a surface ⟨coins with dates *effaced* by wear⟩ ⟨regrowth has *effaced* the worst scars from the fire⟩ **2 :** to make (oneself) modestly or shyly inconspicuous — **ef·face·able** \-ˈfā-sə-bəl\ *adj* — **ef·face·ment** \-ˈfā-smənt\ *n* — **ef·fac·er** *n*

[1]ef·fect \i-ˈfekt\ *n* [ME, fr. MF & L; MF, fr. L *effectus,* fr. *effectus,* pp. of *efficere* to bring about, fr. *ex-* + *facere* to make, do — more at DO] (14c) **1 :** something that inevitably follows an antecedent (as a cause or agent) **2 a :** PURPORT, INTENT **b :** basic meaning **:** ESSENCE **3 :** an outward sign **:** APPEARANCE **4 :** ACCOMPLISHMENT, FULFILLMENT **5 :** power to bring about a result **:** INFLUENCE ⟨the content itself of television . . . is therefore less important than its ~ —*Current Biog.*⟩ **6** *pl* **:** movable property **:** GOODS ⟨personal ~*s*⟩ **7 a :** a distinctive impression ⟨the color gives the ~ of being warm⟩ **b :** the creation of a desired impression ⟨her tears were purely for ~⟩ **c :** something designed to produce a distinctive or desired impression ⟨special lighting ~*s*⟩ **8 :** the quality or state of being operative **:** OPERATION ⟨the law goes into ~ next week⟩

syn EFFECT, CONSEQUENCE, RESULT, EVENT, ISSUE, OUTCOME mean a condition or occurrence traceable to a cause. EFFECT designates something that necessarily and directly follows or occurs by reason of a cause; CONSEQUENCE implies a looser or remoter connection with a cause and usu. implies that the cause is no longer operating; RESULT applies often to the last in a series of effects; an EVENT is a result that cannot be foreseen or is at least partly determined by conditions beyond human control; an ISSUE is often a result that ends or solves a difficulty; an OUTCOME is the final result of complex or conflicting causes or forces.

— **in effect :** in substance **:** VIRTUALLY ⟨the . . . committee agreed to what was *in effect* a reduction in the hourly wage —*Current Biog.*⟩ — **to the effect :** with the meaning ⟨issued a statement *to the effect* that he would resign⟩

[2]effect *vt* (1589) **1 :** to cause to come into being **2 a :** to bring about often by surmounting obstacles **:** ACCOMPLISH ⟨~ a settlement of a dispute⟩ **b :** to put into effect ⟨the duty of the legislature to ~ the will of the citizens⟩ ***syn*** see PERFORM

usage The confusion of the verbs *affect* and *effect* is not only quite common but has a long history. *Effect* was used in place of [3]*affect* as early as 1494 and in place of [2]*affect* as early as 1652. If you think you want to use the verb *effect* but are not certain, check the definitions in this dictionary. The noun *affect* is sometimes mistakenly used for *effect.* Except when your topic is psychology, you will seldom need the noun *affect.*

[1]ef·fec·tive \i-ˈfek-tiv\ *adj* (14c) **1 a :** producing a decided, decisive, or desired effect **b :** IMPRESSIVE, STRIKING ⟨a gold lamé fabric studded with ~ . . . precious stones —Stanley Marcus⟩ **2 :** ready for service or action ⟨~ manpower⟩ **3 :** ACTUAL ⟨the need to increase ~ demand for goods⟩ **4 :** being in effect **:** OPERATIVE ⟨the tax becomes ~ next year⟩ **5** *of a rate of interest* **:** equal to the rate of simple interest that yields the same increase in one monetary unit when the interest is paid once at the end of the interest period as a quoted rate of interest does when calculated at compound interest over the same period — compare NOMINAL 4 — **ef·fec·tive·ly** *adv* — **ef·fec·tive·ness** *n* — **ef·fec·tiv·i·ty** \ˌef-ˌek-ˈtiv-ət-ē, i-ˌfek-\ *n*

syn EFFECTIVE, EFFECTUAL, EFFICIENT, EFFICACIOUS mean producing or capable of producing a result. EFFECTIVE stresses the actual production of or the power to produce an effect ⟨an *effective* rebuttal⟩ EFFECTUAL suggests the accomplishment of a desired result esp. as viewed after the fact ⟨the measures to halt crime proved *effectual*⟩ EFFICIENT suggests an acting or a potential for action or use in such a way as to avoid loss or waste of energy in effecting, producing, or functioning ⟨an *efficient* small car⟩ EFFICACIOUS suggests possession of a special quality or virtue that gives effective power ⟨a detergent that is *efficacious* in removing grease⟩

[2]effective *n* (1610) **:** one that is effective; *esp* **:** a soldier equipped for duty

ef·fec·tor \i-ˈfek-tər, -ˌtȯ(ə)r\ *n* (1906) **1 :** a bodily organ (as a gland or muscle) that becomes active in response to stimulation **2 :** a substance that induces protein synthesis by combining allosterically with a genetic repressor

ef·fec·tu·al \i-ˈfek-chə(-wə)l, -ˈfeksh-wəl\ *adj* (14c) **:** producing or able to produce a desired effect ***syn*** see EFFECTIVE — **ef·fec·tu·al·i·ty** \-ˌfek-chə-ˈwal-ət-ē\ *n* — **ef·fec·tu·al·ness** \-ˈfek-chə(-wə)l-nəs, -ˈfeksh-wəl-\ *n*

ef·fec·tu·al·ly \i-ˈfek-chə(-wə)-lē, -ˈfeksh-wə-\ *adv* (14c) **1 :** in an effectual manner **2 :** with great effect **:** COMPLETELY

ef·fec·tu·ate \i-ˈfek-chə-ˌwāt\ *vt* **-at·ed; -at·ing** (1580) **:** EFFECT 2 — **ef·fec·tu·a·tion** \-ˌfek-chə-ˈwā-shən\ *n*

ef·fem·i·na·cy \ə-ˈfem-ə-nə-sē\ *n* (1602) **:** the quality of being effeminate

[1]ef·fem·i·nate \-nət\ *adj* [ME, fr. L *effeminatus,* fr. pp. of *effeminare* to make effeminate, fr. *ex-* + *femina* woman — more at FEMININE] (15c) **1 :** having feminine qualities untypical of a man **:** not manly in appearance or manner **2 :** marked by an unbecoming delicacy or overrefinement ⟨~ art⟩ ⟨an ~ civilization⟩

[2]effeminate *n* (1597) **:** an effeminate person

ef·fen·di \e-ˈfen-dē, ə-\ *n* [Turk *efendi* master, fr. NGk *aphentēs,* alter. of Gk *authentēs* — more at AUTHENTIC] (1614) **:** a man of property, authority, or education in an eastern Mediterranean country

ef·fer·ent \ˈef-ə-rənt; ˈef-ˌer-ənt, ˈē-ˌfer-\ *adj* [F *efférent,* fr. L *efferent-, efferens,* prp. of *efferre* to carry outward, fr. *ex-* + *ferre* to carry — more at BEAR] (1856) **:** conducting outward from a part or organ; *specif* **:** conveying nervous impulses to an effector — compare AFFERENT — **efferent** *n* — **ef·fer·ent·ly** *adv*

ef·fer·vesce \ˌef-ər-ˈves\ *vi* **-vesced; -vesc·ing** [L *effervescere,* fr. *ex-* + *fervescere* to begin to boil, incho. of *fervēre* to boil — more at BURN] (1702) **1 :** to bubble, hiss, and foam as gas escapes **2 :** to show liveliness or exhilaration — **ef·fer·ves·cence** \-ˈves-ᵊn(t)s\ *n* — **ef·fer·ves·cent** \-ᵊnt\ *adj* — **ef·fer·ves·cent·ly** *adv*

ef·fete \e-ˈfēt, i-\ *adj* [L *effetus,* fr. *ex-* + *fetus* fruitful — more at FEMININE] (1660) **1 :** no longer fertile **2 a :** worn out with age **:** EXHAUSTED **b :** marked by weakness or decadence **c :** OUTMODED ⟨an old but by no means ~ statute —Edward Jenks⟩ **3 :** EFFEMINATE ⟨a good-humored, ~ boy brought up by maiden aunts —Herman Wouk⟩ — **ef·fete·ly** *adv* — **ef·fete·ness** *n*

ef·fi·ca·cious \ˌef-ə-ˈkā-shəs\ *adj* [L *efficac-, efficax,* fr. *efficere*] (1528) **:** having the power to produce a desired effect ***syn*** see EFFECTIVE — **ef·fi·ca·cious·ly** *adv* — **ef·fi·ca·cious·ness** *n*

ef·fi·cac·i·ty \ˌef-ə-ˈkas-ət-ē\ *n* (15c) **:** EFFICACY

ef·fi·ca·cy \ˈef-i-kə-sē\ *n, pl* **-cies** (13c) **:** the power to produce an effect

ef·fi·cien·cy \i-ˈfish-ən-sē\ *n, pl* **-cies** (1633) **1 :** the quality or degree of being efficient **2 a :** efficient operation **b (1) :** effective operation as measured by a comparison of production with cost (as in energy, time, and money) **(2) :** the ratio of the useful energy delivered by a dynamic system to the energy supplied to it **3 :** EFFICIENCY APARTMENT

efficiency apartment *n* (1930) **:** a small usu. furnished apartment with minimal kitchen and bath facilities

efficiency engineer *n* (1913) **:** one who analyzes methods, procedures, and jobs in order to secure maximum efficiency — called also *efficiency expert*

ef·fi·cient \i-ˈfish-ənt\ *adj* [ME, fr. MF or L; MF, fr. L *efficient-, efficiens,* fr. prp. of *efficere* to bring about — more at EFFECT] (14c) **1 :** being or involving the immediate agent in producing an effect ⟨the ~ action of heat in changing water to steam⟩ **2 :** productive of desired effects; *esp* **:** productive without waste ***syn*** see EFFECTIVE — **ef·fi·cient·ly** *adv*

ef·fi·gy \ˈef-ə-jē\ *n, pl* **-gies** [MF *effigie,* fr. L *effigies,* fr. *effingere* to form, fr. *ex-* + *fingere* to shape — more at DOUGH] (1539) **:** an image or representation esp. of a person; *specif* **:** a crude figure representing a hated person — **in effigy :** publicly in the form of an effigy ⟨the football coach was burned *in effigy*⟩

ef·flo·resce \ˌef-lə-ˈres\ *vi* **-resced; -resc·ing** [L *efflorescere,* fr. *ex-* + *florescere* to begin to blossom — more at FLORESCENCE] (1775) **1 :** to burst forth **:** BLOOM **2 a :** to change to a powder from loss of water of crystallization **b :** to form or become covered with a powdery crust ⟨bricks may ~ owing to the deposition of soluble salts⟩

ef·flo·res·cence \-ˈres-ᵊn(t)s\ *n* (1626) **1 :** the period or state of flowering **2 a :** the action or process of developing and unfolding as if coming into flower **:** BLOSSOMING ⟨periods of . . . intellectual and artistic ~ —Julian Huxley⟩ **b :** an instance of such development **c :** fullness of manifestation **:** CULMINATION **3 :** the process or product of efflorescing chemically **4 :** a redness of the skin **:** ERUPTION — **ef·flo·res·cent** \-ᵊnt\ *adj*

ef•flu•ence \ˈef-ˌlü-ən(t)s; e-ˈflü-, ə-ˈ\ *n* (1603) **1** : something that flows out **2** : an action or process of flowing out

[1]**ef•flu•ent** \-ənt\ *adj* [L *effluent-, effluens,* prp. of *effluere* to flow out, fr. *ex-* + *fluere* to flow — more at FLUID] (1726) : flowing out : EMANATING, OUTGOING ⟨an ~ river⟩

[2]**effluent** *n* (1859) : something that flows out: as **a** : an outflowing branch of a main stream or lake **b** : waste material (as smoke, liquid industrial refuse, or sewage) discharged into the environment esp. when serving as a pollutant

ef•flu•vi•um \e-ˈflü-vē-əm\ *also* **ef•flu•via** \-vē-ə\ *n, pl* **-via** *or* **-vi•ums** [L *effluvium* act of flowing out, fr. *effluere*] (1646) **1** : an invisible emanation; *esp* : an offensive exhalation or smell **2** : a by-product esp. in the form of waste

ef•flux \ˈef-ˌləks\ *n* [L *effluxus,* pp. of *effluere*] (1641) **1** : EFFLUENCE **2** : a passing away : EXPIRATION — **ef•flux•ion** \e-ˈflək-shən\ *n*

ef•fort \ˈef-ərt, -ˌȯ(ə)rt\ *n* [ME, fr. MF, fr. OF *esfort,* fr. *esforcier* to force, fr. *ex-* + *forcier* to force] (15c) **1** : conscious exertion of power : hard work **2** : a serious attempt : TRY **3** : something produced by exertion or trying ⟨the novel was his most ambitious ~⟩ **4** : effective force as distinguished from the possible resistance called into action by such a force **5** : the total work done to achieve a particular end ⟨the war ~⟩

ef•fort•ful \-ərt-fəl\ *adj* (ca. 1895) : showing or requiring effort — **ef•fort•ful•ly** \-fə-lē\ *adv* — **ef•fort•ful•ness** \-fəl-nəs\ *n*

ef•fort•less \-ərt-ləs\ *adj* (1801) : showing or requiring little or no effort *syn* see EASY — **ef•fort•less•ly** *adv* — **ef•fort•less•ness** *n*

ef•fron•tery \i-ˈfrənt-ə-rē, e-\ *n, pl* **-ter•ies** [F *effronterie,* deriv. of LL *effront-, effrons* shameless, fr. L *ex-* + *front-, frons* forehead — more at BRINK] (1697) : shameless boldness : INSOLENCE ⟨the ~ to propound three such heresies —*Times Lit. Supp.*⟩ *syn* see TEMERITY

ef•ful•gence \i-ˈfu̇l-jən(t)s, e-, -ˈfəl-\ *n* [LL *effulgentia,* fr. L *effulgent-, effulgens,* prp. of *effulgēre* to shine forth, fr. *ex-* + *fulgēre* to shine — more at FULGENT] (1667) : radiant splendor : BRILLIANCE — **ef•ful•gent** \-jənt\ *adj*

[1]**ef•fuse** \i-ˈfyüz, e-\ *vb* **ef•fused; ef•fus•ing** [L *effusus,* pp. of *effundere,* fr. *ex-* + *fundere* to pour — more at FOUND] *vt* (1526) **1** : to pour out (a liquid) **2** : EMIT, RADIATE ~ *vi* : to flow out : EMANATE

[2]**ef•fuse** \-ˈfyüs\ *adj* (ca. 1530) **1** : poured out freely : OVERFLOWING **2** : DIFFUSE; *specif* : spread out flat without definite form ⟨~ lichens⟩

ef•fu•sion \i-ˈfyü-zhən, e-\ *n* (15c) **1** : an act of effusing **2** : unrestrained expression of words or feelings ⟨greeted her with great ~ —Olive H. Prouty⟩ **3 a** (1) : the escape of a fluid from anatomical vessels by rupture or exudation (2) : the flow of a gas through an aperture whose diameter is small as compared with the distance between the molecules of the gas **b** : the fluid that escapes

ef•fu•sive \i-ˈfyü-siv, e-, -ziv\ *adj* (1662) **1** *archaic* : pouring freely **2** : excessively demonstrative : GUSHING **3** : characterized or formed by a nonexplosive outpouring of lava ⟨~ rocks⟩ — **ef•fu•sive•ly** *adv* — **ef•fu•sive•ness** *n*

eft \ˈeft\ *n* [ME *evete, ewte,* fr. OE *efete*] (bef. 12c) : NEWT; *esp* : the terrestrial phase of a predominantly aquatic newt

eft•soons \eft-ˈsünz\ *adv* [ME *eftsones,* alter. of OE *eftsōna,* fr. OE *eft* after + *sōna* soon; akin to OE *æfter* after] *archaic* (bef. 12c) : soon after

egad \i-ˈgad\ *or* **egads** \-ˈgadz\ *interj* [prob. euphemism for *oh God*] (1673) — used as a mild oath

egal \ˈē-gəl\ *adj* [ME, fr. MF, fr. L *aequalis*] *obs* (14c) : EQUAL

egal•i•tar•i•an \i-ˌgal-ə-ˈter-ē-ən\ *adj* [F *égalitaire,* fr. *égalité* equality, fr. L *aequalitat-, aequalitas,* fr. *aequalis* equal] (1885) : asserting, promoting, or marked by egalitarianism — **egalitarian** *n*

egal•i•tar•i•an•ism \-ē-ə-ˌniz-əm\ *n* (1905) **1** : a belief in human equality esp. with respect to social, political, and economic rights and privileges **2** : a social philosophy advocating the removal of inequalities among people

éga•li•té \ā-gȧ-lē-tā\ *n* [F] (1794) : social or political equality

Eg•e•ria \i-ˈjir-ē-ə\ *n* [L, a nymph who advised the legendary Roman king Numa Pompilius] (1621) : a woman adviser or companion

eges•ta \i-ˈjes-tə\ *n pl* [NL, fr. L, neut. pl. of *egestus*] (1727) : something egested

eges•tion \i-ˈjes(h)-chən\ *n* [ME *egestioun,* fr. MF or L; MF *egestion,* fr. L *egestion-, egestio,* fr. *egestus,* pp. of *egerere* to carry outside, discharge, fr. *e-* + *gerere* to carry — more at CAST] (1670) : the act or process of discharging undigested or waste material from a cell or organism; *specif* : DEFECATION — **egest** \i-ˈjest\ *vt* — **eges•tive** \-ˈjes-tiv\ *adj*

[1]**egg** \ˈeg, ˈāg\ *vt* [ME *eggen,* fr. ON *eggja;* akin to OE *ecg* edge — more at EDGE] (13c) : to incite to action — usu. used with *on* ⟨~*ed* the mob on to riot⟩

[2]**egg** *n, often attrib* [ME *egge,* fr. ON *egg;* akin to OE *ǣg* egg, L *ovum,* Gk *ōion*] (14c) **1 a** : the hard-shelled reproductive body produced by a bird and esp. by domestic poultry **b** : an animal reproductive body consisting of an ovum together with its nutritive and protective envelopes and having the capacity to develop into a new individual capable of independent existence **c** : OVUM **2** : something resembling an egg **3** : PERSON ⟨he's a good ~⟩ — **egg•less** *adj* — **eggy** \-ē\ *adj* — **with egg on one's face** : in a state of embarrassment or humiliation

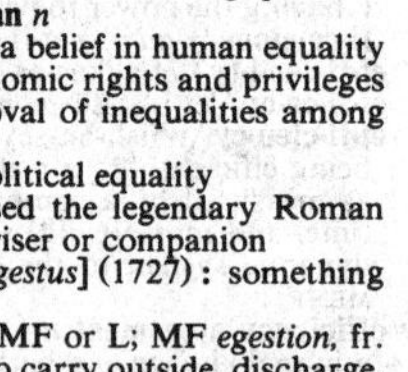

egg 1a: *1* shell, *2* shell membrane, *3* egg membrane, *4* air space, *5* chalaza, *6* albumen or white layers, *7* yolk layers, *8* blastodisc, *9* vitelline membrane

[3]**egg** *vt* (1833) **1** : to cover with egg **2** : to pelt with eggs

egg and dart *n* (ca. 1864) : a carved ornamental design in relief consisting of an egg-shaped figure alternating with a figure somewhat like an elongated javelin or arrowhead

egg•beat•er \ˈeg-ˌbēt-ər, ˈāg-\ *n* (1828) **1** : a hand-operated kitchen utensil used for beating, stirring, or whipping; *esp* : a rotary device for these purposes **2** : HELICOPTER

egg case *n* (1847) : a protective case enclosing eggs : OOTHECA — called also *egg capsule*

egg cell *n* (1880) : OVUM

egg cream *n* (1954) : a drink consisting of milk, a flavoring syrup, and soda water

egg•cup \ˈeg-ˌkəp, ˈāg-\ *n* (1833) : a cup for holding an egg that is to be eaten from the shell

egg•head \-ˌhed\ *n* (1952) : INTELLECTUAL, HIGHBROW ⟨practical men who disdain the schemes and dreams of ~*s* —W. L. Miller⟩

egg•head•ed \-ˈhed-əd\ *adj* (1950) : having the characteristics of an egghead — **egg•head•ed•ness** *n*

egg•nog \-ˌnäg\ *n* (1775) : a drink consisting of eggs beaten up with sugar, milk or cream, and often alcoholic liquor

egg•plant \-ˌplant\ *n* (1767) **1 a** : a widely cultivated perennial herb (*Solanum melongena*) yielding edible fruit **b** : the usu. smooth ovoid fruit of the eggplant **2** : a dark grayish or blackish purple

egg roll *n* (1941) : a thin egg-dough casing filled with minced vegetables and often bits of meat (as shrimp or chicken) and usu. fried in deep fat

eggs Ben•e•dict \-ˈben-ə-ˌdikt\ *n pl but sing or pl in constr* [prob. fr. the name *Benedict*] (1928) : poached eggs and broiled ham placed on toasted halves of English muffin and covered with hollandaise sauce

[1]**egg•shell** \ˈeg-ˌshel, ˈāg-\ *n* (14c) **1** : the hard exterior covering of an egg **2** : something resembling an eggshell esp. in fragility

[2]**eggshell** *adj* (1835) **1** : thin and fragile **2** : slightly glossy **3** : yellowish white

egg timer *n* (1884) : a small sandglass running about three minutes for timing the boiling of eggs

egg tooth *n* (1893) : a hard sharp prominence on the beak of an unhatched bird or the nose of an unhatched reptile that is used to break through the eggshell

egis \ˈē-jəs\ *var of* AEGIS

eg•lan•tine \ˈeg-lən-ˌtīn, -ˌtēn\ *n* [ME *eglentyn,* fr. MF *aiglent,* fr. (assumed) VL *aculentum,* fr. L *acus* needle; akin to L *acer* sharp — more at EDGE] (14c) : SWEETBRIER

ego \ˈē-(ˌ)gō *also* ˈeg-(ˌ)ō\ *n, pl* **egos** [NL, fr. L, I — more at I] (1789) **1** : the self esp. as contrasted with another self or the world **2 a** : EGOTISM **b** : SELF-ESTEEM 1 **3** : the one of the three divisions of the psyche in psychoanalytic theory that serves as the organized conscious mediator between the person and reality esp. by functioning both in the perception of and adaptation to reality — compare [1]ID, SUPEREGO — **egoless** *adj*

ego•cen•tric \ˌē-gō-ˈsen-trik *also* ˌeg-ō-\ *adj* (1894) **1** : concerned with the individual rather than society **2** : taking the ego as the starting point in philosophy **3 a** : limited in outlook or concern to one's own activities or needs **b** : SELF-CENTERED, SELFISH — **egocentric** *n* — **ego•cen•tri•cal•ly** \-tri-k(ə-)lē\ *adv* — **ego•cen•tric•i•ty** \-ˌsen-ˈtris-ət-ē\ *n* — **ego•cen•trism** \-ˈsen-ˌtriz-əm\ *n*

ego–defense \ˌē-(ˌ)gō-di-ˈfen(t)s *also* ˌeg-(ˌ)ō-\ *n* (1946) : a psychological mechanism designed consciously or unconsciously to protect one's self-image or self-esteem

ego ideal *n* (1922) : the positive standards, ideals, and ambitions that according to psychoanalytic theory are assimilated from the superego

ego–in•volve•ment *n* \-in-ˈvälv-mənt, -ˈvȯlv- *also* -ˈväv- *or* -ˈvōv-\ (1936) : an involvement of one's self-esteem in the performance of a task or in an object

ego•ism \ˈē-gə-ˌwiz-əm *also* ˈeg-ə-\ *n* (1785) **1 a** : a doctrine that individual self-interest is the actual motive of all conscious action **b** : a doctrine that individual self-interest is the valid end of all actions **2** : excessive concern for oneself usu. without exaggerated feelings of self-importance — compare EGOTISM 2

ego•ist \-wəst\ *n* (1785) **1** : a believer in egoism **2** : an egocentric or egotistic person — **ego•is•tic** \ˌē-gə-ˈwis-tik *also* ˌeg-ə-\ *also* **ego•is•ti•cal** \-ti-kəl\ *adj* — **ego•is•ti•cal•ly** \-ti-k(ə-)lē\ *adv*

egoistic hedonism *n* (1874) : the ethical theory that the valid aim of right conduct is one's own happiness

ego•ma•nia \ˌē-gō-ˈmā-nē-ə, -nyə\ *n* (1825) : the quality or state of being extremely egocentric — **ego•ma•ni•ac** \-nē-ˌak\ *n* — **ego•ma•ni•a•cal** \-mə-ˈnī-ə-kəl\ *adj* — **ego•ma•ni•a•cal•ly** \-k(ə-)lē\ *adv*

ego•tism \ˈē-gə-ˌtiz-əm *also* ˈeg-ə-\ *n* [L *ego* + E *-tism* (as in *idiotism*)] (1714) **1 a** : excessive use of the first person singular personal pronoun **b** : the practice of talking about oneself too much **2** : an exaggerated sense of self-importance : CONCEIT — compare EGOISM 2 — **ego•tist** \-təst\ *n* — **ego•tis•tic** \ˌē-gə-ˈtis-tik *also* ˌeg-ə-\ *or* **ego•tis•ti•cal** \-ˈtis-ti-kəl\ *adj* — **ego•tis•ti•cal•ly** \-k(ə-)lē\ *adv*

ego–trip \ˈē-gō-ˌtrip *also* ˈeg-ō-\ *vi* (1967) : to behave in a self-seeking manner ⟨never overplayed, never *ego-tripped,* never grabbed the spotlight —Bob Palmer⟩

ego trip *n* (1967) : an act or course of action that enhances and satisfies one's ego

egre•gious \i-ˈgrē-jəs\ *adj* [L *egregius,* fr. *e-* + *greg-, grex* herd — more at GREGARIOUS] (1578) **1** *archaic* : DISTINGUISHED **2** : conspicuously bad : FLAGRANT ⟨an ~ mistake⟩ — **egre•gious•ly** *adv* — **egre•gious•ness** *n*

[1]**egress** \ˈē-ˌgres\ *n* [L *egressus,* fr. *egressus,* pp. of *egredi* to go out, fr. *e-* + *gradi* to go — more at GRADE] (1538) **1** : the act or right of going or coming out; *specif* : the emergence of a celestial object from eclipse, occultation, or transit **2** : a place or means of going out : EXIT

[2]**egress** \ē-ˈgres\ *vi* (1578) : to go out : ISSUE

egres•sion \ē-ˈgresh-ən\ *n* (15c) : EGRESS, EMERGENCE

egret \ˈē-grət, -ˌgret *also* i-ˈgret, ˈeg-rət\ *n* [ME, fr. MF *aigrette,* fr. OProv *aigreta,* of Gmc origin; akin to OHG *heigaro* heron] (14c) : any of various herons that bear long plumes during the breeding season

[1]**Egyp•tian** \i-ˈjip-shən\ *adj* (14c) : of, relating to, or characteristic of Egypt or the Egyptians

[2]**Egyptian** *n* (14c) **1** : a native or inhabitant of Egypt **2** : the Afro-Asiatic language of the ancient Egyptians from earliest times to about the 3d century A.D. **3** *often not cap* : a typeface having little contrast between thick and thin strokes and squared serifs

Egyptian alfalfa weevil *n* (1943) : an Old World weevil (*Hypera brunneipennis*) established in western No. America where it feeds on alfalfa and various clovers

Egyptian clover *n* (ca. 1900) : BERSEEM

Egyptian cotton *n* (1896) : a fine long-staple often somewhat brownish cotton grown chiefly in Egypt

Egypto- *comb form* [prob. fr. F *Égypto-,* fr. Gk *Aigypto-,* fr. *Aigyptos*] : Egypt ⟨*Egypto*logy⟩

Egyp·tol·o·gy \ˌē-(ˌ)jip-'täl-ə-jē\ *n* (1862) **:** the study of Egyptian antiquities — **Egyp·tol·o·gist** \-jəst\ *n*

eh \'ā, 'e, 'a(i), *also with* h *preceding and/or with nasalization*\ *interj* [ME *ey*] (13c) — used to ask for confirmation or repetition or to express inquiry

ei·der \'īd-ər\ *n* [D, G, or Sw, fr. Icel *æthur*, fr. ON *æthr*] (1743) **1 :** any of several large northern sea ducks (*Somateria* or related genera) having fine soft down that is used by the female for lining the nest — called also *eider duck* **2 :** EIDERDOWN 1

ei·der·down \-ˌdau̇n\ *n* [prob. fr. G *eiderdaune*, fr. Icel *æthardūnn*, fr. *æthur* + *dūnn* [7]down] (1774) **1 :** the down of the eider **2 :** a comforter filled with eiderdown **3 :** a soft lightweight clothing fabric knitted or woven and napped on one or both sides

ei·det·ic \ī-'det-ik\ *adj* [Gk *eidētikos* of a form, fr. *eidos* form — more at WISE] (ca. 1923) **:** marked by or involving extraordinarily accurate and vivid recall esp. of visual images ⟨an ~ memory⟩ — **ei·det·i·cal·ly** \-i-k(ə-)lē\ *adv*

ei·do·lon \ī-'dō-lən\ *n, pl* **-lons** \-lənz\ *or* **-la** \-lə\ [Gk *eidōlon* — more at IDOL] (1828) **1 :** an unsubstantial image **:** PHANTOM **2 :** IDEAL

ei·gen·val·ue \'ī-gən-ˌval-(ˌ)yü, -yə(-w)\ *n* [part trans. of G *eigenwert*, fr. *eigen* own, peculiar, characteristic (fr. OHG *eigan*) + *wert* value — more at OWN] (1927) **:** a scalar associated with a given linear transformation of a vector space and having the property that there is some nonzero vector which when multiplied by the scalar is equal to the vector obtained by letting the transformation operate on the vector; *esp* **:** a root of the characteristic equation of a matrix — called also *characteristic root, characteristic value*

ei·gen·vec·tor \-ˌvek-tər\ *n* [ISV *eigen-* (fr. G *eigen*) + *vector* vector] (1941) **:** a nonzero vector that is mapped by a given linear transformation of a vector space onto a vector that is the product of a scalar multiplied by the original vector — called also *characteristic vector*

eight \'āt\ *n* [ME *eighte*, fr. *eighte*, adj., fr. OE *eahta;* akin to OHG *ahto* eight, L *octo*, Gk *oktō*] (bef. 12c) **1** — see NUMBER table **2 :** the eighth in a set or series ⟨the ~ of spades⟩ **3 :** something having eight units or members: as **a :** an 8-oared racing boat or its crew **b :** an 8-cylinder engine or automobile — **eight** *adj or pron*

eight ball *n* (1932) **1 :** a black pool ball numbered 8 **2 :** MISFIT ⟨tried to weed out the *eight balls*⟩ — **behind the eight ball :** in a highly disadvantageous position or baffling situation

eigh·teen \(')ā(t)-'tēn\ *n* [ME *eightetene*, adj., fr. OE *eahtatīene*, fr. *eahta* + *-tīene* (akin to OE *tīen* ten) — more at TEN] (bef. 12c) — see NUMBER table — **eighteen** *adj or pron* — **eigh·teenth** \-'tēn(t)th\ *adj or n*

eight·fold \'āt-ˌfōld, -'fōld\ *adj* (bef. 12c) **1 :** having eight units or members **2 :** being eight times as great or as many — **eight·fold** \-'fōld\ *adv*

eightfold way *n* (1928) **:** a unified theoretical scheme for classifying the relationship among strongly interacting elementary particles on the basis of isospin and hypercharge

eighth \'ātth, 'āth\ *n, pl* **eighths** \'āt(th)s, 'āths\ (bef. 12c) **1** — see NUMBER table **2 :** OCTAVE — **eighth** *adj or adv*

eighth note *n* (ca. 1864) **:** a musical note with the time value of 1/8 of a whole note

eighth rest *n* (ca. 1890) **:** a musical rest corresponding in time value to an eighth note

eight·pen·ny nail \ˌāt-ˌpen-ē-\ *n* [fr. its original price per hundred] (15c) **:** a nail typically 2 1/2 inches long

eighty \'āt-ē\ *n, pl* **eight·ies** [ME *eighty*, adj., fr. OE *eahtatig*, short for *hundeahtatig*, n., group of eighty, fr. *hund-* group of ten (akin to Goth *taihun* ten) + *eahta* eight + *-tig* group of ten; — more at TEN] (bef. 12c) **1** — see NUMBER table **2** *pl* **:** the numbers 80 to 89; *specif* **:** the years 80 to 89 in a lifetime or century — **eight·i·eth** \'āt-ē-əth\ *adj or n* — **eighty** *adj or pron*

eighty–six *or* **86** \ˌāt-ē-'siks\ *vt* [prob. rhyming slang for [4]*nix*] *slang* (ca. 1967) **:** to refuse to serve (a customer); *also* **:** EJECT

-ein *or* **-eine** *n suffix* [ISV, alter. of *-in, -ine*] **:** compound distinguished from a compound with a similar name ending in *-in* or *-ine* ⟨phthalein⟩

ein·korn \'īn-ˌkȯ(ə)rn\ *n* [G, fr. OHG, fr. *ein* one + *korn* grain — more at ONE, CORN] (ca. 1901) **:** a one-grained wheat (*Triticum monococcum*) sometimes considered the most primitive wheat and grown esp. in poor soils in central Europe — called also *einkorn wheat*

ein·stei·ni·um \īn-'stī-nē-əm\ *n* [NL, fr. Albert *Einstein*] (1955) **:** a radioactive element produced artificially — see ELEMENT table

ei·re·nic *var of* IRENIC

eis·ege·sis \ˌī-sə-'jē-səs\ *n, pl* **-ege·ses** \-ˌsēz\ [Gk *eis* into (akin to Gk *en* in) + E *exegesis* — more at IN] (1878) **:** the interpretation of a text (as of the Bible) by reading into it one's own ideas — compare EXEGESIS

ei·stedd·fod \ī-'steth-ˌvȯd, ā-\ *n, pl* **-fods** \-ˌvȯdz\ *or* **-fod·au** \-ˌsteth-'vȯd-ˌī\ [W, lit., session, fr. *eistedd* to sit + *bod* being] (1822) **:** a usu. Welsh competitive festival of the arts esp. in poetry and singing — **ei·stedd·fod·ic** \ˌī-ˌsteth-'vȯd-ik, ā-\ *adj*

[1]ei·ther \'ē-thər *also* 'ī-\ *adj* [ME, fr. OE *ǣghwæther* both, each, fr. *ā* always + *ge-*, collective prefix + *hwæther* which of two, whether — more at AYE, CO-] (bef. 12c) **1 :** being the one and the other of two **:** EACH ⟨flowers blooming on ~ side of the walk⟩ **2 :** being the one or the other of two ⟨take ~ road⟩

[2]either *pron* (bef. 12c) **:** the one or the other

[3]either *conj* (bef. 12c) — used as a function word before two or more coordinate words, phrases, or clauses joined usu. by *or* to indicate that what immediately follows is the first of two or more alternatives

[4]either *adv* (15c) **1 :** LIKEWISE, MOREOVER — used for emphasis after a negative ⟨not wise or handsome ~⟩ **2 :** for that matter — used for emphasis after an alternative following a question or conditional clause esp. where negation is implied ⟨who answers for the Irish parliament? or army ~? —Robert Browning⟩

[1]ei·ther–or \ˌē-thə-'rȯ(ə)r *also* ˌī-\ *n* (1922) **:** an unavoidable choice or exclusive division between only two alternatives ⟨never a matter of knowledge versus proficiency, never a simple ~ — H. J. Muller⟩

[2]either–or *adj* (1926) **:** of or marked by either-or **:** BLACK-AND-WHITE ⟨an ~ situation⟩

[1]ejac·u·late \i-'jak-yə-ˌlāt\ *vb* **-lat·ed; -lat·ing** [L *ejaculatus*, pp. of *ejaculari* to throw out, fr. *e-* + *jaculari* to throw, fr. *jaculum* dart, fr. *jacere* to throw — more at JET] *vt* (1576) **1 :** to eject from a living body; *specif* **:** to eject (semen) in orgasm **2 :** to utter suddenly and vehemently ~ *vi* **:** to eject a fluid — **ejac·u·la·tor** \-ˌlāt-ər\ *n*

[2]ejac·u·late \-lət\ *n* (1927) **:** the semen released by one ejaculation

ejac·u·la·tion \i-ˌjak-yə-'lā-shən\ *n* (1603) **1 :** an act of ejaculating; *specif* **:** a sudden discharging of a fluid from a duct **2 :** something ejaculated; *esp* **:** a short sudden emotional utterance

ejac·u·la·to·ry \i-'jak-yə-lə-ˌtōr-ē, -ˌtȯr-\ *adj* (1655) **1 :** casting or throwing out; *specif* **:** associated with or concerned in physiological ejaculation ⟨~ vessels⟩ **2 :** marked by or given to vocal ejaculation

ejaculatory duct *n* (1751) **:** a duct through which semen is ejaculated; *specif* **:** either of the paired ducts in the human male that are formed by the junction of the duct from the seminal vesicle with the vas deferens, pass through the prostate, and open into or close to the prostatic utricle

eject \i-'jekt\ *vt* [ME *ejecten*, fr. L *ejectus*, pp. of *eicere*, fr. *e-* + *jacere*] (15c) **1 a :** to drive out esp. by physical force **b :** to evict from property **2 :** to throw out or off from within ⟨~*s* the empty cartridges⟩ — **eject·able** \-'jek-tə-bəl\ *adj* — **ejec·tion** \-'jek-shən\ *n* — **ejec·tive** \-'jek-tiv\ *adj*

syn EJECT, EXPEL, OUST, EVICT, DISMISS mean to drive or force out. EJECT carries an esp. strong implication of throwing or thrusting out from within as a physical action; EXPEL stresses a thrusting out or driving away esp. permanently which need not be physical; OUST implies removal or dispossession by power of the law or by compulsion of necessity; EVICT chiefly applies to turning out of house and home; DISMISS implies a getting rid of something unpleasant or troublesome simply by refusing to consider it further.

ejec·ta \i-'jek-tə\ *n pl but sing or pl in constr* [NL, fr. L, neut. pl. of *ejectus*] (1886) **:** material thrown out (as from a volcano)

ejection seat *n* (1945) **:** an emergency escape seat for propelling an occupant out and away from an airplane by means of an explosive charge

eject·ment \i-'jek(t)-mənt\ *n* (1567) **1 :** the act or an instance of ejecting **:** DISPOSSESSION **2 :** an action for the recovery of possession of real property and damages and costs

ejec·tor \i-'jek-tər\ *n* (1640) **1 :** one that ejects **2 :** a jet pump for withdrawing a gas, fluid, or powdery substance from a space

eka- \ˌek-ə, ˌā-kə\ *comb form* [Skt *eka* one — more at ONE] **:** standing or assumed to stand next in order beyond (a specified element) in the same family of the periodic table — in names of chemical elements esp. when not yet discovered ⟨*eka*cesium (now called francium)⟩

[1]eke \'ēk\ *adv* [ME, fr. OE *ēac;* akin to OHG *ouh* also, L *aut* or, Gk *au* again] *archaic* (bef. 12c) **:** ALSO

[2]eke *vt* **eked; ek·ing** [ME *eken*, fr. OE *īecan, ēcan;* akin to OHG *ouhhōn* to add, L *augēre* to increase, Gk *auxein*] (bef. 12c) **1** *archaic* **:** INCREASE, LENGTHEN **2 :** to get with great difficulty — usu. used with *out* ⟨~ out a living⟩

eke out *vt* (1596) **1 :** to make up for the deficiencies of **:** SUPPLEMENT ⟨*eked out* his income by getting a second job⟩ **2 :** to make (a supply) last by economy

ekis·tics \i-'kis-tiks\ *n pl but sing in constr* [NGk *oikistikē*, fr. fem. of *oikistikos* relating to settlement, fr. Gk, fr. *oikizein* to settle, colonize, fr. *oikos* house — more at VICINITY] (1958) **:** a science dealing with human settlements and drawing on the research and experience of professionals in various fields (as architecture, engineering, city planning, and sociology) — **ekis·tic** \-tik\ *adj*

Ek·man dredge \ˌek-mən-\ *n* [prob. fr. V. W. *Ekman* †1954 Swed. oceanographer] (1948) **:** a dredge that has opposable jaws operated by a messenger traveling down a cable to release a spring catch and that is used in ecology for sampling the bottom of a body of water

ekt·ex·ine \(')ek-'tek-ˌsēn, -ˌsīn\ *n* [Gk *ekto-* ect- + E *exine*] (1947) **:** a structurally variable outer layer of the exine

ekue·le \ā-'kwā-(ˌ)lā\ *also* **ek·pwe·le** \ek-'pwā-\ *n, pl* **ekuele** *also* **ek·pweles** [native name in Equatorial Guinea] (ca. 1973) **:** the basic monetary unit of Equatorial Guinea 1975–85

[1]el \'el\ *n* (14c) **:** the letter *l*

[2]el *n, often cap* (1906) **:** ELEVATED RAILROAD

[1]elab·o·rate \i-'lab-(ə-)rət\ *adj* [L *elaboratus*, fr. pp. of *elaborare* to work out, acquire by labor, fr. *e-* + *laborare* to work — more at LABORATORY] (1592) **1 :** planned or carried out with great care ⟨took ~ precautions⟩ **2 :** marked by complexity, fullness of detail, or ornateness ⟨~ space suits⟩ ⟨an ~ recipe⟩ — **elab·o·rate·ly** *adv* — **elab·o·rate·ness** *n*

[2]elab·o·rate \i-'lab-ə-ˌrāt\ *vb* **-rat·ed; -rat·ing** *vt* (1611) **1 :** to produce by labor **2 :** to build up (as complex organic compounds) from simple ingredients **3 :** to work out in detail **:** DEVELOP ~ *vi* **1 :** to become elaborate **2 :** to expand something in detail ⟨would you care to ~ on that statement⟩ — **elab·o·ra·tion** \-ˌlab-ə-'rā-shən\ *n* — **elab·o·ra·tive** \-'lab-ə-ˌrāt-iv\ *adj*

Elaine \i-'lān\ *n* **:** any of several women in Arthurian legend; *esp* **:** one who dies for unrequited love of Lancelot

Elam·ite \'ē-lə-ˌmīt\ *n* (1894) **:** a language of unknown affinities used in Elam approximately from the 25th to the 4th centuries B.C.

élan \ā-'läⁿ\ *n* [F, fr. MF *eslan* rush, fr. *(s')eslancer* to rush, fr. *ex-* + *lancer* to hurl — more at LANCE] (1864) **:** vigorous spirit or enthusiasm

eland \'ē-lənd, -ˌland\ *n, pl* **eland** *also* **elands** [Afrik, elk, fr. D, fr. obs. G *elend*, fr. Lith *elnis;* akin to OHG *elaho* elk — more at ELK] (1600) **:** either of two large African antelopes (*Taurotragus oryx* and *T. derbianus*) bovine in form with short spirally twisted horns in both sexes

élan vi·tal \ā-läⁿ-vē-tȧl\ *n* [F] (1907) **:** the vital force or impulse of life; *specif* **:** a creative principle held by Bergson to be immanent in all organisms and responsible for evolution

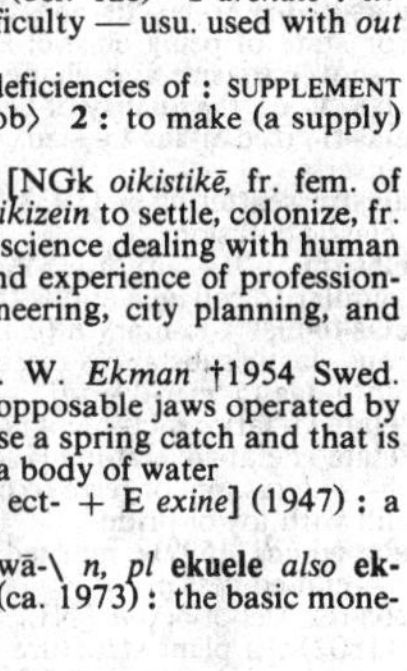

eland

\ə\ abut \ᵊ\ kitten, F table \ər\ further \a\ ash \ā\ ace \ä\ cot, cart \au̇\ out \ch\ chin \e\ bet \ē\ easy \g\ go \i\ hit \ī\ ice \j\ job \ŋ\ sing \ō\ go \ȯ\ law \ȯi\ boy \th\ thin \t͟h\ the \ü\ loot \u̇\ foot \y\ yet \zh\ vision \à, k̲, ⁿ, œ, œ̄, ue, ue̅, ʸ\ see Guide to Pronunciation

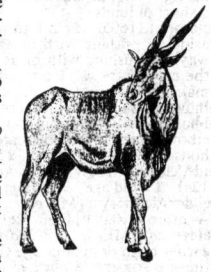

el·a·pid \'el-ə-pəd\ *n* [NL *Elap-, Elaps,* genus of snakes, fr. MGk, a fish, alter. of Gk *elops*] (1885) : any of a family (Elapidae) of venomous snakes with grooved fangs
[1]**elapse** \i-'laps\ *vi* **elapsed; elaps·ing** [L *elapsus,* pp. of *elabi,* fr. *e-* + *labi* to slip — more at SLEEP] (1644) : to slip or glide away : PASS ⟨four years *elapsed* before he returned⟩
[2]**elapse** *n* (1677) : PASSAGE ⟨returned after an ~ of 15 years⟩
elapsed time *n* (ca. 1909) : the actual time taken (as by a boat or automobile) to travel over a specified course (as in racing)
elas·mo·branch \i-'laz-mə-,braŋk\ *n, pl* **-branchs** [deriv. of Gk *elasmos* metal plate (fr. *elaunein*) + L *branchia* gill; akin to Gk *bronchos* trachea — more at CRAW] (1872) : any of a class (Chondrichthyes) of fishes with lamellate gills that comprise the sharks, rays, chimaeras, and various extinct related fishes — **elasmobranch** *adj*
elas·tase \i-'las-,tās, -,tāz\ *n* [*elastin* + *-ase*] (1949) : an enzyme esp. of pancreatic juice that digests elastin
[1]**elas·tic** \i-'las-tik\ *adj* [NL *elasticus,* fr. LGk *elastos* ductile, beaten, fr. Gk *elaunein* to drive, beat out; akin to OIr *luid* he went] (1653) **1 a** *of a solid* : capable of recovering size and shape after deformation **b** *of a gas* : capable of indefinite expansion **2** : capable of recovering quickly esp. from depression or disappointment **3** : capable of being easily stretched or expanded and resuming former shape : FLEXIBLE **4 a** : capable of ready change or easy expansion or contraction **b** : receptive to new ideas : ADAPTABLE — **elas·ti·cal·ly** \-ti-k(ə-)lē\ *adv*
syn ELASTIC, RESILIENT, SPRINGY, FLEXIBLE, SUPPLE mean able to endure strain without being permanently injured. ELASTIC implies the property of resisting deformation by stretching; RESILIENT implies the ability to recover shape quickly when the deforming force or pressure is removed; SPRINGY stresses both the ease with which something yields to pressure and the quickness of its return to original shape; FLEXIBLE applies to something which may or may not be resilient or elastic but which can be bent or folded without breaking; SUPPLE applies to something that can be readily bent, twisted, or folded without any sign of injury.
[2]**elastic** *n* (1835) **1 a** : an elastic fabric usu. made of yarns containing rubber **b** : something made from this fabric **2 a** : easily stretched rubber usu. prepared in cords, strings, or bands **b** : RUBBER BAND
elastic collision *n* (1923) : a collision in which the total kinetic energy of the colliding particles remains unchanged
elastic fiber *n* (1849) : a thick very elastic smooth yellowish connective tissue fiber that contains elastin and that branches and anastomoses with other similar fibers
elas·tic·i·ty \i-,las-'tis-ət-ē, ,ē-,las-, -'tis-tē\ *n, pl* **-ties** (1664) : the quality or state of being elastic: as **a** : the capability of a strained body to recover its size and shape after deformation : SPRINGINESS **b** : RESILIENCE **c** : the quality of being adaptable
elas·ti·cized \i-'las-tə-,sīzd\ *adj* (ca. 1909) : made with elastic thread or inserts
elastic scattering *n* (1933) : a scattering of particles as the result of elastic collision
elas·tin \i-'las-tən\ *n* [ISV, fr. NL *elasticus*] (1875) : a protein that is similar to collagen and is the chief constituent of elastic fibers
elas·to·mer \-tə-mər\ *n* [*elastic* + *-o-* + *-mer*] (ca. 1939) : any of various elastic substances resembling rubber ⟨polyvinyl ~*s*⟩ — **elas·to·mer·ic** \i-,las-tə-'mer-ik\ *adj*
[1]**elate** \i-'lāt\ *adj* (14c) : ELATED
[2]**elate** *vt* **elat·ed; elat·ing** [L *elatus* (pp. of *efferre* to carry out, elevate), fr. *e-* + *latus,* pp. of *ferre* to carry — more at TOLERATE, BEAR] (1619) : to fill with joy or pride
elat·ed *adj* (1599) : marked by high spirits : EXULTANT — **elat·ed·ly** *adv* — **elat·ed·ness** *n*
el·a·ter \'el-ət-ər\ *n* [NL, fr. Gk *elatēr* driver, fr. *elaunein* to drive] (1802) : a plant structure functioning in the distribution of spores: as **a** : one of the elongated filaments among the spores in the capsule of a liverwort **b** : one of the filamentous appendages of the spores in the scouring rushes
elat·er·ite \i-'lat-ə-,rīt\ *n* [G *elaterit,* fr. Gk *elatēr*] (1826) : a dark brown elastic mineral resin occurring in soft flexible masses
ela·tion \i-'lā-shən\ *n* (14c) **1** : the quality or state of being elated **2** : pathological euphoria
E layer *n* (1933) : a layer of the ionosphere occurring at about 65 miles (110 kilometers) above the earth's surface during daylight hours and capable of reflecting shortwave frequencies
[1]**el·bow** \'el-,bō\ *n* [ME *elbowe,* fr. OE *elboga,* fr. *el-* (akin to *eln* ell) + OE *boga* bow — more at ELL, BOW] (bef. 12c) **1 a** : the joint of the arm **b** : a corresponding joint in the anterior limb of a lower vertebrate **2** : something resembling an elbow; *specif* : an angular pipe fitting — **out at elbows** *or* **out at the elbows 1** : shabbily dressed **2** : short of funds
[2]**elbow** *vt* (1605) **1 a** : to push with the elbow : JOSTLE **b** : to shove aside by pushing with or as if with the elbow **2** : to force (as one's way) by pushing with or as if with the elbow ⟨~*ing* our way through the crowd⟩ ~ *vi* **1** : to advance by pushing with the elbow **2** : to make an angle : TURN
elbow grease *n* (1672) : energy vigorously exerted esp. in physical labor
el·bow·room \'el-,bō-,rüm, -,ru̇m\ *n* (1540) **1 a** : room for moving the elbows freely **b** : adequate space for work or operation ⟨the large house gives plenty of ~⟩ **2** : free scope ⟨~ to try new ideas⟩
eld \'eld\ *n* [ME, fr. OE *ieldo;* akin to OE *eald* old — more at OLD] (bef. 12c) **1** : old age **2** *archaic* : old times : ANTIQUITY
[1]**el·der** \'el-dər\ *n* [ME *eldre,* fr. OE *ellærn;* prob. akin to OE *alor* alder — more at ALDER] (bef. 12c) : ELDERBERRY 2
[2]**elder** *adj* [ME, fr. OE *ieldra,* compar. of *eald* old] (bef. 12c) **1** : of earlier birth or greater age ⟨his ~ brother⟩ **2** : of or relating to earlier times : FORMER **3** *obs* : of or relating to a more advanced time of life **4** : prior or superior in rank, office, or validity
[3]**elder** *n* (bef. 12c) **1** : one living in an earlier period **2 a** : one who is older : SENIOR ⟨the child trying to please his ~*s*⟩ **b** : an aged person **3** : one having authority by virtue of age and experience ⟨the village ~*s*⟩ **4** : any of various church officers: as **a** : PRESBYTER 1 **b** : a permanent officer elected by a Presbyterian congregation and ordained to serve on the session and assist the pastor at communion **c** : MINISTER 2a, 2b **d** : a Mormon ordained to the Melchizedek priesthood — **el·der·ship** \-,ship\ *n*
el·der·ber·ry \'el-də(r)-,ber-ē\ *n* (1589) **1** : the edible black or red berrylike drupe of any of a genus (*Sambucus*) of shrubs or trees of the honeysuckle family bearing flat clusters of small white or pink flowers **2** : a tree or shrub bearing elderberries
[1]**el·der·ly** \'el-dər-lē\ *adj* (1611) **1 a** : rather old; *specif* : being past middle age **b** : OLD-FASHIONED **2** : of, relating to, or characteristic of later life or elderly persons — **el·der·li·ness** *n*
[2]**elderly** *n, pl* **-ly** *or* **-lies** (1965) : an elderly person
elder statesman *n* (1904) : an eminent senior member of a group or organization; *esp* : a retired statesman who unofficially advises current leaders
el·dest \'el-dəst\ *adj* (bef. 12c) : of the greatest age or seniority : OLDEST
eldest hand *n* (1599) : the card player who first receives cards in the deal
El Do·ra·do \,el-də-'räd-(,)ō, -'rād-\ *n* [Sp, lit., the gilded one] (1596) **1** : a city or country of fabulous riches held by 16th century explorers to exist in So. America **2** : a place of fabulous wealth, abundance, or opportunity
el·dritch \'el-drich\ *adj* [perh. fr. (assumed) ME *elfriche* fairyland, fr. ME *elf* + *riche* kingdom, fr. OE *rīce* — more at RICH] (1508) : WEIRD, EERIE
El·e·at·ic \,el-ē-'at-ik\ *adj* [L *Eleaticus,* fr. Gk *Eleatikos,* fr. *Elea* (Velia), ancient town in southern Italy] (1695) : of or relating to a school of Greek philosophers founded by Parmenides and developed by Zeno and marked by belief in the unity of being and the unreality of motion or change — **Eleatic** *n* — **El·e·at·i·cism** \-'at-ə-,siz-əm\ *n*
ele·cam·pane \,el-i-,kam-'pān\ *n* [ME *elena campana,* fr. ML *enula campana,* lit., field elecampane, fr. *inula, enula* elecampane + *campana* of the field] (14c) : a large coarse European composite herb (*Inula helenium*) that has yellow ray flowers and is naturalized in the U.S.
[1]**elect** \i-'lekt\ *adj* [ME, fr. L *electus* choice, fr. pp. of *eligere* to select, fr. *e-* + *legere* to choose — more at LEGEND] (15c) **1** : carefully selected : CHOSEN **2** : chosen for salvation through divine mercy **3 a** : chosen for office or position but not yet installed ⟨the president-*elect*⟩ **b** : chosen for marriage at some future time to a specific person ⟨the bride-*elect*⟩
[2]**elect** *n, pl* **elect** (15c) **1** : one chosen or set apart (as by divine favor) **2** *pl* : a select or exclusive group of people
[3]**elect** *vt* [ME *electen,* fr. L *electus*] (15c) **1** : to select by vote for an office, position, or membership ⟨~*ed* him class president⟩ **2** : to make a selection of ⟨will ~ a heavy academic program⟩ **3** : to choose esp. by preference : decide on ⟨might ~ to sell the business⟩ ~ *vi* : to make a selection
elect·able \i-'lek-tə-bəl\ *adj* (1879) : capable of being elected (as to public office) — **elect·abil·i·ty** \-,lek-tə-'bil-ət-ē\ *n*
elec·tion \i-'lek-shən\ *n* (13c) **1 a** : an act or process of electing **b** : the fact of being elected **2** : predestination to eternal life **3** : the right, power, or privilege of making a choice ***syn*** see CHOICE
Election Day *n* (1651) : a day legally established for the election of public officials; *esp* : the first Tuesday after the first Monday in November in an even year designated for national elections in the U.S. and observed as a legal holiday in many states
elec·tion·eer \i-,lek-shə-'ni(ə)r\ *vi* [*election* + *-eer* (as in *privateer,* v.)] (1789) : to take an active part in an election; *specif* : to work for the election of a candidate or party — **elec·tion·eer·er** *n*
[1]**elec·tive** \i-'lek-tiv\ *adj* (1530) **1 a** : chosen or filled by popular election ⟨an ~ official⟩ **b** : of or relating to election **c** : based on the right or principle of election ⟨the presidency is an ~ office⟩ **2** : permitting a choice : OPTIONAL ⟨an ~ course in school⟩ **3 a** : tending to operate on one substance rather than another **b** : favorably inclined to one more than to another : SYMPATHETIC ⟨an ~ affinity⟩ — **elec·tive·ly** *adv* — **elec·tive·ness** *n*
[2]**elective** *n* (1850) : an elective course or subject
elec·tor \i-'lek-tər, -,tȯ(ə)r\ *n* (15c) **1** : one qualified to vote in an election **2** : one entitled to participate in an election: as **a** : one of the German princes entitled to take part in choosing the Holy Roman Emperor **b** : a member of the electoral college in the U.S.
elec·tor·al \i-'lek-t(ə-)rəl\ *adj* (1675) **1** : of or relating to an elector ⟨the ~ vote⟩ **2** : of or relating to election ⟨an ~ system⟩
electoral college *n* (1691) : a body of electors; *esp* : one that elects the president and vice-president of the U.S.
elec·tor·ate \i-'lek-t(ə-)rət\ *n* (1675) **1** : the territory, jurisdiction, or dignity of a German elector **2** : a body of people entitled to vote
electr- *or* **electro-** *comb form* [NL *electricus*] **1 a** : electricity ⟨*electrometer*⟩ **b** : electric ⟨*electrode*⟩ : electric and ⟨*electrochemical*⟩ : electrically ⟨*electropositive*⟩ **2** : electrolytic ⟨*electroanalysis*⟩ **3** : electron ⟨*electrovalence*⟩
Elec·tra \i-'lek-trə\ *n* [L, fr. Gk *Ēlektra*] : a sister of Orestes who aids him in killing their mother Clytemnestra
Electra complex *n* (1913) : the Oedipus complex when it occurs in a female
elec·tress \i-'lek-trəs\ *n* (1618) : the wife or widow of a German elector
elec·tret \i-'lek-trət, -,tret\ *n* [*electricity* + *magnet*] (1885) : a dielectric body in which a permanent state of electric polarization has been set up
[1]**elec·tric** \i-'lek-trik\ *adj* [NL *electricus* produced from amber by friction, electric, fr. ML, of amber, fr. L *electrum* amber, electrum, fr. Gk *ēlektron;* akin to Gk *ēlektōr* beaming sun, Skt *ulkā* meteor] (1646) **1** *or* **elec·tri·cal** \-tri-kəl\ : of, relating to, or operated by electricity **2** : exciting as if by electric shock ⟨an ~ performance⟩ ⟨a ~ personality⟩; *also* : charged with strong emotion ⟨the room was ~ with tension⟩ **3 a** : ELECTRONIC 3a **b** : amplifying sound by electronic means — used of a musical instrument ⟨an ~ guitar⟩ **4** : very bright ⟨~ blue⟩ ⟨~ orange⟩ — **elec·tri·cal·ly** \-tri-k(ə-)lē\ *adv*
[2]**electric** *n* (1646) **1** *archaic* : a nonconductor of electricity used to excite or accumulate electricity **2** : something (as a light, automobile, or train) operated by electricity
electrical storm *n* (1941) : THUNDERSTORM — called also *electric storm*
electric chair *n* (1889) **1** : a chair used in legal electrocution **2** : the penalty of death by electrocution
electric eel *n* (1802) : a large eel-shaped fish (*Electrophorus electricus*) of the Orinoco and Amazon basins that is capable of giving a severe shock with its electric organs
electric eye *n* (1898) **1** : PHOTOELECTRIC CELL **2** : a miniature cathode-ray tube used to determine a condition (as of radio tuning)

elec·tri·cian \i-ˌlek-ˈtrish-ən\ *n* (1751) **1 :** a specialist in electricity **2 :** one who installs, maintains, operates, or repairs electrical equipment

elec·tric·i·ty \i-ˌlek-ˈtris-ət-ē, -ˈtris-tē\ *n, pl* **-ties** (1646) **1 a :** a fundamental entity of nature consisting of negative and positive kinds composed respectively of electrons and protons or possibly of electrons and positrons, observable in the attractions and repulsions of bodies electrified by friction and in natural phenomena (as lightning or the aurora borealis), and usu. utilized in the form of electric currents **b :** electric current or power **2 :** a science that deals with the phenomena and laws of electricity **3 :** keen contagious excitement

electric organ *n* (1773) **:** a specialized tract of tissue (as in the electric eel) in which electricity is generated

electric ray *n* (1774) **:** any of various round-bodied short-tailed rays (family Torpedinidae) of warm seas with a pair of electric organs

elec·tri·fi·ca·tion \i-ˌlek-trə-fə-ˈkā-shən\ *n* (1748) **1 :** an act or process of electrifying **2 :** the state of being electrified

elec·tri·fy \i-ˈlek-trə-ˌfī\ *vt* **-fied; -fy·ing** (1745) **1 a :** to charge with electricity **b** (1) **:** to equip for use of electric power (2) **:** to supply with electric power (3) **:** to amplify (music) electronically **2 :** to excite intensely or suddenly as if by electric shock

elec·tro·acous·tics \i-ˌlek-trō-ə-ˈkü-stiks\ *n pl but sing in constr* (1927) **:** a science that deals with the transformation of acoustic energy into electric energy or vice versa — **elec·tro·acous·tic** \-tik\ *adj* — **elec·tro·acous·ti·cal·ly** \-ti-k(ə-)lē\ *adv*

elec·tro·anal·y·sis \-ə-ˈnal-ə-səs\ *n* (1903) **:** chemical analysis by electrolytic methods — **elec·tro·an·a·lyt·ic** \-ˌan-ᵊl-ˈit-ik\ *or* **elec·tro·an·a·lyt·i·cal** \-ˈit-i-kəl\ *adj*

elec·tro·car·dio·gram \-ˈkärd-ē-ə-ˌgram\ *n* (ca. 1904) **:** the tracing made by an electrocardiograph

elec·tro·car·dio·graph \-ˌgraf\ *n* (1913) **:** an instrument for recording the changes of electrical potential occurring during the heartbeat used esp. in diagnosing abnormalities of heart action — **elec·tro·car·dio·graph·ic** \-ˌkärd-ē-ə-ˈgraf-ik\ *adj* — **elec·tro·car·dio·graph·i·cal·ly** \-i-k(ə-)lē\ *adv* — **elec·tro·car·di·og·ra·phy** \-ē-ˈäg-rə-fē\ *n*

elec·tro·chem·is·try \-ˈkem-ə-strē\ *n* (1814) **:** a science that deals with the relation of electricity to chemical changes and with the interconversion of chemical and electrical energy — **elec·tro·chem·i·cal** \-ˈkem-i-kəl\ *adj* — **elec·tro·chem·i·cal·ly** \-k(ə-)lē\ *adv*

elec·tro·con·vul·sive \i-ˌlek-trō-kən-ˈvəl-siv\ *adj* (1947) **:** of, relating to, or involving convulsive response to electroshock ⟨impaired learning ability in rats due to ~ shocks⟩

electroconvulsive therapy *n* (1948) **:** ELECTROSHOCK THERAPY

elec·tro·cor·ti·co·gram \i-ˌlek-trō-ˈkȯrt-i-kə-ˌgram\ *n* (1939) **:** an electroencephalogram made with the electrodes in direct contact with the brain

elec·tro·cute \i-ˈlek-trə-ˌkyüt\ *vt* **-cut·ed; -cut·ing** [*electr-* + *-cute* (as in *execute*)] (1889) **1 :** to execute (a criminal) by electricity **2 :** to kill by electric shock — **elec·tro·cu·tion** \-ˌlek-trə-ˈkyü-shən\ *n*

elec·trode \i-ˈlek-ˌtrōd\ *n* (1834) **1 :** a conductor used to establish electrical contact with a nonmetallic part of a circuit **2 :** a semiconductor device element that emits or collects electrons or holes or that controls their movements

[1]**elec·tro·de·pos·it** \i-ˌlek-trō-di-ˈpäz-ət\ *n* (1864) **:** a deposit formed in or at an electrode by electrolysis

[2]**electrodeposit** *vt* (1882) **:** to deposit (as a metal or rubber) by electrolysis — **elec·tro·de·po·si·tion** \-ˌdep-ə-ˈzish-ən, -ˌdē-pə-\ *n*

elec·tro·der·mal \i-ˌlek-trō-ˈdər-məl\ *adj* (1946) **:** of or relating to electrical activity in or electrical properties of the skin

elec·tro·di·al·y·sis \i-ˌlek-trō-dī-ˈal-ə-səs\ *n* (1921) **:** dialysis accelerated by an electromotive force applied to electrodes adjacent to the membranes — **elec·tro·di·a·lyt·ic** \-ˌdī-ə-ˈlit-ik\ *adj*

elec·tro·dy·nam·ics \-dī-ˈnam-iks\ *n pl but sing in constr* (1827) **:** a branch of physics that deals with the effects arising from the interactions of electric currents with magnets, with other currents, or with themselves — **elec·tro·dy·nam·ic** \-ik\ *adj*

elec·tro·dy·na·mom·e·ter \-ˌdī-nə-ˈmäm-ət-ər\ *n* [ISV] (1876) **:** an instrument that measures current by indicating the strength of the forces between a current flowing in fixed coils and one flowing in movable coils

elec·tro·en·ceph·a·lo·gram \-in-ˈsef-ə-lə-ˌgram\ *n* [ISV] (1934) **:** the tracing of brain waves made by an electroencephalograph

elec·tro·en·ceph·a·lo·graph \-ˌgraf\ *n* [ISV] (1936) **:** an apparatus for detecting and recording brain waves — **elec·tro·en·ceph·a·log·ra·pher** \-ˌsef-ə-ˈläg-rə-fər\ *n* — **elec·tro·en·ceph·a·lo·graph·ic** \-ˌsef-ə-lə-ˈgraf-ik\ *adj* — **elec·tro·en·ceph·a·lo·graph·i·cal·ly** \-i-k(ə-)lē\ *adv* — **elec·tro·en·ceph·a·log·ra·phy** \-ˈläg-rə-fē\ *n*

elec·tro·fish·ing \i-ˈlek-trō-ˌfish-iŋ\ *n* (1950) **:** the taking of fish by a system based on their tendency to respond positively to a source of direct electric current

elec·tro·form \i-ˈlek-trə-ˌfȯrm\ *vt* (1931) **:** to form (shaped articles) by electrodeposition on a mold — **electroform** *n*

elec·tro·gen·e·sis \i-ˌlek-trə-ˈjen-ə-səs\ *n* (ca. 1890) **:** the production of electrical activity esp. in living tissue

elec·tro·gen·ic \-ˈjen-ik\ *adj* (ca. 1891) **:** of or relating to the production of electrical activity in living tissue ⟨an ~ pump causing movement of sodium ions across a membrane⟩

elec·tro·gram \i-ˈlek-trə-ˌgram\ *n* (ca. 1935) **:** a tracing of the electrical potentials of a tissue (as the brain or heart) made by means of electrodes placed directly in the tissue instead of on the surface of the body

elec·tro·hy·drau·lic \i-ˌlek-trō-hī-ˈdrȯ-lik\ *adj* (1922) **1 :** of or relating to a combination of electric and hydraulic mechanisms **2 :** involving or produced by the action of very brief but powerful pulse discharges of electricity under a liquid resulting in the generation of shock waves and highly reactive chemical species ⟨an ~ effect⟩ — **elec·tro·hy·drau·li·cal·ly** \-li-k(ə-)lē\ *adv*

elec·tro·jet \i-ˈlek-trə-ˌjet\ *n* (1955) **:** an overhead concentration of electric current found in the regions of strong auroral displays and along the aclinic line

elec·tro·ki·net·ic \i-ˌlek-trō-kə-ˈnet-ik, -kī-\ *adj* (1881) **:** of or relating to the motion of particles or liquids that results from or produces a difference of electric potential

elec·tro·ki·net·ics \-iks\ *n pl but sing in constr* (ca. 1925) **:** a branch of physics that deals with the motion of electric currents or charged particles

elec·tro·less \i-ˈlek-ˌtrō-ləs, -trə-\ *adj* (1947) **:** being or involving chemical deposition of metal instead of electrodeposition

elec·trol·o·gist \i-ˌlek-ˈträl-ə-jəst\ *n* [blend of *electrolysis* and *-logist* (fr. *-logy* + *-ist*)] (ca. 1902) **:** one that removes hair, warts, moles, and birthmarks by means of an electric current applied to the body with a needle-shaped electrode — **elec·trol·o·gy** \-ə-jē\ *n*

elec·tro·lu·mi·nes·cence \i-ˌlek-trō-ˌlü-mə-ˈnes-ᵊn(t)s\ *n* (ca. 1902) **:** luminescence resulting from a high-frequency discharge through a gas or from application of an alternating current to a layer of phosphor — **elec·tro·lu·mi·nes·cent** \-ᵊnt\ *adj*

elec·trol·y·sis \i-ˌlek-ˈträl-ə-səs\ *n* (1834) **1 a :** the producing of chemical changes by passage of an electric current through an electrolyte **b :** subjection to this action **2 :** the destruction of hair roots with an electric current

elec·tro·lyte \i-ˈlek-trə-ˌlīt\ *n* (1834) **1 :** a nonmetallic electric conductor in which current is carried by the movement of ions **2 :** a substance that when dissolved in a suitable solvent or when fused becomes an ionic conductor

elec·tro·lyt·ic \i-ˌlek-trə-ˈlit-ik\ *adj* (1842) **:** of or relating to electrolysis or an electrolyte; *also* **:** involving or produced by electrolysis — **elec·tro·lyt·i·cal·ly** \-i-k(ə-)lē\ *adv*

elec·tro·lyze \i-ˈlek-trə-ˌlīz\ *vt* **-lyzed; -lyz·ing** (1834) **:** to subject to electrolysis

elec·tro·mag·net \i-ˌlek-trō-ˈmag-nət\ *n* (1831) **:** a core of magnetic material surrounded by a coil of wire through which an electric current is passed to magnetize the core

elec·tro·mag·net·ic \-mag-ˈnet-ik\ *adj* (1821) **:** of, relating to, or produced by electromagnetism — **elec·tro·mag·net·i·cal·ly** \-i-k(ə-)lē\ *adv*

electromagnetic pulse *n* (1981) **:** high-intensity electromagnetic radiation generated by a nuclear blast high above the earth's surface and held to disrupt electronic and electrical systems

electromagnetic radiation *n* (1939) **:** a series of electromagnetic waves

electromagnetic spectrum *n* (ca. 1934) **:** the entire range of wavelengths or frequencies of electromagnetic radiation extending from gamma rays to the longest radio waves and including visible light

electromagnetic unit *n* (ca. 1911) **:** any of a system of electrical units based primarily on the magnetic properties of electrical currents

electromagnetic wave *n* (1905) **:** one of the waves that are propagated by simultaneous periodic variations of electric and magnetic field intensity and that include radio waves, infrared, visible light, ultraviolet, X rays, and gamma rays

elec·tro·mag·ne·tism \i-ˌlek-trō-ˈmag-nə-ˌtiz-əm\ *n* (1828) **1 :** magnetism developed by a current of electricity **2 :** a branch of physical science that deals with the physical relations between electricity and magnetism

elec·tro·me·chan·i·cal \-mə-ˈkan-i-kəl\ *adj* (1888) **:** of, relating to, or being a mechanical process or device actuated or controlled electrically; *specif* **:** being a transducer for converting mechanical energy to electrical energy or vice versa — **elec·tro·me·chan·i·cal·ly** \-k(ə-)lē\ *adv*

elec·tro·met·al·lur·gy \-ˈmet-ᵊl-ˌər-jē, *esp Brit* -mə-ˈtal-ər-\ *n* (1840) **:** a branch of metallurgy that deals with the application of electric current either for electrolytic deposition or as a source of heat

elec·trom·e·ter \i-ˌlek-ˈträm-ət-ər\ *n* (1749) **:** any of various instruments for detecting or measuring electric-potential differences or ionizing radiations by means of the forces of attraction or repulsion between charged bodies

elec·tro·mo·tive force \i-ˌlek-trō-ˌmōt-iv-, -trə-\ *n* (1827) **:** something that moves or tends to move electricity **:** the amount of energy derived from an electrical source per unit quantity of electricity passing through the source (as a cell or generator)

elec·tro·myo·gram \i-ˌlek-trō-ˈmī-ə-ˌgram\ *n* (1917) **:** a tracing made with an electromyograph

elec·tro·myo·graph \-ˌgraf\ *n* [*electr-* + *my-* + *-graph*] (1948) **:** an instrument that converts the electrical activity associated with functioning skeletal muscle into a visual record or into sound and has been used to diagnose neuromuscular disorders and in biofeedback training — **elec·tro·myo·graph·ic** \-ˌmī-ə-ˈgraf-ik\ *adj* — **elec·tro·myo·graph·i·cal·ly** \-i-k(ə-)lē\ *adv* — **elec·tro·my·og·ra·phy** \-mī-ˈäg-rə-fē\ *n*

elec·tron \i-ˈlek-ˌträn\ *n* [*electr-* + [2]*-on*] (1891) **:** an elementary particle consisting of a charge of negative electricity equal to about 1.602 $\times 10^{-19}$ coulomb and having a mass when at rest of about 9.109534 $\times$ 10^{-28} gram or about $\frac{1}{1836}$ that of a proton

elec·tro·neg·a·tive \i-ˌlek-trō-ˈneg-ət-iv\ *adj* (1810) **1 :** charged with negative electricity **2 :** capable of acting as the negative electrode of a voltaic cell **3 :** having a tendency to attract electrons — **elec·tro·neg·a·tiv·i·ty** \-ˌneg-ə-ˈtiv-ət-ē\ *n*

electron gas *n* (ca. 1929) **:** a population of free electrons in a vacuum or in a metallic conductor

electron gun *n* (1930) **:** the electron-emitting cathode and its surrounding assembly in a cathode-ray tube for directing, controlling, and focusing the stream of electrons to a spot of desired size

elec·tron·ic \i-ˌlek-ˈträn-ik\ *adj* (1902) **1 :** of or relating to electrons **2 :** of, relating to, or utilizing devices constructed or working by the methods or principles of electronics **3 a :** generating musical tones by electronic means ⟨an ~ organ⟩ **b :** of, relating to, or being music that consists of sounds electronically generated or modified **4 :** of or relating to a medium (as television) transmitted electronically ⟨~ journalism⟩ — **elec·tron·i·cal·ly** \-i-k(ə-)lē\ *adv*

electronic mail *n* (1979) **:** messages sent and received electronically (as between terminals linked by telephone lines or microwave relays)

elec·tron·ics \i-ˌlek-ˈträn-iks\ *n pl* (1910) **1** *sing in constr* **:** a branch of physics that deals with the emission, behavior, and effects of electrons (as in electron tubes and transistors) and with electronic devices **2 :** electronic devices or equipment

\ə\ abut \ᵊ\ kitten, F table \ər\ further \a\ ash \ā\ ace \ä\ cot, cart
\au̇\ out \ch\ chin \e\ bet \ē\ easy \g\ go \i\ hit \ī\ ice \j\ job
\ŋ\ sing \ō\ go \ȯ\ law \ȯi\ boy \th\ thin \t͟h\ the \ü\ loot \u̇\ foot
\y\ yet \zh\ vision \à, k̲, ⁿ, œ, œ̄, ue, u̅e, ʸ\ *see* Guide to Pronunciation

electron lens *n* (1931) : a device for focusing a beam of electrons by means of an electric or a magnetic field

electron micrograph *n* (1941) : a micrograph made with an electron microscope — **electron micrography** \-mī-ˈkräg-rə-fē\ *n*

electron microscope *n* (1932) : an electron-optical instrument in which a beam of electrons focused by means of an electron lens is used to produce an enlarged image of a minute object on a fluorescent screen or photographic plate — **electron microscopist** *n* — **electron microscopy** *n*

electron multiplier *n* (1936) : a device utilizing secondary emission of electrons for amplifying a current of electrons

electron optics *n pl but sing in constr* (1916) : a branch of physics in which the principles of optics are applied to beams of electrons — **electron–op·ti·cal** \i-ˌlek-ˌträ-ˈnäp-ti-kəl\ *adj*

electron transport *n* (1951) : the sequential transfer of electrons esp. by cytochromes in cellular respiration from an oxidizable substrate to molecular oxygen by a series of oxidation-reduction reactions

electron tube *n* (1922) : an electronic device in which conduction by electrons takes place through a vacuum or a gaseous medium within a sealed glass or metal container and which has various common uses based on the controlled flow of electrons

electron volt *n* (1930) : a unit of energy equal to the energy gained by an electron in passing from a point of low potential to a point one volt higher in potential : 1.60×10^{-19} joule

elec·tro·oc·u·lo·gram \i-ˌlek-trō-ˈäk-yə-lə-ˌgram\ *n* [*electr-* + *ocul-* + *-gram*] (1947) : a record of the standing voltage between the front and back of the eye that is correlated with eyeball movement (as in REM sleep) and obtained by electrodes suitably placed on the skin near the eye

elec·tro·oc·u·log·ra·phy \-ˌäk-yə-ˈläg-rə-fē\ *n, pl* **-phies** (1951) : the preparation and study of electrooculograms

elec·tro–op·tics \-trō-ˈäp-tiks\ *n pl but sing in constr* (ca. 1891) : a branch of physics that deals with the effects of an electric field on light traversing it — **elec·tro–op·tic** \-tik\ *or* **elec·tro–op·ti·cal** \-ti-kəl\ *adj* — **elec·tro–op·ti·cal·ly** \-ti-k(ə-)lē\ *adv*

elec·tro·os·mo·sis \i-ˌlek-trō-äz-ˈmō-səs, -äs-\ *n* (1906) : the movement of a liquid out of or through a porous diaphragm or a biological membrane under the influence of an electric field — **elec·tro·os·mot·ic** \-ˈmät-ik\ *adj*

elec·tro·phe·ro·gram \-trə-ˈfir-ə-ˌgram, -ˈfer-\ *n* [*electr-* + ISV *phero-* (fr. Gk *pherein* to carry) + *-gram*] (1951) : ELECTROPHORETOGRAM

elec·tro·phil·ic \i-ˌlek-trə-ˈfil-ik\ *adj* (1936) : involving or having an affinity for electrons : electron-seeking ⟨~ reagents⟩ — **elec·tro·phi·lic·i·ty** \-trō-fil-ˈis-ət-ē\ *n*

elec·tro·pho·re·sis \-trə-fə-ˈrē-səs\ *n* [NL] (1911) : the movement of suspended particles through a fluid or gel under the action of an electromotive force applied to electrodes in contact with the suspension — **elec·tro·pho·rese** \-ˈrēs, -ˈrēz\ *vt* — **elec·tro·pho·ret·ic** \-ˈret-ik\ *adj* — **elec·tro·pho·ret·i·cal·ly** \-i-k(ə-)lē\ *adv*

elec·tro·pho·reto·gram \-ˈret-ə-ˌgram\ *n* [*electrophoretic* + *-o-* + *-gram*] (1954) : a record that consists of the separated components of a mixture (as of proteins) produced by electrophoresis in a supporting medium (as filter paper)

elec·troph·o·rus \i-ˌlek-ˈträf-ə-rəs\ *n, pl* **-ri** \-ˌrī, -ˌrē\ [NL, fr. *electr-* + *-phorus* -phore] (1778) : an instrument for the production of electric charges by induction consisting of a disk that is negatively electrified by friction and a metal plate that becomes charged by induction when placed on the disk

elec·tro·pho·tog·ra·phy \i-ˌlek-trō-fə-ˈtäg-rə-fē\ *n* (1894) : photography in which images are produced by electrical means (as in xerography) — **elec·tro·pho·to·graph·ic** \-trə-ˌfōt-ə-ˈgraf-ik\ *adj*

elec·tro·phys·i·ol·o·gy \i-ˌlek-trō-ˌfiz-ē-ˈäl-ə-jē\ *n* (1838) **1** : physiology that is concerned with the electrical aspects of physiological phenomena **2** : electrical phenomena associated with a physiological process (as the function of a body or bodily part) ⟨~ of the eye⟩ — **elec·tro·phys·i·o·log·i·cal** \-ē-ə-ˈläj-i-kəl\ *also* **elec·tro·phys·i·o·log·ic** \-ik\ *adj* — **elec·tro·phys·i·o·log·i·cal·ly** \-i-k(ə-)lē\ *adv* — **elec·tro·phys·i·ol·o·gist** \-ē-ˈäl-ə-jəst\ *n*

elec·tro·plate \i-ˈlek-trə-ˌplāt\ *vt* (ca. 1859) : to plate with an adherent continuous coating by electrodeposition

elec·tro·pos·i·tive \i-ˌlek-trō-ˈpäz-ət-iv, -ˈpäz-tiv\ *adj* (1813) **1 a** : charged with positive electricity **b** : capable of acting as the positive electrode of a voltaic cell **2** : having a tendency to release electrons

elec·tro·ret·i·no·gram \-ˈret-ᵊn-ə-ˌgram\ *n* (1936) : a graphic record of electrical activity of the retina used esp. in the diagnosis of retinal conditions

elec·tro·ret·i·no·graph \-ˌgraf\ *n* (1962) : an instrument for recording electrical activity in the retina — **elec·tro·ret·i·no·graph·ic** \-ˌret-ᵊn-ə-ˈgraf-ik\ *adj* — **elec·tro·ret·i·nog·ra·phy** \-ᵊn-ˈäg-rə-fē\ *n*

elec·tro·scope \i-ˈlek-trə-ˌskōp\ *n* [prob. fr. F *électroscope*] (1810) : any of various instruments for detecting the presence of an electric charge on a body, for determining whether the charge is positive or negative, or for indicating and measuring intensity of radiation

elec·tro·shock \-trō-ˌshäk\ *n* (1941) **1** : ^{3}SHOCK 5 **2** : ELECTROSHOCK THERAPY

electroshock therapy *n* (1942) : the treatment of mental disorder and esp. depression by the induction of unconsciousness and convulsions through the use of an electric current now usu. on an anesthetized patient — called also *electroconvulsive therapy*

elec·tro·stat·ic \i-ˌlek-trə-ˈstat-ik\ *adj* [ISV] (1867) **1** : of or relating to static electricity or electrostatics **2** : of or relating to painting with a spray that utilizes electrically charged particles to ensure complete coating — **elec·tro·stat·i·cal·ly** \-ˈstat-i-k(ə-)lē\ *adv*

electrostatic generator *n* (ca. 1931) : an apparatus for the production of electrical discharges at high voltage commonly consisting of an insulated hollow conducting sphere that accumulates in its interior the charge continuously conveyed from a source of direct current by an endless belt of flexible nonconducting material

electrostatic precipitator *n* (1949) : an electrostatic device in chimney flues that removes particles from escaping gases

elec·tro·stat·ics \i-ˌlek-trə-ˈstat-iks\ *n pl but sing in constr* (1827) : physics that deals with phenomena due to attractions or repulsions of electric charges but not dependent upon their motion

electrostatic unit *n* (ca. 1909) : any of a system of electrical units based primarily on forces of interaction between electric charges

elec·tro·sur·gery \i-ˌlek-trō-ˈsərj-(ə-)rē\ *n* (ca. 1909) : surgery by means of diathermy — **elec·tro·sur·gi·cal** \-ˈsər-ji-kəl\ *adj*

elec·tro·ther·a·py \-ˈther-ə-pē\ *n* (1881) : treatment of disease by means of electricity (as in diathermy)

elec·tro·ther·mal \-ˈthər-məl\ *or* **elec·tro·ther·mic** \-mik\ *adj* (1884) : relating to or combining electricity and heat; *specif* : relating to the generation of heat by electricity — **elec·tro·ther·mal·ly** \-mə-lē\ *adv*

elec·tro·ton·ic \i-ˌlek-trə-ˈtän-ik\ *adj* (ca. 1864) **1** : of, induced by, relating to, or constituting electrotonus **2** : of, relating to, or being the spread of electrical activity through living tissue or cells in the absence of repeated action potentials ⟨an ~ junction between cells⟩ — **elec·tro·ton·i·cal·ly** \-i-k(ə-)lē\ *adv*

elec·trot·o·nus \i-ˌlek-ˈträt-ᵊn-əs\ *n* [NL] (1860) : the altered sensitivity of a nerve when a constant current of electricity passes through any part of it

elec·tro·type \i-ˈlek-trə-ˌtīp\ *n* (1840) **1** : a duplicate printing surface made by an electroplating process **2** : a copy of a coin made by an electroplating process — **electrotype** *vt* — **elec·tro·typ·er** \-ˌtī-pər\ *n*

elec·tro·va·lence \i-ˌlek-trō-ˈvā-lən(t)s\ *n* (1921) : valence characterized by the transfer of electrons from one atom to another with the formation of ions; *also* : the number of charges acquired by an atom by the loss or gain of electrons — **elec·tro·va·lent** \-lənt\ *adj*

elec·tro·va·len·cy \-lən-sē\ *n* (1923) : ELECTROVALENCE

electrovalent bond *n* (1943) : a chemical bond formed between ions of opposite charge

elec·tro·win·ning \i-ˈlek-trō-ˌwin-iŋ\ *n* (1924) : the recovery esp. of metals from solutions by electrolysis

elec·trum \i-ˈlek-trəm\ *n* [ME, fr. L — more at ELECTRIC] (14c) : a natural pale yellow alloy of gold and silver

elec·tu·ary \i-ˈlek-chə-ˌwer-ē\ *n, pl* **-ar·ies** [ME *electuarie*, fr. L *electuarium*, prob. fr. Gk *ekleikton*, fr. *ekleichein* to lick up, fr. *ex-* + *leichein* to lick — more at LICK] (14c) : CONFECTION 2b

el·e·doi·sin \ˌel-ə-ˈdȯis-ᵊn\ *n* [irreg. fr. NL *Eledone*, fr. Gk *eledōnē*, a kind of octopus] (1965) : a small protein $C_{54}H_{85}N_{13}O_{15}S$ from the salivary glands of several octopuses (genus *Eledone*) that is a powerful vasodilator and hypotensive agent

el·ee·mo·sy·nary \ˌel-i-ˈmäs-ᵊn-ˌer-ē, -ˈmäz-, -ˈmōs-\ *adj* [ML *eleemosynarius*, fr. LL *eleemosyna* alms — more at ALMS] (1620) : of, relating to, or supported by charity

el·e·gance \ˈel-i-gən(t)s\ *n* (1510) **1 a** : refined grace or dignified propriety : URBANITY **b** : tasteful richness of design or ornamentation ⟨the sumptuous ~ of the furnishings⟩ **c** : dignified gracefulness or restrained beauty of style : POLISH ⟨the essay is marked by lucidity, wit, and ~⟩ **d** : scientific precision, neatness, and simplicity ⟨the ~ of a mathematical proof⟩ **2** : something that is elegant

el·e·gan·cy \-gən-sē\ *n, pl* **-cies** (15c) : ELEGANCE

el·e·gant \ˈel-i-gənt\ *adj* [MF or L; MF, fr. L *elegant-, elegans;* akin to L *eligere* to select — more at ELECT] (15c) **1** : marked by elegance **2** : of a high grade or quality : SPLENDID ⟨~ gems priced at hundreds of thousands of dollars⟩ ***syn*** see CHOICE — **el·e·gant·ly** *adv*

ele·gi·ac \ˌel-ə-ˈjī-ək, -ˌak *also* i-ˈlē-jē-ˌak\ *also* **el·e·gi·a·cal** \ˌel-ə-ˈjī-ə-kəl\ *adj* [LL *elegiacus*, fr. Gk *elegeiakos*, fr. *elegeion*] (1542) **1 a** : of, relating to, or consisting of two dactylic hexameter lines the second of which lacks the arses in the third and sixth feet **b (1)** : written in or consisting of elegiac couplets **(2)** : noted for having written poetry in such couplets **c** : of or relating to the period in Greece about the seventh century B.C. when poetry written in such couplets flourished **2** : of, relating to, or comprising elegy or an elegy; *esp* : expressing sorrow often for something now past ⟨an ~ lament for departed youth⟩ — **elegiac** *n* — **el·e·gi·a·cal·ly** \ˌel-ə-ˈjī-ə-k(ə-)lē\ *adv*

ele·git \i-ˈlē-jət\ *n* [L, lit., he has chosen, fr. *eligere*] (1503) : a judicial writ of execution by which a defendant's goods and if necessary his lands are delivered for debt to the plaintiff until the debt is paid

el·e·gize \ˈel-ə-ˌjīz\ *vb* **-gized; -giz·ing** *vi* (1702) : to write an elegy ~ *vt* : to write an elegy on

el·e·gy \ˈel-ə-jē\ *n, pl* **-gies** [L *elegia* poem in elegiac couplets, fr. Gk *elegeia, elegeion*, fr. *elegos* song of mourning] (1501) **1** : a poem in elegiac couplets **2 a** : a song or poem expressing sorrow or lamentation esp. for one who is dead **b** : something (as a speech) resembling such a song or poem **3 a** : a pensive or reflective poem that is usu. nostalgic or melancholy **b** : a short pensive musical composition

el·e·ment \ˈel-ə-mənt\ *n* [ME, fr. OF & L; OF, fr. L *elementum*] (13c) **1 a** : one of the four substances air, water, fire, and earth formerly believed to compose the physical universe **b** *pl* : weather conditions caused by activities of the elements; *esp* : violent or severe weather **c** : the state or sphere natural or suited to a person or thing ⟨at school she was in her ~⟩ **2** : a constituent part: as **a** *pl* : the simplest principles of a subject of study : RUDIMENTS **b (1)** : a part of a geometric magnitude ⟨an infinitesimal ~ of volume⟩ **(2)** : a generator of a geometric figure; *also* : a line or line segment contained in the surface of a cone or cylinder **(3)** : a basic member of a mathematical or logical class or set **(4)** : one of the individual entries in a mathematical matrix or determinant **c** : one of a number of distinct groups composing a human community ⟨the criminal ~ in the city⟩ **d (1)** : one of the necessary data or values on which calculations or conclusions are based **(2)** : one of the factors determining the outcome of a process **e** : any of more than 100 fundamental substances that consist of atoms of only one kind and that singly or in combination constitute all matter **f** : a distinct part of a composite device **g** : a subdivision of a military unit **3** *pl* : the bread and wine used in the Eucharist

syn ELEMENT, COMPONENT, CONSTITUENT, INGREDIENT, FACTOR mean one of the parts of a compound or complex whole. ELEMENT applies to any such part and often connotes irreducible simplicity; COMPONENT and CONSTITUENT may designate any of the substances (whether elements or compounds) or the qualities that enter into the makeup of a complex product; COMPONENT stresses its separate entity or distinguishable character; CONSTITUENT stresses its essential and formative character; INGREDIENT applies to any of the substances which when combined form a particular mixture (as a medicine or alloy); FACTOR applies to any constituent or element whose presence helps actively to perform a certain kind of work or produce a definite result.

CHEMICAL ELEMENTS

ELEMENT & SYMBOL	ATOMIC NUMBER	ATOMIC WEIGHT (C = 12)
actinium (Ac)	89	227.0278
aluminum (Al)	13	26.98154
americium (Am)	95	
antimony (Sb)	51	121.75
argon (Ar)	18	39.948
arsenic (As)	33	74.9216
astatine (At)	85	
barium (Ba)	56	137.33
berkelium (Bk)	97	
beryllium (Be)	4	9.01218
bismuth (Bi)	83	208.9804
boron (B)	5	10.81
bromine (Br)	35	79.904
cadmium (Cd)	48	112.41
calcium (Ca)	20	40.08
californium (Cf)	98	
carbon (C)	6	12.011
cerium (Ce)	58	140.12
cesium (Cs)	55	132.9054
chlorine (Cl)	17	35.453
chromium (Cr)	24	51.996
cobalt (Co)	27	58.9332
copper (Cu)	29	63.546
curium (Cm)	96	
dysprosium (Dy)	66	162.50
einsteinium (Es)	99	
erbium (Er)	68	167.26
europium (Eu)	63	151.96
fermium (Fm)	100	
fluorine (F)	9	18.998403
francium (Fr)	87	
gadolinium (Gd)	64	157.25
gallium (Ga)	31	69.72
germanium (Ge)	32	72.59
gold (Au)	79	196.9665
hafnium (Hf)	72	178.49
helium (He)	2	4.00260
holmium (Ho)	67	164.9304
hydrogen (H)	1	1.0079
indium (In)	49	114.82
iodine (I)	53	126.9045
iridium (Ir)	77	192.22
iron (Fe)	26	55.847
krypton (Kr)	36	83.80
lanthanum (La)	57	138.9055
lawrencium (Lr)	103	
lead (Pb)	82	207.2
lithium (Li)	3	6.941
lutetium (Lu)	71	174.967
magnesium (Mg)	12	24.305
manganese (Mn)	25	54.9380
mendelevium (Md)	101	
mercury (Hg)	80	200.59
molybdenum (Mo)	42	95.94
neodymium (Nd)	60	144.24
neon (Ne)	10	20.179
neptunium (Np)	93	237.0482
nickel (Ni)	28	58.69
niobium (Nb)	41	92.9064
nitrogen (N)	7	14.0067
nobelium (No)	102	
osmium (Os)	76	190.2
oxygen (O)	8	15.9994
palladium (Pd)	46	106.42
phosphorus (P)	15	30.97376
platinum (Pt)	78	195.08
plutonium (Pu)	94	
polonium (Po)	84	
potassium (K)	19	39.0983
praseodymium (Pr)	59	140.9077
promethium (Pm)	61	
protactinium (Pa)	91	231.0359
radium (Ra)	88	226.0254
radon (Rn)	86	
rhenium (Re)	75	186.207
rhodium (Rh)	45	102.9055
rubidium (Rb)	37	85.4678
ruthenium (Ru)	44	101.07
samarium (Sm)	62	150.36
scandium (Sc)	21	44.9559
selenium (Se)	34	78.96
silicon (Si)	14	28.0855
silver (Ag)	47	107.868
sodium (Na)	11	22.98977
strontium (Sr)	38	87.62
sulfur (S)	16	32.06
tantalum (Ta)	73	180.9479
technetium (Tc)	43	
tellurium (Te)	52	127.60
terbium (Tb)	65	158.9254
thallium (Tl)	81	204.383
thorium (Th)	90	232.0381
thulium (Tm)	69	168.9342
tin (Sn)	50	118.69
titanium (Ti)	22	47.88
tungsten (W)	74	183.85

ELEMENT & SYMBOL	ATOMIC NUMBER	ATOMIC WEIGHT (C = 12)
unnilhexium (Unh)	106	
unnilpentium (Unp)	105	
unnilquadium (Unq)	104	
uranium (U)	92	238.0289
vanadium (V)	23	50.9415
xenon (Xe)	54	131.29
ytterbium (Yb)	70	173.04
yttrium (Y)	39	88.9059
zinc (Zn)	30	65.38
zirconium (Zr)	40	91.22

el·e·men·tal \,el-ə-'ment-ᵊl\ adj (15c)   **1 a** : of, relating to, or being an element; specif : existing as an uncombined chemical element   **b** : of, relating to, or being the basic or ultimate constituent of something : FUNDAMENTAL ⟨~ biological and social realities⟩   **c** : of, relating to, or dealing with the rudiments of something : ELEMENTARY ⟨taught ~ crafts to the children⟩   **d** : forming an integral part : INHERENT ⟨an ~ sense of rhythm⟩   **2** : of, relating to, or resembling a great force of nature ⟨the rains come with ~ violence⟩ ⟨~ passions⟩ — **elemental** n — **el·e·men·tal·ly** \-ᵊl-ē\ adv
el·e·men·ta·ry \,el-ə-'ment-ə-rē, -'men-trē\ adj (14c)   **1 a** : of, relating to, or dealing with the simplest elements or principles of something ⟨avoids the most ~ decision-making⟩   **b** : of or relating to an elementary school ⟨an ~ curriculum⟩   **2** : ELEMENTAL 1a, 1b   **3** : ELEMENTAL 2 — **el·e·men·ta·ri·ly** \-,men-'ter-ə-lē, -'men-trə-lē\ adv — **el·e·men·ta·ri·ness** \-'ment-ə-rē-nəs, -'men-trē-\ n
elementary body n (ca. 1911) : a distinguishable unit that makes up an inclusion body and probably is the infective particle of some viruses
elementary particle n (1934) : any of the particles of which matter and energy are composed; esp : one whose existence has not been attributed to the combination of other more fundamental entities
elementary school n (1841) : a school including usu. the first four to the first eight grades and often a kindergarten
el·e·mi \'el-ə-mē\ n [NL elimi] (1543) : any of various fragrant oleoresins obtained from tropical trees (family Burseraceae) and used chiefly in varnishes, lacquers, and printing inks
elen·chus \i-'leŋ-kəs\ n, pl **-chi** \-,kī, -(,)kē\ [L, fr. Gk elenchos] (1663) : REFUTATION; esp : one in syllogistic form
el·e·phant \'el-ə-fənt\ n, often attrib [ME, fr. MF & L; MF olifant, fr. L elephantus, fr. Gk elephant-, elephas] (14c)   **1** : any of a family (Elephantidae, the elephant family) of thickset mostly very large nearly hairless four-footed mammals that have the snout prolonged into a muscular trunk and two incisors in the upper jaw developed esp. in the male into large tusks which furnish ivory and that include two living forms and various extinct relatives: as   **a** : a tall large-eared mammal (Loxodonta africana) of tropical Africa — called also African elephant   **b** : a relatively small-eared mammal (Elephas maximus) of forests of southeastern Asia — called also Asiatic elephant, Indian elephant   **2** : an animal or fossil related to the elephants

elephant: 1 African, 2 Indian

elephant grass n (1832)   **1** : an Old World cattail (Typha elephantina) used esp. in making baskets   **2** : NAPIER GRASS
el·e·phan·ti·a·sis \,el-ə-fən-'tī-ə-səs, -,fan-\ n, pl **-a·ses** \-,sēz\ [NL, fr. L, a kind of leprosy, fr. Gk, fr. elephant-, elephas] (1581)   **1** : enlargement and thickening of tissues; specif : the enormous enlargement of a limb or the scrotum caused by obstruction of lymphatics by filarial worms (esp. Wuchereria bancrofti)   **2** : an undesirable usu. enormous growth, enlargement, or overdevelopment ⟨~ of intellect and atrophy of emotion —Michael Lerner⟩
el·e·phan·tine \,el-ə-'fan-,tēn, -,tīn, 'el-ə-fən-\ adj (1630)   **1 a** : having enormous size or strength : MASSIVE   **b** : CLUMSY, PONDEROUS   **2** : of or relating to an elephant
elephant seal n (1841) : a nearly extinct large seal (Mirounga angustirostris) with a long inflatable proboscis that was formerly abundant along the coasts of California and Lower California; also : a related seal (M. leonina) formerly abundant on coasts of the southern hemisphere
El·eu·sin·i·an mysteries \,el-yü-,sin-ē-ən-\ n pl (1643) : religious mysteries celebrated at ancient Eleusis in worship of Demeter and Persephone
¹el·e·vate \'el-ə-,vāt\ adj, archaic (14c) : ELEVATED
²el·e·vate \-,vāt\ vt **-vat·ed; -vat·ing** [ME elevaten, fr. L elevatus, pp. of elevare, fr. e- + levare to raise — more at LEVER] (15c)   **1** : to lift up : RAISE   **2** : to raise in rank or status : EXALT   **3** : to improve morally, intellectually, or culturally   **4** : to raise the spirits of : ELATE   syn see LIFT

\ə\ abut \ᵊ\ kitten, F table \ər\ further \a\ ash \ā\ ace \ä\ cot, cart
\aů\ out \ch\ chin \e\ bet \ē\ easy \g\ go \i\ hit \ī\ ice \j\ job
\ŋ\ sing \ō\ go \ȯ\ law \ȯi\ boy \th\ thin \th\ the \ü\ loot \ů\ foot
\y\ yet \zh\ vision \ä, k̲, ⁿ, œ, œ̄, ūe, ūē, ᵞ\ see Guide to Pronunciation

el·e·vat·ed \-ˌvāt-əd\ *adj* (1553) **1 a :** raised esp. above the ground or other surface ⟨an ~ highway⟩ **b :** increased esp. abnormally (as in degree or amount) ⟨~ blood pressure⟩ **2 a :** being morally or intellectually on a high plane ⟨an ~ mind⟩ **b :** FORMAL, DIGNIFIED ⟨~ diction⟩ **3 :** exhilarated in mood or feeling

elevated railroad *n* (1868) **:** an urban or interurban railroad operating chiefly on an elevated structure — called also *elevated railway*

el·e·va·tion \ˌel-ə-ˈvā-shən\ *n* (14c) **1 :** the height to which something is elevated: as **a :** the angular distance of a celestial object above the horizon **b :** the degree to which a gun is aimed above the horizon **c :** the height above the level of the sea **:** ALTITUDE **2 :** a ballet dancer's or a skater's leap and seeming suspension in the air; *also* **:** the ability to achieve an elevation **3 :** an act or instance of elevating **4 :** something that is elevated: as **a :** an elevated place **b :** a swelling esp. on the skin **5 :** the quality or state of being elevated **6 :** a geometrical projection (as of a building) on a vertical plane ***syn*** see HEIGHT

el·e·va·tor \ˈel-ə-ˌvāt-ər\ *n* (15c) **1 :** one that raises or lifts something up: as **a :** an endless belt or chain conveyor with cleats, scoops, or buckets for raising material **b :** a cage or platform and its hoisting machinery for conveying something to different levels **c :** a building for elevating, storing, discharging, and sometimes processing grain **2 :** a movable auxiliary airfoil usu. attached to the tail plane of an airplane for producing motion up or down — see AIRPLANE illustration

elev·en \i-ˈlev-ən\ *n* [ME *enleven,* fr. *enleven,* adj., fr. OE *endleofan,* fr. *end-* (akin to OE *ān* one) + *-leofan;* perh. akin to OE *lēon* to lend — more at ONE, LOAN] (bef. 12c) **1** — see NUMBER table **2 :** the 11th in a set or series **3 :** something having 11 units or members; *esp* **:** a football team — **eleven** *adj or pron* — **elev·enth** \-ən(t)th\ *adj or n*

eleven–plus \i-ˌlev-ən-ˈpləs\ *n, Brit* (1937) **:** an examination taken between the ages of 11 and 12 that determines the type of secondary education to which a student is assigned

elev·ens·es \-ən-zəz\ *n pl but sometimes sing in constr* [irreg. pl. of *eleven* (o'clock)] *Brit* (ca. 1819) **:** light refreshment (as a snack) taken in the middle of the morning

eleventh hour *n* (1826) **:** the latest possible time ⟨won his reprieve at the *eleventh hour*⟩

el·e·von \ˈel-ə-ˌvän\ *n* [*elevator* + *aileron*] (1944) **:** an airplane control surface that combines the functions of elevator and aileron

elf \ˈelf\ *n, pl* **elves** \ˈelvz\ [ME, fr. OE *ælf;* akin to ON *alfr* elf & prob. to L *albus* white — more at ALB] (bef. 12c) **1 :** a small often mischievous fairy **2 a :** a small lively creature; *esp* **:** a mischievous child **b :** a usu. lively mischievous or malicious person — **elf·ish** \ˈel-fish\ *adj* — **elf·ish·ly** *adv*

elf·in \ˈel-fən\ *adj* [irreg. fr. *elf*] (1596) **1 a :** of, relating to, or produced by an elf **b :** resembling an elf **2 :** having an otherworldly or magical quality or charm

elf·lock \ˈel-ˌfläk\ *n* (1592) **:** hair matted as if by elves — usu. used in pl.

el–hi \(ˈ)el-ˈhī\ *adj* [*el*ementary (school) + *hi*gh (school)] (1948) **:** of, relating to, or designed for use in grades 1 to 12

Eli \ˈē-ˌlī\ *n* [Heb *ʽĒlī*] **:** a judge and priest of Israel who according to the account in I Samuel was entrusted with the care of the boy Samuel

Eli·as \i-ˈlī-əs\ *n* [LL, fr. Gk *Ēlias,* fr. Heb *Ēlīyāh*] **:** ELIJAH

elic·it \i-ˈlis-ət\ *vt* [L *elicitus,* pp. of *elicere,* fr. *e-* + *lacere* to allure — more at DELIGHT] (1605) **1 a :** to draw forth or bring out (something latent or potential) **b :** to derive (as a truth) by logical processes **2 :** to call forth or draw out (a response or reaction) ***syn*** see EDUCE — **elic·i·ta·tion** \ i-ˌlis-ə-ˈtā-shən, ˌē-\ *n* — **elic·i·tor** \i-ˈlis-ət-ər\ *n*

elide \i-ˈlīd\ *vt* **elid·ed; elid·ing** [L *elidere* to strike out, fr. *e-* + *laedere* to injure by striking] (1796) **1 a :** to suppress or alter (as a vowel or syllable) by elision **b :** to strike out (as a written word or passage) **2 a :** to leave out of consideration **:** OMIT **b :** CURTAIL, ABRIDGE

el·i·gi·ble \ˈel-ə-jə-bəl\ *adj* [ME, fr. MF & LL; MF, fr. LL *eligibilis,* fr. L *eligere* to choose — more at ELECT] (15c) **1 a :** qualified to be chosen **:** ENTITLED ⟨~ for sophomore standing⟩ ⟨~ to retire⟩ **b :** permitted under football rules to catch a forward pass ⟨an ~ receiver⟩ **2 :** worthy of being chosen **:** DESIRABLE ⟨an ~ young bachelor⟩ — **el·i·gi·bil·i·ty** \ˌel-ə-jə-ˈbil-ət-ē\ *n* — **eligible** *n* — **el·i·gi·bly** \ˈel-ə-jə-blē\ *adv*

Eli·jah \i-ˈlī-jə\ *n* [Heb *Ēlīyāh*] **:** a Hebrew prophet of the 9th century B.C. who according to the account in I Kings championed the worship of Jehovah as against Baal

elim·i·nate \i-ˈlim-ə-ˌnāt\ *vt* **-nat·ed; -nat·ing** [L *eliminatus,* pp. of *eliminare,* fr. *e-* + *limin-, limen* threshold — more at LIMB] (1568) **1 a :** to cast out or get rid of **:** REMOVE, ERADICATE ⟨the need to ~ poverty⟩ **b :** to set aside as unimportant **:** IGNORE **2 :** to expel (as waste) from the living body **3 :** to cause to disappear by combining two or more equations — **elim·i·na·tion** \-ˌlim-ə-ˈnā-shən\ *n* — **elim·i·na·tive** \-ˈlim-ə-ˌnāt-iv\ *adj* — **elim·i·na·tor** \-ˌnāt-ər\ *n*

Eli·sha \i-ˈlī-shə\ *n* [Heb *Ĕlīshāʽ*] **:** a Hebrew prophet and disciple and successor of Elijah

eli·sion \i-ˈlizh-ən\ *n* [LL *elision-, elisio,* fr. L *elisus,* pp. of *elidere*] (1581) **1 a :** the use of a speech form that lacks a final or initial sound which a variant speech form has ⟨the use of *'s* instead of *is* in *there's* is an example of ~⟩ **b :** the omission of an unstressed vowel or syllable in a verse to achieve a uniform metrical pattern **2 :** the act or an instance of omitting something **:** OMISSION

elite \ā-ˈlēt, i-\ *n* [F *élite,* fr. OF *eslite,* fr. fem. of *eslit,* pp. of *eslire* to choose, fr. L *eligere*] (1823) **1 a :** the choice part or segment; *esp* **:** a socially superior group **b :** a powerful minority group ⟨a power ~ inside the government⟩ **2 :** a typewriter type providing 12 characters to the linear inch — **elite** *adj*

elit·ism \-ˈlēt-ˌiz-əm\ *n* (1947) **1 a :** leadership or rule by an elite **b :** belief in or advocacy of such elitism **2 :** consciousness of being or belonging to an elite — **elit·ist** \-ˈlēt-əst\ *n or adj*

elix·ir \i-ˈlik-sər\ *n* [ME, fr. ML, fr. Ar *al-iksīr* the elixir, fr. *al* the + *iksīr* elixir, prob. fr. Gk *xērion* desiccative powder, fr. *xēros* dry — more at SERENE] (14c) **1 a :** a substance held capable of changing base metals into gold **:** PHILOSOPHERS' STONE **b** (1) **:** a substance held capable of prolonging life indefinitely (2) **:** CURE-ALL (3) **:** a sweetened liquid usu. containing alcohol that is used as a vehicle for medicinal agents **2 :** the essential principle

Eliz·a·be·than \i-ˌliz-ə-ˈbē-thən\ *adj* (1817) **:** of, relating to, or characteristic of Elizabeth I of England or her age — **Elizabethan** *n*

elk \ˈelk\ *n, pl* **elks** [ME, prob. fr. OE *eolh;* akin to OHG *elaho* elk, Gk *elaphos* deer] (bef. 12c) **1** *pl usu* **elk a :** the largest existing deer (*Alces alces*) of Europe and Asia resembling but not so large as the moose of No. America **b :** a No. American deer (*Cervus canadensis*) similar to the red deer of Europe and related forms — called also *wapiti* **c :** any of various large Asian deer **2 :** soft tanned rugged leather **3** *cap* [Benevolent and Protective Order of *Elks*] **:** a member of a major benevolent and fraternal order

elk·hound \ˈelk-ˌhau̇nd, ˈel-ˌkau̇nd\ *n* (1835) **:** NORWEGIAN ELKHOUND

[1]**ell** \ˈel\ *n* [ME *eln,* fr. OE; akin to OHG *elina* ell, L *ulna* elbow, arm, Gk *ōlenē* elbow, Skt *āni* linchpin, thigh] (bef. 12c) **1 :** a former English unit of length (as for cloth) equal to 45 inches **2 :** any of various units of length similar in use to the English ell

[2]**ell** *n* [alter. of [1]*el*] (1773) **1 :** an extension at right angles to the length of a building **2 :** an elbow in a pipe or conduit

el·lag·ic acid \ə-ˌlaj-ik-, e-\ *n* [F *ellagique,* fr. *ellag,* anagram of *galle* gall] (1810) **:** a crystalline phenolic compound $C_{14}H_6O_8$ with two lactone groupings that is obtained esp. from oak galls and some tannins and is used medicinally as a hemostatic

el·lipse \i-ˈlips, e-\ *n* [Gk *elleipsis*] (1753) **1 a :** OVAL **b :** a closed plane curve generated by a point moving in such a way that the sums of its distances from two fixed points is a constant **:** a plane section of a right circular cone that is a closed curve **2 :** ELLIPSIS

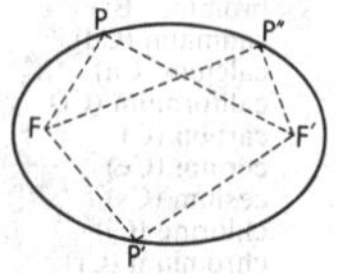

ellipse 1b: *F, F′* foci; *P, P′, P″* any point on the curve; *FP + PF′ = FP″ + P″F′ = FP′ + P′F′*

el·lip·sis \i-ˈlip-səs, e-\ *n, pl* **el·lip·ses** \-ˌsēz\ [L, fr. Gk *elleipsis* ellipsis, ellipse, fr. *elleipein* to leave out, fall short, fr. *en* in + *leipein* to leave — more at IN, LOAN] (1540) **1 a :** the omission of one or more words that are obviously understood but that must be supplied to make a construction grammatically complete ⟨"the man that he sees" may be changed by ~ to "the man he sees"⟩ **b :** a leap or sudden passage without logical connectives from one topic to another **2 :** marks or a mark (as . . . or *** or —) indicating an omission (as of words) or a pause

el·lip·soid \i-ˈlip-ˌsȯid, e-\ *n* (1721) **:** a surface all plane sections of which are ellipses or circles — **ellipsoid** *or* **el·lip·soi·dal** \i-ˌlip-ˈsȯid-ᵊl, (ˌ)e-\ *adj*

el·lip·tic \i-ˈlip-tik, e-\ *or* **el·lip·ti·cal** \-ti-kəl\ *adj* [Gk *elleiptikos* defective, marked by ellipsis, fr. *elleipein*] (1656) **1 :** of, relating to, or shaped like an ellipse **2 a :** of, relating to, or marked by ellipsis or an ellipsis **b** (1) **:** of, relating to, or marked by extreme economy of speech or writing (2) **:** of or relating to deliberate obscurity (as of literary or conversational style) — **el·lip·ti·cal·ly** \-ti-k(ə-)lē\ *adv*

el·lip·tic·i·ty \i-ˌlip-ˈtis-ət-ē, (ˌ)e-\ *n* (1753) **:** deviation of an ellipse or a spheroid from the form of a circle or a sphere

elm \ˈelm\ *n* [ME, fr. OE; akin to OHG *elme* elm, L *ulmus*] (bef. 12c) **1 :** any of a genus (*Ulmus* of the family Ulmaceae, the elm family) comprising large graceful trees with alternate stipulate leaves and small apetalous flowers **2 :** the wood of an elm

elm bark beetle *n* (1909) **:** either of two beetles that are vectors for the fungus causing Dutch elm disease: **a :** a beetle (*Hylurgopinus rufipes*) native to eastern No. America **b :** a European beetle (*Scolytus multistriatus*) that is established in eastern No. America

elm leaf beetle *n* (1881) **:** a small orange-yellow black-striped Old World chrysomelid beetle (*Pyrrhalta luteola*) that is a leaf-eating pest of elms in eastern No. America as a larva and as an adult

El Ni·ño \el-ˈnēn-yō\ *n* [Sp, lit., the child] (1925) **:** an irregularly occurring flow of unusually warm surface water along the western coast of South America that is accompanied by abnormally high rainfall in usu. arid areas and that prevents upwelling of nutrient-rich cold deep water causing a decline in the regional fish population

el·o·cu·tion \ˌel-ə-ˈkyü-shən\ *n* [ME *elocucioun,* fr. L *elocution-, elocutio,* fr. *elocutus,* pp. of *eloqui*] (15c) **1 :** the art of effective public speaking **2 :** a style of speaking esp. in public — **el·o·cu·tion·ary** \-shə-ˌner-ē\ *adj* — **el·o·cu·tion·ist** \-sh(ə-)nəst\ *n*

elo·dea \i-ˈlōd-ē-ə\ *n* [NL, fr. Gk *helōdēs* marshy, fr. *helos* marsh; akin to Skt *saras* pond] (ca. 1868) **:** any of a small American genus (*Elodea*) of submerged aquatic monocotyledonous herbs

eloign \i-ˈlȯin\ *vt* [ME *eloynen,* fr. MF *esloigner,* fr. OF, fr. *es-* ex- (fr. L *ex-*) + *loing* (adv.) far, fr. L *longe,* fr. *longus* long] (1500) **1** *archaic* **:** to take (oneself) far away **2** *archaic* **:** to remove to a distant or unknown place **:** CONCEAL

[1]**elon·gate** \i-ˈlȯŋ-ˌgāt\ *vb* **-gat·ed; -gat·ing** [LL *elongatus,* pp. of *elongare,* to withdraw, fr. L *e-* + *longus*] *vt* (1578) **:** to extend the length of ~ *vi* **:** to grow in length

[2]**elongate** *or* **elon·gat·ed** *adj* (1828) **1 :** stretched out **2 :** SLENDER

elon·ga·tion \(ˌ)ē-ˌlȯŋ-ˈgā-shən\ *n* (14c) **1 a :** the angular distance of a celestial body from another around which it revolves or from a particular point in the sky **b :** the daily extreme east or west position of a star with reference to the north celestial pole **2 a :** the state of being elongated or lengthened; *also* **:** the process of growing or increasing in length **b :** something that is elongated

elope \i-ˈlōp\ *vi* **eloped; elop·ing** [AF *aloper*] (1628) **1 a :** to run away from one's husband with a lover **b :** to run away secretly with the intention of getting married usu. without parental consent **2 :** to slip away **:** ESCAPE — **elope·ment** \-ˈlōp-mənt\ *n* — **elop·er** *n*

el·o·quence \ˈel-ə-kwən(t)s\ *n* (14c) **1 :** discourse marked by force and persuasiveness; *also* **:** the art or power of using such discourse **2 :** the quality of forceful or persuasive expressiveness

el·o·quent \-kwənt\ *adj* [ME, fr. MF, fr. L *eloquent-, eloquens,* fr. prp. of *eloqui* to speak out, fr. *e-* + *loqui* to speak] (14c) **1 :** marked by forceful and fluent expression ⟨an ~ preacher⟩ **2 :** vividly or movingly expressive or revealing ⟨an ~ monument⟩ — **el·o·quent·ly** *adv*

[1]**else** \ˈel(t)s\ *adv* [ME *elles,* fr. OE; akin to L *alius* other, *alter* other of two, Gk *allos* other] (bef. 12c) **1 a :** in a different manner or place or at a different time ⟨how ~ could he have acted⟩ ⟨here and nowhere ~⟩ **b :** in an additional manner or place or at an additional time ⟨where ~ is gold found⟩ **2 :** if not **:** OTHERWISE ⟨leave or ~ you'll be sorry⟩ — used absolutely to express a threat ⟨do what I tell you or ~⟩

[2]**else** *adj* (bef. 12c) **:** OTHER: **a :** being different in identity ⟨it must have been somebody ~⟩ **b :** being in addition ⟨what ~ did he say⟩

else·where \-ˌ(h)we(ə)r, -ˌ(h)wa(ə)r\ *adv* [ME *elleswher,* fr. OE *elles hwær*] (bef. 12c) **:** in or to another place ⟨took his business ~⟩

el·u·ant *or* **el·u·ent** \'el-yə-wənt\ *n* [L *eluent-, eluens,* prp. of *eluere*] (1941) : a solvent used in eluting

el·u·ate \'el-yə-wət, -ˌwāt\ *n* [L *eluere* + E *-ate*] (1932) : the washings obtained by eluting

elu·ci·date \i-'lü-sə-ˌdāt\ *vb* **-dat·ed; -dat·ing** [LL *elucidatus,* pp. of *elucidare,* fr. L *e-* + *lucidus* lucid] *vt* (1568) : to make lucid esp. by explanation or analysis ~ *vi* : to give a clarifying explanation — syn see EXPLAIN — **elu·ci·da·tion** \-ˌlü-sə-'dā-shən\ *n* — **elu·ci·da·tive** \-'lü-sə-ˌdāt-iv\ *adj* — **elu·ci·da·tor** \-ˌdāt-ər\ *n*

elu·cu·brate \i-'lü-k(y)ə-ˌbrāt\ *vt* **-brat·ed; -brat·ing** [L *elucubratus,* pp. of *elucubrare* to compose by lamplight, fr. *e-* + *lucubrare* to work by lamplight — more at LUCUBRATION] (ca. 1623) : to work out or express by studious effort — **elu·cu·bra·tion** \-ˌlü-k(y)ə-'brā-shən\ *n*

elude \ē-'lüd\ *vt* **elud·ed; elud·ing** [L *eludere,* fr. *e-* + *ludere* to play — more at LUDICROUS] (1612) **1** : to avoid adroitly : EVADE ⟨the mice *eluded* the traps⟩ ⟨managed to ~ capture⟩ **2** : to escape the perception, understanding, or grasp of ⟨subtlety simply ~s them⟩ ⟨victory continued to ~ us⟩ **3** : DEFY 4 ⟨it ~s explanation⟩ — syn see ESCAPE

Elul \e-'lül\ *n* [Heb *Ēlūl*] (1535) : the 12th month of the civil year or the 6th month of the ecclesiastical year in the Jewish calendar — see MONTH table

elu·sion \ē-'lü-zhən\ *n* [ML *elusion-, elusio,* fr. LL, deception, fr. L *elusus,* pp. of *eludere*] (1624) : an act of eluding: as **a** : an adroit escape **b** : an evasion esp. of a problem or an order

elu·sive \ē-'lü-siv, -'lü-ziv\ *adj* (1719) : tending to elude: as **a** : tending to evade grasp or pursuit ⟨an eligible though ~ bachelor⟩ **b** : hard to comprehend or define ⟨an ~ concept that means many things to many people⟩ **c** : hard to isolate or identify ⟨a haunting ~ aroma⟩ — **elu·sive·ly** *adv* — **elu·sive·ness** *n*

elute \ē-'lüt\ *vt* **elut·ed; elut·ing** [L *elutus,* pp. of *eluere* to wash out, fr. *e-* + *lavere* to wash — more at LYE] (1731) : EXTRACT; *specif* : to remove (adsorbed material) from an adsorbent by means of a solvent — **elu·tion** \-'lü-shən\ *n*

elu·tri·ate \ē-'lü-trē-ˌāt\ *vt* **-at·ed; -at·ing** [L *elutriatus,* pp. of *elutriare,* irreg. fr. *elutus*] (ca. 1727) : to purify, separate, or remove by washing — **elu·tri·a·tor** \-ˌāt-ər\ *n*

elu·vi·al \ē-'lü-vē-əl\ *adj* (1862) **1** : of, relating to, or composed of eluvium **2** : of or relating to eluviation or to eluviated materials or areas

elu·vi·ate \-vē-ˌāt\ *vi* **-at·ed; -at·ing** (1926) : to undergo eluviation

elu·vi·a·tion \(ˌ)ē-ˌlü-vē-'ā-shən\ *n* (1899) : the transportation of dissolved or suspended material within the soil by the movement of water when rainfall exceeds evaporation

elu·vi·um \ē-'lü-vē-əm\ *n* [NL, fr. L *eluere*] (1882) **1** : rock debris produced by the weathering and disintegration of rock in situ **2** : fine soil or sand deposited by wind

el·ver \'el-vər\ *n* [alter. of *eelfare* (migration of eels)] (1640) : a young eel

elves *pl of* ELF

el·vish \'el-vish\ *adj* (13c) **1** : of or relating to elves **2** : MISCHIEVOUS

ely·sian \i-'lizh-ən\ *adj, often cap* (1579) **1** : of or relating to Elysium **2** : BLISSFUL, DELIGHTFUL

elysian fields *n pl, often cap E* (1579) : ELYSIUM

Ely·si·um \i-'liz(h)-ē-əm\ *n, pl* **-si·ums** *or* **-sia** \-ē-ə\ [L, fr. Gk *Elysion*] (1590) **1** : the abode of the blessed after death in classical mythology **2** : PARADISE 2

elytr- *or* **elytri-** *or* **elytro-** *comb form* [NL *elytron*] : elytron ⟨elytroid⟩ ⟨elytriferous⟩

el·y·tron \'el-ə-ˌträn\ *also* **el·y·trum** \-trəm\ *n, pl* **-tra** \-trə\ [NL, fr. Gk, sheath, wing cover, fr. *eilyein* to roll, wrap — more at VOLUBLE] (1774) : one of the anterior wings in beetles and some other insects that serve to protect the posterior pair of functional wings

em \'em\ *n* (13c) **1** : the letter *m* **2** : the width of a piece of type about as wide as it is tall used as a unit of measure of typeset matter

em- — see EN-

'em \əm\ *pron* [ME *hem,* fr. OE *heom, him,* dat. pl. of *hē* he] (bef. 12c) : THEM

ema·ci·ate \i-'mā-shē-ˌāt\ *vb* **-at·ed; -at·ing** [L *emaciatus,* pp. of *emaciare,* fr. *e-* + *macies* leanness, fr. *macer* lean — more at MEAGER] *vt* (1650) **1** : to cause to lose flesh so as to become very thin **2** : to make feeble ~ *vi* : to waste away physically — **ema·ci·a·tion** \-ˌmā-s(h)ē-'ā-shən\ *n*

emalangeni *pl of* LILANGENI

em·a·nate \'em-ə-ˌnāt\ *vb* **-nat·ed; -nat·ing** [L *emanatus,* pp. of *emanare,* fr. *e-* + *manare* to flow] *vi* (1756) : to come out from a source ~ *vt* : EMIT syn see SPRING

em·a·na·tion \ˌem-ə-'nā-shən\ *n* (1570) **1 a** : the action of emanating **b** : the origination of the world by a series of hierarchically descending radiations from the Godhead through intermediate stages to matter **2 a** : something that emanates or is produced by emanation : EFFLUENCE **b** : a heavy gaseous element produced by radioactive disintegration ⟨radium ~⟩ — **em·a·na·tion·al** \-shnəl, -shən-ᵊl\ *adj* — **em·a·na·tive** \'em-ə-ˌnāt-iv\ *adj*

eman·ci·pate \i-'man(t)-sə-ˌpāt\ *vt* **-pat·ed; -pat·ing** [L *emancipatus,* pp. of *emancipare,* fr. *e-* + *mancipare* to transfer ownership of, fr. *mancip-, manceps* purchaser, fr. *manus* hand + *capere* to take — more at MANUAL, HEAVE] (1625) **1** : to free from restraint, control, or the power of another; *esp* : to free from bondage **2** : to release from paternal care and responsibility and make sui juris **3** : to free from any controlling influence (as traditional mores or beliefs) — syn see FREE — **eman·ci·pa·tor** \-ˌpāt-ər\ *n*

eman·ci·pa·tion \i-ˌman(t)-sə-'pā-shən\ *n* (1631) : the act or process of emancipating — **eman·ci·pa·tion·ist** \-sh(ə-)nəst\ *n*

emar·gin·ate \(ˈ)ē-'mär-jə-nət, -ˌnāt\ *adj* [L *emarginatus,* pp. of *emarginare* to deprive of a margin, fr. *e-* + *margin-, margo* margin] (1794) : having the margin notched — **emar·gi·na·tion** \(ˌ)ē-ˌmär-jə-'nā-shən\ *n*

emas·cu·late \i-'mas-kyə-ˌlāt\ *vt* **-lat·ed; -lat·ing** [L *emasculatus,* pp. of *emasculare,* fr. *e-* + *masculus* male — more at MALE] (1607) **1** : to deprive of virile or procreative power : CASTRATE **2** : to deprive of strength, vigor, or spirit : WEAKEN **3** : to remove the androecium of (a flower) in the process of artificial cross-pollination syn see UNNERVE — **emas·cu·late** \-lət\ *adj* — **emas·cu·la·tion** \-ˌmas-kyə-'lā-shən\ *n* — **emas·cu·la·tor** \-'mas-kyə-ˌlāt-ər\ *n*

em·balm \im-'bä(l)m, *NEng also* -'bäm\ *vt* [ME *embaumen,* fr. MF *embaumer,* fr. OF *embasmer,* fr. *en-* + *basme* balm — more at BALM] (14c) **1** : to treat (a dead body) so as to protect from decay **2** : to fill with sweet odors : PERFUME **3** : to protect from decay or oblivion : PRESERVE **4** : to fix in a static condition — **em·balm·er** *n* — **em·balm·ment** \-'bä(l)m-mənt, -'bäm-\ *n*

em·bank \im-'baŋk\ *vt* (1700) : to enclose or confine by an embankment

em·bank·ment \-mənt\ *n* (1786) **1** : a raised structure to hold back water or to carry a roadway **2** : the action of embanking

em·bar·ca·de·ro \(ˌ)em-ˌbär-kə-'de(ə)r-(ˌ)ō\ *n, pl* **-ros** [Sp, fr. *embarcado,* pp. of *embarcar* to embark, fr. *en-* (fr. L *in-*) + *barca* bark, fr. LL] *West* (1846) : a landing place esp. on an inland waterway

¹em·bar·go \im-'bär-(ˌ)gō\ *n, pl* **-goes** [Sp, fr. *embargar* to bar, (assumed) VL *imbarricare,* fr. L *in-* + (assumed) VL *barra* bar] (1593) **1** : an order of a government prohibiting the departure of commercial ships from its ports **2** : a legal prohibition on commerce ⟨an ~ on arms shipments⟩ **3** : STOPPAGE, IMPEDIMENT; *esp* : PROHIBITION ⟨I lay no ~ on anybody's words —Jane Austen⟩ **4** : an order by a common carrier or public regulatory agency prohibiting or restricting freight transportation

²embargo *vt* **-goed; -go·ing** (1755) : to place an embargo on (as ships or commerce)

em·bark \im-'bärk\ *vb* [MF *embarquer,* fr. OProv *embarcar,* fr. *em-* (fr. L *im-*) + *barca* bark] *vt* (1550) **1** : to cause to go on board (as a boat or airplane) **2** : to engage, enlist, or invest in an enterprise ~ *vi* **1** : to go on board a vehicle for transportation **2** : to make a start : COMMENCE ⟨~ed on a new career⟩ — **em·bar·ka·tion** \ˌem-ˌbär-'kā-shən, -bər-\ *n* — **em·bark·ment** \im-'bärk-mənt\ *n*

em·bar·rass \im-'bar-əs\ *vt* [F *embarrasser,* fr. Sp *embarazar,* fr. Pg *embaraçar*] (1672) **1 a** : to place in doubt, perplexity, or difficulties **b** : to involve in financial difficulties **c** : to cause to experience a state of self-conscious distress ⟨bawdy stories ~ed her⟩ **2 a** : to hamper the movement of **b** : HINDER, IMPEDE **3** : to make intricate : COMPLICATE **4** : to impair the activity of (a bodily function) or the function of (a bodily part) ⟨digestion ~ed by overeating⟩ — **em·bar·rass·able** \-ə-bəl\ *adj*

em·bar·rassed·ly \-əst-lē, -ə-səd-lē\ *adv* (1883) : with embarrassment ⟨giggled ~⟩

em·bar·rass·ing·ly \-ə-siŋ-lē\ *adv* (ca. 1864) : to an embarrassing degree

em·bar·rass·ment \im-'bar-ə-smənt\ *n* (ca. 1676) **1** : the state of being embarrassed: as **a** : confusion or disturbance of mind **b** : difficulty arising from the want of money to pay debts **c** : difficulty in functioning as a result of disease ⟨cardiac ~⟩ **2** : something that embarrasses : IMPEDIMENT **b** : an excessive quantity from which to select — used esp. in the phrase *embarrassment of riches*

em·bas·sage \'em-bə-sij\ *n* (1526) **1** : the message or commission entrusted to an ambassador **2** *archaic* : EMBASSY

em·bas·sy \'em-bə-sē\ *n, pl* **-sies** [MF *ambassee,* of Gmc origin; akin to OHG *ambaht* service] (1579) **1 a** : the function or position of an ambassador **b** : a mission abroad undertaken officially esp. by an ambassador **2** : EMBASSAGE 1 **3** : a body of diplomatic representatives; *specif* : one headed by an ambassador **4** : the official residence and offices of an ambassador

em·bat·tle \im-'bat-ᵊl\ *vt* **em·bat·tled; em·bat·tling** \-'bat-liŋ, -ᵊl-iŋ\ [ME *embatailen,* fr. MF *embatailler,* fr. *en-* + *bataille* to battle] (14c) **1** : to arrange in order of battle : prepare for battle **2** : FORTIFY

em·bat·tled *adj* (15c) **1 a** : ready to fight : prepared to give battle ⟨here once the ~ farmers stood —R. W. Emerson⟩ **b** : engaged in battle, conflict, or controversy ⟨an ~ official accused of extortion⟩ **2 a** : being a site of battle, conflict, or controversy ⟨the ~ capital⟩ **b** : characterized by conflict or controversy ⟨his ... often ~ experience as an educator —Nat Hentoff⟩

¹em·bat·tle·ment \-'bat-ᵊl-mənt\ *n* (15c) : BATTLEMENT

²embattlement *n* (1971) : the state of being embattled

em·bay \im-'bā\ *vt* (1600) : to shut or shelter esp. in a bay ⟨an ~ed fleet⟩

em·bay·ment \-'bā-mənt\ *n* (1815) **1** : formation of a bay **2** : a bay or a conformation resembling a bay

Emb·den \'em-dən\ *n* [*Emden,* West Germany] (1903) : a breed of large white domestic geese with an orange bill and deep orange shanks and toes

em·bed \im-'bed\ *vb* **em·bed·ded; em·bed·ding** *vt* (1794) **1 a** : to enclose closely in or as if in a matrix ⟨fossils *embedded* in stone⟩ **b** : to make something an integral part of ⟨inflation was *embedded* in the economic system⟩ **c** : to prepare (a microscopy specimen) for sectioning by infiltrating with and enclosing in a supporting substance **2** : to surround closely ⟨a sweet pulp ~s the plum seed⟩ ~ *vi* : to become embedded — **em·bed·ment** \-'bed-mənt\ *n*

em·bel·lish \im-'bel-ish\ *vt* [ME *embelisshen,* fr. MF *embeliss-,* stem of *embelir,* fr. *en-* + *bel* beautiful — more at BEAUTY] (14c) **1** : to make beautiful with ornamentation : DECORATE **2** : to heighten the attractiveness of by adding ornamental details : ENHANCE ⟨events in his life, heavily ~ed by his biographers —Marvin Reznikoff⟩ syn see ADORN — **em·bel·lish·er** *n*

em·bel·lish·ment \-ish-mənt\ *n* (1623) **1** : the act or process of embellishing **2** : something serving to embellish **3** : ORNAMENT 5

em·ber \'em-bər\ *n* [ME *eymere,* fr. ON *eimyrja;* akin to OE *ǣmerge* ashes, L *urere* to burn] (14c) **1** : a glowing fragment (as of coal) from a fire; *esp* : one smoldering in ashes **2** *pl* : the smoldering remains of a fire **3** *pl* : slowly cooling emotions, memories, ideas, or responses still capable of being enlivened

ember day \'em-bər-\ *n* [ME, fr. OE *ymbrendæg,* fr. *ymbrene* circuit, anniversary + *dæg* day] (bef. 12c) : a Wednesday, Friday, or Saturday following the first Sunday in Lent, Whitsunday, September 14, or December 13 and set apart for fasting and prayer in Western churches

---

\ə\ abut \ᵊ\ kitten, F table \ər\ further \a\ ash \ā\ ace \ä\ cot, cart \aú\ out \ch\ chin \e\ bet \ē\ easy \g\ go \i\ hit \ī\ ice \j\ job \ŋ\ sing \ō\ go \ó\ law \ói\ boy \th\ thin \t̲h̲\ the \ü\ loot \ú\ foot \y\ yet \zh\ vision \ä, k̲, ⁿ, œ, œ̄, ᵫ, ᵫ̄, �\ see Guide to Pronunciation

em·bez·zle \im-'bez-əl\ *vt* **em·bez·zled; em·bez·zling** \-(ə-)liŋ\ [ME *embesilen,* fr. AF *embeseiller,* fr. MF *en-* + *besillier* to destroy] (15c) **:** to appropriate (as property entrusted to one's care) fraudulently to one's own use — **em·bez·zle·ment** \-əl-mənt\ *n* — **em·bez·zler** \-(ə-)lər\ *n*

em·bit·ter \im-'bit-ər\ *vt* (1603) **1 :** to make bitter **2 :** to excite bitter feelings in — **em·bit·ter·ment** \-mənt\ *n*

[1]em·blaze \im-'blāz\ *vt* **em·blazed; em·blaz·ing** [*en-* + *blaze* (to blazon)] (1593) **1** *archaic* **:** EMBLAZON 1 **2 :** to adorn sumptuously ⟨with gems and golden luster rich *emblazed* —John Milton⟩

[2]emblaze *vt* **em·blazed; em·blaz·ing** (1634) **1 :** to illuminate esp. by a blaze **2 :** to set ablaze

em·bla·zon \im-'blāz-ᵊn\ *vt* **em·bla·zoned; em·bla·zon·ing** \-'blāz-niŋ, -ᵊn-iŋ\ (1592) **1 a :** to inscribe or adorn with or as if with heraldic bearings or devices **b :** to inscribe (as heraldic bearings) on a surface **2 :** CELEBRATE, EXTOL ⟨have his . . . deeds ~*ed* by a poet —Thomas Nash⟩ — **em·bla·zon·er** \-'blāz-nər, -ᵊn-ər\ *n* — **em·bla·zon·ment** \-'blāz-ᵊn-mənt\ *n*

em·bla·zon·ry \-ᵊn-rē\ *n* (1667) **1 :** the act or art of emblazoning **2 :** emblazoned figures **:** brilliant decoration

[1]em·blem \'em-bləm\ *n* [ME, fr. L *emblema* inlaid work, fr. Gk *emblēmat-, emblēma,* fr. *emballein* to insert, fr. *en-* + *ballein* to throw — more at DEVIL] (15c) **1 :** a picture with a motto or set of verses intended as a moral lesson **2 :** an object or the figure of an object symbolizing and suggesting another object or an idea **3 a :** a symbolic object used as a heraldic device **b :** a device, symbol, or figure adopted and used as an identifying mark

[2]emblem *vt* (1584) **:** EMBLEMATIZE

em·blem·at·ic \,em-blə-'mat-ik\ *also* **em·blem·at·i·cal** \-i-kəl\ *adj* (1645) **:** of, relating to, or constituting an emblem **:** SYMBOLIC — **em·blem·at·i·cal·ly** \-i-k(ə-)lē\ *adv*

em·blem·a·tize \em-'blem-ə-,tīz\ *vt* **-tized; -tiz·ing** (1615) **:** to represent by or as if by an emblem **:** SYMBOLIZE

em·ble·ments \'em-blə-mən(t)s\ *n pl* [ME *emblayment,* fr. MF *emblaement,* fr. *emblaer* to sow with grain, fr. *en-* + *blee* grain] (15c) **:** crops from annual cultivation legally belonging to the tenant

em·bodi·ment \im-'bäd-i-mənt\ *n* (1828) **1 :** one that embodies something ⟨the ~ of all our hopes⟩ **2 :** the act of embodying **:** the state of being embodied

em·body \im-'bäd-ē\ *vt* **em·bod·ied; em·body·ing** (1548) **1 :** to give a body to (a spirit) **:** INCARNATE **2 a :** to deprive of spirituality **b :** to make concrete and perceptible **3 :** to cause to become a body or part of a body **:** INCORPORATE **4 :** to represent in human or animal form **:** PERSONIFY ⟨men who greatly *embodied* the idealism of American life —A. M. Schlesinger *b*1917⟩ — **em·bodi·er** *n*

embol- *or* **emboli-** *or* **embolo-** *comb form* [NL, fr. *embolus*] **:** embolus ⟨*embolectomy*⟩

em·bold·en \im-'bōl-dən\ *vt* (15c) **:** to instill with boldness or courage

em·bo·lec·to·my \,em-bə-'lek-tə-mē\ *n, pl* **-mies** (1923) **:** surgical removal of an embolus

em·bol·ic \em-'bäl-ik, im-\ *adj* (ca. 1864) **:** of or relating to an embolus or embolism

em·bo·lism \'em-bə-,liz-əm\ *n* [ME *embolisme,* fr. ML *embolismus,* fr. Gk *embol-* (fr. *emballein* to insert, intercalate) — more at EMBLEM] (14c) **1 :** the insertion of one or more days in a calendar **:** INTERCALATION **2 a :** the sudden obstruction of a blood vessel by an embolus **b :** EMBOLUS — **em·bo·lis·mic** \,em-bə-'liz-mik\ *adj*

em·bo·li·za·tion \,em-bə-lə-'zā-shən\ *n* (1942) **:** the process or state in which a blood vessel or organ is obstructed by the lodgment of a material mass (as an embolus)

em·bo·lus \'em-bə-ləs\ *n, pl* **-li** \-,lī\ [NL, fr. Gk *embolos* wedge-shaped object, stopper, fr. *emballein*] (1859) **:** an abnormal particle (as an air bubble) circulating in the blood — compare THROMBUS

em·bon·point \ä^n-bō^n-pwa^n\ *n* [F, fr. MF, fr. *en bon point* in good condition] (1670) **:** plumpness of person **:** STOUTNESS

em·bo·som \im-'bu̇z-əm *also* -'büz-\ *vt* (1590) **1** *archaic* **:** to take into or place in the bosom **2 :** to shelter closely **:** ENCLOSE ⟨his house ~*ed* in the grove —Alexander Pope⟩

[1]em·boss \im-'bäs, -'bȯs\ *vt* [ME *embosen,* fr. MF *embocer,* fr. *en-* + *boce* boss] (15c) **1 :** to raise the surface of into bosses; *esp* **:** to ornament with raised work **2 :** to raise in relief from a surface **3 :** ADORN, EMBELLISH — **em·boss·able** \-ə-bəl\ *adj* — **em·boss·er** \-ər\ *n* — **em·boss·ment** \-mənt\ *n*

[2]emboss *vt* [ME *embosen* to become exhausted fr. being hunted, deriv. of MF *bois* woods] *obs* (1590) **:** to drive (as a hunted animal) to bay

em·bou·chure \,äm-bü-'shu̇(ə)r\ *n* [F, fr. (*s'*)*emboucher* to flow into, fr. *en-* + *bouche* mouth — more at DEBOUCH] (1760) **1 :** the position and use of the lips, tongue, and teeth in playing a wind instrument **2 :** the mouthpiece of a musical instrument

em·bowed \im-'bōd\ *adj* (15c) **:** bent like a bow: as **a :** ARCHED, VAULTED ⟨an ~ ceiling⟩ **b :** curved outward to form a projecting recess

em·bow·el \im-'bau̇(-ə)l\ *vt* **-eled** *or* **-elled; -el·ing** *or* **-el·ling** (1521) **1 :** DISEMBOWEL **2** *obs* **:** ENCLOSE

em·bow·er \im-'bau̇(-ə)r\ *vt* (1580) **:** to shelter or enclose in or as if in a bower ⟨like a rose ~*ed* in its own green leaves —P. B. Shelley⟩

[1]em·brace \im-'brās\ *vb* **em·braced; em·brac·ing** [ME *embracen,* fr. MF *embracer,* fr. OF *embracier,* fr. *en-* + *brace* two arms — more at BRACE] *vt* (14c) **1 a :** to clasp in the arms **:** HUG **b :** CHERISH, LOVE **2 :** ENCIRCLE, ENCLOSE **3 a :** to take up esp. readily or gladly ⟨~ a cause⟩ **b :** to avail oneself of **:** WELCOME ⟨*embraced* the opportunity to study further⟩ **4 a :** to take in or include as a part, item, or element of a more inclusive whole ⟨charity ~*s* all acts that contribute to human welfare⟩ **b :** to be equal or equivalent to ⟨his assets *embraced* $10⟩ ~ *vi* **:** to participate in an embrace ***syn*** see ADOPT, INCLUDE — **em·brace·able** \-'brā-sə-bəl\ *adj* — **em·brace·ment** \-'brā-smənt\ *n* — **em·brac·er** *n* — **em·brac·ing·ly** \-'brā-siŋ-lē\ *adv*

[2]embrace *n* (1592) **1 :** a close encircling with the arms and pressure to the bosom esp. as a sign of affection **:** HUG **2 :** GRIP, ENCIRCLEMENT ⟨in the ~ of terror⟩ **3 :** ACCEPTANCE ⟨her ~ of new ideas⟩

em·bra·ceor \im-'brā-sər\ *n* [AF, fr. MF *embraseor* instigator, fr. *embraser* to set on fire, fr. *en-* + *brase, brese* live coals] (15c) **:** one guilty of embracery

em·brac·ery \im-'brās-(ə-)rē\ *n, pl* **-er·ies** [ME, fr. AF *embraceor*] (15c) **:** an attempt to influence a jury corruptly (as by bribes or threats)

em·brac·ive \-'brā-siv\ *adj* (1855) **1 :** disposed to embrace **2 :** INCLUSIVE, COMPREHENSIVE

em·branch·ment \im-'branch-mənt\ *n* [F *embranchement,* fr. (*s'*)*embrancher* to branch out, fr. *en-* + *branche* branch] (1830) **1 :** a branching off or out (as of a valley) **2 :** BRANCH

em·bran·gle \im-'braŋ-gəl\ *vt* **-gled; -gling** \-g(ə-)liŋ\ [*en-* + *brangle* (squabble)] (1664) **:** EMBROIL — **em·bran·gle·ment** \-gəl-mənt\ *n*

em·bra·sure \im-'brā-zhər\ *n* [F, fr. obs. *embraser* to widen an opening] (1702) **1 :** a recess of a door or window **2 :** an opening with sides flaring outward in a wall or parapet of a fortification usu. for allowing the firing of cannon

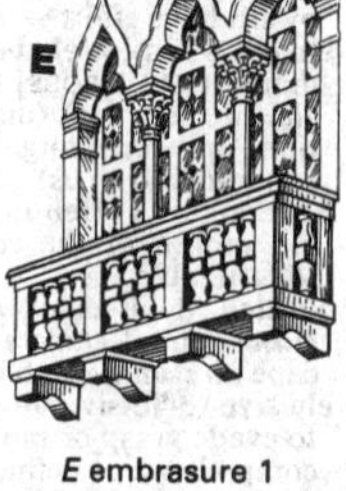

E embrasure 1

em·brit·tle \im-'brit-ᵊl\ *vb* **-brit·tled; -brit·tling** \-'brit-liŋ, -ᵊl-iŋ\ *vt* (1902) **:** to make brittle ~ *vi* **:** to become brittle — **em·brit·tle·ment** \-'brit-ᵊl-mənt\ *n*

em·bro·ca·tion \,em-brə-'kā-shən\ *n* [LL *embrocatus,* pp. of *embrocare* to rub with lotion, fr. Gk *embroche* lotion, fr. deriv. of *en-* + *brechein* to wet] (ca. 1610) **:** LINIMENT

embroglio *var of* IMBROGLIO

em·broi·der \im-'brȯid-ər\ *vb* **em·broi·dered; em·broi·der·ing** \-(ə-)riŋ\ [ME *embroderen,* fr. MF *embroder,* fr. *en-* + *broder* to embroider, of Gmc origin; akin to OE *brord* point — more at BRISTLE] *vt* (14c) **1 a :** to ornament with needlework **b :** to form with needlework **2 :** to elaborate on **:** EMBELLISH ~ *vi* **1 :** to make embroidery **2 :** to provide embellishments **:** ELABORATE — **em·broi·der·er** \-'brȯid-ər-ər\ *n*

em·broi·dery \im-'brȯid-(ə-)rē\ *n, pl* **-der·ies** (14c) **1 a :** the art or process of forming decorative designs with hand or machine needlework **b :** a design or decoration so formed **c :** an object decorated with embroidery **2 :** elaboration by use of decorative and often fictitious detail **3 :** something pleasing or desirable but unimportant ⟨considered the humanities mere educational ~⟩

em·broil \im-'brȯi(ə)l\ *vt* [F *embrouiller,* fr. MF, fr. *en-* + *brouiller* to broil] (1603) **1 :** to throw into disorder or confusion **2 :** to involve in conflict or difficulties — **em·broil·ment** \-mənt\ *n*

em·brown \im-'brau̇n\ *vt* (1667) **1 :** DARKEN **2 :** to cause to turn brown

embrue *var of* IMBRUE

embry- *or* **embryo-** *comb form* [LL, fr. Gk, fr. *embryon*] **:** embryo ⟨*embryogeny*⟩

em·bryo \'em-brē-,ō\ *n, pl* **em·bry·os** [ML *embryon-, embryo,* fr. Gk *embryon,* fr. *en-* + *bryein* to swell; akin to Gk *bryon* moss] (1548) **1 a** *archaic* **:** a vertebrate at any stage of development prior to birth or hatching **b :** an animal in the early stages of growth and differentiation that are characterized by cleavage, the laying down of fundamental tissues, and the formation of primitive organs and organ systems; *esp* **:** the developing human individual from the time of implantation to the end of the eighth week after conception **2 :** the young sporophyte of a seed plant usu. comprising a rudimentary plant with plumule, radicle, and cotyledons **3 a :** something as yet undeveloped **b :** a beginning or undeveloped state of something ⟨productions seen in ~ during their out-of-town tryout period —Henry Hewes⟩

em·bryo·gen·e·sis \,em-brē-ō-'jen-ə-səs\ *n* (1830) **:** the formation and development of the embryo — **em·bryo·ge·net·ic** \-jə-'net-ik\ *adj*

em·bry·og·e·ny \,em-brē-'äj-ə-nē\ *n, pl* **-nies** (1835) **:** EMBRYOGENESIS — **em·bryo·gen·ic** \-brē-ō-'jen-ik\ *adj*

em·bry·oid \'em-brē-,ȯid\ *n* (ca. 1927) **:** a mass of plant or animal tissue that resembles an embryo — **embryoid** *adj*

em·bry·ol·o·gy \,em-brē-'äl-ə-jē\ *n* [F *embryologie*] (ca. 1847) **1 :** a branch of biology dealing with embryos and their development **2 :** the features and phenomena exhibited in the formation and development of an embryo — **em·bry·o·log·i·cal** \-brē-ə-'läj-i-kəl\ *adj* — **em·bry·o·log·i·cal·ly** \-i-k(ə-)lē\ *adv* — **em·bry·ol·o·gist** \-brē-'äl-ə-jəst\ *n*

embryon- *or* **embryoni-** *comb form* [ML *embryon-, embryo*] **:** embryo ⟨*embryonic*⟩

em·bry·o·nal \em-'brī-ən-ᵊl\ *adj* (1652) **:** EMBRYONIC 1

em·bry·o·nat·ed \'em-brē-ə-,nāt-əd\ *adj* (1697) **:** having an embryo

em·bry·on·ic \,em-brē-'än-ik\ *adj* (ca. 1847) **1 :** of or relating to an embryo **2 :** being in an early stage of development **:** INCIPIENT, RUDIMENTARY — **em·bry·on·i·cal·ly** \-i-k(ə-)lē\ *adv*

embryonic disk *n* (ca. 1938) **1 a :** BLASTODISC **b :** BLASTODERM **2 :** the part of the inner cell mass of a blastocyst from which the embryo of a placental mammal develops — called also *embryonic shield*

embryonic membrane *n* (1947) **:** a structure (as the amnion) that derives from the fertilized ovum but does not form a part of the embryo

em·bryo·phyte \'em-brē-ə-,fīt\ *n* (ca. 1909) **:** a plant (as a fern) producing an embryo and developing vascular tissues

embryo sac *n* (1872) **:** the female gametophyte of a seed plant consisting of a thin-walled sac within the nucellus that contains the egg nucleus and others which give rise to endosperm on fertilization

em·bry·ot·ic \,em-brē-'ät-ik\ *adj* [*embryo* + *-tic* (as in *patriotic*)] (1761) **:** EMBRYONIC 2

[1]em·cee \'em-'sē\ *n* [*M. C.*] (1933) **:** MASTER OF CEREMONIES

[2]emcee *vb* **em·ceed; em·cee·ing** *vt* (1937) **:** to act as master of ceremonies of ~ *vi* **:** to act as master of ceremonies

Em·den *var of* EMBDEN

-eme \,ēm\ *n suffix* [F *-ème* (fr. *phonème* speech sound, phoneme)] **:** significantly distinctive unit of language structure ⟨*taxeme*⟩

emend \ē-'mend\ *vt* [ME *emenden,* fr. L *emendare* — more at AMEND] (15c) **:** to correct usu. by textual alterations ***syn*** see CORRECT — **emend·able** \-'men-də-bəl\ *adj* — **emend·er** *n*

emen·da·tion \,ē-,men-'dā-shən; ,em-ən-, -,en-\ *n* (1536) **1 :** the act or practice of emending **2 :** an alteration designed to correct or improve

[1]em·er·ald \'em-(ə-)rəld\ *n* [ME *emeralde,* fr. MF *esmeralde,* fr. (assumed) VL *smaralda,* fr. L *smaragdus,* fr. Gk *smaragdos*] (14c) **1 :** a rich green variety of beryl prized as a gemstone **2 :** any of various green gemstones (as synthetic corundum or demantoid)

[2]emerald *adj* (1572) **:** brightly or richly green

emerald green *n* (1646) **1 :** a clear bright green resembling that of the emerald **2 :** any of various strong greens

emerge \i-ˈmərj\ *vi* **emerged; emerg·ing** [L *emergere,* fr. *e-* + *mergere* to plunge — more at MERGE] (1563) **1 :** to become manifest **2 :** to rise from or as if from an enveloping fluid : come out into view **3 :** to rise from an obscure or inferior condition **4 :** to come into being through evolution

emer·gence \i-ˈmər-jən(t)s\ *n* (1704) **1 :** the act or an instance of emerging **2 :** any of various superficial outgrowths of plant tissue usu. formed from both epidermis and immediately underlying tissues

emer·gen·cy \i-ˈmər-jən-sē\ *n, pl* **-cies** *often attrib* (1631) **1 :** an unforeseen combination of circumstances or the resulting state that calls for immediate action **2 :** an urgent need for assistance or relief ⟨the governor declared a state of ~ after the flood⟩ ***syn*** see JUNCTURE

¹emer·gent \i-ˈmər-jənt\ *adj* [ME, fr. L *emergent-, emergens,* prp. of *emergere*] (1593) **1 a :** arising unexpectedly **b :** calling for prompt action : URGENT **2 :** rising out of or as if out of a fluid **3 :** arising as a natural or logical consequence **4 :** newly formed or prominent ⟨the ~ nations of Africa⟩

²emergent *n* (1620) **1 :** something emergent **2 a :** a tree that rises above the surrounding forest **b :** a plant rooted in shallow water and having most of the vegetative growth above water

emergent evolution *n* (1915) **:** evolution which according to some biological and philosophical theories involves the appearance of new characters and qualities (as life and consciousness) at more complex levels of organization (as the cell or organism) which cannot be predicted solely from the study of less complex levels (as the atom or molecule) — compare CREATIVE EVOLUTION

emerg·ing *adj* (1946) **:** EMERGENT 4

emer·i·ta \i-ˈmer-ət-ə\ *adj* [L, fem. of *emeritus*] (1928) **:** EMERITUS — used of a woman ⟨Professor *Emerita* Mary Smith⟩

¹emer·i·tus \i-ˈmer-ət-əs\ *n, pl* **-i·ti** \-ə-ˌtī, -ˌtē\ (1750) **:** one retired from professional life but permitted to hold the rank of his last office as an honorary title

²emeritus *adj* [L, pp. of *emereri* to serve out one's term, fr. *e-* + *mereri, merēre* to earn, deserve, serve — more at MERIT] (1794) **1 :** holding after retirement an honorary title corresponding to that held last during active service **2 :** retired from an office or position ⟨professor ~⟩ — converted to *emeriti* after a plural substantive ⟨professors *emeriti*⟩

emersed \(ˈ)ē-ˈmərst\ *adj* (1686) **:** standing out of or rising above a surface (as of a fluid) ⟨~ aquatic weeds⟩

emer·sion \(ˈ)ē-ˈmər-zhən, -shən\ *n* [L *emersus,* pp. of *emergere*] (1633) **:** an act of emerging **:** EMERGENCE

em·ery \ˈem-(ə-)rē\ *n, pl* **em·er·ies** *often attrib* [ME, fr. MF *emeri,* fr. OIt *smiriglio,* fr. ML *smiriglum,* fr. Gk *smyrid-, smyris*] (15c) **:** a dark granular mineral that consists essentially of corundum and is used for grinding and polishing; *also* **:** a hard abrasive powder

emery board *n* (1725) **:** a nail file made of cardboard covered with powdered emery

eme·sis \ˈem-ə-səs, i-ˈmē-\ *n, pl* **eme·ses** \-ˌsēz\ [NL, fr. Gk, fr. *emein*] (1847) **:** an act or instance of vomiting

emet·ic \i-ˈmet-ik\ *n* [L *emetica,* fr. Gk *emetikē,* fr. fem. of *emetikos* causing vomiting, fr. *emein* to vomit — more at VOMIT] (1657) **:** an agent that induces vomiting — **emetic** *adj* — **emet·i·cal·ly** \-i-k(ə-)lē\ *adv*

em·e·tine \ˈem-ə-ˌtēn\ *n* (1819) **:** an amorphous alkaloid $C_{29}H_{40}N_2O_4$ extracted from ipecac root and used as an emetic and expectorant

émeute \ā-mœ̄t\ *n, pl* **émeutes** *same*\ [F, fr. OF *esmeute* act of starting, fr. fem. of *esmeut,* pp. of *esmovoir* to start — more at EMOTION] (1782) **:** UPRISING

-emia *or* **-ae·mia** \ˈē-mē-ə\ *also* **-he·mia** *or* **-hae·mia** \ˈhē-\ *n comb form* [NL *-emia, -aemia,* fr. Gk *-aimia,* fr. *haima* blood — more at HEM-] **1 :** condition of having (such) blood ⟨leuk*emia*⟩ **2 :** condition of having (a specified thing) in the blood ⟨ur*emia*⟩

emic \ˈē-mik\ *adj* [phon*emic*] (1954) **:** of, relating to, or involving analysis of linguistic or behavioral phenomena in terms of the internal structural or functional elements of a particular system — compare ETIC

¹em·i·grant \ˈem-i-grənt\ *n* (1754) **1 :** one who emigrates **2 :** a migrant plant or animal

²emigrant *adj* (1794) **:** departing or having departed from a country to settle elsewhere

em·i·grate \ˈem-ə-ˌgrāt\ *vi* **-grat·ed; -grat·ing** [L *emigratus,* pp. of *emigrare,* fr. *e-* + *migrare* to migrate] (1778) **:** to leave one's place of residence or country to live elsewhere — **em·i·gra·tion** \ˌem-ə-ˈgrā-shən\ *n*

émi·gré *also* **emi·gré** \ˈem-i-ˌgrā, ˌem-i-ˈ\ *n* [F *émigré,* fr. pp. of *émigrer* to emigrate, fr. L *emigrare*] (1792) **:** EMIGRANT; *esp* **:** a person forced to emigrate for political reasons

em·i·nence \ˈem-ə-nən(t)s\ *n* (15c) **1 :** a position of prominence or superiority **2 :** something eminent, prominent, or lofty: as **a :** a person of high rank or attainments — used as a title for a cardinal **b :** a natural elevation

émi·nence grise \ā-mē-näⁿ-sə-grēz\ *n, pl* **éminences grises** *same*\ [F, lit., gray eminence, nickname of Père Joseph (François du Tremblay) †1638 Fr. monk and diplomat, confidant of Cardinal Richelieu who was known as *Éminence Rouge* red eminence; fr. the colors of their respective habits] (1925) **:** a confidential agent; *esp* **:** one exercising unsuspected or unofficial power

em·i·nen·cy \ˈem-ə-nən-sē\ *n, pl* **-cies** (1604) **:** EMINENCE

em·i·nent \ˈem-ə-nənt\ *adj* [ME, fr. MF or L; MF, fr. L *eminent-, eminens,* prp. of *eminēre* to stand out, fr. *e-* + *-minēre* (akin to L *mont-, mons* mountain) — more at MOUNT] (15c) **1 :** standing out so as to be readily perceived or noted **:** CONSPICUOUS **2 :** jutting out **:** PROJECTING **3 :** exhibiting eminence esp. in standing above others in some quality or position **:** PROMINENT ***syn*** see FAMOUS — **em·i·nent·ly** *adv*

eminent domain *n* (1853) **:** a right of a government to take private property for public use by virtue of the superior dominion of the sovereign power over all lands within its jurisdiction

emir \i-ˈmi(ə)r, ā-\ *n* [Ar *amīr* commander] (1612) **:** a native ruler in parts of Asia and Africa

emir·ate \ˈem-ə-rət, -ˌrāt\ *n* (1863) **:** the state or jurisdiction of an emir

em·is·sary \ˈem-ə-ˌser-ē\ *n, pl* **-sar·ies** [L *emissarius,* fr. *emissus,* pp. of *emittere*] (1616) **1 :** one sent on a mission as the agent of another **2 :** a secret agent

emis·sion \ē-ˈmish-ən\ *n* (1607) **1 a :** an act or instance of emitting **:** EMANATION **b** *archaic* **:** PUBLICATION **c :** a putting into circulation **2 a :** something sent forth by emitting: as **(1) :** electrons discharged from a surface **(2) :** electromagnetic waves radiated by an antenna or a celestial body **(3) :** substances discharged into the air (as by a smokestack or an automobile gasoline engine) **b :** EFFLUVIUM — **emis·sive** \-ˈmis-iv\ *adj*

emis·siv·i·ty \ˌem-ə-ˈsiv-ət-ē, ˌē-ˌmis-ˈiv-\ *n, pl* **-ties** (1880) **:** the relative power of a surface to emit heat by radiation **:** the ratio of the radiant energy emitted by a surface to that emitted by a blackbody at the same temperature

emit \ē-ˈmit\ *vt* **emit·ted; emit·ting** [L *emittere* to send out, fr. *e-* + *mittere* to send — more at SMITE] (1626) **1 a :** to throw or give off or out (as light) **b :** to send out **:** EJECT **2 a :** to issue with authority; *esp* **:** to put (as money) into circulation **b** *obs* **:** PUBLISH **3 :** to give utterance or voice to ⟨*emitted* a groan⟩ — **emit·ter** *n*

emit·tance \ē-ˈmit-ᵊn(t)s\ *n* (1940) **1 :** the energy radiated by the surface of a body per second per unit area **2 :** EMISSIVITY

Emmanuel *var of* IMMANUEL

em·men·a·gogue \ə-ˈmen-ə-ˌgäg, e-\ *n* [Gk *emmēna* menses (fr. neut. pl. of *emmēnos* monthly, fr. *en-* + *mēn* month) + E *-agogue* — more at MOON] (ca. 1731) **:** an agent that promotes the menstrual discharge

Em·men·ta·ler *or* **Em·men·tha·ler** \ˈem-ən-ˌtäl-ər\ *or* **Em·men·thal** \-ˌtäl\ *n* [G, fr. *Emmental,* Switzerland] (1902) **:** SWISS CHEESE

em·mer \ˈem-ər\ *n* [G, fr. OHG *amari*] (ca. 1900) **:** a wheat (*Triticum dicoccum*) having spikelets with two hard red kernels that remain in the glumes after threshing; *broadly* **:** a tetraploid wheat — called also *emmer wheat*

em·met \ˈem-ət\ *n* [ME *emete,* fr. OE *ǣmette* ant — more at ANT] *chiefly dial* (bef. 12c) **:** ANT

Em·my \ˈem-ē\ *n, pl* **Emmys** [fr. alter. of *Immy,* nickname for *image orthicon* (a camera tube used in television)] (1949) **:** a statuette awarded annually by a professional organization for notable achievement in television

em·o·din \ˈem-ə-dən\ *n* [ISV *emodi-* (fr. NL *Rheum emodi,* species of rhubarb) + *-in*] (1858) **:** an orange crystalline phenolic compound $C_{15}H_{10}O_5$ that is obtained from plants (as rhubarb and cascara buckthorn) and is used as a laxative

¹emol·lient \i-ˈmäl-yənt\ *adj* [L *emollient-, emolliens,* prp. of *emollire* to soften, fr. *e-* + *mollis* soft — more at MELT] (1643) **1 :** making soft or supple; *also* **:** soothing esp. to the skin or mucous membrane **2 :** making less intense or harsh **:** MOLLIFYING ⟨soothe us in our agonies with ~ words —H. L. Mencken⟩

²emollient *n* (1656) **:** something that softens or soothes

emol·u·ment \i-ˈmäl-yə-mənt\ *n* [ME, fr. L *emolumentum,* lit., miller's fee, fr. *emolere* to grind up, fr. *e-* + *molere* to grind — more at MEAL] (15c) **1 :** the returns arising from office or employment usu. in the form of compensation or perquisites **2** *archaic* **:** ADVANTAGE

emote \i-ˈmōt\ *vi* **emot·ed; emot·ing** [back-formation fr. *emotion*] (1917) **:** to give expression to emotion esp. in or as if in acting

emo·tion \i-ˈmō-shən\ *n* [F, fr. MF *emouvoir* to stir up, fr. OF *esmovoir,* fr. L *exmovēre* to move away, disturb, fr. *ex-* + *movēre* to move] (1660) **1 a** *obs* **:** DISTURBANCE **b :** EXCITEMENT **2 a :** the affective aspect of consciousness **:** FEELING **b :** a state of feeling **c :** a psychic and physical reaction (as anger or fear) subjectively experienced as strong feeling and physiologically involving changes that prepare the body for immediate vigorous action ***syn*** see FEELING

emo·tion·al \-shnəl, -shən-ᵊl\ *adj* (1834) **1 :** of or relating to emotion ⟨an ~ disorder⟩ **2 :** dominated by or prone to emotion ⟨an ~ person⟩ **3 :** appealing to or arousing emotion ⟨an ~ sermon⟩ **4 :** markedly aroused or agitated in feeling or sensibilities ⟨gets ~ at weddings⟩ — **emo·tion·al·i·ty** \-ˌmō-shə-ˈnal-ət-ē\ *n* — **emo·tion·al·ly** \-ˈmō- shnə-lē, -shən- ᵊl-ē\ *adv*

emo·tion·al·ism \i-ˈmō-shnə-ˌliz-əm, -shən-ᵊl-ˌiz-\ *n* (1865) **1 :** undue indulgence in or display of emotion **2 :** a tendency to regard things emotionally

emo·tion·al·ist \-shnə-ləst, -shən-ᵊl-əst\ *n* (1866) **1 :** one who bases a theory or policy on an emotional conviction **2 :** one prone to emotionalism — **emo·tion·al·is·tic** \-ˌmō-shnə-ˈlis-tik, -shən-ᵊl-ˈis-\ *adj*

emo·tion·al·ize \i-ˈmō-shnə-ˌlīz, -shən-ᵊl-ˌīz\ *vt* **-ized; -iz·ing** (1879) **:** to give an emotional quality to

emo·tion·less \i-ˈmō-shən-ləs\ *adj* (1862) **:** showing or expressing no emotion — **emo·tion·less·ness** *n*

emo·tive \i-ˈmōt-iv\ *adj* (1830) **1 :** of or relating to the emotions **2 :** appealing to or expressing emotion ⟨the ~ use of language⟩ — **emo·tive·ly** *adv* — **emo·tiv·i·ty** \i-ˌmō-ˈtiv-ət-ē, ˌē-ˌmō-\ *n*

em·pa·na·da \ˌem-pə-ˈnäd-ə\ *n* [AmSp, fr. Sp, fem. of *empanado,* pp. of *empanar* to bread, fr. *em-* (fr. L *en-*) + *pan* bread, fr. L *panis* — more at FOOD] (1922) **:** a turnover with a sweet or savory filling (as ground meat)

empanel *var of* IMPANEL

em·pa·thet·ic \ˌem-pə-ˈthet-ik\ *adj* (1932) **:** EMPATHIC — **em·pa·thet·i·cal·ly** \-i-k(ə-)lē\ *adv*

em·path·ic \em-ˈpath-ik, im-\ *adj* (1909) **:** involving, characterized by, or based on empathy

em·pa·thize \ˈem-pə-ˌthīz\ *vi* **-thized; -thiz·ing** (ca. 1921) **:** to experience empathy ⟨adults unable to ~ with a child's frustrations⟩

em·pa·thy \ˈem-pə-thē\ *n* (1904) **1 :** the imaginative projection of a subjective state into an object so that the object appears to be infused with it **2 :** the action of understanding, being aware of, being sensitive to, and vicariously experiencing the feelings, thoughts, and experience of another of either the past or present without having the feelings, thoughts, and experience fully communicated in an objectively explicit manner; *also* **:** the capacity for this

em·pen·nage \ˌäm-pə-ˈnäzh, ˌem-\ *n* [F, feathers of an arrow, empennage, fr. *empenner* to feather an arrow, fr. *em-* ¹en- + *penne* feather, fr. MF — more at PEN] (1909) **:** the tail assembly of an airplane

\ə\ **abut** \ᵊ\ **kitten, F table** \ər\ **further** \a\ **ash** \ā\ **ace** \ä\ **cot, cart**
\au̇\ **out** \ch\ **chin** \e\ **bet** \ē\ **easy** \g\ **go** \i\ **hit** \ī\ **ice** \j\ **job**
\ŋ\ **sing** \ō\ **go** \ȯ\ **law** \ȯi\ **boy** \th\ **thin** \th̲\ **the** \ü\ **loot** \u̇\ **foot**
\y\ **yet** \zh\ **vision** \á, k̟, ⁿ, œ, œ̄, ue, ue̅, ʸ\ *see* **Guide to Pronunciation**

em·per·or \'em-pər-ər, -prər\ *n* [ME, fr. OF *empereor,* fr. L *imperator,* lit., commander, fr. *imperatus,* pp. of *imperare* to command, fr. *in-* + *parare* to prepare, order — more at PARE] (13c) **:** the sovereign or supreme monarch of an empire — **em·per·or·ship** \-,ship\ *n*
em·pery \'em-p(ə-)rē\ *n, pl* **em·per·ies** [ME *emperie,* fr. OF, fr. *emperer* to command, fr. L *imperare*] (13c) **:** wide dominion **:** EMPIRE
em·pha·sis \'em(p)-fə-səs\ *n, pl* **-pha·ses** \-,sēz\ [L, fr. Gk, exposition, emphasis, fr. *emphainein* to indicate, fr. *en-* + *phainein* to show — more at FANCY] (1573) **1 a :** force or intensity of expression that gives special impressiveness or importance to something ⟨writing with ~ on the need for reform⟩ **b :** a particular prominence given in reading or speaking to one or more words or syllables **2 :** special consideration of or stress or insistence on something ⟨their ~ on discipline⟩
em·pha·size \'em(p)-fə-,sīz\ *vt* **-sized; -siz·ing** (ca. 1828) **:** to place emphasis on **:** STRESS ⟨*emphasized* the need for reform⟩
em·phat·ic \im-'fat-ik, em-\ *adj* [Gk *emphatikos,* fr. *emphainein*] (1708) **1 :** uttered with or marked by emphasis **2 :** tending to express oneself in forceful speech or to take decisive action **3 :** attracting special attention **4 :** constituting or belonging to a set of tense forms in English consisting of the auxiliary *do* followed by an infinitive without *to* that are used to facilitate rhetorical inversion or to emphasize something — **em·phat·i·cal·ly** \-'fat-i-k(ə-)lē\ *adv*
em·phy·se·ma \,em(p)-fə-'zē-mə, -'sē-\ *n* [NL, fr. Gk *emphysēma* bodily inflation, fr. *emphysan* to inflate, fr. *em-* [2]en- + *physan* to blow — more at FOG] (1661) **:** a condition characterized by air-filled expansions of body tissues; *specif* **:** a condition of the lung marked by abnormal dilation of its air spaces and distension of its walls and frequently by impairment of heart action — **em·phy·se·ma·tous** \-'zem-ət-əs, -'sem-, -'zēm-, -'sēm-\ *adj* — **em·phy·se·mic** \-'zē-mik, -'sē-\ *adj*
em·pire \'em-,pī(ə)r\ *n* [ME, fr. OF *empire, emperie,* fr. L *imperium* absolute authority, empire, fr. *imperare*] (13c) **1 a (1) :** a major political unit having a territory of great extent or a number of territories or peoples under a single sovereign authority; *esp* **:** one having an emperor as chief of state **(2) :** the territory of such a political unit **b :** something held to resemble a political empire; *esp* **:** an extensive territory or enterprise under single domination or control ⟨the beautiful heiress to a meat-packing ~ —*Punch*⟩ **2 :** imperial sovereignty, rule, or dominion
Em·pire \'äm-,pi(ə)r, 'em-,pī(ə)r\ *adj* [F, fr. (*le premier*) *Empire* the first Empire of France] (1869) **:** of, relating to, or characteristic of a style (as of clothing or furniture) popular in early 19th century France
Empire Day \'em-,pī(ə)r-\ *n* (1902) **:** COMMONWEALTH DAY — used before the official adoption of *Commonwealth Day* in 1958
em·pir·ic \im-'pir-ik, em-\ *n* [L *empiricus,* fr. Gk *empeirikos* doctor relying on experience alone, fr. *empeiria* experience, fr. *em-* [2]en- + *peiran* to attempt — more at FEAR] (1527) **1 :** CHARLATAN **2 :** one who relies on practical experience
em·pir·i·cal \-i-kəl\ *also* **em·pir·ic** \-ik\ *adj* (1569) **1 :** relying on experience or observation alone often without due regard for system and theory **2 :** originating in or based on observation or experience ⟨~ data⟩ **3 :** capable of being verified or disproved by observation or experiment ⟨~ laws⟩ — **em·pir·i·cal·ly** \-i-k(ə-)lē\ *adv*
empirical formula *n* (1885) **:** a chemical formula showing the simplest ratio of elements in a compound rather than the total number of atoms in the molecule ⟨CH_2O is the *empirical formula* for glucose⟩
em·pir·i·cism \im-'pir-ə-,siz-əm, em-\ *n* (1657) **1 a :** a former school of medical practice founded on experience without the aid of science or theory **b :** QUACKERY, CHARLATANRY **2 a :** the practice of relying on observation and experiment esp. in the natural sciences **b :** a tenet arrived at empirically **3 a :** a theory that all knowledge originates in experience **b :** LOGICAL POSITIVISM — **em·pir·i·cist** \-səst\ *n*
em·place \im-'plās\ *vt* [back-formation fr. *emplacement*] (1865) **:** to put into position ⟨missiles *emplaced* around the city⟩
em·place·ment \-'plā-smənt\ *n* [F, fr. MF *emplacer* to emplace, fr. *en-* + *place*] (1802) **1 :** the situation or location of something **2 :** a prepared position for weapons or military equipment ⟨radar ~*s*⟩ **3 :** a putting into position **:** PLACEMENT
em·plane \im-'plān\ *var of* ENPLANE
[1]**em·ploy** \im-'plȯi\ *vt* [ME *emploien,* fr. MF *emploier,* fr. L *implicare* to enfold, involve, implicate, fr. *in-* + *plicare* to fold — more at PLY] (15c) **1 a :** to make use of (someone or something inactive) ⟨~ a pen for sketching⟩ **b :** to use (as time) advantageously **c (1) :** to use or engage the services of **(2) :** to provide with a job that pays wages or a salary **2 :** to devote to or direct toward a particular activity or person ⟨~*ed* all her energies to help the poor⟩ ***syn*** see USE — **em·ploy·er** *n*
[2]**employ** *n* (1666) **1** *archaic* **a :** USE **b :** OCCUPATION **2 :** the state of being employed ⟨in the government's ~⟩
[1]**em·ploy·able** \im-'plȯi-ə-bəl\ *adj* (1691) **:** capable of being employed — **em·ploy·abil·i·ty** \-,plȯi-ə-'bil-ət-ē\ *n*
[2]**employable** *n* (1934) **:** one who is employable
em·ploy·ee *or* **em·ploye** \im-,plȯ(i)-'ē, (,)em-; im-'plȯ(i)-,ē, em-\ *n* (1822) **:** one employed by another usu. for wages or salary and in a position below the executive level
em·ploy·ment \im-'plȯi-mənt\ *n* (15c) **1 :** USE, PURPOSE **2 a :** activity in which one engages or is employed **b :** an instance of such activity **3 :** the act of employing **:** the state of being employed ***syn*** see WORK
employment agency *n* (1888) **:** an agency whose business is to find jobs for people seeking them or to find people to fill jobs that are open
em·poi·son \im-'pȯiz-[ə]n\ *vt* [ME *empoysonen,* fr. MF *empoisoner,* fr. *en-* + *poison* poison, fr. OF] (14c) **1** *archaic* **:** POISON **2 :** EMBITTER ⟨a look of ~*ed* acceptance —Saul Bellow⟩ — **em·poi·son·ment** \-mənt\ *n*
em·po·ri·um \im-'pȯr-ē-əm, em-, -'pȯr-\ *n, pl* **-ri·ums** *also* **-ria** \-ē-ə\ [L, fr. Gk *emporion,* fr. *emporos* traveler, trader, fr. *em-* [2]en- + *poros* passage, journey — more at FARE] (1586) **1 a :** a place of trade; *esp* **:** a commercial center **b :** a usu. sizable place of business that serves customers **2 :** a store carrying a diversity of merchandise
em·pow·er \im-'paù(-ə)r\ *vt* (1648) **:** to give official authority or legal power to — **em·pow·er·ment** \-mənt\ *n*
em·press \'em-prəs\ *n* [ME *emperesse,* fr. OF, fem. of *empereor* emperor] (12c) **1 :** the wife or widow of an emperor **2 :** a woman who holds an imperial title in her own right
em·presse·ment \äⁿ-pres-(ə-)mäⁿ\ *n* [F, fr. (*s'*)*empresser* to hurry, fr. *en-* + *presser* to press] (1709) **:** demonstrative warmth or cordiality
em·prise \em-'prīz\ *n* [ME, fr. MF, fr. OF, fr. *emprendre* to undertake, fr. (assumed) VL *imprehendere,* fr. L *in-* + *prehendere* to seize — more at PREHENSILE] (14c) **:** an adventurous, daring, or chivalric enterprise
[1]**emp·ty** \'em(p)-tē\ *adj* **emp·ti·er; -est** [ME, fr. OE *ǣmettig* unoccupied, fr. *ǣmetta* leisure, perh. fr. *ǣ-* without + *-metta* (akin to *mōtan* to have to) — more at MUST] (bef. 12c) **1 a :** containing nothing **b :** not occupied or inhabited **c :** UNFREQUENTED **d :** not pregnant ⟨~ heifer⟩ **e :** NULL 4a ⟨the ~ set⟩ **2 a :** lacking reality, substance, or value **:** HOLLOW ⟨an ~ pleasure⟩ **b :** destitute of effect or force **c :** devoid of sense **:** FOOLISH **3 :** HUNGRY **4 a :** IDLE ⟨~ hours⟩ **b :** having no purpose or result **:** USELESS **5 :** marked by the absence of human life, activity, or comfort — **emp·ti·ly** \-tə-lē\ *adv* — **emp·ti·ness** \-tē-nəs\ *n*
syn EMPTY, VACANT, BLANK, VOID, VACUOUS mean lacking contents which could or should be present. EMPTY suggests a complete absence of contents ⟨an *empty* bucket⟩ VACANT suggests an absence of appropriate contents or occupants ⟨a *vacant* apartment⟩ BLANK stresses the absence of any significant, relieving, or intelligible features on a surface ⟨a *blank* wall⟩ VOID suggests absolute emptiness as far as the mind or senses can determine ⟨a statement *void* of meaning⟩ VACUOUS suggests the emptiness of a vacuum and esp. the lack of intelligence or significance ⟨a *vacuous* facial expression⟩ ***syn*** see in addition VAIN
[2]**empty** *vb* **emp·tied; emp·ty·ing** *vt* (bef. 12c) **1 a :** to make empty **:** remove the contents of **b :** DEPRIVE, DIVEST **c :** to discharge (itself) of contents **2 :** to remove from what holds or encloses ⟨~ the grain from sacks⟩ ~ *vi* **1 :** to become empty **2 :** to discharge contents ⟨the river *empties* into the ocean⟩
[3]**empty** *n, pl* **emp·ties** (1535) **:** something (as a container) that is empty
emp·ty–hand·ed \,em(p)-tē-'han-dəd\ *adj* (1613) **1 :** having or bringing nothing **2 :** having acquired or gained nothing ⟨came back ~⟩
emp·ty–head·ed \-'hed-əd\ *adj* (1650) **:** SCATTERBRAINED
empty nest·er \-'nes-tər\ *n* (1971) **:** a parent whose children have grown and moved away from home
em·pur·ple \im-'pər-pəl\ *vb* **em·pur·pled; em·pur·pling** \-'pər-p(ə-)liŋ\ *vt* (1590) **:** to tinge or color purple ~ *vi* **:** to become purple
em·py·ema \,em-,pī-'ē-mə\ *n, pl* **-ema·ta** \-mət-ə\ *or* **-emas** [LL, fr. Gk *empyēma*] (1615) **:** the presence of pus in a bodily cavity — **em·py·emic** \-mik\ *adj*
em·py·re·al \,em-,pī-'rē-əl, -pə-; em-'pir-ē-əl, -'pī-rē-\ *adj* [LL *empyrius, empyreus,* fr. LGk *empyrios,* fr. Gk *em-* [2]en- + *pyr* fire] (15c) **1 :** of or relating to the empyrean **:** CELESTIAL **2 :** SUBLIME
[1]**em·py·re·an** \-ən\ *adj* (15c) **:** EMPYREAL
[2]**empyrean** *n* (1667) **1 a :** the highest heaven or heavenly sphere in ancient and medieval cosmology usu. consisting of fire or light **b :** the true and ultimate heavenly paradise **2 :** FIRMAMENT, HEAVENS
EMT \'ē-'em-'tē\ *n* [emergency medical technician] (1972) **:** a person trained and certified to provide basic medical services before and during transportation to a hospital
emu \'ē-(,)myü\ *n* [modif. of Pg *ema* rhea] (1613) **1 :** any of various tall flightless birds (as the rhea) **2 :** a swift-running Australian bird (*Dromiceius novaehollandiae*) with undeveloped wings that is related to and smaller than the ostrich

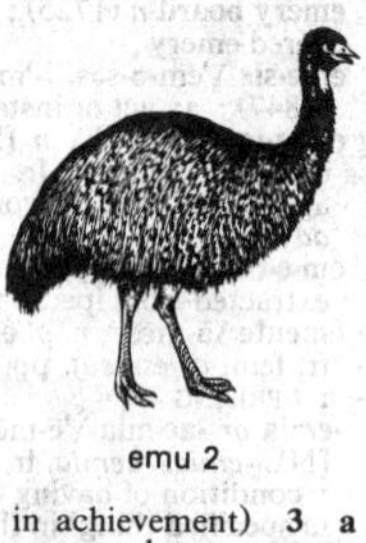

emu 2

[1]**em·u·late** \'em-yə-,lāt\ *vt* **-lat·ed; -lat·ing** [L *aemulatus,* pp. of *aemulari,* fr. *aemulus* rivaling — more at ETIOLOGY] (1589) **1 a :** to strive to equal or excel **b :** IMITATE; *esp* **:** to imitate by means of an emulator **2 :** to equal or approach equality with
[2]**em·u·late** \-lət\ *adj, obs* (1602) **:** EMULOUS 1a ⟨pricked on by a most ~ pride —Shak.⟩
em·u·la·tion \,em-yə-'lā-shən\ *n* (1542) **1** *obs* **:** ambitious or envious rivalry **2 :** ambition or endeavor to equal or excel others (as in achievement) **3 a :** IMITATION **b :** the use of or technique of using an emulator — **em·u·la·tive** \'em-yə-,lāt-iv\ *adj* — **em·u·la·tive·ly** *adv*
em·u·la·tor \'em-yə-,lāt-ər\ *n* (1589) **1 :** one that emulates **2 :** hardware or software that permits programs written for one computer to be run on another usu. newer computer
em·u·lous \'em-yə-ləs\ *adj* (1667) **1 a :** ambitious or eager to emulate **b :** inspired by or deriving from a desire to emulate **2** *obs* **:** JEALOUS — **em·u·lous·ly** *adv* — **em·u·lous·ness** *n*
emul·si·ble \i-'məl-sə-bəl\ *adj* (1944) **:** capable of being emulsified — **emul·si·bil·i·ty** \i-,məl-sə-'bil-ət-ē\ *n*
emul·si·fi·er \i-'məl-sə-,fī(-ə)r\ *n* (1888) **:** one that emulsifies; *esp* **:** a surface-active agent (as a soap) promoting the formation and stabilization of an emulsion
emul·si·fy \-,fī\ *vt* **-fied; -fy·ing** (1859) **:** to convert (as an oil) into an emulsion — **emul·si·fi·abil·i·ty** \i-,məl-sə-,fī-ə-'bil-ət-ē\ *n* — **emul·si·fi·able** \i-'məl-sə-,fī-ə-bəl\ *adj* — **emul·si·fi·ca·tion** \i-,məl-sə-fə-'kā-shən\ *n*
emul·sion \i-'məl-shən\ *n* [NL *emulsion-, emulsio,* fr. L *emulsus,* pp. of *emulgēre* to milk out, fr. *e-* + *mulgēre* to milk; akin to OE *melcan* to milk, Gk *amelgein*] (1612) **1 a :** a system (as fat in milk) consisting of a liquid dispersed with or without an emulsifier in an immiscible liquid usu. in droplets of larger than colloidal size **b :** the state of such a system **2 :** SUSPENSION 2b(3); *esp* **:** a suspension of a sensitive silver salt or a mixture of silver halides in a viscous medium (as a gelatin solution) forming a coating on photographic plates, film, or paper — **emul·sive** \-'məl-siv\ *adj*
emul·soid \i-'məl-,sȯid\ *n* (ca. 1909) **1 :** a colloidal system consisting of a liquid dispersed in a liquid **2 :** a lyophilic sol (as a gelatin solution) — **emul·soi·dal** \-,məl-'sȯid-[ə]l\ *adj*
emunc·to·ry \i-'məŋ(k)-t(ə-)rē\ *n, pl* **-ries** [NL *emunctorium,* fr. L *emunctus,* pp. of *emungere* to clean the nose, fr. *e-* + *-mungere* (akin to *mucus*) — more at MUCUS] (14c) **:** an organ (as a kidney) or part of the body (as the skin) that carries off body wastes
en \'en\ *n* (1792) **1 :** the width of a piece of type half the width of an em **2 :** the letter *n*
[1]**en-** *also* **em-** \e *also occurs in these prefixes although only* i *may be shown as in* "engage"\ *prefix* [ME, fr. OF, fr. L *in-, im-,* fr. *in*] **1 :** put into or onto ⟨encradle⟩ ⟨enthrone⟩ **:** cover with ⟨enverdure⟩ **:** go into or on to ⟨embus⟩ — in verbs formed from nouns **2 :** cause to be ⟨enslave⟩ — in

verbs formed from adjectives or nouns **3** : provide with ⟨*empower*⟩ — in verbs formed from nouns **4** : so as to cover ⟨*enwrap*⟩ : thoroughly ⟨*entangle*⟩ — in verbs formed from verbs; in all senses usu. *em-* before *b, m,* or *p*

[2]**en-** *also* **em-** *prefix* [ME, fr. L, fr. Gk, fr. *en* in — more at IN] : in : within ⟨*enzootic*⟩ — usu. *em-* before *b, m,* or *p* ⟨*empathy*⟩

[3]**en-** *comb form* [ISV, fr. *-ene*] : chemically unsaturated; *esp* : having one double bond ⟨*enamine*⟩

[1]**-en** \ən, ən\ *also* **-n** \n\ *adj suffix* [ME, fr. OE; akin to OHG *-in* made of, L *-inus* of or belonging to, Gk *-inos* made of, of or belonging to] : made of : consisting of ⟨*earthen*⟩ ⟨*silvern*⟩

[2]**-en** *vb suffix* [ME *-nen,* fr. OE *-nian;* akin to OHG *-inōn* -en] **1 a** : cause to be ⟨*sharpen*⟩ **b** : cause to have ⟨*lengthen*⟩ **2 a** : come to be ⟨*steepen*⟩ **b** : come to have ⟨*lengthen*⟩

en·able \in-'ā-bəl\ *vt* **en·abled; en·abling** \-b(ə-)liŋ\ (15c) **1 a** : to provide with the means or opportunity ⟨training that ~*s* people to earn a living⟩ **b** : to make possible, practical, or easy **2** : to give legal power, capacity, or sanction to ⟨a law *enabling* admission of a state⟩

en·act \in-'akt\ *vt* (15c) **1** : to establish by legal and authoritative act; *specif* : to make (as a bill) into law **2** : ACT OUT ⟨~ a role⟩ — **en·ac·tor** \-'ak-tər\ *n*

en·act·ment \-'ak(t)-mənt\ *n* (1817) **1** : the act of enacting : the state of being enacted **2** : something (as a law) that has been enacted

[1]**enam·el** \in-'am-əl\ *vt* **-eled** *or* **-elled; -el·ing** *or* **-el·ling** \-(ə-)liŋ\ [ME *enamelen,* fr. MF *enamailler,* fr. *en-* + *esmail* enamel, of Gmc origin; akin to OHG *smelzan* to melt — more at SMELT] (14c) **1** : to cover, inlay, or decorate with enamel **2** : to beautify with a colorful surface **3** : to form a glossy surface on (as paper, leather, or cloth) — **enam·el·er** \-(ə-)lər\ *n* — **enam·el·ist** \-ə-ləst\ *n*

[2]**enamel** *n* (15c) **1** : a usu. opaque vitreous composition applied by fusion to the surface of metal, glass, or pottery **2** : a surface or outer covering that resembles enamel **3 a** : something that is enameled **b** : ENAMELWARE **4** : a cosmetic intended to give a smooth or glossy appearance **5** : a hard calcareous substance that forms a thin layer capping the teeth — see TOOTH illustration **6** : a paint that flows out to a smooth coat when applied and that dries with a glossy appearance

enam·el·ware \in-'am-əl-ˌwa(ə)r, -ˌwe(ə)r\ *n* (1903) : metalware (as kitchen utensils) coated with enamel

en·amine \'en-ə-ˌmēn\ *n* (1942) : an amine containing the double bond linkage C=C–N

en·am·or \in-'am-ər\ *vt* **-ored; -or·ing** \-(ə-)riŋ\ [ME *enamouren,* fr. MF *enamourer,* fr. *en-* + *amour* love — more at AMOUR] (14c) : to inflame with love : CHARM — usu. used in the passive with *of*

en·am·our *chiefly Brit var of* ENAMOR

en·an·tio·mer \in-'ant-ē-ə-mər\ *n* [Gk *enantios* + E *-mer*] (ca. 1929) : ENANTIOMORPH — **en·an·tio·mer·ic** \-ˌant-ē-ə-'mer-ik\ *adj*

en·an·tio·morph \in-'ant-ē-ə-ˌmȯrf\ *n* [Gk *enantios* opposite (fr. *enanti* facing, fr. *en* in + *anti* against) + ISV *-morph* -morph] (1885) : either of a pair of chemical compounds or crystals whose molecular structures have a mirror-image relationship to each other — **en·an·tio·mor·phic** \-ˌant-ē-ə-'mȯr-fik\ *adj* — **en·an·tio·mor·phism** \-'mȯr-ˌfiz-əm\ *n* — **en·an·tio·mor·phous** \-'mȯr-fəs\ *adj*

en·ar·thro·sis \ˌen-ˌär-'thrō-səs\ *n, pl* **-thro·ses** \-ˌsēz\ [NL, fr. Gk *enarthrōsis,* fr. *en* + *arthrōsis* articulation] (1634) : BALL-AND-SOCKET JOINT 2

ena·tion \i-'nā-shən\ *n* [L *enatus,* pp. of *enasci* to rise out of, fr. *e-* + *nasci* to be born — more at NATION] (ca. 1842) : an outgrowth from the surface of an organ ⟨a plant virus forming ~*s* on leaves⟩

en bloc \än-'bläk\ *adv or adj* [F] (1861) : as a whole : in a mass

en bro·chette \ˌän-brō-'shet\ *adj* [F] *of food* (ca. 1909) : cooked or served in small pieces on a skewer ⟨beef *en brochette*⟩

En·cae·nia \en-'sē-nyə\ *n pl but sing or pl in constr* [NL, fr. L, dedication festival, fr. Gk *enkainia,* fr. *en* + *kainos* new — more at RECENT] (1691) : an annual university ceremony (as at Oxford) of commemoration with recital of poems and essays and conferring of degrees

en·cage \in-'kāj\ *vt* (1593) : CAGE 1

en·camp \in-'kamp\ *vt* (1568) : to place or establish in a camp ~ *vi* : to set up or occupy a camp

en·camp·ment \-mənt\ *n* (1598) **1** : the act of encamping : the state of being encamped **2 a** : the place where a group (as a body of troops) is encamped **b** : the individuals that make up an encampment

en·cap·su·late \in-'kap-sə-ˌlāt\ *vb* **-lat·ed; -lat·ing** *vt* (ca. 1902) **1** : to enclose in or as if in a capsule **2** : EPITOMIZE, CONDENSE ⟨~ a period of history⟩ ~ *vi* : to become encapsulated — **en·cap·su·la·tion** \-ˌkap-sə-'lā-shən\ *n*

en·cap·su·lat·ed *adj* (1894) : surrounded by a gelatinous or membranous envelope ⟨~ water bacteria⟩

en·cap·sule \in-'kap-səl, -(ˌ)sül\ *vt* **-suled; -sul·ing** (1877) : ENCAPSULATE

en·case \in-'kās\ *vt* (1633) : to enclose in or as if in a case

en·case·ment \in-'kā-smənt\ *n* (1741) : the act or process of encasing : the state of being encased; *also* : CASE, COVERING

en·cash \in-'kash\ *vt, Brit* (1861) : CASH — **en·cash·ment** \-mənt\ *n, Brit*

en·caus·tic \in-'kȯ-stik\ *n* [*encaustic,* adj., fr. L *encausticus,* fr. Gk *enkaustikos,* fr. *enkaiein* to burn in, fr. *en-* + *kaiein* to burn — more at CAUSTIC] (1601) **1** : a paint made from pigment mixed with melted beeswax and resin and after application fixed by heat **2** : the method involving the use of encaustic; *also* : a work produced by this method — **encaustic** *adj*

-ence \ən(t)s, ən(t)s\ *n suffix* [ME, fr. OF, fr. L *-entia,* fr. *-ent-, -ens,* prp. ending + *-ia* -y] **1** : action or process ⟨*emergence*⟩ : instance of an action or process ⟨*reference*⟩ **2** : quality or state ⟨*despondence*⟩

[1]**en·ceinte** \än(n)-'sant\ *adj* [MF, fr. (assumed) VL *incienta,* alter. of L *incient-, inciens* being with young, fr. *in* + *-cient-, -ciens* (akin to Gk *kyein* to be pregnant) — more at CAVE] (1599) : PREGNANT 3

[2]**enceinte** *n* [F, fr. OF, enclosing wall, fr. *enceindre* to surround, fr. L *incingere,* fr. *in-* + *cingere* to gird — more at CINCTURE] (1708) : a line of fortification enclosing a castle or town; *also* : the area or town so enclosed

encephal- *or* **encephalo-** *comb form* [F *encéphal-,* fr. Gk *enkephal-,* fr. *enkephalos,* fr. *en-* + *kephalē* head — more at CEPHALIC] : brain ⟨*encephalitis*⟩ ⟨*encephalocele*⟩

en·ceph·a·li·tis \in-ˌsef-ə-'līt-əs\ *n, pl* **-lit·i·des** \-'lit-ə-ˌdēz\ (1843) : inflammation of the brain — **en·ceph·a·lit·ic** \-'lit-ik\ *adj*

en·ceph·a·li·to·gen·ic \-ˌlīt-ə-'jen-ik\ *adj* (1923) : tending to cause encephalitis ⟨an ~ strain of a virus⟩ — **en·ceph·a·li·to·gen** \-'līt-ə-jən, -ˌjen\ *n*

en·ceph·a·lo·gram \in-'sef-ə-lə-ˌgram\ *n* [ISV] (1928) : an X-ray picture of the brain made by encephalography

en·ceph·a·lo·graph \-ˌgraf\ *n* (1928) **1** : ENCEPHALOGRAM **2** : ELECTROENCEPHALOGRAPH

en·ceph·a·log·ra·phy \in-ˌsef-ə-'läg-rə-fē\ *n* [ISV] (1824) : roentgenography of the brain after the cerebrospinal fluid has been replaced by a gas (as air)

en·ceph·a·lo·my·eli·tis \in-ˌsef-ə-lō-ˌmī-ə-'līt-əs\ *n, pl* **-elit·i·des** \-ə-'lit-ə-ˌdēz\ [NL] (1908) : concurrent inflammation of the brain and spinal cord; *specif* : any of several virus diseases of horses

en·ceph·a·lo·myo·car·di·tis \-ˌmī-ə-kär-'dīt-əs\ *n* (1948) : an acute febrile virus disease characterized by degeneration and inflammation of skeletal and cardiac muscle and lesions of the central nervous system

en·ceph·a·lon \in-'sef-ə-ˌlän, -lən\ *n, pl* **-la** \-lə\ [NL, fr. Gk *enkephalos*] (1741) : the vertebrate brain

en·ceph·a·lop·a·thy \in-ˌsef-ə-'läp-ə-thē\ *n* (1866) : a disease of the brain; *esp* : one involving alterations of brain structure — **en·ceph·a·lo·path·ic** \-lə-'path-ik\ *adj*

en·chain \in-'chān\ *vt* [ME *encheynen,* fr. MF *enchainer,* fr. OF, fr. *en-* + *chaeine* chain] (14c) : to bind or hold with or as if with chains — **en·chain·ment** \-mənt\ *n*

en·chant \in-'chant\ *vt* [ME *enchanten,* fr. MF *enchanter,* fr. L *incantare,* fr. *in-* + *cantare* to sing — more at CHANT] (14c) **1** : to influence by charms and incantation : BEWITCH **2** : to attract and move deeply : rouse to ecstatic admiration ⟨the scene ~*ed* her to the point of tears —Elinor Wylie⟩ ***syn*** see ATTRACT

en·chant·er *n* (13c) : one that enchants; *esp* : SORCERER

en·chant·ing *adj* (1606) : CHARMING — **en·chant·ing·ly** \-iŋ-lē\ *adv*

en·chant·ment \in-'chant-mənt\ *n* (13c) **1 a** : the act or art of enchanting **b** : the quality or state of being enchanted **2** : something that enchants

en·chant·ress \in-'chan-trəs\ *n* (14c) **1** : a woman who practices magic : SORCERESS **2** : a fascinating woman

en·chase \in-'chās\ *vt* [ME *enchasen* to emboss, fr. MF *enchasser* to enshrine, set, fr. *en-* + *chasse* reliquary, fr. L *capsa* case — more at CASE] (15c) **1** : ORNAMENT: as **a** : to cut or carve in relief **b** : INLAY **2** : SET ⟨~ a gem⟩

en·chi·la·da \ˌen-chə-'läd-ə\ *n* [AmerSp] (1887) : a tortilla spread with a meat or cheese filling, rolled up, and covered with chili-seasoned tomato sauce

en·chi·rid·i·on \ˌen-ˌkī-'rid-ē-ən\ *n, pl* **-rid·ia** \-ē-ə\ [LL, fr. Gk *encheiridion,* fr. *en* in + *cheir* hand — more at IN, CHIR-] (15c) : HANDBOOK, MANUAL

-en·chy·ma \'eŋ-kə-mə\ *n comb form, pl* **-en·chy·ma·ta** \ən-'kim-ət-ə, -'kī-mət-\ *or* **-enchymas** [NL, fr. *parenchyma*] : cellular tissue ⟨*collenchyma*⟩

en·ci·pher \in-'sī-fər, en-\ *vt* (1577) : to convert (a message) into cipher — **en·ci·pher·er** \-fər-ər\ *n* — **en·ci·pher·ment** \-fər-mənt\ *n*

en·cir·cle \in-'sər-kəl\ *vt* [ME *enserclе*] (15c) **1** : to form a circle around : SURROUND **2** : to pass completely around — **en·cir·cle·ment** \-mənt\ *n*

en·clasp \in-'klasp\ *vt* (1596) : to seize and hold : EMBRACE

en·clave \'en-ˌklāv; 'än-ˌklāv, 'äŋ-, -ˌkläv\ *n* [F, fr. MF, fr. *enclaver* to enclose, fr. (assumed) VL *inclavare* to lock up, fr. L *in-* + *clavis* key — more at CLAVICLE] (1868) : a territorial or culturally distinct unit enclosed within foreign territory ⟨ethnic ~*s*⟩

en·clit·ic \en-'klit-ik\ *adj* [LL *encliticus,* fr. Gk *enklitikos,* fr. *enklinesthai* to lean on, fr. *en-* + *klinein* to lean — more at LEAN] *of a word or particle* (1750) : being without independent accent and treated in pronunciation as forming a part of the preceding word ⟨*thee* in *prithee* and *not* in *cannot* are ~⟩ — **enclitic** *n*

en·close \in-'klōz\ *vt* [ME *enclosen,* prob. fr. *enclos* enclosed, fr. MF, pp. of *enclore* to enclose, fr. (assumed) VL *inclaudere,* alter. of L *includere* — more at INCLUDE] (14c) **1 a** (1) : to close in : SURROUND ⟨~ a porch with glass⟩ (2) : to fence off (common land) for individual use **b** : to hold in : CONFINE **2** : to include along with something else in a parcel or envelope ⟨a check is *enclosed* herewith⟩

en·clo·sure \in-'klō-zhər\ *n* (15c) **1** : the act or action of enclosing : the quality or state of being enclosed **2** : something that encloses **3** : something enclosed ⟨a letter with two ~*s*⟩

en·code \in-'kōd, en-\ *vt* (ca. 1919) : to convert (as a body of information) from one system of communication into another; *esp* : to convert (a message) into code — **en·cod·er** *n*

en·co·mi·ast \en-'kō-mē-ˌast, -mē-əst\ *n* [Gk *enkōmiastēs,* fr. *enkōmiazein* to praise, fr. *enkōmion*] (1610) : one that praises : EULOGIST — **en·co·mi·as·tic** \-ˌkō-mē-'as-tik\ *adj*

en·co·mi·um \en-'kō-mē-əm\ *n, pl* **-mi·ums** *or* **-mia** \-mē-ə\ [L, fr. Gk *enkōmion,* fr. *en* in + *kōmos* revel, celebration] (1589) : glowing and warmly enthusiastic praise; *also* : an expression of this

syn ENCOMIUM, EULOGY, PANEGYRIC, TRIBUTE, CITATION mean a formal expression of praise. ENCOMIUM implies enthusiasm and warmth in praising a person or a thing; EULOGY applies to a prepared speech or writing extolling the virtues and services of a person; PANEGYRIC suggests an elaborate often poetic compliment; TRIBUTE implies deeply felt praise conveyed either through words or through a significant act; CITATION applies to the formal praise accompanying the mention of a person in a military dispatch or in awarding an honorary degree.

en·com·pass \in-'kəm-pəs *also* -'käm-\ *vt* [ME *encompassen*] (14c) **1 a** : to form a circle about : ENCLOSE **b** *obs* : to go completely around **2 a** : ENVELOP **b** : INCLUDE ⟨a plan that ~*es* a number of aims⟩ **3** : BRING ABOUT, ACCOMPLISH ⟨~ a task⟩ — **en·com·pass·ment** \-pə-smənt\ *n*

[1]**en·core** \ˈän-ˌkō(ə)r, -ˌkȯ(ə)r\ *n* [F, still, again] (1712) **:** a demand for repetition or reappearance made by an audience; *also* **:** a reappearance or additional performance in response to such a demand

[2]**encore** *vt* **en·cored; en·cor·ing** (1748) **:** to request an encore of or by

[1]**en·coun·ter** \in-ˈkau̇nt-ər\ *n* (13c) **1 a :** a meeting between hostile factions or persons **b :** a sudden often violent clash **:** COMBAT **2 a :** a chance meeting **b :** a direct often momentary meeting **3 :** a coming into the vicinity of a celestial body ⟨the Martian ~ of a spacecraft⟩

[2]**encounter** *vb* **en·coun·tered; en·coun·ter·ing** \-ˈkau̇nt-ə-riŋ, -ˈkau̇n-triŋ\ [ME *encountren,* fr. MF *encontrer,* fr. ML *incontrare,* fr. LL *incontra* toward, fr. L *in-* + *contra* against — more at COUNTER] *vt* (14c) **1 a :** to meet as an adversary or enemy **b :** to engage in conflict with **2 :** to come upon face-to-face **3 :** to come upon unexpectedly ~ *vi* **:** to meet esp. by chance

encounter group *n* (1969) **:** a usu. unstructured group that seeks to develop the capacity of the individual to express feelings and to form emotional ties by unrestrained confrontation of individuals

en·cour·age \in-ˈkər-ij, -ˈkə-rij\ *vt* **-aged; -ag·ing** [ME *encoragen,* fr. MF *encoragier,* fr. OF, fr. *en-* + *corage* courage] (15c) **1 :** to inspire with courage, spirit, or hope **:** HEARTEN **2 :** to spur on **:** STIMULATE **3 :** to give help or patronage to **:** FOSTER — **en·cour·ag·er** *n*

en·cour·age·ment \-ij-mənt, -rij-\ *n* (1568) **1 :** the act of encouraging **:** the state of being encouraged **2 :** something that encourages

en·cour·ag·ing *adj* (1663) **:** giving hope or promise **:** INSPIRITING — **en·cour·ag·ing·ly** \-iŋ-lē\ *adv*

en·crim·son \in-ˈkrim-zən\ *vt* (1597) **:** to make or dye crimson

en·croach \in-ˈkrōch\ *vi* [ME *encrochen* to get, seize, fr. MF *encrochier,* fr. OF, fr. *en-* + *croc, croche* hook — more at CROCHET] (1534) **1 :** to enter by gradual steps or by stealth into the possessions or rights of another **2 :** to advance beyond the usual or proper limits ⟨the gradually ~*ing* sea⟩ ***syn*** see TRESPASS — **en·croach·er** *n* — **en·croach·ment** \-ˈkrōch-mənt\ *n*

en·crust \in-ˈkrəst\ *vb* [prob. fr. L *incrustare,* fr. *in-* + *crusta* crust] *vt* (1641) **:** to cover, line, or overlay with a crust ~ *vi* **:** to form a crust

en·crus·ta·tion \(ˌ)in-ˌkrəs-ˈtā-shən, ˌen-\ *var of* INCRUSTATION

en·crypt \in-ˈkript, en-\ *vt* (1944) **1 :** ENCIPHER **2 :** ENCODE — **en·cryp·tion** \-ˈkrip-shən\ *n*

en·cum·ber \in-ˈkəm-bər\ *vt* **en·cum·bered; en·cum·ber·ing** \-b(ə-)riŋ\ [ME *encombren,* fr. MF *encombrer,* fr. OF, fr. *en-* + (assumed) OF *combre* abatis] (14c) **1 :** WEIGH DOWN, BURDEN **2 :** to impede or hamper the function or activity of **:** HINDER **3 :** to burden with a legal claim (as a mortgage) ⟨~ an estate⟩

en·cum·brance \in-ˈkəm-brən(t)s\ *n* (1535) **1 :** something that encumbers **:** IMPEDIMENT **2 :** a claim (as a mortgage) against property

en·cum·branc·er \-brən-sər\ *n* (1858) **:** one that holds an encumbrance

-en·cy \ən-sē, ᵊn-\ *n suffix* [ME *-encie,* fr. L *-entia* — more at -ENCE] **:** quality or state ⟨despondency⟩

[1]**en·cyc·li·cal** \in-ˈsik-li-kəl, en-\ *adj* [LL *encyclicus,* fr. Gk *enkyklios* circular, general, fr. *en* in + *kyklos* circle — more at IN, WHEEL] (1647) **:** addressed to all the individuals of a group **:** GENERAL

[2]**encyclical** *n* (1837) **:** an encyclical letter; *specif* **:** a papal letter to the bishops of the church as a whole or to those in one country

en·cy·clo·pe·dia *also* **en·cy·clo·pae·dia** \in-ˌsī-klə-ˈpēd-ē-ə\ *n* [ML *encyclopaedia* course of general education, fr. Gk *enkyklios* + *paideia* education, child-rearing, fr. *paid-, pais* child — more at FEW] (1644) **:** a work that contains information on all branches of knowledge or treats comprehensively a particular branch of knowledge usu. in articles arranged alphabetically often by subject

en·cy·clo·pe·dic *also* **en·cy·clo·pae·dic** \-ˈpēd-ik\ *adj* (1824) **:** of, relating to, or suggestive of an encyclopedia or its methods of treating or covering a subject **:** COMPREHENSIVE ⟨an ~ mind⟩ — **en·cy·clo·pe·di·cal·ly** \-i-k(ə-)lē\ *adv*

en·cy·clo·pe·dism \-ˈpē-ˌdiz-əm\ *n* (1833) **:** encyclopedic knowledge

en·cy·clo·pe·dist \-ˈpēd-əst\ *n* (1651) **1 :** one who compiles or writes for an encyclopedia **2** *often cap* **:** one of the writers of a French encyclopedia (1751-80) who were identified with the Enlightenment and advocated deism and scientific rationalism

en·cyst \in-ˈsist, en-\ *vt* (ca. 1828) **:** to enclose in or as if in a cyst ~ *vi* **:** to form or become enclosed in a cyst — **en·cyst·ment** \-ˈsis(t)-mənt\ *n*

[1]**end** \ˈend\ *n* [ME *ende,* fr. OE; akin to OHG *enti* end, L *ante* before, Gk *anti* against] (bef. 12c) **1 a :** the part of an area that lies at the boundary **b** (1) **:** a point that marks the extent of something (2) **:** the point where something ceases to exist ⟨world without ~⟩ **c :** the extreme or last part lengthwise **:** TIP **d :** the terminal unit of something spatial that is marked off by units **e :** a player stationed at the extremity of a line (as in football) **2 a :** cessation of a course of action, pursuit, or activity **b :** DEATH, DESTRUCTION **c** (1) **:** the ultimate state (2) **:** RESULT, ISSUE **3 :** something incomplete, fragmentary, or undersized **:** REMNANT **4 a :** the goal toward which an agent acts or should act **b :** the object by virtue of or for the sake of which an event takes place **5 a :** a share in an undertaking ⟨kept your ~ up⟩ **b :** a particular operation or aspect of an undertaking or organization ⟨the advertising ~ of a business⟩ **6 :** something that is extreme **:** ULTIMATE — used with *the* **7 :** a period of action or turn in any of various sports events (as archery or lawn bowling) — **end·ed** \ˈen-dəd\ *adj*

syn END, TERMINATION, ENDING, TERMINUS mean the point or line beyond which something does not or cannot go. END is the inclusive term, implying the final limit in time or space, in extent of influence, or range of possibility; TERMINATION and ENDING apply to the end of something having predetermined limits or being complete or finished; ENDING often includes the portion leading to the actual final point; TERMINUS applies commonly to the point to which one moves or progresses. ***syn*** see in addition INTENTION

— **in the end :** AFTER ALL, ULTIMATELY — **no end :** EXCEEDINGLY — **on end :** without a stop or letup ⟨it rained for days *on end*⟩

[2]**end** *vt* (bef. 12c) **1 a :** to bring to an end **b :** DESTROY **2 :** to make up the end of ~ *vi* **1 a :** to come to an end **b :** to reach a specified ultimate rank or situation — often used with *up* ⟨~*ed* up as a colonel⟩ **2 :** DIE ***syn*** see CLOSE

[3]**end** *adj* (13c) **:** FINAL, ULTIMATE ⟨~ results⟩ ⟨~ markets⟩ ⟨~ user⟩

[4]**end** *vt* [prob. alter. of E dial. *in* (to harvest)] *dial Eng* (1607) **:** to put (grain or hay) into a barn or stack

end- *or* **endo-** *comb form* [F, fr. Gk, fr. *endon* within, fr. *en* in + *-don* (akin to L *domus* house) — more at IN, TIMBER] **1 :** within **:** inside ⟨*endo*skeleton⟩ — compare ECT-, EXO- **2 :** taking in ⟨*endo*thermal⟩ **3** *endo-* **:** forming a bridge between two atoms in a cyclic system

en·dam·age \in-ˈdam-ij\ *vt* [ME *endamagen*] (14c) **:** to cause loss or damage to

end·amoe·ba \ˌen-də-ˈmē-bə\ *n* [NL, genus name] (ca. 1879) **:** any of a genus (*Endamoeba*) comprising amoebas parasitic in the intestines of insects — compare ENTAMOEBA — **end·amoe·bic** \-bik\ *adj*

en·dan·ger \in-ˈdān-jər\ *vb* **en·dan·gered; en·dan·ger·ing** \-ˈdānj-(ə-)riŋ\ *vt* (1509) **:** to bring into danger or peril ~ *vi* **:** to create a dangerous situation ⟨driving to ~⟩ — **en·dan·ger·ment** \-ˈdān-jər-mənt\ *n*

en·dan·gered *adj* (1597) **:** threatened with extinction ⟨~ species⟩

en·darch \ˈen-ˌdärk\ *adj* (ca. 1900) **:** formed or taking place from inner cells outward ⟨~ xylem⟩

end around *n* (1926) **:** a football play in which an offensive end comes behind the line of scrimmage to take a handoff and attempts to carry the ball around the opposite flank

end·ar·ter·ec·to·my \ˌen-ˌdärt-ə-ˈrek-tə-mē\ *n, pl* **-mies** [NL *endarterium* intima of an artery (fr. *end-* + *arteria* artery) + E *-ectomy*] (1959) **:** surgical removal of the inner layer of an artery when thickened and atheromatous or occluded (as by intimal plaques)

end·brain \ˈen(d)-ˌbrān\ *n* (1927) **:** TELENCEPHALON

end brush *n* (ca. 1884) **:** END PLATE

en·dear \in-ˈdi(ə)r\ *vt* (1580) **1** *obs* **:** to make higher in cost, value, or estimation **2 :** to cause to become beloved or admired — **en·dear·ing·ly** \-iŋ-lē\ *adv*

en·dear·ment \in-ˈdi(ə)r-mənt\ *n* (1611) **1 :** the act or process of endearing **2 :** a word or an act (as a caress) expressing affection

[1]**en·deav·or** \in-ˈdev-ər\ *vb* **en·deav·ored; en·deav·or·ing** \-(ə-)riŋ\ [ME *endeveren* to exert oneself, fr. *en-* + *dever* duty — more at DEVOIR] *vt* (15c) **1** *archaic* **:** to strive to achieve or reach **2 :** to attempt (as the fulfillment of an obligation) by exertion of effort ⟨~*s* to finish the race⟩ ~ *vi* **:** to work with set purpose ***syn*** see ATTEMPT

[2]**endeavor** *n* (15c) **1 :** serious determined effort **2 :** activity directed toward a goal **:** ENTERPRISE ⟨fields of ~⟩

[1]**en·dem·ic** \en-ˈdem-ik, in-\ *adj* [F *endémique,* fr. *endémie* endemic disease, fr. Gk *endēmia* action of dwelling, fr. *endēmos* endemic, fr. *en* in + *dēmos* people, populace — more at DEMAGOGUE] (1759) **1 :** belonging or native to a particular people or country **2 :** restricted or peculiar to a locality or region ⟨~ diseases⟩ ⟨an ~ species⟩ ***syn*** see NATIVE — **en·dem·i·cal·ly** \-ˈdem-i-k(ə-)lē\ *adv* — **en·de·mic·i·ty** \ˌen-ˌdem-ˈis-ət-ē, -də-ˈmis-\ *n* — **en·de·mism** \ˈen-də-ˌmiz-əm\ *n*

[2]**endemic** *n* (1926) **:** an endemic organism; *esp* **:** one that is a plant

end·er·gon·ic \ˌen-ˌdər-ˈgän-ik\ *adj* [*end-* + Gk *ergon* work — more at WORK] (1940) **:** requiring expenditure of energy ⟨photosynthesis is an ~ chemical reaction⟩

end·ex·ine \(ˈ)en-ˈdek-ˌsēn, -ˌsīn\ *n* (1947) **:** an inner membranous layer of the exine

end·game \ˈen(d)-ˌgām\ *n* (1884) **:** the last stage in various games; *esp* **:** the stage of a chess game after major reduction of forces

end·ing \ˈen-diŋ\ *n* (bef. 12c) **:** a thing that constitutes an end; *esp* **:** one or more letters or syllables added to a word base esp. in inflection ***syn*** see END

endite *archaic var of* INDITE

en·dive \ˈen-ˌdīv\ *n* [ME, fr. MF, fr. LL *endivia,* fr. LGk *entubion,* fr. L *intubus*] (14c) **1 :** an annual or biennial composite herb (*Cichorium endivia*) widely cultivated as a salad plant — called also *escarole* **2 :** the developing crown of chicory when blanched for use as salad by growing in darkness or semidarkness

end·leaf \ˈen-ˌdlēf\ *n* (1888) **:** ENDPAPER

end·less \ˈen-(d)ləs\ *adj* (bef. 12c) **1 :** being or seeming to be without end **2 :** extremely numerous ⟨all the multiplied, ~, nameless iniquities —Edmund Burke⟩ **3 :** joined at the ends ⟨an ~ chain⟩ — **end·less·ly** *adv* — **end·less·ness** *n*

end line *n* (ca. 1920) **:** a line marking an end or boundary esp. of a playing area: as **a :** a line at either end of a football field 10 yards beyond and parallel to the goal line **b :** a line at either end of a court (as in basketball or tennis) perpendicular to the sidelines

end·long \ˈen-ˌdlȯŋ\ *adv* [ME *endelong,* alter. of *andlong,* fr. OE *andlang* along, fr. *andlang,* prep. — more at ALONG] *archaic* (bef. 12c) **:** LENGTHWISE

end man *n* (1865) **:** a man at each end of the line of performers in a minstrel show who engages in comic repartee with the interlocutor

end·most \ˈen(d)-ˌmōst\ *adj* (bef. 12c) **:** situated at the very end

end·note \ˈen(d)-ˌnōt\ *n* (1926) **:** a note placed at the end of the text (as of an article, chapter, or book)

en·do·bi·ot·ic \ˌen-dō-ˌbī-ˈät-ik, -bē-\ *adj* [ISV] (ca. 1900) **:** dwelling within the cells or tissues of a host ⟨~ fungi⟩

en·do·car·di·al \ˌen-dō-ˈkärd-ē-əl\ *adj* (1847) **1 :** situated within the heart **2 :** of or relating to the endocardium

en·do·car·di·tis \-ˌkär-ˈdīt-əs\ *n* (1836) **:** inflammation of the lining of the heart and its valves

en·do·car·di·um \-ˈkärd-ē-əm\ *n, pl* **-dia** [NL, fr. *end-* + Gk *kardia* heart] (ca. 1864) **:** a thin serous membrane lining the cavities of the heart

en·do·carp \ˈen-də-ˌkärp\ *n* [F *endocarpe*] (1830) **:** the inner layer of the pericarp of a fruit (as an apple or orange) when it consists of two or more layers of different texture or consistency

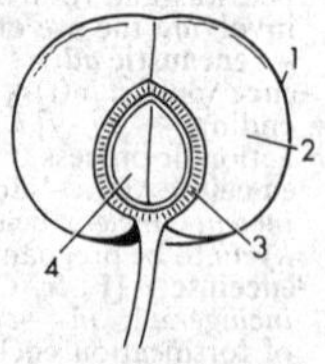

endocarp (cross section of a cherry): *1* exocarp, *2* mesocarp, *3* endocarp, *4* seed; *1, 2,* and *3* together form the pericarp

en·do·cast \ˈen-dō-ˌkast\ *n* (1949) **:** ENDOCRANIAL CAST

en·do·chon·dral \ˌen-də-ˈkän-drəl\ *adj* (1882) **:** relating to, formed by, or being ossification that takes place from centers arising in cartilage and involves deposition of lime salts in the cartilage matrix followed by secondary absorption and replacement by true bony tissue

en·do·cra·ni·al cast \ˌen-də-ˌkrā-nē-əl-\ *n* (1923) **:** a cast of the cranial cavity showing the approximate shape of the brain

[1]**en·do·crine** \ˈen-də-krən, -ˌkrīn, -ˌkrēn\ *adj* [ISV *end-* + Gk *krinein* to separate — more at CER-

TAIN] (ca. 1911) **1 :** secreting internally; *specif* **:** producing secretions that are distributed in the body by way of the bloodstream ⟨an ~ system⟩ **2 :** of, relating to, affecting, or resembling an endocrine gland or secretion ⟨~ tumors⟩

²endocrine *n* (1922) **1 :** HORMONE **2 :** ENDOCRINE GLAND

endocrine gland *n* (1914) **:** a gland (as the thyroid or the pituitary) that produces an endocrine secretion — called also *ductless gland*

en·do·cri·no·log·ic \ˌen-də-ˌkrin-ᵊl-ˈäj-ik, -ˌkrīn-, -ˌkrēn-\ *or* **en·do·cri·no·log·i·cal** \-i-kəl\ *adj* (ca. 1934) **:** involving or relating to the endocrine glands or secretions or to endocrinology

en·do·cri·nol·o·gy \ˌen-də-kri-ˈnäl-ə-jē, -ˌkrī-\ *n* [ISV] (ca. 1913) **:** a science dealing with the endocrine glands — **en·do·cri·nol·o·gist** \-jəst\ *n*

en·do·cy·to·sis \-sī-ˈtō-səs\ *n* [NL, fr. *end-* + *-cytosis* (as in *phagocytosis*)] (1963) **:** incorporation of substances into a cell by phagocytosis or pinocytosis — **en·do·cy·tot·ic** \-ˈtät-ik\ *adj*

en·do·derm \ˈen-də-ˌdərm\ *n* [F *endoderme,* fr. *end-* + Gk *derma* skin — more at DERM-] (1861) **:** the innermost of the germ layers of an embryo that is the source of the epithelium of the digestive tract and its derivatives **:** HYPOBLAST; *also* **:** a tissue that is derived from this germ layer — **en·do·der·mal** \ˌen-də-ˈder-məl\ *adj*

en·do·der·mis \ˌen-də-ˈdər-məs\ *n* [NL] (1884) **:** the innermost tissue of the cortex in many roots and stems

end·odon·tia \ˌen-də-ˈdän-ch(ē-)ə\ *n* [NL] (1946) **:** ENDODONTICS

end·odon·tics \-ˈdänt-iks\ *n pl but sing in constr* (1946) **:** a branch of dentistry concerned with diseases of the pulp — **end·odon·tic** \-ˈdänt-ik\ *adj* — **end·odon·ti·cal·ly** \-ˈdänt-i-k(ə-)lē\ *adv* — **end·odon·tist** \-ˈdänt-əst\ *n*

en·do·en·zyme \ˌen-dō-ˈen-ˌzīm\ *n* [ISV] (ca. 1909) **:** an enzyme that functions inside the cell

en·do·er·gic \ˌen-dō-ˈər-jik\ *adj* (1940) **:** absorbing energy **:** ENDOTHERMIC ⟨~ nuclear reactions⟩

en·dog·a·my \en-ˈdäg-ə-mē\ *n* (1865) **:** marriage within a specific group as required by custom or law — **en·dog·a·mous** \-məs\ *adj*

en·do·gen·ic \ˌen-də-ˈjen-ik\ *adj* (ca. 1904) **1 :** of or relating to metamorphism taking place within the earth **2 :** ENDOGENOUS

en·dog·e·nous \en-ˈdäj-ə-nəs\ *adj* (1830) **1 :** growing or produced by growth from deep tissue ⟨~ plant roots⟩ **2 a :** caused by factors inside the organism or system ⟨an ~ psychic depression⟩ ⟨~ business cycles⟩ **b :** produced or synthesized within the organism or system ⟨an ~ hormone⟩ — **en·dog·e·nous·ly** *adv*

en·do·lith·ic \ˌen-də-ˈlith-ik\ *adj* (1886) **:** living within or penetrating deeply into stony substances (as rocks, coral, or mollusk shells) ⟨~ lichens⟩

en·do·lymph \ˈen-də-ˌlim(p)f\ *n* [ISV] (1836) **:** the watery fluid in the membranous labyrinth of the ear — **en·do·lym·phat·ic** \ˌen-də-lim-ˈfat-ik\ *adj*

en·do·me·tri·osis \ˌen-dō-ˌmē-trē-ˈō-səs\ *n* (1925) **:** the presence of functioning endometrial tissue in places where it is not normally found

en·do·me·tri·um \-ˈmē-trē-əm\ *n, pl* **-tria** \-trē-ə\ [NL, fr. *end-* + Gk *mētra* uterus, fr. *mētr-, mētēr* mother — more at MOTHER] (ca. 1882) **:** the mucous membrane lining the uterus — **en·do·me·tri·al** \-trē-əl\ *adj*

en·do·mi·to·sis \-mī-ˈtō-səs\ *n* (1942) **:** division of chromosomes that is not followed by nuclear division and that results in an increased number of chromosomes in the cell — **en·do·mi·tot·ic** \-mī-ˈtät-ik\ *adj*

en·do·mix·is \-ˈmik-səs\ *n* [NL, fr. *end-* + Gk *mixis* act of mixing, fr. *mignynai* to mix — more at MIX] (1914) **:** a periodic nuclear reorganization in ciliated protozoans

en·do·morph \ˈen-də-ˌmȯrf\ *n* [*endo*derm + *-morph*] (1940) **:** an endomorphic individual

en·do·mor·phic \ˌen-də-ˈmȯr-fik\ *adj* [*endo*derm + *-morphic;* fr. the predominance in such types of structures developed from the endoderm] (1888) **1 :** of or relating to the component in W. H. Sheldon's classification of body types that measures the massiveness of the digestive viscera and the body's degree of roundedness and softness **2 :** having a heavy rounded body build often with a marked tendency to become fat — **en·do·mor·phy** \ˈen-də-ˌmȯr-fē\ *n*

en·do·mor·phism \ˌen-də-ˈmȯr-ˌfiz-əm\ *n* (1955) **:** a homomorphism that maps a mathematical set into itself — compare ISOMORPHISM

en·do·nu·cle·ase \ˌen-dō-ˈn(y)ü-klē-ˌās, -ˌāz\ *n* (1965) **:** an enzyme that breaks down a nucleotide chain into two or more shorter chains by attacking it at points not adjacent to the end — compare EXONUCLEASE

en·do·nu·cleo·lyt·ic \-ˌn(y)ü-klē-ō-ˈlit-ik\ *adj* [*end-* + *nucleo-* + *-lytic*] (1967) **:** cleaving a nucleotide chain at an internal point ⟨~ nicks⟩

en·do·par·a·site \-ˈpar-ə-ˌsīt\ *n* [ISV] (ca. 1882) **:** a parasite that lives in the internal organs or tissues of its host — **en·do·par·a·sit·ic** \-ˌpar-ə-ˈsit-ik\ *adj* — **en·do·par·a·sit·ism** \-ˈpar-ə-ˌsīt-ˌiz-əm, -sə-ˌtiz-\ *n*

en·do·pep·ti·dase \-ˈpep-tə-ˌdās, -ˌdāz\ *n* (1936) **:** any of a group of enzymes that hydrolyze peptide bonds inside the long chains of protein molecules **:** PROTEINASE — compare EXOPEPTIDASE

en·do·per·ox·ide \-pə-ˈräk-ˌsīd\ *n* (1962) **:** any of various biosynthetic intermediates in the formation of prostaglandins

en·do·phyte \ˈen-də-ˌfīt\ *n* [ISV] (1835) **:** a plant living within another plant — **en·do·phyt·ic** \ˌen-də-ˈfit-ik\ *adj*

en·do·plasm \ˈen-də-ˌplaz-əm\ *n* [ISV] (1882) **:** the inner relatively fluid part of the cytoplasm — **en·do·plas·mic** \ˌen-də-ˈplaz-mik\ *adj*

endoplasmic reticulum *n* (1947) **:** a system of interconnected vesicular and lamellar cytoplasmic membranes that functions esp. in the transport of materials within the cell and that is studded with ribosomes in some places — see CELL illustration

en·dop·o·dite \en-ˈdäp-ə-ˌdīt\ *n* [ISV] (1870) **:** the mesial or internal branch of a typical limb of a crustacean

en·do·poly·ploi·dy \ˌen-dō-ˈpäl-i-ˌplȯid-ē\ *n* (1947) **:** a polyploid state in which the chromosomes have divided repeatedly without subsequent division of the nucleus or cell — **en·do·poly·ploid** \-ˌplȯid\ *adj*

end organ *n* (1878) **:** a structure forming the end of a neural path and consisting of an effector or a receptor with its associated nerve terminations

en·dor·phin \en-ˈdȯr-fən\ *n* [*end-* + *morphine*] (1978) **:** any of a group of proteins with potent analgesic properties that occur naturally in the brain — compare ENKEPHALIN

en·dorse \in-ˈdȯ(ə)rs\ *vt* **en·dorsed; en·dors·ing** [alter. of obs. *endoss,* fr. ME *endosen,* fr. MF *endosser,* fr. OF, to put on the back, fr. *en-* + *dos* back, fr. L *dorsum*] (14c) **1 a :** to write on the back of; *esp* **:** to sign one's name as payee on the back of (a check) in order to obtain the cash or credit represented on the face **b :** to inscribe (one's signature) on a check, bill, or note **c :** to inscribe (as an official document) with a title or memorandum **d :** to make over to another (the value represented in a check, bill, or note) by inscribing one's name on the document **e :** to acknowledge receipt of (a sum specified) by one's signature on a document **2 :** to express approval of publicly and definitely ⟨~ a mayoral candidate⟩ ***syn*** see APPROVE — **en·dors·able** \-ˈdȯr-sə-bəl\ *adj* — **en·dors·ee** \in-ˌdȯr-ˈsē, ˌen-\ *n* — **en·dors·er** \in-ˈdȯr-sər\ *n*

en·dorse·ment \in-ˈdȯr-smənt\ *n* (15c) **1 :** the act or process of endorsing **2 a :** something that is written in the process of endorsing **b :** a provision added to an insurance contract altering its scope or application **3 :** SANCTION, APPROVAL

en·do·scope \ˈen-də-ˌskōp\ *n* [ISV] (1861) **:** an instrument for visualizing the interior of a hollow organ (as the rectum or urethra) — **en·dos·co·py** \en-ˈdäs-kə-pē\ *n*

en·do·scop·ic \ˌen-də-ˈskäp-ik\ *adj* (1861) **:** of, relating to, or performed by means of the endoscope or endoscopy — **en·do·scop·i·cal·ly** \-i-k(ə-)lē\ *adv*

en·do·skel·e·ton \ˌen-dō-ˈskel-ət-ᵊn\ *n* (1839) **:** an internal skeleton or supporting framework in an animal — **en·do·skel·e·tal** \-ət-ᵊl\ *adj*

end·os·mo·sis \ˌen-ˌdäs-ˈmō-səs, -ˌdäz-\ *n* [alter. of obs. *endosmose,* fr. F, fr. *end-* + Gk *ōsmos* act of pushing, fr. *ōthein* to push; akin to Skt *vadhati* he strikes] (1836) **:** passage (as of a surface-active substance) through a membrane from a region of lower to a region of higher concentration — **end·os·mot·ic** \-ˈmät-ik\ *adj* — **end·os·mot·i·cal·ly** \-i-k(ə-)lē\ *adv*

en·do·sperm \ˈen-də-ˌspərm\ *n* [F *endosperme,* fr. *end-* + Gk *sperma* seed — more at SPERM] (ca. 1850) **:** a nutritive tissue in seed plants formed within the embryo sac

endosperm nucleus *n* (ca. 1902) **:** the triploid nucleus formed in the embryo sac of a seed plant by fusion of a sperm nucleus with two polar nuclei or with a nucleus formed by the prior fusion of the polar nuclei

en·do·spore \ˈen-də-ˌspō(ə)r, -ˌspȯ(ə)r\ *n* [ISV] (1875) **:** an asexual spore developed within the cell esp. in bacteria

end·os·te·al \en-ˈdäs-tē-əl\ *adj* (1878) **1 :** of or relating to the endosteum **2 :** located within bone or cartilage — **end·os·te·al·ly** \-ə-lē\ *adv*

end·os·te·um \en-ˈdäs-tē-əm\ *n, pl* **-tea** \-tē-ə\ [NL, fr. *end-* + Gk *osteon* bone — more at OSSEOUS] (ca. 1881) **:** the layer of vascular connective tissue lining the medullary cavities of bone

en·do·style \ˈen-də-ˌstīl\ *n* [ISV *end-* + Gk *stylos* pillar — more at STEER] (1854) **:** a pair of parallel longitudinal folds projecting into the pharyngeal cavity and bounding a furrow lined with glandular ciliated cells in lower chordates (as the tunicates)

en·do·sul·fan \ˌen-də-ˈsəl-fən, -ˌfan\ *n* [*endo-* + *sulf-* + *-an*] (1962) **:** a brownish crystalline insecticide $C_9H_6Cl_6O_3S$ that is used in the control of numerous crop insects and some mites

en·do·sym·bi·o·sis \ˌen-dō-ˌsim-bī-ˈō-səs, -bē-\ *n* (1940) **:** symbiosis in which a symbiont dwells within the body of its symbiotic partner — **en·do·sym·bi·ont** \-ˈsim-bī-ˌänt, -bē-\ *also* **en·do·sym·bi·ote** \-ˌōt\ *n* — **en·do·sym·bi·ot·ic** \-ˌsim-bī-ˈät-ik, -bē-\ *adj*

en·do·the·ci·um \ˌen-dō-ˈthē-s(h)ē-əm\ *n, pl* **-cia** \-s(h)ē-ə\ [NL] (ca. 1832) **:** the inner lining of a mature anther

endotheli- *or* **endothelio-** *comb form* [ISV, fr. NL *endothelium*] **:** endothelium ⟨*endothelio*ma⟩

en·do·the·li·o·ma \-ˌthē-lē-ˈō-mə\ *n, pl* **-o·mas** *or* **-o·ma·ta** \-mət-ə\ [NL] (ca. 1880) **:** a tumor developing from endothelial tissue

en·do·the·li·um \ˌen-də-ˈthē-lē-əm\ *n, pl* **-lia** \-lē-ə\ [NL, fr. *end-* + *-thelium* (as in *epithelium*)] (1872) **1 :** an epithelium of mesodermal origin composed of a single layer of thin flattened cells that lines internal body cavities **2 :** the inner layer of the seed coat of some plants — **en·do·the·li·al** \-lē-əl\ *adj*

en·do·therm \ˈen-də-ˌthərm\ *n* (1946) **:** a warm-blooded animal

en·do·ther·mic \ˌen-də-ˈthər-mik\ *also* **en·do·ther·mal** \-məl\ *adj* [ISV] (1884) **1 :** characterized by or formed with absorption of heat **2 :** WARM-BLOODED

en·do·ther·my \ˈen-də-ˌthər-mē\ *n* (1922) **:** physiological regulation of body temperature by metabolic means; *esp* **:** the property or state of being warm-blooded

en·do·tox·in \ˌen-dō-ˈtäk-sən\ *n* [ISV] (1904) **:** a toxin of internal origin; *specif* **:** a poisonous substance present in bacteria (as the causative agent of typhoid fever) but separable from the cell body only on its disintegration — **en·do·tox·ic** \-sik\ *adj*

en·do·tra·che·al \-ˈtrā-kē-əl\ *adj* (1910) **1 :** placed within the trachea ⟨an ~ tube⟩ **2 :** applied or effected through the trachea

en·do·tro·phic \ˌen-də-ˈtrō-fik\ *adj, of a mycorrhiza* (1904) **:** penetrating into the associated root and ramifying between the cells — compare ECTOTROPHIC

en·dow \in-ˈdau̇\ *vt* [ME *endowen,* fr. AF *endouer,* fr. MF *en-* + *douer* to endow, fr. L *dotare,* fr. *dot-, dos* gift, dowry — more at DATE] (15c) **1 :** to furnish with an income ⟨~ a hospital⟩ **2 :** to furnish with a dower **3 a :** to provide or equip gratuitously **:** ENRICH **b :** CREDIT 5a

en·dow·ment \-mənt\ *n* (15c) **1 :** the act or process of endowing **2 :** something that is endowed; *specif* **:** the part of an institution's income derived from donations **3 :** natural capacity, power, or ability

en·do·zo·ic \ˌen-də-ˈzō-ik\ *adj* [ISV] (ca. 1938) **:** living within or involving passage through an animal ⟨~ distribution of weeds⟩

end·pa·per \ˈen(d)-ˌpā-pər\ *n* (1818) **:** a once-folded sheet of paper having one leaf pasted flat against the inside of the front or back cover of a book and the other pasted at the base to the first or last page

end plate *n* (1878) **:** a complex terminal arborization of a motor nerve cell

end point *n* (1899) **1 :** a point marking the completion of a process or stage of a process **2** *usu* **end·point :** either of two points or values that mark the ends of a line segment or interval; *also* **:** a point that marks the end of a ray

\ə\ abut \ᵊ\ kitten, F table \ər\ further \a\ ash \ā\ ace \ä\ cot, cart
\au̇\ out \ch\ chin \e\ bet \ē\ easy \g\ go \i\ hit \ī\ ice \j\ job
\ŋ\ sing \ō\ go \ȯ\ law \ȯi\ boy \th\ thin \t͟h\ the \ü\ loot \u̇\ foot
\y\ yet \zh\ vision \á, k̲, ⁿ, œ, œ̄, ue, ue̅, ʸ\ *see* Guide to Pronunciation

end product *n* (1903) **:** the final product of a series of processes or activities

en·drin \'en-drən\ *n* [*end-* + diel*drin*] (ca. 1952) **:** a chlorinated hydrocarbon insecticide $C_{12}H_8Cl_6O$ that is a stereoisomer of dieldrin and resembles dieldrin in toxicity

end run *n* (1902) **1 :** a football play in which the ballcarrier attempts to run wide around the end of the line **2 :** an evasive trick

end–stopped \'en(d)-,stäpt\ *adj* (1877) **:** marked by a logical or rhetorical pause at the end ⟨an ~ line of verse⟩ — compare RUN-ON

end table *n* (1851) **:** a small table that is usu. about the height of the arm of a chair and is used beside a larger piece of furniture (as a sofa)

[1]**en·due** \in-'d(y)ü\ *vt* **en·dued; en·du·ing** [ME *enduen,* fr. L *induere,* fr. *ind-* in (fr. OL *indu*) + *-uere* to put on — more at INDIGENOUS] (15c) **:** PUT ON, DON

[2]**endue** *vt* **en·dued; en·du·ing** [ME *enduen,* fr. MF *enduire* to bring in, introduce, fr. L *inducere* — more at INDUCE] (15c) **1 :** PROVIDE, ENDOW **2 :** IMBUE, TRANSFUSE

en·dur·able \in-'d(y)u̇r-ə-bəl\ *adj* (1800) **:** capable of being endured **:** BEARABLE — **en·dur·ably** \-blē\ *adv*

en·dur·ance \in-'d(y)u̇r-ən(t)s\ *n* (15c) **1 :** PERMANENCE, DURATION **2 :** the ability to withstand hardship, adversity, or stress **3 :** SUFFERING

en·dure \in-'d(y)u̇(ə)r\ *vb* **en·dured; en·dur·ing** [ME *enduren,* fr. MF *endurer,* fr. (assumed) VL *indurare,* fr. L, to harden, fr. *in-* + *durare* to harden, endure — more at DURING] *vi* (14c) **1 :** to continue in the same state **:** LAST **2 :** to remain firm under suffering or misfortune without yielding **~** *vt* **1 :** to undergo (as a hardship) esp. without giving in **:** SUFFER **2 :** TOLERATE, PERMIT ***syn*** see BEAR, CONTINUE

en·dur·ing *adj* (1532) **:** LASTING, DURABLE — **en·dur·ing·ly** \-'d(y)u̇r-iŋ-lē\ *adv* — **en·dur·ing·ness** *n*

en·duro \in-'d(y)u̇(ə)r-(,)ō\ *n, pl* **en·dur·os** [irreg. fr. *endurance*] (1930) **:** a long race (as for automobiles or motorcycles) stressing endurance rather than speed

end user *n* (ca. 1945) **:** the ultimate consumer of a finished product

end·ways \'en-,dwāz\ *adv or adj* (1575) **1 :** with the end forward (as toward the observer) **2 :** in or toward the direction of the ends **:** LENGTHWISE ⟨~ pressure⟩ **3 :** on end **:** UPRIGHT ⟨boxes set ~⟩

end·wise \'en-,dwīz\ *adv or adj* (1657) **:** ENDWAYS

En·dym·i·on \en-'dim-ē-ən\ *n* [L, fr. Gk *Endymiōn*] **:** a beautiful youth loved by Selene

end zone *n* (1928) **:** the area at either end of a football field between the goal line and the end line

-ene \,ēn\ *n suffix* [ISV, fr. Gk *-ēnē,* fem. of *-ēnos,* adj. suffix] **:** unsaturated carbon compound ⟨benz*ene*⟩; *esp* **:** carbon compound with one double bond ⟨ethyl*ene*⟩

en·e·ma \'en-ə-mə\ *n, pl* **enemas** *also* **ene·ma·ta** \,en-ə-'mät-ə, 'en-ə-mət-ə\ [LL, fr. Gk, fr. *enienai* to inject, fr. *en-* + *hienai* to send — more at JET] (15c) **1 :** the injection of liquid into the intestine by way of the anus **2 :** material for injection as an enema

en·e·my \'en-ə-mē\ *n, pl* **-mies** [ME *enemi,* fr. OF, fr. L *inimicus,* fr. *in-* [1]in- + *amicus* friend — more at AMIABLE] (13c) **1 :** one that is antagonistic to another; *esp* **:** one seeking to injure, overthrow, or confound an opponent **2 :** something harmful or deadly **3 a :** a military adversary **b :** a hostile unit or force

en·er·get·ic \,en-ər-'jet-ik\ *adj* [Gk *energētikos,* fr. *energein* to be active, fr. *energos*] (1652) **1 :** operating with or marked by vigor or effect **2 :** marked by energy **:** STRENUOUS **3 :** of or relating to energy ⟨~ equation⟩ ***syn*** see VIGOROUS — **en·er·get·i·cal·ly** \-i-k(ə-)lē\ *adv*

en·er·get·ics \-iks\ *n pl but sing in constr* (1855) **1 :** a branch of mechanics that deals primarily with energy and its transformations **2 :** the total energy relations and transformations of a physical, chemical, or biological system ⟨the ~ of an ecological community⟩

en·er·gize \'en-ər-,jīz\ *vb* **-gized; -giz·ing** *vi* (1752) **:** to put forth energy **:** ACT **~** *vt* **1 :** to impart energy to **2 :** to make energetic or vigorous **3 :** to apply voltage to — **en·er·gi·za·tion** \,en-ər-jī-'zā-shən\ *n*

en·er·giz·er \-,jī-zər\ *n* (1750) **:** one that energizes; *esp* **:** ANTIDEPRESSANT

en·er·gy \'en-ər-jē\ *n, pl* **-gies** [LL *energia,* fr. Gk *energeia* activity, fr. *energos* active, fr. *en* in + *ergon* work — more at WORK] (1599) **1 :** vigorous exertion of power **:** EFFORT ⟨investing time and ~⟩ **2 a :** the capacity of acting or being active ⟨intellectual ~⟩ **b :** dynamic quality ⟨narrative ~⟩ **3 :** the capacity for doing work **4 :** usable power (as heat or electricity); *also* **:** the resources for producing such power ***syn*** see POWER

energy level *n* (1910) **:** one of the stable states of constant energy that may be assumed by a physical system — used esp. of the quantum states of electrons in atoms and of nuclei; called also *energy state*

[1]**ener·vate** \i-'nər-vət\ *adj* (1603) **:** lacking physical, mental, or moral vigor **:** ENERVATED

[2]**en·er·vate** \'en-ər-,vāt\ *vt* **-vat·ed; -vat·ing** [L *enervatus,* pp. of *enervare,* fr. *e-* + *nervus* sinew — more at NERVE] (1614) **1 :** to lessen the vitality or strength of **2 :** to reduce the mental or moral vigor of ***syn*** see UNNERVE — **en·er·va·tion** \,en-ər-'vā-shən\ *n*

en·fant ter·ri·ble \äⁿ-fäⁿ-te-rēblᵊ\ *n, pl* **enfants terribles** *same*\ [F, lit., terrifying child] (1851) **1 :** one whose inopportune remarks or unconventional actions cause embarrassment **2 :** one who is strikingly unorthodox, innovative, or avant-garde

en·fee·ble \in-'fē-bəl\ *vt* **en·fee·bled; en·fee·bling** \-b(ə-)liŋ\ [ME *enfeblen,* fr. MF *enfeblir,* fr. OF, fr. *en-* + *feble* feeble] (14c) **:** to make feeble **:** deprive of strength ***syn*** see WEAKEN — **en·fee·ble·ment** \-bəl-mənt\ *n*

en·feoff \in-'fef, -'fēf\ *vt* [ME *enfeoffen,* fr. AF *enfeoffer,* fr. OF *en-* + *fief* fief] (15c) **:** to invest with a fief, fee, or other possession — **en·feoff·ment** \-mənt\ *n*

en·fet·ter \in-'fet-ər\ *vt* (1604) **:** to bind in fetters **:** ENCHAIN

en·fe·ver \in-'fē-vər\ *vt* (1647) **:** FEVER

En·field rifle \,en-,fēld-\ *n* [*Enfield,* England] (1854) **:** a .30 caliber bolt-action repeating rifle used by U.S. and British troops in World War I

[1]**en·fi·lade** \'en-fə-,lād, -,läd\ *n* [F, fr. *enfiler* to thread, enfilade, fr. OF, to thread, fr. *en-* + *fil* thread — more at FILE] (1705) **1 :** an arrangement (as of rooms) in opposite and parallel rows **2 :** gunfire directed along the length of an enemy battle line

[2]**enfilade** *vt* **-lad·ed; -lad·ing** (1706) **:** to rake or be in a position to rake with gunfire in a lengthwise direction

enflame *var of* INFLAME

en·fleu·rage \,äⁿ-,flər-'äzh\ *n* [F, fr. *enfleurer* to saturate with the perfume of flowers, fr. *en-* [1]en- + *fleur* flower, fr. OF *flor* — more at FLOWER] (ca. 1855) **:** a process of extracting perfumes by exposing absorbents to the exhalations of flowers

en·fold \in-'fōld\ *vt* (1592) **1 a :** to cover with or as if with folds **:** ENVELOP **b :** to surround with a covering **:** CONTAIN **2 :** to clasp within the arms **:** EMBRACE

en·force \in-'fō(ə)rs, -'fȯ(ə)rs\ *vt* [ME *enforcen,* fr. MF *enforcier,* fr. OF, fr. *en-* + *force* force] (14c) **1 :** to give force to **:** STRENGTHEN **2 :** to urge with energy **3 :** CONSTRAIN, COMPEL **4** *obs* **:** to effect or gain by force **5 :** to carry out effectively ⟨~ laws⟩ — **en·force·abil·i·ty** \-,fōr-sə-'bil-ət-ē, -,fȯr-\ *n* — **en·force·able** \-'fōr-sə-bəl, -'fȯr-\ *adj* — **en·force·ment** \-'fōr-smənt, -'fȯr-\ *n* — **en·forc·er** *n*

en·fran·chise \in-'fran-,chīz\ *vt* **-chised; -chis·ing** [ME *enfranchisen,* fr. MF *enfranchiss-,* stem of *enfranchir,* fr. OF, fr. *en-* + *franc* free — more at FRANK] (15c) **1 :** to set free (as from slavery) **2 :** to endow with a franchise: as **a :** to admit to the privileges of a citizen; *specif* **:** to admit to the right of suffrage **b :** to admit (a municipality) to political privileges or rights — **en·fran·chise·ment** \-,chīz-mənt, -chəz-\ *n*

en·gage \in-'gāj\ *vb* **en·gaged; en·gag·ing** [ME *engagen,* fr. MF *engagier,* fr. OF, fr. *en-* + *gage* token, gage] *vt* (15c) **1 :** to offer (as one's word) as security for a debt or cause **2 a** *obs* **:** to entangle or entrap in or as if in a snare or bog **b :** to attract and hold by influence or power **c :** to interlock with **:** MESH; *also* **:** to cause (mechanical parts) to mesh **3 :** to bind (as oneself) to do something; *esp* **:** to bind by a pledge to marry **4 a :** to provide occupation for **:** INVOLVE ⟨~ him in a new project⟩ **b :** to arrange to obtain the use or services of **:** HIRE **5 a :** to hold the attention of **:** ENGROSS ⟨her work ~s her completely⟩ **b :** to induce to participate ⟨*engaged* the shy boy in conversation⟩ **6 a :** to enter into contest with **b :** to bring together or interlock (weapons) **7 :** to deal with esp. at length **~** *vi* **1 a :** to pledge oneself **:** PROMISE **b :** GUARANTEE ⟨he ~s for the honesty of his brother⟩ **2 a :** to begin and carry on an enterprise ⟨he *engaged* in trade for a number of years⟩ **b :** to take part **:** PARTICIPATE ⟨at college he *engaged* in gymnastics⟩ **3 :** to enter into conflict **4 :** to come together and interlock (as of machinery parts) **:** be or become in gear

en·ga·gé \,äⁿ-,gazh-'ā\ *adj* [F, pp. of *engager* to engage, fr. MF *engagier*] (1946) **:** being actively involved in or committed esp. to political concerns

en·gaged \in-'gājd\ *adj* (1615) **1 :** involved in activity **:** OCCUPIED **2 :** pledged to be married **:** BETROTHED **3 :** greatly interested **:** COMMITTED **4 :** involved esp. in a hostile encounter **5 :** partly embedded in a wall ⟨an ~ column⟩ **6 :** being in gear **:** MESHED

en·gage·ment \in-'gāj-mənt\ *n* (1624) **1 a :** a promise to be present at a specified time and place **b :** employment esp. for a stated time **2 :** something that engages **:** PLEDGE **3 a :** the act of engaging **:** the state of being engaged **b :** BETROTHAL **4 :** the state of being in gear **5 :** a hostile encounter between military forces

en·gag·ing *adj* (1673) **:** tending to draw favorable attention **:** ATTRACTIVE — **en·gag·ing·ly** \-'gā-jiŋ-lē\ *adv*

en·gar·land \in-'gär-lənd\ *vt* (1581) **:** to adorn with or as if with a garland

En·gel·mann spruce \,eŋ-gəl-mən-\ *n* [George *Engelmann* †1884 Am. botanist] (1866) **:** a large spruce (*Picea engelmannii*) of the Rocky mountain region and British Columbia that yields a light-colored wood

en·gen·der \in-'jen-dər\ *vb* **en·gen·dered; en·gen·der·ing** \-d(ə-)riŋ\ [ME *engendren,* fr. MF *engendrer,* fr. L *ingenerare,* fr. *in-* + *generare* to generate] *vt* (14c) **1 :** BEGET, PROCREATE **2 :** to cause to exist or to develop **:** PRODUCE ⟨angry words ~ strife⟩ **~** *vi* **:** to assume form **:** ORIGINATE

en·gild \in-'gild\ *vt* (15c) **:** to make bright with or as if with light

[1]**en·gine** \'en-jən\ *n* [ME *engin,* fr. MF, fr. L *ingenium* natural disposition, talent, fr. *in-* + *gignere* to beget — more at KIN] (14c) **1** *obs* **a :** INGENUITY **b :** evil contrivance **:** WILE **2 :** something used to effect a purpose **:** AGENT, INSTRUMENT ⟨mournful and terrible ~ of horror and of crime —E. A. Poe⟩ **3 a :** a mechanical tool: as **(1) :** an instrument or machine of war **(2)** *obs* **:** a torture implement **b :** MACHINERY **c :** any of various mechanical appliances — compare FIRE ENGINE **4 :** a machine for converting any of various forms of energy into mechanical force and motion **5 :** a railroad locomotive

[2]**engine** *vt* **en·gined; en·gin·ing** (1868) **:** to equip with engines

-en·gined \'en-jənd\ *adj comb form* **:** having (such or so many) engines ⟨front-*engined* cars⟩ ⟨four-*engined* planes⟩

[1]**en·gi·neer** \,en-jə-'ni(ə)r\ *n* [alter. (influenced by *-eer*) of earlier *enginer,* fr. ME, alter. of *engynour,* fr. MF *engigneur,* fr. OF *engignier* to contrive, fr. *engin*] (14c) **1 :** a member of a military group devoted to engineering work **2** *obs* **:** a crafty schemer **:** PLOTTER **3 a :** a designer or builder of engines **b :** a person who is trained in or follows as a profession a branch of engineering **c :** a person who carries through an enterprise by skillful or artful contrivance **4 :** a person who runs or supervises an engine or an apparatus

[2]**engineer** *vt* (1843) **1 :** to lay out, construct, or manage as an engineer **2 a :** to contrive or plan out usu. with more or less subtle skill and craft **b :** to guide the course of **3 :** to modify or produce by genetic engineering ⟨insulin made by genetically ~*ed* bacteria — *Technical Survey*⟩ ***syn*** see GUIDE

en·gi·neer·ing *n* (1720) **1 :** the activities or function of an engineer: as **a :** the art of managing engines **b :** calculated manipulation or direction (as of behavior) ⟨social ~⟩ — compare GENETIC ENGINEERING **2 :** the application of science and mathematics by which the properties of matter and the sources of energy in nature are made useful to people in structures, machines, products, systems, and processes — compare BIOENGINEERING

en·gine·ry \'en-jən-rē\ *n* (1641) **1 :** instruments of war **2 :** machines and tools **:** MACHINERY

en·gird \in-'gərd\ *vt, archaic* (1566) **:** GIRD, ENCOMPASS

en·gir·dle \in-'gərd-ᵊl\ *vt* (1602) **:** to encircle with or as if with a girdle

en·gla·cial \en-'glā-shəl\ *adj* (ca. 1891) **:** embedded in a glacier

[1]**En·glish** \'iŋ-glish, 'iŋ-lish\ *adj* [ME, fr. OE *englisc,* fr. *Engle* (pl.) Angles] (bef. 12c) **:** of, relating to, or characteristic of England, the English people, or the English language — **En·glish·ness** *n*

²**English** *n* (bef. 12c) **1 a :** the language of the people of England and the U.S. and many areas now or formerly under British control **b :** a particular variety of English distinguished by peculiarities (as of pronunciation) **c :** English language, literature, or composition when a subject of study **2** *pl in constr* **:** the people of England **3 a :** an English translation **b :** idiomatic or intelligible English **4 :** spin around the vertical axis deliberately imparted to a ball that is driven or rolled — compare DRAW, FOLLOW; BODY ENGLISH

³**English** *vt* (14c) **1 :** to translate into English **2 :** to adopt into English **:** ANGLICIZE

English breakfast *n* (1877) **:** CONGOU; *broadly* **:** any similar black tea

English cocker spaniel *n* (1950) **:** any of a breed of spaniels that have square muzzles, wide well-developed noses, and distinctive heads which are ideally half muzzle and half skull with the forehead and skull arched and slightly flattened

English daisy *n* (ca. 1890) **:** DAISY 1a

English foxhound *n* (1938) **:** any of a breed of foxhounds developed in England and characterized by a large heavily boned form, rather short ears, and lightly fringed tail

English horn *n* [trans. of It *corno inglese*] (1838) **:** a double-reed woodwind instrument resembling the oboe in design but having a longer tube and a range a fifth lower than that of the oboe

En·glish·man \ˈiŋ-glish-mən, ˈiŋ-lish-\ *n* (bef. 12c) **:** a native or inhabitant of England

English muffin *n* (1926) **:** bread dough rolled and cut into rounds, baked on a griddle, and split and toasted just before eating

English saddle *n* (ca. 1934) **:** a saddle with long side bars, steel cantle and pommel, no horn, and a leather seat supported by webbing stretched between the saddlebow and cantle — see SADDLE illustration

English setter *n* (1859) **:** any of a breed of bird dogs characterized by a moderately long flat silky coat of white or white with color and by feathering on the tail and legs

English shepherd *n* (1950) **:** any of a breed of vigorous medium-sized working dogs with a long and glossy black coat usu. with tan to brown markings that was developed in England for herding sheep and cattle

English sonnet *n* (ca. 1903) **:** a sonnet consisting of three quatrains and a couplet with a rhyme scheme of *abab cdcd efef gg* — called also *Shakespearean sonnet*

English sparrow *n* (1876) **:** a sparrow (*Passer domesticus*) native to most of Europe and parts of Asia that has been intentionally introduced into America, Australia, New Zealand and elsewhere to destroy insects although it feeds largely on grain seeds — called also *house sparrow*

English springer spaniel *n* (ca. 1934) **:** any of a breed of springer spaniels having a deep-bodied muscular build and a moderately long silky coat usu. of black and white or liver and white hair — called also *English springer*

English system *n* (1927) **:** the foot-pound-second system of units

English toy spaniel *n* (ca. 1934) **:** any of a breed of small blocky spaniels with well-rounded upper skull projecting forward toward the short turned-up nose

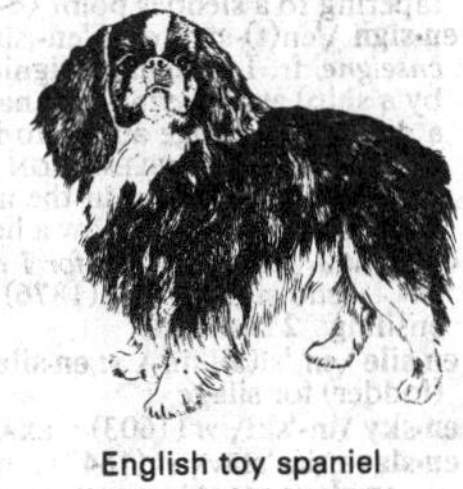
English toy spaniel

English walnut *n* (1772) **:** a Eurasian walnut (*Juglans regia*) valued for its large edible nut and its hard richly figured wood; *also* **:** its nut

En·glish·wom·an \ˈiŋ-glish-ˌwu̇m-ən *also* ˈiŋ-lish-\ *n* (15c) **:** a woman of English birth, nationality, or origin

English yew *n* (1930) **:** YEW 1a(1)

en·gorge \in-ˈgȯ(ə)rj\ *vb* [MF *engorgier,* fr. OF, to devour, fr. *en-* + *gorge* throat — more at GORGE] *vt* (1515) **:** GORGE, GLUT; *specif* **:** to fill with blood to the point of congestion ~ *vi* **:** to suck blood to the limit of body capacity — **en·gorge·ment** \-mənt\ *n*

en·graft \in-ˈgraft\ *vt* (1585) **1 :** to join or fasten as if by grafting **2 :** GRAFT 1, 3 ⟨~*ed* embryonic gill tissue into the back⟩ — **en·graft·ment** \-ˈgraf(t)-mənt\ *n*

en·grailed \in-ˈgrā(ə)ld\ *adj* [ME *engreled,* fr. MF *engreslé,* fr. *en-* + *gresle* slender, fr. L *gracilis*] (15c) **1 :** indented with small concave curves ⟨an ~ heraldic bordure⟩ **2 :** made of or bordered by a circle of raised dots ⟨an ~ coin⟩

en·grain \in-ˈgrān\ *vt* (1641) **:** INGRAIN

en·gram *also* **en·gramme** \ˈen-ˌgram\ *n* [ISV] (1908) **:** a hypothetical change in neural tissue postulated in order to account for persistence of memory

en·grave \in-ˈgrāv\ *vt* **en·graved; en·grav·ing** [MF *engraver,* fr. *en-* + *graver* to grave, of Gmc origin; akin to OE *grafan* to grave] (1513) **1 a :** to form by incision (as on wood or metal) **b :** to impress deeply as if with a graver ⟨the incident was *engraved* in his memory⟩ **2 a :** to cut figures, letters, or devices on for printing; *also* **:** to print from an engraved plate **b :** PHOTOENGRAVE — **en·grav·er** *n*

en·grav·ing *n* (1601) **1 :** the act or process of one that engraves **2 :** something that is engraved: as **a :** an engraved printing surface **b :** engraved work **3 :** an impression from an engraved printing surface

en·gross \in-ˈgrōs\ *vt* [ME *engrossen,* fr. AF *engrosser,* prob. fr. ML *ingrossare,* fr. L *in* + ML *grossa* large handwriting, fr. L, fem. of *grossus* thick] (15c) **1 a :** to copy or write in a large hand **b :** to prepare the usu. final handwritten or printed text of (an official document) **2** [ME *engrossen,* fr. MF *en gros* in large quantities] **a :** to purchase large quantities of (as for speculation) **b** *archaic* **:** AMASS, COLLECT **c :** to take or engage the whole attention of **:** occupy completely ⟨ideas that have ~*ed* the minds of scholars for generations⟩ — **en·gross·er** *n*

en·gross·ing \-ˈgrō-siŋ\ *adj* (1825) **:** taking up the attention completely **:** ABSORBING — **en·gross·ing·ly** \-siŋ-lē\ *adv*

en·gross·ment \in-ˈgrō-smənt\ *n* (1526) **1 :** the act of engrossing **2 :** the state of being absorbed or occupied **:** PREOCCUPATION

en·gulf \in-ˈgəlf\ *vt* (1555) **1 :** to flow over and enclose **:** OVERWHELM ⟨the mounting seas threatened to ~ the island⟩ **2 :** to take in (food) by or as if by flowing over and enclosing — **en·gulf·ment** \-mənt\ *n*

en·ha·lo \in-ˈhā-(ˌ)lō\ *vt* (1842) **:** to surround with or as if with a halo

en·hance \in-ˈhan(t)s\ *vt* **en·hanced; en·hanc·ing** [ME *enhauncen,* fr. AF *enhauncer,* alter. of OF *enhaucier,* fr. (assumed) VL *inaltiare,* fr. L *in* + *altus* high — more at OLD] (13c) **1** *obs* **:** RAISE **2 :** to add or contribute to: as **a :** IMPROVE **b :** INCREASE ***syn*** see INTENSIFY — **en·hance·ment** \-ˈhan(t)-smənt\ *n* — **en·hanc·er** \-ˈhan(t)-sər\ *n*

en·har·mon·ic \ˌen-(ˌ)här-ˈmän-ik\ *adj* [F *enharmonique,* fr. MF, of a scale employing quarter tones, fr. Gk *enarmonios,* fr. *en* in + *harmonia* harmony, scale] (1794) **:** of, relating to, or being notes that are written differently (as A flat and G sharp) but sound the same in the tempered scale — **en·har·mon·i·cal·ly** \-i-k(ə-)lē\ *adv*

enig·ma \i-ˈnig-mə\ *n* [L *aenigma,* fr. Gk *ainigmat-, ainigma,* fr. *ainissesthai* to speak in riddles, fr. *ainos* fable] (15c) **1 :** an obscure speech or writing **2 :** something hard to understand or explain **3 :** an inscrutable or mysterious person ***syn*** see MYSTERY

enig·mat·ic \ˌen-(ˌ)ig-ˈmat-ik *also* ˌē-(ˌ)nig-\ *also* **enig·mat·i·cal** \-i-kəl\ *adj* (1628) **:** of, relating to, or resembling an enigma **:** MYSTERIOUS ***syn*** see OBSCURE — **enig·mat·i·cal·ly** \-i-k(ə-)lē\ *adv*

en·isle \in-ˈī(ə)l\ *vt* (1612) **1 :** to place apart **:** ISOLATE **2 :** to make an island of

en·jamb·ment \in-ˈjam-mənt\ *or* **en·jambe·ment** *same, or* än-zhäⁿb(ə-)mäⁿ\ *n* [F *enjambement,* fr. MF, encroachment, fr. *enjamber* to straddle, encroach on, fr. *en-* + *jambe* leg — more at JAMB] (1837) **:** the running over of a sentence from one verse or couplet into another so that closely related words fall in different lines — compare RUN-ON

en·join \in-ˈjȯin\ *vt* [ME *enjoinen,* fr. OF *enjoindre,* fr. L *injungere,* fr. *in-* + *jungere* to join — more at YOKE] (13c) **1 :** to direct or impose by authoritative order or with urgent admonition **2 :** FORBID, PROHIBIT ⟨was ~*ed* by conscience from telling a lie⟩ ***syn*** see COMMAND

en·joy \in-ˈjȯi\ *vb* [ME *enjoie,* fr. MF *enjoir,* fr. OF, fr. *en-* + *joir* to enjoy, fr. L *gaudēre* to rejoice — more at JOY] *vi* (15c) **:** to have a good time ~ *vt* **1 :** to have for one's use, benefit, or lot **:** EXPERIENCE ⟨~*ed* great success⟩ **2 :** to take pleasure or satisfaction in — **en·joy·able** \-ə-bəl\ *adj* — **en·joy·able·ness** *n* — **en·joy·ably** \-blē\ *adv* — **enjoy oneself :** to have a good time

en·joy·ment \in-ˈjȯi-mənt\ *n* (1553) **1 a :** the action or state of enjoying **b :** possession and use ⟨the ~ of civic rights⟩ **2 :** something that gives keen satisfaction

en·keph·a·lin \in-ˈkef-ə-lən, -(ˌ)lin\ *n* [*enkephal-* (alter. of *encephal-*) + *-in*] (1977) **:** either of two pentapeptides with opiate and analgesic activity that occur naturally in the brain and have a marked affinity for opiate receptors — compare ENDORPHIN

en·kin·dle \in-ˈkin-dᵊl\ *vt* (1542) **1 :** to set (as fuel) on fire **2 :** to make bright and glowing ~ *vi* **:** to take fire **:** FLAME

en·lace \in-ˈlās\ *vt* [ME *enlacen,* fr. MF *enlacier,* fr. OF, fr. *en-* + *lacier* to lace] (14c) **1 :** ENCIRCLE, ENFOLD **2 :** ENTWINE, INTERLACE

en·lace·ment \in-ˈlā-smənt\ *n* (1830) **1 :** the process or result of interlacing **2 :** a pattern of interlacing elements

en·large \in-ˈlärj\ *vb* **en·larged; en·larg·ing** [ME *enlargen,* fr. MF *enlargier,* fr. OF, fr. *en-* + *large* large, abundant] *vt* (14c) **1 :** to make larger **:** EXTEND **2 :** to give greater scope to **:** EXPAND **3 :** to set free (as a captive) ~ *vi* **1 :** to grow larger **2 :** to speak or write at length **:** ELABORATE ⟨let me ~ upon that point⟩ ***syn*** see INCREASE — **en·larg·er** *n*

en·large·ment \in-ˈlärj-mənt\ *n* (1540) **1 :** an act or instance of enlarging **:** the state of being enlarged **2 :** a photographic print larger than the negative that is made by projecting the negative image through a lens onto a photographic printing surface

en·light·en \in-ˈlīt-ᵊn\ *vt* **en·light·ened; en·light·en·ing** \-ˈlīt-niŋ, -ᵊn-iŋ\ (1587) **1** *archaic* **:** ILLUMINATE **2 a :** to furnish knowledge to **:** INSTRUCT **b :** to give spiritual insight to

en·light·ened *adj* (1663) **1 :** freed from ignorance and misinformation ⟨an ~ people⟩ **2 :** based on full comprehension of the problems involved ⟨issued an ~ ruling⟩

en·light·en·ment \in-ˈlīt-ᵊn-mənt\ *n* (1669) **1 :** the act or means of enlightening **:** the state of being enlightened **2** *cap* **:** a philosophic movement of the 18th century marked by a rejection of traditional social, religious, and political ideas and an emphasis on rationalism — used with *the* **3** *Buddhism* **:** a final blessed state marked by the absence of desire or suffering

en·list \in-ˈlist\ *vt* (1698) **1 :** to engage (a person) for duty in the armed forces **2 a :** to secure the support and aid of **:** employ in advancing an interest ⟨~ all the available resources⟩ ⟨~ the community in an experiment⟩ **b :** to win over **:** ATTRACT ⟨trying to ~ my sympathies⟩ ~ *vi* **1 :** to enroll oneself in the armed forces **2 :** to participate heartily (as in a cause, drive, or crusade) — **en·list·ee** \-ˌlis-ˈtē\ *n* — **en·list·ment** \-ˈlis(t)-mənt\ *n*

en·list·ed \-ˈlis-təd\ *adj* (1724) **:** of, relating to, or constituting the part of a military or naval force below commissioned or warrant officers

enlisted man *n* (1724) **:** a man or woman in the armed forces ranking below a commissioned or warrant officer; *specif* **:** one ranking below a noncommissioned officer or petty officer

en·liv·en \in-ˈlī-vən\ *vt* (1604) **:** to give life, action, or spirit to **:** ANIMATE ***syn*** see QUICKEN

en masse \äⁿ(n)-ˈmas\ *adv* [F] (1795) **:** in a body **:** as a whole

en·mesh \in-ˈmesh\ *vt* (1604) **:** to catch or entangle in or as if in meshes — **en·mesh·ment** \-mənt\ *n*

en·mi·ty \ˈen-mət-ē\ *n, pl* **-ties** [ME *enmite,* fr. MF *enemité,* fr. OF *enemisté,* irreg. fr. *enemi* enemy] (14c) **:** positive, active, and typically mutual hatred or ill will

syn ENMITY, HOSTILITY, ANTIPATHY, ANTAGONISM, ANIMOSITY, RANCOR, ANIMUS mean deep-seated dislike or ill will. ENMITY suggests positive hatred which may be open or concealed; HOSTILITY suggests an enmity showing itself in attacks or aggression; ANTIPATHY and ANTAGONISM imply a natural or logical basis for one's hatred or dislike, ANTIPATHY suggesting repugnance, a desire to avoid or reject, and ANTAGONISM suggesting a clash of temperaments leading readily to hostility; ANI-

\ə\ abut \ᵊ\ kitten, F table \ər\ further \a\ ash \ā\ ace \ä\ cot, cart
\au̇\ out \ch\ chin \e\ bet \ē\ easy \g\ go \i\ hit \ī\ ice \j\ job
\ŋ\ sing \ō\ go \ȯ\ law \ȯi\ boy \th\ thin \th\ the \ü\ loot \u̇\ foot
\y\ yet \zh\ vision \à, k, ⁿ, œ, œ̄, ue, u̅e, ʸ\ see Guide to Pronunciation

MOSITY and RANCOR suggest intense ill will and vindictiveness that threaten to kindle hostility; RANCOR is esp. applied to bitter brooding over a wrong; ANIMUS adds to animosity the implication of strong prejudice.

en·ne·ad \ˈen-ē-ˌad\ *n* [Gk *ennead-, enneas,* fr. *ennea* nine — more at NINE] (1653) **:** a group of nine

en·no·ble \in-ˈō-bəl\ *vt* **en·no·bled; en·no·bling** \-b(ə-)liŋ\ [ME *ennobelen,* fr. MF *ennoblir,* fr. OF, fr. *en-* + *noble* noble] (15c) **1 :** to make noble **:** ELEVATE ⟨he seemed *ennobled* by his suffering⟩ **2 :** to raise to the rank of nobility — **en·no·ble·ment** \-bəl-mənt\ *n*

en·nui \ˈän-ˈwē\ *n* [F, fr. OF *enui* annoyance, fr. *enuier* to annoy — more at ANNOY] (1732) **:** a feeling of weariness and dissatisfaction **:** BOREDOM ⟨that ~ . . . that comes on those to whom life denies nothing —Oscar Wilde⟩

Enoch \ˈē-nək, -nik\ *n* [Gk *Enōch,* fr. Heb *Hănōkh*] **:** an Old Testament patriarch and father of Methuselah

enol \ˈē-ˌnȯl, -ˌnōl\ *n* [ISV *ene-* (fr. *-ene*) + *-ol*] (ca. 1909) **:** an organic compound that contains a hydroxyl group bonded to a carbon atom having a double bond and that is usu. characterized by the grouping C=C(OH) — **eno·lic** \ē-ˈnō-lik, -ˈnäl-ik\ *adj*

eno·lase \ˈē-nə-ˌlās, -ˌlāz\ *n* [ISV *enol* + *-ase*] (1942) **:** a crystalline enzyme that is found esp. in muscle and yeast and is important in the metabolism of carbohydrates

enol·o·gy \ē-ˈnäl-ə-jē\ *n* [Gk *oinos* wine + E *-logy* — more at WINE] (1814) **:** a science that deals with wine and wine making — **eno·log·i·cal** \ˌē-nᵊl-ˈäj-i-kəl\ *adj* — **enol·o·gist** \ē-ˈnäl-ə-jəst\ *n*

enor·mi·ty \i-ˈnȯr-mət-ē\ *n, pl* **-ties** (15c) **1 :** a grave offense against order, right, or decency **2 :** the quality or state of being immoderate, monstrous, or outrageous; *esp* **:** great wickedness **3 :** the quality or state of being huge **:** IMMENSITY

usage *Enormity,* some people insist, is improperly used to denote large size and is properly used only to denote wickedness, outrage, or crime. They recommend *enormousness* for large size. *Enormousness,* however, is simply not a popular word. It developed later than *enormity* and in about the same way: its first sense (equivalent to *enormity* 2) appears to have dropped out of use; its second sense is used less frequently than sense 3 of *enormity. Enormity*'s third sense has continued in use from the end of the eighteenth century; it has been stigmatized as incorrect, for unknown reasons, since the end of the nineteenth. *Enormity* is used with more subtleness than is usu. indicated. In sense 1 it need not carry overtones of moral transgression, although it most often does. It regularly denotes a considerable departure from the expected or normal ⟨they awakened; they sat up; and then the *enormity* of their situation burst upon them. "How did the fire start?" —John Steinbeck⟩ ⟨a man able to have made the world grow pale with the *enormity* of his learned acquisitions —Thomas DeQuincey⟩ While it is used neutrally to denote great size, more often it is used of something so large as to be overwhelming ⟨the *enormity* of population pressures in India —M.T. Kaufman⟩ ⟨the *enormity* of the task of teachers in slum schools —J. B. Conant⟩ and may even be used to suggest both great size and deviation from morality ⟨the *enormity* of existing stockpiles of atomic weapons —*New Republic*⟩

enor·mous \i-ˈnȯr-məs\ *adj* [L *enormis,* fr. *e, ex* out of + *norma* rule] (15c) **1 a** *archaic* **:** ABNORMAL, INORDINATE **b :** exceedingly wicked **:** SHOCKING ⟨an ~ sin⟩ **2 :** marked by extraordinarily great size, number, or degree; *esp* **:** exceeding usual bounds or accepted notions — **enor·mous·ly** *adv* — **enor·mous·ness** *n*

syn ENORMOUS, IMMENSE, HUGE, VAST, GIGANTIC, COLOSSAL, MAMMOTH mean exceedingly large. ENORMOUS and IMMENSE both suggest an exceeding of all ordinary bounds in size or amount or degree, but ENORMOUS often adds an implication of abnormality or monstrousness; HUGE commonly suggests an immensity of bulk or amount; VAST usu. suggests immensity of extent; GIGANTIC stresses the contrast with the size of others of the same kind; COLOSSAL applies esp. to a human creation of stupendous or incredible dimensions; MAMMOTH suggests both hugeness and ponderousness of bulk.

eno·sis \i-ˈnō-səs\ *n* [NGk *henōsis,* fr. Gk, union, fr. *henoun* to unite, fr. *hen-, heis* one — more at SAME] (1938) **:** a movement to secure the political union of Greece and Cyprus

[1]**enough** \i-ˈnəf; *after* t, d, s, z *often* ᵊn-ˈəf\ *adj* [ME *ynough,* fr. OE *genōg* (akin to OHG *ginuog* enough), fr. *ge-* (perfective prefix) + *-nōg;* akin to L *nancisci* to get, Gk *enenkein* to carry — more at CO-] (bef. 12c) **:** occurring in such quantity, quality, or scope as to fully satisfy demands or needs ***syn*** see SUFFICIENT

[2]**enough** *adv* (bef. 12c) **1 :** in or to a degree or quantity that satisfies or that is sufficient or necessary for satisfaction **:** SUFFICIENTLY **2 :** FULLY, QUITE **3 :** in a tolerable degree

[3]**enough** *pron* (bef. 12c) **:** a sufficient number, quantity, or amount ⟨~ were present to constitute a quorum⟩ ⟨had ~ of their foolishness⟩

enounce \ē-ˈnau̇n(t)s\ *vt* **enounced; enounc·ing** [F *énoncer,* fr. L *enuntiare* to report — more at ENUNCIATE] (1805) **1 :** to set forth or state (as a proposition) **2 :** to pronounce distinctly **:** ARTICULATE

enow \i-ˈnau̇\ *adv or adj* [ME *inow,* fr. OE *genōg*] *archaic* (bef. 12c) **:** ENOUGH

en pas·sant \ˌän-ˌpä-ˈsän, -pə-\ *adv* [F] (1818) **1 :** in passing **2** — used in chess of the capture of a pawn as it makes a first move of two squares by an enemy pawn in a position to threaten the first of these squares

en·plane \in-ˈplān\ *vi* (1923) **:** to board an airplane

en prise \än-ˈprēz\ *adj* [F, lit., engaged, within grasp] *of a chess piece* (1899) **:** exposed to capture

en·quire \in-ˈkwī(ə)r\, **en·qui·ry** \ˈin-ˌkwī(ə)r-ē, in-ˈ; ˈin-kwə-rē, ˈiŋ-\ *var of* INQUIRE, INQUIRY

en·rage \in-ˈrāj\ *vt* [MF *enrager* to become mad, fr. OF *enragier,* fr. *en-* + *rage* rage] (1500) **:** to fill with rage **:** ANGER

en rap·port \ˌän-rə-ˈpō(ə)r, -ˈpȯ(ə)r\ *adj* [F] (1818) **:** being in a state of mutual accord and harmony

en·rapt \in-ˈrapt\ *adj* (1606) **:** wholly absorbed with rapture

en·rap·ture \in-ˈrap-chər\ *vt* **en·rap·tured; en·rap·tur·ing** \-ˈrap-chə-riŋ, -ˈrap-shriŋ\ (1742) **:** to fill with delight

en·reg·is·ter \in-ˈrej-ə-stər\ *vt* [MF *enregistrer,* fr. OF, fr. *en-* + *registre* register] (1523) **:** to put on record **:** REGISTER

en·rich \in-ˈrich\ *vt* [ME *enrichen,* fr. MF *enrichir,* fr. OF, fr. *en-* + *riche* rich] (14c) **:** to make rich or richer by the addition or increase of some desirable quality, attribute, or ingredient ⟨the experience will ~ your life⟩: as **a :** to add beauty to **:** ADORN **b :** to enhance the taste of ⟨butter will ~ the sauce⟩ **c :** to make (a soil) more fertile **d :** to improve the nutritive value of (a food) by adding nutrients (as vitamins or amino acids) and esp. by restoring part of the nutrients lost in processing ⟨~*ed* flour⟩ **e :** to process so as to add or increase the proportion of a desirable ingredient ⟨~*ed* uranium⟩ ⟨~*ed* natural gas⟩ — **en·rich·er** *n* — **en·rich·ment** \-ˈrich-mənt\ *n*

en·robe \in-ˈrōb\ *vt* (1593) **1 :** to cover with or as if with a robe **2 :** COAT 2

en·roll *or* **en·rol** \in-ˈrōl\ *vb* **en·rolled; en·roll·ing** [ME *enrollen,* fr. MF *enroller,* fr. *en-* + *rolle* roll, register] *vt* (14c) **1 :** to insert, register, or enter in a list, catalog, or roll ⟨the school ~*s* about 800 pupils⟩ **2 :** to prepare a final perfect copy of (a bill passed by a legislature) in written or printed form **3 :** to roll or wrap up ~ *vi* **:** to enroll oneself or cause oneself to be enrolled ⟨he ~*ed* in the history course⟩ — **en·roll·ee** \-rō-ˈlē\ *n* — **en·roll·ment** \-ˈrōl-mənt\ *n*

en·root \in-ˈrüt, -ˈru̇t\ *vt* [ME *enrooten*] (15c) **:** ESTABLISH, IMPLANT

en route \än(n)-ˈrüt, en-, in-\ *adv or adj* [F] (1779) **:** on or along the way ⟨he reads *en route*⟩ ⟨arrived early despite *en route* delays⟩

en·sam·ple \in-ˈsam-pəl\ *n* [ME, fr. MF *ensample, example*] (13c) **:** EXAMPLE, INSTANCE

en·san·guine \in-ˈsaŋ-gwən\ *vt* **-guined; -guin·ing** (1667) **1 :** to make bloody **2 :** CRIMSON

en·sconce \in-ˈskän(t)s\ *vt* **en·sconced; en·sconc·ing** [*en-* + [2]*sconce*] (1598) **1 :** SHELTER, CONCEAL **2 :** ESTABLISH, SETTLE ⟨*ensconced* in a new job⟩

enscroll *vt* (ca. 1909) **:** to write on a scroll **:** RECORD

en·sem·ble \än(n)-ˈsäm-bəl\ *n* [F, fr. *ensemble* together, fr. L *insimul* at the same time, fr. *in-* + *simul* at the same time — more at SAME] (1750) **:** a group constituting an organic whole or producing together a single effect: as **a :** concerted music of two or more parts **b :** a complete costume of harmonizing or complementary clothing and accessories **c (1) :** the musicians engaged in the performance of a musical ensemble **(2) :** a group of supporting players, singers, or dancers; *esp* **:** CORPS DE BALLET

ensemble acting *n* (ca. 1926) **:** a system of theatrical presentation with an emphasis on an integration of all roles rather than on a star performance

en·serf \in-ˈsərf\ *vt* (1882) **:** to make a serf of **:** deprive of liberty and personal rights — **en·serf·ment** \-mənt\ *n*

en·sheathe \in-ˈshēth\ *vt* (1593) **:** to cover with or as if with a sheath

en·shrine \in-ˈshrīn, *esp Southern* -ˈsrīn\ *vt* [ME *enshrinen*] (14c) **1 :** to enclose in or as if in a shrine **2 :** to preserve or cherish as sacred — **en·shrine·ment** \-mənt\ *n*

en·shroud \in-ˈshrau̇d, *esp Southern* -ˈsrau̇d\ *vt* (1583) **:** to cover or enclose with or as if with a shroud

en·si·form \ˈen(t)-sə-ˌfȯrm\ *adj* [F *ensiforme,* fr. L *ensis* sword + F *-forme* -form; akin to Skt *asi* sword] (1541) **:** having sharp edges and tapering to a slender point ⟨~ leaves of the gladiolus⟩

en·sign \ˈen(t)-sən, *also* ˈen-ˌsīn *for 1, 2, & 3a*\ *n* [ME *ensigne,* fr. MF *enseigne,* fr. L *insignia* insignia, flags] (15c) **1 :** a flag that is flown (as by a ship) as the symbol of nationality and that may also be flown with a distinctive badge added to its design **2 a :** a badge of office, rank, or power **b :** EMBLEM, SIGN **3 a** *archaic* **:** STANDARD-BEARER **b :** a commissioned officer in the navy or coast guard ranking above a chief warrant officer and below a lieutenant junior grade

en·si·lage \ˈen(t)-s(ə-)lij, *for 1 also* in-ˈsī-lij\ *n* [Fr, fr. *ensiler* to ensile, fr. *en-* + *silo* silo, fr. Sp] (1876) **1 :** the process of preserving fodder by ensiling **2 :** SILAGE

en·sile \en-ˈsī(ə)l, in-\ *vt* **en·siled; en·sil·ing** (1883) **:** to prepare and store (fodder) for silage

en·sky \in-ˈskī\ *vt* (1603) **:** EXALT

en·slave \in-ˈslāv\ *vt* (1643) **:** to reduce to or as if to slavery **:** SUBJUGATE — **en·slave·ment** \-mənt\ *n* — **en·slav·er** *n*

en·snare \in-ˈsna(ə)r, -ˈsne(ə)r\ *vt* (1593) **:** to take in or as if in a snare ***syn*** see CATCH

en·snarl \in-ˈsnär(-ə)l\ *vt* (1593) **:** to involve in a snarl

en·sor·cell *or* **en·sor·cel** \in-ˈsȯr-səl\ *vt* **-celled** *or* **-celed; -cell·ing** *or* **-cel·ing** [MF *ensorceler,* alter. of OF *ensorcerer,* fr. *en-* + *-sorcerer,* fr. *sorcier* sorcerer — more at SORCERY] (1541) **:** BEWITCH, ENCHANT — **en·sor·cell·ment** \-mənt\ *n*

en·soul \in-ˈsōl\ *vt* (1652) **:** to endow or imbue with a soul

en·sphere \in-ˈsfi(ə)r\ *vt* (1612) **:** to enclose in or as if in a sphere

en·sue \in-ˈsü\ *vb* **en·sued; en·su·ing** [ME *ensuen,* fr. MF *ensuivre,* fr. OF, fr. *en-* + *suivre* to follow — more at SUE] *vt* (15c) **:** to strive to attain **:** PURSUE ⟨I wander, seeking peace, and *ensuing* it —Rupert Brooke⟩ ~ *vi* **:** to take place afterward or as a result ***syn*** see FOLLOW

en suite \än-ˈswēt\ *adv or adj* [F] (1818) **:** in a succession, series, or set

en·sure \in-ˈshu̇(ə)r\ *vt* **en·sured; en·sur·ing** [ME *ensuren,* fr. AF *enseurer,* prob. alter. of OF *aseürer* — more at ASSURE] (1704) **:** to make sure, certain, or safe **:** GUARANTEE

syn ENSURE, INSURE, ASSURE, SECURE mean to make a thing or person sure. ENSURE, INSURE, and ASSURE are interchangeable in many contexts where they indicate the making certain or inevitable of an outcome, but INSURE sometimes stresses the taking of necessary measures beforehand, and ASSURE distinctively implies the removal of doubt and suspense from a person's mind; SECURE implies action taken to guard against attack or loss.

en·swathe \in-ˈswäth, -ˈswȯth, -ˈswāth\ *vt* (1597) **:** to enfold or enclose with or as if with a covering **:** SWATHE

ent- *or* **ento-** *comb form* [NL, fr. Gk *entos* within; akin to L *intus* within, Gk *en* in — more at IN] **:** inner **:** within ⟨entoblast⟩

en·tab·la·ture \in-ˈtab-lə-ˌchu̇(ə)r, -ˌt(y)u̇(ə)r\ *n* [obs. F, modif. of It *intavolatura,* fr. *intavolare* to put on a board or table, fr. *in-* (fr. L) + *tavola* board,

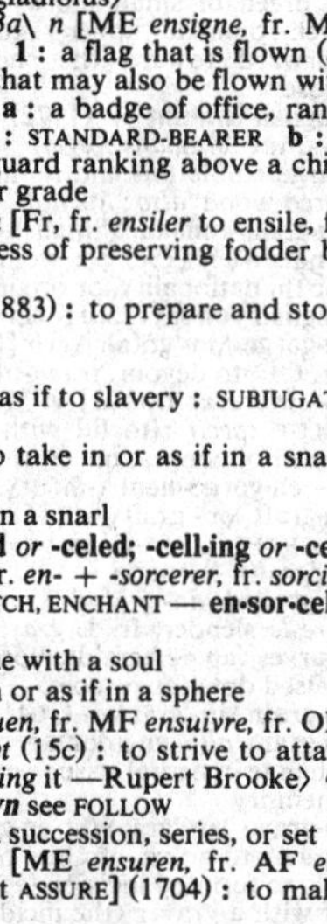

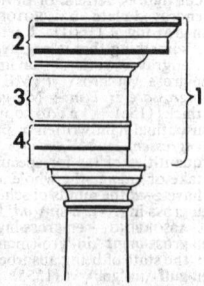

1 entablature, *2* cornice, *3* frieze, *4* architrave

table, fr. L *tabula*] (1611) **:** a horizontal part in classical architecture that rests on the columns and consists of architrave, frieze, and cornice

[1]**en·tail** \in-ˈtā(ə)l\ *vt* [ME *entailen, entaillen,* fr. [1]*en-* + *taile, taille* limitation — more at TAIL] (14c) **1 :** to restrict (property) by limiting the inheritance to the owner's lineal descendants or to a particular class thereof (as his male children) **2 a :** to confer, assign, or transmit as if by entail **:** FASTEN ⟨~*ed* on them indelible disgrace —Robert Browning⟩ **b :** to fix (a person) permanently in some condition or status ⟨~ him and his heirs unto the crown —Shak.⟩ **3 :** to impose, involve, or imply as a necessary accompaniment or result ⟨the project will ~ considerable expense⟩ — **en·tail·er** \-ˈtā-lər\ *n* — **en·tail·ment** \-ˈtā(ə)l-mənt\ *n*

[2]**entail** \ˈen-ˌtāl, in-ˈtā(ə)l\ *n* (14c) **1 a :** an entailing esp. of lands **b :** an entailed estate **2 :** something (as a quality) transmitted as if by entail

ent·amoe·ba \ˌent-ə-ˈmē-bə\ *n* (1914) **:** any of a genus (*Entamoeba*) comprising various amoebas parasitic in vertebrates and including one (*E. histolytica*) that causes amebic dysentery in humans — compare ENDAMOEBA

en·tan·gle \in-ˈtaŋ-gəl\ *vt* (15c) **1 a :** to wrap or twist together **:** INTERWEAVE **b :** ENSNARE **2 a :** to make tangled, complicated, or confused ⟨my explanation only served to ~ the question further⟩ **b :** to involve in a tangle ⟨*entangled* in a lawsuit⟩ — **en·tan·gler** \-g(ə-)lər\ *n*

en·tan·gle·ment \in-ˈtaŋ-gəl-mənt\ *n* (1637) **1 :** the condition of being deeply involved **2 a :** the action of entangling **:** the state of being entangled **b :** something that entangles, confuses, or ensnares

en·tel·e·chy \en-ˈtel-ə-kē, in-\ *n, pl* **-chies** [LL *entelechia,* fr. Gk *entelecheia,* fr. *entelēs* complete (fr. *telos* end) + *echein* to have — more at WHEEL, SCHEME] (1603) **1 :** the actualization of form-giving cause as contrasted with potential existence **2 :** a hypothetical agency not demonstrable by scientific methods that in some vitalist doctrines is considered an inherent regulating and directing force in the development and functioning of an organism

en·tente \än-ˈtänt\ *n* [F, fr. OF, intent, understanding — more at INTENT] (1854) **1 :** an international understanding providing for a common course of action **2** [F *entente cordiale*] **:** a coalition of parties to an entente

en·tente cor·diale \(ˌ)än-ˈtänt-ˌkȯrd-ˈyäl\ *n* [F, lit., cordial understanding] (1844) **1 :** ENTENTE 1 **2 :** a friendly agreement or working relationship

en·ter \ˈent-ər\ *vb* **en·tered; en·ter·ing** \ˈent-ə-riŋ, ˈen-triŋ\ [ME *entren,* fr. OF *entrer,* fr. L *intrare,* fr. *intra* within; akin to L *inter* between — more at INTER-] *vi* (13c) **1 :** to go or come in **2 :** to come or gain admission into a group **:** JOIN — often used with *into* **3 a :** to make a beginning ⟨~*ing* upon a career⟩ **b :** to begin to consider a subject — usu. used with *into* or *upon* **4 :** to go upon land for the purpose of taking possession **5 :** to play a part **:** be a factor ⟨your personal prejudices shouldn't ~ into the discussion⟩ ~ *vt* **1 :** to come or go into ⟨~ a room⟩ **2 :** INSCRIBE, REGISTER ⟨~ the names of qualified voters⟩ **3 :** to cause to be received or admitted ⟨~ a child at a school⟩ **4 :** to put in **:** INSERT ⟨~ the new data into the computer⟩ **5 a :** to make a beginning in **:** TAKE UP ⟨~ politics⟩ **b :** to pass within the limits of (a particular period of time) ⟨was famous by the time he ~*ed* his early thirties⟩ **6 :** to become a member of or an active participant in ⟨~ the university⟩ ⟨~ a race⟩ **7 :** to make report of (a ship or its cargo) to customs authorities **8 :** to place in proper form before a court of law or upon record ⟨~ a writ⟩ **9 :** to go into or upon and take actual possession of (as land) **10 :** to put formally on record ⟨~*ing* a complaint⟩ — **en·ter·able** \ˈent-ə-rə-bəl, ˈen-trə-\ *adj*

syn ENTER, PENETRATE, PIERCE, PROBE mean to make way into something. ENTER is the most general of these and may imply either going in or forcing a way in; PENETRATE carries a strong implication of an impelling force or compelling power that achieves entrance; PIERCE adds to PENETRATE a clear implication of an entering point; PROBE implies penetration to investigate or explore something hidden from sight or knowledge.

— **enter into 1 :** to make oneself a party to or in ⟨*enter into* an important agreement⟩ **2 :** to form a constituent part of ⟨tin *enters into* the composition of pewter⟩ **3 a :** to participate or share in ⟨cheerfully *entering into* the household tasks⟩ **b :** to be in tune or sympathy with ⟨couldn't *enter into* the festive spirit of the occasion⟩

enter- *or* **entero-** *comb form* [Gk, fr. *enteron* — *more at* INTER-] **:** intestine ⟨*enteritis*⟩

en·ter·al \ˈent-ə-rəl\ *adj* (1903) **:** ENTERIC — **en·ter·al·ly** \-rə-lē\ *adv*

en·ter·ic \en-ˈter-ik, in-\ *adj* (ca. 1859) **1 :** of or relating to the intestines; *broadly* **:** ALIMENTARY **2 :** of, relating to, or being a medicinal preparation treated to pass through the stomach unaltered and disintegrate in the intestines

en·ter·i·tis \ˌent-ə-ˈrīt-əs\ *n* (1808) **1 :** inflammation of the intestines and esp. of the human ileum **2 :** a disease of domestic animals (as panleucopenia of cats) marked by enteritis and diarrhea

en·tero·bac·te·ri·um \ˌent-ə-rō-bak-ˈtir-ē-əm\ *n* (ca. 1951) **:** any of a family (Enterobacteriaceae) of gram-negative straight rod bacteria (as a salmonella or a colon bacillus) that ferment glucose and include saprophytes as well as some serious pathogens of man, lower animals, and plants — **en·tero·bac·te·ri·al** \-ē-əl\ *adj*

en·tero·bi·a·sis \-ˈbī-ə-səs\ *n, pl* **-a·ses** \-ˌsēz\ [NL, fr. *Enterobius,* genus name + *-iasis*] (ca. 1927) **:** infestation with or disease caused by pinworms (genus *Enterobius*) that occurs esp. in children

en·tero·chro·maf·fin \-ˈkrō-mə-fən\ *adj* (ca. 1941) **:** of or relating to epithelial cells of the intestinal mucosa that stain esp. with chromium salts and usu. contain serotonin

en·tero·coc·cus \-ˈkäk-əs\ *n,* **-coc·ci** \-ˈkäk-ˌ(s)ī, -ˈkäk-(ˌ)(s)ē\ [NL, genus name] (1908) **:** STREPTOCOCCUS; *esp* **:** a streptococcus (as *Streptococcus faecalis*) normally present in the intestine — **en·tero·coc·cal** \-ˈkäk-əl\ *adj*

en·tero·coele *or* **en·tero·coel** \ˈent-ə-rō-ˌsēl\ *n* (1877) **:** a coelom originating by outgrowth from the archenteron — **en·tero·coe·lous** \ˌent-ə-rō-ˈsē-ləs\ *or* **en·tero·coe·lic** \-lik\ *adj*

en·tero·co·li·tis \ˌent-ə-rō-kə-ˈlīt-əs\ *n* [NL] (ca. 1857) **:** enteritis affecting both the large and small intestine

en·tero·gas·trone \-ˈgas-ˌtrōn\ *n* [*enter-* + *gastr-* + hor*mone*] (ca. 1930) **:** a hormone that is produced by the duodenal mucosa and has an inhibitory action on gastric motility and secretion

en·tero·hep·a·ti·tis \-ˌhep-ə-ˈtīt-əs\ *n* [NL] (1895) **:** BLACKHEAD 2

en·tero·ki·nase \ˌent-ə-rō-ˈkī-ˌnās, -ˌnāz\ *n* [ISV] (ca. 1902) **:** an enzyme esp. of the upper intestinal mucosa that activates trypsinogen by converting it to trypsin

en·ter·on \ˈent-ə-ˌrän, -rən\ *n* [NL, fr. Gk, intestine — more at INTER-] (ca. 1842) **:** the alimentary canal or system — used esp. of the embryo

en·tero·patho·gen·ic \ˌent-ə-rō-ˌpath-ə-ˈjen-ik\ *adj* (ca. 1865) **:** tending to produce disease in the intestinal tract ⟨~ bacteria⟩

en·ter·op·a·thy \ˌent-ə-ˈräp-ə-thē\ *n* (ca. 1891) **:** a disease of the intestinal tract

en·ter·os·to·my \ˌent-ə-ˈräs-tə-mē\ *n, pl* **-mies** [ISV] (1878) **:** a surgical formation of an opening into the intestine through the abdominal wall — **en·ter·os·to·mal** \-tə-məl\ *adj*

en·tero·tox·in \ˌent-ə-rō-ˈtäk-sən\ *n* (ca. 1928) **:** a toxic substance that is produced by microorganisms (as some staphylococci) and causes gastrointestinal symptoms (as in some forms of food poisoning or cholera)

en·tero·vi·rus \-ˈvī-rəs\ *n* [NL] (1957) **:** any of a group of picornaviruses (as the causative agent of poliomyelitis) that typically occur in the gastrointestinal tract but may be involved in respiratory ailments, meningitis, and neurological disorders — **en·tero·vi·ral** \-rəl\ *adj*

en·ter·prise \ˈent-ə(r)-ˌprīz\ *n* [ME *enterprise,* fr. MF *entreprise,* fr. OF *entreprendre* to undertake, fr. *entre-* inter- + *prendre* to take — more at PRIZE] (15c) **1 :** a project or undertaking that is esp. difficult, complicated, or risky **2 :** readiness to engage in daring action **:** INITIATIVE **3 a :** a unit of economic organization or activity; *esp* **:** a business organization **b :** a systematic purposeful activity ⟨agriculture is the main economic ~ among these people⟩

en·ter·pris·er \-ˌprī-zər\ *n* (1523) **:** one who undertakes an enterprise; *specif* **:** ENTREPRENEUR

en·ter·pris·ing \-ˌprī-ziŋ\ *adj* (1611) **:** marked by an independent energetic spirit and by readiness to undertake or experiment

en·ter·tain \ˌent-ər-ˈtān\ *vb* [ME *entertinen,* fr. MF *entretenir,* fr. *entre-* inter- + *tenir* to hold — more at TENABLE] *vt* (15c) **1 a** *archaic* **:** MAINTAIN **b** *obs* **:** RECEIVE **2 :** to show hospitality to **3 a :** to keep, hold, or maintain in the mind ⟨I ~ grave doubts about her sincerity⟩ **b :** to receive and take into consideration ⟨refused to ~ our plea⟩ **4 :** to provide entertainment for **5 :** to play against (an opposing team) on one's home field or court ~ *vi* **:** to provide entertainment esp. for guests ***syn*** see AMUSE — **en·ter·tain·er** *n*

en·ter·tain·ing *adj* (1568) **:** providing entertainment **:** DIVERTING — **en·ter·tain·ing·ly** \-ˈtā-niŋ-lē\ *adv*

en·ter·tain·ment \ˌent-ər-ˈtān-mənt\ *n* (15c) **1 :** the act of entertaining **2 a** *archaic* **:** MAINTENANCE, PROVISION **b** *obs* **:** EMPLOYMENT **3 :** something diverting or engaging: as **a :** a public performance **b :** a usu. light comic or adventure novel

en·thal·py \ˈen-ˌthal-pē, en-ˈ\ *n* [*en-* + Gk *thalpein* to heat] (ca. 1924) **:** the sum of the internal energy of a body and the product of its volume multiplied by the pressure

en·thrall *or* **en·thral** \in-ˈthrȯl\ *vt* **en·thralled; en·thrall·ing** [ME *enthrallen*] (15c) **1 :** to hold spellbound **:** CHARM **2 :** to hold in or reduce to slavery — **en·thrall·ment** \-ˈthrȯl-mənt\ *n*

en·throne \in-ˈthrōn\ *vt* (1606) **1 a :** to seat ceremonially on a throne **b :** to seat in a place associated with a position of authority or influence **2 :** to assign supreme virtue or value to **:** EXALT — **en·throne·ment** \-mənt\ *n*

en·thuse \in-ˈth(y)üz\ *vb* **en·thused; en·thus·ing** [back-formation fr. *enthusiasm*] *vt* (1827) **1 :** to make enthusiastic **2 :** to express with enthusiasm ~ *vi* **:** to show enthusiasm ⟨a splendid performance, and I was *enthusing* over it —Julian Huxley⟩

usage *Enthuse* is apparently American in origin, although the earliest known example of its use occurs in a letter written in 1827 by a young Scotsman who spent about two years in the Pacific Northwest. It has been disapproved since about 1870. Current evidence shows it to be flourishing nonetheless on both sides of the Atlantic esp. in journalistic prose.

en·thu·si·asm \in-ˈth(y)ü-zē-ˌaz-əm\ *n* [Gk *enthousiasmos,* fr. *enthousiazein* to be inspired, fr. *entheos* inspired, fr. *en-* + *theos* god] (1603) **1 a :** belief in special revelations of the Holy Spirit **b :** religious fanaticism **2 a :** strong excitement of feeling **:** ARDOR **b :** something inspiring zeal or fervor ***syn*** see PASSION

en·thu·si·ast \-ˌast, -əst\ *n* (1609) **:** a person filled with enthusiasm: as **a :** one who is ardently attached to a cause, object, or pursuit ⟨a sports car ~⟩ **b :** one who tends to become ardently absorbed in an interest

en·thu·si·as·tic \in-ˌth(y)ü-zē-ˈas-tik\ *adj* (1603) **:** filled with or marked by enthusiasm — **en·thu·si·as·ti·cal·ly** \-ti-k(ə-)lē\ *adv*

en·thy·meme \ˈen(t)-thi-ˌmēm\ *n* [L *enthymema,* fr. Gk *enthymēma,* fr. *enthymeisthai* to keep in mind, fr. *en-* + *thymos* mind, soul — more at FUME] (1552) **:** a syllogism in which one of the premises is implicit

en·tice \in-ˈtīs\ *vt* **en·ticed; en·tic·ing** [ME *enticen,* fr. MF *enticier*] (14c) **:** to attract artfully or adroitly or by arousing hope or desire **:** TEMPT ***syn*** see LURE — **en·tice·ment** \-ˈtī-smənt\ *n* — **en·tic·ing·ly** \-ˈtī-siŋ-lē\ *adv*

[1]**en·tire** \in-ˈtī(ə)r, ˈen-ˌ\ *adj* [ME, fr. MF *entir,* fr. L *integer,* lit., untouched, fr. *in-* + *tangere* to touch — more at TANGENT] (14c) **1 :** having no element or part left out **:** WHOLE ⟨was alone the ~ day⟩ **2 :** complete in degree **:** TOTAL ⟨their ~ devotion to their family⟩ **3 a :** consisting of one piece **b :** HOMOGENEOUS, UNMIXED **c :** INTACT ⟨strove to keep the collection ~⟩ **4 :** not castrated **5 :** having the margin continuous or free from indentations ⟨an ~ leaf⟩ ***syn*** see WHOLE, PERFECT — **entire** *adv* — **en·tire·ness** *n*

[2]**entire** *n* (1597) **1** *archaic* **:** the whole **:** ENTIRETY **2 :** STALLION

en·tire·ly *adv* (14c) **1 :** to the full or entire extent **:** COMPLETELY ⟨agreed with me ~⟩ ⟨you are ~ welcome⟩ **2 :** to the exclusion of others **:** SOLELY ⟨it is our fault ~⟩

en·tire·ty \in-ˈtī-rət-ē, -ˈtī(-ə)rt-ē\ *n, pl* **-ties** (1548) **1 :** the state of being entire or complete **2 :** SUM TOTAL, WHOLE

en·ti·tle \in-ˈtīt-^{ə}l\ *vt* **en·ti·tled; en·ti·tling** \-ˈtīt-liŋ, -^{ə}l-iŋ\ [ME *entitlen*, fr. MF *entituler*, fr. LL *intitulare*, fr. L *in-* + *titulus* title] (14c) **1 :** to give a title to : DESIGNATE **2 :** to furnish with proper grounds for seeking or claiming something ⟨this ticket ~*s* the bearer to free admission⟩

en·ti·tle·ment \-ˈtīt-^{ə}l-mənt\ *n* (1944) **1 a :** the state or condition of being entitled : RIGHT **b :** a right to benefits specified esp. by law or contract **2 :** a government program providing benefits to members of a specified group; *also* **:** funds supporting or distributed by such a program

en·ti·ty \ˈen(t)-ət-ē\ *n, pl* **-ties** [ML *entitas*, fr. L *ent-, ens* existing thing, fr. coined prp. of *esse* to be — more at IS] (1596) **1 a :** BEING, EXISTENCE; *esp* **:** independent, separate, or self-contained existence **b :** the existence of a thing as contrasted with its attributes **2 :** something that has separate and distinct existence and objective or conceptual reality

ento- — see ENT-

en·to·blast \ˈent-ə-ˌblast\ *n* (ca. 1864) **:** HYPOBLAST

en·to·derm \ˈent-ə-ˌdərm\ *n* (ca. 1879) **:** ENDODERM — **en·to·der·mal** \ˌent-ə-ˈdər-məl\ *or* **en·to·der·mic** \-mik\ *adj*

en·toil \in-ˈtȯi(ə)l\ *vt* (1621) **:** ENTRAP, ENMESH

entom- *or* **entomo-** *comb form* [F, fr. Gk *entomon*] **:** insect ⟨*entomophagous*⟩

en·tomb \in-ˈtüm\ *vt* [ME *entoumben*, fr. MF *entomber*, fr. *en-* + *tombe* tomb] (1576) **1 :** to deposit in a tomb : BURY **2 :** to serve as a tomb for — **en·tomb·ment** \-ˈtüm-mənt\ *n*

en·to·mo·fau·na \ˌent-ə-mō-ˈfȯn-ə, -ˈfän-\ *n* [NL] (1951) **:** a fauna of insects **:** the insects of an environment or region

en·to·mol·o·gy \ˌent-ə-ˈmäl-ə-jē\ *n* [F *entomologie*, fr. Gk *entomon* insect (fr. neut. of *entomos* cut up, fr. *en-* + *temnein* to cut) + F *-logie* -logy — more at TOME] (1766) **:** a branch of zoology that deals with insects — **en·to·mo·log·i·cal** \-mə-ˈläj-i-kəl\ *adj* — **en·to·mo·log·i·cal·ly** \-k(ə-)lē\ *adv* — **en·to·mol·o·gist** \ˌent-ə-ˈmäl-ə-jəst\ *n*

en·to·moph·a·gous \ˌent-ə-ˈmäf-ə-gəs\ *adj* (1839) **:** feeding on insects

en·to·moph·i·lous \ˌent-ə-ˈmäf-ə-ləs\ *adj* (ca. 1880) **:** being normally pollinated by insects — compare ZOOPHILOUS — **en·to·moph·i·ly** \-lē\ *n*

en·to·mos·tra·can \ˌent-ə-ˈmäs-tri-kən\ *n* [deriv. of *entom-* + Gk *ostrakon* shell — more at OYSTER] (1847) **:** any of numerous simple typically small crustaceans (as branchiopods, ostracods, copepods, and barnacles) sometimes placed in a subclass (Entomostraca)

en·to·proct \ˈent-ə-ˌpräkt\ *n* [deriv. of *ent-* + Gk *prōktos* anus] (1940) **:** any of a phylum (Entoprocta) of animals lacking a true coelom and having the anus adjacent to the mouth — **entoproct** *adj*

en·tou·rage \ˌän-tü-ˈräzh\ *n* [F, fr. MF, fr. *entourer* to surround, fr. *entour* around, fr. *en* in (fr. L *in*) + *tour* circuit — more at TURN] (1832) **1 :** one's attendants or associates **2 :** SURROUNDINGS

en·to·zoa \ˌent-ə-ˈzō-ə\ *n pl* [NL] (ca. 1847) **:** internal animal parasites; *esp* **:** the intestinal worms — **en·to·zo·an** \-ˈzō-ən\ *adj or n*

en·to·zo·ic \-ˈzō-ik\ *adj* (1861) **:** living within an animal ⟨an ~ amoeba⟩

en·tr'acte \ˈä^n(n)-ˌtrakt, -ˌträkt, ä^n(n)-ˈ\ *n* [F, fr. *entre-* inter- + *acte* act] (1842) **1 :** a dance, piece of music, or interlude performed between two acts of a play **2 :** the interval between two acts of a play

en·trails \ˈen-ˌtrālz, -trəlz\ *n pl* [ME *entrailles*, fr. MF, fr. ML *intralia*, alter. of L *interanea*, pl. of *interaneum* intestine, fr. neut. of *interaneus* interior] (14c) **:** BOWELS, VISCERA; *broadly* **:** internal parts

[1]**en·train** \in-ˈtrān\ *vt* [MF *entrainer*, fr. *en-* + *trainer* to draw, drag — more at TRAIN] (1568) **1 :** to draw along with or after oneself **2 :** to draw in and transport (as solid particles or gas) by the flow of a fluid **3 :** to incorporate (air bubbles) into concrete **4 :** to determine or modify the phase or period of ⟨circadian rhythms ~*ed* by a light cycle⟩ — **en·train·er** *n* — **en·train·ment** \-ˈtrān-mənt\ *n*

[2]**entrain** *vt* (1881) **:** to put aboard a train ~ *vi* **:** to go aboard a train

[1]**en·trance** \ˈen-trən(t)s\ *n* (15c) **1 :** the means or place of entry **2 :** the act of entering **3 :** power or permission to enter : ADMISSION **4 :** the point at which a voice or instrument part begins in ensemble music **5 :** the first appearance of an actor in a scene

[2]**en·trance** \in-ˈtran(t)s\ *vt* **en·tranced; en·tranc·ing** (1593) **1 :** to carry away with delight, wonder, or rapture **2 :** to put into a trance — **en·trance·ment** \-ˈtran(t)-smənt\ *n*

en·trance·way \ˈen-trən(t)-ˌswā\ *n* (1865) **:** ENTRYWAY

en·trant \ˈen-trənt\ *n* (1635) **:** one that enters; *esp* **:** one that enters a contest

en·trap \in-ˈtrap\ *vt* [MF *entraper*, fr. *en-* + *trape* trap] (1534) **1 :** to catch in or as if in a trap **2 :** to lure into a compromising statement or act ***syn*** see CATCH — **en·trap·ment** \-mənt\ *n*

en·treat \in-ˈtrēt\ *vb* [ME *entreten*, fr. MF *entraitier*, fr. *en-* + *traitier* to treat] *vt* (14c) **1 :** to plead with esp. in order to persuade **:** ask urgently ⟨~*ed* his boss for another chance⟩ **2** *archaic* **:** to deal with : TREAT ~ *vi* **1** *obs* **a :** NEGOTIATE **b :** INTERCEDE **2 :** to make an earnest request : PLEAD ***syn*** see BEG — **en·treat·ing·ly** \-iŋ-lē\ *adv* — **en·treat·ment** \-mənt\ *n*

en·treaty \in-ˈtrēt-ē\ *n, pl* **-treat·ies** (15c) **:** an act of entreating : PLEA

en·tre·chat \ˈä^n(n)-trə-ˌshä\ *n* [F, modif. of It (*capriola*) *intrecciata*, lit., intertwined caper] (1775) **:** a leap in which a ballet dancer repeatedly crosses the legs and sometimes beats them together

en·tre·cote \ˈä^n(n)-trə-ˌkōt\ *n* [F *entrecôte*, fr. *entre-* inter- + *côte* rib, fr. L *costa* — more at INTER-, COAST] (1841) **:** a steak cut from between the ribs

en·trée *or* **en·tree** \ˈän-ˌtrā *also* än-ˈ\ *n* [F *entrée*, fr. OF] (1759) **1 :** the principal dish of the meal in the U.S. **2 a :** the act or manner of entering : ENTRANCE **b :** freedom of entry or access

en·tre·mets *as sing* ˌä^n(n)-trə-ˈmā, *as pl* -ˈmā(z)\ *n pl but sing or pl in constr* [ME, fr. MF, fr. OF *entremes*, fr. L *intermissus*, pp. of *intermittere* to intermit] (15c) **:** dishes served in addition to the main course of a meal; *esp* **:** DESSERT

en·trench \in-ˈtrench\ *vt* (1555) **1 a :** to place within or surround with a trench esp. for defense **b :** to place (oneself) in a strong defensive position **c :** to establish solidly ⟨~*ed* themselves in the business⟩ **2 :** to cut into : FURROW; *specif* **:** to erode downward so as to form a trench ~ *vi* **1 :** to dig or occupy a trench for defensive purposes **2 :** to enter upon or take over something unfairly, improperly, or unlawfully : ENCROACH — used with *on* or *upon* ***syn*** see TRESPASS — **en·trench·ment** \-mənt\ *n*

en·tre·pôt \ˈä^n(n)-trə-ˌpō\ *n* [F] (1758) **:** an intermediary center of trade and transshipment

en·tre·pre·neur \ˌä^{n}n-trə-p(r)ə-ˈnər, -ˈn(y)u̇(ə)r\ *n* [F, fr. OF, fr. *entreprendre* to undertake — more at ENTERPRISE] (1852) **:** one who organizes, manages, and assumes the risks of a business or enterprise — **en·tre·pre·neur·ial** \-ˈn(y)u̇r-ē-əl, -ˈnər-\ *adj* — **en·tre·pre·neur·ial·ly** \-ē-ə-lē\ *adv* — **en·tre·pre·neur·ship** \-ˈnər-ˌship, -ˈn(y)u̇(ə)r-\ *n*

en·tre·sol \ˈä^n(n)-trə-ˌsäl, -ˌsȯl\ *n* [F] (1711) **:** MEZZANINE

en·tro·py \ˈen-trə-pē\ *n, pl* **-pies** [G *entropie*, fr. Gk *en-* + *trepein* to turn, change — more at TROPE] (1868) **1 a :** a measure of the unavailable energy in a closed thermodynamic system so related to the state of the system that a change in the measure varies with change in the ratio of the increment of heat taken in to the absolute temperature at which it is absorbed **b :** a measure of the disorder of a closed thermodynamic system in terms of a constant multiple of the natural logarithm of the probability of the occurrence of a particular molecular arrangement of the system that by suitable choice of a constant reduces to the measure of unavailable energy **2 :** a measure of the amount of information in a message that is based on the logarithm of the number of possible equivalent messages **3 :** the degradation of the matter and energy in the universe to an ultimate state of inert uniformity **4 :** the steady degradation or disorganization of a system or society — **en·tro·pic** \en-ˈtrō-pik, -ˈträp-ik\ *adj* — **en·tro·pi·cal·ly** \-pi-k(ə-)lē, -i-k(ə-)lē\ *adv*

en·trust \in-ˈtrəst\ *vt* (1602) **1 :** to confer a trust on; *esp* **:** to deliver something in trust to **2 :** to commit to another with confidence ***syn*** see COMMIT — **en·trust·ment** \-ˈtrəs(t)-mənt\ *n*

en·try \ˈen-trē\ *n, pl* **entries** [ME *entre*, fr. OF *entree*, fr. fem. of *entré*, pp. of *entrer* to enter] (13c) **1 :** the right or privilege of entering : ENTRÉE **2 :** the act of entering : ENTRANCE **3 :** a place of entrance: as **a :** VESTIBULE, PASSAGE **b :** DOOR, GATE **4 a :** the act of making or entering a record **b :** something entered: as **(1) :** a record or notation of an occurrence, transaction, or proceeding **(2) :** a descriptive record (as in a card catalog or an index) **(3) :** HEADWORD **(4) :** a headword with its definition or identification **(5) :** VOCABULARY ENTRY **5 :** a person, thing, or group entered in a contest

en·try·way \-trē-ˌwā\ *n* (1746) **:** a passage for entrance

entry word *n* (ca. 1908) **:** HEADWORD

en·twine \in-ˈtwīn\ *vt* (1597) **:** to twine together or around ~ *vi* **:** to become twisted or twined

en·twist \in-ˈtwist\ *vt* (1590) **:** ENTWINE

enu·cle·ate \(ˈ)ē-ˈn(y)ü-klē-ˌāt\ *vt* **-at·ed; -at·ing** [L *enucleatus*, pp. of *enucleare*, lit., to remove the kernel from, fr. *e-* + *nucleus* kernel — more at NUCLEUS] (1548) **1** *archaic* **:** EXPLAIN **2 :** to deprive of a nucleus **3 :** to remove without cutting into ⟨~ a tumor⟩ ⟨~ the eyeball⟩ — **enu·cle·ation** \(ˌ)ē-ˌn(y)ü-klē-ˈā-shən\ *n*

enu·mer·a·ble \i-ˈn(y)üm-(ə-)rə-bəl\ *adj* (ca. 1889) **:** DENUMERABLE — **enu·mer·a·bil·i·ty** \-ˌn(y)üm-(ə-)rə-ˈbil-ət-ē\ *n*

enu·mer·ate \i-ˈn(y)ü-mə-ˌrāt\ *vt* **-at·ed; -at·ing** [L *enumeratus*, pp. of *enumerare*, fr. *e-* + *numerare* to count, fr. *numerus* number — more at NIMBLE] (1647) **1 :** to ascertain the number of : COUNT **2 :** to specify one after another : LIST — **enu·mer·a·tion** \-ˌn(y)ü-mə-ˈrā-shən\ *n* — **enu·mer·a·tive** \-ˈn(y)ü-mə-ˌrāt-iv, -ˈn(y)üm-(ə-)rət-\ *adj*

enu·mer·a·tor \-ˈn(y)ü-mə-ˌrāt-ər\ *n* (1856) **:** one that enumerates; *esp* **:** a census taker

enun·ci·ate \ē-ˈnən(t)-sē-ˌāt\ *vb* **-at·ed; -at·ing** [L *enuntiatus*, pp. of *enuntiare* to report, declare, fr. *e-* + *nuntiare* to report — more at ANNOUNCE] *vt* (1623) **1 a :** to make a definite or systematic statement of : FORMULATE **b :** ANNOUNCE, PROCLAIM ⟨*enunciated* the principles to be followed by the new administration⟩ **2 :** ARTICULATE, PRONOUNCE ⟨~ your words clearly⟩ ~ *vi* **:** to utter articulate sounds — **enun·cia·ble** \-ˈnən(t)-sē-ə-bəl, -nən-ch(ē-)ə-\ *adj* — **enun·ci·a·tion** \-ˌnən(t)-sē-ˈā-shən\ *n* — **enun·ci·a·tor** \-ˈnən(t)-sē-ˌāt-ər\ *n*

enure *var of* INURE

en·ure·sis \ˌen-yu̇-ˈrē-səs\ *n* [NL, fr. Gk *enourein* to urinate in, wet the bed, fr. *en-* + *ourein* to urinate — more at URINE] (1800) **:** an involuntary discharge of urine : incontinence of urine — **en·uret·ic** \-ˈret-ik\ *adj or n*

en·vel·op \in-ˈvel-əp\ *vt* [ME *envolupen*, fr. MF *envoluper, enveloper*, fr. OF *envoloper*, fr. *en-* + *voloper* to wrap] (14c) **1 :** to enclose or enfold completely with or as if with a covering **2 :** to mount an attack on (an enemy's flank) — **en·vel·op·ment** \-mənt\ *n*

en·ve·lope \ˈen-və-ˌlōp, ˈän-\ *n* (1714) **1 :** a flat usu. paper container (as for a letter) **2 :** something that envelops : WRAPPER ⟨the ~ of air around the earth⟩ **3 a :** the outer covering of an aerostat **b :** the bag containing the gas in a balloon or airship **4 :** a natural enclosing covering (as a membrane, shell, or integument) **5 a :** a curve tangent to each of a family of curves **b :** a surface tangent to each of a family of surfaces

en·ven·om \in-ˈven-əm\ *vt* [ME *envenimen*, fr. OF *envenimer*, fr. *en-* + *venim* venom] (13c) **1 :** to make poisonous **2 :** EMBITTER

en·ven·om·iza·tion \in-ˌven-ə-mə-ˈzā-shən\ *n* (1960) **:** a poisoning caused by a bite or sting

en·vi·able \ˈen-vē-ə-bəl\ *adj* (1602) **:** highly desirable — **en·vi·able·ness** *n* — **en·vi·ably** \-blē\ *adv*

en·vi·er \ˈen-vē-ər\ *n* (15c) **:** one that envies

en·vi·ous \ˈen-vē-əs\ *adj* (14c) **1 :** feeling or showing envy ⟨~ of her neighbor's success⟩ ⟨~ looks⟩ **2** *archaic* **a :** EMULOUS **b :** ENVIABLE — **en·vi·ous·ly** *adv* — **en·vi·ous·ness** *n*

en·vi·ron \in-ˈvī-rən, -ˈvī(-ə)rn\ *vt* [ME *envirounen*, fr. MF *environner*, fr. *environ* around, fr. *en* in (fr. L *in*) + *viron* circle, fr. *virer* to turn, fr. (assumed) VL *virare*] (14c) **:** ENCIRCLE, SURROUND

en·vi·ron·ment \in-ˈvī-rə(n)-mənt, -ˈvī(-ə)r(n)-\ *n* (1603) **1 :** the circumstances, objects, or conditions by which one is surrounded **2 a :** the complex of physical, chemical, and biotic factors (as climate, soil, and living things) that act upon an organism or an ecological community and ultimately determine its form and survival **b :** the aggregate of social and cultural conditions that influence the life of an individual or community — **en·vi·ron·men·tal** \-ˌvī-rə(n)-ˈment-^{ə}l, -ˌvī(-ə)r(n)-\ *adj* — **en·vi·ron·men·tal·ly** \-^{ə}l-ē\ *adv*

en·vi·ron·men·tal·ism \-ˌvī-rə(n)-ˈment-^{ə}l-ˌiz-əm, -ˌvī(-ə)r(n)-\ *n* (ca. 1922) **1 :** a theory that views environment rather than heredity as the important factor in the development and esp. the cultural and intellectual development of an individual or group **2 :** advocacy of the preservation or improvement of the natural environment; *esp* **:** the movement to control pollution

en·vi·ron·men·tal·ist \-ᵊl-əst\ *n* (1916) **1 :** an advocate of environmentalism **2 :** one concerned about the quality of the human environment; *specif* **:** a specialist in human ecology

en·vi·rons \in-ˈvī-rənz, -ˈvī(-ə)rnz\ *n pl* (1761) **1 :** the districts around a city **2 a :** environing things **:** SURROUNDINGS **b :** an adjoining region or space **:** VICINITY

en·vis·age \in-ˈviz-ij\ *vt* **-aged; -ag·ing** [F *envisager,* fr. *en-* + *visage* face] (1837) **1 :** to view or regard in a certain way ⟨~*s* himself as a sincere young man⟩ **2 :** to have a mental picture of esp. in advance of realization ⟨~*s* an entirely new system of education⟩ ***syn*** see THINK

en·vi·sion \in-ˈvizh-ən\ *vt* (1921) **:** to picture to oneself ⟨~*s* a career dedicated to promoting peace⟩ ***syn*** see THINK

en·voi *or* **en·voy** \ˈen-ˌvȯi, ˈän-\ *n* [ME *envoye,* fr. MF *envoi,* lit., message, fr. OF *envei,* fr. *envoier* to send on one's way, fr. (assumed) VL *inviare,* fr. L *in-* + *via* way — more at VIA] (14c) **:** the usu. explanatory or commendatory concluding remarks to a poem, essay, or book; *specif* **:** a short fixed final stanza of a ballade serving as a summary or dedication

en·voy \ˈen-ˌvȯi, ˈän-\ *n* [F *envoyé,* fr. pp. of *envoyer* to send, fr. OF *envoier*] (1660) **1 a :** a minister plenipotentiary accredited to a foreign government who ranks between an ambassador and a minister resident — called also *envoy extraordinary* **b :** a person delegated to represent one government in its dealings with another **2 :** MESSENGER, REPRESENTATIVE

¹en·vy \ˈen-vē\ *n, pl* **envies** [ME *envie,* fr. OF, fr. L *invidia,* fr. *invidus* envious, fr. *invidēre* to look askance at, envy, fr. *in-* + *vidēre* to see — more at WIT] (13c) **1** *obs* **:** MALICE **2 :** painful or resentful awareness of an advantage enjoyed by another joined with a desire to possess the same advantage **3 :** an object of envious notice or feeling ⟨his new car made him the ~ of his friends⟩

²envy *vb* **en·vied; en·vy·ing** *vt* (14c) **1 :** to feel envy toward or on account of **2** *obs* **:** BEGRUDGE ~ *vi, obs* **:** to feel or show envy — **en·vy·ing·ly** \-vē-iŋ-lē\ *adv*

en·wheel \in-ˈhwē(ə)l, -ˈwē(ə)l\ *vt, obs* (1604) **:** ENCIRCLE

en·wind \in-ˈwīnd\ *vt* **en·wound** \-ˈwau̇nd\; **en·wind·ing** (1598) **:** to wind in or about **:** ENFOLD

en·womb \in-ˈwüm\ *vt* (1591) **:** to shut up as if in a womb

en·wrap \in-ˈrap\ *vt* (14c) **1 :** to wrap in a covering **:** ENFOLD **2 a :** ENVELOP **b :** to preoccupy or absorb mentally **:** ENGROSS

en·wreathe \in-ˈrēth\ *vt* (1620) **:** to encircle with or as if with a wreath **:** ENVELOP

en·zo·ot·ic \ˌen-zə-ˈwät-ik\ *adj* [*en-* + *zo-* + ¹*-otic*] *of animal diseases* (ca. 1890) **:** peculiar to or constantly present in a locality — **enzootic** *n*

en·zy·mat·ic \ˌen-zə-ˈmat-ik\ *also* **en·zy·mic** \en-ˈzī-mik\ *adj* (1900) **:** of, relating to, or produced by an enzyme — **en·zy·mat·i·cal·ly** \ˌen-zə-ˈmat-i-k(ə-)lē\ *also* **en·zy·mi·cal·ly** \en-ˈzī-mi-k(ə-)lē\ *adv*

en·zyme \ˈen-ˌzīm\ *n* [G *enzym,* fr. MGk *enzymos* leavened, fr. Gk *en-* + *zymē* leaven — more at JUICE] (ca. 1881) **:** any of numerous complex proteins that are produced by living cells and catalyze specific biochemical reactions at body temperatures

en·zy·mol·o·gy \ˌen-ˌzī-ˈmäl-ə-jē, -zə-\ *n* [ISV] (ca. 1900) **:** a branch of science that deals with enzymes, their nature, activity, and significance — **en·zy·mol·o·gist** \-jəst\ *n*

eo- *comb form* [Gk *ēō-* dawn, fr. *ēōs* — more at EAST] **:** earliest **:** oldest ⟨*eo*lithic⟩

Eo·cene \ˈē-ə-ˌsēn\ *adj* (1831) **:** of, relating to, or being an epoch of the Tertiary between the Paleocene and the Oligocene or the corresponding system of rocks — **Eocene** *n*

eo·hip·pus \ˌē-ō-ˈhip-əs\ *n* [NL, fr. *eo-* + Gk *hippos* horse — more at EQUINE] (1879) **:** any of a genus (*Eohippus*) of small primitive 4-toed horses from the Lower Eocene of the western U.S.

eo·lian \ē-ˈō-lē-ən, -ˈōl-yən\ *adj* [L *Aeolus,* Aeolus] (ca. 1921) **:** borne, deposited, produced, or eroded by the wind

eo·lith \ˈē-ə-ˌlith\ *n* (1895) **:** a very crudely chipped flint

Eo·lith·ic \ˌē-ə-ˈlith-ik\ *adj* (1890) **:** of or relating to the early period of the Stone Age marked by the use of eoliths

eon \ˈē-ən, ˈē-ˌän\ *var of* AEON

eo no·mi·ne \ˌē-ō-ˈnäm-ə-nē\ [L] (1627) **:** by or under that name

Eos \ˈē-ˌäs\ *n* [Gk *Ēōs*] **:** the Greek goddess of dawn — compare AURORA

eo·sin \ˈē-ə-sən\ *or* **eo·sine** \-sən, -ˌsēn\ *n* [ISV, fr. Gk *ēōs* dawn] (1866) **1 :** a red fluorescent dye $C_{20}H_8Br_4O_5$ obtained by the action of bromine on fluorescein and used esp. in cosmetics and as a toner; *also* **:** its red to brown sodium or potassium salt used esp. as a biological stain for cytoplasmic structures **2 :** any of several dyes related to eosin

¹eo·sin·o·phil \ˌē-ə-ˈsin-ə-ˌfil\ *or* **eo·sin·o·phile** *adj* (ca. 1882) **:** EOSINOPHILIC 1

²eosinophil *also* **eosinophile** \-ˈfīl\ *n* (1886) **:** a leukocyte or other granulocyte with cytoplasmic inclusions readily stained by eosin

eo·sin·o·phil·ia \-ˌsin-ə-ˈfil-ē-ə\ *n* (ca. 1904) **:** abnormal increase in the number of eosinophils in the blood that is characteristic of allergic states and various parasitic infections

eo·sin·o·phil·ic \-ˌsin-ə-ˈfil-ik\ *adj* (ca. 1900) **1 :** staining readily with eosin **2 :** of, relating to, or characterized by eosinophilia

epact \ˈē-ˌpakt, ˈep-ˌakt\ *n* [MF *epacte,* fr. LL *epacta,* fr. Gk *epaktē,* fr. *epagein* to bring in, intercalate, fr. *epi-* + *agein* to drive — more at AGENT] (1552) **:** a period added to harmonize the lunar with the solar calendar

ep·ar·chy \ˈep-ˌär-kē\ *n, pl* **-chies** [Gk *eparchia* province, fr. *eparchos* prefect, fr. *epi-* + *archos* ruler — more at ARCH-] (1796) **:** a diocese of an Eastern church

ep·au·let *also* **ep·au·lette** \ˌep-ə-ˈlet; ˈep-ə-ˌlet, -lət\ *n* [F *épaulette,* dim. of *épaule* shoulder, fr. LL *spatula* shoulder blade, spoon, dim. of L *spatha* spoon, sword — more at SPADE] (1783) **:** something that ornaments or protects the shoulder; *specif* **:** an ornamental fringed shoulder pad formerly worn as part of a military uniform

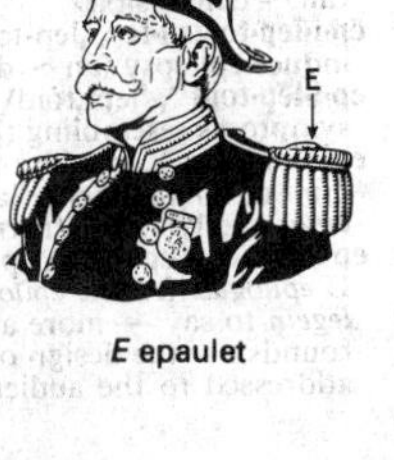

E epaulet

ep·a·zote \ˈep-ə-ˌzōt\ *n* [AmSp, fr. Nahuatl *epazotl*] (1975) **:** WORMSEED b

épée \ˈep-ˌā, ā-ˈpā\ *n* [F, fr. L *spatha*] (1889) **1 :** a fencing or dueling sword having a bowl-shaped guard and a rigid blade of triangular section with no cutting edge that tapers to a sharp point blunted for fencing — compare FOIL, SABER **2 :** the art or sport of fencing with the épée

épée·ist \-əst\ *n* (1910) **:** one who fences with an épée

ep·ei·rog·e·ny \ˌep-ˌī-ˈräj-ə-nē\ *n, pl* **-nies** [Gk *ēpeiros* mainland, continent + E *-geny*] (ca. 1890) **:** the deformation of the earth's crust by which the broader features of relief are produced — **epei·ro·gen·ic** \i-ˌpī-rə-ˈjen-ik\ *adj* — **epei·ro·gen·i·cal·ly** \-i-k(ə-)lē\ *adv*

epen·the·sis \i-ˈpen(t)-thə-səs, e-\ *n, pl* **-the·ses** \-ˌsēz\ [LL, fr. Gk, fr. *epentithenai* to insert a letter, fr. *epi-* + *entithenai* to put in, fr. *en-* + *tithenai* to put — more at DO] (1543) **:** the insertion or development of a sound or letter in the body of a word (as \ə\ in \ˈath-ə-ˌlēt\ *athlete*) — **ep·en·thet·ic** \ˌep-ən-ˈthet-ik\ *adj*

epergne \i-ˈpərn, ā-\ *n* [prob. fr. F *épargne* saving] (1761) **:** an often ornate tiered centerpiece consisting typically of a frame of wrought metal (as silver or gold) bearing dishes, vases, or candle holders or a combination of these

ep·ex·e·ge·sis \ˌep-ˌek-sə-ˈjē-səs\ *n, pl* **-ge·ses** \-ˌsēz\ [Gk *epexēgēsis,* fr. *epi-* + *exēgēsis* exegesis] (1621) **:** additional explanation or explanatory matter — **ep·ex·e·get·i·cal** \-ˈjet-i-kəl\ *or* **ep·ex·e·get·ic** \-ˈjet-ik\ *adj* — **ep·ex·e·get·i·cal·ly** \-ˈjet-i-k(ə-)lē\ *adv*

ephah \ˈē-fə, ˈef-ə\ *n* [ME *ephi,* fr. LL, fr. Heb *ēphāh,* fr. Egypt *ipt*] (14c) **:** an ancient Hebrew unit of dry measure equal to $^1/_{10}$ homer or a little over a bushel

ephebe \ˈef-ˌēb, i-ˈfēb\ *n* [L *ephebus*] (1697) **:** a young man; *esp* **:** EPHEBUS

ephe·bic \-bik\ *adj* (1865) **:** of or relating to the ephebi ⟨~ education⟩

ephe·bus \i-ˈfē-bəs, e-\ *n, pl* **-bi** \-ˌbī\ [L, fr. Gk *ephēbos,* fr. *epi-* + *hēbē* youth, puberty] (1889) **:** a youth of ancient Greece; *esp* **:** an Athenian 18 or 19 years old in training for full citizenship

ephe·dra \i-ˈfed-rə, ˈef-ə-drə\ *n* [NL, genus name] (ca. 1891) **:** any of a large genus (*Ephedra* of the family Gnetaceae) of jointed nearly leafless desert shrubs with the leaves reduced to scales at the nodes

ephed·rine \i-ˈfed-rən, *Brit also* ˈef-ə-drən\ *n* [NL *Ephedra,* genus of shrubs, fr. L, horsetail plant, fr. Gk, fr. *ephedros* sitting upon, fr. *epi-* + *hedra* seat — more at SIT] (1889) **:** a crystalline alkaloid $C_{10}H_{15}NO$ extracted from Chinese ephedras or synthesized and used in the form of a salt for relief of hay fever, asthma, and nasal congestion

¹ephem·er·al \i-ˈfem-(ə-)rəl\ *adj* [Gk *ephēmeros* lasting a day, daily, fr. *epi-* + *hēmera* day] (1576) **1 :** lasting one day only ⟨an ~ fever⟩ **2 :** lasting a very short time ⟨~ pleasures⟩ ***syn*** see TRANSIENT — **ephem·er·al·ly** \-rə-lē\ *adv*

²ephemeral *n* (1817) **:** something ephemeral; *specif* **:** a plant that grows, flowers, and dies in a few days

ephem·er·al·i·ty \i-ˌfem-ə-ˈral-ət-ē\ *n, pl* **-ties** (1822) **1 :** the quality or state of being ephemeral **2** *pl* **:** ephemeral things

ephem·er·id \i-ˈfem-ə-rəd\ *n* [deriv. of Gk *ephēmeron*] (1872) **:** MAYFLY

ephem·er·is \-ə-rəs\ *n, pl* **eph·e·mer·i·des** \ˌef-ə-ˈmer-ə-ˌdēz\ [L, diary, ephemeris, fr. Gk *ephēmeris,* fr. *ephēmeros*] (1508) **1 :** a tabular statement of the assigned places of a celestial body for regular intervals **2 :** EPHEMERAL

ephemeris time *n* (ca. 1950) **:** a uniform measure of time defined by the orbital motions of the planets

ephem·er·on \i-ˈfem-ə-ˌrän\ *n, pl* **ephem·era** \-ˈfem-(ə-)rə\ [NL, fr. Gk *ephēmeron* mayfly, fr. neut. of *ephēmeros*] (1626) **1** *pl also* **ephem·er·ons** \-ˈfem-ə-ˌränz\ **:** an insect (as a mayfly) that lives only a very short time **2** *pl* **:** matter of no lasting significance; *esp* **:** collectibles (as posters, broadsides, and tickets) that were orig. intended to have only ephemeral value

Ephe·sians \i-ˈfē-zhənz\ *n pl but sing in constr* [short for *Epistle to the Ephesians*] **:** a letter addressed to early Christians and included as a book in the New Testament — see BIBLE table

eph·od \ˈef-ˌäd, ˈē-ˌfäd\ *n* [ME, fr. LL, fr. Heb *ēphōdh*] (14c) **1 :** a linen apron worn in ancient Hebrew rites; *esp* **:** a vestment for the high priest **2 :** an ancient Hebrew instrument of priestly divination

eph·or \ˈef-ər, -ˌȯ(ə)r\ *n* [L *ephorus,* fr. Gk *ephoros,* fr. *ephoran* to oversee, fr. *epi-* + *horan* to see — more at WARY] (1579) **1 :** one of five ancient Spartan magistrates having power over the king **2 :** a government official in modern Greece; *esp* **:** one who oversees public works — **eph·or·ate** \ˈef-ə-ˌrāt\ *n*

Ephra·im \ˈē-frē-əm\ *n* [Heb *Ephrayim*] **:** a son of Joseph and the traditional eponymous ancestor of one of the tribes of Israel

Ephra·im·ite \-ə-ˌmīt\ *n* (1611) **1 :** a member of the Hebrew tribe of Ephraim **2 :** a native or inhabitant of the biblical northern kingdom of Israel

epi- *or* **ep-** *prefix* [ME, fr. MF & L; MF, fr. L, fr. Gk, fr. *epi* on, at, besides, after; akin to OE *eofot* crime] **1 :** upon ⟨*epi*phyte⟩ **:** besides ⟨*epi*phenomenon⟩ **:** attached to ⟨*epi*didymis⟩ **:** over ⟨*epi*center⟩ **:** outer ⟨*epi*blast⟩ **:** after ⟨*epi*genesis⟩ **2 a :** chemical entity related to (such) another ⟨*epi*cholesterol⟩ **b :** chemical entity distinguished from (such) another by having a bridge connection ⟨*epi*chlorohydrin⟩

epi·blast \ˈep-ə-ˌblast\ *n* (1875) **:** the outer layer of the blastoderm **:** ECTODERM — **epi·blas·tic** \ˌep-ə-ˈblas-tik\ *adj*

epib·o·ly \i-ˈpib-ə-lē\ *n, pl* **-lies** [Gk *epibolē* addition, fr. *epiballein* to throw on, fr. *epi-* + *ballein* to throw — more at DEVIL] (1875) **:** the growing of one part about another; *esp* **:** such growth of the dorsal lip area during gastrulation — **ep·i·bol·ic** \ˌep-ə-ˈbäl-ik\ *adj*

¹ep·ic \ˈep-ik\ *adj* [L *epicus,* fr. Gk *epikos,* fr. *epos* word, speech, poem — more at VOICE] (1589) **1 :** of, relating to, or having the characteristics of an epic **2 a :** extending beyond the usual or ordinary esp. in size or scope ⟨his genius was ~ —*Times Lit. Supp.*⟩ **b :** HEROIC — **ep·i·cal** \-i-kəl\ *adj* — **ep·i·cal·ly** \-i-k(ə-)lē\ *adv*

²epic *n* (1706) **1 :** a long narrative poem in elevated style recounting the deeds of a legendary or historical hero ⟨the *Iliad* and the *Odyssey* are ~*s*⟩ **2 :** a work of art (as a novel or drama) that resembles or suggests an epic **3 :** a series of events or body of legend or tradition thought to form the proper subject of an epic ⟨the winning of the West was a great American ~⟩

epi·ca·lyx \ˌep-i-ˈkā-liks *also* -ˈkal-iks\ *n* (ca. 1870) **:** an involucre resembling the calyx but consisting of a whorl of bracts that is exterior to the calyx or results from the union of the sepal appendages

epi·can·thic fold \ˌep-ə-ˌkan(t)-thik-\ *n* [NL *epicanthus* epicanthic fold, fr. *epi-* + *canthus* canthus] (1913) **:** a prolongation of a fold of the skin of the upper eyelid over the inner angle or both angles of the eye — called also *Mongolian fold*

epi·car·di·um \ˌep-ə-ˈkard-ē-əm\ *n, pl* **-dia** \-ē-ə\ [NL, fr. *epi-* + Gk *kardia* heart] (ca. 1865) **:** the visceral part of the pericardium that closely envelops the heart — **epi·car·di·al** \-ē-əl\ *adj*

epi·carp \ˈep-i-ˌkärp\ *n* [F *épicarpe*, fr. *épi-* epi- + *-carpe* -carp] (1835) **:** EXOCARP

ep·i·cene \ˈep-ə-ˌsēn\ *adj* [ME, fr. L *epicoenus*, fr. Gk *epikoinos*, fr. *epi-* + *koinos* common — more at CO-] (15c) **1** *of a noun* **:** having but one form to indicate either sex **2 a :** having characteristics typical of the other sex **:** INTERSEXUAL **b :** EFFEMINATE **3 :** lacking characteristics of either sex — **epicene** *n* — **ep·i·cen·ism** \-ˌsē-ˌniz-əm, ˌep-ə-ˈ\ *n*

epi·cen·ter \ˈep-i-ˌsent-ər\ *n* [NL *epicentrum*, fr. *epi-* + L *centrum* center] (1887) **1 :** the part of the earth's surface directly above the focus of an earthquake **2 :** CENTER 2a, 2c — **epi·cen·tral** \ˌep-i-ˈsen-trəl\ *adj*

epi·chlo·ro·hy·drin \ˌep-i-ˌklōr-ə-ˈhī-drən, -ˌklȯr-\ *n* (ca. 1891) **:** a volatile liquid toxic epoxide C_3H_5ClO having a chloroform odor and used esp. in making epoxy resins and rubbers

epi·con·ti·nen·tal \ˌep-i-ˌkänt-ᵊn-ˈent-ᵊl\ *adj* (1900) **:** lying upon a continent or a continental shelf ⟨~ seas⟩

epi·cot·yl \ˈep-i-ˌkät-ᵊl\ *n* [*epi-* + *cotyle*don] (ca. 1880) **:** the portion of the axis of a plant embryo or seedling above the cotyledonary node

ep·i·crit·ic \ˌep-ə-ˈkrit-ik\ *adj* [Gk *epikritikos* determinative, fr. *epikrinein* to decide, fr. *epi-* + *krinein* to judge — more at CERTAIN] (ca. 1905) **:** of, relating to, being, or mediating cutaneous sensory reception marked by accurate discrimination between small degrees of sensation

epic simile *n* (ca. 1941) **:** an extended simile that is used typically in epic poetry to intensify the heroic stature of the subject and to serve as decoration

ep·i·cure \ˈep-i-ˌkyu̇(ə)r\ *n* [*Epicurus*] (1565) **1** *archaic* **:** one devoted to sensual pleasure **:** SYBARITE **2 :** one with sensitive and discriminating tastes esp. in food or wine

syn EPICURE, GOURMET, GASTRONOME, BON VIVANT mean one who takes pleasure in eating and drinking. EPICURE implies fastidiousness and voluptuousness of taste; GOURMET implies being a connoisseur in food and drink and the discriminating enjoyment of them; GASTRONOME implies that one has studied extensively the history and rituals of haute cuisine; BON VIVANT stresses the enjoyment of fine food and drink in company.

ep·i·cu·re·an \ˌep-i-kyu̇-ˈrē-ən, -ˈkyu̇r-ē-\ *adj* (1586) **1** *cap* **:** of or relating to Epicurus or Epicureanism **2 :** of, relating to, or suited to an epicure

Epicurean *n* (14c) **1 :** a follower of Epicurus **2** *often not cap* **:** EPICURE 2

ep·i·cu·re·an·ism \-ə-ˌniz-əm\ *n* (1751) **1** *cap* **a :** the philosophy of Epicurus who subscribed to a hedonistic ethics that considered an imperturbable emotional calm the highest good, held intellectual pleasures superior to others, and advocated the renunciation of momentary in favor of more permanent pleasures **b :** a mode of life in consonance with Epicureanism **2 :** EPICURISM

ep·i·cur·ism \ˈep-i-ˌkyu̇(ə)r-ˌiz-əm, ˌep-i-ˈ\ *n* (1586) **:** the practices or tastes of an epicure or an epicurean

epi·cu·ti·cle \ˌep-i-ˈkyüt-i-kəl\ *n* (1929) **:** an outermost waxy layer of the insect exoskeleton — **epi·cu·tic·u·lar** \-kyu̇-ˈtik-yə-lər\ *adj*

epi·cy·cle \ˈep-ə-ˌsī-kəl\ *n* [ME *epicicle*, fr. LL *epicyclus*, fr. Gk *epikyklos*, fr. *epi-* + *kyklos* circle — more at WHEEL] (14c) **1** *in Ptolemaic astron* **:** a circle in which a planet moves and which has a center that is itself carried around at the same time on the circumference of a larger circle **2 :** a process going on within a larger one — **epi·cy·clic** \ˌep-ə-ˈsī-klik, -ˈsik-lik\ *adj*

epicyclic train *n* (ca. 1890) **:** a train (as of gear wheels) designed to have one or more parts travel around the circumference of another fixed or revolving part

epi·cy·cloid \ˌep-ə-ˈsī-ˌklȯid\ *n* (ca. 1790) **:** a curve traced by a point on a circle that rolls on the outside of a fixed circle — **epi·cy·cloi·dal** \-sī-ˈklȯid-ᵊl\ *adj*

¹ep·i·dem·ic \ˌep-ə-ˈdem-ik\ *adj* [F *épidémique*, fr. MF, fr. *epidemie*, n., epidemic, fr. LL *epidemia*, fr. Gk *epidēmia* visit, epidemic, fr. *epidēmos* visiting, epidemic, fr. *epi-* + *dēmos* people] (1603) **1 :** affecting or tending to affect many individuals within a population, community, or region at the same time ⟨typhoid was ~⟩ **2 a :** excessively prevalent **b :** CONTAGIOUS 4 ⟨~ laughter⟩ **3 :** of, relating to, or constituting an epidemic ⟨the practice had reached ~ proportions⟩ — **ep·i·dem·i·cal** \-i-kəl\ *adj* — **ep·i·dem·i·cal·ly** \-i-k(ə-)lē\ *adv* — **ep·i·de·mic·i·ty** \-də-ˈmis-ət-ē\ *n*

²epidemic *n* (1799) **1 :** an outbreak of epidemic disease **2 :** an outbreak or product of sudden rapid spread, growth, or development; *specif* **:** a natural population suddenly and greatly enlarged

ep·i·de·mi·ol·o·gy \ˌep-ə-ˌdē-mē-ˈäl-ə-jē, -ˌdem-ē-\ *n* [LL *epidemia* + ISV *-logy*] (ca. 1864) **1 :** a branch of medical science that deals with the incidence, distribution, and control of disease in a population **2 :** the sum of the factors controlling the presence or absence of a disease or pathogen — **ep·i·de·mi·o·log·i·cal** \-ˌdē-mē-ə-ˈläj-i-kəl, -ˌdem-ē-\ *also* **ep·i·de·mi·o·log·ic** \-ik\ *adj* — **ep·i·de·mi·o·log·i·cal·ly** \-i-k(ə-)lē\ *adv* — **ep·i·de·mi·ol·o·gist** \-ˌdē-mē-ˈäl-ə-jəst, -ˌdem-ē-\ *n*

ep·i·den·drum \ˌep-ə-ˈden-drəm\ *n* [NL, fr. Gk *epi-* + *dendron* tree — more at DENDR-] (1791) **:** any of a large genus (*Epidendrum*) of chiefly epiphytic orchids found esp. in tropical America

epiderm- *or* **epidermo-** *comb form* [*epidermis*] **:** epidermis ⟨*epidermal*⟩

epi·der·mal \ˌep-ə-ˈdər-məl\ *also* **epi·der·mic** \-mik\ *adj* (1816) **:** of, relating to, or arising from the epidermis

epi·der·mis \-məs\ *n* [LL, fr. Gk, fr. *epi-* + *derma* skin — more at DERM-] (1626) **1 a :** the outer epithelial layer of the external integument of the animal body that is derived from the embryonic epiblast; *specif* **:** the outer nonsensitive and nonvascular layer of the skin of a vertebrate that overlies the dermis **b :** any of various animal integuments **2 :** a thin surface layer of tissue in higher plants formed by growth of a primary meristem

epi·der·moid \-ˌmȯid\ *adj* (1835) **:** resembling epidermis or epidermal cells **:** made up of elements like those of epidermis ⟨~ cancer of the lung⟩

epi·dia·scope \ˌep-ə-ˈdī-ə-ˌskōp\ *n* [ISV] (1903) **1 :** a projector for images of opaque objects or for images or transparencies **2 :** EPISCOPE

ep·i·did·y·mis \ˌep-ə-ˈdid-ə-məs\ *n, pl* **-mi·des** \-mə-ˌdēz\ [NL, fr. Gk, fr. *epi-* + *didymos* testicle, twin, fr. *dyo* two — more at TWO] (1610) **:** an elongated mass of convoluted efferent tubules at the back of the testis — **ep·i·did·y·mal** \-məl\ *adj*

ep·i·dote \ˈep-ə-ˌdōt\ *n* [F *épidote*, fr. Gk *epididonai* to give in addition, fr. *epi-* + *didonai* to give — more at DATE] (1808) **:** a yellowish green mineral $Ca_2(Al,Fe)_3Si_3O_{12}OH$ usu. occurring in grains or columnar masses and sometimes used as a gemstone

epi·du·ral \ˌep-i-ˈd(y)u̇r-əl\ *adj* (1882) **:** situated upon or administered outside the dura mater ⟨~ anesthesia⟩ ⟨~ structures⟩

epi·fau·na \-ˈfȯn-ə, -ˈfän-\ *n* [NL] (ca. 1914) **:** benthic fauna living on the substrate (as a hard sea floor) or on other organisms — compare INFAUNA — **epi·fau·nal** \-ˈfȯn-ᵊl, -ˈfän-\ *adj*

epi·gas·tric \ˌep-i-ˈgas-trik\ *adj* (1656) **1 :** lying upon or over the stomach **2 :** of, relating to, supplying, or draining the anterior walls of the abdomen ⟨~ arteries⟩

epi·ge·al \ˌep-i-ˈjē-əl\ *also* **epi·ge·ous** \-ˈjē-əs\ *adj* [Gk *epigaios* upon the earth, fr. *epi-* + *gē* earth] (ca. 1864) **1** *of a cotyledon* **:** forced above ground by elongation of the hypocotyl **2 :** marked by the production of epigeal cotyledons ⟨~ germination⟩

epi·ge·an \ˌep-i-ˈjē-ən\ *also* **epi·ge·ic** \-ˈjē-ik\ *or* **epi·ge·ous** \-ˈjē-əs\ *adj* (ca. 1900) **:** living on or near the surface of the ground; *also* **:** relating to or being the environment near the surface of the ground

epi·gen·e·sis \ˌep-ə-ˈjen-ə-səs\ *n* [NL] (1798) **1 :** development of new characters (as of a whole new plant) in an initially undifferentiated entity (as a fertilized egg or spore) **2 :** change in the mineral character of a rock owing to outside influences

epi·ge·net·ic \-jə-ˈnet-ik\ *adj* (1883) **1 :** of, relating to, or produced by epigenesis ⟨genetic versus ~ influences⟩ **2** *of deposit or structure* **:** formed after the laying down of the enclosing rock — **epi·ge·net·i·cal·ly** \-i-k(-ə)lē\ *adv*

epi·glot·tal \ˌep-ə-ˈglät-ᵊl\ *also* **epi·glot·tic** \-ˈglät-ik\ *adj* (1926) **:** of, relating to, or produced with the aid of the epiglottis

epi·glot·tis \-ˈglät-əs\ *n* [NL, fr. Gk *epiglōttis*, fr. *epi-* + *glōttis* glottis] (1615) **:** a thin plate of flexible cartilage in front of the glottis that folds back over and protects the glottis during swallowing

ep·i·gone \ˈep-ə-ˌgōn\ *n* [G, fr. L *epigonus* successor, fr. Gk *epigonos*, fr. *epigignesthai* to be born after, fr. *epi-* + *gignesthai* to be born — more at KIN] (1865) **:** an imitative follower; *esp* **:** an inferior imitator of a creative thinker or artist — **ep·i·gon·ic** \ˌep-ə-ˈgän-ik\ *or* **epig·o·nous** \i-ˈpig-ə-nəs, e-\ *adj* — **epig·o·nism** \-ˈpig-ə-ˌniz-əm\ *n*

epig·o·nus \i-ˈpig-ə-nəs, e-\ *n, pl* **-ni** \-ˌnī, -ˌnē\ [L] (1922) **:** EPIGONE

ep·i·gram \ˈep-ə-ˌgram\ *n* [ME *epigrame*, fr. L *epigrammat-, epigramma*, fr. Gk, fr. *epigraphein* to write on, inscribe, fr. *epi-* + *graphein* to write — more at CARVE] (15c) **1 :** a concise poem dealing pointedly and often satirically with a single thought or event and often ending with an ingenious turn of thought **2 :** a terse, sage, or witty and often paradoxical saying **3 :** epigrammatic expression — **ep·i·gram·ma·tism** \ˌep-ə-ˈgram-ə-ˌtiz-əm\ *n* — **ep·i·gram·ma·tist** \-ˈgram-ət-əst\ *n*

ep·i·gram·mat·ic \ˌep-ə-grə-ˈmat-ik\ *adj* (1704) **1 :** of, relating to, or resembling an epigram **2 :** marked by or given to the use of epigrams — **ep·i·gram·mat·i·cal** \-i-kəl\ *adj* — **ep·i·gram·mat·i·cal·ly** \-i-k(ə-)lē\ *adv*

ep·i·gram·ma·tize \-ˈgram-ə-ˌtīz\ *vb* **-tized; -tiz·ing** *vt* (1691) **1 :** to express in the form of an epigram **2 :** to make an epigram about ~ *vi* **:** to make an epigram — **ep·i·gram·ma·tiz·er** *n*

ep·i·graph \ˈep-ə-ˌgraf\ *n* [Gk *epigraphē*, fr. *epigraphein*] (1624) **1 :** an engraved inscription **2 :** a quotation set at the beginning of a literary work or a division of it to suggest its theme

epig·ra·pher \i-ˈpig-rə-fər, e-\ *n* (1887) **:** EPIGRAPHIST

ep·i·graph·ic \ˌep-ə-ˈgraf-ik\ *also* **ep·i·graph·i·cal** \-i-kəl\ *adj* (1858) **:** of or relating to epigraphs or epigraphy — **ep·i·graph·i·cal·ly** \-i-k(ə-)lē\ *adv*

epig·ra·phist \i-ˈpig-rə-fəst, e-\ *n* (ca. 1864) **:** a specialist in epigraphy

epig·ra·phy \-fē\ *n* (1851) **1 :** EPIGRAPHS, INSCRIPTIONS **2 :** the study of inscriptions; *esp* **:** the deciphering of ancient inscriptions

epig·y·nous \i-ˈpij-ə-nəs, e-\ *adj* (ca. 1830) **1** *of a floral organ* **:** adnate to the surface of the ovary and appearing to grow from the top of it **2 :** having epigynous floral organs — **epig·y·ny** \-nē\ *n*

ep·i·la·tion \ˌep-ə-ˈlā-shən\ *n* [F *épilation*, fr. *épiler* to remove hair, fr. *é-* + L *pilus* hair — more at PILE] (1878) **:** the loss or removal of hair

ep·i·lep·sy \ˈep-ə-ˌlep-sē\ *n, pl* **-sies** [MF *epilepsie*, fr. LL *epilepsia*, fr. Gk *epilēpsia*, fr. *epilambanein* to seize, fr. *epi-* + *lambanein* to take, seize — more at LATCH] (1543) **:** any of various disorders marked by disturbed electrical rhythms of the central nervous system and typically manifested by convulsive attacks usu. with clouding of consciousness

epilept- *or* **epilepti-** *or* **epilepto-** *comb form* [Gk *epilēpt-*, fr. *epilēptos* seized by epilepsy, fr. *epilambanein*] **:** epilepsy ⟨*epileptoid*⟩

ep·i·lep·tic \ˌep-ə-ˈlep-tik\ *adj* (1608) **:** relating to, affected with, or having the characteristics of epilepsy — **epileptic** *n* — **ep·i·lep·ti·cal·ly** \-ti-k(ə-)lē\ *adv*

ep·i·lep·ti·form \-ˈlep-tə-ˌfȯrm\ *adj* (1861) **:** resembling that of epilepsy ⟨an ~ convulsion⟩

ep·i·lep·to·gen·ic \-ˌlep-tə-ˈjen-ik\ *adj* (ca. 1882) **:** inducing or tending to induce epilepsy ⟨an ~ drug⟩

ep·i·lep·toid \-ˈlep-ˌtȯid\ *adj* (1866) **1 :** EPILEPTIFORM **2 :** exhibiting symptoms resembling those of epilepsy ⟨the ~ person⟩

epi·lim·ni·on \ˌep-ə-ˈlim-nē-ˌän, -nē-ən\ *n* [NL, fr. *epi-* + Gk *limnion*, dim. of *limnē* marshy lake — more at LIMNETIC] (ca. 1910) **:** the water layer overlying the thermocline of a lake

ep·i·logue *or* **ep·i·log** \ˈep-ə-ˌlȯg, -ˌläg\ *n* [ME *epiloge*, fr. MF *epilogue*, fr. L *epilogus*, fr. Gk *epilogos*, fr. *epilegein* to say in addition, fr. *epi-* + *legein* to say — more at LEGEND] (15c) **1 :** a concluding section that rounds out the design of a literary work **2 a :** a speech often in verse addressed to the audience by an actor at the end of a play **b :** the actor speaking such an epilogue **c :** the final scene of a play that comments on or summarizes the main action **3 :** the concluding section of a musical composition **:** CODA

epi·mer \ˈep-i-mər\ *n* [*epi-* + *isomer*] (ca. 1911) **:** either of the stereoisomers of a sugar or sugar derivative that differ in the arrangement of the hydrogen atom and the hydroxyl group on the first asymmetric carbon atom of a chain — **epi·mer·ic** \ˌep-i-ˈmer-ik\ *adj*

epim·er·ase \i-ˈpim-ə-ˌrās, e-, -ˌrāz\ *n* (1960) **:** any of various isomerases that catalyze the inversion of asymmetric groups in a substrate with several centers of asymmetry

ep·i·mere \ˈep-ə-ˌmi(ə)r\ *n* [ISV] (ca. 1882) **:** the dorsal part of a mesodermal segment of a chordate embryo

epi·my·si·um \ˌep-ə-ˈmiz(h)-ē-əm\ *n, pl* **-sia** \-ē-ə\ [NL, fr. *epi-* + Gk *mys* mouse, muscle — more at MOUSE] (ca. 1900) **:** the external connective-tissue sheath of a muscle

epi·nas·ty \ˈep-ə-ˌnas-tē\ *n* (1880) **:** a nastic movement in which a plant part (as a flower petal) is bent outward and often downward

epi·neph·rine *also* **epi·neph·rin** \ˌep-ə-ˈnef-rən\ *n* [ISV *epi-* + Gk *nephros* kidney — more at NEPHRITIS] (1899) **:** a colorless crystalline feebly basic sympathomimetic hormone $C_9H_{13}NO_3$ that is the principal blood-pressure raising hormone secreted by the adrenal medulla and is used medicinally esp. as a heart stimulant, a vasoconstrictor in controlling hemorrhages of the skin, and a muscle relaxant in bronchial asthma — called also *adrenaline*

epi·neu·ri·um \ˌep-ə-ˈn(y)u̇r-ē-əm\ *n* [NL] (ca. 1882) **:** the external connective-tissue sheath of a nerve trunk

epi·pe·lag·ic \ˌep-i-pə-ˈlaj-ik\ *adj* (1940) **:** of, relating to, or constituting the part of the oceanic zone into which enough light penetrates for photosynthesis

ep·i·phan·ic \ˌep-ə-ˈfan-ik\ *adj* (1951) **:** of or having the character of an epiphany

epiph·a·nous \i-ˈpif-ə-nəs\ *adj* (1823) **:** EPIPHANIC

epiph·a·ny \i-ˈpif-ə-nē\ *n, pl* **-nies** [ME *epiphanie,* fr. MF, fr. LL *epiphania,* fr. LGk, pl., prob. alter. of Gk *epiphaneia* appearance, manifestation, fr. *epiphainein* to manifest, fr. *epi-* + *phainein* to show — more at FANCY] (14c) **1** *cap* **:** January 6 observed as a church festival in commemoration of the coming of the Magi as the first manifestation of Christ to the Gentiles or in the Eastern Church in commemoration of the baptism of Christ **2 :** an appearance or manifestation esp. of a divine being **3 a** (1) **:** a usu. sudden manifestation or perception of the essential nature or meaning of something (2) **:** an intuitive grasp of reality through something (as an event) usu. simple and striking **b :** a literary representation of an epiphany

epi·phe·nom·e·nal \ˌep-i-fi-ˈnäm-ən-ᵊl\ *adj* (1899) **:** of or relating to an epiphenomenon **:** DERIVATIVE — **epi·phe·nom·e·nal·ly** \-ᵊl-ē\ *adv*

epi·phe·nom·e·nal·ism \-ᵊl-ˌiz-əm\ *n* (1899) **:** a doctrine that mental processes are epiphenomena of brain processes

epi·phe·nom·e·non \-ˈnäm-ə-ˌnän, -nən\ *n* (ca. 1706) **:** a secondary phenomenon accompanying another and caused by it

ep·i·phragm \ˈep-ə-ˌfram\ *n* [Gk *epiphragma* covering] (ca. 1854) **:** a closing membrane or septum (as of a snail shell or a moss capsule)

epiph·y·se·al \i-ˌpif-ə-ˈsē-əl\ *also* **ep·i·phys·i·al** \ˌep-ə-ˈfiz-ē-əl\ *adj* (ca. 1841) **:** of or relating to an epiphysis

epiph·y·sis \i-ˈpif-ə-səs\ *n, pl* **-y·ses** \-ˌsēz\ [NL, fr. Gk, growth, fr. *epiphyesthai* to grow on, fr. *epi-* + *phyesthai* to grow, pass. of *phyein* to bring forth — more at BE] (1634) **1 :** a part or process of a bone that ossifies separately and later becomes ankylosed to the main part of the bone; *esp* **:** an end of a long bone **2 :** PINEAL GLAND

epi·phyte \ˈep-ə-ˌfīt\ *n* (ca. 1847) **:** a plant that derives its moisture and nutrients from the air and rain and grows usu. on another plant

epi·phyt·ic \ˌep-ə-ˈfit-ik\ *adj* (1830) **1 :** of, relating to, or being an epiphyte **2 :** living on the surface of plants — **epi·phyt·i·cal·ly** \-ˈfit-i-k(ə-)lē\ *adv* — **epi·phyt·ism** \ˈep-ə-ˌfit-ˌiz-əm\ *n*

ep·i·phy·tol·o·gy \ˌep-ə-ˌfī-ˈtäl-ə-jē\ *n* [*epiphytotic* + *-logy*] (1940) **1 :** a science that deals with character, ecology, and causes of outbreak of plant diseases **2 :** the sum of the factors controlling the occurrence of a disease or pathogen of plants

ep·i·phy·tot·ic \-ˈtät-ik\ *adj* [*epi-* + Gk *phyton* plant, fr. *phyein*] (ca. 1899) **:** of, relating to, or being a plant disease that tends to recur sporadically and to affect large numbers of susceptible plants — **epiphytotic** *n*

epi·ro·gen·ic, epi·rog·e·ny *var of* EPEIROGENIC, EPEIROGENY

epi·scia \i-ˈpish-(ē-)ə\ *n* [NL, fr. Gk *episkios* shaded, fr. *epi-* + *skia* shadow — more at SHINE] (ca. 1868) **:** any of a genus (*Episcia*) of tropical American herbs that have hairy foliage and are related to the African violet

epis·co·pa·cy \i-ˈpis-kə-pə-sē\ *n, pl* **-cies** (1647) **1 :** government of the church by bishops or by a hierarchy **2 :** EPISCOPATE

epis·co·pal \i-ˈpis-kə-pəl, -bəl\ *adj* [ME, fr. LL *episcopalis,* fr. *episcopus* bishop — more at BISHOP] (15c) **1 :** of or relating to a bishop **2 :** of, having, or constituting government by bishops **3** *cap* **:** of or relating to the Protestant Episcopal Church representing the Anglican communion in the U.S. — **epis·co·pal·ly** \-p(ə-)lē\ *adv*

Episcopal *n* (1752) **:** EPISCOPALIAN

Epis·co·pa·lian \i-ˌpis-kə-ˈpāl-yən\ *n* (1690) **1 :** an adherent of the episcopal form of church government **2 :** a member of an episcopal church (as the Protestant Episcopal Church) — **Episcopalian** *adj* — **Epis·co·pa·lian·ism** \-yə-ˌniz-əm\ *n*

epis·co·pate \i-ˈpis-kə-pət, -ˌpāt\ *n* (1641) **1 :** the rank, office, or term of bishop **2 :** DIOCESE **3 :** the body of bishops (as in a country)

epi·scope \ˈep-ə-ˌskōp\ *n* [ISV] (ca. 1909) **:** a projector for images of opaque objects (as photographs)

epi·si·ot·o·my \i-ˌpiz-ē-ˈät-ə-mē, -ˌpēz-\ *n* [NL *episio-* vulva (fr. Gk *epision* pubic region) + *-tomy*] (1878) **:** surgical enlargement of the vulval orifice for obstetrical purposes during parturition

ep·i·sode \ˈep-ə-ˌsōd *also* -ˌzōd\ *n* [Gk *epeisodion,* fr. neut. of *epeisodios* coming in besides, fr. *epi-* + *eisodios* coming in, fr. *eis* into (akin to Gk *en* in) + *hodos* road, journey — more at IN, CEDE] (1678) **1 :** a usu. brief unit of action in a dramatic or literary work: as **a :** the part of an ancient Greek tragedy between two choric songs **b :** a developed situation that is integral to but separable from a continuous narrative **:** INCIDENT **c :** one of a series of loosely connected stories or scenes **d :** the part of a serial presented at one performance **2 :** an event that is distinctive and separate although part of a larger series **3 :** a digressive subdivision in a musical composition ***syn*** see OCCURRENCE

ep·i·sod·ic \ˌep-ə-ˈsäd-ik *also* -ˈzäd-\ *also* **ep·i·sod·i·cal** \-i-kəl\ *adj* (1773) **1 :** made up of separate esp. loosely connected episodes **2 :** having the form of an episode **3 :** of or limited in duration or significance to a particular episode **:** TEMPORARY ⟨may be able to establish whether the sea-floor spreading is continuous or ~ —A. I. Hammond⟩ **4 :** occurring, appearing, or changing at usu. irregular intervals **:** OCCASIONAL, CAPRICIOUS ⟨~ care of his patients⟩ — **ep·i·sod·i·cal·ly** \-i-k(ə-)lē\ *adv*

epi·some \ˈep-ə-ˌsōm, -ˌzōm\ *n* (ca. 1931) **:** a genetic determinant (as the DNA of some bacteriophages) that can replicate autonomously in bacterial cytoplasm or as an integral part of the chromosomes — **epi·som·al** \ˌep-ə-ˈsō-məl, -ˈzō-\ *adj* — **epi·som·al·ly** \-mə-lē\ *adv*

epis·ta·sis \i-ˈpis-tə-səs\ *n, pl* **-ta·ses** \-ˌsēz\ [NL, fr. Gk, act of stopping, fr. *ephistanai* to stop, fr. *epi-* + *histanai* to cause to stand — more at STAND] (ca. 1917) **:** suppression of the effect of a gene by a nonallelic gene — **ep·i·stat·ic** \ˌep-ə-ˈstat-ik\ *adj*

ep·i·stax·is \ˌep-ə-ˈstak-səs\ *n, pl* **-stax·es** \-ˌsēz\ [NL, fr. Gk, fr. *epistazein* to drip on, to bleed at the nose again, fr. *epi-* + *stazein* to drip — more at STAGNATE] (1793) **:** NOSEBLEED

ep·i·ste·mic \ˌep-ə-ˈstē-mik, -ˈstem-ik\ *adj* (1922) **:** of or relating to knowledge or knowing **:** COGNITIVE — **ep·i·ste·mi·cal·ly** \-(m)i-k(ə-)lē\ *adv*

epis·te·mol·o·gy \i-ˌpis-tə-ˈmäl-ə-jē\ *n* [Gk *epistēmē* knowledge, fr. *epistanai* to understand, know, fr. *epi-* + *histanai* to cause to stand — more at STAND] (ca. 1856) **:** the study or a theory of the nature and grounds of knowledge esp. with reference to its limits and validity — **epis·te·mo·log·i·cal** \-mə-ˈläj-i-kəl\ *adj* — **epis·te·mo·log·i·cal·ly** \-k(ə-)lē\ *adv* — **epis·te·mol·o·gist** \-ˈmäl-ə-jəst\ *n*

epi·ster·num \ˌep-i-ˈstər-nəm\ *n* [NL] (1855) **:** a lateral division or piece of a somite of an arthropod

epis·tle \i-ˈpis-əl\ *n* [ME, letter, Epistle, fr. OF, fr. L *epistula, epistola* letter, fr. Gk *epistolē* message, letter, fr. *epistellein* to send to, fr. *epi-* + *stellein* to send — more at STALL] (13c) **1** *cap* **a :** one of the letters adopted as books of the New Testament **b :** a liturgical lection usu. from one of the New Testament Epistles **2 a :** LETTER; *esp* **:** a formal or elegant letter **b :** a composition in the form of a letter — **epis·tler** \-ˈpis-(ə-)lər\ *n*

[1]**epis·to·lary** \i-ˈpis-tə-ˌler-ē\ *adj* (ca. 1656) **1 :** of, relating to, or suitable to a letter **2 :** contained in or carried on by letters ⟨an endless sequence of . . . ~ love affairs —*Times Lit. Supp.*⟩ **3 :** written in the form of a series of letters ⟨~ novel⟩

[2]**epistolary** *n, pl* **-lar·ies** (ca. 1909) **:** a lectionary containing a body of liturgical epistles

epis·to·ler \i-ˈpis-tə-lər\ *n* (1530) **:** the reader of the liturgical Epistle esp. in Anglican churches

ep·i·stome \ˈep-ə-ˌstōm\ *n* [NL *epistoma*] (1852) **:** any of several structures or regions situated above or covering the mouth of various invertebrates

epis·tro·phe \i-ˈpis-trə-(ˌ)fē\ *n* [Gk *epistrophē,* lit., turning about, fr. *epi-* + *strophē* turning — more at STROPHE] (ca. 1854) **:** repetition of a word or expression at the end of successive phrases, clauses, sentences, or verses esp. for rhetorical or poetic effect ⟨Lincoln's "of the people, by the people, for the people" is an example of ~⟩ — compare ANAPHORA

epi·style \ˈep-ə-ˌstīl\ *n* [L *epistylium,* fr. Gk *epistylion,* fr. *epi-* + Gk *stylos* pillar — more at STEER] (1615) **:** ARCHITRAVE 1

ep·i·taph \ˈep-ə-ˌtaf\ *n* [ME *epitaphe,* fr. MF & ML; MF, fr. ML *epitaphium,* fr. L, funeral oration, fr. Gk *epitaphion,* fr. *epi-* + *taphos* tomb, funeral] (14c) **1 :** an inscription on or at a tomb or a grave in memory of the one buried there **2 :** a brief statement commemorating or epitomizing a deceased person or something past — **ep·i·taph·ial** \ˌep-ə-ˈtaf-ē-əl\ *or* **ep·i·taph·ic** \-ˈtaf-ik\ *adj*

epit·a·sis \i-ˈpit-ə-səs\ *n, pl* **-a·ses** \-ˌsēz\ [Gk, increased intensity, fr. *epiteinein* to stretch tighter, fr. *epi-* + *teinein* to stretch — more at THIN] (1589) **:** the part of a play developing the main action and leading to the catastrophe

ep·i·taxy \ˈep-ə-ˌtak-sē\ *n* [*epi-* + *-taxy* (fr. Gk *-taxia* -taxis)] (ca. 1931) **:** the growth on a crystalline substrate of a crystalline substance that mimics the orientation of the substrate — **ep·i·tax·i·al** \ˌep-ə-ˈtak-sē-əl\ *adj* — **ep·i·tax·i·al·ly** \-sē-ə-lē\ *adv*

ep·i·tha·la·mi·um \ˌep-ə-thə-ˈlā-mē-əm\ *or* **ep·i·tha·la·mi·on** \-mē-ən\ *n, pl* **-mi·ums** *or* **-mia** \-mē-ə\ [L & Gk; L *epithalamium,* fr. Gk *epithalamion,* fr. *epi-* + *thalamos* room, bridal chamber; akin to Gk *tholos* rotunda — more at DALE] (1589) **:** a song or poem in honor of a bride and bridegroom — **ep·i·tha·lam·ic** \-ˈlam-ik\ *adj*

epitheli- *or* **epithelio-** *comb form* [NL *epithelium*] **:** epithelium

ep·i·the·li·al \ˌep-ə-ˈthē-lē-əl\ *adj* (1845) **:** of or relating to epithelium

ep·i·the·li·oid \-lē-ˌȯid\ *adj* (1878) **:** resembling epithelium ⟨~ cells⟩

ep·i·the·li·o·ma \-ˌthē-lē-ˈō-mə\ *n* (1872) **:** a benign or malignant tumor derived from epithelial tissue — **ep·i·the·li·o·ma·tous** \-mət-əs\ *adj*

ep·i·the·li·um \ˌep-ə-ˈthē-lē-əm\ *n, pl* **-lia** \-lē-ə\ [NL, fr. *epi-* + Gk *thēlē* nipple — more at FEMININE] (1748) **1 :** a membranous cellular tissue that covers a free surface or lines a tube or cavity of an animal body and serves esp. to enclose and protect the other parts of the body, to produce secretions and excretions, and to function in assimilation **2 :** a usu. thin layer of parenchyma that lines a cavity or tube of a plant

ep·i·the·li·za·tion \ˌep-ə-ˌthē-lə-ˈzā-shən\ *or* **ep·i·the·li·al·iza·tion** \-ˌthē-lē-ə-\ *n* (ca. 1934) **:** the process of becoming covered with or converted to epithelium — **ep·i·the·lize** \ˌep-ə-ˈthē-ˌlīz\ *or* **ep·i·the·li·al·ize** \-ˈthē-lē-ə-ˌlīz\ *vt*

ep·i·thet \ˈep-ə-ˌthet *also* -thət\ *n* [L *epitheton,* fr. Gk, fr. neut. of *epithetos* added, fr. *epitithenai* to put on, add, fr. *epi-* + *tithenai* to put — more at DO] (1579) **1 a :** a characterizing word or phrase accompanying or occurring in place of the name of a person or thing **b :** a disparaging or abusive word or phrase **c :** the part of a taxonomic name identifying a subordinate unit within a genus **2** *obs* **:** EXPRESSION — **ep·i·thet·ic** \ˌep-ə-ˈthet-ik\ *or* **ep·i·thet·i·cal** \-i-kəl\ *adj*

\ə\ abut \ᵊ\ kitten, F table \ər\ further \a\ ash \ā\ ace \ä\ cot, cart \au̇\ out \ch\ chin \e\ bet \ē\ easy \g\ go \i\ hit \ī\ ice \j\ job \ŋ\ sing \ō\ go \ȯ\ law \ȯi\ boy \th\ thin \t͟h\ the \ü\ loot \u̇\ foot \y\ yet \zh\ vision \á, k̲, ⁿ, œ, œ̄, ue, ue̅, ʸ\ see Guide to Pronunciation

epit·o·me \i-ˈpit-ə-mē\ *n* [L, fr. Gk *epitomē*, fr. *epitemnein* to cut short, fr. *epi-* + *temnein* to cut — more at TOME] (1520) **1 a :** a summary of a written work **b :** a brief presentation or statement of something **2 :** a typical or ideal example : EMBODIMENT ⟨the British monarchy itself is the ~ of tradition —Richard Joseph⟩ **3 :** brief or miniature form — usu. used with *in*

epit·o·mize \-ˌmīz\ *vt* **-mized; -miz·ing** (1599) **1 :** to make or give an epitome of **2 :** to serve as the typical or ideal example of

epi·zo·ic \ˌep-ə-ˈzō-ik\ *adj* (ca. 1857) **:** dwelling upon the body of an animal ⟨an ~ plant⟩ — **epi·zo·ite** \-ˌīt\ *n*

epi·zo·ot·ic \ˌep-ə-zə-ˈwät-ik\ *n* (1748) **:** a disease that affects many animals of one kind at the same time — **epizootic** *adj* — **epi·zo·ot·i·cal·ly** \-i-k(ə-)lē\ *adv*

epi·zo·ot·i·ol·o·gy \ˌep-ə-zə-ˌwät-ē-ˈäl-ə-jē\ *also* **epi·zo·otol·o·gy** \-ˌzō-ə-ˈtäl-ə-jē\ *n* (1910) **1 :** the sum of the factors controlling the occurrence of a disease or pathogen of animals **2 :** a science that deals with the character, ecology, and causes of outbreaks of animal diseases — **epi·zo·oti·o·log·i·cal** \-zə-ˌwōt-ē-ə-ˈläj-i-kəl, -ˌwät-\ *also* **epi·zo·oti·o·log·ic** \-ik\ *adj*

ep·och \ˈep-ək, ˈep-ˌäk, *US also & Brit usu* ˈē-ˌpäk\ *n* [ML *epocha*, fr. Gk *epochē* cessation, fixed point, fr. *epechein* to pause, hold back, fr. *epi-* + *echein* to hold — more at SCHEME] (1614) **1 :** an instant of time or a date selected as a point of reference (as in astronomy) **2 a :** an event or a time marked by an event that begins a new period or development **b :** a memorable event or date **3 a :** an extended period of time usu. characterized by a distinctive development or by a memorable series of events **b :** a division of geologic time less than a period and greater than an age ***syn*** see PERIOD

ep·och·al \ˈep-ə-kəl, ˈep-ˌäk-əl\ *adj* (1685) **1 :** of or relating to an epoch **2 :** uniquely or highly significant : MOMENTOUS ⟨his fights to advance . . . democracy during his three ~ years in the assembly —C. G. Bowers⟩; *also* **:** UNPARALLELED ⟨the . . . delegates . . . have fallen for it out of their almost ~ dumbness —J. T. Flynn⟩ — **ep·och·al·ly** \-ē\ *adv*

ep·ode \ˈep-ˌōd\ *n* [L *epodos*, fr. Gk *epōidos*, fr. *epōidos* sung or said after, fr. *epi-* + *aidein* to sing — more at ODE] (1598) **1 :** a lyric poem in which a long verse is followed by a shorter one **2 :** the third part of a triadically constructed Greek ode following the strophe and the antistrophe

ep·onym \ˈep-ə-ˌnim\ *n* [Gk *epōnymos*, fr. *epōnymos* eponymous, fr. *epi-* + *onyma* name — more at NAME] (ca. 1846) **1 :** the person for whom something is or is believed to be named **2 :** a name (as of a drug or a disease) based on or derived from an eponym — **ep·onym·ic** \ˌep-ə-ˈnim-ik\ *adj*

epon·y·mous \i-ˈpän-ə-məs, e-\ *adj* (1846) **:** of, relating to, or being the person for whom something is or is believed to be named

epon·y·my \-mē\ *n, pl* **-mies** (1865) **:** the explanation of a proper name (as of a town or tribe) by supposing a fictitious eponym

ep·o·pee \ˈep-ə-ˌpē\ *n* [F *épopée*, fr. Gk *epopoiia*, fr. *epos* + *poiein* to make — more at POET] (1697) **:** EPIC; *esp* **:** an epic poem

ep·os \ˈep-ˌäs\ *n* [Gk, word, epic poem] (ca. 1828) **1 :** EPIC **2 :** a number of poems that treat an epic theme but are not formally united

ep·ox·ide \(ˈ)ep-ˈäk-ˌsīd\ *n* (1930) **:** an epoxy compound

¹ep·oxy \i-ˈpäk-sē\ *adj* [*epi-* + *oxygen*] (ca. 1916) **1 :** containing oxygen attached to two different atoms already united in some other way; *specif* **:** containing a 3-membered ring consisting of one oxygen and two carbon atoms **2 :** of or relating to an epoxide

²epoxy *vt* **ep·ox·ied** *or* **ep·oxyed; ep·oxy·ing** (1966) **:** to glue with epoxy resin

epoxy resin *n* (1950) **:** a flexible usu. thermosetting resin made by polymerization of an epoxide and used chiefly in coatings and adhesives — called also *epoxy*

ep·si·lon \ˈep-sə-ˌlän, -lən\ *n* [Gk *e psilon*, lit., simple e] (15c) **1 :** the 5th letter of the Greek alphabet — see ALPHABET table **2 :** an arbitrarily small positive quantity in mathematical analysis — **ep·si·lon·ic** \ˌep-sə-ˈlän-ik\ *adj*

Ep·som salt \ˌep-səm-\ *n* (1770) **:** EPSOM SALTS

Epsom salts *n pl but sing in constr* [*Epsom*, England] (1876) **:** a bitter colorless or white crystalline salt $MgSO_4 \cdot 7H_2O$ that is a hydrated magnesium sulfate with cathartic properties

Ep·stein–Barr virus \ˌep-ˌstīn-ˌbär-\ *n* [Michael Anthony *Epstein* b1921 and Y.M. *Barr* fl 1964 Eng. pathologists] (1968) **:** a herpesvirus that causes infectious mononucleosis and is associated with Burkitt's lymphoma and nasopharyngeal carcinoma

equa·ble \ˈek-wə-bəl, ˈē-kwə-\ *adj* [L *aequabilis*, fr. *aequare* to make level or equal, fr. *aequus*] (1643) **1 :** marked by lack of variation or change : UNIFORM **2 :** marked by lack of noticeable, unpleasant, or extreme variation or inequality ***syn*** see STEADY — **equa·bil·i·ty** \ˌek-wə-ˈbil-ət-ē, ˌē-kwə-\ *n* — **equa·ble·ness** \ˈek-wə-bəl-nəs, ˈē-kwə-\ *n* — **equa·bly** \-blē\ *adv*

¹equal \ˈē-kwəl\ *adj* [ME, fr. L *aequalis*, fr. *aequus* level, equal] (14c) **1 a** (1) **:** of the same measure, quantity, amount, or number as another (2) **:** identical in mathematical value or logical denotation : EQUIVALENT **b :** like in quality, nature, or status **c :** like for each member of a group, class, or society ⟨provide ~ employment opportunities⟩ **2 :** regarding or affecting all objects in the same way : IMPARTIAL **3 :** free from extremes: as **a :** tranquil of mind or mood **b :** not showing variation in appearance, structure, or proportion **4 a :** capable of meeting the requirements of a situation or a task **b :** SUITABLE ⟨bored with work not ~ to his abilities⟩ ***syn*** see SAME

²equal *vt* **equaled** *or* **equalled; equal·ing** *or* **equal·ling** (1590) **1 :** to be equal to; *esp* **:** to be identical in value to **2** *archaic* **:** EQUALIZE **3 :** to make or produce something equal to

³equal *n* (1753) **1 :** one that is equal ⟨insists that women can be absolute ~s with men —Anne Bernays⟩ **2 :** an equal quantity

equal–area *adj, of a map projection* (ca. 1929) **:** maintaining constant ratio of size between quadrilaterals formed by the meridians and parallels and the quadrilaterals of the globe thereby preserving true areal extent of forms represented

equal·i·tar·i·an \i-ˌkwäl-ə-ˈter-ē-ən\ *adj or n* (1799) **:** EGALITARIAN — **equal·i·tar·i·an·ism** \-ē-ə-ˌniz-əm\ *n*

equal·i·ty \i-ˈkwäl-ət-ē\ *n, pl* **-ties** (15c) **1 :** the quality or state of being equal **2 :** EQUATION 2a

equal·ize \ˈē-kwə-ˌlīz\ *vt* **-ized; -iz·ing** (1622) **1 :** to make equal **2 a :** to compensate for **b :** to make uniform; *specif* **:** to distribute evenly or uniformly ⟨~ the tax burden⟩ **c :** to adjust or correct the frequency characteristics of (an electronic signal) by restoring to their original level high frequencies that have been attenuated — **equal·iza·tion** \ˌē-kwə-lə-ˈzā-shən\ *n*

equal·iz·er \-ˌlī-zər\ *n* (1792) **:** one that equalizes: as **a :** a device that provides for equal distribution (as of force) **b :** a score that ties a game

equal·ly \ˈē-kwə-lē\ *adv* (14c) **1 :** in an equal or uniform manner : EVENLY **2 :** to an equal degree : ALIKE ⟨respected ~ by young and old⟩

equal opportunity employer *n* (1965) **:** an employer who agrees not to discriminate against any employee or job applicant because of race, color, religion, national origin, sex, physical or mental handicap, or age

equal sign *n* (ca. 1909) **:** a sign = indicating mathematical or logical equivalence — called also *equality sign, equals sign*

equa·nim·i·ty \ˌē-kwə-ˈnim-ət-ē, ˌek-wə-\ *n, pl* **-ties** [L *aequanimitas*, fr. *aequo animo* with even mind] (1663) **1 :** evenness of mind esp. under stress **2 :** right disposition : BALANCE

equate \i-ˈkwāt, ˈē-ˌ\ *vb* **equat·ed; equat·ing** [ME *equaten*, fr. L *aequatus*, pp. of *aequare*] *vt* (15c) **1 a :** to make equal : EQUALIZE **b :** to make such an allowance or correction in as will reduce to a common standard or obtain a correct result **2 :** to treat, represent, or regard as equal, equivalent, or comparable ⟨~s disagreement with disloyalty⟩ ~ *vi* **:** to correspond as equal

equa·tion \i-ˈkwā-zhən *also* -shən\ *n* (14c) **1 a :** the act or process of equating **b** (1) **:** an element affecting a process : FACTOR (2) **:** a complex of variable factors **c :** a state of being equated; *specif* **:** a state of association or identification of two or more things ⟨bring governmental enterprises and payment for them into immediate ~ —R. G. Tugwell⟩ **2 a :** a usu. formal statement of the equality or equivalence of mathematical or logical expressions **b :** an expression representing a chemical reaction quantitatively by means of chemical symbols

equa·tion·al \i-ˈkwāzh-nəl, -ən-ᵊl *also* -ˈkwāsh-\ *adj* (1864) **1 :** of, using, or involving equation or equations **2 :** dividing into two equal parts — used esp. of the mitotic cell division usu. following reduction in meiosis — **equa·tion·al·ly** \-ē\ *adv*

equation of time (ca. 1847) **:** the difference between apparent time and mean time usu. expressed as a correction which is to be added to apparent time to give local mean time

equa·tor \i-ˈkwāt-ər, ˈē-ˌ\ *n* [ME, fr. ML *aequator*, lit., equalizer, fr. L *aequatus*] (14c) **1 :** the great circle of the celestial sphere whose plane is perpendicular to the axis of the earth **2 :** a great circle of the earth or a celestial body that is everywhere equally distant from the two poles and divides the surface into the northern and southern hemispheres **3 a :** a circle or circular band dividing the surface of a body into two usu. equal and symmetrical parts **b :** EQUATORIAL PLANE ⟨the ~ of a dividing cell⟩ **4 :** GREAT CIRCLE

¹equa·to·ri·al \ˌē-kwə-ˈtōr-ē-əl, ˌek-wə-, -ˈtȯr-\ *adj* (1664) **1 a :** of, relating to, or located at the equator or an equator; *also* **:** being in the plane of the equator ⟨an ~ orbit of a satellite⟩ **b :** of, originating in, or suggesting the region around the geographic equator **2 a :** being or having a support that includes two axles at right angles to each other with one parallel to the earth's axis of rotation ⟨an ~ telescope⟩ **b :** extending in a direction essentially in the plane of a cyclic structure (as of cyclohexane) ⟨~ hydrogens⟩ — compare AXIAL

²equatorial *n* (1793) **:** an equatorial telescope

equatorial plane *n* (ca. 1892) **:** the plane perpendicular to the spindle of a dividing cell and midway between the poles

equatorial plate *n* (1887) **1 :** METAPHASE PLATE **2 :** EQUATORIAL PLANE

equa·tor·ward \i-ˈkwāt-ər-wərd\ *adv or adj* (1875) **:** toward or near the equator ⟨currents flowing ~⟩ ⟨~ winds⟩

equer·ry \ˈek-wə-rē, i-ˈkwer-ē\ *n, pl* **-ries** [obs. *escurie, equerry* stable, fr. MF *escuirie* office of a squire, stable, fr. *escuier* squire — more at ESQUIRE] (1591) **1 :** an officer of a prince or noble charged with the care of horses **2 :** one of the officers of the British royal household in personal attendance on the sovereign or another member of the royal family

¹eques·tri·an \i-ˈkwes-trē-ən\ *adj* [L *equestr-*, *equester* of a horseman, fr. *eques* horseman, fr. *equus* horse — more at EQUINE] (ca. 1656) **1 a :** of, relating to, or featuring horseback riding **b** *archaic* **:** riding on horseback : MOUNTED **c :** representing a person on horseback ⟨an ~ statue⟩ **2 :** of, relating to, or composed of knights

²equestrian *n* (1791) **:** one who rides on horseback

eques·tri·enne \i-ˌkwes-trē-ˈen\ *n* [²*equestrian* + *-enne* (as in *tragedienne*)] (ca. 1864) **:** a female rider on horseback

equi- *comb form* [ME, fr. MF, fr. L *aequi-*, fr. *aequus* equal] **:** equal ⟨*equi*poise⟩ **:** equally ⟨*equi*probable⟩

equi·an·gu·lar \ˌē-kwi-ˈaŋ-gyə-lər, ˌek-wi-\ *adj* (1660) **:** having all or corresponding angles equal ⟨an ~ triangle⟩ ⟨mutually ~ parallelograms⟩

equi·ca·lor·ic \ˌē-kwə-kə-ˈlȯr-ik, ˌek-wə-, -ˈlär-\ *adj* (1940) **:** capable of yielding equal amounts of energy in the body ⟨~ diets⟩

equi·dis·tant \-ˈdis-tənt\ *adj* [MF or LL; MF, fr. LL *aequidistant-*, *aequidistans*, fr. L *aequi-* + *distant-*, *distans*, prp. of *distare* to stand apart — more at DISTANT] (1570) **1 :** equally distant **2 :** representing map distances true to scale in all directions — **equi·dis·tant·ly** *adv*

equi·lat·er·al \ˌē-kwə-ˈlat-ə-rəl, ˌek-wə-, -ˈla-trəl\ *adj* [LL *aequilateralis*, fr. L *aequi-* + *later-*, *latus* side — more at LATERAL] (1570) **1 :** having all sides equal ⟨an ~ triangle⟩ — see TRIANGLE illustration **2 :** having all the faces equal ⟨an ~ polyhedron⟩

equilateral hyperbola *n* (1880) **:** a hyperbola with its asymptotes at right angles

equil·i·brate \i-ˈkwil-ə-ˌbrāt\ *vb* **-brat·ed; -brat·ing** *vt* (1635) **:** to bring into or keep in equilibrium : BALANCE ~ *vi* **:** to bring about, come to, or be in equilibrium — **equil·i·bra·tion** \-ˌkwil-ə-ˈbrā-shən\ *n* — **equil·i·bra·tor** \-ˈkwil-ə-ˌbrāt-ər\ *n* — **equil·i·bra·to·ry** \-brə-ˌtōr-ē, -ˌtȯr-\ *adj*

equi·li·brist \ˌē-kwə-ˈlib-rəst, ˌek-wə-; i-ˈkwil-ə-brəst\ *n* (1760) **:** one who balances himself in unnatural positions and hazardous movements — **equil·i·bris·tic** \i-ˌkwil-ə-ˈbris-tik\ *adj*

equi·lib·ri·um \ˌē-kwə-ˈlib-rē-əm, ˌek-wə-\ *n, pl* **-ri·ums** *or* **-ria** \-rē-ə\ [L *aequilibrium,* fr. *aequilibris* being in equilibrium, fr. *aequi-* + *libra* weight, balance] (1608) **1 a :** a state of adjustment between opposing or divergent influences or elements **b :** a state of intellectual or emotional balance : POISE **2 :** a state of balance between opposing forces or actions that is either static (as in a body acted on by forces whose resultant is zero) or dynamic (as in a reversible chemical reaction when the velocities in both directions are equal)

equi·mol·al \-ˈmō-ləl\ *adj* (1936) **1 :** having equal molal concentration **2 :** EQUIMOLAR 1

equi·mo·lar \-ˈmō-lər\ *adj* (ca. 1909) **1 :** of or relating to an equal number of moles ⟨an ~ mixture⟩ **2 :** having equal molar concentration

equine \ˈē-ˌkwīn, ˈek-ˌwīn\ *adj* [L *equinus,* fr. *equus* horse; akin to OE *eoh* horse, Gk *hippos*] (1778) **:** of, relating to, or resembling a horse or the horse family — **equine** *n* — **equine·ly** *adv*

[1]**equi·noc·tial** \ˌē-kwə-ˈnäk-shəl, ˌek-wə-\ *adj* (14c) **1 :** relating to an equinox or to a state or the time of equal day and night **2 :** relating to the regions or climate on or near the equator **3 :** relating to the time when the sun passes an equinoctial point

[2]**equinoctial** *n* (14c) **1 :** EQUATOR 1 **2 :** an equinoctial storm

equi·nox \ˈē-kwə-ˌnäks, ˈek-wə-\ *n* [ME, fr. MF or ML; MF *equinoxe,* fr. ML *equinoxium,* alter. of L *aequinoctium,* fr. *aequi-* equi- + *noct-, nox* night — more at NIGHT] (14c) **1 :** either of the two points on the celestial sphere where the celestial equator intersects the ecliptic **2 :** either of the two times each year when the sun crosses the equator and day and night are everywhere of equal length, being about March 21 and September 23

equip \i-ˈkwip\ *vt* **equipped; equip·ping** [MF *equiper,* alter. of OF *esciper* to equip a ship, of Gmc origin; akin to OE *scip* ship] (1523) **1 :** to furnish for service or action : make ready by appropriate provisioning **2 :** DRESS, ARRAY ***syn*** see FURNISH

eq·ui·page \ˈek-wə-pij\ *n* (1579) **1 a :** material or articles used in equipment : OUTFIT **b** *archaic* (1) **:** a set of small articles (as for table service) (2) **:** ETUI **c :** TRAPPINGS **2** *archaic* **:** RETINUE **3 :** a horse-drawn carriage with its servants; *also* **:** such a carriage alone

equip·ment \i-ˈkwip-mənt\ *n* (1717) **1 a :** the set of articles or physical resources serving to equip a person or thing: as (1) **:** the implements used in an operation or activity : APPARATUS (2) **:** all the fixed assets other than land and buildings of a business enterprise (3) **:** the rolling stock of a railway **b :** a piece of such equipment **2 a :** the equipping of a person or thing **b :** the state of being equipped **3 :** mental or emotional traits or resources : ENDOWMENT

[1]**equi·poise** \ˈek-wə-ˌpȯiz, ˈē-kwə-\ *vt* (1664) **1 :** to serve as an equipoise to **2 :** to put or hold in equipoise

[2]**equipoise** *n* (1665) **1 :** a state of equilibrium **2 :** COUNTERBALANCE

equi·pol·lence \ˌē-kwə-ˈpäl-ən(t)s, ˌek-wə-\ *n* (15c) **:** the quality of being equipollent

equi·pol·lent \-ənt\ *adj* [ME, fr. MF, fr. L *aequipollent-, aequipollens,* fr. *aequi-* equi- + *pollent-, pollens,* prp. of *pollēre* to be able] (15c) **1 :** equal in force, power, or validity **2 :** the same in effect or signification — **equipollent** *n* — **equi·pol·lent·ly** *adv*

equi·pon·der·ant \-ˈpän-d(ə-)rənt\ *adj* (1630) **:** evenly balanced

equi·po·ten·tial \ˌē-kwə-pə-ˈten-chəl, ˌek-wə-\ *adj* (ca. 1865) **:** having the same potential : of uniform potential throughout ⟨~ points⟩ ⟨an ~ surface⟩

equi·prob·a·ble \-ˈpräb-(ə-)bəl\ *adj* (1921) **:** having the same degree of logical or mathematical probability ⟨~ alternatives⟩

eq·ui·se·tum \ˌek-wə-ˈsēt-əm\ *n, pl* **-se·tums** *or* **-se·ta** \-ˈsēt-ə\ [NL, fr. L *equisaetum* horsetail plant, fr. *equus* horse + *saeta* bristle — more at SINEW] (1830) **:** any of a genus (*Equisetum*) of lower tracheophytes comprising perennial plants that spread by creeping rhizomes, are homosporous and asexual, and have leaves reduced to nodal sheaths on the hollow jointed grooved shoots — called also *scouring rush*

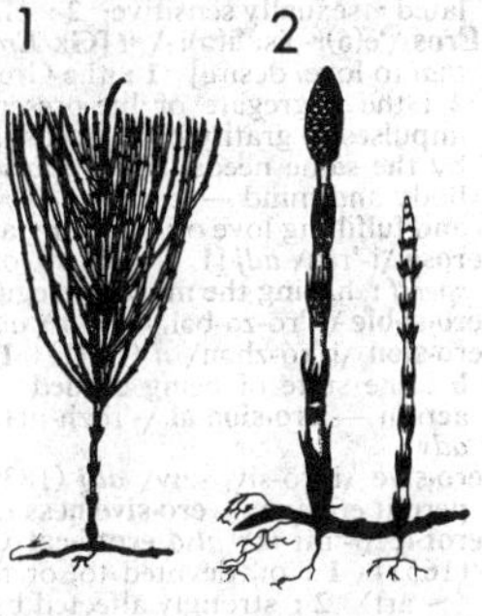

equisetum: *1* vegetative plant, *2* fertile plant

eq·ui·ta·ble \ˈek-wət-ə-bəl\ *adj* (1646) **1 :** having or exhibiting equity : dealing fairly and equally with all concerned **2 :** existing or valid in equity as distinguished from law ***syn*** see FAIR — **eq·ui·ta·bil·i·ty** \ˌek-wət-ə-ˈbil-ət-ē\ *n* — **eq·ui·ta·ble·ness** \ˈek-wət-ə-bəl-nəs\ *n* — **eq·ui·ta·bly** \-blē\ *adv*

eq·ui·ta·tion \ˌek-wə-ˈtā-shən\ *n* (1562) **:** the act or art of riding on horseback

eq·ui·ty \ˈek-wət-ē\ *n, pl* **-ties** [ME *equite,* fr. MF *equité,* fr. L *aequitat-, aequitas,* fr. *aequus* equal, fair] (14c) **1 a :** justice according to natural law or right; *specif* **:** freedom from bias or favoritism **b :** something that is equitable **2 a :** a system of law originating in the English chancery and comprising a settled and formal body of legal and procedural rules and doctrines that supplement, aid, or override common and statute law and are designed to protect rights and enforce duties fixed by substantive law **b :** trial or remedial justice under or by the rules and doctrines of equity **c :** a body of legal doctrines and rules developed to enlarge, supplement, or override a narrow rigid system of law **3 a :** a right, claim, or interest existing or valid in equity **b :** the money value of a property or of an interest in a property in excess of claims or liens against it **c :** a risk interest or ownership right in property

equity capital *n* (1942) **:** VENTURE CAPITAL

equiv·a·lence \i-ˈkwiv(-ə)-lən(t)s\ *n* (15c) **1 a :** the state or property of being equivalent **b :** the relation holding between two statements if they are either both true or both false so that to affirm one and to deny the other would result in a contradiction **2 :** a presentation of terms as equivalent **3 :** equality in metrical value of a regular foot and one in which there are substitutions

equivalence class *n* (1952) **:** a set for which an equivalence relation holds between every pair of elements

equivalence relation *n* (1949) **:** a relation (as equality) between elements of a set (as the real numbers) that is symmetric, reflexive, and transitive and for any two elements either holds or does not hold

equiv·a·len·cy \i-ˈkwiv(-ə)-lən-sē\ *n, pl* **-cies** (1535) **:** EQUIVALENCE

equiv·a·lent \-lənt\ *adj* [ME, fr. MF or LL; MF, fr. LL *aequivalent-, aequivalens,* prp. of *aequivalēre* to have equal power, fr. L *aequi-* + *valēre* to be strong — more at WIELD] (15c) **1 :** equal in force, amount, or value; *also* **:** equal in area or volume but not admitting of superposition ⟨a square ~ to a triangle⟩ **2 a :** like in signification or import **b :** having logical equivalence ⟨~ statements⟩ **3 :** corresponding or virtually identical esp. in effect or function **4** *obs* **:** equal in might or authority **5 :** having the same chemical combining capacity ⟨~ quantities of two elements⟩ **6 a :** having the same solution set ⟨~ equations⟩ **b :** capable of being placed in one-to-one correspondence ⟨~ sets⟩ **c :** related by an equivalence relation ***syn*** see SAME — **equivalent** *n* — **equiv·a·lent·ly** *adv*

equivalent weight *n* (ca. 1929) **:** the weight of a substance esp. in grams that combines with or is chemically equivalent to eight grams of oxygen or one gram of hydrogen : the atomic or molecular weight divided by the valence

equiv·o·cal \i-ˈkwiv-ə-kəl\ *adj* [LL *aequivocus,* fr. *aequi-* equi- + *voc-, vox* voice — more at VOICE] (1601) **1 a :** subject to two or more interpretations and usu. used to mislead or confuse ⟨he did not lie but his story of the party was certainly ~⟩ **b :** uncertain as an indication or sign **2 a :** of uncertain nature or classification **b :** of uncertain disposition toward a person or thing : UNDECIDED **c :** of doubtful advantage, genuineness, or moral rectitude ⟨~ behavior⟩ ***syn*** see OBSCURE — **equiv·o·cal·i·ty** \-ˌkwiv-ə-ˈkal-ət-ē\ *n* — **equiv·o·cal·ly** \-ˈkwiv-ə-k(ə-)lē\ *adv* — **equiv·o·cal·ness** \-kəl-nəs\ *n*

equiv·o·cate \i-ˈkwiv-ə-ˌkāt\ *vi* **-cat·ed; -cat·ing** (1590) **1 :** to use equivocal language esp. with intent to deceive **2 :** to avoid committing oneself in what one says ***syn*** see LIE — **equiv·o·ca·tion** \-ˌkwiv-ə-ˈkā-shən\ *n* — **equiv·o·ca·tor** \-ˈkwiv-ə-ˌkāt-ər\ *n*

equi·voque *also* **equi·voke** \ˈek-wə-ˌvōk, ˈē-kwə-\ *n* [F *équivoque,* fr. *équivoque* equivocal, fr. LL *aequivocus*] (1599) **1 :** an equivocal word or phrase; *specif* **:** PUN **2 a :** double meaning **b :** WORDPLAY

[1]**-er** \ər; *after some vowels, often* r; *after* ŋ, *usu* gər\ *adj suffix or adv suffix* [ME *-er, -ere, -re,* fr. OE *-ra* (in adjectives), *-or* (in adverbs); akin to OHG *-iro,* adj. compar. suffix, L *-ior,* Gk *-iōn*] — used to form the comparative degree of adjectives and adverbs of one syllable ⟨hott*er*⟩ ⟨dri*er*⟩ and of some adjectives and adverbs of two syllables ⟨complet*er*⟩ and sometimes of longer ones ⟨divineli*er*⟩

[2]**-er** \ər; *after some vowels, often* r\ *also* **-ier** \ē-ər, yər\ *or* **-yer** \yər\ *n suffix* [ME *-er, -ere, -ier, -iere;* partly fr. OE *-ere* (fr. L *-arius*); partly fr. OF *-ier, -iere,* fr. L *-arius, -aria, -arium* -ary; partly fr. MF *-ere,* fr. L *-ator* -or — more at -ARY, -OR] **1 a :** person occupationally connected with ⟨hatt*er*⟩ ⟨furri*er*⟩ ⟨law*yer*⟩ **b :** person or thing belonging to or associated with ⟨head*er*⟩ ⟨old-tim*er*⟩ **c :** native of : resident of ⟨cottag*er*⟩ ⟨New York*er*⟩ **d :** one that has ⟨three-deck*er*⟩ **e :** one that produces or yields ⟨pork*er*⟩ **2 a :** one that does or performs (a specified action) ⟨report*er*⟩ — sometimes added to both elements of a compound ⟨build*er*-upp*er*⟩ **b :** one that is a suitable object of (a specified action) ⟨broil*er*⟩ **3 :** one that is ⟨foreign*er*⟩ — *-yer* in a few words after *w, -ier* in a few words after other letters, otherwise *-er*

era \ˈir-ə, ˈer-ə, ˈē-rə\ *n* [LL *aera,* fr. L, counters, pl. of *aer-, aes* copper, money — more at ORE] (1615) **1 a :** a fixed point in time from which a series of years is reckoned **b :** a memorable or important date or event; *esp* **:** one that begins a new period in the history of a person or thing **2 :** a system of chronological notation computed from a given date as basis **3 a :** a period set off or typified by some prominent figure or characteristic feature **b :** a stage in the development of a person or thing; *esp* **:** one of the five major divisions of geologic time ⟨Paleozoic ~⟩ ***syn*** see PERIOD

erad·i·cate \i-ˈrad-ə-ˌkāt\ *vt* **-cat·ed; -cat·ing** [L *eradicatus,* pp. of *eradicare,* fr. *e-* + *radic-, radix* root — more at ROOT] (1564) **1 :** to pull up by the roots **2 :** to do away with as if by pulling up by the roots ⟨~ ignorance by better teaching⟩ ***syn*** see EXTERMINATE — **erad·i·ca·ble** \-ˈrad-i-kə-bəl\ *adj* — **erad·i·ca·tion** \-ˌrad-ə-ˈkā-shən\ *n* — **erad·i·ca·tor** \-ˌkāt-ər\ *n*

erase \i-ˈrās, *Brit* -ˈrāz\ *vb* **erased; eras·ing** [L *erasus,* pp. of *eradere,* fr. *e-* + *radere* to scratch, scrape — more at RAT] *vt* (1605) **1 a :** to rub or scrape out (as written, painted, or engraved letters) **b :** to remove (recorded matter) from a magnetic tape or wire **c :** to delete from a computer storage device **2 a :** to remove from existence or memory as if by erasing **b :** to nullify the effect or force of ~ *vi* **:** to yield to being erased — **eras·abil·i·ty** \-ˌrā-sə-ˈbil-ət-ē\ *n* — **eras·able** \-ˈrā-sə-bəl\ *adj*

eras·er \i-ˈrā-sər\ *n* (1790) **:** one that erases; *specif* **:** a device (as a sharp instrument, a piece of rubber, or a felt pad) used to erase marks (as of ink or chalk)

Eras·tian \i-ˈras-tē-ən, -ˈras-chən\ *adj* [Thomas *Erastus* †1583 German-Swiss physician and Zwinglian theologian] (1837) **:** of, characterized by, or advocating the doctrine of state supremacy in ecclesiastical affairs — **Erastian** *n* — **Eras·tian·ism** \-ˌiz-əm\ *n*

era·sure \i-ˈrā-shər *also* -zhər\ *n* (1734) **:** an act or instance of erasing

Er·a·to \ˈer-ə-ˌtō\ *n* [Gk *Eratō*] **:** the Greek Muse of lyric and love poetry

er·bi·um \ˈər-bē-əm\ *n* [NL, fr. *Ytterby,* Sweden] (1843) **:** a metallic element of the rare-earth group that occurs with yttrium — see ELEMENT table

[1]**ere** \(ˌ)e(ə)r, (ˌ)a(ə)r\ *prep* [ME *er,* fr. OE *ǣr,* fr. *ǣr,* adv., early, soon; akin to OHG *ēr* earlier, Gk *ēri* early] (bef. 12c) **:** [2]BEFORE 2 ⟨contrived ~ the beginning of the world —Norman Douglas⟩

[2]**ere** *conj* (bef. 12c) **:** [3]BEFORE ⟨I will be thrown into Etna . . . ~ I will leave her —Shak.⟩

\ə\ abut \ᵊ\ kitten, F table \ər\ further \a\ ash \ā\ ace \ä\ cot, cart \au̇\ out \ch\ chin \e\ bet \ē\ easy \g\ go \i\ hit \ī\ ice \j\ job \ŋ\ sing \ō\ go \ȯ\ law \ȯi\ boy \th\ thin \t͟h\ the \ü\ loot \u̇\ foot \y\ yet \zh\ vision \á, k̲, ⁿ, œ, œ̄, ue, ue̅, ʸ\ see Guide to Pronunciation

Er·e·bus \'er-ə-bəs\ *n* [L, fr. Gk *Erebos*] (1582) **1 :** a personification of darkness in Greek mythology **2 :** a place of darkness in the underworld on the way to Hades

[1]**erect** \i-'rekt\ *adj* [ME, fr. L *erectus,* pp. of *erigere* to erect, fr. *e-* + *regere* to lead straight, guide — more at RIGHT] (14c) **1 a :** vertical in position; *specif* **:** not spread out or decumbent ⟨an ~ plant stem⟩ **b :** standing up or out from the body ⟨~ hairs⟩ **c :** characterized by firm or rigid straightness in bodily posture ⟨an ~ bearing⟩ **2** *archaic* **:** directed upward **3** *obs* **:** ALERT, WATCHFUL **4 :** being in a state of physiological erection — **erect·ly** \-'rek-(t)lē\ *adv* — **erect·ness** \-'rek(t)-nəs\ *n*

[2]**erect** *vt* (15c) **1 a** (1) **:** to put up by the fitting together of materials or parts **:** BUILD (2) **:** to fix in an upright position (3) **:** to cause to stand up or stand out **b** *archaic* **:** to direct upward **c :** to change (an image) from an inverted to a normal position **2 :** to elevate in status **3 :** SET UP, ESTABLISH **4** *obs* **:** ENCOURAGE, EMBOLDEN **5 :** to draw or construct (as a perpendicular or figure) upon a given base — **erect·able** \-'rek-tə-bəl\ *adj*

erec·tile \i-'rek-tᵊl, -,tīl\ *adj* (1830) **:** capable of becoming erect ⟨~ tissue⟩ — compare CAVERNOUS 3 — **erec·til·i·ty** \-,rek-'til-ət-ē\ *n*

erec·tion \i-'rek-shən\ *n* (15c) **1 a :** the state marked by firm turgid form and erect position of a previously flaccid bodily part containing cavernous tissue when that tissue becomes dilated with blood **b :** an occurrence of such a state in the penis or clitoris **2 :** the act or process of erecting something **:** CONSTRUCTION **3 :** something erected

erec·tor \i-'rek-tər\ *n* (1538) **:** one that erects; *esp* **:** a muscle that raises or keeps a part erect

E region *n* (1936) **:** the part of the ionosphere occurring between 55 and 80 miles (90 and 130 kilometers) above the surface of the earth and containing the daytime E layer and the sporadic E layer

ere·long \e(ə)r-'lȯŋ, a(ə)r-\ *adv* (1577) **:** before long **:** SOON

er·e·mite \'er-ə-,mīt\ *n* [ME — more at HERMIT] (13c) **:** HERMIT; *esp* **:** a religious recluse — **er·e·mit·ic** \,er-ə-'mit-ik\ *or* **er·e·mit·i·cal** \-i-kəl\ *adj* — **er·e·mit·ism** \'er-ə-,mīt-,iz-əm\ *n*

er·em·urus \,er-ə-'myu̇r-əs\ *n, pl* **-uri** \-'myu̇(ə)r-,ī\ [NL, fr. Gk *erēmos* solitary + *oura* tail — more at RETINA, SQUIRREL] (1829) **:** any of a genus (*Eremurus*) of perennial herbs of the lily family that produce tall racemes of showy blooms — called also *foxtail lily*

ere·now \e(ə)r-'nau̇, a(ə)r-\ *adv* (14c) **:** before now **:** HERETOFORE

erep·sin \i-'rep-sən\ *n* [ISV *er-* (prob. fr. L *eripere* to sweep away, fr. *e-* + *rapere* to sweep) + *pepsin* — more at RAPID] (1902) **:** a proteolytic fraction obtained esp. from the intestinal juice and known to be a mixture of exopeptidases

er·e·thism \'er-ə-,thiz-əm\ *n* [F *éréthisme,* fr. Gk *erethismos* irritation, fr. *erethizein* to irritate; akin to Gk *ornynai* to rouse — more at RISE] (1800) **:** abnormal irritability or responsiveness to stimulation — **ereth·ic** \ə-'reth-ik\ *adj*

ere·while \e(ə)r-'(h)wī(ə)l, a(ə)r-\ *also* **ere·whiles** \-'(h)wī(ə)lz\ *adv, archaic* (14c) **:** HERETOFORE

erg \'ərg\ *n* [Gk *ergon* work — more at WORK] (ca. 1873) **:** a cgs unit of work equal to the work done by a force of one dyne acting through a distance of one centimeter and equivalent to 10^{-7} joule

erg- *or* **ergo-** *comb form* [Gk, fr. *ergon*] **:** work ⟨ergophobia⟩

er·gas·tic \(,)ər-'gas-tik\ *adj* [Gk *ergastikos* able to work, fr. *ergazesthai* to work, fr. *ergon* work] (ca. 1896) **:** constituting the nonliving by-products of protoplasmic activity ⟨~ substances⟩

er·gas·to·plasm \-tə-,plaz-əm\ *n* [ISV *ergastic* + *-o-* + *-plasm*] (1902) **:** ribosome-studded endoplasmic reticulum — **er·gas·to·plas·mic** \-,gas-tə-'plaz-mik\ *adj*

-er·gic \(,)ər-jik\ *adj comb form* [E *-ergy* work (fr. LL *-ergia,* fr. Gk, fr. *ergon* work) + E *-ic* — more at WORK] **:** exhibiting or stimulating activity ⟨synergic⟩

er·go \'e(ə)r-(,)gō, 'ər-\ *adv* [ME, fr. L, fr. OL, because of, fr. (assumed) OL *e rogo* from the direction (of)] (14c) **:** THEREFORE, HENCE

ergo- *comb form* [F, fr. *ergot*] **:** ergot ⟨ergosterol⟩

er·go·dic \(,)ər-'gäd-ik, -'gōd-\ *adj* [G *ergodenhypothese,* lit., hypothesis of the path of energy, fr. *erg-* + Gk *hodos* path, road — more at CEDE] (1926) **1 :** of or relating to a process in which every sequence or sizable sample is equally representative of the whole (as in regard to a statistical parameter) **2 :** involving or relating to the probability that any state will recur; *esp* **:** having zero probability that any state will never recur — **er·go·dic·i·ty** \,ər-gə-'dis-ət-ē\ *n*

er·go·graph \'ər-gə-,graf\ *n* [ISV] (1892) **:** an apparatus for measuring the work capacity of a muscle

er·gom·e·ter \(,)ər-'gäm-ət-ər\ *n* (ca. 1879) **:** an apparatus for measuring the work performed by a group of muscles — **er·go·met·ric** \,ər-gə-'me-trik\ *adj*

er·go·nom·ics \,ər-gə-'näm-iks\ *n pl but sing or pl in constr* [*erg-* + *-nomics* (as in *bionomics*)] (1949) **:** an applied science concerned with the characteristics of people that need to be considered in designing and arranging things that they use in order that people and things will interact most effectively and safely — called also *human engineering* — **er·go·nom·ic** \-ik\ *adj* — **er·go·nom·i·cal·ly** \-i-k(ə-)lē\ *adv* — **er·gon·o·mist** \(,)ər-'gän-ə-məst\ *n*

er·go·no·vine \,ər-gə-'nō-,vēn\ *n* [*ergo-* + L *novus* new — more at NEW] (ca. 1936) **:** an alkaloid $C_{19}H_{23}N_3O_2$ from ergot with similar pharmacological action but reduced toxicity

er·gos·ter·ol \(,)ər-'gäs-tə-,rȯl, -,rōl\ *n* [ISV] (1889) **:** a crystalline steroid alcohol $C_{28}H_{44}O$ that occurs esp. in yeast, molds, and ergot and is converted by ultraviolet irradiation ultimately into vitamin D_2

er·got \'ər-gət, -,gät\ *n* [F, lit., cock's spur] (1683) **1 :** the black or dark purple sclerotium of fungi (genus *Claviceps*) that occurs as a club-shaped body replacing the seed of a grass (as rye); *also* **:** a fungus bearing ergots **2 :** a disease of rye and other cereals caused by an ergot fungus **3 a :** the dried sclerotia of an ergot fungus grown on rye and containing several alkaloids (as ergonovine and ergotamine) **b :** any of such alkaloids used medicinally for their contractile effect on smooth muscle (as of peripheral arterioles) — **er·got·ic** \(,)ər-'gät-ik\ *adj*

er·got·a·mine \(,)ər-'gät-ə-,mēn\ *n* [ISV] (1921) **:** an alkaloid $C_{33}H_{35}N_5O_5$ from ergot that has the pharmacological action of ergot and is used esp. in treating migraine

er·got·ism \'ər-gət-,iz-əm\ *n* (ca. 1847) **:** a toxic condition produced by eating grain, grain products (as rye bread), or grasses infected with ergot fungus or by chronic excessive use of an ergot drug

er·got·ized \-,īzd\ *adj* (1860) **:** infected with ergot ⟨~ grain⟩; *also* **:** poisoned by ergot ⟨~ cattle⟩

er·i·ca \'er-i-kə\ *n* [NL, fr. L *erice* heather, fr. Gk *ereikē* — more at BRIER] (1826) **:** any of a large genus (*Erica*) of the heath family of low much-branched evergreen shrubs

er·i·ca·ceous \,er-ə-'kā-shəs\ *adj* (ca. 1859) **:** of, relating to, or being a heath or the heath family

er·i·coid \'er-ə-,kȯid\ *adj* (1900) **:** resembling heath

Erie \'i(ə)r-ē\ *n* (ca. 1909) **1 :** a member of an American Indian people of the Lake Erie region **2 :** the language of the Erie people

erig·er·on \ə-'rij-ə-,rän\ *n* [NL, fr. L, groundsel, fr. Gk *ērigerōn,* fr. *ēri* early + *gerōn* old man; fr. the hoary down of some species — more at ERE, GERONT-] (1601) **:** any of a widely distributed genus (*Erigeron*) of composite herbs with flower heads that resemble asters but have fewer and narrower involucral bracts

Eri·nys \i-'rin-əs, -'rī-nəs\ *n, pl* **Erin·y·es** \-'rin-ē-,ēz\ [Gk] (1590) **:** FURY 2a

er·i·o·phy·id \,er-ē-'äf-ē-əd, -ē-ə-'fī-əd\ *n* [deriv. of Gk *erion* wool + *phyē* growth; akin to Gk *physis* growth — more at PHYSICS] (1942) **:** any of a large family (Eriophyidae) of minute plant-feeding mites that have two pairs of legs placed far anterior and lack a respiratory system — **eriophyid** *adj*

[1]**eris·tic** \i-'ris-tik, e-\ *also* **eris·ti·cal** \-ti-kəl\ *adj* [Gk — *eristokos* fond of wrangling, fr. *erizein* to wrangle, fr. *eris* strife; akin to Gk *ornynai* to rouse — more at RISE] (1637) **:** characterized by disputatious and often subtle and specious reasoning — **eris·ti·cal·ly** \-ti-k(ə-)lē\ *adv*

[2]**eristic** *n* (1659) **1 :** a person devoted to logical disputation **2 :** the art or practice of disputation and polemics

Er·len·mey·er flask \,ər-lən-,mī(-ə)r-, ,er-lən-\ *n* [Emil *Erlenmeyer* (ca. 1890)] **:** a flat-bottomed conical laboratory flask

er·mine \'ər-mən\ *n, pl* **ermines** [ME, fr. OF, of Gmc origin; akin to OHG *harmo* weasel] (13c) **1** *or pl* **ermine a :** any of several weasels that assume white winter pelage usu. with more or less black on the tail; *esp* **:** a large European weasel (*Mustela erminea*) **b :** the white fur of the ermine in winter pelage **2 :** a rank or office whose ceremonial or official robe is ornamented with ermine

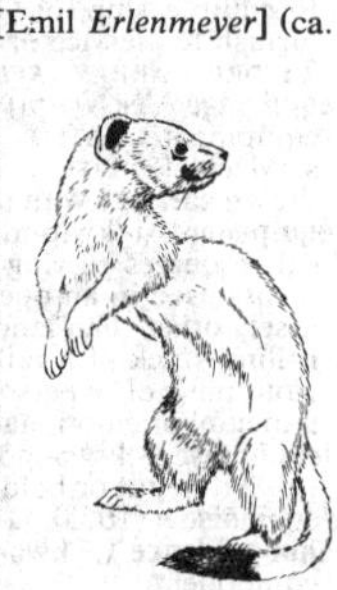
ermine 1a

er·mined \-mənd\ *adj* (15c) **:** clothed or adorned with ermine

erne *or* **ern** \'ərn, 'e(ə)rn\ *n* [ME, fr. OE *earn;* akin to OHG *arn* eagle, Gk *ornis* bird] (bef. 12c) **:** EAGLE; *esp* **:** a long-winged sea eagle (*Haliäetus albicilla*)

erode \i-'rōd\ *vb* **erod·ed; erod·ing** [L *erodere* to eat away, fr. *e-* + *rodere* to gnaw — more at RAT] *vt* (1612) **1 :** to diminish or destroy by degrees: **a :** to eat into or away by slow destruction of substance **:** CORRODE **b :** to wear away by the action of water, wind, or glacial ice **c :** to cause to deteriorate or disappear as if by eating or wearing away ⟨buying power is *eroded* with each inflationary year —R. H. McDonough⟩ **2 :** to produce or form by eroding ⟨glaciers ~ U-shaped valleys⟩ ~ *vi* **:** to undergo erosion — **erod·ibil·i·ty** \-,rōd-ə-'bil-ət-ē\ *n* — **erod·ible** \-'rōd-ə-bəl\ *adj*

erog·e·nous \i-'räj-ə-nəs\ *adj* [Gk *erōs* + E *-genous, -genic*] (ca. 1909) **1 :** producing sexual excitement or libidinal gratification when stimulated **:** sexually sensitive **2 :** of, relating to, or arousing sexual feelings

Eros \'e(ə)r-,äs, 'i(ə)r-\ *n* [Gk *Erōs,* fr. *erōs* sexual love; akin to Gk *erasthai* to love, desire] **1 :** the Greek god of erotic love — compare CUPID **2 :** the aggregate of life-preserving instincts that are manifested as impulses to gratify basic needs (as sex), sublimated impulses motivated by the same needs, and impulses serving to protect and preserve the body and mind — compare DEATH INSTINCT **3** *often not cap* **:** aspiring and fulfilling love often having a sensual quality **:** DESIRE, YEARNING

erose \i-'rōs\ *adj* [L *erosus,* pp. of *erodere*] (1793) **:** IRREGULAR, UNEVEN; *specif* **:** having the margin irregularly notched as if gnawed ⟨an ~ leaf⟩

ero·si·ble \i-'rō-zə-bəl, -'rō-sə-\ *adj* (ca. 1909) **:** capable of being eroded

ero·sion \i-'rō-zhən\ *n* (1541) **1 a :** the action or process of eroding **b :** the state of being eroded **2 :** an instance or product of erosive action — **ero·sion·al** \-'rōzh-nəl, -'rō-zhən-ᵊl\ *adj* — **ero·sion·al·ly** \-ē\ *adv*

ero·sive \i-'rō-siv, -ziv\ *adj* (1830) **:** tending to erode or to induce or permit erosion — **ero·sive·ness** *n* — **ero·siv·i·ty** \i-,rō-'siv-ət-ē\ *n*

erot·ic \i-'rät-ik\ *also* **erot·i·cal** \-i-kəl\ *adj* [Gk *erōtikos,* fr. *erōt-, erōs*] (1651) **1 :** of, devoted to, or tending to arouse sexual love or desire ⟨~ art⟩ **2 :** strongly affected by sexual desire — **erotic** *n* — **erot·i·cal·ly** \-i-k(ə-)lē\ *adv*

erot·i·ca \i-'rät-i-kə\ *n pl but sing or pl in constr* [NL, fr. Gk *erōtika,* neut. pl. of *erōtikos*] (1854) **:** literary or artistic works having an erotic theme or quality

erot·i·cism \i-'rät-ə-,siz-əm\ *n* (1881) **1 :** an erotic theme or quality **2 :** a state of sexual arousal **3 :** insistent sexual impulse or desire — **erot·i·cist** \-səst\ *n*

erot·i·cize \-,sīz\ *vt* **-cized; -ciz·ing** (ca. 1914) **:** to make erotic ⟨a film version that ~s the original story⟩ — **erot·i·ci·za·tion** \i-,rät-ə-sə-'zā-shən\ *n*

er·o·tism \'er-ə-,tiz-əm\ *n* (1849) **:** EROTICISM

er·o·tize \'er-ə-,tīz\ *vt* **-tized; -tiz·ing** (1936) **:** to invest with erotic significance or sexual feeling — **er·o·ti·za·tion** \,er-ət-ə-'zā-shən\ *n*

eroto- *comb form* [NL, fr. Gk *erōto-,* fr. *erōt-, erōs*] **:** sexual desire ⟨erotomania⟩

ero·to·gen·ic \i-,rät-ə-'jen-ik, -,rät-\ *adj* (ca. 1909) **:** EROGENOUS

err \'e(ə)r, 'ər\ *vi* [ME *erren,* fr. MF *errer,* fr. L *errare;* akin to OE *ierre* wandering, angry, ON *rās* race — more at RACE] (14c) **1** *archaic* **:** STRAY **2 a :** to make a mistake **b :** to violate an accepted standard of conduct

er·ran·cy \'er-ən-sē\ *n, pl* **-cies** (1621) **:** the state or an instance of erring

er·rand \'er-ənd\ *n* [ME *erend* message, business, fr. OE *ǣrend;* akin to OHG *ārunti* message] (bef. 12c) **1** *archaic* **a :** an oral message entrusted to a person **b :** EMBASSY, MISSION **2 a :** a short trip taken to attend to some business often for another ⟨was on an ~ for his mother⟩ **b :** the object or purpose of such a trip

er·rant \'er-ənt\ *adj* [ME *erraunt*, fr. MF *errant*, prp. of *errer* to err & *errer* to travel, fr. ML *iterare*, fr. L *iter* road, journey — more at ITINERANT] (14c) **1** : traveling or given to traveling ⟨an ~ knight⟩ **2 a** : straying outside the proper path or bounds ⟨an ~ calf⟩ **b** : moving about aimlessly or irregularly ⟨an ~ breeze⟩ **c** : deviating from a standard (as of truth or propriety) ⟨an ~ child⟩ **d** : FALLIBLE — **errant** *n* — **er·rant·ly** *adv*

er·rant·ry \'er-ən-trē\ *n, pl* **-ries** (1654) : the quality, condition, or fact of wandering; *esp* : a roving in search of chivalrous adventure

er·ra·ta \e-'rät-ə, -'rāt-, -'rat-\ *n* [L, pl. of *erratum*] (1589) : a list of corrigenda; *also* : a page bearing such a list

1**er·rat·ic** \ir-'at-ik\ *adj* [ME, fr. MF or L; MF *erratique*, fr. L *erraticus*, fr. *erratus*, pp. of *errare*] (14c) **1 a** : having no fixed course : WANDERING ⟨an ~ comet⟩ **b** *archaic* : NOMADIC **2** : transported from an original resting place esp. by a glacier ⟨~ boulder⟩ **3 a** : characterized by lack of consistency, regularity, or uniformity **b** : deviating from what is ordinary or standard : ECCENTRIC ⟨an ~ genius⟩ ***syn*** see STRANGE — **er·rat·i·cal** \-i-kəl\ *adj* — **er·rat·i·cal·ly** \-i-k(ə-)lē\ *adv* — **er·rat·i·cism** \-'at-ə-,siz-əm\ *n*

2**erratic** *n* (ca. 1623) : one that is erratic; *esp* : an erratic boulder or block of rock

er·ra·tum \e-'rät-əm, -'rāt-, -'rat-\ *n, pl* **-ta** \-ə\ [L, fr. neut. of *erratus*] (1589) : ERROR; *esp* : CORRIGENDUM

er·ro·ne·ous \ir-'ō-nē-əs, e-'rō-\ *adj* [ME, fr. L *erroneus*, fr. *erron-*, *erro* wanderer, fr. *errare*] (15c) **1** : containing or characterized by error : MISTAKEN ⟨~ assumptions⟩ **2** *archaic* : WANDERING — **er·ro·ne·ous·ly** *adv* — **er·ro·ne·ous·ness** *n*

er·ror \'er-ər\ *n* [ME *errour*, fr. MF, fr. L *error*, fr. *errare*] (14c) **1 a** : an act or condition of ignorant or imprudent deviation from a code of behavior **b** : an act involving an unintentional deviation from truth or accuracy **c** : an act that through ignorance, deficiency, or accident departs from or fails to achieve what should be done: as (1) : a defensive misplay other than a wild pitch or passed ball made by a baseball player when normal play would have resulted in an out or prevented an advance by a base runner (2) : the failure of a player (as in tennis) to make a successful return of a ball during play **d** : a mistake in the proceedings of a court of record in matters of law or of fact **2 a** : the quality or state of erring **b** *Christian Science* : illusion about the nature of reality that is the cause of human suffering : the contradiction of truth **c** : an instance of false belief **3** : something produced by mistake; *esp* : a postage stamp exhibiting a consistent flaw (as a wrong color) in its manufacture **4 a** : the difference between an observed or calculated value and a true value; *specif* : variation in measurements, calculations, or observations of a quantity due to mistakes or to uncontrollable factors **b** : the amount of deviation from a standard or specification **5** : a deficiency or imperfection in structure or function ⟨an ~ of metabolism⟩ — **er·ror·less** \'er-ər-ləs\ *adj*

syn ERROR, MISTAKE, SLIP, BLUNDER, LAPSE mean a departure from what is true, right, or proper. ERROR suggests the existence of a standard or guide and a straying from the right course through failure to make effective use of this ⟨one *error* in judgment lost the battle⟩ MISTAKE implies misconception or inadvertence and usu. expresses less criticism than *error* ⟨dialed the wrong number by *mistake*⟩ BLUNDER regularly imputes stupidity or ignorance as a cause and connotes some degree of blame ⟨a political campaign noted mostly for its series of *blunders*⟩ SLIP stresses inadvertence or accident and applies esp. to trivial but embarrassing mistakes ⟨during the speech I made several *slips*⟩ LAPSE stresses forgetfulness, weakness, or inattention as a cause ⟨apart from a few grammatical *lapses*, the paper is good⟩

er·satz \'e(ə)r-,säts, -,zäts, er-'; 'ər-,sats\ *adj* [G *ersatz-*, fr. *ersatz*, n., substitute] (1875) : being a usu. artificial and inferior substitute or imitation ⟨~ flour made from potatoes⟩ — **ersatz** *n*

Erse \'ərs\ *n* [ME (Sc) *Erisch*, adj., Irish, alter. of *Irish*] (14c) **1** : SCOTTISH GAELIC **2** : IRISH GAELIC — **Erse** *adj*

erst \'ərst\ *adv* [ME *erest* earliest, formerly, fr. OE *ǣrest*, superl. of *ǣr* early — more at ERE] *archaic* (bef. 12c) : ERSTWHILE

1**erst·while** \'ərst-,(h)wīl\ *adv* (15c) : in the past : FORMERLY ⟨cultures, ~ unknown to each other — Robert Plank⟩

2**erstwhile** *adj* (1903) : FORMER, PREVIOUS ⟨his ~ students⟩

eru·cic acid \i-,rü-sik-\ *n* [NL *Eruca*, genus of herbs, fr. L, colewort] (1869) : a crystalline fatty acid $C_{22}H_{42}O_2$ found in the form of glycerides esp. in rapeseed oil

eruct \i-'rəkt\ *vb* [L *eructare*, fr. *e-* + *ructare* to belch, fr. *-ructus*, pp. of *-rugere* to belch; akin to L *rugire* to roar] (1666) : BELCH

eruc·ta·tion \i-,rək-'tā-shən, ,ē-\ *n* (15c) : an act or instance of belching

er·u·dite \'er-(y)ə-,dīt\ *adj* [ME *erudit*, fr. L *eruditus*, fr. pp. of *erudire* to instruct, fr. *e-* + *rudis* rude, ignorant] (15c) : possessing or displaying erudition : LEARNED ⟨an ~ scholar⟩ — **er·u·dite·ly** *adv*

er·u·di·tion \,er-(y)ə-'dish-ən\ *n* (15c) : extensive knowledge acquired chiefly from books : profound, recondite, or bookish learning ***syn*** see KNOWLEDGE

erum·pent \i-'rəm-pənt\ *adj* [L *erumpent-*, *erumpens*, prp. of *erumpere*] (1650) : bursting forth ⟨~ fungi⟩

erupt \i-'rəpt\ *vb* [L *eruptus*, pp. of *erumpere* to burst forth, fr. *e-* + *rumpere* to break — more at REAVE] *vi* (1657) **1 a** : to force out or release suddenly and often violently something (as lava or steam) that is pent up **b** (1) : to burst from limits or restraint (2) *of a tooth* : to emerge through the gum **c** : to become active or violent : EXPLODE ⟨violence ~*ed* in the ghetto⟩ **2** : to break out (as with a skin eruption) ~ *vt* : to force out or release usu. suddenly and violently — **erupt·ible** \-'rəp-tə-bəl\ *adj* — **erup·tive** \-tiv\ *adj* — **erup·tive·ly** *adv*

erup·tion \i-'rəp-shən\ *n* (1555) **1 a** : an act, process, or instance of erupting **b** : the breaking out of a rash on the skin or mucous membrane **2** : a product of erupting (as a skin rash)

-ery \(ə-)rē\ *n suffix* [ME *-erie*, fr. OF, fr. *-ier* -er + *-ie* -y] **1** : qualities collectively : character : -NESS ⟨snobb*ery*⟩ **2** : art : practice ⟨quack*ery*⟩ **3** : place of doing, keeping, producing, or selling (the thing specified) ⟨fish*ery*⟩ ⟨bak*ery*⟩ **4** : collection : aggregate ⟨fin*ery*⟩ **5** : state or condition ⟨slav*ery*⟩

eryn·go \i-'riŋ-(,)gō\ *n, pl* **-goes** *or* **-gos** [modif. of L *eryngion* sea holly, fr. Gk *ēryngion*] (1598) **1** *obs* : candied sea-holly root made to be used as an aphrodisiac **2** : any of various plants (genus *Eryngium*) that have elongate spinulose-margined leaves and flowers in dense bracted heads

ery·sip·e·las \,er-ə-'sip-(ə-)ləs, ,ir-\ *n* [ME *erisipila*, fr. L *erysipelas*, fr. Gk, fr. *erysi-* (akin to Gk *erythros* red) + *-pelas* (akin to L *pellis* skin) — more at RED, FELL] (14c) : an acute febrile disease associated with intense edematous local inflammation of the skin and subcutaneous tissues caused by a hemolytic streptococcus

er·y·the·ma \,er-ə-'thē-mə\ *n* [NL, fr. Gk *erythēma*, fr. *erythainein* to redden, fr. *erythros*] (1766) : abnormal redness of the skin due to capillary congestion — **er·y·them·a·tous** \-'them-ət-əs\ *adj*

er·y·thor·bate \,er-ə-'thȯr-,bāt\ *n* (1963) : a salt of erythorbic acid that is used in foods as an antioxidant

er·y·thor·bic acid \-,thȯr-bik-\ *n* [*erythr-* + ascorbic acid] (1964) : a diastereoisomer of ascorbic acid with optical activity

erythr- *or* **erythro-** *comb form* [Gk, fr. *erythros* — more at RED] **1** : red ⟨*erythro*cyte⟩ **2** : erythrocyte ⟨*erythr*oid⟩

er·y·thre·mia \,er-ə-'thrē-mē-ə\ *n* [NL] (ca. 1908) : POLYCYTHEMIA VERA

er·y·thrism \'er-ə-,thriz-əm\ *n* (1864) : a condition marked by exceptional prevalence of red pigmentation (as in skin or hair) — **er·y·thris·tic** \,er-ə-'thris-tik\ *also* **er·y·thris·mal** \-'thriz-məl\ *adj*

er·y·thrite \'er-ə-,thrīt\ *n* (1844) : a mineral $Co_3(AsO_4)_2 \cdot 8H_2O$ consisting of a hydrous cobalt arsenate occurring esp. in monoclinic crystals

eryth·ro·blast \i-'rith-rə-,blast\ *n* [ISV] (ca. 1890) : a polychromatic nucleated cell of red marrow that is the first specifically identifiable stage in red blood cell formation; *broadly* : a cell ancestral to red blood cells — **eryth·ro·blas·tic** \-,rith-rə-'blas-tik\ *adj*

eryth·ro·blas·to·sis \i-,rith-rə-,blas-'tō-səs\ *n, pl* **-to·ses** \-,sēz\ [NL] (ca. 1923) : abnormal presence of erythroblasts in the circulating blood; *esp* : ERYTHROBLASTOSIS FETALIS

erythroblastosis fe·ta·lis \-fi-'tal-əs\ *n* [NL, fetal erythroblastosis] (ca. 1934) : a hemolytic disease of the fetus and newborn that occurs when the system of an Rh-negative mother produces antibodies to an antigen in the blood of an Rh-positive fetus which cross the placenta and destroy fetal erythrocytes and that is characterized by an increase in circulating erythroblasts and by jaundice

eryth·ro·cyte \i-'rith-rə-,sīt\ *n* [ISV] (ca. 1900) : RED BLOOD CELL — **eryth·ro·cyt·ic** \-,rith-rə-'sit-ik\ *adj*

ery·throid \i-'rith-,rȯid, 'er-ə-,thrȯid\ *adj* (1927) : relating to erythrocytes or their precursors

eryth·ro·my·cin \i-,rith-rə-'mīs-ᵊn\ *n* (ca. 1952) : a broad-spectrum antibiotic produced by an actinomycete (*Streptomyces erythreus*)

er·y·thron \'er-ə-,thrän\ *n* [NL, fr. Gk, neut. of *erythros*] (ca. 1935) : the red blood cells and their precursors in the bone marrow

eryth·ro·poi·e·sis \i-,rith-rō-pȯi-'ē-səs\ *n* [NL, fr. *erythr-* + Gk *poiēsis* creation — more at POESY] (1918) : the production of red blood cells (as from the bone marrow) — **eryth·ro·poi·et·ic** \-'et-ik\ *adj*

eryth·ro·poi·e·tin \-'pȯi-ət-ᵊn\ *n* [*erythropoietic* + *-in*] (1948) : a hormonal substance that is prob. formed in the kidney and stimulates red blood cell formation

eryth·ro·sin \i-'rith-rə-sən\ *also* **eryth·ro·sine** \-sən, -,sēn\ *n* [ISV *erythr-* + *eosin*] (ca. 1882) : any of several dyes made by iodination of fluorescein that yield reddish shades

1**-es** \əz, iz *after* s, z, sh, ch; z *after* v *or a vowel*\ *n pl suffix* [ME *-es*, *-s* — more at 1-s] — used to form the plural of most nouns that end in *s* ⟨glass*es*⟩, *z* ⟨fuzz*es*⟩, *sh* ⟨bush*es*⟩, *ch* ⟨peach*es*⟩, or a final *y* that changes to *i* ⟨lad*ies*⟩ and of some nouns ending in *f* that changes to *v* ⟨loav*es*⟩; compare 1-S

2**-es** *adv suffix* [ME *-es*, *-s* — more at 2-s] : 2-S

3**-es** *vb suffix* [ME — more at 3-s] — used to form the third person singular present of most verbs that end in *s* ⟨bless*es*⟩, *z* ⟨fizz*es*⟩, *sh* ⟨hush*es*⟩, *ch* ⟨catch*es*⟩, or a final *y* that changes to *i* ⟨def*ies*⟩ ; compare 3-S

Esau \'ē-(,)sȯ\ *n* [L, fr. Gk *Ēsau*, fr. Heb *'Ēsāw*] : the elder son of Isaac and Rebekah who sold his birthright to his twin brother Jacob

es·ca·drille \'es-kə-,dril, -,drē\ *n* [F, flotilla, escadrille, fr. Sp *escuadrilla*, dim. of *escuadra* squadron, squad — more at SQUAD] (1912) : a unit of a European air command containing usu. six airplanes

es·ca·lade \'es-kə-,lād, -,läd\ *n* [F, fr. It *scalata*, fr. *scalare* to scale, fr. *scala* ladder, fr. LL — more at SCALE] (ca. 1598) : an act of scaling esp. the walls of a fortification — **escalade** *vt* — **es·ca·lad·er** *n*

es·ca·late \'es-kə-,lāt, ÷-kyə-\ *vb* **-lat·ed; -lat·ing** [back-formation fr. *escalator*] *vi* (1944) : to increase in extent, volume, number, amount, intensity, or scope ⟨a little war threatens to ~ into a huge ugly one — Arnold Abrams⟩ ~ *vt* : EXPAND 2 — **es·ca·la·tion** \,es-kə-'lā-shən, ÷-kyə-\ *n* — **es·ca·la·to·ry** \'es-kə-lə-,tōr-ē, -,tȯr-, ÷ -kyə-\ *adj*

1**es·ca·la·tor** \'es-kə-,lāt-ər, ÷ -kyə-\ *n* [fr. *Escalator*, a trademark] (1900) **1 a** : a power-driven set of stairs arranged like an endless belt that ascend or descend continuously **b** : an upward course suggestive of an escalator ⟨a never-stopping ~ of economic progress —D. W. Brogan⟩ **2** : an escalator clause or provision

2**escalator** *adj* (1930) : providing for a periodic proportional upward or downward adjustment (as of prices or wages) ⟨an ~ arrangement tying the base pay . . . to living costs —*N. Y. Times*⟩

es·cal·lop \is-'käl-əp, -'kal-\ *var of* SCALLOP

es·cap·able \is-'kā-pə-bəl\ *adj* (ca. 1864) : capable of being escaped : AVOIDABLE

es·ca·pade \'es-kə-,pād\ *n* [F, action of escaping, fr. Sp. *escapada*, fr. *escapar* to escape, fr. (assumed) VL *excappare*] (1672) : a usu. adventurous action that runs counter to approved or conventional conduct ⟨childish ~*s*⟩

1**es·cape** \is-'kāp\ *vb* **es·caped; es·cap·ing** [ME *escapen*, fr. ONF *escaper*, fr. (assumed) VL *excappare*, fr. L *ex-* + LL *cappa* head covering, cloak] *vi* (13c) **1 a** : to get away (as by flight) ⟨*escaped* from prison⟩ **b** : to issue from confinement ⟨gas is *escaping*⟩ **c** *of a plant* : to run wild from cultivation **2** : to avoid a threatening evil ~ *vt* **1** : to get or stay out of the way of : AVOID **2** : to fail to be noticed or recallable by ⟨his name ~*s* me⟩ **3 a** : to issue from **b** : to be uttered involuntarily by — **es·cap·er** *n*

syn ESCAPE, AVOID, EVADE, ELUDE, SHUN, ESCHEW mean to get away or keep away from something. ESCAPE stresses the fact of getting away or being passed by not necessarily through effort or by conscious intent; AVOID stresses forethought and caution in keeping clear of danger or difficulty; EVADE implies adroitness, ingenuity, or lack of scruple in escaping or avoiding; ELUDE implies a slippery or baffling quality in the person or thing that escapes; SHUN often implies an avoiding as a matter of habitual practice or policy and may imply repugnance or abhorrence; ESCHEW implies an avoiding or abstaining from as unwise or distasteful.

²**escape** *n* (14c) **1 :** an act or instance of escaping: as **a :** flight from confinement **b :** evasion of something undesirable **c :** leakage or outflow esp. of a fluid **d :** distraction or relief from routine or reality **2 :** a means of escape **3 :** a cultivated plant run wild

³**escape** *adj* (1751) **1 :** providing a means of escape ⟨an ~ hatch⟩ ⟨~ literature⟩ **2 :** providing a means of evading a regulation, claim, or commitment ⟨an ~ clause in a contract⟩

escape artist *n* (1943) **:** one (as a showman or criminal) unusually adept at escaping from confinement

es·cap·ee \is-ˌkā-ˈpē, ˌes-(ˌ)kā-, ˌes-kə-\ *n* (1865) **:** one that has escaped; *esp* **:** an escaped prisoner

escape mechanism *n* (1927) **:** a mode of behavior or thinking adopted to evade unpleasant facts or responsibilities

es·cape·ment \is-ˈkāp-mənt\ *n* (1755) **1 a :** a device in a timepiece which controls the motion of the train of wheelwork and through which the energy of the power source is delivered to the pendulum or balance by means of impulses that permit a tooth to escape from a pallet at regular intervals **b :** a ratchet device (as the spacing mechanism of a typewriter) that permits motion in one direction only in equal steps **2 a :** the act of escaping **b :** a way of escape **:** VENT

escape velocity *n* (1934) **:** the minimum velocity that a moving body (as a rocket) must have to escape from the gravitational field of the earth or of a celestial body and move outward into space

es·cap·ism \is-ˈkā-ˌpiz-əm\ *n* (1933) **:** habitual diversion of the mind to purely imaginative activity or entertainment as an escape from reality or routine — **es·cap·ist** \-pəst\ *adj or n*

es·cap·ol·o·gy \is-ˌkā-ˈpäl-ə-jē, ˌes-(ˌ)\ *n* (1939) **:** the art or practice of escaping — **es·cap·ol·o·gist** \-jəst\ *n*

es·car·got \ˌes-ˌkär-ˈgō\ *n, pl* **-gots** \-ˈgō(z)\ [F, snail, fr. MF, fr. OProv *escaragol*] (ca. 1892) **:** a snail prepared for use as food

es·ca·role \ˈes-kə-ˌrōl\ *n* [F, fr. LL *escariola*, fr. L *escarius* of food, fr. *esca* food, fr. *edere* to eat — more at EAT] (1899) **:** ENDIVE 1

es·carp \is-ˈkärp\ *n or vt* [F *escarpe*, n., fr. It *scarpa*] (1728) **:** SCARP

es·carp·ment \-mənt\ *n* (1802) **1 :** a steep slope in front of a fortification **2 :** a long cliff or steep slope separating two comparatively level or more gently sloping surfaces and resulting from erosion or faulting

-es·cence \ˈes-ᵊn(t)s\ *n suffix* [MF, fr. L *-escentia*, fr. *-escent-*, *-escens* + *-ia* -y] **:** process of becoming ⟨hyal*escence*⟩

-es·cent \ˈes-ᵊnt\ *adj suffix* [MF, fr. L *-escent-*, *-escens*, prp. suffix of incho. verbs in *-escere*] **1 :** beginning **:** beginning to be **:** slightly ⟨frut*escent*⟩ **2 :** reflecting or emitting light (in a specified way) ⟨opal*escent*⟩

¹**es·char** \ˈes-ˌkär\ *n* [ME *escare* — more at SCAR] (1543) **:** a scab formed esp. after a burn

²**es·char** \ˈes-kər\ *var of* ESKER

es·cha·rot·ic \ˌes-kə-ˈrät-ik\ *adj* [F or LL; F *escharotique*, fr. LL *escharoticus*, fr. Gk *escharōtikos*, fr. *escharoun* to form an eschar, fr. *eschara* eschar] (1612) **:** producing an eschar — **escharotic** *n*

es·cha·to·log·i·cal \(ˌ)es-ˌkat-ᵊl-ˈäj-i-kəl, ˌes-kət-\ *adj* (1854) **1 :** of or relating to eschatology or an eschatology **2 :** of or relating to the end of the world or the events associated with it in eschatology — **es·cha·to·log·i·cal·ly** \-i-k(ə-)lē\ *adv*

es·cha·tol·o·gy \ˌes-kə-ˈtäl-ə-jē\ *n, pl* **-gies** [Gk *eschatos* last, farthest] (1844) **1 :** a branch of theology concerned with the final events in the history of the world or of mankind **2 :** a belief concerning death, the end of the world, or the ultimate destiny of mankind; *specif* **:** any of various Christian doctrines concerning the Second Coming, the resurrection of the dead, or the Last Judgment

¹**es·cheat** \is(h)-ˈchēt\ *n* [ME *eschete*, fr. OF, reversion of property, fr. *escheoir* to fall, devolve, fr. (assumed) VL *excadēre*, fr. L *ex-* + (assumed) VL *cadēre* to fall, fr. L *cadere* — more at CHANCE] (14c) **1 :** escheated property **2 a :** the reversion of lands in English feudal law to the lord of the fee when there are no heirs capable of inheriting under the original grant **b :** the reversion of property to the crown in England or to the state in the U.S. when there are no legal heirs

²**escheat** *vt* (14c) **:** to cause to revert by escheat ~ *vi* **:** to revert by escheat — **es·cheat·able** \-ə-bəl\ *adj*

es·chew \is(h)-ˈchü\ *vt* [ME *eschewen*, fr. MF *eschiuver*, of Gmc origin; akin to OHG *sciuhen* to frighten off — more at SHY] (14c) **:** to avoid habitually esp. on moral or practical grounds **:** SHUN ***syn*** see ESCAPE — **es·chew·al** \-əl\ *n*

es·co·lar \ˌes-kə-ˈlär\ *n, pl* **escolar** *or* **escolars** [Sp, lit., scholar, fr. ML *scholaris* — more at SCHOLAR] (1890) **:** a large widely distributed rough-scaled fish (*Ruvettus pretiosus*) that resembles a mackerel

¹**es·cort** \ˈes-ˌkȯ(ə)rt\ *n* [F *escorte*, fr. It *scorta*, fr. *scorgere* to guide, fr. (assumed) VL *excorrigere*, fr. L *ex-* + *corrigere* to make straight, correct — more at CORRECT] (1579) **1 a** (1) **:** a person or group of persons accompanying another to give protection or as a courtesy (2) **:** the man who goes on a date with a woman **b :** a protective screen of warships or fighter planes or a single ship or plane used to fend off enemy attack from one or more vulnerable craft **2 :** accompaniment by a person or an armed protector (as a ship)

²**es·cort** \is-ˈkȯ(ə)rt, es-, ˈes-ˌ\ *vt* (1708) **:** to accompany as an escort ***syn*** see ACCOMPANY

es·cot \is-ˈkät\ *vt* [MF *escoter*, fr. *escot* contribution, of Gmc origin; akin to ON *skot* contribution, shot — more at SHOT] *obs* (1602) **:** SUPPORT, MAINTAIN

es·cri·toire \ˈes-krə-ˌtwär\ *n* [obs. F, writing desk, scriptorium, fr. ML *scriptorium*] (1694) **:** a writing table or desk; *specif* **:** SECRETARY 4b

¹**es·crow** \ˈes-ˌkrō, es-ˈ\ *n* [MF *escroue* scroll] (1594) **1 :** a deed, a bond, money, or a piece of property held in trust by a third party to be turned over to the grantee only upon the fulfillment of a condition **2 :** a fund or deposit designed to serve as an escrow — **in escrow :** in trust as an escrow ⟨have over $1000 *in escrow* to pay taxes⟩

²**es·crow** \es-ˈkrō, ˈes-ˌ\ *vt* (1949) **:** to place in escrow

es·cu·do \is-ˈküd-(ˌ)ō\ *n, pl* **-dos** [Sp & Pg, lit., shield, fr. L *scutum*] (ca. 1821) **1 :** any of various former gold or silver coins of Hispanic countries **2** — see MONEY table **3 :** the basic monetary unit of Chile between 1960 and 1975 **4 :** the peso of Guinea-Bissau

es·cu·lent \ˈes-kyə-lənt\ *adj* [L *esculentus*, fr. *esca* food, fr. *edere* to eat — more at EAT] (1626) **:** EDIBLE — **esculent** *n*

es·cutch·eon \is-ˈkəch-ən\ *n* [ME *escochon*, fr. MF *escuchon*, fr. (assumed) VL *scution-*, *scutio*, fr. L *scutum* shield — more at ESQUIRE] (15c) **1 :** a defined area on which armorial bearings are displayed and which usu. consists of a shield **2 :** a protective or ornamental plate or flange (as around a keyhole) **3 :** the part of a ship's stern on which the name is displayed

Es·dras \ˈez-drəs\ *n* [LL, fr. Gk, fr. Heb *ʿEzrā*] **1 :** either of two books of the Roman Catholic canon of the Old Testament — see BIBLE table **2 :** either of two uncanonical books of Scripture included in the Protestant Apocrypha — see BIBLE table

¹**-ese** \ˈēz, ˈēs\ *adj suffix* [Pg *-ês* & It *-ese*, fr. L *-ensis*] **:** of, relating to, or originating in (a certain place or country) ⟨Japan*ese*⟩

²**-ese** *n suffix, pl* **-ese 1 :** native or resident of (a specified place or country) ⟨Chin*ese*⟩ **2 a :** language of (a particular place, country, or nationality) ⟨Siam*ese*⟩ **b :** speech, literary style, or diction peculiar to (a specified place, person, or group) — usu. in words applied in depreciation ⟨journal*ese*⟩

es·em·plas·tic \ˌes-ˌem-ˈplas-tik, -əm-\ *adj* [Gk *es hen* into one + E *plastic*] (1817) **:** shaping or having the power to shape disparate things into a unified whole ⟨the ~ power of the poetic imagination —W. H. Gardner⟩

es·er·ine \ˈes-ə-ˌrēn\ *n* [F *ésérine*] (1879) **:** PHYSOSTIGMINE

es·ker \ˈes-kər\ *n* [IrGael *eiscir* ridge] (1848) **:** a long narrow ridge or mound of sand, gravel, and boulders deposited by a stream flowing on, within, or beneath a stagnant glacier

Es·ki·mo \ˈes-kə-ˌmō\ *n* [Dan, of Algonquian origin; akin to Cree *askimowew* he eats it raw] (1689) **1** *pl* **Eskimo** *or* **Eskimos a :** a group of peoples of northern Canada, Greenland, Alaska, and eastern Siberia **b :** a member of such people **2 :** the language of the Eskimo people — **Es·ki·mo·an** \ˌes-kə-ˈmō-ən\ *adj*

Eskimo curlew *n* (1813) **:** a New World curlew (*Numenius borealis*) that breeds in northern No. America and winters in So. America and is now extremely rare

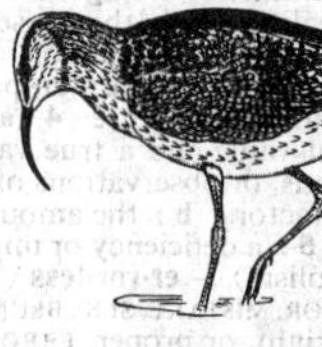
Eskimo curlew

Eskimo dog *n* (1774) **:** a sled dog of American origin

ESOP \ˌē-ˌes-(ˌ)ō-ˈpē, ˈē-ˌsäp\ *n* [*em*ployee *s*tock *o*wnership *p*lan] (1975) **:** a program by which a corporation's employees acquire its capital stock

esophag- *or* **esophago-** *comb form* **:** esophagus ⟨*esophag*ectomy⟩ **:** esophageal and ⟨*esophago*gastric⟩

esoph·a·ge·al \i-ˌsäf-ə-ˈjē-əl\ *adj* (1807) **:** of or relating to the esophagus

esoph·a·gus \i-ˈsäf-ə-gəs\ *n, pl* **-gi** \-ˌgī, -ˌjī\ [ME *ysophagus*, fr. Gk *oisophagos*, fr. *oisein* to be going to carry + *phagein* to eat — more at BAKSHEESH] (14c) **:** a muscular tube that in man is about nine inches long and passes from the pharynx down the neck between the trachea and the spinal column and behind the left bronchus where it pierces the diaphragm slightly to the left of the middle line and joins the cardiac end of the stomach

es·o·ter·ic \ˌes-ə-ˈter-ik\ *adj* [LL *esotericus*, fr. Gk *esōterikos*, fr. *esōterō*, compar. of *eisō*, *esō* within, fr. *eis* into, fr. *en* in — more at IN] (1655) **1 a :** designed for or understood by the specially initiated alone ⟨a body of ~ legal doctrine —B. N. Cardozo⟩ **b :** of or relating to knowledge that is restricted to a small group **2 a :** limited to a small circle ⟨~ pursuits⟩ **b :** PRIVATE, CONFIDENTIAL ⟨an ~ purpose⟩ — **es·o·ter·i·cal·ly** \-i-k(ə-)lē\ *adv*

es·o·ter·i·ca \-i-kə\ *n pl* [NL, fr. Gk *esōterika*, neut. pl. of *esōterikos*] (1929) **:** esoteric items

es·o·ter·i·cism \-ˈter-ə-ˌsiz-əm\ *n* (1846) **1 :** esoteric doctrines or practices **2 :** the quality or state of being esoteric

ESP \ˌē-ˌes-ˈpē\ *n* [*e*xtra*s*ensory *p*erception] (1934) **:** extrasensory perception

es·pa·drille \ˈes-pə-ˌdril\ *n* [F, alter. of *espardille*, deriv. of L *spartum*] (1892) **:** a flat sandal usu. having a fabric upper and a flexible sole

¹**es·pal·ier** \is-ˈpal-yər, -ˌyā\ *n* [F, deriv. of It *spalla* shoulder, fr. LL *spatula* shoulder blade — more at EPAULET] (1662) **1 :** a plant (as a fruit tree) trained to grow flat against a support (as a wall or trellis) **2 :** a railing or trellis on which fruit trees or shrubs are trained to grow flat

²**espalier** *vt* (1810) **1 :** to train as an espalier **2 :** to furnish with an espalier

es·par·to \is-ˈpärt-(ˌ)ō\ *n, pl* **-tos** [Sp, fr. L *spartum*, fr. Gk *sparton* — more at SPIRE] (1845) **1 :** either of two Spanish and Algerian grasses (*Stipa tenacissima* and *Lygeum spartum*) used esp. to make cordage, shoes, and paper — called also *esparto grass* **2 :** the fiber of esparto

es·pe·cial \is-ˈpesh-əl\ *adj* [ME, fr. MF — more at SPECIAL] (14c) **:** being distinctive: as **a :** directed toward a particular individual, group, or end ⟨sent ~ greetings to his son⟩ ⟨took ~ care to speak clearly⟩ **b :** of special note or importance **:** unusually great or significant ⟨a decision of ~ relevance⟩ **c :** highly distinctive or personal **:** PECULIAR ⟨had an ~ dislike for music⟩ **d :** CLOSE, INTIMATE ⟨his ~ crony⟩ **e :** SPECIFIC, PARTICULAR ⟨had no ~ destination in mind⟩ ***syn*** see SPECIAL — **es·pe·cial·ly** \-ˈpesh-(ə-)lē\ *adv* — **in especial :** in particular

es·per·ance \ˈes-p(ə-)rən(t)s\ *n* [ME *esperaunce*, fr. MF *esperance*] *obs* (15c) **:** HOPE, EXPECTATION

Es·pe·ran·to \ˌes-pə-ˈrant-(ˌ)ō, -ˈrän-(ˌ)tō\ *n* [Dr. *Esperanto*, pseudonym of L. L. Zamenhof †1917 Pol. oculist, its inventor] (1892) **:** an artificial international language based as far as possible on words common to the chief European languages — **Es·pe·ran·tist** \-ˈrant-əst, -ˈränt-\ *n or adj*

es·pi·al \is-ˈpī(-ə)l\ *n* (14c) **1 :** OBSERVATION **2 :** an act of noticing **:** DISCOVERY

es·piè·gle \es-pyeglᵊ\ *adj* [F, after *Ulespiegle* (Till Eulenspiegel), peasant prankster] (1816) **:** FROLICSOME, ROGUISH

es·piè·gle·rie \es-pyeg-lə-rē\ *n* [F, fr. *espiègle*] (1816) **:** the quality or state of being roguish or frolicsome
es·pi·o·nage \'es-pē-ə-ˌnäzh, -ˌnäj, -nij, *Canad also* -ˌnazh; ˌes-pē-ə-'näzh; is-'pē-ə-nij\ *n* [F *espionnage,* fr. MF, fr. *espionner* to spy, fr. *espion* spy, fr. OIt *spione,* fr. *spia,* of Gmc origin; akin to OHG *spehōn* to spy — more at SPY] (1793) **:** the practice of spying or the use of spies to obtain information about the plans and activities esp. of a foreign government or a competing company ⟨industrial ~⟩
es·pla·nade \'es-plə-ˌnäd, ˌes-plə-' *also* -'nād *or* -ˌnād\ *n* [MF, fr. It *spianata,* fr. *spianare* to level, fr. L *explanare* — more at EXPLAIN] (1591) **:** a level open stretch of paved or grassy ground; *esp* **:** one designed for walking or driving along a shore
es·pous·al \is-'pau̇-zəl *also* -səl\ *n* (14c) **1 a :** BETROTHAL **b :** WEDDING **c :** MARRIAGE **2 :** a taking up or adopting of a cause or belief
es·pouse \is-'pau̇z *also* -'pau̇s\ *vt* **es·poused; es·pous·ing** [ME *espousen,* fr. MF *espouser,* fr. LL *sponsare* to betroth, fr. L *sponsus* betrothed — more at SPOUSE] (15c) **1 :** MARRY **2 :** to take up and support as a cause **:** become attached to ⟨~ the problems of minority groups⟩ ***syn*** see ADOPT — **es·pous·er** *n*
es·pres·so \e-'spres-(ˌ)ō\ *n, pl* **-sos** [It *(caffè) espresso,* lit., pressed out coffee] (1945) **:** coffee brewed by forcing steam through finely ground darkly roasted coffee beans
es·prit \is-'prē\ *n* [F, fr. L *spiritus* spirit] (1591) **1 :** vivacious cleverness or wit **2 :** ESPRIT DE CORPS
es·prit de corps \is-ˌprēd-ə-'kō(ə)r, -'kȯ(ə)r\ *n* [F] (1780) **:** the common spirit existing in the members of a group and inspiring enthusiasm, devotion, and strong regard for the honor of the group
es·py \is-'pī\ *vt* **es·pied; es·py·ing** [ME *espien,* fr. OF *espier* — more at SPY] (14c) **:** to catch sight of ⟨among the several horses . . . she *espied* the white mustang —Zane Grey⟩
-esque \'esk\ *adj suffix* [F, fr. It *-esco,* of Gmc origin; akin to OHG *-isc* -ish — more at -ISH] **:** in the manner or style of **:** like ⟨statuesque⟩
Es·qui·mau \'es-kə-ˌmō\ *n, pl* **Esquimau** *or* **Es·qui·maux** \-ˌmō(z)\ [F, of Algonquian origin] (1584) **:** ESKIMO
es·quire \'es-ˌkwī(ə)r, is-'\ *n* [ME, fr. MF *esquier* squire, fr. LL *scutarius,* fr. L *scutum* shield; akin to OHG *sceida* sheath] (15c) **1 :** a member of the English gentry ranking below a knight **2 :** a candidate for knighthood serving as shield bearer and attendant to a knight **3** — used as a title of courtesy usu. placed in its abbreviated form after the surname ⟨John R. Smith, *Esq.*⟩ **4** *archaic* **:** a landed proprietor
ess \'es\ *n* (1540) **1 :** the letter *s* **2 :** something resembling the letter *S* in shape; *esp* **:** an S-shaped curve in a road
-ess \əs, is, *also* ˌes\ *n suffix* [ME *-esse,* fr. OF, fr. LL *-issa,* fr. Gk] **:** female ⟨giantess⟩
1es·say \e-'sā, ə-'sā, 'es-ˌā\ *vt* (14c) **1 a :** to put to a test **b :** 2ASSAY 2a **2 :** to make an often tentative or experimental effort to perform **:** TRY ***syn*** see ATTEMPT — **es·say·er** *n*
2es·say \'es-ˌā; *senses 1, 2 & 4 also* e-'sā\ *n* [MF *essai,* fr. LL *exagium* act of weighing, fr. *ex-* + *agere* to drive — more at AGENT] (14c) **1 :** TRIAL, TEST **2 a :** EFFORT, ATTEMPT; *esp* **:** an initial tentative effort **b :** the result or product of an attempt **3 a :** an analytic or interpretative literary composition usu. dealing with its subject from a limited or personal point of view **b :** something resembling such a composition ⟨a photographic ~⟩ **4 :** a proof of an unaccepted design for a stamp or piece of paper money
es·say·ist \'es-ˌā-əst\ *n* (1601) **:** a writer of essays
es·say·is·tic \ˌes-(ˌ)ā-'is-tik\ *adj* (1855) **1 :** of or relating to an essay or an essayist **2 :** resembling an essay in quality or character
essay question *n* (1947) **:** an examination question that requires an answer in a sentence, paragraph, or short composition
es·sence \'es-ᵊn(t)s\ *n* [ME, fr. MF & L; MF, fr. L *essentia,* fr. *esse* to be — more at IS] (14c) **1 a :** the permanent as contrasted with the accidental element of being **b :** the individual, real, or ultimate nature of a thing esp. as opposed to its existence **c :** the properties or attributes by means of which something can be placed in its proper class or identified as being what it is **2 :** something that exists **:** ENTITY **3 a** (1) **:** a volatile substance or constituent (as of perfume) (2) **:** a constituent or derivative (as an extract or essential oil) possessing the special qualities (as of a plant or drug) in concentrated form; *also* **:** a preparation (as an alcoholic solution) of such an essence or a synthetic substitute **b :** ODOR, PERFUME **4 :** one that possesses or exhibits a quality in abundance as if in concentrated form ⟨she was the ~ of punctuality⟩ — **in essence :** in or by its very nature **:** ESSENTIALLY, BASICALLY ⟨was *in essence* an honest person⟩ — **of the essence :** of the utmost importance **:** ESSENTIAL ⟨time was *of the essence*⟩
Es·sene \is-'ēn, 'es-ˌēn\ *n* [Gk *Essēnos*] (1553) **:** a member of a monastic brotherhood of Jews in Palestine from the 2d century B.C. to the 2d century A.D. — **Es·se·ni·an** \is-'ē-nē-ən, es-\ *or* **Es·se·nic** \-'en-ik, -'ē-nik\ *adj* — **Es·se·nism** \-'ē-ˌniz-əm\ *n*
1es·sen·tial \i-'sen-chəl\ *adj* (14c) **1 :** of, relating to, or constituting essence **:** INHERENT **2 :** of the utmost importance **:** BASIC, INDISPENSABLE, NECESSARY ⟨~ foods⟩ ⟨an ~ requirement for admission to college⟩ **3 :** IDIOPATHIC ⟨~ disease⟩ — **es·sen·tial·ly** \-'sench-(ə-)lē\ *adv* — **es·sen·tial·ness** \-'sen-chəl-nəs\ *n*
syn ESSENTIAL, FUNDAMENTAL, VITAL, CARDINAL mean so important as to be indispensable. ESSENTIAL implies belonging to the very nature of a thing and therefore being incapable of removal without destroying the thing itself or its character; FUNDAMENTAL applies to something that is a foundation without which an entire system or complex whole would collapse; VITAL suggests something that is necessary to a thing's continued existence or operation; CARDINAL suggests something on which an outcome turns or depends.
2essential *n* (15c) **1 :** something basic ⟨the ~s of astronomy⟩ **2 :** something necessary, indispensable, or unavoidable
essential amino acid *n* (1938) **:** an amino acid (as lysine) that is required for normal health and growth, is manufactured in the body in insufficient quantities or not at all, and is usu. supplied by dietary protein
es·sen·tial·ism \-ˌliz-əm\ *n* (1927) **1 :** an educational theory that ideas and skills basic to a culture should be taught to all alike by time-tested methods — compare PROGRESSIVISM **2 :** a philosophical theory ascribing ultimate reality to essence embodied in a thing perceptible to the senses — compare NOMINALISM — **es·sen·tial·ist** \-ləst\ *adj or n*
es·sen·ti·al·i·ty \i-ˌsen-chē-'al-ət-ē\ *n, pl* **-ties** (1616) **1 a :** essential nature **:** ESSENCE **b :** an essential quality, property, or aspect **2 :** the quality or state of being essential ⟨the ~ of freedom and justice —P. G. Hoffman⟩
es·sen·tial·ize \i-'sen-chə-ˌlīz\ *vt* **-ized; -iz·ing** (1913) **:** to express or formulate in essential form **:** reduce to essentials
essential oil *n* (1674) **:** any of a class of volatile oils that impart the characteristic odors to plants and are used esp. in perfumes and flavorings — compare FIXED OIL
es·soin \is-'ȯin\ *n* [ME *essoine,* fr. MF, fr. ML *essonium,* fr. L *ex-* + LL *sonium* care, worry] (14c) **1 :** an excuse for not appearing in an English law court at the appointed time **2** *obs* **:** EXCUSE, DELAY
es·so·nite \'es-ᵊn-ˌīt\ *n* [F, fr. Gk *hēsson* inferior; fr. its being less hard than true hyacinth] (1820) **:** a yellow to brown garnet
1-est \əst, ist\ *adj suffix or adv suffix* [ME, fr. OE *-st, -est, -ost;* akin to OHG *-isto* (adj. superl. suffix), Gk *-istos*] — used to form the superlative degree of adjectives and adverbs of one syllable ⟨fattest⟩ ⟨latest⟩, of some adjectives and adverbs of two syllables ⟨luckiest⟩ ⟨oftenest⟩, and less often of longer ones ⟨beggarliest⟩
2-est \əst, ist\ *or* **-st** \st\ *vb suffix* [ME, fr. OE *-est, -ast, -st;* akin to OHG *-ist, -ōst, -ēst,* 2d sing. ending] — used to form the archaic 2d person singular of English verbs (with *thou*) ⟨gettest⟩ ⟨didst⟩
es·tab·lish \is-'tab-lish\ *vt* [ME *establissen,* fr. MF *establiss-,* stem of *establir,* fr. L *stabilire,* fr. *stabilis* stable] (15c) **1 a :** to make firm or stable **b :** to introduce and cause to grow and multiply ⟨~ grass on pasturelands⟩ **2 :** to institute (as a law) permanently by enactment or agreement **3** *obs* **:** SETTLE 7 **4 a :** to bring into existence **:** FOUND ⟨~*ed* a republic⟩ **b :** BRING ABOUT, EFFECT ⟨~*ed* friendly relations⟩ **5 a :** to put on a firm basis **:** SET UP ⟨~ his son in business⟩ **b :** to put into a favorable position **c :** to gain full recognition or acceptance of ⟨the performance ~*ed* her as a good actress⟩ **6 :** to make (a church) a national institution **7 :** to put beyond doubt **:** PROVE ⟨~*ed* my innocence⟩
established church *n* (1660) **:** a church recognized by law as the official church of a nation and supported by civil authority
es·tab·lish·ment \is-'tab-lish-mənt\ *n* (15c) **1 :** something established: as **a :** a settled arrangement; *esp* **:** a code of laws **b :** ESTABLISHED CHURCH **c :** a permanent civil or military organization **d :** a place of business or residence with its furnishings and staff **e :** a public or private institution **2 :** an established order of society: as **a** *often cap* **:** a group of social, economic, and political leaders who form a ruling class (as of a nation) **b** *often cap* **:** a controlling group ⟨the literary ~⟩ **3 a :** the act of establishing **b :** the state of being established
es·tab·lish·men·tar·i·an \is-ˌtab-lish-mən-'ter-ē-ən, -ˌmen-\ *adj* (1847) **:** of, relating to, or favoring the social or political establishment — **establishmentarian** *n* — **es·tab·lish·men·tar·i·an·ism** \-ē-ə-ˌniz-əm\ *n*
es·ta·mi·net \e-stá-mē-nā\ *n, pl* **-nets** \-nā(z)\ [F] (1814) **:** a small café **:** BISTRO
es·tate \is-'tāt\ *n* [ME *estat,* fr. OF — more at STATE] (13c) **1 :** STATE, CONDITION **2 :** social standing or rank esp. of a high order **3 :** a social or political class; *specif* **:** one of the great classes (as the nobility, the clergy, and the commons) formerly vested with distinct political powers **4 a :** the degree, quality, nature, and extent of one's interest in land or other property **b** (1) **:** POSSESSIONS, PROPERTY; *esp* **:** a person's property in land and tenements ⟨a man of small ~⟩ (2) **:** the assets and liabilities left by a person at death **c :** a landed property usu. with a large house on it **5** *Brit* **:** ESTATE CAR
estate agent *n, Brit* (1880) **:** a real estate broker or manager
estate car *n, Brit* (1950) **:** STATION WAGON
estate tax *n* (ca. 1910) **:** an excise in the form of a percentage of the net estate that is levied on the privilege of an owner of property of transmitting his property to others after his death — compare INHERITANCE TAX 1
1es·teem \is-'tēm\ *n* (14c) **1** *archaic* **:** WORTH, VALUE **2** *archaic* **:** OPINION, JUDGMENT **3 :** the regard in which one is held; *esp* **:** high regard ⟨the ~ we all feel for her⟩
2esteem *vt* [ME *estemen* to estimate, fr. MF *estimer,* fr. L *aestimare*] (15c) **1** *archaic* **:** APPRAISE **2 a :** to view as **:** CONSIDER ⟨~ it a privilege⟩ **b :** THINK, BELIEVE **3 :** to set a high value on **:** regard highly and prize accordingly ***syn*** see REGARD
es·ter \'es-tər\ *n* [G, fr. *essigäther* ethyl acetate, fr. *essig* vinegar (fr. OHG *ezzīh,* fr. L *acetum*) + *äther* ether — more at ACETIC] (ca. 1852) **:** any of a class of often fragrant compounds formed by the reaction between an acid and an alcohol usu. with elimination of water
es·ter·ase \'es-tə-ˌrās, -ˌrāz\ *n* (1910) **:** an enzyme that accelerates the hydrolysis or synthesis of esters
es·ter·i·fy \e-'ster-ə-ˌfī\ *vt* **-fied; -fy·ing** (ca. 1905) **:** to convert into an ester — **es·ter·i·fi·ca·tion** \-ˌster-ə-fə-'kā-shən\ *n*
Es·ther \'es-tər\ *n* [L, fr. Heb *Estēr*] **1 :** the Jewish heroine of the Old Testament book of Esther **2 :** a narrative book of canonical Jewish and Christian Scripture — see BIBLE table
es·the·sia \es-'thē-zh(ē-)ə\ *n* [NL, back-formation fr. *anesthesia*] (1879) **:** capacity for sensation and feeling **:** SENSIBILITY
esthesio- *or* **aesthesio-** *comb form* [Gk *aisthēsis*] **:** sensation ⟨*esthesio*logy⟩
es·the·sis \es-'thē-səs\ *n* [NL, fr. Gk *aisthēsis,* fr. *aisthanesthai* to perceive — more at AUDIBLE] (ca. 1851) **:** SENSATION; *esp* **:** rudimentary sensation
esthete, esthetic, esthetician, estheticism, esthetics *var of* AESTHETE, AESTHETIC, AESTHETICIAN, AESTHETICISM, AESTHETICS
es·ti·ma·ble \'es-tə-mə-bəl\ *adj* (15c) **1 :** capable of being estimated **2** *archaic* **:** VALUABLE **3 :** worthy of esteem — **es·ti·ma·ble·ness** *n*
1es·ti·mate \'es-tə-ˌmāt\ *vt* **-mat·ed; -mat·ing** [L *aestimatus,* pp. of *aestimare* to value, estimate, fr. *aes* copper — more at ORE] (1532) **1** *archaic* **a :** ESTEEM **b :** APPRAISE **2 a :** to judge tentatively or approximately the value, worth, or significance of **b :** to determine roughly

the size, extent, or nature of **c** : to produce a statement of the approximate cost of **3** : JUDGE, CONCLUDE — **es·ti·ma·tive** \-,māt-iv\ *adj*
syn ESTIMATE, APPRAISE, EVALUATE, VALUE, RATE ASSESS mean to judge something with respect to its worth or significance. ESTIMATE implies a judgment, considered or casual, that precedes or takes the place of actual measuring or counting or testing out; APPRAISE commonly implies the fixing by an expert of the monetary worth of a thing, but it may be used of any critical judgment; EVALUATE suggests an attempt to determine either the relative or intrinsic worth of something in terms other than monetary; VALUE equals APPRAISE but without implying expertness of judgment; RATE adds to ESTIMATE the notion of placing a thing according to a scale of values; ASSESS implies a critical appraisal for the purpose of understanding or interpreting, or as a guide in taking action.

2es·ti·mate \'es-tə-mət\ *n* (1563) **1** : the act of appraising or valuing : CALCULATION **2** : an opinion or judgment of the nature, character, or quality of a person or thing ⟨had a high ~ of his abilities⟩ **3 a** : a rough or approximate calculation **b** : a numerical value obtained from a statistical sample and assigned to a population parameter **4** : a statement of the cost of work to be done

es·ti·ma·tion \,es-tə-'mā-shən\ *n* (14c) **1** : JUDGMENT, OPINION **2 a** : the act of estimating something **b** : the value, amount, or size arrived at in an estimate **3** : ESTEEM, HONOR

es·ti·ma·tor \'es-tə-,māt-ər\ *n* (1611) **1** : one that estimates **2** : ESTIMATE 3b; *also* : a statistical function whose value for a sample furnishes an estimate of a population parameter

es·ti·val \'es-tə-vəl\ *adj* [ME, fr. MF or L; MF, fr. L *aestivalis,* fr. *aestivus* of summer, fr. *aestas* summer — more at EDIFY] (14c) : of or relating to the summer

es·ti·vate \-,vāt\ *vi* **-vat·ed; -vat·ing** (1626) **1** : to spend the summer usu. at one place **2** : to pass the summer in a state of torpor — compare HIBERNATE

es·ti·va·tion \,es-tə-'vā-shən\ *n* (1625) : the state of one that estivates

Es·to·nian \e-'stō-nē-ən, -nyən\ *n* (1795) **1** : a member of a Finno-Ugric-speaking people of Estonia **2** : the Finno-Ugric language of the Estonian people — **Estonian** *adj*

es·top \e-'stäp\ *vt* **es·topped; es·top·ping** [ME *estoppen,* fr. MF *estouper* fr. (assumed) VL *stuppare* to stop with a tow — more at STOP] (15c) **1** *archaic* : to stop up **2** : STOP, BAR; *specif* : to impede by estoppel

es·top·pel \e-'stäp-əl\ *n* [prob. fr. MF *estoupail* bung, fr. *estouper*] (1531) : a legal bar to alleging or denying a fact because of one's own previous actions or words to the contrary

estr- *or* **estro-** *or* **oestr-** *or* **oestro-** *comb form* : estrus ⟨*estr*ogen⟩

es·tra·di·ol \,es-trə-'dī-,ȯl, -,ōl\ *n* [ISV *estra-* (fr. *estrin*) + *di-* + *-ol*] (1934) : an estrogenic hormone that is a phenolic steroid alcohol $C_{18}H_{24}O_2$ usu. made synthetically and that is often used combined as an ester esp. in treating menopausal symptoms

es·tral cycle \,es-trəl-\ *n* (1941) : ESTROUS CYCLE

es·trange \is-'trānj\ *vt* **es·tranged; es·trang·ing** [ME *estrangen,* fr. MF *estranger,* fr. ML *extraneare,* fr. L *extraneus* strange — more at STRANGE] (15c) **1** : to remove from customary environment or associations **2** : to arouse esp. mutual enmity or indifference in where there had formerly been love, affection, or friendliness : ALIENATE — **es·trange·ment** \-'trānj-mənt\ *n* — **es·trang·er** *n*
syn ESTRANGE, ALIENATE, DISAFFECT, WEAN mean to cause one to break a bond of affection or loyalty. ESTRANGE implies the development of indifference or hostility with consequent separation or divorcement; ALIENATE may or may not suggest separation but always implies loss of affection or interest; DISAFFECT refers esp. to those from whom loyalty is expected and stresses the effects (as rebellion or discontent) of alienation without actual separation; WEAN implies separation from something having a strong hold on one.

1es·tray \is-'trā\ *vi* [MF *estraier*] *archaic* (1535) : STRAY

2estray *n* (1581) : STRAY 1

es·trin \'es-trən\ *n* [NL *estrus*] (ca. 1926) : an estrogenic hormone; *esp* : ESTRONE

es·tri·ol \'es-,trī-,ȯl, e-'strī-, -,ōl\ *n* [*estrin* + *tri-* + *-ol*] (1933) : a crystalline estrogenic hormone that is a glycol $C_{18}H_{24}O_3$ usu. obtained from the urine of pregnant women

es·tro·gen \'es-trə-jən\ *n* [NL *estrus* + ISV *-o-* + *-gen*] (1927) : a substance (as a sex hormone) tending to promote estrus and stimulate the development of female secondary sex characteristics

es·tro·gen·ic \,es-trə-'jen-ik\ *adj* (1930) **1** : promoting estrus **2** : of, relating to, caused by, or being an estrogen — **es·tro·gen·i·cal·ly** \-i-k(ə-)lē\ *adv*

es·trone \'es-,trōn\ *n* [ISV, fr. *estrin*] (1933) : an estrogenic hormone that is a ketone $C_{18}H_{22}O_2$, is usu. obtained from the urine of pregnant females, and is used similarly to estradiol

es·trous \'es-trəs\ *adj* (1900) **1** : of, relating to, or characteristic of estrus **2** : being in heat

estrous cycle *n* (1900) : the correlated phenomena of the endocrine and generative systems of a female mammal from the beginning of one period of estrus to the beginning of the next — called also *estral cycle*

es·tru·al \'es-trə-wəl\ *adj* (ca. 1857) : ESTROUS

es·trus \'es-trəs\ *or* **es·trum** \-trəm\ *n* [NL, fr. L *oestrus* gadfly, frenzy, fr. Gk *oistros* — more at IRE] (ca. 1890) **1 a** : a regularly recurrent state of sexual excitability during which the female of most mammals will accept the male and is capable of conceiving : HEAT **b** : a single occurrence of this state **2** : ESTROUS CYCLE

es·tu·ar·i·al \,es(h)-chə-'wer-ē-əl\ *adj* (1883) : ESTUARINE

es·tu·a·rine \'es(h)-chə-wə-,rīn, -,rēn\ *adj* (1849) : of, relating to, or formed in an estuary ⟨~ currents⟩ ⟨~ animals⟩ ⟨~ environment⟩

es·tu·ary \'es(h)-chə-,wer-ē\ *n, pl* **-ar·ies** [L *aestuarium,* fr. *aestus* boiling, tide; akin to L *aestas* summer — more at AESTIVAL] (1538) : a water passage where the tide meets a river current; *esp* : an arm of the sea at the lower end of a river

esu·ri·ence \i-'su̇r-ē-ən(t)s, -'zu̇r-\ *n* (1825) : the quality or state of being esurient

esu·ri·ent \-ənt\ *adj* [L *esurient-, esuriens,* prp. of *esurire* to be hungry; akin to L *edere* to eat — more at EAT] (1672) : HUNGRY, GREEDY — **esu·ri·ent·ly** *adv*

et \'et\ *dial past and past part of* EAT

1-et \'et, ,et, ət, it\ *n suffix* [ME, fr. OF *-et,* masc., & *-ete,* fem., fr. LL *-itus* & *-ita*] : small one ⟨baron*et*⟩ ⟨cellar*et*⟩

2-et *n suffix* [as in *duet*] : group ⟨oct*et*⟩

eta \'āt-ə, 'ēt-ə\ *n* [ME, fr. LL, fr. Gk *ēta,* of Sem origin; akin to Heb *ḥēth* heth] (15c) : the 7th letter of the Greek alphabet — see ALPHABET table

éta·gère *or* **eta·gere** \,ā-,tä-'zhe(ə)r, ,āt-ə-\ *n* [F *étagère,* fr. MF *estagiere,* fr. *estage* floor of a building, station, fr. OF — more at STAGE] (1851) : a piece of furniture consisting of a set of open shelves for displaying small objects and sometimes having an enclosed cabinet as a base

eta·mine \'at-ə-,mēn\ *n* [F *étamine*] (1714) : a light cotton or worsted fabric with an open mesh

etat·ism \ā-'tät-,iz-əm\ *n* [F *étatisme,* fr. *état* state, fr. OF *estat* — more at STATE] (1923) : STATE SOCIALISM — **etat·ist** \-'tät-əst\ *adj*

et·cet·era \et-'set-ə-rə, -'se-trə *also* it-\ *n* (1656) **1** : a number of unspecified additional persons or things **2** *pl* : unspecified additional items : ODDS AND ENDS

et cet·era \et-'set-ə-rə, -'se-trə *also* it-\ [L] (bef. 12c) : and others esp. of the same kind : and so forth

1etch \'ech\ *vb* [D *etsen,* fr. G *ätzen,* to corrode, to eat into, fr. OHG *azzen* to cause to eat; akin to OHG *ezzan* to eat — more at EAT] *vt* (1634) **1 a** : to produce esp. on metal or glass by the corrosive action of an acid **b** : to subject to such etching **2** : to delineate or impress clearly ⟨scenes ~*ed* in our minds⟩ ⟨pain was ~*ed* on his features⟩ ~ *vi* : to practice etching — **etch·er** *n*

2etch *n* (1896) **1** : the action or effect of an etching acid on a surface **2** : a chemical agent used in etching

etch·ing *n* (1634) **1 a** : the act or process of etching **b** : the art of producing pictures or designs by printing from an etched metal plate **2 a** : an etched design **b** : an impression from an etched plate

1eter·nal \i-'tərn-ᵊl\ *adj* [ME, fr. MF, fr. LL *aeternalis,* fr. L *aeternus* eternal; akin to L *aevum* age, eternity — more at AYE] (14c) **1 a** : having infinite duration : EVERLASTING **b** : of or relating to eternity **c** : characterized by abiding fellowship with God ⟨good teacher, what must I do to inherit ~ life? —Mk 10:17 (RSV)⟩ **2 a** : continued without intermission : PERPETUAL **b** : seemingly endless **3** *archaic* : INFERNAL **4** : valid or existing at all times : TIMELESS ⟨~ verities⟩ — **eter·nal·ize** \-ᵊl-,īz\ *vt* — **eter·nal·ly** \-ᵊl-ē\ *adv* — **eter·nal·ness** *n*

2eternal *n* (1582) **1** *cap* : GOD 1 — used with *the* **2** : something eternal

eterne \i-'tərn\ *adj* [ME, fr. MF, fr. L *aeternus*] *archaic* (14c) : ETERNAL

eter·ni·ty \i-'tər-nət-ē\ *n, pl* **-ties** [ME *eternite,* fr. MF *eternité,* fr. L *aeternitat-, aeternitas,* fr. *aeternus*] (14c) **1** : the quality or state of being eternal **2** : infinite time **3** *pl* : AGE 2c **4** : the state after death : IMMORTALITY **5** : a seemingly endless or immeasurable time ⟨the speaker droned on for an ~⟩

eter·nize \i-'tər-,nīz\ *vt* **-nized; -niz·ing** (1580) **1 a** : to make eternal **b** : to prolong indefinitely **2** : IMMORTALIZE — **eter·ni·za·tion** \-,tər-nə-'zā-shən\ *n*

ete·sian \i-'tē-zhən\ *adj, often cap* [L *etesius,* fr. Gk *etēsios,* fr. *etos* year — more at WETHER] (1601) : recurring annually — used of summer winds that blow over the Mediterranean — **etesian** *n, often cap*

eth \'eth\ *var of* EDH

eth- *or* **etho-** *comb form* [ISV] : ethyl ⟨*eth*aldehyde⟩ ⟨*etho*chloride⟩

1-eth \əth, ith\ *or* **-th** \th\ *vb suffix* [ME, fr. OE *-eth, -ath, -th;* akin to OHG *-it, -ōt, -ēt,* 3d sing. ending, L *-t, -it*] — used to form the archaic third person singular present of verbs ⟨go*eth*⟩ ⟨do*th*⟩

2-eth — see -TH

eth·a·cryn·ic acid \,eth-ə-,krin-ik-\ *n* [perh. fr. *eth-* + *acetic* + *butyryl* + *phenol*] (1964) : a potent synthetic diuretic $C_{13}H_{12}Cl_2O_4$ used esp. in the treatment of edema

eth·am·bu·tol \eth-'am-byu̇-,tȯl, -,tōl\ *n* [*ethylene* + *amine* + *butanol*] (1965) : a compound $C_{10}H_{24}N_2O_2$ used esp. in the treatment of tuberculosis

eth·ane \'eth-,ān\ *n* [ISV, fr. *ethyl*] (ca. 1890) : a colorless odorless gaseous hydrocarbon C_2H_6 found in natural gas and used esp. as a fuel

eth·a·nol \'eth-ə-,nȯl, -,nōl\ *n* (1900) : ALCOHOL 1

eth·a·nol·amine \,eth-ə-'näl-ə-,mēn, -'nōl-\ *n* (1897) : a colorless liquid amino alcohol C_2H_7NO used esp. as a solvent in synthesis of detergents and in gas purification

eth·ene \'eth-,ēn\ *n* (ca. 1873) : ETHYLENE

eth·e·phon \'eth-ə-,fän\ *n* [*ethyl* + *phos*phonic acid (a dibasic organic acid)] (1971) : a synthetic plant growth regulator $C_2H_6ClO_3P$ that induces flowering and abscission by promoting the release of ethylene and has been used to cause early ripening (as of apples on the tree)

ether \'ē-thər\ *n* [ME, fr. L *aether,* fr. Gk *aithēr,* fr. *aithein* to ignite, blaze; akin to Gk *aithos* fire, OE *ād* pyre — more at EDIFY] (14c) **1 a** : the rarefied element formerly believed to fill the upper regions of space **b** : the upper regions of space : HEAVENS **2 a** : a medium that in the undulatory theory of light permeates all space and transmits transverse waves **b** : the medium that transmits radio waves **3 a** : a light volatile flammable liquid $C_4H_{10}O$ used chiefly as a solvent and anesthetic **b** : any of various organic compounds characterized by an oxygen atom attached to two carbon atoms — **ethe·ric** \i-'ther-ik, -'thir-\ *adj*

ethe·re·al \i-'thir-ē-əl\ *adj* (1513) **1 a** : of or relating to the regions beyond the earth **b** : CELESTIAL, HEAVENLY **c** : UNWORLDLY, SPIRITUAL **2 a** : lacking material substance : IMMATERIAL, INTANGIBLE **b** : marked by unusual delicacy and refinement ⟨this smallest, most ~, and daintiest of birds —William Beebe⟩ **3** : relating to, containing, or resembling a chemical ether — **ethe·re·al·i·ty** \-,thir-ē-'al-ət-ē\ *n* — **ethe·re·al·iza·tion** \-ē-ə-lə-'zā-shən\ *n* — **ethe·re·al·ize** \-'thir-ē-ə-,līz\ *vt* — **ethe·re·al·ly** \-ē-ə-lē\ *adv* — **ethe·re·al·ness** *n*

ether extract *n* (ca. 1900) : the part of a complex organic material that is soluble in ether and consists chiefly of fats and fatty acids

ether·ize \'ē-thə-,rīz\ *vt* **-ized; -iz·ing** (1853) **1** : to treat or anesthetize with ether **2** : to make numb as if by anesthetizing — **ether·iza·tion** \,ē-thə-rə-'zā-shən\ *n* — **ether·iz·er** *n*

eth·ic \'eth-ik\ *n* [ME *ethik,* fr. MF *ethique,* fr. L *ethice,* fr. Gk *ēthikē,* fr. *ēthikos*] (14c) **1** *pl but sing or pl in constr* : the discipline dealing with what is good and bad and with moral duty and obligation **2 a** : a set of moral principles or values **b** : a theory or system of moral values ⟨the present-day materialistic ~⟩ **c** *pl but sing or pl in constr* : the principles of conduct governing an individual or a group ⟨professional ~*s*⟩

[1]**eth·i·cal** \'eth-i-kəl\ *also* **eth·ic** \-ik\ *adj* [ME *etik,* fr. L *ethicus,* fr. Gk *ēthikos,* fr. *ēthos* character — more at SIB] (1607) **1 :** of or relating to ethics **2 :** involving or expressing moral approval or disapproval **3 :** conforming to accepted professional standards of conduct **4** *of a drug* **:** restricted to sale only on a doctor's prescription **syn** see MORAL — **eth·i·cal·i·ty** \,eth-ə-'kal-ət-ē\ *n* — **eth·i·cal·ly** \'eth-i-k(ə-)lē\ *adv* — **eth·i·cal·ness** \-kəl-nəs\ *n*

[2]**ethical** *n* (1952) **:** an ethical drug

ethi·cian \e-'thish-ən\ *n* (1629) **:** ETHICIST

eth·i·cist \'eth-ə-səst\ *n* (ca. 1890) **:** a specialist in ethics

ethid·ium bromide \e-'thid-ē-əm-\ *n* [*ethyl* + *-id* + *-ium*] (1965) **:** a biological dye used to block nucleic acid synthesis (as in mitochondria) and to destroy trypanosomes

ethinyl *var of* ETHYNYL

eth·i·on \'eth-ē-,än\ *n* [blend of *eth-* and *thion-*] (ca. 1960) **:** an organophosphate $C_9H_{22}O_4P_2S_4$ used as a pesticide

eth·i·on·amide \,eth-ē-'än-ə-,mīd\ *n* (1962) **:** a compound $C_8H_{10}N_2S$ used against mycobacteria (as in tuberculosis and leprosy)

ethi·o·nine \e-'thī-ə-,nēn\ *n* (1938) **:** an amino acid $C_6H_{13}NO_2S$ that is the ethyl homologue of methionine and is biologically antagonistic to methionine

Ethi·op \'ē-thē-,äp\ *or* **Ethi·ope** \-,ōp\ *n* [ME *Ethiope,* fr. L *Aethiops,* fr. Gk *Aithiops*] *archaic* (13c) **:** ETHIOPIAN

[1]**Ethi·o·pi·an** \,ē-thē-'ō-pē-ən\ *n* (13c) **1 :** a member of any of the mythical or actual peoples usu. described by the ancient Greeks as dark-skinned and living far to the south **2** *archaic* **:** NEGRO **3 :** a native or inhabitant of Ethiopia

[2]**Ethiopian** *adj* (1578) **1 :** of, relating to, or characteristic of the inhabitants or the country of Ethiopia **2 :** of, relating to, or being the biogeographic region that includes Africa south of the Sahara, southern Arabia, and sometimes Madagascar and the adjacent islands

[1]**Ethi·o·pic** \-'äp-ik, -'ō-pik\ *adj* (1659) **1 :** ETHIOPIAN **2 a :** of, relating to, or constituting Ethiopic **b :** of, relating to, or constituting a group of related Semitic languages spoken in Ethiopia

[2]**Ethiopic** *n* (ca. 1864) **1 :** a Semitic language formerly spoken in Ethiopia and still used as the liturgical language of the Christian church in Ethiopia **2 :** the Ethiopic group of Semitic languages

eth·moid \'eth-,mȯid\ *or* **eth·moi·dal** \eth-'mȯid-ᵊl\ *adj* [F *ethmoïde,* fr. Gk *ēthmoeidēs,* lit., like a strainer, fr. *ēthmos* strainer] (1741) **:** of, relating to, adjoining, or being one or more bones of the walls and septum of the nasal cavity — **ethmoid** *n*

[1]**eth·nic** \'eth-nik\ *n* (14c) **:** a member of an ethnic group; *esp* **:** a member of a minority group who retains the customs, language, or social views of his group

[2]**ethnic** *adj* [ME, fr. LL *ethnicus,* fr. Gk *ethnikos* national, gentile, fr. *ethnos* nation, people] (15c) **1 :** HEATHEN **2 a :** of or relating to large groups of people classed according to common racial, national, tribal, religious, linguistic, or cultural origin or background ⟨~ minorities⟩ ⟨~ enclaves⟩ **b :** being a member of an ethnic group **c :** of, relating to, or characteristic of ethnics ⟨~ neighborhoods⟩ ⟨~ foods⟩

eth·ni·cal \'eth-ni-kəl\ *adj* (15c) **1 :** ETHNIC **2 :** of or relating to ethnology **:** ETHNOLOGIC — **eth·ni·cal·ly** \-k(ə-)lē\ *adv*

eth·nic·i·ty \eth-'nis-ət-ē\ *n* (1950) **:** ethnic quality or affiliation

ethno- *comb form* [F, fr. Gk *ethno-, ethn-,* fr. *ethnos*] **:** race **:** people **:** cultural group ⟨*ethnocentric*⟩

eth·no·bot·a·ny \,eth-nō-'bät-ᵊn-ē, -'bät-nē\ *n* (1890) **:** the plant lore of a race or people; *also* **:** the systematic study of such lore — **eth·no·bo·tan·i·cal** \-bə-'tan-i-kəl\ *adj* — **eth·no·bo·tan·i·cal·ly** \-i-k(ə-)lē\ *adv* — **eth·no·bot·a·nist** \-'bät-ᵊn-əst, -'bät-nəst\ *n*

eth·no·cen·tric \,eth-nō-'sen-trik\ *adj* (ca. 1890) **1 :** having race as a central interest **2 :** characterized by or based on the attitude that one's own group is superior — **eth·no·cen·tric·i·ty** \-sen-'tris-ət-ē\ *n* — **eth·no·cen·trism** \-'sen-,triz-əm\ *n*

eth·nog·ra·phy \eth-'näg-rə-fē\ *n* [F *ethnographie,* fr. *ethno-* + *-graphie* -graphy] (1834) **:** the systematic recording of human cultures — **eth·nog·ra·pher** \-fər\ *n* — **eth·no·graph·ic** \,eth-nə-'graf-ik\ *or* **eth·no·graph·i·cal** \-i-kəl\ *adj* — **eth·no·graph·i·cal·ly** \-i-k(ə-)lē\ *adv*

eth·no·his·to·ry \,eth-nō-'his-t(ə-)rē\ *n* (1943) **:** a study of the development of cultures; *specif* **:** the interpretation of the significance of archaeological findings by means of documentary material — **eth·no·his·to·ri·an** \-(h)is-'tōr-ē-ən, -'tȯr-, -'tär-\ *n* — **eth·no·his·to·ric** \-(h)is-'tȯr-ik, -'tär-\ *or* **eth·no·his·to·ri·cal** \-i-kəl\ *adj*

eth·nol·o·gy \eth-'näl-ə-jē\ *n* (ca. 1828) **1 :** a science that deals with the division of mankind into races and their origin, distribution, relations, and characteristics **2 :** anthropology dealing chiefly with the comparative and analytical study of cultures **:** CULTURAL ANTHROPOLOGY — **eth·no·log·i·cal** \,eth-nə-'läj-i-kəl\ *also* **eth·no·log·ic** \-ik\ *adj* — **eth·nol·o·gist** \eth-'näl-ə-jəst\ *n*

eth·no·meth·od·ol·o·gy \,eth-nō-,meth-ə-'däl-ə-jē\ *n* (1967) **:** a branch of sociology dealing with nonspecialists' commonsense understanding of the structure and organization of society — **eth·no·meth·od·ol·o·gist** \-'däl-ə-jəst\ *n*

eth·no·mu·si·col·o·gy \,eth-nō-,myü-zi-'käl-ə-jē\ *n* (1950) **1 :** the study of music that is outside the European art tradition **2 :** the study of music in a sociocultural context — **eth·no·mu·si·co·log·i·cal** \-kə-'läj-i-kəl\ *adj* — **eth·no·mu·si·col·o·gist** \-'käl-ə-jəst\ *n*

eth·no·sci·ence \'eth-nō-,sī-ən(t)s\ *n* (1961) **:** the nature lore (as folk taxonomy of plants and animals) of primitive peoples

etho- — see ETH-

ethol·o·gy \ē-'thäl-ə-jē\ *n* (ca. 1843) **1 :** a branch of knowledge dealing with human ethos and with its formation and evolution **2 :** the scientific and objective study of animal behavior esp. under natural conditions — **etho·log·i·cal** \,ē-thə-'läj-i-kəl, ,eth-ə-\ *adj* — **ethol·o·gist** \ē-'thäl-ə-jəst\ *n*

ethos \'ē-,thäs\ *n* [NL, fr. Gk *ēthos* custom, character — more at SIB] (1851) **:** the distinguishing character, sentiment, moral nature, or guiding beliefs of a person, group, or institution

eth·oxy \e-'thäk-sē\ *adj* (ca. 1909) **:** relating to or containing ethoxyl

eth·ox·yl \e-'thäk-səl\ *n* [ISV *eth-* + *ox-* + *-yl*] (ca. 1900) **:** the univalent radical C_2H_5O composed of ethyl united with oxygen

eth·yl \'eth-əl\ *n* [ISV *ether* + *-yl*] (1838) **:** a univalent hydrocarbon radical C_2H_5 — **eth·yl·ic** \e-'thil-ik\ *adj*

ethyl acetate *n* (1874) **:** a colorless fragrant volatile flammable liquid ester $C_4H_8O_2$ used esp. as a solvent

ethyl alcohol *n* (1869) **:** ALCOHOL 1

ethyl cellulose *n* (1936) **:** any of various thermoplastic substances used esp. in plastics and lacquers

ethyl chloride *n* (ca. 1891) **:** a colorless pungent flammable gaseous or volatile liquid C_2H_5Cl used esp. as a local surface anesthetic

eth·yl·ene \'eth-ə-,lēn\ *n* (ca. 1852) **1 :** a colorless flammable gaseous unsaturated hydrocarbon C_2H_4 that is found in coal gas, can be produced by pyrolysis of petroleum hydrocarbons, and occurs in plants functioning esp. as a natural growth regulator that promotes the ripening of fruit **2 :** a divalent hydrocarbon group C_2H_4 derived from ethane — **eth·yl·enic** \,eth-ə-'lē-nik, -'len-ik\ *adj* — **eth·yl·eni·cal·ly** \-(n)i-k(ə-)lē\ *adv*

ethylene glycol *n* (1901) **:** a thick liquid alcohol $C_2H_6O_2$ used esp. as an antifreeze and in making polyester fibers

ethylene oxide *n* (1898) **:** a colorless flammable toxic gaseous or liquid compound C_2H_4O used esp. in synthesis (as of ethylene glycol) and in sterilization and fumigation

ethyl ether *n* (1878) **:** ETHER 3a

ethy·nyl \e-'thīn-ᵊl, 'eth-ə-,nil\ *n* [*ethyne* (fr. *ethyl* + *-ine*) + *-yl*] (1929) **:** a univalent unsaturated group $HC{\equiv}C$ derived from acetylene by removal of one hydrogen atom

et·ic \'et-ik\ *adj* [phon*etic*] (1954) **:** of, relating to, or involving description of linguistic or behavioral phenomena considered in isolation from a particular system or in relation to predetermined general concepts — compare EMIC

-et·ic \'et-ik\ *adj suffix* [L & Gk; L *-eticus,* fr. Gk *-etikos, -ētikos,* fr. *-etos, -ētos,* ending of certain verbals] **:** -IC ⟨limn*etic*⟩ — often in adjectives corresponding to nouns ending in *-esis* ⟨gen*etic*⟩

eti·o·late \'ēt-ē-ə-,lāt\ *vt* **-lat·ed; -lat·ing** [F *étioler*] (1791) **1 :** to bleach and alter the natural development of (a green plant) by excluding sunlight **2 a :** to make pale and sickly **b :** to take away the natural vigor or inhibit the potential for growth of (as by undue sheltering or pampering) — **eti·o·la·tion** \,ēt-ē-ə-'lā-shən\ *n*

eti·o·log·ic \,ēt-ē-ə-'läj-ik\ *or* **eti·o·log·i·cal** \-i-kəl\ *adj* (1902) **1 :** assigning or seeking to assign a cause **2 :** of or relating to etiology — **eti·o·log·i·cal·ly** \-i-k(ə-)lē\ *adv*

eti·ol·o·gy \,ēt-ē-'äl-ə-jē\ *n, pl* **-gies** [ML *aetiologia* statement of causes, fr. Gk *aitiologia,* fr. *aitia* cause; akin to L *aemulus* rivaling] (1555) **1 :** CAUSE, ORIGIN; *specif* **:** all of the causes of a disease or abnormal condition **2 :** a branch of knowledge concerned with the causes of particular phenomena; *specif* **:** a branch of medical science concerned with the causes and origins of diseases

et·i·quette \'et-i-kət, -,ket\ *n* [F *étiquette,* lit., ticket — more at TICKET] (1750) **:** the conduct or procedure required by good breeding or prescribed by authority to be observed in social or official life

Eton collar \,ēt-ᵊn-\ *n* [*Eton* College, English public school] (1895) **:** a large stiff turnover collar

Eton jacket *n* (1881) **:** a short black jacket with long sleeves, wide lapels, and an open front

Etru·ri·an \i-'trůr-ē-ən\ *n* [*Etruria*] (1623) **:** ETRUSCAN — **Etrurian** *adj*

[1]**Etrus·can** \i-'trəs-kən\ *adj* [L *etruscus;* akin to L *Etruria,* ancient country] (1706) **:** of, relating to, or characteristic of Etruria, the Etruscans, or the Etruscan language

[2]**Etruscan** *n* (1773) **1 :** the language of the Etruscans which is of unknown affiliation **2 :** a native or inhabitant of ancient Etruria

-ette \'et, ,et, ət, it\ *n suffix* [ME, fr. MF, fem. dim. suffix, fr. OF *-ete* — more at -ET] **1 :** little one ⟨kitchen*ette*⟩ **2 :** female ⟨farmer*ette*⟩ **3 :** imitation ⟨beaver*ette*⟩

étude \'ā-,t(y)üd\ *n* [F, lit., study, fr. MF *estude, estudie,* fr. OF — more at STUDY] (ca. 1837) **1 :** a piece of music for the practice of a point of technique **2 :** a composition built on a technical motive but played for its artistic value

etui \ā-'twē, 'ā-,\ *n, pl* **etuis** [F *étui*] (1611) **:** a small ornamental case

et·y·mol·o·gist \,et-ə-'mäl-ə-jəst\ *n* (1635) **:** a specialist in etymology

et·y·mol·o·gize \-,jīz\ *vb* **-gized; -giz·ing** *vt* (1530) **:** to discover, formulate, or state an etymology for ~ *vi* **:** to study or formulate etymologies

et·y·mol·o·gy \-jē\ *n, pl* **-gies** [ME *ethimologie,* fr. L *etymologia,* fr. Gk, fr. *etymon* + *-logia* -logy] (14c) **1 :** the history of a linguistic form (as a word) shown by tracing its development since its earliest recorded occurrence in the language where it is found, by tracing its transmission from one language to another, by analyzing it into its component parts, by identifying its cognates in other languages, or by tracing it and its cognates to a common ancestral form in an ancestral language **2 :** a branch of linguistics concerned with etymologies — **et·y·mo·log·i·cal** \-mə-'läj-i-kəl\ *adj* — **et·y·mo·log·i·cal·ly** \-k(ə-)lē\ *adv*

et·y·mon \'et-ə-,män\ *n, pl* **-ma** \-mə\ *also* **-mons** [L, fr. Gk, literal meaning of a word according to its origin, fr. *etymos* true; akin to Gk *eteos* true — more at SOOTH] (1570) **1 a :** an earlier form of a word in the same language or an ancestral language **b :** a word in a foreign language that is the source of a particular loanword **2 :** a word or morpheme from which words are formed by composition or derivation

eu- *comb form* [ME, fr. L, fr. Gk, fr. *ey, eu,* fr. neut. of *eys* good; perh. akin to L *esse* to be] **1 a :** well **:** easily ⟨*eu*plastic⟩ — compare DYS- **b :** good ⟨*eu*daemon⟩ — compare DYS- **2 a :** true ⟨*eu*chromosome⟩ ⟨*eu*globulin⟩ **b :** truly ⟨*eu*coelomate⟩

eu·ca·lypt \'yü-kə-,lipt\ *n* (1885) **:** EUCALYPTUS

eu·ca·lyp·tol *also* **eu·ca·lyp·tole** \,yü-kə-'lip-,tōl, -,tȯl\ *n* (ca. 1879) **:** CINEOLE

eu·ca·lyp·tus \,yü-kə-'lip-təs\ *n, pl* **-ti** \-,tī, -,tē\ *or* **-tus·es** [NL, fr. *eu-* + Gk *kalyptos* covered, fr. *kalyptein* to conceal; fr. the conical covering of the buds — more at HELL] (1809) **:** any of a genus (*Eucalyptus*) of mostly Australian evergreen trees or rarely shrubs of the myrtle family that have rigid entire leaves and umbellate flowers and are widely cultivated for their gums, resins, oils, and useful woods

eu·cary·ote, eucaryotic *var of* EUKARYOTE, EUKARYOTIC

\ə\ abut \ᵊ\ kitten, F table \ər\ further \a\ ash \ā\ ace \ä\ cot, cart \aů\ out \ch\ chin \e\ bet \ē\ easy \g\ go \i\ hit \ī\ ice \j\ job \ŋ\ sing \ō\ go \ȯ\ law \ȯi\ boy \th\ thin \th\ the \ü\ loot \ů\ foot \y\ yet \zh\ vision \à, k, ⁿ, œ, œ̄, ue, ue̅, ʸ\ *see* Guide to Pronunciation

Eu·cha·rist \'yü-k(ə-)rəst\ *n* [ME *eukarist,* fr. MF *eucharistie,* fr. LL *eucharistia,* fr. Gk, Eucharist, gratitude, fr. *eucharistos* grateful, fr. *eu-* + *charizesthai* to show favor, fr. *charis* favor, grace, gratitude; akin to Gk *chairein* to rejoice — more at YEARN] (14c) **1 :** COMMUNION 2a **2** *Christian Science* **:** spiritual communion with God — **eu·cha·ris·tic** \,yü-kə-'ris-tik\ *adj, often cap*

[1]eu·chre \'yü-kər\ *n* [origin unknown] (1841) **:** a card game in which each player is dealt five cards and the player making trump must take three tricks to win a hand

[2]euchre *vt* **eu·chred; eu·chring** \-k(ə-)riŋ\ (ca. 1864) **1 :** to prevent from winning three tricks in euchre **2 :** CHEAT, TRICK ⟨*euchred* out of their life savings —Pete Martin⟩

eu·chro·ma·tin \(')yü-'krō-mət-ən\ *n* [G, fr. *eu-* + *chromatin*] (1932) **:** the genetically active portion of chromatin that is largely composed of genes — **eu·chro·mat·ic** \,yü-krō-'mat-ik\ *adj*

eu·clase \'yü-,klās, -,klāz\ *n* [F, fr. *eu-* (fr. L) + Gk *klasis* breaking, fr. *klan* to break — more at HALT] (1804) **:** a mineral $BeAlSiO_4(OH)$ that consists of a brittle silicate of beryllium and aluminum in pale-yellow, green, or blue prismatic crystals and is used esp. as a gemstone

eu·clid·e·an *also* **eu·clid·i·an** \yü-'klid-ē-ən\ *adj, often cap* (1660) **:** of, relating to, or based on the geometry of Euclid or a geometry with similar axioms

Euclidean algorithm *n* (ca. 1955) **:** a method of finding the greatest common divisor of two numbers by dividing the larger by the smaller, the smaller by the remainder, the first remainder by the second remainder, and so on until exact division is obtained whence the greatest common divisor is the exact divisor

euclidean geometry *n, often cap E* (1865) **1 :** geometry based on Euclid's axioms **2 :** the geometry of a euclidean space

euclidean space *n, often cap E* (1883) **:** a space in which Euclid's axioms and definitions (as of straight and parallel lines and angles of plane triangles) apply

Eu·clid's algorithm \,yü-klədz-\ *n* (1928) **:** EUCLIDEAN ALGORITHM

eu·crite \'yü-,krīt\ *n* [G *eukrit,* fr. Gk *eukritos* easily discerned, fr. *eu-* + *kritos* separated, fr. *krinein* to separate — more at CERTAIN] (ca. 1899) **1 :** a stony meteorite composed essentially of plagioclase and pigeonite **2 :** a rock consisting of a very basic gabbro — **eu·crit·ic** \yü-'krit-ik\ *adj*

eu·dae·mo·nism \yu̇-'dē-mə-,niz-əm\ *or* **eu·dai·mo·nism** \-'dī-\ *n* [Gk *eudaimonia* happiness, fr. *eudaimōn* having a good attendant spirit, happy, fr. *eu-* + *daimōn* spirit] (1827) **:** a theory that the highest ethical goal is happiness and personal well-being — **eu·dae·mo·nist** \-nəst\ *n* — **eu·dae·mo·nis·tic** \-,dē-mə-'nis-tik\ *adj*

eu·di·om·e·ter \,yüd-ē-'äm-ət-ər\ *n* [modif. of It *eudiometro,* fr. Gk *eudia* fair weather (fr. *eu-* + *-dia* weather — akin to L *dies* day) + It *-metro* -meter, fr. Gk *metron* measure] (1777) **:** an instrument for the volumetric measurement and analysis of gases — **eu·dio·met·ric** \,yüd-ē-ə-'me-trik\ *adj* — **eu·dio·met·ri·cal·ly** \-tri-k(ə-)lē\ *adv*

eu·gen·ic \yu̇-'jen-ik\ *adj* [Gk *eugenēs* wellborn, fr. *eu-* + *-genēs* born — more at -GEN] (1883) **1 :** relating to or fitted for the production of good offspring **2 :** of or relating to eugenics — **eu·gen·i·cal·ly** \-i-k(ə-)lē\ *adv*

eu·gen·i·cist \-'jen-ə-səst\ *n* (ca. 1909) **:** a student or advocate of eugenics

eu·gen·ics \yu̇-'jen-iks\ *n pl but sing or pl in constr* (ca. 1883) **:** a science that deals with the improvement (as by control of human mating) of hereditary qualities of a race or breed

eu·ge·nol \'yü-jə-,nȯl, -,nōl\ *n* [F *eugénol,* fr. NL *Eugenia,* genus of tropical trees] (1886) **:** a colorless aromatic liquid phenol $C_{10}H_{12}O_2$ found esp. in clove oil and used chiefly in flavors and perfumes

eu·geo·syn·cline \(,)yü-,jē-ō-'sin-,klīn\ *n* (1944) **:** a narrow rapidly subsiding geosyncline usu. with volcanic materials mingled with clastic sediments — **eu·geo·syn·cli·nal** \-(,)sin-'klīn-ᵊl\ *adj*

eu·gle·na \yu̇-'glē-nə\ *n* [NL, fr. *eu-* + Gk *glēnē* eyeball, socket of a joint; prob. akin to Gk *glainoi* ornaments — more at CLEAN] (ca. 1900) **:** any of a genus (*Euglena*) of green freshwater flagellates often classed as algae

eu·gle·noid \-,nȯid\ *n* (1890) **:** any of a taxon (Euglenoidina or Euglenophyta) of varied flagellates (as a euglena) that are typically green or colorless stigma-bearing solitary organisms with one or two flagella emerging from a well-defined gullet — **euglenoid** *adj*

euglenoid movement *n* (1940) **:** writhing usu. nonprogressive protoplasmic movement of plastic-bodied euglenoid flagellates

eu·glob·u·lin \yü-'gläb-yə-lən\ *n* [ISV] (ca. 1904) **:** a simple protein that does not dissolve in pure water

eu·he·mer·ism \yu̇-'hē-mə-,riz-əm, -'hem-ə-\ *n* [*Euhemerus,* 4th cent. B.C. Gk mythographer] (1846) **:** interpretation of myths as traditional accounts of historical persons and events — **eu·he·mer·ist** \-rəst\ *n* — **eu·he·mer·is·tic** \-,hē-mə-'ris-tik, -,hem-ə-\ *adj*

eu·kary·ote \(')yü-'kar-ē-,ōt, -ē-ət\ *n* [*eu-* + *kary-* + *-ote* (as in *zygote*)] (1943) **:** an organism composed of one or more cells with visibly evident nuclei — compare PROKARYOTE — **eu·kary·ot·ic** \-,kar-ē-'ät-ik\ *adj*

eu·la·chon \'yü-lə-,kän, -li-kən\ *n, pl* **eulachon** *or* **eulachons** [Chinook Jargon *ulâkân*] (1836) **:** a marine food fish (*Thaleichthys pacificus*) of the north Pacific coast related to the smelt — called also *candlefish*

eu·lo·gist \'yü-lə-jəst\ *n* (1808) **:** one who eulogizes

eu·lo·gi·um \yu̇-'lō-jē-əm\ *n, pl* **-gia** \-jē-ə\ *or* **-gi·ums** [ML] (1621) **:** EULOGY

eu·lo·gize \'yü-lə-,jīz\ *vt* **-gized; -giz·ing** (1810) **:** to speak or write in high praise of **:** EXTOL — **eu·lo·giz·er** *n*

eu·lo·gy \'yü-lə-jē\ *n, pl* **-gies** [ME *euloge,* fr. ML *eulogium,* fr. Gk *eulogia* praise, fr. *eu-* + *-logia* -logy] (15c) **1 :** a commendatory formal statement or set oration **2 :** high praise ***syn*** see ENCOMIUM — **eu·lo·gis·tic** \,yü-lə-'jis-tik\ *adj* — **eu·lo·gis·ti·cal·ly** \-ti-k(ə-)lē\ *adv*

Eu·men·i·des \yü-'men-ə-,dēz\ *n pl* [L, fr. Gk, lit., the gracious ones] **:** the Furies in Greek mythology

eu·nuch \'yü-nək, -nik\ *n* [ME *eunuk,* fr. L *eunuchus,* fr. Gk *eunouchos,* fr. *eunē* bed + *echein* to have, have charge of — more at SCHEME] (14c) **1 :** a castrated man placed in charge of a harem or employed as a chamberlain in a palace **2 :** a man or boy deprived of the testes or external genitals — **eu·nuch·ism** \-,iz-əm\ *n*

eu·nuch·oid \-,ȯid\ *n* (1906) **:** a sexually deficient individual; *esp* **:** one lacking in sexual differentiation and tending toward the intersex state — **eunuchoid** *adj*

eu·on·y·mus \yu̇-'än-ə-məs\ *n* [NL, genus name, fr. L *euonymos* spindle tree, fr. Gk *euōnymos,* fr. *euōnymos* having an auspicious name, fr. *eu-* + *onyma* name — more at NAME] (1767) **:** SPINDLE TREE

eu·pa·trid \yu̇-'pa-trəd, 'yü-pə-\ *n, pl* **eu·pat·ri·dae** \yu̇-'pa-trə-,dē\ *often cap* [Gk *eupatridēs,* fr. *eu-* + *patr-, patēr* father — more at FATHER] (1836) **:** one of the hereditary aristocrats of ancient Athens

eu·pep·tic \yu̇-'pep-tik\ *adj* (1831) **1 :** of, relating to, or having good digestion **2 :** CHEERFUL, OPTIMISTIC

eu·phau·si·id \yu̇-'fȯ-zē-əd\ *n* [NL *Euphausia,* genus of crustaceans] (1926) **:** any of an order (Euphausiacea) of small usu. luminescent malacostracan crustaceans that resemble shrimps and in some areas form an important element in marine plankton — **euphausiid** *adj*

eu·phe·mism \'yü-fə-,miz-əm\ *n* [Gk *euphēmismos,* fr. *euphēmos* auspicious, sounding good, fr. *eu-* + *phēmē* speech, fr. *phanai* to speak — more at BAN] (ca. 1656) **:** the substitution of an agreeable or inoffensive expression for one that may offend or suggest something unpleasant; *also* **:** the expression so substituted — **eu·phe·mis·tic** \,yü-fə-'mis-tik\ *adj* — **eu·phe·mis·ti·cal·ly** \-ti-k(ə-)lē\ *adv*

eu·phen·ics \yu̇-'fen-iks\ *n pl but sing in constr* [*eu-* + *phen-* (fr. *phenotype*) + *-ics;* after E *genotype: eugenics*] (1963) **:** a science that deals with the biological improvement of human beings after birth — **eu·phen·ic** \-ik\ *adj*

eu·pho·ni·ous \yu̇-'fō-nē-əs\ *adj* (1774) **:** pleasing to the ear — **eu·pho·ni·ous·ly** *adv* — **eu·pho·ni·ous·ness** *n*

eu·pho·ni·um \yu̇-'fō-nē-əm\ *n* [Gk *euphōnos* + E *-ium* (as in *harmonium*)] (1862) **:** a brass instrument smaller than but resembling a tuba and having a range from B flat below the bass staff upward for three octaves

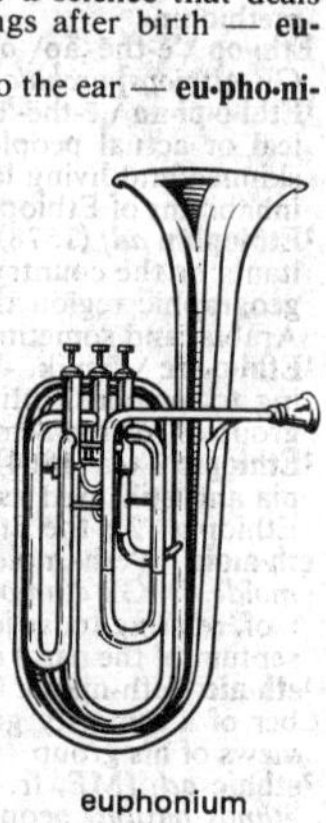
euphonium

eu·pho·ny \'yü-fə-nē\ *n, pl* **-nies** [F *euphonie,* fr. LL *euphonia,* fr. Gk *euphōnia,* fr. *euphōnos* sweet-voiced, musical, fr. *eu-* + *phōnē* voice — more at BAN] (ca. 1623) **1 :** pleasing or sweet sound; *esp* **:** the acoustic effect produced by words so formed or combined as to please the ear **2 :** a harmonious succession of words having a pleasing sound — **eu·phon·ic** \yu̇-'fän-ik\ *adj* — **eu·phon·i·cal·ly** \-i-k(ə-)lē\ *adv*

eu·phor·bia \yu̇-'fȯr-bē-ə\ *n* [NL, alter. of L *euphorbea,* fr. *Euphorbus,* 1st cent. A.D. physician] (1525) **:** any of a large genus (*Euphorbia* of the family Euphorbiaceae) of plants that have a milky juice and flowers lacking a calyx and included in an involucre which surrounds a group of several staminate flowers and a central pistillate flower with 3-lobed pistils; *broadly* **:** SPURGE

eu·pho·ria \yu̇-'fōr-ē-ə, -'fȯr-\ *n* [NL, fr. Gk, fr. *euphoros* healthy, fr. *eu-* + *pherein* to bear — more at BEAR] (1706) **:** a feeling of well-being or elation — **eu·phor·ic** \-'fȯr-ik, -'fär-\ *adj* — **eu·phor·i·cal·ly** \-i-k(ə-)lē\ *adv*

eu·pho·ri·ant \yu̇-'fōr-ē-ənt, -'fȯr-\ *n* (1947) **:** a drug that tends to induce euphoria — **euphoriant** *adj*

eu·pho·tic \yü-'fōt-ik\ *adj* [ISV] (1909) **:** of, relating to, or constituting the upper layers of a body of water into which sufficient light penetrates to permit growth of green plants

Eu·phros·y·ne \yu̇-'fräs-ᵊn-(,)ē, -'fräz-\ *n* [L, fr. Gk *Euphrosynē*] **:** one of the three Graces

eu·phu·ism \'yü-fyə-,wiz-əm\ *n* [*Euphues,* character in prose romances by John Lyly] (1592) **1 :** an elegant Elizabethan literary style marked by excessive use of balance, antithesis, and alliteration and by frequent use of similes drawn from mythology and nature **2 :** artificial elegance of language — **eu·phu·ist** \-wəst\ *n* — **eu·phu·is·tic** \,yü-fyə-'wis-tik\ *adj* — **eu·phu·is·ti·cal·ly** \-ti-k(ə-)lē\ *adv*

eu·ploid \'yü-,plȯid\ *adj* [ISV] (1926) **:** having a chromosome number that is an exact multiple of the monoploid number — compare ANEUPLOID — **euploid** *n* — **eu·ploi·dy** \-,plȯid-ē\ *n*

eup·nea *also* **eup·noea** \yüp-'nē-ə\ *n* [NL, fr. Gk *eupnoia,* fr. *eupnous* breathing freely, fr. *eu-* + *pnein* to breathe — more at SNEEZE] (ca. 1706) **:** normal respiration — **eup·ne·ic** \-'nē-ik\ *adj*

Eur- *or* **Euro-** *comb form* [*Europe*] **:** European and ⟨*Euramerican*⟩ **:** European

Eur·amer·i·can \,yu̇r-ə-'mer-ə-kən\ *or* **Eu·ro–Amer·i·can** \,yu̇r-ō-ə-'mer-\ *adj* (1941) **:** common to Europe and America

Eur·asian \yu̇-'rā-zhən, -shən\ *adj* (1844) **1 :** of a mixed European and Asian origin **2 :** of or relating to Europe and Asia — **Eurasian** *n*

eu·re·ka \yu̇-'rē-kə\ *interj* [Gk *heurēka* I have found, fr. *heuriskein* to find; fr. the exclamation attributed to Archimedes on discovering a method for determining the purity of gold — more at HEURISTIC] (1603) — used to express triumph on a discovery

eu·ro \'yu̇(ə)r-(,)ō\ *n, pl* **euros** [native name in Australia] (1898) **:** WALLAROO

Eu·ro·bond \'yu̇r-ō-,bänd\ *n* (1967) **:** a bond of a U.S. corporation that is sold outside the U.S. and that is denominated and paid for in dollars and yields interest in dollars

Eu·ro·cen·tric \,yu̇r-ə-'sen-trik\ *adj, chiefly Brit* (1961) **:** EUROPOCENTRIC

Eu·ro·com·mu·nism \,yu̇r-ō-'käm-yə-,niz-əm\ *n* (1981) **:** the communism esp. of western European Communist parties that is marked by a willingness to reach power through coalitions and by independence from Soviet leadership — **Eurocommunist** *n or adj*

Eu·ro·crat \'yu̇r-ə-,krat\ *n* [*European Common Market* + *-crat*] (1962) **:** a staff member of the administrative commission of the European Common Market

Eu·ro·cur·ren·cy \,yu̇r-ō-'kər-ən-sē, -'kə-rən-\ *n* (ca. 1976) **:** moneys (as of the U.S. and Japan) held outside their countries of origin and used in the money markets of Europe

Eu·ro·dol·lar \'yu̇r-ō-,däl-ər\ *n* (1960) **:** a U.S. dollar held as Eurocurrency

Eu·ro·pa \yu̇-'rō-pə\ *n* [L, fr. Gk *Eurōpē*] **:** a Phoenician princess carried off by Zeus in the form of a white bull and by him mother of Minos, Rhadamanthus, and Sarpedon

Eu·ro·pe·an \,yu̇r-ə-'pē-ən\ *n* (1632) **1 :** a native or inhabitant of Europe **2 :** a person of European descent — **European** *adj* — **Eu·ro·pe·an·iza·tion** \-,pē-ə-nə-'zā-shən\ *n* — **Eu·ro·pe·an·ize** \-'pē-ə-,nīz\ *vt*

European chafer *n* (1947) **:** an Old World beetle (*Amphimallon majalis*) now established in parts of eastern No. America where its larva is a destructive pest on the roots of turf grasses
European corn borer *n* (1920) **:** an Old World moth (*Ostrinia nubilalis*) that is widespread in eastern No. America where its larva is a major pest esp. in the stems and crowns of Indian corn, dahlias, and potatoes
European plan *n* (1834) **:** a hotel plan whereby the daily rates cover only the cost of the room — compare AMERICAN PLAN
European red mite *n* (1966) **:** a small bright or brownish red oval mite (*Panonychus ulmi*) that is a destructive orchard pest
eu·ro·pi·um \yu̇-ˈrō-pē-əm\ *n* [NL, fr. *Europa* Europe] (1901) **:** a bivalent and trivalent metallic element of the rare-earth group found in monazite sand — see ELEMENT table
Eu·ro·po·cen·tric \yu̇-ˌrō-pə-ˈsen-trik\ *adj* [*Europe* + E *-o-* + *-centric*] (1926) **:** centered on Europe and the Europeans ⟨world history texts . . . showed a markedly ~ orientation —J. W. Hall⟩ — **Eu·ro·po·cen·trism** \-ˌtriz-əm\ *n*
eury- *comb form* [NL, fr. Gk, fr. *eurys;* akin to Skt *uru* broad, wide] **:** broad **:** wide ⟨*eury*haline⟩
eu·ry·bath·ic \ˌyu̇r-i-ˈbath-ik\ *adj* [*eury-* + Gk *bathos* depth] (1902) **:** capable of living on the bottom in both deep and shallow water ⟨~ gastropods⟩
Eu·ryd·i·ce \yu̇-ˈrid-ə-(ˌ)sē\ *n* [L, fr. Gk *Eurydikē*] **:** the wife of Orpheus whom he attempts to bring back from Hades
eu·ry·ha·line \ˌyu̇r-i-ˈhā-ˌlīn, -ˈhal-ˌīn\ *adj* [ISV *eury-* + Gk *halinos* of salt, fr. *hals* salt — more at SALT] (1888) **:** able to live in waters of a wide range of salinity
eu·ryp·ter·id \yu̇-ˈrip-tə-rəd\ *n* [deriv. of Gk *eury-* + *pteron* wing — more at FEATHER] (1871) **:** any of an order (Eurypterida) of usu. large aquatic Paleozoic arthropods related to the horseshoe crabs — **eurypterid** *adj*
eu·ry·therm \ˈyu̇r-i-ˌthərm\ *n* [prob. fr. G *eurytherm* eurythermal, fr. *eury-* + Gk *thermē* heat] (1953) **:** an organism that tolerates a wide range of temperature — **eu·ry·ther·mal** \ˌyu̇r-i-ˈthər-məl\ *or* **eu·ry·ther·mic** \-mik\ *or* **eu·ry·ther·mous** \-məs\ *adj*
eu·ryth·mic *or* **eu·rhyth·mic** \yu̇-ˈrith-mik\ *adj* (ca. 1901) **1 :** HARMONIOUS **2 :** of or relating to eurythmy or eurythmics
eu·ryth·mics *or* **eu·rhyth·mics** \-miks\ *n pl but sing or pl in constr* (1925) **:** the art of harmonious bodily movement esp. through expressive timed movements in response to improvised music
eu·ryth·my *or* **eu·rhyth·my** \-mē\ *n* [G *eurhythmie,* fr. L *eurythmia* rhythmical movement, fr. Gk, fr. *eurythmos* rhythmical, fr. *eu-* + *rhythmos* rhythm] (1949) **:** a system of harmonious body movement to the rhythm of spoken words
eu·ry·top·ic \ˌyu̇r-i-ˈtäp-ik\ *adj* [prob. fr. G *eurytop,* fr. *eury-* + Gk *topos* place] (ca. 1945) **:** tolerant of wide variation in one or more physical factors of the environment
eu·sta·chian tube \yu̇-ˌstā-sh(ē-)ən- *also* -ˌstā-kē-ən-\ *n, often cap E* [Bartolommeo *Eustachio*] (1741) **:** a bony and cartilaginous tube connecting the middle ear with the nasopharynx and equalizing air pressure on both sides of the tympanic membrane — see EAR illustration
eu·stat·ic \yu̇-ˈstat-ik\ *adj* [ISV] (1906) **:** relating to or characterized by worldwide change of sea level
eu·stele \ˈyü-ˌstēl, yu̇-ˈstē-lē\ *n* (ca. 1920) **:** a stele typical of dicotyledonous plants that consists of vascular bundles of xylem and phloem strands with parenchymal cells between the bundles
eu·tec·tic \yu̇-ˈtek-tik\ *adj* [Gk *eutēktos* easily melted, fr. *eu-* + *tēktos* melted, fr. *tēkein* to melt — more at THAW] (1904) **1** *of an alloy or solution* **:** having the lowest melting point possible **2 :** of or relating to a eutectic alloy or solution or its melting or freezing point — **eutectic** *n* — **eu·tec·toid** \-ˌtȯid\ *adj or n*
Eu·ter·pe \yu̇-ˈtər-pē\ *n* [L, fr. Gk *Euterpē*] **:** the Greek Muse of music
eu·tha·na·sia \ˌyü-thə-ˈnā-zh(ē-)ə\ *n* [Gk, easy death, fr. *euthanatos,* fr. *eu-* + *thanatos* death — more at THANATOS] (1742) **:** the act or practice of killing or permitting the death of hopelessly sick or injured individuals (as persons or domestic animals) in a relatively painless way for reasons of mercy — **eu·tha·na·sic** \-zik, -sik\ *adj*
eu·than·a·tize \yu̇-ˈthan-ə-ˌtīz\ *also* **eu·tha·nize** \ˈyü-thə-ˌnīz\ *vt* **-tized** *also* **-nized; -tiz·ing** *also* **-niz·ing** [Gk *euthanatos*] (1961) **:** to subject to euthanasia
eu·then·ics \yu̇-ˈthen-iks\ *n pl but sing or pl in constr* [Gk *euthenein* to thrive, fr. *eu-* + *-thenein* (akin to Skt *āhanas* swelling)] (1905) **:** a science that deals with development of human well-being by improvement of living conditions — **eu·the·nist** \yu̇-ˈthen-əst, ˈyü-thə-nəst\ *n*
eu·the·ri·an \yu̇-ˈthir-ē-ən\ *adj* [deriv. of NL *eu-* + Gk *thērion* beast — more at TREACLE] (1880) **:** of or relating to a major division (Eutheria) of mammals comprising the placental mammals — **eutherian** *n*
eu·thy·roid \(ˈ)yü-ˈthī-ˌrȯid\ *adj* (1924) **:** characterized by normal thyroid function
eu·tro·phic \yu̇-ˈtrō-fik\ *adj* [prob. fr. G *eutroph* eutrophic, fr. Gk *eutrophos* well-nourished, nourishing, fr. *eu-* + *trephein* to nourish — more at ATROPHY] *of a body of water* (1928) **:** characterized by the state resulting from eutrophication — compare MESOTROPHIC, OLIGOTROPHIC — **eu·tro·phy** \ˈyü-trə-fē\ *n*
eu·tro·phi·ca·tion \yu̇-ˌtrō-fə-ˈkā-shən\ *n* (1946) **:** the process by which a body of water becomes either naturally or by pollution rich in dissolved nutrients (as phosphates) and often shallow with a seasonal deficiency in dissolved oxygen
evac·u·ate \i-ˈvak-yə-ˌwāt\ *vb* **-at·ed; -at·ing** [L *evacuatus,* pp. of *evacuare,* fr. *e-* + *vacuus* empty — more at VACUUM] *vt* (1533) **1 :** to remove the contents of **:** EMPTY **2 :** to discharge from the body as waste **:** VOID **3 :** to remove something (as gas or water) from esp. by pumping **4 a :** to remove esp. from a military zone or dangerous area **b :** to withdraw from military occupation of **c :** VACATE ⟨were ordered to ~ the building⟩ ~ *vi* **1 :** to withdraw from a place in an organized way esp. for protection **2 :** to pass urine or feces from the body — **evac·u·a·tive** \-ˌwāt-iv\ *adj*
evac·u·a·tion \i-ˌvak-yə-ˈwā-shən\ *n* (15c) **1 :** the act or process of evacuating **2 :** something evacuated or discharged
evac·u·ee \i-ˌvak-yə-ˈwē\ *n* (1918) **:** an evacuated person
evade \i-ˈvād\ *vb* **evad·ed; evad·ing** [MF & L; MF *evader,* fr. L *evadere,* fr. *e-* + *vadere* to go, walk — more at WADE] *vi* (1513) **1 :** to slip away **2 :** to take refuge in evasion ~ *vt* **1 :** to elude by dexterity or stratagem **2 a :** to avoid facing up to ⟨*evaded* the real issues⟩ **b :** to avoid the performance of **:** DODGE, CIRCUMVENT; *esp* **:** to fail to pay (taxes) **c :** to avoid answering directly **:** turn aside **3 :** to be elusive to **:** BAFFLE ⟨the simple, personal meaning *evaded* them —C. D. Lewis⟩ ***syn*** see ESCAPE — **evad·able** \-ˈvād-ə-bəl\ *adj* — **evad·er** *n*
evag·i·na·tion \i-ˌvaj-ə-ˈnā-shən\ *n* [LL *evagination-, evaginatio,* act of unsheathing, fr. L *evaginatus,* pp. of *evaginare* to unsheathe, fr. *e-* + *vagina* sheath] (1663) **1 :** an act or instance of everting **2 :** a product of eversion **:** OUTGROWTH
eval·u·ate \i-ˈval-yə-ˌwāt\ *vt* **-at·ed; -at·ing** [back-formation fr. *evaluation*] (1842) **1 :** to determine or fix the value of **2 :** to determine the significance or worth of usu. by careful appraisal and study ⟨~ a new antibiotic⟩ ***syn*** see ESTIMATE — **eval·u·a·tion** \-ˌval-yə-ˈwā-shən\ *n* — **eval·u·a·tive** \-ˈval-yə-ˌwāt-iv\ *adj* — **eval·u·a·tor** \-ˌwāt-ər\ *n*
ev·a·nesce \ˌev-ə-ˈnes\ *vi* **-nesced; -nesc·ing** [L *evanescere* — more at VANISH] (1822) **:** to dissipate like vapor
ev·a·nes·cence \ˌev-ə-ˈnes-ᵊn(t)s\ *n* (1751) **1 :** the process or fact of evanescing **2 :** evanescent quality
ev·a·nes·cent \-ᵊnt\ *adj* [L *evanescent-, evanescens,* prp. of *evanescere*] (1717) **:** tending to vanish like vapor ***syn*** see TRANSIENT
[1]**evan·gel** \i-ˈvan-jəl\ *n* [ME *evangile,* fr. MF, fr. LL *evangelium,* fr. Gk *euangelion* good news, gospel, fr. *euangelos* bringing good news, fr. *eu-* + *angelos* messenger] (14c) **:** GOSPEL
[2]**evangel** *n* (1614) **:** EVANGELIST
evan·gel·i·cal \ˌē-ˌvan-ˈjel-i-kəl, ˌev-ən-\ *also* **evan·gel·ic** \-ik\ *adj* (1531) **1 :** PROTESTANT **2 :** of, relating to, or being in agreement with the Christian gospel esp. as it is presented in the four Gospels **3 :** emphasizing salvation by faith in the atoning death of Jesus Christ through personal conversion, the authority of Scripture, and the importance of preaching as contrasted with ritual **4 a** *cap* **:** of or relating to the Evangelical Church in Germany **b** *often cap* **:** of, adhering to, or marked by fundamentalism **:** FUNDAMENTALIST **c** *often cap* **:** LOW CHURCH **5 :** marked by militant or crusading zeal **:** EVANGELISTIC, ZEALOUS ⟨the ~ ardor of the movement's leaders —Amos Vogel⟩ — **Evan·gel·i·cal·ism** \-i-kə-ˌliz-əm\ *n* — **evan·gel·i·cal·ly** \-i-k(ə-)lē\ *adv*
Evangelical *n* (1532) **:** one holding evangelical principles or belonging to an evangelical party or church
evan·ge·lism \i-ˈvan-jə-ˌliz-əm\ *n* (1626) **1 :** the winning or revival of personal commitments to Christ **2 :** militant or crusading zeal — **evan·ge·lis·tic** \-ˌvan-jə-ˈlis-tik\ *adj* — **evan·ge·lis·ti·cal·ly** \-ti-k(ə-)lē\ *adv*
evan·ge·list \i-ˈvan-jə-ləst\ *n* (12c) **1** *often cap* **:** a writer of any of the four Gospels **2 :** one who evangelizes; *specif* **:** a Protestant minister or layman who preaches at special services
evan·ge·lize \i-ˈvan-jə-ˌlīz\ *vb* **-lized; -liz·ing** *vt* (14c) **1 :** to preach the gospel to **2 :** to convert to Christianity ~ *vi* **:** to preach the gospel — **evan·ge·li·za·tion** \-ˌvan-jə-lə-ˈzā-shən\ *n*
evap·o·rate \i-ˈvap-ə-ˌrāt\ *vb* **-rat·ed; -rat·ing** [ME *evaporaten,* fr. L *evaporatus,* pp. of *evaporare,* fr. *e-* + *vapor* steam, vapor] *vt* (15c) **1 a :** to convert into vapor; *also* **:** to dissipate or draw off in vapor or fumes **b :** to deposit (as a metal) in the form of a film by sublimation **2 a :** to expel moisture from **b :** EXPEL ⟨~ electrons from a hot wire⟩ ~ *vi* **1 a :** to pass off in vapor or in invisible minute particles **b** (1) **:** to pass off or away **:** DISAPPEAR ⟨my despair *evaporated* —J. F. Wharton⟩ (2) **:** to diminish quickly **2 :** to give forth vapor — **evap·o·ra·tion** \-ˌvap-ə-ˈrā-shən\ *n* — **evap·o·ra·tive** \-ˈvap-ə-ˌrāt-iv\ *adj* — **evap·o·ra·tive·ly** *adv* — **evap·o·ra·tiv·i·ty** \-ˌvap-ə-rə-ˈtiv-ət-ē\ *n* — **evap·o·ra·tor** \-ˈvap-ə-ˌrāt-ər\ *n*
evaporated milk *n* (1870) **:** unsweetened milk concentrated by partial evaporation
evap·o·rite \i-ˈvap-ə-ˌrīt\ *n* [*evapora*tion + *-ite*] (1924) **:** a sedimentary rock (as gypsum) that originates by evaporation of seawater in an enclosed basin — **evap·o·rit·ic** \-ˌvap-ə-ˈrit-ik\ *adj*
evapo·trans·pi·ra·tion \i-ˈvap-ō-ˌtran(t)-spə-ˈrā-shən\ *n* [*evaporation* + *transpiration*] (1938) **:** loss of water from the soil both by evaporation and by transpiration from the plants growing thereon
eva·sion \i-ˈvā-zhən\ *n* [ME, fr. MF or LL; MF, fr. LL *evasion-, evasio,* fr. L *evasus,* pp. of *evadere* to evade] (15c) **1 :** the act or an instance of evading **:** ESCAPE ⟨suspected of tax ~⟩ **2 :** a means of evading **:** DODGE
eva·sive \i-ˈvā-siv, -ziv\ *adj* (1725) **:** tending or intended to evade **:** EQUIVOCAL ⟨~ answers⟩ — **eva·sive·ly** *adv* — **eva·sive·ness** *n*
eve \ˈēv\ *n* [ME *eve, even*] (13c) **1 :** EVENING **2 :** the evening or the day before a special day **3 :** the period immediately preceding
Eve \ˈēv\ *n* [OE *Ēfe,* fr. LL *Eva,* fr. Heb *Ḥawwāh*] **:** the first woman and wife of Adam
evec·tion \i-ˈvek-shən\ *n* [L *evection-, evectio* rising, fr. *evectus,* pp. of *evehere* to carry out, raise up, fr. *e-* + *vehere* to carry — more at WAY] (1706) **:** perturbation of the moon's orbital motion due to the attraction of the sun
[1]**even** \ˈē-vən, ˈēb-ᵊm\ *n* [ME, *even, eve,* fr. OE *ǣfen*] *archaic* (bef. 12c) **:** EVENING
[2]**even** *adj* [ME, fr. OE *efen;* akin to OHG *eban* even] (bef. 12c) **1 a :** having a horizontal surface **:** FLAT ⟨~ ground⟩ **b :** being without break, indentation, roughness, or other irregularity **:** SMOOTH **c :** being in the same plane or line **2 a :** free from irregularity or variation **:** UNIFORM ⟨his disposition was ~⟩ **b :** LEVEL 4 **3 a** *obs* **:** CANDID **b :** EQUAL, FAIR ⟨an ~ exchange⟩ **c** (1) **:** leaving nothing due on either side **:** SQUARE ⟨we will not be ~ until you repay my visit⟩ (2) **:** fully revenged **d :** being in equilibrium **:** BALANCED; *specif* **:** showing neither profit nor loss **4 a :** being one of the sequence of natural numbers beginning with two and counting by twos that are exactly divisible by two **b :** marked by an even number **c :** being a mathematical function such that $f(x) = f(-x)$ where the value remains unchanged if the sign of the independent variable is reversed **5 :** EXACT, PRECISE ⟨an ~ dollar⟩ **6 :** as likely as not **:** FIFTY-FIFTY ⟨an ~ chance of winning⟩

syn see LEVEL, STEADY — **even·ly** *adv* — **even·ness** \-vən-nəs\ *n* — **on an even keel** *also* **on even keel** : in a sound or stable condition

[3]**even** *adv* [ME, fr. OE *efne,* fr. *efen,* adj.] (bef. 12c) **1 a** : EXACTLY, PRECISELY **b** : to a degree that extends : FULLY, QUITE ⟨faithful ~ unto death⟩ **c** : at the very time **2 a** — used as an intensive to emphasize the identity or character of something ⟨he looked content, ~ happy⟩ **b** — used as an intensive to indicate something unexpected ⟨refused ~ to look at her⟩ **c** — used as an intensive to stress the comparative degree ⟨he did ~ better⟩

[4]**even** *vb* **evened; even·ing** \ˈēv-(ə-)niŋ\ *vt* (13c) : to make even ~ *vi* : to become even — **even·er** \-(ə-)nər\ *n*

even·fall \ˈē-vən-ˌfȯl\ *n* (1814) : the beginning of evening : DUSK

even·hand·ed \ˌē-vən-ˈhan-dəd\ *adj* (1605) : FAIR, IMPARTIAL — **even·hand·ed·ly** *adv* — **even·hand·ed·ness** *n*

eve·ning \ˈēv-niŋ\ *n, often attrib* [ME, fr. OE *ǣfnung,* fr. *ǣfnian* to grow toward evening, fr. *ǣfen* evening; akin to OHG *āband* evening and perh. to Gk *epi* on] (bef. 12c) **1 a** : the latter part and close of the day and early part of the night **b** *chiefly Southern & Midland* : AFTERNOON **c** : the period from sunset or the evening meal to bedtime **2** : the latter portion **3** : the period of an evening's entertainment

evening dress *n* (1797) : dress for evening social occasions

evening prayer *n, often cap E&P* (1598) : the daily evening office of the Anglican liturgy

evening primrose *n* (1806) : any of several dicotyledonous plants of a family (Onagraceae, the evening-primrose family) and esp. of the type genus (*Oenothera*); *esp* : a coarse biennial herb (*O. biennis*) with yellow flowers that open in the evening

eve·nings \ˈēv-niŋz\ *adv* (1870) : in the evening repeatedly : on any evening ⟨goes bowling ~⟩

evening star *n* (1535) **1** : a bright planet (as Venus) seen esp. in the western sky at or after sunset **2** : a planet that rises before midnight

even permutation *n* (ca. 1932) : a permutation that is produced by the successive application of an even number of interchanges of pairs of elements

even·song \ˈē-vən-ˌsȯŋ\ *n, often cap* [ME, fr. OE *ǣfensang,* fr. *ǣfen* even + *sang* song] (bef. 12c) **1** : VESPERS 1 **2** : EVENING PRAYER

event \i-ˈvent\ *n* [MF or L; MF, fr. L *eventus,* fr. *eventus,* pp. of *evenire* to happen, fr. *e-* + *venire* to come — more at COME] (1573) **1 a** *archaic* : OUTCOME **b** : the final outcome or determination of a legal action **c** : a postulated outcome, condition, or eventuality ⟨in the ~ that I am not there, call the house⟩ **2 a** : something that happens : OCCURRENCE **b** : a noteworthy happening **c** : a social occasion or activity **3** : any of the contests in a program of sports **4** : the fundamental entity of observed physical reality represented by a point designated by three coordinates of place and one of time in the space-time continuum postulated by the theory of relativity **5** : a subset of the possible outcomes of an experiment ⟨7 is an ~ in the throwing of two dice⟩ *syn* see EFFECT, OCCURRENCE — **event·less** \-ləs\ *adj* — **at all events** : in any case — **in any event** : in any case — **in the event** *Brit* : as it turns out

event·ful \i-ˈvent-fəl\ *adj* (1600) **1** : full of or rich in events **2** : MOMENTOUS — **event·ful·ly** \-fə-lē\ *adv* — **event·ful·ness** *n*

even·tide \ˈē-vən-ˌtīd\ *n* (bef. 12c) : the time of evening : EVENING

even·tu·al \i-ˈvench-(ə-)wəl, -ˈven-chəl\ *adj* (1683) **1** *archaic* : CONTINGENT, CONDITIONAL **2** : taking place at an unspecified later time : ultimately resulting ⟨they counted on our ~ success⟩ *syn* see LAST

even·tu·al·ly \-ē\ *adv* (1680) : at an unspecified later time : in the end

even·tu·al·i·ty \i-ˌven-chə-ˈwal-ət-ē\ *n, pl* **-ties** (1759) : a possible event or outcome : POSSIBILITY

even·tu·ate \i-ˈven-chə-ˌwāt\ *vi* **-at·ed; -at·ing** (1789) : to come out finally : RESULT ⟨emotional growth . . . ~s in balance and control — *Encyc. Americana*⟩

ev·er \ˈev-ər\ *adv* [ME, fr. OE *ǣfre*] (bef. 12c) **1** : ALWAYS ⟨~ striving to improve⟩ ⟨the *ever*-increasing population⟩ **2 a** : at any time ⟨more than ~ before⟩ **b** : in any way ⟨how can I ~ thank you⟩ **3** — used as an intensive esp. with *so* ⟨looks ~ so angry⟩

ev·er·bloom·ing \ˌev-ər-ˈblü-miŋ\ *adj* (ca. 1891) : blooming more or less continuously throughout the growing season

ev·er·glade \ˈev-ər-ˌglād\ *n* [the *Everglades,* Fla.] (1823) : a swampy grassland esp. in southern Florida usu. containing saw grass and at least seasonally covered by slowly moving water — usu. used in pl.

[1]**ev·er·green** \ˈev-ər-ˌgrēn\ *n* (1644) **1** : an evergreen plant; *also* : CONIFER **2** *pl* : twigs and branches of evergreen plants used for decoration **3** : something that retains its freshness, interest, or popularity

[2]**evergreen** *adj* (1671) **1** : having foliage that remains green and functional through more than one growing season — compare DECIDUOUS **2** : ever retaining its freshness, interest, or popularity : PERENNIAL, ENDURING

evergreen oak *n* (1775) : any of various oaks (as a live oak, a holm oak, or a tan oak) with foliage that persists for two years so that the plant is more or less continuously green

[1]**ev·er·last·ing** \ˌev-ər-ˈlas-tiŋ\ *adj* (13c) **1** : lasting or enduring through all time : ETERNAL **2 a** (1) : continuing long or indefinitely (2) *of a plant* : retaining its form or color for a long time when dried **b** : tediously persistent ⟨the ~ sympathy-seeker who demands attention — H. A. Overstreet⟩ **3** : wearing indefinitely — **ev·er·last·ing·ly** \-tiŋ-lē\ *adv* — **ev·er·last·ing·ness** *n*

[2]**everlasting** *n* (14c) **1** : ETERNITY ⟨from ~ ⟩ **2** *cap* : GOD 1 — used with *the* **3 a** : any of several chiefly composite plants (as cudweed) with flowers that can be dried without loss of form or color — compare PEARLY EVERLASTING **b** : the flower of an everlasting

ev·er·more \ˌev-ər-ˈmō(ə)r, -ˈmȯ(ə)r\ *adv* (13c) **1** : FOREVER, ALWAYS **2** : in the future

ever·sion \i-ˈvər-zhən, -shən\ *n* (1751) **1** : the act of turning inside out : the state of being turned inside out ⟨~ of the bladder⟩ **2** : the condition (as of the foot) of being turned or rotated outward — **ever·si·ble** \-ˈvər-sə-bəl\ *adj*

evert \i-ˈvərt\ *vt* [L *evertere,* fr. *e-* + *vertere* to turn — more at WORTH] (1533) **1** : OVERTHROW, UPSET **2** : to subject (as an anatomical part) to eversion

ev·ery \ˈev-rē\ *adj* [ME *everich, every,* fr. OE *ǣfre ǣlc,* fr. *ǣfre* ever + *ǣlc* each] (bef. 12c) **1** : being each individual or part of a group without exception **2** *obs* : being all taken severally **3** : being each within a range of possibilities ⟨was given ~ chance⟩ **4** : COMPLETE, ENTIRE — **every now and then** *or* **every now and again** *or* **every so often** : at intervals : OCCASIONALLY

ev·ery·body \ˈev-ri-ˌbäd-ē, -bəd-\ *pron* (1530) : every person : EVERYONE

ev·ery·day \ˌev-rē-ˌdā\ *adj* (1632) : encountered or used routinely or typically : ORDINARY ⟨clothes for ~ wear⟩ — **ev·ery·day·ness** \-ˈdā-nəs\ *n*

ev·ery·man \ˈev-rē-ˌman\ *n* [*Everyman,* allegorical character in *The Summoning of Everyman,* 15th cent. Eng. morality play] *often cap* (1906) : the typical or ordinary person ⟨an *Everyman,* always tempted, always guileless, always rueful —Walter Terry⟩

ev·ery·one \-(ˌ)wən\ *pron* (13c) : EVERYBODY

ev·ery·place \-ˌplās\ *adv* (ca. 1917) : EVERYWHERE

ev·ery·thing \ˈev-rē-ˌthiŋ\ *pron* (14c) **1 a** : all that exists **b** : all that relates to the subject **2** : something that is most important or excellent : all that counts ⟨you mean ~ to me⟩

ev·ery·where \ˈev-rē-ˌ(h)we(ə)r, -ˌ(h)wa(ə)r\ *adv* (13c) : in every place or part

every which way \ˌev-rē-ˈhwich-ˌwā, -ˈwich-\ *adv* [prob. by folk etymology fr. ME *everich way* every way] (1824) **1** : in every direction **2** : in a disorderly manner : IRREGULARLY ⟨toys scattered about *every which way*⟩

evict \i-ˈvikt\ *vt* [ME *evicten,* fr. LL *evictus,* pp. of *evincere,* fr. L, to vanquish, win a point — more at EVINCE] (15c) **1 a** : to recover (property) from a person by legal process **b** : to put (a tenant) out by legal process **2** : to force out : EXPEL *syn* see EJECT — **evic·tion** \-ˈvik-shən\ *n* — **evic·tor** \-ˈvik-tər\ *n*

evict·ee \i-ˌvik-ˈtē\ *n* (1879) : an evicted person

[1]**ev·i·dence** \ˈev-əd-ən(t)s, -ə-ˌden(t)s\ *n* (14c) **1 a** : an outward sign : INDICATION **b** : something that furnishes proof : TESTIMONY; *specif* : something legally submitted to a tribunal to ascertain the truth of a matter **2** : one who bears witness; *esp* : one who voluntarily confesses a crime and testifies for the prosecution against his accomplices — **in evidence 1** : to be seen : CONSPICUOUS ⟨trim lawns . . . are everywhere *in evidence* —*Amer. Guide Series: N.C.*⟩ **2** : as evidence

[2]**evidence** *vt* **-denced; -denc·ing** (1619) : to offer evidence of : PROVE, EVINCE *syn* see SHOW

ev·i·dent \ˈev-əd-ənt, -ə-ˌdent\ *adj* [ME, fr. MF, fr. L *evident-, evidens,* fr. *e-* + *vident-, videns,* prp. of *vidēre* to see — more at WIT] (14c) : clear to the vision or understanding

syn EVIDENT, MANIFEST, PATENT, DISTINCT, OBVIOUS, APPARENT, PLAIN, CLEAR mean readily perceived or apprehended. EVIDENT implies presence of visible signs that lead one to a definite conclusion; MANIFEST implies an external display so evident that little or no inference is required; PATENT applies to a cause, effect, or significant feature that is clear and unmistakable once attention has been directed to it; DISTINCT implies such sharpness of outline or definition that no unusual effort to see or hear or comprehend is required; OBVIOUS implies such ease in discovering or accounting for that it often suggests conspicuousness or little need for perspicacity in the observer; APPARENT is very close to EVIDENT except that it may imply more conscious exercise of inference; PLAIN and CLEAR imply the quality of being unmistakable, PLAIN because of lack of intricacy, complexity, or elaboration, CLEAR because of an absence of anything that confuses the mind or obscures the pattern.

ev·i·den·tial \ˌev-ə-ˈden-chəl\ *adj* (1641) : being, relating to, or affording evidence ⟨photographs of ~ value⟩ — **ev·i·den·tial·ly** \-ˈdench-(ə-)lē\ *adv*

ev·i·den·tia·ry \ˌev-ə-ˈden-chə-rē, -chē-ˌer-ē\ *adj* (1810) **1** : EVIDENTIAL **2** : conducted so that evidence may be presented ⟨an ~ hearing⟩

ev·i·dent·ly \ˈev-əd-ənt-lē, -ə-ˌdent-, *esp for 2 often* ˌev-ə-ˈdent-\ *adv* (14c) **1** : in an evident manner : CLEARLY, OBVIOUSLY ⟨any style that is . . . so ~ bad or second-rate —T. S. Eliot⟩ **2** : on the basis of available evidence ⟨he was born . . . ~ in Texas —Robert Coughlan⟩

[1]**evil** \ˈē-vəl, *Brit often & US also* ˈē-(ˌ)vil\ *adj* **evil·er** *or* **evil·ler; evil·est** *or* **evil·lest** [ME, fr. OE *yfel;* akin to OHG *ubil* evil] (bef. 12c) **1 a** : morally reprehensible : SINFUL, WICKED ⟨an ~ impulse⟩ **b** : arising from actual or imputed bad character or conduct ⟨a man of ~ reputation⟩ **2 a** *archaic* : INFERIOR **b** : causing discomfort or repulsion : OFFENSIVE ⟨an ~ odor⟩ **c** : DISAGREEABLE ⟨woke late and in an ~ temper⟩ **3 a** : causing harm : PERNICIOUS ⟨the ~ institution of slavery⟩ **b** : marked by misfortune : UNLUCKY *syn* see BAD — **evil** *adv, archaic* — **evil·ly** \-(l)ē\ *adv* — **evil·ness** \-nəs\ *n*

[2]**evil** *n* (bef. 12c) **1** : something that brings sorrow, distress, or calamity **2 a** : the fact of suffering, misfortune, and wrongdoing **b** : a cosmic evil force

evil·do·er \ˌē-vəl-ˈdü-ər\ *n* (14c) : one who does evil

evil·do·ing \-ˈdü-iŋ\ *n* (14c) : the act or action of doing evil

evil eye *n* (bef. 12c) : an eye or glance held capable of inflicting harm; *also* : a person believed to have such an eye or glance

evil–mind·ed \ˌē-vəl-ˈmīn-dəd, -vil-\ *adj* (1531) : having an evil disposition or evil thoughts — **evil–mind·ed·ly** *adv* — **evil–mind·ed·ness** *n*

evince \i-ˈvin(t)s\ *vt* **evinced; evinc·ing** [L *evincere* to vanquish, win a point, fr. *e-* + *vincere* to conquer — more at VICTOR] (1621) **1** : to constitute outward evidence of **2** : to display clearly : REVEAL *syn* see SHOW — **evinc·ible** \-ˈvin(t)-sə-bəl\ *adj*

evis·cer·ate \i-ˈvis-ə-ˌrāt\ *vb* **-at·ed; -at·ing** [L *evisceratus,* pp. of *eviscerare,* fr. *e-* + *viscera* viscera] *vt* (1621) **1 a** : to take out the entrails of : DISEMBOWEL **b** : to deprive of vital content or force **2** : to remove an organ from (a patient) or the contents of (an organ) ~ *vi* : to protrude through a surgical incision or suffer protrusion of a part through an incision — **evis·cer·a·tion** \-ˌvis-ə-ˈrā-shən\ *n*

ev·i·ta·ble \ˈev-ət-ə-bəl\ *adj* [L *evitabilis,* fr. *evitare* to avoid, fr. *e-* + *vitare* to shun] (1502) : capable of being avoided

evo·ca·ble \ˈev-ə-kə-bəl, i-ˈvō-kə-\ *adj* (1886) : capable of being evoked

evo·ca·tion \ˌē-vō-ˈkā-shən, ˌev-ə-\ *n* [L *evocation-, evocatio,* fr. *evocatus,* pp. of *evocare*] (1574) **1** : the act or fact of evoking : SUMMONING: as **a** : the summoning of a spirit **b** : imaginative recreation ⟨a contemporary film rather than an ~ of the past —R. M. Coles⟩ **2** : INDUCTION 4e — **evo·ca·tor** \ˈē-vō-ˌkāt-ər, ˈev-ə-\ *n*

evoc·a·tive \i-ˈväk-ət-iv\ *adj* (1657) : tending or serving to evoke ⟨settings . . . so ~ that they bring tears to the eyes —Eric Malpass⟩ — **evoc·a·tive·ly** *adv* — **evoc·a·tive·ness** *n*

evoke \i-ˈvōk\ *vt* **evoked; evok·ing** [F *évoquer,* fr. L *evocare,* fr. *e-* + *vocare* to call — more at VOCATION] (1623) **1 :** to call forth or up: as **a :** CONJURE 2a ⟨~ evil spirits⟩ **b :** to cite esp. with approval or for support : INVOKE **c :** to bring to mind or recollection ⟨this place ~*s* memories of happier years⟩ **2 :** to recreate imaginatively ***syn*** see EDUCE

evo·lute \ˈev-ə-ˌlüt *also* ˈē-və-\ *n* (1730) **:** the locus of the center of curvature or the envelope of the normals of a curve

evo·lu·tion \ˌev-ə-ˈlü-shən, ˌē-və-\ *n* [L *evolution-, evolutio* unrolling, fr. *evolutus,* pp. of *evolvere*] (1622) **1 a :** a process of change in a certain direction : UNFOLDING **b :** the action or an instance of forming and giving something off : EMISSION **c (1) :** a process of continuous change from a lower, simpler, or worse to a higher, more complex, or better state : GROWTH **(2) :** a process of gradual and relatively peaceful social, political, and economic advance **d :** something evolved **2 :** one of a set of prescribed movements **3 :** the process of working out or developing **4 :** the extraction of a mathematical root **5 a :** the historical development of a biological group (as a race or species) : PHYLOGENY **b :** a theory that the various types of animals and plants have their origin in other preexisting types and that the distinguishable differences are due to modifications in successive generations **6 :** a process in which the whole universe is a progression of interrelated phenomena — **evo·lu·tion·ari·ly** \-shə-ˌner-ə-lē\ *adv* — **evo·lu·tion·ary** \-shə-ˌner-ē\ *adj* — **evo·lu·tion·ism** \-shə-ˌniz-əm\ *n* — **evo·lu·tion·ist** \-sh(ə-)nəst\ *n or adj*

evolve \i-ˈvälv, -ˈvȯlv *also* -ˈväv *or* -ˈvȯv\ *vb* **evolved; evolv·ing** [L *evolvere* to unroll, fr. *e-* + *volvere* to roll — more at VOLUBLE] *vt* (1641) **1 a :** DERIVE, EDUCE **b :** DEVELOP, WORK OUT ⟨~ social, political, and literary philosophies —L. W. Doob⟩ **c :** to produce by natural evolutionary processes **2 :** EMIT ~ *vi* **:** to undergo evolutionary change — **evolv·able** \-ˈväl-və-bəl, -ˈvȯl- *also* -ˈväv-ə- *or* -ˈvȯv-ə-\ *adj* — **evolve·ment** \-ˈvälv-mənt, -ˈvȯlv- *also* -ˈväv- *or* -ˈvȯv-\ *n*

evul·sion \i-ˈvəl-shən\ *n* [L *evulsion-, evulsio,* fr. *evulsus,* pp. of *evellere* to pluck out, fr. *e-* + *vellere* to pluck — more at VULNERABLE] (1611) **:** EXTRACTION

ev·zone \ˈev-ˌzōn\ *n* [NGk *euzōnos,* fr. Gk, active, lit., well girt, fr. *eu-* + *zōnē* girdle — more at ZONE] (1897) **:** a member of a select Greek infantry unit

ewe \ˈyü, ˈyō\ *n* [ME, fr. OE *ēowu;* akin to OHG *ouwi* ewe, L *ovis* sheep, GK *ois*] (bef. 12c) **:** the female of the sheep esp. when mature; *also* **:** the female of various related animals

Ewe \ˈā-ˌwā, ˈā-ˌvā\ *n* (1890) **:** a Kwa language of Ghana and Togo

ewe–neck \-ˈnek\ *n* (1820) **:** a thin neck with a concave arch occurring as a defect in dogs and horses — **ewe–necked** \-ˈnekt\ *adj*

ew·er \ˈyü-ər, ˈyu̇(-ə)r\ *n* [ME, fr. AF, fr. OF *evier,* fr. (assumed) VL *aquarium,* fr. L, neut. of *aquarius* of water, fr. *aqua* water — more at ISLAND] (14c) **:** a vase-shaped pitcher or jug

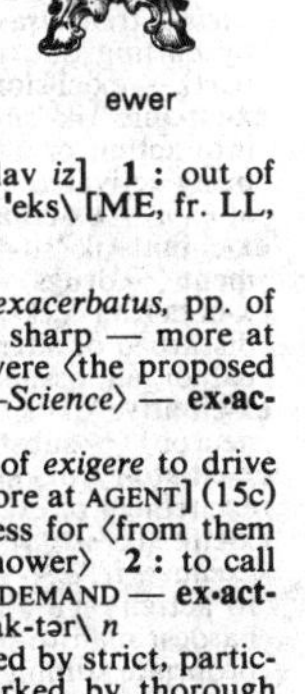

ewer

¹ex \ˈeks\ *n* (bef. 12c) **:** the letter *x*

²ex \(ˌ)eks\ *prep* [L] (ca. 1795) **1 :** out of : FROM: as **a :** from a specified place or source **b :** from a specified dam ⟨a promising calf by Eric XVI ~ Heatherbell⟩ **2 :** free from : WITHOUT: as **a :** without an indicated value or right — used esp. of securities **b :** free of charges precedent to removal from the specified place with purchaser to provide means of subsequent transportation ⟨~ dock⟩

³ex \ˈeks\ *n* [¹*ex-*] (1827) **:** one that formerly held a specified position or place; *esp* **:** a former spouse

¹ex- \e *also occurs in this prefix where only* i *is shown below (as in "express") and* ks *sometimes occurs where only* gz *is shown (as in "exact")*\ *prefix* [ME, fr. OF & L; OF, fr. L (also, intensive prefix), fr. *ex* out of, from; akin to Gk *ex, ex-* out of, from, OSlav *iz*] **1 :** out of : outside ⟨*ex*clave⟩ **2 :** not ⟨*ex*stipulate⟩ **3** \(ˌ)eks, ˈeks\ [ME, fr. LL, fr. L] **:** former ⟨*ex*-president⟩ ⟨*ex*-child actor⟩

²ex- — see EXO-

ex·ac·er·bate \ig-ˈzas-ər-ˌbāt\ *vt* **-bat·ed; -bat·ing** [L *exacerbatus,* pp. of *exacerbare,* fr. *ex-* + *acerbus* harsh, bitter, fr. *acer* sharp — more at EDGE] (1582) **:** to make more violent, bitter, or severe ⟨the proposed shutdown . . . would ~ unemployment problems —*Science*⟩ — **ex·ac·er·ba·tion** \-ˌzas-ər-ˈbā-shən\ *n*

¹ex·act \ig-ˈzakt\ *vt* [ME *exacten,* fr. L *exactus,* pp. of *exigere* to drive out, demand, measure, fr. *ex-* + *agere* to drive — more at AGENT] (15c) **1 :** to call for forcibly or urgently and obtain : press for ⟨from them has been ~*ed* the ultimate sacrifice —D. D. Eisenhower⟩ **2 :** to call for as necessary, appropriate, or desirable ***syn*** see DEMAND — **ex·act·able** \-ˈzak-tə-bəl\ *adj* — **ex·ac·tor** *also* **ex·act·er** \-ˈzak-tər\ *n*

²exact *adj* [L *exactus*] (1533) **1 :** exhibiting or marked by strict, particular, and complete accordance with fact **2 :** marked by thorough consideration or minute measurement of small factual details ***syn*** see CORRECT — **ex·act·ness** \-ˈzak(t)-nəs\ *n*

ex·ac·ta \ig-ˈzak-tə\ *n* [AmerSp *quiniela exacta* exact quiniela] (ca. 1964) **:** PERFECTA

exact differential *n* (1825) **:** a differential expression of the form $X_1dx_1 + \ldots + X_ndx_n$ where the *X's* are the partial derivatives of a function $f(x_1, \ldots, x_n)$ with respect to $x_1, \ldots, x_n$ respectively

ex·act·ing \ig-ˈzak-tiŋ\ *adj* (1583) **1 :** tryingly or unremittingly severe in making demands **2 :** requiring careful attention and precise accuracy ***syn*** see ONEROUS — **ex·act·ing·ly** \-tiŋ-lē\ *adv* — **ex·act·ing·ness** *n*

ex·ac·tion \ig-ˈzak-shən\ *n* (14c) **1 a :** the act or process of exacting **b :** EXTORTION **2 :** something exacted; *esp* **:** a fee, reward, or contribution demanded or levied with severity or injustice

ex·ac·ti·tude \ig-ˈzak-tə-ˌt(y)üd\ *n* (1734) **:** the quality or an instance of being exact : EXACTNESS

ex·act·ly \ig-ˈzak-(t)lē\ *adv* (1612) **1 a :** in a manner or to a degree that strictly conforms to a fact or condition ⟨it's ~ 3 o'clock⟩ ⟨do ~ as you're told⟩ ⟨these two pieces are ~ the same size⟩ **b :** in every respect : ALTOGETHER, ENTIRELY ⟨that was ~ the wrong thing to do⟩ ⟨not ~ what I had in mind⟩ **2 :** quite so — used to express agreement

exact science *n* (1898) **:** a science (as physics, chemistry, or astronomy) whose laws are capable of accurate quantitative expression

ex·ag·ger·ate \ig-ˈzaj-ə-ˌrāt\ *vb* **-at·ed; -at·ing** [L *exaggeratus,* pp. of *exaggerare,* lit., to heap up, fr. *ex-* + *agger* heap, fr. *aggerere* to carry toward, fr. *ad-* + *gerere* to carry — more at CAST] *vt* (1563) **1 :** to enlarge beyond bounds or the truth : OVERSTATE ⟨a friend ~*s* a man's virtues —Joseph Addison⟩ **2 :** to enlarge or increase esp. beyond the normal : OVEREMPHASIZE ~ *vi* **:** to make an overstatement — **ex·ag·ger·at·ed·ly** *adv* — **ex·ag·ger·at·ed·ness** *n* — **ex·ag·ger·a·tion** \-ˌzaj-ə-ˈrā-shən\ *n* — **ex·ag·ger·a·tive** \-ˈzaj-ə-ˌrāt-iv, ˈ-zaj-(ə-)rət-\ *adj* — **ex·ag·ger·a·tor** \-ˈzaj-ə-ˌrāt-ər\ *n* — **ex·ag·ger·a·to·ry** \-ˈzaj-(ə-)rə-ˌtōr-ē, -ˌtȯr-\ *adj*

ex·alt \ig-ˈzȯlt\ *vb* [ME *exalten,* fr. MF & L; MF *exalter,* fr. L *exaltare,* fr. *ex-* + *altus* high — more at OLD] *vt* (15c) **1 :** to raise high : ELEVATE **2 :** to raise in rank, power, or character **3 :** to elevate by praise or in estimation : GLORIFY **4** *obs* **:** ELATE **5 :** to enhance the activity of : INTENSIFY ⟨rousing and ~*ing* the imagination —George Eliot⟩ ~ *vi* **:** to induce exaltation — **ex·alt·ed·ly** *adv* — **ex·alt·er** *n*

ex·al·ta·tion \ˌeg-ˌzȯl-ˈtā-shən, ˌek-ˌsȯl-\ *n* (14c) **1 :** an act of exalting **:** the state of being exalted **2 :** an excessively intensified sense of well-being, power, or importance **3 :** an increase in degree or intensity ⟨~ of virulence of a virus⟩

ex·am \ig-ˈzam\ *n* (1877) **:** EXAMINATION

ex·a·men \ig-ˈzā-mən\ *n* [L, tongue of a balance, examination, fr. *exigere* — more at EXACT] (1606) **1 :** EXAMINATION **2 :** a critical study

ex·am·i·nant \-ˈzam-ə-nənt\ *n* (1588) **1 :** EXAMINEE **2 :** one who examines : EXAMINER

ex·am·i·na·tion \ig-ˌzam-ə-ˈnā-shən\ *n* (14c) **1 :** the act or process of examining **:** the state of being examined **2 :** an exercise designed to examine progress or test qualification or knowledge **3 :** a formal interrogation — **ex·am·i·na·tion·al** \-shnəl, -shən-ᵊl\ *adj*

ex·am·i·na·to·ri·al \-nə-ˈtōr-ē-əl, -ˈtȯr-\ *adj* (1866) **:** of or relating to an examiner or examination

ex·am·ine \ig-ˈzam-ən\ *vb* **ex·am·ined; ex·am·in·ing** \-(ə-)niŋ\ [ME *examinen,* fr. MF *examiner,* fr. L *examinare,* fr. *examen*] *vt* (14c) **1 a :** to inspect closely **b :** to test the condition of **c :** to inquire into carefully : INVESTIGATE **2 a :** to interrogate closely ⟨~ a prisoner⟩ **b :** to test by questioning in order to determine progress, fitness, or knowledge ~ *vi* **:** to make or give an examination ***syn*** see SCRUTINIZE — **ex·am·in·able** \-ˈzam-ə-nə-bəl\ *adj* — **ex·am·in·er** \-ˈzam-(ə-)nər\ *n*

ex·am·in·ee \ig-ˌzam-ə-ˈnē\ *n* (1788) **:** a person who is examined

¹ex·am·ple \ig-ˈzam-pəl\ *n* [ME, fr. MF, fr. L *exemplum,* fr. *eximere* to take out, fr. *ex-* + *emere* to take — more at REDEEM] (14c) **1 :** one that serves as a pattern to be imitated or not to be imitated ⟨a good ~⟩ ⟨a bad ~⟩ **2 :** a punishment inflicted on someone as a warning to others; *also* **:** an individual so punished **3 :** a particular single item, fact, incident, or aspect that is representative of all of a group or type **4 :** a parallel or closely similar case esp. when serving as a precedent or model **5 :** an instance (as a problem to be solved) serving to illustrate a rule or precept or to act as an exercise in the application of a rule ***syn*** see INSTANCE, MODEL — **for example** \fər-ig-ˈzam-pəl, frig-\ **:** as an example ⟨there are many sources of air pollution; exhaust fumes, *for example*⟩

²example *vt* **ex·am·pled; ex·am·pling** \-p(ə-)liŋ\ (15c) **1 :** to serve as an example of **2** *archaic* **:** to be or set an example to

ex·an·i·mate \eg-ˈzan-ə-mət\ *adj* [L *exanimatus,* pp. of *exanimare* to deprive of life or spirit, fr. *ex-* + *anima* breath, soul — more at ANIMATE] (1534) **1 :** lacking animation : SPIRITLESS **2 :** lifeless or appearing lifeless

ex·an·them \eg-ˈzan(t)-thəm, ˈek-ˌsan-ˌthem\ *also* **ex·an·the·ma** \ˌeg-ˌzan-ˈthē-mə\ *n, pl* **-thems** *also* **-them·a·ta** \ˌeg-ˌzan-ˈthem-ət-ə\ *or* **-themas** [LL *exanthema,* fr. Gk *exanthēma,* fr. *exanthein* to bloom, break out, fr. *ex-* + *anthos* flower — more at ANTHOLOGY] (1656) **:** an eruptive disease (as measles) or its symptomatic eruption — **ex·an·them·a·tous** \ˌeg-ˌzan-ˈthem-ət-əs\ *or* **ex·an·the·mat·ic** \-ˌzan-thə-ˈmat-ik\ *adj*

¹ex·arch \ˈek-ˌsärk\ *n* [LL *exarchus,* fr. LGk *exarchos,* fr. Gk, leader, fr. *exarchein* to begin, take the lead, fr. *ex-* + *archein* to rule, begin — more at ARCH-] (1588) **1 :** a Byzantine viceroy **2 :** an Eastern bishop ranking below a patriarch and above a metropolitan; *specif* **:** the head of an independent church — **ex·ar·chal** \ek-ˈsär-kəl\ *adj* — **ex·arch·ate** \ˈek-ˌsär-kət\ *n* — **ex·ar·chy** \ˈek-ˌsär-kē\ *n*

²exarch *adj* [*exo-* + *-arch*] (1926) **:** formed or taking place from the periphery toward the center ⟨~ xylem⟩

¹ex·as·per·ate \ig-ˈzas-pə-ˌrāt\ *vt* **-at·ed; -at·ing** [L *exasperatus,* pp. of *exasperare,* fr. *ex-* + *asper* rough] (1534) **1 a :** to excite or inflame the anger of : ENRAGE **b :** to cause irritation or annoyance to **2** *obs* **:** to make grievous or more grievous or malignant — **ex·as·per·at·ed·ly** *adv* — **ex·as·per·at·ing·ly** \-ˌrāt-iŋ-lē\ *adv*

²ex·as·per·ate \-p(ə-)rət\ *adj* (1540) **1 :** irritated or annoyed esp. to the point of injudicious action : EXASPERATED **2 :** roughened with irregular prickles or elevations ⟨~ seed coats⟩

ex·as·per·a·tion \ig-ˌzas-pə-ˈrā-shən\ *n* (1547) **1 :** the state of being exasperated **2 :** the act or an instance of exasperating

Ex·cal·i·bur \ek-ˈskal-ə-bər\ *n* [ME *Excalaber,* fr. OF *Escalibor,* fr. ML *Caliburnus*] **:** the sword of King Arthur

ex ca·the·dra \ˌek-skə-ˈthē-drə\ *adv or adj* [NL, lit., from the chair] (1818) **:** by virtue of or in the exercise of one's office or position ⟨*ex cathedra* pronouncements⟩

ex·ca·vate \ˈek-skə-ˌvāt\ *vb* **-vat·ed; -vat·ing** [L *excavatus,* pp. of *excavare,* fr. *ex-* + *cavare* to make hollow — more at CAVATINA] *vt* (1599) **1 :** to form a cavity or hole in **2 :** to form by hollowing **3 :** to dig out and remove **4 :** to expose to view by or as if by digging away a covering ⟨~ the remains of an ancient civilization⟩ ⟨another writer whose work I *excavated* —William Zinsser⟩ ~ *vi* **:** to make excavations

ex·ca·va·tion \ˌek-skə-ˈvā-shən\ *n* (1611) **1 :** the action or process of excavating **2 :** a cavity formed by cutting, digging, or scooping — **ex·ca·va·tion·al** \-shnəl, -shən-ᵊl\ *adj*

\ə\ abut \ᵊ\ kitten, F table \ər\ further \a\ ash \ā\ ace \ä\ cot, cart \au̇\ out \ch\ chin \e\ bet \ē\ easy \g\ go \i\ hit \ī\ ice \j\ job \ŋ\ sing \ō\ go \ȯ\ law \ȯi\ boy \th\ thin \t͟h\ the \ü\ loot \u̇\ foot \y\ yet \zh\ vision \à, k̟, ⁿ, œ, œ̄, ue, ue̅, ʸ\ see Guide to Pronunciation

ex·ca·va·tor \'ek-skə-,vāt-ər\ *n* (ca. 1815) : one that excavates; *esp* : a power-operated shovel

ex·ceed \ik-'sēd\ *vb* [ME *exceden,* fr. MF *exceder,* fr. L *excedere,* fr. *ex-* + *cedere* to go — more at CEDE] *vt* (14c) **1** : to extend outside of ⟨the river will ~ its banks⟩ **2** : to be greater than or superior to **3** : to go beyond a limit set by ⟨~*ed* his authority⟩ ~ *vi* **1** *obs* : OVERDO **2** : PREDOMINATE

syn EXCEED, SURPASS, TRANSCEND, EXCEL, OUTDO, OUTSTRIP mean to go or be beyond a stated or implied limit, measure, or degree. EXCEED implies going beyond a limit set by authority or established by custom or by prior achievement ⟨*exceed* the speed limit⟩ SURPASS suggests superiority in quality, merit, or skill ⟨the book *surpassed* our expectations⟩ TRANSCEND implies a rising or extending notably above or beyond ordinary limits ⟨*transcended* the values of their culture⟩ EXCEL implies preeminence in achievement or quality and may suggest superiority to all others ⟨*excels* in mathematics⟩ OUTDO applies to a bettering or exceeding what has been done before ⟨*outdid* herself this time⟩ OUTSTRIP suggests surpassing in a race or competition ⟨*outstripped* other firms in selling the new plastic⟩

ex·ceed·ing *adj* (1547) : exceptional in amount, quality, or degree

ex·ceed·ing·ly \-iŋ-lē\ *or* **ex·ceed·ing** *adv* (1535) : to an extreme degree : EXTREMELY

ex·cel \ik-'sel\ *vb* **ex·celled; ex·cel·ling** [ME *excellen,* fr. L *excellere,* fr. *ex-* + *-cellere* to rise, project; akin to L *collis* hill — more at HILL] *vt* (15c) : to be superior to : surpass in accomplishment or achievement ~ *vi* : to be distinguishable by superiority : surpass others ⟨~ in mathematics⟩ ***syn*** see EXCEED

ex·cel·lence \'ek-s(ə-)lən(t)s\ *n* (14c) **1** : the quality of being excellent **2** : an excellent or valuable quality : VIRTUE **3** : EXCELLENCY 2

ex·cel·len·cy \-s(ə-)lən-sē\ *n, pl* **-cies** (15c) **1** : EXCELLENCE; *esp* : outstanding or valuable quality — usu. used in pl. ⟨so crammed, as he thinks, with *excellencies* —Shak.⟩ **2** — used as a title for certain high dignitaries of state (as a governor or an ambassador) and church (as a Roman Catholic archbishop or bishop)

ex·cel·lent \'ek-s(ə-)lənt\ *adj* [ME, fr. MF, fr. L *excellent-, excellens,* fr. prp. of *excellere*] (14c) **1** *archaic* : SUPERIOR **2** : very good of its kind : eminently good : FIRST-CLASS — **ex·cel·lent·ly** *adv*

ex·cel·si·or \ik-'sel-sē-ər\ *n* [trade name, fr. L, higher, compar. of *excelsus* high, fr. pp. of *excellere*] (1868) : fine curled wood shavings used esp. for packing fragile items

1ex·cept \ik-'sept\ *also* **ex·cept·ing** \-'sep-tiŋ\ *prep* (14c) : with the exclusion or exception of ⟨daily ~ Sundays⟩

2except *vb* [ME *excepten,* fr. MF *excepter,* fr. L *exceptare,* fr. *exceptus,* pp. of *excipere* to take out, except, fr. *ex-* + *capere* to take — more at HEAVE] *vt* (15c) : to take or leave out from a number or a whole : EXCLUDE ~ *vi* : to take exception : OBJECT

3except *also* **excepting** *conj* (15c) **1** : on any other condition than that : UNLESS ⟨~ you repent⟩ **2** : ONLY ⟨I would go ~ it's too far⟩

except for *prep* (ca. 1894) : but for ⟨*except for* you I would be dead⟩

ex·cep·tion \ik-'sep-shən\ *n* (14c) **1** : the act of excepting : EXCLUSION **2** : one that is excepted; *esp* : a case to which a rule does not apply **3** : QUESTION, OBJECTION ⟨witnesses whose authority is beyond ~ —T. B. Macaulay⟩ **4** : an oral or written legal objection (as to a court's ruling)

ex·cep·tion·able \ik-'sep-sh(ə-)nə-bəl\ *adj* (1691) : being likely to cause objection : OBJECTIONABLE ⟨visitors even drink the ~ beer —W. D. Howells⟩ — **ex·cep·tion·abil·i·ty** \-,sep-sh(ə-)nə-'bil-ət-ē\ *n* — **ex·cep·tion·ably** \-'sep-sh(ə-)nə-blē\ *adv*

ex·cep·tion·al \ik-'sep-shnəl, -shən-ᵊl\ *adj* (ca. 1846) **1** : forming an exception : RARE ⟨an ~ number of rainy days⟩ **2** : better than average : SUPERIOR ⟨~ skill⟩ **3** : deviating from the norm: as **a** : having above or below average intelligence **b** : physically handicapped — **ex·cep·tion·al·i·ty** \-,sep-shə-'nal-ət-ē\ *n* — **ex·cep·tion·al·ness** *n*

ex·cep·tion·al·ly \ik-'sep-shnə-lē, -shən-ᵊl-ē\ *adv* (1848) : in an exceptional manner : to an exceptional degree; *esp* : more than average or usual ⟨an ~ difficult task⟩

ex·cep·tive \ik-'sep-tiv\ *adj* (ca. 1860) **1** : relating to, containing, or constituting exception **2** *archaic* : CAPTIOUS

1ex·cerpt \ek-'sərpt, eg-'zərpt, 'ek-, , 'eg-,\ *vt* [L *excerptus,* pp. of *excerpere,* fr. *ex-* + *carpere* to gather, pluck — more at HARVEST] (15c) **1** : to select (a passage) for quoting : EXTRACT **2** : to take or publish extracts from (as a book) — **ex·cerpt·er** *also* **ex·cerp·tor** *n* — **ex·cerp·tion** \ek-'sərp-shən, eg-'zərp-\ *n*

2ex·cerpt \'ek-,sərpt, 'eg-,zərpt\ *n* (1627) : a passage (as from a book or musical composition) selected, performed, or copied : EXTRACT

1ex·cess \ik-'ses, 'ek-,\ *n* [ME, fr. MF or LL; MF *exces,* fr. LL *excessus,* fr. L, departure, projection, fr. *excessus,* pp. of *excedere* to exceed] (14c) **1 a** : the state or an instance of surpassing usual, proper, or specified limits : SUPERFLUITY **b** : the amount or degree by which one thing or quantity exceeds another ⟨an ~ of 10 bushels⟩ **2** : undue or immoderate indulgence : INTEMPERANCE ⟨prevent ~*es* and abuses by newly created local powers —Albert Shanker⟩ — **in excess of** : to an amount or degree beyond : OVER

2excess *adj* (15c) : more than the usual, proper, or specified amount ⟨charges for ~ baggage⟩

3excess *vt* (1974) : to eliminate the position of ⟨~*ed* several teachers because of budget cutbacks⟩

ex·ces·sive \ik-'ses-iv\ *adj* (14c) : exceeding the usual, proper, or normal — **ex·ces·sive·ly** *adv* — **ex·ces·sive·ness** *n*

syn EXCESSIVE, IMMODERATE, INORDINATE, EXTRAVAGANT, EXORBITANT, EXTREME mean going beyond a normal limit. EXCESSIVE implies an amount or degree too great to be reasonable or acceptable; IMMODERATE implies lack of desirable or necessary restraint; INORDINATE implies an exceeding of the limits dictated by reason or good judgment; EXTRAVAGANT implies an indifference to restraints imposed by truth, prudence, or good taste; EXORBITANT implies a departure from accepted standards regarding amount or degree; EXTREME may imply an approach to the farthest limit possible or conceivable but commonly means only to a notably high degree.

1ex·change \iks-'chānj, 'eks-,\ *n, often attrib* [ME *exchaunge,* fr. MF *eschange,* fr. *eschangier* to exchange, fr. (assumed) VL *excambiare,* fr. L *ex-* + *cambiare* to exchange — more at CHANGE] (14c) **1** : the act of giving or taking one thing in return for another : TRADE ⟨an ~ of prisoners⟩ **2 a** : the act of substituting one thing for another **b** : reciprocal giving and receiving **3** : something offered, given, or received in an exchange **4 a** : funds payable currently at a distant point either in a foreign currency or in domestic currency **b** (1) : interchange or conversion of the money of two countries or of current and uncurrent money with allowance for difference in value (2) : EXCHANGE RATE (3) : the amount of the difference in value between two currencies or between values of a particular currency at two places **c** : instruments (as checks or bills of exchange) presented in a clearinghouse for settlement **5** : a place where things or services are exchanged: as **a** : an organized market or center for trading in securities or commodities **b** : a store or shop specializing in merchandise usu. of a particular type **c** : a cooperative store or society **d** : a central office in which telephone lines are connected to permit communication — **in exchange** : as a substitute

2exchange *vb* **ex·changed; ex·chang·ing** *vt* (15c) **1 a** : to part with, give, or transfer in consideration of something received as an equivalent **b** : to have replaced by other merchandise ⟨*exchanged* the shirt for one in a larger size⟩ **2** : to part with for a substitute ⟨*exchanging* future security for immediate pleasure⟩ **3** : BARTER, SWAP ~ *vi* **1** : to pass or become received in exchange **2** : to engage in an exchange — **ex·change·abil·i·ty** \iks-,chān-jə-'bil-ət-ē\ *n* — **ex·change·able** \iks-'chān-jə-bəl\ *adj* — **ex·chang·er** \iks-'chān-jər, eks-,\ *n*

exchange rate *n* (1896) : the ratio at which the principal unit of two currencies may be traded

exchange student *n* (ca. 1930) : a student from one country received into an institution in another country in exchange for one sent to an institution in the home country of the first

Ex·chang·ite \iks-'chān-,jīt\ *n* [(*National*) *Exchange* (*club*)] (ca. 1934) : a member of a major national service club

ex·che·quer \'eks-,chek-ər, iks-'\ *n* [ME *escheker,* fr. AF, fr. OF *eschequier* chessboard, counting table — more at CHECKER] (14c) **1** *cap* : a department or office of state in medieval England charged with the collection and management of the royal revenue and judicial determination of all revenue causes **2** *cap* : a former superior court having jurisdiction in England and Wales primarily over revenue matters and now merged with King's Bench **3** *often cap* **a** : the department or office of state in Great Britain and Northern Ireland charged with the receipt and care of the national revenue **b** : the national banking account of this realm **4** : TREASURY; *esp* : a national or royal treasury **5** : pecuniary resources : FUNDS

ex·cip·i·ent \ik-'sip-ē-ənt\ *n* [L *excipient-, excipiens,* prp. of *excipere* to take out, take up — more at EXCEPT] (ca. 1909) : an inert substance (as gum arabic or starch) that forms a vehicle (as for a drug)

ex·ci·ple \'ek-sə-pəl\ *n* [NL *excipulum,* fr. L, receptacle, fr. *excipere*] (ca. 1866) : a saucer-shaped rim around the hymenium of various lichens

ex·cis·able \'ek-,sī-zə-bəl, -,sī-sə-, ek-'\ *adj* (1689) : subject to excise

1ex·cise \'ek-,sīz, -,sīs\ *n* [obs. D *excijs* (now *accijus*), fr. MD, prob. modif. of OF *assise* session, assessment — more at ASSIZE] (15c) **1** : an internal tax levied on the manufacture, sale, or consumption of a commodity within a country **2** : any of various taxes on privileges often assessed in the form of a license or fee

2ex·cise \'ek-,sīz, -,sīs, ik-'sīz\ *vt* **ex·cised; ex·cis·ing** (1652) : to impose an excise on

3ex·cise \ik-'sīz\ *vt* **ex·cised; ex·cis·ing** [L *excisus,* pp. of *excidere,* fr. *ex-* + *caedere* to cut — more at CONCISE] (1634) : to remove by or as if by excision : RESECT

ex·cise·man \'ek-,sīz-mən, -,sīs-, -,man, ek-'\ *n* (1647) : an officer who inspects and rates articles liable to excise under British law

ex·ci·sion \ik-'sizh-ən\ *n* [ME *excysion,* fr. MF *excision,* fr. L *excision-, excisio,* fr. *excisus*] (1541) : the act or procedure of removing by or as if by cutting out; *esp* : surgical removal or resection (as of a diseased part) — **ex·ci·sion·al** \-'sizh-nəl, -ᵊn-əl\ *adj*

ex·cit·able \ik-'sīt-ə-bəl\ *adj* (1609) : capable of being readily roused into action or a state of excitement or irritability; *specif* : capable of being activated by and reacting to stimuli — **ex·cit·abil·i·ty** \-,sīt-ə-'bil-ət-ē\ *n* — **ex·cit·able·ness** \-'sīt-ə-bəl-nəs\ *n*

ex·ci·tant \ik-'sīt-ᵊnt, 'ek-sət-ənt\ *adj* (1607) : tending to excite or augment ⟨~ drugs⟩ — **excitant** *n*

ex·ci·ta·tion \,ek-,sī-'tā-shən, ,ek-sə-\ *n* (15c) : EXCITEMENT; *esp* : the disturbed or altered condition resulting from stimulation of an individual, organ, tissue, or cell

ex·cit·ative \ik-'sīt-ət-iv\ *adj* (15c) : tending to induce excitation (as of a neuron) ⟨~ substances⟩

ex·cit·ato·ry \ik-'sīt-ə-,tōr-ē, -,tȯr-\ *adj* (15c) : exhibiting or produced by excitement or excitation

ex·cite \ik-'sīt\ *vt* **ex·cit·ed; ex·cit·ing** [ME *exciten,* fr. MF *exciter,* fr. L *excitare,* fr. *ex-* + *citare* to rouse — more at CITE] (14c) **1 a** : to call to activity **b** : to rouse to an emotional response ⟨scenes to ~ the hardest man to pity⟩ **c** : to arouse (as an emotional response) by appropriate stimuli ⟨~ enthusiasm for the new regime —Arthur Knight⟩ **2 a** : ENERGIZE ⟨~ an electromagnet⟩ **b** : to produce a magnetic field in ⟨~ a dynamo⟩ **3** : to increase the activity of (as a living organism) : STIMULATE **4** : to raise (as an atomic nucleus, an atom, or a molecule) to a higher energy level ***syn*** see PROVOKE

ex·cit·ed *adj* (ca. 1828) : having or showing strong feelings — **ex·cit·ed·ly** *adv*

excited state *n* (ca. 1909) : a state of a physical system (as an atomic nucleus, an atom, or a molecule) that is higher in energy than the ground state

ex·cite·ment \ik-'sīt-mənt\ *n* (1604) **1** : something that excites or rouses **2** : the action of exciting : the state of being excited

ex·cit·er \ik-'sīt-ər\ *n* (14c) **1** : one that excites **2 a** : a dynamo or battery that supplies the electric current used to produce the magnetic field in another dynamo or motor **b** : an electrical oscillator that generates the carrier frequency (as for a radio transmitter)

ex·cit·ing \ik-'sīt-iŋ\ *adj* (ca. 1811) : producing excitement — **ex·cit·ing·ly** \-iŋ-lē\ *adv*

ex·ci·ton \'ek-sə-,tän, -,sī-\ *n* [ISV *excitation* + *-on*] (1936) : a mobile combination of an electron and a hole in an excited crystal (as of a semiconductor) — **ex·ci·ton·ic** \,ek-sə-'tän-ik, -,sī-\ *adj*

ex·ci·tor \ik-'sīt-ər\ *n* (1816) : an afferent nerve arousing increased action of the part that it supplies

ex·claim \iks-'klām\ *vb* [MF *exclamer,* fr. L *exclamare,* fr. *ex-* + *clamare* to cry out — more at CLAIM] *vi* (ca. 1570) **1 :** to cry out or speak in strong or sudden emotion ⟨~*ed* in delight⟩ **2 :** to speak loudly or vehemently ⟨~*ed* against immorality⟩ ~ *vt* **:** to utter sharply, passionately, or vehemently **:** PROCLAIM — **ex·claim·er** *n*

ex·cla·ma·tion \,eks-klə-'mā-shən\ *n* (14c) **1 :** a sharp or sudden utterance **2 :** vehement expression of protest or complaint

exclamation point *n* (1824) **:** a mark ! used esp. after an interjection or exclamation to indicate forceful utterance or strong feeling

ex·clam·a·to·ry \iks-'klam-ə-,tōr-ē, -,tȯr-\ *adj* (1593) **:** containing, expressing, using, or relating to exclamation ⟨an ~ phrase⟩

ex·clave \'eks-,klāv, -,kläv\ *n* [*ex-* + *-clave* (as in *enclave*)] (1888) **:** a portion of a country separated from the main part and constituting an enclave in respect to the surrounding territory

ex·clo·sure \eks-'klō-zhər\ *n* [*ex-* + *-closure* (as in *enclosure*)] (1920) **:** an area from which intruders (as animals) are excluded esp. by fencing

ex·clud·able *or* **ex·clud·ible** \iks-'klüd-ə-bəl\ *adj* (1916) **:** subject to exclusion ⟨~ income⟩ — **ex·clud·abil·i·ty** \-,klüd-ə-'bil-ət-ē\ *n*

ex·clude \iks-'klüd\ *vt* **ex·clud·ed; ex·clud·ing** [ME *excluden,* fr. L *excludere,* fr. *ex-* + *claudere* to close — more at CLOSE] (14c) **1 a :** to prevent or restrict the entrance of ⟨draw the shade to ~ the sunlight⟩ **b :** to bar from participation, consideration, or inclusion **2 :** to expel or bar esp. from a place or position previously occupied — **ex·clud·er** *n*

ex·clu·sion \iks-'klü-zhən\ *n* [L *exclusion-, exclusio,* fr. *exclusus,* pp. of *excludere*] (15c) **1 :** the act or an instance of excluding **2 :** the state of being excluded — **ex·clu·sion·ary** \-zhə-,ner-ē\ *adj*

ex·clu·sion·ist \iks-'klüzh-(ə-)nəst\ *n* (1822) **:** one who would exclude another from some right or privilege — **exclusionist** *adj*

exclusion principle *n* (1928) **:** a principle in physics: no two electrons in an atom or molecule will be exactly equivalent

1**ex·clu·sive** \iks-'klü-siv, -ziv\ *adj* (1515) **1 a :** excluding or having power to exclude **b :** limiting or limited to possession, control, or use by a single individual or group **2 a :** excluding others from participation **b :** snobbishly aloof **3 a :** accepting or soliciting only a socially restricted patronage (as of the upper class) **b :** STYLISH, FASHIONABLE **c :** restricted in distribution, use, or appeal because of expense **4 a :** SINGLE, SOLE ⟨~ jurisdiction⟩ **b :** WHOLE, UNDIVIDED ⟨his ~ attention⟩ — **ex·clu·sive·ly** *adv* — **ex·clu·sive·ness** *n*

2**exclusive** *n* (1533) **:** something exclusive: as **a :** a newspaper story at first released to or printed by only one newspaper **b :** an exclusive right (as to sell a particular product in a certain area)

exclusive disjunction *n* (1942) **:** a compound proposition in logic that is true when one and only one of its constituent statements is true — see TRUTH TABLE table

exclusive of *prep* (1698) **:** not taking into account ⟨there were four of us *exclusive of* the guide⟩

ex·clu·siv·ism \iks-'klü-sə-,viz-əm, -'klü-zə-\ *n* (ca. 1834) **:** the practice of excluding or of being exclusive

ex·clu·siv·i·ty \,eks-,klü-'siv-ət-ē, iks-, -'ziv-\ *n, pl* **-ties** (1926) **1 :** the quality or state of being exclusive **2 :** exclusive rights or services

ex·cog·i·tate \ek-'skäj-ə-,tāt\ *vt* [L *excogitatus,* pp. of *excogitare,* fr. *ex-* + *cogitare* to cogitate] (1531) **:** to think out **:** DEVISE — **ex·cog·i·ta·tion** \(,)ek-,skäj-ə-'tā-shən\ *n* — **ex·cog·i·ta·tive** \ek-'skäj-ə-,tāt-iv\ *adj*

1**ex·com·mu·ni·cate** \,ek-skə-'myü-nə-,kāt\ *vt* [ME *excommunicaten,* fr. LL *excommunicatus,* pp. of *excommunicare,* fr. L *ex-* + LL *communicare* to communicate] (15c) **:** to subject to excommunication — **ex·com·mu·ni·ca·tor** \-,kāt-ər\ *n*

2**ex·com·mu·ni·cate** \-ni-kət\ *adj* (1551) **:** excluded from the rites of the church **:** EXCOMMUNICATED — **excommunicate** *n*

ex·com·mu·ni·ca·tion \-,myü-nə-'kā-shən\ *n* (15c) **1 :** an ecclesiastical censure depriving a person of the rights of church membership **2 :** exclusion from fellowship in a group or community — **ex·com·mu·ni·ca·tive** \-'myü-nə-,kāt-iv, -ni-kət-\ *adj*

ex·co·ri·ate \ek-'skōr-ē-,āt, -'skȯr-\ *vt* **-at·ed; -at·ing** [ME *excoriaten,* fr. LL *excoriatus,* pp. of *excoriare,* fr. L *ex-* + *corium* skin, hide — more at CUIRASS] (15c) **1 :** to wear off the skin of **:** ABRADE **2 :** to censure scathingly — **ex·co·ri·a·tion** \(,)ek-,skōr-ē-'ā-shən, -,skȯr-\ *n*

ex·cre·ment \'ek-skrə-mənt\ *n* [L *excrementum,* fr. *excernere*] (1533) **:** waste matter discharged from the body; *esp* **:** waste discharged from the alimentary canal — **ex·cre·men·tal** \,ek-skrə-'ment-ᵊl\ *adj* — **ex·cre·men·ti·tious** \-,men-'tish-əs, -mən-\ *adj*

ex·cres·cence \ik-'skres-ᵊn(t)s\ *n* (15c) **:** an often immoderate or abnormal projection, outgrowth, or enlargement ⟨warty ~*s* in the colon⟩ ⟨some assurance that the liberal arts are to be freed of some current ~*s* —*Newsweek*⟩

ex·cres·cen·cy \-ᵊn-sē\ *n, pl* **-cies** (1545) **:** EXCRESCENCE

ex·cres·cent \-ᵊnt\ *adj* [L *excrescent-, excrescens,* prp. of *excrescere* to grow out, fr. *ex-* + *crescere* to grow — more at CRESCENT] (1633) **1 :** forming an abnormal, excessive, or useless outgrowth **2 :** of, relating to, or constituting epenthesis — **ex·cres·cent·ly** *adv*

ex·cre·ta \ik-'skrēt-ə\ *n pl* [NL, fr. L, neut. pl. of *excretus*] (ca. 1855) **:** waste matter eliminated or separated from an organism; *esp* **:** EXCRETIONS — **ex·cre·tal** \-'skrēt-ᵊl\ *adj*

ex·crete \ik-'skrēt\ *vt* **ex·cret·ed; ex·cret·ing** [L *excretus,* pp. of *excernere* to sift out, discharge, fr. *ex-* + *cernere* to sift — more at CERTAIN] (1620) **:** to separate and eliminate or discharge (waste) from the blood or tissues or from the active protoplasm — **ex·cret·er** *n*

ex·cre·tion \ik-'skrē-shən\ *n* (1603) **1 :** the act or process of excreting **2 :** something excreted; *esp* **:** useless, superfluous, or harmful material (as urea) that is eliminated from the body and that differs from a secretion in not being produced to perform a useful function

ex·cre·to·ry \'ek-skrə-,tōr-ē, -,tȯr-\ *adj* (1681) **:** of, relating to, or functioning in excretion ⟨~ ducts⟩

ex·cru·ci·ate \ik-'skrü-shē-,āt\ *vt* **-at·ed; -at·ing** [L *excruciatus,* pp. of *excruciare,* fr. *ex-* + *cruciare* to crucify, fr. *cruc-, crux* cross — more at RIDGE] (ca. 1570) **1 :** to inflict intense pain on **:** TORTURE **2 :** to subject to intense mental distress

ex·cru·ci·at·ing *adj* (1664) **1 :** causing great pain or anguish **:** AGONIZING ⟨the nation's most ~ dilemma —W. H. Ferry⟩ **2 :** very intense **:** EXTREME ⟨~ pain⟩ ⟨the characters are paired off with an ~ regard for balance —Douglas Watt⟩ — **ex·cru·ci·at·ing·ly** \-,āt-iŋ-lē\ *adv*

ex·cru·ci·a·tion \ik-,skrü-s(h)ē-'ā-shən\ *n* (1618) **:** the act of excruciating **:** the state or an instance of being excruciated

ex·cul·pate \'ek-(,)skəl-,pāt, (')ek-'\ *vt* **-pat·ed; -pat·ing** [(assumed) ML *exculpatus,* pp. of *exculpare,* fr. L *ex-* + *culpa* blame] (1656) **:** to clear from alleged fault or guilt — **ex·cul·pa·tion** \,ek-(,)skəl-'pā-shən\ *n*

syn EXCULPATE, ABSOLVE, EXONERATE, ACQUIT, VINDICATE mean to free from a charge. EXCULPATE implies a clearing from blame or fault often in a matter of small importance; ABSOLVE implies a release either from an obligation that binds the conscience or from the consequences of disobeying the law or committing a sin; EXONERATE implies a complete clearance from an accusation or charge and from any attendant suspicion of blame or guilt; ACQUIT implies a formal decision in one's favor with respect to a definite charge; VINDICATE may refer to things as well as persons that have been subjected to critical attack or imputation of guilt, weakness, or folly, and implies a clearing effected by proving the unfairness of such criticism or blame.

ex·cul·pa·to·ry \ek-'skəl-pə-,tōr-ē, -,tȯr-\ *adj* (1779) **:** tending or serving to exculpate

ex·cur·rent \(')ek-'skər-ənt, -'skə-rənt\ *adj* [L *excurrent-, excurrens,* prp. of *excurrere* to run out, extend, fr. *ex-* + *currere* to run — more at CAR] (1605) **1 a :** having the axis prolonged to form an undivided main stem or trunk (as in conifers) — compare DELIQUESCENT 2 **b :** projecting beyond the apex — used esp. of the midrib of a mucronate leaf **2 :** characterized by a current that flows outward ⟨~ canals of a sponge⟩

ex·cur·sion \ik-'skər-zhən\ *n* [L *excursion-, excursio,* fr. *excursus,* pp. of *excurrere*] (1577) **1 a :** a going out or forth **:** EXPEDITION **b (1) :** a usu. brief pleasure trip **(2) :** a trip at special reduced rates **2 :** deviation from a direct, definite, or proper course; *esp* **:** DIGRESSION ⟨needless ~*s* into abstruse theory⟩ **3 a :** a movement outward and back or from a mean position or axis; *also* **:** the distance traversed **:** AMPLITUDE ⟨the ~ of a piston⟩ **b :** one complete movement of expansion and contraction of the lungs and their membranes (as in breathing)

ex·cur·sion·ist \-'skərzh-(ə-)nəst\ *n* (1830) **:** a person who goes on an excursion

ex·cur·sive \-'skər-siv\ *adj* (1673) **:** constituting a digression **:** characterized by digression — **ex·cur·sive·ly** *adv* — **ex·cur·sive·ness** *n*

ex·cur·sus \ik-'skər-səs\ *n, pl* **ex·cur·sus·es** *also* **ex·cur·sus** \-səs, -,süs\ [L, digression, fr. *excursus,* pp.] (1803) **:** an appendix or digression that contains further exposition of some point or topic

ex·cu·sa·to·ry \ik-'skyü-zə-,tōr-ē, -,tȯr-\ *adj* (1535) **:** making or containing excuse

1**ex·cuse** \ik-'skyüz, *imperatively often* 'skyüz\ *vt* **ex·cused; ex·cus·ing** [ME *excusen,* fr. OF *excuser,* fr. L *excusare,* fr. *ex-* + *causa* cause, explanation] (13c) **1 a :** to make apology for ⟨quietly *excused* his clumsiness⟩ **b :** to try to remove blame from ⟨*excused* himself for being so careless⟩ **2 :** to forgive entirely or overlook as of trivial import **:** regard as excusable ⟨she graciously *excused* his thoughtlessness⟩ **3 :** to grant exemption or release to ⟨the class was *excused*⟩ **4 :** to serve as excuse for **:** JUSTIFY ⟨nothing can ~ such heedlessness⟩ — **ex·cus·able** \ik-'skyü-zə-bəl\ *adj* — **ex·cus·able·ness** *n* — **ex·cus·ably** \-blē\ *adv* — **ex·cus·er** *n*

syn EXCUSE, CONDONE, PARDON, FORGIVE mean to exact neither punishment nor redress. Both EXCUSE and CONDONE imply a passing over without censure or meet punishment. Distinctively, one may EXCUSE specific acts esp. in social or conventional situations or the person responsible for these ⟨*excuse* an interruption⟩ ⟨*excused* her for interrupting⟩ Often the term implies extenuating circumstances ⟨injustice *excuses* strong responses⟩ or in some contexts self-justification ⟨always ready to *excuse* himself from any responsibility for the results of his behavior⟩ One more often CONDONES a kind of behavior (as dishonesty, folly, or violence) and esp. one that constitutes a grave breach (as of a moral or legal code) or a person or institution responsible for such behavior ⟨a culture that *condones* drink but not drugs⟩ PARDON and FORGIVE are often interchangeable, but their implications can be distinct. One PARDONS when one remits a penalty due for an admitted or established offense ⟨*pardon* a criminal⟩ ⟨*pardon* the noisy enthusiasm of a child⟩ One FORGIVES when one gives up all claim to requital and to resentment or vengeful feelings ⟨to err is human, to *forgive* divine —Alexander Pope⟩

2**ex·cuse** \ik-'skyüs\ *n* (14c) **1 :** the act of excusing **2 a :** something offered as justification or as grounds for being excused **b** *pl* **:** an expression of regret for failure to do something **c :** a note of explanation of an absence **3 :** JUSTIFICATION, REASON ***syn*** see APOLOGY

ex–di·rec·to·ry \,eks-də-'rek-t(ə-)rē, -dī-\ *adj* [L *ex* out of — more at EX-] *Brit* (1936) **:** not listed in a telephone directory **:** UNLISTED

ex·ec \ig-'zek\ *n* (1942) **1 :** EXECUTIVE OFFICER **2 :** EXECUTIVE

ex·e·cra·ble \'ek-si-krə-bəl\ *adj* (14c) **1 :** deserving to be execrated **:** DETESTABLE ⟨~ crimes⟩ **2 :** very bad **:** WRETCHED ⟨~ hotel food⟩ — **ex·e·cra·ble·ness** *n* — **ex·e·cra·bly** \-blē\ *adv*

ex·e·crate \'ek-sə-,krāt\ *vt* **-crat·ed; -crat·ing** [L *exsecratus,* pp. of *exsecrari* to put under a curse, fr. *ex* + *sacr-, sacer* sacred] (1561) **1 :** to declare to be evil or detestable **:** DENOUNCE **2 :** to detest utterly — **ex·e·cra·tive** \-,krāt-iv\ *adj* — **ex·e·cra·tor** \-,krāt-ər\ *n*

syn EXECRATE, CURSE, DAMN, ANATHEMATIZE mean to denounce violently. EXECRATE implies intense loathing and usu. passionate fury; CURSE and DAMN imply angry denunciation by blasphemous oaths or profane imprecations; ANATHEMATIZE implies solemn denunciation of an evil or an injustice.

ex·e·cra·tion \,ek-sə-'krā-shən\ *n* (14c) **1 :** the act of cursing or denouncing; *also* **:** the curse so uttered **2 :** an object of curses **:** something detested

ex·ec·u·tant \ig-'zek-(y)ət-ənt\ *n* (1858) **:** one who executes or performs; *esp* **:** one skilled in the technique of an art **:** PERFORMER

ex·e·cute \'ek-si-,kyüt\ *vt* **-cut·ed; -cut·ing** [ME *executen,* fr. MF *executer,* back-formation fr. *execution*] (14c) **1 :** to carry out fully **:** put completely into effect ⟨is a soldier morally responsible for a command that he ~*s*⟩ **2 :** to do what is provided or required by ⟨~ a decree⟩ **3 :** to put to death esp. in compliance with a legal sentence **4 :** to make or produce (as a work of art) esp. by carrying out a design 5 : to perform what is required to give validity to ⟨~ a deed⟩ 6 : PLAY ⟨~ a piece of music⟩ — **ex·e·cut·able** \-ˌkyüt-ə-bəl\ *adj*

syn EXECUTE, ADMINISTER mean to carry out the declared intent of another. EXECUTE stresses the enforcing of the specific provisions of a law, will, commission, or a command; ADMINISTER implies the continuing exercise of delegated authority in pursuance of only generally indicated goals rather than specif. prescribed means of attaining them. ***syn*** see in addition KILL, PERFORM

ex·e·cu·tion \ˌek-si-ˈkyü-shən\ *n* [ME, fr. MF, fr. L *exsecution-, exsecutio,* fr. *exsecutus,* pp. of *exsequi* to execute, fr. *ex-* + *sequi* to follow — more at SUE] (14c) 1 : the act or process of executing : PERFORMANCE 2 : a putting to death esp. as a legal penalty 3 : a judicial writ empowering an officer to carry out a judgment 4 : the act or mode or result of performance 5 *archaic* : effective or destructive action ⟨his brandished steel, which smoked with bloody ~ —Shak.⟩ — usu. used with *do* ⟨as soon as day came, we went out to see what ~ we had done —Daniel Defoe⟩

ex·e·cu·tion·er \-sh(ə-)nər\ *n* (1594) : one who executes; *esp* : one who puts to death

¹**ex·ec·u·tive** \ig-ˈzek-(y)ət-iv\ *adj* (1649) 1 a : designed for or relating to execution or carrying into effect ⟨~ board⟩ b : having administrative or managerial responsibility ⟨~ director⟩ 2 a : of or relating to the execution of the laws and the conduct of public and national affairs b : belonging to the branch of government that is charged with such powers as diplomatic representation, superintendence of the execution of the laws, and appointment of officials and that usu. has some power over legislation (as through veto) — compare JUDICIAL, LEGISLATIVE 3 : of or relating to an executive ⟨the ~ offices⟩

²**executive** *n* (1787) 1 : the executive branch of a government; *also* : the person or persons who constitute the executive magistracy of a state 2 : one that exercises administrative or managerial control

executive agreement *n* (1942) : an agreement between the U.S. and a foreign government made by the executive branch of the government alone and dealing usu. with routine matters

executive council *n* (1778) 1 : a council constituted to advise or share in the functions of a political executive 2 : a council that exercises supreme executive power

executive officer *n* (1790) : the officer second in command of a military or naval organization

executive order *n* (1883) : REGULATION 2b

executive privilege *n* (1940) : exemption from legally enforced disclosure of communications within the executive branch of government when such disclosure would adversely affect the functions and decision-making processes of the executive branch

executive secretary *n* (1950) : a secretary having administrative duties; *specif* : an official responsible for administering the activities and business affairs of an organization

executive session *n* (1840) : a usu. closed session (as of a legislative body) that functions as an executive council (as of the U.S. Senate when considering appointments or the ratification of treaties)

ex·ec·u·tor \ig-ˈzek-(y)ət-ər *or in sense 1* ˈek-sə-ˌkyüt-\ *n* [ME, fr. OF, fr. L *exsecutor,* fr. *exsecutus*] (13c) 1 a : one who executes something b *obs* : EXECUTIONER 2 a : the person appointed by a testator to execute his will b : LITERARY EXECUTOR — **ex·ec·u·to·ri·al** \ig-ˌzek-(y)ə-ˈtōr-ē-əl, -ˈtȯr-\ *adj*

ex·ec·u·to·ry \ig-ˈzek-(y)ə-ˌtōr-ē, -ˌtȯr-\ *adj* (15c) 1 : relating to administration 2 : designed or of such a nature as to be executed in time to come or to take effect on a future contingency

ex·ec·u·trix \ig-ˈzek-(y)ə-(ˌ)triks\ *n, pl* **ex·ec·u·tri·ces** \-ˌzek-(y)ə-ˈtrī-(ˌ)sēz\ *or* **ex·ec·u·trix·es** \-ˈzek-(y)ə-ˌtrik-səz\ (15c) : a woman who is an executor

ex·e·dra \ˈek-sə-drə\ *n, pl* **-drae** \-ˌdrē, -ˌdrī\ [L, fr. Gk, fr. *ex-* + *hedra* seat — more at SIT] (ca. 1706) 1 *in ancient Greece and Rome* : a room for conversation formed by an open or columned recess often semicircular in shape and furnished with seats 2 : a large outdoor nearly semicircular seat with a solid back

ex·e·ge·sis \ˌek-sə-ˈjē-səs\ *n, pl* **-ge·ses** \-ˈjē-(ˌ)sēz\ [NL, fr. Gk *exēgēsis,* fr. *exēgeisthai* to explain, interpret, fr. *ex-* + *hēgeisthai* to lead — more at SEEK] (1619) : EXPOSITION, EXPLANATION; *esp* : an explanation or critical interpretation of a text

ex·e·gete \ˈek-sə-ˌjēt\ *n* [Gk *exēgētēs,* fr. *exēgeisthai*] (1730) : one who practices exegesis

ex·e·get·i·cal \ˌek-sə-ˈjet-i-kəl\ *or* **ex·e·get·ic** \-ik\ *adj* [Gk *exēgētikos,* fr. *exēgeisthai*] (1623) : of or relating to exegesis : EXPLANATORY

ex·e·get·ist \-ˈjet-əst\ *n* (1848) : EXEGETE

ex·em·plar \ig-ˈzem-ˌplär, -plər\ *n* [ME, fr. L, fr. *exemplum* example] (15c) : something that serves as a model or example: as a : an ideal model b : a typical or standard specimen c : a copy of a book or writing d : IDEA 1a ***syn*** see MODEL

ex·em·pla·ry \ig-ˈzem-plə-rē\ *adj* (1589) 1 a : serving as a pattern b : deserving imitation : COMMENDABLE ⟨his courage was ~⟩ 2 : serving as a warning : MONITORY 3 : serving as an example, instance, or illustration — **ex·em·plar·i·ly** \ˌeg-ˌzem-ˈpler-ə-lē\ *adv* — **ex·em·pla·ri·ness** \ig-ˈzem-plə-rē-nəs\ *n* — **ex·em·plar·i·ty** \ˌeg-ˌzem-ˈplar-ət-ē\ *n*

ex·em·pli·fi·ca·tion \ig-ˌzem-plə-fə-ˈkā-shən\ *n* (1542) 1 : an exemplified copy of a document 2 a : the act or process of exemplifying b : EXAMPLE, CASE IN POINT

ex·em·pli·fy \ig-ˈzem-plə-ˌfī\ *vt* **-fied; -fy·ing** [ME *exemplifien,* fr. MF *exemplifier,* fr. ML *exemplificare,* fr. L *exemplum*] (15c) 1 : to show or illustrate by example 2 : to make an attested copy or transcript of (a document) under seal 3 a : to be an instance of or serve as an example : EMBODY b : to be typical of

ex·em·pli gra·tia \ig-ˌzem-(ˌ)plē-ˈgrät-ē-ˌä, -ˈgrā-sh(ē-)ə\ *adv* [L] (1569) : for example

ex·em·plum \ig-ˈzem-pləm\ *n, pl* **-pla** \-plə\ [L] (14c) 1 : EXAMPLE, MODEL 2 : an anecdote or short narrative used to point a moral or sustain an argument

¹**ex·empt** \ig-ˈzem(p)t\ *adj* [ME, fr. L *exemptus,* pp. of *eximere* to take out — more at EXAMPLE] (14c) 1 *obs* : set apart 2 : free or released from some liability or requirement to which others are subject ⟨was ~ from jury duty⟩

²**exempt** *vt* (15c) 1 : to release or deliver from some liability or requirement to which others are subject : EXCUSE ⟨a man ~*ed* from military service⟩ 2 *obs* : to set apart

³**exempt** *n* (1532) : one exempted or freed from duty

ex·emp·tion \ig-ˈzem(p)-shən\ *n* (14c) 1 : the act of exempting or state of being exempt : IMMUNITY 2 : one that exempts or is exempted; *esp* : a source or amount of income exempted from taxation

ex·en·ter·ate \ig-ˌzent-ə-ˌrāt\ *vt* **-at·ed; -at·ing** [L *exenteratus,* pp. of *exenterare* to disembowel, modif. of Gk *exenterizein,* fr. *ex-* + *enteron* intestine — more at INTER-] (1607) : to remove the contents of (as the orbit or pelvis) — **ex·en·ter·a·tion** \-ˌzent-ə-ˈrā-shən\ *n*

¹**ex·er·cise** \ˈek-sər-ˌsīz\ *n* [ME, fr. MF *exercice,* fr. L *exercitium,* fr. *exercitus,* pp. of *exercēre* to drive on, keep busy, fr. *ex-* + *arcēre* to enclose, hold off — more at ARK] (14c) 1 a : the act of bringing into play or realizing in action : USE b : the discharge of an official function or professional occupation c : the act or an instance of carrying out the terms of an agreement (as an option) 2 a : regular or repeated use of a faculty or bodily organ b : bodily exertion for the sake of developing and maintaining physical fitness 3 : something performed or practiced in order to develop, improve, or display a specific power or skill ⟨arithmetic ~*s*⟩ 4 : a performance having a strongly marked secondary or ulterior aspect ⟨party politics has always been an ~ in compromise —H.S. Ashmore⟩ 5 a : a maneuver, operation, or drill carried out for training and discipline b *pl* : a program including speeches, announcements of awards and honors, and various traditional practices of secular or religious character ⟨commencement ~*s*⟩

²**exercise** *vb* **-cised; -cis·ing** *vt* (14c) 1 a : to make effective in action : USE ⟨didn't ~ good judgment⟩ b : to bring to bear : EXERT ⟨~ influence⟩ c : to implement the terms of (as an option) 2 a : to use repeatedly in order to strengthen or develop b : to train (as troops) by drills and maneuvers c : to put through exercises ⟨~ the horses⟩ 3 a : to engage the attention and effort of b : to cause anxiety, alarm, or indignation in ⟨citizens *exercised* about pollution⟩ ~ *vi* : to take exercise — **ex·er·cis·able** \-ˌsī-zə-bəl\ *adj*

ex·er·cis·er \ˈek-sər-ˌsī-zər\ *n* (1552) 1 : one that exercises 2 : an apparatus for use in physical exercise

ex·er·ci·ta·tion \ig-ˌzər-sə-ˈtā-shən\ *n* [ME *exercitacioun,* fr. L *exercitation-, exercitatio,* fr. *exercitatus,* pp. of *exercitare* to exercise diligently, fr. *exercitus,* pp. of *exercēre*] (14c) : EXERCISE

ex·er·gon·ic \ˌek-(ˌ)sər-ˈgän-ik\ *adj* [*exo-* + Gk *ergon* work — more at WORK] (1940) : liberating energy ⟨an ~ biochemical reaction⟩

ex·ergue \ˈek-ˌsərg, ˈeg-ˌzərg\ *n* [F, fr. NL *exergum,* fr. Gk *ex* out of + *ergon* work] (1697) : a space on a coin, token, or medal usu. on the reverse below the central part of the design

ex·ert \ig-ˈzərt\ *vt* [L *exsertus,* pp. of *exserere* to thrust out, fr. *ex-* + *serere* to join — more at SERIES] (1660) 1 a : to put forth (as strength) b : to put (oneself) into action or to tiring effort 2 : to bring to bear esp. with sustained effort or lasting effect 3 : EMPLOY, WIELD ⟨~*ed* his leadership abilities intelligently⟩

ex·er·tion \ig-ˈzər-shən\ *n* (1677) : the act or an instance of exerting; *esp* : a laborious or perceptible effort

ex·e·unt \ˈek-sē-(ˌ)ənt, -ˌünt\ [L, they go out, fr. *exire* to go out — more at EXIT] (15c) — used as a stage direction to specify that all or certain named characters leave the stage

ex·fo·li·ate \(ˌ)eks-ˈfō-lē-ˌāt\ *vb* **-at·ed; -at·ing** [LL *exfoliatus,* pp. of *exfoliare* to strip of leaves, fr. L *ex-* + *folium* leaf — more at BLADE] *vt* (1612) 1 : to cast off in scales, laminae, or splinters 2 : to remove the surface of in scales or laminae 3 : to spread or extend by or as if by opening out leaves ~ *vi* 1 : to split into or give off scales, laminae, or body cells 2 : to come off in thin layers or scales 3 : to grow by or as if by producing or unfolding leaves — **ex·fo·li·a·tion** \(ˌ)eks-ˌfō-lē-ˈā-shən\ *n* — **ex·fo·li·a·tive** \eks-ˈfō-lē-ˌāt-iv\ *adj*

ex gra·tia \(ˌ)eks-ˈgrā-sh(ē-)ə\ *adj or adv* [NL] (1769) : as a favor : not compelled by legal right ⟨*ex gratia* pension payments⟩

ex·hal·ant *or* **ex·hal·ent** \eks-ˈ(h)ā-lənt\ *adj* (1771) : bearing out or outward : EMISSIVE ⟨an ~ siphon of a clam⟩

ex·ha·la·tion \ˌeks-(h)ə-ˈlā-shən\ *n* (14c) 1 : something exhaled or given off : EMANATION 2 : an act of exhaling

ex·hale \eks-ˈ(h)ā(ə)l\ *vb* **ex·haled; ex·hal·ing** [ME *exalen,* fr. L *exhalare,* fr. *ex-* + *halare* to breathe; akin to L *anima* breath — more at ANIMATE] *vi* (15c) 1 : to rise or be given off as vapor 2 : to emit breath or vapor ~ *vt* 1 a : to breathe out b : to give forth (gaseous matter) : EMIT 2 *archaic* : to cause to be emitted in vapor

¹**ex·haust** \ig-ˈzȯst\ *vb* [L *exhaustus,* pp. of *exhaurire,* fr. *ex-* + *haurire* to draw; akin to MHG *œsen* to empty, Gk *auein* to take] *vt* (1533) 1 a : to consume entirely : USE UP ⟨~*ed* our funds in a week⟩ b : to tire extremely or completely ⟨~*ed* by overwork⟩ c : to deprive of a valuable quality or constituent ⟨~ a photographic developer⟩ ⟨~ a soil of fertility⟩ 2 a : to draw off or let out completely b : to empty by drawing off the contents; *specif* : to create a vacuum in 3 a : to develop (a subject) completely b : to try out the whole number of ⟨~*ed* all the possibilities⟩ ~ *vi* : DISCHARGE, EMPTY ⟨the engine ~*s* through the muffler⟩ ***syn*** see DEPLETE, TIRE — **ex·haust·er** *n* — **ex·haust·ibil·i·ty** \-ˌzȯ-stə-ˈbil-ət-ē\ *n* — **ex·haust·ible** \-ˈzȯ-stə-bəl\ *adj*

²**exhaust** *n* (1848) 1 a : the escape of used gas or vapor from an engine b : the gas or vapor thus escaping 2 a : the conduit through which used gases escape b : an arrangement for withdrawing fumes, dusts, or odors from an enclosure 3 : EXHAUSTION

ex·haus·tion \ig-ˈzȯs-chən\ *n* (1646) : the act or process of exhausting : the state of being exhausted

ex·haus·tive \ig-ˈzȯ-stiv\ *adj* (1786) : testing all possibilities or considering all elements : THOROUGH ⟨conducted an ~ investigation⟩ — **ex·haus·tive·ly** *adv* — **ex·haus·tive·ness** *n* — **ex·haus·tiv·i·ty** \-ˌzȯ-ˈstiv-ət-ē\ *n*

ex·haust·less \ig-ˈzȯst-ləs\ *adj* (1712) : not to be exhausted : INEXHAUSTIBLE — **ex·haust·less·ly** *adv* — **ex·haust·less·ness** *n*

¹**ex·hib·it** \ig-ˈzib-ət\ *vb* [ME *exhibiten,* fr. L *exhibitus,* pp. of *exhibēre,* fr. *ex-* + *habēre* to have, hold — more at GIVE] *vt* (15c) 1 : to present to view: as a : to show or display outwardly esp. by visible signs or actions ⟨~*ed* no fear⟩ b : to have as a readily discernible quality or feature ⟨in all cultures we know, men ~ an aesthetic sense —H. J. Muller⟩ c : to show publicly esp. for purposes of competition or demonstration 2 : to submit (as a document) to a court or officer in

course of proceedings; *also* : to present or offer officially or in legal form **3** : to administer for medical purposes ⟨the patient should fast . . . before chloroform is ~*ed* —A. B. Garrod⟩ ~ *vi* : to display something for public inspection ***syn*** see SHOW — **ex·hib·i·tive** \-ət-iv\ *adj* — **ex·hib·i·tor** \-ət-ər\ *n* — **ex·hib·i·to·ry** \-ə-ˌtōr-ē, -ˌtȯr-\ *adj*

[2]**exhibit** *n* (1626) **1** : a document or material object produced and identified in court or before an examiner for use as evidence **2** : something exhibited **3** : an act or instance of exhibiting

ex·hi·bi·tion \ˌek-sə-ˈbish-ən\ *n* (1663) **1** : an act or instance of exhibiting **2** *Brit* : a grant drawn from the funds of a school or university to help maintain a student **3** : a public showing (as of works of art, objects of manufacture, or athletic skill)

ex·hi·bi·tion·er \-ˈbish-(ə-)nər\ *n*, *Brit* (1679) : one who holds a grant from a school or university

ex·hi·bi·tion·ism \-ˈbish-ə-ˌniz-əm\ *n* (1893) **1 a** : a perversion marked by a tendency to indecent exposure **b** : an act of such exposure **2** : the act or practice of behaving so as to attract attention to oneself — **ex·hi·bi·tion·ist** \-ˈbish-(ə-)nəst\ *n or adj* — **ex·hi·bi·tion·is·tic** \-ˌbish-ə-ˈnis-tik\ *adj* — **ex·hi·bi·tion·is·ti·cal·ly** \-ti-k(ə-)lē\ *adv*

ex·hil·a·rate \ig-ˈzil-ə-ˌrāt\ *vt* **-rat·ed; -rat·ing** [L *exhilaratus*, pp. of *exhilarare*, fr. *ex-* + *hilarare* to gladden, fr. *hilarus* cheerful — more at HILARIOUS] (1540) **1 a** : to make cheerful **b** : ENLIVEN, EXCITE **2** : REFRESH, STIMULATE — **ex·hil·a·rat·ing·ly** \ig-ˈzil-ə-ˌrāt-iŋ-lē\ *adv* — **ex·hil·a·ra·tive** \-ˌrāt-iv\ *adj*

ex·hil·a·ra·tion \ig-ˌzil-ə-ˈrā-shən\ *n* (1623) **1** : the action of exhilarating **2** : the feeling or the state of being exhilarated

ex·hort \ig-ˈzȯ(ə)rt\ *vb* [ME *exhorten*, fr. MF *exhorter*, fr. L *exhortari*, fr. *ex-* + *hortari* to incite — more at YEARN] *vt* (15c) : to incite by argument or advice : urge strongly ~ *vi* : to give warnings or advice : make urgent appeals — **ex·hort·er** *n*

ex·hor·ta·tion \ˌeks-ˌȯr-ˈtā-shən, ˌegz-, -ər-\ *n* (14c) **1** : an act or instance of exhorting **2** : language intended to incite and encourage

ex·hor·ta·tive \ig-ˈzȯrt-ət-iv\ *adj* (15c) : serving to exhort

ex·hor·ta·to·ry \-ə-ˌtōr-ē, -ˌtȯr-\ *adj* (15c) : using exhortation : EXHORTATIVE ⟨an ~ appeal⟩

ex·hume \igz-ˈ(y)üm, iks-ˈ(h)yüm\ *vt* **ex·humed; ex·hum·ing** [F or ML; F *exhumer*, fr. ML *exhumare*, fr. L *ex* out of + *humus* earth — more at EX-, HUMBLE] (1783) **1** : DISINTER **2** : to bring back from neglect or obscurity — **ex·hu·ma·tion** \ˌeks-(h)yü-ˈmā-shən, ˌegz-(y)ü-\ *n* — **ex·hum·er** \igz-ˈ(y)ü-mər, iks-ˈ(h)yü-\ *n*

ex·i·gence \ˈek-sə-jən(t)s\ *n* (1589) : EXIGENCY

ex·i·gen·cy \ˈek-sə-jən-sē, ig-ˈzij-ən-\ *n*, *pl* **-cies** (1581) **1 a** : the quality or state of being exigent **b** : a state of affairs that makes urgent demands ⟨a leader must act in any sudden ~⟩ **2** : that which is required in a particular situation — usu. used in pl. ***syn*** see JUNCTURE

ex·i·gent \ˈek-sə-jənt\ *adj* [L *exigent-*, *exigens*, prp. of *exigere* to demand — more at EXACT] (1670) **1** : requiring immediate aid or action **2** : requiring or calling for much : DEMANDING — **ex·i·gent·ly** *adv*

ex·i·gu·ity \ˌeg-zi-ˈgyü-ət-ē\ *n*, *pl* **-ities** (ca. 1623) : the quality or state of being exiguous : SCANTINESS

ex·ig·u·ous \ig-ˈzig-yə-wəs\ *adj* [L *exiguus*, fr. *exigere*] (1651) : excessively scanty : INADEQUATE ⟨attempting to build up their ~ navy⟩ — **ex·ig·u·ous·ly** *adv* — **ex·ig·u·ous·ness** *n*

[1]**ex·ile** \ˈeg-ˌzīl, ˈek-ˌsīl\ *n* [ME *exil*, fr. MF, fr. L *exilium*] (14c) **1 a** : forced removal from one's country or home **b** : voluntary absence from one's country or home **2 a** : a person expelled from his country or home by authority **b** : one who separates himself from his home — **ex·il·ic** \eg-ˈzil-ik\ *adj*

[2]**exile** *vt* **ex·iled; ex·il·ing** (14c) : to banish or expel from one's own country or home ***syn*** see BANISH

ex·im·i·ous \eg-ˈzim-ē-əs\ *adj* [L *eximius*, fr. *eximere* to take out — more at EXAMPLE] *archaic* (1547) : CHOICE, EXCELLENT

ex·ine \ˈek-ˌsēn, -ˌsīn\ *n* [prob. fr. G, fr. *ex-* + NL *in-* fibrous tissue, fr. Gk *in-*, *is* tendon] (ca. 1884) : the outer of the two major layers forming the walls of some spores and esp. pollen grains

ex·ist \ig-ˈzist\ *vi* [L *exsistere* to come into being, exist, fr. *ex-* + *sistere* to stand; akin to L *stare* to stand — more at STAND] (1602) **1 a** : to have real being whether material or spiritual ⟨do unicorns ~⟩ **b** : to have being in space and time ⟨the greatest poet who ever ~*ed*⟩ **c** : to have being in a specified place or with respect to understood limitations or conditions ⟨strange ideas ~*ed* in his mind⟩ **2** : to continue to be ⟨racism still ~*s* in society⟩ **3 a** : to have life or the functions of vitality ⟨we cannot ~ without oxygen⟩ **b** : to live at an inferior level or under adverse circumstances ⟨the hungry ~*ing* from day to day⟩

ex·is·tence \ig-ˈzis-tən(t)s\ *n* (14c) **1 a** *obs* : reality as opposed to appearance **b** : reality as presented in experience **c** (1) : the totality of existent things (2) : a particular being ⟨all the fair ~*s* of heaven —John Keats⟩ **d** : sentient or living being : LIFE **2 a** : the state or fact of having being esp. independently of human consciousness and as contrasted with nonexistence **b** : the manner of being that is common to every mode of being **c** : being with respect to a limiting condition or under a particular aspect **3** : continued or repeated manifestation

ex·is·tent \-tənt\ *adj* [L *exsistent-*, *exsistens*, prp. of *exsistere*] (15c) **1** : having being : EXISTING **2** : existing now : PRESENT — **existent** *n*

ex·is·ten·tial \ˌeg-(ˌ)zis-ˈten-chəl, ˌek-(ˌ)sis-\ *adj* (1693) **1** : of, relating to, or affirming existence ⟨~ propositions⟩ **2 a** : grounded in existence or the experience of existence : EMPIRICAL **b** : having being in time and space **3** [trans. of Dan *eksistentiel* & G *existential*] : EXISTENTIALIST — **ex·is·ten·tial·ly** \-ˈtench-(ə-)lē\ *adv*

ex·is·ten·tial·ism \-ˈten-chə-ˌliz-əm\ *n* (1930) : a chiefly 20th century philosophical movement embracing diverse doctrines but centering on analysis of individual existence in an unfathomable universe and the plight of the individual who must assume ultimate responsibility for his acts of free will without any certain knowledge of what is right or wrong or good or bad

[1]**ex·is·ten·tial·ist** \-ləst\ *n* (1931) : an adherent of existentialism

[2]**existentialist** *adj* (1946) : of or relating to existentialism or existentialists — **ex·is·ten·tial·is·tic** \-ˌten-chə-ˈlis-tik\ *adj* — **ex·is·ten·tial·is·ti·cal·ly** \-ti-k(ə-)lē\ *adv*

existential quantifier *n* (1940) : a quantifier that asserts that there exists at least one value of a variable ⟨in the statement "for some *x*, $2x + 5 = 8$" the phrase *for some* is an *existential quantifier*⟩ — called also *existential operator*

[1]**ex·it** \ˈeg-zət, ˈek-sət\ [L, he goes out, fr. *exire* to go out, fr. *ex-* + *ire* to go — more at ISSUE] (1538) — used as a stage direction to specify who goes off stage

[2]**exit** *n* [L *exitus*, fr. *exitus*, pp. of *exire*] (1588) **1** [[1]*exit*] : a departure from a stage **2 a** : the act of going out or going away **b** : DEATH **3** : a way out of an enclosed place or space **4** : one of the designated points of departure from an expressway — **ex·it·less** *adj*

[3]**exit** *vi* (1607) **1** : to go out or away : DEPART **2** : DIE ~ *vt* : LEAVE 3a

exit poll *n* (1980) : a poll that is taken (as by news media) of voters as they leave the voting place and that is usu. used for predicting the winners

ex li·bris \ek-ˈslē-brəs, -ˌbrēs\ *n*, *pl* **ex libris** [NL, from the books; used before the owner's name on bookplates] (1880) : BOOKPLATE

Ex·moor \ˈek-ˌsmu̇(ə)r, -ˌsmō(ə)r, -ˌsmȯ(ə)r\ *n* [*Exmoor*, England] (1808) **1** : any of a breed of horned sheep of Devonshire in England valued esp. for mutton **2** : any of a breed of hardy ponies native to the Exmoor district and having a mealy-colored muzzle

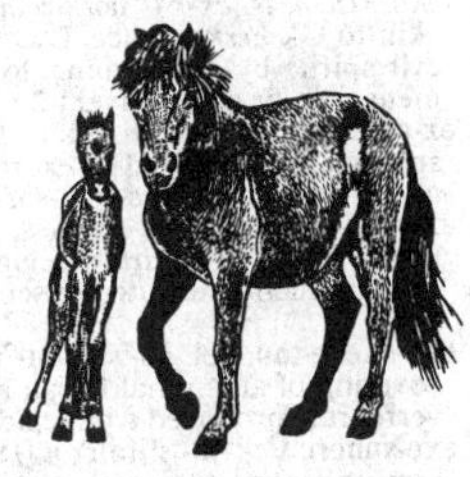

Exmoor 2

ex ni·hi·lo \(ˈ)eks-ˈnē-(h)ə-ˌlō, -ˈni-, -ˈnī-\ *adv or adj* [L] (1656) : from or out of nothing ⟨creation *ex nihilo*⟩

exo- *or* **ex-** *comb form* [Gk *exō* out, outside, fr. *ex* out of — more at EX-] **1** : outside ⟨*exo*gamy⟩ : outer ⟨*exo*skeleton⟩ — compare ECT-, END- **2** : turning out ⟨*exo*ergic⟩

exo·bi·ol·o·gy \ˌek-sō-bī-ˈäl-ə-jē\ *n* (1960) : a branch of biology concerned with the search for life outside the earth and with the effects of extraterrestrial environments on living organisms — **exo·bi·o·log·i·cal** \-ˌbī-ə-ˈläj-i-kəl\ *adj* — **exo·bi·ol·o·gist** \-bī-ˈäl-ə-jəst\ *n*

exo·carp \ˈek-sō-ˌkärp\ *n* [ISV] (1870) : the outermost layer of the pericarp of a fruit — see ENDOCARP illustration

exo·crine \ˈek-sə-krən, -ˌkrīn, -ˌkrēn\ *adj* [ISV *exo-* + Gk *krinein* to separate — more at CERTAIN] (ca. 1913) : producing, being, or relating to a secretion that is released outside its source ⟨~ pancreatic cells⟩

exocrine gland *n* (ca. 1927) : a gland (as a sweat gland or a kidney) that releases a secretion external to or at the surface of an organ by means of a canal or duct

exo·cy·clic \ˌek-sō-ˈsī-klik, -ˈsik-lik\ *adj* (1888) : situated outside of a ring in a chemical structure

exo·cy·to·sis \ˌek-sō-sī-ˈtō-səs\ *n*, *pl* **-to·ses** \-ˌsēz\ [NL, fr. *exo-* + *cyt-* + *-osis*] (1963) : the release of cellular substances (as secretory products) contained in cell vesicles by fusion of the vesicular membrane with the plasma membrane and subsequent release of the contents to the exterior of the cell — **exo·cy·tot·ic** \-ˈtät-ik\ *adj*

exo·der·mis \ˌek-sō-ˈdər-məs\ *n* [NL] (ca. 1900) : a layer of the outer living cortical cells of plants that takes over the functions of the epidermis in roots lacking secondary thickening

ex·odon·tia \ˌek-sə-ˈdän-ch(ē-)ə\ *n* [NL, fr. *ex-* + *-odontia*] (1913) : a branch of dentistry that deals with the extraction of teeth — **ex·odon·tist** \-ˈdänt-əst\ *n*

ex·o·dus \ˈek-səd-əs, ˈeg-zəd-\ *n* [L, fr. Gk *Exodos*, lit., road out, fr. *ex-* + *hodos* road — more at CEDE] **1** *cap* : the mainly narrative second book of canonical Jewish and Christian Scripture — see BIBLE table **2** : a mass departure : EMIGRATION

exo·en·zyme \ˌek-sō-ˈen-ˌzīm\ *n* [ISV] (ca. 1923) : an extracellular enzyme

exo·er·gic \ˌek-sō-ˈər-jik\ *adj* (1942) : releasing energy : EXOTHERMIC

exo·eryth·ro·cyt·ic \ˌek-sō-i-ˌrith-rə-ˈsit-ik\ *adj* (1942) : occurring outside the red blood cells — used esp. of stages of malaria parasites

ex of·fi·cio \ˌek-sə-ˈfish-ē-ˌō, -ˈfis-\ *adv or adj* [LL] (1533) : by virtue or because of an office ⟨the Vice President serves *ex officio* as president of the Senate⟩

ex·og·a·my \ek-ˈsäg-ə-mē\ *n*, *pl* **-mies** (1865) : marriage outside of a specific group esp. as required by custom or law — **ex·og·a·mous** \ek-ˈsäg-ə-məs\ *or* **exo·gam·ic** \ˌek-sə-ˈgam-ik\ *adj*

ex·og·e·nous \ek-ˈsäj-ə-nəs\ *adj* [F *exogène* exogenous, fr. *exo-* + *-gène* (fr. Gk *-genēs* born) — more at -GEN] (1830) **1** : produced by growth from superficial tissue ⟨~ roots produced by leaves⟩ **2 a** : caused by factors (as food or a traumatic factor) or an agent (as a disease-producing organism) from outside the organism or system ⟨~ obesity⟩ ⟨~ psychic depression⟩ **b** : introduced from or produced outside the organism or system; *specif* : not synthesized within the organism or system — **ex·og·e·nous·ly** *adv*

ex·on \ˈek-ˌsän\ *n* [expressed sequence + [2]*-on*] (ca. 1978) : a sequence of nucleotides in DNA or RNA that is expressed as all or part of the polypeptide chain of a protein — compare INTRON — **ex·on·ic** \ek-ˈsän-ik\ *adj*

ex·on·er·ate \ig-ˈzän-ə-ˌrāt\ *vt* **-at·ed; -at·ing** [ME *exoneraten*, fr. L *exoneratus*, pp. of *exonerare* to unburden, fr. *ex-* + *oner-*, *onus* load] (1524) **1** : to relieve of a responsibility, obligation, or hardship **2** : to clear from accusation or blame ***syn*** see EXCULPATE — **ex·on·er·a·tion** \-ˌzän-ə-ˈrā-shən\ *n* — **ex·on·er·a·tive** \-ˈzän-ə-ˌrāt-iv\ *adj*

exo·nu·cle·ase \ˌek-sō-ˈn(y)ü-klē-ˌās, -ˌāz\ *n* (1963) : an enzyme that breaks down a nucleic acid by removing nucleotides one by one from the end of a chain — compare ENDONUCLEASE

exo·nu·mia \ˌek-sə-ˈn(y)ü-mē-ə\ *n pl* [NL, fr. *exo-* + E *numismatic* + NL *-ia* -ia] (1966) : numismatic items (as tokens, medals, or scrip) other than coins and paper money

exo·pep·ti·dase \-ˈpep-tə-ˌdās, -ˌdāz\ *n* (1936) : any of a group of enzymes that hydrolyze peptide bonds formed by the terminal amino acids of peptide chains : PEPTIDASE — compare ENDOPEPTIDASE

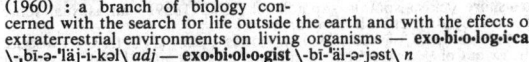

ex·oph·thal·mos *also* **ex·oph·thal·mus** \ˌek-säf-ˈthal-məs, -səf-, -säp-\ *n* [NL, fr. Gk *exophthalmos* having prominent eyes, fr. *ex* out + *ophthalmos* eye; akin to Gk *ōps* eye — more at EYE] (1872) **:** abnormal protrusion of the eyeball — **ex·oph·thal·mic** \-mik\ *adj*

ex·or·bi·tance \ig-ˈzȯr-bət-ən(t)s\ *n* (1611) **1 :** an exorbitant action or procedure; *esp* **:** excessive or gross deviation from rule, right, or propriety **2 :** the tendency or disposition to be exorbitant

ex·or·bi·tant \-ənt\ *adj* [ME, fr. MF, fr. LL *exorbitant-, exorbitans,* prp. of *exorbitare* to deviate, fr. L *ex-* + *orbita* track, rut — more at ORB] (15c) **1 :** not coming within the scope of the law **2 :** exceeding in intensity, quality, amount, or size the customary or appropriate limits ***syn*** see EXCESSIVE — **ex·or·bi·tant·ly** *adv*

ex·or·cise *also* **ex·or·cize** \ˈek-ˌsȯr-ˌsīz, -sər-\ *vt* **-cised** *also* **-cized; -cis·ing** *also* **-ciz·ing** [ME *exorcisen,* fr. MF *exorciser,* fr. LL *exorcizare,* fr. Gk *exorkizein,* fr. *ex-* + *horkizein* to bind by oath, adjure, fr. *horkos* oath; akin to Gk *herkos* fence, L *sarcire* to mend] (1546) **1 a :** to expel (an evil spirit) by adjuration **b :** to get rid of (something troublesome, menacing, or oppressive) **2 :** to free of an evil spirit — **ex·or·cis·er** *n*

ex·or·cism \-ˌsiz-əm\ *n* (14c) **1 :** the act or practice of exorcising **2 :** a spell or formula used in exorcising — **ex·or·cist** \-ˌsist, -səst\ *n* — **ex·or·cis·tic** \ˌek-ˌsȯr-ˈsis-tik, -sər-\ *or* **ex·or·cis·ti·cal** \-ti-kəl\ *adj*

ex·or·di·um \eg-ˈzȯrd-ē-əm\ *n, pl* **-diums** *or* **-dia** \-ē-ə\ [L, fr. *exordiri* to begin, fr. *ex-* + *ordiri* to begin — more at ORDER] (1577) **:** a beginning or introduction esp. to a discourse or composition — **ex·or·di·al** \-ē-əl\ *adj*

exo·skel·e·ton \ˌek-sō-ˈskel-ət-ᵊn\ *n* (1847) **1 :** an external supportive covering of an animal (as an arthropod) **2 :** bony or horny parts of a vertebrate produced from epidermal tissues — **exo·skel·e·tal** \-ət-ᵊl\ *adj*

exo·sphere \ˈek-sō-ˌsfi(ə)r\ *n* [ISV] (1949) **:** the outer fringe region of the atmosphere of the earth or a planet — **exo·spher·ic** \ˌek-sō-ˈsfi(ə)r-ik, -ˈsfer-\ *adj*

exo·spore \ˈek-sə-ˌspō(ə)r, -ˌspȯ(ə)r\ *n* [ISV] (1859) **:** an asexual spore formed by abstriction from a parent cell

ex·os·to·sis \ˌek-(ˌ)säs-ˈtō-səs\ *n, pl* **-to·ses** \-ˌsēz\ [NL, fr. Gk *exostōsis,* fr. *ex* out of + *osteon* bone — more at EX-, OSSEOUS] (1736) **:** a spur or bony outgrowth from a bone or the root of a tooth

ex·o·ter·ic \ˌek-sə-ˈter-ik\ *adj* [L & Gk; L *exotericus,* fr. Gk *exōterikos,* lit., external, fr. *exōterō* more outside, compar. of *exō* outside — more at EXO-] (1655) **1 a :** suitable to be imparted to the public ⟨the ~ doctrine⟩ — compare ESOTERIC **b :** belonging to the outer or less initiate circle **2 :** relating to the outside **:** EXTERNAL — **ex·o·ter·i·cal·ly** \-i-k(ə-)lē\ *adv*

exo·ther·mic \ˌek-sō-ˈthər-mik\ *or* **exo·ther·mal** \-məl\ *adj* [ISV] (1884) **:** characterized by or formed with evolution of heat — **exo·ther·mi·cal·ly** \-mi-k(ə-)lē\ *adv* — **exo·ther·mi·ci·ty** \-ˌthər-ˈmis-ət-ē\ *n*

¹ex·ot·ic \ig-ˈzät-ik\ *adj* [L *exoticus,* fr. Gk *exōtikos,* fr. *exō*] (1599) **1 :** introduced from another country **:** not native to the place where found **2** *archaic* **:** OUTLANDISH, ALIEN **3 :** strikingly or excitingly different or unusual **4 :** of or relating to striptease ⟨~ dancing⟩ — **ex·ot·i·cal·ly** \-i-k(ə-)lē\ *adv* — **ex·ot·ic·ness** \-ik-nəs\ *n*

²exotic *n* (1645) **1 :** one (as a plant or animal) that is exotic **2 :** STRIPTEASER

ex·ot·i·ca \ig-ˈzät-i-kə\ *n pl* [NL, fr. L, neut. pl. of *exoticus*] (1876) **:** things excitingly different or unusual; *esp* **:** literary or artistic items having an exotic theme or nature

ex·ot·i·cism \ig-ˈzät-ə-ˌsiz-əm\ *also* **ex·o·tism** \ˈeg-zə-ˌtiz-əm, ˈek-sə-\ *n* (1827) **:** the quality or state of being exotic

exo·tox·in \ˌek-sō-ˈtäk-sən\ *n* [ISV] (ca. 1923) **:** a soluble poisonous substance produced during growth of a microorganism and released into the surrounding medium

ex·pand \ik-ˈspand\ *vb* [ME *expaunden,* fr. L *expandere,* fr. *ex-* + *pandere* to spread — more at FATHOM] *vt* (15c) **1 :** to open up **:** UNFOLD **2 :** to increase the extent, number, volume, or scope of **:** ENLARGE **3 a :** to express at length or in greater detail **b :** to write out in full ⟨~ all abbreviations⟩ **c :** to subject to mathematical expansion ⟨~ a function in a power series⟩ ~ *vi* **1 :** to open out **:** SPREAD **2 :** to increase in extent, number, volume, or scope **3 :** to speak or write fully or in detail ⟨intend to ~ on this theme⟩ **4 :** to feel generous or optimistic — **ex·pand·able** \-ˈspan-də-bəl\ *adj*

syn EXPAND, AMPLIFY, SWELL, DISTEND, INFLATE, DILATE mean to increase in size or volume. EXPAND may apply whether the increase comes from within or without and regardless of manner (as growth, unfolding, addition of parts); AMPLIFY implies the extension or enlargement of something inadequate; SWELL implies gradual expansion beyond a thing's original or normal limits; DISTEND implies outward extension caused by pressure from within; INFLATE implies expanding by introduction of air or something insubstantial and suggests a resulting vulnerability and liability to sudden collapse; DILATE applies esp. to expansion of circumference.

ex·pand·ed *adj, of a typeface* (1923) **:** EXTENDED

expanded metal *n* (1890) **:** sheet metal cut and expanded into a lattice and used esp. as lath

expanded plastic *n* (1945) **:** lightweight cellular plastic used esp. as insulation and protective packing material — called also *foamed plastic, plastic foam*

ex·pand·er \ik-ˈspan-dər\ *n* (1862) **:** one that expands; *specif* **:** any of several colloidal substances (as dextran) of high molecular weight used as a blood or plasma substitute for increasing the blood volume

ex·panse \ik-ˈspan(t)s\ *n* [NL *expansum,* fr. L, neut. of *expansus,* pp. of *expandere*] (1667) **1 :** FIRMAMENT **2 :** great extent of something spread out ⟨an ~ of calm ocean⟩

ex·pan·si·ble \ik-ˈspan(t)-sə-bəl\ *adj* (1691) **:** capable of being expanded — **ex·pan·si·bil·i·ty** \-ˌspan(t)-sə-ˈbil-ət-ē\ *n*

ex·pan·sile \ik-ˈspan(t)-səl, -ˈspan-ˌsīl\ *adj* (1776) **:** of, relating to, or capable of expansion

ex·pan·sion \ik-ˈspan-chən\ *n* (1611) **1 :** EXPANSE **2 :** the act or process of expanding ⟨territorial ~⟩ **3 :** the quality or state of being expanded **4 :** the increase in volume of working fluid (as steam) in an engine cylinder after cutoff or in an internal-combustion engine after explosion **5 a :** an expanded part **b :** something that results from an act of expanding ⟨the book is an ~ of a lecture series⟩ **6 :** the result of carrying out an indicated mathematical operation **:** the expression of a function in the form of a series — **ex·pan·sion·al** \-ˈspanch-nəl, -ən-ᵊl\ *adj*

ex·pan·sion·ary \ik-ˈspan-chə-ˌner-ē\ *adj* (1936) **:** tending toward expansion ⟨an ~ economy⟩

ex·pan·sion·ism \ik-ˈspan-chə-ˌniz-əm\ *n* (1899) **:** a policy or practice of expansion and esp. of territorial expansion by a nation — **ex·pan·sion·ist** \-ˈspanch-(ə-)nəst\ *n* — **expansionist** *or* **ex·pan·sion·is·tic** \-ˌspan-chə-ˈnis-tik\ *adj*

ex·pan·sive \ik-ˈspan(t)-siv\ *adj* (1651) **1 :** having a capacity or a tendency to expand **2 :** causing or tending to cause expansion **3 a :** characterized by high spirits, generosity, or readiness to talk **:** OPEN ⟨grew ~ after dinner⟩ **b :** marked by or indicative of exaggerated euphoria and delusions of self-importance ⟨an ~ patient⟩ **4 :** marked by expansion: as **a :** having a great expanse **:** SIZABLE **b :** EXTENSIVE, DETAILED **5 :** characterized by richness, abundance, or magnificence ⟨~ living⟩ — **ex·pan·sive·ly** *adv* — **ex·pan·sive·ness** *n*

ex·pan·siv·i·ty \ˌek-ˌspan-ˈsiv-ət-ē, ik-\ *n* (1837) **:** the quality or state of being expansive; *esp* **:** the capacity to expand

ex par·te \(ˈ)ek-ˈspärt-ē\ *adv or adj* [ML] (1672) **1 :** on or from one side or party only — used of legal proceedings **2 :** from a one-sided or partisan point of view

ex·pa·ti·ate \ek-ˈspā-shē-ˌāt\ *vi* **-at·ed; -at·ing** [L *exspatiatus,* pp. of *exspatiari* to wander, digress, fr. *ex-* + *spatium* space, course — more at SPEED] (1535) **1 :** to move about freely or at will **:** WANDER **2 :** to speak or write at length or in detail ⟨was *expatiating* upon the value of the fabric —Thomas Hardy⟩ — **ex·pa·ti·a·tion** \(ˌ)ek-ˌspā-shē-ˈā-shən\ *n*

¹ex·pa·tri·ate \ek-ˈspā-trē-ˌāt\ *vb* **-at·ed; -at·ing** [ML *expatriatus,* pp. of *expatriare* to leave one's own country, fr. L *ex-* + *patria* native country, fr. fem. of *patrius* of a father, fr. *patr-, pater* father — more at FATHER] *vt* (1784) **1 :** to withdraw (oneself) from residence in or allegiance to one's native country **2 :** BANISH, EXILE ~ *vi* **:** to leave one's native country to live elsewhere; *also* **:** to renounce allegiance to one's native country — **ex·pa·tri·ate** \-ˌāt, -ət\ *n* — **ex·pa·tri·a·tion** \(ˌ)ek-ˌspā-trē-ˈā-shən\ *n*

²ex·pa·tri·ate \ek-ˈspā-trē-ˌāt, -trē-ət\ *adj* (1829) **:** living in a foreign land

ex·pa·tri·a·tism \ek-ˈspā-trē-ə-ˌtiz-əm\ *n* (1937) **:** the fact or state of being an expatriate

ex·pect \ik-ˈspekt\ *vb* [L *exspectare* to look forward to, fr. *ex-* + *spectare* to look at, fr. *spectus,* pp. of *specere* to look — more at SPY] *vi* (1560) **1** *archaic* **:** WAIT, STAY **2 :** to look forward **3 :** to be pregnant **:** await the birth of one's child — used in progressive tenses ⟨she's ~*ing* next month⟩ ~ *vt* **1** *archaic* **:** AWAIT **2 :** SUPPOSE, THINK **3 :** to anticipate or look forward to the coming or occurrence of ⟨we ~ them any minute now⟩ ⟨~*ed* a telephone call⟩ **4 a :** to consider probable or certain ⟨~ to be forgiven⟩ ⟨~ that things will improve⟩ **b :** to consider reasonable, due, or necessary ⟨~*ed* respect from the students⟩ **c :** to consider bound in duty or obligated ⟨they ~ you to pay your dues⟩ — **ex·pect·able** \-ˈspek-tə-bəl\ *adj* — **ex·pect·ably** \-blē\ *adv* — **ex·pect·ed·ly** *adv* — **ex·pect·ed·ness** *n*

syn EXPECT, HOPE, LOOK mean to await some occurrence or outcome. EXPECT implies a high degree of certainty and usu. involves the idea of preparing or envisioning; HOPE implies little certainty but suggests confidence or assurance in the possibility that what one desires or longs for will happen; LOOK suggests a degree of expectancy and watchfulness rather than confidence or certainty.

ex·pec·tance \ik-ˈspek-tən(t)s\ *n* (1603) **:** EXPECTANCY

ex·pec·tan·cy \-tən-sē\ *n, pl* **-cies** (1600) **1 a :** the act, action, or state of expecting **b :** the state of being expected **2 a :** something expected **b :** the expected amount (as of the number of years of life) based on statistical probability ⟨life ~⟩

¹ex·pec·tant \-tənt\ *adj* (14c) **1 :** characterized by expectation **2 :** expecting the birth of a child ⟨~ mothers⟩ — **ex·pec·tant·ly** *adv*

²expectant *n* (1625) **:** one who is looking forward to something

ex·pec·ta·tion \ˌek-ˌspek-ˈtā-shən, ik-\ *n* (1550) **1 :** the act or state of expecting **:** ANTICIPATION **2 a :** something expected ⟨not up to ~s⟩ **b :** basis for expecting **:** ASSURANCE ⟨they have every ~ of success⟩ **c :** prospects of inheritance — usu. used in pl. **3 :** the state of being expected **4 a :** EXPECTANCY 2b **b :** EXPECTED VALUE

ex·pec·ta·tive \ik-ˈspek-tət-iv\ *adj* (1560) **:** of, relating to, or constituting an object of expectation

expected value *n* (1947) **1 :** the sum of the values of a random variable with each value multiplied by its probability of occurrence **2 :** the integral of the product of a probability density function of a continuous random variable and the random variable itself when taken over all possible values of the variable

ex·pec·to·rant \ik-ˈspek-t(ə-)rənt\ *n* (1782) **:** an agent that promotes the discharge or expulsion of mucus from the respiratory tract; *broadly* **:** an antitussive agent — **expectorant** *adj*

ex·pec·to·rate \-tə-ˌrāt\ *vb* **-rat·ed; -rat·ing** [prob. fr. (assumed) NL *expectoratus,* pp. of *expectorare,* fr. L, to cast out of the mind, fr. *ex-* + *pector-, pectus* breast, soul — more at PECTORAL] *vt* (1601) **1 :** to eject from the throat or lungs by coughing or hawking and spitting **2 :** SPIT ~ *vi* **1 :** to discharge matter from the throat or lungs by coughing or hawking and spitting **2 :** SPIT — **ex·pec·to·ra·tion** \-ˌspek-tə-ˈrā-shən\ *n*

ex·pe·di·ence \ik-ˈspēd-ē-ən(t)s\ *n* (1593) **:** EXPEDIENCY

ex·pe·di·en·cy \-ən-sē\ *n, pl* **-cies** (1612) **1** *obs* **a :** HASTE, DISPATCH **b :** an enterprise requiring haste or caution **2 :** the quality or state of being suited to the end in view **:** SUITABILITY, FITNESS **3 :** adherence to expedient means and methods ⟨put more emphasis on ~ than on principle —W. H. Jones⟩ **4 :** a means of achieving a particular end **:** EXPEDIENT — **ex·pe·di·en·tial** \-ˌspēd-ē-ˈen-chəl\ *adj*

¹ex·pe·di·ent \ik-ˈspēd-ē-ənt\ *adj* [ME, fr. MF or L; MF, fr. L *expedient-, expediens,* prp. of *expedire* to extricate, arrange, be advantageous, fr. *ex-* + *ped-, pes* foot — more at FOOT] (14c) **1 :** suitable for achieving a particular end in a given circumstance **2 :** characterized by concern with what is opportune; *specif* **:** governed by self-interest — **ex·pe·di·ent·ly** *adv*

syn EXPEDIENT, POLITIC, ADVISABLE mean dictated by practical or prudent motives. EXPEDIENT usu. implies what is immediately advantageous without regard for ethics or consistent principles; POLITIC stresses judiciousness and tactical value but usu. implies some lack of candor or sincerity; ADVISABLE applies to what is practical, prudent, or advantageous but lacks the derogatory implication of EXPEDIENT and POLITIC.

[2]**expedient** *n* (1653) **:** something expedient **:** a temporary means to an end *syn* see RESOURCE

ex·pe·dite \'ek-spə-ˌdīt\ *vt* **-dit·ed; -dit·ing** [L *expeditus,* pp. of *expedire*] (15c) **1 :** to execute promptly **2 :** to accelerate the process or progress of **:** speed up **3 :** ISSUE, DISPATCH

ex·pe·dit·er *also* **ex·pe·di·tor** \-ˌdīt-ər\ *n* (1891) **:** one that expedites; *specif* **:** one employed to ensure efficient movement of goods or supplies in a business

ex·pe·di·tion \ˌek-spə-'dish-ən\ *n* (15c) **1 a :** a journey or excursion undertaken for a specific purpose **b :** the group of persons making such a journey **2 :** efficient promptness **:** SPEED **3 :** a sending or setting forth *syn* see HASTE

ex·pe·di·tion·ary \-'dish-ə-ˌner-ē\ *adj* (1817) **:** of, relating to, or being an expedition; *also* **:** sent on military service abroad ⟨an ~ force⟩

ex·pe·di·tious \ˌek-spə-'dish-əs\ *adj* (1559) **:** characterized by or acting promptly and efficiently *syn* see FAST — **ex·pe·di·tious·ly** *adv* — **ex·pe·di·tious·ness** *n*

ex·pel \ik-'spel\ *vt* **ex·pelled; ex·pel·ling** [ME *expellen,* fr. L *expellere,* fr. *ex-* + *pellere* to drive — more at FELT] (14c) **1 :** to force out **:** EJECT ⟨*expelled* the smoke from her lungs⟩ **2 :** to force to leave (as a place or organization) by official action **:** take away rights or privileges of membership ⟨*expelled* from college⟩ *syn* see EJECT — **ex·pel·la·ble** \-'spel-ə-bəl\ *adj* — **ex·pel·ler** *n*

ex·pel·lee \ˌek-ˌspel-'ē, ik-\ *n* (1888) **:** one who is expelled; *specif* **:** one transferred from the country of residence for resettlement in the country with which he is ethnically associated

ex·pend \ik-'spend\ *vt* [ME *expenden,* fr. L *expendere* to weigh out, expend, fr. *ex-* + *pendere* to weigh — more at SPIN] (15c) **1 :** to pay out **:** SPEND ⟨the social services upon which public revenue is ~*ed* —J. A. Hobson⟩ **2 :** to make use of for a specific purpose **:** UTILIZE ⟨projects on which they ~*ed* great energy⟩; *also* **:** USE UP — **ex·pend·er** *n*

[1]**ex·pend·able** \ik-'spen-də-bəl\ *adj* (1805) **:** that may be expended: as **a :** normally used up or consumed in service ⟨~ supplies like pencils and paper⟩ **b :** more economically replaced than rescued, salvaged, or protected — **ex·pend·abil·i·ty** \-ˌspen-də-'bil-ət-ē\ *n*

[2]**expendable** *n* (1942) **:** one that is expendable — usu. used in pl.

ex·pen·di·ture \ik-'spen-di-chər, -də-ˌchu̇(ə)r, -də-ˌt(y)u̇(ə)r\ *n* [irreg. fr. *expend*] (1769) **1 :** the act or process of expending ⟨an ~ of energy⟩ **2 :** something expended **:** DISBURSEMENT, EXPENSE ⟨income should exceed ~*s*⟩

[1]**ex·pense** \ik-'spen(t)s\ *n* [ME, fr. AF or LL; AF, fr. LL *expensa,* fr. L, fem. of *expensus,* pp. of *expendere*] (14c) **1 a :** something expended to secure a benefit or bring about a result **b :** financial burden or outlay **:** COST ⟨built the monument at their own ~⟩ **c :** an item of business outlay chargeable against revenue for a specific period **2** *archaic* **:** the act or an instance of expending **:** EXPENDITURE **3 :** a cause or occasion of expenditure ⟨an estate is a great ~⟩ **4 :** a loss, detriment, or embarrassment that results from some action or gain **:** SACRIFICE ⟨everyone had a good laugh at my ~⟩ — usu. used in the phrase *at the expense of* ⟨develop a boy's physique at the ~ of his intelligence —Bertrand Russell⟩

[2]**expense** *vt* **ex·pensed; ex·pens·ing** (ca. 1909) **1 :** to charge with expenses **2 a :** to charge to an expense account **b :** to write off as an expense

expense account *n* (ca. 1872) **:** an account of expenses reimbursable to an employee

ex·pen·sive \ik-'spen(t)-siv\ *adj* (1634) **1 :** involving high cost or sacrifice ⟨an ~ hobby⟩ **2 a :** commanding a high price and esp. one that is not based on intrinsic worth or is beyond a prospective buyer's means **b :** characterized by high prices ⟨~ shops⟩ — **ex·pen·sive·ly** *adv* — **ex·pen·sive·ness** *n*

[1]**ex·pe·ri·ence** \ik-'spir-ē-ən(t)s\ *n* [ME, fr. MF, fr. L *experientia* act of trying, fr. *experient-, experiens,* prp. of *experiri* to try, fr. *ex-* + *-periri* (akin to *periculum* attempt) — more at FEAR] (14c) **1 a :** direct observation of or participation in events as a basis of knowledge **b :** the fact or state of having been affected by or gained knowledge through direct observation or participation **2 a :** practical knowledge, skill, or practice derived from direct observation of or participation in events or in a particular activity **b :** the length of such participation ⟨has 10 years ~ in the job⟩ **3 a :** the conscious events that make up an individual life **b :** the events that make up the conscious past of a community or nation or mankind generally **4 :** something personally encountered, undergone, or lived through **5 :** the act or process of directly perceiving events or reality

[2]**experience** *vt* **-enced; -enc·ing** (1580) **1 :** to learn by experience ⟨I have *experienced* that a landscape and the sky unfold the deepest beauty —Nathaniel Hawthorne⟩ **2 :** to have experience of **:** UNDERGO ⟨*experienced* severe hardships as a child⟩ — **experience religion :** to undergo religious conversion

ex·pe·ri·enced \-ən(t)st\ *adj* (1576) **:** made skillful or wise through observation of or participation in a particular activity or in affairs generally **:** PRACTICED ⟨an ~ driver⟩

ex·pe·ri·en·tial \ik-ˌspir-ē-'en-chəl\ *adj* (1816) **:** relating to, derived from, or providing experience **:** EMPIRICAL ⟨~ knowledge⟩ ⟨~ lessons⟩ — **ex·pe·ri·en·tial·ly** \-'ench-(ə-)lē\ *adv*

[1]**ex·per·i·ment** \ik-'sper-ə-mənt *also* -'spir-\ *n* [ME, fr. MF, fr. L *experimentum,* fr. *experiri*] (14c) **1 a :** TEST, TRIAL ⟨make another ~ of his suspicion —Shak.⟩ **b :** a tentative procedure or policy **c :** an operation carried out under controlled conditions in order to discover an unknown effect or law, to test or establish a hypothesis, or to illustrate a known law **2** *obs* **:** EXPERIENCE **3 :** the process of testing **:** EXPERIMENTATION

[2]**ex·per·i·ment** \-ˌment\ *vi* (1787) **:** to carry out experiments **:** try out a new procedure, idea, or activity — **ex·per·i·men·ta·tion** \ik-ˌsper-ə-mən-'tā-shən, -ˌmen- *also* -ˌspir-\ *n* — **ex·per·i·ment·er** \-'sper-ə-ˌment-ər *also* -'spir-\ *n*

ex·per·i·men·tal \ik-ˌsper-ə-'ment-ᵊl *also* -ˌspir-\ *adj* (15c) **1 :** of, relating to, or based on experience or experiment **2 a :** serving the ends of or used as a means of experimentation ⟨an ~ school⟩ **b :** relating to or having the characteristics of experiment **:** TENTATIVE ⟨still in the ~ stage⟩ — **ex·per·i·men·tal·ly** \-ᵊl-ē\ *adv*

ex·per·i·men·tal·ism \-ᵊl-ˌiz-əm\ *n* (1834) **:** reliance on or advocacy of experimental or empirical principles and procedures; *specif* **:** INSTRUMENTALISM

ex·per·i·men·tal·ist \-ᵊl-əst\ *n* (1762) **:** one who experiments; *specif* **:** a person conducting scientific experiments

experiment station *n* (1874) **:** an establishment for scientific research (as in agriculture) where experiments are carried out, studies of practical application are made, and information is disseminated

[1]**ex·pert** \'ek-ˌspərt, ik-'\ *adj* [ME, fr. MF & L; MF, fr. L *expertus,* fr. pp. of *experiri*] (14c) **1** *obs* **:** EXPERIENCED **2 :** having, involving, or displaying special skill or knowledge derived from training or experience *syn* see PROFICIENT — **ex·pert·ly** *adv* — **ex·pert·ness** *n*

[2]**ex·pert** \'ek-ˌspərt\ *n* [F, fr. *expert,* adj.] (1825) **:** one with the special skill or knowledge representing mastery of a particular subject

[3]**ex·pert** \'ek-ˌspərt\ *vi* (ca. 1889) **:** to serve as an expert

ex·per·tise \ˌek-(ˌ)spər-'tēz, -'tēs\ *n* [F, fr. MF, expertness, fr. *expert*] (1868) **1 :** expert opinion or commentary **2 :** the skill of an expert

ex·pert·ism \'ek-ˌspərt-ˌiz-əm\ *n* (1886) **:** EXPERTISE 2

ex·pert·ize \'ek-spər-ˌtīz\ *vb* **-ized; -iz·ing** *vi* (1889) **:** to give a professional opinion usu. after careful study ~ *vt* **:** to examine and give expert judgment on

expert system *n* (1980) **:** computer software that attempts to mimic the reasoning of a human specialist

ex·pi·ate \'ek-spē-ˌāt\ *vb* **-at·ed; -at·ing** [L *expiatus,* pp. of *expiare* to atone for, fr. *ex-* + *piare* to atone for, appease — more at PIOUS] *vt* (1594) **1** *obs* **:** to put an end to **2 a :** to extinguish the guilt incurred by **b :** to make amends for ⟨permission to ~ their offences by their assiduous labours —Francis Bacon⟩ ~ *vi* **:** to make expiation — **ex·pi·a·ble** \'ek-spē-ə-bəl\ *adj* — **ex·pi·a·tor** \-spē-ˌāt-ər\ *n*

ex·pi·a·tion \ˌek-spē-'ā-shən\ *n* (15c) **1 :** the act of making atonement **2 :** the means by which atonement is made

ex·pi·a·to·ry \'ek-spē-ə-ˌtōr-ē, -ˌtȯr-\ *adj* (15c) **:** serving to expiate

ex·pi·ra·tion \ˌek-spə-'rā-shən\ *n* (1526) **1 a** *archaic* **:** the last emission of breath **:** DEATH **b** (1) **:** the act or process of releasing air from the lungs through the nose or mouth (2) **:** the escape of carbon dioxide from the body protoplasm (as through the blood and lungs or by diffusion) **2 :** the fact of coming to an end or the point at which something ends **:** TERMINATION

ex·pi·ra·to·ry \ik-'spī-rə-ˌtōr-ē, ek-', -ˌtȯr-; 'ek-sp(ə-)rə-\ *adj* (ca. 1847) **:** of, relating to, or employed in the expiration of air from the lungs

ex·pire \ik-'spī(ə)r, *oftenest for vi 3 and vt 2* ek-\ *vb* **ex·pired; ex·pir·ing** [ME *expiren,* fr. MF or L; MF *expirer,* fr. L *exspirare,* fr. *ex-* + *spirare* to breathe — more at SPIRIT] *vi* (15c) **1 :** to breathe one's last breath **:** DIE **2 :** to come to an end **3 :** to emit the breath ~ *vt* **1** *obs* **:** CONCLUDE **2 :** to breathe out from or as if from the lungs **3** *archaic* **:** EMIT

ex·pi·ry \ik-'spī(ə)r-ē, 'ek-spə-rē\ *n, pl* **-ries** (1790) **:** EXPIRATION: as **a :** exhalation of breath **b :** DEATH **c :** TERMINATION; *esp* **:** the termination of a time or period fixed by law, contract, or agreement

ex·plain \ik-'splān\ *vb* [ME *explanen,* fr. L *explanare,* lit., to make level, fr. *ex-* + *planus* level, flat — more at FLOOR] *vt* (1513) **1 a :** to make known **b :** to make plain or understandable ⟨footnotes that ~ the terms⟩ **2 :** to give the reason for or cause of **3 :** to show the logical development or relationships of ~ *vi* **:** to make something plain or understandable — **ex·plain·able** \-'splā-nə-bəl\ *adj* — **ex·plain·er** *n*

syn EXPLAIN, EXPOUND, EXPLICATE, ELUCIDATE, INTERPRET mean to make something clear or understandable. EXPLAIN implies a making plain or intelligible what is not immediately obvious or entirely known; EXPOUND implies a careful often elaborate explanation; EXPLICATE adds the idea of a developed or detailed analysis; ELUCIDATE stresses the throwing of light upon as by offering details or motives previously obscure or only implicit; INTERPRET adds to EXPLAIN the need for imagination or sympathy or special knowledge in dealing with something.

— **explain oneself :** to clarify one's statements or the reasons for one's conduct

explain away *vt* (1704) **1 :** to get rid of by or as if by explanation **2 :** to minimize the significance of by or as if by explanation

ex·pla·na·tion \ˌek-splə-'nā-shən\ *n* (14c) **1 :** the act or process of explaining **2 :** something that explains ⟨gave no ~⟩

ex·plan·a·tive \ik-'splan-ət-iv\ *adj* (1750) **:** EXPLANATORY — **ex·plan·a·tive·ly** *adv*

ex·plan·a·to·ry \ik-'splan-ə-ˌtōr-ē, -ˌtȯr-\ *adj* (1618) **:** serving to explain ⟨~ notes⟩ — **ex·plan·a·to·ri·ly** \-ˌsplan-ə-'tōr-ə-lē, -'tȯr-\ *adv*

[1]**ex·plant** \(ˈ)ek-'splant\ *vt* [*ex-* + *-plant* (as in *implant*)] (1915) **:** to remove (living tissue) esp. to a medium for tissue culture — **ex·plan·ta·tion** \ˌek-ˌsplan-'tā-shən\ *n*

[2]**ex·plant** \'ek-ˌsplant\ *n* (1917) **:** living tissue removed from an organism and placed in a medium for tissue culture

[1]**ex·ple·tive** \'ek-splət-iv\ *n* (1612) **1 a :** a syllable, word, or phrase inserted to fill a vacancy (as in a sentence or a metrical line) without adding to the sense; *esp* **:** a word (as *it* in "make it clear which you prefer") that occupies the position of the subject or object of a verb in normal English word order and anticipates a subsequent word or phrase that supplies the needed meaningful content **b :** an exclamatory word or phrase; *esp* **:** one that is obscene or profane **2 :** one that serves to fill out or as a filling

[2]**expletive** *adj* [LL *expletivus,* fr. L *expletus,* pp. of *explēre* to fill out, fr. *ex-* + *plēre* to fill — more at FULL] (1656) **1 :** serving to fill up ⟨~ phrases⟩ **2 :** marked by the use of expletives

ex·ple·to·ry \'ek-splə-ˌtōr-ē, -ˌtȯr-\ *adj* (1672) **:** EXPLETIVE

ex·pli·ca·ble \ek-'splik-ə-bəl, 'ek-(ˌ)splik-\ *adj* (1556) **:** capable of being explained — **ex·pli·ca·bly** \-blē\ *adv*

ex·pli·cate \'ek-splə-ˌkāt\ *vt* **-cat·ed; -cat·ing** [L *explicatus,* pp. of *explicare,* lit., to unfold, fr. *ex-* + *plicare* to fold — more at PLY] (1531) **1 :** to give a detailed explanation of **2 :** to develop the implications of **:** analyze logically *syn* see EXPLAIN — **ex·pli·ca·tion** \ˌek-splə-'kā-shən\ *n* — **ex·pli·ca·tor** \'ek-splə-ˌkāt-ər\ *n*

ex·pli·ca·tion de texte \ek-splē-kä-syō^{n}-də-tekst\ *n, pl* **explications de texte** *same*\ [F, lit., explanation of text] (1935) **:** a method of literary criticism involving a detailed analysis of a work

\ə\ abut \ᵊ\ kitten, F table \ər\ further \a\ ash \ā\ ace \ä\ cot, cart \au̇\ out \ch\ chin \e\ bet \ē\ easy \g\ go \i\ hit \ī\ ice \j\ job \ŋ\ sing \ō\ go \ȯ\ law \ȯi\ boy \th\ thin \t͟h\ the \ü\ loot \u̇\ foot \y\ yet \zh\ vision \à, k̲, ^{n}, œ, œ̄, ue, ue̅, ʸ\ *see* Guide to Pronunciation

[1]**ex·pli·ca·tive** \ek-ˈsplik-ət-iv, ˈek-splə-ˌkāt-\ *adj* (1649) **:** serving to explicate; *specif* **:** serving to explain logically what is contained in the subject ⟨an ~ proposition⟩ — **ex·pli·ca·tive·ly** *adv*

[2]**explicative** *n* (1775) **:** an explicative expression

ex·pli·ca·to·ry \ek-ˈsplik-ə-ˌtōr-ē, -ˈek-(ˌ)splik-, -ˌtȯr-\ *adj* (1625) **:** EXPLICATIVE

ex·plic·it \ik-ˈsplis-ət\ *adj* [F or ML; F *explicite,* fr. ML *explicitus,* fr. L, pp. of *explicare*] (ca. 1613) **1 :** fully revealed or expressed without vagueness, implication, or ambiguity **:** leaving no question as to meaning or intent ⟨~ instructions⟩ **2 :** fully developed or formulated ⟨an ~ plan⟩ ⟨an ~ notion of our objective⟩ **3 :** unambiguous in expression ⟨was very ~ on how we are to behave⟩ **4** *of a mathematical function* **:** defined by an expression containing only independent variables — compare IMPLICIT 1c — **ex·plic·it·ly** *adv* — **ex·plic·it·ness** *n*

syn EXPLICIT, DEFINITE, EXPRESS, SPECIFIC mean perfectly clear in meaning. EXPLICIT implies such verbal plainness and distinctness that there is no need for inference and no room for difficulty in understanding; DEFINITE stresses precise, clear statement or arrangement that leaves no doubt or indecision; EXPRESS implies both explicitness and direct and positive utterance; SPECIFIC applies to what is precisely and fully treated in detail or particular.

ex·plode \ik-ˈsplōd\ *vb* **ex·plod·ed; ex·plod·ing** [L *explodere* to drive off the stage by clapping, fr. *ex-* + *plaudere* to clap] *vt* (ca. 1611) **1** *archaic* **:** to drive from the stage by noisy disapproval **2 :** to bring into disrepute or discredit ⟨~ a theory⟩ **3 :** to cause to explode or burst noisily ⟨~ dynamite⟩ ⟨~ a bomb⟩ ~ *vi* **1 :** to burst forth with sudden violence or noise from internal energy: as **a :** to undergo a rapid chemical or nuclear reaction with the production of noise, heat, and violent expansion of gases ⟨dynamite ~*s*⟩ ⟨an atom bomb ~*s*⟩ **b :** to burst violently as a result of pressure from within **2 :** to give forth a sudden strong and noisy outburst of emotion ⟨*exploded* in anger⟩ — **ex·plod·er** *n*

ex·plod·ed *adj* (1944) **:** showing the parts separated but in correct relationship to each other ⟨an ~ view of a carburetor⟩

[1]**ex·ploit** \ˈek-ˌsplȯit, ik-ˈ\ *n* [ME, outcome, success, fr. MF, fr. L *explicitum,* neut. of *explicitus,* pp.] (1538) **:** DEED, ACT; *esp* **:** a notable or heroic act ***syn*** see FEAT

[2]**ex·ploit** \ik-ˈsplȯit, ˈek-ˌ\ *vt* (1838) **1 a :** to put to productive use ⟨~ the country's natural resources⟩ **b :** to take advantage of **:** UTILIZE ⟨~*ing* your talents⟩ ⟨~ your opponent's weakness⟩ **2 :** to make use of meanly or unjustly for one's own advantage ⟨~*ing* the peasants with long hours and abysmally low wages⟩ — **ex·ploit·able** \-ə-bəl\ *adj* — **ex·ploit·er** *n*

ex·ploi·ta·tion \ˌek-ˌsplȯi-ˈtā-shən\ *n* (1803) **1 :** an act of exploiting: as **a :** utilization or working of a natural resource **b :** an unjust or improper use of another person for one's own profit or advantage **c :** coaction between organisms in which one is benefited at the expense of the other **2 :** PUBLICITY, ADVERTISING — **ex·ploit·ative** \ik-ˈsplȯit-ət-iv\ *adj* — **ex·ploit·ative·ly** *adv*

ex·ploit·ive \ik-ˈsplȯit-iv\ *adj* (1885) **:** of, relating to, or being exploitation

ex·plo·ra·tion \ˌek-splə-ˈrā-shən, -ˌsplȯ-\ *n* (1543) **:** the act or an instance of exploring — **ex·plo·ra·tion·al** \-shnəl, -shən-ᵊl\ *adj*

ex·plor·ative \ik-ˈsplōr-ət-iv, -ˈsplȯr-\ *adj* (1738) **:** EXPLORATORY — **ex·plor·ative·ly** *adv*

ex·plor·ato·ry \-ə-ˌtōr-ē, -ˌtȯr-\ *adj* (1651) **:** of, relating to, or being exploration ⟨~ surgery⟩ ⟨~ drilling for oil⟩

ex·plore \ik-ˈsplō(ə)r, -ˈsplȯ(ə)r\ *vb* **ex·plored; ex·plor·ing** [L *explorare,* fr. *ex-* + *plorare,* lit., to cry out] *vt* (1585) **1 a :** to investigate, study, or analyze **:** look into ⟨~ the relationship between social class and learning ability⟩ ⟨*explored* ways to settle their differences⟩ — sometimes used with indirect questions ⟨to ~ where ethical issues arise — R.T. Blackburn⟩ **b :** to become familiar with by testing or experimenting ⟨~ new cuisines⟩ ⟨*exploring* a variety of musical idioms⟩ **2 :** to travel over (new territory) for adventure or discovery **3 :** to examine minutely esp. for diagnostic purposes ⟨~ the wound⟩ ~ *vi* **:** to make or conduct a systematic search ⟨~ for oil⟩

ex·plor·er \ik-ˈsplōr-ər, -ˈsplȯr-\ *n* (1740) **1 :** one that explores; *esp* **:** a person who travels in search of geographical or scientific information **2** *cap* **:** a member of the scouting program of the Boy Scouts of America for young people 14 to 20 years of age

ex·plo·si·ble \ik-ˈsplō-zə-bəl, -ˈsplō-sə-\ *adj* (1799) **:** capable of being exploded — **ex·plo·si·bil·i·ty** \-ˌsplō-zə-ˈbil-ət-ē, -sə-\ *n*

ex·plo·sion \ik-ˈsplō-zhən\ *n* [L *explosion-, explosio* act of driving off by clapping, fr. *explosus,* pp. of *explodere*] (1667) **1 :** the act or an instance of exploding **2 :** a large-scale, rapid, and spectacular expansion, outbreak, or upheaval ⟨the population ~⟩ **3 :** the release of occluded breath that occurs in one kind of articulation of stop consonants

[1]**ex·plo·sive** \ik-ˈsplō-siv, -ziv\ *adj* (1667) **1 a :** relating to, characterized by, or operated by explosion ⟨an ~ engine⟩ **b :** resulting from or as if from an explosion ⟨~ population growth⟩ **2 a :** tending to explode ⟨an ~ person⟩ **b :** likely to erupt in or produce hostile reaction or violence ⟨an ~ ghetto situation⟩ — **ex·plo·sive·ly** *adv* — **ex·plo·sive·ness** *n*

[2]**explosive** *n* (1874) **1 :** an explosive substance **2 :** a consonant characterized by explosion in its articulation when it occurs in certain environments **:** STOP

ex·po \ˈek-(ˌ)spō\ *n, pl* **expos** (1913) **:** EXPOSITION 3

ex·po·nent \ik-ˈspō-nənt, ˈek-ˌ\ *n* [L *exponent-, exponens,* prp. of *exponere* — more at EXPOSE] (1706) **1 :** a symbol written above and to the right of a mathematical expression to indicate the operation of raising to a power ⟨in the expression a^3, the ~ *3* indicates that the product of *a* used three times as a factor is to be found⟩ **2 a :** one that expounds or interprets **b :** one that champions, advocates, or exemplifies

ex·po·nen·tial \ˌek-spə-ˈnen-chəl\ *adj* (1704) **1 :** of or relating to an exponent **2 :** involving a variable in an exponent ⟨10^x is an ~ expression⟩ **3 :** expressible or approximately expressible by an exponential function ⟨an ~ growth rate⟩ — **ex·po·nen·tial·ly** \-ˈnench-(ə-)lē\ *adv*

exponential function *n* (ca. 1894) **:** a mathematical function in which an independent variable appears in one of the exponents — called also *exponential*

ex·po·nen·ti·a·tion \ˌek-spə-ˌnen-chē-ˈā-shən\ *n* [*exponent* + *-iation* (as in *differentiation*)] (1903) **:** the act or process of raising a quantity to a power — called also *involution*

[1]**ex·port** \ek-ˈspō(ə)rt, -ˈspȯ(ə)rt, ˈek-ˌ\ *vb* [L *exportare,* fr. *ex-* + *portare* to carry — more at FARE] *vt* (15c) **1 :** to carry away **:** REMOVE **2 :** to carry or send (as a commodity) to some other place (as another country) ~ *vi* **:** to export something abroad — **ex·port·abil·i·ty** \(ˌ)ek-ˌspōrt-ə-ˈbil-ət-ē, -ˌspȯrt-\ *n* — **ex·port·able** \ek-ˈspōrt-ə-bəl, -ˈspȯrt-, ˈek-ˌ\ *adj*

[2]**ex·port** \ˈek-ˌspō(ə)rt, -ˌspȯ(ə)rt\ *n* (1690) **1 :** something exported; *specif* **:** a commodity conveyed from one country or region to another for purposes of trade **2 :** an act of exporting **:** EXPORTATION ⟨the ~ of wheat⟩

[3]**ex·port** \ˈek-ˌ\ *adj* (1795) **:** of or relating to exportation or exports ⟨~ duties⟩

ex·por·ta·tion \ˌek-ˌspōr-ˈtā-shən, -ˌspȯr-, -spər-\ *n* (1610) **:** an act of exporting; *also* **:** a commodity exported

ex·port·er \ek-ˈspōrt-ər, -ˈspȯrt-, ˈek-ˌ\ *n* (1691) **:** one that exports; *specif* **:** a wholesaler who sells to merchants or industrial consumers in foreign countries

ex·pose \ik-ˈspōz\ *vt* **ex·posed; ex·pos·ing** [ME *exposen,* fr. MF *exposer,* fr. L *exponere* to set forth, explain (perf. indic. *exposui*), fr. *ex-* + *ponere* to put, place — more at POSITION] (15c) **1 a :** to deprive of shelter, protection, or care **:** subject to risk from a harmful action or condition ⟨~ troops needlessly⟩ ⟨has not yet been *exposed* to measles⟩ **b :** to submit or make accessible to a particular action or influence ⟨~ children to good books⟩; *specif* **:** to subject (a sensitive photographic film, plate, or paper) to radiant energy **c :** to abandon (an infant) esp. by leaving in the open **2 :** to cause to be visible or open to view **:** DISPLAY: as **a :** to offer publicly for sale **b :** to exhibit for public veneration **c :** to reveal the face of (a playing card) or the cards of (a player's hand) **3 a :** to make known **:** bring to light (as something shameful) **b :** to disclose the faults or crimes of ⟨~ a murderer⟩ ***syn*** see SHOW — **ex·pos·er** *n*

ex·po·sé *or* **ex·po·se** \ˌek-spō-ˈzā, -spə-\ *n* [F *exposé,* fr. pp. of *exposer*] (1803) **1 :** a formal statement of facts **2 :** an exposure of something discreditable ⟨a newspaper ~ of crime conditions⟩

ex·posed \ik-ˈspōzd\ *adj* (1630) **1 :** open to view **2 :** not shielded or protected ⟨an ~ electric wire⟩ ***syn*** see LIABLE

ex·pos·it \ik-ˈspäz-ət\ *vt* [L *expositus,* pp. of *exponere*] (1882) **:** EXPOUND

ex·po·si·tion \ˌek-spə-ˈzish-ən\ *n* (14c) **1 :** a setting forth of the meaning or purpose (as of a writing) **2 a :** discourse or an example of it designed to convey information or explain what is difficult to understand **b (1) :** the first part of a musical composition in sonata form in which the thematic material of the movement is presented **(2) :** the opening section of a fugue **3 :** a public exhibition or show — **ex·po·si·tion·al** \-ˈzish-nəl, -ən-ᵊl\ *adj*

ex·pos·i·tive \ik-ˈspäz-ət-iv\ *adj* (1535) **:** DESCRIPTIVE, EXPOSITORY

ex·pos·i·tor \-ət-ər\ *n* [ME *expositour,* fr. MF *expositeur,* fr. LL *expositor,* fr. L *expositus*] (14c) **:** one who explains **:** COMMENTATOR

ex·pos·i·to·ry \-ə-ˌtōr-ē, -ˌtȯr-\ *adj* (1628) **:** of, relating to, or containing exposition ⟨~ writing⟩

[1]**ex post fac·to** \ˌek-ˌspōst-ˈfak-(ˌ)tō\ *adv* [LL, lit., from a thing done afterward] (1632) **:** after the fact **:** RETROACTIVELY

[2]**ex post facto** *adj* (1789) **:** done, made, or formulated after the fact **:** RETROACTIVE ⟨*ex post facto* approval⟩ ⟨*ex post facto* laws⟩

ex·pos·tu·late \ik-ˈspäs-chə-ˌlāt\ *vb* [L *expostulatus,* pp. of *expostulare* to demand, dispute, fr. *ex-* + *postulare* to ask for — more at POSTULATE] *vt, obs* (1534) **:** DISCUSS, EXAMINE ~ *vi* **:** to reason earnestly with a person for purposes of dissuasion or remonstrance

ex·pos·tu·la·tion \-ˌspäs-chə-ˈlā-shən\ *n* (1540) **:** an act or an instance of expostulating — **ex·pos·tu·la·to·ry** \-ˈspäs-chə-lə-ˌtōr-ē, -ˌtȯr-\ *adj*

ex·po·sure \ik-ˈspō-zhər\ *n* (1606) **1 :** the fact or condition of being exposed: as **a :** the condition of being presented to view or made known ⟨a politician seeks a lot of ~⟩ **b :** the condition of being unprotected esp. from severe weather ⟨died of ~⟩ **c :** the condition of being subject to some effect or influence ⟨risk ~ to the flu⟩ **2 :** the act or an instance of exposing: as **a :** disclosure of something secret ⟨the ~ of fraud brought about several indictments⟩ **b :** the treating of sensitized material (as film) to controlled amounts of radiant energy; *also* **:** the amount of such energy or length of such treatment ⟨a 3-second ~⟩ **3 a :** the manner of being exposed **b :** the position (as of a house) with respect to weather influences or compass points ⟨a window with a southern ~⟩ **4 :** a piece or section of sensitized material (as film) on which an exposure is or can be made ⟨20 ~*s* to the roll⟩

exposure meter *n* (1891) **:** a device for indicating correct photographic exposure under varying conditions of illumination

ex·pound \ik-ˈspau̇nd\ *vb* [ME *expounden,* fr. MF *expondre,* fr. L *exponere* to explain — more at EXPOSE] *vt* (14c) **1 a :** to set forth **:** STATE **b :** to defend with argument **2 :** to explain by setting forth in careful and often elaborate detail ⟨~ a law⟩ ~ *vi* **:** to make a statement **:** COMMENT ***syn*** see EXPLAIN — **ex·pound·er** *n*

[1]**ex·press** \ik-ˈspres\ *adj* [ME, fr. MF *expres,* fr. L *expressus,* pp. of *exprimere* to press out, express, fr. *ex-* + *premere* to press — more at PRESS] (14c) **1 a :** directly, firmly, and explicitly stated ⟨he disobeyed my ~ orders⟩ **b :** EXACT, PRECISE **2 a :** designed for or adapted to its purpose **b :** of a particular sort **:** SPECIFIC ⟨he came for that ~ purpose⟩ **3 a :** traveling at high speed; *specif* **:** traveling with few or no stops along the way ⟨~ train⟩ **b :** adapted or suitable for travel at high speed ⟨an ~ highway⟩ **c** *Brit* **:** designated to be delivered without delay by special messenger ⟨~ mail⟩ ***syn*** see EXPLICIT

[2]**express** *adv* (14c) **1** *obs* **:** EXPRESSLY **2 :** by express ⟨send a package ~⟩

[3]**express** *n* (1619) **1 a** *Brit* **:** a messenger sent on a special errand **b** *Brit* **:** a dispatch conveyed by a special messenger **c (1) :** a system for the prompt and safe transportation of parcels, money, or goods at rates higher than standard freight charges **(2) :** a company operating such a merchandise freight service **(3) :** the goods or shipments so transported **d** *Brit* **:** SPECIAL DELIVERY **2 :** an express vehicle

[4]**express** *vt* [ME *expressen,* fr. MF & L; MF *expresser,* fr. OF, fr. *expres,* adj., fr. L *expressus,* pp.] (14c) **1 a :** DELINEATE, DEPICT **b :** to represent in words **:** STATE **c :** to give or convey a true impression of **:** SHOW, REFLECT **d :** to make known the opinions or feelings of (one-

self) ⟨~*ed* himself very strongly on that subject⟩ **e** : to give expression to the artistic or creative impulses or abilities of (oneself) **f** : to represent by a sign or symbol : SYMBOLIZE **2 a** : to force out (as the juice of a fruit) by pressure **b** : to subject to pressure so as to extract something **3** : to send by express — **ex·press·er** *n* — **ex·press·ible** \-ə-bəl\ *adj*

syn EXPRESS, VENT, UTTER, VOICE, BROACH, AIR mean to make known what one thinks or feels. EXPRESS suggests an impulse to reveal in words, gestures, actions, or what one creates or produces; VENT stresses a strong inner compulsion to express esp. in words; UTTER implies the use of the voice not necessarily in articulate speech; VOICE does not necessarily imply vocal utterance but does imply expression or formulation in words; BROACH adds the implication of disclosing for the first time something long thought over or reserved for a suitable occasion; AIR implies an exposing or parading of one's views often in order to gain relief or sympathy or attention.

ex·press·age \ik-ˈspres-ij\ *n* (1857) : a carrying of parcels by express; *also* : a charge for such carrying

ex·pres·sion \ik-ˈspresh-ən\ *n* (15c) **1 a** : an act, process, or instance of representing in a medium (as words) : UTTERANCE ⟨freedom of ~⟩ **b** (1) : something that manifests, embodies, or symbolizes something else ⟨this gift is an ~ of my admiration for you⟩ (2) : a significant word or phrase (3) : a mathematical or logical symbol or a meaningful combination of symbols (4) : the detectable effect of a gene; *also* : EXPRESSIVITY **2 a** : a mode, means, or use of significant representation or symbolism; *esp* : felicitous or vivid indication or depiction of mood or sentiment ⟨read the poem with ~⟩ **b** (1) : the quality or fact of being expressive (2) : facial aspect or vocal intonation as indicative of feeling **3** : an act or product of pressing out — **ex·pres·sion·al** \-ˈspresh-nəl, -ən-ᵊl\ *adj*

ex·pres·sion·ism \ik-ˈspresh-ə-ˌniz-əm\ *n, often cap* (ca. 1901) : a theory or practice in art of seeking to depict not objective reality but the subjective emotions and responses that objects and events arouse in the artist — **ex·pres·sion·ist** \-ˈspresh-(ə-)nəst\ *n or adj, often cap* — **ex·pres·sion·is·tic** \-ˌspresh-ə-ˈnis-tik\ *adj* — **ex·pres·sion·is·ti·cal·ly** \-ti-k(ə-)lē\ *adv*

ex·pres·sion·less \ik-ˈspresh-ən-ləs\ *adj* (1831) : lacking expression ⟨an ~ face⟩ — **ex·pres·sion·less·ly** *adv* — **ex·pres·sion·less·ness** *n*

ex·pres·sive \ik-ˈspres-iv\ *adj* (15c) **1** : of or relating to expression ⟨the ~ function of language⟩ **2** : serving to express, utter, or represent ⟨he used foul and novel terms ~ of rage —H. G. Wells⟩ **3** : full of expression : SIGNIFICANT ⟨an ~ silence⟩ — **ex·pres·sive·ly** *adv* — **ex·pres·sive·ness** *n*

ex·pres·siv·i·ty \ˌek-ˌspres-ˈiv-ət-ē\ *n, pl* **-ties** (1934) **1** : the relative capacity of a gene to affect the phenotype of the organism of which it is a part **2** : the quality of being expressive

ex·press·ly \ik-ˈspres-lē\ *adv* (1526) **1** : in an express manner : EXPLICITLY ⟨he ~ rejected the proposal⟩ **2** : for the express purpose : PARTICULARLY ⟨needed a clinic ~ for the treatment of addicts⟩

ex·press·man \ik-ˈspres-ˌman, -mən\ *n* (1839) : a person employed in the express business

ex·pres·so \ik-ˈspres-(ˌ)ō\ *var of* ESPRESSO

ex·press·way \ik-ˈspres-ˌwā\ *n* (1938) : a high-speed divided highway for through traffic with access partially or fully controlled and grade separations at important intersections with other roads

ex·pro·pri·ate \ek-ˈsprō-prē-ˌāt\ *vt* **-at·ed; -at·ing** [ML *expropriatus,* pp. of *expropriare,* fr. L *ex-* + *proprius* own] (1611) **1** : to deprive of possession or proprietary rights **2** : to transfer (the property of another) to one's own possession — **ex·pro·pri·a·tor** \-ˌāt-ər\ *n*

ex·pro·pri·a·tion \(ˌ)ek-ˌsprō-prē-ˈā-shən\ *n* (15c) : the act of expropriating or the state of being expropriated; *specif* : the action of the state in taking or modifying the property rights of an individual in the exercise of its sovereignty

ex·pulse \ik-ˈspəls\ *vt* **ex·pulsed; ex·puls·ing** (15c) : EXPEL

ex·pul·sion \ik-ˈspəl-shən\ *n* [ME, fr. L *expulsion-, expulsio,* fr. *expulsus,* pp. of *expellere* to expel] (15c) : the act of expelling : the state of being expelled — **ex·pul·sive** \-ˈspəl-siv\ *adj*

ex·punc·tion \ik-ˈspəŋ(k)-shən\ *n* [L *expunctus,* pp. of *expungere*] (1606) : the act of expunging : the state of being expunged : ERASURE

ex·punge \ik-ˈspənj\ *vt* **ex·punged; ex·pung·ing** [L *expungere* to mark for deletion by dots, fr. *ex-* + *pungere* to prick — more at PUNGENT] (1602) **1** : to strike out, obliterate, or mark for deletion **2** : to efface completely : DESTROY — **ex·pung·er** *n*

ex·pur·gate \ˈek-spər-ˌgāt\ *vt* **-gat·ed; -gat·ing** [L *expurgatus,* pp. of *expurgare,* fr. *ex-* + *purgare* to purge] (1678) : to cleanse of something morally harmful, offensive, or erroneous; *esp* : to expunge objectionable parts from before publication or presentation ⟨~ a book⟩ — **ex·pur·ga·tion** \ˌek-spər-ˈgā-shən\ *n* — **ex·pur·ga·tor** \ˈek-spər-ˌgāt-ər\ *n*

ex·pur·ga·to·ri·al \(ˌ)ek-ˌspər-gə-ˈtōr-ē-əl, -ˈtȯr-\ *adj* (1807) : relating to expurgation or an expurgator : EXPURGATORY

ex·pur·ga·to·ry \ek-ˈspər-gə-ˌtōr-ē, -ˌtȯr-\ *adj* (1625) : serving to purify from something morally harmful, offensive, or erroneous

¹ex·qui·site \ek-ˈskwiz-ət, ˈek-(ˌ)\ *adj* [ME *exquisit,* fr. L *exquisitus,* pp. of *exquirere* to search out, fr. *ex-* + *quaerere* to seek] (15c) **1** : carefully selected : CHOICE **2** *archaic* : ACCURATE **3 a** : marked by flawless craftsmanship or by beautiful, ingenious, delicate, or elaborate execution **b** : keenly appreciative : DISCRIMINATING ⟨~ taste⟩ **c** : ACCOMPLISHED, PERFECTED ⟨an ~ gentleman⟩ **4 a** : pleasing through beauty, fitness, or perfection ⟨an ~ white blossom⟩ **b** : ACUTE, INTENSE ⟨~ pain⟩ **c** : having uncommon or esoteric appeal ***syn*** see CHOICE — **ex·qui·site·ly** *adv* — **ex·qui·site·ness** *n*

²exquisite *n* (1819) : one who is overly fastidious in dress or ornament

ex·san·gui·na·tion \(ˌ)ek(s)-ˌsaŋ-gwə-ˈnā-shən\ *n* [NL *exsanguination-, exsanguinatio,* fr. L *exsanguinatus* bloodless, fr. *ex-* + *sanguin-, sanguis* blood] (ca. 1909) : the action or process of draining or losing blood — **ex·san·gui·nate** \ek(s)-ˈsaŋ-gwə-ˌnāt\ *vt*

ex·scind \ek-ˈsind\ *vt* [L *exscindere,* fr. *ex-* + *scindere* to cut, tear — more at SHED] (1662) : to cut off or out : EXCISE

ex·sert \ek-ˈsərt\ *vt* [L *exsertus,* pp. of *exserere* — more at EXERT] (1665) : to thrust out — **ex·ser·tile** \-ˈsərt-ᵊl, -ˈsər-ˌtīl\ *adj* — **ex·ser·tion** \-ˈsər-shən\ *n*

ex·sert·ed *adj* (1816) : projecting beyond an enclosing organ or part

ex·sic·cate \ˈek-si-ˌkāt\ *vt* **-cat·ed; -cat·ing** [L *exsiccatus,* pp. of *exsiccare,* fr. *ex-* + *siccare* to dry, fr. *siccus* dry — more at SACK] (1545) : to remove moisture from : DRY — **ex·sic·ca·tion** \ˌek-si-ˈkā-shən\ *n*

ex·stip·u·late \(ˈ)ek(s)-ˈstip-yə-lət\ *adj* (1830) : having no stipules

ex·tant \ˈek-stənt; ek-ˈstant, ˈek-ˌ\ *adj* [L *exstant-, exstans,* prp. of *exstare* to stand out, be in existence, fr. *ex-* + *stare* to stand — more at STAND] (1545) **1** *archaic* : standing out or above **2 a** : currently or actually existing ⟨~ and projected programs⟩ ⟨the most charming writer ~ —G. W. Johnson⟩ **b** : not destroyed or lost ⟨~ manuscripts⟩

ex·tem·po·ral \ek-ˈstem-p(ə-)rəl\ *adj* [L *extemporalis,* fr. *ex tempore*] *archaic* (1570) : EXTEMPORANEOUS — **ex·tem·po·ral·ly** \-ē\ *adv*

ex·tem·po·ra·ne·ity \(ˌ)ek-ˌstem-pə-rə-ˈnē-ət-ē, -ˈnā-\ *n* (1937) : the quality or state of being extemporaneous

ex·tem·po·ra·ne·ous \(ˌ)ek-ˌstem-pə-ˈrā-nē-əs\ *adj* [LL *extemporaneus,* fr. L *ex tempore*] (ca. 1656) **1 a** (1) : composed, performed, or uttered on the spur of the moment : IMPROMPTU (2) : carefully prepared but delivered without notes or text **b** : skilled at or given to extemporaneous utterance **c** : happening suddenly and often unexpectedly and usu. without clearly known causes or relationships ⟨a great deal of criminal and delinquent behavior is . . . ~ —W. C. Reckless⟩ **2** : provided, made, or put to use as an expedient : MAKESHIFT — **ex·tem·po·ra·ne·ous·ly** *adv* — **ex·tem·po·ra·ne·ous·ness** *n*

ex·tem·po·rary \ik-ˈstem-pə-ˌrer-ē\ *adj* (1610) : EXTEMPORANEOUS — **ex·tem·po·rar·i·ly** \-ˌstem-pə-ˈrer-ə-lē\ *adv*

ex·tem·po·re \ik-ˈstem-pə-(ˌ)rē\ *adv* [L *ex tempore,* fr. *ex* + *tempore,* abl. of *tempus* time] (1553) : in an extemporaneous manner ⟨speaking ~⟩

ex·tem·po·ri·za·tion \ik-ˌstem-pə-rə-ˈzā-shən\ *n* (ca. 1860) **1** : the act of extemporizing : IMPROVISATION **2** : something extemporized

ex·tem·po·rize \ik-ˈstem-pə-ˌrīz\ *vb* **-rized; -riz·ing** *vi* (1644) **1** : to do something extemporaneously : IMPROVISE; *esp* : to speak extemporaneously **2** : to get along in a makeshift manner ~ *vt* : to compose, perform, or utter extemporaneously : IMPROVISE — **ex·tem·po·riz·er** *n*

ex·tend \ik-ˈstend\ *vb* [ME *extenden,* fr. MF or L; MF *estendre,* fr. L *extendere,* fr. *ex-* + *tendere* to stretch — more at THIN] *vt* (14c) **1** : to spread or stretch forth : UNBEND ⟨~*ed* both her arms⟩ **2 a** : to stretch out to fullest length **b** : to cause (as a horse) to move at full stride **c** : to exert (oneself) to full capacity ⟨could work long and hard without seeming to ~ himself⟩ **d** (1) : to increase the bulk of (as by the addition of a cheaper substance or a modifier) (2) : ADULTERATE **3** [ME *extenden,* fr. ML *extendere* (fr. L) or AF *estendre,* fr. OF] **a** *Brit* : to take possession of (as lands) by a writ of extent **b** *obs* : to take by force **4 a** : to make the offer of : PROFFER ⟨~*ing* aid to the needy⟩ **b** : to make available ⟨~*ing* credit to customers⟩ **5 a** : to cause to reach (as in distance or scope) ⟨national authority was ~*ed* over new territories⟩ **b** : to cause to be longer : PROLONG ⟨~ the side of a triangle⟩ ⟨~*ed* their visit another day⟩; *also* : to prolong the time of payment of **c** : ADVANCE, FURTHER ⟨~*ing* his potential through job training⟩ **6 a** : to cause to be of greater area or volume : ENLARGE **b** : to increase the scope, meaning, or application of : BROADEN ⟨beauty, I suppose, opens the heart, ~*s* the consciousness —Algernon Blackwood⟩ **c** *archaic* : EXAGGERATE ~ *vi* **1** : to stretch out in distance, space, or time : REACH ⟨his jurisdiction ~*ed* over the whole area⟩ **2** : to reach in scope or application ⟨his concern ~*s* beyond mere business to real service to his customers⟩ — **ex·tend·able** *or* **ex·tend·ible** \-ˈsten-də-bəl\ *adj*

syn EXTEND, LENGTHEN, PROLONG, PROTRACT mean to draw out or add to so as to increase in length. EXTEND and LENGTHEN imply a drawing out in space or time but EXTEND may also imply increase in width, scope, area, or range ⟨*extend* a vacation⟩ ⟨*extend* welfare services⟩ ⟨*lengthen* a skirt⟩ ⟨*lengthen* the workweek⟩ PROLONG suggests chiefly increase in duration esp. beyond usual limits ⟨*prolonged* illness⟩ PROTRACT adds to PROLONG implications of needlessness, vexation, or indefiniteness ⟨*protracted* litigation⟩

ex·tend·ed *adj* (15c) **1** : INTENSIVE ⟨~ efforts⟩ **2** : having spatial magnitude : being larger than a point ⟨an ~ source of light⟩ **3** : EXTENSIVE ⟨made available ~ information —Ruth G. Strickland⟩ **4** : DERIVATIVE 1, SECONDARY 2a ⟨an ~ sense of a word⟩ **5** *of a typeface* : having a wider face than that of a typeface not so characterized — **ex·tend·ed·ly** *adv* — **ex·tend·ed·ness** *n*

extended family *n* (ca. 1935) : a family that includes in one household near relatives in addition to a nuclear family

extended play *n* (ca. 1952) : a 45-rpm phonograph record with a playing time of about 6 to 8 minutes

ex·tend·er \ik-ˈsten-dər\ *n* (ca. 1611) : one that extends; *esp* : a substance added to a product esp. in the capacity of a diluent, adulterant, or modifier

ex·ten·si·ble \ik-ˈsten(t)-sə-bəl\ *adj* (ca. 1611) : capable of being extended — **ex·ten·si·bil·i·ty** \-ˌsten(t)-sə-ˈbil-ət-ē\ *n*

ex·ten·sile \ik-ˈsten(t)-səl, -ˈsten-ˌsīl\ *adj* (1744) : EXTENSIBLE

ex·ten·sion \ik-ˈsten-chən\ *n* [ME, fr. MF or LL; MF, fr. LL *extension-, extensio,* fr. L *extensus,* pp. of *extendere*] (15c) **1 a** : the action of extending : state of being extended **b** : an enlargement in scope or operation ⟨tools are ~*s* of human hands⟩ **2 a** : the total range over which something extends : COMPASS **b** : DENOTATION 2 **3 a** : the stretching of a fractured or dislocated limb so as to restore it to its natural position **b** : an unbending movement around a joint in a limb (as the knee or elbow) that increases the angle between the bones of the limb at the joint — compare FLEXION 4a **4** : a property whereby something occupies space **5** : an increase in length of time; *specif* : an increase in time allowed under agreement or concession ⟨was granted an ~⟩ **6** : a program that geographically extends the educational resources of an institution by special arrangements (as correspondence courses) to persons otherwise unable to take advantage of such resources **7 a** : a part constituting an addition **b** : a section or line segment forming an additional length **c** : an extra telephone connected to the principal line **8** : a mathematical set (as a field or group) that includes a given and similar set as a subset

ex·ten·sion·al \ik-'stench-nəl, -'sten-chən-ᵊl\ *adj* (1647) **1 :** of, relating to, or marked by extension; *specif* **:** DENOTATIVE **2 :** concerned with objective reality — **ex·ten·sion·al·i·ty** \-ˌsten-chə-'nal-ət-ē\ *n* — **ex·ten·sion·al·ly** \-'stench-nə-lē, -'sten-chən-ᵊl-ē\ *adv*

extension cord *n* (1946) **:** an electric cord fitted with a plug at one end and a receptacle at the other

ex·ten·si·ty \ik-'sten(t)-sət-ē\ *n, pl* **-ties** (1834) **1 a :** the quality of having extension **b :** degree of extension **:** RANGE **2 :** an attribute of sensation whereby space or size is perceived

ex·ten·sive \ik-'sten(t)-siv\ *adj* (1605) **1 :** EXTENSIONAL **2 :** having wide or considerable extent ⟨~ reading⟩ **3 :** of, relating to, or constituting farming in which large areas of land are utilized with minimum outlay and labor — **ex·ten·sive·ly** *adv* — **ex·ten·sive·ness** *n*

ex·ten·som·e·ter \ˌek-ˌsten-'säm-ət-ər\ *n* [*extension* + *-o-* + *-meter*] (1887) **:** an instrument for measuring minute deformations of test specimens caused by tension, compression, bending, or twisting

ex·ten·sor \ik-'sten(t)-sər\ *n* (1713) **:** a muscle serving to extend a bodily part (as a limb)

ex·tent \ik-'stent\ *n* [ME, fr. AF & MF; AF *extente* land valuation, fr. MF, area, surveying of land, fr. *extendre* to extend] (14c) **1** *archaic* **:** valuation (as of land) in Great Britain esp. for taxation **2 a :** seizure (as of land) in execution of a writ of extent in Great Britain **:** the condition of being so seized **b :** a writ giving to a creditor temporary possession of his debtor's property **3 a :** the range over which something extends **:** SCOPE ⟨the ~ of his authority⟩ **b :** the point, degree, or limit to which something extends ⟨using talents to the greatest ~⟩ **c :** the amount of space or surface that something occupies or the distance over which it extends **:** MAGNITUDE ⟨the ~ of the forest⟩

ex·ten·u·ate \ik-'sten-yə-ˌwāt\ *vt* **-at·ed; -at·ing** [L *extenuatus,* pp. of *extenuare,* fr. *ex-* + *tenuis* thin — more at THIN] (1529) **1 a** *archaic* **:** to make light of **b :** to lessen or to try to lessen the seriousness or extent of by making partial excuses **:** MITIGATE **c** *obs* **:** DISPARAGE **2 a** *archaic* **:** to make thin or emaciated **b :** to lessen the strength or effect of — **ex·ten·u·a·tor** \-ˌwāt-ər\ *n* — **ex·ten·u·a·to·ry** \-wə-ˌtōr-ē, -ˌtȯr-\ *adj*

ex·ten·u·a·tion \ik-ˌsten-yə-'wā-shən\ *n* (1542) **1 :** the act of extenuating or state of being extenuated; *esp* **:** partial justification **2 :** something extenuating; *esp* **:** a partial excuse

¹ex·te·ri·or \ek-'stir-ē-ər\ *adj* [L, compar. of *exter, exterus* being on the outside, foreign, fr. *ex*] (1528) **1 :** being on an outside surface **:** situated on the outside **2 :** observable by outward signs ⟨his ~ quietness is belied by an occasional nervous twitch —*Current Biog.*⟩ **3 :** suitable for use on outside surfaces — **ex·te·ri·or·ly** *adv*

²exterior *n* (1591) **1 a :** an exterior part or surface **:** OUTSIDE **b :** outward manner or appearance **2 :** a representation (as on stage or film) of an outdoor scene

exterior angle *n* (1890) **1 :** the angle between a side of a polygon and an extended adjacent side **2 :** an angle formed by a transversal as it cuts one of two lines and situated on the outside of the line

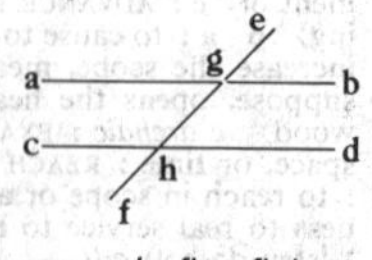

ega, egb, fhc, fhd exterior angle 2

ex·te·ri·or·i·ty \(ˌ)ek-ˌstir-ē-'ȯr-ət-ē, -'är-\ *n* (1611) **:** the quality or state of being exterior or exteriorized **:** EXTERNALITY

ex·te·ri·or·ize \ek-'stir-ē-ə-ˌrīz\ *vt* **-ized; -iz·ing** (1879) **1 :** EXTERNALIZE **2 :** to bring out of the body (as for surgery) — **ex·te·ri·or·iza·tion** \-ˌstir-ē-ə-rə-'zā-shən\ *n*

ex·ter·mi·nate \ik-'stər-mə-ˌnāt\ *vt* **-nat·ed; -nat·ing** [L *exterminatus,* pp. of *exterminare,* fr. *ex-* + *terminus* boundary — more at TERM] (1591) **:** to get rid of completely usu. by killing off ⟨~ crabgrass from a lawn⟩ — **ex·ter·mi·na·tion** \-ˌstər-mə-'nā-shən\ *n* — **ex·ter·mi·na·tor** \-'stər-mə-ˌnāt-ər\ *n*

syn EXTERMINATE, EXTIRPATE, ERADICATE, UPROOT mean to effect the destruction or abolition of something. EXTERMINATE implies complete and immediate extinction by killing off all individuals; EXTIRPATE implies extinction of a race, family, species, or sometimes an idea or doctrine by destruction or removal of its means of propagation; ERADICATE implies the driving out or elimination of something that has established itself; UPROOT implies a forcible or violent removal and stresses displacement or dislodgment rather than immediate destruction.

ex·ter·mi·na·to·ry \ik-'stərm-(ə-)nə-ˌtōr-ē, -ˌtȯr-\ *adj* (1790) **:** of, relating to, or marked by extermination

ex·ter·mine \ik-'stər-mən\ *vt* **-mined; -min·ing** *obs* (1539) **:** EXTERMINATE

¹ex·tern \ek-'stərn, 'ek-ˌ\ *adj* [MF or L; MF *externe,* fr. L *externus*] *archaic* (1533) **:** EXTERNAL

²ex·tern *also* **ex·terne** \'ek-ˌstərn\ *n* (1610) **:** a person connected with an institution but not living or boarding in it; *specif* **:** a nonresident doctor or medical student at a hospital

¹ex·ter·nal \ek-'stərn-ᵊl\ *adj* [L *externus* external, fr. *exter*] (1556) **1 a :** capable of being perceived outwardly ⟨~ signs of a disease⟩ ⟨~ reality⟩ **b (1) :** having merely the outward appearance of something **:** SUPERFICIAL **(2) :** not intrinsic or essential ⟨~ circumstances⟩ **2 a :** of, relating to, or connected with the outside or an outer part **b :** applied or applicable to the outside **3 a (1) :** situated outside, apart, or beyond; *specif* **:** situated near or toward the surface of the body **(2) :** arising or acting from outside ⟨~ force⟩ **b :** of or relating to dealings or relationships with foreign countries **c :** having existence independent of the mind ⟨~ reality⟩ — **ex·ter·nal·ly** \-ᵊl-ē\ *adv*

²external *n* (1600) **:** something that is external: as **a** *archaic* **:** an outer part **b :** an external feature or aspect — usu. used in pl. ⟨the ~*s* of religion⟩

external–combustion engine *n* (1915) **:** a heat engine (as a steam engine) that derives its heat from fuel consumed outside the engine cylinder

external degree *n* (1928) **:** a degree conferred on a student who has not attended the university but has passed the qualifying examination

ex·ter·nal·ism \ek-'stərn-ᵊl-ˌiz-əm\ *n* (1856) **1 :** EXTERNALITY 1 **2 :** attention to externals; *esp* **:** excessive preoccupation with externals

ex·ter·nal·i·ty \ˌek-ˌstər-'nal-ət-ē\ *n, pl* **-ties** (1673) **1 :** the quality or state of being external or externalized **2 :** something that is external **3 :** a secondary or unexpected consequence ⟨increased air pollution was one ~ of the new design⟩

ex·ter·nal·iza·tion \ek-ˌstərn-ᵊl-ə-'zā-shən\ *n* (1803) **1 a :** the action or process of externalizing **b :** the quality or state of being externalized **2 :** something externalized **:** EMBODIMENT

ex·ter·nal·ize \ek-'stərn-ᵊl-ˌīz\ *vt* **-ized; -iz·ing** (1852) **1 :** to make external or externally manifest **:** EMBODY **2 :** to attribute to causes outside the self **:** RATIONALIZE ⟨~ his failure⟩

external respiration *n* (1940) **:** exchange of gases between the external environment and a distributing system of the animal body (as the lungs of higher vertebrates or the tracheal tubes of insects) or between the alveoli of the lungs and the blood — compare INTERNAL RESPIRATION

ex·tern·ship \'ek-ˌstərn-ˌship\ *n* [*external* + *-ship* (as in *internship*)] (1945) **:** a training program that is part of a course of study of an educational institution and is taken in private business

ex·tero·cep·tive \ˌek-stə-rō-'sep-tiv\ *adj* [L *exter* + E *-o-* + *-ceptive* (as in *receptive*)] (ca. 1921) **:** activated by, relating to, or being stimuli received by an organism from outside

ex·tero·cep·tor \-tər\ *n* [NL, fr. L *exter* + NL *-o-* + *-ceptor* (as in *receptor*)] (1906) **:** a sense organ excited by exteroceptive stimuli

ex·ter·ri·to·ri·al \ˌek-ˌster-ə-'tōr-ē-əl, -'tȯr-\ *adj* (ca. 1880) **:** EXTRATERRITORIAL — **ex·ter·ri·to·ri·al·i·ty** \-ˌtōr-ē-'al-ət-ē, -ˌtȯr-\ *n*

¹ex·tinct \ik-'stiŋ(k)t, 'ek-ˌ\ *adj* [ME, fr. L *exstinctus,* pp. of *exstinguere*] (15c) **1 a :** no longer burning **b :** no longer active ⟨an ~ volcano⟩ **2 :** no longer existing ⟨an ~ animal⟩ **3 a :** gone out of use **:** SUPERSEDED **b :** having no qualified claimant ⟨an ~ title⟩

²extinct *vt, archaic* (15c) **:** EXTINGUISH

ex·tinc·tion \ik-'stiŋ(k)-shən\ *n* (15c) **1 :** the act of making extinct or causing to be extinguished **2 :** the condition or fact of being extinct or extinguished; *also* **:** the process of becoming extinct ⟨~ of a species⟩ **3 :** the process of eliminating or reducing a conditioned response by not reinforcing it

ex·tinc·tive \ik-'stiŋ(k)-tiv\ *adj* (1600) **:** tending or serving to extinguish or make extinct

ex·tin·guish \ik-'stiŋ-(g)wish\ *vt* [L *exstinguere* (fr. *ex-* + *stinguere* to extinguish) + E *-ish* (as in *abolish*); akin to L *instigare* to incite — more at STICK] (1551) **1 a :** to cause to cease burning **:** QUENCH **b (1) :** to bring to an end **:** make an end of ⟨hope for their safety was slowly ~*ed*⟩ **(2) :** to reduce to silence or ineffectiveness **c :** to cause extinction of (a conditioned response) **d :** to dim the brightness of **:** ECLIPSE **2 a :** to cause to be void **:** NULLIFY ⟨~ a claim⟩ **b :** to get rid of usu. by payment ⟨~ a debt⟩ — **ex·tin·guish·able** \-ə-bəl\ *adj* — **ex·tin·guish·er** \-ər\ *n* — **ex·tin·guish·ment** \-mənt\ *n*

ex·tir·pate \'ek-stər-ˌpāt\ *vt* **-pat·ed; -pat·ing** [L *exstirpatus,* pp. *exstirpare,* fr. *ex-* + *stirp-, stirps* trunk, root — more at TORPID] (1539) **1 a :** to pull up by the root **b :** to destroy completely **:** WIPE OUT **2 :** to cut out by surgery ***syn*** see EXTERMINATE — **ex·tir·pa·tion** \ˌek-stər-'pā-shən\ *n* — **ex·tir·pa·tor** \'ek-stər-ˌpāt-ər\ *n*

ex·tol *also* **ex·toll** \ik-'stōl\ *vt* **ex·tolled; ex·tol·ling** [ME *extollen,* fr. L *extollere,* fr. *ex-* + *tollere* to lift up — more at TOLERATE] (15c) **:** to praise highly **:** GLORIFY — **ex·tol·ler** *n* — **ex·tol·ment** \-'stōl-mənt\ *n*

ex·tor·sion \ek-'stȯr-shən, 'ek-ˌ\ *n* (1899) **:** outward rotation (as of a body part) about an axis or fixed point

ex·tort \ik-'stȯ(ə)rt\ *vt* [L *extortus,* pp. of *extorquēre* to wrench out, extort, fr. *ex-* + *torquēre* to twist — more at TORTURE] (1529) **:** to obtain from a person by force, intimidation, or undue or illegal power **:** WRING; *also* **:** to gain esp. by ingenuity or compelling argument ***syn*** see EDUCE — **ex·tort·er** *n* — **ex·tor·tive** \-'stȯrt-iv\ *adj*

ex·tor·tion \ik-'stȯr-shən\ *n* (14c) **1 :** the act or practice of extorting esp. money or other property; *specif* **:** the offense committed by an official engaging in such practice **2 :** something extorted; *esp* **:** a gross overcharge — **ex·tor·tion·er** \-sh(ə-)nər\ *n* — **ex·tor·tion·ist** \-sh(ə-)nəst\ *n*

ex·tor·tion·ary \-shə-ˌner-ē\ *adj, archaic* (1805) **:** EXTORTIONATE 1

ex·tor·tion·ate \ik-'stȯr-sh(ə-)nət\ *adj* (1789) **1 :** characterized by extortion **2 :** EXCESSIVE, EXORBITANT — **ex·tor·tion·ate·ly** *adv*

¹ex·tra \'ek-strə\ *adj* [prob. short for *extraordinary*] (1776) **1 a :** more than is due, usual, or necessary **:** ADDITIONAL ⟨~ work⟩ **b :** subject to an additional charge ⟨room service is ~⟩ **2 :** SUPERIOR ⟨~ quality⟩

²extra *n* (ca. 1793) **1 :** something extra or additional: as **a :** an added charge **b :** a special edition of a newspaper **c :** an additional worker; *specif* **:** one hired to act in a group scene in a motion picture or stage production **2 :** something of superior quality or grade

³extra *adv* (1823) **:** beyond the usual size, extent, or degree ⟨~ large⟩

extra- *prefix* [ME, fr. L, fr. *extra,* adv. & prep., outside, except, beyond, fr. *exter* being on the outside — more at EXTERIOR] **:** outside **:** beyond ⟨*extra*judicial⟩

extra–base hit *n* (ca. 1949) **:** a hit in baseball that lets the batter reach more than one base

ex·tra·cel·lu·lar \ˌek-strə-'sel-yə-lər\ *adj* (1867) **:** situated or occurring outside a cell or the cells of the body ⟨~ digestion⟩ ⟨~ enzymes⟩ — **ex·tra·cel·lu·lar·ly** *adv*

ex·tra·chro·mo·som·al \-ˌkrō-mə-'sō-məl, -'zō-\ *adj* (1940) **:** situated or controlled by factors outside the chromosome ⟨~ inheritance⟩

ex·tra·cor·po·re·al \-kȯr-'pōr-ē-əl, -'pȯr-\ *adj* (1865) **:** occurring or based outside the living body ⟨heart surgery employing ~ circulation⟩ — **ex·tra·cor·po·re·al·ly** \-ē-ə-lē\ *adv*

ex·tra·cra·ni·al \-'krā-nē-əl\ *adj* (1887) **:** situated or occurring outside the cranium

¹ex·tract \ik-'strakt, *oftenest in sense* 5 'ek-ˌ\ *vt* [ME *extracten,* fr. L *extractus,* pp. of *extrahere,* fr. *ex-* + *trahere* to draw — more at DRAW] (15c) **1 a :** to draw forth (as by research) ⟨~ data⟩ **b :** to pull or take out forcibly ⟨~*ed* a wisdom tooth⟩ **c :** to obtain by much effort from someone unwilling ⟨~*ed* a confession⟩ **2 :** to withdraw (as a juice or fraction) by physical or chemical process; *also* **:** to treat with a solvent so as to remove a soluble substance **3 :** to separate (a metal) from an ore **4 :** to determine (a mathematical root) by calculation **5 :** to select (excerpts) and copy out or cite ***syn*** see EDUCE — **ex·tract·abil·i·ty** \ik-ˌstrak-tə-'bil-ət-ē, (ˌ)ek-\ *n* — **ex·tract·able** \ik-'strak-tə-bəl, 'ek-ˌ\ *adj*

²ex·tract \'ek-ˌstrakt\ *n* (15c) **1 :** a selection from a writing or discourse **:** EXCERPT **2 :** a product (as an essence or concentrate) prepared by extracting; *esp* **:** a solution (as in alcohol) of essential constituents of a complex material (as meat or an aromatic plant)

ex·trac·tion \ik-'strak-shən\ *n* (15c) **1 :** the act or process of extracting something **2 :** ANCESTRY, ORIGIN **3 :** something extracted

[1]**ex·trac·tive** \ik-ˈstrak-tiv, ˈek-ˌ\ *adj* (1599) **1 a :** of, relating to, or involving extraction **b :** tending toward or resulting in withdrawal of natural resources by extraction with no provision for replenishment ⟨~ agriculture⟩ **2 :** capable of being extracted — **ex·trac·tive·ly** *adv*

[2]**extractive** *n* (1844) **:** something extracted or extractable **:** EXTRACT

ex·trac·tor \ik-ˈstrak-tər\ *n* (1611) **:** one that extracts; *specif* **:** the mechanism in a firearm that dislodges a spent cartridge from the chamber

ex·tra·cur·ric·u·lar \ˌek-strə-kə-ˈrik-yə-lər\ *adj* (1925) **1 :** not falling within the scope of a regular curriculum; *specif* **:** of or relating to officially or semiofficially approved and usu. organized student activities (as athletics) connected with school and usu. carrying no academic credit **2 a :** lying outside one's regular duties or routine **b :** EXTRAMARITAL — **extracurricular** *n*

ex·tra·dit·able \ˈek-strə-ˌdīt-ə-bəl\ *adj* (1881) **1 :** subject or liable to extradition **2 :** making liable to extradition ⟨an ~ offense⟩

ex·tra·dite \ˈek-strə-ˌdīt\ *vt* **-dit·ed; -dit·ing** [back-formation fr. *extradition*] (1864) **1 :** to deliver up to extradition **2 :** to obtain the extradition of

ex·tra·di·tion \ˌek-strə-ˈdish-ən\ *n* [F, fr. *ex-* + L *tradition-, traditio* act of handing over — more at TRADITION] (1839) **:** the surrender of an alleged criminal usu. under the provisions of a treaty or statute by one state or other authority to another having jurisdiction to try the charge

ex·tra·dos \ˈek-strə-ˌdäs, -ˌdō; ek-ˈstrā-ˌdäs\ *n, pl* **ex·tra·dos** \-ˌdōz, -ˌdäs\ *or* **ex·tra·dos·es** \-ˌdäs-əz\ [F, fr. L *extra* + F *dos* back — more at DOSSIER] (1772) **:** the exterior curve of an arch — see ARCH illustration

ex·tra·ga·lac·tic \ˌek-strə-gə-ˈlak-tik\ *adj* [ISV] (1851) **:** lying or coming from outside the Milky Way

ex·tra·he·pat·ic \-hi-ˈpat-ik\ *adj* (1926) **:** situated or originating outside the liver

ex·tra·ju·di·cial \-jü-ˈdish-əl\ *adj* (1630) **1 a :** not forming a valid part of regular legal proceedings ⟨an ~ investigation⟩ **b :** delivered without legal authority **:** PRIVATE 2a(2) ⟨the judge's ~ statements⟩ **2 :** done in contravention of due process of law ⟨an ~ execution⟩ — **ex·tra·ju·di·cial·ly** \-ˈdish-(ə-)lē\ *adv*

ex·tra·le·gal \ˌek-strə-ˈlē-gəl\ *adj* (1644) **:** not regulated or sanctioned by law — **ex·tra·le·gal·ly** \-gə-lē\ *adv*

ex·tra·lim·it·al \-ˈlim-ət-ᵊl\ *adj* (1874) **:** not present in a given area — used of kinds of organisms (as species)

ex·tra·lin·guis·tic \-liŋ-ˈgwis-tik\ *adj* (1927) **:** lying outside the province of linguistics — **ex·tra·lin·guis·ti·cal·ly** \-ti-kə-lē\ *adv*

ex·tra·lit·er·ary \-ˈlit-ə-ˌrer-ē\ *adj* (1945) **:** lying outside the field of literature

ex·tral·i·ty \ek-ˈstral-ət-ē\ *n* [by contr.] (ca. 1925) **:** EXTRATERRITORIALITY

ex·tra·mar·i·tal \ˌek-strə-ˈmar-ət-ᵊl\ *adj* (1925) **:** of or relating to a married person's sexual intercourse with other than his or her spouse **:** ADULTEROUS

ex·tra·mun·dane \ˌek-strə-ˌmən-ˈdān, -ˈmən-ˌ\ *adj* [LL *extramundanus*, fr. L *extra* + *mundus* the world] (1665) **:** situated in or relating to a region beyond the material world

ex·tra·mu·ral \-ˈmyu̇r-əl\ *adj* (1854) **1 :** existing or functioning outside or beyond the walls, boundaries, or precincts of an organized unit (as a school or hospital) **2** *chiefly Brit* **:** of, relating to, or taking part in extension courses or facilities — **ex·tra·mu·ral·ly** \-ə-lē\ *adv*

ex·tra·mu·si·cal \-ˈmyü-zi-kəl\ *adj* (1923) **:** lying outside the province of music

ex·tra·ne·ous \ek-ˈstrā-nē-əs\ *adj* [L *extraneus* — more at STRANGE] (1638) **1 :** existing on or coming from the outside **2 a :** not forming an essential or vital part ⟨an ~ scene that added nothing to the play⟩ **b :** having no relevance ⟨~ points that do not serve his argument⟩ **3 :** being a number obtained in solving an equation that is not a solution of the equation ⟨~ roots⟩ *syn* see EXTRINSIC — **extra·ne·ous·ly** *adv* — **ex·tra·ne·ous·ness** *n*

ex·tra·nu·cle·ar \ˌek-strə-ˈn(y)ü-klē-ər, ÷-kyə-lər\ *adj* (1887) **1 :** situated in or affecting the parts of a cell external to the nucleus **:** CYTOPLASMIC **2 :** situated outside the nucleus of an atom

ex·tra·oc·u·lar muscle \ˌek-strə-ˈäk-yə-lər-\ *n* (1939) **:** any of six small voluntary muscles that pass between the eyeball and the orbit and control the movement of the eyeball in relation to the orbit

ex·traor·di·naire \ik-ˌstrȯr(d)-ᵊn-ˈer, ek-\ *adj* [F] (1945) **:** EXTRAORDINARY — used postpositively ⟨a chef ~⟩

ex·traor·di·nary \ik-ˈstrȯrd-ᵊn-ˌer-ē, ˌek-strə-ˈȯrd-\ *adj* [ME *extraordinarie*, fr. L *extraordinarius*, fr. *extra ordinem* out of course, fr. *extra* + *ordinem*, acc. of *ordin-, ordo* order] (15c) **1 a :** going beyond what is usual, regular, or customary ⟨~ powers⟩ **b :** exceptional to a very marked extent **:** REMARKABLE ⟨~ beauty⟩ **2 :** employed for or sent on a special function or service ⟨an ambassador ~⟩ — **ex·traor·di·nari·ly** \ik-ˌstrȯrd-ᵊn-ˈer-ə-lē, ˌek-strə-ˌȯrd-\ *adv* — **ex·traor·di·nari·ness** \ik-ˈstrȯrd-ᵊn-ˌer-ē-nəs, ˌek-strə-ˈȯrd-\ *n*

extra point *n* (ca. 1949) **:** a point gained on a conversion in football

ex·trap·o·late \ik-ˈstrap-ə-ˌlāt\ *vb* **-lat·ed; -lat·ing** [L *extra* outside + E *-polate* (as in *interpolate*) — more at EXTRA-] *vt* (1874) **1 :** to infer (values of a variable in an unobserved interval) from values within an already observed interval **2 a :** to project, extend, or expand (known data or experience) into an area not known or experienced so as to arrive at a usu. conjectural knowledge of the unknown area ⟨~s present trends to construct an image of the future⟩ **b :** to predict by projecting past experience or known data ⟨~ public sentiment on one issue from known public reaction on others⟩ ~ *vi* **:** to perform the act or process of extrapolating — **ex·trap·o·la·tion** \-ˌstrap-ə-ˈlā-shən\ *n* — **ex·trap·o·la·tive** \-ˈstrap-ə-ˌlāt-iv\ *adj* — **ex·trap·o·la·tor** \-ˌlāt-ər\ *n*

ex·tra·py·ra·mi·dal \ˌek-strə-pə-ˈram-əd-ᵊl, -ˌpir-ə-ˈmid-ᵊl\ *adj* (ca. 1902) **:** situated outside of and esp. involving other descending nerve tracts than the pyramidal tracts

ex·tra·sen·so·ry \ˌek-strə-ˈsen(t)s-(ə-)rē\ *adj* (1934) **:** residing beyond or outside the ordinary senses ⟨instances of ~ perception⟩

ex·tra·sys·to·le \-ˈsis-tə-(ˌ)lē\ *n* [NL] (1900) **:** a premature beat of one of the chambers of the heart that leads to momentary arrhythmia

[1]**ex·tra·ter·res·tri·al** \-tə-ˈres-trē-əl, -ˈres(h)-chəl\ *adj* (1868) **:** originating or existing outside the earth or its atmosphere ⟨~ life⟩; *also* **:** of or relating to extraterrestrial space ⟨~ exploration⟩

[2]**extraterrestrial** *n* (1921) **:** an extraterrestrial being

ex·tra·ter·ri·to·ri·al \-ˌter-ə-ˈtōr-ē-əl, -ˈtȯr-\ *adj* (1869) **:** existing or taking place outside the territorial limits of a jurisdiction

ex·tra·ter·ri·to·ri·al·i·ty \-ˌtor-ē-ˈal-ət-ē, -ˌtȯr-\ *n* (1839) **:** exemption from the application or jurisdiction of local law or tribunals

ex·tra·trop·i·cal cyclone \ˌek-strə-ˌträp-i-kəl-\ *n* (1923) **:** a cyclone in the middle latitudes often being 1500 miles in diameter and usu. containing a cold front that extends toward the equator for hundreds of miles

ex·tra·uter·ine \ˌek-strə-ˈyüt-ə-rən, -ˌrīn\ *adj* [ISV] (1709) **:** situated or occurring outside the uterus ⟨~ pregnancy⟩

ex·trav·a·gance \ik-ˈstrav-i-gən(t)s\ *n* (1650) **1 a :** an instance of excess or prodigality; *specif* **:** an excessive outlay of money **b :** something extravagant **2 :** the quality or fact of being extravagant

ex·trav·a·gan·cy \-gən-sē\ *n, pl* **-cies** (1625) **:** EXTRAVAGANCE

ex·trav·a·gant \ik-ˈstrav-i-gənt\ *adj* [ME, fr. MF, fr. ML *extravagant-, extravagans*, fr. L *extra-* + *vagant-, vagans*, prp. of *vagari* to wander about — more at VAGARY] (15c) **1 a** *archaic* **:** WANDERING **b** *obs* **:** STRANGE, CURIOUS **2 a :** exceeding the limits of reason or necessity ⟨~ claims⟩ **b :** lacking in moderation, balance, and restraint ⟨~ praise⟩ **c :** extremely or excessively elaborate **3 a :** spending much more than necessary **b :** PROFUSE, LAVISH **4 :** unreasonably high in price *syn* see EXCESSIVE — **ex·trav·a·gant·ly** *adv*

ex·trav·a·gan·za \ik-ˌstrav-ə-ˈgan-zə\ *n* [It *estravaganza*, lit., extravagance, fr. *estravagante* extravagant, fr. ML *extravagant-, extravagans*] (1754) **1 :** a literary or musical work marked by extreme freedom of style and structure and usu. by elements of burlesque or parody **2 :** a lavish or spectacular show or event **3 :** something extravagant

ex·trav·a·gate \ik-ˈstrav-ə-ˌgāt\ *vi* **-gat·ed; -gat·ing** *archaic* (ca. 1795) **:** to go beyond proper limits

[1]**ex·trav·a·sate** \ik-ˈstrav-ə-ˌsāt, -ˌzāt\ *vb* **-sat·ed; -sat·ing** [L *extra* + *vas* vessel — more at VASE] *vt* (1668) **:** to force out or cause to escape from a proper vessel or channel ~ *vi* **:** to pass by infiltration or effusion from a proper vessel or channel (as a blood vessel) into surrounding tissue — **ex·trav·a·sa·tion** \-ˌstrav-ə-ˈsā-shən, -ˈzā-\ *n*

[2]**extravasate** *n* (ca. 1909) **:** an extravasated fluid (as blood)

ex·tra·vas·cu·lar \ˌek-strə-ˈvas-kyə-lər\ *adj* (1804) **:** destitute of or not contained in body vessels ⟨~ plant fibers⟩ ⟨~ tissue fluids⟩

ex·tra·ve·hic·u·lar \-vē-ˈhik-yə-lər\ *adj* (1965) **:** taking place outside a vehicle (as a spacecraft) ⟨~ activity⟩

[1]**ex·treme** \ik-ˈstrēm\ *adj* [ME, fr. MF, fr. L *extremus*, superl. of *exter, exterus* being on the outside — more at EXTERIOR] (15c) **1 a :** existing in a very high degree ⟨~ poverty⟩ **b :** going to great or exaggerated lengths **:** RADICAL ⟨went on an ~ diet⟩ **c :** exceeding the ordinary, usual, or expected ⟨~ weather conditions⟩ **2** *archaic* **:** LAST **3 :** situated at the farthest possible point from a center ⟨the country's ~ north⟩ **4 a :** most advanced or thoroughgoing ⟨the ~ political left⟩ **b :** MAXIMUM *syn* see EXCESSIVE — **ex·treme·ness** *n*

[2]**extreme** *n* (1593) **1 a :** something situated at or marking one end or the other of a range ⟨~s of heat and cold⟩ **b :** the first term or the last term of a mathematical proportion **c :** the major term or minor term of a syllogism **2 a :** a very pronounced or excessive degree ⟨his enthusiasm was carried to an ~⟩ **b :** highest degree **:** MAXIMUM **3 :** an extreme measure or expedient ⟨going to ~s⟩ — **in the extreme :** to the greatest possible extent

ex·treme·ly *adv* (1533) **1 :** to an extreme extent **2 :** in an extreme manner

extremely high frequency *n* (1952) **:** a radio frequency in the highest range of the radio spectrum — see RADIO FREQUENCY table

extremely low frequency *n* (1966) **:** a radio frequency in the lowest range of the radio spectrum — see RADIO FREQUENCY table

extreme unction \ik-ˌstrē-ˈməŋ(k)-shən, ˌek-(ˌ)strē-\ *n* (1579) **:** a sacrament in which a priest anoints a critically ill or injured person and prays for his recovery and salvation

ex·trem·ism \ik-ˈstrē-ˌmiz-əm\ *n* (1865) **1 :** the quality or state of being extreme **2 :** advocacy of extreme political measures **:** RADICALISM — **ex·trem·ist** \-məst\ *n or adj*

ex·trem·i·ty \ik-ˈstrem-ət-ē\ *n, pl* **-ties** (14c) **1 a :** the farthest or most remote part, section, or point **b :** a limb of the body; *esp* **:** a human hand or foot **2 a :** extreme danger or critical need **b :** a moment marked by imminent destruction or death **3 a :** an intense degree ⟨the ~ of his participation — *Saturday Rev.*⟩ **b :** the utmost degree (as of emotion or pain) **4 :** a drastic or desperate act or measure ⟨driven to *extremities*⟩

ex·tre·mum \ik-ˈstrē-məm\ *n, pl* **-ma** \-mə\ [NL, fr. L, neut. of *extremus*] (1904) **:** a maximum or a minimum of a mathematical function — called also *extreme value*

ex·tri·cate \ˈek-strə-ˌkāt\ *vt* **-cat·ed; -cat·ing** [L *extricatus*, pp. of *extricare*, fr. *ex-* + *tricae* trifles, perplexities] (1614) **1 a** *archaic* **:** UNRAVEL **b :** to distinguish from a related thing **2 :** to free or remove from an entanglement or difficulty — **ex·tri·ca·ble** \ik-ˈstrik-ə-bəl, ek-ˈ, ˈek-(ˌ)\ *adj* — **ex·tri·ca·tion** \ˌek-strə-ˈkā-shən\ *n*

syn EXTRICATE, DISENTANGLE, UNTANGLE, DISENCUMBER, DISEMBARRASS mean to free from what binds or holds back. EXTRICATE implies the use of care or ingenuity in freeing from a difficult position or situation; DISENTANGLE and UNTANGLE suggest painstaking separation of a thing from other things; DISENCUMBER implies a release from something that clogs or weighs down; DISEMBARRASS suggests a release from something that impedes or hinders.

ex·trin·sic \ek-ˈstrin-zik, -ˈstrin(t)-sik\ *adj* [F & LL; F *extrinsèque*, fr. LL *extrinsecus*, fr. L, adv., from without; akin to L *exter* outward and to L *sequi* to follow — more at EXTERIOR, SUE] (1613) **1 a :** not forming part of or belonging to a thing **:** EXTRANEOUS **b :** originating from or on the outside; *esp* **:** originating outside a part and acting upon the part as a whole ⟨~ muscles of the tongue⟩ **2 :** EXTERNAL — **ex·trin·si·cal·ly** \-zi-k(ə-)lē, -si-\ *adv*

syn EXTRINSIC, EXTRANEOUS, FOREIGN, ALIEN mean external to a thing, its essential nature, or its original character. EXTRINSIC applies to what is distinctly outside the thing in question or is not contained in or derived from its essential nature; EXTRANEOUS applies to what is on or

\ə\ abut \ᵊ\ kitten, F table \ər\ further \a\ ash \ā\ ace \ä\ cot, cart \au̇\ out \ch\ chin \e\ bet \ē\ easy \g\ go \i\ hit \ī\ ice \j\ job \ŋ\ sing \ō\ go \ȯ\ law \ȯi\ boy \th\ thin \t͟h\ the \ü\ loot \u̇\ foot \y\ yet \zh\ vision \à, k̲, ⁿ, œ, œ̄, ue, ue̅, ʸ\ *see* Guide to Pronunciation

comes from the outside and may or may not be capable of becoming an essential part; FOREIGN applies to what is so different as to be rejected or repelled or, if admitted, to be incapable of becoming identified or assimilated by the thing in question; ALIEN is stronger than FOREIGN in suggesting opposition, repugnance, or irreconcilability.

extrinsic factor *n* (ca. 1930) : VITAMIN B_{12}

extro- *prefix* [alter. of L *extra-*] : outward ⟨*extro*vert⟩ — compare INTRO-

ex·trorse \'ek-ˌstrȯ(ə)rs\ *adj* [prob. fr. (assumed) NL *extrorsus,* fr. LL, adv., outward, fr. L *extra-* + *-orsus* (as in *introrsus*) — more at INTRORSE] (1858) : turned away from the axis of growth ⟨an ~ anther⟩ — **ex·trorse·ly** *adv*

ex·tro·ver·sion *or* **ex·tra·ver·sion** \ˌek-strə-'vər-zhən, -shən\ *n* [G *extraversion,* fr. L *extra-* + *versus,* pp. of *vertere* to turn — more at WORTH] (1915) : the act, state, or habit of being predominantly concerned with and obtaining gratification from what is outside the self — **ex·tro·ver·sive** \-siv, -ziv\ *adj*

¹ex·tro·vert *or* **ex·tra·vert** \'ek-strə-ˌvərt\ *adj* (1918) : EXTROVERTED

²extrovert *or* **extravert** *n* [modif. of G *extravertiert, fr. L extra-* + *vertere*] (1918) : one whose attention and interests are directed wholly or predominantly toward what is outside the self

ex·tro·vert·ed *or* **ex·tra·vert·ed** *adj* (1923) : marked by or suggesting extroversion; *esp* : FRIENDLY, UNINHIBITED

ex·trude \ik-'strüd\ *vb* **ex·trud·ed; ex·trud·ing** [L *extrudere,* fr. *ex-* + *trudere* to thrust — more at THREAT] *vt* (1566) **1** : to force, press, or push out **2** : to shape (as metal or plastic) by forcing through a die ~ *vi* : to become extruded — **ex·trud·abil·i·ty** \-ˌstrüd-ə-'bil-ət-ē\ *n* — **ex·trud·able** \-'strüd-ə-bəl\ *adj* — **ex·trud·er** \-'strüd-ər\ *n*

ex·tru·sion \ik-'strü-zhən\ *n* [ML *extrusion-, extrusio,* fr. L *extrusus,* pp. of *extrudere*] (1540) : the act or process of extruding; *also* : a form or product produced by this process

ex·tru·sive \ik-'strü-siv, -ziv\ *adj* (1816) : relating to or formed by geological extrusion from the earth in a molten state or as volcanic ash

ex·u·ber·ance \ig-'zü-b(ə-)rən(t)s\ *n* (1631) **1** : the quality or state of being exuberant **2** : an exuberant act or expression

ex·u·ber·ant \-b(ə-)rənt\ *adj* [ME, fr. MF, fr. L *exuberant-, exuberans,* prp. of *exuberare* to be abundant, fr. *ex-* + *uber* fruitful, fr. *uber* udder — more at UDDER] (15c) **1 a** : joyously unrestrained and enthusiastic **b** : lacking compactness and discipline : flamboyantly overdone ⟨writing spoiled by ~ overdrawn metaphors⟩ **2** : extreme or excessive in degree, size, or extent **3** : produced in extreme abundance : PLENTIFUL *syn* see PROFUSE — **ex·u·ber·ant·ly** *adv*

ex·u·ber·ate \-bə-ˌrāt\ *vi* **-at·ed; -at·ing** (15c) **1** *archaic* : to have something in abundance : OVERFLOW **2** : to become exuberant : show exuberance ⟨*exuberated* over his victory⟩

ex·u·date \'ek-s(y)ü-ˌdāt, -shü-\ *n* (1876) : exuded matter

ex·u·da·tion \ˌek-s(y)ü-'dā-shən, -shü-\ *n* (1612) **1** : the process of exuding **2** : EXUDATE — **ex·u·da·tive** \ig-'züd-ət-iv; 'ek-s(y)ü-ˌdāt-iv, -shü-\ *adj*

ex·ude \ig-'züd\ *vb* **ex·ud·ed; ex·ud·ing** [L *exsudare,* fr. *ex-* + *sudare* to sweat — more at SWEAT] *vi* (1574) **1** : to ooze out **2** : to undergo diffusion ~ *vt* **1** : to cause to ooze or spread out in all directions **2** : to display conspicuously or abundantly ⟨~*s* charm⟩

ex·ult \ig-'zəlt\ *vi* [MF *exulter,* fr. L *exsultare,* lit., to leap up, fr. *ex-* + *saltare* to leap — more at SALTATION] (1570) **1** *obs* : to leap for joy **2** : to be extremely joyful : REJOICE — **ex·ult·ing·ly** \-'zəl-tiŋ-lē\ *adv*

ex·ul·tance \ig-'zəlt-ᵊn(t)s\ *n* (15c) : EXULTATION

ex·ul·tan·cy \-'zəlt-ᵊn-sē\ *n* (1621) : EXULTATION

ex·ul·tant \ig-'zəlt-ᵊnt\ *adj* (1653) : filled with or expressing great joy or triumph : JUBILANT — **ex·ul·tant·ly** *adv*

ex·ul·ta·tion \ˌek-(ˌ)səl-'tā-shən, ˌeg-(ˌ)zəl-\ *n* (15c) : the act of exulting : the state of being exultant

ex·urb \'ek-ˌsərb, 'eg-ˌzərb\ *n* [*ex-* + *-urb* (as in *suburb*)] (1955) : a region or district that lies outside a city and usu. beyond its suburbs and that often is inhabited chiefly by well-to-do families — **ex·ur·ban** \ek-'sər-bən; eg-'zər-, ig-\ *adj*

ex·ur·ban·ite \ek-'sər-bə-ˌnīt; eg-'zər-, ig-\ *n* (1955) : one who lives in an exurb

ex·ur·bia \-bē-ə\ *n* (1955) : the generalized region of exurbs

ex·u·vi·ae \ig-'zü-vē-ˌē, -vē-ˌī\ *n pl* [L, fr. *exuere* to take off, fr. *ex-* + *-uere* to put on] (1653) : sloughed off natural animal coverings (as the skins of snakes) — **ex·u·vi·al** \-vē-əl\ *adj*

ex·u·vi·a·tion \-ˌzü-vē-'ā-shən\ *n* (1839) : the process of molting

¹ex–vo·to \(ˈ)eks-'vōt-(ˌ)ō\ *n, pl* **ex–votos** [L *ex voto* according to a vow] (1787) : a votive offering

²ex–voto *adj* (1823) : VOTIVE

-ey — see -Y

ey·as \'ī-əs\ *n* [ME, alter. (by incorrect division of *a neias*) of *neias,* fr. MF *niais* fresh from the nest, fr. (assumed) VL *nidax* nestling, fr. L *nidus* nest — more at NEST] (15c) : an unfledged bird; *specif* : a nestling hawk

¹eye \'ī\ *n* [ME, fr. OE *ēage;* akin to OHG *ouga* eye, L *oculus,* Gk *ōps* eye, face] (bef. 12c) **1 a** : an organ of sight; *esp* : a nearly spherical hollow organ that is lined with a sensitive retina, is lodged in a bony orbit in the skull, is the vertebrate organ of sight, and is normally paired **b** : all the visible structures within and surrounding the orbit and including eyelids, eyelashes, and eyebrows **c (1)** : the faculty of seeing with eyes **(2)** : the faculty of intellectual or aesthetic perception or appreciation ⟨an ~ for beauty⟩ **d** : LOOK, GLANCE ⟨cast an eager ~⟩ **e (1)** : an attentive look ⟨kept an ~ on his valuables⟩ **(2)** : ATTENTION, NOTICE ⟨caught his ~⟩ **(3)** : close observation : SCRUTINY ⟨works under the ~ of her boss⟩ **f** : POINT OF VIEW, JUDGMENT ⟨beauty is in the ~ of the beholder⟩ — often used in pl. ⟨an offender in the ~*s* of the law⟩ **g** : VIEW 5 ⟨with an ~ to the future⟩ **2** : something having an appearance suggestive of an eye: as **a** : the hole through the head of a needle **b** : a usu. circular marking (as on a peacock's tail) **c** : LOOP; *esp* : a loop or catch to receive a hook **d** : an undeveloped bud (as on a potato) **e** : an area like a hole in the center of a tropical cyclone marked by only light winds or complete calm with no precipitation **f** : the center of a flower esp. when differently colored or marked; *specif* : the disk of a composite **g (1)** : a triangular piece of beef cut from between the top and bottom of a round **(2)** : the chief muscle of a chop **(3)** : a compact mass of muscular tissue usu. embedded in fat in a rib or loin cut of meat **h** : a device (as a photoelectric cell) that functions in a manner analogous to human vision **3** : something central : CENTER ⟨the ~ of the problem —Norman Mailer⟩ **4** : the direction from which the wind is blowing — **eye·less** \'ī-ləs\ *adj* — **eye·like** \-ˌlīk\ *adj* — **my eye** — used to express mild disagreement or sometimes surprise ⟨a diamond, *my eye!* That's glass⟩

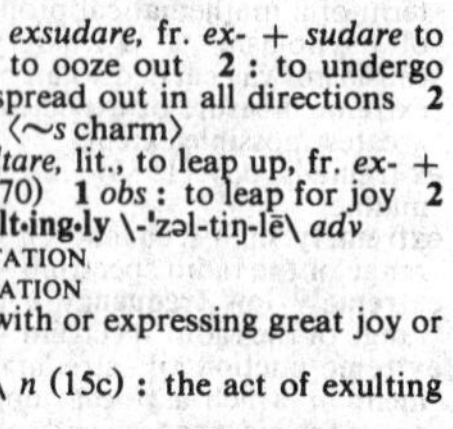

eye 1a: *1* optic nerve, *2* blind spot, *3* fovea, *4* sclera, *5* choroid, *6* retina, *7* ciliary body, *8* posterior chamber, *9* anterior chamber, *10* cornea, *11* lens, *12* iris, *13* suspensory ligament, *14* conjunctiva, *15* vitreous humor

²eye *vb* **eyed; eye·ing** *or* **ey·ing** *vt* (15c) **1 a** : to fix the eyes on : look at **b** : to watch closely **2** : to furnish with an eye ~ *vi, obs* : SEEM, LOOK — **ey·er** \'ī(-ə)r\ *n*

¹eye·ball \'ī-ˌbȯl\ *n* (1590) : the more or less globular capsule of the vertebrate eye formed by the sclera and cornea together with their contained structures

²eyeball *vt* (1901) : to look at intently

eyeball–to–eyeball *adv or adj* (1962) : FACE-TO-FACE

eye bank *n* (1944) : a storage place for human corneas from the newly dead for transplanting to the eyes of those blind through corneal defects

eye·bolt \'ī-'bōlt\ *n* (1769) : a bolt with a looped head

eye·bright \'ī-ˌbrīt\ *n* (1533) : any of several herbs (genus *Euphrasia*) of the figwort family with opposite toothed or cut leaves

eye·brow \'ī-ˌbrau̇\ *n* (15c) : the ridge over the eye or hair growing on it

eyebrow pencil *n* (1895) : a cosmetic pencil for the eyebrows

eye–catch·er \'ī-ˌkach-ər, -ˌkech-\ *n* (1923) : something strongly attracting the eye — **eye–catch·ing** \-iŋ\ *adj*

eye chart *n* (1943) : a chart that is read at a fixed distance for purposes of testing sight; *esp* : one with rows of letters or objects of decreasing size

eye contact *n* (1965) : visual contact with another person's eyes

eye·cup \'ī-ˌkəp\ *n* (1857) **1** : a small oval cup with a rim curved to fit the orbit of the eye used for applying liquid remedies to the eyes **2** : OPTIC CUP

eyed \'īd\ *adj* (14c) : having an eye or eyes esp. of a specified kind or number — often used in combination ⟨an almond-*eyed* girl⟩

eyed·ness \'īd-nəs\ *n* [*-eyed* (as in *right-eyed, left-eyed*)] (1924) : preference for the use of one eye instead of the other (as in using a monocular microscope)

eye·drop·per \'ī-ˌdräp-ər\ *n* (1937) : DROPPER 2

eye·ful \'ī-ˌfu̇l\ *n* (ca. 1864) **1** : a full or completely satisfying view **2** : one that is visually attractive; *esp* : a strikingly beautiful woman

eye·glass \'ī-ˌglas\ *n* (1664) **1 a** : EYEPIECE **b** : a lens worn to aid vision; *specif* : MONOCLE **c** *pl* : GLASSES, SPECTACLES **2** : EYECUP 1

eye·hole \'ī-ˌhōl\ *n* (1637) **1** : ¹ORBIT **2** : PEEPHOLE

eye·lash \'ī-ˌlash\ *n* (1752) **1** : the fringe of hair edging the eyelid — usu. used in pl. **2** : a single hair of the eyelashes

eye lens *n* (1871) : the lens nearest the eye in an eyepiece

eye·let \'ī-lət\ *n* [alter. of ME *oilet,* fr. MF *oillet,* dim. of *oil* eye, fr. L *oculus*] (14c) **1 a** : a small hole designed to receive a cord or used for decoration (as in embroidery) **b** : a small typically metal ring to reinforce an eyelet : GROMMET **2** : PEEPHOLE, LOOPHOLE

eye·lid \'ī-ˌlid\ *n* (13c) : either of the movable lids of skin and muscle that can be closed over the eyeball

eye·lin·er \'ī-ˌlī-nər\ *n* (1947) : makeup used to emphasize the contour of the eyes

ey·en \'ī(-ə)n\ *archaic pl of* EYE

eye–open·er \'ī-ˌōp(-ə)-nər\ *n* (1818) **1** : a drink intended to wake one up **2** : something startling, surprising, or enlightening — **eye–open·ing** \-niŋ\ *adj*

eye·piece \'ī-ˌpēs\ *n* (1790) : the lens or combination of lenses at the eye end of an optical instrument

eye·point \'ī-ˌpȯint\ *n* (1827) : the point at which the eye is placed in using an optical instrument (as a microscope)

eye·pop·per \'ī-ˌpäp-ər\ *n* (1941) : something that excites or astonishes — **eye–pop·ping** \-ˌpäp-iŋ\ *adj*

eye rhyme *n* (1871) : an imperfect rhyme that appears to have identical vowel sounds from similarity of spelling (as *move* and *love*)

eye·shade \'ī-ˌshād\ *n* (1845) : a visor that shields the eyes from strong light and is fastened on with a headband

eye shadow *n* (1937) : a cosmetic cream or powder in one of various colors that is applied to the eyelids to accent the eyes

eye·shot \'ī-ˌshät\ *n* (1599) : the range of the eye : VIEW

eye·sight \'ī-ˌsīt\ *n* (13c) **1** : SIGHT 4a **2** *archaic* : OBSERVATION 1

eye·sore \'ī-ˌsō(ə)r, -ˌsȯ(ə)r\ *n* (1530) : something offensive to view

eye·spot \'ī-ˌspät\ *n* (1877) **1 a** : a simple visual organ of pigment or pigmented cells covering a sensory termination : OCELLUS **b** : a small pigmented body of various unicellular algae **2** : a spot of color **3** : any of several fungous diseases of plants characterized by yellowish oval lesions on the leaves and stem; *esp* : a disease of various grasses (as sugarcane) caused by a fungus (*Helminthosporium sacchari*)

eye·stalk \'ī-ˌstȯk\ *n* (1854) : one of the movable peduncles bearing an eye at the tip in a decapod crustacean

eye·strain \'ī-ˌstrān\ *n* (1874) : weariness or a strained state of the eye

eye·strings \'ī-ˌstriŋz\ *n pl, obs* (1601) : organic eye attachments formerly believed to break at death or blindness

eye·tooth \'ī-'tüth\ *n* (ca. 1545) : a canine tooth of the upper jaw

eye·wash \'ī-ˌwȯsh, -ˌwäsh\ *n* (ca. 1859) **1** : an eye lotion **2** : misleading or deceptive statements, actions, or procedures

eye·wink \'ī-ˌwiŋk\ *n* (1598) : LOOK, GLANCE

eye·wit·ness \'ī-'wit-nəs\ *n* (1539) : one who sees an occurrence or an object; *esp* : one who gives a report on what he has seen

eyre \'a(ə)r, 'e(ə)r\ *n* [ME *eire,* fr. AF, fr. OF *erre* trip, fr. *errer* to travel — more at ERRANT] (13c) : a circuit traveled by an itinerant justice in medieval England or the court he presided over

ey·rie \'ī(ə)r-ē, *or like* AERIE\ *var of* AERIE

ey·rir \'ā-ˌri(ə)r\ *n, pl* **au·rar** \'au̇-ˌrär, 'œi-\ [Icel, fr. ON, money (in pl.), prob. fr. L *aureus* a gold coin] (ca. 1927) — see *krona* at MONEY table

Eze·chiel \i-'zē-kyəl, -kē-əl\ *n* [LL] : EZEKIEL
Eze·kiel \i-'zē-kyəl, -kē-əl\ *n* [LL *Ezechiel*, fr. Heb *Yĕḥezqēl*] **1** : a Hebrew priest and prophet of the 6th century B.C. **2** : a prophetic book of canonical Jewish and Christian Scripture written by Ezekiel — see BIBLE table

Ez·ra \'ez-rə\ *n* [LL, fr. Heb *Ezrā*] **1** : a Hebrew priest, scribe, and reformer of Judaism of the 5th century B.C. in Babylon and Jerusalem **2** : a narrative book of canonical Jewish and Christian Scripture — see BIBLE table

F

f \'ef\ *n, pl* **f's** *or* **fs** \'efs\ *often cap, often attrib* **1 a** : the 6th letter of the English alphabet **b** : a graphic representation of this letter **c** : a speech counterpart of orthographic *f* **2** : the 4th tone of a C-major scale **3** : a graphic device for reproducing the letter *f* **4** : one designated *f* esp. as the 6th in order or class **5 a** : a grade rating a student's work as failing **b** : one graded or rated with an F **6** : something shaped like the letter F
fa \'fä\ *n* [ME, fr. ML, fr. the syllable sung to this note in a medieval hymn to St. John the Baptist] (13c) : the 4th tone of the diatonic scale in solmization
fa·ba·ceous \fə-'bā-shəs\ *adj* [NL *Fabaceae*, family of legumes, fr. *Faba*, type genus, fr. L, bean] (ca. 1727) **1** : of or relating to the legume family : LEGUMINOUS **2** : relating to, resembling, or being a bean
Fa·bi·an \'fā-bē-ən\ *adj* (1777) **1 a** : of, relating to, or in the manner of the Roman general Quintus Fabius Maximus known for his defeat of Hannibal in the Second Punic War by the avoidance of decisive contests **b** : CAUTIOUS, DILATORY **2** [the *Fabian* Society; fr. the members' belief in slow rather than revolutionary change in government] : of, relating to, or being a society of socialists organized in England in 1884 to spread socialist principles gradually — **Fabian** *n* — **Fa·bi·an·ism** \-ə-ˌniz-əm\ *n*
¹fa·ble \'fā-bəl\ *n* [ME, fr. MF, fr. L *fabula* conversation, story, play, fr. *fari* to speak — more at BAN] (14c) : a fictitious narrative or statement: as **a** : a legendary story of supernatural happenings **b** : a narration intended to enforce a useful truth; *esp* : one in which animals speak and act like human beings **c** : FALSEHOOD, LIE
²fable *vb* **fa·bled; fa·bling** \-b(ə-)liŋ\ *vi, archaic* (14c) : to tell fables ~ *vt* : to talk or write about as if true — **fa·bler** \-b(ə-)lər\ *n*
fa·bled \'fā-bəld\ *adj* (1606) **1** : FICTITIOUS **2** : told or celebrated in fables **3** : RENOWNED, FAMOUS
fab·li·au \'fab-lē-ˌō\ *n, pl* **-aux** \-ˌō(z)\ [F, fr. OF, dim. of *fable*] (1804) : a short, usu. comic, frankly coarse, and often cynical tale in verse popular in the 12th and 13th centuries
fab·ric \'fab-rik\ *n* [MF *fabrique*, fr. L *fabrica* workshop, structure — more at FORGE] (15c) **1 a** : STRUCTURE, BUILDING **b** : underlying structure : FRAMEWORK ⟨the ~ of society⟩ **2** : an act of constructing : ERECTION; *specif* : the construction and maintenance of a church building **3 a** : structural plan or style of construction **b** : TEXTURE, QUALITY — used chiefly of textiles **c** : the arrangement of physical components (as of soil) in relation to each other **4 a** : CLOTH **1a b** : a material that resembles cloth **5** : the appearance or pattern produced by the shapes and arrangement of the crystal grains in a rock
fab·ri·cant \'fab-ri-kənt\ *n* (1757) : MANUFACTURER
fab·ri·cate \'fab-ri-ˌkāt\ *vt* **-cat·ed; -cat·ing** [ME *fabricaten*, fr. L *fabricatus*, pp. of *fabricari*, fr. *fabrica*] (15c) **1** : CONSTRUCT, MANUFACTURE; *specif* : to construct from diverse and usu. standardized parts **2 a** : INVENT, CREATE **b** : to make up for the purpose of deception *syn* see MAKE — **fab·ri·ca·tor** \-ˌkāt-ər\ *n*
fab·ri·ca·tion \ˌfab-ri-'kā-shən\ *n* (15c) **1** : the act or process of fabricating **2** : a product of fabrication; *esp* : LIE, FALSEHOOD
fab·u·lar \'fab-yə-lər\ *adj* (1684) : of, relating to, or having the form of a fable
fab·u·list \'fab-yə-ləst\ *n* (1593) **1** : a creator or writer of fables **2** : LIAR — **fabulist** *or* **fab·u·lis·tic** \ˌfab-yə-'lis-tik\ *adj*
fab·u·lous \'fab-yə-ləs\ *adj* [L *fabulosus*, fr. *fabula*] (15c) **1 a** : resembling a fable esp. in incredible, astonishing, or exaggerated quality **b** : WONDERFUL, MARVELOUS ⟨had a ~ time⟩ **2** : told in or based on fable *syn* see FICTITIOUS — **fab·u·lous·ly** *adv* — **fab·u·lous·ness** *n*
fa·cade *also* **fa·çade** \fə-'säd\ *n* [F *façade*, fr. It *facciata*, fr. *faccia* face, fr. (assumed) VL *facia*] (ca. 1656) **1** : the front of a building; *also* : any other face (as on a street or court) of a building given special architectural treatment **2** : a false, superficial, or artificial appearance or effect : FACE
¹face \'fās\ *n, often attrib* [ME, fr. OF, fr. (assumed) VL *facia*, fr. L *facies* make, form, face, fr. *facere* to make, do — more at DO] (13c) **1 a** : the front part of the human head including the chin, mouth, nose, cheeks, eyes, and usu. the forehead **b** : the face as a means of identification : COUNTENANCE ⟨would know that ~ anywhere⟩ **2** *archaic* : PRESENCE, SIGHT **3 a** : facial expression **b** : GRIMACE **c** : MAKEUP **3a**(1) **4 a** : outward appearance ⟨suspicious on the ~ of it⟩ **b** : DISGUISE, PRETENSE **c** (1) : ASSURANCE, CONFIDENCE ⟨maintaining a firm ~ in spite of adversity⟩ (2) : EFFRONTERY ⟨how anyone could have the ~ to ask that question⟩ **d** : DIGNITY, PRESTIGE ⟨afraid to lose ~⟩ **5** : SURFACE: **a** (1) : a front, upper, or outer surface (2) : the front of something having two or four sides (3) : FACADE (4) : an exposed surface of rock (5) : any of the plane surfaces that bound a geometric solid **b** : a surface specially prepared: as (1) : the principal dressed surface (as of a disk) (2) : the right side (as of cloth or leather) (3) : an inscribed, printed, or marked side **c** (1) : the surface (as of type) that receives the ink and transfers it to the paper (2) : a style of type **6** : the end or wall of a mine tunnel, drift, or excavation at which work is progressing **7** : FACE VALUE **8** : PERSON ⟨lots of new ~s around here⟩ — **face·less** \-ləs\ *adj* — **face·less·ness** *n* — **in the face of** *also* **in face of** : face-to-face with : DESPITE ⟨succeed *in the face of* great difficulties⟩ — **to one's face** : in one's presence or so that one is fully aware of what is going on : FRANKLY
²face *vb* **faced; fac·ing** *vi* (15c) **1** : to confront impudently **2 a** : to line near the edge esp. with a different material **b** : to cover the front or surface of ⟨*faced* the building with marble⟩ **3** : to meet face-to-face or in competition **4 a** : to stand or sit with the face toward **b** : to front on ⟨a house *facing* the park⟩ **5 a** : to recognize and deal with straightforwardly ⟨~ the facts⟩ **b** : to master by confronting with determination — used with *down* ⟨*faced* down his critics⟩ **6 a** : to have as a prospect : be confronted by ⟨~ a grim future⟩ **b** : to be a prospect or a source of concern for ⟨the problems that ~ us⟩ **c** : to bring face-to-face ⟨he was *faced* with ruin⟩ **7** : to make the surface of (as a stone) flat or smooth **8** : to cause (troops) to face in a particular direction on command ~ *vi* **1** : to have the face or front turned in a specified direction **2** : to turn the face in a specified direction — **face the music** : to meet an unpleasant situation, a danger, or the consequences of one's actions
face angle *n* (1913) : an angle formed by two edges of a polyhedral angle
face card *n* (1826) : a king, queen, or jack in a deck of cards
face·cloth \'fās-ˌklȯth\ *n* (1602) : WASHCLOTH
face cord *n* (ca. 1926) : a unit of wood cut for fuel equal to a stack 4 x 8 feet with lengths of pieces from about 12 to 16 inches
-faced \ˌfāst\ *adj comb form* : having (such) a face or (so many) faces ⟨rosy-*faced*⟩ ⟨two-*faced*⟩
face·down \'fās-ˌdau̇n\ *adv* (1949) : with the face down ⟨sliding ~⟩
face fly *n* (1961) : a European fly (*Musca autumnalis*) that is similar to the housefly, is widely established in No. America, and causes great distress in livestock by clustering about the face
face–hard·en \'fās-ˌhärd-ᵊn\ *vt* (1896) : to harden the surface of (as steel)
face–lift \'fā-ˌslift\ *n* (1934) : FACE-LIFTING — **face–lift** *vt*
face–lift·ing \'fā-ˌslif-tiŋ\ *n* (1922) **1** : a plastic operation for removal of facial defects (as wrinkles) typical of aging **2** : an alteration or restyling intended esp. to modernize
face–off \'fās-ˌȯf\ *n* (1896) **1** : a method of putting a puck in play in ice hockey by dropping it between two opposing players each of whom attempts to gain control of the puck or hit it to a teammate **2** : CONFRONTATION
face·plate \'fā-ˌsplāt\ *n* (1841) **1** : a disk fixed with its face at right angles to the live spindle of a lathe for the attachment of the work **2** : a protective cover for the human face (as of a diver) **3** : the glass front of a kinescope on which the image is seen
fac·er \'fā-sər\ *n* (15c) **1** : one that faces; *specif* : a cutter for facing a surface **2** : a stunning check or defeat
face–sav·er \'fās-ˌsā-vər\ *n* (1923) : something (as a compromise) that saves face — **face–sav·ing** \-ˌsā-viŋ\ *adj or n*
fac·et \'fas-ət\ *n* [F *facette*, dim. of *face*] (1625) **1** : a small plane surface (as on a cut gem) — see BRILLIANT illustration **2** : any of the definable aspects that make up a subject (as of contemplation) or an object (as of consideration) **3** : the external corneal surface of an ommatidium **4** : a smooth flat circumscribed anatomical surface (as of a bone) **5** : a fillet between the flutes of a column — **fac·et·ed** *or* **fac·et·ted** \'fas-ət-əd\ *adj*
fa·cete \fə-'sēt\ *adj* [L *facetus*] *archaic* (1603) : FACETIOUS, WITTY
fa·ce·ti·ae \fə-'sē-shē-ˌē, -ˌī\ *n pl* [L, fr. pl. of *facetia* jest, fr. *facetus* elegant, witty] (1529) : witty or humorous writings or sayings
fa·ce·tious \fə-'sē-shəs\ *adj* [MF *facetieux*, fr. *facetie* jest, fr. L *facetia*] (1599) **1** : jocular in an often clumsy or inappropriate manner **2** : characterized by pleasantry or levity : JOCOSE ⟨a ~ remark⟩ *syn* see WITTY — **fa·ce·tious·ly** *adv* — **fa·ce·tious·ness** *n*

facade 1

face–to–face *adv or adj* (14c) **1 :** within each other's sight or presence ⟨met and talked ~⟩ ⟨a ~ consultation⟩ **2 :** in or into direct contact or confrontation ⟨came ~ with the problem⟩

face·up \'fā-'səp\ *adv* (1920) **:** with the face up

face up *vi* (1920) **:** to meet something or someone without shrinking — usu. used with *to* ⟨*faced up* to the situation⟩

face value *n* (1876) **1 :** the value indicated on the face (as of a postage stamp or a stock certificate) **2 :** the apparent value or significance ⟨if their results may be taken at *face value*⟩

facia *var of* FASCIA

1**fa·cial** \'fā-shəl\ *adj* (1818) **1 :** of or relating to the face **2 :** concerned with or used in improving the appearance of the face — **fa·cial·ly** \-shə-lē\ *adv*

2**facial** *n* (1914) **:** a facial treatment

facial index *n* (ca. 1889) **:** the ratio of the breadth of the face to its length multiplied by 100

facial nerve *n* (ca. 1818) **:** either of the 7th pair of cranial nerves that supply motor fibers esp. to the muscles of the face and jaw and send a separate mixed branch to the tongue

-fa·cient \'fā-shənt\ *adj comb form* [L *-facient-, -faciens* (as in *calefacient-, calefaciens* making warm, prp. of *calefacere* to warm)] **:** making **:** causing ⟨somni*facient*⟩

fa·cies \'fā-sh(ē-,)ēz\ *n, pl* **facies** [NL, fr. L, face] (1684) **1 :** an appearance and expression of the face characteristic of a particular condition esp. when abnormal ⟨adenoid ~⟩ **2 :** general appearance ⟨a plant species with a particularly distinct ~⟩ **3 :** a part of a rock or group of rocks that differs from the whole formation (as in composition, age, or fossil content)

fac·ile \'fas-əl\ *adj* [MF, fr. L *facilis,* fr. *facere* to do — more at DO] (15c) **1 a** (1) **:** easily accomplished or attained ⟨a ~ victory⟩ (2) **:** SPECIOUS, SUPERFICIAL ⟨I am not concerned . . . with offering any ~ solution for so complex a problem —T. S. Eliot⟩ **b :** used or comprehended with ease **c :** readily manifested and often lacking sincerity or depth ⟨~ tears⟩ **2** *archaic* **:** mild or pleasing in manner or disposition **3 a :** READY, FLUENT ⟨~ prose⟩ **b :** POISED, ASSURED ***syn*** see EASY — **fac·ile·ly** \-ə(l)-lē\ *adv* — **fac·ile·ness** \-əl-nəs\ *n*

fa·cil·i·tate \fə-'sil-ə-,tāt\ *vt* **-tat·ed; -tat·ing** (1611) **:** to make easier — **fa·cil·i·ta·tive** \-,tāt-iv\ *adj* — **fa·cil·i·ta·tor** \-,tāt-ər\ *n*

fa·cil·i·ta·tion \fə-,sil-ə-'tā-shən\ *n* (1619) **1 :** the act of facilitating **:** the state of being facilitated **2 a :** the lowering of the threshold for reflex conduction along a particular neural pathway esp. from repeated use of that pathway **b :** the increasing of the ease or intensity of a response by repeated stimulation

fa·cil·i·ta·to·ry \fə-'sil-ə-tə-,tōr-ē, -,tȯr-\ *adj* (1944) **:** inducing or involved in facilitation esp. of a reflex action

fa·cil·i·ty \fə-'sil-ət-ē\ *n, pl* **-ties** (1531) **1 :** the quality of being easily performed **2 :** ease in performance **:** APTITUDE **3 :** readiness of compliance **4 a :** something that makes an action, operation, or course of conduct easier — usu. used in pl. ⟨provide books and other *facilities* for study⟩ **b :** something (as a hospital) that is built, installed, or established to serve a particular purpose

fac·ing \'fā-siŋ\ *n* (1566) **1 a :** a lining at the edge esp. of a garment **b** *pl* **:** the collar, cuffs, and trimmings of a uniform coat **2 :** an ornamental or protective layer **3 :** material for facing

fac·sim·i·le \fak-'sim-ə-lē\ *n* [L *fac simile* make similar] (1691) **1 :** an exact copy **2 :** the transmission of graphic matter (as printing or still pictures) by wire or radio and its reproduction ***syn*** see REPRODUCTION — **facsimile** *vt*

fact \'fakt\ *n* [L *factum,* fr. neut. of *factus,* pp. of *facere*] (1539) **1 :** a thing done: as **a :** CRIME ⟨accessory after the ~⟩ **b** *obs* **:** FEAT **c** *archaic* **:** ACTION **2** *archaic* **:** PERFORMANCE, DOING **3 :** the quality of being actual **:** ACTUALITY ⟨a question of ~ hinges on evidence⟩ **4 a :** something that has actual existence ⟨space travel is now a ~⟩ **b :** an actual occurrence **:** EVENT ⟨prove the ~ of damage⟩ **5 :** a piece of information presented as having objective reality — **in fact :** in truth

fact finder *n* (1926) **:** one that tries to determine the realities of a case, situation, or relationship; *esp* **:** an impartial examiner designated by a government agency to appraise the facts underlying a particular matter (as a labor dispute) — **fact–find·ing** *n or adj*

fac·tic·i·ty \fak-'tis-ət-ē\ *n* [F or G; F *facticité,* fr. G *faktizität,* fr. *factum* fact, fr. L *factum*] (1945) **:** the quality or state of being a fact

fac·tion \'fak-shən\ *n* [MF & L; MF, fr. L *faction-, factio* act of making, faction — more at FASHION] (1509) **1 :** a party or group (as within a government) that is often contentious or self-seeking **:** CLIQUE **2 :** party spirit esp. when marked by dissension — **fac·tion·al** \-shnəl, -shən-ᵊl\ *adj* — **fac·tion·al·ism** \-shnə-,liz-əm, -shən-ᵊl-,iz-\ *n* — **fac·tion·al·ly** \-ē\ *adv*

-fac·tion \'fak-shən\ *n comb form* [ME *-faccioun,* fr. MF & L; MF *-faction,* fr. L *-faction-, -factio* (as in *satisfaction-, satisfactio* satisfaction)] **:** making **:** -FICATION ⟨petri*faction*⟩

fac·tious \'fak-shəs\ *adj* [MF or L; MF *factieux,* fr. L *factiosus,* fr. *factio*] (1532) **:** of or relating to faction: as **a :** caused by faction ⟨~ disputes⟩ **b :** inclined to faction or the formation of factions **c :** SEDITIOUS — **fac·tious·ly** *adv* — **fac·tious·ness** *n*

fac·ti·tious \fak-'tish-əs\ *adj* [L *facticius,* fr. *factus,* pp. of *facere* to make, do — more at DO] (1646) **1 :** produced by man rather than by natural forces **2 a :** formed by or adapted to an artificial or conventional standard **b :** produced by special effort **:** SHAM ⟨created a ~ demand by spreading rumors of shortage⟩ — **fac·ti·tious·ly** *adv* — **fac·ti·tious·ness** *n*

fac·ti·tive \'fak-tət-iv\ *adj* [NL *factitivus,* irreg. fr. L *factus*] (1846) **:** of, relating to, or being a transitive verb that in some constructions requires an objective complement as well as an object — **fac·ti·tive·ly** *adv*

-fac·tive \'fak-tiv\ *adj comb form* [MF *-factif,* fr. *-faction*] **:** making **:** causing ⟨petri*factive*⟩

fact of life (1854) **1 :** something that exists and must be taken into consideration **2** *pl* **:** the fundamental physiological processes and behavior involved in sex and reproduction

1**fac·tor** \'fak-tər\ *n* [ME, fr. MF *facteur,* fr. L *factor* doer, fr. *factus*] (15c) **1 :** one who acts or transacts business for another: as **a :** BROKER 1b **b :** one that lends money to producers and dealers (as on the security of accounts receivable) **2 a** (1) **:** one that actively contributes to the production of a result **:** INGREDIENT ⟨cost wasn't a ~ in his purchase⟩ (2) **:** a substance that functions in or promotes the function of a particular physiological process or bodily system **b :** a good or service used in the process of production **3 :** GENE **4 a :** any of the numbers or symbols in mathematics that when multiplied together form a product; *also* **:** a number or symbol that divides another number or symbol **b :** a quantity by which a given quantity is multiplied or divided in order to indicate a difference in measurement ⟨costs increased by a ~ of 10⟩ ***syn*** see ELEMENT — **fac·tor·ship** \-,ship\ *n*

2**factor** *vb* **fac·tored; fac·tor·ing** \-t(ə-)riŋ\ *vi* (1621) **:** to work as a factor ~ *vt* **1 :** to resolve into factors **2 :** to include or admit as a factor — used with *into* ⟨~ inflation into our calculations⟩ — **fac·tor·able** \-t(ə-)rə-bəl\ *adj*

fac·tor·age \-t(ə-)rij\ *n* (1613) **1 :** the charges made by a factor for his services **2 :** the business of a factor

factor analysis *n* (1931) **:** the analytical process of transforming statistical data (as measurements) into linear combinations of usu. independent variables — **factor analytic** *adj*

factor VIII \-'āt\ *n* (1965) **:** ANTIHEMOPHILIC FACTOR

factor group *n* (1897) **:** QUOTIENT GROUP

1**fac·to·ri·al** \fak-'tōr-ē-əl, -'tȯr-\ *adj* (1837) **:** of, relating to, or being a factor or a factorial

2**factorial** *n* (1869) **1 :** the product of all the positive integers from 1 to *n* — symbol *n!* **2 :** the quantity *0!* arbitrarily defined as equal to 1

factor in *vt* (1972) **:** FIGURE IN

fac·tor·iza·tion \,fak-tə-rə-'zā-shən\ *n* (1886) **:** the operation of resolving a quantity into factors; *also* **:** a product obtained by factorization — **fac·tor·ize** \'fak-tə-,rīz\ *vt*

fac·to·ry \'fak-t(ə-)rē\ *n, pl* **-ries** (1582) **1 :** a station where resident factors trade **2 a :** a building or set of buildings with facilities for manufacturing **b :** the seat of some kind of production ⟨the vice *factories* of the slums⟩ — **fac·to·ry·like** \-,līk\ *adj*

fac·to·tum \fak-'tōt-əm\ *n* [NL, lit., do everything, fr. L *fac* (imper. of *facere* do) + *totum* everything] (1566) **1 :** a person having many diverse activities or responsibilities **2 :** a general servant

fac·tu·al \'fak-chə(-wə)l, 'faksh-wəl\ *adj* (1834) **1 :** of or relating to facts **2 :** restricted to or based on fact — **fac·tu·al·i·ty** \,fak-chə-'wal-ət-ē\ *n* — **fac·tu·al·ly** \'fak-chə(-wə)-lē, 'faksh-wə-\ *adv* — **fac·tu·al·ness** *n*

fac·tu·al·ism \'fak-chə(-wə)-,liz-əm, 'faksh-wə-\ *n* (1936) **:** adherence or dedication to facts — **fac·tu·al·ist** \-ləst\ *n*

fac·ture \'fak-chər\ *n* [ME, fr. MF, fr. L *factura* action of making, fr. *factus*] (15c) **:** the manner in which something (as an artistic work) is made **:** EXECUTION

fac·u·la \'fak-yə-lə\ *n, pl* **-lae** \-,lē, -,lī\ [NL, fr. L, dim. of *fac-, fax* torch] (1706) **:** any of the bright regions of the sun's photosphere seen most easily near the sun's edge

fac·ul·ta·tive \'fak-əl-,tāt-iv\ *adj* (1820) **1 a :** of or relating to the grant of permission, authority, or privilege ⟨~ legislation⟩ **b :** OPTIONAL **2 :** of or relating to a mental faculty **3 a :** taking place under some conditions but not under others ⟨~ diapause⟩ **b :** exhibiting an indicated life-style under some environmental conditions but not under others ⟨~ anaerobes⟩ — **fac·ul·ta·tive·ly** *adv*

fac·ul·ty \'fak-əl-tē\ *n, pl* **-ties** [ME *faculte,* fr. MF *faculté,* fr. ML & L; ML *facultat-, facultas* branch of learning or teaching, fr. L, ability, abundance, fr. *facilis* facile] (14c) **1 :** ABILITY, POWER: as **a :** innate or acquired ability to act or do **b :** an inherent capability, power, or function ⟨the ~ of hearing⟩ **c :** one of the powers of the mind formerly held by psychologists to form a basis for the explanation of all mental phenomena **d :** natural aptitude ⟨he has a ~ for saying the right things⟩ **2 a :** a branch of teaching or learning in an educational institution **b** *archaic* **:** something in which one is trained or qualified **3 a :** the members of a profession **b :** the teaching and administrative staff and those members of the administration having academic rank in an educational institution **c** *pl* **faculty :** a member of a faculty **4 :** power, authority, or prerogative given or conferred ***syn*** see GIFT

fad \'fad\ *n* [origin unknown] (1867) **:** a practice or interest followed for a time with exaggerated zeal **:** CRAZE ***syn*** see FASHION — **fad·dish** \'fad-ish\ *adj* — **fad·dish·ness** *n* — **fad·dism** \'fad-,iz-əm\ *n* — **fad·dist** \'fad-əst\ *n* — **fad·dy** \-ē\ *adj*

FAD \,ef-,ā-'dē\ *n* (1944) **:** FLAVIN ADENINE DINUCLEOTIDE

1**fade** \'fād\ *vb* **fad·ed; fad·ing** [ME *faden,* fr. MF *fader,* fr. *fade* feeble, insipid, fr. (assumed) VL *fatidus,* alter. of L *fatuus* fatuous, insipid] *vi* (14c) **1 :** to lose freshness or vitality **:** WITHER **2 :** to lose freshness or brilliance of color **3 :** to sink away **:** VANISH **4 :** to change gradually in loudness, strength, or visibility — used of a motion-picture image or of an electronics signal and usu. with *in* or *out* **5** *of an automobile brake* **:** to lose braking power gradually **6 :** to move back from the line of scrimmage — used of a quarterback ~ *vt* **:** to cause to fade — **fad·er** *n*

2**fade** *n* (1918) **1 :** a gradual changing of one picture to another in a motion-picture or television sequence **2 :** a fading of an automobile brake

3**fade** \'fäd\ *adj* [ME, fr. MF] (15c) **:** INSIPID, COMMONPLACE

fade·away \'fād-ə-,wā\ *n* (1909) **1 a :** SCREWBALL 1 **b :** a slide in which a base runner throws his body sideways to avoid the tag **2 :** an act or instance of fading away

fade·less \'fād-ləs\ *adj* (1652) **:** not susceptible to fading

fade–out \'fā-,dau̇t\ *n* (1917) **:** an act or instance of fading out; *esp* **:** a gradual decrease in a motion-picture or television image's visibility at the end of a sequence

fa·do \'fäth-(,)ü, 'fath-\ *n, pl* **fados** [Pg, lit., fate, fr. L *fatum*] (1902) **:** a plaintive Portuguese folk song

fae·cal, fae·ces *var of* FECAL, FECES

fa·e·na \fä-'ā-(,)nä\ *n* [Sp, lit., task, fr. obs. Catal, fr. L *facienda* things to be done, fr. *facere* to do — more at DO] (1927) **:** a series of final passes leading to the kill made by the matador in a bullfight

fa·er·ie *also* **fa·ery** \'fā-(ə-)rē, 'fa(ə)r-ē, 'fe(ə)r-ē\ *n, pl* **fa·er·ies** [ME, fr. MF *faerie* — more at FAIRY] (1590) **1 :** FAIRYLAND **2 :** FAIRY — **faery** *adj*

Faero·ese \,far-ə-'wēz, ,fer-, -'wēs\ *n, pl* **Faeroese** (1855) **1 :** a member of the Germanic people inhabiting the Faeroes **2 :** the Germanic language of the Faeroese people — **Faeroese** *adj*

Faf·nir \ˈfäv-nər, ˈfäf-, -ˌni(ə)r\ *n* [ON *Fāfnir*] **:** a dragon in Norse myth that guards the Nibelungs' gold hoard until slain by Sigurd

1fag \ˈfag\ *vb* **fagged; fag·ging** [obs. *fag* to droop, perh. fr. *fag* (fag end)] *vi* (1772) **1 :** to work hard **:** TOIL **2 :** to act as a fag esp. in an English public school ⟨*fagging* for older boys during his first year⟩ ~ *vt* **:** to tire by strenuous activity **:** EXHAUST ***syn*** see TIRE

2fag *n* (1780) **1** *chiefly Brit* **:** TOIL, DRUDGERY **2 a :** an English public-school boy who acts as servant to an older schoolmate **b :** DRUDGE

3fag *n* [*fag end*] (ca. 1888) **:** CIGARETTE

4fag *n* [prob. by shortening] (1931) **:** FAGGOT — often used disparagingly

fag end *n* [earlier *fag*, fr. ME *fagge* flap] (ca. 1721) **1 a :** the last part or coarser end of a web of cloth **b :** the untwisted end of a rope **2 a :** a poor or worn-out end **:** REMNANT **b :** the extreme end

fag·got \ˈfag-ət\ *n* [origin unknown] (1914) **:** a male homosexual — often used disparagingly — **fag·goty** \-ət-ē\ *adj*

fa·gin \ˈfā-gən\ *n* [*Fagin*, character in Charles Dickens' *Oliver Twist* (1839)] (1847) **:** an adult who instructs others (as children) in crime

1fag·ot *or* **fag·got** \ˈfag-ət\ *n* [ME *fagot*, fr. MF] (14c) **:** BUNDLE: as **a :** a bundle of sticks **b :** a bundle of pieces of wrought iron to be shaped by rolling or hammering at high temperature

2fagot *or* **faggot** *vt* (ca. 1598) **:** to make a fagot of **:** bind together into a bundle ⟨~*ed* sticks⟩

fag·ot·ing *or* **fag·got·ing** *n* (1885) **1 :** an embroidery produced by pulling out horizontal threads from a fabric and tying the remaining cross threads into groups of an hourglass shape **2 :** an openwork stitch joining hemmed edges

Fahr·en·heit \ˈfar-ən-ˌhīt\ *adj* [Gabriel D. *Fahrenheit*] (1753) **:** relating or conforming to a thermometric scale on which under standard atmospheric pressure the boiling point of water is at 212 degrees above the zero of the scale, the freezing point is at 32 degrees above zero, and the zero point approximates the temperature produced by mixing equal quantities by weight of snow and common salt

fa·ience *or* **fa·ïence** \fā-ˈän(t)s, fī-, -ˈäⁿs\ *n* [F, fr. *Faenza*, Italy] (1714) **:** earthenware decorated with opaque colored glazes

1fail \ˈfā(ə)l\ *vb* [ME *failen*, fr. OF *faillir*, fr. (assumed) VL *fallire*, alter. of L *fallere* to deceive, disappoint; prob. akin to Gk *phēlos* deceitful] *vi* (13c) **1 a :** to lose strength **:** WEAKEN ⟨her health was ~*ing*⟩ **b :** to fade or die away ⟨until our family line ~*s*⟩ **c :** to stop functioning ⟨the patient's heart ~*ed*⟩ **2 a :** to fall short ⟨~*ed* in his duty⟩ **b :** to be or become absent or inadequate ⟨the water supply ~*ed*⟩ **c :** to be unsuccessful (as in passing an examination) **d :** to become bankrupt or insolvent ~ *vt* **1 a :** to disappoint the expectations or trust of ⟨his friends ~*ed* him⟩ **b :** to miss performing an expected service or function for ⟨for once his wit ~*ed* him⟩ **2 :** to be deficient in **:** LACK ⟨our youth . . . never ~*ed* an invincible courage —Douglas MacArthur⟩ **3 :** to leave undone **:** NEGLECT ⟨~ to lock the door⟩ **4 a :** to be unsuccessful in passing (as a test) **b :** to grade (as a student) as not passing — **fail·ing·ly** \ˈfā-liŋ-lē\ *adv*

2fail *n* (13c) **1 :** FAILURE — usu. used in the phrase *without fail* **2 :** a failure (as by a security dealer) to deliver or receive securities within a prescribed period after purchase or sale

1fail·ing \ˈfā-liŋ\ *n* (1590) **:** a usu. slight or insignificant defect in character, conduct, or ability ***syn*** see FAULT

2failing *prep* (1810) **:** in absence or default of ⟨~ specific instructions, use your own judgment⟩

faille \ˈfī(ə)l\ *n* [F] (1869) **:** a somewhat shiny closely woven silk, rayon, or cotton fabric characterized by slight ribs in the weft

fail–safe \ˈfā(ə)l-ˌsāf\ *adj* (1946) **1 :** incorporating some feature for automatically counteracting the effect of an anticipated possible source of failure **2 :** being or relating to a safeguard that prevents continuing on a bombing mission according to a preconceived plan **3 :** having no chance of failure **:** infallibly problem-free

fail·ure \ˈfā(ə)l-yər\ *n* [alter. of earlier *failer*, fr. AF, fr. OF *faillir* to fail] (1643) **1 a :** omission of occurrence or performance; *specif* **:** a failing to perform a duty or expected action **b :** a state of inability to perform a normal function ⟨kidney ~⟩ — compare HEART FAILURE **c :** a fracturing or giving way under stress ⟨structure ~⟩ **2 a :** lack of success **b :** a failing in business **:** BANKRUPTCY **3 a :** a falling short **:** DEFICIENCY ⟨a crop ~⟩ **b :** DETERIORATION, DECAY **4 :** one that has failed

1fain \ˈfān\ *adj* [ME *fagen*, *fayn*, fr. OE *fægen*; akin to ON *fegiun* happy, OE *fæger* fair] (bef. 12c) **1** *archaic* **:** HAPPY, PLEASED **2** *archaic* **:** INCLINED, DESIROUS **3** *archaic* **a :** WILLING **b :** being obliged or constrained **:** COMPELLED

2fain *adv* (12c) **1** *archaic* **:** with pleasure **2** *archaic* **:** RATHER

1fai·né·ant \fā-nā-äⁿ\ *n, pl* **fainéants** \-äⁿ(z)\ [F, fr. MF *fait-nient*, lit., does nothing, by folk etymology fr. *faignant*, fr. prp. of *faindre*, *feindre* to feign] (1619) **:** an irresponsible idler

2fai·né·ant \fā-nā-äⁿ\ *or* **fai·ne·ant** \ˈfā-nē-ənt\ *adj* (1855) **:** idle and ineffectual **:** INDOLENT

1faint \ˈfānt\ *adj* [ME *faint*, *feint*, fr. MF, fr. pp. of *faindre*, *feindre* to feign, shirk — more at FEIGN] (14c) **1 :** lacking courage and spirit **:** COWARDLY **2 :** weak, dizzy, and likely to faint **3 :** lacking strength or vigor **:** performed, offered, or accomplished weakly or languidly **4 :** producing a sensation of faintness **:** OPPRESSIVE ⟨the ~ atmosphere of a tropical port⟩ **5 :** lacking distinctness **:** DIM — **faint·ish** \-ish\ *adj* — **faint·ish·ness** *n* — **faint·ly** *adv* — **faint·ness** *n*

2faint *vi* (14c) **1** *archaic* **:** to lose courage or spirit **2** *archaic* **:** to become weak **3 :** to lose consciousness because of a temporary decrease in the blood supply to the brain **4 :** to lose brightness

3faint *n* (1808) **:** the physiological action of fainting; *also* **:** the resulting condition **:** SYNCOPE 1

faint·heart·ed \ˈfānt-ˈhärt-əd\ *adj* (15c) **:** lacking courage or resolution **:** TIMID — **faint·heart·ed·ly** *adv* — **faint·heart·ed·ness** *n*

1fair \ˈfa(ə)r, ˈfe(ə)r\ *adj* [ME *fager*, *fair*, fr. OE *fæger*; akin to OHG *fagar* beautiful and perh. to Lith *puošti* to decorate] (bef. 12c) **1 :** pleasing to the eye or mind esp. because of fresh, charming, or flawless quality **2 :** superficially pleasing **:** SPECIOUS ⟨she trusted his ~ promises⟩ **3 a :** CLEAN, PURE ⟨~ sparkling water⟩ ⟨a man of ~ fame⟩ **b :** CLEAR, LEGIBLE **4 :** not stormy or foul **:** FINE ⟨~ weather⟩ **5 :** AMPLE ⟨a ~ estate⟩ **6 a :** marked by impartiality and honesty **:** free from self-interest, prejudice, or favoritism ⟨a very ~ man to do business with⟩ **b** (1) **:** conforming with the established rules **:** ALLOWED (2) **:** consonant with merit or importance **:** DUE ⟨a ~ share⟩ **c :** open to legitimate pursuit, attack, or ridicule ⟨~ game⟩ **7 a :** PROMISING, LIKELY ⟨he was in a ~ way to win⟩ **b :** favorable to a ship's course ⟨a ~ wind⟩ **8** *archaic* **:** free of obstacles **9 :** not dark **:** BLOND **10 :** sufficient but not ample **:** ADEQUATE ⟨a ~ understanding of the work⟩ **11 :** being such to the utmost **:** UTTER ⟨a ~ treat to watch him —*New Republic*⟩ — **fair·ness** *n*

syn FAIR, JUST, EQUITABLE, IMPARTIAL, UNBIASED, DISPASSIONATE, OBJECTIVE mean free from favor toward either or any side. FAIR implies an elimination of one's own feelings, prejudices, and desires so as to achieve a proper balance of conflicting interests; JUST implies an exact following of a standard of what is right and proper; EQUITABLE implies a less rigorous standard than JUST and usu. suggests equal treatment of all concerned; IMPARTIAL stresses an absence of favor or prejudice; UNBIASED implies even more strongly an absence of all prejudice; DISPASSIONATE suggests freedom from the influence of strong feeling and often implies cool or even cold judgment; OBJECTIVE stresses a tendency to view events or persons as apart from oneself and one's own interest or feelings. ***syn*** see in addition BEAUTIFUL

2fair *n* (bef. 12c) **1** *obs* **:** BEAUTY, FAIRNESS **2 :** something that is fair or fortunate **3** *archaic* **:** WOMAN; *esp* **:** SWEETHEART — **for fair :** to the greatest extent or degree **:** FULLY ⟨the rush was on *for fair* —R. L. Neuberger⟩ — **no fair :** something that is not according to the rules ⟨that's *no fair*⟩

3fair *adv* (bef. 12c) **:** FAIRLY

4fair *vi, of the weather* (1836) **:** CLEAR ~ *vt* **:** to join so that the external surfaces blend smoothly

5fair *n* [ME *feire*, fr. OF, fr. ML *feria* weekday, fair, fr. LL, festal day, fr. L *feriae* (pl.) holidays — more at FEAST] (13c) **1 :** a gathering of buyers and sellers at a particular place and time for trade **2 a :** a competitive exhibition (as of farm products) usu. with accompanying entertainment and amusements **b :** an exhibition designed to acquaint prospective buyers or the general public with a product **3 :** a sale of assorted articles usu. for a charitable purpose

fair ball *n* (1856) **:** a batted baseball that lands within the foul lines or that is within the foul lines when bounding to the outfield past first or third base or when going beyond the outfield for a home run

fair catch *n* (ca. 1876) **:** a catch of a kicked football by a player who gives a prescribed signal, may not advance the ball, and may not be tackled

fair copy *n* (1709) **:** a neat and exact copy esp. of a corrected draft

fair·ground \ˈfa(ə)r-ˌgrau̇nd, ˈfe(ə)r-\ *n* (1851) **:** an area where outdoor fairs, circuses, or exhibitions are held — often used in pl. with sing. constr. ⟨what a spot for a ~*s* —W. L. Gresham⟩

1fair·ing \ˈfa(ə)r-iŋ, ˈfe(ə)r-\ *n* (1574) **1** *Brit* **a :** a present bought or given at a fair **b :** GIFT **2** *Brit* **:** 3DESERT 2

2fairing *n* (1914) **:** a member or structure whose primary function is to produce a smooth outline and to reduce drag or air resistance (as on an airplane)

fair·ish \ˈfa(ə)r-ish, ˈfe(ə)r-\ *adj* (1611) **:** fairly good ⟨a ~ wage for those days⟩ — **fair·ish·ly** *adv*

fair·lead \ˈfa(ə)r-ˌlēd, ˈfe(ə)r-\ *n* (1841) **1** *also* **fair·lead·er** \-ər\ **:** a block, ring, or strip of plank with holes that serves as a guide for the running rigging or any ship's rope and keeps it from chafing **2 :** a course of running ship's rope that avoids all chafing

fair·ly \ˈfa(ə)r-lē, ˈfe(ə)r-\ *adv* (15c) **1 :** in a handsome manner ⟨a table ~ set⟩ **2** *obs* **a :** in a gentle manner **:** QUIETLY **b :** in a courteous manner **3 :** in a manner of speaking **:** QUITE ⟨~ bursting with pride⟩ **4 a :** in a proper or legal manner ⟨~ priced stocks⟩ **b :** without bias or distortion **:** IMPARTIALLY ⟨a story told ~ and objectively⟩ **5 :** to a full degree or extent **:** PLAINLY, DISTINCTLY ⟨had ~ caught sight of him⟩ **6 :** for the most part **:** RATHER ⟨a ~ easy job⟩

fair market value *n* (1926) **:** a price at which both buyers and sellers are willing to do business

fair–mind·ed \ˈfa(ə)r-ˈmīn-dəd, ˈfe(ə)r-\ *adj* (1874) **:** JUST, UNPREJUDICED — **fair–mind·ed·ness** *n*

fairness doctrine *n* (1967) **:** a tenet of licensed broadcasting that ensures a reasonable opportunity for the airing of conflicting viewpoints on controversial issues

fair play *n* (1595) **:** equitable or impartial treatment **:** JUSTICE

fair shake *n* (1830) **:** a fair chance or fair treatment ⟨give the negative side a *fair shake* —S. L. Payne⟩

fair–spo·ken \ˈfa(ə)r-ˈspō-kən, ˈfe(ə)r-\ *adj* (15c) **:** pleasant and courteous in speech ⟨a ~ youth⟩

fair–trade \ˈfa(ə)r-ˈtrād, ˈfe(ə)r-\ *vt* (1941) **:** to market (a commodity) in compliance with the provisions of a fair-trade agreement — **fair trader** *n*

fair trade *n* (1941) **:** trade in conformity with a fair-trade agreement

fair–trade agreement *n* (1937) **:** an agreement between a producer and a seller that commodities bearing a trademark, label, or brand name belonging to the producer be sold at or above a specified price

fair·way \ˈfa(ə)r-ˌwā, ˈfe(ə)r-\ *n* (1584) **1 a :** a navigable part of a river, bay, or harbor **b :** an open path or space **2 :** the mowed part of a golf course between a tee and a green

fair–weather *adj* (1736) **1 :** loyal only during a time of success ⟨a ~ friend⟩ **2 :** suitable for, done during, or made in fair weather ⟨a ~ sail⟩

fairy \ˈfa(ə)r-ē, ˈfe(ə)r-\ *n, pl* **fairies** [ME *fairie* fairyland, fairy people, fr. OF *faerie*, fr. *feie*, *fee* fairy, fr. L *Fata*, goddess of fate, fr. *fatum* fate] (14c) **1 :** a mythical being of folklore and romance usu. having diminutive human form and magic powers **2 :** a male homosexual — often used disparagingly — **fairy** *adj* — **fairy·like** \-ˌlīk\ *adj*

fairy godmother *n* (1851) **:** a generous friend or benefactor

fairy·ism \-ˌiz-əm\ *n, archaic* (1715) **:** the power to enchant

fairy·land \-ˌland\ *n* (1590) **1 :** the land of fairies **2 :** a place of delicate beauty or magical charm

fairy ring *n* [fr. the folk belief that such rings were dancing places of the fairies] (1599) **1 :** a ring of mushrooms produced at the periphery of a body of mycelium which has grown centrifugally from an initial growth point; *also* **:** a ring of luxuriant vegetation esp. when associated with these mushrooms **2 :** a mushroom (esp. *Marasmius oreades*) that commonly grows in fairy rings

fairy shrimp *n* (1857) **:** any of several delicate transparent freshwater branchiopod crustaceans (order Anostraca)

fairy–tale *adj* (1819) **:** characteristic of or suitable to a fairy tale; *esp* **:** marked by unusual grace or beauty

fairy tale *n* (1749) **1 :** a narrative of adventures involving fantastic forces and beings (as fairies, wizards, and goblins) — called also *fairy story* **2 :** a made-up story usu. designed to mislead

fait ac·com·pli \ˈfāt-ə-ˌkäm-ˈplē, ˈfet-ə-, ˈfe-ˌta-, -ˌkōⁿ(m)-, *Brit usu* -ˈkäm-(ˌ)plē\ *n, pl* **faits accomplis** *same, or* -ˈplēz\ [F, accomplished fact] (1845) **:** a thing accomplished and presumably irreversible

¹faith \ˈfāth\ *n, pl* **faiths** \ˈfāths, ˈfāt͟hz\ [ME *feith,* fr. OF *feid, foi,* fr. L *fides;* akin to L *fidere* to trust — more at BIDE] (13c) **1 a :** allegiance to duty or a person **:** LOYALTY **b** (1) **:** fidelity to one's promises (2) **:** sincerity of intentions **2 a** (1) **:** belief and trust in and loyalty to God (2) **:** belief in the traditional doctrines of a religion **b** (1) **:** firm belief in something for which there is no proof (2) **:** complete trust **3 :** something that is believed esp. with strong conviction; *esp* **:** a system of religious beliefs ***syn*** see BELIEF — **in faith :** without doubt or question **:** VERILY

²faith *vt, archaic* (15c) **:** BELIEVE, TRUST

¹faith·ful \ˈfāth-fəl\ *adj* (14c) **1** *obs* **:** full of faith **2 :** steadfast in affection or allegiance **:** LOYAL **3 :** firm in adherence to promises or in observance of duty **:** CONSCIENTIOUS **4 :** given with strong assurance **:** BINDING ⟨~ promise⟩ **5 :** true to the facts, to a standard, or to an original ⟨a ~ copy⟩ — **faith·ful·ly** \-fə-lē\ *adv* — **faith·ful·ness** *n*

syn FAITHFUL, LOYAL, CONSTANT, STAUNCH, STEADFAST, RESOLUTE mean firm in adherence to whatever one owes allegiance. FAITHFUL implies unswerving adherence to a person or thing or to the oath or promise by which a tie was contracted; LOYAL implies a firm resistance to any temptation to desert or betray; CONSTANT stresses continuing firmness of emotional attachment without necessarily implying strict obedience to promises or vows; STAUNCH suggests fortitude and resolution in adherence and imperviousness to influences that would weaken it; STEADFAST implies a steady and unwavering course in love, allegiance, or conviction; RESOLUTE implies firm determination to adhere to a cause or purpose.

²faithful *n, pl* **faithful** *or* **faithfuls** (1558) **:** one that is faithful: as **a :** church members in full communion and good standing — used with *the* **b :** the body of adherents of the Muslim religion — used with *the* **c :** a loyal follower, member, or fan ⟨party ~*s*⟩

faith healing *n* (1885) **:** a method of treating diseases by prayer and exercise of faith in God — **faith healer** *n*

faith·less \ˈfāth-ləs\ *adj* (14c) **1 :** not true to allegiance or duty **:** TREACHEROUS, DISLOYAL ⟨a ~ servant⟩ **2 :** not to be relied on **:** UNTRUSTWORTHY ⟨a ~ tool⟩ — **faith·less·ly** *adv* — **faith·less·ness** *n*

syn FAITHLESS, FALSE, DISLOYAL, TRAITOROUS, TREACHEROUS, PERFIDIOUS mean untrue to what should command one's fidelity or allegiance. FAITHLESS applies to any failure to keep a promise or pledge or any breach of allegiance or loyalty; FALSE stresses the fact of failing to be true in any manner ranging from fickleness to cold treachery; DISLOYAL implies a lack of complete faithfulness in thought or words or actions to a friend, cause, leader, or country; TRAITOROUS implies either actual treason or a serious betrayal of trust; TREACHEROUS implies readiness to betray trust or confidence; PERFIDIOUS adds to FAITHLESS the implication of an incapacity for fidelity or reliability.

fai·tour \ˈfāt-ər\ *n* [ME, fr. AF, fr. OF *faitor* perpetrator, fr. L *factor* doer — more at FACTOR] *archaic* (14c) **:** CHEAT, IMPOSTER

fa·ji·ta \fə-ˈhē-tə, fä-\ *n* [MexSp] (1984) **:** marinated beef or chicken or sometimes shrimp grilled or broiled and served usu. with a flour tortilla and various spicy sauces

¹fake \ˈfāk\ *vt* **faked; fak·ing** [ME *faken*] (15c) **:** to coil in fakes

²fake *n* (1627) **:** one loop of a coil (as of ship's rope or a fire hose) coiled free for running

³fake *adj* [origin unknown] (1775) **:** COUNTERFEIT, SHAM

⁴fake *n* (1827) **:** one that is not what it purports to be: as **a :** a worthless imitation passed off as genuine **b :** IMPOSTOR, CHARLATAN **c :** a simulated movement in a sports contest (as a pretended kick, pass, or jump or a quick movement in one direction before going in another) designed to deceive an opponent **d :** a device or apparatus used by a magician to achieve the illusion of magic in a trick ***syn*** see IMPOSTURE

⁵fake *vb* **faked; fak·ing** *vt* (1851) **1 :** to alter, manipulate, or treat so as to give a spuriously genuine appearance to **:** DOCTOR ⟨*faked* the lab results⟩ **2 :** COUNTERFEIT, SIMULATE, CONCOCT **3 :** to deceive (an opponent) in a sports contest by means of a fake **4 :** IMPROVISE, AD-LIB ⟨whistle a few bars . . . and I'll ~ the rest —Robert Sylvester⟩ ~ *vi* **1 :** to engage in faking something **:** PRETEND **2 :** to give a fake to an opponent — **fak·er** *n* — **fak·ery** \ˈfā-k(ə-)rē\ *n*

fa·kir *n* [Ar *faqīr,* lit., poor man] (1609) **1** \fə-ˈki(ə)r, fä-, fa-; ˈfā-kər\ **a :** a Muslim mendicant **:** DERVISH **b :** an itinerant Hindu ascetic or wonder-worker **2** \ˈfā-kər\ **:** IMPOSTOR; *esp* **:** SWINDLER

fa la \fä-ˈlä\ *n* [*fa-la,* meaningless syllables often occurring in its refrain] (1595) **:** a 16th and 17th century part-song

fa·la·fel \fə-ˈläf-əl\ *n, pl* **falafel** [Ar *falāfil*] (1950) **:** a spicy mixture of ground vegetables (as chick-peas or fava beans) formed into balls or patties and then fried

Fa·lan·gist \fə-ˈlan-jəst, ˈfā-ˌ\ *n* [Sp *Falangista,* fr. *Falange española* Spanish Phalanx, a fascist organization] (1936) **:** a member of the fascist political party governing Spain after the civil war of 1936–39

Fa·la·sha \fə-ˈläsh-ə\ *n, pl* **-sha** *or* **-shas** [Amharic *fälasha,* fr. *fälasi* sojourner, stranger] (1710) **:** a member of a Jewish people in Ethiopia similar in biological type to the Galla

fal·cate \ˈfal-ˌkāt, ˈfȯl-\ *adj* [L *falcatus,* fr. *falc-, falx* sickle, scythe] (1826) **:** hooked or curved like a sickle

fal·chion \ˈfȯl-chən\ *n* [ME *fauchoun,* fr. MF *fauchon,* fr. *fauchier* to mow, fr. (assumed) VL *falcare,* fr. L *falc-, falx*] (14c) **1 :** a broad-bladed slightly curved sword of medieval times **2** *archaic* **:** SWORD

fal·ci·form \ˈfal-sə-ˌfȯrm, ˈfȯl-\ *adj* [L *falc-, falx* + E *-iform*] (1766) **:** having the shape of a scythe or sickle

fal·con \ˈfal-kən, ˈfȯl- *also* ˈfȯ-kən\ *n* [ME, fr. OF, fr. LL *falcon-, falco,* perh. of Gmc origin; akin to OHG *falcho* falcon] (13c) **1 a :** any of various hawks trained for use in falconry; *esp* **:** PEREGRINE — used technically only of a female; compare TIERCEL **b :** any of various hawks (family Falconidae) with long wings, dark eyes, and a V-shaped projection on the upper mandible which is accommodated by a notch in the lower mandible **:** HAWK 1 **2 :** a light cannon used from the 15th to the 17th centuries

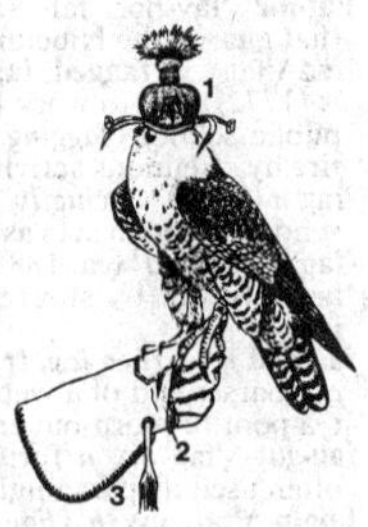

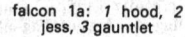

falcon 1a: *1* hood, *2* jess, *3* gauntlet

fal·con·er \-kə-nər\ *n* (12c) **1 :** one who hunts with or trains hawks **2 :** a breeder or trainer of hawks for hunting

fal·con·et \ˌfal-kə-ˈnet, ˌfȯl- *also* ˌfȯ-\ *n* (1559) **1 :** a very small cannon used in the 16th and 17th centuries **2 :** any of several very small Asian falcons constituting a genus (*Microhierax*)

fal·con–gen·tle \-kən-ˈjent-ᵊl\ *n* [ME *faucon gentil* peregrine falcon, fr. MF, lit., noble falcon] (15c) **:** the female peregrine falcon

fal·co·nine \ˈfal-kə-ˌnīn, ˈfȯl- *also* ˈfȯ-\ *adj* (ca. 1889) **:** belonging to or resembling a falcon ⟨a ~ face⟩

fal·con·ry \ˈfal-kən-rē, ˈfȯl- *also* ˈfȯ-kən-\ *n* (1575) **1 :** the art of training hawks to hunt in cooperation with a person **2 :** the sport of hunting with hawks

fal·de·ral \ˈfäl-də-ˌräl\ *var of* FOLDEROL

fald·stool \ˈfȯl(d)-ˌstül\ *n* [ML *faldistolium,* of Gmc origin; akin to OHG *faltistuol* folding chair, fr. *falt* (akin to OHG *faldan* to fold) + *stuol* chair — more at FOLD, STOOL] (1603) **1 :** a folding stool or chair; *specif* **:** one used by a bishop **2 :** a folding stool or small desk at which one kneels during devotions; *esp* **:** one used by the sovereign of England at his coronation **3 :** the desk from which the litany is read in Anglican churches

¹fall \ˈfȯl\ *vb* **fell** \ˈfel\; **fall·en** \ˈfȯ-lən\; **fall·ing** [ME *fallen,* fr. OE *feallan;* akin to OHG *fallan* to fall and perh. to Lith *pulti*] *vi* (bef. 12c) **1 a :** to descend freely by the force of gravity **b :** to hang freely ⟨her hair ~*s* over her shoulders⟩ **c :** to drop oneself to a lower position ⟨*fell* to his knees⟩ **d :** to come or go as if by falling ⟨darkness ~*s* early in the winter⟩ ⟨her sadness *fell* from her⟩ **2 :** to become born — usu. used of lambs **3 a :** to become lower in degree or level ⟨the temperature *fell* 10°⟩ **b :** to drop in pitch or volume ⟨their voices *fell* to a whisper⟩ **c :** ISSUE ⟨wisdom that *fell* from his lips⟩ **d :** to become lowered ⟨her eyes *fell*⟩ **4 a :** to leave an erect position suddenly and involuntarily ⟨slipped and *fell* on the ice⟩ **b :** to enter as if unawares **:** STUMBLE, STRAY ⟨*fell* into error⟩ **c :** to drop down wounded or dead; *esp* **:** to die in battle **d :** to suffer military capture ⟨after a long siege the city *fell*⟩ **e :** to lose office ⟨the party *fell* from power⟩ **f :** to suffer ruin, defeat, or failure ⟨we must stand or ~ together⟩ ⟨the deal *fell* through⟩ **5 :** to commit an immoral act; *esp* **:** to lose one's chastity **6 a :** to move or extend in a downward direction ⟨the land ~*s* away to the east⟩ **b :** SUBSIDE, ABATE ⟨the wind is ~*ing*⟩ **c :** to decline in quality, activity, or quantity ⟨production *fell* off because of the strike⟩ **d :** to lose weight — used with *off* or *away* **e :** to assume a look of shame, disappointment, or dejection ⟨his face *fell*⟩ **f :** to decline in financial value or price ⟨stocks *fell* sharply after the President's speech⟩ **7 a :** to occur at a certain time **b :** to come by chance ⟨it *fell* into my mind to write you⟩ ⟨*fell* in with a fast crowd⟩ **c :** to come or pass by lot, assignment, or inheritance **:** DEVOLVE ⟨it *fell* to him to break the news⟩ **d :** to have a certain or proper position, place, or station ⟨the accent ~*s* on the second syllable⟩ **8 :** to come within the limits, scope, or jurisdiction of something ⟨this word ~*s* into the class of verbs⟩ **9 :** to pass suddenly and passively into a state of body or mind or a new state or condition ⟨~ asleep⟩ ⟨~ in love⟩ **10 :** to set about heartily or actively ⟨*fell* to work⟩ **11 :** STRIKE, IMPINGE ⟨music ~*ing* on the ear⟩ ~ *vt* **:** FELL 1 — **fall apart 1 :** DISINTEGRATE **2 :** to succumb to mental or emotional stress **:** BREAK DOWN — **fall behind 1 :** to lag behind **2 :** to be in arrears — **fall between two stools :** to fail because of inability to choose between or reconcile two alternative or conflicting courses of action — **fall flat :** to produce no response or result ⟨the joke *fell flat*⟩ — **fall for 1 :** to fall in love with **2 :** to become a victim of ⟨he *fell for* the trick⟩ — **fall foul 1 :** to have a collision — used chiefly of ships **2 :** to have a quarrel **:** CLASH — often used with *of* — **fall from grace :** BACKSLIDE — **fall home :** to curve inward — used of the timbers or upper parts of a ship's side — **fall into line :** to comply with a certain course of action — **fall on** *or* **fall upon :** to meet with ⟨he *fell on* hard times⟩ — **fall over oneself** *or* **fall over backward :** to display excessive eagerness — **fall short 1 :** to be deficient **2 :** to fail to attain something (as a goal or target)

²fall *n* (13c) **1 :** the act of falling by the force of gravity **2 a :** a falling out, off, or away **:** DROPPING ⟨the ~ of leaves⟩ ⟨a ~ of snow⟩ **b :** the season when leaves fall from trees **:** AUTUMN **c :** a thing or quantity that falls or has fallen ⟨a ~ of rock at the base of the cliff⟩; *specif* **:** one or more meteorites or their fragments that have fallen together **d** (1) **:** BIRTH (2) **:** the quantity born — usu. used of lambs **3 a :** a costume decoration of lace or thin fabric arranged to hang loosely and gracefully **b :** a very wide turned-down collar worn in the 17th century **c :** the part of a turnover collar from the crease to the outer edge **d :** a wide front flap on trousers (as those worn by sailors) **e :** the freely hanging lower edge of the skirt of a coat **f :** one of the three outer and often drooping segments of the flower of an iris **g :** long hair overhanging the face of dogs of some breeds **h :** a usu. long straight portion of hair that is attached to a person's own hair **4 :** a hoisting-tackle rope or chain; *esp* **:** the part of it to which the power is applied **5 a :** loss of greatness **:** COLLAPSE ⟨the ~ of the Roman Empire⟩ **b :** the surrender or capture of a besieged place ⟨the ~ of Troy⟩ **c :** lapse or departure from innocence or goodness **d :** loss of a woman's chastity **6 a :** the downward slope (as of a hill) **:** DECLIVITY **b :** a precipitous descent of water **:** WATERFALL — usu. used in pl. but sing. or pl. in constr. **c :** a musical cadence **d :** a falling-pitch intonation in speech **7 :** a decrease in size, quantity, degree, or value **8 a**

: the distance which something falls **b** : INCLINATION, PITCH **9** **a** : the act of felling something **b** : the quantity of trees cut down **c** (1) : an act of forcing a wrestler's shoulders to the mat for a specified time (as one second) (2) : a bout of wrestling **10** *Scot* : DESTINY, LOT

[3]**fall** *adj* (1677) : of, relating to, or suitable for autumn ⟨a new ~ coat⟩

fal·la·cious \fə-ˈlā-shəs\ *adj* (1509) **1** : embodying a fallacy **2** : tending to deceive or mislead : DELUSIVE — **fal·la·cious·ly** *adv* — **fal·la·cious·ness** *n*

fal·la·cy \ˈfal-ə-sē\ *n, pl* **-cies** [L *fallacia,* fr. *fallac-, fallax* deceitful, fr. *fallere* to deceive — more at FAIL] (14c) **1** **a** *obs* : GUILE, TRICKERY **b** : deceptive appearance : DECEPTION **2** **a** : a false or mistaken idea ⟨the popular ~ that poets are impractical⟩ **b** : erroneous or fallacious character : ERRONEOUSNESS **3** : an often plausible argument using false or invalid inference

fal–lal \fa-ˈlal, ˈfal-ˌ(l)al\ *n* [perh. alter. of *falbala* (furbelow)] (1706) : a fancy ornament esp. in dress — **fal·lal·ery** \fa-ˈlal-ə-rē\ *n*

fall armyworm *n* (ca. 1881) : a migratory American moth (*Spodoptera frugiperda*) that is esp. destructive to small grains and grasses as a larva

fall away *vi* (1535) **1** **a** : to withdraw friendship or support **b** : to renounce one's faith **2** **a** : to diminish gradually in size **b** : to drift off a course

fall·back \ˈfȯl-ˌbak\ *n* (1851) **1** : something on which one can fall back : RESERVE **2** : a falling back : RETREAT **3** : something that falls back ⟨the ~ from an explosion⟩

fall back \-ˈbak\ *vi* (1607) : RETREAT, RECEDE — **fall back on** *or* **fall back upon** : to have recourse to ⟨when facts were scarce he *fell back on* his imagination⟩

fall down *vi* (1873) : to fail to meet expectations or requirements ⟨he *fell down* on the job⟩

fall·er \ˈfȯ-lər\ *n* (1677) **1** : a machine part that acts by falling **2** : a logger who fells trees

fall·fish \ˈfȯl-ˌfish\ *n* (1811) : a common cyprinid fish (*Semotilus corporalis*) of the streams of northeastern No. America — compare CHUB

fall guy *n* (1906) **1** : one that is easily duped **2** : SCAPEGOAT

fal·li·bil·i·ty \ˌfal-ə-ˈbil-ət-ē\ *n* (1634) : liability to err

fal·li·ble \ˈfal-ə-bəl\ *adj* [ME, fr. ML *fallibilis,* fr. L *fallere*] (15c) **1** : liable to be erroneous ⟨a ~ generalization⟩ **2** : capable of making a mistake ⟨all men are ~⟩ — **fal·li·bly** \-blē\ *adv*

fall in *vi* (1719) **1** : to sink inward ⟨the roof *fell in*⟩ **2** : to take one's proper place in a military formation — **fall in with** **1** : to concur with ⟨had to *fall in with* her wishes⟩ **2** : to harmonize with ⟨it *falls in* exactly *with* my views⟩

falling diphthong *n* (1888) : a diphthong with less stress on the second element than on the first (as \ȯi\ in \ˈnȯiz\ *noise*)

fall·ing–out \ˌfȯ-liŋ-ˈau̇t\ *n, pl* **fallings–out** *or* **falling–outs** (1568) : an instance of falling out : QUARREL

falling rhythm *n* (1918) : rhythm with stress occurring regularly on the first syllable of each foot — compare RISING RHYTHM

falling star *n* (1563) : METEOR 2a

fall line *n* (1882) **1** : a line joining the waterfalls on numerous rivers that marks the point where each river descends from the upland to the lowland and the limit of the navigability of each river **2** : the natural downhill course (as for skiing) between two points on a slope

fall·off \ˈfȯ-ˌlȯf\ *n* (1880) : a decline esp. in quantity or quality ⟨a ~ in exports⟩ ⟨a ~ of light intensity⟩

fall off \(ˈ)fȯ-ˈlȯf\ *vi* (1605) **1** : TREND 1b **2** *of a ship* : to deviate to leeward of the point to which the bow was directed

fal·lo·pi·an tube \fə-ˈlō-pē-ən-\ *n, often cap F* [Gabriel *Fallopius* †1562 Ital. anatomist] (ca. 1706) : either of the pair of tubes conducting the egg from the ovary to the uterus

fall·out \ˈfȯ-ˌlau̇t\ *n* (1949) **1** **a** : the often radioactive particles stirred up by or resulting from a nuclear explosion and descending through the atmosphere; *also* : other polluting particles (as volcanic ash) descending likewise **b** : descent (as of fallout) through the atmosphere **2** : an incidental result : BY-PRODUCT ⟨the war . . . produced its own literary ~ —a profusion of books —*Newsweek*⟩

fall out \(ˈ)fȯ-ˈlau̇t\ *vi* (15c) **1** : QUARREL ⟨friends who have *fallen out*⟩ **2** : TURN OUT, HAPPEN ⟨as it *fell out* we couldn't have made it on time⟩ **3** **a** : to leave one's place in the ranks **b** : to leave a building in order to take one's place in a military formation

[1]**fal·low** \ˈfal-(ˌ)ō, -ə(-w)\ *adj* [ME *falow,* fr. OE *fealu;* akin to OHG *falo* pale, fallow, L *pallēre* to be pale, Gk *polios* gray] (bef. 12c) : of a light yellowish brown color

[2]**fallow** *n* [ME *falwe, falow,* fr. OE *fealg* — more at FELLY] (bef. 12c) **1** *obs* : plowed land **2** : usu. cultivated land that is allowed to lie idle during the growing season **3** : the state or period of being fallow **4** : the tilling of land without sowing it for a season

[3]**fallow** *vt* (15c) : to plow, harrow, and break up (land) without seeding to destroy weeds and conserve soil moisture

[4]**fallow** *adj* (15c) **1** : left untilled or unsown after plowing **2** : DORMANT, INACTIVE — used esp. in the phrase *to lie fallow* ⟨at this very moment there are probably important inventions lying ~ —*Harper's*⟩ — **fal·low·ness** *n*

fallow deer *n* [[1]*fallow*] (15c) : a small deer (*Dama dama*) with broad antlers and a pale yellow coat spotted with white in the summer that was orig. found in Europe and Asia Minor but has been introduced elsewhere

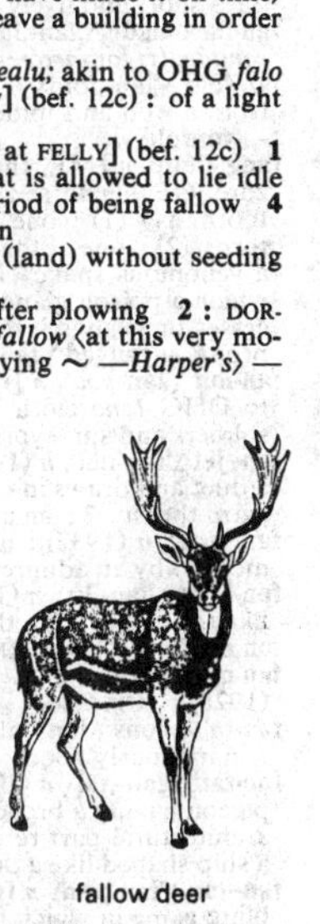

fallow deer

fall to \ˈfȯl-ˈtü\ *vi* (1593) : to begin doing something (as working or eating) esp. vigorously — often used in invitation or command

[1]**false** \ˈfȯls\ *adj* **fals·er; fals·est** [ME *fals,* fr. OF & L; OF, fr. L *falsus,* fr. pp. of *fallere* to deceive] (12c) **1** : not genuine ⟨~ documents⟩ ⟨~ teeth⟩ **2** **a** : intentionally untrue ⟨~ testimony⟩ **b** : adjusted or made so as to deceive ⟨~ scales⟩ ⟨a trunk with a ~ bottom⟩ **c** : tending to mislead ⟨a ~ promise⟩ **3** : not true ⟨~ concepts⟩ **4** **a** : not faithful or loyal : TREACHEROUS **b** *obs* : not solid **5** **a** : not essential or permanent — used of parts of a structure that are temporary or supplemental **b** : fitting over a main part to strengthen it, to protect it, or to disguise its appearance ⟨a ~ ceiling⟩ **c** : appearing forced or artificial : UNCONVINCING ⟨a ~ scene in a movie⟩ **6** : of a kind related to or resembling another kind that is usu. designated by the unqualified vernacular ⟨~ oats⟩ **7** : inaccurate in pitch ⟨a ~ note⟩ **8** **a** : based on mistaken ideas ⟨~ pride⟩ **b** : inconsistent with the facts ⟨a ~ position⟩ ⟨a ~ sense of security⟩ **9** : IMPRUDENT, UNWISE ⟨don't make a ~ move⟩ ***syn*** see FAITHLESS — **false·ly** *adv* — **false·ness** *n*

[2]**false** *adv* (14c) : in a false or faithless manner : TREACHEROUSLY ⟨his wife played him ~⟩

false alarm *n* (1579) **1** : an alarm (as a fire or burglar alarm) that is set off needlessly **2** : one that excites but fails to meet expectations

false arrest *n* (1926) : an arrest not justifiable under law

false·hood \ˈfȯls-ˌhu̇d\ *n* (13c) **1** : an untrue statement : LIE **2** : absence of truth or accuracy : FALSITY **3** : the practice of lying : MENDACITY

false horizon *n* (1812) : HORIZON 1c

false imprisonment *n* (14c) : imprisonment of a person contrary to law

false mi·ter·wort \-ˈmīt-ər-ˌwərt, -ˌwȯ(ə)rt\ *n* (1868) : FOAMFLOWER

false positive *n* (1946) : an individual who is wrongly diagnosed as having a condition or wrongly classified in a particular reference category because of imperfect testing methods or procedures — **false–positive** *adj*

false pregnancy *n* (ca. 1860) : PSEUDOCYESIS, PSEUDOPREGNANCY

false rib *n* (15c) : a rib whose cartilages unite indirectly or not at all with the sternum — compare FLOATING RIB

false Solomon's–seal *also* **false Solomonseal** *n* (ca. 1856) : any of a genus (*Smilacina*) of herbs of the lily family that differ from Solomon's seal in having flowers in a terminal raceme or panicle

false start *n* (1815) **1** : a premature start (as of a race) **2** : an unsuccessful attempt to begin an endeavor (as a career)

[1]**fal·set·to** \fȯl-ˈset-(ˌ)ō\ *n, pl* **-tos** [It, fr. dim. of *falso* false, fr. L *falsus*] (1774) **1** : an artificially high voice; *specif* : an artificially produced singing voice that overlaps and extends above the range of the full voice esp. of a tenor **2** : a singer who uses falsetto

[2]**falsetto** *adv* (1940) : in falsetto

fals·ie \ˈfȯl-sē\ *n* (1943) : an artificial addition to a bodily part worn to enhance appearance; *specif* : a breast-shaped usu. fabric or rubber cup used to pad a brassiere — usu. used in pl.

fal·si·fy \ˈfȯl-sə-ˌfī\ *vb* **-fied; -fy·ing** [ME *falsifien,* fr. MF *falsifier,* fr. ML *falsificare,* fr. L *falsus*] *vt* (15c) **1** : to prove or declare false **2** : to make false: as **a** : to make false by mutilation or addition ⟨his accounts were *falsified* to conceal a theft⟩ **b** : to represent falsely : MISREPRESENT **3** : to prove unsound by experience ~ *vi* : to tell lies : LIE — **fal·si·fi·ca·tion** \ˌfȯl-sə-fə-ˈkā-shən\ *n* — **fal·si·fi·er** \ˈfȯl-sə-ˌfī(-ə)r\ *n*

fal·si·ty \ˈfȯl-sət-ē\ *n, pl* **-ties** (13c) **1** : something false : LIE **2** : the quality or state of being false

Fal·staff \ˈfȯl-ˌstaf\ *n* : a convivial roguish character in Shakespeare's *Merry Wives of Windsor* and *Henry IV* — **Fal·staff·ian** \fȯl-ˈstaf-ē-ən\ *adj*

falt·boat \ˈfält-ˌbōt, ˈfȯlt-\ *n* [part trans. of G *faltboot* folding boat, fr. *falten* to fold (fr. OHG *faldan*) + *boot* boat] (1926) : FOLDBOAT

[1]**fal·ter** \ˈfȯl-tər\ *vb* **fal·tered; fal·ter·ing** \-t(ə-)riŋ\ [ME *falteren*] *vi* (14c) **1** **a** : to walk unsteadily : STUMBLE **b** : to give way : TOTTER ⟨could feel my legs *~ing*⟩ **c** : to move waveringly or hesitatingly ⟨forced to bail out of *~ing* airplanes —*Nat'l Geographic*⟩ **2** : to speak brokenly or weakly : STAMMER **3** **a** : to hesitate in purpose or action : WAVER **b** : to lose drive or effectiveness : FAIL, WEAKEN ⟨the business was *~ing*⟩ ~ *vt* : to utter hesitatingly or brokenly ***syn*** see HESITATE — **fal·ter·er** \-tər-ər\ *n* — **fal·ter·ing·ly** \-t(ə-)riŋ-lē\ *adv*

[2]**falter** *n* (1834) : an act or instance of faltering

[1]**fame** \ˈfām\ *n* [ME, fr. OF, fr. L *fama* report, fame; akin to L *fari* to speak — more at BAN] (13c) **1** **a** : public estimation : REPUTATION **b** : popular acclaim : RENOWN **2** *archaic* : RUMOR

[2]**fame** *vt* **famed; fam·ing** (14c) **1** *archaic* : REPORT, REPUTE **2** : to make famous

famed \ˈfāmd\ *adj* (1533) : known widely and well : FAMOUS

fa·mil·ial \fə-ˈmil-yəl\ *adj* [F, fr. L *familia*] (ca. 1900) **1** : tending to occur in more members of a family than expected by chance alone ⟨a ~ disorder⟩ **2** : of, relating to, or characteristic of a family

[1]**fa·mil·iar** \fə-ˈmil-yər\ *n* (13c) **1** : a member of the household of a high official **2** : an intimate associate : COMPANION **3** : a spirit often embodied in an animal and held to attend and serve or guard a person **4** **a** : one who is well acquainted with something **b** : one who frequents a place

[2]**familiar** *adj* [ME *familier,* fr. MF, fr. L *familiaris,* fr. *familia*] (14c) **1** : closely acquainted : INTIMATE ⟨a ~ family friend⟩ **2** *obs* : AFFABLE, SOCIABLE **3** **a** : of or relating to a family ⟨remembering past ~ celebrations⟩ **b** : frequented by families ⟨a ~ resort⟩ **4** **a** : being free and easy ⟨the ~ association of old friends⟩ **b** : marked by informality ⟨a ~ essay⟩ **c** : overly free and unrestrained : PRESUMPTUOUS ⟨grossly ~ behavior⟩ **d** : moderately tame ⟨~ animals⟩ **5** **a** : frequently seen or experienced : easily recognized **b** : of everyday occurrence **6** : closely acquainted through personal knowledge or study ⟨~ with the facts of the case⟩ — **fa·mil·iar·ly** *adv* — **fa·mil·iar·ness** *n*

syn FAMILIAR, INTIMATE mean closely acquainted. FAMILIAR suggests the ease, informality, absence of reserve or constraint natural among members of a family or acquaintances of long standing; INTIMATE stresses the closeness and intensity rather than the mere frequency of personal association and suggests either deep mutual understanding or the sharing of deeply personal thoughts and feelings. ***syn*** see in addition COMMON

fa·mil·iar·i·ty \fə-ˌmil-ˈyar-ət-ē, -ˌmil-ē-ˈ(y)ar-\ *n, pl* **-ties** (13c) **1** **a** : the quality or state of being familiar **b** : a state of close relationship : INTIMACY **2** **a** : absence of ceremony : INFORMALITY **b** : an unduly informal act or expression : IMPROPRIETY **c** : a sexual liberty **3** : close acquaintance with something ⟨my ~ with American history⟩

\ə\ abut \$^{ə}$\ kitten, F table \ər\ further \a\ ash \ā\ ace \ä\ cot, cart
\au̇\ out \ch\ chin \e\ bet \ē\ easy \g\ go \i\ hit \ī\ ice \j\ job
\ŋ\ sing \ō\ go \ȯ\ law \ȯi\ boy \th\ thin \t͟h\ the \ü\ loot \u̇\ foot
\y\ yet \zh\ vision \à, k̟, ^{n}, œ, œ̄, ue, ue̅, ^{y}\ see Guide to Pronunciation

fa·mil·iar·ize \fə-ˈmil-yə-ˌrīz\ *vt* **-ized; -iz·ing** (1608) **1** : to make known or familiar ⟨Shakespeare . . . ~*s* the wonderful —Samuel Johnson⟩ **2** : to make well acquainted ⟨~ students with good literature⟩ — **fa·mil·iar·iza·tion** \-ˌmil-yə-rə-ˈzā-shən\ *n*

familiar spirit *n* (1565) **1** : a spirit or demon that serves or prompts an individual **2** : the spirit of a dead person invoked by a medium to advise or prophesy

fam·i·lism \ˈfam-ə-ˌliz-əm\ *n* (1925) : a social pattern in which the family assumes a position of ascendance over individual interests — **fam·i·lis·tic** \ˌfam-ə-ˈlis-tik\ *adj*

1**fam·i·ly** \ˈfam-(ə-)lē\ *n, pl* **-lies** [ME *familie,* fr. L *familia* household (including servants as well as kin of the householder), fr. *famulus* servant; perh. akin to Skt *dhāman* dwelling place] (15c) **1** : a group of individuals living under one roof and usu. under one head : HOUSEHOLD **2 a** : a group of persons of common ancestry : CLAN **b** : a people or group of peoples regarded as deriving from a common stock : RACE **3 a** : a group of people united by certain convictions or a common affiliation : FELLOWSHIP **b** : the staff of a high official (as the President) **4** : a group of things related by common characteristics: as **a** : a closely related series of elements or chemical compounds **b** : a group of soils that have similar profiles and include one or more series **c** : a group of related languages descended from a single ancestral language **5** : the basic unit in society having as its nucleus two or more adults living together and cooperating in the care and rearing of their own or adopted children **6 a** : a group of related plants or animals forming a category ranking above a genus and below an order and usu. comprising several to many genera **b** *in livestock breeding* (1) : the descendants or line of a particular individual esp. of some outstanding female (2) : an identifiable strain within a breed **7** : a set of curves or surfaces whose equations differ only in parameters **8** : a unit of a crime syndicate (as the Mafia) operating within a geographical area

2**family** *adj* (1602) **1** : of or relating to a family **2** : designed or suitable for both children and adults ⟨~ restaurants⟩ ⟨~ movies⟩

family Bible *n* (1740) : a large Bible usu. having special pages for recording births, marriages, and deaths

family circle *n* (1868) : a gallery in a theater or opera house usu. located above or behind a gallery containing more expensive seats

family court *n* (ca. 1931) : COURT OF DOMESTIC RELATIONS

family doctor *n* (1846) : a doctor regularly called by a family in time of medical need — called also *family physician*

family man *n* (1856) **1** : a man with a wife and children dependent on him **2** : a responsible man of domestic habits

family name *n* (1699) : SURNAME 2

family planning *n* (1939) : planning intended to determine the number and spacing of one's children through effective methods of birth control

family room *n* (1853) : a large room designed as a recreation center for members of a family

family style *adv or adj* (1932) : with the food placed on the table in serving dishes from which those eating may help themselves ⟨meals are served *family style*⟩

family tree *n* (1807) **1** : a genealogical diagram **2** : GENEALOGY

family way *n* (1796) : condition of being pregnant — used with *in* and *the* or *a* ⟨she is in the *family way* again⟩

fam·ine \ˈfam-ən\ *n* [ME, fr. MF, fr. (assumed) VL *famina,* fr. L *fames* hunger] (14c) **1** : an extreme scarcity of food **2** *archaic* : STARVATION **3** *archaic* : a ravenous appetite **4** : a great shortage

fam·ish \ˈfam-ish\ *vb* [ME *famishen,* prob. alter. of *famen,* fr. MF *afamer,* fr. (assumed) VL *affamare,* fr. L *ad-* + *fames*] *vt* (15c) **1** : to cause to suffer severely from hunger **2** *archaic* : to cause to starve to death ~ *vi* **1** *archaic* : STARVE **2** : to suffer for lack of something necessary ⟨this invention of language, at a moment when French poetry in particular was ~*ing* for such invention —T. S. Eliot⟩ — **fam·ish·ment** \-mənt\ *n*

fa·mous \ˈfā-məs\ *adj* [ME, fr. MF *fameux,* fr. L *famosus,* fr. *fama* fame] (14c) **1 a** : widely known **b** : honored for achievement **2** : EXCELLENT, FIRST-RATE ⟨~ weather for a walk⟩ — **fa·mous·ness** *n*

syn FAMOUS, RENOWNED, CELEBRATED, NOTED, NOTORIOUS, DISTINGUISHED, EMINENT, ILLUSTRIOUS mean known far and wide. FAMOUS implies little more than the fact of being, sometimes briefly, widely and popularly known; RENOWNED implies more glory and acclamation, CELEBRATED more notice and attention esp. in print; NOTED suggests well-deserved public attention; NOTORIOUS frequently adds to FAMOUS an implication of questionableness or evil; DISTINGUISHED implies acknowledged excellence or superiority; EMINENT implies even greater conspicuousness for outstanding quality or character; ILLUSTRIOUS stresses enduring honor and glory attached to a deed or person.

fa·mous·ly *adv* (1579) **1** : in a celebrated manner **2** : in a superlative fashion **3** : to an unusual degree : VERY

fam·u·lus \ˈfam-yə-ləs\ *n, pl* **-li** \-ˌlī, -ˌlē\ [G, assistant to a professor, fr. L, servant] (1837) : a private secretary or attendant

1**fan** \ˈfan\ *n* [ME, fr. OE *fann,* fr. L *vannus* — more at WINNOW] (bef. 12c) **1** : any of various devices for winnowing grain **2** : an instrument for producing a current of air: as **a** : a device for cooling the person that is usu. shaped like a segment of a circle and is composed of material (as feathers or paper) mounted on thin rods or slats moving about a pivot so that the device may be closed compactly when not in use **b** : a device that consists of a series of vanes radiating from a hub rotated on its axle by a motor **c** *slang* : an airplane propeller **3** : something resembling an open fan **4** : a gently sloping fan-shaped body of detritus; *esp* : ALLUVIAL FAN — **fan·like** \-ˌlīk\ *adj*

2**fan** *vb* **fanned; fan·ning** *vt* (bef. 12c) **1 a** : to drive away the chaff of (grain) by means of a current of air **b** : to eliminate (as chaff) by winnowing **2** : to move or impel (air) with a fan **3** : to blow or breathe upon ⟨the breeze *fanning* her hair⟩ **4 a** : to direct a current of air upon with a fan **b** : to stir up to activity as if by fanning : STIMULATE ⟨he was *fanning* her antagonism with insults⟩ **5** *archaic* : WAVE **6** *slang* : SPANK **7** : to spread like a fan ⟨the peacock *fanned* his tail⟩ **8** : to strike (a batter) out in baseball **9** : to fire a series of shots from (a single-action revolver) by holding the trigger back and successively striking the hammer to the rear with the free hand ~ *vi* **1** : to move like a fan : FLUTTER **2** : to spread like a fan — often used with *out* ⟨deputies *fanning* out on the hunt⟩ **3** : STRIKE OUT 3 — **fan·ner** \ˈfan-ər\ *n*

3**fan** *n* [prob. short for *fanatic*] (1682) **1** : an enthusiastic devotee (as of a sport or a performing art) usu. as a spectator **2** : an ardent admirer or enthusiast (as of a celebrity or a pursuit) ⟨science-fiction ~*s*⟩

fa·nat·ic \fə-ˈnat-ik\ *or* **fa·nat·i·cal** \-i-kəl\ *adj* [L *fanaticus* inspired by a deity, frenzied, fr. *fanum* temple — more at FEAST] (1550) : marked by excessive enthusiasm and often intense uncritical devotion ⟨they're ~ about politics⟩ — **fanatic** *n* — **fa·nat·i·cal·ly** \fə-ˈnat-i-k(ə-)lē\ *adv* — **fa·nat·i·cal·ness** \-kəl-nəs\ *n*

fa·nat·i·cism \fə-ˈnat-ə-ˌsiz-əm\ *n* (1652) : fanatic outlook or behavior

fa·nat·i·cize \-ˌsīz\ *vt* **-cized; -ciz·ing** (1812) : to cause to become fanatic

fan·ci·er \ˈfan(t)-sē-ər\ *n* (1765) **1** : one that has a special liking or interest **2** : a person who breeds or grows a particular animal or plant for points of excellence ⟨a pigeon ~⟩

fan·ci·ful \ˈfan(t)-si-fəl\ *adj* (1627) **1** : marked by fancy or unrestrained imagination rather than by reason and experience **2** : existing in fancy only **3** : marked by or as if by fancy or whim ⟨gave ~ names to their children⟩ ***syn*** see IMAGINARY — **fan·ci·ful·ly** \-f(ə-)lē\ *adv* — **fan·ci·ful·ness** \-fəl-nəs\ *n*

fan·ci·ly \ˈfan(t)-sə-lē\ *adv* (1937) **1** : with fancy or imagination esp. when studied or affected **2** : in an elaborate or ornate manner

fan·ci·ness \-sē-nəs\ *n* (1943) : fancy quality or form

1**fan·cy** \ˈfan(t)-sē\ *n, pl* **fancies** [ME *fantasie, fantsy* fantasy, fancy, fr. MF *fantasie,* fr. L *phantasia,* fr. Gk, appearance, imagination, fr. *phantazein* to present to the mind (middle voice, to imagine), fr. *phainein* to show; akin to OE *gebōned* polished, Gk *phōs* light] (14c) **1 a** : a liking formed by caprice rather than reason : INCLINATION ⟨took a ~ to the strange little animal⟩ **b** : amorous fondness : LOVE **2 a** : NOTION, WHIM **b** : an image or representation of something formed in the mind **3** *archaic* : fantastic quality or state **4 a** : imagination esp. of a capricious or delusive sort **b** : the power of conception and representation used in artistic expression (as by a poet) **5** : TASTE, JUDGMENT **6 a** : devotees of some particular art, practice, or amusement **b** : the object of interest of such a fancy; *esp* : PUGILISM

2**fancy** *vt* **fan·cied; fan·cy·ing** (14c) **1** : to have a fancy for : LIKE **2** : to form a conception of : IMAGINE ⟨~ our embarrassment⟩ **3 a** : to believe mistakenly or without evidence **b** : to believe without being certain ⟨she *fancied* she had met him before⟩ **4** : to visualize or interpret as ⟨*fancied* myself a child again⟩ ***syn*** see THINK

3**fancy** *adj* **fan·ci·er; -est** (1646) **1** : dependent or based on fancy : WHIMSICAL **2 a** : not plain : ORNAMENTAL ⟨a ~ hairdo⟩ **b** : of particular excellence or highest grade ⟨~ tuna⟩ **c** *of an animal or plant* : bred esp. for bizarre or ornamental qualities that lack practical utility **3** : based on conceptions of the fancy ⟨~ sketches⟩ **4 a** : dealing in fancy goods **b** : above real value or the usual market price; *esp* : EXTRAVAGANT ⟨paying ~ prices for inferior goods⟩ **5** : executed with technical skill and superior grace ⟨~ diving⟩ **6** : PARTI-COLOR ⟨~ carnations⟩

fancy dress *n* (1770) : a costume (as for a masquerade) chosen to suit the wearer's fancy

fan·cy–free \ˈfan(t)-sē-ˈfrē\ *adj* (1590) **1** : free from amorous attachment or engagement **2** : free to imagine or fancy

fancy man *n* (ca. 1811) : a woman's paramour; *also* : PIMP

fancy up *vt* (1934) : to add superficial adornment to ⟨*fancy up* an old dress with ruffles⟩

fancy woman *n* (1812) : a woman of questionable morals; *specif* : PROSTITUTE

fan·cy·work \ˈfan(t)-sē-ˌwərk\ *n* (1810) : decorative needlework

fan·dan·go \fan-ˈdaŋ-(ˌ)gō\ *n, pl* **-gos** [Sp] (1774) **1** : a lively Spanish or Spanish-American dance in triple time that is usu. performed by a man and a woman to the accompaniment of guitar and castanets; *also* : music for this dance **2** : TOMFOOLERY

fan·dom \ˈfan-dəm\ *n* (1903) : all the fans (as of a sport)

fane \ˈfān\ *n* [ME, fr. L *fanum* — more at FEAST] (15c) **1** : TEMPLE **2** : CHURCH

fan·fare \ˈfan-ˌfa(ə)r, -ˌfe(ə)r\ *n* [F] (1605) **1** : a showy outward display **2** : a short and lively sounding of trumpets

fan·far·o·nade \ˌfan-ˌfar-ə-ˈnād, -ˈnäd\ *n* [F *fanfaronnade,* fr. Sp *fanfarronada,* fr. *fanfarrón* braggart] (1652) : empty boasting : BLUSTER

fan·fold \ˈfan-ˌfōld\ *n* (1925) : paper (as business forms or tape) made from a web and folded like a fan lengthwise and sometimes crosswise — **fanfold** *vt*

fang \ˈfaŋ\ *n* [ME, that which is taken, fr. OE; akin to OHG *fang* seizure, OE *fōn* to seize — more at PACT] (1555) **1 a** : a long sharp tooth: as (1) : one by which an animal's prey is seized and held or torn (2) : one of the long hollow or grooved and often erectile teeth of a venomous snake **b** : one of the chelicerae of a spider at the tip of which a poison gland opens **2** : the root of a tooth or one of the processes or prongs into which a root divides **3** : a projecting tooth or prong — **fanged** \ˈfaŋd\ *adj*

fan·ion \ˈfan-yən\ *n* [F, fr. *fanon* maniple, pennon, of Gmc origin; akin to OHG *fano* cloth — more at VANE] (1706) : a small flag used by soldiers and surveyors to mark positions

fan–jet \ˈfan-ˌjet\ *n* (1962) **1** : a jet engine having a fan that operates in a duct and draws in extra air whose compression and expulsion provide extra thrust **2** : an airplane powered by a fan-jet engine

fan letter *n* (1932) : a letter sent to a public figure (as in sports or the movies) by an admirer

fan·light \ˈfan-ˌlīt\ *n* (1819) : a semicircular window with radiating bars like the ribs of a fan that is placed over a door or window

fan mail *n* (1924) : FAN LETTERS

fan·ny \ˈfan-ē\ *n, pl* **fannies** [perh. fr. *Fanny,* nickname of *Frances*] (1928) : BUTTOCKS

fan·tab·u·lous \fan-ˈtab-yə-ləs\ *adj* [*fan*tastic + *fabulous*] *slang* (1959) : marvelously good

fan·tail \ˈfan-ˌtāl\ *n* (1728) **1** : a fan-shaped tail or end **2** : a domestic pigeon having a broad rounded tail often with 30 or 40 feathers **3** : an architectural part resembling a fan **4** : a counter or after overhang of a ship shaped like a duck's bill

fan–tan \ˈfan-ˌtan\ *n* [Chin (Pek) *fan*1-*t'an*1] (1878) **1** : a Chinese gambling game in which the banker divides a pile of objects (as beans) into fours and players bet on what number will be left at the end of the count **2 :** a card game in which players must build in sequence upon sevens and attempt to be the first one out of cards

fan·ta·sia \fan-ˈtā-zhə, -z(h)ē-ə; ˌfant-ə-ˈzē-ə\ *also* **fan·ta·sie** \ˌfant-ə-ˈzē, ˌfänt-\ *n* [It *fantasia* & G *fantasie,* lit., fancy, fr. L *phantasia* — more at FANCY] (1724) **1 :** a free usu. instrumental composition not in strict form **2 a :** a work (as a poem or play) in which the author's fancy roves unrestricted **b :** something possessing grotesque, bizarre, or unreal qualities

fan·ta·sied \ˈfant-ə-sēd, -zēd\ *adj* (1561) **1 :** existing only in the imagination **:** FANCIED **2** *obs* **:** full of fancies or strange whims

fan·ta·sist \-səst, -zəst\ *n* (1923) **:** one who creates fantasias or fantasies

fan·ta·size \-ˌsīz\ *vb* **-sized; -siz·ing** *vt* (1926) **:** FANTASY ⟨likes to ~ herself as very wealthy⟩ ~ *vi* **:** to indulge in reverie **:** create or develop imaginative and often fantastic views or ideas ⟨doing things I'd *fantasized* about in my sheltered childhood —Diane Arbus⟩ — **fan·ta·siz·er** \-ˌsī-zər\ *n*

fantasm *var of* PHANTASM

fan·tast \ˈfan-ˌtast\ *n* [G, fr. ML *fantasta,* prob. back-formation fr. LL *phantasticus*] (1588) **1 :** VISIONARY **2 :** a fantastic or eccentric person **3 :** FANTASIST

¹fan·tas·tic \fan-ˈtas-tik, fən-\ *also* **fan·tas·ti·cal** \-ti-kəl\ *adj* [ME *fantastic, fantastical,* fr. MF & LL; MF *fantastique,* fr. LL *phantasticus,* fr. Gk *phantastikos* producing mental images, fr. *phantazein* to present to the mind] (14c) **1 a :** based on fantasy **:** not real **b :** conceived or seemingly conceived by unrestrained fancy **c :** so extreme as to challenge belief **:** UNBELIEVABLE; *broadly* **:** exceedingly large or great **2 :** marked by extravagant fantasy or extreme individuality **:** ECCENTRIC — **fan·tas·ti·cal·i·ty** \(ˌ)fan-ˌtas-tə-ˈkal-ət-ē, fən-\ *n* — **fan·tas·ti·cal·ly** \fan-ˈtas-ti-k(ə-)lē, fən-\ *adv* — **fan·tas·ti·cal·ness** \-kəl-nəs\ *n*

syn FANTASTIC, BIZARRE, GROTESQUE mean conceived, made, or carried out without adherence to truth or reality. FANTASTIC may connote unrestrained extravagance in conception or merely ingenuity of decorative invention; BIZARRE applies to the sensationally queer or strange and implies violence of contrast or incongruity of combination; GROTESQUE may apply to what is conventionally ugly but artistically effective or it may connote ludicrous awkwardness or incongruity often with sinister or tragic overtones. ***syn*** see in addition IMAGINARY

²fantastic *n* (14c) **:** ECCENTRIC 2

fan·tas·ti·cate \fan-ˈtas-tə-ˌkāt, fən-\ *vt* **-cat·ed; -cat·ing** (1600) **:** to make fantastic — **fan·tas·ti·ca·tion** \(ˌ)fan-ˌtas-tə-ˈkā-shən, fən-\ *n*

fan·tas·ti·co \fan-ˈtas-ti-ˌkō, fən-\ *n, pl* **-coes** [It, fantastic (adj.), fr. LL *phantasticus*] (1591) **:** a ridiculously fantastic individual

¹fan·ta·sy \ˈfant-ə-sē, -zē\ *n, pl* **-sies** [ME *fantasie* — more at FANCY] (14c) **1** *obs* **:** HALLUCINATION **2 :** FANCY; *esp* **:** the free play of creative imagination **3 :** a creation of the imaginative faculty whether expressed or merely conceived: as **a :** a fanciful design or invention **b :** a chimerical or fantastic notion **c :** FANTASIA 1 **d :** imaginative fiction featuring esp. strange settings and grotesque characters — called also *fantasy fiction* **4 :** CAPRICE **5 :** the power or process of creating esp. unrealistic or improbable mental images in response to psychological need ⟨an object of ~⟩; *also* **:** a mental image or a series of mental images (as a daydream) so created ⟨sexual *fantasies* of adolescence⟩ **6 :** a coin usu. not intended for circulation as currency and often issued by a dubious authority (as a government-in-exile)

²fantasy *vb* **-sied; -sy·ing** *vt* (15c) **:** to portray in the mind **:** FANCY ~ *vi* **:** to indulge in a fantasy or reverie **:** DAYDREAM

fan·ta·sy·land \-ˌland\ *n* (1967) **:** an imaginary or ideal place or situation

fan·toc·ci·ni \ˌfänt-ə-ˈchē-nē, ˌfant-\ *n pl* [It, pl. of *fantoccino,* dim. of *fantoccio* doll, aug. of *fante* child, fr. L *infant-, infans* infant] (1771) **:** a puppet show using puppets operated by strings or mechanical devices; *also* **:** such puppets

fan·tod \ˈfan-ˌtäd\ *n* [perh. alter. of E dial. *fantique, fanteeg*] (1839) **1** *pl* **a :** a state of irritability and tension **b :** FIDGETS **2 :** an emotional outburst **:** FIT

fantom *var of* PHANTOM

fan tracery *n* (1815) **:** decorative tracery on vaulting in which the ribs diverge like the rays of a fan

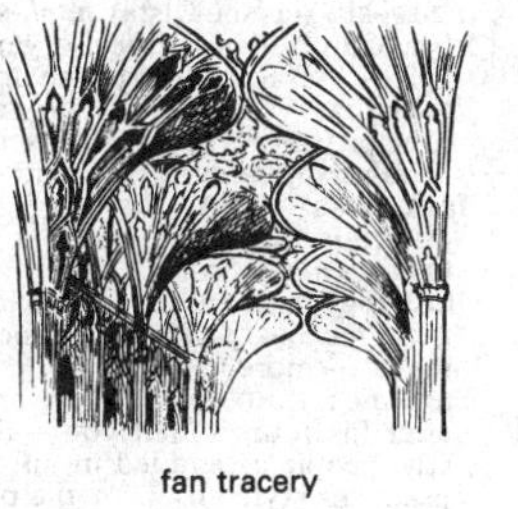

fan tracery

fan·wise \ˈfan-ˌwīz\ *adv or adj* (1882) **:** in the manner or position of the slats of an open fan ⟨boats anchored ~ at the pier⟩

fan·zine \(ˈ)fan-ˈzēn\ *n* [¹*fan* + *magazine*] (1949) **:** a magazine written by and for fans esp. of science fiction or fantasy writing

¹far \ˈfär\ *adv* **far·ther** \-thər\ *or* **fur·ther** \ˈfər-\; **far·thest** *or* **fur·thest** \-thəst\ [ME *fer,* fr. OE *feorr;* akin to OHG *ferro* far, OE *faran* to go — more at FARE] (bef. 12c) **1 :** at or to a considerable distance in space ⟨wandered ~ from home⟩ **2 a :** to a great extent **:** MUCH ⟨~ better methods⟩ **b :** by a broad interval **:** WIDELY ⟨the ~ distant future⟩ **c :** of a distinctly different quality — usu. used with *from* ⟨the trip was ~ from a failure⟩ **3 :** to or at a definite distance, point, or degree ⟨as ~ as I know⟩ **4 :** to an advanced point or extent ⟨a bright student will go ~⟩ ⟨worked ~ into the night⟩ **5 :** at a considerable distance in time ⟨not ~ from the year 1870⟩ — **by far :** far and away ⟨is *by far* the best runner⟩ — **far and away :** by a considerable margin ⟨was *far and away* the superior team⟩ — **how far :** to what extent, degree, or distance ⟨didn't know *how far* to trust them⟩ — **so far 1 :** to a certain extent, degree, or distance ⟨when the water rose *so far,* the villagers sought higher ground⟩ **2 :** up to the present ⟨has written just one novel *so far*⟩ — **thus far :** so far ⟨*thus far* our findings have been negative⟩

²far *adj* **farther** *or* **further; farthest** *or* **furthest** (bef. 12c) **1 a :** remote in space **b :** distinctly different in quality or relationship **c :** remote in time **2 a :** LONG ⟨a ~ journey⟩ **b :** of notable extent **:** COMPREHENSIVE ⟨a man of ~ vision⟩ **3 :** the more distant of two **4 :** EXTREME ⟨the ~ left⟩ ⟨a ~ right political organization⟩

far·ad \ˈfa(ə)r-ˌad, ˈfar-əd\ *n* [Michael *Faraday*] (1861) **:** the unit of capacitance equal to the capacitance of a capacitor between whose plates there appears a potential of one volt when it is charged by one coulomb of electricity

far·a·day \ˈfar-ə-ˌdā, -əd-ē\ *n* [Michael *Faraday*] (1904) **:** the quantity of electricity transferred in electrolysis per equivalent weight of an element or ion equal to about 96,500 coulombs

fa·rad·ic \fə-ˈrad-ik, far-ˈad-\ *also* **far·a·da·ic** \ˌfar-ə-ˈdā-ik\ *adj* (1875) **:** of or relating to an asymmetric alternating current of electricity produced by an induction coil

far·a·dism \ˈfar-ə-ˌdiz-əm\ *n* (1876) **:** the application of a faradic current of electricity (as for therapeutic purposes)

far·an·dole \ˈfar-ən-ˌdōl\ *n* [F *farandole,* fr. Prov *farandoulo*] (1863) **1 :** a lively Provençal dance in which men and women hold hands, form a chain, and follow a leader through a serpentine course **2 :** music in sextuple time for a farandole

far and wide *adv* (bef. 12c) **:** in every direction **:** EVERYWHERE ⟨advertised the event *far and wide*⟩

far·away \ˌfär-ə-ˌwā\ *adj* (1735) **1 :** lying at a great distance **:** REMOTE **2 :** DREAMY, ABSTRACTED ⟨a ~ look in her eyes⟩

¹farce \ˈfärs\ *vt* **farced; farc·ing** [ME *farsen,* fr. MF *farcir,* fr. L *farcire;* akin to Gk *phrassein* to enclose] (14c) **1 :** STUFF **2 :** to make more acceptable (as a literary work) by padding or spicing

²farce *n* [ME *farse,* fr. MF *farce,* fr. (assumed) VL *farsa,* fr. L, fem. of *farsus,* pp. of *farcire*] (14c) **1 :** a savory stuffing **:** FORCEMEAT **2 :** a light dramatic composition marked by broadly satirical comedy and improbable plot **3 :** the broad humor characteristic of farce or pretense **4 a :** ridiculous or empty show **b :** MOCKERY ⟨the upholding of this law became a ~⟩

far·ceur \fär-ˈsər\ *n* [F, fr. MF, fr. *farcer* to joke, fr. OF, fr. *farce*] (1781) **1 :** JOKER, WAG **2 :** a writer or actor of farce

far·ci *or* **far·cie** \fär-ˈsē\ *adj* [F, fr. pp. of *farcir*] (1903) **:** stuffed esp. with forcemeat ⟨oysters ~⟩

far·ci·cal \ˈfär-si-kəl\ *adj* (1716) **1 :** of, relating to, or resembling farce **:** LUDICROUS **2 :** laughably inept **:** ABSURD — **far·ci·cal·i·ty** \ˌfär-sə-ˈkal-ət-ē\ *n* — **far·ci·cal·ly** \ˈfär-si-k(ə-)lē\ *adv*

far·cy \ˈfär-sē\ *n* [ME *farsin, farsi,* fr. MF *farcin,* fr. LL *farcimen,* fr. L, sausage, fr. *farcire*] (14c) **:** GLANDERS; *esp* **:** cutaneous glanders

¹fard \ˈfärd\ *vt* [ME *farden,* fr. MF *farder,* of Gmc origin; akin to OHG *faro* colored — more at PERCH] (15c) **1 :** to paint (the face) with cosmetics **2** *archaic* **:** to gloss over

²fard *n, archaic* (1540) **:** paint used on the face

far·del \ˈfärd-ᵊl\ *n* [ME, fr. MF, prob. fr. Ar *fardah*] (14c) **1 :** BUNDLE **2 :** BURDEN

¹fare \ˈfa(ə)r, ˈfe(ə)r\ *vi* **fared; far·ing** [ME *faren,* fr. OE *faran;* akin to OHG *faran* to go, L *portare* to carry, Gk *peran* to pass through, *poros* passage, journey] (bef. 12c) **1 :** GO, TRAVEL **2 :** GET ALONG, SUCCEED ⟨how did you ~ on your exam?⟩ **3 :** EAT, DINE

²fare *n* [ME, journey, passage, supply of food, fr. OE *faru, fær;* akin to OE *faran* to go] (15c) **1 a :** the price charged to transport a person **b :** a paying passenger on a public conveyance **2 a :** range of food **:** DIET **b :** material provided for use, consumption, or enjoyment

fare–thee–well \ˌfa(ə)r-(ˌ)thē-ˌwel, ˈfe(ə)r-\ *or* **fare–you–well** \-yə-, -yü-, -yē-\ *n* (1816) **1 :** a state of perfection ⟨imitated the speaker's pompous manner to a ~⟩ **2 :** the utmost degree ⟨drubbed the burglar to a ~⟩

¹fare·well \fa(ə)r-ˈwel, fe(ə)r-\ *vb imper* (14c) **:** get along well — used interjectionally to or by one departing

²farewell *n* (14c) **1 :** a wish of well-being at parting **:** GOOD-BYE **2 a :** an act of departure **:** LEAVE-TAKING **b :** a formal occasion honoring a person about to leave or retire

³fare·well \fa(ə)r-ˈwel, fe(ə)r-\ *vt* (1580) **:** to bid farewell to

⁴fare·well \ˌfa(ə)r-ˌwel, ˌfe(ə)r-\ *adj* (1711) **:** of or relating to leave-taking **:** FINAL ⟨a ~ appearance⟩

far·fel *or* **far·fal** \ˈfär-fəl\ *n* [Yiddish *farfl* (pl.), fr. MHG *varveln*] (1892) **:** noodles in the form of small pellets or granules

far·fetched \ˈfär-ˈfecht\ *adj* (1583) **1 :** brought from a remote time or place **2 :** not easily or naturally deduced or introduced **:** IMPROBABLE ⟨a ~ story⟩ — **far·fetched·ness** \-ˈfech(t)-nəs, -ˈfech-əd-nəs\ *n*

far–flung \-ˈfləŋ\ *adj* (1895) **1 :** widely spread or distributed ⟨~ trading operations⟩ **2 :** REMOTE ⟨~ sections of the city⟩

far–gone \ˈfär-ˈgȯn *also* -ˈgän\ *adj* (1778) **:** nearing an end ⟨was too ~ to be saved⟩

fa·ri·na \fə-ˈrē-nə\ *n* [L, meal, flour, fr. *far* spelt — more at BARLEY] (14c) **1 :** a fine meal of vegetable matter (as cereal grains) used chiefly for puddings or as a breakfast cereal **2 :** any of various powdery or mealy substances

far·i·na·ceous \ˌfar-ə-ˈnā-shəs\ *adj* (1656) **1 :** containing or rich in starch **2 :** having a mealy texture or surface

fa·ri·nha \fə-ˈrēn-yə\ *n* [Pg, flour, cassava meal, fr. L *farina*] (1726) **:** cassava meal

far·kle·ber·ry \ˈfär-kəl-ˌber-ē\ *n* [origin unknown] (1765) **:** a shrub or small tree (*Vaccinium arboreum*) of the heath family of the southeastern U.S. having a black berry with stony seeds

farl *or* **farle** \ˈfär(-ə)l\ *n* [contr. of Sc *fardel,* lit., fourth part, fr. ME (Sc), fr. *ferde del;* fr. *ferde* fourth + *del* part] *Scot* (1686) **:** a small scone

¹farm \ˈfärm\ *n, often attrib* [ME *ferme* rent, lease, fr. OF, lease, fr. *fermer* to fix, make a contract, fr. L *firmare* to make firm, fr. *firmus* firm] (14c) **1** *obs* **:** a sum or due fixed in amount and payable at fixed intervals **2 :** a letting out of revenues or taxes for a fixed sum to one authorized to collect and retain them **3 :** a district or division of a country leased out for the collection of government revenues **4 :** a tract of land devoted to agricultural purposes **5 a :** a plot of land devoted to the raising of animals and esp. domestic livestock **b :** a tract of water reserved for the artificial cultivation of some aquatic life form **6 :** a minor-league team (as in baseball) associated with a major-league team as a subsidiary to which recruits are assigned until needed or for further training

\ə\ abut \ᵊ\ kitten, F table \ər\ further \a\ ash \ā\ ace \ä\ cot, cart \au̇\ out \ch\ chin \e\ bet \ē\ easy \g\ go \i\ hit \ī\ ice \j\ job \ŋ\ sing \ō\ go \ȯ\ law \ȯi\ boy \th\ thin \th\ the \ü\ loot \u̇\ foot \y\ yet \zh\ vision \à, k, ⁿ, œ, œ̄, ue, ue̅, ʸ\ see Guide to Pronunciation

²**farm** *vt* (15c) **1** *obs* : RENT **2** : to collect and take the fees or profits of (an occupation or business) on payment of a fixed sum **3** : to give up (as an estate or a business) to another on condition of receiving in return a fixed sum **4 a** : to devote to agriculture **b** : to manage and cultivate as a farm **c** : to grow or cultivate in quantity ⟨~ shellfish⟩ ⟨~ rice⟩ ~ *vi* : to engage in raising crops, animals, or fish
farm·er \ˈfär-mər\ *n* (14c) **1** : a person who pays a fixed sum for some privilege or source of income **2** : a person who cultivates land or crops or raises animals or fish **3** : YOKEL, BUMPKIN
farmer cheese *n* (1949) : a pressed unripened cheese similar to but drier and firmer than cottage cheese — called also *farm cheese*
farm·er·ette \ˌfär-mə-ˈret\ *n* (1902) : a woman who is a farmer or farmhand
farmer's lung *n* (ca. 1945) : an acute pulmonary disorder that is characterized by sudden onset, fever, cough, expectoration, and breathlessness and that results from the inhalation of dust from moldy hay or straw
farm·hand \ˈfärm-ˌhand\ *n* (1843) : a farm laborer; *esp* : a hired laborer on a farm
farm·house \-ˌhau̇s\ *n* (1598) : a dwelling on a farm
farm·ing *n* (1733) : the practice of agriculture
farm·land \ˈfärm-ˌland\ *n* (1638) : land used or suitable for farming
farm out *vt* (1607) **1** : to turn over for performance (as a job) or use usu. on contract **2 a** : to put (as children or prisoners) into the hands of a private individual for care in return for a fee **b** : to send (as a baseball player) to a farm team **3** : to exhaust (land) by farming esp. by continuously raising one crop
farm·stead \ˈfärm-ˌsted\ *also* **farm·stead·ing** \-iŋ\ *n* (1807) : the buildings and adjacent service areas of a farm
farm·yard \-ˌyärd\ *n* (1748) : space around or enclosed by farm buildings; *esp* : BARNYARD
faro \ˈfa(ə)r-(ˌ)ō, ˈfe(ə)r-\ *n, pl* **faros** [prob. alter. of earlier *pharaoh*, trans. of F *pharaon*] (1735) : a gambling game in which players bet on cards drawn from a dealing box
Faro·ese *var of* FAEROESE
far–off \ˈfär-ˈȯf\ *adj* (15c) : remote in time or space
fa·rouche \fə-ˈrüsh\ *adj* [F, wild, shy, fr. LL *forasticus* belonging outside, fr. L *foras* outdoors; akin to L *fores* door — more at DOOR] (1755) **1** : WILD **2** : marked by shyness and lack of social graces
far–out \ˈfär-ˈau̇t\ *adj* (1954) : marked by a considerable departure from the conventional or traditional ⟨~ clothes⟩ — **far–out·ness** *n*
far·rag·i·nous \fə-ˈraj-ə-nəs\ *adj* (1615) : formed of various materials
far·ra·go \fə-ˈräg-(ˌ)ō, -ˈrā-(ˌ)gō\ *n, pl* **-goes** [L *farragin-, farrago* mixed fodder, mixture, fr. *far* spelt — more at BARLEY] (1632) : a confused mixture : HODGEPODGE
far–reach·ing \ˈfär-ˈrē-chiŋ\ *adj* (1824) : having a wide range or effect
far–red \-ˈred\ *adj* (1951) **1** : lying in the part of the infrared spectrum farthest from the red — used of radiations with wavelengths between 30 and about 1000 microns **2** : lying in the part of the infrared spectrum nearest to the red — used of radiations with wavelengths starting at about .8 micron
far·ri·er \ˈfar-ē-ər\ *n* [alter. of ME *ferrour*, fr. MF *ferrour* blacksmith, fr. OF *ferreor*, fr. *ferrer* to fit with iron, fr. (assumed) VL *ferrare*, fr. L *ferrum* iron] (15c) : one that shoes horses
¹**far·row** \ˈfar-(ˌ)ō, -ə(-w)\ *vb* [ME *farwen*, fr. (assumed) OE *feargian*, fr. OE *fearh* young pig; akin to OHG *farah* young pig, L *porcus* pig] *vt* (bef. 12c) : to give birth to (a farrow) ~ *vi, of swine* : to bring forth young — often used with *down*
²**farrow** *n* (1577) **1** : a litter of pigs **2** : an act of farrowing
³**farrow** *adj* [ME (Sc) *ferow;* prob. akin to OE *fearr* bull, ox — more at PARE] *of a cow* (15c) : not pregnant
far·see·ing \ˈfär-ˈsē-iŋ\ *adj* (1837) : FARSIGHTED 1
Far·si \ˈfär-sē\ *n* [Per *fārsī*, fr. *Fārs* Persia] (ca. 1885) : PERSIAN 2b
far side *n* (15c) : the farther side — **on the far side of** : BEYOND ⟨just *on the far side of* 40⟩
far·sight·ed \ˈfär-ˈsīt-əd\ *adj* (1609) **1 a** : seeing or able to see to a great distance **b** : having foresight or good judgment : SAGACIOUS **2** : affected with hyperopia — **far·sight·ed·ly** *adv*
far·sight·ed·ness *n* (1824) **1** : the quality or state of being farsighted **2** : HYPEROPIA
¹**fart** \ˈfärt\ *vi* [ME *ferten, farten;* akin to OHG *ferzan* to break wind, ON *freta*, Gk *perdesthai*, Skt *pardate* he breaks wind] (13c) : to expel intestinal gas from the anus — usu. considered vulgar
²**fart** *n* (14c) **1** : an expulsion of intestinal gas — usu. considered vulgar **2** : a foolish or contemptible person — usu. considered vulgar
¹**far·ther** \ˈfär-t͟hər\ *adv* [ME *ferther*, alter. of *further*] (14c) **1** : at or to a greater distance or more advanced point ⟨~ down the corridor⟩ **2** : to a greater degree or extent ⟨we do not extend the one-man idea any ~ than we have to —G. F. Eliot⟩

usage *Farther* and *further* have been used more or less interchangeably throughout most of their history, but currently they are showing signs of diverging. As adverbs they continue to be used interchangeably whenever spatial, temporal, or metaphorical distance is involved. But where there is no notion of distance, *further* is used ⟨our techniques can be *further* refined⟩ *Further* is also used as a sentence modifier ⟨*further*, the workshop participants were scarcely optimistic about some brave new world of higher education —L. B. Mayhew⟩ but *farther* is not. A polarizing process appears to be taking place in their adjective use. *Farther* is taking over the meaning of distance ⟨the *farther* shore⟩ and *further* the meaning of addition ⟨needed no *further* invitation⟩

²**farther** *adj* (14c) **1** : more distant : REMOTER **2** : ³FURTHER 2 ⟨clearing his throat preparatory to ~ revelations —Edith Wharton⟩
far·ther·most \-ˌmōst\ *adj* (15c) : most distant : FARTHEST
¹**far·thest** \ˈfär-t͟həst\ *adj* (14c) : most distant esp. in space or time
²**farthest** *adv* (15c) **1** : to or at the greatest distance in space or time ⟨who can jump the ~⟩ **2** : to the most advanced point ⟨goes ~ toward answering the question⟩ **3** : by the greatest degree or extent : MOST ⟨the painting ~ removed from reality⟩
far·thing \ˈfär-t͟hiŋ\ *n* [ME *ferthing*, fr. OE *fēorthung* (akin to MHG *vierdunc* fourth part), fr. OE *fēortha* fourth + *-ung* ²-ing] (bef. 12c) **1 a** : a former British monetary unit equal to ¼ of a penny **b** : a coin representing this unit **2** : something of small value : MITE
far·thin·gale \ˈfär-t͟hən-ˌgāl, -t͟hiŋ-\ *n* [modif. of MF *verdugale*, fr. OSp *verdugado*, fr. *verdugo* young shoot of a tree, fr. *verde* green, fr. L *viridis* — more at VERDANT] (1552) : a support (as of hoops) worn esp. in the 16th century beneath a skirt to expand it at the hipline
fas·ces \ˈfas-ˌēz\ *n pl but sing or pl in constr* [L, fr. pl. of *fascis* bundle; akin to L *fascia*] (1598) : a bundle of rods and among them an ax with projecting blade borne before ancient Roman magistrates as a badge of authority
fas·cia *1b, 1c, & 4 are usu* ˈfāsh-(ē-)ə, *other senses are usu* ˈfash-\ *n, pl* **-ci·ae** \-ē-ˌē\ *or* **-cias** [It, fr. L, band, bandage; akin to MIr *basc* necklace] (1563) **1** *or* **fa·cia** \ˈfāsh(-ē)-ə\ : a flat horizontal member of an order or building having the form of a flat band or broad fillet: as **a** : one of the three bands making up the architrave in the Ionic order **b** *or* **fascia board** : a horizontal piece (as a board) covering the joint between the top of a wall and the projecting eaves **c** : a nameplate over the front of a shop **2** : a broad and well-defined band of color **3** : a sheet of connective tissue covering or binding together body structures; *also* : tissue of this character **4** *or* **fa·cia** \ˈfāsh(-ē)-ə\ *Brit* : the dashboard of an automobile — **fas·cial** \ˈfash-(ē-)əl\ *adj*
fas·ci·at·ed \ˈfash-ē-ˌāt-əd\ *adj* (ca. 1835) **1** : exhibiting fasciation **2** : arranged in fascicles
fas·ci·a·tion \ˌfas(h)-ē-ˈā-shən\ *n* (1677) : a malformation of plant stems commonly manifested as enlargement and flattening as if several were fused
fas·ci·cle \ˈfas-i-kəl\ *n* [L *fasciculus*, dim. of *fascis*] (15c) **1** : a small bundle: as **a** : an inflorescence consisting of a compacted cyme less capitate than a glomerule **b** : FASCICULUS 1 **2** : one of the divisions of a book published in parts — **fas·ci·cled** \-kəld\ *adj*
fas·cic·u·lar \fə-ˈsik-yə-lər, fa-\ *adj* (1805) : of, relating to, or consisting of fascicles or fasciculi — **fas·cic·u·lar·ly** *adv*
fas·cic·u·late \-lət\ *adj* (1794) : FASCICULAR
fas·cic·u·la·tion \fə-ˌsik-yə-ˈlā-shən, fa-\ *n* [NL *fasciculus* + E *-ation* (as in *fibrillation*)] (1938) : muscular twitching involving the simultaneous contraction of contiguous groups of muscle fibers
fas·ci·cule \ˈfas-i-ˌkyü(ə)l\ *n* [F, fr. L *fasciculus*] (1880) : FASCICLE 2
fas·cic·u·lus \fə-ˈsik-yə-ləs, fa-\ *n, pl* **-li** \-ˌlī\ [NL, fr. L] (1713) **1** : a slender bundle of anatomical fibers **2** : FASCICLE 2
fas·ci·nate \ˈfas-ᵊn-ˌāt\ *vb* **-nat·ed; -nat·ing** [L *fascinatus*, pp. of *fascinare*, fr. *fascinum* witchcraft] *vt* (1598) **1** *obs* : BEWITCH **2 a** : to transfix and hold spellbound by an irresistible power ⟨believed that the serpent could ~ its prey⟩ **b** : to command the interest of : ALLURE ⟨was *fascinated* by her personality⟩ ~ *vi* : to be irresistibly attractive ***syn*** see ATTRACT
fas·ci·nat·ing *adj* (1648) : extremely interesting or charming : CAPTIVATING — **fas·ci·nat·ing·ly** \-ˌnāt-iŋ-lē\ *adv*
fas·ci·na·tion \ˌfas-ᵊn-ˈā-shən\ *n* (1605) **1** : the quality or power of fascinating **2** : the state of being fascinated
fas·ci·na·tor \ˈfas-ᵊn-ˌāt-ər\ *n* (1750) **1** : one that fascinates **2** : a woman's lightweight head scarf usu. of crochet or lace
fas·cine \fa-ˈsēn, fə-\ *n* [F, fr. L *fascina*, fr. *fascis*] (1688) : a long bundle of sticks of wood bound together and used for such purposes as filling ditches and making revetments for riverbanks
fa·sci·o·li·a·sis \fə-ˌsē-ə-ˈlī-ə-səs, -ˌsī-\ *n, pl* **-a·ses** \-ˌsēz\ [NL, fr. *Fasciola*, genus of flukes + *-iasis*] (1890) : infestation with or disease caused by liver flukes (genus *Fasciola*)
fas·cism \ˈfash-ˌiz-əm *also* ˈfas-ˌiz-\ *n* [It *fascismo*, fr. *fascio* bundle, fasces, group, fr. L *fascis* bundle & *fasces* fasces] (1921) **1** *often cap* : a political philosophy, movement, or regime (as that of the Fascisti) that exalts nation and often race above the individual and that stands for a centralized autocratic government headed by a dictatorial leader, severe economic and social regimentation, and forcible suppression of opposition **2** : a tendency toward or actual exercise of strong autocratic or dictatorial control ⟨early instances of army ~ and brutality —J. W. Aldridge⟩ — **fas·cist** \-əst\ *n or adj, often cap* — **fas·cis·tic** \fa-ˈshis-tik *also* -ˈsis-\ *adj, often cap* — **fas·cis·ti·cal·ly** \-ti-k(ə-)lē\ *adv, often cap*
Fa·sci·sta \fä-ˈshē-(ˌ)stä\ *n, pl* **-sti** \-(ˌ)stē\ [It, fr. *fascio*] (1921) : a member of an Italian political organization under Mussolini governing Italy 1922–1943 according to the principles of fascism
fas·cist·ize \ˈfash-ə-ˌstīz *also* ˈfas-ə-\ *vt* **-ized; -iz·ing** (1925) : to make over or transform into a Fascista : convert to the principles of fascism — **fas·cist·iza·tion** \ˌfash-ə-stə-ˈzā-shən *also* ˌfas-ə-\ *n*
fash \ˈfash\ *vb* [MF *fascher*, fr. (assumed) VL *fastidiare* to disgust, fr. L *fastidium* disgust — more at FASTIDIOUS] *chiefly Scot* (1533) : VEX — **fash** *n, chiefly Scot*
¹**fash·ion** \ˈfash-ən\ *n* [ME *facioun, fasoun* shape, manner, fr. MF *façon*, fr. L *faction-, factio* act of making, faction, fr. *factus*, pp. of *facere* to make — more at DO] (14c) **1 a** : the make or form of something **b** *archaic* : KIND, SORT **2 a** : an often personal manner or way ⟨he will, after his sour ~, tell you —Shak.⟩ **b** : mode of action or operation ⟨the people assembled in an orderly ~⟩ **3 a** : a prevailing custom, usage, or style **b** (1) : the prevailing style (as in dress) during a particular time (2) : a garment in such a style ⟨always wears the latest ~s⟩ **c** : social standing or prominence esp. as signalized by dress or conduct

syn FASHION, STYLE, MODE, VOGUE, FAD, RAGE, CRAZE mean the usage accepted by those who want to be up-to-date. FASHION is the most general term and applies to any way of dressing, behaving, writing, or performing that is favored at any one time or place; STYLE often implies a distinctive fashion adopted by people of wealth or taste; MODE suggests the fashion of the moment among those anxious to appear elegant and sophisticated; VOGUE stresses the wide acceptance of a fashion; FAD suggests caprice in taking up or in dropping a fashion; RAGE and CRAZE stress intense enthusiasm in adopting a fad. ***syn*** see in addition METHOD

— **after a fashion** : in an approximate or rough way ⟨became an artist *after a fashion*⟩
²**fashion** *vt* **fash·ioned; fash·ion·ing** \ˈfash-(ə-)niŋ\ (15c) **1 a** : to give shape or form to : MOLD **b** : ALTER, TRANSFORM **c** : to mold into a particular character by influencing or training **d** : to make or construct usu. with the use of imagination and ingenuity ⟨~ a lamp from an old churn⟩ **2** : FIT, ADAPT **3** *obs* : CONTRIVE ***syn*** see MAKE — **fash·ion·er** \-(ə-)nər\ *n*

1fash·ion·able \'fash-(ə-)nə-bəl\ *adj* (1606) **1 :** conforming to the custom, fashion, or established mode **2 :** of or relating to the world of fashion — **fash·ion·abil·i·ty** \,fash-(ə-)nə-'bil-ət-ē\ *n* — **fash·ion·able·ness** \'fash-(ə-)nə-bəl-nəs\ *n* — **fash·ion·ably** \-blē\ *adv*

2fashionable *n* (1800) **:** a fashionable person

fash·ion·mon·ger \'fash-ən-,məŋ-gər, -,mäŋ-\ *n* (1599) **:** one that studies, imitates, or sets the fashion

fashion plate *n* (1851) **1 :** an illustration of a clothing style **2 :** a person who dresses in the newest fashion

1fast \'fast\ *adj* [ME, fr. OE *fæst;* akin to OHG *festi* firm, ON *fastr,* Arm *hast*] (bef. 12c) **1 a :** firmly fixed ⟨roots that are ~ in the ground⟩ **b :** tightly shut ⟨all the drawers were ~⟩ **c :** adhering firmly ⟨the glued sheets became ~⟩ **d :** not easily freed **:** STUCK ⟨a shell ~ in the chamber of a gun⟩ **e :** STABLE ⟨movable items were made ~ to the deck⟩ **2 :** firmly loyal ⟨became ~ friends over the years⟩ **3 a :** characterized by quick motion, operation, or effect: **(1) :** moving or able to move rapidly **:** SWIFT **(2) :** taking a comparatively short time **(3) :** imparting quickness of motion ⟨a ~ bowler⟩ **(4) :** accomplished quickly **(5) :** agile of mind; *esp* **:** quick to learn ⟨a special class for ~ students⟩ **b :** conducive to rapidity of play or action ⟨a ~ track⟩ **c (1)** *of a timepiece or weighing device* **:** indicating in advance of what is correct **(2) :** according to daylight saving time **d :** contributing to a shortening of exposure time ⟨~ film⟩ **e :** acquired with unusually little effort and often by shady or dishonest methods ⟨made some ~ money on the numbers⟩ **4 a :** securely attached ⟨a rope ~ to the wharf⟩ **b :** TENACIOUS ⟨kept a ~ hold on her purse⟩ **5 a** *archaic* **:** sound asleep **b** *of sleep* **:** not easily disturbed **6 :** permanently dyed **7 a :** WILD ⟨runs around with a pretty ~ bunch⟩ **b :** sexually promiscuous **8 :** resistant to change (as from destructive action or fading) — often used in combination ⟨sun*fast*⟩ ⟨acid-*fast* bacteria⟩

syn FAST, RAPID, SWIFT, FLEET, QUICK, SPEEDY, HASTY, EXPEDITIOUS mean moving, proceeding, or acting with celerity. FAST and RAPID are very close in meaning, but FAST applies particularly to the thing that moves ⟨*fast* horse⟩ RAPID to the movement itself ⟨*rapid* current⟩ SWIFT suggests great rapidity coupled with ease of movement ⟨returned the ball with one *swift* stroke⟩ FLEET adds the implication of lightness and nimbleness ⟨*fleet* runners⟩ QUICK suggests promptness and the taking of little time ⟨a *quick* wit⟩ SPEEDY implies quickness of successful accomplishment ⟨*speedy* delivery of the mail⟩ and may also suggest unusual velocity; HASTY suggests hurry and precipitousness and often connotes carelessness; EXPEDITIOUS suggests efficiency together with rapidity of accomplishment.

2fast *adv* (bef. 12c) **1 :** in a firm or fixed manner **2 :** in a sound manner **:** DEEPLY ⟨fell ~ asleep⟩ **3 a :** in a rapid manner **:** QUICKLY **b :** in quick succession ⟨kaleidoscopic impressions that come so thick and ~ —M. B. Tucker⟩ **4 :** in a reckless manner **:** DISSIPATEDLY **5 :** ahead of a correct time or posted schedule **6** *archaic* **:** CLOSE, NEAR

3fast *vi* [ME *fasten,* fr. OE *fæstan;* akin to OHG *fastēn* to fast] (bef. 12c) **1 :** to abstain from food **2 :** to eat sparingly or abstain from some foods

4fast *n* (bef. 12c) **1 :** the practice of fasting **2 :** a time of fasting

5fast *n* [alter. of ME *fest,* fr. ON *festr* rope, mooring cable, fr. *fastr* firm] (15c) **:** something that fastens or holds a fastening

fast and loose *adv* (1595) **1 :** in a craftily deceitful way ⟨manipulated evidence ... and played *fast and loose* with the truth —C. V. Woodward⟩ **2 :** in a reckless or irresponsible manner ⟨playing *fast and loose* with his wife's money⟩

fast·back \'fas(t)-,bak\ *n* (1954) **:** an automobile roof with a long curving downward slope to the rear; *also* **:** an automobile with such a roof

fast·ball \'fas(t)-,bȯl\ *n* (1912) **:** a baseball pitch thrown at full speed and often rising slightly as it nears the plate

fast break *n* (1948) **:** a quick offensive drive toward a goal (as in basketball) in an attempt to score before the opponent's defense is set up — **fast–break** *vi*

fas·ten \'fas-ᵊn\ *vb* **fas·tened; fas·ten·ing** \'fas-niŋ, -ᵊn-iŋ\ [ME *fastnen,* fr. OE *fæstnian* to make fast; akin to OHG *festinōn* to make fast, OE *fæst* 1fast] *vt* (bef. 12c) **1 a :** to attach esp. by pinning, tying, or nailing **b :** to make fast and secure **c :** to fix firmly or securely **d :** to secure against opening **2 :** to fix or set steadily ⟨~*ed* his attention on the main problem⟩ **3 :** to take a firm grip with ⟨the dog ~*ed* his teeth in the old shoe⟩ **4 a :** to attach (oneself) persistently and usu. objectionably **b :** IMPOSE ⟨~*ed* the blame on the wrong man⟩ ~ *vi* **1 :** to become fast or fixed **2 :** to take a firm grip or hold **b :** to focus attention — **fas·ten·er** \'fas-nər, -ᵊn-ər\ *n*

syn FASTEN, FIX, ATTACH, AFFIX mean to make something stay firmly in place. FASTEN implies an action such as tying, buttoning, nailing, locking, or otherwise securing; FIX usu. implies a driving in, implanting, or embedding; ATTACH suggests a connecting or uniting by a bond, link, or tie in order to keep things together; AFFIX implies an imposing of one thing on another by gluing, impressing, or nailing.

fas·ten·ing *n* (bef. 12c) **:** something that fastens **:** FASTENER

fast–food \,fas(t)-,füd\ *adj* (1969) **:** specializing in food that can be prepared and served quickly ⟨a ~ restaurant⟩

fast–for·ward \,fas(t)-'fȯr-,wərd\ *n* (1948) **:** a function of a tape player by which the tape is advanced at a higher speed than when it is playing normally

fas·tid·i·ous \fa-'stid-ē-əs, fə-\ *adj* [ME, fr. L *fastidiosus,* fr. *fastidium* disgust, prob. fr. *fastus* arrogance (akin to L *fastigium* top) + *taedium* irksomeness — more at TEDIUM] (15c) **1** *archaic* **:** SCORNFUL **2 a :** having high and often capricious standards **:** difficult to satisfy or please ⟨highbrow critics ... so ~ that they can talk only to a small circle of initiates —Granville Hicks⟩ **b :** showing or demanding excessive delicacy or care **c :** reflecting a meticulous, sensitive, or demanding attitude ⟨~ workmanship⟩ **3 :** having complex nutritional requirements ⟨~ microorganisms⟩ — **fas·tid·i·ous·ly** *adv* — **fas·tid·i·ous·ness** *n*

fas·ti·gi·ate \fa-'stij-ē-ət\ *adj* [prob. fr. (assumed) NL *fastigiatus,* fr. L *fastigium*] (1662) **:** narrowing toward the top; *esp* **:** having upright usu. clustered branches

fast lane *n* (1980) **:** a way of life marked by fast living and the ready flow of money — used esp. in the phrase *life in the fast lane*

fast·ness \'fas(t)-nəs\ *n* (bef. 12c) **1 :** the quality or state of being fast: as **a :** the quality or state of being fixed **b :** the quality or state of being swift **c :** colorfast quality **d :** resistance (as of an organism) to the action of a usu. toxic substance **2 a :** a fortified or secure place **b :** a remote and secluded place ⟨vacationed in his mountain ~⟩

Fast of Esther (ca. 1901) **:** a Jewish fast day observed the day before Purim in commemoration of a fast proclaimed by Queen Esther

fast–talk \'fas(t)-'tȯk\ *vt* (1946) **:** to influence or persuade by fluent, facile, and usu. deceptive or tricky talk ⟨~*ed* him into buying a lemon⟩

fast track *n* (1980) **:** a course leading to rapid advancement or success — **fast–track** *adj*

fas·tu·ous \'fas-chə-wəs\ *adj* [L *fastuosus,* fr. *fastus* arrogance] (1638) **1 :** HAUGHTY, ARROGANT ⟨a ~ air of finality —Carl Van Vechten⟩ **2 :** OSTENTATIOUS, SHOWY ⟨disdained ~ ceremonies⟩

1fat \'fat\ *adj* **fat·ter; fat·test** [ME, fr. OE *fætt,* pp. of *fǣtan* to cram; akin to OHG *feizit* fat, L *opimus* fat, copious] (bef. 12c) **1 :** notable for having an unusual amount of fat: **a :** PLUMP **b :** OBESE **c** *of a meat animal* **:** fattened for market **d** *of food* **:** OILY, GREASY **2 a :** well filled out **:** THICK, BIG ⟨a ~ volume of verse⟩ **b :** FULL, RICH ⟨a gorgeous ~ bass voice —*Irish Digest*⟩ **c :** well stocked ⟨a ~ refrigerator⟩ **d :** PROSPEROUS, WEALTHY ⟨grew ~ on the war —*Time*⟩ **e :** being substantial and impressive ⟨a ~ bank account⟩ **3 a :** richly rewarding or profitable ⟨a ~ part in a new play⟩ ⟨accepted a ~ contract⟩ **b :** practically nonexistent ⟨a ~ chance⟩ **4 :** PRODUCTIVE, FERTILE ⟨a ~ year for crops⟩ **5 a** *of soil* **:** containing minerals that cause a greasy feel **b** *of wood* **:** having a high resin content **6 :** STUPID, FOOLISH **7 :** being swollen ⟨got a ~ lip from the fight⟩ — **fat·ness** *n*

2fat *n* (bef. 12c) **1 :** animal tissue consisting chiefly of cells distended with greasy or oily matter **2 a :** oily or greasy matter making up the bulk of adipose tissue and often abundant in seeds **b :** any of numerous compounds of carbon, hydrogen, and oxygen that are glycerides of fatty acids, the chief constituents of plant and animal fat, and a major class of energy-rich food, that are soluble in organic solvents (as ether) but not in water, and that are widely used industrially **c :** a solid or semisolid fat as distinguished from an oil **3 :** the best or richest part **4 :** OBESITY **5 :** something in excess **:** SUPERFLUITY

3fat *vt* **fat·ted; fat·ting** (14c) **:** to make fat **:** FATTEN

fa·tal \'fāt-ᵊl\ *adj* [ME, fr. MF & L; MF, fr. L *fatalis,* fr. *fatum*] (14c) **1** *obs* **:** FATED **2 :** FATEFUL ⟨a ~ hour⟩ **3 a :** of or relating to fate **b :** resembling fate in proceeding according to a fixed sequence **c :** determining one's fate **4 a :** causing death **b :** bringing ruin ***syn*** see DEADLY

fa·tal·ism \-,iz-əm\ *n* (1678) **:** a doctrine that events are fixed in advance for all time in such a manner that human beings are powerless to change them; *also* **:** a belief in or attitude determined by this doctrine — **fa·tal·ist** \-əst\ *n* — **fa·tal·is·tic** \,fāt-ᵊl-'is-tik\ *adj* — **fa·tal·is·ti·cal·ly** \-ti-k(ə-)lē\ *adv*

fa·tal·i·ty \fā-'tal-ət-ē, fə-\ *n, pl* **-ties** [ME, fr. MF *fatalité,* fr. LL *fatalitat-, fatalitas,* fr. L *fatalis*] (15c) **1 a :** the quality or state of causing death or destruction **:** DEADLINESS **b :** the quality or condition of being destined for disaster **2 :** something established by fate **3 a :** FATE 1 **b :** FATALISM **4 :** the agent or agency of fate **5 a :** death resulting from a disaster **b :** one that experiences or is subject to a fatal outcome ⟨one of the *fatalities* was a small child⟩

fa·tal·ly \'fāt-ᵊl-ē\ *adv* (15c) **1 :** in a way determined by fate **2 :** in a manner suggesting fate or an act of fate: as **a :** in a manner resulting in death **:** MORTALLY ⟨~ wounded⟩ **b :** beyond repair **:** IRREVOCABLY **c :** in a manner resulting in ruin or evil ⟨it is ~ easy to pass off our prejudices as our opinions —W. F. Hambly⟩ **d :** in a manner that cannot be easily resisted ⟨thinks she is ~ attractive —J. W. Krutch⟩

fa·ta mor·ga·na \,fät-ə-mȯr-'gän-ə, -'gan-\ *n* [It, lit., Morgan the fay] (1818) **:** MIRAGE

fat·back \'fat-,bak\ *n* (1903) **:** the strip of fat from the back of a hog carcass usu. cured by drying and salting — see PORK illustration

fat body *n* (1869) **:** an insect fatty tissue esp. of nearly mature larvae that serves as a food reserve

fat cat *n* (1928) **1 a :** a wealthy contributor to a political campaign fund **b :** a wealthy and privileged person **c :** BIG SHOT **2 :** a lethargic complacent person

fat cell *n* (1845) **:** one of the fat-laden cells making up adipose tissue

fat depot *n* (1946) **:** ADIPOSE TISSUE

1fate \'fāt\ *n* [ME, fr. MF or L; MF, fr. L *fatum,* lit., what has been spoken, fr. neut. of *fatus,* pp. of *fari* to speak — more at BAN] (14c) **1 :** the principle or determining cause or will by which things in general are believed to come to be as they are or events to happen as they do **:** DESTINY **2 a :** an inevitable and often adverse outcome, condition, or end **b :** DISASTER; *esp* **:** DEATH **3 a :** final outcome **b :** the expected result of normal development ⟨prospective ~ of embryonic cells⟩ **4** *pl, cap* **:** the three goddesses who determine the course of human life in classical mythology

syn FATE, DESTINY, LOT, PORTION, DOOM mean a predetermined state or end. FATE implies an inevitable and usu. an adverse outcome; DESTINY implies something foreordained and often suggests a great or noble course or end; LOT and PORTION imply a distribution by fate or destiny, LOT suggesting blind chance, PORTION implying the apportioning of good and evil; DOOM distinctly implies a grim or calamitous fate.

2fate *vt* **fat·ed; fat·ing** (1601) **:** DESTINE; *also* **:** DOOM ⟨the deep antipathy ... seeming to ~ them to antagonism —Les Savage⟩

fat·ed *adj* (1715) **:** decreed, controlled, or marked by fate

fate·ful \'fāt-fəl\ *adj* (1715) **1 :** having a quality of ominous prophecy ⟨a ~ remark⟩ **2 a :** involving momentous consequences **:** DECISIVE ⟨made his ~ decision to declare war —W. L. Shirer⟩ **b :** DEADLY, CATASTROPHIC **3 :** controlled by fate **:** FOREORDAINED ***syn*** see OMINOUS — **fate·ful·ly** \-fə-lē\ *adv* — **fate·ful·ness** *n*

fat·head \'fat-,hed\ *n* (1842) **:** a slow-witted or stupid person **:** FOOL — **fat·head·ed** \-'hed-əd\ *adj* — **fat·head·ed·ly** *adv* — **fat·head·ed·ness** *n*

1fa·ther \'fäth-ər, 'fäth-\ *n* [ME *fader,* fr. OE *fæder;* akin to OHG *fater* father, L *pater,* Gk *patēr*] (bef. 12c) **1 a :** a man who has begotten a child; *also* **:** SIRE 3 **b** *cap* **(1) :** GOD 1 **(2) :** the first person of the Trinity **2 :** FOREFATHER **3 a :** one related to another in a way suggesting that of father to child **b** : an old man — used as a respectful form of address **4** *often cap* : a pre-Scholastic Christian writer accepted by the church as an authoritative witness to its teaching and practice — called also *church father* **5 a** : one that originates or institutes ⟨the ~ of modern science⟩ **b** : SOURCE ⟨the sun, the ~ of warmth and light — Lena M. Whitney⟩ **c** : PROTOTYPE **6** : a priest of the regular clergy; *broadly* : PRIEST — used esp. as a title **7** : one of the leading men (as of a city) — usu. used in pl. — **fa·ther·hood** \-ˌhu̇d\ *n* — **fa·ther·less** \-ləs\ *adj*

²**father** *vb* **fa·thered; fa·ther·ing** \ˈfät͟h-(ə-)riŋ, ˈfät͟h-\ *vt* (15c) **1 a** : BEGET **b** : to make oneself the founder, producer, or author of ⟨~*ed* a plan for improving the city's schools⟩ **c** : to accept responsibility for **2** : to fix the paternity or origin of **3** : FOIST, IMPOSE ~ *vi* : to care for or look after someone as a father might

Father Christmas *n, Brit* : SANTA CLAUS

father figure *n* (1934) : one often of particular power or influence who serves as an emotional substitute for a father

father image *n* (1937) : an idealization of one's father often projected onto someone to whom one looks for guidance and protection

father–in–law \ˈfät͟h-(ə-)rən-ˌlȯ, -ərn-ˌlȯ, ˈfät͟h-\ *n, pl* **fa·thers–in–law** \-ər-zən-\ (14c) **1** : the father of one's spouse **2** *archaic* : STEPFATHER

fa·ther·land \ˈfät͟h-ər-ˌland, ˈfät͟h-\ *n* (1623) **1** : one's native land or country **2** : the native land or country of one's father or ancestors

fa·ther·like \-ˌlīk\ *adj or adv* (1570) : FATHERLY

fa·ther·li·ness \-lē-nəs\ *n* (1551) : paternal quality

fa·ther·ly \ˈfät͟h-ər-lē, fät͟h-\ *adj* (bef. 12c) **1** : of, relating to, or befitting a father ⟨~ responsibilities⟩ **2** : resembling a father (as in affection or care) ⟨a ~ old man⟩ — **fatherly** *adv*

Father's Day *n* (1927) : the third Sunday in June appointed for the honoring of fathers

¹**fath·om** \ˈfat͟h-əm\ *n* [ME *fadme,* fr. OE *fæthm* outstretched arms, length of the outstretched arms; akin to ON *fathmr* fathom, L *patēre* to be open, *pandere* to spread out, Gk *petannynai*] (bef. 12c) **1** : a unit of length equal to six feet used esp. for measuring the depth of water **2** : COMPREHENSION

²**fathom** *vt* (1634) **1** : to measure by a sounding line **2** : to penetrate and come to understand ⟨couldn't ~ the problem⟩ ~ *vi* **1** : to take soundings **2** : PROBE — **fath·om·able** \ˈfat͟h-ə-mə-bəl\ *adj*

Fa·thom·e·ter \fa-ˈt͟häm-ət-ər, ˈfat͟h-ə(m)-ˌmēt-\ *trademark* — used for a sonic depth finder

fath·om·less \ˈfat͟h-əm-ləs\ *adj* (1638) : incapable of being fathomed — **fath·om·less·ly** *adv* — **fath·om·less·ness** *n*

fa·tid·ic \fā-ˈtid-ik, fə-\ *or* **fa·tid·i·cal** \-i-kəl\ *adj* [L *fatidicus,* fr. *fatum* fate + *dicere* to say — more at DICTION] (1671) : of or relating to prophecy

fa·ti·ga·bil·i·ty \fə-ˌtē-gə-ˈbil-ət-ē, ˌfat-i-gə-\ *n* (1908) : susceptibility to fatigue

fa·ti·ga·ble \fə-ˈtē-gə-bəl, ˈfat-i-gə-\ *adj* (1608) : susceptible to fatigue

¹**fa·tigue** \fə-ˈtēg\ *n* [F, fr. MF, fr. *fatiguer* to fatigue, fr. L *fatigare;* akin to L *affatim* sufficiently and prob. to L *fames* hunger] (1669) **1 a** : LABOR **b** : manual or menial work performed by military personnel **c** *pl* : the uniform or work clothing worn on fatigue and in the field **2 a** (1) : weariness from labor or exertion (2) : nervous exhaustion **b** : the temporary loss of power to respond induced in a sensory receptor or motor end organ by continued stimulation **3** : the tendency of a material to break under repeated stress

²**fatigue** *vb* **fa·tigued; fa·tigu·ing** *vt* (1693) **1** : to weary with labor or exertion **2** : to induce a condition of fatigue in ~ *vi* : to suffer fatigue ***syn*** see TIRE — **fa·tigu·ing·ly** \-ˈtē-giŋ-lē\ *adv*

³**fatigue** *adj* (1774) **1** : consisting of, done, or used in fatigue ⟨~ detail⟩ **2** : belonging to fatigues ⟨a ~ cap⟩

fat·ling \ˈfat-liŋ\ *n* (1526) : a young animal fattened for slaughter

fat·ly *adv* (15c) **1** : RICHLY **2** : in the manner of one that is fat **3** : in a smug manner : COMPLACENTLY ⟨snickered ~ at his wife's mistake⟩

fats·hed·era \fats-ˈ(h)ed-ə-rə\ *n* [NL *Fatsia,* genus of shrubs + *Hedera,* genus of vines, fr. L, ivy] (1948) : a vigorous upright hybrid ornamental foliage plant (*Hedera helix* × *Aralia elata*) with glossy deeply lobed palmate leaves

fat·so \ˈfat-(ˌ)sō\ *n, pl* **fatsoes** [prob. fr. *Fats,* nickname for a fat person + *-o*] (1944) : a fat person — often used as a disparaging form of address

fat–sol·u·ble \ˈfat-ˌsäl-yə-bəl\ *adj* (1921) : soluble in fats or fat solvents

fat·stock \-ˌstäk\ *n, chiefly Brit* (1880) : livestock that is fat and ready for market

fat–tailed sheep \ˌfat-ˌtāld-\ *n* (1842) : a coarse-wooled mutton sheep that has great quantities of fat on each side of the tail bones

fat·ten \ˈfat-ᵊn\ *vb* **fat·tened; fat·ten·ing** \ˈfat-niŋ, -ᵊn-iŋ\ *vt* (bef. 12c) **1 a** : to make fat, fleshy, or plump; *esp* : to feed (as a stock animal) for slaughter **b** : to make more substantial **2** : to make fertile ~ *vi* : to become fat — **fat·ten·er** \ˈfat-nər, -ᵊn-ər\ *n*

fat·tish \ˈfat-ish\ *adj* (14c) : somewhat fat

¹**fat·ty** \ˈfat-ē\ *adj* **fat·ti·er; -est** (14c) **1** : containing fat esp. in unusual amounts; *also* : unduly stout : CORPULENT **2** : GREASY **3** : derived from or chemically related to fat — **fat·ti·ness** *n*

²**fatty** *n, pl* **fatties** (1797) : one that is fat; *esp* : an overweight person

fatty acid *n* (ca. 1863) **1** : any of numerous saturated aliphatic monocarboxylic acids $C_nH_{2n+1}COOH$ (as acetic acid) including many that occur naturally usu. in the form of esters in fats, waxes, and essential oils **2** : any of the saturated or unsaturated monocarboxylic acids (as palmitic acid) usu. with an even number of carbon atoms that occur naturally in the form of glycerides in fats and fatty oils

fa·tu·ity \fə-ˈt(y)ü-ət-ē, fa-, -ˈchü-\ *n, pl* **-ities** [MF *fatuité* foolishness, fr. L *fatuitat-, fatuitas,* fr. *fatuus*] (1538) **1 a** : something foolish or stupid **b** : STUPIDITY, FOOLISHNESS **2** *archaic* : IMBECILITY, DEMENTIA

fat·u·ous \ˈfach-(ə-)wəs\ *adj* [L *fatuus* foolish — more at BATTLE] (1633) : complacently or inanely foolish : SILLY ***syn*** see SIMPLE — **fat·u·ous·ly** *adv* — **fat·u·ous·ness** *n*

fat–wit·ted \ˈfat-ˈwit-əd\ *adj* (1596) : STUPID, IDIOTIC

fau·bourg \fō-ˈbu̇(ə)r\ *n* [ME *fabour,* fr. MF *fauxbourg,* alter. of *forsbourg,* fr. OF *forsborc,* fr. *fors* outside + *borc* town — more at BOURG] (15c) **1** : SUBURB; *esp* : a suburb of a French city **2** : a city quarter

fau·ces \ˈfȯ-ˌsēz\ *n pl but sing or pl in constr* [L, pl., throat, fauces] (1541) : the narrow passage from the mouth to the pharynx situated between the soft palate and the base of the tongue — **fau·cial** \ˈfȯ-shəl\ *adj*

fau·cet \ˈfȯs-ət, ˈfäs-\ *n* [ME, bung, faucet, fr. MF *fausset* bung, fr. *fausser* to damage, fr. LL *falsare* to falsify, fr. L *falsus* false] (15c) : a fixture for drawing a liquid from a pipe, cask, or other vessel

faugh *a strong* p-*sound or lip trill; often read as* ˈfȯ(k)\ *interj* (1542) — used to express contempt, disgust, or abhorrence

¹**fault** \ˈfȯlt\ *n* [ME *faute,* fr. MF, fr. (assumed) VL *fallita,* fr. fem. of *fallitus,* pp. of L *fallere* to deceive, disappoint — more at FAIL] (14c) **1** *obs* : LACK **2 a** : WEAKNESS, FAILING; *esp* : a moral weakness less serious than a vice **b** : a physical or intellectual imperfection or impairment **c** : an error esp. in service in a net or racket game **3 a** : MISDEMEANOR **b** : MISTAKE **4** : responsibility for wrongdoing or failure ⟨the accident was the driver's ~⟩ **5** : a fracture in the earth's crust accompanied by a displacement of one side of the fracture with respect to the other and in a direction parallel to the fracture

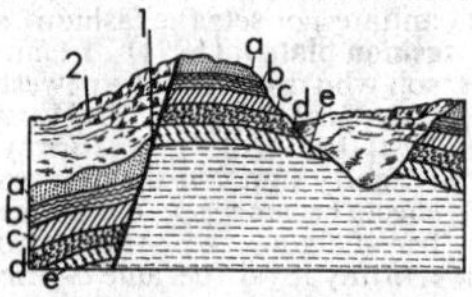

fault 5: *1* fault with displaced strata *a, b, c, d, e; 2* scarp

syn FAULT, FAILING, FRAILTY, FOIBLE, VICE mean an imperfection or weakness of character. FAULT implies a failure, not necessarily culpable, to reach some standard of perfection in disposition, action, or habit; FAILING suggests a minor shortcoming in character; FRAILTY implies a general or chronic proneness to yield to temptation; FOIBLE applies to a harmless or endearing weakness or idiosyncrasy; VICE can be a general term for any imperfection or weakness, but it often suggests violation of a moral code or the giving of offense to the moral sensibilities of others.

— **at fault 1** : unable to find the scent and continue chase **2** : open to blame : RESPONSIBLE ⟨couldn't determine who was really *at fault*⟩ — **to a fault** : to an excessive degree ⟨particular *to a fault*⟩

²**fault** *vi* (15c) **1** : to commit a fault : ERR **2** : to fracture so as to produce a geologic fault ~ *vt* **1** : to find a fault in ⟨equally easy to praise this book and to ~ it —H. G. Roepke⟩ **2** : to produce a geologic fault in **3** : BLAME, CENSURE ⟨one cannot ~ him for publishing as much as he did —R. M. Elman⟩

fault·find·er \ˈfȯlt-ˌfīn-dər\ *n* (1561) : one given to faultfinding

¹**fault·find·ing** \-diŋ\ *adj* (1622) : disposed to find fault : captiously critical ***syn*** see CRITICAL

²**faultfinding** *n* (1626) : CRITICISM; *esp* : petty, nagging, or unreasonable censure

fault·less \ˈfȯlt-ləs\ *adj* (14c) : having no fault : IRREPROACHABLE ⟨~ workmanship⟩ — **fault·less·ly** *adv* — **fault·less·ness** *n*

faulty \ˈfȯl-tē\ *adj* **fault·i·er; -est** (14c) : marked by fault, blemish, or defect : IMPERFECT — **fault·i·ly** \-tə-lē\ *adv* — **fault·i·ness** \-tē-nəs\ *n*

faun \ˈfȯn, ˈfän\ *n* [ME, fr. L *faunus,* fr. *Faunus*] (14c) : a figure in Roman mythology similar to the satyr

fau·na \ˈfȯn-ə, ˈfän-\ *n, pl* **faunas** *also* **fau·nae** \-ˌē, -ˌī\ [NL, fr. LL *Fauna,* sister of Faunus] (1771) : animal life; *esp* : the animals characteristic of a region, period, or special environment — compare FLORA — **fau·nal** \-ᵊl\ *adj* — **fau·nal·ly** \-ᵊl-ē\ *adv*

fau·nis·tic \fȯ-ˈnis-tik, fä-\ *adj* (1881) : of or relating to zoogeography : FAUNAL — **fau·nis·ti·cal·ly** \-ti-k(ə-)lē\ *adv*

Fau·nus \ˈfȯn-əs, ˈfän-\ *n* [L] : the Roman god of animals

Faust \ˈfau̇st\ *or* **Fau·stus** \ˈfau̇-stəs, ˈfȯ-\ *n* [G] : a magician of German legend who enters into a compact with the devil

Faust·ian \ˈfau̇-stē-ən, ˈfȯ-\ *adj* (1876) : of, belonging to, resembling, or befitting Faust or Faustus: as **a** : sacrificing spiritual values for material gains **b** : striving insatiably for knowledge and mastery **c** : constantly troubled and tormented by spiritual dissatisfaction or spiritual striving

faute de mieux \ˌfōt-də-ˈmyə(r), -ˈmyœ\ *adv* [F] (1766) : for lack of something better or more desirable ⟨sherry made him dopey but he drank it *faute de mieux* —F. T. Marsh⟩

fau·vism \ˈfō-ˌviz-əm\ *n, often cap* [F *fauvisme,* fr. *fauve* wild animal, fr. *fauve* tawny, wild, of Gmc origin; akin to OHG *falo* fallow — more at FALLOW] (1922) : a movement in painting typified by the work of Matisse and characterized by vivid colors, free treatment of form, and a resulting vibrant and decorative effect — **fau·vist** \-vəst\ *n, often cap*

faux \ˈfō\ *adj* [F, false] (1975) : IMITATION, ERSATZ ⟨~ marble⟩

faux pas \ˈfō-ˌpä, fō-ˈ\ *n, pl* **faux pas** \-ˌpä(z), -ˈpä(z)\ [F, lit., false step] (1676) : BLUNDER; *esp* : a social blunder

fa·va bean \ˌfäv-ə-\ *n* [It *fava,* fr. L *faba* bean] (ca. 1943) : BROAD BEAN

fa·vo·ni·an \fə-ˈvō-nē-ən\ *adj* [L *favonianus,* fr. *Favonius,* the west wind] (ca. 1656) : of or relating to the west wind : MILD

¹**fa·vor** \ˈfā-vər\ *n* [ME, friendly regard, attractiveness, fr. OF *favor* friendly regard, fr. L, fr. *favēre* to be favorable; akin to OHG *gouma* attention, OSlav *gověti* to revere] (14c) **1 a** (1) : friendly regard shown toward another esp. by a superior (2) : approving consideration or attention : APPROBATION **b** : PARTIALITY **c** *archaic* : LENIENCY **d** *archaic* : PERMISSION **e** : POPULARITY **2** *archaic* **a** : APPEARANCE **b** (1) : FACE (2) : a facial feature **3 a** : gracious kindness; *also* : an act of such kindness **b** *archaic* : AID, ASSISTANCE **c** *pl* : effort in one's behalf or interest : ATTENTION **4 a** : a token of love (as a ribbon) usu. worn conspicuously **b** : a small gift or decorative item given out at a party **c** : BADGE **5 a** : a special privilege or right granted or conceded **b** : sexual privileges — usu. used in pl. **6** *archaic* : LETTER **7** : BEHALF, INTEREST — **in favor of 1 a** : in accord or sympathy with **b** : for the acquittal of ⟨returned a verdict *in favor of* the accused⟩ **c** : in support of **2** : to the order of **3** : in order to choose : out of preference for ⟨was offered athletic scholarships . . . but he turned them down *in favor of* a career in professional baseball —*Current Biog.*⟩ — **in one's favor 1** : in one's good graces ⟨doing extra work to get back *in the teacher's favor*⟩ **2** : to one's advantage ⟨the odds were *in his favor*⟩ — **out of favor** : UNPOPULAR, DISLIKED ⟨was *out of favor* with his neighbors⟩

²**favor** *vt* **fa·vored; fa·vor·ing** \ˈfāv-(ə-)riŋ\ (14c) **1 a** : to regard or treat with favor **b** (1) : to do a kindness for : OBLIGE (2) : ENDOW **c** : to treat gently or carefully : SPARE ⟨~*ed* his injured leg⟩ **2** : to show partiality toward : PREFER **3 a** : to give support or confirmation to : SUSTAIN **b** : to afford advantages for success to : FACILITATE ⟨good

weather ~*ed* the outing⟩ **4 :** to bear a resemblance to ⟨he ~*s* his father⟩ — **fa·vor·er** \ˈfā-vər-ər\ *n*

fa·vor·able \ˈfāv-(ə-)rə-bəl, ˈfā-vər-bəl\ *adj* (14c) **1 a :** disposed to favor : PARTIAL **b :** expressing approval : COMMENDATORY **c :** giving a result that is in one's favor ⟨a ~ comparison⟩ **d :** AFFIRMATIVE **2 :** winning approval : PLEASING **3 a :** tending to promote or facilitate : ADVANTAGEOUS ⟨~ wind⟩ **b :** marked by success — **fa·vor·able·ness** *n* — **fa·vor·ably** \-blē\ *adv*

syn FAVORABLE, AUSPICIOUS, PROPITIOUS mean pointing toward a happy outcome. FAVORABLE implies that the persons involved are approving or helpful or that the circumstances are advantageous; AUSPICIOUS applies to something taken as a sign or omen promising success before or at the beginning of an event; PROPITIOUS may also apply to beginnings but often implies a continuing favorable condition.

fa·vored \ˈfā-vərd\ *adj* (15c) **1 :** having an appearance or features of a particular kind ⟨hard-*favored*⟩ **2 :** endowed with special advantages or gifts **3 :** providing preferential treatment

¹fa·vor·ite \ˈfāv-(ə-)rət, ˈfā-vərt, *chiefly substand* ˈfāv-(ə-),rīt\ *n* [It *favorito,* pp. of *favorire* to favor, fr. *favore* favor, fr. L *favor*] (1583) **1 :** one that is treated or regarded with special favor or liking; *specif* **:** one unusually loved, trusted, or provided with favors by a person of high rank or authority **2 :** a competitor (as a horse in a race) judged most likely to win

²favorite *adj* (1711) **:** constituting a favorite; *specif* **:** markedly popular

favorite son *n* (1788) **1 :** one favored by the delegates of his state as presidential candidate at a national political convention **2 :** a famous person who is popular with hometown people

fa·vor·it·ism \ˈfāv-(ə-)rət-,iz-əm, ˈfā-vərt-,iz-\ *n* (1763) **1 :** the showing of special favor : PARTIALITY **2 :** the state or fact of being a favorite

fa·vour *chiefly Brit var of* FAVOR

fa·vus \ˈfā-vəs\ *n* [NL, fr. L, honeycomb] (ca. 1706) **:** a contagious skin disease caused by a fungus (as *Achorion schoenleinii*) occurring in man and many domestic animals and fowls

¹fawn *vi* [ME *faunen,* fr. OE *fagnian* to rejoice, fr. *fægen, fagan* glad — more at FAIN] (13c) **1 :** to show affection — used esp. of a dog **2 :** to court favor by a cringing or flattering manner — **fawn·er** *n* — **fawn·ing·ly** \-iŋ-lē\ *adv*

syn FAWN, TOADY, TRUCKLE, CRINGE, COWER mean to behave abjectly before a superior. FAWN implies seeking favor by servile flattery or exaggerated attention; TOADY suggests the attempt to ingratiate oneself by an abjectly menial or subservient attitude; TRUCKLE implies the subordination of onself and one's desires or judgment to those of a superior; CRINGE suggests a bowing or shrinking in fear or servility; COWER suggests a display of abject fear in the company of threatening or domineering people.

²fawn \ˈfȯn, ˈfän\ *n* [ME *foun,* fr. MF *feon, faon* young of an animal, fr. (assumed) VL *feton-, feto,* fr. L *fetus* offspring — more at FETUS] (14c) **1 :** a young deer; *esp* **:** one still unweaned or retaining a distinctive baby coat **2 :** KID 1 **3 :** a variable color averaging a light grayish brown

fawn lily *n* (ca. 1894) **:** DOGTOOTH VIOLET

fawny \ˈfȯn-ē, ˈfän-\ *adj* (1849) **:** of a color approximating fawn

fax \ˈfaks\ *n* [by shortening & alter.] (1948) **:** FACSIMILE 2 — **fax** *vt*

¹fay \ˈfā\ *vb* [ME *feien,* fr. OE *fēgan;* akin to OHG *fuogen* to fit, L *pangere* to fasten — more at PACT] (bef. 12c) **:** to fit or join closely or tightly

²fay *n* [ME *fai, fei,* fr. OF *feid, fei* — more at FAITH] *obs* (13c) **:** FAITH

³fay *n* [ME *faie,* fr. MF *feie, fee* — more at FAIRY] (14c) **:** FAIRY, ELF

⁴fay *adj* (14c) **:** resembling an elf

⁵fay *n* (1927) **:** OFAY

faze \ˈfāz\ *vt* **fazed; faz·ing** [alter. of *feeze* (to drive away, frighten), fr. ME *fesen,* fr. OE *fēsian* to drive away] (1830) **:** to disturb the composure of : DISCONCERT, DAUNT

F clef *n* (1596) **:** BASS CLEF

F distribution *n* [Sir Ronald *Fisher* †1962 Eng. geneticist and statistician] (1947) **:** a probability density function that is used esp. in analysis of variance and is a function of the ratio of two independent random variables (as the variances of two random samples) each of which has a chi-square distribution and is divided by its number of degrees of freedom

fe·al·ty \ˈfē(-ə)l-tē\ *n, pl* **-ties** [alter. of ME *feute,* fr. OF *feelté, fealté,* fr. L *fidelitat-, fidelitas* — more at FIDELITY] (14c) **1 a :** the fidelity of a vassal or feudal tenant to his lord **b :** the obligation of such fidelity **2 :** intense fidelity ***syn*** see FIDELITY

¹fear \ˈfi(ə)r\ *vt* (bef. 12c) **1** *archaic* **:** FRIGHTEN **2** *archaic* **:** to feel fear in (oneself) **3 :** to have a reverential awe of ⟨~ God⟩ **4 :** to be afraid of : consider or expect with alarm ~ *vi* **:** to be afraid or apprehensive — **fear·er** *n*

²fear *n* [ME *fer,* fr. OE *fǣr* sudden danger; akin to L *periculum* attempt, peril, Gk *peiran* to attempt, OE *faran* to go — more at FARE] (12c) **1 a :** an unpleasant often strong emotion caused by anticipation or awareness of danger **b (1) :** an instance of this emotion **(2) :** a state marked by this emotion **2 :** anxious concern : SOLICITUDE **3 :** profound reverence and awe esp. toward God **4 :** reason for alarm : DANGER

syn FEAR, DREAD, FRIGHT, ALARM, PANIC, TERROR, TREPIDATION mean painful agitation in the presence or anticipation of danger. FEAR is the most general term and implies anxiety and usu. loss of courage; DREAD usu. adds the idea of intense reluctance to face or meet a person or situation and suggests aversion as well as anxiety; FRIGHT implies the shock of sudden, startling fear; ALARM suggests a sudden and intense awareness of immediate danger; PANIC implies unreasoning and overmastering fear causing hysterical activity; TERROR implies the most extreme degree of fear; TREPIDATION adds to DREAD the implications of timidity, trembling, and hesitation.

fear·ful \ˈfi(ə)r-fəl\ *adj* (14c) **1 :** causing or likely to cause fear, fright, or alarm esp. because of dangerous quality ⟨a ~ storm⟩ **2 a :** full of fear **b :** indicating or arising from fear ⟨a ~ glance⟩ **c :** inclined to fear : TIMOROUS **3 :** being extreme (as in badness, intensity, or size) ⟨a ~ waste⟩ ⟨~ slum conditions⟩ — **fear·ful·ly** \-f(ə-)lē\ *adv* — **fear·ful·ness** \-fəl-nəs\ *n*

syn FEARFUL, APPREHENSIVE, AFRAID mean disturbed by fear. FEARFUL implies often a timorous or worrying temperament ⟨the child is *fearful* of loud noises⟩ APPREHENSIVE suggests a state of mind and implies a premonition of evil or danger ⟨*apprehensive* that war would break out⟩ AFRAID often suggests weakness or cowardice and regularly implies inhibition of action or utterance ⟨*afraid* to speak the truth⟩

fear·less \ˈfi(ə)r-ləs\ *adj* (1591) **:** free from fear : BRAVE — **fear·less·ly** *adv* — **fear·less·ness** *n*

fear·some \ˈfi(ə)r-səm\ *adj* (1768) **1 :** causing fear **2 :** TIMID, TIMOROUS — **fear·some·ly** *adv* — **fear·some·ness** *n*

fea·si·ble \ˈfē-zə-bəl\ *adj* [ME *faisible,* fr. MF, fr. *fais-,* stem of *faire* to make, do, fr. L *facere* — more at DO] (15c) **1 :** capable of being done or carried out ⟨a ~ plan⟩ **2 :** capable of being used or dealt with successfully : SUITABLE **3 :** REASONABLE, LIKELY ***syn*** see POSSIBLE — **fea·si·bil·i·ty** \,fē-zə-ˈbil-ət-ē\ *n* — **fea·si·bly** \ˈfē-zə-blē\ *adv*

¹feast \ˈfēst\ *n* [ME *feste* festival, feast, fr. MF, festival, fr. L *festa,* pl. of *festum* festival, fr. neut. of *festus* solemn, festal; akin to L *feriae* holidays, *fanum* temple, Arm *dikʻ* gods] (13c) **1 a :** an elaborate meal often accompanied by a ceremony or entertainment : BANQUET **b :** something that gives unusual or abundant pleasure **2 :** a periodic religious observance commemorating an event or honoring a deity, person, or thing

²feast *vi* (14c) **1 :** to take part in a feast **2 :** to enjoy some unusual pleasure or delight ~ *vt* **1 :** to give a feast for **2 :** DELIGHT, GRATIFY — **feast·er** *n*

Feast of Tabernacles (14c) **:** SUKKOTH

¹feat \ˈfēt\ *n* [ME *fait,* fr. MF, fr. L *factum,* fr. neut. of *factus,* pp. of *facere* to make, do — more at DO] (14c) **1 :** ACT, DEED **2 a :** a deed notable esp. for courage **b :** an act or product of skill, endurance, or ingenuity

syn FEAT, EXPLOIT, ACHIEVEMENT mean a remarkable deed. FEAT implies strength or dexterity or daring; EXPLOIT suggests an adventurous or heroic act; ACHIEVEMENT implies hard-won success in the face of difficulty or opposition.

²feat *adj* [ME *fete, fayt,* fr. MF *fait,* pp. of *faire*] (15c) **1** *archaic* **:** BECOMING, NEAT **2** *archaic* **:** SMART, DEXTEROUS

¹feath·er \ˈfeth-ər\ *n* [ME *fether,* fr. OE; akin to OHG *federa* wing, L *petere* to go to, seek, Gk *petesthai* to fly, *piptein* to fall, *pteron* wing] (bef. 12c) **1 a :** one of the light horny epidermal outgrowths that form the external covering of the body of birds and that consist of a shaft bearing on each side a series of barbs which bear barbules which in turn bear barbicels commonly ending in hooked hamuli and interlocking with the barbules of an adjacent barb to link the barbs into a continuous vane **b :** PLUME **c :** the vane of an arrow **2 a :** PLUMAGE **b :** KIND, NATURE ⟨birds of a ~ flock together⟩ **c :** ATTIRE, DRESS **d :** CONDITION, MOOD **3 :** FEATHERING 2 **4 :** a projecting strip, rib, fin, or flange **5 :** a feathery flaw in the eye or in a precious stone **6 :** the act of feathering an oar — **feath·ered** \-ərd\ *adj* — **feath·er·less** *adj* — **a feather in one's cap :** a mark of distinction : HONOR

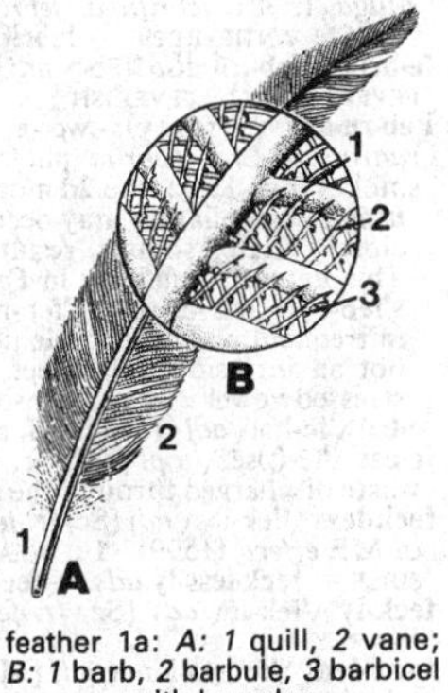

feather 1a: *A: 1* quill, *2* vane; *B: 1* barb, *2* barbule, *3* barbicel with hamulus

²feather *vb* **feath·ered; feath·er·ing** \-(ə-)riŋ\ *vt* (bef. 12c) **1 a :** to furnish (as an arrow) with a feather **b :** to cover, clothe, or adorn with feathers **2 a :** to turn (an oar blade) almost horizontal when lifting from the water at the end of a stroke to reduce air resistance **b (1) :** to change the angle of (airplane propeller blades) so that the chords become approximately parallel to the line of flight; *also* **:** to change the angle of airplane propeller blades of (an engine) in such a manner **(2) :** to change the angle of (a rotor blade of a rotorcraft) periodically in forward flight **3 :** to reduce the edge of to a featheredge **4 :** to cut (as air) with or as if with a wing **5 :** to join by a tongue and groove ~ *vi* **1 :** to grow or form feathers **2 :** to have or take on the appearance of a feather or something feathered **3 :** to soak in and spread : BLUR — used of ink or a printed impression **4 :** to feather an oar or an airplane propeller blade — **feather one's nest :** to provide for oneself esp. while in a position of trust

¹feath·er·bed \ˈfeth-ər-,bed\ *adj* (1938) **:** calling for, sanctioning, or resulting from featherbedding

²featherbed *vi* (1947) **1 a :** to require that more workers be hired than are needed **b :** to limit production under a featherbed rule **2 :** to do featherbed work or put in time under a featherbed rule ~ *vt* **1 :** to bring under a featherbed rule **2 :** to assist (as an industry) by government aid

feather bed *n* (bef. 12c) **1 :** a feather mattress **2 :** a bed having a feather mattress

feath·er·bed·ding *n* (1921) **:** the requiring of an employer usu. under a union rule or safety statute to hire more employees than are needed or to limit production

feath·er·brain \-,brān\ *n* (1839) **:** a foolish scatterbrained person — **feath·er·brained** \-,brānd\ *adj*

feath·er·edge \ˈfeth-ə-,rej, ,feth-ə-ˈ\ *n* (1616) **:** a very thin sharp edge; *esp* **:** one that is easily broken or bent over — **featheredge** *vt*

feath·er·head \ˈfeth-ər-,hed\ *n* (1831) **:** FEATHERBRAIN — **feath·er·head·ed** \,feth-ər-ˈhed-əd\ *adj*

feath·er·ing \ˈfeth-(ə-)riŋ\ *n* (1530) **1 a :** a covering of feathers : PLUMAGE **b :** a style in which feathers are attached to arrows; *also* **:** the feathers of an arrow **2 :** a fringe of hair (as on the legs of a dog) — see DOG illustration

feather star *n* (1862) **:** COMATULID

\ə\ **abut** \ᵊ\ **kitten, F table** \ər\ **further** \a\ **ash** \ā\ **ace** \ä\ **cot, cart** \au̇\ **out** \ch\ **chin** \e\ **bet** \ē\ **easy** \g\ **go** \i\ **hit** \ī\ **ice** \j\ **job** \ŋ\ **sing** \ō\ **go** \ȯ\ **law** \ȯi\ **boy** \th\ **thin** \th\ **the** \ü\ **loot** \u̇\ **foot** \y\ **yet** \zh\ **vision** \à, k̲, ⁿ, œ, œ̄, ue, ue̅, ʸ\ *see* Guide to Pronunciation

feath·er·stitch \ˈfet͟h-ər-ˌstich\ *n* (1835) : an embroidery stitch consisting of a line of diagonal blanket stitches worked alternately to the left and right — **featherstitch** *vb*

feath·er·weight \-ˌwāt\ *n* (1812) **1** : one that is very light in weight; *specif* : a boxer in a weight division having a maximum limit of 126 pounds for professionals and 125 pounds for amateurs — compare BANTAMWEIGHT, LIGHTWEIGHT **2** : a person not very intelligent or effective

feath·ery \ˈfet͟h-(ə-)rē\ *adj* (1580) : resembling, suggesting, or covered with feathers

1feat·ly \ˈfēt-lē\ *adv* [ME *fetly*, fr. *fete* feat (adj.)] (14c) **1** : in a suitable manner : PROPERLY **2** : in a graceful manner : NIMBLY **3** : with skill and ingenuity

2featly *adj* (1801) : GRACEFUL, NEAT

1fea·ture \ˈfē-chər\ *n* [ME *feture*, fr. MF, fr. L *factura* act of making, fr. *factus*, pp. of *facere* to make — more at DO] (14c) **1 a** : the structure, form, or appearance esp. of a person **b** *obs* : physical beauty **2 a** : the makeup or appearance of the face or its parts **b** : a part of the face : LINEAMENT **3** : a prominent part or characteristic **4** : a special attraction: as **a** : the principal motion picture shown on a program with other pictures **b** : a featured article, story, or department in a newspaper or magazine **c** : something offered to the public or advertised as particularly attractive — **fea·ture·less** \-ləs\ *adj*

2feature *vb* **fea·tured; fea·tur·ing** \ˈfēch-(ə-)riŋ\ *vt* (ca. 1755) **1** *chiefly dial* : to resemble in features **2** : to picture or portray in the mind : IMAGINE **3 a** : to give special prominence to **b** : to have as a characteristic or feature ~ *vi* : to play an important part

fea·tured \ˈfē-chərd\ *adj* (1790) **1** : having facial features of a particular kind — used in combination ⟨a heavy-*featured* lout⟩ **2** : displayed, advertised, or presented as a special attraction

feaze \ˈfēz, ˈfāz\ *var of* FAZE

febri- *comb form* [LL, fr. L *febris*] : fever ⟨*febrific*⟩

fe·brif·ic \fi-ˈbrif-ik\ *adj, archaic* (1710) : FEVERISH

feb·ri·fuge \ˈfeb-rə-ˌfyüj\ *n* [F *fébrifuge*, prob. fr. (assumed) NL *febrifuga*, fr. LL *febrifuga*, *febrifugia* centaury, fr. *febri-* + *-fuga* -fuge] (1686) : ANTIPYRETIC — **febrifuge** *adj*

fe·brile \ˈfeb-ˌrīl *also* ˈfēb-\ *adj* [ML *febrilis*, fr. L *febris* fever — more at FEVER] (1651) : FEVERISH

Feb·ru·ary \÷ˈfeb-(y)ə-ˌwer-ē, ˈfeb-rə-\ *n* [ME *Februarie*, fr. OE *Februarius*, fr. L, fr. *Februa*, pl., feast of purification; perh. akin to L *fumus* smoke] (bef. 12c) : the 2d month of the Gregorian calendar

usage Dissimilation may occur when a word contains two identical or closely related sounds, resulting in the change or loss of one of them. This happens regularly in *February*, which is more often pronounced \ˈfeb-(y)ə-ˌwer-ē\ than \ˈfeb-rə-ˌwer-ē\, though all of these variants are in frequent and acceptable use. The \y\ heard from many speakers is not an intrusion but rather an alternative pronunciation of the unstressed vowel *u* after a consonant, as in *January* and *annual*.

fe·cal \ˈfē-kəl\ *adj* (1541) : of, relating to, or constituting feces

fe·ces \ˈfē-(ˌ)sēz\ *n pl* [ME, fr. L *faec-*, *faex* (sing.) dregs] (14c) : bodily waste discharged through the anus : EXCREMENT

feck·less \ˈfek-ləs\ *adj* [Sc, fr. *feck* effect, majority, fr. ME (Sc) *fek*, alter. of ME *effect*] (1599) **1** : WEAK, INEFFECTIVE **2** : WORTHLESS, IRRESPONSIBLE — **feck·less·ly** *adv* — **feck·less·ness** *n*

feck·ly \ˈfek-lē\ *adv* [Sc, fr. *feck* + *-ly*] *chiefly Scot* (1768) : ALMOST, NEARLY

fec·u·lent \ˈfek-yə-lənt\ *adj* [ME, fr. L *faeculentus*, fr. *faec-*, *faex*] (15c) : foul with impurities : FECAL — **fec·u·lence** \-lən(t)s\ *n*

fe·cund \ˈfek-ənd, ˈfēk-\ *adj* [ME, fr. MF *fecond*, fr. L *fecundus* — more at FEMININE] (15c) **1** : fruitful in offspring or vegetation : PROLIFIC **2** : intellectually productive or inventive to a marked degree ***syn*** see FERTILE — **fe·cun·di·ty** \fi-ˈkən-dət-ē, fe-\ *n*

fe·cun·date \ˈfek-ən-ˌdāt, ˈfē-kən-\ *vt* **-dat·ed; -dat·ing** [L *fecundatus*, pp. of *fecundare*, fr. *fecundus*] (1631) **1** : to make fecund **2** : IMPREGNATE — **fe·cun·da·tion** \ˌfek-ən-ˈdā-shən, ˌfē-kən-\ *n*

fed \ˈfed\ *n, often cap* (1788) : a federal agent or officer — usu. used in pl.

fe·da·yee \fi-ˌda-ˈ(y)ē, -ˌdä-\ *n, pl* **fe·da·yeen** \-ˈ(y)ēn\ [Ar *fidāʼī*, lit., one who sacrifices himself] (1955) : a member of an Arab commando group operating esp. against Israel

fed·er·al \ˈfed(-ə)-rəl\ *adj* [L *foeder-*, *foedus* compact, league; akin to L *fidere* to trust — more at BIDE] (1645) **1** *archaic* : of or relating to a compact or treaty **2 a** : formed by a compact between political units that surrender their individual sovereignty to a central authority but retain limited residuary powers of government **b** : of or constituting a form of government in which power is distributed between a central authority and a number of constituent territorial units **c** : of or relating to the central government of a federation as distinguished from the governments of the constituent units **3** *cap* : advocating or friendly to the principle of a federal government with strong centralized powers; *esp* : of or relating to the American Federalists **4** *often cap* : of, relating to, or loyal to the federal government or the Union armies of the U.S. in the American Civil War — **fed·er·al·ly** \-rə-lē\ *adv*

Federal *n* (1861) **1** : a supporter of the government of the U.S. in the Civil War; *specif* : a soldier in the federal armies **2** : FED — usu. used in pl.

federal court *n* (1789) : a court established by authority of a federal government; *esp* : one established under the constitution and laws of the U.S.

federal district *n* (ca. 1934) : a district set apart as the seat of the central government of a federation

federal district court *n* (ca. 1932) : a district trial court of law and equity that hears cases under federal jurisdiction

fed·er·al·ism \ˈfed(-ə)-rə-ˌliz-əm\ *n* (1789) **1 a** *often cap* : the distribution of power in an organization (as a government) between a central authority and the constituent units — compare CENTRALISM **b** : support or advocacy of this principle **2** *cap* : the principles of the Federalists

fed·er·al·ist \-ləst\ *n* (1787) **1** : an advocate of federalism: as **a** *often cap* : an advocate of a federal union between the American colonies after the Revolution and of the adoption of the U.S. Constitution **b** *often cap* : WORLD FEDERALIST **2** *cap* : a member of a major political party in the early years of the U.S. favoring a strong centralized national government — **federalist** *adj, often cap*

fed·er·al·iza·tion \ˌfed(-ə)-rə-lə-ˈzā-shən\ *n* (ca. 1864) **1** : the act of federalizing **2** : the state of being federalized

fed·er·al·ize \ˈfed(-ə)-rə-ˌlīz\ *vt* **-ized; -iz·ing** (ca. 1801) **1** : to unite in or under a federal system **2** : to bring under the jurisdiction of a federal government

Federal Reserve bank *n* (1914) : one of 12 reserve banks set up under the Federal Reserve Act to hold reserves and discount commercial paper for affiliated banks in their respective districts

1fed·er·ate \ˈfed(-ə)-rət\ *adj* [L *foederatus*, fr. *foeder-*, *foedus*] (1710) : united in an alliance or federation : FEDERATED

2fed·er·ate \ˈfed-ə-ˌrāt\ *vt* **-at·ed; -at·ing** (1814) : to join in a federation

federated church *n* (ca. 1926) : a local church uniting two or more congregations that maintain different denominational ties — compare UNION CHURCH

fed·er·a·tion \ˌfed-ə-ˈrā-shən\ *n* (ca. 1721) **1** : the act of federating; *esp* : the forming of a federal union **2** : something formed by federation: as **a** : a federal government **b** : a union of organizations

fed·er·a·tive \ˈfed-ə-ˌrāt-iv, ˈfed(-ə)-rət-\ *adj* (1690) : FEDERAL — **fed·er·a·tive·ly** *adv*

fe·do·ra \fi-ˈdōr-ə, -ˈdȯr-\ *n* [*Fédora* (1882), drama by V. Sardou] (1895) : a low soft felt hat with the crown creased lengthwise

fed up *adj* (1882) : tired, sated, or disgusted beyond endurance ⟨*fed up* with things as they are⟩

1fee \ˈfē\ *n* [ME, fr. MF *fé*, *fief*, fr. OF, of Gmc origin; akin to OE *feoh* cattle, property, OHG *fihu* cattle; akin to L *pecus* cattle, *pecunia* money, *pectere* to comb] (14c) **1 a** (1) : an estate in land held in feudal law from a lord on condition of homage and service (2) : a piece of land so held **b** : an inherited or heritable estate in land **2 a** (1) : a fixed charge (2) : a charge for a professional service **b** : TIP — **in fee** : in absolute and legal possession

2fee *vt* **feed; fee·ing** (15c) **1** *chiefly Scot* : HIRE **2** : 9TIP 2

fee·ble \ˈfē-bəl\ *adj* **fee·bler** \-b(ə-)lər\; **fee·blest** \-b(ə-)ləst\ [ME *feble*, fr. OF, fr. L *flebilis* lamentable, wretched, fr. *flēre* to weep — more at BLEAT] (12c) **1 a** : markedly lacking in strength **b** : indicating weakness **2 a** : deficient in qualities or resources that indicate vigor, authority, force, or efficiency **b** : INADEQUATE, INFERIOR ***syn*** see WEAK — **fee·ble·ness** \-bəl-nəs\ *n* — **fee·bly** \-blē\ *adv*

fee·ble·mind·ed \ˌfē-bəl-ˈmīn-dəd\ *adj* (1534) **1** *obs* : IRRESOLUTE, VACILLATING **2** : mentally deficient **3** : FOOLISH, STUPID — **fee·ble·mind·ed·ly** *adv* — **fee·ble·mind·ed·ness** *n*

fee·blish \ˈfē-b(ə-)lish\ *adj* (1674) : somewhat feeble

1feed \ˈfēd\ *vb* **fed** \ˈfed\; **feed·ing** [ME *feden*, fr. OE *fēdan*; akin to OE *fōda* food — more at FOOD] *vt* (bef. 12c) **1 a** : to give food to **b** : to give as food **2 a** : to furnish something essential to the growth, sustenance, maintenance, or operation of **b** : to supply (material to be operated on) to a machine **3** : to produce or provide food for **4 a** : SATISFY, GRATIFY **b** : SUPPORT, ENCOURAGE **5 a** (1) : to supply for use or consumption (2) : CHANNEL, ROUTE **b** (1) : to supply (a signal) to an electronic circuit (2) : to send by wire to a transmitting station for broadcast **6** : to supply with cues and situations that make a role more effective **7** : to pass or throw a ball or puck to (a teammate) esp. for a shot at the goal ~ *vi* **1 a** : to consume food : EAT **b** : PREY — used with *on*, *upon*, or *off* **2** : to become nourished or satisfied as if by food **3 a** : to become channeled or directed **b** : to move into a machine or opening in order to be used or processed

2feed *n* (1614) **1 a** : an act of eating **b** : MEAL; *esp* : a large meal **2 a** : food for livestock; *specif* : a mixture or preparation for feeding livestock **b** : the amount given at each feeding **3 a** : material supplied (as to a furnace or machine) **b** : a mechanism by which the action of feeding is effected **c** : the motion or process of carrying forward the material to be operated upon (as in a machine) **d** : the process of feeding a television program (as to a local station) **4** : ASSIST 2

feed·back \ˈfēd-ˌbak\ *n* (1920) **1** : the return to the input of a part of the output of a machine, system, or process (as for producing changes in an electronic circuit that improve performance or in an automatic control device that provide self-corrective action) **2 a** : the partial reversion of the effects of a process to its source or to a preceding stage **b** : the return to a point of origin of evaluative or corrective information about an action or process ⟨student ~ was solicited to help revise the curriculum⟩; *also* : the information so transmitted

feedback inhibition *n* (1963) : inhibition of an enzyme controlling an early stage of a series of biochemical reactions by the end product when it reaches a critical concentration

feed·er \ˈfēd-ər\ *n* (14c) : one that feeds: as **a** : a device or apparatus for supplying food **b** (1) : TRIBUTARY (2) : a source of supply (3) : a heavy wire conductor supplying electricity at some point of an electric distribution system (as from a substation) (4) : a transmission line running from a radio transmitter to an antenna (5) : BRANCH; *esp* : a branch transportation line **c** : an animal being fattened or suitable for fattening

feed·lot \ˈfēd-ˌlät\ *n* (1889) : a plot of land on which livestock are fattened for market

feed·stock \-ˌstäk\ *n* (1932) : raw material supplied to a machine or processing plant

feed·stuff \-ˌstəf\ *n* (1856) : FEED 2a; *also* : any of the constituent nutrients of an animal ration

1feel \ˈfē(ə)l\ *vb* **felt** \ˈfelt\; **feel·ing** [ME *felen*, fr. OE *fēlan*; akin to OHG *fuolen* to feel, L *palpare* to caress, and perh. to Gk *pallein* to brandish — more at POLEMIC] *vt* (bef. 12c) **1 a** : to handle or touch in order to examine, test, or explore some quality ⟨*felt* the coat to see if it was wet⟩ **b** : to perceive by a physical sensation coming from discrete end organs (as of the skin or muscles) **2 a** : to undergo passive experience of **b** : to have one's sensibilities markedly affected by **3** : to ascertain by cautious trial — often used with *out* **4 a** : to be aware of by instinct or inference **b** : BELIEVE, THINK ~ *vi* **1 a** : to receive or be able to receive a tactile sensation **b** : to search for something by using the sense of touch **2** : to be conscious of an inward impression, state of mind, or physical condition **3** : to seem esp. to the sense of touch **4** : to have sympathy or pity — **feel like** : to have an inclination for

2feel *n* (13c) **1** : the sense of touch **2** : SENSATION, FEELING **3 a** : the quality of a thing as imparted through or as if through touch **b** : typical or peculiar quality or atmosphere; *also* : an awareness of such a quality or atmosphere **4** : intuitive knowledge or ability

feel·er \'fē-lər\ *n* (15c) : one that feels: as **a** : a tactile process (as a tentacle) of an animal **b** : something (as a proposal) ventured to ascertain the views of others

1feel·ing \'fē-liŋ\ *n* (12c) **1 a** (1) : the one of the basic physical senses of which the skin contains the chief end organs and of which the sensations of touch and temperature are characteristic : TOUCH (2) : a sensation experienced through this sense **b** : generalized bodily consciousness or sensation **c** : appreciative or responsive awareness or recognition **2 a** : an emotional state or reaction ⟨had a kindly ~ toward the child⟩ **b** *pl* : susceptibility to impression : SENSITIVITY ⟨the remark hurt her ~s⟩ **3 a** : the undifferentiated background of one's awareness considered apart from any identifiable sensation, perception, or thought **b** : the overall quality of one's awareness **c** : conscious recognition : SENSE **4 a** : often unreasoned opinion or belief : SENTIMENT **b** : PRESENTIMENT **5** : capacity to respond emotionally esp. with the higher emotions ⟨a man of noble ~⟩ **6** : the character ascribed to something : ATMOSPHERE **7 a** : the quality of a work of art that embodies and conveys the emotion of the artist **b** : sympathetic aesthetic response **8** : FEEL 4 ⟨a ~ for words⟩

syn FEELING, EMOTION, AFFECTION, SENTIMENT, PASSION mean a subjective response to a person, thing, or situation. FEELING denotes any partly mental, partly physical response marked by pleasure, pain, attraction, or repulsion; it may suggest the mere existence of a response but imply nothing about the nature or intensity of it; EMOTION carries a strong implication of excitement or agitation but, like FEELING, encompasses both positive and negative responses; AFFECTION applies to feelings that are also inclinations or likings; SENTIMENT often implies an emotion inspired by an idea; PASSION suggests a very powerful or controlling emotion.

2feeling *adj* (15c) **1 a** : SENTIENT, SENSITIVE **b** : easily moved emotionally **2** *obs* : deeply felt **3** : expressing emotion or sensitivity — **feel·ing·ly** \-liŋ-lē\ *adv* — **feel·ing·ness** *n*

feel up *vt* (1930) : to touch or fondle (someone) for sexual pleasure

fee simple *n, pl* **fees simple** (14c) : a fee without limitation to any class of heirs or restrictions on transfer of ownership

fee splitting *n* (1943) : payment by a specialist (as a doctor or a lawyer) of a part of his fee to the person who made the referral

feet *pl of* FOOT

fee tail *n, pl* **fees tail** (15c) : a fee limited to a particular class of heirs

feet·first \'fēt-'fərst\ *adv* (1949) : with the feet foremost ⟨jumped into the water ~⟩

feet of clay [fr. the feet of the idol in Dan 2:33] (1859) : a flaw of character that is usu. not readily apparent ⟨a towering figure, posthumously judged to have *feet of clay* —*Times Lit. Supp.*⟩

feeze \'fēz, 'fāz\ *n* [ME *veze*, fr. *fesen*, *vesen* to drive away — more at FAZE] (14c) **1** *chiefly dial* : RUSH **2** *dial* : a state of alarm or excitement

Feh·ling's solution \'fā-liŋ(z)-\ *n* [Hermann *Fehling* †1885 Ger. chemist] (1873) : a blue solution of Rochelle salt and copper sulfate used as an oxidizing agent in a test for sugars and aldehydes in which the precipitation of a red oxide of copper indicates a positive result

feign \'fān\ *vb* [ME *feignen*, fr. OF *feign-*, stem of *feindre*, fr. L *fingere* to shape, feign — more at DOUGH] *vt* (13c) **1 a** : to give a false appearance of : induce as a false impression ⟨~ death⟩ **b** : to assert as if true : PRETEND **2** *archaic* **a** : INVENT, IMAGINE **b** : to give fictional representation to **3** *obs* : DISGUISE, CONCEAL ~ *vi* : PRETEND, DISSEMBLE ***syn*** see ASSUME — **feign·er** *n*

feigned *adj* (14c) **1** : FICTITIOUS **2** : not genuine or real

1feint \'fānt\ *n* [F *feinte*, fr. OF, fr. *feint*, pp. of *feindre*] (1679) : something feigned; *specif* : a mock blow or attack on or toward one part in order to distract attention from the point one really intends to attack ***syn*** see TRICK

2feint *vi* (1810) : to make a feint ~ *vt* **1** : to lure or deceive with a feint **2** : to make a pretense of

fei·rie \'fē-rē\ *adj* [ME (Sc) *fery*, fr. ME *fere* strong, fr. OE *fēre* able to go; akin to OE *faran* to travel, fare] *Scot* (bef. 12c) : NIMBLE, STRONG

feist \'fīst\ *n* [obs. *fisting hound*, fr. obs. *fist* (to break wind)] *chiefly dial* (1770) : a small dog

feisty \'fī-stē\ *adj* **feist·i·er; -est** (1896) **1** *chiefly Southern & Midland* **a** : full of nervous energy : FIDGETY **b** : being touchy and quarrelsome **c** : being frisky and exuberant **2** : having or showing a lively aggressiveness : SPUNKY — **feist·i·ness** *n*

fe·la·fel \fə-'läf-əl\ *var of* FALAFEL

feld·sher \'fel(d)-shər\ *n* [Russ *fel'dsher*, fr. G *feldscher*, *feldscherer* field surgeon, fr. *feld* field (fr. OHG) + *scherer* barber, surgeon, deriv. of OHG *skeran* to cut; akin to ON *skera* to cut — more at FIELD, SHEAR] (1877) : a medical or surgical practitioner without full professional qualifications or status in some east European countries and esp. Russia

feld·spar \'fel(d)-,spär\ *n* [modif. of obs. G *feldspath* (now *feldspat*), fr. G *feld* field + obs. G *spath* (now *spat*) spar] (1757) : any of a group of crystalline minerals that consist of aluminum silicates with either potassium, sodium, calcium, or barium and that are an essential constituent of nearly all crystalline rocks (hardness 6–6.5, sp. gr. 2.5–2.9)

feld·spath·ic \fel(d)-'spath-ik\ *adj* [*feldspath* (var. of *feldspar*), fr. obs. G] (ca. 1828) : relating to or containing feldspar — used esp. of a porcelain glaze

fe·li·cif·ic \,fē-lə-'sif-ik\ *adj* [L *felic-*, *felix*] (1865) : causing or intended to cause happiness

felicific calculus *n* (1945) : a method of determining the rightness of an action by balancing the probable pleasures and pains that it would produce

1fe·lic·i·tate \fi-'lis-ə-,tāt\ *adj* [LL *felicitatus*, pp. of *felicitare* to make happy, fr. L *felicitas*] *obs* (1605) : made happy

2felicitate *vt* **-tat·ed; -tat·ing** (1628) **1** *archaic* : to make happy **2 a** : to consider happy or fortunate **b** : to offer congratulations to — **fe·lic·i·ta·tion** \-,lis-ə-'tā-shən\ *n* — **fe·lic·i·ta·tor** \-'lis-ə-,tāt-ər\ *n*

fe·lic·i·tous \fi-'lis-ət-əs\ *adj* (1789) **1** : very well suited or expressed : APT ⟨a ~ remark⟩ **2** : PLEASANT, DELIGHTFUL ***syn*** see FIT — **fe·lic·i·tous·ly** *adv* — **fe·lic·i·tous·ness** *n*

fe·lic·i·ty \fi-'lis-ət-ē\ *n, pl* **-ties** [ME *felicite*, fr. MF *felicité*, fr. L *felicitat-*, *felicitas*, fr. *felic-*, *felix* fruitful, happy — more at FEMININE] (14c) **1 a** : the quality or state of being happy; *esp* : great happiness **b** : an instance of happiness **2** : something that causes happiness **3** : a pleasing manner or quality esp. in art or language : APTNESS **4** : an apt expression

fe·lid \'fē-ləd\ *n* [NL *Felidae*, family name, fr. *Felis*, genus of cats, fr. L, cat] (ca. 1895) : CAT 1b — **felid** *adj*

fe·line \'fē-,līn\ *adj* [L *felinus*, fr. *felis*] (1681) **1** : of or relating to cats or the cat family **2** : resembling a cat: as **a** : sleekly graceful **b** : SLY, TREACHEROUS **c** : STEALTHY — **feline** *n* — **fe·line·ly** *adv* — **fe·lin·i·ty** \fē-'lin-ət-ē\ *n*

feline distemper *n* (1942) : PANLEUKOPENIA

feline panleukopenia *n* (ca. 1943) : PANLEUKOPENIA

1fell \'fel\ *n* [ME, fr. OE; akin to OHG *fel* skin, L *pellis*] (bef. 12c) **1** : SKIN, HIDE, PELT **2** : a thin tough membrane covering a carcass directly under the hide

2fell *vt* [ME *fellen*, fr. OE *fellan*; akin to OE *feallan* to fall — more at FALL] (bef. 12c) **1 a** : to cut, beat, or knock down **b** : KILL **2** : to sew (a seam) by folding one raw edge under the other and sewing flat on the wrong side — **fell·able** \'fel-ə-bəl\ *adj* — **fell·er** *n*

3fell *past of* FALL

4fell *adj* [ME *fel*, fr. MF, fr. OF — more at FELON] (14c) **1 a** : FIERCE, CRUEL, TERRIBLE **b** : SINISTER, MALEVOLENT ⟨a ~ purpose⟩ **c** : very destructive : DEADLY ⟨a ~ disease⟩ **2** *Scot* : SHARP, PUNGENT — **fell·ness** *n* — **fel·ly** \'fel-lē\ *adv* — **at one fell swoop** : all at once; *also* : with a single concentrated effort

5fell *n* [ME, fr. ON *fell*, *fjall* mountain; akin to OHG *felis* rock] *dial Brit* (14c) : a high barren field or moor

fel·la \'fel-ə\ *var of* FELLOW

fel·lah \'fel-ə, fə-'lä\ *n, pl* **fel·la·hin** *or* **fel·la·heen** \,fel-ə-'hēn, fə-,lä-'hēn\ [Ar *fallāḥ*] (1743) : a peasant or agricultural laborer in an Arab country (as Egypt)

fel·late \'fel-,āt, fə-'lāt\ *vb* **fel·lat·ed; fel·lat·ing** [L *fellatus*, pp. of *fellare*] *vt* (1965) : to perform fellatio on ~ *vi* : to fellate someone — **fel·la·tor** \-ər\ *n*

fel·la·tio \fə-'lā-shē-,ō, fe-, -'lät-ē-\ *also* **fel·la·tion** \-'lā-shən\ *n* [NL *fellation-*, *fellatio*, fr. L *fellatus*, pp. of *felare*, *fellare*, lit., to suck — more at FEMININE] (1887) : oral stimulation of the penis

fell·mon·ger \'fel-,məŋ-gər, -,mäŋ-\ *n* [1*fell*] *Brit* (1530) : one who removes hair or wool from hides in preparation for leather making — **fell·mon·gered** \-gərd\ *adj, Brit* — **fell·mon·ger·ing** \-g(ə-)riŋ\ *or* **fell·mon·gery** \-g(ə-)rē\ *n, Brit*

fel·low \'fel-(,)ō, -ə(-w)\ *n, often attrib* [ME *felawe*, fr. OE *fēolaga*, fr. ON *fēlagi*, fr. *fēlag* partnership, fr. *fē* cattle, money (akin to OE *feoh*) + *lag* act of laying; akin to OE *licgan* to lie — more at FEE, LIE] (bef. 12c) **1** : COMRADE, ASSOCIATE **2 a** : an equal in rank, power, or character : PEER **b** : one of a pair : MATE **3** : a member of a group having common characteristics; *specif* : a member of an incorporated literary or scientific society **4 a** *obs* : a person of one of the lower social classes **b** : a worthless man or boy **c** : MAN, BOY **d** : BOYFRIEND, BEAU **5** : an incorporated member of a college or collegiate foundation esp. in a British university **6** : a person appointed to a position granting a stipend and allowing for advanced study or research

fellow feeling *n* (1613) : a feeling of community of interest or of mutual understanding ⟨*fellow feeling* . . . in the face of the impersonality of urban life —Richard Poirier⟩

fel·low·ly \-ō-lē, -ə-lē\ *adj* (13c) : SOCIABLE — **fellowly** *adv*

fel·low·man \,fel-ō-'man, -ə-\ *n* (1667) : a kindred human being

fellow servant *n* (1900) : an employee working with another employee under such circumstances that each one if negligent may expose the other to harm which the employer cannot reasonably be expected to guard against or be held legally liable for

1fel·low·ship \'fel-ō-,ship, -ə-\ *n* (bef. 12c) **1** : COMPANIONSHIP, COMPANY **2 a** : community of interest, activity, feeling, or experience **b** : the state of being a fellow or associate **3** : a company of equals or friends : ASSOCIATION **4** : the quality or state of being comradely **5** *obs* : MEMBERSHIP, PARTNERSHIP **6 a** : the position of a fellow (as of a university) **b** : the stipend of a fellow **c** : a foundation for the providing of such a stipend

2fellowship *vb* **-shipped** *also* **-shiped** \-,shipt\; **-ship·ping** *also* **-ship·ing** \-,ship-iŋ\ *vi* (14c) : to join in fellowship esp. with a church member ~ *vt* : to admit to fellowship (as in a church)

fellow traveler *n* [trans. of Russ *poputchik*] (1936) : one that sympathizes with and often furthers the ideals and program of an organized group (as the Communist party) without membership in the group or regular participation in its activities — **fel·low–trav·el·ing** *adj*

fel·ly \'fel-ē\ *or* **fel·loe** \-(,)ō\ *n, pl* **fellies** *or* **felloes** [ME *fely*, *felive*, fr. OE *felg*; akin to OHG *felga* felly, OE *fealg* piece of plowed land] (bef. 12c) : the exterior rim or a segment of the rim of a wheel supported by the spokes

felo–de–se \,fel-ōd-ə-'sā, -'sē\ *n, pl* **fe·lo·nes–de–se** \fə-,lō-(,)nēz-də-\ *or* **felos–de–se** \,fel-ōz-də-\ [ML *felo de se*, *fello de se*, lit., evildoer upon himself] (1651) **1** : one who deliberately kills himself or who dies from the effects of his commission of an unlawful malicious act **2** : an act of deliberate self-destruction : SUICIDE

1fel·on \'fel-ən\ *n* [ME, fr. MF *felon*, *fel*, fr. ML *fellon-*, *fello* evildoer, villain] (13c) **1** : one who has committed a felony **2** *archaic* : VILLAIN **3** : WHITLOW

2felon *adj* (14c) **1** *archaic* **a** : CRUEL **b** : EVIL **2** *archaic* : WILD

fe·lo·ni·ous \fə-'lō-nē-əs\ *adj* (1575) **1** *archaic* : very evil : VILLAINOUS **2** : of, relating to, or having the nature of a felony — **fe·lo·ni·ous·ly** *adv* — **fe·lo·ni·ous·ness** *n*

fel·on·ry \'fel-ən-rē\ *n* (1837) : FELONS; *specif* : the convict population of a penal colony

fel·o·ny \'fel-ə-nē\ *n, pl* **-nies** (14c) **1 :** an act on the part of a feudal vassal involving the forfeiture of his fee **2 a :** a grave crime formerly differing from a misdemeanor under English common law by involving forfeiture in addition to any other punishment **b :** a grave crime declared to be a felony by the common law or by statute regardless of the punishment actually imposed **c :** a crime declared a felony by statute because of the punishment imposed **d :** a crime for which the punishment in federal law may be death or imprisonment for more than one year

fel·site \'fel-,sīt\ *n* [*felspar* + *-ite*] (1794) **:** a dense igneous rock consisting almost entirely of feldspar and quartz — **fel·sit·ic** \fel-'sit-ik\ *adj*

fel·spar *var of* FELDSPAR

[1]**felt** \'felt\ *n* [ME, fr. OE; akin to OHG *filz* felt, L *pellere* to drive, beat, Gk *pelas* near] (bef. 12c) **1 a :** a cloth made of wool and fur often mixed with natural or synthetic fibers through the action of heat, moisture, chemicals, and pressure **b :** a firm woven cloth of wool or cotton heavily napped and shrunk **2 :** an article made of felt **3 :** a material resembling felt: as **a :** a heavy paper of organic or asbestos fibers impregnated with asphalt and used in building construction **b :** semirigid pressed fiber insulation used in building

[2]**felt** *vt* (14c) **1 :** to make out of or cover with felt **2 :** to cause to adhere and mat together **3 :** to make into felt or a similar substance

[3]**felt** *past and past part of* FEEL

felt·ing \'fel-tiŋ\ *n* (1686) **1 :** the process of making felt **2 :** FELT

fe·luc·ca \fə-'lü-kə, -'lək-ə\ *n* [It *feluca*] (1615) **:** a narrow fast lateen-rigged sailing vessel chiefly of the Mediterranean area

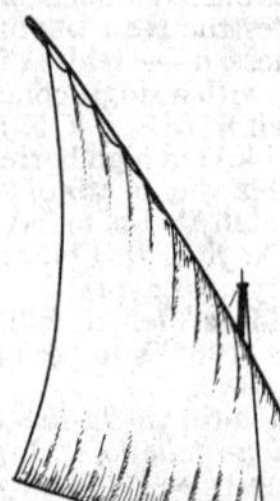
felucca

[1]**fe·male** \'fē-,māl\ *n* [ME, alter. of *femel, femelle,* fr. MF & ML; MF *femelle,* fr. ML *femella,* fr. L, girl, dim. of *femina*] (14c) **1 :** an individual that bears young or produces eggs as distinguished from one that begets young; *esp* **:** a woman or girl as distinguished from a man or boy **2 :** a pistillate plant

[2]**female** *adj* (14c) **1 a :** of, relating to, or being the sex that bears young or produces eggs **b :** PISTILLATE **2 :** having some quality (as gentleness or delicacy) associated with the female sex **3 :** designed with a hollow or groove into which a corresponding male part fits ⟨~ coupling of a hose⟩ — **fe·male·ness** *n*

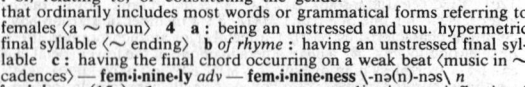

[1]**fem·i·nine** \'fem-ə-nən\ *adj* [ME, fr. MF *feminin,* fr. L *femininus,* fr. *femina* woman; akin to OE *delu* nipple, L *filius* son, *felix, fetus,* & *fecundus* fruitful, *felare* to suck, Gk *thēlē* nipple] (14c) **1 :** FEMALE 1a **2 :** characteristic of or appropriate or peculiar to women **3 :** of, relating to, or constituting the gender that ordinarily includes most words or grammatical forms referring to females ⟨a ~ noun⟩ **4 a :** being an unstressed and usu. hypermetric final syllable ⟨~ ending⟩ **b** *of rhyme* **:** having an unstressed final syllable **c :** having the final chord occurring on a weak beat ⟨music in ~ cadences⟩ — **fem·i·nine·ly** *adv* — **fem·i·nine·ness** \-nə(n)-nəs\ *n*

[2]**feminine** *n* (15c) **1 a :** a noun, pronoun, adjective, or inflectional form or class of the feminine gender **b :** the feminine gender **2 :** the female principle ⟨eternal ~⟩

fem·i·nin·i·ty \,fem-ə-'nin-ət-ē\ *n* (14c) **1 :** the quality or nature of the female sex **2 :** EFFEMINACY **3 :** WOMEN, WOMANKIND

fem·i·nism \'fem-ə-,niz-əm\ *n* (1895) **1 :** the theory of the political, economic, and social equality of the sexes **2 :** organized activity on behalf of women's rights and interests — **fem·i·nist** \-nəst\ *n or adj* — **fem·i·nis·tic** \,fem-ə-'nis-tik\ *adj*

fe·min·i·ty \fe-'min-ət-ē, fə-\ *n* (14c) **:** FEMININITY

fem·i·nize \'fem-ə-,nīz\ *vt* **-nized; -niz·ing** (1652) **1 :** to give a feminine quality to **2 :** to cause (a male or castrate) to take on feminine characters (as by implantation of ovaries or administration of estrogenic substances) — **fem·i·ni·za·tion** \,fem-ə-nə-'zā-shən\ *n*

femme *also* **fem** \'fem\ *n* [prob. fr. F *femme* woman, fr. L *femina*] (1958) **:** a lesbian who plays the female role in a homosexual relationship

femme fa·tale \,fem-fə-'tal, ,fam-, -'täl\ *n, pl* **femmes fa·tales** \-'tal(z), -'täl(z)\ [F, lit., disastrous woman] (1912) **1 :** a seductive woman who lures men into dangerous or compromising situations **:** SIREN **2 :** a woman who attracts men by an aura of charm and mystery

fem·o·ral \'fem-(ə-)rəl\ *adj* (ca. 1771) **:** of or relating to the femur or thigh

femoral artery *n* (ca. 1771) **:** the chief artery of the thigh lying in its anterior inner part

fem·to- \,fem(p)-tō\ *comb form* [ISV, fr. Dan or Norw *femten* fifteen, fr. ON *fimmtān;* akin to OE *fiftēne* fifteen] **:** one quadrillionth (10^{-15}) part of ⟨*femto*second⟩

fe·mur \'fē-mər\ *n, pl* **fe·murs** *or* **fem·o·ra** \'fem-(ə-)rə\ [NL *femor-, femur,* fr. L, thigh] (ca. 1771) **1 :** the proximal bone of the hind or lower limb — called also *thighbone* **2 :** the segment of an insect's leg that is third from the body

[1]**fen** \'fen\ *n* [ME, fr. OE *fenn;* akin to OHG *fenna* fen, Skt *paṅka* mud] (bef. 12c) **:** low land covered wholly or partly with water unless artificially drained

[2]**fen** \'fən\ *n, pl* **fen** [Chin (Pek) *fên*[1]] (ca. 1945) — see *yuan* at MONEY table

[1]**fence** \'fen(t)s\ *n, often attrib* [ME *fens,* short for *defens* defense] (14c) **1** *archaic* **:** a means of protection **:** DEFENSE **2 :** a barrier intended to prevent escape or intrusion or to mark a boundary; *esp* **:** such a barrier made of posts and wire or boards **3 :** FENCING 1 **4 a :** a receiver of stolen goods **b :** a place where stolen goods are bought — **fence·less** \-ləs\ *adj* — **fence·less·ness** *n* — **on the fence :** in a position of neutrality or indecision

[2]**fence** *vb* **fenced; fenc·ing** *vt* (15c) **1 a :** to enclose with a fence **b** (1) **:** to keep in or out with a fence (2) **:** to ward off **2 :** to provide a defense for **3 :** to sell (stolen property) to a fence ~ *vi* **1 a :** to practice fencing **b** (1) **:** to use tactics of attack and defense resembling those of fencing (2) **:** to parry arguments by shifting ground **2** *archaic* **:** to provide protection — **fenc·er** *n*

fence–mend·ing \'fen(t)-,smen-diŋ\ *n* (1947) **:** the rehabilitating of a deteriorated political relationship

fence·row \'fen(t)s-,rō\ *n* (1842) **:** the land occupied by a fence including the uncultivated area on each side

fence–sit·ting \'fen(t)s-,sit-iŋ\ *n* (1904) **:** a state of indecision or neutrality with respect to conflicting positions — **fence sitter** *n*

fenc·ing *n* (1581) **1 :** the art or practice of attack and defense with the foil, épee, or saber **2 a** (1) **:** FENCE 2 (2) **:** the fences of a property or region **b :** material used for building fences

[1]**fend** \'fend\ *vb* [ME *fenden,* short for *defenden*] *vt* (14c) **1 :** DEFEND **2 :** to keep or ward off **:** REPEL — often used with *off* **3** *dial Brit* **:** to provide for **:** SUPPORT ~ *vi* **1** *dial Brit* **:** to make an effort **:** STRUGGLE **2 a :** to try to get along without help **:** SHIFT **b :** to provide a livelihood

[2]**fend** *n, chiefly Scot* (1721) **:** an effort or attempt esp. for oneself

fend·er \'fen-dər\ *n* (13c) **:** a device that protects: as **a :** a cushion (as foam rubber, a bundle of rope, or a wood float) between a boat and a dock or between two boats that lessens shock and prevents chafing **b :** RAILING **c :** a device in front of locomotives and streetcars to lessen injury to animals or pedestrians in case of collision **d :** a guard over the wheel of a motor vehicle **e :** a low metal frame or a screen before an open fireplace **f :** an oblong or triangular shield of leather attached to the stirrup leather of a saddle to protect a rider's legs — **fend·ered** \-dərd\ *adj* — **fend·er·less** *adj*

fender bender *n* (1962) **:** a minor automobile accident

fe·nes·tra \fə-'nes-trə\ *n, pl* **-trae** \-,trē, -,trī\ [NL, fr. L, window] (ca. 1737) **1 :** a small anatomical opening (as in a bone): as **a :** an oval opening between the middle ear and the vestibule having the base of the stapes or columella attached to its membrane — called also *fenestra ova·lis* \-ō-'vā-ləs\, *fenestra ves·tib·u·li* \-ves-'tib-yə-(,)lē\, *oval window* **b :** a round opening between the middle ear and the cochlea — called also *fenestra cochleae, fenestra ro·tun·da* \-rō-'tən-də\, *round window* **2 :** an opening cut in bone — **fe·nes·tral** \-trəl\ *adj*

fe·nes·trate \fə-'nes-,trāt, 'fen-ə-,strāt\ *adj* [L *fenestratus,* fr. *fenestra*] (1835) **:** FENESTRATED 2

fen·es·trat·ed \'fen-ə-,strāt-əd\ *adj* (1849) **1 :** provided with or characterized by windows **2 :** having one or more openings or pores ⟨~ blood capillaries⟩

fen·es·tra·tion \,fen-ə-'strā-shən\ *n* (1846) **1 :** the arrangement, proportioning, and design of windows and doors in a building **2 :** an opening in a surface (as a wall or membrane) **3 :** the operation of cutting an opening in the bony labyrinth between the inner ear and tympanum to replace natural fenestrae that are not functional

Fe·ni·an \'fē-nē-ən\ *n* [IrGael *Fēinne,* pl. of *Fiann,* legendary band of Irish warriors] (1816) **1 :** one of a legendary band of warriors defending Ireland in the 2d and 3d centuries A.D. **2 :** a member of a secret 19th century Irish and Irish-American organization dedicated to the overthrow of British rule in Ireland — **Fenian** *adj* — **Fe·ni·an·ism** \-ə-,niz-əm\ *n*

fen·nec \'fen-ik\ *n* [Ar *fanak*] (1790) **:** a small pale-fawn African fox (*Fennecus zerda*) with large ears

fen·nel \'fen-ᵊl\ *n* [ME *fenel,* fr. OE *finugl,* fr. (assumed) VL *fenuculum,* fr. L *feniculum* fennel, dim. of *fenum* hay; perh. akin to L *fetus* fruitful — more at FEMININE] (bef. 12c) **:** a perennial European herb (*Foeniculum vulgare*) of the carrot family adventive in No. America and cultivated for its foliage and aromatic seeds

fen·ny \'fen-ē\ *adj* [ME, fr. OE *fennig,* fr. *fenn* fen] (bef. 12c) **1 :** having the characteristics of a fen **:** BOGGY **2 :** peculiar to or found in a fen

fenu·greek \'fen-yə-,grēk\ *n* [ME *fenugrek,* fr. MF *fenugrec,* fr. L *fenum Graecum,* lit., Greek hay] (bef. 12c) **:** a leguminous annual Asian herb (*Trigonella foenumgraecum*) with aromatic seeds

feoff·ee \fe-'fē, fē-'fē\ *n* (15c) **:** one to whom a feoffment is made

feoff·ment \'fef-mənt, 'fēf-\ *n* [ME *feoffement,* fr. AF, fr. *feoffer* to invest with a fee, fr. OF *fief* fee] (14c) **:** the granting of a fee

feof·for \'fef-ər, 'fēf-; fe-'fó(ə)r, fē-\ *or* **feoff·er** \'fef-ər, 'fēf-\ *n* (15c) **:** one who makes a feoffment

-fer \fər\ *n comb form* [F & L; F *-fère,* fr. L *-fer* bearing, one that bears, fr. *ferre* to carry — more at BEAR] **:** one that bears ⟨*aquifer*⟩

fe·rae na·tu·rae \'fer-,ī-nə-'tü(ə)r-,ī\ *adj* [L, of a wild nature] (1661) **:** wild by nature and not usu. tamed

fe·ral \'fir-əl, 'fer-\ *adj* [ML *feralis,* fr. L *fera* wild animal, fr. fem. of *ferus* wild — more at FIERCE] (1604) **1 :** of, relating to, or suggestive of a wild beast **:** SAVAGE **2 a :** not domesticated or cultivated **:** WILD **b :** having escaped from domestication and become wild

fer–de–lance \'ferd-ᵊl-'an(t)s, -'än(t)s\ *n, pl* **fer–de–lance** [F, lit., lance iron, spearhead] (1880) **:** a large extremely venomous pit viper (*Bothrops atrox*) of Central and So. America

fere \'fi(ə)r\ *n* [ME, fr. OE *gefēra;* akin to OE *faran* to go, travel — more at FARE] (bef. 12c) **1** *archaic* **:** COMPANION, COMRADE **2** *archaic* **:** SPOUSE

[1]**fe·ria** \'fir-ē-ə, 'fer-\ *n* [ML — more at FAIR] (15c) **:** a weekday of a church calendar on which no feast falls — **fe·ri·al** \-ē-əl\ *adj*

[2]**fe·ria** \'fer-ē-ə, -ē-,ä\ *n* [Sp, fair, market, fr. ML — more at FAIR] (1844) **:** an Hispanic market festival often in observance of a religious holiday

fe·rine \'fi(ə)r-,īn\ *adj* [L *ferinus,* fr. *fera*] (1640) **:** FERAL

fer·i·ty \'fer-ət-ē\ *n* [L *feritas,* fr. *ferus*] (1534) **:** the quality or state of being feral

fer·lie *also* **fer·ly** \'fer-lē\ *n, pl* **ferlies** [ME, fr. *ferly* strange, fr. OE *fǣrlic* unexpected, fr. *fǣr* sudden danger — more at FEAR] *Scot* (13c) **:** WONDER

fer·ma·ta \fer-'mät-ə\ *n* [It, lit., stop, fr. *fermare* to stop, fr. L *firmare* to make firm] (1842) **:** a prolongation at the discretion of the performer of a musical note, chord, or rest beyond its given time value; *also* **:** the sign denoting such a prolongation — called also *hold*

[1]**fer·ment** \(,)fər-'ment\ *vi* (14c) **1 :** to undergo fermentation **2 :** to be in a state of agitation or intense activity ~ *vt* **1 :** to cause to undergo fermentation **2 :** to work up (as into a state of agitation) **:** FOMENT — **fer·ment·able** \-ə-bəl\ *adj*

[2]**fer·ment** \'fər-,ment *also* (,)fər-'\ *n* [ME, fr. L *fermentum* yeast — more at BARM] (15c) **1 a :** a living organism (as a yeast) that causes fermentation by virtue of its enzymes **b :** ENZYME **2 a :** a state of unrest **:** AGITATION **b :** a process of active often disorderly development ⟨the great period of creative ~ in literature —William Barrett⟩

fer·men·ta·tion \,fər-mən-'tā-shən, -,men-\ *n* (1601) **1 a :** a chemical change with effervescence **b :** an enzymatically controlled anaerobic breakdown of an energy-rich compound (as a carbohydrate to carbon dioxide and alcohol or to an organic acid); *broadly* : an enzymatically controlled transformation of an organic compound **2** : FERMENT 2

fer·men·ta·tive \(,)fər-'ment-ət-iv\ *adj* (1661) **1** : causing or producing a substance that causes fermentation ⟨~ organisms⟩ **2** : of, relating to, or produced by fermentation

fer·men·ter \(,)fər-'ment-ər\ *n* (1918) **1** : an organism that causes fermentation **2** *or* **fer·men·tor** : an apparatus for carrying out fermentation

fer·mi \'fe(ə)r-(,)mē, 'fər-\ *n* [Enrico *Fermi*] (1955) : a unit of length equal to 10^{-13} centimeter

fer·mi·on \'fer-mē-,än, 'fər-\ *n* [Enrico *Fermi* + E [2]*-on*] (1947) : a particle (as an electron, proton, or neutron) whose spin quantum number is an odd multiple of $1/2$

fer·mi·um \'fer-mē-əm, 'fər-\ *n* [Enrico *Fermi*] (1955) : a radioactive metallic element artificially produced (as by bombardment of plutonium with neutrons) — see ELEMENT table

fern \'fərn\ *n* [ME, fr. OE *fearn;* akin to OHG *farn* fern, Skt *parṇa* wing, leaf] (bef. 12c) : any of numerous flowerless seedless plants constituting a class (Filicineae) of lower vascular plants; *esp* : any of an order (Filicales) resembling seed plants in being differentiated into root, stem, and leaflike fronds and in having vascular tissue but differing in reproducing by spores — **fern·like** \-,līk\ *adj* — **ferny** \'fər-nē\ *adj*

fern·ery \'fərn-(ə-)rē\ *n, pl* **-er·ies** (1840) **1** : a place or stand where ferns grow **2** : a collection of growing ferns

fern seed *n* (1596) : the dustlike asexual spores of ferns formerly taken for seeds and thought to make the possessor invisible

fe·ro·cious \fə-'rō-shəs\ *adj* [L *feroc-, ferox,* lit., fierce looking, fr. *ferus* + *-oc-, -ox* (akin to Gk *ōps* eye) — more at EYE] (1646) **1** : exhibiting or given to extreme fierceness and unrestrained violence and brutality **2** : extremely intense ⟨~ heat⟩ ***syn*** see FIERCE — **fe·ro·cious·ly** *adv* — **fe·ro·cious·ness** *n*

fe·roc·i·ty \fə-'räs-ət-ē\ *n* (1606) : the quality or state of being ferocious

-f·er·ous \f-(ə-)rəs\ *adj comb form* [ME, fr. MF & L; MF *-fere* -fer, fr. L *-fer*] : bearing : producing ⟨carboni*ferous*⟩

fer·rate \'fe(ə)r-,āt\ *n* [ISV, fr. L *ferrum* iron + [1]*-ate*] (1854) : a compound containing iron and oxygen in the anion; *esp* : a red salt analogous to the chromates and sulfates

fer·re·dox·in \,fer-ə-'däk-sən\ *n* [L *ferrum* + E *redox* + *-in*] (1962) : any of a group of iron-containing plant proteins that function as electron carriers in photosynthetic organisms and in some anaerobic bacteria

[1]**fer·ret** \'fer-ət\ *n* [ME *furet, ferret,* fr. MF *furet,* fr. (assumed) VL *furittus,* lit., little thief, dim. of L *fur* thief — more at FURTIVE] (14c) **1** : a partially domesticated usu. albino European polecat that is sometimes classed as a separate species (*Mustela furo*) and is used esp. for hunting rodents **2** : an active and persistent searcher — **fer·rety** \-ət-ē\ *adj*

[2]**ferret** *vi* (15c) **1** : to hunt with ferrets **2** : to search about ~ *vt* **1 a** (1) : to hunt (as rabbits) with ferrets (2) : to drive esp. from covert **b** : to find and bring to light by searching — usu. used with *out* ⟨~ out the answers⟩ **2** : HARRY, WORRY — **fer·ret·er** *n*

[3]**ferret** *n* [prob. modif. of It *fioretti* floss silk, fr. pl. of *fioretto,* dim. of *fiore* flower, fr. L *flor-, flos* — more at BLOW] (1649) : a narrow cotton, silk, or wool tape — called also *ferreting*

ferri- *comb form* [L, fr. *ferrum*] **1** : iron ⟨*ferri*ferous⟩ **2** : ferric iron ⟨*ferri*cyanic⟩

fer·ri·age \'fer-ē-ij\ *n* [ME] (14c) **1** : the fare paid for a ferry passage **2** : the act or business of transporting by ferry

fer·ric \'fer-ik\ *adj* (1799) **1** : of, relating to, or containing iron **2** : being or containing iron usu. with a valence of three

ferric ammonium citrate *n* (1938) : a complex salt containing varying amounts of iron and used esp. for making blueprints

ferric chloride *n* (ca. 1895) : a deliquescent dark salt $FeCl_3$ that readily hydrates to the yellow-orange form and that is used in sewage treatment and as an astringent

ferric hydroxide *n* (ca. 1909) : a hydrate $Fe_2O_3{\cdot}nH_2O$ of ferric oxide that is capable of acting both as a base and as a weak acid

ferric oxide *n* (1882) : the red or black oxide of iron Fe_2O_3 found in nature as hematite and as rust and also obtained synthetically and used as a pigment and for polishing

fer·ri·cy·a·nide \,fer-,ī-'sī-ə-,nīd, ,fer-i-\ *n* [ISV] (1845) **1** : the negative trivalent radical $Fe(CN)_6$ **2** : a compound containing the negative trivalent radical $Fe(CN)_6$; *esp* : the red salt $K_3Fe(CN)_6$ used in making blue pigments

fer·rif·er·ous \fə-'rif-(ə-)rəs, fe-\ *adj* (1811) : containing or yielding iron

fer·ri·mag·net·ic \'fer-,ī-mag-'net-ik, ,fer-i-\ *adj* (1951) : of or relating to a substance (as ferrite) characterized by magnetization in which one group of magnetic ions is polarized in a direction opposite to the other — **fer·ri·mag·net** \'fer-,ī-,mag-nət, 'fer-i-\ *n* — **fer·ri·mag·net·i·cal·ly** \'fer-,ī-mag-'net-i-k(ə-)lē, ,fer-i-\ *adv* — **fer·ri·mag·ne·tism** \-'mag-nə-,tiz-əm\ *n*

Fer·ris wheel \'fer-əs-\ *n* [G. W. G. *Ferris* †1896 Am. engineer] (1893) : an amusement device consisting of a large upright power-driven wheel carrying seats that remain horizontal around its rim

fer·rite \'fe(ə)r-,īt\ *n* (1851) **1** : any of several magnetic substances that consist essentially of an iron oxide combined with one or more metals (as manganese, nickel, or zinc), have high magnetic permeability and high electrical resistivity, and are used esp. in computer memories **2** : a solid solution in which alpha iron is the solvent — **fer·rit·ic** \fə-'rit-ik, fe-\ *adj*

fer·ri·tin \'fer-ət-ᵊn\ *n* [*ferrite* + *-in*] (1937) : a crystalline iron-containing protein that functions in the storage of iron and is found esp. in the liver and spleen

ferro- *comb form* [ML, fr. L *ferrum*] **1** : iron ⟨*ferro*concrete⟩ **2** : iron and ⟨*ferro*nickel⟩ — chiefly in names of alloys **3** : ferrous iron ⟨*ferro*cyanic⟩

fer·ro·cene \'fer-ō-,sēn\ *n* [*ferro-* + cyclopentadi*ene*] (1952) : a crystalline stable organometallic coordination compound $(C_5H_5)_2Fe$; *also* : an analogous compound with a heavy metal (as chromium)

fer·ro·con·crete \,fer-ō-'kän-,krēt, -kän-'\ *n* (1900) : REINFORCED CONCRETE

fer·ro·cy·a·nide \-'sī-ə-,nīd\ *n* (1845) **1** : the negative tetravalent radical $Fe(CN)_6$ **2** : a compound containing the negative tetravalent radical $Fe(CN)_6$; *esp* : the salt $K_4Fe(CN)_6$ used in making blue pigments (as Prussian blue)

fer·ro·elec·tric \,fer-ō-i-'lek-trik\ *adj* (1935) : of or relating to crystalline substances having spontaneous electric polarization reversible by an electric field — **ferroelectric** *n* — **fer·ro·elec·tric·i·ty** \-,lek-'tris-ət-ē, -'tris-tē\ *n*

fer·ro·mag·ne·sian \-mag-'nē-zhən, -shən\ *adj* (1899) : containing iron and magnesium ⟨~ minerals⟩

fer·ro·mag·net·ic \-'net-ik\ *adj* (1850) : of or relating to substances with an abnormally high magnetic permeability, a definite saturation point, and appreciable residual magnetism and hysteresis — **fer·ro·mag·net** \'fer-ə-,mag-nət\ *n* — **fer·ro·mag·ne·tism** \,fer-ō-'mag-nə-,tiz-əm\ *n*

[1]**fer·ro·type** \'fer-ə-,tīp\ *n* (1844) **1** : a positive photograph made by a collodion process on a thin iron plate having a darkened surface **2** : the process by which a ferrotype is made

[2]**ferrotype** *vt* (ca. 1890) : to give a gloss to (a photographic print) by squeegeeing facedown while wet on a ferrotype plate and allowing to dry

fer·rous \'fer-əs\ *adj* [NL *ferrosus,* fr. L *ferrum*] (1865) **1** : of, relating to, or containing iron **2** : being or containing iron with a valence of two

ferrous oxide *n* (1873) : a black easily oxidizable powder FeO that is the monoxide of iron

ferrous sulfate *n* (1865) : a salt $FeSO_4$; *esp* : COPPERAS

fer·ru·gi·nous \fə-'rü-jə-nəs, fe-\ *also* **fer·ru·gin·e·ous** \,fer-(y)ù-'jin-ē-əs\ *adj* [L *ferrugineus, ferruginus,* fr. *ferrugin-, ferrugo* iron rust, fr. *ferrum*] (1661) **1** : of, relating to, or containing iron ⟨a ~ soil⟩ **2** : resembling iron rust in color

[1]**fer·rule** \'fer-əl\ *n* [alter. of ME *virole,* fr. MF, fr. L *viriola,* dim. of *viria* bracelet, of Celtic origin; akin to OIr *fiar* oblique — more at VEER] (15c) **1** : a ring or cap usu. of metal put around a slender shaft (as a cane or a tool handle) to strengthen it or prevent splitting **2** : a short tube or bushing for making a tight joint (as between pipes)

[2]**ferrule** *vt* **fer·ruled; fer·rul·ing** (15c) : to supply with a ferrule

[1]**fer·ry** \'fer-ē\ *vb* **fer·ried; fer·ry·ing** [ME *ferien,* fr. OE *ferian* to carry, convey; akin to OE *faran* to go — more at FARE] *vt* (bef. 12c) **1 a** : to carry by boat over a body of water **b** : to cross by a ferry **2 a** : to convey (as by aircraft or motor vehicle) from one place to another : TRANSPORT **b** : to fly (an airplane) from the factory or other shipping point to a designated delivery point or from one base to another ~ *vi* : to cross water in a boat

[2]**ferry** *n, pl* **ferries** (13c) **1** : a place where persons or things are carried across a body of water (as a river) in a boat **2** : FERRYBOAT **3** : a franchise or right to operate a ferry service across a body of water **4** : an organized service and route for flying airplanes esp. across a sea or continent for delivery to the user

fer·ry·boat \'fer-ē-,bōt\ *n* (14c) : a boat used to ferry passengers, vehicles, or goods

fer·ry·man \-mən\ *n* (12c) : a person who operates a ferry

fer·tile \'fərt-ᵊl\ *adj* [ME, fr. MF & L; MF, fr. L *fertilis,* fr. *ferre* to carry, bear — more at BEAR] (15c) **1 a** : producing or bearing fruit in great quantities : PRODUCTIVE **b** : characterized by great resourcefulness of thought or imagination : INVENTIVE ⟨a ~ mind⟩ **c** *obs* : PLENTIFUL **2 a** (1) : capable of sustaining abundant plant growth ⟨~ soil⟩ (2) : affording abundant possibilities for development ⟨a ~ area for research⟩ **b** : capable of growing or developing ⟨~ egg⟩ **c** (1) : capable of producing fruit (2) *of an anther* : containing pollen (3) : developing spores or spore-bearing organs **d** : capable of breeding or reproducing **3** : capable of being converted into fissionable material ⟨~ uranium 238⟩ — **fer·tile·ly** \-ᵊl-(l)ē\ *adv* — **fer·tile·ness** \-ᵊl-nəs\ *n*

syn FERTILE, FECUND, FRUITFUL, PROLIFIC mean producing or capable of producing offspring or fruit. FERTILE implies the power to reproduce in kind or to assist in reproduction and growth; applied figuratively, it suggests readiness of invention and development; FECUND emphasizes abundance or rapidity in bearing fruit or offspring; FRUITFUL adds to FERTILE and FECUND the implication of desirable or useful results; PROLIFIC stresses rapidity of spreading or multiplying by or as if by natural reproduction.

fer·til·i·ty \(,)fər-'til-ət-ē\ *n* (15c) **1** : the quality or state of being fertile **2** : the birthrate of a population

fer·til·iza·tion \,fərt-ᵊl-ə-'zā-shən\ *n* (ca. 1787) : an act or process of making fertile: as **a** : the application of fertilizer **b** (1) : an act or process of fecundation, insemination, impregnation, or pollination (2) : the process of union of two germ cells whereby the somatic chromosome number is restored and the development of a new individual is initiated

fertilization membrane *n* (1931) : a resistant membranous layer of many eggs that prevents multiple fertilization by separating from the surface immediately after entry of a sperm

fer·til·ize \'fərt-ᵊl-,īz\ *vt* **-ized; -iz·ing** (1648) : to make fertile: as **a** : to cause the fertilization of **b** : to apply a fertilizer to ⟨~ land⟩ — **fer·til·iz·able** \-,ī-zə-bəl\ *adj*

fer·til·iz·er \-,ī-zər\ *n* (1661) : one that fertilizes; *specif* : a substance (as manure or a chemical mixture) used to make soil more fertile

fer·ule \'fer-əl\ *also* **fer·u·la** \'fer-(y)ə-lə\ *n* [L *ferula* giant fennel, ferule] (1599) **1** : an instrument (as a flat piece of wood) used to punish children **2** : school discipline

fe·ru·lic acid \fə-,rü-lik-\ *n* [*ferula*] (1876) : a white crystalline acid that is structurally related to vanillin and is obtained esp. from plant sources (as aspen bark)

fer·ven·cy \'fər-vən-sē\ *n, pl* **-cies** (15c) : FERVOR

fer·vent \'fər-vənt\ *adj* [ME, fr. MF & L; MF, fr. L *fervent-, fervens,* prp. of *fervēre* to boil, glow — more at BURN] (14c) **1** : very hot : GLOWING **2** : exhibiting or marked by great intensity of feeling : ZEALOUS ⟨~ prayers⟩ ***syn*** see IMPASSIONED — **fer·vent·ly** *adv*

\ə\ **abut** \ᵊ\ **kitten, F table** \ər\ **further** \a\ **ash** \ā\ **ace** \ä\ **cot, cart**
\aù\ **out** \ch\ **chin** \e\ **bet** \ē\ **easy** \g\ **go** \i\ **hit** \ī\ **ice** \j\ **job**
\ŋ\ **sing** \ō\ **go** \ȯ\ **law** \ȯi\ **boy** \th\ **thin** \t͟h\ **the** \ü\ **loot** \ù\ **foot**
\y\ **yet** \zh\ **vision** \à, k̲, ⁿ, œ, œ̄, ue, ue̅, ʸ\ *see* Guide to Pronunciation

fer·vid \'fər-vəd\ *adj* [L *fervidus,* fr. *fervēre*] (1599) **1 :** very hot : BURNING **2 :** marked by often extreme fervor ⟨a ~ crusader⟩ ***syn*** see IMPASSIONED — **fer·vid·ly** *adv* — **fer·vid·ness** *n*

fer·vor \'fər-vər\ *n* [ME *fervour,* fr. MF & L; MF *ferveur,* fr. L *fervor,* fr. *fervēre*] (14c) **1 :** intense heat **2 :** intensity of feeling or expression ⟨booing and cheering with almost equal ~ —Alan Rich⟩ ***syn*** see PASSION

fer·vour *chiefly Brit var of* FERVOR

fes·cen·nine \'fes-ᵊn-,īn, -,ēn\ *adj* [L *fescennini (versus),* ribald songs sung at rustic weddings, prob. fr. *fescinninus* of Fescennium, fr. *Fescennium,* town in Etruria] (1601) : SCURRILOUS, OBSCENE

fes·cue \'fes-(,)kyü\ *n* [ME *festu* stalk, straw, fr. MF, fr. LL *festucum,* fr. L *festuca*] (1513) **1 :** a small pointer (as a stick) used to point out letters to children learning to read **2 :** any of a genus (*Festuca*) of tufted perennial grasses with panicled spikelets

fescue foot *n* (1949) **:** a disease of the feet of cattle resembling ergotism that is associated with feeding on fescue grass and esp. tall fescue

[1]**fess** *also* **fesse** \'fes\ *n* [ME *fesse,* fr. MF *faisse,* fr. L *fascia* band] (15c) **1 :** a broad horizontal bar across the middle of a heraldic field **2 :** the center point of an armorial escutcheon

[2]**fess** \'fes\ *vi* [short for *confess*] (1840) **:** to own up : CONFESS — usu. used with *up*

-fest \,fest\ *n comb form* [G, fr. *fest* celebration, fr. L *festum* — more at FEAST] **:** meeting or occasion marked by (such) activity ⟨song*fest*⟩

fes·tal \'fest-ᵊl\ *adj* [L *festum*] (15c) **:** of or relating to a feast or festival : FESTIVE — **fes·tal·ly** \-ᵊl-ē\ *adv*

[1]**fes·ter** \'fes-tər\ *n* [ME, fr. MF *festre,* fr. L *fistula* pipe, fistulous ulcer] (14c) **:** a suppurating sore : PUSTULE

[2]**fester** *vb* **fes·tered; fes·ter·ing** \-t(ə-)riŋ\ *vi* (14c) **1 :** to generate pus **2 :** PUTREFY, ROT **3 a :** to cause increasing poisoning, irritation, or bitterness : RANKLE ⟨dissent ~*ed* unchecked⟩ **b :** to undergo or exist in a state of progressive deterioration ⟨allowed slums to ~⟩ ~ *vt* **:** to make inflamed or corrupt

[1]**fes·ti·nate** \'fes-tə-nət, -,nāt\ *adj* [L *festinatus,* pp. of *festinare* to hasten — more at BORZOI] (1605) : HASTY — **fes·ti·nate·ly** *adv*

[2]**fes·ti·nate** \-,nāt\ *vb* **-nat·ed; -nat·ing** (1652) : HASTEN

[1]**fes·ti·val** \'fes-tə-vəl\ *adj* [ME, fr. MF, fr. L *festivus* festive] (14c) **:** of, relating to, appropriate to, or set apart as a festival

[2]**festival** *n* (1589) **1 a :** a time of celebration marked by special observances **b :** FEAST 2 **2 :** a periodic season or program of cultural events or entertainment **3 :** GAIETY, CONVIVIALITY

fes·ti·val·go·er \-,gō(-ə)r\ *n* (1959) **:** one who attends a festival

fes·tive \'fes-tiv\ *adj* [L *festivus,* fr. *festum*] (1651) **1 :** of, relating to, or suitable for a feast or festival **2 :** JOYFUL, GAY — **fes·tive·ly** *adv* — **fes·tive·ness** *n*

fes·tiv·i·ty \fes-'tiv-ət-ē, fəs-\ *n, pl* **-ties** (14c) **1 :** FESTIVAL 1 **2 :** the quality or state of being festive : GAIETY **3 :** festive activity

[1]**fes·toon** \fes-'tün\ *n* [F *feston,* fr. It *festone,* fr. *festa* festival, fr. L — more at FEAST] (1630) **1 :** a decorative chain or strip hanging between two points **2 :** a carved, molded, or painted ornament representing a decorative chain

[2]**festoon** *vt* (1800) **1 :** to hang or form festoons on **2 :** to shape into festoons

fes·toon·ery \fes-'tü-nə-rē\ *n* (1836) **:** an arrangement of festoons

fest·schrift \'fest-,shrift\ *n, pl* **fest·schrif·ten** \-,shrif-tən\ *or* **festschrifts** *often cap* [G, fr. *fest* celebration + *schrift* writing, fr. OHG *scrift,* fr. *scriban* to write, fr. L *scribere* — more at -FEST, SCRIBE] (1901) **:** a volume of writings by different authors presented as a tribute or memorial esp. to a scholar

fe·ta \'fet-ə, 'fe-,tä\ *n* [NGk *(tyri) pheta,* fr. *tyri* cheese + *pheta* slice, fr. It *fetta*] (1940) **:** a white semisoft Greek cheese made from sheep's or goat's milk and cured in brine

fe·tal \'fēt-ᵊl\ *adj* (1811) **:** of, relating to, or being a fetus

fetal hemoglobin *n* (1950) **:** a hemoglobin variant that predominates in the blood of a newborn and persists in increased proportions in some forms of anemia (as thalassemia)

fetal position *n* (1963) **:** a resting position in which the body is curved, the legs and arms are bent and drawn toward the chest, and the head is bowed forward and which is assumed in some forms of psychic regression

[1]**fetch** \'fech\ *vb* [ME *fecchen,* fr. OE *fetian, feccan;* akin to OE *fōt* foot — more at FOOT] *vt* (bef. 12c) **1 a :** to go or come after and bring or take back **b :** DERIVE, DEDUCE **2 a :** to cause to come **b :** to bring in (as a price) : REALIZE **c :** INTEREST, ATTRACT **3 a :** to give (a blow) by striking : DEAL **b** *chiefly dial* **:** BRING ABOUT, ACCOMPLISH **c** (1) **:** to take in (as a breath) : DRAW (2) **:** to bring forth (as a sound) : HEAVE ⟨~ a sigh⟩ **4 a :** to reach by sailing esp. against the wind or tide **b :** to arrive at : REACH ~ *vi* **1 :** to get and bring something; *specif* **:** to retrieve killed game **2 :** to take a roundabout way : CIRCLE **3 a :** to hold a course on a body of water **b :** VEER — **fetch·er** *n*

[2]**fetch** *n* (1530) **1 :** TRICK, STRATAGEM **2 :** an act or instance of fetching **3 a :** the distance along open water or land over which the wind blows **b :** the distance traversed by waves without obstruction

[3]**fetch** *n* [origin unknown] (ca. 1787) **1 :** DOPPELGÄNGER **2 :** GHOST

fetch·ing *adj* (1880) : ATTRACTIVE, PLEASING — **fetch·ing·ly** \-iŋ-lē\ *adv*

fetch up *vt* (1599) **1 :** to bring up or out : PRODUCE **2 :** to make up (as lost time) **3 :** to bring to a stop ~ *vi* **:** to reach a standstill, stopping place, or goal : end up ⟨may have *fetched up* running a village store — Geoffrey Household⟩

[1]**fete** *or* **fête** \'fāt, 'fet\ *n* [ME *fete,* fr. MF, fr. OF *feste* — more at FEAST] (15c) **1 :** FESTIVAL **2 a :** a lavish often outdoor entertainment **b :** a large elaborate party

[2]**fete** *or* **fête** *vt* **fet·ed** *or* **fêt·ed; fet·ing** *or* **fêt·ing** (1819) **1 :** to honor or commemorate with a fete **2 :** to pay high honor to

fête cham·pê·tre \,fāt-,shäⁿ(m)-'petrᵊ, ,fet-\ *n, pl* **fêtes champêtres** *same*\ [F, lit., rural festival] (1774) **:** an outdoor entertainment

fet·er·i·ta \,fet-ə-'rēt-ə\ *n* [Sudanese Ar] (1913) **:** any of various grain sorghums with compact oval heads of large soft white seeds

fe·ti·cide \'fēt-ə-,sīd\ *n* (ca. 1844) **:** the act of causing the death of a fetus

fet·id \'fet-əd, *esp Brit* 'fē-tid\ *adj* [ME, fr. L *fetidus,* fr. *foetēre* to stink; akin to L *fumus* smoke — more at FUME] (15c) **:** having a heavy offensive smell ***syn*** see MALODOROUS — **fet·id·ly** *adv* — **fet·id·ness** *n*

fe·tish *also* **fe·tich** \'fet-ish *also* 'fēt-\ *n* [F & Pg; F *fétiche,* fr. Pg *feitiço,* fr. *feitiço* artificial, false, fr. L *facticius* factitious] (1613) **1 a :** an object believed among a primitive people to have magical power to protect or aid its owner; *broadly* **:** a material object regarded with superstitious or extravagant trust or reverence **b :** an object of irrational reverence or obsessive devotion : PREPOSSESSION **c :** an object or bodily part whose real or fantasied presence is psychologically necessary for sexual gratification and that is an object of fixation to the extent that it may interfere with complete sexual expression **2 :** a rite or cult of fetish worshipers **3 :** FIXATION

fe·tish·ism *also* **fe·tich·ism** \-ish-,iz-əm\ *n* (1801) **1 :** belief in magical fetishes **2 :** extravagant irrational devotion **3 :** the pathological displacement of erotic interest and satisfaction to a fetish — **fe·tish·ist** \-ish-əst\ *n* — **fe·tish·is·tic** \,fet-ish-'is-tik *also* ,fēt-\ *adj* — **fe·tish·is·ti·cal·ly** \-ti-k(ə-)lē\ *adv*

fet·lock \'fet-,läk\ *n* [ME *fitlok, fetlak;* akin to OE *fōt* foot] (14c) **1 a :** a projection bearing a tuft of hair on the back of the leg above the hoof of a horse or similar animal — see HORSE illustration **b :** the tuft of hair itself **2 :** the joint of the limb at the fetlock

feto- *or* **feti-** *also* **foeto-** *or* **foeti-** *comb form* [NL *fetus*] **:** fetus ⟨*feti*cide⟩ **:** fetal and ⟨*feto*placental⟩

fe·tol·o·gy \fē-'täl-ə-jē\ *n* (1965) **:** a branch of medical science concerned with the study and treatment of the fetus in the uterus — **fe·tol·o·gist** \-jəst\ *n*

fe·to·pro·tein \,fēt-ō-'prō-,tēn, -'prōt-ē-ən\ *n* (1966) **:** a fetal antigen that is also associated with some malignant conditions (as hepatoma) in the adult

fe·tor \'fēt-ər, 'fē-,tò(ə)r\ *n* [ME *fetoure,* fr. L *foetor,* fr. *foetēre*] (15c) **:** a strong offensive smell : STENCH

fe·tos·co·py \fēt-'äs-kə-pē\ *n, pl* **-pies** (1971) **:** examination of the pregnant uterus by means of a fiber-optic tube — **fe·to·scope** \'fēt-ə-,skōp\ *n*

[1]**fet·ter** \'fet-ər\ *n* [ME *feter,* fr. OE; akin to OE *fōt* foot] (bef. 12c) **1 :** a chain or shackle for the feet **2 :** something that confines : RESTRAINT

[2]**fetter** *vt* (bef. 12c) **1 :** to put fetters on : SHACKLE **2 :** to restrain from motion or action ***syn*** see HAMPER

[1]**fet·tle** \'fet-ᵊl\ *n* (1740) **1 a :** a state of physical fitness or order : CONDITION **b :** state of mind : SPIRITS ⟨the good news put us in fine ~⟩ **2 :** FETTLING

[2]**fettle** *vt* **fet·tled; fet·tling** \'fet-liŋ, -ᵊl-iŋ\ [ME *fetlen* to shape, prepare; prob. akin to OE *fæt* vessel — more at VAT] (1881) **:** to cover or line the hearth of (as a reverberatory furnace) with fettling

fet·tling \'fet-liŋ, -ᵊl-iŋ\ *n* (1864) **:** loose material (as ore or sand) thrown on the hearth of a furnace to protect it

fet·tuc·ci·ne *or* **fet·tu·ci·ne** *or* **fet·tu·ci·ni** \,fet-ə-'chē-nē\ *n pl but sing or pl in constr* [It, pl. of *fettuccina,* dim. of *fettuccia* small slice, ribbon, dim. of *fetta* slice] (1912) **:** pasta in the form of narrow ribbons; *also* **:** a dish of which fettuccine forms the base

fettuccine Al·fre·do \-(,)al-'frād-(,)ō, -äl-\ *or* **fettuccine all'·Al·fre·do** \-,al-(,)al-, -,äl-(,)äl-\ *n* [fr. *Alfredo all'Augusteo,* restaurant in Rome where it originated] (1961) **:** a dish consisting of butter, fettuccine, Parmesan cheese, cream, and seasonings

fe·tus \'fēt-əs\ *n* [ME, fr. L, act of bearing young, offspring; akin to L *fetus* newly delivered, fruitful — more at FEMININE] (14c) **:** an unborn or unhatched vertebrate esp. after attaining the basic structural plan of its kind; *specif* **:** a developing human from usu. three months after conception to birth

[1]**feud** \'fyüd\ *n* [ME *feud,* fr. ML *feodum, feudum,* of Gmc origin; akin to OE *feoh* cattle, property — more at FEE] (13c) **:** FEE 1a

[2]**feud** *n* [alter. of ME *feide,* fr. MF, of Gmc origin; akin to OHG *fēhida* hostility, feud, OE *fāh* hostile — more at FOE] (14c) **:** a mutual enmity or quarrel that is often prolonged or inveterate; *esp* **:** a lasting state of hostilities between families or clans marked by violent attacks for revenge — **feud** *vi*

feu·dal \'fyüd-ᵊl\ *adj* (1612) **1 :** of, relating to, or having the characteristics of a medieval fee **2 :** of, relating to, or suggestive of feudalism ⟨~ law⟩ — **feu·dal·ly** \-ᵊl-ē\ *adv*

feu·dal·ism \'fyüd-ᵊl-,iz-əm\ *n* (ca. 1828) **1 :** the system of political organization prevailing in Europe from the 9th to about the 15th centuries having as its basis the relation of lord to vassal with all land held in fee and as chief characteristics homage, the service of tenants under arms and in court, wardship, and forfeiture **2 :** any of various political or social systems similar to medieval feudalism — **feu·dal·ist** \-ᵊl-əst\ *n* — **feu·dal·is·tic** \,fyüd-ᵊl-'is-tik\ *adj*

feu·dal·i·ty \fyü-'dal-ət-ē\ *n, pl* **-ties** (1790) **1 :** the quality or state of being feudal **2 :** a feudal holding, domain, or concentration of power

feu·dal·ize \'fyüd-ᵊl-,īz\ *vt* **-ized; -iz·ing** (1828) **:** to make feudal — **feu·dal·iza·tion** \,fyüd-ᵊl-ə-'zā-shən\ *n*

[1]**feu·da·to·ry** \'fyüd-ə-,tōr-ē, -,tòr-\ *adj* [ML *feudatorius,* fr. *feudatus,* pp. of *feudare* to enfeoff, fr. *feudum*] (1592) **1 :** owing feudal allegiance **2 :** being under the overlordship of a foreign state

[2]**feudatory** *n, pl* **-ries** (1765) **1 :** one holding lands by feudal tenure **2 :** a dependent lordship : FEE

[1]**feud·ist** \'fyüd-əst\ *n* (1607) **:** a specialist in feudal law

[2]**feudist** *n* (1901) **:** one who feuds

feuil·le·ton \,fə(r)-yə-'tōⁿ, ,fœ-yə-\ *n* [F, fr. *feuillet* sheet of paper, fr. OF *foillet,* dim. of *foille* leaf — more at FOIL] (1845) **1 :** a part of a European newspaper or magazine devoted to material designed to entertain the general reader **2 :** something (as an installment of a novel) printed in a feuilleton **3 a :** a novel printed in installments **b :** a work of fiction catering to popular taste **4 :** a short literary composition often having a familiar tone and reminiscent content — **feuil·le·ton·ism** \-'tō(ⁿ)-,niz-əm\ *n* — **feuil·le·ton·ist** \-nəst\ *n*

Feul·gen \'fòil-gən\ *adj* (1928) **:** of, relating to, utilizing, or staining by the Feulgen reaction ⟨positive ~ mitochondria⟩

Feulgen reaction *n* [Robert *Feulgen* †1955 Ger. physiologist] (1928) **:** the development of a brilliant purple color by DNA in a microscopic preparation stained with a modified Schiff's reagent

[1]**fe·ver** \'fē-vər\ *n* [ME, fr. OE *fēfer,* fr. L *febris;* akin to L *fovēre* to warm] (bef. 12c) **1 a :** a rise of body temperature above the normal **b :** any of various diseases of which fever is a prominent symptom **2 a :** a state of heightened or intense emotion or activity **b :** a contagious usu. transient enthusiasm : CRAZE

2fever *vb* **fe·vered; fe·ver·ing** \'fēv-(ə-)riŋ\ *vt* (1606) : to throw into a fever : AGITATE ~ *vi* : to contract or be in a fever : be or become feverish

fever blister *n* (ca. 1884) : COLD SORE

fe·ver·few \'fē-vər-ˌfyü\ *n* [ME, fr. OE *feferfuge,* fr. LL *febrifugia* centaury — more at FEBRIFUGE] (bef. 12c) : a perennial European composite herb (*Chrysanthemum parthenium*)

fe·ver·ish \'fēv-(ə-)rish\ *adj* (14c) **1 a :** having the symptoms of a fever **b :** indicating or relating to fever **c :** tending to cause fever **2 :** marked by intense emotion, activity, or instability — **fe·ver·ish·ly** *adv* — **fe·ver·ish·ness** *n*

fe·ver·ous \'fēv-(ə-)rəs\ *adj* (14c) : FEVERISH

fever pitch *n* (ca. 1915) : a state of intense excitement and agitation

fever tree *n* (1868) : any of several shrubs or trees that are thought to indicate regions free from fever or that yield remedies for fever: as **a :** a blue gum (*Eucalyptus globulus*) **b :** an African acacia (*Acacia xanthlophloea*)

fe·ver·wort \'fē-vər-ˌwərt, -ˌwȯ(ə)rt\ *n* (ca. 1611) : a coarse American herb (*Triosteum perfoliatum*) of the honeysuckle family — called also *horse gentian*

1**few** \'fyü\ *pron, pl in constr* [ME *fewe,* pron. & adj., fr. OE *fēawa;* akin to OHG *fō* little, L *paucus* little, *pauper* poor, Gk *paid-, pais* child, Skt *putra* son] (bef. 12c) : not many persons or things ⟨~ were present⟩ ⟨~ of his stories are true⟩

2**few** *adj* (bef. 12c) **1 :** consisting of or amounting to only a small number ⟨one of our ~ pleasures⟩ **2 :** at least some but indeterminately small in number — used with *a* ⟨caught a ~ fish⟩ — **few·ness** *n*

3**few** *n, pl in constr* (bef. 12c) **1 :** a small number of units or individuals ⟨a ~ of them⟩ **2 :** a special limited number ⟨the discriminating ~⟩

1**few·er** \'fyü-ər, 'fyü(ə)r\ *pron, pl in constr* (bef. 12c) : a smaller number of persons or things

2**fewer** *adj, comparative of* FEW ***usage*** see LESS

few·trils \'fyü-trəlz\ *n pl* [origin unknown] *dial Eng* (ca. 1750) : things of little value : TRIFLES

fey \'fā\ *adj* [ME *feye,* fr. OE *fǣge;* akin to OHG *feigi* fey and perh. to OE *fāh* hostile, outlawed — more at FOE] (bef. 12c) **1 a** *chiefly Scot* **:** fated to die : DOOMED **b :** marked by a foreboding of death or calamity **2 a :** able to see into the future : VISIONARY **b :** marked by an otherworldly air or attitude **c :** CRAZY, TOUCHED — **fey·ly** *adv* — **fey·ness** *n*

fez \'fez\ *n, pl* **fez·zes** *also* **fez·es** [F, fr. *Fez,* Morocco] (1802) : a brimless cone-shaped flat-crowned hat that usu. has a tassel, is usu. made of red felt, and is worn esp. by men in eastern Mediterranean countries — **fezzed** \'fezd\ *adj*

fez

fi·acre \fē-'äkrᵊ\ *n, pl* **fi·acres** *same, or* -'äk-rəz\ [F, fr. the Hotel St. *Fiacre,* Paris] (1699) : a small hackney coach

fi·an·cé \ˌfē-ˌän-'sā, fē-'än-ˌ\ *n* [F, fr. MF, fr. pp. of *fiancer* to promise, betroth, fr. OF *fiancier,* fr. *fiance* promise, trust, fr. *fier* to trust, fr. (assumed) VL *fidare,* alter. of L *fidere* — more at BIDE] (1864) : a man engaged to be married

fi·an·cée \ˌfē-ˌän-'sā, fē-'än-ˌ\ *n* [F, fem. of *fiancé*] (1853) : a woman engaged to be married

fi·an·chet·to \ˌfē-ən-'ket-(ˌ)ō, -'chet-\ *vb* [*fianchetto* (an opening in chess), fr. It, dim. of *fianco* side, flank, fr. OF *flanc* — more at FLANK] *vt* (1848) : to develop (a bishop) in a chess game to the second square on the adjacent knight's file ~ *vi* : to fianchetto a bishop in a chess game

1**fi·as·co** \fē-'as-(ˌ)kō *also* -'äs-\ *n, pl* **-coes** [F, fr. It, prob. fr. *fare fiasco,* lit., to make a bottle] (1853) : a complete failure

2**fi·as·co** \fē-'äs-(ˌ)kō, -'as-\ *n, pl* **-coes** *also* **fi·as·chi** \-(ˌ)kē\ [It, fr. LL *flasco* bottle — more at FLASK] (1887) : BOTTLE, FLASK; *esp* : a bulbous long-necked straw-covered bottle for wine

fi·at \'fē-ət, -ˌat, -ˌät; 'fī-ət, -ˌat\ *n* [L, let it be done, 3d sing. pres. subj. of *fieri* to become, be done — more at BE] (1630) **1 :** a command or act of will that creates something without or as if without further effort **2 :** an authoritative decision of consciousness ⟨a ~ of conscience⟩ **3 :** an authoritative or arbitrary order : DECREE ⟨government by ~⟩

fiat money *n* (1874) : money (as paper currency) not convertible into coin or specie of equivalent value

1**fib** \'fib\ *n* [perh. by shortening & alter. fr. *fable*] (1611) : a trivial or childish lie

2**fib** *vi* **fibbed; fib·bing** (1690) : to tell a fib ***syn*** see LIE — **fib·ber** *n*

3**fib** *vb* **fibbed; fib·bing** [origin unknown] *Brit* (1665) : BEAT, PUMMEL

fi·ber *or* **fi·bre** \'fī-bər\ *n* [F *fibre,* fr. L *fibra*] (1607) **1 :** a thread or a structure or object resembling a thread: as **a** (1) **:** a slender root (as of a grass) (2) **:** an elongated tapering thick-walled plant cell void at maturity that imparts elasticity, flexibility, and tensile strength **b** (1) **:** a strand of nerve tissue : AXON, DENDRITE (2) **:** one of the filaments composing most of the intercellular matrix of connective tissue (3) **:** one of the elongated contractile cells of muscle tissue **c :** a slender and greatly elongated natural or synthetic filament (as of wool, cotton, asbestos, gold, glass, or rayon) typically capable of being spun into yarn **d :** ROUGHAGE **2 :** material made of fibers; *specif* : VULCANIZED FIBER **3 a :** an element that gives texture or substance **b :** basic toughness : STRENGTH, FORTITUDE **c :** essential structure or character ⟨the very ~ of a person's being⟩ — **fi·bered** \-bərd\ *adj*

fi·ber·board *also* **fi·bre·board** \-ˌbō(ə)rd, -ˌbȯ(ə)rd\ *n* (1897) : a material made by compressing fibers (as of wood) into stiff sheets; *also* : PAPERBOARD

fi·ber·fill \-ˌfil\ *n* (1962) : man-made fibers used as a filling material (as for cushions)

fi·ber·glass \-ˌglas\ *n* (1937) : glass in fibrous form used in making various products (as glass wool, yarns, textiles, and structures)

fi·ber·ize \'fī-bə-ˌrīz\ *vt* **-ized; -iz·ing** (ca. 1934) : to break into fibers — **fi·ber·iza·tion** \ˌfī-b(ə-)rə-'zā-shən\ *n*

fi·ber–op·tic \'fī-bə-ˌräp-tik\ *adj* (1961) : of, relating to, or using fiber optics

fiber optics *n pl* (1956) **1 :** thin transparent fibers of glass or plastic that are enclosed by material of a lower index of refraction and that transmit light throughout their length by internal reflections; *also* : a bundle of such fibers used in an instrument (as for viewing body cavities) **2** *sing in constr* **:** the technique of the use of fiber optics

fi·ber·scope \'fī-bər-ˌskōp\ *n* (1954) : a flexible instrument utilizing fiber optics and used esp. in medicine for examination of inaccessible areas (as the stomach)

Fi·bo·nac·ci number \ˌfē-bə-ˌnäch-ē-, ˌfib-ə-\ *n* [Leonardo *Fibonacci* †*ab* 1250 Ital. mathematician] (1914) : an integer in the infinite sequence 1, 1, 2, 3, 5, 8, 13, . . . of which the first two terms are 1 and 1 and each succeeding term is the sum of the two immediately preceding

fibr- *or* **fibro-** *comb form* [L *fibra*] : fiber : fibrous tissue ⟨*fibr*oid⟩ : fibrous and ⟨*fibro*vascular⟩

fi·branne \'fī-ˌbran, fī-'\ *n* [F, viscose rayon, fr. *fibre*] (1941) : a fabric made of spun-rayon yarn

fi·bril \'fīb-rəl, 'fib-\ *n* [NL *fibrilla,* dim. of L *fibra*] (1664) : a small filament or fiber: as **a :** ROOT HAIR **b** (1) **:** one of the fine threads into which a striated muscle fiber can be longitudinally split (2) **:** NEUROFIBRIL — **fi·bril·lar** \'fib-rə-lər, 'fīb-\ *adj* — **fi·bril·lose** \'fib-rə-ˌlōs, 'fīb-\ *adj*

fi·bril·late \'fib-rə-ˌlāt, 'fīb-\ *vb* **-lat·ed; -lat·ing** *vi* (1839) : to undergo or exhibit fibrillation ~ *vt* : to cause to undergo fibrillation

fi·bril·la·tion \ˌfib-rə-'lā-shən, ˌfīb-\ *n* (1839) **1 :** an act or process of forming fibers or fibrils **2 a :** a muscular twitching involving individual muscle fibers acting without coordination **b :** very rapid irregular contractions of the muscle fibers of the heart resulting in a lack of synchronism between heartbeat and pulse

fi·brin \'fī-brən\ *n* (1800) : a white insoluble fibrous protein formed from fibrinogen by the action of thrombin esp. in the clotting of blood

fi·brin·o·gen \fī-'brin-ə-jən\ *n* [ISV] (1872) : a globulin that is produced in the liver, that is present esp. in the blood plasma, and that is converted into fibrin during clotting of blood

fi·bri·noid \'fīb-rə-ˌnȯid, 'fīb-\ *n, often attrib* (1910) : a homogeneous acidophilic refractile material that somewhat resembles fibrin and is formed in the walls of blood vessels and in connective tissue in some pathological conditions and normally in the placenta

fi·bri·no·ly·sin \ˌfī-brən-ᵊl-'īs-ᵊn\ *n* [ISV] (1915) : any of several proteolytic enzymes that promote the dissolution of blood clots; *esp* : PLASMIN

fi·bri·no·ly·sis \-'ī-səs, -brə-'näl-ə-səs\ *n* [NL] (1907) : the usu. enzymatic breakdown of fibrin — **fi·bri·no·lyt·ic** \-brən-ᵊl-'it-ik\ *adj*

fi·bri·no·pep·tide \ˌfī-brə-nō-'pep-ˌtīd\ *n* (1967) : any of the vertebrate proteins that are split off from fibrinogen by thrombin during clotting of the blood, comprise two in each species, and exhibit great interspecific variability

fi·bro·blast \'fīb-rə-ˌblast, 'fib-\ *n* [ISV] (ca. 1876) : an undifferentiated mesenchyme cell giving rise to connective tissue — **fi·bro·blas·tic** \ˌfīb-rə-'blas-tik, ˌfib-\ *adj*

fi·bro·cys·tic \ˌfīb-rə-'sis-tik, ˌfib-\ *adj* (1854) : characterized by the presence or development of fibrous tissue and cysts

1**fi·broid** \'fīb-ˌrȯid, 'fib-\ *adj* (1852) : resembling, forming, or consisting of fibrous tissue

2**fibroid** *n* (1872) : a benign tumor made up of fibrous and muscular tissue that occurs esp. in the uterine wall

fi·bro·in \'fīb-rə-wən, 'fib-\ *n* [F *fibroïne,* fr. *fibr-* + *-ine* -in] (1861) : an insoluble protein comprising the filaments of the raw silk fiber

fi·bro·ma \fī-'brō-mə\ *n, pl* **-mas** *also* **-ma·ta** \-mət-ə\ (1847) : a benign tumor consisting mainly of fibrous tissue — **fi·bro·ma·tous** \-mət-əs\ *adj*

fi·bro·sar·co·ma \ˌfīb-rə-sär-'kō-mə, ˌfib-\ *n* (1878) : a sarcoma of relatively low malignancy made up chiefly of spindle-shaped cells that tend to form collagenous fibrils

fi·bro·sis \fī-'brō-səs\ *n* (1873) : a condition marked by increase of interstitial fibrous tissue — **fi·brot·ic** \-'brät-ik\ *adj*

fi·bro·si·tis \ˌfīb-rə-'sīt-əs, ˌfib-\ *n* [NL, fr. *fibrosus* fibrous, fr. ISV *fibrous*] (1904) : a rheumatic disorder of fibrous tissue

fi·brous \'fī-brəs\ *adj* [modif. of F *fibreux,* fr. *fibre* fiber] (1626) **1 a :** containing, consisting of, or resembling fibers **b :** characterized by fibrosis **c :** capable of being separated into fibers ⟨a ~ mineral⟩ **2 :** TOUGH, SINEWY ⟨~ texture⟩

fibrous root *n* (1626) : a root (as in most grasses) that has no prominent central axis and that branches in all directions

fi·bro·vas·cu·lar \'fīb-rō-'vas-kyə-lər, ˌfib-\ *adj* (ca. 1845) : having or consisting of fibers and conducting cells ⟨~ bundles in leaves⟩

fibrovascular bundle *n* (ca. 1911) : VASCULAR BUNDLE

fib·u·la \'fib-yə-lə\ *n, pl* **-lae** \-lē, -lī\ *or* **-las** [L; akin to L *figere* to fasten] (1673) **1 :** a clasp resembling a safety pin used esp. by the ancient Greeks and Romans **2 :** the outer and usu. the smaller of the two bones of the hind limb of tetrapod vertebrates between the knee and ankle — **fib·u·lar** \-lər\ *adj*

-fic \fik\ *adj suffix* [MF & L; MF *-fique,* fr. L *-ficus,* fr. *facere* to make — more at DO] : making : causing ⟨felici*fic*⟩

-fi·ca·tion \fə-'kā-shən\ *n comb form* [ME *-ficacioun,* fr. MF & L; MF *-fication,* fr. L *-fication-, -ficatio,* fr. *-ficatus,* pp. ending of verbs ending in *-ficare* to make, fr. *-ficus*] : making : production ⟨rei*fication*⟩

fice \'fīs\ *var of* FEIST

fiche \'fēsh *also* 'fish\ *n, pl* **fiche** *also* **fiches** [F, peg, tag, slide, fr. OF, fr. *ficher*] (1926) : MICROFICHE

fi·chu \'fish-(ˌ)ü, 'fēsh-\ *n* [F, fr. pp. of *ficher* to stick in, throw on, fr. (assumed) VL *figicare,* fr. L *figere* to fasten, pierce — more at DIKE] (1803) : a woman's light triangular scarf that is draped over the shoulders and fastened in front or worn to fill in a low neckline

fi·cin \'fīs-ᵊn\ *n* [L *ficus* fig] (1930) : a proteinase that is obtained from the latex of fig trees and is used as an anthelmintic and protein digestive

fick·le \'fik-əl\ *adj* [ME *fikel* deceitful, inconstant, fr. OE *ficol* deceitful; akin to OE *befician* to deceive, L *pigēre* to irk and prob. to OE *fāh* hostile — more at FOE] (bef. 12c) : marked by lack of steadfastness,

\ə\ abut \ᵊ\ kitten, F table \ər\ further \a\ ash \ā\ ace \ä\ cot, cart \au̇\ out \ch\ chin \e\ bet \ē\ easy \g\ go \i\ hit \ī\ ice \j\ job \ŋ\ sing \ō\ go \ȯ\ law \ȯi\ boy \th\ thin \th\ the \ü\ loot \u̇\ foot \y\ yet \zh\ vision \á, k̲, ⁿ, œ, œ̄, ue, ue̅, ʸ\ *see* Guide to Pronunciation

constancy, or stability : given to erratic changeableness ***syn*** see INCONSTANT — **fick·le·ness** *n* — **fick·ly** \'fik-(ə-)lē\ *adv*

fi·co \'fē-(,)kō\ *n, pl* **ficoes** [obs. *fico,* obscene gesture of contempt, modif. of It *fica* fig, vulva, gesture of contempt, fr. (assumed) VL *fica* fig — more at FIG] (1577) : FIG 2

fic·tile \'fik-tᵊl, -,tīl\ *adj* [L *fictilis* molded of clay, fr. *fictus*] (1626) **1** : molded or moldable of earth, clay, or other soft material **2** : of or relating to pottery

fic·tion \'fik-shən\ *n* [ME *ficcioun,* fr. MF *fiction,* fr. L *fiction-, fictio* act of fashioning, fiction, fr. *fictus,* pp. of *fingere* to shape, fashion, feign — more at DOUGH] (14c) **1 a** : something invented by the imagination or feigned; *specif* : an invented story **b** : fictitious literature (as novels or short stories) **2** : an assumption of a possibility as a fact irrespective of the question of its truth ⟨a legal ~⟩ **3** : the action of feigning or of creating with the imagination — **fic·tion·al** \-shnəl, -shən-ᵊl\ *adj* — **fic·tion·al·i·ty** \,fik-shə-'nal-ət-ē\ *n* — **fic·tion·al·ly** \'fik-shnə-lē, -shən-ᵊl-ē\ *adv*

fic·tion·al·ize \'fik-shnə-,līz, -shən-ᵊl-,īz\ *vt* **-ized; -iz·ing** (ca. 1918) : to make into or treat in the manner of fiction ⟨~ a biography⟩ — **fic·tion·al·iza·tion** \,fik-shnə-lə-'zā-shən, -shən-ᵊl-ə-\ *n*

fic·tion·eer \,fik-shə-'ni(ə)r\ *n* (1923) : one who writes fiction esp. in quantity and without high standards — **fic·tion·eer·ing** *n*

fic·tion·ist \'fik-sh(ə-)nəst\ *n* (1829) : a writer of fiction; *esp* : NOVELIST

fic·tion·ize \'fik-shə-,nīz\ *vt* **-ized; -iz·ing** (1831) : FICTIONALIZE — **fic·tion·iza·tion** \,fik-shə-nə-'zā-shən\ *n*

fic·ti·tious \fik-'tish-əs\ *adj* [L *ficticius* artificial, feigned, fr. *fictus*] (1621) **1** : of, relating to, or characteristic of fiction : IMAGINARY **2 a** : conventionally or hypothetically assumed or accepted ⟨a ~ concept⟩ **b** *of a name* : FALSE, ASSUMED **3** : not genuinely felt — **fic·ti·tious·ly** *adv* — **fic·ti·tious·ness** *n*

syn FICTITIOUS, FABULOUS, LEGENDARY, MYTHICAL, APOCRYPHAL mean having the nature of something imagined or invented. FICTITIOUS implies fabrication and suggests artificiality or contrivance more than deliberate falsification or deception; FABULOUS stresses the marvelous or incredible character of something without necessarily implying impossibility or actual nonexistence; LEGENDARY suggests the elaboration of invented details and distortion of historical facts produced by popular tradition; MYTHICAL implies a purely fanciful explanation of facts or the creation of beings and events out of the imagination; APOCRYPHAL implies an unknown or dubious source or origin or may imply that the thing itself is dubious or inaccurate.

fic·tive \'fik-tiv\ *adj* (15c) **1** : not genuine : FEIGNED **2** : of, relating to, or capable of imaginative creation **3** : of, relating to, or having the characteristics of fiction : FICTIONAL — **fic·tive·ly** *adv* — **fic·tive·ness** *n*

fi·cus \'fī-kəs\ *n, pl* **ficus** *or* **fi·cus·es** [NL, fr. L, fig] (1864) : FIG 1b

fid \'fid\ *n* [origin unknown] (1615) **1** : a sturdy pin used in opening the strands of a rope **2** : a square bar of wood or iron used to support a topmast

-fid \fəd, ,fid\ *adj comb form* [L *-fidus,* fr. *findere* to split — more at BITE] : divided into (so many) parts ⟨sexi*fid*⟩ or (such) parts ⟨pinnati*fid*⟩

[1]**fid·dle** \'fid-ᵊl\ *n* [ME *fidel,* fr. (assumed) OE *fithele,* prob. fr. ML *vitula*] (bef. 12c) **1** : VIOLIN **2** : a device (as a slat, rack, or light railing of cords) to keep dishes from sliding off a table aboard ship **3** : FIDDLESTICKS — used as an interjection **4** : SWINDLE

[2]**fiddle** *vb* **fid·dled; fid·dling** \'fid-liŋ, -ᵊl-iŋ\ *vi* (14c) **1** : to play on a fiddle **2 a** : to move the hands or fingers restlessly **b** : to spend time in aimless or fruitless activity : PUTTER ⟨*fiddled* around with the engine for hours⟩ **c** : MEDDLE, TAMPER ⟨*fiddled* clandestinely in other governments⟩ ~ *vt* **1** : to play (as a tune) on a fiddle **2** : CHEAT, SWINDLE **3** : to alter or manipulate deceptively for fraudulent gain ⟨accountants *fiddling* the books —Stanley Cohen⟩ — **fid·dler** \'fid-lər, -ᵊl-ər\ *n*

fiddle away *vt* (1667) : to fritter away ⟨*fiddled away* his time⟩

fid·dle·back \'fid-ᵊl-,bak\ *n* (1890) : something resembling a fiddle

fid·dle–fad·dle \'fid-ᵊl-,fad-ᵊl\ *n* [redupl. of *fiddle* (fiddlesticks)] (1577) : NONSENSE — often used as an interjection

fid·dle–foot·ed \,fid-ᵊl-'fu̇t-əd\ *adj* (1946) **1** : SKITTISH, JUMPY ⟨a ~ horse⟩ **2** : prone to wander ⟨the nameless ~ drifters, the shifty riders who traveled the back trails —Luke Short⟩

fid·dle·head \'fid-ᵊl-,hed\ *n* (1599) **1** : an ornament on a ship's bow curved like the scroll at the head of a violin **2** : one of the young unfurling fronds of some ferns that are often eaten as greens

fiddler crab *n* (1843) : a burrowing crab (genus *Uca*) that has one claw much enlarged in the male

fid·dle·stick \'fid-ᵊl-,stik\ *n* (15c) **1 a** *archaic* : a violin bow **b** *Southern* : a small stick or switch used to strike the strings of a fiddle in time to the music while the fiddler plays with a bow — usu. used in pl. **2 a** : something of little value : TRIFLE ⟨didn't care a ~ for that⟩ **b** *pl* : NONSENSE — used as an interjection

fid·dling \'fid-liŋ, -lən\ *adj* (1660) : TRIFLING, PETTY ⟨a ~ excuse⟩

fi·de·ism \'fēd-(,)ā-,iz-əm\ *n* [prob. fr. F *fidéisme,* fr. L *fides*] (ca. 1885) : reliance on faith rather than reason in pursuit of religious truth — **fi·de·ist** \-,ā-əst\ *n* — **fi·de·is·tic** \,fēd-(,)ā-'is-tik\ *adj*

Fi·del·ism \'fēd-ᵊl-,iz-əm, fi-'del-\ *n* [*Fidel* Castro] (1959) : CASTROISM — **Fi·del·ist** \-əst\ *n or adj*

Fi·del·is·ta \,fēd-ᵊl-'ē-stə\ *n* [AmSp, fr. *Fidel* Castro + *-ista* -ist] (1960) : an adherent of Fidelism

fi·del·i·ty \fə-'del-ət-ē, fī-\ *n, pl* **-ties** [ME *fidelite,* fr. MF *fidelité,* fr. L *fidelitat-, fidelitas,* fr. *fidelis* faithful, fr. *fides* faith, fr. *fidere* to trust — more at BIDE] (15c) **1 a** : the quality or state of being faithful **b** : accuracy in details : EXACTNESS **2** : the degree to which an electronic device (as a record player, radio, or television) accurately reproduces its effect (as sound or picture)

syn FIDELITY, ALLEGIANCE, FEALTY, LOYALTY, DEVOTION, PIETY mean faithfulness to something to which one is bound by pledge or duty. FIDELITY implies strict and continuing faithfulness to an obligation, trust, or duty; ALLEGIANCE suggests an adherence like that of a citizen to his country; FEALTY implies a fidelity acknowledged by the individual and as compelling as a sworn vow; LOYALTY implies a faithfulness that is steadfast in the face of any temptation to renounce, desert, or betray; DEVOTION stresses zeal and service amounting to self-dedication; PIETY stresses fidelity to obligations regarded as natural and fundamental.

fidge \'fij\ *vi* **fidged; fidg·ing** [prob. alter. of E dial. *fitch,* fr. ME *fichen*] *chiefly Scot* (1575) : FIDGET

[1]**fidg·et** \'fij-ət\ *n* [irreg. fr. *fidge*] (1674) **1** : uneasiness or restlessness as shown by nervous movements — usu. used in pl. **2** [[2]*fidget*] : one that fidgets

[2]**fidget** *vi* (1754) : to move or act restlessly or nervously ~ *vt* : to cause to move or act nervously

fidg·ety \'fij-ət-ē\ *adj* (1730) **1** : inclined to fidget **2** : making unnecessary fuss : FUSSY — **fidg·et·i·ness** *n*

fi·do \'fīd-(,)ō\ *n, pl* **fidos** [*f*reaks + *i*rregulars + *d*efects + *o*ddities] (1966) : a coin having a minting error

fi·du·cial \fə-'d(y)ü-shəl, fī-\ *adj* (1571) **1** : taken as standard of reference ⟨a ~ mark⟩ **2** : founded on faith or trust **3** : having the nature of a trust : FIDUCIARY — **fi·du·cial·ly** \-,d(y)üsh-(ə-)lē\ *adv*

[1]**fi·du·cia·ry** \-'d(y)ü-shē-,er-ē, -shə-rē\ *n, pl* **-ries** (1631) : one that holds a fiduciary relation or acts in a fiduciary capacity

[2]**fiduciary** *adj* [L *fiduciarius,* fr. *fiducia* confidence, trust, fr. *fidere*] (1641) : of, relating to, or involving a confidence or trust: as **a** : held or founded in trust or confidence **b** : holding in trust **c** : depending on public confidence for value or currency ⟨~ fiat money⟩

fie \'fī\ *interj* [ME *fi,* fr. OF] (13c) — used to express disgust or disapproval

fief \'fēf\ *n* [F, fr. OF — more at FEE] (ca. 1611) **1** : a feudal estate : FEE **2** : something over which one has rights or exercises control ⟨a politician's ~⟩ — **fief·dom** \-dəm\ *n*

[1]**field** \'fē(ə)ld\ *n* [ME, fr. OE *feld;* akin to OHG *feld* field, OE *flōr* floor — more at FLOOR] (bef. 12c) **1 a** : an open land area free of woods and buildings **b** (1) : an area of cleared enclosed land used for cultivation or pasture ⟨a ~ of wheat⟩ (2) : land containing a natural resource **c** : the place where a battle is fought; *also* : BATTLE **d** : a large unbroken expanse (as of ice) **2 a** : an area or division of an activity **b** : the sphere of practical operation outside a laboratory, office, or factory ⟨geologists working in the ~⟩ **c** : an area for military exercises or maneuvers **d** (1) : an area constructed, equipped, or marked for sports (2) : the portion of an indoor or outdoor sports area enclosed by the running track and on which field events are conducted (3) : either of the three sections of a baseball outfield ⟨hits to all ~*s*⟩ **3** : a space on which something is drawn or projected: as **a** : the space on the surface of a coin, medal, or seal that does not contain the design **b** : the ground of each division in a flag **c** : the whole surface of an escutcheon **4** : the individuals that make up all or part of the participants in a sports activity; *esp* : all participants with the exception of the favorite or the winner in a contest where more than two are entered **5** : a complex of forces that serve as causative agents in human behavior **6 a** : a set of mathematical elements that is subject to two binary operations the second of which is distributive relative to the first and that constitutes a commutative group under the first operation and also under the second if the zero or unit element under the first is omitted **b** : a region of embryonic tissue capable of a particular type of differentiation ⟨a morphogenetic ~⟩ **c** : a region or space in which a given effect (as magnetism) exists **7** : the area visible through the lens of an optical instrument **8** : a series of drain tiles and an absorption area **9** : a particular area (as a column or set of columns on a punch card) in which the same type of information is regularly recorded

[2]**field** *adj* (13c) : of or relating to a field: as **a** : growing in or inhabiting the fields or open country **b** : made, conducted, or used in the field **c** : operating or active in the field

[3]**field** *vt* (1823) **1 a** : to catch or pick up (a batted ball) and usu. throw to a teammate **b** : to give an impromptu answer or solution to ⟨the senator ~*ed* the reporters' questions⟩ **2** : to put into the field ⟨~ an army⟩ ⟨~ a team⟩; *also* : to enter in competition ~ *vi* : to play as a fielder

field artillery *n* (1644) : artillery other than antiaircraft artillery used with armies in the field

field corn *n* (1856) : an Indian corn (as dent corn or flint corn) with starchy kernels grown for feeding stock or for market grain

field crop *n* (1860) : an agricultural crop (as hay, grain, or cotton) grown on large areas

field day *n* (1747) **1 a** : a day for military exercises or maneuvers **b** : an outdoor meeting or social gathering **c** : a day of sports and athletic competition **2** : a time of extraordinary pleasure or opportunity ⟨the newspaper had a *field day* with the scandal⟩

field·er \'fēl-dər\ *n* (1832) : one that fields; *esp* : a defensive player stationed in the field (as in baseball)

fielder's choice *n* (1902) : a situation in baseball in which a batter reaches base safely because the fielder attempts to put out another base runner on the play

field event *n* (1899) : an event (as weight-throwing or jumping) in a track-and-field meet other than a race

field·fare \'fē(ə)l(d)-,fa(ə)r, -,fe(ə)r\ *n* [ME *feldefare,* fr. OE, fr. *feld* + *-fare;* prob. akin to OE *fara* companion; akin to OE *faran* to go — more at FARE] (bef. 12c) : a medium-sized Eurasian thrush (*Turdus pilaris*) with ash-colored head and chestnut wings

field glass *n* (1836) : a binocular without prisms esp. for use outdoors — usu. used in pl.

field goal *n* (1902) **1** : a score in football made by drop-kicking or place-kicking the ball over the crossbar from ordinary play **2** : a goal in basketball made while the ball is in play

field grade *n* (1948) : the rank of a field officer

field hand *n* (1826) : an outdoor farm laborer

field hockey *n* (1903) : a game played on a turfed field between two teams of 11 players each whose object is to direct a ball into the opponent's goal with a hockey stick

field house *n* (1895) **1** : a building at an athletic field for housing equipment or providing dressing facilities **2** : a building enclosing a large area suitable for various forms of athletics and usu. providing seats for spectators

fielding average *n* (ca. 1947) : the average (as of a baseball fielder) determined by dividing the number of putouts and assists by the number of chances — compare BATTING AVERAGE

field judge *n* (ca. 1929) : a football official whose duties include covering action on kicks and forward passes and timing intermission periods and time-outs

field lens n (1837) : the lens in a compound eyepiece that is nearer the objective

field magnet n (1891) : a magnet for producing and maintaining a magnetic field esp. in a generator or electric motor

field marshal n (1614) : the highest ranking military officer (as in the British army)

field mouse n (15c) : any of various mice that inhabit fields; esp : VOLE

field officer n (1656) : a commissioned officer in the army, air force, or marine corps of the rank of colonel, lieutenant colonel, or major — compare COMPANY OFFICER, GENERAL OFFICER

field of force (1850) : FIELD 6c

field of honor (1824) **1** : a place where a duel is fought **2** : BATTLEFIELD

field of view (1812) : FIELD 7

field of vision (1862) : VISUAL FIELD

field pea n (1709) : a small-seeded pea (Pisum sativum var. arvense) widely grown for forage and food

field-piece \'fē(ə)l(d)-ˌpēs\ n (1590) : a gun or howitzer for use in the field

field spaniel n (1867) : any of a breed of medium-sized hunting and retrieving spaniels that have a flat dense usu. black coat

field-stone \'fē(ə)l(d)-ˌstōn\ n (1799) : stone (as in building) in usu. unaltered form as taken from the field

field-strip \-ˌstrip\ vt (1947) : to take apart (a weapon) to the extent authorized for routine cleaning, lubrication, and minor repairs

field-test \-ˌtest\ vt (1948) : to test (as a procedure or product) in a natural environment — **field test** n

field theory n (1901) : a detailed mathematical description of the assumed physical properties of a region under some influence (as gravitation)

field trial n (ca. 1896) **1** : a trial of sporting dogs in actual performance **2** : a trial of a new product in actual situations for which it is intended

field trip n (1926) : a visit (as to a factory, farm, or museum) made (as by students and a teacher) for purposes of firsthand observation

field winding n (1893) : the winding of the field magnet of a dynamo or motor

field-work \'fē(ə)l-ˌdwərk\ n (1743) **1** : a temporary fortification thrown up by an army in the field **2** : work done in the field (as by students) to gain practical experience through firsthand observation **3** : the gathering of anthropological or sociological data through the interviewing and observation of subjects in the field — **field-work-er** n

fiend \'fēnd\ n [ME, fr. OE fēond; akin to OHG fīant enemy, Skt pīyati he scorns] (bef. 12c) **1 a** : DEVIL 1 **b** : DEMON **2** : a person of great wickedness or maliciousness **3** : a person excessively devoted to a pursuit or study : FANATIC ⟨a golf ~⟩ **3** : a person who uses immoderate quantities of something : ADDICT ⟨a dope ~⟩ **4** : WIZARD 3 ⟨a ~ at mathematics⟩

fiend-ish \'fēn-dish\ adj (1529) **1** : perversely diabolical ⟨took a ~ pleasure in hurting people⟩ **2** : extremely cruel or wicked **3** : excessively bad, unpleasant, or difficult ⟨~ weather⟩ — **fiend-ish-ly** adv — **fiend-ish-ness** n

fierce \'fi(ə)rs\ adj **fierc-er; fierc-est** [ME fiers, fr. MF, fr. L ferus wild, savage; akin to Gk thēr wild animal] (14c) **1 a** : violently hostile or aggressive in temperament **b** : given to fighting or killing : PUGNACIOUS **2 a** : marked by unrestrained zeal or vehemence ⟨a ~ argument⟩ **b** : extremely vexatious, disappointing, or intense ⟨~ pain⟩ **3** : furiously active or determined ⟨make a ~ effort⟩ **4** : wild or menacing in appearance — **fierce-ly** adv — **fierce-ness** n

syn FIERCE, FEROCIOUS, BARBAROUS, SAVAGE, CRUEL mean showing fury or malignity in looks or actions. FIERCE applies to humans and animals that inspire terror by their wild and menacing aspect or fury in attack; FEROCIOUS implies extreme fierceness and unrestrained violence and brutality; BARBAROUS implies a ferocity or mercilessness regarded as unworthy of civilized people; SAVAGE implies the absence of inhibitions restraining civilized people filled with rage, lust, or other violent passion; CRUEL implies indifference to suffering and even positive pleasure in inflicting it.

fi-eri fa-cias \ˌfī-(ə-)rē-'fā-sh(ē-)əs\ n [L, cause (it) to be done] (15c) : a writ authorizing the sheriff to obtain satisfaction of a judgment in debt or damages from the goods and chattels of the defendant

fi-ery \'fī(-ə)-rē\ adj **fi-er-i-er; -est** [ME, fr. fire, fier fire] (13c) **1 a** : consisting of fire **b** : BURNING, BLAZING **c** : using or carried out with fire **d** : liable to catch fire or explode : FLAMMABLE ⟨a ~ vapor⟩ **2 a** : hot like a fire **b** (1) : being in an inflamed state or condition ⟨a ~ boil⟩ (2) : feverish and flushed ⟨a ~ forehead⟩ **3** : of the color of fire : RED ⟨a ~ sunset⟩ **4 a** : full of or exuding emotion or spirit ⟨a ~ sermon⟩ **b** : easily provoked : IRRITABLE — **fi-eri-ly** \-rə-lē\ adv — **fi-eri-ness** \-rē-nəs\ n — **fiery** adj

fi-es-ta \fē-'es-tə\ n [Sp, fr. L festa — more at FEAST] (1844) : FESTIVAL; specif : a saint's day celebrated in Spain and Latin America with processions and dances

fife \'fīf\ n [G pfeife pipe, fife, fr. OHG pfīfa, fr. (assumed) VL pipa pipe — more at PIPE] (1555) : a small transverse flute with six to eight finger holes and usu. no keys that is used chiefly to accompany drums in a marching band

fife rail n (ca. 1721) : a rail about the mast near the deck to which rigging is belayed

fif-teen \(ˌ)fif-'tēn\ n [ME fiftene, adj., fr. OE fīftēne, fr. fīf five + -tiene (akin to OE tien ten) — more at FIVE, TEN] (bef. 12c) **1** — see NUMBER table **2** : the first point scored by a side in a game of tennis — called also five — **fifteen** adj or pron — **fif-teenth** \-'tēn(t)th\ adj or n

fifth \'fif(t)th, 'fiftth, 'fift\ n, pl **fifths** \'fif(t)ths, 'fif(t)s\ (bef. 12c) **1** — see NUMBER table **2 a** : the musical interval embracing five diatonic degrees **b** : a tone at this interval; specif : DOMINANT 1 **c** : the harmonic combination of two tones at this interval **3** : a unit of measure for liquor equal to one fifth of a U.S. gallon **4** cap : the Fifth Amendment of the U.S. Constitution — **fifth** adj or adv — **fifth-ly** adv

fifth column n [name applied to rebel sympathizers in Madrid in 1936 when four rebel columns were advancing on the city] (1936) : a group of secret sympathizers or supporters of an enemy that engage in espionage or sabotage within defense lines or national borders — **fifth col-um-nism** \-'käl-əm-ˌ(n)iz-əm\ n — **fifth col-um-nist** \-(n)əst\ n

fifth wheel n (1874) **1 a** : a horizontal wheel or segment of a wheel that consists of two parts rotating on each other above the fore axle of a carriage and that forms support to prevent tipping **b** : a similar coupling between tractor and trailer of a semitrailer **2** : a spare wheel **3** : one that is superfluous, unnecessary, or burdensome

fif-ty \'fif-tē\ n, pl **fifties** [ME, fr. fifty, adj., fr. OE fīftig, fr. fīftig, n., group of 50, fr. fīf five + -tig group of ten — more at TEN] (bef. 12c) **1** — see NUMBER table **2** : the numbers 50 to 59; specif : the years 50 to 59 in a lifetime or century **3** : a 50-dollar bill — **fif-ti-eth** \-tē-əth\ adj or n — **fifty** adj or pron

fif-ty–fif-ty \ˌfif-tē-'fif-tē\ adj (1913) **1** : shared, assumed, or borne equally ⟨a ~ proposition⟩ **2** : half favorable and half unfavorable ⟨a ~ chance⟩ — **fifty–fifty** adv

¹fig \'fig\ n [ME fige, fr. OF, fr. OProv figa, fr. (assumed) VL fica, fr. L ficus fig tree, fig] (13c) **1 a** : an oblong or pear-shaped fruit that is a syconium **b** : any of a genus (Ficus) of trees of the mulberry family bearing fruits that are syconia; esp : a widely cultivated tree (F. carica) that produces edible figs **2** : a contemptibly worthless trifle ⟨not worth a ~⟩

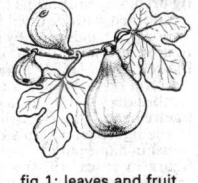
fig 1: leaves and fruit

²fig n [fig, vb. (to adorn)] (1835) : DRESS, ARRAY ⟨a young woman in dazzling royal full ~ —Mollie Panter-Downes⟩

¹fight \'fīt\ vb **fought** \'fòt\; **fight-ing** [ME fighten, fr. OE feohtan; akin to OHG fehtan to fight, L pectere to comb — more at FEE] vi (bef. 12c) **1 a** : to contend in battle or physical combat; esp : to strive to overcome a person by blows or weapons **b** : to engage in boxing **2** : to put forth a determined effort ~ vt **1 a** (1) : to contend against in or as if in battle or physical combat (2) : to box against in the ring **b** (1) : to attempt to prevent the success or effectiveness of ⟨the company fought the takeover attempt⟩ (2) : to oppose the passage or development of ⟨~ a bill in Congress⟩ **2 a** : WAGE, CARRY ON ⟨~ a battle⟩ **b** : to take part in (as a boxing match) **3** : to struggle to endure or surmount ⟨~ a cold⟩ **4 a** : to gain by struggle ⟨~s his way through⟩ **b** : to resolve by struggle ⟨fought out their differences in court⟩ **5 a** : to manage (a ship) in a battle or storm **b** : to cause to struggle or contend **c** : to manage in an unnecessarily rough or awkward manner — **fight shy of** : to avoid facing or meeting

²fight n (bef. 12c) **1 a** : a hostile encounter : BATTLE, COMBAT **b** : a boxing match **c** : a verbal disagreement : ARGUMENT **2** : a struggle for a goal or an objective ⟨a ~ for justice⟩ **3** : strength or disposition for fighting : PUGNACITY ⟨still full of ~⟩

fight-er \'fīt-ər\ n (bef. 12c) : one that fights: **a** (1) : WARRIOR, SOLDIER (2) : a pugnacious or game individual (3) : BOXER **b** : an airplane of high speed and maneuverability with armament designed to destroy enemy aircraft

fighting chair n (1950) : a chair from which a salt-water angler plays a hooked fish

fighting chance n (1889) : a chance that may be realized by a struggle ⟨the patient had a fighting chance to live⟩

fig leaf n (14c) **1** : the leaf of a fig tree **2** [fr. the use by Adam and Eve of fig leaves to cover their nakedness after eating the forbidden fruit (Gen. 3:7)] : something that conceals or camouflages usu. inadequately or dishonestly

fig marigold n (1731) : any of several carpetweeds (genus Mesembryanthemum) with showy white or pink flowers

fig-ment \'fig-mənt\ n [ME, fr. L figmentum, fr. fingere to shape — more at DOUGH] (15c) : something made up or contrived

fig-ur-al \'fig-(y)ə-rəl\ adj (1813) : of, relating to, or consisting of human or animal figures ⟨a ~ composition⟩

fig-u-ra-tion \ˌfig-(y)ə-'rā-shən\ n (14c) **1** : FORM, OUTLINE **2** : the act or process of creating or providing a figure ⟨Dante's unique ~ of the underworld⟩ **3** : an act or instance of representation in figures and shapes ⟨cubism was explained as a synthesis of colored ~s of objects —Janet Flanner⟩ **4** : ornamentation of a musical passage by using decorative and usu. repetitive figures

fig-u-ra-tive \'fig-(y)ə-rat-iv\ adj (14c) **1 a** : representing by a figure or resemblance : EMBLEMATIC **b** : of or relating to representation of form or figure in art ⟨~ sculpture⟩ **2 a** : expressing one thing in terms normally denoting another with which it may be regarded as analogous : METAPHORICAL ⟨~ language⟩ **b** : characterized by figures of speech ⟨a ~ description⟩ — **fig-u-ra-tive-ly** adv — **fig-u-ra-tive-ness** n

¹fig-ure \'fig-yər, Brit & often US 'fig-ər\ n [ME, fr. OF, fr. L figura, fr. fingere] (13c) **1 a** : a number symbol : NUMERAL, DIGIT ⟨a salary running into six ~s⟩ **b** pl : arithmetical calculations ⟨good at ~s⟩ **c** : a written or printed character **d** : value esp. as expressed in numbers : PRICE ⟨sold at a low ~⟩ **2 a** : a geometric form (as a line, triangle, or sphere) esp. when considered as a set of geometric elements (as points) in space of a given number of dimensions ⟨a square is a plane ~⟩ **b** : bodily shape or form esp. of a person ⟨a slender ~⟩ **c** : an object noticeable only as a shape or form ⟨~s moving in the dusk⟩ **3 a** : the graphic representation of a form esp. of a person or geometric entity **b** : a diagram or pictorial illustration of textual matter **4** : a person, thing, or action representative of another **5** : an intentional deviation from the ordinary form or syntactical relation of words **6** : the form of a syllogism with respect to the relative position of the middle term **7** : an often repetitive pattern or design in a manufactured article (as cloth) or natural product (as wood) ⟨a polka-dot ~⟩ **8** : appearance made : impression produced ⟨the couple cut quite a ~⟩ **9 a** : a series of movements in a dance **b** : an outline representation of a form traced by a series of evolutions (as with skates on an ice surface or by an airplane in the air) **10** : a prominent personality : PERSONAGE ⟨great ~s of history⟩ **11** : a short coherent group of notes or chords that may constitute part of a phrase, theme, or composition *syn* see FORM

[2]**figure** *vb* **fig·ured; fig·ur·ing** \'fig-yə-riŋ, 'fig(-ə)-\ *vt* (14c) **1 :** to represent by or as if by a figure or outline **:** PORTRAY **2 :** to decorate with a pattern; *also* **:** to write figures over or under (the bass) in order to indicate the accompanying chords **3 :** to indicate or represent by numerals **4 a :** CALCULATE **b :** CONCLUDE, DECIDE ⟨*figured* there was no use in further effort⟩ **c :** REGARD, CONSIDER ⟨*figured* him an upright man⟩ ~ *vi* **1 a :** to be or appear important or conspicuous **b :** to be involved or implicated ⟨persons who *figured* in a robbery⟩ **2 :** to perform a figure in dancing **3 :** COMPUTE, CALCULATE **4 :** to seem rational, normal, or expected ⟨that ~*s*⟩ — **fig·ur·er** \-(y)ər-ər\ *n* — **figure on 1 :** to take into consideration ⟨*figuring on* $50 a month extra income⟩ **2 :** to rely on **3 :** PLAN ⟨I *figure on* going into town⟩

fig·ured \-(y)ərd\ *adj* (1552) **1 :** being represented **:** PORTRAYED **2 :** adorned with, formed into, or marked with a figure ⟨~ muslin⟩ ⟨~ wood⟩ **3 :** indicated by figures

figured bass *n* (1801) **:** CONTINUO

figure eight *n* (1887) **:** something resembling the Arabic numeral eight in form or shape: as **a :** a small knot — see KNOT illustration **b :** an embroidery stitch **c :** a dance pattern **d :** a skater's figure

fig·ure·head \'fig-(y)ər-,hed\ *n* (1765) **1 :** the figure on a ship's bow **2 :** a head or chief in name only

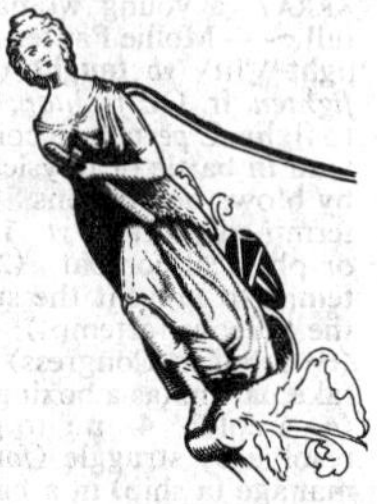
figurehead 1

figure in *vt* (ca. 1934) **:** to include esp. in a reckoning ⟨*figure in* occasional expenses⟩

figure of speech (1824) **:** a form of expression (as a simile or metaphor) used to convey meaning or heighten effect often by comparing or identifying one thing with another that has a meaning or connotation familiar to the reader or listener

figure out *vt* (1833) **1 :** DISCOVER, DETERMINE ⟨try to *figure out* a way to do it⟩ **2 :** SOLVE, FATHOM ⟨*figure out* a problem⟩

figure skating *n* (1869) **:** skating in which the skater describes or outlines prescribed figures — **figure skater** *n*

fig·u·rine \,fig-(y)ə-'rēn\ *n* [F, fr. It *figurina,* dim. of *figura* figure, fr. L — more at FIGURE] (1854) **:** a small carved or molded figure **:** STATUETTE

fig wasp *n* (1883) **:** a minute wasp (*Blastophaga psenes* of the family Agaontidae) that breeds in the caprifig and is the agent of caprification; *broadly* **:** a wasp of the same family

fig·wort \'fig-,wərt, -,wȯ(ə)rt\ *n* (1548) **:** any of a genus (*Scrophularia* of the family Scrophulariaceae, the figwort family) of chiefly herbaceous plants with leaves having no stipules, an irregular bilabiate corolla, and a 2-celled ovary

Fi·ji·an \'fē-(,)jē-ən, fi-'\ *n* (1809) **1 :** a member of a Melanesian people of the Fiji islands **2 :** the Austronesian language of the Fijians — **Fijian** *adj*

fila *pl of* FILUM

fil·a·ment \'fil-ə-mənt\ *n* [MF, fr. ML *filamentum,* fr. LL *filare* to spin — more at FILE] (1594) **:** a single thread or a thin flexible threadlike object, process, or appendage: as **a :** a tenuous conductor (as of carbon or metal) made incandescent by the passage of an electric current; *specif* **:** a cathode in the form of a metal wire in an electron tube **b** (1) **:** a thin and fine elongated constituent part of a gill (2) **:** an elongated thin series of cells attached one to another or a very long thin cylindrical single cell (as of some algae, fungi, or bacteria) **c :** the anther-bearing stalk of a stamen — see FLOWER illustration — **fil·a·men·ta·ry** \,fil-ə-'ment-ə-rē, -'men-trē\ *adj* — **fil·a·men·tous** \-'ment-əs\ *adj*

fi·lar \'fī-lər\ *adj* [L *filum* thread] (1874) **:** of or relating to a thread or line; *esp* **:** having threads across the field of view ⟨a ~ eyepiece⟩

fi·lar·ia \fə-'lar-ē-ə, -'ler-\ *n, pl* **-i·ae** \-ē-,ē, -ē-,ī\ [NL, fr. L *filum*] (1883) **:** any of numerous slender filamentous nematodes (of *Filaria* and related genera) that as adults are parasites in the blood or tissues of mammals and as larvae usu. develop in biting insects — **fi·lar·i·al** \-ē-əl\ *adj* — **fi·lar·i·id** \-ē-əd\ *adj or n*

fil·a·ri·a·sis \,fil-ə-'rī-ə-səs\ *n, pl* **-a·ses** \-,sēz\ (1879) **:** infestation with or disease caused by filariae

fil·a·ture \'fil-ə-,chu̇(ə)r, -chər, -,t(y)u̇(ə)r\ *n* [F, fr. LL *filatus,* pp. of *filare*] (1759) **1 :** a factory where silk is reeled **2 :** the reeling of silk from cocoons **3 :** a reel for drawing off silk from cocoons

fil·bert \'fil-bərt\ *n* [ME, fr. AF *philber,* fr. St. *Philibert* †684 Frankish abbot whose feast day falls in the nutting season] (15c) **1 :** either of two European hazels (*Corylus avellana pontica* and *C. maxima*); *also* **:** the sweet thick-shelled nut of the filbert **2 :** HAZELNUT

filch \'filch\ *vt* [ME *filchen*] (14c) **:** to appropriate furtively or casually ⟨~ a cookie⟩ *syn* see STEAL

[1]**file** \'fī(ə)l\ *n* [ME, fr. OE *fēol;* akin to OHG *fīla* file] (bef. 12c) **1 :** a tool usu. of hardened steel with cutting ridges for forming or smoothing surfaces esp. of metal **2 :** a shrewd or crafty person

[2]**file** *vt* **filed; fil·ing** (13c) **:** to rub, smooth, or cut away with or as if with a file

[3]**file** *vt* **filed; fil·ing** [ME *filen,* fr. OE *fȳlan,* fr. *fūl* foul] *chiefly dial* (bef. 12c) **:** DEFILE, CORRUPT

[4]**file** *vb* **filed; fil·ing** [ME *filen,* fr. MF *filer* to string documents on a string or wire, fr. *fil* thread, fr. OF, fr. L *filum;* akin to Arm *jil* sinew] *vt* (15c) **1 :** to arrange in order for preservation and reference ⟨~ letters⟩ **2 a :** to place among official records as prescribed by law ⟨~ a mortgage⟩ **b :** to send (copy) to a newspaper ⟨*filed* a good story⟩ **c :** to return to the office of the clerk of a court without action on the merits **3 :** to perform the first act of (as a lawsuit) ⟨threatened to ~ charges against him⟩ ~ *vi* **1 :** to register as a candidate esp. in a primary election **2 :** to place items in a file

[5]**file** *n* (1525) **1 :** a device (as a folder, case, or cabinet) by means of which papers are kept in order **2 a** *archaic* **:** ROLL, LIST **b :** a collection of papers or publications usu. arranged or classified **c :** a collection of related data records (as for a computer) — **on file :** in or as if in a file for ready reference

[6]**file** *n* [MF, fr. *filer* to spin, fr. LL *filare,* fr. L *filum*] (1598) **1 :** a row of persons, animals, or things arranged one behind the other **2 :** any of the rows of squares that extend across a chessboard from white's side to black's side

[7]**file** *vi* **filed; fil·ing** (1616) **:** to march or proceed in file

filé \fə-'lā, (')fi-'lā, (')fē-'lā\ *n* [AmerF (Louisiana), fr. F, pp. of *filer* to twist, spin] (1806) **:** powdered young leaves of sassafras used to thicken soups or stews

file clerk *n* (1919) **:** a clerk who works on files

file·fish \'fī(ə)l-,fish\ *n* (1814) **:** any of various bony fishes (order Tetraodontiformes and esp. genera *Aluterus, Cantherhines,* and *Monacanthus* of the family Balistidae) with rough granular leathery skins

fi·let \fi-'lā\ *n* [F, lit., net] (1881) **:** a lace with a square mesh and geometric designs

fi·let mi·gnon \,fil-(,)ā-mēn-'yōⁿ, fi-,lā-\ *n, pl* **filets mignons** \-(,)ā-mēn-'yōⁿz, -,lā-\ [F, lit., dainty fillet] (1906) **:** a thick slice of beef cut from the narrow end of a beef tenderloin

fili- *or* **filo-** *comb form* [L *filum*] **:** thread ⟨*filiform*⟩

fil·ial \'fil-ē-əl, 'fil-yəl\ *adj* [ME, fr. LL *filialis,* fr. L *filius* son — more at FEMININE] (14c) **1 :** of, relating to, or befitting a son or daughter ⟨~ obedience⟩ **2 :** having or assuming the relation of a child or offspring — **fil·ial·ly** \-ē-ə-lē, -yə-lē\ *adv*

filial generation *n* (1909) **:** a generation in a breeding experiment that is successive to a parental generation

fil·i·a·tion \,fil-ē-'ā-shən\ *n* (15c) **1 a :** filial relationship esp. of a son to his father **b :** the adjudication of paternity **2 a :** descent or derivation esp. from a culture or language **b :** the act or process of determining such relationship

[1]**fil·i·bus·ter** \'fil-ə-,bəs-tər\ *n* [Sp *filibustero,* lit., freebooter] (1587) **1 :** an irregular military adventurer; *specif* **:** an American engaged in fomenting insurrections in Latin America in the mid-19th century **2** [[2]*filibuster*] **a :** the use of extreme dilatory tactics in an attempt to delay or prevent action esp. in a legislative assembly **b :** an instance of this practice

[2]**filibuster** *vb* **-tered; -ter·ing** \-t(ə-)riŋ\ *vi* (1853) **1 :** to carry out insurrectionist activities in a foreign country **2 :** to engage in a filibuster ~ *vt* **:** to subject to a filibuster — **fil·i·bus·ter·er** \-tər-ər\ *n*

fil·i·form \'fil-ə-,fȯrm, 'fī-lə-\ *adj* (1757) **:** shaped like a filament

[1]**fil·i·gree** \'fil-ə-,grē\ *n* [F *filigrane,* fr. It *filigrana,* fr. L *filum* + *granum* grain — more at CORN] (1693) **1 :** ornamental work esp. of fine wire of gold, silver, or copper applied chiefly to gold and silver surfaces **2 a :** ornamental openwork of delicate or intricate design **b :** a pattern or design resembling such openwork ⟨a ~ of frost⟩

[2]**filigree** *vt* **fil·i·greed; fil·i·gree·ing** (1831) **:** to adorn with or as if with filigree

fil·ing \'fī-liŋ\ *n* (14c) **1 :** an act or instance of using a file **2 :** a fragment rubbed off in filing ⟨iron ~*s*⟩

fil·io·pi·etis·tic \'fil-ē-ō-,pī-ə-'tis-tik\ *adj* [*filial* + *-o-* + *pietistic*] (1893) **:** of or relating to an often excessive veneration of ancestors or tradition

Fil·i·pi·no \,fil-ə-'pē-(,)nō\ *n, pl* **Filipinos** [Sp] (1898) **1 :** a native of the Philippine islands; *specif* **:** a member of a Christianized Philippine people **2 :** a citizen of the Republic of the Philippines — **Filipino** *adj*

[1]**fill** \'fil\ *vb* [ME *fillen,* fr. OE *fyllan;* akin to OE *full* full] *vt* (bef. 12c) **1 a :** to put into as much as can be held or conveniently contained ⟨~ a cup with water⟩ **b :** to supply with a full complement ⟨the class is already ~*ed*⟩ **c** (1) **:** to cause to swell or billow ⟨wind ~*ed* the sails⟩ (2) **:** to trim (a sail) to catch the wind **d :** to raise the level of with fill ⟨~*ed* land⟩ **e :** to repair the cavities of (teeth) **f :** to stop up **:** OBSTRUCT, PLUG ⟨wreckage ~*ed* the channel⟩ **g :** to stop up the interstices, crevices, or pores of (as cloth, wood, or leather) with a foreign substance **2 a :** FEED, SATIATE **b :** SATISFY, FULFILL ⟨~*s* all requirements⟩ **c :** MAKE OUT, COMPLETE — often used with *out* or *in* ⟨~ out a form⟩ ⟨~ in the blanks⟩ **3 a :** to occupy the whole of ⟨smoke ~*ed* the room⟩ **b :** to spread through **c :** to make full ⟨a mind ~*ed* with fantasies⟩ **4 a :** to possess and perform the duties of **:** HOLD ⟨~ an office⟩ **b :** to place a person in ⟨~ a vacancy⟩ **5 :** to supply as directed ⟨~ a prescription⟩ **6 :** to cover the surface of with a layer of precious metal ~ *vi* **:** to become full — **fill one's shoes :** to take over one's job, position, or responsibilities

[2]**fill** *n* (bef. 12c) **1 :** a full supply; *esp* **:** a quantity that satisfies or satiates ⟨eat your ~⟩ **2 :** material used to fill a receptacle, cavity, passage, or low place

fill away *vi* (1840) **1 :** to trim a sail to catch the wind **2 :** to proceed on the course esp. after being brought up in the wind

filled milk *n* (ca. 1924) **:** skim milk with fat content increased by the addition of vegetable oils

[1]**fill·er** \'fil-ər\ *n* (15c) **:** one that fills: as **a :** a substance added to a product (as to increase bulk, weight, viscosity, opacity, or strength) **b :** a composition used to fill the pores and grain esp. of a wood surface before painting or varnishing **c :** a piece used to cover or fill in a space between two parts of a structure **d :** tobacco used to form the core of a cigar **e :** material used to fill extra space in a column or page of a newspaper or magazine **f :** a pack of paper for a loose-leaf notebook

[2]**fil·ler** \'fil-,e(ə)r\ *n, pl* **fillers** *or* **filler** [Hung *fillér*] (1904) — see *forint* at MONEY table

[1]**fil·let** \'fil-ət, *in sense 2b also* fi-'lā, 'fil-(,)ā\ *also* **fi·let** \fi-'lā, 'fil-(,)ā\ *n* [ME *filet,* fr. MF, dim. of *fil* thread — more at FILE] (14c) **1 :** a ribbon or narrow strip of material used esp. as a headband **2 :** a thin narrow strip of material: as **a :** a band of anatomical fibers; *specif* **:** LEMNISCUS **b :** a piece or slice of boneless meat or fish; *esp* **:** the tenderloin of beef **3 a :** a concave junction formed where two surfaces meet **b :** a curved strip forming such a junction **4 :** a narrow flat architectural member: **a :** a flat molding separating others **b :** the space between two flutings in a shaft

[2]**fil·let** \'fil-ət, *in sense 2 also* fi-'lā, 'fil-(,)ā\ *vt* (1604) **1 :** to bind, furnish, or adorn with or as if with a fillet **2 :** to cut into fillets

fill–in \'fil-,in\ *n* (ca. 1917) **:** someone or something that fills in

fill in \(')fil-'in\ *vt* (1840) **1 :** to give necessary or recently acquired information to ⟨I'll *fill* you *in*⟩ **2 :** to enrich (as a design) with detail ~ *vi* **:** to fill a vacancy usu. temporarily

fill·ing \'fil-iŋ\ *n* (14c) **1 :** an act or instance of filling **2 :** something used to fill a cavity, container, or depression ⟨a ~ for a tooth⟩ **3**

: something that completes: as **a :** the yarn interlacing the warp in a fabric; *also* **:** yarn for the shuttle **b :** a food mixture used to fill pastry or sandwiches
filling station *n* (1921) **:** SERVICE STATION 1
1fil·lip \ˈfil-əp\ *vt* [prob. of imit. origin] (15c) **1 a :** to strike or tap with a fillip ⟨~*ed* him on the nose⟩ **b :** to make a filliping motion with ⟨~*ed* his fingers⟩ **2 :** to project quickly by or as if by a fillip ⟨~ crumbs off the table⟩ **3 :** STIMULATE ⟨with this to ~ his spirits —Robert Westerby⟩
2fillip *n* (ca. 1530) **1 a :** a blow or gesture made by the sudden forcible straightening of a finger curled up against the thumb **b :** a short sharp blow **:** BUFFET **2 :** something tending to arouse or excite
fill out *vi* (1888) **:** to put on flesh
fil·ly \ˈfil-ē\ *n, pl* **fillies** [ME *fyly,* fr. ON *fylja;* akin to OE *fola* foal] (15c) **1 :** a young female horse usu. of less than four years **2 :** a young woman **:** GIRL
1film \ˈfilm\ *n, often attrib* [ME *filme,* fr. OE *filmen;* akin to Gk *pelma* sole of the foot, OE *fell* skin — more at FELL] (bef. 12c) **1 a :** a thin skin or membranous covering **:** PELLICLE **b :** an abnormal growth on or in the eye **2 :** a thin covering or coating ⟨a ~ of ice on the pond⟩ **3 a :** an exceedingly thin layer **:** LAMINA **b** (1) **:** a thin flexible transparent sheet (as of plastic) used as a wrapping (2) **:** such a sheet of cellulose acetate or cellulose nitrate coated with a radiation-sensitive emulsion for taking photographs or making roentgenograms **4 :** MOTION PICTURE
2film *vt* (1602) **1 :** to cover with or as if with a film **2 :** to make a motion picture of or from ⟨~ a scene⟩ ~ *vi* **1 :** to become covered or obscured with or as if with a film **2 :** to make a motion picture
film badge *n* (1945) **:** a small pack of sensitive photographic film worn as a badge for indicating exposure to radiation
film·card \ˈfilm-ˌkärd\ *n* (1965) **:** MICROFICHE
film·dom \ˈfilm-dəm\ *n* (1916) **:** the motion-picture industry
film·ic \ˈfil-mik\ *adj* (ca. 1930) **:** of, relating to, or resembling motion pictures — **film·i·cal·ly** \-mi-k(ə-)lē\ *adv*
film·mak·er \ˈfilm-ˌmā-kər\ *n* (1908) **:** MOVIEMAKER
film·mak·ing \-ˌmā-kiŋ\ *n* (1913) **:** the making of movies
film noir \-ˈnwär\ *n* [F, lit., black film] (1958) **:** a type of crime film featuring cynical malevolent characters in a sleazy setting and an ominous atmosphere that is conveyed by shadowy photography and foreboding background music; *also* **:** a film of this type
film·og·ra·phy \fil-ˈmäg-rə-fē\ *n, pl* **-phies** [*film* + *-ography* (as in *bibliography*)] (1962) **:** a list of motion pictures featuring the work of a prominent film figure or relating to a particular topic
film·set·ting \ˈfilm-ˌset-iŋ\ *n* (1961) **:** PHOTOCOMPOSITION — **film·set** *adj* — **filmset** *vt* — **film·set·ter** *n*
film·strip \ˈfilm-ˌstrip\ *n* (1930) **:** a strip of usu. 35 millimeter film bearing photographs, diagrams, or graphic matter for still projection
filmy \ˈfil-mē\ *adj* **film·i·er; -est** (1604) **1 :** of, resembling, or composed of film **:** GAUZY ⟨~ draperies⟩ **2 :** covered with a haze or film — **film·i·ly** \-mə-lē\ *adv* — **film·i·ness** \-mē-nəs\ *n*
filo- — see FILI-
fils \ˈfils\ *n, pl* **fils** [Ar] (1931) — see *dinar, dirham, rial* at MONEY table
1fil·ter \ˈfil-tər\ *n* [ME *filtre,* fr. ML *filtrum* piece of felt used as a filter, of Gmc origin; akin to OHG *filz* felt — more at FELT] (1563) **1 :** a porous article or mass (as of paper or sand) through which a gas or liquid is passed to separate out matter in suspension **2 :** an apparatus containing a filter medium **3 a :** a device or material for suppressing or minimizing waves or oscillations of certain frequencies (as of electricity, light, or sound) **b :** a transparent material (as colored glass) that absorbs light of certain wavelengths or colors selectively and is used for modifying light that reaches a sensitized photographic material — called also *color filter*
2filter *vb* **fil·tered; fil·ter·ing** \-t(ə-)riŋ\ *vt* (1576) **1 :** to subject to the action of a filter **2 :** to remove by means of a filter ~ *vi* **1 :** to pass or move through or as if through a filter **2 :** to come or go in small units over a period of time ⟨people began ~*ing* in⟩
fil·ter·able *also* **fil·tra·ble** \ˈfil-t(ə-)rə-bəl\ *adj* (1908) **:** capable of being filtered or of passing through a filter — **fil·ter·abil·i·ty** \ˌfil-t(ə-)rə-ˈbil-ət-ē\ *n*
filterable virus *n* (1911) **:** any of the infectious agents that remain virulent after a fluid containing them passes through a filter of diatomite or unglazed porcelain and that include the viruses as presently understood and various other groups (as the mycoplasmas and rickettsias) which were orig. considered viruses before their cellular nature was established
filter bed *n* (ca. 1874) **:** a sand or gravel bed for filtering water or sewage
filter feeder *n* (1928) **:** an animal that obtains its food by filtering organic matter or minute organisms from a current of water that passes through some part of its system
filter paper *n* (ca. 1846) **:** porous unsized paper used esp. for filtering
filter tip *n* (1932) **:** a cigar or cigarette tip designed to filter the smoke before it enters the smoker's mouth; *also* **:** a cigar or cigarette provided with such a tip — **fil·ter–tipped** \ˌfil-tər-ˈtipt\ *adj*
filth \ˈfilth\ *n* [ME, fr. OE *fȳlth,* fr. *fūl* foul] (bef. 12c) **1 :** foul or putrid matter; *esp* **:** loathsome dirt or refuse **2 a :** moral corruption or defilement **b :** something that tends to corrupt or defile
filthy \ˈfil-thē\ *adj* **filth·i·er; -est** (14c) **1 :** covered with or containing filth **:** offensively dirty **2 a :** UNDERHAND, VILE **b :** OBSCENE ***syn*** see DIRTY — **filth·i·ly** \-thə-lē\ *adv* — **filth·i·ness** \-thē-nəs\ *n*
fil·trate \ˈfil-ˌtrāt\ *n* (1845) **:** material that has passed through a filter
fil·tra·tion \fil-ˈtrā-shən\ *n* (1605) **1 :** the process of filtering **2 :** the process of passing through or as if through a filter; *also* **:** DIFFUSION
fi·lum \ˈfī-ləm\ *n, pl* **fi·la** \-lə\ [NL, fr. L — more at FILE] (ca. 1860) **:** a filamentous structure **:** FILAMENT
fim·bria \ˈfim-brē-ə\ *n, pl* **-bri·ae** \-brē-ˌē, -ˌī\ [NL, fr. L, fringe] (ca. 1737) **:** a bordering fringe esp. at the entrance of the fallopian tubes — **fim·bri·al** \-brē-əl\ *adj*
fim·bri·at·ed \ˈfim-brē-ˌāt-əd\ *also* **fim·bri·ate** \-ˌāt\ *adj* (15c) **:** having the edge or extremity bordered by slender processes **:** FRINGED — **fim·bri·a·tion** \ˌfim-brē-ˈā-shən\ *n*
1fin \ˈfin\ *n* [ME *finn,* fr. OE; akin to L *spina* thorn, spine] (bef. 12c) **1 :** an external membranous process of an aquatic animal (as a fish) used in propelling or guiding the body — see FISH illustration **2 :** something resembling a fin esp. in appearance or function: **a :** HAND, ARM **b** (1) **:** an appendage of a boat (as a submarine) (2) **:** an airfoil attached to an airplane for directional stability **c :** FLIPPER 1b **d :** any of the projecting ribs on a radiator or an engine cylinder — **fin·like** \-ˌlīk\ *adj* — **finned** \ˈfind\ *adj*
2fin *vb* **finned; fin·ning** *vt* (1933) **:** to equip with fins ~ *vi* **:** to show the fins above the water
3fin *n* [Yiddish *finf* five, fr. OHG — more at FIVE] *slang* (1925) **:** a 5-dollar bill
fi·na·gle \fə-ˈnā-gəl\ *vb* **fi·na·gled; fi·na·gling** \-g(ə-)liŋ\ [perh. alter. of *fainaigue* (to renege)] *vt* (ca. 1924) **1 :** to obtain by indirect or involved means **2 :** to obtain by trickery **:** SWINDLE ~ *vi* **:** to use devious and often dishonest methods to achieve one's ends — **fi·na·gler** \-g(ə-)lər\ *n*
1fi·nal \ˈfīn-ᵊl\ *adj* [ME, fr. MF, fr. L *finalis,* fr. *finis* boundary, end] (14c) **1 a :** not to be altered or undone ⟨all sales are ~⟩ **b :** of or relating to a concluding court action or proceeding ⟨~ decree⟩ **2 :** being the last in a series, process, or progress ⟨the ~ chapter⟩ **3 :** of or relating to the ultimate purpose or result of a process ⟨the ~ goal of life⟩ **4 :** relating to or occurring at the end or conclusion ***syn*** see LAST — **fi·nal·ly** \ˈfīn-ᵊl-ē, ˈfīn-lē\ *adv*
2final *n* (1609) **:** something that is final: as **a :** a deciding match, game, heat, or trial — usu. used in pl. **b :** the last examination in a course — often used in pl.
fi·na·le \fə-ˈnal-ē, fi-ˈnäl-\ *n* [It, fr. *finale,* adj., final, fr. L *finalis*] (1783) **:** the close or termination of something: as **a :** the last section of an instrumental musical composition **b :** the closing part, scene, or number in a public performance **c :** the last and often climactic event or item in a sequence
fi·nal·ist \ˈfīn-ᵊl-əst\ *n* (1898) **:** a contestant in the finals of a competition
fi·nal·i·ty \fī-ˈnal-ət-ē, fə-\ *n, pl* **-ties** (1833) **1 a :** the character or condition of being final, settled, irrevocable, or complete **b :** the condition of being at an ultimate point esp. of development or authority **2 :** something final; *esp* **:** a fundamental fact, action, or belief
fi·nal·ize \ˈfīn-ᵊl-ˌīz\ *vt* **-ized; -iz·ing** (1922) **1 :** to put in final or finished form ⟨soon my conclusion will be *finalized* —D. D. Eisenhower⟩ **2 :** to give final approval to ⟨*finalizing* the papers prepared and presented by his staff —*Newsweek*⟩ — **fi·nal·iza·tion** \ˌfīn-ᵊl-ə-ˈzā-shən\ *n*
usage *Finalize* has been frequently castigated as an unnecessary neologism or as U.S. government gobbledygook. It appears to have originated in Australia (where it has been acceptable all along) in the early 1920s. The U.S. Navy picked it up in the late 20s, and from there it came into widespread use. It is a standard formation (see -IZE). Our current evidence indicates it is most frequently used in government, business dealings, and child adoption; it usu. is not found in belles-lettres.
1fi·nance \fə-ˈnan(t)s, ˈfī-ˌ, fī-ˈ\ *n* [ME, payment, ransom, fr. MF, fr. *finer* to end, pay, fr. *fin* end — more at FINE] (1739) **1** *pl* **:** money or other liquid resources of a government, business, group, or individual **2 :** the system that includes the circulation of money, the granting of credit, the making of investments, and the provision of banking facilities **3 :** the science or study of the management of funds **4 :** the obtaining of funds or capital **:** FINANCING
2finance *vt* **fi·nanced; fi·nanc·ing** (1866) **1 a :** to raise or provide funds or capital for ⟨~ a new house⟩ **b :** to furnish with necessary funds ⟨~ a son through college⟩ **2 :** to sell something to on credit
finance company *n* (1924) **:** a company that makes usu. small short-term loans usu. to individuals
fi·nan·cial \fə-ˈnan-chəl, fī-\ *adj* (1769) **:** relating to finance or financiers — **fi·nan·cial·ly** \-ˈnanch-(ə-)lē\ *adv*
fi·nan·cier \ˌfin-ən-ˈsi(ə)r; fə-ˌnan-, ˌfī-\ *n* (1618) **1 :** one who specializes in raising and expending public moneys **2 :** one who deals with finance and investment on a large scale
fi·nanc·ing *n* (1827) **:** the act or process or an instance of raising or providing funds; *also* **:** the funds thus raised or provided
fin·back \ˈfin-ˌbak\ *n* (1725) **:** a common whalebone whale (*Balaenoptera physalus*) of the Atlantic coast of the U.S. that attains a length of over 60 feet; *broadly* **:** RORQUAL

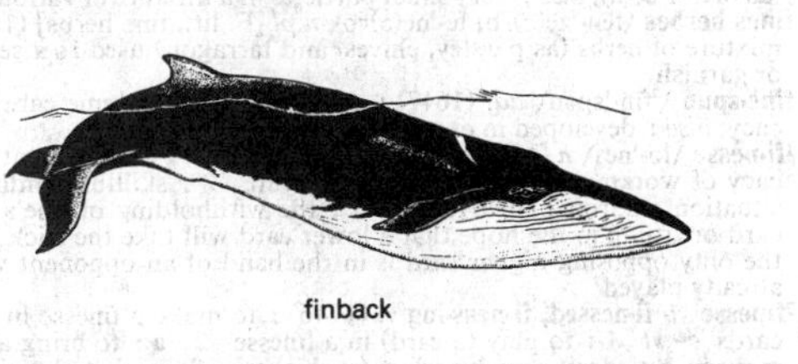

finback

finch \ˈfinch\ *n* [ME, fr. OE *finc;* akin to OHG *fincho* finch, Gk *spiza* chaffinch] (bef. 12c) **:** any of numerous songbirds (as the sparrows, grosbeaks, crossbills, goldfinches, linnets, and buntings of the family Fringillidae) having a short stout conical bill adapted for crushing seeds
1find \ˈfīnd\ *vb* **found** \ˈfau̇nd\; **find·ing** [ME *finden,* fr. OE *findan;* akin to OHG *findan* to find, L *pont-, pons* bridge, Gk *pontos* sea, Skt *patha* way, course] *vt* (bef. 12c) **1 a :** to come upon often accidentally **:** ENCOUNTER **b :** to meet with (a particular reception) ⟨hoped to ~ favor⟩ **2 a :** to come upon by searching or effort ⟨must ~ a suitable person for the job⟩ **b :** to discover by study or experiment ⟨~ an answer⟩ **c :** to obtain by effort or management ⟨~ the time to study⟩ **d :** ATTAIN, REACH ⟨the bullet *found* its mark⟩ **e :** to discover by

sounding ⟨∼ bottom in a lake⟩ **3 a :** EXPERIENCE, DETECT ⟨∼ much pleasure in your company⟩ **b :** to perceive (oneself) to be in a certain place or condition **c :** to gain or regain the use or power of ⟨trying to ∼ his tongue⟩ **d :** to bring (oneself) to a realization of one's powers or of one's proper sphere of activity ⟨must help the student to ∼ himself as an individual —N. M. Pusey⟩ **4 a :** PROVIDE, SUPPLY **b :** to furnish (room and board) esp. as a condition of employment **5 :** to settle upon and make a statement about (as a conclusion) ⟨∼ a verdict⟩ **∼** *vi* **:** to determine a case judicially by a verdict ⟨∼ for the defendant⟩ — **find fault :** to criticize unfavorably

[2]**find** *n* (1825) **1 :** an act or instance of finding **2 :** something found: as **a :** a valuable item ⟨an archaeological ∼⟩ **b :** a person whose ability proves to be unexpectedly good

find·er \ˈfīn-dər\ *n* (15c) **1 :** one that finds **2 :** a small astronomical telescope of low power and wide field attached to a larger telescope for finding an object **3 :** a device on a camera for showing the area of the subject to be included in the picture

fin de siè·cle \ˌfa^{n}-də-sē-ˈekl^{ə}\ *adj* [F, end of the century] (1890) **:** of, relating to, or characteristic of the close of the 19th century and esp. its literary and artistic climate of sophistication, world-weariness, and fashionable despair

find·ing \ˈfīn-diŋ\ *n* (14c) **1 a :** the act of one that finds **b :** FIND 2 **2** *pl* **:** small tools and supplies used by an artisan (as a dressmaker, jeweler, or shoemaker) **3 a :** the result of a judicial examination or inquiry **b :** the results of an investigation — usu. used in pl.

find out *vt* (1552) **1 :** to learn by study, observation, or search **:** DISCOVER **2 a :** to catch in an offense (as a crime) ⟨the culprits were soon *found out*⟩ **b :** to ascertain the true character or identity of ⟨if you pretend, you may be *found out*⟩ **∼** *vi* **:** to discover, learn, or verify something ⟨I don't know, but I'll *find out* for you⟩

[1]**fine** \ˈfīn\ *n* [ME, fr. OF *fin,* fr. L *finis* boundary, end] (13c) **1** *obs* **:** END, CONCLUSION **2 :** a compromise of a fictitious suit used as a form of conveyance of lands **3 a :** a sum imposed as punishment for an offense **b :** a forfeiture or penalty paid to an injured party in a civil action — **in fine :** in short

[2]**fine** *vt* **fined; fin·ing** (15c) **:** to impose a fine on **:** punish by a fine

[3]**fine** *adj* **fin·er; fin·est** [ME *fin,* fr. OF, fr. L *finis,* n., end, limit] (13c) **1 a :** free from impurity **b** *of a metal* **:** having a stated proportion of pure metal in the composition expressed in parts per thousand ⟨a gold coin .9166 ∼⟩ **2 a (1) :** very thin in gauge or texture ⟨∼ thread⟩ **(2) :** not coarse ⟨∼ sand⟩ **(3) :** very small ⟨∼ print⟩ **(4) :** KEEN ⟨a knife with a ∼ edge⟩ **b :** physically trained or hardened close to the limit of efficiency — used of an athlete or animal **3 a (1) :** having a delicate or subtle quality ⟨a wine of ∼ bouquet⟩ **(2) :** subtle or sensitive in perception or discrimination ⟨a ∼ distinction⟩ **b :** performed with extreme care and accuracy ⟨a ∼ adjustment⟩ **4 :** superior in quality, conception, or appearance **:** EXCELLENT **5 :** marked by or affecting elegance or refinement ⟨∼ manners⟩ **6 :** very well ⟨feel ∼⟩ **7** — used as an intensive ⟨the leader, in a ∼ frenzy, beheaded one of his wives —Brian Crozier⟩ — **fine·ness** \ˈfīn-nəs\ *n*

[4]**fine** *adv* (14c) **:** FINELY

[5]**fine** *vb* **fined; fin·ing** *vt* (14c) **1 :** PURIFY, CLARIFY ⟨∼ and filter wine⟩ **2 :** to make finer in quality or size **∼** *vi* **1 :** to become pure or clear ⟨the ale will ∼⟩ **2 :** to become smaller in lines or proportions **:** DIMINISH

[6]**fi·ne** \ˈfē-(ˌ)nā\ *n* [It, fr. L *finis* end] (ca. 1798) **:** END — used as a direction in music to mark the closing point after a repeat

fine art *n* (1767) **1 a :** art (as painting, sculpture, or music) concerned primarily with the creation of beautiful objects — usu. used in pl. **b :** objects of fine art **2 :** an activity requiring a fine skill

fine·ly \ˈfīn-lē\ *adv* (14c) **:** in a fine manner: as **a :** extremely well **:** EXCELLENTLY ⟨you did ∼⟩ **b :** with close discrimination **:** PRECISELY **c :** with delicacy or subtlety **:** SENSITIVELY ⟨a leader ∼ attuned to the needs of the people⟩ **d :** MINUTELY ⟨∼ ground meal⟩

fine print *n* (1951) **:** something thoroughly and often deliberately obscure; *esp* **:** a part of an agreement (as a contract) spelling out restrictions and limitations often in small type or obscure language

fin·ery \ˈfīn-(ə-)rē\ *n, pl* **-er·ies** (1680) **:** ORNAMENT, DECORATION; *esp* **:** dressy or showy clothing and jewels

fines \ˈfīnz\ *n pl* [[3]*fine*] (ca. 1909) **:** finely crushed or powdered material (as ore or coal); *also* **:** very small particles in a mixture of various sizes

fines herbes \fēn-ˈze(ə)rb, fē-ˈne(ə)rb\ *n pl* [F, lit., fine herbs] (1846) **:** a mixture of herbs (as parsley, chives, and tarragon) used as a seasoning or garnish

fine·spun \ˈfīn-ˈspən\ *adj* (1647) **:** developed with extreme care or delicacy; *also* **:** developed in excessively fine or subtle detail

[1]**fi·nesse** \fə-ˈnes\ *n* [ME, fr. MF, fr. *fin*] (1528) **1 :** refinement or delicacy of workmanship, structure, or texture **2 :** skillful handling of a situation **:** adroit maneuvering **3 :** the withholding of one's highest card or trump in the hope that a lower card will take the trick because the only opposing higher card is in the hand of an opponent who has already played

[2]**finesse** *vb* **fi·nessed; fi·ness·ing** *vi* (1746) **:** to make a finesse in playing cards **∼** *vt* **1 :** to play (a card) in a finesse **2 a :** to bring about or manage by adroit maneuvering ⟨∼ his way through tight places —Marquis James⟩ **b :** EVADE, TRICK

fin·est \ˈfī-nəst\ *n, pl in constr* [superl. of [3]*fine*] (1951) **:** POLICEMEN — usu. used with the possessive form of a city or area ⟨the city's ∼⟩

fine structure *n* (1935) **:** microscopic structure of a biological entity or one of its parts esp. as studied in preparations for the electron microscope — **fine structural** *adj*

fine–tooth comb \ˌfīn-ˌtüth-\ *n* (1839) **1 :** a comb with close-set teeth used esp. for clearing parasites or foreign matter from the hair **2 :** an attitude or system of thorough searching or scrutinizing ⟨went over the report with a *fine-tooth comb*⟩

fine–tune \(ˈ)fīn-ˈtün\ *vt* (1924) **1 :** to make small adjustments so as to bring to the highest level of performance or effectiveness ⟨∼ a TV set⟩ ⟨∼ an engine⟩ ⟨∼ the format⟩ **2 :** to stabilize (an economy) by small-scale fiscal and monetary manipulations

fin·fish \ˈfin-ˌfish\ *n* (1694) **:** a true fish — compare SHELLFISH

[1]**fin·ger** \ˈfiŋ-gər\ *n* [ME, fr. OE; akin to OHG *fingar* finger] (bef. 12c) **1 :** any of the five terminating members of the hand **:** a digit of the forelimb; *esp* **:** one other than the thumb **2 a :** something that resembles a finger ⟨a narrow ∼ of land⟩ **b :** a part of a glove into which a finger is inserted **c :** a projecting piece (as a pawl for a ratchet) brought into contact with an object to affect its motion **3 :** the breadth of a finger **4 :** INTEREST, SHARE — often used in the phrase *have a finger in the pie* **5 :** BIRD 9 — **fin·ger·like** \-ˌlīk\ *adj*

[2]**finger** *vb* **fin·gered; fin·ger·ing** \-g(ə-)riŋ\ *vt* (15c) **1 a :** to play (a musical instrument) with the fingers **b :** to play (as notes or chords) with a specific fingering **c :** to mark the notes of (a music score) as a guide in playing **2 :** to touch or feel with the fingers **3 :** to point out **:** IDENTIFY **4 :** to extend into or penetrate in the shape of a finger **∼** *vi* **1 :** to touch or handle something **2 a :** to use the fingers in playing a musical instrument **b :** to have a certain fingering — used of a musical instrument ⟨∼*s* like a clarinet⟩ **3 :** to extend in the shape or manner of a finger

fin·ger·board \ˈfiŋ-gər-ˌbō(ə)rd, -ˌbȯ(ə)rd\ *n* (1672) **:** the part of a stringed instrument against which the fingers press the strings to vary the pitch — see VIOLIN illustration

finger bowl *n* (ca. 1860) **:** a small water bowl for rinsing the fingers at the table

fin·gered \ˈfiŋ-gərd\ *adj* (1529) **1 :** having fingers esp. of a specified kind or number — used in combination ⟨stubby-*fingered*⟩ ⟨five-*fingered*⟩ **2 :** having projections or processes like fingers ⟨a ∼ cranberry scoop⟩

finger hole *n* (1854) **1 :** any of several holes in the side of a wind instrument (as a recorder) which may be covered or left open by the fingers to change the pitch of the tone **2 :** a hole (as in a telephone dial or a bowling ball) into which the finger is placed to provide a grip

fin·ger·ing \ˈfiŋ-g(ə-)riŋ\ *n* (14c) **1 a :** the act or method of using the fingers in playing an instrument **b :** the marking (as by figures on a musical score) of the method of fingering **2 :** the act or process of handling or touching with the fingers

fin·ger·ling \ˈfiŋ-gər-liŋ\ *n* (1836) **:** a small fish esp. up to one year of age

fin·ger·nail \ˈfiŋ-gər-ˌnāl, ˌfiŋ-gər-ˈnā(ə)l\ *n* (13c) **:** the nail of a finger

finger painting *n* (1937) **:** a technique of spreading pigment on wet paper chiefly with the fingers; *also* **:** a picture so produced

fin·ger·post \ˈfiŋ-gər-ˌpōst\ *n* (1785) **1 :** a post bearing one or more signs often terminating in a pointing finger **2 :** something serving as a guide to understanding or knowledge

fin·ger·print \-ˌprint\ *n* (1859) **1 :** the impression of a fingertip on any surface; *esp* **:** an ink impression of the lines upon the fingertip taken for purpose of identification **2 :** chromatographic, electrophoretic, or spectrographic evidence of the presence or identity of a substance; *esp* **:** the chromatogram or electrophoretogram obtained by cleaving a protein by enzymatic action and subjecting the resulting collection of peptides to two-dimensional chromatography or electrophoresis — **fingerprint** *vt* — **fin·ger·print·ing** *n*

[1]**fin·ger·tip** \-ˌtip\ *n* (1842) **1 :** the tip of a finger **2 :** a protective covering for the end of a finger — **at one's fingertips :** instantly or readily available

[2]**fingertip** *adj* (ca. 1926) **1 :** readily accessible **:** being in close proximity ⟨∼ information⟩ ⟨∼ controls⟩ **2 :** extending from head or shoulders to mid-thigh — used of clothing

finger wave *n* (ca. 1934) **:** a method of setting hair by dampening with water or wave solution and forming waves or curls with the fingers and a comb

fin·i·al \ˈfin-ē-əl\ *n* [ME, fr. *final, finial* final] (15c) **1 :** a usu. foliated ornament forming an upper extremity esp. in Gothic architecture **2 :** a crowning ornament or detail (as a decorative knob)

fin·i·cal \ˈfin-i-kəl\ *adj* [prob. fr. [3]*fine*] (1592) **:** FINICKY — **fin·i·cal·ly** \-k(ə-)lē\ *adv* — **fin·i·cal·ness** \-kəl-nəs\ *n*

fin·ick·ing \-kiŋ, -kən\ *adj* [alter. of *finical*] (1661) **:** FINICKY

fin·icky \ˈfin-i-kē\ *adj* [alter. of *finicking*] (ca. 1825) **:** excessively nice, exacting, or meticulous in taste or standards — **fin·ick·i·ness** *n*

fi·nis \ˈfin-əs, ˈfī-nəs\ *n* [ME, fr. L] (15c) **:** END, CONCLUSION

[1]**fin·ish** \ˈfin-ish\ *vb* [ME *finisshen,* fr. MF *finiss-,* stem of *finir,* fr. L *finire,* fr. *finis*] *vt* (14c) **1 a :** to bring to an end **:** TERMINATE ⟨∼*ed* his speech and sat down⟩ **b :** to use or dispose of entirely ⟨her sandwich ∼*ed* the loaf⟩ **2 a :** to bring to completion or issue **:** PERFECT ⟨hope to ∼ their new home before winter⟩ **b :** to provide with a finish; *esp* **:** to put a final coat or surface on ⟨∼ a table with varnish⟩ **3 a :** to bring to an end the significance or effectiveness of ⟨the scandal ∼*ed* his career⟩ **b :** to bring about the death of **∼** *vi* **1 :** to come to an end **:** TERMINATE **2 :** to come to the end of a course, task, or undertaking **3 :** to end a competition in a specified manner or position ⟨∼*ed* third in the race⟩ ***syn*** see CLOSE — **fin·ish·er** *n*

[2]**finish** *n* (1779) **1 :** something that completes or perfects: as **a :** the fine or decorative work required for a building or one of its parts **b :** a finishing material used in painting **c :** the final treatment or coating of a surface **d** *of a beverage* **:** the taste in the mouth upon or after swallowing **2 a :** the final stage **:** END **b :** the cause of one's ruin **3 :** the result or product of a finishing process **4 :** the quality or state of being perfected

fin·ished *adj* (1709) **:** marked by the highest quality **:** CONSUMMATE

finishing school *n* (1836) **:** a private school for girls that emphasizes cultural studies and prepares students esp. for social activities

finish line *n* (1899) **:** a line marking the end of a racecourse

fi·nite \ˈfī-ˌnīt\ *adj* [ME *finit,* fr. L *finitus,* pp. of *finire*] (15c) **1 a :** having definite or definable limits ⟨∼ number of possibilities⟩ ⟨a ∼ community⟩ **b :** having a limited nature or existence ⟨∼ beings⟩ **2 :** completely determinable in theory or in fact by counting, measurement, or thought **:** neither infinite nor infinitesimal ⟨a ∼ distance⟩ ⟨the ∼ velocity of light⟩ **3 a :** less than an arbitrary positive integer and greater than the negative of that integer **b :** having a finite number of elements ⟨a ∼ set⟩ **4 :** of, relating to, or being a verb or verb form that can function as a predicate or as the initial element of one and that is limited (as in tense, person, and number) — **finite** *n* — **fi·nite·ly** *adv* — **fi·nite·ness** *n*

fi·ni·tude \ˈfī-nə-ˌt(y)üd, ˈfin-ə-\ *n* (1644) **:** finite quality or state

fink \ˈfiŋk\ *n* [origin unknown] (1903) **1 :** one who is disapproved of or is held in contempt **2 :** STRIKEBREAKER **3 :** INFORMER 2

fink out *vi* (1956) **1 :** to fail miserably **2 :** BACK OUT, COP OUT

Fin•land•iza•tion \ˌfin-lən-də-ˈzā-shən, (ˌ)fin-ˌlan-\ *n* [*Finland*] (1969) **:** a foreign policy of neutrality that makes a non-Communist country susceptible to the influence of the Soviet Union; *also* **:** the conversion to such a policy

Finn \ˈfin\ *n* [Sw *Finne*] (bef. 12c) **1 :** a member of a people speaking Finnish or a Finnic language **2 a :** a native or inhabitant of Finland **b :** one who is of Finnish descent

fin•nan had•die \ˌfin-ən-ˈhad-ē\ *n* [alter. of *findon haddock*, fr. *Findon*, Scotland] (1707) **:** smoked haddock — called also *finnan haddock*

Finn•ic \ˈfin-ik\ *adj* (1668) **1 :** of or relating to the Finns **2 :** of, relating to, or constituting the branch of the Finno-Ugric subfamily of the Uralic family of languages that includes Finnish, Estonian, and Lapp

[1]**Finn•ish** \ˈfin-ish\ *adj* (1699) **:** of, relating to, or characteristic of Finland, the Finns, or Finnish

[2]**Finnish** *n* (1845) **:** a Finno-Ugric language spoken in Finland, Karelia, and small areas of Sweden and Norway

Fin•no–Ugric \ˌfin-ō-ˈ(y)ü-grik\ *adj* (1879) **1 :** of or relating to any of various peoples of northern and eastern Europe and northwestern Siberia speaking related languages and including the Finnish and Hungarian peoples and the Lapps and Estonians **2 :** of, relating to, or constituting a subfamily of the Uralic family of languages comprising various languages spoken in Hungary, Lapland, Finland, Estonia, and northwestern U.S.S.R. — **Finno–Ugric** *n*

fin•ny \ˈfin-ē\ *adj* (1590) **1 :** provided with or characterized by fins **2 :** relating to or being fish

fin whale *n* (1885) **:** FINBACK

fiord *var of* FJORD

fio•ri•tu•ra \fē-ˌȯr-ə-ˈtu̇r-ə\ *n, pl* **-tu•re** \-ˈtu̇r-ē\ [It, lit., flowering, fr. *fiorito*, pp. of *fiorire* to flower, fr. (assumed) VL *florire* — more at FLOURISH] (1841) **:** ORNAMENT 5

fip•ple flute \ˌfip-əl-\ *n* [origin unknown] (1911) **:** any of a group of wind instruments (as a flageolet or recorder) having a straight tubular shape, a whistle mouthpiece, and finger holes

fir \ˈfər\ *n* [ME, fr. OE *fyrh*; akin to OHG *forha* fir, L *quercus* oak] (bef. 12c) **1 :** any of a genus (*Abies*) of north temperate evergreen trees of the pine family that have flattish leaves, smooth circular leaf scars, and erect cones and are valued for their wood; *also* **:** any of various conifers (as the Douglas fir) of other genera **2 :** the wood of a fir

[1]**fire** \ˈfī(ə)r\ *n, often attrib* [ME, fr. OE *fȳr*; akin to OHG *fiur* fire, Gk *pyr*] (bef. 12c) **1 a (1) :** the phenomenon of combustion manifested in light, flame, and heat **(2) :** one of the four elements of the alchemists **b (1) :** burning passion **:** ARDOR **(2) :** liveliness of imagination **:** INSPIRATION **2 :** fuel in a state of combustion (as on a hearth) **3 a :** a destructive burning (as of a building) **b (1) :** death or torture by fire **(2) :** severe trial or ordeal **4 :** BRILLIANCY, LUMINOSITY ⟨the ~ of a gem⟩ **5 a :** the discharge of firearms **b :** intense verbal attack **c :** a rapidly delivered series (as of remarks) — **fire•less** \-ləs\ *adj* — **on fire 1 :** being consumed by fire **:** AFLAME **2 :** EAGER, BURNING — **under fire 1 :** exposed to the firing of an enemy's weapons **2 :** under attack

[2]**fire** *vb* **fired; fir•ing** *vt* (13c) **1 a :** to set on fire **:** KINDLE; *also* **:** IGNITE ⟨~ a rocket engine⟩ **b (1) :** to give life or spirit to **:** INSPIRE **(2) :** to fill with passion **:** INFLAME **c :** to light up as if by fire **2 a :** to drive out or away by or as if by fire **b :** to dismiss from a position **3 a (1) :** to cause to explode **:** DETONATE **(2) :** to propel from or as if from a gun **:** DISCHARGE, LAUNCH ⟨~ a rocket⟩ **(3) :** to score (a number) in a game or contest **b :** to throw with speed **:** HURL **c :** to utter with force and rapidity **4 :** to apply fire or fuel to: as **a :** to process by applying heat **b :** to feed or serve the fire of ~ *vi* **1 a :** to take fire **:** KINDLE, IGNITE **b** *of an internal-combustion engine* **:** to have the explosive charge ignite at the proper time **2 a :** to become irritated or angry — often used with *up* **b :** to become filled with excitement or enthusiasm **3 a :** to discharge a firearm **b :** to emit or let fly an object **4 :** to tend a fire — **fir•er** *n*

fire ant *n* (1796) **:** any of a genus (*Solenopsis*) of fiercely stinging omnivorous ants; *esp* **:** IMPORTED FIRE ANT

fire•arm \ˈfī(ə)r-ˌärm\ *n* (1646) **:** a weapon from which a shot is discharged by gunpowder — usu. used only of small arms

fire•ball \ˈfī(ə)r-ˌbȯl\ *n* (1555) **1 :** a ball of fire; *also* **:** something resembling such a ball ⟨the primordial ~ associated with the beginning of the universe —*Scientific American*⟩ **2 :** a brilliant meteor that may trail bright sparks **3 :** the highly luminous cloud of vapor and dust created by a nuclear explosion **4 :** a highly energetic person **:** HUSTLER

fire blight *n* (1817) **:** a destructive highly infectious disease of apples, pears, and related fruits caused by a bacterium (*Erwinia amylovora*)

fire•boat \ˈfī(ə)r-ˌbōt\ *n* (1849) **:** a ship equipped with fire-fighting apparatus

fire•bomb \-ˌbäm\ *n* (1895) **:** an incendiary bomb — **firebomb** *vt*

fire•box \-ˌbäks\ *n* (1791) **1 :** a chamber (as of a furnace or steam boiler) that contains a fire **2 :** a box containing an apparatus for transmitting an alarm to a fire station

fire•brand \-ˌbrand\ *n* (13c) **1 :** a piece of burning wood **2 :** one that creates unrest or strife **:** AGITATOR

fire•break \-ˌbrāk\ *n* (1841) **:** a barrier of cleared or plowed land intended to check a forest or grass fire

fire•brick \-ˌbrik\ *n* (1793) **:** a refractory brick capable of sustaining high temperature that is used esp. for lining furnaces or fireplaces

fire brigade *n* (1838) **:** a body of fire fighters: as **a :** a private, institutional, or temporary fire-fighting organization **b** *Brit* **:** FIRE DEPARTMENT

fire•bug \ˈfī(ə)r-ˌbəg\ *n* (1872) **:** INCENDIARY, PYROMANIAC

fire•clay \-ˌklā\ *n* (1819) **:** clay capable of withstanding high temperatures that is used esp. for firebrick and crucibles

fire control *n* (1864) **1 :** the planning, preparation, and delivery of gunfire on targets **2 :** the control or extinction of fires

fire•crack•er \ˈfī(ə)r-ˌkrak-ər\ *n* (1829) **:** a usu. paper cylinder containing an explosive and a fuse and usu. discharged to make a noise

fire•damp \-ˌdamp\ *n* (1677) **:** a combustible mine gas that consists chiefly of methane; *also* **:** the explosive mixture of this gas with air

fire department *n* (1825) **1 :** an organization for preventing or extinguishing fires; *esp* **:** a government division (as in a municipality) having these duties **2 :** the members of a fire department

fire•dog \-ˌdȯg\ *n, chiefly Southern & Midland* (1792) **:** ANDIRON

fire•drake \ˈfī(ə)r-ˌdrāk\ *n* [ME *firdrake*, fr. OE *fȳrdraca*, fr. *fȳr* + *draca* dragon — more at DRAKE] (bef. 12c) **:** a fire-breathing dragon esp. in Teutonic mythology

fire drill *n* (ca. 1890) **:** a practice drill in extinguishing fires or in the conduct and manner of exit in case of fire

fire–eat•er \ˈfī(ə)r-ˌēt-ər\ *n* (1672) **1 :** a performer who pretends to eat fire **2 a :** a violent or pugnacious person **b :** one who displays very militant or aggressive partisanship

fire–eat•ing \-ˌēt-iŋ\ *adj* (1819) **:** violent or highly militant in disposition, bearing, or policy ⟨a ~ radical⟩

fire engine *n* (1680) **:** a usu. mobile apparatus for directing an extinguishing agent upon fires

fire escape *n* (1788) **:** a device for escape from a burning building; *esp* **:** a metal stairway attached to the outside of a building

fire extinguisher *n* (1849) **:** a portable or wheeled apparatus for putting out small fires by ejecting fire-extinguishing chemicals

fire•fight \ˈfī(ə)r-ˌfīt\ *n* (1899) **:** a usu. brief intense exchange of fire between opposing infantry units

fire fighter *n* (1903) **:** one who fights fires **:** FIREMAN 1 — **fire fighting** *n*

fire•fly \ˈfī(ə)r-ˌflī\ *n* (1658) **:** any of various winged nocturnal beetles (esp. family Lampyridae) that produce a bright soft intermittent light by oxidation of luciferin esp. for courtship purposes

fire•guard \-ˌgärd\ *n* (1833) **1 :** one who watches for the outbreak of fire; *also* **:** one whose duty is to extinguish fires **2 :** FIRE SCREEN **3 :** FIREBREAK

fire hall *n* (1881) **:** FIRE STATION

fire•house \ˈfī(ə)r-ˌhau̇s\ *n* (ca. 1900) **:** FIRE STATION

fire irons *n pl* (1648) **:** utensils (as tongs) for tending a fire esp. in a fireplace

fire•light \ˈfī(ə)r-ˌlīt\ *n* (bef. 12c) **:** the light of a fire (as in a fireplace)

fire•lock \-ˌläk\ *n* (1547) **1 :** a gunlock employing a slow match to ignite the powder charge; *also* **:** a gun having such a lock **2 a :** FLINTLOCK **b :** WHEEL LOCK

fire•man \-mən\ *n* (14c) **1 :** one who tends or feeds fires **:** STOKER **2 :** a member of a company organized to fight fires **:** FIRE FIGHTER **3 :** an enlisted man in the navy who works with engineering machinery **4 :** a relief pitcher in baseball

fire opal *n* (1816) **:** GIRASOLE 2

fire•place \ˈfī(ə)r-ˌplās\ *n* (1698) **1 :** a framed opening made in a chimney to hold an open fire **:** HEARTH; *also* **:** a metal container with a smoke pipe used for the same purpose **2 :** an outdoor structure of brick, stone, or metal for an open fire

fire•plug \-ˌpləg\ *n* (1713) **:** HYDRANT

fire•pow•er \-ˌpau̇(-ə)r\ *n* (1913) **1 :** the capacity (as of a military unit) to deliver effective fire on a target **2 :** the aggregate of effective missiles that can be placed upon a target **3 :** the scoring action or potential of a team

[1]**fire•proof** \-ˈprüf\ *adj* (1638) **:** proof against or resistant to fire

[2]**fireproof** *vt* (1867) **:** to make fireproof

fire•room \ˈfī(ə)r-ˌrüm, -ˌru̇m\ *n* (1836) **:** STOKEHOLD 1

fire sale *n* (1891) **:** a sale of merchandise damaged in a fire

fire screen *n* (15c) **:** a protective and often ornamental screen before a fireplace

fire ship *n* (1588) **:** a ship carrying combustibles or explosives sent among the enemy's ships or works to set them on fire

[1]**fire•side** \ˈfī(ə)r-ˌsīd\ *n* (1563) **1 :** a place near the fire or hearth **2 :** HOME

[2]**fireside** *adj* (1740) **:** having an informal or intimate quality

fire station *n* (ca. 1900) **:** a building housing fire apparatus and usu. firemen

fire•stone \ˈfī(ə)r-ˌstōn\ *n* (bef. 12c) **1 :** pyrite formerly used for striking fire; *also* **:** FLINT **2 :** a stone that will endure high heat

fire–stop \-ˌstäp\ *n* (1897) **:** material used to close open parts of a structure (as a building) for preventing the spread of fire — **fire–stop** *vt*

fire tower *n* (1827) **:** a tower (as in a forest) from which a watch for fires is maintained

fire•trap \ˈfī(ə)r-ˌtrap\ *n* (1881) **:** a place (as a building) apt to catch on fire or difficult to escape from in case of fire

fire truck *n* (1935) **:** an automotive vehicle equipped with fire-fighting apparatus

fire wall *n* (1759) **:** a wall constructed to prevent the spread of fire

fire•wa•ter \ˈfī(ə)r-ˌwȯt-ər, -ˌwät-\ *n* (1817) **:** strong alcoholic beverage

fire•weed \-ˌwēd\ *n* (ca. 1784) **:** any of several plants that grow esp. in clearings or burned districts: as **a :** a weedy composite (*Erechtites hieracifolia*) that has clusters of brush-shaped flower heads with no ray flowers **b :** a tall perennial (*Epilobium angustifolium*) of the evening-primrose family that has long spikes of pinkish purple flowers and is an important honey plant in some areas — called also *willow herb*

fire•wood \-ˌwu̇d\ *n* (14c) **:** wood cut for fuel

fire•work \-ˌwərk\ *n* (1575) **1 :** a device for producing a striking display by the combustion of explosive or flammable compositions **2** *pl* **:** a display of fireworks **3** *pl* **a :** a display of temper or intense conflict **b :** a spectacular display (as of artistic brilliance)

fir•ing \ˈfī(ə)r-iŋ\ *n* (14c) **1 :** the act or process of one that fires **2 :** the process of maturing ceramic products by the application of heat **3 :** FIREWOOD, FUEL **4 :** the scorching of plants esp. by unfavorable soil conditions

firing line *n* (1881) **1 :** a line from which fire is delivered against a target **2 :** the forefront of an activity — used esp. in the phrase *on the firing line*

firing pin *n* (1874) **:** the pin that strikes the cartridge primer in the breech mechanism of a firearm

firing squad *n* (1904) **1 :** a detachment detailed to fire volleys over the grave of one buried with military honors **2 :** a detachment detailed to carry out a sentence of death by shooting

\ə\ abut \ᵊ\ kitten, F table \ər\ further \a\ ash \ā\ ace \ä\ cot, cart \au̇\ out \ch\ chin \e\ bet \ē\ easy \g\ go \i\ hit \ī\ ice \j\ job \ŋ\ sing \ō\ go \ȯ\ law \ȯi\ boy \th\ thin \t͟h\ the \ü\ loot \u̇\ foot \y\ yet \zh\ vision \à, k̟, ⁿ, œ, œ̄, ue, ue̅, ʸ\ see Guide to Pronunciation

fir·kin \'fər-kən\ *n* [ME, deriv. of MD *veerdel* fourth, fr. *veer* four; akin to OE *fēower* — more at FOUR] (14c) **1 :** a small wooden vessel or cask **2 :** any of various British units of capacity usu. equal to 1/4 barrel

¹firm \'fərm\ *adj* [ME *ferm,* fr. MF, fr. L *firmus;* akin to Gk *thronos* chair, throne] (14c) **1 a :** securely or solidly fixed in place **b :** not weak or uncertain : VIGOROUS **c :** having a solid or compact structure that resists stress or pressure **2 a** (1) **:** not subject to change or revision (2) **:** not subject to price weakness : STEADY **b :** not easily moved or disturbed : STEADFAST **c :** WELL-FOUNDED **3 :** indicating firmness or resolution ⟨a ~ mouth⟩ — **firm·ly** *adv* — **firm·ness** *n*

syn FIRM, HARD, SOLID mean having a texture or consistency that resists deformation. FIRM implies such compactness and coherence and often elasticity of substance as to resist pulling, distorting, or pressing; HARD implies impenetrability and nearly complete but inelastic resistance to pressure or tension; SOLID implies a texture of uniform density so as to be not only firm but heavy.

²firm *adv* (14c) **:** in a firm manner : STEADFASTLY, FIXEDLY

³firm *vt* (14c) **1 a :** to make secure or fast : TIGHTEN ⟨~*ing* his grip on the racquet⟩ — often used with *up* **b :** to make solid or compact ⟨~ the soil⟩ **2 :** to put into final form : SETTLE ⟨~ a contract⟩ — often used with *up* **3 :** to give additional support to : STRENGTHEN — usu. used with *up* ~ *vi* **1 :** to become firm : HARDEN — often used with *up* **2 :** to recover from a decline : IMPROVE — often used with *up*

⁴firm *n* [G *firma,* fr. It, signature, deriv. of L *firmare* to make firm, confirm, fr. *firmus*] (1744) **1 :** the name or title under which a company transacts business **2 :** a partnership of two or more persons not recognized as a legal person distinct from the members composing it **3 :** a business unit or enterprise

fir·ma·ment \'fər-mə-mənt\ *n* [ME, fr. LL & L; LL *firmamentum,* fr. L, support, fr. *firmare*] (13c) **1 :** the vault or arch of the sky : HEAVENS **2** *obs* **:** BASIS **3 :** the field or sphere of an interest or activity ⟨the international fashion ~⟩ — **fir·ma·men·tal** \,fər-mə-'ment-ᵊl\ *adj*

fir·mer chisel \'fər-mər-\ *n* [F *fermoir* chisel, alter. of MF *formoir,* fr. *former* to form, fr. OF *forme* form] (1823) **:** a woodworking chisel with a thin flat blade

firm·ware \'fərm-,mwa(ə)r, -,mwe(ə)r\ *n* (1967) **:** computer programs contained permanently in a hardware device (as a read-only memory)

firn \'fi(ə)rn\ *n* [G, fr. OHG *firni* old; akin to OE *faran*] (1853) **:** NÉVÉ

¹first \'fərst\ *adj* [ME, fr. OE *fyrst;* akin to OHG *furist* first, OE *faran* to go — more at FARE] (bef. 12c) **:** preceding all others in time, order, or importance: as **a :** EARLIEST **b :** being the lowest forward gear or speed of a motor vehicle **c :** relating to or having the highest or most prominent part among a group of similar voices or instruments in concerted or ensemble music ⟨~ tenor⟩ ⟨~ violins⟩

²first *adv* (bef. 12c) **1 a :** before another in time, space, or importance **b :** for the first time **2 :** in preference to something else : SOONER

³first *n* (14c) **1** — see NUMBER table **2 :** something that is first: as **a :** the first occurrence or item of a kind **b :** the first forward gear or speed of a motor vehicle **c :** the highest or chief voice or instrument of a group **d :** an article of commerce of the finest grade **e :** the winning or highest place in a competition, examination, or contest **3 :** FIRST BASE — **at first :** at the beginning : INITIALLY

first aid *n* (1882) **:** emergency care or treatment given to an ill or injured person before regular medical aid can be obtained

first base *n* (1845) **1 :** the base that must be touched first by a base runner in baseball **2 :** the player position for defending the area around first base **3 :** the first step or stage in a course of action ⟨plans never got to *first base*⟩ — **first base·man** \-'bā-smən\ *n*

first·born \'fərs(t)-'bȯ(ə)rn\ *adj* (14c) **:** first brought forth : ELDEST — **firstborn** *n*

first cause *n* (14c) **:** the self-created ultimate source of all being

first class *n* (1750) **:** the first or highest group in a classification: as **a :** the highest of usu. three classes of travel accommodations **b :** a class of mail that comprises letters, postcards, or matter sealed against inspection — **first-class** *adj or adv*

first class·man \'fərs(t)-'klas-mən\ *n* (1886) **:** a fourth-year student in a military school (as West Point)

first consonant shift *n* (1934) **:** CONSONANT SHIFT a

first day cover *n* (1932) **:** a philatelic cover franked with a newly issued postage stamp and postmarked on the first day of issue at a city officially chosen for first day sale

first-degree burn *n* (ca. 1924) **:** a mild burn characterized by heat, pain, and reddening of the burned surface but not exhibiting blistering or charring of tissues

first down *n* (1897) **1 :** the first of a series of four downs in which a football team must net a 10-yard gain to retain possession of the ball **2 :** a gain of a total of 10 or more yards within four downs giving the team the right to start a new series of downs

first edition *n* (ca. 1828) **:** the copies of a literary work first printed from the same type and issued at the same time; *also* **:** a single copy from a first edition

first estate *n, often cap F&E* (1935) **:** the first of the traditional political estates; *specif* **:** CLERGY

first floor *n* (15c) **1 :** GROUND FLOOR **2** *chiefly Brit* **:** the floor next above the ground floor

first·fruits \'fərs(t)-'früts\ *n pl* (14c) **1 :** the earliest gathered fruits offered to the Deity in acknowledgment of the gift of fruitfulness **2 :** the earliest products or results of an endeavor

first·hand \'fərst-'hand\ *adj* (1748) **:** coming directly from the original source — **firsthand** *adv*

first lady *n, often cap F&L* (1853) **1 :** the wife or hostess of the chief executive of a country or jurisdiction **2 :** the leading woman of an art or profession

first lieutenant *n* (1782) **1 :** a commissioned officer in the army, air force, or marine corps ranking above a second lieutenant and below a captain **2 :** a naval officer responsible for a ship's upkeep

first·ling \'fərst-liŋ\ *n* (1535) **1 :** the first of a class or kind **2 :** the first produce or result of something

first·ly \-lē\ *adv* (ca. 1532) **:** in the first place : FIRST

first mortgage *n* (1855) **:** a mortgage that has priority as a lien over all mortgages and liens except those imposed by law

first name *n* (13c) **:** the name that stands first in one's full name

first night *n* (1711) **:** the night on which a theatrical production is first performed at a given place; *also* **:** the performance itself

first-night·er \'fərs(t)-'nīt-ər\ *n* (1882) **:** a spectator at a first-night performance

first off *adv* (1880) **:** in the first place : FIRST

first offender *n* (1849) **:** one legally convicted of an offense for the first time

first papers *n pl* (1912) **:** papers declaring intention filed by an applicant for citizenship as the first step in the naturalization process

first person *n* (1520) **1 a :** a set of linguistic forms (as verb forms, pronouns, and inflectional affixes) referring to the speaker or writer of the utterance in which they occur **b :** a linguistic form belonging to such a set **c :** reference of a linguistic form to the speaker or writer of the utterance in which it occurs **2 :** a style of discourse marked by general use of verbs and pronouns of the first person

¹first-rate \'fər-'strāt\ *adj* (1671) **:** of the first order of size, importance, or quality — **first-rate·ness** *n* — **first-rat·er** \-'strāt-ər\ *n*

²first-rate *adv* (1842) **:** very well

First Reader *n* (1896) **:** a Christian Scientist chosen to conduct meetings for a specified time and specif. to read aloud from the writings of Mary Baker Eddy

first reading *n* (1702) **:** the first submitting of a bill before a quorum of a legislative assembly usu. by title or number only

first sergeant *n* (ca. 1860) **1 :** a noncommissioned officer serving as the chief assistant to the commander of a military unit (as a company or squadron) **2 :** the rank of a first sergeant; *specif* **:** a rank in the army above a platoon sergeant and below a command sergeant major and in the marine corps above a gunnery sergeant and below a sergeant major

first-string \'fərs(t)-'striŋ\ *adj* (1917) **1 :** being a regular as distinguished from a substitute (as on a team) **2 :** FIRST-RATE

first water *n* (1753) **1 :** the purest luster — used of gems **2 :** the highest grade, degree, or quality

first world *n, often cap F&W* [after *third world*] (1967) **:** the Western industrialized non-Communist nations

firth \'fərth\ *n* [ME, fr. ON *fjǫrthr* — more at FORD] (14c) **:** ESTUARY

fisc \'fisk\ *n* [L *fiscus*] (1598) **:** a state or royal treasury

¹fis·cal \'fis-kəl\ *adj* [L *fiscalis,* fr. *fiscus* basket, treasury; akin to Gk *pithos* wine jar] (1563) **1 :** of or relating to taxation, public revenues, or public debt ⟨~ policy⟩ **2 :** of or relating to financial matters ⟨~ agent⟩ — **fis·cal·ly** \-kə-lē\ *adv*

²fiscal *n* (1929) **1 :** REVENUE STAMP **2 :** FISCAL YEAR

fiscal year *n* (1843) **:** an accounting period of 12 months

¹fish \'fish\ *n, pl* **fish** *or* **fish·es** *often attrib* [ME, fr. OE *fisc;* akin to OHG *fisc* fish, L *piscis*] (bef. 12c) **1 a :** an aquatic animal — usu. used in combination ⟨star*fish*⟩ ⟨cuttle*fish*⟩ **b :** any of numerous cold-blooded strictly aquatic craniate vertebrates that include the teleosts and usu. the elasmobranchs and cyclostomes and that have typically an elongated somewhat spindle-shaped body terminating in a broad caudal fin, limbs in the form of fins when present at all, and a 2-chambered heart by which blood is sent through thoracic gills to be oxygenated **c** *fishes pl, cap* **:** PISCES **2 :** the flesh of fish used as food **3 :** FELLOW, CHAP ⟨a queer ~⟩ **4 :** something that resembles a fish; *esp* **:** a piece of wood or iron fastened alongside another member to strengthen it — **fish·less** \'fish-ləs\ *adj* — **fish·like** \-,līk\ *adj* — **fish out of water :** a person who is out of his proper sphere or element — **neither fish nor fowl :** one that does not belong to a particular class or category

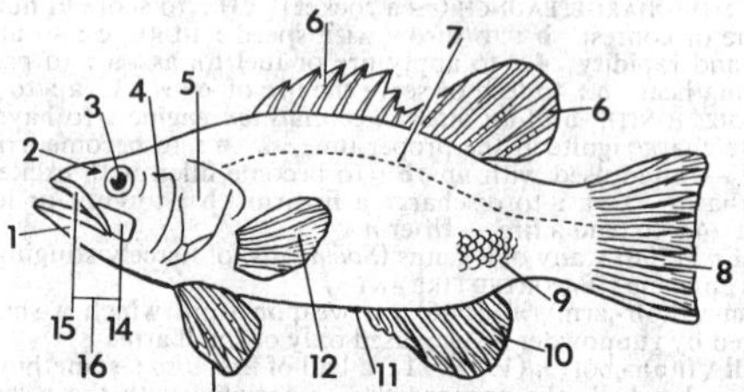

fish 1b: *1* mandible, *2* external naris, *3* eye, *4* cheek, *5* operculum, *6* dorsal fins, *7* lateral line, *8* caudal fin, *9* scales, *10* anal fin, *11* anus, *12* pectoral fin, *13* pelvic fin, *14* maxilla, *15* premaxilla, *16* upper jaw

²fish *vi* (bef. 12c) **1 :** to attempt to catch fish **2 :** to seek something by roundabout means ⟨~*ing* for a compliment⟩ **3 a :** to search for something underwater ⟨~ for pearls⟩ **b :** to engage in a search by groping or feeling ⟨~*ing* around in her purse for her keys⟩ ~ *vt* **1 a :** to try to catch fish in **b :** to fish with : use (as a boat, net, or bait) in fishing **2 a :** to go fishing for ⟨~ salmon⟩ **b :** to pull or draw as if fishing ⟨~*ed* the ball from under the car⟩ ⟨~ wires through a conduit⟩ — **fish·abil·i·ty** \,fish-ə-'bil-ət-ē\ *n* — **fish·able** \'fish-ə-bəl\ *adj* — **fish or cut bait :** to make a choice between alternatives

fish-and-chips \,fish-ən-'chips\ *n pl* (1876) **:** fried fish and french fried potatoes

fish·bowl \'fish-,bōl\ *n* (1906) **1 :** a bowl for the keeping of live fish **2 :** a place or condition that affords no privacy

fish cake *n* (1854) **:** a round fried cake made of shredded fish and mashed potato

fish duck *n* (1858) **:** MERGANSER

fish·er \'fish-ər\ *n* (bef. 12c) **1 :** one that fishes **2 a :** a large dark brown No. American arboreal carnivorous mammal (*Martes pennanti*) related to the weasels **b :** the fur or pelt of this animal

fish·er·man \-mən\ *n* (15c) **1 :** one who engages in fishing as an occupation or for pleasure **2 :** a ship used in commercial fishing

fisherman's bend *n* (1823) **:** a knot made by passing the end twice round a spar or through a ring and then back under both turns — see KNOT illustration

fish·ery \'fish-(ə-)rē\ *n, pl* **-er·ies** (1677) **1 :** the act, process, occupation, or season of taking fish or other sea animals (as sponges or seals) : FISHING **2 :** a place for catching fish or taking other sea animals (as

sponges or seals) **3 :** a fishing establishment; *also* **:** its fishermen **4 :** the legal right to take fish at a particular place or in particular waters **5 :** the technology of fishery — usu. used in pl.
fish–eye \ˈfish-ˌī\ *adj* (1942) **:** being, having, or produced by a wide-angle photographic lens that has a highly curved protruding front, that covers an angle of about 180 degrees, and that gives a circular image ⟨a ~ lens⟩
fish farm *n* (1865) **:** a commercial facility for raising aquatic animals for human food — **fish–farm** \(ˈ)fish-ˈfärm\ *vt*
fish fry *n* (1824) **1 :** a meal (as a picnic) featuring fried fish **2 :** fried fish
fish hawk *n* (1709) **:** OSPREY 1
fish•hook \ˈfish-ˌhu̇k\ *n* (14c) **:** a usu. barbed hook for catching fish
fish•ing *n* (13c) **1 :** the sport or business of catching fish **2 :** a place for catching fish
fishing expedition *n* (ca. 1925) **1 :** a legal interrogation or examination to discover information for a later proceeding **2 :** an investigation that does not stick to a stated objective but hopes to uncover incriminating or newsworthy evidence
fish joint *n* (1849) **:** a butt joint of timbers or rails in which the two abutting members are held in alignment by one or more fishplates
fish ladder *n* (1865) **:** a series of pools arranged like steps by which fish can pass over a dam in going upstream
fish meal *n* (1854) **:** ground dried fish and fish waste used as fertilizer and animal food
fish•mong•er \ˈfish-ˌməŋ-gər, -ˌmäŋ-\ *n, chiefly Brit* (14c) **:** a fish dealer
fish•net \-ˌnet\ *n* (bef. 12c) **1 :** netting fitted with floats and weights or a supporting frame for catching fish **2 :** a coarse open-mesh fabric
fish out *vt* (1955) **:** to exhaust the supply of fish in by fishing
fish•plate \-ˌplāt\ *n* (1855) **:** a steel plate used to lap a butt joint
fish protein concentrate *n* (1961) **:** a protein-rich food additive obtained as a nearly colorless and tasteless powder from ground whole fish
fish stick *n* (1953) **:** a small elongated breaded fillet of fish
fish story *n* [fr. the traditional exaggeration by fishermen of the size of fish almost caught] (1819) **:** an extravagant or incredible story
fish•tail \ˈfish-ˌtāl\ *vi* (1927) **1 :** to swing the tail of an airplane from side to side to reduce speed esp. when landing **2 :** to have the rear end slide from side to side out of control while moving forward ⟨the car ~*ed* on the icy curve⟩
fish•way \-ˌwā\ *n* (1845) **:** a contrivance for enabling fish to pass around a fall or dam in a stream; *specif* **:** FISH LADDER
fish•wife \-ˌwīf\ *n* [ME] (15c) **1 :** a woman who sells fish **2 :** a vulgar abusive woman
fishy \ˈfish-ē\ *adj* **fish•i•er; -est** (1547) **1 :** of or resembling fish esp. in taste or odor **2 :** creating doubt or suspicion **:** QUESTIONABLE
fishy•back \-ˌbak\ *n* [*fish* + *-y* + *-back* (as in *piggyback*)] (ca. 1950) **:** the movement of truck trailers or freight containers by barge or ship — compare BIRDYBACK, PIGGYBACK
fis•sile \ˈfis-əl, ˈfis-ˌīl\ *adj* [L *fissilis,* fr. *fissus*] (1661) **1 :** capable of being split or divided in the direction of the grain or along natural planes of cleavage ⟨~ wood⟩ ⟨~ crystals⟩ **2 :** FISSIONABLE — **fis•sil•i•ty** \fis-ˈil-ət-ē\ *n*
¹fis•sion \ˈfish-ən *also* ˈfizh-\ *n* [L *fission-, fissio,* fr. *fissus,* pp. of *findere* to split — more at BITE] (1841) **1 :** reproduction by spontaneous division of the body into two or more parts each of which grows into a complete organism **2 :** a splitting or breaking up into parts **3 a :** the splitting of a molecule into simpler molecules **b :** the splitting of an atomic nucleus resulting in the release of large amounts of energy — **fis•sion•al** \-ᵊl\ *adj*
²fission *vb* **fis•sioned; fis•sion•ing** \ˈfish-(ə-)niŋ, ˈfizh-\ *vt* (1929) **:** to cause to undergo fission ~ *vi* **:** to undergo fission
fis•sion•able \ˈfish-(ə-)nə-bəl, ˈfizh-\ *adj* (1945) **:** capable of undergoing fission — **fis•sion•abil•i•ty** \ˌfish-(ə-)nə-ˈbil-ət-ē, ˌfizh-\ *n* — **fissionable** *n*
fission bomb *n* (1941) **:** ATOM BOMB 1
fis•sip•a•rous \fis-ˈip-ə-rəs\ *adj* [L *fissus* + E *-parous*] (1874) **:** tending to break up into parts **:** DIVISIVE — **fis•sip•a•rous•ness** *n*
¹fis•sure \ˈfish-ər\ *n* [ME, fr. MF, fr. L *fissura,* fr. *fissus*] (15c) **1 :** a narrow opening or crack of considerable length and depth usu. occurring from some breaking or parting **2 a :** a natural cleft between body parts or in the substance of an organ **b :** a break or slit in tissue usu. at the junction of skin and mucous membrane **3 :** a separation or disagreement in thought or viewpoint **:** SCHISM ⟨~*s* in a political party⟩
²fissure *vb* **fis•sured; fis•sur•ing** *vt* (1656) **:** to break into fissures **:** CLEAVE ~ *vi* **:** CRACK, DIVIDE
¹fist \ˈfist\ *n* [ME, fr. OE *fȳst;* akin to OHG *fūst* fist, OSlav *pęstĭ*] (bef. 12c) **1 :** the hand clenched with the fingers doubled into the palm and the thumb doubled inward across the fingers **2 :** the hand closed as in grasping **:** CLUTCH **3 :** INDEX 5
²fist *vt* (1607) **1 :** to grip with the fist **:** HANDLE **2 :** to clench into a fist
-fist•ed \ˈfis-təd\ *comb form* **:** having (such or so many) fists ⟨two-*fisted*⟩ ⟨tight*fisted*⟩
fist•fight \ˈfist-ˌfīt\ *n* (1603) **:** a usu. spontaneous fight with bare fists
fist•ful \-ˌfu̇l\ *n* (1611) **1 :** HANDFUL ⟨a ~ of coins⟩ **2 :** a considerable number ⟨a whole ~ of musicians —Thomas Lask⟩
fist•ic \ˈfis-tik\ *adj* (1806) **:** of or relating to boxing or to fighting with the fists
fist•i•cuffs \ˈfis-ti-ˌkəfs\ *n pl* [alter. of *fisty cuff,* fr. *fisty* (fistic) + *cuff*] (1605) **:** a fight with the fists
fist•note \ˈfis(t)-ˌnōt\ *n* (ca. 1934) **:** matter in a text to which attention is directed by means of an index mark
fis•tu•la \ˈfis(h)-chə-lə\ *n, pl* **-las** *or* **-lae** \-ˌlē, -ˌlī\ [ME, fr. L, pipe, fistula] (14c) **:** an abnormal passage leading from an abscess or hollow organ to the body surface or from one hollow organ to another and permitting passage of fluids or secretions
fis•tu•lous \-ləs\ *adj* (15c) **1 :** of, relating to, or having the form or nature of a fistula **2 :** hollow like a pipe or reed
fistulous withers *n pl but sing or pl in constr* (1900) **:** a deep-seated chronic inflammation of the withers of the horse in which bloody fluid is discharged
¹fit \ˈfit\ *n* [ME, fr. OE *fitt;* akin to OS *fittea* division of a poem, OHG *fizza* skein] *archaic* (bef. 12c) **:** a division of a poem or song
²fit *adj* **fit•ter; fit•test** [ME; akin to ME *fitten*] (14c) **1 a** (1) **:** adapted to an end or design **:** suitable by nature or by art (2) **:** adapted to the environment so as to be capable of surviving **b :** acceptable from a particular viewpoint (as of competence or morality) **:** PROPER ⟨not ~ to be a father⟩ ⟨a movie ~ for the whole family⟩ ⟨saw ~ to make changes⟩ **2 a :** put into a suitable state **:** made ready ⟨get the house ~ for company⟩ **b :** being in such a state as to be or seem ready to do or suffer something ⟨fair ~ to cry I was —Bryan MacMahon⟩ ⟨laughing ~ to burst⟩ **3 :** sound physically and mentally **:** HEALTHY — **fit•ly** *adv* — **fit•ness** *n*
syn FIT, SUITABLE, MEET, PROPER, APPROPRIATE, FITTING, APT, HAPPY, FELICITOUS mean right with respect to some end, need, use, or circumstance. FIT stresses adaptability and sometimes special readiness for use or action; SUITABLE implies an answering to requirements or demands; MEET suggests a just proportioning; PROPER suggests a suitability through essential nature or accordance with custom; APPROPRIATE implies eminent or distinctive fitness; FITTING implies harmony of mood or tone; APT connotes a fitness marked by nicety and discrimination; HAPPY suggests what is effectively or successfully appropriate; FELICITOUS suggests an aptness that is opportune, telling, or graceful.
— **fit to be tied :** extremely angry or irritated — **fit to kill :** to a striking degree ⟨dressed *fit to kill*⟩
³fit *n* [ME, fr. OE *fitt* strife] (ca. 1536) **1 a :** a sudden violent attack of a disease (as epilepsy) esp. when marked by convulsions or unconsciousness **:** PAROXYSM **b :** a sudden but transient attack of a physical disturbance **2 :** a sudden burst or flurry (as of activity) ⟨cleaned the whole house in a ~ of efficiency⟩ **3 :** an emotional reaction (as in anger or frustration) ⟨has a ~ when I show up late⟩ — **by fits** *or* **by fits and starts :** in an impulsive and irregular manner
⁴fit *vb* **fit•ted** *also* **fit; fit•ting** [ME *fitten* to marshal troops, fr. or akin to MD *vitten* to be suitable; akin to OHG *fizza* skein] *vt* (1586) **1 a :** to be suitable for or to **:** harmonize with **b** *archaic* **:** to be seemly or proper for ⟨it ~*s* us then to be as provident as fear may teach us —Shak.⟩ **2 a :** to conform correctly to the shape or size of ⟨it doesn't ~ me anymore⟩ **b** (1) **:** to insert or adjust until correctly in place ⟨~ the mechanism into the box⟩ (2) **:** to make or adjust to the right shape and size ⟨*fitting* the jacket to the customer⟩ **c :** to make a place or room for **:** ACCOMMODATE **3 :** to be in agreement or accord with ⟨the theory ~*s* all the facts⟩ **4 a :** to put into a condition of readiness **b :** to cause to conform to or suit something **5 :** SUPPLY, EQUIP ⟨*fitted* the ship with new engines⟩ — often used with *out* **6 :** to adjust (a smooth curve of a specified type) to a given set of points ~ *vi* **1** *archaic* **:** to be seemly, proper, or suitable **2 :** to conform to a particular shape or size; *also* **:** to be accommodated ⟨will we all ~ into the car?⟩ **3 :** to be in harmony or accord **:** BELONG — often used with *in* — **fit•ter** *n*
⁵fit *n* (1688) **:** the fact, condition, or manner of fitting or being fitted: as **a :** the way clothing fits the wearer **b :** the degree of closeness between surfaces in an assembly of parts **c :** the conformity between an experimental result and theoretical expectation or between data and an approximating curve ⟨a statistical test of goodness of ~⟩
⁶fit *dial past of* FIGHT
fitch \ˈfich\ *or* **fitch•ew** \ˈfich-(ˌ)ü\ *n* [ME *fiche, ficheux,* fr. MF or MD; MF *fichau,* fr. MD *vitsau*] (15c) **1 :** the fur or pelt of the polecat **2 :** POLECAT 1
fitch•et \ˈfich-ət\ *n* (1535) **:** POLECAT 1
fit•ful \ˈfit-fəl\ *adj* (1605) **1** *obs* **:** characterized by fits or paroxysms **2 :** having a spasmodic or intermittent character **:** IRREGULAR ⟨~ sleep⟩ — **fit•ful•ly** \-fə-lē\ *adv* — **fit•ful•ness** *n*
syn FITFUL, SPASMODIC, CONVULSIVE mean lacking steadiness or regularity in movement. FITFUL implies intermittence, a succession of starts and stops or risings and fallings; SPASMODIC adds to FITFUL the implication of violent activity alternating with inactivity; CONVULSIVE suggests the breaking of regularity or quiet by uncontrolled movement.
fit•ment \ˈfit-mənt\ *n* [⁴*fit*] (ca. 1864) **1** *pl* **:** FITTINGS **2 :** EQUIPMENT, FURNITURE
¹fit•ting \ˈfit-iŋ\ *adj* (15c) **:** APPROPRIATE, SUITABLE, PROPER ***syn*** see FIT — **fit•ting•ly** \-iŋ-lē\ *adv* — **fit•ting•ness** *n*
²fitting *n* (1607) **1 :** an action or act of one that fits; *specif* **:** a trying on of clothes which are in the process of being made or altered **2 :** a small often standardized part ⟨an electrical ~⟩
five \ˈfīv\ *n* [ME, fr. *five,* adj., fr. OE *fīf;* akin to OHG *finf* five, L *quinque,* Gk *pente*] (bef. 12c) **1** — see NUMBER table **2 :** the fifth in a set or series ⟨the ~ of clubs⟩ **3 :** something having five units or members; *esp* **:** a basketball team **4 :** a 5-dollar bill **5 :** FIFTEEN 2 — **five** *adj or pron*
five–and–ten \ˌfī-vən-ˈten\ *n* [fr. the fact that all articles in such stores were formerly priced at either 5 or 10 cents] (1880) **:** a retail store that carries chiefly inexpensive merchandise (as notions and household goods) — called also *five-and-dime*
five–fin•ger \ˈfīv-ˌfiŋ-gər\ *n* (bef. 12c) **:** CINQUEFOIL 1
five•fold \ˈfīv-ˌfōld, -ˈfōld\ *adj* (bef. 12c) **1 :** having five units or members **2 :** being five times as great or as many — **five•fold** \-ˈfōld\ *adv*
five of a kind (1897) **:** four cards of the same rank plus a wild card in one hand — see POKER illustration
fiv•er \ˈfī-vər\ *n* (1843) **1** *slang* **:** a 5-dollar bill **2** *Brit* **:** a 5-pound note
fives \ˈfīvz\ *n pl* (1636) **:** a British handball game
five–star \ˌfīv-ˈstär\ *adj* (1913) **:** of first class or quality
¹fix \ˈfiks\ *vb* [ME *fixen,* fr. L *fixus,* pp. of *figere* to fasten — more at DIKE] *vt* (14c) **1 a :** to make firm, stable, or stationary **b :** to give a permanent or final form to: as (1) **:** to change into a stable compound or available form ⟨bacteria that ~ nitrogen⟩ (2) **:** to kill, harden, and preserve for microscopic study (3) **:** to make the image of (a photographic film) permanent by removing unused salts **c :** AFFIX, ATTACH **2 a :** to hold or direct steadily ⟨~*es* his eyes on the horizon⟩ **b :** to

capture the attention of ⟨~*ed* her with a stare⟩ **3 a :** to set or place definitely : ESTABLISH **b :** to make an accurate determination of : DISCOVER ⟨~*ing* our location on the chart⟩ **c :** ASSIGN ⟨~ the blame⟩ **4 :** to set in order : ADJUST **5 :** to get ready : PREPARE ⟨~ lunch⟩ **6 a :** REPAIR, MEND ⟨~ the clock⟩ **b :** RESTORE, CURE ⟨the doctor ~*ed* him up⟩ **c :** SPAY, CASTRATE **7 a :** to get even with **b :** to influence the actions, outcome, or effect of by improper or illegal methods ⟨the jury had been ~*ed*⟩ ~ *vi* **1 :** to become firm, stable, or fixed **2 :** to get set : be on the verge ⟨we're ~*ing* to leave soon⟩ **3 :** to direct one's attention or efforts : FOCUS; *also* : DECIDE, SETTLE — usu. used with *on* ***syn*** see FASTEN — **fix·able** \'fik-sə-bəl\ *adj*

²fix *n* (1809) **1 :** a position of difficulty or embarrassment : PREDICAMENT **2 a :** the position (as of a ship) determined by bearings, observations, or radio; *also* : a determination of one's position **b :** an accurate determination or understanding esp. by observation or analysis **3 :** an act or instance of obtaining special privilege or immunity from the law or of exerting improper or illegal influence on the outcome of something **4 :** a shot of a narcotic **5 :** FIXATION **6 :** something that fixes or restores

fix·ate \'fik-,sāt\ *vb* **fix·at·ed; fix·at·ing** *vt* (1885) **1 :** to make fixed, stationary, or unchanging **2 :** to focus one's gaze on **3 :** to direct (the libido) toward an infantile form of gratification ~ *vi* **1 :** to focus or concentrate one's gaze or attention **2 :** to undergo arrestment at a stage of development

fix·at·ed *adj* (1926) **:** arrested in development or adjustment; *esp* : arrested at a pregenital level of psychosexual development

fix·a·tion \fik-'sā-shən\ *n* (14c) **:** the act, process, or result of fixing, fixating, or becoming fixated: as **a :** a persistent concentration of libidinal energies upon objects characteristic of psychosexual stages of development preceding the genital stage **b :** stereotyped behavior (as in response to frustration) **c :** an obsessive or unhealthy preoccupation or attachment

fix·a·tive \'fik-sət-iv\ *n* (ca. 1855) **:** something that fixes or sets: as **a :** a substance added to a perfume esp. to prevent too rapid evaporation **b :** a varnish used esp. for the protection of crayon drawings **c :** a substance used to fix living tissue — **fixative** *adj*

fixed \'fikst\ *adj* (14c) **1 a :** securely placed or fastened : STATIONARY **b (1) :** NONVOLATILE **(2) :** formed into a chemical compound **c (1) :** not subject to change or fluctuation : SETTLED ⟨a ~ income⟩ **(2) :** firmly set in the mind ⟨a ~ idea⟩ **(3) :** having a final or crystallized form or character **(4) :** recurring on the same date from year to year ⟨~ holidays⟩ **d :** IMMOBILE, CONCENTRATED ⟨a ~ stare⟩ **2 :** supplied with something (as money) needed or desirable ⟨comfortably ~ by the standards of his class — Frederick Lane⟩ — **fixed·ly** \'fik-səd-lē, 'fiks-tlē\ *adv* — **fixed·ness** \'fik-səd-nəs, 'fiks(t)-nəs\ *n*

fixed charge *n* (ca. 1901) **:** a regularly recurring expense (as rent, taxes, or interest) that must be met when due

fixed oil *n* (ca. 1800) **:** a nonvolatile oil; *esp* : a fatty oil — compare ESSENTIAL OIL

fixed–point *adj* (1960) **:** involving or being a mathematical notation (as in a decimal system) in which the point separating whole numbers and fractions is fixed — compare FLOATING-POINT

fixed star *n* (14c) **:** a star so distant that its motion can be measured only by very precise observations over long periods

fix·er \'fik-sər\ *n* (1849) **:** one that fixes: as **a :** one that intervenes to enable a person to circumvent the law or obtain a political favor **b :** one that adjusts matters or disputes by negotiation

fix·ing \-siŋ\ *n* (1605) **1 :** the act or process of one that fixes **2** *pl* *often* -sənz\ : TRIMMINGS ⟨a turkey dinner with all the ~*s*⟩

fix·i·ty \'fik-sət-ē\ *n, pl* **-ties** (1666) **1 :** the quality or state of being fixed or stable **2 :** something that is fixed

fix·ture \'fiks-chər\ *n* [modif. of LL *fixura,* fr. L *fixus*] (1598) **1 :** the act or process of fixing : the state of being fixed **2 a :** something that is fixed or attached (as to a building) as a permanent appendage or as a structural part ⟨a plumbing ~⟩ **b :** a device for supporting work during machining **c :** an item of movable property so incorporated into real property that it may be regarded as legally a part of it **3 :** a familiar or invariably present element or feature in some particular setting; *esp* : a person long associated with a place or activity **4 :** a settled date or time esp. for a sporting or festive event; *also* : such an event esp. as a regularly scheduled affair

fix up *vt* (1871) **1 :** to set right : SETTLE ⟨*fixed up* their dispute⟩ **2 :** REFURBISH ⟨*fix up* the attic⟩ **3 :** to provide with something needed or wanted; *esp* : to arrange a date for

¹fizz \'fiz\ *vi* [prob. of imit. origin] (1685) **1 :** to make a hissing or sputtering sound **2 :** to show excitement or exhilaration

²fizz *n* (1842) **1 a :** a hissing sound **b :** SPIRIT, LIVELINESS **2 :** an effervescent beverage — **fizzy** \-ē\ *adj*

¹fiz·zle \'fiz-əl\ *vi* **fiz·zled; fiz·zling** \-(ə-)liŋ\ [prob. alter. of *fist* (to break wind)] (ca. 1841) **1 :** FIZZ **2 :** to fail or end feebly esp. after a promising start — often used with *out*

²fizzle *n* (1842) **:** an abortive effort : FAILURE

fjeld \fē-'el\ *n* [Dan, fr. ON *fjall* mountain — more at FELL] (1860) **:** a barren plateau of the Scandinavian upland

fjord \fē-'ō(ə)rd\ *n* [Norw *fjord,* fr. ON *fjǫrthr* — more at FORD] (1674) **:** a narrow inlet of the sea between cliffs or steep slopes

flab \'flab\ *n* [back-formation fr. *flabby*] (1951) **:** soft flabby body tissue

flab·ber·gast \'flab-ər-,gast\ *vt* [origin unknown] (1772) **:** to overwhelm with shock, surprise, or wonder : DUMBFOUND ***syn*** see SURPRISE — **flab·ber·gast·ing·ly** \-,gas-tiŋ-lē\ *adv*

flab·by \'flab-ē\ *adj* **flab·bi·er; -est** [alter. of *flappy*] (1598) **1 :** lacking resilience or firmness : FLACCID **2 :** weak and ineffective : FEEBLE — **flab·bi·ly** \'flab-ə-lē\ *adv* — **flab·bi·ness** \'flab-ē-nəs\ *n*

fla·bel·late \flə-'bel-ət, 'flab-ə-,lāt\ *adj* (1819) **:** shaped like a fan

flabelli- *comb form* [L, fr. *flabellum*] **:** fan ⟨*flabelli*form⟩

fla·bel·li·form \flə-'bel-ə-,fȯrm\ *adj* (1777) **:** FLABELLATE

fla·bel·lum \flə-'bel-əm\ *n, pl* **-la** \-ə\ [NL, fr. L, fan] (1900) **:** a body organ or part resembling a fan

flac·cid \'flas-əd, 'flak-səd\ *adj* [L *flaccidus,* fr. *flaccus* flabby] (1620) **1 a :** not firm or stiff; *also* : lacking normal or youthful firmness ⟨~ muscles⟩ **b** *of a plant part* : deficient in turgor **2 :** lacking vigor or force ⟨~ leadership⟩ — **flac·cid·i·ty** \fla(k)-'sid-ət-ē\ *n* — **flac·cid·ly** \'flak-səd-lē, 'flas-əd-\ *adv*

¹flack \'flak\ *n* [origin unknown] (1939) **:** one who provides publicity; *esp* : PRESS AGENT — **flack·ery** \-(ə-)rē\ *n*

²flack *var of* FLAK

fla·con \'flak-ən, -,än; fla-'kōⁿ\ *n* [F, fr. MF, bottle — more at FLAGON] (1824) **:** a small usu. ornamental bottle with a tight cap

¹flag \'flag\ *n* [ME *flagge* reed, rush] (14c) **:** any of various monocotyledonous plants with long ensiform leaves: as **a :** IRIS; *esp* : a wild iris **b :** SWEET FLAG

²flag *n, often attrib* [perh. fr. *¹flag*] (15c) **1 :** a usu. rectangular piece of fabric of distinctive design that is used as a symbol (as of a nation) or as a signaling device **2 a :** the tail of some dogs (as a setter or hound); *also* : the long hair fringing a setter's tail **b :** the tail of a deer **3 a :** something used like a flag to signal or attract attention **b :** one of the cross strokes of a musical note less than a quarter note in value **4 :** something represented by a flag: as **a :** FLAGSHIP **b :** an admiral functioning in his office of command **c :** NATIONALITY; *esp* : the nationality of registration of a ship or aircraft

³flag *vt* **flagged; flag·ging** (1856) **1 :** to signal with or as if with a flag; *esp* : to signal to stop ⟨*flagged* the train⟩ — often used with *down* **2 :** to put a flag on (as for identification) ⟨*flagged* the important pages⟩

⁴flag *vi* **flagged; flag·ging** [origin unknown] (1545) **1 :** to hang loose without stiffness **2 a :** to become unsteady, feeble, or spiritless **b :** to decline in interest or attraction

⁵flag *n* [ME *flagge* turf, fr. ON *flaga* slab; akin to OE *flōh* chip — more at PLEASE] (1604) **:** a hard evenly stratified stone that splits into flat pieces suitable for paving; *also* : a piece of such stone

⁶flag *vt* **flagged; flag·ging** (1615) **:** to lay (as a pavement) with flags

flag day *n* (1894) **1** *cap F&D* : June 14 observed in various states in commemoration of the adoption in 1777 of the official U.S. flag **2** *Brit* **:** a day on which charitable contributions are solicited in exchange for small flags

fla·gel·lant \'flaj-ə-lənt, flə-'jel-ənt\ *n* (1563) **:** one that whips: as **a :** a person who scourges himself as a public penance **b :** a person who responds sexually to being beaten by or to beating another person — **flagellant** *adj* — **fla·gel·lant·ism** \-,iz-əm\ *n*

fla·gel·lar \flə-'jel-ər, 'flaj-ə-lər\ *adj* (ca. 1889) **:** of or relating to a flagellum

¹flag·el·late \'flaj-ə-,lāt\ *vt* **-lat·ed; -lat·ing** [L *flagellatus,* pp. of *flagellare,* fr. *flagellum,* dim. of *flagrum* whip; akin to ON *blaka* to wave] (ca. 1623) **1 :** WHIP, SCOURGE **2 :** to drive or punish as if by whipping

²fla·gel·late \'flaj-ə-lət, -,lāt; flə-'jel-ət\ *adj* [NL *flagellatus,* fr. *flagellum*] (ca. 1864) **1 a** *or* **flag·el·lat·ed** \'flaj-ə-,lāt-əd\ **:** having flagella **b :** shaped like a flagellum **2** [*³flagellate*] **:** of, relating to, or caused by flagellates ⟨~ diarrhea⟩

³flagellate *like²*\ *n* [NL *Flagellata,* class of unicellular organisms, fr. neut. pl. of *flagellatus*] (1879) **:** a flagellate protozoan or alga

flag·el·la·tion \,flaj-ə-'lā-shən\ *n* (15c) **:** the act or practice of flagellating; *esp* : the practice of a flagellant

fla·gel·lin \flə-'jel-ən\ *n* [*flagell*um + ¹-*in*] (1955) **:** a polymeric protein that is the chief constituent of bacterial flagella and is believed to be responsible for the specificity of their flagellar antigens

fla·gel·lum \flə-'jel-əm\ *n, pl* **-la** \-ə\ *also* **-lums** [NL, fr. L, whip, shoot of a plant] (1852) **:** any of various elongated filiform appendages of plants or animals: as **a :** the slender distal part of an antenna **b :** a long tapering process that projects singly or in groups from a cell and is the primary organ of motion of many microorganisms

fla·geo·let \,flaj-ə-'let, -'lā\ *n* [F, fr. OF *flajolet,* fr. *flajol* flute, fr. (assumed) VL *flabeolum,* fr. L *flare* to blow — more at BLOW] (1659) **:** a small fipple flute resembling the treble recorder

flag football *n* (1954) **:** a variation of football in which a player must remove a flag attached to the ballcarrier's clothing to stop the play

¹flag·ging \'flag-iŋ\ *adj* (1545) **1 :** LANGUID, WEAK **2 :** becoming progressively less : DWINDLING — **flag·ging·ly** \-iŋ-lē\ *adv*

²flagging *n* (1622) **:** a pavement or walk of flagstones

fla·gi·tious \flə-'jish-əs\ *adj* [ME *flagicious,* fr. L *flagitiosus,* fr. *flagitium* shameful thing; akin to L *flagrum* whip] (14c) **:** marked by outrageous or scandalous crime or vice : VILLAINOUS — **fla·gi·tious·ly** *adv* — **fla·gi·tious·ness** *n*

flag·man \'flag-mən\ *n* (1832) **:** one who signals with or as if with a flag

flag officer *n* [fr. his being entitled to display a flag with one or more stars indicating his rank] (1665) **:** any of the officers in the navy or coast guard above captain — compare GENERAL OFFICER

flag of truce (1627) **:** a white flag carried or displayed to an enemy as an invitation to conference or parley

flag·on \'flag-ən\ *n* [ME, fr. MF *flascon, flacon* bottle, fr. LL *flascon-, flasco* — more at FLASK] (15c) **1 a :** a large usu. metal or pottery vessel (as for wine) with handle and spout and often a lid **b :** a large bulging short-necked bottle **2 :** the contents of a flagon

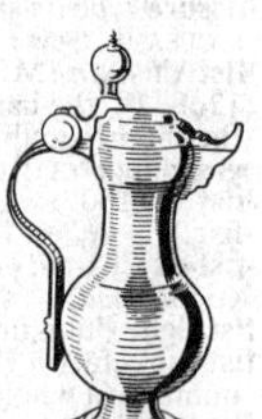
flagon 1a

flag·pole \'flag-,pōl\ *n* (1884) **:** a pole on which to raise a flag

fla·grance \'flā-grən(t)s *also* 'flag-rən(t)s\ *n* (1612) **:** FLAGRANCY

fla·gran·cy \'flā-grən-sē *also* 'flag-rən-\ *n* (1599) **:** the quality or state of being flagrant

flag rank *n* (1894) **:** the rank of a flag officer

fla·grant \'flā-grənt *also* 'flag-rənt\ *adj* [L *flagrant-, flagrans,* prp. of *flagrare* to burn — more at BLACK] (1513) **1** *archaic* **:** fiery hot : BURNING **2 :** conspicuously offensive ⟨~ errors⟩; *esp* : so obviously inconsistent with what is right or proper as to appear to be a flouting of law or morality ⟨~ violations of human rights⟩ — **fla·grant·ly** *adv*

syn FLAGRANT, GLARING, GROSS, RANK mean conspicuously bad or objectionable. FLAGRANT applies usu. to offenses or errors so bad that they can neither escape notice nor be condoned ⟨*flagrant* abuse of the office of president⟩ GLARING implies painful or damaging obtrusiveness of something that is conspicuously wrong, faulty, or improper ⟨this evil is so *glaring,* so inexcusable — G. B. Shaw⟩ GROSS implies the exceeding of reasonable or excusable limits ⟨even illness cannot excuse such unfilial behavior and such *gross* folly —Robert Graves⟩ RANK applies to what is openly and extremely objectionable and utterly condemned ⟨O, my offense is *rank,* it smells to heaven —Shak.⟩

fla·gran·te de·lic·to \flə-ˌgrant-ē-di-ˈlik-(ˌ)tō\ *adv* [ML, lit., while the crime is blazing] (1826) **:** in the very act of committing a misdeed **:** RED-HANDED
flag·ship \ˈflag-ˌship\ *n* (1672) **1 :** the ship that carries the commander of a fleet or subdivision of a fleet and flies his flag **2 :** the finest, largest, or most important one of a series, network, or chain ⟨a ~ store⟩
flag·staff \-ˌstaf\ *n* (1613) **:** a staff on which a flag is hoisted
flag·stick \-ˌstik\ *n* (1926) **:** a staff for a flag marking the location of the cup on a golf putting green
flag·stone \-ˌstōn\ *n* (1730) **:** [5]FLAG
flag stop *n* (1941) **:** a point at which a vehicle in public transportation stops only on prearrangement or signal
flag–wav·er \ˈflag-ˌwā-vər\ *n* (1925) **1 :** one who waves a flag in signaling **2 :** one who is intensely and conspicuously patriotic **3 :** a song intended to rouse patriotic sentiment
flag–wav·ing \-viŋ\ *n* (1892) **:** passionate appeal to patriotic or partisan sentiment **:** CHAUVINISM
[1]**flail** \ˈflā(ə)l\ *n* [ME *fleil, flail,* partly fr. (assumed) OE *flegel,* fr. LL *flagellum* flail, fr. L, whip & partly fr. MF *flaiel,* fr. LL *flagellum* — more at FLAGELLATE] (bef. 12c) **:** a hand threshing implement consisting of a wooden handle at the end of which a stouter and shorter stick is so hung as to swing freely
[2]**flail** *vt* (15c) **1 a :** to strike with or as if with a flail ⟨arms *~ing* the water⟩ **b :** to move, swing, or beat as if wielding a flail ⟨*~ing* a club to drive away the insects⟩ **2 :** to thresh (grain) with a flail **~** *vi* **:** to move, swing, or beat like a flail
flair \ˈfla(ə)r, ˈfle(ə)r\ *n* [F, lit., sense of smell, fr. OF, odor, fr. *flairier* to give off an odor, fr. LL *flagrare,* alter. of L *fragrare* — more at FRAGRANT] (1881) **1 :** a skill or instinctive ability to appreciate or make good use of something **:** TALENT ⟨a ~ for color and style⟩; *also* **:** INCLINATION, TENDENCY ⟨a ~ for the dramatic⟩ **2 :** a uniquely attractive quality (as elegance, smartness, or sophistication) **:** STYLE ⟨fashionable dresses with a ~ all their own⟩
flak \ˈflak\ *n, pl* **flak** [G, fr. *flie*ger*a*bwehr*k*anonen, fr. *flieger* flyer + *abwehr* defense + *kanonen* cannons] (1938) **1 :** antiaircraft guns **2 :** the bursting shells fired from flak **3 :** CRITICISM, OPPOSITION
[1]**flake** \ˈflāk\ *n* [ME, of Scand origin; akin to Norw *flak* disk] (14c) **1 :** a small loose mass or bit ⟨snow *~s*⟩ **2 :** a thin flattened piece or layer **:** CHIP **3** [prob. fr. *flaky*] **:** one who is flaky **:** ODDBALL **4** *slang* **:** COCAINE
[2]**flake** *vb* **flaked; flak·ing** *vi* (1627) **:** to separate into flakes; *also* **:** to peel in flakes **~** *vt* **1 :** to form or break into flakes **:** CHIP **2 :** to cover with or as if with flakes — **flak·er** *n*
[3]**flake** *n* [ME, hurdle, fr. ON *flaki;* akin to OHG *flah* smooth, Gk *pelagos* sea, L *placēre* to please — more at PLEASE] (1623) **:** a stage, platform, or tray for drying fish or produce
flake out *vi* (1939) **1** *slang* **:** to fall asleep **2** *slang* **:** to be overcome esp. by exhaustion
flake tool *n* (1947) **:** a Stone-Age tool that is a flake of stone struck off from a larger piece
flak jacket *n* (1950) **:** a jacket of heavy fabric containing metal plates for protection against flak; *broadly* **:** a bulletproof vest — called also *flak vest*
flaky *also* **flak·ey** \ˈflā-kē\ *adj* **flak·i·er; -est** (1580) **1 :** consisting of flakes ⟨~ snow⟩ **2 :** tending to flake ⟨a ~ piecrust⟩ **3** [prob. fr. *flake out*] **:** distinctly and often amusingly eccentric **:** OFFBEAT, WACKY — **flak·i·ness** *n*
flam \ˈflam\ *n* [prob. imit.] (1819) **:** a drumbeat of two strokes of which the first is a very quick grace note
[1]**flam·bé** \fläm-ˈbā, flä^n-\ *adj* [F *flambé,* fr. pp. of *flamber* to flame, singe, fr. OF, fr. *flambe* flame] (1914) **:** dressed or served covered with flaming liquor — usu. used postpositively ⟨crepe suzettes ~⟩
[2]**flambé** *vt* **flam·béed; flam·bé·ing** (ca. 1934) **:** to douse with a liquor (as brandy, rum, or cognac) and ignite
flam·beau \ˈflam-ˌbō\ *n, pl* **flam·beaux** \-ˌbōz\ *or* **flambeaus** [F, fr. MF, fr. *flambe* flame] (1632) **:** a flaming torch; *broadly* **:** TORCH
flam·boy·ance \flam-ˈbȯi-ən(t)s\ *n* (1891) **:** the quality or state of being flamboyant
flam·boy·an·cy \-ən-sē\ *n* (ca. 1889) **:** FLAMBOYANCE
[1]**flam·boy·ant** \-ənt\ *adj* [F, fr. prp. of *flamboyer* to flame, fr. OF, fr. *flambe*] (1832) **1** *often cap* **:** characterized by waving curves suggesting flames ⟨~ tracery⟩ **2 :** marked by or given to strikingly elaborate, ornate, or colorful display or behavior — **flam·boy·ant·ly** *adv*
[2]**flamboyant** *n* (1879) **:** ROYAL POINCIANA
[1]**flame** \ˈflām\ *n* [ME *flaume, flaumbe,* fr. MF *flamme* (fr. L *flamma*) & *flambe,* fr. OF, fr. *flamble,* fr. L *flammula,* dim. of *flamma* flame; akin to L *flagrare* to burn — more at BLACK] (14c) **1 :** the glowing gaseous part of a fire **2 a :** a state of blazing combustion ⟨the car burst into ~⟩ **b :** a condition or appearance suggesting a flame or burning: as (1) **:** burning zeal or passion (2) **:** a strong reddish orange color **3 :** BRILLIANCE, BRIGHTNESS **4 :** SWEETHEART
[2]**flame** *vb* **flamed; flam·ing** *vi* (14c) **1 :** to burn with a flame **:** BLAZE **2 :** to burst or break out violently or passionately ⟨*flaming* with indignation⟩ **3 :** to shine brightly **:** GLOW ⟨color *flaming* up in her cheeks⟩ **~** *vt* **1 :** to send or convey by means of flame ⟨~ a message by signal fires⟩ **2 :** to treat or affect with flame: as **a :** to sear, sterilize, or destroy by fire **b :** FLAMBÉ — **flam·er** *n*
flame cell *n* (1888) **:** a hollow cell that has a tuft of vibratile cilia and is part of the excretory system of various lower invertebrates (as a flatworm)
fla·men \ˈflā-mən\ *n, pl* **flamens** *or* **flam·i·nes** \ˈflam-ə-ˌnēz\ [ME *flamin,* fr. L *flamin-, flamen*] (14c) **:** a priest esp. in ancient Rome
fla·men·co \flə-ˈmeŋ-(ˌ)kō\ *n, pl* **-cos** [Sp, lit., Flemish, like a Gypsy, fr. MD *Vlaminc* Fleming] (1896) **1 :** a vigorous rhythmic dance style of the Andalusian Gypsies; *also* **:** a dance in flamenco style **2 :** music or song suitable to accompany a flamenco dance
flame·out \ˈflā-ˌmau̇t\ *n* (ca. 1950) **:** the unintentional cessation of operation of a jet airplane engine
flame photometer *n* (1945) **:** a spectrophotometer in which a spray of metallic salts in solution is vaporized in a very hot flame and subjected to quantitative analysis by measuring the intensities of the spectral lines of the metals present — **flame photometric** *adj* — **flame photometry** *n*
flame·proof \ˈflām-ˈprüf\ *adj* (1886) **:** resistant to damage or burning on contact with flame — **flameproof** *vt* — **flame·proof·er** *n*
flame–retardant *adj* (1947) **:** made or treated so as to resist burning ⟨~ sleepwear⟩
flame·throw·er \-ˌthrō(-ə)r\ *n* (1917) **:** a device that expels from a nozzle a burning stream of liquid or semiliquid fuel under pressure
flame tree *n* (ca. 1866) **:** any of several trees or shrubs with showy scarlet or yellow flowers: as **a :** a tree (*Brachychiton acerifolium*) of southern Australia with panicles of brilliant scarlet flowers **b :** ROYAL POINCIANA
flam·ing \ˈflā-miŋ\ *adj* (14c) **1 :** being on fire **:** BLAZING **2 :** resembling or suggesting a flame in color, brilliance, or wavy outline ⟨the ~ sunset sky⟩ ⟨~ red hair⟩ **3 :** INTENSE, PASSIONATE ⟨~ youth⟩ — **flam·ing·ly** \-miŋ-lē\ *adv*
fla·min·go \flə-ˈmiŋ-(ˌ)gō\ *n, pl* **-gos** *also* **-goes** [Pg, fr. Sp *flamenco,* prob. fr. OProv *flamenc,* fr. *flama* flame (fr. L *flamma*) + *-enc* [2]-ing] (1565) **:** any of several aquatic birds (family Phoenicopteridae) with long legs and neck, webbed feet, a broad lamellate bill resembling that of a duck but abruptly bent downward, and usu. rosy-white plumage with scarlet wing coverts and black wing quills

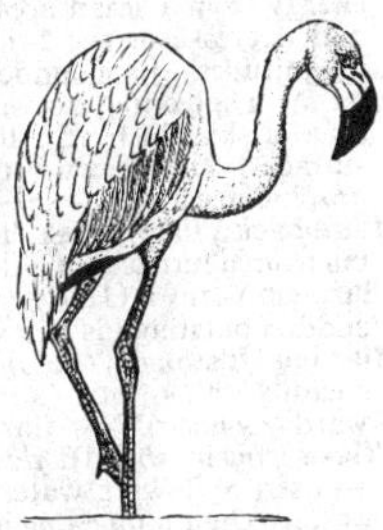
flamingo

flam·ma·bil·i·ty \ˌflam-ə-ˈbil-ət-ē\ *n* (1646) **:** ability to support combustion; *esp* **:** a high capacity for combustion
flam·ma·ble \ˈflam-ə-bəl\ *adj* [L *flammare* to flame, set on fire, fr. *flamma*] (1813) **:** capable of being easily ignited and of burning quickly — **flammable** *n*
flan \ˈflan, ˈflä^n(n)\ *n* [F, fr. OF *flaon,* fr. LL *fladon-, flado* flat cake] (1846) **1 :** an open case of pastry or sponge cake containing a filling and often covered with a fruit glaze **2 :** the metal disk of a coin, token, or medal as distinguished from the design and lettering stamped on it
fla·neur \flä-ˈnər\ *n* [F *flâneur*] (1854) **:** LOAFER
[1]**flange** \ˈflanj\ *n* [perh. alter. of *flanch* (a curving charge on a heraldic shield)] (ca. 1735) **:** a rib or rim for strength, for guiding, or for attachment to another object ⟨a ~ on a pipe⟩ ⟨a ~ on a wheel⟩
[2]**flange** *vt* **flanged; flang·ing** (ca. 1859) **:** to furnish with a flange — **flang·er** *n*
[1]**flank** \ˈflaŋk\ *n* [ME, fr. OF *flanc,* of Gmc origin; akin to OHG *hlanca* loin, flank — more at LANK] (12c) **1 a :** the fleshy part of the side between the ribs and the hip; *broadly* **:** the side of a quadruped **b :** a cut of meat from this part of an animal — see BEEF illustration **2 a :** SIDE **b :** the right or left of a formation **3 :** the area along either side of a heraldic shield
[2]**flank** *vt* (1596) **1 :** to protect a flank of **2 :** to attack or threaten the flank of (as a body of troops) **3 a :** to be situated at the side of; *esp* **:** to be situated on both sides of ⟨a road *~ed* with linden trees⟩ **b :** to place something on each side of
flan·ken \ˈflaŋ-kən\ *n* [prob. fr. Yiddish *flanken;* akin to OHG *hlanca* flank] (1950) **:** flank steak boiled in stock with spices and vegetables
flank·er \ˈflaŋ-kər\ *n* (1948) **:** a football player stationed wide of the formation slightly behind the line of scrimmage as a pass receiver — called also *flanker back*
flank steak *n* (1902) **:** a pear-shaped muscle of the beef flank; *also* **:** a steak cut from this muscle — see BEEF illustration
flan·nel \ˈflan-^{ə}l\ *n* [ME *flaunneol* woolen cloth or garment] (1503) **1 a :** a soft twilled wool or worsted fabric with a loose texture and a slightly napped surface **b :** a napped cotton fabric of soft yarns simulating the texture of wool flannel **c :** a stout cotton fabric usu. napped on one side **2** *pl* **a :** flannel underwear **b :** outer garments of flannel; *esp* **:** men's trousers — **flannel** *adj* — **flan·nel·ly** \-^{ə}l-ē\ *adj*
flan·nel·ette \ˌflan-^{ə}l-ˈet\ *n* (ca. 1882) **:** a lightweight cotton flannel
flan·nel·mouthed \ˈflan-^{ə}l-ˌmau̇tht, -ˌmau̇t͟hd\ *adj* (1884) **1 :** speaking indistinctly **2 :** speaking in a tricky or ingratiating way
[1]**flap** \ˈflap\ *n* [ME *flappe*] (14c) **1 :** a stroke with something broad **:** SLAP **2** *obs* **:** something broad and flat used for striking **3 :** something that is broad, limber, or flat and usu. thin and that hangs loose or projects freely: as **a :** a piece on a garment that hangs free **b :** a part of a book jacket that folds under the book's cover **c :** a piece of tissue partly severed from its place of origin for use in surgical grafting **d :** an extended part forming the closure (as of an envelope or carton) **e :** a movable auxiliary airfoil usu. attached to an airplane wing's trailing edge to increase lift or drag — see AIRPLANE illustration **4 :** the motion of something broad and limber (as a sail or wing) **5 a :** a state of excitement **:** FUSS, TIZZY **b :** a state of panicky confusion **:** UPROAR
[2]**flap** *vb* **flapped; flap·ping** *vt* (14c) **1 :** to beat with or as if with a flap **2 :** to toss sharply **:** FLING **3 :** to move or cause to move in flaps **~** *vi* **1 :** to sway loosely usu. with a noise of striking and esp. when moved by wind **2 a :** to beat or pulsate wings or something suggesting wings **b :** to progress by flapping **c :** to flutter ineffectively **3 :** to talk foolishly and persistently
flap·doo·dle \ˈflap-ˌdüd-^{ə}l\ *n* [origin unknown] (1878) **:** NONSENSE
flap·jack \-ˌjak\ *n* (1600) **:** PANCAKE
flap·pa·ble \ˈflap-ə-bəl\ *adj* (1968) **:** lacking self-assurance **:** easily upset
flap·per \ˈflap-ər\ *n* (ca. 1570) **1 a :** one that flaps **b :** something (as a flyswatter) used in flapping or striking **c :** FLIPPER 1 **2 :** a young woman; *specif* **:** a young woman of the period of World War I and the following decade who showed freedom from conventions (as in conduct)
flap·py \ˈflap-ē\ *adj* (1905) **:** flapping or tending to flap

[1]**flare** \'fla(ə)r, 'fle(ə)r\ *vb* **flared; flar·ing** [origin unknown] *vi* (ca. 1700) **1 a :** to stream in the wind **b :** to burn with an unsteady flame **2 a :** to shine with a sudden light ⟨a match ~*s* in the darkness⟩ **b** (1) **:** to become suddenly excited or angry — usu. used with *up* ⟨she ~*s* up at the slightest thing⟩ (2) **:** to break out or intensify usu. suddenly or violently — often used with *up* ⟨ground fighting *flared* up after a two-week lull⟩ **c :** to express strong emotion (as anger) ⟨*flaring* out at such abuses⟩ **3 :** to open or spread outward ⟨the pants ~ gently at the bottom⟩ ~ *vt* **1 :** to display conspicuously ⟨*flaring* her scarf to attract attention⟩ **2 :** to cause to flare ⟨the breeze ~*s* the candle⟩ **3 :** to signal with a flare or by flaring **4 :** to burn (a jet of waste gas) in the open air

[2]**flare** *n* (1814) **1 :** an unsteady glaring light **2 a :** a fire or blaze of light used to signal, illuminate, or attract attention; *also* **:** a device or composition used to produce such a flare **b :** a temporary outburst of energy from a small area of the sun's surface; *also* **:** a sudden increase and decrease in the brightness of a star often amounting to several magnitudes **3 :** a sudden outburst (as of sound, excitement, or anger) **4 a :** a spreading outward; *also* **:** a place or part that spreads **b :** an area of skin flush **5 :** light resulting from reflection (as between lens surfaces) or an effect of this light (as a fogged or dense area in a photographic negative)

flare·back \'fla(ə)r-,bak, 'fle(ə)r-\ *n* (1905) **:** a burst of flame back or out (as from a furnace) in a direction opposite to that of normal operation

flare–up \-,əp\ *n* (1837) **1 :** a sudden outburst or intensification **2 :** a sudden bursting (as of a smoldering fire) into flame or light

flar·ing \'fla(ə)r-iŋ, 'fle(ə)r-\ *adj* (1593) **1 a :** flaming brightly or unsteadily **b :** GAUDY ⟨a ~ resort hotel⟩ **2 :** opening or spreading outward ⟨~ nostrils⟩ — **flar·ing·ly** \-iŋ-lē\ *adv*

[1]**flash** \'flash\ *vb* [ME *flaschen,* of imit. origin] *vi* (13c) **1 :** RUSH, DASH — used of flowing water **2 :** to break forth in or like a sudden flame or flare ⟨lightning ~*ing* in the sky⟩ **3 a :** to appear suddenly ⟨an idea ~*es* into her mind⟩ **b :** to move with great speed ⟨the days ~ by⟩ **4 a :** to break forth or out so as to make a sudden display ⟨the sun ~*ed* from behind a cloud⟩ **b :** to act or speak vehemently and suddenly esp. in anger **5 a :** to give off light suddenly or in transient bursts **b :** to glow or gleam esp. with animation or passion ⟨her eyes ~*ed* with anger⟩ **6 :** to change suddenly or violently into vapor ⟨hot water ~*ing* to steam under reduced pressure⟩ **7 :** to expose one's genitals usu. suddenly and briefly in public **8 :** to have sudden insight — often used with *on* ~ *vt* **1 a** *archaic* **:** SPLASH **b :** to fill by a sudden inflow of water **2 a :** to cause the sudden appearance of (light) **b :** to cause to burst violently into flame; *also* **:** to burn for determining character of residue **c** (1) **:** to cause (light) to reflect (2) **:** to cause (as a mirror) to reflect light (3) **:** to cause (a lamp) to flash **d :** to convey by means of flashes of light **3 a :** to make known or cause to appear with great speed ⟨~ a message on the screen⟩ **b :** to display obtrusively and ostentatiously ⟨always ~*ing* a roll of bills⟩ **c :** to expose to view suddenly and briefly ⟨~*ing* a shy smile⟩ **4 :** to cover with or form into a thin layer: as **a :** to protect against rain by covering with sheet metal or a substitute **b :** to coat (as glass) with a thin layer (as of metal or a differently colored glass) **5 :** to subject (an exposed photographic negative or positive) to a supplementary uniform exposure to light before development in order to modify detail or tone

syn FLASH, GLEAM, GLANCE, GLINT, SPARKLE, GLITTER, GLISTEN, GLIMMER, SHIMMER mean to send forth light. FLASH implies a sudden and transient outburst of bright light; GLEAM suggests a steady light seen through an obscuring medium or against a dark background; GLANCE suggests a bright darting light reflected from a quickly moving surface; GLINT implies a cold glancing light; SPARKLE suggests innumerable moving points of bright light; GLITTER connotes a brilliant sparkling or gleaming; GLISTEN applies to the soft sparkle from a wet or oily surface; GLIMMER suggests a faint or wavering gleam; SHIMMER implies a soft tremulous gleaming or a blurred reflection.

[2]**flash** *n* (1566) **1 a :** a sudden burst of light **b :** a movement of a flag in signaling **2 :** a sudden and often brilliant burst ⟨a ~ of wit⟩ **3 :** a brief time ⟨I'll be back in a ~⟩ **4 a :** SHOW, DISPLAY; *esp* **:** a vulgar ostentatious display **b** *archaic* **:** a showy ostentatious person **c :** one that attracts notice; *esp* **:** an outstanding athlete **5** *obs* **:** thieves' slang **6 :** a rush of water released to permit passage of a boat **7 :** something flashed: as **a :** GLIMPSE, LOOK **b :** SMILE **c :** a first brief news report **d :** FLASHLIGHT 2,3 **e :** a quick-spreading flame or momentary intense outburst of radiant heat **8 :** RUSH 7 **9 :** the rapid conversion of a liquid into vapor

[3]**flash** *adj* (1700) **1 a :** FLASHY, SHOWY **b :** of, relating to, or characteristic of flashy people or things ⟨~ behavior⟩ **c :** of, relating to, or characteristic of persons considered social outcasts ⟨~ language⟩ **2 a :** of sudden origin and short duration ⟨a ~ fire⟩ **b :** involving very brief exposure to an intense altering agent (as heat or cold) ⟨~ drying of milk⟩ ⟨~ freezing of food⟩

flash·back \'flash-,bak\ *n* (1902) **1 :** a recession of flame to an unwanted position (as into a blowpipe) **2 :** interruption of chronological sequence (as in a literary work) by interjection of events of earlier occurrence; *also* **:** an instance of a flashback

flash·board \-,bō(ə)rd, -,bȯ(ə)rd\ *n* (1768) **:** one or more boards projecting above the top of a dam to increase the depth of the water

flash·bulb \-,bəlb\ *n* (1935) **:** an electric flash lamp in which metal foil or wire is burned

flash card *n* (1923) **:** a card bearing words, numbers, or pictures that is briefly displayed (as by a teacher to a class) usu. as a learning aid

flash·cube \'flash-,kyüb\ *n* (1965) **:** a cubical device that incorporates four flashbulbs, is usu. attached to a camera, and can be turned for taking four pictures in rapid succession

flash·er \'flash-ər\ *n* (1686) **:** one that flashes: as **a :** a light (as a traffic signal or automobile light) that catches the attention by flashing **b :** a device for automatically flashing a light **c :** an exhibitionist who flashes

flash flood *n* (1940) **:** a local flood of great volume and short duration generally resulting from heavy rainfall in the immediate vicinity — **flash flood** *vt*

flash–for·ward \'flash-'fȯr-wərd\ *n* (1949) **:** interruption of chronological sequence (as in a literary work) by interjection of events of future occurrence; *also* **:** an instance of a flash-forward

flash·gun \-,gən\ *n* (1925) **1 :** a device for holding and igniting flashlight powder **2 :** a device for holding and operating a flashbulb or a flashtube

flash·ing \'flash-iŋ\ *n* (1742) **:** sheet metal used in waterproofing roof valleys or hips or the angle between a chimney and a roof

flash in the pan [fr. the firing of the priming in the pan of a flintlock musket without discharging the piece] (1792) **1 :** a sudden spasmodic effort that accomplishes nothing **2 :** one that appears promising but turns out to be disappointing or worthless

flash lamp *n* (1908) **:** a lamp for producing a brief but intense flash of light used esp. for taking photographs

flash·light \'flash-,līt\ *n* (1886) **1 :** a flash of light or a light that flashes; *esp* **:** a scintillating light or a light of regularly varying brightness in a lighthouse **2 a :** a sudden bright artificial light used in taking photographic pictures **b :** a photograph taken by such a light **3 :** a small battery-operated portable electric light

flash·over \-,ō-vər\ *n* (1892) **1 :** an abnormal electrical discharge (as through the air to the ground from a high potential source or between two conducting portions of a structure) **2 :** the sudden spread of flame over an area when it becomes heated to the flash point

flash point *n* (ca. 1878) **1 :** the lowest temperature at which vapors above a volatile combustible substance ignite in air when exposed to flame **2 :** a point at which someone or something bursts suddenly into action or being **3 :** TINDERBOX 2

flash·tube \'flash-,t(y)üb\ *n* (1945) **:** a gas discharge tube that produces very brief intense flashes of light and is used esp. in photography

flashy \'flash-ē\ *adj* **flash·i·er; -est** (1597) **1** *chiefly dial* **:** lacking in substance or flavor **:** INSIPID **2 :** momentarily dazzling **3 a :** superficially attractive **:** BRIGHT **b :** ostentatious or showy often beyond the bounds of good taste; *esp* **:** marked by gaudy brightness ***syn*** see GAUDY — **flash·i·ly** \'flash-ə-lē\ *adv* — **flash·i·ness** \'flash-ē-nəs\ *n*

flask \'flask\ *n* [MF *flasque* powder flask, deriv. of LL *flascon-, flasco* bottle, prob. of Gmc origin; akin to OHG *flaska* bottle] (1549) **1 :** a container often somewhat narrowed toward the outlet and often fitted with a closure; *esp* **:** a broad flattened necked vessel used esp. to carry alcoholic beverages on the person **2 :** a frame that holds molding sand used in a foundry

[1]**flat** \'flat\ *n* (13c) **1 :** a level surface of land — often used in pl. ⟨sagebrush ~*s*⟩ ⟨tidal ~*s*⟩ **2 :** a flat part or surface ⟨the ~ of one's hand⟩ **3 a :** a musical note or tone one half step lower than a specified note or tone **b :** a character on a line or space of the musical staff indicating a half step drop in pitch **4 :** something flat: as **a :** a shallow box in which seedlings are started **b :** a flat-bottomed boat **c :** a flat piece of theatrical scenery **d :** a shoe or slipper having a flat heel or no heel **5 :** a floor or story in a building **6 :** an apartment on one floor **7 :** a deflated tire **8 :** the area to either side of an offensive football formation

[2]**flat** *adj* **flat·ter; flat·test** [ME, fr. ON *flatr;* akin to OHG *flaz* flat, Gk *platys* — more at PLACE] (14c) **1 a :** lying at full length or spread out upon the ground **:** PROSTRATE **b :** resting with a surface against something **2 a :** having a continuous horizontal surface **b :** being or characterized by a horizontal line or tracing without peaks or depressions ⟨the EEG is ominously ~, indicating that her brain function is gone —Don Gold⟩ **3 :** having a relatively smooth or even surface **4 :** arranged or laid out so as to be level or even **5 :** having the major surfaces essentially parallel and distinctly greater than the minor surfaces ⟨a ~ piece of wood⟩ **6 a :** clearly unmistakable **:** DOWNRIGHT ⟨a ~ denial⟩ **b** (1) **:** ABSOLUTE, FIXED ⟨a ~ rate⟩ (2) **:** having no fraction either lacking or in excess **:** EXACT ⟨in four minutes ~⟩ (3) **:** *of a frequency response* **:** not varying significantly throughout its range **7 a :** lacking in animation, zest, or vigor **:** DULL ⟨how weary, stale, ~ and unprofitable, seem to me all the uses of this world —Shak.⟩ **b :** lacking flavor **:** TASTELESS **c :** lacking effervescence or sparkle ⟨~ ginger ale⟩ **d :** commercially inactive ⟨the stock market continues to be ~⟩ **e :** lacking air **:** DEFLATED — used of tires **8 a** (1) *of a tone* **:** lowered a half step in pitch (2) **:** lower than the proper pitch **b** *of the vowel a* **:** pronounced as in *bad* or *bat* **9 a :** having a low trajectory **b** *of a tennis stroke* **:** made so as to give little or no spin to the ball **10** *of a sail* **:** TAUT **11 a :** uniform in hue or shade **b** *of a painting* **:** having little or no illusion of depth **c** *of a photograph or negative* **:** lacking contrast **d** *of a photographic lighting arrangement* **:** not emphasizing shadows or contours **e :** free from gloss ⟨a ~ paint⟩ ***syn*** see LEVEL, INSIPID — **flat·ly** *adv* — **flat·ness** *n*

[3]**flat** *adv* (1531) **1 :** in a flat manner **:** DIRECTLY, POSITIVELY **2 a :** on or against a flat surface ⟨lying ~ on his back⟩ **b :** at full length ⟨fell ~ on his face⟩ **3 :** in a complete manner **:** ABSOLUTELY ⟨~ broke⟩ **4 :** below the proper musical pitch **5 :** without interest charge; *esp* **:** without allowance or charge for accrued interest ⟨bonds sold ~⟩

[4]**flat** *vb* **flat·ted; flat·ting** *vt* (1603) **1 :** FLATTEN **2 :** to lower in pitch esp. by a half step ~ *vi* **:** to sing or play below the true pitch

[1]**flat·bed** \'flat-,bed\ *n* (1875) **:** a motortruck or trailer with a body in the form of a platform or shallow box

[2]**flat·bed** \,flat-,bed\ *adj* (1892) **:** having a horizontal bed on which the work rests ⟨~ printing press⟩ ⟨~ plotter⟩

flat·boat \-,bōt\ *n* (1660) **:** a boat with a flat bottom and square ends used for transportation of bulky freight esp. in shallow waters

flat·cap \-,kap\ *n* (1598) **1 :** a round low-crowned cap worn esp. in 16th and 17th century London **2 :** a wearer of a flatcap; *esp* **:** a Londoner

flat·car \-,kär\ *n* (1881) **:** a railroad freight car without permanent raised sides, ends, or covering

flat–coated retriever \,flat-,kōt-əd-\ *n* (1950) **:** any of an English breed of medium-sized sporting dogs that have a dense smooth black or liver-colored coat

flat·fish \'flat-,fish\ *n* (1710) **:** any of an order (Heterosomata) of marine teleost fishes (as the halibuts, flounders, turbots, and soles) that as adults swim on one side of the laterally compressed body and have both eyes on the upper side

flat·foot \-,fu̇t (*always so in sense 3*), -'fu̇t\ *n, pl* **flat·feet** \-,fēt, -'fēt\ (1870) **1 :** a condition in which the arch of the instep is flattened so that the entire sole rests upon the ground **2 :** a foot affected with flatfoot **3 a** *or pl* **flatfoots** *slang* **:** POLICEMAN; *esp* **:** a patrolman walking a regular beat **b** *slang* **:** SAILOR

1flat-foot·ed \-ˈfu̇t-əd\ *adj* (1601) **1** : affected with flatfoot; *broadly* : walking with a dragging or shambling gait **2** **a** : firm and well balanced on the feet **b** : free from reservation : FORTHRIGHT ⟨had an honest ~ way of saying a thing⟩ **3** : found unprepared : UNREADY — used chiefly in the phrase *catch one flat-footed* **4** : proceeding in a plodding way ⟨a ~ movie⟩ — **flat–foot·ed·ly** *adv* — **flat–foot·ed·ness** *n*

2flat–footed *adv* (1828) : in an open and determined manner : FLATLY

flat–hat \ˈflat-ˌhat\ *vi* [fr. an alleged incident in which a pedestrian's hat was crushed by a low-flying plane] (1940) : to fly low in an airplane in a reckless manner : HEDGEHOP — **flat–hat·ter** *n*

Flat·head \-ˌhed\ *n, pl* **Flatheads** *or* **Flathead** (1709) **1** : a member of any of several No. American Indian peoples that practiced head-flattening **2** : an American Indian people of Montana **3** *not cap* : any of various fishes with more or less flat heads; *esp* : any of a family (Percophididae) of mostly Australian and East Indian marine food fishes that resemble sculpins

flat·head catfish \ˌflat-ˌhed-\ *n* (1945) : a large yellowish brown-mottled catfish (*Pylodictis olivaris*) of the central and Gulf states of the U.S.

flat·iron \ˈflat-ˌī(-ə)rn\ *n* (1744) : IRON 2d

flat knot *n* (ca. 1955) : REEF KNOT

flat·land \ˈflat-ˌland\ *n* (1735) **1** : a region in which the land is predominantly flat — usu. used in pl. **2** : land that lacks significant variation in elevation — **flat·land·er** \-ˌlan-dər\ *n*

flat·let \ˈflat-lət\ *n, Brit* (1925) : EFFICIENCY APARTMENT

flat·ling \ˈflat-liŋ\ *or* **flat·lings** \-liŋz\ *adv, dial Brit* (15c) : with a flat side or edge

flat–out \ˈflat-ˌau̇t\ *adj* (1925) **1** : being or going at maximum effort or speed **2** : OUT-AND-OUT, DOWNRIGHT ⟨it was a ~ lie⟩

flat out \-ˈau̇t\ *adv* (1932) **1** : in a blunt and direct manner : OPENLY ⟨called *flat out* for revolution —*Nat'l Review*⟩ **2** : at top speed or peak performance ⟨the car does 180 m.p.h. *flat out*⟩

flat race *n* (1848) : a race (as for horses) on a level course without obstacles (as hurdles) — compare STEEPLECHASE

flat silver *n* (1928) : eating or serving utensils (as knives, forks, and spoons) made of or plated with silver

flat·ten \ˈflat-ᵊn\ *vb* **flat·tened; flat·ten·ing** \ˈflat-niŋ, -ᵊn-iŋ\ *vt* (1630) **1** : to make flat: as **a** : to make level or smooth **b** : to lay low : RUIN **c** : to make dull or uninspired — often used with *out* **2** : to make (as paint) lusterless ~ *vi* **1** : to become flat or flatter: as **a** : to become dull or spiritless **b** : to extend in or into a flat position or form **c** : to become uniform or stabilized often at a new lower level — usu. used with *out* **2** **a** : to manipulate an airplane so as to bring its longitudinal axis parallel with the ground — used with *out* **b** *of an airplane* : to assume such a position — **flat·ten·er** \ˈflat-nər, -ᵊn-ər\ *n*

1flat·ter \ˈflat-ər\ *vb* [ME *flateren*, fr. OF *flater* to lick, flatter, of Gmc origin; akin to OHG *flaz* flat] *vt* (13c) **1** : to praise excessively esp. from motives of self-interest **2** **a** *archaic* : SOOTHE, BEGUILE **b** : to encourage or gratify esp. usu. with the assurance that something is right ⟨I ~ myself that my interpretation is correct⟩ **3** **a** : to portray too favorably ⟨the portrait ~*s* him⟩ **b** : to display to advantage ⟨candlelight often ~*s* the face⟩ ~ *vi* : to use flattery — **flat·ter·er** \-ər-ər\ *n* — **flat·ter·ing·ly** \-ə-riŋ-lē\ *adv*

2flatter *n* (1714) : one that flattens: as **a** : a drawplate with a narrow rectangular orifice for drawing flat strips **b** : a flat-faced swage used in smithing

flat·tery \ˈflat-ə-rē\ *n, pl* **-ter·ies** (14c) **1** **a** : the act or practice of flattering **b** (1) : something that flatters (2) : insincere or excessive praise **2** *obs* : a pleasing self-deception

flat·tish \ˈflat-ish\ *adj* (1611) : somewhat flat

flat·top \ˈflat-ˌtäp\ *n* (1817) : something with a flat or flattened upper surface: as **a** : AIRCRAFT CARRIER **b** : a modified crew cut

flat·u·lence \ˈflach-ə-lən(t)s\ *n* (1711) : the quality or state of being flatulent

flat·u·len·cy \-lən-sē\ *n* (1660) : FLATULENCE

flat·u·lent \-lənt\ *adj* [MF, fr. L *flatus* act of blowing, wind, fr. *flatus*, pp. of *flare* to blow — more at BLOW] (1599) **1** **a** : marked by or affected with gases generated in the intestine or stomach **b** : likely to cause digestive flatulence **2** : pretentious without real worth or substance : TURGID — **flat·u·lent·ly** *adv*

fla·tus \ˈflāt-əs\ *n* [L, act of blowing, act of breaking wind] (1651) : gas generated in the stomach or bowels

flat·ware \ˈflat-ˌwa(ə)r, -ˌwe(ə)r\ *n* (ca. 1896) : tableware more or less flat and usu. formed or cast in a single piece; *esp* : eating and serving utensils (as knives, forks, and spoons) — compare HOLLOWWARE

flat·ways \-ˌwāz\ *adv* (1692) : FLATWISE

flat·wise \-ˌwīz\ *adv* (1601) : with the flat surface presented in some expressed or implied position

flat·work \-ˌwərk\ *n* (1925) : laundry that can be finished mechanically and does not require hand ironing

flat·worm \-ˌwərm\ *n* (1896) : PLATYHELMINTH; *esp* : TURBELLARIAN

flaunt \ˈflȯnt, ˈflänt\ *vb* [prob. of Scand origin; akin to ON *flana* to rush around — more at PLANET] *vi* (1566) **1** : to display or obtrude oneself to public notice **2** : to wave or flutter showily ⟨the flag ~*s* in the breeze⟩ ~ *vt* **1** : to display ostentatiously or impudently : PARADE ⟨~*ing* his superiority⟩ **2** : to treat contemptuously ⟨~*ed* the rules —Louis Untermeyer⟩ ***syn*** see SHOW — **flaunt** *n* — **flaunt·ing·ly** \-iŋ-lē\ *adv* — **flaunty** \-ē\ *adj*

usage Although transitive sense 2 of *flaunt* undoubtedly arose from confusion with *flout*, the contexts in which it appears cannot be called substandard ⟨meting out punishment to the occasional mavericks who operate rigged games, tolerate rowdyism, or otherwise *flaunt* the law —Oscar Lewis⟩ ⟨observed with horror the *flaunting* of their authority in the suburbs, where men . . . put up buildings that had no place at all in a Christian commonwealth —Marchette Chute⟩ ⟨in our profession we never excommunicate a colleague, never defrock or disbar . . . ; very rarely do we publicly chastise a colleague who has *flaunted* our most basic principles —R. T. Blackburn, *AAUP Bull.*⟩ If you use it, however, you should be aware that many people will consider it a mistake. Use of *flout* in the sense of *flaunt* 1 is occas. found but is relatively infrequent.

flau·tist \ˈflȯt-əst, ˈflau̇t-\ *n* [It *flautista*, fr. *flauto* flute, fr. OProv *flaut*] (1860) : FLUTIST

fla·va·none \ˈflā-və-ˌnōn\ *n* [L *flavus* + ISV *-ane* + *-one*] (1949) : a colorless crystalline ketone $C_{15}H_{12}O_2$; *also* : any of the derivatives of this ketone many of which occur in plants often in the form of glycosides

fla·vin \ˈflā-vən\ *n* [ISV, fr. L *flavus* yellow — more at BLUE] (ca. 1853) : any of a class of yellow water-soluble nitrogenous pigments derived from isoalloxazine and occurring in the form of nucleotides as coenzymes of flavoproteins; *esp* : RIBOFLAVIN

flavin adenine dinucleotide *n* (1960) : a coenzyme $C_{27}H_{33}N_9O_{15}P_2$ of some flavoproteins

fla·vine \ˈflā-ˌvēn\ *n* [ISV, fr. L *flavus*] (1853) : any of a series of yellow acridine dyes (as acriflavine) often used medicinally for their antiseptic properties

flavin mononucleotide *n* (ca. 1953) : FMN

fla·vone \ˈflā-ˌvōn\ *n* [ISV, fr. L *flavus*] (1897) : a colorless crystalline ketone $C_{15}H_{10}O_2$ found in the leaves, stems, and seed capsules of many primroses; *also* : any of the derivatives of this ketone many of which occur as yellow plant pigments in the form of glycosides and are used as dyestuffs

fla·vo·noid \ˈflā-və-ˌnȯid\ *n* [*flavone* + *-oid*] (1947) : any of a group of aromatic compounds that includes many common pigments (as the anthocyanins and flavones)

fla·vo·nol \ˈflā-və-ˌnȯl, -ˌnōl\ *n* (1898) : any of various hydroxy derivatives of flavone

fla·vo·pro·tein \ˌflā-vō-ˈprō-ˌtēn, -ˈprōt-ē-ən\ *n* [ISV *flavin* + *-o-* + *protein*] (1936) : a dehydrogenase that contains a flavin and often a metal and plays a major role in biological oxidations

1fla·vor \ˈflā-vər\ *n* [ME, fr. MF *flaor, flavor*, fr. (assumed) VL *flator*, fr. L *flare* to blow — more at BLOW] (14c) **1** **a** *archaic* : ODOR, FRAGRANCE **b** : the quality of something that affects the sense of taste : SAVOR ⟨condiments give ~ to food⟩ **c** : the blend of taste and smell sensations evoked by a substance in the mouth ⟨the ~ of ripe fruit⟩ **2** : a substance that flavors ⟨hard candy with artificial ~⟩ **3** : characteristic or predominant quality ⟨the newspaper retains a community ~⟩ **4** : a property that distinguishes different types of quarks and different kinds of leptons (as the electron, muon, and tau particle) — **fla·vored** \-vərd\ *adj* — **fla·vor·ful** \-vər-fəl\ *adj* — **fla·vor·ful·ly** \-fə-lē\ *adv* — **fla·vor·less** \-vər-ləs\ *adj* — **fla·vor·some** \-səm\ *adj*

2flavor *vt* **fla·vored; fla·vor·ing** \ˈflāv-(ə-)riŋ\ (1542) : to give or add flavor to

fla·vor·ing *n* (1542) : FLAVOR 2

fla·vour *chiefly Brit var of* FLAVOR

1flaw \ˈflȯ\ *n* [of Scand origin; akin to Norw *flaga* gust; akin to L *plangere* to beat — more at PLAINT] (1513) **1** : a sudden brief burst of wind; *also* : a spell of stormy weather **2** *obs* : an outburst esp. of passion

2flaw *n* [ME, flake, prob. of Scand origin; akin to Sw *flaga* flake, flaw; akin to OE *flōh* flat stone — more at PLEASE] (1586) **1** : an often hidden defect that may cause failure under stress: as **a** : a faulty part (as a crack or break) ⟨the axle broke at a ~⟩ **b** : a usu. immaterial defect or weakness in something ⟨vanity was the great ~ in his character⟩ ⟨a ~ in the book's plot⟩ **c** : a fault in a legal paper that may nullify it **2** *obs* : FRAGMENT ***syn*** see BLEMISH — **flaw·less** \-ləs\ *adj* — **flaw·less·ly** *adv* — **flaw·less·ness** *n*

3flaw *vt* (1613) : to make flaws in ~ *vi* : to become defective

flax \ˈflaks\ *n, often attrib* [ME, fr. OE *fleax*; akin to OHG *flahs* flax, L *plectere* to braid — more at PLY] (bef. 12c) **1** : any of a genus (*Linum* of the family Linaceae, the flax family) of herbs; *esp* : a slender erect annual (*L. usitatissimum*) with blue flowers commonly cultivated for its bast fiber and seed **2** : the fiber of the flax plant esp. when prepared for spinning **3** : any of several plants resembling flax

flax·en \ˈflak-sən\ *adj* (1521) **1** : made of flax **2** : resembling flax esp. in pale soft strawy color ⟨~ hair⟩

flax·seed \ˈflak(s)-ˌsēd\ *n* (1562) : the seed of flax used as a source of oil and medicinally as a demulcent and emollient

flaxy \ˈflak-sē\ *adj* **flax·i·er; -est** (1634) : resembling flax esp. in texture

flay \ˈflā\ *vt* [ME *flen*, fr. OE *flēan*; akin to ON *flā* to flay, *flekkr* spot, Lith *plėšti* to tear] (bef. 12c) **1** : to strip off the skin or surface of : SKIN **2** : to criticize harshly : EXCORIATE **3** : LASH ⟨the wind whipped up to gale fury, ~*ing* his face —Richard Kent⟩

F layer *n* (1940) : the highest and most densely ionized regular layer of the ionosphere occurring at night within the F region

flea \ˈflē\ *n* [ME *fle*, fr. OE *flēa*; akin to OHG *flōh* flea, OE *flēon* to flee] (bef. 12c) : any of an order (Siphonaptera) of wingless bloodsucking insects that have a hard laterally compressed body and legs adapted to leaping and that feed on warm-blooded animals — **flea in one's ear** : an irritating hint or warning : REBUKE

flea·bag \ˈflē-ˌbag\ *n* (1932) : an inferior hotel or rooming house

flea·bane \-ˌbān\ *n* (1548) : any of various composite plants (as of the genus *Erigeron*) that were once believed to drive away fleas

flea beetle *n* (1842) : any of a subfamily (Alticinae, esp. genera *Alticia* and *Epitrix*) of small chrysomelid beetles with legs adapted for leaping that feed on foliage and sometimes serve as vectors of virus diseases of plants

flea·bite \ˈflē-ˌbīt\ *n* (ca. 1570) **1** : the bite of a flea; *also* : the red spot caused by such a bite **2** : a trifling pain or annoyance

flea–bit·ten \-ˌbit-ᵊn\ *adj* (1570) **1** *of a horse* : having a white or gray coat flecked with a darker color **2** : bitten by or infested with fleas

flea collar *n* (1970) : a collar for animals that contains insecticide for killing fleas

flea·hop·per \-ˌhäp-ər\ *n* (1902) : any of various small jumping bugs that feed on cultivated plants

flea market *n* [trans. of F *Marché aux Puces*, a market in Paris] (1922) : a usu. open-air market for secondhand articles and antiques

flea·pit \-ˌpit\ *n, Brit* (1937) : a dilapidated building usu. housing a movie theater

flea·wort \ˈflē-ˌwərt, -ˌwȯ(ə)rt\ *n* [ME *flewort,* fr. OE *flēawyrt,* fr. *flēa* + *wyrt* herb, root — more at ROOT] (bef. 12c) : any of three Old World plantains (esp. *Plantago psyllium*) whose seeds are sometimes used as a mild laxative — compare PSYLLIUM SEED

flèche \ˈflāsh, ˈflesh\ *n* [F, lit., arrow] (1848) : SPIRE; *esp* : a slender spire above the intersection of the nave and transepts of a church

flé·chette \flā-ˈshet, fle-\ *n* [F, fr. dim. of *flèche* arrow, fr. OF *fleche,* of Gmc origin; akin to MD *vlieke* arrow, OE *flēogan* to fly] (1915) : a small dart-shaped projectile that is clustered in an explosive warhead, dropped as a missile from an airplane, or fired from a hand-held gun

[1]fleck \ˈflek\ *vt* [back-formation fr. *flecked* spotted, fr. ME, prob. fr. ON *flekkóttr,* fr. *flekkr* spot — more at FLAY] (14c) : STREAK, SPOT ⟨white-caps ~*ed* the blue sea⟩

[2]fleck *n* (1598) **1** : SPOT, MARK ⟨a brown tweed with ~*s* of yellow⟩ **2** : FLAKE, PARTICLE ⟨~*s* of snow drifted down⟩

flec·tion *var of* FLEXION

fledge \ˈflej\ *vb* **fledged; fledg·ing** [*fledge* (capable of flying), fr. ME *flegge,* fr. OE *-flycge;* akin to OHG *flucki* capable of flying, OE *flēogan* to fly — more at FLY] *vi, of a bird* (1566) : to acquire the feathers necessary for flight ~ *vt* **1** : to rear until ready for flight or independent activity **2** : to cover with or as if with feathers or down **3** : to furnish (as an arrow) with feathers

fledg·ling \ˈflej-liŋ\ *n* (1830) **1** : a young bird just fledged **2** : an immature or inexperienced person **3** : one that is new ⟨a ~ company in the industry⟩

flee \ˈflē\ *vb* **fled** \ˈfled\; **flee·ing** [ME *flen,* fr. OE *flēon;* akin to OHG *fliohan* to flee] *vi* (bef. 12c) **1 a** : to run away often from danger or evil : FLY **b** : to hurry toward a place of security **2** : to pass away swiftly : VANISH ⟨mists ~*ing* before the rising sun⟩ ~ *vt* : to run away from : SHUN

[1]fleece \ˈflēs\ *n* [ME *flees,* fr. OE *flēos;* akin to MHG *vlius* fleece, L *pluma* feather, down] (bef. 12c) **1 a** : the coat of wool covering a wool-bearing animal (as a sheep) **b** : the wool obtained from a sheep at one shearing **2 a** : any of various soft or woolly coverings **b** : a soft bulky deep-piled knitted or woven fabric used chiefly for clothing

[2]fleece *vt* **fleeced; fleec·ing** (1537) **1 a** : to strip of money or property by fraud or extortion **b** : to charge excessively for goods or services **2** : to remove the fleece from : SHEAR **3** : to dot or cover with fleecy masses

fleeced \ˈflēst\ *adj* (1580) **1** : covered with or as if with a fleece **2** *of a textile* : having a soft nap

fleech \ˈflēch\ *vb* [ME (Sc) *flechen*] *dial* (14c) : COAX, WHEEDLE

fleecy \ˈflē-sē\ *adj* **fleec·i·er; -est** (1590) : covered with, made of, or resembling fleece ⟨a ~ winter coat⟩

[1]fleer \ˈfli(ə)r\ *vi* [ME *fleryen,* of Scand origin; akin to Norw *flire* to giggle — more at FLIMFLAM] (15c) : to laugh or grimace in a coarse derisive manner : SNEER *syn* see SCOFF — **fleer·ing·ly** \-iŋ-lē\ *adv*

[2]fleer *n* (1604) : a word or look of derision or mockery

[1]fleet \ˈflēt\ *vb* [ME *fleten,* fr. OE *flēotan;* akin to OHG *fliozzan* to float, OE *flōwan* to flow] *vi* (bef. 12c) **1** *obs* : DRIFT **2 a** *archaic* : FLOW **b** : to fade away : VANISH **3** : to fly swiftly ~ *vt* **1** : to cause (time) to pass usu. quickly or imperceptibly **2** [alter. of *flit*] : to move or change in position ⟨~ a hawser⟩

[2]fleet *n* [ME *flete,* fr. OE *flēot* ship, fr. *flēotan*] (13c) **1** : a number of warships under a single command; *specif* : an organization of ships and aircraft under the command of a flag officer **2** : a group (as of ships, planes, or trucks) operated under unified control

[3]fleet *adj* [prob. fr. [1]*fleet*] (1529) **1** : swift in motion : NIMBLE **2** : EVANESCENT, FLEETING *syn* see FAST — **fleet·ly** *adv* — **fleet·ness** *n*

fleet admiral *n* (1946) : an admiral of the highest rank in the navy whose insignia is five stars

fleet–foot·ed \-ˈfu̇t-əd\ *adj* (1743) : able to run fast

fleet·ing *adj* (1563) : passing swiftly : TRANSITORY *syn* see TRANSIENT — **fleet·ing·ly** \-iŋ-lē\ *adv* — **fleet·ing·ness** *n*

Fleet Street \ˈflēt-\ *n* [*Fleet Street,* London, England, center of the London newspaper district] (1882) : the London press

flei·shig \ˈflā-shik\ *adj* [Yiddish, fr. MHG *vleischic* meaty, fr. *vleisch* flesh, meat, fr. OHG *fleisk*] (1943) : made of, prepared with, or used for meat or meat products — compare MILCHIG, PAREVE

Flem·ing \ˈflem-iŋ\ *n* [ME, fr. MD *Vlaminc* (akin to MD *Vlander* Flanders)] (12c) : a member of the Germanic people inhabiting northern Belgium and a small section of northern France

[1]Flem·ish \ˈflem-ish\ *adj* (14c) : of, relating to, or characteristic of Flanders or the Flemings or their language

[2]Flemish *n* (1727) **1** : the Dutch language used by the Flemings **2** *pl in constr* : FLEMINGS

Flemish giant *n* (ca. 1898) : a rabbit of a breed prob. of Belgian origin that is characterized by large size, vigor, and solid coat color in black, white, or gray

flense \ˈflen(t)s\ *vt* **flensed; flens·ing** [D *flensen* or Dan & Norw *flense*] (1814) : to strip (as a whale) of blubber or skin

[1]flesh \ˈflesh\ *n* [ME, fr. OE *flǣsc;* akin to OHG *fleisk* flesh and prob. to ON *flā* to flay — more at FLAY] (bef. 12c) **1 a** : the soft parts of the body of an animal and esp. of a vertebrate; *esp* : the parts composed chiefly of skeletal muscle as distinguished from visceral structures, bone, and integuments **b** : sleek well-fatted condition of body **c** : SKIN **2 a** : edible parts of an animal **b** : flesh of a mammal or fowl that is an article of diet ⟨abstain from ~ during religious fasts⟩ **3 a** : the physical being of man ⟨the spirit indeed is willing, but the ~ is weak —Mt 26:41 (AV)⟩ **b** : HUMAN NATURE **4 a** : human beings : MANKIND **b** : living beings **c** : STOCK, KINDRED **5** : a fleshy plant part used as food; *also* : the fleshy part of a fruit **6** *Christian Science* : an illusion that matter has sensation **7** : SUBSTANCE ⟨insights buried in the ~ of the narrative —Jan Carew⟩ — **in the flesh** : in person and alive

[2]flesh *vt* (1530) **1** : to initiate or habituate esp. by giving a foretaste **2** *archaic* : GRATIFY **3** : to clothe or cover with or as if with flesh; *broadly* : to give substance to — usu. used with *out* **4** : to free from flesh ~ *vi* : to become fleshy — often used with *up* or *out*

flesh and blood *n* (bef. 12c) **1** : corporeal nature as composed of flesh and of blood **2** : near kindred — used chiefly in the phrase *one's own flesh and blood* **3** : SUBSTANCE, REALITY

fleshed \ˈflesht\ *adj* (15c) : having flesh esp. of a specified kind — often used in combination ⟨pink-*fleshed*⟩ ⟨thick-*fleshed*⟩

flesh fly *n* (14c) : a two-winged fly whose maggots feed on flesh; *esp* : any of a family (Sarcophagidae) of flies some of which cause myiasis

flesh·i·ness \ˈflesh-ē-nəs\ *n* (15c) : the state of being fleshy : CORPULENCE

flesh·ings \ˈflesh-iŋz\ *n pl* (1838) : material removed in fleshing a hide or skin

flesh·ly \ˈflesh-lē\ *adj* (bef. 12c) **1 a** : CORPOREAL, BODILY **b** : of, relating to, or characterized by indulgence of bodily appetites; *esp* : LASCIVIOUS ⟨~ desires⟩ **c** : not spiritual : WORLDLY **2** : FLESHY, PLUMP **3** : having a sensuous quality ⟨~ art⟩ *syn* see CARNAL

flesh·ment \ˈflesh-mənt\ *n* [[2]*flesh*] *obs* (1605) : excitement associated with a successful beginning

flesh·pot \ˈflesh-ˌpät\ *n* (1592) **1** *pl* : bodily comfort : LUXURY **2** : a place of lascivious entertainment — usu. used in pl.

flesh wound *n* (1674) : an injury involving penetration of the body musculature without damage to bones or internal organs

fleshy \ˈflesh-ē\ *adj* **flesh·i·er; -est** (14c) **1 a** : marked by, consisting of, or resembling flesh **b** : marked by abundant flesh; *esp* : CORPULENT **2 a** : SUCCULENT, PULPY ⟨the rich ~ texture of a perfectly ripe melon⟩ **b** : not thin, dry, or membranous ⟨~ fungi⟩

fleshy fruit *n* (1929) : a fruit (as a berry, drupe, or pome) consisting largely of soft succulent tissue

fletch \ˈflech\ *vt* [back-formation fr. *fletcher*] (1635) : FEATHER ⟨~ an arrow⟩

fletch·er \ˈflech-ər\ *n* [ME *fleccher,* fr. OF *flechier,* fr. *fleche* arrow — more at FLÉCHETTE] (14c) : a maker of arrows

fleur de coin \ˌflərd-ə-ˈkwaⁿ\ *adj* [F *à fleur de coin,* lit., with the bloom of the die] (ca. 1889) : being in the preserved mint condition

fleur–de–lis *or* **fleur–de–lys** \ˌflərd-ᵊl-ˈē, ˌflu̇rd-\ *n, pl* **fleurs–de–lis** *or* **fleur–de–lis** *or* **fleurs–de–lys** *or* **fleur–de–lys** \ˌflərd-ᵊl-ˈē(z), ˌflu̇rd-\ [ME *flourdelis,* fr. MF *flor de lis,* lit., lily flower] (14c) **1** : IRIS 3 **2** : a conventionalized iris in artistic design and heraldry

fleur-de-lis 2

fleu·ry \ˈflu̇(ə)r-ē\ *adj* [alter. of ME *flory,* fr. OF *floré,* fr. *flor* flower — more at FLOWER] *of a heraldic cross* (15c) : having the ends of the arms broadening out into the heads of fleurs-de-lis — see CROSS illustration

flew *past of* FLY

flews \ˈflüz\ *n pl* [origin unknown] (1575) : the pendulous lateral parts of a dog's upper lip — see DOG illustration

[1]flex \ˈfleks\ *vb* [L *flexus,* pp. of *flectere*] *vt* (1521) **1** : to bend esp. repeatedly **2 a** : to move muscles so as to cause flexion of (a joint) **b** : to move or tense (a muscle or muscles) by contraction ~ *vi* : BEND — **flex one's muscles** : to demonstrate one's strength ⟨an exaggerated need to *flex his* political *muscles* —J. P. Lash⟩

[2]flex *n* [short for *flexible cord*] *chiefly Brit* (1905) : electric cord

[3]flex *n* (ca. 1934) : an act or instance of flexing

flex·i·ble \ˈflek-sə-bəl\ *adj* (15c) **1** : capable of being flexed : PLIANT **2** : yielding to influence : TRACTABLE **3** : characterized by a ready capability to adapt to new, different, or changing requirements ⟨a ~ foreign policy⟩ ⟨~ public transportation⟩ ⟨a ~ schedule⟩ *syn* see ELASTIC — **flex·i·bil·i·ty** \ˌflek-sə-ˈbil-ət-ē\ *n* — **flex·i·bly** \ˈflek-sə-blē\ *adv*

flex·ile \ˈflek-səl, -ˌsīl\ *adj* (1633) : FLEXIBLE

flex·ion \ˈflek-shən\ *n* [L *flexion-, flexio,* fr. *flexus,* pp. of *flectere*] (1656) **1** : the act of flexing or bending **2** : a part bent : BEND **3** : INFLECTION 3 **4 a** : a bending movement around a joint in a limb (as the knee or elbow) that decreases the angle between the bones of the limb at the joint — compare EXTENSION 3b **b** : a forward raising of the arm or leg by a movement at the shoulder or hip joint

flex·og·ra·phy \flek-ˈsäg-rə-fē\ *n* [*flex*ible + *-o-* + *-graphy*] (1954) : a process of rotary letterpress printing using flexible plates and fast-drying inks — **flexo·graph·ic** \ˌflek-sə-ˈgraf-ik\ *adj* — **flexo·graph·i·cal·ly** \-i-k(ə-)lē\ *adv*

flex·or \ˈflek-sər, -ˌsȯ(ə)r\ *n* (1615) : a muscle serving to bend a body part (as a limb)

flex·time \ˈflek-ˌstīm\ *n* (1973) : a system that allows employees to choose their own times for starting and finishing work within a broad range of available hours

flex·u·ous \ˈfleksh-(ə-)wəs\ *adj* [L *flexuosus,* fr. *flexus* bend, fr. *flexus,* pp.] (1605) **1** : having turns or windings **2** : lacking rigidity in structure or action ⟨its ~ and elastic body⟩

flex·ur·al \ˈflek-sh(ə-)rəl\ *adj* (1879) **1** : of, relating to, or resulting from flexure **2** : characterized by flexure

flex·ure \ˈflek-shər\ *n* (1592) **1** : the quality or state of being flexed : FLEXION **2** : TURN, BEND, FOLD

fley \ˈflā\ *vt* [ME *flayen,* fr. OE *āflēgan,* fr. *ā-,* perfective prefix + *-flēgan* to put to flight] *Scot* (bef. 12c) : FRIGHTEN

flib·ber·ti·gib·bet \ˌflib-ərt-ē-ˈjib-ət\ *n* [ME *flepergebet*] (15c) : a silly flighty person — **flib·ber·ti·gib·bety** \-ət-ē\ *adj*

flic \ˈflēk\ *n* [F] (1899) : a French policeman

[1]flick \ˈflik\ *n* [imit.] (15c) **1** : a light sharp jerky stroke or movement **2** : a sound produced by a flick **3** : FLICKER 1

[2]flick *vt* (1816) **1 a** : to strike lightly with a quick sharp motion ⟨~*ed* the horse with a whip⟩ **b** : to remove with light blows ⟨~*ed* an ash off her sleeve⟩ **2 a** : to move or propel with or as if with a flick ⟨~*ed* her hair back over her shoulder⟩ ⟨~ a switch⟩ ⟨~*ing* cigarette butts into the gutter⟩ **b** : to activate, deactivate, or change by or as if by flicking a switch ⟨~ on a cigarette lighter⟩ ⟨~ off the radio⟩ ~ *vi* **1** : to go or pass quickly or abruptly ⟨a bird ~*ed* by⟩ ⟨~*ing* through some papers⟩ **2** : to direct flicks at something

[3]flick *n* [short for [3]*flicker*] (1926) : MOVIE

[1]flick·er \ˈflik-ər\ *vb* **flick·ered; flick·er·ing** \-(ə-)riŋ\ [ME *flikeren,* fr. OE *flicorian*] *vi* (bef. 12c) **1** : to move irregularly or unsteadily : FLUTTER **2** : to burn or shine fitfully or with a fluctuating light **3** : to appear briefly ~ *vt* **1** : to cause to flicker **2** : to produce by flickering — **flick·er·ing·ly** \-(ə-)riŋ-lē\ *adv*

[2]flicker *n* (1809) : a common large brightly marked woodpecker (*Colaptes auratus*) of eastern No. America; *also* : any of several related birds of the southern and western U.S.

[3]**flicker** *n* (1849) **1 a :** an act of flickering **b :** a sudden brief movement **c :** a momentary quickening ⟨a ~ of anger⟩ **d :** a slight indication : HINT ⟨a ~ of recognition⟩ **2 :** a wavering light **3 :** MOVIE — often used in pl. — **flick·ery** \'flik-(ə-)rē\ *adj*

flick·er·tail \'flik-ər-ˌtāl\ *n* (1890) **:** a ground squirrel (*Citellus richardsoni*) chiefly of the north-central U.S. and adjacent Canada

flied *past of* [3]FLY

fli·er \'flī(-ə)r\ *n* (15c) **1 :** one that flies; *specif* **:** AIRMAN **2 :** a reckless or speculative venture **3 :** an advertising circular **4 :** a step in a straight flight of steps

[1]**flight** \'flīt\ *n, often attrib* [ME, fr. OE *flyht;* akin to MD *vlucht* flight, OE *flēogan* to fly] (bef. 12c) **1 a :** an act or instance of passing through the air by the use of wings ⟨the ~ of a bee⟩ **b :** the ability to fly ⟨~ is natural to birds⟩ **2 a :** a passing through the air or through space outside the earth's atmosphere ⟨~ of an arrow⟩ ⟨~ of a rocket to the moon⟩ **b :** the distance covered in such a flight **c :** swift movement **3 a :** a trip made by or in an airplane or spacecraft **b :** a scheduled airplane flight **4 :** a group of similar beings or objects flying through the air together **5 :** a brilliant, imaginative, or unrestrained exercise or display ⟨a ~ of fancy⟩ **6 a :** a continuous series of stairs from one landing or floor to another **b :** a series (as of terraces or conveyors) resembling a flight of stairs **7 :** a unit of the U.S. Air Force below a squadron — **flight·less** \-ləs\ *adj*

[2]**flight** *vi* (1879) **:** to rise, settle, or fly in a flock ⟨geese ~*ing* on the marsh⟩ ~ *vt* **:** [1]FLUSH

[3]**flight** *n* [ME *fluht, fliht;* akin to OHG *fluht* flight, OE *flēon* to flee] (13c) **:** an act or instance of running away

flight attendant *n* (1956) **:** a person who attends passengers on an airplane

flight bag *n* [[1]*flight*] (1943) **1 :** a lightweight traveling bag with zippered outside pockets **2 :** a small canvas satchel

flight control *n* (1944) **1 :** the control from a ground station of an airplane or spacecraft esp. by radio **2 :** the system of control devices of an airplane

flight deck *n* (1924) **1 :** the uppermost complete deck of an aircraft carrier **2 :** the forward compartment in some airplanes

flight engineer *n* (1944) **:** a flight crewman responsible for mechanical operation

flight feather *n* (1735) **:** one of the quills of a bird's wing or tail that support it in flight — compare CONTOUR FEATHER

flight lieutenant *n* (1914) **:** a commissioned officer in the British air force who ranks with a captain in the army

flight line *n* (1943) **1 :** a parking and servicing area for airplanes **2 :** the line in air or space along which something (as an airplane or missile) travels or is intended to travel

flight path *n* (1911) **:** the path in the air or space made or followed by something (as a particle, an airplane, or a spacecraft) in flight

flight pay *n* (1928) **:** an additional allowance paid to military personnel on flight status

flight plan *n* (ca. 1936) **:** a usu. written statement (as by a pilot) of the details of an intended flight (as of an airplane or spacecraft) usu. filed with an authority

flight status *n* (1956) **:** the status of a person in the military participating in regular authorized aircraft flights

flight strip *n* (1939) **:** an emergency landing field beside a highway

flight surgeon *n* (1925) **:** an air force medical officer trained in aeromedicine

flight–test \'flīt-ˌtest\ *vt* (1930) **:** to test (as an airplane or spacecraft) in flight

flighty \'flīt-ē\ *adj* **flight·i·er; -est** (ca. 1552) **1 :** SWIFT **2 :** lacking stability or steadiness: **a :** easily upset **:** VOLATILE ⟨a ~ temper⟩ **b :** easily excited **:** SKITTISH ⟨a ~ horse⟩ **c :** IRRESPONSIBLE, SILLY ⟨a ~ young girl⟩ — **flight·i·ly** \'flīt-ᵊl-ē\ *adv* — **flight·i·ness** \'flīt-ē-nəs\ *n*

[1]**flim-flam** \'flim-ˌflam\ *n* [prob. of Scand origin; akin to ON *flim* mockery] (1538) **1 :** DECEPTION, FRAUD **2 :** deceptive nonsense

[2]**flimflam** *vt* **flim·flammed; flim·flam·ming** (1660) **:** to subject to a flimflam — **flim·flam·mer** *n* — **flim·flam·mery** \-ˌflam(-ə)-rē\ *n*

[1]**flim·sy** \'flim-zē\ *adj* **flim·si·er; -est** [perh. alter. of [1]*film* + *-sy* (as in *tricksy*)] (1702) **1 a :** lacking in physical strength or substance ⟨~ silks⟩ **b :** of inferior materials and workmanship **2 :** having little worth or plausibility — **flim·si·ly** \-zə-lē\ *adv* — **flim·si·ness** \-zē-nəs\ *n*

[2]**flimsy** *n, pl* **flimsies** *chiefly Brit* (1857) **:** a lightweight paper used esp. for multiple copies; *also* **:** a document printed on flimsy

flinch \'flinch\ *vi* [MF *flenchir* to bend] (1579) **:** to shrink from or as if from physical pain **:** WINCE; *esp* **:** to tense the muscles involuntarily in fear ***syn*** see RECOIL — **flinch** *n* — **flinch·er** *n*

flin·ders \'flin-dərz\ *n pl* [ME *flendris*] (15c) **:** SPLINTERS, FRAGMENTS

[1]**fling** \'fliŋ\ *vb* **flung** \'fləŋ\; **fling·ing** \'fliŋ-iŋ\ [ME *flingen,* of Scand origin; akin to ON *flengja* to whip, *flā* to flay — more at FLAY] *vi* (14c) **1 :** to move in a brusque or headlong manner ⟨~*ing* out of the room in a rage⟩ **2** *of an animal* **:** to kick or plunge vigorously **3** *Scot* **:** CAPER ~ *vt* **1 a :** to throw forcefully, impetuously, or casually ⟨~*ing* the door open⟩ ⟨*flung* herself down on the sofa⟩ ⟨clothes were *flung* on the floor⟩ **b :** to cast as if by throwing ⟨~*ing* a challenge⟩ ⟨*flung* off all restraint⟩ **2 :** to place or send suddenly and unceremoniously ⟨was arrested and *flung* into prison⟩ **3 :** to give unrestrainedly ⟨*flung* himself into music⟩ ***syn*** see THROW — **fling·er** \'fliŋ-ər\ *n*

[2]**fling** *n* (1550) **1 :** an act or instance of flinging **2 a :** a casual try or involvement **b :** a casual or brief love affair **3 :** a period devoted to self-indulgence

flint \'flint\ *n* [ME, fr. OE; akin to OHG *flins* pebble, hard stone and prob. to OHG *spaltan* to split — more at SPILL] (bef. 12c) **1 :** a massive hard quartz that produces a spark when struck by steel **2 :** an implement of flint used by primitive man **3 :** a material used for producing a spark; *esp* **:** an alloy (as of iron and cerium) used in lighters **4 :** something resembling flint in hardness — **flint·like** \-ˌlīk\ *adj*

flint corn *n* (1705) **:** an Indian corn (*Zea mays indurata*) having hard horny usu. rounded kernels with the soft endosperm enclosed by a hard outer layer

flint glass *n* (1683) **:** heavy brilliant glass that contains lead oxide, has a relatively high index of refraction, and is used for optical structures

flint·lock \'flint-ˌläk\ *n* (1683) **1 :** a lock for a gun or pistol having a flint in the hammer for striking a spark to ignite the charge **2 :** a firearm fitted with a flintlock

flinty \'flint-ē\ *adj* **flint·i·er; -est** (1536) **1 :** resembling flint; *esp* **:** STERN, UNYIELDING **2 :** composed of or covered with flint — **flint·i·ly** \'flint-ᵊl-ē\ *adv* — **flint·i·ness** \'flint-ē-nəs\ *n*

[1]**flip** \'flip\ *vb* **flipped; flip·ping** [prob. imit.] *vt* (1616) **1 :** to toss so as to cause to turn over in the air ⟨~ a coin⟩; *also* **:** TOSS ⟨~ me the ball⟩ ⟨~ one end of the scarf over your shoulder⟩ **2 :** to cause to turn and esp. to turn over ⟨~ the dial⟩ ⟨hit a ditch and *flipped* the car⟩ ⟨*flipping* the pages of a book⟩ ~ *vi* **1 :** to make a twitching or flicking movement ⟨the fish *flipped* and flopped on the deck⟩; *also* **:** to change from one position to another and esp. turn over ⟨the car *flipped*⟩ **2 :** LEAF 2 ⟨*flipped* through the pages⟩ **3** *slang* **a :** to lose one's mind or composure — often used with *out* **b :** to become extremely enthusiastic

[2]**flip** *n* (1692) **1 :** an act or instance of flipping **2 :** the motion used in flipping **3 :** a somersault esp. when performed in the air **4 :** a mixed drink usu. consisting of a sweetened spiced liquor (as beer, wine, or rum) to which beaten eggs have been added

[3]**flip** *adj* (ca. 1847) **:** FLIPPANT, IMPERTINENT

flip–flop \'flip-ˌfläp\ *n* (1529) **1 :** the sound or motion of something flapping loosely **2 a :** a backward handspring **b :** a sudden reversal of direction or point of view **3 :** a usu. electronic device or a circuit (as in a computer) capable of assuming either of two stable states — **flip–flop** *vi*

flip·pan·cy \'flip-ən-sē\ *n, pl* **-cies** (1747) **:** unbecoming levity or pertness esp. in respect to grave or sacred matters

flip·pant \'flip-ənt\ *adj* [prob. fr. [1]*flip*] (1605) **1** *archaic* **:** GLIB, TALKATIVE **2 :** lacking proper respect or seriousness — **flip·pant·ly** *adv*

flip·per \'flip-ər\ *n* (1822) **1 a :** a broad flat limb (as of a seal) adapted for swimming **b :** a flat rubber shoe with the front expanded into a paddle used in skin diving **2 :** one that flips

flip side *n* [[1]*flip*] (1949) **:** the reverse and usu. less popular side of a phonograph record; *broadly* **:** the reverse or opposite side

[1]**flirt** \'flərt\ *vb* [origin unknown] *vt* (1583) **1 :** FLICK **2 :** to move in a jerky manner ~ *vi* **1 :** to move erratically **:** FLIT **2 a :** to behave amorously without serious intent **b :** to show superficial or casual interest or liking ⟨~*ed* with the idea⟩ ***syn*** see TRIFLE — **flir·ta·tion** \ˌflər-'tā-shən\ *n* — **flirt·er** *n* — **flirty** \'flərt-ē\ *adj*

[2]**flirt** *n* (1590) **1 :** an act or instance of flirting **2 :** a person who flirts

flir·ta·tious \ˌflər-'tā-shəs\ *adj* (1834) **:** inclined to flirt **:** COQUETTISH — **flir·ta·tious·ly** *adv* — **flir·ta·tious·ness** *n*

flit \'flit\ *vi* **flit·ted; flit·ting** [ME *flitten,* of Scand origin; akin to ON *flytjask* to move, OE *flēotan* to float] (13c) **1 :** to pass quickly or abruptly from one place or condition to another **2** *archaic* **:** ALTER, SHIFT **3 :** to move in an erratic fluttering manner — **flit** *n*

flitch \'flich\ *n* [ME *flicche,* fr. OE *flicce;* akin to OHG *fleisk* flesh — more at FLESH] (bef. 12c) **1 :** a side of pork cured and smoked as bacon **2 a :** a longitudinal section of a log **b :** a bundle of sheets of veneer laid together in sequence **3 :** one of the parts secured together to make a girder or beam

[1]**flit·ter** \'flit-ər\ *vi* [freq. of *flit*] (1534) **:** FLUTTER, FLICKER

[2]**flitter** *n* (1554) **:** one that flits

fliv·ver \'fliv-ər\ *n* [origin unknown] (1910) **:** a small cheap usu. old automobile

[1]**float** \'flōt\ *n* [ME *flote* boat, float, fr. OE *flota* ship; akin to OHG *flōz* raft, stream, OE *flēotan* to float — more at FLEET] (bef. 12c) **1 :** an act or instance of floating **2 :** something that floats in or on the surface of a fluid: as **a :** a device (as a cork) buoying up the baited end of a fishing line **b :** a floating platform anchored near a shoreline for use by swimmers or boats **c :** a hollow ball that floats at the end of a lever in a cistern, tank, or boiler and regulates the liquid level **d :** a sac containing air or gas and buoying up the body of a plant or animal **:** PNEUMATOPHORE **e :** a watertight structure giving an airplane buoyancy on water **3 :** a tool or apparatus for smoothing a surface **4 :** a government grant of a fixed amount of land not yet located by survey out of a larger specific tract **5 a :** a vehicle with a platform used to carry an exhibit in a parade **b :** the vehicle and exhibit together **6 a :** an amount of money represented by checks outstanding and in process of collection **b :** the time between a transaction (as the writing of a check or a purchase on credit) and the actual withdrawal of funds to cover it **7 :** a soft drink with ice cream floating in it — **floaty** \'flōt-ē\ *adj*

[2]**float** *vi* (bef. 12c) **1 :** to rest on the surface of or be suspended in a fluid **2 a :** to drift on or through or as if on or through a fluid ⟨yellow leaves ~*ed* down⟩ **b :** WANDER **3** *of a currency* **:** to find a level in the international exchange market in response to the law of supply and demand and without any restrictive effect of artificial support or control ~ *vt* **1 a :** to cause to float in or on the surface of a fluid **b :** to cause to float as if in a fluid **2 :** to support (a structure) on a mat or raft foundation when the ground gives poor support **3 :** FLOOD ⟨~ a cranberry bog⟩ **4 :** to smooth (as plaster or cement) with a float **5 a :** to put forth (as a proposal) for acceptance **b :** to place (an issue of securities) on the market **c :** to obtain money for the establishment or development of (an enterprise) by issuing and selling securities **d :** NEGOTIATE ⟨~ a loan⟩

float·age *var of* FLOTAGE

floa·ta·tion *var of* FLOTATION

float·er \'flōt-ər\ *n* (1717) **1 a :** one that floats **b :** a person who floats something **2 :** a person who votes illegally in various polling places **3 :** a person who floats or drifts: as **a :** a person without a permanent residence or regular employment **b :** an employee without a specific job **4 :** a policy insuring specific items of personal property (as jewelry or art)

float·ing *adj* (1600) **1 :** buoyed on or in a fluid **2 :** located out of the normal position ⟨a ~ kidney⟩ **3 a :** continually drifting or changing

position ⟨the ~ population⟩ **b :** not presently committed or invested ⟨~ capital⟩ **c :** short-term and usu. not funded ⟨~ debt⟩ **d :** having no fixed value or rate ⟨~ currencies⟩ ⟨~ interest rates⟩ **4 :** connected or constructed so as to operate and adjust smoothly ⟨a ~ axle⟩
floating dock *n* (1838) **:** a dock that floats on the water and can be partly submerged to permit entry of a ship and raised to keep the ship high and dry — called also *floating drydock*
floating island *n* (1771) **:** a dessert consisting of custard with floating masses of beaten egg whites
floating–point *adj* (1948) **:** involving or being a mathematical notation in which a quantity is denoted by one number multiplied by a power of the number base ⟨the fixed-point value 99.9 could be expressed in a ~ system as .999 × 10^2⟩ — compare FIXED-POINT
floating point *n* (1958) **:** a floating-point system or notation; *also* **:** a point used in such a system or notation
floating rib *n* (1831) **:** a rib (as one of either of the last two pairs in man) that has no attachment to the sternum — compare FALSE RIB
float·plane \ˈflōt-ˌplān\ *n* (1922) **:** a seaplane supported on the water by one or more floats
[1]**floc** \ˈfläk\ *n* [short for *floccule*] (1921) **1 :** a flocculent mass formed by the aggregation of a number of fine suspended particles **2 :** [3]FLOCK 1,2,3
[2]**floc** *vb* **flocced** \ˈfläkt\; **floc·cing** \ˈfläk-iŋ\ *vi* (1956) **:** to aggregate into flocs ~ *vt* **:** to cause to floc
[1]**floc·cu·late** \ˈfläk-yə-ˌlāt\ *vb* **-lat·ed; -lat·ing** *vt* (1877) **:** to cause to aggregate into a flocculent mass ⟨~ clay⟩ ~ *vi* **:** to become flocculated — **floc·cu·lant** \-lənt\ *n* — **floc·cu·la·tion** \ˌfläk-yə-ˈlā-shən\ *n* — **floc·cu·la·tor** \ˈfläk-yə-ˌlāt-ər\ *n*
[2]**floc·cu·late** \-lət, -ˌlāt\ *n* (ca. 1909) **:** something that has flocculated
floc·cule \ˈfläk-(ˌ)yü(ə)l\ *n* [LL *flocculus*] (1845) **:** a small loosely aggregated bit of material suspended in or precipitated from a liquid
floc·cu·lent \-lənt\ *adj* [L *floccus* + E *-ulent*] (1800) **1 :** resembling wool esp. in loose fluffy organization **2 :** made up of flocs or floccules ⟨a ~ precipitate⟩
floc·cu·lus \-ləs\ *n, pl* **-li** \-ˌlī, -ˌlē\ [LL, dim. of L *floccus* flock of wool; akin to OHG *blaha* coarse linen] (1799) **1 :** a small loosely aggregated mass **2 :** a bright or dark patch on the sun
[1]**flock** \ˈfläk\ *n* [ME, fr. OE *flocc* crowd, band; akin to ON *flokkr* crowd, band] (bef. 12c) **1 :** a group of birds or mammals assembled or herded together **2 :** a group under the guidance of a leader; *specif* **:** a church congregation in relation to the pastor **3 :** a large number ⟨a whole ~ of tourists⟩
[2]**flock** *vi* (14c) **:** to gather or move in a flock ⟨they ~*ed* to the beach⟩
[3]**flock** *n* [ME] (13c) **1 :** a tuft of wool or cotton fiber **2 :** woolen or cotton refuse used for stuffing furniture and mattresses **3 :** very short or pulverized fiber used esp. to form a velvety pattern on cloth or paper or a protective covering on metal **4 :** FLOC
[4]**flock** *vt* (1530) **1 :** to fill with flock **2 :** to decorate with flock
flock·ing \ˈfläk-iŋ\ *n* (1874) **:** a design in flock
floe \ˈflō\ *n* [prob. fr. Norw *flo* flat layer] (ca. 1817) **1 :** floating ice formed in a large sheet on the surface of a body of water **2 :** ICE FLOE
flog \ˈfläg\ *vt* **flogged; flog·ging** [perh. modif. of L *flagellare* to whip — more at FLAGELLATE] (ca. 1676) **1 :** to beat with a rod or whip **:** LASH **2 :** to criticize harshly **3 :** to force into action **:** DRIVE **4 :** SELL: **a** *chiefly Brit* **:** to sell stolen goods **b :** PLUG, PUBLICIZE — **flog·ger** *n* — **flog a dead horse :** to attempt to revive interest in a worn-out or forgotten subject
flo·ka·ti \flō-ˈkät-ē\ *n* [NGk *phlokatē* peasant's blanket] (1967) **:** a hand-woven Greek woolen rug with a thick shaggy pile
[1]**flood** \ˈfləd\ *n* [ME, fr. OE *flōd;* akin to OHG *fluot* flood, OE *flōwan* to flow] (bef. 12c) **1 a :** a rising and overflowing of a body of water esp. onto normally dry land **b** *cap* **:** a flood described in the Bible as covering the earth in the time of Noah **2 :** the flowing in of the tide **3 :** an overwhelming quantity or volume **4 :** FLOODLIGHT
[2]**flood** *vt* (1663) **1 :** to cover with a flood **:** INUNDATE **2 a :** to fill abundantly or excessively ⟨~ the market⟩ **b :** to supply to (the carburetor of an internal-combustion engine) an excess of fuel so that engine operation is hampered ~ *vi* **1 :** to pour forth, go, or come in a flood **2 :** to become filled with a flood — **flood·er** *n*
flood·gate \ˈfləd-ˌgāt\ *n* [ME *flodgate*] (13c) **1 :** a gate for shutting out, admitting, or releasing a body of water **:** SLUICE **2 :** something serving to restrain an outburst
[1]**flood·light** \-ˌlīt\ *vt* (1923) **:** to illuminate by means of one or more floodlights
[2]**floodlight** *n* (1924) **1 a :** artificial illumination in a broad beam **b :** a source of such illumination **2 :** a lighting unit for projecting a beam of light
flood·plain \ˈfləd-ˌplān\ *n* (1873) **1 :** level land that may be submerged by floodwaters **2 :** a plain built up by stream deposition
flood tide *n* (1719) **1 :** a rising tide **2 a :** an overwhelming quantity **b :** a high point **:** PEAK
flood·wall \ˈfləd-ˌwȯl\ *n* (1952) **:** a wall (as a levee) built to prevent inundation by high water
flood·wa·ter \-ˌwȯt-ər, -ˌwät-\ *n* (1791) **:** the water of a flood
flood·way \-ˌwā\ *n* (1915) **:** a channel for diverting floodwaters
floo·ey \ˈflü-ē\ *adj* [origin unknown] (1920) **:** AWRY, ASKEW
[1]**floor** \ˈflō(ə)r, ˈflȯ(ə)r\ *n, often attrib* [ME *flor,* fr. OE *flōr;* akin to OHG *fluor* meadow, L *planus* level, Gk *planasthai* to wander] (bef. 12c) **1 :** the level base of a room **2 a :** the lower inside surface of a hollow structure (as a cave or bodily part) **b :** a ground surface ⟨the ocean ~⟩ **3 a :** a structure dividing a building into stories; *also* **:** STORY **b :** the occupants of such a floor **4 :** the surface of a structure on which one travels ⟨the ~ of a bridge⟩ **5 a :** a main level space (as in a stock exchange or legislative chamber) distinguished from a platform or gallery **b :** the members of an assembly ⟨took questions from the ~⟩ **c :** the right to address an assembly ⟨the senator from Utah has the ~⟩ **6 :** a lower limit **:** BASE — **floored** *adj*
[2]**floor** *vt* (15c) **1 :** to cover with a floor or flooring **2 a :** to knock to the floor **b :** SHOCK, OVERWHELM **c :** to reduce to silence or defeat **3 :** to press (the accelerator of a vehicle) to the floorboard — **floor·er** *n*
floor·age \ˈflōr-ij, ˈflȯr-\ *n* (1734) **:** floor space
floor·board \ˈflō(ə)r-ˌbō(ə)rd, ˈflȯ(ə)r-ˌbȯ(ə)rd\ *n* (1881) **1 :** a board in a floor **2 :** the floor of an automobile
floor exercise *n* (ca. 1974) **:** an event in gymnastics competition consisting of various ballet and tumbling movements (as jumps, somersaults, and handstands) performed without apparatus
floor furnace *n* (1955) **:** a small furnace located close below the floor
floor·ing \ˈflōr-iŋ, ˈflȯr-\ *n* (1624) **1 :** FLOOR, BASE **2 :** material for floors ⟨the disadvantages of softwood ~⟩
floor lamp *n* (1892) **:** a tall lamp that stands on the floor
floor leader *n* (1899) **:** a member of a legislative body chosen by his party to have charge of its organization and strategy on the floor
floor–length *adj* (1939) **:** reaching to the floor ⟨a ~ gown⟩
floor manager *n* (1887) **:** a person who directs something (as the activities in support of a candidate at a nominating convention) from the floor
floor sample *n* (1957) **:** an article offered for sale at a reduced price because it has been used for display or demonstration
floor show *n* (1927) **:** a series of acts presented in a nightclub
floor–through \ˈflōr-ˌthrü, ˈflȯr-\ *n* (1967) **:** an apartment that occupies an entire floor of a building
floor·walk·er \ˈflōr-ˌwȯ-kər, ˈflȯr-\ *n* (1876) **:** a person employed in a retail store to oversee the salespeople and aid customers
floo·zy *or* **floo·zie** \ˈflü-zē\ *n, pl* **floozies** [origin unknown] (1911) **:** a tawdry or immoral woman; *specif* **:** PROSTITUTE
[1]**flop** \ˈfläp\ *vb* **flopped; flop·ping** [alter. of [2]*flap*] *vi* (1602) **1 :** to swing or bounce loosely **2 :** to throw or move oneself in a heavy, clumsy, or relaxed manner ⟨*flopped* into the chair with a sigh of relief⟩ **3 :** to change suddenly **4 :** to go to bed ⟨so tired I had to ~⟩ **5 :** to fail completely ⟨in spite of good reviews the play *flopped*⟩ ~ *vt* **:** to move or drop heavily and noisily ⟨*flopped* the bundles down with a thud⟩ — **flop·per** *n*
[2]**flop** *adv* (1728) **:** RIGHT, SQUARELY ⟨fell ~ on his face⟩
[3]**flop** *n* (1823) **1 :** an act or sound of flopping **2 :** a complete failure **:** DUD **3** *slang* **:** a place to sleep
flop·house \ˈfläp-ˌhau̇s\ *n* (1916) **:** a cheap rooming house or hotel
flop·over \-ˌō-vər\ *n* (1952) **:** a defect in television reception in which a succession of frames appears to traverse the screen vertically
[1]**flop·py** \ˈfläp-ē\ *adj* **flop·pi·er; -est** (1858) **:** tending to flop; *esp* **:** being both soft and flexible — **flop·pi·ly** \ˈfläp-ə-lē\ *adv* — **flop·pi·ness** \ˈfläp-ē-nəs\ *n*
[2]**floppy** *n, pl* **-pies** (1976) **:** FLOPPY DISK
floppy disk *n* (1973) **:** a small flexible plastic disk coated with magnetic material on which data for a computer can be stored
flo·ra \ˈflōr-ə, ˈflȯr-\ *n, pl* **floras** *also* **flo·rae** \ˈflō(ə)r-ˌē, ˈflȯ(ə)r-, -ˌī\ [NL, fr. L *Flora,* Roman goddess of flowers, fr. L *flor-, flos*] (1717) **1 :** a treatise on or list of the plants of an area or period **2 :** plant life; *esp* **:** the plants characteristic of a region, period, or special environment — compare FAUNA
flo·ral \ˈflōr-əl, ˈflȯr-\ *adj* [L *flor-, flos* flower — more at BLOW] (1753) **:** of or relating to flowers or a flora
floral envelope *n* (1830) **:** PERIANTH
Flor·ence flask \ˌflȯr-ən(t)s-, ˌflär-\ *n* [*Florence,* Italy; fr. the use of flasks of this shape for certain Italian wines] (1744) **:** a round usu. flat-bottomed laboratory vessel with a long neck
flo·res·cence \flō-ˈres-ᵊn(t)s, flə-\ *n* [NL *florescentia,* fr. L *florescent-, florescens,* prp. of *florescere,* incho. of *florēre* to blossom, flourish — more at FLOURISH] (1793) **:** a state or period of flourishing — **flo·res·cent** \-ᵊnt\ *adj*
flo·ret \ˈflōr-ət, ˈflȯr-\ *n* [ME *flourette,* fr. MF *flouret,* dim. of *flour* flower] (1671) **:** a small flower; *esp* **:** one of the small flowers forming the head of a composite plant
flori- *comb form* [L, fr. *flor-, flos*] **:** flower or flowers ⟨*flori*culture⟩
flo·ri·at·ed \ˈflōr-ē-ˌāt-əd, ˈflȯr-\ *adj* (1845) **:** having floral ornaments or a floral form — **flo·ri·a·tion** \ˌflōr-ē-ˈā-shən, ˌflȯr-\ *n*
flo·ri·bun·da \ˌflōr-ə-ˈbən-də, ˌflȯr-\ *n* [NL, fem. of *floribundus* flowering freely] (1898) **:** any of various bush roses with large flowers in open clusters that derive from crosses of polyantha and tea roses
flo·ri·cul·ture \ˈflōr-ə-ˌkəl-chər, ˈflȯr-\ *n* (1822) **:** the cultivation and management of ornamental and flowering plants — **flo·ri·cul·tur·al** \ˌflōr-ə-ˈkəlch-(ə-)rəl, ˌflȯr-\ *adj* — **flo·ri·cul·tur·ist** \-rəst\ *n*
flor·id \ˈflȯr-əd, ˈflär-\ *adj* [L *floridus* blooming, flowery, fr. *florēre*] (ca. 1656) **1 a** *obs* **:** covered with flowers **b :** excessively flowery in style **:** ORNATE **2 :** tinged with red **:** RUDDY ⟨a ~ complexion⟩ **3** *archaic* **:** HEALTHY **4 :** fully developed **:** manifesting a complete and typical clinical syndrome ⟨the ~ stage of a disease⟩ — **flo·rid·i·ty** \flə-ˈrid-ət-ē, flȯ-\ *n* — **flor·id·ly** \ˈflȯr-əd-lē, ˈflär-\ *adv*
flo·rif·er·ous \flȯ-ˈrif-(ə-)rəs\ *adj* [L *florifer,* fr. *flori-* + *-fer* fer] (ca. 1656) **:** bearing flowers; *esp* **:** blooming freely — **flo·rif·er·ous·ness** *n*
flo·ri·gen \ˈflōr-ə-jən, ˈflȯr-\ *n* [ISV] (1936) **:** a hormone or hormonal agent that promotes flowering — **flo·ri·gen·ic** \ˌflōr-ə-ˈjen-ik, ˌflȯr-\ *adj*
flo·ri·le·gium \ˌflōr-ə-ˈlē-j(ē-)əm, ˌflȯr-\ *n, pl* **-gia** \-j(ē-)ə\ [NL, fr. L *florilegus* culling flowers, fr. *flori-* + *legere* to gather — more at LEGEND] (1647) **:** a volume of writings **:** ANTHOLOGY
flo·rin \ˈflȯr-ən, ˈflär-, ˈflōr-\ *n* [ME, fr. MF, fr. OIt *fiorino,* fr. *fiore* flower, fr. L *flor-, flos;* fr. the lily on the coins] (14c) **1 a :** an old gold coin first struck at Florence in 1252 **b :** any of various European gold coins patterned after the Florentine florin **2 a :** a British silver coin worth two shillings **b :** any of several similar coins issued in British Commonwealth countries **3 :** GULDEN **4 :** FORINT
flo·rist \ˈflōr-əst, ˈflȯr-\ *n* (1623) **:** one who sells or grows for sale flowers and ornamental plants — **flo·rist·ry** \-ə-strē\ *n*
flo·ris·tic \flȯ-ˈris-tik\ *adj* (1898) **:** of or relating to flowers, a flora, or the phytogeographical study of plants and plant groups — **flo·ris·ti·cal·ly** \-ti-k(ə-)lē\ *adv*
-flo·rous \ˈflōr-əs, ˈflȯr-\ *adj comb form* [LL *-florus,* fr. L *flor-, flos*] **:** having or bearing (such or so many) flowers ⟨uni*florous*⟩
flo·ru·it \ˈflȯr-(y)ə-wət, ˈflär-\ *n* [L, he flourished, fr. *florēre* to flourish] (1843) **:** a period of flourishing (as of a person or movement)
[1]**floss** \ˈfläs, ˈflȯs\ *n* [fr. or akin to D *vlos;* akin to MHG *vlus, vlius* fleece — more at FLEECE] (1759) **1 :** waste or short silk fibers that cannot be reeled **2 a :** soft thread of silk or mercerized cotton for embroidery **b :** DENTAL FLOSS **c :** a lightweight wool knitting yarn **3 :** fluffy fibrous material; *esp* **:** SILK COTTON
[2]**floss** *vt* (1974) **:** to use dental floss on ~ *vi* **:** to use dental floss
floss·flow·er \-ˌflau̇(-ə)r\ *n* (ca. 1928) **:** AGERATUM

flossy \'fläs-ē, 'flȯs-\ *adj* **floss·i·er; -est** (1839) **1 a :** of, relating to, or having the characteristics of floss **b :** DOWNY **2 :** stylish or glamorous esp. at first impression ⟨slick ~ writing⟩ — **floss·i·ly** \'fläs-ə-lē\ *adv*
flo·ta \'flōt-ə\ *n* [Sp] (1527) **:** a fleet of Spanish ships
flo·tage \'flōt-ij\ *n* [[2]*float*] (1626) **1 :** FLOTATION 1 **2 :** material that floats **:** FLOTSAM **3** *usu* **floatage :** the charge for transferring railroad cars on a barge
flo·ta·tion \flō-'tā-shən\ *n* [[2]*float*] (1806) **1 :** the act, process, or state of floating **2 :** an act or instance of financing (as an issue of stock) **3 :** the separation of the particles of a mass of pulverized ore according to their relative capacity for floating on a given liquid; *also* **:** any of various similar processes involving the relative capacity of materials for floating **4 :** the ability (as of a tire) to stay on the surface of soft ground or snow
flo·til·la \flō-'til-ə\ *n* [Sp, dim. of *flota* fleet, fr. OF *flote,* fr. ON *floti;* akin to OE *flota* ship, fleet — more at FLOAT] (1711) **1 :** a fleet of ships; *esp* **:** a navy organizational unit consisting of two or more squadrons of small warships **2 :** a large force of moving things
flot·sam \'flät-səm\ *n* [AF *floteson,* fr. OF *floter* to float, of Gmc origin; akin to OE *flotian* to float, *flota* ship] (ca. 1607) **1 :** floating wreckage of a ship or its cargo; *broadly* **:** floating debris **2 a :** vagrant impoverished people **b :** unimportant miscellaneous material
[1]**flounce** \'flau̇n(t)s\ *vi* **flounced; flounc·ing** [perh. of Scand origin; akin to Norw *flunsa* to hurry] (1542) **1 a :** to move with exaggerated jerky motions ⟨little girls *flouncing* about in their mothers' clothes⟩ **b :** to go with sudden determination ⟨*flounced* out of the room in a huff⟩ **2 :** FLOUNDER, STRUGGLE
[2]**flounce** *n* (1583) **:** an act or instance of flouncing — **flouncy** \'flau̇n(t)-sē\ *adj*
[3]**flounce** *vt* **flounced; flounc·ing** [alter. of earlier *frounce,* fr. ME *frouncen* to curl] (1711) **:** to trim with flounces
[4]**flounce** *n* (1713) **:** a strip of fabric attached by one edge; *also* **:** a wide ruffle — **flouncy** \'flau̇n(t)-sē\ *adj*
flounc·ing \'flau̇n(t)-siŋ\ *n* (1873) **:** material used for flounces
[1]**floun·der** \'flau̇n-dər\ *n, pl* **flounder** *or* **flounders** [ME, of Scand origin; akin to ON *flythra* flounder, *flatr* flat — more at FLAT] (14c) **:** FLATFISH; *esp* **:** one of either of two families (Pleuronectidae and Bothidae) that include important marine food fishes
[2]**flounder** *vi* **floun·dered; floun·der·ing** \-d(ə-)riŋ\ [prob. alter. of *founder*] (1592) **1 :** to struggle to move or obtain footing **2 :** to proceed or act clumsily or ineffectually
[1]**flour** \'flau̇(ə)r\ *n* [ME — more at FLOWER] (13c) **1 :** finely ground meal of wheat usu. largely freed from bran; *also* **:** a similar meal of another material (as a cereal grain, an edible seed, or dried processed fish) **2 :** a fine soft powder — **flour·less** *adj* — **floury** \-ē\ *adj*
[2]**flour** *vt* (1651) **:** to coat with or as if with flour ~ *vi* **:** to break up into particles
[1]**flour·ish** \'flər-ish, 'flə-rish\ *vb* [ME *florisshen,* fr. MF *floriss-,* stem of *florir,* fr. (assumed) VL *florire,* alter. of L *florēre,* fr. *flor-, flos* flower] *vi* (14c) **1 :** to grow luxuriantly **:** THRIVE **2 a :** to achieve success **:** PROSPER **b :** to be in a state of activity or production ⟨~*ed* around 1850⟩ **c :** to reach a height of development or influence **3 :** to make bold and sweeping gestures ~ *vt* **:** to wield with dramatic gestures **:** BRANDISH ***syn*** see SWING — **flour·ish·er** *n* — **flour·ish·ing·ly** \-iŋ-lē\ *adv*
[2]**flourish** *n* (1597) **1 :** a period of thriving **2 a :** an extraneous florid embellishment or passage **b :** an act or instance of brandishing **:** WAVE **c :** a studied or ostentatious action
[1]**flout** \'flau̇t\ *vb* [prob. fr. ME *flouten* to play the flute, fr. *floute* flute] *vt* (1551) **:** to treat with contemptuous disregard **:** SCORN ⟨~*ing* the rules⟩ ~ *vi* **:** to indulge in scornful behavior ***syn*** see SCOFF ***usage*** see FLAUNT — **flout·er** *n*
[2]**flout** *n* (ca. 1570) **1 :** INSULT **2 :** MOCKERY
[1]**flow** \'flō\ *vb* [ME *flowen,* fr. OE *flōwan;* akin to OHG *flouwen* to rinse, wash, L *pluere* to rain, Gk *plein* to sail, float] *vi* (bef. 12c) **1 a** (1) **:** to issue or move in a stream (2) **:** CIRCULATE **b :** to move with a continual change of place among the constituent particles ⟨the molasses ~*ed* slowly⟩ **2 :** RISE ⟨the tide ebbs and ~*s*⟩ **3 :** ABOUND **4 a :** to proceed smoothly and readily ⟨conversation ~*ed* easily⟩ **b :** to have a smooth continuity ⟨the ~*ing* lines of the car⟩ **5 :** to hang loose and billowing **6 :** to derive from a source **:** COME ⟨the wealth that ~*s* from our industries⟩ **7 :** to deform under stress without cracking or rupturing — used esp. of minerals and rocks **8 :** MENSTRUATE ~ *vt* **1 a :** to cause to flow **b :** to cover with water **:** FLOOD **2 :** to discharge in a flow ***syn*** see SPRING — **flow·ing·ly** \-iŋ-lē\ *adv*
[2]**flow** *n* (15c) **1 :** an act of flowing **2 :** FLOOD 1a, 2 **3 a :** a smooth uninterrupted movement ⟨a constant ~ of information⟩ **b :** STREAM; *also* **:** a mass of material which has flowed when molten ⟨an old lava ~⟩ **c :** the direction of movement or apparent movement (as of a play in football) **4 :** the quantity that flows in a certain time **5 a :** MENSTRUATION **b :** YIELD, PRODUCTION **6 a :** the motion characteristic of fluids **b :** a continuous transfer of energy
flow·age \'flō-ij\ *n* (1830) **1 a :** an overflowing onto adjacent land **b :** a body of water formed by overflowing or damming **c :** floodwater esp. of a stream **2 :** gradual deformation of a body of plastic solid (as rock) by intermolecular shear
flow·chart \-ˌchärt\ *n* (1920) **:** a diagram that shows step-by-step progression through a procedure or system esp. using connecting lines and a set of conventional symbols — **flow·chart·ing** \-iŋ\ *n*
flow diagram *n* (1943) **:** FLOWCHART
[1]**flow·er** \'flau̇(-ə)r\ *n* [ME *flour* flower, best of anything, flour, fr. OF *flor, flour,* fr. L *flor-, flos* — more at BLOW] (13c) **1 a :** BLOSSOM, INFLORESCENCE **b :** a shoot of the sporophyte of a higher plant that is modified for reproduction and consists of a shortened axis bearing modified leaves **c :** a plant cultivated for its blossoms **2 a :** the best part or example ⟨the ~ of our youth⟩ **b :** the finest most vigorous period **c :** a state of blooming or flourishing **3** *pl* **:** a finely divided powder produced esp. by condensation or sublimation ⟨~*s* of sulfur⟩ — **flow·ered** \'flau̇(-ə)rd\ *adj* — **flow·er·ful** \'flau̇(-ə)r-fəl\ *adj* — **flow·er·less** \-ləs\ *adj* — **flow·er·like** \-ˌlīk\ *adj*

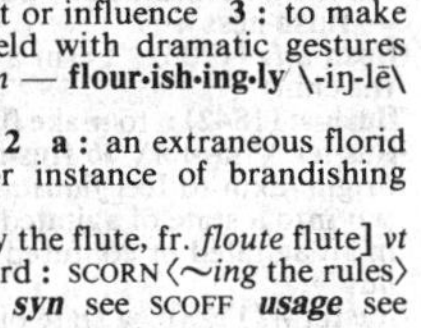

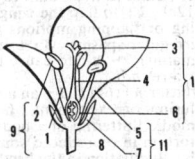

cross section of flower 1b: *1* filament, *2* anther, *3* stigma, *4* style, *5* petal, *6* ovary, *7* sepal, *8* pedicel, *9* stamen, *10* pistil, *11* perianth

[2]**flower** *vi* (13c) **1 a :** DEVELOP ⟨~*ed* into young womanhood⟩ **b :** FLOURISH **2 :** to produce flowers **:** BLOSSOM ~ *vt* **1 :** to cause to bear flowers **2 :** to decorate with floral designs — **flow·er·er** \'flau̇(-ə)r-ər\ *n*
flow·er·age \'flau̇(-ə)r-ij\ *n* (1840) **:** a flowering state
flower bud *n* (ca. 1847) **:** a plant bud that produces only a flower
flower bug *n* (ca. 1889) **:** any of various small mostly black-and-white predaceous bugs (family Anthocoridae) that frequent flowers and feed on pest insects (as aphids and thrips)
flower child *n* [fr. his displaying of flowers as a symbol of his sentiments] (1967) **:** a hippie who advocates love, beauty, and peace
flow·er·et \'flau̇(-ə)r-ət\ *n* (15c) **:** FLORET
flower girl *n* (1924) **:** a little girl who carries flowers at a wedding
flower head *n* (1845) **:** a capitulum (as of a composite) having sessile flowers so arranged that the whole inflorescence looks like a single flower
flowering dogwood *n* (1843) **:** a common spring-flowering white-bracted dogwood (*Cornus florida*)
flowering plant *n* (1861) **1 :** a plant that produces flowers, fruit, and seed **:** ANGIOSPERM **2 :** a plant notable for or cultivated for its ornamental flowers
flower people *n pl* (1967) **:** FLOWER CHILDREN
flow·er·pot \'flau̇(-ə)r-ˌpät\ *n* (1598) **:** a pot in which to grow plants
flow·ery \'flau̇(-ə)r-ē\ *adj* (14c) **1 :** of, relating to, or resembling flowers **2 :** marked by or given to rhetorical elegance — **flow·er·i·ness** *n*
[1]**flown** \'flōn\ *past part of* FLY
[2]**flown** *adj* [archaic pp. of [1]*flow*] (1626) **:** filled to excess
flow sheet *n* (1912) **:** FLOWCHART
flow·stone \'flō-ˌstōn\ *n* (1928) **:** travertine found where water flowing in a very thin sheet over rocks has deposited mineral matter
flu \'flü\ *n* [by shortening] (1839) **1 :** INFLUENZA **2 :** any of several virus diseases marked esp. by respiratory symptoms
[1]**flub** \'fləb\ *vb* **flubbed; flub·bing** [origin unknown] *vt* (ca. 1904) **:** to make a mess of **:** BOTCH ⟨*flubbed* the test⟩ ~ *vi* **:** BLUNDER
[2]**flub** *n* (1944) **:** an act or instance of flubbing
flub·dub \'fləb-ˌdəb\ *n* [origin unknown] (1888) **:** CLAPTRAP, BUNKUM
fluc·tu·ant \'flək-chə-wənt\ *adj* (1560) **1 :** moving in waves **2 :** VARIABLE, UNSTABLE **3 :** being movable and compressible ⟨a ~ abscess⟩
fluc·tu·ate \'flək-chə-ˌwāt\ *vb* **-at·ed; -at·ing** [L *fluctuatus,* pp. of *fluctuare,* fr. *fluctus* flow, wave, fr. *fluctus,* pp. of *fluere — more at* FLUID] *vi* (ca. 1656) **1 :** to ebb and flow in waves **2 :** to shift back and forth uncertainly ~ *vt* **:** to cause to fluctuate ***syn*** see SWING — **fluc·tu·a·tion** \ˌflək-chə-'wā-shən\ *n* — **fluc·tu·a·tion·al** \-'wā-shnəl, -shən-ᵊl\ *adj*
flue \'flü\ *n* [origin unknown] (1582) **:** an enclosed passageway for directing a current: as **a :** a channel in a chimney for conveying flame and smoke to the outer air **b :** a pipe for conveying flame and hot gases around or through water in a steam boiler **c :** an air channel leading to the lip of a wind instrument **d :** FLUE PIPE
flue–cured \-ˌkyu̇(ə)rd\ *adj* (1848) **:** cured with heat transmitted through a flue without exposure to smoke or fumes ⟨~ tobacco⟩
flu·en·cy \'flü-ən-sē\ *n* (1636) **:** the quality or state of being fluent
flu·ent \'flü-ənt\ *adj* [L *fluent-, fluens,* prp. of *fluere*] (1599) **1 a :** capable of flowing **:** FLUID **b :** capable of moving with ease and grace ⟨the ~ body of a dancer⟩ **2 a :** ready or facile in speech ⟨~ in Spanish⟩ **b :** effortlessly smooth and rapid **:** POLISHED ⟨a ~ performance⟩ — **flu·ent·ly** *adv*
flue pipe *n* (1852) **:** an organ pipe whose tone is produced by an air current striking the lip and causing the air within to vibrate — compare REED PIPE
flu·er·ic \flü-'er-ik\ *adj* (1967) **:** FLUIDIC — **flu·er·ics** \-iks\ *n pl but sing in constr*
flue stop *n* (1855) **:** an organ stop made up of flue pipes
[1]**fluff** \'fləf\ *n* [prob. alter. of *flue* (fluff)] (1790) **1 :** NAP, DOWN **2 :** something fluffy **3 :** something inconsequential **4 :** BLUNDER; *esp* **:** an actor's lapse of memory
[2]**fluff** *vi* (1875) **1 :** to become fluffy **2 :** to make a mistake; *esp* **:** to forget or bungle one's lines in a play ~ *vt* **1 :** to make fluffy **2 a :** to spoil by a mistake **:** BOTCH **b :** to deliver badly or forget (one's lines) in a play
fluffy \'fləf-ē\ *adj* **fluff·i·er; -est** (1825) **1 a :** covered with or resembling fluff **b :** being light and soft or airy ⟨a ~ omelet⟩ **2 :** lacking in intellectual content or decisive quality ⟨vague, ~, uncertain policies — Geoffrey Crowther⟩ — **fluff·i·ly** \'fləf-ə-lē\ *adv* — **fluff·i·ness** \'fləf-ē-nəs\ *n*
flü·gel·horn *or* **flue·gel·horn** \'flü-gəl-ˌhȯ(ə)rn, 'flᵫe-\ *n* [G, fr. *flügel* wing, flank + *horn* horn; fr. its use to signal the flanking drivers in a battue] (1854) **:** a valved brass instrument resembling a cornet but having a larger bore — **flü·gel·horn·ist** \-əst\ *n*
[1]**flu·id** \'flü-əd\ *adj* [F or L; F *fluide,* fr. L *fluidus,* fr. *fluere* to flow; akin to Gk *phlyzein* to boil over] (1603) **1 a :** having particles that easily move and change their relative position without a separation of the mass and that easily yield to pressure **:** capable of flowing **b :** likely or tending to change or move ⟨boundaries became ~⟩ **2 :** characterized by or employing a smooth easy style ⟨the ballerina's ~ movements⟩ **3 a :** available for a different use **b :** easily converted into cash ⟨~ assets⟩ — **flu·id·ly** *adv* — **flu·id·ness** *n*
[2]**fluid** *n* (1661) **:** a substance (as a liquid or gas) tending to flow or conform to the outline of its container — **flu·id·al** \-əd-ᵊl\ *adj* — **flu·id·al·ly** \-ᵊl-ē\ *adv*
fluid drive *n* (1941) **:** an automotive power coupling that operates on a hydraulic turbine principle with the flywheel having a set of turbine blades connected directly to it and driving them in oil thereby turning another set of turbine blades attached to the transmission gears

\ə\ abut \ᵊ\ kitten, F table \ər\ further \a\ ash \ā\ ace \ä\ cot, cart \au̇\ out \ch\ chin \e\ bet \ē\ easy \g\ go \i\ hit \ī\ ice \j\ job \ŋ\ sing \ō\ go \ȯ\ law \ȯi\ boy \th\ thin \t͟h\ the \ü\ loot \u̇\ foot \y\ yet \zh\ vision \à, k̲, ⁿ, œ, ᵫ, ue, ᵫe, ʸ\ *see* Guide to Pronunciation

flu·id·ex·tract \ˌflü-ə-ˈdek-ˌstrakt\ *n* (1851) **:** an alcohol preparation of a vegetable drug containing the active constituents of one gram of the dry drug in each milliliter

flu·id·ic \flü-ˈid-ik\ *adj* (1960) **:** of, relating to, or being a device (as an amplifier or control) that depends for operation on the pressures and flows of a fluid in precisely shaped channels — **fluidic** *n* — **flu·id·ics** \-iks\ *n pl but sing in constr*

flu·id·i·ty \flü-ˈid-ət-ē\ *n* (1603) **1 :** the quality or state of being fluid **2 :** the physical property of a substance that enables it to flow

flu·id·ize \ˈflü-ə-ˌdīz\ *vt* **-ized; -iz·ing** (ca. 1855) **1 :** to cause to flow like a fluid **2 :** to suspend (as solid particles) in a rapidly moving stream of gas or vapor to induce flowing motion of the whole; *esp* **:** to fluidize the particles of (a loose bed of material) in an upward flow (as of a gas) for enhancing a chemical or physical reaction — **flu·id·iza·tion** \ˌflü-əd-ə-ˈzā-shən\ *n* — **flu·id·iz·er** \ˈflü-ə-ˌdī-zər\ *n*

fluid mechanics *n pl but sing or pl in constr* (ca. 1944) **:** a branch of mechanics dealing with the properties of liquids and gases

flu·id·ounce \ˌflü-ə-ˈdau̇n(t)s\ *n* (ca. 1882) **1 :** a U.S. unit of liquid capacity equal to 1/16 pint — see WEIGHT table **2 :** a British unit of liquid capacity equal to 1/20 pint — see WEIGHT table

flu·idram \ˌflü-ə(d)-ˈdram\ *n* [blend of [1]*fluid* and *dram*] (1880) **:** a unit of liquid capacity equal to 1/8 fluidounce — see WEIGHT table

[1]**fluke** \ˈflük\ *n* [ME, fr. OE *flōc;* akin to OHG *flah* smooth — more at FLAKE] (bef. 12c) **1 :** FLATFISH **2 :** a flattened digenetic trematode worm; *broadly* **:** TREMATODE — compare LIVER FLUKE

[2]**fluke** *n* [perh. fr. [1]*fluke*] (1561) **1 :** the part of an anchor that fastens in the ground — see ANCHOR illustration **2 :** a barbed head (as of a harpoon) **3 :** one of the lobes of a whale's tail

[3]**fluke** *n* [origin unknown] (1857) **1 :** an accidentally successful stroke at billiards or pool **2 :** a stroke of luck ⟨the discovery was a ~⟩

fluky *also* **fluk·ey** \ˈflü-kē\ *adj* **fluk·i·er; -est** (1867) **1 :** happening by or depending on chance **2 :** being unsteady or uncertain

flume \ˈflüm\ *n* [prob. fr. ME *flum* river, fr. OF, fr. L *flumen,* fr. *fluere* — more at FLUID] (1748) **1 :** an inclined channel for conveying water (as for power) **2 :** a ravine or gorge with a stream running through it

flum·mery \ˈfləm-(ə-)rē\ *n, pl* **-mer·ies** [W *llymru*] (ca. 1623) **1 a :** a soft jelly or porridge made with flour or meal **b :** any of several sweet desserts **2 :** MUMMERY, MUMBO JUMBO

flum·mox \ˈfləm-əks, -iks\ *vt* [origin unknown] (1837) **:** CONFUSE

[1]**flump** \ˈfləmp\ *vi* [imit.] (1816) **:** to move or fall suddenly and heavily ⟨~*ed* down into his chair⟩ ~ *vt* **:** to place or drop with a flump

[2]**flump** *n* (1832) **:** a dull heavy sound (as of a fall)

flung *past and past part of* FLING

[1]**flunk** \ˈfləŋk\ *vb* [perh. blend of *flinch* and *funk*] *vi* (1823) **:** to fail esp. in an examination or course ~ *vt* **1 :** to give a failing grade to **2 :** to get a failing grade in — **flunk·er** *n*

[2]**flunk** *n* (1846) **:** an act or instance of flunking

flunk out *vi* (1920) **:** to be dismissed from a school or college for failure ~ *vt* **:** to dismiss from a school or college for failure

flun·ky *or* **flun·key** \ˈfləŋ-kē\ *n, pl* **flunkies** *or* **flunkeys** [Sc, of unknown origin] (ca. 1782) **1 a :** a liveried servant **b :** one performing menial duties ⟨worked as a ~ in a lumber camp⟩ **2 :** YES-MAN

flu·o·cin·o·lone ac·e·to·nide \ˌflü-ə-ˈsin-ᵊl-ˌōn-ˌas-ə-ˈtō-ˌnīd\ *n* [*fluor-* + *cin-* (of unknown origin) + *-ol* + cortisone + *acetone* + *-ide*] (ca. 1966) **:** a glucocorticoid steroid $C_{24}H_{30}F_2O_6$ used esp. as an anti-inflammatory agent in the treatment of skin diseases

flu·or \ˈflü-ˌȯ(ə)r, ˈflü-ər\ *n* [NL, mineral belonging to a group used as fluxes and including fluorite, fr. L, flow, fr. *fluere* — more at FLUID] (1661) **:** FLUORITE

fluor- *or* **fluoro-** *comb form* [F, fr. *fluorine*] **1 :** fluorine ⟨*fluor*ide⟩ **2** *also* **fluori- :** fluorescence ⟨*fluoro*scope⟩ ⟨*fluori*meter⟩

flu·o·resce \ˌflu̇(-ə)r-ˈes, flōr-, flȯr-\ *vi* **-resced; -resc·ing** [back-formation fr. *fluorescence*] (1874) **:** to produce, undergo, or exhibit fluorescence — **flu·o·resc·er** *n*

flu·o·res·ce·in \-ˈes-ē-ən\ *n* (ca. 1876) **:** a yellow or red crystalline dye $C_{20}H_{12}O_5$ with a bright yellow-green fluorescence in alkaline solution

flu·o·res·cence \-ˈes-ᵊn(t)s\ *n* (1852) **:** emission of or the property of emitting electromagnetic radiation usu. as visible light resulting from and occurring only during the absorption of radiation from some other source; *also* **:** the radiation emitted

flu·o·res·cent \-ˈes-ᵊnt\ *adj* (1853) **1 :** having or relating to fluorescence **2 :** bright and glowing as a result of fluorescence ⟨a ~ pink⟩ — **fluorescent** *n*

fluorescent lamp *n* (1896) **:** a tubular electric lamp having a coating of fluorescent material on its inner surface and containing mercury vapor whose bombardment by electrons from the cathode provides ultraviolet light which causes the material to emit visible light

flu·o·ri·date \ˈflu̇r-ə-ˌdāt, ˈflōr-, ˈflȯr-\ *vt* **-dat·ed; -dat·ing** (1949) **:** to add a fluoride to (as drinking water) to reduce tooth decay — **flu·o·ri·da·tion** \ˌflu̇r-ə-ˈdā-shən, ˌflōr-, ˌflȯr-\ *n*

flu·o·ride \ˈflu̇(-ə)r-ˌīd\ *n* (1826) **1 :** a compound of fluorine with a more electropositive element or group **2 :** the monovalent anion of fluorine — **fluoride** *adj*

flu·o·ri·nate \ˈflu̇r-ə-ˌnāt, ˈflōr-, ˈflȯr-\ *vt* **-nat·ed; -nat·ing** (1929) **:** to treat or cause to combine with fluorine or a compound of fluorine — **flu·o·ri·na·tion** \ˌflu̇r-ə-ˈnā-shən, ˌflōr-, ˌflȯr-\ *n*

flu·o·rine \ˈflu̇(-ə)r-ˌēn, -ən\ *n* [F, fr. NL *fluor*] (1813) **:** a nonmetallic halogen element that is isolated as a pale yellowish flammable irritating toxic diatomic gas — see ELEMENT table

flu·o·rite \ˈflu̇(-ə)r-ˌīt\ *n* [It, fr. NL *fluor*] (1868) **:** a transparent or translucent mineral CaF_2 of different colors that consists of a fluoride of calcium and is used as a flux and in the making of opalescent and opaque glasses

flu·o·ro·car·bon \ˌflu̇(-ə)r-ō-ˈkär-bən\ *n* (ca. 1937) **:** any of various chemically inert compounds containing carbon and fluorine used chiefly as lubricants, refrigerants, nonstick coatings, and formerly aerosol propellants and in making resins and plastics

flu·o·ro·chrome \ˈflu̇(-ə)r-ə-ˌkrōm\ *n* (1943) **:** any of various fluorescent substances used in biological staining to produce fluorescence in a specimen

flu·o·rog·ra·phy \ˌflu̇(-ə)r-ˈäg-rə-fē\ *n* (1941) **:** PHOTOFLUOROGRAPHY — **flu·o·ro·graph·ic** \ˌflu̇(-ə)r-ə-ˈgraf-ik\ *adj*

flu·o·rom·e·ter \ˌflu̇(-ə)r-ˈäm-ət-ər\ *or* **flu·o·rim·e·ter** \-ˈim-\ *n* (1897) **:** an instrument for measuring fluorescence and related phenomena (as intensity of radiation) — **flu·o·ro·met·ric** *or* **flu·o·ri·met·ric** \ˌflu̇(-ə)r-ə-ˈme-trik\ *adj* — **flu·o·rom·e·try** \ˌflu̇(-ə)r-ˈäm-ə-trē\ *or* **flu·o·rim·e·try** \-ˈim-\ *n*

[1]**flu·o·ro·scope** \ˈflu̇r-ə-ˌskōp\ *n* [ISV] (1896) **:** an instrument used for observing the internal structure of an opaque object (as the living body) by means of X rays — **flu·o·ro·scop·ic** \ˌflu̇r-ə-ˈskäp-ik\ *adj* — **flu·o·ro·scop·i·cal·ly** \-i-k(ə-)lē\ *adv* — **flu·o·ros·co·pist** \ˌflu̇(-ə)r-ˈäs-kə-pəst\ *n* — **flu·o·ros·co·py** \-pē\ *n*

[2]**fluoroscope** *vt* **-scoped; -scop·ing** (1898) **:** to examine by fluoroscopy

flu·o·ro·sis \ˌflu̇(-ə)r-ˈō-səs\ *n* (1927) **:** an abnormal condition (as of the teeth) caused by fluorine or its compounds — **flu·o·rot·ic** \-ˈät-ik\ *adj*

flu·o·ro·ura·cil \ˌflu̇(-ə)r-ō-ˈyu̇r-ə-ˌsil, -ˌsəl\ *n* [*fluor-* + *uracil*] (ca. 1958) **:** a fluorine-containing pyrimidine base $C_4H_3FN_2O_2$ used to treat some kinds of cancer

flu·or·spar \ˈflu̇(-ə)r-ˌspär\ *n* (1794) **:** FLUORITE

flu·phen·azine \flü-ˈfen-ə-ˌzēn\ *n* [*fluor-* + *phenazine*] (ca. 1960) **:** a tranquilizing compound $C_{22}H_{26}F_3N_3OS$ used esp. combined as a salt

[1]**flur·ry** \ˈflər-ē, ˈflə-rē\ *n, pl* **flurries** [prob. fr. *flurr* (to throw scatteringly)] (1698) **1 a :** a gust of wind **b :** a brief light snowfall **2 :** a sudden agitated rush or disturbance ⟨a ~ of publicity⟩ ⟨caused a ~ at the meeting⟩ **3 :** a brief advance or decline in prices **:** a short-lived outburst of trading activity

[2]**flurry** *vb* **flur·ried; flur·ry·ing** *vt* (1757) **:** to cause to become agitated and confused ~ *vi* **:** to move in an agitated or confused manner

[1]**flush** \ˈfləsh\ *vb* [ME *flusshen*] *vi* (13c) **:** to take wing suddenly ~ *vt* **1 :** to cause (a bird) to flush **2 :** to expose or chase from a place of concealment ⟨~*ed* the boys from their hiding place⟩

[2]**flush** *n* [MF *flus, fluz,* fr. L *fluxus* flow, flux] (1529) **1 :** a hand of playing cards all of the same suit; *specif* **:** a poker hand containing five cards of the same suit but not in sequence — see POKER illustration **2 :** a series of three or more slalom gates set vertically on a slope

[3]**flush** *n* [perh. modif. of L *fluxus*] (1529) **1 :** a sudden flow (as of water); *also* **:** a rinsing or cleansing with or as if with a flush of water **2 a :** a sudden increase or expansion; *esp* **:** sudden and usu. abundant new plant growth **b :** a surge of emotion ⟨felt a ~ of anger at the insult⟩ **3 a :** a tinge of red **:** BLUSH **b :** a fresh and vigorous state ⟨in the first ~ of womanhood⟩ **4 :** a transitory sensation of extreme heat — compare HOT FLASH

[4]**flush** *vi* (1548) **1 :** to flow and spread suddenly and freely **2 a :** to glow brightly **b :** BLUSH ⟨~*ed* when she saw the picture⟩ **3 :** to produce new growth ⟨the plants ~*ed* twice during the year⟩ ~ *vt* **1 a :** to cause to flow **b :** to pour liquid over or through; *esp* **:** to cleanse or wash out with or as if with a rush of liquid ⟨~ the toilet⟩ ⟨~ the lungs with air⟩ **2 :** INFLAME, EXCITE — usu. used passively ⟨~*ed* with victory⟩ **3 :** to cause to blush

[5]**flush** *adj* (1594) **1 a :** full of life and vigor **:** LUSTY **b :** of a ruddy healthy color **2 a :** filled to overflowing **b :** AFFLUENT **3 :** readily available **:** ABUNDANT **4 a :** having or forming a continuous plane or unbroken surface ⟨~ paneling⟩ **b :** directly abutting or immediately adjacent: as **(1) :** set even with an edge of a type page or column **:** having no indention **(2) :** arranged edge to edge so as to fit snugly — **flush·ness** *n*

[6]**flush** *adv* (1700) **1 :** in a flush manner **2 :** SQUARELY ⟨hit him ~ on the chin⟩

[7]**flush** *vt* (1842) **:** to make flush ⟨~ the headings on a page⟩

[1]**flus·ter** \ˈfləs-tər\ *vb* **flus·tered; flus·ter·ing** \-t(ə-)riŋ\ [prob. of Scand origin; akin to Icel *flaustur* hurry] *vt* (1604) **1 :** to make tipsy **2 :** to put into a state of agitated confusion **:** UPSET ~ *vi* **:** to move or behave in an agitated or confused manner ***syn*** see DISCOMPOSE — **flus·tered·ly** *adv*

[2]**fluster** *n* (1728) **:** a state of agitated confusion

[1]**flute** \ˈflüt\ *n* [ME *floute,* fr. MF *flahute,* fr. OProv *flaut*] (14c) **1 a :** RECORDER 3 **b :** a keyed woodwind instrument consisting of a cylindrical tube which is stopped at one end and which has a side hole over which air is blown to produce the tone and having a range from middle C upward for three octaves **2 :** something shaped like a flute: as **a :** a tall slender wineglass **b :** a grooved pleat (as on a hat brim) **3 :** a rounded groove; *specif* **:** one of the vertical parallel grooves on a classical architectural column — **flute·like** \-ˌlīk\ *adj* — **fluty** *or* **flut·ey** \-ē\ *adj*

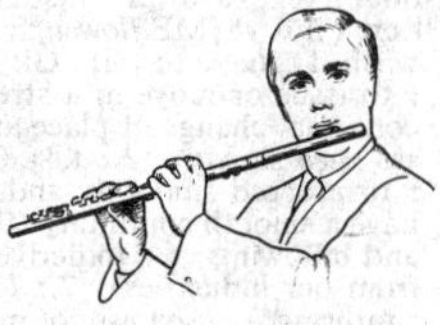

flute 1b

[2]**flute** *vb* **flut·ed; flut·ing** *vi* (14c) **1 :** to play a flute **2 :** to produce a flutelike sound ~ *vt* **1 :** to utter with a flutelike sound **2 :** to form flutes in — **flut·er** *n*

flut·ed *adj* (1611) **:** having or marked by grooves

flut·ing \ˈflüt-iŋ\ *n* (1728) **1 :** a series of flutes **:** FLUTE ⟨the ~ of a column⟩ **2 :** fluted material

flut·ist \ˈflüt-əst\ *n* (1603) **:** one who plays a flute

[1]**flut·ter** \ˈflət-ər\ *vb* [ME *floteren* to float, flutter, fr. OE *floterian,* freq. of *flotian* to float; akin to OE *flēotan* to float — more at FLEET] *vi* (bef. 12c) **1 :** to flap the wings rapidly **2 a :** to move with quick wavering or flapping motions ⟨flags ~*ing* in the wind⟩ **b :** to vibrate in irregular spasms **3 :** to move about or behave in an agitated aimless manner ~ *vt* **:** to cause to flutter — **flut·ter·er** \-ər-ər\ *n* — **flut·tery** \-ə-rē\ *adj*

[2]**flutter** *n* (1641) **1 :** an act of fluttering **2 a :** a state of nervous confusion or excitement **b :** FLURRY, COMMOTION **c :** abnormal spasmodic fluttering of a body part ⟨treatment of atrial ~⟩ **3 a :** a distortion in reproduced sound similar to but of a higher pitch than wow **b :** fluctuation in the brightness of a television image **4 :** an unwanted oscillation (as of an aileron or a bridge) set up by natural forces **5** *chiefly Brit* **:** a small speculative venture or gamble ⟨took a ~ on the ponies⟩

flut·ter·board \ˈflət-ər-ˌbō(ə)rd, -ˌbȯ(ə)rd\ *n* (1950) **:** a rectangular board used by swimmers in practicing leg strokes

flutter kick *n* (ca. 1934) **:** an alternating whipping motion of the legs used in various swimming styles (as the crawl)

flu·vi·al \ˈflü-vē-əl\ *adj* [L *fluvialis,* fr. *fluvius* river, fr. *fluere*] (14c) **1** : of, relating to, or living in a stream or river **2** : produced by stream action

flu·vi·a·tile \ˈflü-vē-ə-ˌtīl\ *adj* [MF, fr. L *fluviatilis,* irreg. fr. *fluvius*] (1599) : FLUVIAL

[1]**flux** \ˈfləks\ *n* [ME, fr. MF & ML; MF, fr. ML *fluxus,* fr. L, flow, fr. *fluxus,* pp. of *fluere* to flow — more at FLUID] (14c) **1** : a flowing of fluid from the body; *esp* : an excessive abnormal discharge from the bowels **2** : a continuous moving on or passing by (as of a stream) **3** : a continued flow : FLOOD **4 a** : INFLUX **b** : CHANGE, FLUCTUATION ⟨the program was in a state of ~⟩ **5 a** : a substance used to promote fusion esp. of metals or minerals **b** : a substance (as rosin) applied to surfaces to be joined by soldering, brazing, or welding to clean and free them from oxide and promote their union **6** : the rate of transfer of fluid, particles, or energy across a given surface

[2]**flux** *vt* (15c) **1** : to cause to become fluid **2** : to treat with a flux ~ *vi* : to become fluid : FUSE

flux gate *n* (1944) : a device used to indicate the direction and intensity of the magnetic field (as on a planet)

flux·ion \ˈflək-shən\ *n* (1606) **1** : the action of flowing or changing; *also* : something subjected to such action **2** : the derivative of a mathematical function — compare METHOD OF FLUXIONS — **flux·ion·al** \-shnəl, -shən-ᵊl\ *adj*

[1]**fly** \ˈflī\ *vb* **flew** \ˈflü\; **flown** \ˈflōn\; **fly·ing** [ME *flien,* fr. OE *flēogan;* akin to OHG *fliogan* to fly, OE *flōwan* to flow] *vi* (bef. 12c) **1 a** : to move in or pass through the air with wings **b** : to move through the air or before the wind ⟨clouds ~*ing* across the sky⟩; *also* : to move through outer space **c** : to float, wave, or soar in the air ⟨flags ~*ing* at half-mast⟩ **2 a** : to take flight : FLEE **b** : to fade and disappear : VANISH **3 a** : to move, pass, or spread quickly **b** : to be moved with sudden extreme emotion ⟨*flew* into a rage⟩ **c** : to seem to pass quickly ⟨our vacation simply *flew*⟩ **4** : to become expended or dissipated rapidly **5** : to pursue or attack in flight **6** : to operate or travel in an airplane or spacecraft **7** : to work successfully : win popular acceptance ⟨knew from past campaigns that a pure human-rights approach would not ~ —Charles Brydon⟩ ~ *vt* **1 a** : to cause to fly, float, or hang in the air ⟨~*ing* a kite⟩ **b** : to operate (as a balloon, aircraft, rocket, or spacecraft) in flight **c** : to journey over or through by flying **2 a** : to flee or escape from **b** : AVOID, SHUN **3** : to transport by aircraft or spacecraft — **fly at** : to assail suddenly and violently — **fly blind** : to fly an airplane solely by instruments — **fly contact** : to fly an airplane with the aid of visible landmarks or reference points — **fly high** : to be elated — **fly in the face of** *or* **fly in the teeth of** : to stand or act forthrightly or brazenly in defiance or contradiction of

[2]**fly** *n, pl* **flies** (bef. 12c) **1** : the action or process of flying : FLIGHT **2 a** : a device consisting of two or more radial vanes capable of rotating on a spindle to act as a fan or to govern the speed of clockwork or very light machinery **b** : FLYWHEEL **3** *pl* : the space over a theater stage where scenery and equipment can be hung **4** : something attached by one edge: as **a** : a garment closing concealed by a fold of cloth extending over the fastener **b** (1) : the length of an extended flag from its staff or support (2) : the outer or loose end of a flag **5** : a baseball hit high into the air **6** : FLYLEAF **7** : a sheet of material (as canvas) that is attachable to a tent for use as a double top or as a rooflike extension **8** : a football pass pattern in which the receiver runs straight downfield — **on the fly 1** : in motion : BUSY **2** : while still in the air : without the ball bouncing ⟨hit a long home run that carried 450 feet *on the fly*⟩

[3]**fly** *vi* **flied; fly·ing** (1893) : to hit a fly in baseball

[4]**fly** *n, pl* **flies** [ME *flie,* fr. OE *flēoge;* akin to OHG *flioga* fly, OE *flēogan* to fly] (bef. 12c) **1** : a winged insect — used chiefly in combination ⟨may*flies*⟩ ⟨butter*fly*⟩ **2** : TWO-WINGED FLY; *esp* : one that is large and stout-bodied **3** : a fishhook dressed (as with feathers or tinsel) to suggest an insect — **fly in the ointment** : a detracting factor or element

[5]**fly** *adj* [prob. fr. [1]*fly*] *chiefly Brit* (1811) : KEEN, ARTFUL

fly·able \ˈflī-ə-bəl\ *adj* (1936) : suitable for flying or for being flown

fly agaric *n* (1862) : a poisonous mushroom (*Amanita muscaria*) with a usu. bright red cap

fly ash *n* (1931) : fine solid particles of ashes, dust, and soot carried out from burning fuel (as coal or oil) by the draft

fly·away \ˈflī-ə-ˌwā\ *adj* (1775) **1** : lacking in order and practical sense : FLIGHTY ⟨an irresponsible, careless, ~ sort of person⟩ **2** : made loose and flowing esp. because of unconfined fullness at the back ⟨a ~ jacket⟩ **3 a** : ready to fly ⟨~ aircraft⟩ **b** : of or relating to an airplane that is ready to fly ⟨~ price⟩

fly ball *n* (1867) : [2]FLY 5

fly·belt \ˈflī-ˌbelt\ *n* (1894) : an area infested with tsetse fly

[1]**fly·blow** \-ˌblō\ *vt* **-blew; -blown** [[4]*fly* + [1]*blow*] (1603) **1** : to deposit eggs or young larvae of a flesh fly or blowfly in **2** : TAINT, CONTAMINATE

[2]**flyblow** *n* (ca. 1909) : FLY-STRIKE

fly·blown \ˈflī-ˌblōn\ *adj* (1529) **1 a** : not pure : TAINTED ⟨a world ~ with the vices of irresponsible power —V. L. Parrington⟩ **b** : not bright and new : SEEDY, MOTH-EATEN **c** : TRITE, HACKNEYED ⟨a long list of ~ metaphors —*Horizon*⟩ **2 a** : infested with eggs or young larvae of a flesh fly or blowfly **b** : covered with flyspecks

fly·boat \-ˌbōt\ *n* [modif. of D *vlieboot,* fr. *Vlie,* channel between North Sea & Wadden Zee + *boot* boat] (1577) : any of various fast boats

fly book *n* (1848) : a case usu. in the form of a book for fishing flies

fly–boy \ˈflī-ˌbȯi\ *n* (1946) : a member of the air force

fly bridge *n* (1965) : an open deck on a cabin cruiser located above the bridge on the cabin roof and usu. having a duplicate set of navigating equipment

fly·by \ˈflī-ˌbī\ *n, pl* **flybys** (1953) **1** : FLYOVER 1 **2 a** : a flight of a spacecraft past a celestial body (as Mars) close enough to obtain scientific data **b** : a spacecraft that makes a flyby

[1]**fly–by–night** \ˈflī-bə-ˌnīt\ *n* (1822) **1** : one that seeks to evade responsibilities and esp. creditors by flight **2** : one without established reputation or standing; *esp* : a shaky business enterprise

[2]**fly–by–night** *adj* (1914) **1** : given to making a quick profit usu. by shady or irresponsible acts **2** : TRANSITORY, PASSING ⟨~ fashions⟩

fly–by–night·er \ˌflī-bə-ˈnīt-ər\ *n* (1946) : FLY-BY-NIGHT

fly casting *n* (ca. 1889) : the casting of artificial flies in fly-fishing or as a competitive sport

fly·catch·er \ˈflī-ˌkach-ər, -ˌkech-\ *n* (1678) : a bird (order Passeriformes) that feeds on insects taken on the wing

fly dope *n* (1897) **1** : an insect repellent **2** : a dressing that makes fishing flies water-resistant so that they will float

fly·er *var of* FLIER

fly–fish·ing \ˈflī-ˌfish-iŋ\ *n* (1653) : a method of fishing in which an artificial fly is cast by use of a long flexible rod, a reel, and a relatively heavy oiled or treated line

fly front *n* (1893) : a concealed closing on the front of coats, skirts, shirts, dresses, or pants

fly gallery *n* (1888) : a narrow raised platform at the side of a theater stage from which flying scenery lines are operated

[1]**fly·ing** \ˈflī-iŋ\ *adj* (bef. 12c) **1 a** : moving or capable of moving in the air **b** : rapidly moving ⟨~ feet⟩ **c** : very brief **2** : intended for ready movement or action ⟨a ~ squad car⟩ **3** : having stylized wings — used esp. of livestock brand marks **4** : of or relating to the operation of aircraft ⟨belongs to a ~ club⟩ **5** : traversed or to be traversed (as in speed-record trials) after a running start ⟨~ kilometer⟩ ⟨~ mile⟩ — **with flying colors** : with complete or eminent success

[2]**flying** *n* (1565) **1** : travel by air **2** : the operation of an aircraft or spacecraft

flying boat *n* (1903) : a seaplane with a hull adapted for floating

flying bomb *n* (1944) : ROBOT BOMB

flying bridge *n* (1909) **1** : the highest navigational bridge on a ship **2** : FLY BRIDGE

flying buttress *n* (1669) : a masonry structure that typically consists of a straight inclined bar carried on an arch and a solid pier or buttress against which it abuts and that receives the thrust of a roof or vault

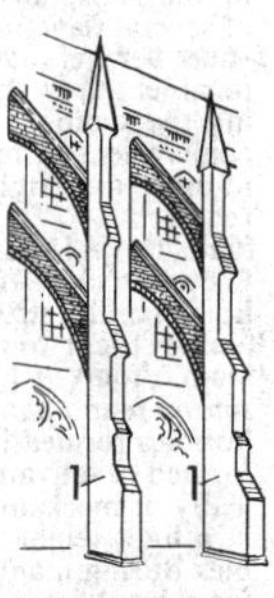

1 flying buttress

flying column *n* (1869) : a strong military detachment that operates at a distance from the main force

Flying Dutchman *n* **1** : a legendary Dutch mariner condemned to sail the seas until Judgment Day **2** : a spectral ship that according to legend haunts the seas near the Cape of Good Hope

flying field *n* (1916) : a field with a graded area for airplane landings and takeoffs

flying fish *n* (1511) : any of numerous fishes (family Exocoetidae) chiefly of tropical and warm seas that have long pectoral fins suggesting wings and are able to move some distance through the air

flying fox *n* (ca. 1759) : FRUIT BAT

flying gurnard *n* (ca. 1884) : any of several marine fishes (family Dactylopteridae) that resemble gurnards and have large pectoral fins allowing them to glide above the water for short distances

flying jib *n* (1711) : a sail outside the jib on an extension of the jibboom — see SAIL illustration

flying lemur *n* (ca. 1883) : either of two East Indian or Philippine arboreal nocturnal mammals (*Cynocephalus volans* and *C. variegatus*) that are about the size of a cat with a broad fold of skin from the neck to the tail on each side that embraces the limbs and forms a parachute used in making long sailing leaps and that is usu. isolated in a distinct order (Dermoptera)

flying machine *n* (1736) : an apparatus for navigating the air

flying mare *n* (1754) : a wrestling maneuver in which the aggressor seizes his opponent's wrist, turns about, and jerks him over his back

flying officer *n* (1913) : a commissioned officer in the British air force who ranks with a first lieutenant in the army

flying saucer *n* (1947) : any of various unidentified moving objects repeatedly reported as seen in the air and usu. described as being saucer-shaped or disk-shaped — called also *flying disk*

flying spot *n* (1933) : a spot of light that is moved over a surface (as one bearing printing or an image) so that light reflected from or transmitted by different parts of the surface is translated into electrical signals for transmission (as in television or computers)

flying squad *n* (1927) : a usu. small standby group of people ready to move or act swiftly; *esp* : a police unit formed to respond quickly in an emergency

flying squirrel *n* (1624) : either of two small nocturnal No. American squirrels (*Glaucomys volans* and *G. sabrinus*) with folds of skin connecting the forelegs and hind legs that enable it to make long gliding leaps; *also* : any of several similar squirrels

flying start *n* (ca. 1890) : a start in racing in which the participants are already moving when they cross the starting line or receive the starting signal

flying wedge *n* (1909) : a moving formation (as of guards or police) resembling a wedge

fly·leaf \ˈflī-ˌlēf\ *n* (1832) : one of the free endpapers of a book

fly·man \-mən, -ˌman\ *n* (1883) : a worker in the flies of a theater who manipulates curtains and scenery

fly net *n* (bef. 12c) : a net to exclude or keep off insects (as from a harness horse)

fly·over \ˈflī-ˌō-vər\ *n* (1931) **1** : a usu. low-altitude flight over a predesignated place by one or more airplanes **2** *Brit* : OVERPASS

fly·pa·per \-ˌpā-pər\ *n* (1847) : paper coated with a sticky often poisonous substance for killing flies

fly·past \-ˌpast\ *n, chiefly Brit* (1914) : FLYOVER 1

fly rod *n* (1684) : a light springy fishing rod used in fly casting

flysch \ˈflish\ *n* [G dial.] (ca. 1853) : a thick and extensive deposit largely of sandstone that is formed in a geosyncline adjacent to a rising mountain belt and is esp. common in the Alpine region of Europe

fly sheet *n* (1833) **1 :** a small loose advertising sheet : HANDBILL **2 :** a sheet of a folder, booklet, or catalog giving directions for the use of or information about the material that follows
fly·speck \ˈflī-ˌspek\ *n* (ca. 1847) **1 :** a speck made by fly excrement **2 :** something small and insignificant — **flyspeck** *vt*
fly–strike \-ˌstrīk\ *n* (1940) **:** infestation with fly maggots — **fly–struck** \-ˌstrək\ *adj*
fly·swat·ter \-ˌswät-ər\ *n* (1917) **:** a device for killing insects that consists of a flat piece of perforated rubber or plastic or fine-mesh wire netting attached to a handle
fly·ti·er \ˈflī-ˌtī(-ə)r\ *n* [*fly* + *tier* (one that ties)] (1881) **:** a maker of flies for fishing
flyt·ing \ˈflīt-iŋ\ *n* [ME, gerund of *fliten, flyten* to contend, argue, fr. OE *flītan;* akin to OHG *flīzan* to argue] (13c) **:** a dispute or exchange of personal abuse in verse form (as in an epic)
fly·way \ˈflī-ˌwā\ *n* (1891) **:** an established air route of migratory birds
fly·weight \-ˌwāt\ *n* (1911) **:** a boxer in a weight division having a maximum limit of 112 pounds — compare BANTAMWEIGHT
fly·wheel \-ˌhwēl, -ˌwēl\ *n* (1784) **:** a heavy wheel for opposing and moderating by its inertia any fluctuation of speed in the machinery with which it revolves; *also* **:** a similar wheel used for storing kinetic energy (as for motive power)
fly whisk *n* (1841) **:** a whisk for brushing away flies
FM \ˌef-ˌem\ *n* [*f*requency *m*odulation] (1940) **:** a broadcasting system using frequency modulation; *also* **:** a radio receiver of such a system — **FM** *adj*
FMN \ˌef-ˌem-ˈen\ *n* [*f*lavin *m*ono*n*ucleotide] (ca. 1953) **:** a yellow crystalline phosphoric ester $C_{17}H_{21}N_4O_9P$ of riboflavin that is a coenzyme of several flavoprotein enzymes — called also *flavin mononucleotide*
f–num·ber \ˈef-ˌnəm-bər\ *n* [*f*ocal length] (ca. 1903) **1 :** the ratio of the focal length to the aperture in an optical system **2 :** a number following the symbol f/ that expresses the effectiveness of the aperture of a camera lens in relation to brightness of image so that the smaller the number the brighter the image and therefore the shorter the exposure required
1foal \ˈfōl\ *n* [ME *fole,* fr. OE *fola;* akin to L *pullus* young of an animal, Gk *pais* child — more at FEW] (bef. 12c) **:** the young of an animal of the horse family; *esp* **:** one under one year
2foal *vi* (14c) **:** to give birth to a foal
1foam \ˈfōm\ *n* [ME *fome,* fr. OE *fām;* akin to OHG *feim* foam, L *spuma* foam, *pumex* pumice] (bef. 12c) **1 :** a light frothy mass of fine bubbles formed in or on the surface of a liquid: as **a :** a frothy mass formed in salivating or sweating **b :** a stabilized froth produced chemically or mechanically and used esp. in fighting oil fires **c :** a material in a lightweight cellular form resulting from introduction of gas bubbles during manufacture **2 :** SEA **3 :** something resembling foam — **foam·less** \-ləs\ *adj*
2foam *vi* (bef. 12c) **1 a :** to produce or form foam **b :** to froth at the mouth esp. in anger; *broadly* **:** to be angry **2 :** to gush out in foam **3 :** to become covered with or as if with foam ⟨streets . . . ~*ing* with life —Thomas Wolfe⟩ ~ *vt* **1 :** to cause to foam; *specif* **:** to cause air bubbles to form in **2 :** to convert (as a plastic) into a foam — **foam·able** \ˈfō-mə-bəl\ *adj* — **foam·er** \ˈfō-mər\ *n*
foamed plastic *n* (1937) **:** EXPANDED PLASTIC
foam·flow·er \ˈfōm-ˌflau̇(-ə)r\ *n* (1895) **:** an American woodland spring-flowering herb (*Tiarella cordifolia*) that has white flowers with very long stamens and no stem leaves — called also *false miterwort*
foam rubber *n* (ca. 1939) **:** spongy rubber of fine texture made from latex by foaming (as by whipping) before vulcanization
foamy \ˈfō-mē\ *adj* **foam·i·er; -est** (bef. 12c) **1 :** covered with foam **:** FROTHY **2 :** full of, consisting of, or resembling foam — **foam·i·ly** \-mə-lē\ *adv* — **foam·i·ness** \-mē-nəs\ *n*
1fob \ˈfäb\ *vt* **fobbed; fob·bing** [ME *fobben*] *archaic* (14c) **:** DECEIVE, CHEAT
2fob *n* [perh. akin to G dial. *fuppe* pocket] (1653) **1 :** WATCH POCKET **2 :** a short strap, ribbon, or chain attached esp. to a pocket watch **3 :** an ornament attached to a fob chain
fob off *vt* (1597) **1 :** to put off with a trick, excuse, or inferior substitute **2 :** to pass or offer (something spurious) as genuine **3 :** to put aside ⟨now *fob off* what once they would have welcomed eagerly —Walter Lippmann⟩
fo·cal \ˈfō-kəl\ *adj* (1693) **:** of, relating to, being, or having a focus — **fo·cal·ly** \-kə-lē\ *adv*
focal infection *n* (1923) **:** a persistent bacterial infection of some organ or region; *esp* **:** one causing symptoms elsewhere in the body
fo·cal·ize \ˈfō-kə-ˌlīz\ *vb* **-ized; -iz·ing** *vt* (1845) **1 :** to bring to a focus **2 :** LOCALIZE ~ *vi* **1 :** to come to a focus **:** CONCENTRATE **2 :** LOCALIZE — **fo·cal·iza·tion** \ˌfō-kə-lə-ˈzā-shən\ *n*
focal length *n* (1753) **:** the distance of a focus from the surface of a lens or concave mirror
focal plane *n* (1895) **:** a plane that is perpendicular to the axis of a lens or mirror and passes through the focus
focal point *n* (1928) **:** FOCUS 1a, 5a
focal ratio *n* (1926) **:** F-NUMBER 1
fo'c'sle *var of* FORECASTLE
1fo·cus \ˈfō-kəs\ *n, pl* **fo·ci** \ˈfō-ˌsī *also* -ˌkī\ *also* **fo·cus·es** [NL, fr. L, hearth] (1644) **1 a :** a point at which rays (as of light, heat, or sound) converge or from which they diverge or appear to diverge; *specif* **:** the point where the geometrical lines or their prolongations conforming to the rays diverging from or converging toward another point intersect and give rise to an image after reflection by a mirror or refraction by a lens or optical system **b :** a point of convergence of a beam of particles (as electrons) **2 a :** FOCAL LENGTH **b :** adjustment for distinct vision; *also* **:** the area that may be seen distinctly or resolved into a clear image **c :** a position in which something must be placed for clarity of perception ⟨tried to bring the issues into ~⟩ **d :** DIRECTION 6c **3 :** one of the fixed points that with the corresponding directrix defines a conic section **4 :** a localized area of disease or the chief site of a generalized disease or infection **5 a :** a center of activity, attraction, or attention ⟨the ~ of the meeting was drug abuse⟩ **b :** a point of concentration **6 :** the place of origin of an earthquake or moonquake **7 :** directed attention **:** EMPHASIS — **fo·cus·less** \-ləs\ *adj* — **in focus :** having or giving the proper sharpness of outline due to good focusing — **out of focus :** not in focus

2focus *vb* **fo·cused** *also* **fo·cussed; fo·cus·ing** *also* **fo·cus·sing** *vt* (1807) **1 :** to bring (as light rays) to a focus **:** CONCENTRATE **2 :** to cause to be concentrated ⟨~*ed* their attention on the most urgent problems⟩ **3 a :** to adjust the focus of (as the eye or a lens) **b :** to bring into focus ~ *vi* **1 :** to come to a focus **:** CONVERGE **2 :** to adjust one's eye or a camera to a particular range **3 :** to concentrate attention or effort — **fo·cus·able** \-kəs-ə-bəl\ *adj* — **fo·cus·er** *n*
fod·der \ˈfäd-ər\ *n* [ME, fr. OE *fōdor;* akin to OHG *fuotar* food — more at FOOD] (bef. 12c) **1 :** something fed to domestic animals; *esp* **:** coarse food for cattle, horses, or sheep **2 :** an often inferior person or thing that is used to supply a heavy demand ⟨routine entertainment ~⟩ — **fodder** *vt*
fod·gel \ˈfäj-əl\ *adj* [origin unknown] *Scot* (1724) **:** BUXOM
foe \ˈfō\ *n* [ME *fo,* fr. OE *fāh,* fr. *fāh,* adj., hostile; akin to OHG *gifēh* hostile] (bef. 12c) **1 :** one who has personal enmity for another **2 :** an enemy in war **:** ADVERSARY **3 :** one who opposes on principle ⟨a ~ of needless expenditures⟩ **4 :** something prejudicial or injurious
foehn *or* **föhn** \ˈfə(r)n, ˈfœn, ˈfān\ *n* [G *föhn*] (1865) **:** a warm dry wind blowing down the side of a mountain
foe·man \ˈfō-mən\ *n* (bef. 12c) **:** an enemy in war **:** FOE
foe·tal, foe·tus *chiefly Brit var of* FETAL, FETUS
foe·tid *var of* FETID
foeto- *or* **foeti-** — see FETO-
1fog \ˈfȯg, ˈfäg\ *n* [prob. of Scand origin; akin to Dan *fog* spray, shower; akin to L *pustula* blister, pimple, Gk *physan* to blow] (1544) **1 a :** vapor condensed to fine particles of water suspended in the lower atmosphere that differs from cloud only in being near the ground **b :** a fine spray or a foam for fire fighting **2 :** a murky condition of the atmosphere or a substance causing it **3 a :** a state of confusion or bewilderment **b :** something that confuses or obscures ⟨hid behind a ~ of rhetoric⟩ **4 :** cloudiness or partial opacity in a developed photographic image caused by chemical action or stray radiation — **fog·less** \-ləs\ *adj*
2fog *vb* **fogged; fog·ging** *vt* (1599) **1 :** to cover, envelop, or suffuse with or as if with fog ⟨~ the barns with pesticide⟩ **2 :** to make obscure or confusing ⟨accusations which *fogged* the real issues⟩ **3 :** to make confused **4 :** to produce fog on (as a photographic film) during development ~ *vi* **1 :** to become covered or thick with fog **2 a :** to become blurred by a covering of fog or mist **b :** to become indistinct through exposure to light or radiation
fog·bound \ˈfȯg-ˌbau̇nd, ˈfäg-\ *adj* (1855) **1 :** covered with or surrounded by fog ⟨~ coast⟩ **2 :** unable to move because of fog ⟨~ ship⟩
fog·bow \-ˌbō\ *n* (1831) **:** a nebulous arc or circle of white or yellowish light sometimes seen in fog
fog·dog \-ˌdȯg\ *n* (1867) **:** FOGBOW
fog·gage \ˈfȯg-ij, ˈfäg-\ *n, chiefly Scot* (15c) **:** MOSS
fog·gy \ˈfȯg-ē, ˈfäg-\ *adj* **fog·gi·er; -est** (1544) **1 a :** filled or abounding with fog **b :** covered or made opaque by moisture or grime **2 :** blurred or obscured as if by fog ⟨hadn't the *foggiest* notion⟩ — **fog·gi·ly** \ˈfȯg-ə-lē, ˈfäg-\ *adv* — **fog·gi·ness** \ˈfȯg-ē-nəs, ˈfäg-\ *n*
Foggy Bottom *n* [*Foggy Bottom,* district in Washington, D.C.] (1951) **:** the U.S. Department of State
fog·horn \ˈfȯg-ˌhȯ(ə)rn, ˈfäg-\ *n* (1858) **1 :** a horn (as on a ship) sounded in a fog to give warning **2 :** a loud hoarse voice
fo·gy *also* **fo·gey** \ˈfō-gē\ *n, pl* **fogies** *also* **fogeys** [origin unknown] (1780) **:** a person with old-fashioned ideas — usu. used with *old* — **fo·gy·ish** \-gē-ish\ *adj* — **fo·gy·ism** \-ˌiz-əm\ *n*
foi·ble \ˈfȯi-bəl\ *n* [obs. F (now *faible*), fr. obs. *foible* weak, fr. OF *feble* feeble] (1648) **1 :** the part of a sword or foil blade between the middle and point **2 :** a minor flaw or shortcoming in character or behavior **:** WEAKNESS ***syn*** see FAULT
foie gras \ˈfwä-ˈgrä\ *n* [F] (1818) **:** the fatted liver of an animal and esp. of a goose usu. served as a pâté
1foil \ˈfȯi(ə)l\ *vt* [ME *foilen* to trample, full cloth, fr. MF *fouler* — more at FULL] (14c) **1** *obs* **:** TRAMPLE **2 a :** to prevent from attaining an end **:** DEFEAT **b :** to bring to naught **:** THWART ***syn*** see FRUSTRATE
2foil *n* (1576) **1** *archaic* **:** DEFEAT **2** *archaic* **:** the track or trail of an animal **3 a :** a light fencing sword having a usu. circular guard and a flexible blade of rectangular section tapering to a blunted point — compare ÉPÉE, SABER **b :** the art or sport of fencing with the foil — often used in pl.
3foil *n* [ME, leaf, fr. MF *foille* (fr. L *folia,* pl. of *folium*) & *foil,* fr. L *folium* — more at BLADE] (14c) **1 a :** an indentation between cusps in Gothic tracery **b :** one of several arcs that enclose a complex figure **2 a :** very thin sheet metal **b :** a thin coat of tin or silver laid on the back of a mirror **3 :** a thin piece of material (as metal) put under an inferior or paste stone to add color or brilliance **4 :** one that serves as a contrast to another ⟨acted as a ~ for a comedian⟩ **5 :** HYDROFOIL 1
4foil *vt* (1611) **1 :** to back or cover with foil **2 :** to enhance by contrast
foiled \ˈfȯi(ə)ld\ *adj* (1835) **:** ornamented with foils ⟨a ~ arch⟩
foils·man \ˈfȯi(ə)lz-mən\ *n* (1927) **:** one who fences with a foil
1foin \ˈfȯin\ *vi* [ME *foinen,* fr. *foin* fork for spearing fish, fr. MF *foisne*] *archaic* (14c) **:** to thrust with a pointed weapon **:** LUNGE
2foin *n, archaic* (15c) **:** a pass in fencing **:** LUNGE
foi·son \ˈfȯiz-ᵊn\ *n* [ME *foisoun,* fr. MF *foison,* fr. L *fusion-, fusio* pouring, effusion — more at FUSION] (14c) **1** *archaic* **:** rich harvest **2** *chiefly Scot* **:** physical energy or strength **3** *pl, obs* **:** RESOURCES
foist \ˈfȯist\ *vt* [prob. fr. obs. D *vuisten* to take into one's hand, fr. MD *vuysten,* fr. *vuyst* fist; akin to OE *fȳst* fist] (1563) **1 a :** to introduce or insert surreptitiously or without warrant **b :** to force another to accept esp. by stealth or deceit **2 :** to pass off as genuine or worthy ⟨~ costly and valueless products on the public —Jonathan Spivak⟩
fo·la·cin \ˈfō-lə-sən\ *n* [*fol*ic *ac*id + *-in*] (ca. 1949) **:** FOLIC ACID
fo·late \ˈfō-ˌlāt\ *n* (1951) **:** FOLIC ACID
1fold \ˈfōld\ *n* [ME, fr. OE *falod;* akin to MLG *vālt* enclosure] (bef. 12c) **1 :** an enclosure for sheep **2 a :** a flock of sheep **b :** a group of people or institutions that share a common faith, belief, activity, or enthusiasm
2fold *vt* (bef. 12c) **:** to pen up or confine (as sheep) in a fold
3fold *vb* [ME *folden,* fr. OE *fealdan;* akin to OHG *faldan* to fold, Gk *diplasios* twofold] *vt* (bef. 12c) **1 :** to lay one part over another part of ⟨~ a letter⟩ **2 :** to reduce the length or bulk of by doubling over ⟨~ a

tent⟩ 3 : to clasp together : ENTWINE ⟨~ the hands⟩ 4 : to clasp or enwrap closely : EMBRACE 5 : to bend (as a layer of rock) into folds 6 a : to incorporate (a food ingredient) into a mixture by repeated gentle overturnings without stirring or beating b : to incorporate closely 7 : to bring to an end ~ *vi* 1 : to become doubled or pleated 2 : to fail completely : COLLAPSE; *esp* : to go out of business — **fold·able** \ˈfōl-də-bəl\ *adj*

⁴fold *n* (13c) 1 : a part doubled or laid over another part : PLEAT 2 : something that is folded together or that enfolds 3 a : a bend or flexure produced in rock by forces operative after the depositing or consolidation of the rock b *chiefly Brit* : an undulation in the landscape 4 : a margin apparently formed by the doubling upon itself of a flat anatomical structure (as a membrane) 5 : a crease made by folding something (as a newspaper)

-fold \ˌfōld, ˈfōld\ *suffix* [ME, fr. OE *-feald;* akin to OHG *-falt* -fold, L *-plex, -plus,* OE *fealdan*] 1 : multiplied by (a specified number) : times — in adjectives ⟨a twelve*fold* increase⟩ and adverbs ⟨repay you ten*fold*⟩ 2 : having (so many) parts ⟨three*fold* aspect of the problem⟩

fold·away \ˈfōl-də-ˌwā\ *adj* (1948) : designed to fold out of the way or out of sight ⟨~ doors⟩ ⟨~ bed⟩

fold·boat \ˈfōl(d)-ˌbōt\ *n* [trans. of G *faltboot*] (1938) : a small collapsible canoe made of rubberized sailcloth stretched over a framework

fold·boat·ing \-iŋ\ *n* (ca. 1961) : the sport of shooting rapids and cruising on swift water in a foldboat — **fold·boat·er** \-ər\ *n*

fold·er \ˈfōl-dər\ *n* (1552) 1 : one that folds 2 : a folded printed circular 3 : a folded cover or large envelope for holding or filing loose papers

fol·de·rol \ˈfäl-də-ˌräl\ *n* [*fol-de-rol,* a refrain in some old songs] (1820) 1 : a useless ornament or accessory : TRIFLE 2 : NONSENSE

folding door *n* (1611) : a door with jointed sections that can be folded together like an accordion

folding money *n* (1930) : PAPER MONEY

fold·out \ˈfōl-ˌdau̇t\ *n* (1950) : a folded leaf in a publication (as a book) that is larger in some dimension than the page

fo·li·a·ceous \ˌfō-lē-ˈā-shəs\ *adj* (1658) 1 : of, relating to, or resembling a foliage leaf 2 : consisting of thin laminae ⟨~ spar⟩

fo·liage \ˈfō-l(ē-)ij *also* -lyij\ *n* [MF *fuellage,* fr. *foille* leaf — more at FOIL] (1598) 1 : a representation of leaves, flowers, and branches for architectural ornamentation 2 : the aggregate of leaves of one or more plants produced in nature 3 : a cluster of leaves, flowers, and branches — **fo·liaged** \-l(ē-)ijd *also* -lyijd\ *adj*

foliage plant *n* (1862) : a plant grown primarily for its decorative foliage

fo·li·ar \ˈfō-lē-ər\ *adj* (ca. 1864) : of, by, relating to, or applied to leaves ⟨~ sprays⟩

¹fo·li·ate \ˈfō-lē-ət, -ˌāt\ *adj* [L *foliatus* leafy fr. *folium* leaf — more at BLADE] (1658) 1 : shaped like a leaf ⟨a ~ sponge⟩ 2 : FOLIATED

²foliate *n* (ca. 1920) : a foliated rock or stone tool ⟨bifacial ~*s*⟩

-fo·li·ate \-ət, -ˌāt\ *adj comb form* : having (such or so many) leaves or leaflets ⟨tri*foliate*⟩

fo·li·at·ed \-ˌāt-əd\ *adj* (1650) 1 : composed of or separable into layers ⟨a ~ rock⟩ 2 : ornamented with foils or a leaf design

fo·li·a·tion \ˌfō-lē-ˈā-shən\ *n* (1623) 1 a : the process of forming into a leaf b : the state of being in leaf c : VERNATION 2 : the numbering of the leaves of a manuscript or early printed book 3 a : ornamentation with foliage b : a decoration resembling a leaf 4 : the enrichment of an opening by foils 5 : the act of beating a metal into a thin plate or foil 6 : foliated texture

fo·lic acid \ˌfō-lik-\ *n* [L *folium*] (1941) : a crystalline vitamin $C_{19}H_{19}N_7O_6$ of the B complex that is used esp. in the treatment of nutritional anemias — called also *pteroylglutamic acid*

fo·lie à deux \fȯ-lē-ȧ-dœ̄, ˌfäl-ē-ˌäd-ˈə(r)\ *n* [F, lit., double madness] (ca. 1892) : the presence of the same or similar delusional ideas in two persons closely associated with one another

¹fo·lio \ˈfō-lē-ˌō\ *n, pl* **fo·li·os** [ME, fr. L, abl. of *folium*] (1533) 1 a : a leaf esp. of a manuscript or book b : a leaf number c : a page number d : an identifying reference in accounting used in posting 2 a : a sheet of paper folded once b : a case or folder for loose papers 3 a : the size of a piece of paper cut two from a sheet; *also* : paper or a page of this size b : a book printed on folio pages c : a book of the largest size 4 : a certain number of words taken as a unit or division in a document for purposes of measurement or reference

²folio *vt* (1858) : to put a serial number on each leaf or page of

-fo·li·o·late \ˈfō-lē-ə-ˌlāt\ *adj comb form* [LL *foliolum* leaflet, dim. of L *folium*] : having (such or so many) leaflets ⟨tri*foliolate*⟩

fo·li·ose \ˈfō-lē-ˌōs\ *adj* [L *foliosus* leafy] (ca. 1889) : having a flat, thin, and usu. lobed thallus attached to the substratum ⟨~ lichens⟩ — compare CRUSTOSE, FRUTICOSE

fo·li·um \ˈfō-lē-əm\ *n, pl* **fo·lia** \-lē-ə\ [NL, fr. L, leaf] (ca. 1889) : a thin layer occurring esp. in metamorphic rocks

¹folk \ˈfōk\ *n, pl* **folk** *or* **folks** [ME, fr. OE *folc;* akin to OHG *folc* people] (bef. 12c) 1 *archaic* : a group of kindred tribes forming a nation : PEOPLE 2 : the great proportion of the members of a people that determines the group character and that tends to preserve its characteristic form of civilization and its customs, arts and crafts, legends, traditions, and superstitions from generation to generation 3 *pl* : a certain kind or class of people ⟨old ~*s*⟩ ⟨just plain ~⟩ 4 *folks pl* : people generally 5 *folks pl* : the persons of one's own family; *esp* : PARENTS

²folk *adj* (bef. 12c) 1 : originating or traditional with the common people of a country or region and typically reflecting their life-style 2 : of or relating to the common people or to the study of the common people ⟨~ sociology⟩

folk etymology *n* (1882) : the transformation of words so as to give them an apparent relationship to other better-known or better-understood words (as in the change of Spanish *cucaracha* to English *cockroach*)

¹folk·ie *also* **folky** \ˈfō-kē\ *n, pl* **folkies** (1965) : a folk singer or instrumentalist

²folkie *or* **folky** *adj* (1965) : of or relating to folk music

folk·ish \ˈfō-kish\ *adj* (1938) : FOLKLIKE — **folk·ish·ness** *n*

folk·like \ˈfō-ˌklīk\ *adj* (1939) : having a folk character

folk·lore \ˈfō-ˌklō(ə)r, -ˌklȯ(ə)r\ *n* (1846) 1 : traditional customs, tales, sayings, or art forms preserved among a people 2 : a branch of knowledge that deals with folklore 3 : a widely held unsupported notion or body of notions — **folk·lor·ic** \-ˌklōr-ik, -ˌklȯr-\ *adj* — **folk·lor·ish** \-ish\ *adj* — **folk·lor·ist** \-əst\ *n* — **folk·lor·is·tic** \ˌfō-ˌklōr-ˈis-tik, -ˌklȯr-\ *adj*

folk mass *n* (1966) : a mass in which traditional liturgical music is replaced by folk music

folk medicine *n* (1878) : traditional medicine as practiced nonprofessionally by people isolated from modern medical services and involving esp. the use of vegetable remedies on an empirical basis

folk·moot \ˈfōk-ˌmüt\ *or* **folk·mote** \-ˌmōt\ *n* [alter. of OE *folcmōt, folcgemōt,* fr. *folc* people + *mōt, gemōt* meeting — more at MOOT] (bef. 12c) : a general assembly of the people (as of a shire) in early England

folk·sing·er \-ˌsiŋ-ər\ *n* (1884) : one who sings folk songs or sings in a style associated with folk songs — **folk·sing·ing** \-ˌsiŋ-iŋ\ *n*

folk song *n* (1870) : a traditional or composed song typically characterized by stanzaic form, refrain, and simplicity of melody

folksy \ˈfōk-sē\ *adj* **folks·i·er; -est** [*folks* + *-y*] (1852) 1 : SOCIABLE, FRIENDLY 2 : informal, casual, or familiar in manner or style ⟨~ humor⟩ — **folks·i·ly** \-sə-lē\ *adv* — **folks·i·ness** \-sē-nəs\ *n*

folk·tale \ˈfōk-ˌtāl\ *n* (1852) : a characteristically anonymous, timeless, and placeless tale circulated orally among a people

folk·way \ˈfō-ˌkwā\ *n* (ca. 1906) : a mode of thinking, feeling, or acting common to a given group of people; *esp* : a traditional social custom

fol·li·cle \ˈfäl-i-kəl\ *n* [NL *folliculus,* fr. L, dim. of *follis* bag — more at FOOL] (1646) 1 a : a small anatomical cavity or deep narrow-mouthed depression b : a small lymph node c : a vesicle in the mammalian ovary that contains a developing egg surrounded by a covering of cells; *esp* : GRAAFIAN FOLLICLE 2 : a dry dehiscent one-celled many-seeded fruit that has a single carpel and opens along only one suture — **fol·lic·u·lar** \fə-ˈlik-yə-lər, fä-\ *adj*

follicle mite *n* (ca. 1925) : any of several minute mites (genus *Demodex*) parasitic in hair follicles

follicle–stimulating hormone *n* (ca. 1943) : a hormone from an anterior lobe of the pituitary gland that stimulates the growth of the ovum-containing follicles in the ovary and activates sperm-forming cells

fol·lic·u·lin \fə-ˈlik-yə-lən, fä-\ *n* [NL *folliculus* + E *-in*] (1928) : ESTROGEN; *esp* : ESTRONE

¹fol·low \ˈfäl-(ˌ)ō, -ə(-w)\ *vb* [ME *folwen,* fr. OE *folgian;* akin to OHG *folgēn* to follow] *vt* (bef. 12c) 1 : to go, proceed, or come after ⟨~*ed* the guide⟩ 2 a : to pursue in an effort to overtake b : to seek to attain ⟨~ knowledge⟩ 3 a : to accept as authority : OBEY ⟨~*ed* his conscience⟩ b : to be or act in accordance with ⟨~ directions⟩ 4 : to copy after : IMITATE 5 a : to walk or proceed along ⟨~ a path⟩ b : to engage in as a calling or way of life : PURSUE ⟨wheat-growing is generally ~*ed* here⟩ 6 a : to come or take place after in time, sequence, or order b : to cause to be followed ⟨~*ed* dinner with a liqueur⟩ 7 : to come into existence or take place as a result or consequence of ⟨disaster ~*ed* the blunder⟩ 8 a : to watch steadily ⟨~*ed* the ball over the fence⟩ b : to keep the mind on ⟨~ a speech⟩ c : to attend closely to : keep abreast of ⟨she ~*ed* his career with interest⟩ d : to understand the sense or logic of (as a line of thought) ~ *vi* 1 : to go or come after a person or thing in place, time, or sequence 2 : to result or occur as a consequence, effect, or inference

syn FOLLOW, SUCCEED, ENSUE, SUPERVENE mean to come after something or someone. FOLLOW may apply to a coming after in time, position, or logical sequence; SUCCEED implies a coming after immediately in a sequence determined by natural order, inheritance, election, or laws of rank; ENSUE commonly suggests a logical consequence or naturally expected development; SUPERVENE suggests the following or beginning of something unforeseen or unpredictable. ***syn*** see in addition CHASE

— **follow one's nose** 1 : to go in a straight or obvious course 2 : to proceed without plan or reflection : obey one's instincts — **follow suit** 1 : to play a card of the same suit as the card led 2 : to follow an example set

²follow *n* (1870) 1 : the act or process of following 2 : forward spin given to a ball by striking it above center — compare DRAW

fol·low·er \ˈfäl-ə-wər\ *n* (bef. 12c) 1 a : one in the service of another : RETAINER b : one that follows the opinions or teachings of another c : one that imitates another 2 *archaic* : one that chases 3 : a sheet added to the first sheet of an indenture or other deed 4 : a machine part that receives motion from another part 5 : a spring-loaded plate at the bottom of a firearm's magazine that angles cartridges for proper insertion into the chamber 6 : FAN, DEVOTEE

syn FOLLOWER, ADHERENT, DISCIPLE, PARTISAN mean one who attaches himself to another. FOLLOWER may apply to a person who attaches himself either to the person or beliefs of another; ADHERENT suggests a close and persistent attachment; DISCIPLE implies a devoted allegiance to the teachings of one chosen as a master; PARTISAN suggests a zealous often prejudiced attachment.

fol·low·er·ship \-ˌship\ *n* (ca. 1928) 1 : FOLLOWING 2 : the capacity or willingness to follow a leader

¹fol·low·ing \ˈfäl-ə-wiŋ\ *adj* (14c) 1 : being next in order or time ⟨the ~ day⟩ 2 : listed or shown next ⟨trains will leave at the ~ times⟩

²following *n* (15c) : a group of followers, adherents, or partisans

³following *prep* (ca. 1926) : subsequent to ⟨~ the lecture tea was served⟩

fol·low–on \ˈfäl-ə-ˌwȯn, -ˌwän\ *adj* (1926) : being or relating to something (as an object, technique, or event) held to be a second or later generation in development of the thing ⟨a ~ bomber⟩ — **follow–on** *n*

follow out *vt* (1762) 1 : to follow to the end or to a conclusion 2 : CARRY OUT, EXECUTE ⟨*followed out* his orders⟩

follow shot *n* (ca. 1909) 1 : a shot in billiards or pool made by striking the cue ball above its center to cause it to continue forward after striking the object ball 2 : a camera shot in which the camera follows the movement of the subject

fol·low–through \ˈfäl-ō-ˌthrü, ˌfäl-ō-ˈ, -ə-\ *n* (1897) 1 : the act or an instance of following through 2 : the part of the stroke following the striking of a ball

\ə\ abut \ᵊ\ kitten, F table \ər\ further \a\ ash \ā\ ace \ä\ cot, cart \au̇\ out \ch\ chin \e\ bet \ē\ easy \g\ go \i\ hit \ī\ ice \j\ job \ŋ\ sing \ō\ go \ȯ\ law \ȯi\ boy \th\ thin \t͟h\ the \ü\ loot \u̇\ foot \y\ yet \zh\ vision \ȧ, k̟, ⁿ, œ, œ̄, ue, ue̅, ʸ\ *see* Guide to Pronunciation

follow through *vi* (1897) **1 :** to continue a stroke or motion to the end of its arc **2 :** to press on in an activity or process esp. to a conclusion

[1]**fol·low–up** \ˈfäl-ə-ˌwəp\ *n* (1795) **1 a :** the act or an instance of following up **b :** something that follows up **2 :** maintenance of contact with or reexamination of a person (as a patient) esp. following treatment **3 :** a news story presenting new information on a story published earlier

[2]**follow–up** \ˌfäl-ə-ˌwəp\ *adj* (1915) **1 :** of, relating to, or being something that follows up ⟨~ action by the police —Frank Faulkner⟩ **2 :** done, conducted, or administered in the course of following up persons esp. after institutionalization ⟨~ care for discharged hospital patients⟩

follow up \ˌfäl-ə-ˈwəp\ *vt* (1792) **1 :** to follow with something similar, related, or supplementary ⟨*following up* his convictions with action —G. P. Merrill⟩ **2 :** to maintain contact with (a person) so as to monitor the effects of earlier activities or treatments **3 :** to pursue in an effort to take further action ⟨the police *follow up* leads⟩ **~** *vi* **:** to take appropriate action ⟨*follow up* on . . . complaints, and customer suggestions — *Marketing*⟩

fol·ly \ˈfäl-ē\ *n, pl* **follies** [ME *folie,* fr. OF, fr. *fol* fool] (13c) **1 :** lack of good sense or normal prudence and foresight **2 :** a foolish act or idea **3 a** *obs* **:** EVIL, WICKEDNESS; *esp* **:** lewd behavior **b :** criminally or tragically foolish actions or conduct **4 :** an excessively costly or unprofitable undertaking **5 :** an often extravagant picturesque building erected to suit a fanciful taste

Fol·som \ˈfōl-səm\ *adj* [*Folsom,* N.M.] (1928) **:** of or relating to a prehistoric culture of No. America on the east side of the Rocky mountains that is characterized by flint projectile points having a concave base with side projections and a longitudinal groove on each face

fo·ment \ˈfō-ˌment, fō-ˈ\ *vt* [ME *fomenten,* fr. LL *fomentare,* fr. L *fomentum* fomentation, fr. *fovēre* to warm, fondle, foment — more at FEVER] (14c) **1 :** to treat with moist heat (as for easing pain) **2 :** to promote the growth or development of **:** ROUSE, INCITE ⟨~ a rebellion⟩ ***syn*** see INCITE — **fo·ment·er** *n*

fo·men·ta·tion \ˌfō-mən-ˈtā-shən, -ˌmen-\ *n* (15c) **1 a :** the application of hot moist substances to the body to ease pain **b :** the material so applied **2 :** the act of fomenting **:** INSTIGATION

[1]**fond** \ˈfänd\ *adj* [ME, fr. *fonne* fool] (14c) **1 :** FOOLISH, SILLY ⟨~ pride⟩ **2 a :** prizing highly **:** DESIROUS ⟨~ of praise⟩ **b :** having an affection or liking — used with *of* ⟨~ of music⟩ **3 a :** foolishly tender **:** INDULGENT ⟨a ~ mother⟩ **b :** AFFECTIONATE, LOVING ⟨a ~ wife⟩ ⟨absence makes the heart grow *~er*⟩ **4 :** cherished with great affection **:** doted on ⟨our *~est* hopes⟩

[2]**fond** *vi, obs* (1530) **:** to be foolish **:** DOTE

[3]**fond** \ˈfōⁿ\ *n, pl* **fonds** \ˈfōⁿ(z)\ [F, fr. L *fundus* bottom, piece of property — more at BOTTOM] (1664) **1 :** BACKGROUND, BASIS **2** *obs* **:** FUND

fon·dant \ˈfän-dənt\ *n* [F, fr. prp. of *fondre* to melt — more at FOUND] (1877) **1 :** a soft creamy preparation of sugar, water, and flavorings that is used as a basis for candies or icings **2 :** a candy consisting chiefly of fondant

fon·dle \ˈfän-dᵊl\ *vb* **fon·dled; fon·dling** \-(d)liŋ, -dᵊl-iŋ\ [freq. of obs. *fond* to fondle] *vt* (1694) **1** *obs* **:** PAMPER **2 :** to handle tenderly, lovingly, or lingeringly **:** CARESS **~** *vi* **:** to show affection or desire by caressing — **fon·dler** \-(d)lər, -dᵊl-ər\ *n*

fond·ly \ˈfän-(d)lē\ *adv* (14c) **1** *archaic* **:** in a foolish manner **:** FOOLISHLY **2 :** in a fond manner **:** AFFECTIONATELY **3 :** in a willingly credulous manner ⟨~ imagine that human beings today think faster — Warwick Braithwaite⟩

fond·ness \ˈfän(d)-nəs\ *n* (14c) **1** *obs* **:** FOOLISHNESS, FOLLY **2 :** tender affection **3 :** APPETITE, RELISH ⟨had a ~ for argument⟩

fon·due *also* **fon·du** \fän-ˈd(y)ü, ˈfän-ˌ\ *n* [F *fondue,* fr. fem. of *fondu,* pp. of *fondre* to melt, fr. MF — more at FOUND] (1878) **1 a (1) :** a preparation of melted cheese (as Swiss cheese and Gruyère) usu. flavored with white wine and kirsch **(2) :** a dish that consists of small pieces of food (as meat or fruit) cooked in or dipped into a hot liquid ⟨beef ~⟩ ⟨chocolate ~⟩ **b :** a chafing dish in which fondue is made **2 :** a baked dish similar to a soufflé usu. made with cheese and bread crumbs

F_1 layer \ˈef-ˈwən-\ *n* (1933) **:** the lower of the two layers into which the F region of the ionosphere splits in the daytime occurring at varying heights from about 80 to 120 miles (130 to 200 kilometers) above the earth's surface

[1]**font** \ˈfänt\ *n* [ME, fr. OE, fr. LL *font-, fons,* fr. L, fountain] (bef. 12c) **1 a :** a receptacle for baptismal water **b :** a receptacle for holy water **c :** a receptacle for various liquids **2 :** SOURCE, FOUNTAIN ⟨a ~ of information⟩ — **font·al** \ˈfänt-ᵊl\ *adj*

[2]**font** *n* [MF *fonte* act of founding, fr. (assumed) VL *fundita,* fem. of *funditus,* pp. of L *fundere* to found, pour — more at FOUND] (1683) **:** an assortment or set of type all of one size and style

fon·ta·nel *or* **fon·ta·nelle** \ˌfänt-ᵊn-ˈel, ˈfänt-ᵊn-ˌ\ *n* [ME *fontinelle* a bodily hollow or pit, fr. MF *fontenele,* dim. of *fontaine* fountain] (1741) **:** a membrane-covered opening in bone or between bones; *specif* **:** any of the spaces closed by membranous structures between the uncompleted angles of the parietal bones and the neighboring bones of a fetal or young skull

fon·ti·na \fän-ˈtē-nə\ *n, often cap* [It] (1938) **:** a cheese that is semisoft to hard in texture and mild to medium sharp in flavor

food \ˈfüd\ *n, often attrib* [ME *fode,* fr. OE *fōda;* akin to OHG *fuotar* food, fodder, L *panis* bread, *pascere* to feed] (bef. 12c) **1 a :** material consisting essentially of protein, carbohydrate, and fat used in the body of an organism to sustain growth, repair, and vital processes and to furnish energy; *also* **:** such food together with supplementary substances (as minerals, vitamins, and condiments) **b :** inorganic substances absorbed by plants in gaseous form or in water solution **2 :** nutriment in solid form **3 :** something that nourishes, sustains, or supplies ⟨~ for thought⟩ — **food·less** \-ləs\ *adj* — **food·less·ness** *n*

food chain *n* (1926) **:** an arrangement of the organisms of an ecological community according to the order of predation in which each uses the next usu. lower member as a food source

food cycle *n* (1925) **:** a group of food chains constituting all or most of the food relations that enable an ecological community to survive

food poisoning *n* (1887) **:** an acute gastrointestinal disorder caused by bacteria or their toxic products or by chemical residues in food

food processor *n* (1974) **:** an electric kitchen appliance with a set of interchangeable blades revolving inside a container

food pyramid *n* (1949) **:** an ecological hierarchy of food relationships esp. when expressed quantitatively (as in mass, numbers, or energy) in which a chief predator is at the top, each level preys on the next lower level, and usu. green plants are at the bottom

food stamp *n* (1940) **:** a government-issued coupon that is sold or given to low-income persons and is redeemable for food

food·stuff \ˈfüd-ˌstəf\ *n* (1872) **:** a substance with food value; *specif* **:** the raw material of food before or after processing

food vacuole *n* (ca. 1889) **:** a vacuole (as in an amoeba) in which ingested food is digested

food web *n* (1949) **:** the totality of interacting food chains in an ecological community

foo·fa·raw \ˈfü-fə-ˌrȯ\ *n* [origin unknown] (ca. 1934) **1 :** frills and flashy finery **2 :** a disturbance or to-do over a trifle **:** FUSS

[1]**fool** \ˈfül\ *n* [ME, fr. OF *fol,* fr. LL *follis,* fr. L, bellows, bag; akin to L *flare* to blow — more at BLOW] (13c) **1 :** a person lacking in judgment or prudence **2 a :** a retainer formerly kept in great households to provide casual entertainment and commonly dressed in motley with cap, bells, and bauble **b :** one who is victimized or made to appear foolish **:** DUPE **3 a :** a harmlessly deranged person or one lacking in common powers of understanding **b :** one with a marked propensity or fondness for something ⟨a dancing ~⟩ ⟨a ~ for candy⟩ **4 :** a cold dessert of pureed fruit mixed with whipped cream or custard

[2]**fool** *adj* (13c) **:** FOOLISH, SILLY ⟨barking his ~ head off⟩

[3]**fool** *vt* (1548) **1 :** to spend on trifles or without advantage **:** FRITTER — used with *away* **2 :** to make a fool of **:** DECEIVE **3** *obs* **:** INFATUATE **~** *vi* **1 a :** to spend time idly or aimlessly ⟨just *~ing* around all day⟩ **b :** to meddle, tamper, or experiment esp. thoughtlessly or ignorantly ⟨don't ~ with that gun⟩ **2 a :** to play or improvise a comic role **b :** to speak in jest **:** JOKE ⟨I was only *~ing*⟩ **3 :** to contend or fight without serious intent or with less than full strength **:** TOY ⟨a dangerous man to ~ with⟩

fool around *vi* (1837) **:** to engage in casual sexual activity

fool·ery \ˈfül-(ə-)rē\ *n, pl* **-er·ies** (1552) **1 :** a foolish act, utterance, or belief **2 :** foolish behavior

fool·har·dy \ˈfül-ˌhärd-ē\ *adj* (13c) **:** foolishly adventurous and bold **:** RASH ***syn*** see ADVENTUROUS — **fool·har·di·ly** \-ˌhärd-ᵊl-ē\ *adv* — **fool·har·di·ness** \-ˌhärd-ē-nəs\ *n*

fool·ish \ˈfü-lish\ *adj* (14c) **1 :** marked by or proceeding from folly **2 a :** ABSURD, RIDICULOUS **b :** marked by a loss of composure **:** NONPLUSSED, ABASHED **3 :** INSIGNIFICANT, TRIFLING, HUMBLE ***syn*** see SIMPLE — **fool·ish·ly** *adv*

fool·ish·ness *n* (15c) **1 :** foolish behavior **:** FOLLY **2 :** a foolish act or idea

fool·proof \ˈfül-ˈprüf\ *adj* (1902) **:** so simple, plain, or reliable as to leave no opportunity for error, misuse, or failure ⟨a ~ plan⟩

fools·cap *or* **fool's cap** \ˈfül-ˌskap\ *n* (1632) **1 :** a cap or hood usu. with bells worn by jesters **2 :** a conical cap for slow or lazy students **3** [fr. the watermark of a foolscap formerly applied to such paper] *usu foolscap* **:** a size of paper formerly standard in Great Britain; *broadly* **:** a piece of writing paper

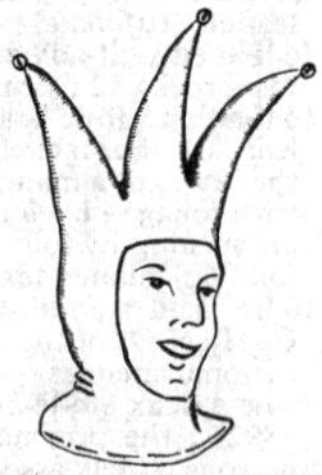

foolscap 1

fool's gold *n* (1872) **1 :** PYRITE **2 :** CHALCOPYRITE

fool's paradise *n* (15c) **:** a state of delusory happiness

fool's parsley *n* (ca. 1836) **:** a poisonous European weed (*Aethusa cynapium*) of the carrot family resembling parsley

[1]**foot** \ˈfu̇t\ *n, pl* **feet** \ˈfēt\ *also* **foot** [ME *fot,* fr. OE *fōt;* akin to OHG *fuot* foot, L *ped-, pes,* Gk *pod-, pous*] (bef. 12c) **1 :** the terminal part of the vertebrate leg upon which an individual stands **2 :** an invertebrate organ of locomotion or attachment; *esp* **:** a ventral muscular surface or process of a mollusk **3 :** any of various units of length based on the length of the human foot; *esp* **:** a unit equal to $^1/_3$ yard and comprising 12 inches — *pl foot* used between a number and a noun ⟨a 10-*foot* pole⟩; *pl feet* or *foot* used between a number and an adjective ⟨6 *feet* tall⟩; see WEIGHT table **4 :** the basic unit of verse meter consisting of any of various fixed combinations or groups of stressed and unstressed or long and short syllables **5 a :** motion or power of walking or running **:** STEP ⟨fleet of ~⟩ **b :** SPEED, SWIFTNESS ⟨showed early ~⟩ **6 :** something resembling a foot in position or use **:** BASE: as **a :** the lower end of the leg of a chair or table **b (1) :** the basal portion of the sporogonium in mosses **(2) :** a specialized outgrowth by which the embryonic sporophyte of many ferns and related plants and some seed plants absorbs nourishment from the gametophyte **c :** a piece on a sewing machine that presses the cloth against the feed **7** *foot pl, chiefly Brit* **:** INFANTRY **8 :** the lower edge (as of a sail) **9 :** the lowest part **:** BOTTOM ⟨the ~ of the hill⟩ **10 a :** the end that is lower or opposite the head ⟨the ~ of the bed⟩ **b :** the part (as of a stocking) that covers the foot **11 foots** *pl but sing or pl in constr* **:** material deposited esp. in aging or refining **:** DREGS **12 foots** *pl* **:** FOOTLIGHTS — **at one's feet :** under one's spell or influence — **foot in the door :** the initial step toward a goal — **off one's feet :** in a sitting or lying position — **on foot :** by walking or running ⟨tour the campus *on foot*⟩ — **on one's feet 1 :** in a standing position **2 :** in an established position or state **3 :** in a recovered condition (as from illness) **4 :** in an extemporaneous manner ⟨good debaters can think *on their feet*⟩ — **to one's feet :** to a standing position

[2]**foot** *vi* (15c) **1 :** DANCE **2 :** to go on foot **3** *of a sailboat* **:** to make speed **:** MOVE **~** *vt* **1 a :** to perform the movements of (a dance) **b :** to walk, run, or dance on, over, or through **2** *archaic* **a :** KICK **b :** REJECT **3** *archaic* **:** ESTABLISH **4 a :** to add up **b :** to pay or stand credit for ⟨agreed to ~ the bill⟩ **5 :** to make or renew the foot of (as a stocking)

foot·age \ˈfu̇t-ij\ *n* (1892) **:** length or quantity expressed in feet: as **a :** BOARD FEET **b :** the total number of running feet of motion-picture film used (as for a scene or subject); *also* **:** the material contained on such footage

foot–and–mouth disease *n* (1862) **:** an acute contagious febrile virus disease esp. of cloven-footed animals marked by ulcerating vesicles in

the mouth, about the hoofs, and on the udder and teats — called also *foot-and-mouth, hoof-and-mouth disease*
foot·ball \'fu̇t-ˌbȯl\ *n* (15c) **1 :** any of several games played between two teams on a rectangular field having two goalposts at each end and whose object is to get the ball over a goal line or between goalposts by running, passing, or kicking: as **a** *Brit* **:** SOCCER **b** *Brit* **:** RUGBY **c :** an American game played between two teams of 11 players each in which the ball is in possession of one side at a time and is advanced by running or passing **d** *Austral* **:** AUSTRALIAN RULES FOOTBALL **e** *Canad* **:** CANADIAN FOOTBALL **2 a :** an inflated oval ball used in the game of football **b** *Brit* **:** a soccer ball **3 :** something tossed or kicked about **:** PLAYTHING ⟨the bill became a political ~ in Congress⟩ — **foot·ball·er** \-ˌbȯ-lər\ *n*
foot·bath \'fu̇t-ˌbath, -ˌbȧth\ *n* (1599) **:** a bath (as at the entrance to an indoor swimming pool) for cleansing, warming, or disinfecting the feet
foot·board \'fu̇t-ˌbō(ə)rd, -ˌbȯ(ə)rd\ *n* (1766) **1 :** a narrow platform on which to stand or brace the feet **2 :** a board forming the foot of a bed
foot·boy \-ˌbȯi\ *n* (1590) **:** a serving boy **:** PAGE, ATTENDANT
foot·bridge \'fu̇t-ˌbrij\ *n* (1506) **:** a bridge for pedestrians
foot–can·dle \-'kan-dᵊl\ *n* (1906) **:** a unit of illuminance on a surface that is everywhere one foot from a uniform point source of light of one candle and equal to one lumen per square foot
foot·cloth \-ˌklȯth\ *n* (14c) **1** *archaic* **:** an ornamental cloth draped over the back of a horse to reach the ground on each side **2 :** CARPET
foot–drag·ging \-ˌdrag-iŋ\ *n* (1952) **:** failure to act with the necessary promptness or vigor
foot·ed \'fu̇t-əd\ *adj* (14c) **:** having a foot or feet esp. of a specified kind or number — often used in combination ⟨a four-*footed* animal⟩
foot·er \'fu̇t-ər\ *n, archaic* (1608) **:** PEDESTRIAN
-foot·er \'fu̇t-ər\ *comb form* **:** one that is a specified number of feet in height, length, or breadth ⟨a six-*footer*⟩
foot·fall \'fu̇t-ˌfȯl\ *n* (1610) **:** the sound of a footstep
foot fault *n* (1886) **:** an infraction of the service rules (as in tennis, racquetball, or volleyball) that results from illegal placement of the server's feet — **foot–fault** \'fu̇t-ˌfȯlt\ *vi*
foot·gear \'fu̇t-ˌgi(ə)r\ *n* (1837) **:** FOOTWEAR
foot·hill \-ˌhil\ *n* (1850) **1 :** a hill at the foot of higher hills **2** *pl* **:** a hilly region at the base of a mountain range
foot·hold \-ˌhōld\ *n* (1625) **1 :** a hold for the feet **:** FOOTING **2 :** a position usable as a base for further advance
foot·ing \'fu̇t-iŋ\ *n* (14c) **1 :** a stable position or placing of the feet **2 :** a surface or its condition with respect to one walking or running on it; *specif* **:** the condition of a racetrack **3 :** the act of moving on foot **:** STEP, TREAD **4 a :** a place or space for standing **:** FOOTHOLD **b :** established position **:** STATUS; *esp* **:** position or rank in relation to others ⟨they all started off on an equal ~⟩ **5 :** BASIS **6 :** terms of social intercourse **7 :** an enlargement at the lower end of a foundation wall, pier, or column to distribute the load **8 :** the sum of a column of figures
foo·tle \'fü-tᵊl\ *vi* **foo·tled; foo·tling** \'füt-liŋ, -ᵊl-iŋ\ [alter. of *footer* (to footle)] (1892) **1 :** to talk or act foolishly **2 :** to waste time **:** TRIFLE, FOOL — **footle** *n* — **foo·tler** \'füt-lər, -ᵊl-ər\ *n*
foot·less \'fu̇t-ləs\ *adj* (14c) **1 a :** having no feet **b :** lacking foundation **:** UNSUBSTANTIAL **2 :** STUPID, INEPT — **foot·less·ly** *adv* — **foot·less·ness** *n*
foot·lights \-ˌlīts\ *n pl* (1836) **1 :** a row of lights set across the front of a stage floor **2 :** the stage as a profession
foo·tling \'füt-liŋ, -ᵊl-iŋ\ *adj* [*footle*] (1896) **1 :** lacking judgment or ability **:** INEPT ⟨~ amateurs who understand nothing —E. R. Bentley⟩ **2 :** lacking use or value **:** TRIVIAL
foot·lock·er \'fu̇t-ˌläk-ər\ *n* (ca. 1942) **:** a small trunk designed to be placed at the foot of a bed (as in a barracks)
foot·loose \-ˌlüs\ *adj* (1873) **:** having no ties **:** free to move about
foot·man \-mən\ *n* (13c) **1 a** *archaic* **:** a traveler on foot **:** PEDESTRIAN **b :** INFANTRYMAN **2 a :** a servant in livery formerly attending a rider or required to run in front of his master's carriage **b :** a servant who serves at table, tends the door, and runs errands
foot·mark \-ˌmärk\ *n* (1826) **:** FOOTPRINT
[1]**foot·note** \-ˌnōt\ *n* (1822) **1 :** a note of reference, explanation, or comment usu. placed below the text on a printed page **2 :** something that is subordinately related to a larger event or work **:** COMMENTARY ⟨that biography is an illuminating ~ to our times⟩
[2]**footnote** *vt* (1893) **:** to furnish with a footnote **:** ANNOTATE
foot·pace \'fu̇t-ˌpās\ *n* (1538) **1 :** a walking pace **2 :** PLATFORM, DAIS
[1]**foot·pad** \-ˌpad\ *n* [*foot* + *pad* (highwayman)] (1683) **:** one who robs a pedestrian
[2]**footpad** *n* [*foot* + [1]*pad*] (1966) **:** a flattish foot on the leg of a spacecraft for distributing weight to minimize sinking into a surface
foot·path \'fu̇t-ˌpath, -ˌpȧth\ *n* (1526) **:** a narrow path for pedestrians
foot–pound \-'pau̇nd\ *n, pl* **foot–pounds** (1850) **:** a unit of work equal to the work done by a force of one pound acting through a distance of one foot in the direction of the force
foot–pound·al \-'pau̇n-dᵊl\ *n* (ca. 1890) **:** an absolute unit of work equal to the work done by a force of one poundal acting through a distance of one foot in the direction of the force
foot–pound–second *adj* (1892) **:** being or relating to a system of units based upon the foot as the unit of length, the pound as the unit of weight and the second as the unit of time — abbr. *fps*
foot·print \'fu̇t-ˌprint\ *n* (1552) **1 :** an impression of the foot on a surface **2 :** an area within which a spacecraft is intended to land
foot·race \-ˌrās\ *n* (1663) **:** a race run by humans on foot
foot·rest \-ˌrest\ *n* (1861) **:** a support for the feet
foot·rope \-ˌrōp\ *n* (1772) **1 :** the part of a boltrope sewed to the lower edge of a sail **2 :** a rope rigged below a yard for men to stand on
foot rot *n* (1807) **1 :** a progressive inflammation of the feet of sheep or cattle **2 :** a plant disease marked by rot of the stem near the ground
foot·slog \'fu̇t-ˌsläg\ *vi* (1899) **:** to march or tramp through mud — **foot·slog·ger** *n*
foot soldier *n* (1622) **:** INFANTRYMAN
foot·sore \'fu̇t-ˌsō(ə)r, -ˌsȯ(ə)r\ *adj* (1719) **:** having sore or tender feet (as from much walking) — **foot·sore·ness** *n*
foot·stall \-ˌstȯl\ *n* (1585) **:** the plinth, base, or pedestal of a pillar
foot·step \-ˌstep\ *n* (13c) **1 :** the mark of the foot **:** TRACK **2 a :** TREAD **b :** distance covered by a step **:** PACE **3 :** a step on which to ascend or descend **4 :** a way of life, conduct, or action ⟨followed in his father's ~*s*⟩
foot·stone \-ˌstōn\ *n* (1724) **:** a stone placed at the foot of a grave
foot·stool \-ˌstül\ *n* (1530) **:** a low stool used to support the feet
foot·wall \-ˌwȯl\ *n* (1869) **1 :** the lower underlying wall of a vein, ore deposit, or coal seam in a mine **2 :** the lower wall of an inclined fault
foot·way \-ˌwā\ *n* (15c) **:** a narrow way or path for pedestrians
foot·wear \-ˌwa(ə)r, -ˌwe(ə)r\ *n* (1584) **:** wearing apparel (as shoes or boots) for the feet
foot·work \-ˌwərk\ *n* (1895) **1 :** the management of the feet (as in boxing); *also* **:** the work done with them **2 :** the activity of moving from place to place ⟨the investigation entailed a lot of ~⟩ **3 :** DEALING, TACTICS ⟨fancy political ~⟩
foo·ty \'füt-ē\ *adj* [F *foutu*, fr. pp. of *foutre* to copulate, fr. L *futuere*; prob. akin to L *-futare* to beat — more at BEAT] (1752) **1** *chiefly dial* **:** INSIGNIFICANT, PALTRY **2** *chiefly dial* **:** poorly kept **:** SHABBY
[1]**foo·zle** \'fü-zəl\ *n* (1890) **:** an act of foozling; *esp* **:** a bungling golf stroke
[2]**foozle** *vt* **foo·zled; foo·zling** \'füz-(ə-)liŋ\ [perh. fr. G dial. *fuseln* to work carelessly] (1892) **:** to manage or play awkwardly **:** BUNGLE
[1]**fop** \'fäp\ *n* [ME; akin to ME *fobben* to deceive, MHG *voppen*] (15c) **1** *obs* **:** a foolish or silly person **2 :** a man who is devoted to or vain about his appearance or dress **:** COXCOMB, DANDY
[2]**fop** *vt* **fopped; fop·ping** *obs* (1602) **:** FOOL, DUPE
fop·pery \'fäp-(ə-)rē\ *n, pl* **-per·ies** (1546) **1 :** foolish character or action **:** FOLLY **2 :** the behavior or dress of a fop
fop·pish \'fäp-ish\ *adj* (1599) **1** *obs* **:** FOOLISH, SILLY **2 a :** characteristic of a fop ⟨a ~ dressing gown⟩ **b :** behaving or dressing in the manner of a fop — **fop·pish·ly** *adv* — **fop·pish·ness** *n*
[1]**for** \fər, (')fȯ(ə)r, *Southern also* (')fär\ *prep* [ME, fr. OE; akin to L *per* through, *prae* before, *pro* before, for, ahead, Gk *pro*, OE *faran* to go — more at FARE] (bef. 12c) **1 a** — used as a function word to indicate purpose ⟨a grant ~ studying medicine⟩ **b** — used as a function word to indicate an intended goal ⟨left ~ home⟩ ⟨acted ~ the best⟩ **c** — used as a function word to indicate the object or recipient of a perception, desire, or activity ⟨now ~ a good rest⟩ ⟨run ~ your life⟩ ⟨an eye ~ a bargain⟩ **2 a :** as being or constituting ⟨take him ~ a fool⟩ ⟨eggs ~ breakfast⟩ **b** — used as a function word to indicate an actual or implied enumeration or selection ⟨~ one thing, the price is too high⟩ **3 :** because of ⟨cried ~ joy⟩ **4** — used as a function word to indicate suitability or fitness ⟨it is not ~ the president to make that decision⟩ ⟨ready ~ action⟩ **5 a :** in place of **b (1) :** on behalf of **:** REPRESENTING **(2) :** in favor of **6 :** in spite of — usu. used with *all* ⟨~ all his large size, he moves gracefully⟩ **7 :** with respect to **:** CONCERNING ⟨a stickler ~ detail⟩ **8** — used as a function word to indicate equivalence in exchange ⟨$10 ~ a hat⟩, equality in number or quantity ⟨point ~ point⟩, or correspondence or correlation ⟨~ one good one, you'll find five that don't work⟩ **9** — used as a function word to indicate duration of time or extent of space **10 :** in honor of **:** AFTER
[2]**for** *conj* (12c) **:** for the reason that **:** on this ground **:** BECAUSE
for- *prefix* [ME, fr. OE; akin to OHG *fur-* for-, OE *for*] **1 :** so as to involve prohibition, exclusion, omission, failure, neglect, or refusal ⟨*for*say⟩ **2 :** destructively or detrimentally ⟨*for*do⟩ **3 :** completely **:** excessively **:** to exhaustion **:** to pieces ⟨*for*spent⟩
fora *pl of* FORUM
[1]**for·age** \'fȯr-ij, 'fär-\ *n* [ME, fr. OF, fr. *forre* fodder, of Gmc origin; akin to OHG *fuotar* food, fodder — more at FOOD] (13c) **1 :** food for animals esp. when taken by browsing or grazing **2** [[2]*forage*] **:** the act of foraging **:** search for provisions
[2]**forage** *vb* **for·aged; for·ag·ing** *vt* (15c) **1 :** to strip of provisions **:** collect forage from **2 :** to secure by foraging ⟨*foraged* a chicken for the feast⟩ ~ *vi* **1 :** to wander in search of forage or food **2 :** to secure forage (as for horses) by stripping the country **3 :** RAVAGE, RAID **4 :** to make a search **:** RUMMAGE — **for·ag·er** *n*
fo·ram \'fōr-əm, 'fȯr-\ *n* (1927) **:** FORAMINIFER
fo·ra·men \fə-'rā-mən\ *n, pl* **fo·ram·i·na** \-'ram-ə-nə\ *or* **fo·ra·mens** \-'rā-mənz\ [L *foramin-, foramen*, fr. *forare* to bore — more at BORE] (1671) **:** a small opening, perforation, or orifice **:** FENESTRA — **fo·ram·i·nal** \fə-'ram-ən-ᵊl\ *or* **fo·ram·i·nous** \-ə-nəs\ *adj*
fo·ra·men mag·num \fə-ˌrā-mən-'mag-nəm\ *n* [NL, lit., great opening] (1882) **:** the opening in the skull through which the spinal cord passes to become the medulla oblongata
foramen ova·le \-ō-'val-ē, -'väl-, -'vāl-\ *n* [NL, lit., oval opening] (ca. 1889) **:** an opening in the septum between the two atria of the heart that is normally present only in the fetus
for·a·min·i·fer \ˌfȯr-ə-'min-ə-fər, ˌfär-\ *n* (1841) **:** any of an order (Foraminifera) of large chiefly marine rhizopods usu. having calcareous shells that often are perforated with minute holes for protrusion of slender pseudopodia and form the bulk of chalk and nummulitic limestone — **fo·ra·mi·nif·er·al** \fə-ˌram-ə-'nif-(ə-)rəl; ˌfȯr-ə-mə-'nif-, ˌfär-\ *adj*
fo·ra·mi·nif·era \fə-ˌram-ə-'nif-(ə-)rə; ˌfȯr-ə-mə-'nif-, ˌfär-\ *n pl* [NL, fr. L *foramin-, foramen* + *-fera*, neut. pl. of *-fer* -fer] (ca. 1847) **:** organisms that are foraminifers
fo·ra·mi·nif·er·an \-(ə-)rən\ *n* (1929) **:** FORAMINIFER
for and *conj, obs* (1529) **:** and also
for·as·much as \'fȯr-əz-ˌməch-əz\ *conj* (13c) **:** in view of the fact that **:** SINCE
[1]**for·ay** \'fȯr-ˌā, 'fōr-, 'fär- *also* fȯ-'rā *or* fə-\ *vb* [ME *forrayen*, fr. MF *forrer*, fr. *forre* fodder — more at FORAGE] *vt, archaic* (14c) **:** to ravage in search of spoils **:** PILLAGE ~ *vi* **:** to make a raid or brief invasion ⟨~*ed* into enemy territory⟩ — **for·ay·er** *n*
[2]**foray** *n* (14c) **1 :** a sudden or irregular invasion or attack for war or spoils **:** RAID **2 :** a brief excursion or attempt esp. outside one's accustomed sphere ⟨the teacher's ~ into politics⟩
forb \'fȯ(ə)rb\ *n* [Gk *phorbē* fodder, food, fr. *pherbein* to graze] (1924) **:** an herb other than grass

---

\ə\ abut \ᵊ\ kitten, F table \ər\ further \a\ ash \ā\ ace \ä\ cot, cart
\au̇\ out \ch\ chin \e\ bet \ē\ easy \g\ go \i\ hit \ī\ ice \j\ job
\ŋ\ sing \ō\ go \ȯ\ law \ȯi\ boy \th\ thin \th\ the \ü\ loot \u̇\ foot
\y\ yet \zh\ vision \à, k, ⁿ, œ, œ̄, ue, ue̅, ʸ\ see Guide to Pronunciation

1for·bear \fȯr-ˈba(ə)r, fər-, -ˈbe(ə)r\ *vb* **-bore** \-ˈbō(ə)r, -ˈbȯ(ə)r\; **-borne** \-ˈbō(ə)rn, -ˈbȯ(ə)rn\; **-bear·ing** [ME *forberen,* fr. OE *forberan* to endure, do without, fr. *for-* + *beran* to bear] *vt* (bef. 12c) **1** *obs* **:** to leave alone **:** SHUN ⟨∼ his presence —Shak.⟩ **2** *obs* **:** to do without **3 :** to hold oneself back from esp. with an effort of self-restraint ∼ *vi* **1 :** HOLD BACK, ABSTAIN **2 :** to control oneself when provoked **:** be patient — **for·bear·er** *n*

2forbear *var of* FOREBEAR

for·bear·ance \fȯr-ˈbar-ən(t)s, fər-, -ˈber-\ *n* (1576) **1 :** a refraining from the enforcement of something (as a debt, right, or obligation) that is due **2 :** the act of forbearing **:** PATIENCE **3 :** the quality of being forbearing **:** LENIENCY

1for·bid \fər-ˈbid, fȯr-\ *vt* **-bade** \-ˈbad, -ˈbād\ *or* **-bad** \-ˈbad\; **-bid·den** \-ˈbid-ᵊn\; **-bid·ding** [ME *forbidden,* fr. OE *forbēodan,* fr. *for-* + *bēodan* to bid — more at BID] (bef. 12c) **1 :** to proscribe from or as if from the position of one in authority **:** command against ⟨the law ∼*s* stores to sell liquor to minors⟩ ⟨her mother ∼*s* her to go⟩ **2 :** to hinder or prevent as if by an effectual command ⟨space ∼*s* further treatment here⟩ — **for·bid·der** *n*

syn FORBID, PROHIBIT, INTERDICT, INHIBIT mean to debar one from doing something or to order that something not to be done. FORBID implies that the order is from one in authority and that obedience is expected; PROHIBIT suggests the issuing of laws, statutes, or regulations; INTERDICT implies prohibition by civil or ecclesiastical authority usu. for a given time or a declared purpose; INHIBIT implies the imposition of restraints or restrictions that amount to prohibitions, not only by authority but also by the exigencies of the time or situation.

2forbid *adj, archaic* (1606) **:** ACCURSED ⟨he shall live a man ∼ —Shak.⟩

for·bid·dance \fər-ˈbid-ᵊn(t)s, fȯr-\ *n* (1608) **:** the act of forbidding

for·bid·den \-ˈbid-ᵊn\ *adj* (1923) **:** not conforming to the usual selection principles — used of quantum phenomena ⟨∼ transition⟩ ⟨∼ radiation⟩ ⟨∼ spectral line⟩

forbidden fruit *n* [fr. the forbidden fruit of the Garden of Eden in Gen 3: 2–19] (1662) **:** an immoral or illegal pleasure

for·bid·ding *adj* (1712) **1 :** such as to make approach or passage difficult or impossible ⟨∼ walls⟩ **2 :** DISAGREEABLE, REPELLENT ⟨a ∼ task⟩ **3 :** GRIM, MENACING — **for·bid·ding·ly** \-ˈbid-iŋ-lē\ *adv*

forbode *var of* FOREBODE

1for·by *or* **for·bye** \fȯr-ˈbī\ *prep* [ME *forby,* prep. & adv., fr. *fore-* + *by*] (14c) **1** *archaic* **a :** PAST **b :** NEAR **2** *chiefly Scot* **:** BESIDES

2forby *or* **forbye** *adv, chiefly Scot* (1590) **:** BESIDES **:** in addition

1force \ˈfō(ə)rs, ˈfȯ(ə)rs\ *n* [ME, fr. MF, fr. (assumed) VL *fortia,* fr. L *fortis* strong] (14c) **1 a :** strength or energy exerted or brought to bear **:** cause of motion or change **:** active power ⟨the ∼*s* of nature⟩ ⟨the love of justice has been a powerful motivating ∼ in his life⟩ **b :** moral or mental strength **c :** capacity to persuade or convince ⟨couldn't resist the ∼ of his argument⟩ **2 a :** military strength **b** (1) **:** a body (as of troops or ships) assigned to a military purpose (2) *pl* **:** the whole military strength (as of a nation) **c :** a body of persons or things available for a particular end ⟨a labor ∼⟩ ⟨the missile ∼⟩ **d :** an individual or group having the power of effective action ⟨police and citizens must join ∼*s* to prevent violence⟩ ⟨he was a ∼ behind the passing of that bill⟩ **3 :** violence, compulsion, or constraint exerted upon or against a person or thing **4 :** an agency or influence that if applied to a free body results chiefly in an acceleration of the body and sometimes in elastic deformation and other effects **5 :** the quality of conveying impressions intensely in writing or speech ***syn*** see POWER — **force·less** \-ləs\ *adj* — **in force 1 :** in great numbers ⟨police were summoned *in force*⟩ **2 :** VALID, OPERATIVE ⟨his suspension from school must remain *in force*⟩

2force *vt* **forced; forc·ing** (14c) **1 :** to do violence to; *esp* **:** RAPE **2 :** to compel by physical, moral, or intellectual means **3 :** to make or cause through natural or logical necessity ⟨*forced* to admit he was right⟩ **4 a :** to press, drive, attain to, or effect against resistance or inertia ⟨∼ a bill through the legislature⟩ **b :** to impose or thrust urgently, importunately, or inexorably ⟨∼ unwanted attentions on a woman⟩ **5 :** to achieve or win by strength in struggle or violence: **a :** to win one's way into ⟨∼ a castle⟩ ⟨*forced* the mountain passes⟩ **b :** to break open or through ⟨∼ a lock⟩ **6 a :** to raise or accelerate to the utmost ⟨*forcing* the pace⟩ **b :** to produce only with unnatural or unwilling effort ⟨she *forced* a smile in spite of her distress⟩ **c :** to wrench, strain, or use (language) with marked unnaturalness and lack of ease **7 a :** to hasten the rate of progress or growth of **b :** to bring (as plants) to maturity out of the normal season ⟨*forcing* lilies for the Easter trade⟩ **8 :** to induce (as a particular bid or play by another player) in a card game by some conventional act, play, bid, or response **9 a :** to cause (a runner in baseball) to be put out on a force play **b :** to cause (a run) to be scored in baseball by giving a base on balls when the bases are full — **forc·er** *n* — **force one's hand :** to cause one to act precipitously **:** force one to reveal his purpose or intention

forced \ˈfō(ə)rst, ˈfȯ(ə)rst\ *adj* (ca. 1537) **1 :** compelled by force **:** INVOLUNTARY ⟨a ∼ landing⟩ **2 :** done or produced with effort, exertion, or pressure ⟨a ∼ laugh⟩ — **forced·ly** \ˈfōr-səd-lē, ˈfȯr-\ *adv*

force–feed *vt* (1901) **1 :** to feed (as an animal) by forcible administration of food **2 :** to force to take in ⟨∼ students the classics⟩

force·ful \ˈfōrs-fəl, ˈfȯrs-\ *adj* (1571) **:** possessing or filled with force **:** EFFECTIVE — **force·ful·ly** \-fə-lē\ *adv* — **force·ful·ness** *n*

force ma·jeure \ˌfōr-smä-ˈzhər, ˌfȯr-, -smə-\ *n* [F, superior force] (1883) **1 :** superior or irresistible force **2 :** an event or effect that cannot be reasonably anticipated or controlled — compare ACT OF GOD

force·meat \ˈfōr-ˌsmēt, ˈfȯr-\ *n* [*force* (alter. of ²*farce*) + *meat*] (1688) **:** finely chopped and highly seasoned meat or fish that is either served alone or used as a stuffing — called also *farce*

force of habit (ca. 1925) **:** behavior made involuntary or automatic by repeated practice

force–out \ˈfōr-ˌsau̇t, ˈfȯr-\ *n* (1896) **:** FORCE PLAY

force play *n* (1897) **:** a play in baseball in which a runner is put out when he is forced to advance to the next base but fails to do so safely

for·ceps \ˈfȯr-səps, -ˌseps\ *n, pl* **forceps** [L, fr. *formus* warm + *capere* to take — more at WARM, HEAVE] (1670) **:** an instrument for grasping, holding firmly, or exerting traction upon objects esp. for delicate operations (as by jewelers or surgeons) — **for·ceps·like** \-ˌlīk\ *adj*

force pump *n* (1659) **:** a pump with a solid piston for drawing and forcing through valves a liquid (as water) to a considerable height above the pump or under a considerable pressure

forc·ible \ˈfōr-sə-bəl, ˈfȯr-\ *adj* (14c) **1 :** effected by force used against opposition or resistance **2 :** characterized by force, efficiency, or energy **:** POWERFUL — **forc·ible·ness** *n* — **forc·ibly** \-blē\ *adv*

1ford \ˈfō(ə)rd, ˈfȯ(ə)rd\ *n* [ME, fr. OE; akin to ON *fjorthr* fjord, L *portus* port, OE *faran* to go — more at FARE] (bef. 12c) **:** a shallow part of a body of water that may be crossed by wading

2ford *vt* (1614) **:** to cross (a body of water) by wading — **ford·able** \ˈfōrd-ə-bəl, ˈfȯrd-\ *adj*

for·do \fȯr-ˈdü, fōr-\ *vt* **-did** \-ˈdid\; **-done** \-ˈdən\; **-do·ing** \-ˈdü-iŋ\ [ME *fordon,* fr. OE *fordōn,* fr. *for-* + *dōn* to do] (bef. 12c) **1** *archaic* **:** to do away with **:** DESTROY **2 :** to overcome with fatigue — used only as past participle ⟨quite *fordone* with the heat⟩

1fore \ˈfō(ə)r, ˈfȯ(ə)r\ *adv* [ME, fr. OE; akin to OE *for*] (bef. 12c) **1** *obs* **:** at an earlier time or period **2 :** in, toward, or adjacent to the front **:** FORWARD

2fore *also* **'fore** *prep* (bef. 12c) **1** *chiefly dial* **:** BEFORE **2 :** in the presence of

3fore *adj* [*fore-*] (15c) **1 :** situated in front of something else **:** FORWARD **2 :** prior in order of occurrence **:** FORMER

4fore *n* (1842) **:** something that occupies a front position — **to the fore :** in or into a position of prominence **:** FORWARD

5fore *interj* [prob. short for *before*] (1878) — used by a golfer to warn anyone within range of the probable line of flight of his ball

fore- *comb form* [ME *for-, fore-,* fr. OE *fore-,* fr. *fore,* adv.] **1 a :** earlier **:** beforehand ⟨*fore*see⟩ **b :** occurring earlier **:** occurring beforehand ⟨*fore*shock⟩ **2 a :** situated at the front **:** in front ⟨*fore*leg⟩ **b :** front part of (something specified) ⟨*fore*arm⟩

fore–and–aft \ˌfōr-ə-ˈnaft, ˌfȯr-\ *adj* (1820) **1 :** lying, running, or acting in the general line of the length of a construction (as a ship or a house) **:** LONGITUDINAL **2 :** having no square sails

fore and aft *adv* (1618) **1 :** lengthwise of a ship **:** from stem to stern **2 :** in, at, or toward both the bow and stern **3 :** in or at the front and back

fore–and–aft·er \-ˈnaf-tər\ *n* (1823) **:** a ship with a fore-and-aft rig; *esp* **:** SCHOONER

fore–and–aft rig *n* (1879) **:** a sailing-ship rig in which most or all of the sails are not attached to yards but are bent to gaffs or set on the masts or on stays in a fore-and-aft line

1fore·arm \(ˈ)fōr-ˈärm, (ˈ)fȯr-\ *vt* (1592) **:** to arm in advance **:** PREPARE

2fore·arm \ˈfōr-ˌärm, ˈfȯr-\ *n* (1741) **:** the part of the arm between the elbow and the wrist; *also* **:** the corresponding part in other vertebrates

fore·bay \ˈfō(ə)r-ˌbā, ˈfȯ(ə)r-\ *n* (1770) **:** a reservoir or canal from which water is taken to run equipment (as a waterwheel or turbine)

fore·bear \-ˌba(ə)r, -ˌbe(ə)r\ *n* [ME (Sc) *forebear,* fr. *fore-* + *-bear* (fr. *been* to be)] (15c) **:** ANCESTOR, FOREFATHER — usu. used in pl.

fore·bode \(ˈ)fōr-ˈbōd, (ˈ)fȯr-\ *vt* (1603) **1 :** to have an inward conviction of (as coming ill or misfortune) **2 :** FORETELL, PORTEND ∼ *vi* **:** AUGUR, PREDICT — **fore·bod·er** *n*

1fore·bod·ing \-ˈbōd-iŋ\ *n* (14c) **:** the act of one who forebodes; *also* **:** an omen, prediction, or presentiment esp. of coming evil **:** PORTENT

2foreboding *adj* (1679) **:** indicative of or marked by foreboding — **fore·bod·ing·ly** \-iŋ-lē\ *adv* — **fore·bod·ing·ness** *n*

fore·brain \ˈfō(ə)r-ˌbrān, ˈfȯ(ə)r-\ *n* (1879) **:** the anterior of the three primary divisions of the developing vertebrate brain or the corresponding part of the adult brain that includes rostrally esp. the cerebral hemispheres and more caudally esp. the thalamus and hypothalamus — called also *prosencephalon;* compare DIENCEPHALON, TELENCEPHALON

fore·cad·die \-ˌkad-ē\ *n* (1792) **:** a golf caddie who is stationed in the fairway and who indicates the position of balls on the course

1fore·cast \-ˌkast; fōr-ˈkast, fȯr-\ *vb* **forecast** *also* **fore·cast·ed; fore·cast·ing** *vt* (15c) **1 a :** to calculate or predict (some future event or condition) usu. as a result of rational study and analysis of available pertinent data; *esp* **:** to predict (weather conditions) on the basis of correlated meteorological observations **b :** to indicate as likely to occur **2 :** to serve as a forecast of **:** PRESAGE ⟨such events may ∼ peace⟩ ∼ *vi* **:** to calculate the future ***syn*** see FORETELL — **fore·cast·able** \-ə-bəl\ *adj* — **fore·cast·er** *n*

2fore·cast \ˈfō(ə)r-ˌkast, ˈfȯ(ə)r-\ *n* (1541) **1** *archaic* **:** foresight of consequences and provision against them **:** FORETHOUGHT **2 :** a prophecy, estimate, or prediction of a future happening or condition

fore·cas·tle \ˈfōk-səl; ˈfōr-ˌkas-əl, ˈfȯr-\ *n* (15c) **1 :** the part of the upper deck of a ship forward of the foremast or of the fore channels **2 :** the forward part of a merchantman where the crew is housed

fore–check \ˈfō(ə)r-ˌchek, ˈfȯ(ə)r-\ *vi* (1951) **:** to guard an opponent in ice hockey in his own defensive zone

fore·close \(ˈ)fōr-ˈklōz, (ˈ)fȯr-\ *vb* [ME *forclosen,* fr. MF *forclos,* pp. of *forclore,* fr. *fors* outside (fr. L *foris*) + *clore* to close — more at FORUM] *vt* (15c) **1 :** to shut out **:** PRECLUDE **2 :** to hold exclusively **3 :** to deal with or close in advance **4 :** to subject to foreclosure proceedings ∼ *vi* **:** to foreclose a mortgage

fore·clo·sure \-ˈklō-zhər\ *n* (1728) **:** an act or instance of foreclosing; *specif* **:** a legal proceeding that bars or extinguishes a mortgagor's right of redeeming a mortgaged estate

fore·deck \ˈfō(ə)r-ˌdek, ˈfȯ(ə)r-\ *n* (1565) **:** the forepart of a ship's main deck

foredo *var of* FORDO

fore·doom \(ˈ)fōr-ˈdüm, (ˈ)fȯr-\ *vt* (1608) **:** to doom beforehand

fore·face \ˈfō(ə)r-ˌfās, ˈfȯ(ə)r-\ *n* (1545) **:** the part of the head of a quadruped that is in front of the eyes

fore·fa·ther \-ˌfät͟h-ər, -ˌfät͟h-\ *n* (14c) **1 :** ANCESTOR 1a **2 :** a person of an earlier period and common heritage

fore·feel \(ˈ)fōr-ˈfē(ə)l, (ˈ)fȯr-\ *vt* **-felt** \-ˈfelt\; **-feel·ing** (1580) **:** to have a presentiment of

forefend *var of* FORFEND

fore·fin·ger \ˈfō(ə)r-ˌfiŋ-gər, ˈfȯ(ə)r-\ *n* (15c) **:** the finger next to the thumb — called also *index finger*

fore·foot \-ˌfu̇t\ *n* (14c) **1 :** one of the anterior feet esp. of a quadruped **2 :** the forward part of a ship where the stem and keel meet

fore·front \-ˌfrənt\ *n* (15c) **:** the foremost part or place **:** VANGUARD

fore·gath·er *var of* FORGATHER

1fore·go \fōr-ˈgō, fȯr-\ *vt* **-went** \-ˈwent\; **-gone** \-ˈgȯn *also* -ˈgän\; **-go·ing** \-ˈgō-iŋ, -ˈgȯ(-)iŋ\ (bef. 12c) : to go before : PRECEDE — **fore·go·er** \-ˈgō(-ə)r\ *n*

2forego *var of* FORGO

fore·go·ing \-ˈgō-iŋ, -ˈgȯ(-)iŋ\ *adj* (15c) : listed, mentioned, or occurring before ⟨the ~ statement can be proven⟩ ***syn*** see PRECEDING

fore·gone \ˌfōr-ˌgȯn, ˌfȯr- *also* -ˌgän\ *adj* (1600) : PREVIOUS, PAST

foregone conclusion *n* (1604) **1** : a conclusion that has preceded argument or examination **2** : an inevitable result : CERTAINTY ⟨the victory was a *foregone conclusion*⟩

fore·ground \ˈfō(ə)r-ˌgrau̇nd, ˈfȯ(ə)r-\ *n* (1695) **1** : the part of a scene or representation that is nearest to and in front of the spectator **2** : a position of prominence : FOREFRONT

fore·gut \-ˌgət\ *n* (ca. 1889) : the anterior part of the alimentary canal of a vertebrate embryo that develops into the pharynx, esophagus, stomach, and extreme anterior part of the intestine

1fore·hand \-ˌhand\ *n* (1557) **1** *archaic* : superior position : ADVANTAGE **2** : the part of a horse that is before the rider **3** : a forehand stroke (as in tennis or racquets); *also* : the side on which such strokes are made

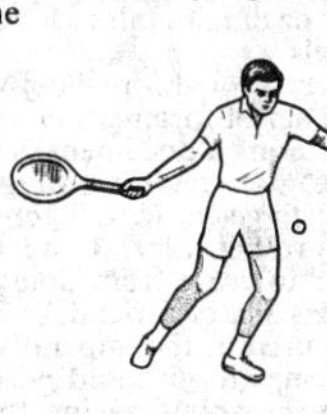
forehand 3

2forehand *adj* (1598) **1** *obs* : done or given in advance : PRIOR **2** : made with the palm of the hand turned in the direction in which the hand is moving ⟨a ~ tennis stroke⟩

3forehand *adv* (1925) : with a forehand stroke

fore·hand·ed \(ˈ)fōr-ˈhan-dəd, (ˈ)fȯr-\ *adj* (1650) **1 a** : mindful of the future : PRUDENT **b** : WELL-TO-DO **2** : FOREHAND 2 — **fore·hand·ed·ly** *adv* — **fore·hand·ed·ness** *n*

fore·head \ˈfär-əd, ˈfȯr-; ˈfō(ə)r-ˌhed, ˈfȯ(ə)r- *also* -ˌed\ *n* (bef. 12c) **1** : the part of the face above the eyes **2** : the front or forepart of something ⟨flames in the ~ of the morning sky —John Milton⟩

fore·hoof \ˈfō(ə)r-ˌhu̇f, ˈfȯ(ə)r-, -ˌhüf\ *n* (1770) : the hoof of a forefoot

for·eign \ˈfȯr-ən, ˈfär-\ *adj* [ME *forein,* fr. OF, fr. LL *foranus* on the outside, fr. L *foris* outside — more at FORUM] (13c) **1** : situated outside a place or country; *esp* : situated outside one's own country **2** : born in, belonging to, or characteristic of some place or country other than the one under consideration **3** : of, relating to, or proceeding from some other person or material thing than the one under consideration **4** : alien in character : not connected or pertinent **5** : related to or dealing with other nations **6** : occurring in an abnormal situation in the living body and often introduced from outside **7** : not being within the jurisdiction of a political unit (as a state) ***syn*** see EXTRINSIC — **for·eign·ness** \-ən-nəs\ *n*

foreign affairs *n pl* (1659) : matters having to do with international relations and with the interests of the home country in foreign countries

foreign aid *n* (1949) : assistance (as economic aid) provided by one nation to another

foreign bill *n* (1682) : a bill of exchange that is not both drawn and payable within a particular jurisdiction

for·eign–born \ˌfȯr-ən-ˈbȯ(ə)rn, ˌfär-\ *adj* (1856) : foreign by birth

foreign correspondent *n* (1948) : a correspondent employed to send news or comment from a foreign country

for·eign·er \ˈfȯr-ə-nər, ˈfär-\ *n* (15c) **1** : a person belonging to or owing allegiance to a foreign country **2** *chiefly dial* : STRANGER 1c

foreign exchange *n* (1691) **1** : a process of settling accounts or debts between persons residing in different countries **2** : foreign currency or current short-term credit instruments payable in such currency

for·eign·ism \ˈfȯr-ə-ˌniz-əm, ˈfär-\ *n* (1855) : something peculiar to a foreign language or people; *specif* : a foreign idiom or custom

foreign minister *n* (1709) : a governmental minister for foreign affairs

foreign office *n* (1859) : a government office (as a ministry) having to do with foreign affairs

foreign policy *n* (ca. 1909) : the policy of a sovereign state in its interaction with other sovereign states

foreign service *n* (1927) : the field force of a foreign office comprising diplomatic and consular personnel

1fore·judge \fər-ˈjəj, fōr-, fȯr-\ *vt* [ME *forjuggen,* fr. MF *forjugier,* fr. *fors* outside (fr. L *foris*) + *jugier* to judge] (15c) : to expel, oust, or put out by judgment of a court

2fore·judge \(ˈ)fōr-ˈjəj, (ˈ)fȯr-\ *vt* (1561) : PREJUDGE

fore·know \(ˈ)fōr-ˈnō, (ˈ)fȯr-\ *vt* **-knew** \-ˈn(y)ü\; **-known** \-ˈnōn\; **-know·ing** (14c) : to have previous knowledge of : know beforehand esp. by paranormal means or by revelation ***syn*** see FORESEE — **fore·knowl·edge** \-ˈnäl-ij\ *n*

fore·la·dy \ˈfō(ə)r-ˌlād-ē, ˈfȯ(ə)r-\ *n* (1889) : a woman who acts as a foreman

fore·land \ˈfōr-lənd, ˈfȯr-\ *n* (14c) : PROMONTORY, HEADLAND

fore·leg \ˈfō(ə)r-ˌleg, ˈfȯ(ə)r-, -ˌlāg\ *n* (15c) : a front leg

fore·limb \-ˌlim\ *n* (1794) : an arm, fin, wing, or leg that is or is homologous to a foreleg ⟨the ~ of a bat⟩

fore·lock \-ˌläk\ *n* (bef. 12c) : a lock of hair growing from the front of the head

fore·man \ˈfōr-mən, ˈfȯr-\ *n* (14c) : a first or chief man: as **a** : a member of a jury who acts as chairman and spokesman **b (1)** : a chief and often specially trained workman who works with and commonly leads a gang or crew **(2)** : a person in authority over a group of workers, a particular operation, or a section of a plant — **fore·man·ship** \-ˌship\ *n*

fore·mast \ˈfō(ə)r-ˌmast, ˈfȯ(ə)r-, -məst\ *n* (1582) : the mast nearest the bow of a ship

1fore·most \-ˌmōst\ *adj* [ME *formest,* fr. OE, superl. of *forma* first; akin to OHG *fruma* advantage, OE *fore* fore] (bef. 12c) **1** : first in a series or progression **2** : of first rank or position : PREEMINENT

2foremost *adv* (bef. 12c) **1** : in the first place **2** : most importantly ⟨first and ~⟩

fore·moth·er \ˈfō(ə)r-ˌmət͟h-ər, ˈfȯ(ə)r-\ *n* (1582) : a female ancestor

fore·name \-ˌnām\ *n* (1533) : a name that precedes one's surname

fore·named \-ˌnāmd\ *adj* (13c) : named previously : AFORESAID

fore·noon \ˈfō(ə)r-ˌnün, ˈfȯ(ə)r-, fōr-ˈ, fȯr-ˈ\ *n* (15c) : the early part of the day ending with noon : MORNING

1fo·ren·sic \fə-ˈren(t)-sik, -ˈren-zik\ *adj* [L *forensis* public, forensic, fr. *forum* forum] (1659) **1** : belonging to, used in, or suitable to courts of judicature or to public discussion and debate **2** : ARGUMENTATIVE, RHETORICAL **3** : specializing in or relating to forensic medicine ⟨~ pathologist⟩ ⟨~ breakthrough⟩ — **fo·ren·si·cal·ly** \-si-k(ə-)lē, -zi-\ *adv*

2forensic *n* (1814) **1** : an argumentative exercise **2** *pl but sing or pl in constr* : the art or study of argumentative discourse

forensic medicine *n* (1845) : a science that deals with the relation and application of medical facts to legal problems

fore·or·dain \ˌfōr-ȯr-ˈdān, ˌfȯr-\ *vt* (15c) : to dispose or appoint in advance : PREDESTINE — **fore·or·di·na·tion** \-ˌȯrd-ᵊn-ˈā-shən\ *n*

fore·part \ˈfō(ə)r-ˌpärt, ˈfȯ(ə)r-\ *n* (15c) **1** : the anterior part of something **2** : the earlier part of a period of time

fore·passed *or* **fore·past** \-ˌpast\ *adj* (1557) : BYGONE

fore·paw \-ˌpȯ\ *n* (1825) : the paw of a foreleg

fore·peak \-ˌpēk\ *n* (1693) : the extreme forward lower compartment or tank used for trimming or storage in a ship

fore·play \-ˌplā\ *n* (1929) : erotic stimulation preceding sexual intercourse

fore·quar·ter \-ˌkwȯ(r)t-ər\ *n* (15c) : the front half of a lateral half of the body or carcass of a quadruped ⟨a ~ of beef⟩

fore·reach \fōr-ˈrēch, fȯr-\ *vi, of a ship* (1644) : to gain ground in tacking ~ *vt* : to gain on or overhaul and go ahead of (a ship) when close-hauled

fore·run \-ˈrən\ *vt* **-ran** \-ˈran\; **-run; -run·ning** (bef. 12c) **1** : to run before **2** : to come before as a token of something to follow **3** : FORESTALL, ANTICIPATE

fore·run·ner \ˈfō(ə)r-ˌrən-ər, ˈfȯ(ə)r-\ *n* (14c) **1** : one that precedes and indicates the approach of another: as **a** : a premonitory sign or symptom **b** : a skier who runs the course before the start of a race **2** : PREDECESSOR, FOREBEAR

syn FORERUNNER, PRECURSOR, HARBINGER, HERALD mean one who goes before or announces the coming of another. FORERUNNER is applicable to anything that serves as a sign or presage; PRECURSOR applies to a person or thing paving the way for the success or accomplishment of another; HARBINGER and HERALD both apply, chiefly figuratively, to one that proclaims or announces the coming or arrival of a notable event.

fore·sad·dle \-ˌsad-ᵊl\ *n* (1924) : a wholesale cut of mutton, lamb, or veal that consists of the undivided forequarters of a carcass

fore·said \-ˌsed\ *adj, archaic* (bef. 12c) : AFORESAID

fore·sail \ˈfō(ə)r-ˌsāl, ˈfȯ(ə)r-, -səl\ *n* (15c) **1** : a sail carried on the foreyard of a square-rigged ship that is the lowest sail on the foremast **2** : the lower sail set abaft a schooner's foremast — see SAIL illustration **3** : FORESTAYSAIL

fore·see \fōr-ˈsē, fȯr-\ *vt* **-saw** \-ˈsȯ\; **-seen** \-ˈsēn\; **-see·ing** (bef. 12c) : to see (as a development) beforehand — **fore·see·able** \-ˈsē-ə-bəl, fər-\ *adj* — **fore·se·er** \fōr-ˈsē-ər, fȯr-, -ˈsi(-ə)r\ *n*

syn FORESEE, FOREKNOW, DIVINE, APPREHEND, ANTICIPATE mean to know beforehand. FORESEE implies nothing about how the knowledge is derived and may apply to ordinary reasoning and experience; FOREKNOW usu. implies supernatural assistance, as through revelation; DIVINE adds to FORESEE the suggestion of exceptional wisdom or discernment; APPREHEND implies foresight mingled with uncertainty, anxiety, or dread; ANTICIPATE implies taking action about or responding emotionally to something before it happens.

fore·shad·ow \-ˈshad-(ˌ)ō, -ə(-w)\ *vt* (1577) : to represent, indicate, or typify beforehand : PREFIGURE — **fore·shad·ow·er** \-ə-wər\ *n*

fore·shank \ˈfō(ə)r-ˌshaŋk, ˈfȯ(ə)r-\ *n* (1924) : the upper part of the foreleg of cattle; *also* : meat cut from this part

fore·sheet \-ˌshēt\ *n* (1667) **1** : one of the sheets of a foresail **2** *pl* : the forward part of an open boat

fore·shore \-ˌshō(ə)r, -ˌshȯ(ə)r\ *n* (1764) **1** : a strip of land margining a body of water **2** : the part of a seashore between high-water and low-water marks

fore·short·en \fōr-ˈshȯrt-ᵊn, fȯr-\ *vt* (1606) **1** : to shorten by proportionately contracting in the direction of depth so that an illusion of projection or extension in space is obtained **2** : to make more compact : ABRIDGE

fore·side \ˈfō(ə)r-ˌsīd, ˈfȯ(ə)r-\ *n* (15c) : the front side or part : FRONT

fore·sight \ˈfō(ə)r-ˌsīt, ˈfȯ(ə)r-\ *n* (14c) **1** : an act or the power of foreseeing : PRESCIENCE **2** : an act of looking forward; *also* : a view forward **3** : provident care : PRUDENCE ⟨had the ~ to invest his money wisely⟩ — **fore·sight·ed** \-əd\ *adj* — **fore·sight·ed·ly** *adv* — **fore·sight·ed·ness** *n* — **fore·sight·ful** \-ˌsīt-fəl\ *adj*

fore·skin \-ˌskin\ *n* (1535) : a fold of skin that covers the glans of the penis — called also *prepuce*

fore·speak \fōr-ˈspēk, fȯr-\ *vt* **-spoke** \-ˈspōk\; **-spo·ken** \-ˈspō-kən\; **-speak·ing** (14c) **1** : FORETELL, PREDICT **2** : to arrange for in advance

1for·est \ˈfȯr-əst, ˈfär-\ *n, often attrib* [ME, fr. OF, fr. ML *forestis,* fr. L *foris* outside — more at FORUM] (13c) **1** : a tract of wooded land in England formerly owned by the sovereign and used for game **2** : a dense growth of trees and underbrush covering a large tract **3** : something resembling a forest esp. in profusion ⟨a ~ of TV antennas⟩ — **for·est·al** \-əs-tᵊl\ *or* **fo·res·tial** \fə-ˈres-tē-əl, fō-, -ˈres(h)-chəl\ *adj* — **for·est·ed** \ˈfȯr-ə-stəd, ˈfär-\ *adj*

2forest *vt* (1818) : to cover with trees or forest — **for·es·ta·tion** \ˌfȯr-ə-ˈstā-shən, ˌfär-\ *n*

fore·stage \ˈfō(ə)r-ˌstāj, ˈfȯ(ə)r-\ *n* (1923) : APRON 2g

fore·stall \fōr-ˈstȯl, fȯr-\ *vt* [ME *forstallen,* fr. *forstall* act of waylaying, fr. OE *foresteall,* fr. *fore-* + *steall* position, stall] (bef. 12c) **1** *archaic* : INTERCEPT **2** : to exclude, hinder, or prevent by prior occupation or measures **3** : to get ahead of : ANTICIPATE **4** *obs* : OBSTRUCT, BESET **5** : to prevent the normal trading in by buying or diverting goods or by persuading persons to raise prices ***syn*** see PREVENT — **fore·stall·er** *n* — **fore·stall·ment** \-ˈstȯl-mənt\ *n*

\ə\ abut \ᵊ\ kitten, F table \ər\ further \a\ ash \ā\ ace \ä\ cot, cart \au̇\ out \ch\ chin \e\ bet \ē\ easy \g\ go \i\ hit \ī\ ice \j\ job \ŋ\ sing \ō\ go \ȯ\ law \ȯi\ boy \th\ thin \t͟h\ the \ü\ loot \u̇\ foot \y\ yet \zh\ vision \à, k̲, ⁿ, œ, œ̄, ue, ue̅, ʸ\ *see* Guide to Pronunciation

fore·stay \ˈfō(ə)r-ˌstā, ˈfȯ(ə)r-\ *n* (13c) **:** a stay from the foremast head to the deck of a ship
fore·stay·sail \-ˌsāl, -səl\ *n* (1742) **:** the triangular aftermost headsail of a schooner, ketch, or yawl set on hanks on the forestay — see SAIL illustration
for·est·er \ˈfȯr-ə-stər, ˈfär-\ *n* [ME *forster, forester,* fr. OF *forestier,* fr. *forest*] (13c) **1 :** a person trained in forestry **2 :** an inhabitant of a forest **3 :** any of various woodland moths (family Agaristidae) **4** *cap* **:** a member of a major benevolent and fraternal order
forest floor *n* (1849) **:** the richly organic layer of soil and debris characteristic of forested land
forest green *n* (1810) **:** a dark yellowish or moderate olive green
for·est·land \ˈfȯr-əst-ˌland, ˈfär-\ *n* (1649) **:** land covered with forest or reserved for the growth of forests
forest ranger *n* (1830) **:** an officer charged with the patrolling and guarding of a forest; *esp* **:** one in charge of the management and protection of a portion of a public forest
for·est·ry \ˈfȯr-ə-strē, ˈfär-\ *n* (1823) **1 :** FORESTLAND **2 a :** the science of developing, caring for, or cultivating forests **b :** the management of growing timber
forest tent caterpillar *n* (1854) **:** a moth (*Malacosoma disstria* of the family Lasiocampidae) whose orange-marked larva is a tent caterpillar and a serious defoliator of deciduous trees
foreswear, foresworn *var of* FORSWEAR, FORSWORN
[1]**fore·taste** \ˈfō(ə)r-ˌtāst, ˈfȯ(ə)r-\ *n* (15c) **1 :** an advance indication or warning **2 :** a small anticipatory sample ***syn*** see PROSPECT
[2]**fore·taste** \fōr-ˈtāst, fȯr-ˈ, ˈfō(ə)r-ˌ, ˈfȯ(ə)r-ˌ\ *vt* (15c) **:** to taste beforehand **:** ANTICIPATE
fore·tell \fōr-ˈtel, fȯr-\ *vt* **-told** \-ˈtōld\; **-tell·ing** (14c) **:** to tell beforehand **:** PREDICT — **fore·tell·er** *n*
syn FORETELL, PREDICT, FORECAST, PROPHESY, PROGNOSTICATE mean to tell beforehand. FORETELL applies to the telling of the coming of a future event by any procedure or any source of information; PREDICT commonly implies inference from facts or accepted laws of nature; FORECAST adds the implication of anticipating eventualities and differs from PREDICT in being usually concerned with probabilities rather than certainties; PROPHESY connotes inspired or mystic knowledge of the future esp. as the fulfilling of divine threats or promises; PROGNOSTICATE suggests the learned or skilled interpretation of signs or symptoms.
[1]**fore·thought** \ˈfō(ə)r-ˌthȯt, ˈfȯ(ə)r-\ *n* (14c) **1 :** a thinking or planning out in advance **:** PREMEDITATION **2 :** consideration for the future
[2]**forethought** *adj* (15c) **:** thought of or planned beforehand **:** DELIBERATE
fore·thought·ful \-fəl\ *adj* (1809) **:** full of or having forethought — **fore·thought·ful·ly** \-fə-lē\ *adv* — **fore·thought·ful·ness** *n*
fore·time \ˈfō(ə)r-ˌtīm, ˈfȯ(ə)r-\ *n* (1540) **:** former or past time **:** the time before the present
[1]**fore·to·ken** \ˈfō(ə)r-ˌtō-kən, ˈfȯ(ə)r-\ *n* (14c) **:** a premonitory sign
[2]**fore·to·ken** \fōr-ˈtō-kən, fȯr-\ *vt* **fore·to·kened; fore·to·ken·ing** \-ˈtōk-(ə-)niŋ\ (1500) **:** to indicate or warn of in advance
fore·top \ˈfō(ə)r-ˌtäp, ˈfȯ(ə)r-; ˈfōrt-əp, ˈfȯrt-\ *n* (1509) **:** the platform at the head of a ship's foremast
fore–top·gal·lant \ˈfōr-ˌtäp-ˌgal-ənt, ˈfȯr-; ˈfōrt-ə-ˌgal-, ˈfȯrt-\ *adj* (1627) **:** being the part next above the fore-topmast
fore·top·man \ˈfōr-ˌtäp-mən, ˈfȯr-; ˈfōrt-əp-, ˈfȯrt-\ *n* (1816) **:** a sailor on duty on the foremast and above
fore–top·mast \ˈfōr-ˌtäp-məst, ˈfȯr-; ˈfōrt-əp-ˌmast, ˈfȯrt-\ *n* (1626) **:** a mast next above the foremast
fore–top·sail \ˈfōr-ˌtäp-səl, ˈfȯr-; ˈfōrt-əp-, ˈfȯrt-\ *n* (1582) **:** the sail above the foresail
[1]**for·ev·er** \fə-ˈrev-ər, fō; *Southern often* fə-ˈev-ə\ *adv* (14c) **1 :** for a limitless time ⟨wants to live ~⟩ **2 :** at all times **:** CONTINUALLY ⟨is ~ making bad puns⟩
[2]**forever** *n* (1858) **:** a seemingly interminable time **:** excessively long ⟨it took her ~ to find the answer⟩
for·ev·er·more \-ˌrev-ə(r)-ˈmō(ə)r, -ˈmȯ(ə)r\ *adv* (14c) **:** FOREVER
for·ev·er·ness \-ˈrev-ər-nəs\ *n* (1945) **:** ETERNITY
fore·warn \fōr-ˈwȯ(ə)rn, fȯr-\ *vt* (14c) **:** to warn in advance
fore·wing \ˈfō(ə)r-ˌwiŋ, ˈfȯ(ə)r-\ *n* (ca. 1889) **:** either of the anterior wings of a 4-winged insect
fore·wom·an \ˈfō(ə)r-ˌwu̇m-ən, ˈfȯ(ə)r-\ *n* (1709) **:** FORELADY
fore·word \ˈfōr-(ˌ)wərd, ˈfȯr-\ *n* (1842) **:** prefatory comments (as for a book) esp. when written by someone other than the author
foreworn *archaic var of* FORWORN
fore·yard \ˈfō(ə)r-ˌyärd, ˈfȯ(ə)r-\ *n* (1627) **:** the lowest yard on a foremast
[1]**for·feit** \ˈfȯr-fət\ *n* [ME *forfait,* fr. MF, fr. pp. of *forfaire* to commit a crime, forfeit, prob. fr. *fors* outside (fr. L *foris*) + *faire* to do, fr. L *facere* — more at FORUM, DO] (14c) **1 :** something forfeited or subject to being forfeited (as for a crime, offense, or neglect of duty) **:** PENALTY **2 :** forfeiture esp. of civil rights **3 a :** something deposited (as for making a mistake in a game) and then redeemed on payment of a fine **b** *pl* **:** a game in which forfeits are exacted
[2]**forfeit** *vt* (14c) **1 :** to lose or lose the right to by some error, offense, or crime **2 :** to subject to confiscation as a forfeit — **for·feit·able** \-ə-bəl\ *adj* — **for·feit·er** *n*
[3]**forfeit** *adj* (14c) **:** forfeited or subject to forfeiture
for·fei·ture \ˈfȯr-fə-ˌchu̇(ə)r, -chər, -ˌt(y)u̇(ə)r\ *n* (14c) **1 :** the act of forfeiting **:** the loss of property or money because of a breach of a legal obligation **2 :** something (as money or property) that is forfeited **:** PENALTY
for·fend \fȯr-ˈfend, fōr-\ *vt* (14c) **1 a** *archaic* **:** FORBID **b :** to ward off **:** PREVENT **2 :** PROTECT, PRESERVE
for·gath·er \fȯr-ˈgath-ər, fōr-, -ˈgeth-\ *vi* (1513) **1 :** to come together **:** ASSEMBLE **2 :** to meet someone usu. by chance
[1]**forge** \ˈfō(ə)rj, ˈfȯ(ə)rj\ *n* [ME, fr. OF, fr. L *fabrica,* fr. *fabr-, faber*

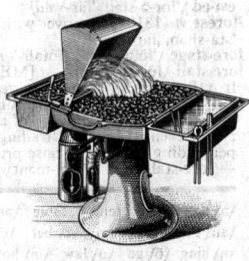

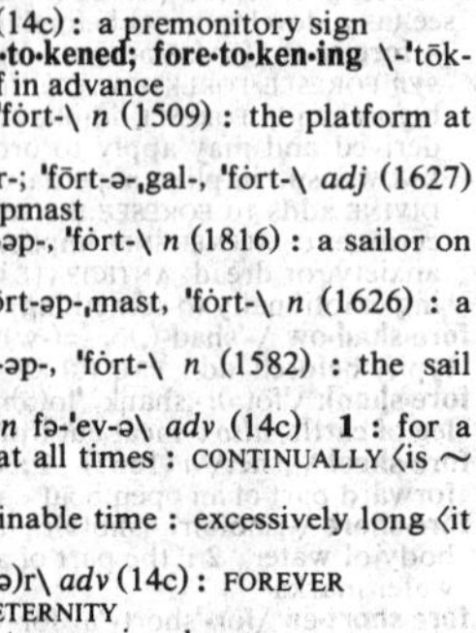
forge 1

smith — more at DAFT] (13c) **1 :** a furnace or a shop with its furnace where metal is heated and wrought **:** SMITHY **2 :** a workshop where wrought iron is produced or where iron is made malleable
[2]**forge** *vb* **forged; forg·ing** *vt* (14c) **1 a :** to form (as metal) by heating and hammering **b :** to form (metal) by a mechanical or hydraulic press with or without heat **2 :** to form or bring into being esp. by an expenditure of effort ⟨working to ~ party unity⟩ **3 :** to make or imitate falsely esp. with intent to defraud **:** COUNTERFEIT ~ *vi* **1 :** to work at a forge **2 :** to commit forgery ***syn*** see MAKE — **forge·abil·i·ty** \ˌfōr-jə-ˈbil-ət-ē, ˌfȯr-\ *n* — **forge·able** \ˈfōr-jə-bəl, ˈfȯr-\ *adj*
[3]**forge** *vi* **forged; forg·ing** [origin unknown] (1611) **1 :** to move forward slowly and steadily ⟨the great ship *forged* ahead through the waves⟩ **2 :** to move with a sudden increase of speed and power ⟨the horse *forged* into the lead in the homestretch⟩
forg·er \ˈfōr-jər, ˈfȯr-\ *n* [[2]*forge*] (14c) **1 a :** one that falsifies; *specif* **:** a creator of false tales **b :** a person guilty of forgery **2 :** one that forges metals
forg·ery \ˈfōrj-(ə-)rē, ˈfȯrj-\ *n, pl* **-er·ies** (1583) **1** *archaic* **:** INVENTION **2 :** an act of forging; *esp* **:** the crime of falsely and fraudulently making or altering a document (as a check) **3 :** something forged
for·get \fər-ˈget, fȯr-\ *vb* **-got** \-ˈgät\; **-got·ten** \-ˈgät-ᵊn\ *or* **-got; -get·ting** [ME *forgeten,* fr. OE *forgietan,* fr. *for-* + *-gietan* (akin to ON *geta* to get)] *vt* (bef. 12c) **1 a :** to lose the remembrance of ⟨I ~ his name⟩ **b** *obs* **:** to cease from doing **2 :** to treat with inattention or disregard ⟨*forgot* his old friends⟩ **3 :** to disregard intentionally **:** OVERLOOK — usu. used in the imperative ⟨~ it⟩ ~ *vi* **1 :** to cease remembering or noticing ⟨forgive and ~⟩ **2 :** to fail to become mindful at the proper time ⟨~ about paying the bill⟩ ***syn*** see NEGLECT — **for·get·ter** *n* — **forget oneself :** to lose one's dignity, temper, or self-control
for·get·ful \-ˈget-fəl\ *adj* (14c) **1 :** likely to forget **2 :** characterized by negligent failure to remember **:** NEGLECTFUL **3 :** inducing oblivion ⟨~ sleep⟩ — **for·get·ful·ly** \-fə-lē\ *adv* — **for·get·ful·ness** *n*
for·ge·tive \ˈfōr-jət-iv, ˈfȯr-\ *adj* [prob. fr. [2]*forge* + *-tive* (as in *inventive*)] *archaic* (1597) **:** INVENTIVE, IMAGINATIVE
for·get–me–not \fər-ˈget-mē-ˌnät, fȯr-\ *n* (1532) **:** any of a genus (*Myosotis*) of small herbs of the borage family having bright-blue or white flowers usu. arranged in a curving spike
for·get·ta·ble \fər-ˈget-ə-bəl, fȯr-\ *adj* (1845) **:** fit or likely to be forgotten
forg·ing \ˈfōr-jiŋ, ˈfȯr-\ *n* (14c) **1 :** the art or process of forging **2 :** a piece of forged work **3 :** FORGERY 2
for·give \fər-ˈgiv, fȯr-\ *vb* **-gave** \-ˈgāv\; **-giv·en** \-ˈgiv-ən\; **-giv·ing** [ME *forgiven,* fr. OE *forgifan,* fr. *for-* + *gifan* to give] *vt* (bef. 12c) **1 :** to cease to feel resentment against (an offender) **:** PARDON ⟨~ one's enemies⟩ **2 a :** to give up resentment of or claim to requital for ⟨~ an insult⟩ **b :** to grant relief from payment of ⟨~ a debt⟩ ~ *vi* **:** to grant forgiveness ***syn*** see EXCUSE — **for·giv·able** \-ˈgiv-ə-bəl\ *adj* — **for·giv·ably** \-blē\ *adv* — **for·giv·er** *n*
for·give·ness \-ˈgiv-nəs\ *n* (bef. 12c) **:** the act of forgiving **:** PARDON
for·giv·ing *adj* (1690) **1 :** willing or able to forgive **2 :** allowing room for error or weakness ⟨designed to be a ~ tennis racquet⟩ — **for·giv·ing·ly** \-ˈgiv-iŋ-lē\ *adv* — **for·giv·ing·ness** *n*
for·go \fȯr-ˈgō, fōr-\ *vt* **-went** \-ˈwent\; **-gone** \-ˈgȯn *also* -ˈgän\; **-go·ing** \-ˈgō-iŋ, -ˈgȯ(-)iŋ\ [ME *forgon,* fr. OE *forgān* to pass by, forgo, fr. *for-* + *gān* to go] (bef. 12c) **1** *archaic* **:** FORSAKE **2 :** to abstain from **:** RENOUNCE — **for·go·er** \-ˈgō(-ə)r\ *n*
for·got·ten man \fər-ˌgät-ᵊn-, fȯr-\ *n* (1925) **:** a person or category of persons that receives less attention than is merited
fo·rint \ˈfō(ə)r-ˌint\ *n, pl* **forints** *also* **forint** [Hung] (ca. 1916) — see MONEY table
forjudge *var of* FOREJUDGE
[1]**fork** \ˈfō(ə)rk\ *n* [ME *forke,* fr. OE & ONF; OE *forca* & ONF *forque,* fr. L *furca*] (bef. 12c) **1 :** an implement with two or more prongs used esp. for taking up (as in eating), pitching, or digging **2 :** a forked part, tool, or piece of equipment **3 a :** a division into branches or the place where something divides into branches **b :** CONFLUENCE **4 :** one of the branches into which something forks **5 :** an attack by one chess piece (as a knight) on two pieces simultaneously — **fork·ful** \-ˌfu̇l\ *n*
[2]**fork** *vi* (15c) **1 :** to divide into two or more branches ⟨where the road ~*s*⟩ **2 a :** to use or work with a fork **b :** to make a turn into or travel a fork ~ *vt* **1 :** to give the form of a fork to ⟨~*ing* her fingers⟩ **2 :** to raise, pitch, dig, or work with a fork ⟨~ hay⟩ **3 :** to attack (two chessmen) simultaneously **4 :** PAY, CONTRIBUTE ⟨had to ~ out $5000 to keep the matter quiet⟩ — **fork·er** *n*
forked \ˈfō(ə)rkt, ˈfȯr-kəd\ *adj* (14c) **1 :** resembling a fork esp. in having one end divided into two or more branches or points ⟨~ lightning⟩ **2 :** shaped like a fork or having a forked part ⟨a ~ road⟩
fork·lift \ˈfȯr-ˌklift\ *n* (1944) **:** a self-propelled machine for hoisting and transporting heavy objects by means of steel fingers inserted under the load
forky \ˈfȯr-kē\ *adj* **fork·i·er; -est** (1697) **:** FORKED ⟨a ~ beard⟩
for·lorn \fər-ˈlȯ(ə)rn, fȯr-\ *adj* [ME *forloren,* fr. OE, pp. of *forlēosan* to lose, fr. *for-* + *lēosan* to lose — more at LOSE] (bef. 12c) **1 a :** BEREFT, FORSAKEN ⟨left quite ~ of hope⟩ **b :** sad and lonely because of isolation or desertion **:** DESOLATE **2 :** being in poor condition **:** MISERABLE, WRETCHED ⟨~ tumbledown buildings⟩ **3 :** nearly hopeless ⟨a ~ attempt⟩ ***syn*** see ALONE — **for·lorn·ly** *adv* — **for·lorn·ness** \-ˈlȯ(ə)rn-nəs\ *n*
forlorn hope *n* [by folk etymology fr. D *verloren hoop,* lit., lost band] (1579) **1 :** a body of men selected to perform a perilous service **2 :** a desperate or extremely difficult enterprise
[1]**form** \ˈfō(ə)rm\ *n* [ME *forme,* fr. OF, fr. L *forma* form, beauty] (13c) **1 a :** the shape and structure of something as distinguished from its material **b :** a body (as of a person) esp. in its external appearance or as distinguished from the face **:** FIGURE **c** *archaic* **:** BEAUTY **2 :** the essential nature of a thing as distinguished from its matter: as **a :** IDEA 1a **b :** the component of a thing that determines its kind **3 a :** established method of expression or proceeding **:** procedure according to rule or rote **b :** a prescribed and set order of words **:** FORMULA ⟨the ~ of the marriage service⟩ **4 :** a printed or typed document with blank spaces for insertion of required or requested information ⟨tax ~*s*⟩ **5 a (1) :** conduct regulated by extraneous controls (as of cus-

tom or etiquette) : CEREMONY (2) : show without substance **b** : manner or conduct as tested by a prescribed or accepted standard ⟨rudeness is simply bad ∼⟩ **c** : manner or style of performing or accomplishing according to recognized standards of technique ⟨a strong swimmer but weak on ∼⟩ **6 a** : the resting place of a hare **b** : a long seat : BENCH **7 a** : a supporting frame model of the human figure or part (as the torso) of the human figure usu. used for displaying apparel **b** : a proportioned and often adjustable model for fitting clothes **c** : a mold in which concrete is placed to set **8** : the printing type or other matter arranged and secured in a chase ready for printing **9 a** : one of the different modes of existence, action, or manifestation of a particular thing or substance : KIND ⟨one ∼ of respiratory disorder⟩ ⟨a ∼ of art⟩ **b** : a distinguishable group of organisms **10 a** (1) : orderly method of arrangement (as in the presentation of ideas) : manner of coordinating elements (as of an artistic production or course of reasoning) (2) : a particular kind or instance of such arrangement ⟨the sonnet is a poetical ∼⟩ **b** : PATTERN, SCHEMA ⟨arguments of the same logical ∼⟩ **c** : the structural element, plan, or design of a work of art — compare CONTENT 2c **d** : a visible and measurable unit defined by a contour : a bounded surface or volume **11** : a grade in a British secondary school or in some American private schools **12 a** (1) : the past performance of a race horse (2) : RACING FORM **b** : known ability to perform ⟨a singer at the top of his ∼⟩ **c** : condition suitable for performing (as in athletic competition) **13 a** : LINGUISTIC FORM **b** : one of the different aspects a word may take as a result of inflection or change of spelling or pronunciation ⟨verbal ∼*s*⟩ **14** : a mathematical expression of a particular type ⟨an equation in parametric ∼⟩

syn FORM, FIGURE, SHAPE, CONFORMATION, CONFIGURATION mean outward appearance. FORM usu. suggests reference to both internal structure and external outline and often the principle that gives unity to the whole; FIGURE applies chiefly to the form as determined by bounding or enclosing lines; SHAPE like FIGURE suggests an outline but carries a stronger implication of the enclosed body or mass; CONFORMATION implies structure composed of related parts; CONFIGURATION refers to the disposition and arrangement of component parts.

²**form** *vt* (13c) **1** : to give form or shape to : FASHION **2 a** : to give a particular shape to : shape or mold into a certain state or after a particular model : ARRANGE ⟨∼ the dough into a ball⟩ ⟨a state ∼*ed* along republican lines⟩ **b** : to arrange themselves in ⟨the women ∼*ed* a line⟩ **c** : to model by instruction and discipline ⟨a mind ∼*ed* by classical education⟩ **3** : DEVELOP, ACQUIRE ⟨∼ a habit⟩ **4** : to serve to make up or constitute : be a usu. essential or basic element of **5 a** : to assume an inflection so as to produce (as a tense) ⟨∼*s* the past in *-ed*⟩ **b** : to combine to make (a compound word) **6** : to arrange in order : DRAW UP ∼ *vi* **1** : to become formed or shaped **2** : to take form : come into existence : ARISE **3** : to take on a definite form, shape, or arrangement ***syn*** see MAKE — **form·abil·i·ty** \ˌfȯr-mə-ˈbil-ət-ē\ *n* — **form·able** \ˈfȯr-mə-bəl\ *adj* — **form on** : to take up a formation next to

form- *or* **formo-** *comb form* [*formic*] : formic acid ⟨*form*ate⟩

-form \ˌfȯrm\ *adj comb form* [MF & L; MF *-forme*, fr. L *-formis*, fr. *forma*] : in the form or shape of : resembling ⟨ovi*form*⟩

¹**for·mal** \ˈfȯr-məl\ *adj* [ME, fr. MF or L; MF, fr. L *formalis*, fr. *forma*] (14c) **1 a** : belonging to or constituting the form or essence of a thing ⟨∼ cause⟩ **b** : relating to or involving the outward form, structure, relationships, or arrangement of elements rather than content ⟨∼ logic⟩ ⟨∼ style of painting⟩ ⟨∼ approach to comparative linguistics⟩ **2 a** : following or according with established form, custom, or rule : CONVENTIONAL ⟨lacked ∼ schooling⟩ **b** : done in due or lawful form ⟨a ∼ contract⟩ **3 a** : characterized by punctilious respect for form : METHODICAL ⟨very ∼ in all his dealings⟩ **b** : rigidly ceremonious : PRIM **4** : having the appearance without the substance ⟨∼ Christians who go to church only at Easter⟩ ***syn*** see CEREMONIAL — **for·mal·ly** \-mə-lē\ *adv* — **for·mal·ness** *n*

²**formal** *n* (1605) : something (as a dance or a dress) formal in character

³**formal** *adj* [*formula* + *-al*] (ca. 1934) : ⁴MOLAR

form·al·de·hyde \fȯr-ˈmal-də-ˌhīd, fər-\ *n* [ISV *form-* + *aldehyde*] (1872) : a colorless pungent irritating gas CH_2O used chiefly as a disinfectant and preservative and in synthesizing other compounds and resins

for·ma·lin \ˈfȯr-mə-lən, -ˌlēn\ *n* [*Formalin*, a trademark] (1893) : a clear aqueous solution of formaldehyde containing a small amount of methanol

for·mal·ism \ˈfȯr-mə-ˌliz-əm\ *n* (ca. 1840) : the practice or the doctrine of strict adherence to prescribed or external forms (as in religion or art); *also* : an instance of this — **for·mal·ist** \-ləst\ *n or adj* — **for·mal·is·tic** \ˌfȯr-mə-ˈlis-tik\ *adj*

for·mal·i·ty \fȯr-ˈmal-ət-ē\ *n, pl* **-ties** (1597) **1** : the quality or state of being formal **2** : compliance with formal or conventional rules : CEREMONY **3** : an established form or procedure that is required or conventional

for·mal·ize \ˈfȯr-mə-ˌlīz\ *vt* **-ized; -iz·ing** (1646) **1** : to give a certain or definite form to : SHAPE **2 a** : to make formal **b** : to give formal status or approval to — **for·mal·iz·able** \-ˌlī-zə-bəl\ *adj* — **for·mal·iza·tion** \ˌfȯr-mə-lə-ˈzā-shən\ *n* — **for·mal·iz·er** \ˈfȯr-mə-ˌlī-zər\ *n*

for·mant \ˈfȯr-mənt, -ˌmant\ *n* (1901) : a characteristic component of the quality of a speech sound; *specif* : any of several resonance bands held to determine the phonetic quality of a vowel

¹**for·mat** \ˈfȯ(ə)r-ˌmat\ *n* [F or G; F, fr. G, fr. L *formatus*, pp. of *formare* to form, fr. *forma*] (1840) **1** : the shape, size, and general makeup (as of something printed) **2** : general plan of organization or arrangement (as of a television show)

²**format** *vt* **for·mat·ted; for·mat·ting** (1964) : to produce in a specified form or style ⟨*formatted* output of a computer⟩

for·mate \ˈfȯ(ə)r-ˌmāt\ *n* (1807) : a salt or ester of formic acid

for·ma·tion \fȯr-ˈmā-shən\ *n* (15c) **1** : an act of giving form or shape to something or of taking form : DEVELOPMENT **2** : something that is formed ⟨new word ∼*s*⟩ **3** : the manner in which a thing is formed : STRUCTURE ⟨the peculiar ∼ of the heart⟩ **4** : the largest unit in an ecological community comprising two or more associations and their precursors **5 a** : any igneous, sedimentary, or metamorphic rock represented as a unit **b** : any sedimentary bed or consecutive series of beds sufficiently homogeneous or distinctive to be a unit **6** : an arrangement of a body or group of persons or things in some prescribed manner or for a particular purpose — **for·ma·tion·al** \-shnəl, -shən-ᵊl\ *adj*

¹**for·ma·tive** \ˈfȯr-mət-iv\ *adj* (15c) **1 a** : giving or capable of giving form : CONSTRUCTIVE ⟨a ∼ influence⟩ **b** : used in word formation or inflection **2** : capable of alteration by growth and development; *also* : producing new cells and tissues **3** : of, relating to, or characterized by formative effects or formation ⟨∼ years⟩ — **for·ma·tive·ly** *adv*

²**formative** *n* (1816) **1** : the element in a word that serves to give the word appropriate form and is not part of the base **2** : the minimal syntactically functioning element in a transformational grammar

form class *n* (1933) : a class of linguistic forms that can be used in the same position in a construction and that have one or more morphological or syntactical features in common

form critical *adj* (1933) : based on or applying form criticism

form criticism *n* (1928) : a method of criticism for determining the sources and historicity of esp. biblical writings through analysis of the writings in terms of traditional literary forms (as love poems, parables, and sayings) — **form critic** *n*

formed \ˈfȯrmd\ *adj* (1605) : organized in a way characteristic of living matter ⟨mitochondria are ∼ bodies of the cell⟩

for·mée \ˈfȯr-ˌmā, fȯr-ˈ\ *adj* [F, fem. pp. of *former* to form, fr. L *formare*] *of a heraldic cross* (1610) : having the arms narrow at the center and expanding toward the ends — see CROSS illustration

¹**for·mer** \ˈfȯr-mər\ *adj* [ME, fr. *forme* first, fr. OE *forma* — more at FOREMOST] (12c) **1 a** : coming before in time **b** : of, relating to, or occurring in the past ⟨∼ correspondence⟩ **2** : preceding in place or arrangement : FOREGOING ⟨∼ part of the chapter⟩ **3** : first mentioned or in order of two things mentioned or understood ⟨of these two evils the ∼ is the lesser⟩ **4** : having been previously : ONETIME ⟨a ∼ athlete⟩ ***syn*** see PRECEDING

²**form·er** \ˈfȯr-mər\ *n* (14c) **1** : one that forms **2** *chiefly Brit* : a member of a school form — usu. used in combination ⟨sixth ∼⟩

for·mer·ly \ˈfȯr-mə(r)-lē\ *adv* (1590) **1** *obs* : just before **2** : at an earlier time : PREVIOUSLY

form·fit·ting \ˈfȯrm-ˌfit-iŋ\ *adj* (1897) : conforming to the outline of the body : fitting snugly ⟨a ∼ sweater⟩

form·ful \ˈfȯrm-fəl\ *adj* (1950) : exhibiting or notable for form

form genus *n* (1873) : an artificial taxonomic category established for organisms (as imperfect fungi) of obscure true relationships

for·mic \ˈfȯr-mik\ *adj* [L *formica* ant — more at PISMIRE] (1791) : derived from formic acid

For·mi·ca \fȯr-ˈmī-kə, fər-\ *trademark* — used for any of various laminated plastic products used esp. for surface finish

formic acid *n* (1791) : a colorless pungent fuming vesicant liquid acid CH_2O_2 found esp. in ants and in many plants and used chiefly in dyeing and finishing textiles

for·mi·cary \ˈfȯr-mə-ˌker-ē\ *n, pl* **-car·ies** [ML *formicarium*, fr. L *formica*] (1816) : an ant nest

for·mi·da·ble \ˈfȯr-məd-ə-bəl *also* fȯr-ˈmid- *or* fər-ˈmid-\ *adj* [ME, fr. L *formidabilis*, fr. *formidare* to fear, fr. *formido* fear; akin to Gk *mormō* she-monster] (15c) **1** : causing fear, dread, or apprehension ⟨a ∼ prospect⟩ **2** : having qualities that discourage approach or attack **3** : tending to inspire awe or wonder — **for·mi·da·bil·i·ty** \ˌfȯr-məd-ə-ˈbil-ət-ē; fȯr-ˌmid-, fər-ˌ\ *n* — **for·mi·da·ble·ness** \ˈfȯr-məd-ə-bəl-nəs; fȯr-ˈmid-, fər-ˈ\ *n* — **for·mi·da·bly** \-blē\ *adv*

form·less \ˈfȯrm-ləs\ *adj* (1591) **1** : having no regular form or shape **2** : lacking order or arrangement **3** : having no physical existence — **form·less·ly** *adv* — **form·less·ness** *n*

form letter *n* (1909) **1** : a letter on a subject of frequent recurrence that can be sent to different people without essential change except in the address **2** : a letter that is printed in many copies, has a very general salutation (as *Dear Friend*), and is sent to a usu. large number of people

formo- — see FORM-

¹**for·mu·la** \ˈfȯr-myə-lə\ *n, pl* **-las** *or* **-lae** \-ˌlē, -ˌlī\ [L, dim. of *forma* form] (1618) **1 a** : a set form of words for use in a ceremony or ritual **b** : a conventionalized statement intended to express some fundamental truth or principle esp. as a basis for negotiation or action **2 a** (1) : RECIPE (2) : PRESCRIPTION **b** : a milk mixture or substitute for feeding an infant **3 a** : a general fact, rule, or principle expressed in usu. mathematical symbols **b** : a symbolic expression of the chemical composition or constitution of a substance **c** : a group of numerical symbols associated to express concisely facts or data (as the number and kinds of teeth in the jaw) **d** : a combination of signs in a logical calculus **4** : a prescribed or set form or method (as of writing) : an established rule or custom — often used derogatorily ⟨television programs that were unimaginative ∼ works⟩ — **for·mu·la·ic** \ˌfȯr-myə-ˈlā-ik\ *adj* — **for·mu·la·ical·ly** \-ˈlā-ə-k(ə-)lē\ *adv*

²**formula** *adj, of a racing car* (1927) : conforming to prescribed specifications as to size, weight, and engine displacement and usu. having a long narrow body, open wheels, a single-seat open cockpit, and the engine in the rear

for·mu·la·rize \ˈfȯr-myə-lə-ˌrīz\ *vt* **-rized; -riz·ing** (1852) : to state in or reduce to a formula : FORMULATE — **for·mu·la·ri·za·tion** \ˌfȯr-myə-lə-rə-ˈzā-shən\ *n* — **for·mu·la·riz·er** \ˈfȯr-myə-lə-ˌrī-zər\ *n*

for·mu·lary \ˈfȯr-myə-ˌler-ē\ *n, pl* **-lar·ies** (1541) **1** : a book or other collection of stated and prescribed forms (as oaths or prayers) **2** : a prescribed form or model : FORMULA **3** : a book containing a list of medicinal substances and formulas — **formulary** *adj*

for·mu·late \ˈfȯr-myə-ˌlāt\ *vt* **-lat·ed; -lat·ing** (1860) **1 a** : to reduce to or express in a formula **b** : to put into a systematized statement or expression **c** : DEVISE ⟨∼ policy⟩ **2 a** : to develop a formula for the preparation of (as a soap or plastic) **b** : to prepare according to a formula — **for·mu·la·tor** \-ˌlāt-ər\ *n*

for·mu·la·tion \ˌfȯr-myə-ˈlā-shən\ *n* (1876) : an act or the product of formulating

formula weight *n* (ca. 1920) : MOLECULAR WEIGHT — used esp. of ionic compounds

for·mu·li·za·tion \ˌfȯr-myə-lə-ˈzā-shən\ *n* (1881) **:** FORMULATION
for·mu·lize \ˈfȯr-myə-ˌlīz\ *vt* **-lized; -liz·ing** (1842) **:** FORMULATE 1
form word *n* (1875) **:** FUNCTION WORD
for·myl \ˈfȯr-ˌmil\ *n* [ISV] (ca. 1864) **:** the radical HCO of formic acid that is also characteristic of aldehydes
for·ni·cate \ˈfȯr-nə-ˌkāt\ *vb* **-cat·ed; -cat·ing** [LL *fornicatus,* pp. of *fornicare,* fr. L *fornic-, fornix* arch, vault, brothel] *vi* (1552) **:** to commit fornication ~ *vt* **:** to commit fornication with — **for·ni·ca·tor** \-ˌkāt-ər\ *n*
for·ni·ca·tion \ˌfȯr-nə-ˈkā-shən\ *n* [ME *fornicacioun,* fr. MF & LL; MF *fornication,* fr. LL *fornication-, fornicatio,* fr. *fornicatus,* pp.] (14c) **1 :** human sexual intercourse other than between a man and his wife **:** sexual intercourse between a spouse and an unmarried person **:** sexual intercourse between unmarried people **2 :** sexual intercourse on the part of an unmarried person accomplished with consent and not deemed adultery ***syn*** see ADULTERY
for·nix \ˈfȯr-niks\ *n, pl* **for·ni·ces** \-nə-ˌsēz\ [NL, fr. L] (1681) **:** an anatomical arch or fold
for·rad·er *also* **for·rard·er** \ˈfär-əd-ər\ *adv* [E dial., compar. of E *forward*] *chiefly Brit* (1888) **:** further ahead
for·sake \fər-ˈsāk, fȯr-\ *vt* **for·sook** \-ˈsu̇k\; **for·sak·en** \-ˈsā-kən\; **for·sak·ing** [ME *forsaken,* fr. OE *forsacan,* fr. *for-* + *sacan* to dispute; akin to OE *sacu* action at law — more at SAKE] (bef. 12c) **1 :** to renounce (as something once cherished) without intent to recover or resume ⟨~ a bad habit⟩ **2 :** to quit or leave entirely **:** withdraw from ⟨*forsook* the theater for politics⟩ ***syn*** see ABANDON
for·sooth \fər-ˈsüth\ *adv* [ME *for soth,* fr. OE *forsōth,* fr. *for* + *sōth* sooth] (bef. 12c) **:** in truth **:** INDEED — often used to imply contempt or doubt
for·spent \fər-ˈspent, fȯr-\ *adj, archaic* (1563) **:** WORN-OUT, EXHAUSTED
for·swear \fȯr-ˈswa(ə)r, fōr-, -ˈswe(ə)r\ *vb* **-swore** \-ˈswō(ə)r, -ˈswȯ(ə)r\; **-sworn** \-ˈswō(ə)rn, -ˈswȯ(ə)rn\; **-swear·ing** *vt* [ME *forsweren,* fr. OE *forswerian,* fr. *for-* + *swerian* to swear] (bef. 12c) **1 a :** to reject or renounce under oath **b :** to renounce earnestly **2 :** to deny under oath **3 :** to make a liar of (oneself) under or as if under oath ~ *vi* **:** to swear falsely ***syn*** see ABJURE
for·sworn \-ˈswō(ə)rn, -ˈswȯ(ə)rn\ *adj* (bef. 12c) **:** guilty of perjury **:** marked by perjury
for·syth·ia \fər-ˈsith-ē-ə, *chiefly Brit* -ˈsīth-\ *n* [NL, genus name, fr. William *Forsyth* †1804 Brit. botanist] (1814) **:** any of a genus (*Forsythia*) of ornamental shrubs of the olive family with opposite leaves and yellow bell-shaped flowers appearing before the leaves in early spring
fort \ˈfō(ə)rt, ˈfȯ(ə)rt\ *n* [ME *forte,* fr. MF *fort,* fr. *fort,* adj., strong, fr. L *fortis;* akin to OE *beorg* mound — more at BARROW] (15c) **1 :** a strong or fortified place; *esp* **:** a fortified place occupied only by troops and surrounded with such works as a ditch, rampart, and parapet **:** FORTIFICATION **2 :** a permanent army post — often used in place names
for·ta·lice \ˈfȯrt-ᵊl-əs\ *n* [ME, fr. ML *fortalitia,* fr. L *fortis*] (15c) **1** *archaic* **:** FORTRESS **2** *archaic* **:** a small fort
[1]**forte** \ˈfō(ə)rt, ˈfȯ(ə)rt; *1 is often* ˈfȯr-ˌtā *or* fȯr-ˈtā *or* ˈfȯrt-ē\ *n* [F *fort,* fr. *fort,* adj., strong] (1682) **1 :** one's strong point **2 :** the part of a sword or foil blade that is between the middle and the hilt and that is the strongest part of the blade
[2]**for·te** \ˈfȯr-ˌtā, ˈfȯrt-ē\ *adv or adj* [It, fr. *forte* strong, fr. L *fortis*] (1724) **:** in a loud and often forceful manner — used as a direction in music
[3]**for·te** \ˈfȯr-ˌtā, ˈfȯrt-ē\ *n* (1759) **:** a tone or passage played forte
for·te–pi·a·no \ˌfȯr-ˌtā-pē-ˈän-(ˌ)ō, ˌfȯrt-ē-\ *adv or adj* (ca. 1897) **:** loud then immediately soft — used as a direction in music
[1]**forth** \ˈfō(ə)rth, ˈfȯ(ə)rth\ *adv* [ME, fr. OE; akin to OE *for*] (bef. 12c) **1 :** onward in time, place, or order **:** FORWARD ⟨from that day ~⟩ **2 :** out into notice or view ⟨put ~ leaves⟩ **3** *obs* **:** AWAY, ABROAD
[2]**forth** *prep, archaic* (bef. 12c) **:** forth from **:** OUT OF
forth·com·ing \(ˈ)fōrth-ˈkəm-iŋ, (ˈ)fȯrth-\ *adj* [obs. *forthcome* (to come forth)] (1521) **1 :** being about to appear **:** APPROACHING ⟨the ~ holidays⟩ **2 a :** readily available ⟨funds will be ~ soon⟩ **b :** SOCIABLE, AFFABLE ⟨a ~ and courteous man⟩ **c :** RESPONSIVE, COOPERATIVE
forth of *prep, archaic* (bef. 12c) **:** out from **:** OUT OF
[1]**forth·right** \ˈfōr-ˌthrīt, ˈfȯr-\ *adv* [ME, fr. OE *forthriht,* fr. *forth* + *riht* right] (bef. 12c) **1 a :** directly forth or ahead **b :** without hesitation **:** FRANKLY **2** *archaic* **:** at once
[2]**forthright** *adj* (bef. 12c) **1** *archaic* **:** proceeding straight on **2 :** free from ambiguity or evasiveness **:** going straight to the point ⟨a ~ critic⟩ ⟨a ~ appraisal of a problem⟩ — **forth·right·ly** *adv* — **forth·right·ness** *n*
[3]**forthright** *n, archaic* (1606) **:** a straight path
forth·with \(ˈ)fōrth-ˈwith, (ˈ)fȯrth-, -ˈwith\ *adv* (14c) **:** IMMEDIATELY
for·ti·fi·ca·tion \ˌfȯrt-ə-fə-ˈkā-shən\ *n* (15c) **1 :** an act or process of fortifying **2 :** something that fortifies, defends, or strengthens; *esp* **:** works erected to defend a place or position
fortified wine *n* (1906) **:** a wine (as sherry) to which alcohol usu. in the form of grape brandy has been added during or after fermentation
for·ti·fi·er \ˈfȯrt-ə-ˌfī(-ə)r\ *n* (ca. 1552) **:** one that fortifies
for·ti·fy \-ˌfī\ *vb* **-fied; -fy·ing** [ME *fortifien,* fr. MF *fortifier,* fr. LL *fortificare,* fr. L *fortis* strong] *vt* (15c) **:** to make strong: as **a :** to strengthen and secure (as a town) by forts or batteries **b :** to give physical strength, courage, or endurance to **:** INVIGORATE ⟨*fortified* himself with a glass of wine⟩ **c :** to add mental or moral strength to **:** ENCOURAGE ⟨*fortified* by prayer⟩ **d :** to add material to for strengthening or enriching ~ *vi* **:** to erect fortifications
for·tis \ˈfȯrt-əs\ *adj* [NL, fr. L, strong] (ca. 1909) **:** produced with relatively great articulatory tenseness and strong expiration ⟨\t\ in *toe* is ~, \d\ in *doe* is lenis⟩
[1]**for·tis·si·mo** \fȯr-ˈtis-ə-ˌmō\ *adv or adj* [It, superl. of *forte*] (1724) **:** very loud — used as a direction in music
[2]**fortissimo** *n, pl* **-mos** *or* **-mi** \-ˌmē\ (1856) **:** a very loud passage, sound, or tone
for·ti·tude \ˈfȯrt-ə-ˌt(y)üd\ *n* [ME, fr. L *fortitudin-, fortitudo,* fr. *fortis*] (12c) **1** *obs* **:** STRENGTH **2 :** strength of mind that enables a person to encounter danger or bear pain or adversity with courage
fort·night \ˈfȯrt-ˌnīt, ˈfȯrt-\ *n* [ME *fourtenight,* alter. of *fourtene night,* fr. OE *fēowertȳne niht* fourteen nights] (bef. 12c) **:** a period of 14 days **:** two weeks
[1]**fort·night·ly** \-lē\ *adj* (1800) **:** occurring or appearing once in a fortnight
[2]**fortnightly** *adv* (1820) **:** once in a fortnight **:** every fortnight
[3]**fortnightly** *n, pl* **-lies** (1940) **:** a publication issued fortnightly
FOR·TRAN *or* **For·tran** \ˈfȯ(ə)r-ˌtran\ *n* [*for*mula *tran*slation] (1956) **:** an algebraic and logical language for programming a computer
for·tress \ˈfȯr-trəs\ *n* [ME *forteresse,* fr. MF *forteresce,* fr. ML *fortalitia* fortalice] (14c) **:** a fortified place **:** STRONGHOLD; *esp* **:** a large and permanent fortification sometimes including a town
for·tu·itous \fȯr-ˈt(y)ü-ət-əs, fər-\ *adj* [L *fortuitus;* akin to L *fort-, fors*] (1653) **1 :** occurring by chance **2 :** FORTUNATE, LUCKY ***syn*** see ACCIDENTAL — **for·tu·itous·ly** *adv* — **for·tu·itous·ness** *n*
for·tu·ity \-ət-ē\ *n, pl* **-ities** [irreg. fr. *fortuitous*] (1747) **1 :** the quality or state of being fortuitous **2 :** a chance event or occurrence
for·tu·nate \ˈfȯrch-(ə-)nət\ *adj* (14c) **1 :** bringing some good thing not foreseen as certain **:** AUSPICIOUS **2 :** receiving some unexpected good ***syn*** see LUCKY — **for·tu·nate·ly** *adv* — **for·tu·nate·ness** *n*
[1]**for·tune** \ˈfȯr-chən\ *n* [ME, fr. MF, fr. L *fortuna;* akin to L *fort-, fors* chance, luck, *ferre* to carry — more at BEAR] (14c) **1** *often cap* **:** a hypothetical force or personified power that unpredictably determines events and issues favorably or unfavorably **2** *obs* **:** ACCIDENT, INCIDENT **3 a :** prosperity attained partly through luck **:** SUCCESS **b :** LUCK 1 **c** *pl* **:** the turns and courses of luck accompanying one's progress (as through life) ⟨her ~s varied but she never gave up⟩ **4 :** DESTINY, FATE ⟨tell his ~ with cards⟩; *also* **:** a prediction of fortune **5 a :** possession of material goods **:** WEALTH ⟨a man of ~⟩ **b :** a store of material possessions ⟨the family ~⟩ **c :** a very large sum of money ⟨won a ~ playing the races⟩
[2]**fortune** *vb* **for·tuned; for·tun·ing** *vt* (14c) **1** *obs* **:** to give good or bad fortune to **2** *archaic* **:** to endow with a fortune ~ *vi, archaic* **:** HAPPEN, CHANCE
fortune cookie *n* (1962) **:** a thin folded cookie containing a slip of paper on which is printed a fortune, proverb, or humorous statement
fortune hunter *n* (1689) **:** a person who seeks wealth esp. by marriage
for·tune–tell·er \-ˌtel-ər\ *n* (1590) **:** one that professes to foretell future events — **for·tune–tell·ing** \-iŋ\ *n or adj*
for·ty \ˈfȯrt-ē\ *n, pl* **forties** [ME *fourty,* adj., fr. OE *fēowertig,* fr. *fēowertig* group of 40, fr. *fēower* four + *-tig* group of 10 — more at TEN] (bef. 12c) **1** — see NUMBER table **2** *pl* **:** the numbers 40 to 49; *specif* **:** the years 40 to 49 in a lifetime or century **3 :** the third point scored by a side in a game of tennis — **for·ti·eth** \ˈfȯrt-ē-əth\ *adj or n* — **forty** *adj or pron*
for·ty–five \ˌfȯrt-ē-ˈfīv\ *n* (bef. 12c) **1** — see NUMBER table **2 :** a .45 caliber handgun — usu. written .45 **3 :** a microgroove phonograph record designed to be played at 45 revolutions per minute — usu. written 45 — **forty–five** *adj or pron*
Forty Hours *n pl but sing or pl in constr* (1759) **:** a Roman Catholic devotion in which the churches of a diocese in two-day turns have the Blessed Sacrament exposed on the altar for continuous daytime veneration
for·ty–nin·er \ˌfȯrt-ē-ˈnī-nər\ *n* (1853) **:** one taking part in the rush to California for gold in 1849
forty winks *n pl but sing or pl in constr* (1872) **:** a short sleep **:** NAP
fo·rum \ˈfōr-əm, ˈfȯr-\ *n, pl* **forums** *also* **fo·ra** \-ə\ [L; akin to L *foris* outside, *fores* door — more at DOOR] (15c) **1 a :** the marketplace or public place of an ancient Roman city forming the center of judicial and public business **b :** a public meeting place for open discussion **c :** a medium (as a newspaper) of open discussion or expression of ideas **2 :** a judicial body or assembly **:** COURT **3 a :** a public meeting or lecture involving audience discussion **b :** a program (as on radio or television) involving discussion of a problem usu. by several authorities
[1]**for·ward** \ˈfȯr-wərd, *Southern also* ˈfär-\ *adj* [ME, fr. OE *foreweard* fr. *fore-* + *-weard* -ward] (bef. 12c) **1 a :** near, being at, or belonging to the forepart **b :** situated in advance **2 a :** strongly inclined **:** READY **b :** lacking modesty or reserve **:** BRASH **3 :** notably advanced or developed **:** PRECOCIOUS **4 :** moving, tending, or leading toward a position in front; *also* **:** moving toward an opponent's goal **5 a :** advocating an advanced policy in the direction of what is considered progress **b :** EXTREME, RADICAL **6 :** of, relating to, or getting ready for the future ⟨~ buying of produce⟩ — **for·ward·ly** *adv* — **for·ward·ness** *n*
[2]**forward** *adv* (bef. 12c) **:** to or toward what is ahead or in front ⟨from that time ~⟩ ⟨moved slowly ~ through the mud⟩
[3]**forward** *vt* (1596) **1 :** to help onward **:** PROMOTE ⟨~*ed* his friend's career⟩ **2 a :** to send forward **:** TRANSMIT ⟨will ~ the goods on receipt of his check⟩ **b :** to send or ship onward from an intermediate post or station in transit ⟨~ mail to the new address⟩ ***syn*** see ADVANCE
[4]**forward** *n* (1879) **:** a player in any of several games who plays at the front of his team's formation near the goal at which his team is attempting to score
for·ward·er \-wərd-ər\ *n* (1549) **:** one that forwards; *esp* **:** an agent who performs services (as receiving, transshipping, or delivering) designed to assure and facilitate the passage of goods of his principal to their destination
for·ward·ing \-wərd-iŋ\ *n* (1635) **:** the act of one that forwards; *esp* **:** the business of a forwarder of goods
for·ward–look·ing \ˈfȯr-wərd-ˌlu̇k-iŋ\ *adj* (1800) **:** concerned with or planning for the future
forward pass *n* (ca. 1903) **:** a pass in football thrown in the direction of the opponents' goal
for·wards \ˈfȯr-wərdz\ *adv* (15c) **:** FORWARD
for·worn \fər-ˈwō(ə)rn, -ˈwȯ(ə)rn\ *adj, archaic* (1528) **:** WORN-OUT
for·zan·do \fȯrt-ˈsän-(ˌ)dō\ *adj or adv* [It] (ca. 1828) **:** SFORZANDO
fos·sa \ˈfäs-ə\ *n, pl* **fos·sae** \-ˌē, -ˌī\ [NL, fr. L, ditch] (1771) **:** an anatomical pit, groove, or depression
fosse *or* **foss** \ˈfäs\ *n* [ME *fosse,* fr. OF, fr. L *fossa,* fr. fem. of *fossus*] (15c) **:** DITCH, MOAT
fos·sick \ˈfäs-ik\ *vb* [E dial. *fussick, fussock* to potter, irreg. fr. E *fuss*] *vi* (1852) **1** *Austral* **:** to search for gold typically by picking over abandoned workings **2** *chiefly Austral* **:** to search about **:** RUMMAGE ~ *vt, chiefly Austral* **:** to search for, by, or as if by rummaging **:** ferret out — **fos·sick·er** *n, chiefly Austral*
[1]**fos·sil** \ˈfäs-əl\ *adj* [L *fossilis* dug up, fr. *fossus,* pp. of *fodere* to dig — more at BED] (1654) **1 :** having the characteristics of a fossil: as **a :** preserved in a mineralized or petrified form from a past geologic age ⟨~ imprint of a raindrop⟩ **b :** being water that accumulated in an

underground reservoir in a past geologic age **2 :** being or resembling a fossil **3 :** of or relating to fossil fuel

[2]**fossil** *n* (1736) **1 :** a remnant, impression, or trace of an animal or plant of past geologic ages that has been preserved in the earth's crust **2 a :** one whose views are outmoded : FOGY **b :** something (as a theory) that has become rigidly fixed **3 :** an old word or word element preserved only by idiom (as *fro* in *to and fro*)

fossil fuel *n* (1835) **:** a fuel (as coal, oil, or natural gas) that is formed in the earth from plant or animal remains

fos·sil·if·er·ous \\ˌfäs-ə-ˈlif-(ə-)rəs\\ *adj* (1847) **:** containing fossils

fos·sil·ize \\ˈfäs-ə-ˌlīz\\ *vb* **-ized; -iz·ing** *vt* (1794) **1 :** to convert into a fossil **2 :** to make outmoded, rigid, or fixed ~ *vi* **:** to become changed into a fossil — **fos·sil·iza·tion** \\ˌfäs-ə-lə-ˈzā-shən\\ *n*

fos·so·ri·al \\fä-ˈsōr-ē-əl, -ˈsȯr-\\ *adj* [ML *fossorius,* fr. L *fossus,* pp.] (1836) **:** adapted to digging ⟨a ~ foot⟩

[1]**fos·ter** \\ˈfȯs-tər, ˈfäs-\\ *adj* [ME, fr. OE *fōstor-,* fr. *fōstor* food, feeding; akin to OE *fōda* food] (bef. 12c) **:** affording, receiving, or sharing nurture or parental care though not related by blood or legal ties

[2]**foster** *vt* **fos·tered; fos·ter·ing** \\-t(ə-)riŋ\\ (bef. 12c) **1 :** to give parental care to : NURTURE **2 :** to promote the growth or development of : ENCOURAGE — **fos·ter·er** \\-tər-ər\\ *n*

fos·ter·age \\-tə-rij\\ *n* (1614) **1 :** the act of fostering **2 :** a custom once prevalent in Ireland, Wales, and Scotland of entrusting one's child to foster parents to be brought up

fos·ter·ling \\-tər-liŋ\\ *n* (bef. 12c) **:** a foster child

fou \\ˈfü\\ *adj* [ME (Sc) *fow* full, fr. ME *full*] *Scot* (1535) **:** DRUNK

Fou·cault pendulum \\ˌfü-ˌkō-\\ *n* [J.B.L. *Foucault*] (1931) **:** a device that consists of a heavy weight hung by a long wire and that swings in a constant direction which appears to change showing that the earth rotates

fought *past and past part of* FIGHT

[1]**foul** \\ˈfau̇(ə)l\\ *adj* [ME, fr. OE *fūl;* akin to OHG *fūl* rotten, L *pus* pus, *putēre* to stink, Gk *pyon* pus] (bef. 12c) **1 a :** offensive to the senses : LOATHSOME **b :** filled or covered with offensive matter **2 :** full of dirt or mud **3 a :** morally or spiritually odious : DETESTABLE ⟨a ~ crime⟩ **b :** notably unpleasant or distressing : WRETCHED, HORRID ⟨in a ~ mood⟩ **4 :** OBSCENE, ABUSIVE ⟨~ language⟩ **5 a :** being wet and stormy **b :** obstructive to navigation ⟨a ~ tide⟩ **6** *dial Brit* **:** HOMELY, UGLY **7 a :** TREACHEROUS, DISHONORABLE ⟨fair means or ~⟩ **b :** constituting an infringement of rules in a game or sport ⟨a ~ blow in boxing⟩ **8 :** containing marked-up corrections ⟨~ manuscript⟩ ⟨~ proofs⟩ **9 :** encrusted, clogged, or choked with a foreign substance ⟨the chimney was ~ and smoked badly⟩ **10 :** being odorous and impure : POLLUTED ⟨~ air⟩ **11 :** placed in a situation that impedes physical movement : ENTANGLED **12 :** being outside the foul lines in baseball *syn* see DIRTY — **foul·ly** \\ˈfau̇(l)-lē\\ *adv* — **foul·ness** *n*

[2]**foul** *n* (bef. 12c) **1** *archaic* **:** bad luck **2 :** an entanglement or collision esp. in angling or sailing **3 a :** an infringement of the rules in a game or sport **b :** FREE THROW **4 :** FOUL BALL

[3]**foul** *vi* (bef. 12c) **1 :** to become or be foul: as **a :** DECOMPOSE, ROT **b :** to become encrusted, clogged, or choked with a foreign substance **c :** to become entangled or come into collision **2 :** to commit a violation of the rules in a sport or game **3 :** to hit a foul ball ~ *vt* **1 :** to make foul: as **a :** to make dirty : POLLUTE **b :** to become entangled or come into collision with **c :** to encrust with a foreign substance ⟨a ship's bottom ~*ed* with barnacles⟩ **d :** OBSTRUCT, BLOCK **2 :** DISHONOR, DISCREDIT **3 :** to commit a foul against **4 :** to hit (a baseball) foul

[4]**foul** *adv* (13c) **:** in a foul manner **:** so as to be foul

fou·lard \\fü-ˈlärd\\ *n* [F] (1830) **1 a :** a lightweight plain-woven or twilled silk usu. decorated with a printed pattern **b :** an imitation of this fabric **2 :** an article of clothing made of foulard

foul ball *n* (1860) **:** a baseball batted into foul territory

foul·brood \\ˈfau̇l-ˌbrüd\\ *n* (1863) **:** a destructive bacterial disease of the larvae of the honeybee

foul·ing *n* (14c) **:** DEPOSIT, INCRUSTATION ⟨~ on a ship's bottom⟩

foul line *n* (1878) **1 :** either of two straight lines extending from the rear corner of home plate through the outer corners of first and third base respectively and prolonged to the boundary of a baseball field **2 :** a line across a bowling alley that a player must not step over when delivering the ball **3 :** either of two lines on a basketball court parallel to and 15 feet from the backboards behind which a player must stand while shooting a free throw

foul·mouthed \\ˈfau̇l-ˈmau̇t͟hd, -ˈmau̇tht\\ *adj* (1596) **:** given to the use of obscene, profane, or abusive language

foul out *vi* (ca. 1897) **:** to be put out of a basketball game for exceeding the number of fouls permitted

foul play *n* (15c) **:** VIOLENCE; *esp* **:** MURDER

foul tip *n* [[1]*foul* + *tip* (tap)] (1870) **:** a pitched ball in baseball that is slightly deflected by the bat; *specif* **:** a tipped pitch legally caught by the catcher and counting as a full strike with the ball remaining in play

foul–up \\ˈfau̇-ˌləp\\ *n* (1950) **1 :** a state of confusion caused by ineptitude, carelessness, or mismanagement ⟨~*s* in transportation⟩ **2 :** a mechanical difficulty ⟨a ~ in the steering mechanism — *Springfield (Mass.) Union*⟩

foul up \\(ˈ)fau̇-ˈləp\\ *vt* (1950) **1 :** to make dirty : CONTAMINATE **2 :** to spoil by making mistakes or using poor judgment : CONFUSE **3 :** ENTANGLE, BLOCK ⟨*fouled up* communications⟩ ~ *vi* **:** to become confused : get into difficulty : BUNGLE ⟨it was his fault. He had *fouled up* — Pat Frank⟩

[1]**found** \\ˈfau̇nd\\ *past and past part of* FIND

[2]**found** *adj* (1793) **1 :** having all usual, standard, or reasonably expected equipment ⟨the boat comes fully ~, ready to go — *Holiday*⟩ **2 :** presented as or incorporated into an artistic work essentially as found ⟨sculpture of fabric, wood, and other ~ materials — Hilton Kramer⟩

[3]**found** *n* (1830) **:** free food and lodging in addition to wages ⟨they're paid $175 a month and ~ — *New Yorker*⟩

[4]**found** *vt* [ME *founden,* fr. OF *fonder,* fr. L *fundare,* fr. *fundus* bottom — more at BOTTOM] (13c) **1 :** to take the first steps in building **2 :** to set or ground on something solid : BASE **3 :** to establish (as an institution) often with provision for future maintenance

[5]**found** *vt* [MF *fondre* to pour, melt, fr. L *fundere;* akin to OE *gēotan* to pour, Gk *chein*] (1562) **:** to melt (metal) and pour into a mold

foun·da·tion \\fau̇n-ˈdā-shən\\ *n* (14c) **1 :** the act of founding **2 :** a basis (as a tenet, principle, or axiom) upon which something stands or is supported ⟨the ~*s* of geometry⟩ ⟨the rumor is without ~ in fact⟩ **3 a :** funds given for the permanent support of an institution : ENDOWMENT **b :** an organization or institution established by endowment with provision for future maintenance **4 :** an underlying natural or prepared base or support; *esp* **:** the whole masonry substructure of a building **5 a :** a body or ground upon which something is built up or overlaid **b :** a woman's supporting undergarment : CORSET — **foun·da·tion·al** \\-shnəl, -shən-ᵊl\\ *adj* — **foun·da·tion·al·ly** \\-ē\\ *adv* — **foun·da·tion·less** \\-shən-ləs\\ *adj*

foundation stone *n* (1651) **1 :** a stone in the foundation of a building; *esp* **:** such a stone laid with public ceremony — compare CORNERSTONE **2 :** BASIS, GROUNDWORK

[1]**found·er** \\ˈfau̇n-dər\\ *n* [[4]*found*] (14c) **:** one that founds or establishes

[2]**foun·der** \\ˈfau̇n-dər\\ *vb* **foun·dered; foun·der·ing** \\-d(ə-)riŋ\\ [ME *foundren* to send to the bottom, collapse, fr. MF *fondrer,* deriv. of L *fundus*] *vi* (14c) **1 :** to become disabled; *esp* **:** to go lame **2 :** to give way : COLLAPSE **3 :** to sink below the surface of the water **4 :** to come to grief : FAIL ~ *vt* **:** to disable (an animal) esp. by excessive feeding

[3]**foun·der** *n* (ca. 1547) **:** the condition of a foundered horse; *esp* **:** inflammation of a horse's hoof accompanied by pain and lameness

[4]**found·er** *n* [[5]*found*] (15c) **:** one that founds metal; *specif* **:** TYPEFOUNDER

foun·der·ous *or* **foun·drous** \\ˈfau̇n-d(ə-)rəs\\ *adj* (1767) **:** likely to cause one to founder : MIRY

founding father *n* (1914) **1 :** an originator of an institution or movement : FOUNDER **2** *cap both Fs* **:** a member of the American Constitutional Convention of 1787

found·ling \\ˈfau̇n-(d)liŋ\\ *n* (14c) **:** an infant found after its unknown parents have abandoned it

found object *n* (1959) **:** OBJET TROUVÉ

found·ry \\ˈfau̇n-drē\\ *n, pl* **foundries** (1601) **1 :** the act, process, or art of casting metals; *also* **:** CASTINGS **2 :** an establishment where founding is carried on

[1]**fount** \\ˈfau̇nt\\ *n* [ME, fr. MF *font,* fr. L *font-, fons*] (15c) **:** SOURCE, FOUNTAIN

[2]**fount** \\ˈfänt, ˈfau̇nt\\ *n* [F *fonte,* fr. MF — more at FONT] *Brit* (ca. 1683) **:** a type font

[1]**foun·tain** \\ˈfau̇nt-ᵊn\\ *n* [ME, fr. MF *fontaine,* fr. LL *fontana,* fr. L, fem. of *fontanus* of a spring, fr. *font-, fons*] (15c) **1 :** a spring of water issuing from the earth **2 :** SOURCE **3 :** an artificially produced jet of water; *also* **:** the structure from which it rises **4 :** a reservoir containing a liquid that can be drawn off as needed

[2]**fountain** *vi* (1903) **:** to flow or spout like a fountain ~ *vt* **:** to cause to flow like a fountain

foun·tain·head \\-ˌhed\\ *n* (1585) **1 :** a spring that is the source of a stream **2 :** principal source : ORIGIN

fountain pen *n* (1710) **:** a pen containing a reservoir that automatically feeds the writing point with ink

four \\ˈfō(ə)r, ˈfȯ(ə)r\\ *n* [ME, fr. *four* adj., fr. OE *fēower;* akin to OHG *fior* four, L *quattuor,* Gk *tessares, tettares*] (bef. 12c) **1** — see NUMBER table **2 :** the fourth in a set or series ⟨the ~ of hearts⟩ **3 :** something having four units or members: as **a :** a 4-oared racing shell or its crew **b :** a 4-cylinder engine or automobile — **four** *adj or pron*

four–bag·ger \\-ˈbag-ər\\ *n* (1926) **:** HOME RUN

four–ball \\-ˌbȯl\\ *adj* (1904) **:** relating to or being a golf match in which the best individual score of one partnership is matched against the best individual score of another partnership for each hole

four–channel *adj* (1971) **:** of or relating to quadriphony

four·chée \\fu̇(ə)r-ˈshā\\ *adj* [F (fem.), lit., forked] *of a heraldic cross* (1706) **:** having the end of each arm forked — see CROSS illustration

four–dimensional *adj* (1886) **:** relating to or having four dimensions ⟨~ space-time continuum⟩; *esp* **:** consisting of or relating to elements requiring four coordinates to determine them

four·dri·nier \\ˌfōr-drə-ˈni(ə)r, ˌfȯr-; fu̇r-ˈdrin-ē-ər, fōr-, fȯr-\\ *n, often cap* [Henry & Sealy *Fourdrinier*] (1839) **:** a machine for making paper in an endless web

four–flush *vi* (1896) **:** to bluff in poker holding a four flush; *broadly* **:** to make a false claim : BLUFF — **four–flush·er** \\-ˈfləsh-ər\\ *n*

four flush *n* (1887) **:** four cards of the same suit in a 5-card poker hand

four·fold \\ˈfō(ə)r-ˌfōld, ˈfȯ(ə)r-, -ˈfōld\\ *adj* [ME, fr. OE *fēowerfeald,* fr. *fēower* + *-feald* -fold] (bef. 12c) **1 :** being four times as great or as many **2 :** having four units or members — **four·fold** \\-ˈfōld\\ *adv*

four–foot·ed \\-ˈfu̇t-əd\\ *adj* (14c) **:** having four feet : QUADRUPED

four·gon \\fu̇(ə)r-ˈgōⁿ\\ *n, pl* **fourgons** \\-ˈgōⁿ(z)\\ [F] (1848) **:** a wagon for carrying baggage

4–H \\(ˈ)fō(ə)r-ˈāch, (ˈ)fȯ(ə)r-\\ *adj* [fr. the fourfold aim of improving the head, heart, hands, and health] (1926) **:** of or relating to a program set up by the U.S. Department of Agriculture orig. in rural areas to help young people become productive citizens by instructing them in useful skills (as in agriculture, animal husbandry, and carpentry), community service, and personal development — **4–H'·er** \\-ˈā-chər\\ *n*

four–hand \\ˈfō(ə)r-ˌhand, ˈfȯ(ə)r-\\ *adj* (ca. 1909) **:** FOUR-HANDED

four–hand·ed \\-ˈhan-dəd\\ *adj* (1774) **1 :** designed for four hands ⟨a ~ musical composition⟩ **2 :** engaged in by four persons ⟨a ~ card game⟩

Four Horsemen *n pl* [fr. the apocalyptic vision in Rev 6:2–8] (1925) **:** war, famine, pestilence, and death personified as the four major plagues of mankind

Four Hundred *or* **400** *n* (1888) **:** the exclusive social set of a community — used with *the*

Fou·ri·er analysis \\ˌfu̇r-ē-ˌā-\\ *n* [Baron J.B.J. *Fourier* †1830 Fr. geometrician & physicist] (ca. 1928) **:** the process of using the terms of a Fourier series to find a function that approximates periodic data

Fou·ri·er·ism \\ˈfu̇r-ē-ə-ˌriz-əm, -ē-ˌā-ˌiz-\\ *n* [F *fouriérisme,* fr. F.M.C. *Fourier*] (1841) **:** a system for reorganizing society into cooperative communities of small groups living in common — **Fou·ri·er·ist** \\-ē-ə-rəst, -ē-ˌā-əst\\ *n*

\\ə\\ abut \\ᵊ\\ kitten, F table \\ər\\ further \\a\\ ash \\ā\\ ace \\ä\\ cot, cart \\au̇\\ out \\ch\\ chin \\e\\ bet \\ē\\ easy \\g\\ go \\i\\ hit \\ī\\ ice \\j\\ job \\ŋ\\ sing \\ō\\ go \\ȯ\\ law \\ȯi\\ boy \\th\\ thin \\t͟h\\ the \\ü\\ loot \\u̇\\ foot \\y\\ yet \\zh\\ vision \\ȧ, k̟, ⁿ, œ, œ̄, ue, ue̅, ʸ\\ *see* Guide to Pronunciation

Fou·ri·er series \\,fu̇r-ē-,ā-\\ *n* [Baron J.B.J. *Fourier*] (ca. 1909) **:** an infinite series in which the terms are constants multiplied by sine or cosine functions of integer multiples of the variable and which is used in the analysis of periodic functions

Fourier's theorem *n* (1880) **:** a theorem in mathematics: under suitable conditions any periodic function can be represented by a Fourier series

Fourier transform *n* (1948) **:** a function (as *F(u)*) that under suitable conditions can be obtained from a given function (as *f(x)*) by multiplying by e^{iux} and integrating over all values of *x*

four–in–hand \\'fōr-ən-,hand, 'fȯr-\\ *n* (1793) **1 :** a necktie tied in a slipknot with long ends overlapping vertically in front **2 a :** a team of four horses driven by one person **b :** a vehicle drawn by such a team

four–letter *adj* (1923) **:** of, relating to, or being four-letter words **:** OBSCENE, PORNOGRAPHIC

four–letter word *n* (1934) **:** any of a group of vulgar or obscene words typically made up of four letters

four–line octave *n* [fr. the four accent marks appended to the letters representing its notes] (1931) **:** the musical octave that begins on the third C above middle C — see PITCH illustration

four–o'clock \\'fōr-ə-,kläk, 'fȯr-\\ *n* (1756) **:** any of a genus (*Mirabilis*) of chiefly American annual or perennial herbs (family Nyctaginaceae, the four-o'clock family) having apetalous flowers with a showy involucre simulating a calyx; *esp* **:** a garden plant (*M. jalapa*) with fragrant yellow, red, or white flowers opening late in the afternoon

four of a kind (ca. 1934) **:** four cards of the same rank in one hand — see POKER illustration

four·pen·ny nail \\,fōr-,pen-ē-, ,fȯr-\\ *n* (15c) **:** a nail 1 3/8 inches long

four–post·er \\(')fōr-'pō-stər, (')fȯr-\\ *n* (1836) **:** a bed with tall often carved corner posts orig. designed to support curtains or a canopy

four·ra·gère \\,fu̇r-ə-'zhe(ə)r\\ *n* [F, fr. *fourrager*, adj., yielding forage, fr. *fourrage* forage] (1919) **:** a braided cord worn usu. around the left shoulder; *esp* **:** such a cord awarded as a decoration to a military unit

four·score \\'fōr-'skō(ə)r, 'fȯr-'skȯ(ə)r\\ *adj* (13c) **:** being four times twenty **:** EIGHTY

four·some \\'fōr-səm, 'fȯr-\\ *n* (14c) **1 a :** a group of four persons or things **:** QUARTET **b :** two couples **2 :** a golf match between two pairs of partners

four·square \\-'skwa(ə)r, -'skwe(ə)r\\ *adj* (14c) **1 :** SQUARE **2 :** marked by boldness and conviction **:** FORTHRIGHT — **foursquare** *adv*

four–star \\-'stär\\ *adj* [fr. the number of asterisks used to denote relative excellence in guidebooks] (1921) **:** of a superior degree of excellence ⟨a ~ French restaurant⟩

four·teen \\(')fōr(t)-'tēn, (')fȯr(t)-\\ *n* [ME *fourtene*, fr. OE *fēowertīene*, fr. *fēowertiene*, adj., fr. *fēower* + *-tīene* (akin to OE *tīen* ten) — more at TEN] (bef. 12c) — see NUMBER table — **fourteen** *adj or pron* — **four·teenth** \\-'tēn(t)th\\ *adj or n*

four·teen·er \\-'tē-nər\\ *n* (1884) **:** a verse consisting of 14 syllables or esp. of 7 iambic feet

fourth \\'fō(ə)rth, 'fȯ(ə)rth\\ *n, pl* **fourths** \\'fō(ə)r(th)s, 'fȯ(ə)r(th)s\\ (bef. 12c) **1** — see NUMBER table **2 a :** a musical interval embracing four tones of the diatonic scale **b :** a tone at this interval; *specif* **:** SUBDOMINANT **a c :** the harmonic combination of two tones a fourth apart **3 :** the 4th forward gear or speed of a motor vehicle **4** *cap* **:** INDEPENDENCE DAY — **fourth** *adj or adv* — **fourth·ly** *adv*

fourth class *n* (1862) **1 :** a class or group ranking fourth in a series **2 :** a class of mail in the U.S. that comprises merchandise and non-second-class printed matter and is not sealed against inspection

fourth dimension *n* (1875) **1 :** a dimension in addition to length, breadth, and depth; *specif* **:** a coordinate in addition to three rectangular coordinates esp. when interpreted as the time coordinate in a space-time continuum **2 :** something outside the range of ordinary experience — **fourth–dimensional** *adj*

fourth estate *n, often cap F&E* (1837) **:** the public press

Fourth of July (1779) **:** INDEPENDENCE DAY

fourth world *n, often cap F&W* [after *third world*] (1974) **:** a group of nations esp. in Africa and Asia characterized by extremely low per capita income and an absence of valuable natural resources

four–way \\'fōr-'wā, 'fȯr-\\ *adj* (1824) **1 :** allowing passage in any of four directions **2 :** including four participants

four–wheel \\,fōr-,hwēl, ,fȯr-, -,wēl\\ *or* **four–wheeled** \\'fōr-'hwē(ə)ld, 'fȯr-, -'wē(ə)ld\\ *adj* (1622) **1 :** having four wheels **2 :** acting on or by means of four wheels of an automotive vehicle ⟨~ drive⟩

four–wheel·er \\-'hwē-lər, -'wē-\\ *n* (1846) **:** a vehicle with four wheels

fo·vea \\'fō-vē-ə\\ *n, pl* **fo·ve·ae** \\-vē-,ē, -vē-,ī\\ [NL, fr. L, pit] (1849) **:** a small fossa; *esp* **:** a small rodless area of the retina that affords acute vision — see EYE illustration — **fo·ve·al** \\-vē-əl\\ *adj* — **fo·ve·ate** \\-vē-,āt, -ət\\ *adj*

fovea cen·tra·lis \\-sen-'tral-əs, -'träl-, -'trāl-\\ *n* [NL, central fovea] (1858) **:** the fovea of the retina of the eye

¹fowl \\'fau̇(ə)l\\ *n, pl* **fowl** *or* **fowls** [ME *foul*, fr. OE *fugel*; akin to OHG *fogal* bird] (bef. 12c) **1 :** a bird of any kind — compare WATERFOWL, WILDFOWL **2 a :** a cock or hen of the domestic chicken (*Gallus gallus*); *esp* **:** an adult hen **b :** any of several domesticated or wild gallinaceous birds — compare GUINEA FOWL, JUNGLE FOWL **3 :** the meat of fowls used as food

²fowl *vi* (bef. 12c) **:** to seek, catch, or kill wildfowl — **fowl·er** *n*

fowling piece *n* (1596) **:** a shotgun for shooting birds or small quadrupeds

¹fox \\'fäks\\ *n, pl* **fox·es** *also* **fox** *often attrib* [ME, fr. OE; akin to OHG *fuhs* fox, Skt *puccha* tail] (bef. 12c) **1 a :** any of various alert carnivorous mammals (esp. genus *Vulpes*) of the dog family related to but smaller than wolves with shorter legs, more pointed muzzle, large erect ears, and long bushy tail **b :** the fur of a fox **2 :** a clever crafty person **3** *archaic* **:** SWORD **4** *cap* **:** a member of an American Indian people formerly living in Wisconsin **5 :** rope yarns twisted and tarred to make small cordage used for lashings or for weaving mats **6 :** an attractive young woman

²fox *vt* (1602) **1 a :** to trick by ingenuity or cunning **:** OUTWIT **b :** BAFFLE **2** *obs* **:** INTOXICATE **3 a :** to repair (a shoe) by renewing the upper **b :** to add a strip to; *esp* **:** to trim (a shoe) with a strip of material (as leather)

foxed \\'fäkst\\ *adj* (1847) **:** discolored with yellowish brown stains ⟨~ leaves of old books⟩

fox fire *n* (15c) **:** an eerie phosphorescent light (as of decaying wood); *also* **:** a luminous fungus (as *Armillaria mellea*) that causes decaying wood to glow

fox·glove \\'fäks-,gləv\\ *n* (bef. 12c) **:** any of a genus (*Digitalis*) of erect herbs of the figwort family; *esp* **:** a common European biennial or perennial (*D. purpurea*) cultivated for its showy racemes of dotted white or purple tubular flowers and as a source of digitalis

fox grape *n* (1657) **:** any of several native grapes (esp. *Vitis labrusca*) of eastern No. America with sour or musky fruit

fox·hole \\'fäks-,hōl\\ *n* (1919) **:** a pit dug usu. hastily for individual cover from enemy fire

fox·hound \\-,hau̇nd\\ *n* (1528) **:** any of various large swift powerful hounds of great endurance used in hunting foxes and developed to form several breeds and many distinctive strains — compare AMERICAN FOXHOUND, ENGLISH FOXHOUND

fox·tail \\'fäk-,stāl\\ *n* (14c) **1 a :** the tail of a fox **b :** something resembling the tail of a fox **2 :** any of several grasses (esp. genera *Alopecurus*, *Hordeum*, and *Setaria*) with spikes resembling brushes — called also *foxtail grass*

foxtail lily *n* (1946) **:** EREMURUS

foxtail millet *n* (ca. 1899) **:** a coarse drought-resistant but frost-sensitive annual grass (*Setaria italica*) grown for grain, hay, and forage

fox terrier *n* (1823) **:** any of a breed of small lively terriers formerly used to dig out foxes and known in smooth-haired and wirehaired varieties

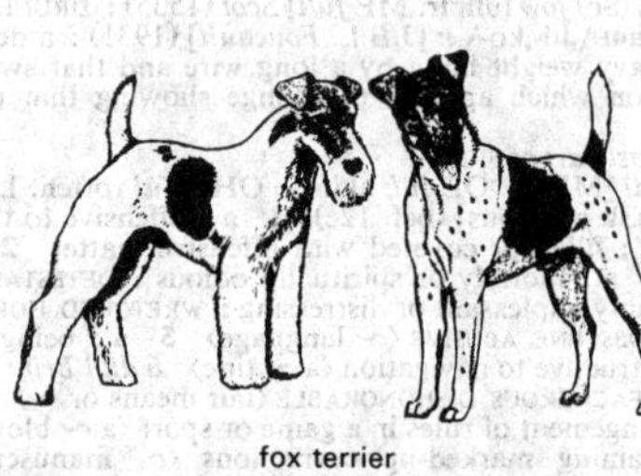

fox terrier

Foxtrot (1952) — a communications code word for the letter *f*

¹fox–trot \\'fäk-,strät\\ *n* (1872) **1 :** a short broken slow trotting gait in which the hind foot of the horse hits the ground a trifle before the diagonally opposite forefoot **2 :** a ballroom dance in duple time that includes slow walking steps, quick running steps, and the step of the two-step

²fox–trot *vi* (1917) **:** to dance the fox-trot

foxy \\'fäk-sē\\ *adj* **fox·i·er; -est** (1528) **1 :** resembling or suggestive of a fox ⟨a narrow ~ face⟩ **:** as **a :** cunningly shrewd in conniving and contriving **:** warily guileful **b :** of a warm reddish brown color ⟨~ eyebrows⟩ **2 :** having a sharp brisk flavor ⟨~ grapes⟩ ⟨~ wine⟩ **3 :** physically attractive ⟨a ~ lady⟩ ***syn*** see SLY — **fox·i·ly** \\'fäk-sə-lē\\ *adv* — **fox·i·ness** \\-sē-nəs\\ *n*

foy \\'fȯi\\ *n* [D dial. *fooi* feast at end of the harvest] *chiefly Scot* (15c) **:** a farewell feast or gift

foy·er \\'fȯi(-ə)r, 'fȯi-,(y)ā *also* 'fwä-,yā\\ *n* [F, lit., fireplace, fr. ML *focarius*, fr. L *focus* hearth] (1859) **:** an anteroom or lobby esp. of a theater; *also* **:** an entrance hallway **:** VESTIBULE

Fra \\(,)frä\\ *n* [It, short for *frate*, fr. L *frater* — more at BROTHER] (ca. 1890) **:** BROTHER — used as a title preceding the name of an Italian monk or friar

fra·cas \\'frāk-əs, 'frak-, *Brit* 'frak-,ä\\ *n, pl* **fra·cas·es** \\-ə-səz\\ *or Brit* **fracas** \\-,äz\\ [F, din, row, fr. It *fracasso*, fr. *fracassare* to shatter] (1727) **:** a noisy quarrel **:** BRAWL

frac·tal \\'frak-tᵊl\\ *n* [alter. of *fractional*] (1975) **:** any of various extremely irregular curves or shapes that repeat themselves at any scale on which they are examined and are assigned fractional dimensions

fract·ed \\'frak-təd\\ *adj* [L *fractus*] *obs* (1547) **:** BROKEN

frac·tion \\'frak-shən\\ *n* [ME *fraccioun*, fr. LL *fraction-*, *fractio* act of breaking, fr. L *fractus*, pp. of *frangere* to break — more at BREAK] (14c) **1 a :** a numerical representation (as 3/4, 5/8, 3.234) indicating the quotient of two numbers **b (1) :** a piece broken off **:** FRAGMENT **(2) :** a discrete unit **:** PORTION **2 :** BIT, LITTLE ⟨a ~ closer⟩ **3 :** one of several portions (as of a distillate) separable by fractionation

frac·tion·al \\-shnəl, -shən-ᵊl\\ *adj* (1675) **1 :** of, relating to, or being a fraction **2 :** relatively small **:** INCONSIDERABLE **3 :** of, relating to, or being fractional currency **4 :** of, relating to, or involving a process for separating components of a mixture through differences in physical or chemical properties ⟨~ distillation⟩ — **frac·tion·al·ly** \\-ē\\ *adv*

fractional currency *n* (1862) **1 :** paper money in denominations of less than one dollar issued by the U.S. 1863–76 **2 :** currency in denominations less than the basic monetary unit

frac·tion·al·ize \\'frak-shnə-,līz, -shən-ᵊl-,īz\\ *vt* **-ized; -iz·ing** (1924) **:** to break up into parts or sections — **frac·tion·al·iza·tion** \\,frak-shnə-lə-'zā-shən, -shən-ᵊl-ə-'zā-\\ *n*

frac·tion·ate \\'frak-shə-,nāt\\ *vt* **-at·ed; -at·ing** (1867) **1 :** to separate (as a mixture) into different portions **2 :** to divide or break up — **frac·tion·ation** \\,frak-shə-'nā-shən\\ *n* — **frac·tion·ator** \\'frak-shə-,nāt-ər\\ *n*

frac·tious \\'frak-shəs\\ *adj* [*fraction* (discord) + *-ous*] (1725) **1 :** tending to be troublesome **:** UNRULY **2 :** QUARRELSOME, IRRITABLE — **frac·tious·ly** *adv* — **frac·tious·ness** *n*

¹frac·ture \\'frak-chər, -shər\\ *n* [ME, fr. L *fractura*, fr. *fractus*] (15c) **1 a :** the act or process of breaking or the state of being broken; *specif* **:** the breaking of hard tissue (as bone) **b :** the rupture (as by tearing) of soft tissue ⟨kidney ~⟩ **2 :** the result of fracturing **:** BREAK **3 :** the general appearance of a freshly broken surface of a mineral

²fracture *vb* **frac·tured; frac·tur·ing** \\-chə-riŋ, -shriŋ\\ *vt* (1612) **1 a :** to cause a fracture in **:** BREAK ⟨~ a rib⟩ **b :** RUPTURE, TEAR **2 a :** to damage or destroy as if by rupturing **b :** to cause great disorder in **c :** to break up **:** FRACTIONATE **d :** to go beyond the limits of (as rules) **:** VIOLATE ⟨*fractured* the English language with malaprops —Goodman Ace⟩ ~ *vi* **:** to undergo fracture

frae \(')frā\ *prep* [ME (northern) *fra, frae,* fr. ON *frā;* akin to OE *fram* from] *Scot* (1700) : FROM

frag·ile \'fraj-əl, -,īl\ *adj* [MF, fr. L *fragilis* — more at FRAIL] (1607) **1 a** : easily broken or destroyed : FRAIL **b** : constitutionally delicate : lacking in physical vigor **2** : TENUOUS, SLIGHT — **fra·gil·i·ty** \frə-'jil-ət-ē\ *n*

syn FRAGILE, FRANGIBLE, BRITTLE, CRISP, FRIABLE mean breaking easily. FRAGILE implies extreme delicacy of material or construction and need for careful handling; FRANGIBLE implies susceptibility to being broken without implying weakness or delicacy; BRITTLE implies hardness together with lack of elasticity or flexibility or toughness; CRISP implies a firmness and brittleness desirable esp. in some foods; FRIABLE applies to substances that are easily crumbled or pulverized.

1**frag·ment** \'frag-mənt\ *n* [ME, fr. L *fragmentum,* fr. *frangere* to break — more at BREAK] (15c) : a part broken off, detached, or incomplete ***syn*** see PART

2**frag·ment** \-,ment\ *vb* (1818) : FRAGMENTIZE

frag·men·tal \frag-'ment-ᵊl\ *adj* (1798) : FRAGMENTARY — **frag·men·tal·ly** \-ᵊl-ē\ *adv*

frag·men·tary \'frag-mən-,ter-ē\ *adj* (1611) : consisting of fragments : INCOMPLETE — **frag·men·tari·ly** \,frag-mən-'ter-ə-lē\ *adv* — **frag·men·tari·ness** \-,ter-ē-nəs\ *n*

frag·men·tate \'frag-mən-,tāt\ *vb* **-tat·ed; -tat·ing** (1945) : FRAGMENTIZE — **frag·men·ta·tion** \,frag-mən-'tā-shən, -,men-\ *n*

fragmentation bomb *n* (1918) : a bomb or shell whose relatively thick casing is splintered upon explosion and thrown in fragments in all directions

frag·men·tize \'frag-mən-,tīz\ *vb* **-tized; -tiz·ing** *vt* (1815) : to break up or apart into fragments ~ *vi* : to fall to pieces — **frag·men·tiz·er** *n*

fra·grance \'frā-grən(t)s\ *n* (1667) **1** : the quality or state of having a sweet odor **2 a** : a sweet or delicate odor (as of fresh flowers, pine trees, or perfume) **b** : something (as a perfume) compounded to give off a sweet or pleasant odor

syn FRAGRANCE, PERFUME, SCENT, INCENSE, REDOLENCE mean a sweet or pleasant odor. FRAGRANCE suggests the odors of flowers or other growing things; PERFUME may suggest a stronger or heavier odor and applies esp. to a prepared or synthetic liquid; SCENT is very close to PERFUME but of wider application because more neutral in connotation; INCENSE applies to the smoke from burning spices and gums and suggests an esp. pleasing odor; REDOLENCE implies a mixture of fragrant or pungent odors.

fra·gran·cy \-grən-sē\ *n* (1578) : FRAGRANCE

fra·grant \'frā-grənt\ *adj* [ME, fr. L *fragrant-, fragrans,* fr. prp. of *fragrare* to be fragrant; akin to MHG *bræhen* to smell] (15c) : marked by fragrance ***syn*** see ODOROUS — **fra·grant·ly** *adv*

frail \'frā(ə)l\ *adj* [ME, fr. MF *fraile,* fr. L *fragilis* fragile, fr. *frangere*] (14c) **1** : easily led into evil ⟨~ humanity⟩ **2** : easily broken or destroyed : FRAGILE **3 a** : physically weak **b** : SLIGHT, UNSUBSTANTIAL ***syn*** see WEAK — **frail·ly** \'frā(ə)l-lē\ *adv* — **frail·ness** *n*

frail·ty \'frā(-ə)l-tē\ *n, pl* **frailties** (14c) **1** : the quality or state of being frail **2** : a fault due to weakness esp. of moral character ***syn*** see FAULT

fraise \'frāz\ *n* [F] (1775) : an obstacle of pointed stakes driven into the ramparts of a fortification in a horizontal or inclined position

Frak·tur \fräk-'tu̇(ə)r\ *n* [G, fr. L *fractura* fracture] (1904) **1** : a German style of black letter **2** *often not cap* : a piece of very decorative calligraphy done in a traditional Pennsylvania Dutch style

fram·able *or* **frame·able** \'frā-mə-bəl\ *adj* (1577) : capable of being framed

fram·be·sia \fram-'bē-zh(ē-)ə\ *n* [NL, fr. F *framboise* raspberry; fr. the appearance of the lesions] (1803) : YAWS

1**frame** \'frām\ *vb* **framed; fram·ing** [ME *framen* to benefit, construct, fr. OE *framian* to benefit, make progress; akin to ON *fram* forward, OE *fram* from] *vi* (bef. 12c) **1** *archaic* : PROCEED, GO **2** *obs* : MANAGE ~ *vt* **1 a** : PLAN, CONTRIVE ⟨*framed* a new method of achieving their purpose⟩ **b** : to give expression to : FORMULATE **c** : SHAPE, CONSTRUCT **d** : to draw up (as a document) **2** : to fit or adjust esp. to something or for an end : ARRANGE **3** *obs* : PRODUCE **4** : to construct by fitting and uniting the parts of the skeleton of (a structure) **5** : to enclose in a frame; *also* : to enclose as if in a frame **6 a** : to devise falsely (as a criminal charge) **b** : to contrive the evidence against (an innocent man) so that a verdict of guilty is assured **c** : to prearrange (as a contest) so that a particular outcome is assured — **fram·er** *n*

2**frame** *n* (14c) **1 a** : something composed of parts fitted together and united **b** : the physical makeup of an animal and esp. a human body : PHYSIQUE, FIGURE **2 a** : the constructional system that gives shape or strength (as to a building); *also* : a frame dwelling **b** : such a skeleton not filled in or covered **3 a** : an open case or structure made for admitting, enclosing, or supporting something ⟨a window ~⟩ **b** : a machine built upon or within a framework ⟨a spinning ~⟩ **c** : a structural unit in an automobile chassis supported on the axles and supporting the rest of the chassis and the body **d (1)** : a part of a pair of glasses that holds one of the lenses **(2)** *pl* : that part of a pair of glasses other than the lenses **4** *obs* : the act or manner of framing **5** : a particular state or disposition (as of the mind) : MOOD **6 a** : an enclosing border **b** : the matter or area enclosed in such a border: as **(1)** : one of the squares in which scores for each round are recorded (as in bowling); *also* : a round in bowling **(2)** : an individual drawing in a comic strip usu. enclosed by a bordering line **(3)** : one picture of the series on a length of motion-picture or other film **(4)** : a complete image being transmitted by television **c** : an inning in baseball **d** : a limiting, typical, or esp. appropriate set of circumstances ⟨studies made within the ~ of our society and culture⟩ **e** : an event that forms the background for the action of a novel or play **7** : FRAME-UP **8** : a minimal unit of instruction or stimulus in a programmed instruction routine

3**frame** *adj* (1775) : having a wood frame ⟨~ houses⟩

frame of reference (1897) **1** : an arbitrary set of axes with reference to which the position or motion of something is described or physical laws are formulated **2** : a set or system (as of facts or ideas) serving to orient or give particular meaning : VIEWPOINT, THEORY

frame·shift \'frām-,shift\ *adj* (1967) : relating to, being, or causing a mutation in which a number of nucleotides not divisible by three is inserted or deleted so that some triplet codons are read incorrectly during genetic translation — **frameshift** *n*

frame–up \'frā-,məp\ *n* (1900) **1** : an act or series of actions in which someone is framed **2** : an action that is framed

1**frame·work** \'frām-,wərk\ *n* (1644) **1 a** : a skeletal, openwork, or structural frame **b** : a basic structure (as of ideas) **2** : FRAME OF REFERENCE **3** : the larger branches of a tree that determine its shape

2**framework** *vt* (1945) : to graft scions of another variety on the framework of (a tree)

fram·ing \'frā-miŋ\ *n* (15c) : FRAME, FRAMEWORK

franc \'fraŋk\ *n* [F] (14c) — see MONEY table

1**fran·chise** \'fran-,chīz\ *n* [ME, fr. MF, fr. *franchir* to free, fr. OF *franc* free — more at FRANK] (14c) **1** : freedom or immunity from some burden or restriction vested in a person or group **2 a** : a special privilege granted to an individual or group; *esp* : the right to be and exercise the powers of a corporation **b** : a constitutional or statutory right or privilege; *esp* : the right to vote **c (1)** : the right or license granted to an individual or group to market a company's goods or services in a particular territory **(2)** : the territory involved in such a right

2**franchise** *vt* **fran·chised; fran·chis·ing** (14c) **1** *archaic* : FREE **2** : to grant a franchise to

fran·chi·see \,fran-,chī-'zē, -chə-\ *n* (1954) : one that is granted a franchise

fran·chis·er \'fran-,chī-zər\ *n* [in sense 1, fr. 1*franchise;* in sense 2, fr. 2*franchise*] (1843) **1** : FRANCHISEE **2** : FRANCHISOR

fran·chi·sor \,fran-,chī-'zȯ(ə)r, -chə-\ *n* [2*franchise* + *-or*] (1967) : one that grants a franchise

Fran·cis·can \fran-'sis-kən\ *n* [ML *Franciscus* Francis] (1592) : a member of the Order of Friars Minor founded by St. Francis of Assisi in 1209 and dedicated esp. to preaching, missions, and charities — **Franciscan** *adj*

fran·ci·um \'fran(t)-sē-əm\ *n* [NL, fr. *France*] (ca. 1946) : a radioactive element of the alkali-metal group discovered as a disintegration product of actinium and obtained artificially by the bombardment of thorium with protons — see ELEMENT table

Franco- *comb form* [ML, fr. *Francus* Frenchman, fr. LL, Frank] **1** : French and ⟨*Franco*-German⟩ **2** : French ⟨*Franco*phile⟩

Fran·co–Amer·i·can \,fraŋ-kō-ə-'mer-ə-kən\ *n* (1859) : an American of French or esp. French-Canadian descent — **Franco–American** *adj*

fran·co·lin \'fraŋ-k(ə-)lən\ *n* [F, fr. It *francolino*] (1653) : any of numerous partridges (*Francolinus* and related genera) of southern Asia and Africa

Fran·co·phile \'fraŋ-kə-,fīl\ *or* **Fran·co·phil** \-,fil\ *adj* (1889) : markedly friendly to France or French culture — **Francophile** *n*

Fran·co·phobe \-,fōb\ *adj* (1891) : marked by a fear or strong dislike of France or French culture or customs — **Francophobe** *n*

fran·co·phone \-,fōn\ *adj, often cap* (1900) : consisting of or belonging to a French-speaking population — **Francophone** *n*

franc–ti·reur \,fräⁿ-(,)tē-'rər\ *n* [F, fr. *franc* free + *tireur* shooter] (1808) : a civilian fighter or sniper

fran·gi·ble \'fran-jə-bəl\ *adj* [ME, fr. MF & ML; MF, fr. ML *frangibilis,* fr. L *frangere* to break — more at BREAK] (15c) : readily or easily broken ***syn*** see FRAGILE — **fran·gi·bil·i·ty** \,fran-jə-'bil-ət-ē\ *n*

fran·gi·pane \'fran-jə-,pān, fräⁿ-zhē-pán\ *n* [F, frangipani (perfume), fragipane, fr. It] (1844) : a custard usu. flavored with almonds

fran·gi·pa·ni *also* **fran·gi·pan·ni** \,fran-jə-'pan-ē, -'pän-\ *n, pl* **-pani** *or* **-panis** [modif. of It *frangipane,* fr. Marquis Muzio *Frangipane,* 16th cent. Ital. nobleman] (1676) **1** : a perfume derived from or imitating the odor of the flower of the red jasmine **2** : any of several shrubs or small trees (genus *Plumeria*) of the dogbane family (as red jasmine) native to the American tropics but introduced elsewhere

fran·glais \fräⁿ-'glā\ *n, often cap* [F, blend of *français* French and *anglais* English] (1964) : French marked by a considerable number of borrowings from English

1**frank** \'fraŋk\ *adj* [ME, free, fr. OF *franc,* fr. ML *francus,* fr. LL *Francus* Frank] (1548) **1** : marked by free, forthright, and sincere expression ⟨a ~ reply⟩ **2** : clinically evident : UNMISTAKABLE ⟨~ pus⟩ — **frank·ness** *n*

syn FRANK, CANDID, OPEN, PLAIN mean showing willingness to tell what one feels or thinks. FRANK stresses lack of shyness or secretiveness or of evasiveness from considerations of tact or expedience; CANDID suggests expression marked by sincerity and honesty esp. in offering unwelcome criticism or opinion; OPEN implies frankness but suggests more indiscretion than FRANK and less earnestness than CANDID; PLAIN suggests outspokenness and freedom from affectation or subtlety in expression.

2**frank** *vt* (1708) **1 a** : to mark (a piece of mail) with an official signature or sign indicating the right of the sender to free mailing **b** : to mail free **c** : to affix to (mail) a stamp or a marking indicating the payment of postage **2** : to enable to pass or go freely or easily — **frank·able** \'fraŋ-kə-bəl\ *adj* — **frank·er** *n*

3**frank** *n* (1713) **1 a** : the signature of the sender on a piece of franked mail serving in place of a postage stamp **b** : a mark or stamp on a piece of mail indicating postage paid **c** : a franked envelope **2** : the privilege of sending mail free of charge

4**frank** *n* (1904) : FRANKFURTER

Frank \'fraŋk\ *n* [ME, partly fr. OE *Franca;* partly fr. OF *Franc,* fr. LL *Francus,* of Gmc origin; akin to OHG *Franko* Frank, OE *Franca*] (bef. 12c) : a member of a West Germanic people that entered the Roman provinces in A.D. 253, occupied the Netherlands and most of Gaul, and established themselves along the Rhine

Fran·ken·stein \'fraŋ-kən-,stīn *also* -,stēn\ *n* **1** : a student of physiology in Mary W. Shelley's novel *Frankenstein* whose life is ruined by a monster he creates **2** : a work or agency that ruins its originator **3** : a monster in the shape of a man — **Fran·ken·stein·ian** \,fraŋ-kən-'stī-nē-ən, -'stin-ē-\ *adj*

frank·furt·er *or* **frank·fort·er** \ˈfraŋk-fə(r)t-ər, -ˌfərt-\ *or* **frank·furt** *or* **frank·fort** \-fərt\ *n* [G *Frankfurter* of Frankfurt, fr. *Frankfurt am Main,* Germany] (1894) **:** a cured cooked sausage (as of beef or beef and pork) that may be skinless or stuffed in a casing

frank·in·cense \ˈfraŋ-kən-ˌsen(t)s\ *n* (14c) **:** a fragrant gum resin from chiefly East African or Arabian trees (genus *Boswellia* of the family Burseraceae) that is an important incense resin

1**Frank·ish** \ˈfraŋ-kish\ *adj* (14c) **:** of or relating to the Franks

2**Frankish** *n* (1863) **:** the Germanic language of the Franks

frank·lin \ˈfraŋ-klən\ *n* [ME *frankeleyn,* fr. AF *fraunclein,* fr. OF *franc*] (13c) **:** a medieval English landowner of free but not noble birth

frank·lin·ite \-klə-ˌnīt\ *n* [*Franklin,* N.J.] (1820) **:** a black slightly magnetic mineral $ZnFe_2O_4$ consisting of an oxide of iron and zinc

Frank·lin stove \ˌfraŋ-klən-\ *n* [Benjamin *Franklin,* its inventor] (1787) **:** a metal heating stove resembling an open fireplace but designed to be set out in a room

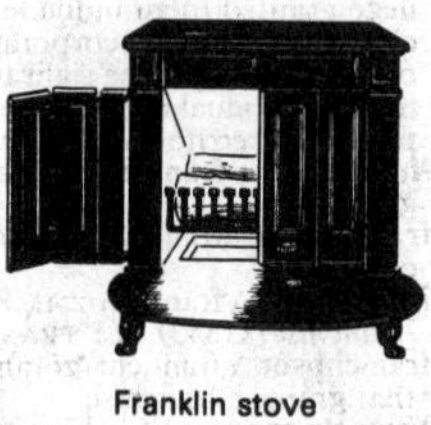

Franklin stove

frank·ly \ˈfraŋ-klē\ *adv* (1540) **1 :** in a frank manner **2 :** in truth **:** INDEED

frank·pledge \ˈfraŋk-ˌplej\ *n* [ME *frankeplegge,* fr. AF *fraunc plege* (prob. trans. of ME *friborg* peace pledge), fr. *fraunc* free (fr. OF *franc*) + *plege* pledge] (15c) **:** an Anglo-Saxon system under which each adult male member of a tithing was responsible for the good conduct of the others; *also* **:** the member himself or the tithing

fran·se·ria \fran-ˈsir-ē-ə\ *n* [NL, fr. Antonio *Franseri,* 18th cent. Span. botanist] (1900) **:** any of a genus (*Franseria*) of annual or perennial composite herbs or shrubs

fran·tic \ˈfrant-ik\ *adj* [ME *frenetik, frantik* — more at FRENETIC] (14c) **1 a** *archaic* **:** mentally deranged **b :** emotionally out of control ⟨~ with anger and frustration⟩ **2 :** marked by fast and nervous, disordered, or anxiety-driven activity ⟨made a ~ search for the lost child⟩ — **fran·ti·cal·ly** \-i-k(ə-)lē\ *adv* — **fran·tic·ly** \-i-klē\ *adv* — **fran·tic·ness** \-ik-nəs\ *n*

frap \ˈfrap\ *vt* **frapped; frap·ping** [ME *frapen* to strike, beat, fr. MF *fraper*] (1548) **:** to draw tight (as with ropes or cables)

1**frap·pé** *or* **frap·pe** \fra-ˈpā\ *adj* [F *frappé,* fr. pp. of *frapper* to strike, chill, fr. MF *fraper* to strike] *of a beverage* (1848) **:** chilled or partly frozen

2**frap·pé** \fra-ˈpā\ *or* **frappe** \ˈfrap, fra-ˈpā\ *n* (1848) **1 a :** a partly frozen drink (as of fruit juice) **b :** a liqueur served over shaved ice **2 :** a thick milk shake

frat \ˈfrat\ *n* (1895) **:** FRATERNITY

fra·ter·nal \frə-ˈtərn-ᵊl\ *adj* [ME, fr. ML *fraternalis,* fr. L *fraternus,* fr. *frater* brother — more at BROTHER] (15c) **1 a :** of, relating to, or involving brothers **b :** of, relating to, or being a fraternity or society ⟨a ~ order⟩ **2 :** derived from two ova **:** DIZYGOTIC ⟨~ twins⟩ **3 :** FRIENDLY, BROTHERLY — **fra·ter·nal·ism** \-ᵊl-ˌiz-əm\ *n* — **fra·ter·nal·ly** \-ᵊl-ē\ *adv*

fra·ter·ni·ty \frə-ˈtər-nət-ē\ *n, pl* **-ties** (14c) **1 :** a group of people associated or formally organized for a common purpose, interest, or pleasure: as **a :** a fraternal order **b :** GUILD **c :** a men's student organization formed chiefly for social purposes having secret rites and a name consisting of Greek letters **d :** a student organization for scholastic, professional, or extracurricular activities ⟨a debating ~⟩ **2 :** the quality or state of being brothers **:** BROTHERLINESS **3 :** men of the same class, profession, character, or tastes ⟨the racetrack ~⟩

frat·er·nize \ˈfrat-ər-ˌnīz\ *vi* **-nized; -niz·ing** (1611) **1 :** to associate or mingle as brothers or on fraternal terms **2 a :** to associate on close terms with members of a hostile group esp. when contrary to military orders ⟨*fraternizing* with the enemy⟩ **b :** to be friendly or amiable — **frat·er·ni·za·tion** \ˌfrat-ər-nə-ˈzā-shən\ *n* — **frat·er·niz·er** \ˈfrat-ər-ˌnī-zər\ *n*

frat·ri·cide \ˈfra-trə-ˌsīd\ *n* [in sense 1, fr. ME, fr. MF or L; MF, fr. L *fratricida,* fr. *fratr-, frater* brother + *-cida* -cide; in sense 2, fr. MF or L; MF, fr. L *fratricidium,* fr. *fratr-, frater* + *-cidium* -cide] (15c) **1 :** one that murders or kills his own brother or sister or an individual having a relationship with him like that of a brother or sister **2 :** the act of a fratricide — **frat·ri·cid·al** \ˌfra-trə-ˈsīd-ᵊl\ *adj*

Frau \ˈfrau̇\ *n, pl* **Frau·en** \ˈfrau̇(-ə)n\ [G, woman, wife, fr. OHG *frouwa* mistress, lady; akin to OE *frēa* lord, OHG *fruma* advantage — more at FOREMOST] (1813) **:** a German married woman **:** WIFE — used as a title equivalent to *Mrs.*

fraud \ˈfrȯd\ *n* [ME *fraude,* fr. MF, fr. L *fraud-, fraus;* akin to Skt *dhvarati* he bends, injures] (14c) **1 a :** DECEIT, TRICKERY; *specif* **:** intentional perversion of truth in order to induce another to part with something of value or to surrender a legal right **b :** an act of deceiving or misrepresenting **:** TRICK **2 a :** one who is not what he pretends to be **:** IMPOSTOR; *also* **:** one who defrauds **:** CHEAT **b :** one that is not what it seems or is represented to be ***syn*** see DECEPTION, IMPOSTURE

fraud·u·lence \ˈfrȯ-jə-lən(t)s\ *n* (1610) **:** the quality or state of being fraudulent

fraud·u·lent \-lənt\ *adj* (15c) **:** characterized by, based on, or done by fraud **:** DECEITFUL — **fraud·u·lent·ly** *adv* — **fraud·u·lent·ness** *n*

1**fraught** \ˈfrȯkt\ *n* [ME, freight, load, fr. MD or MLG *vracht, vrecht*] *chiefly Scot* (13c) **:** LOAD, CARGO

2**fraught** *vt* **fraught·ed** *or* **fraught; fraught·ing** [ME *fraughten,* fr. 1*fraught*] *chiefly Scot* (14c) **:** LOAD, FREIGHT

3**fraught** \ˈfrȯt\ *adj* [ME, fr. pp. of *fraughten*] (14c) **1** *archaic* **a :** LADEN **b :** well supplied or provided **2 :** full of or accompanied by something specified **:** CHARGED — used with *with* ⟨the situation . . . is ~ with a very high violence potential —Harvey Wheeler⟩

fräu·lein \ˈfrȯi-ˌlīn\ *n* [G, dim of *frau*] (1689) **1** *cap* **:** an unmarried German woman — used as a title equivalent to *Miss* **2 :** a German governess

frax·i·nel·la \ˌfrak-sə-ˈnel-ə\ *n* [NL, dim. of L *fraxinus* ash tree — more at BIRCH] (1664) **:** a Eurasian perennial herb (*Dictamnus albus*) of the rue family with flowers that exhale a flammable vapor in hot weather — called also *gas plant*

1**fray** \ˈfrā\ *vt* [ME *fraien,* short for *affraien* to affray] *archaic* (14c) **:** SCARE; *also* **:** to frighten away

2**fray** *n* (14c) **:** BRAWL, FIGHT; *also* **:** DISPUTE, DEBATE

3**fray** *vb* [ME *fraien,* fr. MF *froyer, frayer* to rub, fr. L *fricare* — more at FRICTION] *vt* (15c) **1 a :** to wear (as an edge of cloth) by or as if by rubbing **:** FRET **b :** to separate the threads at the edge of **2 :** STRAIN, IRRITATE ⟨his temper became a bit *~ed*⟩ ~ *vi* **:** to wear out or into shreds

4**fray** *n* (1630) **:** a raveled place or worn spot (as on fabric)

fray·ing *n* (1637) **:** something rubbed or worn off by fraying

1**fraz·zle** \ˈfraz-əl\ *vb* **fraz·zled; fraz·zling** \ˈfraz-(ə-)liŋ\ [alter. of E dial. *fazle* (to tangle, fray)] *vt* (1825) **1 :** 3FRAY **2 a :** to put in a state of extreme physical or nervous fatigue **b :** UPSET ~ *vi* **:** to become frazzled

2**frazzle** *n* (1872) **1 :** the state of being frazzled **2 :** a condition of fatigue or nervous exhaustion ⟨worn to a ~⟩

1**freak** \ˈfrēk\ *n* [origin unknown] (1563) **1 a :** a sudden and odd or seemingly pointless idea or turn of the mind **b :** a seemingly capricious action or event **2** *archaic* **:** a whimsical quality or disposition **3 :** one that is markedly unusual or abnormal ⟨by some ~ of the storm one car in the line was completely buried⟩: as **a :** a person or animal with a physical oddity who appears in a circus sideshow **b** *slang* (1) **:** a sexual deviate (2) **:** a person who uses an illicit drug **c :** HIPPIE **d :** an ardent enthusiast ⟨film *~s*⟩ **e :** an atypical postage stamp usu. caused by a unique defect in paper (as a crease) or a unique event in the manufacturing process (as a speck of dirt on the plate) that does not produce a constant or systematic effect

2**freak** *adj* (ca. 1887) **:** having the character of a freak ⟨a ~ accident⟩

3**freak** *vi* (1965) **1 :** to withdraw from reality esp. by taking drugs — often used with *out* **2 :** to experience nightmarish hallucinations as a result of taking drugs — often used with *out* **3 :** to behave irrationally or unconventionally under or as if under the influence of drugs — often used with *out* ~ *vt* **1 :** to put under the influence of a psychedelic drug — often used with *out* **2 :** to disturb the composure of **:** UPSET — often used with *out* — **freaked** *adj* — **freaked–out** *adj*

4**freak** *vt* [perh. fr. or akin to 1*freckle*] (1637) **:** to streak esp. with color ⟨silver and mother-of-pearl *~ing* the intense azure —Robert Bridges †1930⟩

freak·ish \ˈfrē-kish\ *adj* (1653) **1 :** WHIMSICAL, CAPRICIOUS **2 :** being or befitting a freak — **freak·ish·ly** *adv* — **freak·ish·ness** *n*

freak of nature (1847) **:** FREAK 3a

freak–out \ˈfrē-ˌkau̇t\ *n* (1966) **1 :** a withdrawal from reality esp. by means of drugs **2 a :** a drug-induced state of mind characterized by nightmarish hallucinations **:** a bad trip **b :** an irrational act **3 :** a gathering of hippies **4 :** one who freaks out

freak show *n* (ca. 1887) **:** an exhibition (as a sideshow) featuring freaks of nature

freaky \ˈfrē-kē\ *adj* **freak·i·er; -est** (1824) **:** FREAKISH — **freak·i·ness** *n*

1**freck·le** \ˈfrek-əl\ *n* [ME *freken, frekel,* of Scand origin; akin to ON *freknōttr* freckled; akin to OE *spearca* spark] (15c) **:** one of the small brownish spots in the skin that are usu. due to precipitation of pigment and that increase in number and intensity on exposure to sunlight — **freck·ly** \ˈfrek-(ə-)lē\ *adj*

2**freckle** *vb* **freck·led; freck·ling** \ˈfrek-(ə-)liŋ\ *vt* (1613) **:** to sprinkle or mark with freckles or small spots ~ *vi* **:** to become marked with freckles

1**free** \ˈfrē\ *adj* **fre·er; fre·est** [ME, fr. OE *frēo;* akin to OHG *frī* free, Gk *prays* gentle] (bef. 12c) **1 a :** having the legal and political rights of a citizen **b :** enjoying civil and political liberty ⟨~ citizens⟩ **c :** enjoying political independence or freedom from outside domination **d :** enjoying personal freedom **:** not subject to the control or domination of another **2 a :** not determined by anything beyond its own nature or being **:** choosing or capable of choosing for itself **b :** determined by the choice of the actor or performer ⟨~ actions⟩ **c :** made, done, or given voluntarily or spontaneously **3 a :** exempt, relieved, or released from something unpleasant or burdensome ⟨~ from pain⟩ **b :** not bound, confined, or detained by force **4 a :** having no trade restrictions **b :** not subject to government regulation **c** *of foreign exchange* **:** not subject to restriction or official control **5 a :** having no obligations (as to work) or commitments (as to duty or custom) ⟨I'll be ~ this evening⟩ **b :** not taken up with commitments or obligations ⟨a ~ evening⟩ **6 :** having a scope not restricted by qualification ⟨a ~ variable⟩ **7 a** (1) **:** not obstructed or impeded **:** CLEAR ⟨a ~ and open highway⟩ (2) **:** not being used or occupied ⟨waved with his ~ hand⟩ **b :** not hampered or restricted in its normal operation **8 a :** not fastened ⟨the ~ end of the rope⟩ **b :** not confined to a particular position or place; *also* **:** not having a specific opponent to cover in football ⟨a ~ safety⟩ **c :** capable of moving or turning in any direction ⟨a ~ particle⟩ **d :** performed without apparatus ⟨~ tumbling⟩ **9 a :** not parsimonious ⟨~ spending⟩ **b :** OUTSPOKEN **c :** availing oneself of something without stint **d :** FRANK, OPEN **e :** overly familiar or forward in action or attitude **f :** LICENTIOUS **10 :** not costing or charging anything **11 a** (1) **:** not united with, attached to, combined with, or mixed with something else **:** SEPARATE ⟨~ ores⟩ ⟨a ~ surface of a bodily part⟩ (2) **:** FREESTANDING ⟨a ~ column⟩ **b :** chemically uncombined ⟨~ oxygen⟩ ⟨~ acids⟩ **c :** not permanently attached but able to move about ⟨a ~ electron in a metal⟩ **d :** capable of being used alone as a meaningful linguistic form ⟨the word *hats* is a ~ form⟩ — compare 4BOUND 7 **12 a :** not literal or exact ⟨~ translation⟩ **b :** not restricted by or conforming to conventional forms ⟨~ skating⟩ **13 :** FAVORABLE — used of a wind blowing from a direction more than six points from dead ahead **14 :** not allowing slavery **15 :** open to all comers — **free·ly** *adv*

syn FREE, INDEPENDENT, SOVEREIGN, AUTONOMOUS mean not subject to the rule or control of another. FREE stresses the complete absence of external rule and the full right to make all of one's own decisions; INDEPENDENT implies a standing alone; applied to a state it implies lack of connection with any other having power to interfere with its citizens, laws, or policies; SOVEREIGN stresses the absence of a superior power and implies supremacy within a thing's own domain or sphere; AUTONOMOUS stresses independence in matters pertaining to self-government.

— for free : without charge

[2]**free** *vt* **freed; free·ing** (bef. 12c) **1 a :** to cause to be free **b :** to relieve or rid of what restrains, confines, restricts, or embarrasses ⟨~ a person from debt⟩ **c :** DISENTANGLE, CLEAR **2** *obs* **:** BANISH — **free·er** *n*
syn FREE, RELEASE, LIBERATE, EMANCIPATE, MANUMIT mean to set loose from restraint or constraint. FREE implies a usu. permanent removal from whatever binds, confines, entangles, or oppresses; RELEASE suggests a setting loose from confinement, restraint, or a state of pressure or tension, often without implication of permanent liberation; LIBERATE stresses particularly the resulting state of liberty; EMANCIPATE implies the liberation of a person from subjection or domination; MANUMIT implies emancipation from slavery.

[3]**free** *adv* (1559) **1 :** in a free manner **2 :** without charge ⟨admitted ~⟩ **3 :** with the wind more than six points from dead ahead ⟨sailing ~⟩

free agent *n* (1955) **:** a professional athlete (as a football player) who is free to negotiate a contract with any team — **free agency** *n*

free alongside ship *adv or adj* (ca. 1903) **:** with delivery at the side of the ship free of charges and the buyer's liability then beginning

free alongside vessel *adv or adj* (ca. 1923) **:** FREE ALONGSIDE SHIP

free and easy *adj* (1699) **1 :** marked by informality and lack of constraint ⟨the *free and easy,* open-air life of the plains —Allan Murray⟩ **2 :** not observant of strict demands ⟨his *free and easy* judgments⟩ — **free–and–eas·i·ness** \ˌfrē-ən-ˈ(d)ē-zē-nəs\ *n* — **free and easy** *adv*

free association *n* (1899) **1 a :** the verbal or written expression of all the content of consciousness without censorship or control as an aid in gaining access to unconscious processes esp. in psychoanalysis **b :** the reporting of the first thought that comes to mind in response to a given stimulus (as a word) **2 :** an idea or image elicited by free association **3 :** a method using free association — **free–as·so·ci·ate** \ˌfrē-ə-ˈsō-s(h)ē-ˌāt\ *vi*

free·base \ˈfrē-ˌbās\ *vi* (1980) **:** to prepare or use free base cocaine ~ *vt* **:** to prepare or use (cocaine) as free base

free base *n* (1980) **:** cocaine freed from impurities by treatment (as with ether) and heated to produce vapors for inhalation

free beach *n* (1975) **:** a beach at which nudity is permitted

free·bie *or* **free·bee** \ˈfrē-bē\ *n* [by alter. fr. obs. slang *freeby* gratis, irreg. fr. *free*] (1942) **:** something (as a theater ticket) given or received without charge

free·board \ˈfrē-ˌbō(ə)rd, -ˌbȯ(ə)rd\ *n* (1726) **1 :** the distance between the waterline and the freeboard deck of a ship or between the level of the water and the upper edge of the side of a small boat **2 :** the height above the recorded high-water mark of a structure (as a dam) associated with the water **3 :** the space between the surface of the ground and the undercarriage of an automobile

freeboard deck *n* (ca. 1953) **:** the deck below which all bulkheads are made watertight

free·boo·ter \ˈfrē-ˌbüt-ər\ *n* [by folk etymology fr. D *vrijbuiter,* fr. *vrijbuit* plunder, fr. *vrij* free + *buit* booty] (1570) **:** PIRATE, PLUNDERER — **free·boot** \-ˌbüt\ *vi*

free·born \ˈfrē-ˈbȯ(ə)rn\ *adj* (13c) **1 :** not born in vassalage or slavery **2 :** of, relating to, or befitting one that is freeborn

free diver *n* (1953) **:** one who engages in skin diving — **free diving** *n*

freed·man \ˈfrēd-mən, -ˌman\ *n* (1601) **:** a man freed from slavery

free·dom \ˈfrēd-əm\ *n* [ME *fredom,* fr. OE *frēodōm,* fr. *frēo* free + *-dōm* -dom] (bef. 12c) **1 :** the quality or state of being free: as **a :** the absence of necessity, coercion, or constraint in choice or action **b :** liberation from slavery or restraint or from the power of another **:** INDEPENDENCE **c :** the quality or state of being exempt or released usu. from something onerous ⟨~ from care⟩ **d :** EASE, FACILITY ⟨spoke the language with ~⟩ **e :** the quality of being frank, open, or outspoken ⟨answered the questions with ~⟩ **f :** improper familiarity **g :** boldness of conception or execution **h :** unrestricted use ⟨gave him the ~ of their home⟩ **2 a :** a political right **b :** FRANCHISE, PRIVILEGE
syn FREEDOM, LIBERTY, LICENSE mean the power or condition of acting without compulsion. FREEDOM has a broad range of application from total absence of restraint to merely a sense of not being unduly hampered or frustrated; LIBERTY suggests release from former restraint or compulsion; LICENSE implies freedom specially granted or conceded and may connote an abuse of freedom.

freedom of the seas (1917) **:** the right of a merchant ship to travel any waters except territorial waters either in peace or war

freedom ride *n, often cap F&R* (1961) **:** a ride made by civil rights workers through states of the southern U.S. to ascertain whether public facilities (as bus terminals) are desegregated — **freedom rider** *n*

freed·wom·an \ˈfrēd-ˌwu̇m-ən\ *n* (1866) **:** a woman freed from slavery

free enterprise *n* (1890) **:** freedom of private business to organize and operate for profit in a competitive system without interference by government beyond regulation necessary to protect public interest and keep the national economy in balance

free–fall \ˈfrē-ˈfȯl\ *n* (1919) **1 :** the condition of unrestrained motion in a gravitational field; *also* **:** such motion **2 :** the part of a parachute jump before the parachute opens — **free–fall** *vi*

free–float·ing \-ˈflōt-iŋ\ *adj* (1921) **1 :** relatively uncommitted (as to a particular purpose) ⟨was not sure how the ~ intellectuals would vote⟩ **2 :** felt as an emotion without apparent cause ⟨~ anxiety⟩

free–for–all \ˈfrē-fə-ˌrȯl\ *n* (1881) **:** a competition, dispute, or fight open to all comers and usu. with no rules **:** BRAWL — **free–for–all** *adj*

free–form \(ˈ)frē-ˈfȯ(ə)rm\ *adj* (1950) **1 :** having or being an irregular or asymmetrical shape or design ⟨~ furniture⟩ **2 :** not conforming to or constrained by set rules, conventions, or traditions ⟨~ dancing⟩

free·hand \ˈfrē-ˌhand\ *adj* (ca. 1862) **:** done without mechanical aids or devices ⟨~ drawing⟩ — **freehand** *adv*

free hand \-ˈhand\ *n* (1929) **:** freedom of action or decision

free·hand·ed \ˈfrē-ˈhan-dəd\ *adj* (1656) **:** GENEROUS, OPENHANDED — **free·hand·ed·ly** *adv* — **free·hand·ed·ness** *n*

free·heart·ed \-ˈhärt-əd\ *adj* (14c) **1 :** FRANK, UNRESERVED **2 :** GENEROUS — **free·heart·ed·ly** *adv*

free·hold \ˈfrē-ˌhōld\ *n* (15c) **1 :** a tenure of real property by which an estate of inheritance in fee simple or fee tail or for life is held; *also* **:** an estate held by such tenure — compare FEE 1 **2 :** a tenure of an office or dignity similar to a freehold — **free·hold·er** \-ˌhōl-dər\ *n*

free kick *n* (1882) **:** a kick (as in football, soccer, or rugby) with which an opponent may not interfere; *specif* **:** an unhindered kick (as in soccer) in any direction awarded because of an infraction of the rules by an opponent

[1]**free–lance** *adj* (1901) **:** of, relating to, or being a free lance **:** INDEPENDENT ⟨a ~ photographer⟩

[2]**free–lance** *vi* (1902) **:** to act as a free lance ~ *vt* **:** to produce and submit (as for publication) in the manner of a free lance — **free–lanc·er** *n*

free lance *n* (1820) **1 a :** a knight or roving soldier available for hire by a state or commander **b :** one who acts independently without regard to party lines or deference to authority **2 :** one who pursues a profession without long-term commitments to any one employer

free–liv·ing \ˈfrē-ˈliv-iŋ\ *adj* (1818) **1 :** marked by more than usual freedom in the gratification of appetites **2 a :** not fixed to the substrate but capable of motility ⟨a ~ protozoan⟩ **b :** being metabolically independent **:** neither parasitic nor symbiotic

free·load \-ˈlōd\ *vi* (ca. 1934) **:** to impose upon another's generosity or hospitality without sharing in the cost or responsibility involved **:** SPONGE — **free·load·er** *n*

free love *n* (1822) **1 :** the practice of living openly with one of the opposite sex without marriage **2 :** sexual relations without any commitments by either partner

free lunch *n* (1975) **:** something given entirely free of charge or obligation ⟨in politics there is no *free lunch*⟩

free·man \ˈfrē-mən, -ˌman\ *n* [ME *freman,* fr. OE *frēoman,* fr. *frēo* free + *man* man] (bef. 12c) **1 :** one enjoying civil or political liberty **2 :** one having the full rights of a citizen

free market *n* (1907) **:** an economic market operating by free competition

free·mar·tin \ˈfrē-ˌmärt-ᵊn\ *n* [origin unknown] (1681) **:** a sexually imperfect usu. sterile female calf twinborn with a male

Free·ma·son \-ˈmās-ᵊn\ *n* (1646) **:** a member of a major fraternal organization called Free and Accepted Masons or Ancient Free and Accepted Masons that has certain secret rituals

free·ma·son·ry \-rē\ *n* (1741) **1** *cap* **:** the principles, institutions, or practices of Freemasons — called also *Masonry* **2 :** natural or instinctive fellowship or sympathy

free·ness *n* (14c) **:** FREEDOM

free on board *adv or adj* (1924) **:** without charge for delivery to and placing on board a carrier at a specified point

free port *n* (1711) **:** an enclosed port or section of a port where goods are received and shipped free of customs duty

freer *comparative of* FREE

free radical *n* (1900) **:** an esp. reactive atom or group of atoms that has one or more unpaired electrons

free reed *n* (1855) **:** a reed in a musical instrument (as a harmonium) that vibrates in an air opening just large enough to allow the reed to move freely — compare BEATING REED

free rein *n* (1952) **:** unrestricted liberty of action or decision

free ride *n* (1899) **:** something (as entertainment, acclaim, or a profit) obtained without the usual cost or effort — **free ride** *vi* — **free rider** *n*

free·sia \ˈfrē-zh(ē-)ə, -zē-ə\ *n* [NL, fr. F. H. T. *Freese* †1876 Ger. physician] (ca. 1882) **:** any of a genus (*Freesia*) of the iris family of sweet-scented African herbs with red, white, or yellow flowers

free–soil *adj* (1848) **1 :** characterized by free soil ⟨~ states⟩ **2** *cap F&S* **:** opposing the extension of slavery into U.S. territories and the admission of slave states into the Union prior to the Civil War; *specif* **:** of, relating to, or constituting a minor U.S. political party having these aims — **Free–Soil·er** \-ˈsȯi-lər\ *n*

free soil *n* (1848) **:** U.S. territory where prior to the Civil War slavery was prohibited

free–spo·ken \ˈfrē-ˈspō-kən\ *adj* (1625) **:** speaking freely **:** OUTSPOKEN

freest *superlative of* FREE

free·stand·ing \ˈfrē-ˈstan-diŋ\ *adj* (1876) **1 :** standing alone or on its own foundation free of support or attachment ⟨a ~ wall⟩ **2 :** not part of or affiliated with another establishment ⟨a ~ clinic⟩ ⟨a ~ school⟩

free·stone \ˈfrē-ˌstōn\ *n* (13c) **1 :** a stone that may be cut freely without splitting **2 a :** a fruit stone to which the flesh does not cling **b :** a fruit having such a stone

free·style \ˈfrē-ˌstīl\ *n, often attrib* (ca. 1934) **:** a competition in which a contestant uses a style (as of swimming) of his choice instead of a specified style — **free·styl·er** *n*

free–swim·ming \-ˈswim-iŋ\ *adj* (ca. 1890) **:** able to swim about **:** not attached ⟨the ~ larva of the barnacle⟩

free–swing·ing \-ˈswiŋ-iŋ\ *adj* (1949) **:** bold, forthright, and heedless of personal consequences ⟨a ~ soldier of fortune —Will Herberg⟩

free·think·er \-ˈthiŋ-kər\ *n* (1692) **:** one that forms opinions on the basis of reason independently of authority; *esp* **:** one who doubts or denies religious dogma — **free·think·ing** \-kiŋ\ *n or adj*

free thought *n* (1711) **:** unorthodox attitudes or beliefs; *specif* **:** 18th century deism

free throw *n* (ca. 1929) **:** an unhindered shot in basketball made from behind a set line and awarded because of a foul by an opponent

free throw lane *n* (ca. 1929) **:** a 12 or 16 foot wide lane on a basketball court that extends from underneath the goal to a line 15 feet in front of the backboard and that players may not enter during a free throw

free trade *n* (1606) **:** trade based on the unrestricted international exchange of goods with tariffs used only as a source of revenue

free trader *n* (1698) **:** one that practices or advocates free trade

free university *n* (1966) **:** an unaccredited autonomous free institution established within a university by students to present and discuss subjects not usu. dealt with in the academic curriculum

free verse *n* (1908) **:** verse whose meter is irregular in some respect or whose rhythm is not metrical

free·way \ˈfrē-ˌwā\ *n* (1930) **1 :** an expressway with fully controlled access **2 :** a toll-free highway

[1]**free·wheel** \-ˈ(h)wē(ə)l\ *n* (1899) **1 :** a power-transmission system in a motor vehicle with a device that permits the propeller shaft to run freely when its speed is greater than that of the engine shaft **2 :** a clutch fitted in the rear hub of a bicycle that permits the rear wheel to run on free from the rear sprocket when the pedals are stopped

²**freewheel** *vi* (1911) **:** to move, live, or drift along freely or irresponsibly — **free·wheel·er** *n* — **free·wheel·ing** *adj* — **free·wheel·ing·ness** *n*
free·will \ˌfrē-ˌwil\ *adj* (1535) **:** VOLUNTARY, SPONTANEOUS
free will *n* (13c) **1 :** voluntary choice or decision ⟨I do this of my own *free will*⟩ **2 :** freedom of humans to make choices that are not determined by prior causes or by divine intervention
Freewill Baptist *n* (1732) **:** a member of a Baptist group holding to Arminian doctrine and practicing open communion
free world *n* (1949) **:** the part of the world where democracy and capitalism or moderate socialism rather than totalitarian or Communist political and economic systems prevail
¹**freeze** \ˈfrēz\ *vb* **froze** \ˈfrōz\; **fro·zen** \ˈfrōz-ᵊn\; **freez·ing** [ME *fresen*, fr. OE *frēosan;* akin to OHG *friosan* to freeze, L *pruina* hoarfrost, OE *frost* frost] *vi* (bef. 12c) **1 a :** to become congealed into ice by cold **b :** to solidify as a result of abstraction of heat **2 a :** to become chilled with cold ⟨almost *froze* to death⟩ **b :** to become coldly formal in manner **3 :** to adhere solidly by or as if by freezing ⟨pressure caused the metals to ~⟩ **4 :** to become clogged with ice ⟨the water pipes *froze*⟩ **5 :** to become fixed or motionless; *esp* **:** to become incapable of acting or speaking ~ *vt* **1 a :** to harden into ice **b :** to convert from a liquid to a solid by cold **2 a :** to make extremely cold **:** CHILL **b :** to act toward in a stiff and formal way **3 a :** to act on usu. destructively by frost **b :** to anesthetize by cold **4 :** to cause to grip tightly or remain in immovable contact **5 a :** to cause to become fixed, immovable, or unalterable ⟨wanted to ~ interest rates⟩ **b :** to forbid further manufacture, use, or sale of (a raw material) **c :** to immobilize by governmental regulation the expenditure, withdrawal, or exchange of ⟨foreign-owned bank balances⟩ **6 :** to attempt to retain continuous possession of (a ball or puck) without an attempt to score usu. in order to protect a small lead — **freez·ing·ly** *adv*
²**freeze** *n* (15c) **1 :** a state of weather marked by low temperature esp. when below the freezing point **2 a :** an act or instance of freezing **b :** the state of being frozen
freeze–dry \ˈfrēz-ˈdrī\ *vt* (1949) **:** to dry (as food) in a frozen state under high vacuum esp. for preservation — **freeze–dried** *adj*
freeze–etch·ing \ˈfrē-ˈzech-iŋ\ *n* (1968) **:** preparation of a specimen (as of tissue) for electron microscopic examination by freezing, fracturing along natural structural lines, and preparing a replica (as by simultaneous vapor deposition of carbon and platinum) — **freeze–etch** \-ˈzech\ *or* **freeze–etched** \-ˈzecht\ *adj*
freeze fracture *n* (1973) **:** FREEZE-ETCHING
freeze–frame \ˈfrēz-ˈfrām\ *n* (1948) **:** a frame of a motion-picture film that is repeated so as to give the illusion of a static picture
freez·er \ˈfrē-zər\ *n* (1847) **:** one that freezes or keeps cool; *esp* **:** a compartment, room, or device for freezing food or keeping it frozen
freezer burn *n* (1926) **:** light-colored spots developed in frozen foods as a result of surface evaporation and drying when inadequately wrapped or packaged
freezing point *n* (1747) **:** the temperature at which a liquid solidifies ⟨the *freezing point* of water is 0° Celsius or 32° Fahrenheit⟩
free zone *n* (1901) **:** an area within which goods may be received and stored without payment of duty
F region *n* (1923) **:** the highest region of the ionosphere occurring from 80 miles (130 kilometers) to more than 300 miles (500 kilometers)
¹**freight** \ˈfrāt\ *n, often attrib* [ME, fr. MD or MLG *vracht, vrecht*] (15c) **1 a :** the compensation paid for the transportation of goods **b :** COST ⟨help pay the ~⟩ **2 a :** goods to be shipped **:** CARGO **b :** LOAD, BURDEN **3 a :** the ordinary transportation of goods by a common carrier and distinguished from express **b :** a train designed or used for such transportation
²**freight** *vt* (15c) **1 a :** to load with goods for transportation **b :** BURDEN, CHARGE **2 :** to transport or ship by freight
freight·age \ˈfrāt-ij\ *n* (1694) **:** FREIGHT
freight·er \-ər\ *n* (1622) **1 :** one that loads or charters and loads a ship **2 :** SHIPPER **3 :** a ship or airplane used chiefly to carry freight
freight ton *n* (ca. 1909) **:** TON 1c
frem·i·tus \ˈfrem-ət-əs\ *n* [NL, fr. L, murmur, fr. *fremitus,* pp. of *fremere* to murmur; akin to OE *bremman* to roar] (1879) **:** a sensation felt by a hand placed on a part of the body (as the chest) that vibrates during speech
french \ˈfrench\ *vt, often cap* (1941) **:** to cut (snap beans) in thin lengthwise strips before cooking
¹**French** \ˈfrench\ *adj* [ME, fr. OE *frencisc,* fr. *Franca* Frank] (bef. 12c) **:** of, relating to, or characteristic of France, its people, or their language — **French·ness** *n*
²**French** *n* (12c) **1 :** a Romance language that developed out of the Vulgar Latin of Transalpine Gaul and became the literary and official language of France **2** *pl in constr* **:** the French people
French bean *n* (1634) **1** *chiefly Brit* **:** a bean (as a green bean) of which the whole young pod is eaten **2** *chiefly Brit* **:** KIDNEY BEAN 2
French bulldog *n* (1875) **:** any of a breed of small compact heavy-boned dogs developed in France and having erect ears
French Canadian *n* (1758) **:** one of the descendants of French settlers in Lower Canada
French chalk *n* (1728) **:** a soft white granular variety of steatite used esp. for drawing lines on cloth and for removing grease in dry cleaning
French chop *n* (ca. 1923) **:** a rib chop with the meat trimmed from the end of the rib
French cuff *n* (1916) **:** a soft double cuff that is made by turning back part of a wide cuff band and that fastens by cuff links
french curve *n, often cap F* (1885) **:** a curved piece of flat often plastic material used as a guide in drawing curves
French door *n* (1923) **:** a door with rectangular glass panes extending the full length; *also* **:** FRENCH WINDOW
French dressing *n* (1876) **1 :** a salad dressing made with oil and vinegar or lemon juice, and spices **2 :** a commercial salad dressing that is tomato-flavored and of creamy consistency
¹**french fry** *n, often cap 1st F* (1918) **:** a strip of potato fried in deep fat — usu. used in pl.
²**french fry** *vt, often cap 1st F* [back-formation fr. *French fried (potatoes)*] (ca. 1930) **:** to fry (as strips of potato) in deep fat until brown
French horn *n* (1742) **:** a circular valved brass instrument having a conical bore, a funnel-shaped mouthpiece, and a usual range from B below the bass staff upward for more than three octaves

french·ify \ˈfren-chə-ˌfī\ *vt* **-ified; -ify·ing** (1592) *often cap* **:** to make French in qualities, traits, or typical practices
French kiss *n* (1923) **:** an open-mouth kiss usu. involving tongue-to-tongue contact — **French–kiss** *vb*
French leave *n* [fr. an 18th cent. French custom of leaving a reception without taking leave of the host or hostess] (1771) **:** an informal, hasty, or secret departure
French·man \ˈfrench-mən\ *n* (bef. 12c) **1 :** a native or inhabitant of France **2 :** one who is of French descent
French pastry *n* (1922) **:** a rich pastry filled esp. with custard or fruit

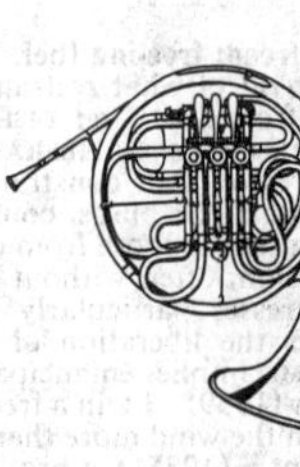

French horn

French provincial *n, often cap P* (ca. 1945) **:** a style of furniture, architecture, or fabric originating in or characteristic of the 17th and 18th century French provinces
French telephone *n* (1932) **:** HANDSET
French toast *n* (1871) **:** bread dipped in a mixture of egg and milk and sautéed
French window *n* (1801) **:** a pair of casement windows that reaches to the floor, opens in the middle, and is placed in an exterior wall
French·wom·an \ˈfrench-ˌwu̇m-ən\ *n* (1593) **1 :** a woman who is a native or inhabitant of France **2 :** a woman of French descent
fre·net·ic \fri-ˈnet-ik\ *adj* [ME *frenetik* insane, fr. MF *frenetique,* fr. L *phreneticus,* modif. of Gk *phrenitikos,* fr. *phrenitis* inflammation of the brain, fr. *phren-, phrēn* diaphragm, mind] (14c) **:** FRENZIED, FRANTIC — **fre·net·i·cal·ly** \-i-k(ə-)lē\ *adv* — **fre·net·i·cism** \-ˈnet-ə-ˌsiz-əm\ *n*
fren·u·lum \ˈfren-yə-ləm\ *n, pl* **-la** \-lə\ [NL, dim. of L *frenum*] (ca. 1706) **1 :** a connecting fold of membrane serving to support or restrain a part (as the tongue) **2 :** a bristle or group of bristles on the front edge of the posterior wings of some lepidoptera that unites the wings by interlocking with the retinaculum of the forewings
fre·num \ˈfrē-nəm\ *n, pl* **frenums** *or* **fre·na** \-nə\ [L, lit., bridle; akin to L *firmus* firm] (1741) **:** FRENULUM 1
fren·zied \ˈfren-zēd\ *adj* (1796) **:** marked by frenzy — **fren·zied·ly** *adv*
¹**fren·zy** \ˈfren-zē\ *n, pl* **frenzies** [ME *frenesie,* fr. MF, fr. ML *phrenesia,* alter. of L *phrenesis,* fr. *phreneticus*] (14c) **1 a :** a temporary madness **b :** a violent mental or emotional agitation **2 :** intense usu. wild and often disorderly compulsive or agitated activity
²**frenzy** *vt* **fren·zied; fren·zy·ing** (1795) **:** to affect with frenzy
Fre·on \ˈfrē-ˌän\ *trademark* — used for any of various nonflammable gaseous and liquid fluorocarbons used as refrigerants and as propellants for aerosols
fre·quence \ˈfrē-kwən(t)s\ *n* (1603) **:** FREQUENCY
fre·quen·cy \ˈfrē-kwən-sē\ *n, pl* **-cies** (1641) **1 :** the fact or condition of occurring frequently **2 a :** the number of times that a periodic function repeats the same sequence of values during a unit variation of the independent variable **b :** the number of individuals in a single class when objects are classified according to variations in a set of one or more specified attributes **3 :** the number of repetitions of a periodic process in a unit of time: as **a :** the number of complete alternations per second of an alternating current **b :** the number of sound waves per second produced by a sounding body **c :** the number of complete oscillations per second of an electromagnetic wave
frequency distribution *n* (1895) **:** an arrangement of statistical data that exhibits the frequency of the occurrence of the values of a variable
frequency modulation *n* (1922) **:** modulation of the frequency of the carrier wave in accordance with speech or a signal; *also* **:** a broadcasting system using such modulation
frequency response *n* (1926) **:** the ability of a device (as an audio amplifier) to handle the frequencies applied to it; *also* **:** a graph representing this ability
¹**fre·quent** \ˈfrē-kwənt\ *adj* [ME, fr. MF or L; MF, fr. L *frequent-, frequens*] (15c) **1** *obs* **:** FULL, THRONGED **2 a :** COMMON, USUAL **b :** happening at short intervals **:** often repeated or occurring **3 :** HABITUAL, PERSISTENT **4** *archaic* **:** INTIMATE, FAMILIAR — **fre·quent·ness** *n*
²**fre·quent** \frē-ˈkwent, ˈfrē-kwənt\ *vt* (15c) **1 :** to associate with, be in, or resort to often or habitually **2** *archaic* **:** to read systematically or habitually — **fre·quen·ta·tion** \ˌfrē-ˌkwen-ˈtā-shən, -kwən-\ *n* — **fre·quent·er** *n*
fre·quen·ta·tive \frē-ˈkwent-ət-iv\ *adj* (1533) **:** denoting repeated or recurrent action or state — used of a verb aspect, verb form, or meaning — **frequentative** *n*
fre·quent·ly \ˈfrē-kwənt-lē\ *adv* (1531) **:** at frequent or short intervals
fres·co \ˈfres-(ˌ)kō\ *n, pl* **frescoes** [It, fr. *fresco* fresh, of Gmc origin; akin to OHG *frisc* fresh] (1598) **1 :** the art of painting on freshly spread moist lime plaster with water-based pigments **2 :** a painting executed in fresco — **fresco** *vt*
¹**fresh** \ˈfresh\ *adj* [ME, fr. OF *freis,* of Gmc origin; akin to OHG *frisc* fresh, OE *fersc* fresh] (13c) **1 a :** not salt ⟨~ water⟩ **b (1) :** free from taint **:** PURE ⟨~ air⟩ **(2)** *of wind* **:** STRONG **2 a :** not altered by processing ⟨~ vegetables⟩ **b :** having its original qualities unimpaired: as **(1) :** full of or renewed in vigor or readiness for action **:** REFRESHED ⟨rose ~ from a good night's sleep⟩ **(2) :** not stale, sour, or decayed ⟨~ bread⟩ **(3) :** not faded ⟨the lessons remain ~ in her memory⟩ **(4) :** not worn or rumpled ⟨a ~ white shirt⟩ **3 a (1) :** experienced, made, or received newly or anew ⟨form ~ friendships⟩ **(2) :** ADDITIONAL, ANOTHER ⟨make a ~ start⟩ **b :** ORIGINAL, VIVID ⟨a ~, historically accurate portrayal⟩ **c :** lacking experience **:** RAW **d :** newly or just come or arrived ⟨~ from school⟩ **e :** having the milk flow recently established ⟨a ~ cow⟩ **4** [prob. by folk etymology fr. G *frech*] **:** disposed to take liberties **:** IMPUDENT **syn** see NEW — **fresh·ly** *adv* — **fresh·ness** *n*
²**fresh** *adv* (14c) **:** just recently **:** NEWLY ⟨we're ~ out of eggs⟩ ⟨~ caught fish⟩
³**fresh** *n* (1538) **1 :** an increased flow or rush (as of water) **:** FRESHET **2 :** a stream of fresh water running into salt water
fresh breeze *n* (ca. 1805) **:** wind having a speed of 19 to 24 miles per hour

fresh·en \ˈfresh-ən\ *vb* **fresh·ened; fresh·en·ing** \-(ə-)niŋ\ *vi* (1697) **1** : to grow or become fresh: as **a** *of wind* : to increase in strength **b** : to become fresh in appearance or vitality — usu. used with *up* ⟨~ up with a shower⟩ **c** *of water* : to lose saltiness **2** *of a milk animal* : to begin lactating ~ *vt* : to make fresh; *also* : REFRESH, REVIVE — **fresh·en·er** \-(ə-)nər\ *n*

fresh·et \ˈfresh-ət\ *n* (1596) **1** *archaic* : STREAM 1 **2 a** : a great rise or overflowing of a stream caused by heavy rains or melted snow **b** : something resembling or suggesting a freshet ⟨a ~ of anger⟩ ⟨a ~ of visitors⟩

fresh gale *n* (1582) : wind having a speed of 39 to 46 miles per hour

fresh·man \ˈfresh-mən\ *n, often attrib* (1550) **1** : BEGINNER, NEWCOMER **2** : a first-year student

fresh·wa·ter \ˌfresh-ˌwȯt-ər, -ˌwät-\ *adj* (1528) **1** : of, relating to, or living in fresh water **2** : accustomed to navigating only in fresh waters ⟨a ~ sailor⟩; *also* : UNSKILLED **3** : inland and usu. provincial ⟨a ~ college⟩

freshwater drum *n* (1945) : a croaker (*Aplodinotus grunniens*) of the Great Lakes and Mississippi valley that sometimes attains a weight of 50 pounds or more — called also *sheepshead, white perch*

Fres·nel lens \ˌfrez-nəl-, frā-ˌnel-\ *n* [Augustin J. *Fresnel*] (1848) : a lens that has a surface consisting of a concentric series of simple lens sections so that a thin lens with a short focal length and large diameter is possible and that is used esp. for spotlights

1fret \ˈfret\ *vb* **fret·ted; fret·ting** [ME *freten* to devour, fret, fr. OE *fretan* to devour; akin to OHG *frezzan* to devour, *ezzan* to eat — more at EAT] *vt* (13c) **1** : to cause to suffer emotional strain : VEX **2 a** : to eat or gnaw into : CORRODE; *also* : FRAY **b** : RUB, CHAFE **c** : to make by wearing away a substance ⟨the stream *fretted* a channel⟩ **3** : to pass (as time) in fretting **4** : AGITATE, RIPPLE ~ *vi* **1 a** : to eat into something **b** : to affect something as if by gnawing or biting : GRATE **2 a** : WEAR, CORRODE **b** : CHAFE **c** : FRAY **3 a** : to become vexed or worried **b** *of running water* : to become agitated

2fret *n* (1545) **1 a** : the action of wearing away : EROSION **b** : a worn or eroded spot **2** : an agitation of mind : IRRITATION

3fret *vt* **fret·ted; fret·ting** [ME *fretten*, fr. MF *freter* to bind with a ferrule, fret, fr. OF, fr. *frete* ferrule] (14c) **1 a** : to decorate with interlaced designs **b** : to form a pattern upon **2** : to enrich with embossed or pierced carved patterns

4fret *n* (14c) **1** : an ornamental network; *esp* : a medieval metallic or jeweled net for a woman's headdress **2** : an ornament or ornamental work often in relief consisting of small straight bars intersecting one another in right or oblique angles

fret 2

5fret *n* [prob. fr. MF *frete* ferrule] (1500) : one of a series of ridges fixed across the fingerboard of a stringed musical instrument (as a guitar) — **fret·less** *adj* — **fret·ted** *adj*

6fret *vt* **fret·ted; fret·ting** (1600) : to press (the strings of a stringed instrument) against the frets

fret·ful \ˈfret-fəl\ *adj* (1602) : disposed to fret : IRRITABLE — **fret·ful·ly** \-fə-lē\ *adv* — **fret·ful·ness** *n*

fret·saw \ˈfret-ˌsȯ\ *n* (1865) : a narrow-bladed fine-toothed saw held under tension in a frame and used for cutting curved outlines

fret·work \-ˌwərk\ *n* (1601) **1** : decoration consisting of work adorned with frets **2** : ornamental openwork or work in relief

Freud·ian \ˈfrȯid-ē-ən\ *adj* (1910) : of, relating to, or according with the psychoanalytic theories or practices of Freud — **Freudian** *n* — **Freud·ian·ism** \-ə-ˌniz-əm\ *n*

Freudian slip *n* (1953) : a slip of the tongue that is motivated by and reveals some unconscious aspect of the mind

Freund's adjuvant \ˈfrȯin(d)z-, ˈfrȯin(t)s-\ *n* [Jules T. *Freund* †1960 Am. immunologist] (1950) : any of various substances (as killed tubercle bacilli) added to an antigen to increase its antigenicity

Frey \ˈfrā\ *n* [ON *Freyr*] : the Norse god of fertility, crops, peace, and prosperity

Freya \ˈfrā-ə\ *n* [ON *Freyja*] : the Norse goddess of love and beauty

fri·a·ble \ˈfrī-ə-bəl\ *adj* [MF or L; MF, fr. L *friabilis*, fr. *friare* to crumble — more at FRICTION] (1563) : easily crumbled or pulverized ⟨~ soil⟩ ***syn*** see FRAGILE — **fri·a·bil·i·ty** \ˌfrī-ə-ˈbil-ət-ē\ *n*

fri·ar \ˈfrī(-ə)r\ *n* [ME *frere, fryer*, fr. OF *frere*, lit., brother, fr. L *fratr-, frater* — more at BROTHER] (13c) : a member of a mendicant order

fri·ar·ly \-lē\ *adj* (1549) : resembling a friar : relating to friars

friar's lantern *n* (1632) : IGNIS FATUUS

fri·ary \ˈfrī(-ə)r-ē\ *n, pl* **-ar·ies** (1538) : a monastery of friars

1frib·ble \ˈfrib-əl\ *vb* **frib·bled; frib·bling** \-(ə-)liŋ\ [origin unknown] *vi* (1633) **1** : TRIFLE **2** *obs* : DODDER ~ *vt* : to trifle or fool away

2fribble *n* (1664) : a frivolous person, thing, or idea : TRIFLER — **fribble** *adj*

fric·an·deau \ˈfrik-ən-ˌdō\ *n* [F, fr. MF, irreg. fr. *friccasser*] (1706) : larded veal roasted and glazed in its own juices

1fric·as·see \ˈfrik-ə-ˌsē, ˌfrik-ə-ˈ\ *n* [MF, fr. fem. of *fricassé*, pp. of *fricasser* to fricassee] (1568) : a dish of cut-up pieces of meat (as chicken or veal) stewed in stock and served in a white sauce

2fricassee *vt* **-seed; -see·ing** (1657) : to cook as a fricassee

fric·a·tive \ˈfrik-ət-iv\ *n* [L *fricatus*, pp. of *fricare*] (1863) : a consonant characterized by frictional passage of the expired breath through a narrowing at some point in the vocal tract ⟨\f v th t͟h s z sh zh h\ are ~*s*⟩ — **fricative** *adj*

fric·tion \ˈfrik-shən\ *n* [ME, fr. MF or L; MF, fr. L *friction-, frictio*, fr. *frictus*, pp. of *fricare* to rub; akin to L *friare* to crumble, Skt *bhrīṇanti* they injure] (15c) **1 a** : the rubbing of one body against another **b** : the force that resists relative motion between two bodies in contact **2** : the clashing between two persons or parties of opposed views : DISAGREEMENT — **fric·tion·less** \-ləs\ *adj* — **fric·tion·less·ly** *adv*

fric·tion·al \ˈfrik-shnəl, -shən-ᵊl\ *adj* (1847) **1** : of or relating to friction **2** : moved or produced by friction — **fric·tion·al·ly** \-ē\ *adv*

friction clutch *n* (ca. 1842) : a clutch in which connection is made through sliding friction

friction drive *n* (1907) : an automobile power-transmission system that transmits motion by surface friction instead of teeth and provides a full range of variation in desired speed ratios

friction match *n* (1839) : 3MATCH 2

friction tape *n* (1920) : a usu. cloth tape impregnated with water-resistant insulating material and an adhesive and used esp. to protect, insulate, and support electrical conductors

Fri·day \ˈfrīd-ē, -ˌdā\ *n* [ME, fr. OE *frigedæg* (akin to OHG *friatag* Friday), fr. (assumed) *Frīg* Frigga + *dæg* day, prehistoric trans. of L *dies Veneris* Venus' day] (bef. 12c) : the sixth day of the week — **Fri·days** \-ēz, -ˌdāz\ *adv*

fridge *also* **frig** \ˈfrij\ *n* [by shortening & alter.] (1926) : REFRIGERATOR

fried·cake \ˈfrīd-ˌkāk\ *n* (1857) : DOUGHNUT, CRULLER

1friend \ˈfrend\ *n* [ME *frend*, fr. OE *frēond*; akin to OHG *friunt* friend, OE *frēon* to love, *frēo* free] (bef. 12c) **1 a** : one attached to another by affection or esteem **b** : ACQUAINTANCE **2 a** : one that is not hostile **b** : one that is of the same nation, party, or group **3** : one that favors or promotes something (as a charity) **4** : a favored companion **5** *cap* : a member of a Christian sect that stresses Inner Light, rejects sacraments and an ordained ministry, and opposes war — called also *Quaker* — **friend·less** \ˈfren-(d)ləs\ *adj* — **friend·less·ness** *n*

2friend *vt* (13c) : to act as the friend of : BEFRIEND

1friend·ly \ˈfren-(d)lē\ *adj* **friend·li·er; -est** (bef. 12c) : of, relating to, or befitting a friend: as **a** : showing kindly interest and goodwill **b** : not hostile **c** : inclined to favor **d** : CHEERFUL, COMFORTING ***syn*** see AMICABLE — **friend·li·ly** \ˈfren-(d)lə-lē\ *adv* — **friend·li·ness** *n*

2friendly *adv* (12c) : in a friendly manner : AMICABLY

3friendly *n, pl* **friendlies** (1861) : one that is friendly; *esp* : a native who is friendly to settlers or invaders

friend of the court (1944) : AMICUS CURIAE

friendship \ˈfren(d)-ˌship\ *n* (bef. 12c) **1** : the state of being friends **2** : the quality or state of being friendly : FRIENDLINESS **3** *obs* : AID

fri·er *var of* FRYER

Frie·sian \ˈfrē-zhən\ *n, chiefly Brit* (1923) : HOLSTEIN

1frieze \ˈfrēz *or* (*compare* FRISÉ) frē-ˈzā\ *n* [ME *frise*, fr. MF, fr. MD *vriese*] (14c) **1** : a heavy durable coarse wool and shoddy fabric with a rough surface **2** : a pile surface of uncut loops or of patterned cut and uncut loops

2frieze \ˈfrēz\ *n* [MF *frise*, perh. fr. ML *phrygium, frisium* embroidered cloth, fr. L *phrygium*, fr. neut. of *Phrygius* Phrygian, fr. *Phrygia* Phrygia] (1563) **1** : the part of an entablature between the architrave and the cornice — see ENTABLATURE illustration **2** : a sculptured or richly ornamented band (as on a building) **3** : a band, line, or series suggesting a frieze ⟨a constant ~ of visitors wound its way around the . . . ruins —Mollie Panter-Downes⟩

frig \ˈfrig\ *vi* **frigged; frig·ging** [prob. fr. E dial. *frig* to rub, masturbate] (1598) : COPULATE — usu. considered vulgar; sometimes used in present participle as meaningless intensive

frig·ate \ˈfrig-ət\ *n* [MF, fr. OIt *fregata*] (1585) **1** : a light boat propelled orig. by oars but later by sails **2** : a square-rigged war vessel intermediate between a corvette and a ship of the line **3** : a warship that is smaller than a destroyer and is used for escort, antisubmarine, and patrol duties

frigate bird *n* (1738) : any of several strong-winged seabirds (family Fregatidae) noted for their rapacious habits

Frig·ga \ˈfrig-ə\ *n* [ON *Frigg*] : the wife of Odin and Norse goddess of married love and of the hearth

1fright \ˈfrīt\ *n* [ME, fr. OE *fyrhto, fryhto*; akin to OHG *forhta* fear] (bef. 12c) **1** : fear excited by sudden danger : ALARM ⟨screeching brakes give us a *fright*⟩ **2** : something strange, ugly, or shocking ⟨his beard was a ~⟩ ***syn*** see FEAR

2fright *vt* (bef. 12c) : to alarm suddenly : FRIGHTEN

fright·en \ˈfrīt-ᵊn\ *vb* **fright·ened; fright·en·ing** \ˈfrīt-niŋ, -ᵊn-iŋ\ *vt* (1666) **1** : to make afraid : TERRIFY **2** : to drive or force by frightening ⟨~*ed* the boy into confessing⟩ ~ *vi* : to become frightened — **fright·en·ing·ly** \-niŋ-lē, -ᵊn-iŋ-\ *adv*

fright·ful \ˈfrīt-fəl\ *adj* (1607) **1** : causing intense fear or alarm : TERRIFYING **2** : causing shock or horror : STARTLING **3** : EXTREME ⟨~ thirst⟩ — **fright·ful·ly** \-fə-lē\ *adv* — **fright·ful·ness** *n*

fright wig *n* (1930) : a wig with hair that stands out from the head

frig·id \ˈfrij-əd\ *adj* [L *frigidus*, fr. *frigēre* to be cold; akin to L *frigus* frost, cold, Gk *rhigos*] (1622) **1 a** : intensely cold **b** : lacking warmth or ardor : INDIFFERENT **2** : lacking imaginative qualities : INSIPID **3 a** : abnormally averse to sexual intercourse — used esp. of women **b** *of a female* : unable to achieve orgasm during sexual intercourse — **frig·id·ly** *adv* — **frig·id·ness** *n*

Frig·i·daire \ˌfrij-ə-ˈda(ə)r, -ˈde(ə)r\ *trademark* — used for a mechanical refrigerator

fri·gid·i·ty \frij-ˈid-ət-ē\ *n* (15c) : the quality or state of being frigid; *specif* : marked or abnormal sexual indifference esp. in a woman

frigid zone *n* (1622) : the area or region between the arctic circle and the north pole or between the antarctic circle and the south pole

frig·o·rif·ic \ˌfrig-ə-ˈrif-ik\ *adj* [L *frigorificus*, fr. *frigor-, frigus* frost] (1667) : causing cold : CHILLING

fri·jo·le \frē-ˈhō-lē\ *also* **fri·jol** \frē-ˈhōl, ˈfrē-ˌ\ *n, pl* **fri·jo·les** \frē-ˈhō-lēz, ˈfrē-ˌ\ [AmerSp *frijol*] *chiefly Southwest* (1577) : BEAN 1b — usu. used in pl.

1frill \ˈfril\ *vt* (1574) : to provide or decorate with a frill

2frill *n* [perh. fr. Flem *frul*] (1591) **1 a** : a gathered, pleated, or bias-cut fabric edging used on clothing **b** : a strip of paper curled at one end and rolled to be slipped over the bone end (as of a chop) in serving **2** : a ruff of hair or feathers about the neck of an animal **3 a** : AFFECTATION, AIR — usu. used in pl. ⟨an honest . . . man who had no ~*s*, . . . no nonsense about him —W. A. White⟩ **b** : something decorative or desirable but not essential : LUXURY — **frilly** \ˈfril-ē\ *adj*

1fringe \ˈfrinj\ *vt* **fringed; fring·ing** \ˈfrin-jiŋ\ (13c) **1** : to furnish or adorn with a fringe **2** : to serve as a fringe for : BORDER

2fringe *n, often attrib* [ME *frenge*, fr. MF, fr. (assumed) VL *frimbia*, fr. L *fimbriae* (pl.)] (14c) **1** : an ornamental border consisting of short straight or twisted threads or strips hanging from cut or raveled edges or from a separate band **2 a :** something resembling a fringe : EDGE, PERIPHERY — often used in pl. ⟨operated on the ~*s* of the law⟩ **b :** one of various light or dark bands produced by the interference or diffraction of light **3 a :** something that is marginal, additional, or secondary to some activity, process, or subject **b :** a group with marginal or extremist views **c :** FRINGE BENEFIT — **fringy** \'frin-jē\ *adj*

fringe area *n* (1950) **:** a region in which reception from a given broadcasting station is weak or subject to serious distortion

fringe benefit *n* (1948) **1 :** an employment benefit (as a pension, a paid holiday, or health insurance) granted by an employer that involves a money cost without affecting basic wage rates **2 :** any additional benefit

fringe tree *n* (1730) **:** a small tree (*Chionanthus virginicus*) of the olive family that has clusters of white flowers and occurs in the southern U.S. but is widely planted elsewhere

frip·pery \'frip-(ə-)rē\ *n, pl* **-per·ies** [MF *friperie,* deriv. of ML *faluppa* piece of straw] (1568) **1** *obs* **a :** cast-off clothes **b** *archaic* **:** a place where old clothes are sold **2 a :** FINERY **b :** something showy, frivolous, or nonessential **:** LUXURY, TRIFLE **c :** OSTENTATION; *esp* **:** something foolish or affectedly elegant

Fris·bee \'friz-bē\ *trademark* — used for a plastic disk several inches in diameter sailed between players by a flip of the wrist

fri·sé \frē-'zā\ *n* [F, fr. pp. of *friser* to curl] (1884) **:** 1FRIEZE

Frise aileron \'frēz-\ *n* [Leslie George *Frise* b1897 Eng. engineer] (ca. 1934) **:** an aileron having a nose portion projecting ahead of the hinge axis and a lower surface in line with the lower surface of the wing

fri·sette \frē-'zet\ *n* [F, fr. *friser*] *archaic* (1818) **:** a fringe of hair or curls worn on the forehead by women

fri·seur \frē-'zər\ *n* [F, fr. *friser*] (1750) **:** HAIRDRESSER

1**Fri·sian** \'frizh-ən, 'frē-zhən\ *n* [ME *Fresan,* fr. OE *Frisan*] (bef. 12c) **1 :** a member of a people that inhabit principally the Netherlands province of Friesland and the Frisian islands in the North sea **2 :** the Germanic language of the Frisian people

2**Frisian** *adj* (1598) **:** of, relating to, or characteristic of Friesland, the Frisians, or Frisian

1**frisk** \'frisk\ *vb* [obs. *frisk* (lively)] *vi* (1519) **:** to leap, skip, or dance in a lively or playful way **:** GAMBOL ~ *vt* **:** to search (a person) for something (as a concealed weapon) by running the hand rapidly over the clothing and through the pockets — **frisk·er** *n*

2**frisk** *n* (1525) **1 a** *archaic* **:** CAPER **b :** GAMBOL, ROMP **c :** DIVERSION **2 :** an act of frisking

frisky \'fris-kē\ *adj* **frisk·i·er; -est** (1500) **:** inclined to frisk **:** LIVELY, PLAYFUL — **frisk·i·ly** \'fris-kə-lē\ *adv* — **frisk·i·ness** \-kē-nəs\ *n*

fris·son \frē-'sō^{n}\ *n, pl* **frissons** \-'sō^{n}(z)\ [F, fr. LL *friction-, frictio,* irreg. fr. L *frigēre* to be cold — more at FRIGID] (1777) **:** a brief moment of emotional excitement **:** SHUDDER, THRILL

1**frit** \'frit\ *n* [It *fritta,* fr. fem. of *fritto,* pp. of *friggere* to fry, fr. L *frigere* — *more at* FRY] (1662) **1 :** the calcined or partly fused materials of which glass is made **2 :** any of various chemically complex glasses used ground esp. to introduce soluble or unstable ingredients into glazes or enamels

2**frit** *vt* **frit·ted; frit·ting** (1805) **1 :** to prepare (materials for glass) by heat **:** FUSE **2 :** to convert into a frit

frith \'frith\ *n* (14c) **:** FIRTH

frit·il·lar·ia \,frit-ᵊl-'er-ē-ə, -'ar-\ *n* [NL, fr. L *fritillus* dice cup; fr. the markings of the petals] (1664) **:** any of a genus (*Fritillaria*) of bulbous herbs of the lily family with mottled or checkered flowers

frit·il·lary \'frit-ᵊl-,er-ē\ *n, pl* **-lar·ies** [NL *fritillaria*] (1633) **1 :** FRITILLARIA **2 :** any of numerous nymphalid butterflies (esp. genera *Argynnis* and *Speyeria*) that usu. are orange with black spots on the upper side of both wings and silver spotted on the underside of the hind wing

frit·ta·ta \frē-'tät-ə\ *n* [It, omlette, fr. *fritto*] (1931) **:** an unfolded omelet often containing chopped vegetables or meats

frit·ted *adj* [2*frit*] (ca. 1909) **:** being porous glass made of sintered powdered glass or fiberglass

1**frit·ter** \'frit-ər\ *n* [ME *fritour,* fr. MF *friture,* fr. (assumed) VL *frictura,* fr. *frictus,* pp. of *frigere* to fry] (14c) **:** a small mass of fried or sautéed batter often containing fruit or meat

2**fritter** *vb* [*fritter,* n. (fragment, shred)] *vt* (1728) **1 :** to spend or waste bit by bit, on trifles, or without commensurate return — usu. used with *away* **2 :** to break into small fragments ~ *vi* **:** DISSIPATE, DWINDLE — **frit·ter·er** \-ər-ər\ *n*

fritz \'fritz\ *n* [origin unknown] (1902) **:** a state of disorder or disrepair — used in the phrase *on the fritz*

friv·ol \'friv-əl\ *vi* **-oled** *or* **-olled; -ol·ing** *or* **-ol·ling** \-(ə-)liŋ\ [back-formation fr. *frivolous*] (1866) **:** to act frivolously **:** TRIFLE — **friv·ol·er** *or* **friv·ol·ler** \-(ə-)lər\ *n*

fri·vol·i·ty \friv-'äl-ət-ē\ *n, pl* **-ties** (1796) **1 :** the quality or state of being frivolous **2 :** a frivolous act or thing

friv·o·lous \'friv-(ə-)ləs\ *adj* [ME, fr. L *frivolus*] (15c) **1 :** of little weight or importance **2 a :** lacking in seriousness **b :** marked by unbecoming levity — **friv·o·lous·ly** *adv* — **friv·o·lous·ness** *n*

1**frizz** \'friz\ *vb* [F *friser*] *vt* (1620) **:** to form into small tight curls ~ *vi, of hair* **:** to form a mass of tight curls

2**frizz** *n* (1668) **1 :** a tight curl **2 :** hair that is tightly curled

3**frizz** *vb* [alter. of 1FRY] *vt* (1835) **:** to fry or sear with a sizzling noise ~ *vi* **:** SIZZLE

1**friz·zle** \'friz-əl\ *vb* **friz·zled; friz·zling** \-(ə-)liŋ\ [prob. akin to OFris *frisle* curl] (1565) **:** FRIZZ, CURL

2**frizzle** *n* (1613) **:** a crisp curl

3**frizzle** *vb* **friz·zled; friz·zling** [1*fry* + *sizzle*] *vt* (1839) **1 :** to fry until crisp and curled **2 :** BURN, SCORCH ~ *vi* **:** to cook with a sizzling noise

frizzy \'friz-ē\ *adj* **frizz·i·er; -est** (ca. 1864) **:** tightly curled — **frizz·i·ness** *n*

1**fro** \frə, (')frō\ *prep* [ME, fr. ON *frā;* akin to OE *fram* from] *dial Brit* (13c) **:** FROM

2**fro** \'frō\ *adv* (14c) **:** BACK, AWAY — used in the phrase *to and fro*

1**frock** \'fräk\ *n* [ME *frok,* fr. MF *froc,* of Gmc origin; akin to OHG *hroch* mantle, coat] (14c) **1 :** an outer garment worn by monks and friars **:** HABIT **2 :** an outer garment worn chiefly by men: **a :** a long loose mantle **b :** a workman's outer shirt; *esp* **:** SMOCK FROCK **c :** a woolen jersey worn esp. by sailors **3 :** a woman's dress

2**frock** *vt* (1828) **1 :** to clothe in a frock **2 :** to make a cleric of

frock coat *n* (1744) **:** a man's usu. double-breasted coat having knee-length skirts front and back

froe \'frō\ *n* [perh. alter. of obs. *froward* turned away, fr. ME; fr. the position of the handle] (1574) **:** a cleaving tool for splitting cask staves and shingles from the block

frog \'frög, 'fräg\ *n* [ME *frogge,* fr. OE *frogga;* akin to OHG *frosk* frog, Skt *pravate* he jumps up] (bef. 12c) **1 :** any of various smooth-skinned web-footed largely aquatic tailless agile leaping amphibians (as of the suborder Diplasiocoela) — compare TOAD **2 :** the triangular elastic horny pad in the middle of the sole of the foot of a horse — see HOOF illustration **3 a :** a loop attached to a belt to hold a weapon or tool **b :** an ornamental braiding for fastening the front of a garment that consists of a button and a loop through which it passes **4** *often cap* **:** FRENCHMAN — usu. taken to be offensive **5 :** a device permitting the wheels on one rail of a track to cross an intersecting rail **6 :** a condition in the throat that produces hoarseness ⟨had a ~ in his throat⟩ **7 :** the nut of a violin bow **8 :** a small holder (as of metal, glass, or plastic) with perforations or spikes for holding flowers in place in a bowl or vase

frog·eye \-,ī\ *n* (ca. 1909) **:** any of numerous leaf diseases characterized by concentric rings about the diseased spots

frog·hop·per \-,häp-ər\ *n* (1711) **:** SPITTLEBUG

frog kick *n* (1940) **:** a breaststroke kick that is executed with the knees pointed outward

frog·man \'frög-,man, 'fräg-, -mən\ *n* (1945) **:** a person equipped (as with face mask, flippers, and air supply) for extended periods of underwater swimming; *esp* **:** a person so equipped for military reconnaissance and demolition

frog spit *n* (1825) **1 :** CUCKOO SPIT 1 **2 :** an alga that forms slimy masses on quiet water

1**frol·ic** \'fräl-ik\ *adj* [D *vroolijk,* fr. MD *vrolijc,* fr. *vro* happy; akin to OHG *frō* happy] (1538) **:** full of fun **:** MERRY

2**frolic** *vi* **frol·icked; frol·ick·ing** (1593) **1 :** to make merry **2 :** to play and run about happily **:** ROMP

3**frolic** *n* (1616) **1 :** a playful or mischievous action **2 a :** FUN, MERRIMENT **b :** PARTY

frol·ic·some \'fräl-ik-səm\ *adj* (1699) **:** full of gaiety **:** SPORTIVE

from \(')frəm, 'främ *also* fəm\ *prep* [ME, fr. OE *from, fram;* akin to OHG *fram,* adv., forth, away, OE *faran* to go — more at FARE] (bef. 12c) **1** — used as a function word to indicate a starting point: as (1) a place where a physical movement begins ⟨came here ~ the city⟩ (2) a starting point in measuring or reckoning or in a statement of limits ⟨a week ~ today⟩ ⟨cost ~ $5 to $10⟩ **2** — used as a function word to indicate separation: as (1) physical separation (2) an act or condition of removal, abstention, exclusion, release, subtraction, or differentiation ⟨protection ~ the sun⟩ ⟨relief ~ anxiety⟩ **3** — used as a function word to indicate the source, cause, agent, or basis ⟨we conclude ~ this⟩ ⟨a call ~ my lawyer⟩ ⟨inherited a love of music ~ his father⟩ ⟨read ~ his new book of poems⟩ ⟨worked hard ~ necessity⟩

frond \'fränd\ *n* [L *frond-, frons* foliage] (1785) **1 :** a large leaf (esp. of a palm or fern) usu. with many divisions **2 :** a thallus or thalloid shoot (as of a lichen or seaweed) resembling a leaf — **frond·ed** \'frän-dəd\ *adj*

fron·deur \frō^{n}-'dər\ *n* [F, lit., slinger, participant in a 17th cent. revolt in which the rebels were compared to schoolboys using slings only when the teacher was not looking] (1798) **:** REBEL, MALCONTENT

1**front** \'frənt\ *n* [ME, fr. OF, fr. L *front-, frons* — more at BRINK] (13c) **1 a :** FOREHEAD; *also* **:** the whole face **b :** external and often feigned appearance esp. in the face of danger or other trial **2 a** (1) **:** VANGUARD (2) **:** a line of battle (3) a zone of conflict between armies **b** (1) **:** a stand on an issue **:** POLICY (2) **:** an area of activity (as study or debate) ⟨progress on the educational ~⟩ (3) **:** a movement linking divergent elements to achieve common objectives; *esp* **:** a political coalition **3 :** a side of a building; *esp* **:** the side that contains the principal entrance **4 a :** the forward part or surface **b** (1) **:** FRONTAGE (2) **:** a beach promenade at a seaside resort **c :** DICKEY 1a **d :** the boundary between two dissimilar air masses **5** *archaic* **:** BEGINNING **6 a** (1) **:** a position ahead of a person or of the foremost part of a thing (2) — used as a call by a hotel desk clerk in summoning a bellhop **b :** a position of leadership or superiority **7 a :** a person, group, or thing used to mask the identity or true character or activity of the actual controlling agent **b :** a person who serves as the nominal head or spokesman of an enterprise or group to lend it prestige — **in front of :** directly before or ahead of ⟨watching the road *in front of* him⟩ — **out front :** in the audience

2**front** *vi* (1523) **1 :** FACE ⟨a ten-acre plot ~*ing* on a lake —*Current Biog.*⟩ **2 :** to serve as a front ⟨~*ing* for special interests⟩ ~ *vt* **1 a :** CONFRONT ⟨went to the woods because I wished . . . to ~ only the essential facts of life —H. D. Thoreau⟩ **b :** to appear before ⟨daily ~*ed* him in some fresh splendor —Alfred Tennyson⟩ **2 a :** to be in front of ⟨lawn ~*ing* the house⟩ **b :** to be the leader of (a musical group) ⟨appeared as a soloist and ~*ed* bands⟩ **3 :** to supply a front to ⟨~*ed* the building with bricks⟩ **4 :** to face toward ⟨the house ~*s* the street⟩ **5 :** to articulate (a sound) with the tongue farther forward

3**front** *adj* (1600) **1 a :** of, relating to, or situated at the front **b :** acting as a front ⟨~ company⟩ **2 :** articulated at or toward the front of the oral passage ⟨~ vowels⟩ **3 :** constituting the first nine holes of an 18-hole golf course — **front** *adv*

front·age \'frənt-ij\ *n* (1622) **1 a :** a piece of land that fronts **b :** the land between the front of a building and the street **c :** the length of a frontage ⟨the house has a ~ of 100 feet⟩ **2 :** the front side of a building **3 :** the act or fact of facing a given way

frontage road *n* (1949) **:** a local street that parallels an expressway or through street and that provides access to property near to the expressway — called also *service road*

1**fron·tal** \'frənt-ᵊl\ *n* (14c) **1** [ME *frontel,* fr. ML *frontellum,* dim. of L *front-, frons*] **:** a cloth hanging over the front of an altar **2 :** FACADE

2**frontal** *adj* [NL *frontalis,* fr. L *front-, frons*] (1656) **1 :** of, relating to, or adjacent to the forehead or the frontal bone **2 a :** of, relating to, or situated at the front **b :** directed against the front or at the main point or issue **:** DIRECT ⟨~ assault⟩ **3 :** parallel to the main axis of the body and at right angles to the sagittal plane **4 :** of or relating to a meteorological front — **fron·tal·ly** \-ᵊl-ē\ *adv*

frontal bone *n* (1741) : either of a pair of membrane bones forming the forehead

fron·tal·i·ty \,frən-'tal-ət-ē\ *n* (1905) **1** *sculpture* : a schematic composition of the front view that is complete without lateral movement **2** *painting* : the depiction of an object, figure, or scene in a plane parallel to the plane of the picture surface

frontal lobe *n* (1879) : the anterior division of each cerebral hemisphere

front bench *n* (1891) : either of the two benches nearest the chair in a British legislature (as the House of Commons) occupied by government and opposition leaders — compare BACK BENCH — **front–bench·er** \-'ben-chər\ *n*

front burner *n* (1973) : the condition of being in active consideration or development ⟨energy questions that are on the world's *front burner*⟩ — compare BACK BURNER

front·court \'frənt-'kō(ə)rt, -'kȯ(ə)rt\ *n* (ca. 1949) : a basketball team's offensive half of the court; *also* : the positions of forward and center on a basketball team

front dive *n* (ca. 1934) : a dive from a position facing the water

front–end *adj* (1967) : relating to or required at the beginning of an undertaking ⟨no ~ charge at the time of investment⟩

front–end load *n* (ca. 1964) : the part of the total commission and expenses taken out of early payments under a contract plan for the periodic purchase of investment-company shares

fron·te·nis \,frən-'ten-əs, frän-\ *n* [AmerSp, blend of *frontón* pelota court and *tenis* tennis] (1944) : a game of Mexican origin played with rackets and a rubber ball on a 3-walled court

fron·tier \,frən-'ti(ə)r, 'frən-, , frän-', 'frän-,\ *n* [ME *fronter*, fr. MF *frontiere*, fr. *front*] (15c) **1 a** : a border between two countries **b** *obs* : a stronghold on a frontier **2 a** : a region that forms the margin of settled or developed territory **b** : the farthermost limits of knowledge or achievement in a particular subject **c** : a new field for exploitative or developmental activity — **frontier** *adj*

fron·tiers·man \,frən-'ti(ə)rz-mən, frän-\ *n* (1782) : one who lives or works on a frontier

fron·tis·piece \'frənt-ə-,spēs\ *n* [MF *frontispice*, fr. LL *frontispicium*, lit., view of the front, fr. L *front-, frons* + *-i-* + *specere* to look at — more at SPY] (1597) **1 a** : the principal front of a building **b** : a decorated pediment over a portico or window **2** : an illustration preceding and usu. facing the title page of a book or magazine

front·less \'frənt-ləs\ *adj, archaic* (1605) : SHAMELESS

front·let \-lət\ *n* [ME *frontlette*, fr. MF *frontelet*, dim. of *frontel*, fr. L *frontale*, fr. *front-, frons*] (15c) **1** : a band or phylactery worn on the forehead **2** : FOREHEAD; *esp* : the forehead of a bird when distinctively marked

front·line \,frənt-,līn\ *adj* (1915) **1** : situated or suitable for use at a military front ⟨~ ambulances⟩ **2 a** : of or relating to the most advanced, demanding, or significant activity or procedure in a field or enterprise **b** : relating to or being proficient or competent in a field ⟨~ teachers⟩; *also* : FIRST-STRING ⟨~ catchers⟩

front line \(')frənt-'līn\ *n* (1917) **1** : a military line formed by the most advanced tactical combat units; *also* : FRONT **2** : the most advanced, responsible, or visible position in a field or activity

front–load *vt* (1976) : to assign costs or benefits to the early stages of (as a contract, project, or time period)

front man *n* (1927) **1** : a person serving as a front or figurehead **2** : the lead performer in a musical group

front matter *n* (ca. 1909) : matter preceding the main text of a book

front money *n* (ca. 1928) : money that is paid in advance for a promised service or product

fronto- *comb form* [ISV, fr. L *front-, frons*] **1** : frontal and ⟨*fronto*parietal⟩ **2** [[1]*front*] : boundary of an air mass ⟨*fronto*genesis⟩

front office *n, often attrib* (1900) : the policy-making officials of an organization

front·o·gen·e·sis \,frənt-ō-'jen-ə-səs\ *n* [NL] (1931) : the coming together into a distinct front of two dissimilar air masses that commonly react upon each other to induce cloud and precipitation

front·ol·y·sis \,frənt-'äl-ə-səs\ *n* [NL] (ca. 1938) : a process tending to destroy a meteorological front

fron·ton \'frän-,tän\ *n* [Sp *frontón* gable, wall of a pelota court, fronton, fr. aug. of *frente* forehead, fr. L *front-, frons*] (1896) : a jai alai arena

[1]**front–page** \'frənt-'pāj\ *adj* (1917) : printed on the front page of a newspaper; *also* : very newsworthy

[2]**front–page** *vt* (1929) : to print or report on the front page

front room *n* (1853) : LIVING ROOM, PARLOR

front–run·ner \'frənt-'rən-ər\ *n* (1914) **1** : a contestant who runs best when in the lead **2** : a leading contestant in a rivalry or competition

front·ward \'frənt-wərd\ *or* **front·wards** \-wərdz\ *adv or adj* (1865) : toward the front

frore \'frō(ə)r, 'frȯ(ə)r\ *adj* [ME *froren*, fr. OE, pp. of *frēosan* to freeze] (bef. 12c) : FROSTY, FROZEN

frosh \'fräsh\ *n, pl* **frosh** [by shortening & alter.] (1915) : FRESHMAN

[1]**frost** \'frȯst\ *n* [ME, fr. OE; akin to OHG *frost* — more at FREEZE] (bef. 12c) **1 a** : the process of freezing **b** : the temperature that causes freezing **c** : a covering of minute ice crystals on a cold surface; *also* : ice particles formed from a gas **2 a** : coldness of deportment or temperament : an indifferent, reserved, or unfriendly manner **b** : FAILURE ⟨the play was . . . a most dreadful ~ —Arnold Bennett⟩

[2]**frost** *vt* (1635) **1 a** : to cover with or as if with frost; *esp* : to put icing on (cake) **b** : to produce a fine-grained slightly roughened surface on (as metal or glass) **2** : to injure or kill (as plants) by frost ~ *vi* : to become frosted : FREEZE

frost·belt \-,belt\ *n, often cap* (1978) : the northern and northeastern states of the U.S. — compare SUNBELT

[1]**frost·bite** \'frȯs(t)-,bīt\ *vt* **-bit** \-,bit\; **-bit·ten** \-,bit-ᵊn\; **-bit·ing** \-,bīt-iŋ\ (1601) : to affect or injure by frost or frostbite

[2]**frostbite** *n* (1813) : the freezing or the local effect of a partial freezing of some part of the body

[3]**frostbite** *adj* (1953) : done in cold weather ⟨~ sailing⟩; *also* : of or relating to cold-weather sailing ⟨~ sailors⟩

frost·bit·ing \-,bīt-iŋ\ *n* (1965) : the sport of sailing in cold weather

frost·ed \'frȯ-stəd\ *adj* (1946) **1** : QUICK-FROZEN ⟨~ vegetables⟩ **2** : having undergone frosting ⟨~ hair⟩

frost heave *n* (1941) : an upthrust of ground or pavement caused by freezing of moist soil — called also *frost heaving*

frost·ing \'frȯ-stiŋ\ *n* (1756) **1 a** : ICING **b** : TRIMMING, ORNAMENTATION **2** : lusterless finish of metal or glass : MAT; *also* : a white finish produced on glass (as by etching) **3** : the lightening (as by chemicals) of small strands of hair throughout the entire head to produce a two-tone effect — compare STREAKING

frost·work \'frȯs-,twərk\ *n* (1729) **1** : the figures that moisture sometimes forms in freezing (as on a windowpane) **2** : ornamentation (as on silver, glass, or paper) imitative of the figures of frostwork

frosty \'frȯ-stē\ *adj* **frost·i·er; -est** (bef. 12c) **1 a** : attended with or producing frost : FREEZING **b** : briskly cold : CHILLY **2** : covered or appearing as if covered with frost : HOARY ⟨a man of 65, with ~ eyebrows and hair —Nan Robertson⟩ **3** : marked by coolness or extreme reserve in manner ⟨his smile was distinctly ~ —Erle Stanley Gardner⟩ — **frost·i·ly** \-stə-lē\ *adv* — **frost·i·ness** \-stē-nəs\ *n*

[1]**froth** \'frȯth\ *n, pl* **froths** \'frȯths, 'frȯthz\ [ME, fr. ON *frotha*; akin to OE *āfrēothan* to froth, Gk *prēthein* to blow up] (14c) **1 a** : bubbles formed in or on a liquid : FOAM **b** : a foamy slaver sometimes accompanying disease or exhaustion **2** : something unsubstantial or of little value ⟨swayed by popular fads and ~ —Gay Talese⟩

[2]**froth** \'frȯth, 'frȯth\ *vt* (14c) **1** : to cause to foam **2** : VENT, VOICE **3** : to cover with froth ~ *vi* **1** : to foam at the mouth **2** : to throw froth out or up

frothy \'frȯ-thē, -thē\ *adj* **froth·i·er; -est** (15c) **1** : full of or consisting of froth ⟨~ surf⟩ ⟨a ~ milk shake⟩ **2 a** : gaily frivolous or light in content or treatment : SHALLOW ⟨~ poetry⟩ ⟨a ~ romantic comedy⟩ **b** : made of light thin material ⟨~ garments⟩ — **froth·i·ly** \-thə-lē, -thə-\ *adv* — **froth·i·ness** \-thē-nəs, -thē-\ *n*

frot·tage \frȯ-'täzh\ *n* [F, fr. *frotter* to rub] (1935) : the technique of creating a design by rubbing (as with a pencil) over an object placed underneath the paper; *also* : a composition so made

frou·frou \'frü-(,)frü\ *n* [F, of imit. origin] (1870) **1** : a rustling esp. of a woman's skirts **2** : frilly ornamentation esp. in women's clothing

frow \'frō\ *var of* FROE

fro·ward \'frō-(w)ərd\ *adj* [ME, turned away, froward, fr. *fro* from + *-ward* -ward] (13c) **1** : habitually disposed to disobedience and opposition **2** *archaic* : ADVERSE — **fro·ward·ly** *adv* — **fro·ward·ness** *n*

[1]**frown** \'fraün\ *vb* [ME *frounen*, fr. MF *froigner* to snort, frown, of Celt origin; akin to W *ffroen* nostril] *vi* (14c) **1** : to contract the brow in displeasure or concentration **2** : to give evidence of displeasure or disapproval by or as if by facial expression ⟨critics ~ on the idea⟩ ~ *vt* : to show displeasure with or disapproval of esp. by facial expression — **frown·er** *n* — **frown·ing·ly** \'fraü-niŋ-lē\ *adv*

[2]**frown** *n* (1605) **1** : a wrinkling of the brow in displeasure or concentration **2** : an expression of displeasure

frows·ty \'fraü-stē\ *adj* **frowst·i·er; -est** [alter. of *frowsy*] *chiefly Brit* (1865) : MUSTY

frow·sy *or* **frow·zy** \'fraü-zē\ *adj* **frow·si·er** *or* **frow·zi·er; -est** [origin unknown] (1681) **1** : having a slovenly or uncared-for appearance ⟨a couple of ~ stuffed chairs —R.M. Williams⟩ **2** : MUSTY, STALE ⟨a ~ smell of stale beer and stale smoke —W.S. Maugham⟩

froze *past of* FREEZE

fro·zen \'frōz-ᵊn\ *adj* (14c) **1 a** : treated, affected, or crusted over by freezing **b** : subject to long and severe cold ⟨~ north⟩ **2 a** (1) : drained or incapable of emotion (2) : expressing or characterized by cold unfriendliness **b** : incapable of being changed, moved, or undone : FIXED; *specif* : debarred by official action from movement or from change in status ⟨~ wages⟩ **c** : not available for present use ⟨~ capital⟩ — **fro·zen·ly** *adv* — **fro·zen·ness** \-ᵊn-(n)əs\ *n*

frozen food *n* (ca. 1940) : food that has been subjected to rapid freezing and is kept frozen until used

fruc·ti·fi·ca·tion \,frək-tə-fə-'kā-shən, ,frük-\ *n* (1604) **1** : the forming or producing of fruit **2** : SPOROPHORE

fruc·ti·fy \'frək-tə-,fī, 'frük-\ *vb* **-fied; -fy·ing** [ME *fructifien*, fr. MF *fructifier*, fr. L *fructificare*, fr. *fructus* fruit] *vi* (14c) : to bear fruit ⟨its seeds shall ~ —Amy Lowell⟩ ⟨no partnership can ~ without candor on both sides —D. M. Ogilvy⟩ ~ *vt* : to make fruitful or productive

fruc·tose \'frək-,tōs, 'frük-, 'frük-, -,tōz\ *n* (ca. 1864) **1** : a sugar $C_6H_{12}O_6$ known in three forms that are optically different with respect to polarized light **2** : the very sweet soluble levorotatory D-form of fructose that occurs esp. in fruit juices and honey — called also *levulose*

fruc·tu·ous \'frək-chə-wəs, 'frük-\ *adj* (14c) : FRUITFUL ⟨a ~ land⟩

fru·gal \'frü-gəl\ *adj* [MF or L; MF, fr. L *frugalis* virtuous, frugal, alter. of *frugi*, fr. dat. of *frug-, frux* fruit, value; akin to L *frui* to enjoy] (1598) : characterized by or reflecting economy in the expenditure of resources ***syn*** see SPARING — **fru·gal·i·ty** \frü-'gal-ət-ē\ *n* — **fru·gal·ly** \'frü-gə-lē\ *adv*

fru·giv·o·rous \frü-'jiv-ə-rəs\ *adj* [L *frug-, frux* + E *-vorous*] (1713) : feeding on fruit

[1]**fruit** \'früt\ *n, often attrib* [ME, fr. OF, fr. L *fructus* fruit, use, fr. *fructus*, pp. of *frui* to enjoy, have the use of — more at BROOK] (12c) **1 a** : a product of plant growth (as grain, vegetables, or cotton) ⟨the ~s of the field⟩ **b** (1) : the usu. edible reproductive body of a seed plant; *esp* : one having a sweet pulp associated with the seed ⟨the ~ of the tree⟩ (2) : a succulent plant part used chiefly in a dessert or sweet course **c** : a dish, quantity, or diet of fruits ⟨please pass the ~⟩ **d** : a product of fertilization in a plant with its modified envelopes or appendages; *specif* : the ripened ovary of a seed plant and its contents **e** : the flavor or aroma of fresh fruit in mature wine **2** : OFFSPRING, PROGENY **3 a** : the state of bearing fruit ⟨a tree in ~⟩ **b** : the effect or consequence of an action or operation : PRODUCT, RESULT ⟨the ~s of our labor⟩ **4** : a male homosexual — often used disparagingly — **fruit·ed** \-əd\ *adj*

[2]**fruit** *vi* (14c) : to bear fruit ~ *vt* : to cause to bear fruit

fruit·age \'früt-ij\ *n* (1578) **1 a** : the condition or process of bearing fruit **b** : FRUIT **2** : the product or result of an action

fruit bat *n* (1877) : any of a suborder (Megachiroptera) of large Old World fruit-eating bats of warm regions — called also *flying fox*

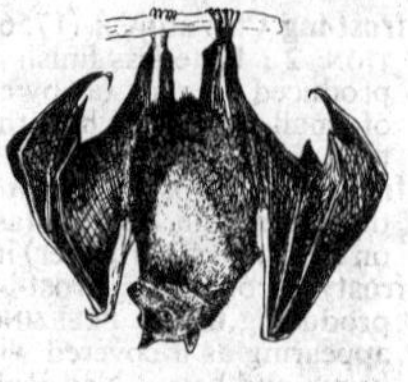
fruit bat

fruit·cake \ˈfrüt-ˌkāk\ *n* (1848) **1 :** a rich cake containing nuts, dried or candied fruits, and spices **2 :** NUT 8a

fruit·er·er \ˈfrüt-ər-ər\ *n* [ME, modif. of MF *fruitier*, fr. *fruit*] *chiefly Brit* (15c) : one who deals in fruit

fruit fly *n* (ca. 1753) : any of various small two-winged flies (as a drosophila) whose larvae feed on fruit or decaying vegetable matter

fruit·ful \ˈfrüt-fəl\ *adj* (14c) **1 a :** yielding or producing fruit **b :** conducive to an abundant yield **2 :** abundantly productive — **fruit·ful·ly** \-fə-lē\ *adv* — **fruit·ful·ness** *n*

fruiting body *n* (1918) : a plant organ specialized for producing spores

fru·ition \frü-ˈish-ən\ *n* [ME *fruicioun*, fr. MF or LL; MF *fruition*, fr. LL *fruition-, fruitio*, fr. L *fruitus*, alter. of *fructus*, pp.] (15c) **1 :** pleasurable use or possession : ENJOYMENT **2 a :** the state of bearing fruit **b :** REALIZATION, ACCOMPLISHMENT

fruit·less \ˈfrüt-ləs\ *adj* (14c) **1 :** UNSUCCESSFUL **2 :** lacking or not bearing fruit — **fruit·less·ly** *adv* — **fruit·less·ness** *n*

fruit·let \-lət\ *n* (1882) **1 :** a small fruit **2 :** a unit of a collective fruit

fruit sugar *n* (ca. 1889) : FRUCTOSE 2

fruity \ˈfrüt-ē\ *adj* **fruit·i·er; -est** (1657) **1 a :** relating to or resembling a fruit **b** *of wine* : having the flavor or aroma of ripe fruit **2 a :** extremely effective, interesting, or enjoyable **b :** sweet or sentimental esp. to excess **3** *slang* **a :** CRAZY, SILLY **b :** HOMOSEXUAL — **fruit·i·ness** *n*

fru·men·ty \ˈfrü-mən-tē\ *n, pl* **-ties** [ME, fr. MF *frumentee*, fr. *frument* grain, fr. L *frumentum*, fr. *frui* to enjoy — more at BROOK] (14c) : a dish of wheat boiled in milk usu. with sugar, spice, and raisins

frump \ˈfrəmp\ *n* [prob. fr. *frumple* (to wrinkle)] (1817) **1 :** a dowdy unattractive girl or woman **2 :** a staid, drab, old-fashioned person — **frump·ish** \ˈfrəm-pish\ *adj*

frumpy \ˈfrəm-pē\ *adj* **frump·i·er; -est** (1746) : generally uninteresting and unattractive : DRAB, DOWDY

1**frus·trate** \ˈfrəs-ˌtrāt\ *vt* **frus·trat·ed; frus·trat·ing** [ME *frustraten*, fr. L *frustratus*, pp. of *frustrare* to deceive, frustrate, fr. *frustra* in error, in vain; akin to L *fraus* fraud — more at FRAUD] (15c) **1 a :** to balk or defeat in an endeavor **b :** to induce feelings of discouragement in **2 a :** to make ineffectual : bring to nothing ⟨nagging daily cares that ~ a person's aspirations⟩ **b :** to make invalid or of no effect : NULLIFY

syn FRUSTRATE, THWART, FOIL, BAFFLE, BALK, CIRCUMVENT, OUTWIT mean to check or defeat another's plan or block achievement of a goal. FRUSTRATE implies making vain or ineffectual all efforts however vigorous or persistent; THWART suggests frustration or checking by deliberately crossing or opposing; FOIL implies checking or defeating so as to discourage further effort; BAFFLE implies frustration by confusing or puzzling; BALK suggests the interposing of obstacles or hindrances; CIRCUMVENT implies frustration by a particular stratagem; OUTWIT suggests craft and cunning.

2**frustrate** *adj* (15c) : FRUSTRATED

frus·trat·ed *adj* (1641) **1 :** balked or discouraged in some endeavor or purpose : DISAPPOINTED ⟨looked upon the critics as merely ~ writers⟩ **2 :** filled with a sense of frustration ⟨learned not to resort to aggressiveness when ~ —Ashley Montagu⟩

frus·trat·ing \-ˌtrāt-iŋ\ *adj* (1871) : tending to produce or characterized by frustration — **frus·trat·ing·ly** \-iŋ-lē\ *adv*

frus·tra·tion \(ˌ)frəs-ˈtrā-shən\ *n* (1555) **1 :** the act of frustrating **2 a :** the state or an instance of being frustrated **b :** a deep chronic sense or state of insecurity and dissatisfaction arising from unresolved problems or unfulfilled needs **3 :** something that frustrates

frus·tule \ˈfrəs-(ˌ)chü(ə)l, -(ˌ)t(y)ü(ə)l\ *n* [F, fr. L *frustulum*, dim. of *frustum*] (1857) : the 2-valved siliceous shell of a diatom

frus·tum \ˈfrəs-təm\ *n, pl* **frustums** *or* **frus·ta** \-tə\ [NL, fr. L, piece, bit — more at BRUISE] (1658) : the part of a solid cone or pyramid next to the base that is formed by cutting off the top by a plane parallel to the base; *also* : the part of a solid intersected between two usu. parallel planes

fru·tes·cent \frü-ˈtes-ᵊnt\ *adj* [L *frutex* + E *-escent*] (1709) : having or approaching the habit or appearance of a shrub : SHRUBBY

fru·ti·cose \ˈfrüt-i-ˌkōs\ *adj* [L *fruticosus*, fr. *frutic-, frutex* shrub; akin to OHG *broz* bud, OIr *broth* whisker] (1668) : having a shrubby bushy thallus with flattened or cylindrical branches ⟨~ lichens⟩ — compare CRUSTOSE, FOLIOSE

1**fry** \ˈfrī\ *vb* **fried; fry·ing** [ME *frien*, fr. OF *frire*, fr. L *frigere*; akin to Gk *phrygein* to roast, fry, Skt *bhṛjjati* he roasts] *vt* (13c) : to cook in a pan or on a griddle over a fire esp. with the use of fat ~ *vi* : to undergo frying

2**fry** *n, pl* **fries** (1833) **1 :** a dish of something fried **2 :** a social gathering or picnic where food is fried and eaten ⟨a fish ~⟩

3**fry** *n, pl* **fry** [ME, prob. fr. ONF *fri*, fr. OF *frier, froyer* to rub, spawn — more at FRAY] (13c) **1 a :** recently hatched fishes **b :** the young of other animals **2 :** very small adult fishes **3 :** members of a group or class : INDIVIDUALS ⟨small ~⟩ ⟨a great part of the earth is peopled with these ~ —Katherine Mansfield⟩

fry·er \ˈfrī(-ə)r\ *n* (1884) : something intended for or used in frying: as **a :** a young chicken **b :** a deep utensil for frying foods

frying pan *n* (14c) : a metal pan with a handle that is used for frying foods — called also *fry pan* — **out of the frying pan into the fire :** clear of one difficulty only to fall into a greater one

f–stop \ˈef-ˌstäp\ *n* (1946) : a camera lens aperture setting indicated by an f-number

F_2 layer \ˈef-ˈtü-\ *n* (1933) : the upper of the two layers into which the F region of the ionosphere splits in the daytime at varying heights from about 120 miles (200 kilometers) to more than 300 miles (500 kilometers) above the earth

fubsy \ˈfəb-zē\ *adj* [obs. E *fubs* (chubby person)] (1780) : being chubby and somewhat squat

fuch·sia \ˈfyü-shə\ *n* [NL, fr. Leonhard *Fuchs* †1566 Ger. botanist] (1852) **1 :** any of a genus (*Fuchsia*) of decorative shrubs of the evening-primrose family having showy nodding flowers usu. in deep pinks, reds, and purples **2 :** a vivid reddish purple

fuch·sin *or* **fuch·sine** \ˈfyük-sən, -ˌsēn\ *n* [F *fuchsine*, prob. fr. NL *Fuchsia*; fr. its color] (1865) : a dye that is produced by oxidation of a mixture of aniline and toluidines and yields a brilliant bluish red

1**fuck** \ˈfək\ *vb* [of Gmc origin, prob. fr. or akin to D *fokken* to breed (cattle), fr. MD, push, thrust, copulate; akin to Sw dial. *fock* penis] *vi* (15c) **1 :** COPULATE — usu. considered obscene; sometimes used in the present participle as a meaningless intensive **2 :** MESS 3 — used with *with*; usu. considered vulgar ~ *vt* **1 :** to engage in coitus with — usu. considered obscene; sometimes used interjectionally with an object (as a personal or reflexive pronoun) to express anger, contempt, or disgust **2 :** to deal with unfairly or harshly : CHEAT, DO IN — usu. considered vulgar — **fuck·er** *n*

2**fuck** *n* (1680) **1 :** an act of copulation — usu. considered obscene **2 :** a sexual partner — usu. considered obscene **3 a :** DAMN 2 — usu. considered vulgar **b** — used esp. with *the* as a meaningless intensive; usu. considered vulgar ⟨what the ~ do they want from me⟩

fuck up \(ˈ)fək-ˈəp\ *vi* (1951) : to act foolishly or stupidly : BLUNDER — usu. considered vulgar ~ *vt* : to ruin or spoil esp. through stupidity, ignorance, or carelessness : BUNGLE — usu. considered vulgar — **fuck-up** \ˈfək-ˌəp\ *n*

1**fu·coid** \ˈfyü-ˌkȯid\ *adj* [NL *Fucus*, fr. L] (1839) : relating to or resembling the rockweeds

2**fucoid** *n* (ca. 1847) : a fucoid seaweed or fossil

fu·cose \ˈfyü-ˌkōs, -ˌkōz\ *n* [ISV *fuc-* (fr. L *fucus*) + *-ose*] (ca. 1890) : an aldose sugar that occurs in bound form in the dextrorotatory D-form in various glycosides and in the levorotatory L-form in some brown algae and in mammalian polysaccharides typical of some blood groups

fu·co·xan·thin \ˌfyü-kō-ˈzan-thən\ *n* (ca. 1873) : a brown carotenoid pigment $C_{40}H_{60}O_6$ occurring esp. in the ova of brown algae

fu·cus \ˈfyü-kəs\ *n* [L, archil, rouge, fr. Gk *phykos* seaweed, archil, rouge, of Sem origin; akin to Heb *pūkh* antimony used as a cosmetic] (1599) **1** *obs* : a face paint **2** [NL, genus name, fr. L] : any of a genus (*Fucus*) of cartilaginous brown algae used in the kelp industry; *broadly* : any of various brown algae

fud \ˈfəd\ *n* (1913) : FUDDY-DUDDY

fud·dle \ˈfəd-ᵊl\ *vb* **fud·dled; fud·dling** \ˈfəd-liŋ, -ᵊl-iŋ\ [origin unknown] *vi* (1588) : to take part in a drinking bout : TIPPLE ~ *vt* **1 :** to make drunk : INTOXICATE **2 :** to make confused : MUDDLE

fud·dy–dud·dy \ˈfəd-ē-ˌdəd-ē\ *n, pl* **-dies** [perh. redupl. of Sc *fuddy* short-tailed animal, tail, fr. *fud* tail] (1904) : one who is old-fashioned, pompous, unimaginative, or concerned about trifles — **fuddy–duddy** *adj*

1**fudge** \ˈfəj\ *vb* **fudged; fudg·ing** [origin unknown] *vi* (1674) **1 :** to exceed the proper bounds or limits of something ⟨feel that the author has *fudged* a little on the . . . rules for crime fiction —*Newsweek*⟩; *also* : CHEAT ⟨*fudging* on an exam⟩ **2 :** to fail to live up to something : fail to perform as expected **3 :** to avoid commitment : HEDGE ⟨the government's tendency to ~ on delicate matters of policy —Claire Sterling⟩ ~ *vt* **1 a :** to devise as a substitute or without adequate basis : FAKE **b :** EXAGGERATE, FALSIFY ⟨*fudged* the figures⟩ **2 :** to fail to come to grips with ⟨has too often blessed war, condoned injustice, *fudged* the racial issue —M. A. Kapp⟩

2**fudge** *n* (1766) **1 :** foolish nonsense — often used interjectionally to express annoyance, disappointment, or disbelief **2 :** a soft creamy candy made typically of sugar, milk, butter, and flavoring

1**fu·el** \ˈfyü(-ə)l\ *n, often attrib* [ME *fewel*, fr. OF *fouaille*, fr. *feu* fire, fr. LL *focus*, fr. L, hearth — more at FOCUS] (13c) **1 a :** a material used to produce heat or power by burning **b :** nutritive material **c :** a material from which atomic energy can be liberated esp. in a reactor **2 :** a source of sustenance or incentive

2**fuel** *vb* **-eled** *or* **-elled; -el·ing** *or* **-el·ling** *vt* (1592) **1 :** to provide with fuel **2 :** SUPPORT, STIMULATE ⟨movement is ~*ed* by massive grants-in-aid —Allen Schick⟩ ~ *vi* : to take in fuel — often used with *up*

fuel cell *n* (1922) : a cell that continuously changes the chemical energy of a fuel and oxidant to electrical energy

fuel oil *n* (1893) : an oil that is used for fuel and that usu. has a higher flash point than kerosene

fuel·wood \ˈfyü(-ə)l-ˌwu̇d\ *n* (1668) : FIREWOOD

1**fug** \ˈfəg\ *n* [prob. alter. of 1*fog*] (1888) : an odorous emanation; *esp* : the stuffy atmosphere of a poorly ventilated space — **fug·gy** \ˈfəg-ē\ *adj*

2**fug** *vb* **fugged; fug·ging** *vi* (1889) : to loll indoors in a stuffy atmosphere ~ *vt* : to make stuffy and odorous

fu·ga·cious \fyü-ˈgā-shəs\ *adj* [L *fugac-, fugax*, fr. *fugere*] (1634) **1 :** lasting a short time : EVANESCENT **2 :** disappearing before the usual time — used chiefly of plant parts (as stipules) other than floral organs — **fu·gac·i·ty** \-ˈgas-ət-ē\ *n*

fu·gal \ˈfyü-gəl\ *adj* (1854) : of, relating to, or being in the style of a musical fugue — **fu·gal·ly** \-gə-lē\ *adv*

-fuge \ˌfyüj\ *n comb form* [F, fr. LL *-fuga*, fr. L *fugare* to put to flight, fr. *fuga*] : one that drives away ⟨insecti*fuge*⟩

1**fu·gi·tive** \ˈfyü-jət-iv\ *n* (14c) **1 :** one who flees or tries to escape; *specif* : REFUGEE **2 :** something elusive or hard to find

2**fugitive** *adj* [ME, fr. MF & L; MF *fugitif*, fr. L *fugitivus*, fr. *fugitus*, pp. of *fugere* to flee; akin to Gk *pheugein* to flee] (15c) **1 :** running away or intending flight ⟨~ slave⟩ ⟨~ debtor⟩ **2 :** moving from place to place : WANDERING **3 a :** being of short duration **b :** difficult to grasp or retain : ELUSIVE **c :** likely to evaporate, deteriorate, change, fade, or disappear **4 :** being of transient interest ***syn*** see TRANSIENT — **fu·gi·tive·ly** *adv* — **fu·gi·tive·ness** *n*

fu·gle \ˈfyü-gəl\ *vi* [back-formation fr. *fugleman*] *archaic* (1834) : to act as fugleman

fu·gle·man \ˈfyü-gəl-mən\ *n* [modif. of G *flügelmann*, fr. *flügel* wing + *mann* man] (1804) **1 :** a trained soldier formerly posted in front of a line of men at drill to serve as a model in their exercises **2 :** one who heads a group; *specif* : a political manager

fu·gu \ˈf(y)ü-(ˌ)gü\ *n* [Jp] (1909) : any of various globefishes that contain a heat-stable toxic principle resembling curare and that are used as food in Japan after toxin-containing organs are removed

fugue \ˈfyüg\ *n* [prob. fr. It *fuga* flight, fugue, fr. L, flight, fr. *fugere*] (1597) **1 :** a polyphonic musical composition in which one or two themes are repeated or imitated by successively entering voices and contrapuntally developed in a continuous interweaving of the voice parts **2 :** a disturbed state of consciousness in which the one affected performs acts of which he appears to be conscious but of which on recovery he has no recollection — **fugue** *vb* — **fugu·ist** \ˈfyü-gəst\ *n*

füh·rer *or* **fueh·rer** \ˈfyu̇r-ər, ˈfir-\ *n* [G *führer* leader, guide, fr. MHG *vüerer*, fr. *vüeren* to lead, bear, fr. OHG *fuoren* to lead; akin to OE *faran* to go — more at FARE] (1934) **1 a :** LEADER — used chiefly of the leader of the German Nazis **b :** a lesser Nazi party official **2 :** a leader exercising tyrannical authority

fu·ji \ˈf(y)ü-(ˌ)jē\ *n* [*Fuji* mountain, Japan] (1925) **:** a spun silk clothing fabric in plain weave orig. made in Japan

1-ful \fəl\ *adj suffix, sometimes* **-ful·ler;** *sometimes* **-ful·lest** [ME, fr. OE, fr. *full*, adj] **1 :** full of ⟨event*ful*⟩ **2 :** characterized by ⟨peace*ful*⟩ **3 :** having the qualities of ⟨master*ful*⟩ **4 :** tending, given, or liable to ⟨mourn*ful*⟩

2-ful \ˌfu̇l\ *n suffix* **:** number or quantity that fills or would fill ⟨room*ful*⟩

Fu·la *or* **Fu·lah** \ˈfü-lə\ *n, pl* **Fula** *or* **Fulas** *or* **Fulah** *or* **Fulahs** (1832) **1 :** a Sudanese people of African Negroid stock and Mediterranean Caucasoid admixture **2 :** a member of the Fula people

Fu·la·ni \ˈfü-ˌlän-ē, fü-ˈ\ *n, pl* **-ni** *or* **-nis** (1855) **1 a :** FULA 1; *esp* **:** the Fula of northern Nigeria and adjacent areas **b :** a member of the Fulani people **2 :** the language of the Fula people

ful·crum \ˈfu̇l-krəm, ˈfəl-\ *n, pl* **fulcrums** *or* **ful·cra** \-krə\ [LL, fr. L, bedpost, fr. *fulcire* to prop — more at BALK] (1674) **1 a :** PROP; *specif* **:** the support about which a lever turns **b :** one that supplies capability for action **2 :** a part of an animal that serves as a hinge or support

ful·fill *or* **ful·fil** \fu̇(l)-ˈfil *also* fə-\ *vt* **ful·filled; ful·fill·ing** [ME *fulfillen*, fr. OE *fullfyllan*, fr. *full* + *fyllan* to fill] (bef. 12c) **1** *archaic* **:** to make full **:** FILL ⟨her subtle, warm, and golden breath . . . ~*s* him with beatitude —Alfred Tennyson⟩ **2 a :** to put into effect **b :** to bring to an end **c :** to measure up to **:** SATISFY **3 a :** to convert into reality **b :** to develop the full potentialities of ***syn*** see PERFORM — **ful·fill·er** *n* — **ful·fill·ment** \-mənt\ *n*

ful·gent \ˈfu̇l-jənt, ˈfəl-\ *adj* [ME, fr. L *fulgent-, fulgens*, prp. of *fulgēre* to shine; akin to L *flagrare* to burn — more at BLACK] (15c) **:** dazzlingly bright **:** RADIANT — **ful·gent·ly** *adv*

ful·gu·rant \ˈfu̇l-g(y)ə-rənt, ˈfu̇l-jə-, ˈfəl-\ *adj* (1647) **:** flashing like lightning **:** DAZZLING

ful·gu·ra·tion \ˌfu̇l-g(y)ə-ˈrā-shən, ˌfu̇l-jə-, fəl-\ *n* [L *fulguration-, fulguratio* sheet lightning, fr. *fulguratus*, pp. of *fulgurare* to flash with lightning, fr. *fulgur* lightning, fr. *fulgēre*] (1633) **1 :** the act or process of flashing like lightning **2 :** the drying up of tissue by use of a high-frequency electric current applied with a needle electrode — **ful·gu·rate** \ˈfu̇l-g(y)ə-ˌrāt, ˈfu̇l-jə-, ˈfəl-\ *vt*

ful·gu·rite \ˈfu̇l-g(y)ə-ˌrīt, ˈfu̇l-jə-, ˈfəl-\ *n* [ISV, fr. L *fulgur*] (1834) **:** an often tubular vitrified crust produced by the fusion of sand or rock by lightning

ful·gu·rous \-rəs\ *adj* [L *fulgur*] (1865) **:** emitting flashes of or like lightning

ful·ham \ˈfu̇l-əm\ *n* [alter. of earlier *fullan*, perh. fr. *full* + *one*] *archaic* (1550) **:** a loaded die

fu·lig·i·nous \fyu̇-ˈlij-ə-nəs\ *adj* [LL *fuliginosus*, fr. L *fuligin-, fuligo* soot; akin to L *fumus* smoke — more at FUME] (1621) **1 a :** SOOTY **b :** OBSCURE, MURKY **2 :** having a dark or dusky color — **fu·lig·i·nous·ly** *adv*

1full \ˈfu̇l\ *adj* [ME, fr. OE; akin to OHG *fol* full, L *plenus* full, *plēre* to fill, Gk *plērēs* full, *plēthein* to be full] (bef. 12c) **1 :** containing as much or as many as is possible or normal ⟨a bin ~ of corn⟩ **2 a :** complete esp. in detail, number, or duration ⟨a ~ report⟩ ⟨my ~ share⟩ ⟨gone a ~ hour⟩ **b :** lacking restraint, check, or qualification ⟨~ retreat⟩ ⟨~ support⟩ **c :** having all distinguishing characteristics **:** enjoying all authorized rights and privileges ⟨~ member⟩ ⟨~ professor⟩ **d :** not lacking in any essential **:** PERFECT ⟨in ~ control of your senses⟩ **3 a :** being at the highest or greatest degree **:** MAXIMUM ⟨~ speed⟩ ⟨~ strength⟩ **b :** being at the height of development ⟨~ bloom⟩ **4 :** rounded in outline ⟨a ~ figure⟩ **5 a :** possessing or containing a great number or amount — used with *of* ⟨a room ~ of pictures⟩ ⟨~ of hope⟩ **b :** having an abundance of material esp. in the form of gathered, pleated, or flared parts ⟨a ~ skirt⟩ **c :** rich in experience ⟨a ~ life⟩ **6 a :** satisfied esp. with food or drink **b :** large enough to satisfy ⟨a ~ meal⟩ **7** *archaic* **:** completely weary **8 :** having both parents in common ⟨~ sisters⟩ **9 :** having volume or depth of sound ⟨~ tones⟩ **10 :** completely occupied esp. with a thought or plan ⟨~ of their own concerns⟩ **11 :** possessing a rich or pronounced quality ⟨a food of ~ flavor⟩ — **full·ness** *also* **ful·ness** \ˈfu̇l-nəs\ *n*

syn FULL, COMPLETE, PLENARY, REPLETE mean containing all that is wanted or needed or possible. FULL implies the presence or inclusion of everything that is wanted or required by something or that can be held, contained, or attained by it; COMPLETE applies when all that is needed is present; PLENARY adds to COMPLETE the implication of fullness without qualification; REPLETE implies being filled to the brim or to satiety.

— **full of it :** not to be believed

2full *adv* (bef. 12c) **1 a :** VERY, EXTREMELY ⟨knew ~ well they had lied to me⟩ **b :** ENTIRELY ⟨swung ~ around —Morley Callaghan⟩ **2 :** STRAIGHT, SQUARELY ⟨got hit ~ in the face⟩ **3** — used as an intensive ⟨wound up winning by a ~ four strokes —William Johnson⟩

3full *n* (14c) **1 a :** the utmost extent ⟨enjoy to the ~⟩ **b :** the highest or fullest state or degree ⟨the ~ of the moon⟩ **2 :** the requisite or complete amount ⟨paid in ~⟩

4full *vi, of the moon* (14c) **:** to become full ~ *vt* **:** to make full in sewing

5full *vt* [ME *fullen*, fr. MF *fouler* to trample under foot, fr. ML *fullare* to walk, trample, full, fr. L *fullo* fuller] (14c) **:** to shrink and thicken (woolen cloth) by moistening, heating, and pressing

full·back \ˈfu̇l-ˌbak\ *n* (1887) **1 :** an offensive football back used primarily for line plunges and blocking **2 :** a primarily defensive player usu. stationed nearest the defended goal (as in soccer, field hockey, or rugby)

full blast *adv* (1909) **:** at full capacity **:** with great intensity

full–blood *n* (1812) **1** \ˈfu̇l-ˈbləd\ **:** descent from parents both of one pure breed **2** \-ˌbləd\ **:** an individual of full-blood

full–blood·ed \ˈfu̇l-ˈbləd-əd\ *adj* (1774) **1 :** of unmixed ancestry **:** PUREBRED **2 :** FLORID, RUDDY ⟨of ~ face⟩ **3 :** FORCEFUL ⟨~ prose style⟩ **4 a :** lacking no particulars **:** GENUINE **b :** containing fullness of substance **:** RICH — **full–blood·ed·ness** *n*

full–blown \-ˈblōn\ *adj* (1635) **1 a :** being at the height of bloom **b :** fully mature **2 :** possessing all the usual or necessary features ⟨a general philosophy, if not a ~ ideology, is emerging —W. H. Jones⟩

full–bod·ied \-ˈbäd-ēd\ *adj* (1686) **1 :** having a large body **2** *of a beverage* **:** imparting to the palate the general impression of substantial weight and rich texture **3 :** having importance, significance, or meaningfulness ⟨~ study of literature⟩

full circle *adv* (1879) **:** through a series of developments that lead back to the original source, position, or situation or to a complete reversal of the original position — usu. used in the phrase *come full circle*

full–dress *adj* (1761) **1 :** complete down to the last formal detail ⟨a ~ rehearsal⟩ **2 :** carried out by all possible means

full dress *n* (1790) **:** the style of dress prescribed for ceremonial or formal social occasions

1full·er \ˈfu̇l-ər\ *n* [ME, fr. OE *fullere*, fr. L *fullo*] (bef. 12c) **:** one that fulls cloth

2ful·ler \ˈfu̇l-ər\ *n* [*fuller* (to form a groove in)] (ca. 1864) **:** a blacksmithing hammer for grooving and spreading iron

fuller's earth *n* [*1fuller;* fr. its earlier use as fulling agent] (15c) **:** an earthy substance that consists chiefly of clay mineral but lacks plasticity and that is used as an adsorbent, a filter medium, and a carrier for catalysts

ful·ler's teasel *n* (15c) **:** TEASEL 1a

full–fash·ioned \ˈfu̇l-ˈfash-ənd\ *adj* (1883) **:** employing or produced by a knitting process for shaping to conform to body lines ⟨~ hosiery⟩

full–fledged \-ˈflejd\ *adj* (1883) **1 :** fully developed **:** TOTAL, COMPLETE ⟨a ~ debate⟩ **2 :** having full plumage **3 :** having attained complete status ⟨~ lawyer⟩

full house *n* (1887) **:** a poker hand containing three of a kind and a pair — see POKER illustration

full–length \ˈfu̇l-ˈleŋ(k)th\ *adj* (1760) **1 :** showing or adapted to the entire length esp. of the human figure ⟨a ~ mirror⟩ ⟨a ~ dress⟩ **2 :** having a length as great as that which is normal or standard for an object of its kind ⟨a ~ play⟩

full marks *n pl, chiefly Brit* (1916) **:** due credit or commendation

full moon *n* (bef. 12c) **:** the moon with its whole apparent disk illuminated

full·mouthed \ˈfu̇l-ˈmau̇t͟hd, -ˈmau̇tht\ *adj* (1577) **1 a :** having a full mouth **b :** having a full complement of teeth ⟨~ ewes⟩ **2 :** uttered with full power or sound **:** LOUD

full nelson *n* (ca. 1922) **:** a wrestling hold in which both arms are thrust under the corresponding arms of an opponent and the hands clasped behind the opponent's head — compare HALF NELSON

full–out \-ˈau̇t\ *adj* (14c) **:** COMPLETE, TOTAL

full–scale \-ˈskā(ə)l\ *adj* (1933) **1 :** identical to an original in proportion and size ⟨~ drawing⟩ **2 a :** involving full use of available resources ⟨a ~ biography⟩ ⟨~ war⟩ **b :** TOTAL, COMPLETE ⟨a ~ musical renaissance —*Current Biog.*⟩

full–ser·vice \-ˈsər-vəs\ *adj* (1957) **:** providing comprehensive service of a particular kind ⟨a ~ bank⟩

full–size \-ˈsīz\ *adj* (1832) **1 :** having the usual or normal size of its kind **2 :** having the dimensions 54 inches by 75 inches — used of a bed; compare KING-SIZE, QUEEN-SIZE, TWIN-SIZE

full stop *n* (1596) **:** PERIOD 5a

full tilt *adv* [*3tilt*] (1600) **:** at high speed

full–time *adj* (1898) **:** employed for or involving full time ⟨~ employees⟩ ⟨~ work⟩ — **full–time** *adv*

full time *n* (1898) **:** the amount of time considered the normal or standard amount for working during a given period

ful·ly \ˈfu̇l-(l)ē\ *adv* (bef. 12c) **1 :** in a full manner or degree **:** COMPLETELY **2 :** at least ⟨~ nine tenths of us⟩

ful·mar \ˈfu̇l-mər, -ˌmär\ *n* [of Scand origin; akin to ON *fūlmār* fulmar, fr. *fūll* foul + *mār* gull — more at MEW] (1698) **:** an arctic seabird (*Fulmarus glacialis*) closely related to the petrels; *also* **:** any of several related birds of southern seas

ful·mi·nant \ˈfu̇l-mə-nənt, ˈfəl-\ *adj* (1602) **:** FULMINATING 3

1ful·mi·nate \-ˌnāt\ *vb* **-nat·ed; -nat·ing** [ME *fulminaten*, fr. ML *fulminatus*, pp. of *fulminare*, fr. L, to flash with lightning, strike with lightning, fr. *fulmin-, fulmen* lightning; akin to L *flagrare* to burn — more at BLACK] *vt* (15c) **1 :** to utter or send out with denunciation **2 :** to cause to explode ~ *vi* **1 :** to send forth censures or invectives **2 :** to make a sudden loud noise **:** EXPLODE — **ful·mi·na·tion** \ˌfu̇l-mə-ˈnā-shən, ˌfəl-\ *n* — **ful·mi·na·tor** \ˈfu̇l-mə-ˌnāt-ər, ˈfəl-\ *n*

2fulminate *n* [*fulminic acid*] (1826) **:** an often explosive salt (as mercury fulminate) containing the radical CNO

ful·mi·nat·ing *adj* (1626) **1 :** exploding with a vivid flash **2 :** hurling denunciations or menaces **3 :** coming on suddenly with great severity

ful·mine \ˈfu̇l-mən, ˈfəl-\ *vb, archaic* (1590) **:** FULMINATE

ful·some \ˈfu̇l-səm\ *adj* [ME *fulsom* copious, cloying, fr. *full* + *-som* -some] (13c) **1 :** characterized by abundance **:** COPIOUS ⟨describes in ~ detail —G. N. Shuster⟩ **2 :** offensive to the senses or to moral or aesthetic sensibility **:** DISGUSTING **3 a :** excessively complimentary or flattering **:** LAVISH ⟨an admiration whose extent I did not express, lest I be thought ~ —A. J. Liebling⟩ **b :** OBSEQUIOUS **4 :** exceeding the bounds of good taste **:** OVERDONE ⟨the ~ chromium glitter of the escalators dominating the central hall —Lewis Mumford⟩ **5 :** being completely developed **:** FULL, WELL-ROUNDED ⟨she was in generally ~, limpid voice —Thor Eckert, Jr.⟩ — **ful·some·ly** *adv* — **ful·some·ness** *n*

usage Many commentators condemn the modern use of *fulsome* without pejorative overtones as misuse or ignorance. This use (sense 1) is, however, the earliest and etymologically purest sense of the word. But since the pejorative senses continue to flourish, expressions like "fulsome praise" can be ambiguous; the reader or hearer may not be sure whether sense 1 or sense 3 is intended.

ful·vous \'fu̇l-vəs, 'fəl-\ *adj* [L *fulvus;* perh. akin to L *flavus* yellow — more at BLUE] (1664) : of a dull brownish yellow : TAWNY

Fu Man·chu mustache \,fü-(,)man-'chü-\ *n* [*Fu Manchu,* Chinese villain in stories by "Sax Rohmer" (A. S. Ward †1955)] (ca. 1936) : a long mustache with ends that turn down to the chin

fu·ma·rase \'fyü-mə-,rās, -,rāz\ *n* (ca. 1936) : an enzyme that catalyzes the interconversion (as in the Krebs cycle) of fumaric acid and malic acid or their salts

fu·ma·rate \-,rāt\ *n* (1864) : a salt or ester of fumaric acid

fu·mar·ic acid \fyu̇-,mar-ik-\ *n* [ISV, fr. NL *Fumaria,* genus of herbs, fr. LL, fumitory, fr. L *fumus*] (1876) : a crystalline acid $C_4H_4O_4$ found in various plants or made synthetically and used esp. in making resins

fu·ma·role \'fyü-mə-,rōl\ *n* [It *fumarola,* modif. of LL *fumariolum,* fr. L *fumarium* smoke chamber for aging wine, fr. *fumus*] (1811) : a hole in a volcanic region from which hot gases and vapors issue — **fu·ma·rol·ic** \,fyü-mə-'rō-lik\ *adj*

1**fum·ble** \'fəm-bəl\ *vb* **fum·bled; fum·bling** \-b(ə-)liŋ\ [prob. of Scand origin; akin to Sw *fumla* to fumble] *vi* (1534) **1 a :** to grope for or handle something clumsily or aimlessly **b :** to make awkward attempts to do or find something ⟨*fumbled* in his pocket for a coin⟩ **c :** to search by trial and error **d :** BLUNDER **2 :** to feel one's way or move awkwardly **3 a :** to drop or juggle or fail to play cleanly a grounder **b :** to lose hold of a football while handling or running with it ~ *vt* **1 :** to bring about by clumsy manipulation **2 a :** to feel or handle clumsily **b :** to deal with in a blundering way : BUNGLE **3 :** to make (one's way) in a clumsy manner **4 a :** MISPLAY ⟨~ a grounder⟩ **b :** to lose hold of (a football) while handling or running — **fum·bler** \-b(ə-)lər\ *n* — **fum·bling·ly** \-b(ə-)liŋ-lē\ *adv*

2**fumble** *n* (1634) **1 :** an act or instance of fumbling **2 :** a fumbled ball

1**fume** \'fyüm\ *n* [ME, fr. MF *fum,* fr. L *fumus;* akin to OHG *toumen* to be fragrant, Gk *thymos* mind, spirit] (14c) **1 a :** a smoke, vapor, or gas esp. when irritating or offensive ⟨engine exhaust ~s⟩ **b :** an often noxious suspension of particles in a gas (as air) **2 :** something (as an emotion) that impairs one's reasoning ⟨sometimes his head gets a little hot with the ~s of patriotism —Matthew Arnold⟩ **3 :** a state of excited irritation or anger — usu. used in the phrase *in a fume* — **fumy** \'fyü-mē\ *adj*

2**fume** *vb* **fumed; fum·ing** *vt* (15c) **1 :** to expose to or treat with fumes **2 :** to give off in fumes ⟨*fuming* thick black smoke⟩ **3 :** to utter while in a state of excited irritation or anger ~ *vi* **1 a :** to emit fumes **b :** to be in a state of excited irritation or anger ⟨he fretted and *fumed* over the delay⟩ **2 :** to rise in or as if in fumes

fu·mi·gant \'fyü-mi-gənt\ *n* (1890) : a substance used in fumigating

fu·mi·gate \'fyü-mə-,gāt\ *vt* **-gat·ed; -gat·ing** [L *fumigatus,* pp. of *fumigare,* fr. *fumus* + *-igare* (akin to L *agere* to drive) — more at AGENT] (1781) : to apply smoke, vapor, or gas to esp. for the purpose of disinfecting or of destroying pests — **fu·mi·ga·tion** \,fyü-mə-'gā-shən\ *n* — **fu·mi·ga·tor** \'fyü-mə-,gāt-ər\ *n*

fu·mi·to·ry \'fyü-mə-,tōr-ē, -,tȯr-\ *n* [ME *fumeterre,* fr. MF, fr. ML *fumus terrae,* lit., smoke of the earth, fr. L *fumus* + *terrae,* gen. of *terra* earth — more at TERRACE] (14c) : any of a genus (*Fumaria* of the family Fumariaceae, the fumitory family) of erect or climbing herbs; *esp* : a common European herb (*F. officinalis*)

1**fun** \'fən\ *n* [E dial. *fun* to hoax, perh. alter. of ME *fonnen,* fr. *fonne* dupe] (1727) **1 :** what provides amusement or enjoyment; *specif* : playful often boisterous action or speech ⟨a lively person full of ~⟩ **2 :** a mood for finding or making amusement ⟨the teasing was all in ~⟩ **3 a :** AMUSEMENT, ENJOYMENT ⟨sickness takes all the ~ out of life⟩ **b :** derisive jest : SPORT, RIDICULE ⟨made him a figure of ~⟩ **4 :** violent or excited activity or argument ⟨let a snake loose in the classroom; then the ~ began⟩

syn FUN, JEST, SPORT, GAME, PLAY mean action or speech that provides amusement or arouses laughter. FUN usu. implies laughter or gaiety but may imply merely a lack of serious or ulterior purpose; JEST implies lack of earnestness in what is said or done and may suggest a hoaxing or teasing; SPORT applies esp. to the arousing of laughter against someone; GAME is close to SPORT, and often stresses mischievous or malicious fun; PLAY stresses the opposition to *earnest* without implying any element of malice or mischief.

2**fun** *vi* **funned; fun·ning** (1833) : to indulge in banter or play : JOKE

3**fun** *adj* (1846) : providing entertainment, amusement, or enjoyment ⟨a ~ party⟩ ⟨a ~ person to be with⟩

fu·nam·bu·lism \fyu̇-'nam-byə-,liz-əm\ *n* [L *funambulus* ropewalker, fr. *funis* rope + *ambulare* to walk] (1824) **1 :** tightrope walking **2 :** a show esp. of mental agility — **fu·nam·bu·list** \-ləst\ *n*

fun and games *n pl but sing or pl in constr* (1920) : light amusement : DIVERSION

1**func·tion** \'fəŋ(k)-shən\ *n* [L *function-, functio* performance, fr. *functus,* pp. of *fungi* to perform; prob. akin to Skt *bhuṅkte* he enjoys] (1533) **1 :** professional or official position : OCCUPATION **2 :** the action for which a person or thing is specially fitted or used or for which a thing exists : PURPOSE **3 :** any of a group of related actions contributing to a larger action; *esp* : the normal and specific contribution of a bodily part to the economy of a living organism **4 :** an impressive, elaborate, or formal ceremony or social gathering **5 a :** a mathematical correspondence that assigns exactly one element of one set to each element of the same or another set **b :** a variable (as a quality, trait, or measurement) that depends on and varies with another ⟨height is a ~ of age⟩ **6 :** characteristic behavior of a chemical compound due to a particular reactive unit — **func·tion·less** \-ləs\ *adj*

syn FUNCTION, OFFICE, DUTY, PROVINCE mean the acts or operations expected of a person or thing. FUNCTION implies a definite end or purpose that the one in question serves or a particular kind of work it is intended to perform ⟨the *function* of language is two-fold: to communicate emotion and to give information —Aldous Huxley⟩ OFFICE is typically applied to the function or service expected of a person by reason of his trade or profession or his special relationship to others ⟨they exercise the *offices* of the judge, the priest, the counsellor —W.E. Gladstone⟩ DUTY applies to a task or responsibility imposed by one's occupation, rank, status, or calling ⟨it is the judicial *duty* of the court, to examine the whole case —R. B. Taney⟩ PROVINCE applies to a function, office, or duty that naturally or logically falls to one ⟨nursing does not belong to a man; it is not his *province* —Jane Austen⟩

2**function** *vi* **func·tioned; func·tion·ing** \-sh(ə-)niŋ\ (1856) **1 :** to have a function : SERVE ⟨an attributive noun ~s as an adjective⟩ **2 :** to be in action : OPERATE ⟨a government ~s through numerous divisions⟩

func·tion·al \'fəŋ(k)-shnəl, -shən-ᵊl\ *adj* (1631) **1 a :** of, connected with, or being a function **b :** affecting physiological or psychological functions but not organic structure ⟨~ heart disease⟩ **2 :** used to contribute to the development or maintenance of a larger whole ⟨~ and practical school courses⟩; *also* : designed or developed chiefly from the point of view of use ⟨~ clothing⟩ **3 :** performing or able to perform a regular function — **func·tion·al·ity** \,fəŋ(k)-shə-'nal-ət-ē\ *n* — **func·tion·al·ly** \'fəŋ(k)-shnə-lē, -shən-ᵊl-ē\ *adv*

functional calculus *n* (1933) : PREDICATE CALCULUS

functional group *n* (ca. 1939) : a characteristic reactive unit of a chemical compound esp. in organic chemistry

functional illiterate *n* (1947) : a person having had some schooling but not meeting a minimum standard of literacy

func·tion·al·ism \'fəŋ(k)-shnə-,liz-əm, -shən-ᵊl-,iz-\ *n* (1914) **1 :** a philosophy of design (as in architecture) holding that form should be adapted to use, material, and structure **2 :** a theory that stresses the interdependence of the patterns and institutions of a society and their interaction in maintaining cultural and social unity **3 :** a doctrine or practice that emphasizes practical utility or functional relations — **func·tion·al·ist** \-shnə-ləst, -shən-ᵊl-əst\ *n* — **functionalist** *or* **func·tion·al·is·tic** \,fəŋ(k)-shnə-'lis-tik, -shən-ᵊl-'is-\ *adj*

functional shift *n* (1942) : the process by which a word or form comes to be used in a second or third grammatical function ⟨the *functional shift* of "go" from verb to adjective as in "all systems are go"⟩

func·tion·ary \'fəŋ(k)-shə-,ner-ē\ *n, pl* **-ar·ies** (1791) **1 :** one who serves in a certain function **2 :** one holding office in a government or political party

function word *n* (1940) : a word (as a preposition, auxiliary verb, or conjunction) expressing primarily grammatical relationship

func·tor \'fəŋ(k)-tər\ *n* (1935) : something that performs a function or an operation

1**fund** \'fənd\ *n* [L *fundus* bottom, piece of landed property — more at BOTTOM] (1682) **1 :** an available quantity of material or intangible resources : SUPPLY **2 a :** a sum of money or other resources whose principal or interest is set apart for a specific objective **b :** money on deposit on which checks or drafts can be drawn — usu. used in pl. **c :** CAPITAL **d** *pl* : the stock of the British national debt — usu. used with *the* **3** *pl* : available pecuniary resources **4 :** an organization administering a special fund

2**fund** *vt* (1776) **1 a :** to make provision of resources for discharging the interest or principal of **b :** to provide funds for ⟨a science program federally ~*ed*⟩ **2 :** to place in a fund : ACCUMULATE **3 :** to convert into a debt that is payable either at a distant date or at no definite date and that bears a fixed interest ⟨~ a floating debt⟩

fun·da·ment \'fən-də-mənt\ *n* [ME, fr. OF *fondement,* fr. L *fundamentum,* fr. *fundare* to found, fr. *fundus*] (13c) **1 :** an underlying ground, theory, or principle **2 a :** BUTTOCKS **b :** ANUS **3 :** the part of a land surface that has not been altered by human activities

1**fun·da·men·tal** \,fən-də-'ment-ᵊl\ *adj* (15c) **1 a :** serving as an original or generating source : PRIMARY ⟨a discovery ~ to scientific progress⟩ **b :** serving as a basis supporting existence or determining essential structure or function : BASIC **2 a :** of or relating to essential structure, function, or facts : RADICAL ⟨~ change⟩; *specif* : of or dealing with general principles rather than practical application ⟨~ science⟩ **b :** adhering to fundamentalism **3 :** of, relating to, or produced by the lowest component of a complex vibration **4 :** of central importance : PRINCIPAL ⟨~ purpose⟩ **5 :** belonging to one's innate or ingrained characteristics : DEEP-ROOTED ⟨hard to spoil his ~ good humor⟩ ***syn*** see ESSENTIAL — **fun·da·men·tal·ly** \-ᵊl-ē\ *adv*

2**fundamental** *n* (1633) **1 :** something fundamental; *esp* : one of the minimum constituents without which a thing or a system would not be what it is **2 a :** the principal musical tone produced by vibration (as of a string or column of air) on which a series of higher harmonics is based **b :** the root of a chord **3 :** the harmonic component of a complex wave that has the lowest frequency and commonly the greatest amplitude

fun·da·men·tal·ism \-ᵊl-,iz-əm\ *n* (1922) **1 a** *often cap* : a movement in 20th century Protestantism emphasizing the literally interpreted Bible as fundamental to Christian life and teaching **b :** the beliefs of this movement **c :** adherence to such beliefs **2 :** a movement or attitude stressing strict and literal adherence to a set of basic principles — **fun·da·men·tal·ist** \-ᵊl-əst\ *n* — **fundamentalist** *or* **fun·da·men·tal·is·tic** \-,ment-ᵊl-'is-tik\ *adj*

fundamental law *n* (ca. 1914) : the organic or basic law of a political unit as distinguished from legislative acts; *specif* : CONSTITUTION

fundamental particle *n* (ca. 1934) : ELEMENTARY PARTICLE

fundamental tissue *n* (1887) : plant tissue other than dermal and vascular tissues that consists typically of relatively undifferentiated parenchymatous and supportive cells

fun·dic \'fən-dik\ *adj* (1927) : of or relating to a fundus

fund–rais·er \'fən-,drā-zər\ *n* (1957) **1 :** a person employed to raise funds **2 :** a social event (as a cocktail party) held for the purpose of raising funds

fund–rais·ing \-ziŋ\ *n* (1940) : the organized activity of raising funds (as for an institution or political cause)

fun·dus \'fən-dəs\ *n, pl* **fun·di** \-,dī, -,dē\ [NL, fr. L, bottom] (1754) : the bottom of or part opposite the aperture of the internal surface of a hollow organ: as **a :** the greater curvature of the stomach **b :** the lower back part of the bladder **c :** the large upper end of the uterus **d :** the part of the eye opposite the pupil

1**fu·ner·al** \'fyün-(ə-)rəl\ *adj* [ME, fr. LL *funeralis,* fr. L *funer-, funus* funeral (n.); perh. akin to ON *deyja* to die — more at DIE] (14c) **1 :** of, relating to, or constituting a funeral **2 :** FUNEREAL 2

2**funeral** *n* [ME *funerelles* (pl.), fr. MF *funerailles* (pl.), fr. ML *funeralia* (pl.), fr. LL, neut. pl. of *funeralis,* adj.] (1512) **1 :** the observances held for a dead person usu. before burial or cremation **2** *chiefly dial*

: a funeral sermon **3** : a funeral procession **4** : an end of something's existence **5** : a matter of concern to one : WORRY ⟨if you get lost in the desert, that's your ~⟩

funeral director *n* (1886) : one whose profession is the management of funerals and who is usu. an embalmer

funeral home *n* (1926) : an establishment with facilities for the preparation of the dead for burial or cremation, for the viewing of the body, and for funerals — called also *funeral parlor*

fu·ner·ary \'fyü-nə-ˌrer-ē\ *adj* (1693) : of, used for, or associated with burial ⟨a pharaoh's ~ chamber⟩

fu·ne·re·al \fyü-'nir-ē-əl\ *adj* [L *funereus*, fr. *funer-, funus*] (1725) **1** : of or relating to a funeral **2** : befitting or suggesting a funeral (as in solemnity) — **fu·ne·re·al·ly** \-ə-lē\ *adv*

fun·fair \'fən-ˌfa(ə)r, -ˌfe(ə)r\ *n, chiefly Brit* (1925) : an amusement park

fun·gal \'fəŋ-gəl\ *adj* (1835) **1** : of, relating to, or having the characteristics of fungi **2** : caused by a fungus

fungi- *comb form* [L *fungus*] : fungus ⟨*fungi*form⟩

1fun·gi·ble \'fən-jə-bəl\ *n* (1765) : something that is fungible — usu. used in pl.

2fungible *adj* [NL *fungibilis*, fr. L *fungi* to perform — more at FUNCTION] (1818) **1** : of such a kind or nature that one specimen or part may be used in place of another specimen or equal part in the satisfaction of an obligation **2** : INTERCHANGEABLE — **fun·gi·bil·i·ty** \ˌfən-jə-'bil-ət-ē\ *n*

fun·gi·cid·al \ˌfən-jə-'sīd-ᵊl, ˌfəŋ-gə-\ *adj* (1905) : destroying fungi; *broadly* : inhibiting the growth of fungi — **fun·gi·cid·al·ly** \-ᵊl-ē\ *adv*

fun·gi·cide \'fən-jə-ˌsīd, 'fəŋ-gə-\ *n* [ISV] (1889) : an agent that destroys fungi or inhibits their growth

fun·gi·form \'fən-jə-ˌfȯrm, 'fəŋ-gə-\ *adj* (1823) : shaped like a mushroom

fun·go \'fəŋ-(ˌ)gō\ *n, pl* **fungoes** [origin unknown] (1867) : a fly ball hit esp. for practice fielding by a player who tosses a ball in the air and hits it as it comes down

fun·goid \'fəŋ-ˌgȯid\ *adj* (1836) : resembling, characteristic of, or being a fungus ⟨a ~ growth⟩ — **fungoid** *n*

fun·gous \'fəŋ-gəs\ *adj* (15c) : FUNGAL

fun·gus \'fəŋ-gəs\ *n, pl* **fun·gi** \'fən-ˌjī, 'fəŋ-ˌgī\ *also* **fun·gus·es** \'fəŋ-gə-səz\ *often attrib* [L] (1527) **1** : any of a major group (Fungi) of saprophytic and parasitic lower plants that lack chlorophyll and include molds, rusts, mildews, smuts, mushrooms, and yeasts **2** : infection with a fungus

fun house *n* (1948) : a building in an amusement park that contains various devices designed to startle or amuse

1fu·nic·u·lar \fyü-'nik-yə-lər, fə-\ *adj* [L *funiculus*] (1664) **1** : dependent on the tension of a cord or cable **2** : having the form of or associated with a cord **3** [NL *funiculus*] : of, relating to, or being a funiculus

2funicular *n* (1911) : a cable railway ascending a mountain; *esp* : one in which an ascending car counterbalances a descending car

fu·nic·u·lus \-ləs\ *n, pl* **-li** \-ˌlī, -ˌlē\ [NL, fr. L, dim. of *funis* rope] (1830) **1** : a bodily structure suggesting a cord: as **a** : a bundle of nerve fibers **b** : SPERMATIC CORD **2** : the stalk of a plant ovule

1funk \'fəŋk\ *vi* (1737) : to become frightened and shrink back ~ *vt* **1** : to be afraid of : DREAD **2** : to shrink from undertaking or facing

2funk *n* [prob. fr. obs. Flem *fonck*] (1743) **1** **a** : a state of paralyzing fear **b** : a depressed state of mind **2** : one that funks : COWARD

3funk *n* [back-formation fr. *2funky*] (1959) **1** : funky music **2** : the quality or state of being funky ⟨jeans ... have lost much of their ~ — Tom Wolfe⟩

funk hole *n* (1900) **1** : DUGOUT 2 **2** : a place of safe retreat

fun·kia \'fəŋ-kē-ə, 'fu̇ŋ-\ *n* [NL, genus name, fr. C. H. *Funck* †1839 Ger. botanist] (1839) : PLANTAIN LILY

1funky \'fəŋ-kē\ *adj* (1837) : being in a state of funk : PANICKY

2funky *adj* **funk·i·er; -est** [*funk* (offensive odor)] (1899) **1** : having an offensive odor : FOUL **2** : having an earthy unsophisticated style and feeling; *esp* : having the style and feeling of blues ⟨~ piano playing⟩ **3** : odd or quaint in appearance or style — **funk·i·ness** *n*

1fun·nel \'fən-ᵊl\ *n* [ME *fonel*, fr. OProv *fonilh*, fr. ML *fundibulum*, short for L *infundibulum*, fr. *infundere* to pour in, fr. *in-* + *fundere* to pour — more at FOUND] (15c) **1** **a** : a utensil that is usu. a hollow cone with a tube extending from the smaller end and that is designed to catch and direct a downward flow **b** : something shaped like a funnel **2** : a stack or flue for the escape of smoke or for ventilation

2funnel *vb* **-neled** *also* **-nelled; -nel·ing** *also* **-nel·ling** *vi* (1594) **1** : to have or take the shape of a funnel **2** : to pass through or as if through a funnel ~ *vt* **1** : to form in the shape of a funnel ⟨~*ed* his hands and shouted through them⟩ **2** : to move to a focal point or into a central channel ⟨contributions were ~*ed* into one account⟩

fun·nel·form \'fən-ᵊl-ˌfȯrm\ *adj* (ca. 1828) : INFUNDIBULIFORM

1fun·ny \'fən-ē\ *adj* **fun·ni·er; -est** (1756) **1** **a** : affording light mirth and laughter : AMUSING **b** : seeking or intended to amuse : FACETIOUS **2** : differing from the ordinary in a suspicious, perplexing, quaint, or eccentric way : QUEER **3** : involving trickery or deception ⟨told his prisoner not to try anything ~⟩ — **fun·ni·ly** \'fən-ᵊl-ē\ *adv* — **fun·ni·ness** \'fən-ē-nəs\ *n* — **funny** *adv*

2funny *n, pl* **funnies** (1852) : a comic strip or comic section of a periodical — usu. used in pl.

funny bone *n* [fr. the tingling felt when it is struck] (1840) **1** : the place at the back of the elbow where the ulnar nerve rests against a prominence of the humerus **2** : a sense of humor ⟨tickled his *funny bone*⟩

funny book *n* (1947) : COMIC BOOK

funny car *n* (1969) : a specialized dragster that has a one-piece molded body resembling the body of a mass-produced car

funny farm *n, slang* (1963) : a psychiatric hospital

fun·ny·man \'fən-ē-ˌman\ *n* (1852) : one noted for humor : COMEDIAN 2

funny money *n* (1943) **1** : artificially inflated currency **2** : counterfeit money

funny paper *n* (1847) : a comic section of a newspaper

1fur \'fər\ *vb* **furred; fur·ring** [ME *furren*, fr. MF *fourrer*, fr. OF *forrer*, fr. *fuerre* sheath, of Gmc origin; akin to OHG *fuotar* sheath; akin to Gk *pōy* herd, Skt *pāti* he protects] *vt* (14c) **1** : to cover, line, trim, or clothe with fur **2** : to coat or clog as if with fur **3** : to apply furring to ~ *vi* : to become coated or clogged as if with fur

2fur *n, often attrib* (14c) **1** : a piece of the dressed pelt of an animal used to make, trim, or line wearing apparel **2** : an article of clothing made of or with fur **3** : the hairy coat of a mammal esp. when fine, soft, and thick; *also* : such a coat with the skin **4** : a coating resembling fur: as **a** : a coat of epithelial debris on the tongue **b** : the thick pile of a fabric (as chenille) — **fur·less** \'fər-ləs\ *adj*

fu·ran \'fyu̇(ə)r-ˌan, fyu̇-'ran\ *also* **fu·rane** \'fyu̇(ə)r-ˌān, fyu̇-'rān\ *n* [ISV, fr. *furfural*] (1894) : a flammable liquid C_4H_4O that is obtained from wood oils of pines or made synthetically and is used esp. in organic synthesis

fu·ra·nose \'fyu̇r-ə-ˌnōs, -ˌnōz\ *n* (1927) : a sugar having an oxygen-containing ring of five atoms

fu·ran·o·side \fyu̇-'ran-ə-ˌsīd\ *n* (1932) : a glycoside containing the ring characteristic of furanose

fu·ra·zol·i·done \ˌfyu̇r-ə-'zäl-ə-ˌdōn\ *n* [*furfural* + *azole* + *-ide* + *-one*] (1955) : an antimicrobial drug $C_8H_7N_3O_5$ used against bacteria and some protozoa esp. in infections of the gastrointestinal tract

fur·bear·er \'fər-ˌbar-ər, -ˌber-\ *n* (1906) : an animal that bears fur esp. of a commercially desired quality

fur·be·low \'fər-bə-ˌlō\ *n* [by folk etymology fr. F dial. *farbella*] (1706) **1** : a pleated or gathered piece of material; *specif* : a flounce on women's clothing **2** : something that suggests a furbelow esp. in being showy or superfluous — **furbelow** *vt*

fur·bish \'fər-bish\ *vt* [ME *furbisshen*, fr. MF *fourbiss-*, stem of *fourbir*, of Gmc origin; akin to OHG *furben* to polish] (14c) **1** : to make lustrous : POLISH **2** : to give a new look to : RENOVATE — often used with *up* — **fur·bish·er** *n*

fur·ca·tion \ˌfər-'kā-shən\ *n* [ML *furcation-, furcatio*, fr. *furcatus*, pp. of *furcare* to branch, fr. L *furca* fork] (1646) **1** : something that is branched : FORK **2** : the act or process of branching

fur·cu·la \'fər-kyə-lə\ *n, pl* **-lae** \-ˌlē, -ˌlī\ [NL, fr. L, forked prop, dim. of *furca*] (1859) : a forked process or part: as **a** : WISHBONE **b** : the forked leaping appendage arising from the fourth abdominal segment of a collembolan

fur·fu·ra·ceous \ˌfər-f(y)ə-'rā-shəs\ *adj* [LL *furfuraceus*, fr. L *furfur* bran] (1650) : consisting of or covered with flaky particles ⟨~ eczema⟩

fur·fu·ral \'fər-f(y)ə-ˌral\ *n* [L *furfur* + ISV *-al*] (1879) : a liquid aldehyde $C_5H_4O_2$ of penetrating odor that is usu. made from plant materials and used esp. in making furan or phenolic resins and as a solvent

fur·fur·al·de·hyde \ˌfər-f(y)ə-'ral-də-ˌhīd\ *n* [L *furfur* + ISV *aldehyde* — more at GRIT] (1879) : FURFURAL

fur·fu·ran \'fər-f(y)ə-ˌran\ *n* (1877) : FURAN

fu·ri·o·so \ˌfyu̇r-ē-'ō-(ˌ)sō, -(ˌ)zō\ *adv or adj* [It, lit., furious] (1823) : with great force or vigor — used as a direction in music

fu·ri·ous \'fyu̇r-ē-əs\ *adj* [ME, fr. MF *furieus*, fr. L *furiosus*, fr. *furia* madness, fury] (14c) **1** **a** : exhibiting or goaded by anger **b** : giving a stormy or turbulent appearance ⟨~ bursts of flame from the wind-swept fire⟩ **c** : marked by noise, excitement, or activity **2** : INTENSE 1a ⟨the ~ growth of tropical vegetation⟩ — **fu·ri·ous·ly** *adv*

1furl \'fər(-ə)l\ *vb* [MF *ferler*, fr. ONF *ferlier* to tie tightly, fr. OF *fer, ferm* tight (fr. L *firmus* firm) + *lier* to tie, fr. L *ligare* — more at LIGATURE] *vt* (1556) : to wrap or roll (as a sail or a flag) close to or around something ~ *vi* : to curl or fold as in being furled

2furl *n* (1643) **1** : a furled coil **2** : the act of furling

fur·long \'fər-ˌlȯŋ\ *n* [ME, fr. OE *furlang*, fr. *furh* furrow + *lang* long] (14c) : a unit of distance equal to 220 yards

1fur·lough \'fər-(ˌ)lō\ *n* [D *verlof*, lit., permission, fr. MD, fr. *ver-* for- + *lof* permission; akin to MHG *loube* permission — more at FOR-, LEAVE] (1625) : a leave of absence from duty granted esp. to a soldier; *also* : a document authorizing such a leave of absence

2furlough *vt* (1781) **1** : to grant a furlough to **2** : to lay off from work

fur·mi·ty \'fər-mət-ē\ *var of* FRUMENTY

fur·nace \'fər-nəs\ *n* [ME *furnas*, fr. OF *fornaise*, fr. L *fornac-, fornax*; akin to L *formus* warm — more at WARM] (13c) : an enclosed structure in which heat is produced (as for heating a house or for reducing ore)

fur·nish \'fər-nish\ *vt* [ME *furnisshen*, fr. MF *fourniss-*, stem of *fournir* to complete, equip, of Gmc origin; akin to OHG *frummen* to further, *fruma* advantage — more at FOREMOST] (15c) **1** : to provide with what is needed; *esp* : to equip with furniture **2** : SUPPLY, GIVE ⟨~*ed* food and shelter for the refugees⟩ — **fur·nish·er** *n*

syn FURNISH, EQUIP, OUTFIT, APPOINT, ACCOUTRE, ARM mean to supply one with what is needed. FURNISH implies the provision of any or all essentials for performing a function; EQUIP suggests the provision of something making for efficiency in action or use; OUTFIT implies provision of a complete list or set of articles as for a journey, an expedition, a special occupation; APPOINT implies provision of complete and usu. elegant or elaborate equipment or furnishings; ACCOUTRE suggests the supplying of personal dress or equipment for a special activity; ARM implies provision for effective action or operation esp. in war.

fur·nish·ing *n* (1594) **1** : an article or accessory of dress — usu. used in pl. **2** : an object that tends to increase comfort or utility; *specif* : an article of furniture for the interior of a building — usu. used in pl.

fur·ni·ture \'fər-ni-chər\ *n* [MF *fourniture*, fr. *fournir*] (1542) : equipment that is necessary, useful, or desirable: as **a** *archaic* : the trappings of a horse **b** : movable articles used in readying an area (as a room or patio) for occupancy or use

fu·ror \'fyu̇(ə)r-ˌȯ(ə)r, -ˌō(ə)r, -ər\ *n* [MF & L; MF, fr. L, fr. *furere* to rage — more at DUST] (15c) **1** : an angry or maniacal fit : RAGE **2** : FURY 4 **3** : a fashionable craze : VOGUE **4** **a** : furious or hectic activity **b** : an outburst of public excitement or indignation : UPROAR

fu·rore \'fyu̇(ə)r-ˌō(ə)r, -ˌȯ(ə)r, -ər, *esp Brit* fyu̇-'rō-ri\ *n* [It, fr. L *furor*] (1815) **1** : FUROR 3 **2** : FUROR 4b

fu·ro·se·mide \fyu̇-'rō-sə-ˌmīd\ *n* [*furfural* + *-o-* + *sulf-* + *emide*, prob. alter. of *amide*] (1965) : a powerful diuretic $C_{12}H_{11}ClN_2O_5S$ used esp. to treat edema — called also *fursemide*

furred \'fərd\ *adj* [ME] (14c) **1** : lined, trimmed, or faced with fur **2** : coated as if with fur; *specif* : having a coating consisting chiefly of mucus and dead epithelial cells ⟨a ~ tongue⟩ **3** : bearing or wearing fur **4** : provided with furring ⟨~ wall⟩

\ə\ **abut** \ᵊ\ **kitten**, F **table** \ər\ **further** \a\ **ash** \ā\ **ace** \ä\ **cot, cart**
\au̇\ **out** \ch\ **chin** \e\ **bet** \ē\ **easy** \g\ **go** \i\ **hit** \ī\ **ice** \j\ **job**
\ŋ\ **sing** \ō\ **go** \ȯ\ **law** \ȯi\ **boy** \th\ **thin** \t͟h\ **the** \ü\ **loot** \u̇\ **foot**
\y\ **yet** \zh\ **vision** \à, ḵ, ⁿ, œ, œ̄, ue, ue̅, ʸ\ *see* Guide to Pronunciation

fur·ri·er \ˈfər-ē-ər, ˈfə-rē-\ *n* [alter. of ME *furrer,* fr. AF *furrere,* fr. OF *forrer* to fur — more at FUR] (14c) **1 :** a fur dealer **2 a :** one that dresses furs **b :** one that makes, repairs, alters, or cleans fur garments

fur·ri·ery \-ə-rē\ *n* (1784) **1 :** the fur business **2 :** fur craftsmanship

fur·rin·er \ˈfər-ə-nər\ *n* [alter. of *foreigner*] *chiefly dial* (1849) **:** one not native to a community ⟨that was a ~ come from outside —Muriel E. Sheppard⟩

fur·ring \ˈfər-iŋ\ *n* (14c) **1 :** a fur trimming or lining **2 a :** the application of thin wood, brick, or metal to joists, studs, or walls to form a level surface (as for attaching wallboard) or an air space **b :** the material used in this process

[1]**fur·row** \ˈfər-(ˌ)ō, -ə(-w); ˈfə-(ˌ)rō, -rə(-w)\ *n* [ME *furgh, forow,* fr. OE *furh;* akin to OHG *furuh* furrow, L *porca*] (bef. 12c) **1 a :** a trench in the earth made by a plow **b :** rural land **:** FIELD **2 :** something that resembles the track of a plow: as **a :** a marked narrow depression **:** GROOVE **b :** a deep wrinkle ⟨~*s* in his brow⟩

[2]**furrow** *vt* (15c) **:** to make furrows, grooves, wrinkles, or lines in ~ *vi* **:** to make or form furrows, grooves, wrinkles, or lines

fur·ry \ˈfər-ē\ *adj* **fur·ri·er; -est** (1674) **1 :** consisting of or resembling fur ⟨animals with ~ coats⟩ **2 :** covered with fur **3 :** thick in quality ⟨spoke with a ~ voice⟩

fur seal *n* (1775) **:** any of various eared seals that have a double coat with a dense soft underfur used esp. for clothing and trimmings

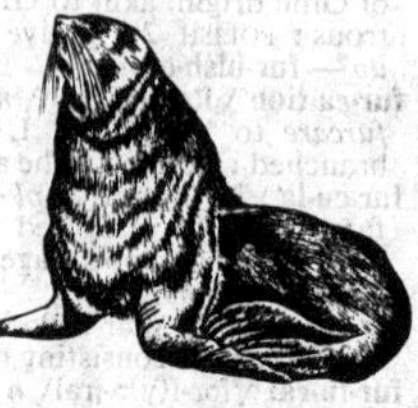

fur seal

fur·se·mide \ˈfər-sə-ˌmīd\ *n* (1965) **:** FUROSEMIDE

[1]**fur·ther** \ˈfər-t͟hər\ *adv* [ME, fr. OE *furthor* (akin to OHG *furthar* further), compar., fr. the root of OE *forth* forth] (bef. 12c) **1 :** [1]FARTHER 1 ⟨my ponies are tired, and I have ~ to go —Thomas Hardy⟩ **2 :** in addition **:** MOREOVER **3 :** to a greater degree or extent ⟨~ annoyed by a second intrusion⟩ ***usage*** see FARTHER

[2]**further** *vt* **fur·thered; fur·ther·ing** \ˈfərt͟h-(ə-)riŋ\ (bef. 12c) **:** to help forward **:** PROMOTE ⟨~*ed* his education in graduate school⟩ ***syn*** see ADVANCE — **fur·ther·er** \ˈfər-t͟hər-ər\ *n*

[3]**further** *adj* (13c) **1 :** [2]FARTHER 1 ⟨rode . . . across the valley and up the ~ slopes —T. E. Lawrence⟩ **2 :** going or extending beyond **:** ADDITIONAL ⟨~ volumes⟩ ⟨~ education⟩ ***usage*** see FARTHER

fur·ther·ance \ˈfərt͟h-(ə-)rən(t)s\ *n* (15c) **:** the act of furthering **:** ADVANCEMENT

further education *n, Brit* (1898) **:** ADULT EDUCATION

fur·ther·more \ˈfər-t͟hə(r)-ˌmō(ə)r, -ˌmȯ(ə)r\ *adv* (13c) **:** in addition to what precedes **:** BESIDES

fur·ther·most \-ər-ˌmōst\ *adj* (15c) **:** most distant **:** FARTHEST

fur·thest \ˈfər-t͟həst\ *adv or adj* (14c) **:** FARTHEST

fur·tive \ˈfərt-iv\ *adj* [F or L; F *furtif,* fr. L *furtivus,* fr. *furtum* theft, fr. *fur* thief; akin to Gk *phōr* thief, L *ferre* to carry — more at BEAR] (1612) **1 a :** done by stealth **:** SURREPTITIOUS **b :** expressive of stealth **:** SLY ⟨had the ~ look of one with something to hide⟩ **2 :** obtained underhandedly **:** STOLEN ***syn*** see SECRET — **fur·tive·ly** *adv* — **fur·tive·ness** *n*

fu·run·cle \ˈfyu̇(ə)r-ˌəŋ-kəl\ *n* [L *furunculus* petty thief, sucker, furuncle, dim. of *furon-, furo* ferret, thief, fr. *fur*] (1676) **:** a localized inflammatory swelling of the skin and underlying tissues that is caused by infection by a bacterium in a hair follicle or skin gland and that discharges pus and a central core of dead tissue **:** BOIL

fu·run·cu·lo·sis \fyu̇-ˌrəŋ-kyə-ˈlō-səs\ *n, pl* **-lo·ses** \-ˌsēz\ (1861) **1 :** the condition of having or tending to develop multiple furuncles **2 :** a highly infectious disease of various salmonoid fishes (as trout) that is caused by a bacterium (*Bacterium salmonicida*) and is esp. virulent in dense fish populations (as in hatcheries)

fu·ry \ˈfyu̇(ə)r-ē\ *n, pl* **furies** [ME *furie,* fr. MF & L; MF, fr. L *furia,* fr. *furere* to rage — more at DUST] (14c) **1 :** intense, disordered, and often destructive rage **2 a** *cap* **:** any of the avenging deities in Greek mythology who torment criminals and inflict plagues **b :** an avenging spirit **c :** one who resembles an avenging spirit; *esp* **:** a spiteful woman **3 :** extreme fierceness or violence **4 :** a state of inspired exaltation **:** FRENZY ***syn*** see ANGER

furze \ˈfərz\ *n* [ME *firse,* fr. OE *fyrs*] (bef. 12c) **:** GORSE — **furzy** \ˈfər-zē\ *adj*

fus·cous \ˈfəs-kəs\ *adj* [L *fuscus* —more at DUSK] (1662) **:** of any of several colors averaging a brownish gray

[1]**fuse** \ˈfyüz\ *vb* **fused; fus·ing** [L *fusus,* pp. of *fundere* to pour, melt — more at FOUND] *vt* (1592) **1 :** to reduce to a liquid or plastic state by heat **2 :** to blend thoroughly by or as if by melting together ⟨in her richest work she ~*s* comedy and tragedy —T.A. Gullason⟩ **3 :** to stitch by applying heat and pressure with or without the use of an adhesive ~ *vi* **1 :** to become fluid with heat; *also* **:** to fail because of the blowing of a fuse **2 :** to become blended by or as if by melting together ***syn*** see MIX

[2]**fuse** *n* (1884) **:** an electrical safety device consisting of or including a wire or strip of fusible metal that melts and interrupts the circuit when the current exceeds a particular amperage

[3]**fuse** *n* [It *fuso* spindle, fr. L *fusus,* of unknown origin] (1664) **1 :** a continuous train of a combustible substance enclosed in a cord or cable for setting off an explosive charge by transmitting fire to it **2** *usu* **fuze :** a mechanical or electrical detonating device for setting off the bursting charge of a projectile, bomb, or torpedo

[4]**fuse** *or* **fuze** \ˈfyüz\ *vt* **fused** *or* **fuzed; fus·ing** *or* **fuz·ing** (1802) **:** to equip with a fuse

fused quartz *n* (1925) **:** QUARTZ GLASS — called also *fused silica*

fu·see \fyü-ˈzē\ *n* [F *fusée,* lit., spindleful of yarn, fr. OF, fr. *fus* spindle, fr. L *fusus*] (1622) **1 :** a conical spirally grooved pulley in a timepiece from which a cord or chain unwinds onto a barrel containing the spring and which by its increasing diameter compensates for the lessening power of the spring **2 :** [3]FUSE 1 **3 :** a friction match with a bulbous head not easily blown out **4 :** a red signal flare used esp. for protecting stalled trains and trucks

fu·se·lage \ˈfyü-sə-ˌläzh, -zə-\ *n* [F, fr. *fuselé* spindle-shaped, fr. MF, fr. *fusel,* dim. of *fus*] (1909) **:** the central body portion of an airplane designed to accommodate the crew and the passengers or cargo

fu·sel oil \ˈfyü-zəl-\ *n* [G *fusel* bad liquor] (ca. 1859) **:** an acrid oily liquid occurring in insufficiently distilled alcoholic liquors, consisting chiefly of amyl alcohol, and used esp. as a source of alcohols and as a solvent

fusi- *comb form* [L *fusus*] **:** spindle ⟨*fusi*form⟩

fus·ible \ˈfyü-zə-bəl\ *adj* (14c) **:** capable of being fused and esp. liquefied by heat — **fus·ibil·i·ty** \ˌfyü-zə-ˈbil-ət-ē\ *n*

fu·si·form \ˈfyü-zə-ˌfȯrm\ *adj* (1746) **:** tapering toward each end ⟨~ bacteria⟩

[1]**fu·sil** \ˈfyü-zəl\ *or* **fu·sile** \ˈfyü-zəl, -ˌzīl\ *adj* [ME, fr. L *fusilis,* fr. *fusus,* pp.] (14c) **1** *archaic* **a :** made by melting and pouring into forms **:** CAST **b :** liquefied by heat **2** *archaic* **:** FUSIBLE

[2]**fusil** *n* [F, lit., steel for striking fire, fr. OF *foisil,* fr. (assumed) VL *focilis,* fr. LL *focus* fire — more at FUEL] (1680) **:** a light flintlock musket

fu·sil·ier *or* **fu·sil·eer** \ˌfyü-zə-ˈli(ə)r\ *n* [F *fusilier,* fr. *fusil*] (1680) **1 :** a soldier armed with a fusil **2 :** a member of a British regiment formerly armed with fusils

[1]**fu·sil·lade** \ˈfyü-sə-ˌläd, -ˌlād, ˌfyü-sə-ˈ, -zə-\ *n* [F, fr. *fusiller* to shoot, fr. *fusil*] (1801) **1 a :** a number of shots fired simultaneously or in rapid succession **b :** something that gives the effect of a fusillade ⟨a ~ of rocks and bottles⟩ **2 :** a spirited outburst esp. of criticism

[2]**fusillade** *vt* **-lad·ed; -lad·ing** (1816) **:** to attack or shoot down by a fusillade

fu·sion \ˈfyü-zhən\ *n, often attrib* [L *fusion-, fusio,* fr. *fusus,* pp.] (1555) **1 a :** the act or process of liquefying or rendering plastic by heat **b :** the liquid or plastic state induced by heat **2 :** a union by or as if by melting: as **a :** a merging of diverse elements into a unified whole **b :** a political partnership ⟨a ~ of the major parties⟩ **c :** the union of atomic nuclei to form heavier nuclei resulting in the release of enormous quantities of energy when certain light elements unite

fusion bomb *n* (1950) **:** a bomb in which nuclei of a light chemical element unite to form nuclei of heavier elements with a release of energy; *esp* **:** HYDROGEN BOMB

fu·sion·ist \ˈfyüzh-(ə-)nəst\ *n* (1851) **:** one who promotes or takes part in a coalition esp. of political parties

[1]**fuss** \ˈfəs\ *n* [origin unknown] (1701) **1 a :** needless bustle or excitement **:** COMMOTION **b :** a show of flattering attention ⟨made a big ~ over his favorite niece⟩ **2 a :** a state of agitation esp. over a trivial matter **b :** OBJECTION, PROTEST **c :** an often petty controversy or quarrel ⟨ended up having a pretty good ~ with my wife —Mac Hyman⟩

[2]**fuss** *vi* (1792) **1 a :** to create or be in a state of restless activity; *specif* **:** to shower flattering attentions ⟨doting grandparents ~*ing* over the grandchildren⟩ **b :** to pay close or undue attention to small details ⟨~*ed* with her hair⟩ **2 a :** to become upset **:** WORRY **b :** to express annoyance or pique **:** COMPLAIN ⟨a mother who has to cope with ~*ing* children⟩ ~ *vt* **:** AGITATE, UPSET — **fuss·er** *n*

fuss·bud·get \ˈfəs-ˌbəj-ət\ *n* (1904) **:** one who fusses esp. about trifles — **fuss·bud·gety** \-ət-ē\ *adj*

fuss·pot \ˈfəs-ˌpät\ *n* (1921) **:** FUSSBUDGET

fussy \ˈfəs-ē\ *adj* **fuss·i·er; -est** (1831) **1 :** easily upset **:** IRRITABLE **2 :** overly decorative **:** ORNATE ⟨a ~ wallpaper pattern⟩ **3 a :** requiring or giving close attention to details ⟨~ bookkeeping procedures⟩ **b :** revealing a sometimes extreme concern for niceties **:** FASTIDIOUS ⟨not ~ about food⟩ — **fuss·i·ly** \ˈfəs-ə-lē\ *adv* — **fuss·i·ness** \ˈfəs-ē-nəs\ *n*

fus·tian \ˈfəs-chən\ *n* [ME, fr. OF *fustaine,* fr. ML *fustaneum,* prob. fr. *fustis* tree trunk, fr. L, club — more at BEAT] (13c) **1 a :** a strong cotton and linen fabric **b :** a class of cotton fabrics usu. having a pile face and twill weave **2 :** pretentious and banal writing or speech — **fustian** *adj*

fus·tic \ˈfəs-tik\ *n* [ME *fustik,* fr. MF *fustoc,* fr. Ar *fustuq,* fr. Gk *pistakē* pistachio tree — more at PISTACHIO] (15c) **1 :** the wood of a tropical American tree (*Chlorophora tinctoria*) of the mulberry family that yields a yellow dye; *also* **:** any of several similar dyewoods **2 :** a tree yielding fustic

fus·ti·gate \ˈfəs-tə-ˌgāt\ *vt* **-gat·ed; -gat·ing** [LL *fustigatus,* pp. of *fustigare,* fr. L *fustis* + *-igare* (as in *fumigare* to fumigate)] (1656) **1 :** CUDGEL **2 :** to criticize severely — **fus·ti·ga·tion** \ˌfəs-tə-ˈgā-shən\ *n*

fus·ty \ˈfəs-tē\ *adj* **fus·ti·er; -est** [ME, fr. *fust* wine cask, fr. MF, club, cask, fr. L *fustis*] (14c) **1** *Brit* **:** impaired by age or dampness **:** MOLDY **2 :** saturated with dust and stale odors **:** MUSTY **3 :** rigidly old-fashioned or reactionary ***syn*** see MALODOROUS — **fus·ti·ly** \-tə-lē\ *adv* — **fus·ti·ness** \-tē-nəs\ *n*

fu·thark \ˈfü-ˌthärk\ *also* **fu·thorc** *or* **fu·thork** \-ˌthȯ(ə)rk\ *n* [fr. the first six letters, *f, u, þ* (*th*), *o* (or *a*), *r, c* (=k)] (1851) **:** the runic alphabet

fu·tile \ˈfyüt-ᵊl, ˈfyü-ˌtīl\ *adj* [MF or L; MF, fr. L *futilis* that pours out easily, useless, fr. *fut-* (akin to *fundere* to pour) — more at FOUND] (1555) **1 :** serving no useful purpose **:** completely ineffective ⟨efforts to convince him were ~⟩ **2 :** occupied with trifles **:** FRIVOLOUS — **fu·tile·ly** \-ᵊl-(l)ē, -ˌtīl-lē\ *adv* — **fu·tile·ness** \-ᵊl-nəs, -ˌtīl-nəs\ *n*

syn FUTILE, VAIN, FRUITLESS mean producing no result. FUTILE may connote completeness of failure or unwisdom of undertaking; VAIN usu. implies simple failure to achieve a desired result; FRUITLESS comes close to VAIN but often suggests long and arduous effort or severe disappointment.

fu·til·i·tar·i·an \fyü-ˌtil-ə-ˈter-ē-ən, ˌfyü-\ *n* [blend of *futile* and *utilitarian*] (1827) **:** one who believes that human striving is futile — **futilitarian** *adj* — **fu·til·i·tar·i·an·ism** \-ē-ə-ˌniz-əm\ *n*

fu·til·i·ty \fyü-ˈtil-ət-ē\ *n, pl* **-ties** (1623) **1 :** the quality or state of being futile **:** USELESSNESS **2 :** a useless act or gesture ⟨the *futilities* of debate for its own sake —W. A. White⟩

fu·ton \ˈfü-ˌtän\ *n, pl* **futons** *also* **futon** [Jp] (1876) **:** a mattress filled usu. with cotton that is placed on the floor for use as a bed

fut·tock \ˈfət-ək\ *n* [prob. alter. of *foothook* (futtock)] (1611) **:** one of the curved timbers scarfed together to form the lower part of the compound rib of a ship

futtock shroud *n* (1840) **:** a short iron rod connecting the topmast rigging with the lower mast

[1]**fu·ture** \ˈfyü-chər\ *adj* [ME, fr. MF & L; MF *futur,* fr. L *futurus* about to be — more at BE] (14c) **1 :** that is to be; *specif* **:** existing after death **2 :** of, relating to, or constituting a verb tense expressive of time yet to come **3 :** existing or occurring at a later time ⟨met his ~ wife⟩

²**future** n (14c) **1 a :** time that is to come **b :** what is going to happen **2 :** an expectation of advancement or progressive development **3 :** something (as a bulk commodity) bought for future acceptance or sold for future delivery — usu. used in pl. ⟨the use of grain ∼s as a hedge against price changes⟩ **4 a :** the future tense of a language **b :** a verb form in the future tense

fu·ture·less \ˈfyü-chər-ləs\ adj (ca. 1855) : having no prospect of future success

future perfect adj (ca. 1898) : of, relating to, or constituting a verb tense that is traditionally formed in English with will have and shall have and that expresses completion of an action by a specified time that is yet to come — **future perfect** n

future shock n (1970) : the physical and psychological distress suffered by one who is unable to cope with the rapidity of social and technological changes

fu·tur·ism \ˈfyü-chə-ˌriz-əm\ n (ca. 1909) **1 :** a movement in art, music, and literature begun in Italy about 1909 and marked esp. by an effort to give formal expression to the dynamic energy and movement of mechanical processes **2 :** a point of view that finds meaning or fulfillment in the future rather than in the past or present

fu·tur·ist \ˈfyü-chə-rəst\ n (1842) **1 :** one who is a believer in or practitioner of futurism **2 :** one who is a believer in or practitioner of futurology — **futurist** adj

fu·tur·is·tic \ˌfyü-chə-ˈris-tik\ adj (1915) : of, relating to, or characteristic of the future, futurism, or futurology; also : very modern — **fu·tur·is·ti·cal·ly** \-ti-k(ə-)lē\ adv

fu·tur·is·tics \-tiks\ n pl but sing in constr (1969) : FUTUROLOGY

fu·tu·ri·ty \fyü-ˈt(y)ùr-ə-tē, -ˈchùr-\ n, pl **-ties** (1637) **1 :** time to come : FUTURE **2 :** the quality or state of being future **3** pl : future events

or prospects **4 a :** a horse race usu. for two-year-olds in which the competitors are nominated at birth or before **b :** a race or competition for which entries are made well in advance of the event

fu·tur·ol·o·gy \ˌfyü-chə-ˈräl-ə-jē\ n (1946) : a study that deals with future possibilities based on current trends — **fu·tur·o·log·i·cal** \-rə-ˈläj-i-kəl\ adj — **fu·tur·ol·o·gist** \-ˈräl-ə-jəst\ n

futz \ˈfəts\ vi [prob. fr. Yiddish; akin to OHG ferzan to fart — more at FART] slang (1932) : FOOL 1a — often used with around ⟨∼ around without producing any worthwhile music —John Koegel⟩

fuze, fu·zee var of FUSE, FUSEE

¹**fuzz** \ˈfəz\ n [prob. back-formation fr. fuzzy] (1674) **1 :** fine light particles or fibers (as of down or fluff) **2 :** a blurred effect

²**fuzz** vi (1702) **1 :** to fly off in or become covered with fluffy particles **2 :** to become blurred ⟨her frame of reference ∼ing at the edges —Jane O'Reilly⟩ ∼ vt **1 :** to make fuzzy **2 :** to envelop in a haze : BLUR

³**fuzz** [origin unknown] (1927) : POLICE; also : a police officer

fuzzy \ˈfəz-ē\ adj **fuzz·i·er; -est** [perh. fr. LG fussig loose, spongy; akin to OHG fūl rotten — more at FOUL] (1713) **1 :** marked by or giving a suggestion of fuzz ⟨a ∼ covering of felt⟩ **2 :** lacking in clarity or definition ⟨moving the camera causes ∼ photos⟩ ⟨∼ thinking⟩ — **fuzz·i·ly** \ˈfəz-ə-lē\ adv — **fuzz·i·ness** \ˈfəz-ē-nəs\ n

-fy \ˌfī\ vb suffix [ME -fien, fr. OF -fier, fr. L -ficare, fr. -ficus -fic] **1 :** make : form into ⟨dandify⟩ **2 :** invest with the attributes of : make similar to ⟨citify⟩

fyce \ˈfīs\ var of FEIST

fyke \ˈfīk\ n [D fuik] (1832) : a long bag net kept open by hoops

fyl·fot \ˈfil-ˌfät\ n [ME, device used to fill the lower part of a painted glass window (fr. a conjectural MS reading)] (1842) : SWASTIKA

g \ˈjē\ n, pl **g's** or **gs** \ˈjēz\ often cap, often attrib **1 a :** the 7th letter of the English alphabet **b :** a graphic representation of this letter **c :** a speech counterpart of orthographic g **2 :** the 5th tone of a C-major scale **3 :** a graphic device for reproducing the letter **4 :** one designated g esp. as the 7th in order or class **5** [gravity] : a unit of force equal to the force exerted by gravity on a body at rest and used to indicate the force to which a body is subjected when accelerated **6** [grand] slang : a sum of $1000 **7 :** something shaped like the letter G

G adj [general] of a motion picture (1968) : of such a nature that all ages may be allowed admission — compare PG, PG-13, R, X

¹**gab** \ˈgab\ vi **gabbed; gab·bing** [prob. short for gabble] (1786) : to talk in a rapid or thoughtless manner : CHATTER — **gab·ber** n

²**gab** n (1790) : TALK; esp : idle talk

gab·ar·dine \ˈgab-ər-ˌdēn\ n [MF gaverdine] (1520) **1 :** GABERDINE 1 **2 a :** a firm hard-finish durable fabric (as of wool or rayon) twilled with diagonal ribs on the right side **b :** a garment of gabardine

gab·ble \ˈgab-əl\ vb **gab·bled; gab·bling** \-(ə-)liŋ\ [prob. of imit. origin] vi (1577) **1 :** to talk fast or foolishly : JABBER **2 :** to utter inarticulate or animal sounds ∼ vt : to say with incoherent rapidity : BABBLE — **gab·ble** n — **gab·bler** \-(ə-)lər\ n

gab·bro \ˈgab-(ˌ)rō\ n, pl **gabbros** [It, prob. modif. of L glaber smooth — more at GLAD] (ca. 1828) : a granular igneous rock composed essentially of calcic plagioclase, a ferromagnesian mineral, and accessory minerals — **gab·bro·ic** \ga-ˈbrō-ik\ adj

gab·broid \ˈgab-ˌrȯid\ adj (1900) : resembling gabbro

gab·by \ˈgab-ē\ adj **gab·bi·er; -est** (1719) : TALKATIVE, GARRULOUS

ga·belle \gə-ˈbel\ n [ME, fr. MF, fr. OIt gabella tax, fr. Ar qabālah] (15c) : a tax on salt levied in France prior to 1790

gab·er·dine \ˈgab-ər-ˌdēn\ n [MF gaverdine] (1520) **1 :** a coarse long coat or smock worn chiefly by Jews in medieval times **b :** an English laborer's smock **c :** GARMENT **2 :** GABARDINE 2

gab·fest \ˈgab-ˌfest\ n (1897) **1 :** an informal gathering for general talk ⟨political ∼s⟩ **2 :** an extended conversation

ga·bi·on \ˈgā-bē-ən, ˈgab-ē-\ n [MF, fr. OIt gabbione, lit., large cage, aug. of gabbia cage, fr. L cavea — more at CAGE] (1579) : a basket or cage filled with earth or rocks and used esp. in building a support or abutment

ga·ble \ˈgā-bəl\ n [ME, fr. MF, of Gmc origin; akin to ON gafl gable — more at CEPHALIC] (14c) **1 a :** the vertical triangular end of a building from cornice or eaves to ridge **b :** the similar end of a gambrel roof **c :** the end wall of a building **2 :** a triangular part or structure

ga·bled \-bəld\ adj (1849) : built with a gable

gable roof n (1850) : a double-sloping roof that forms a gable at each end

gab·oon \ga-ˈbün, gə-\ n [alter. of ¹gob + -oon (as in spittoon)] dial (1929) : SPITTOON

Ga·bri·el \ˈgā-brē-əl\ n [Heb Gabhrī'ēl] : one of the four archangels named in Hebrew tradition

ga·by \ˈgā-bē\ n, pl **gabies** [perh. of Scand origin; akin to ON gapa to gape — more at GAPE] dial chiefly Eng (ca. 1796) : SIMPLETON

¹**gad** \ˈgad\ n [ME, spike, fr. ON gaddr; akin to OE geard rod — more at YARD] (13c) **1 :** a chisel or pointed iron or steel bar for loosening ore or rock **2** chiefly dial : ROD, STICK

²**gad** vi **gad·ded; gad·ding** [ME gadden] (15c) : to be on the go to little purpose — usu. used with about — **gad·der** n

³**gad** interj [euphemism for God] (1608) — used as a mild oath

Gad \ˈgad\ n [Heb Gādh] : a son of Jacob and the traditional eponymous ancestor of one of the tribes of Israel — **Gad·ite** \-ˌīt\ n

gad·about \ˈgad-ə-ˌbaùt\ n (1837) : a person who flits about in social activity — **gadabout** adj

gad·a·rene \ˈgad-ə-ˌrēn\ adj, often cap [fr. the demon-possessed Gadarene swine in Mt 8:28 that rushed into the sea] (1820) : HEADLONG, PRECIPITATE ⟨a ∼ rush to the cities⟩

gad·fly \ˈgad-ˌflī\ n [¹gad] (1626) **1 :** any of various flies (as a horsefly, botfly, or warble fly) that bite or annoy livestock **2 :** a usu. intentionally annoying person who stimulates or provokes others esp. by persistent irritating criticism

gad·get \ˈgaj-ət\ n [origin unknown] (1886) : an often small mechanical or electronic device with a practical use but often thought of as a novelty — **gad·get·eer** \ˌgaj-ə-ˈti(ə)r\ n — **gad·get·ry** \ˈgaj-ə-trē\ n — **gad·gety** \-ət-ē\ adj

ga·doid \ˈgād-ˌȯid, ˈgad-\ adj [NL Gadus, genus of fishes, fr. Gk gados, a fish] (ca. 1842) : resembling or related to the cods — **gadoid** n

gad·o·lin·ite \ˈgad-ᵊl-ə-ˌnīt\ n [G gadolinit, fr. Johann Gadolin †1852 Finn. chemist] (1802) : a black or brown mineral $Be_2FeY_2Si_2O_{10}$ that is a source of rare earths and consists of silicate of iron, beryllium, yttrium, cerium, and erbium

gad·o·lin·i·um \ˌgad-ᵊl-ˈin-ē-əm\ n [NL, fr. J. Gadolin] (1886) : a magnetic metallic element of the rare-earth group occurring in combination in gadolinite and several other minerals — see ELEMENT table

ga·droon \gə-ˈdrün\ n [F godron round plait, gadroon] (1723) **1 :** the ornamental notching or carving of a rounded molding **2 :** a short often oval fluting or reeding used in decoration — **gadroon** vt — **ga·droon·ing** n

gad·wall \ˈgad-ˌwȯl\ n, pl **gadwalls** or **gadwall** [origin unknown] (1666) : a grayish brown dabbling duck (Anas strepera) about the size of the mallard

gad·zooks \gad-ˈzüks, -ˈzùks\ interj, often cap [perh. fr. God's hooks, swearing by the Crucifixion nails] archaic (1694) —used as a mild oath

Gaea \ˈjē-ə\ n [Gk Gaia] : the Greek earth goddess and mother of the Titans

Gael \ˈgā(ə)l\ n [ScGael Gàidheal & IrGael Gaedheal] (1753) **1 :** a Scottish Highlander **2 :** a Celtic esp. Gaelic-speaking inhabitant of Ireland, Scotland, or the Isle of Man

Gael·ic \ˈgā-lik, ˈgal-, ˈgäl-\ adj [ScGael Gàidhealach & IrGael Gaedhealach, fr. Gaedheal] (1741) **1 :** of or relating to the Gaels and esp. the Celtic Highlanders of Scotland **2 :** of, relating to, or constituting the Goidelic speech of the Celts in Ireland, the Isle of Man, and the Scottish Highlands — **Gaelic** n

¹**gaff** \ˈgaf\ n [ME, fr. MF gaffe, fr. Prov gaf] (14c) **1 a :** a spear or spearhead for taking fish or turtles **b :** a handled hook for holding or lifting heavy fish **c :** a metal spur for a gamecock **d :** a butcher's hook **e :** a climbing iron or its steel point used by a telephone lineman

\ə\ abut \ᵊ\ kitten, F table \ər\ further \a\ ash \ā\ ace \ä\ cot, cart \aù\ out \ch\ chin \e\ bet \ē\ easy \g\ go \i\ hit \ī\ ice \j\ job \ŋ\ sing \ō\ go \ȯ\ law \ȯi\ boy \th\ thin \th\ the \ü\ loot \ù\ foot \y\ yet \zh\ vision \ä, k̲, ⁿ, œ, œ̄, ᵫ, ūᴇ, ᵩ\ see Guide to Pronunciation

2 : the spar on which the head of a fore-and-aft sail is extended 3 a : HOAX, FRAUD b : GIMMICK, TRICK 4 a : something painful or difficult to bear : ORDEAL — usu. used in the phrase *stand the gaff; esp* : persistent raillery or criticism b : rough treatment : ABUSE 5 : GAFFE

[2]**gaff** *vt* (1844) 1 a : to strike or secure with a gaff b : to fit (a gamecock) with a gaff 2 : DECEIVE, TRICK; *also* : FLEECE 3 : to fix for the purpose of cheating : GIMMICK ⟨~ the dice⟩

[3]**gaff** *n* [origin unknown] *Brit* (1812) : a cheap theater or music hall

gaffe \ˈgaf\ *n* [F, gaff, gaffe] (1909) : a social or diplomatic blunder : FAUX PAS

gaf·fer \ˈgaf-ər\ *n* [prob. alter. of *godfather*] (1589) 1 : an old man — compare GAMMER 2 *Brit* a : EMPLOYER b : FOREMAN, OVERSEER 3 : a head glassblower 4 : a lighting electrician on a motion-picture or television set

gaff–top·sail \ˈgaf-ˈtäp-ˌsāl, -səl\ *n* (1794) : a usu. triangular topsail with its foot extended upon the gaff — see SAIL illustration

[1]**gag** \ˈgag\ *vb* **gagged; gag·ging** [ME *gaggen* to strangle, of imit. origin] *vt* (1509) 1 a : to stop the mouth of with something inserted b : to pry or hold open with a gag c : to prevent from exercising freedom of speech or expression 2 : to choke or cause to retch 3 : to provide or write quips or pranks for ⟨~ a show⟩ ~ *vi* 1 a : CHOKE; *also* : to suffer a throat spasm that makes swallowing or breathing difficult b : RETCH 2 : to be unable to endure something : BALK 3 : to make quips

[2]**gag** *n* (1553) 1 : something thrust into the mouth to keep it open or to prevent speech or outcry 2 : an official check or restraint on debate or free speech ⟨~ rule⟩ 3 : a laugh-provoking remark or act 4 : PRANK, TRICK

ga·ga \ˈgä-(ˌ)gä\ *adj* [F, fr. *gaga* fool, of imit. origin] (1920) 1 : CRAZY, FOOLISH 2 : marked by wild enthusiasm : INFATUATED, DOTING

[1]**gage** \ˈgāj\ *n* [ME, fr. MF, of Gmc origin; akin to OHG *wetti* pledge — more at WED] (14c) 1 : a token of defiance; *specif* : a glove or cap cast on the ground to be taken up by an opponent as a pledge of combat 2 : something deposited as a pledge of performance

[2]**gage** *vt* (15c) 1 *archaic* : PLEDGE 2 *archaic* : STAKE, RISK

[3]**gage** *var of* GAUGE

[4]**gage** *n* (1847) : GREENGAGE

gag·ger \ˈgag-ər\ *n* (1624) 1 : one that gags 2 : GAGMAN

gag·gle \ˈgag-əl\ *n* [ME *gagyll,* fr. *gagelen* to cackle] (15c) 1 : FLOCK; *esp* : a flock of geese when not in flight — compare SKEIN 2 : AGGREGATION, CLUSTER ⟨a ~ of reporters and photographers⟩

gag·man \ˈgag-ˌman\ *n* (1928) 1 : a gag writer 2 : a comedian who uses gags

gag·ster \ˈgag-stər\ *n* (1935) : GAGMAN; *also* : one who plays practical jokes

gahn·ite \ˈgän-ˌīt\ *n* [G *gahnit,* fr. J. G. *Gahn* †1818 Swed. chemist] (ca. 1808) : a usu. dark green mineral $ZnAl_2O_4$ consisting of an oxide of zinc and aluminum

gai·ety \ˈgā-ət-ē\ *n, pl* **-eties** [F *gaieté*] (1634) 1 : MERRYMAKING; *also* : festive activity — often used in pl. 2 : high spirits : MERRIMENT 3 : ELEGANCE, FINERY

gail·lar·dia \gə-ˈlärd-(ē-)ə\ *n* [NL, fr. *Gaillard* de Marentonneau, 18th cent. Fr. botanist] (1888) : any of a genus (*Gaillardia*) of chiefly western American composite herbs with showy flower heads

gai·ly \ˈgā-lē\ *adv* (14c) : in a gay manner : marked by gaiety

[1]**gain** \ˈgān\ *n* [ME *gayne,* fr. MF *gaigne, gain,* fr. OF *gaaigne, gaaing,* fr. *gaaignier* to till, earn, gain, of Gmc origin; akin to OHG *weidanōn* to hunt for food, L *vis* power — more at VIM] (14c) 1 : resources or advantage acquired or increased : PROFIT ⟨made substantial ~s last year⟩ 2 : the act or process of gaining 3 a : an increase in amount, magnitude, or degree ⟨a ~ in efficiency⟩ b : the ratio of increase of output over input in an amplifier c : the effectiveness of a directional antenna expressed as the ratio in decibels of standard antenna input power to the directional antenna input power that will produce the same field strength in the desired direction

[2]**gain** *vt* (14c) 1 a : to acquire or get possession of usu. by industry, merit, or craft ⟨~ an advantage⟩ ⟨he stood to ~ a fortune⟩ b : to win in competition or conflict ⟨the attackers ~*ed* the day⟩ c : to get by a natural development or process ⟨~ strength⟩ d : to establish a specific relationship with ⟨~ a friend⟩ e (1) : to arrive at : REACH, ATTAIN ⟨~*ed* the river that night⟩ (2) : TRAVERSE, COVER ⟨~*ed* 10 yards on the play⟩ 2 : to win to one's side : PERSUADE ⟨~ adherents to a cause⟩ 3 : to cause to be obtained or given : ATTRACT ⟨~ attention⟩ 4 a : to increase in (a particular quality) ⟨~ momentum⟩ b : to make an increase of (a specified amount) ⟨~*ed* 3% in the past month⟩ 5 *of a timepiece* : to run fast by the amount of ⟨the clock ~*s* a minute a day⟩ ~ *vi* 1 : to get advantage : PROFIT ⟨hoped to ~ from his crime⟩ 2 a : INCREASE ⟨the day was ~*ing* in warmth⟩ b : to increase in weight c : to improve in health or ability 3 *of a timepiece* : to run fast — **gain·er** *n* — **gain ground** : to make progress

[3]**gain** *n* [origin unknown] (1679) 1 : a beveled shoulder above a tenon 2 : a notch or mortise for insertion of a girder or joist

gain·ful \ˈgān-fəl\ *adj* (1555) : productive of gain : PROFITABLE ⟨~ employment⟩ — **gain·ful·ly** \-fə-lē\ *adv* — **gain·ful·ness** *n*

gain·giv·ing \ˈgān-ˌgiv-iŋ, (ˈ)gān-ˈ\ *n* [*gain-* (against) + *giving*] *archaic* (1602) : MISGIVING

gain·say \gān-ˈsā\ *vt* **-said** \-ˈsād, -ˈsed\; **-say·ing** \-ˈsā-iŋ\; **-says** \-ˈsāz, -ˈsez\ [ME *gainsayen,* fr. *gain-* against (fr. OE *gēan-*) + *sayen* to say — more at AGAIN] (14c) 1 : DENY, DISPUTE ⟨couldn't ~ the statistics⟩ 2 : CONTRADICT, OPPOSE *syn* see DENY — **gain·say·er** *n*

[1]**gait** \ˈgāt\ *n* [ME *gait, gate* gate, way] (1509) 1 : a manner of walking or moving on foot 2 : a sequence of foot movements (as a walk, trot, pace, or canter) by which a horse or a dog moves forward 3 : a manner or rate of movement or progress ⟨the leisurely ~ of summer⟩

[2]**gait** *vt* (1900) 1 : to train (a horse) to use a particular gait or set of gaits 2 : to lead (a show dog) before a judge to display carriage and movement

gait·ed \ˈgāt-əd\ *adj* (1588) : having a particular gait or so many gaits ⟨slow-*gaited*⟩

gai·ter \ˈgāt-ər\ *n* [F *guêtre*] (1775) 1 : a cloth or leather leg covering reaching from the instep to above the ankle or to mid-calf or knee 2 a : an ankle-high shoe with elastic gores in the sides b : an overshoe with fabric upper

[1]**gal** \ˈgal\ *n* [by alter.] (1795) : GIRL, WOMAN

[2]**gal** *n* [*Galileo* Galilei] (1914) : a unit of acceleration equivalent to one centimeter per second per second — used esp. for values of gravity

ga·la \ˈgā-lə, ˈgal-ə, ˈgäl-ə\ *n* [It, fr. MF *gale* festivity, pleasure — more at GALLANT] (1716) : a festive celebration; *esp* : a public entertainment marking a special occasion — **gala** *adj*

ga·la·bia *or* **ga·la·bi·eh** *or* **ga·la·bi·ya** \jə-ˈläb(-ē)-ə\ *n* [Ar *jallabīyah*] (1725) : DJELLABA

galact- *or* **galacto-** *comb form* [L *galact-,* fr. Gk *galakt-, galakto-,* fr. *galakt-, gala*] 1 : milk ⟨*galacto*poiesis⟩ 2 : related to galactose ⟨*galacto*mannan⟩

ga·lac·tic \gə-ˈlak-tik\ *adj* (1839) 1 : of or relating to a galaxy and esp. the Milky Way galaxy 2 : HUGE ⟨a ~ sum of money⟩

ga·lac·tor·rhea \gə-ˌlak-tə-ˈrē-ə\ *n* (ca. 1860) : a spontaneous flow of milk from the nipple

ga·lac·tos·amine \gə-ˌlak-ˈtō-sə-ˌmēn, -zə-\ *n* (1900) : an amino derivative $C_6H_{13}O_5N$ of galactose that occurs in cartilage

ga·lac·tose \gə-ˈlak-ˌtōs, -ˌtōz\ *n* [F, fr. *galact-*] (1869) : a sugar $C_6H_{12}O_6$ less soluble and less sweet than glucose

ga·lac·tos·emia \gə-ˌlak-tə-ˈsē-mē-ə\ *n* (1934) : an inherited metabolic disorder in which galactose accumulates in the blood due to deficiency of an enzyme catalyzing its conversion to glucose — **ga·lac·tos·emic** \-mik\ *adj*

ga·lac·to·si·dase \gə-ˌlak-ˈtō-sə-ˌdās, -zə-ˌdāz\ *n* (1917) : an enzyme (as lactase) that hydrolyzes a galactoside

ga·lac·to·side \gə-ˈlak-tə-ˌsīd\ *n* (1862) : a glycoside that yields galactose on hydrolysis

ga·lac·to·syl \gə-ˈlak-tə-ˌsil\ *n* (1950) : a glycosyl radical $C_6H_{11}O_5$ that is derived from galactose

ga·lact·uron·ic acid \gə-ˌlak-t(y)u̇-ˌrän-ik-\ *n* [ISV] (1917) : a crystalline aldehyde-acid $C_6H_{10}O_7$ that occurs esp. in polymerized form in pectin

ga·la·go \gə-ˈlā-(ˌ)gō, -ˈläg-(ˌ)ō\ *n, pl* **-gos** [NL, perh. fr. Wolof *golokh* monkey] (ca. 1848) : any of several small active nocturnal arboreal African primates (*Galago* and related genera) with long ears, a long tail, and elongated hind limbs that enable them to leap with great agility — called also *bush baby*

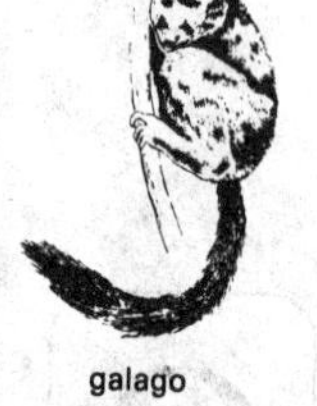
galago

ga·lah \gə-ˈlä\ *n* [native name in Australia] (1890) : a showy Australian cockatoo (*Kakatoë roseicapilla*) that is a destructive pest in wheat-growing areas and is often kept as a cage bird

Gal·a·had \ˈgal-ə-ˌhad\ *n* 1 : the knight of the Round Table who successfully seeks the Holy Grail 2 : one who is pure, noble, and unselfish

gal·an·tine \ˈgal-ən-ˌtēn\ *n* [F, fr. OF *galentine, galatine* fish sauce, fr. ML *galatina,* prob. fr. L *gelatus,* pp. of *gelare* to congeal, freeze — more at COLD] (1725) : a cold dish consisting of boned meat or fish that has been stuffed, poached, and covered with aspic

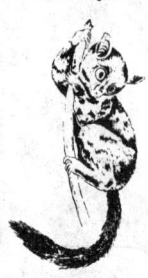

Gal·a·tea \ˌgal-ə-ˈtē-ə\ *n* [L, fr. Gk *Galateia*] : a female figure sculpted by Pygmalion and given life by Aphrodite in fulfillment of his prayer

Ga·la·tians \gə-ˈlā-shənz\ *n pl but sing in constr* : an argumentative letter of St. Paul written to the Christians of Galatia and included as a book in the New Testament — see BIBLE table

gal·a·vant *var of* GALLIVANT

ga·lax \ˈgā-ˌlaks\ *n* [NL] (1753) : any of a genus (*Galax*) of evergreen herbs related to the true heaths with leaves widely used for decorations

gal·axy \ˈgal-ək-sē\ *n, pl* **-ax·ies** [ME *galaxie, galaxias,* fr. LL *galaxias,* fr. Gk, fr. *galakt-, gala* milk; akin to L *lac* milk] (14c) 1 a *often cap* : MILKY WAY GALAXY — used with *the* b : one of billions of systems each including stars, nebulae, star clusters, globular clusters, and interstellar matter that make up the universe 2 : an assemblage of brilliant or notable persons or things

gal·ba·num \ˈgal-bə-nəm, ˈgȯl-\ *n* [ME, fr. L, fr. Gk *chalbanē,* fr. Heb *ḥelbĕnāh*] (12c) : a yellowish to green or brown aromatic bitter gum resin derived from several Asian plants (as *Ferula galbaniflua*) and used for medicinal purposes and in incense

gale \ˈgā(ə)l\ *n* [origin unknown] (1547) 1 a : a strong current of air: (1) : a wind from 32 to 63 miles per hour (2) : FRESH GALE — see BEAUFORT SCALE table b *archaic* : BREEZE 2 : an emotional outburst ⟨~*s* of laughter⟩

ga·lea \ˈgā-lē-ə\ *n* [NL, fr. L, helmet, prob. fr. Gk *galē* weasel] (1834) : an anatomical part suggesting a helmet: as a : the upper lip of the corolla of a mint b : the outer or lateral lobe of the maxilla in mandibulate insects — **ga·le·ate** \-lē-ˌāt\ *adj*

ga·le·na \gə-ˈlē-nə\ *n* [L, lead ore] (1601) : a bluish gray mineral PbS with metallic luster consisting of lead sulfide, showing highly perfect cubic cleavage, and constituting the principal ore of lead

ga·len·i·cal \gə-ˈlen-i-kəl, gā-\ *n* [*Galen* + *-ic* + *-al*] (1768) : a medicine prepared by extracting one or more active constituents of a plant

Ga·len·ism \ˈgā-lə-ˌniz-əm\ *n* [*Galen*] (1727) : the Galenic system of medical practice

ga·lère \ga-ˈle(ə)r\ *n* [F, lit., galley, fr. MF, fr. Catal *galera,* fr. MGk *galea*] (1756) : a group of people having an attribute in common

gal Friday *n* (1958) : GIRL FRIDAY

Ga·li·bi \gə-ˈlē-bē, ˈgal-ə-bē\ *n, pl* **Galibi** *or* **Galibis** (ca. 1895) 1 : a member of a Carib people of French Guiana 2 : the language of the Galibi people

Gal·i·le·an \ˌgal-ə-ˈlē-ən, -ˈlā-\ *adj* (1727) : of, relating to, or discovered by Galileo Galilei

gal·i·lee \ˈgal-ə-ˌlē\ *n* [AF, fr. ML *galilaea*] (15c) : a chapel or porch at the entrance of an English church

gal·in·gale \ˈgal-ən-ˌgāl, -iŋ-\ *n* [ME, a kind of ginger, fr. MF *galingal,* fr. Ar *khalanjān*] (1578) : an Old World sedge (*Cyperus longus*) that is used for papermaking and basket-weaving and has an aromatic root; *broadly* : any of various plants related to galingale

gal·i·ot *var of* GALLIOT

[1]**gall** \ˈgȯl\ *n* [ME, fr. OE *gealla;* akin to Gk *cholē, cholos* gall, wrath, OE *geolu* yellow — more at YELLOW] (bef. 12c) 1 a : BILE; *esp* : bile obtained from an animal and used in the arts or medicine b : something bitter to endure c : bitterness of spirit : RANCOR 2 : brazen

boldness coupled with impudent assurance and insolence *syn* see TEMERITY

2**gall** *n* [ME *galle,* fr. OE *gealla,* fr. L *galla* gallnut] (bef. 12c) **1 a :** a skin sore caused by chronic irritation **b :** a cause or state of exasperation **2** *archaic* **:** FLAW

3**gall** *vt* (14c) **1 :** to fret and wear away by friction **:** CHAFE ⟨the loose saddle ~*ed* the horse's back⟩ ⟨the ~*ing* of a metal bearing⟩ **2 :** IRRITATE, VEX ⟨sarcasm ~*s* her⟩ ~ *vi* **1 :** to become sore or worn by rubbing **2 :** SEIZE 2

4**gall** *n* [ME *galle,* fr. MF, fr. L *galla*] (14c) **:** a swelling of plant tissue usu. due to fungi or insect parasites and sometimes forming an important source of tannin

Gal·la \'gal-ə\ *n, pl* **Galla** *or* **Gallas** (1875) **1 :** a member of any of several groups of Cushitic-speaking peoples of Kenya and southern Ethiopia **2 :** the Cushitic language of the Galla

gal·la·mine tri·eth·io·dide \'gal-ə-,mēn-,trī-,eth-'ī-ə-,dīd\ *n* [pyro*gall*ol + *amine* + *triethyl* + *iodide*] (1951) **:** a substituted ammonium salt $C_{30}H_{60}I_3N_3O_3$ that is used to produce muscle relaxation esp. during anesthesia — called also *gallamine*

1**gal·lant** \gə-'lant, gə-'länt, 'gal-ənt\ *n* (14c) **1 :** a young man of fashion **2 a :** LADIES' MAN **b :** SUITOR **c :** PARAMOUR

2**gal·lant** \'gal-ənt (*usu in sense 2*); gə-'lant, gə-'länt (*usu in sense 3*)\ *adj* [ME *galaunt,* fr. MF *galant,* fr. prp. of *galer* to have a good time, fr. *gale* pleasure, of Gmc origin; akin to OE *wela* weal — more at WEAL] (15c) **1 :** showy in dress or bearing **:** SMART **2 a :** SPLENDID, STATELY ⟨a ~ ship⟩ **b :** SPIRITED, BRAVE ⟨~ efforts against the enemy⟩ **c :** nobly chivalrous and often self-sacrificing **3 :** courteously and elaborately attentive esp. to ladies *syn* see CIVIL — **gal·lant·ly** *adv*

3**gal·lant** \gə-'lant, -'länt\ *vt* (1672) **1 :** to pay court to (a lady) **:** ATTEND **2** *obs* **:** to manipulate (a fan) in a modish manner ~ *vi* **:** to pay court to ladies

gal·lant·ry \'gal-ən-trē\ *n, pl* **-ries** (1613) **1** *archaic* **:** gallant appearance **2 a :** an act of marked courtesy **b :** courteous attention to a lady **c :** amorous attention or pursuit **3 :** spirited and conspicuous bravery

gal·late \'gal-,āt, 'gȯl-\ *n* (1794) **:** a salt or ester of gallic acid

gall·blad·der \'gȯl-,blad-ər\ *n* (1676) **:** a membranous muscular sac in which bile from the liver is stored

gal·le·ass \'gal-ē-əs\ *n* [MF *galeasse,* fr. OF *galie* galley] (1544) **:** a large fast war galley of southern Europe in the 16th and 17th centuries

gal·lein \'gal-ē-ən, 'gal-,ēn\ *n* [*gall*ic acid + phthal*ein*] (1871) **:** a metallic-green crystalline phthalein dye $C_{20}H_{12}O_7$ used esp. in dyeing textiles violet and as an indicator

gal·le·on \'gal-ē-ən\ *n* [OSp *galeón,* fr. MF *galion,* fr. OF *galie*] (1529) **:** a heavy square-rigged sailing ship of the 15th to early 18th centuries used for war or commerce esp. by the Spanish

gal·le·ria \,gal-ə-'rē-ə\ *n* [It, gallery, fr. ML *galeria*] (ca. 1901) **:** a roofed and usu. glass-enclosed promenade or court (as at a shopping mall)

gal·lery \'gal(-ə)-rē\ *n, pl* **-ler·ies** [ME *galerie,* fr. ML *galeria*] (15c) **1 a :** a roofed promenade **:** COLONNADE **b :** CORRIDOR **2 a :** an outdoor balcony **b** *Southern & Midland* **:** PORCH, VERANDA **c** (1) **:** a platform at the quarters or stern of a ship (2) **:** a gun platform or emplacement on a ship **d :** a railed walk around the upper part of an engine to facilitate oiling or inspection **3 a :** a long and narrow passage, apartment, or corridor **b :** a subterranean passageway in a cave or military mining system; *also* **:** a working drift or level in mining **c :** an underground passage made by a mole or ant or a passage made in wood by an insect **4 a :** a room or building devoted to the exhibition of works of art **b :** an institution or business exhibiting or dealing in works of art **c :** COLLECTION, AGGREGATION ⟨the rich ~ of characters in this novel —H. S. Canby⟩ **5 a :** a structure projecting from one or more interior walls of an auditorium to accommodate additional people; *esp* **:** the highest balcony in a theater commonly having the cheapest seats **b :** the part of a theater audience seated in the top gallery **c :** the undiscriminating general public **d :** the spectators at a tennis or golf match **6 :** a photographer's studio — **gal·ler·ied** \-rēd\ *adj* — **gal·lery·ite** \-rē-,īt\ *n*

gallery forest *n* (1920) **:** a forest growing along a watercourse in a region otherwise devoid of trees

gal·lery·go·er \'gal(-ə)-rē-,gō(-ə)r\ *n* (1888) **:** one who frequently goes to art galleries

ga·lle·ta \gə-'yet-ə, gī-'et-ə\ *n* [Sp, hardtack] (1872) **:** either of two perennial forage grasses (*Hilaria rigida* and *H. jamesii*) used for hay in the southwestern U.S. and in Mexico

gal·ley \'gal-ē\ *n, pl* **galleys** [ME *galeie,* fr. OF *galie,* deriv. of MGk *galea*] (13c) **1 :** a large low medieval ship propelled by sails and oars and used in the Mediterranean for war and trading **2 :** a seagoing ship of classical antiquity propelled chiefly by oars **3 :** a large open rowing boat formerly used in England **4 :** the kitchen and cooking apparatus esp. of a ship or airplane **5 :** an oblong tray to hold esp. a single column of set type **b :** a proof of typeset matter esp. in a single column before being made into pages

gal·ley–west \,gal-ē-'west\ *adv* [prob. alter. of E dial. *collywest* (badly askew)] (1875) **:** into destruction or confusion ⟨was knocked ~⟩

gall·fly \'gȯl-,flī\ *n* (1822) **:** an insect (as a gall wasp) that deposits its eggs in plants and causes galls in which the larvae feed

1**gal·liard** \'gal-yərd\ *adj* [ME *gaillard,* fr. MF] *archaic* (14c) **:** GAY, LIVELY

2**galliard** *n* (1533) **:** a sprightly dance with five steps to a phrase popular in the 16th and 17th centuries

Gal·lic \'gal-ik\ *adj* [L *Gallicus,* fr. *Gallia* Gaul] (1672) **:** of or relating to Gaul or France

gal·lic acid \,gal-ik-, ,gȯ-lik-\ *n* [F *gallique,* fr. *galle* gall] (1791) **:** a white crystalline acid $C_7H_6O_5$ found widely in plants or combined in tannins and used esp. in dyes and writing ink and as a photographic developer

Gal·li·can \'gal-i-kən\ *adj* (14c) **1 :** GALLIC **2** *often not cap* **:** of or relating to Gallicanism — **Gallican** *n*

Gal·li·can·ism \-kə-,niz-əm\ *n* (1858) **:** a movement originating in France and advocating administrative independence from papal control for the Roman Catholic Church in each nation

gal·li·cism \'gal-ə-,siz-əm\ *n, often cap* (ca. 1656) **1 :** a characteristic French idiom or expression appearing in another language **2 :** a French trait

gal·li·cize \-,sīz\ *vt* **-cized; -ciz·ing** (1773) **:** to cause to conform to a French mode or idiom — **gal·li·ci·za·tion** \,gal-ə-sə-'zā-shən\ *n*

gal·li·gas·kins \,gal-i-'gas-kənz\ *n pl* [prob. modif. of MF *garguesques,* fr. OSp *gregüescos,* fr. *griego* Greek, fr. L *Graecus*] (1577) **1 a :** loose wide hose or breeches worn in the 16th and 17th centuries **b :** very loose trousers **2** *chiefly dial* **:** LEGGINGS

gal·li·mau·fry \,gal-ə-'mȯ-frē\ *n, pl* **-fries** [MF *galimafree* hash] (1551) **:** HODGEPODGE

gal·li·na·ceous \,gal-ə-'nā-shəs\ *adj* [L *gallinaceus* of domestic fowl, fr. *gallina* hen, fr. *gallus* cock] (1783) **:** of or relating to an order (Galliformes) of heavy-bodied largely terrestrial birds including the pheasants, turkeys, grouse, and the common domestic fowl

gall·ing \'gȯ-liŋ\ *adj* [3*gall*] (1583) **:** markedly irritating **:** VEXING ⟨a most ~ defeat⟩ — **gall·ing·ly** \-liŋ-lē\ *adv*

gal·li·nip·per \'gal-ə-,nip-ər\ *n* [origin unknown] (1709) **:** any of various insects (as a large mosquito) that bite or are thought to bite

gal·li·nule \'gal-ə-,n(y)ü(ə)l\ *n* [NL *Gallinula,* genus of birds, fr. L, pullet, dim. of *gallina*] (1776) **:** any of several aquatic birds of the rail family with long thin feet and a platelike frontal area on the head; *esp* **:** one (*Gallinula chloropus*) widespread in the New World, Eurasia, and Africa that has a largely red bill, red frontal area on the head, and a white band on the flanks

gal·li·ot \'gal-ē-ət\ *n* [ME *galiote,* fr. MF, fr. ML *galeota,* dim. of *galea* galley, fr. MGk] (14c) **1 :** a small swift galley formerly used in the Mediterranean **2** [D *galjoot,* fr. MF *galiote*] **:** a long narrow light-draft Dutch merchant sailing ship

gal·li·pot \'gal-i-,pät\ *n* [ME *galy pott*] (15c) **1 :** a small usu. ceramic vessel **2** *archaic* **:** DRUGGIST

gal·li·um \'gal-ē-əm\ *n* [NL, fr. L *gallus* cock (intended as trans. of surname of Paul *Lecoq* de Boisbaudran †1912 Fr. chemist)] (1875) **:** a rare bluish white metallic element that is hard and brittle at low temperatures but melts just above room temperature and expands on freezing — see ELEMENT table

gallium arsenide *n* (1962) **:** a synthetic compound GaAs used esp. as a semi-conducting material

gal·li·vant \'gal-ə-,vant\ *vi* [perh. alter. of 3*gallant*] (1823) **1 :** to go about usu. ostentatiously or indiscreetly with members of the opposite sex **2 :** to travel or roam about for pleasure

gall midge *n* (1902) **:** any of numerous minute two-winged flies (family Cecidomyiidae) most of which cause gall formation in plants

gall mite *n* (1881) **:** any of various minute 4-legged mites (family Eriophyidae) that form galls on plants

gall·nut \'gȯl-,nət\ *n* [4*gall*] (1572) **:** a gall resembling a nut

gal·lon \'gal-ən\ *n* [ME *galon,* a liquid measure, fr. ONF, fr. ML *galeta* pail, a liquid measure] (13c) **:** a unit of liquid capacity equal to 231 cubic inches or four quarts — see WEIGHT table

gal·lon·age \'gal-ə-nij\ *n* (ca. 1909) **:** amount in gallons

gal·loon \gə-'lün\ *n* [F *galon*] (1604) **:** a narrow trimming esp. of lace, embroidery, or braid with metallic threads

1**gal·lop** \'gal-əp\ *vi* (15c) **1 :** to progress or ride at a gallop **2 :** to run fast ~ *vt* **1 :** to cause to gallop **2 :** to transport at a gallop — **gal·lop·er** *n*

2**gallop** *n* [MF *galop*] (1523) **1 :** a bounding gait of a quadruped; *specif* **:** a fast natural 3-beat gait of the horse — compare 3CANTER, RUN **2 :** a ride or run at a gallop **3 :** a rapid or hasty progression or pace

gal·lo·pade \,gal-ə-'pād, -'päd\ *n* (1831) **:** GALOP

Gal·lo·phile \'gal-ə-,fīl\ *adj* [L *Gallus* Gaul + E *-phile*] (ca. 1909) **:** FRANCOPHILE — **Gallophile** *n*

gal·lop·ing *adj* (1642) **:** progressing, developing, or increasing rapidly ⟨~ inflation⟩ ⟨a ~ farce⟩ ⟨~ alcoholism⟩

Gal·lo·way \'gal-ə-,wā\ *n* [*Galloway,* Scotland] (1805) **:** any of a breed of hardy medium-sized hornless chiefly black beef cattle native to southwestern Scotland

gal·low·glass \'gal-ō-,glas\ *n* [by folk etymology fr. IrGael *gallóglach,* fr. *gall* foreigner + *óglach* soldier] (1515) **1 :** a mercenary or retainer of an Irish chief **2 :** an armed Irish foot soldier

1**gal·lows** \'gal-(,)ōz, -əz, *in sense 3 also* -əs\ *n, pl* **gallows** *or* **gal·lows·es** [ME *galwes,* pl. of *galwe,* fr. OE *gealga;* akin to OHG *galgo* gallows, Arm *jałk* twig] (bef. 12c) **1 a :** a frame usu. of two upright posts and a crossbeam from which criminals are hanged — called also *gallows tree* **b :** the punishment of hanging ⟨got the ~ for murder⟩ **2 :** a structure consisting of an upright frame with a crosspiece **3** *chiefly dial* **:** SUSPENDER 2a

2**gallows** *adj* (15c) **:** deserving the gallows

gallows bird *n* (ca. 1785) **:** a person who deserves hanging

gallows humor *n* [trans. of G *galgenhumor*] (1901) **:** humor that makes fun of a very serious or terrifying situation

gall·stone \'gȯl-,stōn\ *n* (1758) **:** a calculus formed in the gallbladder or biliary passages

gal·lus \'gal-əs\ *n* [alter. of 1*gallows*] *chiefly dial* (1835) **:** SUSPENDER 2a — usu. used in pl.

gal·lused \'gal-əst\ *adj, chiefly dial* (1927) **:** wearing galluses

gall wasp *n* (1879) **:** any of a family (Cynipidae) of hymenopterous gall-flies

gal·ly \'gal-ē\ *vt* **gal·lied; gal·ly·ing** [origin unknown] *chiefly dial* (1605) **:** FRIGHTEN, TERRIFY

Ga·lois theory \'gal-,wä-\ *n* [Évariste *Galois*] (1893) **:** a part of the theory of mathematical groups concerned esp. with the conditions under which a solution to a polynomial equation with coefficients in a given mathematical field can be obtained in the field by the repetition of operations and the extraction of nth roots

ga·loot \gə-'lüt\ *n* [origin unknown] *slang* (1866) **:** FELLOW; *esp* **:** one that is strange or foolish

ga·lop \'gal-əp, ga-'lō\ *n* [F] (1831) **:** a lively dance in duple measure; *also* **:** the music of a galop

ga·lore \gə-'lō(ə)r, -'lȯ(ə)r\ *adj* [IrGael *go leor* enough] (1628) **:** ABUNDANT, PLENTIFUL — used postpositively ⟨bargains ~⟩

\ə\ abut \ᵊ\ kitten, F table \ər\ further \a\ ash \ā\ ace \ä\ cot, cart
\au̇\ out \ch\ chin \e\ bet \ē\ easy \g\ go \i\ hit \ī\ ice \j\ job
\ŋ\ sing \ō\ go \ȯ\ law \ȯi\ boy \th\ thin \t͟h\ the \ü\ loot \u̇\ foot
\y\ yet \zh\ vision \à, k̲, ⁿ, œ, œ̄, ue, ue̅, ʸ\ *see* Guide to Pronunciation

ga·losh \gə-ˈläsh\ *n* [ME *galoche,* fr. MF] (14c) **1** *obs* : a shoe with a heavy sole **2** : a high overshoe worn esp. in snow and slush — **ga·loshed** \-ˈläsht\ *adj*

ga·lumph \gə-ˈləm(p)f\ *vi* [prob. alter. of ¹*gallop*] (1872) : to move with a clumsy heavy tread

gal·van·ic \gal-ˈvan-ik\ *adj* (1797) **1** : of, relating to, or producing a direct current of electricity ⟨a ~ cell⟩ **2 a** : having an electric effect ⟨a ~ performance⟩ **b** : produced as if by an electric shock ⟨had a ~ effect on the audience⟩ — **gal·van·i·cal·ly** \-i-k(ə-)lē\ *adv*

galvanic couple *n* (ca. 1897) : a pair of dissimilar substances (as metals) capable of acting together as an electric source when brought in contact with an electrolyte

galvanic skin response *n* (1942) : a change in the electrical resistance of the skin that is a physiochemical response to a change in emotional state

galvanise *Brit var of* GALVANIZE

gal·va·nism \ˈgal-və-ˌniz-əm\ *n* [F or It; F *galvanisme,* fr. It *galvanismo,* fr. Luigi *Galvani*] (1797) **1** : a direct current of electricity esp. when produced by chemical action **2** : the therapeutic use of direct electric current **3** : vital or forceful activity

gal·va·nize \ˈgal-və-ˌnīz\ *vb* **-nized; -niz·ing** *vt* (1802) **1 a** : to subject to the action of an electric current esp. for the purpose of stimulating physiologically ⟨~ a muscle⟩ **b** : to stimulate or excite as if by an electric shock ⟨an issue that would ~ public opinion⟩ **2** : to coat (iron or steel) with zinc; *esp:* to immerse in molten zinc to produce a coating of zinc-iron alloy ~ *vi* : to react as if stimulated by an electric shock ⟨they *galvanized* into action⟩ — **gal·va·ni·za·tion** \ˌgal-və-nə-ˈzā-shən\ *n* — **gal·va·niz·er** \ˈgal-və-ˌnī-zər\ *n*

galvano- *comb form* [*galvanic*] : galvanic current ⟨*galvano*meter⟩

gal·va·nom·e·ter \ˌgal-və-ˈnäm-ət-ər\ *n* (1802) : an instrument for detecting or measuring a small electric current by movements of a magnetic needle or of a coil in a magnetic field — **gal·va·no·met·ric** \-nō-ˈme-trik\ *adj*

gal·va·no·scope \gal-ˈvan-ə-ˌskōp, ˈgal-və-nə-\ *n* (1832) : an instrument for detecting the presence and direction of an electric current by the deflection of a magnetic needle

¹**gam** \ˈgam\ *n* [prob. fr. F dial. *gambe,* fr. ONF, fr. LL *gamba*] *slang* (1781) : LEG

²**gam** *n* [perh. short for obs. *gammon* (talk)] (1846) **1** : a visit or friendly conversation at sea or ashore esp. between whalers **2** : a school of whales

³**gam** *vb* **gammed; gam·ming** *vi* (1849) : to engage in a gam ~ *vt* **1** : to have a gam with **2** : to spend or pass (as time) talking

gam- *or* **gamo-** *comb form* [NL, fr. Gk, marriage, fr. *gamos* — more at BIGAMY] **1** : united : joined ⟨*gamo*sepalous⟩ **2** : sexual : sexuality ⟨*gam*ic⟩ ⟨*gamo*genesis⟩

gama grass \ˈgam-ə-\ *n* [prob. alter. of *grama*] (1833) : a tall coarse American grass (*Tripsacum dactyloides*) valuable for forage — called also *gama*

ga·may \ga-ˈmā, ˈgam-ˌā\ *n, often cap* [F, fr. *Gamay,* town in So. Burgundy] (ca. 1948) : any of various wines produced from the same grape as the French Beaujolais ⟨~ rosé⟩

gam·ba \ˈgäm-bə, ˈgam-\ *n* (1598) : VIOLA DA GAMBA

¹**gam·ba·do** \gam-ˈbād-(ˌ)ō\ *n, pl* **-does** *also* **-dos** [perh. modif. of It *gambale,* fr. *gamba* leg] (ca. 1656) : a horseman's legging

²**gambado** *n, pl* **-does** *also* **-dos** [modif. of F *gambade* — more at GAMBOL] (1820) **1** : a spring of a horse **2** : CAPER, GAMBOL

gam·bier *also* **gam·bir** \ˈgam-ˌbi(ə)r\ *n* [Malay *gambir*] (1830) : a yellowish catechu that is obtained from a Malayan woody vine (*Uncaria gambir*) of the madder family and is used for chewing with the betel nut and for tanning and dyeing

gam·bit \ˈgam-bət\ *n* [It *gambetto,* lit., act of tripping someone, fr. *gamba* leg, fr. LL *gamba, camba,* modif. of Gk *kampē* bend — more at CAMP] (1656) **1** : a chess opening in which a player risks one or more minor pieces to gain an advantage in position **2 a** (1) : a remark intended to start a conversation or make a telling point (2) : TOPIC **b** : a calculated move : STRATAGEM

¹**gam·ble** \ˈgam-bəl\ *vb* **gam·bled; gam·bling** \-b(ə-)liŋ\ [prob. back-formation fr. *gambler,* prob. alter. of obs. *gamner,* fr. obs. *gamen* (to play)] *vi* (ca. 1775) **1 a** : to play a game for money or property **b** : to bet on an uncertain outcome **2** : to stake something on a contingency : take a chance ~ *vt* **1** : to risk by gambling : WAGER **2** : VENTURE, HAZARD — **gam·bler** \-blər\ *n*

²**gamble** *n* (1823) **1 a** : an act having an element of risk **b** : something chancy **2** : the playing of a game of chance for stakes

gam·boge \gam-ˈbōj, -ˈbüzh\ *n* [NL *gambogium,* alter. of *cambugium,* irreg. fr. *Cambodia*] (1712) **1** : an orange to brown gum resin from southeast Asian trees (genus *Garcinia,* family Guttiferae) that is used as a yellow pigment and cathartic **2** : a strong yellow

¹**gam·bol** \ˈgam-bəl\ *vi* **-boled** *or* **-bolled; -bol·ing** *or* **-bol·ling** \-b(ə-)liŋ *also* -bliŋ\ (1508) : to skip about in play : FRISK

²**gambol** *n* [modif. of MF *gambade* spring of a horse, gambol, prob. fr. OProv *camba* leg, fr. LL] (ca. 1510) : a skipping or leaping about in play

gam·brel \ˈgam-brəl\ *n* [ONF *gamberel,* fr. *gambe* leg, fr. LL *gamba*] (1547) **1** : a stick or iron for suspending slaughtered animals **2** : the hock of an animal

gambrel roof *n* (1765) : a curb roof with a lower steeper slope and an upper flatter one on each of its two sides — see ROOF illustration

gam·bu·sia \gam-ˈb(y)ü-zh(ē-)ə\ *n* [NL, modif. of AmerSp *gambusino* gambusia] (ca. 1902) : any of a genus (*Gambusia*) of live-bearers (family Poeciliidae) introduced as valuable exterminators of mosquito larvae in warm fresh waters

¹**game** \ˈgām\ *n* [ME, fr. OE *gamen;* akin to OHG *gaman* amusement] (bef. 12c) **1 a** (1) : activity engaged in for diversion or amusement : PLAY (2) : the equipment for a game **b** : often derisive or mocking jesting : FUN, SPORT ⟨make ~ of a nervous player⟩ **2 a** : a procedure or strategy for gaining an end : TACTIC **b** (1) : an illegal or shady scheme or maneuver : RACKET (2) : a field of gainful activity : LINE ⟨the newspaper ~⟩ (3) : a specified type of activity or mode of behavior ⟨the dating ~⟩ ⟨the ~ of politics⟩ **3 a** (1) : a physical or mental competition conducted according to rules with the participants in direct opposition to each other (2) : a division of a larger contest (3) : the number of points necessary to win (4) : points scored in certain card games (as in all fours) by a player whose cards count up the highest (5) : the manner of playing in a contest (6) : the set of rules governing a game **b** *pl* : organized athletics **c** : a situation that involves contest, rivalry, or struggle ⟨got into aviation early in the ~⟩; *esp* : one in which opposing interests given specific information are allowed a choice of moves with the object of maximizing their wins and minimizing their losses **4 a** (1) : animals under pursuit or taken in hunting; *esp* : wild animals hunted for sport or food (2) : the flesh of game animals **b** *archaic* : PLUCK **c** : an object of ridicule or attack — often used in the phrase *fair game* **syn** see FUN

²**game** *vb* **gamed; gam·ing** *vi* (1610) : to play for a stake ~ *vt, archaic* : to lose or squander by gambling

³**game** *adj* (ca. 1787) **1** : having a resolute unyielding spirit ⟨~ to the end⟩ **2** : of or relating to game ⟨~ laws⟩ — **game·ly** *adv* — **game·ness** *n*

⁴**game** *adj* [perh. fr. ³*game*] (1677) : LAME ⟨a ~ leg⟩

game bird *n* (1841) : a bird that may be legally hunted according to the laws esp. of a state of the U.S.

game·cock \ˈgām-ˌkäk\ *n* (1873) : a rooster of the domestic chicken trained for fighting

game fish *n* (1883) **1** : a fish of a family (Salmonidae) including salmons, trouts, chars, and whitefishes **2** : SPORT FISH; *esp* : a fish made a legal catch by law

game·keep·er \ˈgām-ˌkē-pər\ *n* (1670) : a person in charge of the breeding and protection of game animals or birds on a private preserve

gam·elan \ˈgam-ə-ˌlan\ *n* [Jav] (1817) : an Indonesian orchestra consisting chiefly of percussion instruments (as gongs, xylophones, and drums)

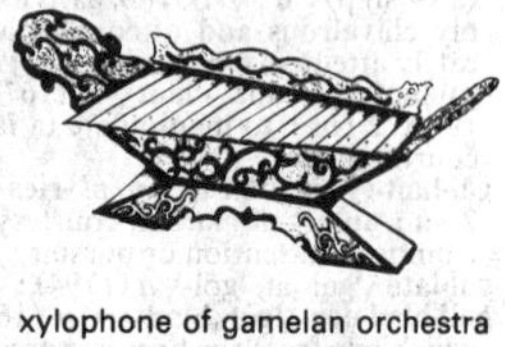
xylophone of gamelan orchestra

game of chance (1925) : a game (as a dice game) in which chance rather than skill determines the outcome

game plan *n* (1970) : a strategy for achieving an objective

game point *n* (ca. 1949) : a situation (as in tennis) in which one player will win the game by winning the next point; *also* : the point itself

games·man·ship \ˈgāmz-mən-ˌship\ *n* (1947) **1** : the art or practice of winning games by questionable expedients without actually violating the rules **2** : the use of ethically dubious methods to gain an objective

game·some \ˈgām-səm\ *adj* [ME] (14c) : MERRY, FROLICSOME — **game·some·ly** *adv* — **game·some·ness** *n*

game·ster \ˈgām-stər\ *n* (1581) : one who plays games; *esp* : GAMBLER

gamet- *or* **gameto-** *comb form* [NL, fr. *gameta*] : gamete ⟨*gameto*phore⟩

gam·etan·gi·um \ˌgam-ə-ˈtan-jē-əm\ *n, pl* **-gia** \-jē-ə\ [NL, fr. *gamet-* + Gk *angeion* vessel — more at ANGI-] (1886) : a cell or organ in which gametes are developed

ga·mete \ˈgam-ˌēt *also* gə-ˈmēt\ *n* [NL *gameta,* fr. Gk *gametēs* husband, fr. *gamein* to marry, fr. *gamos* marriage — more at BIGAMY] (1886) : a mature male or female germ cell usu. possessing a haploid chromosome set and capable of initiating formation of a new diploid individual by fusion with a gamete of the opposite sex — **ga·met·ic** \gə-ˈmet-ik, -ˈmēt-\ *adj* — **ga·met·i·cal·ly** \-i-k(ə-)lē\ *adv*

game theory *n* (1949) : the analysis of a situation involving conflicting interests (as in business or military strategy) in terms of gains and losses among opposing players

ga·me·to·cyte \gə-ˈmēt-ə-ˌsīt\ *n* [ISV] (ca. 1925) : a cell that divides to produce gametes

ga·me·to·gen·e·sis \gə-ˌmēt-ə-ˈjen-ə-səs, ˌgam-ət-ə-\ *n* [NL] (ca. 1900) : the production of gametes — **ga·me·to·gen·ic** \-ˈjen-ik\ *or* **gam·etog·e·nous** \ˌgam-ə-ˈtäj-ə-nəs\ *adj*

ga·me·to·phore \gə-ˈmēt-ə-ˌfō(ə)r, -ˌfȯ(ə)r\ *n* (1890) : a modified branch (as of a moss) bearing gametangia

ga·me·to·phyte \gə-ˈmēt-ə-ˌfīt\ *n* [ISV] (1890) : the individual or generation of a plant exhibiting alternation of generations that bears sex organs — compare SPOROPHYTE — **ga·me·to·phyt·ic** \-ˌmēt-ə-ˈfit-ik\ *adj*

gam·ic \ˈgam-ik\ *adj* (1864) : requiring fertilization : SEXUAL

-gam·ic \ˈgam-ik\ *adj comb form* [ISV, fr. Gk *-gamos* -gamous] : having (such) reproductive organs ⟨cleisto*gamic*⟩

gam·in \ˈgam-ən\ *n* [F] (1840) **1** : a boy who hangs out on the streets : URCHIN **2** : GAMINE 2

ga·mine \ga-ˈmēn\ *n* [F, fem. of *gamin*] (1889) **1** : a girl who hangs out on the streets **2** : a small playfully mischievous girl

gam·ing \ˈgā-miŋ\ *n* (1501) **1** : the practice of gambling **2** : the playing of games that simulate actual conditions (as of business or war) esp. for training or testing purposes

¹**gam·ma** \ˈgam-ə\ *n* [ME, fr. LL, fr. Gk, of Sem origin; akin to Heb *gīmel* gimel] (15c) **1** : the 3d letter of the Greek alphabet — see ALPHABET table **2** : the degree of contrast of a developed photographic image or of a television image **3** : a unit of magnetic intensity equal to 0.00001 oersted **4** : GAMMA RAY **5** : MICROGRAM

²**gamma** *or* **γ-** *adj* (1896) **1** : of, relating to, or being one of three or more closely related chemical substances **2** : third in position in the structure of an organic molecule from a particular group or atom

gam·ma–ami·no·bu·tyr·ic acid *also* **γ-ami·no·bu·tyr·ic acid** \ˌgam-ə-ə-ˌmē-(ˌ)nō-byü-ˌtir-ik-, ˌgam-ə-ˌam-ə-(ˌ)nō-\ *n* (1964) : an amino acid $C_4H_9NO_2$ that is a neurotransmitter in the central nervous system

gamma globulin *n* (1937) **1 a** : a protein fraction of blood rich in antibodies **b** : a sterile solution of gamma globulin from pooled human blood administered esp. for passive immunity against measles, German measles, infectious hepatitis, or poliomyelitis **2** : any of numerous globulins of blood plasma or serum that have less electrophoretic mobility at alkaline pH than serum albumins, alpha globulins, or beta globulins and that include most antibodies — compare IMMUNOGLOBULIN

gamma ray *n* (1903) **1** : a photon or radiation quantum emitted spontaneously by a radioactive substance; *also* : a high-energy photon **2** : a continuous stream of gamma rays — called also *gamma radiation*

gam·mer \ˈgam-ər\ *n* [prob. alter. of *godmother*] *archaic* (1575) : an old woman — compare GAFFER

¹**gam·mon** \ˈgam-ən\ *n* [ME, fr. ONF *gambon* ham, aug. of *gambe* leg — more at GAM] (15c) **1** *chiefly Brit* : HAM 2 **2** *chiefly Brit* **a** : a side of bacon **b** : the lower end of a side of bacon

2gammon *n* [perh. alter. of ME *gamen* game] (1730) **1** *archaic* **:** BACKGAMMON **2 :** the winning of a backgammon game before the loser removes any men from the board
3gammon *vt* (1735) **:** to beat by scoring a gammon
4gammon *n* [obs. *gammon* (talk)] (1720) **:** talk intended to deceive **:** HUMBUG
5gammon *vi* (1789) **1 :** to talk gammon **2 :** PRETEND, FEIGN ~ *vt* **:** DECEIVE, FOOL
gamo- — see GAM-
gamo·pet·al·ous \ˌgam-ə-ˈpet-ə̇l-əs\ *adj* (1830) **:** having the corolla composed of united petals ⟨the morning glory is ~⟩
-g·a·mous \g-ə-məs\ *adj comb form* [Gk *-gamos,* fr. *gamos* marriage — more at BIGAMY] **1 :** characterized by having or practicing (such) a marriage or (such or so many) marriages ⟨exo*gamous*⟩ **2 :** -GAMIC ⟨hetero*gamous*⟩
gamp \ˈgamp\ *n* [Sarah *Gamp,* nurse with a large umbrella in *Martin Chuzzlewit* by Charles Dickens] *Brit* (1864) **:** a large umbrella
gam·ut \ˈgam-ət\ *n* [ML *gamma,* lowest note of a medieval scale (fr. LL, 3d letter of the Greek alphabet) + *ut* ut] (15c) **1 :** the whole series of recognized musical notes **2 :** an entire range or series ⟨ran the ~ from praise to contempt⟩ ***syn*** see RANGE
gamy *or* **gam·ey** \ˈgā-mē\ *adj* **gam·i·er; -est** (1844) **1 :** BRAVE, PLUCKY — used esp. of animals **2 a :** having the flavor of game; *esp* **:** having the flavor of game near tainting **b :** SMELLY **3 a :** SORDID, SCANDALOUS ⟨gave her all the ~ details⟩ **b :** CORRUPT, DISREPUTABLE ⟨a ~ character⟩ **c :** sexually suggestive ⟨~ witticisms⟩ — **gam·i·ly** \-mə-lē\ *adv* — **gam·i·ness** \-mē-nəs\ *n*
-g·a·my \g-ə-mē\ *n comb form* [ME *-gamie,* fr. LL *-gamia,* fr. Gk — more at BIGAMY] **1 :** marriage ⟨exo*gamy*⟩ **2 :** union for propagation or reproduction ⟨allo*gamy*⟩ **3 :** possession of (such) reproductive organs or (such) a mode of fertilization ⟨cleisto*gamy*⟩
gan *past of* GIN
Gan·da \ˈgan-də\ *n, pl* **Ganda** *or* **Gandas** (1934) **1 :** a member of a Bantu-speaking people of Uganda **2 :** the Bantu language of the Ganda people used as the official language of Uganda
1gan·der \ˈgan-dər\ *n* [ME, fr. OE *gandra;* akin to OE *gōs* goose] (bef. 12c) **1 :** the adult male goose **2 :** SIMPLETON
2gander *vi, dial* (1687) **:** WANDER, RAMBLE
3gander *n* [prob. fr. *1gander;* fr. the outstretched neck of a person craning to look at something] (1914) **:** LOOK, GLANCE
gan·dy dancer \ˈgan-dē-\ *n* [perh. fr. the *Gandy* Manufacturing Company, Chicago, Ill., toolmakers] (1923) **1 :** a laborer in a railroad section gang **2 :** an itinerant or seasonal laborer
ga·nef \ˈgä-nəf\ *n* [Yiddish, fr. Heb *gannābh* thief] *slang* (1923) **:** THIEF, RASCAL
Ga·ne·lon \ˌgan-ə-ˈlōⁿ\ *n* [F] **:** the traitor in the Charlemagne romances who is responsible for the death of Roland
1gang \ˈgaŋ\ *n* [ME, fr. OE; akin to OHG *gang* act of going, Skt *jaṅghā* shank] (bef. 12c) **1 a (1) :** a set of articles **:** OUTFIT ⟨a ~ of oars⟩ **(2) :** a combination of similar implements or devices arranged for convenience to act together ⟨a ~ of saws⟩ **b :** GROUP: as **(1) :** a group of persons working together **(2) :** a group of persons working to unlawful or antisocial ends; *esp* **:** a band of antisocial adolescents **2 :** a group of persons having informal and usu. close social relations
2gang *vt* (1856) **1 a :** to assemble or operate simultaneously as a group **b :** to arrange in or produce as a gang **2 :** to attack in a gang ~ *vi* **:** to move or act as a gang
3gang *vi* [ME *gangen,* fr. OE *gangan;* akin to OE *gang*] *Scot* (bef. 12c) **:** GO
gang·bust·er \ˈgaŋ-ˌbəs-tər\ *n* (1940) **:** one engaged in the aggressive breakup of organized criminal gangs — **like gangbusters :** with great vigor or enthusiasm
gang·er \ˈgaŋ-ər\ *n, Brit* (1849) **:** the foreman of a gang of workers
gang hook *n* (ca. 1934) **:** two or three fishhooks with their shanks joined together
gang·land \ˈgaŋ-ˌland, -lənd\ *n* (1912) **:** the world of organized crime
gangli- *or* **ganglio-** *comb form* [NL, fr. Gk *ganglion*] **:** ganglion ⟨*gangl*iectomy⟩ ⟨*ganglio*plexus⟩
gan·gling \ˈgaŋ-gliŋ, -glən\ *adj* [perh. irreg. fr. Sc *gangrel* vagrant, lanky person] (ca. 1808) **:** loosely and awkwardly built **:** LANKY
gan·gli·on \ˈgaŋ-glē-ən\ *n, pl* **-glia** \-glē-ə\ *also* **-gli·ons** [LL, fr. Gk; akin to L *galla* gallnut] (1671) **1 :** a small cystic tumor connected either with a joint membrane or tendon sheath **2 :** a mass of nerve tissue containing nerve cells external to the brain or spinal cord; *also* **:** NUCLEUS 2b — **gan·gli·on·at·ed** \ˈgaŋ-glē-ə-ˌnāt-əd\ *adj* — **gan·gli·on·ic** \ˌgaŋ-glē-ˈän-ik\ *adj*
gan·gli·o·side \ˈgaŋ-glē-ə-ˌsīd\ *n* [ISV *ganglion* + *2-ose* + *-ide*] (1943) **:** any of a group of glycolipids that yield a hexose sugar on hydrolysis and are found esp. in the plasma membrane of cells of the gray matter
gan·gly \ˈgaŋ-glē\ *adj* **gan·gli·er; -est** (1872) **:** GANGLING
gang·plank \ˈgaŋ-ˌplaŋk\ *n* (1846) **:** a movable bridge used in boarding or leaving a ship at a pier
gang·plow \-ˌplau̇\ *n* (1850) **:** a plow designed to turn two or more furrows at one time
gang·rel \ˈgaŋ-(ə-)rəl\ *n* [ME, irreg. fr. *gangen* to go, fr. OE *gangan;* akin to OE *gang*] *Scot* (14c) **:** VAGRANT
1gan·grene \ˈgaŋ-ˌgrēn, gaŋ-ˈ, ˈgan-, gan-ˈ\ *n* [L *gangraena,* fr. Gk *gangraina;* akin to Gk *gran* to gnaw] (1543) **1 :** local death of soft tissues due to loss of blood supply **2 :** a pervasive moral evil — **gan·gre·nous** \ˈgaŋ-grə-nəs\ *adj*
2gangrene *vb* **gan·grened; gan·gren·ing** *vt* (1607) **:** to make gangrenous ~ *vi* **:** to become gangrenous
gang·ster \ˈgaŋ-stər\ *n* (1896) **:** a member of a gang of criminals **:** RACKETEER — **gang·ster·ism** \-stə-ˌriz-əm\ *n*
gangue \ˈgaŋ\ *n* [F, fr. G *gang* vein of metal, fr. OHG, act of going] (1806) **:** the worthless rock or vein matter in which valuable metals or minerals occur
gang up *vi* (1925) **1 :** to combine for a specific purpose ⟨*ganged up* to raise prices⟩ **2 :** to make a joint assault ⟨*ganged up* on him and beat him up⟩ **3 :** to exert group pressure ⟨the class *ganged up* against the teacher⟩
gang·way \ˈgaŋ-ˌwā\ *n* (bef. 12c) **1 :** PASSAGEWAY; *esp* **:** a temporary way of planks **2 a :** either of the sides of the upper deck of a ship **b :** the opening by which a ship is boarded **c :** GANGPLANK **3** *Brit* **:** AISLE **4 :** a main level or haulageway in a mine **5 a :** a cross aisle dividing the front benches from the back benches in the British House of Commons **b :** an aisle in the British House of Commons that separates government and opposition benches **6 :** a clear passage through a crowd — often used as an interjection
gan·is·ter *or* **gan·nis·ter** \ˈgan-ə-stər\ *n* [origin unknown] (1811) **1 :** a fine-grained quartzite used in the manufacture of refractory brick **2 :** a mixture of ground quartz and fireclay used for lining metallurgical furnaces
gan·ja \ˈgän-jə, ˈgan-\ *n* [Hindi *gā̃jā,* fr. Skt *gañjā*] (1689) **:** a potent and selected preparation of marijuana used esp. for smoking
gan·net \ˈgan-ət\ *n, pl* **gannets** *also* **gannet** [ME *ganet,* fr. OE *ganot;* akin to OE *gōs* goose] (bef. 12c) **:** any of several large fish-eating seabirds (family Sulidae) that breed in large colonies chiefly on offshore islands
gan·oid \ˈgan-ˌȯid\ *adj* [deriv. of Gk *ganos* brightness; akin to Gk *gēthein* to rejoice — more at JOY] (ca. 1847) **:** of or relating to a subclass (Ganoidei) of living and extinct teleost fishes (as the sturgeons) with usu. hard rhombic enameled scales — **ganoid** *n*
gante·lope *or* **gant·lope** \ˈgant-ˌlōp\ *n* [modif. of Sw *gatlopp,* fr. OSw *gatulop,* fr. *gata* road + *lop* course] *archaic* (1646) **:** 2GAUNTLET
1gant·let \ˈgȯnt-lət, ˈgänt-\ *var of* GAUNTLET
2gantlet *n* [*2gauntlet*] (1902) **:** a stretch of railroad track where two lines of track overlap so that one rail of each track is within the rails of the other in order to obviate switching
gant·line \ˈgant-ˌlīn, -lən\ *n* [perh. alter. of *girtline* (gantline)] (1840) **:** a line rove through a block aloft on a ship and used for hoisting
gan·try \ˈgan-trē\ *n, pl* **gantries** [perh. modif. of ONF *gantier,* fr. L *cantherius* trellis] (1574) **1 :** a frame for supporting barrels **2 :** a frame structure raised on side supports so as to span over or around something: as **a :** a platform made to carry a traveling crane and supported by towers or side frames running on parallel tracks; *also* **:** a movable structure with platforms at different levels used for erecting and servicing rockets before launching **b :** a structure spanning several railroad tracks and displaying signals for each
Gan·y·mede \ˈgan-i-ˌmēd\ *n* [L *Ganymedes,* fr. Gk *Ganymēdēs*] **1 :** a beautiful youth in classical mythology carried off to Olympus to be the cupbearer of the gods **2 :** a satellite of Jupiter
gaol \ˈjā(ə)l\, **gaol·er** \ˈjā-lər\ *chiefly Brit var of* JAIL, JAILER
1gap \ˈgap\ *n* [ME, fr. ON, chasm, hole; akin to ON *gapa* gape] (14c) **1 a :** a break in a barrier (as a wall, hedge, or line of military defense) **b :** an assailable position **2 a :** a mountain pass **b :** RAVINE **3 :** SPARK GAP **4 :** a separation in space **5 :** a break in continuity **:** HIATUS ⟨unexplained ~s in his story⟩ **6 :** a break in the vascular cylinder of a plant where a vascular trace departs from the central cylinder **7 :** lack of balance **:** DISPARITY ⟨the ~ between imports and exports⟩ **8 :** a wide difference in character or attitude ⟨the generation ~⟩ **9 :** a problem caused by some disparity ⟨a communication ~⟩ ⟨credibility ~⟩ — **gap·py** \-ē\ *adj*
2gap *vb* **gapped; gap·ping** *vt* (1879) **:** to make an opening in ~ *vi* **:** to fall or stand open
1gape \ˈgāp *sometimes* ˈgap\ *vi* **gaped; gap·ing** [ME *gapen,* fr. ON *gapa;* akin to L *hiare* to gape, yawn — more at YAWN] (13c) **1 a :** to open the mouth wide **b :** to open or part widely ⟨holes *gaped* in the pavement⟩ **2 :** to gaze stupidly or in openmouthed surprise or wonder **3 :** YAWN ***syn*** see GAZE — **gap·ing·ly** \ˈgā-piŋ-lē, ˈgap-iŋ-\ *adv*
2gape *n* (1535) **1 :** an act of gaping: **a :** YAWN **b :** an openmouthed stare **2 :** an unfilled space or extent **3 a :** the median margin-to-margin length of the open mouth **b :** the line along which the mandibles of a bird close **c :** the width of an opening **4** *pl but sing in constr* **a :** a disease of young birds in which gapeworms invade and irritate the trachea **b :** a fit of yawning
gap·er \ˈgā-pər *sometimes* ˈgap-ər\ *n* (1637) **1 :** one that gapes **2 :** any of several large sluggish burrowing clams (family Myacidae) including several used for food
gape·worm \ˈgā-ˌpwərm *sometimes* ˈgap-ˌwərm\ *n* (1873) **:** a nematode worm (*Syngamus trachea*) that causes gapes of birds
gapped scale *n* (1910) **:** a musical scale derived from a larger system of tones by omitting certain tones
1gar \ˈgär\ *interj* [euphemism for *God*] (1598) — used as a mild oath
2gar *n* [short for *garfish*] (1765) **:** any of various fishes that have an elongate body resembling that of a pike and long and narrow jaws: as **a :** NEEDLEFISH **b :** any of several predaceous No. American freshwater ganoid fishes (family Lepisosteidae) with rank tough flesh
1ga·rage *n* \gə-ˈräzh, -ˈräj; *chiefly NewEng* -ˈrazh, -ˈraj; *Canad also* -ˈrazh, -ˈraj; *Brit usu* ˈgar-(ˌ)äzh, -(ˌ)äj, -ij\ [F, act of docking, garage, fr. *garer* to dock, of Gmc origin; akin to OHG *biwarōn* to protect — more at WARE] (1902) **:** a shelter or repair shop for automotive vehicles
2garage *vt* **ga·raged; ga·rag·ing** (1905) **:** to keep or put in a garage
ga·rage·man \-ˌman\ *n* (1919) **:** one who works in a garage
garage sale *n* (1964) **:** a sale of used household or personal articles (as furniture, tools, or clothing) held on the seller's own premises
Ga·rand rifle \gə-ˈrand-, ˌgar-ənd-\ *n* [John C. *Garand*] (ca. 1939) **:** M1 RIFLE
garb \ˈgärb\ *n* [MF or OIt; MF *garbe* graceful contour, grace, fr. OIt *garbo* grace] (1599) **1** *obs* **:** FASHION, MANNER **2 a :** style of apparel **b :** outward form **:** APPEARANCE — **garb** *vt*
gar·bage \ˈgär-bij\ *n* [ME, animal entrails] (15c) **1 a :** food waste **:** REFUSE **b :** unwanted or useless material **2 a :** TRASH 1b **b :** inaccurate or useless data
gar·bage·man \-ˌman\ *n* (1888) **:** one who collects and hauls away garbage
gar·ban·zo \gär-ˈbän-(ˌ)zō\ *n, pl* **-zos** [Sp] (1759) **:** CHICK-PEA — called also *garbanzo bean*
1gar·ble \ˈgär-bəl\ *vt* **gar·bled; gar·bling** \-b(ə-)liŋ\ [ME *garbelen,* fr. OIt *garbellare* to sift, fr. Ar *ghirbāl* sieve, fr. LL *cribellum;* akin to L *cernere*

to sift — more at CERTAIN] (15c) 1 *archaic* : CULL 2 : to sift impurities from 3 a : to so alter or distort as to create a wrong impression or change the meaning ⟨~ a story in repeating it⟩ b : to introduce textual error into (a message) by inaccurate encipherment, transmission, or decipherment — **gar·bler** \-b(ə-)lər\ *n*

[2]garble *n* (1502) 1 : the impurities removed from spices in sifting 2 : an act or an instance of garbling

gar·board \'gär-ˌbō(ə)rd, -ˌbȯ(ə)rd\ *n* [obs. D *gaarboord*] (1626) : the strake next to a ship's keel

gar·boil \-ˌbȯil\ *n* [MF *garbouil*] *archaic* (1548) : a confused disordered state : TURMOIL

gar·çon \gär-'sōⁿ\ *n, pl* **garçons** \-'sōⁿ(z)\ [F, boy, servant, fr. OF, prob. of Gmc origin; akin to OHG *recchio* banished man] (1788) : WAITER

garde–man·ger \ˌgärd-(ə-)ˌmäⁿ-'zhā\ *n, pl* **garde–mangers** \-'zhā(z)\ [F] (1928) : a cook who specializes in the preparation of cold foods (as meats, fish, and salads)

[1]gar·den \'gärd-ᵊn\ *n* [ME *gardin*, fr. ONF, of Gmc origin; akin to OHG *gart* enclosure — more at YARD] (13c) 1 a : a plot of ground where herbs, fruits, flowers, or vegetables are cultivated b : a rich well-cultivated region c : a container (as a window box) planted with usu. a variety of small plants ⟨herb ~*s*⟩ 2 a : a public recreation area or park usu. ornamented with plants and trees ⟨a botanical ~⟩ b : an open-air eating or drinking place c : a large hall for public entertainment — **gar·den·ful** \-ˌfu̇l\ *n*

[2]garden *vb* **gar·dened; gar·den·ing** \'gärd-niŋ, -ᵊn-iŋ\ *vi* (1577) : to lay out or work in a garden ~ *vt* 1 : to make into a garden 2 : to ornament with gardens — **gar·den·er** \'gärd-nər, -ᵊn-ər\ *n*

[3]garden *adj* (1622) 1 : of, relating to, or frequenting a garden 2 a : of a kind grown in the open as distinguished from one more delicate ⟨~ plant⟩ b : GARDEN-VARIETY

garden apartment *n* (1946) : a multiple-unit low-rise dwelling having considerable lawn or garden space

garden city *n* (1848) : a planned residential community with park and planted areas

garden cress *n* (1577) : an annual herb (*Lepidium sativum*) of the mustard family sometimes cultivated for its pungent basal leaves

garden heliotrope *n* (1902) : a tall rhizomatous Old World valerian (*Valeriana officinalis*) widely cultivated for its fragrant tiny flowers and for its roots which yield the drug valerian

gar·de·nia \gär-'dē-nyə\ *n* [NL, fr. Alexander *Garden* †1791 Scot. naturalist] (1760) : any of a large genus (*Gardenia*) of Old World tropical trees and shrubs of the madder family with showy fragrant white or yellow flowers

Garden of Eden : EDEN

garden rocket *n* (ca. 1832) : a yellowish flowered European herb (*Eruca sativa*) of the mustard family that is sometimes grown for salad — called also *rocket, rugola*

garden–variety *adj* (1928) : ORDINARY, COMMONPLACE

garde·robe \'gär-ˌdrōb\ *n* [ME, fr. MF; akin to ONF *warderobe* wardrobe] (15c) 1 : a wardrobe or its contents 2 : a private room : BEDROOM 3 : PRIVY 2

gar·dy·loo \ˌgärd-ē-'lü\ *interj* [perh. fr. F *garde à l'eau!* look out for the water!] (1622) — used in Edinburgh as a warning cry when it was customary to throw slops from the windows into the streets

Gar·eth \'gar-əth\ *n* : a knight of the Round Table and nephew of King Arthur

gar·fish \'gär-ˌfish\ *n* [ME *garfysshe*] (15c) : GAR

Gar·gan·tua \gär-'ganch-(ə-)wə\ *n* [F] : a gigantic king in Rabelais' *Gargantua* having a great capacity for food and drink

gar·gan·tuan \-wən\ *adj, often cap* [*Gargantua*] (1596) : of tremendous size or volume : GIGANTIC, COLOSSAL ⟨entire cities fleeing before ~ walls of water —William Cleary⟩

gar·get \'gär-gət\ *n* [prob. fr. ME, throat, fr. MF *gargate;* akin to MF *gargouiller*] (1587) : mastitis of domestic animals; *esp* : chronic bovine mastitis with gross changes in the form and texture of the udder — **gar·gety** \-gət-ē\ *adj*

[1]gar·gle \'gär-gəl\ *vb* **gar·gled; gar·gling** \-g(ə-)liŋ\ [MF *gargouiller* to gargle, of imit. origin] *vt* (1527) 1 a : to hold (a liquid) in the mouth or throat and agitate with air from the lungs b : to cleanse or disinfect (the oral cavity) in this manner 2 : to utter with a gargling sound ~ *vi* 1 : to use a gargle 2 : to speak or sing as if gargling

[2]gargle *n* (1657) 1 : a liquid used in gargling 2 : a gargling sound

gar·goyle \'gär-ˌgȯil\ *n* [ME *gargoyl*, fr. MF *gargouille;* akin to MF *gargouiller*] (13c) 1 a : a spout in the form of a grotesque human or animal figure projecting from a roof gutter to throw rainwater clear of a building b : a grotesquely carved figure 2 : a person with an ugly face — **gar·goyled** \-ˌgȯild\ *adj*

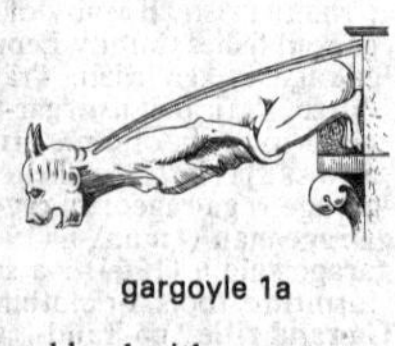

gargoyle 1a

gar·i·bal·di \ˌgar-ə-'bȯl-dē\ *n* (1862) : a woman's blouse copied from the red shirt worn by the Italian patriot Garibaldi

ga·rigue \gə-'rēg\ *n* [F] (1896) : a low open scrubland with many evergreen shrubs, low trees, and bunchgrasses found in poor land in the Mediterranean region

gar·ish \'ga(ə)r-ish, 'ge(ə)r-\ *adj* [origin unknown] (1545) 1 : clothed in vivid colors 2 a : excessively vivid : FLASHY b : offensively or distressingly bright : GLARING 3 : tastelessly showy ***syn*** see GAUDY — **gar·ish·ly** *adv* — **gar·ish·ness** *n*

[1]gar·land \'gär-lənd\ *n* [ME, fr. MF *garlande*] (14c) 1 : WREATH, CHAPLET 2 : a grommet or ring of rope used aboard ship in hoisting or to prevent chafing 3 : ANTHOLOGY, COLLECTION

[2]garland *vt* (15c) 1 : to form into a garland 2 : to adorn with or as if with a garland

gar·lic \'gär-lik\ *n* [ME *garlek*, fr. OE *gārlēac*, fr. *gār* spear + *lēac* leek — more at GORE] (bef. 12c) : a European bulbous herb (*Allium sativum*) of the lily family widely cultivated for its pungent compound bulbs much used in cookery; *also* : one of the bulbs — **gar·licked** \-likt\ *adj* — **gar·licky** \-li-kē\ *adj*

garlic salt *n* (1927) : a seasoning of ground dried garlic and salt

[1]gar·ment \'gär-mənt\ *n* [ME, fr. MF *garnement*, fr. OF, fr. *garnir* to equip — more at GARNISH] (14c) : an article of clothing

[2]garment *vt* (1547) : to clothe with or as if with a garment

[1]gar·ner \'gär-nər\ *n* [ME, fr. OF *grenier*, fr. L *granarium*, fr. *granum* grain — more at CORN] (12c) 1 a : GRANARY b : a grain bin 2 : something that is collected : ACCUMULATION

[2]garner *vt* **gar·nered; gar·ner·ing** \'gärn-(ə-)riŋ\ (14c) 1 a : to gather into storage b : to deposit as if in a granary ⟨volumes in which he has ~*ed* the fruits of his lifetime labors —Reinhold Niebuhr⟩ 2 a : to acquire by effort : EARN b : ACCUMULATE, COLLECT

gar·net \'gär-nət\ *n* [ME *grenat*, fr. MF, fr. *grenat*, adj., red like a pomegranate, fr. *(pomme) grenate* pomegranate] (14c) 1 : a brittle and more or less transparent usu. red silicate mineral that has a vitreous luster, occurs mainly in crystals but also in massive form and in grains, is found commonly in gneiss and mica schist, and is used as a semiprecious stone and as an abrasive (hardness 6.5–7.5, sp. gr. 3.15–4.3) 2 : a variable color averaging a dark red

gar·net·if·er·ous \ˌgär-nət-'if-(ə-)rəs\ *adj* (1852) : containing garnets

garnet paper *n* (ca. 1902) : an abrasive paper with crushed garnet as the abrasive

gar·ni·er·ite \'gär-nē-ə-ˌrīt\ *n* [Jules *Garnier* †1904 Fr. geologist] (1875) : a soft mineral prob. $(Mg, Ni)_3Si_2O_5(OH)_4$ consisting of hydrous nickel magnesium silicate and constituting an important ore of nickel

[1]gar·nish \'gär-nish\ *vt* [ME *garnishen*, fr. MF *garniss-*, stem of *garnir* to warn, equip, garnish, of Gmc origin; akin to OHG *warnōn* to take heed — more at WARN] (14c) 1 a : DECORATE, EMBELLISH b : to add decorative or savory touches to (food) 2 : to equip with accessories : FURNISH 3 : GARNISHEE ***syn*** see ADORN

[2]garnish *n* (1596) 1 : EMBELLISHMENT, ORNAMENT 2 : a savory or decorative condiment (as watercress or parsley) 3 a : an unauthorized fee formerly extorted from a new inmate of an English jail b : a similar payment required of a new worker

[1]gar·nish·ee \ˌgär-nə-'shē\ *n* (1627) : one who is served with a garnishment

[2]garnishee *vt* **-eed; -ee·ing** (ca. 1890) 1 : to serve with a garnishment 2 : to take (as a debtor's wages) by legal authority

gar·nish·ment \'gär-nish-mənt\ *n* (1550) 1 : GARNISH 2 : a legal summons or warning concerning the attachment of property to satisfy a debt 3 : a stoppage of a specified sum from wages to satisfy a creditor

gar·ni·ture \'gär-ni-chər, -nə-ˌchu̇(ə)r\ *n* [MF, equipment, alter. of OF *garnesture*, fr. *garnir*] (1667) : EMBELLISHMENT, TRIMMING

gar·pike \'gär-ˌpīk\ *n* (1776) : GAR b

gar·ret \'gar-ət\ *n* [ME *garette* watchtower, fr. MF *garite*, watchtower, refuge, deriv. of OF *garir*] (14c) : a room or unfinished part of a house just under the roof

[1]gar·ri·son \'gar-ə-sən\ *n* [ME *garisoun* protection, fr. OF *garison*, fr. *garir* to protect, of Gmc origin; akin to OHG *werien* to defend — more at WEIR] (15c) 1 : a military post; *esp* : a permanent military installation 2 : the troops stationed at a garrison

[2]garrison *vt* **gar·ri·soned; gar·ri·son·ing** \'gar-ə-s(ə-)niŋ\ (1569) 1 : to station troops in 2 a : to assign as a garrison b : to occupy with troops

garrison cap *n* (1944) : a visorless folding cap worn as part of a military uniform — compare SERVICE CAP

Gar·ri·son finish \ˌgar-ə-sən-\ *n* [prob. fr. Edward "Snapper" *Garrison*, 19th cent. Am. jockey] (1935) : a finish in which the winner comes from behind at the end

garrison house *n* (1676) 1 : a house fortified against Indian attack 2 : BLOCKHOUSE 3 : a house having the second story overhanging the first in the front

garrison state *n* (1937) : a state organized on a primarily military basis; *esp* : one whose military preparations threaten to convert it into a totalitarian state

gar·ron \'gar-ən, gə-'rȯn\ *n* [IrGael *gearrān* & ScGael *gearran*, gelding] *Scot & Irish* (1540) : a small sturdy workhorse

[1]gar·rote *or* **ga·rotte** \gə-'rät, -'rōt; 'gar-ət\ *n* [Sp *garrote*] (1622) 1 a : a method of execution by strangling with an iron collar b : the iron collar used 2 a : strangulation esp. with robbery as the motive b : an implement for this purpose

[2]garrote *or* **garotte** *vt* **gar·rot·ed** *or* **ga·rott·ed; gar·rot·ing** *or* **ga·rott·ing** (1851) 1 : to execute with or as if with a garrote 2 : to strangle and rob — **gar·rot·er** *n*

gar·ru·li·ty \gə-'rü-lət-ē, ga-\ *n* (1581) : the quality or state of being talkative

gar·ru·lous \'gar-ə-ləs *also* 'gar-yə-\ *adj* [L *garrulus*, fr. *garrire* to chatter — more at CARE] (1611) : given to prosy, rambling, or tedious loquacity : pointlessly or annoyingly talkative ***syn*** see TALKATIVE — **gar·ru·lous·ly** *adv* — **gar·ru·lous·ness** *n*

[1]gar·ter \'gärt-ər\ *n* [ME, fr. ONF *gartier*, fr. *garet* bend of the knee, of Celt origin; akin to OIr *gairri* calves of the legs] (14c) 1 a : a band worn to hold up a stocking or sock b : a strap hanging from a girdle or corset to support a stocking c : a band worn to hold up a shirt sleeve 2 *cap* a : the British Order of the Garter b : the blue velvet garter that is its badge c : membership in the order

[2]garter *vt* (15c) : to support with or as if with a garter

garter snake *n* (1769) : any of numerous harmless viviparous American snakes (genus *Thamnophis*) with longitudinal stripes on the back

garth \'gärth\ *n* [ME, fr. ON *garthr* yard; akin to OHG *gart* enclosure — more at YARD] (14c) : a small yard or enclosure : CLOSE

gar·vey \'gär-vē\ *n, pl* **garveys** [prob. fr. the name *Garvey*] (ca. 1896) : a small scow of the New Jersey coast

[1]gas \'gas\ *n, pl* **gas·es** *also* **gas·ses** [NL, alter. of L *chaos* space, chaos] (1779) 1 : a fluid (as air) that has neither independent shape nor volume but tends to expand indefinitely 2 a : a gas or gaseous mixture with the exception of atmospheric air: as (1) : a gas or gaseous mixture used to produce anesthesia (2) : a combustible gaseous mixture (as for fuel) b : a substance that can be used to produce a poisonous, asphyxiating, or irritant atmosphere 3 : empty talk : BOMBAST 4 : GASOLINE 5 *slang* : one that is very appealing or enjoyable ⟨the party was a ~⟩

[2]gas *vb* **gassed; gas·sing** *vt* (1852) 1 : to supply with gas or esp. gasoline ⟨~ up the automobile⟩ 2 a : to treat chemically with gas b : to poison or otherwise affect adversely with gas ~ *vi* 1 : to give off gas 2 : to talk idly 3 : to fill the tank (as of an automobile) with gasoline — often used with *up*

gas·bag \'gas-ˌbag\ *n* (1827) **1** : a bag for holding gas **2** : an idle talker

gas chamber *n* (1945) : a chamber in which prisoners are executed by poison gas

gas chromatograph *n* (1958) : an instrument used to separate a sample into components in gas chromatography

gas chromatography *n* (1952) : chromatography in which the sample mixture is vaporized and injected into a stream of carrier gas (as nitrogen or helium) moving through a column containing a stationary phase composed of a liquid or particulate solid and is separated into its component compounds according to their affinity for the stationary phase — **gas chromatographic** *adj*

gas·con \'gas-kən\ *n* (14c) **1** *cap* : a native of Gascony **2** : a boastful swaggering person — **Gascon** *adj*

gas·con·ade \ˌgas-kə-'nād\ *n* [F *gasconnade,* fr. *gasconner* to boast, fr. *gascon* gascon, boaster] (1709) : BRAVADO, BOASTING — **gasconade** *vi* — **gas·con·ad·er** *n*

gas·eous \'gas-ē-əs, 'gash-əs\ *adj* (1799) **1 a** : having the form of or being gas; *also* : of or relating to gases **b** : heated so as to remain free from suspended liquid droplets — used of a vapor not in contact with its own liquid **2** : lacking substance or solidity : TENUOUS — **gas·eous·ness** *n*

gas fitter *n* (ca. 1858) : a worker who installs or repairs gas pipes and appliances

gas gangrene *n* (1914) : progressive gangrene marked by impregnation of the dead and dying tissue with gas and caused by one or more toxin-producing clostridia

gas–guz·zler \'gas-'gəz(-ə)-lər\ *n* (1977) : a usu. large automobile that gets relatively poor mileage — **gas–guz·zling** \-'gəz(-ə)-liŋ\ *adj*

[1]gash \'gash\ *n* (13c) **1** : a deep long cut esp. in flesh **2** : a deep narrow depression in land whether natural or man-made

[2]gash *vb* [ME *garsen,* fr. ONF *garser,* fr. (assumed) VL *charissare,* fr. Gk *charassein* to scratch, engrave — more at CHARACTER] *vt* (14c) : to make a gash in ~ *vi* : to make a gash : CUT

[3]gash *adj* [origin unknown] (1706) **1** *chiefly Scot* : KNOWING, WITTY **2** *chiefly Scot* : well-dressed : TRIM

gas·hold·er \'gas-ˌhōl-dər\ *n* (1802) : a container for gas; *esp* : a large cylindrical tank for storing fuel gas under pressure

gas·house \-ˌhau̇s\ *n* (1880) : GASWORKS

gas·ify \'gas-ə-ˌfī\ *vb* **-ified; -ify·ing** *vt* (ca. 1828) : to convert into gas ⟨~ coal⟩ ~ *vi* : to become gaseous — **gas·ifi·ca·tion** \ˌgas-ə-fə-'kā-shən\ *n* — **gas·ifi·er** \'gas-ə-ˌfī(-ə)r\ *n*

gas·ket \'gas-kət\ *n* [perh. modif. of F *garcette*] (1622) **1** : a line or band used to lash a furled sail **2 a** : plaited hemp or tallowed rope for packing pistons or making pipe or other joints fluid-tight **b** : packing for the same purpose made of other material (as rubber, asbestos, or metal); *also* : sealing material over a crack

gas·kin \'gas-kən\ *n* [prob. short for *galligaskins*] (1573) **1** *pl, obs* : HOSE, BREECHES **2** : a part of the hind leg of a quadruped between the stifle and the hock — see HORSE illustration

gas·light \'gas-ˌlīt, -'līt\ *n* (1808) **1** : light made by burning illuminating gas **2** : a gas flame or gas lighting fixture

gas–liquid chromatography *n* (1952) : gas chromatography in which the stationary phase is a liquid — **gas–liquid chromatographic** *adj*

gas·lit \-ˌlit, -'lit\ *adj* (1837) : illuminated by gaslight

gas log *n* (1885) : a hollow perforated imitation log used as a gas burner in a fireplace

gas mask *n* (1915) : a mask connected to a chemical air filter and used to protect the face and lungs against poison gases; *broadly* : RESPIRATOR 1

gas·o·gene \'gas-ə-ˌjēn\ *n* [F *gazogène,* fr. *gaz* gas (fr. NL *gas*) + *-o-* + *-gène* -gen] (1853) **1** : a portable apparatus for carbonating liquids **2** : an apparatus carried by a vehicle to produce gas for fuel by partial burning of charcoal or wood

gas·o·hol \'gas-ə-ˌhȯl\ *n* [blend of *gasoline* and *alcohol*] (1977) : a fuel consisting of 10 percent ethyl alcohol and 90 percent gasoline

gas oil *n* (1901) : a hydrocarbon oil used as a fuel oil; *esp* : a petroleum distillate intermediate in boiling range and viscosity between kerosene and lubricating oil

gas·olier \ˌgas-ə-'li(ə)r\ *n* [alter. of *gaselier,* fr. *gas* + *-elier* (as in *chandelier*)] (1905) : a gaslight chandelier

gas·o·line *also* **gas·o·lene** \'gas-ə-ˌlēn, ˌgas-ə-' *also* 'gaz- *or* ˌgaz-\ *n* [[1]*gas* + *-ol* + *-ine* or *-ene*] (1865) : a volatile flammable liquid hydrocarbon mixture used as a fuel esp. for internal-combustion engines and blended from several products of natural gas and petroleum — **gas·o·lin·ic** \ˌgas-ə-'lē-nik, -'lin-ik\ *adj*

gas·om·e·ter \ga-'säm-ət-ər\ *n* [F *gazomètre,* fr. *gaz* + *-o-* + *-mètre* -meter] (1790) **1** : a laboratory apparatus for holding and measuring gases **2** : GASHOLDER

gas–operated *adj, of a firearm* (1944) : using part of the force of expanding propellant gases to operate the action

gasp \'gasp\ *vb* [ME *gaspen;* akin to ON *geispa* to yawn] *vi* (14c) **1** : to catch the breath convulsively and audibly (as with shock) **2** : to breathe laboriously ~ *vt* : to utter in a gasping manner — **gasp** *n*

gasp·er \'gäs-pə(r)\ *n, slang Brit* (1914) : CIGARETTE

gas plant *n* (ca. 1909) : FRAXINELLA

gas·ser \'gas-ər\ *n* (1892) **1** : an oil well that yields gas **2** *slang* : a talkative person **3** *slang* : something outstanding

gas station *n* (1925) : SERVICE STATION 1

gas·sy \'gas-ē\ *adj* **gas·si·er; -est** (1757) **1** : full of or containing gas **2** : having the characteristics of gas **3** : full of boastful or insincere talk — **gas·si·ness** *n*

gast \'gast\ *vt* [ME *gasten,* fr. *gast, gost* ghost — more at GHOST] (14c) *obs* : SCARE ⟨~*ed* by the noise I made, full suddenly he fled —Shak.⟩

gas·ter \'gas-tər\ *n* [Gk *gastēr*] (ca. 1909) : the enlarged part of the abdomen behind the pedicel in hymenopterous insects (as ants)

gas·tight \'gas-'tīt\ *adj* (1831) : impervious to gas — **gas·tight·ness** *n*

gast·ness \'gas(t)-nəs\ *n, obs* (14c) : FRIGHT, TERROR

gastr- *or* **gastro-** *also* **gastri-** *comb form* [Gk, fr. *gastr-, gastēr*] **1** : belly ⟨*Gastro*poda⟩ : stomach ⟨*gastr*itis⟩ **2** : gastric and ⟨*gastro*intestinal⟩

gas·tral \'gas-trəl\ *adj* (1828) : of or relating to the stomach or digestive tract

gas·trea *also* **gas·traea** \ga-'strē-ə\ *n* [NL, fr. Gk *gastr-, gastēr*] (1879) : a hypothetical metazoan ancestral form corresponding in organization to a simple invaginated gastrula

gas·trec·to·my \ga-'strek-tə-mē\ *n, pl* **-mies** [ISV] (1886) : surgical removal of all or part of the stomach

gas·tric \'gas-trik\ *adj* [Gk *gastr-, gastēr,* alter. of (assumed) Gk *grastēr,* fr. Gk *gran* to gnaw, eat] (1656) : of or relating to the stomach

gastric gland *n* (ca. 1900) : any of various glands in the walls of the stomach that secrete gastric juice

gastric juice *n* (ca. 1730) : a thin watery acid digestive fluid secreted by glands in the mucous membrane of the stomach

gastric ulcer *n* (ca. 1910) : a peptic ulcer situated in the stomach

gas·trin \'gas-trən\ *n* (1905) : a polypeptide hormone that is secreted by the gastric mucosa and induces secretion of gastric juice

gas·tri·tis \ga-'strīt-əs\ *n* (1806) : inflammation esp. of the mucous membrane of the stomach

gas·troc·ne·mi·us \ˌgas-(ˌ)träk-'nē-mē-əs, -trək-\ *n, pl* **-mii** \-mē-ˌī\ [NL, fr. Gk *gastroknēmē* calf of the leg, fr. *gastr-* + *knēmē* shank — more at HAM] (1676) : the largest and most superficial muscle of the calf of the leg arising by two heads from the condyles of the femur and having its tendon of insertion incorporated as part of the Achilles tendon

gas·tro·coel *also* **gas·tro·coele** \'gas-trə-ˌsēl\ *n* [F *gastrocèle,* fr. *gastr-* + *-cèle* -coele] (ca. 1900) : ARCHENTERON

gas·tro·du·o·de·nal \'gas-trō-ˌd(y)ü-ə-'dēn-ᵊl, -d(y)u̇-'äd-ᵊn-əl\ *adj* (ca. 1854) : of, relating to, or involving both the stomach and the duodenum

gas·tro·en·ter·i·tis \ˌgas-trō-ˌent-ə-'rīt-əs\ *n* (1822) : inflammation of the lining membrane of the stomach and the intestines

gas·tro·en·ter·ol·o·gy \-ˌent-ə-'räl-ə-jē\ *n* [ISV] (1904) : the study of the diseases and pathology of the stomach and intestines — **gas·tro·en·ter·o·log·i·cal** \-rə-'läj-i-kəl\ *adj* — **gas·tro·en·ter·ol·o·gist** \-ˌent-ə-'räl-ə-jəst\ *n*

gas·tro·esoph·a·ge·al \'gas-trō-i-ˌsäf-ə-'jē-əl\ *adj* (ca. 1909) : of, relating to, or involving the stomach and esophagus

gas·tro·in·tes·ti·nal \ˌgas-trō-in-'tes-tən-ᵊl, -'tes(t)-nəl\ *adj* (1831) : of, relating to, affecting, or including both stomach and intestine ⟨~ tract⟩ ⟨~ distress⟩

gas·tro·lith \'gas-trə-ˌlith\ *n* (1854) : a stone or pebble found in some fish or reptile stomachs and thought to function in grinding food

gas·tro·nome \'gas-trə-ˌnōm\ *n* [F, back-formation fr. *gastronomie*] (1823) : a lover of good food; *esp* : one with a serious interest in gastronomy **syn** see EPICURE

gas·tron·o·mist \ga-'strän-ə-məst\ *n* (1825) : GASTRONOME

gas·tron·o·my \-mē\ *n* [F *gastronomie,* fr. Gk *Gastronomia,* title of a 4th cent. B.C. poem, fr. *gastro-* belly + *-nomia* -nomy] (1814) **1** : the art or science of good eating **2** : culinary customs or style — **gas·tro·nom·ic** \ˌgas-trə-'näm-ik\ *also* **gas·tro·nom·i·cal** \-i-kəl\ *adj* — **gas·tro·nom·i·cal·ly** \-i-k(ə-)lē\ *adv*

gas·tro·pod \'gas-trə-ˌpäd\ *n* [NL *Gastropoda,* fr. *gastr-* + *-pod*] (1826) : any of a large class (Gastropoda) of mollusks (as snails) with a univalve shell or none and usu. with a distinct head bearing sensory organs — **gastropod** *adj*

gas·tro·scope \'gas-trə-ˌskōp\ *n* [ISV] (1888) : an instrument for viewing the interior of the stomach — **gas·tro·scop·ic** \ˌgas-trə-'skäp-ik\ *adj* — **gas·tros·co·pist** \ga-'sträs-kə-pəst\ *n* — **gas·tros·co·py** \-pē\ *n*

gas·tro·trich \'gas-trə-ˌtrik\ *n* [deriv. of Gk *gastr-* + *trich-, thrix* hair — more at TRICH-] (1940) : any of a small group (Gastrotricha) of minute freshwater multicellular animals superficially resembling infusorians

gas·tro·vas·cu·lar \ˌgas-trō-'vas-kyə-lər\ *adj* [ISV] (1876) : functioning in both digestion and circulation ⟨the ~ cavity of a coelenterate⟩

gas·tru·la \'gas-trə-lə\ *n, pl* **-las** *or* **-lae** \-ˌlē, -ˌlī\ [NL, fr. *gastr-*] (1877) : an early metazoan embryo consisting of a hollow 2-layered cellular cup made up of an outer epiblast and an inner hypoblast that meet along the marginal line of a blastopore opening into the archenteron — compare BLASTULA, MORULA — **gas·tru·lar** \-lər\ *adj*

gas·tru·la·tion \ˌgas-trə-'lā-shən\ *n* (1879) : the process of becoming or of forming a gastrula

gas turbine *n* (1904) : an internal-combustion engine in which expanding gases from the combustion chamber drive the blades of a turbine

gas·works \'gas-ˌwərks\ *n pl but sing in constr* (1819) : a plant for manufacturing gas and esp. illuminating gas

[1]gat \(ˈ)gat\ *archaic past of* GET

[2]gat \'gat\ *n* [prob. fr. D, lit., hole; akin to OE *geat* gate] (1723) : a natural or artificial channel or passage

[3]gat \'gat\ *n* [short for *Gatling gun*] *slang* (ca. 1904) : HANDGUN

[1]gate \'gāt\ *n* [ME, fr. OE *geat;* akin to ON *gat* opening, Gk *chezein* to defecate] (bef. 12c) **1** : an opening in a wall or fence **2** : a city or castle entrance often with defensive structures (as towers) **3** : the frame or door that closes a gate **4 a** : a means of entrance or exit **b** : a pass or defile in mountains **c** : a space between two markers through which a competitor must pass in the course of a slalom race **d** : a mechanically operated barrier used as a starting device for a race (as in skiing) **5 a** : a door, valve, or other device for controlling the passage esp. of fluid **b** : a signal that makes an electronic circuit operative for a short period **c** : a device (as in a computer) that outputs a signal when specified input conditions are met ⟨logic ~⟩ **6** : a channel in a foundry mold through which the molten metal flows into the cavity made by the pattern **7** : the total admission receipts or the number of spectators esp. at a sports event **8** *slang* : DISMISSAL ⟨gave him the ~⟩

[2]gate *vt* **gat·ed; gat·ing** (1901) **1** : to supply with a gate **2** *Brit* : to punish by confinement to a campus or dormitory **3** : to control by means of a gate

[3]gate *n* [ME, fr. ON *gata* road; akin to OHG *gazza* road] (13c) **1** *archaic* : WAY, PATH **2** *dial* : METHOD, STYLE

gate–crash·er \'gāt-ˌkrash-ər\ *n* (1926) : one who enters, attends, or participates without ticket or invitation — **gate–crash** *vb*

gate·fold \-ˌfōld\ *n* (1946) **:** FOLDOUT; *esp* **:** one with a single fold that opens out like a gate

gate·keep·er \-ˌkē-pər\ *n* (1572) **1 :** one that tends or guards a gate **2 :** SUPERVISOR, MONITOR — **gate·keep·ing** \-piŋ\ *adj*

gate·leg table \ˌgāt-ˌleg-, -ˌlāg-\ *n* (1926) **:** a table with drop leaves supported by movable paired legs

gate·post \'gāt-ˌpōst\ *n* (1522) **:** the post to which a gate is hung or the one against which it closes

gate·way \-ˌwā\ *n* (1707) **1 :** an opening for a gate **2 :** GATE 4a

1gath·er \'ga*th*-ər, 'ge*th*-\ *vb* **gath·ered; gath·er·ing** \-(ə-)riŋ\ [ME *gaderen,* fr. OE *gaderian;* akin to Skt *gadh* to hold fast — more at GOOD] *vt* (bef. 12c) **1 :** to bring together **:** COLLECT **2 a :** PICK, HARVEST **b :** to pick up little by little **c :** to accumulate and place in readiness ⟨~*ed* up his tools⟩ **d :** to assemble (volume signatures) in sequence for binding **3 :** to serve as a center of attraction for **4 :** to effect the collection of (as tax) **5 a :** to summon up ⟨~*ed* his courage⟩ **b :** to gain by gradual increase **:** ACCUMULATE ⟨~ speed⟩ **c :** to prepare (as oneself) by mustering strength **6 a :** to bring together the parts of **b :** to draw about or close to something ⟨~*ing* his cloak about him⟩ **c :** to pull (fabric) along a line of stitching so as to draw into puckers **d :** to haul in **7 :** to reach a conclusion often intuitively from hints or through inferences ⟨I ~ that you want to leave⟩ ~ *vi* **1 a :** to come together in a body **b :** to cluster around a focus of attraction **2 a :** to swell and fill with pus **b :** GROW, INCREASE — **gath·er·er** \-ər-ər\ *n*

syn GATHER, COLLECT, ASSEMBLE, CONGREGATE mean to come or bring together into a group, mass, or unit. GATHER is the most general term for bringing or coming together from a spread-out or scattered state; COLLECT often implies careful selection or orderly arrangement; ASSEMBLE implies an ordered union or organization of persons or things often for a definite purpose; CONGREGATE implies a spontaneous flocking together into a crowd or huddle. ***syn*** see in addition INFER

2gather *n* (1555) **1 :** something gathered: as **a :** a puckering in cloth made by gathering **b :** a mass of molten glass collected for use in glassblowing **2 :** an act or instance of gathering

gath·er·ing *n* (bef. 12c) **1 :** ASSEMBLY, MEETING **2 :** a suppurating swelling **:** ABSCESS **3 :** the collecting of food and raw materials from the wild **4 :** COLLECTION, COMPILATION **5 :** a gather in cloth

Gat·ling gun \ˌgat-liŋ-\ *n* [Richard J. *Gatling* †1903 Am. inventor] (1867) **:** an early machine gun with a crank-operated revolving cluster of barrels fired once each per revolution

ga·tor \'gāt-ər\ *n* (1844) **:** ALLIGATOR

gauche \'gōsh\ *adj* [F, lit., left] (1751) **1 :** lacking social experience or grace **:** CRUDE **2 :** not planar ⟨~ conformation of molecules⟩ ***syn*** see AWKWARD — **gauche·ly** *adv* — **gauche·ness** *n*

gau·che·rie \ˌgōsh-(ə-)'rē\ *n* (1798) **:** a tactless or awkward act

gau·cho \'gau̇-(ˌ)chō\ *n, pl* **gauchos** [AmerSp] (1824) **:** a cowboy of the So. American pampas

gaud \'gȯd, 'gäd\ *n* [ME *gaude*] (15c) **:** ORNAMENT, TRINKET

gaud·ery \-ə-rē\ *n* (1597) **:** showy ornamentation; *esp* **:** personal finery

1gau·dy \'gȯd-ē, 'gäd-\ *adj* **gaud·i·er; -est** (1583) **:** ostentatiously or tastelessly ornamented — **gaud·i·ly** \'gȯd-ᵊl-ē, 'gäd-\ *adv* — **gaud·i·ness** \'gȯd-ē-nəs, 'gäd-\ *n*

syn GAUDY, TAWDRY, GARISH, FLASHY, MERETRICIOUS mean vulgarly or cheaply showy. GAUDY implies a tasteless use of overly bright, often clashing colors or excessive ornamentation ⟨false eloquence, like the prismatic glass, its *gaudy* colors spreads on every place —Alexander Pope⟩ TAWDRY applies to what is at once gaudy and cheap and sleazy ⟨the woman . . . big, bovine in a motley of cheap and *tawdry* clothes —William Styron⟩ GARISH describes what is distressingly or offensively bright ⟨hide me from day's *garish* eye —John Milton⟩ FLASHY implies an effect of brilliance quickly and easily seen to be shallow or vulgar ⟨two painted *flashy* women with fine legs —Graham Greene⟩ MERETRICIOUS stresses falsity and may describe a tawdry show that beckons with a false allure or promise ⟨soldiers . . . circled displays of colored postcards, and picked up *meretricious* mementos —James Baldwin⟩

2gaudy *n, pl* **gaudies** [prob. fr. L *gaudium* joy — more at JOY] (1651) **:** a feast or entertainment esp. in the form of an annual college dinner in a British university

gauf·fer \'gäf-ər, 'gȯf-, 'gōf-\ *var of* GOFFER

1gauge \'gāj\ *n* [ME *gauge,* fr. ONF] (15c) **1 a :** measurement according to some standard or system **b :** DIMENSIONS, SIZE **2** *usu* **gage :** an instrument for or a means of measuring or testing: as **a :** an instrument for measuring a dimension or for testing mechanical accuracy **b :** an instrument with a graduated scale or dial for measuring or indicating quantity **3 :** relative position of a ship with reference to another ship and the wind **4 a :** the distance between the rails of a railroad **b :** the distance between a pair of wheels on an axle **5 :** the quantity of plaster of paris used with mortar to accelerate its setting **6 :** the size of a shotgun barrel's interior diameter nominally expressed as the number of lead balls each just fitting the interior diameter of the barrel required to make a pound ⟨a 12-*gauge* shotgun⟩ **7 a :** the thickness of a thin material (as sheet metal or plastic film) **b :** the diameter of a slender object (as wire, a hypodermic needle, or a screw) **c :** the fineness of a knitted fabric expressed by the number of loops per 1½ inch so that the higher the number the finer the texture ***syn*** see STANDARD

2gauge *vt* **gauged; gaug·ing** (15c) **1 a :** to measure the size, dimensions, or other measurable quantity of exactly **b :** to determine the capacity or contents of **c :** ESTIMATE, JUDGE ⟨hard to ~ his moods⟩ **2 a :** to check for conformity to specifications or limits **b :** to measure off or set out **3 :** to mix (plaster) in definite proportions **4 :** to dress (as bricks) to size by rubbing or chipping — **gauge·able** \'gā-jə-bəl\ *adj* — **gauge·ably** \-blē\ *adv*

gaug·er \'gā-jər\ *n* (15c) **1 :** one that gauges **2** *chiefly Brit* **:** an exciseman who inspects dutiable bulk goods

Gaul \'gȯl\ *n* (1630) **1 :** a Celt of ancient Gaul **2 :** FRENCHMAN

1Gaul·ish \'gȯ-lish\ *adj* (1659) **:** of or relating to the Gauls or their language or land

2Gaulish *n* (1668) **:** the Celtic language of the ancient Gauls — see INDO-EUROPEAN LANGUAGES table

Gaull·ism \'gō-ˌliz-əm, 'gȯ-\ *n* [Charles de *Gaulle*] (1943) **1 :** a French political movement during World War II led by Charles de Gaulle in opposition to the Vichy regime **2 :** a postwar French political movement led by Charles de Gaulle — **Gaull·ist** \-ləst\ *adj or n*

gault \'gȯlt\ *n* [prob. of Scand origin; akin to ON *gald* hard-packed snow] (1575) **:** a heavy thick clay soil

gaum \'gȯm, 'gäm\ *vt* [perh. alter. of 4*gum*] *dial* (1796) **:** SMUDGE, SMEAR

gaunt \'gȯnt, 'gänt\ *adj* [ME] (15c) **1 :** excessively thin and angular often as a result of suffering **2 :** BARREN, DESOLATE ***syn*** see LEAN — **gaunt·ly** *adv* — **gaunt·ness** *n*

1gaunt·let \'gȯnt-lət, 'gänt-\ *n* [ME, fr. MF *gantelet,* dim. of *gant* glove, of Gmc origin; akin to MD *want* mitten, ON *vöttr* gloves] (15c) **1 :** a glove worn with medieval armor to protect the hand **2 :** any of various protective gloves used esp. in industry **3 :** a challenge to combat **4 :** a dress glove extending above the wrist — **gaunt·let·ed** \-lət-əd\ *adj*

2gauntlet *n* [by folk etymology fr. *gantelope*] (1661) **1 :** a double file of men facing each other and armed with clubs or other weapons with which to strike at an individual who is made to run between them **2 :** CROSS FIRE; *also* **:** ORDEAL ⟨ran the ~ of criticism and censure⟩

gaur \'gau̇(ə)r\ *n* [Hindi, fr. Skt *gaura;* akin to Skt *go* bull, cow — more at COW] (1806) **:** a large East Indian wild ox (*Bibos gaurus*) with a broad forehead and short thick conical horns

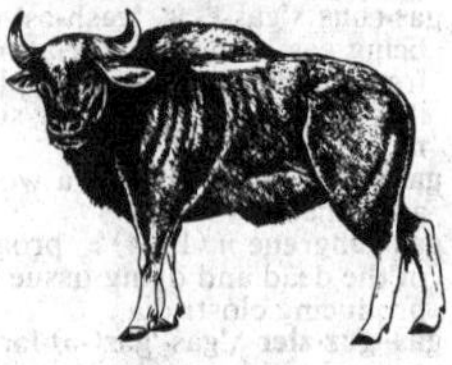
gaur

gauss \'gau̇s\ *n, pl* **gauss** *also* **gauss·es** [Karl F. *Gauss*] (1882) **:** the cgs unit of magnetic flux density that is equal to 1 × 10⁻⁴ tesla

Gauss·ian curve \ˌgau̇-sē-ən-\ *n* [Karl F. *Gauss*] (1905) **:** NORMAL CURVE

Gaussian distribution *n* (1905) **:** NORMAL DISTRIBUTION

gauze \'gȯz\ *n* [MF *gaze*] (1561) **1 a :** a thin often transparent fabric used chiefly for clothing or draperies **b :** a loosely woven cotton surgical dressing **c :** a firm woven fabric of metal or plastic filaments **2 :** HAZE, MIST — **gauze·like** \-ˌlīk\ *adj* — **gauz·i·ly** \'gȯ-zə-lē\ *adv* — **gauzy** \-zē\ *adj*

ga·vage \gə-'väzh, gä-\ *n* [F, fr. *garer* to stuff, force-feed] (1889) **:** introduction of material into the stomach by a tube

gave *past of* GIVE

1gav·el \'gav-əl\ *n* [ME, fr. OE *gafol;* akin to OE *giefan* to give] (bef. 12c) **:** rent or tribute in medieval England

2gavel *n* [origin unknown] (ca. 1860) **:** a mallet used (as by a presiding officer or auctioneer) for commanding attention or confirming an action (as a vote or sale)

3gavel *vt* **-eled** *or* **-elled; -el·ing** *or* **-el·ling** \'gav-(ə-)liŋ\ (1925) **:** to bring or force by use of a gavel ⟨~*ed* the audience to silence⟩ ⟨~*ed* through an adjournment motion⟩

gav·el·kind \'gav-əl-ˌkīnd\ *n* [ME *gavelkynde,* fr. 1*gavel* + *kinde* kind] (13c) **:** a tenure of land existing chiefly in Kent from Anglo-Saxon times until 1925 and providing for division of an intestate's estate equally among the sons or other heirs

gavel-to-gavel *adj* (1968) **:** extending from the beginning to the end of a meeting or session ⟨~ television coverage⟩

ga·vi·al \'gā-vē-əl\ *n* [F, modif. of Hindi or Nepali *ghariyāl,* fr. or akin to Skt *ghaṇṭika* alligator, perh. fr. *ghaṇṭa* throat] (ca. 1825) **:** a large harmless crocodilian (*Gavialis gangeticus*) of India

ga·votte \gə-'vät\ *n* [F, fr. MF, fr. OProv *gavato,* fr. *gavot* Alpine dweller] (1696) **1 :** a dance of French peasant origin marked by the raising rather than sliding of the feet **2 :** a tune for the gavotte in moderately quick 4/4 time — **gavotte** *vi*

Ga·wain \gə-'wān, 'gä-ˌwān, 'gau̇-ən\ *n* **:** a knight of the Round Table and nephew of King Arthur

1gawk \'gȯk\ *n* [prob. fr. E dial. *gawk* (left-handed)] (1757) **:** a clumsy stupid person **:** LOUT

2gawk *vi* [perh. alter. of obs. *gaw* (to stare)] (1785) **:** to gape or stare stupidly — **gawk·er** *n*

gawk·ish \'gȯ-kish\ *adj* (1876) **:** GAWKY — **gawk·ish·ly** *adv* — **gawk·ish·ness** *n*

gawky \'gȯ-kē\ *adj* **gawk·i·er; -est** (1759) **:** AWKWARD, CLUMSY ⟨a ~ child with long arms and legs⟩ — **gawk·i·ly** \-kə-lē\ *adv* — **gawky** *n*

1gay \'gā\ *adj* [ME, fr. MF *gai*] (14c) **1 a :** happily excited **:** MERRY **b :** keenly alive and exuberant **:** having or inducing high spirits ⟨he turned from a sober traditional style to one more timely and ~⟩ **2 a :** BRIGHT, LIVELY ⟨~ sunny meadows⟩ **b :** brilliant in color **3 :** given to social pleasures; *also* **:** LICENTIOUS **4 a :** HOMOSEXUAL **b :** of, relating to, or used by homosexuals ⟨~ liberation⟩ ⟨a ~ bar⟩ ***syn*** see LIVELY — **gay** *adv* — **gay·ness** *n*

2gay *n* (1953) **:** HOMOSEXUAL

gay·ety, gayly *var of* GAIETY, GAILY

1gaze \'gāz\ *vi* **gazed; gaz·ing** [ME *gazen*] (14c) **:** to fix the eyes in a steady and intent look and often with eagerness or studious attention — **gaz·er** *n*

syn GAZE, GAPE, STARE, GLARE, PEER mean to look (at) long and attentively. GAZE implies fixed and prolonged attention (as in wonder, admiration, or abstractedness); GAPE suggests an openmouthed often stupid wonder; STARE implies a direct open-eyed gazing denoting curiosity, disbelief, or insolence; GLARE is a fierce or angry staring; PEER suggests a looking narrowly and curiously as if through a small opening.

2gaze *n* (1566) **:** a fixed intent look

ga·ze·bo \gə-'zā-(ˌ)bō, -'zē-\ *n, pl* **-bos** [perh. fr. 1*gaze* + L *-ebo* (as in *videbo* I shall see)] (1752) **1 :** BELVEDERE **2 :** a freestanding roofed structure usu. open on the sides

gaze·hound \'gāz-ˌhau̇nd\ *n* (1570) **:** a dog that hunts by sight rather than by scent; *esp* **:** GREYHOUND

ga·zelle \gə-'zel\ *n, pl* **gazelles** *also* **gazelle** [F, fr. MF, fr. Ar *ghazāl*] (1600) **:** any of numerous small, graceful, and swift African and Asian antelopes (*Gazella* and related genera) noted for their soft lustrous eyes

1ga·zette \gə-'zet\ *n* [F, fr. It *gazetta*] (1605) **1 :** NEWSPAPER **2 :** an official journal **3** *Brit* **:** an announcement in an official gazette

2gazette *vt* **ga·zett·ed; ga·zett·ing** (1678) **1** *chiefly Brit* **:** to announce or publish in a gazette **2** *Brit* **:** to announce the appointment or status of in an official gazette

gaz·et·teer \ˌgaz-ə-'ti(ə)r\ *n* (1611) **1** *archaic* **:** JOURNALIST, PUBLICIST **2** [*The Gazetteer's: or, Newsman's Interpreter,* a geographical index edited by Laurence Echard †1730 Eng. historian] : a geographical dictionary; *also* : a book in which something (as wines or restaurants) is treated esp. in regard to geographic distribution and regional specialization

gaz·o·gene \'gaz-ə-ˌjēn\ *var of* GASOGENE

gaz·pa·cho \gəz-'päch-(ˌ)ō, gəs-\ *n, pl* **-chos** [Sp] (1845) : a spicy soup that is usu. made from chopped raw vegetables (as tomato, onion, pepper, and cucumber) and that is served cold

GB \(')jē-'bē\ *n* [code name] (1961) : SARIN

G clef *n* (1596) : TREBLE CLEF

ge- *or* **geo-** *comb form* [ME *geo-*, fr. MF & L; MF, fr. L, fr. Gk *gē-*, *geō-*, fr. *gē*] **1** : earth : ground : soil ⟨geanticline⟩ ⟨geophyte⟩ **2** : geographic : geography and ⟨geopolitics⟩

ge·an·ti·cline \jē-'ant-i-ˌklīn\ *also* **ge·an·ti·cli·nal** \(ˌ)jē-ˌant-i-'klīn-ᵊl\ *n* (1874) : a great upward flexure of the earth's crust — compare GEOSYNCLINE

[1]**gear** \'gi(ə)r\ *n* [ME *gere*, fr. ON *gørvi*; akin to OHG *garuwi* equipment, clothing, OE *gearu* ready — more at YARE] (14c) **1 a** : CLOTHING, GARMENTS **b** : movable property : GOODS **2** : EQUIPMENT, PARAPHERNALIA ⟨fishing ~⟩ **3 a** : the rigging of a ship or boat **b** : the harness esp. of horses **4** *dial chiefly Brit* : absurd talk : NONSENSE **5** *dial chiefly Brit* : DOINGS **6 a (1)** : a mechanism that performs a specific function in a complete machine ⟨steering ~⟩ **(2)** : a toothed wheel **(3)** : working relation, position, or adjustment ⟨in ~⟩ **b** : one of two or more adjustments of a transmission (as of a bicycle or motor vehicle) that determine mechanical advantage, relative speed, and direction of travel — **gear·less** \-ləs\ *adj*

[2]**gear** *vt* (1851) **1 a** : to provide (as machinery) with gearing **b** : to connect by gearing **c** : to put into gear **2 a** : to make ready for effective operation **b** : to adjust so as to match, blend with, or satisfy something ⟨an institution ~*ed* to the needs of the blind⟩ ~ *vi* **1** *of machinery* : to be in or come into gear **2** : to become adjusted so as to match, blend, or harmonize

gear·box \'gi(ə)r-ˌbäks\ *n* (1902) **1** : TRANSMISSION 3 **2** : GEARING 2

gear·ing \'gi(ə)r-iŋ\ *n* (1833) **1** : the act or process of providing or fitting with gears **2** : the parts by which motion is transmitted from one portion of machinery to another; *esp* : a train of gear wheels

gear·shift \'gi(ə)r-ˌshift\ *n* (1904) : a mechanism by which the transmission gears in a power-transmission system are engaged and disengaged

gear wheel *n* (ca. 1874) : a toothed wheel that gears with another piece of a mechanism; *specif* : COGWHEEL

Geat \'gēt, 'gā-ət, 'yaət\ *n* [OE *Gēat*] (bef. 12c) : a member of a Scandinavian people of southern Sweden subjugated by the Swedes in the 6th century — **Geat·ish** \-ish\ *adj*

gecko \'gek-(ˌ)ō\ *n, pl* **geck·os** *or* **geck·oes** [Malay *ge'kok*, of imit. origin] (1711) : any of numerous small harmless chiefly tropical and nocturnal insectivorous lizards (family Gekkonidae)

[1]**gee** \'jē\ *vb imper* [origin unknown] (1628) — used as a direction to turn to the right or move ahead; compare [5]HAW ~ *vi* **geed; gee·ing** : to turn to the right side

[2]**gee** *interj* [euphemism for *Jesus*] (1895) — used as an introductory expletive or to express surprise or enthusiasm

[3]**gee** *n* (1926) **1** : the letter *g* **2** [*grand*] *slang* : a thousand dollars

gee·gaw \'jē-(ˌ)gȯ, 'gē-\ *var of* GEWGAW

geek \'gēk\ *n* [prob. fr. E dial. *geek*, *geck* fool, fr. LG *geck*, fr. MLG] (ca. 1942) : a carnival performer often billed as a wild man whose act usu. includes biting the head off a live chicken or snake

geese *pl of* GOOSE

geest \'gāst, 'gēst\ *n* [G] (ca. 1828) **1** : alluvial matter not of recent origin on the surface of land **2** : loose material (as earth or soil) formed by decay of rocks in a place

gee–whiz \(')jē-'(h)wiz\ *adj* (ca. 1934) **1** : designed to arouse wonder or excitement or to amplify the merits or significance of something esp. by the use of clever or sensational language ⟨play-by-play specialists who wallow in ~ banality — Jack Gould⟩ **2** : marked by spectacular or astonishing qualities or achievement ⟨some people still look upon atom power as in the ~ stage —*Kiplinger Washington Letter*⟩ **3** : characterized by wide-eyed enthusiasm, excitement, and wonder

gee whiz *interj* (1885) : [2]GEE

Ge·ez \gē-'ez\ *n* [Ethiopic *ge'ez*] (1790) : ETHIOPIC 1

gee·zer \'gē-zər\ *n* [prob. alter. of Sc *guiser* (one in disguise)] (1885) : a queer, odd, or eccentric man

ge·fil·te fish \gə-'fil-tə-\ *n* [Yiddish, lit., filled fish] (1892) : balls or cakes of seasoned minced fish simmered in a fish stock or baked in a tomato sauce

ge·gen·schein \'gā-gən-ˌshīn\ *n, often cap* [G, fr. *gegen* against, counter- + *schein* shine] (1880) : a faint light about 20° across on the celestial sphere opposite the sun probably associated in origin with the zodiacal light

Ge·hen·na \gi-'hen-ə\ *n* [LL, fr. Gk *Geenna*, fr. Heb *Gê' Hinnōm*, lit., valley of Hinnom] (1594) **1** : a place or state of misery **2** : HELL 1a(2)

Gei·ger counter \'gī-gər-\ *or* **Geiger–Mül·ler counter** \-'myül-ər-, -'mil-, -'məl-\ *n* [Hans *Geiger* †1945 Ger. physicist & W. *Müller*, 20th cent. Ger. physicist] (1924) : an instrument for detecting the presence and intensity of radiations (as cosmic rays or particles from a radioactive substance) by means of the ionizing effect on an enclosed gas which results in a pulse that is amplified and fed to a device giving a visible or audible indication

gei·sha \'gā-shə, 'gē-\ *n, pl* **geisha** *or* **geishas** [Jp, fr. *gei* art + *-sha* person] (1887) : a Japanese girl who is trained to provide entertaining and lighthearted company esp. for a man or a group of men

[1]**gel** \'jel\ *n* [*gelatin*] (1899) **1** : a colloid in a more solid form than a sol **2** : JELLY 2 **3** : GELATIN 3

[2]**gel** *vi* **gelled; gel·ling** (1917) : to change into or take on the form of a gel — **gel·able** \'jel-ə-bəl\ *adj*

ge·län·de·läu·fer \gə-'len-də-ˌlȯi-fər\ *n* [G, fr. *gelände* (deriv. of OHG *lant* land) open fields + *läufer* runner, fr. *laufen* to run, fr. OHG *hloufan* — more at LAND, LEAP] (1933) : a skier making a cross-country run : LANGLAUFER

ge·län·de·sprung \-ˌs(h)prùŋ\ *n* [G, fr. *gelände* + *sprung* jump; akin to OHG *springan* to jump — more at SPRING] (1931) : a jump in skiing made from a low crouching position with the aid of both ski poles and usu. over an obstacle

gel·ate \'jel-ˌāt\ *vi* **gel·at·ed; gel·at·ing** (1915) : GEL

gel·a·tin *also* **gel·a·tine** \'jel-ət-ᵊn\ *n* [F *gélatine* edible jelly, gelatin, fr. It *gelatina*, fr. *gelato*, pp. of *gelare* to freeze, fr. L — more at COLD] (1800) **1** : glutinous material obtained from animal tissues by boiling; *esp* : a colloidal protein used as a food, in photography, and in medicine **2 a** : any of various substances (as agar) resembling gelatin **b** : an edible jelly made with gelatin **3** : a thin colored transparent sheet used over a stage light to color it

ge·la·ti·ni·za·tion \jə-ˌlat-ᵊn-ə-'zā-shən, ˌjel-ət-ᵊn-\ *n* (1843) : the process of converting into a gelatinous form or into a jelly — **ge·la·ti·nize** \jə-'lat-ᵊn-ˌīz, 'jel-ət-ᵊn-\ *vb*

ge·lat·i·nous \jə-'lat-nəs, -ᵊn-əs\ *adj* (ca. 1724) **1** : resembling gelatin or jelly : VISCOUS ⟨a ~ precipitate⟩ **2** : of, relating to, or containing gelatin — **ge·lat·i·nous·ly** *adv* — **ge·lat·i·nous·ness** *n*

[1]**ge·la·tion** \ji-'lā-shən\ *n* [L *gelation-*, *gelatio*, fr. *gelatus*, pp. of *gelare*] (1854) : the action or process of freezing

[2]**gel·ation** \je-'lā-shən\ *n* [[1]*gel* + *-ation*] (1902) : the formation of a gel from a sol

ge·la·to \jel-'ä-(ˌ)tō\ *n, pl* **-ti** \-tē\ *also* **-tos** [It, lit., frozen] (1929) : a soft rich ice cream containing little or no air

[1]**geld** \'geld\ *n* [OE *gield*, *geld* service, tribute; akin to OE *gieldan* to pay, yield — more at YIELD] (bef. 12c) : the crown tax paid under Anglo-Saxon and Norman kings

[2]**geld** *vt* [ME *gelden*, fr. ON *gelda*; akin to OE *gelte* young sow, Gk *gallos* eunuch, priest of Cybele] (14c) **1** : CASTRATE **2** : to deprive of a natural or essential part ⟨sick of workingmen being ~*ed* of their natural expression . . . A workingman bereft of his profanity is a silent man — *Atlantic*⟩

geld·ing \'gel-diŋ\ *n* [ME, fr. ON *geldingr*, fr. *gelda*] (14c) **1** : a castrated animal; *specif* : a castrated male horse **2** *archaic* : EUNUCH

ge·lée \zhə-'lā\ *n* [F, jelly, fr. MF — more at JELLY] (1966) : a cosmetic gel

gel·id \'jel-əd\ *adj* [L *gelidus*, fr. *gelu* frost, cold — more at COLD] (1599) : extremely cold : ICY ⟨~ water⟩ ⟨a man of ~ reserve — *New Yorker*⟩ — **ge·lid·i·ty** \jə-'lid-ət-ē, je-\ *n* — **gel·id·ly** \'jel-əd-lē\ *adv*

gel·ig·nite \'jel-ig-ˌnīt\ *n* [*gelatin* + L *ignis* fire + E *-ite* — more at IGNITE] (1889) : a dynamite in which the adsorbent base is largely potassium nitrate or a similar nitrate usu. with some wood pulp

gel·lant *also* **gel·ant** \'jel-ənt\ *n* (1956) : a substance used to produce gelling

gelt \'gelt\ *n* [D & G *geld* & Yiddish *gelt*; all akin to OE *geld* [1]geld] *slang* (1529) : MONEY

[1]**gem** \'jem\ *n* [ME *gemme*, fr. MF, fr. L *gemma* bud, gem] (bef. 12c) **1 a** : JEWEL **b** : a precious or sometimes semiprecious stone cut and polished for ornament **2 a** : something prized esp. for great beauty or perfection **b** : a highly prized or well-beloved person **3** : MUFFIN

[2]**gem** *vt* **gemmed; gem·ming** (1610) : to adorn with or as if with gems

gem- \(')jem\ *comb form* : geminal ⟨gemdichloride⟩

Ge·ma·ra \gə-'mär-ə, -'mȯr-\ *n* [Aram *gĕmārā* completion] (1613) : a commentary on the Mishnah forming the second part of the Talmud — **Ge·ma·ric** \-ik\ *adj* — **Ge·ma·rist** \-əst\ *n*

ge·mein·schaft \gə-'mīn-ˌshäft\ *n* [G, community, fr. *gemein* common, general (fr. OHG *gimeini*) + *-schaft* -ship — more at MEAN] (1937) : a spontaneously arising organic social relationship characterized by strong reciprocal bonds of sentiment and kinship within a common tradition; *also* : a community or society characterized by this relationship — compare GESELLSCHAFT

gem·i·nal \'jem-ən-ᵊl\ *adj* [L *geminus* twin] (1967) : relating to or characterized by two usu. similar substituents on the same atom — **gem·i·nal·ly** \-ᵊl-ē\ *adv*

[1]**gem·i·nate** \'jem-ə-nət, -ˌnāt\ *adj* [L *geminatus*, pp. of *geminare* to double, fr. *geminus* twin] (15c) : arranged in pairs : DUPLICATE

[2]**gem·i·nate** \-ˌnāt\ *vb* **-nat·ed; -nat·ing** *vt* (1637) : DOUBLE ~ *vi* : to become double or paired — **gem·i·na·tion** \ˌjem-ə-'nā-shən\ *n*

Gem·i·ni \'jem-ə-(ˌ)nē, -ˌnī; 'gem-ə-ˌnē\ *n pl but sing in constr* [L (gen. *Geminorum*), lit., the twins (Castor and Pollux)] **1** : the 3d zodiacal constellation pictorially represented as the twins Castor and Pollux sitting together and located on the opposite side of the Milky Way from Taurus and Orion **2 a** : the 3d sign of the zodiac in astrology — see ZODIAC table **b** : one born under this sign

gem·ma \'jem-ə\ *n, pl* **gem·mae** \-ˌē\ [L] (1770) : BUD; *broadly* : an asexual reproductive body that becomes detached from a parent plant

gem·ma·tion \je-'mā-shən\ *n* (1836) : reproduction by gemmae

gem·mule \'jem-(ˌ)yü(ə)l\ *n* [F, fr. L *gemmula*, dim. of *gemma*] (ca. 1841) : a small bud: **a** : a minute particle that in the theory of pangenesis mediates the production in a new individual of cells like that in which it originated **b** : an internal resistant reproductive bud (as of a sponge)

gem·my \'jem-ē\ *adj* (15c) **1** : having the characteristics desired in a gemstone **2** : BRIGHT, GLITTERING

gem·ol·o·gist *or* **gem·mol·o·gist** \je-'mäl-ə-jəst, jə-\ *n* (1931) : a specialist in gems; *specif* : one who appraises gems

gem·ol·o·gy *or* **gem·mol·o·gy** \-jē\ *n* [L *gemma* gem] (1811) : the science of gems — **gem·olog·i·cal** \ˌjem-ə-'läj-i-kəl\ *adj*

ge·mot *or* **ge·mote** \gə-'mōt, yə-\ *n* [OE *gemōt*, fr. *ge-* (perfective prefix) + *mōt* assembly — more at CO-, MOOT] (bef. 12c) : a judicial or legislative assembly in Anglo-Saxon England

gems·bok \'gemz-ˌbäk\ *n* [Afrik, lit., male chamois, fr. G *gemsbock*, fr. *gems* chamois + *bock* male goat, fr. OHG *boc* — more at BUCK] (1777) : a large and strikingly marked oryx (*Oryx gazella*) formerly abundant in southern Africa

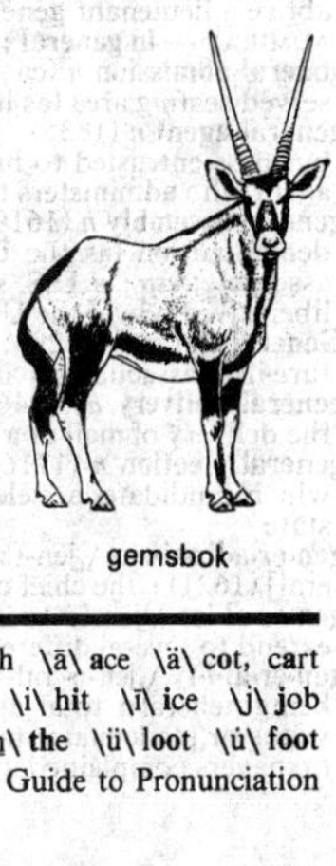

gemsbok

gem·stone \'jem-ˌstōn\ *n* (bef. 12c) **:** a mineral or petrified material that when cut and polished can be used in jewelry
ge·müt·lich \gə-'mu̅e̅t-lik̲, -'müt-lik\ *adj* [G, fr. MHG *gemüetlich* cheerful] (1852) **:** agreeably pleasant **:** COMFORTABLE
ge·müt·lich·keit \gə-'mu̅e̅t-lik̲-ˌkīt, -'müt-lik-\ *n* [G, fr. *gemütlich* + *-keit*, alter. of *-heit* -hood] (1892) **:** CORDIALITY, FRIENDLINESS
[1]**gen-** *or* **geno-** *comb form* [Gk *genos* birth, race, kind — more at KIN] **1 :** race ⟨*geno*cide⟩ **2 :** genus **:** kind ⟨*geno*type⟩
[2]**gen-** *or* **geno-** *comb form* **:** gene ⟨*geno*cline⟩
-gen \jən *also esp when two unstressed syllables precede* ˌjen\ *also* **-gene** \ˌjēn\ *n comb form* [F *-gène*, fr. Gk *-genēs* born; akin to Gk *genos* birth] **1 :** producer ⟨andro*gen*⟩ **2 :** one that is (so) produced ⟨culti*gen*⟩ ⟨phos*gene*⟩
gen·darme \'zhän-ˌdärm *also* 'jän-\ *n* [F, fr. MF, back-formation fr. *gensdarmes*, pl. of *gent d'armes*, lit., armed people] (1796) **1 :** one of a body of soldiers esp. in France serving as an armed police force for the maintenance of public order **2 :** POLICEMAN
gen·dar·mer·ie *or* **gen·dar·mery** \jän-'därm-ə-rē, zhän-\ *n, pl* **-mer·ies** [MF *gendarmerie*, fr. *gendarme*] (1792) **:** a body of gendarmes
[1]**gen·der** \'jen-dər\ *n* [ME *gendre*, fr. MF *genre*, *gendre*, fr. L *gener-*, *genus* birth, race, kind, gender — more at KIN] (14c) **1 :** SEX ⟨black divinities of the feminine ~ —Charles Dickens⟩ **2 a :** a subclass within a grammatical class (as noun, pronoun, adjective, or verb) of a language that is partly arbitrary but also partly based on distinguishable characteristics (as shape, social rank, manner of existence, or sex) and that determines agreement with and selection of other words or grammatical forms **b :** membership of a word or a grammatical form in such a subclass **c :** an inflectional form showing membership in such a subclass
[2]**gender** *vb* **gen·dered; gen·der·ing** \-d(ə-)riŋ\ [ME *gendren*, fr. MF *gendrer*, fr. L *generare* — more at GENERATE] (14c) **:** ENGENDER
gene \'jēn\ *n* [G *gen*, short for *pangen*, fr. *pan-* + *-gen*] (1911) **:** an element of the germ plasm having a specific function in inheritance that is determined by a specific sequence of purine and pyrimidine bases in DNA or sometimes in RNA and that serves to control the transmission of a hereditary character by specifying the structure of a particular protein or by controlling the function of other genetic material
ge·ne·al·o·gist \ˌjē-nē-'äl-ə-jəst, ˌjen-ē-, -'al-\ *n* (1605) **:** a person who traces or studies the descent of persons or families
ge·ne·al·o·gy \-jē\ *n, pl* **-gies** [ME *genealogie*, fr. MF, fr. LL *genealogia*, fr. Gk, fr. *genea* race, family + *-logia* -logy; akin to Gk *genos* race] (14c) **1 :** an account of the descent of a person, family, or group from an ancestor or from older forms **2 :** regular descent of a person, family, or group of organisms from a progenitor or older form **:** PEDIGREE **3 :** the study of family pedigrees — **ge·ne·a·log·i·cal** \ˌjē-nē-ə-'läj-i-kəl, ˌjen-ē-\ *adj* — **ge·ne·a·log·i·cal·ly** \-k(ə-)lē\ *adv*
gene conversion *n* (1955) **:** the production of gametes by a heterozygote esp. in fungi in unequal numbers and often in a 3:1 ratio that is thought to occur by selective copying during chromatid replication of one member of the gene pair in preference to the other
gene flow *n* (1947) **:** the passage and establishment of genes typical of one breeding population into the gene pool of another by hybridization and backcrossing
gene frequency *n* (1930) **:** the frequency of occurrence of a specified gene in a population compared to its alleles
gene mutation *n* (1928) **:** POINT MUTATION
gene pool *n* (1946) **:** the collection of genes in an interbreeding population that includes each gene at a certain frequency in relation to its alleles
genera *pl of* GENUS
gen·er·a·ble \'jen-(ə-)rə-bəl\ *adj* (14c) **:** capable of being generated
[1]**gen·er·al** \'jen-(ə-)rəl\ *adj* [ME, fr. MF, fr. L *generalis*, fr. *gener-*, *genus* kind, class — more at KIN] (14c) **1 :** involving, applicable to, or affecting the whole **2 :** involving, relating to, or applicable to every member of a class, kind, or group ⟨the ~ equation of a straight line⟩ **3 a :** applicable to or characteristic of the majority of individuals involved **:** PREVALENT **b :** concerned or dealing with universal rather than particular aspects **4 :** relating to, determined by, or concerned with main elements rather than limited details ⟨bearing a ~ resemblance to the original⟩ **5 :** not confined by specialization or careful limitation **6 :** belonging to the common nature of a group of like individuals **:** GENERIC **7 :** holding superior rank or taking precedence over others similarly titled ⟨the ~ manager⟩ ⟨~ secretary⟩ ***syn*** see UNIVERSAL
[2]**general** *n* (14c) **1 :** something (as a concept, principle, or statement) that involves or is applicable to the whole **2** *archaic* **:** the general public **:** PEOPLE **3 :** SUPERIOR GENERAL **4 a :** GENERAL OFFICER **b :** a commissioned officer in the army, air force, or marine corps who ranks above a lieutenant general and whose insignia is four stars — compare ADMIRAL — **in general :** for the most part **:** GENERALLY
general admission *n* (ca. 1949) **:** a fee paid for admission to a usu. unreserved seating area (as in an auditorium or stadium)
general agent *n* (1835) **1 :** one employed to transact generally all legal business entrusted to him by his principal **2 :** an insurance company agent who administers the company's business within a specified area
general assembly *n* (1619) **1 :** the highest governing body in a religious denomination (as the United Presbyterian Church) **2 :** a legislative assembly; *esp* **:** a U.S. state legislature **3** *cap G&A* **:** the supreme deliberative body of the United Nations
General Court *n* (1629) **:** a legislative assembly; *specif* **:** the state legislature in Massachusetts and New Hampshire
general delivery *n* (1846) **:** a department of a post office that handles the delivery of mail at a post office window to persons who call for it
general election *n* (1716) **:** an election usu. held at regular intervals in which candidates are elected in all or most constituencies of a nation or state
gen·er·a·lis·si·mo \ˌjen-(ə-)rə-'lis-ə-ˌmō\ *n, pl* **-mos** [It, fr. *generale* general] (1621) **:** the chief commander of an army **:** COMMANDER IN CHIEF
gen·er·al·ist \'jen-(ə-)rə-ləst\ *n* (1611) **:** one whose skills or interests extend to several different fields
gen·er·al·i·ty \ˌjen-ə-'ral-ət-ē\ *n, pl* **-ties** (15c) **1 :** the quality or state of being general **:** total applicability **2 a :** GENERALIZATION 2 **b :** a vague or inadequate statement **3 :** the greatest part **:** BULK ⟨the ~ of taxpayers complained about the increase⟩
gen·er·al·iza·tion \ˌjen-(ə-)rə-lə-'zā-shən\ *n* (1761) **1 :** the act or process of generalizing **2 :** a general statement, law, principle, or proposition **3 :** the act or process whereby a response is made to a stimulus similar to but not identical with a reference stimulus
gen·er·al·ize \'jen-(ə-)rə-ˌlīz\ *vb* **-ized; -iz·ing** *vt* (1751) **1 :** to give a general form to **2 a :** to derive or induce (a general conception or principle) from particulars **b :** to draw a general conclusion from **3 :** to give general applicability to ⟨~ a law⟩; *also* **:** to make indefinite ~ *vi* **1 :** to form generalizations; *also* **:** to make vague or indefinite statements **2 :** to spread or extend throughout the body — **gen·er·al·iz·able** \-ˌlī-zə-bəl\ *adj* — **gen·er·al·iz·er** *n*
gen·er·al·ized *adj* (1842) **:** made general; *esp* **:** not highly differentiated biologically nor strictly adapted to a particular environment
gen·er·al·ly \'jen-(ə-)rə-lē, 'jen-ər-lē\ *adv* (14c) **:** in a general manner: as **a :** in disregard of specific instances and with regard to an overall picture ⟨~ speaking⟩ **b :** as a rule **:** USUALLY
general officer *n* (1681) **:** any of the officers in the army, air force, or marine corps above colonel — compare COMPANY OFFICER, FIELD OFFICER
general of the air force (1949) **:** a general of the highest rank in the air force whose insignia is five stars
general of the army (1945) **:** a general of the highest rank in the army whose insignia is five stars
general paresis *n* (1874) **:** insanity caused by syphilitic alteration of the brain that leads to dementia and paralysis — called also *general paralysis of the insane*
general practitioner *n* (ca. 1885) **:** a physician or veterinarian who does not limit his practice to a specialty; *broadly* **:** GENERALIST
general–purpose *adj* (1894) **:** suitable to be used for two or more basic purposes
general semantics *n pl but sing or pl in constr* (1933) **:** a doctrine and educational discipline intended to improve habits of response of human beings to their environment and one another esp. by training in the more critical use of words and other symbols
gen·er·al·ship \'jen-(ə-)rəl-ˌship\ *n* (1610) **1 :** office or tenure of office of a general **2 :** military skill in a high commander **3 :** LEADERSHIP
general store *n* (1835) **:** a retail store located usu. in a small or rural community that carries a wide variety of goods including groceries but is not divided into departments
general theory of relativity (ca. 1934) **:** RELATIVITY 3b
general will *n* (ca. 1902) **:** the collective will of a community that is the embodiment or expression of its common interest
gen·er·ate \'jen-ə-ˌrāt\ *vt* **-at·ed; -at·ing** [L *generatus*, pp. of *generare*, fr. *gener-*, *genus* birth — more at KIN] (1509) **1 :** to bring into existence: as **a :** PROCREATE, BEGET **b :** to originate by a vital, chemical, or physical process **:** PRODUCE ⟨~ electricity⟩ **2 :** to define or originate (as a mathematical or linguistic set or structure) by the application of one or more rules or operations to given quantities; *esp* **:** to trace out (as a curve) by a moving point or trace out (as a surface) by a moving curve **3 :** to be the cause of (a situation, action, or state of mind) ⟨these stories . . . ~ a good deal of psychological suspense —*Atlantic*⟩
gen·er·a·tion \ˌjen-ə-'rā-shən\ *n* (14c) **1 a :** a body of living beings constituting a single step in the line of descent from an ancestor **b :** a group of individuals born and living contemporaneously **c :** a group of individuals having contemporaneously a status (as that of students in a school) which each one holds only for a limited period **d :** a type or class of objects usu. developed from an earlier type ⟨first of the . . . new ~ of powerful supersonic fighters — Kenneth Koyen⟩ **2 :** the average span of time between the birth of parents and that of their offspring **3 a :** the action or process of producing offspring **:** PROCREATION **b :** origination by a mathematical, chemical, or other process **:** PRODUCTION; *specif* **:** formation of a geometric figure by motion of another **c :** the process of coming or bringing into being ⟨~ of income⟩ — **gen·er·a·tion·al** \-shnəl, -shən-ᵊl\ *adj*
gen·er·a·tive \'jen-ə-ˌrāt-iv, -(ə-)rət-\ *adj* (14c) **:** having the power or function of generating, originating, producing, or reproducing
generative cell *n* (ca. 1892) **:** a sexual reproductive cell **:** GAMETE
generative grammar *n* (1959) **1 :** a description in the form of an ordered set of rules for producing the grammatical sentences of a language **2 :** TRANSFORMATIONAL GRAMMAR
generative nucleus *n* (ca. 1892) **:** the one of the two nuclei resulting from the first division in the pollen grain of a seed plant that gives rise to sperm nuclei — compare TUBE NUCLEUS
gen·er·a·tor \'jen-ə-ˌrāt-ər\ *n* (1646) **1 :** one that generates **2 :** an apparatus in which vapor or gas is formed **3 :** a machine by which mechanical energy is changed into electrical energy **4 :** a mathematical entity that when subjected to one or more operations yields another mathematical entity or its elements; *specif* **:** GENERATRIX
gen·er·a·trix \ˌjen-ə-'rā-triks\ *n, pl* **-er·a·tri·ces** \-trə-ˌsēz, -ə-rə-'trī-(ˌ)sēz\ (1840) **:** a point, line, or surface whose motion generates a line, surface, or solid
[1]**ge·ner·ic** \jə-'ner-ik\ *adj* [F *générique*, fr. L *gener-*, *genus* birth, kind, class] (1676) **1 a :** relating to or characteristic of a whole group or class **:** GENERAL **b :** being or having a nonproprietary name **2 :** relating to or having the rank of a biological genus ***syn*** see UNIVERSAL — **ge·ner·i·cal·ly** \-i-k(ə-)lē\ *adv* — **ge·ner·ic·ness** *n*
[2]**generic** *n* (1967) **:** a generic product (as a drug)
gen·er·os·i·ty \ˌjen-ə-'räs-ət-ē, -'räs-tē\ *n, pl* **-ties** (1623) **1 a :** liberality in spirit or act; *esp* **:** liberality in giving **b :** a generous act **2 :** ABUNDANCE
gen·er·ous \'jen-(ə-)rəs\ *adj* [MF or L; MF *genereus*, fr. L *generosus*, fr. *gener-*, *genus*] (1588) **1** *archaic* **:** HIGHBORN **2 a :** characterized by a noble or forbearing spirit **:** MAGNANIMOUS, KINDLY **b :** liberal in giving **:** OPENHANDED **c :** marked by abundance or ample proportions **:** COPIOUS **d :** full-flavored ⟨~ wine⟩ ***syn*** see LIBERAL — **gen·er·ous·ly** *adv* — **gen·er·ous·ness** *n*
gen·e·sis \'jen-ə-səs\ *n, pl* **-e·ses** \-ˌsēz\ [L, fr. Gk, fr. *gignesthai* to be born — more at KIN] (ca. 1604) **:** the origin or coming into being of something
Genesis *n* [Gk] **:** the mainly narrative first book of canonical Jewish and Christian Scriptures — see BIBLE table
gene–splic·ing \'jēn-'splī-siŋ\ *n* (ca. 1978) **:** the technique by which recombinant DNA is produced and made to function in an organism

gen·et \ˈjen-ət\ *n* [ME *genete,* fr. MF, fr. Ar *jarnayt*] (15c) **:** any of several small Old World carnivorous mammals (genus *Genetta*) related to the civets but with scent glands less developed and claws fully retractile
ge·net·ic \jə-ˈnet-ik\ *also* **ge·net·i·cal** \-i-kəl\ *adj* [*genesis*] (1831) **1 :** relating to or determined by the origin, development, or causal antecedents of something **2 a :** of, relating to, or involving genetics **b :** of, relating to, or being a gene — **ge·net·i·cal·ly** \-i-k(ə-)lē\ *adv*
-ge·net·ic \jə-ˈnet-ik\ *adj comb form* **:** -GENIC 1, 2 ⟨psycho*genetic*⟩ ⟨spermato*genetic*⟩
genetic code *n* (1961) **:** the biochemical basis of heredity consisting of codons in DNA and RNA that determine the specific amino acid sequence in proteins and that are uniform for the forms of life studied so far
genetic drift *n* (1945) **:** changes of gene frequency in small populations due to chance preservation or extinction of particular genes
genetic engineering *n* (1966) **:** the directed alteration of genetic material by intervention in genetic processes; *esp* **:** GENE-SPLICING — **genetic engineer** *n*
genetic map *n* (ca. 1960) **:** MAP 3
genetic marker *n* (1950) **:** a usu. dominant gene or trait that serves esp. to identify genes or traits linked with it
ge·net·ics \jə-ˈnet-iks\ *n pl but sing in constr* (1905) **1 a :** a branch of biology that deals with the heredity and variation of organisms **b :** a treatise or textbook on genetics **2 :** the genetic makeup and phenomena of an organism, type, group, or condition — **ge·net·i·cist** \-ˈnet-ə-səst\ *n*
ge·ne·va \jə-ˈnē-və\ *n* [modif. of obs. D *genever* (now *jenever*), lit., juniper, deriv. of L *juniperus*] (1706) **:** a highly aromatic bitter gin orig. made in the Netherlands
Ge·ne·va bands \jə-ˌnē-və-\ *n pl* [*Geneva,* Switzerland; fr. their use by the Calvinist clergy of Geneva] (1882) **:** two strips of white cloth suspended from the front of a clerical collar and sometimes used by Protestant clergymen — called also *Geneva tabs*
Geneva convention *n* (1880) **:** one of a series of agreements concerning the treatment of prisoners of war and of the sick, wounded, and dead in battle first made at Geneva, Switzerland in 1864 and subsequently accepted in later revisions by most nations
Geneva cross *n* [fr. its adoption by the Geneva convention] (ca. 1889) **:** RED CROSS
Geneva gown *n* [fr. its use by the Calvinist clergy of Geneva] (1820) **:** a loose large-sleeved black academic gown widely used as a vestment by members of the Protestant clergy
Ge·ne·van \jə-ˈnē-vən\ *adj* (1573) **1 :** of or relating to Geneva, Switzerland **2 :** of or relating to Geneva about the time of the beginning of the Reformation; *specif* **:** of or relating to Calvinism — **Genevan** *n*
¹ge·nial \ˈjēn-yəl\ *adj* [L *genialis,* fr. *genius*] (1566) **1** *obs* **:** of or relating to marriage or generation ⟨the ~ bed —John Milton⟩ **2 a :** favorable to growth or comfort **:** MILD ⟨~ sunshine⟩ **b :** marked by or diffusing sympathy or friendliness **:** KINDLY **3** *obs* **:** INBORN, NATIVE **4 :** displaying or marked by genius *syn* see GRACIOUS — **ge·nial·i·ty** \ˌjē-nē-ˈal-ət-ē, jēn-ˈyal-\ *n* — **ge·nial·ly** \ˈjē-nyə-lē\ *adv*
²ge·ni·al \ji-ˈnī(-ə)l\ *adj* [Gk *geneion* chin, fr. *genys* jaw — more at CHIN] (1831) **:** of or relating to the chin
gen·ic \ˈjēn-ik, ˈjen-\ *adj* (1918) **:** GENETIC 2b — **gen·i·cal·ly** \-i-k(ə-)lē\ *adv*
-gen·ic \ˈjen-ik *sometimes* ˈjē-nik\ *adj comb form* [ISV *-gen* & *-geny* + *-ic*] **1 :** producing **:** forming ⟨ero*genic*⟩ **2 :** produced by **:** formed from ⟨phyto*genic*⟩ **3** [*photogenic*] **:** suitable for production or reproduction by (such) a medium ⟨tele*genic*⟩
ge·nic·u·late \jə-ˈnik-yə-lət\ *or* **ge·nic·u·lat·ed** \-ˌlāt-əd\ *adj* [L *geniculatus,* fr. *geniculum,* dim. of *genu* knee — more at KNEE] (1657) **:** bent abruptly at an angle like a bent knee
ge·nie \ˈjē-nē *sometimes* ˈjen-ē\ *n, pl* **ge·nies** *also* **ge·nii** \ˈjē-nē(-ˌī)\ [F *génie,* fr. Ar *jinnīy*] (1748) **:** JINNI
gen·i·tal \ˈjen-ə-tᵊl\ *adj* [ME, fr. L *genitalis,* fr. *genitus,* pp. of *gignere* to beget — more at KIN] (14c) **1 :** GENERATIVE **2 :** of, relating to, or being a sexual organ **3 :** of, relating to, or characterized by the stage of psychosexual development in which oral and anal impulses are subordinated to adaptive interpersonal mechanisms — **gen·i·tal·ly** \-tə-lē\ *adv*
gen·i·ta·lia \ˌjen-ə-ˈtāl-yə\ *n pl* [L, fr. neut. pl. of *genitalis*] (1876) **:** the organs of the reproductive system; *esp* **:** the external genital organs — **gen·i·ta·lic** \-ˈtal-ik, -ˈtāl-\ *adj*
gen·i·tals \ˈjen-ə-tᵊlz\ *n pl* (14c) **:** GENITALIA
gen·i·ti·val \ˌjen-ə-ˈtī-vəl\ *adj* (1818) **:** of, relating to, or formed with or from the genitive case — **gen·i·ti·val·ly** \-və-lē\ *adv*
gen·i·tive \ˈjen-ət-iv\ *adj* [ME, fr. L *genetivus, genitivus,* lit., of generation (erroneous translation of Gk *genikos* genitive), fr. *genitus*] (14c) **1 :** of, relating to, or constituting a grammatical case marking typically a relationship of possessor or source — compare POSSESSIVE **2 :** not characterized by case inflection but nevertheless expressing a relationship that in some inflected languages is often marked by a genitive case — used esp. of English prepositional phrases introduced by *of* — **genitive** *n*
genito- *comb form* [*genital*] **:** genital and ⟨*genito*urinary⟩
gen·i·to·uri·nary \ˌjen-ə-tō-ˈyu̇r-ə-ˌner-ē\ *adj* (1835) **:** of or relating to the genital and urinary organs or functions
gen·i·ture \ˈjen-ə-ˌchu̇(ə)r, -chər, -ˌt(y)u̇(ə)r\ *n* (1500) **:** NATIVITY, BIRTH
ge·nius \ˈjēn-yəs, ˈjē-nē-əs\ *n, pl* **ge·nius·es** *or* **ge·nii** \-nē-ˌī\ [L, tutelary spirit, fondness for social enjoyment, fr. *gignere* to beget] (14c) **1 a** *pl* **genii :** an attendant spirit of a person or place **b** *pl usu* **genii :** a person who influences another for good or bad **2 :** a strong leaning or inclination **:** PENCHANT **3 a :** a peculiar, distinctive, or identifying character or spirit **b :** the associations and traditions of a place **c :** a personification or embodiment esp. of a quality or condition **4** *pl usu* **genii :** SPIRIT, JINN **5** *pl usu* **geniuses a :** a single strongly marked capacity or aptitude ⟨had a ~ for getting along with boys — Mary Ross⟩ **b :** extraordinary intellectual power esp. as manifested in creative activity **c :** a person endowed with transcendent mental superiority; *specif* **:** a person with a very high intelligence quotient *syn* see GIFT
genius lo·ci \-ˈlō-ˌsī, -ˌkē\ *n* [L] (1771) **1 :** a tutelary deity of a place **2 :** the pervading spirit of a place
geno- — see GEN-
geno·cide \ˈjen-ə-ˌsīd\ *n* (1944) **:** the deliberate and systematic destruction of a racial, political, or cultural group — **geno·cid·al** \ˌjen-ə-ˈsīd-ᵊl\ *adj*
ge·nome \ˈjē-ˌnōm\ *n* [G *genom,* fr. *gen-* ²gen- + chromosom chromosome] (1930) **:** one haploid set of chromosomes with the genes they contain — **ge·no·mic** \ji-ˈnō-mik, -ˈnäm-ik\ *adj*
ge·no·type \ˈjē-nə-ˌtīp, ˈjen-ə-\ *n* (1897) **1** [¹*gen-*] **:** TYPE SPECIES **2** [²*gen-*] **:** all or part of the genetic constitution of an individual or group — compare PHENOTYPE — **ge·no·typ·ic** \ˌjē-nə-ˈtip-ik, ˌjen-ə-\ *also* **ge·no·typ·i·cal** \-i-kəl\ *adj* — **ge·no·typ·i·cal·ly** \-i-k(ə-)lē\ *adv*
-g·e·nous \j-ə-nəs\ *adj comb form* [*-gen* + *-ous*] **1 :** producing **:** yielding ⟨pyro*genous*⟩ **2 :** having (such) an origin ⟨hypo*genous*⟩
genre \ˈzhäⁿ-rə, ˈzhäⁿ-, ˈzhäⁿ-; ˈzhäⁿr; ˈjän-rə\ *n* [F, fr. MF *genre* kind, gender — more at GENDER] (1816) **1 :** KIND, SORT **2 :** a category of artistic, musical, or literary composition characterized by a particular style, form, or content **3 :** painting that depicts scenes or events from everyday life usu. realistically
gen·ro \ˈgen-ˈrō\ *n pl, often cap* [Jp *genrō*] (1876) **:** the elder statesmen of Japan who formerly advised the emperor
gens \ˈjenz, ˈgen(t)s\ *n, pl* **gen·tes** \ˈjen-ˌtēz, ˈgen-ˌtās\ [L *gent-, gens* — more at GENTLE] (1847) **1 :** a Roman clan embracing the families of the same stock in the male line with the members having a common name and being united in worship of their common ancestor **2 :** CLAN; *esp* **:** a patrilineal clan **3 :** a distinguishable group of related organisms
¹gent \ˈjent\ *adj* [ME, noble, graceful, fr. OF, fr. L *genitus,* pp. of *gignere* to beget — more at KIN] *archaic* (13c) **:** PRETTY, GRACEFUL
²gent *n* (1564) **:** GENTLEMAN
gen·ta·mi·cin \ˌjent-ə-ˈmīs-ᵊn\ *n* [alter. of earlier *gentamycin,* fr. *genta-* (prob. irreg. fr. *gentian violet;* fr. the color of the organism from which it is produced) + *-mycin*] (1963) **:** a broad-spectrum antibiotic that is derived from an actinomycete (*Micromonospora purpurea* or *M. echinospora*) and is extensively used as the sulfate in treating infections esp. of the urinary tract
gen·teel \jen-ˈtē(ə)l\ *adj* [MF *gentil* gentle] (1599) **1 a :** having an aristocratic quality or flavor **:** STYLISH **b :** of or relating to the gentry or upper class **c :** elegant or graceful in manner, appearance, or shape **d :** free from vulgarity or rudeness **:** POLITE **2 a :** maintaining or striving to maintain the appearance of superior or middle-class social status or respectability **b (1) :** marked by false delicacy, prudery, or affectation **(2) :** conventionally or insipidly pretty ⟨timid and ~ artistic style⟩ — **gen·teel·ly** \-ˈtē(ə)l-lē\ *adv* — **gen·teel·ness** *n*
gen·teel·ism \-ˈtē(ə)l-ˌiz-əm\ *n* (1908) **:** a word believed by its user to be genteel (as *stomach* for *belly*)
gen·tian \ˈjen-chən\ *n* [ME *gencian,* fr. MF *gentiane,* fr. L *gentiana*] (14c) **1 :** any of two genera (*Gentiana* and *Dasystephana*) of herbs of a family (Gentianaceae, the gentian family) with opposite smooth leaves and showy usu. blue flowers **2 :** the rhizome and roots of a yellow-flowered gentian (*Gentiana lutea*) of southern Europe that is used as a tonic and stomachic
gentian violet *n, often cap G&V* (1897) **:** any of several dyes or dye mixtures consisting of one or more methyl derivatives of pararosaniline; *esp* **:** a dark green or greenish mixture used esp. as a bactericide, fungicide, and anthelmintic
¹gen·tile \ˈjen-ˌtīl\ *n* [ME, fr. LL *gentilis,* fr. L *gent-, gens* nation] (14c) **1** *often cap* **:** a person of a non-Jewish nation or of non-Jewish faith; *esp* **:** a Christian as distinguished from a Jew **2 :** HEATHEN, PAGAN **3** *often cap* **:** a non-Mormon
²gentile *adj* (15c) **1** *often cap* **a :** of or relating to the nations at large as distinguished from the Jews; *also* **:** of or relating to Christians as distinguished from the Jews **b :** of or relating to non-Mormons **2 :** HEATHEN, PAGAN **3** [L *gentilis*] **:** relating to a tribe or clan
gen·ti·lesse \ˌjent-ᵊl-ˈes\ *n* [ME, fr. MF, fr. *gentil*] *archaic* (14c) **:** decorum of conduct befitting a member of the gentry
gen·til·i·ty \jen-ˈtil-ət-ē\ *n, pl* **-ties** (14c) **1 a :** the condition of belonging to the gentry **b :** the members of the upper class **:** GENTRY **2 a (1) :** decorum of conduct **:** COURTESY **(2) :** attitudes or activity marked by false delicacy, prudery, or affectation **b (1) :** superior social status or prestige evidenced by manners, possessions, or mode of life **(2) :** the maintenance of the appearance of superior or middle-class social status esp. in the face of decayed prosperity
gen·tis·ic acid \jen-ˌtis-ik-, -ˌtiz-\ *n* [ISV, fr. *gentisin* (a pigment obtained from gentian root)] (1879) **:** a crystalline acid $C_7H_6O_4$ used medicinally as an analgesic and diaphoretic
¹gen·tle \ˈjent-ᵊl\ *adj* **gen·tler** \ˈjent-lər, -ᵊl-ər\; **gen·tlest** \ˈjent-ləst, -ᵊl-əst\ [ME *gentil,* fr. OF, fr. L *gentilis* of a clan, of the same clan, fr. *gent-, gens* clan, nation; akin to L *gignere* to beget — more at KIN] (13c) **1 a :** belonging to a family of high social station **b** *archaic* **:** CHIVALROUS **c :** HONORABLE, DISTINGUISHED; *specif* **:** of or relating to a gentleman **d :** KIND, AMIABLE — used esp. in address as a complimentary epithet ⟨~ reader⟩ **e :** suited to a person of high social station **2 a :** TRACTABLE, DOCILE **b :** free from harshness, sternness, or violence **3 :** SOFT, DELICATE ⟨heard a ~ knock on the door⟩ **4 :** MODERATE — **gent·ly** \ˈjent-lē\ *adv*
²gentle *n* (14c) **:** a person of gentle birth or status
³gentle *vt* **gen·tled; gen·tling** \ˈjent-liŋ, -ᵊl-iŋ\ (14c) **1 :** to raise from the commonalty **:** ENNOBLE **2 a :** to make gentler **b :** MOLLIFY, PLACATE **c :** to stroke soothingly **:** PET
gentle breeze *n* (ca. 1902) **:** wind having a speed of 8 to 12 miles per hour
gen·tle·folk \ˈjent-ᵊl-ˌfōk\ *also* **gen·tle·folks** \-ˌfōks\ *n pl* (1594) **:** persons of gentle or good family and breeding
gen·tle·man \ˈjen(t)-ᵊl-mən, *in rapid speech also* ˈjen(t)-ə-mən\ *n, often attrib* [ME *gentilman*] (13c) **1 a :** a man of noble or gentle birth **b :** a man belonging to the landed gentry **c (1) :** a man who combines gentle birth or rank with chivalrous qualities **(2) :** a man whose con

duct conforms to a high standard of propriety or correct behavior   **d** (1) : a man of independent means who does not engage in any occupation or profession for gain   (2) : a man who does not engage in a menial occupation or in manual labor for gain   **2** : VALET — often used in the phrase *gentleman's gentleman*   **3** : a man of any social class or condition — often used in a courteous reference ⟨show this ~ to a seat⟩ or usu. in the pl. in address ⟨ladies and *gentlemen*⟩ — **gen·tle·man·like** \-mən-ˌlīk\ *adj* — **gen·tle·man·like·ness** *n*

gentleman-at-arms *n, pl* **gentlemen-at-arms** (1859) : one of a military corps of 40 gentlemen who attend the British sovereign on state occasions

gentleman–commoner *n, pl* **gentlemen–commoners** (1687) : one of a privileged class of commoners formerly required to pay higher fees than ordinary commoners at the universities of Oxford and Cambridge

gentleman farmer *n, pl* **gentlemen farmers** (1749) : a man of superior social position and wealth who farms mainly for pleasure rather than for profit

gen·tle·man·ly \-lē\ *adj* (15c) : characteristic of or having the character of a gentleman — **gen·tle·man·li·ness** *n*

gentleman of fortune (1883) : ADVENTURER

gentleman's agreement *or* **gentlemen's agreement** *n* (1886) : an agreement secured only by the honor of the participants

gen·tle·ness \'jent-ᵊl-nəs\ *n* (14c) : the quality or state of being gentle; *esp* : mildness of manners or disposition

gen·tle·per·son \'jent-ᵊl-ˌpərs-ᵊn\ *n* (1975) : a gentleman or lady

gentle sex *n* (1583) : the female sex : women in general

gen·tle·wom·an \'jent-ᵊl-ˌwùm-ən\ *n* (13c) **1 a** : a woman of noble or gentle birth   **b** : a woman attendant upon a lady of rank   **2** : a woman of refined manners or good breeding : LADY

Gen·too \'jen-(ˌ)tü\ *n, pl* **Gentoos** [Pg *gentio,* lit., gentile, fr. LL *gentilis*] *archaic* (1638) : HINDU

gen·trice \'jen-trəs\ *n* [ME *gentrise,* fr. OF *genterise,* alter. of *gentelise,* fr. *gentil* gentle] *archaic* (13c) : gentility of birth : RANK

gen·tri·fi·ca·tion \ˌjen-trə-fə-'kā-shən\ *n* (1964) : the immigration of middle-class people into a deteriorating or recently renewed city area — **gen·tri·fy** \'jen-trə-ˌfī\ *vt*

gen·try \'jen-trē\ *n, pl* **gentries** [ME *gentrie,* alter. of *gentrise*] (14c) **1 a** *obs* : the qualities appropriate to a person of gentle birth; *esp* : COURTESY   **b** : the condition or rank of a gentleman   **2 a** : upper or ruling class : ARISTOCRACY   **b** : a class whose members are entitled to bear a coat of arms though not of noble rank; *esp* : the landed proprietors having such status   **3** : people of a specified class or kind : FOLKS ⟨no real heroes or heroines among the academic ~ —R. G. Hanvey⟩

gen·u·flect \'jen-yə-ˌflekt\ *vi* [LL *genuflectere,* fr. L *genu* knee + *flectere* to bend — more at KNEE] (1630) **1 a** : to bend the knee   **b** : to touch the knee to the floor or ground esp. in worship   **2** : to be servilely obedient or respectful : KOWTOW — **gen·u·flec·tion** \ˌjen-yə-'flek-shən\ *n*

gen·u·ine \'jen-yə-wən, -,(ˌ)win, ÷-,win\ *adj* [L *genuinus* native, genuine; akin to L *gignere* to beget — more at KIN] (1596) **1 a** : actually having the reputed or apparent qualities or character ⟨~ vintage wines⟩   **b** : actually produced by or proceeding from the alleged source or author ⟨the signature is ~⟩   **c** : sincerely and honestly felt or experienced ⟨a deep and ~ love⟩   **d** : ACTUAL, TRUE ⟨a ~ improvement⟩   **2** : free from

GEOLOGIC TIME AND FORMATIONS

ERAS	PERIODS AND SYSTEMS	EPOCHS AND SERIES	APPROXIMATE NO. OF YEARS AGO	EARLIEST RECORD OF	
				ANIMALS	PLANTS
Cenozoic	Quaternary	Holocene (Recent)			
		Pleistocene (Glacial)		mankind	
	Tertiary	Pliocene	70,000,000		
		Miocene			
		Oligocene			
		Eocene			
		Paleocene			
Mesozoic	Cretaceous	Upper		placental mammals	
		Lower			grasses and cereals flowering plants
	Jurassic		160,000,000	birds	
				mammals	
	Triassic				ginkgoes
Paleozoic	Permian		230,000,000		cycads and conifers
	Pennsylvanian			insects	
	Mississippian			reptiles	primitive gymnosperms
	Devonian		390,000,000	amphibians	vascular plants: lycopodiums, equisetums, ferns, etc.
	Silurian				
	Ordovician		500,000,000	fishes	mosses
	Cambrian		620,000,000		
Proterozoic	not divided into periods		1,420,000,000	invertebrates	spores of uncertain relationship marine algae
Archeozoic			3,800,000,000		

hypocrisy or pretense : SINCERE ***syn*** see AUTHENTIC — **gen·u·ine·ly** *adv* — **gen·u·ine·ness** \-wən-(n)əs\ *n*

usage The objection which some commentators make to the pronunciation \ˈjen-yə-ˌwīn\ is perhaps occasioned by the fact that it is more frequent among those with less schooling. However, this variant is heard in the speech of cultured or highly educated speakers sufficiently frequently for it to be recognized as a widespread pronunciation at all social levels. This variant was recorded as early as 1890 and appears to be simply a long-standing spelling pronunciation.

ge·nus \ˈjē-nəs, ˈjen-əs\ *n, pl* **gen·era** \ˈjen-ə-rə\ [L *gener-, genus* birth, race, kind — more at KIN] (1551) **1 :** a class, kind, or group marked by common characteristics or by one common characteristic; *specif* **:** a category of biological classification ranking between the family and the species, comprising structurally or phylogenetically related species or an isolated species exhibiting unusual differentiation, and being designated by a Latin or latinized capitalized singular noun **2 :** a class of objects divided into several subordinate species

-g·e·ny \j-ə-nē\ *n comb form* [Gk *-geneia* act of being born, fr. *-genēs* born — more at -GEN] **:** generation **:** production ⟨*biogeny*⟩

geo- — see GE-

geo·bot·a·ny \ˌjē-ō-ˈbät-ᵊn-ē, -ˈbät-nē\ *n* (1904) **:** PHYTOGEOGRAPHY — **geo·bo·tan·i·cal** \-bə-ˈtan-i-kəl\ *also* **geo·bo·tan·ic** \-ik\ *adj* — **geo·bot·a·nist** \-ˈbät-ᵊn-əst, -ˈbät-nəst\ *n*

geo·cen·tric \ˌjē-ō-ˈsen-trik\ *adj* (1686) **1 a :** relating to, measured from, or as if observed from the earth's center — compare TOPOCENTRIC **b :** having or relating to the earth as center — compare HELIOCENTRIC **2 :** taking or based on the earth as the center of perspective and valuation — **geo·cen·tri·cal·ly** \-tri-k(ə-)lē\ *adv*

geo·chem·is·try \ˌjē-ō-ˈkem-ə-strē\ *n* (ca. 1902) **1 :** a science that deals with the chemical composition of and chemical changes in the solid matter of the earth or a celestial body (as the moon) **2 :** the related chemical and geological properties of a substance — **geo·chem·i·cal** \-ˈkem-i-kəl\ *adj* — **geo·chem·i·cal·ly** \-k(ə-)lē\ *adv* — **geo·chem·ist** \-ˈkem-əst\ *n*

geo·chro·nol·o·gy \-krə-ˈnäl-ə-jē\ *n* (1893) **1 :** the chronology of the past as indicated by geologic data **2 :** the study of geochronology — **geo·chro·no·log·ic** \-ˌkrän-ᵊl-ˈäj-ik, -ˌkrōn-\ *or* **geo·chro·no·log·i·cal** \-i-kəl\ *adj* — **geo·chro·no·log·i·cal·ly** \-i-k(ə-)lē\ *adv* — **geo·chro·nol·o·gist** \-krə-ˈnäl-ə-jəst\ *n*

ge·ode \ˈjē-ˌōd\ *n* [L *geodes,* a gem, fr. Gk *geōdēs* earthlike, fr. *gē* earth] (1619) **1 :** a nodule of stone having a cavity lined with crystals or mineral matter **2 :** the cavity in a geode

[1]**geo·de·sic** \ˌjē-ə-ˈdes-ik, -ˈdēs-, -ˈdez-, -ˈdēz-\ *adj* (1821) **1 :** GEODETIC **2 :** made of light straight structural elements mostly in tension ⟨a ~ dome⟩

[2]**geodesic** *n* (1883) **:** the shortest line between two points that lies in a given surface

ge·od·e·sy \jē-ˈäd-ə-sē\ *n* [Gk *geōdaisia,* fr. *geō-* ge- + *daiesthai* to divide — more at TIDE] (1570) **:** a branch of applied mathematics concerned with the determination of the size and shape of the earth and the exact positions of points on its surface and with the description of variations of its gravity field — **ge·od·e·sist** \-ə-səst\ *n*

geo·det·ic \ˌjē-ə-ˈdet-ik\ *also* **geo·det·i·cal** \-i-kəl\ *adj* [*geodesy;* after such pairs as *heresy: heretic*] (ca. 1828) **1 :** of, relating to, or determined by geodesy **2 :** relating to the geometry of geodetic lines

geodetic line *n* (ca. 1864) **:** a geodesic on the earth's surface

geodetic survey *n* (1880) **:** a survey of a large land area in which corrections are made for the curvature of the earth's surface

Geo·dim·e·ter \ˌjē-ə-ˈdim-ət-ər\ *trademark* — used for an electronic-optical device that measures distance on the basis of the velocity of light

geo·duck \ˈgü-ē-ˌdək\ *n* [Chinook Jargon *go-duck*] (1883) **:** a large edible clam (*Panope generosa*) of the Pacific coast that sometimes weighs over five pounds

geo–eco·nom·ic \ˈjē-ō-ˌek-ə-ˈnäm-ik, -ˌē-kə-\ *adj* (1941) **:** of, relating to, or characterized by economic conditions or policies that are influenced by geographic factors and are international in scope

ge·og·ra·pher \jē-ˈäg-rə-fər\ *n* (1542) **:** a specialist in geography

geo·graph·ic \ˌjē-ə-ˈgraf-ik\ *or* **geo·graph·i·cal** \-i-kəl\ *adj* (1559) **1 :** of or relating to geography **2 :** belonging to or characteristic of a particular region — **geo·graph·i·cal·ly** \-i-k(ə-)lē\ *adv*

geographical mile *n* (1823) **:** NAUTICAL MILE a

ge·og·ra·phy \jē-ˈäg-rə-fē\ *n, pl* **-phies** [L *geographia,* fr. Gk *geōgraphia,* fr. *geōgraphein* to describe the earth's surface, fr. *geō-* + *graphein* to write — more at CARVE] (1542) **1 :** a science that deals with the earth and its life; *esp* **:** the description of land, sea, air, and the distribution of plant and animal life including man and his industries **2 :** the geographic features of an area **3 :** a treatise on geography **4 :** a delineation or systematic arrangement of constituent elements **:** CONFIGURATION ⟨the philosophers . . . have tried to construct *geographies* of human reason —*Times Lit. Supp.*⟩

geo·hy·drol·o·gy \ˌjē-ō-hī-ˈdräl-ə-jē\ *n* (ca. 1909) **:** a science that deals with the character, source, and mode of occurrence of underground water — **geo·hy·dro·log·ic** \-ˌhī-drə-ˈläj-ik\ *adj*

ge·oid \ˈjē-ˌȯid\ *n* [G, fr. Gk *geoeidēs* earthlike, fr. *gē*] (1881) **:** the surface within or around the earth that is everywhere normal to the direction of gravity and coincides with mean sea level in the oceans — **ge·oi·dal** \jē-ˈȯid-ᵊl\ *adj*

geo·log·ic \ˌjē-ə-ˈläj-ik\ *or* **geo·log·i·cal** \-i-kəl\ *adj* (1795) **:** of, relating to, or based on geology — **geo·log·i·cal·ly** \-i-k(ə-)lē\ *adv*

geologic time *n* (ca. 1909) **:** the long period of time occupied by the earth's geologic history

ge·ol·o·gize \jē-ˈäl-ə-ˌjīz\ *vi* **-gized; -giz·ing** (1831) **:** to study geology or make geologic investigations

ge·ol·o·gy \jē-ˈäl-ə-jē\ *n, pl* **-gies** [NL *geologia,* fr. *ge-* + *-logia* -logy] (1735) **1 a :** a science that deals with the history of the earth and its life esp. as recorded in rocks **b :** a study of the solid matter of a celestial body (as the moon) **2 :** geologic features **3 :** a treatise on geology — **ge·ol·o·gist** \-jəst\ *n*

geo·mag·net·ic \ˌjē-ō-mag-ˈnet-ik\ *adj* (ca. 1904) **:** of or relating to terrestrial magnetism — **geo·mag·net·i·cal·ly** \-i-k(ə-)lē\ *adv* — **geo·mag·ne·tism** \-ˈmag-nə-ˌtiz-əm\ *n*

geomagnetic storm *n* (1941) **:** MAGNETIC STORM

geo·man·cy \ˈjē-ə-ˌman(t)-sē\ *n* [ME *geomancie,* fr. MF, fr. ML *geomantia,* fr. LGk *geōmanteia,* fr. Gk *geō-* + *-manteia* -mancy] (14c) **:** divination by means of figures or lines or geographic features — **geo·man·cer** \-sər\ *n* — **geo·man·tic** \ˌjē-ə-ˈmant-ik\ *adj*

ge·om·e·ter \jē-ˈäm-ət-ər\ *n* (15c) **1 :** a specialist in geometry **2 :** GEOMETRID

geo·met·ric \ˌjē-ə-ˈme-trik\ *or* **geo·met·ri·cal** \-ˈme-tri-kəl\ *adj* (14c) **1 a :** of, relating to, or according to the methods or principles of geometry **b :** increasing in a geometric progression ⟨~ population growth⟩ **2** *cap* **:** of or relating to a style of ancient Greek pottery characterized by geometric decorative motifs **3 a :** utilizing rectilinear or simple curvilinear motifs or outlines in design **b :** of or relating to art based on simple geometric shapes (as straight lines, circles, or squares) ⟨~ abstractions⟩ — **geo·met·ri·cal·ly** \-tri-k(ə-)lē\ *adv*

ge·om·e·tri·cian \(ˌ)jē-ˌäm-ə-ˈtrish-ən, ˌjē-ə-mə-\ *n* (15c) **:** GEOMETER 1

geometric mean *n* (1901) **:** the nth root of the product of *n* numbers; *specif* **:** a number that is the second term of three consecutive terms of a geometric progression ⟨the *geometric mean* of 9 and 4 is 6⟩

geometric progression *also* **geometrical progression** *n* (ca. 1909) **:** a sequence (as 1, $1/2$, $1/4$) in which the ratio of a term to its predecessor is always the same — called also *geometric sequence*

geometric series *n* (ca. 1909) **:** a series (as $1 + x + x^2 + x^3 + \ldots$) whose terms form a geometric progression

geo·me·trid \jē-ˈäm-ə-trəd, ˌjē-ə-ˈme-trəd\ *n* [deriv. of Gk *geōmetrēs* geometer, fr. *geōmetrein*] (1876) **:** any of a family (Geometridae) of usu. medium-sized moths with large wings and larvae that are loopers — **geometrid** *adj*

ge·om·e·trize \jē-ˈäm-ə-ˌtrīz\ *vb* **-trized; -triz·ing** *vi* (1658) **:** to work by or as if by geometric methods or laws ~ *vt* **1 :** to represent geometrically **2 :** to make conform to geometric principles and laws — **ge·om·e·tri·za·tion** \-ˌäm-ə-trə-ˈzā-shən\ *n*

ge·om·e·try \jē-ˈäm-ə-trē\ *n, pl* **-tries** [ME *geometrie,* fr. MF, fr. L *geometria,* fr. Gk *geōmetria,* fr. *geōmetrein* to measure the earth, fr. *geō-* ge- + *metron* measure — more at MEASURE] (14c) **1 a :** a branch of mathematics that deals with the measurement, properties, and relationships of points, lines, angles, surfaces, and solids; *broadly* **:** the study of properties of given elements that remain invariant under specified transformations **b :** a particular type or system of geometry **c :** a treatise on geometry **2 a :** CONFIGURATION **b :** surface shape **3 :** an arrangement of objects or parts that suggests geometric figures

geo·mor·phic \ˌjē-ə-ˈmȯr-fik\ *adj* (1894) **:** of or relating to the form of the earth or a celestial body (as the moon) or its solid surface features

geo·mor·phol·o·gy \-mȯr-ˈfäl-ə-jē\ *n, pl* **-gies** [ISV] (1893) **1 :** a science that deals with the land and submarine relief features of the earth's surface or the comparable relief features of a celestial body (as the moon) and seeks a genetic interpretation of them **2 a :** the features dealt with in geomorphology **b :** a treatise on geomorphology — **geo·mor·pho·log·ic** \-ˌmȯr-fə-ˈläj-ik\ *or* **geo·mor·pho·log·i·cal** \-i-kəl\ *adj* — **geo·mor·pho·log·i·cal·ly** \-i-k(ə-)lē\ *adv* — **geo·mor·phol·o·gist** \-mȯr-ˈfäl-ə-jəst\ *n*

ge·oph·a·gy \jē-ˈäf-ə-jē\ *n* [ISV] (1850) **:** a practice of eating earthy substances (as clay) widespread among primitive or economically depressed peoples on a scanty or unbalanced diet — compare [1]PICA

geo·phone \ˈjē-ə-ˌfōn\ *n* (1919) **:** an instrument for detecting vibrations passing through rocks, soil, or ice

geo·phys·ics \ˌjē-ə-ˈfiz-iks\ *n pl but sing or pl in constr* [ISV] (ca. 1889) **:** the physics of the earth including the fields of meteorology, hydrology, oceanography, seismology, volcanology, magnetism, radioactivity, and geodesy — **geo·phys·i·cal** \-i-kəl\ *adj* — **geo·phys·i·cal·ly** \-i-k(ə-)lē\ *adv* — **geo·phys·i·cist** \-ˈfiz-(ə-)səst\ *n*

geo·phyte \ˈjē-ə-ˌfīt\ *n* (ca. 1900) **:** a perennial plant that bears its overwintering buds below the surface of the soil

geo·pol·i·ti·cian \ˌjē-ō-ˌpäl-ə-ˈtish-ən\ *n* (1941) **:** a specialist in geopolitics

geo·pol·i·tics \-ˈpäl-ə-ˌtiks\ *n pl but sing in constr* (1904) **1 :** a study of the influence of such factors as geography, economics, and demography on the politics and esp. the foreign policy of a state **2 :** a governmental policy guided by geopolitics **3 :** a combination of political and geographic factors relating to something (as a state or particular resources) — **geo·po·lit·i·cal** \-pə-ˈlit-i-kəl\ *adj* — **geo·po·lit·i·cal·ly** \-i-k(ə-)lē\ *adv*

geo·pres·sured \ˌjē-ō-ˈpresh-ərd\ *adj* (1968) **:** subjected to great pressure from geologic forces ⟨~ methane⟩

Geor·die \ˈjȯrd-ē\ *n* [Sc, dim. of the name *George*] *chiefly Brit* (1866) **:** an inhabitant of Newcastle-upon-Tyne or its environs; *also* **:** the dialect of English spoken by Geordies

George \ˈjȯ(ə)rj\ *n* [St. *George*] (1506) **1 :** either of two of the insignia of the British Order of the Garter **2 :** a British coin bearing the image of St. George

geor·gette \jȯr-ˈjet\ *n* [fr. *Georgette,* a trademark] (1915) **:** a thin strong clothing crepe of fibers woven from hard-twisted yarns to produce a dull pebbly surface

[1]**Geor·gian** \ˈjȯr-jən\ *n* (15c) **1 :** a native or inhabitant of Georgia in the Caucasus **2 :** the language of the Georgian people

[2]**Georgian** *adj* (1607) **:** of, relating to, or constituting Georgia in the Caucasus, the Georgians, or Georgian

[3]**Georgian** *n* (1741) **:** a native or resident of the state of Georgia

[4]**Georgian** *adj* (1762) **:** of, relating to, or characteristic of the state of Georgia or its people

[5]**Georgian** *adj* (1875) **1 :** of, relating to, or characteristic of the reigns of the first four Georges of Great Britain **2 :** of, relating to, or characteristic of the reign of George V of Great Britain

[6]**Georgian** *n* (1901) **1 :** one belonging to either of the Georgian periods **2 :** Georgian taste or style

Geor·gia pine \ˌjȯr-jə-\ *n* (1796) **:** LONGLEAF PINE

[1]**geor·gic** \ˈjȯr-jik\ *n* [the *Georgics,* poem by Vergil, fr. L *georgicus*] (1513) **:** a poem dealing with agriculture

---

\ə\ **abut** \ᵊ\ **kitten, F table** \ər\ **further** \a\ **ash** \ā\ **ace** \ä\ **cot, cart**
\au̇\ **out** \ch\ **chin** \e\ **bet** \ē\ **easy** \g\ **go** \i\ **hit** \ī\ **ice** \j\ **job**
\ŋ\ **sing** \ō\ **go** \ȯ\ **law** \ȯi\ **boy** \th\ **thin** \t͟h\ **the** \ü\ **loot** \u̇\ **foot**
\y\ **yet** \zh\ **vision** \à, k̲, ⁿ, œ, ᵫ, ue, ue̅, ʸ\ *see* **Guide to Pronunciation**

[2]**georgic** *adj* [L *georgicus,* fr. Gk *geōrgikos,* fr. *geōrgos* farmer, fr. *geō-* ge- + *ergon* work — more at WORK] (1711) : of or relating to agriculture

geo·sci·ence \ˌjē-ō-ˈsī-ən(t)s\ *n* (1942) **1** : the sciences (as geology, geophysics, and geochemistry) dealing with the earth **2** : any of the geosciences — **geo·sci·en·tist** \-ənt-əst\ *n*

geo·sta·tion·ary \-ˈstā-shə-ˌner-ē\ *adj* (1961) : of, relating to, or being an artificial satellite that travels above the equator and at the same speed as the earth rotates so that the satellite seems to remain in the same place

geo·strat·e·gy \-ˈstrat-ə-jē\ *n* (1942) **1** : a branch of geopolitics that deals with strategy **2** : the combination of geopolitical and strategic factors characterizing a particular geographic region **3** : the use by a government of strategy based on geopolitics — **geo·stra·te·gic** \-strə-ˈtē-jik\ *adj* — **geo·strat·e·gist** \-ˈstrat-ə-jəst\ *n*

geo·stroph·ic \ˌjē-ə-ˈsträf-ik\ *adj* [*ge-* + Gk *strophikos* turned, fr. *strophē* turning — more at STROPHE] (1916) : of, relating to, or arising from the deflective forces caused by the rotation of the earth — **geo·stroph·i·cal·ly** \-i-k(ə-)lē\ *adv*

geo·syn·chro·nous \ˌjē-ō-ˈsiŋ-krə-nəs, -ˈsin-\ *adj* (1969) : GEOSTATIONARY

geo·syn·cline \-ˈsin-ˌklīn\ *or* **geo·syn·cli·nal** \-sin-ˈklīn-ᵊl\ *n* (ca. 1879) : a great downward flexure of the earth's crust — compare GEANTICLINE — **geosynclinal** *adj*

geo·tac·tic \ˌjē-ō-ˈtak-tik\ *adj* (1899) : of or relating to geotaxis

geo·tax·is \-ˈtak-səs\ *n* [NL] (1899) : a taxis in which the force of gravity is the directive factor

geo·tec·ton·ic \-tek-ˈtän-ik\ *adj* (1882) : of or relating to the form, arrangement, and structure of rock masses of the earth's crust resulting from folding or faulting — **geo·tec·ton·i·cal·ly** \-i-k(ə-)lē\ *adv*

geo·ther·mal \-ˈthər-məl\ *also* **geo·ther·mic** \-mik\ *adj* [ISV] (1875) : of, relating to, or utilizing the heat of the earth's interior; *also* : produced or permeated by such heat ⟨~ steam⟩ ⟨~ region⟩ — **geo·ther·mal·ly** \-mə-lē\ *adv*

geo·tro·pic \ˌjē-ə-ˈtrō-pik, -ˈträp-ik\ *adj* (1875) : of or relating to geotropism — **geo·tro·pi·cal·ly** \-ˈtrō-pi-k(ə-)lē, -ˈträp-i-\ *adv*

ge·ot·ro·pism \jē-ˈä-trə-ˌpiz-əm\ *n* [ISV] (1875) : a tropism (as of plant roots) in which gravity is the orienting factor

ge·rah \ˈgir-ə\ *n* [Heb *gērāh,* lit., grain] (1534) : an ancient Hebrew unit of weight equal to 1/20 shekel

ge·ra·ni·ol \jə-ˈrā-nē-ˌȯl, -ˌōl\ *n* [ISV, fr. NL *Geranium*] (1871) : a fragrant liquid unsaturated alcohol $C_{10}H_{18}O$ used chiefly in perfumes and soap

ge·ra·ni·um \jə-ˈrā-nē-əm, -nyəm\ *n* [NL, fr. L, geranium, fr. Gk *geranion,* fr. dim. of *geranos* crane — more at CRANE] (1548) **1** : any of a widely distributed genus (*Geranium* of the family Geraniaceae, the geranium family) of plants having regular flowers without spurs and with glands that alternate with the petals **2** : PELARGONIUM **3** : a vivid or strong red

ge·rar·dia \jə-ˈrärd-ē-ə\ *n* [NL, fr. John *Gerard* †1612 Eng. botanist] (1851) : any of a genus (*Gerardia*) of often root-parasitic herbs of the figwort family having showy pink, purple, or yellow flowers

ger·bera \ˈgər-bə-rə, ˈjər-\ *n* [NL, fr. Traugott *Gerber* †1743 Ger. naturalist] (1889) : any of a genus (*Gerbera*) of Old World composite herbs having basal tufted leaves and showy heads of yellow, pink, or orange flowers with prominent rays

ger·bil *also* **ger·bille** \ˈjər-bəl\ *n* [F *gerbille,* fr. NL *Gerbillus,* dim. of *gerboa, jerboa* jerboa] (1849) : any of numerous Old World burrowing desert rodents (of *Gerbillus* and related genera) with long hind legs adapted for leaping

ge·rent \ˈjir-ənt\ *n* [L *gerent-, gerens* prp. of *gerere* to bear, carry on — more at CAST] (1576) : one that rules or manages

ge·re·nuk \ˈger-ə-ˌnu̇k, gə-ˈren-ək\ *n, pl* **gerenuk** *or* **gerenuks** [Somali *garanug*] (1895) : a large-eyed antelope (*Litocranius walleri*) of eastern Africa with a long neck and limbs

gerfalcon *var of* GYRFALCON

[1]**ge·ri·at·ric** \ˌjer-ē-ˈa-trik, ˌjir-\ *n* (1909) **1** *pl but sing in constr* : a branch of medicine that deals with the problems and diseases of old age and aging people — compare GERONTOLOGY **2** : an aged person

[2]**geriatric** *adj* [Gk *gēras* old age + E *-iatric* — more at CORN] (1926) : of or relating to geriatrics, the aged, or the process of aging

ger·i·a·tri·cian \ˌjer-ē-ə-ˈtrish-ən, ˌjir-\ *n* (1926) : a specialist in geriatrics

ge·ri·a·trist \ˌjer-ē-ˈa-trəst, ˌjir-; jə-ˈrī-ə-\ *n* (1928) : GERIATRICIAN

germ \ˈjərm\ *n* [F *germe,* fr. L *germin-, germen,* fr. *gignere* to beget — more at KIN] (1644) **1 a** : a small mass of living substance capable of developing into an organism or one of its parts **b** : the embryo with the scutellum of a cereal grain that is usu. separated from the starchy endosperm during milling **2** : something that serves as an origin : RUDIMENTS **3** : MICROORGANISM; *esp* : a microorganism causing disease

[1]**ger·man** \ˈjər-mən\ *adj* [ME *germain,* fr. MF, fr. L *germanus* having the same parents, irreg. fr. *germen*] (14c) : having the same parents or the same grandparents on either the maternal or paternal side — usu. used after the noun which it modifies and joined to it by a hyphen ⟨brother-german⟩ ⟨cousin-german⟩

[2]**german** *n, obs* (15c) : a near relative

[1]**Ger·man** \ˈjər-mən\ *n* [ML *Germanus,* fr. L, any member of the Germanic peoples] (14c) **1 a** : a native or inhabitant of Germany **b** : a person of German descent **c** : one whose native language is German and who is a native of a country other than Germany **2 a** : the Germanic language spoken mainly in Germany, Austria, and parts of Switzerland **b** : the literary and official language of Germany **3** *often not cap* **a** : a dance consisting of intricate figures that are improvised and intermingled with waltzes **b** *chiefly Midland* : a dancing party; *specif* : one at which the german is danced

[2]**German** *adj* (1552) : of, relating to, or characteristic of Germany, the Germans, or German

German cockroach *n* (1896) : a small active winged cockroach (*Blattella germanica*) prob. of African origin but now common in many urban buildings in the U.S. — called also *Croton bug*

ger·man·der \(ˌ)jər-ˈman-dər\ *n* [deriv. of Gk *chamaidrys,* fr. *chamai* on the ground + *drys* tree — more at HUMBLE, TREE] (15c) : any of a genus (*Teucrium*) of plants of the mint family with flowers having four exserted stamens, a short corolla tube, and a prominent lower lip

ger·mane \(ˌ)jər-ˈmān\ *adj* [ME *germain,* lit., having the same parents, fr. MF] (14c) **1** *obs* : closely akin **2** : being at once relevant and appropriate : FITTING ⟨omit details that are not ~ to the discussion⟩ ***syn*** see RELEVANT — **ger·mane·ly** *adv*

[1]**Ger·man·ic** \(ˌ)jər-ˈman-ik\ *adj* (1633) **1** : of, relating to, or characteristic of Germany, the Germans, or German **2** : of, relating to, or characteristic of the Germanic-speaking peoples **3** : of, relating to, or constituting Germanic

[2]**Germanic** *n* (1892) : a branch of the Indo-European language family containing English, German, Dutch, Afrikaans, Flemish, Frisian, the Scandinavian languages, and Gothic — see INDO-EUROPEAN LANGUAGES table

Ger·man·ism \ˈjər-mə-ˌniz-əm\ *n* (1611) **1** : a characteristic feature of German occurring in another language **2** : partiality for Germany or German customs **3** : the practices or objectives characteristic of the Germans

Ger·man·ist \-nəst\ *n* (1831) : a specialist in German or Germanic language, literature, or culture

ger·ma·ni·um \(ˌ)jər-ˈmā-nē-əm\ *n* [NL, fr. ML *Germania* Germany] (1886) : a grayish white hard brittle metalloid element that resembles silicon and is used as a semiconductor — see ELEMENT table

ger·man·ize \ˈjər-mə-ˌnīz\ *vb* **-ized; -iz·ing** *often cap, vt* (1598) **1** *archaic* : to translate into German **2** : to cause to acquire German characteristics ~ *vi* : to have or acquire German customs or leanings — **ger·man·iza·tion** \ˌjər-mə-nə-ˈzā-shən\ *n, often cap*

German measles *n pl but sing or pl in constr* (ca. 1875) : an acute contagious virus disease that is milder than typical measles but is damaging to the fetus when occurring early in pregnancy

Ger·mano- *comb form* **1** \(ˌ)jər-ˈman-ō, -ə\ : German ⟨*Germano*phile⟩ **2** \-ō\ : German and ⟨*Germano*-Russian⟩

[1]**Ger·mano·phile** \(ˌ)jər-ˈman-ə-ˌfīl\ *adj* (1898) : approving or favoring the German people and their institutions and customs

[2]**Germanophile** *n* (1898) : one that is Germanophile

German shepherd *n* (1934) : a working dog of a breed originating in northern Europe that is intelligent and responsive and is often used in police work and as a guide dog for the blind

German shorthaired pointer *n* (ca. 1934) : any of a German breed of liver or liver and white gundogs

German silver *n* (1856) : NICKEL SILVER

German wirehaired pointer *n* (ca. 1964) : any of a German breed of liver or liver and white gundogs that have a flat-lying wiry coat

germ cell *n* (ca. 1855) : an egg or sperm cell or one of their antecedent cells

ger·men \ˈjər-mən\ *n* [L] *archaic* (1605) : GERM 1a, 2

germ·free \ˈjərm-ˌfrē\ *adj* (1926) : free of microorganisms : AXENIC

ger·mi·cid·al \ˌjər-mə-ˈsīd-ᵊl\ *adj* (1888) : of or relating to a germicide; *also* : destroying germs

ger·mi·cide \ˈjər-mə-ˌsīd\ *n* (1881) : an agent that destroys germs

ger·mi·na·bil·i·ty \ˌjər-mə-nə-ˈbil-ət-ē\ *n* (1896) : the capacity to germinate

ger·mi·nal \ˈjərm-nəl, -ən-ᵊl\ *adj* [F, fr. L *germin-, germen* — more at GERM] (1808) **1 a** : being in the earliest stage of development **b** : CREATIVE, PRODUCTIVE **2** : of, relating to, or having the characteristics of a germ cell or early embryo — **ger·mi·nal·ly** \-ē\ *adv*

germinal vesicle *n* (1851) : the enlarged nucleus of the egg before completion of meiosis

ger·mi·nate \ˈjər-mə-ˌnāt\ *vb* **-nat·ed; -nat·ing** [L *germinatus,* pp. of *germinare* to sprout, fr. *germin-, germen* bud, germ] *vt* (1610) : to cause to sprout or develop ~ *vi* **1** : to begin to grow : SPROUT **2** : to come into being : EVOLVE ⟨before Western civilization began to ~ —A. L. Kroeber⟩ — **ger·mi·na·tion** \ˌjər-mə-ˈnā-shən\ *n* — **ger·mi·na·tive** \ˈjər-mə-ˌnāt-iv, -mə-nət-\ *adj*

germ layer *n* (1879) : any of the three primary layers of cells differentiated in most embryos during and immediately following gastrulation

germ plasm *n* (1889) **1** : germ cells and their precursors serving as the bearers of heredity and being fundamentally independent of other cells **2** : the hereditary material of the germ cells : GENES

germ·proof \ˈjərm-ˈprüf\ *adj* (1902) : impervious to the penetration or action of germs

germ theory *n* (1871) : a theory in medicine: infections, contagious diseases, and various other conditions result from the action of microorganisms

germ warfare *n* (1938) : the use of harmful microorganisms (as bacteria) as weapons in war

germy \ˈjər-mē\ *adj* **germ·i·er; -est** (1912) : full of germs ⟨~ river water⟩

geront- *or* **geronto-** *comb form* [F *géront-, géronto-,* fr. Gk *geront-, geronto-,* fr. *geront-, gerōn* old man; akin to Gk *gēras* old age — more at CORN] : aged one : old age ⟨*geronto*logy⟩

ge·ron·tic \jə-ˈrän-tik\ *adj* (1885) : of or relating to decadence or old age

ger·on·toc·ra·cy \ˌjer-ən-ˈtäk-rə-sē\ *n, pl* **-cies** [F *gérontocratie,* fr. *géront-* geront- + *-cratie* -cracy] (1830) : rule by elders; *specif* : a form of social organization in which a group of old men or a council of elders dominates or exercises control — **ge·ron·to·crat** \jə-ˈränt-ə-ˌkrat\ *n* — **ge·ron·to·crat·ic** \-ˌränt-ə-ˈkrat-ik\ *adj*

ger·on·tol·o·gy \ˌjer-ən-ˈtäl-ə-jē\ *n* [ISV] (1903) : a branch of knowledge dealing with aging and the problems of the aged — compare GERIATRIC 1 — **ge·ron·to·log·i·cal** \jə-ˌränt-ᵊl-ˈäj-i-kəl\ *or* **ge·ron·to·log·ic** \-ik\ *adj* — **ger·on·tol·o·gist** \ˌjer-ən-ˈtäl-ə-jəst\ *n*

ge·ron·to·mor·phic \jə-ˌränt-ə-ˈmȯr-fik\ *adj* (1939) : characterized by physical specialization most fully developed in the old male of a species ⟨~ traits⟩

-g·er·ous \j-(ə-)rəs\ *adj comb form* [L *-ger,* fr. *gerere* to bear — more at CAST] : bearing : producing ⟨denti*gerous*⟩

[1]**ger·ry·man·der** \ˈjer-ē-ˌman-dər, ˌjer-ē-ˈ *also* ˈger-, ˌger-\ *n* [Elbridge *Gerry* + sala*mander*; fr. the shape of an election district formed during Gerry's governorship of Mass.] (1812) **1** : the act or method of gerrymander-

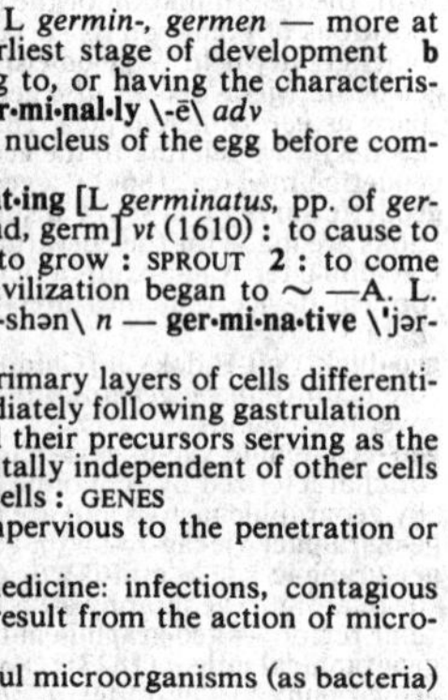

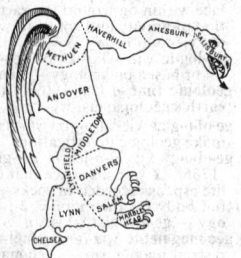

gerrymander 2

ing **2 :** a district or pattern of districts varying greatly in size or population as a result of gerrymandering

[2]**gerrymander** *vt* **-dered; -der·ing** \-d(ə-)riŋ\ (1812) **1 :** to divide (a territorial unit) into election districts to give one political party an electoral majority in a large number of districts while concentrating the voting strength of the opposition in as few districts as possible **2 :** to divide (an area) into political units to give special advantages to one group ⟨~ a school district⟩

ger·und \ˈjer-ənd\ *n* [LL *gerundium,* fr. L *gerundus,* gerundive of *gerere* to bear, carry on — more at CAST] (1513) **1 :** a verbal noun in Latin that expresses generalized or uncompleted action **2 :** any of several linguistic forms analogous to the Latin gerund in languages other than Latin; *esp* **:** the English verbal noun in *-ing* that has the function of a substantive and at the same time shows the verbal features of tense, voice, and capacity to take adverbial qualifiers and to govern objects

ge·run·dive \jə-ˈrən-div\ *n* (15c) **1 :** the Latin future passive participle that functions as the verbal adjective, that expresses the fitness or necessity of the action to be performed, and that has the same suffix as the gerund **2 :** a verbal adjective in a language other than Latin analogous to the gerundive

ge·sell·schaft \gə-ˈzel-ˌshäft\ *n* [G, companionship, society, fr. OHG *giselliscaft,* fr. *gisellio* one that rooms with another (fr. *sal* room, hall) + *-scaft* -ship — more at SALOON, -SHIP] (1887) **:** a rationally developed mechanistic type of social relationship characterized by impersonally contracted associations between persons; *also* **:** a community or society characterized by this relationship — compare GEMEINSCHAFT

ges·so \ˈjes-(ˌ)ō\ *n, pl* **gessoes** [It, lit., gypsum, fr. L *gypsum*] (1596) **1 :** plaster of paris or gypsum prepared with glue for use in painting or making bas-reliefs **2 :** a paste prepared by mixing whiting with size or glue and spread upon a surface to fit it for painting or gilding — **gessoed** \-(ˌ)ōd\ *adj*

gest *or* **geste** \ˈjest\ *n* [ME *geste* — more at JEST] (14c) **1 :** ADVENTURE, EXPLOIT **2 :** a tale of adventures; *esp* **:** a romance in verse

ge·stalt \gə-ˈs(h)tält, -ˈs(h)tȯlt\ *n, pl* **ge·stalt·en** \-^{ə}n\ *or* **gestalts** [G, lit., shape, form] (1922) **:** a structure, configuration, or pattern of physical, biological, or psychological phenomena so integrated as to constitute a functional unit with properties not derivable by summation of its parts

ge·stalt·ist \gə-ˈs(h)täl-təst, -ˈs(h)tȯl-\ *n, often cap* (1931) **:** a specialist in Gestalt psychology

Gestalt psychology *n* (1924) **:** the study of perception and behavior from the standpoint of an organism's response to configurational wholes with stress on the uniformity of psychological and physiological events and rejection of analysis into discrete events of stimulus, percept, and response

ge·sta·po \gə-ˈstäp-(ˌ)ō\ *n, pl* **-pos** [G, fr. *Ge*heime *Sta*ats*po*lizei, lit., secret state police] (1934) **:** a secret-police organization operating esp. against persons suspected of treason or sedition and often employing underhanded and terrorist methods

ges·tate \ˈjes-ˌtāt\ *vb* **ges·tat·ed; ges·tat·ing** [back-formation fr. *gestation*] *vt* (1866) **1 :** to carry in the uterus during pregnancy **2 :** to conceive and gradually develop in the mind ~ *vi* **:** to be in the process of gestation

ges·ta·tion \je-ˈstā-shən\ *n* [L *gestation-, gestatio,* fr. *gestatus,* pp. of *gestare* to bear, fr. *gestus,* pp. of *gerere* to bear — more at CAST] (1615) **1 :** the carrying of young in the uterus **:** PREGNANCY **2 :** conception and development esp. in the mind — **ges·ta·tion·al** \-shnəl, -shən-^{ə}l\ *adj*

geste *also* **gest** \ˈjest\ *n* [MF *geste,* fr. L *gestus,* fr. *gestus,* pp. of *gerere*] (14c) **1** *archaic* **:** DEPORTMENT **2** *archaic* **:** GESTURE

ges·tic \ˈjes-tik\ *adj* (1764) **:** relating to or consisting of bodily movements or gestures

ges·tic·u·lant \je-ˈstik-yə-lənt\ *adj* (1877) **:** making gesticulations ⟨the little wiry man ~ and wild —William Faulkner⟩

ges·tic·u·late \je-ˈstik-yə-ˌlāt\ *vi* **-lat·ed; -lat·ing** [L *gesticulatus,* pp. of *gesticulari,* fr. (assumed) L *gesticulus,* dim. of L *gestus*] (1613) **:** to make gestures esp. when speaking — **ges·ti·cu·la·tive** \je-ˈstik-yə-ˌlāt-iv\ *adj* — **ges·tic·u·la·tor** \-ˌlāt-ər\ *n* — **ges·tic·u·la·to·ry** \-lə-ˌtōr-ē, -ˌtȯr-\ *adj*

ges·tic·u·la·tion \je-ˌstik-yə-ˈlā-shən\ *n* (15c) **1 :** the act of making gestures **2 :** GESTURE; *esp* **:** an expressive gesture made in showing strong feeling or in enforcing an argument

[1]**ges·ture** \ˈjes(h)-chər\ *n* [ME, fr. ML *gestura* mode of action, fr. L *gestus,* pp.] (15c) **1** *archaic* **:** CARRIAGE, BEARING **2 :** the use of motions of the limbs or body as a means of expression **3 :** a movement usu. of the body or limbs that expresses or emphasizes an idea, sentiment, or attitude **4 :** something said or done by way of formality or courtesy, as a symbol or token, or for its effect on the attitudes of others ⟨a political ~ to draw popular support —V. L. Parrington⟩ — **ges·tur·al** \-chə-rəl\ *adj* — **ges·tur·al·ly** \-chə-rə-lē\ *adv*

[2]**gesture** *vb* **ges·tured; ges·tur·ing** *vi* (1542) **:** to make a gesture ~ *vt* **:** to express or direct by a gesture

gesture language *n* (ca. 1901) **:** communication by gestures; *esp* **:** SIGN LANGUAGE

ge·sund·heit \gə-ˈzu̇nt-ˌhīt\ *interj* [G, lit., health, fr. *gesund* healthy (fr. OHG *gisunt*) + *-heit* -hood — more at SOUND] (1914) — used to wish good health esp. to one who has just sneezed

[1]**get** \(ˈ)get, ÷(ˈ)git\ *vb* **got** \(ˈ)gät\; **got** *or* **got·ten** \ˈgät-^{ə}n\; **get·ting** [ME *geten,* fr. ON *geta* to get, beget; akin to OE *bigietan* to beget, L *prehendere* to seize, grasp, Gk *chandanein* to hold, contain] *vt* (13c) **1 a :** to gain possession of **b :** to receive as a return **:** EARN ⟨he *got* a bad reputation for carelessness⟩ **2 a :** to obtain or receive by way of benefit or advantage ⟨he *got* little for his trouble⟩ ⟨~ the better of an enemy⟩ **b :** to achieve as a result of military activity **3 a :** to obtain by concession or entreaty ⟨~ your mother's permission to go⟩ **b :** to become affected by (a disease or bodily condition) **:** CATCH ⟨*got* measles from his sister⟩ **4 a :** to seek out and obtain ⟨hoped to ~ dinner at the inn⟩ **b :** to obtain and bring where wanted or needed ⟨~ a pencil from the desk⟩ **5 :** BEGET **6 a :** to cause to come or go ⟨quickly *got* his luggage through customs⟩ **b :** to cause to move ⟨~ it out of the house⟩ **c :** to cause to be in a certain position or condition ⟨*got* his feet wet⟩ **d :** to make ready **:** PREPARE **7 a :** SEIZE **b :** OVERCOME **c :** to have an emotional effect on ⟨the strain was beginning to ~ me⟩ **d :** PUZZLE **e :** IRRITATE **f :** to take vengeance on; *specif* **:** KILL **g :** HIT **8 a :** to be subjected to ⟨*got* a bad fall⟩ **b :** to receive by way of punishment **c :** to suffer a specified injury to **9 a :** MEMORIZE ⟨*got* the verse by heart⟩ **b :** to find out by calculation ⟨~ the answer to a problem⟩ **c :** HEAR **d :** UNDERSTAND **10 :** to prevail on **:** CAUSE ⟨finally *got* them to tidy up their room⟩ **11 a :** HAVE — used in the present perfect tense form with present meaning ⟨I've *got* no money⟩ **b :** to have as an obligation or necessity — used in the present perfect tense form with present meaning ⟨he has *got* to come⟩ **12 :** to establish communication with **13 :** to put out in baseball ~ *vi* **1 a :** to succeed in coming or going ⟨~ to the city⟩ **b :** to reach or enter into a certain condition ⟨*got* to sleep after midnight⟩ **2 :** to acquire wealth **3 :** to be able ⟨never *got* to go to college⟩ **4 a :** to succeed in becoming ⟨how to ~ clear of all the debts I owe —Shak.⟩ **b :** to become involved ⟨people who ~ into trouble with the law⟩ **5 :** to leave immediately ⟨told them to ~⟩ ~ *verbal auxiliary* — used with the past participle of transitive verbs as a passive voice auxiliary ⟨they *got* caught in the act⟩

usage The pronunciation \(ˈ)git\ has been noted as a feature of some British and American dialects since the 16th century. In the phonetic spelling of his own speech Benjamin Franklin records *git.* However, since at least 1687 some grammarians and teachers have deprecated this pronunciation. It nonetheless remains in widespread and unpredictable use in many dialects, often, but not exclusively, in weakly stressed positions followed by a strong stress, as in "get up!"

— **get after :** to pursue with exhortation, reprimand, or attack — **get ahead :** to achieve success ⟨determined to *get ahead* in life⟩ — **get at 1 :** to reach effectively **2 :** to influence corruptly **:** BRIBE **3 :** to turn one's attention to **4 :** to try to prove or make clear ⟨what is he *getting at*⟩ — **get away with :** to avoid criticism or punishment for or the consequences of (as a reprehensible act) — **get cracking :** to make a start **:** get going ⟨ought to *get cracking* on that assignment⟩ — **get even :** to get revenge — **get even with :** to repay in kind — **get going :** to make a start — **get into :** to become strongly involved with or deeply interested in — **get it :** to receive a scolding or punishment — **get it on 1 :** to become enthusiastic, energetic, or excited **2 :** to engage in sexual intercourse — **get on :** to produce an unfortunate effect on **:** UPSET ⟨the noise *got on* my nerves⟩ — **get one's goat :** to make one angry or annoyed — **get over 1 a :** OVERCOME, SURMOUNT **b :** to recover from **2 :** to move or travel across — **get somewhere :** to be successful — **get there :** to be successful — **get through 1 :** to reach the end of **:** COMPLETE **2 :** to while away ⟨hardly knew how to *get through* his days⟩ — **get to 1 a :** BEGIN ⟨she *gets to* worrying over nothing at all⟩ **b :** to be ready to begin or deal with ⟨I'll *get to* the accounts as soon as I can⟩ **2 :** to have an effect on **:** INFLUENCE — **get together 1 :** to bring together **:** ACCUMULATE **2 :** to come together **:** ASSEMBLE **3 :** to reach agreement — **get wind of :** to become aware of — **get with it :** to become alert or aware **:** show sophisticated consciousness

[2]**get** \ˈget\ *n* (14c) **1 a :** something begotten: (1) **:** OFFSPRING (2) **:** the entire progeny of a male animal **b :** LINEAGE **2 :** a return of a difficult shot in a game (as tennis)

ge·ta \ˈge-(ˌ)tä, ˈget-ə\ *n, pl* **geta** *or* **getas** [Jp] (1884) **:** a Japanese wooden clog for outdoor wear

get about *vi* (1859) **1 :** to be up and about **:** begin to walk ⟨has recovered from his injuries and is able to *get about* again⟩ **2 :** to become current **:** CIRCULATE

get across *vi* (1913) **:** to become clear or convincing ~ *vt* **:** to make clear or convincing ⟨we couldn't *get* our point *across*⟩

get along *vi* (1768) **1 a :** to proceed toward a destination **:** PROGRESS **b :** to approach an advanced stage; *esp* **:** to approach old age **2 :** to meet one's needs **:** MANAGE ⟨we *got along* on a minimum of clothing⟩ **3 :** to be or remain on congenial terms

get around *vt* (1848) **1 :** to get the better of **:** CIRCUMVENT **2 :** EVADE ~ *vi* **1 :** to go from place to place **2 :** to become known or current ⟨word *got around* that he was resigning⟩ **3 a :** to find or take the necessary time or effort — used with *to* **b :** to give attention or consideration — used with *to*

get·at·able \get-ˈat-ə-bəl\ *adj* (1799) **:** ACCESSIBLE, APPROACHABLE

get·away \ˈget-ə-ˌwā\ *n* (1890) **1 :** an act or instance of getting away: as **a :** START **b :** ESCAPE **2 :** a place suitable for a vacation

get back *vi* (1605) **1 :** to come or go again to a person, place, or condition **:** RETURN, REVERT ⟨*getting back* to the main topic of the lecture⟩ **2 :** to gain revenge **:** RETALIATE — used with *at*

get by *vi* (1918) **1 :** to make ends meet **:** SURVIVE **2 :** to succeed with the least possible effort or accomplishment **3 :** to proceed without being discovered, criticized, or punished

get down *vi* (1581) **1 :** to alight esp. from a vehicle **:** DESCEND **2 :** to give one's attention or consideration — used with *to* ⟨*get down* to business⟩ ~ *vt* **1 :** to cause to be physically, mentally, or emotionally exhausted **:** DEPRESS ⟨the weather was *getting* her *down*⟩ **2 :** to manage to swallow **3 :** to commit to writing **:** DESCRIBE

Geth·sem·a·ne \geth-ˈsem-ə-nē\ *n* [Gk *Gethsēmanē*] **1 :** the garden outside Jerusalem mentioned in Mk 14 as the scene of the agony and arrest of Jesus **2 :** a place or occasion of great mental or spiritual suffering

get in *vi* (1533) **1 a :** ENTER **b :** ARRIVE **2 a :** to become friendly **b :** to become involved **3 :** to become accepted for membership or chosen for office ~ *vt* **1 :** to include in one's schedule **2 :** to succeed in doing, making, or delivering **3 :** to cause to become involved

get off *vi* (1748) **1 :** START, LEAVE ⟨intended to *get off* on his trip early in the morning⟩ **2 :** to avoid the most serious consequences of a dangerous situation or punishment ⟨*got off* with a light prison term⟩ **3 :** to leave work with permission ⟨*got off* early and went to the ball game⟩ **4 :** to get high on a drug **5 :** to experience orgasm **6 :** to experience great pleasure ~ *vt* **1 :** to secure the release of or procure a modified penalty for ⟨his lawyers *got* him *off* with little difficulty⟩ **2 a :** UTTER ⟨*get off* a joke⟩ **b :** to write and send **:** DISPATCH **3 :** to succeed in doing, making, or delivering **4 :** to cause to get off

\ə\ abut \$^{ə}$\ kitten, F table \ər\ further \a\ ash \ā\ ace \ä\ cot, cart
\au̇\ out \ch\ chin \e\ bet \ē\ easy \g\ go \i\ hit \ī\ ice \j\ job
\ŋ\ sing \ō\ go \ȯ\ law \ȯi\ boy \th\ thin \t͟h\ the \ü\ loot \u̇\ foot
\y\ yet \zh\ vision \à, k̟, ^{n}, œ, œ̄, ue, u̅e, ^{y}\ see Guide to Pronunciation

get on *vi* (1768) **1 :** GET ALONG ⟨was *getting on* in years⟩ ⟨*got on* well with the boss⟩ ⟨*get on* with the game⟩ **2 :** to gain knowledge or understanding ⟨*got on* to the racket⟩

get out *vi* (14c) **1 :** LEAVE, ESCAPE ⟨doubted that he would *get out* alive⟩ **2 :** to become known : leak out ⟨their secret *got out*⟩ ~ *vt* **1 :** to cause to leave or escape **2 :** to bring before the public; *esp* **:** PUBLISH

get·ter \'get-ər\ *n* (15c) **1 :** one that gets **2 :** a substance introduced into a vacuum tube or electric lamp to remove traces of gas

get–to·geth·er \'get-tə-ˌgeth-ər\ *n* (1911) **:** MEETING; *esp* **:** an informal social gathering

get·up \'get-ˌəp\ *n* (1847) **1 :** general composition or structure **2 :** OUTFIT, COSTUME

get up \get-'əp, git-\ *vi* (14c) **1 a :** to arise from bed **b :** to rise to one's feet **c :** CLIMB, ASCEND **2 :** to go ahead or faster — used in the imperative as a command esp. to driven animals ~ *vt* **1 :** to make preparations for **:** ORGANIZE ⟨*got up* a party for the newcomers⟩ **2 :** to arrange as to external appearance **:** DRESS **3 :** to acquire a knowledge of **4 :** to create in oneself ⟨cannot *get up* the courage to tell them⟩

get–up–and–go \ˌget-ˌəp-ən-'gō, ˌgit-, -ᵊm-, -ᵊŋ-\ *n* (1906) **:** energy displayed in initiation of action

ge·um \'jē-əm\ *n* [L] (ca. 1548) **:** AVENS

gew·gaw \'g(y)ü-(ˌ)gȯ\ *n* [origin unknown] (1529) **:** a showy trifle **:** BAUBLE, TRINKET

ge·würz·tra·mi·ner \gə-'vü(ə)rt-ˌstram-ə-nər, -ˌsträm-\ *n, often cap* [G, fr. *gewürz* spice + *Traminer* of or relating to Tramin (Termeno, Italy)] (ca. 1950) **:** a light dry Alsatian white wine with a spicy bouquet; *also* **:** a similar wine made elsewhere

gey \(ˈ)gā\ *adv* [alter. of *gay*, adv.] *chiefly Scot* (1796) **:** VERY, QUITE

gey·ser \'gī-zər, *Brit sometimes* 'gā- *or* 'gē- *for 1 & usu* 'gē- *for 2*\ *n* [Icel *geysir* gusher, fr. *geysa* to rush forth, fr. ON; akin to OE *gēotan* to pour — more at FOUND] (1780) **1 :** a spring that throws forth intermittent jets of heated water and steam **2** *Brit* **:** an apparatus for heating water rapidly with a gas flame (as for a bath)

gey·ser·ite \-zə-ˌrīt\ *n* [F *geysérite*, fr. *geyser*, fr. Icel *geysir*] (1814) **:** a hydrous silica that constitutes one variety of opal and is deposited around some hot springs and geysers in white or grayish concretions

ghar·ry \'gar-ē, 'gär-\ *n, pl* **gharries** [Hindi *gāṛī*] (1810) **:** a horse-drawn cab used esp. in India and Egypt

ghast \'gast\ *adj, archaic* (1622) **:** GHASTLY

ghast·ful \-fəl\ *adj, archaic* (14c) **:** FRIGHTFUL — **ghast·ful·ly** *adv, archaic*

ghast·ly \'gast-lē\ *adj* **ghast·li·er; -est** [ME *gastly*, fr. *gasten* to terrify] (14c) **1 a :** terrifyingly horrible to the senses **:** FRIGHTENING ⟨a ~ crime⟩ **b :** intensely unpleasant, disagreeable, or objectionable ⟨such a life seems ~ in its emptiness and sterility —Aldous Huxley⟩ **2 :** resembling a ghost **3** *obs* **:** filled with fear **4 :** very great ⟨~ mistake⟩ — **ghast·li·ness** *n* — **ghastly** *adv*

syn GHASTLY, GRISLY, GRUESOME, MACABRE, LURID mean horrifying and repellent in appearance or aspect. GHASTLY suggests the terrifying aspects of corpses and ghosts; GRISLY and GRUESOME suggest additionally the results of extreme violence or cruelty; MACABRE implies a morbid preoccupation with the physical aspects of death; LURID adds to GRUESOME the suggestion of shuddering fascination with violent death and esp. with murder.

ghat \'gȯt, 'gät\ *n* [Hindi *ghāṭ*] (1783) **:** a broad flight of steps that is situated on an Indian riverbank and that provides access to the water esp. for bathing

ghee *or* **ghi** \'gē\ *n* [Hindi, *ghī*, fr. Skt *ghṛta*; akin to MIr *gert* milk] (1665) **:** a semifluid clarified butter made esp. in India

gher·kin \'gər-kən\ *n* [D *gurken*, pl. of *gurk* cucumber, deriv. of Pol *ogurek*, fr. MGk *agouros*] (1661) **1 :** a small prickly fruit used for pickling; *also* **:** the slender annual vine (*Cucumis anguria*) of the gourd family that bears it **2 :** the immature fruit of the cucumber

¹ghet·to \'get-(ˌ)ō\ *n, pl* **ghettos** *or* **ghettoes** [It] (1611) **1 :** a quarter of a city in which Jews were formerly required to live **2 :** a quarter of a city in which members of a minority group live esp. because of social, legal, or economic pressure

²ghetto *vt* (1936) **:** GHETTOIZE

ghetto blaster *n* (1983) **:** a large portable radio or tape player that is often played loudly in public places

ghet·to·ize \'get-ō-ˌīz\ *vt* **-ized; -iz·ing** (1939) **:** to isolate in or as if in a ghetto — **ghet·to·iza·tion** \ˌget-ō-ə-'zā-shən\ *n*

Ghib·el·line \'gib-ə-ˌlēn, -ˌlīn, -lən\ *n* [It *Ghibellino*] (1573) **:** a member of an aristocratic political party in medieval Italy supporting the authority of the German emperors — compare GUELF

ghib·li \'gib-lē\ *n* [Ar *gibliy* south wind] (1942) **:** a hot desert wind of northern Africa

ghillie *var of* GILLIE

¹ghost \'gōst\ *n* [ME *gost, gast*, fr. OE *gāst*; akin to OHG *geist* spirit, Skt *heḍa* anger] (bef. 12c) **1 :** the seat of life or intelligence **:** SOUL ⟨give up the ~⟩ **2 :** a disembodied soul; *esp* **:** the soul of a dead person believed to be an inhabitant of the unseen world or to appear to the living in bodily likeness **3 :** SPIRIT, DEMON **4 a :** a faint shadowy trace ⟨a ~ of a smile⟩ **b :** the least bit ⟨not a ~ of a chance⟩ **5 :** a false image in a photographic negative or on a television screen caused esp. by reflection **6 :** one who ghostwrites **7 :** a red blood cell that has lost its hemoglobin — **ghost·like** \-ˌlīk\ *adj* — **ghosty** \'gō-stē\ *adj*

²ghost *vt* (1606) **1 :** to haunt like a ghost **2 :** GHOSTWRITE ~ *vi* **1 :** to move silently like a ghost **2 :** GHOSTWRITE

ghost dance *n* (1890) **:** a group dance for communication with the spirits of the dead characteristic of an American Indian messianic cult

ghost·ing *n* (ca. 1957) **:** a false image on a television screen; *also* **:** the formation of such images

ghost·ly \'gōst-lē\ *adj* **ghost·li·er; -est** (bef. 12c) **1 :** of or relating to the soul **:** SPIRITUAL **2 :** of, relating to, or having the characteristics of a ghost **:** SPECTRAL — **ghost·li·ness** *n* — **ghostly** *adv*

ghost story *n* (1819) **1 :** a story about ghosts **2 :** a tale based on imagination rather than fact

ghost town *n* (1931) **:** a once-flourishing town wholly or nearly deserted usu. as a result of the exhaustion of some natural resource (as gold)

ghost word *n* (1886) **:** a word form never in established usage; *esp* **:** one arising from an editorial or typographical error or a mistaken pronunciation

ghost·write \'gō-ˌstrīt\ *vb* **-wrote** \-ˌstrōt\; **-writ·ten** \-ˌstrit-ᵊn\ [back-formation fr. *ghostwriter*] *vi* (1927) **:** to write for and in the name of another ~ *vt* **:** to write (as a speech) for another who is the presumed author — **ghost·writ·er** *n*

ghoul \'gül\ *n* [Ar *ghūl*] (1786) **1 :** a legendary evil being that robs graves and feeds on corpses **2 :** one suggestive of a ghoul — **ghoul·ish** \'gü-lish\ *adj* — **ghoul·ish·ly** *adv* — **ghoul·ish·ness** *n*

¹GI \(ˈ)jē-'ī\ *adj* [galvanized *iron*; fr. abbr. used in listing such articles as garbage cans, but taken as abbr. for *government issue*] (ca. 1935) **1 :** provided by an official U.S. military supply department ⟨~ shoes⟩ **2 :** of, relating to, or characteristic of U.S. military personnel **3 :** conforming to military regulations or customs ⟨a ~ haircut⟩

²GI *n, pl* **GI's** *or* **GIs** \-'īz\ (1943) **:** a member or former member of the U.S. armed forces; *esp* **:** a man enlisted in the army

³GI *adv* (1949) **:** in strict conformity with military regulations or customs

⁴GI *vt* **GI'd** \-'īd\; **GI'·ing** \-'ī-iŋ\ (1951) **:** to clean thoroughly (as floors) in preparation for or as if for a military inspection

¹gi·ant \'jī-ənt\ *n* [ME *giaunt*, fr. OF *geant*, fr. L *gigant-, gigas*, fr. Gk] (13c) **1 :** a legendary manlike being of great stature and strength **2 a :** a living being of great size **b :** a person of extraordinary powers ⟨a literary ~⟩ **3 :** something unusually large or powerful — **gi·ant·like** \-ˌlīk\ *adj*

²giant *adj* (15c) **:** characterized by extremely large size, proportion, or power

giant·ess \'jī-ənt-əs\ *n* (14c) **:** a female giant

gi·ant·ism \'jī-ənt-ˌiz-əm\ *n* (1639) **1 :** the quality or state of being a giant ⟨~ in industry⟩ **2 :** GIGANTISM 2

giant panda *n* (1920) **:** PANDA 2

giant reed *n* (ca. 1900) **:** a tall European grass (*Arundo donax*) with woody stems used esp. in making organ reeds, baskets, and shelters

giant schnauzer *n* (ca. 1934) **:** any of a breed of powerful heavyset schnauzers that attain a height of 23½ to 27½ inches

giant sequoia *n* (ca. 1931) **:** BIG TREE

giant slalom *n* (1952) **:** a slalom race for skiers on a longer and steeper course than that used for the regular slalom

giant star *n* (1912) **:** a star of great intrinsic luminosity and of large mass

giaour \'jau̇(ə)r\ *n* [Turk *gâvur*] (1564) **:** one outside the Muslim faith **:** INFIDEL 2a

giar·di·a·sis \(ˌ)jē-ˌär-'dī-ə-səs, jē-ər-, jär-\ *n, pl* **-a·ses** [NL, fr. *Giardia*, fr. Alfred M. *Giard* †1908 Fr. biologist] (1919) **:** infestation with or disease caused by a flagellate protozoan (genus *Giardia* and esp. *G. lamblia* in man) that is often characterized by diarrhea

¹gib \'gib\ *n* [ME, fr. *Gib*, nickname for *Gilbert*] (1561) **:** a male cat; *specif* **:** a castrated male cat

²gib *n* [origin unknown] (1795) **:** a plate of metal or other material machined to hold other parts in place, to afford a bearing surface, or to provide means for overcoming looseness

³gib *vt* **gibbed; gib·bing** (ca. 1864) **:** to fasten with a gib

gib·ber \'jib-ər\ *vi* **gib·bered; gib·ber·ing** \-(ə-)riŋ\ [imit.] (1604) **:** to speak rapidly, inarticulately, and often foolishly — **gibber** *n*

gib·ber·el·lic acid \ˌjib-ə-ˌrel-ik-\ *n* (1954) **:** a crystalline acid $C_{19}H_{22}O_6$ that is a gibberellin used esp. in the malting of barley

gib·ber·el·lin \-'rel-ən\ *n* [NL, fr. *Gibberella fujikoroi*, fungus from which it was first isolated] (1939) **:** any of several plant-growth regulators that in low concentrations promote shoot growth

gib·ber·ish \'jib-(ə-)rish, 'gib-\ *n* [prob. fr. *gibber*] (1554) **:** unintelligible or meaningless language: **a :** a technical or esoteric language **b :** pretentious or needlessly obscure language

¹gib·bet \'jib-ət\ *n* [ME *gibet*, fr. OF] (13c) **1 :** GALLOWS **2 :** an upright post with a projecting arm for hanging the bodies of executed criminals as a warning

²gibbet *vt* (1646) **1 a :** to hang on a gibbet **b :** to expose to infamy or public scorn **2 :** to execute by hanging on a gibbet

gib·bon \'gib-ən\ *n* [F] (1770) **:** any of several tailless apes (genera *Hylobates* and *Symphalangus*) of southeastern Asia and the East Indies that are the smallest and most arboreal anthropoid apes

gib·bos·i·ty \jib-'äs-ət-ē, gib-\ *n, pl* **-ties** (15c) **:** PROTUBERANCE, SWELLING

gib·bous \'jib-əs, 'gib-\ *adj* [ME, fr. MF *gibbeux*, fr. LL *gibbosus* humpbacked, fr. L *gibbus* hump; akin to ON *keikr* bent backwards] (15c) **1 a :** marked by convexity or swelling **:** PROTUBERANT **b** *of the moon or a planet* **:** seen with more than half but not all of the apparent disk illuminated **2 :** having a hump **:** HUMPBACKED

gibe \'jīb\ *vb* **gibed; gib·ing** [perh. fr. MF *giber* to shake, handle roughly] *vi* (1567) **:** to utter taunting words ~ *vt* **:** to deride or tease with taunting words ***syn*** see SCOFF — **gibe** *n* — **gib·er** *n*

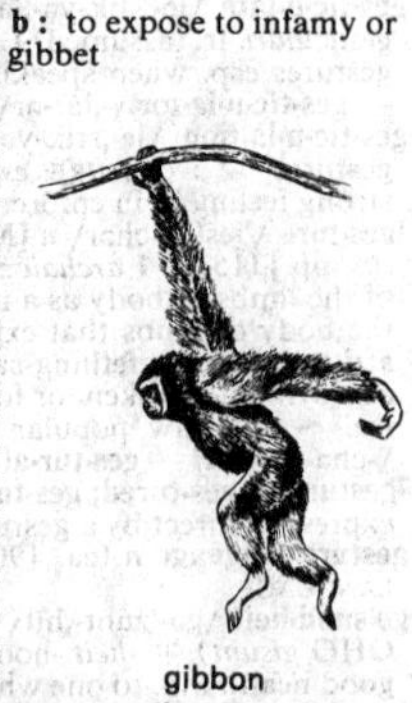

gibbon

gib·lets \'jib-ləts *also* 'gib-\ *n pl* [ME *gibelet* entrails, garbage, fr. MF, stew of wildfowl] (15c) **:** the edible viscera of a fowl

Gi·bral·tar \jə-'brȯl-tər\ *n* [*Gibraltar*, fortress in the Brit. colony of Gibraltar] (1856) **:** an impregnable stronghold

Gib·son \'gib-sən\ *n* [fr. the name *Gibson*] (1949) **:** a martini garnished with a cocktail onion

Gibson girl *adj* [Charles D. *Gibson*] (1936) **:** of or relating to a style esp. in women's clothing characterized by high necks, full sleeves, and wasp waists

gid \'gid\ *n* [back-formation fr. *giddy*] (1601) **:** a disease esp. of sheep caused by the larva of a tapeworm (*Multiceps multiceps*) in the brain

gid·dap \gid-'ap, -'əp\ *also* **gid·dy·ap** \ˌgid-ē-'ap, -'əp\ *vb imper* [alter. of *get up*] (ca. 1897) **—** a command to a horse to go ahead or go faster

¹gid·dy \'gid-ē\ *adj* **gid·di·er; -est** [ME *gidy* mad, foolish, fr. OE *gydig* possessed, mad; akin to OE *god* god] (14c) **1 a :** DIZZY ⟨~ from the unaccustomed exercise⟩ **b :** causing dizziness ⟨a ~ height⟩ **c :** whirling rapidly **2 :** lightheartedly silly **:** FRIVOLOUS — **gid·di·ly** \'gid-ᵊl-ē\ *adv* — **gid·di·ness** \'gid-ē-nəs\ *n*

[2]**giddy** *vb* **gid·died; gid·dy·ing** *vt* (1602) **:** to make giddy ~ *vi* **:** to become giddy

Gid·e·on \'gid-ē-ən\ *n* [Heb *Gidh'ōn*] **1 :** an early Hebrew hero noted for his defeat of the Midianites **2 :** a member of an interdenominational organization whose activities include the placing of Bibles in hotel rooms

gie \'gē\ *chiefly Scot var of* GIVE

Gi·em·sa stain \gē-,em-zə-\ *also* **Giemsa's stain** *n* [Gustav *Giemsa* †1948 Ger. chemotherapist] (ca. 1909) **:** a stain consisting of eosin and a blue dye and used chiefly in the differential staining of blood films — called also *Gi·em·sa* \gē-'em-zə\

[1]**gift** \'gift\ *n* [ME, fr. ON, something given, talent; akin to OE *giefan* to give] (13c) **1 :** a notable capacity, talent, or endowment **2 :** something voluntarily transferred by one person to another without compensation **3 :** the act, right, or power of giving
syn GIFT, FACULTY, APTITUDE, BENT, TALENT, GENIUS, KNACK mean a special ability for doing something. GIFT often implies special favor by God or nature; FACULTY applies to an innate or less often acquired ability for a particular accomplishment or function; APTITUDE implies a natural liking for some activity and the likelihood of success in it; BENT is nearly equal to APTITUDE but it stresses inclination perhaps more than specific ability; TALENT suggests a marked natural ability that needs to be developed; GENIUS suggests impressive inborn creative ability; KNACK implies a comparatively minor but special ability making for ease and dexterity in performance.

[2]**gift** *vt* (ca. 1550) **1 :** to endow with some power, quality, or attribute **2 :** PRESENT ⟨generously ~*ed* us with a copy —*Saturday Rev.*⟩

gift certificate *n* (1942) **:** a certified statement entitling the recipient to select merchandise in the establishment of the issuer to the amount stated thereon

gift·ed \'gif-təd\ *adj* (1644) **1 :** having great natural ability **:** TALENTED ⟨~ children⟩ **2 :** revealing a special gift ⟨~ voices⟩ — **gift·ed·ly** *adv* — **gift·ed·ness** *n*

gift of gab (1695) **:** the ability to talk glibly and persuasively

gift of tongues [fr. the gifts of the Spirit in 1 Cor 12:1-13] (1560) **:** the charismatic gift of ecstatic speech

gift·ware \'gif-,twa(ə)r, -,twe(ə)r\ *n* ['*gift* + *-ware* (as in *silverware*)] (1904) **:** wares or goods suitable for gifts

gift wrap *vt* (1936) **:** to wrap (merchandise intended as a gift) decoratively

[1]**gig** \'gig\ *n* [ME *gigg* top, perh. of Scand origin; akin to ON *geiga* to turn aside; akin to OE *geonian* to yawn — more at YAWN] (15c) **1 :** something that whirls or is whirled: as **a** *obs* **:** TOP, WHIRLIGIG **b :** a 3-digit selection in a numbers game **2 :** a person of odd or grotesque appearance **3 a :** a long light ship's boat propelled by oars, sail, or motor **b :** a rowboat designed for speed rather than for work **4 :** a light two-wheeled one-horse carriage

[2]**gig** *vi* **gigged; gig·ging** (1807) **:** to travel in a gig

[3]**gig** *n* [short for earlier *fizgig, fishgig,* of unknown origin] (1722) **1 :** a pronged spear for catching fish **2 :** an arrangement of hooks to be drawn through a school of fish when they will not bite in order to hook them in the bodies

[4]**gig** *vb* **gigged; gig·ging** *vt* (1803) **1 :** to spear with a gig **2 a** *chiefly West* **:** SPUR, JAB **b :** GOAD, PROVOKE ~ *vi* **:** to fish with a gig

[5]**gig** *n* [origin unknown] (1927) **:** JOB; *esp* **:** an entertainer's engagement for a specified time

[6]**gig** *vi* **gigged; gig·ging** (1939) **:** to work as a musician ⟨*gigged* with various bands —*Downbeat*⟩

[7]**gig** *n* [origin unknown] (ca. 1941) **:** a military demerit

[8]**gig** *vt* **gigged; gig·ging** (ca. 1941) **:** to give a military gig to

giga- \'jig-ə, 'gig-ə\ *comb form* [ISV, fr. Gk *gigas* giant] **:** billion ⟨*giga*ton⟩ ⟨*giga*volt⟩

giga·bit \-,bit\ *n* (1970) **:** a unit of information equal to one billion bits

giga·cy·cle \-,sī-kəl\ *n* (1960) **:** GIGAHERTZ

giga·hertz \-,hərts, -,he(ə)rts\ *n* (1964) **:** a unit of frequency equal to one billion hertz

gigant- *or* **giganto-** *comb form* [Gk, fr. *gigant-, gigas*] **:** giant ⟨*gigant*ism⟩

gi·gan·tesque \,jī-,gan-'tesk, -gən-\ *adj* (1834) **:** of enormous or grotesquely large proportions

gi·gan·tic \jī-'gant-ik, jə-\ *adj* (1612) **:** exceeding the usual or expected (as in size, force, or prominence) ⟨a man of ~ stature⟩ ⟨made a last ~ effort⟩ ⟨the growth of ~ industrial combines⟩ *syn* see ENORMOUS — **gi·gan·ti·cal·ly** \-i-k(ə-)lē\ *adv*

gi·gan·tism \jī-'gan-,tiz-əm, jə-; 'jī-gən-\ *n* (ca. 1885) **1 :** the quality or state of being gigantic **:** GIANTISM 1 **2 :** development to abnormally large size **3 :** excessive vegetative growth often accompanied by the inhibiting of reproduction

gi·gas \'jī-gəs\ *adj* [NL, fr. L, giant, fr. Gk] *of a polyploid plant* (1915) **:** having thicker stem, taller growth, darker thicker leaves, and larger flowers and seeds than a corresponding diploid

giga·watt \'jig-ə-,wät, 'gig-\ *n* (ca. 1962) **:** a unit of power equal to one billion watts

gig·gle \'gig-əl\ *vb* **gig·gled; gig·gling** \-(ə-)liŋ\ [imit.] *vi* (1509) **:** to laugh with repeated short catches of the breath ~ *vt* **:** to utter with a giggle — **giggle** *n* — **gig·gler** \-(ə-)lər\ *n* — **gig·gling·ly** \-(ə-)liŋ-lē\ *adv* — **gig·gly** \-(ə-)lē\ *adj*

gig·o·lo \'jig-ə-,lō, 'zhig-\ *n, pl* **-los** [F, alter. of *gigolette* girl who frequents public dances, prostitute, fr. MF *giguer* to dance — more at JIG] (1922) **1 :** a man supported by a woman usu. in return for his attentions **2 :** a professional dancing partner or male escort

gi·got \'jig-ət, zhē-'gō\ *n, pl* **gi·gots** \-əts, -'gō(z)\ [MF, dim. of *gigue* fiddle; fr. its shape — more at JIG] (1526) **1 :** a leg of meat (as lamb) esp. when cooked **2 :** a leg-of-mutton sleeve

gigue \'zhēg\ *n* [F, fr. MF] (1685) **:** a lively dance movement (as of a suite) having compound triple rhythm and composed in fugal style

Gi·la monster \,hē-lə-\ *n* [*Gila* river, Ariz.] (1877) **:** a large orange and black venomous lizard (*Heloderma suspectum*) of the southwestern U.S.; *also* **:** a related lizard (*H. horridum*) of Mexico

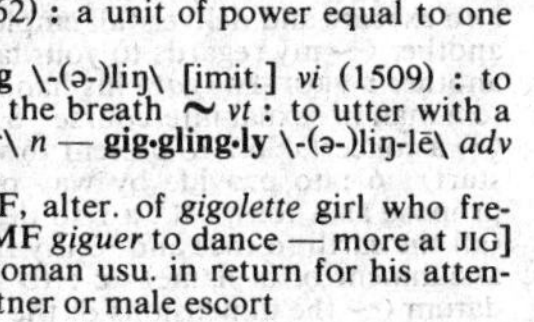
Gila monster

gil·bert \'gil-bərt\ *n* [William *Gilbert*] (1893) **:** the centimeter-gram-second unit of magnetomotive force equivalent to $10 \div 4\pi$ ampere-turn

[1]**gild** \'gild\ *vt* **gild·ed** \'gil-dəd\ *or* **gilt** \'gilt\; **gild·ing** [ME *gilden,* fr. OE *gyldan;* akin to OE *gold* gold] (13c) **1 :** to overlay with or as if with a thin covering of gold **2 a :** to give money to **b :** to give an attractive but often deceptive appearance to **c** *archaic* **:** to make bloody — **gild·er** *n* — **gild·ing** *n* — **gild the lily :** to add unnecessary ornamentation to something beautiful in its own right

[2]**gild** *var of* GUILD

Gil·ga·mesh \'gil-gə-,mesh\ [Sumerian *Gil-ga-meš*] **:** a legendary Sumerian king and hero of the *Gilgamesh Epic*

[1]**gill** \'jil\ *n* [ME *gille,* prob. fr. ML *gillo* wine vessel] (13c) — see WEIGHT table

[2]**gill** \'gil\ *n* [ME *gile, gille,* of Scand origin; akin to ON *gjǫnar* gills; akin to Gk *chelynē* lip, jawbone] (14c) **1 :** an organ (as of a fish) for obtaining oxygen from water **2 a :** WATTLE 2 **b :** the flesh under or about the chin or jaws — usu. used in pl. **c :** one of the radiating plates forming the undersurface of the cap of a mushroom fungus — **gilled** \'gild\ *adj* — **to the gills :** as full as possible

[3]**gill** \'gil\ *vt* (1884) **:** GILLNET ~ *vi, of fish* **:** to become entangled in a gill net — **gill·er** *n*

[4]**gill** \'gil\ *n* [ME *gille,* fr. ON *gil;* akin to OHG *gil* hernia] (15c) **1** *Brit* **:** RAVINE **2** *Brit* **:** a narrow stream or rivulet

[5]**gill** \'jil\ *n, often cap* [ME, fr. *Gill,* nickname for *Gillian*] (15c) **:** GIRL, SWEETHEART

gill arch *n* (1879) **1 :** one of the bony or cartilaginous arches or curved bars extending dorsoventrally and placed one behind the other on each side of the pharynx and supporting the gills of fishes and amphibians **2 :** one of the rudimentary ridges in the embryos of all higher vertebrates that correspond to the gill arches

gill cleft *n* (ca. 1890) **:** GILL SLIT 1, 2

gill cover *n* (1776) **:** OPERCULUM 2b

gill fungus *n* (ca. 1926) **:** a basidiomycete (as an agaric) having gills

[1]**gil·lie** \'gil-ē\ *n* [ScGael *gille* & IrGael *giolla* boy] (1705) **1 :** a male attendant on a Scottish Highland chief; *broadly* **:** ATTENDANT **2** *Scot & Irish* **:** a fishing and hunting guide **3 :** a shoe with a low top and decorative lacing

[2]**gillie** *vi* **gil·lied; gil·ly·ing** (1900) **:** to serve as a gillie

gill·net \'gil-,net\ *vt* (1949) **:** to catch (fish) with a gill net

gill net *n* (1796) **:** a flat net suspended vertically in the water with meshes that allow the head of a fish to pass but entangle it as it seeks to withdraw

gill–net·ter \-,net-ər\ *n* (ca. 1889) **:** a boat equipped for or engaged in fishing with gill nets; *also* **:** a person who fishes with a gill net

gill raker *n* (1880) **:** one of the bony processes on a gill arch that divert solid substances from the gills

gill slit *n* (1854) **1 :** one of the openings or clefts between the gill arches in vertebrates that breathe by gills through which water taken in at the mouth passes to the exterior and so bathes the gills **2 :** one of the rudimentary grooves in the neck region of the embryos of air-breathing vertebrates that correspond to the gill slits **3 :** the external opening to the cavity containing the gills when a protective covering of the gills is present

gil·ly·flow·er \'jil-ē-,flau̇(-ə)r\ *n* [by folk etymology fr. ME *gilofre* clove, fr. MF *girofle, gilofre,* fr. L *caryophyllum,* fr. Gk *karyophyllon,* fr. *karyon* nut + *phyllon* leaf — more at CAREEN, BLADE] (14c) **:** CARNATION 2

Gil·son·ite \'gil-sə-,nīt\ *trademark* — used for uintaite

[1]**gilt** \'gilt\ *adj* [ME, fr. pp. of *gilden* to gild] (14c) **:** covered with gold or gilt **:** of the color of gold

[2]**gilt** *n* (15c) **1 :** gold or something that resembles gold laid on a surface **2** *slang* **:** MONEY **3 :** superficial brilliance

[3]**gilt** *n* [ME *gylte,* fr. ON *gyltr;* akin to OE *gelte* young sow — more at GELD] (14c) **:** a young female swine

gilt–edged \'gil-'tejd\ *or* **gilt–edge** \-'tej\ *adj* (1818) **1 :** having a gilt edge **2 :** of the best quality ⟨~ securities⟩

[1]**gim·bal** \'gim-bəl, 'jim-\ *n* [alter. of obs. *gemel* (double ring)] (1780) **:** a device that permits a body to incline freely in any direction or suspends it so that it will remain level when its support is tipped — usu. used in pl.; called also *gimbal ring*

[2]**gimbal** *vt* **-balled** *or* **-baled; -bal·ling** *or* **-bal·ing** (1875) **:** to provide with or support on gimbals

gim·crack \'jim-,krak\ *n* [origin unknown] (1676) **:** a showy object of little use or value **:** GEWGAW — **gimcrack** *adj* — **gim·crack·ery** \-(ə-)rē\ *n*

gi·mel \'gim-əl\ *n* [Heb *gīmel*] (ca. 1899) **:** the 3d letter of the Hebrew alphabet — see ALPHABET table

[1]**gim·let** \'gim-lət\ *n* [ME, fr. MF *guimbelet,* modif of MD *wimmelkijn,* fr. *wimmel* wimble] (14c) **:** a small tool with a screw point, grooved shank, and cross handle for boring holes

[2]**gimlet** *adj* (1752) **:** having a piercing or penetrating quality

[3]**gimlet** *vt* (1840) **:** to pierce with or as if with a gimlet

[4]**gimlet** *n* [prob. fr. [1]*gimlet*] (1928) **:** a drink consisting of sweetened lime juice and gin or vodka and sometimes carbonated or plain water

gim·let–eyed \-'īd\ *adj* (1752) **:** SHARP-SIGHTED

gim·mal \'gim-əl, 'jim-\ *n* [alter. of obs. *gemel* (double ring)] (1598) **1** *pl* **:** joined work (as in a clock) whose parts move within each other **2 :** a pair or series of interlocked rings

[1]**gim·mick** \'gim-ik\ *n* [origin unknown] (ca. 1926) **1 a :** a mechanical device for secretly and dishonestly controlling gambling apparatus **b :** an ingenious or novel mechanical device **:** GADGET **2 a :** an important feature that is not immediately apparent **:** CATCH ⟨what's the ~ . . . what's in it for you —Maxwell Griffith⟩ **b :** an ingenious and usu. new scheme or angle — **gim·micky** \-i-kē\ *adj*

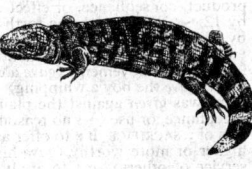

[2]gimmick *vt* (1928) **1 :** to alter or influence by means of a gimmick **2 :** to provide with a gimmick (as an attention-getting device, a novel twist, or a gadget) — often used with *up*

gim·mick·ry \'gim-i-krē\ *n, pl* **-ries** (1948) **:** an array or profusion of gimmicks; *also* **:** use of gimmicks

[1]gimp \'gimp\ *n* [perh. fr. D] (1664) **:** an ornamental flat braid or round cord used as a trimming

[2]gimp *n* [origin unknown] (1901) **:** SPIRIT, VIM

[3]gimp *n* [origin unknown] (1929) **1 :** CRIPPLE **2 :** LIMP ⟨walks with a ~ —Damon Runyon⟩ — **gimpy** \'gim-pē\ *adj*

[4]gimp *vi* (1948) **:** LIMP, HOBBLE ⟨came ~*ing* across the floor on three legs —Nelson Algren⟩

[1]gin \'gin\ *vb* **gan** \'gan\; **gin·ning** [ME *ginnen,* short for *beginnen*] *archaic* (13c) **:** BEGIN

[2]gin \'jin\ *n* [ME *gin,* modif. of OF *engin* — more at ENGINE] (13c) **:** any of various tools or mechanical devices: as **a :** a snare or trap for game **b :** a machine for raising or moving heavy weights **c :** COTTON GIN

[3]gin \'jin\ *vt* **ginned; gin·ning** (1625) **1 :** SNARE **2 :** to separate (cotton fiber) from seeds and waste material — **gin·ner** *n* — **gin·ning** *n*

[4]gin \(,)gin\ *conj* [perh. alter. of Sc & E dial. *gif,* fr. ME *yif, if*] *dial* (1674) **:** IF

[5]gin \'jin\ *n* [by shortening & alter. fr. *geneva*] (1714) **1 :** a colorless alcoholic beverage made from distilled or redistilled neutral grain spirits flavored with juniper berries and aromatics (as anise and caraway seeds) **2 a :** GIN RUMMY **b :** the act of laying down a full hand of matched cards in gin rummy — **gin·ny** \'jin-ē\ *adj*

gin and tonic *n* (1935) **:** a drink that consists of gin and quinine water garnished with a wedge of lime or lemon

[1]gin·ger \'jin-jər\ *n* [ME, fr. OE *gingifer,* fr. ML *gingiber,* alter. of L *zingiber,* fr. Gk *zingiberi,* perh. deriv. of Skt *sṛngavera*] (bef. 12c) **1 a** (1) **:** a thickened pungent aromatic rhizome that is used as a spice and sometimes in medicine (2) **:** the spice usu. prepared by drying and grinding ginger **b :** any of a genus (*Zingiber* of the family Zingiberaceae, the ginger family) of herbs with pungent aromatic rhizomes; *esp* **:** a widely cultivated tropical herb (*Z. officinale*) that supplies most of the ginger of commerce **2 :** high spirit **:** PEP ⟨the ~ to care hard and work hard —Willa Cather⟩ **3 :** a strong brown — **gin·gery** \'jinj-(ə-)rē\ *adj*

[2]ginger *vt* **gin·gered; gin·ger·ing** \'jinj-(ə-)riŋ\ (1849) **:** to make lively **:** pep up ⟨~ up the tourist trade —*N.Y. Times*⟩

ginger ale *n* (1886) **:** a sweetened carbonated nonalcoholic beverage flavored mainly with ginger extract

ginger beer *n* (1809) **:** a sweetened carbonated nonalcoholic beverage heavily flavored with ginger or capsicum or both

gin·ger·bread \'jin-jər-,bred\ *n* (15c) **1 :** a cake whose ingredients include molasses and ginger **2** [fr. the fancy shapes and gilding formerly often applied to gingerbread] **:** lavish or superfluous ornament esp. in architecture — **gingerbread** *adj* — **gin·ger·bready** \-ē\ *adj*

ginger group *n, chiefly Brit* (1925) **:** a group that serves as an energizing force within a larger body (as a political party)

gin·ger·ly \'jin-jər-lē\ *adj* [perh. fr. [1]*ginger*] (1594) **:** very cautious or careful — **gin·ger·li·ness** *n* — **gingerly** *adv*

gin·ger·root \'jin-jər-,(r)üt, -,(r)u̇t\ *n* (1831) **:** GINGER 1a(1)

gin·ger·snap \-,snap\ *n* (1805) **:** a thin brittle cookie sweetened with molasses and flavored with ginger

ging·ham \'giŋ-əm\ *n* [modif. of Malay *genggang* checkered cloth] (1615) **:** a clothing fabric usu. of yarn-dyed cotton in plain weave

gingiv- *or* **gingivo-** *comb form* [L *gingiva*] **:** gum **:** gums ⟨*gingiv*itis⟩

gin·gi·va \'jin-jə-və, jin-'jī-\ *n, pl* **-vae** \-,vē\ [L — more at CONGER EEL] (1889) **:** [1]GUM — **gin·gi·val** \'jin-jə-vəl\ *adj*

gin·gi·vec·to·my \,jin-jə-'vek-tə-mē\ *n, pl* **-mies** (ca. 1927) **:** the excision of a portion of the gingiva

gin·gi·vi·tis \,jin-jə-'vīt-əs\ *n* (1874) **:** inflammation of the gums

gink \'giŋk\ *n* [origin unknown] *slang* (1910) **:** PERSON, GUY

gink·go *also* **ging·ko** \'giŋ-(,)kō *also* 'giŋk-(,)gō\ *n, pl* **ginkgoes** *or* **ginkgos** [NL *Ginkgo,* fr. Jp *ginkyo*] (1773) **:** a showy gymnospermous tree (*Ginkgo biloba*) of eastern China with fan-shaped leaves and yellow fruit often grown as a shade tree

gin mill *n* (1865) **:** BAR, SALOON

gin rummy *n* [[5]*gin*] (1941) **:** a rummy game for two players in which each player is dealt 10 cards and in which a player may win a hand by matching all his cards or may end play when his unmatched cards count up to 10 or less

gin·seng \'jin-,saŋ, -,seŋ, -(,)siŋ\ *n* [Chin (Pek) *jen²-shen¹*] (1654) **1 :** the root of a ginseng **2 a :** a Chinese perennial herb (*Panax schinseng* of the family Araliaceae, the ginseng family) having 5-foliolate leaves, scarlet berries, and an aromatic root valued locally as a medicine **b :** any of several plants related to ginseng; *esp* **:** a No. American herb (*P. quinquefolius*)

Gipsy *var of* GYPSY

gi·raffe \jə-'raf\ *n, pl* **giraffes** [It *giraffa,* fr. Ar *zirāfah*] (1594) **1** *or pl* **giraffe :** a large fleet African ruminant mammal (*Giraffa camelopardalis*) that is the tallest of living quadrupeds and has a very long neck and a short coat with dark blotches separated by pale lines **2** *cap* **:** CAMELOPARDALIS — **gi·raff·ish** \-'raf-ish\ *adj*

gir·an·dole \'jir-ən-,dōl\ *n* [F & It; F, fr. It *girandola,* fr. *girare* to turn, fr. LL *gyrare,* fr. L *gyrus* gyre] (1634) **1 :** a radiating and showy composition (as a cluster of skyrockets fired together) **2 :** an ornamental branched candlestick

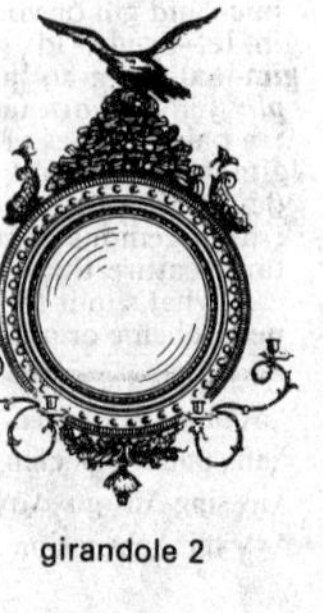

girandole 2

gir·a·sole *also* **gir·a·sol** \'jir-ə-,sȯl, -,sōl, -,säl\ *n* [It *girasole* sunflower, fr. *girare* + *sole* sun, fr. L *sol* — more at SOLAR] (1586) **1 :** JERUSALEM ARTICHOKE **2** *usu* **girasol :** an opal of varying color that gives out fiery reflections in bright light

[1]gird \'gərd\ *vb* **gird·ed** \'gərd-əd\ *or* **girt** \'gərt\; **gird·ing** [ME *girden,* fr. OE *gyrdan;* akin to OE *geard* yard — more at YARD] *vt* (bef. 12c) **1 a :** to encircle or bind with a flexible band (as a belt) **b :** to make fast (as a sword by a belt or clothing with a cord) **c :** SURROUND **2 :** PROVIDE, EQUIP; *esp* **:** to invest with the sword of knighthood **3 :** to prepare (oneself) for action **~** *vi* **:** to prepare for action — **gird one's loins :** to prepare for action **:** muster up one's resources

[2]gird *vb* [ME *girden* to strike, thrust] *vt* (1546) **:** to sneer at **:** MOCK **~** *vi* **:** GIBE, RAIL

[3]gird *n* (1566) **:** a sarcastic remark

gird·er \'gərd-ər\ *n* [[1]*gird*] (1611) **:** a horizontal main structural member (as in a building or bridge) that supports vertical loads and that consists of a single piece or of more than one piece bound together

[1]gir·dle \'gərd-ᵊl\ *n* [ME *girdel,* fr. OE *gyrdel;* akin to OHG *gurtil* girdle, OE *gyrdan* to gird] (bef. 12c) **1 :** something that encircles or confines: as **a :** an article of dress encircling the body usu. at the waist **b :** a woman's close-fitting undergarment often boned and usu. elasticized that extends from the waist to below the hips **c :** either of two more or less complete bony rings at the anterior and posterior ends of the vertebrate trunk supporting the arms and legs respectively: (1) **:** PECTORAL GIRDLE (2) **:** PELVIC GIRDLE **2 :** the edge of a brilliant that is grasped by the setting — see BRILLIANT illustration

[2]girdle *vt* **gir·dled; gir·dling** \'gərd-liŋ, -ᵊl-iŋ\ (1582) **1 :** to encircle with or as if with girdle **2 :** to move around **:** CIRCLE ⟨*girdled* the world⟩ **3 :** to cut away the bark and cambium in a ring around (a plant) usu. to kill by interrupting the circulation of water and nutrients

girl \'gər(-ə)l\ *n* [ME *gurle, girle* young person of either sex] (13c) **1 a :** a female child **b :** a young unmarried woman **c :** a single or married woman of any age — sometimes taken to be offensive **2 a :** a female servant or employee — sometimes taken to be offensive **b :** SWEETHEART **c :** DAUGHTER — **girl·hood** \-,hu̇d\ *n*

girl Friday *n* [*girl* + *Friday* (as in *man Friday*)] (1940) **:** a female assistant (as in an office) entrusted with a wide variety of tasks

girl·friend \'gər(-ə)l-,frend\ *n* (1859) **1 :** a female friend **2 :** a frequent or regular female companion of a boy or man **3 :** MISTRESS 5a

Girl Guide *n* (1909) **:** a member of a worldwide scouting movement for girls 7 to 18 years of age

girl·ie *also* **girly** \'gər-lē\ *adj* (1942) **:** featuring scantily clothed women ⟨~ magazines⟩ ⟨~ show⟩

girl·ish \'gər-lish\ *adj* (1565) **:** of, relating to, or having the characteristics of a girl or girlhood ⟨~ laughter⟩ — **girl·ish·ly** *adv* — **girl·ish·ness** *n*

Girl Scout *n* (1909) **:** a member of any of the scouting programs of the Girl Scouts of the United States of America for girls ages 6 through 17

girn \'gi(ə)rn\ *vi* [ME *girnen,* alter. of *grinnen* to grin, snarl] *chiefly Scot* (13c) **:** SNARL — **girn** *n, chiefly Scot*

gi·ro \'ji(ə)r-(,)ō, 'zhi(ə)r-; 'jē-(,)rō, 'zhē-, *esp Brit* 'jī-\ *n* [G, fr. It, turn, transfer, fr. L *gyrus* gyre] (1890) **:** a service of many European banks that permits authorized direct transfer of funds among account holders as well as conventional transfers by check

giron *var of* GYRON

Gi·rond·ist \jə-'rän-dəst, zhi-\ *n* [F *girondiste,* fr. *Gironde,* a political party, fr. *Gironde,* department of France represented by its leaders] (1795) **:** a member of the moderate republican party in the French legislative assembly in 1791

girsh \'kərsh, 'gərsh, 'gi(ə)rsh\ *n, pl* **girsh** [Ar *qirsh*] (1946) **:** QURSH

girt \'gərt\ *vb* [ME *girten,* alter. of *girden*] *vt* (15c) **1 :** GIRD **2 :** to fasten by means of a girth **~** *vi* **:** to measure in girth

[1]girth \'gərth\ *n* [ME, fr. ON *gjörth;* akin to OE *gyrdan* to gird] (14c) **1 :** a band or strap that encircles the body of an animal to fasten something (as a saddle) on its back **2 a :** a measure around a body ⟨for the man of more than average ~ —Agnes M. Miall⟩ **b :** SIZE, DIMENSIONS ⟨the river was twice its usual ~⟩

[2]girth *vt* (15c) **1 :** ENCIRCLE **2 :** to bind or fasten with a girth **3 :** to measure the girth of

gi·sarme \giz-'ärm\ *n* [ME, fr. OF] (13c) **:** a medieval weapon consisting of a sharpened blade mounted on a long staff and carried by foot soldiers

gist \'jist\ *n* [AF, it lies, fr. MF, fr. *gesir* to lie, fr. L *jacēre* — more at ADJACENT] (1726) **1 :** the ground of a legal action **2 :** the main point of a matter **:** ESSENCE ⟨the ~ of an argument⟩

git·tern \'git-ərn\ *n* [ME *giterne,* fr. MF *guiterne,* modif. of OSp *guitarra* guitar] (14c) **:** a medieval guitar

[1]give \'giv\ *vb* **gave** \'gāv\; **giv·en** \'giv-ən\; **giv·ing** [ME *given,* of Scand origin; akin to OSw *giva* to give; akin to OE *giefan, gifan* to give, L *habēre* to have, hold] *vt* (13c) **1 :** to make a present of ⟨~ a doll to a child⟩ **2 a :** to grant or bestow by formal action ⟨the law ~*s* citizens the right to vote⟩ **b :** to accord or yield to another ⟨*gave* him her confidence⟩ **3 a :** to put into the possession of another for his use **b** (1) **:** to administer as a sacrament (2) **:** to administer as a medicine **c :** to commit to another as a trust or responsibility and usu. for an expressed reason ⟨*gave* her his coat to hold⟩ **d :** to transfer from one's authority or custody ⟨the sheriff *gave* the prisoner to the warden⟩ **e :** to execute and deliver ⟨all employees must ~ bond⟩ **f :** to convey to another ⟨~ my regards to your family⟩ **4 a :** to offer to the action of another **:** PROFFER ⟨*gave* his hand to the visitor⟩ **b :** to yield (oneself) to a man in sexual intercourse **5 a :** to present in public performance ⟨~ a concert⟩ **b :** to present to view or observation ⟨*gave* the signal to start⟩ **6 :** to provide by way of entertainment ⟨~ a party⟩ **7 :** to propose as a toast **8 a :** to designate as a share or portion **:** ALLOT ⟨all the earth to thee and to thy race I ~ —John Milton⟩ **b :** to make assignment of (a name) **c :** to set forth as an actual or hypothetical datum ⟨~ the dimensions of the room⟩ **d :** to attribute in thought or utterance **:** ASCRIBE ⟨*gave* all the glory to God⟩ **9 a :** to yield as a product, consequence, or effect **:** PRODUCE ⟨cows ~ milk⟩ ⟨84 divided by 12 ~*s* 7⟩ **b :** to bring forth **:** BEAR **10 a :** to yield possession of by way of exchange **:** PAY **b :** to dispose of for a price **:** SELL **11 a :** to deliver by some bodily action ⟨*gave* him a push⟩ **b :** to carry out (as a bodily movement) ⟨*gave* a cynical smile⟩ **c :** to inflict as punishment ⟨*gave* the boy a whipping⟩ **d :** to award by formal verdict ⟨judgment was *given* against the plaintiff⟩ **12 :** to offer for consideration, acceptance, or use ⟨~*s* no reason for his absence⟩ **13 a :** to suffer the loss of **:** SACRIFICE **b :** to offer as appropriate or due esp. to something higher or more worthy ⟨*gave* his spirit to God⟩ ⟨~ one's time to the service of others⟩ **c :** to apply freely or fully ⟨children *giving* themselves to their play⟩ **d :** to offer as a pledge ⟨I ~ you my word⟩ **14 a**

: to cause a person to catch by contagion, infection, or exposure **15 a** : to allow one to have or take ⟨~ me time to consider your plan⟩ **b** : to be the cause of — used with an infinitive phrase as object ⟨you *gave* me to understand that you would be late⟩ **16** : to care to the extent of ⟨didn't ~ a hang⟩ ~ *vi* **1** : to make gifts or presents **2 a** : to yield to physical force or strain **b** : to collapse from the application of force or pressure **c** : to undergo or submit to change ⟨if the plan is to succeed, stubborn objections will have to ~⟩ **3 a** *of weather* : to become mild **b** *of frozen ground* : THAW **4** : to afford a view or passage : OPEN **5** : to enter wholeheartedly into an activity **6** *slang* : GO ON, HAPPEN ⟨he demanded to know what *gave*⟩

syn GIVE, PRESENT, DONATE, BESTOW, CONFER, AFFORD mean to convey to another as his possession. GIVE, the general term, is applicable to any passing over of anything by any means ⟨*give* alms⟩ ⟨*give* a boy a ride on a pony⟩ ⟨*give* my love to your mother and sisters —John Keats⟩ PRESENT carries a note of formality and ceremony ⟨*present* an award⟩ ⟨pray, *present* my respects to Lady Scott —Lord Byron⟩ DONATE is likely to imply a publicized giving (as to charity) ⟨*donate* a piano to the orphanage⟩ BESTOW implies the conveying of something as a gift and may suggest condescension on the part of the giver ⟨*bestow* unwanted advice⟩ ⟨large gifts have I *bestowed* on learned clerks —Shak.⟩ CONFER implies a gracious giving (as of a favor or honor) ⟨the Queen *confers* her titles and degrees —Alexander Pope⟩ AFFORD implies a giving or bestowing usu. as a natural or legitimate consequence of the character of the giver ⟨do the laws of his country *afford* him a remedy? —John Marshall⟩ ⟨the trees *afforded* us a welcome shade⟩

— **give a good account of** : to acquit (oneself) well — **give birth to 1** : to produce as offspring ⟨*gave birth to* a son⟩ **2** : to be the source of — **give ground** : to withdraw before superior force : RETREAT — **give or take** : to add or subtract (a specified small amount) without material alteration — **give rise to** : BRING ABOUT — **give the gun** : to open the throttle of : speed up — **give the lie to 1** : to accuse of falsehood **2** : to show to be false, inaccurate, or invalid — **give tongue** *of hounds* : to begin barking on the scent — **give way 1 a** : RETREAT **b** : to yield the right of way **2** : to yield oneself without restraint or control **3 a** : to yield to or as if to physical stress ⟨the wind caused the roof to *give way*⟩ **b** : to yield to entreaty or insistence **4** : to yield place **5** : to begin to row

[2]**give** *n* (1868) **1** : capacity or tendency to yield to force or strain **2** : the quality or state of being springy

give–and–take \ˌgiv-ən-ˈtāk\ *n* (1778) **1** : the practice of making mutual concessions : COMPROMISE **2** : good-natured exchange of ideas

give·away \ˈgiv-ə-ˌwā\ *n* (1882) **1** : an unintentional revelation or betrayal **2** : something given away free; *specif* : PREMIUM **3** : a radio or television program on which prizes are given away

give away *vt* (15c) **1** : to make a present of **2** : to deliver (a bride) to the bridegroom at a wedding **3 a** : BETRAY **b** : DISCLOSE, REVEAL **4** : to give (as weight) by way of a handicap

give back *vi* (1548) : RETIRE, RETREAT ~ *vt* : to send in return or reply : RESTORE, RETURN

give in *vt* (1602) : DELIVER, SUBMIT ⟨*gave in* his resignation⟩ ~ *vi* : to yield under insistence or entreaty : SURRENDER

[1]**giv·en** \ˈgiv-ən\ *adj* (14c) **1** : presented as a gift : bestowed without compensation **2** : PRONE, DISPOSED ⟨~ to swearing⟩ **3** *of an official document* : having been executed : DATED **4 a** : FIXED, SPECIFIED ⟨at a ~ time⟩ **b** : assumed as actual or hypothetical : GRANTED ⟨~ that all men are equal before the law⟩ **5** : immediately present in experience

[2]**given** *n* (1879) : something taken for granted : a basic assumption

given name *n* (1827) : a name that precedes one's surname; *esp* : FIRST NAME

give off *vt* (1831) **1** : to send out as a branch **2** : EMIT ⟨*gave off* an unpleasant smell⟩ ~ *vi* : to branch off

give out *vt* (14c) **1 a** : DECLARE, PUBLISH ⟨*giving out* that the doctor . . . required a few days of complete rest —Charles Dickens⟩ **b** : to read aloud the words of (a hymn or psalm) for congregational singing **2** : EMIT ⟨*gave out* a constant hum⟩ **3** : ISSUE ⟨*gave out* new uniforms⟩ ~ *vi* **1** : to become exhausted : COLLAPSE **2** : BREAK DOWN, FAIL

give over *vt* (14c) **1** : CEASE **2 a** : to yield without restraint or control : ABANDON ⟨she *gave* herself *over* to laughter before she could go on —H. D. Skidmore⟩ **b** : to set apart for a particular purpose or use **3** *archaic* : to pronounce incurable **4** : ENTRUST ~ *vi* : to bring an activity to an end : STOP ⟨told him to *give over* and let me alone —Brendan Behan⟩

giv·er \ˈgiv-ər\ *n* (14c) : one that gives : DONOR

give up *vt* (13c) **1** : to cease to do (some action) : ABANDON ⟨*gave up* his job⟩ **2** : to desist from ⟨refused to *give up* his efforts⟩ **3 a** : to abandon (oneself) to a particular feeling, influence, or activity ⟨*gave* himself *up* to despair⟩ **b** : to devote to a particular purpose or use **4** : to declare incurable or insoluble **5** : to despair of seeing ⟨we'd *given* you *up*⟩ **6** : to allow (a hit or run in baseball) while pitching ~ *vi* : to withdraw from an activity or course of action : QUIT — often used with *on* ⟨don't *give up* on finishing the project⟩ — **give up the ghost** : to cease to function : DIE

giz·mo *or* **gis·mo** \ˈgiz-(ˌ)mō\ *n, pl* **gizmos** *or* **gismos** [origin unknown] (1943) : GADGET

giz·zard \ˈgiz-ərd\ *n* [alter. of ME *giser,* fr. ONF *guisier,* fr. L *gigeria* (pl.) giblets] (15c) **1 a** : the muscular enlargement of the alimentary canal of birds that when the crop is present follows it and the proventriculus and has usu. thick muscular walls and a tough horny lining for grinding the food **b** : a thickened part of the alimentary canal in some animals (as an insect or an earthworm) that is similar in function to the crop of a bird **2** : INNARDS

gla·bel·la \glə-ˈbel-ə\ *n, pl* **-bel·lae** \-ˈbel-(ˌ)ē, -ˌī\ [NL, fr. L, fem. of *glabellus* hairless, dim. of *glaber*] (ca. 1823) : the smooth prominence between the eyebrows — **gla·bel·lar** \-ˈbel-ər\ *adj*

gla·bres·cent \glā-ˈbres-ᵊnt\ *adj* (1857) **1** : somewhat glabrous **2** : tending to become glabrous

gla·brous \ˈglā-brəs\ *adj* [L *glabr-, glaber* smooth, bald — more at GLAD] (1640) : SMOOTH; *esp* : having a surface without hairs or projections ⟨~ skin⟩

gla·cé \gla-ˈsā\ *adj* [F, fr. pp. of *glacer* to freeze, ice, glaze, fr. L *glaciare,* fr. *glacies*] (1847) **1** : made or finished so as to have a smooth glossy surface ⟨~ silk⟩ **2** : coated with a glaze : CANDIED ⟨~ cherries⟩

gla·cial \ˈglā-shəl\ *adj* [L *glacialis,* fr. *glacies*] (1656) **1 a** : extremely cold : FRIGID ⟨a ~ wind⟩ **b** : devoid of warmth and cordiality ⟨a ~ handshake⟩ **c** : coldly imperturbable ⟨maintained a ~ calm⟩ **2 a** : of, relating to, or produced by glaciers **b** : suggestive of the very slow movement of glaciers ⟨progress on the bill has been ~⟩ **c** (1) : of, relating to, or being any of those parts of geologic time from Precambrian onward when a much larger portion of the earth was covered by glaciers than at present (2) *cap* : PLEISTOCENE **3** : resembling ice in appearance ⟨~ acetic acid⟩ — **gla·cial·ly** \-shə-lē\ *adv*

gla·ci·ate \ˈglā-shē-ˌāt\ *vt* **-at·ed; -at·ing** (ca. 1656) **1** : FREEZE **2 a** : to cover with a glacier **b** : to subject to glacial action; *also* : to produce glacial effects in or on — **gla·ci·a·tion** \ˌglā-s(h)ē-ˈā-shən\ *n*

gla·cier \ˈglā-shər *also* -zhər, *esp Brit* ˈglas-ē-ər *or* ˈglās-ē-\ *n* [F dial., fr. MF dial., fr. MF *glace* ice, fr. L *glacies;* akin to L *gelu* frost — more at COLD] (1744) : a large body of ice moving slowly down a slope or valley or spreading outward on a land surface

glacio- *comb form* **1** : glacier ⟨*glacio*logy⟩ **2** \ˌglā-sh(ē-)ō, -sē-ō\ : glacial and ⟨*glacio*fluvial⟩

gla·ci·ol·o·gy \ˌglā-s(h)ē-ˈäl-ə-jē\ *n* [ISV] (1889) **1** : any of the branches of science dealing with snow or ice accumulation, glaciation, or glacial epochs **2** : the glacial features of a region — **gla·ci·o·log·ic** \-ə-ˈläj-ik\ *or* **gla·ci·o·log·i·cal** \-i-kəl\ *adj* — **gla·ci·ol·o·gist** \-ˈäl-ə-jəst\ *n*

gla·cis \gla-ˈsē, ˈglas-ē\ *n, pl* **glacis** \-ˈsēz, -ēz\ [F, fr. *glacer* to freeze, slide] (1672) **1 a** : a gentle slope : INCLINE **b** : a slope that runs downward from a fortification **2** : BUFFER STATE; *also* : BUFFER ZONE

[1]**glad** \ˈglad\ *adj* **glad·der; glad·dest** [ME, shining, glad, fr. OE *glæd;* akin to OHG *glat* shining, smooth, L *glaber* smooth, bald] (bef. 12c) **1** *archaic* : having a cheerful or happy disposition by nature **2 a** : experiencing pleasure, joy, or delight : made happy **b** : marked by a feeling of pleased or satisfied gratification **c** : very willing ⟨~ to do it⟩ **3 a** : marked by, expressive of, or caused by happiness and joy ⟨a ~ shout⟩ **b** : causing happiness and joy : PLEASANT ⟨~ tidings⟩ **4** : full of brightness and cheerfulness ⟨a ~ spring morning⟩ — **glad·ly** *adv* — **glad·ness** *n*

[2]**glad** *vb* **glad·ded; glad·ding** *archaic* (bef. 12c) : GLADDEN

[3]**glad** *n* (1923) : GLADIOLUS 1

glad·den \ˈglad-ᵊn\ *vb* **glad·dened; glad·den·ing** \ˈglad-niŋ, -ᵊn-iŋ\ *vt* (13c) : to make glad ~ *vi, archaic* : to be glad

glade \ˈglād\ *n* [perh. fr. [1]*glad*] (14c) : an open space surrounded by woods — **glady** \ˈglād-ē\ *adj*

glad–hand \ˈglad-ˌhand\ *vt* (1903) : to extend a glad hand to ⟨candidates *~ing* everyone they meet⟩ ~ *vi* : to extend a glad hand ⟨*~ing* as if he were running for mayor⟩ — **glad–hand·er** \ˈglad-ˈhan-dər\ *n*

glad hand *n* (ca. 1895) : a warm welcome or greeting often prompted by ulterior reasons

glad·i·a·tor \ˈglad-ē-ˌāt-ər\ *n* [L, fr. *gladius* sword, of Celt origin; akin to W *cleddyf* sword; akin to L *clades* destruction, Gk *klados* sprout, branch — more at HALT] (15c) **1** : a person engaged in a fight to the death as public entertainment for ancient Romans **2** : a person engaging in a public fight or controversy **3** : a trained fighter; *specif* : a professional boxer — **glad·i·a·to·ri·al** \ˌglad-ē-ə-ˈtōr-ē-əl, -ˈtȯr-\ *adj*

glad·i·o·la \ˌglad-ē-ˈō-lə\ *n* [back-formation fr. *gladiolus,* taken as a pl.] (1926) : GLADIOLUS 1

glad·i·o·lus \ˌglad-ē-ˈō-ləs\ *n, pl* **-li** \-(ˌ)lē, -ˌlī\ [NL, fr. L, gladiolus, fr. dim. of *gladius*] (15c) **1** *or pl* **gladiolus** *or* **glad·i·o·lus·es** : any of a genus (*Gladiolus*) of chiefly African plants of the iris family with erect sword-shaped leaves and spikes of brilliantly colored irregular flowers arising from flattened corms **2** : the large middle portion of the sternum

glad rags *n pl* (1900) : dressy clothes

glad·some \ˈglad-səm\ *adj* (14c) : giving or showing joy : CHEERFUL — **glad·some·ly** *adv* — **glad·some·ness** *n*

glad·stone \ˈglad-ˌstōn, *chiefly Brit* -stən\ *n, often cap* [W. E. *Gladstone*] (1889) : a traveling bag with flexible sides on a rigid frame that opens flat into two equal compartments

glai·kit *or* **glai·ket** \ˈglā-kət\ *adj* [ME (Sc) *glaikit*] *chiefly Scot* (15c) : FOOLISH, GIDDY

glair *or* **glaire** \ˈgla(ə)r, ˈgle(ə)r\ *n* [ME *gleyre* egg white, fr. MF *glaire,* modif. of (assumed) VL *claria,* fr. L *clarus* clear — more at CLEAR] (13c) **1** : a sizing liquid made from egg white **2** : a viscid substance suggestive of an egg white

glairy \-ē\ *adj* **glair·i·er; -est** (1662) : having the characteristics of or overlaid with glair

glaive \ˈglāv\ *n* [ME, fr. MF, javelin, sword, modif. of L *gladius* sword] *archaic* (15c) : SWORD; *esp* : BROADSWORD

glam·or·ize *also* **glam·our·ize** \ˈglam-ə-ˌrīz\ *vt* **-ized; -iz·ing** (1936) **1** : to make glamorous ⟨~ the living room⟩ **2** : to look upon as glamorous : ROMANTICIZE ⟨the novel *~s* war⟩ — **glam·or·iza·tion** \ˌglam-ə-rə-ˈzā-shən\ *n* — **glam·or·iz·er** \ˈglam-ə-ˌrī-zər\ *n*

glam·or·ous *also* **glam·our·ous** \ˈglam-(ə-)rəs\ *adj* (1882) : full of glamour — **glam·or·ous·ly** *adv* — **glam·or·ous·ness** *n*

glam·our *or* **glam·or** \ˈglam-ər\ *n* [Sc *glamour,* alter. of E *grammar;* fr. the popular association of erudition with occult practices] (1715) **1** : a magic spell ⟨the girls appeared to be under a ~ —Llewelyn Powys⟩ **2** : an exciting and often illusory and romantic attractiveness; *esp* : alluring or fascinating personal attraction — often used attributively ⟨~ stock⟩ ⟨~ boy⟩ ⟨~ girl⟩ — **glamour** *vt* — **glam·our·less** \-ləs\ *adj*

[1]**glance** \ˈglan(t)s\ *vb* **glanced; glanc·ing** [ME *glencen, glenchen*] *vi* (15c) **1** : to strike a surface obliquely so as to go off at an angle ⟨the bullet *glanced* off the wall⟩ **2 a** : to flash or gleam with quick intermittent rays of light ⟨brooks *glancing* in the sun⟩ **b** : to make sudden quick movements ⟨dragonflies *glancing* over the pond⟩ **3** : to touch on a subject or refer to it briefly or indirectly ⟨the work *~s* at the customs of ancient cultures⟩ **4 a** *of the eyes* : to move swiftly from one thing to another **b** : to take a quick look at something ⟨*glanced* at his watch⟩ ~ *vt* **1** *archaic* **a** : to take a quick look at **b** : to catch a

glimpse of **2 :** to give an oblique path of direction to: **a :** to throw or shoot so that the object glances from a surface **b** *archaic* **:** to aim (as an innuendo) indirectly **:** INSINUATE ***syn*** see FLASH — **glanc·er** *n*

[2]**glance** *n* (1503) **1 a :** a quick intermittent flash or gleam **b** *archaic* **:** a sudden quick movement **2 a** *archaic* **:** a rapid oblique movement **b :** a deflected impact or blow **3 a :** a swift movement of the eyes **b :** a quick or cursory look **4** *archaic* **a :** a brief satirical reference to something **:** GIBE **b :** ALLUSION — **at first glance :** on first consideration ⟨*at first glance* the subject seems harmless enough⟩

[3]**glance** *n* [G *glanz* luster, glance; akin to OHG *glanz* bright — more at GLINT] (1828) **:** any of several mineral sulfides that are usu. dark colored and have a metallic luster

glanc·ing \ˈglan(t)-siŋ\ *adj* (ca. 1536) **1 :** having a slanting direction ⟨a ~ blow⟩ **2 :** INCIDENTAL, INDIRECT ⟨made ~ allusions to her past⟩ — **glanc·ing·ly** \-siŋ-lē\ *adv*

[1]**gland** \ˈgland\ *n* [F *glande,* fr. OF, glandular swelling on the neck, gland, modif. of L *gland-, glans* acorn; akin to Gk *balanos* acorn] (1692) **1 a :** a cell or group of cells that selectively removes materials from the blood, concentrates or alters them, and secretes them for further use in the body or for elimination from the body **b :** any of various animal structures (as lymph nodes) suggestive of glands though not secretory in function **2 :** any of various secreting organs (as a nectary) of plants — **gland·less** \ˈglan-dləs\ *adj*

[2]**gland** *n* [origin unknown] (1825) **1 :** a device for preventing leakage of fluid past a joint in machinery **2 :** the movable part of a stuffing box by which the packing is compressed

glan·dered \ˈglan-dərd\ *adj* (1667) **:** affected with glanders

glan·ders \-dərz\ *n pl but sing or pl in constr* [MF *glandre* glandular swelling on the neck, fr. L *glandulae,* fr. pl. of *glandula,* dim. of *gland-, glans*] (1523) **:** a contagious and destructive disease esp. of horses caused by a bacterium (*Actinobacillus mallei*) and characterized by caseating nodular lesions esp. of the respiratory mucosae and lungs that tend to break down and form ulcers

gland of Bartholin (ca. 1900) **:** BARTHOLIN'S GLAND

glan·du·lar \ˈglan-jə-lər\ *adj* (1740) **1 a :** of, relating to, or involving glands, gland cells, or their products **b :** having the characteristics or function of a gland **2 a :** INNATE, INHERENT ⟨the almost ~ . . . instinct for adventure and romance —*Newsweek*⟩ **b :** PHYSICAL, SEXUAL — **glan·du·lar·ly** *adv*

glandular fever *n* (1902) **:** INFECTIOUS MONONUCLEOSIS

glans \ˈglanz\ *n, pl* **glan·des** \ˈglan-ˌdēz\ [L *gland-, glans,* lit., acorn] (1650) **1 :** a conical vascular body forming the extremity of the penis — called also *glans penis* **2 :** a structure of the clitoris similar to the glans penis — called also *glans cli·to·ri·dis* \-klə-ˈtȯr-əd-əs\

[1]**glare** \ˈgla(ə)r, ˈgle(ə)r\ *vb* **glared; glar·ing** [ME *glaren;* akin to OE *glæs* glass] *vi* (13c) **1 a :** to shine with a harsh uncomfortably brilliant light ⟨light *glaring* from the unshaded bulb⟩ **b :** STAND OUT, OBTRUDE **2 :** to stare angrily or fiercely ~ *vt* **1 :** to express (as hostility) by staring angrily **2** *archaic* **:** to cause to be sharply reflected ***syn*** see GAZE

[2]**glare** *n* (15c) **1 a :** a harsh uncomfortably bright light ⟨the ~ of a neon sign⟩ ⟨the ~ of publicity⟩; *esp* **:** painfully bright sunlight **b :** cheap showy brilliance **:** GARISHNESS **2 :** an angry or fierce stare **3 :** a surface or sheet of ice with a smooth slippery surface

glar·ing \ˈgla(ə)r-iŋ, ˈgle(ə)r-\ *adj* (14c) **1 :** having a fixed look of hostility, fierceness, or anger **2 a :** shining with or reflecting an uncomfortably bright light **b (1) :** GARISH **(2) :** vulgarly ostentatious **3 :** obtrusively and often painfully obvious ⟨a ~ error⟩ ***syn*** see FLAGRANT — **glar·ing·ly** \-iŋ-lē\ *adv* — **glar·ing·ness** *n*

glary \ˈgla(ə)r-ē, ˈgle(ə)r-\ *adj* **glar·i·er; -est** (1632) **:** having a dazzling brightness **:** GLARING

[1]**glass** \ˈglas\ *n, often attrib* [ME *glas,* fr. OE *glæs;* akin to OE *geolu* yellow — more at YELLOW] (bef. 12c) **1 a :** an amorphous inorganic usu. transparent or translucent substance consisting of a mixture of silicates or sometimes borates or phosphates formed by fusion of silica or of oxides of boron or phosphorus with a flux and a stabilizer into a mass that cools to a rigid condition without crystallization **b :** a substance resembling glass esp. in hardness and transparency ⟨organic ~*es* made from plastics⟩ **c :** a substance (as pumice) produced by the quick cooling of an igneous magma **2 a :** something made of glass: as **(1) :** TUMBLER **(2) :** MIRROR **(3) :** BAROMETER **b (1) :** an optical instrument or device that has one or more lenses and is designed to aid in the viewing of objects not readily seen **(2)** *pl* **:** a device used to correct defects of vision or to protect the eyes that consists typically of a pair of glass lenses and the frame by which they are held in place — called also *eyeglasses, spectacles* **3 :** the quantity held by a glass container **4 :** GLASSWARE — **glass·ful** \ˈglas-ˌfu̇l\ *n* — **glass·less** \-ləs\ *adj*

[2]**glass** *vt* (14c) **1 a :** to provide with glass **:** GLAZE 1 **b :** to enclose, case, or wall with glass ⟨the sun porch was ~*ed* in⟩ **c :** to put in a glass container **2 :** to make glassy **3 a :** REFLECT **b :** to see mirrored **4 :** to scan (as for game or forest fires) with an optical instrument ~ *vi* **1 :** to become glassy **2 :** to look for game through an optical instrument

glass·blow·ing \-ˌblō-iŋ\ *n* (1829) **:** the art of shaping a mass of glass that has been softened by heat by blowing air into it through a tube — **glass·blow·er** \-ˌblō(-ə)r\ *n*

glass eye *n* (1687) **1 :** an artificial eye made of glass **2 :** an eye having a pale, whitish, or colorless iris — **glass–eyed** \-ˈīd\ *adj*

glass harmonica *n* (ca. 1909) **:** a musical instrument consisting of a series of rotating hemispherical glasses played by touching the dampened edges with a finger

glass·house \ˈglas-ˌhau̇s\ *n* (14c) **1 :** GLASSWORKS **2** *chiefly Brit* **:** GREENHOUSE **3** *Brit* **:** a military prison

glass·ie \ˈglas-ē\ *or* **glassy** *n, pl* **glass·ies** (1887) **:** a playing marble made of glass

glass·ine \gla-ˈsēn\ *n* (1916) **:** a thin dense transparent or semitransparent paper highly resistant to the passage of air and grease

glass jaw *n* (1921) **:** vulnerability (as of a boxer) to knockout punches

glass·mak·er \ˈglas-ˌmā-kər\ *n* (1576) **:** one that makes glass — **glass·mak·ing** \-kiŋ\ *n*

glass snake *n* (1709) **:** a limbless snakelike lizard (*Ophisaurus ventralis*) of the southern U.S. with a fragile tail that readily breaks into pieces; *also* **:** any of several similar Old World lizards

glass sponge *n* (1875) **:** a siliceous sponge (class Hyalospongiae) with 6-rayed spicules and a skeleton often resembling glass when dried

glass·ware \ˈglas-ˌwa(ə)r, -ˌwe(ə)r\ *n* (1745) **:** articles made of glass

glass wool *n* (1879) **:** glass fibers in a mass resembling wool and being used esp. for thermal insulation and air filters

glass·work \ˈglas-ˌwərk\ *n* (1611) **1 a :** the manufacture of glass or glassware; *also* **:** glaziers' work **b** *pl* **:** a place where glass is made **2 :** GLASSWARE — **glass·work·er** \-ˌwər-kər\ *n*

glass·wort \-ˌwərt, -ˌwȯ(ə)rt\ *n* [fr. its former use in the manufacture of glass] (1597) **:** any of a genus (*Salicornia*) of woody jointed succulent herbs of the goosefoot family with leaves reduced to fleshy sheaths

glassy \ˈglas-ē\ *adj* **glass·i·er; -est** (14c) **1 :** resembling or made of glass **2 :** having little animation **:** DULL, LIFELESS ⟨~ eyes⟩ — **glass·i·ly** \ˈglas-ə-lē\ *adv* — **glass·i·ness** \ˈglas-ē-nəs\ *n*

Glau·ber's salt \ˌglau̇-bər(z)-\ *n* [Johann R. *Glauber* †1668 Ger. chemist] (1736) **:** a colorless crystalline sulfate of sodium $Na_2SO_4 \cdot 10H_2O$ used esp. in dyeing, as a cathartic, and in solar energy systems — called also *Glauber salt;* sometimes used in pl.

glau·co·ma \glau̇-ˈkō-mə, glȯ-\ *n* [L, cataract, fr. Gk *glaukōma,* fr. *glaukos*] (1643) **:** a disease of the eye marked by increased pressure within the eyeball that can result in damage to the optic disk and gradual loss of vision

glau·co·nite \ˈglȯ-kə-ˌnīt\ *n* [G *glaukonit,* irreg. fr. Gk *glaukos*] (1836) **:** a mineral consisting of a dull green earthy iron potassium silicate occurring abundantly in greensand — **glau·co·nit·ic** \ˌglȯ-kə-ˈnit-ik\ *adj*

glau·cous \ˈglȯ-kəs\ *adj* [L *glaucus* gleaming, gray, fr. Gk *glaukos*] (1671) **1 a :** of a pale yellow-green color **b :** of a light bluish gray or bluish white color **2 :** having a powdery or waxy coating that gives a frosted appearance and tends to rub off ⟨~ fruits⟩ — **glau·cous·ness** *n*

[1]**glaze** \ˈglāz\ *vb* **glazed; glaz·ing** [ME *glasen,* fr. *glas* glass] *vt* (14c) **1 :** to furnish or fit with glass **2 a :** to coat with or as if with a glaze ⟨the storm *glazed* trees with ice⟩ **b :** to apply a glaze to ⟨~ doughnuts⟩ **3 :** to give a smooth glossy surface to ~ *vi* **1 :** to become glazed or glassy ⟨his eyes *glazed* over⟩ **2 :** to form a glaze — **glaz·er** *n*

[2]**glaze** *n* (1752) **1 :** a smooth slippery coating of thin ice **2 a (1) :** a liquid preparation applied to food on which it hardens and forms a firm glossy coating **(2) :** a mixture predominantly of oxides (as silica and alumina) applied to the surface of ceramic wares to form a moisture-impervious and often lustrous or ornamental coating **b :** a transparent or translucent color applied to modify the effect of a painted surface **c :** a smooth glossy or lustrous surface or finish **3 :** a glassy film

[3]**glaze** *vi* **glazed; glaz·ing** [prob. blend of *glare* and *gaze*] *archaic* (1601) **:** STARE

glazed \ˈglāzd\ *adj* (15c) **1 :** covered with or as if with a glassy film ⟨~ eyes⟩ **2 :** marked by rigidity of expression **:** grimly set ⟨the ~ faces of the survivors⟩

gla·zier \ˈglā-zhər, -zē-ər\ *n* (14c) **:** one who sets glass — **gla·ziery** \ˈglāzh(-ə)-rē, ˈglā-zē-ə-\ *n*

glaz·ing \ˈglā-ziŋ\ *n* (1677) **1 :** the action, process, or trade of using or applying glaze **2 a :** GLASSWORK **b :** GLAZE **3 :** glass or other transparent material used for windows

[1]**gleam** \ˈglēm\ *n* [ME *gleem,* fr. OE *glǣm;* akin to OE *geolu* yellow — more at YELLOW] (bef. 12c) **1 a :** a transient appearance of subdued or partly obscured light ⟨the ~ of dawn in the east⟩ **b (1) :** a small bright light ⟨the ~ of a match⟩ **(2) :** GLINT ⟨a ~ of anticipation in his eyes⟩ **2 :** a brief or faint appearance or occurrence **:** TRACE ⟨a ~ of hope⟩ — **gleamy** \ˈglē-mē\ *adj*

[2]**gleam** *vi* (13c) **1 :** to shine with or as if with subdued steady light or moderate brightness **2 :** to appear briefly or faintly ⟨a light ~*ed* in the darkness⟩ ~ *vt* **:** to cause to gleam ***syn*** see FLASH

glean \ˈglēn\ *vb* [ME *glenen,* fr. MF *glener,* fr. LL *glennare;* akin to MIr *digliunn* I glean] *vi* (14c) **1 :** to gather grain or other produce left by reapers **2 :** to gather information or other material bit by bit ~ *vt* **1 a :** to pick up after a reaper **b :** to strip (as a field) of the leavings of reapers **2 a :** to gather (as information) bit by bit **b :** to pick over in search of relevant material ⟨~*ing* old letters for information on the founding of the town⟩ **3 :** FIND OUT, LEARN, ASCERTAIN — **glean·able** \ˈglē-nə-bəl\ *adj* — **glean·er** *n*

glean·ings \ˈglē-niŋz\ *n pl* (15c) **:** things acquired by gleaning

glebe \ˈglēb\ *n* [L *gleba* clod, land — more at CLIP] (14c) **1** *archaic* **:** LAND; *specif* **:** a plot of cultivated land **2 :** land belonging or yielding revenue to a parish church or ecclesiastical benefice

glede \ˈglēd\ *n* [ME, fr. OE *glida;* akin to OE *glīdan* to glide] (bef. 12c) **:** any of several birds of prey (as a kite of Europe)

glee \ˈglē\ *n* [ME, fr. OE *glēo* entertainment, music; akin to ON *glȳ* joy, Gk *chleuē* joke] (bef. 12c) **1 :** exultant high-spirited joy **:** MERRIMENT **2 :** a song in homophonic style for three or more unaccompanied usu. male voices ***syn*** see MIRTH

glee club *n* (1814) **:** a chorus organized for singing usu. short choral pieces

gleed \ˈglēd\ *n* [ME, fr. OE *glēd;* akin to OE *glōwan* to glow] *archaic* (bef. 12c) **:** a glowing coal

glee·ful \ˈglē-fəl\ *adj* (1586) **:** full of glee **:** MERRY — **glee·ful·ly** \-fə-lē\ *adv* — **glee·ful·ness** *n*

gleek \ˈglēk\ *vi* [origin unknown] *archaic* (1590) **:** to make a gibe or jest

glee·man \ˈglē-mən\ *n* [ME *gleman,* fr. OE *glēoman,* fr. *glēo* + *man* man] (bef. 12c) **:** JONGLEUR

glee·some \ˈglē-səm\ *adj, archaic* (1603) **:** GLEEFUL

gleet \ˈglēt\ *n* [ME *glet* slimy or mucous matter, fr. MF *glete,* fr. L *glittus* viscous; akin to LL *glut-, glus* glue — more at CLAY] (14c) **:** a chronic inflammation of a bodily orifice usu. accompanied by an abnormal discharge; *also* **:** the discharge itself (as from the urethra in gonorrhea) — **gleety** \-ē\ *adj*

gleg \ˈgleg\ *adj* [ME, fr. ON *glöggr* clear-sighted] *Scot* (14c) **:** QUICK, SHARP

glei·za·tion \glā-ˈzā-shən\ *n* (1938) **:** development of or conversion into gley

glen \ˈglen\ *n* [ME (Sc), valley, fr. (assumed) ScGael *glenn;* akin to MIr *glend* valley] (15c) **:** a secluded narrow valley

glen·gar·ry \glen-ˈgar-ē\ *n, pl* **-ries** *often cap* [*Glengarry,* valley in Scotland] (1841) **:** a woolen cap of Scottish origin

glen plaid \ˈglen-\ *n* [short for *glenurquhart plaid,* fr. *Glen Urquhart,* prob. fr. *Glen Urquhart,* valley in Inverness-shire, Scotland] (1926) **:** a twill pattern of broken checks; *also* **:** a fabric woven in this pattern — called also *glen check*

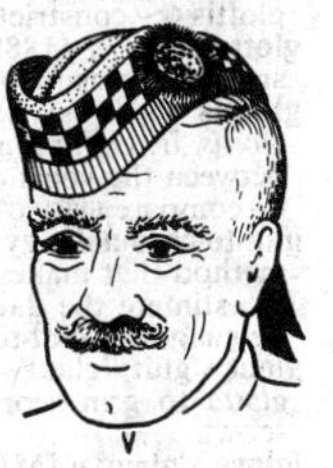
glengarry

gley \ˈglā\ *n* [Russ *gleĭ* clay; akin to OE *clǣg* clay — more at CLAY] (1927) **:** a sticky clay layer formed under the surface of some waterlogged soils

glia \ˈglē-ə, ˈglī-ə\ *n* [NL, fr. MGk, glue] (1891) **:** NEUROGLIA

gli·a·din \ˈglī-əd-ən\ *n* [It *gliadina,* fr. MGk *glia* glue — more at CLAY] (ca. 1828) **:** PROLAMIN; *esp* **:** one obtained by alcoholic extraction of gluten from wheat and rye

gli·al \ˈglē-əl, ˈglī-əl\ *adj* [NL *glia*] (1888) **:** of or relating to neuroglia

glib \ˈglib\ *adj* **glib·ber; glib·best** [prob. modif. of LG *glibberig* slippery] (1599) **1** *archaic* **:** SMOOTH, SLIPPERY **2 a :** marked by ease and informality **:** NONCHALANT **b :** showing little forethought or preparation **:** OFFHAND ⟨~ answers⟩ **c :** lacking depth and substance **:** SUPERFICIAL, PAT ⟨mouthing ~ solutions to knotty problems⟩ **3 :** marked by ease and fluency in speaking or writing often to the point of being insincere or deceitful ⟨a ~ politician⟩ — **glib·ly** *adv* — **glib·ness** *n*

[1]**glide** \ˈglīd\ *vb* **glid·ed; glid·ing** [ME *gliden,* fr. OE *glīdan;* akin to OHG *glītan* to glide] *vi* (bef. 12c) **1 a :** to move smoothly, continuously, and effortlessly ⟨swans *gliding* over the lake⟩ **b :** to move stealthily **:** CREEP ⟨*gliding* along the wall until they were out of sight⟩ **2 :** to pass gradually and imperceptibly ⟨hours *glided* by⟩ **3** *of an airplane* **:** to descend gradually in a controlled way but without engine power sufficient for level flight; *also* **:** to fly in a glider **4 :** to produce a glide (as in music or speech) ~ *vt* **:** to cause to glide

[2]**glide** *n* (1596) **1 :** the act or action of gliding **2 :** a calm stretch of shallow water flowing smoothly **3 a :** PORTAMENTO **b :** a nonsignificant sound and esp. a less prominent vowel sound produced by the passing of the vocal organs to or from the articulatory position of a speech sound — compare DIPHTHONG **4 :** a device for facilitating movement of something; *esp* **:** a circular usu. metal button attached to the bottom of furniture legs to provide a smooth surface

glide path *n* (1936) **:** the path of descent of an airplane as marked out by a radio beam that guides a pilot in landing; *also* **:** the radio beam

glid·er \ˈglīd-ər\ *n* (15c) **1 :** one that glides: as **a :** an aircraft similar to an airplane but without an engine **b :** a porch seat suspended from an upright framework by short chains or straps **2 :** something that aids gliding; *specif* **:** GLIDE 4

glide slope *n* (ca. 1949) **:** GLIDE PATH

glim \ˈglim\ *n* [perh. short for [2]*glimmer*] (ca. 1700) **:** something that furnishes light (as a lantern or candle); *also* **:** illumination given off by such a source

[1]**glim·mer** \ˈglim-ər\ *vi* **glim·mered; glim·mer·ing** \-(ə-)riŋ\ [ME *glimeren;* akin to OE *glǣm* gleam] (15c) **1 a :** to shine faintly or unsteadily **b :** to give off a subdued unsteady reflection **2 :** to appear indistinctly with a faintly luminous quality ***syn*** see FLASH

[2]**glimmer** *n* (1590) **1 a :** a feeble or intermittent light **b :** a subdued unsteady shining or sparkle **2 a :** a dim perception or faint idea **:** INKLING ⟨I had only the vaguest ~ of why I was there⟩ **b :** HINT, SPARK ⟨a ~ of intelligence⟩

glim·mer·ing *n* (15c) **:** GLIMMER

[1]**glimpse** \ˈglim(p)s\ *vb* **glimpsed; glimps·ing** [ME *glimsen;* akin to MHG *glimsen* to glimmer, OE *glǣm* gleam] *vi* (14c) **1** *archaic* **:** GLIMMER **2 :** to take a brief look ~ *vt* **:** to get a brief look at — **glimps·er** *n*

[2]**glimpse** *n* (1540) **1** *archaic* **:** GLIMMER **2 :** a brief fleeting view or look

[1]**glint** \ˈglint\ *vb* [ME *glinten* to dart obliquely, glint, alter. of *glenten,* of Scand origin; akin to Sw dial. *glänta* to clear up; akin to OHG *glanz* bright, OE *geolu* yellow — more at YELLOW] *vi* (14c) **1 a** *archaic* **:** to glance off an object **b** *of rays of light* **:** to be reflected at an angle from a surface **2 :** to give off reflection in brilliant flashes; *also* **:** GLEAM **3 :** to look quickly or briefly **:** GLANCE **4 :** to appear briefly or faintly ~ *vt* **:** to cause to glint ***syn*** see FLASH

[2]**glint** *n* (14c) **1 :** a tiny bright flash of light **2 :** a brief or faint manifestation **:** GLIMMER ⟨a ~ of recognition⟩; *also* **:** a trace of emotion expressed through the eyes ⟨on occasion a steely ~ replaces the twinkle . . . and a hard note of authority comes into his normally soft voice — Roscoe McGowen⟩

gli·o·ma \glē-ˈō-mə, glī-\ *n, pl* **-mas** *or* **-ma·ta** \-mət-ə\ [NL, fr. *glia* neuroglia] (1870) **:** a tumor arising from neuroglia

[1]**glis·sade** \glis-ˈäd, -ˈād\ *vi* **glis·sad·ed; glis·sad·ing** [F, n., slide, glissade, fr. *glisser* to slide, fr. OF *glicier,* alter. of *glier,* of Gmc origin; akin to OHG *glītan* to glide] (1859) **1 :** to slide in a standing or squatting position down a snow-covered slope without the aid of skis **2 :** to perform a ballet glissade — **glis·sad·er** *n*

[2]**glissade** *n* (1862) **1 :** the action of glissading **2 :** a gliding step in ballet

glis·san·do \gli-ˈsän-(ˌ)dō\ *n, pl* **-di** \-(ˌ)dē\ *or* **-dos** [prob. modif. of F *glissade*] (1873) **:** a rapid sliding up or down the musical scale

[1]**glis·ten** \ˈglis-ᵊn\ *vi* **glis·tened; glis·ten·ing** \ˈglis-niŋ, -ᵊn-iŋ\ [ME *glistnen,* fr. OE *glisnian;* akin to OE *glisian* to glitter, *geolu* yellow — more at YELLOW] (bef. 12c) **:** to give off a sparkling or lustrous reflection of or as if of a moist or polished surface ***syn*** see FLASH

[2]**glisten** *n* (1840) **:** GLITTER, SPARKLE

glis·ter \ˈglis-tər\ *vi* **glis·tered; glis·ter·ing** \-t(ə-)riŋ\ [ME *glistren;* akin to OE *glisian*] (14c) **:** GLITTER — **glister** *n*

glitch \ˈglich\ *n* [prob. fr. G *glitschen* to slide, slip; akin to OHG *glītan* to glide — more at GLIDE] (1962) **1 a :** an unwanted brief surge of electric power **b :** a false or spurious electronic signal **2 :** MALFUNCTION ⟨a ~ in a spacecraft's fuel cell⟩ **3 :** a minor problem that causes a temporary setback **:** SNAG

[1]**glit·ter** \ˈglit-ər\ *vi* [ME *gliteren,* fr. ON *glitra;* akin to OE *geolu* yellow] (14c) **1 a :** to shine by reflection with many small flashes of brilliant light **:** SPARKLE ⟨the diamonds ~*ed* in the sunlight⟩ **b :** to shine with strong emotion **:** FLASH ⟨eyes ~*ing* in anger⟩ **2 :** to be brilliantly attractive, lavish, or spectacular; *also* **:** to be superficially attractive or exciting ***syn*** see FLASH — **glit·ter·ing·ly** \-ə-riŋ-lē\ *adv*

[2]**glitter** *n* (1602) **1 a :** sparkling brilliance of something that glitters **b :** a bright usu. superficial attractiveness **c :** the quality of being spectacular **2 :** small glittering objects used for ornamentation — **glit·tery** \ˈglit-ə-rē\ *adj*

glit·te·ra·ti \ˌglit-ə-ˈrät-ē\ *n pl* [[2]*glitter* + *-ati* (as in *literati*)] (1940) **:** CELEBRITIES, BEAUTIFUL PEOPLE

glitter rock *n* (1973) **:** rock music characterized by performers wearing glittering costumes and bizarre often grotesque makeup

glitz \ˈglits\ *n* [prob. modif. of G *glitzern* to glitter, fr. MHG *glitzen;* akin to ON *glitra* to glitter] (1971) **:** extravagant showiness **:** GLITTER, OSTENTATION — **glitzy** \ˈglit-sē\ *adj*

gloam \ˈglōm\ *n* [Sc *gloam* to become twilight, back-formation fr. *gloaming*] *archaic* (1821) **:** TWILIGHT

gloam·ing \ˈglō-miŋ\ *n* [ME (Sc) *gloming,* fr. OE *glōming,* fr. *glōm* twilight; akin to OE *glōwan* to glow] (bef. 12c) **:** TWILIGHT, DUSK

[1]**gloat** \ˈglōt\ *vi* [prob. of Scand origin; akin to ON *glotta* to grin scornfully; akin to OE *geolu* yellow] (1676) **1** *obs* **:** to look or glance admiringly or amorously **2 :** to observe or think about something with triumphant and often malicious satisfaction, gratification, or delight ⟨~ over an enemy's misfortune⟩ — **gloat·er** *n* — **gloat·ing·ly** *adv*

[2]**gloat** *n* (1899) **:** the act or feeling of one who gloats

glob \ˈgläb\ *n* [perh. blend of *globe* and *blob*] (1900) **1 :** a small drop **:** BLOB ⟨little ~*s* of ink⟩ **2 :** a usu. large and rounded mass — **glob·by** \-ē\ *adj*

glob·al \ˈglō-bəl\ *adj* (1676) **1 :** SPHERICAL **2 :** of, relating to, or involving the entire world **:** WORLDWIDE ⟨~ warfare⟩ ⟨a ~ system of communication⟩; *also* **:** of or relating to a celestial body (as the moon) **3 :** of, relating to, or applying to a whole (as a mathematical function or a computer program) ⟨a ~ search for a word in a manuscript⟩ — **glob·al·ly** \ˈglō-bə-lē\ *adv*

glob·al·ism \ˈglō-bə-ˌliz-əm\ *n* (1943) **:** a national policy of treating the whole world as a proper sphere for political influence — compare IMPERIALISM, INTERNATIONALISM — **glob·al·ist** \-ləst\ *n*

glob·al·ize \ˈglō-bə-ˌlīz\ *vt* **-ized; -iz·ing** (1944) **:** to make global; *esp* **:** to make worldwide in scope or application — **glob·al·iza·tion** \ˌglō-bə-lə-ˈzā-shən\ *n*

[1]**globe** \ˈglōb\ *n* [MF, fr. L *globus* — more at CLIP] (15c) **:** something spherical or rounded: as **a :** a spherical representation of the earth, a celestial body, or the heavens **b :** EARTH 4 **c :** ORB 5

[2]**globe** *vt* **globed; glob·ing** *archaic* (1641) **:** to form into a globe

globe artichoke *n* (1858) **:** ARTICHOKE 1

globe·fish \ˈglōb-ˌfish\ *n* (1668) **:** PUFFER 2a

globe·flow·er \-ˌflau̇(-ə)r\ *n* (1597) **:** any of a genus (*Trollius*) of plants of the buttercup family with globose yellow flowers

globe–trot·ter \-ˌträt-ər\ *n* (1875) **:** one that travels widely — **globe–trot·ting** \-ˌträt-iŋ\ *n or adj*

glo·bin \ˈglō-bən\ *n* [ISV, back-formation fr. *hemoglobin*] (1877) **:** a colorless protein obtained by removal of heme from a conjugated protein and esp. hemoglobin

glo·boid \ˈglō-ˌbȯid\ *adj* (1887) **:** shaped like a sphere

glo·bose \ˈglō-ˌbōs\ *adj* (15c) **:** GLOBULAR 1a(1) ⟨~ pollen⟩

glob·u·lar \ˈgläb-yə-lər, *1b is also* ˈglōb-\ *adj* [partly fr. L *glob*us + E *-ular;* partly fr. L *globulus* + E *-ar*] (1656) **1 a (1) :** having the shape of a globe or globule **(2) :** having a compact folded molecular structure ⟨~ proteins⟩ **b :** GLOBAL **2 :** having or consisting of globules

glob·ule \ˈgläb-(ˌ)yü(ə)l\ *n* [F, fr. L *globulus,* dim. of *globus*] (1661) **:** a tiny globe or ball ⟨~*s* of mercury⟩

glob·u·lin \ˈgläb-yə-lən\ *n* (1845) **:** any of a class of simple proteins (as myosin) that are insoluble in pure water but are soluble in dilute salt solutions and that occur widely in plant and animal tissues — compare ALPHA GLOBULIN, BETA GLOBULIN, GAMMA GLOBULIN

glo·chid·i·um \glō-ˈkid-ē-əm\ *n, pl* **-ia** \-ē-ə\ [NL, fr. Gk *glōchis* projecting point + NL *-idium*] (1882) **:** a larval freshwater mussel (family Unionidae) that develops as an external parasite on fish

glock·en·spiel \ˈgläk-ən-ˌs(h)pēl\ *n* [G, fr. *glocke* bell (fr. OHG *glocka,* of Celtic origin; akin to MIr *clocc* bell) + *spiel* play, fr. OHG *spil* — more at CLOCK, SPIEL] (1883) **:** a percussion instrument consisting of a series of graduated metal bars tuned to the chromatic scale and played with two hammers

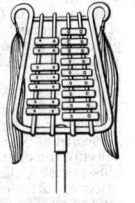

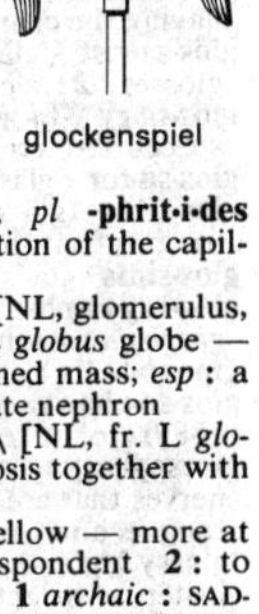
glockenspiel

glom \ˈgläm\ *vt* **glommed; glom·ming** [prob. alter. of E dial. *glaum* to grab] (1907) **1** *slang* **:** TAKE, STEAL **2** *slang* **:** SEIZE, CATCH — **glom on to** *slang* **:** to take possession of

glo·mer·u·lar \glə-ˈmer-(y)ə-lər, glō-\ *adj* (1885) **:** of, relating to, or produced by a glomerulus ⟨~ nephritis⟩ ⟨~ capillaries⟩

glom·er·ule \ˈgläm-ə-ˌrül, -ər-ˌyü(ə)l\ *n* [NL *glomerulus*] (1793) **:** a compacted cyme like the flower head of a composite

glo·mer·u·lo·ne·phri·tis \glə-ˌmer-(y)ə-lō-ni-ˈfrīt-əs\ *n, pl* **-phrit·i·des** \-ˈfrit-ə-ˌdēz\ (1886) **:** nephritis marked by inflammation of the capillaries of the renal glomeruli

glo·mer·u·lus \glə-ˈmer-(y)ə-ləs, glō-\ *n, pl* **-li** \-ˌlī, -ˌlē\ [NL, glomerulus, glomerule, dim. of L *glomer-, glomus* ball; akin to L *globus* globe — more at CLIP] (1856) **:** a small convoluted or intertwined mass; *esp* **:** a tuft of capillaries at the point of origin of each vertebrate nephron

glo·mus \ˈglō-məs\ *n, pl* **glo·mera** \ˈgläm-ə-rə, ˈglōm-\ [NL, fr. L *glomer-, glomus*] (1903) **:** a small arteriovenous anastomosis together with its supporting structures

[1]**gloom** \ˈglüm\ *vb* [ME *gloumen;* akin to OE *geolu* yellow — more at YELLOW] *vi* (14c) **1 :** to look, feel, or act sullen or despondent **2 :** to be or become overcast **3 :** to loom up dimly ~ *vt* **1** *archaic* **:** SADDEN **2 :** to make dark, murky, or somber

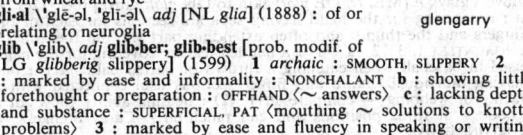

[2]**gloom** *n* (1629) **1 a :** partial or total darkness **b :** a dark or shadowy place **2 a :** lowness of spirits : DEJECTION **b :** an atmosphere of despondency ⟨a ~ fell over the household⟩

gloomy \ˈglü-mē\ *adj* **gloom·i·er; -est** (1588) **1 a :** partially or totally dark; *esp* **:** dismally and depressingly dark ⟨~ weather⟩ **b :** having a frowning or scowling appearance : FORBIDDING ⟨a ~ countenance⟩ **c :** low in spirits : MELANCHOLY ⟨felt ~ after the play⟩ **2 a :** causing gloom : DEPRESSING ⟨a ~ story⟩ ⟨a bleak ~ landscape⟩ **b :** lacking in promise or hopefulness : PESSIMISTIC ⟨~ prophecies⟩ ⟨a ~ future⟩ *syn* see SULLEN — **gloom·i·ly** \-mə-lē\ *adv* — **gloom·i·ness** \-mē-nəs\ *n*

glop \ˈgläp\ *n* [origin unknown] (ca. 1944) **:** a thick semiliquid food or mixture of foods that is unappetizing in appearance; *broadly* **:** something mushy, worthless, or tasteless — **glop·py** \-ē\ *adj*

Glo·ria \ˈglōr-ē-ə, ˈglȯr-\ *n* [L, glory] (13c) **1 :** GLORIA IN EXCELSIS **2 :** GLORIA PATRI

Gloria in Ex·cel·sis \-ˌin-eks-ˈchel-səs, -ek-ˈshel-\ [LL, glory (be to God) on high] (14c) **:** a Christian liturgical hymn having the verse form of the Psalms

Gloria Pa·tri \-ˈpä-(ˌ)trē\ *n* [LL, glory (be) to the Father] (13c) **:** a 2-verse doxology to the Trinity

glo·ri·fy \ˈglōr-ə-ˌfī, ˈglȯr-\ *vt* **-fied; -fy·ing** [ME *glorifien,* fr. MF *glorifier,* fr. LL *glorificare,* fr. *gloria*] (14c) **1 a :** to make glorious by bestowing honor, praise, or admiration **b :** to elevate to celestial glory **2 :** to light up brilliantly ⟨a large chandelier *glorifies* the whole room⟩ **3 a :** to represent as glorious : EXTOL ⟨romantic love is *glorified* in song and literature⟩ **b :** to cause to be or seem to be better than the actual condition ⟨the new position is just a *glorified* version of the old stockroom job⟩ **4 :** to give glory to (as in worship) — **glo·ri·fi·ca·tion** \ˌglōr-ə-fə-ˈkā-shən, ˌglȯr-\ *n* — **glo·ri·fi·er** \ˈglōr-ə-ˌfī(-ə)r, ˈglȯr-\ *n*

glo·ri·ous \ˈglōr-ē-əs, ˈglȯr-\ *adj* [ME, fr. OF & L; OF *glorieus, glorios,* fr. L *gloriosus* glorious, vainglorious, fr. *gloria*] (13c) **1 a :** possessing or deserving glory : ILLUSTRIOUS **b :** entitling one to glory ⟨a ~ victory⟩ **2 :** marked by great beauty or splendor : MAGNIFICENT **3 :** DELIGHTFUL, WONDERFUL ⟨had a ~ weekend⟩ *syn* see SPLENDID — **glo·ri·ous·ly** *adv* — **glo·ri·ous·ness** *n*

[1]**glo·ry** \ˈglōr-ē, ˈglȯr-\ *n, pl* **glories** [ME *glorie,* fr. MF & L; MF, fr. L *gloria*] (14c) **1 a :** praise, honor, or distinction extended by common consent : RENOWN **b :** worshipful praise, honor, and thanksgiving ⟨giving ~ to God⟩ **2 a :** something that secures praise or renown ⟨the ~ of a brilliant career⟩ **b :** a distinguished quality or asset **3 a (1) :** great beauty and splendor : MAGNIFICENCE ⟨the ~ that was Greece and the grandeur that was Rome —E. A. Poe⟩ **(2) :** something marked by beauty or resplendence ⟨a perfect ~ of a day⟩ **b :** the splendor and beatific happiness of heaven; *broadly* **:** ETERNITY **4 a :** a state of great gratification or exaltation ⟨when she's acting she's in her ~⟩ **b :** a height of prosperity or achievement **5 :** a ring or spot of light: as **a :** AUREOLE **b :** CORONA 2a, 2b

[2]**glory** *vi* **glo·ried; glo·ry·ing** (14c) **:** to rejoice proudly — used with *in*

[3]**glory** *or* **glory be** *interj* (1816) — used to express surprise or delight

[1]**gloss** \ˈgläs, ˈglȯs\ *n* [prob. of Scand origin; akin to Icel *glossa* to glow; akin to OE *geolu* yellow] (1538) **1 :** a surface luster or brightness : SHINE **2 :** a deceptively attractive appearance : SEMBLANCE ⟨selfishness that had a ~ of humanitarianism about it⟩ **3 :** a transparent cosmetic preparation for adding shine and usu. color to the lips

[2]**gloss** *vt* (1656) **1 a :** to mask the true nature of : give a deceptively attractive appearance to — used with *over* ⟨the misery was general, where not ~*ed* over by liberal application of alcohol —Marston Bates⟩ **b :** to deal with (a subject or problem) too lightly or not at all — used with *over* ⟨he ~*es* over scholarly controversies rather than confronting them head-on —John Israel⟩ **2 :** to give a gloss to

[3]**gloss** *n* [ME *glose,* fr. MF, fr. L *glossa* unusual word requiring explanation, fr. Gk *glōssa, glōtta* tongue, language, unusual word; akin to Gk *glōchis* projecting point] (14c) **1 a :** a brief explanation (as in the margin or between the lines of a text) of a difficult or obscure word or expression **b :** a false and often willfully misleading interpretation (as of a text) **2 a :** GLOSSARY **b :** an interlinear translation **c :** a continuous commentary accompanying a text

[4]**gloss** *vt* (14c) **1 a :** to provide a gloss for : EXPLAIN, DEFINE **b :** INTERPRET **2 :** to dispose of (as a difficult problem) by false or perverse interpretation ⟨trying to ~ away the irrationalities of the universe —Irwin Edman⟩

gloss- *or* **glosso-** *comb form* [L, fr. Gk *glōss-, glōsso-,* fr. *glōssa*] **1 :** tongue ⟨*gloss*algia⟩ **2 :** language ⟨*glosso*logy⟩

glos·sa \ˈgläs-ə, ˈglȯs-\ *n, pl* **glos·sae** \-ˌē, -ˌī\ *also* **glossas** [NL, fr. Gk *glōssa*] (ca. 1889) **:** a tongue or lingual structure esp. in an insect; *esp* **:** the median distal lobe of the labium of an insect

glos·sal \-əl\ *adj* (ca. 1860) **:** of or relating to the tongue

glos·sar·i·al \glä-ˈsar-ē-əl, glȯ-, -ˈser-\ *adj* (1821) **:** of, relating to, or having the characteristics of a glossary

glos·sa·rist \ˈgläs-ə-rəst, ˈglȯs-\ *n* (1774) **1 :** one that makes textual glosses **2 :** a compiler of a glossary

glos·sa·ry \-(ə-)rē\ *n, pl* **-ries** (14c) **:** a collection of textual glosses or of specialized terms with their meanings

glos·sa·tor \ˈgläs-ˌāt-ər, ˈglȯs-\ *n* (14c) **:** GLOSSARIST

glos·si·na \glä-ˈsī-nə, glȯ-, -ˈsē-\ *n* [NL, genus name, fr. Gk *glōssa* tongue; fr. its long proboscis] (ca. 1889) **:** TSETSE FLY

glos·si·tis \glä-ˈsīt-əs, ˈglȯ-\ *n* (1822) **:** inflammation of the tongue

glos·sog·ra·pher \glä-ˈsäg-rə-fər, glȯ-\ *n* [Gk *glōssographos,* fr. *glōssa* + *graphein* to write — more at CARVE] (1607) **:** GLOSSARIST

glos·so·la·lia \ˌgläs-ə-ˈlā-lē-ə, ˌglȯs-\ *n* [NL] (1879) **:** TONGUE 4c(1)

glos·so·pha·ryn·geal \ˌgläs-ō-ˌfar-ən-ˈjē-əl, ˌglȯs-, -fə-ˈrin-j(ē-)əl\ *adj* (ca. 1889) **:** of or relating to both tongue and pharynx

glossopharyngeal nerve *n* (ca. 1889) **:** either of the 9th pair of cranial nerves that are mixed nerves and supply chiefly the pharynx, posterior tongue, and parotid gland

[1]**glossy** \ˈgläs-ē, ˈglȯs-\ *adj* **gloss·i·er; -est** (1556) **1 :** having a surface luster or brightness ⟨rich ~ leather⟩ ⟨~ paper⟩ **2 :** attractive in an artificially opulent, sophisticated, or smoothly captivating manner : SLICK ⟨lots of ~ and phony chatter⟩ *syn* see SLEEK — **gloss·i·ly** \-ə-lē\ *adv* — **gloss·i·ness** \-ē-nəs\ *n*

[2]**glossy** *n, pl* **gloss·ies** (1928) **1** *chiefly Brit* **:** SLICK 3 **2 :** a photograph printed on smooth shiny paper

glott- *or* **glotto-** *comb form* [Gk *glōtt-, glōtto-* tongue, fr. *glōssa, glōtta*] **:** language ⟨*glotto*logy⟩

glot·tal \ˈglät-ᵊl\ *adj* (1846) **:** of, relating to, or produced in or by the glottis ⟨~ constriction⟩

glottal stop *n* (1888) **:** the interruption of the breath stream during speech by closure of the glottis

glot·tis \ˈglät-əs\ *n, pl* **glot·tis·es** *or* **glot·ti·des** \-ə-ˌdēz\ [Gk *glōttid-, glōttis,* fr. *glōtta* tongue — more at GLOSS] (1578) **:** the elongated space between the vocal cords; *also* **:** the structures that surround this space — compare EPIGLOTTIS

glot·to·chro·nol·o·gy \ˌglät-ō-krə-ˈnäl-ə-jē\ *n* (1953) **:** a linguistic method that makes use of the rate of vocabulary replacement in order to estimate the date of divergence for distinct but genetically related languages — **glot·to·chro·no·log·i·cal** \-ˌkrän-ᵊl-ˈäj-i-kəl, -ˌkrōn-\ *adj*

glout \ˈglüt, ˈglau̇t\ *vi* [ME *glouten,* prob. of Scand origin; akin to ON *glotta* to grin scornfully — more at GLOAT] *archaic* (14c) **:** FROWN, SCOWL

[1]**glove** \ˈgləv\ *n* [ME, fr. OE *glōf;* akin to ON *glōfi* glove] (bef. 12c) **1 a :** a covering for the hand having separate sections for each of the fingers and the thumb and often extending part way up the arm **b :** [1]GAUNTLET 1, 3 **2 a (1) :** a padded leather covering for the hand used in baseball when catching a thrown or batted ball; *specif* **:** one having individual thumb and finger sections usu. connected with a lacing or webbing — compare MITT **(2) :** fielding ability ⟨he's got a good ~ at three positions and can pinch-hit —Casey Stengel⟩ **b :** BOXING GLOVE

[2]**glove** *vt* **gloved; glov·ing** (15c) **1 a :** to cover with or as if with a glove **b :** to furnish with gloves **2 :** to catch (a baseball) in one's gloved hand

glove box *n* (1946) **1** *chiefly Brit* **:** GLOVE COMPARTMENT **2 :** a sealed protectively lined compartment having holes to which are attached gloves for use in handling dangerous materials inside the compartment

glove compartment *n* (1939) **:** a small storage cabinet in the dashboard of an automobile

glov·er \ˈgləv-ər\ *n* (14c) **:** one that makes or sells gloves

[1]**glow** \ˈglō\ *vi* [ME *glowen,* fr. OE *glōwan;* akin to OE *geolu* yellow — more at YELLOW] (bef. 12c) **1 a :** to shine with or as if with an intense heat ⟨the fire ~*ing* in the darkness⟩ **b (1) :** to have a rich warm typically ruddy color ⟨cheeks ~*ing* with health⟩ **(2) :** FLUSH, BLUSH ⟨the children ~*ed* with excitement⟩ **2 a :** to experience a sensation of or as if of heat ⟨~*ing* with rage⟩ **b :** to show exuberance or elation ⟨~ with pride⟩ — **glow·ing·ly** \-iŋ-lē\ *adv*

[2]**glow** *n* (1600) **1 :** brightness or warmth of color; *esp* **:** REDNESS ⟨the ~ of his cheeks⟩ **2 a :** warmth of feeling or emotion **b :** a sensation of warmth ⟨the drug produces a sustained ~⟩ **3 a :** the state of glowing with heat and light **b :** light such as is emitted by a solid body heated to luminosity : INCANDESCENCE

[1]**glow·er** \ˈglau̇(-ə)r, ÷ˈglō(-ə)r\ *vi* [ME (Sc) *glowren;* perh. of Scand origin; akin to Norw dial. *glyra* to look askance, Icel *glossa* to glow — more at GLOSS] (15c) **:** to look or stare with sullen annoyance or anger

[2]**glower** *n* (1715) **:** a sullen brooding look indicative of annoyance or anger

glow lamp *n* (1884) **:** a gas-discharge electric lamp in which most of the light proceeds from the glow of the gas near the cathode

glow plug n (ca. 1941) **:** a heating element in a diesel-engine cylinder to preheat the air and facilitate starting; *also* **:** a similar element for ignition in other internal-combustion engines

glow·worm \ˈglō-ˌwərm\ *n* [ME] (14c) **:** any of various luminous insect larvae or adults with wings rudimentary or lacking; *esp* **:** a larva or wingless female of a firefly (family Lampyridae) that emits light from the abdomen

glox·in·ia \gläk-ˈsin-ē-ə\ *n* [NL, genus name, fr. B. P. *Gloxin* 18th cent. Ger. botanist] (1816) **:** any of a genus (*Sinningia*) of Brazilian tuberous herbs of a family (Gesneriaceae, the gloxinia family); *esp* **:** a plant (*S. speciosa*) widely cultivated for its showy bell-shaped or slipper-shaped flowers

[1]**gloze** \ˈglōz\ *vt* **glozed; gloz·ing** [ME *glosen* to gloss, flatter, fr. *glose* gloss] *archaic* (14c) **:** [4]GLOSS 1

[2]**gloze** *vt* **glozed; gloz·ing** (1820) **:** [2]GLOSS 1 — often used with *over*

gluc- *or* **gluco-** *comb form* [ISV] **1 a :** glucose **b :** related to or containing glucose **2 :** GLYC-

glu·ca·gon \ˈglü-kə-ˌgän\ *n* [*gluc-* + *-agon* (perh. fr. Gk *agōn,* prp. of *agein* to lead, drive) — more at AGENT] (1923) **:** a protein hormone that is produced esp. by the islets of Langerhans and that promotes an increase in the sugar content of the blood by increasing the rate of glycogen breakdown in the liver

glu·co·cor·ti·coid \ˌglü-kō-ˈkȯrt-i-ˌkȯid\ *n* (1950) **:** any of a group of corticoids (as hydrocortisone) that are involved esp. in carbohydrate, protein, and fat metabolism, that are anti-inflammatory and immunosuppressive, and that are used widely in medicine (as in the alleviation of the symptoms of rheumatoid arthritis) — compare MINERALOCORTICOID

glu·co·ki·nase \-ˈkī-ˌnās, -ˌnāz\ *n* (1950) **:** a hexokinase found esp. in the liver that catalyzes the phosphorylation of glucose

glu·co·nate \ˈglü-kə-ˌnāt\ *n* (1884) **:** a salt or ester of gluconic acid

glu·co·neo·gen·e·sis \ˌglü-kə-ˌnē-ə-ˈjen-ə-səs\ *n* [NL] (1912) **:** formation of glucose within the animal body esp. by the liver from substances (as fats and proteins) other than carbohydrates

glu·con·ic acid \(ˌ)glü-ˌkän-ik-\ *n* [ISV, irreg. fr. *glucose* + *-ic*] (1871) **:** a crystalline acid $C_6H_{12}O_7$ obtained by oxidation of glucose and used chiefly in cleaning metals

glu·cos·amine \glü-ˈkō-sə-ˌmēn, -zə-\ *n* (1884) **:** an amino derivative $C_6H_{13}NO_5$ of glucose that occurs esp. as a constituent of polysaccharides (as chitin) in animal supporting structures and some plant cell walls

glu·cose \ˈglü-ˌkōs, -ˌkōz\ *n* [F, modif. of Gk *gleukos* must, sweet wine; akin to Gk *glykys* sweet — more at DULCET] (1840) **1 :** a sugar $C_6H_{12}O_6$ known in dextrorotatory, levorotatory, and racemic forms; *esp* **:** the sweet colorless soluble dextrorotatory form that occurs widely in nature and is the usual form in which carbohydrate is assimilated by animals **2 :** a light-colored syrup made from cornstarch

glucose–1–phosphate *n* [fr. the position at which the phosphate group is attached] (1938) **:** an ester $C_6H_{13}O_9P$ that reacts in the presence of a phosphorylase with aldoses and ketoses to yield disaccharides or with itself in liver and muscle to yield glycogen and phosphoric acid

glucose phosphate *n* (1927) : a phosphate ester of glucose: as **a** : GLUCOSE-1-PHOSPHATE **b** : GLUCOSE-6-PHOSPHATE

glucose–6–phosphate *n* [fr. the position at which the phosphate group is attached] (1964) : an ester $C_6H_{13}O_9P$ that is formed from glucose and ATP in the presence of a glucokinase and that is an essential early stage in glucose metabolism

glu·co·si·dase \glü-ˈkō-sə-ˌdās, -zə-ˌdāz\ *n* (ca. 1926) : an enzyme (as maltase) that hydrolyzes a glucoside

glu·co·side \ˈglü-kə-ˌsīd\ *n* (1857) : GLYCOSIDE; *esp* : a glycoside that yields glucose on hydrolysis — **glu·co·sid·ic** \ˌglü-kə-ˈsid-ik\ *adj*

gluc·uron·ic acid \ˌglü-kyə-ˌrän-ik-\ *n* (1911) : a compound $C_6H_{10}O_7$ that occurs esp. as a constituent of mucopolysaccharides (as hyaluronic acid) and combined as a glucuronide

gluc·uron·i·dase \-ˈrän-ə-ˌdās, -ˌdāz\ *n* (1945) : an enzyme that hydrolyzes a glucuronide; *esp* : one that occurs widely (as in liver and spleen) and hydrolyzes the beta form of a glucuronide

gluc·uro·nide \glü-ˈkyu̇r-ə-ˌnīd\ *n* (1934) : any of various derivatives of glucuronic acid that are formed esp. as combinations with often toxic aromatic hydroxyl compounds (as phenols) and are excreted in the urine

¹glue \ˈglü\ *n* [ME *glu,* fr. MF, fr. LL *glut-, glus* —more at CLAY] (14c) **1** : any of various strong adhesive substances; *esp* : a hard protein chiefly gelatinous substance that absorbs water to form a viscous solution with strong adhesive properties and that is obtained by cooking down collagenous materials (as hides or bones) **2** : a solution of glue used for sticking things together — **glu·ey** \ˈglü-ē\ *adj* — **glu·i·ly** \ˈglü-ə-lē\ *adv*

²glue *vt* **glued; glu·ing** *also* **glue·ing** (14c) **1** : to cause to stick tightly with glue ⟨*gluing* the wings onto the model airplane⟩ **2** : to fix (as the eyes) on an object steadily or with deep concentration ⟨kept his eyes *glued* to the TV screen⟩

glum \ˈgləm\ *adj* **glum·mer; glum·mest** [prob. akin to ME *gloumen* to gloom] (1547) **1** : broodingly morose ⟨became ~ when they heard the news⟩ **2** : DREARY, GLOOMY ⟨a ~ countenance⟩ ***syn*** see SULLEN — **glum·ly** *adv* — **glum·ness** *n*

glu·ma·ceous \glü-ˈmā-shəs\ *adj* (ca. 1828) : consisting or having the character of glumes ⟨~ flowers⟩

glume \ˈglüm\ *n* [NL *gluma,* fr. L, hull, husk; akin to L *glubere* to peel — more at CLEAVE] (1789) : a chaffy bract; *specif* : either of two empty bracts at the base of the spikelet in grasses

glu·on \ˈglü-ˌän\ *n* [¹*glue* + ²*-on*] (1974) : a hypothetical neutral massless particle held to bind together quarks to form hadrons

¹glut \ˈglət\ *vb* **glut·ted; glut·ting** [ME *glouten,* prob. fr. MF *gloutir* to swallow, fr. L *gluttire* — more at GLUTTON] *vt* (14c) **1** : to fill esp. with food to satiety : SATIATE **2** : to flood (the market) with goods so that supply exceeds demand ~ *vi* : to eat gluttonously ***syn*** see SATIATE

²glut *n* (1594) **1** *archaic* : the act or process of glutting **2** : an excessive quantity : OVERSUPPLY

³glut *vt* **glut·ted; glut·ting** [prob. fr. obs. *glut,* n. (swallow)] *archaic* (1600) : to swallow greedily

glu·ta·mate \ˈglüt-ə-ˌmāt\ *n* (1876) : a salt or ester of glutamic acid; *esp* : MONOSODIUM GLUTAMATE

glu·tam·ic acid \(ˌ)glü-ˌtam-ik-\ *n* [ISV *gluten* + *amino* + *-ic*] (1871) : a crystalline amino acid $C_5H_9NO_4$ widely distributed in plant and animal proteins and used in the form of a sodium salt as a seasoning

glu·ta·min·ase \ˈglüt-ə-mə-ˌnās, glü-ˈtam-ə-, -ˌnāz\ *n* (1938) : an enzyme that hydrolyzes glutamine to glutamic acid and ammonia

glu·ta·mine \ˈglüt-ə-ˌmēn\ *n* [ISV *gluten* + *amine*] (ca. 1885) : a crystalline amino acid $C_5H_{10}N_2O_3$ that is found both free and in proteins in plants and animals and that yields glutamic acid and ammonia on hydrolysis

glu·tar·al·de·hyde \ˌglüt-ə-ˈral-də-ˌhīd\ *n* [*glutaric* acid + *aldehyde*] (1951) : a compound $C_5H_8O_2$ that contains two aldehyde groups and is used esp. in tanning leather and in the fixation of biological tissues

glu·tar·ic acid \glü-ˌtar-ik-\ *n* [prob. fr. *gluten* + *-aric* (as in *tartaric acid*)] (ca. 1885) : a crystalline acid $C_5H_8O_4$ used esp. in organic synthesis

glu·ta·thi·one \ˌglüt-ə-ˈthī-ˌōn\ *n* [ISV *gluta-* (fr. *glutamic acid*) + *thi-* + *-one*] (1921) : a peptide $C_{10}H_{17}N_3O_6S$ that contains one amino-acid residue each of glutamic acid, cysteine, and glycine, that occurs widely in plant and animal tissues, and that plays an important role in biological oxidation-reduction processes and as a coenzyme

glu·te·al \ˈglüt-ē-əl, glü-ˈtē-\ *adj* (1804) : of or relating to the gluteus muscles

glu·ten \ˈglüt-ᵊn\ *n* [L *glutin-, gluten* glue; akin to LL *glut-, glus* glue — more at CLAY] (1803) : a tenacious elastic protein substance esp. of wheat flour that gives cohesiveness to dough — **glu·ten·ous** \ˈglüt-nəs, -ᵊn-əs\ *adj*

glu·teth·i·mide \glü-ˈteth-ə-ˌmīd, -məd\ *n* [*gluten* + *eth-* + *imide*] (1955) : a sedative-hypnotic drug $C_{13}H_{15}NO_2$ that induces sleep with less depression of respiration than occurs with comparable doses of barbiturates

glu·te·us \ˈglüt-ē-əs, glü-ˈtē-\ *n, pl* **glu·tei** \ˈglüt-ē-ˌī, -ē-ˌē; glü-ˈtē-ˌī\ [NL *glutaeus, gluteus,* fr. Gk *gloutos* buttock — more at CLOUD] (ca. 1681) : any of the large muscles of the buttocks; *esp* : GLUTEUS MAXIMUS

gluteus max·i·mus \-ˈmak-sə-məs\ *n, pl* **glutei max·i·mi** \-ˈmak-sə-ˌmī\ [NL, lit., largest gluteus] (1886) : the outermost muscle of the three glutei found in each of the human buttocks

glu·ti·nous \ˈglüt-nəs, -ᵊn-əs\ *adj* [MF or L; MF *glutineux,* fr. L *glutinosus,* fr. *glutin-, gluten*] (15c) : having the quality of glue : GUMMY — **glu·ti·nous·ly** *adv*

glut·ton \ˈglət-ᵊn\ *n* [ME *glotoun,* fr. OF *gloton,* fr. L *glutton-, glutto;* akin to L *gluttire* to swallow, *gula* throat, OE *ceole*] (13c) **1 a** : one given habitually to greedy and voracious eating and drinking **b** : one that has a great capacity for accepting or enduring something ⟨he's a ~ for punishment⟩ **2** : WOLVERINE 1a; *esp* : one occurring in the Old World

glut·ton·ous \ˈglət-nəs, -ᵊn-əs\ *adj* (14c) : marked by or given to gluttony ***syn*** see VORACIOUS — **glut·ton·ous·ly** *adv* — **glut·ton·ous·ness** *n*

glut·tony \ˈglət-nē, -ᵊn-ē\ *n, pl* **-ton·ies** (13c) : excess in eating or drinking

glyc- *or* **glyco-** *comb form* [ISV, fr. Gk *glyk-* sweet, fr. *glykys*] **1** : sugar ⟨*glyco*protein⟩ **2** : glycine ⟨*glyc*yl⟩

gly·can \ˈglī-ˌkan\ *n* (1953) : POLYSACCHARIDE

glycer- *or* **glycero-** *comb form* [ISV, fr. *glycerin*] **1** : glycerol ⟨*glycer*yl⟩ **2** : related to glycerol or glyceric acid ⟨*glycer*aldehyde⟩

glyc·er·al·de·hyde \ˌglis-ə-ˈral-də-ˌhīd\ *n* (1882) : a sweet crystalline compound $C_3H_6O_3$ that is formed as an intermediate in carbohydrate metabolism by the breakdown of sugars and that yields glycerol on reduction

gly·cer·ic acid \glis-ˌer-ik-\ *n* [ISV, fr. *glycerin*] (ca. 1864) : a syrupy acid $C_3H_6O_4$ obtainable by oxidation of glycerol or glyceraldehyde

glyc·er·ide \ˈglis-ə-ˌrīd\ *n* (ca. 1864) : an ester of glycerol esp. with fatty acids — **glyc·er·id·ic** \ˌglis-ə-ˈrid-ik\ *adj*

glyc·er·in *or* **glyc·er·ine** \ˈglis-(ə-)rən\ *n* [F *glycérine,* fr. Gk *glykeros* sweet; akin to Gk *glykys*] (1838) : GLYCEROL

glyc·er·in·ate \ˈglis-(ə-)rə-ˌnāt\ *vt* **-at·ed; -at·ing** (1897) : to treat with or preserve in glycerin — **glyc·er·in·ation** \ˌglis-(ə-)rə-ˈnā-shən\ *n*

glyc·er·ol \ˈglis-ə-ˌrȯl, -ˌrōl\ *n* [*glycerin* + *-ol*] (1884) : a sweet syrupy hygroscopic trihydroxy alcohol $C_3H_8O_3$ usu. obtained by the saponification of fats and used esp. as a solvent and plasticizer

glyc·er·yl \ˈglis-(ə-)rəl\ *n* (1845) : a radical derived from glycerol by removal of hydroxide; *esp* : a trivalent radical CH_2CHCH_2

gly·cine \ˈglī-ˌsēn, ˈglīs-ᵊn\ *n* (1851) : a sweet crystalline amino acid $C_2H_5NO_2$ obtained esp. by hydrolysis of proteins

gly·co·gen \ˈglī-kə-jən\ *n* (ca. 1864) : a white amorphous tasteless polysaccharide $(C_6H_{10}O_5)_x$ that is the principal form in which carbohydrate is stored in animal tissues

gly·co·gen·e·sis \ˌglī-kə-ˈjen-ə-səs\ *n* [NL] (ca. 1897) : the formation and storage of glycogen

gly·co·gen·ol·y·sis \ˌglī-kə-jə-ˈnäl-ə-səs\ *n, pl* **-y·ses** \-ˌsēz\ [NL] (ca. 1902) : the breakdown of glycogen esp. to glucose in the animal body — **gly·co·gen·o·lyt·ic** \-jən-ᵊl-ˈit-ik, -ˌjen-\ *adj*

gly·col \ˈglī-ˌkȯl, -ˌkōl\ *n* [ISV *glyc-* + *-ol*] (1858) : ETHYLENE GLYCOL; *broadly* : a related alcohol containing two hydroxyl groups

gly·col·ic acid *also* **gly·col·lic acid** \(ˌ)glī-ˌkäl-ik-\ *n* [ISV *glycol* + *-ic*] (1852) : a translucent crystalline compound $C_2H_4O_3$ found esp. in unripe grapes and sugar beets and used esp. in textile and leather processing

gly·co·lip·id \ˌglī-kō-ˈlip-əd\ *n* (1940) : a lipid (as a ganglioside or a cerebroside) that contains a carbohydrate radical

gly·col·y·sis \glī-ˈkäl-ə-səs\ *n* [NL] (1892) : the enzymatic breakdown of a carbohydrate (as glycogen) by way of phosphate derivatives with the production of pyruvic or lactic acid and energy stored in high-energy phosphate bonds of ATP — **gly·co·lyt·ic** \ˌglī-kə-ˈlit-ik\ *adj*

gly·co·pep·tide \ˌglī-kō-ˈpep-ˌtīd\ *n* (1959) : GLYCOPROTEIN

gly·co·pro·tein \-ˈprō-ˌtēn, -ˈprōt-ē-ən\ *n* (ca. 1908) : a conjugated protein in which the nonprotein group is a carbohydrate

gly·cos·ami·no·gly·can \ˌglī-kō-sə-ˌmē-nō-ˈglī-ˌkan, -kō-ˌsam-ə-nō-\ *n* [*glycose* + *amino* + *glycan*] (1978) : MUCOPOLYSACCHARIDE

gly·co·si·dase \glī-ˈkō-sə-ˌdās, -zə-ˌdāz\ *n* (1944) : an enzyme that catalyzes the hydrolysis of a bond joining a sugar of a glycoside to an alcohol or another sugar unit

gly·co·side \ˈglī-kə-ˌsīd\ *n* (1930) : any of numerous sugar derivatives that contain a nonsugar group attached through an oxygen or nitrogen bond and that on hydrolysis yield a sugar (as glucose) — **gly·co·sid·ic** \ˌglī-kə-ˈsid-ik\ *adj* — **gly·co·sid·i·cal·ly** \-i-k(ə-)lē\ *adv*

gly·cos·uria \ˌglī-kō-ˈshu̇r-ē-ə, -kəs-ˈyu̇r-\ *n* [NL] (1860) : the presence in the urine of abnormal amounts of sugar

gly·co·syl \ˈglī-kə-ˌsil\ *n* (1945) : a univalent radical derived from a cyclic form of glucose by removal of the hemiacetal hydroxyl group

gly·cyl \ˈglī-səl\ *n* (1901) : the univalent acyl radical C_2H_4NO of glycine

glyph \ˈglif\ *n* [Gk *glyphē* carved work, fr. *glyphein* to carve — more at CLEAVE] (ca. 1727) **1** : an ornamental vertical groove esp. in a Doric frieze **2** : a symbolic figure or a character usu. incised or carved in relief **3** : a symbol (as a curved arrow on a road sign) that conveys information nonverbally — **glyph·ic** \-ik\ *adj*

Glyp·tal \ˈglip-tᵊl\ *trademark* — used for an alkyd

glyp·tic \ˈglip-tik\ *n* [prob. fr. F *glyptique,* fr. Gk *glyptikē,* fr. *glyphein*] (ca. 1818) : the art or process of carving or engraving esp. on gems

G–man \ˈjē-ˌman\ *n* [prob. fr. government *man*] (1917) : a special agent of the Federal Bureau of Investigation

gnar *or* **gnarr** \ˈnär\ *vi* **gnarred; gnar·ring** [imit.] (15c) : SNARL, GROWL

¹gnarl \ˈnär(-ə)l\ *vi* [prob. freq. of *gnar*] (1593) : SNARL, GROWL

²gnarl *vt* [back-formation fr. *gnarled*] (1814) : to twist into a state of deformity

³gnarl *n* (1824) : a hard protuberance with twisted grain on a tree

gnarled \ˈnär(-ə)ld\ *adj* [prob. alter. of *knurled*] (1603) **1** : full of knots or gnarls : KNOTTY **2** : crabbed in disposition, aspect, or character

gnarly \ˈnär-lē\ *adj* (1829) : GNARLED

gnash \ˈnash\ *vt* [alter. of ME *gnasten*] (15c) : to strike or grind (as the teeth) together — **gnash** *n*

gnat \ˈnat\ *n* [ME, fr. OE *gnæt;* akin to OE *gnagan* to gnaw] (bef. 12c) : any of various small usu. biting two-winged flies — **gnat·ty** \-ē\ *adj*

gnat·catch·er \ˈnat-ˌkach-ər, -ˌkech-\ *n* (1844) : any of a genus (*Polioptila* of the family Sylviidae) of several very small No. and So. American insectivorous warblers

gnath- *or* **gnatho-** *comb form* [NL, fr. Gk *gnath-,* fr. *gnathos;* akin to Gk *genys* jaw — more at CHIN] : jaw ⟨*gnatho*plasty⟩

gnath·ic \ˈnath-ik\ *or* **gna·thal** \ˈnā-thəl, ˈnath-əl\ *adj* (1882) : of or relating to the jaw

-gna·thous *adj comb form* [NL *-gnathus,* fr. Gk *gnathos*] : having (such) a jaw ⟨opistho*gnathous*⟩

gnaw \ˈnȯ\ *vb* [ME *gnawen,* fr. OE *gnagan;* akin to OHG *gnagan* to gnaw] *vt* (bef. 12c) **1 a** : to bite or chew on with the teeth; *esp* : to wear away by persistent biting or nibbling ⟨a dog ~*ing* a bone⟩ **b** : to make by gnawing ⟨rats ~*ed* a hole⟩ **2 a** : to be a source of vexation to : PLAGUE ⟨anxiety always ~*ing* him⟩ **b** : to affect like gnawing ⟨hunger ~*ing* his vitals⟩ **3** : ERODE, CORRODE ~ *vi* **1** : to bite or nibble persistently ⟨~*ing* at her under lip⟩ **2** : to produce an effect of

\ə\ abut \ᵊ\ kitten, F table \ər\ further \a\ ash \ā\ ace \ä\ cot, cart \au̇\ out \ch\ chin \e\ bet \ē\ easy \g\ go \i\ hit \ī\ ice \j\ job \ŋ\ sing \ō\ go \ȯ\ law \ȯi\ boy \th\ thin \t͟h\ the \ü\ loot \u̇\ foot \y\ yet \zh\ vision \à, k̟, ⁿ, œ, œ̄, ue, ue̅, ʸ\ *see* Guide to Pronunciation

or as if of gnawing ⟨waves ~*ing* away at the cliffs⟩ — **gnaw·er** \'nȯ(-ə)r\ *n*

gneiss \'nīs\ *n* [G *gneis,* alter. of MHG *gneiste* spark, fr. OHG *gneisto;* akin to OE *fȳrgnāst* spark] (1757) : a foliated metamorphic rock corresponding in composition to granite or some other feldspathic plutonic rock — **gneiss·ic** \'nī-sik\ *adj* — **gneiss·oid** \-ˌsȯid\ *adj* — **gneiss·ose** \-ˌsōs\ *adj*

[1]**gnome** \'nōm\ *n* [Gk *gnōmē,* fr. *gignōskein* to know — more at KNOW] (1577) : MAXIM, APHORISM

[2]**gnome** *n* [F, fr. NL *gnomus*] (1712) **1 :** an ageless and often deformed dwarf of folklore who lives in the earth and usu. guards precious ores or treasure **2 :** an elemental being in the theory of Paracelsus that inhabits earth — **gnom·ish** \'nō-mish\ *adj*

gno·mic \'nō-mik\ *adj* (1815) **1 :** characterized by aphorism ⟨~ poetry⟩ **2 :** given to the composition of gnomic poetry ⟨a ~ poet⟩

gno·mon \'nō-mən, -ˌmän\ *n* [L, fr. Gk *gnōmōn* interpreter, pointer on a sundial, fr. *gignōskein*] (1546) **1 :** an object that by the position or length of its shadow serves as an indicator esp. of the hour of the day: as **a :** the style of an ordinary sundial **b :** a column or shaft erected perpendicular to the horizon **2 :** the remainder of a parallelogram after the removal of a similar parallelogram containing one of its corners

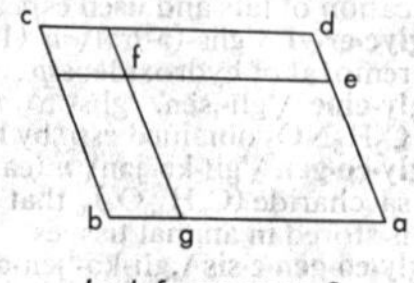

bcdefg gnomon 2

gno·mon·ic \nō-'män-ik\ *adj* (1601) : of or relating to the gnomon or its use in telling time

gno·sis \'nō-səs\ *n* [Gk *gnōsis,* lit., knowledge, fr. *gignōskein*] (1703) : esoteric knowledge of spiritual truth held by the ancient Gnostics to be essential to salvation

Gnos·tic \'näs-tik\ *n* [LL *gnosticus,* fr. Gk *gnōstikos* of knowledge, fr. *gignōskein*] (1585) : an adherent of gnosticism — **Gnostic** *adj*

gnos·ti·cism \'näs-tə-ˌsiz-əm\ *n, often cap* (1664) : the thought and practice esp. of various cults of late pre-Christian and early Christian centuries distinguished by the conviction that matter is evil and that emancipation comes through gnosis

gno·to·bi·ot·ic \ˌnōt-ō-bī-'ät-ik, -bē-\ *adj* [Gk *gnōtos* known (fr. *gignōskein* to know) + *biotē* life, way of life — more at KNOW, BIOTA] (1949) : of, relating to, living in, or being a controlled environment containing one or a few kinds of organisms; *also* : AXENIC — **gno·to·bi·ot·i·cal·ly** \-i-k(ə-)lē\ *adv*

gnu \'n(y)ü\ *n, pl* **gnu** *or* **gnus** [modif. of Bushman *nqu*] (1777) : either of two large African antelopes (*Connochaetes gnou* and *C. taurinus*) with a head like that of an ox, short mane, long tail, and horns in both sexes that curve downward and outward

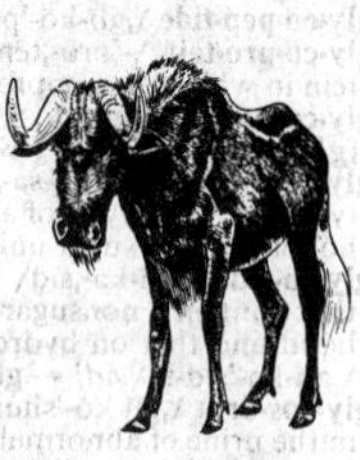
gnu

[1]**go** \'gō\ *vb* **went** \'went\; **gone** \'gȯn *also* 'gän\; **go·ing** \'gō-iŋ, 'gȯ(-)iŋ; *"going to" in sense 13 is often* 'gō-nə *or* 'gȯn-ə *or* 'gən-ə\; **goes** \'gōz\ [ME *gon,* fr. OE *gān;* akin to OHG *gān* to go, Gk *kichanein* to reach, attain] *vi* (bef. 12c) **1 :** to move on a course : PROCEED ⟨~ slow⟩ ⟨*went* by train⟩ — compare STOP **2 :** to move out of or away from a place expressed or implied : LEAVE, DEPART ⟨they *went* from school to the party⟩ ⟨she is *going* away for the summer⟩ **3 a :** to take a certain course or follow a certain procedure ⟨reports ~ through channels to the president⟩ **b :** to pass by means of a process like journeying ⟨the message *went* by wire⟩ **c :** to proceed without delay and often in a thoughtless or reckless manner — used esp. to intensify a complementary verb ⟨why did he have to ~ and spoil everything⟩ **d** (1) **:** to extend from point to point or in a certain direction : RUN ⟨his land ~*es* almost to the river⟩ (2) **:** to give access : LEAD ⟨that door ~*es* to the cellar⟩ **4** *obs* : WALK **5 :** to be habitually in a certain state or condition ⟨~ bareheaded⟩ ⟨~ armed after dark⟩ **6 a :** to become lost, consumed, or spent ⟨the time allotted me was *gone*⟩ **b :** DIE **c :** to slip away : ELAPSE ⟨the evening *went* pleasantly enough⟩ **d :** to come to be given up or discarded ⟨these slums have to ~⟩ **e :** to pass by sale ⟨*went* for a good price⟩ **f :** to become impaired or weakened ⟨his hearing started to ~⟩ **g :** to give way esp. under great force or pressure : BREAK **7 a :** to move along in a specified manner : FARE ⟨everything was ~*ing* well⟩ **b :** to be in general or on an average ⟨cheap, as yachts ~⟩ **c :** to be or become esp. as the result of a contest ⟨decision *went* against him⟩ **d :** to turn out well : SUCCEED ⟨worked hard to make the party ~⟩ **8 a :** to apply oneself ⟨*went* to fighting among themselves⟩ **b :** to put or subject oneself ⟨*went* to unnecessary expense⟩ **c** *chiefly Southern & Midland* : INTEND ⟨I didn't ~ to do it⟩ **9 :** to have recourse to another for corroboration, vindication, or decision : RESORT ⟨~ to court to recover damages⟩ **10 a :** to begin an action or motion ⟨here ~*es*⟩ **b :** to maintain or perform a certain action or motion ⟨drums had been ~*ing* strong⟩ **c :** to function in the proper or expected manner ⟨trying to get the motor to ~⟩ **11 a :** to have currency ⟨now ~*es* by another name⟩ **b :** to pass from person to person : CIRCULATE ⟨the story ~*es* that the expedition was a failure⟩ **12 a :** to act in accordance or harmony ⟨a good rule to ~ by⟩ **b :** to come to be determined ⟨dreams ~ by contraries⟩ **c :** to come to be applied or appropriated ⟨part of the budget ~*es* for military purposes⟩ **d :** to pass by award, assignment, or lot ⟨the prize *went* to a sophomore⟩ **e :** to contribute to an end or result ⟨qualities that ~ to make a hero⟩ **13 :** to be about, intending, or expecting something — used in a progressive tense before an infinitive ⟨is ~*ing* to leave town⟩ **14 a :** EXTEND ⟨his knowledge fails to ~ very deep⟩ **b :** to come or arrive at a certain state or condition ⟨~ to sleep⟩ **c :** to come to be ⟨the tire *went* flat⟩ **15 a :** to be in phrasing or expression : READ ⟨as the phrase ~*es*⟩ **b :** to be capable of being sung or played ⟨the tune ~*es* like this⟩ **16 :** to be compatible, suitable, or becoming : HARMONIZE ⟨claret ~*es* with beef⟩ **17 a :** to be capable of passing, extending, or being contained or inserted ⟨will these clothes ~ in your suitcase⟩ **b :** to have a usual or proper place or position : BELONG ⟨these books ~ on the top shelf⟩ **18 :** to have a tendency : CONDUCE ⟨it ~*es* to show he can be trusted⟩ **19 a** (1) **:** to carry authority ⟨what she said *went*⟩ (2) **:** to be acceptable, satisfactory, or adequate ⟨anything ~*es* here⟩ **b :** to hold true : be valid **20 :** to empty the bladder or bowels ~ *vt* **1 :** to proceed along or according to : FOLLOW ⟨if I were ~*ing* his way⟩ **2 :** to travel through or along : TRAVERSE ⟨*went* the length of the street⟩ **3 a :** to make a wager of : BET ⟨~ a dollar on the outcome⟩ **b :** to make an offer of : BID ⟨willing to ~ $50 for the clock⟩ **4 a :** to assume the function or obligation of ⟨promised to ~ bail for his friend⟩ **b :** to participate to the extent of ⟨decided to ~ halves if either of them found the treasure⟩ **5 :** YIELD, WEIGH ⟨striped bass that would ~ a hundred pounds⟩ **6 a :** to put up with : TOLERATE — usu. used negatively ⟨left because he couldn't ~ the noise⟩ **b :** AFFORD ⟨can't ~ the price⟩ **c :** ENJOY ⟨I could ~ a soda⟩ **7 :** SAY — used chiefly in oral narration of speech — **go·er** \'gō(-ə)r\ *n* — **go about :** to set about : UNDERTAKE — **go after :** SEEK, PURSUE — **go all the way 1 :** to enter into complete agreement **2 :** to engage in sexual intercourse — **go ape 1 :** to become extremely angry or upset : lose control **2 :** to become highly excited or enthusiastic — **go at 1 a :** to make an attack on **b :** to make an approach to **2 :** UNDERTAKE — **go back on 1 :** ABANDON **2 :** BETRAY **3 :** FAIL — **go begging :** to be in little demand — **go by the board 1 :** to be carried over a ship's side **2 :** to be discarded — **go down the line :** to give wholehearted support — **go fly a kite :** to stop being an annoyance or disturbance ⟨got mad and told him to *go fly a kite*⟩ — **go for 1 :** to pass for or serve as **2 :** to try to secure ⟨he *went for* the last penny⟩ **3 a :** FAVOR, ACCEPT ⟨cannot *go for* your idea⟩ **b :** to have an interest in or liking for ⟨she *went for* him in a big way —Chandler Brossard⟩ **4 :** ATTACK, ASSAIL ⟨*went for* him when his back was turned⟩ — **go for broke :** to put forth all one's strength or resources — **go great guns :** to achieve great success — **go hang :** to cease to be of interest or concern — **go into :** to be contained in ⟨5 *goes into* 60 12 times⟩ — **go it 1 :** to behave in a reckless, excited, or impromptu manner **2 :** to proceed in a rapid or furious manner **3 :** to conduct one's affairs : ACT ⟨insists on *going it* alone⟩ — **go one better :** OUTDO, SURPASS — **go over 1 :** EXAMINE **2 a :** REPEAT **b :** STUDY, REVIEW — **go places :** to be on the way to success — **go public** *of a close corporation* : to offer shares for sale to the general public — **go steady :** to date one person exclusively and frequently — **go the distance :** to complete a course of action : finish a contest in a specified capacity ⟨the pitcher *went the distance* allowing only three runs on nine hits⟩ — **go the vole :** to risk all for great gains — **go through 1 :** to subject to thorough examination, consideration, or study **2 :** EXPERIENCE, UNDERGO **3 :** CARRY OUT, PERFORM ⟨*went through* his work in a daze⟩ — **go to bat for :** to give active support or assistance to : DEFEND, CHAMPION — **go to one's head 1 :** to cause one to become confused, excited, or dizzy **2 :** to cause one to become conceited or overconfident — **go to pieces :** to become shattered (as in nerves or health) — **go to town 1 :** to work or act rapidly or efficiently **2 :** to be markedly successful **3 :** to indulge oneself excessively — **go with :** DATE — **go without saying :** to be self-evident

[2]**go** \'gō\ *n, pl* **goes** (1727) **1 :** the act or manner of going **2 :** the height of fashion : RAGE ⟨elegant shawls labeled . . . "quite the ~" —R. S. Surtees⟩ **3 :** an often unexpected turn of affairs : OCCURRENCE **4 :** the quantity used or furnished at one time ⟨you can obtain a ~ of brandy for sixpence —C. B. Fairbanks⟩ **5 :** ENERGY, VIGOR **6 a :** a turn in an activity (as a game) ⟨told his opponent that it was his ~⟩ **b :** ATTEMPT, TRY ⟨have a ~ at painting⟩ **7 :** a spell of activity ⟨finished the job at one ~⟩ **8 :** SUCCESS ⟨made a ~ of the business⟩ **9 :** permission to proceed : GO-AHEAD ⟨gave the astronauts a ~ for another orbit⟩ — **no go :** to no avail : USELESS — **on the go :** constantly or restlessly active

[3]**go** *adj* (1961) : functioning properly : being in good and ready condition ⟨declared all systems ~⟩

[4]**go** *n* [Jp] (1890) : an oriental game played between two players who alternately place black and white stones on a board checkered by 19 vertical lines and 19 horizontal lines in an attempt to enclose the larger area on the board

[1]**goad** \'gōd\ *n* [ME *gode,* fr. OE *gād* spear, goad; akin to Langobardic *gaida* spear, Skt *hinoti* he urges on] (bef. 12c) **1 a :** something that pricks like a goad : THORN **b :** something that urges or stimulates into action : SPUR **2 :** a pointed rod used to urge on an animal ***syn*** see MOTIVE

[2]**goad** *vt* (1579) **1 :** to drive (as cattle) with a goad **2 :** to incite or rouse as if with a goad

[1]**go–ahead** \'gō-ə-ˌhed\ *adj* (1834) **1 :** marked by energy and enterprise : PROGRESSIVE ⟨a vigorous ~ company⟩ **2 :** indicating that one may proceed ⟨~ signal⟩

[2]**go–ahead** *n* (1840) **1 a :** ENERGY, SPIRIT ⟨had a great deal of courage and ~⟩ **b :** one possessing go-ahead **2 :** a sign, signal, or authority to proceed : GREEN LIGHT

goal \'gōl, *chiefly Northern esp in 1b & 3a also* 'gül\ *n* [ME *gol* boundary, limit] (1531) **1 a :** the terminal point of a race **b :** an area to be reached safely in children's games **2 :** the end toward which effort is directed : AIM **3 a :** an area or object toward which players in various games attempt to advance a ball or puck and usu. through or into which it must go in order to score points **b :** the act or action of causing a ball or puck to go through or into such a goal **c :** the score resulting from such an act ***syn*** see INTENTION — **goal** *vi*

goal·ie \'gō-lē\ *n* (1921) : GOALKEEPER

goal·keep·er \'gōl-ˌkē-pər\ *n* (1658) : a player who defends the goal in any of various games (as hockey, lacrosse, or soccer)

goal kick *n* (1909) : a free kick in soccer awarded to a defensive player when the ball is driven out of bounds over the end line by an opposing player

goal line *n* (1867) : a line at either end and usu. running the width of a playing area on which a goal or goalpost is situated

goal·mouth \'gōl-ˌmau̇th\ *n* (1882) : the area directly in front of the goal (as in soccer or hockey)

go along *vi* (1602) **1 :** to move along : PROCEED **2 :** to go or travel as a companion **3 :** to act in cooperation

goal·post \'gōl-ˌpōst\ *n* (1857) : one of usu. two vertical posts that with or without a crossbar constitute the goal in various games

goal·tend·er \'gōl-ˌten-dər\ *n* (ca. 1909) : GOALKEEPER

goal·tend·ing \-diŋ\ *n* (1968) **1 :** the act of guarding a goal (as in hockey) **2 :** the act of touching or deflecting a basketball that is on its downward path toward the basket or that is within the rim of the basket

go·an·na \gō-'an-ə\ *n* [alter. of *iguana*] (1891) **:** any of several large monitor lizards (family Varanidae)

Goa powder \ˌgō-ə-\ *n* [*Goa*, India] (1874) **:** a bitter powder found in the wood of a Brazilian leguminous tree (*Vataireopsis araroba*) and valued as the chief source of the drug chrysarobin

go–around \'gō-ə-ˌrau̇nd\ *n* (1891) **1 a :** ROUND ⟨reached an apparent agreement during the first ∼⟩ **b :** a heated argument or struggle ⟨had a real ∼ with her about it⟩ **2 :** RUNAROUND ⟨he's been giving me the ∼⟩ **3 :** an act or instance of going around (as in an air traffic pattern)

go around \ˌgō-ə-'rau̇nd\ *vi* (1500) **1 a :** to pass from place to place **:** go here and there **b :** to have currency **:** CIRCULATE ⟨an amusing story is *going around*⟩ **2 :** to satisfy demand **:** fill the need ⟨not enough jobs to *go around*⟩

goat \'gōt\ *n, pl* **goats** [ME *gote*, fr. OE *gāt*; akin to OHG *geiz* goat, ON *geit*, L *haedus* kid] (bef. 12c) **1 a** *or pl* **goat :** any of various hollow-horned ruminant mammals (esp. of the genus *Capra*) related to the sheep but of lighter build and with backwardly arching horns, a short tail, and usu. straight hair **b** *cap* **:** CAPRICORN **2 :** a licentious man **:** LECHER **3 :** SCAPEGOAT — **goat·ish** \'gōt-ish\ *adj* — **goat·like** \-ˌlīk\ *adj*

goa·tee \gō-'tē\ *n* [fr. its resemblance to the beard of a he-goat] (1844) **:** a small pointed or tufted beard on a man's chin

goat·fish \'gōt-ˌfish\ *n* (1639) **:** MULLET 2

goat·herd \-ˌhərd\ *n* [ME *goteherd*, fr. OE *gāthyrd*] (bef. 12c) **:** one who tends goats

goat·skin \-ˌskin\ *n* (14c) **1 :** the skin of a goat **2 :** leather made from goatskin

goat·suck·er \-ˌsək-ər\ *n* (1611) **:** any of a family (Caprimulgidae) of medium-sized long-winged crepuscular or nocturnal birds (as the whip-poorwills and nighthawks) having a short wide bill, short legs, and soft mottled plumage and feeding on insects which they catch on the wing

1**gob** \'gäb\ *n* [ME *gobbe*, fr. MF *gobe* large piece of food, back-formation fr. *gobet*] (14c) **1 :** LUMP **2 :** a large amount — usu. used in pl. ⟨∼*s* of money⟩

2**gob** *n* [origin unknown] (1915) **:** SAILOR

gob·bet \'gäb-ət\ *n* [ME *gobet*, fr. MF, mouthful, piece] (14c) **1 :** a piece or portion (as of meat) **2 :** LUMP, MASS **3 :** a small quantity of liquid **:** DROP

1**gob·ble** \'gäb-əl\ *vt* **gob·bled; gob·bling** \-(ə-)liŋ\ [prob. irreg. fr. 1*gob*] (1601) **1 :** to swallow or eat greedily **2 :** to take eagerly **:** GRAB — often used with *up* **3 :** to read rapidly or greedily — often used with *up*

2**gobble** *vi* **gob·bled; gob·bling** \-(ə-)liŋ\ [imit.] (1680) **1 :** to make the natural guttural noise of a male turkey **2 :** to make a sound resembling the gobble of a turkey — **gobble** *n*

gob·ble·dy·gook *or* **gob·ble·de·gook** \'gäb-əl-dē-ˌgu̇k, -ˌgük\ *n* [irreg. fr. *gobble*, n.] (1944) **:** wordy and generally unintelligible jargon

gob·bler \'gäb-lər\ *n* (1737) **:** a male turkey

Go·be·lin \'gō-bə-lən, ˌgō-bə-'laⁿ\ *adj* [*Gobelin* dye and tapestry works, Paris, France] (1821) **:** of, relating to, or characteristic of tapestry produced at the Gobelin works in Paris — **Gobelin** *n*

go–be·tween \'gō-bə-ˌtwēn\ *n* (1598) **:** an intermediate agent **:** BROKER

gob·let \'gäb-lət\ *n* [ME *gobelet*, fr. MF] (14c) **1** *archaic* **:** a bowl-shaped drinking vessel without handles **2 :** a drinking vessel (as of glass) with a foot and stem — compare TUMBLER

goblet cell *n* [fr. its shape] (1878) **:** a mucus-secreting epithelial cell (as of intestinal columnar epithelium) that is distended at the free end

gob·lin \'gäb-lən\ *n* [ME *gobelin*, fr. MF, fr. ML *gobelinus*, deriv. of Gk *kobalos* rogue] (14c) **:** an ugly or grotesque sprite that is mischievous and sometimes evil and malicious

go·bo \'gō-(ˌ)bō\ *n, pl* **gobos** *also* **goboes** [origin unknown] (ca. 1930) **1 :** a dark strip (as of wallboard) to shield a motion-picture or television camera from light **2 :** a device to shield a microphone from sound

go·by \'gō-bē\ *n, pl* **gobies** *also* **goby** [L *gobius* gudgeon, fr. Gk *kōbios*] (1769) **:** any of numerous spiny-finned fishes (family Gobiidae) that usu. have the pelvic fins united to form a ventral sucking disk

go by *vi* (1508) **1 :** PASS ⟨as time *goes by*⟩ **2 :** to make a brief visit **:** CALL ⟨all the family was at home when we *went by* yesterday⟩

go–cart \'gō-ˌkärt\ *n* (1689) **1 a :** WALKER **b :** STROLLER **2 :** HANDCART **3 :** a light open carriage

1**god** \'gäd *also* 'gȯd\ *n* [ME, fr. OE; akin to OHG *got* god] (bef. 12c) **1** *cap* **:** the supreme or ultimate reality: as **a :** the Being perfect in power, wisdom, and goodness whom men worship as creator and ruler of the universe **b** *Christian Science* **:** the incorporeal divine Principle ruling over all as eternal Spirit **:** infinite Mind **2 :** a being or object believed to have more than natural attributes and powers and to require man's worship; *specif* **:** one controlling a particular aspect or part of reality **3 :** a person or thing of supreme value **4 :** a powerful ruler

2**god** *vt* **god·ded; god·ding** (1595) **:** to treat as a god **:** IDOLIZE, DEIFY

god–aw·ful \gäd-'ȯ-fəl\ *adj* [*goddamned* + *awful*] (1878) **:** extremely unpleasant or disagreeable **:** ABOMINABLE ⟨∼ explosions of violence —*Playboy*⟩

god·child \'gäd-ˌchīld *also* 'gȯd-\ *n* (13c) **:** a person for whom another person becomes sponsor at baptism

1**god·damn** *or* **god·dam** \'gäd-'dam\ *n, often cap* (1647) **:** DAMN ⟨they were in no mood to give a good ∼ about anything —Robert Lowry⟩

2**goddamn** *or* **goddam** *vb, often cap* (1928) **:** DAMN

god·damned \ˌgäd-ˌdam(d)\ *or* **god·damn** *or* **god·dam** \-ˌdam\ *adj or adv* (1918) **:** DAMNED

god·daugh·ter \'gäd-ˌdȯt-ər *also* 'gȯd-\ *n* (bef. 12c) **:** a female godchild

god·dess \'gäd-əs\ *n* (14c) **1 :** a female god **2 :** a woman whose great charm or beauty arouses adoration

go–dev·il \'gō-ˌdev-əl\ *n* (1852) **:** any of various devices: as **a :** a weight formerly dropped in a bored hole (as of an oil well) to explode a cartridge previously lowered **b :** a cleaning scraper rotated and propelled through a pipeline by the force of the flowing fluid **c :** a handcar or small gasoline car used on a railroad for transporting laborers and supplies

1**god·fa·ther** \'gäd-ˌfäth-ər, -ˌfäth-, *also* 'gȯd-\ *n* (bef. 12c) **1 :** a man who sponsors a person at baptism **2 :** one having a relation to someone or something analogous to that of a male sponsor to his godchild ⟨made him the ∼ of a whole generation of rebels —*Times Lit. Supp.*⟩

2**godfather** *vt* (1780) **:** to act as godfather to

God–fear·ing \-ˌfi(ə)r-iŋ\ *adj* (1835) **:** having a reverent feeling toward God **:** DEVOUT

god·for·sak·en \-fər-ˌsā-kən\ *adj* (1856) **1 :** pitiable in circumstances **:** MISERABLE ⟨poor ∼ orphans⟩ **2 :** situated in a remote or desolate place ⟨a ∼ deserted road⟩ **3 :** neglected in appearance **:** DISMAL ⟨the toughest, dreariest, most ∼ looking country —Richard Bissell⟩

god·head \-ˌhed\ *n* [ME *godhed*, fr. *god* + *-hed* -hood; akin to ME *-hod* -hood] (13c) **1 :** divine nature or essence **:** DIVINITY **2** *cap* **a :** GOD 1 **b :** the nature of God esp. as existing in three persons — used with *the*

god·hood \-ˌhu̇d\ *n* [ME *godhod*, fr. OE *godhād*, fr. *god* + *-hād* -hood] (bef. 12c) **:** DIVINITY

Go·di·va \gə-'dī-və\ *n* **:** an English earl's wife who in legend rode naked through Coventry to save its citizens from a tax

god·less \'gäd-ləs *also* 'gȯd-\ *adj* (1528) **:** not acknowledging a deity or divine law — **god·less·ness** *n*

god·like \-ˌlīk\ *adj* (bef. 12c) **:** resembling or having the qualities of God or a god **:** DIVINE — **god·like·ness** *n*

god·ling \-liŋ\ *n* (1570) **:** an inferior or local god

god·ly \-lē\ *adj* **god·li·er; -est** (14c) **1 :** DIVINE **2 :** PIOUS, DEVOUT — **god·li·ness** *n* — **godly** *adv*

god·moth·er \-ˌməth-ər\ *n* (bef. 12c) **:** a woman who sponsors a person at baptism

go·down \'gō-ˌdau̇n\ *n* [by folk etymology fr. Malay *gudang*] (1588) **:** a warehouse in an oriental country

go down *vi* (14c) **1 a :** to fall to or as if to the ground ⟨the plane *went down* in flames⟩ **b :** to go below the horizon **:** SET ⟨the sun *went down*⟩ **c :** to become submerged **:** SINK ⟨the ship *went down* with all hands⟩ **2 :** to admit of being swallowed ⟨the medicine *went down* easily⟩ **3 :** to undergo defeat **4 a :** to find acceptance ⟨will the plan *go down* with the farmers⟩ **b :** to come to be remembered esp. in posterity ⟨he will *go down* in history as a great president⟩ **5 :** to undergo a decline or decrease ⟨the fever *went down*⟩ ⟨the market is *going down*⟩ **6** *Brit* **:** to leave a university **7** *slang* **:** to take place **:** HAPPEN — **go down on :** to perform fellatio or cunnilingus on

god·par·ent \'gäd-ˌpar-ənt, -ˌper- *also* 'gȯd-\ *n* (1865) **:** a sponsor at baptism

God's acre *n* (1617) **:** CHURCHYARD

god·send \'gäd-ˌsend *also* 'gȯd-\ *n* [back-formation fr. *god-sent*] (1820) **:** a desirable or needed thing or event that comes unexpectedly

god·son \-ˌsən\ *n* (bef. 12c) **:** a male godchild

God·speed \-'spēd\ *n* [ME *God speid*, fr. the phrase *God spede you* God prosper you] (1526) **:** a prosperous journey **:** SUCCESS ⟨bade him ∼⟩

god·wit \'gäd-ˌwit\ *n* [origin unknown] (1552) **:** any of a genus (*Limosa*) of long-billed wading birds related to the snipes but resembling curlews

goes *pres 3d sing of* GO, *pl of* GO

goe·thite \'gə(r)-ˌtīt\ *n* [G *göthit*, fr. J. W. von *Goethe*] (ca. 1823) **:** a mineral $HFeO_2$ that consists of an iron hydrogen oxide and is the commonest constituent of many forms of natural rust

go·fer \'gō-fər\ *n* [alter. of *go for*] (1970) **:** an employee whose duties include running errands

gof·fer \'gäf-ər, 'gȯf-\ *vt* [F *gaufrer*, fr. *gaufre* honeycomb, waffle, fr. OF, of Gmc origin; akin to MD *wafel* waffle] (1706) **:** to crimp, plait, or flute (as linen or lace) esp. with a heated iron — **goffer** *n*

go–get·ter \'gō-ˌget-ər, -ˌget-\ *n* (1921) **:** an aggressively enterprising person **:** HUSTLER — **go–get·ting** \-ˌget-iŋ\ *adj or n*

1**gog·gle** \'gäg-əl\ *vi* **gog·gled; gog·gling** \-(ə-)liŋ\ [ME *gogelen* to squint] (14c) **:** to stare with wide or protuberant eyes — **gog·gler** \-(ə-)lər\ *n*

2**goggle** *adj* (1540) **:** PROTUBERANT, STARING ⟨∼ eyes⟩ — **gog·gly** \'gäg-(ə-)lē\ *adj*

gog·gle–eye \'gäg-ə-ˌlī\ *n* (1840) **1 :** ROCK BASS 1 **2 :** WARMOUTH

gog·gle–eyed \ˌgäg-ə-'līd\ *adj* (14c) **:** having bulging or rolling eyes

gog·gles \'gäg-əlz\ *n pl* (1715) **:** protective glasses set in a flexible frame (as of rubber or plastic) that fits snugly against the face — **gog·gled** \-əld\ *adj*

go–go \'gō-(ˌ)gō\ *adj* [*a-go-go*] (1965) **1 a :** of, relating to, or being a discotheque or the music or dances performed there **b :** employed to entertain in a discotheque ⟨∼ dancers⟩ **2 :** marked by spirited or aggressive action ⟨∼ baseball⟩ **3 a :** relating to or dealing in popular often speculative investment expected to yield high returns ⟨∼ mutual funds⟩ **b :** marked by ready and often speculative investment or fast-paced growth and modernization ⟨the ∼ years⟩

1**Goi·del·ic** \gȯi-'del-ik\ *adj* [MIr *Gōidel* Gael] (1882) **1 :** of, relating to, or characteristic of the Gaels **2 :** of, relating to, or constituting Goidelic

2**Goidelic** *n* (1882) **:** the branch of the Celtic languages that includes Irish Gaelic, Scottish Gaelic, and Manx — see INDO-EUROPEAN LANGUAGES table

go in *vi* (bef. 12c) **1 :** to make an approach (as in attacking) **2 a :** to take part in a game or contest **b :** to call the opening bet in poker **:** STAY **3** *of a celestial body* **:** to become obscured by a cloud **4 :** to form a union or alliance **:** JOIN — often used with *with* ⟨asked the rest of us to *go in* with them⟩ — **go in for 1 :** to give support to **:** ADVOCATE **2 :** to have or show an interest in or a liking for **3 :** to engage in **:** take part in

1**go·ing** \'gō-iŋ, 'gȯ(-)iŋ\ *n* (14c) **1 :** an act or instance of going **2** *pl* **:** BEHAVIOR, ACTIONS ⟨for his eyes are upon the ways of man, and he seeth all his ∼*s* —Job 34:21 (AV)⟩ **3 :** the condition of the ground (as for walking) **4 :** advance toward an objective **:** PROGRESS ⟨found the ∼ too slow and gave up the job⟩

[2]**going** *adj* (14c) **1 a :** that goes — often used in combination ⟨easy*going*⟩ ⟨out*going*⟩ **b :** WORKING, MOVING ⟨everything was in ~ order⟩ **2 :** LIVING, EXISTING ⟨the best novelist ~⟩ **3 :** CURRENT, PREVAILING ⟨~ price⟩ **4 :** conducting business with the expectation of indefinite continuance ⟨~ concern⟩ — **going on :** drawing near to **:** APPROACHING ⟨is six years old *going on* seven⟩

go·ing–over \ˌgō-iŋ-ˈō-vər, ˌgȯ(-)iŋ-\ *n, pl* **go·ings–over** (1872) **1 a :** a severe scolding **b :** BEATING **2 :** a thorough examination or investigation

go·ings–on \ˌgō-iŋ-ˈzȯn, (ˈ)gȯ(-)iŋ-, -ˈzän\ *n pl* (1775) **1 :** ACTIONS, EVENTS **2 :** irregular or reprehensible happenings or conduct ⟨titillating stories about the ~ of the carefree millionaires —Eleanor Early⟩

goi·ter \ˈgȯit-ər\ *n* [F *goitre,* fr. MF, back-formation fr. *goitron* throat, fr. (assumed) VL *guttrion-, guttrio,* fr. L *guttur* — more at COT] (1625) **:** an enlargement of the thyroid gland visible as a swelling of the front of the neck — compare HYPERTHYROIDISM, HYPOTHYROIDISM — **goi·trous** \ˈgȯi-trəs, ˈgȯit-ə-rəs\ *adj*

goitre *chiefly Brit var of* GOITER

goi·tro·gen \ˈgȯi-trə-jən\ *n* (1946) **:** a substance (as thiourea or thiouracil) that induces goiter formation

goi·tro·gen·ic \ˌgȯi-trə-ˈjen-ik\ *adj* (1929) **:** producing or tending to produce goiter — **goi·tro·ge·nic·i·ty** \ˌgȯi-trə-jə-ˈnis-ət-ē\ *n*

Gol·con·da \gäl-ˈkän-də\ *n* [*Golconda,* India, famous for its diamonds] (1884) **:** a rich mine; *broadly* **:** a source of great wealth

gold \ˈgōld\ *n, often attrib* [ME, fr. OE; akin to OHG *gold* gold, OE *geolu* yellow — more at YELLOW] (bef. 12c) **1 :** a malleable ductile yellow metallic element that occurs chiefly free or in a few minerals and is used esp. in coins, jewelry, and dentures — see ELEMENT table **2 a (1) :** gold coins **(2) :** a gold piece **b :** MONEY **c :** GOLD STANDARD **3 :** a variable color averaging deep yellow **4 :** something resembling gold; *esp* **:** something valued as the finest of its kind ⟨a heart of ~⟩

[1]**gold·brick** \ˈgōl(d)-ˌbrik\ *n* (1881) **1 a :** a worthless brick that appears to be of gold **b :** something that appears to be valuable but is actually worthless **2 :** a person (as a soldier) who shirks assigned work

[2]**goldbrick** *vt* (1902) **:** SWINDLE ~ *vi* **:** to shirk duty or responsibility **:** goof off

gold·bug \-ˌbəg\ *n* (1878) **:** a supporter of the gold standard

gold coast *n, often cap G&C* (1909) **:** an exclusive residential district

Gold Democrat *n* (1896) **:** a member of the Democratic party favoring the gold standard; *esp* **:** one supporting an independent ticket in the presidential election of 1896

gold digger *n* (1920) **1 :** one who digs for gold **2 :** a woman who uses feminine charm to extract money or gifts from men

gold·en \ˈgōl-dən\ *adj* [ME] (13c) **1 :** consisting of, relating to, or containing gold **2 a :** having the color of gold **b :** BLOND 1a **3 :** LUSTROUS, SHINING **4 :** of a high degree of excellence **:** SUPERB **5 :** PROSPEROUS, FLOURISHING ⟨~ days⟩ **6 a :** radiantly youthful and vigorous **b :** possessing talents that promise worldly success — often used with *boy* **c :** highly favored **:** POPULAR **7 :** FAVORABLE, ADVANTAGEOUS ⟨a ~ opportunity⟩ **8 :** of, relating to, or marking a 50th anniversary **9 :** MELLOW, RESONANT ⟨a smooth ~ tenor⟩ — **gold·en·ly** *adv* — **gold·en·ness** \-dən-(n)əs\ *n*

golden age *n* (1555) **:** a period of great happiness, prosperity, and achievement

gold·en–ag·er \ˈgōl-də-ˌnā-jər\ *n* (1961) **:** an elderly and often retired person usu. engaging in club activities

golden al·ex·an·ders \-ˌal-ig-ˈzan-dərz, -ˌel-\ *n pl but sing or pl in constr, often cap A* [ML *alexandrum*] (ca. 1923) **:** a showy No. American yellow-flowered perennial herb (*Zizia aurea*) of the carrot family that occurs in moist woods and meadows; *also* **:** any of several related herbs

golden–brown alga *n* (ca. 1957) **:** any of a major group (Chrysophyta) of algae (as diatoms) with yellowish green to golden brown pigments obscuring the chlorophyll — called also *chrysophyte, golden alga*

golden club *n* (1837) **:** an American aquatic plant (*Orontium aquaticum*) of the arum family with a spadix of minute yellow flowers

golden eagle *n* (1839) **:** a large eagle (*Aquila chrysaëtos*) of the northern hemisphere with brownish yellow tips on the head and neck feathers

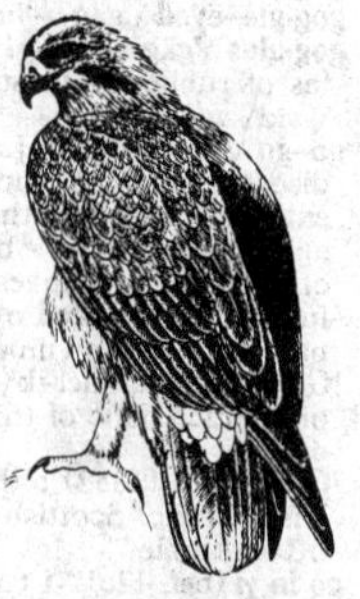

golden eagle

gold·en·eye \ˈgōl-də-ˌnī\ *n* (1678) **1 :** either of two diving ducks (genus *Bucephala*); *esp* **:** a large-headed swift-flying Holarctic diving duck (*B. clangula*) having the male strikingly marked in black and white **2 :** a lacewing (family Chrysopidae) with yellow eyes

Golden Fleece *n* (15c) **:** a fleece of gold placed by the king of Colchis in a dragon-guarded grove and recovered by the Argonauts

golden glow *n* (1902) **:** a tall branching composite herb (*Rudbeckia laciniata hortensia*) with showy yellow much-doubled flower heads

golden hamster *n* (ca. 1947) **:** a small tawny hamster (*Mesocricetus auratus*) native to Asia Minor but kept as a pet or used as a lab animal elsewhere — called also *Syrian hamster*

Golden Horde *n* [fr. the golden tent of the Mongol ruler] (1863) **:** a body of Mongol Tatars that overran eastern Europe in the 13th century and dominated Russia until 1486

golden mean *n* (1587) **:** the medium between extremes **:** MODERATION

golden nematode *n* (1946) **:** a small yellowish Old World nematode worm (*Heterodera rostochiensis*) established locally as a pest of potatoes in eastern No. America

golden oldie *n* (1970) **:** one that was a hit in the past

golden plover *n* (1785) **:** either of two gregarious plovers (genus *Pluvialis*); *esp* **:** one (*P. dominica*) that breeds in arctic America and Siberia and winters in Hawaii and the southern hemisphere

gold·en·rain tree \ˌgōl-dən-ˈrān-\ *n* (1926) **:** a roundheaded tree (*Koelreuteria paniculata* of the family Sapindaceae) that has very long showy clusters of yellow flowers

golden retriever *n* (1919) **:** any of a breed of medium-sized retrievers having a flat moderately long golden coat

gold·en·rod \ˈgōl-dən-ˌräd\ *n* (1568) **:** any of numerous chiefly No. American composite biennial or perennial plants (esp. of the genus *Solidago*) with stems resembling wands and heads of small yellow or sometimes white flowers often clustered in panicles — compare RAYLESS GOLDENROD

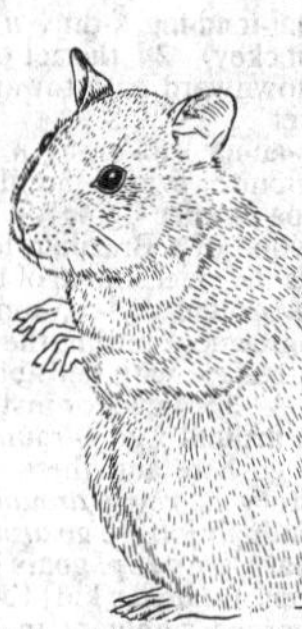

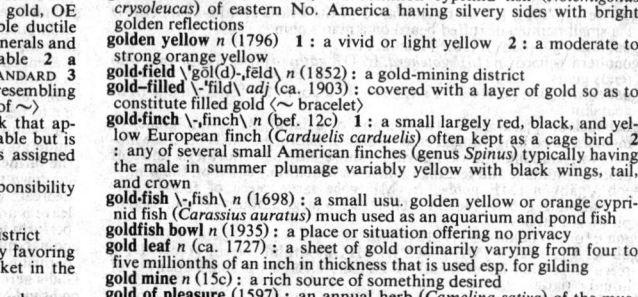

golden hamster

golden rule *n* (1807) **1 :** a guiding principle **2** *cap G&R* **:** a rule of ethical conduct referring to Mt 7:12 and Lk 6:31 and stating that one should do to others as he would have others do to him

gold·en·seal \ˈgōl-dən-ˌsēl\ *n* (1839) **:** a perennial American herb (*Hydrastis canadensis*) of the buttercup family with large rounded leaves and a thick knotted yellow rootstock sometimes used in pharmacy

golden section *n* (1875) **:** a proportion (as one involving a line divided into two segments or the length and width of a rectangle and their sum) in which the ratio of the whole to the larger part is the same as the ratio of the larger part to the smaller

golden shiner *n* (ca. 1903) **:** a common cyprinid fish (*Notemigonus crysoleucas*) of eastern No. America having silvery sides with bright golden reflections

golden yellow *n* (1796) **1 :** a vivid or light yellow **2 :** a moderate to strong orange yellow

gold·field \ˈgōl(d)-ˌfēld\ *n* (1852) **:** a gold-mining district

gold–filled \-ˈfild\ *adj* (ca. 1903) **:** covered with a layer of gold so as to constitute filled gold ⟨~ bracelet⟩

gold·finch \-ˌfinch\ *n* (bef. 12c) **1 :** a small largely red, black, and yellow European finch (*Carduelis carduelis*) often kept as a cage bird **2 :** any of several small American finches (genus *Spinus*) typically having the male in summer plumage variably yellow with black wings, tail, and crown

gold·fish \-ˌfish\ *n* (1698) **:** a small usu. golden yellow or orange cyprinid fish (*Carassius auratus*) much used as an aquarium and pond fish

goldfish bowl *n* (1935) **:** a place or situation offering no privacy

gold leaf *n* (ca. 1727) **:** a sheet of gold ordinarily varying from four to five millionths of an inch in thickness that is used esp. for gilding

gold mine *n* (15c) **:** a rich source of something desired

gold of pleasure (1597) **:** an annual herb (*Camelina sativa*) of the mustard family that produces oil-rich seeds

gold rush *n* (1876) **1 :** a rush to newly discovered goldfields in pursuit of riches **2 :** the headlong pursuit of sudden wealth in a new or lucrative field — **gold rush·er** \-ˈrəsh-ər\ *n*

gold·smith \ˈgōl(d)-ˌsmith\ *n* (bef. 12c) **:** one who makes or deals in articles of gold

gold standard *n* (1831) **:** a monetary standard under which the basic unit of currency is defined by a stated quantity of gold and which is usu. characterized by the coinage and circulation of gold, unrestricted convertibility of other money into gold, and the free export and import of gold for the settlement of international obligations

gold·stone \ˈgōl(d)-ˌstōn\ *n* (1626) **:** aventurine glass spangled close and fine with particles of gold-colored material

go·lem \ˈgō-ləm, ˈgȯi-, ˈgā-\ *n* [Yiddish *goylem,* fr. Heb *gōlem* shapeless mass] (1897) **1 :** an artificial human being in Hebrew folklore endowed with life **2 :** something resembling a golem: as **a :** AUTOMATON **b :** BLOCKHEAD

golf \ˈgälf, ˈgȯlf, ˈgäf, ˈgȯf *sometimes* ˈgəlf\ *n, often attrib* [ME (Sc)] (15c) **:** a game in which a player using special clubs attempts to sink a ball with as few strokes as possible into each of the 9 or 18 successive holes on a course — **golf** *vi* — **golf·er** *n*

Golf (1957) — a communications code word for the letter *g*

golf ball *n* (1637) **1 :** a small hard dimpled ball used in golf **2 :** the spherical printing element of an electric typewriter

golf cart *n* (1899) **1 :** a small cart for wheeling a golf bag around a golf course **2 :** a motorized cart for carrying a golfer and his equipment over a golf course — called also *golf car*

golf course *n* (1890) **:** an area of land laid out for the game of golf with a series of 9 or 18 holes each including tee, fairway, and putting green and often one or more natural or artificial hazards — called also *golf links*

golf widow *n* (ca. 1927) **:** a woman whose husband spends much time on the golf course

Gol·gi \ˈgȯl-(ˌ)jē\ *adj* (1891) **:** of or relating to the Golgi apparatus, Golgi bodies, or a method of staining for them ⟨~ vesicles⟩

Golgi apparatus *n* [Camillo *Golgi*] (1916) **:** a cytoplasmic organelle that appears in electron microscopy as a series of parallel sometimes vesicular membranes without ribosomes and is prob. active in cellular secretion — called also *Golgi complex;* see CELL illustration

Golgi body *n* (1925) **:** a discrete particle of the Golgi apparatus as observed in a stained preparation — called also *dictyosome*

go·liard \ˈgōl-yərd, -ˌyärd\ *n* [ME, fr. MF, goliard, glutton, deriv. of L *gula* throat — more at GLUTTON] (15c) **:** a wandering student of the 12th or 13th century given to the writing of satiric Latin verse and to convivial living and minstrelsy — **go·liar·dic** \gōl-ˈyärd-ik\ *adj*

Go·li·ath \gə-ˈlī-əth\ *n* [Heb *Golyath*] **1 :** a Philistine champion who in I Samuel 17 is killed by David **2 :** GIANT

gol·li·wog *or* **gol·li·wogg** \ˈgäl-ē-ˌwäg\ *n* [*Golliwogg,* an animated doll in children's fiction by Bertha Upton †1912 Am. writer] (1895) **1 :** a grotesque black doll **2 :** a person resembling a golliwog

gol·ly \ˈgäl-ē\ *interj* [euphemism for *God*] (1775) — used as a mild oath or to express surprise

gon- *or* **gono-** *comb form* [Gk, fr. *gonos* procreation, seed, fr. *gignesthai* to be born — more at KIN] **:** sexual **:** generative **:** semen **:** seed ⟨*gono*duct⟩

-gon \ˌgän *also* -gən\ *n comb form* [NL *-gonum,* fr. Gk *-gōnon,* fr. *gōnia* angle; akin to Gk *gony* knee — more at KNEE] **:** figure having (so many) angles ⟨deca*gon*⟩

go·nad \ˈgō-ˌnad\ *n* [NL *gonad-, gonas,* fr. Gk *gonos*] (1880) **:** any of the reproductive glands that produce gametes and include the ovaries and testes — **go·nad·al** \gō-ˈnad-ᵊl\ *adj*

go·nad·ec·to·my \ˌgō-nə-ˈdek-tə-mē\ *n, pl* **-mies** (1915) : surgical removal of an ovary or testis — **go·nad·ec·to·mized** \-ˌmīzd\ *adj*
go·nad·o·trop·ic \gō-ˌnad-ə-ˈträp-ik\ *or* **go·nad·o·tro·phic** \-ˈtrō-fik, -ˈträf-ik\ *adj* (1931) : acting on or stimulating the gonads
go·nad·o·tro·pin \-ˈtrō-pən\ *or* **go·nad·o·tro·phin** \-fən\ *n* (1931) : a gonadotropic hormone (as follicle-stimulating hormone)
Gond \ˈgänd\ *n* (1795) : a member of a Dravidian or pre-Dravidian people of central India
Gon·di \ˈgän-dē\ *n* (1855) : the Dravidian language of the Gonds
gon·do·la \ˈgän-də-lə (*usual for sense 1*), gän-ˈdō-\ *n* [It, fr. MGk *kondoura* small vessel] (1549) **1** : a long narrow flat-bottomed boat with a high prow and stern used on the canals of Venice **2** : a heavy flat-bottomed boat used on New England rivers and on the Ohio and Mississippi rivers **3** : a railroad car with no top, a flat bottom, and fixed sides that is used chiefly for hauling heavy bulk commodities **4 a** : an elongated car attached to the underside of an airship **b** : an often spherical airtight enclosure suspended from a balloon for carrying passengers or instruments **c** : an enclosed car suspended from a cable and used for transporting passengers; *esp* : one used as a ski lift **5** : a motortruck or trailer having a large hopper-shaped container for transporting mixed concrete
gon·do·lier \ˌgän-də-ˈli(ə)r\ *n* (1603) : one who propels a gondola
gone \ˈgȯn *also* ˈgän\ *adj* [fr. pp. of *go*] (1598) **1 a** : DEAD **b** : LOST, RUINED ⟨lost looks and ~ faculties —Penelope Gilliatt⟩ **c** : characterized by sinking or dropping ⟨the empty or ~ feeling in the abdomen so common in elevators —H. G. Armstrong⟩ **2 a** : INVOLVED, ABSORBED ⟨far ~ in hysteria⟩ **b** : possessed with a strong attachment or a foolish or unreasoning love or desire : INFATUATED — often used with *on* ⟨was real ~ on that man —Pete Martin⟩ **c** : PREGNANT ⟨she's six months ~⟩ **3** : PAST ⟨memories of ~ summers —John Cheever⟩ **4** *slang* : GREAT ⟨a real ~ fashion reporter —Inez Robb⟩
G_1 phase \ˌjē-ˈwən-\ *n* [growth] (1973) : the period in the cell cycle from the end of cell division to the beginning of DNA replication — compare G_2 PHASE, M PHASE, S PHASE
gon·er \ˈgȯn-ər *also* ˈgän-ər\ *n* (1854) : one whose case is hopeless
gon·fa·lon \ˈgän-fə-ˌlän, -lən\ *n* [It *gonfalone*] (1595) **1** : the ensign of certain princes or states (as the medieval republics of Italy) **2** : a flag that hangs from a crosspiece or frame
gong \ˈgäŋ, ˈgȯŋ\ *n* [Malay & Jav, of imit. origin] (1590) **1** : a disk-shaped percussion instrument that produces a resounding tone when struck with a usu. padded hammer **2 a** : a saucer-shaped bell (as in a fire alarm) that is struck by a mechanical hammer **b** : a wire rod wound in a flat spiral for sounding the time or chime or alarm (as in a clock) **3** *Brit* : MEDAL — **gong** *vi*
Gon·go·rism \ˈgäŋ-gə-ˌriz-əm\ *n* [Sp *gongorismo*, fr. Luis de *Góngora* y Argote †1627 Span. poet] (1813) : a literary style characterized by studied obscurity and by the use of various ornate devices — **gon·go·ris·tic** \ˌgäŋ-gə-ˈris-tik\ *adj*
goni- *or* **gonio-** *comb form* [Gk *gōnia*] : corner : angle ⟨*goniometer*⟩
go·nid·i·al \gō-ˈnid-ē-əl\ *adj* (1845) : of or relating to a gonidium
go·nid·i·um \-ē-əm\ *n, pl* **-ia** \-ē-ə\ [NL, fr. *gon-* + *-idium*] (1845) **1** : an asexual reproductive cell or group of cells in or on a gametophyte **2** : a chlorophyll-bearing algal cell within the thallus of a lichen
gon·if, gon·iff \ˈgän-əf\ *var of* GANEF
go·ni·om·e·ter \ˌgō-nē-ˈäm-ət-ər\ *n* (1766) **1** : an instrument for measuring angles **2** : DIRECTION FINDER — **go·nio·met·ric** \-nē-ə-ˈme-trik\ *adj* — **go·ni·om·e·try** \-nē-ˈäm-ə-trē\ *n*
gono·coc·cus \ˌgän-ə-ˈkäk-əs\ *n, pl* **-coc·ci** \-ˈkäk-ˌ(s)ī, -ˈkäk-(ˌ)(s)ē\ [NL] (1889) : a pus-producing bacterium (*Neisseria gonorrhoeae*) that causes gonorrhea — **gono·coc·cal** \-ˈkäk-əl\ *or* **gono·coc·cic** \-ˈkäk-(s)ik\ *adj*
gono·cyte \ˈgän-ə-ˌsīt\ *n* [ISV] (1900) : a cell that produces gametes; *esp* : GAMETOCYTE
go–no–go \ˈgō-ˈnō-ˌgō\ *adj* (ca. 1945) **1** : being or relating to a required decision to continue or stop a course of action **2** : being or relating to a point at which a go-no-go decision must be made
gono·phore \ˈgän-ə-ˌfō(ə)r, -ˌfȯ(ə)r\ *n* [ISV] (1835) : an attached reproductive zooid of a hydroid colony
gono·pore \ˈgän-ə-ˌpō(ə)r, -ˌpȯ(ə)r\ *n* (1897) : a genital pore
gon·or·rhea \ˌgän-ə-ˈrē-ə\ *n* [NL, fr. LL, morbid loss of semen, fr. Gk *gonorrhoia*, fr. *gon-* + *-rrhoia* -rrhea] (1547) : a contagious inflammation of the genital mucous membrane caused by the gonococcus — called also *clap* — **gon·or·rhe·al** \-ˈrē-əl\ *adj*
-g·o·ny \g-ə-nē\ *n comb form* [L *-gonia*, fr. Gk, fr. *gonos*] : generation : reproduction : manner of coming into being ⟨*sporogony*⟩
gon·zo \ˈgän-(ˌ)zō\ *adj* [perh. fr. It *gonzo* simpleton] (1971) : idiosyncratically subjective but engagé ⟨~ journalism⟩; *also* : BIZARRE
goo \ˈgü\ *n* [perh. alter. of *glue*] (1911) **1** : a viscid or sticky substance **2** : sentimental tripe — **goo·ey** \-ē\ *adj*
goo·ber \ˈgü-bər, ˈgu̇b-ər\ *n* [of African origin; akin to Kongo *nguba* peanut] *Southern & Midland* (1833) : PEANUT
[1]**good** \ˈgu̇d\ *adj* **bet·ter** \ˈbet-ər\; **best** \ˈbest\ [ME, fr. OE *gōd*; akin to OHG *guot* good, Skt *gadh* to hold fast] (bef. 12c) **1 a (1)** : of a favorable character or tendency ⟨~ news⟩ **(2)** : BOUNTIFUL, FERTILE ⟨~ land⟩ **(3)** : HANDSOME, ATTRACTIVE ⟨~ looks⟩ **b (1)** : SUITABLE, FIT ⟨~ to eat⟩ **(2)** : free from injury or disease ⟨one ~ arm⟩ **(3)** : not depreciated ⟨bad money drives out ~⟩ **(4)** : commercially sound ⟨a ~ risk⟩ **(5)** : certain to last or live ⟨~ for another year⟩ **(6)** : certain to pay or contribute ⟨~ for a hundred dollars⟩ **(7)** : certain to elicit a specified result ⟨always ~ for a laugh⟩ **(8)** : PROFITABLE, ADVANTAGEOUS ⟨made a very ~ deal⟩ **c (1)** : AGREEABLE, PLEASANT ⟨had a ~ time⟩ **(2)** : SALUTARY, WHOLESOME ⟨~ for a cold⟩ **(3)** : AMUSING, CLEVER ⟨a ~ joke⟩ **d** : of a noticeably large size or quantity : CONSIDERABLE ⟨won by a ~ margin⟩ ⟨a ~ bit of the time⟩ ⟨a ~ many of us⟩ **e (1)** : WELL-FOUNDED, COGENT ⟨~ reasons⟩ **(2)** : TRUE ⟨holds ~ for society at large⟩ **(3)** : deserving of respect : HONORABLE ⟨in ~ standing⟩ **(4)** : legally valid or effectual ⟨~ title⟩ **f (1)** : ADEQUATE, SATISFACTORY ⟨~ care⟩ — often used in faint praise ⟨his serve is only ~ —Frank Deford⟩ **(2)** : conforming to a standard ⟨~ English⟩ **(3)** : CHOICE, DISCRIMINATING ⟨~ taste⟩ **(4)** : containing less fat and being less tender than higher grades — used of meat and esp. of beef **2 a (1)** : VIRTUOUS, JUST, COMMENDABLE ⟨a ~ man⟩ **(2)** : RIGHT ⟨~ conduct⟩ **(3)** : KIND, BENEVOLENT ⟨~ intentions⟩ **b** : UPPER-CLASS ⟨a ~ family⟩ **c** : COMPETENT, SKILLFUL ⟨a ~ doctor⟩ **d** : LOYAL ⟨a ~ party man⟩ ⟨a ~ Catholic⟩ — **good·ish** \ˈgu̇d-ish\ *adj* — **as good as** : in effect : VIRTUALLY ⟨*as good as* dead⟩ — **as good as gold 1** : of the highest worth or reliability ⟨his promise is *as good as gold*⟩ **2** : well-behaved ⟨the child was *as good as gold*⟩ — **good and** \ˌgu̇d-ᵊn\ : VERY, ENTIRELY ⟨was *good and* mad⟩
[2]**good** *n* (bef. 12c) **1 a** : something that is good **b (1)** : something conforming to the moral order of the universe **(2)** : praiseworthy character : GOODNESS **c** : a good element or portion **2** : advancement of prosperity or health ⟨the ~ of the community⟩ ⟨it's for your own ~⟩ **3 a** : something that has economic utility or satisfies an economic want **b** *pl* : personal property having intrinsic value but usu. excluding money, securities, and negotiable instruments **c** *pl* : CLOTH **d** *pl* : WARES, COMMODITIES, MERCHANDISE ⟨canned ~*s*⟩ **4** : good persons — used with *the* **5** *pl* : proof of wrongdoing ⟨didn't have the ~s on him —T. G. Cooke⟩ — **for good** : FOREVER, PERMANENTLY — **in good with** : in a favored position with — **to the good 1** : for the best : BENEFICIAL ⟨efforts to restrict credit were all *to the good* —*Time*⟩ **2** : in a position of net gain or profit ⟨wound up $10 *to the good*⟩
[3]**good** *adv* (13c) **1** : WELL ⟨he showed me how ~ I was doing —Herbert Gold⟩ **2** — used as an intensive ⟨a ~ 200 pounds⟩ ⟨a ~ long time⟩
usage *Good* as an adverb occurs chiefly in speech and is considered by some to be less than standard; it is seldom found in edited prose except in representations of speech. *Good* is an adjective and standard after verbs like *feel* and *taste* ⟨the heat feels *good*⟩ ⟨the soup tastes *good*⟩ Both *good* and *well* are used to express good health, but "I feel good" may connote good spirits in addition to good health.
good book *n, often cap G&B* (1860) : BIBLE
good–bye *or* **good–by** \gu̇d-ˈbī, gə(d)-\ *n* [alter. of *God be with you*] (1573) : a concluding remark or gesture at parting
good deal \(ˈ)gu̇(d)-ˈdē(ə)l\ *n* (1881) : a considerable quantity or extent : LOT ⟨a *good deal* is known about heart disease⟩ ⟨a *good deal* faster⟩
good faith *n* (1893) : honesty or lawfulness of purpose
good fellow *n* (13c) : an affable companionable person — **good–fel·low·ship** \ˈgu̇d-ˈfel-ō-ˌship, -ˈfel-ə-\ *n*
good–for–noth·ing \ˈgu̇d-fər-ˌnəth-iŋ\ *adj* (1711) : of no use or value — **good–for–nothing** *n*
Good Friday *n* [fr. its special sanctity] (13c) : the Friday before Easter observed in churches as the anniversary of the crucifixion of Christ and in some states of the U.S. as a legal holiday
good–heart·ed \ˈgu̇d-ˈhärt-əd\ *adj* (1552) : having a kindly generous disposition — **good–heart·ed·ly** *adv* — **good–heart·ed·ness** *n*
good–hu·mored \-ˈ(h)yü-mərd\ *adj* (1662) : GOOD-NATURED, CHEERFUL — **good–hu·mored·ly** *adv* — **good–hu·mored·ness** *n*
good life *n* (1946) : a life marked by a high standard of living
good–look·ing \ˈgu̇d-ˈlu̇k-iŋ\ *adj* (1780) : having a pleasing or attractive appearance — **good–look·er** \-ˈlu̇k-ər\ *n*
good·ly \ˈgu̇d-lē\ *adj* **good·li·er; -est** (bef. 12c) **1** : pleasantly attractive **2** : significantly large : CONSIDERABLE ⟨a ~ number⟩
good·man \ˈgu̇d-mən\ *n* (13c) **1** *archaic* : the master of a household **2** *archaic* : MR.
good–na·tured \-ˈnā-chərd\ *adj* (1577) : of a pleasant cheerful cooperative disposition ***syn*** see AMIABLE — **good–na·tured·ly** *adv* — **good–na·tured·ness** *n*
good–neighbor *adj* (1937) : marked by principles of friendship, cooperation, and noninterference in the internal affairs of another country ⟨a ~ policy⟩
good·ness \ˈgu̇d-nəs\ *n* (bef. 12c) **1** : the quality or state of being good **2** — used interjectionally to express mild surprise or shock **3** : the nutritious, flavorful, or beneficial part of something
good offices *n pl* (1904) : services as a mediator
good old boy *n* (1972) : a usu. rural white Southerner who conforms to the social behavior of his peers
Good Sa·mar·i·tan \-sə-ˈmar-ət-ᵊn, -ˈmer-\ *n* (1846) : SAMARITAN 2
good–tem·pered \ˈgu̇d-ˈtem-pərd\ *adj* (1768) : not easily vexed — **good–tem·pered·ly** *adv* — **good–tem·pered·ness** *n*
good·wife \ˈgu̇d-ˌwīf\ *n* (13c) **1** *archaic* : the mistress of a household **2** *archaic* : MRS.
good·will \ˈgu̇d-ˈwil\ *n* (bef. 12c) **1 a** : a kindly feeling of approval and support : benevolent interest or concern **b (1)** : the favor or prestige that a business has acquired beyond the mere value of what it sells **(2)** : the value of projected earnings increases of a business esp. as part of its purchase price **(3)** : the value of other intangible assets (as tax credits) of a business esp. as part of its purchase price **2 a** : cheerful consent **b** : willing effort — **good·willed** \-ˈwild\ *adj*
[1]**goody** \ˈgu̇d-ē\ *n* [alter. of *goodwife*] *archaic* (1559) : a usu. married woman of lowly station — used as a title preceding a surname
[2]**goody** *or* **good·ie** *n, pl* **good·ies** (1756) : something that is particularly attractive, pleasurable, good, or desirable
goody–goody \ˌgu̇d-ē-ˈgu̇d-ē\ *adj* (1871) : affectedly or ingratiatingly good or proper — **goody–goody** *n*
[1]**goof** \ˈgüf\ *n* [prob. alter. of E dial. *goff* (simpleton)] (1915) **1** : a ridiculous stupid person **2** : BLUNDER
[2]**goof** *vi* (1941) **1** : to make a usu. foolish or careless mistake : BLUNDER **2** *slang* : to spend time idly or foolishly — often used with *off* ~ *vt* : to make a mess of : BUNGLE — usu. used with *up* — **goof on** *slang* : to make fun of : KID, PUT ON ⟨you're *goofing on* me, right?⟩
goof·ball \ˈgüf-ˌbȯl\ *n* (ca. 1951) **1** *slang* : a barbiturate sleeping pill **2** *slang* : a goofy person
go off *vi* (1579) **1** : EXPLODE **2** : to burst forth or break out suddenly or noisily **3** : to go forth, out, or away : LEAVE **4** : to undergo decline or deterioration **5** : to follow the expected or desired course : PROCEED ⟨the party *went off* well⟩ **6** : to make a characteristic noise : SOUND — **go off the deep end 1** : to enter recklessly on a course **2** : to become very much excited
goof–off \ˈgü-ˌfȯf\ *n* (1932) : one who evades work or responsibility

\ə\ abut \ᵊ\ kitten, F table \ər\ further \a\ ash \ā\ ace \ä\ cot, cart \au̇\ out \ch\ chin \e\ bet \ē\ easy \g\ go \i\ hit \ī\ ice \j\ job \ŋ\ sing \ō\ go \ȯ\ law \ȯi\ boy \th\ thin \t͟h\ the \ü\ loot \u̇\ foot \y\ yet \zh\ vision \ȧ, k̟, ⁿ, œ, œ̄, ue, ue̅, ʸ\ see Guide to Pronunciation

goofy \'gü-fē\ *adj* **goof·i·er; -est** (1921) : CRAZY, SILLY — **goof·i·ly** \-fə-lē\ *adv* — **goof·i·ness** \-fē-nəs\ *n*

goo·gol \'gü-ˌgȯl\ *n* [coined by Milton Sirotta *b ab* 1929 nephew of Edward Kasner †1955 Am. mathematician] (1938) : the figure 1 followed by 100 zeroes equal to 10^{100}

goo·gol·plex \-ˌpleks\ *n* [*googol* + *-plex* (as in *duplex*)] (1938) : the figure 1 followed by a googol of zeroes equal to

$$10^{googol} \text{ or } 10^{10^{100}}$$

[1]**goo–goo** \'gü-(ˌ)gü\ *adj* [prob. alter. of [2]*goggle*] (1900) : LOVING, ENTICING — used chiefly in the phrase *goo-goo eyes*

[2]**goo–goo** *n, pl* **goo–goos** [fr. *good* government] (1912) : a member or advocate of a political reform movement

[1]**gook** \'gu̇k, 'gük\ *n* [origin unknown] (1935) : a native belonging usu. to a brown or yellow race — usu. used disparagingly

[2]**gook** *var of* GUCK

goon \'gün\ *n* [prob. short for E dial. *gooney* (simpleton)] (1921) **1** : a stupid person **2** : a man hired to terrorize or eliminate opponents

go on *vi* (15c) **1 a** : to continue on or as if on a journey ⟨life *goes on*⟩ ⟨*went on* to greater things⟩ **b** : to keep on : CONTINUE ⟨*went on* smoking⟩ **c** : PROCEED ⟨*went on* to win the election⟩ **2** : to take place : HAPPEN ⟨what's *going on*⟩ **3** : to talk esp. in an effusive manner ⟨the way people *go on* about their ancestors —Hamilton Basso⟩

goo·ney *also* **goo·ny** *or* **goo·nie** \'gü-nē\ *n, pl* **gooneys** *or* **goonies** [prob. fr. E dial. *gooney* (simpleton)] (1850) : BLACK-FOOTED ALBATROSS

gooney bird *n* (1947) : BLACK-FOOTED ALBATROSS

goop \'güp\ *n* [prob. alter. of *goo*] (ca. 1958) : GOO, GUNK

goo·san·der \gü-'san-dər\ *n* [origin unknown] (1622) : the common merganser (*Mergus merganser*) of the northern hemisphere

[1]**goose** \'güs\ *n, pl* **geese** \'gēs\ [ME *gos,* fr. OE *gōs;* akin to OHG *gans* goose, L *anser*] (bef. 12c) **1 a** : any of numerous large waterfowl (family Anatidae) that are intermediate between the swans and ducks and have long necks, feathered lores, and reticulate tarsi **b** : a female goose as distinguished from a gander **2** : SIMPLETON, DOLT **3** *pl* **goos·es** : a tailor's smoothing iron with a gooseneck handle **4** *pl* **goos·es** : a poke between the buttocks

[2]**goose** *vt* **goosed; goos·ing** (1879) **1** : to poke between the buttocks with an upward thrust **2** : to incite to action or accelerated growth : SPUR ⟨an effort to ~ newsstand sales⟩

goose·ber·ry \'güs-ˌber-ē, 'güz-, -b(ə-)rē, *chiefly Brit* 'gu̇z-\ *n* (1532) **1 a** : the acid usu. prickly fruit of any of several shrubs (genus *Ribes*) of the saxifrage family **b** : a shrub bearing gooseberries **2** : CURRANT 2

goose bumps *n pl* (1933) : GOOSEFLESH

goose egg *n* (1866) : ZERO, NOTHING; *esp* : a score of zero in a game or contest

goose·flesh \'güs-ˌflesh\ *n* (1810) : a roughness of the skin produced by erection of its papillae usu. from cold or fear

goose·foot \-ˌfu̇t\ *n, pl* **goose·foots** (1548) : any of a genus (*Chenopodium*) or family (Chenopodiaceae, the goosefoot family) of glabrous herbs with utricular fruit

goose grass *n* (1530) **1** : CLEAVERS **2** : YARD GRASS

goose·neck \'güs-ˌnek\ *n, often attrib* (1688) : something (as a flexible jointed metal pipe) curved like the neck of a goose or U-shaped — **goose·necked** \-ˌsnekt\ *adj*

goose pimples *n pl* (ca. 1889) : GOOSEFLESH

goose–step \'güs-'step\ *vi* (1879) **1** : to march in a goose step **2** : to practice an unthinking conformity

goose step *n* (1806) : a straight-legged stiff-kneed step used by troops of some armies when passing in review

goos·ey \'gü-sē\ *adj* **goos·i·er; -est** (1811) **1** : resembling a goose **2 a** : affected with gooseflesh : SCARED **b** : very nervous **c** : susceptible to or reacting strongly to goosing (as by jumping in the air)

go out *vi* (bef. 12c) **1 a** : to go forth, abroad, or outdoors; *specif* : to leave one's house **b** (1) : to take the field as a soldier (2) : to participate as a principal in a duel **c** : to travel as or as if a colonist or immigrant **d** : to work away from home **2 a** : to come to an end **b** : to become extinguished ⟨the hall light *went out*⟩ **c** : to give up office : RESIGN **d** : to become obsolete or unfashionable **e** (1) : to play the last card of one's hand (2) : to reach or exceed the total number of points required for game in cards **3** : to go on strike **4** : BREAK, COLLAPSE **5** : to become a candidate ⟨*went out* for the football team⟩

go over *vi* (15c) **1** : to go on a journey **2** : to become converted **3** : to receive approval : SUCCEED ⟨his plan *went over* well⟩

[1]**go·pher** \'gō-fər\ *n* [origin unknown] (1791) **1** : a burrowing edible land tortoise (*Gopherus polyphemus*) of the southern U.S.; *broadly* : any of several related land tortoises **2 a** : any of several burrowing rodents (family Geomyidae) of western No. America, Central America, and the southern U.S. that are the size of a large rat and have large cheek pouches opening beside the mouth **b** : any of numerous small ground squirrels (genus *Citellus*) of the prairie region of No. America closely related to the chipmunks **3** : GOPHER BALL

[2]**gopher** *var of* GOFER

gopher ball *n* (ca. 1949) : a pitched baseball hit for a home run

gopher snake *n* (1837) **1** : INDIGO SNAKE **2** : BULL SNAKE

Gor·di·an knot \ˌgȯrd-ē-ən-\ *n* (1611) **1** : a knot tied by Gordius, king of Phrygia, held to be capable of being untied only by the future ruler of Asia, and cut by Alexander the Great with his sword **2** : an intricate problem; *esp* : a problem insoluble in its own terms

Gor·don setter \ˌgȯrd-ᵊn-\ *n* [Alexander, 4th Duke of *Gordon* †1827 Scot. sportsman] (1865) : any of a breed of large bird dogs that have a long flat black-and-tan coat

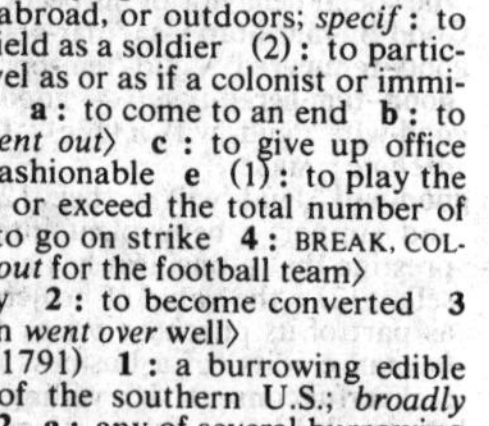

Gordon setter

[1]**gore** \'gō(ə)r, 'gȯ(ə)r\ *n* [ME, filth, fr. OE *gor*] (bef. 12c) : BLOOD; *esp* : clotted blood

[2]**gore** *n* [ME, fr. OE *gāra;* akin to OE *gār* spear, Gk *chaios* shepherd's staff] (bef. 12c) **1** : a small usu. triangular piece of land **2** : a tapering or triangular piece (as of cloth in a skirt)

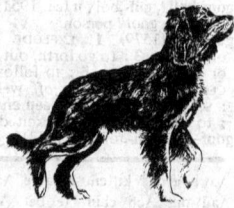

[3]**gore** *vt* **gored; gor·ing** (1548) **1** : to cut into a tapering triangular form **2** : to provide with a gore

[4]**gore** *vt* **gored; gor·ing** [ME *goren*] (1523) : to pierce or wound with something pointed (as a horn or knife) ⟨*gored* by a bull⟩

[1]**gorge** \'gȯ(ə)rj\ *n* [ME, fr. MF, fr. LL *gurga,* alter. of *gurges,* fr. L, whirlpool — more at VORACIOUS] (14c) **1** : THROAT — often used with *rise* to indicate revulsion accompanied by a sensation of constriction ⟨my ~ rises at the sight of blood⟩ **2 a** : a hawk's crop **b** : STOMACH, BELLY **3** : the entrance into an outwork (as a bastion) of a fort **4** : a narrow passage through land; *esp* : a narrow steep-walled canyon or part of a canyon **5** : a primitive device used instead of a fishhook that consists of an object (as a piece of bone attached in the middle of a line) easy to swallow but difficult to eject **6** : a mass choking a passage ⟨a river dammed by an ice ~⟩

[2]**gorge** *vb* **gorged; gorg·ing** *vi* (14c) : to eat greedily or to repletion ~ *vt* **1 a** : to stuff to capacity : GLUT **b** : to fill completely or to the point of distension ⟨veins *gorged* with blood⟩ **2** : to consume greedily ***syn*** see SATIATE — **gorg·er** *n*

gor·geous \'gȯr-jəs\ *adj* [ME *gorgayse,* fr. MF *gorgias* elegant, fr. *gorgias* wimple, fr. *gorge* gorget] (15c) : splendidly or showily brilliant or magnificent ***syn*** see SPLENDID — **gor·geous·ly** *adv* — **gor·geous·ness** *n*

gor·get \'gȯr-jət\ *n* [ME, fr. MF, fr. *gorge*] (15c) **1** : a piece of armor protecting the throat — see ARMOR illustration **2 a** : an ornamental collar **b** : a part of a wimple covering the throat and shoulders

gor·gon \'gȯr-gən\ *n* [L *Gorgon-, Gorgo,* fr. Gk *Gorgōn*] (14c) **1** *cap* : any of three snake-haired sisters in Greek mythology whose appearance turns the beholder to stone **2** : an ugly or repulsive woman — **Gor·go·ni·an** \gȯr-'gō-nē-ən\ *adj*

gor·go·ni·an \gȯr-'gō-nē-ən\ *n* [deriv. of L *gorgonia* coral, fr. *Gorgon-, Gorgo*] (1835) : any of an order (Gorgonacea) of colonial anthozoans with a usu. horny and branching axial skeleton — **gorgonian** *adj*

gor·gon·ize \'gȯr-gə-ˌnīz\ *vt* **-ized; -iz·ing** (1609) : to have a paralyzing or mesmerizing effect on : STUPEFY, PETRIFY

Gor·gon·zo·la \ˌgȯr-gən-'zō-lə\ *n* [It, fr. *Gorgonzola,* Italy] (1878) : a pungent blue cheese of Italian origin

go·ril·la \gə-'ril-ə\ *n* [deriv. of Gk *Gorillai,* believed to be the name of an alleged African tribe of hairy women] (1853) **1** : an anthropoid ape (*Gorilla gorilla*) of western equatorial Africa related to the chimpanzee but less erect and much larger **2 a** : an ugly or brutal man **b** : THUG, GOON

gor·man·dize \'gȯr-mən-ˌdīz\ *vb* **-dized; -diz·ing** [*gormand,* alter. of *gourmand*] *vi* (1548) : to eat gluttonously or ravenously ~ *vt* : to eat greedily : DEVOUR — **gor·man·diz·er** *n*

gorm·less \'gȯrm-ləs\ *adj* [alter. of E dial. *gaumless,* fr. *gaum* attention, understanding (fr. ME *gome,* fr. ON *gaum, gaumr*) + *-less*] *chiefly Brit* (1883) : lacking intelligence : STUPID

go–round \'gō-ˌrau̇nd\ *n* (1891) : GO-AROUND

gorp \'gȯ(ə)rp\ *n* [origin unknown] (1968) : a snack consisting of high-energy food (as raisins and nuts)

gorse \'gȯ(ə)rs\ *n* [ME *gorst,* fr. OE — more at HORROR] (bef. 12c) : a spiny yellow-flowered European shrub (*Ulex europaeus*); *broadly* : any of several related plants (genera *Ulex* and *Genista*) — **gorsy** \'gȯr-sē\ *adj*

gory \'gō(ə)r-ē, 'gȯ(ə)r-\ *adj* **gor·i·er; -est** (15c) **1** : covered with gore : BLOODSTAINED **2** : BLOODCURDLING, SENSATIONAL

gosh \'gäsh, 'gȯsh\ *interj* [euphemism for *God*] (1757) — used as a mild oath or to express surprise

gos·hawk \'gäs-ˌhȯk\ *n* [ME *goshawke,* fr. OE *gōshafoc,* fr. *gōs* goose + *hafoc* hawk] (bef. 12c) : any of several long-tailed accipitrine hawks with short rounded wings; *esp* : a hawk (*Accipiter gentilis*) of the northern parts of both the Old and the New World that is larger than a crow and has a white stripe above and behind the eye

gos·ling \'gäz-liŋ, 'gȯz-, -lən\ *n* [ME, fr. *gos* goose] (14c) **1** : a young goose **2** : a foolish or callow person

[1]**gos·pel** \'gäs-pəl\ *n* [ME, fr. OE *gōdspel,* fr. *gōd* good + *spell* tale, trans. of LL *evangelium* — more at SPELL] (bef. 12c) **1 a** *often cap* : the message concerning Christ, the kingdom of God, and salvation **b** *cap* : one of the first four New Testament books telling of the life, death, and resurrection of Jesus Christ; *also* : a similar apocryphal book **c** : an interpretation of the Christian message ⟨the social ~⟩ **2** *cap* : a lection from one of the New Testament Gospels **3** : the message or teachings of a religious teacher **4** : something accepted as infallible truth or as a guiding principle ⟨the ~ of conservation —R. M. Hodesh⟩ **5** : gospel music

[2]**gospel** *adj* (bef. 12c) **1 a** : having a basis in or being in accordance with the gospel : EVANGELICAL ⟨ordained to the ~ ministry —*Christian Century*⟩ **b** : marked by special or fervid emphasis on the gospel ⟨a ~ meeting⟩ **2** : of, relating to, or being religious songs of American origin associated with evangelism and popular devotion and marked by simple melody and harmony and elements of folk songs and blues

gos·pel·er *or* **gos·pel·ler** \'gäs-pə-lər\ *n* (1673) **1** : one who preaches or propounds a gospel **2** : one who reads or sings the liturgical Gospel

gospel side *n, often cap G* [fr. the custom of reading the Gospel from this side] (1891) : the left side of an altar or chancel as one faces it

Gos·plan \'gäs-ˌplan, 'gȯs-ˌplän\ *n* [Russ *Gosudarstvennaya Planovaya* (Komissiya) State Planning Commission] (1923) : a Soviet agency that makes long-term economic and social plans and generally supervises their execution

gos·port \'gäs-ˌpō(ə)rt, -ˌpȯ(ə)rt\ *n* [*Gosport,* England] (1942) : a flexible one-way speaking tube for communication between separate cockpits of an airplane

gos·sa·mer \'gäs-ə-mər *also* 'gäz(-ə)-mər\ *n* [ME *gossomer,* fr. *gos* goose + *somer* summer] (14c) **1** : a film of cobwebs floating in air in calm clear weather **2** : something light, delicate, insubstantial, or tenuous ⟨the ~ of youth's dreams —Andrea Parke⟩ — **gossamer** *adj* — **gos·sa·mery** \-mə-rē\ *adj*

gos·san \'gäs-ᵊn\ *n* [Corn *gossen,* fr. *gōs* blood] (1776) : decomposed rock or vein material of reddish or rusty color that results from oxidized pyrites

[1]**gos·sip** \'gäs-əp\ *n* [ME *gossib,* fr. OE *godsibb,* fr. *god* god + *sibb* kinsman, fr. *sibb* related] (bef. 12c) **1 a** *dial Brit* : GODPARENT **b** : COMPANION, CRONY **c** : a person who habitually reveals personal or sensational facts **2 a** : rumor or report of an intimate nature **b** : a chatty

talk **c** : the subject matter of gossip ***syn*** see REPORT — **gos·sip·ry** \-ə-prē\ *n*

²**gossip** *vi* (1627) : to relate gossip — **gos·sip·er** *n*

gos·sipy \ˈgäs-ə-pē\ *adj* (1818) : full of or given to gossip ⟨a ~ letter⟩ ⟨~ neighbors⟩

gos·sy·pol \ˈgäs-ə-ˌpȯl, -ˌpōl\ *n* [ISV, deriv. of L *gossypion* cotton] (1899) : a toxic phenolic pigment $C_{30}H_{30}O_8$ in cottonseed

got *past and past part of* GET

Goth \ˈgäth\ *n* [ME *Gothes, Gotes* (pl.), partly fr. OE *Gotan* (pl.); partly fr. LL *Gothi* (pl.)] (bef. 12c) : a member of a Germanic people that overran the Roman Empire in the early centuries of the Christian era

¹**Goth·ic** \ˈgäth-ik\ *adj* (1611) **1 a** : of, relating to, or resembling the Goths, their civilization, or their language **b** : TEUTONIC, GERMANIC **c** (1) : MEDIEVAL (2) : UNCOUTH, BARBAROUS **2 a** : of, relating to, or having the characteristics of a style of architecture developed in northern France and spreading through western Europe from the middle of the 12th century to the early 16th century that is characterized by the converging of weights and strains at isolated points upon slender vertical piers and counterbalancing buttresses and by pointed arches and vaulting **b** : of or relating to an architectural style reflecting the influence of the medieval Gothic **3** *often not cap* : of or relating to a style of fiction characterized by the use of desolate or remote settings and macabre, mysterious, or violent incidents — **goth·i·cal·ly** \-i-k(ə-)lē\ *adv* — **Goth·ic·ness** \-ik-nəs\ *n*

²**Gothic** *n* (1644) **1 a** : BLACK LETTER **b** : SANS SERIF **2** : the East Germanic language of the Goths — see INDO-EUROPEAN LANGUAGES table **3** : Gothic art style or decoration; *specif* : the Gothic architectural style **4** : a work of fiction in the gothic style

Gothic arch *n* (1739) : a pointed arch; *esp* : one with a joint instead of a keystone at its apex

Goth·i·cism \ˈgäth-ə-ˌsiz-əm\ *n* (1710) **1** : barbarous lack of taste or elegance **2** : conformity to or practice of Gothic style — **Goth·i·cist** \-səst\ *n*

goth·i·cize \-ˌsīz\ *vt* **-cized; -ciz·ing** *often cap* (1712) : to make Gothic

gö·thite *var of* GOETHITE

go through *vi* (1568) **1** : to continue firmly or obstinately to the end ⟨I was *going through* with it if it killed me —A. W. Long⟩ **2 a** : to receive approval or sanction : PASS **b** : to come to a desired or satisfactory conclusion

go to *vi* (15c) **1** *archaic* — used interjectionally as an exhortation ⟨and they said one to another, *go to*, let us make brick —Gen 11:3 (AV)⟩ **2** *archaic* — used interjectionally to express disapproval or disbelief ⟨*go to, go to;* you have known what you should not —Shak.⟩

gotten *past part of* GET

Göt·ter·däm·mer·ung \ˌgə(r)t-ər-ˈdem-ə-ˌru̇ŋ, -ˈdam-\ *n* [fr. *Götterdämmerung* (1876), opera by Richard Wagner, fr. G, lit., twilight of the gods (trans. of ON *ragnarǫk*), fr. *götter* (pl. of *gott* god) + *dämmerung* twilight] (1909) : a collapse (as of a society or regime) marked by catastrophic violence and disorder

gouache \ˈgwäsh\ *n* [F, fr. It *guazzo* gouache, puddle, fr. L *aquatio* act of fetching water, fr. *aquatus*, pp. of *aquari* to fetch water, fr. *aqua* water — more at ISLAND] (1882) **1** : a method of painting with opaque watercolors **2 a** : a picture painted by gouache **b** : the pigment used in gouache

Gou·da \ˈgüd-ə\ *n* [*Gouda*, Netherlands] (1885) : a mild cheese of Dutch origin that is similar to Edam but contains more fat

¹**gouge** \ˈgau̇j\ *n* [ME *gowge*, fr. MF *gouge*, fr. LL *gulbia*, of Celt origin; akin to OIr *gulban* sting] (14c) **1** : a chisel with a concavo-convex cross section **2 a** : the act of gouging **b** : a groove or cavity scooped out **3** : an excessive or improper exaction : EXTORTION

²**gouge** *vt* **gouged; goug·ing** (1570) **1** : to scoop out with or as if with a gouge **2 a** : to force out (an eye) with the thumb **b** : to thrust the thumb into the eye of **3** : to subject to extortion or undue exaction : OVERCHARGE — **goug·er** *n*

gou·lash \ˈgü-ˌläsh, -ˌlash\ *n* [Hung *gulyás* herdsman's stew] (1866) **1** : a stew made with meat (as beef), assorted vegetables, and paprika **2** : a round in bridge played with hands produced by a redistribution of previously dealt cards **3** : a mixture of heterogeneous elements : JUMBLE

go under *vi* (1848) : to be overwhelmed, destroyed, or defeated : FAIL

go up *vi* (15c) **1** *chiefly Brit* : to attend a university **2** *of an actor* : to become confused — **go up in flames** : BURN — **go up in smoke** : to be destroyed by or as if by burning

gourd \ˈgō(ə)rd, ˈgȯ(ə)rd, ˈgu̇(ə)rd\ *n* [ME *gourde*, fr. MF, fr. L *cucurbita*] (14c) **1** : any of a family (Cucurbitaceae, the gourd family) of chiefly herbaceous tendril-bearing vines including the cucumber, melon, squash, and pumpkin **2** : the fruit of a gourd : PEPO; *esp* : any of various hard-rinded inedible fruits of plants of two genera (*Lagenaria* and *Cucurbita*) often used for ornament or for vessels and utensils — **out of one's gourd** *also* **off one's gourd** : CRAZY

gourde \ˈgü(ə)rd\ *n* [AmerF] (ca. 1858) — see MONEY table

gour·mand \ˈgu̇(ə)r-ˌmänd, -mənd\ *n* [ME, fr. MF *gourmant*] (15c) **1** : one who is excessively fond of eating and drinking **2** : one who is heartily interested in good food and drink — **gour·mand·ism** \ˈgu̇(ə)r-ˌmän-ˌdiz-əm, -mən-\ *n* — **gour·man·dize** \-ˌdīz\ *vi*

gour·met \ˈgu̇(ə)r-ˌmā, gu̇r-ˈ\ *n* [F, fr. MF, alter. of *gromet* boy servant, vintner's assistant, fr. ME *grom* groom] (1820) : a connoisseur of food and drink ***syn*** see EPICURE — **gourmet** *adj*

gout \ˈgau̇t\ *n* [ME *goute*, fr. OF, gout, drop, fr. L *gutta* drop] (13c) **1** : a metabolic disease marked by a painful inflammation of the joints, deposits of urates in and around the joints, and usu. an excessive amount of uric acid in the blood **2** : a mass or aggregate esp. of something fluid — **gouty** \-ē\ *adj*

gov·ern \ˈgəv-ərn\ *vb* [ME *governen*, fr. OF *governer*, fr. L *gubernare* to steer, govern, fr. Gk *kybernan*] *vt* (13c) **1 a** : to exercise continuous sovereign authority over; *esp* : to control and direct the making and administration of policy in **b** : to rule without sovereign power and usu. without having the authority to determine basic policy **2 a** *archaic* : MANIPULATE **b** : to control the speed of (as a machine) esp. by automatic means **3 a** : to control, direct, or strongly influence the actions and conduct of **b** : to exert a determining or guiding influence in or over ⟨income must ~ expenditure⟩ ⟨availability often ~s choice⟩ **c** : to hold in check : RESTRAIN **4** : to require (a word) to be in a certain case **5** : to serve as a precedent or deciding principle for ⟨habits and customs that ~ human decisions⟩ ~ *vi* **1** : to prevail or have decisive influence : CONTROL **2** : to exercise authority — **gov·ern·able** \-ər-nə-bəl\ *adj*

syn GOVERN, RULE mean to exercise power or authority in controlling others. GOVERN implies the aim of keeping in a straight course or smooth operation for the good of the individual and the whole; RULE may imply no more than laying down laws or issuing commands that must be obeyed but often suggests the exercise of despotic or arbitrary power.

gov·er·nance \ˈgəv-ər-nən(t)s\ *n* (14c) : GOVERNMENT

gov·ern·ess \ˈgəv-ər-nəs\ *n* (15c) **1** : a woman who governs **2** : a woman entrusted with the care and supervision of a child esp. in a private household — **gov·ern·essy** \-ē\ *adj*

gov·ern·ment \ˈgəv-ər(n)-mənt, -ə-mənt; ˈgəb-ᵊm-ənt, ˈgəv-\ *n, often attrib* [ME *governement*, fr. MF, fr. *governer*] (14c) **1** : the act or process of governing; *specif* : authoritative direction or control **2** *obs* : moral conduct or behavior : DISCRETION **3 a** : the office, authority, or function of governing **b** *obs* : the term during which a governing official holds office **4** : the continuous exercise of authority over and the performance of functions for a political unit : RULE **5 a** : the organization, machinery, or agency through which a political unit exercises authority and performs functions and which is usu. classified according to the distribution of power within it **b** : the complex of political institutions, laws, and customs through which the function of governing is carried out **6** : the body of persons that constitutes the governing authority of a political unit or organization: as **a** : the officials comprising the governing body of a political unit and constituting the organization as an active agency **b** *cap* : the executive branch of the U.S. federal government **c** *cap* : a small group of persons holding simultaneously the principal political executive offices of a nation or other political unit and being responsible for the direction and supervision of public affairs: (1) : such a group in a parliamentary system constituted by the cabinet or by the ministry (2) : ADMINISTRATION 4b **7** : POLITICAL SCIENCE — **gov·ern·men·tal** \ˌgəv-ər(n)-ˈment-ᵊl\ *adj* — **gov·ern·men·tal·ize** \-ᵊl-ˌīz\ *vt* — **gov·ern·men·tal·ly** \-ᵊl-ē\ *adv*

gov·ern·men·tal·ism \ˌgəv-ər(n)-ˈment-ᵊl-ˌiz-əm\ *n* (1848) **1** : a theory advocating extension of the sphere and degree of government activity **2** : the tendency toward extension of the role of government — **gov·ern·men·tal·ist** \-ᵊl-əst\ *n*

government note *n* (ca. 1909) : TREASURY NOTE 2

gov·er·nor \ˈgəv(-ə)-nər *also* ˈgəv-ər-nər\ *n* [ME *governour*, fr. MF *governeor*, fr. L *gubernator* steersman — more at GUBERNATORIAL] (14c) **1** : one that governs: as **a** : one that exercises authority esp. over an area or group **b** : an official elected or appointed to act as ruler, chief executive, or nominal head of a political unit **c** : COMMANDANT **d** : the managing director and usu. the principal officer of an institution or organization **e** : a member of a group that directs or controls an institution or society **2** : TUTOR **3 a** *slang* : one looked upon as governing **b** : MISTER, SIR — usu. used as a term of address **4 a** : an attachment to a machine (as a gasoline engine) for automatic control or limitation of speed **b** : a device giving automatic control (as of pressure or temperature) — **gov·er·nor·ate** \-ət, -ˌāt\ *n*

governor–general *n, pl* **governors–general** *or* **governor–generals** (1586) : a governor of high rank; *esp* : one who governs a large territory or has deputy governors under him

gov·er·nor·ship \ˈgəv(-ə)-nər-ˌship *also* ˈgəv-ər-\ *n* (1658) **1** : the office of governor **2** : the period of incumbency of a governor

gow·an \ˈgau̇-ən\ *n* [prob. alter. of ME *gollan*] *chiefly Scot* (1570) : DAISY 1; *broadly* : a white or yellow field flower — **gow·any** \-ə-nē\ *adj, chiefly Scot*

gown \ˈgau̇n\ *n* [ME, fr. MF *goune*, fr. LL *gunna* a fur or leather garment] (14c) **1 a** : a loose flowing outer garment formerly worn by men **b** : a distinctive robe worn by a professional or academic person **c** : a woman's dress **d** (1) : DRESSING GOWN (2) : NIGHTGOWN **e** : a coverall worn in an operating room **2** : the body of students and faculty of a college or university ⟨rivalry between town and ~⟩ — **gown** *vt*

gowns·man \ˈgau̇nz-mən\ *n* (1627) : a professional or academic person

gox \ˈgäks\ *n* [gaseous oxygen] (1959) : gaseous oxygen

goy \ˈgȯi\ *n, pl* **goy·im** \ˈgȯi-əm\ *or* **goys** [Yiddish, fr. Heb *gōy* people, nation] (1841) : GENTILE 1 — sometimes used disparagingly — **goy·ish** \ˈgȯi-ish\ *adj*

graaf·ian follicle \ˌgräf-ē-ən-, ˌgraf-\ *n, often cap G* [Regnier de *Graaf* †1673 Du. anatomist] (1883) : a vesicle in a mammal ovary enclosing a developing egg

¹**grab** \ˈgrab\ *vb* **grabbed; grab·bing** [obs. D or LG *grabben;* akin to ME *graspen* to grasp, Skt *gṛbhṇāti* he seizes] *vt* (ca. 1581) **1** : to take or seize by or as if by a sudden motion or grasp ⟨~ up an ax⟩ ⟨*grabbed* the opportunity⟩ ⟨~ attention⟩ **2** : to obtain unscrupulously ⟨~ public lands⟩ **3** : to take hastily ⟨~ a bite to eat⟩ ⟨~ a cab⟩ **4** : to forcefully engage the attention of ⟨the technique of *grabbing* an audience —Pauline Kael⟩ ~ *vi* : to make a grab ***syn*** see TAKE — **grab·ber** *n*

²**grab** *adj* (1608) **1** : intended to be grabbed ⟨a ~ rail⟩ **2** : taken at random ⟨~ samples of rocks⟩

³**grab** *n* (1824) **1 a** : a sudden snatch **b** : an unlawful or unscrupulous seizure **c** : something grabbed **2 a** : a device for clutching an object **b** : CLAMSHELL — **up for grabs** : available for anyone to take or win

grab bag *n* (1855) **1** : a receptacle (as a bag) containing small articles which are to be drawn (as at a party or fair) without being seen **2** : something resembling a grab bag

grab·ble \ˈgrab-əl\ *vi* **grab·bled; grab·bling** \-(ə-)liŋ\ [D *grabbelen*, fr. MD, freq. of *grabben*] (1579) **1** : to search with the hand : GROPE **2** : to lie or fall prone : SPRAWL — **grab·bler** \-(ə-)lər\ *n*

grab·by \ˈgrab-ē\ *adj* **grab·bi·er; -est** (1910) : tending to grab : GRASPING, GREEDY

\ə\ abut \ᵊ\ kitten, F table \ər\ further \a\ ash \ā\ ace \ä\ cot, cart \au̇\ out \ch\ chin \e\ bet \ē\ easy \g\ go \i\ hit \ī\ ice \j\ job \ŋ\ sing \ō\ go \ȯ\ law \ȯi\ boy \th\ thin \t͟h\ the \ü\ loot \u̇\ foot \y\ yet \zh\ vision \á, k̲, ⁿ, œ, œ̄, ue, ue̅, ʸ\ *see* Guide to Pronunciation

gra·ben \'gräb-ən\ *n* [G, ditch, fr. OHG *grabo,* fr. *graban* to dig — more at GRAVE] (1896) **:** a depressed segment of the crust of the earth or a celestial body (as the moon) bounded on at least two sides by faults

¹grace \'grās\ *n* [ME, fr. OF, fr. L *gratia* favor, charm, thanks, fr. *gratus* pleasing, grateful; akin to OHG *queran* to sigh, Skt *gṛṇāti* he praises] (12c) **1 a :** unmerited divine assistance given man for his regeneration or sanctification **b :** a state of sanctification enjoyed through divine grace **c :** a virtue coming from God **2 :** a short prayer at a meal asking a blessing or giving thanks **3 a :** disposition to or an act or instance of kindness or clemency **b** *archaic* **:** MERCY, PARDON **c :** a special favor **:** PRIVILEGE ⟨each in his place, by right, not ~, shall rule his heritage —Rudyard Kipling⟩ **d :** a temporary exemption **:** REPRIEVE **e :** APPROVAL, FAVOR ⟨stayed in his good ~*s*⟩ **4 a :** a charming trait or accomplishment **b :** a pleasingly graceful appearance or effect **:** CHARM **c :** ease and suppleness of movement or bearing **5 :** a musical trill, turn, or appoggiatura **6** — used as a title of address or reference for a duke, a duchess, or an archbishop **7 a :** sense of propriety or right **b :** the quality or state of being considerate or thoughtful **8** *pl, cap* **:** three sister goddesses in Greek mythology who are the givers of charm and beauty ***syn*** see MERCY

²grace *vt* **graced; grac·ing** (1585) **1 :** to confer dignity or honor on **2 :** ADORN, EMBELLISH

grace·ful \'grās-fəl\ *adj* (1586) **:** displaying grace in form or action **:** pleasing or attractive in line, proportion, or movement — **grace·ful·ly** \-fə-lē\ *adv* — **grace·ful·ness** *n*

grace·less \'grā-sləs\ *adj* (14c) **1 :** lacking in divine grace **:** IMMORAL, UNREGENERATE **2 a :** lacking a sense of propriety **b :** devoid of attractive qualities **3 :** artistically inept or unbeautiful — **grace·less·ly** *adv* — **grace·less·ness** *n*

grace note *n* (ca. 1823) **1 :** a musical note added as an ornament; *esp* **:** APPOGGIATURA **2 :** a small addition or embellishment

grac·ile \'gras-əl, -ˌīl\ *adj* [L *gracilis;* akin to ON *horr* starvation, Skt *kṛśá* emaciated] (1623) **1 :** SLENDER, SLIGHT **2 :** GRACEFUL — **grac·ile·ness** *n* — **gra·cil·i·ty** \grə-'sil-ət-ē\ *n*

gra·ci·o·so \ˌgräs-ē-'ō-(ˌ)sō, -(ˌ)zō\ *n, pl* **-sos** [Sp, fr. *gracioso,* adj., agreeable, amusing, fr. L *gratiosus*] (1749) **:** a buffoon in Spanish comedy

gra·cious \'grā-shəs\ *adj* [ME, fr. MF *gracieus,* fr. L *gratiosus* enjoying favor, agreeable, fr. *gratia*] (14c) **1 a** *obs* **:** GODLY **b** *archaic* **:** PLEASING, ACCEPTABLE **2 a :** marked by kindness and courtesy **b :** GRACEFUL **c :** marked by tact and delicacy **:** URBANE **d :** characterized by charm, good taste, and generosity of spirit **3 :** MERCIFUL, COMPASSIONATE — used conventionally of royalty and high nobility — **gra·cious·ly** *adv* — **gra·cious·ness** *n*

syn GRACIOUS, CORDIAL, AFFABLE, GENIAL, SOCIABLE mean markedly pleasant and easy in social intercourse. GRACIOUS implies courtesy and kindly consideration; CORDIAL stresses warmth and heartiness; AFFABLE implies easy approachability and readiness to respond pleasantly to conversation or requests or proposals; GENIAL stresses cheerfulness and even joviality; SOCIABLE suggests a genuine liking for the companionship of others.

grack·le \'grak-əl\ *n* [deriv. of L *graculus* jackdaw; akin to OE *crāwan* to crow — more at CROW] (1772) **1 :** any of various Old World starlings (as the hill mynahs) **2 :** any of several rather large American blackbirds (family Icteridae) having glossy iridescent black plumage

¹grad \'grad\ *n or adj* [by shortening] (ca. 1871) **:** GRADUATE

²grad *n* [F *grade* degree, fr. L *gradus*] (1898) **:** one hundredth of a right angle

gra·da·tion \grā-'dā-shən, grə-\ *n* (1549) **1 a :** a series forming successive stages **b :** a step or place in an ordered scale **2 :** an advance by regular degrees **3 :** the act or process of grading **4 :** a gradual passing from one tint or shade to another (as in a painting) **5 :** ABLAUT — **gra·da·tion·al** \-shnəl, -shən-ᵊl\ *adj* — **gra·da·tion·al·ly** \-ē\ *adv*

¹grade \'grād\ *vb* **grad·ed; grad·ing** *vt* (1659) **1 a :** to arrange in grades **:** SORT **b :** to arrange in a scale or series **c :** to assign to a grade or assign a grade to **2 :** to level off to a smooth horizontal or sloping surface ~ *vi* **1 a :** to form a series **b :** BLEND **2 :** to be of a particular grade — **grad·able** \'grād-ə-bəl\ *adj*

²grade *n* [F, fr. L *gradus* step, degree; akin to L *gradi* to step, go, Lith *gridyti* to go, wander] (1796) **1 a (1) :** a stage in a process **(2) :** a position in a scale of ranks or qualities **b :** a class organized for the work of a particular year of a school course **c :** a military or naval rank **d :** a degree of severity in illness ⟨~ III carcinoma⟩ **2 a :** a class of things of the same stage or degree **b :** a mark indicating a degree of accomplishment in school **c :** a standard of food quality **3 a :** the degree of inclination of a road or slope; *also* **:** a sloping road **b :** a datum or reference level; *esp* **:** ground level **c :** ELEVATION 1c **4 :** a domestic animal with one parent purebred and the other of inferior breeding **5** *pl* **:** the elementary school system ⟨taught in the ~*s* for 19 years⟩ — **grade·less** \-ləs\ *adj*

³grade *adj* (1852) **:** being, involving, or yielding domestic animals of improved but not pure stock ⟨~ ewes⟩ ⟨~ breeding⟩

-grade \ˌgrād\ *adj comb form* [F, fr. L *-gradus,* fr. *gradi*] **:** walking ⟨plantigrade⟩

grade crossing *n* (ca. 1890) **:** a crossing of highways, railroad tracks, or pedestrian walks or combinations of these on the same level

grade point *n* (1951) **:** one of the points assigned to each course credit (as in a college) in accordance with the letter grade earned in the course — called also *quality point*

grade point average *n* (1966) **:** the average obtained by dividing the total number of grade points earned by the total number of credits attempted — called also *quality point average*

grad·er \'grād-ər\ *n* (1832) **1 :** one that grades **2 :** a machine for leveling earth **3 :** a pupil in a school grade ⟨a fifth ~⟩

grade school *n* (1869) **:** ELEMENTARY SCHOOL — **grade–school·er** \'grād-ˌskü-lər\ *n*

grade separation *n* (ca. 1949) **:** a highway or railroad crossing using an underpass or overpass

grade up *vt* (1903) **:** to improve by breeding females to purebred males

gra·di·ent \'grād-ē-ənt\ *n* [L *gradient-, gradiens,* prp. of *gradi*] (1835) **1 a :** the rate of regular or graded ascent or descent **:** INCLINATION **b :** a part sloping upward or downward **2 :** change in the value of a quantity (as temperature, pressure, or concentration) with change in a given variable and esp. per unit distance in a specified direction **3 :** the vector sum of the partial derivatives with respect to the three coordinate variables *x, y,* and *z* of a scalar quantity whose value varies from point to point **4 :** a graded difference in physiological activity along an axis (as of the body or an embryonic field) **5 :** change in response with distance from the stimulus

gra·di·om·e·ter \ˌgrād-ē-'äm-ət-ər\ *n* [*gradi*ent + *-o-* + *-meter*] (1809) **:** an instrument for measuring the gradient of a physical quantity (as the earth's magnetic field)

¹grad·u·al \'graj-(ə-)wəl, 'graj-əl\ *n, often cap* [ME, fr. ML *graduale,* fr. L *gradus* step, fr. its being sung on the steps of the altar] (15c) **1 :** a book containing the choral parts of the Mass **2 :** a pair of verses (as from the Psalms) proper after the Epistle in the Mass

²gradual *adj* [ML *gradualis,* fr. L *gradus*] (1541) **1 :** proceeding by steps or degrees **2 :** moving, changing, or developing by fine, slight, or often imperceptible degrees — **grad·u·al·ly** *adv* — **grad·u·al·ness** *n*

grad·u·al·ism \-ˌiz-əm\ *n* (1835) **:** the policy of approaching a desired end by gradual stages — **grad·u·al·ist** \-əst\ *n or adj*

grad·u·and \ˌgraj-ə-'wand\ *n* [ML *graduandus,* gerundive of *graduare*] *Brit* (1882) **:** one about to graduate **:** a candidate for a degree

¹grad·u·ate \'graj-(ə-)wət, -ə-ˌwāt\ *n* (15c) **1 :** a holder of an academic degree or diploma **2 :** a graduated cup, cylinder, or flask

²graduate *adj* (15c) **1 :** holding an academic degree or diploma **2 :** of, relating to, or engaged in studies beyond the first or bachelor's degree ⟨~ school⟩ ⟨a ~ student⟩

³grad·u·ate \'graj-ə-ˌwāt\ *vb* **-at·ed; -at·ing** [ML *graduare,* fr. L *gradus* step, degree] *vt* (15c) **1 a :** to grant an academic degree or diploma to **b :** to be graduated from **2 :** to admit to a particular standing or grade **3 a :** to mark with degrees of measurement **b :** to divide into grades or intervals ~ *vi* **1 :** to receive an academic degree or diploma **2 :** to pass from one stage of experience, proficiency, or prestige to a usu. higher one **3 :** to change gradually — **grad·u·a·tor** \-ˌwāt-ər\ *n*

usage In the 19th century the transitive sense (1a) was prescribed; the intransitive ⟨I *graduated* from college⟩ was condemned. The intransitive, however, has prevailed and is currently the most common use of the verb. The newer transitive sense (1b), while no longer nonstandard, is still objected to by absolutists.

grad·u·at·ed *adj, of a tax* (1861) **:** increasing in rate with increase in taxable base **:** PROGRESSIVE ⟨~ income tax⟩

grad·u·a·tion \ˌgraj-ə-'wā-shən\ *n* (1594) **1 :** a mark on an instrument or vessel indicating degrees or quantity; *also* **:** these marks **2 a :** the award or acceptance of an academic degree or diploma **b :** COMMENCEMENT **3 :** arrangement in degrees or ranks

Graeco- — see GRECO-

graf·fi·to \grə-'fēt-(ˌ)ō, grə-, grä-\ *n, pl* **-ti** \-(ˌ)ē\ [It, dim. of *graffio* scratch, fr. *graffiare* to scratch, prob. fr. *grafio* stylus, fr. L *graphium*] (1851) **:** an inscription or drawing made on some public surface (as a rock or wall); *also* **:** a message or slogan written as or as if as a graffito — **graf·fi·tist** \-'fēt-əst\ *n*

usage The plural *graffiti* is sometimes used with a singular verb as a mass noun ⟨the *graffiti* is being covered with fresh paint —*Springfield (Mass.) Union*⟩ ⟨*graffiti* comes in various styles —S.K. Oberbeck⟩ but this use is not yet as well established as the mass-noun use of *data.* Use of *graffiti* as a singular count noun is less common and is not standard.

¹graft \'graft\ *n* [ME *graffe, grafte,* fr. MF *grafe,* fr. ML *graphium,* fr. L, stylus, fr. Gk *grapheion,* fr. *graphein* to write — more at CARVE] (14c) **1 a :** a grafted plant **b :** SCION 1 **c :** the point of insertion of a scion upon a stock **2 a :** the act of grafting **b :** something grafted; *specif* **:** living tissue used in grafting **3 :** the acquisition of gain (as money) in dishonest or questionable ways; *also* **:** illegal or unfair gain

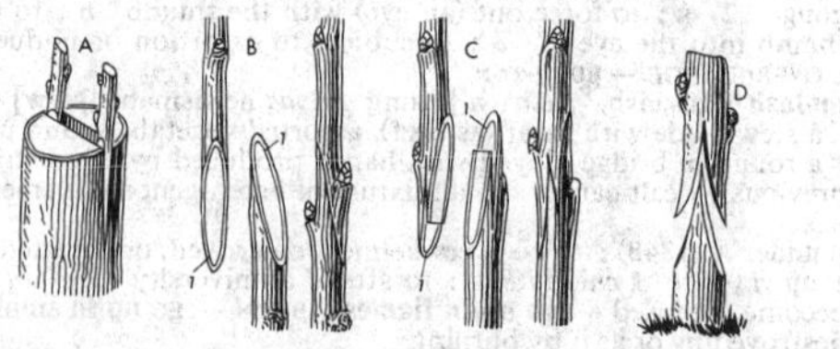

graft 1c: *A* cleft, *B* splice, *C* whip, *D* saddle, *1* cambium

²graft *vt* (15c) **1 a :** to cause (a scion) to unite with a stock; *also* **:** to unite (plants or scion and stock) to form a graft **b :** to propagate (a plant) by grafting **2 a :** to join or unite as if by grafting **b :** to attach (a chemical unit) to a main molecular chain **3 :** to implant (living tissue) surgically **4 :** to get (illicit gain) by graft ~ *vi* **1 :** to become grafted **2 :** to perform grafting **3 :** to practice graft — **graft·er** *n*

³graft *n* [E dial. *graft,* vb, to work, alter. of ¹*grave* (to dig)] *chiefly Brit* (1853) **:** WORK, LABOR

graft·age \'graf-tij\ *n* (ca. 1895) **:** the principles and practice of grafting

graft–versus–host *adj* (1972) **:** relating to or being the bodily condition that results when cells from a tissue or organ transplant mount an immunological attack against the cells or tissues of the host

gra·ham cracker \ˌgrā-əm-, ˌgra(-ə)m-\ *n* [*graham flour*] (1882) **:** a slightly sweet cracker made of whole wheat flour

graham flour *n* [Sylvester *Graham* †1851 Am. dietary reformer] (1834) **:** whole wheat flour

grail \'grā(ə)l\ *n* [ME *graal,* fr. MF, bowl, grail, fr. ML *gradalis*] (14c) **1** *cap* **:** the cup or platter used according to medieval legend by Christ at the Last Supper and thereafter the object of knightly quests **2 :** the object of an extended or difficult quest

¹grain \'grān\ *n* [ME, partly fr. MF *grain* cereal grain, fr. L *granum;* partly fr. MF *graine* seed, kermes, fr. L *grana,* pl. of *granum* — more at CORN] (14c) **1 a (1)** *obs* **:** a single small hard seed **(2) :** a seed or fruit of a cereal grass **:** CARYOPSIS **b :** the seeds or fruits of various food plants including the cereal grasses and in commercial and statutory usage other plants (as the soybean) **c :** plants producing grain **2 a :** a small hard particle or crystal (as of sand or salt) **b :** a minute portion or particle **c** : the least amount possible ⟨not a ~ of truth in what he said⟩ **d** : fine crystallization (as of sugar) **3 a** : kermes or a scarlet dye made from it **b** : cochineal or a brilliant scarlet dye made from it **c** : a fast dye **d** *archaic* : COLOR, TINT **4 a** : a granulated surface or appearance **b** : the outer or hair side of a skin or hide **5** : a unit of weight based on the weight of a grain of wheat taken as an average of the weight of grains from the middle of the ear — see WEIGHT table **6 a** : the stratification of the wood fibers in a piece of wood **b** : a texture due to constituent particles or fibers ⟨the ~ of a rock⟩ **c** : the direction of threads in cloth **7** : tactile quality **8 a** : natural disposition : TEMPER ⟨goes against my ~⟩ **b** : a basic or characteristic quality ⟨anti-intellectual . . . doctrines are very much in the American ~ —R. W. Noland⟩ — **grained** \ˈgrānd\ *adj*

2**grain** *vt* (1530) **1** : INGRAIN **2** : to form into grains : GRANULATE **3** : to paint in imitation of the grain of wood or stone ~ *vi* : to become granular : GRANULATE — **grain·er** *n*

grain alcohol *n* (1922) : ALCOHOL 1

grain elevator *n* (1852) : ELEVATOR 1c

grain·field \ˈgrān-ˌfēld\ *n* (1817) : a field where grain is grown

grain of salt (1647) : a skeptical attitude ⟨took the prediction with a *grain of salt*⟩

grains of paradise (15c) : the pungent seeds of a West African plant (*Aframomum melegueta* of the family Zingiberaceae) that are used as a spice

grain sorghum *n* (1920) : any of several sorghums cultivated primarily for grain — compare SORGO

grainy \ˈgrā-nē\ *adj* **grain·i·er; -est** (15c) **1** : resembling or having some characteristic of grain : not smooth or fine **2** *of a photograph* : appearing to be composed of grain-like particles — **grain·i·ness** *n*

1**gram** \ˈgram\ *n* [obs. Pg (now *grão*), grain, fr. L *granum*] (1702) : any of several leguminous plants (as a chick-pea) grown esp. for their seed

2**gram** *or* **gramme** \ˈgram\ *n* [F *gramme*, fr. LL *gramma*, a small weight, fr. Gk *grammat-*, *gramma* letter, writing, a small weight, fr. *graphein* to write — more at CARVE] (1797) : a metric unit of mass and weight equal to $^{1}/_{1000}$ kilogram and nearly equal to one cubic centimeter of water at its maximum density — see METRIC SYSTEM table

3**gram** *n* [by shortening & alter.] (ca. 1934) : GRANDMOTHER

-gram \ˌgram\ *n comb form* [L *-gramma*, fr. Gk, fr. *gramma*] : drawing : writing : record ⟨chronogram⟩ ⟨telegram⟩

grama \ˈgram-ə\ *n* [Sp, fr. L *gramina*, pl. of *gramen* grass] (1828) : any of several pasture grasses (genus *Bouteloua*) of the western U.S. — called also *grama grass*

gram–atomic weight *n* (ca. 1927) : the mass of one mole of an element equal in grams to the atomic weight— called also *gram-atom*

gram calorie *n* (1902) : CALORIE 1a

gram equivalent *n* (ca. 1897) : the quantity of an element, group, or compound that has a weight in grams equal to the equivalent weight

gra·mer·cy \grə-ˈmər-sē\ *interj* [ME *grand mercy*, fr. MF *grand merci* great thanks] *archaic* (14c) — used to express gratitude or astonishment

gram·i·ci·din \ˌgram-ə-ˈsīd-ᵊn\ *n* [*gram*-positive + *-i-* + *-cide* + *-in*] (1940) : any of several toxic crystalline polypeptide antibiotics produced by a soil bacterium (*Bacillus brevis*) and used against gram-positive bacteria in local infections

gra·min·e·ous \grə-ˈmin-ē-əs\ *adj* [L *gramineus*, fr. *gramin-*, *gramen* grass] (1658) : of or relating to a grass

gram·i·niv·o·rous \ˌgram-ə-ˈniv-(ə-)rəs\ *adj* [L *gramin-*, *gramen*] (1739) : feeding on grass ⟨~ locusts⟩

gram·mar \ˈgram-ər\ *n* [ME *gramere*, fr. MF *gramaire*, modif. of L *grammatica*, fr. Gk *grammatikē*, fr. fem. of *grammatikos* of letters, fr. *grammat-*, *gramma* — more at GRAM] (14c) **1 a** : the study of the classes of words, their inflections, and their functions and relations in the sentence **b** : a study of what is to be preferred and what avoided in inflection and syntax **2 a** : the characteristic system of inflections and syntax of a language **b** : a system of rules that defines the grammatical structure of a language **3 a** : a grammar textbook **b** : speech or writing evaluated according to its conformity to grammatical rules **4** : the principles or rules of an art, science, or technique ⟨a ~ of the theater⟩ — **gram·mar·i·an** \grə-ˈmer-ē-ən, -ˈmar-\ *n*

grammar school *n* (14c) **1 a** : a secondary school emphasizing Latin and Greek in preparation for college **b** : a British college preparatory school **2** : a school intermediate between primary school and high school **3** : ELEMENTARY SCHOOL

gram·mat·i·cal \grə-ˈmat-i-kəl\ *adj* (1530) **1** : of or relating to grammar **2** : conforming to the rules of grammar — **gram·mat·i·cal·i·ty** \-ˌmat-ə-ˈkal-ət-ē\ *n* — **gram·mat·i·cal·ly** \-ˈmat-i-k(ə-)lē\ *adv* — **gram·mat·i·cal·ness** \-kəl-nəs\ *n*

grammatical meaning *n* (1769) : the part of meaning that varies from one inflectional form to another (as from *plays* to *played* to *playing*) — compare LEXICAL MEANING

gram molecular weight *n* (ca. 1902) : the mass of one mole of a compound equal in grams to the molecular weight — called also *gram-molecule*

Gram·my \ˈgram-ē\ *service mark* — used for the annual presentation of a statuette for notable achievement in the recording industry

gram–neg·a·tive \ˈgram-ˈneg-ət-iv\ *adj* (1907) : not holding the purple dye when stained by Gram's stain — used chiefly of bacteria

gram·o·phone \ˈgram-ə-ˌfōn\ *n* [fr. *Gramophone*, a trademark] (1887) : PHONOGRAPH

gramp \ˈgramp\ *or* **gramps** \ˈgram(p)s\ *n, pl* **gramps** [by shortening & alter.] (ca. 1898) : GRANDFATHER

gram–pos·i·tive \ˈgram-ˈpäz-ət-iv, -ˈpäz-tiv\ *adj* (1907) : holding the purple dye when stained by Gram's stain — used chiefly of bacteria

gram·pus \ˈgram-pəs\ *n* [alter. of ME *graspey*, *grapay*, fr. MF *graspeis*, fr. *gras* fat (fr. L *crassus*) + *peis* fish, fr. L *piscis* — more at CRASS, FISH] (1529) **1** : a cetacean (*Grampus griseus*) related to the blackfish; *broadly* : any of various small cetaceans (as the blackfish or killer whale) **2** : the giant whip scorpion (*Mastigoproctus giganteus*) of the southern U.S.

Gram's stain \ˈgramz-\ *or* **Gram stain** \ˈgram-\ *n* [Hans C. J. *Gram* †1938 Dan. physician] (ca. 1903) **1** : a method for the differential staining of bacteria by which some species remain colored and some are decolorized by treatment with a watery solution of iodine and the iodide of potassium after staining with gentian violet — called also *Gram's method* **2** : the chemicals used in Gram's stain

gram–vari·able \ˈgram-ˈver-ē-ə-bəl, -ˈvar-\ *adj* (ca. 1956) : staining irregularly or inconsistently by Gram's stain

grana *pl of* GRANUM

gran·a·dil·la \ˌgran-ə-ˈdil-ə, -ˈdē-(y)ə\ *n* [Sp, dim. of *granada* pomegranate, fr. LL *granata* — more at GRENADE] (1613) : the oblong fruit of various passionflowers (esp. *Passiflora quadrangularis* of tropical America) used as a dessert; *also* : a plant that produces granadillas

gra·na·ry \ˈgrān-(ə-)rē, ˈgran-\ *n, pl* **-ries** [L *granarium*, fr. *granum* grain] (1530) **1 a** : a storehouse for threshed grain **b** : a region producing grain in abundance **2** : a chief source or storehouse

1**grand** \ˈgrand\ *adj* [MF, large, great, grand, fr. L *grandis*] (1584) **1 a** : having more importance than others : FOREMOST **b** : having higher rank than others bearing the same general designation ⟨the ~ champion⟩ **2 a** : INCLUSIVE, COMPREHENSIVE ⟨the ~ total of all money paid out⟩ **b** : DEFINITIVE, INCONTROVERTIBLE ⟨~ example⟩ **3** : CHIEF, PRINCIPAL **4** : large and striking in size, scope, extent, or conception ⟨~ design⟩ **5 a** : LAVISH, SUMPTUOUS ⟨a ~ celebration⟩ **b** : marked by a regal form and dignity **c** : fine or imposing in appearance or impression **d** : LOFTY, SUBLIME ⟨writing in the ~ style⟩ **6 a** : pretending to social superiority : SUPERCILIOUS **b** : intended to impress ⟨a person of ~ gestures and pretentious statements⟩ **7** : very good : WONDERFUL ⟨a ~ time⟩ — **grand·ly** \ˈgran-(d)lē\ *adv* — **grand·ness** \ˈgran(d)-nəs\ *n*

syn GRAND, MAGNIFICENT, IMPOSING, STATELY, MAJESTIC, GRANDIOSE mean large and impressive. GRAND adds to greatness of size the implications of handsomeness and dignity; MAGNIFICENT implies an impressive largeness proportionate to scale without sacrifice of dignity or good taste; IMPOSING implies great size and dignity but esp. stresses impressiveness; STATELY may suggest poised dignity, erectness of bearing, handsomeness of proportions, ceremonious deliberation of movement; MAJESTIC combines the implications of IMPOSING and STATELY and usu. adds a suggestion of solemn grandeur; GRANDIOSE implies a size or scope exceeding ordinary experience but is most commonly applied derogatorily to inflated pretension or absurd exaggeration.

2**grand** *n* (1840) **1** : GRAND PIANO **2** *slang* : a thousand dollars

gran·dam \ˈgran-ˌdam, -dəm\ *or* **gran·dame** \-ˌdām, -dəm\ *n* [ME *graundam*, fr. AF *graund dame*, lit., great lady] (13c) **1** : GRANDMOTHER **2** : an old woman

grand·aunt \ˈgran-ˈdant, -ˈdȧnt\ *n* (1826) : the aunt of one's father or mother — called also *great-aunt*

grand·ba·by \ˈgran(d)-ˌbā-bē\ *n* (1916) : an infant grandchild

grand·child \-ˌchīld\ *n* (1587) : the child of one's son or daughter

grand·dad *or* **gran·dad** \ˈgran-ˌdad\ *n* (1782) : GRANDFATHER

grand·dad·dy \-ˌdad-ē\ *also* **gran·dad·dy** *n* (1769) **1** : GRANDFATHER **2** : one that is the first, earliest, most ancient, or most venerable of its kind ⟨the ~ of . . . modern technical analysis —J. W. Schulz⟩

grand·daugh·ter \-ˌdȯt-ər\ *n* (1611) : the daughter of one's son or daughter

grand duchess *n* (1757) **1** : the wife or widow of a grand duke **2** : a woman who rules a grand duchy in her own right

grand duchy *n* (1835) : the territory or dominion of a grand duke or grand duchess

grand duke *n* (1693) **1** : the sovereign duke of any of various European states **2** : a male descendant of a Russian czar in the male line

grande dame \ˈgrän-ˈdäm, grãⁿd-dȧm\ *n, pl* **grandes dames** \-ˈdäm(z), -dȧm(z)\ *also* **grande dames** *same*\ [F, lit., great lady] (1775) : a usu. elderly woman of great prestige or ability

gran·dee \gran-ˈdē\ *n* [Sp *grande*, fr. *grande*, adj., large, great, fr. L *grandis*] (1598) : a man of elevated rank or station; *esp* : a Spanish or Portuguese nobleman of the first rank

gran·deur \ˈgran-jər, -ˌju̇(ə)r, -ˌd(y)u̇(ə)r, -d(y)ər\ *n* [ME, fr. MF, fr. *grand*] (1600) **1** : the quality or state of being grand : MAGNIFICENCE ⟨the glory that was Greece and the ~ that was Rome —E. A. Poe⟩ **2** : an instance or example of grandeur

grand·fa·ther \ˈgran(d)-ˌfäth-ər, -ˌfȧth-\ *n* (15c) : the father of one's father or mother; *also* : ANCESTOR 1a — **grand·fa·ther·ly** \-lē\ *adj*

grandfather clause *n* (1900) : a clause creating an exemption based on circumstances previously existing; *esp* : a provision in several southern state constitutions designed to enfranchise poor whites and disfranchise Negroes by waiving high voting requirements for descendants of men voting before 1867

grandfather clock *n* [fr. the song *My Grandfather's Clock* (1876) by Henry C. Work †1884 Am. songwriter] (1909) : a tall pendulum clock standing directly on the floor — called also *grandfather's clock*

grand finale *n* (1874) : a climactic finale (as of an opera or sports meet)

grand fir *n* (1897) : a lofty tree (*Abies grandis*) of the northwestern Pacific coastal region of No. America with cylindrical greenish cones and soft wood

Grand Gui·gnol \ˌgrän-gēn-ˈyȯl, -ˈyōl\ *n* [*Le Grand Guignol*, small theater in Montmartre, Paris, specializing in such performances] (1908) : dramatic entertainment featuring the gruesome or horrible — **Grand Guignol** *adj*

gran·di·flo·ra \ˌgran-də-ˈflōr-ə, -ˈflȯr-\ *n* [NL, fr. L *grandis* great + *flor-*, *flos* flower — more at BLOW] (1944) : a bush rose derived from crosses of floribunda and hybrid tea roses and characterized by production of blooms both singly and in clusters on the same plant

gran·dil·o·quence \gran-ˈdil-ə-kwən(t)s\ *n* [prob. fr. MF, fr. L *grandiloquus* using lofty language, fr. *grandis* + *loqui* to speak] (1589) : lofty or pompous eloquence : BOMBAST — **gran·dil·o·quent** \-kwənt\ *adj* — **gran·dil·o·quent·ly** *adv*

gran·di·ose \ˈgran-dē-ˌōs, ˌgran-dē-ˈōs\ *adj* [F, fr. It *grandioso*, fr. *grande* great, fr. L *grandis*] (1840) **1** : characterized by affectation of grandeur or splendor or by absurd exaggeration **2** : impressive because of uncommon largeness, scope, effect, or grandeur ***syn*** see GRAND — **gran·di·ose·ly** *adv* — **gran·di·ose·ness** *n* — **gran·di·os·i·ty** \ˌgran-dē-ˈäs-ət-ē\ *n*

\ə\ abut \ᵊ\ kitten, F table \ər\ further \a\ ash \ā\ ace \ä\ cot, cart \au̇\ out \ch\ chin \e\ bet \ē\ easy \g\ go \i\ hit \ī\ ice \j\ job \ŋ\ sing \ō\ go \ȯ\ law \ȯi\ boy \th\ thin \th\ the \ü\ loot \u̇\ foot \y\ yet \zh\ vision \à, k, ⁿ, œ, œ̄, ue, ue̅, ʸ\ *see* Guide to Pronunciation

gran·di·o·so \ˌgrän-dē-ˈō-(ˌ)sō, ˌgran-, -(ˌ)zō\ *adv or adj* [It] (ca. 1900) : in a broad and noble style — used as a direction in music
grand jury *n* (15c) : a jury that examines accusations against persons charged with crime and if the evidence warrants makes formal charges on which the accused persons are later tried
Grand Lama *n* (ca. 1934) : DALAI LAMA
grand larceny *n* (ca. 1847) : larceny of property of a value greater than that fixed as constituting petit larceny
grand·ma \ˈgran(d)-ˌmä, -ˌmȯ; ˈgram-ˌä, -ˌȯ\ *n* (1867) : GRANDMOTHER
grand mal \ˈgrän(d)-ˌmäl, ˈgräⁿ-ˌmäl, -ˌmal; ˈgran(d)-ˌmal\ *n* [F, lit., great illness] (1897) : severe epilepsy
grand manner *n* (1925) : an elevated or grand style (as in music or literature)
grand march *n* (1928) : an opening ceremony at a ball that consists of a march participated in by all the guests
grand master *n* (1927) : an expert player (as of chess) who has consistently scored high in international competition
grand·moth·er \ˈgran(d)-ˌməth-ər\ *n* (15c) : the mother of one's father or mother; *also* : a female ancestor — **grand·moth·er·ly** \-lē\ *adj*
grand·neph·ew \ˈgran(d)-ˈnef-(ˌ)yü, *chiefly Brit* -ˈnev-\ *n* (1639) : a grandson of one's brother or sister
grand·niece \-ˈnēs\ *n* (ca. 1830) : a granddaughter of one's brother or sister
grand opera *n* (1803) : opera in which the plot is serious or tragic and the entire text is set to music
grand·pa \ˈgran(d)-ˌpä, -ˌpȯ; ˈgram-ˌpä, -ˌpȯ\ *n* (1889) : GRANDFATHER
grand·par·ent \ˈgran(d)-ˌpar-ənt, -ˌper-\ *n* (1830) : a parent of one's father or mother — **grand·pa·ren·tal** \ˌgran(d)-pə-ˈrent-ᵊl\ *adj* — **grand·par·ent·hood** \ˈgran(d)-ˈpar-ent-ˌhu̇d, -ˈper-\ *n*
grand piano *n* (1834) : a piano with horizontal frame and strings — compare UPRIGHT PIANO
grand prix \ˈgräⁿ-ˈprē\ *n, pl* **grand prix** \-ˈprē(z)\ *often cap G&P* [F *Grand Prix de Paris,* an international horse race established 1863, lit., grand prize of Paris] (1908) : one of a series of international formula car races
grand·sire \ˈgran(d)-ˌsī(ə)r\ *or* **grand·sir** \ˈgran(t)-sər\ *n* [ME] (13c) **1** *dial* : GRANDFATHER **2** *archaic* : FOREFATHER **3** *archaic* : an aged man
grand slam *n* (1892) **1** : the winning of all the tricks in one hand of a card game (as bridge) **2** : a clean sweep or total success; *specif* : the winning of all the major or specified tournaments on a tour ⟨twice won the tennis *grand slam*⟩ **3** : a home run made with the bases loaded — **grand–slam** *adj*
grand·son \ˈgran(d)-ˌsən\ *n* (1586) : the son of one's son or daughter
[1]**grand·stand** \-ˌstand\ *n* (1834) **1** : a usu. roofed stand for spectators at a racecourse or stadium **2** : AUDIENCE
[2]**grandstand** *vi* (1927) : to play or act so as to impress onlookers — **grand·stand·er** *n*
grand tour *n* (1670) **1** : an extended tour of the Continent that was formerly a usual part of the education of young British gentlemen **2** : an extensive and usu. educational tour
grand touring car *n* (1970) : a usu. 2-passenger coupe — called also *grand tourer*
grand·un·cle \ˈgran-ˈdəŋ-kəl\ *n* (15c) : an uncle of one's father or mother
grange \ˈgrānj\ *n* [ME, fr. MF, fr. ML *granica,* fr. L *granum* grain] (14c) **1** *archaic* : GRANARY, BARN **2** : FARM; *esp* : a farmhouse with outbuildings **3** *cap* : one of the lodges of a national fraternal association orig. comprised of farmers; *also* : the association itself

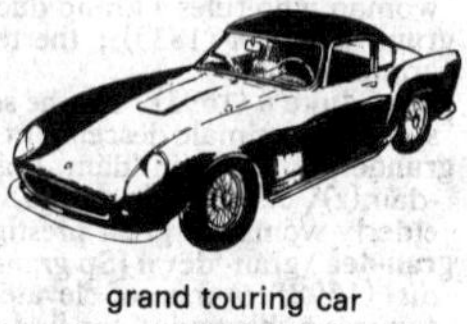

grand touring car

grang·er \ˈgrān-jər\ *n* (1873) **1** *cap* : a member of a Grange **2** *chiefly West* : FARMER, HOMESTEADER
grang·er·ism \ˈgrān-jə-ˌriz-əm\ *n* (1875) : the policy or methods of the grangers
grani- *comb form* [L, fr. *granum*] : grain : seeds ⟨*granivorous*⟩
gran·ite \ˈgran-ət\ *n* [It *granito,* fr. pp. of *granire* to granulate, fr. *grano* grain, fr. L *granum*] (1646) **1** : a very hard natural igneous rock formation of visibly crystalline texture formed essentially of quartz and orthoclase or microcline and used esp. for building and for monuments **2** : unyielding firmness or endurance ⟨the cold ~ of Puritan formalism —V. L. Parrington⟩ — **gran·ite·like** \-ət-ˌlīk\ *adj* — **gra·nit·ic** \grə-ˈnit-ik\ *adj* — **gran·it·oid** \ˈgran-ət-ˌȯid\ *adj*
gran·ite·ware \ˈgran-ət-ˌwa(ə)r, -ˌwe(ə)r\ *n* (1878) : ironware with grayish or bluish mottled enamel
gra·niv·o·rous \grə-ˈniv-(ə-)rəs, grā-\ *adj* (1646) : feeding on seeds or grain ⟨~ rodents⟩
gran·ny *or* **gran·nie** \ˈgran-ē\ *n, pl* **grannies** [by shortening & alter.] (1663) **1 a** : GRANDMOTHER **b** : a fussy person **2** *Southern & Midland* : MIDWIFE
granny dress *n* (1966) : a long loose-fitting dress usu. with high neck and long sleeves
granny knot *n* (1853) : an insecure knot often made instead of a square knot — see KNOT illustration
grano- *comb form* [G, fr. *granit,* fr. It *granito*] : granite : granitic ⟨*granogabbro*⟩
grano·di·o·rite \ˌgran-ō-ˈdī-ə-ˌrīt\ *n* (1893) : a granular intrusive quartzose igneous rock intermediate between granite and quartz-containing diorite with plagioclase predominant over orthoclase — **grano·di·o·rit·ic** \-ˌdī-ə-ˈrit-ik\ *adj*
gra·no·la \grə-ˈnō-lə\ *n* [fr. *Granola,* a trademark] (1971) : a mixture of oatmeal and other ingredients (as brown sugar, raisins, coconut, and nuts) that is eaten esp. for breakfast
grano·lith \ˈgran-ə-ˌlith\ *n* (ca. 1909) : an artificial stone of crushed granite and cement — **grano·lith·ic** \ˌgran-ə-ˈlith-ik\ *adj*
grano·phyre \ˈgran-ə-ˌfī(ə)r\ *n* [ISV, fr. *grano-* + F *-phyre* (as in *porphyre* porphyry)] (1882) : a porphyritic igneous rock chiefly of feldspar and quartz with granular groundmass — **grano·phyr·ic** \ˌgran-ə-ˈfir-ik\ *adj*
[1]**grant** \ˈgrant\ *vt* [ME *granten,* fr. OF *creanter, graanter,* fr. (assumed) VL *credentare,* fr. L *credent-, credens,* prp. of *credere* to believe — more at CREED] (13c) **1 a** : to consent to carry out for a person : allow fulfillment of ⟨~ a request⟩ **b** : to permit as a right, privilege, or favor ⟨luggage allowances ~*ed* to passengers⟩ **2** : to bestow or transfer formally ⟨~ a scholarship to a student⟩; *specif* : to give the possession or title of by a deed **3 a** : to be willing to concede **b** : to assume to be true ⟨~*ing* that you are correct, you may find it hard to prove your point⟩ — **grant·able** \-ə-bəl\ *adj* — **grant·er** \-ər\ *n* — **grant·or** \ˈgrant-ər, -ˌȯ(ə)r; grant-ˈȯ(ə)r\ *n*
syn GRANT, CONCEDE, VOUCHSAFE, ACCORD, AWARD mean to give as a favor or a right. GRANT implies giving to a claimant or petitioner something that could be withheld ⟨acceding to her pleas, he *granted* her another period of six months in which to make good — *Current Biog.*⟩ CONCEDE implies yielding something reluctantly in response to a rightful or compelling claim ⟨even his harshest critics *concede* him a rocklike integrity — *Time*⟩ VOUCHSAFE implies granting something as a courtesy or an act of gracious condescension ⟨occasionally a true poet is *vouchsafed* to the world —Rumer Godden⟩ ACCORD implies giving to another what is due or proper ⟨children easily appreciate justice, and will readily *accord* to others what others *accord* to them —Bertrand Russell⟩ AWARD implies giving what is deserved or merited usu. after a careful weighing of pertinent factors ⟨he was practising law, having been *awarded* his LLB degree with distinction — *Current Biog.*⟩
[2]**grant** *n* (13c) **1** : the act of granting **2** : something granted; *esp* : a gift (as of land or money) for a particular purpose **3 a** : a transfer of property by deed or writing **b** : the instrument by which such a transfer is made; *also* : the property so transferred **4** : a minor territorial division of Maine, New Hampshire, or Vermont orig. granted by the state to an individual or institution
grant·ee \grant-ˈē\ *n* (15c) : one to whom a grant is made
grant–in–aid \ˌgrant-ᵊn-ˈād\ *n, pl* **grants–in–aid** \ˌgran(t)-sə-ˈnād\ (1881) **1** : a grant or subsidy for public funds paid by a central to a local government in aid of a public undertaking **2** : a grant or subsidy to a school or individual for an educational or artistic project
grants·man \ˈgran(t)-smən\ *n* (1966) : a specialist in grantsmanship
grants·man·ship \-ˌship\ *n* [*grants* + *-manship*] (1961) : the art of obtaining grants (as for research)
granul- *or* **granuli-** *or* **granulo-** *comb form* [LL *granulum*] : granule ⟨*granulose*⟩
gran·u·lar \ˈgran-yə-lər\ *adj* (1794) : consisting of or appearing to consist of granules : having a grainy texture — **gran·u·lar·i·ty** \ˌgran-yə-ˈlar-ət-ē\ *n*
gran·u·late \ˈgran-yə-ˌlāt\ *vb* **-lat·ed; -lat·ing** *vt* (1666) : to form or crystallize into grains or granules ~ *vi* **1** : to collect into grains or granules **2** : to form granulations ⟨an open *granulating* wound⟩ — **gran·u·la·tive** \-ˌlāt-iv\ *adj* — **gran·u·la·tor** \-ˌlāt-ər\ *n*
gran·u·la·tion \ˌgran-yə-ˈlā-shən\ *n* (1612) **1** : the act or process of granulating : the condition of being granulated **2** : one of the minute red granules of new capillaries formed on the surface of a wound in healing **3** : GRANULE 2
granulation tissue *n* (1873) : tissue made up of granulations that temporarily replaces lost tissue in a wound
gran·ule \ˈgran-(ˌ)yü(ə)l\ *n* [LL *granulum,* dim. of L *granum* grain] (1652) **1** : a small particle; *esp* : one of numerous particles forming a larger unit **2** : one of the small short-lived brilliant spots on the sun's seething photosphere
gran·u·lite \ˈgran-yə-ˌlīt\ *n* (1849) : a banded or laminated whitish granular rock consisting of feldspar, quartz, and small red garnets and occurring with crystalline schists — **gran·u·lit·ic** \ˌgran-yə-ˈlit-ik\ *adj*
gran·u·lo·cyte \ˈgran-yə-lō-ˌsīt\ *n* [ISV] (1906) : a cell (as a white blood cell) with granule-containing cytoplasm — **gran·u·lo·cyt·ic** \ˌgran-yə-lō-ˈsit-ik\ *adj*
gran·u·lo·cy·to·poi·e·sis \ˈgran-yə-lō-ˌsīt-ə-pȯi-ˈē-səs\ *n* [NL] (1944) : the formation of blood granulocytes typically in the bone marrow
gran·u·lo·ma \ˌgran-yə-ˈlō-mə\ *n, pl* **-mas** *or* **-ma·ta** \-mət-ə\ (1861) : a mass or nodule of chronically inflamed tissue with granulations that is usu. associated with an infective process — **gran·u·lo·ma·tous** \-mət-əs\ *adj*
granuloma in·gui·na·le \-ˌiŋ-gwə-ˈnal-ē, -ˈnäl-, -ˈnāl-\ *n* [NL, lit., inguinal granuloma] (1918) : a venereal disease characterized by ulceration and formation of granulations beginning in the groin and spreading to the buttocks and genitals and caused by a bacterium (*Calymmatobacterium granulomatis,* syn. *Donovania granulomatis*)
granuloma ve·ne·re·um \-və-ˈnir-ē-əm\ *n* [NL, lit., venereal granuloma] (1941) : GRANULOMA INGUINALE
gran·u·lo·sa cell \ˌgran-yə-ˌlō-sə-\ *n* [NL *granulosa,* fr. fem. of *granulosus* granulose] (1936) : one of the cells of the epithelial lining of a graafian follicle
gran·u·lose \ˈgran-yə-ˌlōs\ *adj* (1852) : GRANULAR; *esp* : having the surface roughened with granules
gran·u·lo·sis \ˌgran-yə-ˈlō-səs\ *n, pl* **-lo·ses** \-ˌsēz\ [NL] (1949) : a virus disease of insect larvae distinguished by the presence of minute granular inclusions in infected cells
gra·num \ˈgrā-nəm\ *n, pl* **gra·na** \-nə\ [NL, fr. L, grain — more at CORN] (1894) : one of the lamellar stacks of chlorophyll-containing material in plant chloroplasts
grape \ˈgrāp\ *n, often attrib* [ME, fr. OF *crape, grape* hook, grape stalk, bunch of grapes, grape, of Gmc origin; akin to OHG *krāpfo* hook — more at CRAVE] (13c) **1** : a smooth-skinned juicy greenish white to deep red or purple berry eaten dried or fresh as a fruit or fermented to produce wine **2** : any of numerous woody vines (genus *Vitis* of the family Vitaceae, the grape family) that usu. climb by tendrils, produce clustered fruits that are grapes, and are nearly cosmopolitan in cultivation **3** : GRAPESHOT
grape·fruit \ˈgrāp-ˌfrüt\ *n* (1814) **1** : a large citrus fruit with a bitter yellow rind and inner skin and a highly flavored somewhat acid juicy pulp **2** : a small roundheaded tree (*Citrus paradisi*) that produces grapefruit and is prob. derived from the shaddock
grape hyacinth *n* (1882) : any of several small bulbous spring-flowering herbs (genus *Muscari*) of the lily family with racemes of usu. blue flowers
grape·shot \ˈgrāp-ˌshät\ *n* (1747) : a cluster of small iron balls used as a cannon charge
grape sugar *n* (1831) : DEXTROSE

grape·vine \'grāp-,vīn\ *n* (1736) **1 :** GRAPE 2 **2 a :** an informal person-to-person means of circulating information or gossip ⟨heard about the meeting through the ~⟩ **b :** a secret source of information
grap·ey *or* **grapy** \'grā-pē\ *adj* **grap·i·er; -est** (1594) **1 :** of or relating to grapes or the vine **2** *of a wine* **:** having the taste or aroma of fresh grapes — compare WINY
¹graph \'graf\ *n* [short for *graphic formula*] (1878) **1 :** a diagram (as a series of one or more points, lines, line segments, curves, or areas) that represents the variation of a variable in comparison with that of one or more other variables **2 :** the collection of all points whose coordinates satisfy a given relation (as a function)
²graph *vt* (1898) **1 :** to represent by a graph **2 :** to plot on a graph
³graph *n* [prob. fr. *-graph*] (1945) **1 :** a spelling of a word **2 :** a single occurrence of a letter of an alphabet in any of its various shapes (as D, d) **3 :** a letter or combination of letters taken as a minimum unit in determining the phonemes of a language from written records — compare GRAPHEME
-graph \,graf\ *n comb form* [MF *-graphe,* fr. L *-graphum,* fr. Gk *-graphon,* fr. neut. of *-graphos* written, fr. *graphein* to write — more at CARVE] **1 :** something written ⟨mono*graph*⟩ **2** [F *-graphe,* fr. LL *-graphus*] **:** instrument for making or transmitting records ⟨chrono*graph*⟩
graph·eme \'graf-,ēm\ *n* (1937) **1 :** a unit (as a letter) of a writing system **2 :** the set of units of a writing system (as letters and letter combinations) that represent a phoneme ⟨the *f* of *fin,* the *ph* of *phantom,* and the *gh* of *laugh* are members of one ~⟩ — **gra·phe·mic** \gra-'fē-mik\ *adj* — **gra·phe·mi·cal·ly** \-mi-k(ə-)lē\ *adv*
gra·phe·mics \gra-'fē-miks\ *n pl but sing or pl in constr* (1951) **:** the study and analysis of a writing system in terms of graphemes
-g·ra·pher \g-rə-fər\ *n comb form* [LL *-graphus,* fr. Gk *-graphos,* fr. *graphein*] **:** one that writes about (specified) material or in a (specified) way ⟨cranio*grapher*⟩
¹graph·ic \'graf-ik\ *also* **graph·i·cal** \-i-kəl\ *adj* [L *graphicus,* fr. Gk *graphikos,* fr. *graphein*] (1637) **1 :** formed by writing, drawing, or engraving **2 a :** marked by or capable of clear and lively description or striking imaginative power **b :** sharply outlined or delineated **3 a :** of or relating to the pictorial arts **b :** of, relating to, or involving such reproductive methods as those of engraving, etching, lithography, photography, serigraphy, and woodcut **c :** of or relating to the art of printing **d :** relating or according to graphics **4 :** having mineral crystals resembling written or printed characters **5 :** of, relating to, or represented by a graph **6 :** of or relating to the written or printed word or the symbols or devices used in writing or printing to represent sound or convey meaning — **graph·i·cal·ly** \-i-k(ə-)lē\ *adv* — **graph·ic·ness** \-ik-nəs\ *n*
syn GRAPHIC, VIVID, PICTURESQUE, PICTORIAL mean giving a clear visual impression in words. GRAPHIC stresses the evoking of a clear lifelike picture; VIVID suggests an impressing on the mind the vigorous aliveness of something; PICTURESQUE suggests the presentation of a striking or effective picture composed of features notable for their distinctness and charm; PICTORIAL implies representation in the manner of painting with emphasis upon colors, shapes, and spatial relations.
²graphic *n* (1944) **1 a :** a product of graphic art **b** *pl* **:** the graphic media **2 a :** a graphic representation (as a picture, map, or graph) used esp. for illustration **b** *pl but sing or pl in constr* **:** the art or science of drawing a representation of an object on a two-dimensional surface according to mathematical rules of projection **3** *pl but sing or pl in constr* **:** the process whereby a computer displays graphics on a CRT and an operator can manipulate them (as with a light pen)
-graph·ic \'graf-ik\ *or* **-graph·i·cal** \-i-kəl\ *adj comb form* [LL *-graphicus,* fr. Gk *-graphikos,* fr. *graphikos*] **1 :** written or transmitted in a (specified) way ⟨stylo*graphic*⟩ **2 :** of or relating to writing in a (specified) field or on a (specified) subject ⟨oro*graphic*⟩
graphic arts *n pl* (1882) **:** the fine and applied arts of representation, decoration, and writing or printing on flat surfaces together with the techniques and crafts associated with them
graphics tablet *n* (1980) **:** a device by which graphics information is entered into a computer in a manner similar to drawing
graph·ite \'graf-,īt\ *n* [G *Graphit,* fr. Gk *graphein* to write] (1796) **:** a soft black lustrous carbon that conducts electricity and is used in lead pencils, crucibles, electrolytic anodes, as a lubricant, and as a moderator in atomic-energy plants — **gra·phit·ic** \gra-'fit-ik\ *adj*
graph·i·tize \'graf-ə-,tīz, -,īt-,īz\ *vt* **-tized; -tiz·ing** (1899) **1 :** to convert into graphite **2 :** to impregnate or coat with graphite — **graph·i·tiz·able** \-,tī-zə-bəl, -,īt-,ī-zə-\ *adj* — **graph·i·ti·za·tion** \,graf-ət-ə-'zā-shən, -,īt-\ *n*
grapho- *comb form* [F, fr. MF, fr. Gk, fr. *graphē,* fr. *graphein* to write] **:** writing
gra·phol·o·gist \gra-'fäl-ə-jəst\ *n* (1885) **:** a specialist in graphology
gra·phol·o·gy \-jē\ *n* [F *graphologie,* fr. *grapho-* + *-logie* -logy] (1882) **:** the study of handwriting esp. for the purpose of character analysis — **graph·o·log·i·cal** \,graf-ə-'läj-i-kəl\ *adj*
graph·o·phone \'graf-ə-,fōn\ *n* [fr. *Graphophone,* a trademark] (1886) **:** a phonograph using wax records
graph paper *n* (1927) **:** paper ruled for drawing graphs
-g·ra·phy \g-rə-fē\ *n comb form* [L *-graphia,* fr. Gk, fr. *graphein*] **1 :** writing or representation in a (specified) manner or by a (specified) means or of a (specified) object ⟨steno*graphy*⟩ ⟨photo*graphy*⟩ **2 :** writing on a (specified) subject or in a (specified) field ⟨hagio*graphy*⟩
grap·nel \'grap-nᵊl\ *n* [ME *grapenel,* fr. (assumed) MF *grapinel,* dim. of *grapin,* dim. of *grape* hook — more at GRAPE] (14c) **:** a small anchor with four or five flukes or claws used in dragging or grappling operations and for anchoring a dory or skiff
grap·pa \'gräp-ə\ *n* [It, fr. It dial., grape stalk, of Gmc origin; akin to OHG *krāpfo* hook — more at CRAVE] (ca. 1893) **:** a dry colorless brandy distilled from fermented grape pomace
¹grap·ple \'grap-əl\ *n* [OF *grappelle,* dim. of *grape* hook — more at GRAPE] (13c) **1 a :** an instrument with iron claws used to fasten an enemy ship alongside before boarding **b :** GRAPNEL **2 a :** the act or an instance of grappling **b :** a hand-to-hand struggle **c :** a contest for superiority or mastery **3 :** a bucket similar to a clamshell but usu. having more jaws
²grapple *vb* **grap·pled; grap·pling** \'grap-(ə-)liŋ\ *vt* (1530) **1 :** to seize with or as if with a grapple **2 :** to come to grips with **:** WRESTLE **3 :** to bind closely ~ *vi* **1 :** to make a ship fast with a grapple **2 :** to come to grips **:** WRESTLE **3 :** to use a grapple — **grap·pler** \-(ə-)lər\ *n*
grap·pling *n* (1598) **1 :** GRAPPLE 1a **2 :** GRAPNEL
grappling iron *n* (1538) **:** a hooked iron for anchoring a boat, grappling ships to each other, or recovering sunken objects — called also *grappling hook*
grap·to·lite \'grap-tə-,līt\ *n* [Gk *graptos* painted (fr. *graphein* to write, paint) + E *-lite* — more at CARVE] (1841) **:** any of numerous extinct fossil colonial Paleozoic animals (group Graptolitoidea) with zooids in cups along a chitinous support
¹grasp \'grasp\ *vb* [ME *graspen* — more at GRAB] *vi* (14c) **:** to make the motion of seizing **:** CLUTCH ~ *vt* **1 :** to take or seize eagerly **2 :** to clasp or embrace (as with the fingers or arms) **3 :** to lay hold of with the mind **:** COMPREHEND ***syn*** see TAKE — **grasp·able** \'gras-pə-bəl\ *adj* — **grasp·er** *n*
²grasp *n* (1561) **1 a :** HANDLE **b :** the fluke of an anchor **c :** EMBRACE **2 :** HOLD, CONTROL **3 a :** the reach of the arms **b :** the power of seizing and holding or attaining ⟨perfection always will elude our ~ —A. J. Celebrezze⟩ **4 :** COMPREHENSION ⟨showed a firm ~ of the subject⟩
grasp·ing *adj* (1748) **:** desiring material possessions urgently and excessively and often to the point of ruthlessness ***syn*** see COVETOUS — **grasp·ing·ly** \'gras-piŋ-lē\ *adv* — **grasp·ing·ness** *n*
¹grass \'gras\ *n, often attrib* [ME *gras,* fr. OE *græs;* akin to OHG *gras* grass, OE *grōwan* to grow] (bef. 12c) **1 :** herbage suitable or used for grazing animals **2 :** any of a large family (Gramineae) of monocotyledonous mostly herbaceous plants with jointed stems, slender sheathing leaves, and flowers borne in spikelets of bracts **3 :** land on which grass is grown ⟨keep off the ~⟩ **4** *pl* **:** leaves or plants of grass **5 :** a state or place of retirement ⟨an old horse put out to ~⟩ **6 :** electronic noise on a radarscope that takes the form of vertical lines resembling lawn grass **7 :** MARIJUANA — **grass·like** \-,līk\ *adj*
²grass *vt* (1500) **1 :** to feed (livestock) on grass sometimes without grain or other concentrates **2 :** to cover with grass; *esp* **:** to seed to grass ~ *vi* **:** to produce grass
grass carp *n* (1885) **:** an herbivorous cyprinid fish (*Ctenopharyngodon idella*) of Russia and mainland China that has been introduced elsewhere to control aquatic weeds — called also *white amur*
grass cloth *n* (1857) **:** a lustrous plain textile of usu. loosely woven fibers
grass court *n* (1883) **:** a tennis court with a grass surface
grass·hop·per \'gras-,häp-ər\ *n* (14c) **1 :** any of numerous plant-eating orthopterous insects (suborder Saltatoria) having the hind legs adapted for leaping and sometimes engaging in migratory flights in which whole regions may be stripped of vegetation **2 :** a light unarmed scouting and liaison airplane **3 :** a cocktail made with crème de menthe, crème de cacao, and light cream
grass·land \-,land\ *n* (1682) **1 :** farmland occupied chiefly by forage plants and esp. grasses **2 a :** land on which the natural dominant plant forms are grasses and forbs **b :** an ecological community in which the characteristic plants are grasses
grass roots *n pl but sing or pl in constr, often attrib* (1880) **1 :** society at the local level esp. in rural areas as distinguished from the centers of political leadership ⟨cultural changes occurring at the *grass roots* —C. A. Buss⟩ **2 :** the very foundation or source
grass tree *n* (1802) **:** any of a genus (*Xanthorrhoea*) of Australian plants of the lily family with a thick woody trunk bearing a cluster of stiff linear leaves and a terminal spike of small flowers
grass widow *n* (1528) **1** *chiefly dial* **a :** a discarded mistress **b :** a woman who has had an illegitimate child **2 a :** a woman divorced or separated from her husband **b :** a woman whose husband is temporarily away from her
grass widower *n* (1878) **1 :** a man divorced or separated from his wife **2 :** a man whose wife is temporarily away from him
grassy \'gras-ē\ *adj* **grass·i·er; -est** (15c) **1 a :** covered or abounding with grass ⟨~ lawns⟩ **b :** consisting of or having a flavor or odor of grass ⟨~ butter⟩ **2 :** resembling grass esp. in color
grat *past of* GREET
¹grate \'grāt\ *vb* **grat·ed; grat·ing** [ME *graten,* fr. MF *grater* to scratch, of Gmc origin; akin to OHG *krazzōn* to scratch] *vt* (14c) **1** *archaic* **:** ABRADE **2 :** to reduce to small particles by rubbing on something rough ⟨~ cheese⟩ **3 :** FRET, IRRITATE **4 a :** to gnash or grind noisily **b :** to cause to make a rasping sound **c :** to utter in a harsh voice ~ *vi* **1 :** to rub or rasp noisily **2 :** to cause irritation **:** JAR ⟨dry, cerebral talk that tends to ~ on the nerves —Hollis Alpert⟩ — **grat·er** *n*
²grate *n* [ME, fr. ML *crata, grata* hurdle, modif. of L *cratis* — more at HURDLE] (15c) **1 :** a frame of parallel or crossed bars blocking a passage **2** *obs* **:** CAGE, PRISON **3 a :** a frame or bed of iron bars to hold a stove or furnace fire **b :** FIREPLACE **c :** a barred frame for cooking over a fire **4 :** a screen or sieve for grading ore
³grate *vt* **grat·ed; grat·ing** (1547) **:** to furnish with a grate
grate·ful \'grāt-fəl\ *adj* [obs. *grate* pleasing, thankful, fr. L *gratus* — more at GRACE] (1552) **1 a :** appreciative of benefits received **b :** expressing gratitude **2 a :** affording pleasure or contentment **:** PLEASING **b :** pleasing by reason of comfort supplied or discomfort alleviated — **grate·ful·ly** \-fə-lē\ *adv* — **grate·ful·ness** *n*
grat·i·cule \'grat-ə-,kyü(ə)l\ *n* [F, fr. ML *craticula* fine latticework, dim. of *cratis* wickerwork, hurdle] (1914) **1 :** a scale on transparent material in the focal plane of an optical instrument for the location and measurement of objects **2 :** the network of lines of latitude and longitude upon which a map is drawn
grat·i·fi·ca·tion \,grat-ə-fə-'kā-shən\ *n* (1598) **1 :** the act of gratifying **:** the state of being gratified **2** *archaic* **:** REWARD, RECOMPENSE; *esp* **:** GRATUITY **3 :** a source of satisfaction or pleasure

grat·i·fy \'grat-ə-,fī\ *vt* **-fied; -fy·ing** [MF *gratifier,* fr. L *gratificari,* lit., to make oneself pleasing, fr. *gratus* + *-ificari,* pass. of *-ificare* -ify] (1539) **1** *archaic* : REMUNERATE, REWARD **2** : to be a source of or give pleasure or satisfaction to ⟨it *gratified* him to have his wife wear jewels —Willa Cather⟩ **3** : to give in to : INDULGE, SATISFY ⟨~ a whim⟩

grat·i·fy·ing *adj* (ca. 1611) : giving pleasure esp. through satisfying hope, desire, conscience, or vanity : PLEASING — **grat·i·fy·ing·ly** \-iŋ-lē\ *adv*

gra·tin \'grat-ᵊn, 'grät-\ *n* [F, fr. MF, fr. *grater* to scratch] (1806) : a brown crust formed on food that has been cooked with a topping of buttered crumbs or grated cheese

gra·ti·né *or* **gra·ti·née** \,grat-ᵊn-'ā, ,grät-\ *adj* [F, fr. pp. of *gratiner* to cook au gratin, fr. *gratin*] *of a food* (1931) : having a covering or crust (as of buttered crumbs or grated cheese)

grat·ing \'grāt-iŋ\ *n* (1626) **1** : a partition, covering, or frame of parallel bars or crossbars : GRATE **2** : a wooden or metal lattice used to close or floor any of various openings **3** : a system of close equidistant and parallel lines or bars ruled on a polished surface to produce spectra by diffraction

gra·tis \'grat-əs, 'grät-\ *adv or adj* [ME, fr. L *gratiis, gratis,* fr. abl. pl. of *gratia* favor — more at GRACE] (15c) : without charge or recompense : FREE

grat·i·tude \'grat-ə-,t(y)üd\ *n* [ME, fr. MF or ML; MF, fr. ML *gratitudo,* fr. L *gratus* grateful] (1565) : the state of being grateful : THANKFULNESS

gra·tu·itous \grə-'t(y)ü-ət-əs\ *adj* [L *gratuitus,* fr. *gratus*] (1656) **1 a** : given unearned or without recompense **b** : costing nothing : FREE **c** : not involving a return benefit, compensation, or consideration **2** : not called for by the circumstances : UNWARRANTED ⟨~ insolence⟩ ⟨a ~ assumption⟩ — **gra·tu·itous·ly** *adv* — **gra·tu·itous·ness** *n*

gra·tu·ity \grə-'t(y)ü-ət-ē\ *n, pl* **-ities** (1540) : something given voluntarily or beyond obligation usu. in return for or in anticipation of some service; *esp* : TIP

grat·u·late \'grach-ə-,lāt\ *vt* [L *gratulatus,* pp. of *gratulari* — more at CONGRATULATE] *archaic* (1584) : CONGRATULATE — **grat·u·la·tion** \,grach-ə-'lā-shən\ *n* — **grat·u·la·to·ry** \'grach-ə-lə-,tōr-ē, -,tȯr-\ *adj*

grau·pel \'grau̇-pəl\ *n* [G] (1889) : granular snow pellets — called also *soft hail*

Grau·stark \'grau̇-,stärk, 'grȯ-\ *n* [*Graustark,* imaginary country in the novel *Graustark* (1901) by George B. McCutcheon †1928 Am. novelist] (1941) : an imaginary land of high romance; *also* : a highly romantic piece of writing — **Grau·stark·ian** \grau̇-'stär-kē-ən, grȯ-\ *adj*

gra·va·men \grə-'vā-mən\ *n, pl* **-va·mens** *or* **-vam·i·na** \-'vam-ə-nə\ [LL, burden, fr. L *gravare* to burden, fr. *gravis*] (1647) : the material or significant part of a grievance or complaint

[1]grave \'grāv\ *vt* **graved; grav·en** \'grā-vən\ *or* **graved; grav·ing** [ME *graven,* fr. OE *grafan;* akin to OHG *graban* to dig, OSlav *pogreti* to bury] (bef. 12c) **1** *archaic* : DIG, EXCAVATE **2 a** : to carve or shape with a chisel : SCULPTURE **b** : to carve or cut (as letters or figures) into a hard surface : ENGRAVE **3** : to impress or fix (as a thought) deeply

[2]grave *n* [ME, fr. OE *græf;* akin to OHG *grab* grave, OE *grafan* to dig] (bef. 12c) : an excavation for burial of a body; *broadly* : TOMB

[3]grave *vt* **graved; grav·ing** [ME *graven*] (15c) : to clean and pay with pitch ⟨~ a ship's bottom⟩

[4]grave \'grāv, *in sense 5 often* 'gräv\ *adj* **grav·er; grav·est** [MF, fr. L *gravis* heavy, grave — more at GRIEVE] (1539) **1 a** *obs* : AUTHORITATIVE, WEIGHTY **b** : meriting serious consideration : IMPORTANT ⟨~ problems⟩ **c** : likely to produce great harm or danger ⟨a ~ mistake⟩ **d** : significantly serious : CONSIDERABLE, GREAT ⟨~ importance⟩ **2** : having a serious and dignified quality or demeanor ⟨a ~ and thoughtful look⟩ **3** : drab in color : SOMBER **4** : low-pitched in sound **5 a** *of an accent mark* : having the form ` **b** : marked with a grave accent **c** : of the variety indicated by a grave accent ***syn*** see SERIOUS — **grave·ly** *adv* — **grave·ness** *n*

[5]grave \'grāv, 'gräv\ *n* (1620) : a grave accent ` used to show that a vowel is pronounced with a fall of pitch (as in ancient Greek), that a vowel has a certain quality (as *e* in French), that a final *e* is stressed and close and that a final *o* is stressed and low (as in Italian), that a syllable has a degree of stress between maximum and minimum (as in phonetic transcription), or that the *e* of the English ending *-ed* is to be pronounced (as in "this cursèd day")

[6]gra·ve \'gräv-(,)ā\ *adv or adj* [It, lit., grave, fr. L *gravis*] (1683) : slowly and solemnly — used as a direction in music

[1]grav·el \'grav-əl\ *n* [ME, fr. OF *gravele,* dim. of *grave, greve* pebbly ground, beach] (13c) **1** *obs* : SAND **2 a** : loose rounded fragments of rock **b** : a stratum or deposit of gravel; *also* : a surface covered with gravel ⟨a ~ road⟩ **3** : a deposit of small calculous concretions in the kidneys and urinary bladder

[2]gravel *vt* **-eled** *or* **-elled; -el·ing** *or* **-el·ling** \'grav-(ə-)liŋ\ (1543) **1** : to cover or spread with gravel **2 a** : PERPLEX, CONFOUND **b** : IRRITATE, NETTLE

[3]gravel *adj* (1939) : GRAVELLY 2 — used of the human voice

grav·el–blind \'grav-əl-,blīnd\ *adj* [suggested by *sand-blind*] (1596) : having very weak vision

grave·less \'grāv-ləs\ *adj* (1606) **1** : not buried ⟨these ~ bones⟩ **2** : not requiring graves : DEATHLESS ⟨the ~ home of the blessed⟩

grav·el·ly \'grav-(ə-)lē\ *adj* (14c) **1** : of, containing, or covered with gravel **2** : having a harsh grating sound ⟨a ~ voice⟩

graven image *n* [*graven,* pp. of [1]*grave*] (14c) : an object of worship carved usu. from wood or stone : IDOL

grav·er \'grā-vər\ *n* [ME] (13c) **1** : SCULPTOR, ENGRAVER **2** : any of various cutting or shaving tools used in graving or in hand metal-turning

Graves' disease \'grāvz(-əz)-\ *n* [Robert J. *Graves* †1853 Irish physician] (1868) : HYPERTHYROIDISM; *specif* : exophthalmic goiter

grave·stone \'grāv-,stōn\ *n* (14c) : a burial monument

grave·yard \-,yärd\ *n* (1773) **1** : CEMETERY **2** : one resembling a graveyard; *esp* : a storage place for disused, obsolete, or worn-out things ⟨an automobile ~⟩

graveyard shift *n* (1908) : a work shift beginning late at night (as 11 o'clock); *also* : the workers on such a shift

gravi- *comb form* [MF, fr. L, fr. *gravis*] : heavy

grav·id \'grav-əd\ *adj* [L *gravidus,* fr. *gravis* heavy] (1597) : PREGNANT — **gra·vid·i·ty** \grə-'vid-ət-ē\ *n*

grav·i·da \'grav-əd-ə\ *n, pl* **-i·das** *or* **-i·dae** \-ə-,dē\ [L, fr. fem. of *gravidus*] (1926) : a pregnant woman — often used in combination with a number or figure to indicate the number of pregnancies a woman has had ⟨a 4-*gravida*⟩

gra·vi·me·ter \grə-'vim-ət-ər, 'grav-ə-,mēt-\ *n* [F *gravimètre,* fr. *gravi-* + *-mètre* -meter] (1797) **1** : a device similar to a hydrometer for determining specific gravity **2** : a sensitive weighing instrument for measuring variations in the gravitational field of the earth or moon

gravi·met·ric \,grav-ə-'me-trik\ *adj* (1873) **1** : of or relating to measurement by weight **2** : of or relating to variations in the gravitational field determined by means of a gravimeter — **gravi·met·ri·cal·ly** \-tri-k(ə-)lē\ *adv*

gra·vim·e·try \grə-'vim-ə-trē\ *n* (1858) : the measurement of weight, a gravitational field, or density

graving dock *n* (1840) : DRY DOCK

grav·i·tate \'grav-ə-,tāt\ *vb* **-tat·ed; -tat·ing** *vi* (1692) **1** : to move under the influence of gravitation **2 a** : to move toward something **b** : to become attracted ⟨youngsters . . . ~ toward a strong leader —Rose Friedman⟩ ~ *vt* : to move by gravitation

grav·i·ta·tion \,grav-ə-'tā-shən\ *n* (1645) **1 a** : a force manifested by acceleration toward each other of two free material particles or bodies or of radiant-energy quanta **b** : the action or process of gravitating **2** : an attraction to something — **grav·i·ta·tion·al** \-shnəl, -shən-ᵊl\ *adj* — **grav·i·ta·tion·al·ly** \-ē\ *adv* — **grav·i·ta·tive** \'grav-ə-,tāt-iv\ *adj*

gravitational wave *n* (1899) : a hypothetical wave which travels at the speed of light and by means of which gravitational attraction effect is propagated — called also *gravity wave*

grav·i·ton \'grav-ə-,tän\ *n* [ISV *gravity* + [2]*-on*] (1942) : a hypothetical particle with zero charge and rest mass that is held to be the quantum of the gravitational field

grav·i·ty \'grav-ət-ē\ *n, pl* **-ties** [MF or L; MF *gravité,* fr. L *gravitat-, gravitas,* fr. *gravis*] (1509) **1 a** : dignity or sobriety of bearing **b** : IMPORTANCE, SIGNIFICANCE; *esp* : SERIOUSNESS **c** : a serious situation or problem **2** : the quality of having weight **3** : WEIGHT — used chiefly in the phrase *center of gravity* **4 a** : the gravitational attraction of the mass of the earth, the moon, or a planet for bodies at or near its surface; *broadly* : GRAVITATION **b** : ACCELERATION OF GRAVITY **c** : SPECIFIC GRAVITY — **gravity** *adj*

gra·vure \grə-'vyu̇(ə)r, grā-\ *n* [F, fr. *graver* to grave, of Gmc origin; akin to OHG *graban* to dig, engrave — more at GRAVE] (1893) : PHOTOGRAVURE

gra·vy \'grā-vē\ *n, pl* **gravies** [ME *gravey,* fr. MF *gravé*] (14c) **1** : a sauce made from the thickened and seasoned juices of cooked meat **2 a** : something pleasing or valuable that occurs or is acquired over and above what would ordinarily be expected ⟨with expenses now paid, future money is pure ~ —K. Crossen⟩ **b** : unearned or illicit gain : GRAFT

gravy train *n* (ca. 1927) : a much exploited source of easy money ⟨has him a *gravy train* out there, with these cost-plus contracts and all —*Harper's*⟩; *also* : GRAVY 2a

[1]gray \'grā\ *adj* [ME, fr. OE *grǣg;* akin to OHG *grīs, grāo* gray, OSlav *zirěti* to see] (bef. 12c) **1 a** : of the color gray **b** : tending toward gray ⟨blue-*gray* eyes⟩ **c** : dull in color **2** : having the hair gray : HOARY **3** : clothed in gray **4 a** : lacking cheer or brightness in mood, outlook, style, or flavor; *also* : DISMAL, GLOOMY ⟨a ~ day⟩ **b** : TEDIOUS, UNINTERESTING **5** : intermediate in position, condition, or character **6** *slang* : of or relating to the Caucasian race — **gray·ly** *adv* — **gray·ness** *n*

[2]gray *n* (13c) **1** : something (as an animal, garment, cloth, or spot) of a gray color **2** : any of a series of neutral colors ranging between black and white **3** : one who wears a gray uniform: as **a** : a soldier in the Confederate army during the American Civil War **b** : the Confederate army **4** *slang* : a member of the Caucasian race

[3]gray *vt* (14c) : to make gray ~ *vi* **1** : to become gray **2** : AGE; *also* : to comprise an increasing percentage of older people

gray·beard \'grā-,bi(ə)rd\ *n* (1579) : an old man

gray birch *n* (1851) **1** : a small coarse No. American birch (*Betula populifolia*) that has many lateral branches, grayish white bark, triangular leaves, and soft wood which is worthless as timber and that occurs esp. as a colonizer of old fields which are reverting to woodland **2** : YELLOW BIRCH

gray eminence *n* [trans. of F *Éminence Grise,* nickname of Père Joseph (François Joseph du Tremblay) †1638 Fr. monk and diplomat who was confidant of Cardinal Richelieu, styled *Éminence Rouge* (red eminence); fr. the colors of their respective habits] (1941) : a person who exercises power behind the scenes

gray·fish \'grā-,fish\ *n* (1917) : DOGFISH

gray·ish \'grā-ish\ *adj* (1562) **1** : somewhat gray **2** *of a color* : low in saturation

gray·ling \'grā-liŋ\ *n, pl* **grayling** *also* **graylings** (15c) : any of several freshwater salmonoid fishes (genus *Thymallus*) valued as food and sport fishes

gray matter *n* (1840) **1** : neural tissue esp. of the brain and spinal cord that contains nerve-cell bodies as well as nerve fibers and has a brownish gray color **2** : BRAINS, INTELLECT

gray squirrel *n* (1674) : a common light gray to black squirrel (*Sciurus carolinensis*) that is native to eastern No. America and has been introduced into England

gray·wacke \'grā-,wak(-ə)\ *n* [partial trans. of G *grauwacke*] (1811) : a coarse usu. dark gray sandstone or fine-grained conglomerate composed of firmly cemented rounded fragments (as of quartz and feldspars)

gray whale *n* (1860) : a rather large whalebone whale (*Eschrichtius robustus*) of the northern Pacific

[1]graze \'grāz\ *vb* **grazed; graz·ing** [ME *grasen,* fr. OE *grasian,* fr. *græs* grass] *vi* (bef. 12c) **1** : to feed on growing herbage, attached algae, or phytoplankton **2** : to eat small amounts of various foods several times a day ~ *vt* **1 a** : to crop and eat in the field **b** : to feed on the herbage of **2 a** : to put to graze ⟨*grazed* his cows on the meadow⟩ **b** : to put cattle to graze on **3** : to supply herbage for the grazing of — **graze·able** *or* **graz·able** \'grā-zə-bəl\ *adj* — **graz·er** *n*

[2]graze *n* (1692) **1** : an act of grazing **2** : herbage for grazing

[3]graze *vb* **grazed; graz·ing** [perh. fr. [1]*graze*] *vt* (1604) **1** : to touch lightly in passing **2** : ABRADE, SCRATCH ⟨*grazed* her knee when she fell⟩

~ *vi* : to touch or rub against something in passing

⁴**graze** *n* (1847) : a scraping along a surface or an abrasion made by it; *esp* : a superficial abrasion of the skin

gra·zier \'grā-zhər\ *n* (1674) **1** : a person who grazes cattle; *broadly* : RANCHER **2** *Austral* : a sheep raiser

¹**grease** \'grēs\ *n* [ME *grese,* fr. OF *craisse, graisse,* fr. (assumed) VL *crassia,* fr. L *crassus* fat] (13c) **1 a** : rendered animal fat **b** : oily matter **c** : a thick lubricant **2** : wool as it comes from the sheep retaining the natural oils or fats — **grease·less** \'grē-sləs\ *adj* — **grease·proof** \'grē-'sprüf\ *adj* — **in the grease** *of wool or fur* : in the natural uncleaned condition

²**grease** \'grēs, 'grēz\ *vt* **greased; greas·ing** (14c) **1** : to smear or daub with grease **2** : to lubricate with grease **3** : to soil with grease **4** : to hasten the process or progress of; *also* : FACILITATE **5** *slang* : KILL — **greas·er** *n* — **grease the hand** *or* **grease the palm** : BRIBE

grease monkey *n* (1928) : MECHANIC; *esp* : an airplane mechanic

grease·paint \'grē-,spānt\ *n* (1886) **1** : a melted tallow or grease used in theater makeup **2** : theater makeup

grease pencil *n* (1944) : a pencil in which the marking substance is pigment and grease

greas·er \'grē-zər, -sər\ *n* [¹*grease*] (1846) **1** : a native or inhabitant of Latin America; *esp* : MEXICAN — usu. taken to be offensive **2** : an aggressive swaggering young white male usu. of working-class background

grease·wood \'grē-,swu̇d\ *n* (1838) : a low stiff shrub (*Sarcobatus vermiculatus*) of the goosefoot family common in alkaline soils in the western U.S.; *also* : any of various related or similar shrubs

greasy \'grē-sē, -zē\ *adj* **greas·i·er; -est** (1514) **1 a** : smeared or soiled with grease ⟨~ clothes⟩ **b** : oily in appearance, texture, or manner ⟨his ~ smile —Jack London⟩ **c** : SLIPPERY **2** : containing an unusual amount of grease ⟨~ food⟩ — **greas·i·ly** \-sə-lē, -zə-\ *adv* — **greas·i·ness** \-sē-nəs, -zē-\ *n*

greasy spoon *n* (ca. 1925) : a small cheap usu. unsanitary restaurant

¹**great** \'grāt, *Southern also* 'gre(ə)t\ *adj* [ME *grete,* fr. OE *grēat;* akin to OHG *grōz* large] (bef. 12c) **1 a** : notably large in size : HUGE **b** : of a kind characterized by relative largeness — used in plant and animal names **c** : ELABORATE, AMPLE ⟨~ detail⟩ **2 a** : large in number or measure : NUMEROUS ⟨~ multitudes⟩ **b** : PREDOMINANT ⟨the ~ majority⟩ **3** : remarkable in magnitude, degree, or effectiveness ⟨~ bloodshed⟩ **4** : full of emotion ⟨~ with anger⟩ **5 a** : EMINENT, DISTINGUISHED ⟨a ~ poet⟩ **b** : ARISTOCRATIC, GRAND ⟨~ ladies⟩ **6** : long continued ⟨~ while⟩ **7** : PRINCIPAL, MAIN ⟨a reception in the ~ hall⟩ **8** : more remote in a family relationship by a single generation than a specified relative ⟨*great*-grandfather⟩ **9** : markedly superior in character or quality; *esp* : NOBLE ⟨~ of soul⟩ **10 a** : remarkably skilled ⟨~ at tennis⟩ **b** : marked by enthusiasm : KEEN ⟨~ on science fiction⟩ **11** — used as a generalized term of approval ⟨had a ~ time⟩ ⟨it was just ~⟩ — **great** *adv* — **great·ly** *adv* — **great·ness** *n*

²**great** *n, pl* **great** *or* **greats** (13c) : one that is great

great ape *n* (1949) : any of the recent anthropoid apes

great auk *n* (ca. 1828) : an extinct large flightless auk (*Pinguinus impennis*) formerly abundant along No. Atlantic coasts

great–aunt *n* (1656) : GRANDAUNT

Great Bear *n* : URSA MAJOR

great blue heron *n* (1835) : a large slaty-blue American heron (*Ardea herodias*) with a crested head

great circle *n* (1594) : a circle formed on the surface of a sphere by the intersection of a plane that passes through the center of the sphere; *specif* : such a circle on the surface of the earth an arc of which connecting two terrestrial points constitutes the shortest distance on the earth's surface between them

great·coat \'grāt-,kōt\ *n* (1661) : a heavy overcoat

Great Dane *n* (1774) : any of a breed of tall massive powerful smooth-coated dogs

great divide *n* [the *Great Divide,* No. Am. watershed] (1861) **1** : a watershed between major drainage systems **2** : a significant point of division; *esp* : DEATH ⟨he crossed the *great divide* bravely⟩

great·en \'grāt-ᵊn\ *vb* **great·ened; great·en·ing** \'grāt-niŋ, -ᵊn-iŋ\ *vt* (1614) : to make greater ~ *vi* : to become greater

great·er *adj, often cap* [compar. of *great*] (1882) : consisting of a central city together with adjacent areas that are naturally or administratively connected with it ⟨*Greater* London⟩

greater yellowlegs *n pl but sing or pl in constr* (1928) : a common No. American marsh and shorebird (*Tringa melanoleuca*) that is largely gray above and white below with black or dark gray flecks and yellow legs — compare LESSER YELLOWLEGS

greatest common divisor *n* (ca. 1924) : the largest integer or the polynomial of highest degree that is an exact divisor of each of two or more integers or polynomials — called also *greatest common factor*

great·heart·ed \'grāt-'härt-əd\ *adj* (14c) **1** : characterized by bravery : COURAGEOUS **2** : GENEROUS, MAGNANIMOUS — **great·heart·ed·ly** *adv* — **great·heart·ed·ness** *n*

great horned owl *n* (1812) : a large American owl (*Bubo virginianus*) with conspicuous ear tufts

great laurel *n* (1784) : a large-leaved evergreen rhododendron (*Rhododendron maximum*) of eastern No. America that has rosy bell-shaped flowers more or less speckled with green

Great Mogul *n* (1588) : the sovereign of the empire founded in India by the Moguls in the 16th century

great–nephew *n* (1581) : GRANDNEPHEW

great–niece *n* (1884) : GRANDNIECE

great octave *n* (ca. 1909) : the musical octave that begins on the second C below middle C — see PITCH illustration

great power *n, often cap G&P* (ca. 1890) : one of the nations that figure most decisively in international affairs

Great Pyr·e·nees \-'pir-ə-,nēz\ *n* (1938) : any of a breed of large heavy-coated white dogs that resemble the Newfoundland

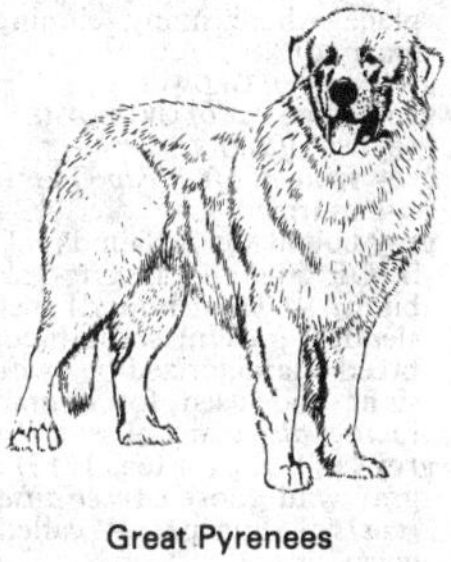

Great Pyrenees

Great Russian *n* (1886) : a member of the Russian-speaking people of the central and northeastern U.S.S.R. — **Great Russian** *adj*

great seal *n* (15c) : a large seal that constitutes an emblem of sovereignty and is used esp. for the authentication of important documents

great skua *n* (ca. 1954) : a large stocky jaeger (*Catharacta skua*) that has dusky plumage and broad rounded wings, breeds chiefly along arctic and antarctic shores, and forages over most cold and temperate seas

great soil group *n* (ca. 1938) : a group of soils that is characterized by common characteristics usu. developed under the influence of environmental factors (as vegetation and climate) active over a considerable geographic range and that comprises one or more families of soil — called also *great group*

great–uncle *n* (1656) : GRANDUNCLE

great white shark *n* (ca. 1934) : WHITE SHARK

great year *n* (ca. 1909) : the period of about 25,800 years required for one complete cycle of the equinoxes around the ecliptic

greave \'grēv\ *n* [ME *greve,* fr. MF] (14c) : armor for the leg below the knee

grebe \'grēb\ *n* [F *grèbe*] (1766) : any of a family (Podicipitidae or Podicipedidae) of swimming and diving birds closely related to the loons but having lobate toes — compare DABCHICK

Gre·cian \'grē-shən\ *adj* [L *Graecia* Greece] (1577) : GREEK — **Grecian** *n* — **gre·cian·ize** \-shə-,nīz\ *vt, often cap*

Gre·cism \'grē-,siz-əm\ *n* (1570) **1** : a Greek idiom **2** : a quality or style imitative of Greek art or culture

gre·cize \-,sīz\ *vt* **gre·cized; gre·ciz·ing** *often cap* (1692) : to make Greek or Hellenistic in character

Gre·co- *or* **Grae·co-** \'grek-ō, 'grē-kō\ *comb form* [L *Graeco-,* fr. *Graecus*] **1** : Greece : Greeks ⟨*Grecophile*⟩ ⟨*Grecomania*⟩ **2** : Greek and ⟨*Graeco-Roman*⟩

¹**gree** \'grē\ *n* [ME, fr. MF *gré* step, degree, fr. L *gradus* — more at GRADE] *Scot* (14c) : MASTERY, SUPERIORITY

²**gree** *vb* **greed; gree·ing** [ME *green,* short for *agreen*] *dial* (14c) : AGREE

greed \'grēd\ *n* [back-formation fr. *greedy*] (1609) : excessive or reprehensible acquisitiveness : AVARICE

greedy \'grēd-ē\ *adj* **greed·i·er; -est** [ME *gredy,* fr. OE *grǣdig;* akin to OHG *grātag* greedy] (bef. 12c) **1** : having a strong desire for food or drink **2** : marked by greed **3** : EAGER, KEEN ⟨elated and ~ for the future — Frances G. Patton⟩ ***syn*** see COVETOUS — **greed·i·ly** \'grēd-ᵊl-ē\ *adv* — **greed·i·ness** \'grēd-ē-nəs\ *n*

¹**Greek** \'grēk\ *n* [ME *Greke,* fr. OE *Grēca,* fr. L *Graecus,* fr. Gk *Graikos*] (bef. 12c) **1 a** : a native or inhabitant of ancient or modern Greece **b** : a person of Greek descent **2 a** : the language used by the Greeks from prehistoric times to the present constituting a branch of Indo-European — see INDO-EUROPEAN LANGUAGES table **b** : ancient Greek as used from the time of the earliest records to the end of the 2d century A.D. — see INDO-EUROPEAN LANGUAGES table **c** *often not cap* [trans. of L *Graecum* (in the medieval phrase *Graecum est; non potest legi* It is Greek; it cannot be read)] : something unintelligible ⟨chemical formulas are *greek* to me⟩ **3** : a member of a Greek-letter fraternity or sorority

²**Greek** *adj* (14c) **1** : of, relating to, or characteristic of Greece, the Greeks, or Greek ⟨~ architecture⟩ **2 a** : EASTERN ORTHODOX **b** : of or relating to an Eastern church using the Byzantine rite in Greek **c** : of or relating to the established Orthodox church of Greece

Greek Catholic *n* (ca. 1909) **1** : a member of an Eastern church **2** : a member of an Eastern rite of the Roman Catholic Church

Greek cross *n* (ca. 1890) : a cross having an upright and a transverse shaft equal in length and intersecting at their middles —see CROSS illustration

Greek fire *n* (13c) : an incendiary composition used in warfare by the Byzantine Greeks and said to have burst into flame on wetting

Greek Orthodox *adj* (ca. 1900) : EASTERN ORTHODOX; *specif* : GREEK 2c

¹**green** \'grēn\ *adj* [ME *grene,* fr. OE *grēne;* akin to OE *grōwan* to grow] (bef. 12c) **1** : of the color green **2 a** : covered by green growth or foliage ⟨~ fields⟩ **b** *of winter* : MILD, CLEMENT **c** : consisting of green plants and usu. edible herbage ⟨a ~ salad⟩ **3** : pleasantly alluring **4** : YOUTHFUL, VIGOROUS **5** : not ripened or matured : IMMATURE ⟨~ apples⟩ ⟨tender ~ grasses⟩ **6** : FRESH, NEW **7 a** : marked by a pale, sickly, or nauseated appearance **b** : affected by intense emotion — used esp. in the phrase *green with envy* **8 a** : not fully processed or treated: as (1) : not aged ⟨~ liquor⟩ (2) : not dressed or tanned ⟨~ hides⟩ (3) : freshly sawed : UNSEASONED **b** : not in condition for a particular use **c** (1) *of a female fish* : not ready to spawn (2) : not quite ready to shed ⟨~ crab⟩ **9 a** : deficient in training, knowledge, or experience **b** : deficient in sophistication and savoir faire : NAIVE **c** : not fully qualified for or experienced in a particular function ⟨~ horse⟩ **10** : indicating that everything is in order and to proceed according to plan ⟨all systems are ~⟩ — **green·ish** \'grē-nish\ *adj* — **green·ish·ness** *n* — **green·ly** *adv* — **green·ness** \'grēn-nəs\ *n* — **green around the gills** : pale or sickly in appearance

²**green** *vi* (bef. 12c) : to become green ~ *vt* **1** : to make green **2** : REJUVENATE, REVITALIZE

³**green** *n* (13c) **1** : a color whose hue is somewhat less yellow than that of growing fresh grass or of the emerald or is that of the part of the spectrum lying between blue and yellow **2** : something of a green color **3** : green vegetation: as **a** *pl* : leafy parts of plants for use as decoration **b** *pl* (1) : leafy herbs (as spinach, dandelions, Swiss chard) that are cooked as a vegetable : POTHERB (2) : GREEN VEGETABLE **4** : a grassy plain or plot: as **a** : a common or park in the center of a town or village **b** : PUTTING GREEN — **greeny** \'grē-nē\ *adj*

green alga *n* (ca. 1903) : an alga in which the chlorophyll is not masked by other pigments; *specif* : such an alga of a division (Chlorophyta)

green·back \'grēn-,bak\ *n* (1862) : a legal-tender note issued by the U.S. government

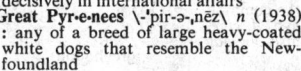

green·back·er \-ər\ *n* (1876) **1** *cap* : a member of a post-Civil War American political party opposing reduction in the amount of paper money in circulation **2** : one who advocates a paper currency backed only by the U.S. government — **green·back·ism** \-ˌiz-əm\ *n*
green bean *n* (1942) : a kidney bean that is used as a snap bean when the pods are colored green
green·belt \ˈgrēn-ˌbelt\ *n* (1932) : a belt of parkways, parks, or farmlands that encircles a community
green·bri·er \-ˌbrī(-ə)r\ *n* (1785) : any of a genus (*Smilax*) of plants of the lily family; *esp* : a prickly vine (*S. rotundifolia*) of the eastern U.S. with umbels of small greenish flowers
green·bug \-ˌbəg\ *n* (1712) : a green aphid (*Schizaphis graminum*) very destructive to small grains
green card *n* [fr. the fact that it was formerly colored green] (1969) : an identity card attesting the permanent resident status of an alien in the U.S. — **green–carder** *n*
green corn *n* (1645) : the young tender ears of Indian corn
green dragon *n* (1817) : an American arum (*Arisaema dracontium*) with digitate leaves, slender greenish yellow spathe, and elongated spadix
green·ery \ˈgrēn-(ə-)rē\ *n, pl* **-er·ies** (1797) **1** : green foliage or plants **2** : GREEN 3a
green–eyed \ˈgrē-ˈnīd\ *adj* (1596) : JEALOUS
green–eyed monster *n* (1604) : JEALOUSY
green·finch \ˈgrēn-ˌfinch\ *n* (1500) : a very common European finch (*Chloris chloris*) having olive-green and yellow plumage
green fingers *n pl* (1934) : GREEN THUMB
green·fly \ˈgrēn-ˌflī\ *n, Brit* (1744) : APHID; *esp* : GREEN PEACH APHID
green·gage \-ˌgāj\ *n* [*green* + Sir William *Gage* †1820 Eng. botanist] (1724) : any of several rather small rounded greenish or greenish yellow cultivated plums
green gland *n* (ca. 1890) : one of a pair of large green glands in some crustaceans (as crayfishes) that have an excretory function and open at the bases of the larger antennae
green·gro·cer \ˈgrēn-ˌgrō-sər\ *n, chiefly Brit* (1723) : a retailer of fresh vegetables and fruit — **green·gro·cery** \-ˌgrōs-(ə-)rē\ *n*
green·heart \-ˌhärt\ *n* (1756) : a tropical So. American evergreen tree (*Nectandra rodioei*) with a hard greenish wood; *also* : its wood
green·horn \-ˌhȯ(ə)rn\ *n* [obs. *greenhorn* (animal with young horns)] (1682) **1** : an inexperienced or unsophisticated person **2** : a newcomer (as to a country) unacquainted with local manners and customs
green·house \-ˌhau̇s\ *n* (1664) **1** : a glassed enclosure used for the cultivation or protection of tender plants **2** : a clear plastic shell covering a section of an airplane
greenhouse effect *n* (1937) : warming of the earth's surface and the lower layers of atmosphere that tends to increase with increasing atmospheric carbon dioxide and that is caused by conversion of solar radiation into heat in a process involving selective transmission of short wave solar radiation by the atmosphere, its absorption by the earth's surface, and reradiation as infrared which is absorbed and partly reradiated back to the surface by carbon dioxide and water vapor in the air
green·ing \ˈgrē-niŋ\ *n* (1664) : any of several green-skinned apples
green·let \ˈgrēn-lət\ *n* (1831) : VIREO
green light *n* [fr. the green traffic light which signals permission to proceed] (1937) : authority or permission to proceed esp. with a project
green·ling \ˈgrēn-liŋ\ *n* (ca. 1900) : any of several food fishes (family Hexagrammidae) of the rocky coasts of the northern Pacific; *esp* : a common food and sport fish (*Hexagrammos decagrammus*)
green–ma·nure \ˌgrēn-mə-ˈn(y)u̇(ə)r\ *vt* (1842) : to fertilize with green manure
green manure *n* (1842) : an herbaceous crop (as clover) plowed under while green to enrich the soil
green mold *n* (1919) : a green or green-spored mold (as of the genera *Penicillium* or *Aspergillus*)
green monkey *n* (1840) : a long-tailed monkey (*Cercopithecus sabaeus*) of West Africa that has greenish-appearing hair and is often used in medical research
gree·nock·ite \ˈgrē-nə-ˌkīt\ *n* [Charles M. Cathcart, Lord *Greenock* †1859 Eng. soldier] (1844) : a mineral CdS consisting of native cadmium sulfide occurring in yellow translucent hexagonal crystals or as an earthy incrustation
green onion *n* (1931) : a young onion pulled before the bulb has enlarged and used esp. in salads
green peach aphid *n* (1922) : a nearly cosmopolitan yellowish green aphid (*Myzus persicae*) that is frequently a vector of plant virus diseases and is destructive esp. to peaches
green pepper *n* (1926) : a sweet pepper before it turns red at maturity
green revolution *n* (1968) : the great increase in production of food grains (as rice and wheat) due to the introduction of high-yielding varieties, to the use of pesticides, and to better management techniques
green·room \ˈgrēn-ˌrüm, -ˌru̇m\ *n* (1701) : a room in a theater or concert hall where performers can relax before, between, or after appearances
green·sand \-ˌsand\ *n* (1796) : a sedimentary deposit that consists largely of dark greenish grains of glauconite often mingled with clay or sand
greens fee \ˈgrēnz-\ *n* (1909) : a fee paid for the privilege of playing on a golf course — called also *green fee*
green·shank \ˈgrēn-ˌshaŋk\ *n* (ca. 1766) : an Old World sandpiper (*Tringa nebularia*) related to the yellowlegs of America
green·sick \-ˌsik\ *adj* [back-formation fr. *greensickness*] (1681) : affected with chlorosis
green·sick·ness *n* (1583) : CHLOROSIS
green snake *n* (1709) : either of two bright green harmless largely insectivorous No. American colubrid snakes (*Liopeltis vernalis* and *Ophiodrys aestivus*)
green soap *n* (1840) : a soft soap made from vegetable oils and used esp. in the treatment of skin diseases
green·stick fracture \ˈgrēn-ˌstik-\ *n* (1885) : a bone fracture in a young individual in which the bone is partly broken and partly bent
green·stone \ˈgrēn-ˌstōn\ *n* (1805) **1** : any of numerous usu. altered dark green compact rocks (as diorite) **2** : NEPHRITE
green·stuff \-ˌstəf\ *n* (1851) : green vegetation used as foodstuff
green sunfish *n* (1902) : a sunfish (*Lepomis cyanellus*) of the Great Lakes region and southwestward to the Rio Grande that is largely greenish above with a blue spot on each scale
green·sward \-ˌswȯ(ə)rd\ *n* (1600) : turf that is green with growing grass
green tea *n* (1704) : tea that is light in color from incomplete fermentation of the leaf before firing
green thumb *n* (1943) : an unusual ability to make plants grow — **green–thumbed** \ˈgrēn-ˈthəmd\ *adj*
green turtle *n* (1657) : a large edible sea turtle (*Chelonia mydas*) with a smooth greenish or olive-colored shell and highly nutritious eggs
green vegetable *n* (1884) : a vegetable whose foliage or foliage-bearing stalks are the chief edible part
Green·wich time \ˈgrin-ij-, ˈgren-, -ich-\ *n* [*Greenwich*, England] (1861) : the mean solar time of the meridian of Greenwich used as the prime basis of standard time throughout the world — called also *Greenwich mean time*
green·wing \ˈgrēn-ˌwiŋ\ *n* (1895) : GREEN-WINGED TEAL
green–winged teal \ˌgrēn-ˌwiŋ(d)-\ *n* (1813) : a small dabbling duck (*Anas crecca*) the male of which has a chestnut head with a green eye patch and a metallic green area on the wing speculum
green·wood \ˈgrēn-ˌwu̇d\ *n* (14c) : a forest green with foliage
1**greet** \ˈgrēt\ *vt* [ME *greten*, fr. OE *grētan*; akin to OE *grǣtan* to weep] (bef. 12c) **1** : to address with expression of kind wishes : HAIL **2 a** : to meet or react to in a specified manner ⟨~*ed* the candidate with boos⟩ **b** : to occur or be perceived as a response to ⟨apathy ~*ed* the plan⟩ **3** : to appear to the perception of ⟨a surprising sight ~*ed* her eyes⟩ — **greet·er** *n*
2**greet** *vi* **grat** \ˈgrat\; **grut·ten** \ˈgrət-ᵊn\ [ME *greten*, fr. OE *grǣtan*; akin to ON *grāta* to weep] *Scot* (bef. 12c) : WEEP, LAMENT
greet·ing *n* (bef. 12c) **1** : a salutation at meeting **2** : an expression of good wishes : REGARDS — usu. used in plural ⟨holiday ~*s*⟩
greeting card *n* (1898) : a card that bears a message of goodwill and is usu. sent or given on a special occasion (as a birthday or a holiday)
greg·a·rine \ˈgreg-ə-ˌrīn\ *n* [deriv. of L *gregarius*] (1867) : any of a large order (Gregarinida) of parasitic vermiform sporozoan protozoans that usu. occur in insects and other invertebrates — **gregarine** *adj*
gre·gar·i·ous \gri-ˈgar-ē-əs, -ˈger-\ *adj* [L *gregarius* of a flock or herd, fr. *greg-*, *grex* flock, herd; akin to Gk *ageirein* to collect, *agora* assembly] (1668) **1 a** : tending to associate with others of one's kind : SOCIAL **b** : marked by or indicating a liking for companionship : SOCIABLE **c** : of or relating to a social group **2 a** *of a plant* : growing in a cluster or a colony **b** : living in contiguous nests but not forming a true colony — used esp. of wasps and bees — **gre·gar·i·ous·ly** *adv* — **gre·gar·i·ous·ness** *n*
1**Gre·go·ri·an** \gri-ˈgōr-ē-ən, -ˈgȯr-\ *adj* (1642) : of or relating to Pope Gregory XIII or the Gregorian calendar
2**Gregorian** *adj* (1653) **1** : of or relating to Pope Gregory I **2** : of, relating to, or having the characteristics of Gregorian chant
3**Gregorian** *adj* [St. *Gregory* the Illuminator †332, apostle of Armenia] (1955) : of or relating to the Armenian national church
Gregorian calendar *n* (ca. 1771) : a calendar in general use introduced in 1582 by Pope Gregory XIII as a revision of the Julian calendar, adopted in Great Britain and the American colonies in 1752, and marked by the suppression of 10 days or after 1700 11 days and the restriction that only those centesimal years divisible by 400 should be leap years — see MONTH table
Gregorian chant *n* (ca. 1751) : a monodic and rhythmically free liturgical chant of the Roman Catholic Church
greige \ˈgrā(zh)\ *adj* [F *grège* raw (of silk), fr. It *greggio*] (1926) : being in an unbleached undyed state as taken from a loom — used of textiles
grei·sen \ˈgrīz-ᵊn\ *n* [G] (1878) : a crystalline rock consisting of quartz and mica that is common in Cornwall and Saxony
grem·lin \ˈgrem-lən\ *n* [perh. modif. of IrGael *gruaimin* ill-humored little fellow] (1941) : a small gnome held to be responsible for malfunction of equipment esp. in aircraft
gre·nade \grə-ˈnād\ *n* [MF, pomegranate, fr. LL *granata*, fr. L, fem. of *granatus* seedy, fr. *granum* grain — more at CORN] (1591) : a small missile that contains an explosive or a chemical agent (as tear gas, a flame producer, or a smoke producer) and that is thrown by hand or projected (as by a rifle or special launcher)
gren·a·dier \ˌgren-ə-ˈdi(ə)r\ *n* [F, fr. *grenade* grenade] (1676) **1 a** : a soldier who carries and throws grenades **b** : a member of a special regiment or corps formerly armed with grenades **2** : any of various deep-sea fishes (family Macruridae) that are related to the cods and have an elongate tapering body and compressed pointed tail — called also *rattail*
gren·a·dine \ˌgren-ə-ˈdēn, ˈgren-ə-ˌ\ *n* [F, fr. *grenade*] (1852) **1** : a plain or figured open-weave fabric of various fibers **2** : a moderate reddish orange **3** : a syrup flavored with pomegranates and used in mixed drinks
Gren·del \ˈgren-dᵊl\ *n* [OE] : a monstrous man-eating descendant of Cain slain by Beowulf in the Old English poem *Beowulf*
Gresh·am's law \ˌgresh-əmz-\ *n* [Sir Thomas *Gresham*] (1858) : an observation in economics: when two coins are equal in debt-paying value but unequal in intrinsic value, the one having the lesser intrinsic value tends to remain in circulation and the other to be hoarded or exported as bullion
Gret·na Green \ˌgret-nə-ˈgrēn\ *n* [*Gretna Green*, Scotland] (1813) : a place where many eloping couples are married
grew *past of* GROW
grew·some *var of* GRUESOME
grey *var of* GRAY
grey friar *n, often cap G&F* (14c) : a Franciscan friar
grey·hound \ˈgrā-ˌhau̇nd\ *n* [ME *grehound*, fr. OE *grīghund*, fr. *grīg-* (akin to ON *grey* bitch) + *hund* hound] (bef. 12c) : a tall slender graceful smooth-coated dog of a breed characterized by swiftness and keen sight and used for coursing game and racing; *also* : any of several related dogs
grey·lag \-ˌlag\ *n* (ca. 1713) : the common gray wild goose (*Anser anser* syn. *A. cinereus*) of Europe — called also *greylag goose*

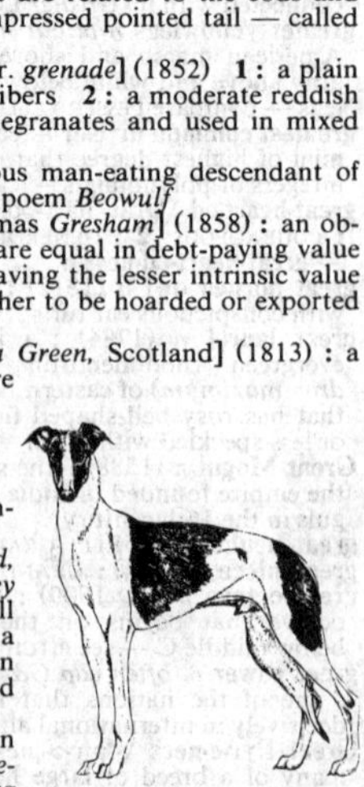
greyhound

grib·ble \'grib-əl\ *n* [prob. dim. of 2*grub*] (1838) **:** a small marine isopod crustacean (*Limnoria lignorum* or *L. terebrans*) that destroys submerged timber

grid \'grid\ *n* [back-formation fr. *gridiron*] (1839) **1 :** GRATING **2 a** (1) **:** a perforated or ridged metal plate used as a conductor in a storage battery (2) **:** an electrode consisting of a mesh or a spiral of fine wire in an electron tube (3) **:** a network of conductors for distribution of electric power; *also* **:** a network of radio or television stations **b :** a network of uniformly spaced horizontal and perpendicular lines (as for locating points on a map); *also* **:** something resembling such a network ⟨a road ~⟩ **c :** GRIDIRON 2; *broadly* **:** FOOTBALL **3 :** the starting positions of cars on a racecourse **4 :** a device (as of glass) in a photocomposer on which are located the characters to be exposed on the film as the text is composed

grid·dle \'grid-ᵊl\ *n* [ME *gredil* gridiron, fr. ONF, fr. L *craticulum,* dim. of *cratis* wickerwork — more at HURDLE] (14c) **:** a flat metal surface or pan on which food is cooked by dry heat

griddle cake *n* (1783) **:** PANCAKE

grid·iron \'grid-ˌī(-ə)rn\ *n* [ME *gredire*] (14c) **1 :** a grate for broiling food **2 :** something consisting of or covered with a network **3 :** a football field

grid·lock \-ˌläk\ *n* (1980) **1 :** a traffic jam in which a grid of intersecting streets is so completely congested that no vehicular movement is possible **2 :** a situation resembling a gridlock (as in congestion or lack of movement)

grief \'grēf\ *n* [ME *gref,* fr. MF, heavy, grave, fr. (assumed) VL *grevis,* alter. of L *gravis*] (15c) **1** *obs* **:** GRIEVANCE 3 **2 a :** deep and poignant distress caused by or as if by bereavement **b :** a cause of such suffering **3 a :** MISHAP, MISADVENTURE **b :** TROUBLE, ANNOYANCE ⟨enough ~ for one day⟩ **c :** an unfortunate outcome **:** DISASTER — used chiefly in the phrase *come to grief* ***syn*** see SORROW

griev·ance \'grē-vən(t)s\ *n* (14c) **1** *obs* **:** SUFFERING, DISTRESS **2 :** a cause of distress (as an unsatisfactory working condition) felt to afford reason for complaint or resistance **3 :** the formal expression of a grievance **:** COMPLAINT ***syn*** see INJUSTICE

grievance committee *n* (1927) **:** a committee formed by a labor union or by employer and employees jointly to discuss and where possible to eliminate grievances

griev·ant \-vənt\ *n* (1958) **:** one who submits a grievance for arbitration

grieve \'grēv\ *vb* **grieved; griev·ing** [ME *greven,* fr. OF *grever,* fr. L *gravare* to burden, fr. *gravis* heavy, grave; akin to Goth *kaurjos,* pl., heavy, Gk *barys,* Skt *guru*] *vt* (13c) **:** to cause to suffer **:** DISTRESS ~ *vi* **:** to feel grief **:** SORROW — **griev·er** *n*

griev·ous \'grē-vəs\ *adj* (14c) **1 :** OPPRESSIVE, ONEROUS ⟨~ costs of war⟩ **2 :** causing or characterized by severe pain, suffering, or sorrow ⟨a ~ wound⟩ ⟨a ~ loss⟩ **3 :** SERIOUS, GRAVE ⟨~ fault⟩ — **griev·ous·ly** *adv* — **griev·ous·ness** *n*

grif·fin *or* **grif·fon** \'grif-ən\ *n* [ME *griffon,* fr. MF *grifon,* modif. of L *gryphus,* modif. of Gk *gryps*] (14c) **:** a mythical animal typically having the head, forepart, and wings of an eagle and the body, hind legs, and tail of a lion

grif·fon \'grif-ən\ *n* [F, lit., griffin] (1882) **1 :** BRUSSELS GRIFFON **2 :** WIREHAIRED POINTING GRIFFON

grift \'grift\ *vt* [*grift,* n., perh. alter. of *graft*] *slang* (1915) **:** to obtain (money) illicitly (as in a confidence game) — **grift** *n, slang* — **grift·er** *n, slang*

grig \'grig\ *n* [ME *grege*] (1566) **:** a lively lighthearted usu. small or young person

gri·gri *var of* GRIS-GRIS

1**grill** \'gril\ *vt* (1668) **1 :** to broil on a grill; *also* **:** to fry or toast on a griddle **2 a :** to torment as if by broiling **b :** to question intensely ⟨the police ~*ed* the suspect⟩ ***syn*** see AFFLICT — **grill·er** *n*

2**grill** *n* [F *gril,* fr. L *craticulum* — more at GRIDDLE] (1685) **1 :** a cooking utensil of parallel bars on which food is exposed to heat (as from charcoal or electricity) **2 :** food that is broiled usu. on a grill — compare MIXED GRILL **3 :** a usu. informal restaurant or dining room

gril·lage \'gril-ij\ *n* [F, fr. *griller* to supply with grillwork, fr. *gril*] (1776) **1 :** a framework of timber or steel for support in marshy or treacherous soil **2 :** a framework for supporting a load (as a column)

grille *or* **grill** \'gril\ *n* [F *grille,* alter. of OF *greille,* fr. L *craticula,* dim. of *cratis* wickerwork — more at HURDLE] (1686) **1 :** a grating forming a barrier or screen; *specif* **:** an ornamental one at the front end of an automobile **2 :** an opening covered with a grille

grill·room \'gril-ˌrüm, -ˌru̇m\ *n* (1883) **:** GRILL 3

grill·work \'gril-ˌwərk\ *n* (1896) **:** work constituting or resembling a grille

grilse \'grils\ *n, pl* **grilse** [ME *grills*] (15c) **:** a young mature Atlantic salmon returning to its native river to spawn for the first time after one winter at sea; *broadly* **:** any of various salmon at such a stage of development

grim \'grim\ *adj* **grim·mer; grim·mest** [ME, fr. OE *grimm;* akin to OHG *grimm* fierce, Gk *chromados* action of gnashing] (bef. 12c) **1 :** fierce in disposition or action **:** SAVAGE **2 a :** stern or forbidding in action or appearance ⟨a ~ taskmaster⟩ **b :** SOMBER, GLOOMY **3 :** UNFLINCHING, UNYIELDING ⟨~ determination⟩ **4 :** ghastly, repellent, or sinister in character ⟨a ~ tale⟩ — **grim·ly** *adv* — **grim·ness** *n*

gri·mace \'grim-əs, grim-'ās\ *n* [F, fr. MF, alter. of *grimache,* of Gmc origin; akin to OE *grima* mask] (1651) **:** a facial expression usu. of disgust or disapproval — **grimace** *vi* — **gri·mac·er** *n*

gri·mal·kin \grim-'ō(l)-kən, -'al-\ *n* [*gray* + *malkin*] (1630) **:** CAT 1a; *esp* **:** an old female cat

grime \'grīm\ *n* [Flem *grijm,* fr. MD *grime* soot, mask; akin to OE *grīma* mask, Gk *chriein* to anoint — more at CHRISM] (14c) **:** soot, smut, or dirt adhering to or embedded in a surface; *broadly* **:** accumulated dirtiness and disorder ⟨the ~ of the slums⟩ — **grime** *vt*

Grimm's law \'grimz-\ *n* [Jacob *Grimm*] (1841) **:** a statement in historical linguistics: Proto-Indo-European voiceless stops became Proto-Germanic voiceless fricatives (as in Greek *pyr, treis, kardia* compared with English *fire, three, heart*), Proto-Indo-European voiced stops became Proto-Germanic voiceless stops (as in Latin *duo, genus* compared with English *two, kin*), and Proto-Indo-European voiced aspirated stops became Proto-Germanic voiced fricatives (as in Sanskrit *nābhi, madhya* "mid" compared with English *navel,* Old Norse *mithr* "mid")

grim reaper *n, often cap G&R* (ca. 1927) **:** death esp. when personified as a man or skeleton with a scythe

grimy \'grī-mē\ *adj* **grim·i·er; -est** (1612) **:** full of or covered with grime **:** DIRTY — **grim·i·ness** *n*

grin \'grin\ *vi* **grinned; grin·ning** [ME *grennen,* fr. OE *grennian;* akin to OHG *grennen* to snarl] (bef. 12c) **:** to draw back the lips so as to show the teeth esp. in amusement or laughter; *broadly* **:** SMILE — **grin** *n* — **grin·ner** *n* — **grin·ning·ly** \'grin-iŋ-lē\ *adv*

1**grind** \'grīnd\ *vb* **ground** \'grau̇nd\; **grind·ing** [ME *grinden,* fr. OE *grindan;* akin to L *frendere* to crush, grind, Gk *chondros* grain, OE *grēot* grit] *vt* (bef. 12c) **1 :** to reduce to powder or small fragments by friction (as in a mill or with the teeth) **2 :** to wear down, polish, or sharpen by friction **:** WHET ⟨~ an ax⟩ **3 a :** to rub or press harshly ⟨*ground* the cigarette out with his heel⟩ **b :** to press together with a rotating motion ⟨~ the teeth⟩ **4 a :** OPPRESS, HARASS **b :** to weaken or destroy gradually — used with *down* ⟨poverty *ground* his spirit down⟩ **5 :** to operate or produce by turning a crank ⟨~ a hand organ⟩ ~ *vi* **1 :** to perform the operation of grinding **2 :** to become pulverized, polished, or sharpened by friction **3 :** to move with difficulty or friction esp. so as to make a grating noise ⟨~*ing* gears⟩ **4 :** DRUDGE; *esp* **:** to study hard ⟨~ for an exam⟩ **5 :** to rotate the hips in an erotic manner (as in a burlesque striptease) — **grind·ing·ly** \'grīn-diŋ-lē\ *adv*

2**grind** *n* (13c) **1 a :** an act of grinding **b :** the sound of grinding **2 a :** dreary monotonous labor or routine; *esp* **:** intensive study **b :** one who works or studies excessively **3 :** the result of grinding; *esp* **:** material obtained by grinding to a particular degree of fineness ⟨a percolator ~ of coffee⟩ **4 :** the act of rotating the hips in an erotic manner ***syn*** see WORK

grind·er \'grīn-dər\ *n* (14c) **1 a :** MOLAR **b** *pl* **:** TEETH **2 :** one that grinds **3 :** a machine or device for grinding **4 :** SUBMARINE 2

grind out *vt* (ca. 1947) **:** to produce in a mechanical way ⟨*grind out* hits⟩

grind·stone \'grīn-ˌstōn\ *n* (13c) **1 :** MILLSTONE 1 **2 :** a flat circular stone of natural sandstone that revolves on an axle and is used for grinding, shaping, or smoothing

grin·go \'griŋ-(ˌ)gō\ *n, pl* **gringos** [Sp, alter. of *griego* Greek, stranger, fr. L *Graecus* Greek] (1849) **:** a foreigner in Spain or Latin America esp. when of English or American origin — often used disparagingly

gri·ot \'grē-ˌō\ *n* [F] (ca. 1923) **:** any of a class of musician-entertainers of West Africa whose performances include tribal histories and genealogies

1**grip** \'grip\ *vt* **gripped; grip·ping** [ME *grippen,* fr. OE *grippan;* akin to OE *gripan*] (bef. 12c) **1 :** to seize or hold firmly **2 :** to hold strongly the interest of ⟨a story that ~*s* the reader⟩ — **grip·per** *n* — **grip·ping·ly** \'grip-iŋ-lē\ *adv*

2**grip** *n* (bef. 12c) **1 a :** a strong or tenacious grasp **b :** strength in gripping **c :** manner or style of gripping **2 a :** a firm tenacious hold typically giving control, mastery, or understanding ⟨could not free himself from the ~ of these new ideas⟩ **b :** mental grasp **:** APPREHENSION **3 :** a part or device for gripping **4 :** a part by which something is grasped; *esp* **:** HANDLE **5 :** TRAVELING BAG **6 :** STAGEHAND

1**gripe** \'grīp\ *vb* **griped; grip·ing** [ME *gripen,* fr. OE *grīpan;* akin to OHG *grīfan* to grasp, Lith *griebti*] *vt* (bef. 12c) **1 :** SEIZE, GRASP **2 a :** AFFLICT, DISTRESS **b :** IRRITATE, VEX ⟨*griped* by new income-tax provisions⟩ **3 :** to cause pinching and spasmodic pain in the bowels of ~ *vi* **1 :** to experience gripes **2 :** to complain with grumbling — **grip·er** *n*

2**gripe** *n* (13c) **1 :** CLUTCH, GRASP; *broadly* **:** CONTROL, MASTERY **2 :** GRIEVANCE, COMPLAINT **3 :** a pinching spasmodic intestinal pain — usu. used in pl. **4 :** HANDLE, GRIP **5 :** a device (as a brake) for grasping or holding

grippe \'grip\ *n* [F, lit., seizure] (1776) **:** an acute febrile contagious virus disease identical with or resembling influenza — **grippy** \'grip-ē\ *adj*

grip·sack \'grip-ˌsak\ *n* (1877) **:** TRAVELING BAG

gri·saille \gri-'zī, -'zā(ə)l\ *n* [F, fr. *gris* gray, fr. MF — more at GRIZZLE] (1848) **:** decoration in tones of a single color and esp. gray designed to produce a three-dimensional effect

Gri·sel·da \griz-'el-də\ *n* [ME, fr. It] **:** a woman of humble origins in medieval legend who endures tests of wifely patience laid on her by her wellborn husband

gris·eo·ful·vin \ˌgriz-ē-ō-'fu̇l-vən, ˌgris-, -'fəl-\ *n* [NL *griseofulvum,* specific epithet of *Penicillium griseofulvum,* mold from which it is obtained] (1939) **:** an antibiotic $C_{17}H_{17}ClO_6$ used systemically in treating superficial infections by fungi

gri·sette \gri-'zet\ *n* [F, grisette, cheap unbleached cloth, fr. *gris*] (1723) **1 :** a young French working-class woman **2 :** a young woman combining part-time prostitution with some other occupation

gris–gris \'grē-(ˌ)grē\ *n, pl* **gris–gris** \-(ˌ)grēz\ [F, of African origin; akin to Balante *grigri* amulet] (1698) **:** an amulet or incantation used chiefly by people of African Negro ancestry

gris·ly \'griz-lē\ *adj* **gris·li·er; -est** [ME, fr. OE *grislic,* fr. *gris-* (akin to OE *āgrīsan* to fear); akin to OHG *grīsenlīh* terrible] (bef. 12c) **1 :** inspiring horror or intense fear **:** FORBIDDING ⟨houses that were dark and ~ under the blank, cold sky —D. H. Lawrence⟩ **2 :** inspiring disgust or distaste ⟨a ~ account of the fire⟩ ***syn*** see GHASTLY — **gris·li·ness** *n*

grist \'grist\ *n* [ME, fr. OE *grīst;* akin to OE *grindan* to grind] (bef. 12c) **1 a :** grain or a batch of grain for grinding **b :** the product obtained from a grist of grain including the flour or meal and the grain offals **2 :** a required or usual amount **3 :** matter of interest or value forming the basis of a story or analysis **4 :** something turned to advantage — used esp. in the phrase *grist for one's mill*

gris·tle \'gris-əl\ *n* [ME *gristil,* fr. OE *gristle;* akin to MLG *gristel* gristle] (bef. 12c) **:** CARTILAGE; *broadly* **:** tough cartilaginous, tendinous, or fibrous matter esp. in table meats

gris·tly \'gris-(ə-)lē\ *adj* **gris·tli·er; -est** (14c) **:** consisting of or containing gristle ⟨~ steak⟩ — **gris·tli·ness** *n*

grist·mill \'grist-ˌmil\ *n* (1602) **:** a mill for grinding grain

\ə\ abut \ᵊ\ kitten, F table \ər\ further \a\ ash \ā\ ace \ä\ cot, cart \au̇\ out \ch\ chin \e\ bet \ē\ easy \g\ go \i\ hit \ī\ ice \j\ job \ŋ\ sing \ō\ go \ȯ\ law \ȯi\ boy \th\ thin \t͟h\ the \ü\ loot \u̇\ foot \y\ yet \zh\ vision \á, k̲, ⁿ, œ, œ̄, ue, ue̅, ʸ\ *see* Guide to Pronunciation

1grit \ˈgrit\ *n* [ME *grete,* fr. OE *grēot;* akin to OHG *grioz* sand, L *furfur* bran, Gk *chrōs* skin] (bef. 12c) **1 a** *obs* : SAND, GRAVEL **b** : a hard sharp granule (as of sand); *also* : material (as many abrasives) composed of such granules **2** : any of several sandstones **3** : the structure of a stone that adapts it to grinding **4** : firmness of mind or spirit : unyielding courage in the face of hardship or danger

2grit *vb* **grit·ted; grit·ting** *vi* (1762) : to give forth a grating sound ~ *vt* **1** : to cover or spread with grit; *esp* : to smooth (as marble) by means of a coarse abrasive **2** : to cause (as one's teeth) to grind or grate

grith \ˈgrith\ *n* [ME, fr. OE, fr. ON, security] (bef. 12c) : peace, security, or sanctuary imposed or guaranteed in early medieval England under various special conditions

grits \ˈgrits\ *n pl but sing or pl in constr* [ME *gryt,* fr. OE *grytt;* akin to OE *grēot*] (bef. 12c) : ground hominy with the germ removed

grit·ty \ˈgrit-ē\ *adj* **grit·ti·er; -est** (1598) **1** : containing or resembling grit **2** : courageously persistent : PLUCKY — **grit·ti·ly** \ˈgrit-ᵊl-ē\ *adv* — **grit·ti·ness** \ˈgrit-ē-nəs\ *n*

1griz·zle \ˈgriz-əl\ *n* [ME *grisel,* adj., gray, fr. MF, fr. *gris,* of Gmc origin; akin to OHG *grīs* gray] (1601) **1** *archaic* : gray hair **2 a** : a roan coat pattern or color **b** : a gray or roan animal

2grizzle *vb* **griz·zled; griz·zling** \ˈgriz-(ə-)liŋ\ *vt* (1740) : to make grayish ~ *vi* : to become grayish

griz·zled \ˈgriz-əld\ *adj* (15c) : sprinkled or streaked with gray : GRAYING ⟨a ~ beard⟩

1griz·zly \ˈgriz-lē\ *adj* **griz·zli·er; -est** (1594) : GRIZZLED

2grizzly *var of* GRISLY

grizzly bear *n* (1791) : a very large powerful brown bear (*Ursus horribilis*) of the uplands of western No. America — called also *grizzly*

groan \ˈgrōn\ *vb* [ME *gronen,* fr. OE *grānian;* akin to OHG *grīnan* to growl] *vi* (bef. 12c) **1** : to utter a deep moan indicative of pain, grief, or annoyance **2** : to make a harsh sound (as of creaking) under sudden or prolonged strain ~ *vt* : to utter or express with groaning — **groan** *n* — **groan·er** *n*

1groat \ˈgrōt\ *n* [ME *grotes,* pl., fr. OE *grotan,* pl. of *grot;* akin to OE *grēot* grit] (bef. 12c) **1** *usu pl but sing or pl in constr* : hulled grain broken into fragments larger than grits **2** : a grain (as of oats) exclusive of the hull

2groat *n* [ME *groot,* fr. MD] (14c) : an old British coin worth four pennies

gro·cer \ˈgrō-sər\ *n* [ME, fr. MF *grossier* wholesaler, fr. *gros* coarse, wholesale — more at GROSS] (15c) : a dealer in staple foodstuffs, meats, produce, and dairy products and usu. household supplies

grocer's itch *n* (1799) : an itching dermatitis that results from prolonged contact with some mites (esp. family Acaridae), their products, or materials (as feeds) infested with them

gro·cery \ˈgrōs-(ə-)rē\ *n, pl* **-cer·ies** (15c) **1** *pl* : commodities sold by a grocer — usu. sing. in Brit. usage **2** : a grocer's store

grog \ˈgräg\ *n* [*Old Grog,* nickname of Edward Vernon †1757 Eng. admiral responsible for diluting the sailors' rum] (1770) **1** : alcoholic liquor; *specif* : liquor (as rum) cut with water and now often served hot with lemon juice and sugar sometimes added **2** : refractory materials (as crushed pottery and firebricks) used in the manufacture of refractory products (as crucibles) to reduce shrinkage in drying and firing

grog·gy \ˈgräg-ē\ *adj* **grog·gi·er; -est** [*grog*] (1832) : weak and unsteady on the feet or in action — **grog·gi·ly** \ˈgräg-ə-lē\ *adv* — **grog·gi·ness** \ˈgräg-ē-nəs\ *n*

gro·gram \ˈgräg-rəm, ˈgrōg-\ *n* [MF *gros grain* coarse texture] (1562) : a coarse loosely woven fabric of silk, silk and mohair, or silk and wool — compare GROSGRAIN

grog·shop \ˈgräg-ˌshäp\ *n, chiefly Brit* (1790) : a usu. low-class barroom

1groin \ˈgrȯin\ *n* [alter. of ME *grynde,* fr. OE, abyss; akin to OE *grund* ground] (15c) **1** : the fold or depression marking the juncture of the lower abdomen and the inner part of the thigh; *also* : the region of this line **2 a** : the projecting curved line along which two intersecting vaults meet **b** : a rib that covers this edge **3** : a rigid structure built out from a shore to protect the shore from erosion, to trap sand, or to direct a current for scouring a channel

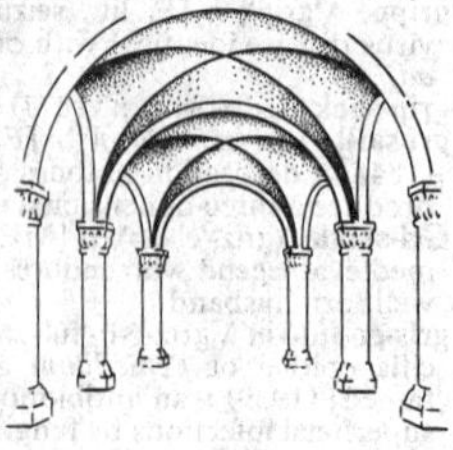
groin 2a

2groin *vt* (1812) : to build or equip with groins

grom·met \ˈgräm-ət, ˈgrəm-\ *n* [perh. fr. obs. F *gormette* curb of a bridle] (1626) **1** : a flexible loop that serves as a fastening, support, or reinforcement **2** : an eyelet of firm material to strengthen or protect an opening or to insulate or protect something passed through it

grom·well \ˈgräm-ˌwel, -wəl\ *n* [ME *gromil,* fr. MF] (14c) : any of a genus (*Lithospermum*) of plants of the borage family having polished white stony nutlets

1groom \ˈgrüm, ˈgru̇m\ *n* [ME *grom*] (14c) **1** *archaic* : MAN, FELLOW **2 a** (1) *archaic* : MANSERVANT (2) : one of several officers of the English royal household **b** : a person responsible for the feeding, exercising, and stabling of horses **3** : BRIDEGROOM

2groom *vt* (1809) **1** : to clean and condition (as a horse or dog) **2** : to make neat or attractive ⟨an impeccably ~*ed* woman⟩ **3** : to get into readiness for a specific objective : PREPARE ⟨was being ~*ed* as a presidential candidate⟩ ~ *vi* : to groom oneself

groom·er \ˈgrü-mər\ *n* (ca. 1884) : one who grooms (as dogs)

grooms·man \ˈgrümz-mən, ˈgru̇mz-\ *n* (1698) : a male friend who attends a bridegroom at his wedding

1groove \ˈgrüv\ *n* [ME *groof;* akin to OE *grafan* to dig — more at GRAVE] (1659) **1** : a long narrow channel or depression **2 a** : a fixed routine : RUT **b** : a situation suited to one's abilities or interests : NICHE **3** : top form ⟨a great talker when he is in the ~⟩ **4** : the line or course to follow for best results ⟨his every pitch was right in the ~⟩ **5** : an enjoyable or exciting experience

2groove *vb* **grooved; groov·ing** *vt* (1686) **1 a** : to make a groove in **b** : to join by a groove **2 a** : to enjoy appreciatively ⟨~*s* exciting experiences⟩ **b** : to excite pleasurably ⟨*grooving* their minds with cannabis —Stephen Nemo⟩ ~ *vi* **1** : to become joined or fitted by a groove **2** : to form a groove **3** : to enjoy oneself intensely **4** : to interact harmoniously ⟨contemporary minds and rock ~ together — Benjamin DeMott⟩ — **groov·er** *n*

groovy \ˈgrü-vē\ *adj* **groov·i·er; -est** (ca. 1937) : MARVELOUS, WONDERFUL, EXCELLENT ⟨felt that this poetry was interesting, enjoyable, not to mention ~ —R. M. Muccigrosso⟩

grope \ˈgrōp\ *vb* **groped; grop·ing** [ME *gropen,* fr. OE *grāpian;* akin to OE *grīpan* to seize] *vi* (bef. 12c) **1** : to feel about blindly or uncertainly in search ⟨*groped* for the light switch⟩ **2** : to look for something blindly or uncertainly ⟨*groping* for the right words⟩ **3** : to feel one's way ~ *vt* **1** : FEEL UP **2** : to find (as one's way) by groping — **grope** *n* — **grop·er** *n*

gros·beak \ˈgrōs-ˌbēk\ *n* [part trans. of F *grosbec,* fr. *gros* thick + *bec* beak] (ca. 1678) : any of several finches of Europe or America having large stout conical bills

gro·schen \ˈgrō-shən, ˈgrȯ-\ *n, pl* **groschen** [G] (1946) — see *schilling* at MONEY table

gros·grain \ˈgrō-ˌgrān\ *n* [F *gros grain* coarse texture] (1869) : a strong close-woven corded fabric usu. of silk or rayon and often with cotton filler — compare GROGRAM

1gross \ˈgrōs\ *adj* [ME, fr. MF *gros* thick, coarse, fr. L *grossus*] (14c) **1 a** *archaic* : immediately obvious **b** (1) : glaringly noticeable usu. because of inexcusable badness or objectionableness ⟨~ error⟩ (2) : OUT-AND-OUT, UTTER ⟨~ injustice⟩ **c** : visible without the aid of a microscope **2 a** : BIG, BULKY; *esp* : excessively fat **b** : growing or spreading with excessive luxuriance **3 a** : of, relating to, or dealing with general aspects or broad distinctions **b** : consisting of an overall total exclusive of deductions ⟨~ income⟩ — compare NET **4** : made up of material or perceptible elements **5** *archaic* : not fastidious in taste : UNDISCRIMINATING **6** : deficient in knowledge : IGNORANT, UNTUTORED **7 a** : coarse in nature or behavior : UNREFINED **b** : gravely deficient in civility or decency : crudely vulgar ⟨merely ~, a scatological rather than a pornographic impropriety —Aldous Huxley⟩ ***syn*** see COARSE, FLAGRANT — **gross·ly** *adv* — **gross·ness** *n*

2gross *n* (1579) **1** *obs* : AMOUNT, SUM **2** : an overall total exclusive of deductions

3gross *vt* (1884) : to earn or bring in (an overall total) exclusive of deductions (as for taxes or expenses) — **gross·er** *n*

4gross *n, pl* **gross** [ME *groce,* fr. MF *grosse,* fr. fem. of *gros*] (14c) : an aggregate of 12 dozen things ⟨~ of pencils⟩

gross anatomy *n* (1888) : a branch of anatomy that deals with the macroscopic structure of tissues and organs

gross national product *n* (1947) : the total value of the goods and services produced by the residents of a nation during a specified period (as a year)

gross out *vt* (1968) : to offend or insult by something gross — **gross–out** *n*

gros·su·lar \ˈgräs(h)-ə-lər, ˈgräs-yə-\ *n* [NL *Grossularia,* genus name of the gooseberry] (1819) : GROSSULARITE

gros·su·la·rite \-lə-ˌrīt\ *n* [G *grossularit,* fr. NL *Grossularia*] (ca. 1847) : a colorless or green, yellow, brown, or red garnet $Ca_3Al_2(SiO_4)_3$

gro·szy \ˈgrȯ-shē\ *also* **grosz** *or* **grosze** \ˈgrȯsh\ *n, pl* **groszy** [Pol] (1949) — see *zloty* at MONEY table

grot \ˈgrät\ *n* [MF *grotte,* fr. It *grotta*] (1506) : GROTTO

1gro·tesque \grō-ˈtesk\ *n* [MF & OIt; MF, fr. OIt (*pittura*) *grottesca,* lit., cave painting, fem. of *grottesco* of a cave, fr. *grotta* grotto] (1561) **1 a** : a style of decorative art characterized by fanciful or fantastic human and animal forms often interwoven with foliage or similar figures that may distort the natural into absurdity, ugliness, or caricature **b** : a piece of work in this style **2** : one that is grotesque **3** : SANS SERIF

2grotesque *adj* (1603) : of, relating to, or having the characteristics of the grotesque: as **a** : FANCIFUL, BIZARRE **b** : absurdly incongruous **c** : departing markedly from the natural, the expected, or the typical ***syn*** see FANTASTIC — **gro·tesque·ly** *adv* — **gro·tesque·ness** *n*

gro·tes·que·rie *also* **gro·tes·que·ry** \grō-ˈtes-kə-rē\ *n, pl* **-ries** [*grotesque* + F *-erie* -ery] (1654) **1** : something that is grotesque **2** : the quality or state of being grotesque : GROTESQUENESS

grot·to \ˈgrät-(ˌ)ō\ *n, pl* **grottoes** *also* **grottos** [It *grotta, grotto,* fr. L *crypta* cavern, crypt] (1617) **1** : CAVE **2** : an artificial recess or structure made to resemble a natural cave

grouch \ˈgrau̇ch\ *n* [prob. alter. of *grutch* (grudge)] (1895) **1 a** : a fit of bad temper **b** : GRUDGE, COMPLAINT ⟨never nursed a ~ five minutes —W. A. White⟩ **2** : a habitually irritable or complaining person : GRUMBLER — **grouch** *vi*

grouchy \ˈgrau̇-chē\ *adj* **grouch·i·er; -est** (1895) : given to grumbling : PEEVISH — **grouch·i·ly** \-chə-lē\ *adv* — **grouch·i·ness** \-chē-nəs\ *n*

1ground \ˈgrau̇nd\ *n* [ME, fr. OE *grund;* akin to OHG *grunt* ground, Gk *chrainein* to touch slightly] (bef. 12c) **1 a** : the bottom of a body of water **b** *pl* (1) : SEDIMENT **1** (2) : ground coffee beans after brewing **2 a** : a basis for belief, action, or argument ⟨~ for complaint⟩ — often used in pl. **b** (1) : a fundamental logical condition (2) : a basic metaphysical cause **3 a** : a surrounding area : BACKGROUND **b** : material that serves as a substratum **4 a** : the surface of the earth **b** : an area used for a particular purpose ⟨parade ~⟩ ⟨fishing ~*s*⟩ **c** *pl* : the area around and belonging to a house or other building **d** : an area to be won or defended in or as if in battle **e** : an area of knowledge or special interest ⟨covered a lot of ~ in his lecture⟩ **5 a** : SOIL, EARTH **b** : a special soil **c** : rock or formation through which mine workings are driven **6 a** : an object that makes an electrical connection with the earth **b** : a large conducting body (as the earth) used as a common return for an electric circuit and as an arbitrary zero of potential **c** : electric connection with a ground **7** : a football offense utilizing primarily running plays — **from the ground up 1** : entirely new or afresh **2** : from top to bottom : THOROUGHLY — **into the ground** : beyond what is necessary or tolerable : to exhaustion ⟨labored an issue *into the ground* —*Newsweek*⟩ — **off the ground** : in or as if in flight : UNDER WAY ⟨the program never got *off the ground*⟩

2ground *vt* (14c) **1** : to bring to or place on the ground **2 a** : to provide a reason or justification for ⟨our fears about technological change may be well ~*ed* —L. K. Williams⟩ **b** : to instruct in fundamentals **3** : to connect electrically with a ground **4** : to restrict to the ground ⟨~ a pilot⟩ **5** : to throw (a football) intentionally to the ground to avoid being tackled for a loss ~ *vi* **1** : to have a ground or basis : RELY **2** : to run aground **3** : to hit a grounder

[3]**ground** *past and past part of* GRIND
ground ball *n* (1942) **:** a batted baseball that bounds or rolls along the ground
ground bass *n* (1699) **:** a short bass passage continually repeated below constantly changing melody and harmony
ground–cher·ry \ˈgrau̇n(d)-ˌcher-ē\ *n* (ca. 1839) **:** a plant (genus *Physalis*) of the nightshade family with pulpy fruits in papery husks; *also* **:** the fruit of this plant
ground cloth *n* (1931) **:** a waterproof sheet placed on the ground for protection (as of a sleeping bag) against soil moisture
ground cover *n* (1900) **1 :** the small plants in a forest except young trees **2 a :** a planting of low plants (as ivy) that covers the ground in place of turf **b :** a plant adapted for use as ground cover
ground crew *n* (1934) **:** the mechanics and technicians who maintain and service an airplane
ground–effect machine *n* [fr. the support provided by the cushion of air as if the vehicle rode on the ground] (ca. 1966) **:** a vehicle for traveling short distances that is supported above the surface of land or water by a cushion of air produced by downwardly directed fans
ground·er \ˈgrau̇n-dər\ *n* (ca. 1867) **:** GROUND BALL
ground·fish \ˈgrau̇n(d)-ˌfish\ *n* (1856) **:** a bottom fish; *esp* **:** any of the commercially important fishes (as cod, haddock, pollack, flounder) that live on the sea bottom
ground floor *n* (1601) **:** the floor of a house most nearly on a level with the ground — compare FIRST FLOOR
ground glass *n* (1848) **:** glass with a light-diffusing surface produced by etching or abrading
ground·hog \ˈgrau̇nd-ˌhȯg, -ˌhäg\ *n* (1784) **:** WOODCHUCK
Groundhog Day *n* [fr. the legend that the groundhog comes out and is frightened back into hibernation if he sees his shadow] (1871) **:** February 2 that traditionally indicates six more weeks of winter if sunny or an early spring if cloudy
ground·ing \ˈgrau̇n-diŋ\ *n* (1644) **:** training or instruction in the fundamentals of a field of knowledge
ground ivy *n* (15c) **:** a trailing mint (*Nepeta hederacea*) with rounded leaves and blue-purple flowers
ground·less \ˈgrau̇n-(d)ləs\ *adj* (1620) **:** having no ground or foundation ⟨~ fears⟩ — **ground·less·ly** *adv* — **ground·less·ness** *n*
ground·ling \ˈgrau̇n-(d)liŋ\ *n* (1602) **1 a :** a spectator who stood in the pit of an Elizabethan theater **b :** a person of unsophisticated taste **2 :** one that lives or works on or near the ground
ground loop *n* (1928) **:** a sharp uncontrollable turn made by an airplane on the ground in landing, taking off, or taxiing
ground·mass \ˈgrau̇n(d)-ˌmas\ *n* (1879) **:** the fine-grained or glassy base of a porphyry in which the larger distinct crystals are embedded
ground meristem *n* (1938) **:** the part of a primary apical meristem remaining after differentiation of dermatogen and procambium
ground·nut \ˈgrau̇n(d)-ˌnət\ *n* (1602) **1 a :** any of several plants having edible tuberous roots; *esp* **:** a No. American leguminous vine (*Apios tuberosa*) with pinnate leaves and clusters of brownish purple fragrant flowers **b :** the root of a groundnut **2** *chiefly Brit* **:** PEANUT
ground·out \ˈgrau̇n-ˌdau̇t\ *n* [*grounder*] (1965) **:** a play in baseball in which a batter is put out after hitting a grounder to an infielder
ground pine *n* (1551) **1 :** a European bugle (*Ajuga chamaepitys*) with a resinous odor **2 :** any of several club mosses (esp. *Lycopodium clavatum* and *L. complanatum*) with long creeping stems and erect branches
ground plan *n* (1731) **1 :** a plan of a floor of a building as distinguished from an elevation **2 :** a first or basic plan
ground rent *n* (1667) **:** the rent paid by a lessee for the use of land esp. for building
ground rule *n* (1890) **1 :** a sports rule adopted to modify play on a particular field, court, or course **2 :** a rule of procedure ⟨*ground rules* for selecting a superintendent —*Amer. School Board Jour.*⟩
[1]**ground·sel** \ˈgrau̇n(d)-səl\ *n* [ME *groundeswele,* fr. OE *grundeswelge,* fr. *grund* ground + *swelgan* to swallow — more at SWALLOW] (bef. 12c) **:** any of a large genus (*Senecio*) of composite plants with mostly yellow flower heads
[2]**groundsel** *n* [ME *ground sille,* fr. *ground* + *sille* sill] (15c) **:** a foundation timber
ground·sheet \ˈgrau̇n(d)-ˌshēt\ *n* (1907) **:** GROUND CLOTH
ground speed *n* (1917) **:** the speed (as of an airplane) with relation to the ground — compare AIRSPEED
ground squirrel *n* (1688) **:** any of various burrowing rodents (as of the genus *Citellus*) that are related to the squirrels and that live in colonies esp. in open areas, often damage crops, and include vectors of plague — called also *spermophile*
ground state *n* (1926) **:** the energy level (as of a system of interacting elementary particles, an atomic nucleus, or an atom) having the least energy of all the possible states — called also *ground level*
ground stroke *n* (1895) **:** a stroke made (as in tennis) by hitting a ball that has rebounded from the ground — compare VOLLEY
ground substance *n* (1882) **:** a more or less homogeneous matrix that forms the background in which the specific differentiated elements of a system are suspended: **a :** the intercellular substance of tissues **b :** HYALOPLASM
ground swell *n* (1818) **1 :** a broad deep undulation of the ocean caused by an often distant gale or seismic disturbance **2 :** a rapid spontaneous growth (as of political opinion) ⟨public *ground swell* of support⟩
ground·wa·ter \ˈgrau̇n-ˌdwȯt-ər, -ˌdwät-\ *n* (1890) **:** water within the earth that supplies wells and springs; *specif* **:** water in the part of the ground that is wholly saturated
ground wave *n* (1925) **:** a radio wave that is propagated along the surface of the earth
ground·wood \ˈgrau̇n-ˌdwu̇d\ *n* [[3]*ground*] (1917) **:** wood ground up and used to make pulp for paper
ground·work \ˈgrau̇n-ˌdwərk\ *n* (15c) **:** FOUNDATION, BASIS ⟨a plan that provides the ~ for a bold new program⟩
ground zero *n* (1946) **:** the point directly above, below, or at which a nuclear explosion occurs
[1]**group** \ˈgrüp\ *n, often attrib* [F *groupe,* fr. It *gruppo,* of Gmc origin; akin to OHG *kropf* craw — more at CROP] (1686) **1 :** two or more figures forming a complete unit in a composition **2 a :** a number of individuals assembled together or having some unifying relationship **b :** an assemblage of objects regarded as a unit **c** (1) **:** a military unit consisting of a headquarters and attached battalions (2) **:** a unit of the U.S. Air Force higher than a squadron and lower than a wing **3 a :** an assemblage of related organisms — often used to avoid taxonomic connotations when the kind or degree of relationship is not clearly defined **b** (1) **:** two or more atoms joined together or sometimes a single atom forming part of a molecule; *esp* **:** FUNCTIONAL GROUP ⟨a methyl ~⟩ (2) **:** an assemblage of elements forming one of the vertical columns of the periodic table **c :** a stratigraphic division comprising rocks deposited during an era **4 :** a mathematical set that is closed under a binary associative operation, contains an identity element, and has an inverse for every element
[2]**group** *vt* (1718) **1 :** to combine in a group **2 :** to assign to a group **:** CLASSIFY ~ *vi* **1 :** to form a group **2 :** to belong to a group **3 :** to make groups of closely spaced hits on a target ⟨the gun ~*ed* beautifully —R. C. Ruark⟩ — **group·able** \ˈgrü-pə-bəl\ *adj*
group captain *n* (1919) **:** a commissioned officer in the British air force who ranks with a colonel in the army
group dynamics *n pl but sing or pl in constr* (1939) **:** the interacting forces within a small human group; *also* **:** the sociological study of these forces
grou·per \ˈgrü-pər\ *n, pl* **groupers** *also* **grouper** [Pg *garoupa*] (1671) **1 :** any of numerous fishes (family Serranidae and esp. genera *Epinephelus* and *Mycteroperca*) that are typically large solitary bottom fishes of warm seas **2 :** any of several rockfishes (family Scorpaenidae)
group·ie \ˈgrü-pē\ *n* (1967) **1 :** a fan of a rock group who usu. follows the group around on concert tours **2 :** an admirer of a celebrity who attends as many of his or her public appearances as possible
group·ing \ˈgrü-piŋ\ *n* (1748) **1 :** the act or process of combining in groups **2 :** a set of objects combined in a group ⟨a furniture ~⟩
group practice *n* (1942) **:** medicine practiced by a group of associated physicians or dentists (as specialists in different fields) working as partners or as partners and employees
group theory *n* (1898) **:** a branch of mathematics concerned with finding all mathematical groups and determining their properties
group therapy *n* (1943) **:** therapy in the presence of a therapist in which several patients discuss and share their personal problems — called also *group psychotherapy* — **group therapist** *n*
group·think \ˈgrüp-ˌthiŋk\ *n* [[1]*group* + *-think* (as in *doublethink*)] (1952) **:** conformity to group values and ethics
[1]**grouse** \ˈgrau̇s\ *n, pl* **grouse** *or* **grouses** [origin unknown] (1531) **:** any of numerous birds (family Tetraonidae) that have a plump body, strong feathered legs, and plumage less brilliant than that of pheasants usu. with reddish brown or other protective color and that include many important game birds
[2]**grouse** *vi* **groused; grous·ing** [origin unknown] (1887) **:** COMPLAIN, GRUMBLE — **grous·er** *n*
[3]**grouse** *n* (1918) **:** COMPLAINT
[1]**grout** \ˈgrau̇t\ *n* [ME, coarse meal, fr. OE *grūt;* akin to OE *grytt* grit] (bef. 12c) **1 :** LEES **2 a :** thin mortar used for filling spaces (as the joints in masonry); *also* **:** any of various other materials (as a mixture of cement and water or chemicals that solidify) used for a similar purpose **b :** PLASTER
[2]**grout** *vt* (1838) **1 :** to fill up or finish with grout **2 :** to fix in place by means of grout ⟨~ a bolt into a wall⟩ — **grout·er** *n*
grove \ˈgrōv\ *n* [ME, fr. OE *grāf*] (bef. 12c) **1 :** a small wood without underbrush ⟨a picnic ~⟩ **2 :** a planting of fruit or nut trees
grov·el \ˈgräv-əl, ˈgrəv-\ *vi* **-eled** *or* **-elled; -el·ing** *or* **-el·ling** \-(ə-)liŋ\ [back-formation fr. *groveling* prone, fr. *groveling,* adv., fr. ME, fr. *gruf,* adv., on the face (fr. ON *ā grūfu*) + *-ling;* akin to OE *crēopan* to creep] (1593) **1 :** to creep with the face to the ground **:** CRAWL **2 a :** to lie or creep with the body prostrate in token of subservience or abasement **b :** to abase oneself **3 :** to give oneself over to what is base or unworthy **:** WALLOW ⟨~*ing* in sentimentality —James Stern⟩ — **grov·el·er** \-(ə-)lər\ *n* — **grov·el·ing·ly** \-(ə-)liŋ-lē\ *adv*
groves of academe [*the olive grove of Academe,* phrase applied to Plato's Academy in John Milton's *Paradise Regained*] (1849) **:** the academic world
grow \ˈgrō\ *vb* **grew** \ˈgrü\; **grown** \ˈgrōn\; **grow·ing** [ME *growen,* fr. OE *grōwan;* akin to OHG *gruowan* to grow] *vi* (bef. 12c) **1 a :** to spring up and develop to maturity **b :** to be able to grow in some place or situation ⟨trees that ~ only in the tropics⟩ **c :** to assume some relation through or as if through a process of natural growth ⟨ferns ~*ing* from the rocks⟩ **2 a :** to increase in size by addition of material either by assimilation into the living organism or by accretion in a nonbiological process (as crystallization) **b :** INCREASE, EXPAND ⟨~*s* in wisdom⟩ **3 :** to develop from a parent source ⟨the book *grew* out of a series of lectures⟩ **4 a :** to pass into a condition **:** BECOME ⟨*grew* pale⟩ **b :** to have an increasing influence ⟨habit ~*s* on a person⟩ **c :** to become increasingly acceptable or attractive ⟨didn't like it at first, but it *grew* on him⟩ ~ *vt* **1 :** to cause to grow **:** PRODUCE ⟨~ wheat⟩ **2 :** DEVELOP 5 — **grow·er** \ˈgrō(-ə)r\ *n* — **grow·ing·ly** \ˈgrō-iŋ-lē\ *adv*
growing pains *n pl* (1810) **1 :** pains in the legs of growing children having no demonstrable relation to growth **2 :** the stresses and strains attending a new project or development
growing point *n* (1882) **:** the undifferentiated end of a plant shoot from which additional shoot tissues differentiate
[1]**growl** \ˈgrau̇(ə)l\ *vb* [prob. imit.] *vi* (14c) **1 a :** RUMBLE ⟨his stomach ~*ed*⟩ **b :** to utter a growl ⟨the dog ~*ed* at the stranger⟩ **2 :** to complain angrily ~ *vt* **:** to utter with a growl
[2]**growl** *n* (1727) **:** a deep guttural inarticulate sound
growl·er \ˈgrau̇-lər\ *n* (1753) **1 :** one that growls **2 :** a container (as a can or pitcher) for beer bought by the measure **3 :** a small iceberg **4**

\ə\ abut \ᵊ\ kitten, F table \ər\ further \a\ ash \ā\ ace \ä\ cot, cart
\au̇\ out \ch\ chin \e\ bet \ē\ easy \g\ go \i\ hit \ī\ ice \j\ job
\ŋ\ sing \ō\ go \ȯ\ law \ȯi\ boy \th\ thin \t͟h\ the \ü\ loot \u̇\ foot
\y\ yet \zh\ vision \à, k̲, ⁿ, œ, œ̄, ue, u̅e, ʸ\ *see* Guide to Pronunciation

: an electromagnetic device with two adjustable pole pieces used for finding short-circuited coils and for magnetizing and demagnetizing

growl·ing \ˈgrau̇-liŋ\ *adj* (1752) : marked by a growl ⟨a low ~ voice⟩ ⟨listened to the ~ thunder⟩ — **growl·ing·ly** \-liŋ-lē\ *adv*

growly \ˈgrau̇-lē\ *adj* **growl·i·er; -est** (1920) : resembling a growl ⟨a ~ voice⟩ — **growl·i·ness** *n*

grown \ˈgrōn\ *adj* (1645) **1** : fully grown : MATURE ⟨~ men and women⟩ **2** : covered or surrounded with vegetation ⟨land well ~ with trees⟩ **3 a** : cultivated or produced in a specified way or locality — used in combination ⟨shade-*grown* tobacco⟩ **b** : overgrown with — used in combination ⟨a weed-*grown* patio⟩

[1]**grown–up** \ˈgrō-ˌnəp\ *adj* (1633) : not childish or immature : ADULT ⟨men and women incapable of ~ behavior⟩

[2]**grown–up** *n* (1813) : ADULT

growth \ˈgrōth\ *n* (1557) **1 a (1)** : a stage in the process of growing : SIZE **(2)** : full growth **b** : the process of growing **c** : progressive development : EVOLUTION **d** : INCREASE, EXPANSION ⟨the ~ of the oil industry⟩ **2 a** : something that grows or has grown **b** : an abnormal proliferation of tissue (as a tumor) **c** : OUTGROWTH **d** : the result of growth : PRODUCT **3** : a producing esp. by growing ⟨fruits of his own ~⟩

growth company *n* (1959) : a company that grows at a greater rate than the economy as a whole and that usu. directs a relatively high proportion of income back into the business

growth factor *n* (1926) : a substance (as a vitamin) that promotes the growth of an organism

growth hormone *n* (1936) **1** : a vertebrate polypeptide hormone that is secreted by the anterior lobe of the pituitary gland and regulates growth — called also *somatotropin* **2** : GROWTH REGULATOR

growth regulator *n* (1936) : any of various synthetic or naturally occurring plant substances (as an auxin or gibberellin) that regulate growth

growth ring *n* (1907) : a layer of wood (as an annual ring) produced during a single period of growth

grow up *vi* (1535) : to grow toward or arrive at full stature or physical or mental maturity ⟨*growing up* intellectually, socially, and physically⟩

groyne \ˈgrȯin\ *n* [by alter.] (1582) : GROIN 3

GR–S \ˌjē-ˌär-ˈes\ *n* [government rubber + styrene] (1943) : a synthetic rubber made by copolymerizing emulsions of butadiene and styrene and used esp. in tires

[1]**grub** \ˈgrəb\ *vb* **grubbed; grub·bing** [ME *grubben;* akin to OE *grafan* to dig — more at GRAVE] *vt* (14c) **1** : to clear by digging up roots and stumps **2** : to dig up by or as if by the roots ~ *vi* **1 a** : to dig in the ground esp. for something that is difficult to find or extract **b** : to search about : RUMMAGE ⟨*grubbed* in the countryside for food and fuel —*Lamp*⟩ **2** : TOIL, DRUDGE ⟨folks who ~ for money —James Street⟩ — **grub·ber** *n*

[2]**grub** *n* [ME *grubbe,* fr. *grubben*] (15c) **1** : a soft thick wormlike larva of an insect **2 a** : one who does menial work : DRUDGE **b** : a slovenly person **3** : FOOD

grub·by \ˈgrə-bē\ *adj* **grub·bi·er; -est** (1725) **1** : infested with fly maggots **2 a** : DIRTY, GRIMY ⟨~ hands⟩ **b** : SLOVENLY, SLOPPY **3** : worthy of contempt : BASE ⟨~ political motives⟩ — **grub·bi·ly** \ˈgrə-bə-lē\ *adv* — **grub·bi·ness** \ˈgrə-bē-nəs\ *n*

[1]**grub·stake** \ˈgrəb-ˌstāk\ *n* (1863) **1** : supplies or funds furnished a mining prospector on promise of a share in his discoveries **2** : material assistance (as a loan) provided for launching an enterprise or for a person in difficult circumstances

[2]**grubstake** *vt* (1879) : to provide with a grubstake — **grub·stak·er** *n*

Grub Street \ˈgrəb-\ *n* [*Grub Street,* London, formerly inhabited by literary hacks] (1630) : the world or category of needy literary hacks

[1]**grudge** \ˈgrəj\ *vt* **grudged; grudg·ing** [ME *grucchen, grudgen* to grumble, complain, fr. MF *groucier,* of Gmc origin; akin to MHG *grogezen* to howl] (15c) : to be unwilling to give or admit : give or allow with reluctance or resentment : BEGRUDGE ⟨*grudged* the money to pay taxes⟩ — **grudg·er** *n*

[2]**grudge** *n* (15c) : a feeling of deep-seated resentment or ill will ***syn*** see MALICE

grudg·ing \ˈgrə-jiŋ\ *adj* (1533) **1** : UNWILLING, RELUCTANT **2** : done, given, or allowed unwillingly, reluctantly, or sparingly ⟨~ compliance with the physical and mental demands —Caryl Chessman⟩ — **grudg·ing·ly** \-jiŋ-lē\ *adv*

gru·el \ˈgrü-əl\ *n* [ME *grewel,* fr. MF *gruel,* of Gmc origin; akin to OE *grūt* grout] (14c) **1** : a thin porridge **2** *chiefly Brit* : PUNISHMENT

gru·el·ing *or* **gru·el·ling** \ˈgrü-ə-liŋ\ *adj* [fr. prp. of obs. *gruel* (to exhaust)] (1852) : trying or taxing to the point of exhaustion : PUNISHING ⟨a ~ race⟩ — **gru·el·ing·ly** \-liŋ-lē\ *adv*

grue·some \ˈgrü-səm\ *adj* [alter. of earlier *growsome,* fr. E dial. *grow, grue* to shiver, fr. ME *gruen,* prob. fr. MD *grūwen;* akin to OHG *ingrūēn* to shiver] (1570) : inspiring horror or repulsion : GRISLY ⟨~ scenes of battle and death —E. J. Fitzgerald⟩ ***syn*** see GHASTLY — **grue·some·ly** *adv* — **grue·some·ness** *n*

[1]**gruff** \ˈgrəf\ *adj* [D *grof;* akin to OHG *grob* coarse, *hruf* scurf — more at DANDRUFF] (1690) **1** : rough, brusque, or stern in manner, speech, or aspect ⟨a ~ reply⟩ **2** : being deep and harsh : HOARSE ⟨a ~ voice⟩ ***syn*** see BLUFF — **gruff·ly** *adv* — **gruff·ness** *n*

[2]**gruff** *vt* (1706) : to utter in a gruff voice or manner

grum·ble \ˈgrəm-bəl\ *vb* **grum·bled; grum·bling** \-b(ə-)liŋ\ [prob. fr. MF *grommeler,* deriv. of MD *grommen;* akin to OHG *grimm* grim] *vi* (1586) **1** : to mutter in discontent **2** : GROWL, RUMBLE ~ *vt* : to express with grumbling — **grumble** *n* — **grum·bler** \-b(ə-)lər\ *n* — **grum·bling·ly** \-b(ə-)liŋ-lē\ *adv* — **grum·bly** \-b(ə-)lē\ *adj*

grum·met \ˈgrəm-ət\ *var of* GROMMET

[1]**grump** \ˈgrəmp\ *n* [obs. E *grumps* (snubs, slights)] (1844) **1** : a fit of ill humor or sulkiness — usu. used in pl. **2** : a person given to complaining

[2]**grump** *vi* (1875) **1** : SULK **2** : GRUMBLE, COMPLAIN ~ *vt* : to utter in a grumpy manner

grumpy \ˈgrəm-pē\ *adj* **grump·i·er; -est** (1778) : moodily cross : SURLY — **grump·i·ly** \-pə-lē\ *adv* — **grump·i·ness** \-pē-nəs\ *n*

grun·gy \ˈgrən-jē\ *adj* **grun·gi·er; -est** [origin unknown] (1967) : shabby or dirty in character or condition

grun·ion \ˈgrən-yən\ *n* [prob. fr. Sp *gruñón* grunter] (1917) : a silversides (*Leuresthes tenuis*) of the California coast notable for the regularity with which it comes inshore to spawn at nearly full moon

[1]**grunt** \ˈgrənt\ *vb* [ME *grunten,* fr. OE *grunnettan,* freq. of *grunian,* of imit. origin] *vi* (bef. 12c) : to utter a grunt ~ *vt* : to utter with a grunt — **grunt·er** *n*

[2]**grunt** *n* (1553) **1 a** : the deep short sound characteristic of a hog **b** : a similar sound **2** [fr. the noise it makes when taken from the water] : any of numerous chiefly tropical marine percoid fishes (family Pomadasidae) related to the snappers **3** : a U.S. army or marine foot soldier esp. in the Vietnam war **4** : one who does routine unglamorous work

grun·tle \ˈgrənt-ᵊl\ *vt* **grun·tled; grun·tling** \ˈgrənt-liŋ, -ᵊl-iŋ\ [back-formation fr. *disgruntle*] (1926) : to put in a good humor ⟨were *gruntled* with a good meal and good conversation —W. P. Webb⟩

grutch \ˈgrəch\ *vt* [ME *grucchen*] *obs* (15c) : BEGRUDGE

grutten *past part of* GREET

Gru·yère \grü-ˈye(ə)r, grē-ˈ(y)e(ə)r\ *n* [*Gruyère,* district in Switzerland] (1802) **1** : a firm cheese with small holes and a nutty flavor that is of Swiss origin and is often used in cooking **2** : a process cheese made from natural Gruyère

gryph·on *var of* GRIFFIN

G–string \ˈjē-ˌstriŋ\ *n* [origin unknown] (1878) : a strip of cloth passed between the legs and supported by a waist cord that is worn esp. by striptease dancers

G suit *n* [gravity *suit*] (1944) : a suit designed to counteract the physiological effects of acceleration on an aviator or astronaut

GT \(ˈ)jē-ˈtē\ *n* [It *Gran Turismo*] (1967) : GRAND TOURING CAR

GTP \ˌjē-(ˌ)tē-ˈpē\ *n* [guanosine *triphosphate*] (1961) : an energy-rich nucleoside triphosphate analogous to ATP that is composed of guanine linked to ribose and three phosphate groups and is necessary for the formation of peptide bonds during protein synthesis — called also *guanosine triphosphate*

G_1 phase \ˌjē-ˈtü-\ *n* [growth] (1973) : the period in the cell cycle from the completion of DNA replication to the beginning of cell division — compare G_1 PHASE, M PHASE, S PHASE

gua·ca·mo·le \ˌgwäk-ə-ˈmō-lē\ *n* [AmerSp, fr. Nahuatl *ahuacamolle*] (1920) : sieved or mashed avocado seasoned with condiments

gua·cha·ro \ˈgwäch-ə-ˌrō\ *n, pl* **-ros** *or* **-roes** [Sp *guácharo*] (1830) : OILBIRD

guai·ac \ˈg(w)ī-ˌak\ *n* [NL *Guaiacum*] (1558) : GUAIACUM 2

guai·a·cum \ˈg(w)ī-ə-kəm\ *n* [NL, fr. Sp *guayaco,* fr. Taino *guayacan*] (1553) **1** : any of a genus (*Guaiacum* of the family Zygophyllaceae) of tropical American trees and shrubs having pinnate leaves, mostly blue flowers, and capsular fruit **2 a** : the hard greenish brown wood of a guaiacum (esp. *Guaiacum officinale*) **b** : a resin with a faint balsamic odor obtained from the trunk of two guaiacums (*G. officinale* and *G. sanctum*)

guan \ˈgwän\ *n* [AmerSp] (1743) : any of various large tropical American lowland forest birds (family Cracidae) that somewhat resemble turkeys

guan

gua·na·co \gwə-ˈnäk-(ˌ)ō\ *n, pl* **-cos** *also* **-co** [Sp, fr. Quechua *huanacu*] (1604) : a So. American mammal (*Lama guanicoe*) with a soft thick fawn-colored coat that is related to the camel but lacks a dorsal hump

gua·neth·i·dine \gwä-ˈneth-ə-ˌdēn\ *n* [*guanidine* + *eth-*] (1959) : a drug $C_{10}H_{22}N_4$ used esp. as the sulfate in treating severe high blood pressure

gua·ni·dine \ˈgwän-ə-ˌdēn\ *n* [ISV, fr. *guanine*] (ca. 1864) : a base CH_5N_3 derived from guanine, found esp. in young tissues, and used in organic synthesis and as a parasympathetic stimulant in medicine esp. as the hydrochloride salt

gua·nine \ˈgwän-ˌēn\ *n* [*guano* + *-ine;* fr. its being found esp. in guano] (1850) : a purine base $C_5H_5N_5O$ that codes genetic information in the polynucleotide chain of DNA or RNA — compare ADENINE, CYTOSINE, THYMINE, URACIL

gua·no \ˈgwän-(ˌ)ō\ *n* [Sp, fr. Quechua *huanu* dung] (1604) : a substance composed chiefly of the excrement of seafowl and used as a fertilizer; *also* : a similar substance (as bat excrement or cannery waste) esp. when used for fertilizer

gua·no·sine \ˈgwän-ə-ˌsēn\ *n* [*guan-* (as in *guanine*) + ribose + *-ine*] (1909) : a nucleoside $C_{10}H_{13}N_5O_5$ that consists of guanine combined with ribose

guanosine triphosphate *n* (ca. 1962) : GTP

guar \ˈgwär\ *n* [Hindi *guār*] (1882) : a drought-tolerant legume (*Cyamopsis tetragonoloba*) grown for forage and for its seeds which produce guar gum

gua·ra·ni \ˌgwär-ə-ˈnē\ *n* [Sp *guaraní*] (1797) **1** *cap* **a** *pl* **guarani** *or* **guaranis** : a member of a Tupi-Guaranian people of Bolivia, Paraguay, and southern Brazil **b** : the language of this people **2** *pl* **guaranies** *also* **guaranis** — see MONEY table

[1]**guar·an·tee** \ˌgar-ən-ˈtē, ˌgär- *also* ˈgar-ən-, *or* ˈgär-ən-,\ *n* [prob. alter. of [1]*guaranty*] (1679) **1** : GUARANTOR **2** : GUARANTY 1 **3** : an assurance for the fulfillment of a condition: as **a** : an agreement by which one person undertakes to secure another in the possession or enjoyment of something **b** : an assurance of the quality of or of the length of use to be expected from a product offered for sale often with a promise of reimbursement **4** : GUARANTY 3

[2]**guarantee** *vt* **-teed; -tee·ing** (1791) **1** : to undertake to answer for the debt, default, or miscarriage of **2** : to engage for the existence, permanence, or nature of : undertake to do or secure (something) ⟨~ the winning of three tricks⟩ **3** : to give security to

guar·an·tor \ˌgar-ən-ˈtȯ(ə)r, ˈgar-ən-tər, ˌgär-, ˈgär-\ *n* (ca. 1828) **1** : one that guarantees **2** : one that makes or gives a guaranty

[1]**guar·an·ty** \ˈgar-ən-tē, ˈgär-\ *n, pl* **-ties** [MF *garantie,* fr. OF, fr. *garantir* to guarantee, fr. *garant* warrant, of Gmc origin; akin to OHG *werēnto* guarantor — more at WARRANT] (1592) **1** : an undertaking to answer for the payment of a debt or the performance of a duty of another in case of the other's default or miscarriage **2** : GUARANTEE 3 **3** : something given as security : PLEDGE **4** : GUARANTOR **5** : the protection of a right afforded by legal provision (as in a constitution)

[2]**guaranty** *vt* **-tied; -ty·ing** (1732) : GUARANTEE

[1]**guard** \ˈgärd\ *n* [ME *garde*, fr. MF, fr. OF, fr. *garder* to guard, defend, of Gmc origin; akin to OHG *wartēn* to watch, take care — more at WARD] (15c) **1 :** one assigned to protect or oversee another: as **a :** a person or a body of persons on sentinel duty **b** *pl* **:** troops attached to the person of the sovereign **c** (1) **:** BRAKEMAN (2) *Brit* **:** CONDUCTOR **2 :** a defensive position (as in boxing) **3 a :** the act or duty of protecting or defending **b :** the state of being protected **:** PROTECTION **4** *archaic* **:** PRECAUTION **5 a :** a position or player next to the center in a football line **b :** a player stationed in the backcourt in basketball **6 :** a protective or safety device; *specif* **:** a device for protecting a machine part or the operator of a machine — **off guard :** in an unprepared or unsuspecting state — **on guard :** defensively watchful **:** ALERT

[2]**guard** *vt* (1500) **1 :** to protect an edge of with an ornamental border **2 a :** to protect from danger esp. by watchful attention **:** make secure ⟨policemen ~*ing* our cities⟩ ⟨a room ~*ed* by locked doors⟩ **b :** to stand at the entrance of as if on guard or as a barrier **c :** to tend to carefully **:** PRESERVE, PROTECT ⟨~*ed* their privacy⟩ **3** *archaic* **:** ESCORT **4 a :** to watch over so as to prevent escape, disclosure, or indiscretion **b :** to attempt to prevent (an opponent) from playing effectively or scoring ~ *vi* **:** to watch by way of caution or defense **:** stand guard *syn* see DEFEND — **guard·er** *n*

[1]**guar·dant** \ˈgärd-ᵊnt\ *adj* [MF *gardant*, prp. of *garder* to guard, look at] (1572) **:** having the head turned toward the spectator — used of a heraldic animal whose body is seen from the side ⟨a lion passant ~⟩

[2]**guardant** *n*, *obs* (1591) **:** GUARDIAN

guard cell *n* (1875) **:** one of the two crescent-shaped epidermal cells that border and open and close a plant stoma

guard·ed \ˈgärd-əd\ *adj* (1709) **:** CAUTIOUS, CIRCUMSPECT — **guard·ed·ly** *adv* — **guard·ed·ness** *n*

guard hair *n* (1913) **:** one of the long coarse hairs forming a protective coating over the underfur of a mammal

guard·house \ˈgärd-ˌhau̇s\ *n* (1592) **1 :** a building occupied by a guard or used as a headquarters by soldiers on guard duty **2 :** a military jail

guard·ian \ˈgärd-ē-ən\ *n* (15c) **1 :** one that guards **:** CUSTODIAN **2 :** a superior of a Franciscan monastery **3 :** one who has the care of the person or property of another — **guard·ian·ship** \-ˌship\ *n*

guard of honor (ca. 1918) **:** HONOR GUARD

guard·rail \ˈgär-ˌdrāl\ *n* (1860) **:** a railing for guarding against danger or trespass; *esp* **:** a barrier (as of steel cables) placed along the edge of a highway at dangerous points

guard·room \ˈgär-ˌdrüm, -ˌdru̇m\ *n* (1762) **1 :** a room occupied by a military guard during its term of duty **2 :** a room where military prisoners are confined

guards·man \ˈgärdz-mən\ *n* (1817) **:** a member of a military body called *guard* or *guards*

guar gum *n* (1950) **:** a gum that consists of the ground endosperm of guar seeds and is used esp. as a thickening agent and as a sizing material for paper and textiles

Guar·ne·ri·us \gwär-ˈnir-ē-əs, -ˈner-\ *n* [NL, fr. It *Guarneri*] (1866) **:** a violin made by one of the Italian Guarneri family in the 17th and 18th centuries

gua·va \ˈgwäv-ə\ *n* [modif. of Sp *guayaba*, of Arawakan origin; akin to Tupi *guayava* guava] (1555) **1 :** any of several tropical American shrubs or small trees (genus *Psidium*) of the myrtle family; *esp* **:** a shrubby tree (*P. guajava*) widely cultivated for its sweet acid yellow fruit **2 :** the fruit of a guava

gua·yu·le \(g)wī-ˈü-lē\ *n* [AmerSp, fr. Nahuatl *cuauhuli*] (1906) **:** a much-branched composite subshrub (*Parthenium argentatum*) of Mexico and the southwestern U.S. that has been cultivated as a source of rubber

gu·ber·na·to·ri·al \ˌgüb-ə(r)-nə-ˈtōr-ē-əl, ˌgyüb-, ˌgüb-, -ˈtȯr-\ *adj* [L *gubernator* governor, steersman, fr. *gubernatus*, pp. of *gubernare* to govern — more at GOVERN] (1734) **:** of or relating to a governor

guck \ˈgək\ *n* [perh. alter. of *goo*] (1949) **:** oozy sloppy dirt or debris **:** GOO, GUNK

[1]**gud·geon** \ˈgəj-ən\ *n* [ME *gudyon*, fr. MF *goujon*] (15c) **1 :** PIVOT, JOURNAL **2 :** a socket for a rudder pintle

[2]**gudgeon** *n* [ME *gojune*, fr. MF *gouvion*, *gougon*, fr. L *gobion-*, *gobio*, alter. of *gobius* — more at GOBY] (15c) **:** a small European freshwater fish (*Gobio gobio*) related to the carps and often used for food or bait

gudgeon pin *n* (1891) **:** WRIST PIN

Gud·run \ˈgu̇d-ˌrün\ *n* [ON *Guthrūn*] **:** the wife of Sigurd and later of Atli in Norse mythology

guel·der rose \ˌgel-də(r)-\ *n* [*Guelderland*, *Gelderland*, Netherlands] (1597) **:** a bush of a cultivated variety of the cranberry bush with large globose heads of sterile flowers

Guelf *or* **Guelph** \ˈgwelf\ *n* [It *Guelfo*] (1579) **:** a member of a papal and popular political party in medieval Italy that opposed the authority of the German emperors in Italy — compare GHIBELLINE

gue·non \gə-ˈnōⁿ\ *n* [F] (1838) **:** any of various long-tailed chiefly arboreal African monkeys (*Cercopithecus* and related genera)

guer·don \ˈgərd-ᵊn\ *n* [ME, fr. MF, fr. OF, of Gmc origin; akin to OHG *widarlōn* recompense] (14c) **:** REWARD, RECOMPENSE — **guerdon** *vt*

guern·sey \ˈgərn-zē\ *n*, *pl* **guernseys** *often cap* [*Guernsey*, Channel islands] (1834) **:** any of a breed of fawn and white dairy cattle that are larger than the jersey and produce rich yellowish milk

guer·ril·la *or* **gue·ril·la** \gə-ˈril-ə, ge-; g(y)ir-ˈil-\ *n* [Sp *guerrilla*, fr. dim. of *guerra* war, of Gmc origin; akin to OHG *werra* strife — more at WAR] (1809) **:** one who engages in irregular warfare esp. as a member of an independent unit carrying out harassment and sabotage

guerrilla theater *n* (1968) **:** STREET THEATER

[1]**guess** \ˈges\ *vb* [ME *gessen*, prob. of Scand origin; akin to ON *geta* to get, guess — more at GET] *vt* (14c) **1 :** to form an opinion of from little or no evidence **2 :** to arrive at a correct conclusion about by conjecture, chance, or intuition ⟨~ the answer⟩ **3 :** BELIEVE, SUPPOSE ⟨I ~ you're right⟩ ~ *vi* **:** to make a guess — **guess·er** *n*

[2]**guess** *n* (14c) **:** CONJECTURE, SURMISE

guess·ti·mate \ˈges-tə-mət\ *n* [blend of *guess* and *estimate*] (1923) **:** an estimate made without adequate information — **guess·ti·mate** \-ˌmāt\ *vt*

guess·work \ˈges-ˌwərk\ *n* (1725) **:** work performed or results obtained by guess **:** CONJECTURE

[1]**guest** \ˈgest\ *n* [ME *gest*, fr. ON *gestr*; akin to OE *gæst* guest, stranger, L *hostis* stranger, enemy] (bef. 12c) **1 a :** a person entertained in one's house **b :** a person to whom hospitality is extended **c :** a person who pays for the services of an establishment (as a hotel or restaurant) **2 :** an organism (as an insect) sharing the dwelling of another; *esp* **:** INQUILINE **3 :** a mineral or rock in a host mineral or rock; *also* **:** a substance that is incorporated in a host substance **4 :** a usu. prominent person not a regular member of a cast or organization who appears in a program or performance

[2]**guest** *vt* (14c) **:** to receive as a guest ~ *vi* **:** to appear as a guest

guff \ˈgəf\ *n* [prob. imit.] (1888) **:** NONSENSE, HUMBUG

guf·faw \(ˌ)gə-ˈfȯ, ˈgəf-ˌȯ\ *n* [imit.] (1720) **:** a loud or boisterous burst of laughter — **guf·faw** \(ˌ)gə-ˈfȯ\ *vi*

gug·gle \ˈgəg-əl\ *vi* **gug·gled; gug·gling** \-(ə-)liŋ\ [imit.] (1611) **:** GURGLE — **guggle** *n*

guid·able \ˈgīd-ə-bəl\ *adj* (1676) **:** capable of being guided

guid·ance \ˈgīd-ᵊn(t)s\ *n* (1590) **1 :** the act or process of guiding **2 :** advice on vocational or educational problems given to students **3 :** the process of controlling the course of a projectile by a built-in mechanism

[1]**guide** \ˈgīd\ *n* [ME, fr. MF, fr. OProv *guida*, of Gmc origin; akin to OE *witan* to look after, *witan* to know — more at WIT] (14c) **1 a :** one who leads or directs another in his way **b :** one who exhibits and explains points of interest **c :** something that provides a person with guiding information **d :** SIGNPOST 1 **e :** one who directs a person in his conduct or course of life **2 a :** a device for steadying or directing the motion of something **b :** a ring or loop for holding the line of a fishing rod in position **c :** a sheet or a card with projecting tab for labeling inserted in a card index to facilitate reference **3 :** a member of a unit on whom the movements or alignments of a military command are regulated — used esp. in commands ⟨~ right⟩

[2]**guide** *vb* **guid·ed; guid·ing** *vt* (14c) **1 :** to act as a guide to **:** direct in a way or course **2 a :** to direct, supervise, or influence usu. to a particular end **b :** to superintend the training or instruction of ~ *vi* **:** to act or work as a guide — **guid·er** *n*

syn GUIDE, LEAD, STEER, PILOT, ENGINEER mean to direct in a course or show the way to be followed. GUIDE implies intimate knowledge of the way and of all its difficulties and dangers; LEAD implies a going ahead to show the way and often to keep those that follow under control and in order; STEER implies an ability to keep to a chosen course and stresses the capacity of maneuvering correctly; PILOT suggests guidance over a dangerous, intricate, or complicated course; ENGINEER implies guidance by one who finds ways to avoid or overcome difficulties in achieving an end or carrying out a plan.

guide·book \ˈgīd-ˌbu̇k\ *n* (1814) **:** HANDBOOK 1; *esp* **:** a book of information for travelers

guided missile *n* (1945) **:** a missile whose course may be altered during flight (as by a target-seeking radar device)

guide·line \ˈgīd-ˌlīn\ *n* (1785) **:** a line by which one is guided: as **a :** a cord or rope to aid a passer over a difficult point or to permit retracing a course **b :** an indication or outline (as by a government) of policy or conduct

guide·post \-ˌpōst\ *n* (1761) **1 :** INDICATION, SIGN **2 :** GUIDELINE b

guide·way \-ˌwā\ *n* (1876) **:** a channel or track for controlling the line of motion of something

guide word *n* (ca. 1928) **:** either of the terms at the head of a page of an alphabetical reference work (as a dictionary) indicating the alphabetically first and last words on the page

gui·don \ˈgīd-ˌän, -ᵊn\ *n* [MF, fr. OProv *guidoo*, fr. *guida* guide] (1548) **1 :** a small flag; *esp* **:** one borne by a military unit as a unit marker **2 :** one who carries a guidon

guid·will·ie \gœd-ˈwil-ē, gid-\ *adj* [Sc *guidwill* goodwill] *Scot* (1788) **:** CORDIAL, CHEERING

guild \ˈgild\ *n* [ME *gilde*, fr. ON *gildi* payment, guild; akin to OE *gield* tribute, guild — more at GELD] (15c) **:** an association of people with similar interests or pursuits; *esp* **:** a medieval association of merchants or craftsmen — **guild·ship** \ˈgil(d)-ˌship\ *n*

guil·der \ˈgil-dər\ *n* [modif. of D *gulden*] (15c) **:** GULDEN

guild·hall \ˈgild-ˌhȯl\ *n* (14c) **:** a hall where a guild or corporation usu. assembles

guilds·man \ˈgil(d)z-mən\ *n* (1873) **1 :** a guild member **2 :** an advocate of guild socialism

guild socialism *n* (1912) **:** an early 20th century English socialistic theory advocating state ownership of industry with control and management by guilds of workers

guile \ˈgī(ə)l\ *n* [ME, fr. OF] (13c) **1 :** deceitful cunning **:** DUPLICITY **2** *obs* **:** STRATAGEM, TRICK — **guile·ful** \-fəl\ *adj* — **guile·ful·ly** \-fə-lē\ *adv* — **guile·ful·ness** *n*

guile·less \ˈgī(ə)l-ləs\ *adj* (1728) **:** INNOCENT, NAIVE — **guile·less·ly** *adv* — **guile·less·ness** *n*

guil·le·mot \ˈgil-ə-ˌmät\ *n* [F, fr. MF, dim. of *Guillaume* William] (1678) **:** any of several narrow-billed auks of northern seas constituting two genera (*Uria* and *Cepphus*)

guil·loche \gil-ˈōsh, gē-ˈ(y)ōsh\ *n* [F *guillochis*] (1857) **:** an architectural ornament formed of two or more interlaced bands with openings containing round devices

guil·lo·tine \ˈgil-ə-ˌtēn; ˌgē-(y)ə-ˈ, ˈgē-(y)ə-ˌ\ *n* [F, fr. Joseph *Guillotin* †1814 Fr. physician] (1793) **1 :** a machine for beheading by means of a heavy blade that slides down in vertical guides **2 :** a shearing machine or instrument (as a paper cutter) that in action resembles a guillotine **3 :** closure by the imposition of a predetermined time limit on the consideration of specific sections of a bill or portions of other legislative business — **guillotine** *vt*

guilt \ˈgilt\ *n* [ME, delinquency, guilt, fr. OE *gylt* delinquency] (bef. 12c) **1 :** the fact of having committed a breach of conduct esp. violating law and involving a penalty; *broadly* **:** guilty conduct **2 a :** the state of one who has committed an offense esp. consciously **b** : feelings of culpability esp. for imagined offenses or from a sense of inadequacy : SELF-REPROACH **3** : a feeling of culpability for offenses

guilt·less \'gilt-ləs\ *adj* (13c) : INNOCENT — **guilt·less·ly** *adv* — **guilt·less·ness** *n*

guilty \'gil-tē\ *adj* **guilt·i·er; -est** (bef. 12c) **1** : justly chargeable with or responsible for a usu. grave breach of conduct **2** *obs* : justly liable to or deserving of a penalty **3 a** : suggesting or involving guilt ⟨~ looks⟩ **b** : aware of or suffering from guilt ⟨~ consciences⟩ ***syn*** see BLAMEWORTHY — **guilt·i·ly** \-tə-lē\ *adv* — **guilt·i·ness** \-tē-nəs\ *n*

guimpe \'gamp, 'gimp\ *n* [F, fr. OF *guimple*, of Gmc origin; akin to OE *wimpel* wimple] (1850) **1** : a blouse worn under a jumper or pinafore **2** : a wide cloth used by some nuns to cover the neck and shoulders **3** [by alter.] : [1]GIMP

guin·ea \'gin-ē\ *n* [*Guinea*, Africa, supposed source of the gold from which it was made] (1664) **1** : an English gold coin issued from 1663 to 1813 and fixed in 1717 at 21 shillings **2** : a unit of value equal to one pound and one shilling

guinea fowl *n* (1788) : a West African bird (*Numida meleagris*) related to the pheasants, raised for food in most parts of the world, and marked by a bare neck and head and slaty plumage speckled with white; *broadly* : any of several related birds of Africa and Madagascar

guinea grass *n* (1785) : a tall African forage grass (*Panicum maximum*) introduced into tropical America and the southern U.S.

guinea hen *n* (1599) : a female guinea fowl; *broadly* : GUINEA FOWL

guinea pepper *n* (1597) : GRAINS OF PARADISE

guinea pig *n* (1664) **1** : a small stout-bodied short-eared nearly tailless domesticated rodent (*Cavia cobaya*) often kept as a pet and widely used in biological research — called also *cavy* **2** : a subject of research, experimentation, or testing

guinea worm *n* (1699) : a slender nematode worm (*Dracunculus medinensis*) attaining a length of several feet and occurring as an adult in the subcutaneous tissues of various mammals including man in warm countries

Guin·e·vere \'gwin-ə-,vi(ə)r\ *n* : the wife of King Arthur and mistress of Lancelot

gui·pure \gi-'p(y)ü(ə)r\ *n* [F] (1843) : a heavy large-patterned decorative lace

gui·ro \'(g)wi(ə)r-(,)ō\ *n* [AmerSp *güiro* calabash, guiro] (1898) : a percussion instrument of Latin-American origin made of a serrated gourd and played by scraping a stick along its surface

gui·sard \'gī-zərd\ *n* [obs. Sc *gyze* to disguise, fr. ME *gyzen* to dress, fr. *guise, gyze* guise] *chiefly Scot* (1626) : MASKER, MUMMER

guise \'gīz\ *n* [ME, fr. OF, of Gmc origin; akin to OHG *wīsa* manner — more at WISE] (13c) **1** : a form or style of dress : COSTUME **2 a** *obs* : MANNER, FASHION **b** *archaic* : a customary way of speaking or behaving **3 a** : external appearance : SEMBLANCE **b** : PRETEXT

gui·tar \gə-'tär, gi-, *esp Southern & Midland also* 'gi-,tär\ *n* [F *guitare*, fr. Sp *guitarra*, fr. Ar *qītār*, fr. Gk *kithara* cithara] (1621) : a flat-bodied stringed instrument with a long fretted neck and usu. six strings plucked with a pick or with the fingers — **gui·tar·ist** \-əst\ *n*

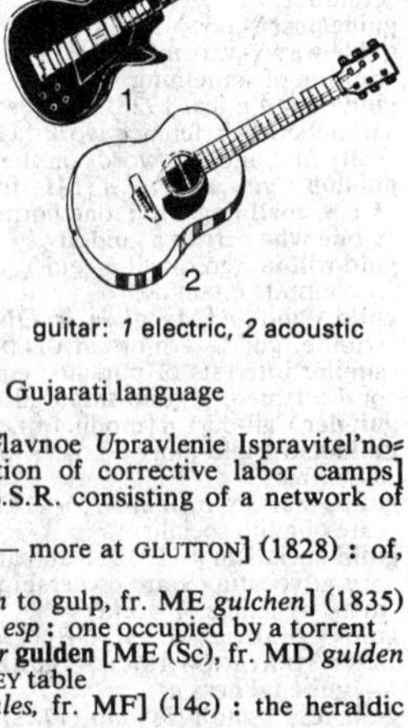

guitar: *1* electric, *2* acoustic

gui·tar·fish \-,fish\ *n* (ca. 1900) : any of several viviparous rays (family Rhinobatidae) somewhat resembling a guitar in outline when viewed from above

Gu·ja·ra·ti \,gü-jə-'rät-ē, ,güj-ə-\ *n*, *pl* **Gujarati** [Hindi *gujarātī*, fr. *Gujarāt* Gujarat] (1808) **1** *or* **Gujerati** : the language of Gujarat and neighboring regions in northwestern India **2** *or* **Guj·ra·ti** \güj-'rät-, güj-'rät-\ : a member of a people chiefly of Gujarat speaking the Gujarati language

gul \'gül\ *n* [Per] (1813) : ROSE

gu·lag \'gü-,läg\ *n*, *often cap* [Russ *G*lavnoe *U*pravlenie Ispravitel'no-trudovykh *Lag*erei chief administration of corrective labor camps] (1974) : the penal system of the U.S.S.R. consisting of a network of labor camps; *also* : LABOR CAMP 1

gu·lar \'g(y)ü-lər\ *adj* [L *gula* throat — more at GLUTTON] (1828) : of, relating to, or situated on the throat

gulch \'gəlch\ *n* [perh. fr. E dial. *gulch* to gulp, fr. ME *gulchen*] (1835) : a deep or precipitous cleft : RAVINE; *esp* : one occupied by a torrent

gul·den \'gül-dən, 'gül-\ *n*, *pl* **guldens** *or* **gulden** [ME (Sc), fr. MD *gulden florijn* golden florin] (16c) — see MONEY table

gules \'gyü(ə)lz\ *n*, *pl* **gules** [ME *goules*, fr. MF] (14c) : the heraldic color red

[1]**gulf** \'gəlf\ *n* [ME *goulf*, fr. MF *golfe*, fr. It *golfo*, fr. LL *colpus*, fr. Gk *kolpos* bosom, gulf; akin to OE *hwealf* vault, OHG *walbo*] (15c) **1** : a part of an ocean or sea extending into the land **2** : a deep chasm : ABYSS **3** : WHIRLPOOL **4** : a wide gap ⟨the ~ between generations⟩

[2]**gulf** *vt* (1807) : ENGULF

gulf·weed \'gəlf-,wēd\ *n* [*Gulf* of Mexico] (1674) : any of several sargassums; *esp* : a branching olive-brown seaweed (*Sargassum bacciferum*) of tropical American seas with numerous berrylike air vesicles

[1]**gull** \'gəl\ *n* [ME, of Celt origin; akin to W *gwylan* gull] (15c) : any of numerous long-winged web-footed aquatic birds (subfamily Larinae of the family Laridae); *esp* : a largely white bird (as of the genus *Larus*) differing from a tern in usu. larger size, stouter build, thicker bill somewhat hooked at the tip, less pointed wings, and short unforked tail

[2]**gull** *vt* [obs. *gull* gullet, fr. ME *golle*, fr. MF *goule*] (1550) : to take advantage of (one who is foolish or unwary) ***syn*** see DUPE

[3]**gull** *n* (1594) : a person who is easily deceived or cheated : DUPE

Gul·lah \'gəl-ə\ *n* (1822) **1** : a member of a group of Negroes inhabiting the sea islands and coastal districts of So. Carolina, Georgia, and northeastern Florida **2** : the English dialect of the Gullahs that is marked by an admixture of vocabulary and grammatical elements from various African languages

gul·let \'gəl-ət\ *n* [ME *golet*, fr. MF *goulet*, dim. of *goule* throat, fr. L *gula* — more at GLUTTON] (14c) **1** : ESOPHAGUS; *broadly* : THROAT **2** : an invagination of the protoplasm in various protozoans (as a paramecium) that sometimes functions in the intake of food **3** : the space between the tips of adjacent saw teeth

gull·ible *also* **gull·able** \'gəl-ə-bəl\ *adj* (1818) : easily duped or cheated — **gull·ibil·i·ty** \,gəl-ə-'bil-ət-ē\ *n* — **gull·ibly** \'gəl-ə-blē\ *adv*

Gul·li·ver \'gəl-ə-vər\ *n* : an Englishman in Jonathan Swift's satire *Gulliver's Travels* who makes voyages to the imaginary lands of the Lilliputians, Brobdingnagians, Laputans, and Houyhnhnms

[1]**gul·ly** \'gül-ē, 'gəl-\ *n*, *pl* **gullies** [short for E dial. *gully knife*] *dial Brit* (1582) : a large knife

[2]**gul·ly** \'gəl-ē\ *n*, *pl* **gullies** [obs. E *gully* (gullet)] (1637) : a trench worn in the earth by running water after rains

[3]**gul·ly** \'gəl-ē\ *vb* **gul·lied; gul·ly·ing** *vt* (1754) : to make gullies in ~ *vi* : to undergo erosion : form gullies

gully erosion *n* (1928) : soil erosion produced by running water

gu·los·i·ty \g(y)ü-'läs-ət-ē\ *n* [ME *gulosite*, fr. LL *gulositas*, fr. L *gulosus* gluttonous, fr. *gula* gullet] (1500) : excessive appetite : GREEDINESS

gulp \'gəlp\ *vb* [ME *gulpen*, fr. a MD or MLG word akin to D & Fris *gulpen* to bubble forth, drink deep; akin to OE *gielpan* to boast — more at YELP] *vt* (14c) **1** : to swallow hurriedly or greedily or in one swallow **2** : to keep back as if by swallowing ⟨~ down a sob⟩ **3** : to take in readily as if by swallowing : DEVOUR ~ *vi* : to catch the breath as if in taking a long drink — **gulp** *n* — **gulp·er** *n*

[1]**gum** \'gəm\ *n* [ME *gome*, fr. OE *gōma* palate; akin to OHG *guomo* palate, Gk *chaos* abyss] (bef. 12c) : the tissue that surrounds the necks of teeth and covers the alveolar parts of the jaws; *broadly* : the alveolar portion of a jaw with its enveloping soft tissues

[2]**gum** *vt* **gummed; gum·ming** (1777) **1** : to enlarge gullets of (a saw) **2** : to chew with the gums

[3]**gum** *n* [ME *gomme*, fr. MF, fr. L *cummi, gummi*, fr. Gk *kommi*, fr. Egypt *qmy.t*] (14c) **1 a** : any of numerous colloidal polysaccharide substances of plant origin that are gelatinous when moist but harden on drying and are salts of complex organic acids — compare MUCILAGE 1 **b** : any of various plant exudates (as a mucilage, oleoresin, or gum resin) **2** : a substance or deposit resembling a plant gum (as in sticky or adhesive quality) **3 a** : a tree (as a sour gum or sapodilla) that yields gum **b** *Austral* : EUCALYPTUS **4** : the wood or lumber of a gum; *esp* : that of the sweet gum **5** : CHEWING GUM

[4]**gum** *vb* **gummed; gum·ming** *vt* (1597) : to clog or impede with or as if with gum ⟨~ up the works⟩ ~ *vi* **1** : to exude or form gum **2** : to become gummy — **gum·mer** *n*

gum ammoniac *n* (14c) : AMMONIAC

gum arabic *n* (15c) : a water-soluble gum obtained from several acacias (esp. *Acacia senegal* and *A. arabica*) and used esp. in the manufacture of adhesives, in confectionery, and in pharmacy

gum·bo \'gəm-(,)bō\ *n*, *pl* **gumbos** [AmerF *gombo*, of Bantu origin; akin to Umbundu *ochinggômbo* okra] (1845) **1** : OKRA 1 **2** : a soup thickened with okra pods and usu. containing vegetables with meat or seafoods **3 a** : any of various fine-grained silty soils esp. of the central U.S. that when wet become impervious and soapy or waxy and very sticky **b** : a heavy sticky mud **4** *often cap* [AmerF *gombo*, perh. fr. Kongo *nkômbô* runaway slave] : a patois used by Negroes and Creoles esp. in Louisiana **5** : MIXTURE, MÉLANGE — **gumbo** *adj*

gum·boil \'gəm-,bȯil\ *n* (1753) : an abscess in the gum

gum·bo–lim·bo \,gəm-bō-'lim-(,)bō\ *n* [perh. fr. *gumbo* + *limbo*, of Bantu origin; akin to Kongo *edimbu* birdlime] (1837) : a tree (*Bursera simaruba*) of southern Florida and the American tropics that has a smooth coppery bark and supplies a reddish resin used locally in cements and varnishes

gum boot *n* (1850) : a rubber boot

gum·drop \'gəm-,dräp\ *n* (1860) : a sugar-coated candy made usu. from corn syrup with gelatin or gum arabic

gum·ma \'gəm-ə\ *n*, *pl* **gummas** *also* **gum·ma·ta** \'gəm-ət-ə\ [NL *gummat-*, *gumma*, fr. LL, gum, alter. of L *gummi* gum] (ca. 1722) : a tumor of gummy or rubbery consistency that is characteristic of the tertiary stage of syphilis — **gum·ma·tous** \-ət-əs\ *adj*

gum·mite \'gəm-,īt\ *n* (1868) : a yellow to reddish brown mixture of hydrous oxides of uranium, thorium, and lead consisting perhaps largely of curite

gum·mo·sis \,gə-'mō-səs\ *n* (1882) : a pathological production of gummy exudate in a plant; *also* : a plant disease marked by gummosis

gum·mous \'gəm-əs\ *adj* (1669) : resembling or composed of gum

gum·my \'gəm-ē\ *adj* **gum·mi·er; -est** (14c) **1** : VISCOUS, STICKY **2 a** : consisting of or containing gum **b** : covered with gum — **gum·mi·ness** *n*

gump·tion \'gəm(p)-shən\ *n* [origin unknown] (1719) **1** : shrewd practical common sense esp. as actively applied to the problems of life **2** : ENTERPRISE, INITIATIVE ***syn*** see SENSE

gum resin *n* (1712) : a product consisting essentially of a mixture of gum and resin usu. obtained by making an incision in a plant and allowing the juice which exudes to solidify

[1]**gum·shoe** \'gəm-,shü\ *n* (1904) : DETECTIVE

[2]**gumshoe** *vi* (1904) : to engage in detective work

gum tragacanth *n* (1573) : TRAGACANTH

gum tree *n* (1676) : [3]GUM 3

gum turpentine *n* (1926) : TURPENTINE 2a

gum·wood \'gəm-,wu̇d\ *n* (1709) : [3]GUM 4

[1]**gun** \'gən\ *n* [ME *gonne, gunne*] (14c) **1 a** : a piece of ordnance usu. with high muzzle velocity and comparatively flat trajectory **b** : a portable firearm (as a rifle or handgun) **c** : a device that throws a projectile **2 a** : a discharge of a gun in a salute or as a signal **b** : a signal marking a beginning or ending **3 a** : HUNTER **b** : GUNMAN **4** : something suggesting a gun in shape or function **5** : THROTTLE — **gunned** \'gənd\ *adj* — **under the gun** : under pressure or attack

[2]**gun** *vb* **gunned; gun·ning** *vi* (1622) : to hunt with a gun ~ *vt* **1 a** : to fire on **b** : SHOOT ⟨*gunned* down by a hit man⟩ **2** : to open up the throttle of so as to increase speed ⟨~ the engine⟩ — **gun for** : to aim at with determination or effort

gun·boat \'gən-,bōt\ *n* (1793) : an armed ship of shallow draft

gunboat diplomacy *n* (1927) : diplomacy backed by the use or threat of military force

gun·cot·ton \-,kät-ᵊn\ *n* (1846) : CELLULOSE NITRATE; *esp* : an explosive highly nitrated product used chiefly in smokeless powder

gun·dog \ˈ-ˌdȯg\ *n* (1744) **:** a dog trained to work with hunters by locating and retrieving game

gun·fight \ˈ-ˌfīt\ *n* (1659) **:** a hostile encounter in which antagonists fire upon each other — **gun·fight·er** \-ər\ *n*

gun·fire \ˈ-ˌfī(ə)r\ *n* (1801) **:** the firing of guns

gun·flint \ˈ-ˌflint\ *n* (1731) **:** a small sharp flint fashioned to ignite the priming in a flintlock

gung ho \ˈgəŋ-ˈhō\ *adj* [*Gung ho!*, motto (interpreted as meaning "work together") of certain U.S. marine raiders in World War II, fr. Chin (Pek) *kung*^{1}*-ho*^{2}, short for *chung*^{1}*-kuo*^{2} *kung*^{1}*-yeh*^{4} *ho*^{2}*-tso*^{4} *she*^{4} Chinese Industrial Cooperatives Society] (1942) **:** extremely or overly zealous or enthusiastic

Gun·ite \ˈgən-ˌīt\ *trademark* — used for a mixture of cement, sand, and water sprayed on a metal mold

gunk \ˈgəŋk\ *n* [origin unknown] (1943) **:** filthy, sticky, or greasy matter — **gunky** \ˈgəŋ-kē\ *adj*

gun lap *n* (ca. 1949) **:** the final lap of a race in track signaled by the firing of a gun as the leader begins the lap

gun·lock \ˈgən-ˌläk\ *n* (1731) **:** a mechanism attached to or integral with a firearm by which the charge is ignited

gun·man \-mən\ *n* (1624) **1 :** a man armed with a gun; *esp* **:** a professional killer **2 :** a man noted for speed or skill in handling a gun

gun·met·al \ˈgən-ˌmet-ᵊl\ *n* (1541) **1 :** a metal used for guns; *specif* **:** a bronze formerly much used as a material for cannon **2 :** an alloy or metal treated to imitate nearly black tarnished copper-alloy gunmetal

gun moll \-ˌmäl, -ˌmȯl\ *n, slang* (ca. 1908) **:** the girlfriend of a gangster

Gun·nar \ˈgu̇n-ˌär, ˈgün-, -ər\ *n* [ON *Gunnarr*] **:** the king of the Nibelungs and husband of Brynhild in Norse mythology

^{1}**gun·nel** \ˈgən-ᵊl\ *var of* GUNWALE

^{2}**gunnel** *n* [origin unknown] (1740) **:** a small slimy elongate north Atlantic blenny (*Pholis gunnellus*); *broadly* **:** any fish of the family (Pholidae) to which the gunnel belongs

gun·ner \ˈgən-ər\ *n* (14c) **1 :** a soldier or airman who operates or aims a gun **2 :** one who hunts with a gun **3 :** a warrant officer who supervises ordnance and ordnance stores

gun·nery \ˈgən-(ə-)rē\ *n* (1605) **:** the use of guns; *specif* **:** the science of the flight of projectiles and of the effective use of guns

gunnery sergeant *n* (ca. 1961) **:** a noncommissioned officer in the marine corps ranking above a staff sergeant and below a master sergeant or first sergeant

gun·ny \ˈgən-ē\ *n* [Hindi *gānī*] (1711) **:** a coarse heavy fabric usu. of jute or hemp used esp. for bagging

gun·ny·sack \-ˌsak\ *n* (1862) **:** a sack made of gunny

gun·play \ˈgən-ˌplā\ *n* (1881) **:** the shooting of small arms with intent to scare or kill

gun·point \ˈ-ˌpȯint\ *n* (1951) **:** the point of a gun — **at gunpoint :** under a threat of death by being shot

gun·pow·der \ˈ-ˌpau̇d-ər\ *n* (15c) **:** an explosive mixture of potassium nitrate, charcoal, and sulfur used in gunnery and blasting; *broadly* **:** any of various powders used in guns as propelling charges

gun room *n* (1626) **:** quarters on a British warship orig. used by the gunner and his mates but now by midshipmen and junior officers

gun·run·ner \ˈgən-ˌrən-ər\ *n* (1899) **:** one that traffics in contraband arms and ammunition — **gun·run·ning** \-ˌrən-iŋ\ *n*

gun·sel \ˈgən(t)-səl\ *n* [slang *gunsel* (stupid person, traitor)] *slang* (1944) **:** GUNMAN

gun·ship \ˈgən-ˌship\ *n* (1966) **:** a helicopter or cargo aircraft armed with rockets and machine guns

gun·shot \ˈgən-ˌshät\ *n* (15c) **1 :** shot or a projectile fired from a gun **2 :** the range of a gun **3 :** the firing of a gun

gun–shy \ˈ-ˌshī\ *adj* (1884) **1 :** afraid of loud noise (as that of a gun) **2 :** markedly distrustful, afraid, or cautious

gun·sling·er \ˈ-ˌsliŋ-ər\ *n* (1928) **:** a person noted for speed and skill in handling and shooting a gun esp. in the American West

gun·sling·ing \ˈ-ˌsliŋ-iŋ\ *n* (1944) **:** the shooting of a gun esp. in a gunfight

gun·smith \ˈ-ˌsmith\ *n* (1588) **:** one who designs, makes, or repairs small firearms — **gun·smith·ing** \-ˌsmith-iŋ\ *n*

Gun·ter's chain \ˌgənt-ərz-\ *n* [Edmund *Gunter*] (ca. 1679) **:** a chain 66 feet long that is the unit of length for surveys of U.S. public lands

Gun·ther \ˈgu̇nt-ər\ *n* [G] **:** a Burgundian king and husband of Brunhild in Germanic legend

gun·wale *also* **gun·nel** \ˈgən-ᵊl\ *n* [ME *gonne-wale*, fr. *gonne* gun + ^{1}*wale*; fr. its former use as a support for guns] (15c) **:** the upper edge of a ship's or boat's side

gup·py \ˈgəp-ē\ *n, pl* **guppies** [R.J.L. *Guppy* †1916 Trinidadian naturalist] (1925) **:** a small live-bearer (*Poecilia reticulata* of the family Poeciliidae) of the Barbados, Trinidad, and Venezuela often kept as an aquarium fish

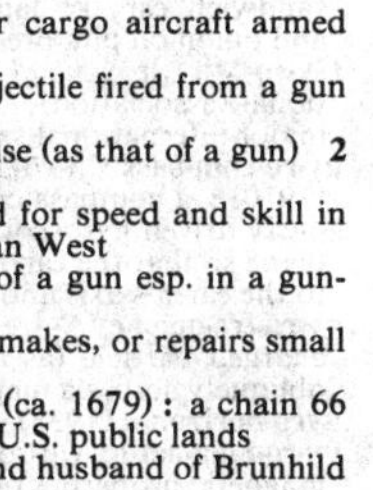

guppy: *1* female, *2* male

gur·gle \ˈgər-gəl\ *vi* **gur·gled; gur·gling** \-g(ə-)liŋ\ [prob. imit.] (1757) **1 :** to flow in a broken irregular current ⟨the brook *gurgling* over the rocks⟩ **2 :** to make a sound like that of a gurgling liquid ⟨the baby *gurgling* in his crib⟩ — **gurgle** *n*

Gur·kha \ˈgu̇(ə)r-kə, ˈgər-\ *n* [*Ghurka*, member of race dominant in Nepal] (1811) **:** a soldier from Nepal in the British or Indian army

gur·nard \ˈgər-nərd\ *n, pl* **gurnard** *or* **gurnards** [ME, fr. MF *gornart*, irreg. fr. *grognier* to grunt, fr. L *grunnire*, of imit. origin] (14c) **:** SEA ROBIN

gur·ney \ˈgər-nē\ *n, pl* **gurneys** [prob. fr. the name *Gurney*] (1939) **:** a wheeled cot or stretcher

gur·ry \ˈgər-ē, ˈgə-rē\ *n* [origin unknown] (1850) **:** fishing offal

gu·ru \gə-ˈrü, ˈgu̇(ə)r-(ˌ)ü\ *n, pl* **gurus** [Hindi *gurū*, fr. Skt *guru*, fr. *guru*, adj., heavy, venerable — more at GRIEVE] (1613) **1 :** a personal religious teacher and spiritual guide in Hinduism **2 a :** a teacher and esp. intellectual guide in matters of fundamental concern **b :** one who is an acknowledged leader or chief proponent

^{1}**gush** \ˈgəsh\ *vb* [ME *guschen*] *vi* (15c) **1 :** to issue copiously or violently **2 :** to emit a sudden copious flow **3 :** to make an effusive display of affection or enthusiasm ⟨an aunt ~*ing* over the baby⟩ ~ *vt* **:** to emit in a copious free flow

^{2}**gush** *n* (1682) **1 a :** a sudden outpouring **b :** something emitted in a gushing forth **2 :** an effusive display or outpouring of sentiment or enthusiasm

gush·er \ˈgəsh-ər\ *n* (1864) **:** one that gushes; *specif* **:** an oil well with a copious natural flow

gushy \ˈgəsh-ē\ *adj* **gush·i·er; -est** (1845) **:** marked by effusive sentimentality — **gush·i·ly** \ˈgəsh-ə-lē\ *adv* — **gush·i·ness** \ˈgəsh-ē-nəs\ *n*

gus·set \ˈgəs-ət\ *n* [ME, piece of armor covering the joints in a suit of armor, fr. MF *gouchet*] (14c) **1 :** a usu. diamond-shaped or triangular insert in a seam (as of a sleeve, pocketbook, or shoe upper) to provide expansion or reinforcement **2 :** a plate or bracket for strengthening an angle in framework (as in a building or bridge) — **gusset** *vt*

gus·sy up \ˌgəs-ē-\ *vt* **gus·sied up; gus·sy·ing up** [origin unknown] (1952) **:** DRESS UP ⟨most of the items are *gussied up* with gold plating — *Newsweek*⟩

^{1}**gust** \ˈgəst\ *n* [ME *guste*, fr. L *gustus*; akin to L *gustare* to taste — more at CHOOSE] (15c) **1** *obs* **a :** the sensation of taste **b :** INCLINATION, LIKING **2 :** keen delight

^{2}**gust** *n* [prob. fr. ON *gustr*; akin to OHG *gussa* flood, OE *gēotan* to pour — more at FOUND] (1588) **1 :** a sudden brief rush of wind **2 :** a sudden outburst **:** SURGE ⟨a ~ of emotion⟩ — **gust·i·ly** \ˈgəs-tə-lē\ *adv* — **gust·i·ness** \-tē-nəs\ *n* — **gusty** \-tē\ *adj*

^{3}**gust** *vi* (1813) **:** to blow in gusts ⟨winds ~*ing* up to 40 mph⟩

gus·ta·tion \ˌgəs-ˈtā-shən\ *n* [L *gustation-*, *gustatio*, fr. *gustatus*, pp. of *gustare*] (1599) **:** the act or sensation of tasting

gus·ta·to·ry \ˈgəs-tə-ˌtōr-ē, -ˌtȯr-\ *adj* (1684) **:** relating to, associated with, or being the sense of taste — **gus·ta·to·ri·ly** \ˌgəs-tə-ˈtōr-ə-lē, -ˈtȯr-\ *adv*

gus·to \ˈgəs-(ˌ)tō\ *n, pl* **gustoes** [Sp, fr. L *gustus*, pp.] (1620) **1 a :** an individual or special taste ⟨we must make allowance for different ~*es*⟩ **b :** enthusiastic and vigorous enjoyment or appreciation **c :** vitality marked by an abundance of vigor and enthusiasm **2** *archaic* **:** artistic style

^{1}**gut** \ˈgət\ *n* [ME, fr. OE *guttas*, pl.; akin to OE *gēotan* to pour] (bef. 12c) **1 a** (1) **:** BOWELS, ENTRAILS — usu. used in pl. (2) **:** the basic visceral or emotional part of a person **b :** the alimentary canal or part of it (as the intestine or stomach) **c :** BELLY, ABDOMEN **d :** CATGUT **2** *pl* **:** the inner essential parts ⟨the ~*s* of a car⟩ **3 :** a narrow passage; *also* **:** a narrow waterway or small creek **4 :** the sac of silk taken from a silkworm ready to spin its cocoon and drawn out into a thread for use as a snell **5** *pl* **:** fortitude and stamina in coping with what alarms, repels, or discourages **:** COURAGE

^{2}**gut** *vt* **gut·ted; gut·ting** (14c) **1 a :** EVISCERATE **b :** to extract all the essential passages or portions from **2 a :** to destroy the inside of ⟨fire *gutted* the building⟩ **b :** to destroy the essential power or effectiveness of ⟨inflation *gutting* the economy⟩ — **gut it out :** PERSEVERE

^{3}**gut** *adj* (1964) **1 :** arising from one's inmost self **:** VISCERAL ⟨a ~ reaction⟩ **2 :** having strong impact or immediate relevance ⟨~ issues⟩

gut·buck·et \ˈgət-ˌbək-ət\ *n* (1929) **1 :** BARRELHOUSE 2 **2 :** a homemade bass fiddle consisting of a stick attached to an inverted washtub and having a single string

gut course *n* (1948) **:** a course (as in college) that is easily passed

gut·less \ˈgət-ləs\ *adj* (1900) **1 :** lacking courage **:** COWARDLY **2 :** lacking significance or vitality — **gut·less·ness** *n*

gutsy \ˈgət-sē\ *adj* **guts·i·er; -est** (1893) **1 :** COURAGEOUS ⟨a ~ little fighter⟩ **2 :** expressing or appealing strongly to the physical senses or passions **:** LUSTY ⟨belting out ~ rock⟩ — **guts·i·ness** *n*

gut·ta \ˈgət-ə, ˈgu̇t-ə\ *n, pl* **gut·tae** \ˈgə-ˌtē, ˈgu̇-, -ˌtī\ [L, lit., drop — more at GOUT] (1563) **:** one of a series of ornaments in the Doric entablature that is usu. in the form of a frustum of a cone

gut·ta–per·cha \ˌgət-ə-ˈpər-chə\ *n* [Malay *gĕtah-pĕrcha*, fr. *gĕtah* sap, latex + *pĕrcha* tree producing gutta-percha] (1845) **:** a tough plastic substance from the latex of several Malaysian trees (genera *Payena* and *Palaquium*) of the sapodilla family that resembles rubber but contains more resin and is used esp. as insulation and in dentistry

gut·ta·tion \ˌgə-ˈtā-shən\ *n* [L *gutta* drop] (ca. 1889) **:** the exudation of liquid water from the uninjured surface of a plant

^{1}**gut·ter** \ˈgət-ər\ *n* [ME *goter*, fr. MF *goutiere*, fr. *goute* drop, fr. L *gutta*] (14c) **1 a :** a trough along the eaves to catch and carry off rainwater **b :** a low area (as at the edge of a street) to carry off surface water (as to a sewer) **c :** a trough or groove to catch and direct something ⟨the ~*s* of a bowling alley⟩ **2 :** a white space formed by the adjoining inside margins of two facing pages (as of a book) **3 :** the lowest or most vulgar level or condition of human life

^{2}**gutter** *vt* (14c) **1 :** to cut or wear gutters in **2 :** to provide with a gutter ~ *vi* **1 a :** to flow in rivulets **b** *of a candle* **:** to melt away through a channel out of the side of the cup hollowed out by the burning wick **2 :** to incline downward in a draft ⟨the candle flame ~*ing* in the breeze⟩

^{3}**gutter** *adj* (15c) **:** of, relating to, or characteristic of the gutter; *esp* **:** marked by extreme vulgarity, cheapness, or indecency ⟨~ journalism⟩ ⟨~ politics⟩

gutter out *vi* (1875) **1 :** to become gradually weaker and then go out ⟨the candle *guttered out*⟩ **2 :** to end feebly or undramatically ⟨his screen career had slowly *guttered out*⟩

gut·ter·snipe \ˈgət-ər-ˌsnīp\ *n* (1869) **1 :** STREET ARAB **2 :** a person of the lowest moral or economic station — **gut·ter·snip·ish** \-ˌsnī-pish\ *adj*

gut·tur·al \ˈgət-ə-rəl, ˈgə-trəl\ *adj* [MF, prob. fr. ML *gutturalis*, fr. L *guttur* throat — more at COT] (1594) **1 :** articulated in the throat ⟨~ sounds⟩ **2 :** VELAR **3 :** being or marked by utterance that is strange, unpleasant, or disagreeable — **guttural** *n* — **gut·tur·al·ism** \ˈgət-ə-rə-ˌliz-əm, ˈgə-trə-\ *n*

gut·ty \ˈgət-ē\ *adj* **gut·ti·er; -est** (1947) **1 :** marked by courage or fortitude ⟨a ~ quarterback⟩ **2 :** having a vigorous challenging quality ⟨~ realism⟩

^{1}**guy** \ˈgī\ *n* [prob. fr. D *gei* brail] (1623) **:** a rope, chain, rod, or wire attached to something as a brace or guide

\ə\ abut \ᵊ\ kitten, F table \ər\ further \a\ ash \ā\ ace \ä\ cot, cart
\au̇\ out \ch\ chin \e\ bet \ē\ easy \g\ go \i\ hit \ī\ ice \j\ job
\ŋ\ sing \ō\ go \ȯ\ law \ȯi\ boy \th\ thin \t͟h\ the \ü\ loot \u̇\ foot
\y\ yet \zh\ vision \à, k̲, ⁿ, œ, œ̄, ue, ue̅, ʸ\ *see* Guide to Pronunciation

[2]guy *vt* (1712) **:** to steady or reinforce with a guy

[3]guy *n* [*Guy* Fawkes] (1806) **1** *often cap* **:** a grotesque effigy of Guy Fawkes traditionally displayed and burned in England on Guy Fawkes Day **2** *chiefly Brit* **:** a person of grotesque appearance **3 a :** MAN, FELLOW **b :** PERSON — used in pl. to refer to the members of a group regardless of sex ⟨saw her and the rest of the ~*s*⟩

[4]guy *vt* (1854) **:** to make fun of **:** RIDICULE

Guy Fawkes Day \ˈgī-ˈfȯks-\ *n* (1825) **:** November 5 observed in England in commemoration of the seizure of Guy Fawkes in 1605 for an attempt to blow up the houses of parliament

guy·ot \ˈgē-(ˌ)ō\ *n* [Arnold H. *Guyot* †1884 Am. geographer & geologist] (1946) **:** a flat-topped seamount

guz·zle \ˈgəz-əl\ *vb* **guz·zled; guz·zling** \-(ə-)liŋ\ [origin unknown] *vi* (1583) **:** to drink esp. liquor greedily, continually, or habitually ~ *vt* **:** to drink greedily or habitually ⟨~ beer⟩ — **guz·zler** \-(ə-)lər\ *n*

gwe·duc \ˈgü-ē-ˌdək\ *var of* GEODUCK

gybe \ˈjīb\ *var of* JIBE

gym \ˈjim\ *n* (ca. 1871) **1 :** GYMNASIUM **2 :** PHYSICAL EDUCATION **3 :** a metal frame supporting an assortment of outdoor play equipment (as a swing, seesaw, and rings)

gym·kha·na \jim-ˈkän-ə, -ˈkan-\ *n* [prob. modif. of Hindi *gend-khāna* racket court] (1877) **:** a meet featuring sports contests or athletic skills: as **a** *Brit* **:** competitive games on horseback **b :** a timed contest for automobiles featuring a series of events designed to test driving skill

gymn- *or* **gymno-** *comb form* [NL, fr. Gk, fr. *gymnos* — more at NAKED] **:** naked **:** bare ⟨*gymno*gynous⟩

gym·na·si·um *sense 1* jim-ˈnā-zē-əm, -zhəm; *sense 2 usu* gim-ˈnä-zē-əm\ *n, pl* **-na·si·ums** *or* **-na·sia** \-ˈnā-zē-ə, -ˈnā-zhə; -ˈnä-zē-ə\ [L, exercise ground, school, fr. Gk *gymnasion*, fr. *gymnazein* to exercise naked, fr. *gymnos*] (1598) **1 a :** a large room used for various indoor sports (as basketball, boxing, or volleyball) and usu. equipped with gymnastic apparatus **b :** a building (as on a college campus) containing space and equipment for various indoor sports activities and usu. including spectator accommodations, locker and shower rooms, offices, classrooms, and a swimming pool **2** [G, fr. L, school] **:** a German secondary school that prepares students for the university

gym·nast \ˈjim-ˌnast, -nəst\ *n* [MF *gymnaste*, fr. Gk *gymnastēs* trainer, fr. *gymnazein*] (1594) **:** one trained in gymnastics

[1]gym·nas·tic \jim-ˈnas-tik\ *adj* (1574) **:** of or relating to gymnastics **:** ATHLETIC — **gym·nas·ti·cal·ly** \-ti-k(ə-)lē\ *adv*

[2]gymnastic *n* (1652) **1** *pl but sing in constr* **a :** physical exercises designed to develop strength and coordination **b :** a competitive sport in which individuals perform optional and prescribed acrobatic feats mostly on special apparatus in order to demonstrate strength, balance, and body control **2 :** an exercise in intellectual or artistic dexterity ⟨my earlier philosophic study had been an intellectual ~ —John Dewey⟩ ⟨mental ~*s*⟩ **3 :** a physical feat or contortion ⟨the ~*s* necessary for the killer to have swung from the fire escape —E.D. Radin⟩

gym·nos·o·phist \jim-ˈnäs-ə-fəst\ *n* [L *gymnosophista*, fr. Gk *gymnosophistēs*, fr. *gymn-* + *sophistēs* wise man, sophist] (15c) **:** one of a sect of ascetics in ancient India who went naked and practiced meditation

gym·no·sperm \ˈjim-nə-ˌspərm\ *n* [deriv. of NL *gymn-* + Gk *sperma* seed — more at SPERM] (ca. 1838) **:** any of a class or subdivision (Gymnospermae) of woody vascular seed plants (as conifers) that produce naked seeds not enclosed in an ovary and that in some instances have motile spermatozoids — **gym·no·sper·mous** \ˌjim-nə-ˈspər-məs\ *adj* — **gym·no·sper·my** \ˈjim-nə-ˌspər-mē\ *n*

gyn- *or* **gyno-** *comb form* [Gk *gyn-*, fr. *gynē* woman — more at QUEEN] **1 :** woman ⟨*gyn*iatrics⟩ ⟨*gyno*cracy⟩ **2 :** female reproductive organ **:** ovary ⟨*gyno*phore⟩ **:** pistil ⟨*gyno*dioecious⟩

gyn·an·dro·morph \(ˈ)gīn-ˈan-drə-ˌmȯrf, (ˈ)jin-\ *n* [ISV, fr. Gk *gynandros* + *-morph*] (ca. 1890) **:** an abnormal individual exhibiting characters of both sexes in various parts of the body **:** a sexual mosaic — **gyn·an·dro·mor·phic** \(ˌ)gīn-ˌan-drə-ˈmȯr-fik, (ˌ)jin-\ *adj* — **gyn·an·dro·mor·phism** \-ˌfiz-əm\ *n* — **gyn·an·dro·mor·phy** \(ˈ)gīn-ˈan-drə-ˌmȯr-fē, (ˈ)jin-\ *n*

gyn·an·drous \(ˈ)gīn-ˈan-drəs, (ˈ)jin-\ *adj* [Gk *gynandros* of doubtful sex, fr. *gynē* woman + *andr-*, *anēr* man — more at ANDR-] (1807) **:** having the androecium and gynoecium united in a column

-gyne \ˌjīn, ˌgīn\ *n comb form* [Gk *gynē*] **1 :** woman **:** female ⟨pseudo*gyne*⟩ **2 :** female reproductive organ ⟨tricho*gyne*⟩

gynec- *or* **gyneco-** *also* **gynaec-** *or* **gynaeco-** *comb form* [Gk *gynaik-*, *gynaiko-*, fr. *gynaik-*, *gynē* woman — more at QUEEN] **:** woman ⟨*gyne*coid⟩

gy·ne·coc·ra·cy \ˌgīn-i-ˈkäk-rə-sē, ˌjin-\ *n, pl* **-cies** [Gk *gynaikokratia*, fr. *gynaik-* + *-kratia* -cracy] (1612) **:** political supremacy of women — **gy·ne·co·crat·ic** \ˌgīn-i-kō-ˈkrat-ik, ˌjin-\ *adj*

gy·ne·coid \ˈgīn-i-ˌkȯid, ˈjin-\ *adj* (1907) **:** typical of the human female ⟨~ pelvis⟩

gy·ne·col·o·gy \ˌgīn-ə-ˈkäl-ə-jē, ˌjin-\ *n* [ISV] (ca. 1847) **:** a branch of medicine that deals with the diseases and hygiene of women — **gy·ne·co·log·ic** \ˌgīn-i-kə-ˈläj-ik, ˌjin-\ *or* **gy·ne·co·log·i·cal** \-i-kəl\ *adj* — **gy·ne·col·o·gist** \ˌgīn-ə-ˈkäl-ə-jəst, ˌjin-\ *n*

gy·neco·mas·tia \ˈgī-nə-kō-ˈmas-tē-ə\ *n* [NL, fr. *gynec-* + *mast-* + NL *-ia*] (1881) **:** excessive development of the breast in the male

gy·noe·ci·um \jin-ˈē-s(h)ē-əm, gīn-\ *n, pl* **-cia** \-s(h)ē-ə\ [NL, alter. of L *gynaeceum* women's apartments, fr. Gk *gynaikeion*, fr. *gynaik-*, *gynē*] (1832) **:** the aggregate of carpels in a flower **:** PISTILS

gy·no·gen·e·sis \ˌgīn-ə-ˈjen-ə-səs\ *n* [NL] (1925) **:** development in which the embryo contains only maternal chromosomes due to activation of an egg by a sperm that degenerates without fusing with the egg nucleus — **gy·no·ge·net·ic** \-jə-ˈnet-ik\ *adj*

gy·no·phore \ˈgīn-ə-ˌfō(ə)r, ˈjin-, -ˌfȯ(ə)r\ *n* (1821) **:** a prolongation of the receptacle (as in a caper flower) that bears the gynoecium at its apex

-g·y·nous \j-ə-nəs\ *adj comb form* [NL *-gynus*, fr. Gk *-gynos*, fr. *gynē* woman — more at QUEEN] **1 :** of, relating to, or having (such or so many) females ⟨hetero*gynous*⟩ **2 a :** having (such or so many) styles or pistils ⟨tetra*gynous*⟩ **b :** situated (in a specified place) in relation to a female organ of a plant ⟨hypo*gynous*⟩

-g·y·ny \j-ə-nē\ *n comb form* **1 :** existence of or condition of having (such or so many) females ⟨poly*gyny*⟩ **2 :** condition of being situated (in a specified place) in relation to a female organ of a plant ⟨epi*gyny*⟩

[1]gyp \ˈjip\ *n* [prob. short for *gypsy*] (1750) **1** *Brit* **:** a college servant **2 a :** CHEAT, SWINDLER **b :** FRAUD, SWINDLE

[2]gyp *vb* **gypped; gyp·ping** (1880) **:** CHEAT

gyp·se·ous \ˈjip-sē-əs\ *adj* (1661) **:** resembling, containing, or consisting of gypsum ⟨~ clay loam⟩

gyp·sif·er·ous \jip-ˈsif-(ə-)rəs\ *adj* (ca. 1847) **:** bearing gypsum

gyp·soph·i·la \jip-ˈsäf-ə-lə\ *n* [NL, fr. L *gypsum* + *-phila* -phil] (1771) **:** any of a large genus (*Gypsophila*) of Old World herbs of the pink family having small delicate paniculate flowers

gyp·sum \ˈjip-səm\ *n* [L, fr. Gk *gypsos*, of Sem origin; akin to Ar *jibs* plaster] (14c) **1 :** a widely distributed mineral $CaSO_4 \cdot 2H_2O$ consisting of hydrous calcium sulfate that is used esp. as a soil amendment and in making plaster of paris **2 :** PLASTERBOARD

gyp·sy \ˈjip-sē\ *vi* **gyp·sied; gyp·sy·ing** (1627) **:** to live or roam like a Gypsy

Gyp·sy \ˈjip-sē\ *n, pl* **Gypsies** [by shortening & alter. fr. *Egyptian*] (1537) **1 :** one of a dark Caucasoid people coming orig. from India to Europe in the 14th or 15th century and living and maintaining a migratory way of life chiefly in Europe and the U.S. **2 :** ROMANY 2 **3** *not cap* **:** one that resembles a Gypsy (as in appearance or mode of life); *esp* **:** WANDERER

gypsy cab *n* (1964) **:** a taxicab licensed only to answer calls; *esp* **:** such a cab that cruises in search of passengers

gypsy moth *n* (1819) **:** an Old World tussock moth (*Porthetria dispar*) that was introduced about 1869 into the U.S. and has a grayish brown mottled hairy caterpillar which is a destructive defoliator of many trees

gyr- *or* **gyro-** *comb form* [prob. fr. MF, fr. L, fr. Gk, fr. *gyros* rounded] **1 :** ring **:** circle **:** spiral ⟨*gyro*magnetic⟩ **2 :** gyroscope ⟨*gyro*compass⟩

[1]gy·rate \ˈjī-ˌrāt\ *adj* (1830) **:** winding or coiled around **:** CONVOLUTED ⟨~ branches of a tree⟩

[2]gyrate *vi* **gy·rat·ed; gy·rat·ing** (1830) **1 :** to revolve around a point or axis **2 :** to oscillate with or as if with a circular or spiral motion — **gy·ra·tor** \-ˌrāt-ər\ *n* — **gy·ra·to·ry** \ˈjī-rə-ˌtōr-ē, -ˌtȯr-\ *adj*

gy·ra·tion \jī-ˈrā-shən\ *n* (1615) **1 :** an act or instance of gyrating **2 :** something (as a coil of a shell) that is gyrate — **gy·ra·tion·al** \-shnəl, -shən-ᵊl\ *adj*

[1]gyre \ˈjī(ə)r\ *vi* **gyred; gyr·ing** [ME *giren*, fr. LL *gyrare*, fr. *gyrus*] (14c) **:** to move in a circle or spiral

[2]gyre *n* [L *gyrus*, fr. Gk *gyros* — more at COWER] (1566) **:** a circular or spiral motion or form; *esp* **:** a giant circular oceanic surface current — **gy·ral** \ˈjī-rəl\ *adj*

gy·rene \jī-ˈrēn\ *n* [prob. alter. of *marine*] *slang* (1944) **:** a U.S. marine

gyr·fal·con \ˈjər-ˌfal-kən, -ˌfȯl- *also* -ˌfō-kən\ *n* [ME *gerfaucun*, fr. OF *girfaucon*, prob. fr. ON *geirfalki*, fr. *geirr* spear (akin to OE *gār*) + *falki* falcon — more at GORE] (13c) **:** an arctic falcon (*Falco rusticolus*) that occurs in several forms, is the largest of all falcons, and is more powerful though less active than the peregrine falcon

gyrfalcon

[1]gy·ro \ˈjī-(ˌ)rō\ *n, pl* **gyros** (1910) **1 :** GYROSCOPE **2 :** GYROCOMPASS

[2]gy·ro \ˈyē-ˌrō, ˈzhir-ō\ *n* [NGk *gyros* turn; fr. the rotation of the meat on a spit] (1971) **:** a sandwich esp. of lamb and beef, tomato, and onion on pita bread

Gy·ro \ˈjī-(ˌ)rō\ *n, pl* **Gyros** [*Gyro* International (association)] (1971) **:** a member of a major international service club

gy·ro·com·pass \ˈjī-rō-ˌkəm-pəs *also* -ˌkäm-\ *n* (1910) **:** a compass consisting of a continuously driven gyroscope whose spinning axis is confined to a horizontal plane so that the earth's rotation causes it to assume a position parallel to the earth's axis and thus point to the true north

gy·ro·fre·quen·cy \-ˌfrē-kwən-sē\ *n* (1938) **:** the frequency with which a charged particle (as an electron) executes spiral gyrations in moving obliquely across a magnetic field

gyro horizon *n* (1938) **:** ARTIFICIAL HORIZON 2

gy·ro·mag·net·ic \ˌjī-rō-mag-ˈnet-ik\ *adj* (1922) **:** of or relating to the magnetic properties of a rotating electrical particle

gyromagnetic ratio *n* (1922) **:** the ratio of the magnetic moment of a spinning charged particle to its angular momentum

gy·ron \ˈjī-rən\ *n* [MF *giron* gore, of Gmc origin; akin to OHG *gēra* wedge-shaped object, OE *gār* spear — more at GORE] (1572) **:** a heraldic charge of triangular form having one side at the edge of the field and the opposite angle usu. at the fess point

gy·ro·plane \ˈjī-rə-ˌplān\ *n* [ISV] (1907) **:** an airplane balanced and supported by the aerodynamic forces acting on rapidly rotating horizontal or slightly inclined airfoils

gy·ro·scope \ˈjī-rə-ˌskōp, *Brit also* ˈgī-\ *n* [F] (1856) **:** a wheel or disk mounted to spin rapidly about an axis and also free to rotate about one or both of two axes perpendicular to each other and to the axis of spin so that a rotation of one of the two mutually perpendicular axes results from application of torque to the other when the wheel is spinning and so that the entire apparatus offers considerable opposition depending on the angular momentum to any torque that would change the direction of the axis of spin — **gy·ro·scop·ic** \ˌjī-rə-ˈskäp-ik\ *adj* — **gy·ro·scop·i·cal·ly** \-i-k(ə-)lē\ *adv*

gy·ro·sta·bi·liz·er \ˌjī-rō-ˈstā-bə-ˌlī-zər\ *n* (1921) **:** a stabilizing device (as for a ship or airplane) that consists of a continuously driven gyro spinning about a vertical axis and pivoted so that its axis of spin may be tipped fore-and-aft in the vertical plane and that serves to oppose sideways motion

gy·ro·stat \ˈjī-rə-ˌstat\ *n* (1879) **:** GYROSTABILIZER

gy·rus \ˈjī-rəs\ *n, pl* **gy·ri** \ˈjī-ˌrī\ [NL, fr. L, circle — more at GYRE] (1846) **:** a convoluted ridge (as a convolution of the brain) between anatomical grooves

gyve \ˈjīv, ˈgīv\ *n* [ME] (13c) **:** FETTER, SHACKLE — **gyve** *vt*

H

h \'āch\ *n, pl* **h's** *or* **hs** \'ā-chəz\ *often cap, often attrib* **1 a :** the 8th letter of the English alphabet **b :** a graphic representation of this letter **c :** a speech counterpart of orthographic *h* **2 :** a graphic device for reproducing the letter *h* **3 :** one designated *h* esp. as the 8th in order or class **4 :** something shaped like the letter H

ha \'hä\ *interj* [ME, fr. OE] (bef. 12c) — used esp. to express surprise or joy

Ha·ba·cuc \'hab-ə-ˌkək, hə-'bak-ək\ *n* [LL, fr. Heb *Hăbhaqqūq*] **:** HABAKKUK

Ha·bak·kuk \'hab-ə-ˌkək, hə-'bak-ək\ *n* [Heb *Hăbhaqqūq*] **1 :** a Hebrew prophet of 7th century B.C. Judah who prophesied an imminent Chaldean invasion **2 :** a prophetic book of canonical Jewish and Christian Scripture — see BIBLE table

ha·ba·ne·ra \ˌ(h)äb-ə-'ner-ə\ *n* [Sp *(danza) habanera,* lit., Havanan dance] (1878) **1 :** a Cuban dance in slow duple time **2 :** the music for the habanera

hab·da·lah \ˌhäv-də-'lä, häv-'dȯ-lə\ *n, often cap* [Heb *habhdālāh* separation] (1733) **:** a Jewish ceremony marking the close of a Sabbath or holy day

ha·be·as cor·pus \ˌhā-bē-əs-'kȯr-pəs\ *n* [ME, fr. ML, lit., you should have the body (the opening words of the writ)] (15c) **1 :** any of several common-law writs issued to bring a party before a court or judge; *esp* **:** HABEAS CORPUS AD SUBJICIENDUM **2 :** the right of a citizen to obtain a writ of habeas corpus as a protection against illegal imprisonment

habeas corpus ad sub·ji·ci·en·dum \-ˌad-səb-ˌyik-ē-'en-dəm\ *n* [NL, lit., you should have the body for submitting] (1768) **:** a writ for inquiring into the lawfulness of the restraint of a person who is imprisoned or detained in another's custody

hab·er·dash·er \'hab-ə(r)-ˌdash-ər\ *n* [ME *haberdassher,* fr. modif. of AF *hapertas* petty merchandise] (14c) **1** *Brit* **:** a dealer in notions **2 :** a dealer in men's clothing and accessories

hab·er·dash·ery \-ˌdash-(ə-)rē\ *n, pl* **-er·ies** (1593) **1 :** goods sold by a haberdasher **2 :** a haberdasher's shop

ha·ber·geon \'hab-ər-jən, hə-'bər-j(ē-)ən\ *n* [ME *haubergeoun,* fr. MF *haubergeon,* dim. of *hauberc* hauberk] (14c) **1 :** a medieval jacket of mail shorter than a hauberk **2 :** HAUBERK

hab·ile \'hab-əl, -ˌīl\ *adj* [F, fr. L *habilis* — more at ABLE] (15c) **:** having general skill **:** ABLE, SKILLFUL

ha·bil·i·ment \hə-'bil-ə-mənt\ *n* [MF *habillement,* fr. *habiller* to dress a log, dress, prob. fr. *bille* log — more at BILLET] (15c) **1** *pl* **:** characteristic apparatus **:** FITTINGS ⟨the ~s of civilization —W. P. Webb⟩ **2 a :** the dress characteristic of an occupation or occasion — usu. used in pl. **b :** CLOTHES — usu. used in pl.

ha·bil·i·tate \hə-'bil-ə-ˌtāt\ *vb* **-tat·ed; -tat·ing** [LL *habilitatus,* pp. of *habilitare,* fr. L *habilitas* ability — more at ABILITY] *vt* (1604) **1** *archaic* **:** to make capable **:** QUALIFY **2 :** CLOTHE, DRESS **~** *vi* **:** to qualify oneself — **ha·bil·i·ta·tion** \-ˌbil-ə-'tā-shən\ *n*

[1]**hab·it** \'hab-ət\ *n* [ME, fr. OF, fr. L *habitus* condition, character, fr. *habitus,* pp. of *habēre* to have, hold — more at GIVE] (13c) **1** *archaic* **:** CLOTHING **2 a :** a costume characteristic of a calling, rank, or function ⟨a nun's ~⟩ **b :** a costume worn for horseback riding **3 :** manner of conducting oneself **:** BEARING **4 :** bodily appearance or makeup esp. as indicative of one's capacities and condition ⟨a man of fleshy ~⟩ **5 :** the prevailing disposition or character of a person's thoughts and feelings **:** mental makeup **6 :** a settled tendency or usual manner of behavior **7 a :** a behavior pattern acquired by frequent repetition or physiologic exposure that shows itself in regularity or increased facility of performance **b :** an acquired mode of behavior that has become nearly or completely involuntary **c :** ADDICTION **8 :** characteristic mode of growth or occurrence **9** *of a crystal* **:** characteristic assemblage of forms at crystallization leading to a usual appearance

syn HABIT, PRACTICE, USAGE, CUSTOM, WONT mean a way of acting fixed through repetition. HABIT implies a doing unconsciously and often compulsively; PRACTICE suggests an act or method followed with regularity and usu. through choice; USAGE suggests a customary action so generally followed that it has become a social norm; CUSTOM applies to a practice or usage so steadily associated with an individual or group as to have almost the force of unwritten law; WONT usu. applies to an habitual manner, method, or practice of an individual or group.

[2]**habit** *vt* (1588) **:** CLOTHE, DRESS

hab·it·able \'hab-ət-ə-bəl *also* hə-'bit-ə-\ *adj* (14c) **:** capable of being lived in **:** suitable for habitation — **hab·it·abil·i·ty** \ˌhab-ət-ə-'bil-ət-ē\ *n* — **hab·it·able·ness** \'hab-ət-ə-bəl-nes\ *n* — **hab·it·ably** \-blē\ *adv*

ha·bi·tant *n* (15c) **1** \'hab-ət-ənt\ **:** INHABITANT, RESIDENT **2** \ˌ(h)ab-i-'tä^{n}\ *also* **ha·bi·tan** \-'tä^{n}\ **:** a settler or descendant of a settler of French origin belonging to the farming class in Canada

hab·i·tat \'hab-ə-ˌtat\ *n* [L, it inhabits, fr. *habitare*] (ca. 1796) **1 a :** the place or type of site where a plant or animal naturally or normally lives and grows **b :** the typical place of residence of a person or a group **c :** a housing for a controlled physical environment in which people can live under surrounding inhospitable conditions (as under the sea) **2 :** the place where something is commonly found

habitat group *n* (1922) **:** a museum exhibit showing plant and animal specimens in such attitudes and with their natural surroundings so reproduced as to picture their habits and habitat

hab·i·ta·tion \ˌhab-ə-'tā-shən\ *n* [ME *habitacioun,* fr. MF *habitation,* fr. L *habitation-, habitatio,* fr. *habitatus,* pp. of *habitare* to inhabit, fr. *habitus,* pp.] (14c) **1 :** the act of inhabiting **:** OCCUPANCY **2 :** a dwelling place **:** RESIDENCE **3 :** SETTLEMENT, COLONY

hab·it–form·ing \'hab-ət-ˌfȯr-miŋ\ *adj* (1899) **:** inducing the formation of an addiction

ha·bit·u·al \hə-'bich-(ə-)wəl, ha-, -'bich-əl\ *adj* (1611) **1 :** having the nature of a habit **:** being in accordance with habit **:** CUSTOMARY ⟨~ smoking⟩ **2 :** doing, practicing, or acting in some manner by force of habit ⟨~ drunkard⟩ **3 :** resorted to on a regular basis ⟨his ~ diet⟩ **4 :** inherent in an individual ⟨~ grace⟩ ***syn*** see USUAL — **ha·bit·u·al·ly** \-ē\ *adv* — **ha·bit·u·al·ness** *n*

ha·bit·u·ate \hə-'bich-ə-ˌwāt, ha-\ *vb* **-at·ed; -at·ing** *vt* (15c) **1 :** to make used to something **:** ACCUSTOM **2** *archaic* **:** FREQUENT **~** *vi* **1 :** to cause habituation **2 :** to undergo habituation ⟨~ to a stimulus⟩

ha·bit·u·a·tion \-ˌbich-ə-'wā-shən\ *n* (15c) **1 :** the act or process of making habitual or accustomed **2 a :** tolerance to the effects of a drug acquired through continued use **b :** psychological dependence on a drug after a period of use — compare ADDICTION **3 :** decrease in responsiveness upon repeated exposure to a stimulus

hab·i·tude \'hab-ə-ˌt(y)üd\ *n* (15c) **1** *archaic* **:** native or essential character **2** *obs* **:** habitual association **3 a :** habitual disposition or mode of behavior or procedure **b :** CUSTOM

ha·bi·tué \hə-'bich-ə-ˌwā, ha-, -ˌbich-ə-'\ *n* [F, fr. pp. of *habituer* to frequent, fr. LL *habituare* to habituate, fr. L *habitus*] (1818) **:** one who frequents a place or numerous places of the same category

hab·i·tus \'hab-ət-əs\ *n, pl* **habitus** \-ət-əs, -ə-ˌtüs\ [NL, fr. L] (1886) **:** HABIT; *specif* **:** body build and constitution esp. as related to predisposition to disease

ha·boob \hə-'büb\ *n* [Ar *habūb* violent storm] (1897) **:** a violent dust storm or sandstorm (as of northern Africa, India, or the southwestern U.S.)

Habs·burg \'haps-, 'häps-\ *var of* HAPSBURG

ha·ček \'häch-ˌek\ *n* [Czech *háček,* lit., little hook] (1953) **:** a diacritic ˇ placed over a letter (as in *č*) to modify it **:** an inverted circumflex

ha·cen·da·do \ˌ(h)äs-ᵊn-'däd-(ˌ)ō\ *also* **ha·ci·en·da·do** \ˌhäs-ē-en-\ *n, pl* **-dos** [Sp, fr. *hacienda*] (1840) **:** the owner or proprietor of a hacienda

[1]**ha·chure** \ha-'shu̇(ə)r\ *n* [F, fr. *hacher* to chop up, hash] (1858) **:** a short line used for shading and denoting surfaces in relief (as in map drawing) and drawn in the direction of slope

[2]**hachure** *vt* **ha·chured; ha·chur·ing** (ca. 1859) **:** to shade with or show by hachures

ha·ci·en·da \ˌ(h)äs-ē-'en-də\ *n* [Sp, fr. OSp *facienda,* fr. L, lit., things to be done, deriv. of *facere* to do, make — more at DO] (1760) **1 :** a large estate esp. in a Spanish-speaking country **:** PLANTATION **2 :** the main dwelling of a hacienda

[1]**hack** \'hak\ *vb* [ME *hakken,* fr. OE *-haccian;* akin to OHG *hacchōn* to hack, OE *hōc* hook] *vt* (bef. 12c) **1 a :** to cut with repeated irregular or unskillful blows **b :** to sever with repeated blows **c :** to cut or reshape by or as if by crude or ruthless strokes ⟨the editor ~*ed* my story to bits⟩ **2 :** to clear by cutting away vegetation ⟨~*ed* his way through the brush⟩ **3 a :** to manage successfully ⟨just couldn't ~ the new job⟩ **b :** TOLERATE ⟨I can't ~ all this noise⟩ **~** *vi* **1 :** to make cutting blows or rough cuts **:** CHOP **2 :** to cough in a short dry manner

[2]**hack** *n* (14c) **1 :** an implement for hacking **2 :** NICK, NOTCH; *esp* **:** a blaze cut in a tree **3 :** a short dry cough **4 :** a hacking blow **5 :** restriction to quarters as punishment for naval officers — usu. used in the phrase *under hack*

[3]**hack** *n* [short for *hackney*] (ca. 1721) **1 a (1) :** a horse let out for common hire **(2) :** a horse used in all kinds of work **b :** a horse worn out in service **:** JADE **c :** a light easy saddle horse; *esp* **:** a three-gaited saddle horse **2 a :** HACKNEY **b (1) :** TAXICAB **(2) :** CABDRIVER **3 :** one who forfeits individual freedom of action or professional integrity in exchange for wages or other assured reward; *esp* **:** a writer who works mainly for hire

[4]**hack** *vt* (1745) **1 :** to make trite and commonplace by frequent and indiscriminate use **2 :** to use as a hack **~** *vi* **1 :** to ride or drive at an ordinary pace or over the roads as distinguished from racing or riding across country **2 :** to operate a taxicab

[5]**hack** *adj* (1749) **1 :** working for hire esp. with loose or easy professional standards **2 :** performed by, suited to, or characteristic of a hack ⟨~ writing⟩ **3 :** HACKNEYED, TRITE

hack·a·more \'hak-ə-ˌmō(ə)r, -ˌmȯ(ə)r\ *n* [by folk etymology fr. Sp *jaquima*] (1850) **:** a bridle with a loop capable of being tightened about the nose in place of a bit or with a slip noose passed over the lower jaw

hack·ber·ry \'hak-ˌber-ē\ *n* [alter. of *hagberry* (a cherry resembling the chokecherry)] (1785) **:** any of a genus (*Celtis*) of trees and shrubs of the elm family with small often edible berries; *also* **:** its wood

[1]**hacker** \'hak-ər\ *n* (1620) **1 :** one that hacks **2 :** a person who is inexperienced or unskilled at a particular activity ⟨a tennis ~⟩

[2]**hacker** *n* [*hack* skillful repair of a computer program + *-er*] (1976) **:** an expert at programming and solving problems with a computer

hack·ie \'hak-ē\ *n* (1935) **:** CABDRIVER

[1]**hack·le** \'hak-əl\ *n* [ME *hakell;* akin to OHG *hāko* hook — more at HOOK] (15c) **1 :** a comb or board with long metal teeth for dressing flax, hemp, or jute **2 a :** one of the long narrow feathers on the neck or saddle of a bird **b :** the neck plumage of the domestic fowl — see COCK illustration **3** *pl* **a :** erectile hairs along the neck and back esp. of a dog **b :** TEMPER, DANDER **4 a :** an artificial fishing fly made chiefly of the filaments of a cock's neck feathers **b :** filaments of cock feather projecting from the head of an artificial fly

[2]**hackle** *vt* **hack·led; hack·ling** \'hak-(ə-)liŋ\ (1616) **:** to comb out with a hackle — **hack·ler** \-(ə-)lər\ *n*

[3]**hackle** *vt* **hack·led; hack·ling** [freq. of [1]*hack*] (1579) **:** to cut or chop up **:** chop off roughly **:** HACK

[4]**hackle** *n* (1941) **:** a fracture resulting in hackly edges

hack·ly \'hak-(ə-)lē\ *adj* (1796) **:** having the appearance of something hacked **:** JAGGED

hack·man \'hak-mən\ *n* (1796) **:** CABDRIVER

hack·ma·tack \'hak-mə-ˌtak\ *n* [of Algonquian origin; akin to Abnaki *akemantak* snowshoe wood] (1792) **:** TAMARACK

[1]**hack·ney** \'hak-nē\ *n, pl* **hackneys** [ME *hakeney*] (14c) **1 a :** a horse suitable for ordinary riding or driving **b :** a trotting horse used chiefly for driving **c :** any of an English breed of rather compact usu. chestnut, bay, or brown high-

hackney 1c

stepping horses **2** *obs* **:** one that works for hire **:** DRUDGE **3 :** a carriage or automobile kept for hire

[2]**hackney** *adj* (1589) **1 :** kept for public hire **2 :** HACKNEYED **3** *archaic* **:** done or suitable for doing by a drudge

[3]**hackney** *vt* **hack·neyed; hack·ney·ing** (1596) **1 a :** to make common or frequent use of **b :** to make trite, vulgar, or commonplace **2** *archaic* **:** to make sophisticated or jaded

hackney coach *n* (1660) **:** a coach kept for hire; *esp* **:** a four-wheeled carriage drawn by two horses and having seats for six persons

hack·neyed \ˈhak-nēd\ *adj* (1749) **:** lacking in freshness or originality *syn* see TRITE

hack·saw \ˈhak-ˌsȯ\ *n* (1654) **:** a fine-tooth saw with a blade under tension in a frame that is used for cutting hard materials (as metal)

hack·work \-ˌwərk\ *n* (1851) **:** literary, artistic, or professional work done on order usu. according to formula and in conformity with commercial standards

had *past and past part of* HAVE

ha·dal \ˈhād-ᵊl\ *adj* [F, fr. *Hadès* Hades] (1959) **:** of, relating to, or being the parts of the ocean below 6000 meters

had·dock \ˈhad-ək\ *n, pl* **haddock** *also* **haddocks** [ME *haddok*] (14c) **:** an important food fish (*Melanogrammus aeglefinus*) that is usu. smaller than the related common cod and that occurs on both sides of the Atlantic

Ha·des \ˈhād-(ˌ)ēz\ *n* [Gk *Haidēs*] **1 :** PLUTO **2 :** the underground abode of the dead in Greek mythology **3 :** SHEOL **4** *often not cap* **:** HELL

hadj, hadji *var of* HAJJ, HAJJI

hadn't \ˈhad-ᵊnt, -ᵊn, *dial also* ˈhat-ᵊn(t) *or* ˈhant\ **:** had not

had·ron \ˈhad-ˌrän\ *n* [ISV *hadr-* thick, heavy (fr. Gk. *hadros* thick) + [2]*-on*] (1962) **:** any of the subatomic particles that take part in the strong interaction — **ha·dron·ic** \ha-ˈdrän-ik\ *adj*

hadst \(ˈ)hadst, hədst, *or t for* d\ *archaic past 2d sing of* HAVE

hae \(ˈ)hā\ *chiefly Scot var of* HAVE

haem *var of* HEME

haem- *or* **haemo-** — see HEM-

haema- — see HEMA-

haemat- *or* **haemato-** — see HEMAT-

hae·ma·tox·y·lon \ˌhē-mə-ˈtäk-sə-ˌlän\ *n* [NL, fr. *hemat-* + Gk *xylon* wood] (1847) **:** the wood or dye of logwood

-haemia — see -EMIA

haemocoele *chiefly Brit var of* HEMOCOEL

haemoglobin *var of* HEMOGLOBIN

haet \ˈhāt\ *n* [contr. of Sc *hae it* (as in *Deil hae it!* Devil take it!)] *chiefly Scot* (1590) **:** a small quantity **:** WHIT, BIT

haf·fet \ˈhaf-ət\ *n* [ME (Sc) *halfheid*, fr. ME *half* half + *hed* head] *Scot* (1513) **:** CHEEK, TEMPLE

haf·ni·um \ˈhaf-nē-əm\ *n* [NL, fr. *Hafnia* (Copenhagen), Denmark] (1923) **:** a metallic element resembling zirconium chemically, occurring in zirconium minerals, and being useful because of its ready absorption of neutrons — see ELEMENT table

[1]**haft** \ˈhaft\ *n* [ME, fr. OE *hæft;* akin to OE *hebban* to lift — more at HEAVE] (bef. 12c) **:** the handle of a weapon or tool

[2]**haft** *vt* (15c) **:** to set in or furnish with a haft

haf·ta·rah *or* **haf·to·rah** \häf-ˈtȯ-rə, ˌhäf-tə-ˈrä\ *n* [Heb *haphṭārāh* conclusion] (1891) **:** one of the biblical selections from the Books of the Prophets read after the parashah in the Jewish synagogue service

[1]**hag** \ˈhag\ *n* [ME *hagge* demon, old woman] (14c) **1 :** an ugly, slatternly, or evil-looking old woman **2** *archaic* **a :** a female demon **b :** an evil or frightening spirit **:** HOBGOBLIN **3 :** WITCH — **hag·gish** \ˈhag-ish\ *adj*

[2]**hag** *n* [E dial., felled timber, of Scand origin; akin to ON *högg* stroke, blow; akin to OE *hēawan* to hew] (1662) **1** *Brit* **:** QUAGMIRE, BOG **2** *Brit* **:** a firm spot in a bog

Ha·gar \ˈhā-ˌgär, -gər\ *n* [Heb *Hāghār*] **:** a concubine of Abraham driven into the desert with her son Ishmael because of Sarah's jealousy according to the account in Genesis

hag·fish \ˈhag-ˌfish\ *n* (1611) **:** any of several marine cyclostomes (order Myxiniformes) that are related to the lampreys and in general resemble eels but have a round mouth surrounded by eight tentacles and that feed upon fishes by boring into their bodies

Hag·ga·dah \hə-ˈgäd-ə, hä-, -ˈgȯd-\ *n, pl* **Hag·ga·doth** \-ˈgäd-ˌōt(h), -ˈgȯd-\ [Heb *haggādhāh*] (1856) **1 :** ancient Jewish lore forming esp. the nonlegal part of the Talmud **2 :** the Jewish ritual for the seder — **hag·ga·dic** \-ˈgad-ik, -ˈgäd-, -ˈgȯd-\ *adj, often cap*

hag·ga·dist \-ˈgäd-əst, -ˈgȯd-\ *n, often cap* (1886) **1 :** a haggadic writer **2 :** a student of the Haggadah — **hag·ga·dis·tic** \ˌhag-ə-ˈdis-tik, ˌhäg-\ *adj, often cap*

Hag·gai \ˈhag-ē-ˌī, ˈhag-ˌī\ *n* [Heb *Haggai*] **1 :** a Hebrew prophet who flourished about 500 B.C. and who advocated that the Temple in Jerusalem be rebuilt **2 :** a prophetic book of canonical Jewish and Christian Scriptures — see BIBLE table

[1]**hag·gard** \ˈhag-ərd\ *adj* [MF *hagard*] (1567) **1** *of a hawk* **:** not tamed **2 a :** wild in appearance **b :** having a worn or emaciated appearance **:** GAUNT ⟨~ faces looked up sadly from out of the straw —W.M. Thackeray⟩ — **hag·gard·ly** *adv* — **hag·gard·ness** *n*

[2]**haggard** *n* (1567) **1 :** an adult hawk caught wild **2** *obs* **:** an intractable person

hag·gis \ˈhag-əs\ *n* [ME *hagese*] (15c) **:** a traditionally Scottish dish that consists of the heart, liver, and lungs of a sheep or a calf minced with suet, onions, oatmeal, and seasonings and that is boiled in the stomach of the animal

[1]**hag·gle** \ˈhag-əl\ *vb* **hag·gled; hag·gling** \-(ə-)liŋ\ [freq. of *hag* (to hew)] *vt* (1599) **1 :** to cut roughly or clumsily **:** HACK **2** *archaic* **:** to annoy or exhaust with wrangling ~ *vi* **:** BARGAIN, WRANGLE — **hag·gler** \-(ə-)lər\ *n*

[2]**haggle** *n* (1858) **:** an act or instance of haggling

hagi- *or* **hagio-** *comb form* [LL, fr. Gk, fr. *hagios*] **1 :** holy ⟨hagioscope⟩ **2 :** saints ⟨*hagiography*⟩

Ha·gi·og·ra·pha \ˌhag-ē-ˈäg-rə-fə, ˌhā-jē-\ *n pl but sing or pl in constr* [LL, fr. LGk, fr. *hagio-* + *graphein* to write — more at CARVE] (1583) **:** the third part of the Jewish scriptures — see BIBLE table

ha·gi·og·ra·pher \-fər\ *n* (1849) **:** a writer of hagiography

ha·gio·graph·ic \ˌhag-ē-ə-ˈgraf-ik, ˌhāj-, ˌhāg-, ˌhaj-\ *also* **ha·gio·graph·i·cal** \-i-kəl\ *adj* (1888) **1 :** of or relating to the Hagiographa **2 :** of or relating to hagiography

ha·gi·og·ra·phy \-ē-ˈäg-rə-fē\ *n* (1821) **1 :** biography of saints or venerated persons **2 :** idealizing or idolizing biography

ha·gi·ol·o·gy \-ē-ˈäl-ə-jē\ *n* (1807) **1 :** literature dealing with venerated persons or writings **2 :** a list of venerated figures — **ha·gi·o·log·ic** \-ē-ə-ˈläj-ik\ *or* **ha·gi·o·log·i·cal** \-i-kəl\ *adj*

ha·gio·scope \ˈhag-ē-ə-ˌskōp, ˈhā-jē-\ *n* (1839) **:** an opening in the interior walls of a cruciform church so placed as to afford a view of the altar to those in the transept — **ha·gio·scop·ic** \ˌhag-ē-ə-ˈskäp-ik, ˌhā-jē-\ *adj*

hag·ride \ˈhag-ˌrīd\ *vt* **-rode** \-ˌrōd\; **-rid·den** \-ˌrid-ᵊn\ (1661) **:** HARASS, TORMENT

hah *var of* HA

[1]**ha–ha** \(ˈ)hä-ˈhä\ *interj* [ME, fr. OE *ha ha*] (bef. 12c) — used to express amusement or derision

[2]**ha–ha** \ˈhä-ˌhä\ *n* [F *haha*] (1712) **:** SUNK FENCE

hahn·ium \ˈhän-ē-əm\ *n* [Otto *Hahn* + *-ium*] (1970) **:** UNNILPENTIUM

haik \ˈhīk\ *n* [Ar *hā'ik*] (1713) **:** a voluminous piece of usu. white cloth worn as an outer garment in northern Africa

haik

hai·ku \ˈhī-(ˌ)kü\ *n, pl* **haiku** [Jp] (1899) **:** an unrhymed verse form of Japanese origin having three lines containing usu. 5, 7, and 5 syllables respectively; *also* **:** a poem in this form usu. having a seasonal reference — compare TANKA

[1]**hail** \ˈhā(ə)l\ *n* [ME, fr. OE *hægl;* akin to OHG *hagal* hail, Gk *kachlēx* pebble] (bef. 12c) **1 :** precipitation in the form of small balls or lumps usu. consisting of concentric layers of clear ice and compact snow **2 :** something that gives the effect of a shower of hail ⟨met a ~ of rifle fire from the ridge⟩

[2]**hail** *vi* (bef. 12c) **1 :** to precipitate hail ⟨it was ~*ing* hard⟩ **2 :** to pour down or strike like hail

[3]**hail** *interj* [ME, fr. ON *heill*, fr. *heill* healthy — more at WHOLE] (13c) **1** — used to express acclamation ⟨~ to the chief —Sir Walter Scott⟩ **2** *archaic* — used as a salutation

[4]**hail** *vt* (13c) **1 a :** SALUTE, GREET **b :** to greet with enthusiastic approval **:** ACCLAIM **2 :** to greet or summon by calling ⟨~ a taxi⟩ ~ *vi* **:** to call out; *esp* **:** to call a greeting to a passing ship — **hail from :** to be or have been a native or resident of

[5]**hail** *n* (1500) **1 :** an exclamation of greeting or acclamation **2 :** a calling to attract attention **3 :** hearing distance ⟨stayed within ~⟩

hail·er \ˈhā-lər\ *n* (1880) **1 :** one that hails **2 :** BULLHORN 1

hail–fel·low \ˈhāl-ˌfel-(ˌ)ō, -ə(-w)\ *adj* (1580) **:** HAIL-FELLOW-WELL-MET — **hail–fellow** *n*

hail–fel·low–well–met \-ō-ˌwel-ˈmet, -ə-ˌwel-\ *adj* [fr. the archaic salutation "Hail, fellow! Well met!"] (1581) **:** heartily informal **:** COMRADELY — **hail–fellow–well–met** *n*

Hail Mary *n* [trans. of ML *Ave, Maria*, fr. the opening words] (14c) **:** a Roman Catholic prayer to the Virgin Mary that consists of salutations and a plea for her intercession

hail·stone \ˈhā(ə)l-ˌstōn\ *n* (bef. 12c) **:** a pellet of hail

hail·storm \-ˌstȯ(ə)rm\ *n* (14c) **:** a storm accompanied by hail

hair \ˈha(ə)r, ˈhe(ə)r\ *n, often attrib* [ME, fr. OE *hǣr;* akin to OHG *hār* hair] (bef. 12c) **1 a :** a slender threadlike outgrowth of the epidermis of an animal; *esp* **:** one of the usu. pigmented filaments that form the characteristic coat of a mammal **b :** the hairy covering of an animal or a body part; *esp* **:** the coating of hairs on a human head **2 :** HAIRCLOTH **3 a :** a minute distance or amount ⟨won by a ~⟩ **b :** a precise degree ⟨aligned to a ~⟩ **4** *obs* **:** NATURE, CHARACTER **5 :** a filamentous structure that resembles hair ⟨leaf ~⟩ — **hair·less** *adj* — **hair·less·ness** *n* — **hair·like** \-ˌlīk\ *adj*

hair ball *n* (1712) **:** a compact mass of hair formed in the stomach esp. of a shedding animal (as a cat) that cleanses its coat by licking

[1]**hair·breadth** \ˈha(ə)r-ˌbretth, ˈhe(ə)r-, -ˌbreth, -ˌbredth\ *or* **hairs·breadth** \ˈha(ə)rz-, ˈhe(ə)rz-\ *n* (1561) **:** a very small distance or margin

[2]**hairbreadth** *adj* (1604) **:** very narrow **:** CLOSE ⟨a ~ escape⟩

hair·brush \ˈha(ə)r-ˌbrəsh, ˈhe(ə)r-\ *n* (1599) **:** a brush for the hair

hair cell *n* (ca. 1890) **:** a cell with hairlike processes; *esp* **:** one of the sensory cells in the auditory epithelium of the organ of Corti

hair·cloth \ˈha(ə)r-ˌklȯth, ˈhe(ə)r-\ *n* (1500) **:** any of various stiff wiry fabrics esp. of horsehair or camel hair used for upholstery or for stiffening in garments

hair·cut \-ˌkət\ *n* (1899) **:** the act, process, or result of cutting and shaping the hair — **hair·cut·ter** \-ˌkət-ər\ *n* — **hair·cut·ting** \-ˌkət-iŋ\ *n*

hair·do \-ˌdü\ *n, pl* **hairdos** (1932) **:** a way of dressing the hair **:** COIFFURE

hair·dress·er \-ˌdres-ər\ *n* (1770) **1 :** one whose occupation is the dressing or cutting of hair **2** *Brit* **:** BARBER

hair·dress·ing \-ˌdres-iŋ\ *n* (1771) **1 a :** the action or process of washing, cutting, curling, or arranging the hair **b :** the occupation of a hairdresser **2 :** a preparation (as a liquid or cream) used in grooming and styling the hair

haired \ˈha(ə)rd, ˈhe(ə)rd\ *adj* (14c) **:** having hair esp. of a specified kind — usu. used in combination ⟨fair-*haired*⟩

hair follicle *n* (1838) **:** the tubular epithelial sheath that surrounds the lower part of the hair shaft and encloses at the bottom a vascular papilla supplying the growing basal part of the hair with nourishment

hair·line \-ˈlīn\ *n* (1846) **1 :** a very slender line: as **a :** a tiny line or crack on a surface **b :** a fine line connecting thicker strokes in a printed letter **2 :** HAIRBREADTH **3 a :** a textile design consisting of lengthwise or crosswise lines usu. one thread wide **b :** a fabric with such a design **4 a :** the outline of scalp hair esp. on the forehead **b :** the way the hair frames the face — **hairline** *adj*

hair·piece \-ˌpēs\ *n* (1926) **1 :** TOUPEE 2 **2 :** supplementary hair (as a switch) used in some feminine coiffures

[1]**hair·pin** \-ˌpin\ *n* (1779) **1 :** a pin to hold the hair in place; *specif* **:** a long U-shaped pin **2 :** something shaped like a hairpin; *specif* **:** a sharp U-shaped turn in a road

[2]**hairpin** *adj* (1887) **:** having the shape of a hairpin ⟨a ~ turn⟩; *also* **:** having hairpin turns ⟨a steep ~ road⟩

hair–rais·er \ˈha(ə)r-ˌrā-zər, ˈhe(ə)r-\ *n* (1897) : THRILLER
hair–rais·ing \-ˌrā-ziŋ\ *adj* (1900) : causing terror, excitement, or astonishment — **hair–rais·ing·ly** \-ziŋ-lē\ *adv*
hair seal *n* (1865) : any of a family (Phocidae, the hair seal family) of seals having a coarse hairy coat, the hind limbs reduced to swimming flippers, and no external ears — compare EARED SEAL
hair shirt *n* (14c) : a shirt made of rough animal hair worn next to the skin as a penance
hair·split·ter \ˈha(ə)r-ˌsplit-ər, ˈhe(ə)r-\ *n* (1849) : one that makes excessively fine distinctions in reasoning : QUIBBLER — **hair·split·ting** \-ˌsplit-iŋ\ *adj or n*
hair·spring \-ˌspriŋ\ *n* (1830) : a slender spiraled recoil spring that regulates the motion of the balance wheel of a timepiece
hair·streak \-ˌstrēk\ *n* (1816) : any of a subfamily (Theclinae of the family Lycaenidae) of small butterflies usu. having striped markings on the underside of the wings and thin filamentous projections from the hind wings
hair·style \ˈha(ə)r-ˌstīl, ˈhe(ə)r-\ *n* (1913) : a way of wearing the hair : COIFFURE
hair·styl·ing \-ˌstī-liŋ\ *n* (1936) : the work of a hairstylist
hair·styl·ist \-ˌstī-ləst\ *n* (1935) : HAIRDRESSER; *esp* : one who does creative styling of coiffures
hair–trigger *adj* (1806) **1** : immediately responsive to the slightest stimulus ⟨a ~ temper⟩ **2** : delicately adjusted or easily disrupted ⟨a ~ balance⟩
hair trigger *n* (1806) : a gun trigger so adjusted as to permit the firearm to be fired by a very slight pressure
hair·worm \ˈha(ə)r-ˌwərm, ˈhe(ə)r-\ *n* (1658) **1** : any of a genus (*Capillaria*) of nematode worms that include serious parasites of the alimentary tract of fowls and tissue and organ parasites of mammals **2** : any of a group (Gordiacea) of very slender elongated worms that are parasitic in arthropods as larvae and are free-living in water as adults
hairy \ˈha(ə)r-ē, ˈhe(ə)r-\ *adj* **hair·i·er; -est** (14c) **1 a** : covered with hair or hairlike material **b** : having a downy fuzz on the stems and leaves **2** : made of or resembling hair **3** : tending to cause nervous tension (as from danger, difficulty, or fear) ⟨a ~ . . . scramble up a steep or tortuous mountain road —R. F. Jones⟩ ⟨a ~ adventure⟩ — **hair·i·ness** \ˈhar-ē-nəs, ˈher-\ *n*
hairy vetch *n* (1901) : a European vetch (*Vicia villosa*) extensively cultivated as a cover and early forage crop
hairy woodpecker *n* (1728) : a common No. American woodpecker (*Picoides villosus*) closely resembling but larger than the downy woodpecker
Hai·tian \ˈhā-shən *also* ˈhāt-ē-ən\ *n* (1805) **1** : a native or inhabitant of Haiti **2** : HAITIAN CREOLE — **Haitian** *adj*
Haitian Creole *n* (1938) : the language that is spoken by the great majority of Haitian inhabitants and that is based on French and various West African languages
hajj \ˈhaj\ *n* [Ar *ḥajj*] (1673) : the pilgrimage to Mecca prescribed as a religious duty for Muslims
hajji \ˈhaj-ē\ *n* [Ar *ḥajjī*, fr. *ḥajj*] (1609) : one who has made a pilgrimage to Mecca — often used as a title
hake \ˈhāk\ *n* [ME] (14c) : any of several marine food fishes (as of the genera *Merluccius* and *Urophycis*) that are related to the common Atlantic cod
ha·ken·kreuz \ˈhäk-ən-ˌkrȯits\ *n, often cap* [G, fr. *haken* hook + *kreuz* cross] (1918) : the swastika used as a symbol of German anti-Semitism or of Nazi Germany
[1]**ha·kim** \hə-ˈkēm\ *n* [Ar *ḥakīm*, lit., wise one] (1585) : a Muslim physician
[2]**ha·kim** \ˈhäk-əm\ *n* [Ar *ḥākim*] (1611) : a Muslim ruler, governor, or judge
hal- *or* **halo-** *comb form* [F, fr. Gk, fr. *hals* — more at SALT] **1** : salt ⟨*halo*phyte⟩ **2** [ISV, fr. *halogen*] : halogen ⟨*hal*ide⟩
ha·la·kah *or* **ha·la·cha** \hä-ˈläk-ə, ˈhä-lə-ˈkä\ *n, often cap* [Heb *halākhāh*, lit., way] (1856) : the body of Jewish law supplementing the scriptural law and forming esp. the legal part of the Talmud — **ha·lak·ic** \hə-ˈlak-ik, hä-ˈläk-\ *adj, often cap*
ha·la·la \hə-ˈläl-ə\ *n, pl* **halala** *or* **halalas** [Ar] (1970) — see *riyal* at MONEY table
ha·la·tion \hā-ˈlā-shən\ *n* [*halo* + *-ation*] (1859) **1** : the spreading of light beyond its proper boundaries in a developed photographic image **2** : a bright ring that sometimes surrounds a bright object on a television screen
hal·berd \ˈhal-bərd, ˈhȯl-\ *or* **hal·bert** \-bərt\ *n* [ME, fr. MF *hallebarde*, fr. MHG *helmbarte*, fr. *helm* handle (fr. OHG *helmo*) + *barte* ax, fr. OHG *barta*; akin to OHG *bart* beard — more at HELM, BEARD] (15c) : a weapon esp. of the 15th and 16th centuries consisting typically of a battle-ax and pike mounted on a handle about six feet long — **hal·berd·ier** \ˌhal-bər-ˈdi(ə)r, ˌhȯl-\ *n*
[1]**hal·cy·on** \ˈhal-sē-ən\ *n* [ME *alceon*, fr. L *halcyon*, fr. Gk *alkyōn*, *halkyōn*] (14c) **1** : a bird identified with the kingfisher and held in ancient legend to nest at sea about the time of the winter solstice and to calm the waves during incubation **2** : KINGFISHER
[2]**halcyon** *adj* (1545) **1** : of or relating to the halcyon or its nesting period **2 a** : CALM, PEACEFUL **b** : HAPPY, GOLDEN **c** : PROSPEROUS, AFFLUENT
[1]**hale** \ˈhā(ə)l\ *adj* [partly fr. ME (northern) *hale*, fr. OE *hāl*; partly fr. ME *hail*, fr. ON *heill* — more at WHOLE] (bef. 12c) : free from defect, disease, or infirmity : SOUND; *also* : retaining exceptional health and vigor ⟨a ~ and hearty old man⟩ ***syn*** see HEALTHY
[2]**hale** *vt* **haled; hal·ing** [ME *halen*, fr. OF *haler* — more at HAUL] (13c) **1** : HAUL, PULL **2** : to compel to go
ha·ler \ˈhäl-ər, -ˌe(ə)r\ *n, pl* **ha·le·ru** \ˈhäl-ə-ˌrü\ [Czech] (ca. 1934) — see *koruna* at MONEY table
[1]**half** \ˈhaf, ˈhȧf\ *n, pl* **halves** \ˈhavz, ˈhȧvz\ [ME, fr. OE *healf*; akin to L *scalpere* to cut, OE *sciell* shell] (bef. 12c) **1 a** : one of two equal parts into which a thing is divisible; *also* : a part of a thing approximately equal to the remainder — often used without *of* ⟨~ the distance⟩ **b** : half an hour — used in designation of time **2** : one of a pair: as **a** : PARTNER **b** : SEMESTER, TERM **c** : one of the two equal periods that together make up the playing time of some games (as football) **3** : HALF-DOLLAR **4** : HALFBACK — **by half** : by a great deal — **by halves** : in part : HALFHEARTEDLY — **half as much again** : one-and-a-half times as much — **in half** : into two equal or nearly equal parts
[2]**half** *adj* (bef. 12c) **1 a** : being one of two equal parts ⟨a ~ share⟩ ⟨a ~ sheet of paper⟩ **b** (1) : amounting to approximately half ⟨a ~ mile⟩ ⟨a ~ million⟩ (2) : falling short of the full or complete thing : PARTIAL ⟨~ measures⟩ ⟨a ~ smile⟩ **2** : extending over or covering only half ⟨a ~ window⟩ ⟨a ~ mask⟩ — **half·ness** *n*
[3]**half** *adv* (12c) **1 a** : in an equal part or degree ⟨the crowd was ~ jeering, ~ respectful⟩ **b** : not completely : PARTIALLY ⟨~ persuaded⟩ ⟨*half*-remembered legends from her childhood⟩ **2** : by any means : AT ALL ⟨her singing isn't ~ bad⟩
half–and–half \ˌhaf-ən-ˈhaf, ˌhȧf-ən-ˈhȧf\ *n* (1756) : something that is approximately half one thing and half another: as **a** : a mixture of two malt beverages (as beer and stout) **b** : a mixture of cream and whole milk — **half–and–half** *adj* — **half–and–half** *adv*
half–assed \ˈhaf-ˈast, ˈhȧf-ˈȧst\ *adj* (ca. 1932) **1** : lacking significance, adequacy, or completeness — often considered vulgar **2** : lacking intelligence, character, or effectiveness — often considered vulgar — **half–assed** *adv*
half·back \ˈhaf-ˌbak, ˈhȧf-\ *n* (1882) **1** : one of the backs stationed near either flank in football **2** : a player stationed immediately behind the forward line (as in field hockey, soccer, or rugby)
half–baked \-ˈbākt\ *adj* (1621) **1** : imperfectly baked : UNDERDONE **2 a** : lacking adequate planning or forethought ⟨a ~ scheme for getting rich⟩ **b** : lacking in judgment, intelligence, or common sense
half–blood \-ˈbləd\ *or* **half–blood·ed** \-ˈbləd-əd\ *adj* (1605) : having half blood or being a half blood
half blood *n* (1553) **1 a** : the relation between persons having only one parent in common **b** : a person so related to another **2** : HALF-BREED **3** : GRADE 4
half boot *n* (1787) : a boot with a top reaching above the ankle and ending below the knee
half–bound \ˈhaf-ˈbau̇nd, ˈhȧf-\ *adj, of a book* (1775) : bound in material of two qualities with the material of better quality on the spine and corners — **half binding** *n*
half–bred \-ˌbred\ *adj* (1701) : having one purebred parent — **half–bred** *n*
half–breed \-ˌbrēd\ *n* (1760) : the offspring of parents of different races; *esp* : the offspring of an American Indian and a Caucasian — **half–breed** *adj*
half brother *n* (14c) : a brother related through one parent only
half–caste \ˈhaf-ˌkast, ˈhȧf-\ *n* (1789) : one of mixed racial descent : HALF-BREED — **half–caste** *adj*
half cock *n* (1745) **1** : the position of the hammer of a firearm when about half retracted and held by the sear so that it cannot be operated by a pull on the trigger **2** : a state of inadequate preparation or mental confusion
half–cocked \ˈhaf-ˈkäkt, ˈhȧf-\ *adj* (1809) **1** : being at half cock **2** : lacking adequate preparation or forethought ⟨go off ~⟩
half crown *n* (1542) : a British coin worth two shillings and sixpence used as legal tender until 1970
half dime *n* (1792) : a silver 5-cent coin struck by the U.S. mint in 1792 and from 1794 to 1873
half disme *n* (1792) : a half dime struck in 1792
half–dol·lar \ˈhaf-ˈdäl-ər, ˈhȧf-\ *n* (1786) **1** : a coin representing one half of a dollar **2** : the sum of 50 cents
half eagle *n* (1786) : a 5-dollar gold piece issued by the U.S. 1795–1916 and in 1929
half–hardy *adj, of a plant* (1824) : able to withstand a moderately low temperature but injured by severe freezing and surviving the winter in cold climates only if carefully protected
half·heart·ed \ˈhaf-ˈhärt-əd, ˈhȧf-\ *adj* (15c) : lacking heart, spirit, or interest ⟨~ attempts to start a conversation⟩ — **half·heart·ed·ly** *adv* — **half·heart·ed·ness** *n*
half hitch *n* (ca. 1769) : a simple knot tied by passing the end of a line around an object, across the main part of the line, and then through the resulting loop — see KNOT illustration
half hour *n* (15c) **1** : thirty minutes **2** : the middle point of an hour — **half–hour·ly** \ˈhaf-ˈau̇(ə)r-lē, ˈhȧf-\ *adv or adj*
half–knot \ˈhaf-ˌnät, ˈhȧf-\ *n* (1933) : a knot intertwining the ends of two cords and used in tying other knots
half–length \ˈhaf-ˈleŋ(k)th, ˈhȧf-\ *n* (1699) : something (as a portrait) that is or represents only half the complete length
half–life \-ˌlīf\ *n* (1907) : the time required for half of something to undergo a process: as **a** : the time required for half of the atoms of a radioactive substance to become disintegrated **b** : the time required for half the amount of a substance (as a drug or radioactive tracer) in or introduced into a living system or ecosystem to be eliminated or disintegrated by natural processes
half–light \-ˌlīt\ *n* (1625) : grayish light (as of a dim interior or evening)
half line *n* (ca. 1914) : a straight line extending from a point indefinitely in one direction only
[1]**half–mast** \-ˈmast\ *n* (1627) : a point some distance but not necessarily halfway down below the top of a mast or staff or the peak of a gaff
[2]**half–mast** *vt* (1891) : to cause to hang at half-mast ⟨~ a flag⟩
half–moon \ˈhaf-ˌmün, ˈhȧf-\ *n* (15c) **1** : the moon when half its disk appears illuminated **2** : something shaped like a crescent **3** : the lunule of a fingernail — **half–moon** *adj*
half nelson *n* (1889) : a wrestling hold in which one arm is thrust under the corresponding arm of an opponent and the hand placed on the back of the opponent's neck — compare FULL NELSON
half note *n* (1597) : a musical note with the time value of $^{1}/_{2}$ of a whole note
half·pen·ny \ˈhāp-(ə-)nē, *US also* ˈhaf-ˌpen-ē, ˈhȧf-\ *n* (13c) **1** *pl* **half·pence** \ˈhā-pən(t)s, *US also* ˈhaf-ˌpen(t)s, ˈhȧf-\ *or* **halfpennies** : a former British coin representing one half of a penny **2** : the sum of half a penny **3** : a small amount — **halfpenny** *adj*

[1]**half–pint** \ˈhaf-ˌpīnt, ˈháf-\ *n* (1611) **1 :** half a pint **2 :** a short, small, or inconsequential person
[2]**half–pint** *adj* (1728) **:** of less than average size **:** DIMINUTIVE
half plane *n* (1891) **:** the part of a plane on one side of an indefinitely extended straight line drawn in the plane
half rest *n* (ca. 1899) **:** a musical rest corresponding in time value to a half note
half sister *n* (13c) **:** a sister related through one parent only
half–slip \ˈhaf-ˌslip, ˈháf-\ *n* (ca. 1948) **:** a topless slip with an elasticized waistband
half–sole *vt* (1795) **:** to put half soles on
half sole *n* (1865) **:** a shoe sole extending from the shank forward
half sovereign *n* (1503) **:** a British gold coin worth 10 shillings
half–space \ˈhaf-ˌspās, ˈháf-\ *n* (1962) **:** the part of three-dimensional euclidean space lying on one side of a plane
half–staff \-ˈstaf\ *n* (1708) **:** HALF-MAST
half step *n* (1904) **1 :** a walking step of 15 inches or in double time of 18 inches **2 :** a musical interval (as E–F or B–C) equivalent to one twelfth of an octave — called also *semitone*
half–timber *or* **half–tim•bered** \ˈhaf-ˈtim-bərd, ˈháf-\ *adj, of a building* (1842) **:** constructed of wood framing with spaces filled with masonry — **half–tim•ber•ing** \-b(ə-)riŋ\ *n*
half•time \-ˌtīm\ *n* (1871) **:** an intermission between halves of a game or contest (as in football or basketball)
half title *n* (1879) **:** the title of a book standing alone on a right-hand page immediately preceding the title page; *also* **:** the page itself
half•tone \ˈhaf-ˌtōn, ˈháf-\ *n* (1651) **1 :** HALF STEP 2 **2 a :** any of the shades of gray between the darkest and the lightest parts of a photographic image **b :** a photoengraving made from an image photographed through a screen and then etched so that the details of the image are reproduced in dots — **halftone** *adj*
half–track \-ˌtrak\ *n* (1927) **1 :** an endless chain-track drive system that propels a vehicle supported in front by a pair of wheels **2 :** a motor vehicle propelled by half-tracks; *specif* **:** one lightly armored for military use — **half–track** *or* **half–tracked** \-ˌtrakt\ *adj*
half–truth \-ˌtrüth\ *n* (1658) **1 :** a statement that is only partially true **2 :** a statement that mingles truth and falsehood with deliberate intent to deceive
half volley *n* (1843) **:** a stroke of a ball (as in tennis) at the instant it rebounds from the ground — **half–volley** *vb*
half•way \ˈhaf-ˈwā, ˈháf-\ *adj* (14c) **1 :** midway between two points **2 :** PARTIAL — **halfway** *adv*
halfway house *n* (1694) **1 a :** a place to stop midway on a journey **b :** a halfway place in a progression **2 :** a center for formerly institutionalized individuals (as mental patients or drug addicts) that is designed to facilitate their readjustment to private life
half–wit \ˈhaf-ˌwit, ˈháf-\ *n* (1755) **:** a foolish or imbecilic person — **half–wit•ted** \-ˈwit-əd\ *adj* — **half–wit•ted•ness** *n*
half–world \-ˌwərld\ *n* (1605) **:** DEMIMONDE
hal•i•but \ˈhal-ə-bət, ˈhäl-\ *n, pl* **halibut** *also* **halibuts** [ME *halybutte,* fr. *haly, holy* holy + *butte* flatfish, fr. MD or MLG *but;* fr. its being eaten on holy days] (14c) **:** a marine food fish that is the largest flatfish and one of the largest teleost fishes, attains a weight of several hundred pounds in the female, and is now usu. classified as an Atlantic species (*Hippoglossus hippoglossus*) and a Pacific one (*H. stenolepis*)
ha•lide \ˈhal-ˌīd, ˈhā-ˌlīd\ *n* (1876) **:** a binary compound of a halogen with a more electropositive element or radical
hal•i•dom \ˈhal-əd-əm\ *or* **hal•i•dome** \-ə-ˌdōm\ *n* [ME, fr. OE *hāligdōm,* fr. *hālig* holy + *-dōm* -dom] *archaic* (bef. 12c) **:** something held sacred
ha•lite \ˈhal-ˌīt, ˈhā-ˌlīt\ *n* (1868) **:** ROCK SALT
hal•i•to•sis \ˌhal-ə-ˈtō-səs\ *n* [NL, fr. L *halitus* breath, fr. *halare* to breathe — more at EXHALE] (1874) **:** a condition of having fetid breath
hall \ˈhȯl\ *n* [ME *halle,* fr. OE *heall;* akin to L *cella* small room, *celare* to conceal — more at HELL] (bef. 12c) **1 a :** the castle or house of a medieval king or noble **b :** the chief living room in such a structure **2 :** the manor house of a landed proprietor **3 :** a large usu. imposing building for public or semipublic purposes **4 a (1) :** a building used by a college or university for some special purpose **(2) :** DORMITORY **b :** a college or a division of a college at some universities **c (1) :** the common dining room of an English college **(2) :** a meal served there **5 a :** the entrance room of a building **:** LOBBY **b :** a corridor or passage in a building **6 :** a large room for assembly **:** AUDITORIUM **7 :** a place used for public entertainment
hal•lah \ˈkäl-ə, ˈhäl-ə\ *var of* CHALLAH
Hal•lel \hä-ˈlā(ə)l\ *n* [Heb *hallēl* praise] (1702) **:** a selection comprising Psalms 113–118 chanted during Jewish feasts (as the Passover)
[1]**hal•le•lu•jah** \ˌhal-ə-ˈlü-yə\ *interj* [Heb *hallĕlūyāh* praise (ye) the Lord] (1535) — used to express praise, joy, or thanks
[2]**hallelujah** *n* (1625) **:** a shout or song of praise or thanksgiving
hal•liard *var of* HALYARD
[1]**hall•mark** \ˈhȯl-ˌmärk\ *n* [Goldsmiths' *Hall,* London, England, where gold and silver articles were assayed and stamped] (1721) **1 a :** an official mark stamped on gold and silver articles in England to attest their purity **b :** a mark or device placed or stamped on an article of trade to indicate origin, purity, or genuineness **2 :** a distinguishing characteristic, trait, or feature ⟨the dramatic flourishes which are the ~ of the trial lawyer —Marion K. Sanders⟩
[2]**hallmark** *vt* (1852) **:** to stamp with a hallmark
hal•lo \hə-ˈlō, ha-\ *or* **hal•loo** \-ˈlü\ *var of* HOLLO
Hall of Fame (ca. 1909) **1 :** a structure housing memorials to famous or illustrious individuals usu. chosen by a group of electors **2 :** a group of individuals in a particular category (as a sport) who have been selected as particularly illustrious —**Hall of Fam•er** \-ˈfā-mər\
hal•low \ˈhal-(ˌ)ō, -ə(-w)\ *vt* [ME *halowen,* fr. OE *hālgian,* fr. *hālig* holy — more at HOLY] (bef. 12c) **1 :** to make holy or set apart for holy use **2 :** to respect greatly **:** VENERATE ***syn*** see DEVOTE
hal•lowed \ˈhal-(ˌ)ōd, ˈhal-əd, *in the Lord's Prayer often* ˈhal-ə-wəd\ *adj* (bef. 12c) **1 :** HOLY, CONSECRATED **2 :** SACRED, REVERED ⟨~ customs⟩
Hal•low•een \ˌhal-ə-ˈwēn, ˌhäl-\ *n* [short for *All Hallow Even* eve of All Saints' Day] (1556) **:** October 31 observed with festivity and the playing of pranks by children during the evening
Hal•low•mas \ˈhal-ō-ˌmas, ˈhal-ə-, -məs\ *n* [short for ME *Alholowmesse,* fr. OE *ealra halgena mæsse,* lit., all saints' mass] (14c) **:** ALL SAINTS' DAY
halls of ivy [fr. the traditional training of ivy on the walls of older college buildings] (1967) **:** an institution of higher education **:** UNIVERSITY, COLLEGE
Hall•statt *or* **Hall•stadt** \ˈhȯl-ˌstat, ˈhäl-ˌs(h)tät\ *adj* [*Hallstatt,* Austria] (1866) **:** of or relating to the earlier period of the Iron Age in Europe
hal•lu•ci•nate \hə-ˈlüs-ᵊn-ˌāt\ *vb* **-nat•ed; -nat•ing** [L *hallucinatus,* pp. of *hallucinari, allucinari* to prate, dream, fr. Gk *alyein* to be distressed, to wander] *vt* (1822) **1 :** to affect with visions or imaginary perceptions **2 :** to perceive or experience as an hallucination **~** *vi* **:** to have hallucinations — **hal•lu•ci•na•tor** \-ˌnāt-ər\ *n*
hal•lu•ci•na•tion \hə-ˌlüs-ᵊn-ˈā-shən\ *n* (1629) **1 a :** perception of objects with no reality usu. arising from disorder of the nervous system or in response to drugs (as LSD) **b :** the object of an hallucinatory perception **2 :** a completely unfounded or mistaken impression or notion **:** DELUSION
hal•lu•ci•na•to•ry \hə-ˈlüs-ᵊn-ə-ˌtōr-ē, -ˈlüs-nə-, -ˌtȯr-\ *adj* (1830) **1 :** tending to produce hallucination ⟨~ drugs⟩ **2 :** resembling, involving, or being an hallucination ⟨~ dreams⟩ ⟨an ~ figure⟩ ⟨an ~ painting⟩
hal•lu•ci•no•gen \hə-ˈlüs-ᵊn-ə-jən\ *n* [*hallucination* + *-o-* + *-gen*] (1954) **:** a substance that induces hallucinations — **hal•lu•ci•no•gen•ic** \-ˌlüs-ᵊn-ə-ˈjen-ik\ *adj or n*
hal•lu•ci•no•sis \hə-ˌlüs-ᵊn-ˈō-səs\ *n* (1905) **:** a pathological mental state characterized by hallucinations
hal•lux \ˈhal-əks\ *n, pl* **hal•lu•ces** \ˈhal-(y)ə-ˌsēz\ [NL, fr. L *hallus, hallux*] (1831) **:** the innermost digit (as the big toe) of the hind or lower limb
hall•way \ˈhȯl-ˌwā\ *n* (1876) **1 :** an entrance hall **2 :** CORRIDOR
[1]**ha•lo** \ˈhā-(ˌ)lō\ *n, pl* **halos** *or* **haloes** [L *halos,* fr. Gk *halōs* threshing floor, disk, halo] (1563) **1 :** a circle of light appearing to surround the sun or moon and resulting from refraction or reflection of light by ice particles in the atmosphere **2 :** something resembling a halo: as **a :** NIMBUS **b :** a swarm of objects (as globular clusters) surrounding a galaxy **c :** a differentiated zone surrounding a central object **3 :** the aura of glory, veneration, or sentiment surrounding an idealized person or thing
[2]**halo** *vt* (1801) **:** to form into or surround with a halo ⟨rainbows ~*ed* the waterfalls —Michael Crawford⟩
halo- — see HAL-
halo•car•bon \-ˈkär-bən\ *n* (1950) **:** any of various compounds (as fluorocarbon) of carbon and one or more halogens
halo•cline \ˈhal-ə-ˌklīn\ *n* (1960) **:** a usu. vertical gradient in salinity
halo effect *n* (ca. 1928) **:** generalization from the perception of one outstanding personality trait to an overly favorable evaluation of the whole personality
halo•gen \ˈhal-ə-jən\ *n* [Sw, fr. *hal-* + *-gen*] (1842) **:** any of the five elements fluorine, chlorine, bromine, iodine, and astatine that form part of group VII A of the periodic table and exist in the free state normally as diatomic molecules — **ha•log•e•nous** \ha-ˈläj-ə-nəs\ *adj*
ha•lo•ge•nate \ˈhal-ə-jə-ˌnāt, ha-ˈläj-ə-\ *vt* **-nat•ed; -nat•ing** (1882) **:** to treat or cause to combine with a halogen — **ha•lo•ge•na•tion** \ˌhal-ə-jə-ˈnā-shən, ha-ˌläj-ə-\ *n*
hal•o•ge•ton \ˌhal-ə-ˈjē-ˌtän\ *n* [NL, fr. *hal-* + Gk *geitōn* neighbor] (1943) **:** a coarse annual herb (*Halogeton glomeratus*) of the goosefoot family that is a noxious weed in western American ranges
halo•mor•phic \ˌhal-ə-ˈmȯr-fik\ *adj, of a soil* (1938) **:** developed in the presence of neutral or alkali salts or both
halo•per•i•dol \ˌhal-ō-ˈper-ə-ˌdȯl, -ˌdōl\ *n* [*hal-* + *piperidine* + *-ol*] (1960) **:** a depressant $C_{21}H_{23}ClFNO_2$ of the central nervous system used esp. as an antipsychotic drug
halo•phile \ˈhal-ə-ˌfīl\ *n* [ISV] (ca. 1844) **:** an organism that flourishes in a salty environment — **halo•phil•ic** \ˌhal-ə-ˈfil-ik\ *adj*
halo•phyte \ˈhal-ə-ˌfīt\ *n* [ISV] (1886) **:** a plant (as saltbush or sea lavender) that grows in salty soil and usu. has a physiological resemblance to a true xerophyte — **halo•phyt•ic** \ˌhal-ə-ˈfit-ik\ *adj*
halo•thane \ˈhal-ə-ˌthān\ *n* [*halo-* + *ethane*] (1957) **:** a nonexplosive inhalational anesthetic $C_2HBrClF_3$
[1]**halt** \ˈhȯlt\ *adj* [ME, fr. OE *healt;* akin to OHG *halz* lame, L *clades* destruction, Gk *klan* to break] (bef. 12c) **:** LAME
[2]**halt** *vi* (bef. 12c) **1 :** to walk or proceed lamely **:** LIMP **2 :** to stand in perplexity or doubt between alternate courses **:** WAVER **3 :** to display weakness or imperfection **:** FALTER
[3]**halt** *n* [G, fr. MHG, fr. *halt,* imper. of *halten* to hold, fr. OHG *haltan* — more at HOLD] (1591) **:** STOP
[4]**halt** *vi* (1656) **1 :** to cease marching or journeying **2 :** DISCONTINUE, TERMINATE ⟨the project ~*ed* for lack of funds⟩ **~** *vt* **1 :** to bring to a stop ⟨the labor conflict has ~*ed* subways and buses⟩ **2 :** to cause the discontinuance of **:** END
[1]**hal•ter** \ˈhȯl-tər\ *n* [ME, fr. OE *hælftre;* akin to OHG *halftra* halter, OE *hielfe* helve] (bef. 12c) **1 a :** a rope or strap for leading or tying an animal **b :** a headstall usu. with noseband and throatlatch to which a lead may be attached **2 :** a rope for hanging criminals **:** NOOSE; *also* **:** death by hanging **3 :** a woman's blouse that leaves the back, arms, and midriff bare and that is typically held in place by straps around the neck and across the back

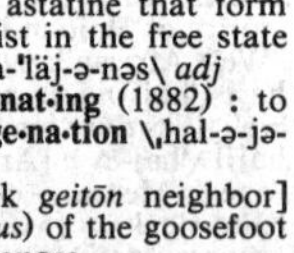
halter 1b

[2]**halter** *vt* **hal•tered; hal•ter•ing** \-t(ə-)riŋ\ (14c) **1 a :** to catch with or as if with a halter; *also* **:** to put a halter on **b :** HANG **2 :** to put restraint upon **:** HAMPER
hal•ter•break \ˈhȯl-tər-ˌbrāk\ *vt* **-broke** \-ˌbrōk\; **-bro•ken** \-ˌbrō-kən\; **-break•ing** (1837) **:** to break (as a colt) to a halter
hal•tere \ˈhȯl-ˌti(ə)r, ˈhal-\ *n, pl* **hal•teres** \ˈhȯl-ˌti(ə)rz, ˈhal-; hȯl-ˈti(ə)r-ēz, hal-\ [NL *halter,* fr. L, jumping weight, fr. Gk *haltēr,* fr. *hallesthai* to leap — more at SALLY] (1823) **:** one of a pair of club-shaped organs in a dipterous insect that are the modified second pair of wings and function as sensory flight instruments
halt•ing \ˈhȯl-tiŋ\ *adj* (1585) **:** marked by a lack of sureness or effectiveness ⟨the witness spoke in a ~ manner⟩ — **halt•ing•ly** \-tiŋ-lē\ *adv*
hal•vah *or* **hal•va** \häl-ˈvä; ˈhäl-(ˌ)vä, -və\ *n* [Yiddish *halva,* fr. Rom, fr. Turk *helva,* fr. Ar *ḥalwā* sweetmeat] (1846) **:** a flaky confection of crushed sesame seeds in a base of syrup (as of honey)

halve \ˈhav, ˈȧv\ *vt* **halved; halv·ing** [ME *halven,* fr. *half* half] (14c) **1 a :** to divide into two equal parts **b :** to reduce to one half ⟨*halving* the present cost⟩ **c :** to share equally **2 :** to play (as a hole in golf) in the same number of strokes as one's opponent

halv·ers \ˈhav-ərz, ˈhȧv-\ *n pl* (1517) **:** half shares **:** HALVES

halves *pl of* HALF

hal·yard \ˈhal-yərd\ *n* [ME *halier,* fr. *halen* to pull — more at HALE] (14c) **:** a rope or tackle for hoisting and lowering something (as sails)

1ham \ˈham\ *n* [ME *hamme,* fr. OE *hamm;* akin to OHG *hamma* ham, Gk *knēmē* shinbone] (bef. 12c) **1 a :** the hollow of the knee **b :** a buttock with its associated thigh — usu. used in pl. **2 :** a cut of meat consisting of a thigh; *esp* **:** one from a hog — see PORK illustration **3** [short for *hamfatter,* fr. "The *Ham-fat* Man," Negro minstrel song] **a :** a showy performer; *esp* **:** an actor performing in an exaggerated theatrical style **b :** a licensed operator of an amateur radio station — **ham** *adj*

2ham *vb* **hammed; ham·ming** *vt* (1933) **:** to execute with exaggerated speech or gestures **:** OVERACT ~ *vi* **:** to overplay a part

Ham \ˈham\ *n* [Heb] **:** a son of Noah held to be the progenitor of the Egyptians, Nubians, and Canaanites

hama·dry·ad \ˌham-ə-ˈdrī-əd, -ˌad\ *n* [L *hamadryad-, hamadryas,* fr. Gk, fr. *hama* together with + *dryad-, dryas* dryad — more at SAME] (14c) **1 :** WOOD NYMPH **2 :** KING COBRA

hama·dry·as baboon \ˌham-ə-ˌdrī-əs-\ *n* [NL *hamadryas,* fr. L *Hamadryas* a wood nymph] (ca. 1890) **:** a baboon (*Pipio hamadryas*) with a reddish pink muzzle and ischial callosities that was venerated by the ancient Egyptians — called also *sacred baboon*

ha·mal *also* **ham·mal** \hə-ˈmäl\ *n* [Ar *ḥammāl* porter] (1766) **:** a porter in eastern countries (as Turkey)

Ha·man \ˈhā-mən\ *n* [Heb *Hāmān*] **:** an enemy of the Jews hanged according to the book of Esther for plotting their destruction

ha·mar·tia \ˌhäm-ˌär-ˈtē-ə\ *n* [Gk, fr. *hamartanein* to miss the mark, err; akin to Gk *memēra* care — more at MEMORY] (1927) **:** TRAGIC FLAW

ha·mate \ˈhā-ˌmāt\ *n* [L *hamatus* hooked, fr. *hamus* hook] (1947) **:** a bone on the inner side of the second row of the carpus in mammals

ham·burg·er \ˈham-ˌbər-gər\ *or* **ham·burg** \-ˌbərg\ *n* [G *Hamburger* of Hamburg, West Germany] (1884) **1 a :** ground beef **b :** a patty of ground beef **2 :** a sandwich consisting of a patty of hamburger in a split round bun

1hame \ˈhām\ *n* [ME] (14c) **:** one of two curved supports which are attached to the collar of a draft horse and to which the traces are fastened

2hame *Scot var of* HOME

ham–fist·ed \ˈham-ˈfis-təd\ *adj* (1928) **:** HAM-HANDED

ham–hand·ed \-ˈhan-dəd\ *adj* (1918) **:** lacking dexterity or grace **:** HEAVY-HANDED

Ham·il·to·ni·an \ˌham-əl-ˈtō-nē-ən\ *n* [Sir William *Hamilton* †1865 Irish mathematician] (1933) **:** a function that is used to describe a dynamic system (as the motion of a particle) in terms of components of momentum and coordinates of space and time and that is equal to the total energy of the system when time is not explicitly part of the function — called also *Hamiltonian function;* compare LAGRANGIAN

Ham·il·to·ni·an·ism \-ˌiz-əm\ *n* (1901) **:** the political principles and ideas held by or associated with Alexander Hamilton that center around a belief in a strong unitary central government, broad interpretation of the federal constitution, encouragement of an industrial and commercial economy, and a general distrust of the political capacity or wisdom of the common man

Ham·ite \ˈham-ˌīt\ *n* [*Ham*] (1854) **:** a member of a group of chiefly northern African peoples that are mostly Muslims and are highly variable in appearance but mainly Caucasoid

1Ham·it·ic \ha-ˈmit-ik, hə-\ *adj* (1844) **:** of, relating to, or characteristic of the Hamites or one of the Hamitic languages

2Hamitic *n* (ca. 1890) **:** HAMITIC LANGUAGES

Hamitic languages *n pl* (ca. 1890) **:** the Berber, Cushitic, and sometimes Egyptian branches of the Afro-Asiatic languages

Ham·i·to–Se·mit·ic \ˌham-ə-(ˌ)tō-sə-ˈmit-ik\ *adj* (1901) **:** of, relating to, or constituting the Afro-Asiatic languages — **Hamito–Semitic** *n*

Hamito–Semitic languages *n pl* (1949) **:** AFRO-ASIATIC LANGUAGES

ham·let \ˈham-lət\ *n* [ME, fr. MF *hamelet,* dim. of *ham* village, of Gmc origin; akin to OE *hām* village, home] (bef. 12c) **:** a small village

Ham·let \ˈham-lət\ *n* **:** a legendary Danish prince and hero of Shakespeare's play *Hamlet*

1ham·mer \ˈham-ər\ *n* [ME *hamer,* fr. OE *hamor;* akin to OHG *hamar* hammer, Gk *akmē* point, edge — more at EDGE] (bef. 12c) **1 a :** a hand tool consisting of a solid head set crosswise on a handle and used for pounding **b :** a power tool that often substitutes a metal block or a drill for the hammerhead **2 :** something that resembles a hammer in form or action: as **a :** a lever with a striking head for ringing a bell or striking a gong **b** (1) **:** an arm that strikes the cap in a percussion lock to ignite the propelling charge (2) **:** a part of the action of a modern gun that strikes the primer of the cartridge in firing or that strikes the firing pin to ignite the cartridge **c :** MALLEUS **d :** GAVEL **e** (1) **:** a padded mallet in a piano action for striking a string (2) **:** a hand mallet for playing on various percussion instruments (as a xylophone) **3 :** a metal sphere that usu. weighs 16 pounds and that is thrown for distance in the hammer throw **4 :** ACCELERATOR b — **under the hammer :** for sale at auction

2hammer *vb* **ham·mered; ham·mer·ing** \ˈham-(ə-)riŋ\ *vi* (14c) **1 :** to strike blows esp. repeatedly with or as if with a hammer **:** POUND **2 :** to make repeated efforts; *esp* **:** to reiterate an opinion or attitude ⟨the lectures all ~*ed* away at the same points⟩ ~ *vt* **1 a :** to beat, drive, or shape with repeated blows of a hammer **b :** to fasten or build with a hammer **2 :** to strike or drive with a force suggesting a hammer blow or repeated blows ⟨~*ed* the ball over the fence⟩ ⟨tried to ~ me into submission⟩ **3 :** to produce or bring about as if by repeated blows ⟨~ out a policy⟩ — **ham·mer·er** \ˈham-ər-ər\ *n*

hammer and sickle *n* (1921) **:** an emblem consisting of a crossed hammer and sickle used chiefly as a symbol of Communism in the Soviet Union

hammer and tongs *adv* (1708) **:** with great force, vigor, or violence ⟨went at each other *hammer and tongs*⟩ — **hammer–and–tongs** *adj*

ham·mered *adj* (1522) **:** having surface indentations produced or appearing to have been produced by hammering ⟨~ copper⟩

ham·mer·head \ˈham-ər-ˌhed\ *n* (1562) **1 :** the striking part of a hammer **2 :** BLOCKHEAD **3 :** any of various active voracious medium-sized sharks that have the eyes at the ends of lateral extensions of the flattened head — see SHARK illustration

ham·mer·less \-ləs\ *adj* (1875) **:** having the hammer concealed ⟨a ~ gun⟩

ham·mer·lock \-ˌläk\ *n* (1897) **:** a wrestling hold in which an opponent's arm is held bent behind his back

hammer mill *n* (1610) **:** a grinder or crusher in which materials are broken up by hammers

hammer throw *n* (1922) **:** a field event in which a metal sphere attached to a flexible handle is thrown for distance

ham·mer·toe \ˌham-ər-ˈtō\ *n* (ca. 1885) **:** a deformed claw-shaped toe and esp. the second that results from permanent angular flexion between one or both phalangeal joints

1ham·mock \ˈham-ək\ *n* [Sp *hamaca,* fr. Taino] (1555) **:** a swinging couch or bed usu. made of netting or canvas and slung by cords from supports at each end

2hammock *n* [origin unknown] (1555) **1 :** HUMMOCK **2 :** a fertile area in the southern U.S. and esp. Florida that is usu. higher than its surroundings and that is characterized by hardwood vegetation and deep humus-rich soil

ham·my \ˈham-ē\ *adj* **ham·mi·er; -est** (1929) **:** marked by exaggerated and usu. self-conscious theatricality — **ham·mi·ly** \ˈham-ə-lē\ *adv* — **ham·mi·ness** \ˈham-ē-nəs\ *n*

1ham·per \ˈham-pər\ *vt* **ham·pered; ham·per·ing** \-p(ə-)riŋ\ [ME *hamperen*] (14c) **1 a :** to restrict the movement of by bonds or obstacles **:** IMPEDE **b :** to interfere with the operation of **:** DISRUPT **2 a :** CURB, RESTRAIN **b :** to interfere with **:** ENCUMBER

syn HAMPER, TRAMMEL, CLOG, FETTER, SHACKLE, MANACLE mean to hinder or impede in moving, progressing, or acting. HAMPER may imply the effect of any impeding or restraining influence; TRAMMEL suggests entangling by or confining within a net; CLOG usu. implies a slowing by something extraneous or encumbering; FETTER suggests a restraining so severe that freedom to move or progress is almost lost; SHACKLE and MANACLE are stronger than FETTER and suggest total loss of freedom.

2hamper *n* [ME *hampere,* alter. of *hanaper,* lit., case to hold goblets, fr. MF *hanapier,* fr. *hanap* goblet, of Gmc origin; akin to OE *hnæpp* bowl] (14c) **:** a large basket usu. with a cover for packing, storing, or transporting articles (as food or laundry)

Hamp·shire \ˈham(p)-ˌshi(ə)r, -shər\ *n* [*Hampshire,* England] (1920) **1 :** any of an American breed of black white-belted swine **2 :** any of a British breed of large hornless mutton-producing sheep — called also *Hampshire Down*

ham·ster \ˈham(p)-stər\ *n* [G, fr. OHG *hamustro,* of Slavic origin; akin to OSlav *chomĕstorŭ* hamster] (1607) **:** any of numerous Old World rodents (*Cricetus* or a related genus) having very large cheek pouches

1ham·string \ˈham-ˌstriŋ\ *n* (1565) **1 a :** either of two groups of tendons at the back of the human knee **b :** HAMSTRING MUSCLE **2 :** a large tendon above and behind the hock of a quadruped

2hamstring *vt* **-strung** \-ˌstrəŋ\; **-string·ing** \-ˌstriŋ-iŋ\ (1641) **1 :** to cripple by cutting the leg tendons **2 :** to make ineffective or powerless **:** CRIPPLE ⟨teachers . . . *hamstrung* by excessive teaching schedules —N. M. Pusey⟩

hamstring muscle *n* (ca. 1888) **:** any of three muscles (as the biceps of the leg) at the back of the thigh that function to flex and rotate the leg and extend the thigh

ham·u·lus \ˈham-yə-ləs\ *n, pl* **-u·li** \-ˌlī, -ˌlē\ [NL, fr. L, dim. of *hamus* hook] (ca. 1727) **:** a hook or hooked process

ham·za *or* **ham·zah** \ˈham-zə\ *n* [Ar *hamzah,* lit., compression] (1938) **:** the sign for a glottal stop in Arabic orthography usu. represented in English by an apostrophe

Han \ˈhän\ *n* [Chin *Han*4] (1736) **1 :** a Chinese dynasty dated 207 B.C.–A.D. 220 and marked by centralized control through an appointive bureaucracy, a revival of learning, and the penetration of Buddhism **2 :** the Chinese peoples esp. as distinguished from Mongol, Manchu, or other non-Chinese elements in the population **:** the Chinese race

1hand \ˈhand\ *n, often attrib* [ME, fr. OE; akin to OHG *hant* hand] (bef. 12c) **1 a** (1) **:** the terminal part of the vertebrate forelimb when modified (as in humans) as a grasping organ (2) **:** the forelimb segment (as the terminal section of a bird's wing) of a vertebrate higher than the fishes that corresponds to the hand irrespective of its form or functional specialization **b :** a part serving the function of or resembling a hand: as (1) **:** the hind foot of an ape (2) **:** the chela of a crustacean **c :** something resembling a hand: as (1) **:** an indicator or pointer on a dial (2) **:** a stylized figure of a hand with forefinger extended to point a direction or call attention to something (3) **:** a cluster of bananas developed from a single flower group (4) **:** a branched rootstock of ginger (5) **:** a bunch of large leaves (as of tobacco) tied together usu. with another leaf **2 a :** personal possession — usu. used in pl. ⟨the documents fell into the ~*s* of the enemy⟩ **b :** CONTROL, SUPERVISION — usu. used in pl. ⟨management of the estate is in the ~*s* of the executor⟩ **3 a :** SIDE, DIRECTION ⟨men fighting on either ~⟩ **b :** one of two sides or aspects of an issue or argument ⟨on the one ~ we can appeal for peace, and on the other, declare war⟩ **4 :** a pledge esp. of betrothal or bestowal in marriage **5 a :** style of penmanship **:** HANDWRITING **b :** SIGNATURE **6 a :** SKILL, ABILITY ⟨tried her ~ at sailing⟩ **b :** an instrumental part ⟨had a ~ in the crime⟩ **7 :** a unit of measure equal to 4 inches used esp. for the height of horses **8 a :** assistance or aid esp. involving physical effort ⟨lend a ~⟩ **b :** PARTICIPATION, INTEREST **c :** a round of applause **9 a** (1) **:** a player in a card game or board game (2) **:** the cards or pieces held by a player **b :** a single round in a game **c :** the force or solidity of one's position (as in negotiations) **10 a :** one who performs or executes a particular work ⟨two portraits by the same ~⟩ **b** (1) **:** one employed at manual labor or general tasks ⟨a ranch ~⟩ (2) **:** WORKER, EMPLOYEE ⟨employed over a hundred ~*s*〉 **c** : a member of a ship's crew 〈all ~*s* on deck〉 **d** : one skilled in a particular action or pursuit **e** : a specialist in a usu. designated activity or region 〈an old China ~〉 **11 a** : HANDIWORK **b** : style of execution : WORKMANSHIP 〈the ~ of a master〉 **c** : the feel of or tactile reaction to something (as silk or leather) — **at hand** : near in time or place : within reach — **at the hands of** *or* **at the hand of** : through the action or process of — **by hand 1** : with the hands or a hand-worked implement (as a tool or pen) rather than with a machine **2** : from one individual directly to another 〈deliver the documents *by hand*〉 — **in hand 1** : in one's possession or control **2** : in preparation — **on all hands** *or* **on every hand** : EVERYWHERE — **on hand 1** : in present possession or readily available **2** : about to appear : PENDING **3** : in attendance : PRESENT — **out of hand 1** : without delay or deliberation; *also* : in a summary or peremptory manner **2** : done with : FINISHED **3** : out of control

[2]hand *adv* (12c) : with the hands rather than by machine

[3]hand *vt* (15c) **1 a** *obs* : to touch or manage with the hands; *also* : to deal with **b** : FURL **2** : to lead, guide, or assist with the hand 〈~ a lady into a bus〉 **3 a** : to give, pass, or transmit with the hand 〈~ a letter to her〉 **b** : PRESENT, PROVIDE 〈~*ed* him a surprise〉 — **hand it to** : to give credit to : concede the excellence of

hand and foot *adv* (bef. 12c) : TOTALLY, ASSIDUOUSLY

hand ax *n* (bef. 12c) **1** : a short-handled ax intended for use with one hand **2** : a prehistoric stone tool having one end pointed for cutting and the other end rounded for holding in the hand

hand•bag \ˈhan(d)-ˌbag\ *n* (1862) **1** : TRAVELING BAG **2** : a bag held in the hand or hung from a shoulder strap and used for carrying small personal articles and money

hand•ball \-ˌbȯl\ *n* (15c) **1** : a small rubber ball used in the game of handball **2** : a game played in a walled court or against a single wall or board by two or four players who use their hands to strike the ball

hand•bar•row \-ˌbar-(ˌ)ō, -ə(-w)\ *n* (15c) : a flat rectangular frame with handles at both ends that is carried by two persons

hand•bill \-ˌbil\ *n* (1753) : a small printed sheet to be distributed (as for advertising) by hand

hand•book \-ˌbu̇k\ *n* (bef. 12c) **1 a** : a book capable of being conveniently carried as a ready reference : MANUAL **b** : a concise reference book covering a particular subject **2 a** : a bookmaker's book of bets **b** : a place where bookmaking is carried on

hand•breadth \-ˌbretth, -ˌbreth, -ˌbredth\ *n* (bef. 12c) : any of various units of length varying from about 2½ to 4 inches based on the breadth of a hand

hand•car \ˈhan(d)-ˌkär\ *n* (1850) : a small four-wheeled railroad car propelled by a hand-operated mechanism or by a small motor

hand•cart \-ˌkärt\ *n* (1810) : a cart drawn or pushed by hand

hand cheese *n* (1890) : a soft cheese that was orig. molded by hand and that has a sharp pungent odor and flavor

hand•clasp \ˈhan(d)-ˌklasp\ *n* (1583) : HANDSHAKE

[1]hand•craft \-ˌkraft\ *n* (bef. 12c) : HANDICRAFT

[2]handcraft *vt* (1933) : to fashion by handicraft

hand•craft•man \-ˌkraf(t)-mən\ *or* **hand•crafts•man** \-ˌkraf(t)-smən\ *n* (15c) : one who is skilled in handicraft

[1]hand•cuff \-ˌkəf\ *n* (1629) : a metal fastening that can be locked around a wrist and is usu. connected by a chain or bar with another such fastening

[2]handcuff *vt* (1720) **1** : to apply handcuffs to : MANACLE **2** : to hold in check : make ineffective or powerless

hand down *vt* (1692) **1** : to transmit in succession (as from father to son) **2** : to make official formulation of and express (the opinion of a court)

hand•ed \ˈhan-dəd\ *adj* (1552) **1** : having a hand or hands esp. of a specified kind or number — usu. used in combination 〈a large-*handed* man〉 **2** : using a specified hand or number of hands — used in combination 〈right-*handed*〉 〈a one-*handed* catch〉

hand•ed•ness \-nəs\ *n* (1915) : a tendency to use one hand rather than the other

hand•fast \ˈhan(d)-ˌfast\ *n* [ME, fr. OE *handfæst*] *archaic* (bef. 12c) : a contract or covenant esp. of betrothal or marriage

hand–feed \ˈhan(d)-ˈfēd\ *vt* **-fed** \-ˈfed\; **-feed•ing** (1805) : to provide and apportion rations to (animals) at regular intervals in quantities sufficient for a single feeding — compare SELF-FEED

hand•ful \ˈhan(d)-ˌfu̇l\ *n, pl* **handfuls** \-ˌfu̇lz\ *also* **hands•ful** \ˈhan(d)z-ˌfu̇l\ (bef. 12c) **1** : as much or as many as the hand will grasp **2** : a small quantity or number **3** : as much as one can manage

hand glass *n* (1882) : a small mirror with a handle

hand•grip \ˈhan(d)-ˌgrip\ *n* (bef. 12c) **1** : a grasping with the hand **2** : HANDLE **3** *pl* : hand-to-hand combat

hand•gun \-ˌgən\ *n* (15c) : a firearm (as a revolver or pistol) designed to be held and fired with one hand

hand•hold \ˈhand-ˌhōld\ *n* (1643) **1** : HOLD, GRIP **2** : something to hold on to (as in mountain climbing)

hand–hold•ing \-ˌhōl-diŋ\ *n* (1967) : the act or condition of providing extremely solicitous care, attention, or detailed instruction

[1]hand•i•cap \ˈhan-di-ˌkap\ *n* [obs. E *handicap* (a game in which forfeits were held in a cap), fr. *hand in cap*] (1660) **1 a** : a race or contest in which an artificial advantage is given or disadvantage imposed on a contestant to equalize chances of winning **b** : an advantage given or disadvantage imposed usu. in the form of points, strokes, weight to be carried, or distance from the target or goal **2** : a disadvantage that makes achievement unusually difficult; *esp* : a physical disability

[2]handicap *vt* **-capped; -cap•ping** (1841) **1 a** : to give a handicap to **b** : to assess the relative winning chances of (contestants) or the likely winner of (a contest) **2** : to put at a disadvantage

hand•i•capped *adj* (1915) : having a physical or mental disability that substantially limits activity esp. in relation to employment or education

hand•i•cap•per \-ˌkap-ər\ *n* (1754) **1** : one who assigns handicaps **2** : one who predicts the winners in a horse race usu. for publication **3** : one who competes with a (specified) handicap — usu. used in combination 〈a 5-*handicapper*〉

hand•i•craft \ˈhan-di-ˌkraft\ *n* [ME *handi-crafte,* alter. of *handcraft*] (13c) **1 a** : manual skill **b** : an occupation requiring skill with the hands **2** : the articles fashioned by those engaged in handicraft — **hand•i•craft•er** \-ˌkraf-tər\ *n*

hand•i•crafts•man \-ˌkraf(t)-smən\ *n* (1551) : one who engages in a handicraft : ARTISAN

Hand•ie–Talk•ie \ˌhan-dē-ˈtȯ-kē\ *trademark* — used for a small portable radio transmitter-receiver

hand•i•ly \ˈhan-də-lē\ *adv* (15c) **1** : in a dexterous manner **2** : EASILY 〈defeated the other candidate ~〉 **3** : conveniently nearby 〈kept the eraser ~ by him while he wrote〉

hand in glove *or* **hand and glove** *adv* (1680) : in extremely close relationship or agreement 〈working *hand in glove* with the racketeers〉

hand in hand *adv* (15c) **1** : with hands clasped (as in intimacy or affection) **2** : in close association

hand•i•work \ˈhan-di-ˌwərk\ *n* [ME *handiwerk,* fr. OE *handgeweorc,* fr. *hand* + *geweorc,* fr. *ge-* (collective prefix) + *weorc* work — more at CO-] (bef. 12c) **1 a** : work done by the hands **b** : work done personally **2** : the product of handiwork

hand•ker•chief \ˈhaŋ-kər-chəf, -(ˌ)chif, -ˌchēf\ *n, pl* **-chiefs** *also* **-chieves** \-chəfs, -(ˌ)chifs, -ˌchēvz (*used by many who have sing.* -chəf *or* -(ˌ)chif), -ˌchēfs, -chəvz, -(ˌ)chivz\ (1530) **1** : a small usu. square piece of cloth used for various usu. personal purposes (as blowing the nose or wiping the eyes) or as an accessory on one's attire **2** : KERCHIEF 1

[1]han•dle \ˈhan-dᵊl\ *n* [ME *handel,* fr. OE *handle;* akin to OE *hand*] (bef. 12c) **1** : a part that is designed esp. to be grasped by the hand **2** : something that resembles a handle **3** : NAME, TITLE **4** : the feel of a textile **5** : the total amount of money bet on a race, game, or event — **han•dled** \-dᵊld\ *adj* — **han•dle•less** \-dᵊl-(l)əs\ *adj* — **off the handle** : into a state of sudden and violent anger

[2]handle *vb* **han•dled; han•dling** \ˈhan-(d)liŋ, -dᵊl-iŋ\ *vt* (bef. 12c) **1 a** : to try or examine (as by touching, feeling, or moving) with the hand 〈~ silk to judge its weight〉 **b** : to manage with the hands 〈~ a horse〉 **2 a** : to deal with in writing or speaking or in the plastic arts **b** : to have overall responsibility for supervising or directing : MANAGE 〈a lawyer ~*s* all my affairs〉 **c** : to train and act as second for (a boxer) **3** : to act on or perform a required function with regard to 〈~ the day's mail〉 **4** : to engage in the buying, selling, or distributing of (a commodity) ~ *vi* : to act, behave, or feel in a certain way when handled or directed 〈car that ~*s* well〉 — **han•dle•able** \-dᵊl-ə-bəl\ *adj*

syn HANDLE, MANIPULATE, WIELD mean to manage dexterously or efficiently. HANDLE implies directing an acquired skill to the accomplishment of immediate ends; MANIPULATE implies adroit handling and in extended use often suggests the use of craft or of fraud; WIELD implies mastery and vigor in handling a tool or a weapon or in exerting influence, authority, or power.

han•dle•bar \ˈhan-dᵊl-ˌbär\ *n* (1887) : a straight or bent bar with a handle at each end; *specif* : one used to steer a bicycle or similar vehicle — usu. used in pl.

handlebar mustache *n* (1933) : a heavy mustache with long sections that curve upward at each end

hand lens *n* (1930) : a magnifying glass to be held in the hand

han•dler \ˈhan-(d)lər, -dᵊl-ər\ *n* (14c) **1** : one that handles something **2 a** : one in immediate physical charge of an animal; *esp* : one who exhibits dogs at shows or field trials **b** : one that helps to train a boxer or acts as his second during a match

hand•less \ˈhan-(d)ləs\ *adj* (13c) **1** : having no hands **2** : inefficient in manual tasks : CLUMSY

han•dling \-(d)liŋ, -dᵊl-iŋ\ *n* (bef. 12c) **1 a** : the action of one that handles something **b** : a process by which something is handled in a commercial transaction; *esp* : the packaging and shipping of an object or material (as to a consumer) **2** : the manner in which something is treated (as in a musical, literary, or art work)

hand•list \ˈhan-ˌ(d)list\ *n* (1859) : a list (as of books) for purposes of reference or checking

hand•made \ˈhan(d)-ˈmād\ *adj* (1613) : made by hand or a hand process

hand•maid•en \-ˌmād-ᵊn\ *or* **hand•maid** \-ˌmād\ *n* (14c) **1** : a personal maid or female servant **2** : something whose essential function is to serve or assist 〈good sense which . . . is the indispensable ~ of the critical art —Carlos Baker〉

hand–me–down \ˈhan(d)-mē-ˌdau̇n\ *adj* (1827) **1** : ready-made and usu. cheap and shoddy **2** : put in use by one person or group after being used, discarded, or handed down by another 〈~ clothes〉 — **hand–me–down** *n*

hand mower *n* (1958) : a motorless lawn mower designed to be pushed by hand

hand off \(ˈ)han-ˈdȯf\ *vt* (1897) : to hand (a football) to a nearby teammate on a play ~ *vi* : to hand off a football — **hand•off** \ˈhan-ˌdȯf\ *n*

hand on *vt* (1642) : HAND DOWN

hand organ *n* (1796) : a barrel organ operated by a hand crank

hand•out \ˈhan-ˌdau̇t\ *n* (1882) **1** : a portion of food, clothing, or money given to or as if to a beggar **2** : a folder or circular of information for free distribution **3** : a prepared statement released to the news media

hand out \(ˈ)han-ˈdau̇t\ *vt* (1877) **1 a** : to give without charge **b** : to give freely **2** : ADMINISTER 〈*handed out* a severe punishment〉

hand over *vt* (1904) : to yield control of

hand over fist *adv* (1825) : quickly and in large amounts

hand•pick \ˈhan(d)-ˈpik\ *vt* (1831) **1** : to pick by hand as opposed to a machine process **2** : to select personally or for personal ends

hand•press \-ˌpres\ *n* (1679) : a hand-operated press

hand•print \-ˌprint\ *n* (1886) : an impression of a hand on a surface

hand puppet *n* (1947) : PUPPET 1a

hand•rail \ˈhan-ˌdrāl\ *n* (1793) : a narrow rail for grasping with the hand as a support

hand running *adv* (1828) : in unbroken succession : CONSECUTIVELY

hand•saw \ˈhan(d)-ˌsȯ\ *n* (14c) : a saw usu. operated with one hand

hands•breadth \ˈhan(d)z-ˌbredth, -ˌbretth\ *var of* HANDBREADTH

hands down \ˈhan(d)z-ˈdau̇n\ *adv* (1867) **1** : without much effort : EASILY **2** : without question — **hands–down** \ˌhan(d)z-ˌdau̇n\ *adj*

[1]hand•sel \ˈhan(t)-səl\ *n* [ME *hansell*] (14c) **1** : a gift made as a token of good wishes or luck esp. at the beginning of a new year **2** : something received first (as in a day of trading) and taken to be a token of good luck **3 a** : a first installment : earnest money **b** : EARNEST, FORETASTE

[2]handsel *vt* **-seled** *or* **-selled; -sel•ing** *or* **-sel•ling** \-s(ə-)liŋ\ (15c) **1** : to give a handsel to **2** : to inaugurate with a token or gesture of luck or pleasure **3** : to use or do for the first time

hand·set \'han(d)-ˌset\ *n* (ca. 1919) **:** a combined telephone transmitter and receiver mounted on a handle
hand·shake \-ˌshāk\ *n* (1873) **:** a clasping of right hands by two people (as in greeting or farewell)
hands–off \'han(d)-'zȯf\ *adj* (1902) **:** characterized by noninterference ⟨a ~ policy toward the internal affairs of other nations⟩
hand·some \'han(t)-səm\ *adj* [ME *handsom* easy to manipulate] (1530) **1** *chiefly dial* **:** APPROPRIATE, SUITABLE **2 :** moderately large **:** SIZABLE ⟨a painting that commanded a ~ price⟩ **3 :** marked by skill or cleverness **:** ADROIT **4 :** marked by graciousness or generosity **:** LIBERAL ⟨~ contributions to charity⟩ **5 :** having a pleasing and usu. impressive or dignified appearance ***syn*** see BEAUTIFUL — **hand·some·ly** *adv* — **hand·some·ness** *n*
hands–on \-'zȯn, -'zän\ *adj* (1969) **:** relating to, being, or providing direct practical experience in the operation or functioning of something ⟨~ training with a new computer system⟩
hand·spike \'han(d)-ˌspīk\ *n* [by folk etymology fr. D *handspaak,* fr. *hand* hand + *spaak* pole; akin to OE *spāca* spoke] (1615) **:** a bar used as a lever
hand·spring \-ˌspriŋ\ *n* (1875) **:** an acrobatic feat in which the body turns forward or backward in a full circle from a standing position and lands first on the hands and then on the feet
hand·stand \-ˌstand\ *n* (1899) **:** an act of supporting the body on the hands with the trunk and legs balanced in the air
hand–to–hand \ˌhan-tə-ˌhand, -də-\ *adj* (1836) **:** involving physical contact
hand to hand \-'hand\ *adv* (15c) **:** in a manner involving physical contact
hand–to–mouth \-ˌmau̇th\ *adj* (1748) **:** having or providing nothing to spare **:** PRECARIOUS ⟨a ~ existence⟩
hand truck *n* (1920) **:** a small hand-propelled truck; *esp* **:** TRUCK 3b
hand·wheel \'han(d)-ˌhwēl, 'han-ˌdwēl\ *n* (1901) **:** a wheel worked by hand
hand·work \'han-ˌdwərk\ *n* (bef. 12c) **:** work done with the hands and not by machines **:** HANDIWORK — **hand·work·er** \-ˌdwər-kər\ *n*
hand·wo·ven \-'dwō-vən\ *adj* (1880) **1 :** produced on a hand-operated loom **2 :** woven by hand ⟨~ baskets⟩
hand–wring·ing \-ˌdriŋ-iŋ\ *n* (1922) **:** an overwrought expression of concern or guilt
hand·write \-ˌdrīt\ *vt* **-wrote** \-ˌdrōt\; **-writ·ten** \-ˌdrit-ᵊn\; **-writ·ing** \-ˌdrīt-iŋ\ [back-formation fr. *handwriting*] (1849) **:** to write by hand
hand·writ·ing \'han-ˌdrīt-iŋ\ *n* (15c) **1 :** writing done by hand; *esp* **:** the form of writing peculiar to a particular person **2 :** something written by hand **:** MANUSCRIPT — **handwriting on the wall :** an omen of one's unpleasant fate
hand·wrought \'han-'drȯt\ *adj* (1876) **:** fashioned by hand or chiefly by hand processes ⟨~ silver⟩
handy \'han-dē\ *adj* **hand·i·er; -est** (1650) **1 a :** conveniently near **b :** convenient for use **c** *of a ship* **:** easily handled **2 :** clever in using the hands esp. in a variety of useful ways ⟨a woman ~ with a gun as well as a needle⟩ — **hand·i·ness** *n*
handy·man \-dē-ˌman\ *n* (1872) **1 :** one who does odd jobs **2 :** one competent in a variety of small skills or inventive or ingenious in repair or maintenance work
[1]**hang** \'haŋ\ *vb* **hung** \'həŋ\ *also* **hanged** \'haŋd\; **hang·ing** \'haŋ-iŋ\ [partly fr. ME *hon,* fr. OE *hōn,* v.t.; partly fr. ME *hangen,* fr. OE *hangian,* v.i. & v.t.; both akin to OHG *hāhan,* v.t., to hang, *hangēn,* v.i. — more at CUNCTATION] *vt* (bef. 12c) **1 a :** to fasten to some elevated point without support from below **:** SUSPEND **b :** to suspend by the neck until dead — often *hanged* in the past; often used as a mild oath ⟨I'll be ~*ed*⟩ **c :** to fasten so as to allow free motion within given limits upon a point of suspension ⟨~ a door⟩ **d :** to fit or fix in position or at a proper angle ⟨~ an ax to its helve⟩ **e :** to adjust the hem of (a skirt) so as to hang evenly and at a proper height **2 :** to furnish with hanging decorations (as flags or bunting) **3 :** to hold or bear in a suspended or inclined manner ⟨*hung* his head in shame⟩ **4 :** to apply to a wall ⟨~ wallpaper⟩ **5 :** to display (pictures) in a gallery **6 :** to throw (as a curve) so that it fails to break properly ~ *vi* **1 a :** to remain suspended or fastened to some point above without support from below **:** DANGLE **b :** to die by hanging — often *hanged* in the past ⟨he ~*ed* for his crimes⟩ **2 :** to remain poised or stationary in the air ⟨clouds ~*ing* low overhead⟩ **3 :** to stay with persistence **4 :** to be imminent **:** IMPEND ⟨doom *hung* over the nation⟩ **5 :** to fall or droop from a usu. tense or taut position **6 :** DEPEND ⟨election ~*s* on one vote⟩ **7 a** (1) **:** to take hold for support **:** CLING ⟨she *hung* on his arm⟩ (2) **:** to keep persistent contact ⟨dogs *hung* to the trail⟩ **b :** to be burdensome or oppressive ⟨time ~*s* on his hands⟩ **8 :** to be uncertain or in suspense ⟨the decision is still ~*ing*⟩ **9 :** to lean, incline, or jut over or downward **10 :** to be in a state of rapt attention ⟨*hung* on his every word⟩ **11 :** to fit or fall from the figure in easy lines ⟨the coat ~*s* loosely⟩ **12** *of a thrown ball* **:** to fail to break or drop as intended — **hang·able** \'haŋ-ə-bəl\ *adj*
usage For both transitive and intransitive senses 1b the past and past participle *hung,* as well as *hanged,* is standard. *Hanged* is most appropriate for official executions ⟨he was to be *hanged,* cut down whilst still alive . . . and his bowels torn out —Louis Allen⟩ but *hung* is also used ⟨gave orders that she should be *hung* —Peter Quennell⟩ *Hung* is more appropriate for less formal hangings ⟨by morning I'll be *hung* in effigy —Ronald Reagan⟩
— **hang fire 1 :** to be slow in the explosion of a charge after its primer has been discharged **2 :** DELAY, HESITATE — **hang one on 1 :** to inflict a blow on **2** *slang* **:** to get very drunk — **hang tough :** to remain resolute in the face of adversity **:** HANG IN
[2]**hang** *n* (1797) **1 :** the manner in which a thing hangs **2 :** DECLIVITY, SLOPE; *also* **:** DROOP **3 a :** the peculiar and significant order or meaning **b :** the special method of doing, using, or dealing with something **:** KNACK **4 :** a hesitation or slackening in motion or in a course — **give a hang** *or* **care a hang :** to be the least bit concerned or worried
[1]**han·gar** \'haŋ-ər, 'haŋ-gər\ *n* [F] (1852) **:** SHELTER, SHED; *esp* **:** a covered and usu. enclosed area for housing and repairing aircraft
[2]**hangar** *vt* (1943) **:** to place or store in a hangar
hang around *vi* (1830) **1 :** to pass time or stay aimlessly **:** loiter idly **2 :** to spend one's time in company
hang back *vi* (1581) **1 :** to drag behind others **2 :** to be reluctant
[1]**hang·dog** \'haŋ-ˌdȯg\ *adj* (1677) **1 :** ASHAMED, GUILTY **2 :** ABJECT, COWED
[2]**hangdog** *n* (1687) **:** a despicable or miserable person
hang·er \'haŋ-ər\ *n* (15c) **1 :** one that hangs or causes to be hung or hanged **2 :** something that hangs, overhangs, or is suspended: as **a :** a decorative strip of cloth **b :** a small sword formerly used by seamen **c** *chiefly Brit* **:** a small wood on steeply sloping land **3 :** a device by which or to which something is hung or hangs: as **a :** a strap on a sword belt by which a sword or dagger can be suspended **b :** a loop by which a garment is hung up **c :** a device that fits inside or around a garment for hanging from a hook or rod
hang·er–on \'haŋ-ə-ˌrȯn, -ˌrän\ *n, pl* **hangers–on** [irreg. fr. *hang on* + *-er*] (1542) **:** one that hangs around a person, place, or institution esp. for personal gain
hang glider *n* (1930) **:** a kitelike glider from which a harnessed rider hangs while gliding down from a cliff or hill — **hang gliding** *n*

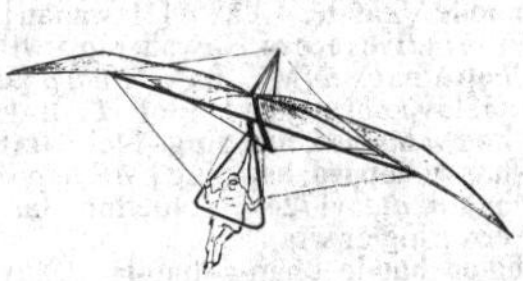
hang glider

hang in *vi* (1966) **:** to refuse to be discouraged or intimidated **:** show pluck **:** PERSIST
[1]**hang·ing** \'haŋ-iŋ\ *adj* (12c) **1 :** situated or lying on steeply sloping ground **2 a :** jutting out **:** OVERHANGING ⟨a ~ rock⟩ **b :** supported only by the wall on one side ⟨a ~ staircase⟩ **3** *archaic* **:** downcast in appearance **4 :** adapted for sustaining a hanging object **5 :** deserving, likely to cause, or prone to inflict death by hanging
[2]**hanging** *n* (14c) **1 :** an execution by strangling or breaking the neck by a suspended noose **2 :** something hung: as **a :** CURTAIN **b :** a covering (as a tapestry) for a wall **3 :** a downward slope **:** DECLIVITY
hanging indention *n* (1904) **:** indention of all the lines of a paragraph except the first
hang·man \'haŋ-mən\ *n* (14c) **:** one who hangs a condemned person; *also* **:** a public executioner
hang·nail \-ˌnāl\ *n* [by folk etymology fr. *agnail* (inflammation about the nail), fr. ME, corn on the foot or toe, fr. OE *angnægl,* fr. *ang-* (akin to *enge* tight, painful) + *nægl* nail — more at ANGER] (1678) **:** a bit of skin hanging loose at the side or root of a fingernail
hang off *vi* (1641) **:** HANG BACK
hang on *vi* (bef. 12c) **1 :** to keep hold **:** hold onto something **2 :** to persist tenaciously ⟨a cold that *hung on* all spring⟩ **3 :** to keep a telephone connection open ⟨*hang on* a second while I look it up⟩ — **hang on to :** to hold, grip, or keep tenaciously ⟨learned to *hang on to* his money⟩
hang·out \'haŋ-ˌau̇t\ *n* (1852) **:** a favorite place for hanging out; *also* **:** a place frequented for entertainment or for socializing
hang out \(ˈ)haŋ-'au̇t\ *vi* (15c) **1 :** to protrude in a downward direction **2 a** *slang* **:** LIVE, RESIDE **b :** to spend one's time idly or in loitering around ~ *vt* **:** to display outside as an announcement to the public
hang·over \'haŋ-ˌō-vər\ *n* (1894) **1 :** something (as a surviving custom) that remains from what is past **2 a :** disagreeable physical effects following heavy consumption of alcohol **b :** disagreeable aftereffects from the use of drugs **c :** a letdown following great excitement or excess
hang·tag \'haŋ-ˌtag\ *n* (1952) **:** a tag attached to an article of merchandise giving information about its material and proper care
hang together *vi* (1551) **1 :** to remain united **:** stand by one another **2 :** to form a consistent or coherent whole
hang–up \'haŋ-ˌəp\ *n* (1960) **:** a source of mental or emotional difficulty; *broadly* **:** PROBLEM
hang up \(ˈ)haŋ-'əp\ *vt* (12c) **1 a :** to place on a hook or hanger designed for the purpose ⟨told the child to *hang up* his coat⟩ **b :** to replace (a telephone receiver) on the cradle so that the connection is broken **2 :** to keep delayed, suspended, or held up ⟨the negotiations were *hung up* for a week⟩ **3 :** to cause to stick or snag immovably ⟨the ship was *hung up* on a sandbar⟩ ~ *vi* **1 :** to terminate a telephone conversation **2 :** to become stuck or snagged so as to be immovable
hank \'haŋk\ *n* [ME, of Scand origin; akin to ON *hönk* hank; akin to OE *hangian* to hang] (14c) **1 :** COIL, LOOP; *specif* **:** a coiled or looped bundle (as of yarn or rope) usu. containing a definite yardage **2 :** a ring attached to the edge of a jib or staysail and running on a stay
han·ker \'haŋ-kər\ *vi* **han·kered; han·ker·ing** \-k(ə-)riŋ\ [prob. fr. Flem *hankeren,* freq. of *hangen* to hang; akin to OE *hangian*] (1642) **:** to have a strong or persistent desire **:** YEARN ***syn*** see LONG — **han·ker·er** \-kər-ər\ *n*
han·ker·ing *n* (1662) **:** a strong or persistent desire
han·kie *or* **han·ky** \'haŋ-kē\ *n, pl* **hankies** [*hand*kerchief + *-ie*] (1895) **:** HANDKERCHIEF
han·ky–pan·ky \ˌhaŋ-kē-'paŋ-kē\ *n* [perh. irreg. fr. *hocus-pocus*] (1841) **1 :** questionable or underhand activity **:** TRICKERY **2 :** sexual dalliance
[1]**Han·o·ve·ri·an** \ˌhan-ə-'vir-ē-ən, -'ver-\ *adj* [*Hanover,* West Germany] (1775) **1 :** of, relating to, or supporting the German ducal house of Hanover **2 :** of or relating to the British royal house that ruled from 1714 to 1901
[2]**Hanoverian** *n* (1936) **:** a member or supporter of the ducal or of the British royal Hanoverian house
Han·sa \'han(t)-sə, 'hän-(ˌ)zä\ *or* **Hanse** \'han(t)s, 'hän-zə\ *n* [*Hansa* fr. ML, fr. MLG *hanse; Hanse* fr. ME, fr. MF, fr. MLG] (12c) **1 :** a medieval merchant guild or trading association **2 :** a league orig. constituted of merchants of various free German cities dealing abroad in the medieval period and later of the cities themselves and organized to secure greater safety and privileges in trading — **Han·se·at·ic** \ˌhan(t)-sē-'at-ik\ *n or adj*

Han·sard \'han(t)-sərd, 'han-,särd\ *n* [Luke *Hansard*] (1876) : the official published verbatim report of proceedings in the British parliament
han·sel *var of* HANDSEL
Han·sen's disease \'han(t)-sənz-\ *n* [Armauer *Hansen* †1912 Norw. physician] (1938) : LEPROSY
han·som \'han(t)-səm\ *n* [Joseph A. *Hansom* †1882 Eng. architect] (1847) : a light 2-wheeled covered carriage with the driver's seat elevated behind — called also *hansom cab*
hant \'hant\ *dial var of* HAUNT
Ha·nuk·kah \'hän-ə-kə, 'kän-\ *n* [Heb *ḥănukkāh* dedication] (1891) : an 8-day Jewish holiday beginning on the 25th of Kislev and commemorating the rededication of the Temple of Jerusalem after its defilement by Antiochus of Syria
hao \'hau̇\ *n, pl* **hao** [Vietnamese *hào*] (1948) : a monetary unit of Vietnam equal to $^1/_{10}$ dong
hao·le \'hau̇-lē, -(,)lā\ *n* [Hawaiian] (1825) : one who is not a member of the native race of Hawaii; *esp* : WHITE — sometimes used disparagingly
¹hap \'hap\ *n* [ME, fr. ON *happ* good luck; akin to OE *gehæp* suitable, OSlav *kobĭ* augury] (13c) **1** : HAPPENING 1 **2** : CHANCE, FORTUNE
²hap *vi* **happed; hap·ping** (14c) : HAPPEN
³hap *vt* **happed; hap·ping** [ME *happen*] *dial* (14c) : CLOTHE, COVER
⁴hap *n, dial* (1724) : something (as a bed quilt or cloak) that serves as a covering or wrap
ha·pa hao·le \,häp-ə-'hau̇-lē, -(,)lā\ *adj* [Hawaiian, fr. *hapa* half (fr. E *half*) + *haole*] (1919) : of part-white ancestry or origin; *esp* : Hawaiian-Caucasian
ha·pax le·go·me·non \,hap-,ak-sli-'gäm-ə-,nän, -nən\ *n, pl* **hapax le·go·me·na** \-nə\ [Gk, something said only once] (1882) : a word or form occurring only once in a document or corpus
ha'·pen·ny \'hāp-(ə-)nē\ *n* [by contr.] (1550) : HALFPENNY
¹hap·haz·ard \(')hap-'haz-ərd\ *n* [¹*hap* + *hazard*] (1575) : CHANCE
²haphazard *adj* (1671) : marked by lack of plan, order, or direction : AIMLESS ***syn*** see RANDOM — **haphazard** *adv* — **hap·haz·ard·ly** *adv* — **hap·haz·ard·ness** *n*
hap·haz·ard·ry \-ər-drē\ *n* (1932) : haphazard character or order
hapl- *or* **haplo-** *comb form* [NL, fr. Gk, fr. *haploos*, fr. *ha-* one (akin to *homos* same) + *-ploos* multiplied by; akin to L *-plex* -fold — more at SAME, FOLD] **1** : single : simple **2** [*haploid*] : of or relating to the haploid generation or condition ⟨*haplosis*⟩
hap·less \'hap-ləs\ *adj* (15c) : having no luck : UNFORTUNATE — **hap·less·ly** *adv* — **hap·less·ness** *n*
hap·loid \'hap-,lȯid\ *adj* [ISV, fr. Gk *haploeidēs* single, fr. *haploos*] (1908) : having the gametic number of chromosomes or half the number characteristic of somatic cells : MONOPLOID — **haploid** *n* — **hap·loi·dy** \-,lȯid-ē\ *n*
hap·lont \'hap-,länt\ *n* [ISV] (1920) : an organism with somatic cells having the haploid chromosome number and only the zygote diploid — compare DIPLONT — **hap·lon·tic** \ha-'plänt-ik\ *adj*
hap·ly \'hap-lē\ *adv* (14c) : by chance, luck, or accident
hap·pen \'hap-ən, -ᵊm\ *vi* **hap·pened; hap·pen·ing** \'hap-(ə-)niŋ\ [ME *happenen*, fr. *hap*] (14c) **1** : to occur by chance — often used with *it* ⟨it so ~s I'm going your way⟩ **2** : to come into being as an event, process, or result ⟨mistakes will ~⟩ ⟨what good things ~*ed* to you?⟩ **3** : to have the luck or fortune : do, encounter, or attain something by or as if by chance ⟨he ~*ed* to overhear the plotters⟩ **4 a** : to meet or discover something by chance ⟨~*ed* upon a system that worked —Richard Corbin⟩ **b** : to come or go casually : make a chance appearance ⟨he ~*ed* into the room just as we were leaving⟩ **5** : to come esp. by way of injury or harm ⟨I promise nothing will ~ to you⟩
hap·pen·chance \'hap-ən-,chan(t)s, 'hap-ᵊm-\ *n* (1876) : HAPPENSTANCE
hap·pen·ing *n* (1551) **1** : something that happens : OCCURRENCE **2** : an event or series of events designed to evoke a spontaneous reaction to sensory, emotional, or spiritual stimuli **3** : something (as an event) that is particularly interesting, entertaining, or important
hap·pen·stance \'hap-ən-,stan(t)s, 'hap-ᵊm-\ *n* [*happen* + circum*stance*] (1897) : a circumstance regarded as due to chance
hap·pi·ly \'hap-ə-lē\ *adv* (14c) **1** : in a fortunate manner : LUCKILY **2** *archaic* : by chance **3** : in a happy manner or state ⟨lived ~ ever after⟩ **4** : in an adequate or fitting manner : SUCCESSFULLY
hap·pi·ness \'hap-i-nəs\ *n* (15c) **1** *obs* : good fortune : PROSPERITY **2 a** : a state of well-being and contentment : JOY **b** : a pleasurable satisfaction **3** : FELICITY, APTNESS
hap·py \'hap-ē\ *adj* **hap·pi·er; -est** [ME, fr. *hap*] (14c) **1** : favored by luck or fortune : FORTUNATE **2** : notably well adapted or fitting : FELICITOUS ⟨a ~ choice⟩ **3 a** : enjoying well-being and contentment : JOYOUS **b** : expressing or suggestive of happiness : PLEASANT **c** : GLAD, PLEASED **d** : having or marked by an atmosphere of good fellowship : FRIENDLY **4 a** : characterized by a dazed irresponsible state ⟨a punch-*happy* prizefighter⟩ **b** : impulsively or obsessively quick to use something ⟨trigger-*happy*⟩ **c** : enthusiastic to the point of obsession : OBSESSED ⟨a nation . . . education-conscious and statistic-*happy* —Helen Rowen⟩ ***syn*** see LUCKY, FIT
hap·py–go–lucky \,hap-ē-gō-'lək-ē\ *adj* (1856) : blithely unconcerned : CAREFREE
happy hour *n* (1970) : a period of time during which the price of drinks (as at a bar) is reduced
happy hunting ground *n* (1837) **1** : the American Indian paradise to which the souls of warriors and hunters pass after death to spend a happy hereafter in hunting and feasting **2** : a choice or profitable area of operation or exploitation ⟨junkyards . . . have become *happy hunting grounds* for the man in search of spare parts —G. H. Waltz⟩
Haps·burg \'haps-,bərg, 'häps-,bu̇(ə)rg\ *adj* [*Habsburg*, Aargau, Switzerland] (ca. 1895) : of or relating to the German royal house to which belong the rulers of Austria from 1278 to 1918, the rulers of Spain from 1516 to 1700, and many of the Holy Roman emperors — **Hapsburg** *n*
hap·ten \'hap-,ten\ *n* [G *hapten*, fr. Gk *haptein* to fasten — more at AP-SIS] (1921) : a small separable part of an antigen that reacts specif. with an antibody but is incapable of stimulating antibody production except in combination with a carrier protein molecule — **hap·ten·ic** \hap-'ten-ik\ *adj*
hap·tic \'hap-tik\ *adj* [ISV, fr. Gk *haptesthai* to touch] (1890) **1** : relating to or based on the sense of touch **2** : characterized by a predilection for the sense of touch ⟨a ~ person⟩
hap·to·glo·bin \'hap-tə-,glō-bən\ *n* [Gk *haptein* + E *-o-* + hemo*globin*] (1941) : any of several carbohydrate-containing serum alpha globulins that can combine with free hemoglobin in the plasma
hara–kiri \,har-i-'kir-ē, -'kar-ē\ *n* [Jp *harakiri*, fr. *hara* belly + *kiri* cutting] (1840) : ritual suicide by disembowelment practiced by the Japanese samurai or formerly decreed by a court in lieu of the death penalty
¹ha·rangue \hə-'raŋ\ *n* [ME *arang*, fr. MF *arenge*, fr. OIt *aringa*, deriv. of *aringo* public square, of Gmc origin; akin to OHG *heri* army and to OHG *hring* ring — more at HARRY, RING] (15c) **1** : a speech addressed to a public assembly **2** : a bombastic ranting speech or writing **3** : LECTURE
²harangue *vb* **ha·rangued; ha·rangu·ing** *vi* (1660) : to make a harangue : DECLAIM ~ *vt* : to address in a harangue ⟨*haranguing* me . . . on the folly of my ways —Jay Jacobs⟩ — **ha·rangu·er** *n*
ha·rass \hə-'ras, 'har-əs\ *vt* [F *harasser*, fr. MF, fr. *harer* to set a dog on, fr. OF *hare*, interj. used to incite dogs, of Gmc origin; akin to OHG *hier* here — more at HERE] (1622) **1** : to worry and impede by repeated raids ⟨~*ed* the enemy⟩ **2 a** : EXHAUST, FATIGUE **b** : to annoy persistently ***syn*** see WORRY — **ha·rass·er** *n* — **ha·rass·ment** \-mənt\ *n*
¹har·bin·ger \'här-bən-jər\ *n* [ME *herbergere*, fr. MF, host, fr. *herberge* hostelry, of Gmc origin; akin to OHG *heriberga*] (14c) **1** *archaic* : a person sent ahead to provide lodgings **2 a** : one that pioneers in or initiates a major change : PRECURSOR **b** : one that presages or foreshadows what is to come ***syn*** see FORERUNNER
²harbinger *vt* (1646) : to be a harbinger of : PRESAGE
¹har·bor \'här-bər\ *n* [ME *herberge, herberwe*, fr. OE *herebeorg* military quarters (akin to OHG *heriberga*), fr. *here* army (akin to OHG *heri*) + *beorg* refuge, defense; akin to OE *burg* fortified town — more at HARRY, BOROUGH] (12c) **1** : a place of security and comfort : REFUGE **2** : a part of a body of water protected and deep enough to furnish anchorage; *esp* : one with port facilities — **har·bor·ful** \-,fu̇l\ *n* — **har·bor·less** \-ləs\ *adj*
²harbor *vb* **har·bored; har·bor·ing** \-b(ə-)riŋ\ *vt* (12c) **1 a** : to give shelter or refuge to **b** : to be the home or habitat of : CONTAIN ⟨the ledges still ~ rattlesnakes⟩ **2** : to hold a thought or feeling of ⟨~*ed* a grudge⟩ ~ *vi* **1** : to take shelter in or as if in a harbor **2** : LIVE — **har·bor·er** \-bər-ər\ *n*
har·bor·age \-bə-rij\ *n* (15c) : SHELTER, HARBOR
har·bor·mas·ter \'här-bər-,mas-tər\ *n* (1769) : an officer who executes the regulations respecting the use of a harbor
harbor seal *n* (1766) : a small seal (*Phoca vitulina*) that occurs along oceanic coasts of the northern hemisphere and often ascends rivers
har·bour *chiefly Brit var of* HARBOR
¹hard \'härd\ *adj* [ME, fr. OE *heard*; akin to OHG *hart* hard, Gk *kratos* strength] (bef. 12c) **1 a** : not easily penetrated : not easily yielding to pressure **b** *of cheese* : not capable of being spread : very firm **2 a** *of liquor* (1) : having a harsh or acid taste (2) : strongly alcoholic **b** : characterized by the presence of salts (as of calcium or magnesium) that prevent lathering with soap ⟨~ water⟩ **3 a** : of or relating to radiation of relatively high penetrating power ⟨~ X rays⟩ **b** : having or producing relatively great photographic contrast ⟨a ~ negative⟩ **4 a** : metallic as distinct from paper ⟨~ money⟩ **b** *of currency* : convertible into gold : stable in value **c** : being high and firm ⟨~ prices⟩ **5 a** : firmly and closely twisted ⟨~ yarns⟩ **b** : having a smooth close napless finish ⟨a ~ worsted⟩ **6 a** : physically fit ⟨in good ~ condition⟩ **b** : resistant to stress (as disease) **c** : free of weakness or defects **7 a** (1) : FIRM, DEFINITE ⟨reached a ~ agreement⟩ (2) : not speculative or conjectural : FACTUAL ⟨~ evidence⟩ **b** : CLOSE, SEARCHING ⟨gave a ~ look⟩ **c** : free from sentimentality or illusion : REALISTIC ⟨good ~ sense⟩ **d** : lacking in responsiveness : OBDURATE, UNFEELING ⟨a ~ heart⟩ **8 a** (1) : difficult to bear or endure ⟨~ luck⟩ ⟨~ times⟩ (2) : OPPRESSIVE, INEQUITABLE ⟨sales taxes are ~ on the poor⟩ ⟨a ~ restriction⟩ **b** (1) : lacking consideration, compassion, or gentleness : CALLOUS ⟨a ~ greedy landlord⟩ (2) : INCORRIGIBLE, TOUGH ⟨a ~ gang⟩ **c** (1) : harsh, severe, or offensive in tendency or effect ⟨said some ~ things⟩ (2) : RESENTFUL ⟨~ feelings⟩ (3) : STRICT, UNRELENTING ⟨drives a ~ bargain⟩ **d** : INCLEMENT ⟨~ winter⟩ **e** (1) : intense in force, manner, or degree ⟨~ blows⟩ (2) : demanding the exertion of energy : calling for stamina and endurance ⟨~ work⟩ (3) : performing or carrying on with great energy, intensity, or persistence ⟨a ~ worker⟩ **9 a** : characterized by sharp or harsh outline, rigid execution, and stiff drawing **b** : sharply defined : STARK ⟨~ shadows⟩ **c** : lacking in shading, delicacy, or resonance ⟨~ singing tones⟩ **d** : sounding as in *arcing* and *geese* respectively — used of *c* and *g* **10 a** (1) : difficult to accomplish or resolve : TROUBLESOME ⟨~ problems⟩ ⟨the true story was ~ to come by⟩ (2) : difficult to comprehend or explain ⟨a ~ concept⟩ **b** : having difficulty in doing something ⟨~ of hearing⟩ **c** : difficult to magnetize or demagnetize **11** : being at once addictive and gravely detrimental to health ⟨such ~ drugs as heroin⟩ **12** : resistant to biodegradation ⟨~ detergents⟩ ⟨~ pesticides like DDT⟩ **13** : being, schooled in, or using the methods of one or more branches of mathematics, the life sciences, or the physical sciences ⟨a ~ scientist⟩

syn HARD, DIFFICULT, ARDUOUS mean demanding great exertion or effort. HARD implies the opposite of all that is easy; DIFFICULT implies the presence of obstacles to be surmounted or puzzles to be resolved and suggests the need of skill, patience, or courage; ARDUOUS stresses the need of laborious and persevering exertion. ***syn*** see in addition FIRM

— **hard up 1** : short of money **2** : poorly provided ⟨he was *hard up* for friends⟩
²hard *adv* (bef. 12c) **1 a** : with great or utmost effort or energy : STRENUOUSLY ⟨were ~ at work⟩ ⟨the children played ~⟩ **b** : in a violent manner : FIERCELY **c** : to the full extent — used in nautical directions ⟨steer ~ aport⟩ **d** : to an immoderate degree ⟨hitting the bottle ~⟩ **e** : in a searching, close, or concentrated manner ⟨stared ~ at him⟩ **2 a** : in such a manner as to cause hardship, difficulty, or pain : SEVERELY **b** : with rancor, bitterness, or grief ⟨took his defeat ~⟩ **3** : in a firm manner : TIGHTLY **4** : to the point of hardness ⟨the water froze ~⟩ **5** : close in time or space ⟨the house stood ~ by the river⟩
hard–and–fast \,härd-ᵊn-'fast\ *adj* (1864) : not to be modified or evaded : STRICT ⟨a ~ rule⟩
hard·back \'härd-,bak\ *n* (1952) : a book bound in hard covers

hard·ball \-ˌbȯl\ *n* (1944) **1 :** BASEBALL **2 :** forceful uncompromising methods employed to gain an end ⟨played political ~ to win the nomination⟩

hard–bit·ten \-ˈbit-ᵊn\ *adj* (1784) **1 :** inclined to bite hard **2 :** seasoned or steeled by difficult experience **:** TOUGH

hard·board \ˈhärd-ˌbō(ə)rd, -ˌbȯ(ə)rd\ *n* (1925) **:** a very dense fiberboard usu. having one smooth face

hard–boil \-ˈbȯi(ə)l\ *vt* [back-formation fr. *hard-boiled*] (1895) **:** to cook (an egg) in the shell until both white and yolk have solidified

hard–boiled \-ˈbȯi(ə)ld\ *adj* (1886) **1 :** devoid of sentimentality **:** TOUGH ⟨a ~ drill sergeant⟩ **2 :** HARDHEADED, PRACTICAL ⟨handle aid programs on a friendly but ~ business basis —*N.Y. Times*⟩

hard·boot \-ˌbüt\ *n* (1922) **:** HORSEMAN

hard·bound \-ˌbau̇nd\ *adj* (1926) **:** HARDCOVER

hard candy *n* (1925) **:** a candy made of sugar and corn syrup boiled without crystallizing and usu. fruit-flavored

hard·case \ˈhärd-ˈkās\ *adj* (1836) **:** HARD-BITTEN, TOUGH

hard case \-ˌkās\ *n* (1836) **:** a tough or hardened person

hard cider *n* (1789) **:** fermented apple juice

hard clam *n* (1799) **:** a clam with a thick hard shell; *specif* **:** QUAHOG

hard coal *n* (1846) **:** ANTHRACITE

hard–coat·ed \ˈhärd-ˈkōt-əd\ *adj, of a dog* (ca. 1898) **:** having a crisp harsh-textured coat

hard copy *n* (1890) **:** readable copy produced on paper in normal size type (as from microfilm or computer storage)

hard–core \-ˈkō(ə)r, -ˈkȯ(ə)r\ *adj* (1936) **1 a :** of, relating to, or being part of a hard core ⟨~ poverty⟩ ⟨the ~ unemployed⟩ **b :** CONFIRMED, DIE-HARD ⟨~ rock fans⟩ ⟨a ~ liberal⟩ **2** *of pornography* **:** containing explicit descriptions of sex acts or scenes of actual sex acts — compare SOFT-CORE **3 :** characterized by or being the purest or most basic form of something **:** FUNDAMENTAL ⟨~ rock music⟩ ⟨a room gussied up in ~ French provincial style —John Canaday⟩

hard core *n* (1936) **1 :** a relatively small enduring core of society marked by apparent resistance to change or inability to escape a persistent wretched condition (as poverty or chronic unemployment) **2 :** a militant or fiercely loyal faction (as of a political unit)

hard·cov·er \ˈhärd-ˈkəv-ər\ *adj* (1949) **1 :** having rigid boards on the sides covered in cloth or paper ⟨~ books⟩ **2 :** of or relating to hardcover books ⟨~ sales⟩ — **hard cover** *n*

hard disk *n* (1978) **:** a rigid metal disk that is sealed against dust and is used as a high-capacity storage device for a microcomputer

hard–edge \ˈhärd-ˈej\ *adj* (1960) **:** of or relating to abstract painting characterized by geometric forms with clearly defined boundaries

hard·en \ˈhärd-ᵊn\ *vb* **hard·ened; hard·en·ing** \ˈhärd-niŋ, -ᵊn-iŋ\ [ME *hardnen,* fr. [1]*hard* + *-nen* [2]-en] *vt* (bef. 12c) **1 :** to make hard or harder **:** INDURATE **2 :** to confirm in disposition, feelings, or action; *esp* **:** to make callous ⟨~*ed* his heart⟩ **3 a :** INURE, TOUGHEN ⟨~ troops⟩ **b :** to inure to cold or other unfavorable environmental conditions — often used with *off* ⟨~ off half-hardy annual plants⟩ **4 :** to protect from possible danger from blast or heat with concrete or earth or by situating underground ⟨~ a missile emplacement⟩ ~ *vi* **1 :** to become hard or harder **2 a :** to become confirmed or strengthened ⟨opposition began to ~⟩ **b :** to assume an appearance of harshness or severity ⟨her face ~*ed* at the word⟩ **3 :** to become higher or less subject to fluctuations downward ⟨prices ~*ed* quickly⟩

hard·en·er \ˈhärd-nər, -ᵊn-ər\ *n* (1611) **:** one that hardens; *esp* **:** a substance added (as to a paint or varnish) to harden the film

hard·en·ing *n* (ca. 1828) **1 :** something that hardens **2 :** SCLEROSIS ⟨~ of the arteries⟩

hard·fist·ed \ˈhärd-ˈfis-təd\ *adj* (1656) **1 :** STINGY, CLOSEFISTED **2 :** HARDHANDED

hard goods *n pl* (1934) **:** DURABLES

hard·hack \ˈhärd-ˌhak\ *n* (1814) **:** a shrubby American spirea (*Spiraea tomentosa*) with rusty hairy leaves and dense terminal panicles of pink or occas. white flowers

hard·hand·ed \-ˈhan-dəd\ *adj* (1590) **1 :** having hands made hard by labor **2 :** STRICT, OPPRESSIVE — **hard·hand·ed·ness** *n*

hard hat *usu* -ˈhat *for 1 and* -ˌhat *for 2 & 3*\ *n* (1926) **1 :** a protective hat made of rigid material (as metal or fiberglass) and worn esp. by construction workers **2 :** a construction worker **3 :** a conservative who is strongly opposed to nonconformists

hard·head \ˈhärd-ˌhed\ *n* (15c) **1 a :** a hardheaded person **b :** BLOCKHEAD **2 :** any of several fishes esp. with a spiny or bony head; *esp* **:** ATLANTIC CROAKER **3 :** any of several knapweeds (esp. *Centaurea nigra*) — usu. used in pl. but sing. or pl. in constr.

hard·head·ed \-ˈhed-əd\ *adj* (1583) **1 :** STUBBORN, WILLFUL **2 :** not moved by sentiment or impulse **:** SOBER, REALISTIC ⟨~ common sense⟩ — **hard·head·ed·ly** *adv* — **hard·head·ed·ness** *n*

hard–heart·ed \ˈhärd-ˈhärt-əd\ *adj* (bef. 12c) **:** lacking in sympathetic understanding **:** UNFEELING, PITILESS — **hard–heart·ed·ly** *adv* — **hard–heart·ed·ness** *n*

hard–hit·ting \-ˈhit-iŋ\ *adj* (1839) **:** strikingly effective in force or result ⟨a ~ sales compaign⟩ ⟨a ~ exposé on political corruption⟩

har·di·hood \ˈhärd-ē-ˌhu̇d\ *n* (1570) **1 a :** resolute courage and fortitude **b :** resolute and self-assured audacity often carried to the point of impudent insolence **2 :** VIGOR, ROBUSTNESS ***syn*** see TEMERITY

har·di·ment \-mənt\ *n* [ME, fr. MF, fr. OF, fr. *hardi* bold, hardy] (14c) **1** *archaic* **:** HARDIHOOD **2** *obs* **:** a bold deed

har·ding·grass \ˈhärd-iŋ-ˌgras\ *n, often cap* [prob. fr. the name *Harding*] (ca. 1922) **:** a perennial grass (*Phalaris tuberosa stenoptera*) of Australia and southern Africa introduced into No. America as a forage grass

hard labor *n* (1853) **:** compulsory labor of imprisoned criminals as a part of the prison discipline

hard–line \ˈhärd-ˈlīn\ *adj* (1962) **:** advocating or involving a persistently firm course of action **:** UNYIELDING ⟨a ~ policy toward polluters⟩ — **hard–lin·er** \-ˈlī-nər\ *n*

hard lines *n pl, chiefly Brit* (1824) **:** hard luck

hard·ly \ˈhärd-lē\ *adv* [ME *hardliche,* fr. OE *heardlice,* fr. *heard* hard] (bef. 12c) **1 :** with force **:** VIGOROUSLY **2 :** in a severe manner **:** HARSHLY **3 :** with difficulty **:** PAINFULLY **4** — used to emphasize a minimal amount ⟨I ~ knew her⟩ ⟨almost new — ~ a scratch on it⟩ **5 :** certainly not ⟨that news is ~ surprising⟩

usage In senses 4 and 5 *hardly* has a negative meaning, and its use with an additional negative is usu. considered substandard. Such use, esp. in *can't hardly,* is generally limited to speech, in which the double negative serves for emphasis. It is seldom found in edited prose except in the transcription of speech.

hardly ever *adv* (1892) **:** almost never **:** very seldom ⟨we *hardly ever* see them anymore⟩

hard maple *n* (1790) **:** SUGAR MAPLE

hard·mouthed \ˈhärd-ˈmau̇t͟hd, -ˈmau̇tht\ *adj* (1617) **1** *of a horse* **:** not sensitive to the bit **2 :** OBSTINATE, STUBBORN

hard·ness \-nəs\ *n* [ME, fr. OE *heardness,* fr. *heard*] (bef. 12c) **1 :** the quality or state of being hard **2 :** the cohesion of the particles on the surface of a mineral as determined by its capacity to scratch another or be itself scratched — compare MOHS' SCALE

hard–nosed \ˈhärd-ˈnōzd\ *adj* (1927) **1 :** HARD-BITTEN, STUBBORN **2 :** HARDHEADED 2 ⟨~ budgeting⟩

hard–of–hear·ing \ˌhärd-ə(v)-ˈhi(ə)r-iŋ\ *adj* (15c) **:** of or relating to a defective but functional sense of hearing

hard–on \ˈhärd-ˌȯn, -ˌän\ *n, pl* **hard–ons** (1860) **:** an erection of the penis — usu. considered vulgar

hard palate *n* (ca. 1847) **:** the bony anterior part of the palate forming the roof of the mouth

hard·pan \ˈhärd-ˌpan\ *n* (1817) **1 :** a cemented or compacted and often clayey layer in soil that is impenetrable by roots **2 :** a fundamental part **:** BEDROCK

hard pine *n* (1884) **:** a pine (as longleaf pine or pitch pine) that has hard wood and leaves usu. in groups of two or three; *also* **:** the wood of a hard pine

hard–pressed \-ˈprest\ *adj* (1825) **:** HARD PUT; *esp.* **:** being under financial strain

hard put *adj* (1893) **:** barely able **:** faced with difficulty or perplexity ⟨was *hard put* to find an explanation⟩

hard rock *n* (1967) **:** rock music marked by a heavy jarring beat, high amplification, and usu. frenzied performances

hard rubber *n* (1860) **:** a firm rubber or rubber product; *esp* **:** a normally black horny substance made by vulcanizing natural rubber with high percentages of sulfur

hard sauce *n* (1880) **:** a creamed mixture of butter and powdered sugar often with added cream and flavoring (as vanilla or rum)

hard·scrab·ble \ˈhärd-ˌskrab-əl\ *adj* (1888) **:** yielding or gaining a meager living by great labor ⟨~ farms⟩

hard sell *n* (1952) **:** aggressive high-pressure salesmanship — compare SOFT SELL

hard–set \ˈhärd-ˈset\ *adj* (15c) **:** RIGID, FIXED

hard–shell \-ˌshel\ *or* **hard–shelled** \-ˌsheld\ *adj* (1838) **:** UNCOMPROMISING, CONFIRMED ⟨a ~ conservative⟩

hard–shell clam \ˌhärd-ˌshel-\ *n* (1799) **:** QUAHOG —called also *hard-shelled clam*

hard–shell crab *n* (1902) **:** a crab that has not recently shed its shell — called also *hard-shelled crab*

hard·ship \ˈhärd-ˌship\ *n* (13c) **1 :** PRIVATION, SUFFERING **2 :** something that causes or entails suffering or privation

hard·stand \-ˌstand\ *n* (1944) **:** a hard-surfaced area for parking an airplane

hard·stand·ing \-ˌstan-diŋ\ *n* (1944) **:** HARDSTAND

hard–sur·face \-ˈsər-fəs\ *vt* (1928) **:** to provide with a paved surface

hard·tack \-ˌtak\ *n* (1836) **1 :** a saltless hard biscuit or bread made of flour and water **2 :** any of several mountain mahoganies

hard–times token *n* (1922) **:** one of the tokens issued during the controversy between the Jacksonian administration and the bank of the U.S.

hard·top \-ˌtäp\ *n* (1949) **:** an automobile or a motorboat having a permanent rigid top; *also* **:** such an automobile styled to resemble a convertible

hard·ware \ˈhär-ˌdwa(ə)r, -ˌdwe(ə)r\ *n* (1515) **1 :** ware (as fittings, cutlery, tools, utensils, or parts of machines) made of metal **2 :** major items of military or police equipment or their components **3 :** the physical components (as electronic and electrical devices) of a vehicle (as a spacecraft) or an apparatus (as a computer); *also* **:** the physical equipment of a system of transportation **4 :** devices (as tape recorders or closed-circuit television) often used as instructional equipment

hardware cloth *n* (1914) **:** rugged galvanized screening commonly in meshes of two, four, or eight squares to the square inch

hard wheat *n* (1812) **:** a wheat with hard flinty kernels that are high in gluten and that yield a strong flour esp. suitable for bread and macaroni

[1]**hard·wood** \ˈhär-ˌdwu̇d\ *n* (1568) **1 :** the wood of an angiospermous tree as distinguished from that of a coniferous tree **2 :** a tree that yields hardwood

[2]**hardwood** *adj* (1817) **1 :** having or made of hardwood ⟨~ floors⟩ **2 :** consisting of mature woody tissue ⟨~ cuttings⟩

hard–wood·ed \ˈhär-ˈdwu̇d-əd\ *adj* (1858) **1 :** having hard wood that is difficult to work or finish **2 :** HARDWOOD 1

hard·work·ing \ˈhär-ˈdwər-kiŋ\ *adj* (1774) **:** INDUSTRIOUS

har·dy \ˈhärd-ē\ *adj* **har·di·er; -est** [ME *hardi,* fr. OF, fr. (assumed) OF *hardir* to make hard, of Gmc origin; akin to OE *heard* hard] (13c) **1 :** BOLD, BRAVE **2 :** AUDACIOUS, BRAZEN **3 a :** inured to fatigue or hardships **:** ROBUST **b :** capable of withstanding adverse conditions (as in living outdoors over winter without artificial protection) ⟨~ plants⟩ ⟨~ cattle⟩ — **har·di·ly** \ˈhärd-ᵊl-ē\ *adv* — **har·di·ness** \ˈhärd-ē-nəs\ *n*

Har·dy–Wein·berg law \ˌhärd-ē-ˈwīn-ˌbərg-\ *n* [G. H. *Hardy* †1947 Eng. mathematician and W. *Weinberg,* 20th cent. Ger. scientist] (1950) **:** a fundamental principle of population genetics: population gene frequencies and population genotype frequencies remain constant from generation to generation if mating is random and if mutation, selection, immigration, and emigration do not occur — called also *Hardy-Weinberg principle*

[1]**hare** \ˈha(ə)r, ˈhe(ə)r\ *n, pl* **hare** *or* **hares** [ME, fr. OE *hara;* akin to OHG *haso* hare, L *canus* hoary, gray] (bef. 12c) **:** any of various swift timid long-eared lagomorph mammals (family Leporidae and esp.

\ə\ abut \ᵊ\ kitten, F table \ər\ further \a\ ash \ā\ ace \ä\ cot, cart
\au̇\ out \ch\ chin \e\ bet \ē\ easy \g\ go \i\ hit \ī\ ice \j\ job
\ŋ\ sing \ō\ go \ȯ\ law \ȯi\ boy \th\ thin \t͟h\ the \ü\ loot \u̇\ foot
\y\ yet \zh\ vision \à, k̟, ⁿ, œ, œ̄, ue, ue̅, ʸ\ see Guide to Pronunciation

genus *Lepus*) that are usu. solitary or sometimes live in pairs and have the young open-eyed and furred at birth — compare RABBIT

[2]hare *vi* **hared; har·ing** (1719) : RUN

hare and hounds *n* (14c) : a game in which some of the players scatter bits of paper for a trail and others try to follow the trail to find and catch them

hare·bell \'ha(ə)r-ˌbel, 'he(ə)r-\ *n* (1611) : a slender blue-flowered herb (*Campanula rotundifolia*) with linear leaves on the stem

hare·brained \-'brānd\ *adj* (1534) : FLIGHTY, FOOLISH

Ha·re Krish·na \ˌhär-ē-'krish-nə, ˌhar-\ *n* [Hindi, fr. *hare* invocation of God + *Krishna* eighth avatar of Vishnu, one of the principal Hindu gods] (1968) : a member of a religious group dedicated to the worship of the Hindu god Krishna

hare·lip \'ha(ə)r-'lip, 'he(ə)r-\ *n* (1567) : a congenital deformity in which the upper lip is split like that of a hare — **hare·lipped** \-'lipt\ *adj*

har·em \'har-əm, 'her-\ *n* [Ar *ḥarīm*, lit., something forbidden & *ḥaram*, lit., sanctuary] (1623) **1 a :** a usu. secluded house or part of a house allotted to women in a Muslim household **b :** the wives, concubines, female relatives, and servants occupying a harem **2 :** a group of women associated with one man **3 :** a group of females associated with one male — used of polygamous animals

harem pants *n* [fr. their oriental appearance] (1952) : women's loose trousers that fit closely at the ankle

har·i·cot \'(h)ar-i-ˌkō\ *n* [F] (1653) : the ripe seed or the unripe pod of any of several beans (genus *Phaseolus* and esp. *P. vulgaris*)

ha·ri·jan \ˌhar-i-'jän\ *n, often cap* [Skt *harijana* one belonging to the god Vishnu, fr. *Hari* Vishnu + *jana* person] (1931) : a member of the outcaste group in India : UNTOUCHABLE

hari–kari \ˌhar-i-'kar-ē, -'kir-\ *var of* HARA-KIRI

hark \'härk\ *vi* [ME *herken*, prob. alter. of OE *heorcnian;* akin to OHG *hōrechen* to listen] (14c) : to pay close attention : LISTEN

hark back *vi* (1834) : to turn back to an earlier topic or circumstance

harken *var of* HEARKEN

har·le·quin \'här-li-k(w)ən\ *n* [alter. (influenced by F *harlequin*, fr. MF *Helquin*) of earlier *harlicken*, modif. of OIt *arlecchino*, fr. MF *Helquin*, a demon] (1590) **1** *a cap* **:** a character in comedy and pantomime with a shaved head, masked face, variegated tights, and wooden sword **b :** BUFFOON **2 a :** a variegated pattern (as of a textile) **b :** a combination of patches on a solid ground of contrasting color (as in the coats of some dogs)

Harlequin

har·le·quin·ade \ˌhär-li-k(w)ə-'nād\ *n* (1790) : a play or pantomime in which Harlequin has a leading role

har·lot \'här-lət\ *n* [ME, fr. OF *herlot* rogue] (15c) : PROSTITUTE

har·lot·ry \-lə-trē\ *n, pl* **-ries** (14c) **1 :** sexual profligacy : PROSTITUTION **2 :** an unprincipled or immoral woman ⟨he sups tonight with a ~ —Shak.⟩

[1]harm \'härm\ *n* [ME, fr. OE *hearm;* akin to OHG *harm* injury, OSlav *sramŭ* shame] (bef. 12c) **1 :** physical or mental damage : INJURY **2 :** MISCHIEF, HURT

[2]harm *vt* (bef. 12c) : to cause harm to ***syn*** see INJURE — **harm·er** *n*

har·ma·line \'här-mə-ˌlēn\ *n* [NL *harmala* (specific epithet of *Peganum harmala*), fr. Gk, rue, of Sem origin; akin to Ar *ḥarmalah* an herb] (1847) : a hallucinogenic alkaloid $C_{13}H_{14}N_2O$ found in several plants (*Peganum harmala* of the family Zygophyllaceae and *Banisteriopsis* spp. of the family Malpighiaceae) and used in medicine as a stimulant of the central nervous system

har·mat·tan \ˌhär-mə-'tan, här-'mat-ᵊn\ *n* [Twi *haramata*] (1671) : a dust-laden wind on the Atlantic coast of Africa in some seasons

harm·ful \'härm-fəl\ *adj* (14c) : of a kind likely to be damaging : INJURIOUS — **harm·ful·ly** \-fə-lē\ *adv* — **harm·ful·ness** *n*

har·mine \'här-ˌmēn\ *n* [NL *harmala* + E *-ine*] (1864) : a hallucinogenic alkaloid $C_{13}H_{12}N_2O$ whose distribution in plants and use in medicine is similar to harmaline

harm·less \'härm-ləs\ *adj* (13c) **1 :** free from harm, liability, or loss **2 :** lacking capacity or intent to injure : INNOCUOUS — **harm·less·ly** *adv* — **harm·less·ness** *n*

[1]har·mon·ic \här-'män-ik\ *adj* [L *harmonicus*, fr. Gk *harmonikos*, fr. *harmonia* harmony] (1570) **1 :** MUSICAL **2 :** of or relating to musical harmony or a harmonic **3 :** pleasing to the ear : HARMONIOUS **4 :** of an integrated nature : CONGRUOUS — **har·mon·i·cal·ly** \-i-k(ə-)lē\ *adv*

[2]harmonic *n* (1727) **1 a :** OVERTONE; *esp* **:** one whose vibration frequency is an integral multiple of that of the fundamental **b :** a flutelike tone produced on a stringed instrument by touching a vibrating string at a nodal point **2 :** a component frequency of a harmonic motion (as of an electromagnetic wave) that is an integral multiple of the fundamental frequency

har·mon·i·ca \här-'män-i-kə\ *n* [It *armonica*, fem. of *armonico* harmonious] (1762) **1 :** GLASS HARMONICA **2 :** a small rectangular wind instrument with free reeds recessed in air slots from which tones are sounded by exhaling and inhaling

harmonic analysis *n* (1867) : the expression of a periodic function as a sum of sines and cosines and specif. by a Fourier series

harmonic mean *n* (1828) : the reciprocal of the arithmetic mean of the reciprocals of a finite set of numbers

harmonic motion *n* (1867) : a periodic motion (as of a sounding violin string or swinging pendulum) that has a single frequency or amplitude or a periodic motion that is composed of two or more such simple periodic motions

harmonic progression *n* (ca. 1864) : a sequence of numbers whose reciprocals form an arithmetic progression

harmonic series *n* (ca. 1828) : a series of the form

$$1 + \frac{1}{2^{\alpha}} + \frac{1}{3^{\alpha}} + \frac{1}{4^{\alpha}} \cdots$$

which diverges for $0 \leq \alpha \leq 1$ and converges for $\alpha > 1$

har·mo·ni·ous \här-'mō-nē-əs\ *adj* (1530) **1 :** musically concordant **2 :** having the parts agreeably related : CONGRUOUS ⟨the flowers blended into a ~ whole⟩ **3 :** marked by accord in sentiment or action — **har·mo·ni·ous·ly** *adv* — **har·mo·ni·ous·ness** *n*

har·mo·ni·um \här-'mō-nē-əm\ *n* [F, fr. MF *harmonie, armonie*] (1847) : REED ORGAN

har·mo·nize \'här-mə-ˌnīz\ *vb* **-nized; -niz·ing** *vi* (15c) **1 :** to play or sing in harmony **2 :** to be in harmony ~ *vt* **1 :** to bring into consonance or accord **2 :** to provide or accompany with harmony — **har·mo·ni·za·tion** \ˌhär-mə-nə-'zā-shən\ *n* — **har·mo·niz·er** \'här-mə-ˌnī-zər\ *n*

har·mo·ny \'här-mə-nē\ *n, pl* **-nies** [ME *armony*, fr. MF *armonie*, fr. L *harmonia*, fr. Gk, joint, harmony, fr. *harmos* joint — more at ARM] (14c) **1** *archaic* **:** tuneful sound : MELODY **2 a :** the combination of simultaneous musical notes in a chord **b :** the structure of music with respect to the composition and progression of chords **c :** the science of the structure, relation, and progression of chords **3 a :** pleasing or congruent arrangement of parts ⟨a painting exhibiting ~ of color and line⟩ **b :** CORRESPONDENCE, ACCORD ⟨lives in ~ with her neighbors⟩ **c :** internal calm : TRANQUILLITY **4 a :** an interweaving of different accounts into a single narrative **b :** a systematic arrangement of parallel literary passages (as of the Gospels) for the purpose of showing agreement or harmony

har·mo·tome \'här-mə-ˌtōm\ *n* [F, fr. Gk *harmos* + *tomē* section, fr. *temnein* to cut — more at TOME] (1804) : a mineral $(Ba,K)(Al,Si)_2Si_6O_{16}{\cdot}6H_2O$ consisting of a hydrous silicate of aluminum, barium, and potassium

[1]har·ness \'här-nəs\ *n* [ME *herneis* baggage, gear, fr. OF] (14c) **1 a :** the gear other than a yoke of a draft animal **b :** GEAR, EQUIPMENT; *esp* **:** military equipment for a horse or man **2 a :** occupational surroundings or routine ⟨get back into ~ after a vacation⟩ **b :** close association ⟨ability to work in ~ with others —R. P. Brooks⟩ **3 a :** something that resembles a harness (as in holding or fastening something) ⟨a parachute ~⟩ ⟨an automobile rider's shoulder ~⟩ **b :** prefabricated wiring with insulation and terminals ready to be attached **4 :** a part of a loom which holds and controls the heddles

[2]harness *vt* (14c) **1 a :** to put a harness on **b :** to attach by means of a harness **2 :** to tie together : YOKE **3 :** UTILIZE ⟨~ nuclear energy⟩

harness horse *n* (1861) : a horse for racing or working in harness

harness racing *n* (1901) : the sport of racing standardbred horses harnessed to 2-wheeled sulkies

[1]harp \'härp\ *n* [ME, fr. OE *hearpe;* akin to OHG *harpha* harp, Gk *karphos* dry stalk] (bef. 12c) **1 :** a plucked stringed instrument consisting of a resonator, an arched or angled neck that may be supported by a post, and strings of graded length that are perpendicular to the soundboard **2 :** something that resembles a harp **3 :** HARMONICA 2 — **harp·ist** \'här-pəst\ *n*

[2]harp *vi* (bef. 12c) **1 :** to play on a harp **2 :** to dwell on or recur to a subject tiresomely or monotonously

harp·er \'här-pər\ *n* (bef. 12c) **1 :** a harp player **2 :** one that harps

har·poon \här-'pün\ *n* [prob. fr. D *harpoen*, fr. OF *harpon* brooch, fr. *harper* to grapple] (1625) : a barbed spear or javelin used esp. in hunting large fish or whales — **harpoon** *vt* — **har·poon·er** *n*

harp·si·chord \'härp-si-ˌkȯ(ə)rd\ *n* [modif. of It *arpicordo*, fr. *arpa* harp + *corda* string] (ca. 1611) : a stringed instrument resembling a grand piano but usu. having two keyboards and two or more strings for each note and producing tones by the plucking of strings with plectra — **harp·si·chord·ist** \-ˌkȯrd-əst\ *n*

har·py \'här-pē\ *n, pl* **harpies** [L *Harpyia*, fr. Gk] (1513) **1** *cap* **:** a foul malign creature in Greek mythology that is part woman and part bird **2 a :** a predatory person : LEECH **b :** a shrewish woman

har·que·bus \'här-kwi-(ˌ)bəs, -kə-bəs\ *n* [MF *harquebuse, arquebuse*, modif. of MD *hakebusse*, fr. *hake* hook + *busse* tube, box, gun, fr. LL *buxis* box — more at BOX] (1532) : a matchlock gun invented in the 15th century which was portable but heavy and was usu. fired from a support — **har·que·bus·ier** \ˌhär-kwi-(ˌ)bə-'si(ə)r, -kə-bə-\ *n*

har·ri·dan \'har-əd-ᵊn\ *n* [perh. modif. of F *haridelle* old horse, gaunt woman] (1700) : SHREW 2

har·ried \'har-ēd\ *adj* (1921) : beset by problems : HARASSED

[1]har·ri·er \'har-ē-ər\ *n* [irreg. fr. [1]*hare*] (1542) **1 :** a hunting dog that resembles a small foxhound and is used esp. for hunting rabbits **2 :** a runner on a cross-country team

[2]harrier *n* [alter. of *harrower*, fr. [1]*harrow*] (1556) : any of various slender hawks (genus *Circus*) having long angled wings and long legs and feeding chiefly on small mammals, reptiles, and insects

[3]harrier *n* (1596) : one that harries

[1]har·row \'har-(ˌ)ō, -ə(-w)\ *vt* [ME *harwen*, fr. OE *hergian*] *archaic* (bef. 12c) : PILLAGE, PLUNDER

[2]harrow *n* [ME *harwe*] (14c) : a cultivating implement set with spikes, spring teeth, or disks and used primarily for pulverizing and smoothing the soil

[3]harrow *vt* (14c) **1 :** to cultivate with a harrow **2 :** TORMENT, VEX — **har·row·er** \'har-ə-wər\ *n*

har·rumph \hə-'rəm(p)f\ *vi* [imit.] (1936) **1 :** to clear the throat in a pompous way **2 :** to comment disapprovingly

har·ry \'har-ē\ *vt* **har·ried; har·ry·ing** [ME *harien*, fr. OE *hergian;* akin to OHG *heriōn* to lay waste, *heri* army, Gk *koiranos* commander] (bef. 12c) **1 :** to make a pillaging or destructive raid on : ASSAULT **2 :** to force (a person) to move along ⟨saga of migratory laborers *harried* across the continent —J. D. Hart⟩ **3 :** to torment by or as if by constant attack ***syn*** see WORRY

harsh \'härsh\ *adj* [ME *harsk*, of Scand origin; akin to Norw *harsk* harsh] (14c) **1 :** having a coarse uneven surface that is rough to the touch **2 a :** causing a disagreeable or painful sensory reaction : IRRITATING **b :** physically discomforting : PAINFUL **3 :** unduly exacting : SEVERE **4 :** lacking in aesthetic appeal or refinement : CRUDE ***syn*** see ROUGH — **harsh·ly** *adv* — **harsh·ness** *n*

harsh·en \'här-shən\ *vb* **harsh·ened; harsh·en·ing** \-sh(ə-)niŋ\ *vt* (1824) : to make (as a voice) harsh ~ *vi* : to become harsh ⟨saw the grain of his skin *~ing* over face bones —Elizabeth Bowen⟩

hart \'härt\ *n* [ME *hert*, fr. OE *heort;* akin to L *cervus* hart, Gk *keras* horn — more at HORN] *chiefly Brit* (bef. 12c) : the male of the red deer esp. when over five years old : STAG — compare HIND

harte·beest \'härt-(ə-)ˌbēst\ *n* [obs. Afrik (now *hartbees*), fr. D, fr. *hart* deer + *beest* beast] (1786) : either of two large African antelopes (*Alcelaphus buselaphus* or *A. lichtensteini*) with annulate divergent horns

harts·horn \'härts-,hȯ(ə)rn\ *n* [fr. the earlier use of hart's horns as the chief source of ammonia] (1685) **:** a preparation of ammonia used as smelling salts

har·um–scar·um \,har-əm-'skar-əm, ,her-əm-'sker-\ *adj* [perh. alter. of *helter-skelter*] (1740) **:** RECKLESS, IRRESPONSIBLE — **harum–scarum** *adv*

ha·rus·pex \hə-'rəs-,peks, 'har-əs-\ *n, pl* **ha·rus·pi·ces** \hə-'rəs-pə-,sēz\ [L, fr. *haru-* (akin to *chordē* gut, cord) + *-spex,* fr. *specere* to look — more at YARN, SPY] (1584) **:** a diviner in ancient Rome basing his predictions on inspection of the entrails of sacrificial animals

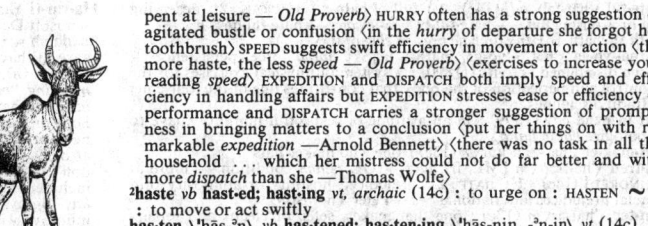

hartebeest

¹har·vest \'här-vəst\ *n, often attrib* [ME *hervest,* fr. OE *hærfest;* akin to L *carpere* to pluck, gather, Gk *karpos* fruit, *keirein* to cut — more at SHEAR] (bef. 12c) **1 :** the season for gathering in agricultural crops **2 :** the act or process of gathering in a crop **3 a :** a mature crop (as of grain or fruit) **:** YIELD **b :** the quantity of a natural product gathered in a single season **4 :** the product or reward of exertion

²harvest *vt* (15c) **1 a :** to gather in (a crop) **:** REAP **b :** to gather (a natural product) as if by harvesting **2 :** to win by achievement ⟨the team *~ed* several awards⟩ **~** *vi* **:** to gather in a crop esp. for food — **har·vest·able** \-və-stə-bəl\ *adj* — **har·vest·er** *n*

harvest fly *n* (1753) **:** CICADA

harvest home *n* (1596) **1 :** the gathering or the time of harvest **2 :** a feast at the close of harvest **3 :** a song sung by the reapers at the close of the harvest

har·vest·man \'här-vəs(t)-mən\ *n* (1830) **:** an arachnid (order Phalangida) that superficially resembles a true spider but has a small rounded body and very long slender legs — called also *daddy longlegs*

harvest mite *n* (1873) **:** CHIGGER 2

harvest moon *n* (1706) **:** the full moon nearest the time of the September equinox

har·vest·time \'här-vəs(t)-,tīm\ *n* (14c) **:** the time during which an annual crop (as wheat) is harvested

has *pres 3d sing of* HAVE

has–been \'haz-,bin, *chiefly Brit* -,bēn\ *n* (1606) **:** one that has passed the peak of effectiveness or popularity ⟨a seedy ~ of an actor traveling a comeback trail —Gordon Allison⟩

ha·sen·pfef·fer \'häz-ᵊn-,(p)fef-ər\ *n* [G, fr. *hase* hare (fr. OHG *haso*) + *pfeffer* pepper — more at HARE] (1892) **:** a highly seasoned stew made of marinated rabbit meat

¹hash \'hash\ *vt* [F *hacher,* fr. OF *hachier,* fr. *hache* battle-ax, of Gmc origin; akin to OHG *hāppa* sickle; akin to Gk *koptein* to cut — more at CAPON] (1590) **1 a :** to chop (as meat and potatoes) into small pieces **b :** CONFUSE, MUDDLE **2 :** to talk about **:** REVIEW — often used with *over*

²hash *n* (1662) **1 :** chopped food; *specif* **:** chopped meat mixed with potatoes and browned **2 :** a restatement of something that is already known **3 a :** HODGEPODGE, JUMBLE **b :** a confused muddle

³hash *n* (1959) **:** HASHISH

hash browns *n pl* (1951) **:** boiled potatoes that have been diced, mixed with chopped onions and shortening, and fried until they form a browned cake — called also *hash brown potatoes, hashed brown potatoes, hashed browns*

Hash·em·ite *or* **Hash·im·ite** \'hash-ə-,mīt\ *n* [*Hashim,* great-grandfather of Muhammad] (1697) **:** a member of an Arab family having common ancestry with Muhammad and founding dynasties in countries of the eastern Mediterranean

hash·ish \'hash-,ēsh, ha-'shēsh\ *n* [Ar *ḥashīsh*] (1598) **:** the concentrated resin from the flowering tops of the female hemp plant (*Cannabis sativa*) that is smoked, chewed, or drunk for its intoxicating effect — called also *charas;* compare BHANG, MARIJUANA

hash mark *n* (1907) **1 :** SERVICE STRIPE **2 :** INBOUNDS LINE

Ha·sid \'has-əd, 'käs-\ *n, pl* **Ha·si·dim** \'has-əd-əm, kä-'sēd-\ [Heb *ḥāsīdh* pious] (1812) **1 :** a member of a Jewish sect of the second century B.C. opposed to Hellenism and devoted to the strict observance of the ritual law **2** *also* **Has·sid :** a member of a Jewish mystical sect founded in Poland about 1750 in opposition to rationalism and ritual laxity — **Ha·sid·ic** *also* **Has·sid·ic** \ha-'sid-ik, hä-, kä-\ *adj*

Ha·si·dism \'has-ə-,diz-əm, 'häs-, 'käs-\ *n* (1904) **1 :** the practices and beliefs of the Hasidim **2 :** the Hasidic movement

Has·mo·nae·an *or* **Has·mo·ne·an** \,haz-mə-'nē-ən\ *n* [LL *Asmonaeus* Hasmon, ancestor of the Maccabees, fr. Gk *Asamōnaios*] (1620) **:** a member of the Maccabees — **Hasmonaean** *or* **Hasmonean** *adj*

hasn't \'haz-ᵊnt, -ᵊn\ **:** has not

hasp \'hasp\ *n* [ME, alter. fr. OE *hæpse;* akin to MHG *haspe* hasp] (bef. 12c) **:** any of several devices for fastening; *esp* **:** a fastener esp. for a door or lid consisting of a hinged metal strap that fits over a staple and is secured by a pin or padlock — **hasp** *vt*

¹has·sle \'has-əl\ *vb* **has·sled; has·sling** \-(ə-)liŋ\ [perh. blend of *harass* + *hustle*] *vi* (1951) **:** ARGUE, FIGHT ⟨*hassled* with the umpire⟩ **~** *vt* **:** to annoy persistently or acutely **:** HARASS ⟨he gets *hassled* in the street because he dresses funny —William Kloman⟩

²hassle *n* (1945) **1 :** a heated often protracted argument **:** WRANGLE **2 :** a violent skirmish **:** FIGHT **3 a :** a state of confusion **:** TURMOIL **b :** an annoying or troublesome concern

has·sock \'has-ək\ *n* [ME, sedge, fr. OE *hassuc*] (bef. 12c) **1 :** TUSSOCK **2 a :** a cushion for kneeling ⟨a church ~⟩ **b :** a padded cushion or low stool that serves as a seat or leg rest

hast \(')hast, (h)əst\ *archaic pres 2d sing of* HAVE

has·tate \'has-,tāt\ *adj* [NL *hastatus,* fr. L *hasta* spear — more at YARD] (1788) **1 :** triangular with sharp basal lobes spreading away from the base of the petiole ⟨~ leaves⟩ **2 :** shaped like a spear or the head of a spear ⟨a ~ spot of a bird⟩

¹haste \'hāst\ *n* [ME, fr. MF, of Gmc origin; akin to OE *hǣst* violence] (14c) **1 :** rapidity of motion **:** SWIFTNESS **2 :** rash or headlong action **:** PRECIPITATENESS ⟨the beauty of speed uncontaminated by ~ —*Harper's*⟩ **3 :** undue eagerness to act

syn HASTE, HURRY, SPEED, EXPEDITION, DISPATCH mean quickness in movement or action. HASTE applies to personal action and implies urgency and precipitancy and often rashness ⟨marry in *haste* and repent at leisure — *Old Proverb*⟩ HURRY often has a strong suggestion of agitated bustle or confusion ⟨in the *hurry* of departure she forgot her toothbrush⟩ SPEED suggests swift efficiency in movement or action ⟨the more haste, the less *speed* — *Old Proverb*⟩ ⟨exercises to increase your reading *speed*⟩ EXPEDITION and DISPATCH both imply speed and efficiency in handling affairs but EXPEDITION stresses ease or efficiency of performance and DISPATCH carries a stronger suggestion of promptness in bringing matters to a conclusion ⟨put her things on with remarkable *expedition* —Arnold Bennett⟩ ⟨there was no task in all the household . . . which her mistress could not do far better and with more *dispatch* than she —Thomas Wolfe⟩

²haste *vb* **hast·ed; hast·ing** *vt, archaic* (14c) **:** to urge on **:** HASTEN **~** *vi* **:** to move or act swiftly

has·ten \'hās-ᵊn\ *vb* **has·tened; has·ten·ing** \'hās-niŋ, -ᵊn-iŋ\ *vt* (14c) **1 :** to urge on ⟨*~ed* her to the door —A. J. Cronin⟩ **2 :** ACCELERATE ⟨~ the coming of a new order —D. W. Brogan⟩ **~** *vi* **:** to move or act quickly — **has·ten·er** \'hās-nər, -ᵊn-ər\ *n*

hast·i·ly \'hā-stə-lē\ *adv* (13c) **:** in haste **:** HURRIEDLY

hasty \'hā-stē\ *adj* **hast·i·er; -est** (14c) **1 a** *archaic* **:** rapid in action or movement **:** SPEEDY **b :** done or made in a hurry **c :** fast and typically superficial ⟨made a ~ examination of the wound⟩ **2 :** EAGER, IMPATIENT **3 :** PRECIPITATE, RASH **4 :** prone to anger **:** IRRITABLE ***syn*** see FAST — **hast·i·ness** *n*

hasty pudding *n* (1599) **1** *Brit* **:** a porridge of oatmeal or flour boiled in water **2** *NewEng* **a :** cornmeal mush **b :** INDIAN PUDDING

¹hat \'hat\ *n* [ME, fr. OE *hæt;* akin to OHG *huot* head covering — more at HOOD] (bef. 12c) **1 :** a covering for the head usu. having a shaped crown and brim **2 a :** a distinctive head covering worn as a symbol of office **b :** an office, position, or role assumed by or as if by the wearing of a special hat — **hat·less** \-ləs\ *adj*

²hat *vb* **hat·ted; hat·ting** *vt* (15c) **:** to furnish or provide with a hat **~** *vi* **:** to make or supply hats

hat·band \'hat-,band\ *n* (15c) **:** a band (as of fabric, leather, or cord) around the crown of a hat just above the brim

hat·box \-,bäks\ *n* (1794) **1 :** a box for holding or storing a hat **2 :** a usu. round piece of luggage designed esp. for carrying hats

¹hatch \'hach\ *n* [ME *hache,* fr. OE *hæc;* akin to MD *hecke* trapdoor] (bef. 12c) **1 :** a small door or opening (as in an airplane or spaceship) ⟨an escape ~⟩ **2 a :** an opening in the deck of a ship or in the floor or roof of a building **b :** the covering for such an opening **c :** HATCHWAY **d :** COMPARTMENT **3 :** FLOODGATE

²hatch *vb* [ME *hacchen;* akin to MHG *hecken* to mate] *vi* (13c) **1 :** to produce young by incubation **2 a :** to emerge from an egg, chrysalis, or pupa **b :** to give forth young or imagoes **3 :** to incubate eggs **:** BROOD **~** *vt* **1 a :** to produce (young) from an egg by applying natural or artificial heat **b :** INCUBATE 1 **2 :** to bring into being **:** ORIGINATE; *esp* **:** to concoct in secret — **hatch·abil·i·ty** \,hach-ə-'bil-ət-ē\ *n* — **hatch·able** \'hach-ə-bəl\ *adj* — **hatch·er** *n*

³hatch *n* (1602) **1 :** an act or instance of hatching **2 :** a brood of hatched young

⁴hatch *vt* [ME *hachen,* fr. MF *hacher* to inlay, chop up, fr. OF *hachier* — more at HASH] (15c) **1 :** to inlay with narrow bands of distinguishable material ⟨a silver handle *~ed* with gold⟩ **2 :** to mark (as a drawing or engraving) with fine closely spaced lines

⁵hatch *n* (1658) **:** LINE; *esp* **:** one used to give the effect of shading

hatch·back \'hach-,bak\ *n* (1970) **1 :** a back on a closed passenger automobile (as a coupe) having an upward-opening hatch **2 :** an automobile having a hatchback

hat·check \'hat-,chek\ *adj* (1917) **1 :** being one that checks hats and articles of outdoor clothing ⟨a ~ girl⟩ **2 :** used in the checking of hats ⟨a ~ stand⟩

hatch·ery \'hach-(ə-)rē\ *n, pl* **-er·ies** (1880) **:** a place for hatching eggs (as of poultry or fish)

hatch·et \'hach-ət\ *n* [ME *hachet,* fr. MF *hachette,* dim. of *hache* battle-ax — more at HASH] (14c) **1 :** a short-handled ax often with a hammerhead to be used with one hand **2 :** TOMAHAWK

hatchet face *n* (1650) **:** a thin sharp face — **hatch·et–faced** \,hach-ət-'fāst\ *adj*

hatchet job *n* (1944) **:** a forceful or malicious verbal attack ⟨a speech that was nothing more than a *hatchet job* on his opponent's character⟩

hatchet man *n* (1755) **1 :** one hired for murder, coercion, or attack **2 a :** a writer specializing in invective **b :** a person hired to perform underhanded or unscrupulous tasks (as ruin reputations)

hatch·ing *n* (1662) **:** the engraving or drawing of fine lines in close proximity chiefly to give an effect of shading; *also* **:** the pattern so created

hatch·ling \'hach-liŋ\ *n* (1899) **:** a recently hatched animal

hatch·ment \'hach-mənt\ *n* [perh. alter. of *achievement*] (1548) **:** a panel on which a coat of arms of a deceased person is temporarily displayed

hatch·way \'hach-,wā\ *n* (1626) **:** a passage giving access usu. by a ladder or stairs to an enclosed space (as a cellar); *also* **:** HATCH 2a

¹hate \'hāt\ *n* [ME, fr. OE *hete;* akin to OHG *haz* hate, Gk *kēdos* grief] (bef. 12c) **1 a :** intense hostility and aversion usu. deriving from fear, anger, or sense of injury **b :** extreme dislike or antipathy **:** LOATHING ⟨had a great ~ of hard work⟩ **2 :** an object of hatred ⟨a generation whose finest ~ had been big business —F. L. Paxson⟩

²hate *vb* **hat·ed; hat·ing** *vt* (bef. 12c) **1 :** to feel extreme enmity toward ⟨*~s* his country's enemies⟩ **2 :** to have a strong aversion to **:** find very distasteful ⟨*hated* to have to meet strangers⟩ ⟨~ hypocrisy⟩ **~** *vi* **:** to express or feel extreme enmity or active hostility — **hat·er** *n*

syn HATE, DETEST, ABHOR, ABOMINATE, LOATHE mean to feel strong aversion or intense dislike for. HATE implies an emotional aversion often coupled with enmity or malice; DETEST suggests violent antipathy; ABHOR implies a deep often shuddering repugnance; ABOMINATE suggests strong detestation and often moral condemnation; LOATHE implies utter disgust and intolerance.

— **hate one's guts :** to hate someone with great intensity

hate·ful \ˈhāt-fəl\ *adj* (14c) **1 :** full of hate : MALICIOUS **2 :** deserving of or arousing hate — **hate·ful·ly** \-fə-lē\ *adv* — **hate·ful·ness** *n*
hath \(ˈ)hath, (h)əth\ *archaic pres 3d sing of* HAVE
hatha–yo·ga \ˈhət-ə-ˈyō-gə, ˈhäth-\ *n* [Skt *hatha* force, persistence + *yoga* disciplined activity] (1890) : a system of physical exercises for the control and perfection of the body that constitutes one of the four chief Hindu disciplines
hat in hand *adv* (1899) : in an attitude of respectful humility ⟨have to apologize *hat in hand*⟩
hat·mak·er \ˈhat-ˌmā-kər\ *n* (15c) : one who makes hats
ha·tred \ˈhā-trəd\ *n* [ME, fr. *hate* + OE *rǣden* condition — more at KINDRED] (14c) **1 :** HATE **2 :** prejudiced hostility or animosity ⟨old racial prejudices and national ∼*s* —Peter Thomson⟩
hat·ter \ˈhat-ər\ *n* (13c) : one that makes, sells, or cleans and repairs hats
hat trick *n* [prob. fr. the former practice of rewarding the feat with the gift of a hat] (1882) **1 :** the retiring of three batsmen with three consecutive balls by a bowler in cricket **2 :** the scoring of three goals in one game (as of hockey or soccer) by a single player
hau·berk \ˈhȯ-(ˌ)bərk\ *n* [ME, fr. OF *hauberc,* of Gmc origin; akin to OE *healsbeorg* neck armor] (13c) : a tunic of chain mail worn as defensive armor from the 12th to the 14th century

1 hauberk

haugh \ˈhȯ(k)\ *n* [ME (Sc) *halch,* fr. OE *healh* corner of land; akin to OE *holh* hole] *Scot* (bef. 12c) : a low-lying meadow by the side of a river
haugh·ty \ˈhȯt-ē, ˈhät-\ *adj* **haugh·ti·er; -est** [obs. *haught,* fr. ME *haute,* fr. MF *haut,* lit., high, fr. L *altus* — more at OLD] (15c) : blatantly and disdainfully proud ***syn*** see PROUD — **haugh·ti·ly** \ˈhȯt-ᵊl-ē, ˈhät-\ *adv* — **haugh·ti·ness** \ˈhȯt-ē-nəs, ˈhät-\ *n*
1**haul** \ˈhȯl\ *vb* [ME *halen* to pull, fr. OF *haler,* of Gmc origin; akin to MD *halen* to pull; akin to OE *geholian* to obtain] *vt* (13c) **1 :** to change the course of (a ship) esp. so as to sail closer to the wind **2 a :** to exert traction on : DRAW ⟨∼ a wagon⟩ **b :** to obtain or move by or as if by hauling ⟨was ∼*ed* to parties night after night by his wife⟩ **c :** to transport in a vehicle : CART **3 :** to bring before an authority for interrogation or judgment : HALE ⟨∼ traffic violators into court⟩ ∼ *vi* **1 :** to exert traction : PULL **2 :** to furnish transportation **3** *of the wind* : SHIFT ***syn*** see PULL
2**haul** *n* (1670) **1 a :** the act or process of hauling : PULL **b :** a device for hauling **2 a :** the result of an effort to collect : TAKE ⟨the burglar's ∼⟩ **b :** the fish taken in a single draft of a net **3 a :** transportation by hauling **b :** the distance or route over which a load is transported ⟨a long ∼⟩ **c :** a quantity transported : LOAD
haul·age \ˈhȯ-lij\ *n* (1826) **1 :** the act or process of hauling **2 :** a charge made for hauling
haul·age·way \-ˌwā\ *n* (ca. 1909) : a passage in a coal mine along which coal is transported
haul·er \ˈhȯ-lər\ *n* (1674) : one that hauls; *esp* : a commercial establishment whose business is hauling or one of its automotive vehicles
haul·ier \ˈhȯl-yər\ *Brit var of* HAULER
haulm \ˈhȯm\ *n* [ME *halm,* fr. OE *healm;* akin to OHG *halm* stem, L *culmus* stalk, Gk *kalamos* reed] (bef. 12c) **1 :** the stems or tops of cultivated plants (as peas, beans, or potatoes) esp. after the crop has been gathered **2 :** a plant stem (as the culm of a grass)
haunch \ˈhȯnch, ˈhänch\ *n* [ME *haunche,* fr. OF *hanche,* of Gmc origin; akin to MD *hanke* haunch] (13c) **1 a :** HIP 1a **b :** HINDQUARTER 2 — usu. used in pl. **2 :** HINDQUARTER 1 **3 :** either side of an arch between the springing and the crown — **on one's haunches :** in a squatting position
1**haunt** \ˈhȯnt, ˈhänt\ *vb* [ME *haunten,* fr. OF *hanter,* of Gmc origin; akin to OE *hām* home] *vt* (13c) **1 a :** to visit often : FREQUENT **b :** to continually seek the company of (a person) **2 a :** to recur constantly and spontaneously to ⟨the tune ∼*ed* her⟩ **b :** to reappear continually in ⟨a sense of tension that ∼*s* his writing⟩ **3 :** to visit or inhabit as a ghost ∼ *vi* **1 :** to stay around or persist : LINGER **2 :** to appear habitually as a ghost — **haunt·er** *n* — **haunt·ing·ly** \-iŋ-lē\ *adv*
2**haunt** \ˈhȯnt, ˈhänt, *2 is usu* ˈhant\ *n* (14c) **1 :** a place habitually frequented **2** *chiefly dial* : GHOST
Hau·sa \ˈhau̇-sə, -zə\ *n, pl* **Hausa** *or* **Hausas** (1820) **1 :** a member of a Negroid people of the Sudan between Lake Chad and the Niger **2 :** the language of the Hausa people widely used in west Africa as a trade language
haus·frau \ˈhau̇s-ˌfrau̇\ *n* [G, fr. *haus* house + *frau* woman, wife — more at FRAU] (1798) : HOUSEWIFE
haus·tel·late \hȯ-ˈstel-ət, ˈhȯ-stə-ˌlāt\ *adj* (1835) : having a haustellum
haus·tel·lum \hȯ-ˈstel-əm\ *n, pl* **-la** \-ə\ [NL, fr. L *haustus,* pp. of *haurire* to drink, draw — more at EXHAUST] (1816) : a proboscis (as of an insect) adapted to suck blood or juices of plants
haus·to·ri·al \hȯ-ˈstōr-ē-əl, -ˈstȯr-\ *adj* (1894) : having a haustorium
haus·to·ri·um \-ē-əm\ *n, pl* **-ria** \-ē-ə\ [NL, fr. L *haustus*] (1875) : a food-absorbing outgrowth of a plant organ (as a hypha or stem)
haut·bois *or* **haut·boy** \ˈ(h)ō-ˌbȯi\ *n, pl* **hautbois** \-ˌbȯiz\ *or* **hautboys** [MF *hautbois,* fr. *haut* high + *bois* wood, of Gmc origin; akin to OHG *busc* bush, forest — more at HAUGHTY] (1575) : OBOE
haute \ˈōt\ *also* **haut** \ˈōt, ˈō\ *adj* [F] (1787) : FASHIONABLE, HIGH-CLASS ⟨∼ interior decorators⟩ ⟨a store filled with ∼ kitsch⟩
haute cou·ture \ˌōt-kü-ˈtu̇(ə)r\ *n* [F, lit., high sewing] (1908) : the houses or designers that create exclusive and often trend-setting fashions for women; *also* : the fashions created
haute cui·sine \-kwi-ˈzēn\ *n* [F, lit., high cooking] (1928) : artful or elaborate cuisine; *esp* : traditionally elaborate French cuisine
haute école \-ā-ˈkȯl, -ˈkəl\ *n* [F, lit., high school] (1858) : a highly stylized form of classical riding : advanced dressage
hau·teur \hȯ-ˈtər, (h)ō-\ *n* [F, fr. *haut* high — more at HAUGHTY] (1628) : ARROGANCE, HAUGHTINESS
haut monde \ō-ˈmänd, ō-mōⁿd\ *also* **haute monde** \ōt-\ *n* [F, lit., high world] (1864) : high society
Ha·vana \hə-ˈvan-ə\ *n* [prob. fr. Sp *habano,* fr. *habano* of Havana, fr. La *Habana* (Havana), Cuba] (1826) **1 :** a cigar made from Cuban tobacco **2 :** a tobacco orig. grown in Cuba
Ha·var·ti \hə-ˈvärt-ē\ *n* [*Havarti,* place-name in Denmark] (1957) : a semisoft Danish cheese having a porous texture and usu. a mild flavor
havdalah *var of* HABDALAH
1**have** \(ˈ)hav, (h)əv, v; *in "have to" meaning "must" usu* ˈhaf\ *vb* **had** \(ˈ)had, (h)əd, d\; **hav·ing** \ˈhav-iŋ\; **has** \(ˈ)haz, (h)əz, z, s; *in "has to" meaning "must" usu* ˈhas\ [ME *haven,* fr. OE *habban;* akin to OHG *habēn* to have, *hevan* to lift — more at HEAVE] *vt* (bef. 12c) **1 a :** to hold or maintain as a possession, privilege, or entitlement ⟨they ∼ a new car⟩ ⟨I ∼ my rights⟩ **b :** to hold in one's use, service, regard, or at one's disposal ⟨the group will ∼ enough tickets for everyone⟩ ⟨we don't ∼ time to stay⟩ ⟨can't ∼ your cake and eat it too⟩ **c :** to hold, include, or contain as a part or whole ⟨the car *has* power brakes⟩ ⟨April *has* 30 days⟩ **2 :** to feel obligation in regard to — usu. used with an infinitive with *to* ⟨we ∼ things to do⟩ ⟨∼ a deadline to meet⟩ **3 :** to stand in a certain relationship to ⟨∼ enemies⟩ ⟨*has* three fine children⟩ ⟨we will ∼ the wind at our backs⟩ **4 a :** to acquire or get possession of : OBTAIN ⟨these shoes are the best to be *had*⟩ **b :** RECEIVE ⟨*had* news⟩ **c :** ACCEPT; *specif* : to accept in marriage **d :** to copulate with **5 a :** to be marked or characterized by (a quality, attribute, or faculty) ⟨∼ red hair⟩ ⟨*has* a way with words⟩ **b :** EXHIBIT, SHOW ⟨*had* the gall to refuse⟩ **c :** USE, EXERCISE ⟨∼ mercy on us⟩ **6 a :** to experience esp. by submitting to, undergoing, or suffering ⟨∼ a cold⟩ **b :** to make the effort to perform (an action) or engage in (an activity) ⟨∼ a look at that cut⟩ ⟨∼ a fight⟩ **c :** to entertain in the mind ⟨∼ an opinion⟩ **7 a :** to cause or command to do something — used with the infinitive without *to* ⟨∼ the children stay⟩ **b :** to cause to be in a certain place or state ⟨*has* people around at all times⟩ **8 :** ALLOW ⟨we'll ∼ no more of that⟩ **9 :** to be competent in ⟨*has* only a little French⟩ **10 a :** to hold in a position of disadvantage or certain defeat ⟨we ∼ him now⟩ **b :** to take advantage of : TRICK, FOOL ⟨been *had* by a partner⟩ **11 :** BEGET, BEAR ⟨∼ a baby⟩ **12 :** to partake of ⟨∼ dinner⟩ **13 :** BRIBE, SUBORN ⟨can be *had* for a price⟩ ∼ *verbal auxiliary* **1 —** used with the past participle to form the present perfect, past perfect, or future perfect ⟨*has* gone home⟩ ⟨*had* already eaten⟩ ⟨will ∼ finished dinner by then⟩ **2 :** to be compelled, obliged, or required — used with an infinitive with *to* or *to* alone ⟨we *had* to go⟩ ⟨do what you *have* to⟩ ⟨it *has* to be said⟩
syn HAVE, HOLD, OWN, POSSESS mean to keep, control, retain, or experience as one's own. HAVE is a general term carrying no specific implication; HOLD suggests stronger control, grasp, or retention; OWN implies a natural or legal right to hold as one's property and under one's full control; POSSESS is often the preferred term when referring to an intangible (as a characteristic, a power, or a quality).
— **have at** \ha-ˈvat\ : to go at or deal with : ATTACK — **have coming :** to deserve or merit what one gets, benefits by, or suffers ⟨he *had* that *coming*⟩ — **have done :** FINISH, STOP — **have done with :** to bring to an end : have no further concern with ⟨let us *have done with* name-calling⟩ — **have had it 1 :** to have had or have done all one is going to be allowed to **2 :** to have experienced, endured, or suffered all one can — **have it :** ASSERT, CLAIM ⟨rumor *has it* that he was drunk⟩ — **have it in for** \ˌhav-ət-ˈin-fər, -ˌfȯ(ə)r\ : to intend to do harm to — **have it out :** to settle a matter of contention by discussion or a fight — **have one's eye on 1 a :** to look at **b :** to watch constantly and attentively **2 :** to have as an objective — **have to do with 1 :** to deal with ⟨the story *has to do with* real people —Alice M. Jordan⟩ **2 :** to have a specified relationship with or effect on ⟨the size of the brain *has* nothing *to do with* intelligence —Ruth Benedict⟩
2**have** \ˈhav\ *n* (1836) : one that is well-endowed esp. in material wealth
have·lock \ˈhav-ˌläk, -lək\ *n* [Sir Henry *Havelock*] (1861) : a covering attached to a cap to protect the neck from the sun or bad weather
ha·ven \ˈhā-vən\ *n* [ME, fr. OE *hæfen;* akin to MHG *habene* harbor, OE *hebban* to lift — more at HEAVE] (bef. 12c) **1 :** HARBOR, PORT **2 :** a place of safety : ASYLUM **3 :** a place offering favorable opportunities or conditions ⟨a tourist's ∼⟩ — **haven** *vt*
have–not \ˈhav-ˌnät, -ˈnät\ *n* (1836) : one that is poor esp. in material wealth
haven't \ˈhav-ənt, ˈhab-ᵊm(t)\ : have not
have on *vt* (13c) **1 :** WEAR ⟨*has on* a new suit⟩ **2 :** to have plans for ⟨what do you *have on* for tomorrow⟩
ha·ver \ˈhā-vər\ *vi* [origin unknown] *chiefly Brit* (1721) : to hem and haw
ha·vers \ˈhā-vərz\ *n pl* [*haver*] *chiefly Scot* (1787) : NONSENSE, POPPYCOCK
hav·er·sack \ˈhav-ər-ˌsak\ *n* [F *havresac,* fr. G *habersack* bag for oats, fr. *haber* oats + *sack* bag] (1749) : a bag similar to a knapsack but worn over one shoulder
ha·ver·sian canal \hə-ˌvər-zhən-\ *n, often cap H* [Clopton *Havers* †1702 Eng. physician & anatomist] (1842) : any of the small canals through which the blood vessels ramify in bone
haversian system *n, often cap H* (1845) : a haversian canal with the concentrically arranged laminae of bone that surround it
1**hav·oc** \ˈhav-ək, -ik\ *n* [ME *havok,* fr. AF, modif. of OF *havot* plunder] (15c) **1 :** wide and general destruction : DEVASTATION **2 :** great confusion and disorder ⟨children can create ∼ in a house⟩ ⟨suspicion played ∼ with her thoughts⟩
2**havoc** *vt* **hav·ocked; hav·ock·ing** (1577) : to lay waste : DESTROY
1**haw** \ˈhȯ\ *n* [ME *hawe,* fr. OE *haga* — more at HEDGE] (bef. 12c) **1 :** a hawthorn berry **2 :** HAWTHORN
2**haw** *n* [origin unknown] (15c) : NICTITATING MEMBRANE; *esp* : an inflamed nictitating membrane of a domesticated mammal
3**haw** *vi* [imit.] (1632) **1 :** to utter the sound represented by *haw* ⟨hemmed and ∼*ed* before answering⟩ **2 :** EQUIVOCATE ⟨the administration hemmed and ∼*ed* over the students' demands⟩
4**haw** *interj* (1679) — often used to indicate a vocalized pause in speaking
5**haw** \ˈhȯ\ *vb imper* [origin unknown] (1777) — used as a direction to turn to the left; compare GEE ∼ *vi* : to turn to the near or left side
Hawaii–Aleutian time *n* (1983) : the time of the 10th time zone west of Greenwich that includes the Hawaiian islands and the Aleutians west of the Fox group
Ha·wai·ian \hə-ˈwä-yən, -ˈwī-(y)ən, -ˈwȯ-yən\ *n* (1864) **1 :** a native or resident of Hawaii; *esp* : one of Polynesian ancestry **2 :** the Polynesian language of the Hawaiians — **Hawaiian** *adj*
Hawaiian goose *n* (ca. 1909) : NENE

Hawaiian guitar *n* (1928) **:** a usu. electric stringed instrument having a long fretted neck and six to eight steel strings that are plucked while being pressed with a movable steel bar for a glissando effect

haw·finch \ˈhȯ-ˌfinch\ *n* [[1]*haw*] (1674) **:** a Eurasian finch (*Coccothraustes coccothraustes*) with a large heavy bill and short thick neck and the male marked with black, white, and brown

[1]hawk \ˈhȯk\ *n* [ME *hauk,* fr. OE *hafoc;* akin to OHG *habuh* hawk, Russ *kobets* a falcon] (bef. 12c) **1 :** any of numerous diurnal birds of prey belonging to a suborder (Falcones of the order Falconiformes) and including all the smaller members of this group; *esp* **:** ACCIPITER — compare OWL **2 :** a small board or metal sheet with a handle on the underside used to hold mortar **3 :** an individual who takes a militant attitude (as in a dispute) and advocates immediate vigorous action; *esp* **:** a supporter of a war or warlike policy — compare DOVE — **hawk·ish** \ˈhȯ-kish\ *adj* — **hawk·ish·ly** *adv* — **hawk·ish·ness** *n*

[2]hawk *vi* (14c) **1 :** to hunt birds by means of a trained hawk **2 :** to soar and strike like a hawk ~ *vt* **:** to hunt on the wing like a hawk

[3]hawk *vb* [imit.] *vi* (1581) **:** to utter a harsh guttural sound in or as if in trying to clear the throat ~ *vt* **:** to raise by hawking ⟨~ up phlegm⟩

[4]hawk *n* (1604) **:** an audible effort to force up phlegm from the throat

[5]hawk *vt* [back-formation fr. [2]*hawker*] (1713) **:** to offer for sale by calling out in the street ⟨~*ing* newspapers⟩; *broadly* **:** SELL

[1]hawk·er \ˈhȯ-kər\ *n* [ME, fr. OE *hafocere,* fr. *hafoc*] (bef. 12c) **:** FALCONER

[2]hawker *n* [by folk etymology fr. LG *höker,* fr. MLG *hōker,* fr. *hōken* to peddle; akin to OE *hēah* high] (1512) **:** one that hawks wares

Hawk·eye \ˈhȯ-ˌkī\ *n* (1823) **:** a native or resident of Iowa — used as a nickname

hawk·moth \ˈhȯk-ˌmȯth\ *n* (1785) **:** any of numerous rather large stout-bodied moths (family Sphingidae) with a long proboscis which at rest is kept coiled, long strong narrow forewings more or less pointed at the ends, and small hind wings — called also *sphinx*

hawks·bill \ˈhȯks-ˌbil\ *n* (1657) **:** a carnivorous sea turtle (*Eretmochelys imbricata*) whose shell yields a valuable tortoiseshell

hawk·shaw \ˈhȯk-ˌshȯ\ *n* [after the comic strip *Hawkshaw the Detective,* by Gus Mager †1956 Am. artist] (1888) **:** DETECTIVE

hawk·weed \ˈhȯ-ˌkwēd\ *n* (1562) **:** any of several composite plants (as of the genera *Hieracium, Picris,* and *Erechtites*) usu. having flower heads with red or orange rays — compare ORANGE HAWKWEED

hawse \ˈhȯz\ *n* [alter. of ME *halse,* fr. ON *hals* neck, hawse — more at COLLAR] (14c) **1 a :** HAWSEHOLE **b :** the part of a ship's bow that contains the hawseholes **2 :** the arrangement of the anchor cables of a ship when both a port and starboard anchor are used **3 :** the distance between a ship's bow and her anchor

hawse·hole \-ˌhōl\ *n* (1664) **:** a hole in the bow of a ship through which a cable passes

haw·ser \ˈhȯ-zər\ *n* [ME, fr. AF *hauceour,* fr. MF *haucier* to hoist, fr. (assumed) VL *altiare,* fr. L *altus* high — more at OLD] (13c) **:** a large rope for towing, mooring, or securing a ship

hawser bend *n* (1897) **:** a method of joining the ends of two heavy ropes by means of seizings

haw·ser–laid \ˌhȯ-zər-ˈlād\ *adj* (1860) **:** CABLE-LAID

haw·thorn \ˈhȯ-ˌthȯ(ə)rn\ *n* [ME *hawethorn,* fr. OE *hagathorn,* fr. *haga* hawthorn + *thorn* — more at HEDGE] (bef. 12c) **:** any of a genus (*Crataegus*) of spring-flowering spiny shrubs (as the European *C. oxyacantha* and the American *C. coccinea*) of the rose family with glossy and often lobed leaves, white or pink fragrant flowers, and small red fruits

Haw·thorne effect \ˈhȯ-ˌthȯrn-\ *n* [fr. the *Hawthorne* Works of the Western Electric Co., Cicero, Ill., where its existence was established by experiment] (1962) **:** the stimulation to output or accomplishment (as in an industrial or educational methods study) that results from the mere fact of being under concerned observation

[1]hay \ˈhā\ *n* [ME *hey,* fr. OE *hieg;* akin to OHG *hewi* hay, OE *hēawan* to hew] (bef. 12c) **1 :** herbage and esp. grass mowed and cured for fodder **2 :** REWARD **3** *slang* **:** BED **4 :** a small sum of money ⟨a saving of . . . $14 million is not ~ —H.C. Schonberg⟩

[2]hay *vi* (1556) **:** to cut, cure, and store hay ~ *vt* **:** to feed with hay

hay·cock \ˈhā-ˌkäk\ *n* (13c) **:** a somewhat rounded conical pile of hay

hay fever *n* (1829) **:** an acute allergic nasal catarrh and conjunctivitis; *esp* **:** POLLINOSIS

hay·fork \ˈhā-ˌfȯ(ə)rk\ *n* (1552) **:** a fork that is mechanically operated or held in the hand and that is used for loading or unloading hay

hay·lage \ˈhā-lij\ *n* [*hay* + *silage*] (1958) **:** a stored forage that is essentially a grass silage wilted to 35 to 50 percent moisture

hay·loft \ˈhā-ˌlȯft\ *n* (1573) **:** a loft esp. for storing hay

hay·mak·er \-ˌmā-kər\ *n* (1912) **:** a powerful blow

hay·mow \-ˌmau̇\ *n* (15c) **:** a mow esp. of or for hay

hay·rack \-ˌrak\ *n* (1825) **1 :** a frame mounted on the running gear of a wagon and used esp. in hauling hay or straw; *also* **:** a wagon equipped with a hayrack **2 :** a feeding rack that holds hay for livestock

hay·rick \-ˌrik\ *n* (15c) **:** a relatively large sometimes thatched outdoor pile of hay **:** HAYSTACK

hay·ride \-ˌrīd\ *n* (1896) **:** a pleasure ride usu. at night by a group in a wagon, sleigh, or open truck partly filled with straw or hay

hay·seed \ˈhā-ˌsēd\ *n, pl* **hayseed** *or* **hayseeds** (1577) **1 a :** seed shattered from hay **b :** clinging bits of straw or chaff from hay **2** *pl* **hayseeds :** BUMPKIN, YOKEL

hay·stack \-ˌstak\ *n* (15c) **:** a stack of hay

hay·wire \-ˌwī(ə)r\ *adv or adj* [fr. the use of baling wire for makeshift repairs] (1905) **:** out of order or control **:** CRAZY ⟨the radio went ~⟩ ⟨is going ~ with grief⟩

ha·zan \kə-ˈzän, ˈkäz-ᵊn\ *n, pl* **ha·za·nim** \kə-ˈzän-əm\ [LHeb *ḥazzān*] (1650) **1 :** an official of a Jewish synagogue or community of the period when the Talmud was compiled **2 :** CANTOR 2

[1]haz·ard \ˈhaz-ərd\ *n* [ME, fr. MF *hasard,* fr. Ar *az-zahr* the die] (14c) **1 :** a game of chance like craps played with two dice **2 :** a source of danger **3 a :** CHANCE **b :** a chance event **:** ACCIDENT **4** *obs* **:** STAKE 3a **5 :** a golf-course obstacle — **at hazard :** at stake

[2]hazard *vt* (1530) **:** VENTURE, RISK ⟨~ a guess as to the outcome⟩

haz·ard·ous \ˈhaz-ərd-əs\ *adj* (1585) **1 :** depending on hazard or chance **2 :** involving or exposing one to risk (as of loss or harm) ⟨a ~ occupation⟩ ⟨handling ~ materials⟩ ***syn*** see DANGEROUS — **haz·ard·ous·ly** *adv* —**haz·ard·ous·ness** *n*

[1]haze \ˈhāz\ *n* [prob. back-formation fr. *hazy*] (1706) **1 a :** fine dust, smoke, or light vapor causing lack of transparency of the air **b :** a cloudy appearance in a transparent liquid or solid; *also* **:** a dullness of finish (as on furniture) **2 :** something suggesting atmospheric haze; *esp* **:** vagueness of mind or mental perception

[2]haze *vb* **hazed; haz·ing** *vi* (1801) **:** to become hazy or cloudy ~ *vt* **:** to make hazy, dull, or cloudy

[3]haze *vt* **hazed; haz·ing** [origin unknown] (1840) **1 a :** to harass by exacting unnecessary or disagreeable work **b :** to harass by banter, ridicule, or criticism **2 :** to haze by way of initiation ⟨~ the fraternity pledges⟩ **3** *West* **:** to drive (as cattle or horses) from horseback — **haz·er** *n* — **haz·ing** *n*

[1]ha·zel \ˈhā-zəl\ *n* [ME *hasel,* fr. OE *hæsel;* akin to OHG *hasal* hazel, L *corulus*] (bef. 12c) **1 :** any of a genus (*Corylus*) of shrubs or small trees of the birch family (esp. the American *C. americana* and the European *C. cornuta*) bearing nuts enclosed in a leafy involucre **2 :** a light brown to strong yellowish brown

[2]hazel *adj* (14c) **1 :** consisting of hazels or of the wood of the hazel **2 :** of the color hazel

hazel hen *n* (1661) **:** a European woodland grouse (*Tetrastes bonasia*) related to the American ruffed grouse — called also *hazel grouse*

ha·zel·nut \ˈhā-zəl-ˌnət\ *n* (bef. 12c) **:** the nut of a hazel

hazy \ˈhā-zē\ *adj* **haz·i·er; -est** [origin unknown] (1625) **1 :** obscured or made dim or cloudy by or as if by haze ⟨a ~ view of the mountains⟩ **2 :** VAGUE, INDEFINITE ⟨has only a ~ recollection⟩; *also* **:** UNCERTAIN ⟨I'm ~ on that point⟩ — **haz·i·ly** \-zə-lē\ *adv* — **haz·i·ness** \-zē-nəs\ *n*

H–bomb \ˈāch-ˌbäm\ *n* (1950) **:** HYDROGEN BOMB

HDL \ˌāch-ˈdē-ˈel\ *n* [*h*igh-*d*ensity *l*ipoprotein] (ca. 1965) **:** a cholesterol-poor protein-rich lipoprotein of blood plasma correlated with reduced risk of atherosclerosis — compare LDL

[1]he \(ˈ)hē, ē\ *pron* [ME, fr. OE *hē;* akin to OE *hēo* she, *hit* it, OHG *hē* he, L *cis, citra* on this side, Gk *ekeinos* that person] (bef. 12c) **1 :** that male one who is neither speaker nor hearer ⟨~ is my father⟩ — compare HIM, HIS, IT, SHE, THEY **2** — used in a generic sense or when the sex of the person is unspecified ⟨~ that hath ears to hear, let him hear —Mt 11:15 (AV)⟩ ⟨one should do the best ~ can⟩

[2]he \ˈhē\ *n* (bef. 12c) **1 :** a male person or animal **2 :** one that is strongly masculine or has strong masculine appeal — usu. used in combination ⟨that's what I call *he*-literature —Sinclair Lewis⟩

[3]he \ˈhā\ *n* [Heb *hē'*] (1639) **:** the 5th letter of the Hebrew alphabet — see ALPHABET table

[1]head \ˈhed\ *n* [ME *hed,* fr. OE *hēafod;* akin to OHG *houbit* head, L *caput*] (bef. 12c) **1 :** the upper or anterior division of the body (as of a man or an insect) that contains the brain, the chief sense organs, and the mouth **2 a :** the seat of the intellect **:** MIND ⟨two ~*s* are better than one⟩ **b :** natural aptitude or talent ⟨a good ~ for figures⟩ **c :** mental or emotional control **:** POISE ⟨a level ~⟩ **d :** HEADACHE **3 :** the obverse of a coin — usu. used in pl. ⟨~*s,* I win⟩ **4 a :** PERSON, INDIVIDUAL ⟨count ~*s*⟩ **b** *pl* **head :** one of a number (as of domestic animals) **5 a :** the end that is upper or higher or opposite the foot ⟨the ~ of the table⟩ ⟨~ of a sail⟩ **b :** the source of a stream **c :** either end of something (as a drum) whose two ends need not be distinguished **d :** a horizontal passage in a coal mine **6 :** DIRECTOR, LEADER: as **a :** HEADMASTER **b :** one in charge of a division or department in an office or institution ⟨the ~ of the English department⟩ **7 a :** CAPITULUM 2 **b :** the foliaged part of a plant esp. when consisting of a compact mass of leaves or close fructification **8 a :** the leading element of a military column or a procession **b :** HEADWAY **9 a :** the uppermost extremity or projecting part of an object **:** TOP **b :** the striking part of a weapon, tool, or implement **c :** the rounded proximal end of a long bone (as the humerus) **d :** the end of a muscle nearest the origin — compare ORIGIN **e :** the oval part of a printed musical note **10 a :** a body of water kept in reserve at a height; *also* **:** the containing bank, dam, or wall **b :** a mass of water in motion **11 a :** the difference in elevation between two points in a body of fluid **b :** the resulting pressure of the fluid at the lower point expressible as this height; *broadly* **:** pressure of a fluid **12 a :** the bow and adjacent parts of a ship **b :** a ship's toilet; *broadly* **:** TOILET **13 :** the approximate length of the head of a horse ⟨won by a ~⟩ **14 :** the place of leadership, honor, or command ⟨at the ~ of his class⟩ **15 a** (1) **:** a word or series of words often in larger letters placed at the beginning of a passage or at the top of a page in order to introduce or categorize (2) **:** a separate part or topic **b :** a portion of a page or sheet that is above the first line of printing **16 :** the foam or scum that rises on a fermenting or effervescing liquid (as beer) **17 a :** the part of a boil, pimple, or abscess at which it is likely to break **b :** culminating point of action **:** CRISIS ⟨events came to a ~⟩ **18 a :** a part or attachment of a machine or machine tool containing a device (as a cutter or drill); *also* **:** the part of an apparatus that performs the chief function or a particular function **b :** MAGNETIC HEAD **19 :** an immediate constituent of a construction that has the same grammatical function as the whole (as *man* in "an old man", "a very old man", or "the man in the street") **20 a :** one who uses a drug (as LSD or marijuana) **b :** DEVOTEE ⟨chili ~*s*⟩ — **by the head :** drawing the greater depth of water forward — **off one's head :** CRAZY, DISTRACTED — **out of one's head :** DELIRIOUS — **over one's head 1 :** beyond one's comprehension or the point of being competent ⟨liked pictures but art criticism was *over his head*⟩ **2 :** so as to pass over one's superior standing or authority ⟨went *over his* supervisor's *head* to complain⟩

[2]head *adj* (bef. 12c) **1 :** of, relating to, or intended for the head **2 :** PRINCIPAL, CHIEF ⟨~ cook⟩ **3 :** situated at the head **4 :** coming from in front ⟨~ sea⟩

[3]head *vt* (14c) **1 :** BEHEAD **2 a :** to cut back the upper or terminal growth of (a plant or plant part) — often used with *back* **b :** to harvest (a cereal grass) by cutting off the heads **3 a :** to put a head on **:** fit a head to ⟨~ an arrow⟩ **b :** to form the head or top of ⟨tower ~*ed* by a spire⟩ **4 :** to act as leader or head to ⟨~ a revolt⟩ **5 a :** to

\ə\ abut \ᵊ\ kitten, F table \ər\ further \a\ ash \ā\ ace \ä\ cot, cart \au̇\ out \ch\ chin \e\ bet \ē\ easy \g\ go \i\ hit \ī\ ice \j\ job \ŋ\ sing \ō\ go \ȯ\ law \ȯi\ boy \th\ thin \t͟h\ the \ü\ loot \u̇\ foot \y\ yet \zh\ vision \à, k̲, ⁿ, œ, œ̄, ue, ue̅, ʸ\ *see* Guide to Pronunciation

face or oppose head-on ⟨~ the waves⟩ **b :** to get in front of so as to hinder, stop, or turn back **c :** to take a lead over (as in a race) : SURPASS **d :** to pass (a stream) by going round above the source **6 a :** to put something at the head of (as a list) **b :** to stand as the first or leading member of ⟨~*s* the list of heroes⟩ **7 :** to set the course of ⟨~ a ship northward⟩ **8 :** to drive (as a soccer ball) with the head **~ *vi* 1 :** to form a head ⟨this cabbage ~*s* early⟩ **2 :** to point or proceed in a certain direction ⟨the fleet was ~*ing* out⟩ **3 :** to have a source : ORIGINATE

head·ache \'hed-,āk\ *n* (bef. 12c) **1 :** pain in the head **2 :** a vexatious or baffling situation or problem — **head·achy** \-,ā-kē\ *adj*

head and shoulders *adv* (1581) **:** beyond comparison : by far ⟨stood *head and shoulders* above the rest in character and ability⟩

head·band \'hed-,band\ *n* (1535) **1 :** a band worn on or around the head **2 :** a narrow strip of cloth sewn or glued by hand to a book at the extreme ends of the backbone

head·board \-,bō(ə)rd, -,bȯ(ə)rd\ *n* (1730) **:** a board forming the head (as of a bed)

head·cheese \-,chēz\ *n* (1841) **:** a jellied loaf or sausage made from edible parts of the head, feet, and sometimes the tongue and heart esp. of a pig

head cold *n* (1937) **:** a common cold centered in the nasal passages and adjacent mucous tissues

head·dress \'hed-,dres\ *n* (1703) **:** an often elaborate covering for the head

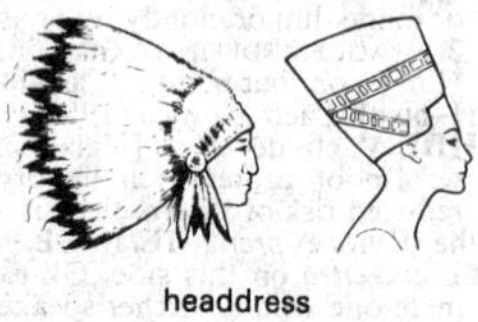

headdress

head·ed \'hed-əd\ *adj* (13c) **1 :** having a head or a heading **2 :** having a head or heads of a specified kind or number — used in combination ⟨became light-*headed* from the fever⟩ ⟨a round*headed* screw⟩

head·er \'hed-ər\ *n* (15c) **1 :** one that removes heads; *esp* **:** a grain-harvesting machine that cuts off the grain heads and elevates them to a wagon **2 a :** a brick or stone laid in a wall with its end toward the face of the wall **b :** a beam fitted at one side of an opening to support free ends of floor joists, studs, or rafters **c :** a horizontal structural or finish piece over an opening : LINTEL **d :** a conduit (as an exhaust pipe for a many-cylindered engine) into which a number of smaller conduits open **e :** a mounting plate through which electrical terminals pass from a sealed device (as a transistor) **3 :** a fall or dive headfirst **4 :** a shot or pass in soccer made by heading the ball

head·first \'hed-'fərst\ *adv* (ca. 1828) **:** with the head foremost : HEADLONG ⟨dove ~ into the waves⟩ — **headfirst** *adj*

head·fore·most \-'fō(ə)r-,mōst, -'fȯ(ə)r-\ *adv* (1697) **:** HEADFIRST, HEADLONG

head·gate \'hed-,gāt\ *n* (1832) **:** a gate for controlling the water flowing into a channel (as an irrigation ditch)

head·gear \-,gi(ə)r\ *n* (15c) **1 :** a covering or protective device for the head **2 :** a harness for a horse's head

head·hunt·er \-,hənt-ər\ *n* (1853) **1 :** one that engages in head-hunting **2 :** a recruiter of personnel esp. at the executive level

head–hunt·ing \-,hənt-iŋ\ *n* (1853) **1 :** the act or custom of seeking out, decapitating, and preserving the heads of enemies as trophies **2 :** a seeking to deprive usu. political enemies of position or influence

head·ing \'hed-iŋ\ *n* (1935) **1 :** the compass direction in which the longitudinal axis of a ship or aircraft points; *broadly* **:** DIRECTION **2 a :** something that forms or serves as a head; *esp* **:** an inscription, headline, or title standing at the top or beginning (as of a letter or chapter) **b :** the address and date at the beginning of a letter showing its place and time of origin **3 :** DRIFT 6

head·lamp \-,lamp\ *n* (1885) **:** HEADLIGHT

head·land \'hed-lənd, -,land\ *n* (bef. 12c) **1 :** unplowed land at the ends of furrows or near a fence **2 :** a point of usu. high land jutting out into a body of water : PROMONTORY

head·less \-ləs\ *adj* (bef. 12c) **1 a :** having no head **b :** having the head cut off : BEHEADED **2 :** having no chief **3 :** lacking good sense or prudence : FOOLISH — **head·less·ness** *n*

head·light \-,līt\ *n* (1861) **1 :** a light with a reflector and special lens mounted on the front of an automotive vehicle to illuminate the road ahead; *also* **:** the beam cast by a headlight **2 :** a light worn on the forehead (as of a miner or physician)

¹head·line \-,līn\ *n* (1824) **1 a :** a head of a newspaper story or article usu. printed in large type and giving the gist of the story or article that follows **b** *pl* **:** front-page news ⟨the scandal made ~*s*⟩ **2 :** words set at the head of a passage or page to introduce or categorize

²headline *vt* (1891) **1 :** to provide with a headline **2 :** to publicize highly **3 :** to be engaged as a leading performer in (a show)

head·lin·er \'hed-,lī-nər\ *n* (1891) **1 :** the principal performer in a show : STAR; *broadly* **:** PERSONALITY 4b **2 :** fabric covering the inside of the roof of an automobile

head linesman *n* (ca. 1949) **:** a football linesman

head·lock \'hed-,läk\ *n* (1905) **:** a hold in which a wrestler encircles his opponent's head with one arm

¹head·long \-'lȯŋ\ *adv* [ME *hedlong,* alter. of *hedling,* fr. *hed* head] (14c) **1 :** HEADFIRST **2 :** without deliberation : RECKLESSLY **3 :** without pause or delay

²head·long \-,lȯŋ\ *adj* (1566) **1 :** lacking in calmness or restraint : PRECIPITATE ⟨releasing the ~ torrent of her emotion in tears⟩ **2 :** plunging headforemost **3** *archaic* **:** STEEP, PRECIPITOUS ***syn*** see PRECIPITATE

head louse *n* (1861) **:** one of a variety (*Pediculus humanus capitis*) of the common louse that lives on the scalp of man

head·man *n* (bef. 12c) **1 a** \'hed-'man\ **:** FOREMAN, OVERSEER **b** \-'man, -,man\ **:** a lesser chief of a primitive community **2** \-mən\ **:** HEADSMAN

head·mas·ter \'hed-,mas-tər, -'mas-\ *n* (1576) **:** a man heading the staff of a private school : PRINCIPAL — **head·mas·ter·ship** \-,ship\ *n*

head·mis·tress \-,mis-trəs, -'mis-\ *n* (1872) **:** a woman heading the staff of a private school

head·most \'hed-,mōst\ *adj* (1628) **:** most advanced : LEADING

head·note \-,nōt\ *n* (1855) **1 :** a prefixed note of comment or explanation **2 :** a note prefixed to the report of a decided legal case

head off *vt* (1841) **:** to turn back or turn aside : BLOCK, PREVENT ⟨*head* them *off* at the pass⟩ ⟨attempts to *head off* the imminent crisis⟩

¹head–on \'hed-'ȯn, -'än\ *adv* (1840) **1 :** with the head or front making the initial contact ⟨the cars collided ~⟩ **2 :** in direct opposition, confrontation, or contradiction ⟨met the problem ~⟩

²head–on *adj* (1903) **1 :** having the front facing in the direction of initial contact or line of sight ⟨a ~ collision⟩ **2 :** FRONTAL

head over heels *adv* (1770) **1 a :** in or as if in a somersault : HELTER-SKELTER **b :** UPSIDE DOWN **2 :** very much : DEEPLY ⟨*head over heels* in love⟩

head·phone \'hed-,fōn\ *n* (1914) **:** an earphone held over the ear by a band worn on the head

head·piece \-,pēs\ *n* (1535) **1 :** a protective or defensive covering for the head **2 :** BRAINS, INTELLIGENCE **3 :** an ornament esp. at the beginning of a chapter

head·pin \-,pin\ *n* (ca. 1934) **:** a bowling pin that stands foremost in the arrangement of pins

head·quar·ter \'hed-,kwȯ(r)t-ər, (')hed-'\ *vt* (1903) **:** to place in headquarters **~ *vi* :** to make one's headquarters

head·quar·ters \-ərz\ *n pl but sing or pl in constr* (1647) **1 :** a place from which a commander performs the functions of command **2 :** the administrative center of an enterprise

head·rest \-,rest\ *n* (1853) **1 :** a support for the head **2 :** a resilient pad at the top of the back of an automobile seat esp. for preventing whiplash injury

head rhyme *n* (ca. 1943) **:** ALLITERATION

head·room \'hed-,rüm, -,rům\ *n* (1851) **:** vertical space in which to stand, sit, or move

head·sail \-,sāl, -səl\ *n* (1627) **:** a sail set forward of the foremast

head·set \-,set\ *n* (1921) **1 :** an attachment for holding an earphone and transmitter at one's head **2 :** a pair of headphones

head·ship \-,ship\ *n* (1582) **:** the position, office, or dignity of a head

head shop *n* (1968) **:** a shop specializing in articles (as hashish pipes and roach clips) of interest to drug users

head·shrink·er \-,shriŋ-kər, *esp Southern* -,sriŋ-\ *n* (1926) **1 :** a headhunter who shrinks the heads of his victims **2 :** a physician who specializes in psychiatry and esp. psychoanalysis

heads·man \'hedz-mən\ *n* (1601) **:** one that beheads : EXECUTIONER

head·space \'hed-,spās\ *n* (1936) **:** the volume above a liquid or solid in a closed container

head·spring \'hed-,spriŋ\ *n* (14c) **:** FOUNTAINHEAD, SOURCE

head·stall \-,stȯl\ *n* (14c) **:** a part of a bridle or halter that encircles the head

head·stand \-,stand\ *n* (ca. 1934) **:** the gymnastic feat of standing on one's head usu. with support from the hands

head start *n* (1886) **1 :** an advantage granted or achieved at the beginning of a race, a chase, or a competition ⟨a 10-minute *head start*⟩ **2 :** a favorable or promising beginning

head·stock \'hed-,stäk\ *n* (1731) **:** a bearing or pedestal for a revolving or moving part; *specif* **:** a part of a lathe that holds the revolving spindle and its attachments

head·stone \-,stōn\ *n* (1775) **:** a memorial stone placed at the head of a grave

head·stream \-,strēm\ *n* (14c) **:** a stream that is the source of a river

head·strong \-,strȯŋ\ *adj* (14c) **1 :** not easily restrained : impatient of control, advice, or suggestions **2 :** directed by ungovernable will ⟨violent ~ actions⟩ ***syn*** see UNRULY

heads–up \,hed-,zəp\ *adj* (1947) **:** ALERT, RESOURCEFUL ⟨fast, aggressive, ~ football⟩

heads up \(')hed-'zəp\ *interj* (ca. 1941) — used as a warning to look out for danger esp. overhead or to clear a passageway

head–to–head *adv or adj* (ca. 1728) **:** in a direct confrontation or encounter usu. between individuals

head·wait·er \'hed-'wāt-ər\ *n* (1805) **:** the head of the dining-room staff of a restaurant or hotel

head·wa·ter \-,wȯt-ər, -,wät-\ *n* (1802) **:** the source of a stream — usu. used in pl.

head·way \-,wā\ *n* (1748) **1 a :** motion or rate of motion in a forward direction **b :** ADVANCE, PROGRESS **2 :** headroom (as under an arch) sufficient to allow passage **3 :** the time interval between two vehicles traveling in the same direction on the same route

head wind *n* (1790) **:** a wind blowing in a direction opposite to a course esp. of a ship or aircraft

head·word \'hed-,wərd\ *n* (1823) **1 :** a word or term placed at the beginning (as of a chapter or an entry in an encyclopedia) **2 :** HEAD 19

head·work \-,wərk\ *n* (1792) **:** mental labor; *esp* **:** clever thinking

heady \'hed-ē\ *adj* **head·i·er; -est** (14c) **1 a :** WILLFUL, RASH ⟨~ opinions⟩ **b :** VIOLENT, IMPETUOUS **2 a :** tending to intoxicate or make giddy ⟨~ wine⟩ ⟨being in such distinguished company was a ~ experience⟩ **b :** GIDDY, EXHILARATED ⟨~ with his success⟩ **c :** RICH ⟨a ~ sauce⟩ ⟨a ~ variety⟩ **d :** IMPRESSIVE ⟨a man of ~ accomplishments⟩ **3 :** marked by or showing good judgment : SHREWD; *also* **:** INTELLECTUAL — **head·i·ly** \'hed-ᵊl-ē\ *adv* — **head·i·ness** \'hed-ē-nəs\ *n*

heal \'hē(ə)l\ *vb* [ME *helen,* fr. OE *hǣlan;* akin to OHG *heilen* to heal, OE *hāl* whole — more at WHOLE] *vt* (bef. 12c) **1 a :** to make sound or whole ⟨~ a wound⟩ **b :** to restore to health **2 a :** to cause (an undesirable condition) to be overcome : MEND ⟨the troubles . . . had not been forgotten, but they had been ~*ed* — William Power⟩ **b :** to patch up (a breach or division) ⟨~ a breach between friends⟩ **3 :** to restore to original purity or integrity ⟨~*ed* of sin⟩ **~ *vi* :** to return to a sound state ***syn*** see CURE

heal·er \'hē-lər\ *n* (bef. 12c) **1 :** one that heals **2 :** a Christian Science practitioner

health \'helth *also* 'heltth\ *n, often attrib* [ME *helthe,* fr. OE *hǣlth,* fr. *hāl*] (bef. 12c) **1 a :** the condition of being sound in body, mind, or spirit; *esp* **:** freedom from physical disease or pain **b :** the general condition of the body ⟨in poor ~⟩ ⟨enjoys good ~⟩ **2 :** flourishing condition : WELL-BEING ⟨the economic ~ of a country⟩ **3 :** a toast to someone's health or prosperity

health food *n* (1882) **:** a food promoted as highly conducive to health

health·ful \'helth-fəl *also* 'heltth-\ *adj* (14c) **1 :** beneficial to health of body or mind **2 :** HEALTHY ⟨he felt incapable of looking into the girl's pretty, ~ face —Saul Bellow⟩ — **health·ful·ness** *n* *syn* HEALTHFUL, WHOLESOME, SALUBRIOUS, SALUTARY mean favorable to the health of mind or body. HEALTHFUL implies a positive contribution to a healthy condition ⟨a *healthful* diet⟩ WHOLESOME applies to what benefits, builds up, or sustains physically, mentally, or spiritually ⟨*wholesome* foods⟩ ⟨the movie is *wholesome* family entertainment⟩ SALUBRIOUS applies chiefly to the helpful effects of climate or air; SALUTARY describes something corrective or beneficially effective, even though it may in itself be unpleasant ⟨a *salutary* warning that resulted in increased production⟩

health insurance *n* (1901) **:** insurance against loss through illness of the insured; *esp* **:** insurance providing compensation for medical expenses

health maintenance organization *n* (ca. 1971) **:** an organization that provides health care to voluntarily enrolled individuals and families in a particular geographic area by member physicians with limited referral to outside specialists and that is financed by fixed periodic payments determined in advance — called also *HMO*

healthy \ˈhel-thē *also* ˈhelt-\ *adj* **health·i·er; -est** (1552) **1 :** enjoying health and vigor of body, mind, or spirit **:** WELL **2 :** evincing health ⟨a ∼ complexion⟩ **3 :** conducive to health ⟨walk three miles every day . . . a beastly bore, but ∼ — G. S. Patton⟩ **4 a :** PROSPEROUS, FLOURISHING **b :** not small or feeble **:** CONSIDERABLE — **health·i·ly** \-thə-lē\ *adv* — **health·i·ness** \-thē-nəs\ *n*

syn HEALTHY, SOUND, WHOLESOME, ROBUST, HALE, WELL mean enjoying or indicative of good health. HEALTHY implies full strength and vigor as well as freedom from signs of disease; SOUND emphasizes the absence of disease, weakness, or malfunction; WHOLESOME implies appearance and behavior indicating soundness and balance; ROBUST implies the opposite of all that is delicate or sickly; HALE applies particularly to robustness in old age; WELL implies merely freedom from disease or illness.

1**heap** \ˈhēp\ *n* [ME *heep,* fr. OE *hēap;* akin to OE *hēah* high] (bef. 12c) **1 :** a collection of things thrown one on another **:** PILE **2 :** a great number or large quantity **:** LOT

2**heap** *vt* (bef. 12c) **1 a :** to throw or lay in a heap **:** pile or collect in great quantity ⟨his sole object was to ∼ up riches⟩ **b :** to form or round into a heap ⟨∼*ed* the dirt into a mound⟩ **2 :** to accord or bestow lavishly or in large quantities ⟨∼*ed* the plates with food⟩ ⟨∼*ed* honors upon them⟩

hear \ˈhi(ə)r\ *vb* **heard** \ˈhərd\; **hear·ing** \ˈhi(ə)r-iŋ\ [ME *heren,* fr. OE *hīeran;* akin to OHG *hōren* to hear, L *cavēre* to be on guard, Gk *akouein* to hear] *vt* (bef. 12c) **1 :** to perceive or apprehend by the ear **2 :** to gain knowledge of by hearing **3 a :** to listen to with attention **:** HEED **b :** ATTEND ⟨∼ mass⟩ **4 a :** to give a legal hearing to **b :** to take testimony from ⟨∼ witnesses⟩ ∼ *vi* **1 :** to have the capacity of apprehending sound **2 a :** to gain information **:** LEARN **b :** to receive communication ⟨haven't *heard* from her lately⟩ **3 :** to entertain the idea — used in the negative ⟨wouldn't ∼ of it⟩ **4** — often used in the expression *Hear! Hear!* to express approval (as during a speech) — **hear·er** \ˈhir-ər\ *n*

hear·ing *n* (13c) **1 a :** the process, function, or power of perceiving sound; *specif* **:** the special sense by which noises and tones are received as stimuli **b :** EARSHOT **2 a :** opportunity to be heard, to present one's side of a case, or to be generally known or appreciated **b (1) :** a listening to arguments **(2) :** a preliminary examination in criminal procedure **c :** a session (as of a legislative committee) in which witnesses are heard and testimony is taken **3** *chiefly dial* **:** a piece of news **:** RUMOR

hearing aid *n* (1922) **:** an electronic device usu. worn by a person for amplifying sound before it reaches the receptor organs

hear·ken \ˈhär-kən\ *vb* **hear·kened; hear·ken·ing** \ˈhärk-(ə-)niŋ\ [ME *herknen,* fr. OE *heorcnian;* akin to OHG *hōrechen* to listen — more at HARK] *vi* (bef. 12c) **1 :** LISTEN **2 :** to give respectful attention ∼ *vt, archaic* **:** to give heed to **:** HEAR

hear·say \ˈhi(ə)r-ˌsā\ *n* (1532) **:** RUMOR

hearsay evidence *n* (1753) **:** evidence based not on a witness's personal knowledge but on matters told him by another

1**hearse** \ˈhərs\ *n* [ME *herse,* fr. MF *herce* harrow, frame for holding candles, fr. L *hirpic-, hirpex* harrow] (15c) **1 a :** a triangular candelabrum for 15 candles used esp. at Tenebrae **b :** an elaborate framework erected over a coffin or tomb to which memorial verses or epitaphs are attached **2 a** *archaic* **:** COFFIN **b** *obs* **:** BIER 2 **3 :** a vehicle for conveying the dead to the grave

2**hearse** *vt* **hearsed; hears·ing** (1592) **1 a** *archaic* **:** to place on or in a hearse **b :** to convey in a hearse **2 :** BURY

1**heart** \ˈhärt\ *n* [ME *hert,* fr. OE *heorte;* akin to OHG *herza* heart, L *cord-, cor,* Gk *kardia*] (bef. 12c) **1 a :** a hollow muscular organ of vertebrate animals that by its rhythmic contraction acts as a force pump maintaining the circulation of the blood **b :** a structure in an invertebrate animal functionally analogous to the vertebrate heart **c :** BREAST, BOSOM **d :** something resembling a heart in shape; *specif* **:** a conventionalized representation of a heart **2 a :** a playing card marked with a conventionalized figure of a heart **b** *pl* **:** the suit comprising cards so marked **c** *pl but sing in constr* **:** a game in which the object is to avoid taking tricks containing hearts **3 a :** PERSONALITY, DISPOSITION ⟨a cold ∼⟩ **b** *obs* **:** INTELLECT **4 :** the emotional or moral as distinguished from the intellectual nature: as **a :** generous disposition **:** COMPASSION ⟨a leader with ∼⟩ **b :** LOVE, AFFECTIONS ⟨won her ∼⟩ **c :** COURAGE, ARDOR ⟨never lost ∼⟩ **5 :** one's innermost character, feelings, or inclinations ⟨knew it in his ∼⟩ ⟨a man after my own ∼⟩ **6 a :** the central or innermost part **:** CENTER **b :** the essential or most vital part of something **c :** the younger central compact part of a leafy rosette (as a head of lettuce) — **at heart :** in essence **:** BASICALLY, ESSENTIALLY — **by heart :** by rote or from memory — **to heart :** with deep concern

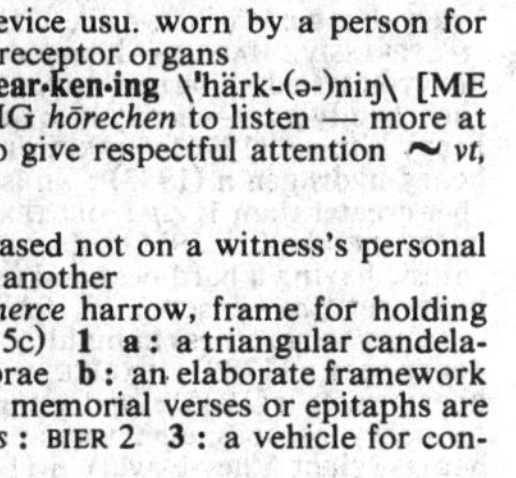

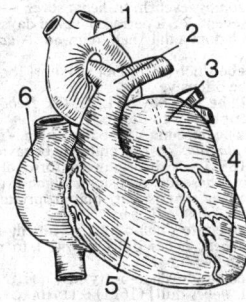

heart 1a: *1* aorta, *2* pulmonary artery, *3* left atrium, *4* left ventricle, *5* right ventricle, *6* right atrium

2**heart** *vt* (bef. 12c) **1** *archaic* **:** HEARTEN **2** *archaic* **:** to fix in the heart

heart·ache \ˈhärt-ˌāk\ *n* (1602) **:** anguish of mind **:** SORROW

heart attack *n* (1928) **:** an acute episode of heart disease (as myocardial infarction) due to insufficient blood supply to the heart muscle itself esp. when caused by a coronary thrombosis or a coronary occlusion

heart·beat \ˈhärt-ˌbēt\ *n* (1850) **1 :** one complete pulsation of the heart **2 :** the vital center or driving impulse

heart block *n* (1903) **:** incoordination of the heartbeat in which the atria and ventricles beat independently and which is marked by decreased cardiac output

heart·break \ˈhärt-ˌbrāk\ *n* (14c) **:** crushing grief

heart·break·er \-ˌbrā-kər\ *n* (1863) **:** one that causes heartbreak

heart·break·ing \-ˌbrā-kiŋ\ *adj* (1599) **1 a :** causing intense sorrow or distress **b :** extremely trying or difficult **2 :** producing an intense emotional reaction or response ⟨∼ beauty⟩ — **heart·break·ing·ly** \-kiŋ-lē\ *adv*

heart·bro·ken \-ˌbrō-kən\ *adj* (1586) **:** overcome by sorrow

heart·burn \-ˌbərn\ *n* (1597) **:** a burning discomfort behind the lower part of the sternum usu. related to spasm of the lower end of the esophagus or of the upper part of the stomach

heart·burn·ing \-ˌbər-niŋ\ *n* (1513) **:** intense or rancorous jealousy or resentment

heart disease *n* (1864) **:** an abnormal organic condition of the heart or of the heart and circulation

heart·ed \ˈhärt-əd\ *adj* (13c) **1 :** having a heart esp. of a specified kind — usu. used in combination ⟨a faint-*hearted* leader⟩ ⟨a light*hearted* wanderer⟩ **2 :** seated in the heart

heart·en \ˈhärt-ᵊn\ *vt* **heart·ened; heart·en·ing** \ˈhärt-niŋ, -ᵊn-iŋ\ (13c) **:** to give heart to **:** ENCOURAGE — **heart·en·ing·ly** \-niŋ-lē, -ᵊn-iŋ-\ *adv*

heart failure *n* (1894) **1 :** a condition in which the heart is unable to pump blood at an adequate rate or in adequate volume **2 :** cessation of heartbeat **:** DEATH

heart·felt \ˈhärt-ˌfelt\ *adj* (1734) **:** deeply felt **:** EARNEST *syn* see SINCERE

heart–free \ˈhärt -ˌfrē\ *adj* (1748) **:** not in love

hearth \ˈhärth\ *n* [ME *herth,* fr. OE *heorth;* akin to OHG *herd* hearth, Skt *kūdayāti* he singes] (bef. 12c) **1 a :** a brick, stone, or cement area in front of a fireplace **b :** the floor of a fireplace **c (1) :** the lowest section of a blast furnace **(2) :** the bottom of a refinery, reverberatory, or open-hearth furnace on which the ore or metal is exposed to the flame **(3) :** the inside bottom of a foundry cupola **2 :** HOME **3 :** a vital or creative center ⟨the central ∼ of occidental civilization —A. L. Kroeber⟩

hearth·stone \-ˌstōn\ *n* (14c) **1 a :** stone forming a hearth **b :** HOME **2 :** a soft stone or composition of powdered stone and pipe clay used to whiten or scour hearths and doorsteps

heart·i·ly \ˈhärt-ᵊl-ē\ *adv* (13c) **1 :** in a hearty manner **2 a :** with all sincerity **:** WHOLEHEARTEDLY **b :** with zest or gusto **3 :** WHOLLY, THOROUGHLY ⟨∼ sick of all this talk⟩

heart·land \ˈhärt-ˌland\ *n* (1904) **:** a central and vital area; *esp* **:** a central land area (as northern Eurasia) held by geopoliticians to have strategic advantages for mastery of the world

heart·less \-ləs\ *adj* (14c) **1** *archaic* **:** SPIRITLESS **2 :** lacking feeling **:** CRUEL — **heart·less·ly** *adv* — **heart·less·ness** *n*

heart–lung machine *n* (1953) **:** a mechanical pump that maintains circulation during heart surgery by shunting blood away from the heart, oxygenating it, and returning it to the body

heart·rend·ing \ˈhärt-ˌren-diŋ\ *adj* (1687) **:** HEARTBREAKING la — **heart·rend·ing·ly** \-diŋ-lē\ *adv*

hearts·ease \ˈhärt-ˌsēz\ *n* (15c) **1 :** peace of mind **:** TRANQUILLITY **2 :** any of various violas; *esp* **:** JOHNNY-JUMP-UP

heart·sick \ˈhärt-ˌsik\ *adj* (1526) **:** very despondent **:** DEPRESSED — **heart·sick·ness** *n*

heart·some \ˈhert-səm\ *adj, chiefly Scot* (1596) **:** giving spirit or vigor **:** ANIMATING, ENLIVENING — **heart·some·ly** *adv, chiefly Scot*

heart·sore \ˈhärt-ˌsō(ə)r, -ˌsȯ(ə)r\ *adj* (1591) **:** HEARTSICK

heart·string \-ˌstriŋ\ *n* (15c) **1** *obs* **:** a nerve once believed to sustain the heart **2 :** the deepest emotions or affections ⟨pulled at his ∼*s*⟩

heart·throb \-ˌthräb\ *n* (1839) **1 :** the throb of a heart **2 a :** sentimental emotion **:** PASSION **b :** SWEETHEART

heart–to–heart \ˌhärt-tə-ˌhärt\ *adj* (1867) **:** SINCERE, FRANK ⟨a ∼ talk⟩

heart·warm·ing \ˈhärt-ˌwȯr-miŋ\ *adj* (1899) **:** inspiring sympathetic feeling **:** CHEERING — **heart–warm·er** *n*

heart–whole \-ˌhōl\ *adj* (1600) **1 :** HEART-FREE **2 :** SINCERE, GENUINE

heart·wood \-ˌwu̇d\ *n* (15c) **:** the older harder nonliving central portion of wood that is usu. darker, denser, less permeable, and more durable than the surrounding sapwood

heart·worm \-ˌwərm\ *n* (1888) **:** a filarial worm (*Dirofilaria immitis*) that is a parasite esp. in the right heart of dogs and is transmitted by mosquitoes; *also* **:** infestation or disease caused by the heartworm

1**hearty** \ˈhärt-ē\ *adj* **heart·i·er; -est** (14c) **1 a :** giving unqualified support **:** THOROUGHGOING **b :** enthusiastically or exuberantly cordial **:** JOVIAL **c :** expressed unrestrainedly **2 a :** exhibiting vigorous good health **b :** ABUNDANT ⟨a ∼ meal⟩ **c :** NOURISHING ⟨a ∼ beef stew⟩ **3 :** VIGOROUS, VEHEMENT *syn* see SINCERE — **heart·i·ness** *n*

2**hearty** *n, pl* **heart·ies** (1803) **:** a bold brave fellow **:** COMRADE; *also* **:** SAILOR

1**heat** \ˈhēt\ *vb* [ME *heten,* fr. OE *hǣtan;* akin to OE *hāt* hot] *vi* (bef. 12c) **1 :** to become warm or hot **2 :** to become hot and start to spoil ∼ *vt* **1 :** to make warm or hot **2 :** EXCITE — **heat·able** \-ə-bəl\ *adj*

2**heat** *n* [ME *hete,* fr. OE *hǣte, hǣtu;* akin to OE *hāt* hot] (bef. 12c) **1 a (1) :** a condition of being hot **:** WARMTH **(2) :** a marked or notable degree of hotness **b :** pathological excessive bodily temperature **c :** a hot place or situation **d (1) :** a period of heat **(2) :** a single com-

plete operation of heating; *also* : the quantity of material so heated **e** (1) : added energy that causes substances to rise in temperature, fuse, evaporate, expand, or undergo any of various other related changes, that flows to a body by contact with or radiation from bodies at higher temperatures, and that can be produced in a body (as by compression) (2) : the energy associated with the random motions of the molecules, atoms, or smaller structural units of which matter is composed **f** : appearance, condition, or color of a body as indicating its temperature **g** : one of a series of intensities of heating **2 a** : intensity of feeling or reaction : PASSION **b** : the height or stress of an action or condition ⟨in the ~ of battle⟩ **c** : sexual excitement esp. in a female mammal; *specif* : ESTRUS **3** : pungency of flavor **4** : a single continuous effort: as **a** : a single round of a contest (as a race) having two or more rounds for each contestant **b** : one of several preliminary contests held to eliminate less competent contenders **5 a** *slang* (1) : the intensification of law-enforcement activity or investigation (2) : POLICE **b** : PRESSURE, COERCION **c** : ABUSE, CRITICISM ⟨took a lot of ~ for his beliefs⟩ — **heat·less** \'hēt-ləs\ *adj* — **heat·proof** \-'prüf\ *adj*

heat cramps *n pl* (1938) : a condition that is marked by sudden development of cramps in skeletal muscles and that results from prolonged work in high temperatures accompanied by profuse perspiration with loss of sodium chloride from the body

heat·ed \'hēt-əd\ *adj* (1593) : marked by anger ⟨a ~ argument⟩ — **heat·ed·ly** *adv*

heat engine *n* (ca. 1895) : a mechanism (as an internal-combustion engine) for converting heat energy into mechanical energy

heat·er \'hēt-ər\ *n* (1500) : one that heats; *esp* : a device that imparts heat or holds something to be heated

heat exchanger *n* (1902) : a device (as an automobile radiator) for transferring heat from one fluid to another without allowing them to mix

heat exhaustion *n* (1939) : a condition marked by weakness, nausea, dizziness, and profuse sweating that results from physical exertion in a hot environment — called also *heat prostration*; compare HEATSTROKE

heath \'hēth\ *n* [ME *heth*, fr. OE *hǣth*; akin to OHG *heida* heather, OW *coit* forest] (bef. 12c) **1 a** : any of a family (Ericaceae, the heath family) of shrubby dicotyledonous and often evergreen plants that thrive on open barren usu. acid and ill-drained soil; *esp* : an evergreen subshrub of either of two genera (*Erica* and *Calluna*) with whorls of needlelike leaves and clusters of small flowers **b** : any of various plants that resemble true heaths **2 a** : a tract of wasteland **b** : an extensive area of rather level open uncultivated land usu. with poor coarse soil, inferior drainage, and a surface rich in peat or peaty humus — **heath·less** \-ləs\ *adj* — **heath·like** \-,līk\ *adj* — **heathy** \'hē-thē\ *adj*

[1]**hea·then** \'hē-t͟hən\ *adj* [ME *hethen*, fr. OE *hǣthen*; akin to OHG *heidan* heathen] (bef. 12c) **1** : of or relating to heathens, their religions, or their customs **2** : STRANGE, UNCIVILIZED

[2]**heathen** *n, pl* **heathens** *or* **heathen** (bef. 12c) **1** : an unconverted member of a people or nation that does not acknowledge the God of the Bible **2** : an uncivilized or irreligious person — **hea·then·dom** \-dəm\ *n* — **hea·then·ism** \-t͟hə-,niz-əm\ *n* — **hea·then·ize** \-t͟hə-,nīz\ *vt*

hea·then·ish \'hē-t͟hə-nish\ *adj* (bef. 12c) : resembling or characteristic of heathens : BARBAROUS — **hea·then·ish·ly** *adv*

[1]**heath·er** \'heth-ər\ *n* [ME (northern) *hather*] (14c) : HEATH 1a; *esp* : a common heath (*Calluna vulgaris*) of northern and alpine regions that has small crowded sessile leaves and racemes of tiny usu. purplish pink flowers

[2]**heather** *adj* (1615) : HEATHERY

heath·ery \'heth-(ə-)rē\ *adj* (1535) **1** : of, relating to, or resembling heather **2** : having flecks of various colors ⟨a soft ~ tweed⟩

heath hen *n* (1644) : a now extinct grouse (*Tympanuchus cupido cupido*) of the northeastern U.S. — compare PRAIRIE CHICKEN

heat lightning *n* (1834) : vivid and extensive flashes of electric light without thunder seen near the horizon esp. at the close of a hot day and ascribed to far-off lightning reflected by high clouds

heat prostration *n* (1938) : HEAT EXHAUSTION

heat pump *n* (1894) : an apparatus for heating or cooling a building by transferring heat by mechanical means from or to a reservoir (as the ground, water, or air) outside the building

heat rash *n* (1887) : PRICKLY HEAT

heat shield *n* (1962) : a barrier of ablative material to protect a space capsule from heat on its reentry into the atmosphere

heat sink *n* (1936) : a substance or device for the absorption or dissipation of unwanted heat (as from a process or an electronic device)

heat·stroke \'hēt-,strōk\ *n* (1888) : a condition marked esp. by cessation of sweating, extremely high body temperature, and collapse that results from prolonged exposure to high temperature — compare HEAT EXHAUSTION

heat–treat \'hēt-,trēt\ *vt* (1907) : to subject to heat; *esp* : to treat (as metals) by heating and cooling in a way that will produce desired properties — **heat treater** *n* — **heat treatment** *n*

heat wave *n* (1878) : a period of unusually hot weather

[1]**heave** \'hēv\ *vb* **heaved** *or* **hove** \'hōv\; **heav·ing** [ME *heven*, fr. OE *hebban*; akin to OHG *hevan* to lift, L *capere* to take] *vt* (bef. 12c) **1** *obs* : ELEVATE **2** : to cause to be lifted upward or onward **3** : THROW, CAST **4** : to utter with obvious effort **5 a** : to cause to swell or rise **b** : to displace (as a rock stratum) esp. by a fault **6** : HAUL, DRAW ~ *vi* **1** : to rise or become thrown or raised up **2** : to strain to do something : LABOR **3 a** : to rise and fall rhythmically **b** : PANT **4** : RETCH **5 a** : PULL, PUSH **b** : to move a ship in a specified direction or manner **c** *of a ship* : to move in an indicated way **syn** see LIFT — **heav·er** *n* — **heave to** : to bring a ship to a stop

[2]**heave** *n* (1571) **1 a** : an effort to heave or raise **b** : HURL, CAST **2** : an upward motion : RISING; *esp* : a rhythmical rising **3** : the horizontal displacement by the faulting of a rock **4** *pl but sing or pl in constr* : chronic pulmonary emphysema of the horse resulting in difficult expiration, heaving of the flanks, and a persistent cough

heave–ho \'hēv-'hō\ *n* [fr. *heave ho!*, interjection used when heaving on a rope] (1944) : DISMISSAL ⟨gave him the old ~⟩

heav·en \'hev-ən\ *n* [ME *heven*, fr. OE *heofon*; perh. akin to OHG *himil* heaven] (bef. 12c) **1** : the expanse of space that seems to be over the earth like a dome : FIRMAMENT — usu. used in pl. **2 a** *often cap* : the dwelling place of the Deity and the joyful abode of the blessed dead **b** : a spiritual state of everlasting communion with God **3** *cap* : GOD 1 **4** : a place or condition of utmost happiness **5** *Christian Science* : a state of thought in which sin is absent and the harmony of divine Mind is manifest

heav·en·ly \-lē\ *adj* (bef. 12c) **1** : of or relating to heaven or the heavens : CELESTIAL ⟨the ~ choirs⟩ ⟨use a telescope to study the ~ bodies⟩ **2 a** : suggesting the blessed state of heaven : BEATIFIC ⟨~ peace⟩ **b** : DELIGHTFUL — **heav·en·li·ness** *n*

heav·en–sent \-,sent\ *adj* (1649) : PROVIDENTIAL

heav·en·ward \-wərd\ *adv or adj* (13c) : toward heaven

heav·en·wards \-wərdz\ *adv* (1650) : HEAVENWARD

heavier–than–air *adj* (1903) : having greater weight than displacement

heavi·ly \'hev-ə-lē\ *adv* (bef. 12c) **1** : in a heavy manner **2** : slowly and laboriously : DULLY **3** *archaic* : with sorrow : GRIEVOUSLY **4** : to a great degree : SEVERELY

[1]**heavy** \'hev-ē\ *adj* **heavi·er; -est** [ME *hevy*, fr. OE *hefig*; akin to OHG *hebic* heavy, OE *hebban* to lift — more at HEAVE] (bef. 12c) **1 a** : having great weight **b** : having a high specific gravity : having great weight in proportion to bulk **c** (1) *of an isotope* : having or being atoms of greater than normal mass (2) *of a compound* : containing heavy isotopes **2** : hard to bear; *specif* : GRIEVOUS, AFFLICTIVE ⟨a ~ sorrow⟩ **3** : of weighty import : SERIOUS **4** : DEEP, PROFOUND **5 a** : borne down by something oppressive : BURDENED **b** : PREGNANT; *esp* : approaching parturition **6 a** : slow or dull from loss of vitality or resiliency : SLUGGISH **b** : lacking sparkle or vivacity : DRAB **c** : lacking mirth or gaiety : DOLEFUL **d** : characterized by declining prices **7** : dulled with weariness : DROWSY **8** : greater in quantity or quality than the average of its kind or class: as **a** : of unusually large size or amount ⟨a ~ turnout⟩ ⟨~ traffic⟩ **b** : of great force ⟨~ seas⟩ **c** : OVERCAST **d** (1) : impeding motion (2) : full of clay and inclined to hold water **e** : coming as if from a depth : LOUD ⟨~ breathing⟩ **f** : THICK, COARSE **g** : OPPRESSIVE ⟨~ odor⟩ **h** : STEEP, ACUTE **i** : LABORIOUS, DIFFICULT ⟨~ going⟩ **j** : IMMODERATE ⟨a ~ smoker⟩ **k** : of large capacity or output **9 a** : digested with difficulty because of excessive richness or seasoning ⟨~ fruitcake⟩ **b** : not properly raised or leavened ⟨~ bread⟩ **10** : producing goods (as coal, steel, or chemicals) used in the production of other goods ⟨~ industry⟩ **11 a** : armed with guns of large caliber **b** : heavily armored **12 a** : having stress ⟨~ rhythm⟩ — used esp. of syllables in accentual verse **b** : being the strongest degree of stress in speech **13** : relating to theatrical parts of a grave or somber nature **14** : LONG 9 ⟨~ on ideas⟩ **15** : IMPORTANT, PROMINENT ⟨a ~ politician⟩ — **heavi·ness** *n*

syn HEAVY, WEIGHTY, PONDEROUS, CUMBROUS, CUMBERSOME mean having great weight. HEAVY implies that something has greater density or thickness than the average of its kind or class; WEIGHTY suggests having actual and not just relative weight; PONDEROUS implies having great weight because of size and massiveness with resulting great inertia; CUMBROUS and CUMBERSOME imply heaviness and bulkiness that make for difficulty in grasping, moving, carrying, or manipulating.

[2]**heavy** *adv* (bef. 12c) : in a heavy manner : HEAVILY

[3]**heavy** *n, pl* **heav·ies** (1841) **1** *pl* : heavy cavalry **2** : HEAVYWEIGHT 2 **3 a** : a theatrical role of a dignified or somber character; *also* : an actor playing such a role **b** : VILLAIN 4 **c** : someone or something influential, serious, or important

heavy chain *n* (1964) : either of the two larger of the four polypeptide chains comprising antibodies — compare LIGHT CHAIN

heavy–du·ty \,hev-ē-'d(y)üt-ē\ *adj* (1914) : able or designed to withstand unusual strain

heavy–foot·ed \-'fu̇t-əd\ *adj* (1625) : heavy and slow in movement

heavy–hand·ed \-'han-dəd\ *adj* (1647) **1** : CLUMSY, UNGRACEFUL **2** : OPPRESSIVE, HARSH — **heavy–hand·ed·ly** *adv* — **heavy–hand·ed·ness** *n*

heavy·heart·ed \-'härt-əd\ *adj* (15c) : DESPONDENT, SADDENED — **heavy·heart·ed·ly** *adv* — **heavy·heart·ed·ness** *n*

heavy hitter *n* (1976) : HEAVYWEIGHT 3

heavy hydrogen *n* (1933) : an isotope of hydrogen having a mass number greater than 1; *esp* : DEUTERIUM

heavy metal *n* (ca. 1975) : energetic and highly amplified electronic rock music having a hard beat and usu. an element of the fantastic

heavy·set \,hev-ē-'set\ *adj* (1922) : stocky and compact and sometimes tending to stoutness in build

heavy spar *n* (1789) : BARITE

heavy water *n* (1933) : water containing more than the usual proportion of heavy isotopes; *esp* : water enriched in deuterium

heavy·weight \'hev-ē-,wāt\ *n* (1857) **1** : one that is above average in weight **2** : one in the usu. heaviest class of contestants: as **a** : a boxer in an unlimited weight division — compare LIGHT HEAVYWEIGHT **b** : a weight lifter weighing more than 198 pounds **3** : BIG SHOT, HEAVY

heb·do·mad \'heb-də-,mad\ *n* [L *hebdomad-*, *hebdomas*, fr. Gk, fr. *hebdomos* seventh, fr. *hepta* seven — more at SEVEN] (1545) **1** : a group of seven **2** : a period of seven days : WEEK

heb·dom·a·dal \heb-'däm-əd-ᵊl\ *adj* (1646) : WEEKLY — **heb·dom·a·dal·ly** \-ᵊl-ē\ *adv*

hebe \'hēb\ *n, often cap* [short for *Hebrew*] (1932) : JEW — usu. taken to be offensive

He·be \'hē-bē\ *n* [L, fr. Gk *Hēbē*] : the Greek goddess of youth and a cupbearer to the gods

he·be·phre·nia \,hē-bə-'frē-nē-ə, -'fren-ē-\ *n* [NL, fr. Gk *hēbē* youth + E *-phrenia*; fr. the childish behavior which is often found with it] (ca. 1883) : a disorganized form of schizophrenia characterized esp. by incoherence, delusions which if present lack an underlying theme, and affect that is flat, inappropriate, or silly — **he·be·phre·nic** \-'fren-ik, -'frē-nik\ *adj or n*

heb·e·tate \'heb-ə-,tāt\ *vt* **-tat·ed; -tat·ing** [L *hebetatus*, pp. of *hebetare*, fr. *hebet-*, *hebes* dull] (1574) : to make dull or obtuse — **heb·e·ta·tion** \,heb-ə-'tā-shən\ *n*

heb·e·tude \'heb-ə-,t(y)üd\ *n* [LL *hebetudo*, fr. *hebēre* to be dull; akin to L *hebes* dull] (1621) : LETHARGY, DULLNESS — **heb·e·tu·di·nous** \,heb-ə-'t(y)üd-nəs, -ᵊn-əs\ *adj*

He·bra·ic \hi-'brā-ik\ *adj* [ME *Ebrayke*, fr. LL *Hebraicus*, fr. Gk *Hebraikos*, fr. *Hebraios*] (14c) : of, relating to, or characteristic of the Hebrews or their language or culture — **He·bra·i·cal·ly** \-'brā-ə-k(ə-)lē\ *adv*

He·bra·ism \'hē-(,)brā-,iz-əm\ *n* (1570) **1** : a characteristic feature of Hebrew occurring in another language **2** : the thought, spirit, or practice characteristic of the Hebrews **3** : a moral theory or emphasis attributed to the Hebrews

He·bra·ist \-ˌbrā-əst\ n (ca. 1755) : a specialist in Hebrew and Hebraic studies

He·bra·is·tic \ˌhē-brā-'is-tik\ adj (1690) 1 : HEBRAIC 2 : marked by Hebraisms

he·bra·ize \'hē-brā-ˌīz\ vb -ized; -iz·ing often cap, vi (1816) : to use Hebraisms ~ vt : to make Hebraic in character or form — he·bra·iza·tion \ˌhē-ˌbrā-ə-'zā-shən\ n, often cap

He·brew \'hē-(ˌ)brü\ n [ME Ebreu, fr. OF, fr. LL Hebraeus, fr. L, adj., fr. Gk Hebraios, fr. Aram 'Ebrai\ (13c) 1 a : the Semitic language of the ancient Hebrews b : any of various later forms of this language 2 : a member of or descendant from one of a group of northern Semitic peoples including the Israelites; esp : ISRAELITE — Hebrew adj

He·brews \-(ˌ)brüz\ n pl but sing in constr : a theological treatise addressed to early Christians and included as a book in the New Testament — see BIBLE table

Hec·ate \'hek-ət-ē, 'hek-ət\ n [L, fr. Gk Hekatē] : a Greek goddess associated esp. with the underworld, night, and witchcraft

hec·a·tomb \'hek-ə-ˌtōm\ n [L hecatombe, fr. Gk hekatombē, fr. hekaton hundred + bē; akin to Gk bous cow — more at HUNDRED, COW] (1592) 1 : an ancient Greek and Roman sacrifice of 100 oxen or cattle 2 : the sacrifice or slaughter of many victims

heck \'hek\ n [euphemism] (1887) : HELL 2a ⟨a ~ of a lot of money⟩

heck·le \'hek-əl\ vt heck·led; heck·ling \-(ə-)liŋ\ [ME hekelen to dress flax, scratch, fr. heckele hackle; akin to OHG hāko hook — more at HOOK] (1808) 1 : to harass and try to disconcert with questions, challenges, or gibes : BADGER — heck·ler \-(ə-)lər\ n

hect- or hecto- comb form [F, irreg. fr. Gk hekaton] : hundred ⟨hectograph⟩

hect·are \'hek-ˌta(ə)r, -ˌte(ə)r, -ˌtär\ n [F, fr. hect- + are ²are] (1810) — see METRIC SYSTEM table

hec·tic \'hek-tik\ adj [ME etyk, fr. MF etique, fr. LL hecticus, fr. Gk hektikos habitual, consumptive, fr. echein to have — more at SCHEME] (14c) 1 : of, relating to, or being a fluctuating but persistent fever (as in tuberculosis) 2 : having a hectic fever 3 : RED, FLUSHED 4 : filled with excitement or confusion ⟨the ~ days before Christmas⟩ — hec·ti·cal·ly \-ti-k(ə-)lē\ adv

hec·to·gram \'hek-tə-ˌgram\ n [F hectogramme, fr. hect- + gramme gram] (1810) — see METRIC SYSTEM table

hec·to·graph \-ˌgraf\ n [G hektograph, fr. hekto- hect- + -graph -graph] (1880) : a machine for making copies of a writing or drawing produced on a gelatin surface — hectograph vt — hec·to·graph·ic \ˌhek-tə-'graf-ik\ adj

hec·to·li·ter \'hek-tə-ˌlēt-ər\ n [F hectolitre, fr. hect- + litre liter] (1810) — see METRIC SYSTEM table

hec·to·me·ter \'hek-tə-ˌmēt-ər, hek-'täm-ət-ər\ n [F hectomètre, fr. hect- + mètre meter] (1810) — see METRIC SYSTEM table

¹hec·tor \'hek-tər\ n [L, fr. Gk Hektōr] 1 cap : a son of Priam, husband of Andromache, and Trojan champion slain by Achilles 2 : BULLY, BRAGGART

²hector vb hec·tored; hec·tor·ing \-t(ə-)riŋ\ vi (1660) : to play the bully : SWAGGER ~ vt : to intimidate or harass by bluster or personal pressure — hec·tor·ing·ly \-t(ə-)riŋ-lē\ adv

Hec·u·ba \'hek-yə-bə\ n [L, fr. Gk Hekabē] : the wife of Priam in Homer's Iliad

he'd \(ˌ)hēd, ēd\: he had : he would

hed·dle \'hed-ᵊl\ n [prob. alter. of ME helde, fr. OE hefeld; akin to ON hafald heddle, OE hebban to lift — more at HEAVE] (bef. 12c) : one of the sets of parallel cords or wires that with their mounting compose the harness used to guide warp threads in a loom

he·der \'kād-ər, 'ked-\ n [Yiddish kheyder, fr. Heb hedher room] (1882) : an elementary Jewish school in which children are taught to read the Pentateuch, the Prayer Book, and other books in Hebrew

¹hedge \'hej\ n [ME hegge, fr. OE hecg; akin to OE haga hedge, hawthorn, L colum sieve] (bef. 12c) 1 a : a fence or boundary formed by a dense row of shrubs or low trees b : BARRIER, LIMIT 2 : a means of protection or defense (as against financial loss) 3 : a calculatedly noncommittal or evasive statement

²hedge vb hedged; hedg·ing vt (14c) 1 : to enclose or protect with or as if with a hedge : ENCIRCLE 2 : to hem in or obstruct with or as if with a barrier : HINDER ⟨hedged about by special regulations and statutes — Sandi Rosenbloom⟩ 3 : to protect oneself from losing by a counterbalancing transaction ⟨~ a bet⟩ ~ vi 1 : to plant, form, or trim a hedge 2 : to evade the risk of commitment esp. by leaving open a way of retreat : TRIM 3 : to protect oneself financially: as a : to buy or sell commodity futures as a protection against loss due to price fluctuation b : to minimize the risk of a bet — hedg·er n — hedg·ing·ly \'hej-iŋ-lē\ adv

³hedge adj (14c) 1 : of, relating to, or designed for a hedge 2 : born, living, or made near or as if near hedges : ROADSIDE 3 : INFERIOR 3

hedge fund n (1967) : an investing group usu. in the form of a limited partnership that employs speculative techniques in the hope of obtaining large capital gains

hedge·hog \'hej-ˌhog, -ˌhäg\ n (15c) 1 a : any of a genus (Erinaceus) of Old World nocturnal insectivorous mammals having both hair and spines that they present outwardly by rolling themselves up b : any of several spiny mammals (as a porcupine) 2 a : a military defensive obstacle (as of barbed wire) b : a well-fortified military stronghold

hedge·hop \-ˌhäp\ vi [back-formation fr. hedgehopper] (1926) : to fly an airplane close to the ground and rise over obstacles as they appear — hedge·hop·per n

hedgehog 1a

hedge·pig \-ˌpig\ n (1605) : HEDGEHOG

hedge·row \-ˌrō\ n (bef. 12c) : a row of shrubs or trees enclosing or separating fields

he·don·ic \hi-'dän-ik\ adj (1656) 1 : of, relating to, or characterized by pleasure 2 : HEDONISTIC — he·don·i·cal·ly \-i-k(ə-)lē\ adv

he·don·ism \'hēd-ᵊn-ˌiz-əm\ n [Gk hēdonē pleasure; akin to Gk hēdys sweet — more at SWEET] (1856) 1 : the doctrine that pleasure or happiness is the sole or chief good in life 2 : a way of life based on or suggesting the principles of hedonism — he·do·nist \-ᵊn-əst\ n — he·do·nis·tic \ˌhēd-ᵊn-'is-tik\ adj — he·do·nis·ti·cal·ly \-ti-k(ə-)lē\ adv

-he·dral \'hē-drəl\ adj comb form [NL -hedron] : having (such) a surface or (such or so many) surfaces ⟨dihedral⟩

-he·dron \'hē-drən\ n comb form, pl -hedrons or -he·dra \-drə\ [NL, fr. Gk -edron, fr. hedra seat — more at SIT] : crystal or geometrical figure having a (specified) form or number of surfaces ⟨pentahedron⟩ ⟨trapezohedron⟩

hee-bie–jee·bies \ˌhē-bē-'jē-bēz\ n pl [coined by Billy DeBeck †1942 Am. cartoonist] (1923) : JITTERS, WILLIES

¹heed \'hēd\ vb [ME heeden, fr. OE hēdan; akin to OHG huota guard, OE hōd hood] vi (bef. 12c) : to pay attention ~ vt : to give consideration or attention to : MIND ⟨~ what he says⟩ ⟨~ the call⟩

²heed n (14c) : ATTENTION, NOTICE

heed·ful \'hēd-fəl\ adj (1548) : taking heed : ATTENTIVE ⟨~ of what they were doing⟩ — heed·ful·ly \-fə-lē\ adv — heed·ful·ness n

heed·less \-ləs\ adj (1579) : not taking heed : INCONSIDERATE, THOUGHTLESS ⟨~ follies of unbridled youth —John DeBruyn⟩ — heed·less·ly adv — heed·less·ness n

hee-haw \'hē-ˌho, -'ho\ n [imit.] (1815) 1 : the bray of a donkey 2 : a loud rude laugh : GUFFAW — hee-haw vi

¹heel \'hē(ə)l\ n [ME, fr. OE hēla; akin to ON hæll heel, OE hōh — more at HOCK] (bef. 12c) 1 a : the back of the human foot below the ankle and behind the arch b : the back of the hind limb of other vertebrates homologous with the human heel 2 : an anatomical structure suggestive of the human heel; esp : the part of the palm of the hand nearest the wrist 3 : one of the crusty ends of a loaf of bread 4 a : the part (as of a shoe) that covers the human heel b : a solid attachment of a shoe or boot forming the back of the sole under the heel of the foot 5 : a rear, low, or bottom part: as a : the after end of a ship's keel or the lower end of a mast b : the base of a tuber or cutting of a plant used for propagation c : the base of a ladder 6 : a contemptible person — heel·less \'hē(ə)l-ləs\ adj — by the heels : in a tight grip — down at heel or down at the heel : in or into a run-down or shabby condition — on the heels of : immediately following — to heel 1 : close behind 2 : into agreement or line — under heel : under control or subjection

²heel vt (1605) 1 a : to furnish with a heel b : to supply esp. with money 2 : to exert pressure on, propel, or strike with the heel ⟨~ed her horse⟩ ~ vi : to move along at someone's heels ⟨a dog that ~s well⟩

³heel vb [alter. of ME heelden, fr. OE hieldan; akin to OHG hald inclined, Lith šalis side, region] vi (bef. 12c) : to lean to one side : TIP; esp, of a boat or ship : to lean temporarily (as from the action of wind or waves) — compare LIST ~ vt : to cause (a boat) to heel

⁴heel n (1760) : a tilt (as of a boat) to one side; also : the extent of such a tilt

heel-and-toe \ˌhē-lən-'tō\ adj (1827) : marked by a stride in which the heel of one foot touches the ground before the toe of the other foot leaves it ⟨~ walking⟩

heel·ball \'hē(ə)l-ˌbol\ n (1822) : a composition of wax and lampblack used by shoemakers for polishing and by antiquarians for making rubbings of inscriptions

heel·er \'hē-lər\ n (1665) 1 : one that heels 2 a : a henchman of a local political boss b : a worker for a local party organization; esp : WARD HEELER

heel fly n (1878) : any of several warble flies (genus Hypoderma) that attack cattle; esp : COMMON CATTLE GRUB

heel·piece \'hē(ə)l-ˌpēs\ n (1709) : a piece designed for or forming the heel (as of a shoe)

heel·tap \-ˌtap\ n (1780) : a small quantity of alcoholic beverage remaining (as in a glass after drinking)

¹heft \'heft\ n [irreg. fr. heave] (15c) 1 a : WEIGHT, HEAVINESS b : IMPORTANCE, INFLUENCE 2 archaic : the greater part of something : BULK

²heft vt (1661) 1 : to heave up : HOIST 2 : to test the weight of by lifting ⟨~ing the rod . . . to get the feel of it —Consumer Reports⟩

hefty \'hef-tē\ adj heft·i·er; -est (1867) 1 : quite heavy 2 a : marked by bigness, bulk, and usu. strength ⟨a ~ football player⟩ b : POWERFUL, MIGHTY c : impressively large : SUBSTANTIAL ⟨~ portions⟩ — heft·i·ly \-tə-lē\ adv — heft·i·ness \-tē-nəs\ n

he·gari \hi-'ga(ə)r-ē, -'ga(ə)r-ə, -'ge(ə)r-; 'hi-ˌgi(ə)r\ n [Ar (Sudan) hegiri] (1919) : any of several Sudanese grain sorghums having chalky white seeds including one grown in the southwestern U.S.

¹He·ge·li·an \hā-'gā-lē-ən, hig-'ā-\ adj (1838) : of, relating to, or characteristic of Hegel, his philosophy, or his dialectic method

²Hegelian (1843) : a follower of Hegel : an adherent of Hegelianism

He·ge·li·an·ism \-lē-ə-ˌniz-əm\ n (1846) : the philosophy of Hegel that places ultimate reality in ideas rather than in things and that uses dialectic to comprehend an absolute idea behind phenomena

he·ge·mo·ny \hi-'jem-ə-nē, -'gem-; 'hej-ə-ˌmō-nē\ n [Gk hēgemonia, fr. hēgemōn leader, fr. hēgeisthai to lead — more at SEEK] (1567) : preponderant influence or authority esp. of one nation over others — heg·e·mon·ic \ˌhej-ə-'män-ik, ˌheg-ə-\ adj

he·gi·ra also he·ji·ra \hi-'ji-rə, 'hej-(ə-)rə\ n [the Hegira, flight of Muhammad from Mecca in A.D. 622, fr. ML, fr. Ar hijrah, lit., flight] (1753) : a journey esp. when undertaken to escape from a dangerous or undesirable situation : EXODUS

Hei·del·berg man \ˌhīd-ᵊl-ˌbərg-, -ˌbe(ə)rg-\ n [Heidelberg, West Germany] (ca. 1920) : an early Pleistocene man known from a massive fossilized jaw with distinctly human dentition and now classified with the pithecanthropines

heif·er \'hef-ər\ n [ME hayfare, fr. OE hēahfore] (bef. 12c) : a young cow; esp : one that has not had a calf

heigh-ho \'hī-'hō, 'hā-\ interj (1553) — used typically to express boredom, weariness, or sadness or sometimes as a cry of encouragement

height \'hīt, 'hīth\ n [ME heighthe, fr. OE hiehthu; akin to OHG hōhida height, OE hēah high] (bef. 12c) 1 a : the highest part : SUMMIT b

: highest or most advanced point : ZENITH ⟨at the ~ of his powers⟩ **2 a :** the distance from the bottom to the top of something standing upright **b :** the extent of elevation above a level **3 :** the condition of being tall or high **4 a :** an extent of land rising to a considerable degree above the surrounding country **b :** a high point or position **5** *obs* : an advanced social rank **6 :** degree of geographical latitude
syn HEIGHT, ALTITUDE, ELEVATION mean vertical distance either between the top and bottom of something or between a base and something above it. HEIGHT refers to something measured vertically whether high or low ⟨a wall two meters in *height*⟩ ALTITUDE and ELEVATION apply to height as measured by angular measurement or atmospheric pressure; ALTITUDE is preferable when referring to vertical distance above the surface of the earth or above sea level; ELEVATION is used esp. in reference to vertical height on land ⟨fly at an *altitude* of 10,000 meters⟩ ⟨Denver is a city with a high *elevation*⟩

height·en \ˈhīt-ᵊn\ *vb* **height·ened; height·en·ing** \ˈhīt-niŋ, -ᵊn-iŋ\ *vt* (1523) **1 a :** to increase the amount or degree of : AUGMENT **b :** to make brighter or more intense : DEEPEN **c :** to bring out more strongly : point up **d :** to make more acute : SHARPEN **2 a :** to raise high or higher : ELEVATE **b :** to raise above the ordinary or trite **3** *obs* : ELATE **~** *vi* **1** *archaic* : GROW, RISE **2 a :** to become great or greater in amount, degree, or extent **b :** to become brighter or more intense
syn see INTENSIFY

height to paper (1683) : the height of printing type standardized at 0.9186 inch in English-speaking countries

Heim·lich maneuver \ˈhīm-lik-\ *n* [Henry J. *Heimlich* b1920 Am. surgeon] (1974) : the manual application of sudden upward pressure on the upper abdomen of a choking victim to force a foreign object from the windpipe

hei·nie \ˈhī-nē\ *n* [alter. of [2]*hinder*] *slang* (1940) : BUTTOCKS

hei·nous \ˈhā-nəs\ *adj* [ME, fr. MF *haineus,* fr. *haine* hate, fr. *hair* to hate, of Gmc origin; akin to OHG *haz* hate — more at HATE] (14c) : hatefully or shockingly evil : ABOMINABLE — **hei·nous·ly** *adv* — **hei·nous·ness** *n*

[1]**heir** \ˈa(ə)r, ˈe(ə)r\ *n* [ME, fr. OF, fr. L *hered-, heres;* akin to Gk *chēros* bereaved, OE *gān* to go] (13c) **1 :** one who inherits or is entitled to inherit property **2 :** one who inherits or is entitled to succeed to a hereditary rank, title, or office ⟨~ to the throne⟩ **3 :** one who receives or is entitled to receive some endowment or quality from a parent or predecessor — **heir·less** \-ləs\ *adj* — **heir·ship** \-ˌship\ *n*

[2]**heir** *vt, chiefly dial* (14c) : INHERIT

heir apparent *n, pl* **heirs apparent** (14c) **1 :** an heir whose right to an inheritance is indefeasible in law if he survives the legal ancestor **2 :** HEIR PRESUMPTIVE **3 :** one whose succession esp. to a position or role appears certain under existing circumstances

heir at law (1729) : an heir in whom an intestate's real property is vested by operation of law

heir·ess \ˈar-əs, ˈer-\ *n* (1607) : a female heir; *esp* : a female heir to great wealth

heir·loom \ˈa(ə)r-ˌlüm, ˈe(ə)r-\ *n* [ME *heirlome,* fr. *heir* + *lome* implement — more at LOOM] (15c) **1 :** a piece of property that descends to the heir as an inseparable part of an inheritance **2 :** something of special value handed on from one generation to another

heir presumptive *n, pl* **heirs presumptive** (1628) : an heir whose legal right to an inheritance may be defeated (as by the birth of a nearer relative)

[1]**heist** \ˈhīst\ *vt* [alter. of [1]*hoist*] (1865) **1** *chiefly dial* : HOIST **2** *slang* **a :** to commit armed robbery on **b :** to steal usu. with violence

[2]**heist** *n, slang* (1930) : armed robbery : HOLDUP; *also* : THEFT

Hel \ˈhel\ *n* [ON] : the Norse goddess of the dead and queen of the underworld

hela cell \ˈhel-ə-\ *n, often cap H&1stL* [*He*nrietta *La*cks, cancer victim who donated such cells in 1951] (1953) : a cell of a continuously cultured strain isolated from a human uterine cervical carcinoma in 1951 and used in biomedical research esp. to culture viruses

held *past and past part of* HOLD

hel·den·te·nor \ˈhel-dən-ˌtā-ˌnȯ(ə)r, -ˌnō(ə)r, -ˌten-ər\ *n, often cap* [G, fr. *held* hero + *tenor* tenor] (1926) : a tenor with a powerful dramatic voice well suited to heroic (as Wagnerian) roles

Helen of Troy \ˌhel-ə-nəv-ˈtrȯi\ : the wife of Menelaus whose abduction by Paris brings about the Trojan War

heli- *or* **helio-** *comb form* [L, fr. Gk *hēli-, hēlio-,* fr. *hēlios* — more at SOLAR] : sun ⟨*helio*centric⟩

he·li·a·cal \hi-ˈlī-ə-kəl\ *adj* [LL *heliacus,* fr. Gk *hēliakos,* fr. *hēlios*] (1607) : relating to or near the sun — used esp. of the last setting of a star before and its first rising after invisibility due to conjunction with the sun — **he·li·a·cal·ly** \-k(ə-)lē\ *adv*

helic- *or* **helico-** *comb form* [Gk *helik-, heliko-,* fr. *helik-, helix* spiral — more at HELIX] : helix : spiral ⟨*helic*al⟩

he·li·cal \ˈhel-i-kəl, ˈhē-li-\ *adj* (1613) : of, relating to, or having the form of a helix; *broadly* : SPIRAL 1a — **he·li·cal·ly** \-k(ə-)lē\ *adv*

he·li·coid \ˈhel-ə-ˌkȯid, ˈhē-lə-\ *or* **he·li·coi·dal** \ˌhel-ə-ˈkȯid-ᵊl, ˌhē-lə-\ *adj* (1704) **1 :** forming or arranged in a spiral **2 :** having the form of a flat coil or flattened spiral ⟨~ snail shell⟩

hel·i·con \ˈhel-ə-ˌkän, -i-kən\ *n* [prob. fr. Gk *helik-, helix* + E *-on* (as in *bombardon*); from its tube's forming a spiral encircling the player's body] (1875) : a large circular tuba similar to a sousaphone but lacking an adjustable bell

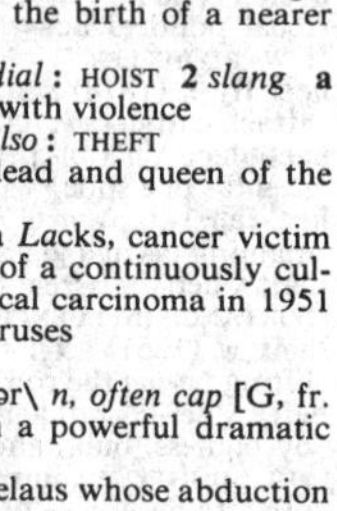
helicon

he·li·copt \ˈhel-ə-ˌkäpt, ˈhē-lə-\ *vb* [back-formation fr. [1]*helicopter*] (1946) : HELICOPTER

[1]**he·li·cop·ter** \ˈhel-ə-ˌkäp-tər, ˈhē-lə-\ *n* [F *hélicoptère,* fr. Gk *heliko-* + *pteron* wing — more at FEATHER] (1887) : an aircraft whose support in the air is derived chiefly from the aerodynamic forces acting on one or more rotors turning about substantially vertical axes

[2]**helicopter** *vi* (1926) : to travel by helicopter **~** *vt* : to transport by helicopter

he·lio·cen·tric \ˌhē-lē-ō-ˈsen-trik\ *adj* (1685) **1 :** referred to or measured from the sun's center or appearing as if seen from it **2 :** having or relating to the sun as center — compare GEOCENTRIC

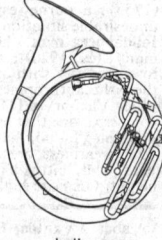

heliocentric parallax *n* (ca. 1864) : the parallax of a star measured using the diameter of the earth's orbit around the sun as a baseline from which observations are made

he·lio·chrome \ˈhē-lē-ə-ˌkrōm\ *n* (1853) : a photograph in natural colors

he·lio·gram \-ˌgram\ *n* (1881) : a message transmitted by a heliograph

[1]**he·lio·graph** \-ˌgraf\ *n* [ISV] (1877) : an apparatus for telegraphing by means of the sun's rays flashed from a mirror

[2]**heliograph** *vt* (1880) : to signal by means of a heliograph — **he·lio·gra·pher** \ˌhē-lē-ˈäg-rə-fər, ˈhē-lē-ə-ˌgraf-ər\ *n*

he·lio·graph·ic \ˌhē-lē-ə-ˈgraf-ik\ *adj* (1706) **1 :** of or relating to heliography or a heliograph **2 :** SOLAR 1 ⟨~ latitude⟩

he·li·og·ra·phy \ˌhē-lē-ˈäg-rə-fē, ˈhē-lē-ə-ˌgraf-ē\ *n* (1840) : the system or practice of signaling with a heliograph

he·li·ol·a·try \ˌhē-lē-ˈäl-ə-trē\ *n* (1828) : sun worship — **he·li·ol·a·trous** \-trəs\ *adj*

he·li·om·e·ter \ˌhē-lē-ˈäm-ət-ər\ *n* [F *héliomètre,* fr. *hélio-* heli- + *-mètre* -meter] (1753) : a visual telescope that has a divided objective designed for measuring the apparent diameter of the sun but later used for measuring angles between celestial bodies or between points on the moon — **he·lio·met·ric** \ˌhē-lē-ō-ˈme-trik\ *adj* — **he·lio·met·ri·cal·ly** \-tri-k(ə-)lē\ *adv*

He·li·os \ˈhē-lē-əs, -ˌ(ˌ)ōs\ *n* [Gk *Hēlios*] : the god of the sun in Greek mythology — compare SOL

he·lio·stat \ˈhē-lē-ə-ˌstat\ *n* [NL *heliostata,* fr. *heli-* + Gk *-statēs* -stat] (1747) : an instrument consisting of a mirror mounted on an axis moved by clockwork by which a sunbeam is steadily reflected in one direction

he·lio·tax·is \ˌhē-lē-ō-ˈtak-səs\ *n* [NL] (1898) : a taxis in which sunlight is the directive factor

he·lio·trope \ˈhē-lē-ə-ˌtrōp, ˈhēl-yə-, *Brit usu* ˈhel-yə-\ *n* [L *heliotropium,* fr. Gk *hēliotropion,* fr. *hēlio-* heli- + *tropos* turn; fr. its flowers' turning toward the sun — more at TROPE] (1626) **1 :** any of a genus (*Heliotropium*) of herbs or shrubs of the borage family — compare GARDEN HELIOTROPE **2 :** BLOODSTONE **3 :** a variable color averaging a moderate to reddish purple

he·li·ot·ro·pism \ˌhē-lē-ˈä-trə-ˌpiz-əm\ *n* (1854) : phototropism in which sunlight is the orienting stimulus — **he·lio·tro·pic** \-lē-ə-ˈtrōp-ik, -ˈträp-\ *adj*

he·lio·zo·an \ˌhē-lē-ə-ˈzō-ən\ *n* [NL *Heliozoa,* fr. *heli-* + *-zoa*] (ca. 1895) : any of an order (Heliozoa) of free-living holozoic usu. freshwater rhizopod protozoans that reproduce by binary fission or budding — **heliozoan** *adj*

he·li·pad \ˈhel-ə-ˌpad, ˈhē-lə-\ *n* (1960) : HELIPORT

he·li·port \-ˌpō(ə)rt, -ˌpȯ(ə)rt\ *n* [*heli*copter + *port*] (1948) : a landing and takeoff place for a helicopter

he·li·stop \-ˌstäp\ *n* (1954) : HELIPORT

he·li·um \ˈhē-lē-əm\ *n* [NL, fr. Gk *hēlios*] (1872) : a light colorless nonflammable gaseous element found esp. in natural gases and used chiefly for inflating airships and balloons, for filling incandescent lamps, and for cryogenic research — see ELEMENT table

he·lix \ˈhē-liks\ *n, pl* **he·li·ces** \ˈhel-ə-ˌsēz, ˈhē-lə-\ *also* **he·lix·es** \ˈhē-lik-səz\ [L, fr. Gk; akin to Gk *eilyein* to roll, wrap — more at VOLUBLE] (1563) **1 :** something spiral in form: as **a :** an ornamental volute **b :** a coil formed by winding wire around a uniform tube **2 :** the incurved rim of the external ear **3 :** a curve traced on a cylinder or cone by the rotation of a point crossing its right sections at a constant oblique angle; *broadly* : SPIRAL 1b

hell \ˈhel\ *n* [ME, fr. OE; akin to OE *helan* to conceal, OHG *helan,* L *celare,* Gk *kalyptein*] (bef. 12c) **1 a** (1) : a nether world in which the dead continue to exist : HADES (2) : the nether realm of the devil and the demons in which the damned suffer everlasting punishment — often used in curses ⟨go to ~⟩ or as a generalized term of abuse ⟨the ~ with it⟩ **b** *Christian Science* : ERROR 2b, SIN **2 a :** a place or state of misery, torment, or wickedness ⟨war is ~ —W. T. Sherman⟩ **b :** a place or state of turmoil or destruction ⟨all ~ broke loose⟩ **c :** a severe scolding ⟨got ~ for coming in late⟩ **d :** unrestrained fun or sportiveness ⟨the kids were full of ~⟩ — often used in the phrase *for the hell of it* **3** *archaic* : a tailor's receptacle **4** — used as an interjection ⟨~, I don't know!⟩ or as an intensive ⟨hurts like ~⟩ ⟨funny as ~⟩ ; often used in the phrase *hell of a* ⟨it was one ~ of a good fight⟩ or with *the* or *in* ⟨moved way the ~ up north⟩ ⟨what in ~ is wrong, now?⟩ — **hell on** : very hard on or destructive to ⟨the constant traveling is *hell on* your digestive system⟩ — **hell or high water :** difficulties of whatever kind or size ⟨will stand by his convictions come *hell or high water*⟩ — **hell to pay :** serious trouble ⟨if he's late there'll be *hell to pay*⟩

he'll \(ˌ)hē(ə)l, hil, ēl, il\ : he will : he shall

hel·la·cious \ˌhel-ˈā-shəs\ *adj* [*hell* + *-acious* (as in *audacious*)] (1943) **1 :** exceptionally powerful or violent **2 :** remarkably good **3 :** extremely difficult **4 :** extraordinarily large — **hel·la·cious·ly** *adv*

hell·ben·der \ˈhel-ˌben-dər\ *n* (1812) : a large aquatic usu. gray salamander (*Cryptobranchus alleganiensis*) of the Ohio valley

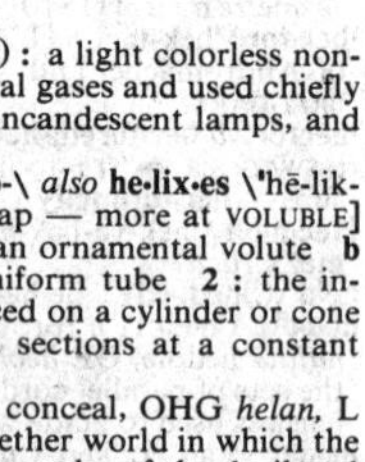
hellbender

hell–bent \-ˌbent\ *adj* (1835) : stubbornly and often recklessly determined ⟨~ to cut taxes again —*New Republic*⟩ — **hell–bent** *adv*

hell·broth \-ˌbrȯth\ *n* (1605) : a brew for working black magic

hell·cat \-ˌkat\ *n* (1605) **1 :** WITCH 2 **2 :** one given to tormenting others; *esp* : SHREW

hel·le·bore \ˈhel-ə-ˌbō(ə)r, -ˌbȯ(ə)r\ *n* [ME *elebre,* fr. L *elleborus, helleborus,* fr. Gk *helleboros*] (15c) **1 :** any of a genus (*Helleborus*) of herbs of the buttercup family having showy flowers with petaloid sepals; *also* : the dried rhizome or an extract or powder of this formerly used in medicine **2 :** a poisonous herb (genus *Veratrum*) of the lily family; *also* : the dried rhizome of a hellebore (*Veratrum album* or *V. viride*) or a powder or extract of this containing alkaloids used as a cardiac and respiratory depressant and as an insecticide

Hel·lene \ˈhel-ˌēn\ *n* [Gk *Hellēn*] (1662) : GREEK 1a

[1]**Hel·len·ic** \he-ˈlen-ik, hə-\ *adj* (1644) : of or relating to Greece, its people, or its language

[2]**Hellenic** *n* (1847) : GREEK 2a

Hel·le·nism \'hel-ə-ˌniz-əm\ *n* (1609) **1 :** GRECISM 1 **2 :** devotion to or imitation of ancient Greek thought, customs, or styles **3 :** Greek civilization esp. as modified in the Hellenistic period by oriental influences **4 :** a body of humanistic and classical ideals associated with ancient Greece and including reason, the pursuit of knowledge and the arts, moderation, civic responsibility, and bodily development

Hel·le·nist \-nəst\ *n* (1613) **1 :** a person living in Hellenistic times who was Greek in language, outlook, and way of life but was not Greek in ancestry; *esp* **:** a hellenized Jew **2 :** a specialist in the language or culture of ancient Greece

Hel·le·nis·tic \ˌhel-ə-'nis-tik\ *adj* (1706) **1 :** of or relating to Greek history, culture, or art after Alexander the Great **2 :** of or relating to the Hellenists — **Hel·le·nis·ti·cal·ly** \-ti-k(ə-)lē\ *adv*

hel·le·nize \'hel-ə-ˌnīz\ *vb* **-nized; -niz·ing** *often cap, vi* (1613) **:** to become Greek or Hellenistic ~ *vt* **:** to make Greek or Hellenistic in form or culture — **hel·le·ni·za·tion** \ˌhel-ə-nə-'zā-shən\ *n, often cap*

hell·er \'hel-ər\ *n* (1895) **:** HELLION

hel·leri \'hel-ə-ˌrī, -(ˌ)rē\ *n* [NL (specific epithet of *Xiphophorus helleri*), fr. C. *Heller*, 20th cent. tropical fish collector] (1909) **1 :** SWORDTAIL **2 :** any of various brightly colored topminnows developed by hybridization of swordtails and platys

hell·fire \'hel-ˌfī(ə)r\ *n* (bef. 12c) **:** the eternal fire of hell that tortures sinners — **hellfire** *adj*

[1]**hell–for–leather** *adv* (1875) **:** in a hell-for-leather manner **:** at full speed ⟨rode ~ down the trail⟩

[2]**hell–for–leather** *adj* (1920) **:** marked by determined recklessness, great speed, or lack of restraint ⟨a cocky, ~ fighting man —H. H. Martin⟩

hell·gram·mite \'hel-grə-ˌmīt\ *n* [origin unknown] (1866) **:** a carnivorous aquatic No. American insect larva that is the young form of a dobsonfly (esp. *Corydalis cornutus*) and is used for fish bait

hell·hole \'hel-ˌhōl\ *n* (1882) **:** a place of extreme misery or squalor

hell·hound \-ˌhau̇nd\ *n* (bef. 12c) **1 :** a dog represented in mythology as a guardian of the underworld **2 :** a fiendish person

hel·lion \'hel-yən\ *n* [prob. alter. (influenced by *hell*) of *hallion* (scamp)] (1787) **:** a troublesome or mischievous person

hell·ish \'hel-ish\ *adj* (1530) **:** of, resembling, or befitting hell ⟨nothing more ~ than warfare within the soul —Frank Yerby⟩; *broadly* **:** TERRIBLE — **hell·ish·ly** *adv* — **hell·ish·ness** *n*

hel·lo \hə-'lō, he-\ *n, pl* **hellos** [alter. of *hollo*] (1893) **:** an expression or gesture of greeting — used interjectionally in greeting, in answering the telephone, or to express surprise

hell–rais·er \'hel-ˌrā-zər\ *n* (1914) **:** one given to wild, boisterous, or intemperate behavior — **hell–rais·ing** \-ˌrā-ziŋ\ *n*

[1]**helm** \'helm\ *n* [ME, fr. OE] (bef. 12c) **:** HELMET 1

[2]**helm** *vt* (bef. 12c) **:** to cover or furnish with a helmet

[3]**helm** *n* [ME *helme*, fr. OE *helma*; akin to OHG *helmo* tiller] (bef. 12c) **1 a :** a lever or wheel controlling the rudder of a ship for steering; *broadly* **:** the entire apparatus for steering a ship **b :** position of the helm with respect to the amidships position ⟨turn the ~ hard alee⟩ **2 :** a position of control **:** HEAD ⟨a new dean is at the ~ of the medical school⟩

[4]**helm** *vt* (1603) **:** to direct with or as if with a helm **:** STEER

hel·met \'hel-mət\ *n* [MF, dim. of *helme* helmet, of Gmc origin; akin to OE *helm* helmet, OHG *helan* to conceal — more at HELL] (15c) **1 :** a covering or enclosing headpiece of ancient or medieval armor **2 :** any of various protective head coverings usu. made of a hard material to resist impact **3 :** something resembling a helmet; *specif* **:** a hood-shaped upper sepal or petal of some flowers — **hel·met·ed** \-mət-əd\ *adj* — **hel·met·like** \-mət-ˌlīk\ *adj*

hel·minth \'hel-ˌmin(t)th\ *n* [Gk *helminth-, helmis*; akin to Gk *eilyein* to roll — more at VOLUBLE] (1852) **:** WORM; *esp* **:** an intestinal worm — used esp. by parasitologists — **hel·min·thic** \hel-'min(t)-thik\ *adj*

hel·min·thi·a·sis \ˌhel-mən-'thī-ə-səs\ *n, pl* **-a·ses** \-ə-ˌsēz\ [NL] (1811) **:** infestation with or disease caused by parasitic worms

hel·min·thol·o·gy \-'thäl-ə-jē\ *n* (1819) **:** a branch of zoology concerned with helminths; *esp* **:** the study of parasitic worms

helms·man \'helmz-mən\ *n* (1622) **:** the person at the helm **:** STEERSMAN — **helms·man·ship** \-ˌship\ *n*

hel·ot \'hel-ət\ *n* [L *Helotes*, pl., fr. Gk *Heilōtes*] (1579) **1** *cap* **:** a member of a class of serfs in ancient Sparta **2 :** SERF, SLAVE — **hel·ot·ry** \'hel-ə-trē\ *n*

hel·ot·ism \'hel-ət-ˌiz-əm\ *n* (1823) **:** a symbiotic relation (as in a lichen) in which one member (as an alga) functions as the slave of the other (as a fungus)

[1]**help** \'help; *Southern often* 'hep *also* 'heəp\ *vb* [ME *helpen*, fr. OE *helpan*; akin to OHG *helfan* to help, Lith *šelpti*] *vt* (bef. 12c) **1 :** to give assistance or support to ⟨~ a child to understand his lesson⟩ **2 a :** to make more pleasant or bearable **:** IMPROVE, RELIEVE ⟨bright curtains will ~ the room⟩ ⟨took an aspirin to ~ her headache⟩ **b** *archaic* **:** RESCUE, SAVE **c :** to get (oneself) out of a difficulty **3 a :** to be of use to **:** BENEFIT **b :** to further the advancement of **:** PROMOTE **4 a :** to change for the better **b :** to refrain from **:** AVOID — used chiefly in the phrases *cannot help* and *cannot help but* **c :** to keep from occurring **:** PREVENT ⟨they couldn't ~ the accident⟩ **5 :** to serve with food or drink esp. at a meal **6 :** to appropriate for the use of (oneself) ~ *vi* **1 :** give assistance or support — often used with *out* **2 :** to be of use or benefit

syn HELP, AID, ASSIST mean to supply what is needed to accomplish an end. HELP carries a strong implication of advance toward an objective; AID suggests the evident need of help or relief and so imputes weakness to the one aided and strength to the one aiding; ASSIST suggests a secondary role in the assistant or a subordinate character in the assistance.

— **so help me :** upon my word **:** believe it or not

[2]**help** *n* (bef. 12c) **1 :** AID, ASSISTANCE **2 :** a source of aid ⟨printed ~s to the memory —C. S. Braden⟩ **3 :** REMEDY, RELIEF **4 a :** one who is in the service of or who assists another **:** HELPER **b :** EMPLOYEE ⟨~ wanted⟩ — often used collectively **5 :** HELPING

help·er *n* (14c) **:** one that helps; *esp* **:** a relatively unskilled worker who assists a skilled worker usu. by manual labor

help·ful \'help-fəl; *Southern often* 'hep- *also* 'heəp-\ *adj* (14c) **:** of service or assistance **:** USEFUL — **help·ful·ly** \-fə-lē\ *adv* — **help·ful·ness** *n*

help·ing *n* (1824) **:** a serving of food

help·ing verb *n* (1824) **:** an auxiliary verb

help·less \'hel-pləs; *Southern often* 'hep-ləs *also* 'heəp-\ *adj* (bef. 12c) **1 :** lacking protection or support **:** DEFENSELESS **2 :** marked by an inability to act or react ⟨the crowd looked on in ~ horror —*Current Biog.*⟩ — **help·less·ly** *adv* — **help·less·ness** *n*

help·mate \'help-ˌmāt; *Southern often* 'hep- *also* 'heəp-\ *n* [by folk etymology fr. *helpmeet*] (1714) **:** one who is a companion and helper; *esp* **:** WIFE

help·meet \-ˌmēt\ *n* [[2]*help* + *meet*, adj.] (1673) **:** HELPMATE

[1]**hel·ter–skel·ter** \ˌhel-tər-'skel-tər\ *adv* [imit.] (1593) **1 :** in undue haste, confusion, or disorder ⟨ran ~, getting in each other's way —F. V. W. Mason⟩ **2 :** in a haphazard manner

[2]**helter–skelter** *n* (1713) **1 :** a disorderly confusion **:** TURMOIL **2** *Brit* **:** a spiral slide around a tower at an amusement park

[3]**helter–skelter** *adj* (1785) **1 :** confusedly hurried **:** PRECIPITATE **2 :** marked by a lack of order or plan **:** HAPHAZARD ⟨the ~ arrangement of the papers, all mussed and frayed —Jean Stafford⟩

helve \'helv\ *n* [ME, fr. OE *hielfe*; akin to OE *healf* half] (bef. 12c) **:** a handle of a tool or weapon **:** HAFT

Hel·ve·tii \hel-'vē-shē-ˌī\ *n pl* [L] (1895) **:** an early Celtic people of western Switzerland in the time of Julius Caesar

[1]**hem** \'hem\ *n* [ME, fr. OE; akin to MHG *hemmen* to hem in, Arm *kamel* to press] (bef. 12c) **1 a :** a border of a cloth article doubled back and stitched down **b :** a similar border on an article of sheet metal, plastic, rubber, or leather **2 :** RIM, MARGIN ⟨bright green ~ of reeds about the ponds —R. M. Lockley⟩

[2]**hem** *vb* **hemmed; hem·ming** *vt* (14c) **1 a :** to finish with a hem **b :** BORDER, EDGE **2 :** to surround in a restrictive manner **:** CONFINE — usu. used with *in* ⟨*hemmed* in by enemy troops⟩ ~ *vi* **:** to make a hem in sewing — **hem·mer** *n*

[3]**hem** \'hem\ *vi* **hemmed; hem·ming** (15c) **1 :** to utter the sound represented by *hem* ⟨*hemmed* and hawed before answering⟩ **2 :** EQUIVOCATE ⟨the administration *hemmed* and hawed over the students' demands⟩

[4]**hem** *usu read as* 'hem\ *interj* [imit.] — often used to indicate a vocalized pause in speaking

hem- *or* **hemo-** *or* **haem-** *or* **haemo-** *comb form* [MF *hemo-*, fr. L *haem-, haemo-*, fr. Gk *haim-, haimo-*, fr. *haima*] **:** blood ⟨*hem*al⟩ ⟨*hemo*flagellate⟩

hema- *or* **haema-** *comb form* [NL, fr. Gk *haima*] **:** HEM- ⟨*hema*cytometer⟩

he·ma·cy·tom·e·ter \ˌhē-mə-sī-'täm-ət-ər\ *n* (1877) **:** an instrument for counting blood cells

hem·ag·glu·ti·na·tion \ˌhē-mə-ˌglüt-ᵊn-'ā-shən\ *n* (ca. 1923) **:** agglutination of red blood cells — **hem·ag·glu·ti·nate** \-'glüt-ᵊn-ˌāt\ *vt*

hem·ag·glu·ti·nin \-'glüt-ᵊn-ən\ *n* [ISV] (ca. 1903) **:** an agglutinin that causes hemagglutination

he–man \'hē-'man\ *n* (1832) **:** a strong virile man

hem·an·gi·o·ma \ˌhē-ˌman-jē-'ō-mə\ *n* [NL, fr. *hem-* + *angioma*] (ca. 1890) **:** a usu. benign tumor made up of blood vessels that typically occurs as a purplish or reddish slightly elevated area of skin

hemat- *or* **hemato-** *or* **haemat-** *or* **haemato-** *comb form* [L *haemat-, haemato-*, fr. Gk *haimat-, haimato-*, fr. *haimat-, haima*] **:** HEM- ⟨*hemat*oid⟩ ⟨*hemato*genous⟩

he·ma·tin \'hē-mə-tən\ *n* (1819) **:** a brownish black or bluish black derivative $C_{34}H_{33}N_4O_5Fe$ of oxidized heme; *also* **:** any of several similar compounds

he·ma·tin·ic \ˌhē-mə-'tin-ik\ *n* (1855) **:** an agent that tends to stimulate blood cell formation or to increase the hemoglobin in the blood — **hematinic** *adj*

he·ma·tite \'hē-mə-ˌtīt\ *n* (1540) **:** a mineral Fe_2O_3 constituting an important iron ore and occurring in crystals or in a red earthy form — **he·ma·ti·tic** \ˌhē-mə-'tit-ik\ *adj*

he·mat·o·crit \hi-'mat-ə-krət, -ˌkrit\ *n* [ISV *hemat-* + Gk *kritēs* judge, fr. *krinein* to judge — more at CERTAIN] (ca. 1903) **1 :** an instrument for determining usu. by centrifugation the relative amounts of plasma and corpuscles in blood **2 :** the ratio of the volume of packed red blood cells to the volume of whole blood as determined by a hematocrit

he·ma·tog·e·nous \ˌhē-mə-'täj-ə-nəs\ *adj* (1886) **1 :** producing blood **2 :** involving, spread by, or arising in the blood ⟨a ~ route of infection⟩

he·ma·to·log·ic \ˌhē-mət-ᵊl-'äj-ik\ *also* **he·ma·to·log·i·cal** \-i-kəl\ *adj* (1854) **:** of or relating to blood or to hematology

he·ma·tol·o·gy \ˌhē-mə-'täl-ə-jē\ *n* (1811) **:** a branch of biology that deals with the blood and blood-forming organs — **he·ma·tol·o·gist** \-jəst\ *n*

he·ma·to·ma \-'tō-mə\ *n, pl* **-mas** *or* **-ma·ta** \-mət-ə\ (1847) **:** a tumor or swelling containing blood

he·ma·toph·a·gous \-'täf-ə-gəs\ *adj* [ISV] (1854) **:** feeding on blood

he·ma·to·poi·e·sis \hi-ˌmat-ə-pȯi-'ē-səs, ˌhē-mət-ō-\ *n* [NL] (1854) **:** the formation of blood or of blood cells in the living body — **he·ma·to·poi·et·ic** \-'et-ik\ *adj*

he·ma·tox·y·lin \ˌhē-mə-'täk-sə-lən\ *n* [ISV, fr. NL *Haematoxylon*, genus of plants] (1847) **:** a crystalline phenolic compound $C_{16}H_{14}O_6$ found in logwood and used chiefly as a biological stain

he·ma·tu·ria \-'t(y)u̇r-ē-ə\ *n* [NL] (1811) **:** the presence of blood or blood cells in the urine

heme \'hēm\ *n* [ISV, fr. *hematin*] (1925) **:** the deep red iron-containing prosthetic group $C_{34}H_{32}N_4O_4Fe$ of hemoglobin

hem·el·y·tron \he-'mel-ə-ˌträn\ *n, pl* **-tra** \-trə\ [NL, fr. *hemi-* + *elytron*] (1826) **:** one of the basally thickened anterior wings of various insects (as true bugs)

hem·ero·cal·lis \ˌhem-ə-rō-'kal-əs\ *n* [NL, fr. Gk *hēmerokalles*, fr. *hēmera* day + *kallos* beauty — more at EPHEMERAL, CALLIGRAPHY] (1625) **:** DAYLILY

hem·er·y·thrin \hē-'mer-ə-thrən\ *n* [*hem-* + *erythr-* + *-in*] (ca. 1909) **:** an iron-containing respiratory pigment in the blood of various invertebrates (as some annelids)

hemi- *prefix* [ME, fr. L, fr. Gk *hēmi-* — more at SEMI-] : half ⟨*hemi*hedral⟩
-hemia — see -EMIA
hemi·ac·e·tal \ˌhem-ē-ˈas-ə-ˌtal\ *n* (1893) : any of a class of compounds characterized by the grouping C(OH)(OR) where R is an alkyl group and usu. formed as intermediates in the preparation of acetals from aldehydes or ketones
he·mic \ˈhē-mik\ *adj* (ca. 1885) : of, relating to, or produced by the blood or the circulation of blood ⟨a ~ murmur⟩
hemi·cel·lu·lose \ˌhem-i-ˈsel-yə-ˌlōs, -ˌlōz\ *n* [ISV] (1891) : any of various plant polysaccharides less complex than cellulose and easily hydrolyzable to simple sugars and other products
hemi·chor·date \-ˈkȯrd-ət, -ˈkȯ(ə)r-ˌdāt\ *n* [NL *Hemichordata,* fr. *hemi-* + *Chordata* chordates] (1885) : any of a division (Hemichordata) of chordates comprising vermiform marine animals (as an acorn worm) that have in the proboscis an outgrowth of the pharyngeal wall which suggests and is probably homologous with the notochord of higher chordates
hemi·cy·cle \ˈhem-i-ˌsī-kəl\ *n* [F *hémicycle,* fr. L *hemicyclium,* fr. Gk *hēmikyklion,* fr. *hēmi-* + *kyklos* circle — more at CYCLE] (1603) : a curved or semicircular structure or arrangement
hemi·demi·semi·qua·ver \ˌhem-i-ˌdem-i-ˈsem-i-ˌkwā-vər\ *n* (1853) : SIXTY-FOURTH NOTE
hemi·he·dral \ˌhem-i-ˈhē-drəl\ *adj* [*hemi-* + *-hedron*] *of a crystal* (1837) : having half the faces required by complete symmetry — compare HOLOHEDRAL, TETARTOHEDRAL — **hemi·he·dral·ly** \-drə-lē\ *adv*
hemi·hy·drate \-ˈhī-ˌdrāt\ *n* (ca. 1901) : a hydrate (as plaster of paris) containing half a mole of water to one mole of the compound forming the hydrate — **hemi·hy·drat·ed** \-ˌdrāt-əd\ *adj*
hemi·me·tab·o·lous \ˌhem-i-mə-ˈtab-ə-ləs\ *adj* (1870) : characterized by incomplete metamorphosis
hemi·mor·phic \ˌhem-i-ˈmȯr-fik\ *adj* [ISV] (1864) : asymmetric in form as regards the two ends of an axis — **hemi·mor·phism** \-ˌfiz-əm\ *n*
hemi·mor·phite \-ˌfīt\ *n* (1868) : a mineral $Zn_4Si_2O_7OH{\cdot}H_2O$ that is a basic zinc silicate in usu. colorless transparent orthorhombic crystals
he·min \ˈhē-mən\ *n* [ISV] (ca. 1890) : a red-brown to blue-black crystalline salt $C_{34}H_{32}N_4O_4FeCl$ derived from oxidized heme but usu. obtained in a characteristic crystalline form from hemoglobin
hemi·o·la \ˌhem-ē-ˈō-lə\ *n* [LL *hemiolia,* fr. Gk *hēmiolia* ratio of one and a half to one, fr. *hēmi-* + *holos* whole — more at SAFE] (1597) : a musical rhythmic alteration consisting of three beats in place of two or two beats in place of three
hemi·ple·gia \ˌhem-i-ˈplē-j(ē-)ə\ *n* [NL, fr. MGk *hēmiplēgia* paralysis, fr. Gk *hēmi-* + *-plēgia* -plegia] (1600) : paralysis of one lateral half of the body or part of it resulting from injury to the motor centers of the brain — **hemi·ple·gic** \-jik\ *adj or n*
he·mip·ter·an \hi-ˈmip-tə-rən\ *n* [deriv. of Gk *hēmi-* + *pteron* wing — more at FEATHER] (1864) : any of a large order (Hemiptera) of insects (as the true bugs) that have mouthparts adapted to piercing and sucking and usu. two pairs of wings, undergo an incomplete metamorphosis, and include many important pests — **he·mip·ter·ous** \-rəs\ *adj*
hemi·sphere \ˈhem-ə-ˌsfi(ə)r\ *n* [ME *hemispere,* fr. L *hemisphaerium,* fr. Gk *hēmisphairion,* fr. *hēmi-* + *sphairion,* dim. of *sphaira* sphere] (14c) **1 a :** a half of the celestial sphere divided into two halves by the horizon, the celestial equator, or the ecliptic **b :** the northern or southern half of the earth divided by the equator or the eastern or western half divided by a meridian **c :** the inhabitants of a terrestrial hemisphere **2 :** REALM, PROVINCE **3 :** one of two half spheres formed by a plane through the sphere's center **4 :** a map or projection of a celestial or terrestrial hemisphere **5 :** CEREBRAL HEMISPHERE — **hemi·spher·ic** \ˌhem-ə-ˈsfi(ə)r-ik, -ˈsfer-\ *or* **hemi·spher·i·cal** \-ˈsfir-i-kəl, -ˈsfer-\ *adj*
hemi·stich \ˈhem-i-ˌstik\ *n* [L *hemistichium,* fr. Gk *hēmistichion,* fr. *hēmi-* + *stichos* line, verse; akin to Gk *steichein* to go — more at STAIR] (1575) : half a poetic line of verse usu. divided by a caesura
hemi·zy·gous \ˌhem-i-ˈzī-gəs\ *adj* (ca. 1921) : having or characterized by one or more genes (as in a genetic deficiency or in an X chromosome paired with a Y chromosome) that have no allelic counterparts
hem·line \ˈhem-ˌlīn\ *n* (1923) : the line formed by the lower edge of a dress, skirt, or coat
hem·lock \ˈhem-ˌläk\ *n* [ME *hemlok,* fr. OE *hemlic*] (bef. 12c) **1 a :** any of several poisonous herbs (as a poison hemlock or a water hemlock) of the carrot family having finely cut leaves and small white flowers **b :** a poisonous drink made from the fruit of the hemlock — compare CONIINE **2 :** any of a genus (*Tsuga*) of evergreen coniferous trees of the pine family; *also* : the soft light splintery wood of a hemlock
hemo- — see HEM-
he·mo·chro·ma·to·sis \ˌhē-mə-ˌkrō-mə-ˈtō-səs\ *n* [NL, fr. *hem-* + *chromat-* + *-osis*] (1899) : a disorder of iron metabolism that occurs usu. in males and that is characterized by bronzing of the skin due to deposition of iron-containing pigments in the tissues and frequently by diabetic symptoms
he·mo·coel \ˈhē-mə-ˌsēl\ *n* (1839) : a body cavity (as in arthropods or some mollusks) that normally contains blood and functions as part of the circulatory system
he·mo·cy·a·nin \ˌhē-mō-ˈsī-ə-nən\ *n* [ISV] (1845) : a colorless copper-containing respiratory pigment in solution in the blood plasma of various arthropods and mollusks
he·mo·cyte \ˈhē-mə-ˌsīt\ *n* [ISV] (ca. 1903) : a blood cell esp. of an invertebrate animal
he·mo·cy·tom·e·ter \ˌhē-mə-sī-ˈtäm-ət-ər\ *n* [ISV] (1877) : HEMACYTOMETER
he·mo·di·al·y·sis \ˌhē-mō-dī-ˈal-ə-səs\ *n* (ca. 1947) : the process of removing blood from an artery (as of a kidney patient), purifying it by dialysis, adding vital substances, and returning it to a vein
he·mo·di·lu·tion \-dī-ˈlü-shən, -də-\ *n* (1939) : decreased concentration (as after hemorrhage) of cells and solids in the blood resulting from gain of fluid from the tissues
he·mo·dy·nam·ic \-dī-ˈnam-ik, -də-\ *adj* (1907) **1 :** of, relating to, or involving hemodynamics **2 :** concerned with or functioning in the mechanics of blood circulation — **he·mo·dy·nam·i·cal·ly** \-i-k(ə-)lē\ *adv*
he·mo·dy·nam·ics \-iks\ *n pl but sing or pl in constr* (ca. 1857) **1 :** a branch of physiology that deals with the circulation of the blood **2 :** the forces or mechanisms involved in circulation (as of a particular body part)
he·mo·fla·gel·late \ˌhē-mō-ˈflaj-ə-lət, -ˌlāt; -flə-ˈjel-ət\ *n* (1909) : a flagellate (as a trypanosome) that is a blood parasite
he·mo·glo·bin \ˈhē-mə-ˌglō-bən\ *n* [ISV, short for earlier *hematoglobulin*] (1869) **1 a :** an iron-containing conjugated protein respiratory pigment occurring in the red blood cells of vertebrates **b :** a dark purplish crystallizable form of hemoglobin found chiefly in the venous blood of vertebrates that is a conjugated protein composed of heme and globin **2 :** any of numerous iron-containing respiratory pigments of invertebrates and some plants (as yeasts) — **he·mo·glo·bin·ic** \ˌhē-mə-glō-ˈbin-ik\ *adj* — **he·mo·glo·bin·ous** \-ˈglō-bə-nəs\ *adj*
he·mo·glo·bin·op·a·thy \ˌhē-mə-ˌglō-bə-ˈnäp-ə-thē\ *n, pl* **-thies** (1957) : a blood disorder (as sickle-cell anemia) caused by a genetically determined change in the molecular structure of hemoglobin
hemoglobin S *n* (1954) : a hemoglobin that occurs in the red blood cells in sickle-cell anemia and sickle-cell trait
he·mo·glo·bin·uria \ˌhē-mə-ˌglō-bə-ˈn(y)u̇r-ē-ə\ *n* [NL] (1866) : the presence of free hemoglobin in the urine — **he·mo·glo·bin·uric** \-ˈn(y)u̇(ə)r-ik\ *adj*
he·mo·lymph \ˈhē-mə-ˌlim(p)f\ *n* (ca. 1885) : the circulatory fluid of various invertebrate animals that is functionally comparable to the blood and lymph of vertebrates
he·mo·ly·sin \ˌhē-mə-ˈlīs-ᵊn\ *n* [ISV] (1900) : a substance that causes the dissolution of red blood cells
he·mo·ly·sis \hi-ˈmäl-ə-səs, ˌhē-mə-ˈlī-səs\ *n* [NL] (ca. 1890) : lysis of red blood cells with liberation of hemoglobin — **he·mo·lyt·ic** \ˌhē-mə-ˈlit-ik\ *adj*
hemolytic anemia *n* (1938) : anemia caused by excessive destruction (as in chemical poisoning, infection, or sickle-cell anemia) of red blood cells
hemolytic disease of the newborn (1948) : ERYTHROBLASTOSIS FETALIS
he·mo·lyze \ˈhē-mə-ˌlīz\ *vb* **-lyzed; -lyz·ing** [irreg. fr. *hemolysis*] *vt* (1902) : to cause hemolysis of ~ *vi* : to undergo hemolysis
he·mo·phil·ia \ˌhē-mə-ˈfil-ē-ə\ *n* [NL] (1854) : a sex-linked hereditary blood defect almost exclusively of males characterized by delayed clotting of the blood and consequent difficulty in controlling hemorrhage even after minor injuries
[1]**he·mo·phil·i·ac** \-ˈfil-ē-ˌak\ *adj* (1896) : of, resembling, or affected with hemophilia
[2]**hemophiliac** *n* (1897) : one affected with hemophilia — called also *bleeder*
he·mo·phil·ic \-ˈfil-ik\ *n or adj* (1864) : HEMOPHILIAC
he·mo·poi·e·sis \ˌhē-mə-pȯi-ˈē-səs\ *n* [NL] (ca. 1900) : HEMATOPOIESIS — **he·mo·poi·et·ic** \-ˈet-ik\ *adj*
he·mo·pro·tein \-ˈprō-ˌtēn, -ˈprōt-ē-ən\ *n* (1948) : a conjugated protein (as hemoglobin or cytochrome) whose prosthetic group is a porphyrin combined with iron
he·mop·ty·sis \hi-ˈmäp-tə-səs\ *n* [NL, fr. *hem-* + Gk *ptysis* act of spitting, fr. *ptyein* to spit — more at SPEW] (1646) : expectoration of blood from some part of the respiratory tract
[1]**hem·or·rhage** \ˈhem-(ə-)rij\ *n* [ME *emoragie,* fr. L *haemorrhagia,* fr. Gk *haimorrhagia,* fr. *haimo-* hem- + *-rrhagia*] (15c) : a copious discharge of blood from the blood vessels — **hem·or·rhag·ic** \ˌhem-ə-ˈraj-ik\ *adj*
[2]**hemorrhage** *vi* **-rhaged; -rhag·ing** (1928) : to undergo heavy or uncontrollable bleeding
hem·or·rhoid \ˈhem-(ə-)ˌrȯid\ *n* [MF *hemorrhoides,* pl., fr. L *haemorrhoidae* fr. Gk *haimorrhoides,* fr. *haimorrhoos* flowing with blood, fr. *haimo-* hem- + *rhein* to flow — more at STREAM] (14c) : a mass of dilated veins in swollen tissue at the margin of the anus or nearby within the rectum — usu. used in pl.; called also *piles*
[1]**hem·or·rhoid·al** \ˌhem-ə-ˈrȯid-ᵊl\ *adj* (1541) **1 :** of, relating to, or involving hemorrhoids **2 :** RECTAL
[2]**hemorrhoidal** *n* (1951) : a hemorrhoidal part (as an artery or vein)
he·mo·sid·er·in \ˌhē-mō-ˈsid-ə-rən\ *n* [ISV] (ca. 1885) : a yellowish brown granular pigment formed by breakdown of hemoglobin and composed essentially of colloidal ferric oxide
he·mo·sta·sis \ˌhē-mə-ˈstā-səs\ *n* [NL, fr. Gk *haimostasis* styptic, fr. *haimo-* hem- + *-stasis*] (1843) : arrest of bleeding
he·mo·stat \ˈhē-mə-ˌstat\ *n* (ca. 1903) : HEMOSTATIC; *esp* : an instrument for compressing a bleeding vessel
[1]**he·mo·stat·ic** \ˌhē-mə-ˈstat-ik\ *n* (1706) : an agent that checks bleeding
[2]**hemostatic** *adj* (1834) **1 :** of or caused by hemostasis **2 :** serving to check bleeding
hemp \ˈhemp\ *n* [ME, fr. OE *hænep;* akin to OHG *hanaf* hemp; both prob. fr. the source of Gk *kannabis* hemp] (bef. 12c) **1 a :** a tall widely cultivated Asian herb (*Cannabis sativa*) of the mulberry family with tough bast fiber used esp. for cordage **b :** the fiber of hemp **c :** a psychoactive drug (as marijuana or hashish) from hemp **2 :** a fiber (as jute) from a plant other than the true hemp; *also* : a plant yielding such fiber
hemp·en \ˈhem-pən\ *adj* (14c) : of, relating to, or resembling hemp
hemp nettle *n* (1801) : any of a genus (*Galeopsis*) of coarse Old World herbs of the mint family; *esp* : a bristly Eurasian herb (*G. tetrahit*) common in the U.S. as a weed
[1]**hem·stitch** \ˈhem-ˌstich\ *vt* (1839) : to decorate (as a border) with hemstitch — **hem·stitch·er** *n*
[2]**hemstitch** *n* (1853) **1 :** decorative needlework similar to drawnwork that is used esp. on or next to the stitching line of hems **2 :** a stitch used in hemstitching
hen \ˈhen\ *n* [ME, fr. OE *henn;* akin to OE *hana* rooster — more at CHANT] (bef. 12c) **1 a :** a female domestic fowl esp. over a year old; *broadly* : a female bird **b :** the female of various mostly aquatic animals (as lobsters or fish) **2 :** WOMAN; *specif* : a fussy middle-aged woman
hen and chickens *n* (1884) : any of several plants having offsets, runners, or proliferous flowers; *esp* : HOUSELEEK
hen·bane \ˈhen-ˌbān\ *n* (13c) : a poisonous fetid Old World herb (*Hyoscyamus niger*) of the nightshade family having sticky hairy dentate leaves and yellowish brown flowers and yielding hyoscyamine and scopolamine
hence \ˈhen(t)s\ *adv* [ME *hennes, henne,* fr. OE *heonan;* akin to OHG *hinnan* away, OE *hēr* here] (bef. 12c) **1 :** from this place : AWAY; *specif* : from this world or life **2 a** *archaic* : HENCEFORTH **b :** from this

time **3 :** because of a preceding fact or premise : THEREFORE **4 :** from this source or origin

hence·forth \'hen(t)s-,fō(ə)rth, -,fȯ(ə)rth, hen(t)s-'\ *adv* (12c) : from this point on

hence·for·ward \hen(t)s-'fȯr-wərd\ *adv* (14c) : HENCEFORTH

hench·man \'hench-mən\ *n* [ME *hengestman* groom, fr. *hengest* stallion (fr. OE) + *man;* akin to OHG *hengist* gelding] (14c) **1** *obs* : a squire or page to a person of high rank **2 a :** a trusted follower : a right-hand man **b :** a political follower whose support is chiefly for personal advantage **c :** an unscrupulous often violent member of a gang

hen·deca·syl·lab·ic \(,)hen-,dek-ə-sə-'lab-ik\ *adj* [L *hendecasyllabus,* fr. Gk *hendeka* eleven (fr. *hen-, heis* one + *deka* ten) + *syllabē* syllable — more at SAME, TEN] (ca. 1727) : consisting of 11 syllables or composed of verses of 11 syllables — **hendecasyllabic** *n* — **hen·deca·syl·la·ble** \hen-'dek-ə-,sil-ə-bəl, (,)hen-,dek-ə-'\ *n*

hen·di·a·dys \hen-'dī-ə-dəs\ *n* [LL *hendiadys, hendiadyoin,* modif. of Gk *hen dia dyoin,* lit., one through two] (1586) : the expression of an idea by the use of usu. two independent words connected by *and* (as *nice and warm*) instead of the usual combination of independent word and its modifier (as *nicely warm*)

hen·e·quen \'hen-i-kən, ,hen-i-'ken\ *n* [Sp *henequén*] (1880) : a strong yellowish or reddish hard fiber obtained from the leaves of a tropical American agave chiefly in Yucatán and used esp. for binder twine; *also* : a plant (*Agave fourcroydes*) that yields henequen

hen·house \'hen-,hau̇s\ *n, pl* **hen·hous·es** \-,hau̇-zəz\ (ca. 1512) : a house or shelter for fowl

Hen·le's loop \,hen-lēz-\ *n* (ca. 1890) : LOOP OF HENLE

1hen·na \'hen-ə\ *n* [Ar *ḥinnā'*] (1600) **1 :** an Old World tropical shrub or small tree (*Lawsonia inermis*) of the loosestrife family with small opposite leaves and axillary panicles of fragrant white flowers **2 :** a reddish brown dye obtained from leaves of the henna plant and used esp. on hair

2henna *vt* (1919) : to dye (as hair) with henna

hen·nery \'hen-ə-rē\ *n, pl* **-ner·ies** (1850) : a poultry farm; *also* : an enclosure for poultry

heno·the·ism \'hen-ə-(,)thē-,iz-əm\ *n* [G *henotheismus,* fr. Gk *hen-, heis* one + *theos* god — more at SAME] (1860) : the worship of one god without denying the existence of other gods — **heno·the·ist** \-,thē-əst\ *n* — **heno·the·is·tic** \,hen-ə-thē-'is-tik\ *adj*

hen party *n* (ca. 1885) : a party for women only

hen·peck \'hen-,pek\ *vt* (1688) : to subject (one's husband) to persistent nagging and domination

hen·ry \'hen-rē\ *n, pl* **henrys** *or* **henries** [Joseph *Henry*] (ca. 1890) : the practical meter-kilogram-second unit of inductance equal to the self-inductance of a circuit or the mutual inductance of two circuits in which the variation of one ampere per second results in an induced electromotive force of one volt

hent \'hent\ *vt* [ME *henten,* fr. OE *hentan* — more at HUNT] *archaic* (bef. 12c) : SEIZE

hen track *n* (1907) : an illegible or scarcely legible mark intended as handwriting — called also *hen scratch*

1hep \'hep, 'həp, 'hət\ *interj* [origin unknown] (1862) — used to mark a marching cadence

2hep \'hep\ *var of* HIP

hep·a·rin \'hep-ə-rən\ *n* [ISV, fr. Gk *hēpar* liver] (1918) : a mucopolysaccharide sulfuric acid ester that is found esp. in liver, that prolongs the clotting time of blood, and that is used medically — **hep·a·rin·ized** \-rə-,nīzd\ *adj*

hepat- *or* **hepato-** *comb form* [L, fr. Gk *hēpat-, hēpato-,* fr. *hēpat-, hēpar*] **1 :** liver ⟨*hepat*ectomy⟩ ⟨*hepato*toxic⟩ **2 :** hepatic and ⟨*hepato*biliary⟩

hep·a·tec·to·my \,hep-ə-'tek-tə-mē\ *n, pl* **-mies** (ca. 1890) : excision of the liver or of part of the liver — **hep·a·tec·to·mized** \-,mīzd\ *adj*

1he·pat·ic \hi-'pat-ik\ *adj* [L *hepaticus,* fr. Gk *hēpatikos,* fr. *hēpat-, hēpar;* akin to L *jecur* liver] (15c) : of, relating to, affecting, associated with, supplying, or draining the liver ⟨a ~ complaint⟩ ⟨~ arteries⟩

2hepatic *n* (1900) : LIVERWORT

he·pat·i·ca \hi-'pat-i-kə\ *n* [NL, fr. ML, liverwort, fr. L, fem. of *hepaticus*] (1578) : a plant of a genus (*Hepatica*) of herbs of the buttercup family with lobed leaves and delicate flowers

hep·a·ti·tis \,hep-ə-'tīt-əs\ *n, pl* **-tit·i·des** \-'tit-ə-,dēz\ (ca. 1727) **1 :** inflammation of the liver **2 :** a disease or condition marked by inflammation of the liver: as **a :** INFECTIOUS HEPATITIS **b :** SERUM HEPATITIS

hepatitis A *n* (1973) : INFECTIOUS HEPATITIS

hepatitis B *n* (1973) : SERUM HEPATITIS

he·pa·to·cel·lu·lar \,hep-ət-ō-'sel-yə-lər, hi-,pat-ə-'sel-\ *adj* (1940) : of or involving hepatocytes ⟨~ carcinoma⟩

he·pa·to·cyte \hi-'pat-ə-,sīt, 'hep-ət-ə-\ *n* (1965) : an epithelial parenchymatous cell of the liver

hep·a·to·ma \,hep-ə-'tō-mə\ *n, pl* **-mas** *or* **-ma·ta** \-mət-ə\ [NL] (1926) : a usu. malignant tumor of the liver

he·pa·to·meg·a·ly \,hep-ət-ō-'meg-ə-lē, hi-pat-ə-'meg-\ *n, pl* **-lies** [*hepat-* + *-megaly* abnormal enlargement, fr. NL *-megalia,* fr. *megal-* megal-] (ca. 1901) : enlargement of the liver

he·pa·to·pan·cre·as \-'paŋ-krē-əs, -'pan-\ *n* (1884) : a glandular structure (as of a crustacean) that combines the digestive functions of the vertebrate liver and pancreas

hep·a·to·tox·ic \-'täk-sik\ *adj* (1926) : relating to or causing injury to the liver ⟨~ drugs⟩

hep·a·to·tox·ic·i·ty \-täk-'sis-ət-ē\ *n* (1952) **1 :** a state of toxic damage to the liver **2 :** a tendency or capacity to cause hepatotoxicity

hep·cat \'hep-,kat\ *n* (ca. 1925) : HIPSTER

He·phaes·tus \hi-'fes-təs, -'fēs-\ *n* [L, fr. Gk *Hēphaistos*] : the Greek god of fire and metalworking — compare VULCAN

hepped up \'hept-'əp\ *adj* (1947) : ENTHUSIASTIC

Hep·ple·white \'hep-əl-,hwīt, -,wīt\ *adj* [George *Hepplewhite*] (1897) : of, relating to, or imitating a style of furniture originating in late 18th century England

hepta- *or* **hept-** *comb form* [Gk, fr. *hepta* — more at SEVEN] **1 :** seven ⟨*hepta*meter⟩ **2 :** containing seven atoms, groups, or equivalents ⟨*hept*ane⟩

hep·ta·chlor \'hep-tə-,klō(ə)r, -,klȯ(ə)r\ *n* [*hepta-* + *chlorine*] (1949) : a persistent cyclodiene chlorinated hydrocarbon pesticide $C_{10}H_5Cl_7$

hep·tad \'hep-,tad\ *n* [Gk *heptad-, heptas,* fr. *hepta*] (1660) : a group of seven

hep·ta·gon \'hep-tə-,gän\ *n* [Gk *heptagōnos* heptagonal, fr. *hepta* + *gōnia* angle — more at -GON] (1570) : a polygon of seven angles and seven sides — **hep·tag·o·nal** \hep-'tag-ən-ᵊl\ *adj*

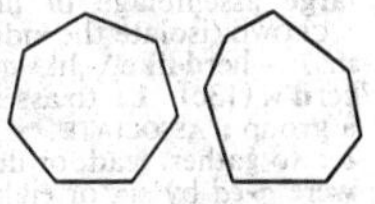

heptagon

hep·tam·e·ter \hep-'tam-ət-ər\ *n* (ca. 1898) : a line of verse consisting of seven metrical feet

hep·tane \'hep-,tān\ *n* (1877) : any of several isomeric hydrocarbons C_7H_{16} of the methane series; *esp* : the liquid normal isomer occurring in petroleum and used esp. as a solvent and in determining octane numbers

hep·tar·chy \'hep-,tär-kē\ *n* (1576) : a hypothetical confederacy of seven Anglo-Saxon kingdoms of the 7th and 8th centuries

Hep·ta·teuch \'hep-tə-,t(y)ük\ *n* [LL *heptateuchos,* fr. Gk, fr. *hepta* + *teuchos* book — more at PENTATEUCH] (1678) : the first seven books of the canonical Jewish and Christian Scriptures

hep·tose \'hep-,tōs, -,tōz\ *n* (1890) : any monosaccharide $C_7H_{14}O_7$ containing seven carbon atoms in the molecule

1her \(h)ər, ,hər\ *adj* [ME *hire,* fr. OE *hiere,* gen. of *hēo* she — more at HE] (bef. 12c) : of or relating to her or herself esp. as possessor, agent, or object of an action ⟨~ house⟩ ⟨~ research⟩ ⟨~ rescue⟩ — compare 1SHE

2her \ər, (')hər\ *pron, objective case of* SHE

He·ra \'hir-ə, 'hē-rə\ *n* [Gk *Hēra, Hērē*] : the sister and consort of Zeus — compare JUNO

Her·a·cles \'her-ə-,klēz\ *n* [Gk *Hēraklēs*] : HERCULES

1her·ald \'her-əld\ *n* [ME, fr. MF *hiraut,* fr. an (assumed) Gmc compound whose first component is akin to OHG *heri* army, and whose second is akin to OHG *waltan* to rule — more at HARRY, WIELD] (14c) **1 a :** an official at a tournament of arms with duties including the making of announcements and the marshaling of combatants **b :** an officer with the status of ambassador acting as official messenger between leaders esp. in war **c** (1) : OFFICER OF ARMS (2) : an officer of arms ranking above a pursuivant and below a king of arms **2 :** an official crier or messenger **3 a :** HARBINGER **b :** one that conveys news or proclaims : ANNOUNCER ⟨it was the lark, the ~ of the morn — Shak.⟩ **c :** one that supports or advocates : SPOKESMAN **syn** see FORERUNNER

2herald *vt* (14c) **1 :** to give notice of : ANNOUNCE **2 a :** to greet esp. with enthusiasm : HAIL **b :** PUBLICIZE **3 :** to signal the approach of : FORESHADOW

he·ral·dic \he-'ral-dik, hə-\ *adj* (1772) : of or relating to heralds or heraldry — **he·ral·di·cal·ly** \-di-k(ə-)lē\ *adv*

her·ald·ry \'her-əl-drē\ *n, pl* **-ries** (1572) **1 :** the practice of devising, blazoning, and granting armorial insignia and of tracing and recording genealogies **2 :** an armorial ensign; *broadly* : INSIGNIA **3 :** PAGEANTRY

herb \'ərb, *US also & Brit usu* 'hərb\ *n, often attrib* [ME *herbe,* fr. OF, fr. L *herba*] (13c) **1 :** a seed-producing annual, biennial, or perennial that does not develop persistent woody tissue but dies down at the end of a growing season **2 :** a plant or plant part valued for its medicinal, savory, or aromatic qualities — **herb·like** \'(h)ər-,blīk\ *adj* — **herby** \'(h)ər-bē\ *adj*

her·ba·ceous \,(h)ər-'bā-shəs\ *adj* (1646) **1 a :** of, relating to, or having the characteristics of an herb **b** *of a stem* : having little or no woody tissue and persisting usu. for a single growing season **2 :** having the texture, color, or appearance of a leaf

herb·age \'(h)ər-bij\ *n* (14c) **1 :** herbaceous vegetation (as grass) esp. when used for grazing **2 :** the succulent parts of herbaceous plants

1herb·al \'(h)ər-bəl\ *n* (1516) **1 :** a book about plants esp. with reference to their medical properties **2** *archaic* : HERBARIUM 1

2herbal *adj* (1612) : of, relating to, or made of herbs

herb·al·ist \(')(h)ər-bə-ləst\ *n* (1594) **1 :** one who collects or grows herbs **2 :** one who practices healing by the use of herbs

her·bar·i·um \,(h)ər-'bar-ē-əm, -'ber-\ *n, pl* **-ia** \-ē-ə\ [LL, fr. *herba* + *-arium* -ary] (1776) **1 :** a collection of dried plant specimens usu. mounted and systematically arranged for reference **2 :** a place that houses an herbarium

herb doctor *n* (1828) : HERBALIST 2

herbed \'(h)ərbd\ *adj* (1950) : seasoned with herbs

her·bi·cide \'(h)ər-bə-,sīd\ *n* [L *herba* + ISV *-cide*] (1899) : an agent used to destroy or inhibit plant growth — **her·bi·cid·al** \,(h)ər-bə-'sīd-ᵊl\ *adj* — **her·bi·cid·al·ly** \-ᵊl-ē\ *adv*

her·bi·vore \'(h)ər-bə-,vō(ə)r, -,vȯ(ə)r\ *n* [NL *Herbivora,* group of mammals, fr. neut. pl. of *herbivorus*] (1854) : a plant-eating animal; *esp* : UNGULATE

her·biv·o·rous \,(h)ər-'biv-ə-rəs\ *adj* [NL *herbivorus,* fr. L *herba* grass + *-vorus* -vorous] (1661) : feeding on plants — **her·biv·o·rous·ly** *adv* — **her·biv·o·ry** \-ə-rē\ *n*

herb Rob·ert \,(h)ərb-'räb-ərt\ *n* [ML *herba Roberti,* prob. fr. *Robertus* (St. Robert) †1067 Fr. ecclesiastic] (13c) : a sticky low geranium (*Geranium robertianum*) with small reddish purple flowers

Her·cu·le·an \,hər-kyə-'lē-ən, ,hər-'kyü-lē-\ *adj* (1596) **1 :** of, relating to, or characteristic of Hercules **2** *often not cap* : of extraordinary power, extent, intensity, or difficulty

Her·cu·les \'hər-kyə-,lēz\ *n* [L, fr. Gk *Hēraklēs*] **1 :** a mythical Greek hero renowned for his great strength and esp. for performing 12 labors imposed on him by Hera **2** [L (gen. *Herculis*)] : a northern constellation between Corona Borealis and Lyra

Her·cu·les'–club \,hər-kyə-,lēz-'kləb\ *n* (1847) **1 :** a small prickly eastern U.S. tree (*Aralia spinosa*) of the ginseng family — called also *angelica tree* **2 :** a prickly shrub or tree (genus *Zanthoxylum,* esp. *Z. clava-herculis*) of the rue family

1herd \'hərd\ *n* [ME, fr. OE *heord;* akin to OHG *herta* herd, Gk *korthys* heap] (bef. 12c) **1 a :** a number of animals of one kind kept together under human control **b :** a congregation of gregarious wild animals

2 **a** (1) : a group of people usu. having a common bond (2) : a large assemblage of like things **b** : the undistinguished masses : CROWD ⟨isolate the individual prophets from the ~ —Norman Cousins⟩ — **herd·like** \-,līk\ *adj*
[2]**herd** *vi* (13c) **1** : to assemble or move in a herd **2** : to place oneself in a group : ASSOCIATE ~ *vt* **1** **a** : to keep or move (animals) together **b** : to gather, lead, or drive as if in a herd ⟨seventy-five boys and girls were ~*ed* by six or eight teachers —W. A. White⟩ **2** : to place in a group
herd·er \'hərd-ər\ *n* (14c) : one that herds; *specif* : HERDSMAN 1
her·dic \'hərd-ik\ *n* [Peter *Herdic* †1888 Am. inventor] (1882) : a small 19th century American horse-drawn cab having side seats and an entrance at the back
herds·man \'hərdz-mən\ *n* (13c) **1** : a manager, breeder, or tender of livestock **2** *cap* : BOÖTES
[1]**here** \'hi(ə)r\ *adv* [ME, fr. OE *hēr;* akin to OHG *hier* here, OE *hē* he] (bef. 12c) **1** **a** : in or at this place ⟨turn ~⟩ — often used interjectionally esp. in answering a roll call **b** : NOW ⟨~ it's morning already⟩ **2** : at or in this point, particular, or case ⟨~ we agree⟩ **3** : in the present life or state **4** : HITHER ⟨come ~⟩ **5** — used interjectionally in rebuke or encouragement — **here goes** — used interjectionally to express resolution or resignation esp. at the beginning of a difficult or unpleasant undertaking — **neither here nor there** : having no interest or relevance : of no consequence ⟨matters of comfort are *neither here nor there* to a real sailing fan⟩
[2]**here** *n* (bef. 12c) : this place
[3]**here** *adj* (15c) **1** — used for emphasis esp. after a demonstrative pronoun or after a noun modified by a demonstrative adjective ⟨this book ~⟩ **2** *substand* — used for emphasis after a demonstrative adjective but before the noun modified ⟨this ~ book⟩
here·abouts \'hi(ə)r-ə-,bau̇ts\ *or* **here·about** \-,bau̇t\ *adv* (13c) : in this vicinity
[1]**here·af·ter** \hi(ə)r-'af-tər\ *adv* (bef. 12c) **1** : after this in sequence or in time **2** : in some future time or state
[2]**hereafter** *n, often cap* (1546) **1** : FUTURE **2** : an existence beyond earthly life
[3]**hereafter** *adj, archaic* (1591) : FUTURE
here and now *n* (1829) : the present time — used with *the* ⟨man's obligation is in the *here and now* —W. H. Whyte⟩
here and there *adv* (14c) **1** : in one place and another **2** : from time to time
here·away \'hi(ə)r-ə-,wā\ *or* **here·aways** \-,wāz\ *adv, dial* (15c) : HEREABOUTS
here·by \hi(ə)r-'bī, 'hi(ə)r-,\ *adv* (14c) : by this means
her·e·dit·a·ment \,her-ə-'dit-ə-mənt\ *n* [ML *hereditamentum,* fr. LL *hereditare* to inherit, fr. L *hered-, heres*] (15c) : heritable property
he·red·i·tar·i·an \hə-,red-ə-'ter-ē-ən\ *n* (1881) : an advocate of the theory that individual differences in human beings can be accounted for primarily on the basis of genetics — **hereditarian** *adj*
he·red·i·tary \hə-'red-ə-,ter-ē\ *adj* [L *hereditarius,* fr. *hereditas*] (15c) **1** **a** : genetically transmitted or transmittable from parent to offspring **b** : characteristic of or fostered by one's predecessors **2** **a** : received or passing by inheritance or required to pass by inheritance or by reason of birth **b** : having title or possession through inheritance or by reason of birth **3** : of a kind established by tradition ⟨~ enemy⟩ **4** : of or relating to inheritance or heredity — **he·red·i·tar·i·ly** \-,red-ə-'ter-ə-lē\ *adv*
he·red·i·ty \hə-'red-ət-ē\ *n* [MF *heredité,* fr. L *hereditat-, hereditas,* fr. *hered-, heres* heir — more at HEIR] (1540) **1** **a** : INHERITANCE **b** : TRADITION **2** **a** : the sum of the qualities and potentialities genetically derived from one's ancestors **b** : the transmission of such qualities from ancestor to descendant through the molecular mechanism lying primarily in the DNA or RNA of the genes
Her·e·ford \'hər-fərd *sometimes* 'her-ə-\ *n* [*Hereford* former county in England] (1805) : any of an English breed of hardy red beef cattle with white faces and markings now extensively raised in the western U.S.
here·in \hi(ə)r-'in\ *adv* (bef. 12c) : in this
here·in·above \(,)hi(ə)r-,in-ə-'bəv\ *adv* (1802) : at a prior point in this writing or document
here·in·af·ter \,hi(ə)r-ə-'naf-tər\ *adv* (1590) : in the following part of this writing or document
here·in·be·fore \(,)hi(ə)r-,in-bi-'fō(ə)r, -'fȯ(ə)r\ *adv* (1687) : in the preceding part of this writing or document
here·in·be·low \-bi-'lō\ *adv* (1946) : at a subsequent point in this writing or document
here·of \hi(ə)r-'əv, -'äv\ *adv* (bef. 12c) : of this
here·on \-'ȯn, -'än\ *adv* (12c) : on this
He·re·ro \hə-'re(ə)r-(,)ō, 'her-ə-,rō\ *n, pl* **Herero** *or* **Hereros** (1862) : a member of a Bantu people of the central part of southwest Africa
he·re·si·arch \hə-'rē-zē-,ärk, 'her-ə-sē-\ *n* [LL *haeresiarcha,* fr. LGk *hairesiarchēs,* fr. *hairesis* + Gk *-archēs* -arch] (1624) : an originator or chief advocate of a heresy
her·e·sy \'her-ə-sē\ *n, pl* **-sies** [ME *heresie,* fr. OF, fr. LL *haeresis,* fr. LGk *hairesis,* fr. Gk, action of taking, choice, sect, fr. *hairein* to take] (13c) **1** **a** : adherence to a religious opinion contrary to church dogma **b** : denial of a revealed truth by a baptized member of the Roman Catholic Church **c** : an opinion or doctrine contrary to church dogma **2** **a** : dissent or deviation from a dominant theory, opinion, or practice **b** : an opinion, doctrine, or practice contrary to the truth or to generally accepted beliefs or standards
her·e·tic \'her-ə-,tik\ *n* (14c) **1** : a dissenter from established church dogma; *esp* : a baptized member of the Roman Catholic Church who disavows a revealed truth **2** : one who dissents from an accepted belief or doctrine : NONCONFORMIST
he·ret·i·cal \hə-'ret-i-kəl\ *also* **he·re·tic** \'her-ə-,tik, hə-'ret-ik\ *adj* (15c) **1** : of, relating to, or characterized by heresy **2** : of, relating to, or characterized by departure from accepted beliefs or standards : UNORTHODOX — **he·ret·i·cal·ly** \hə-'ret-i-k(ə-)lē\ *adv* — **he·ret·i·cal·ness** \-kəl-nəs\ *n*
here·to \hi(ə)r-'tü\ *adv* (12c) : to this writing or document
here·to·fore \'hi(ə)rt-ə-,fō(ə)r, -,fȯ(ə)r, ,hirt-ə-'\ *adv* (14c) : up to this time : HITHERTO
here·un·der \hi(ə)r-'ən-dər\ *adv* (15c) : under or in accordance with this writing or document
here·un·to \hi(ə)r-'ən-(,)tü, ,hi(ə)r-(,)ən-'tü\ *adv* (1509) : to this
here·upon \'hi(ə)r-ə-,pȯn, -,pän, ,hir-ə-'\ *adv* (12c) : on this : immediately after this
here·with \hi(ə)r-'with, -'with\ *adv* (bef. 12c) **1** : with this communication : enclosed in this **2** : HEREBY
her·i·ot \'her-ē-ət\ *n* [ME, fr. OE *heregeatwe,* pl., military equipment, fr. *here* army (akin to OHG *heri* army) + *geatwe* equipment — more at HARRY] (bef. 12c) : a feudal duty or tribute due under English law to a lord on the death of a tenant
her·i·ta·bil·i·ty \,her-ət-ə-'bil-ət-ē\ *n* (1832) **1** : the quality or state of being heritable **2** : the proportion of observed variation in a particular trait (as intelligence) that can be attributed to inherited genetic factors in contrast to environmental ones
her·i·ta·ble \'her-ət-ə-bəl\ *adj* (14c) **1** : capable of being inherited or of passing by inheritance **2** : HEREDITARY
her·i·tage \'her-ət-ij\ *n* [ME, fr. MF, fr. *heriter* to inherit, fr. LL *hereditare,* fr. L *hered-, heres* heir — more at HEIR] (13c) **1** : property that descends to an heir **2** **a** : something transmitted by or acquired from a predecessor : LEGACY, INHERITANCE **b** : TRADITION **3** : something possessed as a result of one's natural situation or birth : BIRTHRIGHT ⟨the nation's ~ of tolerance⟩
her·i·tor \'her-ət-ər\ *n* (15c) : one that inherits : INHERITOR
herky–jerky \'hər-kē-'jər-kē\ *adj* [redupl. of *jerky*] (1957) : characterized by sudden, irregular, or unpredictable movement or style
herm \'hərm\ *n* [L *hermes,* fr. Gk *hermēs* statue of Hermes, herm, fr. *Hermēs*] (1579) : a statue in the form of a square stone pillar surmounted by a bust or head esp. of Hermes
her·ma \'hər-mə\ *n* (1638) : HERM
her·maph·ro·dite \(,)hər-'maf-rə-,dīt\ *n* [ME *hermofrodite,* fr. L *hermaphroditus,* fr. Gk *hermaphroditos,* fr. *Hermaphroditos*] (14c) **1** **a** : an animal or plant having both male and female reproductive organs **b** : HOMOSEXUAL **2** : something that is a combination of diverse elements — **hermaphrodite** *adj* — **her·maph·ro·dit·ic** \(,)hər-,maf-rə-'dit-ik\ *adj* — **her·maph·ro·dit·ism** \-'maf-rə-,dīt-,iz-əm\ *n*
hermaphrodite brig *n* (1840) : a 2-masted vessel square-rigged forward and schooner-rigged aft

hermaphrodite brig

Her·maph·ro·di·tus \(,)hər-,maf-rə-'dīt-əs\ *n* [L, fr. Gk *Hermaphroditos,* fr. *Hermēs* + *Aphroditē* Aphrodite] : a son of Hermes and Aphrodite who becomes joined in one body with a nymph while bathing
her·ma·typ·ic \,hər-mə-'tip-ik\ *adj* [Gk *herma* prop, reef + *typtein* to strike, coin + E *-ic* — more at TYPE] (1950) : building reefs ⟨~ corals⟩
her·me·neu·ti·cal \,hər-mə-'n(y)üt-i-kəl\ *or* **her·me·neu·tic** \-ik\ *adj* [Gk *hermēneutikos,* fr. *hermēneuein* to interpret, fr. *hermēneus* interpreter] (1678) : of or relating to hermeneutics : INTERPRETATIVE — **her·me·neu·ti·cal·ly** \-i-k(ə-)lē\ *adv*
her·me·neu·tics \-iks\ *n pl but sing or pl in constr* (1737) : the study of the methodological principles of interpretation (as of the Bible)
Her·mes \'hər-(,)mēz\ *n* [L, fr. Gk *Hermēs*] : a Greek god of commerce, eloquence, invention, travel, and theft who serves as herald and messenger of the other gods — compare MERCURY
Hermes Tris·me·gis·tus \-,tris-mə-'jis-təs\ *n* [Gk *Hermēs trismegistos,* lit., Hermes thrice greatest] : a legendary author of works embodying magical, astrological, and alchemical doctrines
her·met·ic \(,)hər-'met-ik\ *also* **her·met·i·cal** \-i-kəl\ *adj* [NL *hermeticus,* fr. *Hermet-, Hermes Trismegistus*] (1605) **1** *often cap* **a** : of or relating to the Gnostic writings or teachings arising in the first three centuries A.D. and attributed to Hermes Trismegistus **b** : relating to or characterized by occultism or abstruseness : RECONDITE **2** [fr. the belief that Hermes Trismegistus invented a magic seal to keep vessels airtight] **a** : AIRTIGHT ⟨~ seal⟩ **b** : impervious to external influence ⟨trapped inside the ~ military machine —Jack Newfield⟩ **c** : RECLUSE, SOLITARY ⟨leads a ~ life⟩ — **her·met·i·cal·ly** \-i-k(ə-)lē\ *adv*
her·met·i·cism \-'met-ə-,siz-əm\ *n, often cap* (1897) : HERMETISM
her·me·tism \'hər-mə-,tiz-əm\ *n, often cap* (1894) **1** : a system of ideas based on hermetic teachings **2** : adherence to or practice of hermetic doctrine — **her·me·tist** \-mət-əst\ *n*
her·mit \'hər-mət\ *n* [ME *eremite,* fr. OF, fr. LL *eremita,* fr. LGk *erēmitēs,* fr. Gk, adj., living in the desert, fr. *erēmia* desert, fr. *erēmos* lonely] (12c) **1** **a** : one that retires from society and lives in solitude esp. for religious reasons : RECLUSE **b** *obs* : BEADSMAN **2** : a spiced molasses cookie — **her·mit·ism** \-,iz-əm\ *n*
her·mit·age \'hər-mət-ij\ *n* (13c) **1** **a** : the habitation of a hermit **b** : a secluded residence or private retreat : HIDEAWAY **c** : MONASTERY **2** : the life or condition of a hermit
Her·mi·tage \,(h)er-mi-'täzh\ *n* [Tain-l'*Ermitage,* commune in France] (1680) : a red or white Rhone valley wine
hermit crab *n* (1735) : any of numerous chiefly marine decapod crustaceans (families Paguridae and Parapaguridae) having soft asymmetrical abdomens and occupying the empty shells of gastropods
Her·mi·tian matrix \er-,mē-shən-, ,hər-,mish-ən-\ *n* [Charles *Hermite* †1901 Fr. mathematician] (1935) : a square matrix having the property that each pair of elements in the *i*th row and *j*th column and in the *j*th row and *i*th column are conjugate complex numbers
hern \'he(ə)rn, 'hərn\ *dial var of* HERON
her·nia \'hər-nē-ə\ *n, pl* **-ni·as** *or* **-ni·ae** \-nē-,ē, -nē-,ī\ [L — more at YARN] (14c) : a protrusion of an organ or part through connective tissue or through a wall of the cavity in which it is normally enclosed — called also *rupture* — **her·ni·al** \-nē-əl\ *adj*
her·ni·ate \'hər-nē-,āt\ *vi* **-at·ed; -at·ing** (1876) : to protrude through an abnormal body opening : RUPTURE — **her·ni·a·tion** \,hər-nē-'ā-shən\ *n*
he·ro \'hē-(,)rō, 'hi(ə)r-(,)ō\ *n, pl* **heroes** [L *heros,* fr. Gk *hērōs;* perh. akin to L *servare* to protect] (14c) **1** **a** : a mythological or legendary figure often of divine descent endowed with great strength or ability **b** : an illustrious warrior **c** : a man admired for his achievements and noble qualities **d** : one that shows great courage **2** **a** : the principal male character in a literary or dramatic work **b** : the central figure in an event, period, or movement **3** *pl usu* **heros** : SUBMARINE 2 **4** : an object of extreme admiration and devotion : IDOL

Hero *n* [L, fr. Gk *Hērō*] **:** a legendary priestess of Aphrodite loved by Leander

[1]**he·ro·ic** \hi-'rō-ik *also* her-'ō- *or* hē-'rō-\ *also* **he·ro·ical** \-i-kəl\ *adj* (1549) **1 :** of, relating to, or resembling heroes esp. of antiquity **2 a :** exhibiting or marked by courage and daring **b :** supremely noble or self-sacrificing **3 a :** of impressive size, power, extent, or effect **:** POTENT ⟨~ doses⟩ ⟨a ~ voice⟩ **b :** of great intensity **:** EXTREME, DRASTIC ⟨~ effort⟩ **4 :** of, relating to, or constituting drama written during the Restoration in heroic couplets and concerned with a conflict between love and honor — **he·ro·ical·ly** \-i-k(ə-)lē\ *adv*

[2]**heroic** *n* (ca. 1570) **1 :** a heroic verse or poem **2** *pl* **a :** flamboyantly heroic language or action **b :** heroic action or behavior **c :** determined effort esp. in the face of difficulty

heroic couplet *n* (1903) **:** a rhyming couplet in iambic pentameter

he·roi·com·ic \hi-ˌrō-i-'käm-ik\ *or* **he·roi·com·i·cal** \-'käm-i-kəl\ *adj* [F *héroïcomique*, fr. *héroïque* heroic + *comique* comic] (1756) **:** comic by being ludicrously noble, bold, or elevated

heroic poem *n* (1693) **:** an epic or a poem in epic style

heroic stanza *n* (ca. 1922) **:** a rhymed quatrain in heroic verse with a rhyme scheme of *abab* — called also *heroic quatrain*

heroic verse *n* (1586) **1 :** dactylic hexameter esp. of epic verse of classical times — called also *heroic meter* **2 :** the iambic pentameter used esp. in English epic poetry during the 17th and 18th centuries — called also *heroic line, heroic meter*

her·o·in \'her-ə-wən\ *n* [fr. *Heroin*, a trademark] (1898) **:** a strongly physiologically addictive narcotic $C_{21}H_{23}NO_5$ that is made by acetylation of but is more potent than morphine and that is prohibited for medical use in the U.S. but is used illicitly for its euphoric effects — **her·o·in·ism** \-wə-ˌniz-əm\ *n*

her·o·ine \'her-ə-wən\ *n* [L *heroina*, fr. Gk *hērōinē*, fem. of *hērōs*] (1609) **1 a :** a mythological or legendary woman having the qualities of a hero **b :** a woman admired and emulated for her achievements and qualities **2 a :** the principal female character in a literary or dramatic work **b :** the central female figure in an event or period

her·o·ism \'her-ə-ˌwiz-əm *also* 'hir-\ *n* (1717) **1 :** heroic conduct esp. as exhibited in fulfilling a high purpose or attaining a noble end **2 :** the qualities of a hero

he·ro·ize \'hē-(ˌ)rō-ˌīz, 'hir-(ˌ)ō-; 'her-ə-ˌwīz\ *vt* **-ized; -iz·ing** (1738) **:** to make heroic

her·on \'her-ən\ *n, pl* **herons** *also* **heron** [ME *heiroun*, fr. MF *hairon*, of Gmc origin; akin to OHG *heigaro* heron, Gk *krizein* to creak, OHG *scrīan* to scream] (14c) **:** any of various long-necked wading birds (family Ardeidae) with a long tapering bill, large wings, and soft plumage

her·on·ry \-ən-rē\ *n, pl* **-ries** (1616) **:** a heron rookery

hero–worship *vt* (1857) **:** to feel or express hero worship for — **hero–worshiper** *n*

hero worship *n* (1774) **1 :** veneration of a hero **2 :** foolish or excessive adulation for an individual

her·pes \'hər-(ˌ)pēz\ *n* [L, fr. Gk *herpēs*, fr. *herpein* to creep — more at SERPENT] (14c) **:** any of several inflammatory virus diseases of the skin characterized by clusters of vesicles; *esp* **:** HERPES SIMPLEX — **her·pet·ic** \(ˌ)hər-'pet-ik\ *adj*

her·pes sim·plex \ˌhər-(ˌ)pēz-'sim-ˌpleks\ *n* [NL, lit., simple herpes] (1907) **:** either of two virus diseases marked in one case by groups of watery blisters on the skin or mucous membranes (as of the mouth and lips) above the waist and in the other by such blisters on the genitals

her·pes·vi·rus \-'vī-rəs\ *n* (1925) **:** any of a group of DNA-containing viruses that replicate in cell nuclei and produce herpes

herpes zos·ter \-'zäs-tər\ *n* [NL, lit., girdle herpes] (1807) **:** an acute viral inflammation of the sensory ganglia of spinal and cranial nerves associated with a vesicular eruption and neuralgic pains — called also *shingles*

herpet- *or* **herpeto-** *comb form* [Gk *herpeton*, fr. neut. of *herpetos* creeping, fr. *herpein*] **1 :** reptile or reptiles **2** [L *herpet-, herpes*] **:** herpes

her·pe·tol·o·gy \ˌhər-pə-'täl-ə-jē\ *n* (1824) **:** a branch of zoology dealing with reptiles and amphibians — **her·pe·to·log·i·cal** \-i-kəl\ *adj* — **her·pe·tol·o·gist** \ˌhər-pə-'täl-ə-jəst\ *n*

Herr \(ˌ)he(ə)r\ *n, pl* **Her·ren** \ˌher-ən, (ˌ)he(ə)rn\ [G] (1653) — used among German-speaking people as a title equivalent to *Mr.*

her·ren·volk \'her-ən-ˌfōk, -ˌfōlk\ *n, often cap* [G] (1940) **:** MASTER RACE

her·ring \'her-iŋ\ *n, pl* **herring** *or* **herrings** [ME *hering*, fr. OE *hǣring*; akin to OHG *hārinc* herring] (bef. 12c) **:** a valuable clupeid food fish (*Clupea harengus harengus*) that is abundant in the temperate and colder parts of the north Atlantic and as a different subspecies (*C. h. pallasi*) in the north Pacific and that is preserved in the adult state by smoking or salting and in the young state is extensively canned and sold as sardines; *broadly* **:** a fish of the same family (Clupeidae)

[1]**her·ring·bone** \'her-iŋ-ˌbōn\ *n, often attrib* (1659) **1 :** a pattern made up of rows of parallel lines which in any two adjacent rows slope in opposite directions **2 a :** a twilled fabric with a herringbone pattern; *also* **:** a suit made of this fabric **b :** a herringbone arrangement (as of materials or parts) **3 :** a method in skiing of ascending a slope by herringboning

[2]**herringbone** *vt* (1787) **1 :** to produce a herringbone pattern on **2 :** to arrange in a herringbone pattern ~ *vi* **1 :** to produce a herringbone pattern **2 :** to ascend a slope by toeing out on skis and placing the weight on the inner side

herring gull *n* (1857) **:** a common large gull (*Larus argentatus*) of the northern hemisphere that as an adult is largely white with blue-gray mantle and dark wing tips and pink feet

hers \'hərz\ *pron, sing or pl in constr* **:** that which belongs to her — used without a following noun as a pronoun equivalent in meaning to the adjective *her*

her·self \(h)ər-'self, *Southern also* -'sef\ *pron* (bef. 12c) **1 :** that identical female one — compare [1]SHE; used reflexively, for emphasis, or in absolute constructions ⟨she considers ~ lucky⟩ ⟨she ~ did it⟩ ⟨~ an orphan, she understood the situation⟩ **2 :** her normal, healthy, or sane condition or self **3** *Irish & Scot* **:** a woman of consequence; *esp* **:** the mistress of the house

hertz \'hərts, 'he(ə)rts\ *n, pl* **hertz** [Heinrich R. *Hertz*] (1928) **:** a unit of frequency equal to one cycle per second — abbr. *Hz*

hertz·ian wave \ˌhert-sē-ən-, ˌhərt-\ *n* [Heinrich R. *Hertz*] (1897) **:** an electromagnetic wave produced by the oscillation of electricity in a conductor (as a radio antenna) and of a length ranging from less than a millimeter to many kilometers

he's \(ˌ)hēz, ēz\ **:** he is **:** he has

Hesh·van \'ḵesh-vən\ *n* [Heb *Ḥeshwān*] (ca. 1769) **:** the 2d month of the civil year or the 8th month of the ecclesiastical year in the Jewish calendar — see MONTH table

hes·i·tance \'hez-ə-tən(t)s\ *n* (1601) **:** HESITANCY

hes·i·tan·cy \-tən-sē\ *n, pl* **-cies** (1617) **1 :** the quality or state of being hesitant: as **a :** INDECISION **b :** RELUCTANCE ⟨we are putting our judgment ahead of yours . . . which we do only with the greatest ~ —Gay Talese⟩ **2 :** HESITATION 1

hes·i·tant \'hez-ə-tənt\ *adj* (1647) **:** tending to hesitate ***syn*** see DISINCLINED — **hes·i·tant·ly** *adv*

hes·i·tate \'hez-ə-ˌtāt\ *vb* **-tat·ed; -tat·ing** [L *haesitatus*, pp. of *haesitare* to stick fast, hesitate, fr. *haesus*, pp. of *haerēre* to stick; akin to Lith *gaišti* to loiter] *vi* (1623) **1 :** to hold back in doubt or indecision **2 :** to delay momentarily **:** PAUSE **3 :** STAMMER ~ *vt* **:** to hold back from in doubt or uncertainty ⟨wouldn't ~ to commit herself⟩ — **hes·i·tat·er** *n* — **hes·i·tat·ing·ly** \-ˌtāt-iŋ-lē\ *adv*

syn HESITATE, WAVER, VACILLATE, FALTER mean to show irresolution or uncertainty. HESITATE implies a pause before deciding or acting or choosing; WAVER implies hesitation after seeming to decide and so connotes weakness or a retreat; VACILLATE implies prolonged hesitation from inability to reach a firm decision; FALTER implies a wavering or stumbling and often connotes nervousness, lack of courage, or outright fear.

hes·i·ta·tion \ˌhez-ə-'tā-shən\ *n* (15c) **1 :** an act or instance of hesitating **2 :** a pausing or faltering in speech

Hes·pe·ri·an \he-'spir-ē-ən\ *adj* [L *Hesperia*, the west, fr. Gk, fr. fem. of *hesperios* of the evening, western, fr. *hesperos* evening — more at WEST] (15c) **:** WESTERN, OCCIDENTAL

Hes·per·i·des \he-'sper-ə-ˌdēz\ *n pl* [L, fr. Gk] **1 :** the nymphs in classical mythology who guard with the aid of a dragon a garden in which golden apples grow **2 :** a legendary garden at the western extremity of the world producing golden apples

hes·per·i·din \he-'sper-əd-ᵊn\ *n* [NL *hesperidium* orange, fr. L *Hesperides*] (1838) **:** a crystalline glycoside $C_{28}H_{34}O_{15}$ found in most citrus fruits and esp. in orange peel

hes·per·id·i·um \ˌhes-pə-'rid-ē-əm\ *n, pl* **-id·ia** \-ē-ə\ [NL] (1866) **:** a berry (as an orange or lime) having a leathery rind

Hes·per·us \'hes-p(ə-)rəs\ *n* [ME, fr. L, fr. Gk *Hesperos*] (14c) **:** EVENING STAR 1

hes·sian \'hesh-ən\ *n* (1729) **1** *cap* **a :** a native of Hesse **b :** a German mercenary serving in the British forces during the American Revolution; *broadly* **:** a mercenary soldier **2 :** BURLAP

Hessian boot *n* (1809) **:** a high boot that extends to just below the knee and is commonly ornamented with a tassel and that was introduced into England by the Hessians early in the 19th century

Hessian fly *n* (1787) **:** a small two-winged fly (*Mayetiola destructor*) that is destructive to wheat in America

hess·ite \'hes-ˌīt\ *n* [G *hessit*, fr. Henry *Hess* †1850 Swiss chemist] (1849) **:** a mineral Ag_2Te consisting of a lead-gray sectile silver telluride

hes·so·nite \'hes-ᵊn-ˌīt\ *var of* ESSONITE

hest \'hest\ *n* [ME *hest, hes*, fr. OE *hǣs*; akin to OE *hātan* to command — more at HIGHT] *archaic* (bef. 12c) **:** COMMAND, PRECEPT

Hes·tia \'hes-tē-ə, 'hes(h)-chə\ *n* [Gk] **:** the Greek goddess of the hearth and chief goddess of domestic activity — compare VESTA

he·tae·ra \hi-'tir-ə\ *or* **he·tai·ra** \-'tī-rə\ *n, pl* **he·tae·rae** \-'ti(ə)r-(ˌ)ē\ *or* **hetaeras** *or* **hetairas** *or* **he·tai·rai** \-'tī(ə)r-ˌī\ [Gk *hetaira*, lit., companion, fem. of *hetairos*] (1820) **1 :** one of a class of highly cultivated courtesans in ancient Greece **2 :** DEMIMONDAINE

heter- *or* **hetero-** *comb form* [MF or LL; MF, fr. LL, fr. Gk, fr. *heteros*; akin to Gk *heis* one — more at SAME] **1 :** other than usual **:** other **:** different ⟨*hetero*phyllous⟩ **2 :** containing atoms of different kinds ⟨*hetero*cyclic⟩

het·ero \'het-ə-ˌrō\ *n, pl* **-er·os** (1933) **:** HETEROSEXUAL — **hetero** *adj*

het·ero·at·om \'het-ə-rō-ˌat-əm\ *n* (1900) **:** an atom other than carbon in the ring of a heterocyclic compound

het·ero·aux·in \ˌhet-ə-rō-'ók-sən\ *n* (1935) **:** INDOLEACETIC ACID

het·ero·cer·cal \-'sər-kəl\ *adj* (1838) **1** *of a fish tail fin* **:** having the upper lobe larger than the lower with the end of the vertebral column prolonged and somewhat upturned in the upper lobe **2 :** having or relating to a heterocercal tail fin

het·ero·chro·mat·ic \-krə-'mat-ik\ *adj* (1895) **1 :** of, relating to, or having different colors **2 :** made up of various wavelengths or frequencies **3** [*heterochromatin*] **:** of or relating to heterochromatin

het·ero·chro·ma·tin \-'krō-mət-ən\ *n* [G] (1932) **:** densely staining chromatin that appears as nodules in or along chromosomes and contains relatively few genes

[1]**het·ero·clite** \'het-ə-rə-ˌklīt\ *n* (1580) **1 :** a word irregular in inflection; *esp* **:** a noun irregular in declension **2 :** one that deviates from common rules or forms

[2]**heteroclite** *adj* [MF or LL; MF, fr. LL *heteroclitus*, fr. Gk *heteroklitos*, fr. *heter-* + *klinein* to lean, inflect — more at LEAN] (1598) **:** deviating from common forms or rules

het·ero·cy·clic \ˌhet-ə-rō-'sī-klik, -'sik-lik\ *adj* [ISV] (ca. 1895) **:** relating to, characterized by, or being a ring composed of atoms of more than one kind — **het·ero·cy·cle** \'het-ə-rō-ˌsī-kəl\ *n* — **heterocyclic** *n*

het·ero·cyst \'het-ə-rō-ˌsist\ *n* (1872) **:** a large transparent thick-walled cell that resembles a spore and occurs at intervals along the filament in some blue-green algae — **het·ero·cys·tous** \ˌhet-ə-rō-'sis-təs\ *adj*

het·ero·dox \'het-ə-rə-ˌdäks, 'he-trə-\ *adj* [LL *heterodoxus*, fr. Gk *heterodoxos*, fr. *heter-* + *doxa* opinion — more at DOXOLOGY] (1637) **1 :** contrary to or different from an acknowledged standard or traditional form **:** UNORTHODOX, UNCONVENTIONAL ⟨a ~ sermon⟩ ⟨a ~ notion⟩ **2 :** holding unorthodox opinions or doctrines

het·ero·doxy \-ˌdäk-sē\ *n, pl* **-dox·ies** (1659) **1 :** the quality or state of being heterodox **2 :** a heterodox opinion or doctrine

het·ero·du·plex \ˌhet-ə-rō-ˈd(y)ü-ˌpleks\ *n* (1962) : a nucleic-acid molecule composed of two chains with each derived from a different parent molecule — **heteroduplex** *adj*

[1]**het·ero·dyne** \ˈhet-ə-rə-ˌdīn, ˈhe-trə-\ *adj* (1908) : of or relating to the production of an electrical beat between two radio frequencies of which one usu. is that of a received signal-carrying current and the other that of an uninterrupted current introduced into the apparatus; *also* : of or relating to the production of a beat between two optical frequencies

[2]**heterodyne** *vt* **-dyned; -dyn·ing** (1923) : to combine (as a radio frequency) with a different frequency so that a beat is produced

het·er·oe·cious \ˌhet-ə-ˈrē-shəs\ *adj* [*heter-* + Gk *oikia* house — more at VICINITY] (1882) : passing through the different stages in the life cycle on alternate and often unrelated hosts ⟨~ insects⟩ — **het·er·oe·cism** \-ˈrē-ˌsiz-əm\ *n*

het·ero·ga·mete \ˌhet-ə-rō-gə-ˈmēt, -ˈgam-ˌēt\ *n* [ISV] (1897) : either of a pair of gametes that differ in form, size, or behavior and occur typically as large nonmotile oogametes and small motile sperms — **het·ero·gam·e·ty** \-ˈgam-ət-ē\ *n*

het·ero·ga·met·ic \-gə-ˈmet-ik\ *adj* (1910) : forming two kinds of germ cells of which one produces male offspring and the other female offspring ⟨the human male is ~⟩

het·er·og·a·mous \ˌhet-ə-ˈräg-ə-məs\ *adj* (1839) : having or characterized by fusion of unlike gametes — compare ANISOGAMOUS, ISOGAMOUS

het·er·og·a·my \-mē\ *n* (1894) **1 :** sexual reproduction involving fusion of unlike gametes often differing in size, structure, and physiology **2 :** the condition of reproducing by heterogamy

het·ero·ge·ne·ity \ˌhet-ə-rō-jə-ˈnē-ət-ē, ˌhe-trō-\ *n* (1641) : the quality or state of being heterogeneous

het·ero·ge·neous \ˌhet-ə-rə-ˈjē-nē-əs, ˌhe-trə-, -nyəs\ *adj* [ML *heterogeneus, heterogenus,* fr. Gk *heterogenēs,* fr. *heter-* + *genos* kind — more at KIN] (1630) : consisting of dissimilar or diverse ingredients or constituents : MIXED — **het·er·o·ge·neous·ly** *adv* — **het·er·o·ge·neous·ness** *n*

het·er·og·e·nous \ˌhet-ə-ˈräj-ə-nəs\ *adj* (1916) **1 :** originating in an outside source; *esp* : derived from another species ⟨~ bone graft⟩ **2 :** HETEROGENEOUS

het·er·og·e·ny \-nē\ *n* (1838) : a heterogenous collection or group

het·ero·gon·ic \ˌhet-ə-rə-ˈgän-ik\ *adj* (1924) **1 :** ALLOMETRIC **2 :** being that course of development in which a generation of parasites is succeeded by a free-living generation — used of some nematode worms

het·er·og·o·ny \ˌhet-ə-ˈräg-ə-nē\ *n* (ca. 1887) **1 :** ALTERNATION OF GENERATIONS; *esp* : alternation of a dioecious generation with a parthenogenetic one **2 :** ALLOMETRY

het·ero·graft \ˈhet-ə-rō-ˌgraft\ *n* (1909) : a graft of tissue taken from a donor of one species and grafted into a recipient of another species — compare HOMOGRAFT

het·ero·kary·on \ˌhet-ə-rō-ˈkar-ē-ˌän, -ən\ *n* [NL, fr. *heter-* + *karyon, caryon* nucleus, fr. Gk *karyon* nut, kernel] (ca. 1941) : a cell in the mycelium of a fungus that contains two or more genetically unlike nuclei

het·ero·kary·o·sis \ˌhet-ə-rō-ˌkar-ē-ˈō-səs\ *n* [NL] (1916) : the condition of having cells that are heterokaryons — **het·ero·kary·ot·ic** \-ē-ˈät-ik\ *adj*

het·er·ol·o·gous \-ˈräl-ə-gəs\ *adj* (1822) : derived from a different species ⟨~ DNAs⟩ ⟨~ transplants⟩ — **het·er·ol·o·gous·ly** *adv*

het·ero·ly·sis \ˌhet-ə-ˈräl-ə-səs, -ə-rə-ˈlī-səs\ *n* [NL] (ca. 1909) : decomposition of a compound into two oppositely charged particles or ions — **het·ero·lyt·ic** \-ə-rə-ˈlit-ik\ *adj*

het·ero·mor·phic \ˌhet-ə-rə-ˈmȯr-fik\ *adj* [ISV] (ca. 1859) **1 :** deviating from the usual form **2 :** exhibiting diversity of form or forms ⟨~ pairs of chromosomes⟩ ⟨~ alternation of generations⟩ — **het·ero·mor·phism** \-ˌfiz-əm\ *n*

het·er·on·o·mous \ˌhet-ə-ˈrän-ə-məs\ *adj* (1870) : subject to external controls and impositions

het·er·on·o·my \-mē\ *n* [*heter-* + *-nomy* (as in *autonomy*)] (1798) : subjection to something else; *esp* : a lack of moral freedom or self-determination

het·ero·phile \ˈhet-ə-rə-ˌfīl\ *also* **het·ero·phil** \-ˌfil\ *adj* (1920) : reacting serologically with an antigen of another species

het·er·oph·o·ny \ˌhet-ə-ˈräf-ə-nē\ *n, pl* **-nies** [Gk *heterophōnia* diversity of note, fr. *heter-* + *-phōnia* -phony] (ca. 1890) : independent variation on a single melody by two or more voices

het·ero·phyl·lous \ˌhet-ə-rō-ˈfil-əs\ *adj* (ca. 1828) : having the foliage leaves of more than one form on the same plant or stem — **het·ero·phyl·ly** \ˈhet-ə-rō-ˌfil-ē\ *n*

het·ero·ploid \ˈhet-ə-rə-ˌplȯid\ *adj* [ISV] (1926) : having a chromosome number that is not a simple multiple of the haploid chromosome number — **heteroploid** *n* — **het·ero·ploi·dy** \-ˌplȯid-ē\ *n*

het·ero·po·lar \ˌhet-ə-rə-ˈpō-lər\ *adj* [ISV] (ca. 1895) : POLAR 5, IONIC — **het·ero·po·lar·i·ty** \-rō-pə-ˈlar-ət-ē\ *n*

het·er·op·ter·ous \ˌhet-ə-ˈräp-tə-rəs\ *adj* [deriv. of Gk *heter-* + *pteron* wing — more at FEATHER] (1895) : of or relating to an insect order or suborder (Heteroptera) comprising the true bugs

het·ero·sex·u·al \ˌhet-ə-rō-ˈseksh-(ə-)wəl, -ˈsek-shəl\ *adj* [ISV] (1892) **1 :** of, relating to, or characterized by a tendency to direct sexual desire toward the opposite sex **2 :** of or relating to different sexes — **heterosexual** *n* — **het·ero·sex·u·al·i·ty** \-ˌsek-shə-ˈwal-ət-ē\ *n* — **het·ero·sex·u·al·ly** \-ˈseksh-(ə-)wə-lē, -ˈsek-shə-lē\ *adv*

het·er·o·sis \ˌhet-ə-ˈrō-səs\ *n* [NL] (1914) : a marked vigor or capacity for growth often shown by crossbred animals or plants — called also *hybrid vigor* — **het·er·ot·ic** \-ˈrät-ik\ *adj*

het·ero·spo·rous \ˌhet-ə-rō-ˈspōr-əs, -ˈspȯr-; -ˈräs-pə-rəs\ *adj* (1875) : characterized by heterospory

het·ero·spo·ry \ˈhet-ə-rə-ˌspōr-ē, -ˌspȯr-; ˌhet-ə-ˈräs-pə-rē\ *n* (1898) : the production of microspores and megaspores (as in ferns and seed plants)

het·ero·thal·lic \ˌhet-ə-rō-ˈthal-ik\ *adj* [*heter-* + *thall-* + *-ic*] (1904) **1 :** having two or more morphologically similar haploid phases or types of which individuals from the same type are mutually sterile but individuals from different types are cross-fertile ⟨~ fungi⟩ ⟨~ spores⟩ **2 :** DIOECIOUS — **het·ero·thal·lism** \-ˈthal-ˌiz-əm\ *n*

het·ero·top·ic \-rə-ˈtäp-ik\ *adj* [*heter-* + Gk *topos* place — more at TOPIC] (ca. 1909) : occurring in an abnormal place ⟨~ bone formation⟩ ⟨~ liver transplantation⟩

het·ero·troph \ˈhet-ə-rə-ˌtrōf, -ˌträf\ *n* (ca. 1900) : a heterotrophic individual

het·ero·tro·phic \ˌhet-ə-rə-ˈtrō-fik\ *adj* (1893) : requiring complex organic compounds of nitrogen and carbon for metabolic synthesis — **het·ero·tro·phi·cal·ly** \-fi-k(ə-)lē\ *adv* — **het·ero·tro·phy** \ˌhet-ə-ˈrä-trə-fē, ˈhet-ə-rə-ˌtrō-\ *n*

het·ero·typ·ic \ˌhet-ə-rō-ˈtip-ik\ *adj* (1885) : different in kind, arrangement, or form

het·ero·zy·go·sis \-(ˌ)zī-ˈgō-səs\ *n* [NL] (1902) : HETEROZYGOSITY

het·ero·zy·gos·i·ty \-ˈgäs-ət-ē\ *n* (1912) : the state of being heterozygous

het·ero·zy·gote \-ˈzī-ˌgōt\ *n* (1902) : a heterozygous individual

het·ero·zy·gous \-gəs\ *adj* (1902) : having the two genes at corresponding loci on homologous chromosomes different for one or more loci

heth \ˈkāt(h), ˈk̲et(h)\ *n* [Heb *ḥēth*] (1823) : the 8th letter of the Hebrew alphabet — see ALPHABET table

het·man \ˈhet-mən\ *n, pl* **hetmans** [Pol, commander in chief] (1710) : a cossack leader

het up \ˈhet-ˈəp\ *adj* [*het,* dial. past of *heat*] (1925) : highly excited : UPSET

heu·land·ite \ˈhyü-lən-ˌdīt\ *n* [Henry *Heuland,* 19th cent. Eng. mineral collector] (1822) : a zeolite consisting of a hydrous aluminosilicate of sodium and calcium

[1]**heu·ris·tic** \hyu̇-ˈris-tik\ *adj* [G *heuristisch,* fr. NL *heuristicus,* fr. Gk *heuriskein* to discover; akin to OIr *fūar* I have found] (1821) : involving or serving as an aid to learning, discovery, or problem-solving by experimental and esp. trial-and-error methods ⟨~ techniques⟩ ⟨a ~ assumption⟩; *also* : of or relating to exploratory problem-solving techniques that utilize self-educating techniques (as the evaluation of feedback) to improve performance ⟨a ~ computer program⟩ — **heu·ris·ti·cal·ly** \-ti-k(ə-)lē\ *adv*

[2]**heuristic** *n* (1860) **1 :** the study or practice of heuristic procedure **2 :** heuristic argument **3 :** a heuristic method or procedure

hew \ˈhyü\ *vb* **hewed; hewed** *or* **hewn** \ˈhyün\; **hew·ing** [ME *hewen,* fr. OE *hēawan;* akin to OHG *houwan* to hew, L *cudere* to beat] *vt* (bef. 12c) **1 :** to cut with blows of a heavy cutting instrument **2 :** to fell by blows of an ax ⟨~ a tree⟩ **3 :** to give form or shape to with or as if with heavy cutting blows ⟨~*ed* their farms from the wilderness —J.T. Shotwell⟩ ~ *vi* **1 :** to make cutting blows **2 :** CONFORM, ADHERE — often used in the phrase *hew to the line* ⟨no pressure . . . on newspapers to ~ to the official line —*N.Y. Times Mag.*⟩ — **hew·er** *n*

[1]**hex** \ˈheks\ *vb* [PaG *hexe,* fr. G *hexen,* fr. *hexe* witch, fr. OHG *hagzissa;* akin to ME *hagge* hag] *vi* (1830) : to practice witchcraft ~ *vt* **1 :** to put a hex on **2 :** to affect as if by an evil spell : JINX ⟨giving in to an unscientific fear of ~*ing* the whole project —Daniel Lang⟩ — **hex·er** *n*

[2]**hex** *n* (1856) **1 :** a person who practices witchcraft : WITCH **2 :** SPELL, JINX

[3]**hex** *adj* (1924) : HEXAGONAL ⟨a bolt with a ~ head⟩

[4]**hex** *n* (1970) : a hexadecimal number system

hexa- *or* **hex-** *comb form* [Gk, fr. *hex* six — more at SIX] **1 :** six ⟨*hexamerous*⟩ **2 :** containing six atoms, groups, or equivalents ⟨*hexane*⟩

hexa·bi·ose *or* **hexo·bi·ose** \ˌhek-sə-ˈbī-ˌōs, -ˌōz\ *n* [*hexa-* + *bi-* + *-ose*] (ca. 1901) : a disaccharide (as maltose) yielding two hexose molecules on hydrolysis

hexa·chlo·ride \ˌhek-sə-ˈklō(ə)r-ˌīd, -ˈklȯ(ə)r-\ *n* (ca. 1922) : a chloride containing six atoms of chlorine in a molecule

hexa·chlo·ro·eth·ane \-ˌklōr-ə-ˈweth-ˌān, -ˌklȯr-\ *or* **hexa·chlor·eth·ane** \-ˌklōr-ˈeth-, -ˌklȯr-\ *n* [ISV] (1898) : a toxic crystalline compound C_2Cl_6 used esp. in smoke bombs and in the control of liver flukes in ruminants

hexa·chlo·ro·phene \-ˈklōr-ə-ˌfēn, -ˈklȯr-\ *n* [*hexa-* + *chlor-* + *phenol*] (1948) : a powdered phenolic bacteria-inhibiting agent $C_{13}Cl_6H_6O_2$

hexa·chord \ˈhek-sə-ˌkȯ(ə)rd\ *n* [*hexa-* + Gk *chordē* string — more at YARN] (1730) : a diatonic series of six tones having a semitone between the third and fourth tones

hex·ad \ˈhek-ˌsad\ *or* **hex·ade** \-ˌsād\ *n* [LL *hexad-, hexas,* fr. Gk, fr. *hex*] (1660) : a group or series of six — **hex·ad·ic** \hek-ˈsad-ik\ *adj*

hexa·dec·i·mal \ˌhek-sə-ˈdes-(ə-)məl\ *adj* (1956) : of, relating to, or being a number system with a base of 16 — **hexadecimal** *n*

hexa·gon \ˈhek-sə-ˌgän\ *n* [Gk *hexagōnon,* neut. of *hexagōnos* hexagonal, fr. *hexa-* + *gōnia* angle — more at -GON] (1570) : a polygon of six angles and six sides

hex·ag·o·nal \hek-ˈsag-ən-ᵊl\ *adj* (1571) **1 :** having six angles and six sides **2 :** having a hexagon as section or base **3 :** relating to or being a crystal system characterized by three equal lateral axes intersecting at angles of 60 degrees and a vertical axis of variable length at right angles — **hex·ag·o·nal·ly** \-ᵊl-ē\ *adv*

hexa·gram \ˈhek-sə-ˌgram\ *n* [ISV] (1871) : a figure formed by completing externally an equilateral triangle on each side of a regular hexagon

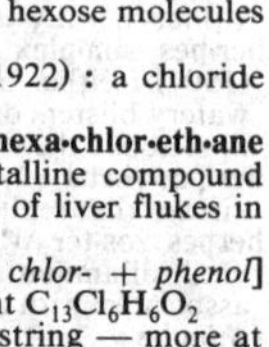
hexagram

hexa·he·dron \ˌhek-sə-ˈhē-drən\ *n, pl* **-drons** *also* **-dra** \-drə\ [LL, fr. Gk *hexaedron,* fr. neut. of *hexaedros* of six surfaces, fr. *hexa-* + *hedra* seat — more at SIT] (1571) : a polyhedron of six faces

hexa·hy·drate \-ˈhī-ˌdrāt\ *n* (ca. 1908) : a chemical compound with six molecules of water — **hexa·hy·drat·ed** \-ˌdrāt-əd\ *adj*

hex·am·e·ter \hek-ˈsam-ət-ər\ *n* [L, fr. Gk *hexametron,* fr. neut. of *hexametros* having six measures, fr. *hexa-* + *metron* measure — more at MEASURE] (1546) : a line of verse consisting of six metrical feet

hexa·me·tho·ni·um \ˌhek-sə-mə-ˈthō-nē-əm\ *n* [*hexa-* + *meth-* + *-onium*] (1949) : either of two compounds $C_{12}H_{30}Br_2N_2$ or $C_{12}H_{30}Cl_2N_2$ used as ganglionic blocking agents in the treatment of hypertension

hexa·meth·y·lene·tet·ra·mine \ˌhek-sə-ˈmeth-ə-ˌlēn-ˈte-trə-ˌmēn\ *n* [ISV] (1888) : a crystalline compound $C_6H_{12}N_4$ used esp. as an accelerator in vulcanizing rubber, as an absorbent for phosgene, and as a urinary antiseptic

hex·ane \ˈhek-ˌsān\ *n* [ISV] (1877) : any of several isomeric volatile liquid paraffin hydrocarbons C_6H_{14} found in petroleum

hex·a·no·ic acid \ˌhek-sə-ˌnō-ik-\ *n* [ISV *hexane* + *-oic*] (1926) : CAPROIC ACID

hexa·ploid \ˈhek-sə-ˌplȯid\ *adj* [ISV] (1912) **:** having or being six times the monoploid chromosome number — **hexaploid** *n* — **hexa·ploi·dy** \-ˌplȯid-ē\ *n*

¹**hexa·pod** \ˈhek-sə-ˌpäd\ *n* [Gk *hexapod-, hexapous* having six feet, fr. *hexa-* + *pod-, pous* foot — more at FOOT] (1668) **:** INSECT 1b

²**hexapod** *adj* (ca. 1847) **1 :** six-footed **2 :** of or relating to insects

Hexa·teuch \ˈhek-sə-ˌt(y)ük\ *n* [*hexa-* + Gk *teuchos* book — more at PENTATEUCH] (1878) **:** the first six books of the Old Testament

hex·en·be·sen \ˈhek-sən-ˌbāz-ᵊn\ *n* [G, fr. *hexen* (pl. of *hexe* witch) + *besen* broom, fr. OHG *besmo* — more at BESOM] (ca. 1900) **:** WITCHES'-BROOM

hex·e·rei \ˌhek-sə-ˈrī\ *n* [PaG, fr. G, fr. *hexe*] (1898) **:** WITCHCRAFT

hexo·bar·bi·tal \ˌhek-sə-ˈbär-bə-ˌtȯl\ *n* [*hexo-* (fr. *hexa-*) + *barbital*] (1941) **:** a barbiturate $C_{12}H_{16}N_2O_3$ used as a sedative and hypnotic and in the form of its soluble sodium salt as an intravenous anesthetic of short duration

hexo·ki·nase \ˌhek-sə-ˈkī-ˌnās, -ˌnāz\ *n* [*hexose* + *kinase*] (1930) **:** any of a group of enzymes that accelerate the phosphorylation of hexoses (as in the formation of glucose-6-phosphate from glucose and ATP) in carbohydrate metabolism

hex·os·a·min·i·dase \ˌhek-ˌsäs-ə-ˈmin-ə-ˌdās, -ˌdāz\ *n* [*hexose* + *amin-* + *-ide* + *-ase*] (1969) **:** either of two hydrolytic enzymes that catalyze the splitting off of a hexose from a ganglioside and are deficient in some metabolic diseases (as a variant of Tay-Sachs disease)

hex·o·san \ˈhek-sə-ˌsan\ *n* (1894) **:** a polysaccharide yielding only hexoses on hydrolysis

hex·ose \ˈhek-ˌsōs, -ˌsōz\ *n* [ISV] (1892) **:** any monosaccharide (as glucose) containing six carbon atoms in the molecule

hex·yl \ˈhek-səl\ *n* [ISV] (1869) **:** an alkyl radical C_6H_{13} derived from a hexane

hex·yl·res·or·cin·ol \ˌhek-səl-rə-ˈzȯrs-ᵊn-ˌȯl, -ˌōl\ *n* (1925) **:** a crystalline phenol $C_{12}H_{18}O_2$ used as an antiseptic and anthelmintic

hey \ˈhā\ *interj* [ME] (13c) — used esp. to call attention or to express interrogation, surprise, or exultation

¹**hey·day** \ˈhā-ˌdā\ *interj* [irreg. fr. *hey*] *archaic* (1526) — used to express elation or wonder

²**heyday** *n* (1590) **1** *archaic* **:** high spirits **2 :** the period of one's greatest strength, vigor, or prosperity

hey presto \(ˈ)hā-ˈpres-(ˌ)tō\ *interj, Brit* (1731) **:** suddenly as if by magic

Hez·e·ki·ah \ˌhez-ə-ˈkī-ə\ *n* [Heb *Ḥizqīyāh*] **:** a king of Judah under whom the kingdom underwent a ruinous Assyrian invasion at the end of the 8th century B.C.

hi \ˈhī(-ē)\ *interj* [ME *hy*] (15c) — used esp. as a greeting

hi·a·tal \hī-ˈāt-ᵊl\ *adj* (1909) **:** of, relating to, or involving a hiatus

hiatal hernia *n* (ca. 1944) **:** a hernia in which an anatomical part (as the stomach) protrudes through the esophageal hiatus of the diaphragm — called also *hiatus hernia*

hi·a·tus \hī-ˈāt-əs\ *n* [L, fr. *hiatus*, pp. of *hiare* to yawn — more at YAWN] (1563) **1 a :** a break in or as if in a material object **:** GAP ⟨the ~ between the theory and the practice of the party —J. G. Colton⟩ **b :** a gap or passage in an anatomical part or organ **2 a :** an interruption in time or continuity **:** BREAK **b :** the occurrence of two vowel sounds without pause or intervening consonantal sound

Hi·a·wa·tha \ˌhī-ə-ˈwō-thə, ˌhē-ə-, -ˈwäth-ə\ *n* **:** the Indian hero of Longfellow's poem *The Song of Hiawatha*

hi·ba·chi \hi-ˈbäch-ē\ *n* [Jp] (1863) **:** a charcoal brazier

hi·ber·nac·u·lum \ˌhī-bər-ˈnak-yə-ləm\ *n, pl* **-la** \-lə\ [NL, fr. L, winter residence, fr. *hibernare*] (1789) **:** a shelter occupied during the winter by a dormant animal (as an insect)

hi·ber·nal \hī-ˈbərn-ᵊl\ *adj* (1646) **:** of, relating to, or occurring in winter

hi·ber·nate \ˈhī-bər-ˌnāt\ *vi* **-nat·ed; -nat·ing** [L *hibernatus*, pp. of *hibernare* to pass the winter, fr. *hibernus* of winter; akin to L *hiems* winter, Gk *cheimōn*] (1802) **1 :** to pass the winter in a torpid or resting state **2 :** to be or become inactive or dormant — **hi·ber·na·tion** \ˌhī-bər-ˈnā-shən\ *n* — **hi·ber·na·tor** \ˈhī-bər-ˌnāt-ər\ *n*

¹**Hi·ber·ni·an** \hī-ˈbər-nē-ən\ *adj* [L *Hibernia* Ireland] (1632) **:** of, relating to, or characteristic of Ireland or the Irish

²**Hibernian** *n* (1709) **:** a native or inhabitant of Ireland

hi·bis·cus \hī-ˈbis-kəs, hə-\ *n* [NL, fr. L, marshmallow] (1706) **:** any of a large genus (*Hibiscus*) of herbs, shrubs, or small trees of the mallow family with dentate leaves and large showy flowers

¹**hic·cup** *also* **hic·cough** \ˈhik-(ˌ)əp\ *n* [imit.] (1580) **1 :** a spasmodic inhalation with closure of the glottis accompanied by a peculiar sound **2 :** an attack of hiccuping — usu. used in pl. but sing or pl. in constr.

²**hiccup** *also* **hiccough** *vi* **hic·cuped** *also* **hic·cupped; hic·cup·ing** *also* **hic·cup·ping** (1586) **:** to make a hiccup; *also* **:** to be affected with hiccups

hic ja·cet \(ˈ)hik-ˈjā-sət, (ˈ)hēk-ˈyäk-ət\ *n* [L, lit., here lies] (1601) **:** EPITAPH

¹**hick** \ˈhik\ *n* [*Hick*, nickname for *Richard*] (1565) **:** an unsophisticated provincial person — **hick·ish** \-ish\ *adj*

²**hick** *adj* (1920) **:** UNSOPHISTICATED, PROVINCIAL ⟨a ~ town⟩

¹**hick·ey** \ˈhik-ē\ *n, pl* **hickeys** [origin unknown] (1907) **1 a :** a threaded coupling between an electrical fixture and an outlet box **b :** a device for bending pipe and conduit **2 :** DEVICE, GADGET

²**hickey** *n, pl* **hickeys** [origin unknown] (1915) **1 :** PIMPLE **2 :** a temporary red mark produced in lovemaking by biting and sucking the skin

hick·o·ry \ˈhik-(ə-)rē\ *n, pl* **-ries** [short for obs. *pokahickory*, fr. *pawcohiccora* food prepared from pounded nuts (in some Algonquian language of Virginia)] (1653) **1 a :** any of a genus (*Carya*) of No. American hardwood trees of the walnut family that often have sweet edible nuts **b :** the usu. tough pale wood of a hickory **2 :** a switch or cane (as of hickory wood) used esp. for punishing a child — **hickory** *adj*

hid \ˈhid\ *adj* (12c) **:** HIDDEN

hi·dal·go \hid-ˈal-(ˌ)gō, ē-ˈt͟häl-\ *n, pl* **-gos** *often cap* [Sp, fr. OSp *fijo dalgo*, lit., son of something, fr. L *filius* son — more at FEMININE] (1594) **:** a member of the lower nobility of Spain

hid·den \ˈhid-ᵊn\ *adj* (13c) **1 :** being out of sight or not readily apparent **:** CONCEALED **2 :** OBSCURE, UNEXPLAINED, UNDISCLOSED

hid·den·ite \ˈhid-ᵊn-ˌīt\ *n* [William E. *Hidden* †1918 Am. mineralogist] (1881) **:** a transparent yellow to green spodumene valued as a gem

hidden tax *n* (1936) **1 :** a tax that is ultimately paid by someone other than the person on whom it is levied **2 :** an economic inequity that reduces one's real income or buying power

¹**hide** \ˈhīd\ *n* [ME, fr. OE *higid, hīd*] (bef. 12c) **:** any of various old English units of land area; *esp* **:** a unit of 120 acres

²**hide** *vb* **hid** \ˈhid\; **hid·den** \ˈhid-ᵊn\ *or* **hid; hid·ing** \ˈhīd-iŋ\ [ME *hiden*, fr. OE *hȳdan*; akin to Gk *keuthein* to conceal, OE *hȳd* hide, skin] *vt* (bef. 12c) **1 a :** to put out of sight **:** SECRETE **b :** to conceal for shelter or protection **:** SHIELD **2 :** to keep secret **3 :** to screen from or as if from view **:** OBSCURE **4 :** to turn (the eyes or face) away in shame or anger ~ *vi* **1 :** to remain out of sight **2 :** to seek protection or evade responsibility — **hid·er** \ˈhīd-ər\ *n*

syn HIDE, CONCEAL, SCREEN, SECRETE, BURY mean to withhold or withdraw from sight. HIDE may or may not suggest intent; CONCEAL usu. does imply intent and often specif. implies a refusal to divulge; SCREEN implies an interposing of something that prevents discovery; SECRETE suggests a depositing in a place unknown to others; BURY implies covering up so as to hide completely.

³**hide** *n, chiefly Brit* (13c) **:** ³BLIND 2

⁴**hide** *n* [ME, fr. OE *hȳd*; akin to OHG *hūt* hide, L *cutis* skin, Gk *kytos* hollow vessel] (bef. 12c) **:** the skin of an animal whether raw or dressed — used esp. of large heavy skins — **hide or hair** *or* **hide nor hair :** a vestige or trace of someone or something ⟨a wife he hadn't seen *hide or hair* of in over 20 years —H. L. Davis⟩

⁵**hide** *vt* **hid·ed; hid·ing** (1825) **:** to give a beating to **:** FLOG

hide–and–seek \ˌhīd-ᵊn-ˈsēk\ *n* (1724) **:** a children's game in which one player covers his eyes while others hide and then goes looking for them

hide·away \ˈhīd-ə-ˌwā\ *n* (1926) **:** RETREAT, HIDEOUT

hide·bound \-ˌbau̇nd\ *adj* (1559) **1** *of a domestic animal* **:** having a dry skin lacking in pliancy and adhering closely to the underlying flesh **2 :** having an inflexible or ultraconservative character

hid·eous \ˈhid-ē-əs\ *adj* [alter. of ME *hidous*, fr. MF, fr. *hisde, hide* terror] (14c) **1 :** offensive to the senses and esp. to sight **:** exceedingly ugly **2 :** morally offensive **:** SHOCKING — **hid·eos·ity** \ˌhid-ē-ˈäs-ət-ē\ *n* — **hid·eous·ly** *adv* — **hid·eous·ness** *n*

hide·out \ˈhī-ˌdau̇t\ *n* (1885) **:** a place of refuge, retreat, or concealment

hid·ey–hole *or* **hidy–hole** \ˈhīd-ē-ˌhōl\ *n* [alter. of earlier *hiding-hole*] (1817) **:** HIDEAWAY

hi·dro·sis \hid-ˈrō-səs, hī-ˈdrō-\ *n* [NL, fr. Gk *hidrōsis*, fr. *hidroun* to sweat, fr. *hidrōs* sweat — more at SWEAT] (ca. 1895) **:** excretion of sweat **:** PERSPIRATION — **hi·drot·ic** \-ˈrät-ik, -ˈdrät-\ *adj*

hie \ˈhī\ *vb* **hied; hy·ing** *or* **hie·ing** [ME *hien*, fr. OE *hīgian* to strive, hasten; akin to OSw *hikka* to pant, Skt *śīghra* quick] (bef. 12c) **:** to go quickly **:** HASTEN

hi·emal \ˈhī-ə-məl\ *adj* [L *hiemalis*, fr. *hiems* winter — more at HIBERNATE] (1560) **:** HIBERNAL

hier- *or* **hiero-** *comb form* [LL, fr. Gk, fr. *hieros* — more at IRE] **:** sacred **:** holy ⟨*hierology*⟩

hi·er·arch \ˈhī-(ə-)ˌrärk\ *n* [MF or ML; MF *hierarche*, fr. ML *hierarcha*, fr. Gk *hierarchēs*, fr. *hier-* + *-archēs* -arch] (15c) **1 :** a religious leader in a position of authority **2 :** a person high in a hierarchy — **hi·er·ar·chal** \ˌhī-(ə-)ˈrär-kəl\ *adj*

hi·er·ar·chi·cal \ˌhī-(ə-)ˈrär-ki-kəl *also* hī-ˈär- *or* hir-ˈär-\ *or* **hi·er·ar·chic** \-kik\ *adj* (15c) **:** of, relating to, or arranged in a hierarchy — **hi·er·ar·chi·cal·ly** \-ki-k(ə-)lē\ *adv*

hi·er·ar·chy \ˈhī-(ə-)ˌrär-kē *also* ˈhī-ˌär- *or* ˈhi(ə)r-ˌär-\ *n, pl* **-chies** (14c) **1 :** a division of angels **2 a :** a ruling body of clergy organized into orders or ranks each subordinate to the one above it; *specif* **:** the bishops of a province or nation **b :** church government by a hierarchy **3 :** a body of persons in authority **4 :** the classification of a group of people according to ability or to economic, social, or professional standing; *also* **:** the group so classified **5 :** a graded or ranked series ⟨Christian ~ of values⟩ ⟨a machine's ~ of responses⟩

hi·er·at·ic \ˌhī-(ə-)ˈrat-ik\ *adj* [L *hieraticus* sacerdotal, fr. Gk *hieratikos*, deriv. of *hieros*] (1669) **1 :** constituting or belonging to a cursive form of ancient Egyptian writing simpler than the hieroglyphic **2 :** SACERDOTAL **3 :** highly stylized or formal — **hi·er·at·i·cal·ly** \-i-k(ə-)lē\ *adv*

hi·ero·dule \ˈhī-(ə-)rō-ˌd(y)ü(ə)l, hī-ˈer-ə-\ *n* [LL *hierodulus*, fr. Gk *hierodoulos*, fr. *hier-* + *doulos* slave] (1835) **:** a slave in the service of a temple — **hi·ero·du·lic** \ˌhī-(ə-)rō-ˈd(y)ü-lik, (ˌ)hī-ˌer-ə-\ *adj*

hi·ero·glyph \ˈhī-(ə-)rə-ˌglif\ *n* [F *hiéroglyphe*, fr. MF, back-formation fr. *hieroglyphique*] (1598) **1 :** a character used in a system of hieroglyphic writing **2 :** something that resembles a hieroglyph

¹**hi·ero·glyph·ic** \ˌhī-(ə-)rə-ˈglif-ik\ *also* **hi·ero·glyph·i·cal** \-i-kəl\ *adj* [MF *hieroglyphique*, fr. LL *hieroglyphicus*, fr. Gk *hieroglyphikos*, fr. *hier-* + *glyphein* to carve — more at CLEAVE] (1585) **1 :** written in, constituting, or belonging to a system of writing mainly in pictorial characters **2 :** inscribed with hieroglyphic **3 :** resembling hieroglyphic in difficulty of decipherment — **hi·ero·glyph·i·cal·ly** \-i-k(ə-)lē\ *adv*

²**hieroglyphic** *n* (1586) **1 :** HIEROGLYPH **2 :** a system of hieroglyphic writing; *specif* **:** the picture script of the ancient Egyptian priesthood — often used in pl. but sing. or pl. in constr. **3 :** something that resembles a hieroglyph esp. in difficulty of decipherment

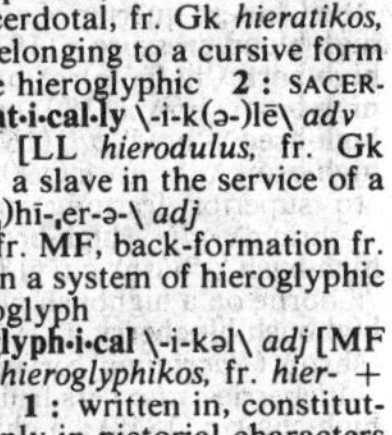

hieroglyphic 2

hi·ero·phant \ˈhī-(ə-)rə-ˌfant, hī-ˈer-ə-fənt\ *n* [LL *hierophanta*, fr. Gk *hierophantēs*, fr. *hier-* + *phainein* to show — more at FANCY] (1677) **1 :** a priest in ancient Greece; *specif* **:** the chief priest of the Eleusinian mysteries **2 a :** EXPOSITOR **b :** ADVOCATE — **hi·ero·phan·tic** \ˌhī-(ə-)rə-ˈfant-ik, (ˌ)hī-ˌer-ə-\ *adj*

hi–fi \ˈhī-ˈfī\ *n* (1948) **1 :** HIGH FIDELITY **2 :** equipment for reproduction of sound with high fidelity

hig·gle \ˈhig-əl\ *vi* **hig·gled; hig·gling** \-(ə-)liŋ\ [prob. alter. of *haggle*] (1633) **:** HAGGLE — **hig·gler** \-(ə-)lər\ *n*

hig·gle·dy–pig·gle·dy \ˌhig-əl-dē-ˈpig-əl-dē\ *adv* [origin unknown] (1598) : in confusion : TOPSY-TURVY, RANDOMLY ⟨tiny hovels piled ~ against each other —Edward Behr⟩ — **higgledy–piggledy** *adj*

1high \ˈhī\ *adj* [ME, fr. OE *hēah;* akin to OHG *hōh* high, L *cacumen* point, top] (bef. 12c) **1 a :** having large extension upward : taller than average, usual, or expected ⟨a ~ hill⟩ ⟨rooms with ~ ceilings⟩ **b :** having a specified elevation : TALL ⟨six feet ~⟩ — often used in combinations ⟨sky-*high*⟩ ⟨waist-*high*⟩ **2 a** (1) **:** advanced toward the acme or culmination ⟨~ summer⟩ (2) **:** advanced toward the most active or culminating period ⟨a vacation on the Riviera during ~ season⟩ (3) **:** constituting the late, most fully developed, or most creative stage or period ⟨~ Gothic⟩ (4) **:** advanced in complexity, development, or elaboration ⟨the ~*er* apes⟩ ⟨~*er* mathematics⟩ **b :** verging on lateness — usu. used in the phrase *high time* **c :** long past : REMOTE ⟨~ antiquity⟩ **3 :** elevated in pitch ⟨a ~ note⟩ **4 :** relatively far from the equator ⟨~ latitude⟩ **5 :** slightly tainted ⟨~ game⟩; *also* : MALODOROUS **6 :** exalted in character : NOBLE ⟨set out with ~ purposes⟩ **7 :** of greater degree, amount, cost, value, or content than average, usual, or expected ⟨~ prices⟩ ⟨food ~ in iron⟩ ⟨submitted a ~ bid⟩ **8 :** of relatively great importance: as **a :** foremost in rank, dignity, or standing ⟨~ officials⟩ **b :** SERIOUS, GRAVE ⟨~ crimes⟩ **c :** observed with the utmost solemnity ⟨~ religious observances⟩ **d :** CRITICAL, CLIMACTIC ⟨the ~ point of the novel is the escape⟩ **e :** marked by sublime, heroic, or stirring events or subject matter ⟨~ tragedy⟩ ⟨~ adventure⟩ **9 :** FORCIBLE, STRONG ⟨~ winds⟩ **10 a :** showing elation or excitement ⟨~ spirits⟩ **b :** INTOXICATED; *also* : excited or stupefied by a drug (as marijuana or heroin) **11 :** articulated with some part of the tongue close to the palate ⟨\ē\ is a ~ vowel⟩ — **high·ly** *adv*

syn HIGH, TALL, LOFTY mean above the average in height. HIGH implies marked extension upward and is applied chiefly to things which rise from a base or foundation or are placed at a conspicuous height above a lower level ⟨a *high* hill⟩ ⟨a *high* ceiling⟩ TALL applies to what grows or rises high by comparison with others of its kind and usu. implies relative narrowness ⟨a *tall* thin man⟩ LOFTY suggests great or imposing altitude ⟨*lofty* mountain peaks⟩

2high *adv* (bef. 12c) **1 :** at or to a high place, altitude, or degree ⟨climbed ~*er* on the ladder⟩ ⟨the bids went too ~⟩ **2 :** WELL, LUXURIOUSLY — often used in the phrases *high off the hog* and *high on the hog*

3high *n* (13c) **1 :** an elevated place or region: as **a :** HILL, KNOLL **b :** the space overhead : SKY — usu. used with *on* **c :** HEAVEN — usu. used with *on* **2 :** a region of high barometric pressure — called also *anticyclone* **3 a :** a high point or level : HEIGHT ⟨sales have reached a new ~⟩ **b :** the transmission gear of an automotive vehicle giving the highest ratio of propeller-shaft to engine-shaft speed and consequently the highest speed of travel **4 :** an excited or stupefied state produced by or as if by a drug (as heroin)

high altar *n* (bef. 12c) : the principal altar in a church

high analysis *adj, of a fertilizer* (1949) : containing more than 20 percent of total plant nutrients

high and dry *adv* (1822) **1 :** out of reach of the current or tide : out of water **2 :** in a helpless or abandoned position : without recourse

high and low *adv* (14c) : EVERYWHERE

high–and–mighty *adj* (13c) : characterized by arrogance : IMPERIOUS

1high·ball \ˈhī-ˌbȯl\ *n* (1897) **1 a :** a railroad signal for a train to proceed at full speed **b :** a fast train **2 :** an iced cocktail containing liquor (as whiskey) and water or a carbonated beverage and served in a tall glass

2highball *vi* (1912) : to go at full or high speed ⟨a ~*ing* express train⟩

high beam *n* (1939) : the long-range focus of a vehicle headlight

high·bind·er \ˈhī-ˌbīn-dər\ *n* [the *Highbinders,* gang of vagabonds in New York City *ab*1806] (1876) **1 :** a professional killer operating in the Chinese quarter of an American city **2 :** a corrupt politician

high blood pressure *n* (1916) : HYPERTENSION

high·born \ˈhī-ˈbȯ(ə)rn\ *adj* (13c) : of noble birth

high·boy \-ˌbȯi\ *n* (1891) : a tall chest of drawers with a legged base

high·bred \-ˈbred\ *adj* (1674) : coming from superior stock

high·brow \-ˌbrau̇\ *n* (1902) : a person who possesses or has pretensions to superior learning or culture — **highbrow** *adj* — **high·browed** \-ˌbrau̇d\ *adj* — **high·brow·ism** \-ˌbrau̇-ˌiz-əm\ *n*

high·bush \-ˈbu̇sh\ *adj* (1805) : forming a notably tall or erect bush; *also* : borne on a highbush plant

highbush blueberry *n* (1913) : a variable moisture-loving No. American shrub (*Vaccinium corymbosum*) that is the source of most cultivated blueberries; *also* : its fruit

high chair *n* (1848) : a child's chair with long legs, a footrest, and usu. a feeding tray

High Church *adj* (1687) : tending esp. in Anglican worship to stress the sacerdotal, liturgical, ceremonial, traditional, and Catholic elements in worship — **High Churchman** *n*

high–class \ˈhī-ˈklas\ *adj* (1864) : SUPERIOR, FIRST-CLASS

high comedy *n* (1895) : comedy employing subtle characterizations and witty dialogue — compare LOW COMEDY

high command *n* (1916) **1 :** the supreme headquarters of a military force **2 :** the highest leaders in an organization

high commissioner *n* (1881) : a principal or a high-ranking commissioner; *esp* : an ambassadorial representative of the government of one country stationed in another

high–count \ˈhī-ˈkau̇nt\ *adj* (1926) : having a large number of warp and weft yarns to the square inch ⟨~ percale sheeting⟩

high court *n* (14c) : SUPREME COURT

high–density lipoprotein *n* (1960) : HDL

high–end \ˈhī-ˈend\ *adj* (1980) : UPSCALE ⟨~ boutiques⟩

high–energy *adj* (1934) **1 a :** having such speed and kinetic energy as to exhibit relativistic departure from classical laws of motion — used esp. of elementary particles whose velocity has been imparted by an accelerator **b :** of or relating to high-energy particles ⟨a ~ reaction⟩ **2 :** yielding a relatively large amount of energy when undergoing hydrolysis ⟨~ phosphate bonds in ATP⟩

high–energy physics *n* (1964) : a branch of physics dealing with the constitution, properties, and interactions of elementary particles esp. as revealed in experiments with particle accelerators

higher criticism *n* (1836) : study of biblical writings to determine their literary history and the purpose and meaning of the authors — compare LOWER CRITICISM — **higher critic** *n*

higher education *n* (1866) : education beyond the secondary level; *esp* : education provided by a college or university

higher law *n* (1844) : a principle of divine or moral law that is considered to be superior to constitutions and enacted legislation

higher learning *n* (13c) : education, learning, or scholarship on the collegiate or university level

high·er–up \ˌhī-ə-ˈrəp, ˈhī-ə-ˌ\ *n* (1911) : a superior officer or official

high explosive *n* (1877) : an explosive (as TNT) that generates gas with extreme rapidity and has a shattering effect

high·fa·lu·tin \ˌhī-fə-ˈlüt-ᵊn\ *adj* [perh. fr. 2*high* + alter. of *fluting,* prp. of *flute*] (1839) **1 :** PRETENTIOUS **2 :** expressed in or marked by the use of high-flown bombastic language : POMPOUS

high fashion *n* (1945) **1 :** HIGH STYLE **2 :** HAUTE COUTURE

high fidelity *n* (1934) : the reproduction of an effect (as sound or an image) with a high degree of faithfulness to the original

high five *n* (1981) : a slapping of upraised right hands by two people (as in celebration) — **high–five** *vb*

high·fli·er \ˈhī-ˈflī(-ə)r\ *n* (ca. 1961) : a stock that trades at many times its earnings

high–flown \ˈhī-ˈflōn\ *adj* (1647) **1 :** exceedingly or excessively high or favorable **2 :** having an excessively embellished or inflated character : PRETENTIOUS ⟨inflated rhetoric and ~ vocabulary —James Yaffe⟩

high–fly·ing \-ˈflī-iŋ\ *adj* (1586) **1 :** rising to considerable height **2 :** marked by extravagance, pretension, or excessive ambition

high frequency *n* (1893) : a radio frequency between very high frequency and medium frequency — see RADIO FREQUENCY table

high gear *n* (1921) **1 :** HIGH 3b **2 :** a state of intense or maximum activity

High German *n* [so called fr. its prevalence in areas near the Alps] (1706) **1 :** German as natively used in southern and central Germany **2 :** GERMAN 2b

high–grade *adj* (1878) **1 :** of superior grade or quality ⟨~ bonds⟩ **2 :** being near the upper or most favorable extreme of a specified range

high–hand·ed \-ˈhan-dəd\ *adj* (1631) : ARBITRARY, OVERBEARING — **high–hand·ed·ly** *adv* — **high–hand·ed·ness** *n*

high–hat \ˈhī-ˈhat\ *adj* (1923) : SUPERCILIOUS, SNOBBISH — **high–hat** *vt*

high hat *n* (1889) **1 :** BEAVER 2 **2 :** a pair of cymbals operated by a foot pedal

High Holiday *n* (1946) : either of two important Jewish holidays: **a :** ROSH HASHANAH **b :** YOM KIPPUR

high horse *n* (14c) : an arrogant and unyielding mood or attitude ⟨wanted to get on her *high horse* and treat him as if he were nothing —William Heuman⟩

high–jack *var of* HIJACK

high jinks *n pl* (1825) : boisterous or rambunctious carryings-on : HORSEPLAY

high jump *n* (1895) : a jump for height in a track-and-field contest

1high·land \ˈhī-lənd\ *n* (bef. 12c) : elevated or mountainous land

2highland *adj* (15c) **1 :** of or relating to a highland **2** *cap* **:** of or relating to the Highlands of Scotland

high·land·er \-lən-dər\ *n* (1610) **1 :** an inhabitant of a highland **2** *cap* **:** an inhabitant of the Highlands of Scotland

Highland fling *n* (1804) : a lively Scottish folk dance

high–lev·el \ˈhī-ˈlev-əl\ *adj* (1876) **1 :** occurring, done, or placed at a high level **2 :** being of high importance or rank ⟨~ diplomats⟩

1high·light \ˈhī-ˌlīt\ *n* (1658) **1 :** the lightest spot or area (as in a painting) : any of several spots in a modeled drawing or painting that receives the greatest amount of illumination **2 :** an event or detail of major significance or special interest

2highlight *vt* **-light·ed; -light·ing** (1927) **1 :** to throw a strong light on **2 a :** to center attention on : EMPHASIZE **b :** to constitute a highlight of

high–low–jack \ˌhī-ˌlō-ˈjak\ *n* (1814) : a card game in which scores are made by winning the highest trump, the lowest trump, the jack of trumps, and either the ten of trumps or the most points

high mass *n, often cap H&M* (12c) : a mass marked by the singing of prescribed parts by the celebrant and the choir or congregation

high–mind·ed \ˈhī-ˈmīn-dəd\ *adj* (1556) : marked by elevated principles and feelings — **high–mind·ed·ly** *adv* — **high–mind·ed·ness** *n*

high–muck–a–muck \ˌhī-ˌmək-i-ˈmək\ *or* **high–muck·e·ty–muck** \ˌhī-ˌmək-ət-ē-ˈmək\ *n* [by folk etymology fr. Chinook Jargon *hiu muckamuck* plenty to eat] (1856) : an important and often arrogant person

high·ness \ˈhī-nəs\ *n* (12c) **1 :** the quality or state of being high **2 —** used as a title for a person of exalted rank (as a king or prince)

high noon *n* (1914) **1 :** precisely noon **2 :** the most advanced, flourishing, or creative stage or period ⟨the *high noon* of his career⟩

high–octane *adj* (1932) **1 :** having a high octane number and hence good antiknock properties ⟨~ gasoline⟩ **2 :** HIGH-POWERED

high–pitched \ˈhī-ˈpicht\ *adj* (1748) **1 :** having a high pitch ⟨a ~ voice⟩ **2 :** marked by or exhibiting strong feeling : AGITATED ⟨a ~, almost frantic campaign —Geoffrey Rice⟩

high place *n* (14c) : a temple or altar used by the ancient Semites and built usu. on a hill or elevation

high polymer *n* (1942) : a substance (as polystyrene) consisting of molecules that are large multiples of units of low molecular weight

high–pow·ered \ˈhī-ˈpau̇(-ə)rd\ *also* **high–pow·er** \-ˈpau̇(-ə)r\ *adj* (1893) : having great drive, energy, or capacity : DYNAMIC

1high–pressure *adj* (1824) **1 a :** having or involving a high or comparatively high pressure esp. greatly exceeding that of the atmosphere **b :** having a high barometric pressure **2 a :** using or involving aggressive and insistent sales techniques **b :** imposing or involving severe strain or tension ⟨~ occupations⟩

2high–pressure *vt* (1926) : to sell or influence by high-pressure tactics

high priest *n* (14c) **1 :** a chief priest esp. of the ancient Jewish Levitical priesthood traditionally traced from Aaron **2 :** a priest of the Melchizedek priesthood in the Mormon Church **3 :** the head of a movement or chief expounder of a doctrine or an art — **high priesthood** *n*

high priestess *n* (1645) : a chief priestess

high relief *n* (1880) : sculptural relief in which at least half of the circumference of the modeled form projects

high–rise \ˈhī-ˈrīz\ *adj* (1954) **1 :** being multistory and equipped with elevators ⟨~ apartments⟩ **2 :** of, relating to, or characterized by high-rise buildings **3 :** of, relating to, or being extra-high bicycle handlebars or a bicycle equipped with them — **high rise** *n*

high·road \'hī-,rōd\ *n* (1709) **1 :** HIGHWAY **2 :** the easiest course
high roller *n* (1881) **1 :** one who spends freely in fast or luxurious living **2 :** one who gambles recklessly or for high stakes
¹**high school** *n* (1824) **:** a school usu. including grades 9–12 or 10–12 — **high school·er** \-'skü-lər\ *n*
²**high school** *n* (1850) **:** a system of advanced exercises in horsemanship
high sea *n* (14c) **:** the open part of a sea or ocean esp. outside territorial waters — usu. used in pl.
high–sound·ing \'hī-'saún-diŋ\ *adj* (1784) **:** POMPOUS, IMPOSING
high–speed \'hī-'spēd\ *adj* (1873) **1 :** operated or adapted for operation at high speed **2 :** relating to the production of short-exposure photographs of rapidly moving objects or events of short duration
high–spir·it·ed \-'spir-ət-əd\ *adj* (1631) **:** characterized by a bold or energetic spirit — **high–spir·it·ed·ly** *adv* — **high–spir·it·ed·ness** *n*
high–stick·ing \-'stik-iŋ\ *n* (1947) **:** the act of carrying the blade of the stick at an illegal height in ice hockey
high street *n, Brit* (bef. 12c) **:** a main or principal street
high–strung \'hī-'strəŋ\ *adj* (1748) **:** having an extremely nervous or sensitive temperament
high style *n* (1939) **:** the newest style in fashion or design usu. adopted by a limited number of people
hight \'hīt\ *adj* [ME, irreg. pp. of *hoten* to command, call, be called, fr. OE *hātan;* akin to OHG *heizzan* to command, call, and prob. to L *ciēre* to move, Gk *kinein*] *archaic* (bef. 12c) **:** being called **:** NAMED
high table *n* (1859) **:** an elevated table in the dining room of a British college for use by the master and fellows of the college and distinguished guests
high·tail \'hī-,tāl\ *vi* (1925) **:** to move at full speed esp. in making a retreat — often used with *it*
high tea *n, Brit* (1831) **:** a fairly substantial late afternoon or early evening meal at which tea is served
high tech \-'tek\ *n* (1973) **1 :** HIGH TECHNOLOGY **2 :** a style of interior design featuring industrial products, materials, or designs
high technology *n* (1968) **:** scientific technology involving the production or use of advanced or sophisticated devices esp. in the fields of electronics and computers
high–tension *adj* (1905) **:** having a high voltage; *also* **:** relating to apparatus to be used at high voltage
high–test *adj* (1923) **:** meeting a high standard; *esp* **:** HIGH-OCTANE
high tide *n* (13c) **1 :** the tide when the water is at its greatest elevation **2 :** culminating point **:** CLIMAX
high–toned \'hī-'tōnd\ *adj* (1807) **1 :** high in social, moral, or intellectual quality **2 :** PRETENTIOUS, POMPOUS
high treason *n* (15c) **:** TREASON 2
high–water *adj* (1856) **:** unusually short ⟨~ pants⟩
high water *n* (15c) **:** a high stage of the water in a river or lake; *also* **:** HIGH TIDE
high·way \'hī-,wā\ *n* (bef. 12c) **:** a public way; *esp* **:** a main direct road
high·way·man \-mən\ *n* (1649) **:** a person who robs travelers on a road
highway robbery *n* (1778) **1 :** robbery committed on or near a public highway usu. against travelers **2 :** excessive profit or advantage derived from a business transaction
high–wrought \'hī-'rȯt\ *adj* (1604) **:** extremely agitated
high yal·ler \-'yal-ər\ *n* [*yaller,* alter. of *yellow*] (1923) **:** a mulatto or Negro of light-brown color — called also *high yellow;* often taken to be offensive
hi·jack \'hī-,jak\ *vt* [origin unknown] (1923) **1 a :** to steal by stopping a vehicle on the highway **b :** to commandeer (a flying airplane) esp. by coercing the pilot at gunpoint **c :** to stop and steal from (a vehicle in transit) **2 a :** to steal or rob as if by hijacking **b :** to subject to extortion or swindling — **hijack** *n* — **hi·jack·er** *n*
¹**hike** \'hīk\ *vb* **hiked; hik·ing** [perh. akin to ¹*hitch*] *vt* (1809) **1 a :** to move, pull, or raise with a sudden motion ⟨*hiked* himself onto the top bunk⟩ **b :** SNAP 6b **c :** to raise in amount sharply or suddenly ⟨~ rents⟩ **2 :** to take on a hike ~ *vi* **1 a :** to go on a hike **b :** to travel by any means **2 :** to rise up; *esp* **:** to work upward out of place ⟨skirt had *hiked* up in back⟩ — **hik·er** *n*
²**hike** *n* (1865) **1 :** a long walk esp. for pleasure or exercise **2 :** an increase esp. in quantity or amount ⟨a new wage ~⟩ **3 :** SNAP 11
hi·lar \'hī-lər\ *adj* (ca. 1864) **:** of, relating to, or located near a hilum
hi·lar·i·ous \hil-'ar-ē-əs, -'er-; hī-'lar-, -'ler-\ *adj* [irreg. fr. L *hilarus, hilaris* cheerful, fr. Gk *hilaros*] (1834) **:** marked by or affording hilarity — **hi·lar·i·ous·ly** *adv* — **hi·lar·i·ous·ness** *n*
hi·lar·i·ty \-ət-ē\ *n* (15c) **:** exhilaration of spirits that may be carried to the point of boisterous conviviality or merriment ***syn*** see MIRTH
Hil·bert space \,hil-bərt-\ *n* [David *Hilbert* †1943 Ger. mathematician] (1939) **:** a vector space for which a scalar product is defined and in which every Cauchy sequence composed of elements in the space converges to a limit in the space
hil·ding \'hil-diŋ\ *n* [*hilding,* adj. (base)] *archaic* (1592) **:** a base contemptible person
¹**hill** \'hil\ *n* [ME, fr. OE *hyll;* akin to L *collis* hill, *culmen* top] (bef. 12c) **1 :** a usu. rounded natural elevation of land lower than a mountain **2 :** an artificial heap or mound (as of earth) **3 :** several seeds or plants planted in a group rather than a row **4 :** SLOPE, INCLINE
²**hill** *vt* (1581) **1 :** to form into a heap **2 :** to draw earth around the roots or base of — **hill·er** *n*
hill·bil·ly \'hil-,bil-ē\ *n, pl* **-lies** [¹*hill* + *Billy,* nickname for *William*] (1900) **:** a person from a backwoods area
hillbilly music *n* (1943) **:** COUNTRY MUSIC
hill climb *n* (1905) **:** a road race for automobiles or motorcycles in which competitors are individually timed up a hill
hill·crest \'hil-,krest\ *n* (ca. 1898) **:** the top line of a hill
hill mynah *n* (ca. 1890) **:** a largely black Asian starling (*Gracula religiosa*) often tamed and taught to pronounce words
hill·ock \'hil-ək\ *n* (14c) **:** a small hill — **hill·ocky** \-ə-kē\ *adj*
Hill reaction \,hil-\ *n* [Robin *Hill,* 20th cent. Brit. biochemist] (1950) **:** the light-dependent transfer of electrons by chloroplasts in photosynthesis that results in the cleavage of water molecules and liberation of oxygen
hill·side \-,sīd\ *n* (14c) **:** a part of a hill between the summit and the foot
hill·top \'hil-,täp\ *n* (15c) **:** the highest part of a hill
hilly \'hil-ē\ *adj* **hill·i·er; -est** (14c) **1 :** abounding in hills **2 :** STEEP
hilt \'hilt\ *n* [ME, fr. OE; akin to OE *healt* lame — more at HALT] (bef. 12c) **:** a handle esp. of a sword or dagger — **to the hilt :** to the very limit **:** COMPLETELY
hi·lum \'hī-ləm\ *n, pl* **hi·la** \-lə\ [NL, fr. L, trifle] (ca. 1753) **1 a :** a scar on a seed (as a bean) marking the point of attachment of the ovule **b :** the nucleus of a starch grain **2 :** a notch in or opening from a bodily part suggesting the hilum of a bean
him \im, (')him\ *pron, objective case of* HE
Hi·ma·la·yan \,him-ə-'lā-ən, him-'äl-(ə-)yən\ *n* [*Himalaya* mountains] (1920) **:** any of a breed of domestic cats developed by crossing the Persian and the Siamese and having the stocky build and long thick coat of the former and the blue eyes and coat patterns of the latter — see CAT illustration
hi·mat·i·on \him-'at-ē-,än, -ən\ *n* [Gk, fr. *hennynai* to clothe — more at WEAR] (1850) **:** a rectangular cloth draped over the left shoulder and about the body and worn as a garment in ancient Greece
him·self \(h)im-'self, *Southern also* -'sef\ *pron* (bef. 12c) **1 a :** that identical male one — compare ¹HE; used reflexively, for emphasis, or in absolute constructions ⟨considers ~ lucky⟩ ⟨he ~ did it⟩ ⟨~ unhappy, he understood the situation⟩ **b** — used reflexively when the sex of the antecedent is unspecified ⟨everyone must fend for ~⟩ **2 :** his normal, healthy, or sane condition or self **3** *chiefly Irish & Scot* **:** a man of consequence; *esp* **:** the master of the house
¹**Him·yar·ite** \'him-yə-,rīt\ *n* [*Himyar,* legendary king in Yemen] (1842) **1 :** a member of an ancient people of southern Arabia **2 :** an Arab of a group of related ancient peoples of southern Arabia
²**Himyarite** *or* **Him·yar·it·ic** \,him-yə-'rit-ik\ *adj* (1843) **:** of or relating to the ancient Himyarites or their language
hin \'hin\ *n* [Heb *hīn,* fr. Egypt *hnw*] (14c) **:** an ancient Hebrew unit of liquid measure equal to about a gallon and a half
Hi·na·ya·na \,hē-nə-'yän-ə\ *n* [Skt *hīnayāna,* lit., lesser vehicle] (1868) **:** THERAVADA — **Hi·na·ya·nist** \-'yän-əst\ *n* — **Hi·na·ya·nis·tic** \-yä-'nis-tik\ *adj*
¹**hind** \'hīnd\ *n, pl* **hinds** *also* **hind** [ME, fr. OE; akin to OHG *hinta* hind, Gk *kemas* young deer] (bef. 12c) **1 :** the female of the red deer — compare HART **2 :** any of various spotted groupers (esp. genus *Epinephelus*)
²**hind** *n* [ME *hine* servant, farmhand, fr. OE *hīna,* gen. of *hīwan,* pl., members of a household; akin to OE *hām* home — more at HOME] (bef. 12c) **1 :** a British farm assistant **2** *archaic* **:** RUSTIC
³**hind** *adj* [ME, prob. back-formation fr. OE *hinder,* adv., behind; akin to OHG *hintar,* prep., behind] (14c) **:** of or forming the part that follows or is behind **:** REAR
hind·brain \'hīn(d)-,brān\ *n* (1888) **1 a :** the posterior of the three primary divisions of the vertebrate brain or the parts developed from it including the cerebellum, pons, and medulla oblongata **b :** METENCEPHALON **c :** MYELENCEPHALON **2 :** the posterior segment of the brain of an invertebrate
¹**hin·der** \'hin-dər\ *vb* **hin·dered; hin·der·ing** \-d(ə-)riŋ\ [ME *hindren,* fr. OE *hindrian;* akin to OE *hinder* behind] *vt* (bef. 12c) **1 :** to make slow or difficult the progress of **:** HAMPER **2 :** to hold back **:** CHECK ~ *vi* **:** to delay, impede, or prevent action — **hin·der·er** \-dər-ər\ *n*
syn HINDER, IMPEDE, OBSTRUCT, BLOCK mean to interfere with the activity or progress of. HINDER stresses causing harmful or annoying delay or interference with progress; IMPEDE implies making forward progress difficult by clogging, hampering, or fettering; OBSTRUCT implies interfering with something in motion or in progress by the sometimes intentional placing of obstacles in the way; BLOCK implies complete obstruction to passage or progress.
²**hind·er** \'hīn-dər\ *adj* [ME, fr. OE *hinder,* adv.] (bef. 12c) **:** situated behind or in the rear **:** POSTERIOR
hind·gut \'hīn(d)-,gət\ *n* (1878) **:** the posterior part of the alimentary canal
Hin·di \'hin-(,)dē\ *n* [Hindi *hindī,* fr. *Hind* India, fr. Per] (1800) **1 :** a literary and official language of northern India **2 :** a complex of Indic dialects of northern India for which Hindi is the usual literary language — **Hindi** *adj*
hind·most \'hīn(d)-,mōst\ *adj* (14c) **:** farthest to the rear **:** LAST
hind·quar·ter \-,kwȯ(r)t-ər\ *n* (1881) **1 :** one side of the back half of the carcass of a quadruped including a leg and usu. one or more ribs **2** *pl* **:** the hind pair of legs of a quadruped; *broadly* **:** all the structures of a quadruped that lie posterior to the attachment of the hind legs to the trunk
hin·drance \'hin-drən(t)s\ *n* (15c) **1 :** the state of being hindered **2 :** the action of hindering **3 :** IMPEDIMENT
hind·sight \'hīn(d)-,sīt\ *n* (1883) **:** perception of the nature and demands of an event after it has happened
¹**Hin·du** *also* **Hin·doo** \'hin-(,)dü\ *n* [Per *Hindū* inhabitant of India, fr. *Hind* India] (1662) **1 :** an adherent of Hinduism **2 :** a native or inhabitant of India
²**Hindu** *also* **Hindoo** *adj* (1698) **:** of, relating to, or characteristic of the Hindus or Hinduism
Hindu–Arabic *adj* (1925) **:** relating to, being, or composed of Arabic numerals ⟨~ numeration system⟩
Hindu calendar *n* (ca. 1909) **:** a lunar calendar usu. dating from 3101 B.C. and used esp. in India
Hin·du·ism \'hin-(,)dü-,iz-əm\ *n* (1829) **:** the dominant cultic religion of India emphasizing dharma with its resulting ritual and social observances and often mystical contemplation and ascetic practices
¹**Hin·du·stani** *also* **Hin·do·stani** \,hin-dú-'stan-ē, -'stän-ē\ *n* [Hindi *Hindūstānī,* fr. Per *Hindūstān* India] (1616) **1 :** a group of Indic dialects of northern India of which literary Hindi and Urdu are considered diverse written forms **2 :** a form of speech allied to Urdu but less divergent from Hindi used in some urban areas
²**Hindustani** *also* **Hindostani** *adj* (1677) **:** of or relating to Hindustan or its people or Hindustani
hind wing *n* (1899) **:** either of the posterior wings of a 4-winged insect

[1]**hinge** \ˈhinj\ *n* [ME *heng;* akin to MD *henge* hook, OE *hangian* to hang] (14c) **1 a :** a jointed or flexible device on which a door, lid, or other swinging part turns **b :** a flexible ligamentous joint **c :** a small piece of thin gummed paper used in fastening a postage stamp in an album **2 :** a determining factor : TURNING POINT

[2]**hinge** *vb* **hinged; hing·ing** *vt* (1606) : to attach by or furnish with hinges ~ *vi* : to be contingent on a single consideration or point — used with *on* or *upon*

hinge joint *n* (1802) : a joint between bones (as at the elbow) that permits motion in only one plane

hin·ny \ˈhin-ē\ *n, pl* **hinnies** [L *hinnus,* fr. Gk *innos*] (1688) : a hybrid between a stallion and a female donkey — compare MULE

[1]**hint** \ˈhint\ *n* [prob. alter. of obs. *hent* act of seizing, fr. *hent* vb.] (1604) **1** *archaic* : OPPORTUNITY, TURN **2 a :** an indirect or summary suggestion ⟨helpful ~*s*⟩ **b :** a statement conveying by implication what it is preferred not to say explicitly **3 :** a slight indication of the existence or nature of something : CLUE **4 :** a very small amount : SUGGESTION

[2]**hint** *vt* (1648) : to convey indirectly and by allusion rather than explicitly ⟨a suspicion that she scarcely dared to ~⟩ ~ *vi* : to give a hint ⟨~ for an invitation⟩ ***syn*** see SUGGEST — **hint·er** *n*

hin·ter·land \ˈhint-ər-ˌland, -lənd\ *n* [G, fr. *hinter* hinder + *land*] (1890) **1 :** a region lying inland from a coast **2 a :** a region remote from urban areas **b :** a region lying beyond major metropolitan or cultural centers

[1]**hip** \ˈhip\ *n* [ME *hipe,* fr. OE *hēope;* akin to OHG *hiafo* hip] (bef. 12c) : the ripened accessory fruit of a rose that consists of a fleshy receptacle enclosing numerous achenes

[2]**hip** *n* [ME, fr. OE *hype;* akin to OHG *huf* hip, L *cubitum* elbow, *cubare* to lie, *-cumbare* to lie down, Gk *kybos* cube, die, OE *hēah* high — more at HIGH] (bef. 12c) **1 a :** the laterally projecting region of each side of the lower or posterior part of the mammalian trunk formed by the lateral parts of the pelvis and upper part of the femur together with the fleshy parts covering them **b :** HIP JOINT **2 :** the external angle formed by the meeting of two sloping sides of a roof that have their wall plates running in different directions

[3]**hip** *vt* **hipped; hip·ping** (1669) : to make (as a roof) with a hip

[4]**hip** *interj* [origin unknown] (1827) — usu. used to begin a cheer ⟨~ ~ hooray⟩

[5]**hip** *also* **hep** *adj* **hip·per; hip·pest** [*hip,* alter. of *hep,* of unknown origin] (1904) : characterized by a keen informed awareness of or interest in the newest developments

[6]**hip** *vt* **hipped; hip·ping** (ca. 1932) : to make aware : TELL, INFORM

[7]**hip** *n* (1952) : HIPNESS

hip and thigh *adv* (1560) : in an overwhelming manner : UNSPARINGLY

hip·bone \ˈhip-ˈbōn, -ˌbōn\ *n* (12c) : INNOMINATE BONE

hip boot *n* (1893) : a boot reaching to the hips that is worn esp. by fishermen

hip joint *n* (1794) : the articulation between the femur and the innominate bone

hip·line \ˈhip-ˌlīn\ *n* (1926) : the line formed by measuring the hip at its fullest part

hip·ness \ˈhip-nəs\ *n* (1946) : the quality or state of being hip

hipp- *or* **hippo-** *comb form* [L, fr. Gk, fr. *hippos* — more at EQUINE] : horse ⟨*hippo*phagous⟩

[1]**hipped** \ˈhipt\ *adj* (15c) : having hips esp. of a specified kind — often used in combination ⟨broad-*hipped*⟩

[2]**hipped** *adj* [*hip* (hypochondria)] (1710) **1 :** DEPRESSED **2 :** absorbed or interested to an extreme degree ⟨~ on astrology⟩

hip·pie *or* **hip·py** \ˈhip-ē\ *n, pl* **hippies** [[5]*hip* + *-ie*] (1953) : a usu. young person who rejects the mores of established society (as by dressing unconventionally or favoring communal living), advocates a nonviolent ethic, and often uses psychedelic drugs or marijuana; *broadly* : a long-haired unconventionally dressed young person — **hip·pie·dom** \-ēd-əm\ *n* — **hip·pie·hood** \-ē-ˌhu̇d\ *n*

hip·po \ˈhip-(ˌ)ō\ *n, pl* **hippos** (1872) : HIPPOPOTAMUS

hip·po·cam·pal \ˌhip-ə-ˈkam-pəl\ *adj* (ca. 1839) : of or relating to the hippocampus

hip·po·cam·pus \-pəs\ *n, pl* **-pi** \-ˌpī, -(ˌ)pē\ [NL, fr. Gk *hippokampos* sea horse, fr. *hipp-* + *kampos* sea monster] (1706) : a curved elongated ridge that extends over the floor of the descending horn of each lateral ventricle of the brain and consists of gray matter covered on the ventricular surface with white matter

hip·po·cras \ˈhip-ə-ˌkras\ *n* [ME *ypocras,* fr. *Ypocras* Hippocrates, to whom its invention was ascribed] (14c) : a mulled wine popular in medieval Europe

Hip·po·crat·ic \ˌhip-ə-ˈkrat-ik\ *adj* (1620) : of or relating to Hippocrates or to the school of medicine that took his name

Hippocratic oath *n* (1747) : an oath embodying a code of medical ethics usu. taken by those about to begin medical practice

Hip·po·crene \ˈhip-ə-ˌkrēn, ˌhip-ə-ˈkrē-nē\ *n* [L, fr. Gk *Hippokrēnē*] (1634) : a fountain on Mount Helicon sacred to the Muses and believed to be a source of poetic inspiration

hip·po·drome \ˈhip-ə-ˌdrōm\ *n* [MF, fr. L *hippodromos,* fr. Gk, fr. *hipp-* + *dromos* racecourse — more at DROMEDARY] (1585) **1 :** an oval stadium for horse and chariot races in ancient Greece **2 :** an arena for equestrian performances

hip·po·griff \-ˌgrif\ *n* [F *hippogriffe,* fr. It *ippogrifo,* fr. *ippo-* hipp- (fr. L *hipp-*) + *grifo* griffin, fr. L *gryphus*] (1656) : a legendary animal having the foreparts of a griffin and the body of a horse

Hip·pol·y·ta \hip-ˈäl-ət-ə\ *n* [L, fr. Gk *Hippolytē*] : a queen of the Amazons given in marriage to Theseus by Hercules

Hip·pol·y·tus \-ət-əs\ *n* [L, fr. Gk *Hippolytos*] : a son of Theseus falsely accused of amorous advances by his stepmother and killed by his father through the agency of Poseidon

Hip·pom·e·nes \hip-ˈäm-ə-ˌnēz\ *n* [L, fr. Gk *Hippomenēs*] : the successful suitor of Atalanta in Greek mythology

hip·po·pot·a·mus \ˌhip-ə-ˈpät-ə-məs\ *n, pl* **-mus·es** *or* **-mi** \-ˌmī, -(ˌ)mē\ [L, fr. Gk *hippopotamos,* fr. *hipp-* + *potamos* river, fr. *petesthai* to fly, rush — more at FEATHER] (14c) : any of several large herbivorous 4-toed chiefly aquatic mammals (family Hippopotamidae and esp. genus *Hippopotamus*) with an extremely large head and mouth, bare and very thick skin, and short legs

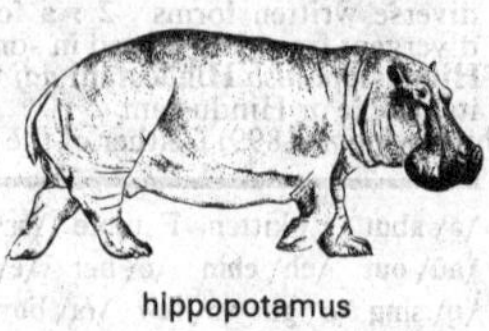

hippopotamus

-hip·pus \ˈhip-əs\ *n comb form* [NL, fr. Gk *hippos* — more at EQUINE] : horse — in generic names esp. in paleontology ⟨*Eohippus*⟩

hip roof *n* (ca. 1727) : a roof having sloping ends and sloping sides — see ROOF illustration

hip·ster \ˈhip-stər\ *n* [[5]*hip*] (1941) : a person who is unusually aware of and interested in new and unconventional patterns esp. in jazz, in the use of stimulants (as drugs), and in exotic religion

hip·ster·ism \-stə-ˌriz-əm\ *n* (1958) **1 :** HIPNESS **2 :** the way of life characteristic of hipsters

[1]**hire** \ˈhī(ə)r\ *n* [ME, fr. OE *hȳr;* akin to MD *hūre* hire] (bef. 12c) **1 a :** payment for the temporary use of something **b :** payment for labor or personal services : WAGES **2 a :** the act of hiring **b :** the state of being hired : EMPLOYMENT

[2]**hire** *vb* **hired; hir·ing** *vt* (bef. 12c) **1 a :** to engage the personal services of for a set sum ⟨~ on a new crew⟩ **b :** to engage the temporary use of for a fixed sum ⟨~ a hall⟩ **2 :** to grant the personal services of or temporary use of for a fixed sum ⟨~ themselves out⟩ **3 :** to get done for pay ⟨~ the mowing done⟩ ~ *vi* : to take employment ⟨~ out as a guide during the tourist season⟩ — **hir·er** *n*

syn HIRE, LET, LEASE, RENT, CHARTER mean to engage or grant for use at a price. HIRE and LET, strictly speaking, are complementary terms, HIRE implying the act of engaging or taking for use and LET the granting of use ⟨we *hired* a car for the summer⟩ ⟨decided to *let* the cottage to a young couple⟩ LEASE strictly implies a letting under the terms of a contract but is often applied to hiring on a lease ⟨the diplomat *leased* an apartment for a year⟩ RENT stresses the payment of money for the full use of property and may imply either hiring or letting ⟨instead of buying a house, they decided to *rent*⟩ ⟨will not *rent* to families with children⟩ CHARTER applies to the hiring or letting of a vehicle usu. for exclusive use ⟨*charter* a bus to go to the game⟩

hire·ling \ˈhī(ə)r-liŋ\ *n* (bef. 12c) : a person who serves for hire esp. for purely mercenary motives

hire purchase *n, chiefly Brit* (1895) : purchase on the installment plan

hiring hall *n* (1934) : a union-operated placement office where registered applicants are referred in rotation to jobs

hir·sute \ˈhər-ˌsüt, ˈhi(ə)r-, ˌhər-ˈ, hi(ə)r-ˈ\ *adj* [L *hirsutus;* akin to L *horrēre* to bristle — more at HORROR] (1621) : roughly hairy; *esp* : pubescent with coarse stiff hairs — **hir·sute·ness** *n*

hir·sut·ism \ˈhər-sə-ˌtiz-əm, ˈhi(ə)r-\ *n* (1926) : excessive growth of hair of normal or abnormal distribution

hir·su·tu·lous \ˌhər-ˈsü-chə-ləs, hi(ə)r-\ *adj* (1893) : minutely or slightly hirsute

hi·ru·din \hir-ˈüd-ᵊn, ˈhir-(y)əd-ən\ *n* [fr. *Hirudin,* a trademark] (1905) : an anticoagulant extracted from the buccal glands of a leech

[1]**his** \(h)iz, ˌhiz\ *adj* [ME, fr. OE, gen. of *hē* he] (bef. 12c) : of or relating to him or himself esp. as possessor, agent, or object of an action ⟨~ house⟩ ⟨~ writings⟩ ⟨~ confirmation⟩ — compare [1]HE

[2]**his** \ˈhiz\ *pron, sing or pl in constr* (bef. 12c) : that which belongs to him — used without a following noun as a pronoun equivalent in meaning to the adjective *his*

His·pan·ic \his-ˈpan-ik\ *adj* [L *hispanicus,* fr. *Hispania* Iberian peninsula, Spain] (1584) : of or relating to the people, speech, or culture of Spain, Spain and Portugal, or Latin America — **Hispanic** *n* — **His·pan·i·cism** \-ˈpan-ə-ˌsiz-əm\ *n* — **His·pan·i·cist** \-səst\ *n* — **His·pan·i·cize** \-ˌsīz\ *vt*

his·pa·ni·dad \ˌis-ˌpan-i-ˈthä(th)\ *n* (1941) : HISPANISM 1

his·pa·nism \ˈhis-pə-ˌniz-əm\ *n, often cap* (1940) **1 :** a movement to reassert the cultural unity of Spain and Latin America **2 :** a characteristic feature of Spanish occurring in another language

His·pa·nist \-nəst\ *n* (1926) : a scholar specially informed in Spanish or Portuguese language, literature, linguistics, or civilization

His·pa·no \his-ˈpan-(ˌ)ō, ˈhis-pə-ˌnō\ *n* [short for *Hispano*-American] (1946) : a native or resident of the southwestern U.S. descended from Spaniards settled there before annexation

Hispano- *comb form* [Sp *hispano,* fr. L *hispanus* Hispanic] : Spanish and ⟨*Hispano*-German⟩ : Spanish ⟨*Hispano*phile⟩

his·pid \ˈhis-pəd\ *adj* [L *hispidus;* prob. akin to L *horrēre*] (1646) : rough or covered with bristles, stiff hairs, or minute spines ⟨~ leaf⟩ — **his·pid·i·ty** \his-ˈpid-ət-ē\ *n*

hiss \ˈhis\ *vb* [ME *hissen,* of imit. origin] *vi* (14c) : to make a sharp sibilant sound ⟨the crowd ~*ed* in disapproval⟩ ⟨water ~*es* from the shower head⟩ ~ *vt* **1 :** to express disapproval of by hissing **2 :** to utter with a hiss — **hiss** *n* — **hiss·er** *n*

[1]**hist** \s *often prolonged and usu with* p *preceding and* t *following; often read as* ˈhist\ *interj* [origin unknown] (1617) — used to attract attention

[2]**hist** \ˈhist\ *dial var of* HOIST

hist- *or* **histo-** *comb form* [F, fr. Gk *histos* mast, loom beam, web, fr. *histanai* to cause to stand — more at STAND] : tissue ⟨*histo*physiology⟩

his·ta·mi·nase \his-ˈtam-ə-ˌnās, ˈhis-tə-mə-, -ˌnāz\ *n* [ISV] (1930) : a widely occurring flavoprotein enzyme that oxidizes histamine and various diamines

his·ta·mine \ˈhis-tə-ˌmēn, -mən\ *n* [ISV] (ca. 1913) : a compound $C_5H_9N_3$ that is found in ergot and many animal tissues or made synthetically and is prob. responsible for the dilatation and increased permeability of blood vessels which play a major role in allergic reactions — **his·ta·min·ic** \ˌhis-tə-ˈmin-ik\ *adj*

his·ta·min·er·gic \ˌhis-tə-mə-ˈnər-jik\ *adj* [ISV *histamine* + *-ergic*] *of autonomic nerve fibers* (1936) : liberating or activated by histamine ⟨~ receptors⟩

his·ti·dine \ˈhis-tə-ˌdēn\ *n* [ISV] (1896) : a crystalline basic amino acid $C_6H_9N_3O_2$ formed in the splitting of most proteins

his·tio·cyte \ˈhis-tē-ə-ˌsīt\ *n* [Gk *histion* web (dim. of *histos*), + ISV *-cyte*] (1924) : MACROPHAGE — **his·tio·cyt·ic** \ˌhis-tē-ə-ˈsit-ik\ *adj*

his·to·chem·i·cal \ˌhis-tō-ˈkem-i-kəl\ *adj* (1874) : of or relating to histochemistry — **his·to·chem·i·cal·ly** \-k(ə-)lē\ *adv*

his·to·chem·is·try \-ˈkem-ə-strē\ *n* [ISV] (1861) : a science that combines the techniques of biochemistry and histology in the study of the chemical constitution of cells and tissues

his·to·com·pat·i·bil·i·ty \ˈhis-(ˌ)tō-kəm-ˌpat-ə-ˈbil-ət-ē\ *n* (1948) : a state of mutual tolerance that allows some tissues to be grafted effectively to others

his·to·gen \ˈhis-tə-jən\ *n* [ISV] (ca. 1925) **:** a zone or clearly delimited region of primary tissue in or from which the specific parts of a plant organ are believed to be produced

his·to·gen·e·sis \ˌhis-tə-ˈjen-ə-səs\ *n* [NL] (1854) **:** the formation and differentiation of tissues — **his·to·ge·net·ic** \-jə-ˈnet-ik\ *adj* — **his·to·ge·net·i·cal·ly** \-i-k(ə-)lē\ *adv*

his·to·gram \ˈhis-tə-ˌgram\ *n* [Gk *histos* mast, web + E *-gram*] (1891) **:** a representation of a frequency distribution by means of rectangles whose widths represent class intervals and whose areas are proportional to the corresponding frequencies

his·tol·o·gy \his-ˈtäl-ə-jē\ *n, pl* **-gies** [F *histologie,* fr. *hist-* + *-logie* -logy] (1847) **1 :** a branch of anatomy that deals with the minute structure of animal and plant tissues as discernible with the microscope **2 :** a treatise on histology **3 :** tissue structure or organization — **his·to·log·i·cal** \ˌhis-tə-ˈläj-i-kəl\ *or* **his·to·log·ic** \-ˈläj-ik\ *adj* — **his·to·log·i·cal·ly** \-i-k(ə-)lē\ *adv* — **his·tol·o·gist** \his-ˈtäl-ə-jəst\ *n*

his·tol·y·sis \his-ˈtäl-ə-səs\ *n* [NL, fr. *hist-* + *-lysis*] (ca. 1857) **:** the breakdown of bodily tissues — **his·to·lyt·ic** \ˌhis-tə-ˈlit-ik\ *adj*

his·tone \ˈhis-ˌtōn\ *n* [ISV] (1885) **:** any of various simple water-soluble proteins that yield a high proportion of basic amino acids on hydrolysis and are found associated with DNA in cell nuclei

his·to·pa·thol·o·gy \ˌhis-tō-pə-ˈthäl-ə-jē, -pa-\ *n* [ISV] (1896) **1 :** a branch of pathology concerned with the tissue changes characteristic of disease **2 :** the tissue changes that affect a part or accompany a disease — **his·to·path·o·log·ic** \-ˌpath-ə-ˈläj-ik\ *or* **his·to·path·o·log·i·cal** \-i-kəl\ *adj* — **his·to·path·o·log·i·cal·ly** \-i-k(ə-)lē\ *adv* — **his·to·pa·thol·o·gist** \-pə-ˈthäl-ə-jəst, -pa-\ *n*

his·to·phys·i·ol·o·gy \-ˌfiz-ē-ˈäl-ə-jē\ *n* (ca. 1886) **1 :** a branch of physiology concerned with the function and activities of tissues **2 :** structural and functional tissue organization — **his·to·phys·i·o·log·i·cal** \-ē-ə-ˈläj-i-kəl\ *or* **his·to·phys·i·o·log·ic** \-ik\ *adj*

his·to·plas·mo·sis \ˌhis-tə-plaz-ˈmō-səs\ *n* [NL, fr. *Histoplasma,* genus of fungi] (ca. 1921) **:** a disease caused by infection with a fungus (*Histoplasma capsulatum*) and marked by benign involvement of lymph nodes of the trachea and bronchi or by severe progressive generalized involvement of the lymph nodes and the reticuloendothelial system

his·to·ri·an \his-ˈtōr-ē-ən, -ˈtȯr-, -ˈtär-\ *n* (15c) **1 :** a student or writer of history; *esp* **:** one that produces a scholarly synthesis **2 :** a writer or compiler of a chronicle

his·tor·ic \his-ˈtȯr-ik, -ˈtär-\ *adj* (1607) **:** HISTORICAL: as **a :** famous in history **b :** having considerable importance ⟨an ~ occasion⟩

his·tor·i·cal \-i-kəl\ *adj* (15c) **1 a :** of, relating to, or having the character of history **b :** based on history **c :** used in the past and reproduced in historical presentations **2 :** famous in history **3 a :** SECONDARY 1c **b :** DIACHRONIC ⟨~ grammar⟩ — **his·tor·i·cal·ly** \-i-k(ə-)lē\ *adv* — **his·tor·i·cal·ness** \-i-kəl-nəs\ *n*

historical materialism *n* (1925) **:** the Marxist theory of history and society that holds that ideas and social institutions develop only as the superstructure of a material economic base — compare DIALECTICAL MATERIALISM

historical present *n* (1867) **:** the present tense used in relating past events

historical school *n* (ca. 1895) **:** a school esp. in economics, legal philosophy, or ethnology emphasizing evolutionary developments and historical methods of research, analysis, and interpretation

his·tor·i·cism \his-ˈtȯr-ə-ˌsiz-əm, -ˈtär-\ *n* (1914) **:** a theory that emphasizes the importance of history as a standard of value or as a determinant of events — **his·tor·i·cist** \-səst\ *adj or n*

his·to·ric·i·ty \ˌhis-tə-ˈris-ət-ē\ *n* (ca. 1875) **:** historical actuality **:** FACT

his·tor·i·cize \his-ˈtȯr-ə-ˌsīz, -ˈtär-\ *vb* **-cized; -ciz·ing** *vt* (1846) **:** to make historical ~ *vi* **:** to use historical material

his·tor·i·co- \his-ˈtȯr-i-(ˌ)kō, -ˈtär-\ *comb form* **:** historical **:** historical and ⟨*historico*philosophical⟩ ⟨*historico*social⟩

his·to·ri·og·ra·pher \his-ˌtōr-ē-ˈäg-rə-fər, -ˌtȯr-\ *n* [MF *historiographeur,* fr. LL *historiographus,* fr. Gk *historiographos,* fr. *historia* + *graphein* to write — more at CARVE] (15c) **:** HISTORIAN

his·to·ri·og·ra·phy \-fē\ *n* (1535) **1 a :** the writing of history; *esp* **:** the writing of history based on the critical examination of sources, the selection of particulars from the authentic materials, and the synthesis of particulars into a narrative that will stand the test of critical methods **b :** the principles, theory, and history of historical writing ⟨a course in ~⟩ **2 :** the product of historical writing **:** a body of historical literature — **his·to·rio·graph·ic** \-ē-ə-ˈgraf-ik\ *or* **his·to·rio·graph·i·cal** \-i-kəl\ *adj* — **his·to·rio·graph·i·cal·ly** \-i-k(ə-)lē\ *adv*

his·to·ry \ˈhis-t(ə-)rē\ *n, pl* **-ries** [L *historia,* fr. Gk, inquiry, history, fr. *histōr, istōr* knowing, learned; akin to Gk *eidenai* to know — more at WIT] (14c) **1 :** TALE, STORY **2 a :** a chronological record of significant events (as affecting a nation or institution) often including an explanation of their causes **b :** a treatise presenting systematically related natural phenomena **c :** an account of a sick person's medical background **3 :** a branch of knowledge that records and explains past events ⟨medieval ~⟩ **4 a :** events that form the subject matter of a history **b :** past events ⟨that's all ~ now⟩ **c :** previous treatment, handling, or experience (as of a metal)

his·tri·on·ic \ˌhis-trē-ˈän-ik\ *adj* [LL *histrionicus,* fr. L *histrion-, histrio* actor, alter. of *hister,* fr. Etruscan] (1648) **1 :** deliberately affected **:** THEATRICAL **2 :** of or relating to actors, acting, or the theater ***syn*** see DRAMATIC — **his·tri·on·i·cal·ly** \-i-k(ə-)lē\ *adv*

his·tri·on·ics \-iks\ *n pl but sing or pl in constr* (1864) **1 :** theatrical performances **2 :** deliberate display of emotion for effect

[1]**hit** \ˈhit\ *vb* **hit; hit·ting** [ME *hitten,* fr. OE *hittan,* fr. ON *hitta* to meet with, hit] *vt* (bef. 12c) **1 a :** to reach with or as if with a blow **b :** to come in contact with ⟨the ball ~ the window⟩ **2 a :** to cause to come into contact **b :** to deliver (as a blow) by action **3 :** to affect esp. detrimentally **4 :** to make a request of ⟨~ his friend for 10 dollars⟩ — often used with *up* **5 :** to discover or meet esp. by chance **6 a :** to accord with **:** SUIT **b :** REACH, ATTAIN ⟨prices ~ a new high⟩ ⟨the best time to ~ the stores⟩ **c** *of fish* **:** to bite at or on **d :** to reflect accurately ⟨~ the right note⟩ **e :** to reach or strike (as a target) esp. for a score in a game or contest ⟨couldn't seem to ~ the basket⟩ **7 :** to indulge in excessively ⟨~ the bottle⟩ ~ *vi* **1 :** to strike a blow **2 a :** to come into contact with something **b :** ATTACK **c** *of a fish* **:** STRIKE *vi* 11b **d :** COME, HAPPEN **3 :** to succeed in attaining something — often used with *on* or *upon* ⟨~ on a solution⟩ **4** *obs* **:** to be in agreement **:** SUIT **5** *of an internal-combustion engine* **:** to fire the charge in the cylinders ***syn*** see STRIKE — **hit·ter** *n* — **hit it big :** to be a success — **hit it off :** to get along well — **hit one's stride :** to reach one's best speed or maximum capability — **hit the books :** to study esp. with intensity — **hit the fan :** to have a major usu. undesirable impact — **hit the hay** *or* **hit the sack :** to go to bed — **hit the high points** *or* **hit the high spots :** to touch on or at the most important points or places — **hit the jackpot :** to become notably and unexpectedly successful — **hit the nail on the head :** to be exactly right — **hit the road :** LEAVE, TRAVEL; *also* **:** to set out — **hit the roof** *or* **hit the ceiling :** to give vent to a burst of anger or angry protest — **hit the spot :** to give complete or special satisfaction — used esp. of food or drink

[2]**hit** *n* (15c) **1 a :** a blow striking an object aimed at **b :** COLLISION **2 a :** a stroke of luck **b :** something that is conspicuously successful **3 :** a telling remark **4 :** BASE HIT **5 :** a single dose of a narcotic drug **6 :** a premeditated murder usu. committed by a member of a crime syndicate — **hit·less** \ˈhit-ləs\ *adj*

hit–and–miss \ˌhit-ᵊn-ˈmis\ *adj* (1897) **:** sometimes successful and sometimes not **:** RANDOM

[1]**hit–and–run** \-ˈrən\ *adj* (1899) **1 :** being or relating to a baseball play in which a base runner starts for the next base as the pitcher starts to pitch and the batter attempts to hit the ball **2 :** being or involving a motor-vehicle driver who does not stop after being involved in an accident **3 :** involving or intended for quick specific action or results

[2]**hit–and–run** *vi* (1966) **:** to execute a hit-and-run play in baseball

[1]**hitch** \ˈhich\ *vb* [ME *hytchen*] *vt* (15c) **1 :** to move by jerks **2 a :** to catch or fasten by or as if by a hook or knot ⟨~*ed* his horse to the fence post⟩ **b** (1) **:** to connect (a vehicle or implement) with a source of motive power ⟨~ a rake to a tractor⟩ (2) **:** to attach (a source of motive power) to a vehicle or instrument ⟨~ the horses to the wagon⟩ **c :** to join in marriage **3 :** HITCHHIKE ~ *vi* **1 :** to move with halts and jerks **:** HOBBLE **2 a :** to become entangled, made fast, or linked **b :** to become joined in marriage **3 :** HITCHHIKE — **hitch·er** *n*

[2]**hitch** *n* (1664) **1 :** LIMP **2 :** a sudden movement or pull **:** JERK ⟨gave his trousers a ~⟩ **3 :** a sudden halt **:** STOPPAGE **4 :** the act or fact of catching hold **5 :** a connection between a vehicle or implement and a detachable source of power (as a tractor or horse) **6 :** a period usu. of military service **7 :** any of various knots used to form a temporary noose in a line or to secure a line temporarily to an object **8 :** LIFT 5b **9 :** CATCH 7

hitch·hike \ˈhich-ˌhīk\ *vi* (1923) **:** to travel by securing free rides from passing vehicles ~ *vt* **:** to solicit and obtain (a free ride) esp. in a passing vehicle — **hitch·hik·er** *n*

hitch up *vi* (1817) **:** to harness and secure a draft animal or team to a vehicle (as a wagon)

[1]**hith·er** \ˈhith-ər\ *adv* [ME *hider, hither,* fr. OE *hider;* akin to Goth *hidre* hither, L *citra* on this side — more at HE] (bef. 12c) **:** to this place

[2]**hither** *adj* (14c) **:** being on the near or adjacent side ⟨the ~ side of the hill⟩

hith·er·most \-ˌmōst\ *adj* (1563) **:** nearest on this side

hith·er·to \-ˌtü, ˌhith-ər-ˈtü\ *adv* (13c) **:** up to this time

hith·er·ward \ˈhith-ə(r)-wərd\ *adv* (12c) **:** HITHER

Hit·ler·ism \ˈhit-lə-ˌriz-əm\ *n* (1930) **:** the nationalistic and totalitarian principles and policies associated with Hitler — **Hit·ler·ite** \-ˌrīt\ *n or adj*

hit list *n* (1972) **:** a list esp. of persons or programs to be opposed or eliminated

hit man *n* (1968) **1 :** a professional assassin who works for a crime syndicate **2 :** HATCHET MAN

hit–or–miss \ˌhit-ər-ˈmis\ *adj* (1654) **:** marked by a lack of care, forethought, system, or plan

hit or miss *adv* (1606) **:** in a hit-or-miss manner **:** HAPHAZARDLY

hit parade *n* (1929) **:** a group or listing of the most popular or noteworthy items of a particular kind (as popular songs)

Hit·tite \ˈhi-ˌtīt\ *n* [Heb *Ḥittī,* fr. Hitt *ḫatti*] (1608) **1 :** a member of a conquering people in Asia Minor and Syria with an empire in the 2d millennium B.C. **2 :** the Indo-European language of the Hittites — see INDO-EUROPEAN LANGUAGES table — **Hittite** *adj*

HIV \ˌāch-ˌī-ˈvē\ *n* [*h*uman *i*mmunodeficiency *v*irus] (1986) **:** AIDS VIRUS

[1]**hive** \ˈhīv\ *n* [ME, fr. OE *hȳf;* akin to Gk *kypellon* cup, OE *hēah* high — more at HIGH] (bef. 12c) **1 :** a container for housing honeybees **2 :** a colony of bees **3 :** a place swarming with busy occupants — **hive·less** \-ləs\ *adj*

[2]**hive** *vb* **hived; hiv·ing** *vt* (15c) **1 :** to collect into a hive **2 :** to store up in or as if in a hive ~ *vi* **1** *of bees* **:** to enter and take possession of a hive **2 :** to reside in close association

hive off *vi* (1931) **:** to break away from a group ~ *vt* **:** to separate from a group ⟨*hived off* the youngest campers into another room⟩

hives \ˈhīvz\ *n pl but sing or pl in constr* [origin unknown] (ca. 1500) **:** URTICARIA

hiz·zon·er \ˌhiz-ˈän-ər\ *n, often cap* [alter. of *his honor*] (ca. 1924) — used as a title for a mayor

HMO \ˌā-(ˌ)chem-ˈō\ *n* (ca. 1972) **:** HEALTH MAINTENANCE ORGANIZATION

ho \ˈhō\ *interj* [ME] (15c) — used esp. to attract attention to something specified ⟨land ~⟩

hoa·gie *also* **hoa·gy** \ˈhō-gē\ *n, pl* **hoagies** [origin unknown] (1955) **:** SUBMARINE 2

[1]**hoar** \ˈhō(ə)r, ˈhȯ(ə)r\ *adj* [ME *hor,* fr. OE *hār;* akin to OHG *hēr* hoary] (bef. 12c) **:** HOARY

[2]**hoar** *n* [ME *hor* hoariness, fr. *hor,* adj.] (1567) **:** FROST 1c

[1]**hoard** \ˈhō(ə)rd, ˈhȯ(ə)rd\ *n* [ME *hord,* fr. OE; akin to Gk *kysthos* vulva, OE *hȳdan* to hide] (bef. 12c) **:** a hidden supply or fund stored up

[2]**hoard** *vt* (bef. 12c) **1 :** to lay up a hoard of **2 :** to keep (as one's thoughts) to oneself ⟨the people outside disperse their affections, you ~ yours —Joseph Conrad⟩ ~ *vi* **:** to lay up a hoard — **hoard·er** *n*

[3]**hoard** *n* (1757) **:** HOARDING 1

\ə\ abut \ᵊ\ kitten, F table \ər\ further \a\ ash \ā\ ace \ä\ cot, cart \au̇\ out \ch\ chin \e\ bet \ē\ easy \g\ go \i\ hit \ī\ ice \j\ job \ŋ\ sing \ō\ go \ȯ\ law \ȯi\ boy \th\ thin \th\ the \ü\ loot \u̇\ foot \y\ yet \zh\ vision \ȧ, k, ⁿ, œ, œ̄, ue, ue̅, ʸ\ *see* Guide to Pronunciation

hoard·ing \'hōrd-iŋ, 'hȯrd-\ *n* [*hourd, hoard* (hoarding)] (1823) **1 :** a temporary board fence put about a building being erected or repaired — called also *hoard* **2** *Brit* **:** BILLBOARD

hoar·frost \'hō(ə)r-,frȯst, 'hȯ(ə)r-\ *n* (13c) **:** FROST 1c

hoarse \'hō(ə)rs, 'hȯ(ə)rs\ *adj* **hoars·er; hoars·est** [ME *hos, hors,* fr. OE *hās;* akin to OE *hāt* hot — more at HOT] (bef. 12c) **1 :** rough or harsh in sound **:** GRATING ⟨~ voice⟩ **2 :** having a hoarse voice ⟨shouted himself ~⟩ — **hoarse·ly** *adv* — **hoarse·ness** *n*

hoars·en \'hōrs-ᵊn, 'hȯrs-\ *vb* **hoars·ened; hoars·en·ing** \'hōrs-niŋ, -ᵊn-iŋ, 'hȯrs-\ *vt* (1748) **:** to make hoarse ~ *vi* **:** to become hoarse

hoary \'hō(ə)r-ē, 'hȯ(ə)r-\ *adj* **hoar·i·er; -est** (1530) **1 a :** gray or white with age **b :** having grayish or whitish usu. pubescent leaves **2 :** impressively or venerably old **:** ANCIENT — **hoar·i·ness** *n*

hoa·tzin \wä(t)-'sēn\ *n* [AmerSp, fr. Nahuatl *uatzin*] (1889) **:** a crested So. American bird (*Opisthocomos hoatzin* of the order Galliformes) smaller than a pheasant with olive-colored plumage marked with white above and with claws on the first and second fingers of the wing

hoatzin

¹hoax \'hōks\ *vt* [prob. contr. of *hocus*] (ca. 1796) **:** to trick into believing or accepting as genuine something false and often preposterous ***syn*** see DUPE — **hoax·er** *n*

²hoax *n* (1808) **1 :** an act intended to trick or dupe **:** IMPOSTURE **2 :** something accepted or established by fraud or fabrication

¹hob \'häb\ *n* [ME *hobbe,* fr. *Hobbe,* nickname for Robert] (15c) **1** *dial Eng* **:** HOBGOBLIN, ELF **2 :** MISCHIEF, TROUBLE ⟨raise ~⟩

²hob *n* [origin unknown] (1511) **1 :** a projection at the back or side of a fireplace on which something may be kept warm **2 :** a cutting tool used for cutting the teeth of worm wheels or gear wheels

³hob *vt* **hobbed; hob·bing** (1874) **1 :** to furnish with hobnails **2 :** to cut with a hob

Hobbes·ian \'häb-zē-ən\ *adj* (1776) **:** of or relating to Hobbes or Hobbism

Hob·bism \'häb-,iz-əm\ *n* (1691) **:** the philosophical system of Hobbes; *esp* **:** the Hobbesian theory that people have a fundamental right to self-preservation and to pursue selfish aims but will relinquish these rights to an absolute monarch in the interest of common safety and happiness — **Hob·bist** \'häb-əst\ *n or adj*

¹hob·ble \'häb-əl\ *vb* **hob·bled; hob·bling** \-(ə-)liŋ\ [ME *hoblen;* akin to MD *hobbelen* to turn, roll] *vi* (14c) **:** to move along unsteadily or with difficulty; *esp* **:** to limp along ~ *vt* **1 :** to cause to limp **:** make lame **:** CRIPPLE **2** [prob. alter. of *hopple* (to hobble)] **a :** to fasten together the legs of (as a horse) to prevent straying **:** FETTER **b :** to place under handicap **:** HAMPER, IMPEDE — **hob·bler** \-(ə-)lər\ *n*

²hobble *n* (1726) **1 :** a hobbling movement **2** *archaic* **:** an awkward situation **3 :** something used to hobble an animal

hob·ble·de·hoy \'häb-əl-di-,hȯi\ *n* [origin unknown] (1540) **:** an awkward gawky youth

hobble skirt *n* (1911) **:** a skirt constricted at the bottom

¹hob·by \'häb-ē\ *n, pl* **hobbies** [ME *hoby,* fr. MF *hobé*] (15c) **:** a small Old World falcon (*Falco subbuteo*) formerly trained to catch small birds (as larks)

²hobby *n, pl* **hobbies** [short for *hobbyhorse*] (1816) **:** a pursuit outside one's regular occupation engaged in esp. for relaxation — **hob·by·ist** \-ē-əst\ *n*

hob·by·horse \'häb-ē-,hȯ(ə)rs\ *n* [*hobby* (small light horse)] (1557) **1 a :** a figure of a horse fastened about the waist in the morris dance **b :** a dancer wearing this figure **2** *obs* **:** BUFFOON **3 a :** a stick having an imitation horse's head at one end that a child pretends to ride **b :** ROCKING HORSE **c :** a toy horse suspended by springs from a frame **4 a :** a topic to which one constantly reverts **b :** ²HOBBY

hob·gob·lin \'häb-,gäb-lən\ *n* (1530) **1 :** a mischievous goblin **2 :** BOGEY 2, BUGABOO

hob·nail \-,nāl\ *n* [²*hob*] (1593) **:** a short large-headed nail for studding shoe soles — **hob·nailed** \-,nāld\ *adj*

hob·nob \-,näb\ *vi* **hob·nobbed; hob·nob·bing** [fr. the obs. phrase *drink hobnob* (to drink alternately to one another)] (1763) **1** *archaic* **:** to drink sociably **2 :** to associate familiarly — **hob·nob·ber** *n*

¹ho·bo \'hō-(,)bō\ *n, pl* **hoboes** *also* **hobos** [perh. alter. of *ho, boy*] (1889) **1 :** a migratory worker **2 :** a homeless and usu. penniless vagrant

²hobo *vi* (1906) **:** to live or travel in the manner of a hobo

Hob·son's choice \,häb-sənz-\ *n* [Thomas *Hobson* †1631 Eng. liveryman, who required every customer to take the horse nearest the door] (1649) **:** an apparently free choice when there is no real alternative

¹hock \'häk\ *n* [ME *hoch, hough,* fr. OE *hōh* heel; akin to ON *hāsin* hock, Skt *kaṅkāla* skeleton] (bef. 12c) **1 a :** the tarsal joint or region in the hind limb of a digitigrade quadruped (as the horse) corresponding to the ankle of man but elevated and bending backward — see HORSE illustration **b :** a joint of a fowl's leg that corresponds to the hock of a quadruped **2 :** a small cut of meat from either the front or hind leg just above the foot ⟨ham ~s⟩

²hock *n, often cap* [modif. of G *hochheimer,* fr. *Hochheim,* Germany] *chiefly Brit* (1625) **:** RHINE WINE 1

³hock *vt* (1878) **:** PAWN — **hock·er** *n*

⁴hock *n* [D *hok* pen, prison] (1883) **1 a :** ²PAWN 2 ⟨got his watch out of ~⟩ **b :** DEBT 3 ⟨in ~ to the bank⟩ **2 :** PRISON

hock·ey \'häk-ē\ *n* [perh. fr. MF *hoquet* shepherd's crook, dim. of *hoc* hook, of Gmc origin; akin to OE *hōc* hook] (1527) **1 :** FIELD HOCKEY **2 :** ICE HOCKEY

hock·shop \'häk-,shäp\ *n* (1871) **:** PAWNSHOP

ho·cus \'hō-kəs\ *vt* **ho·cussed** *or* **ho·cused; ho·cus·sing** *or* **ho·cus·ing** [obs. *hocus,* n., short for *hocus-pocus*] (1675) **1 :** to perpetrate a trick or hoax on **:** DECEIVE **2 :** to befuddle often with drugged liquor; *also* **:** DOPE, DRUG ⟨*hocussed* the favorite before the race⟩

¹ho·cus–po·cus \,hō-kə-'spō-kəs\ *n* [prob. fr. *hocus pocus,* imitation Latin phrase used by jugglers] (1647) **1 :** SLEIGHT OF HAND **2 :** nonsense or sham used esp. to cloak deception

²hocus–pocus *vt* **-cussed** *or* **-cused; -cus·sing** *or* **-cus·ing** (1687) **:** to play tricks on

hod \'häd\ *n* [prob. fr. MD *hodde;* akin to MHG *hotte* cradle] (1573) **1 :** a tray or trough that has a pole handle and that is borne on the shoulder for carrying loads (as of mortar or brick) **2 :** a coal scuttle

hod carrier *n* (1771) **:** a laborer employed in carrying supplies to bricklayers, stonemasons, cement finishers, or plasterers on the job

hodge·podge \'häj-,päj\ *n* [alter. of *hotchpotch*] (15c) **:** a heterogeneous mixture **:** JUMBLE

Hodg·kin's disease \'häj-kənz-\ *n* [Thomas *Hodgkin* †1866 Eng. physician] (1868) **:** a neoplastic disease that is characterized by progressive enlargement of lymph nodes, spleen, and liver and by progressive anemia

ho·do·scope \'häd-ə-,skōp, 'hōd-\ *n* [Gk *hodos* road, path + E *-scope* — more at CEDE] (1915) **:** an instrument for tracing the paths of ionizing particles by means of ion counters in close array

¹hoe \'hō\ *n* [ME *howe,* fr. MF *houe,* of Gmc origin; akin to OHG *houwa* mattock, *houwan* to hew — more at HEW] (14c) **1 :** any of various implements for tilling, mixing, or raking; *esp* **:** an implement with a thin flat blade on a long handle used esp. for cultivating, weeding, or loosening the earth around plants **2 :** BACKHOE

²hoe *vb* **hoed; hoe·ing** *vi* (15c) **:** to use a hoe **:** work with a hoe ~ *vt* **1 :** to weed, cultivate, or thin (a crop) with a hoe **2 :** to remove (weeds) by hoeing **3 :** to dress or cultivate (land) by hoeing — **ho·er** \'hō(-ə)r\ *n*

hoe·cake \'hō-,kāk\ *n* (1745) **:** a small cake made of cornmeal

hoe·down \-,daun\ *n* (1841) **1 :** SQUARE DANCE **2 :** a gathering featuring hoedowns

¹hog \'hȯg, 'häg\ *n, pl* **hogs** *also* **hog** [ME *hogge,* fr. OE *hogg*] (bef. 12c) **1 :** a domestic swine esp. when weighing more than 120 pounds; *broadly* **:** any of various wild and domestic swine **2** *usu* **hogg** *Brit* **:** a young unshorn sheep; *also* **:** wool from such a sheep **3 a :** a selfish, gluttonous, or filthy person **b :** one that uses something to excess ⟨old cars that are gas ~s⟩

²hog *vb* **hogged; hog·ging** *vt* (1798) **1 :** to cause to arch **2 :** to take in excess of one's due ⟨~ the credit⟩ **3 :** to tear up or shred (as waste wood) into bits by machine ~ *vi* **:** to become curved upward in the middle — used of a ship's bottom or keel

³hog *vt* **hogged; hog·ging** [prob. akin to ON *hǫggva* to strike, cut off; akin to OHG *houwan* to hew — more at HEW] (1769) **:** to cut (a horse's mane) short **:** ROACH

ho·gan \'hō-,gän\ *n* [Navaho] (1871) **:** a building usu. made of logs and mud and used as a dwelling by the Navaho Indians

hogan

hog·back \'hȯg-,bak, 'häg-\ *n* (1834) **:** a ridge of land formed by the outcropping edges of tilted strata; *broadly* **:** a ridge with a sharp summit and steeply sloping sides

hog cholera *n* (1859) **:** a highly infectious often fatal virus disease of swine characterized by fever, loss of appetite, weakness, erythematous lesions esp. in light-skinned animals, and severe leukopenia

hog·fish \'hȯg-,fish, 'häg-\ *n* (1734) **1 :** a large West Indian and Florida wrasse (*Lachnolaimus maximus*) often used for food **2 :** PIGFISH

hog·get \'häg-ət, 'hȯg-\ *n* [¹*hog* + *-et*] *chiefly Brit* (15c) **:** HOG 2

hog·gish \'hȯg-ish, 'häg-\ *adj* (15c) **:** grossly selfish, gluttonous, or filthy — **hog·gish·ly** *adv* — **hog·gish·ness** *n*

Hog·ma·nay \,häg-mə-'nā, 'häg-mə-,\ *n* [origin unknown] (1680) **1** *Scot* **:** the eve of New Year's Day **2** *Scot* **:** a gift solicited or given at Hogmanay

hog·nose snake \,hȯg-,nōz-, ,häg-\ *n* (1736) **:** any of several rather small harmless stout-bodied No. American colubrid snakes (genus *Heterodon*) — called also *hog-nosed snake*

hog score *n* [*hog* (curling stone that fails to reach the score)] (1685) **:** a line which is marked across a curling rink seven yards from the tee and beyond which a stone must pass or be removed from the ice — called also *hog line*

hogs·head \'hȯgz-,hed, 'hägz-\ *n* (14c) **1 :** a large cask or barrel; *esp* **:** one containing from 63 to 140 gallons **2 :** any of various units of capacity; *esp* **:** a U.S. unit equal to 63 gallons

hog sucker *n* (1883) **:** a No. American sucker (*Hypentelium nigricans*) that is brassy olive marked with brown and is sometimes used for food

hog–tie \'hȯg-,tī, 'häg-\ *vt* (1894) **1 :** to tie together the feet of **2 :** to make helpless

hog·wash \-,wȯsh, -,wäsh\ *n* (15c) **1 :** SWILL 2a, SLOP 4a **2 :** NONSENSE, BALDERDASH

hog–wild \-'wī(ə)ld\ *adj* (1904) **:** lacking in restraint of judgment or temper ⟨~ enthusiasm⟩ ⟨would go ~ if unconfined by constitutional limitations —Leo Egan⟩

¹Ho·hen·stau·fen \'hō-ən-,s(h)tau-fən\ *n* (ca. 1895) **:** a member of the Hohenstaufen family; *esp* **:** a Hohenstaufen monarch

²Hohenstaufen *adj* (1921) **:** of or relating to a princely German family that reigned over the Holy Roman Empire from 1138–1254 and over Sicily from 1194–1266

¹Ho·hen·zol·lern \'hō-ən-,zäl-ərn\ *n* (ca. 1895) **:** a member of the Hohenzollern family; *esp* **:** a Hohenzollern monarch

²Hohenzollern *adj* (1924) **:** of or relating to a princely German family that reigned in Prussia from 1701–1918 and in Germany from 1871–1918

ho–hum \'hō-'həm\ *adj* (1969) **:** ROUTINE, DULL ⟨a ~ existence⟩

ho hum *interj* [imit.] (1924) — used to express weariness, boredom, or disdain

hoick \'hȯik\ *vt* [prob. alter. of ¹*hike*] (1898) **:** to move or pull abruptly **:** YANK ⟨was ~*ed* out of my job —Vincent Sheean⟩

hoi pol·loi \,hȯi-pə-'lȯi\ *n pl* [Gk, the many; akin to L *plenus* full — more at FULL] (1837) **:** the general populace **:** MASSES

hoise \'hȯiz\ *vt* **hoised** \'hȯizd\ *or* **hoist** \'hȯist\; **hois·ing** \'hȯi-ziŋ\ [origin unknown] (15c) **:** HOIST — **hoist with one's own petard :** victimized or hurt by one's own scheme

¹hoist \'hȯist, *chiefly dial* 'hīst\ *vb* [alter. of *hoise*] *vt* (15c) **:** LIFT, RAISE; *esp* **:** to raise into position by or as if by means of tackle ~ *vi* **:** to become hoisted **:** RISE ***syn*** see LIFT — **hoist·er** *n*

²**hoist** *n* (1654) **1 :** an act of hoisting : LIFT **2 :** an apparatus for hoisting **3 :** the height of a flag when viewed flying

¹**hoi·ty–toi·ty** \ˌhȯit-ē-ˈtȯit-ē, ˌhīt-ē-ˈtīt-ē\ *n* [irreg. redupl. of E dial. *hoit* (to play the fool)] (1668) **:** thoughtless giddy behavior

²**hoity–toity** *adj* (1690) **1 :** thoughtlessly silly or frivolous : FLIGHTY **2 :** marked by an air of assumed importance : HIGHFALUTIN

hoke \ˈhōk\ *vt* **hoked; hok·ing** [*hokum*] (1925) **:** to give an impressive but false value or quality to : FAKE — usu. used with *up* ⟨used parts of B-grade movies to ~ up a film —Robert Sherrill⟩

hok·ey \ˈhō-kē\ *adj* (1927) **1 :** sickly or affectedly sentimental : CORNY, MAWKISH ⟨records on which she *didn't* sing ~ nursery rhymes —G. T. Simon⟩ **2 :** obviously contrived : PHONY ⟨the plots are tricky but not ~ —Cleveland Amory⟩ — **hok·ey·ness** *n*

ho·key·po·key \ˌhō-kē-ˈpō-kē\ *n* (1847) **1 :** HOCUS-POCUS 2 **2 :** ice cream sold by street vendors

hok·ku \ˈhō-(ˌ)kü\ *n, pl* **hokku** [Jp] (1898) **:** HAIKU

ho·kum \ˈhō-kəm\ *n* [prob. fr. *ho*cus-pocus + bun*kum*] (1917) **1 :** a device used (as by showmen) to evoke a desired audience response **2 :** pretentious nonsense : BUNKUM

hol- *or* **holo-** *comb form* [ME, fr. OF, fr. L, fr. Gk, fr. *holos* whole — more at SAFE] **1 :** complete : total ⟨*holo*hedral⟩ **2 :** completely : totally ⟨*hol*andric⟩

hol·an·dric \hō-ˈlan-drik, hä-\ *adj* [ISV, fr. *hol-* + *andr-* + *-ic*] (1930) **:** transmitted by a gene in the nonhomologous portion of the Y chromosome

Hol·arc·tic \hō-ˈlärk-tik, hä-, -ˈlärt-ik\ *adj* (1883) **:** of, relating to, or being the biogeographic region including the northern parts of the Old and the New Worlds and comprising the Nearctic and Palearctic regions or subregions

¹**hold** \ˈhōld\ *vb* **held** \ˈheld \; **hold·ing** [ME *holden*, fr. OE *healdan;* akin to OHG *haltan* to hold, L *celer* rapid, Gk *klonos* agitation] *vt* (bef. 12c) **1 a :** to have possession or ownership of or have at one's disposal ⟨~*s* property worth millions⟩ ⟨the bank ~*s* the title to the car⟩ **b :** to have as a privilege or position of responsibility ⟨~*s* the title of assistant to the president⟩ **c :** to have as a mark of distinction ⟨~*s* the record for the 100-yard dash⟩ ⟨~*s* a Ph.D.⟩ **2 :** to keep under restraint ⟨~ price increases to a minimum⟩: as **a :** to prevent free expression of ⟨~ your temper⟩ — often used in the phrase *hold one's tongue* **b :** to prevent from some action ⟨ordered the troops to ~ fire⟩ ⟨the only restraining motive which may ~ the hand of a tyrant —Thomas Jefferson⟩ **c :** to keep back from use ⟨ask them to ~ a room for us⟩ ⟨I'll have a hot dog, and ~ the mustard⟩ **d :** to delay temporarily the handling of ⟨please ~ all my calls⟩ **3 :** to make liable or accountable or bound to an obligation ⟨I'll ~ you to your promise⟩ **4 a :** to have or maintain in the grasp ⟨~ my hand⟩ ⟨this is how you ~ the racket⟩; *also* : AIM, POINT ⟨*held* a gun on them⟩ **b :** to support or keep from falling or moving ⟨~ me up so I can see⟩ ⟨~ the ladder steady⟩ ⟨a clamp ~*s* the whole thing together⟩ **c :** to bear the pressure of : SUPPORT ⟨the roof cannot ~ all of that weight⟩ **5 :** to prevent from leaving or getting away ⟨~ the train⟩: as **a :** to avoid emitting or letting out ⟨how long can you ~ your breath⟩ **b :** to restrain as or as if a captive ⟨the suspect was *held* without bail⟩ ⟨*held* them at gunpoint⟩ ⟨*held* me for an hour with stories of their adventure⟩; *also* : to have irresistible appeal to ⟨the book *held* my interest throughout⟩ **6 a :** to enclose and keep in a container or within bounds : CONTAIN ⟨the jug ~*s* one gallon⟩ ⟨this corral will not ~ all of the horses⟩ **b :** to be able to consume easily or without undue effect ⟨can't ~ any more pie⟩; *esp* : to be able to drink (alcoholic beverages) without becoming noticeably drunk ⟨can't ~ your liquor⟩ **c :** ACCOMMODATE ⟨the restaurant ~*s* 400 diners⟩ **d :** to have as a principal or essential feature or attribute ⟨the book ~*s* a number of delightful stories⟩; *also* : to have in store ⟨no one knows what the future ~*s*⟩ **7 a :** to have in the mind or express as a judgment, opinion, or belief ⟨I ~ the view that this is wrong⟩ ⟨~ a grudge⟩ ⟨~*ing* that it is nobody's business but his —Jack Olsen⟩ **b :** to think of in a particular way : REGARD ⟨were *held* in high esteem⟩ **8 a :** to assemble for and carry on the activity of ⟨*held* a convention⟩ **b :** to cause to be carried on : CONDUCT ⟨will ~ a seminar⟩ **c :** to produce or sponsor esp. as a public exhibition ⟨will ~ an art show⟩ **9 a :** to maintain occupation, control, or defense of ⟨the troops *held* the ridge⟩; *also* : to resist the offensive efforts or advance of ⟨*held* the opposing team to just two points⟩ **b :** to maintain (a certain condition, situation, or course of action) without change ⟨~ a course due east⟩ **10 a :** to support (the body or a part) in a particular position ⟨~ your arms up⟩ — often used reflexively ⟨~ yourself up straight⟩ **b :** to cover (a part of the body) esp. for protection ⟨had to ~ their ears because of the cold⟩ ~ *vi* **1 a :** to maintain position : refuse to give ground ⟨the defensive line is ~*ing*⟩ **b :** to continue in the same way or to the same degree : LAST ⟨hopes the weather will ~⟩ — often used with *up* **2 :** to maintain a grasp on something : remain fastened to something ⟨the anchor *held* in the rough sea⟩ **3 :** to derive right or title — often used with *of* or *from* **4 :** to bear or carry oneself ⟨asked him to ~ still⟩ **5 :** to be or remain valid : APPLY ⟨the rule ~*s* in most cases⟩ — often used in the phrase *hold true* **6 :** to go ahead as one has been going ⟨*held* south for several miles⟩ **7 :** to forbear an intended or threatened action : HALT, PAUSE — often used as a command **8 :** to stop counting during a countdown **9** *slang* **:** to have illicit drug material in one's possession ***syn*** see HAVE, CONTAIN — **hold a candle to :** to qualify for comparison with — **hold court :** to be the center of attention among friends or admirers ⟨literary or political figures who *hold court* . . . and delight the assembled flatterers with tales of folly and misrule —Lewis Lapham⟩ — **hold forth :** to speak at length : EXPATIATE — **hold hands :** to engage one's hand with another's esp. as an expression of affection — **hold one's own :** to do well in the face of difficulty or opposition — **hold sway :** to have a dominant influence : RULE — **hold the bag 1 :** to be left empty-handed **2 :** to bear alone a responsibility that should have been shared by others — **hold the fort 1 :** to maintain a firm position **2 :** to take care of usual affairs ⟨is *holding the fort* until the manager returns⟩ — **hold the line :** to maintain the current position or situation ⟨*holding the line* on prices —*Current Biog.*⟩ — **hold to :** to give firm assent to : adhere to strongly ⟨*holds to* his promise⟩ — **hold to account :** to hold responsible — **hold water :** to stand up under criticism or analysis — **hold with :** to agree with or approve of

²**hold** *n* (14c) **1 :** STRONGHOLD 1 **2 a :** CONFINEMENT, CUSTODY **b :** PRISON **3 a (1) :** the act or the manner of holding or grasping : GRIP ⟨released his ~ on the handle⟩ **(2) :** a manner of grasping an opponent in wrestling **b :** a nonphysical bond that attaches, restrains, or constrains or by which something is affected, controlled, or dominated ⟨has lost its ~ on the broad public —Oscar Cargill⟩ **c :** full comprehension ⟨get ~ of exactly what is happening —J. P. Lyford⟩ **d :** full or immediate control : POSSESSION ⟨get ~ of yourself⟩ ⟨wants to get ~ of a road map⟩ **4 :** something that may be grasped as a support **5 a :** FERMATA **b :** the time between the onset and the release of a vocal articulation **6 :** a sudden motionless posture at the end of a dance **7 a :** an order or indication that something is to be reserved or delayed **b :** a delay in a countdown (as in launching a spacecraft) — **on hold 1 :** into a state of interruption during a telephone call when one party switches to another line without totally disconnecting the other party **2 :** into a state or period of indefinite suspension ⟨put our plans *on hold*⟩

³**hold** *n* [alter. of *hole*] (1591) **1 :** the interior of a ship below decks; *esp* **:** the cargo deck of a ship **2 :** the cargo compartment of a plane

hold·all \ˈhōl-ˌdȯl\ *n* (1851) **:** a container for miscellaneous articles

hold·back \ˈhōl(d)-ˌbak\ *n* (1581) **1 :** something that retains or restrains **2 a :** the act of holding back **b :** something held back

hold back \(ˈ)hōl(d)-ˈbak\ *vt* (1535) **1 :** to hinder the progress or achievement of : RESTRAIN **2 :** to retain in one's keeping ~ *vi* **1 :** to keep oneself in check **2 :** to refrain from revealing or parting with something

hold–down \ˈhōl-ˌdau̇n\ *n* (1888) **1 :** something used to fasten an object in place **2 a :** an act of holding down **b :** LIMIT ⟨agreed to wage-rate ~*s*⟩

hold down \(ˈ)hōl-ˈdau̇n\ *vt* (1533) **1 :** to keep within limits ⟨*hold* the noise *down*⟩ **2 :** to assume the responsibility for ⟨*holding down* two jobs⟩

hold·en \ˈhōl-dən\ *archaic past part of* HOLD

hold·er \ˈhōl-dər\ *n* (14c) **1 :** a person that holds: **a (1) :** OWNER **(2) :** TENANT **b :** a person in possession of and legally entitled to receive payment of a bill, note, or check **2 :** a device that holds ⟨cigarette ~⟩

holder in due course (1882) **:** one other than the original recipient who holds a legally effective negotiable instrument (as a promissory note) and who has a right to collect from and no responsibility toward the issuer

hold·fast \ˈhōl(d)-ˌfast\ *n* (1841) **1 a :** a part by which a plant clings to a flat surface **b :** an organ by which a parasitic animal attaches itself to its host **2 :** something to which something else may be firmly secured

¹**hold·ing** \ˈhōl-diŋ\ *adj* (14c) **1 :** having the effect of holding back or delaying something ⟨the [war] represented a ~ action against the spread of world Communism —Sidney Offit⟩ **2 :** intended for usu. temporary storage or retention ⟨a ~ tank⟩

²**holding** *n* (15c) **1 a :** land held esp. by a vassal or tenant **b :** property (as land or securities) owned — usu. used in pl. **2 :** a ruling of a court esp. on an issue of law raised in a case — compare DICTUM **3 :** something that holds

holding company *n* (1906) **:** a company whose primary business is holding a controlling interest in the securities of other companies — compare INVESTMENT COMPANY

holding pattern *n* (ca. 1952) **:** the usu. oval course flown (as over an airport) by aircraft awaiting clearance to land

hold off *vt* (15c) **1 :** to fight to a standoff : WITHSTAND **2 :** to block from an objective : DELAY **3 :** to defer action on : POSTPONE ~ *vi* **:** to defer or temporarily stop doing something

hold on *vi* (ca. 1828) **1 a :** to maintain a condition or position : PERSIST **b :** to maintain a grasp on something : HANG ON **2 :** to await something (as a telephone connection) desired or requested; *broadly* : WAIT — **hold on to :** to maintain possession of or adherence to

hold·out \ˈhōl-ˌdau̇t\ *n* (ca. 1893) **:** one that holds out (as in negotiations)

hold out \(ˈ)hōl-ˈdau̇t\ *vt* (1535) **1 :** to present as something realizable : PROFFER **2 :** to represent to be ~ *vi* **1 :** to remain unsubdued or operative : continue to cope or function **2 :** to refuse to go along with others in a concerted action or to come to an agreement ⟨*holding out* for a shorter workweek⟩ — **hold out on :** to withhold something (as information) from

hold·over \ˈhōl-ˌdō-vər\ *n* (1893) **:** one that is held over; *esp* **:** one that continues in office

hold over \(ˈ)hōl-ˈdō-vər\ *vi* (1647) **:** to continue (as in office) for a prolonged period ~ *vt* **1 a :** POSTPONE, DEFER **b :** to retain in a condition or position from an earlier period **2 :** to prolong the engagement of ⟨the film was *held over* another week⟩

hold·up \ˈhōl-ˌdəp\ *n* (1837) **1 :** DELAY **2 :** a robbery carried out at gunpoint

hold up \(ˈ)hōl-ˈdəp\ *vt* (1529) **1 :** DELAY, IMPEDE **2 :** to rob at gunpoint **3 :** to call attention to : single out ⟨his work was *held up* to ridicule⟩ ⟨*hold* this *up* as perfection —*Times Lit. Supp.*⟩ ~ *vi* **:** to continue in the same condition without failing or losing effectiveness or force ⟨you seem to be *holding up* under the strain⟩

¹**hole** \ˈhōl\ *n* [ME, fr. OE *hol* (fr. neut. of *hol*, adj., hollow) & *holh;* akin to OHG *hol*, adj., hollow, L *caulis* stalk, stem, Gk *kaulos*] (bef. 12c) **1 a :** an opening through something : PERFORATION ⟨have a ~ in my coat⟩ **b :** an area where something is missing : GAP: as **(1) :** a serious discrepancy : FLAW, WEAKNESS ⟨there are ~*s* in your logic⟩ **(2) :** an opening in a defensive formation; *esp* : the area of a baseball field between the positions of shortstop and third baseman **(3) :** a defect in a crystal (as of a semiconductor) that is due to an electron's having left its normal position in one of the crystal bonds and that is equivalent in many respects to a positively charged particle **2 :** a cavity, depression, or hollowed-out place: as **a :** a cave, pit, or well in the ground **b :** an unusually deep place in a body of water **c :** BURROW **3 a :** a shallow cylindrical hole in the putting green of a golf course into which the ball is played **b :** a part of the golf course from tee to putting green ⟨just

beginning play on the third ~); *also* : the play on such a hole as a unit of scoring ⟨won the ~ by two strokes⟩ **4** : a wretched or dreary place **5** : an awkward position or circumstance : FIX ⟨got the rebels out of a ~ at the battle —Kenneth Roberts⟩ — **in the hole 1** : having a score below zero; *also* : in a position of owing or losing money **2** : at a disadvantage

²**hole** *vb* **holed; hol·ing** *vt* (bef. 12c) **1** : to make a hole in **2** : to drive into a hole ~ *vi* : to make a hole in something

hole–and–corner *adj* (1835) : being or carried on in a place away from public view; *esp* : carried on in secret ⟨~ whispering, locked doors and stealthy messengers —J. H. Wheelwright⟩

hole card *n* (1908) : a card in stud poker that is properly dealt facedown and that the holder need not expose before the showdown

hole in one (1925) : ACE 4

hole–in–the–wall *n, pl* **holes–in–the–wall** (1856) : a small and often unpretentious out-of-the-way place ⟨one of our more fashionable cuisines, served in . . . expensive restaurants that are far cries from the murky, tacky *holes-in-the-wall* we usually had to rely on —Mimi Sheraton⟩

hole out *vi* (1857) : to play one's ball into the hole in golf

hole up *vi* (1875) : to take refuge or shelter in or as if in a hole or cave ~ *vt* : to place in or as if in a refuge or hiding place

hol·ey \'hō-lē\ *adj* (14c) : having holes

¹**hol·i·day** \'häl-ə-,dā, *Brit usu* 'häl-əd-ē\ *n* [ME, fr. OE *hāligdæg*, fr. *hālig* holy + *dæg* day] (bef. 12c) **1** : HOLY DAY **2** : a day on which one is exempt from work; *specif* : a day marked by a general suspension of work in commemoration of an event **3** *chiefly Brit* : a period of relaxation : VACATION ⟨four weeks' ~ annually plus additional days at Christmas —*advt.*⟩ — often used in the phrase *on holiday;* often used in pl.

²**holiday** *vi* (1869) : to take or spend a holiday esp. in travel or at a resort — **hol·i·day·er** *n*

hol·i·day·mak·er \'häl-əd-ē-,mā-kər, 'häl-ə-,dā-\ *n, chiefly Brit* (1836) : VACATIONER

hol·i·days \-ə-,dāz, *Brit usu* -əd-ēz\ *adv* (1898) : on holidays repeatedly : on any holiday

ho·li·er–than–thou \,hō-lē-ər-t͟hən-'t͟hau̇\ *adj* (1859) : marked by an air of superior piety or morality

¹**ho·li·ness** \'hō-lē-nəs\ *n* [ME *holynesse*, fr. OE *hālignes*, fr. *hālig*] (bef. 12c) **1** : the quality or state of being holy — used as a title for various high religious dignitaries ⟨his *holiness* the pope⟩ **2** : SANCTIFICATION 2

²**holiness** *adj, often cap* (1888) : emphasizing the doctrine of the second blessing; *specif* : of or relating to a perfectionist movement arising in U.S. Protestantism in the late 19th century

ho·lism \'hō-,liz-əm\ *n* [*hol-* + *-ism*] (1926) **1** : a theory that the universe and esp. living nature is correctly seen in terms of interacting wholes (as of living organisms) that are more than the mere sum of elementary particles **2** : a holistic study or method of treatment

ho·lis·tic \hō-'lis-tik\ *adj* (1926) **1** : of or relating to holism **2** : relating to or concerned with wholes or with complete systems rather than with the analysis of, treatment of, or dissection into parts ⟨~ medicine attempts to treat both the mind and the body⟩ ⟨~ ecology views man and the environment as a single system⟩ — **ho·lis·ti·cal·ly** \-ti-k(ə-)lē\ *adv*

hol·land \'häl-ənd\ *n, often cap* [ME *holand*, fr. *Holand*, county in the Netherlands, fr. MD *Holland*] (14c) : a cotton or linen fabric in plain weave usu. heavily sized or glazed and used for window shades, bookbinding, and clothing

hol·lan·daise sauce \,häl-ən-,dāz-\ *n* [F *sauce hollandaise*, lit., Dutch sauce] (ca. 1900) : a rich sauce made of butter, egg yolks, and lemon juice or vinegar

Hol·lands \'häl-ən(d)z\ *n* [D *hollandsch*, fr. *hollandsch genever* Dutch gin] (1788) : gin made in the Netherlands — called also *Holland gin*

¹**hol·ler** \'häl-ər\ *vb* **hol·lered; hol·ler·ing** \-(ə-)riŋ\ [alter. of *hollo*] *vi* (1699) **1** : to cry out (as to attract attention or in pain) : SHOUT **2** : GRIPE, COMPLAIN ~ *vt* : to call out (a word or phrase)

²**holler** *n* (1825) **1** : SHOUT, CRY **2** : COMPLAINT **3** : a freely improvised American Negro work song

³**holler** *chiefly dial var of* HOLLOW

Hol·ler·ith \'häl-ə-,rith\ *n* [Herman *Hollerith* †1929 Am. engineer] (1948) : a system for encoding alphanumeric information on punch cards — called also *Hollerith code*

Hollerith card *n* (1946) : PUNCH CARD

¹**hol·lo** *also* **hol·loa** \'häl-(,)ō, -ə(-w)\ *or* **hol·la** \'häl-ə(-w)\ *vb* (15c) : to cry hollo : HOLLER

²**hollo** *also* **holloa** *or* **holla** *n, pl* **hollos** *also* **holloas** *or* **hollas** (15c) : an exclamation or call of hollo

³**hol·lo** \hä-'lō, hə-; 'häl-(,)ō\ *also* **hol·loa** \hä-'lō, hə-\ *or* **hol·la** \hə-'lä, 'häl-(,)ä\ *interj* [origin unknown] (1588) **1** — used to attract attention **2** — used as a call of encouragement or jubilation

¹**hol·low** \'häl-(,)ō, -ə(-w)\ *adj* **hol·low·er** \'häl-ə-wər\; **hol·low·est** \-ə-wəst\ [ME *holw, holh*, fr. *holh* hole, den, fr. OE *holh* hole, hollow — more at HOLE] (bef. 12c) **1** : having an indentation or inward curve : CONCAVE, SUNKEN **2** : having a cavity within ⟨~ tree⟩ **3** : reverberating like a sound made in or by beating on a large empty enclosure : MUFFLED **4** : lacking in real value, sincerity, or substance : FALSE, MEANINGLESS ⟨~ promises⟩ ⟨his opponent knows . . . that a victory over a weakling is ~ and without triumph —Ernest Beaglehole⟩ *syn* see VAIN — **hol·low·ly** \'häl-ō-lē, -ə-lē\ *adv* — **hol·low·ness** *n*

²**hollow** *n* (bef. 12c) **1** : a depressed or low part of a surface; *esp* : a small valley or basin **2** : an unfilled space : CAVITY, HOLE

³**hollow** *vt* (15c) **1** : to make hollow **2** : to form by a hollowing action — usu. used with *out* ⟨rain barrels ~*ed* out from trees —Robert Shaplen⟩ ~ *vi* : to become hollow

⁴**hollow** *adv* (1601) **1** : so as to have a hollow sound **2** : COMPLETELY, THOROUGHLY ⟨an ongoing story that has the old cowboy-and-Indians genre beat ~ —Barbara Bannon⟩ — often used with *all*

hol·low·ware *or* **hol·lo·ware** \'häl-ə-,wa(ə)r, -,we(ə)r\ *n* (1703) : vessels (as bowls, cups, or vases) usu. of pottery, glass, or metal that have a significant depth and volume — compare FLATWARE

hol·ly \'häl-ē\ *n, pl* **hollies** [ME *holin, holly*, fr. OE *holen;* akin to OHG *hulis* holly, MIr *cuilenn*] (bef. 12c) **1** : any of a genus (*Ilex* of the family Aquifoliaceae, the holly family) of trees and shrubs; *esp* : either of two (*I. opaca* of the eastern U.S. and *I. acquifolium* of Eurasia) with spiny-margined evergreen leaves and usu. red berries often used for Christmas decorations **2** : the foliage or branches of the holly

hol·ly·hock \'häl-ē-,häk, -,hȯk\ *n* [ME *holihoc*, fr. *holi* holy + *hoc* mallow, fr. OE] (13c) : a tall widely cultivated perennial Chinese herb (*Althaea rosea*) of the mallow family with large coarse rounded leaves and tall spikes of showy flowers

Hol·ly·wood \'häl-ē-,wu̇d\ *n* [*Hollywood*, district of Los Angeles, Calif.] (1923) : the American motion-picture industry — **Hol·ly·wood·ish** \-ish\ *adj*

Hollywood bed *n* (1947) : a mattress on a box spring supported by low legs and often having an upholstered headboard

holm \'hō(l)m\ *n* [ME, fr. OE, fr. ON *hōlmr;* akin to OE *hyll* hill] *Brit* (bef. 12c) : a small inland or inshore island; *also* : BOTTOMS

Holmes·ian \'hōm-zē-ən *also* 'hōlm-\ *adj* [Sherlock *Holmes*, detective in stories by Sir Arthur Conan Doyle] (1929) : of, characteristic of, or suggestive of the detective Sherlock Holmes

hol·mi·um \'hō(l)-mē-əm\ *n* [NL, fr. *Holmia* Stockholm, Sweden] (1879) : a metallic element of the rare-earth group that occurs with yttrium and forms highly magnetic compounds — see ELEMENT table

holm oak *n* (1597) : a southern European evergreen oak (*Quercus ilex*)

holo- — see HOL-

ho·lo·blas·tic \,hō-lə-'blas-tik, ,häl-ə-\ *adj* [ISV] (1872) : characterized by cleavage planes that divide the whole egg into distinct and separate though coherent blastomeres ⟨~ eggs⟩ ⟨~ cleavage⟩ — compare MEROBLASTIC

ho·lo·caust \'hō-lə-,kȯst, 'häl-ə- *also* -,käst *or* 'hȯ-lə-kȯst\ *n* [ME, fr. OF *holocauste*, fr. LL *holocaustum*, fr. Gk *holokauston*, fr. neut. of *holokaustos* burnt whole, fr. *hol-* + *kaustos* burnt, fr. *kaiein* to burn — more at CAUSTIC] (13c) **1** : a sacrifice consumed by fire **2** : a thorough destruction esp. involving loss of life ⟨a nuclear ~⟩ **3** *often cap* : the mass slaughter of European civilians and esp. Jews by the Nazis during World War II — usu. used with *the*

Ho·lo·cene \'hō-lə-,sēn, 'häl-ə-\ *adj* [ISV] (1897) : RECENT 2 — **Holocene** *n*

ho·lo·crine \-krən, -,krīn, -,krēn\ *adj* [ISV *hol-* + Gk *krinein* to separate — more at CERTAIN] (ca. 1905) : producing a secretion containing disintegrated secretory cells; *also* : produced by a holocrine gland

ho·lo·en·zyme \,hō-lō-'en-,zīm\ *n* [ISV] (1943) : a complete active enzyme consisting of an apoenzyme combined with its coenzyme

Ho·lo·fer·nes \,häl-ə-'fər-(,)nēz, ,hō-lə-\ *n* [LL, fr. Gk *Holophernēs*] : a general of Nebuchadnezzar's who led an Assyrian army against Israel and was beheaded in his sleep by Judith

ho·lo·gram \'hō-lə-,gram, 'häl-ə-\ *n* (1949) : a three-dimensional picture that is made on a photographic film or plate without the use of a camera, that consists of a pattern of interference produced by a split coherent beam of radiation and esp. light and that for viewing is illuminated with coherent light from behind

ho·lo·graph \'hō-lə-,graf, 'häl-ə-\ *n* [LL *holographus*, fr. LGk *holographos*, fr. Gk *hol-* + *graphein* to write — more at CARVE] (1623) : a document wholly in the handwriting of its author; *also* : the handwriting itself ⟨a letter in the president's ~⟩ — **holograph** *or* **ho·lo·graph·ic** \,hō-lə-'graf-ik, ,häl-ə-\ *adj*

ho·log·ra·phy \hō-'läg-rə-fē\ *n* (1802) : the process of making or using a hologram — **ho·lo·graph** \'hō-lə-,graf, 'häl-ə-\ *vt* — **ho·log·ra·pher** \hō-'läg-rə-fər\ *n* — **ho·lo·graph·ic** \,hō-lə-'graf-ik, ,häl-ə-\ *adj* — **ho·lo·graph·i·cal·ly** \-i-k(ə-)lē\ *adv*

ho·lo·gy·nic \,hō-lə-'jin-ik, ,häl-ə-, -'gī-nik\ *adj* [ISV *hol-* + *-gynic* (fr. Gk *gynē* woman) — more at QUEEN] (1946) : inherited solely in the female line presumably through transmission as a recessive factor in the nonhomologous portion of the X chromosome

ho·lo·he·dral \,hō-lə-'hē-drəl, ,häl-ə-\ *adj* [*hol-* + Gk *hedra* seat — more at SIT] *of a crystal* (1837) : having all the faces required by complete symmetry — compare HEMIHEDRAL, TETARTOHEDRAL

ho·lo·me·tab·o·lous \,hō-lō-mə-'tab-ə-ləs, ,häl-ō-\ *adj* (1870) : characterized by complete metamorphosis ⟨~ insects⟩ — **ho·lo·me·tab·o·lism** \-,liz-əm\ *n*

ho·lo·phras·tic \,hō-lə-'fras-tik, ,häl-ə-\ *adj* [ISV *hol-* + *-phrastic* (fr. Gk *phrazein* to point out, declare)] (1860) : expressing a complex of ideas in a single word or in a fixed phrase

ho·lo·phyt·ic \-'fit-ik\ *adj* (ca. 1885) : obtaining food after the manner of a green plant by photosynthetic activity

ho·lo·thu·ri·an \-'th(y)u̇r-ē-ən\ *n* [deriv. of Gk *holothourion* water polyp] (ca. 1842) : any of a class (Holothurioidea) of echinoderms having an elongate flexible tough muscular body : SEA CUCUMBER — **holothurian** *adj*

ho·lo·type \'hō-lə-,tīp, 'häl-ə-\ *n* (1897) **1** : the single specimen designated by an author as the type of a species or lesser taxon at the time of establishing the group **2** : the type of a species or lesser taxon designated at a date later than that of establishing a group or by another person than the author of the taxon — **ho·lo·typ·ic** \,hō-lə-'tip-ik, ,häl-ə-\ *adj*

ho·lo·zo·ic \,hō-lə-'zō-ik, ,häl-ə-\ *adj* (ca. 1885) : characterized by food procurement after the manner of most animals by the ingestion of complex organic matter : HETEROTROPHIC ⟨~ nutrition⟩

holp \'hō(l)p\ *chiefly dial past of* HELP

hol·pen \'hō(l)-pən\ *chiefly dial past part of* HELP

hol·stein \'hōl-,stēn, -,stīn\ *n* [short for *holstein-friesian*] (1865) : any of a breed of large black-and-white dairy cattle orig. from northern Holland and Friesland that produce large quantities of comparatively low-fat milk

hol·stein–frie·sian \-'frē-zhən\ *n* [*Holstein*, Germany, its later locality + *Friesian* (var. of *Frisian*)] (1889) : HOLSTEIN

hol·ster \'hōl(t)-stər\ *n* [D; akin to OE *heolstor* cover, *helan* to conceal — more at HELL] (1663) : a leather or fabric case for carrying a firearm on the person (as on the hip or shoulder), on a saddle, or in a vehicle

holt \'hōlt\ *n* [ME, fr. OE; akin to OHG *holz* wood, Gk *klados* twig — more at GLADIATOR] *archaic* (bef. 12c) : a small woods : COPSE

ho·lus–bo·lus \,hō-ləs-'bō-ləs\ *adv* [prob. redupl. of *bolus*] (1847) : all at once

ho·ly \'hō-lē\ *adj* **ho·li·er; -est** [ME, fr. OE *hālig;* akin to OE *hāl* whole — more at WHOLE] (bef. 12c) **1** : exalted or worthy of complete devotion as one perfect in goodness and righteousness **2** : DIVINE ⟨for the Lord our God is ~ — *Psalms* 99:9 (AV)⟩ **2** : devoted entirely to the deity or the work of the deity ⟨a ~ temple⟩ ⟨~ prophets⟩ **3 a** : having a divine quality ⟨~ love⟩ **b :** venerated as or as if sacred ⟨~ scripture⟩ ⟨a ~ relic⟩ ⟨lampooning the ~ conventions of playwriting —William Zinsser⟩ **4** — used as an intensive ⟨this is a ~ mess⟩ ⟨he was a ~ terror when he drank —Thomas Wolfe⟩; often used in combination as a mild oath ⟨~ smokes⟩ — **ho•li•ly** \-lə-lē\ *adv*

holy city *n* (14c) **:** a city that is the center of religious worship and traditions

Holy Communion *n* (ca. 1890) **:** COMMUNION 2a

holy day *n* (bef. 12c) **:** a day set aside for special religious observance

holy day of obligation (ca. 1934) **:** a feast on which Roman Catholics are duty-bound to attend mass

Holy Father *n* (15c) **:** POPE 1

Holy Ghost *n* (bef. 12c) **:** the third person of the Trinity **:** HOLY SPIRIT

Holy Grail *n* (1590) **:** GRAIL

Holy Joe \ˌhō-lē-ˈjō\ *n, slang* (1874) **:** PARSON, CHAPLAIN

Holy Office *n* (ca. 1727) **:** a congregation of the curia charged with protecting faith and morals

holy of holies [trans. of LL *sanctum sanctorum,* trans. of Heb *qōdhesh haq-qōdhāshīm*] (1641) **:** the innermost and most sacred chamber of the Jewish tabernacle and temple

holy oil *n* (14c) **:** olive oil blessed by a bishop for use in a sacrament or sacramental

holy order *n, often cap H&O* (14c) **1 a :** MAJOR ORDER — usu. used in pl. **b :** one of the orders of the ministry in the Anglican or Episcopal church **2 :** the rite or sacrament of ordination — usu. used in pl.

Holy Roller *n* (1842) **:** a member of one of the Protestant sects whose worship meetings are characterized by frenzied excitement — often taken to be offensive

Holy Roman Empire *n* (ca. 1895) **:** an empire consisting primarily of a loose confederation of German and Italian territories under the suzerainty of an emperor and existing from the 9th or 10th century to 1806

Holy Saturday *n* (14c) **:** the Saturday before Easter

Holy See *n* (1765) **:** the see of the pope

Holy Spirit *n* (14c) **:** the active presence of God in human life constituting the third person of the Trinity

1**ho•ly•stone** \ˈhō-lē-ˌstōn\ *n* (1823) **:** a soft sandstone used to scrub a ship's decks

2**holystone** *vt* (1828) **:** to scrub with a holystone

Holy Synod *n* (1768) **:** the governing body of a national Eastern church

Holy Thursday *n* (bef. 12c) **1 :** ASCENSION DAY **2 :** MAUNDY THURSDAY

holy war *n* (1691) **:** a war waged by religious partisans to propagate or defend their faith

holy water *n* (bef. 12c) **:** water blessed by a priest and used as a purifying sacramental

Holy Week *n* (bef. 12c) **:** the week before Easter during which the last days of Christ's life are commemorated

holy writ *n, often cap H&W* (bef. 12c) **1 :** BIBLE 1 **2 :** a writing or utterance having unquestionable authority ⟨its financial precepts were not necessarily *Holy Writ* —Herbert Stein⟩

Holy Year *n* (1925) **:** a Roman Catholic jubilee year

hom- *or* **homo-** *comb form* [L, fr. Gk, fr. *homos* — more at SAME] **1 :** one and the same **:** similar **:** alike ⟨*hom*ograph⟩ ⟨*homo*sporous⟩ **2 :** homologous with a (specified) chemical compound ⟨*homo*gentisic acid⟩

hom•age \ˈ(h)äm-ij\ *n* [ME, fr. OF *hommage,* fr. *homme* man, vassal, fr. L *homin-, homo* man; akin to OE *guma* man, L *humus* earth — more at HUMBLE] (13c) **1 a :** a feudal ceremony by which a man acknowledges himself the vassal of a lord **b :** the relationship between a feudal lord and his man **c :** an act done or payment made in meeting the obligations of vassalage **2 a :** reverential regard **:** RESPECT — often used with *pay* **b :** something that shows respect or attests to the worth or influence of another **:** TRIBUTE ⟨his long life filled with international ~*s* to his unique musical talent —*People*⟩ ***syn*** see HONOR

hom•ag•er \ˈ(h)äm-ij-ər\ *n* (15c) **:** VASSAL

homalographic *var of* HOMOLOGRAPHIC

hom•bre \ˈäm-brē, ˈəm-, ˈōm-, -ˌbrā\ *n* [Sp, man, fr. L *homin-, homo*] (1846) **:** GUY, FELLOW

hom•burg \ˈhäm-ˌbərg\ *n* [*Homburg,* Germany] (1901) **:** a man's felt hat with a stiff curled brim and a high crown creased lengthwise

1**home** \ˈhōm\ *n* [ME *hom,* fr. OE *hām* village, home; akin to Gk *kōmē* village, L *civis* citizen, Gk *koiman* to put to sleep — more at CEMETERY] (bef. 12c) **1 a :** one's place of residence **:** DOMICILE **b :** HOUSE **2 :** the social unit formed by a family living together **3 a :** a familiar or usual setting **:** congenial environment; *also* **:** the focus of one's domestic attention ⟨~ is where the heart is⟩ **b :** HABITAT **4 a :** a place of origin ⟨salmon returning to their ~ to spawn⟩; *also* **:** one's own country ⟨having troubles at ~ and abroad⟩ **b :** HEADQUARTERS ⟨~ of the dance company⟩ **5 :** an establishment providing residence and care for people with special needs ⟨~*s* for the elderly⟩ ⟨a ~ for unwed mothers⟩ **6 :** the objective in various games; *esp* **:** HOME PLATE — **home•less** \-ləs\ *adj* — **at home 1 :** relaxed and comfortable **:** at ease ⟨felt completely *at home* on the stage⟩ **2 :** in harmony with the surroundings **3 :** on familiar ground **:** KNOWLEDGEABLE ⟨teachers *at home* in their subject fields⟩

2**home** *adv* (bef. 12c) **1 :** to, from, or at one's home ⟨go ~⟩ ⟨left ~ at the age of 12⟩ **2 a :** to a final, closed, or ultimate position ⟨drive a nail ~⟩ **b :** to or at an ultimate objective (as a goal or finish line) **3 :** to a vital sensitive core ⟨the truth struck ~⟩ — **home free :** out of jeopardy **:** in a comfortable position with respect to some objective

3**home** *adj* (1552) **1 :** of, relating to, or being a home, place of origin, or base of operations ⟨~ office⟩ ⟨checkers in position on their ~ squares⟩ **2 :** prepared, done, or designed for use in a home ⟨~ remedies⟩ ⟨~ cooking⟩ ⟨a ~ videotape system⟩ **3 :** operating or occurring in a home area ⟨the ~ team⟩ ⟨~ games⟩

4**home** *vb* **homed; hom•ing** *vi* (1765) **1 :** to go or return home **2** *of an animal* **:** to return accurately to one's home or natal area from a distance **3 :** to proceed to or toward a source of radiated energy used as a guide ⟨missiles ~ in on radar⟩ **4 :** to proceed or direct attention toward an objective ⟨science is *homing* in on the mysterious human process —Sam Glucksberg⟩ ~ *vt* **:** to send to or provide with a home

home- *or* **homeo-** *also* **homoi-** *or* **homoio-** *comb form* [L & Gk; L *homoeo-,* fr. Gk *homoi-, homoio-,* fr. *homoios,* fr. *homos* same — more at SAME] **:** like **:** similar ⟨*homeo*stasis⟩ ⟨*homoio*thermic⟩

home•body \ˈhōm-ˌbäd-ē\ *n* (1821) **:** one whose life centers in the home

1**home•bound** \ˈhōm-ˌbau̇nd\ *adj* [*home* + 1*bound*] (1834) **:** going homeward **:** bound for home ⟨~ travelers⟩

2**homebound** *adj* [*home* + 4*bound*] (1882) **:** confined to the home ⟨~ invalids⟩

home•boy \ˈhōm-ˌbȯi\ *n* (1964) **:** a man from one's own hometown, community, or region

home•bred \ˈhōm-ˈbred\ *adj* (1587) **:** produced at home **:** INDIGENOUS

home brew *n* (1853) **:** an alcoholic beverage (as beer) made at home

home•built \(ˈ)hōm-ˈbilt\ *adj* (1676) **:** HOMEMADE 1

home•com•ing \ˈhōm-ˌkəm-iŋ\ *n* (14c) **1 :** a return home **2 :** the return of a group of people usu. on a special occasion to a place formerly frequented or regarded as home; *esp* **:** an annual celebration for alumni at a college or university

home computer *n* (1978) **:** a small inexpensive microcomputer

home economics *n pl but sing or pl in constr* (1899) **:** the theory and practice of homemaking — called also *home ec* \-ˈek\ — **home economist** *n*

home fries *n pl* (1951) **:** potatoes that have usu. been parboiled, sliced, and then fried — called also *home fried potatoes*

home front *n* (1919) **:** the sphere of civilian activity in war

home•grown \ˈhōm-ˈgrōn\ *adj* (1827) **1 :** grown or produced at home or in a particular local area ⟨~ vegetables⟩ ⟨~ films⟩ **2 :** native to or characteristic of a particular area ⟨the festival will feature ~ artists⟩ ⟨~ humor⟩

home•land \-ˌland *also* -lənd\ *n* (1670) **1 :** native land **:** FATHERLAND **2 :** a state or area set aside to be a state for a people of a particular national, cultural, or racial origin

home•like \ˈhōm-ˌlīk\ *adj* (1817) **:** characteristic of a home: **a :** CHEERFUL, COZY **b :** SIMPLE, WHOLESOME

home•ly \ˈhōm-lē\ *adj* **home•li•er; -est** (14c) **1 :** suggestive or characteristic of a home **2 :** being something familiar with which one is at home ⟨satisfy themselves with houses, furniture, books and clothes that were worn and ~ and friendly to the touch —Brendan Gill⟩ **3 a :** unaffectedly natural **:** SIMPLE **b :** not elaborate or complex ⟨~ virtues⟩ **4 :** plain or unattractive in appearance — **home•li•ness** *n*

home•made \ˈhōm-ˈ(m)ād\ *adj* (1659) **1 :** made in the home, on the premises, or by one's own efforts **2 :** of domestic manufacture

home•mak•er \ˈhōm-ˌmā-kər\ *n* (1876) **:** one who manages a household esp. as a wife and mother — **home•mak•ing** \-kiŋ\ *n or adj*

ho•meo•mor•phism \ˌhō-mē-ə-ˈmȯr-ˌfiz-əm\ *n* [ISV] (1854) **:** a function that is a one-to-one mapping between sets such that both the function and its inverse are continuous and that in topology exists for geometric figures which can be transformed one into the other by an elastic deformation — **ho•meo•mor•phic** \-ˈmȯr-fik\ *adj*

ho•meo•path•ic \ˌhō-mē-ə-ˈpath-ik\ *adj* (1830) **1 :** of or relating to homeopathy **2 :** of a diluted or insipid nature ⟨a ~ abolitionist —W.A. White⟩ — **ho•meo•path•i•cal•ly** \-i-k(ə-)lē\ *adv*

ho•me•op•a•thy \ˌhō-mē-ˈäp-ə-thē, ˌhäm-ē-\ *n* [G *homöopathie,* fr. *homöo-* home- + *-pathie* -pathy] (1826) **:** a system of medical practice that treats a disease esp. by the administration of minute doses of a remedy that would in healthy persons produce symptoms of the disease treated — **ho•meo•path** \ˈhō-mē-ə-ˌpath\ *n*

ho•meo•sta•sis \ˌhō-mē-ō-ˈstā-səs\ *n* [NL] (1929) **:** a relatively stable state of equilibrium or a tendency toward such a state between the different but interdependent elements or groups of elements of an organism or group — **ho•meo•stat•ic** \-ˈstat-ik\ *adj*

ho•meo•typ•ic \-ˈtip-ik\ *adj* (1889) **:** being or relating to the second or equational meiotic division

home plate *n* (1875) **:** a rubber slab at one corner of a baseball diamond at which a batter stands when batting and which must be touched by a base runner in order to score

home port *n* (ca. 1891) **:** the port from which a ship hails or from which it is documented

1**ho•mer** \ˈhō-mər\ *n* [Heb *ḥōmer*] (1535) **:** an ancient Hebrew unit of capacity equal to about 10½ or later 11½ bushels or 100 gallons

2**hom•er** \ˈhō-mər\ *n* [1*home*] (1880) **1 :** HOMING PIGEON **2 :** HOME RUN

3**hom•er** *vi* (1940) **:** to hit a home run

home range *n* (1884) **:** the area to which the activities of an animal are confined

Ho•mer•ic \hō-ˈmer-ik\ *adj* (1771) **1 :** of, relating to, or characteristic of the Greek poet Homer, his age, or his writings **2 :** of epic proportions **:** HEROIC ⟨~ feats of reporting —Stanley Walker⟩ — **Ho•mer•i•cal•ly** \-i-k(ə-)lē\ *adv*

home•room \ˈhōm-ˌrüm, -ˌru̇m\ *n* (1915) **:** a classroom where pupils report at the beginning of each school day

home rule *n* (1860) **:** self-government or limited autonomy in internal affairs by a dependent political unit (as a territory, county, or municipality)

home run *n* (1856) **:** a hit in baseball that enables the batter to make a complete circuit of the bases and score a run

home screen *n* (1968) **:** TELEVISION 2

home•sick \ˈhōm-ˌsik\ *adj* [back-formation fr. *homesickness*] (1827) **:** longing for home and family while absent from them — **home•sick•ness** *n*

home•site \-ˌsīt\ *n* (1911) **:** a location of or suitable for a home

1**home•spun** \-ˌspən\ *adj* (1591) **1 a :** spun or made at home **b :** made of homespun **2 :** SIMPLE, HOMELY ⟨~ philosophy⟩

2**homespun** *n* (1607) **:** a loosely woven usu. woolen or linen fabric orig. made from homespun yarn

home stand *n* (1965) **:** a series of baseball games played at a team's home field

home•stay \ˈhōm-ˌstā\ *n* (1956) **:** a period during which a visitor in a foreign country lives with a local family

1**home•stead** \ˈhōm-ˌsted, -stəd\ *n* (bef. 12c) **1 a :** the home and adjoining land occupied by a family **b :** an ancestral home **c :** HOUSE **2 :** a tract of land acquired from U.S. public lands by filing a record and living on and cultivating the tract

\ə\ abut \ᵊ\ kitten, F table \ər\ further \a\ ash \ā\ ace \ä\ cot, cart \au̇\ out \ch\ chin \e\ bet \ē\ easy \g\ go \i\ hit \ī\ ice \j\ job \ŋ\ sing \ō\ go \ȯ\ law \ȯi\ boy \th\ thin \t͟h\ the \ü\ loot \u̇\ foot \y\ yet \zh\ vision \à, k̲, ⁿ, œ, œ̄, ue, ue̅, ʸ\ see Guide to Pronunciation

[2]**home·stead** \-ˌsted\ *vt* (1872) **:** to acquire or occupy as a homestead ~ *vi* **:** to acquire or settle on land under a homestead law — **home·stead·er** \-ˌsted-ər\ *n*

homestead law *n* (1850) **1 :** a law exempting a homestead from attachment or sale under execution for general debts **2 :** any of several legislative acts authorizing the sale of public lands in homesteads to settlers

home·stretch \ˈhōm-ˈstrech\ *n* (1841) **1 :** the part of a racecourse between the last turn and the winning post **2 :** a final stage (as of a project)

home·town \-ˈtau̇n\ *n* (1912) **:** the city or town where one was born or grew up; *also* **:** the place of one's principal residence

home truth *n* (1711) **1 :** an unpleasant fact that jars the sensibilities **2 :** a statement of undisputed fact

[1]**home·ward** \ˈhōm-wərd\ *or* **home·wards** \-wərdz\ *adv* (bef. 12c) **:** toward home ⟨look ~, angel —John Milton⟩

[2]**homeward** *adj* (1566) **:** being or going in the direction of home

home·work \ˈhōm-ˌwərk\ *n* (ca. 1683) **1 :** piecework done at home for pay **2 :** an assignment given to a student to be completed outside the regular class period **3 :** preparatory reading or research (as for a discussion)

hom·ey \ˈhō-mē\ *adj* **hom·i·er; -est** (1856) **:** HOMELIKE ⟨a restaurant with a ~ atmosphere⟩— **hom·ey·ness** *or* **hom·i·ness** *n*

ho·mi·cid·al \ˌhäm-ə-ˈsīd-ᵊl, ˌhō-mə-\ *adj* (1725) **:** of, relating to, or tending toward homicide — **ho·mi·cid·al·ly** \-ᵊl-ē\ *adv*

ho·mi·cide \ˈhäm-ə-ˌsīd, ˈhō-mə-\ *n* [in sense 1, fr. ME, fr. MF, fr. L *homicida,* fr. *homo* man + *-cida* -cide; in sense 2, fr. ME, fr. MF, fr. L *homicidium,* fr. *homo* + *-cidium* -cide] (14c) **1 :** a person who kills another **2 :** a killing of one human being by another

hom·i·let·ic \ˌhäm-ə-ˈlet-ik\ *or* **hom·i·let·i·cal** \-i-kəl\ *adj* [LL *homileticus,* fr. Gk *homilētikos* of conversation, fr. *homilein*] (1644) **1 :** of, relating to, or resembling a homily **2 :** of or relating to homiletics — **hom·i·let·i·cal·ly** \-i-k(ə-)lē\ *adv*

hom·i·let·ics \-iks\ *n pl but sing in constr* (1830) **:** the art of preaching

hom·i·ly \ˈhäm-ə-lē\ *n, pl* **-lies** [ME *omelie,* fr. MF, fr. LL *homilia,* fr. LGk, fr. Gk, conversation, discourse, fr. *homilein* to consort with, address, fr. *homilos* crowd, assembly; akin to Gk *homos* same — more at SAME] (14c) **1 :** a religious discourse usu. delivered to a congregation **:** SERMON; *specif* **:** an informal exposition of Scripture **2 :** an inspirational catchphrase; *also* **:** PLATITUDE

homing pigeon *n* (1886) **:** a racing pigeon trained to return home

hom·i·nid \ˈhäm-ə-nəd, -ˌnid\ *n* [deriv. of L *homin-, homo* man] (ca. 1889) **:** any of a family (Hominidae) of bipedal primate mammals comprising recent man, his immediate ancestors, and related forms — **hominid** *adj*

hom·i·ni·za·tion \ˌhäm-ə-nə-ˈzā-shən\ *n* [L *homin-, homo* + E *-ization*] (1952) **:** the evolutionary development of human characteristics that differentiate man from his primate ancestors

hom·i·noid \ˈhäm-ə-ˌnȯid\ *adj* (1925) **:** resembling or related to man — **hominoid** *n*

hom·i·ny \ˈhäm-ə-nē\ *n* [prob. of Algonquian origin; akin to Natick *-minne* grain] (1629) **:** puffed kernels of corn that have been soaked in a lye solution and then washed in order to remove the hulls

hominy grits *n pl but sing or pl in constr* (1879) **:** GRITS

[1]**ho·mo** \ˈhō-(ˌ)mō\ *n, pl* **homos** [NL *Homin-, Homo,* fr. L, man — more at HOMAGE] (1596) **:** any of a genus (*Homo*) of primate mammals that includes modern man (*H. sapiens*) and several extinct related species

[2]**homo** *n, pl* **homos** [by shortening] (1929) **:** HOMOSEXUAL — often used disparagingly

homo- — see HOM-

ho·mo·cer·cal \ˌhō-mə-ˈsər-kəl, ˌhäm-ə-\ *adj* (1838) **1 :** having the upper and lower lobes approximately symmetrical and the vertebral column ending at or near the middle of the base — used of the tail fin of a fish **2 :** having or relating to a homocercal tail fin

ho·mo·chro·mat·ic \-krō-ˈmat-ik\ *adj* (ca. 1909) **:** of or relating to one color

ho·mo·erot·ic \ˌhō-mō-i-ˈrät-ik\ *adj* (1916) **:** HOMOSEXUAL — **ho·mo·erot·i·cism** \-ˈrät-ə-ˌsiz-əm\ *n*

ho·mo·ga·met·ic \ˌhō-mō-gə-ˈmet-ik, ˌhäm-ō-\ *adj* (1910) **:** forming one kind of germ cell; *esp* **:** forming all gametes with one type of sex chromosome

ho·mog·a·my \hō-ˈmäg-ə-mē\ *n* [G *homogamie,* fr. *hom-* + *-gamie* -gamy] (1874) **1 a :** a state of having flowers alike throughout **b :** the maturing of stamens and pistils at the same period **2 :** reproduction within an isolated group perpetuating qualities by which it is differentiated from the larger group of which it is a part; *broadly* **:** the mating of like with like — **ho·mog·a·mous** \-məs\ *adj* — **ho·mo·gam·ic** \ˌhō-mə-ˈgam-ik, ˌhäm-ə-\ *adj*

ho·mog·e·nate \hō-ˈmäj-ə-ˌnāt, hə-\ *n* (1941) **:** a product of homogenizing

ho·mo·ge·ne·ity \ˌhō-mə-jə-ˈnē-ət-ē, -ˈnā-ət- *also* ÷-ˈnī-ət-; *esp Brit* ˈhäm-ə-\ *n* (1625) **1 :** the quality or state of being homogeneous **2 :** the state of having identical distribution functions or values ⟨a test for ~ of variances⟩ ⟨~ of two statistical populations⟩

ho·mo·ge·neous \-ˈjē-nē-əs, -nyəs\ *adj* [ML *homogeneus, homogenus,* fr. Gk *homogenēs,* fr. *hom-* + *genos* kind — more at KIN] (1641) **1 :** of the same or a similar kind or nature **2 :** of uniform structure or composition throughout ⟨a culturally ~ neighborhood⟩ **3 :** having the property that if each variable is replaced by a constant times that variable the constant can be factored out **:** having each term of the same degree if all variables are considered ⟨$x^2 + xy + y^2 = 0$ is a ~ equation⟩ **4 :** HOMOGENOUS 1 — **ho·mo·ge·neous·ly** *adv* — **ho·mo·ge·neous·ness** *n*

ho·mog·e·ni·za·tion \hō-ˌmäj-ə-nə-ˈzā-shən, hə-\ *n* (ca. 1890) **1 :** the act or process of homogenizing **2 :** the quality or state of being homogenized

ho·mog·e·nize \hō-ˈmäj-ə-ˌnīz, hə-\ *vb* **-nized; -niz·ing** *vt* (1886) **1 a :** to blend (diverse elements) into a uniform mixture **b :** to make homogeneous **2 a :** to reduce to small particles of uniform size and distribute evenly usu. in a liquid **b :** to reduce the particles of so that they are uniformly small and evenly distributed; *specif* **:** to break up the fat globules of (milk) into very fine particles esp. by forcing through minute openings ~ *vi* **:** to become homogenized — **ho·mog·e·niz·er** *n*

ho·mog·e·nous \-nəs\ *adj* (1870) **1 :** of, relating to, or exhibiting homogeny **2 :** HOMOPLASTIC 2 **3 :** HOMOGENEOUS

ho·mog·e·ny \-nē\ *n* (1870) **:** correspondence between parts or organs due to descent from the same ancestral type

ho·mo·graft \ˈhō-mə-ˌgraft, ˈhäm-ə-\ *n* (1923) **:** a graft of tissue taken from a donor of the same species as the recipient — compare HETEROGRAFT

ho·mo·graph \ˈhäm-ə-ˌgraf, ˈhō-mə-\ *n* (1873) **:** one of two or more words spelled alike but different in meaning or derivation or pronunciation ⟨the noun *conduct* and the verb *conduct* are ~s⟩ — **ho·mo·graph·ic** \ˌhäm-ə-ˈgraf-ik, ˌhō-mə-\ *adj*

homoi- *or* **homoio-** — see HOME-

ho·moio·therm \hō-ˈmȯi-ə-ˌthərm\ *n* (1891) **:** a homoiothermic organism

ho·moio·ther·mic \-ˌmȯi-ə-ˈthər-mik\ *or* **ho·moio·ther·mal** \-məl\ *adj* (1870) **:** WARM-BLOODED

ho·moi·ou·si·an \hō-ˈmȯi-ˌü-zē-ən, hä-, -ˈü-sē-\ *n* [LGk *homoiousios* of like substance, fr. Gk *homoi-* home- + *ousia* essence, substance, fr. *ont-, ōn,* prp. of *einai* to be — more at IS] (1682) **:** an adherent of an ecclesiastical party of the 4th century holding that the Son is essentially like the Father but not of the same substance

ho·mo·lec·i·thal \ˌhō-mō-ˈles-ə-thəl, ˌhäm-ō-\ *adj* [*hom-* + Gk *lekithos* yolk] *of an egg* (1892) **:** having the yolk small in amount and nearly uniformly distributed

ho·mol·o·gate \hō-ˈmäl-ə-ˌgāt, hə-\ *vt* **-gat·ed; -gat·ing** [ML *homologatus,* pp. of *homologare* to agree, fr. Gk *homologein,* fr. *homologos*] (1593) **:** SANCTION, ALLOW; *esp* **:** to approve or confirm officially — **ho·mol·o·ga·tion** \-ˌmäl-ə-ˈgā-shən\ *n*

ho·mo·log·i·cal \ˌhō-mə-ˈläj-i-kəl, ˌhäm-ə-\ *adj* (ca. 1847) **:** HOMOLOGOUS — **ho·mo·log·i·cal·ly** \-i-k(ə-)lē\ *adv*

ho·mol·o·gize \hō-ˈmäl-ə-ˌjīz, hə-\ *vt* **-gized; -giz·ing** (1811) **1 :** to make homologous **2 :** to demonstrate the homology of — **ho·mol·o·giz·er** *n*

ho·mol·o·gous \hō-ˈmäl-ə-gəs, hə-\ *adj* [Gk *homologos* agreeing, fr. *hom-* + *legein* to say — more at LEGEND] (1660) **1 a :** having the same relative position, value, or structure **b (1) :** exhibiting biological homology **(2) :** having the same or allelic genes with genetic loci usu. arranged in the same order ⟨~ chromosomes⟩ **c :** belonging to or consisting of a chemical series whose members exhibit homology **2 :** derived from or developed in response to organisms of the same species ⟨~ tissue graft⟩

hom·o·lo·graph·ic \ˌhäm-ə-lə-ˈgraf-ik\ *adj* [F *homalographique,* fr. Gk *homalos* even, level (akin to Gk *homos* same) + *graphein* to write — more at SAME, CARVE] (ca. 1864) **:** preserving the mutual relations of parts esp. as to size and form ⟨a ~ map projection⟩

ho·mo·logue *or* **ho·mo·log** \ˈhō-mə-ˌlȯg, ˈhäm-ə-, -ˌläg\ *n* (1848) **:** something (as a chemical compound or a chromosome) exhibiting homology

ho·mol·o·gy \hō-ˈmäl-ə-jē, hə-\ *n, pl* **-gies** (ca. 1656) **1 :** a similarity often attributable to common origin **2 a :** likeness in structure between parts of different organisms due to evolutionary differentiation from the same or a corresponding part of a remote ancestor — compare ANALOGY, HOMOMORPHY **b :** correspondence in structure between different parts of the same individual **3 a :** the relation existing between chemical compounds in a series whose successive members have in composition a regular difference esp. of one carbon and two hydrogen atoms CH_2 **b :** the relation existing among elements in the same group of the periodic table

ho·mo·lo·sine projection \hō-ˌmäl-ə-ˌsīn-\ *n* [irreg. fr. Gk *homalos* even] (1925) **:** an equal-area map projection that combines the sinusoidal projection for latitudes up to 40° with the homolographic for areas poleward of these latitudes

ho·mol·y·sis \hō-ˈmäl-ə-səs\ *n* [NL] (ca. 1932) **:** decomposition of a chemical compound into two uncharged atoms or radicals — **ho·mo·lyt·ic** \ˌhō-mə-ˈlit-ik, ˌhäm-ə-\ *adj*

ho·mo·mor·phism \ˌhō-mə-ˈmȯr-ˌfiz-əm, ˌhäm-ə-\ *n* [ISV] (1869) **1 :** likeness in form: as **a :** HOMOMORPHY **b :** the condition of having perfect flowers of only one type **2 :** a mapping of a mathematical set (as a group, ring, or vector space) into or onto another set or itself in such a way that the result obtained by applying the operations to elements of the first set is mapped onto the result obtained by applying the corresponding operations to their respective images in the second set and such that if there is a unit element in the first set it is mapped onto the unit element of the second set — **ho·mo·mor·phic** \-fik\ *adj*

ho·mo·mor·phy \ˈhō-mə-ˌmȯr-fē, ˈhäm-ə-\ *n* [ISV] (ca. 1874) **:** similarity of form with different fundamental structure; *specif* **:** superficial resemblance between organisms of different groups due to convergence — compare HOMOLOGY, HOMOPHYLY

ho·mo·nu·cle·ar \ˌhō-mə-ˈn(y)ü-klē-ər, ˌhäm-ə-, ÷-kyə-lər\ *adj* (1930) **:** of or relating to a molecule composed of identical nuclei

hom·onym \ˈhäm-ə-ˌnim, ˈhō-mə-\ *n* [L *homonymum,* fr. Gk *homōnymon,* fr. neut. of *homōnymos*] (1697) **1 a :** HOMOPHONE **b :** HOMOGRAPH **c :** one of two or more words spelled and pronounced alike but different in meaning ⟨the noun *quail* and the verb *quail* are ~s⟩ **2 :** NAMESAKE **3 :** a taxonomic designation rejected because the identical term has been used to designate another group of the same rank — compare SYNONYM — **hom·onym·ic** \ˌhäm-ə-ˈnim-ik, ˌhō-mə-\ *adj*

ho·mon·y·mous \hō-ˈmän-ə-məs\ *adj* [L *homonymus* having the same name, fr. Gk *homōnymos,* fr. *hom-* + *onyma, onoma* name — more at NAME] (1621) **1 :** AMBIGUOUS **2 :** having the same designation **3 :** of, relating to, or being homonyms **:** HOMONYMIC — **ho·mon·y·mous·ly** *adv*

ho·mon·y·my \-mē\ *n* (1597) **:** the quality or state of being homonymous

ho·mo·ou·si·an \hō-ˈmō-ˌü-zē-ən, hä-, -ˌü-sē-\ *n* [LGk *homoousios* of the same substance, fr. Gk *hom-* + *ousia* substance — more at HOMOIOUSIAN] (1565) **:** an adherent of an ecclesiastical party of the 4th century holding to the doctrine of the Nicene Creed that the Son is of the same substance with the Father

ho·mo·phile \ˈhō-mə-ˌfīl\ *adj* [*hom-* + [2]*-phil*] (1960) **:** GAY 4b

ho·mo·phobe \-ˌfōb\ *n* (1975) **:** one who hates or fears homosexuals

ho·mo·pho·bia \ˌhō-mə-ˈfō-bē-ə\ *n* [[2]*homo* + *phobia*] (1969) **:** irrational fear of homosexuality or homosexuals — **ho·mo·pho·bic** \-ˈfō-bik\ *adj*

ho·mo·phone \ˈhäm-ə-ˌfōn, ˈhō-mə-\ *n* [ISV] (1843) **1 :** one of two or more words pronounced alike but different in meaning or derivation or spelling ⟨the words *to, too,* and *two* are ~s⟩ **2 :** a character or group of characters pronounced the same as another character or group — **ho·moph·o·nous** \hō-ˈmäf-ə-nəs\ *adj*

ho·mo·pho·nic \ˌhäm-ə-ˈfän-ik, ˌhō-mə-, -ˈfō-nik\ *adj* [Gk *homophōnos* being in unison, fr. *hom-* + *phōnē* sound — more at BAN] (ca. 1879) : CHORDAL — **ho·moph·o·ny** \hō-ˈmäf-ə-nē\ *n*

ho·mo·phy·ly \ˈhō-mə-ˌfī-lē, ˈhäm-ə-; hō-ˈmäf-ə-lē\ *n* [ISV *hom-* + *phyl-* + *-y*] (ca. 1883) : resemblance due to common ancestry — compare HOMOMORPHY

ho·mo·plas·tic \ˌhō-mə-ˈplas-tik, ˌhäm-ə-\ *adj* (1870) **1** : of or relating to homoplasy **2** : of, relating to, or derived from another individual of the same species ⟨~ grafts⟩ — **ho·mo·plas·ti·cal·ly** \-ti-k(ə-)lē\ *adv*

ho·mo·pla·sy \ˈhō-mə-ˌplā-sē, ˈhäm-ə-, -ˌplas-ē; hō-ˈmäp-lə-sē\ *n* (1870) : correspondence between parts or organs acquired as the result of parallel evolution or convergence

ho·mo·po·lar \ˌhō-mə-ˈpō-lər, ˌhäm-ə-\ *adj* (ca. 1883) **1** : of or relating to a union of atoms of like polarity : NONIONIC **2** : having the conductors cut lines of unidirectional flux between poles of a magnet ⟨a ~ generator⟩

ho·mo·pol·y·mer \-ˈpäl-ə-mər\ *n* (1946) : a polymer (as polyethylene) consisting of identical monomer units — **ho·mo·pol·y·mer·ic** \-ˌpäl-ə-ˈmer-ik\ *adj*

ho·mop·ter·an \hō-ˈmäp-tə-rən\ *n* (ca. 1842) : a homopterous insect — **homopteran** *adj*

ho·mop·ter·ous \-rəs\ *adj* [deriv. of Gk *hom-* + *pteron* wing — more at FEATHER] (1826) : of or relating to a large order or suborder (Homoptera) of insects (as cicadas, aphids, and scale insects) that have sucking mouthparts

Ho·mo sa·pi·ens \ˌhō-(ˌ)mō-ˈsap-ē-ənz, -ˈsā-pē-, -ˌenz\ *n* [NL, species name, fr. *Homo*, genus name + *sapiens*, specific epithet, fr. L, wise, intelligent — more at HOMO, SAPIENT] (1802) : MANKIND 1

ho·mo·sce·das·tic \ˌhō-mō-si-ˈdas-tik, ˌhäm-ō-\ *adj* [*hom-* + Gk *skedastikos* able to scatter, fr. *skedannynai* to scatter] (1905) : having equal statistical variances ⟨~ distributions⟩ — **ho·mo·sce·das·tic·i·ty** \-ˌdas-ˈtis-ət-ē\ *n*

ho·mo·sex·u·al \ˌhō-mə-ˈseksh-(ə-)wəl, -ˈsek-shəl\ *adj* (1892) : of, relating to, or characterized by a tendency to direct sexual desire toward another of the same sex — **homosexual** *n* — **ho·mo·sex·u·al·ly** \-ē\ *adv*

ho·mo·sex·u·al·i·ty \ˌhō-mə-ˌsek-shə-ˈwal-ət-ē\ *n* (1892) **1** : the quality or state of being homosexual **2** : erotic activity with another of the same sex

ho·mo·spo·rous \ˌhō-mə-ˈspōr-əs, ˌhäm-ə-, -ˈspȯr-; hō-ˈmäs-pə-rəs\ *adj* (1887) : producing asexual spores of one kind only

ho·mo·spo·ry \ˈhō-mə-ˌspōr-ē, ˈhäm-ə-ˌspȯr-; hō-ˈmäs-pə-rē\ *n* (1902) : the production by various plants (as the club mosses and horsetails) of asexual spores of only one kind

ho·mo·thal·lic \ˌhō-mə-ˈthal-ik\ *adj* [*hom-* + Gk *thallein* to sprout, grow — more at THALLUS] (1904) **1** : having only one haploid phase that produces two kinds of gametes capable of fusing to form a zygote **2** : MONOECIOUS — **ho·mo·thal·lism** \-ˈthal-ˌiz-əm\ *n*

ho·mo·trans·plant \ˌhō-mō-ˈtran(t)-ˌsplant, ˌhäm-ō-\ *n* (1927) : HOMOGRAFT — **ho·mo·trans·plan·ta·tion** \-ˌtran(t)-ˌsplan-ˈtā-shən\ *n*

ho·mo·zy·go·sis \ˌhō-mə-zī-ˈgō-səs, ˌhäm-ə-\ *n* [NL] (1905) : HOMOZYGOSITY

ho·mo·zy·gos·i·ty \-ˈgäs-ət-ē\ *n* (1916) : the state of being homozygous

ho·mo·zy·gote \-ˈzī-ˌgōt\ *n* [ISV] (1902) : a homozygous individual

ho·mo·zy·gous \-ˈzī-gəs\ *adj* (1902) : having the two genes at corresponding loci on homologous chromosomes identical for one or more loci — **ho·mo·zy·gous·ly** *adv*

ho·mun·cu·lus \hō-ˈmən-kyə-ləs\ *n, pl* **-li** \-ˌlī, -ˌlē\ [L, dim. of *homin-*, *homo* man — more at HOMAGE] (1656) : a little man : MANIKIN

homy *var of* HOMEY

hon·cho \ˈhän-(ˌ)chō\ *n, pl* **honchos** [Jp *hanchō* squad leader, fr. *han* squad + *chō* head, chief] (1947) : BOSS, BIG SHOT; *also* : HOTSHOT 2

[1]**hone** \ˈhōn\ *n* [ME, fr. OE *hān* stone; akin to ON *hein* whetstone, L *cot-, cos*, Gk *kōnos* cone] (14c) **1** : a fine-grit stone for sharpening a cutting implement **2** : a tool for enlarging holes to precise tolerances and controlling finishes by means of a mechanically rotated abrasive

[2]**hone** *vt* **honed; hon·ing** (1826) **1** : to sharpen, enlarge, or smooth with a hone **2** : to make more acute, intense, or effective : WHET ⟨helped her ~ her comic timing to perfection —Patricia Bosworth⟩ — **hon·er** *n*

[3]**hone** *vi* **honed; hon·ing** [MF *hoigner* to grumble] (1600) **1** *dial* : GRUMBLE, MOAN **2** *dial* : YEARN

hon·est \ˈän-əst\ *adj* [ME, fr. MF *honeste*, fr. L *honestus* honorable, fr. *honos, honor* honor] (14c) **1** **a** : free from fraud or deception : LEGITIMATE, TRUTHFUL ⟨an ~ plea⟩ **b** : GENUINE, REAL ⟨making ~ stops at stop signs —*Christian Science Monitor*⟩ **c** : HUMBLE, PLAIN ⟨good ~ food⟩ **2** **a** : REPUTABLE, RESPECTABLE ⟨~ decent people⟩ **b** *chiefly Brit* : GOOD, WORTHY **3** : CREDITABLE, PRAISEWORTHY ⟨an ~ day's work⟩ **4** **a** : marked by integrity **b** : FRANK, SINCERE ⟨an ~ appraisal⟩ **c** : INNOCENT, SIMPLE ***syn*** see UPRIGHT — **hon·est** *adv* — **hon·est·ly** *adv*

honest broker *n* (1884) : a neutral mediator ⟨an *honest broker* between the two Democrats —*Christian Science Monitor*⟩

hon·es·ty \ˈän-ə-stē\ *n, pl* **-ties** (14c) **1** *obs* : CHASTITY **2** **a** : fairness and straightforwardness of conduct **b** : adherence to the facts : SINCERITY **3** : any of a genus (*Lunaria*) of European plants of the mustard family with cordate leaves and broad siliques

syn HONESTY, HONOR, INTEGRITY, PROBITY mean uprightness of character or action. HONESTY implies a refusal to lie, steal, or deceive in any way; HONOR suggests an active or anxious regard for the standards of one's profession, calling, or position; INTEGRITY implies trustworthiness and incorruptibility to a degree that one is incapable of being false to a trust, responsibility, or pledge; PROBITY implies tried and proven honesty or integrity.

[1]**hon·ey** \ˈhən-ē\ *n, pl* **honeys** [ME *hony*, fr. OE *hunig*; akin to OHG *honag* honey, L *canicae* bran] (bef. 12c) **1** **a** : a sweet viscid material elaborated out of the nectar of flowers in the honey sac of various bees **b** : a sweet fluid resembling honey that is collected or elaborated by various insects **2** **a** : SWEETHEART, DEAR **b** : a superlative example **3** : the quality or state of being sweet : SWEETNESS

[2]**honey** *vb* **hon·eyed** *also* **hon·ied** \ˈhən-ēd\; **hon·ey·ing** *vt* (14c) **1** : to sweeten with or as if with honey **2** : to speak ingratiatingly to : FLATTER ~ *vi* : to use blandishments or cajolery

[3]**honey** *adj* (14c) **1** : of, relating to, or resembling honey **2** : much loved : DEAR

hon·ey·bee \ˈhən-ē-ˌbē\ *n* (15c) : a social honey-producing bee (*Apis* or related genera); *esp* : a native European bee (*A. mellifera*) kept for its honey and wax

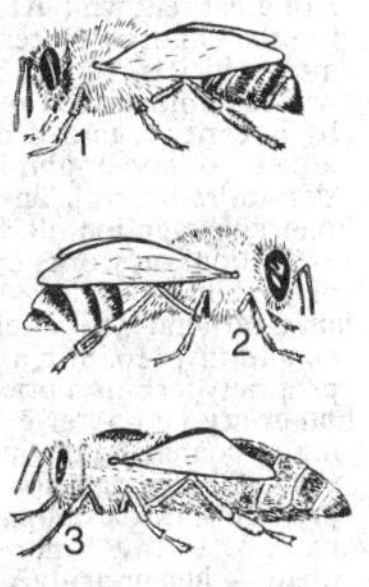

honeybee: *1* worker, *2* drone, *3* queen

[1]**hon·ey·comb** \-ˌkōm\ *n* (bef. 12c) **1** : a mass of hexagonal wax cells built by honeybees in their nest to contain their brood and stores of honey **2** : something that resembles a honeycomb in structure or appearance; *esp* : a strong lightweight cellular structural material

[2]**honeycomb** *vt* (1774) **1** **a** : to cause to be full of cavities like a honeycomb **b** : to make into a checkered pattern : FRET **2** **a** : to penetrate into every part : FILL **b** : SUBVERT, WEAKEN ~ *vi* : to become pitted, checked, or cellular

hon·ey·creep·er \ˈhən-ē-ˌkrē-pər\ *n* (1872) **1** : any of numerous small bright-colored oscine birds (family Coerebidae) of tropical and subtropical America **2** : any of a family (Drepanididae) of oscine birds that are found only in Hawaii

hon·ey·dew \-ˌd(y)ü\ *n* (1577) : a saccharine deposit secreted on the leaves of plants usu. by aphids or scale insects or sometimes by a fungus

honeydew melon *n* (1916) : a pale smooth-skinned muskmelon with greenish sweet flesh

honey eater *n* (1731) : any of several oscine birds (family Meliphagidae) mostly of the South Pacific with a long protrusible tongue adapted for extracting nectar and small insects from flowers

honey guide *n* (1777) : any of several small plainly colored nonpasserine birds (family Indicatoridae and esp. genera *Indicator* and *Prodotiscus*) that inhabit Africa, the Himalayas, and the East Indies and lead men or lower animals to the nests of bees

honey locust *n* (1743) : a tall usu. spiny No. American leguminous tree (*Gleditsia triacanthos*) with very hard durable wood and long twisted pods containing a sweet edible pulp and seeds that resemble beans

hon·ey·moon \ˈhən-ē-ˌmün\ *n* [fr. the idea that the first month of marriage is the sweetest] (1546) **1** : a trip or vacation taken by a newly married couple **2** : a period of harmony immediately following marriage **3** : a period of unusual harmony following the establishment of a new relationship — **honeymoon** *vi* — **hon·ey·moon·er** *n*

honey sac *n* (ca. 1909) : a distension of the esophagus of a bee in which honey is elaborated — called also *honey stomach*

hon·ey·suck·le \ˈhən-ē-ˌsək-əl\ *n* [ME *honysoukel*, alter. of *honysouke*, fr. OE *hunisūce*, fr. *hunig* honey + *sūcan* to suck] (bef. 12c) : any of a genus (*Lonicera* of the family Caprifoliaceae, the honeysuckle family) of shrubs with opposite leaves and often showy flowers rich in nectar; *broadly* : any of various plants (as a columbine or azalea) with tubular flowers rich in nectar

hong \ˈhäŋ, ˈhȯŋ\ *n* [Chin (Cant) *hōng*] (1726) : a commercial establishment or house of foreign trade in China

[1]**honk** \ˈhäŋk, ˈhȯŋk\ *vi* [imit.] (1835) **1** : to make the characteristic cry of a goose **2** : to make a sound resembling the cry of a goose ~ *vt* : to cause (as a horn) to honk — **honk·er** *n*

[2]**honk** *n* (1854) : the characteristic cry of a goose; *also* : a similar sound

hon·kie *or* **hon·ky** *also* **hon·key** \ˈhȯŋ-kē, ˈhäŋ-\ *n, pl* **honkies** *also* **honkeys** [origin unknown] (1967) : a white man — usu. used disparagingly

[1]**hon·ky–tonk** \ˈhäŋ-kē-ˌtäŋk, ˈhȯŋ-kē-ˌtȯŋk\ *n* [origin unknown] (1894) **1** : a tawdry nightclub or dance hall **2** : a district marked by places of cheap entertainment

[2]**honky–tonk** *adj* (1920) **1** : of, used in, or being a form of ragtime piano playing performed typically on an upright piano **2** : marked by or characteristic of honky-tonks

[1]**hon·or** \ˈän-ər\ *n* [ME, fr. OF *honor*, fr. L *honos, honor*] (13c) **1** **a** : good name or public esteem : REPUTATION **b** : a showing of usu. merited respect : RECOGNITION ⟨pay ~ to our founder⟩ **2** : PRIVILEGE **3** : a person of superior standing — now used esp. as a title for a holder of high office ⟨if *Your Honor* please⟩ **4** : one whose worth brings respect or fame : CREDIT ⟨an ~ to the profession⟩ **5** : the center point of the upper half of an armorial escutcheon **6** : an evidence or symbol of distinction: as **a** : an exalted title or rank **b** (1) : BADGE, DECORATION (2) : a ceremonial rite or observance ⟨buried with full military ~s⟩ **c** *archaic* : a gesture of deference : BOW **d** *pl* (1) : an academic distinction conferred on a superior student (2) : a course of study for superior students supplementing or replacing a regular course **e** : an award in a contest or field of competition **7** : CHASTITY, PURITY ⟨fought fiercely for her ~ and her life —Barton Black⟩ **8** **a** : a keen sense of ethical conduct : INTEGRITY **b** : one's word given as a guarantee of performance **9** *pl* : social courtesies or civilities extended by a host ⟨did the ~s at the table⟩ **10** **a** : an ace, king, queen, jack, or ten esp. of the trump suit in bridge **b** : the scoring value of honors held in bridge — usu. used in pl.

syn HONOR, HOMAGE, REVERENCE, DEFERENCE mean respect and esteem shown to another. HONOR may apply to the recognition of one's right to great respect or to any expression of such recognition; HOMAGE adds the implication of accompanying praise; REVERENCE implies profound respect mingled with love, devotion, or awe; DEFERENCE implies a yielding or submitting to another's judgment or preference out of respect or reverence. ***syn*** see in addition HONESTY

[2]**honor** *vt* **hon·ored; hon·or·ing** \-(ə-)riŋ\ (13c) **1** **a** : to regard or treat with honor or respect **b** : to confer honor on **2** **a** : to live up to or fulfill the terms of ⟨~ a commitment⟩ **b** : to accept as payment ⟨~ a credit card⟩ **3** : to salute with a bow in square dancing — **hon·or·ee** \ˌän-ə-ˈrē\ *n* — **hon·or·er** \ˈän-ər-ər\ *n*

hon·or·able \ˈän-(ə-)rə-bəl, ˈän-ər-bəl\ *adj* (14c) **1** : deserving of honor **2** : performed or accompanied with marks of honor or respect **3** **a**

: of great renown : ILLUSTRIOUS **b** : entitled to honor — used as a title for the children of certain British noblemen and for various government officials **4 a** : attesting to creditable conduct **b** : consistent with an untarnished reputation ⟨an ~ withdrawal⟩ **5** : characterized by integrity : guided by a high sense of honor and duty ***syn*** see UPRIGHT — **hon·or·abil·i·ty** \ˌän-(ə-)rə-ˈbil-ət-ē\ *n* — **hon·or·able·ness** \ˈän-(ə-)rə-bəl-nəs, ˈän-ər-bəl-\ *n* — **hon·or·ably** \-blē\ *adv*

honorable mention *n* (1866) : a distinction conferred (as in a contest or exhibition) on works or persons of exceptional merit but not deserving of top honors

hon·o·rar·i·um \ˌän-ə-ˈrer-ē-əm\ *n, pl* **-ia** \-ē-ə\ *also* **-i·ums** [L, fr. neut. of *honorarius*] (1658) : a payment usu. for services on which custom or propriety forbids a price to be set

hon·or·ary \ˈän-ə-ˌrer-ē\ *adj* [L *honorarius*, fr. *honor*] (1614) **1 a** : having or conferring distinction **b** : COMMEMORATIVE **2 a** : conferred or elected in recognition of achievement or service without the usual prerequisites or obligations ⟨an ~ degree⟩ ⟨an ~ member⟩ **b** : UNPAID, VOLUNTARY ⟨an ~ chairman⟩ **3** : dependent on honor for fulfillment — **hon·or·ari·ly** \ˌän-ə-ˈrer-ə-lē\ *adv* — **honorary** *n*

honor guard *n* (1925) : a guard assigned to a ceremonial duty (as to accompany a casket at a military funeral)

hon·or·if·ic \ˌän-ə-ˈrif-ik\ *adj* (1650) **1** : conferring or conveying honor ⟨~ titles⟩ **2** : belonging to or constituting a class of grammatical forms used in speaking to or about a social superior — **honorific** *n* — **hon·or·if·i·cal·ly** \-i-k(ə-)lē\ *adv*

honor roll *n* (1909) : a roster of names of persons deserving honor: as **a** : a list of students achieving academic distinction **b** : a publicly displayed list of the names of local citizens who have served in the armed forces

honor society *n* (1927) : a society for the recognition of scholarly achievement esp. of undergraduates

honor system *n* (1904) : a system (as at a college or prison) whereby persons are trusted to abide by the regulations without supervision or surveillance

hon·our \ˈän-ər\, **hon·our·able** *chiefly Brit var of* HONOR, HONORABLE

[1]**hooch** \ˈhüch\ *n* [short for *hoochinoo* (a distilled liquor made by the Hoochinoo Indians, a Tlingit people)] *slang* (1897) : alcoholic liquor esp. when inferior or illicitly made or obtained

[2]**hooch** *or* **hootch** \ˈhüch\ *n* [modif. of Jp *uchi* house] *slang* (1960) : a usu. thatched hut; *broadly* : DWELLING

[1]**hood** \ˈhu̇d\ *n* [ME, fr. OE *hōd*; akin to OHG *huot* head covering, *huota* guard — more at HEED] (bef. 12c) **1 a** (1) : a flexible covering for the head and neck (2) : a protective covering for the head and face **b** : a covering for a hawk's head and eyes — see FALCON illustration **c** : a covering for a horse's head; *also* : BLINDER **2 a** : an ornamental scarf worn over an academic gown that indicates by its color the wearer's college or university **b** : a color marking or crest on the head of an animal or an expansion of the head that suggests a hood **3 a** : something resembling a hood in form or use **b** : a cover for parts of mechanisms; *specif* : the movable metal covering over the engine of an automobile **c** : a top cover for the body of a vehicle designed to be folded back **d** : an enclosure or canopy provided with a draft for carrying off disagreeable or noxious fumes, sprays, smokes, or dusts **e** : a covering for an opening (as a companion hatch) on a boat — **hood** *vt* — **hood·like** \-ˌlīk\ *adj*

[2]**hood** \ˈhu̇d, ˈhüd\ *n* (1930) : HOODLUM — **hoody** \-ē\ *adj*

-hood \ˌhu̇d\ *n suffix* [ME *-hod*, fr. OE *-hād*; akin to OHG *-heit* state, condition, *heitar* bright, clear] **1** : state : condition : quality : character ⟨boy*hood*⟩ ⟨hardi*hood*⟩ **2** : time : period ⟨child*hood*⟩ ⟨widow*hood*⟩ **3** : instance of a (specified) state or quality ⟨false*hood*⟩ **4** : individuals sharing a (specified) state or character ⟨brother*hood*⟩

hood·ed \ˈhu̇d-əd\ *adj* (15c) **1** : having a hood **2** : shaped like a hood ⟨~ spathes⟩ **3 a** : having the head conspicuously different in color from the rest of the body ⟨~ bird⟩ **b** : having a crest on the head that suggests a hood ⟨~ seals⟩ **c** : having the skin at each side of the neck capable of expansion by movements of the ribs ⟨~ cobra⟩ **4** : half-closed ⟨~ eyes⟩ — **hood·ed·ness** *n*

hood·lum \ˈhüd-ləm, ˈhu̇d-\ *n* [origin unknown] (1871) **1** : THUG; *esp* : one who commits acts of violence **2** : a young ruffian — **hood·lum·ish** \-lə-mish\ *adj* — **hood·lum·ism** \-ˌmiz-əm\ *n*

hood·man–blind \ˌhu̇d-mən-ˈblīnd\ *n, archaic* (1565) : BLINDMAN'S BUFF

[1]**hoo·doo** \ˈhü-(ˌ)dü\ *n, pl* **hoodoos** [of African origin; akin to Hausa *hu[3]ʼdu[3]ʼba[1]* to arouse resentment] (1875) **1** : VOODOO **2** : something that brings bad luck **3** : a natural column of rock in western No. America often in fantastic form — **hoo·doo·ism** \-ˌiz-əm\ *n*

[2]**hoodoo** *vt* (1886) : to cast a spell on; *broadly* : to be a source of misfortune to

hood·wink \ˈhu̇d-ˌwiŋk\ *vt* [[1]*hood* + *wink*] (1562) **1** *archaic* : BLINDFOLD **2** *obs* : HIDE **3** : to deceive by false appearance : DUPE — **hood·wink·er** *n*

hoo·ey \ˈhü-ē\ *n* [origin unknown] (1924) : NONSENSE

[1]**hoof** \ˈhu̇f, ˈhüf\ *n, pl* **hooves** \ˈhüvz, ˈhu̇vz\ *or* **hoofs** [ME, fr. OE *hōf*; akin to OHG *huof* hoof, Skt *śapha*] (bef. 12c) **1** : a curved covering of horn that protects the front of or encloses the ends of the digits of an ungulate mammal and that corresponds to a nail or claw **2** : a hoofed foot esp. of a horse

usage Despite what you might read to the contrary, the plural *hooves* still predominates over *hoofs* in printed text. In speech the singular and plural variant pronunciations exhibit a fairly complex distribution pattern, and often variation occurs unpredictably in the speech of individuals.

— **on the hoof** *of a meat animal* : before butchering : LIVING ⟨10¢ a pound *on the hoof*⟩

hoof 2: *1, 2, 3, 4* parts of wall (*1* toe, *2* side walls, *3* quarters, *4* buttresses), *5* bulbs, *6* sole, *7* white line, *8* frog, *9* bars

[2]**hoof** *vt* (1641) **1** : WALK **2** : KICK, TRAMPLE ~ *vi* : to move on the feet; *esp* : DANCE

hoof–and–mouth disease *n* (1884) : FOOT-AND-MOUTH DISEASE

hoof·beat \ˈhu̇f-ˌbēt, ˈhüf-\ *n* (1847) : the sound of a hoof striking a hard surface (as the ground)

hoofed \ˈhu̇ft, ˈhüft, ˈhüvd, ˈhu̇vd\ *adj* (1513) : furnished with hooves : UNGULATE

hoof·er \ˈhu̇f-ər, ˈhü-fər\ *n* (ca. 1918) : a professional dancer

hoof·print \ˈhu̇f-ˌprint, ˈhüf-\ *n* (1804) : an impression or hollow made by a hoof

hoo–ha \ˈhü-ˌhä\ *n* [imit.] (ca. 1905) : HULLABALLOO

[1]**hook** \ˈhu̇k\ *n* [ME, fr. OE *hōc*; akin to MD *hoec* fishhook, corner, Lith *kengė* hook] (bef. 12c) **1 a** : a curved or bent device for catching, holding, or pulling **b** : something intended to attract and ensnare **2** : something curved or bent like a hook; *esp, pl* : FINGERS **3** : a flight of a ball that deviates from a straight course in a direction opposite to the dominant hand of the player propelling it; *also* : a ball following such a course — compare SLICE **4** : a short blow delivered with a circular motion by a boxer while the elbow remains bent and rigid **5** : HOOK SHOT **6** : BUTTONHOOK — **by hook or by crook** : by any means — **off the hook** : out of trouble — **on one's own hook** : by oneself : INDEPENDENTLY

[2]**hook** *vt* (13c) **1** : to form into a hook : CROOK **2 a** : to seize or make fast by or as if by a hook **b** : to connect by or as if by a hook — often used with *up* **3** : STEAL, PILFER **4** : to make (as a rug) by drawing loops of yarn, thread, or cloth through a coarse fabric with a hook **5** : to hit or throw (a ball) so that a hook results ~ *vi* **1** : to form a hook : CURVE **2** : to become hooked **3** : to work as a prostitute

hoo·kah \ˈhu̇k-ə, ˈhü-kə\ *n* [Ar *ḥuqqah* bottle of a water pipe] (1763) : WATER PIPE

hook and eye *n* (1626) : a 2-part fastening device (as on a garment or a door) consisting of a metal hook that catches over a bar or into a loop

hook and ladder truck *n* (1865) : a piece of mobile fire apparatus carrying ladders and usu. other fire-fighting and rescue equipment — called also *hook and ladder, ladder truck*

hook check *n* (ca. 1939) : an act or instance of attempting to knock the puck away from an opponent in ice hockey by hooking it with the stick

hooked \ˈhu̇kt, *1 is also* ˈhu̇k-əd\ *adj* (bef. 12c) **1** : having the form of a hook **2** : provided with a hook **3** : made by hooking ⟨a ~ rug⟩ **4 a** : addicted to narcotics **b** : fascinated by or devoted to something ⟨~ on skiing⟩

[1]**hook·er** \ˈhu̇k-ər\ *n* (1567) **1** : one that hooks **2** : DRINK ⟨a ~ of Scotch⟩ **3** : PROSTITUTE

[2]**hooker** *n* [D *hoeker*, alter. of MD *hoecboot*, fr. *hoec* fishhook + *boot* boat] (1801) **1** : a one-masted fishing boat used on the English and Irish coasts **2** : an old, outmoded, or clumsy boat

hook·let \ˈhu̇k-lət\ *n* (ca. 1836) : a small hook

hook, line and sinker *adv* [fr. analogy with a well-hooked fish] (1838) : without hesitation or reservation : COMPLETELY ⟨fell for the story *hook, line and sinker*⟩

hook shot *n* (ca. 1932) : a shot in basketball made usu. while standing sideways to the basket by swinging the ball up through an arc with the far hand

hook·up \ˈhu̇k-ˌəp\ *n* (1903) **1** : an assemblage (as of circuits) used for a specific purpose (as radio transmission); *also* : the plan of such an assemblage **2** : an arrangement of mechanical parts; *also* : CONNECTION ⟨a campsite with electric, water, and sewer ~*s*⟩ **3** : a state of cooperation or alliance

hook up \(ˈ)hu̇k-ˈəp\ *vi* (1925) : to become associated esp. in a working or social relationship

hook·worm \ˈhu̇k-ˌwərm\ *n* (1902) **1** : any of several parasitic nematode worms (family Ancylostomatidae) that have strong buccal hooks or plates for attaching to the host's intestinal lining and that include serious bloodsucking pests **2** : ANCYLOSTOMIASIS

hooky *or* **hook·ey** \ˈhu̇k-ē\ *n, pl* **hook·ies** *or* **hookeys** [prob. fr. slang *hook, hook it* (to make off)] (ca. 1848) : TRUANT — used chiefly in the phrase *play hooky*

hoo·li·gan \ˈhü-li-gən\ *n* [perh. fr. Patrick *Hooligan fl*1898 Irish hoodlum in Southwark, London] (1898) : RUFFIAN, HOODLUM — **hoo·li·gan·ism** \-gə-ˌniz-əm\ *n*

[1]**hoop** \ˈhüp, ˈhu̇p\ *n, often attrib* [ME, fr. OE *hōp*; akin to MD *hoep* ring, hoop, OIr *camm* crooked] (bef. 12c) **1** : a circular strip used esp. for holding together the staves of containers or as a plaything **2 a** : a circular figure or object : RING **b** : the rim of a basketball goal; *broadly* : the entire goal **3** : a circle or series of circles of flexible material used to expand a woman's skirt — **hoop·like** \-ˌlīk\ *adj*

[2]**hoop** *vt* (13c) : to bind or fasten with or as if with a hoop — **hoop·er** *n*

hoop·la \ˈhü-ˌplä, ˈhu̇p-ˌlä\ *n* [F *houp-là*, interj.] (1877) **1** : excited commotion : TO-DO; *also* : BALLYHOO **2** : bewildering language

hoo·poe \ˈhü-(ˌ)pü, -(ˌ)pō\ *n* [alter. of obs. *hoop*, fr. MF *huppe*, fr. L *upupa*, of imit. origin] (1668) : any of several Old World nonpasserine birds (family Upupidae) having a slender decurved bill

hoop·skirt \ˈhüp-ˈskərt, ˈhu̇p-\ *n* (1857) : a skirt stiffened with or as if with hoops

hoo·ray \hu̇-ˈrā\ *var of* HURRAH

hoose·gow \ˈhüs-ˌgau̇\ *n* [Sp *juzgado* panel of judges, courtroom, fr. pp. of *juzgar* to judge, fr. L *judicare* — more at JUDGE] *slang* (1911) : JAIL

Hoo·sier \ˈhü-zhər\ *n* [perh. alter. of E dial. *hoozer* anything large of its kind] (1826) : a native or resident of Indiana — used as a nickname — **Hoosier** *adj*

[1]**hoot** \ˈhüt\ *vb* [ME *houten*, of imit. origin] *vi* (13c) **1** : to shout or laugh usu. derisively **2** : to make the natural throat noise of an owl or a similar cry **3** : to make a loud clamorous mechanical sound ~ *vt* **1** : to assail or drive out by hooting ⟨~*ed* down the speaker⟩ **2** : to express in or by hoots ⟨~*ed* their disapproval⟩ — **hoot·er** *n*

[2]**hoot** *n* (15c) **1** : a sound of hooting; *esp* : the cry of an owl **2** : a minimum amount or degree (as of care or consideration) : the least bit ⟨don't give a ~⟩ — **hooty** \-ē\ *adj*

[3]**hoot** \ˈhüt\ *or* **hoots** \ˈhüts\ *interj* [origin unknown] *chiefly Scot* (1540) — used to express impatience, dissatisfaction, or objection

hoo·te·nan·ny \ˈhüt-ᵊn-ˌan-ē\ *n, pl* **-nies** [origin unknown] (1925) **1** *chiefly dial* : GADGET **2** : a gathering at which folksingers entertain often with the audience joining in

Hoo·ver·ville \ˈhü-vər-ˌvil\ *n* [Herbert *Hoover* + *-ville*; fr. the prevalence of such housing during his administration] (1933) : a shantytown of temporary dwellings during the depression years in the U.S.

[1]hop \ˈhäp\ *vb* **hopped; hop·ping** [ME *hoppen,* fr. OE *hoppian;* akin to OE *hype* hip] *vi* (bef. 12c) **1 :** to move by a quick springy leap or in a series of leaps; *also* **:** to move as if by hopping ⟨~ on a plane⟩ **2 :** to make a quick trip esp. by air ~ *vt* **1 :** to jump over ⟨~ a fence⟩ **2 :** to ride on ⟨*hopped* a flight⟩; *esp* **:** to ride surreptitiously and without authorization ⟨~ a freight⟩

[2]hop *n* (1508) **1 a :** a short brisk leap esp. on one leg **b :** BOUNCE, REBOUND ⟨shortstop took it on the first ~⟩ **2 :** DANCE, BALL **3 a :** a flight in an aircraft **b :** a short trip **c :** a free ride

[3]hop *n* [ME *hoppe,* fr. MD; akin to OHG *hopfo* hop, OE *scēaf* sheaf — more at SHEAF] (15c) **1 :** a twining vine (*Humulus lupulus*) of the mulberry family with 3-lobed or 5-lobed leaves and inconspicuous flowers of which the pistillate ones are in glandular cone-shaped catkins **2** *pl* **:** the ripe dried pistillate catkins of a hop used esp. to impart a bitter flavor to malt liquors **3** *slang* **:** a narcotic drug; *esp* **:** OPIUM

[4]hop *vt* **hopped; hop·ping** (1572) **1 :** to impregnate with hops **2 a :** to drug or stimulate with drugs **:** DOPE — usu. used with *up* **b :** EXCITE, ROUSE — used with *up* **3 :** to increase the power of beyond an original rating — used with *up* ⟨~ up an engine⟩ — **hopped–up** \ˈhäp-ˈtəp\ *adj*

[1]hope \ˈhōp\ *vb* **hoped; hop·ing** [ME *hopen,* fr. OE *hopian;* akin to MHG *hoffen* to hope] *vi* (bef. 12c) **1 :** to cherish a desire with expectation of fulfillment ⟨~*s* for a promotion⟩ **2** *archaic* **:** TRUST ~ *vt* **1 :** to long for with expectation of obtainment **2 :** to expect with desire **:** TRUST *syn* see EXPECT — **hop·er** *n* — **hope against hope :** to hope without any basis for expecting fulfillment

[2]hope *n* (bef. 12c) **1** *archaic* **:** TRUST, RELIANCE **2 a :** desire accompanied by expectation of or belief in fulfillment ⟨in ~*s* of an early recovery⟩; *also* **:** expectation of fulfillment or success ⟨not a ~ of winning⟩ **b :** someone or something on which hopes are centered ⟨our only ~ for victory⟩ **c :** something hoped for

hope chest *n* (1911) **:** a young woman's accumulation of clothes and domestic furnishings (as silver and linen) kept in anticipation of her marriage; *also* **:** a chest for such an accumulation

[1]hope·ful \ˈhōp-fəl\ *adj* (13c) **1 :** full of hope **:** inclined to hope **2 :** having qualities which inspire hope — **hope·ful·ness** *n*

[2]hopeful *n* (1720) **:** ASPIRANT ⟨presidential ~*s*⟩

hope·ful·ly \ˈhōp-fə-lē\ *adv* (1639) **1 :** in a hopeful manner **2 :** it is hoped

usage Only the irrationally large amount of critical fire drawn by sense 2 of *hopefully* requires its particular recognition in a dictionary. Similar use of other adverbs (as *interestingly, frankly, clearly*) as sentence modifiers is so commonplace as to excite no notice whatever. While it still arouses occasional objection, *hopefully* as a sentence modifier has been in use at least since 1932 and is well established as standard.

hope·less \ˈhō-pləs\ *adj* (1534) **1 a :** having no expectation of good or success **:** DESPAIRING **b :** not susceptible to remedy or cure **c :** incapable of redemption or improvement **2 a :** giving no ground for hope **:** DESPERATE **b :** incapable of solution, management, or accomplishment **:** IMPOSSIBLE *syn* see DESPONDENT — **hope·less·ly** *adv* — **hope·less·ness** *n*

hop·head \ˈhäp-ˌhed\ *n, slang* (1911) **:** a drug addict

hop hornbeam *n* (1794) **:** an American tree (*Ostrya virginiana*) of the birch family with fruiting clusters resembling hops

Ho·pi \ˈhō-(ˌ)pē\ *n, pl* **Hopi** *also* **Hopis** [Hopi *Hópi,* lit., good, peaceful] (1877) **1 a :** an American Indian people of northeastern Arizona **b :** a member of this people **2 :** the language of the Hopi people

hop·lite \ˈhäp-ˌlīt\ *n* [Gk *hoplitēs,* fr. *hoplon* tool, weapon, fr. *hepein* to care for, work at — more at SEPULCHER] (ca. 1828) **:** a heavily armed infantry soldier of ancient Greece

hop–o'–my–thumb \ˌhäp-ə-mə-ˈthəm\ *n* [earlier *hop on my thumb,* imperative issued to one supposedly small enough to be held in the hand] (1530) **:** a very small person

hop·per \ˈhäp-ər\ *n* (13c) **1 a :** one that hops **b :** a leaping insect; *specif* **:** an immature hopping form of an insect **2** [fr. the shaking motion of hoppers used to feed grain into a mill] **a :** a usu. funnel-shaped receptacle for delivering material (as grain or coal); *also* **:** any of various other receptacles for the temporary storage of material **b :** a freight car with a floor sloping to one or more hinged doors for discharging bulk materials — called also *hopper car* **c :** a box in which a bill to be considered by a legislative body is dropped **d :** a tank holding liquid and having a device for releasing its contents through a pipe

[1]hop·ping \ˈhäp-iŋ\ *adv* (1675) **:** EXTREMELY, VIOLENTLY — used in the phrase *hopping mad*

[2]hopping *adj* (1785) **1 :** intensely active **:** BUSY ⟨they kept us ~⟩ **2 :** extremely angry

hopping John \ˌhäp-ən-ˈjän, -iŋ-\ *or* **hop·pin John** \ˌhäp-ən-\ *n* [perh. by folk etymology fr. F *pois de pigeon,* lit., pigeon peas] (1838) **:** a dish made essentially of cowpeas, rice, and salt pork or bacon

hop·sack \ˈhäp-ˌsak\ *n* [ME *hopsak* sack for hops, fr. *hoppe* [3]hop + *sak* sack] (1888) **:** a rough-surfaced loosely woven clothing fabric

hop·scotch \ˈhäp-ˌskäch\ *n* [[1]*hop* + *scotch* (line)] (1789) **:** a child's game in which a player tosses an object (as a stone) into areas of a figure outlined on the ground and hops through the figure and back to regain the object

hop, skip, and jump *n* (1760) **:** a short distance

hop, step, and jump *n* (1719) **:** TRIPLE JUMP

ho·ra *also* **ho·rah** \ˈhōr-ə, ˈhȯr-ə\ *n* [NHeb *hōrāh,* fr. Rum *horă*] (1878) **:** a circle dance of Romania and Israel

Ho·rae \ˈhō(ə)r-ˌē, ˈhȯ(ə)r-, -ˌī\ *n pl* [L, fr. Gk *Hōrai*] **:** the Greek goddesses of the seasons

ho·ra·ry \ˈhōr-ər-ē, ˈhȯr-, ˈhär-\ *adj* [ML *horarius,* fr. L *hora* hour — more at HOUR] (1632) **:** of or relating to an hour; *also* **:** HOURLY

Ho·ra·tio Al·ger \hə-ˌrā-shō-ˈal-jər\ *adj* (1925) **:** of, relating to, or resembling the fiction of Horatio Alger in which success is achieved through self-reliance and hard work

Ho·ra·tius \hə-ˈrā-sh(ē-)əs\ *n* [L] **:** a hero in Roman legend noted for his defense of a bridge over the Tiber against the Etruscans

horde \ˈhō(ə)rd, ˈhȯ(ə)rd\ *n* [MF, G & Pol; MF & G, fr. Pol *horda,* of Mongolic origin; akin to Mongolian *orda* camp, horde] (1555) **1 a :** a tribal group of Mongolian nomads **b :** a people or tribe of nomadic life **2 :** a teeming crowd or throng **:** SWARM *syn* see CROWD

hore·hound \ˈhō(ə)r-ˌhau̇nd, ˈhȯ(ə)r-\ *n* [ME *horhoune,* fr. OE *hārhūne,* fr. *hār* hoary + *hūne* horehound — more at HOAR] (bef. 12c) **1 a :** a bitter mint (*Marrubium vulgare*) with hoary downy leaves **b :** an extract or confection made from this plant **2 :** any of several mints resembling the horehound

ho·ri·zon \hə-ˈrīz-ᵊn\ *n* [ME *orizon,* fr. LL *horizont-, horizon,* fr. Gk *horizont-, horizōn,* fr. prp. of *horizein* to bound, define, fr. *horos* boundary; akin to L *urvus* circumference of a city] (14c) **1 a :** the apparent junction of earth and sky — called also *apparent horizon* **b (1) :** the plane tangent to the earth's surface at an observer's position — called also *sensible horizon* **(2) :** the plane parallel to the sensible horizon but passing through the earth's center; *also* **:** the great circle formed by the intersection of this plane with the celestial sphere — called also *celestial horizon, rational horizon* **c :** a level mirror (as the surface of mercury in a shallow vessel or a plane reflector adjusted to the true level artificially) used esp. in observing altitudes **d :** range of perception or experience **e :** something that might be attained ⟨new ~*s*⟩ **2 a :** the geological deposit of a particular time usu. identified by distinctive fossils **b :** any of the reasonably distinct layers of soil or its underlying material in a vertical section of land **c :** a cultural area or level of development indicated by separated groups of artifacts — **ho·ri·zon·al** \-ˈrīz-nəl, -ᵊn-əl\ *adj*

hor·i·zon·tal \ˌhȯr-ə-ˈzänt-ᵊl, ˌhär-\ *adj* (1555) **1 a :** of, relating to, or situated near the horizon **b :** parallel to, in the plane of, or operating in a plane parallel to the horizon or to a base line **:** LEVEL ⟨~ distance⟩ ⟨~ engine⟩ **2 :** relating to, directed toward, or consisting of individuals or entities of similar status or on the same level ⟨~ mergers⟩ ⟨~ hostility⟩ — **horizontal** *n* — **hor·i·zon·tal·ly** \-ᵊl-ē\ *adv*

horizontal bar *n* (1827) **1 :** a steel bar supported in a horizontal position approximately eight feet above the floor and used for swinging feats in gymnastics **2 :** an event in gymnastics competition in which the horizontal bar is used

hor·mo·go·ni·um \ˌhȯr-mə-ˈgō-nē-əm\ *n, pl* **-nia** \-nē-ə\ [NL, fr. Gk *hormos* chain, necklace + NL *gonium* — more at SERIES] (1880) **:** a portion of a filament in many blue-green algae that becomes detached as a reproductive body

hor·mon·al \hȯr-ˈmōn-ᵊl\ *adj* (1911) **:** of, relating to, or effected by hormones — **hor·mon·al·ly** \-ᵊl-ē\ *adv*

hor·mone \ˈhȯr-ˌmōn\ *n* [Gk *hormōn,* prp. of *horman* to stir up, fr. *hormē* impulse, assault — more at SERUM] (1905) **1 :** a product of living cells that circulates in body fluids or sap and produces a specific effect on the activity of cells remote from its point of origin; *esp* **:** one exerting a stimulatory effect on a cellular activity **2 :** a synthetic substance that acts like a hormone — **hor·mone·like** \-ˌlīk\ *adj*

horn \ˈhȯ(ə)rn\ *n* [ME, fr. OE; akin to OHG *horn,* L *cornu,* Gk *keras*] (bef. 12c) **1 a :** one of the usu. paired bony processes that arise from the head of many ungulates and that are found in some extinct mammals and reptiles: as **(1) :** one of the permanent paired hollow sheaths of keratin usu. present in both sexes of cattle and their relatives that function chiefly for defense and arise from a bony core anchored to the skull — see COW illustration **(2) :** ANTLER **(3) :** a permanent solid horn of keratin that is attached to the nasal bone of a rhinoceros **(4) :** one of a pair of permanent bone protuberances from the skull of a giraffe or okapi that are covered with hairy skin **b :** a part like an animal's horn attributed esp. to the devil **c :** a natural projection or excrescence from an animal resembling or suggestive of a horn **d (1) :** the tough fibrous material consisting chiefly of keratin that covers or forms the horns of cattle and related animals, hooves, or other horny parts (as claws or nails) **(2) :** a manufactured product (as a plastic) resembling horn **e :** a hollow horn used to hold something **2 :** something resembling or suggestive of a horn: as **a :** one of the curved ends of a crescent **b :** a sharp mountain peak **c :** a body of land or water shaped like a horn **d :** a beak-shaped part of an anvil **e :** a high pommel of a saddle **3 a :** an animal's horn used as a wind instrument **b :** a brass wind instrument: as **(1) :** HUNTING HORN **(2) :** FRENCH HORN **c :** a wind instrument used in a jazz band; *esp* **:** TRUMPET **d :** a usu. electrical device that makes a noise like that of a horn **4 :** a source of strength **5 :** one of the equally disadvantageous alternatives presented by a dilemma **6** *slang* **:** TELEPHONE — **horn** *adj* — **horned** \ˈhȯ(ə)rnd *also* ˈhȯr-nəd\ *adj* — **horned·ness** \ˈhȯr-nəd-nəs, ˈhȯ(ə)rn(d)-nəs\ *n* — **horn·less** \ˈhȯ(ə)rn-ləs\ *adj* — **horn·less·ness** *n* — **horn·like** \-ˌlīk\ *adj*

horn·beam \ˈhȯ(ə)rn-ˌbēm\ *n* (14c) **:** any of a genus (*Carpinus*) of trees of the birch family having smooth gray bark and hard white wood

horn·bill \-ˌbil\ *n* (1773) **:** any of a family (Bucerotidae) of large nonpasserine Old World birds having enormous bills

horn·blende \-ˌblend\ *n* [G] (1770) **:** a mineral approximately $Ca_2Na(Mg,Fe)_4(Al,Fe,Ti)_3Si_6O_{22}(O,OH)_2$ that is the common dark variety of aluminous amphibole; *broadly* **:** AMPHIBOLE 2 — **horn·blend·ic** \hȯrn-ˈblen-dik\ *adj*

horn·book \ˈhȯ(ə)rn-ˌbu̇k\ *n* (1588) **1 :** a child's primer consisting of a sheet of parchment or paper protected by a sheet of transparent horn **2 :** a rudimentary treatise

horned owl *n* (14c) **:** any of various owls having conspicuous tufts of feathers on the head

horned pout *n* (1798) **:** a bullhead (genus *Ameiurus*); *esp* **:** a common bullhead (*A. nebulosus*) of the eastern U.S. that has been introduced into streams of the Pacific coast

horned toad *n* (1806) **:** any of several small harmless insectivorous lizards (genus *Phrynosoma*) of the western U.S. and Mexico having hornlike spines

horned viper *n* (1767) **:** CERASTES

hor·net \ˈhȯr-nət\ *n* [ME *hernet,* fr. OE *hyrnet;* akin to OHG *hornaz* hornet, L *crabro*] (bef. 12c) **:** any of the larger social wasps (family Vespidae) — compare YELLOW JACKET

hornet's nest *n* (1590) **1 :** a troublesome or hazardous situation **2 :** an angry reaction ⟨must have known that his frank comments . . . would stir up a *hornet's nest* —*U.S. Investor*⟩

horn·fels \ˈhȯ(ə)rn-ˌfelz\ *n* [G, fr. *horn* horn + *fels* cliff, rock] (1854) **:** a fine-grained silicate rock produced by metamorphism esp. of slate

\ə\ **abut** \ᵊ\ **kitten,** F **table** \ər\ **further** \a\ **ash** \ā\ **ace** \ä\ **cot, cart**
\au̇\ **out** \ch\ **chin** \e\ **bet** \ē\ **easy** \g\ **go** \i\ **hit** \ī\ **ice** \j\ **job**
\ŋ\ **sing** \ō\ **go** \ȯ\ **law** \ȯi\ **boy** \th\ **thin** \t͟h\ **the** \ü\ **loot** \u̇\ **foot**
\y\ **yet** \zh\ **vision** \à, k̲, ⁿ, œ, ᵫ, ue, u̅e, ʸ\ *see* Guide to Pronunciation

horn fly *n* (1708) : a small black European fly (*Haematobia irritans*) that has been introduced into No. America where it is a blood-sucking pest of cattle

horn in *vi* (1912) : to participate without invitation or consent : IN-TRUDE

horn·ist \'hȯr-nəst\ *n* (1865) : a French horn player

horn–mad \'hȯ(ə)rn-'mad\ *adj* (1579) : furiously enraged

horn of plenty (1586) : CORNUCOPIA

horn·pipe \'hȯ(ə)rn-ˌpip\ *n* (15c) **1** : a single-reed wind instrument consisting of a wooden or bone pipe with finger holes, a bell, and mouthpiece usu. of horn **2** : a lively folk dance of the British Isles orig. accompanied by hornpipe playing

horn–rims \-ˌrimz\ *n pl* (1927) : glasses with horn rims

horn·stone \'hȯ(ə)rn-ˌstȯn\ *n* (1728) : a mineral that is a variety of quartz much like flint but more brittle

horn·swog·gle \-ˌswäg-əl\ *vt* **-swog·gled; -swog·gling** \(-ə-)liŋ\ [origin unknown] *slang* (1829) : BAMBOOZLE, HOAX

horn·tail \-ˌtāl\ *n* (1884) : any of various hymenopterous insects (family Siricidae) related to the typical sawflies but having larvae that burrow in woody plants and on the females a stout hornlike ovipositor for depositing the egg

horn·worm \-ˌwərm\ *n* (1676) : a hawkmoth caterpillar having a horn-like tail process

horn·wort \-ˌwȯrt, -ˌwȯ(ə)rt\ *n* (1805) : any of a genus (*Ceratophyllum*) of rootless thin-stemmed aquatic herbs that have flowers with a sepaloid perianth and a single carpel

horny \'hȯr-nē\ *adj* **horn·i·er; -est** (14c) **1 a** : of or made of horn **b** : HARD, CALLOUS (*horny*-handed) **c** : compact and homogeneous with a dull luster — used of a mineral **2** : having horns **3** [*horn* (erect penis) *+ -y*] **a** : desiring sexual gratification **b** : excited sexually — **horn·i·ness** *n*

hor·o·loge \'hȯr-ə-ˌlōj, 'här-\ *n* [ME, fr. MF, fr. L *horologium*, fr. Gk *hōrologion*, fr. *hōra* hour *+ legein* to gather — more at YEAR, LEGEND] (14c) : a timekeeping device

ho·rol·o·ger \hə-'räl-ə-jər\ *n* (15c) : HOROLOGIST

hor·o·log·ic \ˌhȯr-ə-'läj-ik, ˌhär-\ *also* **hor·o·log·i·cal** \-i-kəl\ *adj* (1593) : of or relating to a horologe or horology

ho·rol·o·gist \hə-'räl-ə-jəst\ *n* (1798) **1** : a person skilled in the practice or theory of horology **2** : a maker of clocks or watches

ho·rol·o·gy \-jē\ *n* [Gk *hōra* + E *-logy*] (14c) **1** : the science of measuring time **2** : the art of making instruments for indicating time

horo·scope \'hȯr-ə-ˌskōp, 'här-\ *n* [ME *oruscope*, fr. MF *horoscope*, fr. L *horoscopus*, fr. Gk *hōroskopos*, fr. *hōra* + *skopos* watcher; akin to Gk *skopein* to look at — more at SPY] (14c) **1** : a diagram of the relative positions of planets and signs of the zodiac at a specific time (as at one's birth) for use by astrologers in inferring individual character and personality traits and in foretelling events of a person's life **2** : an astrological forecast

hor·ren·dous \hȯ-'ren-dəs, hä-, hə-\ *adj* [L *horrendus*, fr. gerundive of *horrēre*] (1659) : perfectly horrid : DREADFUL (the tax rate was ∼) — **hor·ren·dous·ly** *adv*

hor·rent \'hȯr-ənt, 'här-\ *adj* [L *horrent-, horrens*, prp. of *horrēre*] (1667) **1** *archaic* : covered with bristling points : BRISTLED **2** *archaic* : standing up like bristles : BRISTLING

hor·ri·ble \'hȯr-ə-bəl, 'här-\ *adj* [ME *orrible, horrible*, fr. MF, fr. L *horribilis*, fr. *horrēre*] (14c) **1** : marked by or conducive to horror **2** : extremely unpleasant or disagreeable — **horrible** *n* — **hor·ri·ble·ness** *n* — **hor·ri·bly** \-blē\ *adv*

hor·rid \'hȯr-əd, 'här-\ *adj* [L *horridus*, fr. *horrēre*] (1590) **1** *archaic* : ROUGH, BRISTLING **2** : innately offensive or repulsive : a : inspiring horror : SHOCKING **b** : inspiring disgust or loathing : NASTY — **hor·rid·ly** *adv* — **hor·rid·ness** *n*

hor·rif·ic \hȯ-'rif-ik, hä-\ *adj* (1653) : having the power to horrify (a ∼ account of the tragedy) — **hor·rif·i·cal·ly** \-i-k(ə-)lē\ *adv*

hor·ri·fy \'hȯr-ə-ˌfi, 'här-\ *vt* **-fied; -fy·ing** (1791) **1** : to cause to feel horror **2** : to fill with distaste : SHOCK *syn* see DISMAY — **hor·ri·fy·ing·ly** \-ˌfi-iŋ-lē\ *adv*

¹hor·ror \'hȯr-ər, 'här-\ *n* [ME *horrour*, fr. MF *horror*, fr. L, action of trembling, fr. *horrēre* to tremble; akin to OE *gorst* gorse, Gk *chersos* dry land] (14c) **1 a** : painful and intense fear, dread, or dismay : CON-STERNATION (astonishment giving place to ∼ on the faces of the people about me —H. G. Wells) **b** : intense aversion or repugnance **2 a** : the quality of inspiring horror : repulsive, horrible, or dismal quality

or character (contemplating the ∼ of their lives —Liam O'Flaherty) **b** : something that inspires horror **3** *pl* : a state of extreme depression or apprehension

²horror *adj* (1797) : calculated to inspire feelings of dread or horror : BLOODCURDLING (a ∼ story)

hor·ror–struck \-ˌstrək\ *adj* (1821) : struck with horror (stood ∼ as they watched . . . their own city destroyed —*Nashville Tennessean*)

hors de com·bat \ˌȯrd-ə-kōⁿ-'bä\ *adv or adj* [F] (1757) : out of combat : DISABLED

hors d'oeuvre \ȯr-'dərv\ *n, pl* **hors d'oeuvres** *also* **hors d'oeuvre** \-'dərv(z)\ [F *hors-d'oeuvre*, lit., outside of work] (1714) : any of various savory foods usu. served as appetizers

¹horse \'hȯ(ə)rs\ *n, pl* **hors·es** *also* **horse** [ME *hors*, fr. OE; akin to OHG *hros* horse] (bef. 12c) **1 a** (1) : a large solid-hoofed herbivorous mammal (*Equus caballus*, family Equidae, the horse family) domesticated by man since a prehistoric period and used as a beast of burden, a draft animal, or for riding (2) : RACEHORSE (play the ∼s) **b** : a male horse; *esp* : STALLION **c** : a recent or extinct animal of the horse family **2 a** : JACKSTAY **b** : a frame usu. with legs used for supporting something (as planks or staging) **c** (1) : POMMEL HORSE (2) : VAULTING HORSE **3** *horse of* : CAVALRY **4** : a mass of the same geological character as the wall rock occurring within a vein **5** : HORSEPOWER **6** *slang* : HEROIN — **horse·less** \'hȯr-sləs\ *adj* — **horse·like** \'hȯ(ə)r-ˌslik\ *adj* — **from the horse's mouth** : from the original source

²horse *vb* **horsed; hors·ing** *vt* (bef. 12c) **1** : to provide with a horse **2** : to move by brute force ∼ *vi* **1** *of a mare* : to be in heat **2** : to engage in horseplay (*horsing* around too much)

³horse *adj* (15c) **1 a** : of or relating to a horse **b** : hauled or powered by a horse (a ∼ barge) **2** : large or coarse of its kind **3** : mounted on horses (∼ guards)

horse–and–buggy *adj* (1926) **1** : of or relating to the era before the advent of certain socially revolutionizing inventions (as the automobile) **2** : clinging to outdated attitudes or ideas : OLD-FASHIONED

¹horse·back \'hȯrs-ˌbak\ *adv* (14c) : on horseback

²horseback *n* (15c) : the back of a horse

³horseback *adj* (1879) : given without thorough consideration (a ∼ opinion)

horse·bean \'hȯrs-ˌbēn\ *n* (1684) **1** : BROAD BEAN **2** : JERUSALEM THORN 2

horse·car \-ˌkär\ *n* (1833) **1** : a streetcar drawn by horses **2** : a car fitted for transporting horses

horse chestnut *n* (1597) **1** : a large Asian tree (*Aesculus hippocastanum* of the family Hippocastanaceae, the horse-chestnut family) that has palmate leaves and erect conical clusters of showy flowers and is widely cultivated as an ornamental and shade tree and naturalized as an escape; *also* : BUCKEYE **2** : the large glossy brown seed of a horse chestnut

horse coper *n, Brit* (1614) : COPER

horse–feath·ers \'hȯrs-ˌfeth-ərz\ *n pl, slang* (1928) : NONSENSE, BALDER-DASH

horse·flesh \-ˌflesh\ *n* (15c) : horses considered esp. with reference to riding, driving, or racing

horse·fly \-ˌfli\ *n* (14c) : any of a family (Tabanidae) of swift usu. large two-winged flies with bloodsucking females

horse gentian *n* (1843) : FEVERWORT

horse·hair \'hȯrs-ˌha(ə)r, -ˌhe(ə)r\ *n* (14c) **1** : the hair of a horse esp. from the mane or tail **2** : cloth made from horsehair

horsehair worm *n* (ca. 1753) : a free-living adult hairworm — called *also* **horsehair snake**

horse·hide \'hȯrs-ˌhid\ *n* (14c) **1** : the dressed or raw hide of a horse **2** : the ball used in the game of baseball

horse latitudes *n pl* (1777) : either of two belts or regions in the neighborhood of 30° N and 30° S latitude characterized by high pressure, calms, and light baffling winds

horse·laugh \'hȯr-ˌslaf, -ˌsláf\ *n* (1713) : a loud boisterous laugh : GUF-FAW

horseless carriage *n* (1895) : AUTOMOBILE

horse mackerel *n* (1705) **1** : any of several large scombroid fishes (as a bluefin tuna) **2** : any of various large fishes (family Carangidae); *esp* : a large Atlantic food fish (*Trachurus trachurus*)

horse·man \'hȯr-smən\ *n* (14c) **1 a** : a rider on horseback **b** : one skilled in managing horses **2** : a breeder or raiser of horses — **horse·man·ship** \-ˌship\ *n*

horse·mint \'hȯr-ˌsmint\ *n* (13c) : any of various coarse mints; *esp* : MONARDA

horse nettle *n* (1817) : a coarse prickly weed (*Solanum carolinense*) of the nightshade family with bright yellow fruit resembling berries

horse opera *n* (1927) : WESTERN 2

horse·play \'hȯr-ˌsplā\ *n* (1589) : rough or boisterous play

horse·play·er \-ˌər\ *n* (1947) : one who habitually bets on horse races

horse·pow·er \'hȯr-ˌspau̇(-ə)r\ *n* (1806) **1** : the power that a horse exerts in pulling **2** : a unit of power equal in the U.S. to 746 watts and nearly equivalent to the English gravitational unit of the same name that equals 550 foot-pounds of work per second

horsepower–hour *n* (1899) : the work performed or energy consumed by working at the rate of one horsepower for one hour that is equal to 1,980,000 foot-pounds

horse·rad·ish \'hȯrs-ˌrad-ish, -ˌred-\ *n* (1597) **1** : a tall coarse white-flowered herb (*Armoracia lapathifolia*) of the mustard family **2** : a condiment made from ground-up horseradish root

horse's ass \'hȯr-səz-\ *n* (1970) : a stupid or incompetent person : BLOCKHEAD — often considered vulgar

horse sense *n* (1832) : COMMON SENSE

horse·shit \'hȯrs(h)-ˌshit, 'hȯr-\ *n* (1946) : NONSENSE, BUNK — usu. considered vulgar

horse·shoe \'hȯrs(h)-ˌshü, 'hȯr-\ *n* (14c) **1** : a usu. U-shaped band of iron fitted and nailed to the rim of a horse's hoof to protect it **2** : something (as a valley) shaped like a horseshoe **3** *pl* : a game like quoits played with horseshoes or with horseshoe-shaped pieces of metal — **horseshoe** *vt* — **horse·sho·er** \-ˌshü-ər\ *n*

horseshoe arch *n* (1812) : an arch having an intrados that widens above the springing before narrowing to a rounded or pointed crown — see ARCH illustration

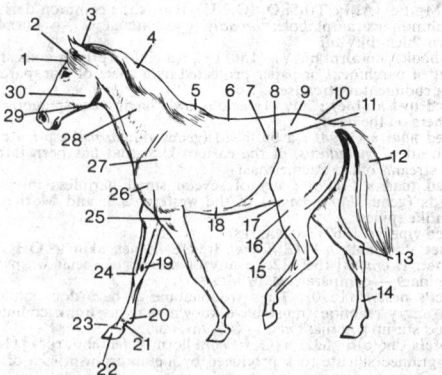

horse 1a(1): *1* forehead, *2* forelock, *3* poll, *4* mane, *5* withers, *6* back, *7* flank, *8* loin, *9* haunch, *10* croup, *11* point of hip, *12* tail, *13* hock, *14* cannon, *15* gaskin, *16* thigh, *17* stifle, *18* barrel, *19* chestnut, *20* fetlock, *21* pastern, *22* hoof, *23* coronet, *24* knee, *25* forearm, *26* chest, *27* shoulder, *28* neck, *29* throatlatch, *30* cheek

horseshoe crab *n* (1797) **:** any of several closely related marine arthropods (order Xiphosura and class Merostomata) with a broad crescentic cephalothorax — called also *king crab*
horse show *n* (1856) **:** an exhibition of horses that usu. includes competition in riding, driving, and jumping
horse·tail \ˈhȯr-ˌstāl\ *n* (14c) **:** any of a genus (*Equisetum*) of perennial flowerless plants related to the ferns — called also *scouring rush*
horse trade *n* (1846) **:** negotiation accompanied by shrewd bargaining and reciprocal concessions ⟨a political *horse trade*⟩ — **horse–trade** *vi* — **horse trader** *n*
horse·weed \ˈhȯr-ˌswēd\ *n* (1790) **1 :** a common No. American fleabane (*Erigeron canadensis*) with linear leaves and small discoid heads of yellowish flowers **2 :** a coarse annual ragweed (*Ambrosia trifida*)
horse·whip \ˈhȯr-ˌswip, ˈhȯrs-ˌhwip\ *vt* (1798) **:** to flog with or as if with a whip made to be used on a horse — **horse·whip·per** *n*
horse·wom·an \ˈhȯr-ˌswu̇m-ən\ *n* (1564) **1 :** a woman horseback rider **2 :** a woman skilled in caring for or managing horses
hors·ey *or* **horsy** \ˈhȯr-sē\ *adj* **hors·i·er; -est** (1591) **1 :** of, relating to, or resembling a horse **2 :** having to do with horses or horse racing **3 :** characteristic of horsemen or horsewomen — **hors·i·ly** \-sə-lē\ *adv* — **hors·i·ness** \-sē-nəs\ *n*
horst \ˈhȯ(ə)rst\ *n* [G] (1893) **:** a block of the earth's crust separated by faults from adjacent relatively depressed blocks
hor·ta·tive \ˈhȯrt-ət-iv\ *adj* [LL *hortativus,* fr. L *hortatus,* pp. of *hortari* to urge — more at YEARN] (1623) **:** giving exhortation **:** ADVISORY — **hor·ta·tive·ly** *adv*
hor·ta·to·ry \ˈhȯrt-ə-ˌtōr-ē, -ˌtȯr-\ *adj* (1586) **:** HORTATIVE, EXHORTATORY
hor·ti·cul·ture \ˈhȯrt-ə-ˌkəl-chər\ *n* [L *hortus* garden + E *-i-* + *culture* — more at YARD] (1678) **:** the science and art of growing fruits, vegetables, flowers, or ornamental plants — **hor·ti·cul·tur·al** \ˌhȯrt-ə-ˈkəlch(-ə)-rəl\ *adj* — **hor·ti·cul·tur·al·ly** \-rə-lē\ *adv* — **hor·ti·cul·tur·ist** \-rəst\ *n*
Ho·rus \ˈhōr-əs, ˈhȯr-\ *n* [LL, fr. Gk *Hōros,* fr. Egypt *Ḥr*] **:** the Egyptian god of light and the son of Osiris and Isis
ho·san·na *also* **ho·san·nah** \hō-ˈzan-ə *also* -ˈzän-\ *interj* [ME *osanna,* fr. OE, fr. LL, fr. Gk *hōsanna,* fr. Heb *hōshīʿāh-nnā* pray, save (us)!] (bef. 12c) — used as a cry of acclamation and adoration — **hosanna** *n*
HO scale \(ˈ)ā-ˈchō-\ *n* [fr. its fitness for rails of HO gauge] (1939) **:** a scale of 3.5 millimeters to one foot used esp. for model toys (as automobiles or trains)
[1]hose \ˈhōz\ *n, pl* **hose** *or* **hos·es** [ME, fr. OE *hosa* stocking, husk; akin to OHG *hosa* leg covering, Gk *kystis* bladder, OE *hȳd* hide] (bef. 12c) **1** *pl* **hose a (1) :** a cloth leg covering that sometimes covers the foot **(2) :** STOCKING, SOCK **b (1) :** a close-fitting garment covering the legs and waist that is usu. attached to a doublet by points **(2) :** short breeches reaching to the knee **2 :** a flexible tube for conveying fluids (as from a faucet or hydrant)
[2]hose *vt* **hosed; hos·ing** (1889) **:** to spray, water, or wash with a hose — often used with *down* ⟨~ down a stable floor⟩
Ho·sea \hō-ˈzā-ə, -ˈzē-\ *n* [Heb *Hōshēaʿ*] **1 :** a Hebrew prophet of the 8th century B.C. **2 :** a prophetic book of canonical Jewish and Christian Scripture — see BIBLE table
ho·sel \ˈhō-zəl\ *n* [dim. of [1]*hose*] (1899) **:** a socket in the head of a golf club into which the shaft is inserted
ho·siery \ˈhōzh(-ə)-rē, ˈhōz(-ə)-\ *n* (1790) **1 :** HOSE 1a **2** *chiefly Brit* **:** KNITWEAR
hos·pice \ˈhäs-pəs\ *n* [F, fr. L *hospitium,* fr. *hospit-, hospes* host — more at HOST] (1818) **1 :** a lodging for travelers, young persons, or the underprivileged esp. when maintained by a religious order **2 :** a facility or program designed to provide a caring environment for supplying the physical and emotional needs of the terminally ill
hos·pi·ta·ble \hä-ˈspit-ə-bəl, ˈhäs-(ˌ)pit-\ *adj* (1570) **1 a :** given to generous and cordial reception of guests **b :** promising or suggesting generous and cordial welcome **c :** offering a pleasant or sustaining environment **2 :** readily receptive **:** OPEN ⟨~ to new ideas⟩ — **hos·pi·ta·bly** \-blē\ *adv*
hos·pi·tal \ˈhäs-ˌpit-ᵊl\ *n, often attrib* [ME, fr. MF, fr. ML *hospitale,* fr. LL, hospice, fr. L, guest room, fr. neut. of *hospitalis* of a guest, fr. *hospit-, hospes*] (14c) **1 :** a charitable institution for the needy, aged, infirm, or young **2 :** an institution where the sick or injured are given medical or surgical care — usu. used in British English without an article in the phrase *in hospital* **3 :** a repair shop for specified small objects ⟨clock ~⟩
Hos·pi·tal·er *or* **Hos·pi·tal·ler** \-ᵊl-ər\ *n* [ME *hospitalier,* fr. MF, fr. ML *hospitalarius,* fr. LL *hospitale*] (14c) **:** a member of a religious military order established in Jerusalem in the 12th century
hos·pi·tal·i·ty \ˌhäs-pə-ˈtal-ət-ē\ *n, pl* **-ties** (14c) **:** hospitable treatment, reception, or disposition
hospitality suite *n* (1963) **:** a room or suite esp. in a hotel set aside as a place for socializing usu. in connection with a business meeting or convention
hos·pi·tal·ize \ˈhäs-ˌpit-ᵊl-ˌīz\ *vt* **-ized; -iz·ing** (1899) **:** to place in a hospital as a patient — **hos·pi·tal·iza·tion** \ˌhäs-ˌpit-ᵊl-ə-ˈzā-shən\ *n*
[1]host \ˈhōst\ *n* [ME, fr. OF, fr. LL *hostis,* fr. L, stranger, enemy — more at GUEST] (13c) **1 :** ARMY **2 :** a very large number **:** MULTITUDE
[2]host *vi* (15c) **:** to assemble in a host usu. for a hostile purpose
[3]host *n* [ME *hoste* host, guest, fr. OF, fr. L *hospit-, hospes,* fr. *hostis*] (13c) **1 a :** one that receives or entertains guests socially, commercially, or officially **b :** one that provides facilities for an event or function ⟨our college served as ~ for the basketball tournament⟩ **2 a :** a living animal or plant affording subsistence or lodgment to a parasite **b :** the larger, stronger, or dominant member of a commensal or symbiotic pair **c :** an individual into which a tissue or part is transplanted from another **3 :** a mineral or rock that is older than the minerals or rocks in it; *also* **:** a substance that contains a usu. small amount of another substance incorporated in its structure **4 :** a radio or television emcee
[4]host *vt* (15c) **1 :** to receive or entertain socially **:** serve as host to **2 a :** to serve as host at **b :** EMCEE ⟨~*ed* a series of TV programs⟩
[5]host *n, often cap* [ME *hoste, oste,* fr. MF *hoiste,* fr. LL & L; LL *hostia* Eucharist, fr. L, sacrifice] (14c) **:** the eucharistic bread
hos·ta \ˈhō-stə, ˈhäs-tə\ *n* [NL, after Nicolaus *Host* †1834 Austrian botanist] (1828) **:** PLANTAIN LILY
hos·tage \ˈhäs-tij\ *n* [ME, fr. OF, fr. *hoste*] (13c) **1 :** a person held by one party in a conflict as a pledge that promises will be kept or terms met by the other party **2 :** one that is involuntarily controlled by an outside influence
[1]hos·tel \ˈhäs-tᵊl\ *n* [ME, fr. OF, fr. LL *hospitale* hospice] (14c) **1 :** INN **2 :** a supervised lodging for usu. young travelers — called also *youth hostel*
[2]hostel *vi* (14c) **:** to stay at hostels overnight in the course of traveling
hos·tel·er \ˈhäs-tə-lər\ *n* (13c) **1 :** one that lodges guests or strangers **2 :** a young traveler who stops at hostels overnight
hos·tel·ry \ˈhäs-tᵊl-rē\ *n, pl* **-ries** (14c) **:** INN, HOTEL
[1]host·ess \ˈhō-stəs\ *n* (13c) **1 :** a woman who entertains socially **2 a :** a woman in charge of a public dining room who seats diners **b :** a female employee on a ship, airplane, bus, or train who manages the provisioning of food and attends passengers **c :** a woman who acts as a dancing partner or companion to male patrons in a dance hall or bar
[2]hostess *vi* (1927) **:** to act as hostess ~ *vt* **:** to serve as hostess to
hos·tile \ˈhäs-tᵊl, -ˌtīl\ *adj* [MF or L; MF, fr. L *hostilis,* fr. *hostis*] (1580) **1 :** of or relating to an enemy **2 :** marked by esp. overt antagonism **:** UNFRIENDLY **3 :** not hospitable ⟨a ~ environment⟩ — **hostile** *n* — **hos·tile·ly** \-tᵊl-(l)ē, -ˌtīl-lē\ *adv*
hos·til·i·ty \hä-ˈstil-ət-ē\ *n, pl* **-ties** (15c) **1 a :** a hostile state **b (1) :** hostile action **(2)** *pl* **:** overt acts of warfare **:** WAR **2 :** conflict, opposition, or resistance in thought or principle ***syn*** see ENMITY
hos·tler \ˈ(h)äs-lər\ *n* [ME, innkeeper, hostler, fr. *hostel*] (14c) **1 :** one who takes care of horses or mules **2 :** one who services a vehicle (as a locomotive or truck) or machine (as a crane)
host·ly \ˈhōst-lē\ *adj* (1893) **:** of or appropriate to a host
host plant *n* (1888) **:** a plant upon which an organism (as an insect or mildew) lodges and subsists
[1]hot \ˈhät\ *adj* **hot·ter; hot·test** [ME, fr. OE *hāt;* akin to OHG *heiz* hot, Lith *kaisti* to get hot] (bef. 12c) **1 a :** having a relatively high temperature **b :** capable of giving a sensation of heat or of burning, searing, or scalding **c :** having heat in a degree exceeding normal body heat **2 a :** ARDENT, FIERY ⟨a ~ temper⟩ **b :** VIOLENT, RAGING ⟨a ~ battle⟩ **c :** sexually excited or receptive **:** LUSTFUL **d :** EAGER ⟨~ for reform⟩ **e** *of jazz* **:** ecstatic and emotionally exciting and marked by strong rhythms and free melodic improvisations **3 :** having or causing the sensation of an uncomfortable degree of body heat ⟨~ and tired⟩ **4 a :** newly made **:** FRESH ⟨a ~ scent⟩ ⟨~ off the press⟩ **b :** close to something sought ⟨guess again, you're getting *hotter*⟩ **5 a :** suggestive of heat or of burning or glowing objects ⟨~ colors⟩ **b :** PUNGENT, PEPPERY **6 a :** of intense and immediate interest ⟨a ~ scandal⟩ **b :** unusually lucky or favorable ⟨~ dice⟩ **c :** temporarily capable of unusual performance (as in a sport) **d :** currently popular (as of merchandise) **e :** very good — used as a generalized term of approval ⟨he's really ~ in math⟩ **f :** ABSURD, UNBELIEVABLE ⟨wants to fight the champ? that's a ~ one⟩ **7 a :** electrically energized esp. with high voltage **b :** RADIOACTIVE; *also* **:** dealing with radioactive material **c** *of an atom* **:** being in an excited state due usu. to nuclear processes **8 a :** recently and illegally obtained ⟨~ jewels⟩ **b :** wanted by the police; *also* **:** unsafe for a fugitive **9** *of a vehicle* **:** FAST **10 :** being full of detail and information and requiring little or no involvement of the listener, viewer, or reader — compare COOL 8 — **hot·ness** *n* — **hot·tish** \ˈhät-ish\ *adj* — **hot under the collar :** extremely exasperated or angry
[2]hot *adv* (bef. 12c) **:** HOTLY
hot air *n* (1854) **:** empty talk
hot·bed \ˈhät-ˌbed\ *n* (1626) **1 :** a bed of soil enclosed in glass, heated esp. by fermenting manure, and used for forcing or for raising seedlings **2 :** an environment that favors rapid growth or development ⟨a ~ of crime⟩
hot·blood \-ˌbləd\ *n* (1798) **1 :** one that is hot-blooded; *esp* **:** one having strong passions or a quick temper **2 :** THOROUGHBRED 1
hot–blood·ed \-ˈbləd-əd\ *adj* (1598) **1 :** easily excited **:** PASSIONATE **2** *of a horse* **:** having Arab or Thoroughbred ancestors — **hot–blood·ed·ness** *n*
hot·box \-ˌbäks\ *n* (1848) **:** a journal bearing (as of a railroad car) overheated by friction
hot·cake \-ˌkāk\ *n* (1683) **:** PANCAKE
hotch \ˈhäch\ *vi* [ME *hotchen,* prob. fr. MF *hocher* to shake, fr. OF *hochier*] (15c) **1** *Scot* **:** WIGGLE, FIDGET **2** *Scot* **:** SWARM
hotch·pot \ˈhäch-ˌpät\ *n* [AF *hochepot,* fr. OF, hotchpotch] (1552) **:** the combining of properties into a common lot to ensure equality of division among heirs
hotch·potch \ˈhäch-ˌpäch\ *n* [ME *hochepot,* fr. MF, fr. OF, fr. *hochier* to shake + *pot*] (1583) **1 a :** a thick soup or stew of vegetables, potatoes, and usu. meat **b :** HODGEPODGE **2 :** HOTCHPOT
hot comb *n* (1970) **:** a metal comb usu. electrically heated for straightening or styling the hair — **hot–comb** *vt*
hot corner *n* (1903) **:** the fielding position of the third baseman in baseball
hot·dog \ˈhät-ˌdȯg\ *vi* [[2]*hot dog*] (1962) **:** to perform in a conspicuous or often ostentatious manner; *esp* **:** to perform fancy stunts and maneuvers (as while surfing or skiing) — **hot·dog·ger** \-ˌdȯg-ər\ *n*
[1]hot dog \ˈhät-ˌdȯg\ *n* (1900) **1 :** FRANKFURTER; *esp* **:** a frankfurter heated and served in a long split roll **2** [prob. fr. [2]*hot dog*] **:** one that hotdogs; *also* **:** SHOW-OFF
[2]hot dog \ˈhät-ˌdȯg, -ˈdȯg\ *interj* (1906) — used to express approval or gratification
ho·tel \hō-ˈtel, ˈhō-ˌ\ *n* [F *hôtel,* fr. OF *hostel* hostel] (1765) **:** an establishment that provides lodging and usu. meals, entertainment, and various personal services for the public **:** INN — **ho·tel·dom** \-dəm\ *n*
Hotel (ca. 1952) — a communications code word for the letter *h*
ho·te·lier \hō-ˈtel-yər; ˌōt-ᵊl-ˈyā, ˌōt-\ *n* [F *hôtelier,* fr. OF *hostelier,* fr. *hostel*] (1905) **:** a proprietor or manager of a hotel
ho·tel·man \hō-ˈtel-ˌman, -mən\ *n* (1920) **:** one who is engaged in the hotel business esp. in a supervisory or managerial capacity

\ə\ **abut** \ᵊ\ **kitten,** F **table** \ər\ **further** \a\ **ash** \ā\ **ace** \ä\ **cot, cart**
\au̇\ **out** \ch\ **chin** \e\ **bet** \ē\ **easy** \g\ **go** \i\ **hit** \ī\ **ice** \j\ **job**
\ŋ\ **sing** \ō\ **go** \ȯ\ **law** \ȯi\ **boy** \th\ **thin** \t͟h\ **the** \ü\ **loot** \u̇\ **foot**
\y\ **yet** \zh\ **vision** \à, k̲, ⁿ, œ, œ̄, ue, ue̅, ʸ\ *see* Guide to Pronunciation

hot flash *n* (1910) **:** a sudden brief flushing and sensation of heat caused by dilation of skin capillaries usu. associated with menopausal endocrine imbalance — called also *hot flush*

1hot·foot \ˈhät-ˌfu̇t\ *adv* (14c) **:** in haste

2hotfoot *vi* (1896) **:** to go hotfoot **:** HURRY — usu. used with *it*

3hotfoot *n, pl* **hotfoots** (1906) **:** a practical joke in which a match is surreptitiously inserted between the upper and the sole of a victim's shoe and lighted

hot·head \ˈhät-ˌhed\ *n* (1884) **:** a hotheaded person

hot·head·ed \-ˈhed-əd\ *adj* (1641) **:** FIERY, IMPETUOUS — **hot·head·ed·ly** *adv* — **hot·head·ed·ness** *n*

1hot·house \-ˌhau̇s\ *n* (1511) **1** *obs* **:** BROTHEL **2 :** a greenhouse maintained at a high temperature esp. for the culture of tropical plants **3 :** HOTBED 2

2hothouse *adj* (1838) **1 :** grown in a hothouse **2 :** having the qualities of a plant raised in a hothouse; *esp* **:** DELICATE

hot line *n* (1955) **1 :** a direct telephone line in constant operational readiness so as to facilitate immediate communication (as between heads of two governments) **2 :** a telephone service by which usu. unidentified callers can talk confidentially about personal problems to a sympathetic listener

hot·ly \ˈhät-lē\ *adv* (15c) **:** in a hot or fiery manner ⟨a ~ debated issue⟩

hot metal *n* (1963) **:** composition in which the type is cast from molten metal

hot money *n* (1936) **:** investment funds having high velocity caused by their seeking the highest short-term rate of return

hot pepper *n* (1945) **1 :** any of various small and usu. thin-walled capsicum fruits of marked pungency **2 :** a pepper plant bearing hot peppers

hot plate *n* (1845) **1 :** a heated iron plate for cooking **2 :** a simple portable appliance for heating or for cooking in limited spaces

hot pot *n* (1851) **:** a stew of meat and vegetables

hot potato *n* (1846) **:** a controversial question or issue that involves unpleasant or dangerous consequences for anyone dealing with it

hot pursuit *n* (ca. 1922) **:** close continuous pursuit of a fleeing suspected lawbreaker or hostile military force esp. across territorial lines

hot rod *n* (1945) **:** an automobile rebuilt or modified for high speed and fast acceleration — **hot–rod** \(ˈ)hät-ˈräd\ *vb* — **hot–rod·der** \ˈhät-ˈräd-ər\ *n*

hots \ˈhäts\ *n pl* (ca. 1947) **:** strong sexual desire — used with *the*

hot seat *n* (1925) **1** *slang* **:** ELECTRIC CHAIR **2 :** a position of uneasiness, embarrassment, or anxiety

hot·shot \ˈhät-ˌshät\ *n* (1925) **1 :** a fast freight **2 :** a showily skillful person ⟨a literary ~⟩ — **hotshot** *adj*

hot spring *n* (1669) **:** THERMAL SPRING; *esp* **:** a spring with water above 37° Celsius

Hot·ten·tot \ˈhät-ᵊn-ˌtät\ *n* [Afrik] (1677) **1 :** a member of a people of southern Africa apparently akin to both the Bushmen and the Bantu **2 :** the language of the Hottentot people

hot tub *n* (1975) **:** a large usu. wooden tub of hot water in which bathers soak and usu. socialize

hot up *vi* (1878) **:** to increase in intensity, pace, or excitement ⟨air raids began to *hot up* about the beginning of February —George Orwell⟩ ~ *vt* **:** to make livelier or speedier

hot war *n* (1947) **:** a conflict involving actual fighting — compare COLD WAR

hot water *n* (14c) **:** a distressing predicament **:** DIFFICULTY ⟨was in *hot water* with the authorities⟩

hot–wire \ˈhät-ˌwī(ə)r\ *vt* (1954) **:** to start (as an automobile) by short-circuiting the ignition system

1hound \ˈhau̇nd\ *n* [ME, fr. OE *hund;* akin to OHG *hunt* dog, L *canis,* Gk *kyōn*] (bef. 12c) **1 a :** DOG **b :** a dog of any of various hunting breeds typically having large drooping ears and a deep voice and following their prey by scent **2 :** a mean or despicable person **3 :** DOGFISH **4 :** one who avidly seeks or collects something ⟨autograph ~*s*⟩

2hound *vt* (1528) **1 :** to pursue with or as if with hounds **2 :** to drive or affect by persistent harassing ⟨~*ed* from office⟩ — **hound·er** *n*

hounds \ˈhau̇n(d)z\ *n pl* [ME *hune,* of Scand origin; akin to ON *hūnn* knob at the top of a masthead, cub — more at CAVE] (15c) **:** the framing at the masthead of a ship that supports the heel of the topmast and the upper parts of the lower rigging

hound's–tongue \ˈhau̇n(d)z-ˌtəŋ\ *n* (bef. 12c) **:** any of various coarse plants (genus *Cynoglossum,* esp. *C. officinale*) of the borage family having tongue-shaped leaves and reddish flowers

hounds·tooth check *or* **hound's–tooth check** \ˌhau̇n(d)z-ˌtüth-\ *n* (1937) **:** a small broken-check textile pattern

hour \ˈau̇(ə)r\ *n* [ME, fr. OF *heure,* fr. LL & L; LL *hora* canonical hour, fr. L, hour of the day, fr. Gk *hōra* — more at YEAR] (13c) **1 :** a time or office for daily liturgical devotion; *esp* **:** CANONICAL HOUR **2 :** the 24th part of a day **:** 60 minutes **3 a :** the time of day reckoned in two 12-hour periods **b** *pl* **:** the time reckoned in one 24-hour period from midnight to midnight using a 4-digit number of which the first two digits indicate the hour and the last two digits indicate the minute ⟨in the military 4:30 p.m. is called 1630 ~*s*⟩ **4 :** a customary or particular time ⟨during our lunch ~⟩ ⟨in our ~ of need⟩ **5 :** an angular unit of right ascension equal to 15 degrees measured along the celestial equator **6 :** the work done or distance traveled at normal rate in an hour ⟨the city was two ~*s* away⟩ **7 a :** a class session **b :** CREDIT HOUR, SEMESTER HOUR

hour angle *n* (ca. 1837) **:** the angle between the celestial meridian of an observer and the hour circle of a celestial object measured westward from the meridian

hour circle *n* (1690) **:** a circle on the celestial sphere that passes through both celestial poles

1hour·glass \ˈau̇(ə)r-ˌglas\ *n* (1515) **:** an instrument for measuring time consisting of a glass vessel having two compartments from the uppermost of which a quantity of sand, water, or mercury runs in an hour into the lower one

2hourglass *adj* (1822) **:** shaped like an hourglass ⟨an ~ figure⟩

hour hand *n* (1669) **:** the short hand that marks the hours on the face of a watch or clock

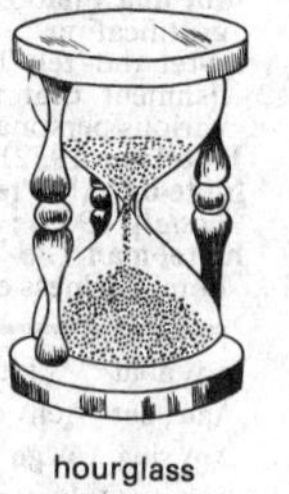

hourglass

hou·ri \ˈhu̇(ə)r-ē, ˈhü-rē\ *n* [F, fr. Per *hūri,* fr. Ar *ḥūrīyah*] (1737) **1 :** one of the beautiful maidens that in Muslim belief live with the blessed in paradise **2 :** a voluptuously beautiful young woman

hour–long \ˈau̇(ə)r-ˈlȯŋ\ *adj* (1803) **:** lasting an hour

1hour·ly \ˈau̇(ə)r-lē\ *adv* (15c) **:** at or during every hour; *also* **:** FREQUENTLY, CONTINUALLY

2hourly *adj* (1530) **1 a :** occurring hour by hour ⟨~ bus service⟩ **b :** FREQUENT, CONTINUAL ⟨in ~ expectation of the rain's stopping⟩ **2 :** computed in terms of an hour ⟨an ~ wage⟩ **3 :** paid by the hour ⟨~ workers⟩

1house \ˈhau̇s\ *n, pl* **hous·es** \ˈhau̇-zəz *also* -səz\ *often attrib* [ME *hous,* fr. OE *hūs;* akin to OHG *hūs* house] (bef. 12c) **1 :** a building that serves as living quarters for one or a few families **:** HOME **2 a** (1) **:** a shelter or refuge (as a nest or den) of a wild animal (2) **:** a natural covering (as a test or shell) that encloses and protects an animal or a colony of zooids **b :** a building in which something is housed ⟨carriage ~⟩ **3 a :** one of the 12 equal sectors in which the celestial sphere is divided in astrology **b :** a zodiacal sign that is the seat of a planet's greatest influence **c :** the circular area 12 feet in diameter surrounding the tee and within which a curling stone must rest in order to count **4 a :** HOUSEHOLD **b :** a family including ancestors, descendants, and kindred ⟨the ~ of Tudor⟩ **5 a :** a residence for a religious community or for students **b :** the community or students in residence **6 a :** a legislative, deliberative, or consultative assembly; *esp* **:** one constituting a division of a bicameral body **b :** the building or chamber where such an assembly meets **c :** a quorum of such an assembly **7 a :** a place of business or entertainment **b** (1) **:** a business organization ⟨a publishing ~⟩ (2) **:** a gambling establishment **c :** the audience in a theater or concert hall ⟨a full ~ on opening night⟩ — **house·ful** \ˈhau̇s-ˌfu̇l\ *n* — **house·less** \ˈhau̇-sləs, ˈhau̇z-ləs\ *adj* — **house·less·ness** *n*

2house \ˈhau̇z\ *vb* **housed; hous·ing** *vt* (bef. 12c) **1 a :** to provide with living quarters or shelter **b :** to store in a house **2 :** to encase, enclose, or shelter as if by putting in a house **3 :** to serve as shelter for **:** CONTAIN ~ *vi* **:** to take shelter **:** LODGE

house arrest *n* (1936) **:** confinement often under guard to one's house or quarters instead of in prison

1house·boat \ˈhau̇s-ˌbōt\ *n* (1790) **:** a boat fitted for use as a dwelling; *esp* **:** a roomy pleasure craft with a broad beam, a usu. shallow draft, and a large superstructure resembling a house

2houseboat *vi* (ca. 1909) **:** to live or cruise on a houseboat — **house·boat·er** \-ər\ *n*

house·bound \ˈhau̇s-ˌbau̇nd\ *adj* (1878) **:** confined to the house

house·boy \-ˌbȯi\ *n* (ca. 1898) **:** HOUSEMAN

1house·break \-ˌbrāk\ *vi* **-broke** \-ˌbrōk\; **-bro·ken** \-ˌbrō-kən\; **-break·ing** [back-formation fr. *housebreaker* & *housebreaking*] (1820) **:** to commit housebreaking — **house·break·er** *n*

2housebreak *vt* **-broke** \-ˌbrōk\; **-bro·ken** \-ˌbrō-kən\; **-break·ing** [back-formation fr. *housebroken*] (1944) **1 :** to make housebroken **2 a :** to teach acceptable social manners to **b :** TAME, SUBDUE

house·break·ing \ˈhau̇s-ˌbrā-kiŋ\ *n* (1617) **:** an act of breaking open and entering the dwelling house of another with a felonious purpose

house·bro·ken \-ˌbrō-kən\ *adj* (1900) **1 :** trained to excretory habits acceptable in indoor living — used of a household pet **2 :** made tractable or polite

house call *n* (1960) **:** a visit (as by a doctor or a repair person) to a home to provide a requested service

house·carl \-ˌkär(-ə)l\ *n* [OE *hūscarl,* fr. ON *hūskarl,* fr. *hūs* house + *karl* man; akin to OE *ceorl* churl] (bef. 12c) **:** a member of the bodyguard of a Danish or early English king or noble

house cat *n* (1607) **:** CAT 1a

house·clean \ˈhau̇s-ˌklēn\ *vb* [back-formation fr. *housecleaning*] *vi* (1863) **1 :** to clean a house and its furniture **2 :** to get rid of unwanted or undesirable items or people ~ *vt* **1 :** to clean the surfaces and furnishings of **2 :** to improve or reform by ridding of undesirable people or practices — **house·clean·ing** *n*

house·coat \ˈhau̇-ˌskōt\ *n* (1913) **:** a woman's often long-skirted informal garment for wear around the house

house cricket *n* (1774) **:** any of various crickets living in or about dwellings; *esp* **:** a widely distributed American cricket (*Acheta domesticus*)

house detective *n* (1898) **:** one who is employed (as by a hotel) to prevent disorderly or improper conduct of patrons

house·dress \ˈhau̇s-ˌdres\ *n* (1897) **:** a dress with simple lines that is suitable for housework and is made usu. of a washable fabric

house·fa·ther \-ˌfä*th*-ər, -ˌfä*th*-\ *n* (1901) **:** a man in charge of a dormitory, hall, or hostel for young people or children

house·fly \ˈhau̇s-ˌflī\ *n* (15c) **:** a cosmopolitan two-winged fly (*Musca domestica*) that is often about human habitations and acts as a mechanical vector of diseases (as typhoid fever); *also* **:** any of various flies of similar appearance or habitat

house·front \-ˌfrənt\ *n* (1838) **:** the facade of a house

house girl *n* (1835) **:** HOUSEMAID

house·guest \ˈhau̇s-ˌgest\ *n* (1917) **:** GUEST 1a

1house·hold \ˈhau̇s-ˌhōld, ˈhau̇-ˌsōld\ *n* (14c) **:** those who dwell under the same roof and compose a family; *also* **:** a social unit comprised of those living together in the same dwelling

2household *adj* (14c) **1 :** of or relating to a household **:** DOMESTIC **2 :** FAMILIAR, COMMON ⟨a ~ name⟩

household art *n* (1924) **:** one of the techniques (as cooking) used in the maintenance and care of a household

house·hold·er \ˈhau̇s-ˌhōl-dər, ˈhau̇-ˌsōl-\ *n* (14c) **:** one who occupies a house or tenement alone or as the head of a household

household troops *n pl* (1711) **:** troops appointed to attend and guard a sovereign or his residence

house·hus·band \ˈhau̇s-ˌhəz-bənd\ *n* (1970) **:** a husband who does housekeeping usu. while his wife earns the family income

house·keep \ˈhau̇-ˌskēp\ *vi* **-kept** \-ˌskept\; **-keep·ing** [back-formation fr. *housekeeper*] (1842) **:** to perform the routine duties (as cooking and cleaning) of managing a house

house·keep·er \-ˌskē-pər\ *n* (15c) **1 :** a woman employed to keep house **2 :** HOUSEWIFE 1

house·keep·ing \-piŋ\ *n* (1550) **1 :** the management of a house and home affairs **2 :** the care and management of property and the provision of equipment and services (as for an industrial organization) **3 :** the routine tasks that must be done in order for a system to function

¹hou·sel \'haù-zəl\ n [ME, fr. OE hūsel sacrifice, Eucharist; akin to Goth hunsl sacrifice] archaic (bef. 12c) : the Eucharist or the act of administering or receiving it

²housel vt, archaic (bef. 12c) : to administer communion to

house·leek \'haù-ˌslēk\ n (15c) : a pink-flowered thick-leaved European plant (Sempervivum tectorum) of the orpine family that tends to form clusters of rosettes and is often grown in rock gardens; broadly : SEMPERVIVUM

house·lights \'haù-ˌslīts\ n pl (1920) : the lights that illuminate the auditorium of a theater

house·maid \'haù-ˌsmād\ n (ca. 1694) : a female servant employed to do housework

housemaid's knee n [so called fr. its frequent occurrence among servant girls who work a great deal on their knees] (1831) : a swelling over the knee due to an enlargement of the bursa in the front of the patella

house·man \'haù-smən, -ˌsman\ n (1798) : a person who performs general work about a house or hotel

house·mate \'haù-ˌsmāt\ n (1809) : one that lives in the same house with another

house·moth·er \'haù-ˌsməth-ər\ n (1834) : a woman acting as hostess, chaperon, and often housekeeper in a residence for young people

house mouse n (1835) : a common nearly cosmopolitan usu. gray mouse (Mus musculus) that lives and breeds about buildings, is a vector of diseases, and is an important experimental animal

house of assembly (1653) : a legislative body or the lower house of a legislature (as in various British colonies, protectorates, and countries of the Commonwealth)

House of Burgesses (1658) : the colonial representative assembly of Virginia

house of cards (1903) : a structure or situation that is insubstantial, shaky, or in constant danger of collapse

House of Commons (1577) : the lower house of the British and Canadian parliaments

house of correction (1632) : an institution where persons who have committed a minor offense and are considered capable of reformation are confined

house of delegates (1783) : HOUSE 6a; esp : the lower house of the state legislature in Maryland, Virginia, and West Virginia

House of Lords (1818) : the upper house of the British Parliament composed of the lords temporal and spiritual

house of representatives (1716) : the lower house of a legislative body (as the U.S. Congress)

house of studies (1929) : an educational institution serving scholars of a religious order — called also house of study

house organ n (1907) : a periodical distributed by a business concern among its employees, sales personnel, or customers

house·paint·er \'haù-ˌspānt-ər\ n (1689) : one whose business or occupation is painting houses

house party n (1876) : a party lasting over one or more nights at a residence (as a home or fraternity house)

house·per·son \'haù-ˌspərs-ᵊn\ n (1974) : a person who does housekeeping

house physician n (1753) : a physician who is employed by and lives in a hospital

house·plant \'haù-ˌsplant\ n (1871) : a plant grown or kept indoors

house–proud \'haù-ˌspraùd\ adj (1849) : proud of one's house or housekeeping

hous·er \'haù-zər\ n (²house] (1940) : one that promotes or administers housing projects

house–rais·ing \'haù-ˌsrā-ziŋ\ n (1704) : the joint erection of a house or its framework by a gathering of neighbors

house·room \-ˌrüm, -ˌrum\ n (1582) : space for accommodation in or as if in a house ⟨given ~ by a family all too eager to have a celebrity in their midst —Walter Kerr⟩

house rule n (1947) : a rule that applies to a game only among a certain group or in a certain place

house seat n (1948) : a theater seat reserved by the management for special guests

house sitter n (1971) : a person who occupies a dwelling to provide security and maintenance while the tenant is away — house–sit \'haùs-ˌ(s)it\ vi — house–sit·ting \-ˌ(s)it-iŋ\ n

house sparrow n (1674) : ENGLISH SPARROW

house–to–house \ˌhaùs-tə-'haùs\ adj (1859) : DOOR-TO-DOOR 1

house·top \'haù-ˌstäp\ n (1526) : ROOF; esp : the level surface of a flat roof — from the housetops : for all to hear : OPENLY ⟨shouting their grievances from the housetops⟩

house trailer n (1937) : TRAILER 3b

house–train \'haù-ˌstrān\ vt, chiefly Brit (1924) : ²HOUSEBREAK

house·wares \'haù-ˌswa(ə)rz, -ˌswe(ə)rz\ n pl (1921) : furnishings for a house; esp : small articles of household equipment (as cooking utensils or small appliances)

house·warm·ing \'haù-ˌswör-miŋ\ n (1577) : a party to celebrate the taking possession of a house or premises

house·wife \'haù-ˌswīf; esp 2 & in early poetry 'həz-əf or 'həs-\ n, pl house·wives \'haù-ˌswīvz also 'haùz-ˌwīvz; 'həz-əfs, 'həs-, -ˌəvz\ (13c) 1 : a married woman in charge of a household 2 : a small container for small articles (as thread) — house·wife·li·ness \-lē-nəs\ n — house·wife·ly \-lē\ adj — house·wif·ery \-ˌwī-f(ə-)rē; Brit -ˌ(ˌ)wif(-ə)-rē also 'həz-ə-frē\ n — house·wif·ey \'haù-ˌswī-fē\ adj

house·work \'haù-ˌswərk\ n (1841) : the work of housekeeping

¹hous·ing \'haù-ziŋ\ n (14c) 1 a : SHELTER, LODGING b : dwellings provided for people 2 : something that covers or protects: as a : a case or enclosure (as for a mechanical part or an instrument) b : a casing (as an enclosed bearing) in which a shaft revolves c : a support (as a frame) for mechanical parts 3 : a portion of a mast that is beneath the deck or of a bowsprit that is inboard 4 a : the space taken out of a structural member (as a timber) to admit the insertion of part of another b : a niche for a sculpture

²housing n [ME, fr. house housing (fr. MF housse, of Gmc origin) + -ing; akin to OE heolstor cover — more at HOLSTER] (15c) : CAPARISON 1

housing development n (1951) : a group of individual dwellings or apartment houses typically of similar design that are usu. built and sold or leased by one management

housing estate n, Brit (1920) : HOUSING DEVELOPMENT

housing project n (ca. 1937) : a publicly supported and administered housing development planned usu. for low-income families

Hou·yhn·hnm \'hwin-əm, hü-'in-əm\ n [imit.] : a member of a race of horses endowed with reason in Swift's Gulliver's Travels

hove past and past part of HEAVE

hov·el \'həv-əl, 'häv-\ n [ME] (15c) 1 : an open shed or shelter 2 : TABERNACLE 3 : a small, wretched, and often dirty house : HUT

hov·er \'həv-ər, 'häv-\ vi hov·ered; hov·er·ing \-(ə-)riŋ\ [ME hoveren, freq. of hoven to hover] (15c) 1 a : to hang fluttering in the air or on the wing b : to remain suspended over a place or object 2 a : to move to and fro near a place b : to be in a state of uncertainty, irresolution, or suspense — hover n — hov·er·er \-ər-ər\ n

Hov·er·craft \-ər-ˌkraft\ trademark — used for a ground-effect machine

¹how \(ˌ)haù\ adv [ME, fr. OE hū; akin to OHG hwuo how, OE hwā who — more at WHO] (bef. 12c) 1 a : in what manner or way b : with what meaning : to what effect c : by what name or title ⟨~ art thou called —Shak.⟩ d : for what reason : WHY 2 : to what degree or extent 3 : in what state or condition ⟨~ are you⟩ 4 : at what price ⟨~ a score of ewes now —Shak.⟩ — how about : what do you say to or think of ⟨how about it, are you going?⟩ — how come : how does it happen that : WHY

²how conj (bef. 12c) 1 a : the way or manner in which ⟨remember ~ they fought⟩; also : the state or condition in which b : THAT ⟨told them ~ he had a situation —Charles Dickens⟩ 2 : HOWEVER, AS ⟨a reader can shift his attention ~ he likes —William Empson⟩

³how \'haù\ n (1533) 1 : a question about manner or method 2 : MANNER, METHOD

¹how·be·it \haù-'bē-ət\ conj (14c) : ALTHOUGH

²howbeit adv (15c) : NEVERTHELESS

how·dah \'haùd-ə\ n [Hindi hauda] (1774) : a seat or covered pavilion on the back of an elephant or camel

how·dy \'haùd-ē\ interj [alter. of how do ye] (1712) — used to express greeting — howdy vb

howe \'haù, 'hò\ n [ME (northern) how, holl, fr. OE hol, fr. hol, adj., hollow — more at HOLE] Scot (bef. 12c) : HOLLOW, VALLEY

¹how·ev·er \haù-'ev-ər\ conj (14c) 1 : in whatever manner or way ⟨can go ~ he likes⟩ 2 archaic : ALTHOUGH

²however adv (14c) 1 a : to whatever degree or extent ⟨has done this for ~ many thousands of years —Emma Hawkridge⟩ b : in whatever manner or way ⟨will help ~ I can⟩ ⟨shall serve you, sir, truly, ~ else —Shak.⟩ 2 : in spite of that : on the other hand : BUT ⟨still seems possible, ~, that conditions will improve⟩ ⟨would like to go; ~, I think I'd better not⟩ 3 : how in the world ⟨~ did you manage to do it⟩

howff or howf \'haùf, 'hòf\ n [D hof enclosure; akin to OE hof enclosure, hȳf hive] Scot (1565) : HAUNT, RESORT

how·it·zer \'haù-ət-sər\ n [D houwitser, deriv. of Czech houfnice ballista] (1695) : a short cannon used to fire projectiles at medium muzzle velocities and with relatively high trajectories

howl \'haù(ə)l\ vb [ME houlen; akin to MHG hiulen to howl, Gk kōkyein to shriek] vi (14c) 1 : to emit a loud sustained doleful sound characteristic of members of the dog family 2 : to cry loudly and without restraint under strong impulse (as pain or grief) 3 : to go on a spree or rampage ~ vt 1 : to utter with unrestrained outcry 2 : to affect, effect, or drive by adverse outcry — used esp. with down ⟨~ed down the speaker⟩ — howl n

howl·er \'haù-lər\ n (1844) 1 : one that howls 2 : a humorous and ridiculous blunder

howler monkey n (1932) : any of a genus (Alouatta) of So. and Central American monkeys that have a long prehensile tail and enlargement of the hyoid and laryngeal apparatus enabling them to make loud howling noises — called also howler

howler monkey

howl·ing \'haù-liŋ\ adj (1599) 1 : producing or marked by howling ⟨a ~ storm⟩ 2 : DESOLATE, WILD ⟨a ~ wilderness⟩ 3 : very great : PRONOUNCED ⟨a ~ success⟩ — howl·ing·ly adv

how·so·ev·er \ˌhaù-sə-'wev-ər\ adv (14c) 1 : in whatever manner 2 : to whatever degree or extent

how–to \'haù-ˌtü\ adj (1926) : giving practical instruction and advice (as on a craft) ⟨~ books on all sorts of hobbies —Harry Milt⟩

¹hoy \'hòi\ interj [ME] (14c) — used in attracting attention or in driving animals

²hoy n [ME, fr. MD hoei] (15c) 1 : a small usu. sloop-rigged coasting ship 2 : a heavy barge for bulky cargo

hoy·den \'hòid-ᵊn\ n [perh. fr. obs D heiden country lout, fr. MD, heathen; akin to OE hǣthen heathen] (1676) : a girl or woman of saucy, boisterous, or carefree behavior — hoy·den·ish \-ish\ adj

hoyle \'hòi(ə)l\ n, often cap [Edmond Hoyle †1769 Eng. writer on games] (1906) : an encyclopedia of the rules of indoor games and esp. card games

Hsia \shē-'ä\ n [Chin (Pek) hsia⁴] (ca. 1909) : the legendary first dynasty of Chinese history traditionally dated from about 2200-1766 B.C.

hua·ra·che \wə-'räch-ē, hə-\ n [MexSp] (1887) : a low-heeled sandal having an upper made of interwoven leather thongs

hub \'həb\ n [prob. alter. of ²hob] (1649) 1 : the central part of a wheel, propeller, or fan 2 : a center of activity : FOCAL POINT 3 : a steel punch from which a working die for a coin or medal is made

hub·ble–bub·ble \'həb-əl-ˌbəb-əl\ n [redupl. of bubble] (1634) 1 : WATER PIPE 2 : a flurry of sound or activity : COMMOTION

hub·bub \'həb-ˌəb\ n [prob. of IrGael origin; akin to ScGael ub ub, interj. of contempt] (1555) 1 : NOISE, UPROAR 2 : CONFUSION, TURMOIL

hub·by \'həb-ē\ n, pl hubbies [by alter.] (1688) : HUSBAND

hub·cap \ˈhəb-ˌkap\ *n* (1903) **:** a removable metal cap over the end of an axle; *esp* **:** one used on the wheel of a motor vehicle
hu·bris \ˈhyü-brəs\ *n* [Gk *hybris* — more at OUT] (1884) **:** exaggerated pride or self-confidence often resulting in retribution — **hu·bris·tic** \hyü-ˈbris-tik\ *adj*
huck \ˈhək\ *n* (1851) **:** HUCKABACK
huck·a·back \ˈhək-ə-ˌbak\ *n* [origin unknown] (1690) **:** an absorbent durable fabric of cotton, linen, or both used chiefly for towels
huck·le·ber·ry \ˈhək-əl-ˌber-ē\ *n* [perh. alter. of *hurtleberry* (huckleberry)] (1670) **1 :** any of a genus (*Gaylussacia*) of American shrubs of the heath family; *also* **:** the edible dark blue to black usu. acid berry (esp. of *G. baccata*) with 10 bony nutlets **2 :** BLUEBERRY
1huck·ster \ˈhək-stər\ *n* [ME *hukster,* fr. MD *hokester,* fr. *hoeken* to peddle; akin to MLG *hōken* to peddle — more at HAWKER] (13c) **1 :** HAWKER, PEDDLER **2 :** one who produces advertising material for commercial clients esp. for radio or television — **huck·ster·ism** \-stə-ˌriz-əm\ *n*
2huckster *vb* **huck·stered; huck·ster·ing** \-st(ə-)riŋ\ *vi* (1592) **:** HAGGLE ~ *vt* **1 :** to deal in or bargain over **2 :** to promote by showmanship
1hud·dle \ˈhəd-ᵊl\ *vb* **hud·dled; hud·dling** \ˈhəd-liŋ, -ᵊl-iŋ\ [prob. fr. or akin to ME *hoderen* to huddle] *vt* (1579) **1** *Brit* **:** to arrange carelessly or hurriedly **2 a :** to crowd together ⟨*huddled* masses of people⟩ **b :** to draw (oneself) together **:** CROUCH **3** *archaic* **:** to herd into or out of a place in a disorderly mass **4 :** to wrap closely in (as clothes) ~ *vi* **1 a :** to gather in a close-packed group **b :** to curl up **:** CROUCH **2 a :** to hold a consultation **b :** to gather in a huddle in football — **hud·dler** \ˈhəd-lər, -ᵊl-ər\ *n*
2huddle *n* (1586) **1 :** a close-packed group **:** BUNCH ⟨~*s* of cattle⟩ ⟨a ~ of cottages⟩ **2 a :** MEETING, CONFERENCE ⟨secret ~*s* were held by five leading Republicans —*Newsweek*⟩ **b :** a brief gathering of football players away from the line of scrimmage to receive instructions (as from the quarterback) for the next down
Hu·di·bras·tic \ˌhyüd-ə-ˈbras-tik\ *adj* [irreg. fr. *Hudibras,* satirical poem by Samuel Butler †1680] (1712) **1 :** written in humorous octosyllabic couplets **2 :** MOCK-HEROIC — **Hudibrastic** *n*
hue \ˈhyü\ *n* [ME *hewe,* fr. OE *hīw;* akin to OE *hār* hoary — more at HOAR] (bef. 12c) **1 :** COMPLEXION, ASPECT ⟨political parties of every ~ —Louis Wasserman⟩ **2 a :** COLOR **b :** gradation of color **c :** the attribute of colors that permits them to be classed as red, yellow, green, blue, or an intermediate between any contiguous pair of these colors — compare BRIGHTNESS, LIGHTNESS, SATURATION
hue and cry *n* [*hue* (outcry)] (15c) **1 a :** a loud outcry formerly used in the pursuit of one who is suspected of a crime **b :** the pursuit of a suspect or a written proclamation for the capture of a suspect **2 :** a clamor of alarm or protest **3 :** HUBBUB
hued \ˈhyüd\ *adj* (bef. 12c) **:** COLORED — usu. used in combination ⟨green-*hued*⟩
1huff \ˈhəf\ *vb* [imit.] *vi* (1583) **1 :** to emit puffs (as of breath or steam) **2 a :** to make empty threats **:** BLUSTER ⟨management ~*ed* about the chances of a lockout⟩ **b :** to react or behave indignantly ⟨refused to agree and ~*ed* off in anger⟩ ~ *vt* **1 :** to puff up **:** INFLATE ⟨their buying ~*ed* low-priced motor shares —*Time*⟩ **2** *archaic* **:** to treat with contempt **:** BULLY **3 :** to make angry
2huff *n* (1599) **:** a usu. peevish and transitory spell of anger or resentment *syn* see OFFENSE
huff·ish \ˈhəf-ish\ *adj* (1755) **:** ARROGANT, SULKY
huffy \ˈhəf-ē\ *adj* **huff·i·er; -est** (1677) **1 :** HAUGHTY, ARROGANT **2 a :** roused to indignation **:** IRRITATED **b :** easily offended **:** TOUCHY — **huff·i·ly** \ˈhəf-ə-lē\ *adv* — **huff·i·ness** \-ē-nəs\ *n*
hug \ˈhəg\ *vt* **hugged; hug·ging** [perh. of Scand origin; akin to ON *hugga* to soothe] (1567) **1 :** to press tightly esp. in the arms **2 a :** CONGRATULATE **b :** to hold fast **:** CHERISH ⟨*hugged* his miseries like a sulky child —John Buchan⟩ **3 :** to stay close to ⟨the road ~*s* the river⟩ — **hug** *n* — **hug·ga·ble** \ˈhəg-ə-bəl\ *adj*
huge \ˈhyüj, ˈyüj\ *adj* **hug·er; hug·est** [ME, fr. OF *ahuge*] (12c) **:** very large or extensive: as **a :** of great size or area **b :** great in scale or degree ⟨~ spending⟩ **c :** great in scope or character ⟨a man of ~ talent⟩ *syn* see ENORMOUS — **huge·ly** *adv* — **huge·ness** *n*
huge·ous \-əs\ *adj* (1529) **:** HUGE — **huge·ous·ly** *adv*
1hug·ger–mug·ger \ˈhəg-ər-ˌməg-ər\ *n* [origin unknown] (1529) **1 :** SECRECY **2 :** CONFUSION, MUDDLE
2hugger–mugger *adj* (1692) **1 :** SECRET **2 :** of a confused or disorderly nature **:** JUMBLED — **hugger–mugger** *adv*
3hugger–mugger *vb* **-mug·gered; -mug·ger·ing** \-ˌməg-(ə-)riŋ\ *vt* (1803) **:** to keep secret **:** hush up ~ *vi* **:** to act or confer stealthily
hug–me–tight \ˈhəg-mē-ˌtīt\ *n* (1860) **:** a woman's short usu. knitted sleeveless close-fitting jacket
Hu·gue·not \ˈhyü-gə-ˌnät\ *n* [MF, French Protestant, fr. MF dial. *huguenot,* adherent of a Swiss political movement, alter. (influenced by Besançon *Hugues* †1532 Swiss political leader) of *eidgnot* confederate, fr. G dial. *eidgenoss*] (1565) **:** a member of the French Reformed communion esp. of the 16th and 17th centuries — **Hu·gue·not·ic** \ˌhyü-gə-ˈnät-ik\ *adj* — **Hu·gue·not·ism** \ˈhyü-gə-ˌnät-ˌiz-əm\ *n*
huh *a short, or a strong* h-*sound followed with varying intonation by an* m-*sound or by* ᵊⁿ; *often read as* ˈhə\ *interj* [imit. of a grunt] (1732) — used typically to express surprise, disbelief, disgust, or interrogation
hu·la \ˈhü-lə\ *also* **hu·la–hu·la** \ˌhü-lə-ˈhü-lə\ *n* [Hawaiian] (1825) **1 :** a sinuous Polynesian dance characterized by rhythmic movement of the hips and mimetic gestures with the hands and often accompanied by chants and rhythmic drumming **2 :** music to which a hula is performed
1hulk \ˈhəlk\ *n* [ME *hulke,* fr. OE *hulc,* prob. fr. ML *holcas,* fr. Gk *holkas,* fr. *helkein* to pull — more at SULCUS] (bef. 12c) **1 a :** a heavy clumsy ship **b :** the body of an old ship unfit for service **c :** an abandoned wreck or shell **d :** a ship used as a prison — usu. used in pl. ⟨every prisoner sent to the ~*s* —Kenneth Roberts⟩ **2 :** one that is bulky or unwieldy ⟨a big ~ of a man⟩
2hulk *vi* (1793) **1** *dial Eng* **:** to move ponderously **2 :** to appear impressively large or massive **:** LOOM
hulk·ing \ˈhəl-kiŋ\ *adj* (1698) **:** PONDEROUS, MASSIVE
1hull \ˈhəl\ *n* [ME, fr. OE *hulu;* akin to OHG *hala* hull, OE *helan* to conceal — more at HELL] (bef. 12c) **1 a :** the outer covering of a fruit or seed **b :** the persistent calyx or involucre that subtends some fruits **2 a :** the frame or body of a ship exclusive of masts, yards, sails, and rigging **b (1) :** the portion of a flying boat which furnishes buoyancy when in contact with the water and to which the main supporting surfaces and other parts are attached **(2) :** the main structure of a rigid airship **3 :** COVERING, CASING — **hull–less** \ˈhəl-ləs\ *adj*
2hull *vt* (14c) **:** to remove the hulls of **:** SHUCK — **hull·er** *n*
hul·la·ba·loo \ˈhəl-ə-bə-ˌlü\ *n, pl* **-loos** [perh. irreg. fr. *hallo* + Sc *balloo,* interj. used to hush children] (1762) **:** a confused noise **:** UPROAR
hull down *adv or adj, of a ship* (1775) **:** at such a distance that only the superstructure is visible
hulled corn *n* (1788) **:** whole grain corn from which the hulls have been removed by soaking or boiling in lye water
hul·lo \(ˌ)hə-ˈlō\ *chiefly Brit var of* HELLO
hum \ˈhəm\ *vb* **hummed; hum·ming** [ME *hummen;* akin to MHG *hummen* to hum, MD *hommel* bumblebee] *vi* (15c) **1 a :** to utter a sound like that of the speech sound \m\ prolonged **b :** to make the natural noise of an insect in motion or a similar sound **:** DRONE **c :** to give forth a low continuous blend of sound **2 :** to be busily active ~ *vt* **1 :** to sing with the lips closed and without articulation **2 :** to affect or express by humming ⟨*hummed* me to sleep⟩ ⟨*hummed* his displeasure⟩ — **hum** *n* — **hum·ma·ble** \ˈhəm-ə-bəl\ *adj*
1hu·man \ˈhyü-mən, ˈyü-\ *adj* [ME *humain,* fr. MF, fr. L *humanus;* akin to L *homo* man — more at HOMAGE] (14c) **1 :** of, relating to, or characteristic of man **2 :** consisting of men **3 a :** having human form or attributes **b :** susceptible to or representative of the sympathies and frailties of man's nature ⟨such an inconsistency is very ~ —P. E. More⟩ — **hu·man·ness** \-mən-nəs\ *n*
2human *n* (1533) **:** a human being — **hu·man·like** \-mən-ˌlīk\ *adj*
hu·mane \hyü-ˈmān, yü-\ *adj* [ME *humain*] (1500) **1 :** marked by compassion, sympathy, or consideration for other human beings or animals **2 :** characterized by or tending to broad humanistic culture **:** HUMANISTIC ⟨~ studies⟩ — **hu·mane·ly** *adv* — **hu·mane·ness** \-ˈmān-nəs\ *n*
human ecology *n* (ca. 1907) **1 :** the ecology of man and of human communities and populations esp. as concerned with preservation of environmental quality (as of air or water) through proper application of conservation and civil engineering practices **2 :** a branch of sociology dealing esp. with the spatial and temporal interrelationships between men and their economic, social, and political organization
human engineering *n* (1920) **1 :** management of human beings and affairs esp. in industry **2 :** ERGONOMICS
human immunodeficiency virus *n* (1986) **:** AIDS VIRUS
hu·man·ism \ˈhyü-mə-ˌniz-əm, ˈyü-\ *n* (1832) **1 a :** devotion to the humanities **:** literary culture **b :** the revival of classical letters, individualistic and critical spirit, and emphasis on secular concerns characteristic of the Renaissance **2 :** HUMANITARIANISM **3 :** a doctrine, attitude, or way of life centered on human interests or values; *esp* **:** a philosophy that usu. rejects supernaturalism and stresses an individual's dignity and worth and capacity for self-realization through reason — **hu·man·ist** \-nəst\ *n or adj* — **hu·man·is·tic** \ˌhyü-mə-ˈnis-tik, ˌyü-\ *adj* — **hu·man·is·ti·cal·ly** \-ti-k(ə-)lē\ *adv*
hu·man·i·tar·i·an \hyü-ˌman-ə-ˈter-ē-ən, yü-\ *n* (1831) **:** a person promoting human welfare and social reform **:** PHILANTHROPIST — **humanitarian** *adj* — **hu·man·i·tar·i·an·ism** \-ē-ə-ˌniz-əm\ *n*
hu·man·i·ty \hyü-ˈman-ət-ē, yü-\ *n, pl* **-ties** (14c) **1 :** the quality or state of being humane **2 a :** the quality or state of being human **b** *pl* **:** human attributes or qualities ⟨his work has the ripeness of the 18th century, and its rough *humanities* —Pamela H. Johnson⟩ **3** *pl* **:** the branches of learning (as philosophy, languages) that investigate human constructs and concerns as opposed to natural processes (as physics or chemistry) **4 :** MANKIND
hu·man·ize \ˈhyü-mə-ˌnīz, ˈyü-\ *vt* **-ized; -iz·ing** (1603) **1 a :** to represent as human **:** attribute human qualities to **b :** to adapt to human nature or use **2 :** to make humane ⟨tried to ~ and regulate war —Vera M. Dean⟩ — **hu·man·iza·tion** \ˌhyü-mə-nə-ˈzā-shən, ˌyü-\ *n* — **hu·man·iz·er** *n*
hu·man·kind \ˈhyü-mən-ˌkīnd, ˈyü-\ *n sing but sing or pl in constr* (1645) **:** the human race
hu·man·ly \ˈhyü-mən-lē, ˈyü-\ *adv* (1581) **1 a :** from the viewpoint of human beings ⟨~ speaking, the process works . . . like this —Elizabeth Janeway⟩ **b :** within the range of human capacity ⟨a ~ impossible task⟩ **2 a :** with regard to or in keeping with human proneness to error or weakness ⟨had the temerity to be ~ inefficient a few times —Leonard Koppett⟩ **b :** with regard to human needs and emotions ⟨provide ~ for those who are not needed in the economy —E. F. Bacon⟩
human nature *n* (1745) **:** the nature of human beings: as **a :** the complex of behavioral patterns, attitudes, and ideas which human beings acquire socially **b :** the complex of fundamental dispositions and traits of human beings
hu·man·oid \ˈhyü-mə-ˌnȯid, ˈyü-\ *adj* (1918) **:** having human form or characteristics ⟨~ dentition⟩ ⟨~ robots⟩ — **humanoid** *n*
human relations *n pl but usu sing in constr* (1916) **1 :** a study of human problems arising from organizational and interpersonal relations (as in industry) **2 :** a course, study, or program designed to develop better interpersonal and intergroup adjustments
hu·mate \ˈhyü-ˌmāt, ˈyü-\ *n* (1844) **:** a salt or ester of a humic acid
1hum·ble \ˈhəm-bəl, ˈəm-\ *adj* **hum·bler** \-b(ə-)lər\; **hum·blest** \-b(ə-)ləst\ [ME, fr. OF, fr. L *humilis* low, humble, fr. *humus* earth; akin to Gk *chthōn* earth, *chamai* on the ground] (13c) **1 :** not proud or haughty **:** not arrogant or assertive **2 :** reflecting, expressing, or offered in a spirit of deference or submission ⟨a ~ apology⟩ **3 :** ranking low in a hierarchy or scale **:** INSIGNIFICANT, UNPRETENTIOUS — **hum·ble·ness** \-bəl-nəs\ *n* — **hum·bly** \-blē\ *adv*
2humble *vt* **hum·bled; hum·bling** \-b(ə-)liŋ\ (14c) **1 :** to make humble in spirit or manner **2 :** to destroy the power, independence, or prestige of — **hum·bler** \-b(ə-)lər\ *n*
hum·ble–bee \ˈhəm-bəl-ˌbē\ *n* [ME *humbylbee,* fr. *humbyl-* (akin to MD *hommel* bumblebee) + *bee* — more at HUM] (15c) **:** BUMBLEBEE
humble pie *n* (1830) **:** submission, apology, or retraction usu. made under pressure — often used in the phrase *eat humble pie*
1hum·bug \ˈhəm-ˌbəg\ *n* [origin unknown] (1751) **1 a :** something designed to deceive and mislead **b :** a person who passes himself off as something that he is not **2 :** an attitude or spirit of pretense and deception **3 :** NONSENSE, DRIVEL *syn* see IMPOSTURE — **hum·bug·gery** \-ˌbəg-(ə-)rē\ *n*

2humbug *vb* **hum·bugged; hum·bug·ging** *vt* (1751) : DECEIVE, HOAX ~ *vi* : to engage in a hoax or deception
hum·ding·er \'həm-'diŋ-ər\ *n* [prob. alter. of *hummer* (humdinger)] (1904) : a striking or extraordinary person or thing
hum·drum \'həm-,drəm\ *adj* [irreg. redupl. of *hum*] (1553) : MONOTONOUS, DULL — **humdrum** *n*
hu·mec·tant \hyü-'mek-tənt\ *n* [L *humectant-, humectans,* prp. of *humectare* to moisten, fr. *humectus* moist, fr. *humēre* to be moist — more at HUMOR] (1771) : a substance that promotes retention of moisture — **humectant** *adj*
hu·mer·al \'hyüm-(ə-)rəl\ *adj* (1615) **1** : of, relating to, or situated in the region of the humerus or shoulder **2** : of, relating to, or being a body part analogous to the humerus or shoulder — **humeral** *n*
humeral veil *n* (1853) : an oblong vestment worn around the shoulders and over the hands by a priest holding a sacred vessel
hu·mer·us \'hyüm-(ə-)rəs\ *n, pl* **hu·meri** \'hyü-mə-,rī, -,rē\ [NL, fr. L *humerus, umerus* upper arm, shoulder; akin to Goth *ams* shoulder, Gk *ōmos*] (15c) : the long bone of the upper arm or forelimb extending from the shoulder to the elbow
hu·mic \'hyü-mik, 'yü-\ *adj* (1844) : of, relating to, or derived at least in part from humus
humic acid *n* (1844) : any of various organic acids obtained from humus
hu·mid \'hyü-məd, 'yü-\ *adj* [F or L; F *humide,* fr. L *humidus,* fr. *humēre*] (15c) : containing or characterized by perceptible moisture esp. to the point of being oppressive ⟨a ~ climate⟩ ***syn*** see WET — **hu·mid·ly** *adv*
hu·mid·i·fi·er \hyü-'mid-ə-,fī(-ə)r, yü-\ *n* (1884) : a device for supplying or maintaining humidity
hu·mid·i·fy \-,fī\ *vt* **-fied; -fy·ing** (1885) : to make humid — **hu·mid·i·fi·ca·tion** \-,mid-ə-fə-'kā-shən\ *n*
hu·mid·i·stat \hyü-'mid-ə-,stat, yü-\ *n* (1904) : an instrument for regulating or maintaining the degree of humidity
hu·mid·i·ty \hyü-'mid-ət-ē, yü-\ *n, pl* **-ties** (15c) : a moderate degree of wetness esp. of the atmosphere : DAMPNESS — compare RELATIVE HUMIDITY
hu·mi·dor \'hyü-mə-,dȯ(ə)r, 'yü-\ *n* [*humid* + *-or* (as in *cuspidor*)] (1903) : a case usu. for storing cigars in which the air is kept properly humidified
hu·mi·fi·ca·tion \,hyü-mə-fə-'kā-shən, ,yü-\ *n* (1897) : formation of or conversion into humus
hu·mi·fied \'hyü-mə-,fīd, 'yü-\ *adj* (1906) : converted into humus
hu·mil·i·ate \hyü-'mil-ē-,āt, yü-\ *vt* **-at·ed; -at·ing** [LL *humiliatus,* pp. of *humiliare,* fr. L *humilis* low — more at HUMBLE] (1533) : to reduce to a lower position in one's own eyes or others' eyes : MORTIFY ***syn*** see ABASE — **hu·mil·i·a·tion** \-,mil-ē-'ā-shən\ *n*
hu·mil·i·at·ing \hyü-'mil-ē-,āt-iŋ, yü-\ *adj* (1757) : extremely destructive to one's self-respect or dignity : HUMBLING — **hu·mil·i·at·ing·ly** \-iŋ-lē\ *adv*
hu·mil·i·ty \hyü-'mil-ət-ē, yü-\ *n* (14c) : the quality or state of being humble
hum·mer \'həm-ər\ *n* (1605) **1** : one that hums **2** : HUMMINGBIRD
hum·ming·bird \'həm-iŋ-,bərd\ *n* (1637) : any of numerous tiny brightly colored nonpasserine birds (family Trochilidae) related to the swifts and like them having narrow wings with long primaries, a slender bill, and a very extensile tongue
hum·mock \'həm-ək\ *n* [alter. of 2*hammock*] (1555) **1** : a rounded knoll or hillock **2** : a ridge of ice **3** : 2HAMMOCK 2 — **hummock** *vb* — **hum·mocky** \-ə-kē\ *adj*
hu·mon·gous \hyü-'məŋ-gəs, yü-, -'mäŋ-\ *adj* [perh. alter. of *huge* + *monstrous*] *slang* (ca. 1967) : extremely large : HUGE
1hu·mor \'(h)yü-mər\ *n* [ME *humour,* fr. MF *humeur,* fr. ML & L; ML *humor,* fr. L, moisture; akin to ON *vǫkr* damp, L *humēre* to be moist, Gk *hygros* wet] (14c) **1 a** : a normal functioning bodily semifluid or fluid (as the blood or lymph) **b** : a secretion (as a hormone) that is an excitant of activity **2 a** *in medieval physiology* : a fluid or juice of an animal or plant; *specif* : one of the four fluids entering into the constitution of the body and determining by their relative proportions a person's health and temperament **b** : characteristic or habitual disposition or bent : TEMPERAMENT ⟨a man of cheerful ~⟩ **c** : an often temporary state of mind imposed esp. by circumstances ⟨was in no ~ to listen to further argument⟩ **d** : a sudden, unpredictable, or unreasoning inclination : WHIM ⟨beset by the uncertain ~*s* of nature⟩ **3 a** : that quality which appeals to a sense of the ludicrous or absurdly incongruous **b** : the mental faculty of discovering, expressing, or appreciating the ludicrous or absurdly incongruous **c** : something that is or is designed to be comical or amusing ***syn*** see WIT — **out of humor** : out of sorts
2humor *vt* **hu·mored; hu·mor·ing** \'(h)yüm-(ə-)riŋ\ (1588) **1** : to soothe or content by indulgence **2** : to adapt oneself to ***syn*** see INDULGE
hu·mor·al \'(h)yüm-(ə-)rəl\ *adj* (15c) : of, relating to, proceeding from, or involving a bodily humor (as a hormone)
hu·mor·esque \,(h)yü-mə-'resk\ *n* [G *humoreske,* fr. *humor,* fr. ML] (1889) : a musical composition typically whimsical or fanciful in character
hu·mor·ist \'(h)yüm-(ə-)rəst\ *n* (1589) **1** *archaic* : a person subject to whims **2** : a person specializing in or noted for humor
hu·mor·is·tic \,(h)yü-mə-'ris-tik\ *adj* (1818) : HUMOROUS
hu·mor·less \'(h)yü-mər-ləs\ *adj* (ca. 1847) **1** : lacking a sense of humor **2** : lacking humorous characteristics — **hu·mor·less·ness** *n*
hu·mor·ous \'(h)yüm-(ə-)rəs\ *adj* (1592) **1** *obs* : HUMID **2 a** : full of or characterized by humor : JOCULAR **b** : indicating or expressive of a sense of humor ***syn*** see WITTY — **hu·mor·ous·ly** *adv* — **hu·mor·ous·ness** *n*
hu·mour *chiefly Brit var of* HUMOR
1hump \'həmp\ *n* [akin to MLG *hump* bump, L *incumbere* to lie down, Gk *kymbē* bowl, OE *hype* hip] (1709) **1** : a rounded protuberance: as **a** : HUMPBACK 1 **b** : a fleshy protuberance on the back of an animal (as a camel, bison, or whale) **c** (1) : MOUND, HUMMOCK (2) : MOUNTAIN, RANGE ⟨the Himalayan ~⟩ **2** *Brit* : a fit of depression or sulking **3** : a difficult, trying, or critical phase — often used in the phrase *over the hump*
2hump *vt* (1835) **1** : to exert (oneself) vigorously **2** : to make humpbacked : HUNCH **3** *chiefly Brit* : to put or carry on the back; *also* : TRANSPORT **4** : to copulate with — usu. considered vulgar ~ *vi* **1** : to exert oneself : HUSTLE **2** : to move swiftly : RACE
hump·back \-,bak, *for 1 also* -'bak\ *n* (1697) **1** : a humped or crooked back; *also* : KYPHOSIS **2** : HUNCHBACK 2 **3** : HUMPBACK WHALE
hump·backed \-'bakt\ *adj* (1681) **1** : having a humped back **2** : convexly curved ⟨a ~ bridge⟩
humpback whale *n* (1725) : a large whalebone whale (*Megaptera novaeangliae*) related to the rorquals but having very long flippers

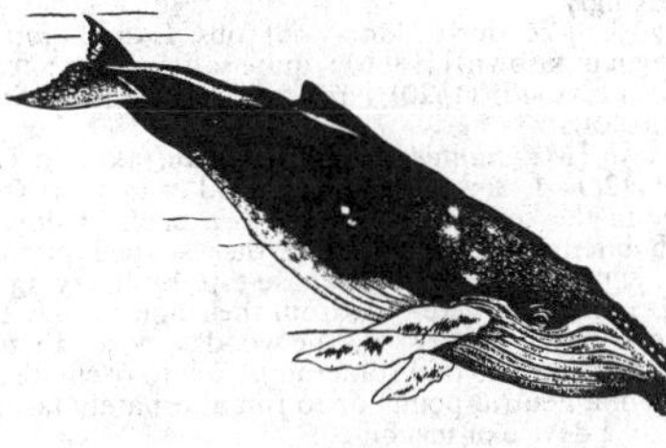
humpback whale

humped \'həm(p)t\ *adj* (1713) : having a hump; *esp* : HUMPBACKED
1humph \'həm(p)f\ *vi* (1814) : to utter a humph ~ *vt* : to utter (as a remark) in a tone suggestive of a humph
2humph *a snort, or* h *followed by* m *or* ᵊn; *often read as* 'həm(p)f\ *interj* [imit. of a grunt] (1815) — used to express doubt or contempt
hump·ty–dump·ty \,həm(p)-tē-'dəm(p)-tē\ *n, pl* **-dumpties** *often cap H&D* [*Humpty-Dumpty,* egg-shaped nursery-rhyme character who fell from a wall and broke into bits] (1883) : something that once damaged can never be repaired or made operative again
humpy \'həm-pē\ *adj* **hump·i·er; -est** (1708) **1** : full of humps **2** : covered with humps
hu·mus \'hyü-məs, 'yü-\ *n* [NL, fr. L, earth — more at HUMBLE] (1796) : a brown or black complex variable material resulting from partial decomposition of plant or animal matter and forming the organic portion of soil
Hun \'hən\ *n* [ME, fr. OE *Hunas,* pl., fr. LL *Hunni,* pl.] (bef. 12c) **1** : a member of a nomadic Mongolian people gaining control of a large part of central and eastern Europe under Attila about A.D. 450 **2 a** *often not cap* : a person who is wantonly destructive : VANDAL **b** : GERMAN; *esp* : a German soldier — usu. used disparagingly
1hunch \'hənch\ *vb* [origin unknown] *vi* (1598) **1** : to thrust oneself forward **2 a** : to assume a bent or crooked posture **b** : to draw oneself into a ball : curl up **c** : HUDDLE, SQUAT ~ *vt* **1** : JOSTLE, SHOVE **2** : to thrust into a hump
2hunch *n* (1630) **1** : an act or instance of hunching : PUSH **2 a** : HUMP **b** : a thick piece : LUMP **3** : a strong intuitive feeling concerning a future event or result
hunch·back \'hənch-,bak\ *n* (1718) **1** : HUMPBACK 1 **2** : a person with a humpback — **hunch·backed** \-'bakt\ *adj*
hun·dred \'hən-drəd, -dərd\ *n, pl* **hundreds** *or* **hundred** [ME, fr. OE, fr. *hund* hundred + *-red* (akin to Goth *rathjo* account, advice); akin to L *centum,* Gk *hekaton,* OE *tien* — more at TEN, REASON] (bef. 12c) **1** — see NUMBER table **2 hundreds** *pl* : the numbers 100 to 999 **3** : a 100-dollar bill **4** : a subdivision of some English and American counties — **hundred** *adj* — **hun·dred·fold** \-,fōld\ *adj or adv* — **hun·dredth** \-drədth, -drətth\ *adj or n*
hun·dred–per·cent·er \,hən-drəd-pər-'sent-ər, -dərd-\ *n* [*hundred-percent (American)*] (1921) : a thoroughgoing nationalist — **hun·dred–per·cent·ism** \-'sent-,iz-əm\ *n*
hundreds digit *n* (1955) : the numeral (as 4 in 456) occupying the hundreds place in a number expressed in the Arabic system of notation
hundreds place *n* (1937) : the place three to the left of the decimal point in a number expressed in the Arabic system of notation
hun·dred·weight \'hən-drə-,dwāt, -dər-,dwāt\ *n, pl* **hundredweight** *or* **hundredweights** (1577) **1** : a unit of weight equal to 100 pounds — called also *short hundredweight;* see WEIGHT table **2** *Brit* : a unit of weight equal to 112 pounds — called also *long hundredweight*
hung *past and past part of* HANG
Hun·gar·i·an \,həŋ-'ger-ē-ən, -'gar-\ *n* (1553) **1 a** : a native or inhabitant of Hungary : MAGYAR **b** : a person of Hungarian descent **2** : MAGYAR 2 — **Hungarian** *adj*
1hun·ger \'həŋ-gər\ *n* [ME, fr. OE *hungor;* akin to OHG *hungar* hunger, Skt *kāṅkṣati* he desires] (bef. 12c) **1 a** : a craving or urgent need for food or a specific nutrient **b** : an uneasy sensation occasioned by the lack of food **c** : a weakened condition brought about by prolonged lack of food **2** : a strong desire : CRAVING
2hunger *vb* **hun·gered; hun·ger·ing** \-g(ə-)riŋ\ *vi* (bef. 12c) **1** : to feel or suffer hunger **2** : to have an eager desire ~ *vt* : to make hungry ***syn*** see LONG
hunger strike *n* (1889) : refusal (as by a prisoner) to eat enough to sustain life
hung jury *n* (ca. 1903) : a jury that fails to reach a verdict
hung over *adj* (1941) : suffering from a hangover
hun·gry \'həŋ-grē\ *adj* **hun·gri·er; -est** [ME, fr. OE *hungrig;* akin to OE *hungor*] (bef. 12c) **1 a** : feeling hunger **b** : characterized by or characteristic of hunger or appetite **2** : EAGER, AVID **3** : not rich or fertile : BARREN — **hun·gri·ly** \-grə-lē\ *adv* — **hun·gri·ness** \-grē-nəs\ *n*
hung up *adj* (1948) **1** : delayed or detained for a time **2** : anxiously nervous **3** : being much involved with: as **a** : being infatuated **b** : ENTHUSIASTIC **c** : PREOCCUPIED

\ə\ abut \ᵊ\ kitten, F table \ər\ further \a\ ash \ā\ ace \ä\ cot, cart \au̇\ out \ch\ chin \e\ bet \ē\ easy \g\ go \i\ hit \ī\ ice \j\ job \ŋ\ sing \ō\ go \ȯ\ law \ȯi\ boy \th\ thin \t͟h\ the \ü\ loot \u̇\ foot \y\ yet \zh\ vision \à, k̲, ⁿ, œ, œ̄, ue, ue̅, ʸ\ see Guide to Pronunciation

hunk \'həŋk\ *n* [Flem *hunke*] (1813) **1 :** a large lump or piece **2 :** an attractive well-built man

hun·ker \'həŋ-kər\ *vi* **hun·kered; hun·ker·ing** \-k(ə-)riŋ\ [perh. of Scand origin; akin to ON *hūka* to squat; akin to MLG *hōken* to squat — more at HAWKER] (1720) **:** CROUCH, SQUAT — usu. used with *down*

hun·kers \'həŋ-kərz\ *n pl* (1756) **:** HAUNCHES

hunks \'həŋ(k)s\ *n pl but sing in constr* [origin unknown] (1602) **:** a surly ill-natured person; *esp* **:** MISER

Hun·ky *also* **Hun·kie** \'həŋ-kē\ *n, pl* **Hunkies** [alter. of *Hungarian*] (ca. 1896) **:** a person of central or east European birth or descent — usu. used disparagingly

hun·ky–do·ry \,həŋ-kē-'dōr-ē, -'dȯr-\ *adj* [obs. E dial. *hunk* (home base) + *-dory* (origin unknown)] (1866) **:** quite satisfactory **:** FINE

Hun·nish \'hən-ish\ *adj* (1820) **:** relating to or resembling the Huns; *specif* **:** BARBAROUS

1hunt \'hənt\ *vb* [ME *hunten*, fr. OE *huntian;* akin to OE *hentan* to seize] *vt* (bef. 12c) **1 a :** to pursue for food or in sport ⟨~ buffalo⟩ **b :** to manage in the search for game ⟨~s a pack of dogs⟩ **2 a :** to pursue with intent to capture ⟨~*ed* the escaped prisoner⟩ **b :** to search out **:** SEEK **3 :** to drive or chase esp. by harrying ⟨members of the colonial council . . . were ~*ed* from their homes —J. T. Adams⟩ **4 :** to traverse in search of prey ⟨~s the woods⟩ ~ *vi* **1 :** to take part in a hunt **2 :** to attempt to find something **3 :** to oscillate alternately to each side (as of a neutral point) or to run alternately faster and slower — used esp. of a device or machine

2hunt *n* (14c) **1 :** the act, the practice, or an instance of hunting **2 :** a group of mounted hunters and their hunting dogs

hunt–and–peck \,hənt-ᵊn-'pek\ *n* (1939) **:** a mode of typing in which one looks at the keyboard and uses random fingering

hunt·er \'hənt-ər\ *n* (13c) **1 a :** a person who hunts game **b :** a dog used or trained for hunting **c :** a horse used or adapted for use in hunting; *esp* **:** a fast strong horse trained for cross-country work and jumping **2 :** one that searches for something

hunt·ing *n* (bef. 12c) **1 :** the act of one that hunts; *specif* **:** the pursuit of game **2 :** the process of hunting **3 a :** a periodic variation in speed of a synchronous electrical machine **b :** a self-induced and undesirable oscillation of a variable above and below the desired value in an automatic control system **c :** a continuous attempt by an automatically controlled system to find a desired equilibrium condition

hunting horn *n* (1694) **:** a signal horn used in the chase; *specif* **:** a long conical tube coiled in a large circle and having a flared bell and a cup-shaped mouthpiece

Hun·ting·ton's chorea \,hənt-iŋ-tənz-\ *n* [George *Huntington* †1916 Am. physician] (1889) **:** hereditary chorea developing in adult life and ending in dementia — called also *Huntington's disease*

hunt·ress \'hən-trəs\ *n* (14c) **:** a woman who hunts game

hunts·man \'hən(t)-smən\ *n* (1567) **1 :** HUNTER 1a **2 :** a person who manages a hunt and looks after the hounds

hup \'həp, 'hət\ *interj* [prob. alter. of *one*] (1951) — used to mark a marching cadence

hur·dies \'hərd-ēz\ *n pl* [origin unknown] *dial Brit* (14c) **:** RUMP

1hur·dle \'hərd-ᵊl\ *n* [ME *hurdel*, fr. OE *hyrdel;* akin to OHG *hurt* hurdle, L *cratis* wickerwork, hurdle] (bef. 12c) **1 a :** a portable panel usu. of wattled withes and stakes used esp. for enclosing land or livestock **b :** a frame or sled formerly used in England for dragging traitors to execution **2 a :** an artificial barrier over which men or horses must leap in a race **b** *pl* **:** any of various track events in which a series of hurdles must be surmounted **3 :** BARRIER, OBSTACLE

2hurdle *vt* **hur·dled; hur·dling** \'hərd-liŋ, -ᵊl-iŋ\ (1896) **1 :** to leap over esp. while running **2 :** OVERCOME, SURMOUNT — **hur·dler** \'hərd-lər, -ᵊl-ər\ *n*

hur·dy–gur·dy \,hərd-ē-'gərd-ē, 'hərd-ē-,\ *n, pl* **-gur·dies** [prob. imit.] (1749) **1 :** a stringed instrument in which sound is produced by the friction of a rosined wheel turned by a crank against the strings and the pitches are varied by keys **2 :** any of various mechanical musical instruments (as the barrel organ)

hurl \'hər(-ə)l\ *vb* **hurled; hurl·ing** \'hər-liŋ\ [ME *hurlen*] *vi* (14c) **1 :** RUSH, HURTLE **2 :** PITCH 5a, 5b ~ *vt* **1 :** to send or thrust with great vigor ⟨the forces that were to be ~*ed* against the Turks —N. T. Gilroy⟩ **2 :** to throw down with violence **3 a :** to throw forcefully **:** FLING ⟨~*ed* the manuscript into the fire⟩ ⟨~*ed* myself over the fence⟩ **b :** PITCH 2a **4 :** to utter with vehemence ⟨~*ed* insults at the police⟩ ***syn*** see THROW — **hurl** *n* — **hurl·er** \'hər-lər\ *n*

hurl·ing \'hər-liŋ\ *n* (1600) **:** an Irish game resembling field hockey played between two teams of 15 players each

hur·ly \'hər-lē\ *n* [prob. short for *hurly-burly*] (1593) **:** UPROAR, TUMULT

hur·ly–bur·ly \,hər-lē-'bər-lē\ *n* [prob. alter. & redupl. of *hurling*, gerund of *hurl*] (1539) **:** UPROAR, TUMULT

Hu·ron \'(h)yu̇r-ən, '(h)yü(ə)r-,än\ *n, pl* **Hurons** *or* **Huron** [F, lit., boor] (1658) **1** *pl* **:** a confederacy of American Indian peoples orig. of the St. Lawrence valley **2 :** a member of any of the Huron peoples

1hur·rah \hu̇-'rō, -'rä, 'hü-,\ *n* (1686) **1 :** EXCITEMENT, FANFARE **2 :** FUSS

2hur·rah \hu̇-'rō, -'rä\ *also* **hur·ray** \hu̇-'rā\ *interj* [perh. fr. G *hurra*] (1716) — used to express joy, approbation, or encouragement

Hur·ri·an \'hu̇r-ē-ən\ *n* (1911) **1 :** a member of an ancient non-Semitic people of northern Mesopotamia, Syria, and eastern Asia Minor about 1500 B.C. **2 :** the language of the Hurrian people

hur·ri·cane \'hər-ə-,kān, -i-kən, 'hə-rə-, 'hə-ri-\ *n* [Sp *huracán*, fr. Taino *hurakán*] (1555) **1 :** a tropical cyclone with winds of 74 miles per hour or greater that is usu. accompanied by rain, thunder, and lightning and that sometimes moves into temperate latitudes — see BEAUFORT SCALE table **2 :** something resembling a hurricane esp. in its turmoil

hurricane lamp *n* (1894) **:** a candlestick or an electric lamp equipped with a glass chimney

hur·ried \'hər-ēd, 'hə-rēd\ *adj* (1667) **1 :** going or working at speed **2 :** done in a hurry **:** HASTY — **hur·ried·ly** \'hər-əd-lē, 'hə-rəd-\ *adv* — **hur·ried·ness** \'hər-ēd-nəs, 'hə-rēd-\ *n*

1hur·ry \'hər-ē, 'hə-rē\ *vb* **hur·ried; hur·ry·ing** [perh. fr. ME *horyen*] *vt* (1592) **1 a :** to carry or cause to go with haste ⟨~ them to the hospital⟩ **b :** to impel to rash or precipitate action **2 a :** to impel to greater speed **:** PROD ⟨used spurs to ~ the horse⟩ **b :** EXPEDITE **c :** to perform with undue haste ⟨~ a minuet⟩ ~ *vi* **:** to move or act with haste ⟨please ~ up⟩ — **hur·ri·er** *n*

2hurry *n* (1600) **1 :** disturbed or disorderly activity **:** COMMOTION **2 a :** agitated and often bustling or disorderly haste **b :** a state of eagerness or urgency **:** RUSH ***syn*** see HASTE — **in a hurry :** without delay **:** as rapidly as possible ⟨the police got there *in a hurry*⟩

hur·ry–scur·ry *or* **hur·ry–skur·ry** \,hər-ē-'skər-ē, ,hə-rē-'skə-rē\ *n* [redupl. of *2hurry*] (1754) **:** a confused rush **:** TURMOIL — **hurry–scurry** *adj or adv*

hurry–up \,hər-ē-,əp, ,hə-rē-\ *adj* (1902) **:** speeded up ⟨~ existence⟩ **:** completed in a hurry ⟨a ~ dinner⟩

1hurt \'hərt\ *vb* **hurt; hurt·ing** [ME *hurten*] *vt* (13c) **1 a :** to inflict with physical pain **:** WOUND **b :** to do substantial or material harm to **:** DAMAGE ⟨the dry summer has ~ the land⟩ **2 a :** to cause pain or anguish to **:** OFFEND **b :** to be detrimental to **:** HAMPER ⟨charges of graft ~ my chances of being elected⟩ ~ *vi* **1 a :** to feel pain **:** SUFFER **b** *chiefly Midland* **:** to be in need **:** WANT **2 :** to cause damage or distress ⟨hit where it ~s⟩ ***syn*** see INJURE — **hurt** *adj* — **hurt·er** *n*

2hurt *n* (13c) **1 :** a cause of injury or damage **:** BLOW **2 a :** a bodily injury or wound **b :** mental distress or anguish **:** SUFFERING **3 :** WRONG, HARM

hurt·ful \'hərt-fəl\ *adj* (1526) **:** causing injury or suffering **:** DAMAGING — **hurt·ful·ly** \-fə-lē\ *adv* — **hurt·ful·ness** *n*

hur·tle \'hərt-ᵊl\ *vb* **hur·tled; hur·tling** \'hərt-liŋ, -ᵊl-iŋ\ [ME *hurtlen* to collide, freq. of *hurten* to cause to strike, hurt] *vi* (14c) **:** to move with or as if with a rushing sound ~ *vt* **:** HURL, FLING — **hurtle** *n*

hurt·less \'hərt-ləs\ *adj* (1549) **:** causing no pain or injury **:** HARMLESS

1hus·band \'həz-bənd\ *n* [ME *husbonde*, fr. OE *hūsbonda* master of a house, fr. ON *hūsbōndi*, fr. *hūs* house + *bōndi* householder; akin to ON *būa* to inhabit; akin to OE *būan* to dwell — more at BOWER] (bef. 12c) **1 :** a married man **2** *Brit* **:** MANAGER, STEWARD **3 :** a frugal manager — **hus·band·ly** *adj*

2husband *vt* (15c) **1 a :** to manage prudently and economically **b :** to use sparingly **:** CONSERVE **2** *archaic* **:** to find a husband for **:** MATE — **hus·band·er** *n*

hus·band·man \'həz-bən(d)-mən\ *n* (14c) **1 :** one that plows and cultivates land **:** FARMER **2 :** a specialist in a branch of farm husbandry

hus·band·ry \'həz-bən-drē\ *n* (13c) **1** *obs* **:** the care of a household **2 :** the control or judicious use of resources **:** CONSERVATION **3 a :** the cultivation or production of plants and animals **:** AGRICULTURE **b :** the scientific control and management of a branch of farming and esp. of domestic animals

1hush \'həsh\ *vb* [back-formation fr. *husht* (hushed), fr. ME *hussht*, fr. *huissht*, interj. used to enjoin silence] *vt* (1546) **1 :** CALM, QUIET ⟨~*ed* the children as they entered the library⟩ **2 :** to put at rest **:** MOLLIFY **3 :** to keep from public knowledge **:** SUPPRESS ⟨~ the story up⟩ ~ *vi* **:** to become quiet

2hush *adj* (1602) **1** *archaic* **:** SILENT, STILL **2 :** intended to prevent the dissemination of certain information ⟨~ money⟩

3hush *n* (1689) **:** a silence or calm esp. following noise **:** QUIET

hush–hush \'həsh-,həsh\ *adj* (1916) **:** SECRET, CONFIDENTIAL

hush puppy *n* [fr. its occasional use as food for dogs] *chiefly Southern* (ca. 1918) **:** cornmeal dough shaped into small balls and fried in deep fat — usu. used in pl.

1husk \'həsk\ *n* [ME] (14c) **1 a :** a typically dry or membranous outer covering (as a pod or hull or one composed of bracts) of a seed or fruit; *also* **:** one of the constituent parts **b :** a carob pod **2 a :** an outer layer **:** SHELL **b :** an emptied shell **:** REMNANT **c :** a supporting framework

2husk *vt* (1562) **:** to strip the husk from — **husk·er** *n*

husk·ing *n* (1693) **:** CORNHUSKING — called also *husking bee*

husk–tomato *n* (1895) **:** GROUND-CHERRY

1husky \'həs-kē\ *adj* **husk·i·er; -est** (1552) **:** resembling, containing, or full of husks

2hus·ky \'həs-kē\ *adj* **hus·ki·er; -est** [prob. fr. *husk* (huskiness), fr. obs. *husk* (to have a dry cough)] (1722) **:** hoarse with or as if with emotion — **hus·ki·ly** \-kə-lē\ *adv* — **hus·ki·ness** \-kē-nəs\ *n*

3hus·ky *n, pl* **huskies** [prob. by shortening & alter. fr. *Eskimo*] (1852) **1 :** a heavy-coated working dog of the New World arctic region **2 :** SIBERIAN HUSKY

4hus·ky *n, pl* **huskies** (1864) **:** one that is husky

5hus·ky *adj* **hus·ki·er; -est** [prob. fr. *1husk*] (1869) **1 :** BURLY, ROBUST **2 :** LARGE

hus·sar \(,)hə-'zär, -'sär\ *n* [Hung *huszár* hussar, (obs.) highway robber, fr. Serb *husar* pirate, fr. ML *cursarius* — more at CORSAIR] (1532) **:** a member of any of various European units orig. modeled on the Hungarian light cavalry of the 15th century

Huss·ite \'həs-,īt, 'hu̇s-\ *n* [NL *Hussita*, fr. John *Huss*] (1532) **:** a member of the Bohemian religious and nationalist movement originating with John Huss — **Hussite** *adj* — **Huss·it·ism** \-,īt-,iz-əm\ *n*

hus·sy \'həs-ē, 'həz-\ *n, pl* **hussies** [alter. of ME *huswif* housewife, fr. *hus* house + *wif* wife, woman] (1647) **1 :** a lewd or brazen woman **2 :** a saucy or mischievous girl

hus·tings \'həs-tiŋz\ *n pl but sing or pl in constr* [ME, fr. OE *hūsting*, fr. ON *hūsthing*, fr. *hūs* house + *thing* assembly] (bef. 12c) **1 a :** a local court formerly held in various English municipalities and still held infrequently in London **b :** a local court in some cities in Virginia **2 a :** a raised platform used until 1872 for the nomination of candidates for the British Parliament and for election speeches **b :** an election platform **:** STUMP **c :** the proceedings or locale of an election campaign

hus·tle \'həs-əl\ *vb* **hus·tled; hus·tling** \'həs-(ə-)liŋ\ [D *husselen* to shake, fr. MD *hutselen*, freq. of *hutsen;* akin to MD *hodde* hod] *vt* (1751) **1 a :** JOSTLE, SHOVE **b :** to convey forcibly or hurriedly **c :** to urge forward precipitately **2 a :** to obtain by energetic activity **b :** to sell something to or obtain something from by energetic and esp. underhanded activity **c :** to sell or promote energetically and aggressively ~ *vi* **1 :** SHOVE, PRESS **2 :** HASTEN, HURRY **3 a :** to make strenuous efforts to secure money or business **b :** to obtain money by fraud or deception **c :** to engage in prostitution **4 :** to play a game or sport in an alert aggressive manner — **hustle** *n* — **hus·tler** \'həs-lər\ *n*

1hut \'hət\ *n* [MF *hutte*, of Gmc origin; akin to OHG *hutta* hut; akin to OE *hȳd* skin, hide] (1658) **1 :** an often small and temporary dwelling of simple construction **:** SHACK **2 :** a simple shelter from the elements — **hut** *vb*

²hut \'hət, 'həp\ *interj* [prob. alter. of *one*] (1948) — used to mark a marching cadence
hutch \'həch\ *n* [ME *huche*, fr. OF] (13c) **1 a :** a chest or compartment for storage **b :** a low cupboard usu. surmounted by open shelves **2 :** a pen or coop for an animal **3 :** SHACK, SHANTY
hut·ment \'hət-mənt\ *n* (1889) **1 :** a collection of huts : ENCAMPMENT **2 :** HUT
Hut·ter·ite \'hət-ə-,rīt, 'hüt-\ *n* [Jakob *Hutter* †1536 Moravian Anabaptist] (1645) **:** a member of a Mennonite sect of northwestern U.S. and Canada living communally and holding property in common — **Hut·te·ri·an** \,hə-'tir-ē-ən, hü-\ *adj*
hutzpah *or* **hutzpa** *var of* CHUTZPAH
huz·zah *or* **huz·za** \(,)hə-'zä\ *n* [origin unknown] (1573) **:** a cheer or shout of acclaim — often used interjectionally to express joy or approbation
hy·a·cinth \'hī-ə-(,)sin(t)th, -sən(t)th\ *n* [L *hyacinthus*, a precious stone, a flowering plant, fr. Gk *hyakinthos*] (1553) **1 a :** a precious stone of the ancients sometimes held to be the sapphire **b :** a gem zircon or essonite **2 a :** a plant of the ancients held to be a lily, iris, larkspur, or gladiolus **b (1) :** any of a genus (*Hyacinthus*) of bulbous herbs of the lily family; *esp* **:** a common garden plant (*H. orientalis*) widely grown for the beauty and fragrance of the flowers **(2) :** any of several other plants of the lily family **3 :** a light violet to moderate purple — **hy·a·cin·thine** \,hī-ə-'sin(t)-thən\ *adj*
Hy·a·cin·thus \,hī-ə-'sin(t)-thəs\ *n* [L, fr. Gk *Hyakinthos*] **:** a youth loved and accidentally killed by Apollo who memorializes him with a hyacinth growing from the youth's blood
Hy·a·des \'hī-ə-,dēz\ *n pl* [L, fr. Gk] (14c) **:** a V-shaped cluster of stars in the head of the constellation Taurus held by the ancients to indicate rainy weather when they rise with the sun
hy·ae·na *var of* HYENA
hyal- *or* **hyalo-** *comb form* [LL, glass, fr. Gk, fr. *hyalos*] **:** glass **:** glassy **:** hyaline ⟨*hyal*escent⟩ ⟨*hyalo*gen⟩
¹**hy·a·line** \'hī-ə-lən, -,līn\ *adj* [LL *hyalinus*, fr. Gk *hyalinos*, fr. *hyalos*] (1661) **1 :** of or relating to glass **2 a :** transparent or nearly so and usu. homogeneous **b** *of a mineral* **(1) :** GLASSY **(2) :** lacking crystallinity **:** AMORPHOUS
²**hy·a·line** \'hī-ə-lən, -,līn, *in sense 2* -lən *or* -,lēn\ *n* (1667) **1 :** something (as the clear atmosphere) that is transparent **2** *or* **hy·a·lin** \-lən\ **:** any of several translucent nitrogenous substances related to chitin, found esp. around cells, and readily stained by eosin
hyaline cartilage *n* (1855) **:** translucent bluish white cartilage with the cells embedded in an apparently homogeneous matrix that is present in joints and respiratory passages and forms most of the fetal skeleton
hy·a·lite \'hī-ə-,līt\ *n* [G *hyalit*, fr. Gk *hyalos*] (1794) **:** a colorless opal that is clear as glass or sometimes translucent or whitish
hy·a·loid \-,lȯid\ *adj* [Gk *hyaloeidēs*, fr. *hyalos*] (1835) **:** GLASSY, TRANSPARENT
hy·a·lo·plasm \hī-'al-ə-,plaz-əm, 'hī-ə-lō-\ *n* [prob. fr. G *hyaloplasma*, fr. *hyal-* + *-plasma* -plasm] (1886) **:** the clear fluid apparently homogeneous matrix of cytoplasm — called also *ground substance*
hy·al·uron·ic acid \,hī-(,)al-yü-,rän-ik-, ,hī-əl-yü-\ *n* [ISV] (1934) **:** a viscous mucopolysaccharide acid that occurs esp. in the vitreous humor, the umbilical cord, and synovial fluid and as a cementing substance in the subcutaneous tissue
hy·al·uron·i·dase \-'rän-ə-,dās, -dāz\ *n* [ISV, irreg. fr. *hyaluronic* (*acid*) + *-ase*] (1940) **:** an enzyme that splits and lowers the viscosity of hyaluronic acid facilitating the spreading of fluids through tissues
hy·brid \'hī-brəd\ *n* [L *hybrida*] (1601) **1 :** an offspring of two animals or plants of different races, breeds, varieties, species, or genera **2 :** a person whose background is a blend of two diverse cultures or traditions **3 a :** something heterogeneous in origin or composition **:** COMPOSITE ⟨artificial ~s of DNA and RNA⟩; *also* **:** something (as a power plant, vehicle, or electronic circuit) that has two different types of components performing essentially the same function **b :** a word composed of elements from different languages — **hybrid** *adj* — **hy·brid·ism** \-brə-,diz-əm\ *n* — **hy·brid·i·ty** \hī-'brid-ət-ē\ *n*
hybrid computer *n* (1968) **:** a computer system consisting of a combination of analog and digital computer systems
hy·brid·ize \'hī-brə-,dīz\ *vb* **-ized; -iz·ing** *vt* (1845) **:** to cause to produce hybrids **:** INTERBREED ~ *vi* **:** to produce hybrids — **hy·brid·iza·tion** \,hī-brəd-ə-'zā-shən\ *n* — **hy·brid·iz·er** *n*
hy·brid·oma \,hī-brə-'dō-mə\ *n* (1978) **:** a hybrid cell produced by the fusion of an antibody-producing lymphocyte with a tumor cell and used to culture continuously a specific antibody of a single molecular species
hybrid perpetual rose *n* (1848) **:** any of numerous vigorous hardy bush roses derived from the bourbon rose and grown esp. for their sometimes recurrent often fragrant bloom
hybrid tea rose *n* (1926) **:** any of numerous moderately hardy cultivated bush roses derived chiefly from tea roses and hybrid perpetual roses and grown esp. for their strongly recurrent bloom of large usu. scentless flowers
hybrid vigor *n* (1918) **:** HETEROSIS
hy·bris \'hī-brəs, 'hē-\ *var of* HUBRIS
hy·da·thode \'hīd-ə-,thōd\ *n* [ISV, fr. Gk *hydat-*, *hydōr* water + *hodos* road — more at CEDE] (1895) **:** an epidermal structure in higher plants functioning in the exudation of water
hy·da·tid \'hīd-ə-təd, -,tid\ *n* [Gk *hydatid-*, *hydatis* watery cyst, fr. *hydat-*, *hydōr*] (1683) **:** a larval tapeworm occurring as a fluid-filled sac containing daughter cysts and scolices or forming a proliferating spongy mass that actively invades and metastasizes in the host's tissues
hydr- *or* **hydro-** *comb form* [ME *ydr-*, *ydro-*, fr. OF, fr. L *hydr-*, *hydro-*, fr. Gk, fr. *hydōr* — more at WATER] **1 a :** water ⟨*hydr*ous⟩ ⟨*hydro*electricity⟩ **b :** liquid ⟨*hydro*kinetics⟩ **2 :** hydrogen **:** containing or combined with hydrogen ⟨*hydro*carbon⟩ ⟨*hydr*oxyl⟩ **3 :** hydroid ⟨*hydro*medusa⟩
Hy·dra \'hī-drə\ *n* [ME *Ydra*, fr. L *Hydra*, fr. Gk] **1 :** a many-headed serpent or monster in Greek mythology slain by Hercules each head of which when cut off was replaced by two others **2** *not cap* **:** a multifarious evil not to be overcome by a single effort **3** [L (gen. *Hydrae*), fr. Gk] **:** a southern constellation of great length that lies south of Cancer, Sextans, Corvus, and Virgo and is represented on old maps by a serpent **4** *not cap* [NL, fr. L, Hydra] **:** any of numerous small tubular freshwater hydrozoan polyps (as of the genus *Hydra*) having at one end a mouth surrounded by tentacles
hy·dra–head·ed \,hī-drə-'hed-əd\ *adj* (1599) **:** having many centers or branches ⟨a ~ organization⟩
hy·dral·azine \hī-'dral-ə-,zēn\ *n* [*hydr-* + phthal*ic* (acid) + *azine*] (1952) **:** a sympatholytic drug $C_8H_8N_4$ used in the treatment of hypertension
hy·dran·gea \hī-'drān-jə\ *n* [NL, fr. *hydr-* + Gk *angeion* vessel — more at ANGI-] (ca. 1753) **:** any of a genus (*Hydrangea*) of shrubs and one woody vine of the saxifrage family with opposite leaves and showy corymbose clusters of usu. sterile white or tinted flowers
hy·drant \'hī-drənt\ *n* (1806) **1 :** a discharge pipe with a valve and spout at which water may be drawn from a water main (as for fighting fires) — called also *fireplug* **2 :** FAUCET
hy·dranth \'hī-,dran(t)th\ *n* [ISV *hydr-* + Gk *anthos* flower — more at ANTHOLOGY] (1874) **:** one of the nutritive zooids of a hydroid colony
hy·drase \'hī-,drās, -,drāz\ *n* (1943) **:** an enzyme that promotes the addition or removal of water to or from its substrate
¹**hy·drate** \'hī-,drāt\ *n* (1802) **1 :** a compound or complex ion formed by the union of water with some other substance **2 :** HYDROXIDE ⟨calcium ~⟩
²**hydrate** *vb* **hy·drat·ed; hy·drat·ing** *vt* (1850) **:** to cause to take up or combine with water or the elements of water ~ *vi* **:** to become a hydrate — **hy·dra·tion** \hī-'drā-shən\ *n* — **hy·dra·tor** \'hī-,drāt-ər\ *n*
hy·drau·lic \hī-'drȯ-lik\ *adj* [L *hydraulicus*, fr. Gk *hydraulikos*, fr. *hydraulis* hydraulic organ, fr. *hydr-* + *aulos* reed instrument — more at ALVEOLUS] (1661) **1 :** operated, moved, or effected by means of water **2 a :** of or relating to hydraulics ⟨~ engineer⟩ **b :** of or relating to water or other liquid in motion ⟨~ erosion⟩ **3 :** operated by the resistance offered or the pressure transmitted when a quantity of liquid (as water or oil) is forced through a comparatively small orifice or through a tube ⟨~ brakes⟩ **4 :** hardening or setting under water ⟨~ cement⟩ — **hy·drau·li·cal·ly** \-li-k(ə-)lē\ *adv*
hydraulic ram *n* (1808) **:** a pump that forces running water to a higher level by utilizing the kinetic energy of flow
hy·drau·lics \hī-'drȯ-liks\ *n pl but sing in constr* (1671) **:** a branch of science that deals with practical applications (as the transmission of energy or the effects of flow) of liquid (as water) in motion
hy·dra·zide \'hī-drə-,zīd\ *n* (1888) **:** any of a class of compounds resulting from the replacement by an acid group of hydrogen in hydrazine or in one of its derivatives
hy·dra·zine \'hī-drə-,zēn\ *n* [ISV] (1887) **:** a colorless fuming corrosive strongly reducing liquid base N_2H_4 used esp. in fuels for rocket and jet engines; *also* **:** an organic base derived from this compound
hy·dra·zo·ic acid \,hī-drə-,zō-ik-\ *n* [*hydr-* + *azo-* + *-ic*] (1894) **:** a colorless volatile poisonous explosive liquid HN_3 that has a foul odor and yields explosive salts of heavy metals
hy·dric \'hī-drik\ *adj* (1926) **:** characterized by, relating to, or requiring an abundance of moisture ⟨a ~ habitat⟩ ⟨a ~ plant⟩ — compare MESIC, XERIC — **hy·dri·cal·ly** \-dri-k(ə-)lē\ *adv*
-hy·dric \'hī-drik\ *adj suffix* **1 :** containing acid hydrogen ⟨mono*hydric*⟩ **2 :** containing hydroxyl ⟨hexa*hydric* alcohols⟩
hy·dride \'hī-,drīd\ *n* (1877) **:** a compound of hydrogen usu. with a more electropositive element or group
hy·dri·od·ic acid \,hī-drē-,äd-ik-\ *n* [ISV] (1819) **:** an aqueous solution of hydrogen iodide HI that is a strong acid resembling hydrochloric acid chemically and that is also a strong reducing agent
¹**hy·dro** \'hī-(,)drō\ *n, pl* **hydros** [short for *hydropathic establishment*] *Brit* (1882) **:** a hydropathic establishment **:** SPA; *also* **:** a hotel catering to people using such an establishment
²**hydro** *adj* (1916) **:** HYDROELECTRIC ⟨~ energy⟩
hy·dro·bi·ol·o·gy \,hī-drō-bī-'äl-ə-jē\ *n* (1926) **:** the biology of bodies or units of water; *esp* **:** LIMNOLOGY — **hy·dro·bi·o·log·i·cal** \-,bī-ə-'läj-i-kəl\ *adj* — **hy·dro·bi·ol·o·gist** \-bī-'äl-ə-jəst\ *n*
hy·dro·bro·mic acid \,hī-drə-,brō-mik-\ *n* [ISV] (1836) **:** an aqueous solution of hydrogen bromide HBr that is a strong acid resembling hydrochloric acid chemically, that is a weak reducing agent, and that is used esp. for making bromides
hy·dro·car·bon \,hī-drə-'kär-bən\ *n* (1826) **:** an organic compound (as acetylene or benzene) containing only carbon and hydrogen and often occurring in petroleum, natural gas, coal, and bitumens — **hy·dro·car·bo·na·ceous** \-,kär-bə-'nā-shəs\ *or* **hy·dro·car·bon·ic** \-kär-'bän-ik\ *or* **hy·dro·car·bon·ous** \-'kär-bə-nəs\ *adj*
hy·dro·cele \'hī-drə-,sēl\ *n* [L, fr. Gk *hydrokēlē*, fr. *hydr-* + *kēlē* tumor — more at -CELE] (1597) **:** an accumulation of serous fluid in a sacculated cavity (as the scrotum)
hy·dro·ce·phal·ic \,hī-drō-sə-'fal-ik\ *adj* (1815) **:** relating to, characterized by, or affected with hydrocephalus — **hydrocephalic** *n*
hy·dro·ceph·a·lus \-'sef-ə-ləs\ *also* **hy·dro·ceph·a·ly** \-lē\ *n* [NL *hydrocephalus*, fr. LL, hydrocephalic, adj., fr. Gk *hydrokephalos*, fr. *hydr-* + *kephalē* head — more at CEPHALIC] (1670) **:** an abnormal increase in the amount of cerebrospinal fluid within the cranial cavity that is accompanied by expansion of the cerebral ventricles, enlargement of the skull and esp. the forehead, and atrophy of the brain
hy·dro·chlo·ric acid \,hī-drə-,klōr-ik-, -,klȯr-\ *n* [ISV] (ca. 1828) **:** an aqueous solution of hydrogen chloride HCl that is a strong corrosive irritating acid, is normally present in dilute form in gastric juice, and is widely used in industry and in the laboratory
hy·dro·chlo·ride \-'klō(ə)r-,īd, -'klȯ(ə)r-\ *n* (1826) **:** a compound of hydrochloric acid esp. with an organic base (as an alkaloid)
hy·dro·chlo·ro·thi·a·zide \-,klōr-ə-'thī-ə-,zīd, -,klȯr-\ *n* [*hydr-* + *chlor-* + *thiazine* + *-ide*] (1958) **:** a diuretic and antihypertensive drug $C_7H_8ClN_3O_4S_2$
hy·dro·col·loid \,hī-drə-'käl-,ȯid\ *n* (1916) **:** a substance that yields a gel with water — **hy·dro·col·loi·dal** \-kə-'lȯid-ᵊl, -kä-\ *adj*
hy·dro·cor·ti·sone \-'kȯrt-ə-,sōn, -,zōn\ *n* (ca. 1951) **:** a glucocorticoid $C_{21}H_{30}O_5$ of the adrenal cortex that is a dihydro derivative of cortisone

and is used in the treatment of rheumatoid arthritis — called also *cortisol*

hy·dro·crack·ing \'hī-drə-,krak-iŋ\ *n* (1940) **:** the cracking of hydrocarbons in the presence of hydrogen — **hy·dro·crack** \-,krak\ *vt* — **hy·dro·crack·er** *n*

hy·dro·cy·an·ic acid \,hī-drō-sī-,an-ik-\ *n* [ISV] (1818) **:** an aqueous solution of hydrogen cyanide HCN that is a poisonous weak acid and is used chiefly in fumigating and in organic synthesis

hy·dro·dy·nam·ic \-dī-'nam-ik\ *also* **hy·dro·dy·nam·i·cal** \-i-kəl\ *adj* [NL *hydrodynamicus,* fr. *hydr-* + *dynamicus* dynamic] (ca. 1828) **:** of, relating to, or involving principles of hydrodynamics — **hy·dro·dy·nam·i·cal·ly** \-i-k(ə-)lē\ *adv*

hy·dro·dy·nam·ics \-iks\ *n pl but sing in constr* (1779) **:** a branch of science that deals with the motion of fluids and the forces acting on solid bodies immersed in fluids and in motion relative to them — compare HYDROSTATICS — **hy·dro·dy·nam·i·cist** \-'nam-ə-səst\ *n*

hy·dro·elec·tric \,hī-drō-i-'lek-trik\ *adj* [ISV] (1827) **:** of or relating to production of electricity by waterpower ⟨constructed a ~ power plant at the dam site⟩ — **hy·dro·elec·tri·cal·ly** \-tri-k(ə-)lē\ *adv* — **hy·dro·elec·tric·i·ty** \-,lek-'tris-ət-ē, -'tris-tē\ *n*

hy·dro·flu·or·ic acid \,hī-drō-flu̇-,ȯr-ik, -,är-\ *n* [ISV] (1822) **:** an aqueous solution of hydrogen fluoride HF that is a weak poisonous acid, that resembles hydrochloric acid chemically but attacks silica and silicates, and that is used esp. in finishing and etching glass

hy·dro·foil \'hī-drə-,fȯil\ *n* (1919) **1 :** a body similar to an airfoil but designed for action in or on water **2 :** a motorboat that has metal plates or fins attached by struts fore and aft for lifting the hull clear of the water as speed is attained

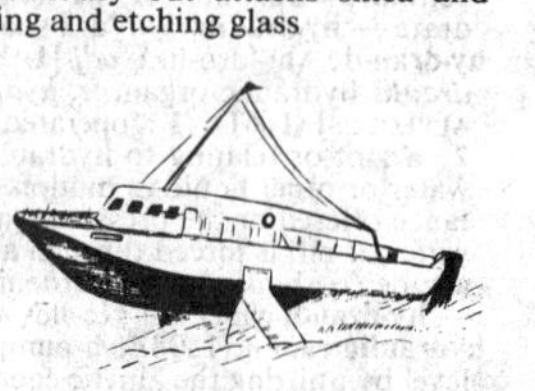

hydrofoil 2

hy·dro·form·ing \-,fȯr-miŋ\ *n* [*hydr-* + re*forming*] (1931) **:** a process for producing high-octane gasoline from petroleum naphthas by catalytic dehydrogenation and aromatization in the presence of hydrogen — **hy·dro·form·er** \-mər\ *n*

hy·dro·gen \'hī-drə-jən, -dər-\ *n* [F *hydrogène,* fr. *hydr-* + *-gène* -gen; fr. the fact that water is generated by its combustion] (1791) **:** a nonmetallic element that is the simplest and lightest of the elements, is normally a colorless odorless highly flammable diatomic gas, and is used esp. in synthesis — compare DEUTERIUM, TRITIUM; see ELEMENT table — **hy·drog·e·nous** \hī-'dräj-ə-nəs\ *adj*

hy·drog·e·nase \hī-'dräj-ə-,nās, -,nāz\ *n* (1900) **:** an enzyme of various microorganisms that promotes the formation and utilization of gaseous hydrogen

hy·dro·ge·nate \hī-'dräj-ə-,nāt, 'hī-drə-jə-\ *vt* **-nat·ed; -nat·ing** (1809) **:** to combine or treat with or expose to hydrogen; *esp* **:** to add hydrogen to the molecule of (an unsaturated organic compound) — **hy·dro·ge·na·tion** \hī-,dräj-ə-'nā-shən, ,hī-drə-jə-\ *n*

hydrogen bomb *n* (1947) **:** a bomb whose violent explosive power is due to the sudden release of atomic energy resulting from the union of light nuclei (as of hydrogen atoms) at very high temperature and pressure to form helium nuclei

hydrogen bond *n* (1923) **:** an electrostatic attraction between a hydrogen atom in one polar molecule (as of water) and a small electronegative atom (as of oxygen, nitrogen, or fluorine) in usu. another molecule of the same or a different polar substance

hydrogen bromide *n* (ca. 1899) **:** a colorless irritating gas HBr that fumes in moist air and yields hydrobromic acid when dissolved in water

hydrogen chloride *n* (1869) **:** a colorless pungent poisonous gas HCl that fumes in moist air and yields hydrochloric acid when dissolved in water

hydrogen cyanide *n* (1882) **1 :** a poisonous usu. gaseous compound HCN that has the odor of bitter almonds **2 :** HYDROCYANIC ACID

hydrogen fluoride *n* (ca. 1909) **:** a colorless corrosive fuming usu. gaseous compound HF that yields hydrofluoric acid when dissolved in water

hydrogen iodide *n* (ca. 1899) **:** an acrid colorless gas HI that fumes in moist air and yields hydriodic acid when dissolved in water

hydrogen ion *n* (1896) **1 :** the cation H^+ of acids consisting of a hydrogen atom whose electron has been transferred to the anion of the acid **2 :** HYDRONIUM

hydrogen peroxide *n* (1872) **:** an unstable compound H_2O_2 used esp. as an oxidizing and bleaching agent, an antiseptic, and a propellant

hydrogen sulfide *n* (1873) **:** a flammable poisonous gas H_2S that has an odor suggestive of rotten eggs and is found esp. in many mineral waters and in putrefying matter

hy·drog·ra·phy \hī-'dräg-rə-fē\ *n* [MF *hydrographie,* fr. *hydr-* + *-graphie* -graphy] (1559) **1 :** the description and study of bodies of water (as seas, lakes, and rivers): as **a :** the measurement of flow and investigation of the behavior of streams esp. with reference to the control of their waters **b :** the charting of bodies of water **2 :** bodies of water — **hy·drog·ra·pher** \-fər\ *n* — **hy·dro·graph·ic** \,hī-drə-'graf-ik\ *adj* — **hy·dro·graph·i·cal·ly** \-i-k(ə-)lē\ *adv*

¹hy·droid \'hī-,drȯid\ *adj* [deriv. of NL *Hydra*] (ca. 1864) **:** of or relating to a hydrozoan; *esp* **:** resembling a typical hydra

²hydroid *n* (1865) **:** HYDROZOAN; *esp* **:** a hydrozoan polyp as distinguished from a medusa

hy·dro·ki·net·ic \,hī-drō-kə-'net-ik, -(,)kī-\ *adj* (1876) **:** of or relating to the motions of fluids or the forces which produce or affect such motions — compare HYDROSTATIC

hy·dro·lase \'hī-drə-,lās, -,lāz\ *n* (1910) **:** a hydrolytic enzyme (as an esterase)

hy·drol·o·gy \hī-'dräl-ə-jē\ *n* [NL *hydrologia,* fr. L *hydr-* + *-logia* -logy] (1762) **:** a science dealing with the properties, distribution, and circulation of water on and below the earth's surface and in the atmosphere — **hy·dro·log·ic** \,hī-drə-'läj-ik\ *or* **hy·dro·log·i·cal** \-i-kəl\ *adj* — **hy·dro·log·i·cal·ly** \-i-k(ə-)lē\ *adv* — **hy·drol·o·gist** \hī-'dräl-ə-jəst\ *n*

hy·dro·ly·sate \hī-'dräl-ə-,sāt, ,hī-drə-'lī-\ *also* **hy·dro·ly·zate** \-,zāt\ *n* (1915) **:** a product of hydrolysis

hy·dro·ly·sis \hī-'dräl-ə-səs, ,hī-drə-'lī-\ *n* [NL] (1880) **:** a chemical process of decomposition involving splitting of a bond and addition of the elements of water — **hy·dro·lyt·ic** \,hī-drə-'lit-ik\ *adj* — **hy·dro·lyt·i·cal·ly** \-i-k(ə-)lē\ *adv*

hy·dro·lyze \'hī-drə-,līz\ *vb* **-lyzed; -lyz·ing** [ISV, fr. NL *hydrolysis*] *vt* (1880) **:** to subject to hydrolysis ~ *vi* **:** to undergo hydrolysis — **hy·dro·lyz·able** \-,lī-zə-bəl\ *adj*

hy·dro·mag·net·ic \,hī-drō-mag-'net-ik\ *adj* [*hydr-* + *magnetic*] (1943) **1 :** MAGNETOHYDRODYNAMIC **2 :** being a wave in an electrically conducting fluid immersed in a magnetic field

hy·dro·man·cy \'hī-drə-,man(t)-sē\ *n* [ME *ydromancie,* fr. MF, fr. L *hydromantia,* fr. *hydr-* + *-mantia* -mancy] (14c) **:** divination by the appearance or motion of liquids (as water)

hy·dro·me·chan·ics \,hī-drō-mi-'kan-iks\ *n pl but sing in constr* (1851) **:** a branch of mechanics that deals with the equilibrium and motion of fluids and of solid bodies immersed in them — **hy·dro·me·chan·i·cal** \-'kan-i-kəl\ *adj*

hy·dro·me·du·sa \,hī-drō-mi-'d(y)ü-sə, -zə\ *n, pl* **-sae** \-,sē, -,zē\ [NL] (ca. 1889) **:** a medusa (as of the orders Anthomedusae and Leptomedusae) produced as a bud from a hydroid — **hy·dro·me·du·san** \-'d(y)üs-ᵊn, -'d(y)üz-\ *adj or n* — **hy·dro·me·du·soid** \-'d(y)ü-,sȯid, -,zȯid\ *adj*

hy·dro·met·al·lur·gy \,hī-drō-'met-ᵊl-,ər-jē\ *n* [ISV] (ca. 1859) **:** the treatment of ores by wet processes (as leaching) — **hy·dro·met·al·lur·gi·cal** \-,met-ᵊl-'ər-ji-kəl\ *adj*

hy·dro·me·te·or \,hī-drō-'mēt-ē-ər, -ē-,ȯ(ə)r\ *n* [ISV] (1857) **:** a product (as fog, rain, or hail) formed by the condensation of atmospheric water vapor

hy·dro·me·te·o·rol·o·gy \-,mēt-ē-ə-'räl-ə-jē\ *n* (ca. 1859) **:** a branch of meteorology that deals with water in the atmosphere esp. as precipitation — **hy·dro·me·te·o·ro·log·i·cal** \-ē-,ȯr-ə-'läj-i-kəl, -,är-ə-, -ə-rə-\ *adj* — **hy·dro·me·te·o·rol·o·gist** \-ē-ə-'räl-ə-jəst\ *n*

hy·drom·e·ter \hī-'dräm-ət-ər\ *n* (1675) **:** an instrument for determining the specific gravity of a liquid (as battery acid or an alcohol solution) and hence its strength — **hy·dro·met·ric** \,hī-drə-'me-trik\ *or* **hy·dro·met·ri·cal** \-tri-kəl\ *adj* — **hy·drom·e·try** \hī-'dräm-ə-trē\ *n*

hy·dro·mor·phic \,hī-drə-'mȯr-fik\ *adj, of a soil* (1938) **:** developed in the presence of an excess of moisture which tends to suppress aerobic factors in soil-building

hy·dron·ic \hī-'drän-ik\ *adj* [*hydr-* + *-onic* (as in *electronic*)] (1946) **:** of, relating to, or being a system of heating or cooling that involves transfer of heat by a circulating fluid (as water or vapor) in a closed system of pipes — **hy·dron·i·cal·ly** \-i-k(ə-)lē\ *adv*

hy·dro·ni·um \hī-'drō-nē-əm\ *n* [ISV *hydr-* + *-onium*] (1908) **:** a hydrated hydrogen ion H_3O^+

hy·drop·a·thy \hī-'dräp-ə-thē\ *n* [ISV] (1843) **:** the empirical use of water in the treatment of disease — compare HYDROTHERAPY — **hy·dro·path·ic** \,hī-drə-'path-ik\ *adj* — **hy·dro·path·i·cal·ly** \-i-k(ə-)lē\ *adv*

hy·dro·per·ox·ide \,hī-drō-pə-'räk-,sīd\ *n* (1922) **:** a compound containing an O_2H group

hy·dro·phane \'hī-drə-,fān\ *n* (1784) **:** a semitranslucent opal that becomes translucent or transparent on immersion in water

hy·dro·phil·ic \,hī-drə-'fil-ik\ *adj* [NL *hydrophilus,* fr. Gk *hydr-* + *-philos* -philous] (1916) **:** of, relating to, or having a strong affinity for water ⟨ionic molecules are ~, dissolving readily in water⟩ — **hy·dro·phi·lic·i·ty** \,hī-drə-fil-'is-ət-ē\ *n*

hy·dro·pho·bia \,hī-drə-'fō-bē-ə\ *n* [LL, fr. Gk, fr. *hydr-* + *-phobia* fear of something — more at PHOBIA] (1547) **1 :** a morbid dread of water **2 :** RABIES

hy·dro·pho·bic \-'fō-bik, -'fäb-ik\ *adj* (1807) **1 :** of, relating to, or suffering from hydrophobia **2 :** lacking affinity for water — **hy·dro·pho·bic·i·ty** \-fō-'bis-ət-ē\ *n*

hy·dro·phone \'hī-drə-,fōn\ *n* (1860) **:** an instrument for listening to sound transmitted through water

hy·dro·phyte \-,fīt\ *n* [ISV] (1832) **1 :** a perennial vascular aquatic plant having its overwintering buds under water **2 :** a plant growing in water or in soil too waterlogged for most plants to survive — **hy·dro·phyt·ic** \,hī-drə-'fit-ik\ *adj*

¹hy·dro·plane \'hī-drə-,plān\ *n* (1901) **1 :** HYDROFOIL **2 a :** a speedboat with hydrofoils or a stepped bottom so that the hull is raised wholly or partly out of the water **b :** a rudder on a horizontal axis on a submarine for steering it upward or downward **3 :** SEAPLANE

²hydroplane *vi* (ca. 1909) **1 a :** to skim over the water with the hull more or less clear of the surface **b :** *of an automobile* **:** to skid on a wet road as a result of a film of fluid that causes tires to lose contact with the road **2 :** to drive or ride in a hydroplane — **hy·dro·plan·er** *n*

hy·dro·pon·ics \,hī-drə-'pän-iks\ *n pl but sing in constr* [*hydr-* + *-ponics* (as in *geoponics*)] (1937) **:** the growing of plants in nutrient solutions with or without an inert medium to provide mechanical support — **hy·dro·pon·ic** \-ik\ *adj* — **hy·dro·pon·i·cal·ly** \-i-k(ə-)lē\ *adv*

hy·dro·pow·er \'hī-drə-,pau̇(-ə)r\ *n* (1933) **:** hydroelectric power

hy·dro·qui·none \,hī-drō-kwin-'ōn, -'kwin-,ōn\ *n* [ISV] (ca. 1865) **:** a white crystalline strongly reducing phenol $C_6H_6O_2$ used esp. as a photographic developer and as an antioxidant and stabilizer

hy·dro·scope \'hī-drə-,skōp\ *n* [ISV] (ca. 1909) **:** a mirror device for enabling a person to see an object at a considerable distance below the surface of water

hy·dro·sere \-,si(ə)r\ *n* (1920) **:** an ecological sere originating in an aquatic habitat

hy·dro–ski \'hī-drō-,skē\ *n* (1952) **:** a hydrofoil attached below the fuselage of a seaplane to accelerate takeoffs

hy·dro·sol \'hī-drə-,säl, -,sȯl\ *n* [*hydr-* + *-sol* (fr. *solution*)] (1864) **:** a sol in which the liquid is water — **hy·dro·sol·ic** \,hī-drə-'säl-ik\ *adj*

hy·dro·space \-,spās\ *n* (1963) **:** the regions beneath the surface of the ocean

hy·dro·sphere \-,sfi(ə)r\ *n* [ISV] (1887) **:** the aqueous vapor of the atmosphere; *broadly* **:** the aqueous envelope of the earth including bodies of water and aqueous vapor in the atmosphere — **hy·dro·spher·ic** \,hī-drə-'sfi(ə)r-ik, -'sfer-\ *adj*

hy·dro·stat·ic \,hī-drə-'stat-ik\ *also* **hy·dro·stat·i·cal** \-i-kəl\ *adj* [prob. fr. NL *hydrostaticus,* fr. *hydr-* + *staticus* static] (1666) **:** of or relating to fluids at rest or to the pressures they exert or transmit — compare HYDROKINETIC — **hy·dro·stat·i·cal·ly** \-i-k(ə-)lē\ *adv*

hy·dro·stat·ics \-iks\ *n pl but sing in constr* (1660) **:** a branch of physics that deals with the characteristics of fluids at rest and esp. with the pressure in a fluid or exerted by a fluid on an immersed body — compare HYDRODYNAMICS

hy·dro·sul·fite \ˌhī-drə-ˈsəl-ˌfīt\ *n* [ISV] (ca. 1864) **:** a salt containing the negative bivalent group S_2O_4; *esp* **:** the sodium salt $Na_2S_2O_4$ used as a reducing and bleaching agent

hy·dro·tax·is \ˌhī-drə-ˈtak-səs\ *n* [NL] (ca. 1900) **:** a taxis in which moisture is the directive factor — **hy·dro·tac·tic** \-ˈtak-tik\ *adj*

hy·dro·ther·a·py \ˌhī-drə-ˈther-ə-pē\ *n* [ISV] (1876) **:** the scientific use of water in the treatment of disease — compare HYDROPATHY

hy·dro·ther·mal \ˌhī-drə-ˈthər-məl\ *adj* [ISV] (1849) **:** of or relating to hot water — used esp. of the formation of minerals by hot solutions rising from a cooling magma — **hy·dro·ther·mal·ly** \-mə-lē\ *adv*

hy·dro·tho·rax \-ˈthō(ə)r-ˌaks, -ˈthȯ(ə)r-\ *n* [NL] (1793) **:** an excess of serous fluid in the pleural cavity; *esp* **:** an effusion resulting from failing circulation (as in heart disease or from lung infection)

hy·drot·ro·pism \hī-ˈdrä-trə-ˌpiz-əm\ *n* [ISV] (ca. 1882) **:** a tropism (as in plant roots) in which water or water vapor is the orienting factor — **hy·dro·tro·pic** \ˌhī-drə-ˈtrō-pik, -ˈträp-ik\ *adj* — **hy·dro·tro·pi·cal·ly** \-ˈtrō-pi-k(ə-)lē, -ˈträp-i-\ *adv*

hy·drous \ˈhī-drəs\ *adj* (1826) **:** containing water usu. chemically combined (as in hydrates)

hy·drox·ide \hī-ˈdräk-ˌsīd\ *n* [ISV] (1851) **1 :** the univalent anion OH— consisting of one atom of hydrogen and one of oxygen — called also *hydroxide ion* **2 a :** an ionic compound of hydroxide with an element or group **b :** any of various hydrated oxides (as of aluminum) regarded as containing hydroxide

hy·droxy \hī-ˈdräk-sē\ *adj* [ISV, fr. *hydroxyl*] (1812) **:** being or containing hydroxyl; *esp* **:** containing hydroxyl esp. in place of hydrogen — often used in combination ⟨*hydroxy*acetic acid⟩

hy·droxy·ap·a·tite \hī-ˌdräk-sē-ˈap-ə-ˌtīt\ *or* **hy·drox·yl·ap·a·tite** \-sə-ˈlap-ə-ˌtīt\ *n* (1912) **:** a complex phosphate of calcium $Ca_5(PO_4)_3OH$ that occurs as a mineral and is the chief structural element of vertebrate bone

hy·droxy·bu·tyr·ic acid \hī-ˌdräk-sē-byü-ˌtir-ik-\ *n* (1879) **:** a hydroxy derivative $C_4H_8O_3$ of butyric acid

hy·drox·yl \hī-ˈdräk-səl\ *n* [*hydr-* + *ox-* + *-yl*] (1869) **1 :** the chemical group or ion OH that consists of one atom of hydrogen and one of oxygen and is neutral or positively charged **2 :** HYDROXIDE 1 — **hy·drox·yl·ic** \ˌhī-ˌdräk-ˈsil-ik\ *adj*

hy·drox·yl·amine \hī-ˌdräk-sə-lə-ˈmēn, ˌhī-ˌdräk-ˈsil-ə-ˌmēn\ *n* [ISV] (1869) **:** a colorless odorless nitrogenous base NH_3O that resembles ammonia in its reactions but is less basic and that is used esp. as a reducing agent

hy·drox·y·lase \hī-ˈdräk-sə-ˌlās, -ˌlāz\ *n* (1953) **:** any of a group of enzymes that catalyze oxidation reactions in which one of the two atoms of molecular oxygen is incorporated into the substrate and the other is used to oxidize NADH or NADPH

hy·drox·yl·ate \hī-ˈdräk-sə-ˌlāt\ *vt* **-at·ed; -at·ing** (ca. 1909) **:** to introduce hydroxyl into — **hy·drox·yl·ation** \-ˌdräk-sə-ˈlā-shən\ *n*

hy·droxy·pro·line \hī-ˌdräk-sē-ˈprō-ˌlēn\ *n* (1905) **:** an amino acid $C_5H_9NO_3$ that occurs naturally as a constituent of collagen

hy·droxy·tryp·ta·mine \-ˈtrip-tə-ˌmēn\ *n* (1949) **:** SEROTONIN

hy·droxy·urea \-yu̇-ˈrē-ə\ *n* (1949) **:** a compound $CH_4N_2O_2$ used to treat some forms of leukemia

hy·droxy·zine \hī-ˈdräk-sə-ˌzēn\ *n* [*hydroxy-* + *piperazine*] (1956) **:** a compound $C_{21}H_{27}ClN_2O_2$ used as an antihistaminic and tranquilizer

hy·dro·zo·an \ˌhī-drə-ˈzō-ən\ *n* [deriv. of Gk *hydr-* + *zōion* animal — more at ZO-] (1877) **:** any of a class (Hydrozoa) of coelenterates that includes simple and compound polyps and jellyfishes having no stomodaeum or gastric tentacles — **hydrozoan** *adj*

hy·e·na \hī-ˈē-nə\ *n* [ME *hyene,* fr. L *hyaena,* fr. Gk *hyaina,* fr. *hys* hog — more at SOW] (14c) **:** any of several large strong nocturnal carnivorous Old World mammals (family Hyaenidae) that usu. feed as scavengers — **hy·e·nic** \-ˈē-nik, -ˈen-ik\ *adj* — **hy·e·noid** \-ˈē-ˌnȯid\ *adj*

hyet- *or* **hyeto-** *comb form* [Gk, fr. *hyetos,* fr. *hyein* to rain — more at SUCK] **:** rain ⟨*hyeto*logy⟩

Hy·ge·ia \hī-ˈjē-(y)ə\ *n* [L, fr. Gk *Hygieia*] **:** the goddess of health in Greek mythology

hy·giene \ˈhī-ˌjēn *also* hī-ˈ\ *n* [F *hygiène* & NL *hygieina,* fr. Gk, neut. pl. of *hygieinos* healthful, fr. *hygiēs* healthy; akin to Skt *su* well and to L *vivus* living — more at QUICK] (1671) **1 :** a science of the establishment and maintenance of health **2 :** conditions or practices (as of cleanliness) conducive to health — **hy·gien·ic** \ˌhī-jē-ˈen-ik, hī-ˈjen-, hī-ˈjēn-\ *adj* — **hy·gien·i·cal·ly** \-i-k(ə-)lē\ *adv* — **hy·gien·ist** \hī-ˈjēn-əst, ˈhī-ˌjēn-, hī-ˈjen-\ *n*

hy·gien·ics \ˌhī-jē-ˈen-iks, hī-ˈjen-, hī-ˈjēn-\ *n pl but sing in constr* (1855) **:** HYGIENE 1

hygr- *also* **hygro-** *comb form* [Gk, fr. *hygros* wet — more at HUMOR] **:** humidity **:** moisture ⟨*hygro*scope⟩

hy·gro·graph \ˈhī-grə-ˌgraf\ *n* [ISV] (ca. 1864) **:** an instrument for recording automatically variations in atmospheric humidity

hy·grom·e·ter \hī-ˈgräm-ət-ər\ *n* [prob. fr. F *hygromètre,* fr. *hygr-* + *-mètre* -meter] (1670) **:** any of several instruments for measuring the humidity of the atmosphere — **hy·gro·met·ric** \ˌhī-grə-ˈme-trik\ *adj* — **hy·grom·e·try** \hī-ˈgräm-ə-trē\ *n*

hy·groph·i·lous \hī-ˈgräf-ə-ləs\ *adj* (1863) **:** living or growing in moist places

hy·gro·phyte \ˈhī-grə-ˌfīt\ *n* [ISV] (1903) **:** HYDROPHYTE — **hy·gro·phyt·ic** \ˌhī-grə-ˈfit-ik\ *adj*

hy·gro·scope \ˈhī-grə-ˌskōp\ *n* (1665) **:** an instrument that shows changes in humidity (as of the atmosphere)

hy·gro·scop·ic \ˌhī-grə-ˈskäp-ik\ *adj* [fr. the use of such materials in the hygroscope] (1790) **1 :** readily taking up and retaining moisture **2 :** taken up and retained under some conditions of humidity and temperature ⟨~ water in clay⟩ — **hy·gro·scop·i·cal·ly** \-i-k(ə-)lē\ *adv* — **hy·gro·scop·ic·i·ty** \-(ˌ)skäp-ˈis-ət-ē\ *n*

hying *pres part of* HIE

Hyk·sos \ˈhik-ˌsäs, -ˌsōs\ *adj* [Gk *Hyksōs,* dynasty ruling Egypt, fr. Egypt *ḥq šsw* ruler of the countries of the nomads] (1899) **:** of or relating to a Semite dynasty that ruled Egypt from about the 18th to the 16th century B.C.

hyl- *or* **hylo-** *comb form* [Gk, fr. *hylē,* lit., wood] **:** matter **:** material ⟨*hylo*morphous⟩

hy·la \ˈhī-lə\ *n* [NL, fr. Gk *hylē*] (1842) **:** any of a genus (*Hyla*) of tree frogs

hy·lo·zo·ism \ˌhī-lə-ˈzō-ˌiz-əm\ *n* [Gk *hylē* + *zōos* alive, living; akin to Gk *zōē* life — more at QUICK] (1678) **:** a doctrine held esp. by early Greek philosophers that all matter has life — **hy·lo·zo·ist** \-ˈzō-əst\ *n* — **hy·lo·zo·is·tic** \-zō-ˈis-tik\ *adj*

hy·men \ˈhī-mən\ *n* [LL, fr. Gk *hymēn* membrane] (1615) **:** a fold of mucous membrane partly closing the orifice of the vagina — **hy·men·al** \-mən-ᵊl\ *adj*

Hymen *n* [L, fr. Gk *Hymēn*] **:** the Greek god of marriage

¹hy·me·ne·al \ˌhī-mə-ˈnē-əl\ *adj* [L *hymenaeus* wedding song, wedding, fr. Gk *hymenaios,* fr. *Hymēn*] (1602) **:** NUPTIAL — **hy·me·ne·al·ly** \-ˈnē-ə-lē\ *adv*

²hymeneal *n* (1655) **1** *pl, archaic* **:** NUPTIALS **2** *archaic* **:** a wedding hymn

hy·me·ni·um \hī-ˈmē-nē-əm\ *n, pl* **-nia** \-nē-ə\ *or* **-ni·ums** [NL, fr. Gk *hymēn*] (1830) **:** a spore-bearing layer in fungi consisting of a group of asci or basidia often interspersed with sterile structures

hy·me·nop·ter·an \ˌhī-mə-ˈnäp-tə-rən\ *n* [NL *Hymenoptera,* fr. Gk, neut. pl. of *hymenopteros* membrane-winged, fr. *hymēn* + *pteron* wing — more at FEATHER] (ca. 1842) **:** any of an order (Hymenoptera) of highly specialized insects with complete metamorphosis that include the bees, wasps, ants, ichneumon flies, sawflies, gall wasps, and related forms, often associate in large colonies with complex social organization, and have usu. four membranous wings and the abdomen generally borne on a slender pedicel — **hymenopteran** *adj* — **hy·me·nop·ter·ous** \-rəs\ *adj*

hy·me·nop·ter·on \-tə-ˌrän, -rən\ *n, pl* **-tera** \-rə\ *also* **-ter·ons** [NL, fr. Gk, neut. of *hymenopteros*] (1877) **:** HYMENOPTERAN

¹hymn \ˈhim\ *n* [ME *ymne,* fr. OE *ymen,* fr. L *hymnus* song of praise, fr. Gk *hymnos*] (bef. 12c) **1 a :** a song of praise to God **b :** a metrical composition adapted for singing in a religious service **2 :** a song of praise or joy **3 :** something resembling a hymn **:** PAEAN

²hymn *vb* **hymned** \ˈhimd\; **hymn·ing** \ˈhim-iŋ\ *vt* (1667) **:** to praise or worship in or as if in hymns ~ *vi* **:** to sing a hymn

hym·nal \ˈhim-nəl\ *n* [ME *hymnale,* fr. ML, fr. L *hymnus*] (15c) **:** a collection of church hymns

hym·na·ry \ˈhim-nə-rē\ *n, pl* **-ries** (1888) **:** HYMNAL

hymn·book \ˈhim-ˌbu̇k\ *n* (1779) **:** HYMNAL

hym·no·dy \ˈhim-nəd-ē\ *n* [LL *hymnodia,* fr. Gk *hymnōidia,* fr. *hymnos* + *aeidein* to sing — more at ODE] (1711) **1 :** hymn singing **2 :** hymn writing **3 :** the hymns of a time, place, or church

hym·nol·o·gy \him-ˈnäl-ə-jē\ *n* [Gk *hymnologia* singing of hymns, fr. *hymnos* + *-logia* -logy] (1638) **1 :** HYMNODY **2 :** the study of hymns

hy·oid \ˈhī-ˌȯid\ *adj* [NL *hyoides* hyoid bone] (1842) **:** of or relating to the hyoid bone

hyoid bone *n* [NL *hyoides,* fr. Gk *hyoeidēs* shaped like the letter upsilon (Υ, υ), being the hyoid bone, fr. *y, hy* upsilon] (ca. 1811) **:** a bone or complex of bones situated at the base of the tongue and supporting the tongue and its muscles

hy·o·scine \ˈhī-ə-ˌsēn\ *n* [ISV *hyoscyamine* + *-ine*] (1872) **:** SCOPOLAMINE; *esp* **:** the levorotatory form of scopolamine

hy·o·scy·a·mine \ˌhī-ə-ˈsī-ə-ˌmēn\ *n* [G *hyoscyamin,* fr. NL *Hyoscyamus,* genus of herbs, fr. L, henbane, fr. Gk *hyoskyamos,* lit., swine's bean, fr. *hyos* (gen. of *hys* swine) + *kyamos* bean — more at SOW] (1858) **:** a poisonous crystalline alkaloid $C_{17}H_{23}NO_3$ of which atropine is a racemic mixture; *esp* **:** its levorotatory form found esp. in the plants belladonna and henbane and used similarly to atropine

hyp- — see HYPO-

hyp·abys·sal \ˌhip-ə-ˈbis-əl, ˌhī-pə-\ *adj* [ISV] (1895) **:** of or relating to a fine-grained igneous rock usu. formed at a moderate distance below the surface — **hyp·abys·sal·ly** \-ə-lē\ *adv*

hy·pae·thral \hī-ˈpē-thrəl\ *adj* [L *hypaethrus* exposed to the open air, fr. Gk *hypaithros,* fr. *hypo-* + *aithēr* ether, air — more at ETHER] (1794) **1 :** having a roofless central space ⟨~ temple⟩ **2 :** open to the sky **3 :** OUTDOOR

hy·pan·thi·um \hī-ˈpan(t)-thē-əm\ *n, pl* **-thia** \-thē-ə\ [NL, fr. *hypo-* + *anth-* + *-ium*] (ca. 1855) **:** an enlargement of the floral receptacle bearing on its rim the stamens, petals, and sepals and often enlarging and surrounding the fruits (as in the rose hip) — **hy·pan·thi·al** \-thē-əl\ *adj*

¹hype \ˈhīp\ *vt* **hyped; hyp·ing** (1926) **1 :** PUT ON, DECEIVE **2 a :** STIMULATE, ENLIVEN — usu. used with *up* **b :** INCREASE ⟨gimmicks designed to ~ attendance at the games⟩ **3 :** to promote or publicize extravagantly — **hyped–up** \ˌhīp-ˈdəp\ *adj*

²hype *n* [by shortening & alter.] (ca. 1936) **1** *slang* **:** HYPODERMIC **2** *slang* **:** a narcotics addict **3 :** DECEPTION, PUT-ON **4 :** extravagant promotion or advertising

hy·per \ˈhī-pər\ *adj* [short for *hyperactive*] (1971) **:** HIGH-STRUNG, EXCITABLE

hyper- *prefix* [ME *iper-,* fr. L *hyper-,* fr. Gk, fr. *hyper* — more at OVER] **1 :** above **:** beyond **:** SUPER- ⟨*hyper*physical⟩ **2 a :** excessively ⟨*hyper*sensitive⟩ **b :** excessive ⟨*hyper*emia⟩ **3 :** that is or exists in a space of more than three dimensions ⟨*hyper*cube⟩ ⟨*hyper*space⟩

hy·per·acu·ity
hy·per·acute
hy·per·ag·gres·sive
hy·per·alert
hy·per·arid
hy·per·arous·al
hy·per·aware
hy·per·aware·ness
hy·per·boom
hy·per·ca·tab·o·lism
hy·per·cau·tious
hy·per·civ·i·lized
hy·per·co·ag·u·la·bil·i·ty
hy·per·co·ag·u·la·ble
hy·per·con·cen·tra·tion
hy·per·con·sci·en·tious
hy·per·con·sci·en·tious·ness
hy·per·con·scious
hy·per·con·scious·ness
hy·per·de·vel·oped
hy·per·de·vel·op·ment
hy·per·emo·tion·al
hy·per·emo·tion·al·i·ty
hy·per·emo·tion·al·ly
hy·per·en·er·get·ic
hy·per·ex·cit·abil·i·ty
hy·per·ex·cit·able
hy·per·ex·cit·ed
hy·per·ex·cite·ment
hy·per·ex·cre·tion
hy·per·fas·tid·i·ous
hy·per·fem·i·nine
hy·per·func·tion
hy·per·func·tion·al
hy·per·func·tion·ing
hy·per·im·mu·ni·za·tion
hy·per·im·mu·nize
hy·per·in·fla·tion
hy·per·in·fla·tion·ary
hy·per·in·ner·va·tion
hy·per·in·tel·lec·tu·al

hy·per·in·tense
hy·per·in·vo·lu·tion
hy·per·ma·nia
hy·per·man·ic
hy·per·mas·cu·line
hy·per·met·a·bol·ic
hy·per·me·tab·o·lism
hy·per·mil·i·tant
hy·per·mod·ern
hy·per·mod·ern·ist
hy·per·mo·der·ni·ty
hy·per·mu·ta·bil·i·ty
hy·per·mu·ta·ble
hy·per·na·tion·al·is·tic
hy·per·phys·i·cal
hy·per·phys·i·cal·ly
hy·per·pig·men·ta·tion
hy·per·pig·ment·ed
hy·per·plu·ral·ism
hy·per·pro·duc·er
hy·per·pro·duc·tion
hy·per·pure
hy·per·rad·i·cal
hy·per·ra·tio·nal
hy·per·re·ac·tive
hy·per·re·ac·tiv·i·ty
hy·per·re·ac·tor
hy·per·re·al·ism
hy·per·re·al·ist
hy·per·re·al·is·tic
hy·per·re·spon·sive
hy·per·ro·man·tic
hy·per·sa·line
hy·per·sa·lin·i·ty
hy·per·sal·i·va·tion
hy·per·se·cre·tion
hy·per·som·no·lence
hy·per·stat·ic
hy·per·stim·u·la·tion
hy·per·sus·cep·ti·bil·i·ty
hy·per·sus·cep·ti·ble
hy·per·sus·pi·cious
hy·per·tech·ni·cal
hy·per·tense
hy·per·typ·i·cal
hy·per·vari·abil·i·ty
hy·per·vari·able
hy·per·vig·i·lance
hy·per·vig·i·lant
hy·per·vir·u·lent
hy·per·vis·cos·i·ty
hy·per·weak

hy·per·acid·i·ty \ˌhī-pə-rə-ˈsid-ət-ē\ *n* (ca. 1890) : the condition of containing more than the normal amount of acid — **hy·per·ac·id** \ˌhī-pə-ˈras-əd\ *adj*

hy·per·ac·tive \ˌhī-pə-ˈrak-tiv\ *adj* (1867) : excessively or pathologically active — **hyperactive** *n* — **hy·per·ac·tiv·i·ty** \-ˌrak-ˈtiv-ət-ē\ *n*

hy·per·aes·the·sia *var of* HYPERESTHESIA

hy·per·al·i·men·ta·tion \ˌhī-pə-ˌral-ə-mən-ˈtā-shən\ *n* (1967) : the administration of nutrients by intravenous feeding esp. to patients who cannot ingest food through the alimentary tract

hy·per·bar·ic \ˌhī-pər-ˈbar-ik\ *adj* [*hyper-* + *bar-* + *-ic*] (1962) : of, relating to, or utilizing greater than normal pressure esp. of oxygen ⟨~ chamber⟩ ⟨~ medicine⟩ — **hy·per·bar·i·cal·ly** \-i-k(ə-)lē\ *adv*

hy·per·bo·la \hī-ˈpər-bə-lə\ *n, pl* **-las** *or* **-lae** \-(ˌ)lē\ [NL, fr. Gk *hyperbolē*] (1579) : a plane curve generated by a point so moving that the difference of the distances from two fixed points is a constant : a curve formed by the intersection of a double right circular cone with a plane that cuts both halves of the cone

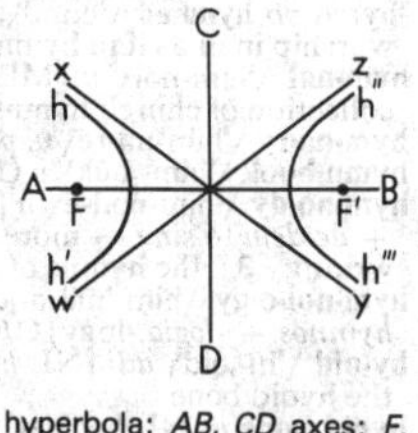

hyperbola: *AB, CD* axes; *F, F′* foci; *xy, zw* asymptotes; *h, h′, h″, h‴* hyperbola

hy·per·bo·le \hī-ˈpər-bə-(ˌ)lē\ *n* [L, fr. Gk *hyperbolē* excess, hyperbole, hyperbola, fr. *hyperballein* to exceed, fr. *hyper-* + *ballein* to throw — more at DEVIL] (15c) : extravagant exaggeration ⟨"mile-high ice-cream cones" is an example of ~⟩ — **hy·per·bo·list** \-ləst\ *n*

¹hy·per·bol·ic \ˌhī-pər-ˈbäl-ik\ *also* **hy·per·bol·i·cal** \-i-kəl\ *adj* (15c) : of or relating to hyperbole — **hy·per·bol·i·cal·ly** \-i-k(ə-)lē\ *adv*

²hyperbolic *also* **hyperbolical** *adj* (1571) **1** : of, relating to, or being analogous to a hyperbola **2** : of, relating to, or being a space in which more than one line parallel to a given line passes through a point ⟨~ geometry⟩

hyperbolic function *n* (ca. 1890) : any of a set of six functions analogous to the trigonometric functions but related to the hyperbola in a way similar to that in which the trigonometric functions are related to a circle

hyperbolic paraboloid *n* (1842) : a saddle-shaped quadric surface whose sections by planes parallel to one coordinate plane are hyperbolas while those sections by planes parallel to the other two are parabolas if proper orientation of the coordinate axes is assumed

hy·per·bo·lize \hī-ˈpər-bə-ˌlīz\ *vb* **-lized; -liz·ing** *vi* (1599) : to indulge in hyperbole ~ *vt* : to exaggerate to a hyperbolic degree

hy·per·bo·loid \-ˌlȯid\ *n* (1743) : a quadric surface whose sections by planes parallel to one coordinate plane are ellipses while those sections by planes parallel to the other two are hyperbolas if proper orientation of the axes is assumed — **hy·per·bo·loi·dal** \(ˌ)hī-ˌpər-bə-ˈlȯid-ᵊl\ *adj*

¹hy·per·bo·re·an \ˌhī-pər-ˈbōr-ē-ən, -ˈbȯr-; -(ˌ)pər-bə-ˈrē-ən\ *adj* (1591) **1** : of or relating to an extreme northern region : FROZEN **2** : of or relating to any of the arctic peoples

²hyperborean *n* [L *Hyperborei* (pl.), fr. Gk *Hyperboreoi*, fr. *hyper-* + *Boreas*] (1601) **1** *often cap* : a member of a people held by the ancient Greeks to live beyond the north wind in a region of perpetual sunshine **2** : an inhabitant of a cool northern climate

hy·per·cal·ce·mia \ˌhī-pər-ˌkal-ˈsē-mē-ə\ *n* [NL] (1925) : an excess of calcium in the blood — **hy·per·cal·ce·mic** \-ˈsē-mik\ *adj*

hy·per·cap·nia \-ˈkap-nē-ə\ *n* [NL, fr. *hyper-* + Gk *kapnos* smoke — more at COVET] (1908) : the presence of excessive amounts of carbon dioxide in the blood — **hy·per·cap·nic** \-nik\ *adj*

hy·per·cat·a·lex·is \-ˌkat-ᵊl-ˈek-səs\ *n, pl* **-lex·es** \-ˈek-ˌsēz\ [NL] (ca. 1890) : the occurrence of an additional syllable after the final complete foot or dipody in a line of verse — **hy·per·cat·a·lec·tic** \-ˈek-tik\ *adj*

hy·per·charge \ˈhī-pər-ˌchärj\ *n* [*hyper*on + *charge*] (1956) : a quantum characteristic of a closely related group of strongly interacting particles represented by a number equal to twice the average value of the electric charge of the group

hy·per·cho·les·ter·ol·emia \ˌhī-pər-kə-ˌles-tə-rə-ˈlē-mē-ə\ *n* [NL] (1916) : the presence of excess cholesterol in the blood — **hy·per·cho·les·ter·ol·emic** \-mik\ *adj*

hy·per·com·plex \ˌhī-pər-ˈkäm-ˌpleks\ *adj* (ca. 1889) : of, relating to, or being the most general form of number that extends the complex number to an expression of the same type involving a finite number of units or components in which addition is by components and multiplication does not have all of the properties of real or complex numbers

hy·per·cor·rect \ˌhī-pər-kə-ˈrekt\ *adj* (1922) : of, relating to, or characterized by the production of a nonstandard linguistic form or construction on the basis of a false analogy ⟨one taught to avoid *it is me* may then create a ~ phrase such as *between you and I*⟩ — **hy·per·cor·rec·tion** \-ˈrek-shən\ *n* — **hy·per·cor·rect·ly** \-ˈrek-(t)lē\ *adv* — **hy·per·cor·rect·ness** \-ˈrek(t)-nəs\ *n*

hy·per·crit·ic \ˌhī-pər-ˈkrit-ik\ *n* [NL *hypercriticus*, fr. *hyper-* + L *criticus* critic] (1633) : a carping or unduly censorious critic — **hy·per·crit·i·cism** \-ˈkrit-ə-ˌsiz-əm\ *n*

hy·per·crit·i·cal \-ˈkrit-i-kəl\ *adj* (1605) : meticulously or excessively critical *syn* see CRITICAL — **hy·per·crit·i·cal·ly** \-k(ə-)lē\ *adv*

hy·per·emia \ˌhī-pə-ˈrē-mē-ə\ *n* [NL] (1836) : excess of blood in a body part : CONGESTION — **hy·per·emic** \-mik\ *adj*

hy·per·es·the·sia \ˌhī-pə-res-ˈthē-zh(ē-)ə\ *n* [NL, fr. *hyper-* + *-esthesia* (as in *anesthesia*)] (1849) : unusual or pathological sensitivity of the skin or of a particular sense — **hy·per·es·thet·ic** \-ˈthet-ik\ *adj*

hy·per·eu·tec·tic \ˌhī-pər-yu̇-ˈtek-tik\ *adj* (1902) : containing the minor component in excess of that contained in the eutectic mixture

hy·per·eu·tec·toid \-ˌtȯid\ *adj* (1908) : containing the minor component in excess of that contained in the eutectoid

hy·per·ex·tend \ˌhī-pə-rik-ˈstend\ *vt* (1883) : to extend so that the angle between bones of a joint is greater than normal — **hy·per·ex·ten·sion** \-ˈsten-chən\ *n*

hy·per·fine \ˈhī-pər-ˌfīn\ *adj* (1926) : being or relating to a fine-structure multiplet occurring in an atomic spectrum that is due to interaction between electrons and nuclear spin

hy·per·fo·cal distance \ˌhī-pər-ˌfō-kəl-\ *n* [ISV] (1905) : the nearest distance upon which a photographic lens may be focused to produce satisfactory definition at infinity

hy·per·ga·my \hī-ˈpər-gə-mē\ *n, pl* **-mies** (1883) : marriage into an equal or higher caste or social group

hy·per·geo·met·ric distribution \ˈhī-pər-ˌjē-ə-ˌme-trik-\ *n* (1950) : a probability function of the form

$$f(x)=\frac{\binom{M}{x}\binom{N-M}{n-x}}{\binom{N}{n}} \text{ where } \binom{M}{x}=\frac{M!}{x!(M-x)!}$$

that gives the probability of obtaining exactly *x* elements of one kind and *n* − *x* elements of another if *n* elements are chosen at random without replacement from a finite population containing *N* elements of which *M* are of the first kind and *N* − *M* are of the second kind

hy·per·gly·ce·mia \ˌhī-pər-glī-ˈsē-mē-ə\ *n* [NL] (1894) : excess of sugar in the blood — **hy·per·gly·ce·mic** \-mik\ *adj*

hy·per·gol·ic \ˌhī-pər-ˈgäl-ik\ *adj* [G *hypergol* (fr. *hyp-* — fr. *hyper-* — + *erg-* + ³*-ol*) + E *-ic*] (1947) **1** : igniting upon contact of components without external aid (as a spark) **2** : of, relating to, or using hypergolic fuel — **hy·per·gol·i·cal·ly** \-i-k(ə-)lē\ *adv*

hy·per·in·su·lin·ism \ˌhī-pə-ˈrin(t)-s(ə-)lə-ˌniz-əm\ *n* [ISV] (1924) : the presence of excess insulin in the body resulting in hypoglycemia

Hy·pe·ri·on \hī-ˈpir-ē-ən\ *n* [L, fr. Gk *Hyperiōn*] : a Titan and the father of Aurora, Selene, and Helios

hy·per·ir·ri·ta·bil·i·ty \ˌhī-pə-ˌrir-ət-ə-ˈbil-ət-ē\ *n* (1913) : abnormally great or uninhibited response to stimuli — **hy·per·ir·ri·ta·ble** \-ˈrir-ət-ə-bəl\ *adj*

hy·per·ker·a·to·sis \ˌhī-pər-ˌker-ə-ˈtō-səs\ *n, pl* **-to·ses** \-ˈtō-ˌsēz\ [NL] (1901) : hypertrophy of the corneous layer of the skin — **hy·per·ker·a·tot·ic** \-ˈtät-ik\ *adj*

hy·per·ki·ne·sia \-kə-ˈnē-zh(ē-)ə, -kī-\ *n* [NL, fr. *hyperkinesis*] (ca. 1848) : HYPERKINESIS

hy·per·ki·ne·sis \-ˈnē-səs\ *n* [NL] (ca. 1855) **1** : abnormally increased and sometimes uncontrollable activity or muscular movements **2** : a condition esp. of childhood characterized by hyperactivity

hy·per·ki·net·ic \-ˈnet-ik\ *adj* (1888) : of, relating to, or marked by hyperkinesis ⟨the ~ child⟩

hy·per·li·pe·mia \ˌhī-pər-lī-ˈpē-mē-ə\ *n* [NL, fr. *hyper-* + *lip-* + *-emia*] (1926) : the presence of excess fat or lipids in the blood — **hy·per·li·pe·mic** \-mik\ *adj*

hy·per·lip·id·emia \-ˌlip-ə-ˈdē-mē-ə\ *n* [NL, fr. *hyper-* + *lipid* + *-emia*] (ca. 1894) : HYPERLIPEMIA

hy·per·mar·ket \ˈhī-pər-ˌmär-kət\ *n, Brit* (1970) : a very large department store that includes a supermarket

hy·per·me·ter \hī-ˈpər-mət-ər\ *n* [LL *hypermetrus* hypercatalectic, fr. Gk *hypermetros* beyond measure, beyond the meter, fr. *hyper-* + *metron* measure, meter] (ca. 1656) **1** : a verse marked by hypercatalexis **2** : a period comprising more than two or three cola — **hy·per·met·ric** \ˌhī-pər-ˈme-trik\ *or* **hy·per·met·ri·cal** \-tri-kəl\ *adj*

hy·per·me·tro·pia \ˌhī-pər-mi-ˈtrō-pē-ə\ *n* [NL, fr. Gk, *hypermetros* + NL *-opia*] (1868) : HYPEROPIA — **hy·per·me·tro·pic** \-ˈtrō-pik, -ˈträp-ik\ *adj*

hy·perm·ne·sia \ˌhī-(ˌ)pərm-ˈnē-zh(ē-)ə\ *n* [NL, fr. *hyper-* + *-mnesia* (as in *amnesia*)] (1882) : abnormally vivid or complete memory or recall of the past — **hy·perm·ne·sic** \-ˈnē-zik, -sik\ *adj*

hy·per·morph \ˈhī-pər-ˌmȯrf\ *n* (1926) : a mutant gene having a similar but greater effect than the corresponding wild-type gene — **hy·per·mor·phic** \ˌhī-pər-ˈmȯr-fik\ *adj*

hy·per·on \ˈhī-pə-ˌrän\ *n* [prob. fr. *hyper-* + *-on*] (1953) : a fundamental particle of the baryon group that is greater in mass than a proton or neutron

hy·per·ope \ˈhī-pə-ˌrōp\ *n* [back-formation fr. *hyperopia*] (1892) : one affected with hyperopia

hy·per·opia \ˌhī-pə-ˈrō-pē-ə\ *n* [NL] (ca. 1886) : a condition in which visual images come to a focus behind the retina of the eye and vision is better for distant than for near objects — called also *farsightedness* — **hy·per·opic** \-ˈrō-pik, -ˈräp-ik\ *adj*

hy·per·os·to·sis \ˌhī-pə-ˌräs-ˈtō-səs\ *n, pl* **-to·ses** \-ˈtō-ˌsēz\ [NL] (1835) : excessive growth or thickening of bone tissue — **hy·per·os·tot·ic** \-ˈtät-ik\ *adj*

hy·per·par·a·site \ˌhī-pər-ˈpar-ə-ˌsīt\ *n* (ca. 1889) : a parasite that is parasitic upon another parasite — **hy·per·par·a·sit·ic** \-ˌpar-ə-ˈsit-ik\ *adj* — **hy·per·par·a·sit·ism** \-ˈpar-ə-ˌsīt-ˌiz-əm, -sə-ˌtiz-\ *n*

hy·per·para·thy·roid·ism \-ˌpar-ə-ˈthī-ˌrȯid-ˌiz-əm\ *n* (1917) : the presence of excess parathyroid hormone in the body resulting in disturbance of calcium metabolism with increase in serum calcium and decrease in inorganic phosphorus, loss of calcium from bone, and renal damage with frequent kidney-stone formation

hy·per·pha·gia \-ˈfā-j(ē-)ə\ *n* [NL] (1941) : abnormally increased appetite for consumption of food frequently associated with injury to the hypothalamus — **hy·per·phag·ic** \-ˈfaj-ik\ *adj*

hy·per·pi·tu·ita·rism \-pə-ˈt(y)ü-ət-ə-ˌriz-əm, -ˈt(y)ü-ə-ˌtriz-\ *n* [ISV] (1909) : excessive production of growth hormones by the pituitary gland — **hy·per·pi·tu·itary** \-ˈt(y)ü-ə-ˌter-ē\ *adj*

hy·per·plane \'hī-pər-ˌplān\ *n* (1903) **:** a figure in hyperspace corresponding to a plane in ordinary space

hy·per·pla·sia \ˌhī-pər-'plā-zh(ē-)ə\ *n* [NL] (1861) **:** an abnormal or unusual increase in the elements composing a part (as tissue cells) — **hy·per·plas·tic** \-'plas-tik\ *adj*

hy·per·ploid \'hī-pər-ˌplȯid\ *adj* [ISV] (1930) **:** having a chromosome number slightly greater than an exact multiple of the monoploid number — **hyperploid** *n* — **hy·per·ploi·dy** \-ˌplȯid-ē\ *n*

hy·per·pnea \ˌhī-pər-'nē-ə, -ˌpərp-'nē-\ *n* [NL] (ca. 1860) **:** abnormally rapid or deep breathing — **hy·per·pne·ic** \-'nē-ik\ *adj*

hy·per·po·lar·ize \ˌhī-pər-'pō-lə-ˌrīz\ *vt* (1950) **:** to produce an increase in potential difference across (a biological membrane) ⟨a *hyperpolarized* nerve cell⟩ ~ *vi* **:** to undergo or produce an increase in potential difference across something — **hy·per·po·lar·iza·tion** \-ˌpō-lə-rə-'zā-shən\ *n*

hy·per·py·rex·ia \-pī-'rek-sē-ə\ *n* [NL] (1866) **:** exceptionally high fever (as in a particular disease)

hy·per·sen·si·tive \ˌhī-pər-'sen(t)-sət-iv, -'sen(t)-stiv\ *adj* (1871) **1 :** excessively or abnormally sensitive **2 :** abnormally susceptible physiologically to a specific agent (as a drug or antigen) — **hy·per·sen·si·tive·ness** *n* — **hy·per·sen·si·tiv·i·ty** \-ˌsen(t)-sə-'tiv-ət-ē\ *n*

hy·per·sex·u·al \-'seksh-(ə-)wəl, -'sek-shəl\ *adj* (1942) **:** exhibiting unusual or excessive concern with or indulgence in sexual activity — **hy·per·sex·u·al·i·ty** \-ˌsek-shə-'wal-ət-ē\ *n*

hy·per·son·ic \-'sän-ik\ *adj* [ISV] (1937) **1 :** of or relating to speed five or more times that of sound in air — compare SONIC **2 :** moving, capable of moving, or utilizing air currents that move at hypersonic speed ⟨~ wind tunnel⟩ — **hy·per·son·i·cal·ly** \-i-k(ə-)lē\ *adv*

hy·per·space \'hī-pər-ˌspās\ *n* (1867) **1 :** space of more than three dimensions **2 :** space other than ordinary euclidean space

hy·per·sthene \'hī-pərs-ˌthēn\ *n* [F *hypersthène*, fr. Gk *hyper-* + *sthenos* strength] (ca. 1808) **:** an orthorhombic grayish or greenish black or dark brown pyroxene $(Mg,Fe)SiO_3$ — **hy·per·sthe·nic** \ˌhī-pərs-'then-ik, -'thē-\ *adj*

hy·per·sur·face \'hī-pər-ˌsər-fəs\ *n* (ca. 1909) **:** a figure that is the analogue in hyperspace of a surface in three-dimensional space

hy·per·ten·sion \'hī-pər-ˌten-chən\ *n* [ISV] (1893) **:** abnormally high blood pressure and esp. arterial blood pressure; *also* **:** the systemic condition accompanying high blood pressure — **hy·per·ten·sive** \ˌhī-pər-'ten(t)-siv\ *adj or n*

hy·per·ther·mia \ˌhī-pər-'thər-mē-ə\ *n* [NL, fr. *hyper-* + *therm-* + *-ia*] (1887) **:** exceptionally high fever esp. when induced artificially for therapeutic purposes — **hy·per·ther·mic** \-mik\ *adj*

hy·per·thy·roid \-'thī-ˌrȯid\ *adj* [back-formation fr. *hyperthyroidism*] (1916) **:** of or relating to hyperthyroidism

hy·per·thy·roid·ism \-ˌrȯid-ˌiz-əm, -rəd-\ *n* [ISV] (ca. 1900) **:** excessive functional activity of the thyroid gland; *also* **:** the resulting condition marked esp. by increased metabolic rate, enlargement of the thyroid gland, rapid heart rate, and high blood pressure

hy·per·to·nia \ˌhī-pər-'tō-nē-ə\ *n* (1842) **:** HYPERTONICITY

hy·per·ton·ic \-'tän-ik\ *adj* [ISV] (1855) **1 :** exhibiting excessive tone or tension ⟨a ~ baby⟩ ⟨a ~ bladder⟩ **2 :** having a higher osmotic pressure than a surrounding medium or a fluid under comparison ⟨animals that produce a ~ urine⟩

hy·per·to·nic·i·ty \-tə-'nis-ət-ē\ *n* (1886) **:** the quality or state of being hypertonic

1**hy·per·tro·phy** \hī-'pər-trə-fē\ *n, pl* **-phies** [prob. fr. NL *hypertrophia*, fr. *hyper-* + *-trophia* -trophy] (1834) **1 :** excessive development of an organ or part; *specif* **:** increase in bulk (as by thickening of muscle fibers) without multiplication of parts **2 :** exaggerated growth or complexity — **hy·per·tro·phic** \ˌhī-pər-'trō-fik\ *adj*

2**hypertrophy** *vi* **-phied; -phy·ing** (1846) **:** to undergo hypertrophy

hy·per·uri·ce·mia \ˌhī-pər-ˌyu̇r-ə-'sē-mē-ə\ *n* [NL, fr. *hyper-* + *uric* + *-emia*] (ca. 1894) **:** excess uric acid in the blood

hy·per·ve·loc·i·ty \-və-'läs-ət-ē, -'läs-tē\ *n* (1949) **:** a high or relatively high velocity; *esp* **:** one greater than 10,000 feet per second

hy·per·ven·ti·la·tion \-ˌvent-ᵊl-'ā-shən\ *n* (1928) **:** excessive ventilation; *specif* **:** excessive rate and depth of respiration leading to abnormal loss of carbon dioxide from the blood — **hy·per·ven·ti·late** \-'vent-ᵊl-ˌāt\ *vb*

hy·per·vi·ta·min·osis \-ˌvīt-ə-mə-'nō-səs\ *n, pl* **-oses** \-'nō-ˌsēz\ [NL, fr. *hyper-* + ISV *vitamin* + NL *-osis*] (1928) **:** an abnormal state resulting from excessive intake of one or more vitamins

hy·pha \'hī-fə\ *n, pl* **hy·phae** \-(ˌ)fē\ [NL, fr. Gk *hyphē* web; akin to Gk *hyphos* web — more at WEAVE] (1866) **:** one of the threads that make up the mycelium of a fungus, increase by apical growth, and are coenocytic or transversely septate — **hy·phal** \-fəl\ *adj*

1**hy·phen** \'hī-fən\ *n* [LL & Gk; LL, fr. Gk, fr. *hyph' hen* under one, fr. *hypo* under + *hen*, neut. of *heis* one — more at UP, SAME] (1620) **:** a punctuation mark - used to divide or to compound words, word elements, or numbers — **hy·phen·less** \-ləs\ *adj*

2**hyphen** *vt* (1814) **:** HYPHENATE

hy·phen·ate \'hī-fə-ˌnāt\ *vt* **-at·ed; -at·ing** (1892) **:** to connect (as two words) or divide (as a word at the end of a line of print) with a hyphen — **hy·phen·ation** \ˌhī-fə-'nā-shən\ *n*

hy·phen·at·ed *adj* [fr. the use of hyphenated words (as German⸗American) to designate foreign-born citizens of the U.S.] (1893) **:** of, relating to, or being an individual or unit of mixed or diverse background or composition ⟨~ citizens formerly suspected of having conflicting loyalties⟩

hypn- *or* **hypno-** *comb form* [F, fr. LL, fr. Gk, fr. *hypnos* — more at SOMNOLENT] **1 :** sleep ⟨*hypno*phobia⟩ **2 :** hypnotism ⟨*hypno*genesis⟩

hyp·na·go·gic *also* **hyp·no·go·gic** \ˌhip-nə-'gäj-ik, -'gō-jik\ *adj* [F *hypnagogique*, fr. Gk *hypn-* + *-agōgos* leading, inducing, fr. *agein* to lead — more at AGENT] (ca. 1886) **:** of, relating to, or associated with the drowsiness preceding sleep

hyp·no·anal·y·sis \ˌhip-nō-ə-'nal-ə-səs\ *n* (1920) **:** the treatment of mental disease by hypnosis and psychoanalytical methods

hyp·noid \'hip-ˌnȯid\ *or* **hyp·noi·dal** \hip-'nȯid-ᵊl\ *adj* (1898) **:** of or relating to sleep or hypnosis

hyp·no·pom·pic \ˌhip-nə-'päm-pik\ *adj* [*hypn-* + Gk *pompē* act of sending — more at POMP] (1901) **:** associated with the semiconsciousness preceding waking ⟨~ illusions⟩

Hyp·nos \'hip-nəs, -ˌnōs\ *n* [Gk] **:** the Greek god of sleep

hyp·no·sis \hip-'nō-səs\ *n, pl* **-no·ses** \-ˌsēz\ [NL] (1882) **1 :** a state that resembles sleep but is induced by a person whose suggestions are readily accepted by the subject **2 :** any of various conditions that resemble sleep **3 :** HYPNOTISM 1

hyp·no·ther·a·py \ˌhip-nō-'ther-ə-pē\ *n* (1897) **1 :** the treatment of disease by hypnotism **2 :** psychotherapy that facilitates suggestion, reeducation, or analysis by means of hypnosis — **hyp·no·ther·a·pist** \-pəst\ *n*

1**hyp·not·ic** \hip-'nät-ik\ *adj* [F or LL; F *hypnotique*, fr. LL *hypnoticus*, fr. Gk *hypnōtikos*, fr. *hypnoun* to put to sleep, fr. *hypnos*] (1625) **1 :** tending to produce sleep **:** SOPORIFIC **2 :** of or relating to hypnosis or hypnotism — **hyp·not·i·cal·ly** \-i-k(ə-)lē\ *adv*

2**hypnotic** *n* (1681) **1 :** a sleep-inducing agent **:** SOPORIFIC **2 :** one that is or can be hypnotized

hyp·no·tism \'hip-nə-ˌtiz-əm\ *n* (1842) **1 :** the study or act of inducing hypnosis — compare MESMERISM **2 :** HYPNOSIS 1 — **hyp·no·tist** \-təst\ *n*

hyp·no·tize \-ˌtīz\ *vt* **-tized; -tiz·ing** (1843) **1 :** to induce hypnosis in **2 :** to dazzle or overcome by or as if by suggestion ⟨a voice that ~s its hearers⟩ ⟨drivers *hypnotized* by speed⟩ — **hyp·no·tiz·abil·i·ty** \ˌhip-nə-ˌtī-zə-'bil-ət-ē\ *n* — **hyp·no·tiz·able** \'hip-nə-ˌtī-zə-bəl\ *adj*

1**hy·po** \'hī-(ˌ)pō\ *n, pl* **hypos** (1711) **:** HYPOCHONDRIA

2**hypo** *n, pl* **hypos** [short for *hyposulfite*] (1861) **:** sodium thiosulfate used as a fixing agent in photography

3**hypo** *n, pl* **hypos** (1925) **1 :** HYPODERMIC SYRINGE **2 :** HYPODERMIC INJECTION **3 :** STIMULUS

4**hypo** *vt* (1942) **:** STIMULATE ⟨do everything possible to ~ the economy —Clem Morgello⟩

hypo- *or* **hyp-** *prefix* [ME *ypo-*, fr. OF, fr. LL *hypo-*, *hyp-*, fr. Gk, fr. *hypo* — more at UP] **1 :** under **:** beneath **:** down ⟨*hypo*blast⟩ ⟨*hypo*dermic⟩ **2 :** less than normal or normally ⟨*hyp*esthesia⟩ ⟨*hypo*tension⟩ **3 :** in a lower state of oxidation **:** in a low and usu. the lowest position in a series of compounds ⟨*hypo*nitrous acid⟩ ⟨*hypo*xanthine⟩

hy·po·blast \'hī-pə-ˌblast\ *n* (1875) **:** the endoderm of an embryo — **hy·po·blas·tic** \ˌhī-pə-'blas-tik\ *adj*

hy·po·cal·ce·mia \ˌhī-pō-ˌkal-'sē-mē-ə\ *n* [NL, fr. *hypo-* + *calc-* + *-emia*] (1925) **:** a deficiency of calcium in the blood — **hy·po·cal·ce·mic** \-mik\ *adj*

hy·po·caust \'hī-pə-ˌkȯst\ *n* [L *hypocaustum*, fr. Gk *hypokauston*, fr. *hypokaiein* to light a fire under, fr. *hypo-* + *kaiein* to burn — more at CAUSTIC] (1678) **:** an ancient Roman central heating system with underground furnace and tile flues to distribute the heat

hy·po·cen·ter \'hī-pə-ˌsent-ər\ *n* (1905) **1 :** the focus of an earthquake **2 :** the point on the earth's surface directly below the center of a nuclear bomb explosion — **hy·po·cen·tral** \ˌhī-pə-'sen-trəl\ *adj*

hy·po·chlo·rite \ˌhī-pə-'klō(ə)r-ˌīt, -'klȯ(ə)r-\ *n* (ca. 1849) **:** a salt or ester of hypochlorous acid

hy·po·chlo·rous acid \-ˌklōr-əs-, -ˌklȯr-\ *n* [ISV] (1841) **:** an unstable strongly oxidizing but weak acid HClO obtained in solution along with hydrochloric acid by reaction of chlorine with water and used esp. in the form of salts as an oxidizing agent, bleaching agent, disinfectant, and chlorinating agent

hy·po·chon·dria \ˌhī-pə-'kän-drē-ə\ *n* [NL, fr. LL, pl., upper abdomen (formerly regarded as the seat of hypochondria), fr. Gk, lit., the parts under the cartilage (of the breastbone), fr. *hypo-* + *chondros* cartilage, grain — more at GRIND] (1668) **:** extreme depression of mind or spirits often centered on imaginary physical ailments; *specif* **:** HYPOCHONDRIASIS

1**hy·po·chon·dri·ac** \-drē-ˌak\ *adj* [F *hypochondriaque*, fr. Gk *hypochondriakos*, fr. *hypochondria*] (1599) **1 :** of, relating to, or being the two regions of the abdomen lying on either side of the epigastric region and above the lumbar regions **2 :** HYPOCHONDRIACAL

2**hypochondriac** *n* (1639) **:** one affected by hypochondria

hy·po·chon·dri·a·cal \-kən-'drī-ə-kəl, -ˌkän-\ *adj* (1621) **:** affected or produced by hypochondria — **hy·po·chon·dri·a·cal·ly** \-k(ə-)lē\ *adv*

hy·po·chon·dri·a·sis \-'drī-ə-səs\ *n, pl* **-a·ses** \-ˌsēz\ [NL, fr. *hypochondria* + *-iasis*] (1766) **:** morbid concern about one's health esp. when accompanied by delusions of physical disease

hy·po·chro·mic anemia \ˌhī-pə-ˌkrō-mik-\ *n* (1935) **:** an anemia marked by deficient hemoglobin and usu. microcytic red blood cells

hy·po·co·rism \hī-'päk-ə-ˌriz-əm; ˌhī-pə-'kō(ə)r-ˌiz-, -'kȯ(ə)r-\ *n* [LL *hypocorisma*, fr. Gk *hypokorisma*, fr. *hypokorizesthai* to call by pet names, fr. *hypo-* + *korizesthai* to caress, fr. *koros* boy, *korē* girl] (1850) **1 :** a pet name **2 :** the use of pet names — **hy·po·co·ris·tic** \ˌhī-pə-kə-'ris-tik\ *or* **hy·po·co·ris·ti·cal** \-ti-kəl\ *adj* — **hy·po·co·ris·ti·cal·ly** \-ti-k(ə-)lē\ *adv*

hy·po·cot·yl \'hī-pə-ˌkät-ᵊl\ *n* [ISV *hypo-* + *cotyl*edon] (1880) **:** the part of the axis of a plant embryo or seedling below the cotyledon

hy·poc·ri·sy \hip-'äk-rə-sē *also* hī-'päk-\ *n, pl* **-sies** [ME *ypocrisie*, fr. OF, fr. LL *hypocrisis*, fr. Gk *hypokrisis* act of playing a part on the stage, hypocrisy, fr. *hypokrinesthai* to answer, act on the stage, fr. *hypo-* + *krinein* to decide — more at CERTAIN] (13c) **1 :** a feigning to be what one is not or to believe what one does not; *esp* **:** the false assumption of an appearance of virtue or religion **2 :** an act or instance of hypocrisy

hyp·o·crite \'hip-ə-ˌkrit\ *n* [ME *ypocrite*, fr. OF, fr. LL *hypocrita*, fr. Gk *hypokritēs* actor, hypocrite, fr. *hypokrinesthai*] (13c) **:** one who affects virtues or qualities he does not have **:** DISSEMBLER — **hypocrite** *adj*

hyp·o·crit·i·cal \ˌhip-ə-'krit-i-kəl\ *adj* (1561) **:** characterized by hypocrisy; *also* **:** being a hypocrite — **hyp·o·crit·i·cal·ly** \-k(ə-)lē\ *adv*

hy·po·cy·cloid \ˌhī-pō-'sī-ˌklȯid\ *n* (1843) **:** a curve traced by a point on the circumference of a circle rolling internally on the circumference of a fixed circle

hy·po·der·mal \ˌhī-pə-'dər-məl\ *adj* (1854) **1 :** of or relating to a hypodermis **2 :** lying beneath an outer skin or epidermis ⟨~ infections of cattle⟩

1**hy·po·der·mic** \-mik\ *adj* [ISV] (1865) **1 :** adapted for use in or administered by injection beneath the skin **2 :** of or relating to the parts beneath the skin 3 : resembling a hypodermic injection in effect : STIMULATING — **hy·po·der·mi·cal·ly** \-mi-k(ə-)lē\ *adv*

[2]**hypodermic** *n* (1875) 1 : HYPODERMIC INJECTION 2 : HYPODERMIC SYRINGE

hypodermic injection *n* (1868) : an injection made into the subcutaneous tissues

hypodermic needle *n* (ca. 1909) 1 : NEEDLE 1c(2) 2 : a hypodermic syringe complete with needle

hypodermic syringe *n* (1893) : a small syringe used with a hollow needle for injection of material into or beneath the skin

hy·po·der·mis \ˌhī-pə-ˈdər-məs\ *n* [NL] (ca. 1866) 1 : the tissue immediately beneath the epidermis of a plant esp. when modified to serve as a supporting and protecting layer 2 : the cellular layer that underlies and secretes the chitinous cuticle (as of an arthropod) 3 : SUPERFICIAL FASCIA

hy·po·dip·loid \ˌhī-pō-ˈdip-ˌlȯid\ *adj* (1966) : having slightly fewer than the diploid number of chromosomes — **hy·po·dip·loi·dy** \-ˌlȯid-ē\ *n*

hy·po·eu·tec·tic \ˌhī-pō-yü-ˈtek-tik\ *adj* (1902) : containing the minor component in an amount less than in the eutectic mixture

hy·po·eu·tec·toid \-ˈtek-ˌtȯid\ *adj* (1911) : containing the minor component in an amount less than that contained in the eutectoid

hy·po·gas·tric \ˌhī-pə-ˈgas-trik\ *adj* [F *hypogastrique*, fr. *hypogastre* hypogastric region, fr. Gk *hypogastrion*, fr. *hypo-* + *gastr-*, *gastēr* belly — more at GASTRIC] (1656) : of or relating to the lower median region of the abdomen

hy·po·ge·al \ˌhī-pə-ˈjē-əl\ *or* **hy·po·ge·an** \-ˈjē-ən\ *or* **hy·po·ge·ous** \-ˈjē-əs\ *adj* [LL *hypogeus* subterranean, fr. Gk *hypogaios*, fr. *hypo-* + *gē* earth] (1686) 1 : growing or living below the surface of the ground 2 *of a cotyledon* : remaining below the ground while the epicotyl elongates

hy·po·gene \ˈhī-pə-ˌjēn\ *adj* [*hypo-* + Gk *-genēs* born, produced — more at -GEN] (1831) : formed, crystallized, or lying at depths below the earth's surface : PLUTONIC — used of various rocks

hy·po·ge·um \ˌhī-pə-ˈjē-əm\ *n, pl* **-gea** \-ˈjē-ə\ [L, fr. Gk *hypogaion*, fr. neut. of *hypogaios*] (1706) : the subterranean part of an ancient building; *also* : an ancient underground burial chamber

hy·po·glos·sal \ˌhī-pə-ˈgläs-əl\ *adj* (1831) : of or relating to the hypoglossal nerves

hypoglossal nerve *n* (1848) : either of the 12th and final pair of cranial nerves which are motor nerves arising from the medulla oblongata and supplying muscles of the tongue in higher vertebrates — called also *hypoglossal*

hy·po·gly·ce·mia \ˌhī-pō-glī-ˈsē-mē-ə\ *n* [NL, fr. *hypo-* + *glyc-* + *-emia*] (ca. 1894) : abnormal decrease of sugar in the blood — **hy·po·gly·ce·mic** \-mik\ *adj or n*

hy·pog·y·nous \hī-ˈpäj-ə-nəs\ *adj* (1821) 1 *of a floral organ* : inserted upon the receptacle or axis below the gynoecium and free from it 2 : having hypogynous floral organs — **hy·pog·y·ny** \-nē\ *n*

hy·po·lim·ni·on \ˌhī-pō-ˈlim-nē-ˌän, -nē-ən\ *n, pl* **-nia** \-nē-ə\ [NL, fr. *hypo-* + Gk *limnion*, dim. of *limnē* lake — more at LIMNETIC] (1928) : the part of a lake below the thermocline made up of water that is stagnant and of essentially uniform temperature except during the period of overturn

hy·po·mag·ne·se·mia \ˌhī-pə-ˌmag-nə-ˈsē-mē-ə\ *n* [NL, fr. *hypo-* + *magnesium* + *-emia*] (1933) : deficiency of magnesium in the blood esp. of cattle

hy·po·ma·nia \ˌhī-pə-ˈmā-nē-ə, -nyə\ *n* [NL] (1882) : a mild mania esp. when part of a manic-depressive cycle — **hy·po·man·ic** \-ˈman-ik\ *adj*

hy·po·morph \ˈhī-pə-ˌmȯrf\ *n* (1926) : a mutant gene having a similar but weaker effect than the corresponding wild-type gene — **hy·po·mor·phic** \ˌhī-pə-ˈmȯr-fik\ *adj*

hy·po·ni·trite \ˌhī-pō-ˈnī-ˌtrīt\ *n* (1846) : a salt or ester of hyponitrous acid

hy·po·ni·trous acid \ˌhī-pō-ˌnī-trəs-\ *n* (1826) : an explosive crystalline weak acid $H_2N_2O_2$ obtained usu. in the form of its salts

hy·po·para·thy·roid·ism \ˈhī-pō-ˌpar-ə-ˈthī-ˌrȯid-ˌiz-əm\ *n* (1910) : deficiency of parathyroid hormone in the body; *also* : the resultant abnormal state marked by low serum calcium and a tendency to chronic tetany

hy·po·phar·ynx \-ˈfar-iŋ(k)s\ *n* [NL] (1826) 1 : an appendage or thickened fold on the floor of the mouth of many insects that resembles a tongue 2 : the laryngeal part of the pharynx extending from the hyoid bone to the lower margin of the cricoid cartilage

hy·po·phy·se·al *also* **hy·po·phy·si·al** \(ˌ)hī-ˌpäf-ə-ˈsē-əl, ˌhī-pə-fə-, ˈzē-; ˌhī-pə-ˈfiz-ē-əl\ *adj* [irreg. fr. NL *hypophysis*] (1882) : of or relating to the hypophysis

hy·poph·y·sec·to·mize \(ˌ)hī-ˌpäf-ə-ˈsek-tə-ˌmīz\ *vt* **-mized; -miz·ing** (1910) : to remove the pituitary gland from

hy·poph·y·sec·to·my \-mē\ *n, pl* **-mies** (1909) : surgical removal of the pituitary gland

hy·poph·y·sis \hī-ˈpäf-ə-səs\ *n, pl* **-y·ses** \-ˌsēz\ [NL, fr. Gk, attachment underneath, fr. *hypophyein* to grow beneath, fr. *hypo-* + *phyein* to grow, produce — more at BE] (ca. 1860) : PITUITARY GLAND

hy·po·pi·tu·ita·rism \ˌhī-pō-pə-ˈt(y)ü-ət-ə-ˌriz-əm, -ˈt(y)ü-ə-ˌtriz-\ *n* [ISV] (1921) : deficient production of growth hormones by the pituitary gland — **hy·po·pi·tu·itary** \-ˈt(y)ü-ə-ˌter-ē\ *adj*

hy·po·pla·sia \-ˈplā-zh(ē-)ə\ *n* [NL] (1889) : a condition of arrested development in which an organ or part remains below the normal size or in an immature state — **hy·po·plas·tic** \-ˈplas-tik\ *adj*

hy·po·ploid \ˈhī-pō-ˌplȯid\ *adj* (1930) : having a chromosome number slightly less than an exact multiple of the monoploid number — **hypoploid** *n*

hy·po·sen·si·ti·za·tion \ˌhī-pō-ˌsen(t)-sət-ə-ˈzā-shən, -ˌsen(t)-stə-ˈzā-\ *n* (1922) : the state or process of being reduced in sensitivity esp. to an allergen : DESENSITIZATION — **hy·po·sen·si·tize** \-ˈsen(t)-sə-ˌtīz\ *vt*

hy·po·spa·di·as \ˌhī-pə-ˈspād-ē-əs\ *n* [NL, fr. Gk, man with hypospadias, fr. *hypo-* + *-spadias*, prob. fr. *spadōn* eunuch, fr. *span* to tear, pluck off — more at SPAN] (1855) : an abnormality of the penis in which the urethra opens on the undersurface

hy·pos·ta·sis \hī-ˈpäs-tə-səs\ *n, pl* **-ta·ses** \-ˌsēz\ [LL, substance, sediment, fr. Gk, support, foundation, substance, sediment, fr. *hyphistasthai* to stand under, support, fr. *hypo-* + *histasthai* to be standing — more at STAND] (1590) 1 a : something that settles at the bottom of a fluid b : the settling of blood in the dependent parts of an organ or body 2 : PERSON 3 3 a : the substance or essential nature of an individual b : something that is hypostatized 4 [NL, fr. LL] : failure of a gene to produce its usual effect when coupled with another gene that is epistatic toward it — **hy·po·stat·ic** \ˌhī-pə-ˈstat-ik\ *adj* — **hy·po·stat·i·cal·ly** \-i-k(ə-)lē\ *adv*

hy·pos·ta·tize \hī-ˈpäs-tə-ˌtīz\ *vt* **-tized; -tiz·ing** [Gk *hypostatos* substantially existing, fr. *hyphistasthai*] (1829) : to attribute real identity to (a concept) — **hy·pos·ta·ti·za·tion** \-ˌpäs-tət-ə-ˈzā-shən\ *n*

hy·po·stome \ˈhī-pə-ˌstōm\ *n* [ISV *hypo-* + *-stome* (fr. Gk *stoma* mouth) — more at STOMACH] (ca. 1862) : any of several structures associated with the mouth: as a : the labrum of a trilobite or crustacean b : the manubrium of a hydrozoan c : a rodlike organ that arises at the base of the beak in various mites and ticks

hy·po·style \ˈhī-pə-ˌstīl\ *adj* [Gk *hypostylos*, fr. *hypo-* + *stylos* pillar — more at STEER] (1831) : having the roof resting on rows of columns — **hypostyle** *n*

hy·po·sul·fite \ˌhī-pō-ˈsəl-ˌfīt\ *n* [*hyposulfurous acid*] (1826) 1 : THIOSULFATE — used esp. in photography 2 : HYDROSULFITE

hy·po·tac·tic \ˌhī-pə-ˈtak-tik\ *adj* [Gk *hypotaktikos*, fr. *hypotassein*] (1896) : of or relating to hypotaxis

hy·po·tax·is \-ˈtak-səs\ *n* [NL, fr. Gk, subjection, fr. *hypotassein* to arrange under, fr. *hypo-* + *tassein* to arrange — more at TACTICS] (1883) : syntactic subordination (as by a conjunction)

hy·po·ten·sion \ˈhī-pō-ˌten-chən\ *n* [ISV] (1893) : abnormally low blood pressure

[1]**hy·po·ten·sive** \ˌhī-pō-ˈten(t)-siv\ *adj* (1904) 1 : characterized by or due to hypotension 2 : causing low blood pressure or a lowering of blood pressure ⟨~ drugs⟩

[2]**hypotensive** *n* (1941) : a person with hypotension

hy·pot·e·nuse \hī-ˈpät-ᵊn-ˌ(y)üs, -ˌ(y)üz\ *also* **hy·poth·e·nuse** \-ˈpäth-ən-\ *n* [L *hypotenusa*, fr. Gk *hypoteinousa*, fr. fem. of *hypoteinōn*, prp. of *hypoteinein* to subtend, fr. *hypo-* + *teinein* to stretch — more at THIN] (1571) 1 : the side of a right-angled triangle that is opposite the right angle 2 : the length of a hypotenuse

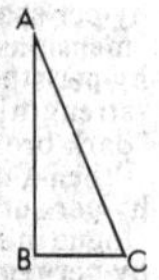

AC hypotenuse

hy·po·tha·lam·ic \ˌhī-pō-thə-ˈlam-ik\ *adj* (1899) : of or relating to the hypothalamus

hy·po·thal·a·mus \-ˈthal-ə-məs\ *n* [NL] (1896) : a basal part of the diencephalon that lies beneath the thalamus on each side, forms the floor of the third ventricle, and includes vital autonomic regulatory centers

[1]**hy·poth·e·cate** \hip-ˈäth-ə-ˌkāt, hīp-\ *vt* **-cat·ed; -cat·ing** [ML *hypothecare* to pledge, fr. LL *hypotheca* pledge, fr. Gk *hypothēkē*, fr. *hypotithenai* to put under, deposit as a pledge] (1681) : to pledge without delivery of title or possession — **hy·poth·e·ca·tion** \-ˌäth-ə-ˈkā-shən\ *n* — **hy·poth·e·ca·tor** \-ˈäth-ə-ˌkāt-ər\ *n*

[2]**hy·poth·e·cate** \hī-ˈpäth-ə-ˌkāt\ *vt* **-cat·ed; -cat·ing** [Gk *hypothēkē* suggestion, fr. *hypotithenai*] (1906) : HYPOTHESIZE

hy·po·ther·mal \ˌhī-pō-ˈthər-məl\ *adj* (1944) : of or relating to a hydrothermal metalliferous ore vein deposited at high temperature

hy·po·ther·mia \-ˈthər-mē-ə\ *n* [NL, fr. *hypo-* + *therm-* + *-ia*] (ca. 1886) : subnormal temperature of the body — **hy·po·ther·mic** \-mik\ *adj*

hy·poth·e·sis \hī-ˈpäth-ə-səs\ *n, pl* **-e·ses** \-ˌsēz\ [Gk, fr. *hypotithenai* to put under, suppose, fr. *hypo-* + *tithenai* to put — more at DO] (1596) 1 : a tentative assumption made in order to draw out and test its logical or empirical consequences 2 a : an assumption or concession made for the sake of argument b : an interpretation of a practical situation or condition taken as the ground for action 3 : the antecedent clause of a conditional statement

syn HYPOTHESIS, THEORY, LAW mean a formula derived by inference from scientific data that explains a principle operating in nature. HYPOTHESIS implies insufficient evidence to provide more than a tentative explanation; THEORY implies a greater range of evidence and greater likelihood of truth; LAW implies a statement of order and relation in nature that has been found to be invariable under the same conditions.

hy·poth·e·size \-ˌsīz\ *vb* **-sized; -siz·ing** *vi* (1738) : to make a hypothesis ~ *vt* : to adopt as a hypothesis

hy·po·thet·i·cal \ˌhī-pə-ˈthet-i-kəl\ *adj* (1588) : being or involving a hypothesis : CONJECTURAL ⟨~ arguments⟩ ⟨a ~ situation⟩ — **hy·po·thet·i·cal·ly** \-i-k(ə-)lē\ *adv*

hy·po·thet·i·co–de·duc·tive \ˌhī-pə-ˈthet-i-ˌkō-di-ˈdək-tiv\ *adj* (1912) : relating to, being, or making use of the method of proposing hypotheses and testing their acceptability or falsity by determining whether their logical consequences are consistent with observed data

hy·po·thy·roid \ˌhī-pō-ˈthī-ˌrȯid\ *adj* (1909) : of, relating to, or affected with hypothyroidism

hy·po·thy·roid·ism \-ˌiz-əm\ *n* [ISV] (1905) : deficient activity of the thyroid gland; *also* : a resultant bodily condition characterized by lowered metabolic rate and general loss of vigor

hy·po·to·nia \ˌhī-pə-ˈtō-nē-ə, -pō-\ *n* [NL] (1886) : the quality or state of being hypotonic

hy·po·ton·ic \ˌhī-pə-ˈtän-ik, -pō-\ *adj* [ISV] (1904) 1 : having deficient tone or tension ⟨~ children⟩ 2 : having a lower osmotic pressure than a surrounding medium or a fluid under comparison ⟨~ organisms⟩

hy·po·to·nic·i·ty \-tə-ˈnis-ət-ē\ *n* (1906) : HYPOTONIA

hy·po·xan·thine \ˌhī-pō-ˈzan-ˌthēn\ *n* [ISV] (1844) : a purine base $C_5H_4N_4O$ found in plant and animal tissues that yields xanthine on oxidation

hyp·ox·emia \ˌhip-ˌäk-ˈsē-mē-ə, ˌhī-ˌpäk-\ *n* [NL, fr. *hypo-* + *ox-* + *-emia*] (ca. 1886) : deficient oxygenation of the blood — **hyp·ox·emic** \-mik\ *adj*

hyp·ox·ia \hip-ˈäk-sē-ə, hī-ˈpäk-\ *n* [NL, fr. *hypo-* + *ox-* + *-ia*] (1941) : a deficiency of oxygen reaching the tissues of the body — **hyp·ox·ic** \-sik\ *adj*

hyps- *or* **hypsi-** *or* **hypso-** *comb form* [Gk, fr. *hypsos* height; akin to OE *ūp* up] : height ⟨*hypso*graphy⟩

hyp·sog·ra·phy \hip-ˈsäg-rə-fē\ *n, pl* **-phies** [ISV] (1885) 1 : a branch of geography that deals with the measurement and mapping of the varying elevations of the earth's surface 2 : topographic relief or the devices (as color shadings) by which it is indicated on maps

hyp·som·e·ter \hip-ˈsäm-ət-ər\ *n* [ISV] (ca. 1864) 1 : an apparatus for estimating elevations in mountainous regions from the boiling points of liquids 2 : any of various instruments for determining the height of trees by triangulation

hyp·som·e·try \hip-'säm-ə-trē\ n (1570) : the measurement of heights (as with reference to sea level) — **hyp·so·met·ric** \,hip-sə-'me-trik\ adj

hy·rax \'hī-,raks\ n, pl **hy·rax·es** \-,rak-səz\ also **hy·ra·ces** \-rə-,sēz\ [Gk hyrak-, hyrax shrew (animal)] (1832) : any of several small ungulate mammals (order Hyracoidea) characterized by thickset body with short legs and ears and rudimentary tail, feet with soft pads and broad nails, and teeth of which the molars resemble those of the rhinoceros and the incisors those of rodents — called also *coney, dassie*

hyrax

hy·son \'hīs-ᵊn\ n [Chin (Pek) hsi¹ ch'un¹, lit., flourishing spring] (1740) : a Chinese green tea made from thinly rolled and twisted leaves

hys·sop \'his-əp\ n [ME ysop, fr. OE ysope, fr. L hyssopus, fr. Gk hyssōpos, of Sem origin; akin to Heb ēzōbh hyssop] (bef. 12c) **1** : a plant used in purificatory sprinkling rites by the ancient Hebrews **2** : a European mint (Hyssopus officinalis) that has highly aromatic and pungent leaves and is sometimes used as a potherb

hyster- or **hystero-** comb form [F or L; F hystér-, fr. L hyster-, fr. Gk, fr. hystera] **1** : womb ⟨hysterotomy⟩ **2** [NL, fr. hysteria] **a** : hysteria ⟨hysterogenic⟩ **b** : hysteria and ⟨hysteroneurasthenia⟩

hys·ter·ec·to·my \,his-tə-'rek-tə-mē\ n, pl **-mies** (ca. 1886) : surgical removal of the uterus — **hys·ter·ec·to·mized** \-tə-,mīzd\ adj

hys·ter·e·sis \,his-tə-'rē-səs\ n, pl **-e·ses** \-,sēz\ [NL, fr. Gk hysterēsis shortcoming, fr. hysterein to be late, fall short, fr. hysteros later — more at OUT] (1801) : a retardation of the effect when the forces acting upon a body are changed (as if from viscosity or internal friction); esp : a lagging in the values of resulting magnetization in a magnetic material (as iron) due to a changing magnetizing force — **hys·ter·et·ic** \-'ret-ik\ adj

hys·te·ria \his-'ter-ē-ə, -'tir-\ n [NL, fr. E hysteric, adj., fr. L hystericus, fr. Gk hysterikos, fr. hystera womb; fr. the former notion that hysteric women were suffering from disturbances of the womb] (1801) **1** : a psychoneurosis marked by emotional excitability and disturbances of the psychic, sensory, vasomotor, and visceral functions **2** : unmanageable fear or emotional excess — **hys·ter·ic** \-'ter-ik\ n — **hys·ter·i·cal** \-'ter-i-kəl\ also **hysteric** adj — **hys·ter·i·cal·ly** \-i-k(ə-)lē\ adv

hys·ter·ics \-'ter-iks\ n pl but sing or pl in constr (1721) : a fit of uncontrollable laughter or crying : HYSTERIA

hys·ter·oid \'his-tə-,ròid\ adj (ca. 1855) : resembling or tending toward hysteria

hys·ter·on prot·er·on \,his-tə-,rän-'prät-ə-,rän, -tə-rən-'prät-ə-rən\ n [LL, fr. Gk, lit., (the) later earlier, (the) latter first] (1565) : a figure of speech consisting of the reversal of a natural or rational order (as in "then came the thunder and the lightning")

hys·ter·ot·o·my \,his-tə-'rät-ə-mē\ n, pl **-mies** [NL hysterotomia, fr. hyster- + -tomia -tomy] (1801) : surgical incision of the uterus; esp : CESAREAN SECTION

I

i \'ī\ n, pl **i's** or **is** \'īz\ often cap, often attrib **1 a** : the 9th letter of the English alphabet **b** : a graphic representation of this letter **c** : a speech counterpart of orthographic i **2** : ONE — see NUMBER table **3** : a graphic device for reproducing the letter i **4** : one designated i esp. as the 9th in order or class **5** : something shaped like the letter I **6** : a unit vector parallel to the x-axis **7** [abbr. for incomplete] **a** : a grade rating a student's work as incomplete **b** : one graded or rated with an I **8** : I FORMATION

¹**I** \(')ī, ə\ pron [ME, fr. OE ic; akin to OHG ih I, L ego, Gk egō] (bef. 12c) : the one who is speaking or writing ⟨~ feel fine⟩ — compare ME, MINE, MY, WE

²**I** \'ī\ n, pl **I's** or **Is** \'īz\ (1529) : someone aware of possessing a personal individuality : SELF

-i- [ME, fr. OF, fr. L, stem vowel of most nouns and adjectives in combination] — used as a connective vowel to join word elements esp. of Latin origin ⟨matrilinear⟩ ⟨raticide⟩

¹**-ia** n suffix [NL, fr. L & Gk, suffix forming feminine nouns] **1** : pathological condition ⟨hysteria⟩ **2** : genus of plants or animals ⟨Fuchsia⟩ **3** : territory : world : society ⟨suburbia⟩

²**-ia** n pl suffix [NL, fr. L (neut. pl. of -ius, adj. ending) & Gk, neut. pl. of -ios, adj. ending] **1** : higher taxon (as class or order) consisting of (such plants or animals) ⟨Sauria⟩ **2** : things derived from or relating to (something specified) ⟨tabloidia⟩

³**-ia** pl of -IUM

Ia·go \ē-'äg-(,)ō\ n : the villain of Shakespeare's tragedy Othello

-ial adj suffix [ME, fr. MF, fr. L -ialis, fr. -i- + -alis -al] : ¹-AL ⟨manorial⟩

iamb \'ī-,am(b)\ or **iam·bus** \ī-'am-bəs\ n, pl **iambs** \'ī-,amz\ or **iam·bus·es** [L iambus, fr. Gk iambos] (1586) : a metrical foot consisting of one short syllable followed by one long syllable or of one unstressed syllable followed by one stressed syllable (as in above) — **iam·bic** \ī-'am-bik\ adj or n

-ian — see -AN

-iana — see -ANA

-i·a·sis \'ī-ə-səs\ n suffix, pl **-i·a·ses** \-,sēz\ [NL, fr. L, fr. Gk, suffix of action, fr. denominative verbs in -ian, -iazein] : disease having characteristics of or produced by (something specified) ⟨hypochondriasis⟩ ⟨ancylostomiasis⟩

-i·at·ric \ē-'a-trik\ also **-i·at·ri·cal** \-tri-kəl\ adj comb form [NL -iatria] : of or relating to (such) medical treatment or healing ⟨pediatric⟩

-i·at·rics \ē-'a-triks\ n pl comb form but sing or pl in constr : medical treatment ⟨pediatrics⟩

iat·ro·gen·ic \(,)ī-,a-trə-'jen-ik\ adj [Gk iatros physician + E -genic] (1924) : induced inadvertently by a physician or his treatment ⟨an ~ rash⟩ — **iat·ro·gen·i·cal·ly** \-i-k(ə-)lē\ adv

-i·a·try \'ī-ə-trē, in a few words ē-,a-trē\ n comb form [F -iatrie, fr. NL -iatria, fr. Gk iatreia art of healing, fr. iatros healer, fr. iasthai to heal] : medical treatment : healing ⟨podiatry⟩

I band \'ī-\ n (1948) : an isotropic band of a striated muscle fiber

I beam n (ca. 1891) : an iron or steel beam that is I-shaped in cross section

¹**Ibe·ri·an** \ī-'bir-ē-ən\ n [Iberia, ancient region of the Caucasus] (1601) : a member of one or more peoples anciently inhabiting the Caucasus in Asia between the Black and Caspian seas — **Iberian** adj

²**Iberian** n [Iberia, peninsula in Europe] (1611) **1 a** : a member of one or more Caucasoid peoples anciently inhabiting the peninsula comprising Spain and Portugal and the Basque region about the Pyrenees and prob. related in origin to peoples of northern Africa **b** : a native or inhabitant of Spain or Portugal or the Basque region **2** : one or more of the languages of the ancient Iberians — **Iberian** adj

ibex \'ī-,beks\ n, pl **ibex** or **ibex·es** [L] (ca. 1607) **1** : any of several wild goats living chiefly in high mountain areas of the Old World and having large recurved horns transversely ridged in front **2** : a wild goat (Capra aegagrus) found in Asia Minor and believed to be the progenitor of the domestic goat

ibi·dem \'ib-ə-,dem, ib-'īd-əm\ adv [L] (1762) : in the same place

-ibil·i·ty \ə-'bil-ət-ē\ — see -ABILITY

ibis \'ī-bəs\ n, pl **ibis** or **ibis·es** [ME, fr. L, fr. Gk, fr. Egypt hby] (14c) : any of several wading birds (family Threskiornithidae) related to the herons but distinguished by a long slender downwardly curved bill

Ibi·zan hound \ī-,vē-thən-, -,bē-, -zən-\ n [Ibiza island] (1948) : any of a breed of slender agile medium-sized hunting dogs developed in the Balearic islands

-ible \ə-bəl\ — see -ABLE

Ibo \'ē-(,)bō\ n, pl **Ibo** or **Ibos** (1732) **1** : a member of a Negro people of the area around the lower Niger **2** : a Kwa language used as a language of trade and education in a large area of southern Nigeria

Ib·sen·ism \'ib-sə-,niz-əm, 'ip-\ n (1890) **1** : dramatic invention or construction characteristic of Ibsen **2** : championship of Ibsen's plays and ideas — **Ib·sen·ite** \-,nīt\ n or adj

ibu·pro·fen \,ī-byü-'prō-fən also ī-'byü-prə-fən\ n [iso- + butyl + propionic acid (a fatty acid) + fen (alter. of phenyl)] (1969) : an antiinflammatory drug $C_{13}H_{18}O_2$ used to relieve pain and fever

Ibizan hound

¹**IC** \(')ī-'sē\ n (1947) : IMMEDIATE CONSTITUENT

²**IC** n (1966) : INTEGRATED CIRCUIT

¹**-ic** \ik\ adj suffix [ME, fr. OF & L; OF -ique, fr. L -icus — more at -Y] **1** : having the character or form of : being ⟨panoramic⟩ : consisting of ⟨runic⟩ **2 a** : of or relating to ⟨aldermanic⟩ **b** : related to, derived from, or containing ⟨alcoholic⟩ **3** : in the manner of : like that of : characteristic of ⟨Byronic⟩ **4** : associated or dealing with ⟨Vedic⟩ : utilizing ⟨electronic⟩ **5** : characterized by : exhibiting ⟨nostalgic⟩ : affected with ⟨allergic⟩ **6** : caused by ⟨amoebic⟩ **7** : tending to produce ⟨analgesic⟩ **8** : having a valence relatively higher than in compounds or ions named with an adjective ending in -ous ⟨ferric iron⟩

²**-ic** n suffix : one having the character or nature of : one belonging to or associated with : one exhibiting or affected by : one that produces

-i·cal \i-kəl\ adj suffix [ME, fr. LL -icalis (as in clericalis clerical, radicalis radical)] : -IC ⟨symmetrical⟩ ⟨geological⟩ — sometimes differing from -ic in that adjectives formed with -ical have a wider or more transferred semantic range than corresponding adjectives in -ic

Ic·a·rus \'ik-ə-rəs\ n [L, fr. Gk Ikaros] : the son of Daedalus who to escape imprisonment flies by means of artificial wings but falls into the sea and drowns when the wax of his wings melts as he flies too near the sun

---

\ə\ abut \ᵊ\ kitten, F table \ər\ further \a\ ash \ā\ ace \ä\ cot, cart \aú\ out \ch\ chin \e\ bet \ē\ easy \g\ go \i\ hit \ī\ ice \j\ job \ŋ\ sing \ō\ go \ò\ law \ói\ boy \th\ thin \th\ the \ü\ loot \ú\ foot \y\ yet \zh\ vision \ä, k, ⁿ, œ, œ̄, ü̇, ᵊ\ see Guide to Pronunciation

ICBM \ˌī-ˌsē-(ˌ)bē-'em\ *n, pl* **ICBM's** *or* **ICBMs** \-'emz\ (1955) **:** an intercontinental ballistic missile
[1]**ice** \'īs\ *n, often attrib* [ME *is,* fr. OE *īs;* akin to OHG *īs* ice, Av *isu-* icy] (bef. 12c) **1 a :** frozen water **b :** a sheet or stretch of ice **2 :** a state of coldness (as from formality or reserve) **3 :** a substance resembling ice; *esp* **:** a substance reduced to the solid state by cold ⟨ammonia ~ in the rings of Saturn⟩ **4 a :** a frozen dessert containing a flavoring (as fruit juice); *esp* **:** one containing no milk or cream **b** *Brit* **:** a serving of ice cream **5** *slang* **:** DIAMONDS; *broadly* **:** JEWELRY **6 :** an undercover premium paid to a theater employee for choice theater tickets — **ice·less** \'ī-sləs\ *adj* — **on ice 1 :** with every likelihood of being won or accomplished **2 :** in reserve or safekeeping
[2]**ice** *vb* **iced; ic·ing** *vt* (15c) **1 a :** to coat with or convert into ice **b :** to chill with ice **c :** to supply with ice **2 :** to cover with or as if with icing **3 :** to put on ice **4 :** to shoot (an ice hockey puck) the length of the rink and beyond the opponents' goal line ~ *vi* **1 :** to become ice-cold **2 a :** to become covered with ice — often used with *up* **b :** to have ice form inside ⟨the carburetor *iced* up⟩
ice age *n* (1873) **1 :** a time of widespread glaciation **2** *cap I&A* **:** the Pleistocene glacial epoch
ice ax *n* (1820) **:** a combination pick and adz with a spiked handle that is used in mountain climbing
ice bag *n* (1883) **:** a waterproof bag to hold ice for local application of cold to the body
ice·berg \'īs-ˌbərg\ *n* [prob. part trans. of Dan or Norw *isberg,* fr. *is* ice + *berg* mountain] (ca. 1820) **1 :** a large floating mass of ice detached from a glacier **2 :** an emotionally cold person **3 :** ICEBERG LETTUCE
iceberg lettuce *n* (1893) **:** any of various crisp light green head lettuces
ice·blink \-ˌbliŋk\ *n* (1817) **:** a glare in the sky over an ice field
ice·boat \-ˌbōt\ *n* (ca. 1819) **1 :** a skeleton boat or frame on runners propelled on ice usu. by sails **2 :** ICEBREAKER 2
ice·boat·ing \-ˌbōt-iŋ\ *n* (1885) **:** the sport of sailing in iceboats — **ice·boat·er** \-ˌbōt-ər\ *n*
ice·bound \-ˌbau̇nd\ *adj* (1641) **:** surrounded or obstructed by ice
ice·box \-ˌbäks\ *n* (1846) **:** REFRIGERATOR
ice·break·er \-ˌbrā-kər\ *n* (1819) **1 :** a structure that protects a bridge pier from floating ice **2 :** a ship equipped to make and maintain a channel through ice **3 :** something that breaks the ice on a project or occasion; *specif* **:** MIXER 1c
ice cap *n* (ca. 1859) **1 :** an ice bag shaped to the head **2 :** a cover of perennial ice and snow; *specif* **:** a glacier forming on an extensive area of relatively level land and flowing outward from its center
ice–cold \'ī-'skōld\ *adj* (bef. 12c) **:** extremely cold
ice–cream *adj* (1890) **:** of a color similar to that of vanilla ice cream
ice cream \(ˈ)ī-'skrēm, 'ī-ˌ\ *n* (1688) **:** a sweet flavored frozen food containing cream or butterfat and usu. eggs
ice–cream chair *n* [fr. its use in ice cream parlors] (1949) **:** a small armless chair with a circular seat for use at a table (as at a sidewalk café)
ice–cream cone *n* (1909) **:** a thin crisp edible cone for holding ice cream; *also* **:** one filled with ice cream
ice·fall \'īs-ˌfȯl\ *n* (1817) **1 :** a frozen waterfall **2 :** the mass of usu. jagged blocks into which a glacier may break when it moves down a steep declivity
ice field *n* (1694) **1 :** an extensive sheet of sea ice **2 :** ICE CAP 2
ice floe *n* (1819) **:** a flat free mass of floating sea ice; *broadly* **:** a large floating fragment of sheet ice
ice fog *n* (1856) **:** a fog composed of ice particles
ice hockey *n* (1883) **:** a game played on an ice rink by two teams of six players on skates whose object is to drive a puck into the opponent's goal with a hockey stick
ice·house \'īs-ˌhau̇s, 'ī-ˌsau̇s\ *n* (1687) **:** a building in which ice is made or stored
[1]**Ice·lan·dic** \ī-'slan-dik\ *adj* (1674) **:** of, relating to, or characteristic of Iceland, the Icelanders, or Icelandic
[2]**Icelandic** *n* (ca. 1824) **:** the North Germanic language of Iceland
Ice·land moss \ˌī-slən(d)-, ˌī-ˌslan(d)-\ *n* (1805) **:** a lichen (*Cetraria islandica*) of mountainous and arctic regions sometimes used in medicine or as food
Iceland poppy *n* (1884) **:** any of various perennial cultivated poppies prob. derived from two species (*Papaver nudicaule* and *P. alpinum*) and characterized by rather small single or double chiefly pastel flowers
Iceland spar *n* (1771) **:** a doubly refracting transparent calcite
ice·man \'ī-ˌsman\ *n* (1851) **1 :** a man skilled in traveling on ice **2 :** one who sells or delivers ice
ice milk *n* (1947) **:** a sweetened frozen food made of skim milk
ice needle *n* (ca. 1934) **:** one of numerous slender ice particles that float in the air in clear cold weather — called also *ice crystal*
Ice·ni \ī-'sē-ˌnī\ *n pl* [L] (ca. 1891) **:** an ancient British people that under their queen Boadicea revolted against the Romans in A.D. 61 — **Ice·ni·an** \-'sē-nē-ən\ *or* **Ice·nic** \-'sē-nik, -'sen-ik\ *adj*
ice pack *n* (1853) **:** an expanse of pack ice
ice pick *n* (1879) **:** a hand tool ending in a spike for chipping ice
ice plant *n* (1753) **:** an Old World annual herb (*Mesembryanthemum crystallinum*) that is related to the carpetweed, has fleshy foliage covered with glistening papillate dots or vesicles, and is widely naturalized in warm regions; *broadly* **:** FIG MARIGOLD
ice point *n* (1903) **:** the temperature of 0° Celsius or 273.15 Kelvin at which ice is in equilibrium with liquid water under air saturated with water at standard atmospheric pressure
ice sheet *n* (1873) **:** ICE CAP 2
ice show *n* (1948) **:** an entertainment consisting of various exhibitions by ice skaters usu. with musical accompaniment
ice–skate \'ī(s)-ˌskāt\ *vi* (1948) **:** to skate on ice — **ice skater** *n*
ice skate *n* (1897) **:** a shoe with a metal runner attached for ice-skating
ice storm *n* (1876) **:** a storm in which falling rain freezes on contact
ice water *n* (1722) **:** chilled or iced water esp. served as a beverage
ichn- *or* **ichno-** *comb form* [Gk, fr. *ichnos*] **:** footprint **:** track ⟨*ichnology*⟩
ich·neu·mon \ik-'n(y)ü-mən\ *n* [L, fr. Gk *ichneumōn,* lit., tracker, fr. *ichneuein* to track, fr. *ichnos* footprint] (15c) **1 :** MONGOOSE **2 :** ICHNEUMON FLY
ichneumon fly *n* (1713) **:** any of a large superfamily (Ichneumonoidea) of hymenopterous insects whose larvae are usu. internal parasites of other insect larvae and esp. of caterpillars
ichor \'ī-ˌkȯ(ə)r, -kər\ *n* [Gk *ichōr*] (15c) **1 :** a thin watery or blood-tinged discharge **2 :** an ethereal fluid taking the place of blood in the veins of the ancient Greek gods — **ichor·ous** \-kə-rəs\ *adj*
ichthy- *or* **ichthyo-** *comb form* [L, fr. Gk, fr. *ichthys;* akin to Arm *jukn* fish] **:** fish ⟨*ichthyic*⟩
ich·thyo·fau·na \ˌik-thē-ō-'fȯn-ə, -'fän-\ *n* [NL] (1883) **:** the fish life of a region — **ich·thyo·fau·nal** \-'fȯn-ᵊl, -'fän-\ *adj*
ich·thy·ol·o·gy \ˌik-thē-'äl-ə-jē\ *n* (1646) **1 :** a branch of zoology that deals with fishes **2 :** a treatise on fishes — **ich·thy·o·log·i·cal** \-thē-ə-'läj-i-kəl\ *adj* — **ich·thy·o·log·i·cal·ly** \-k(ə-)lē\ *adv* — **ich·thy·ol·o·gist** \-thē-'äl-ə-jəst\ *n*
ich·thy·oph·a·gous \ˌik-thē-'äf-ə-gəs\ *adj* [Gk *ichthyophagos,* fr. *ichthy-* + *-phagos* -phagous] (ca. 1828) **:** eating or subsisting on fish
ich·thy·or·nis \ˌik-thē-'ȯr-nəs\ *n* [NL, fr. *ichthy-* + Gk *ornis* bird — more at ERNE] (1884) **:** any of a genus (*Ichthyornis*) of extinct toothed birds
ich·thyo·saur \'ik-thē-ə-ˌsȯ(ə)r\ *n* [deriv. of Gk. *ichthy-* + *sauros* lizard — more at SAURIAN] (1830) **:** any of an order (Ichthyosauria) of extinct marine reptiles with fish-shaped body and elongated snout — **ich·thyo·sau·ri·an** \ˌik-thē-ə-'sȯr-ē-ən\ *adj or n*
-i·cian \'ish-ən\ *n suffix* [ME, fr. OF *-icien,* fr. L *-ica* (as in *rhetorica* rhetoric) + OF *-ien* -ian] **:** specialist **:** practitioner ⟨beaut*ician*⟩
ici·cle \'ī-ˌsik-əl\ *n* [ME *isikel,* fr. *is* ice + *ikel* icicle, fr. OE *gicel;* akin to OHG *ihilla* icicle, MIr *aig* ice] (14c) **1 :** a pendent mass of ice formed by the freezing of dripping water **2 :** an emotionally cold person **3 :** a long narrow strip (as of foil) used to decorate a Christmas tree
[1]**ic·ing** \'ī-siŋ\ *n* (1769) **:** a sweet flavored usu. creamy mixture used to coat baked goods (as cupcakes) — called also *frosting*
[2]**icing** *n* (1948) **:** an act by an ice-hockey player of shooting a puck from within his defensive zone or defensive half of the rink beyond the opponents' goal line but not into the goal
ick·er \'ik-ər\ *n* [deriv. of OE *ēar, eher* — more at EAR] *Scot* (1513) **:** a head of grain
icky \'ik-ē\ *adj* **ick·i·er; -est** [perh. baby talk alter. of *sticky*] (1929) **1 :** offensive to the senses or sensibilities **:** DISTASTEFUL ⟨put off by her ~ triteness —Renata Adler⟩ **2 :** lacking sophistication
icon \'ī-ˌkän\ *n* [L, fr. Gk *eikōn,* fr. *eikenai* to resemble] (1572) **1 :** a usu. pictorial representation **:** IMAGE **2** [LGk *eikōn,* fr. Gk] **:** a conventional religious image typically painted on a small wooden panel and used in the devotions of Eastern Christians **3 :** an object of uncritical devotion **:** IDOL **4 :** EMBLEM, SYMBOL ⟨the house became an ~ of 1860's residential architecture —Paul Goldberger⟩ **5 :** a graphic symbol on a computer display screen that suggests the purpose of an available function — **icon·ic** \ī-'kän-ik\ *adj* — **icon·i·cal·ly** \-i-k(ə-)lē\ *adv* — **ico·nic·i·ty** \ˌī-kə-'nis-ət-ē\ *n*
icon- *or* **icono-** *comb form* [Gk *eikon-, eikono-,* fr. *eikon-, eikōn*] **:** image ⟨*icono*later⟩
icon·o·clasm \ī-'kän-ə-ˌklaz-əm\ *n* (1797) **:** the doctrine, practice, or attitude of an iconoclast
icon·o·clast \-ˌklast\ *n* [ML *iconoclastes,* fr. MGk *eikonoklastēs,* lit., image destroyer, fr. Gk *eikono-* + *klan* to break — more at HALT] (1641) **1 :** one who destroys religious images or opposes their veneration **2 :** one who attacks settled beliefs or institutions — **icon·o·clas·tic** \(ˌ)ī-ˌkän-ə-'klas-tik\ *adj* — **icon·o·clas·ti·cal·ly** \-ti-k(ə-)lē\ *adv*
ico·nog·ra·pher \ˌī-kə-'näg-rə-fər\ *n* (1888) **1 :** a maker of figures or drawings esp. of a conventional type **2 :** a student of iconography
icon·o·graph·ic \(ˌ)ī-ˌkän-ə-'graf-ik\ *or* **icon·o·graph·i·cal** \-i-kəl\ *adj* (ca. 1855) **1 :** of or relating to iconography **2 :** representing something by pictures or diagrams — **icon·o·graph·i·cal·ly** \-i-k(ə-)lē\ *adv*
ico·nog·ra·phy \ˌī-kə-'näg-rə-fē\ *n, pl* **-phies** [ML *iconographia,* fr. Gk *eikonographia* sketch, description, fr. *eikonographein* to describe, fr. *eikon-* + *graphein* to write — more at CARVE] (1678) **1 :** pictorial material relating to or illustrating a subject **2 :** the traditional or conventional images or symbols associated with a subject and esp. a religious or legendary subject **3 :** the imagery or symbolism of a work of art, an artist, or a body of art **4 :** ICONOLOGY
ico·nol·a·try \-'näl-ə-trē\ *n* (1624) **:** the worship of images or icons
ico·nol·o·gy \-'näl-ə-jē\ *n* [F *iconologie,* fr. *icono-* icon- + *-logie* -logy] (ca. 1730) **:** the study of icons or artistic symbolism — **icon·o·log·i·cal** \(ˌ)ī-ˌkän-ᵊl-'äj-i-kəl\ *adj*
icon·o·scope \ī-'kän-ə-ˌskōp\ *n* [fr. *Iconoscope,* a trademark] (1932) **:** a camera tube containing an electron gun and a photoemissive mosaic screen each cell of which produces a charge proportional to the varying light intensity of the image focused on the screen
ico·nos·ta·sis \ˌī-kə-'näs-tə-səs\ *n, pl* **-ta·ses** \-ˌsēz\ [MGk *eikonostasi*] (1833) **:** a screen or partition with doors and tiers of icons that separates the bema from the nave in Eastern churches
ico·sa·he·dral \(ˌ)ī-ˌkō-sə-'hē-drəl, -ˌkäs-ə-\ *adj* (ca. 1828) **:** of or having the form of an icosahedron
ico·sa·he·dron \-drən\ *n, pl* **-drons** *or* **-dra** \-drə\ [Gk *eikosaedron,* fr. *eikosi* twenty + *-edron* -hedron — more at VIGESIMAL] (1570) **:** a polyhedron having 20 faces
-ics \(ˌ)iks\ *n pl suffix but sing or pl in constr* [*-ic* + *-s;* trans. of Gk *-ika,* fr. neut. pl. of *-ikos* -ic] **1 :** study **:** knowledge **:** skill **:** practice ⟨linguist*ics*⟩ ⟨electron*ics*⟩ **2 :** characteristic actions or activities ⟨acrobat*ics*⟩ **3 :** characteristic qualities, operations, or phenomena ⟨mechan*ics*⟩
ic·ter·ic \ik-'ter-ik\ *adj* (1600) **:** of, relating to, or affected with jaundice
ic·ter·us \'ik-tə-rəs\ *n* [NL, fr. Gk *ikteros;* akin to Gk *iktis,* a yellow bird] (1706) **:** JAUNDICE
ic·tus \'ik-təs\ *n* [L, fr. *ictus,* pp. of *icere* to strike; akin to Gk *aichmē* lance] (1752) **:** the recurring stress or beat in a rhythmic or metrical series of sounds
icy \'ī-sē\ *adj* **ic·i·er; -est** (bef. 12c) **1 a :** covered with, abounding in, or consisting of ice **b :** intensely cold **2 :** characterized by coldness **:** FRIGID ⟨an ~ stare⟩ — **ic·i·ly** \-sə-lē\ *adv* — **ic·i·ness** \-sē-nəs\ *n*
[1]**id** \'id\ *n* [NL, fr. L, it] (1924) **:** the one of the three divisions of the psyche in psychoanalytic theory that is completely unconscious and is the source of psychic energy derived from instinctual needs and drives — compare EGO, SUPEREGO
[2]**id** *n* [*-id,* fr. F *-ide,* fr. L *-id-, -is,* fem. patronymic suffix] (1936) **:** a skin rash that is an allergic reaction to an agent causing an infection
[1]**-id** \əd, (ˌ)id\ *n suffix* [in sense 1, fr. L *-ides,* masc. patronymic suffix, fr. Gk *-idēs;* in sense 2, fr. It *-ide,* fr. L *-id-, is,* fem. patronymic suffix, fr. Gk] **1 :** one belonging to a (specified) dynastic line ⟨Fatim*id*⟩ **2**

: meteor associated with or radiating from a (specified) constellation or comet ⟨Perse*id*⟩

²-id *n suffix* [prob. fr. L *-id-, -is,* fem. patronymic suffix, fr. Gk] : body : particle ⟨energ*id*⟩

I'd \(,)īd\ : I had : I should : I would

-i·dae \ə-,dē\ *n pl suffix* [NL, fr. L, fr. Gk *-idai,* pl. of *-idēs*] : members of the family of — in names of zoological families ⟨Fel*idae*⟩

Ida·ho \'īd-ə-,hō\ *n, pl* **Idahos** *or* **Idahoes** (ca. 1934) : an elongated baking potato grown esp. in the state of Idaho

ID card \'ī-'dē-\ *n* (ca. 1945) : a card bearing identifying data (as age or organizational membership) about the individual whose name appears thereon — called also *identification card, identity card*

-ide \,īd\ *also* **-id** \əd, (,)id\ *n suffix* [G & F; G *-id,* fr. F *-ide* (as in *oxide*)] **1** : binary chemical compound — added to the contracted name of the nonmetallic or more electronegative element ⟨hydrogen sulf*ide*⟩ or group ⟨cyan*ide*⟩ **2** : chemical compound derived from or related to another (usu. specified) compound ⟨anhydr*ide*⟩ ⟨glucos*ide*⟩

idea \ī-'dē-ə, 'īd-(,)ē-ə, *also* 'īd-ē\ *n* [L, fr. Gk, fr. *idein* to see — more at WIT] (14c) **1 a** : a transcendent entity that is a real pattern of which existing things are imperfect representations **b** : a standard of perfection : IDEAL **c** : a plan for action : DESIGN **2** *archaic* : a visible representation of a conception : a replica of a pattern **3 a** *obs* : an image recalled by memory **b** : an indefinite or unformed conception **c** : an entity (as a thought, concept, sensation, or image) actually or potentially present to consciousness **4** : a formulated thought or opinion **5** : whatever is known or supposed about something ⟨a child's ~ of time⟩ **6** : the central meaning or chief end of a particular action or situation **7** *Christian Science* : an image in Mind — **idea·less** \ī-'dē-ə-ləs\ *adj*

syn IDEA, CONCEPT, CONCEPTION, THOUGHT, NOTION, IMPRESSION mean what exists in the mind as a representation (as of something comprehended) or as a formulation (as of a plan). IDEA may apply to a mental image or formulation of something seen or known or imagined, to a pure abstraction, or to something assumed or vaguely sensed; CONCEPT may apply to the idea formed by consideration of instances of a species or genus or, more broadly, to any idea of what a thing ought to be; CONCEPTION is often interchangeable with CONCEPT; it may stress the process of imagining or formulating rather than the result; THOUGHT is likely to suggest the result of reflecting, reasoning, or meditating rather than of imagining; NOTION suggests an idea not much resolved by analysis or reflection and may suggest the capricious or accidental; IMPRESSION applies to an idea or notion resulting immediately from some stimulation of the senses.

¹ide·al \ī-'dē(-ə)l, 'ī-,\ *adj* [F or LL; F *idéal,* fr. LL *idealis,* fr. L *idea*] (15c) **1** : existing as an archetypal idea **2 a** : existing as a mental image or in fancy or imagination only; *broadly* : lacking practicality **b** : relating to or constituting mental images, ideas, or conceptions **3 a** : of, relating to, or embodying an ideal **b** : conforming exactly to an ideal, law, or standard : PERFECT **4** : of or relating to philosophical idealism

²ideal *n* (ca. 1623) **1** : a standard of perfection, beauty, or excellence **2** : one regarded as exemplifying an ideal and often taken as a model for imitation **3** : an ultimate object or aim of endeavor : GOAL **4** : a subset of a mathematical ring that is closed under addition and subtraction and contains the products of any given element of the subset with each element of the ring ⟨the integers ending in 0 are an ~ in the ring of all integers⟩ ***syn*** see MODEL — **ide·al·less** \ī-'dē(-ə)l-ləs\ *adj*

ide·al·ism \ī-'dē-(ə),liz-əm, 'ī-(,)dē-\ *n* (1796) **1 a (1)** : a theory that ultimate reality lies in a realm transcending phenomena **(2)** : a theory that the essential nature of reality lies in consciousness or reason **b (1)** : a theory that only the perceptible is real **(2)** : a theory that only mental states or entities are knowable **2 a** : the practice of forming ideals or living under their influence **b** : something that is idealized **3** : literary or artistic theory or practice that affirms the preeminent value of imagination as compared with faithful copying of nature — compare REALISM

¹ide·al·ist \-(ə-)ləst\ *n* (1701) **1 a** : an adherent of a philosophical theory of idealism **b** : an artist or author who advocates or practices idealism in art or writing **2** : one guided by ideals; *esp* : one that places ideals before practical considerations

²idealist *adj* (1875) : IDEALISTIC

ide·al·is·tic \(,)ī-,dē-(ə-)'lis-tik, ,ī-dē-\ *adj* (1829) : of or relating to idealists or idealism — **ide·al·is·ti·cal·ly** \-ti-k(ə-)lē\ *adv*

ide·al·i·ty \,īd-ē-'al-ət-ē\ *n, pl* **-ties** (1817) **1 a** : the quality or state of being ideal **b** : existence only in idea **2** : something imaginary or idealized

ide·al·ize \ī-'dē-(ə-),līz\ *vb* **-ized; -iz·ing** *vi* (1786) **1** : to form ideals **2** : to work idealistically ~ *vt* : to give an ideal form or value to **2** : to treat idealistically — **ide·al·iza·tion** \-,dē-(ə-)lə-'zā-shən\ *n* — **ide·al·iz·er** \-'dē-(ə-),lī-zər\ *n*

ide·al·ly \ī-'dē-ə-lē, -'dē(-ə)l-lē\ *adv* (1598) **1** : in idea or imagination : MENTALLY **2** : in relation to an exemplar **3 a** : conformably to or in respect to an ideal : PERFECTLY **b** : for best results ⟨~, the counselor should vary his techniques for each applicant —T. M. Martinez⟩ **c** : in accordance with an ideal or typical standard : CLASSICALLY

ideal point *n* (1879) : a point added to the plane or to space to eliminate special cases; *specif* : the point at infinity added in projective geometry as the assumed intersection of two parallel lines

ide·ate \'īd-ē-,āt\ *vb* **-at·ed; -at·ing** *vt* (1610) : to form an idea or conception of ~ *vi* : to form an idea

ide·ation \,īd-ē-'ā-shən\ *n* (1829) : the capacity for or the act of forming or entertaining ideas

ide·ation·al \-shnəl, -shən-ᵊl\ *adj* (1853) : of, relating to, or produced by ideation; *broadly* : consisting of or referring to ideas or thoughts of objects not immediately present to the senses — **ide·ation·al·ly** \-ē\ *adv*

idée fixe \(,)ē-,dā-'fēks\ *n, pl* **idées fixes** \-'fēks(-əz)\ [F, fixed idea] (1836) : an idea that dominates one's mind esp. for a prolonged period : OBSESSION

idem \'īd-,em, 'ēd-, 'id-\ *pron* [L, same — more at IDENTITY] (14c) : something previously mentioned : SAME

idem·po·tent \ī-'dem-pət-ənt\ *adj* [ISV *idem-* (fr. L *idem* same) + L *potent-, potens* having power — more at POTENT] (ca. 1870) : relating to or being a mathematical quantity which is not zero and which when applied to itself under a given binary operation (as multiplication) equals itself; *also* : relating to or being an operation under which a mathematical quantity is idempotent — **idempotent** *n*

iden·tic \ī-'dent-ik, ə-\ *adj* (1649) : IDENTICAL: as **a** : constituting a diplomatic action or expression in which two or more governments follow precisely the same course or employ an identical form **b** : constituting an action or expression in which a government follows precisely the same course or employs identical forms with reference to two or more other governments

iden·ti·cal \ī-'dent-i-kəl, ə-\ *adj* [prob. fr. ML *identicus,* fr. LL *identitas*] (1620) **1** : being the same : SELFSAME ⟨the ~ place we stopped before⟩ **2** : having such close resemblance as to be essentially the same ⟨~ hats⟩ ⟨the copy was ~ with the original⟩ **3 a** : having the same cause or origin ⟨the infections appeared to be ~⟩ **b** : MONOZYGOTIC ***syn*** see SAME — **iden·ti·cal·ly** \-i-k(ə-)lē\ *adv* — **iden·ti·cal·ness** \-kəl-nəs\ *n*

iden·ti·fi·ca·tion \ī-,dent-ə-fə-'kā-shən, ə-\ *n* (1644) **1 a** : an act of identifying : the state of being identified **b** : evidence of identity **2 a** : psychological orientation of the self in regard to something (as a person or group) with a resulting feeling of close emotional association **b** : a largely unconscious process whereby an individual models thoughts, feelings, and actions after those attributed to an object that has been incorporated as a mental image

identification card *n* (1908) : ID CARD

iden·ti·fi·er \ī-'dent-ə-,fī(-ə)r, ə-\ *n* (1889) : one that identifies

iden·ti·fy \ī-'dent-ə-,fī, ə-\ *vb* **-fied; -fy·ing** *vt* (1644) **1 a** : to cause to be or become identical **b** : to conceive as united (as in spirit, outlook, or principle) ⟨groups that are *identified* with conservation⟩ **2 a** : to establish the identity of **b** : to determine the taxonomic position of (a biological specimen) ~ *vi* **1** : to be or become the same **2** : to practice psychological identification ⟨~ with the hero of a novel⟩ — **iden·ti·fi·able** \-,fī-ə-bəl\ *adj* — **iden·ti·fi·ably** \-blē\ *adv*

iden·ti·ty \ī-'den(t)-ət-ē, ə-'den(t)-\ *n, pl* **-ties** [MF *identité,* fr. LL *identitat-, identitas,* irreg. fr. L *idem* same, fr. *is* that — more at ITERATE] (1570) **1 a** : sameness of essential or generic character in different instances **b** : sameness in all that constitutes the objective reality of a thing : ONENESS **2 a** : the distinguishing character or personality of an individual : INDIVIDUALITY **b** : the relation established by psychological identification ⟨a symbolic act . . . marking ~ and participation in a collective action —Paul Jacobs⟩ **3** : the condition of being the same with something described or asserted ⟨establish the ~ of stolen goods⟩ **4** : an equation that is satisfied for all values of the symbols **5** : IDENTITY ELEMENT

identity card *n* (1900) : ID CARD

identity crisis *n* (1954) **1** : personal psychosocial conflict esp. in adolescence that involves confusion about one's social role and often a sense of loss of continuity to one's personality **2** : a state of confusion in an institution or organization regarding its nature or direction

identity element *n* (1902) : an element (as 0 in the group of integers under addition) that leaves any element of the set to which it belongs unchanged when combined with it by a specified operation (as addition or multiplication)

identity matrix *n* (ca. 1929) : a square matrix with numeral 1's along the principal diagonal and 0's elsewhere

ideo- *comb form* [F *idéo-,* fr. Gk *idea*] : idea ⟨*ideo*gram⟩

ideo·gram \'id-ē-ə-,gram, 'īd-\ *n* (1838) **1** : a picture or symbol used in a system of writing to represent a thing or an idea but not a particular word or phrase for it; *esp* : one that represents not the object pictured but some thing or idea that the object pictured is supposed to suggest **2** : LOGOGRAM — **ideo·gram·ic** *or* **ideo·gram·mic** \,id-ē-ə-'gram-ik, ,īd-\ *adj* — **ideo·gram·mat·ic** \-ē-ō-grə-'mat-ik\ *adj*

ideo·graph \'id-ē-ə-,graf, 'īd-\ *n* (1835) : IDEOGRAM — **ideo·graph·ic** \,id-ē-ə-'graf-ik, ,īd-\ *adj* — **ideo·graph·i·cal·ly** \-i-k(ə-)lē\ *adv*

ide·og·ra·phy \,id-ē-'äg-rə-fē, ,īd-\ *n* (1836) **1** : the use of ideograms **2** : the representation of ideas by graphic symbols

ideo·log·i·cal \,id-ē-ə-'läj-i-kəl, ,īd-\ *also* **ideo·log·ic** \-'läj-ik\ *adj* (1797) **1** : relating to or concerned with ideas **2** : of, relating to, or based on ideology — **ideo·log·i·cal·ly** \-'läj-i-k(ə-)lē\ *adv*

ideo·logue \'īd-ē-ə-,lȯg, -,läg\ *n* [F *idéologue,* back-formation fr. *idéologie*] (1831) **1** : an impractical idealist : THEORIST **2** : an advocate or adherent of a particular ideology

ide·ol·o·gy \,īd-ē-'äl-ə-jē, ,id-\ *also* **ide·al·o·gy** \-'äl-ə-jē, -'al-\ *n, pl* **-gies** [F *idéologie,* fr. *idéo-* ideo- + *-logie* -logy] (1813) **1** : visionary theorizing **2 a** : a systematic body of concepts esp. about human life or culture **b** : a manner or the content of thinking characteristic of an individual, group, or culture **c** : the integrated assertions, theories, and aims that constitute a sociopolitical program — **ide·ol·o·gist** \-jəst\ *n*

ideo·mo·tor \,id-ē-ə-'mōt-ər, ,īd-\ *adj* [ISV] (1867) : not reflex but resulting from the impingement of ideas on the system

ides \'īdz\ *n pl but sing or pl in constr* [MF, fr. L *idus*] (12c) : the 15th day of March, May, July, or October or the 13th day of any other month in the ancient Roman calendar; *broadly* : this day and the seven days preceding it

-i·din \əd-ən, -ᵊn\ *or* **-i·dine** \ə-,dēn\ *n suffix* [ISV *-ide* + *-in, -ine*] : chemical compound related in origin or structure to another compound ⟨tolu*idine*⟩ ⟨guan*idine*⟩

idio- *comb form* [Gk, fr. *idios* — more at IDIOT] : one's own : personal : separate : distinct ⟨*idio*blast⟩

id·io·blast \'id-ē-ə-,blast\ *n* [ISV] (ca. 1822) : a plant cell (as a sclereid) that differs markedly from neighboring cells — **id·io·blas·tic** \,id-ē-ə-'blas-tik\ *adj*

id·i·o·cy \'id-ē-ə-sē\ *n, pl* **-cies** (1529) **1** : extreme mental deficiency commonly due to incomplete or abnormal development of the brain **2** : something notably stupid or foolish

id·io·graph·ic \,id-ē-ə-'graf-ik\ *adj* [ISV] (ca. 1890) : relating to or dealing with the concrete, individual, or unique

\ə\ abut \ᵊ\ kitten, F table \ər\ further \a\ ash \ā\ ace \ä\ cot, cart \au̇\ out \ch\ chin \e\ bet \ē\ easy \g\ go \i\ hit \ī\ ice \j\ job \ŋ\ sing \ō\ go \ȯ\ law \ȯi\ boy \th\ thin \t͟h\ the \ü\ loot \u̇\ foot \y\ yet \zh\ vision \à, k̟, ⁿ, œ, œ̄, ue, ue̅, ʸ\ *see* Guide to Pronunciation

id·io·lect \'id-ē-ə-ˌlekt\ *n* [*idio-* + *-lect* (as in *dialect*)] (ca. 1948) **:** the language or speech pattern of one individual at a particular period of his life — **id·io·lec·tal** \ˌid-ē-ə-'lek-tᵊl\ *adj*

id·i·om \'id-ē-əm\ *n* [MF & LL; MF *idiome,* fr. LL *idioma* individual peculiarity of language, fr. Gk *idiōmat-, idiōma,* fr. *idiousthai* to appropriate, fr. *idios*] (1588) **1 a :** the language peculiar to a people or to a district, community, or class **:** DIALECT **b :** the syntactical, grammatical, or structural form peculiar to a language **2 :** an expression in the usage of a language that is peculiar to itself either grammatically (as *no, it wasn't me*) or in having a meaning that cannot be derived from the conjoined meanings of its elements (as *Monday week* for "the Monday a week after next Monday") **3 :** a style or form of artistic expression that is characteristic of an individual, a period or movement, or a medium or instrument ⟨the modern jazz ~⟩ **4 :** MANNER, STYLE ⟨a walled, medieval town in the ~ of the Tyrol —Lisa Wyeth⟩

id·i·om·at·ic \ˌid-ē-ə-'mat-ik\ *adj* (1712) **1 :** of, relating to, or conforming to idiom **2 :** peculiar to a particular group, individual, or style — **id·i·om·at·i·cal·ly** \-i-k(ə-)lē\ *adv* — **id·i·om·at·ic·ness** \-ik-nəs\ *n*

id·io·mor·phic \ˌid-ē-ə-'mȯr-fik\ *adj* [Gk *idiomorphos,* fr. *idio-* + *-morphos* -morphous] (1887) **:** having the proper form or shape — used of minerals whose crystalline growth has not been interfered with — **id·io·mor·phi·cal·ly** \-fi-k(ə-)lē\ *adv*

id·io·path·ic \ˌid-ē-ə-'path-ik\ *adj* (1669) **1 :** arising spontaneously or from an obscure or unknown cause **:** PRIMARY **2 :** peculiar to the individual — **id·io·path·i·cal·ly** \-'path-i-k(ə-)lē\ *adv*

id·io·syn·cra·sy \ˌid-ē-ə-'siŋ-krə-sē\ *n, pl* **-sies** [Gk *idiosynkrasia,* fr. *idio-* + *synkerannynai* to blend, fr. *syn-* + *kerannynai* to mingle, mix — more at CRATER] (1604) **1 a :** a peculiarity of constitution or temperament **b :** individual hypersensitiveness (as to a drug or food) **2 :** characteristic peculiarity of habit or structure — **id·io·syn·crat·ic** \ˌid-ē-ō-(ˌ)sin-'krat-ik\ *adj* — **id·io·syn·crat·i·cal·ly** \-'krat-i-k(ə-)lē\ *adv*

id·i·ot \'id-ē-ət\ *n* [ME, fr. L *idiota* ignorant person, fr. Gk *idiōtēs* one in a private station, layman, ignorant person, fr. *idios* one's own, private; akin to L *sed, se* without, *sui* of oneself] (14c) **1 :** a person affected with idiocy; *esp* **:** a feebleminded person having a mental age not exceeding three years and requiring complete custodial care **2 :** a silly or foolish person — **idiot** *adj*

idiot box *n, slang* (ca. 1955) **:** TELEVISION

id·i·ot·ic \ˌid-ē-'ät-ik\ *also* **id·i·ot·i·cal** \-'ät-i-kəl\ *adj* (1713) **1 :** characterized by idiocy **2 :** showing complete lack of thought or common sense **:** FOOLISH — **id·i·ot·i·cal·ly** \-i-k(ə-)lē\ *adv* — **id·i·ot·i·cal·ness** \-i-kəl-nəs\ *n*

1id·i·o·tism \'id-ē-ə-ˌtiz-əm\ *n* [MF *idiotisme,* fr. L *idiotismus* common speech, fr. Gk *idiōtismos,* fr. *idiōtēs*] (1588) **1** *obs* **:** IDIOM 1 **2 :** IDIOM 2

2id·i·ot·ism \'id-ē-ət-ˌiz-əm\ *n* [*idiot* + *-ism*] *archaic* (ca. 1611) **:** IDIOCY 2

idiot light *n* (1966) **:** a colored light on an automobile instrument panel designed to give a warning (as of low oil pressure)

idiot sa·vant \'ē-ˌdyō-sä-'vä^{n}\ *n, pl* **idiots savants** \-ˌdyō-sä-'vä^{n}(z)\ *or* **idiot savants** \-'vä^{n}(z)\ [F, lit., learned idiot] (1927) **:** a mentally defective person who exhibits exceptional skill or brilliance in some limited field

-id·i·um \'id-ē-əm\ *n suffix, pl* **-id·i·ums** *or* **-id·ia** \-ē-ə\ [NL, fr. Gk *-idion,* dim. suffix] **:** small one ⟨anther*idium*⟩

1idle \'īd-ᵊl\ *adj* **idler** \'īd-lər, -ᵊl-ər\; **idlest** \'īd-ləst, -ᵊl-əst\ [ME *idel,* fr. OE *īdel;* akin to OHG *ītal* worthless] (bef. 12c) **1 :** lacking worth or basis **:** USELESS ⟨~ rumor⟩ **2 :** not occupied or employed: as **a :** having no employment **:** INACTIVE ⟨~ workmen⟩ **b :** not turned to appropriate use ⟨~ funds⟩ **c :** not scheduled to compete ⟨the team will be ~ tomorrow⟩ **3 a :** SHIFTLESS, LAZY ⟨~ fellows⟩ **b :** having no evident lawful means of support ⟨the charge of being an ~ person⟩ ***syn*** see VAIN — **idle·ness** \'īd-ᵊl-nəs\ *n* — **idly** \'īd-lē, -ᵊl-ē\ *adv*

2idle *vb* **idled; idling** \'īd-liŋ, -ᵊl-iŋ\ *vi* (1592) **1 a :** to spend time in idleness **b :** to move idly **2 :** to run disconnected so that power is not used for useful work ⟨the engine is *idling*⟩ ~ *vt* **1 :** to pass in idleness **2 :** to make idle ⟨workers *idled* by a strike⟩ **3 :** to cause to idle — **idler** \'īd-lər, -ᵊl-ər\ *n*

idler pulley *n* (ca. 1890) **:** a guide or tightening pulley for a belt or chain

idler wheel *n* (ca. 1842) **1 :** a wheel, gear, or roller used to transfer motion or to guide or support something **2 :** IDLER PULLEY

idlesse \'īd-ləs, īd-'les\ *n* [ME, fr. *idle* + *-esse* (as in *richesse* wealth) — more at RICHES] (15c) **:** the quality or state of being idle **:** IDLENESS

ido·crase \'īd-ə-ˌkrās, 'id-, -ˌkrāz\ *n* [F, fr. Gk *eidos* form + *krasis* mixture, fr. *kerannynai* to mix — more at CRATER] (1804) **:** a mineral $Ca_{10}(Mg,Fe)_2Al_4Si_9O_{34}(OH)_4$ that is a complex silicate of calcium, magnesium, iron, and aluminum

idol \'īd-ᵊl\ *n* [ME, fr. OF *idole,* fr. LL *idolum,* fr. Gk *eidōlon* phantom, idol; akin to Gk *eidos* form — more at IDYLL] (13c) **1 :** a representation or symbol of an object of worship; *broadly* **:** a false god **2 a :** a likeness of something **b** *obs* **:** PRETENDER, IMPOSTOR **3 :** a form or appearance visible but without substance ⟨an enchanted phantom, a lifeless ~ —P. B. Shelley⟩ **4 :** an object of extreme devotion ⟨a movie ~⟩; *also* **:** IDEAL 2 **5 :** a false conception **:** FALLACY

idol·a·ter *or* **idol·a·tor** \ī-'däl-ət-ər\ *n* [ME *idolatrer,* fr. MF *idolatre,* fr. LL *idololatres,* fr. Gk *eidōlolatrēs,* fr. *eidōlon* + *-latrēs* -later] (14c) **1 :** a worshiper of idols **2 :** a person that admires intensely and often blindly one that is not usu. a subject of worship

idol·a·trous \ī-'däl-ə-trəs\ *adj* (1543) **1 :** of or relating to idolatry **2 :** having the character of idolatry ⟨the religion of ~ nationalism —Aldous Huxley⟩ **3 :** given to idolatry — **idol·a·trous·ly** *adv* — **idol·a·trous·ness** *n*

idol·a·try \-trē\ *n, pl* **-tries** (13c) **1 :** the worship of a physical object as a god **2 :** immoderate attachment or devotion to something

idol·ize \'īd-ᵊl-ˌīz\ *vb* **-ized; -iz·ing** *vt* (1598) **:** to worship as a god; *broadly* **:** to love or admire to excess ⟨the common people whom he so *idolized* —*Times Lit. Supp.*⟩ ~ *vi* **:** to practice idolatry — **idol·iza·tion** \ˌīd-ᵊl-ə-'zā-shən\ *n* — **idol·iz·er** \'īd-ᵊl-ˌī-zər\ *n*

idyll *or* **idyl** \'īd-ᵊl, *Brit usu* 'id-(ˌ)il\ *n* [L *idyllium,* fr. Gk *eidyllion,* fr. dim. of *eidos* form; akin to Gk *idein* to see — more at WIT] (1586) **1 a :** a simple descriptive work in poetry or prose that deals with rustic life or pastoral scenes or suggests a mood of peace and contentment **b :** a narrative poem (as Tennyson's *Idylls of the King*) treating an epic, romantic, or tragic theme **2 a :** a lighthearted carefree episode that is a fit subject for an idyll **b :** a romantic interlude

idyl·lic \ī-'dil-ik, *chiefly Brit* i-\ *adj* (1856) **1 :** of, relating to, or being an idyll **2 :** pleasing or picturesque in natural simplicity — **idyl·li·cal·ly** \-i-k(ə-)lē\ *adv*

-ie *also* **-y** \ē\ *n suffix* [ME] **1 :** little one **:** dear little one ⟨bird*ie*⟩ ⟨sonn*y*⟩ **2 :** one belonging to **:** one having to do with ⟨town*y*⟩ **3 :** one of (such) a kind or quality ⟨cut*ie*⟩ ⟨tough*ie*⟩

-ier — see -ER

1if \(ˌ)if, əf\ *conj* [ME, fr. OE *gif;* akin to OHG *ibu* if] (bef. 12c) **1 a :** in the event that **b :** allowing that **c :** on condition that **2 :** WHETHER ⟨asked ~ the mail had come⟩ **3** — used as a function word to introduce an exclamation expressing a wish ⟨~ it would only rain⟩ **4 :** even though ⟨an interesting ~ untenable argument⟩ — **if anything :** on the contrary even **:** perhaps even ⟨*if anything,* you ought to apologize⟩

2if \'if\ *n* (1513) **1 :** CONDITION, STIPULATION ⟨the question . . . depends on too many ~*s* to allow an answer —*Encounter*⟩ **2 :** SUPPOSITION

-if·er·ous \'if-(ə-)rəs\ *adj comb form* [ME, fr. L *-ifer,* fr. *-i-* + *-fer* -ferous] **:** -FEROUS

if·fy \'if-ē\ *adj* ['*if*] (1937) **:** abounding in contingencies or unknown qualities or conditions ⟨the situation is far too ~ for any predictions —*N.Y. Times*⟩ — **if·fi·ness** *n*

-i·form \ə-ˌfȯrm\ *adj comb form* [MF & L; MF *-iforme,* fr. L *-iformis,* fr. *-i-* + *-formis* -form] **:** -FORM ⟨patell*iform*⟩

I formation *n* (1951) **:** an offensive football formation in which the running backs line up in a line directly behind the quarterback — compare T FORMATION

-i·fy \ə-ˌfī\ *vb suffix* [ME *-ifien,* fr. OF *-ifier,* fr. L *-ificare,* fr. *-i-* + *-ficare* -fy] **:** -FY

Ig·bo \'ig-(ˌ)bō\ *var of* IBO

ig·loo \'ig-(ˌ)lü\ *n, pl* **igloos** [Esk *iglu, igdlu* house] (1856) **1 :** an Eskimo house usu. made of sod, wood, or stone when permanent or of blocks of snow or ice in the shape of a dome when built for temporary purposes **2 :** a building or structure shaped like a dome

ig·ne·ous \'ig-nē-əs\ *adj* [L *igneus,* fr. *ignis* fire; akin to Skt *agni* fire] (1664) **1 :** of, relating to, or resembling fire **:** FIERY **2 a :** relating to, resulting from, or suggestive of the intrusion or extrusion of magma or the activity of volcanoes **b :** formed by solidification of magma ⟨~ rock⟩

ig·nes·cent \ig-'nes-ᵊnt\ *adj* [L *ignescent-, ignescens,* prp. of *ignescere* to catch fire, fr. *ignis*] (ca. 1828) **1 :** capable of emitting sparks **2 :** VOLATILE

igni- *comb form* [L, fr. *ignis*] **:** fire **:** burning ⟨*igni*tron⟩

ig·nim·brite \'ig-nəm-ˌbrīt\ *n* [G *ignimbrit,* fr. L *ignis* + *imbr-* (fr. *imber* rain, rain shower) + G *-it* -ite — more at IMBRICATE] (1932) **:** a hard rock formed by solidification of chiefly fine deposits of volcanic ash

ig·nis fat·u·us \ˌig-nəs-'fach-(ə-)wəs\ *n, pl* **ig·nes fat·ui** \-ˌnēz-'fach-ə-ˌwī\ [ML, lit., foolish fire] (ca. 1563) **1 :** a light that sometimes appears in the night over marshy ground and is often attributable to the combustion of gas from decomposed organic matter **2 :** a deceptive goal or hope

ig·nite \ig-'nīt\ *vb* **ig·nit·ed; ig·nit·ing** [L *ignitus,* pp. of *ignire* to ignite, fr. *ignis*] *vt* (1666) **1 :** to subject to fire or intense heat; *esp* **:** to render luminous by heat **2 a :** to set afire; *also* **:** KINDLE **b :** to cause (a fuel mixture) to burn **3 :** to heat up **:** EXCITE ⟨oppression that *ignited* the hatred of the people⟩ ~ *vi* **1 :** to catch fire **2 :** to begin to glow — **ig·nit·able** *also* **ig·nit·ible** \-'nīt-ə-bəl\ *adj* — **ig·nit·er** *or* **ig·ni·tor** \-'nīt-ər\ *n*

ig·ni·tion \ig-'nish-ən\ *n* (1612) **1 :** the act or action of igniting **:** KINDLING **2 :** the process or means (as an electric spark) of igniting a fuel mixture

ig·ni·tron \ig-'nī-ˌträn\ *n* (1933) **:** a mercury-containing rectifier tube in which the arc is struck again at the beginning of each cycle by a special electrode separately energized by an auxiliary circuit

ig·no·ble \ig-'nō-bəl\ *adj* [L *ignobilis,* fr. *in-* + OL *gnobilis* noble] (15c) **1 :** of low birth or common origin **:** PLEBEIAN **2 :** characterized by baseness, lowness, or meanness ***syn*** see MEAN — **ig·no·bil·i·ty** \ˌig-nō-'bil-ət-ē\ *n* — **ig·no·ble·ness** \ig-'nō-bəl-nəs\ *n* — **ig·no·bly** \-blē *also* -bə-lē\ *adv*

ig·no·min·i·ous \ˌig-nə-'min-ē-əs\ *adj* (15c) **1 :** marked with or characterized by disgrace or shame **:** DISHONORABLE **2 :** deserving of shame or infamy **:** DESPICABLE **3 :** HUMILIATING, DEGRADING ⟨suffered an ~ defeat⟩ — **ig·no·min·i·ous·ly** *adv* — **ig·no·min·i·ous·ness** *n*

ig·no·mi·ny \'ig-nə-ˌmin-ē, -mə-nē; ig-'näm-ə-nē\ *n, pl* **-nies** [MF or L; MF *ignominie,* fr. L *ignominia,* fr. *ig-* (as in *ignorare* to be ignorant of, ignore) + *nomin-, nomen* name, repute — more at NAME] (1540) **1 :** deep personal humiliation and disgrace **2 :** disgraceful or dishonorable conduct, quality, or action ***syn*** see DISGRACE

ig·no·ra·mus \ˌig-nə-'rā-məs\ *n, pl* **-mus·es** [*Ignoramus,* ignorant lawyer in *Ignoramus* (1615), play by George Ruggle †1622, Eng. playwright] (1616) **:** an utterly ignorant person **:** DUNCE

ig·no·rance \'ig-n(ə-)rən(t)s\ *n* (13c) **:** the state or fact of being ignorant

ig·no·rant \'ig-n(ə-)rənt\ *adj* (14c) **1 a :** destitute of knowledge or education ⟨an ~ society⟩; *also* **:** lacking knowledge or comprehension of the thing specified ⟨parents ~ of modern mathematics⟩ **b :** resulting from or showing lack of knowledge or intelligence ⟨~ errors⟩ **2 :** UNAWARE, UNINFORMED — **ig·no·rant·ly** *adv* — **ig·no·rant·ness** *n*

syn IGNORANT, ILLITERATE, UNLETTERED, UNTUTORED, UNLEARNED mean not having knowledge. IGNORANT may imply a general condition or it may apply to lack of knowledge or awareness of a particular thing; ILLITERATE applies to either an absolute or a relative inability to read and write; UNLETTERED implies ignorance of the knowledge gained by reading; UNTUTORED may imply lack of schooling in the arts and ways of civilization; UNLEARNED suggests ignorance of advanced subjects.

ig·no·ra·tio elen·chi \ˌig-nə-ˌrät-ē-ˌō-i-'leŋ-ˌkē\ *n* [L, lit., ignorance of proof] (1588) **:** a fallacy in logic of supposing a point proved or disproved by an argument proving or disproving something not at issue

ig·nore \ig-'nō(ə)r, -'nȯ(ə)r\ *vt* **ig·nored; ig·nor·ing** [obs. *ignore* to be ignorant of, fr. F *ignorer,* fr. L *ignorare,* fr. *ignarus* ignorant, unknown, fr. *in-* + *gnoscere, noscere* to know — more at KNOW] (1801) **1 :** to refuse to take notice of **2 :** to reject (a bill of indictment) as ungrounded ***syn*** see NEGLECT — **ig·nor·able** \-'nōr-ə-bəl, -'nȯr-\ *adj* — **ig·nor·er** *n*

Igo·rot \ˌē-gə-ˈrōt\ *n, pl* **Igorot** *or* **Igorots** (1821) **1 :** a member of any of several related peoples of northwestern Luzon, Philippines **2 :** any of the Austronesian languages of the Igorot
Igraine \i-ˈgrān\ *n* **:** the wife of Uther and mother of King Arthur
igua·na \i-ˈgwän-ə\ *n* [Sp, fr. Arawak *iwana*] (1555) **:** any of various large herbivorous typically dark-colored tropical American lizards (family Iguanidae) that have a serrated dorsal crest and are important as human food in their native habitat; *broadly* **:** any of various large lizards

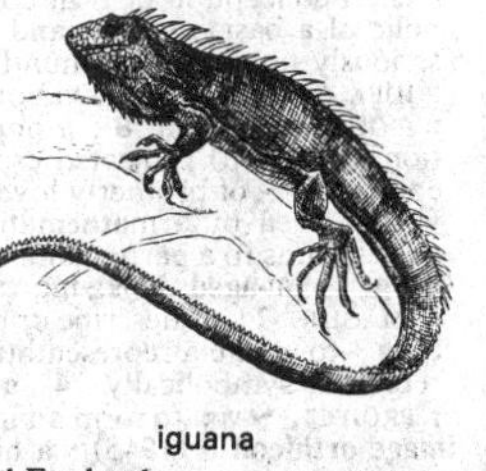
iguana

iguan·odon \i-ˈgwän-ə-ˌdän\ *n* [NL *Iguanodont-, Iguanodon,* fr. Sp *iguana* + Gk *odōn* tooth, fr. *odont-, odous* — more at TOOTH] (1830) **:** any of a genus (*Iguanodon*) of very large herbivorous dinosaurs from the early Cretaceous of Belgium and England
IHS \ˌī-ˌā-ˈches\ [LL, part transliteration of Gk ΙΗΣ, abbreviation for ΙΗΣΟΥΣ *Iēsous* Jesus] (bef. 12c) — used as a Christian symbol and monogram for *Jesus*
ike·ba·na \ˌik-ā-ˈbän-ə, ˌik-i-, ˌēk-\ *n* [Jp, fr. *ikeru* to keep alive, arrange + *hana* flower] (ca. 1901) **:** the Japanese art of flower arranging that emphasizes form and balance
ikon *var of* ICON
il- — see IN-
ilang–ilang *var of* YLANG-YLANG
ile- *also* **ileo-** *comb form* [NL *ileum*] **1 :** ileum ⟨*ile*itis⟩ **2 :** ileal and ⟨*ileo*cecal⟩
1-ile \əl, ᵊl, ˌīl, (ˌ)il\ *adj suffix* [ME, fr. MF, fr. L *-ilis*] **:** of, relating to, or capable of ⟨contract*ile*⟩
2-ile *n suffix* [prob. fr. *-ile* (as in *quartile,* n.)] **:** segment of a (specified) size in a frequency distribution ⟨dec*ile*⟩
il·e·itis \ˌil-ē-ˈīt-əs\ *n* [NL] (ca. 1855) **:** inflammation of the ileum
il·e·um \ˈil-ē-əm\ *n, pl* **il·ea** \-ē-ə\ [ME *ilioun,* fr. L, groin, viscera] (14c) **:** the last division of the small intestine extending between the jejunum and large intestine — **il·e·al** \-ē-əl\ *adj*
il·e·us \ˈil-ē-əs\ *n* [L, fr. Gk *eileos,* fr. *eilyein* to roll — more at VOLUBLE] (1693) **:** mechanical or functional obstruction of the bowel
ilex \ˈī-ˌleks\ *n* [L] (14c) **1 :** HOLM OAK **2 :** HOLLY 1
il·i·ac \ˈil-ē-ˌak\ *also* **il·i·al** \ˈil-ē-əl\ *adj* [LL *iliacus,* fr. L *ilium*] (1541) **:** of, relating to, or located near the ilium
Il·i·ad \ˈil-ē-əd, -ē-ˌad\ *n* [*Iliad,* ancient Greek epic poem attributed to Homer, fr. L *Iliad-, Ilias,* fr. Gk, fr. *Ilion* Troy] (1603) **1 a :** a series of exploits regarded as suitable for an epic **b :** a series of miseries or disastrous events **2 :** a long narrative; *esp* **:** an epic in the Homeric tradition — **Il·i·ad·ic** \ˌil-ē-ˈad-ik\ *adj*
ilio- *comb form* [NL *ilium*] **:** iliac and ⟨*ilio*lumbar⟩
il·i·um \ˈil-ē-əm\ *n, pl* **il·ia** \-ē-ə\ [NL, fr. L *ilium, ileum*] (1706) **:** the dorsal, upper, and largest one of the three bones composing either lateral half of the pelvis
1ilk \ˈilk\ *pron* [ME, fr. OE *ilca,* fr. a prehistoric compound whose constituents are akin respectively to Goth *is* he (akin to L *is* he, that) and OE *gelīc* like — more at ITERATE, LIKE] *chiefly Scot* (bef. 12c) **:** SAME — used with *that* esp. in the names of landed families
2ilk *n* (1790) **:** SORT, KIND ⟨the rejection of these books or others of like ~ —Kathleen Molz⟩
3ilk *pron* [ME, adj. & pron., fr. OE *ylc, ǣlc* — more at EACH] *chiefly Scot* (bef. 12c) **:** EACH
il·ka \ˈil-kə\ *adj* [ME, fr. *ilk* + *a* (indef. art.)] *chiefly Scot* (13c) **:** EACH, EVERY
1ill \ˈil\ *adj* **worse** \ˈwərs\; **worst** \ˈwərst\ [ME, fr. ON *illr*] (12c) **1 a** *chiefly Scot* **:** IMMORAL, VICIOUS **b :** resulting from, accompanied by, or indicative of an evil or malevolent intention ⟨~ deeds⟩ **c :** attributing evil or an objectionable quality ⟨held an ~ opinion of his neighbors⟩ **2 a :** causing suffering or distress ⟨~ weather⟩ **b** *comparative also* **iller** (1) **:** not normal or sound ⟨~ health⟩ (2) **:** not in good health; *also* **:** NAUSEATED **3 a :** not suited to circumstances or not to one's advantage **:** UNLUCKY ⟨an ~ omen⟩ **b :** involving difficulty **:** HARD ⟨an ~ man to please⟩ **4 a :** not meeting an accepted standard ⟨~ manners⟩ **b** *archaic* **:** notably unskillful or inefficient **5 a :** UNFRIENDLY, HOSTILE ⟨~ feeling⟩ **b :** HARSH, CRUEL ⟨~ treatment⟩ ***syn*** see BAD
2ill *adv* **worse; worst** (13c) **1 a :** with displeasure or hostility **b :** in a harsh manner **c :** so as to reflect unfavorably ⟨spoke ~ of the neighbors⟩ **2 :** in a reprehensible manner **3 :** HARDLY, SCARCELY ⟨can ~ afford such extravagances⟩ **4 a :** in an unfortunate manner **:** BADLY, UNLUCKILY ⟨~ fares the land . . . where wealth accumulates, and men decay —Oliver Goldsmith⟩ **b :** in a faulty, inefficient, or unpleasant manner — often used in combination ⟨the methods used may be *ill=* adapted to the aims in view —R. M. Hutchins⟩
3ill *n* (13c) **1 :** the reverse of good **:** EVIL **2 a :** MISFORTUNE, DISTRESS **b** (1) **:** AILMENT, SICKNESS (2) **:** something that disturbs or afflicts **:** TROUBLE ⟨economic and social ~s⟩ **3 :** something that reflects unfavorably ⟨spoke no ~ of him⟩
I'll \(ˌ)ī(ə)l\ **:** I will **:** I shall
ill–ad·vised \ˌil-əd-ˈvīzd\ *adj* (1592) **:** resulting from or showing lack of wise and sufficient counsel or deliberation ⟨an ~ decision⟩ — **ill–ad·vis·ed·ly** \-ˈvī-zəd-lē\ *adv*
ill at ease *adj* (15c) **:** not feeling easy **:** UNCOMFORTABLE
il·la·tion \il-ˈā-shən\ *n* [LL *illation-, illatio,* fr. L, action of bringing in, fr. *illatus* (pp. of *inferre* to bring in), fr. *in-* + *latus,* pp. of *ferre* to carry — more at TOLERATE, BEAR] (1533) **1 :** the action of inferring **:** INFERENCE **2 :** a conclusion inferred
1il·la·tive \ˈil-ət-iv, il-ˈāt-\ *n* (1591) **1 :** a word (as *therefore*) or phrase (as *as a consequence*) introducing an inference **2 :** ILLATION 2
2illative *adj* (1611) **:** INFERENTIAL — **il·la·tive·ly** *adv*
il·laud·able \(ˈ)il-ˈ(l)ōd-ə-bəl\ *adj* [L *illaudabilis,* fr. *in-* + *laudabilis* laudable] (1589) **:** deserving no praise — **il·laud·ably** \-blē\ *adv*
ill–be·ing \ˈil-ˈbē-iŋ\ *n* (1840) **:** a condition of being deficient in health, happiness, or prosperity
ill–bod·ing \-ˈbōd-iŋ\ *adj* (1591) **:** boding evil **:** INAUSPICIOUS
ill–bred \-ˈbred\ *adj* (1604) **:** badly brought up or showing bad upbringing **:** IMPOLITE
1il·le·gal \(ˈ)il-ˈ(l)ē-gəl\ *adj* [F or ML; F *illégal,* fr. ML *illegalis,* fr. L *in-* + *legalis* legal] (1626) **:** not according to or authorized by law **:** UNLAWFUL; *also* **:** not sanctioned by official rules (as of a game) — **il·le·gal·i·ty** \ˌil-i-ˈgal-ət-ē\ *n* — **il·le·gal·ly** \(ˈ)il-ˈ(l)ē-gə-lē\ *adv*
2illegal *n* (1939) **:** an illegal immigrant
il·le·gal·ize \(ˈ)il-ˈ(l)ē-gə-ˌlīz\ *vt* (ca. 1818) **:** to make or declare illegal — **il·le·gal·iza·tion** \(ˌ)il-ˌ(l)ē-gə-lə-ˈzā-shən\ *n*
il·leg·i·ble \(ˈ)il-ˈ(l)ej-ə-bəl\ *adj* (1640) **:** not legible **:** UNDECIPHERABLE ⟨~ writing⟩ — **il·leg·i·bil·i·ty** \(ˌ)il-ˌ(l)ej-ə-ˈbil-ət-ē\ *n* — **il·leg·i·bly** \(ˈ)il-ˈ(l)ej-ə-blē\ *adv*
il·le·git·i·ma·cy \ˌil-i-ˈjit-ə-mə-sē\ *n* (1680) **1 :** the quality or state of being illegitimate **2 :** BASTARDY 2
il·le·git·i·mate \-ˈjit-ə-mət\ *adj* (1536) **1 :** not recognized as lawful offspring; *specif* **:** born of parents not married to each other **2 :** not rightly deduced or inferred **:** ILLOGICAL **3 :** departing from the regular **:** ERRATIC **4 a :** not sanctioned by law **:** ILLEGAL **b :** not authorized by good usage **c** *of a taxon* **:** published either validly or invalidly but not in accordance with the rules of the relevant international code — **il·le·git·i·mate·ly** *adv*
ill–fat·ed \ˈil-ˈfāt-əd\ *adj* (1710) **1 :** having or destined to a hapless fate **:** UNFORTUNATE ⟨an ~ expedition⟩ **2 :** that causes or marks the beginning of misfortune
ill–fa·vored \-ˈfā-vərd\ *adj* (ca. 1530) **1 :** unattractive in physical appearance; *esp* **:** having an ugly face **2 :** OFFENSIVE, OBJECTIONABLE
ill–got·ten \-ˈgät-ᵊn\ *adj* (1552) **:** acquired by illicit or improper means ⟨~ gains⟩
ill–hu·mored \ˈil-ˈ(h)yü-mərd\ *adj* (1687) **:** SURLY, IRRITABLE — **ill–hu·mored·ly** *adv*
il·lib·er·al \(ˈ)il-ˈ(l)ib(-ə)-rəl\ *adj* [MF or L; MF, fr. L *illiberalis* ignoble, stingy, fr. L *in-* + *liberalis* liberal] (1535) **:** not liberal: as **a** *archaic* (1) **:** lacking a liberal education (2) **:** lacking culture and refinement **b :** not requiring the background of a liberal arts education ⟨trades and other ~ occupations⟩ **c** *archaic* **:** not generous **:** STINGY **d** (1) **:** not broad-minded **:** BIGOTED (2) **:** opposed to liberalism — **il·lib·er·al·i·ty** \(ˌ)il-ˌib-ə-ˈral-ət-ē\ *n* — **il·lib·er·al·ly** \(ˈ)il-ˈ(l)ib(-ə)-rə-lē\ *adv* — **il·lib·er·al·ness** \-rəl-nəs\ *n*
il·lib·er·al·ism \-rə-ˌliz-əm\ *n* (1839) **:** opposition to or lack of liberalism
il·lic·it \(ˈ)il-ˈ(l)is-ət\ *adj* [L *illicitus,* fr. *in-* + *licitus* lawful — more at LICIT] (1652) **:** not permitted **:** UNLAWFUL ⟨~ love affairs⟩ — **il·lic·it·ly** *adv*
il·lim·it·able \(ˈ)il-ˈ(l)im-ət-ə-bəl\ *adj* (1596) **:** incapable of being limited or bounded **:** MEASURELESS ⟨the ~ reaches of space and time⟩ — **il·lim·it·abil·i·ty** \(ˌ)il-ˌ(l)im-ət-ə-ˈbil-ət-ē\ *n* — **il·lim·it·able·ness** \(ˈ)il-ˈ(l)im-ət-ə-bəl-nəs\ *n* — **il·lim·it·ably** \-blē\ *adv*
Il·li·nois \ˌil-ə-ˈnȯi *also* -ˈnȯiz\ *n, pl* **Illinois** [F, of Algonquian origin; akin to Shawnee *hilenawe* man] (1703) **1** *pl* **:** a confederacy of American Indian peoples of Illinois, Iowa, and Wisconsin **2 :** a member of any of the Illinois peoples
il·liq·uid \(ˈ)il-ˈ(l)ik-wəd\ *adj* (1913) **1 :** not being cash or readily convertible into cash ⟨~ holdings⟩ **2 :** deficient in liquid assets ⟨the position of the banks . . . was extremely ~. Deposits and cash reserves were falling, advances increasing —J. S. G. Wilson⟩ — **il·li·quid·i·ty** \ˌil-(ˌ)(l)ik-ˈwid-ət-ē\ *n*
il·lite \ˈil-ˌīt\ *n* [*Ill*inois, state of U.S. + 1*-ite*] (ca. 1937) **:** a group of clay minerals having essentially the crystal structure of muscovite; *also* **:** one of these minerals — **il·lit·ic** \il-ˈit-ik\ *adj*
il·lit·er·a·cy \(ˈ)il-ˈ(l)it-ə-rə-sē, -ˈ(l)i-trə-sē\ *n, pl* **-cies** (1660) **1 :** the quality or state of being illiterate; *esp* **:** inability to read or write **2 :** a mistake or crudity (as in speaking) made by or typical of one who is illiterate
il·lit·er·ate \(ˈ)il-ˈ(l)it-ə-rət, -ˈ(l)i-trət\ *adj* [L *illiteratus,* fr. *in-* + *litteratus* literate] (15c) **1 :** having little or no education; *esp* **:** unable to read or write **2 a :** showing or marked by a lack of familiarity with language and literature **b :** violating approved patterns of speaking or writing **3 :** showing or marked by a lack of acquaintance with the fundamentals of a particular field of knowledge ***syn*** see IGNORANT — **illiterate** *n* — **il·lit·er·ate·ly** *adv* — **il·lit·er·ate·ness** *n*
ill–man·nered \ˈil-ˈman-ərd\ *adj* (15c) **:** having bad manners **:** RUDE
ill–na·tured \-ˈnā-chərd\ *adj* (1605) **1 :** MALEVOLENT, SPITEFUL **2 :** having a bad disposition **:** CROSS, SURLY — **ill–na·tured·ly** *adv*
ill·ness \ˈil-nəs\ *n* (1500) **1** *obs* **a :** WICKEDNESS **b :** UNPLEASANTNESS **2 :** an unhealthy condition of body or mind **:** SICKNESS
il·log·ic \(ˈ)il-ˈ(l)äj-ik\ *n* [back-formation fr. *illogical*] (1856) **:** the quality or state of being illogical **:** ILLOGICALITY
il·log·i·cal \-i-kəl\ *adj* (1588) **1 :** not observing the principles of logic **2 :** devoid of logic **:** SENSELESS — **il·log·i·cal·i·ty** \(ˌ)il-ˌ(l)äj-ə-ˈkal-ət-ē\ *n* — **il·log·i·cal·ly** \(ˈ)il-ˈ(l)äj-i-k(ə-)lē\ *adv* — **il·log·i·cal·ness** \-kəl-nəs\ *n*
ill–sort·ed \ˈil-ˈsȯrt-əd\ *adj* (1691) **1 :** not well matched ⟨he and his wife were an ~ pair —Lord Byron⟩ **2** *Scot* **:** much displeased
ill–starred \-ˈstärd\ *adj* (1604) **:** ILL-FATED, UNLUCKY ⟨an ~ venture⟩
ill–tem·pered \-ˈtem-pərd\ *adj* (1601) **:** ILL-NATURED, QUARRELSOME — **ill–tem·pered·ly** \-lē\ *adv*
ill–treat \-ˈtrēt\ *vt* (1689) **:** to treat cruelly or improperly **:** MALTREAT — **ill–treat·ment** \-mənt\ *n*
il·lume \il-ˈüm\ *vt* **il·lumed; il·lum·ing** (1602) **:** ILLUMINATE
il·lu·mi·nance \-mə-nən(t)s\ *n* (ca. 1938) **:** ILLUMINATION 2
il·lu·mi·nant \-nənt\ *n* (1644) **:** an illuminating device or substance
1il·lu·mi·nate \il-ˈü-mə-nət\ *adj* (15c) **1** *archaic* **:** brightened with light **2** *archaic* **:** intellectually or spiritually enlightened
2il·lu·mi·nate \-ˌnāt\ *vt* **-nat·ed; -nat·ing** [L *illuminatus,* pp. of *illuminare,* fr. *in-* + *luminare* to light up, fr. *lumin-, lumen* light — more at LUMINARY] (1500) **1 a** (1) **:** to supply or brighten with light (2) **:** to make luminous or shining **b :** to enlighten spiritually or intellectually **c** *archaic* **:** to set alight **d :** to subject to radiation **2 :** to make clear

\ə\ **abut** \ᵊ\ **kitten,** F **table** \ər\ **further** \a\ **ash** \ā\ **ace** \ä\ **cot, cart** \aü\ **out** \ch\ **chin** \e\ **bet** \ē\ **easy** \g\ **go** \i\ **hit** \ī\ **ice** \j\ **job** \ŋ\ **sing** \ō\ **go** \ȯ\ **law** \ȯi\ **boy** \th\ **thin** \t͟h\ **the** \ü\ **loot** \u̇\ **foot** \y\ **yet** \zh\ **vision** \á, k̲, ⁿ, œ, œ̄, ue, ue̅, ʸ\ *see* Guide to Pronunciation

: ELUCIDATE ⟨~s the theme of her poem⟩ **3** : to make illustrious or resplendent **4** : to decorate (as a manuscript) with gold or silver or brilliant colors or with often elaborate designs or miniature pictures — **il·lu·mi·nat·ing·ly** \-ˌnāt-iŋ-lē\ *adv* — **il·lu·mi·na·tor** \-ˌnāt-ər\ *n*

[3]**il·lu·mi·nate** \-nət\ *n, archaic* (1600) : one having or claiming unusual enlightenment

il·lu·mi·na·ti \il-ˌü-mə-ˈnät-ē\ *n pl* [It & NL; It, fr. NL, fr. L, pl. of *illuminatus*] (1599) **1** *cap* : any of various groups claiming special religious enlightenment **2** : persons who are or who claim to be unusually enlightened

il·lu·mi·na·tion \il-ˌü-mə-ˈnā-shən\ *n* (14c) **1** : the action of illuminating or state of being illuminated: as **a** : spiritual or intellectual enlightenment **b** (1) : a lighting up (2) : decorative lighting or lighting effects **c** : decoration by the art of illuminating **2** : the luminous flux per unit area on an intercepting surface at any given point **3** : one of the decorative features used in the art of illuminating or in decorative lighting

il·lu·mi·na·tive \il-ˈü-mə-ˌnāt-iv\ *adj* (1644) : of, relating to, or producing illumination : ILLUMINATING

il·lu·mine \il-ˈü-mən\ *vt* **-mined; -min·ing** (14c) : ILLUMINATE — **il·lu·min·able** \-mə-nə-bəl\ *adj*

il·lu·mi·nism \-mə-ˌniz-əm\ *n* (1798) **1** : belief in or claim to a personal enlightenment not accessible to mankind in general **2** *cap* : beliefs or claims viewed as forming doctrine or principles of Illuminati — **il·lu·mi·nist** \-nəst\ *n*

ill–us·age \ˈil-ˈyü-sij, -zij\ *n* (1621) : harsh, unkind, or abusive treatment

ill–use \-ˈyüz\ *vt* (1841) : to use badly : MALTREAT, ABUSE

il·lu·sion \il-ˈü-zhən\ *n* [ME, fr. MF, fr. LL *illusion-, illusio,* fr. L, action of mocking, fr. *illusus,* pp. of *illudere* to mock at, fr. *in-* + *ludere* to play, mock — more at LUDICROUS] (14c) **1 a** *obs* : the action of deceiving **b** (1) : the state or fact of being intellectually deceived or misled : MISAPPREHENSION (2) : an instance of such deception **2 a** (1) : a misleading image presented to the vision (2) : something that deceives or misleads intellectually **b** (1) : perception of something objectively existing in such a way as to cause misinterpretation of its actual nature (2) : HALLUCINATION 1 (3) : a pattern capable of reversible perspective **3** : a fine plain transparent bobbinet or tulle usu. made of silk and used for veils, trimmings, and dresses — **il·lu·sion·al** \-ˈüzh-nəl, -ən-ᵊl\ *adj*

il·lu·sion·ary \il-ˈü-zhə-ˌner-ē\ *adj* (1885) : ILLUSORY

il·lu·sion·ism \il-ˈü-zhə-ˌniz-əm\ *n* (1911) : the use of artistic techniques (as perspective or shading) to create the illusion of reality esp. in a work of art

il·lu·sion·ist \il-ˈüzh-(ə-)nəst\ *n* (1850) : one that produces illusory effects: as **a** : one (as an artist) whose work is marked by illusionism **b** : a sleight-of-hand performer or a magician — **il·lu·sion·is·tic** \-ˌü-zhə-ˈnis-tik\ *adj* — **il·lu·sion·is·ti·cal·ly** \-ti-k(ə-)lē\ *adv*

il·lu·sive \il-ˈü-siv, -ˈü-ziv\ *adj* (1679) : ILLUSORY — **il·lu·sive·ly** *adv* — **il·lu·sive·ness** *n*

il·lu·so·ry \il-ˈüs-(ə-)rē, -ˈüz-\ *adj* (1631) : based on or producing illusion : DECEPTIVE ⟨~ hopes⟩ ***syn*** see APPARENT — **il·lu·so·ri·ly** \-(ə-)rə-lē\ *adv* — **il·lu·so·ri·ness** \-(ə-)rē-nəs\ *n*

il·lus·trate \ˈil-əs-ˌtrāt, il-ˈəs-\ *vb* **-trat·ed; -trat·ing** [L *illustratus,* pp. of *illustrare,* fr. *in-* + *lustrare* to purify, make bright — more at LUSTER] *vt* (1526) **1** *obs* **a** : ENLIGHTEN **b** : to light up **2 a** *archaic* : to make illustrious **b** *obs* (1) : to make bright (2) : ADORN **3 a** : to make clear : CLARIFY **b** : to make clear by giving or by serving as an example or instance **c** : to provide with visual features intended to explain or decorate ⟨~ a book⟩ **4** : to show clearly : DEMONSTRATE ~ *vi* : to give an example or instance — **il·lus·tra·tor** \ˈil-əs-ˌtrāt-ər, il-ˈəs-\ *n*

il·lus·tra·tion \ˌil-əs-ˈtrā-shən, il-ˌəs-\ *n* (14c) **1 a** : the action of illustrating : the condition of being illustrated **b** *archaic* : the action of making illustrious or honored or distinguished **2** : something that serves to illustrate: as **a** : an example or instance that helps make something clear **b** : a picture or diagram that helps make something clear or attractive ***syn*** see INSTANCE — **il·lus·tra·tion·al** \-shnəl, -shən-ᵊl\ *adj*

il·lus·tra·tive \il-ˈəs-trət-iv\ *adj* (1643) : serving, tending, or designed to illustrate ⟨~ examples⟩ — **il·lus·tra·tive·ly** *adv*

il·lus·tri·ous \il-ˈəs-trē-əs\ *adj* [L *illustris,* prob. back-formation fr. *illustrare*] (15c) **1** : notably or brilliantly outstanding because of dignity or achievements or actions : EMINENT **2** *archaic* **a** : shining brightly with light **b** : clearly evident ***syn*** see FAMOUS — **il·lus·tri·ous·ly** *adv* — **il·lus·tri·ous·ness** *n*

il·lu·vi·al \(ˈ)il-ˈü-vē-əl\ *adj* (1924) : of, relating to, or marked by illuviation or illuviated materials or areas

il·lu·vi·a·tion \(ˌ)il-ˌü-vē-ˈā-shən\ *n* [*in-* + *-luviation* (as in *eluviation*)] (1928) : accumulation of dissolved or suspended soil materials in one area or horizon as a result of eluviation from another — **il·lu·vi·at·ed** \(ˈ)il-ˈü-vē-ˌāt-əd\ *adj*

ill will *n* (14c) : unfriendly feeling ***syn*** see MALICE

ill–wish·er \ˈil-ˌwish-ər, -ˈwish-\ *n* (1607) : one that wishes ill to another

il·ly \ˈil-(l)ē\ *adv* (15c) : not wisely or well : BADLY, ILL ⟨his ~ concealed pride —Della Lutes⟩

Il·lyr·i·an \il-ˈir-ē-ən\ *n* (1584) **1** : a native or inhabitant of ancient Illyria **2** : the poorly attested Indo-European languages of the Illyrians — see INDO-EUROPEAN LANGUAGES table — **Illyrian** *adj*

il·men·ite \ˈil-mə-ˌnīt\ *n* [G *ilmenit,* fr. *Ilmen* range, Ural Mts., U.S.S.R.] (1827) : a usu. massive iron-black mineral $FeTiO_3$ composed of iron, titanium, and oxygen

Ilo·ca·no *or* **Ilo·ka·no** \ˌē-lə-ˈkän-(ˌ)ō, ˌil-ə-\ *n, pl* **Ilocano** *or* **Ilocanos** *or* **Ilokano** *or* **Ilokanos** (1840) **1 a** : a major people of northern Luzon in the Philippines **b** : a member of this people **2** : the Austronesian language of the Ilocano people

im- — see IN-

I'm \(ˌ)īm\ : I am

[1]**im·age** \ˈim-ij\ *n* [ME, fr. OF, short for *imagene,* fr. L *imagin-, imago;* akin to L *imitari* to imitate] (13c) **1** : a reproduction or imitation of the form of a person or thing; *esp* : an imitation in solid form : STATUE **2 a** : the optical counterpart of an object produced by an optical device (as a lens or mirror) or an electronic device **b** : a likeness of an object produced on a photographic material **3 a** : exact likeness : SEMBLANCE ⟨God created man in his own ~ —Gen 1:27 (RSV)⟩ **b** : a person strikingly like another person ⟨he is the ~ of his father⟩ **4 a** : a tangible or visible representation : INCARNATION ⟨the ~ of filial devotion⟩ **b** *archaic* : an illusory form : APPARITION **5 a** (1) : a mental picture of something not actually present : IMPRESSION (2) : a mental conception held in common by members of a group and symbolic of a basic attitude and orientation ⟨a disorderly courtroom can seriously tarnish a community's ~ of justice —Herbert Brownell⟩ **b** : IDEA, CONCEPT **6** : a vivid or graphic representation or description **7** : FIGURE OF SPEECH **8** : a popular conception (as of a person, institution, or nation) projected esp. through the mass media ⟨promoting a corporate ~ of brotherly love and concern —R. C. Buck⟩ **9** : a set of values given by a mathematical function (as a homomorphism) that corresponds to a particular subset of the domain

[2]**image** *vb* **im·aged; im·ag·ing** *vt* (14c) **1** : to call up a mental picture of : IMAGINE **2** : to describe or portray in language esp. in a vivid manner **3 a** : to create a representation of; *also* : to form an image of **b** : to represent symbolically **4 a** : REFLECT, MIRROR **b** : to make appear : PROJECT ~ *vi* : to form an image — **im·ag·er** \-ər\ *n*

image orthicon *n* (1945) : a highly sensitive television image tube that uses secondary emission and electron multiplication to produce the output signal

im·ag·ery \ˈim-ij-(ə-)rē\ *n, pl* **-er·ies** (14c) **1** : the product of image makers : IMAGES; *also* : the art of making images **2** : figurative language **3** : mental images; *esp* : the products of imagination

image tube *n* (1936) : an electron tube in which incident electromagnetic radiation (as light or infrared) produces a visible image on its fluorescent screen duplicating the original pattern of radiation — called also *image converter*

imag·in·able \im-ˈaj-(ə-)nə-bəl\ *adj* (14c) : capable of being imagined : CONCEIVABLE — **imag·in·able·ness** *n* — **imag·in·ably** \-blē\ *adv*

[1]**imag·i·nal** \im-ˈaj-ən-ᵊl\ *adj* [*imagine* + *-al*] (1647) : of or relating to imagination, images, or imagery

[2]**ima·gi·nal** \im-ˈā-gən-ᵊl, -ˈäg-ən-\ *adj* [NL *imagin-, imago*] (1877) : of or relating to the insect imago

imag·i·nary \im-ˈaj-ə-ˌner-ē\ *adj* (14c) **1 a** : existing only in imagination : lacking factual reality **b** : formed or characterized imaginatively or arbitrarily ⟨his canvases, chiefly ~, somber landscapes —*Current Biog.*⟩ **2** : containing or relating to the imaginary unit ⟨~ roots⟩ — **imag·i·nari·ly** \im-ˌaj-ə-ˈner-ə-lē\ *adv* — **imag·i·nari·ness** \-ˈaj-ə-ˌner-ē-nəs\ *n*

syn IMAGINARY, FANCIFUL, VISIONARY, FANTASTIC, CHIMERICAL, QUIXOTIC mean unreal or unbelievable. IMAGINARY applies to something which is fictitious and purely the product of one's imagination; FANCIFUL suggests the free play of the imagination; VISIONARY stresses impracticality or incapability of realization; FANTASTIC implies incredibility or strangeness beyond belief; CHIMERICAL combines the implication of VISIONARY and FANTASTIC; QUIXOTIC implies a devotion to romantic or chivalrous ideals unrestrained by ordinary prudence and common sense.

imaginary number *n* (ca. 1909) : a complex number (as $2 + 3i$) in which the coefficient of the imaginary unit is not zero — called also *imaginary*

imaginary part *n* (ca. 1929) : the part of a complex number (as $3i$ in $2+3i$) that has the imaginary unit as a factor

imaginary unit *n* (ca. 1909) : the positive square root of minus 1 denoted by i : $+\sqrt{-1}$

imag·i·na·tion \im-ˌaj-ə-ˈnā-shən\ *n* [ME, fr. MF, fr. L *imagination-, imaginatio,* fr. *imaginatus,* pp. of *imaginari*] (14c) **1** : the act or power of forming a mental image of something not present to the senses or never before wholly perceived in reality **2 a** : creative ability **b** : ability to confront and deal with a problem : RESOURCEFULNESS **c** : the thinking or active mind : INTEREST ⟨stories that fired the ~⟩ **3 a** : a creation of the mind; *esp* : an idealized or poetic creation **b** : fanciful or empty assumption

imag·i·na·tive \im-ˈaj-(ə-)nət-iv, -ˈaj-ə-ˌnāt-\ *adj* (14c) **1 a** : of, relating to, or characterized by imagination **b** : devoid of truth : FALSE **2** : given to imagining : having a lively imagination **3** : of or relating to images; *esp* : showing a command of imagery — **imag·i·na·tive·ly** *adv* — **imag·i·na·tive·ness** *n*

imag·ine \im-ˈaj-ən\ *vb* **imag·ined; imag·in·ing** \-ˈaj-(ə-)niŋ\ [ME *imaginen,* fr. MF *imaginer,* fr. L *imaginari,* fr. *imagin-, imago* image] *vt* (14c) **1** : to form a mental image of (something not present) **2** *archaic* : PLAN, SCHEME **3** : SUPPOSE, GUESS ⟨I ~ it will rain⟩ **4** : to form a notion of without sufficient basis : FANCY ⟨~s himself to be the reformer of the world⟩ ~ *vi* **1** : to use the imagination **2** : BELIEVE 3 ***syn*** see THINK

im·ag·ism \ˈim-ij-ˌiz-əm\ *n, often cap* (1912) : a 20th century movement in poetry advocating free verse and the expression of ideas and emotions through clear precise images — **im·ag·ist** \-ij-əst\ *n* — **imagist** *or* **im·ag·is·tic** \ˌim-ij-ˈis-tik\ *adj* — **im·ag·is·ti·cal·ly** \-ti-k(ə-)lē\ *adv*

ima·go \im-ˈā-(ˌ)gō, -ˈäg-(ˌ)ō\ *n, pl* **imagoes** *or* **ima·gi·nes** \-ˈā-gə-ˌnēz, -ˈäg-ə-\ [NL, fr. L, image] (ca. 1797) **1** : an insect in its final, adult, sexually mature, and typically winged state **2** : an idealized mental image of another person or the self

imam \i-ˈmäm, -ˈmam\ *n* [Ar *imām*] (1613) **1** : the prayer leader of a mosque **2** *cap* : a Muslim leader of the line of Ali held by Shiites to be the divinely appointed, sinless, infallible successors of Muhammad **3** : any of various rulers that claim descent from Muhammad and exercise spiritual and temporal leadership over a Muslim region

imam·ate \-ˌāt\ *n, often cap* (1727) **1** : the office of an imam **2** : the region or country ruled over by an imam

ima·ret \i-ˈmär-ət\ *n* [Turk] (ca. 1613) : an inn or hospice in Turkey

Ima·ri \i-ˈmär-ē\ *n* [*Imari,* Japan] (1875) : a multicolored Japanese porcelain usu. characterized by elaborate floral designs — **Imari** *adj*

im·bal·ance \(ˈ)im-ˈbal-ən(t)s\ *n* (ca. 1890) : lack of balance : the state of being out of equilibrium or out of proportion ⟨a vitamin ~⟩ ⟨racial ~ in schools⟩ — **im·bal·anced** \-ən(t)st\ *adj*

im·be·cile \ˈim-bə-səl, -ˌsil\ *n* [F *imbécile,* n., fr. adj., weak, weak-minded, fr. L *imbecillus,* prob. fr. *in-* + *-becillus* (akin to L *baculum* staff) — more at PEG] (1802) **1** : a mentally deficient person; *esp* : a feebleminded person having a mental age of three to seven years and requiring supervision in the performance of routine daily tasks of caring for himself **2** : FOOL, IDIOT — **imbecile** *or* **im·be·cil·ic** \ˌim-bə-ˈsil-ik\ *adj*

im·be·cil·i·ty \ˌim-bə-ˈsil-ət-ē\ *n, pl* **-ties** (1533) **1 :** the quality or state of being imbecile or an imbecile **2 a :** utter foolishness; *also* **:** FUTILITY **b :** something that is foolish or nonsensical
imbed *var of* EMBED
im·bibe \im-ˈbīb\ *vb* **im·bibed; im·bib·ing** [in sense 1, fr. ME *enbiben*, fr. MF *embiber*, fr. L *imbibere* to drink in, conceive, fr. *in-* + *bibere* to drink; in other senses, fr. L *imbibere* — more at POTABLE] *vt* (14c) **1** *archaic* **:** SOAK, STEEP **2 a :** to receive into the mind and retain ⟨~ moral principles⟩ **b :** to assimilate or take into solution **3 a :** DRINK **b :** to take in or up ⟨a sponge ~*s* moisture⟩ ~ *vi* **1 :** DRINK 2 **2 a :** to take in liquid **b :** to absorb or assimilate moisture, gas, light, or heat ***syn*** see ABSORB — **im·bib·er** *n*
im·bi·bi·tion \ˌim-bə-ˈbish-ən\ *n* (15c) **:** the act or action of imbibing; *esp* **:** the taking up of fluid by a colloidal system resulting in swelling — **im·bi·bi·tion·al** \-ˈbish-nəl, -ən-ᵊl\ *adj*
imbitter *var of* EMBITTER
imbosom *var of* EMBOSOM
[1]**im·bri·cate** \ˈim-bri-kət\ *adj* [LL *imbricatus*, pp. of *imbricare* to cover with pantiles, fr. L *imbric-*, *imbrex* pantile, fr. *imbr-*, *imber* rain; akin to Gk *ombros* rain] (ca. 1656) **:** lying lapped over each other in regular order ⟨~ scales⟩
[2]**im·bri·cate** \ˈim-brə-ˌkāt\ *vb* **-cat·ed; -cat·ing** (1784) **:** OVERLAP; *esp* **:** to overlap like roof tiles
im·bri·ca·tion \ˌim-brə-ˈkā-shən\ *n* (1713) **1 :** an overlapping of edges (as of tiles or scales) **2 :** a decoration or pattern showing imbrication

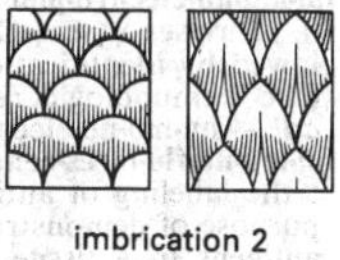
imbrication 2

im·bro·glio \im-ˈbrōl-(ˌ)yō\ *n, pl* **-glios** [It, fr. *imbrogliare* to entangle, fr. MF *embrouiller* — more at EMBROIL] (1750) **1 :** a confused mass **2 a :** an intricate or complicated situation (as in a drama or novel) **b :** an acutely painful or embarrassing misunderstanding **c :** a violently confused or bitterly complicated altercation **:** EMBROILMENT
imbrown *var of* EMBROWN
im·brue \im-ˈbrü\ *vt* **im·brued; im·bru·ing** [ME *enbrewen*, prob. fr. MF *abrevrer*, *embevrer* to soak, drench, deriv. of L *bibere* to drink — more at POTABLE] (15c) **:** STAIN
im·brute \-ˈbrüt\ *vb* **im·brut·ed; im·brut·ing** *vi* (1634) **:** to sink to the level of a brute ~ *vt* **:** to degrade to the level of a brute
im·bue \-ˈbyü\ *vt* **im·bued; im·bu·ing** [L *imbuere*] (1555) **1 :** to permeate or influence as if by dyeing ⟨the spirit that ~*s* the new constitution⟩ **2 :** to tinge or dye deeply ***syn*** see INFUSE
im·id·az·ole \ˌim-ə-ˈdaz-ˌōl\ *n* [ISV] (1892) **:** a white crystalline heterocyclic base $C_3H_4N_2$ that is an antimetabolite related to histidine; *broadly* **:** any of various derivatives of this
im·ide \ˈim-ˌīd\ *n* [ISV, alter. of *amide*] (1865) **:** a compound containing the NH group that is derived from ammonia by replacement of two hydrogen atoms by a metal or an equivalent of acid groups — compare AMIDE — **im·id·ic** \im-ˈid-ik\ *adj*
im·i·do \ˈim-ə-ˌdō\ *adj* (1881) **:** relating to or containing the NH group or its substituted form NR united to one or two groups of acid character
im·ine \ˈim-ˌēn\ *n* [ISV, alter. of *amine*] (1883) **:** a compound containing the NH group or its substituted form NR that is derived from ammonia by replacement of two hydrogen atoms by a hydrocarbon group or other nonacid organic group
im·i·no \ˈim-ə-ˌnō\ *adj* (1903) **:** relating to or containing the NH group or its substituted form NR united to a group other than an acid group
imip·ra·mine \im-ˈip-rə-ˌmēn\ *n* [*imide* + *propyl* + *amine*] (1958) **:** a tricyclic antidepressant drug $C_{19}H_{24}N_2$
im·i·ta·ble \ˈim-ət-ə-bəl\ *adj* (ca. 1598) **:** capable or worthy of being imitated or copied
im·i·tate \ˈim-ə-ˌtāt\ *vt* **-tat·ed; -tat·ing** [L *imitatus*, pp. of *imitari* — more at IMAGE] (1534) **1 :** to follow as a pattern, model, or example **2 :** to be or appear like **:** RESEMBLE **3 :** to produce a copy of **:** REPRODUCE **4 :** MIMIC, COUNTERFEIT ⟨can ~ his father's booming voice⟩ ***syn*** see COPY — **im·i·ta·tor** \-ˌtāt-ər\ *n*
[1]**im·i·ta·tion** \ˌim-ə-ˈtā-shən\ *n* (15c) **1 :** an act or instance of imitating **2 :** something produced as a copy **:** COUNTERFEIT **3 :** a literary work designed to reproduce the style of another author **4 :** the repetition by one voice of a melody, phrase, or motive stated earlier in the composition by a different voice **5 :** the quality of an object in possessing some of the nature or attributes of a transcendent idea **6 :** the assumption of behavior observed in other individuals
[2]**imitation** *adj* (1858) **:** resembling something else that is usu. genuine and of better quality **:** not real ⟨~ leather⟩
im·i·ta·tive \ˈim-ə-ˌtāt-iv\ *adj* (1584) **1 a :** marked by imitation ⟨acting is an ~ art⟩ **b :** reproducing or representing a natural sound **:** ONOMATOPOEIC ⟨"hiss" is an ~ word⟩ **c :** exhibiting mimicry **2 :** inclined to imitate **3 :** imitating something superior **:** COUNTERFEIT — **im·i·ta·tive·ly** *adv* — **im·i·ta·tive·ness** *n*
im·mac·u·la·cy \im-ˈak-yə-lə-sē\ *n* (1799) **:** the quality or state of being immaculate
im·mac·u·late \im-ˈak-yə-lət\ *adj* [ME *immaculat*, fr. L *immaculatus*, fr. *in-* + *maculatus* stained — more at MACULATE] (15c) **1 :** having no stain or blemish **:** PURE **2 :** containing no flaw or error **3 a :** spotlessly clean **b :** having no colored spots or marks ⟨petals ~⟩ — **im·mac·u·late·ly** *adv*
Immaculate Conception *n* (1687) **1 :** the conception of the Virgin Mary in which as decreed in Roman Catholic dogma her soul was preserved free from original sin by divine grace **2 :** December 8 observed as a Roman Catholic festival in commemoration of the Immaculate Conception
im·mane \im-ˈān\ *adj* [L *immanis*, fr. *in-* + *manus* good — more at MATURE] *archaic* (1602) **:** HUGE; *also* **:** monstrous in character
im·ma·nence \ˈim-ə-nən(t)s\ *n* (1816) **:** the quality or state of being immanent **:** INHERENCE
im·ma·nen·cy \-nən-sē\ *n* (1659) **:** IMMANENCE
im·ma·nent \-nənt\ *adj* [LL *immanent-*, *immanens*, prp. of *immanēre* to remain in place, fr. L *in-* + *manēre* to remain — more at MANSION] (1535) **:** remaining or operating within a domain of reality or realm of discourse **:** INHERENT; *specif* **:** having existence or effect only within the mind or consciousness — compare TRANSCENDENT — **im·ma·nent·ly** *adv*
im·ma·nent·ism \-ˌiz-əm\ *n* (1907) **:** any of several theories according to which God or an abstract mind or spirit pervades the world — **im·ma·nent·ist** \-nənt-əst, -ˌnent-\ *n* — **im·ma·nent·is·tic** \ˌim-ə-nənt-ˈis-tik\ *adj*
Im·man·u·el \i-ˈman-y(ə-w)əl\ *n* [Heb] (15c) **:** MESSIAH 1
im·ma·te·ri·al \ˌim-ə-ˈtir-ē-əl\ *adj* [ME *immateriel*, fr. MF, fr. LL *immaterialis*, fr. L *in-* + LL *materialis* material] (14c) **1 :** not consisting of matter **:** INCORPOREAL **2 :** of no substantial consequence **:** UNIMPORTANT
im·ma·te·ri·al·ism \-ē-ə-ˌliz-əm\ *n* (1713) **:** a philosophical theory that material things have no reality except as mental perceptions — **im·ma·te·ri·al·ist** \-ləst\ *n*
im·ma·te·ri·al·i·ty \ˌim-ə-ˌtir-ē-ˈal-ət-ē\ *n, pl* **-ties** (1570) **1 :** the quality or state of being immaterial **2 :** something immaterial
im·ma·te·ri·al·ize \-ˈtir-ē-ə-ˌlīz\ *vt* (1661) **:** to make immaterial or incorporeal
im·ma·ture \ˌim-ə-ˈt(y)u̇(ə)r *also* -ˈchu̇(ə)r\ *adj* [L *immaturus*, fr. *in-* + *maturus* mature] (1548) **1** *archaic* **:** PREMATURE **2 a :** lacking complete growth, differentiation, or development ⟨a thin ~ soil⟩ **b** (1) **:** having the potential capacity to attain a definitive form or state **:** CRUDE, UNFINISHED ⟨a vigorous but ~ school of art⟩ (2) *of a topographic feature* **:** predictably due to undergo further changes — used esp. of valleys and drainages while most of the area is well above base-level **c :** exhibiting less than an expected degree of maturity ⟨emotionally ~ adults⟩ — **immature** *n* — **im·ma·ture·ly** *adv* — **im·ma·tu·ri·ty** \-ˈt(y)u̇r-ət-ē *also* -ˈchu̇r-\ *n*
im·mea·sur·able \(ˌ)im-ˈ(m)ezh-(ə-)rə-bəl, -ˈ(m)ezh-ər-bəl, -ˈ(m)āzh-\ *adj* (14c) **:** incapable of being measured; *broadly* **:** indefinitely extensive — **im·mea·sur·able·ness** *n* — **im·mea·sur·ably** \-blē\ *adv*
im·me·di·a·cy \im-ˈēd-ē-ə-sē, *Brit often* -ˈē-jə-sē\ *n, pl* **-cies** (1605) **1 :** the quality or state of being immediate; *esp* **:** absence of a mediating agent **2 :** something that is immediate — usu. used in pl.
im·me·di·ate \im-ˈēd-ē-ət, *Brit often* -ˈē-jit\ *adj* [LL *immediatus*, fr. L *in-* + LL *mediatus* intermediate — more at MEDIATE] (15c) **1 a :** acting or being without the intervention of another object, cause, or agency **:** DIRECT ⟨the ~ cause of death⟩ **b :** present to the mind independently of other states or factors ⟨~ awareness⟩ **c :** involving or derived from a single premise ⟨an ~ inference⟩ **2 :** being next in line or relation ⟨only the ~ family was present⟩ **3 a :** existing without intervening space or substance ⟨bring the chemicals into ~ contact very carefully⟩ **b :** being near at hand ⟨the ~ neighborhood⟩ **4 a :** occurring, acting, or accomplished without loss or interval of time **:** INSTANT ⟨an ~ need⟩ **b** (1) *of time* **:** near to or related to the present ⟨the ~ past⟩ (2) **:** of or relating to the here and now **:** CURRENT ⟨too busy with ~ concerns to worry about the future⟩ **5 :** directly touching or concerning a person or thing ⟨the child's ~ world is the classroom⟩
immediate constituent *n* (1933) **:** any of the meaningful constituents directly forming a larger linguistic construction (as a phrase or sentence)
[1]**im·me·di·ate·ly** \im-ˈēd-(ē-)ət-lē, *Brit often* -ˈē-jət-\ *adv* (15c) **1 :** in direct connection or relation **:** DIRECTLY ⟨the parties ~ involved in the case⟩ ⟨the house ~ beyond this one⟩ **2 :** without interval of time **:** STRAIGHTWAY
[2]**immediately** *conj* (1839) **:** AS SOON AS
im·me·di·ate·ness *n* (1633) **:** IMMEDIACY 1
im·med·i·ca·ble \(ˈ)im-ˈ(m)ed-i-kə-bəl\ *adj* [L *immedicabilis*, fr. *in-* + *medicabilis* medicable] (1533) **:** INCURABLE ⟨wounds ~ —John Milton⟩ — **im·med·i·ca·bly** \-blē\ *adv*
Im·mel·mann \ˈim-əl-mən\ *n* [Max *Immelmann*] (1917) **:** a turn in which an airplane in flight is first made to complete half of a loop and is then rolled half of a complete turn — called also *Immelmann turn*
im·me·mo·ri·al \ˌim-ə-ˈmōr-ē-əl, -ˈmȯr-\ *adj* [prob. fr. F *immémorial*, fr. MF, fr. *in-* + *memorial*] (1602) **:** extending beyond the reach of memory, record, or tradition ⟨existing from time ~⟩ — **im·me·mo·ri·al·ly** \-ē-ə-lē\ *adv*
im·mense \im-ˈen(t)s\ *adj* [MF, fr. L *immensus* immeasurable, fr. *in-* + *mensus*, pp. of *metiri* to measure — more at MEASURE] (15c) **1 :** marked by greatness esp. in size or degree; *esp* **:** transcending ordinary means of measurement ⟨the ~ and boundless universe⟩ **2 :** supremely good **:** EXCELLENT ⟨her portrayal of the role was ~⟩ ***syn*** see ENORMOUS — **im·mense·ly** *adv* — **im·mense·ness** *n*
im·men·si·ty \im-ˈen(t)-sət-ē\ *n, pl* **-ties** (15c) **1 :** the quality or state of being immense **2 :** something immense
im·men·su·ra·ble \(ˈ)im-ˈ(m)en(t)s-(ə-)rə-bəl, -ˈ(m)ench-(ə-)rə-\ *adj* [LL *immensurabilis*, fr. L *in-* + LL *mensurabilis* measurable] (1500) **:** IMMEASURABLE
im·merge \im-ˈərj\ *vi* **im·merged; im·merg·ing** [L *immergere*] (1706) **:** to plunge into or immerse oneself in something — **im·mer·gence** \-ˈər-jən(t)s\ *n*
im·merse \im-ˈərs\ *vt* **im·mersed; im·mers·ing** [L *immersus*, pp. of *immergere*, fr. *in-* [2]-in + *mergere* to merge] (15c) **1 :** to plunge into something that surrounds or covers; *esp* **:** to plunge or dip into a fluid **2 :** ENGROSS, ABSORB ⟨completely *immersed* in his work⟩ **3 :** to baptize by immersion
im·mers·ible \im-ˈər-sə-bəl\ *adj* (ca. 1846) **:** capable of being totally submerged in water without damage to the heating element ⟨an ~ electric frying pan⟩
im·mer·sion \im-ˈər-zhən, -shən\ *n* (15c) **1 :** an act of immersing **:** a state of being immersed; *specif* **:** baptism by complete submersion of the person in water **2 :** disappearance of a celestial body behind or into the shadow of another
im·mesh \im-ˈesh\ *var of* ENMESH
im·me·thod·i·cal \ˌim-ə-ˈthäd-i-kəl\ *adj* (1605) **:** not methodical — **im·me·thod·i·cal·ly** \-k(ə-)lē\ *adv*
im·mi·grant \ˈim-i-grənt\ *n* (1789) **:** one that immigrates: **a :** a person who comes to a country to take up permanent residence **b :** a plant or

animal that becomes established in an area where it was previously unknown — **immigrant** *adj*

im·mi·grate \'im-ə-ˌgrāt\ *vb* **-grat·ed; -grat·ing** [L *immigratus,* pp. of *immigrare* to remove, go in, fr. *in-* + *migrare* to migrate] *vi* (ca. 1623) : to enter and usu. become established; *esp* : to come into a country of which one is not a native for permanent residence ~ *vt* : to bring in or send as immigrants — **im·mi·gra·tion** \ˌim-ə-'grā-shən\ *n* — **im·mi·gra·tion·al** \-shnəl, -shən-ᵊl\ *adj*

im·mi·nence \'im-ə-nən(t)s\ *n* (1655) **1 :** the quality or state of being imminent **2 :** something imminent; *esp* : impending evil or danger

im·mi·nen·cy \-nən-sē\ *n* (1665) : IMMINENCE 1

im·mi·nent \'im-ə-nənt\ *adj* [L *imminent-, imminens,* prp. of *imminēre* to project, threaten, fr. *in-* + *-minēre* (akin to L *mont-, mons* mountain) — more at MOUNT] (1528) : ready to take place; *esp* : hanging threateningly over one's head ⟨was in ~ danger of being run over⟩ — **im·mi·nent·ly** *adv*

im·min·gle \im-'iŋ-gəl\ *vb* (1606) : BLEND, INTERMINGLE

im·mis·ci·ble \(ˈ)im-'(m)is-ə-bəl\ *adj* (1671) : incapable of mixing or attaining homogeneity — **im·mis·ci·bil·i·ty** \(ˌ)im-ˌ(m)is-ə-'bil-ət-ē\ *n* — **im·mis·ci·bly** \(ˈ)im-'(m)is-ə-blē\ *adv*

im·mit·i·ga·ble \(ˈ)im-'(m)it-i-gə-bəl\ *adj* [LL *immitigabilis,* fr. L *in-* + *mitigare* to mitigate] (1576) : not capable of being mitigated — **im·mit·i·ga·ble·ness** *n* — **im·mit·i·ga·bly** \-blē\ *adv*

im·mit·tance \(ˈ)im-'(m)it-ᵊn(t)s\ *n* [*impedance* + *admittance*] (ca. 1948) : electrical admittance or impedance

im·mix \im-'iks\ *vt* [back-formation fr. *immixed* mixed in, fr. ME *immixte,* fr. L *immixtus,* pp. of *immiscēre,* fr. *in-* + *miscēre* to mix — more at MIX] (15c) : to mix intimately : COMMINGLE — **im·mix·ture** \-'iks-chər\ *n*

im·mo·bile \(ˈ)im-'(m)ō-bəl, -ˌbēl, -ˌbīl\ *adj* [ME *in-mobill,* fr. L *immobilis,* fr. *in-* + *mobilis* mobile] (14c) **1 :** incapable of being moved : FIXED **2 :** not moving : MOTIONLESS ⟨keep the patient ~⟩ — **im·mo·bil·i·ty** \ˌim-(ˌ)ō-'bil-ət-ē\ *n*

im·mo·bi·lize \im-'ō-bə-ˌlīz\ *vt* (1871) : to make immobile: as **a :** to prevent freedom of movement or effective use of ⟨the planes were *immobilized* by bad weather⟩ **b :** to reduce or eliminate motion of (the body or a part) by mechanical means or by strict bed rest **c :** to withhold (money or capital) from circulation — **im·mo·bi·li·za·tion** \-ˌō-bə-lə-'zā-shən\ *n* — **im·mo·bi·liz·er** \-'ō-bə-ˌlī-zər\ *n*

im·mod·er·a·cy \(ˈ)im-'(m)äd-(ə-)rə-sē\ *n* (1682) : lack of moderation

im·mod·er·ate \-(ə-)rət\ *adj* [ME *immoderat,* fr. L *immoderatus,* fr. *in-* + *moderatus,* pp. of *moderare* to moderate] (14c) : exceeding just, usual, or suitable bounds ⟨~ pride⟩ ⟨an ~ appetite⟩ ***syn*** see EXCESSIVE — **im·mod·er·ate·ly** *adv* — **im·mod·er·ate·ness** *n* — **im·mod·er·a·tion** \(ˌ)im-ˌäd-ə-'rā-shən\ *n*

im·mod·est \(ˈ)im-'(m)äd-əst\ *adj* [L *immodestus,* fr. *in-* + *modestus* modest] (ca. 1570) : not modest; *specif* : not conforming to the sexual mores of a particular time or place — **im·mod·est·ly** *adv* — **im·mod·es·ty** \-ə-stē\ *n*

im·mo·late \'im-ə-ˌlāt\ *vt* **-lat·ed; -lat·ing** [L *immolatus,* pp. of *immolare,* fr. *in-* + *mola* spelt grits; fr. the custom of sprinkling victims with sacrificial meal; akin to L *molere* to grind — more at MILL] (1548) **1 :** to offer in sacrifice; *esp* : to kill as a sacrificial victim **2 :** KILL, DESTROY — **im·mo·la·tor** \-ˌlāt-ər\ *n*

im·mo·la·tion \ˌim-ə-'lā-shən\ *n* (15c) **1 :** the act of immolating : the state of being immolated **2 :** something that is immolated

im·mor·al \(ˈ)im-'(m)ȯr-əl, -'(m)är-\ *adj* (1660) : not moral; *broadly* : conflicting with generally or traditionally held moral principles — **im·mor·al·ly** \-ə-lē\ *adv*

im·mor·al·ist \-ə-ləst\ *n* (1697) : an advocate of immorality

im·mo·ral·i·ty \ˌim-(ˌ)ȯ-'ral-ət-ē, ˌim-ə-'ral-\ *n* (1566) **1 :** the quality or state of being immoral; *esp* : UNCHASTITY **2 :** an immoral act or practice

[1]**im·mor·tal** \(ˈ)im-'ȯrt-ᵊl\ *adj* [ME, fr. L *immortalis,* fr. *in-* + *mortalis* mortal] (14c) **1 :** exempt from death ⟨the ~ gods⟩ **2 :** exempt from oblivion : IMPERISHABLE ⟨~ fame⟩ **3 :** connected with or relating to immortality — **im·mor·tal·ly** \-ᵊl-ē\ *adv*

[2]**immortal** *n* (1600) **1 a :** one exempt from death **b** *pl, often cap* : the gods of the Greek and Roman pantheon **2 a :** a person whose fame is lasting **b** *cap* : any of the 40 members of the Académie Française

im·mor·tal·i·ty \ˌim-ˌȯr-'tal-ət-ē\ *n* (14c) : the quality or state of being immortal: **a :** unending existence **b :** lasting fame

im·mor·tal·ize \im-'ȯrt-ᵊl-ˌīz\ *vt* **-ized; -iz·ing** (1566) : to make immortal — **im·mor·tal·iza·tion** \-ˌȯrt-ᵊl-ə-'zā-shən\ *n* — **im·mor·tal·iz·er** \-'ȯrt-ᵊl-ˌī-zər\ *n*

im·mor·telle \ˌim-ˌȯr-'tel\ *n* [F, fr. fem. of *immortel* immortal, fr. L *immortalis*] (1832) : EVERLASTING 3

im·mo·tile \(ˈ)im-'(m)ōt-ᵊl, -'(m)ō-ˌtīl\ *adj* (1872) : lacking motility

[1]**im·mov·able** \(ˈ)im-'(m)ü-və-bəl\ *adj* (14c) **1 :** incapable of being moved; *broadly* : not moving or not intended to be moved **2 a :** STEADFAST, UNYIELDING **b :** not capable of being moved emotionally — **im·mov·abil·i·ty** \(ˌ)im-ˌ(m)ü-və-'bil-ət-ē\ *n* — **im·mov·able·ness** \(ˈ)im-'(m)ü-və-bəl-nəs\ *n* — **im·mov·ably** \-blē\ *adv*

[2]**immovable** *n* (1588) **1 :** one that cannot be moved **2** *pl* : real property

im·mune \im-'yün\ *adj* [L *immunis,* fr. *in-* + *munia* services, obligations; akin to L *munus* service] (15c) **1 a :** FREE, EXEMPT ⟨~ from further taxation⟩ **b :** marked by protection ⟨some criminal leaders are ~ from arrest⟩ **2 :** not susceptible or responsive ⟨~ to all pleas⟩; *esp* : having a high degree of resistance to a disease ⟨~ to diphtheria⟩ **3 a :** having or producing antibodies or lymphocytes capable of reacting with a specific antigen ⟨an ~ serum⟩ **b :** produced by, involved in, or concerned with immunity or an immune response ⟨~ agglutinins⟩ ⟨~ globulins⟩ — **immune** *n*

immune response *n* (1953) : a bodily response to an antigen that involves the interaction of the antigen with lymphocytes to induce the formation of antibodies and lymphocytes capable of reacting with it and rendering it harmless — called also *immune reaction*

im·mu·ni·ty \im-'yü-nət-ē\ *n, pl* **-ties** (14c) : the quality or state of being immune; *specif* : a condition of being able to resist a particular disease esp. through preventing development of a pathogenic microorganism or by counteracting the effects of its products

im·mu·nize \'im-yə-ˌnīz\ *vt* **-nized; -niz·ing** (1892) : to make immune — **im·mu·ni·za·tion** \ˌim-yə-nə-'zā-shən *also* im-ˌyü-nə-\ *n*

immuno- *comb form* [ISV, fr. *immune*] **1 :** physiological immunity ⟨*immuno*logy⟩ **2 :** immunologic ⟨*immuno*chemistry⟩ : immunologically ⟨*immuno*compatible⟩ : immunology and ⟨*immuno*genetics⟩

im·mu·no·as·say \ˌim-yə-nō-'as-ˌā, im-ˌyü-nō-, -a-'sā\ *n* (1959) : the identification of a substance (as a protein) through its capacity to act as an antigen — **im·mu·no·as·say·able** \-a-'sā-ə-bəl\ *adj*

im·mu·no·chem·is·try \-'kem-ə-strē\ *n* [ISV] (1907) : a branch of chemistry that deals with the chemical aspects of immunology — **im·mu·no·chem·i·cal** \-'kem-i-kəl\ *adj* — **im·mu·no·chem·i·cal·ly** \-k(ə-)lē\ *adv* — **im·mu·no·chem·ist** \-'kem-əst\ *n*

im·mu·no·com·pe·tence \-'käm-pət-ən(t)s\ *n* (1967) : the capacity for a normal immune response — **im·mu·no·com·pe·tent** \-ənt\ *adj*

im·mu·no·cy·to·chem·is·try \-ˌsīt-ō-'kem-ə-strē\ *n* (1967) : the biochemistry of cellular immunology — **im·mu·no·cy·to·chem·i·cal** \-'kəm-i-kəl\ *adj* — **im·mu·no·cy·to·chem·i·cal·ly** \-'kem-i-k(ə-)lē\ *adv*

im·mu·no·de·fi·cien·cy \-di-'fish-ən-sē\ *n* (1971) : inability to produce a normal complement of antibodies or immunologically sensitized T cells esp. in response to specific antigens — **im·mu·no·de·fi·cient** \-ənt\ *adj*

im·mu·no·dif·fu·sion \-dif-'yü-zhən\ *n* (1959) : any of several techniques for obtaining a precipitate between an antibody and its specific antigen by suspending one in a gel and letting the other migrate through it from a well or by letting both antibody and antigen migrate through the gel from separate wells to form an area of precipitation

im·mu·no·elec·tro·pho·re·sis \ˌim-yə-nō-ə-ˌlek-trə-fə-'rē-səs, im-ˌyü-nō-\ *n, pl* **-re·ses** \-ˌsēz\ (1958) : electrophoretic separation of proteins followed by identification by the formation of precipitates through specific immunologic reactions — **im·mu·no·elec·tro·pho·ret·ic** \-'ret-ik\ *adj* — **im·mu·no·elec·tro·pho·ret·i·cal·ly** \-i-k(ə-)lē\ *adv*

im·mu·no·flu·o·res·cence \-(ˌ)flu̇(-ə)r-'es-ᵊn(t)s, -flōr-, -flȯr-\ *n* (1960) : the labeling of antigens or antibodies with fluorescent dyes for the purpose of demonstrating the presence of corresponding antibodies or antigens in a tissue preparation or smear — **im·mu·no·flu·o·res·cent** \-ᵊnt\ *adj*

im·mu·no·gen \i-'myü-nə-jən, -ˌjen\ *n* [fr. *Immunogen,* a trademark] (1959) : an antigen that produces an immune response (as antibody production)

im·mu·no·ge·net·ics \ˌim-yə-nō-jə-'net-iks, im-ˌyü-nō-\ *n pl but sing in constr* (1938) : a branch of immunology concerned with the interrelations of heredity, disease, and the immune system and its components (as antibodies) — **im·mu·no·ge·net·ic** \-ik\ *adj* — **im·mu·no·ge·net·i·cal·ly** \-i-k(ə-)lē\ *adv* — **im·mu·no·ge·net·i·cist** \-jə-'net-ə-səst\ *n*

im·mu·no·gen·ic \ˌim-yə-nō-'jen-ik, im-ˌyü-nō-\ *adj* (ca. 1923) : relating to or producing an immune response ⟨~ substances⟩ — **im·mu·no·gen·e·sis** \-'jen-ə-səs\ *n* — **im·mu·no·ge·nic·i·ty** \-jə-'nis-ət-ē\ *n*

im·mu·no·glob·u·lin \-'gläb-yə-lən\ *n* (1953) : any of the vertebrate serum proteins that are made up of light chains and heavy chains usu. linked by disulfide bonds and include all known antibodies

im·mu·no·he·ma·tol·o·gy \-ˌhē-mə-'täl-ə-jē\ *n* (1950) : a branch of immunology that deals with the immunologic properties of blood — **im·mu·no·he·ma·to·log·ic** \-ˌhē-mət-ᵊl-'äj-ik\ *or* **im·mu·no·he·ma·to·log·i·cal** \-'äj-i-kəl\ *adj* — **im·mu·no·he·ma·tol·o·gist** \-ˌhē-mə-'täl-ə-jəst\ *n*

im·mu·no·his·to·chem·i·cal \-ˌhis-tō-'kem-i-kəl\ *adj* (1962) : of or relating to the application of histochemical and immunologic methods to chemical analysis of living cells and tissues — **im·mu·no·his·to·chem·is·try** \-'kem-ə-strē\ *n*

im·mu·nol·o·gy \ˌim-yə-'näl-ə-jē\ *n* [ISV] (1910) : a science that deals with the phenomena and causes of immunity and immune responses — **im·mu·no·log·ic** \-yən-ᵊl-'äj-ik\ *or* **im·mu·no·log·i·cal** \-'äj-i-kəl\ *adj* — **im·mu·no·log·i·cal·ly** \-i-k(ə-)lē\ *adv* — **im·mu·nol·o·gist** \ˌim-yə-'näl-ə-jəst\ *n*

im·mu·no·pa·thol·o·gy \ˌim-yə-nō-pə-'thäl-ə-jē, im-ˌyü-nō-, -pa-\ *n* (1959) : a branch of medicine that deals with immune responses associated with disease — **im·mu·no·path·o·log·ic** \-ˌpath-ə-'läj-ik\ *or* **im·mu·no·path·o·log·i·cal** \-i-kəl\ *adj* — **im·mu·no·pa·thol·o·gist** \-pə-'thäl-ə-jəst, -pa-\ *n*

im·mu·no·pre·cip·i·ta·tion \-pri-ˌsip-ə-'tā-shən\ *n* (1966) : precipitation of a complex of an antibody and its specific antigen — **im·mu·no·pre·cip·i·tate** \-'sip-ət-ət, -ə-ˌtāt\ *n* — **im·mu·no·pre·cip·i·tate** \-ə-ˌtāt\ *vt*

im·mu·no·re·ac·tive \-rē-'ak-tiv\ *adj* (1966) : reacting to particular antigens or haptens ⟨~ lymphocytes⟩ — **im·mu·no·re·ac·tiv·i·ty** \-(ˌ)rē-ˌak-'tiv-ət-ē\ *n*

im·mu·no·sup·pres·sion \-sə-'presh-ən\ *n* (1963) : suppression (as by drugs) of natural immune responses — **im·mu·no·sup·press** \-sə-'pres\ *vt* — **im·mu·no·sup·pres·sant** \-'pres-ᵊnt\ *n or adj* — **im·mu·no·sup·pres·sive** \-'pres-iv\ *adj*

im·mu·no·ther·a·py \-'ther-ə-pē\ *n* [ISV] (ca. 1910) : treatment of or prophylaxis against disease by attempting to produce active or passive immunity — **im·mu·no·ther·a·peu·tic** \-ˌther-ə-'pyüt-ik\ *adj*

im·mure \im-'yu̇(ə)r\ *vt* **im·mured; im·mur·ing** [ML *immurare,* fr. L *in-* + *murus* wall — more at MUNITION] (1583) **1 a :** to enclose within or as if within walls **b :** IMPRISON **2 :** to build into a wall; *esp* : to entomb in a wall — **im·mure·ment** \-'yu̇(ə)r-mənt\ *n*

im·mu·ta·ble \(ˈ)im-'(m)yüt-ə-bəl\ *adj* [ME, fr. L *immutabilis,* fr. *in-* + *mutabilis* mutable] (15c) : not capable of or susceptible to change — **im·mu·ta·bil·i·ty** \(ˌ)im-ˌ(m)yüt-ə-'bil-ət-ē\ *n* — **im·mu·ta·ble·ness** \(ˈ)im-'(m)yüt-ə-bəl-nəs\ *n* — **im·mu·ta·bly** \-blē\ *adv*

[1]**imp** \'imp\ *n* [ME *impe,* fr. OE *impa,* fr. *impian* to imp] (bef. 12c) **1** *obs* : SHOOT, BUD; *also* : GRAFT **2 a :** a small demon : FIEND **b :** a mischievous child : URCHIN

[2]**imp** *vt* [ME *impen,* fr. OE *impian;* akin to OHG *impfōn* to graft; both from a prehistoric WGmc word borrowed fr. (assumed) VL *imputare,* fr. L *in-* + *putare* to prune — more at PAVE] (bef. 12c) **1 :** to graft or repair (a wing, tail, or feather) with a feather to improve a falcon's flying capacity **2 :** to equip with wings

[1]**im·pact** \im-'pakt\ *vb* [L *impactus,* pp. of *impingere* to push against — more at IMPINGE] *vt* (1601) **1 a :** to fix firmly by or as if by packing or wedging **b :** to press together **2 a :** to have an impact on : impinge on **b :** to strike forcefully; *also* : to cause to strike forcefully ~ *vi* **1 :** to have an impact **2 :** to impinge or make contact esp. forcefully — **im·pac·tive** \im-'pak-tiv\ *adj*

[2]**im·pact** \'im-ˌpakt\ *n* (1781) **1 a :** an impinging or striking esp. of one body against another **b :** a forceful contact, collision, or onset; *also* : the impetus communicated in or as if in a collision **2 :** the force

of impression of one thing on another : an impelling or compelling effect ⟨the ~ of modern science on our society⟩

im·pact·ed \im-ˈpak-təd\ *adj* (1876) **1** *of a tooth* : wedged between the jawbone and another tooth **2** : of, relating to, or being an area (as a school district) providing tax-supported services to a population having a large proportion of federal employees and esp. those living or working on tax-exempt federal property ⟨aid to education in ~ areas⟩ **3** : packed or wedged in

im·pac·tion \im-ˈpak-shən\ *n* (1739) : the act of becoming or the state of being impacted; *esp* : lodgment of something (as feces) in a body passage or cavity

im·pac·tor *or* **im·pact·er** \im-ˈpak-tər\ *n* (1916) : one that impacts: as **a** : a machine or part that operates by striking blows **b** : an instrument for collecting samples of suspended particles (as dust in air) by directing a stream of the suspension onto a surface or into a liquid

im·paint \im-ˈpānt\ *vt, obs* (1596) : PAINT, DEPICT

im·pair \im-ˈpa(ə)r, -ˈpe(ə)r\ *vt* [ME *empeiren,* fr. MF *empeirer,* fr. (assumed) VL *impejorare,* fr. L *in-* + LL *pejorare* to make worse — more at PEJORATIVE] (14c) : to damage or make worse by or as if by diminishing in some material respect ⟨his health was ~*ed* by overwork⟩ ⟨the strike seriously ~*ed* community services⟩ ***syn*** see INJURE — **im·pair·er** *n* — **im·pair·ment** \-ˈpa(ə)r-mənt\ *n*

im·pa·la \im-ˈpal-ə, -ˈpäl-\ *n* [Zulu] (ca. 1875) : a large brownish African antelope (*Aepyceros melampus*) that in the male has slender lyrate horns

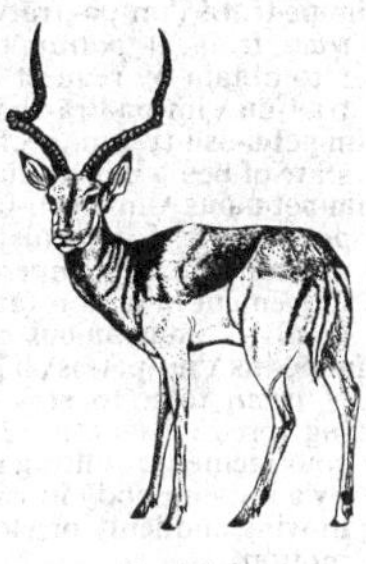

impala

im·pale \im-ˈpā(ə)l\ *vt* **im·paled; im·pal·ing** [MF & ML; MF *empaler,* fr. ML *impalare,* fr. L *in-* + *palus* stake — more at POLE] (1605) **1** : to join (coats of arms) on a heraldic shield divided vertically by a pale **2 a** : to pierce with or as if with something pointed; *esp* : to torture or kill by fixing on a sharp stake **b** : to fix in an inescapable or helpless position — **im·pale·ment** \-mənt\ *n*

im·pal·pa·ble \(ˈ)im-ˈpal-pə-bəl\ *adj* (1509) **1 a** : incapable of being felt by touch : INTANGIBLE ⟨the ~ aura of power that emanated from him —Osbert Sitwell⟩ **b** : so finely divided that no grains or grit can be felt ⟨rock worn to an ~ powder⟩ **2** : not readily discerned by the mind — **im·pal·pa·bil·i·ty** \(ˌ)im-ˌpal-pə-ˈbil-ət-ē\ *n* — **im·pal·pa·bly** \(ˌ)im-ˈpal-pə-blē\ *adv*

im·pan·el \im-ˈpan-ᵊl\ *vt* (15c) : to enroll in or on a panel ⟨~ a jury⟩

im·par·a·dise \im-ˈpar-ə-ˌdīs, -ˌdīz\ *vt* **-dised; -dis·ing** (1592) : ENRAPTURE

im·par·i·ty \(ˈ)im-ˈpar-ət-ē\ *n, pl* **-ties** [LL *imparitas,* fr. L *impar* unequal, fr. *in-* + *par* equal] (1563) : INEQUALITY, DISPARITY

im·part \im-ˈpärt\ *vt* [MF & L; MF *impartir,* fr. L *impartire,* fr. *in-* + *partire* to divide, part] (15c) **1** : to give, convey, or grant from or as if from a store ⟨his assurance ~*ed* authority to his words⟩ ⟨the flavor ~*ed* by herbs⟩ **2** : to communicate the knowledge of : DISCLOSE — **im·par·ta·tion** \ˌim-ˌpär-ˈtā-shən\ *n* — **im·part·ment** \im-ˈpärt-mənt\ *n*

im·par·tial \(ˈ)im-ˈpär-shəl\ *adj* (1587) : not partial or biased : treating or affecting all equally ***syn*** see FAIR — **im·par·tial·i·ty** \(ˌ)im-ˌpär-shē-ˈal-ət-ē, -ˌpär-ˈshal-\ *n* — **im·par·tial·ly** \(ˈ)im-ˈpärsh-(ə-)lē\ *adv*

im·par·ti·ble \(ˈ)im-ˈpärt-ə-bəl\ *adj* [LL *impartibilis,* fr. L *in-* + LL *partibilis* divisible, fr. L *partire*] (14c) : not partible : not subject to partition — **im·par·ti·bly** \-blē\ *adv*

im·pass·able \(ˈ)im-ˈpas-ə-bəl\ *adj* (1568) : incapable of being passed, traveled, crossed, or surmounted — **im·pass·abil·i·ty** \(ˌ)im-ˌpas-ə-ˈbil-ət-ē\ *n* — **im·pass·able·ness** \(ˈ)im-ˈpas-ə-bəl-nəs\ *n* — **im·pass·ably** \-blē\ *adv*

im·passe \ˈim-ˌpas, im-ˈ\ *n* [F, fr. *in-* + *passer* to pass] (1851) **1** : an impassable road or way : CUL-DE-SAC **2 a** : a predicament affording no obvious escape **b** : DEADLOCK

im·pas·si·ble \(ˈ)im-ˈpas-ə-bəl\ *adj* [ME, fr. MF or LL; MF, fr. LL *impassibilis,* fr. L *in-* + LL *passibilis* passible] (14c) **1 a** : incapable of suffering or of experiencing pain **b** : inaccessible to injury **2** : incapable of feeling : IMPASSIVE — **im·pas·si·bil·i·ty** \(ˌ)im-ˌpas-ə-ˈbil-ət-ē\ *n* — **im·pas·si·bly** \(ˈ)im-ˈpas-ə-blē\ *adv*

im·pas·sion \im-ˈpash-ən\ *vt* **im·pas·sioned; im·pas·sion·ing** \-(ə-)niŋ\ [prob. fr. It *impassionare,* fr. *in-* (fr. L) + *passione* passion, fr. LL *passion-, passio*] (1591) : to arouse the feelings or passions of

im·pas·sioned *adj* (1603) : filled with passion or zeal : showing great warmth or intensity of feeling

syn IMPASSIONED, PASSIONATE, ARDENT, FERVENT, FERVID, PERFERVID mean showing intense feeling. IMPASSIONED implies warmth and intensity without violence and suggests fluent verbal expression; PASSIONATE implies great vehemence and often violence and wasteful diffusion of emotion; ARDENT implies an intense degree of zeal, devotion, or enthusiasm; FERVENT stresses sincerity and steadiness of emotional warmth or zeal; FERVID suggests warmly and spontaneously and often feverishly expressed emotion; PERFERVID implies the expression of exaggerated or overwrought feelings.

im·pas·sive \(ˈ)im-ˈpas-iv\ *adj* (1667) **1 a** *archaic* : unsusceptible to pain **b** : unsusceptible to physical feeling : INSENSIBLE **c** : unsusceptible to or destitute of emotion : APATHETIC **2** : giving no sign of feeling or emotion : EXPRESSIONLESS — **im·pas·sive·ly** *adv* — **im·pas·sive·ness** *n* — **im·pas·siv·i·ty** \ˌim-ˌpas-ˈiv-ət-ē\ *n*

syn IMPASSIVE, STOIC, PHLEGMATIC, APATHETIC, STOLID mean unresponsive to something that might normally excite interest or emotion. IMPASSIVE stresses the absence of any external sign of emotion in action or facial expression; STOIC implies an apparent indifference to pleasure or esp. to pain often as a matter of principle or self-discipline; PHLEGMATIC implies a temperament or constitution hard to arouse; APATHETIC may imply a puzzling or deplorable indifference or inertness; STOLID implies an habitual absence of interest, responsiveness, or curiosity.

im·paste \im-ˈpāst\ *vt* [It *impastare,* fr. *in-* (fr. L) + *pasta* paste, fr. LL] *obs* (1576) : to make into a paste or crust

im·pas·to \im-ˈpas-(ˌ)tō, -ˈpäs-\ *n* [It, fr. *impastare*] (1784) **1** : the thick application of a pigment to a canvas or panel in painting; *also* : the body of pigment so applied **2** : raised decoration on ceramic ware usu. of slip or enamel — **im·pas·toed** \-(ˌ)tōd\ *adj*

im·pa·tience \(ˈ)im-ˈpā-shən(t)s\ *n* (13c) : the quality or state of being impatient

im·pa·tiens \im-ˈpā-shənz, -shən(t)s\ *n* [NL, fr. L, impatient] (1885) : any of a widely distributed genus (*Impatiens,* family Balsaminaceae) of watery-juiced annual herbs with irregular spurred or saccate flowers and dehiscent capsules — called also *jewelweed*

im·pa·tient \(ˈ)im-ˈpā-shənt\ *adj* [ME *impacient,* fr. MF, fr. L *impatient-, impatiens,* fr. *in-* + *patient-, patiens* patient] (14c) **1 a** : not patient : restless or short of temper esp. under irritation, delay, or opposition **b** : INTOLERANT ⟨~ of delay⟩ **2** : prompted or marked by impatience ⟨an ~ reply⟩ **3** : eagerly desirous : ANXIOUS ⟨~ to see his sweetheart⟩ — **im·pa·tient·ly** *adv*

im·pawn \im-ˈpȯn, -ˈpän\ *vt, archaic* (1596) : to put in pawn : PLEDGE

[1]**im·peach** \im-ˈpēch\ *vt* [ME *empechen,* fr. MF *empeechier* to hinder, fr. LL *impedicare* to fetter, fr. L *in-* + *pedica* fetter, fr. *ped-, pes* foot — more at FOOT] (14c) **1 a** : to bring an accusation against **b** : to charge with a crime or misdemeanor; *specif* : to charge (a public official) before a competent tribunal with misconduct in office **2** : to cast doubt on; *esp* : to challenge the credibility or validity of ⟨~ the testimony of a witness⟩ — **im·peach·able** \-ˈpē-chə-bəl\ *adj* — **im·peach·ment** \-ˈpēch-mənt\ *n*

[2]**impeach** *n, obs* (1590) : CHARGE, IMPEACHMENT

im·pearl \im-ˈpər(-ə)l\ *vt* [prob. fr. MF *emperler,* fr. *en-* + *perle* pearl] (15c) : to form into pearls; *also* : to form of or adorn with pearls

im·pec·ca·ble \(ˈ)im-ˈpek-ə-bəl\ *adj* [L *impeccabilis,* fr. *in-* + *peccare* to sin] (1531) **1** : not capable of sinning or liable to sin **2** : free from fault or blame : FLAWLESS ⟨spoke ~ French⟩ — **im·pec·ca·bil·i·ty** \(ˌ)im-ˌpek-ə-ˈbil-ət-ē\ *n* — **im·pec·ca·bly** \(ˈ)im-ˈpek-ə-blē\ *adv*

im·pe·cu·nious \ˌim-pi-ˈkyü-nyəs, -nē-əs\ *adj* [*in-* + obs. E *pecunious* (rich), fr. ME, fr. L *pecuniosus,* fr. *pecunia* money — more at FEE] (1596) : having very little or no money usu. habitually : PENNILESS — **im·pe·cu·ni·os·i·ty** \-ˌkyü-nē-ˈäs-ət-ē\ *n* — **im·pe·cu·nious·ly** *adv* — **im·pe·cu·nious·ness** *n*

im·ped·ance \im-ˈpēd-ᵊn(t)s\ *n* (ca. 1886) : something that impedes : HINDRANCE: as **a** : the apparent opposition in an electrical circuit to the flow of an alternating current that is analogous to the actual electrical resistance to a direct current and that is the ratio of effective electromotive force to the effective current **b** : the ratio of the pressure to the volume displacement at a given surface in a sound-transmitting medium

im·pede \im-ˈpēd\ *vt* **im·ped·ed; im·ped·ing** [L *impedire,* fr. *in-* + *ped-, pes* foot — more at FOOT] (1605) : to interfere with or slow the progress of ***syn*** see HINDER — **im·ped·er** *n*

im·ped·i·ment \im-ˈped-ə-mənt\ *n* (14c) **1** : something that impedes; *esp* : an organic obstruction to speech **2** : a bar or hindrance (as lack of sufficient age) to a lawful marriage

im·ped·i·men·ta \(ˌ)im-ˌped-ə-ˈment-ə\ *n pl* [L, pl. of *impedimentum* impediment, fr. *impedire*] (1600) **1** : APPURTENANCES, EQUIPMENT **2** : things that impede

im·pel \im-ˈpel\ *vt* **im·pelled; im·pel·ling** [L *impellere,* fr. *in-* + *pellere* to drive — more at FELT] (15c) **1** : to urge or drive forward or on by or as if by the exertion of strong moral pressure : FORCE **2** : to impart motion to : PROPEL ***syn*** see MOVE

im·pel·ler *also* **im·pel·lor** \im-ˈpel-ər\ *n* (1685) **1** : one that impels **2** : ROTOR; *also* : a blade of a rotor

im·pend \im-ˈpend\ *vi* [L *impendēre,* fr. *in-* + *pendēre* to hang — more at PENDANT] (1599) **1 a** : to hover threateningly : MENACE **b** : to be about to occur **2** *archaic* : to hang suspended

im·pen·dent \im-ˈpen-dənt\ *adj* (1592) : being near at hand : APPROACHING

im·pen·e·tra·bil·i·ty \(ˌ)im-ˌpen-ə-trə-ˈbil-ət-ē\ *n* (1665) **1** : the inability of two portions of matter to occupy the same space at the same time **2** : the quality or state of being impenetrable

im·pen·e·tra·ble \(ˈ)im-ˈpen-ə-trə-bəl\ *adj* [ME *impenetrabel,* fr. MF *impenetrable,* fr. L *impenetrabilis,* fr. *in-* + *penetrabilis* penetrable] (15c) **1 a** : incapable of being penetrated or pierced **b** : inaccessible to knowledge, reason, or sympathy : IMPERVIOUS **2** : incapable of being comprehended : INSCRUTABLE **3** : having the property of impenetrability — **im·pen·e·tra·bly** \-blē\ *adv*

im·pen·i·tence \(ˈ)im-ˈpen-ə-tən(t)s\ *n, archaic* (1624) : the quality or state of being impenitent

im·pen·i·tent \-tənt\ *adj* [ME, fr. LL *impaenitent-, impaenitens,* fr. L *in-* + *paenitent-, paenitens* penitent] (15c) : not penitent — **im·pen·i·tent·ly** *adv*

[1]**im·per·a·tive** \im-ˈper-ət-iv\ *adj* [ME *imperatyf,* fr. LL *imperativus,* fr. L *imperatus,* pp. of *imperare* to command — more at EMPEROR] (15c) **1 a** : of, relating to, or constituting the grammatical mood that expresses the will to influence the behavior of another **b** : expressive of a command, entreaty, or exhortation **c** : having power to restrain, control, and direct **2** : not to be avoided or evaded : NECESSARY ⟨an ~ duty⟩ ***syn*** see MASTERFUL — **im·per·a·tive·ly** *adv* — **im·per·a·tive·ness** *n*

[2]**imperative** *n* (1530) **1** : the imperative mood or a verb form or verbal phrase expressing it **2** : something that is imperative: as **a** : COMMAND, ORDER **b** : RULE, GUIDE **c** : an obligatory act or duty **d** : an imperative judgment or proposition

im·pe·ra·tor \ˌim-pə-ˈrät-ər, -ˈrā-ˌtȯ(ə)r\ *n* [L — more at EMPEROR] (1579) : a commander in chief or emperor of the ancient Romans — **im·per·a·to·ri·al** \(ˌ)im-ˌper-ə-ˈtōr-ē-əl, -ˈtȯr-\ *adj*

im·per·ceiv·able \ˌim-pər-ˈsē-və-bəl\ *adj, archaic* (1617) : IMPERCEPTIBLE

im·per·cep·ti·ble \ˌim-pər-ˈsep-tə-bəl\ *adj* [MF, fr. ML *imperceptibilis,* fr. L *in-* + LL *perceptibilis* perceptible] (15c) : not perceptible by a sense or by the mind : extremely slight, gradual, or subtle — **im·per·cep·ti·bly** \-ˈsep-tə-blē\ *adv*

im·per·cep·tive \ˌim-pər-ˈsep-tiv\ *adj* (1661) : not perceptive — **im·per·cep·tive·ness** *n*

\ə\ abut \ᵊ\ kitten, F table \ər\ further \a\ ash \ā\ ace \ä\ cot, cart \au̇\ out \ch\ chin \e\ bet \ē\ easy \g\ go \i\ hit \ī\ ice \j\ job \ŋ\ sing \ō\ go \ȯ\ law \ȯi\ boy \th\ thin \t͟h\ the \ü\ loot \u̇\ foot \y\ yet \zh\ vision \á, k̟, ⁿ, œ, œ̄, ue, u̅e, ʸ\ *see* Guide to Pronunciation

im·per·cip·i·ence \-ˈsip-ē-ən(t)s\ *n* (1891) **:** the quality or state of being imperceptive — **im·per·cip·i·ent** \-ənt\ *adj*

1im·per·fect \(ˈ)im-ˈpər-fikt\ *adj* [ME *imperfit,* fr. MF *imparfait,* fr. L *imperfectus,* fr. *in-* + *perfectus* perfect] (14c) **1 :** not perfect: as **a :** DEFECTIVE **b** *of a flower* **:** having stamens or pistils but not both **c :** lacking or not involving sexual reproduction ⟨the ~ stage of a fungus⟩ **2 :** of, relating to, or constituting a verb tense used to designate a continuing state or an incomplete action esp. in the past **3 :** not enforceable at law — **im·per·fect·ly** \-fik-(t)lē\ *adv* — **im·per·fect·ness** \-fik(t)-nəs\ *n*

2imperfect *n* (1871) **:** an imperfect tense; *also* **:** the verb form expressing it

imperfect fungus *n* (ca. 1895) **:** any of various fungi (order Fungi Imperfecti, syn. Deuteromycetes) of which only the conidial stage is known

im·per·fec·tion \ˌim-pər-ˈfek-shən\ *n* (14c) **:** the quality or state of being imperfect; *also* **:** FAULT, BLEMISH

im·per·fec·tive \ˌim-pər-ˈfek-tiv *also* (ˈ)im-ˈpər-fik-\ *adj, of a verb form or aspect* (ca. 1887) **:** expressing action as incomplete or without reference to completion or as reiterated — compare PERFECTIVE — **imperfective** *n*

im·per·fo·rate \(ˈ)im-ˈpər-f(ə-)rət, -fə-ˌrāt\ *adj* (1673) **1 :** having no opening or aperture; *specif* **:** lacking the usual or normal opening **2** *of a stamp or a sheet of stamps* **:** lacking perforations or roulettes

1im·pe·ri·al \im-ˈpir-ē-əl\ *adj* [ME, fr. MF, fr. LL *imperialis,* fr. L *imperium* command, empire] (14c) **1 a :** of, relating to, befitting, or suggestive of an empire or an emperor **b (1) :** of or relating to the United Kingdom as distinguished from the constituent parts **(2) :** of or relating to the Commonwealth and British Empire **2 a :** SOVEREIGN **b :** REGAL, IMPERIOUS **3 :** of superior or unusual size or excellence **4 :** belonging to the official British series of weights and measures — see WEIGHT table — **im·pe·ri·al·ly** \-ə-lē\ *adv*

2imperial *n* (1524) **1** *cap* **:** an adherent or soldier of the Holy Roman emperor **2 :** EMPEROR **3** [fr. the beard worn by Napoleon III] **:** a pointed beard growing below the lower lip **4 :** something of unusual size or excellence

im·pe·ri·al·ism \im-ˈpir-ē-ə-ˌliz-əm\ *n* (1851) **1 :** imperial government, authority, or system **2 :** the policy, practice, or advocacy of extending the power and dominion of a nation esp. by direct territorial acquisitions or by gaining indirect control over the political or economic life of other areas; *broadly* **:** the extension or imposition of power, authority, or influence ⟨union ~⟩ — **im·pe·ri·al·ist** \-ləst\ *n or adj* — **im·pe·ri·al·is·tic** \-ˌpir-ē-ə-ˈlis-tik\ *adj* — **im·pe·ri·al·is·ti·cal·ly** \-ti-k(ə-)lē\ *adv*

imperial moth *n* (ca. 1904) **:** a large American moth (*Eacles imperialis*) marked with yellow, lilac, or purplish brown

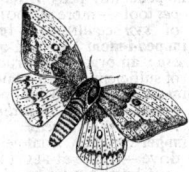

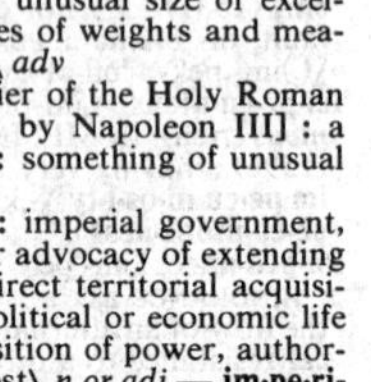
imperial moth

im·per·il \im-ˈper-əl\ *vt* **-iled** *or* **-illed; -il·ing** *or* **-il·ling** (15c) **:** to bring into peril **:** ENDANGER — **im·per·il·ment** \-əl-mənt\ *n*

im·pe·ri·ous \im-ˈpir-ē-əs\ *adj* [L *imperiosus,* fr. *imperium*] (1540) **1 :** befitting or characteristic of one of eminent rank or attainments **:** COMMANDING, DOMINANT ⟨an ~ manner⟩ **b :** marked by arrogant assurance **:** DOMINEERING ⟨her ~ arbitrariness⟩ **2 :** intensely compelling **:** URGENT ⟨the ~ problems of the new age —J. F. Kennedy⟩ ***syn*** see MASTERFUL — **im·pe·ri·ous·ly** *adv* — **im·pe·ri·ous·ness** *n*

im·per·ish·able \(ˈ)im-ˈper-ish-ə-bəl\ *adj* (1648) **1 :** not perishable or subject to decay **2 :** enduring or occurring forever ⟨~ fame⟩ — **im·per·ish·abil·i·ty** \(ˌ)im-ˌper-ish-ə-ˈbil-ət-ē\ *n* — **imperishable** *n* — **im·per·ish·able·ness** \(ˈ)im-ˈper-ish-ə-bəl-nəs\ *n* — **im·per·ish·ably** \-blē\ *adv*

im·pe·ri·um \im-ˈpir-ē-əm\ *n* [L — more at EMPIRE] (1651) **1 a :** supreme power or absolute dominion **:** CONTROL **b :** EMPIRE **2 :** the right to command or to employ the force of the state **:** SOVEREIGNTY

im·per·ma·nence \(ˈ)im-ˈpərm(-ə)-nən(t)s\ *n* (1796) **:** the quality or state of being impermanent

im·per·ma·nen·cy \-nən-sē\ *n* (1648) **:** IMPERMANENCE

im·per·ma·nent \-nənt\ *adj* (1653) **:** not permanent **:** TRANSIENT — **im·per·ma·nent·ly** *adv*

im·per·me·able \(ˈ)im-ˈpər-mē-ə-bəl\ *adj* [LL *impermeabilis,* fr. L *in-* + LL *permeabilis* permeable] (1697) **:** not permitting passage (as of a fluid) through its substance; *broadly* **:** IMPERVIOUS — **im·per·me·abil·i·ty** \(ˌ)im-ˌpər-mē-ə-ˈbil-ət-ē\ *n*

im·per·mis·si·ble \ˌim-pər-ˈmis-ə-bəl\ *adj* (1858) **:** not permissible — **im·per·mis·si·bil·i·ty** \-ˌmis-ə-ˈbil-ət-ē\ *n* — **im·per·mis·si·bly** \-ˈmis-ə-blē\ *adv*

im·per·son·al \(ˈ)im-ˈpərs-nəl, -ᵊn-əl\ *adj* [ME, fr. LL *impersonalis,* fr. L *in-* + LL *personalis* personal] (15c) **1 a :** denoting the verbal action of an unspecified agent and hence used with no expressed subject (as *methinks*) or with a merely formal subject (as *rained* in *it rained*) **b** *of a pronoun* **:** INDEFINITE **2 a :** having no personal reference or connection ⟨~ criticism⟩ **b :** not engaging the human personality or emotion ⟨the machine as compared with the hand tool is an ~ agency —John Dewey⟩ **c :** not existing as a person **:** not having personality — **im·per·son·al·i·ty** \(ˌ)im-ˌpərs-ᵊn-ˈal-ət-ē\ *n* — **im·per·son·al·ly** \(ˈ)im-ˈpərs-nə-lē, -ᵊn-ə-lē\ *adv*

im·per·son·al·ize \(ˈ)im-ˈpərs-nə-ˌlīz, -ᵊn-ə-\ *vt* (1880) **:** to make impersonal — **im·per·son·al·iza·tion** \(ˌ)im-ˌpərs-nə-lə-ˈzā-shən, -ᵊn-ə-\ *n*

im·per·son·ate \im-ˈpərs-ᵊn-ˌāt\ *vt* **-at·ed; -at·ing** (1715) **:** to assume or act the character of **:** PERSONATE — **im·per·son·ation** \-ˌpərs-ᵊn-ˈā-shən\ *n* — **im·per·son·ator** \-ˈpərs-ᵊn-ˌāt-ər\ *n*

im·per·ti·nence \(ˈ)im-ˈpərt-ᵊn-ən(t)s, -ˈpərt-nən(t)s\ *n* (1603) **1 :** the quality or state of being impertinent: as **a :** IRRELEVANCE, INAPPROPRIATENESS **b :** INCIVILITY, INSOLENCE **2 :** an instance of impertinence

im·per·ti·nen·cy \-ən-sē, -nən-\ *n, pl* **-cies** (1589) **:** IMPERTINENCE

im·per·ti·nent \(ˈ)im-ˈpərt-ᵊn-ənt, -ˈpərt-nənt\ *adj* [ME, fr. MF, fr. LL *impertinent-, impertinens,* fr. L *in-* + *pertinent-, pertinens,* prp. of *pertinēre* to pertain] (14c) **1 :** not pertinent **:** IRRELEVANT **2 :** not restrained within due or proper bounds esp. of propriety or good taste ⟨~ curiosity⟩; *also* **:** given to or characterized by insolent rudeness ⟨an ~ answer⟩ — **im·per·ti·nent·ly** *adv*

syn IMPERTINENT, OFFICIOUS, MEDDLESOME, INTRUSIVE, OBTRUSIVE mean given to thrusting oneself into the affairs of others. IMPERTINENT implies exceeding the bounds of propriety in showing interest or curiosity or in offering advice; OFFICIOUS implies the offering of services or attentions that are unwelcome or annoying; MEDDLESOME stresses an annoying and usu. prying interference in others' affairs; INTRUSIVE implies a tactless or otherwise objectionable thrusting into others' affairs; OBTRUSIVE stresses improper or offensive conspicuousness of interfering actions.

im·per·turb·able \ˌim-pər-ˈtər-bə-bəl\ *adj* [ME, fr. LL *imperturbabilis,* fr. L *in-* + *perturbare* to perturb] (15c) **:** marked by extreme calm, impassivity, and steadiness **:** SERENE ***syn*** see COOL — **im·per·turb·abil·i·ty** \-ˌtər-bə-ˈbil-ət-ē\ *n* — **im·per·turb·ably** \-ˈtər-bə-blē\ *adv*

im·per·vi·ous \(ˈ)im-ˈpər-vē-əs\ *adj* [L *impervius,* fr. *in-* + *pervius* pervious] (1650) **1 a :** not allowing entrance or passage **:** IMPENETRABLE ⟨a coat ~ to rain⟩ **b :** not capable of being damaged or harmed ⟨a carpet ~ to rough treatment⟩ **2 :** not capable of being affected or disturbed ⟨~ to criticism⟩ — **im·per·vi·ous·ly** *adv* — **im·per·vi·ous·ness** *n*

im·pe·tig·i·nous \ˌim-pə-ˈtij-ə-nəs\ *adj* (1620) **:** of, relating to, or resembling impetigo

im·pe·ti·go \ˌim-pə-ˈtē-(ˌ)gō, -ˈtī-\ *n* [L, fr. *impetere* to attack — more at IMPETUS] (14c) **:** an acute contagious staphylococcal or streptococcal skin disease characterized by vesicles, pustules, and yellowish crusts

im·pe·trate \ˈim-pə-ˌtrāt\ *vt* **-trat·ed; -trat·ing** [L *impetratus,* pp. of *impetrare,* fr. *in-* + *patrare* to accomplish — more at PERPETRATE] (1533) **1 :** to obtain by request or entreaty **2 :** to ask for **:** ENTREAT — **im·pe·tra·tion** \ˌim-pə-ˈtrā-shən\ *n*

im·pet·u·os·i·ty \im-ˌpech-ə-ˈwäs-ət-ē\ *n, pl* **-ties** (15c) **1 :** the quality or state of being impetuous **2 :** an impetuous action or impulse

im·pet·u·ous \im-ˈpech-(ə-)wəs\ *adj* [ME, fr. MF *impetueux,* fr. LL *impetuosus,* fr. L *impetus*] (14c) **1 :** marked by impulsive vehemence or passion ⟨an ~ temperament⟩ **2 :** marked by force and violence of movement or action ⟨an ~ wind⟩ ***syn*** see PRECIPITATE — **im·pet·u·ous·ly** *adv* — **im·pet·u·ous·ness** *n*

im·pe·tus \ˈim-pət-əs\ *n* [L, assault, impetus, fr. *impetere* to attack, fr. *in-* + *petere* to go to, seek — more at FEATHER] (1641) **1 a (1) :** a driving force **:** IMPULSE **(2) :** INCENTIVE, STIMULUS **b :** stimulation or encouragement resulting in increased activity **2 :** the property possessed by a moving body in virtue of its mass and its motion — used of bodies moving suddenly or violently to indicate the origin and intensity of the motion

im·pi·ety \(ˈ)im-ˈpī-ət-ē\ *n, pl* **-eties** (14c) **1 :** the quality or state of being impious **:** IRREVERENCE **2 :** an impious act

im·pinge \im-ˈpinj\ *vb* **im·pinged; im·ping·ing** [L *impingere,* fr. *in-* + *pangere* to fasten, drive in — more at PACT] *vi* (1605) **1 :** to strike or dash esp. with a sharp collision ⟨I heard the rain ~ upon the earth —James Joyce⟩ **2 :** to have an effect **:** make an impression ⟨waiting for the germ of a new idea to ~ upon my mind —Phyllis Bentley⟩ **3 :** ENCROACH, INFRINGE ⟨~ on other people's rights⟩ ~ *vt* **:** to cause (as a gas or a flame) to strike — **im·pinge·ment** \-ˈpinj-mənt\ *n*

im·pi·ous \ˈim-pē-əs, (ˈ)im-ˈpī-\ *adj* [L *impius,* fr. *in-* + *pius* pious] (1542) **:** not pious **:** lacking in reverence or proper respect (as for God or one's parents) **:** IRREVERENT — **im·pi·ous·ly** *adv*

imp·ish \ˈim-pish\ *adj* (1652) **:** of, relating to, or befitting an imp; *esp* **:** MISCHIEVOUS — **imp·ish·ly** *adv* — **imp·ish·ness** *n*

im·pla·ca·ble \(ˈ)im-ˈplak-ə-bəl, -ˈplā-kə-\ *adj* [MF or L; MF, fr. L *implacabilis,* fr. *in-* + *placabilis* placable] (15c) **:** not placable **:** not capable of being appeased, significantly changed, or mitigated ⟨an ~ enemy⟩ — **im·pla·ca·bil·i·ty** \(ˌ)im-ˌplak-ə-ˈbil-ət-ē, -ˌplā-kə-\ *n* — **im·pla·ca·bly** \(ˈ)im-ˈplak-ə-blē, -ˈplā-kə-\ *adv*

1im·plant \im-ˈplant\ *vt* (15c) **1 a :** to fix or set securely or deeply ⟨a ruby ~*ed* in the idol's forehead⟩ **b :** to set permanently in the consciousness or habit patterns **:** INCULCATE **2 :** to insert in a living site (as for growth, slow release, or formation of an organic union) ⟨subcutaneously ~*ed* hormone pellets⟩ — **im·plant·able** \-ə-bəl\ *adj* — **im·plant·er** \im-ˈplant-ər\ *n*

syn IMPLANT, INCULCATE, INSTILL, INSEMINATE, INFIX mean to introduce into the mind. IMPLANT implies teaching that makes for permanence of what is taught; INCULCATE implies persistent or repeated efforts to impress on the mind; INSTILL stresses gradual, gentle imparting of knowledge over a long period of time; INSEMINATE applies to a sowing of ideas in many minds so that they spread through a class or nation; INFIX stresses firmly inculcating a habit of thought.

2im·plant \ˈim-ˌplant\ *n* (1890) **:** something (as a graft or pellet) implanted in tissue

im·plan·ta·tion \ˌim-ˌplan-ˈtā-shən\ *n* (1578) **1 a :** the act or process of implanting something **b :** the state resulting from being implanted **2** *in placental mammals* **:** the process of attachment of the embryo to the maternal uterine wall

im·plau·si·ble \(ˈ)im-ˈplȯ-zə-bəl\ *adj* (1677) **:** not plausible **:** provoking disbelief — **im·plau·si·bil·i·ty** \(ˌ)im-ˌplȯ-zə-ˈbil-ət-ē\ *n* — **im·plau·si·bly** \(ˈ)im-ˈplȯ-zə-blē\ *adv*

im·plead \im-ˈplēd\ *vt* [ME *empleden,* fr. MF *emplaider,* fr. OF *emplaidier,* fr. *en-* + *plaidier* to plead] (14c) **:** to sue or prosecute at law

1im·ple·ment \ˈim-plə-mənt\ *n* [ME, fr. LL *implementum* action of filling up, fr. L *implēre* to fill up, fr. *in-* + *plēre* to fill — more at FULL] (15c) **1 :** an article serving to equip ⟨the ~*s* of religious worship⟩ **2 :** a tool or utensil forming part of equipment for work **3 :** one that serves as an instrument or tool ⟨the partnership agreement does not seem to be a very potent ~ —H. B. Hoffman⟩

syn IMPLEMENT, TOOL, INSTRUMENT, APPLIANCE, UTENSIL mean a relatively simple device for performing work. IMPLEMENT may apply to anything necessary to perform a task; TOOL suggests an implement adapted to facilitate a definite kind or stage of work and suggests the need of skill more strongly than IMPLEMENT; INSTRUMENT suggests a device capable of delicate or precise work; APPLIANCE refers to a tool or instrument utilizing a power source and suggests portability or temporary attachment; UTENSIL applies to a device used in domestic work or some routine unskilled activity.

2im·ple·ment \-ˌment\ *vt* (1806) **1 :** CARRY OUT, ACCOMPLISH; *esp* **:** to give practical effect to and ensure of actual fulfillment by concrete measures ⟨plans not yet ~*ed* due to lack of funds⟩ **2 :** to provide instruments or means of expression for — **im·ple·men·ta·tion** \ˌim-plə-mən-ˈtā-shən, -ˌmen-\ *n*

im·pli·cate \'im-plə-ˌkāt\ *vt* **-cat·ed; -cat·ing** [L *implicatus,* pp. of *implicare* — more at EMPLOY] (15c) **1** *archaic* **:** to fold or twist together **:** ENTWINE **2 :** to involve as a consequence, corollary, or natural inference **:** IMPLY **3 a :** to bring into intimate or incriminating connection **b :** to involve in the nature or operation of something

im·pli·ca·tion \ˌim-plə-'kā-shən\ *n* (15c) **1 a :** the act of implicating **:** the state of being implicated **b :** close connection; *esp* **:** an incriminating involvement **2 a :** the act of implying **:** the state of being implied **b (1) :** a logical relation between two propositions that fails to hold only if the first is true and the second is false **(2) :** a logical relationship between two propositions in which if the first is true the second is true **(3) :** a statement exhibiting a relation of implication **3 :** something implied: as **a :** SUGGESTION **b :** a possible significance ⟨the book has political ~*s*⟩ — **im·pli·ca·tive** \'im-plə-ˌkāt-iv, im-'plik-ət-\ *adj* — **im·pli·ca·tive·ly** *adv* — **im·pli·ca·tive·ness** *n*

im·plic·it \im-'plis-ət\ *adj* [L *implicitus,* pp. of *implicare*] (1599) **1 a :** capable of being understood from something else though unexpressed **:** IMPLIED ⟨an ~ assumption⟩ **b :** involved in the nature or essence of something though not revealed, expressed, or developed **:** POTENTIAL ⟨a sculptor may see different figures ~ in a block of stone —John Dewey⟩ **c** *of a mathematical function* **:** defined by an expression in which the dependent variable and the one or more independent variables are not separated on opposite sides of an equation ⟨in $x + 3xy + y = 0$, y is an ~ function of x⟩ — compare EXPLICIT 4 **2 :** being without doubt or reserve **:** UNQUESTIONING — **im·plic·it·ly** *adv* — **im·plic·it·ness** *n*

implicit differentiation *n* (ca. 1891) **:** the process of finding the derivative of a dependent variable in an implicit function by differentiating each term separately, by expressing the derivative of the dependent variable as a symbol, and by solving the resulting expression for the symbol

im·plode \im-'plōd\ *vb* **im·plod·ed; im·plod·ing** [*in-* + *-plode* (as in *explode*)] *vi* (1881) **1 a :** to burst inward ⟨a blow causing a vacuum tube to ~⟩ **b :** to undergo violent compression ⟨massive stars which ~⟩ **2 :** to collapse inward as if from external pressure; *also* **:** to become greatly reduced as if from collapsing ~ *vt* **:** to cause to implode

im·plore \im-'plō(ə)r, -'plȯ(ə)r\ *vt* **im·plored; im·plor·ing** [MF or L; MF *implorer,* fr. L *implorare,* fr. *in-* + *plorare* to cry out] (1540) **1 :** to call upon in supplication **:** BESEECH **2 :** to call or pray for earnestly **:** ENTREAT **syn** see BEG — **im·plor·ing·ly** *adv*

im·plo·sion \im-'plō-zhən\ *n* [*in-* + *-plosion* (as in *explosion*)] (1877) **1 :** the inrush of air in forming a suction stop **2 :** the action of imploding **3 :** the act or action of bringing to or as if to a center; *also* **:** INTEGRATION ⟨this ~ of cultures makes realistic for the first time the age-old vision of a world culture —Kenneth Keniston⟩ — **im·plo·sive** \-'plō-siv, -ziv\ *adj or n*

im·ply \im-'plī\ *vt* **im·plied; im·ply·ing** [ME *emplien,* fr. MF *emplier,* fr. L *implicare*] (14c) **1** *obs* **:** ENFOLD, ENTWINE **2 :** to involve or indicate by inference, association, or necessary consequence rather than by direct statement ⟨rights ~ obligations⟩ **3 :** to contain potentially **4 :** to express indirectly ⟨his silence *implied* consent⟩ **syn** see SUGGEST **usage** see INFER

im·po·lite \ˌim-pə-'līt\ *adj* [L *impolitus,* fr. *in-* + *politus* polite] (1739) **:** not polite **:** RUDE — **im·po·lite·ly** *adv* — **im·po·lite·ness** *n*

im·pol·i·tic \(ˈ)im-'päl-ə-ˌtik\ *adj* (1600) **:** not politic **:** RASH — **im·po·lit·i·cal** \ˌim-pə-'lit-i-kəl\ *adj* — **im·po·lit·i·cal·ly** \-'lit-i-k(ə-)lē\ *adv* — **im·pol·i·tic·ly** \(ˈ)im-'päl-ə-ˌtik-lē\ *adv*

im·pon·der·a·ble \(ˈ)im-'pän-d(ə-)rə-bəl\ *adj* [ML *imponderabilis,* fr. L *in-* + LL *ponderabilis* ponderable] (1794) **:** not ponderable **:** incapable of being weighed or evaluated with exactness — **im·pon·der·a·bil·i·ty** \(ˌ)im-ˌpän-d(ə-)rə-'bil-ət-ē\ *n* — **imponderable** *n* — **im·pon·der·a·bly** \(ˈ)im-'pän-d(ə-)rə-blē\ *adv*

im·pone \im-'pōn\ *vt* **im·poned; im·pon·ing** [L *imponere* to put upon, fr. *in-* + *ponere* to put — more at POSITION] *obs* (1529) **:** WAGER, BET

¹im·port \im-'pō(ə)rt, -'pȯ(ə)rt, 'im-ˌ\ *vb* [ME *importen,* fr. L *importare* to bring into, fr. *in-* + *portare* to carry — more at FARE] *vt* (15c) **1 a :** to bear or convey as meaning or portent **:** SIGNIFY **b** *archaic* **:** EXPRESS, STATE **c :** IMPLY **2 :** to bring from a foreign or external source; *esp* **:** to bring (as merchandise) into a place or country from another country **3** *archaic* **:** to be of importance to **:** CONCERN ~ *vi* **:** to be of consequence **:** MATTER — **im·port·able** \im-'pōrt-ə-bəl, -'pȯrt-, 'im-ˌ\ *adj* — **im·port·er** *n*

²im·port \'im-ˌpō(ə)rt, -ˌpȯ(ə)rt\ *n* (1570) **1 :** IMPORTANCE; *esp* **:** relative importance ⟨it is hard to determine the ~ of this decision⟩ **2 :** PURPORT, SIGNIFICATION **3 :** something that is imported **4 :** IMPORTATION

im·por·tance \im-'pȯrt-ᵊn(t)s, *esp Southern & NewEng* -ən(t)s\ *n* (1508) **1 a :** the quality or state of being important **:** CONSEQUENCE **b :** an important aspect or bearing **:** SIGNIFICANCE **2** *obs* **:** IMPORT, MEANING **3** *obs* **:** IMPORTUNITY **4** *obs* **:** a weighty matter

syn IMPORTANCE, CONSEQUENCE, MOMENT, WEIGHT, SIGNIFICANCE mean a quality or aspect having great worth or significance. IMPORTANCE implies a value judgment of the superior worth or influence of something or someone; CONSEQUENCE may imply importance in social rank but more generally implies importance because of probable or possible effects; MOMENT implies conspicuous or self-evident consequence; WEIGHT implies a judgment of the immediate relative importance of something; SIGNIFICANCE implies a quality or character that should mark a thing as important but that is not self-evident and may or may not be recognized.

im·por·tan·cy \-ᵊn-sē, -ən-\ *n, archaic* (1540) **:** IMPORTANCE

im·por·tant \im-'pȯrt-ᵊnt, *esp Southern & NewEng* -ənt\ *adj* [MF, fr. OIt *importante,* fr. L *important-, importans,* prp. of *importare*] (15c) **1 :** marked by or indicative of significant worth or consequence **:** valuable in content or relationship **2** *obs* **:** IMPORTUNATE, URGENT **3 :** giving evidence of a feeling of self-importance — **im·por·tant·ly** *adv*

im·por·ta·tion \ˌim-ˌpōr-'tā-shən, -ˌpȯr-, -pər-\ *n* (1601) **1 :** the act or practice of importing **2 :** something imported

imported cabbageworm *n* (1892) **:** a small cosmopolitan white butterfly (*Pieris rapae*) or its larva which is a pest of cruciferous plants and esp. cabbage

imported fire ant *n* (ca. 1949) **:** either of two mound-building So. American fire ants (*Solenopsis richteri* and *S. invicta*) introduced into the southeastern U.S. that interfere with agriculture and can produce stings requiring medical attention

im·por·tu·nate \im-'pȯrch-(ə-)nət\ *adj* (15c) **1 :** troublesomely urgent **:** overly persistent in request or demand **2 :** TROUBLESOME — **im·por·tu·nate·ly** *adv* — **im·por·tu·nate·ness** *n*

¹im·por·tune \ˌim-pər-'t(y)ün, im-'pȯr-chən\ *adj* [ME, fr. MF & L; MF *importun,* fr. L *importunus,* fr. *in-* + *-portunus* (as in *opportunus* fit) — more at OPPORTUNE] (15c) **:** IMPORTUNATE — **im·por·tune·ly** *adv*

²importune *vb* **-tuned; -tun·ing** *vt* (1530) **1 a :** to press or urge with troublesome persistence **b** *archaic* **:** to request or beg for urgently **2 :** ANNOY, TROUBLE ~ *vi* **:** to beg, urge, or solicit persistently or troublesomely **syn** see BEG — **im·por·tun·er** *n*

im·por·tu·ni·ty \ˌim-pər-'t(y)ü-nət-ē\ *n, pl* **-ties** (15c) **1 :** the quality or state of being importunate **2 :** an importunate request or demand

im·pose \im-'pōz\ *vb* **im·posed; im·pos·ing** [MF *imposer,* fr. L *imponere,* lit., to put upon (perf. indic. *imposui*), fr. *in-* + *ponere* to put — more at POSITION] *vt* (1581) **1 a :** to establish or apply by authority ⟨~ a tax⟩ ⟨~ new restrictions⟩ ⟨~ penalties⟩ **b :** to establish or bring about as if by force ⟨those limits *imposed* by our own inadequacies — C. H. Plimpton⟩ **2 a :** PLACE, SET **b :** to arrange (as pages) in the proper order for printing **3 :** PASS OFF ⟨~ fake antiques on the public⟩ **4 :** to force into the company or on the attention of another ⟨~ oneself on others⟩ ~ *vi* **:** to take unwarranted advantage of something ⟨*imposed* on his good nature⟩ — **im·pos·er** *n*

im·pos·ing \im-'pō-ziŋ\ *adj* (1786) **:** impressive because of size, bearing, dignity, or grandeur **syn** see GRAND — **im·pos·ing·ly** \-ziŋ-lē\ *adv*

im·po·si·tion \ˌim-pə-'zish-ən\ *n* (14c) **1 :** the act of imposing **2 :** something imposed: as **a :** LEVY, TAX **b :** an excessive or uncalled-for requirement or burden **3 :** DECEPTION **4 :** the order of arrangement of imposed pages

im·pos·si·bil·i·ty \(ˌ)im-ˌpäs-ə-'bil-ət-ē\ *n* (14c) **1 :** the quality or state of being impossible **2 :** something impossible

im·pos·si·ble \(ˈ)im-'päs-ə-bəl\ *adj* [ME, fr. MF & L; MF, fr. L *impossibilis,* fr. *in-* + *possibilis* possible] (14c) **1 a :** incapable of being or of occurring **b :** felt to be incapable of being done, attained, or fulfilled **:** insuperably difficult **2 a :** extremely undesirable **:** UNACCEPTABLE **b :** extremely awkward or difficult to deal with — **im·pos·si·ble·ness** *n* — **im·pos·si·bly** \-blē\ *adv*

¹im·post \'im-ˌpōst\ *n* [MF, fr. ML *impositum,* fr. L, neut. of *impositus,* pp. of *imponere*] (1568) **:** something imposed or levied **:** TAX

²impost *n* [F *imposte,* deriv. of L *impositus*] (ca. 1664) **:** a block, capital, or molding from which an arch springs — see ARCH illustration

im·pos·tor *or* **im·pos·ter** \im-'päs-tər\ *n* [LL *impostor,* fr. L *impostus,* pp.] (1586) **:** one that assumes an identity or title not his own for the purpose of deception

im·pos·tume \im-'päs-ˌchüm\ *or* **im·pos·thume** \-ˌth(y)üm\ *n* [ME *emposteme,* deriv. of Gk *apostēma,* fr. *aphistanai* to remove, fr. *apo-* + *histanai* to cause to stand — more at STAND] *archaic* (14c) **:** ABSCESS

im·pos·ture \im-'päs-chər\ *n* [LL *impostura,* fr. L *impositus, impostus,* pp. of *imponere*] (1537) **1 :** the act or practice of deceiving by means of an assumed character or name **2 :** an instance of imposture

syn IMPOSTURE, FRAUD, SHAM, FAKE, HUMBUG, COUNTERFEIT mean a thing made to seem other than it is. IMPOSTURE applies to any situation in which a spurious object or performance is passed off as genuine; FRAUD usu. implies a deliberate perversion of the truth; SHAM applies to fraudulent imitation of a real thing or action; FAKE implies an imitation of or substitution for the genuine but does not necessarily imply dishonesty; HUMBUG suggests elaborate pretense usu. so flagrant as to be transparent; COUNTERFEIT applies esp. to the close imitation of something valuable.

im·po·tence \'im-pət-ən(t)s\ *n* (15c) **:** the quality or state of being impotent

im·po·ten·cy \-ən-sē\ *n* (15c) **:** IMPOTENCE

im·po·tent \'im-pət-ənt\ *adj* [ME, fr. MF & L; MF, fr. L *impotent-, impotens,* fr. *in-* + *potent-, potens* potent] (14c) **1 a :** not potent **:** lacking in power, strength, or vigor **:** HELPLESS **b :** unable to copulate; *broadly* **:** STERILE — usu. used of males **2** *obs* **:** incapable of self-restraint **:** UNGOVERNABLE — **impotent** *n* — **im·po·tent·ly** *adv*

im·pound \im-'paůnd\ *vt* (15c) **1 a :** to shut up in or as if in a pound **:** CONFINE **b :** to seize and hold in the custody of the law **2 :** to collect and confine (water) in or as if in a reservoir

im·pound·ment \-'paůn(d)-mənt\ *n* (1664) **1 :** the act of impounding **:** the state of being impounded **2 :** a body of water formed by impounding

im·pov·er·ish \im-'päv-(ə-)rish\ *vt* [ME *enpoverisen,* fr. MF *empovriss-,* stem of *empovrir,* fr. *en-* + *povre* poor — more at POOR] (15c) **1 :** to make poor **2 :** to deprive of strength, richness, or fertility by depleting or draining of something essential **syn** see DEPLETE — **im·pov·er·ish·er** *n* — **im·pov·er·ish·ment** \-mənt\ *n*

im·pov·er·ished *adj, of a fauna or flora* (1950) **:** represented by few species or individuals

im·prac·ti·ca·ble \(ˈ)im-'prak-ti-kə-bəl\ *adj* (1653) **1 :** not practicable **:** incapable of being performed or accomplished by the means employed or at command **2 :** IMPASSABLE ⟨an ~ road⟩ — **im·prac·ti·ca·bil·i·ty** \(ˌ)im-ˌprak-ti-kə-'bil-ət-ē\ *n* — **im·prac·ti·ca·bly** \(ˈ)im-'prak-ti-kə-blē\ *adv*

im·prac·ti·cal \(ˈ)im-'prak-ti-kəl\ *adj* (1865) **:** not practical: as **a :** not wise to put into or keep in practice or effect **b :** incapable of dealing sensibly or prudently with practical matters **c :** IMPRACTICABLE **d :** IDEALISTIC — **im·prac·ti·cal·i·ty** \(ˌ)im-ˌprak-ti-'kal-ət-ē\ *n* — **im·prac·ti·cal·ly** \(ˈ)im-'prak-ti-k(ə-)lē\ *adv*

im·pre·cate \'im-pri-ˌkāt\ *vb* **-cat·ed; -cat·ing** [L *imprecatus,* pp. of *imprecari,* fr. *in-* + *precari* to pray — more at PRAY] *vt* (1616) **:** to invoke evil on **:** CURSE ~ *vi* **:** to utter curses

im·pre·ca·tion \ˌim-pri-'kā-shən\ *n* (15c) **1 :** the act of imprecating **2 :** CURSE — **im·pre·ca·to·ry** \'im-pri-kə-ˌtōr-ē, im-'prek-ə-, -ˌtȯr-\ *adj*

im·pre·cise \ˌim-pri-'sīs\ *adj* (1805) **:** not precise **:** INEXACT, VAGUE — **im·pre·cise·ly** *adv* — **im·pre·cise·ness** *n* — **im·pre·ci·sion** \-'sizh-ən\ *n*

im·preg·na·ble \im-ˈpreg-nə-bəl\ *adj* [ME *imprenable*, fr. MF, fr. *in-* + *prenable* vulnerable to capture, fr. *prendre* to take — more at PRIZE] (15c) **1** : incapable of being taken by assault : UNCONQUERABLE **2** : UNASSAILABLE; *also* : IMPENETRABLE — **im·preg·na·bil·i·ty** \(,)im-,preg-nə-ˈbil-ət-ē\ *n* — **im·preg·na·ble·ness** \im-ˈpreg-nə-bəl-nəs\ *n* — **im·preg·na·bly** \-blē\ *adv*

im·preg·nant \im-ˈpreg-nənt\ *n* (1926) : a substance used for impregnating another substance

[1]**im·preg·nate** \im-ˈpreg-,nāt, ˈim-,\ *vt* **-nat·ed; -nat·ing** [LL *impraegnatus*, pp. of *impraegnare*, fr. L *in-* + *praegnas* pregnant] (1605) **1 a** : to cause to be filled, imbued, permeated, or saturated **b** : to permeate thoroughly **2** : to make pregnant : FERTILIZE ***syn*** see SOAK — **im·preg·na·tion** \(,)im-,preg-ˈnā-shən\ *n* — **im·preg·na·tor** \im-ˈpreg-,nāt-ər, ˈim-,\ *n*

[2]**im·preg·nate** \im-ˈpreg-nət\ *adj* (1646) : being filled or saturated

im·pre·sa \im-ˈprā-zə, -sə\ *n* [It, lit., undertaking] (1588) : a device with a motto used in the 16th and 17th centuries; *broadly* : EMBLEM

im·pre·sa·rio \,im-prə-ˈsär-ē-,ō, -ˈsar-, -ˈzär-\ *n, pl* **-ri·os** [It, fr. *impresa* undertaking, fr. *imprendere* to undertake, fr. (assumed) VL *imprehendere* — more at EMPRISE] (1746) **1** : the promoter, manager, or conductor of an opera or concert company **2** : one who puts on or sponsors an entertainment (as a television show or sports event) **3** : MANAGER, DIRECTOR

[1]**im·press** \im-ˈpres\ *vb* [ME *impressen*, fr. L *impressus*, pp. of *imprimere*, fr. *in-* + *premere* to press — more at PRESS] *vt* (14c) **1 a** : to apply with pressure so as to imprint **b** : to produce (as a mark) by pressure **c** : to mark by or as if by pressure or stamping **2 a** : to produce a vivid impression of **b** : to affect esp. forcibly or deeply : INFLUENCE **3 a** : TRANSFER, TRANSMIT **b** : to transmit (force or motion) by pressure; *esp* : to apply (as voltage) to a circuit from an outside source ~ *vi* : to produce an impression ***syn*** see AFFECT

[2]**im·press** \ˈim-,pres *also* im-ˈ\ *n* (1590) **1** : a characteristic or distinctive mark : STAMP ⟨the ~ of a fresh and vital intelligence is stamped . . . in his work —Lytton Strachey⟩ **2** : IMPRESSION, EFFECT ⟨have an ~ on history⟩ **3** : the act of impressing **4 a** : a mark made by pressure : IMPRINT **b** : an image of something formed by or as if by pressure: *esp* : SEAL **c** : a product of pressure or influence

[3]**im·press** \im-ˈpres\ *vt* [*in-* + *press*] (1596) **1** : to levy or take by force for public service; *esp* : to force into naval service **2 a** : to procure or enlist by forcible persuasion **b** : FORCE ⟨~*ed* him into a white coat for the Christmas festivities —Nancy Hale⟩

[4]**im·press** \ˈim-,pres *also* im-ˈ\ *n* (1602) : IMPRESSMENT

im·press·ible \im-ˈpres-ə-bəl\ *adj* (15c) : capable of being impressed : SENSITIVE — **im·press·ibil·i·ty** \-,pres-ə-ˈbil-ət-ē\ *n* — **im·press·ibly** \ˈpres-ə-blē\ *adv*

im·pres·sion \im-ˈpresh-ən\ *n* (14c) **1** : the act of impressing: as **a** : an affecting by stamping or pressing **b** : a communicating of a mold, trait, or character by an external force or influence **2** : the effect produced by impressing: as **a** : a stamp, form, or figure resulting from physical contact **b** : an imprint of the teeth and adjacent portions of the jaw for use in dentistry **c** : an esp. marked influence or effect on feeling, sense, or mind **3 a** : a characteristic, trait, or feature resulting from some influence ⟨the ~ on behavior produced by the social milieu⟩ **b** : an effect of alteration or improvement ⟨the settlement left little ~ on the wilderness⟩ **c** : a telling image impressed on the senses or the mind **4 a** : the amount of pressure with which an inked printing surface deposits its ink on the paper **b** : one instance of the meeting of a printing surface and the material being printed; *also* : a single print or copy so made **c** : all the copies (as of a book) printed in one continuous operation from a single makeready **5** : a usu. indistinct or imprecise notion or remembrance **6 a** : the first coat of color in painting **b** : a coat of paint for ornament or preservation **7** : an imitation or representation of salient features in an artistic or theatrical medium; *esp* : an imitation in caricature of a noted personality as a form of theatrical entertainment ***syn*** see IDEA

im·pres·sion·able \im-ˈpresh-(ə-)nə-bəl\ *adj* (1836) : capable of being easily impressed — **im·pres·sion·abil·i·ty** \-,presh-(ə-)nə-ˈbil-ət-ē\ *n*

im·pres·sion·ism \im-ˈpresh-ə-,niz-əm\ *n* (1882) **1** *often cap* : a theory or practice in painting esp. among French painters of about 1870 of depicting the natural appearances of objects by means of dabs or strokes of primary unmixed colors in order to simulate actual reflected light **2 a** : the depiction of scene, emotion, or character by details intended to achieve a vividness or effectiveness more by evoking subjective and sensory impressions than by recreating an objective reality **b** : a style of musical composition designed to create subtle moods and impressions

im·pres·sion·ist \im-ˈpresh-(ə-)nəst\ *n* (1881) **1** *often cap* : one (as a painter) who practices or adheres to the theories of impressionism **2** : an entertainer who does impressions

im·pres·sion·is·tic \(,)im-,presh-ə-ˈnis-tik\ *adj* (1886) **1** *or* **im·pres·sion·ist** \im-ˈpresh-(ə-)nəst\ : of, relating to, or constituting impressionism **2** : based on or involving impression as distinct from knowledge or fact ⟨intuitions and ~ anecdotal accounts —Sidney Hook⟩ — **im·pres·sion·is·ti·cal·ly** \(,)im-,presh-ə-ˈnis-ti-k(ə-)lē\ *adv*

im·pres·sive \im-ˈpres-iv\ *adj* (1598) : making or tending to make a marked impression ***syn*** see MOVING — **im·pres·sive·ly** *adv* — **im·pres·sive·ness** *n*

im·press·ment \im-ˈpres-mənt\ *n* (1787) : the act of seizing for public use or of impressing into public service

im·pres·sure \im-ˈpresh-ər\ *n, archaic* (1600) : a mark made by pressure : IMPRESSION

im·prest \ˈim-,prest\ *n* [obs. *imprest* (to lend), prob. fr. It *imprestare*] (1568) : a loan or advance of money

im·pri·ma·tur \,im-prə-ˈmä-,tu̇(ə)r, im-ˈprim-ə-,t(y)u̇(ə)r\ *n* [NL, let it be printed, fr. *imprimere* to print, fr. L, to imprint, impress — more at IMPRESS] (1640) **1 a** : a license to print or publish esp. by Roman Catholic episcopal authority **b** : approval of a publication under circumstances of official censorship **2 a** : SANCTION, APPROVAL **b** : IMPRINT **c** : a mark of approval or distinction

im·pri·mis \im-ˈprī-məs, -ˈprē-\ *adv* [ME *imprimis*, fr. L *in primis* among the first (things)] (15c) : in the first place — used to introduce a list of items or considerations

[1]**im·print** \im-ˈprint, ˈim-,\ *vt* (14c) **1** : to mark by or as if by pressure : IMPRESS **2 a** : to fix indelibly or permanently (as on the memory) **b** : to subject to or induce by imprinting ⟨an ~*ed* preference⟩ ~ *vi* : to undergo imprinting — **im·print·er** \-ər\ *n*

[2]**im·print** \ˈim-,print\ *n* [MF *empreinte*, fr. fem. of *empreint*, pp. of *empreindre* to imprint, fr. L *imprimere*] (15c) : something imprinted or printed: as **a** : a mark or depression made by pressure ⟨the fossil ~ of a dinosaur's foot⟩ **b** : an identifying name (as of a publisher) placed conspicuously on a product (as at the foot of the title page of a book); *also* : the name under which a publisher issues books **c** : an indelible distinguishing effect or influence

im·print·ing \ˈim-,print-iŋ, im-ˈ\ *n* (ca. 1937) : a rapid learning process that takes place early in the life of a social animal (as a greylag goose) and establishes a behavior pattern (as recognition of and attraction to its own kind or a substitute)

im·pris·on \im-ˈpriz-ᵊn\ *vt* [ME *imprisonen*, fr. OF *emprisoner*, fr. *en-* + *prison* prison] (14c) : to put in or as if in prison : CONFINE — **im·pris·on·able** \-ˈpriz-ᵊn-ə-bəl, -ˈpriz-nə-\ *adj* — **im·pris·on·ment** \im-ˈpriz-ən-mənt\ *n*

im·prob·a·ble \(ˈ)im-ˈpräb(-ə)-bəl\ *adj* [MF or L; MF, fr. L *improbabilis*, fr. *in-* + *probabilis* probable] (1598) : unlikely to be true or to occur; *also* : unlikely but real or true — **im·prob·a·bil·i·ty** \(,)im-,präb-ə-ˈbil-ət-ē\ *n* — **im·prob·a·bly** \(ˈ)im-ˈpräb(-ə)-blē\ *adv*

[1]**im·promp·tu** \im-ˈpräm(p)-(,)t(y)ü\ *n* [F, fr. *impromptu* extemporaneously, fr. L *in promptu* in readiness] (1683) **1** : something that is impromptu **2** : a musical composition suggesting improvisation

[2]**impromptu** *adj* (1764) **1** : made, done, or formed on or as if on the spur of the moment : IMPROVISED **2** : composed or uttered without previous preparation : EXTEMPORANEOUS — **impromptu** *adv*

im·prop·er \(ˈ)im-ˈpräp-ər\ *adj* [MF *impropre*, fr. L *improprius*, fr. *in-* + *proprius* proper] (15c) : not proper: as **a** : not in accord with fact, truth, or right procedure : INCORRECT ⟨~ inference⟩ **b** : not regularly or normally formed or not properly so called **c** : not suited to the circumstances, design, or end ⟨~ medicine⟩ **d** : not in accord with propriety, modesty, good manners, or good taste ***syn*** see INDECOROUS — **im·prop·er·ly** *adv* — **im·prop·er·ness** *n*

improper fraction *n* (1542) : a fraction whose numerator is equal to, larger than, or of equal or higher degree than the denominator

improper integral *n* (ca. 1942) : a definite integral whose region of integration is unbounded or includes a point at which the integrand is undefined or tends to infinity

im·pro·pri·ety \,im-p(r)ə-ˈprī-ət-ē\ *n, pl* **-eties** [F or LL; F *impropriété*, fr. LL *improprietat-, improprietas*, fr. L *improprius*] (1611) **1** : the quality or state of being improper **2** : an improper or indecorous act or remark; *esp* : an unacceptable use of a word or of language

im·prov·able \im-ˈprü-və-bəl\ *adj* (1646) : capable of improving or being improved — **im·prov·abil·i·ty** \-,prü-və-ˈbil-ət-ē\ *n* — **im·prov·ably** \-ˈprü-və-blē\ *adv*

im·prove \im-ˈprüv\ *vb* **im·proved; im·prov·ing** [AF *emprouer* to invest profitably, fr. OF *en-* + *prou* advantage, fr. LL *prode* — more at PROUD] *vt* (15c) **1 a** : to enhance in value or quality : make better **b** : to increase the value of (land or property) by betterment (as cultivation or the erection of buildings) **c** : to grade and drain (a road) and apply surfacing material other than pavement **2** *archaic* : EMPLOY, USE **3** : to use to good purpose ~ *vi* **1** : to advance or make progress in what is desirable **2** : to make useful additions or amendments — **im·prov·er** *n*

im·prove·ment \im-ˈprüv-mənt\ *n* (15c) **1** : the act or process of improving **2 a** : the state of being improved; *esp* : enhanced value or excellence **b** : an instance of such improvement : something that enhances value or excellence

im·prov·i·dence \(ˈ)im-ˈpräv-əd-ən(t)s, -ə-,den(t)s\ *n* (15c) : the quality or state of being improvident

im·prov·i·dent \-əd-ənt, -ə-,dent\ *adj* [LL *improvident-, improvidens*, fr. L *in-* + *provident-, providens* provident] (1514) : not provident : not foreseeing and providing for the future — **im·prov·i·dent·ly** *adv*

im·pro·vi·sa·tion \(,)im-,präv-ə-ˈzā-shən, ,im-prə-və- *also* ,im-prə-(,)vī-\ *n* (1786) **1** : the act or art of improvising **2** : something (as a musical or dramatic composition) improvised — **im·pro·vi·sa·tion·al** \-shnəl, -shən-ᵊl\ *adj* — **im·pro·vi·sa·tion·al·ly** \-ē\ *adv*

im·prov·i·sa·tor \im-ˈpräv-ə-,zāt-ər\ *n* (1795) : one that improvises — **im·prov·i·sa·to·ri·al** \(,)im-,präv-ə-zə-ˈtōr-ē-əl, -ˈtȯr-\ *adj* — **im·pro·vi·sa·to·ry** \im-ˈpräv-ə-zə-,tōr-ē, ,im-prə-ˈvī-zə-, -,tȯr-\ *adj*

im·pro·vi·sa·to·re \(,)im-,präv-ə-zə-ˈtōr-ē, ,im-prə-,vē-zə-, -ˈtȯr-\ *n, pl* **-to·ri** \-ˈtōr-ē, -ˈtȯr-\ *or* **-tores** [It *improvvisatore*, fr. *improvvisare*] (ca. 1765) : one that improvises (as verse) usu. extemporaneously

im·pro·vise \,im-prə-ˈvīz, ˈim-prə-,\ *vb* **-vised; -vis·ing** [F *improviser*, fr. It *improvvisare*, fr. *improvviso* sudden, fr. L *improvisus*, lit., unforeseen, fr. *in-* + *provisus*, pp. of *providēre* to see ahead — more at PROVIDE] *vt* (1826) **1** : to compose, recite, play, or sing extemporaneously **2** : to make, invent, or arrange offhand **3** : to fabricate out of what is conveniently on hand ~ *vi* : to improvise something — **im·pro·vis·er** *or* **im·pro·vi·sor** \-ˈvī-zər, -,vī-\ *n*

im·pru·dence \(ˈ)im-ˈprüd-ᵊn(t)s\ *n* (15c) **1** : the quality or state of being imprudent **2** : an imprudent act

im·pru·dent \-ᵊnt\ *adj* [ME, fr. L *imprudent-, imprudens*, fr. *in-* + *prudent-, prudens* prudent] (14c) : not prudent : lacking discretion — **im·pru·dent·ly** *adv*

im·pu·dence \ˈim-pyəd-ən(t)s\ *n* (14c) : the quality or state of being impudent

im·pu·dent \-ənt\ *adj* [ME, fr. L *impudent-, impudens*, fr. *in-* + *pudent-, pudens*, prp. of *pudēre* to feel shame] (14c) **1** *obs* : lacking modesty **2** : marked by contemptuous or cocky boldness or disregard of others : INSOLENT — **im·pu·dent·ly** *adv*

im·pu·dic·i·ty \,im-pyü-ˈdis-ət-ē\ *n* (1528) : lack of modesty : SHAMELESSNESS

im·pugn \im-ˈpyün\ *vt* [ME *impugnen*, fr. MF *impugner*, fr. L *inpugnare*, fr. *in-* + *pugnare* to fight — more at PUGNACIOUS] (14c) **1** *obs* **a** : ASSAIL **b** : RESIST **2** : to assail by words or arguments : oppose or attack as false or lacking integrity — **im·pugn·able** \-ˈpyü-nə-bəl\ *adj* — **im·pugn·er** \-nər\ *n*

im·puis·sance \(ˈ)im-ˈpwis-ᵊn(t)s, (ˈ)im-ˈpyü-ə-sən(t)s; ,im-pyü-ˈis-ᵊn(t)s\ *n* [ME, fr. MF, fr. *in-* + *puissance* puissance, power] (15c) : WEAKNESS, POWERLESSNESS

im·puis·sant \-ᵊnt, -sənt\ *adj* [F] (1629) : WEAK, POWERLESS

1im·pulse \ˈim-ˌpəls, im-ˈ\ *vt* **im·pulsed; im·puls·ing** [L *impulsus,* fr. *impulsus,* pp. of *impellere* to impel] (1611) : to give an impulse to

2im·pulse \ˈim-ˌpəls\ *n* (1647) **1 a :** INSPIRATION, MOTIVATION **b :** a force so communicated as to produce motion suddenly **c :** INCENTIVE **2 a :** the act of driving onward with sudden force : IMPULSION **b :** motion produced by such an impulsion : IMPETUS **c :** a wave of excitation transmitted through tissues and esp. nerve fibers and muscles that results in physiological activity or inhibition **3 a :** a sudden spontaneous inclination or incitement to some usu. unpremeditated action **b :** a propensity or natural tendency usu. other than rational **4 a :** the product of the average value of a force and the time during which it acts being a quantity equal to the change in momentum produced by the force **b :** PULSE 4a ***syn*** see MOTIVE

im·pul·sion \im-ˈpəl-shən\ *n* (15c) **1 a :** the act of impelling : the state of being impelled **b :** an impelling force **c :** an onward tendency derived from an impulsion : IMPETUS **2 :** IMPULSE 3a **3 :** COMPULSION 2

im·pul·sive \im-ˈpəl-siv\ *adj* (15c) **1 :** having the power of or actually driving or impelling **2 :** actuated by or prone to act on impulse **3 :** acting momentarily ***syn*** see SPONTANEOUS — **im·pul·sive·ly** *adv* — **im·pul·sive·ness** *n* — **im·pul·siv·i·ty** \-ˌpəl-ˈsiv-ət-ē\ *n*

im·pu·ni·ty \im-ˈpyü-nət-ē\ *n* [MF or L; MF *impunité,* fr. L *impunitat-, impunitas,* fr. *impune* without punishment, fr. *in-* + *poena* pain] (1532) : exemption or freedom from punishment, harm, or loss

im·pure \(ˈ)im-ˈpyu̇(ə)r\ *adj* [ME, fr. MF & L; MF, fr. L *impurus,* fr. *in-* + *purus* pure] (15c) : not pure: as **a :** LEWD, UNCHASTE **b :** containing something unclean : FOUL ⟨~ water⟩ **c :** ritually unclean **d :** mixed or impregnated with an extraneous and usu. inferior substance : ADULTERATED ⟨an ~ chemical⟩ — **im·pure·ly** *adv* — **im·pure·ness** *n*

im·pu·ri·ty \(ˈ)im-ˈpyu̇r-ət-ē\ *n, pl* **-ties** (15c) **1 :** something that is impure or makes something else impure **2 :** the quality or state of being impure

im·pu·ta·tion \ˌim-pyə-ˈtā-shən\ *n* (1581) **1 :** the act of imputing: as **a :** ATTRIBUTION, ASCRIPTION **b :** ACCUSATION **c :** INSINUATION **2 :** something imputed — **im·pu·ta·tive** \im-ˈpyüt-ət-iv\ *adj* — **im·pu·ta·tive·ly** *adv*

im·pute \im-ˈpyüt\ *vt* **im·put·ed; im·put·ing** [ME *inputen,* fr. L *imputare,* fr. *in-* + *putare* to consider — more at PAVE] (14c) **1 :** to lay the responsibility or blame for often falsely or unjustly : CHARGE **2 :** to credit to a person or a cause : ATTRIBUTE ⟨our vices as well as our virtues have been *imputed* to bodily derangement —B. N. Cardozo⟩ ***syn*** see ASCRIBE — **im·put·abil·i·ty** \-ˌpyüt-ə-ˈbil-ət-ē\ *n* — **im·put·able** \-ˈpyüt-ə-bəl\ *adj*

1in \(ˈ)in, ən, ᵊn\ *prep* [ME, fr. OE; akin to OHG *in* in, L *in,* Gk *en*] (bef. 12c) **1 a** — used as a function word to indicate inclusion, location, or position within limits ⟨~ the lake⟩ ⟨wounded ~ the leg⟩ ⟨~ the summer⟩ **b :** INTO 1 ⟨went ~ the house⟩ **2** — used as a function word to indicate means, medium, or instrumentality ⟨written ~ pencil⟩ ⟨bound ~ leather⟩ **3 a** — used as a function word to indicate limitation, qualification, or circumstance ⟨alike ~ some respects⟩ ⟨left ~ a hurry⟩ **b :** INTO 2a ⟨broke ~ pieces⟩ **4** — used as a function word to indicate purpose ⟨said ~ reply⟩ **5** — used as a function word to indicate the larger member of a ratio ⟨one ~ six is eligible⟩

2in \ˈin\ *adv* (bef. 12c) **1 a (1) :** to or toward the inside esp. of a house or other building ⟨come ~⟩ **(2) :** to or toward some destination or particular place ⟨flew ~ on the first plane⟩ **(3) :** at close quarters : NEAR ⟨play close ~⟩ **b :** so as to incorporate ⟨mix ~ the flour⟩ — often used in combination ⟨built-*in* bookcases⟩ **c :** to or at its place ⟨fit a piece ~⟩ **2 a :** within a particular place; *esp* : within the customary place of residence or business **b :** in the position of participant, insider, or officeholder **c (1) :** on good terms **(2) :** in a specified relation ⟨~ bad with the boss⟩ **(3) :** in a position of assured or definitive success **d :** in vogue or season **e** *of an oil well* : in production **f :** in one's presence, possession, or control ⟨after harvests are ~⟩ — **in for :** certain to experience ⟨*in for* a rude awakening⟩

3in \ˈin\ *adj* (1599) **1 a :** that is located inside or within ⟨the ~ part⟩ **b :** that is in position, operation, or power ⟨the ~ party⟩ **c :** INSIDE 2 **2 :** that is directed or bound inward : INCOMING ⟨the ~ train⟩ **3 a :** keenly aware of and responsive to what is new and smart ⟨the ~ crowd⟩ **b :** extremely fashionable ⟨the ~ thing to do⟩

4in \ˈin\ *n* (1764) **1 :** one who is in office or power or on the inside ⟨a matter of ~s versus outs⟩ **2 :** INFLUENCE, PULL ⟨enjoyed some sort of ~ with the commandant —Henriette Roosenburg⟩

1in- *or* **il-** *or* **im-** *or* **ir-** *prefix* [ME, fr. MF, fr. L; akin to OE *un-*] : not : NON-, UN- — usu. *il-* before *l* ⟨*il*logical⟩ and *im-* before *b, m,* or *p* ⟨*im*balance⟩ ⟨*im*moral⟩ ⟨*im*practical⟩ and *ir-* before *r* ⟨*ir*reducible⟩ and *in-* before other sounds ⟨*in*conclusive⟩

2in- *or* **il-** *or* **im-** *or* **ir-** *prefix* [ME, fr. MF, fr. L, fr. *in* in, into] **1 :** in : within : into : toward : on ⟨*il*luviation⟩ ⟨*im*mingle⟩ ⟨*ir*radiance⟩ — usu. *il-* before *l, im-* before *b, m,* or *p, ir-* before *r,* and *in-* before other sounds **2 :** 1EN- ⟨*im*brute⟩ ⟨*im*peril⟩ ⟨*in*spirit⟩

1-in \ən, ᵊn, ˌin\ *n suffix* [F *-ine,* fr. L *-ina,* fem. of *-inus* of or belonging to — more at -EN] **1 a :** neutral chemical compound ⟨insul*in*⟩ **b :** enzyme ⟨pancreat*in*⟩ **c :** antibiotic ⟨penicill*in*⟩ **2 :** 2-INE 1a, 1b ⟨epinephr*in*⟩ **3 :** pharmaceutical product ⟨niac*in*⟩

2-in \-ˌin\ *comb form* [2*in* (as in *sit-in*)] **1 :** organized public protest by means of or in favor of : demonstration ⟨teach-*in*⟩ ⟨love-*in*⟩ **2 :** public group activity ⟨sing-*in*⟩

-i·na \ˈē-nə\ *n suffix* [prob. fr. It *-ina,* dim. suffix, fr. L *-īna*] : musical instrument ⟨concert*ina*⟩

in·abil·i·ty \ˌin-ə-ˈbil-ət-ē\ *n* [ME *inabilite,* fr. MF *inhabilité,* fr. *in-* + *habilité* ability] (15c) : lack of sufficient power, resources, or capacity ⟨his ~ to do math⟩

in ab·sen·tia \ˌin-ab-ˈsen-ch(ē-)ə\ *adv* [L] (1886) : in absence ⟨gave him the award *in absentia*⟩

in·ac·ces·si·ble \ˌin-ik-ˈses-ə-bəl, (ˌ)in-ˌak-\ *adj* [MF or LL; MF, fr. LL *inaccessibilis,* fr. L *in-* + LL *accessibilis* accessible] (15c) : not accessible — **in·ac·ces·si·bil·i·ty** \-ˌses-ə-ˈbil-ət-ē\ *n* — **in·ac·ces·si·bly** \-ˈses-ə-blē\ *adv*

in·ac·cu·ra·cy \(ˈ)in-ˈak-yə-rə-sē\ *n, pl* **-cies** (ca. 1755) **1 :** the quality or state of being inaccurate **2 :** MISTAKE, ERROR

in·ac·cu·rate \-yə-rət\ *adj* (1738) : not accurate : FAULTY — **in·ac·cu·rate·ly** \-yə-rət-lē, -yərt-\ *adv*

in·ac·tion \(ˈ)in-ˈak-shən\ *n* (1707) : lack of action or activity : IDLENESS

in·ac·ti·vate \(ˈ)in-ˈak-tə-ˌvāt\ *vt* (1906) : to make inactive — **in·ac·ti·va·tion** \(ˌ)in-ˌak-tə-ˈvā-shən\ *n*

in·ac·tive \(ˈ)in-ˈak-tiv\ *adj* (1664) : not active: as **a (1) :** SEDENTARY **(2) :** INDOLENT, SLUGGISH **b (1) :** being out of use **(2) :** relating to or being members of the armed forces who are not performing or available for military duties **(3)** *of a disease* : QUIESCENT **c (1) :** chemically inert **(2) :** optically neutral in polarized light **d :** biologically inert esp. because of the loss of some quality (as infectivity or antigenicity) — **in·ac·tive·ly** *adv* — **in·ac·tiv·i·ty** \(ˌ)in-ˌak-ˈtiv-ət-ē\ *n*

syn INACTIVE, IDLE, INERT, PASSIVE, SUPINE mean not engaged in work or activity. INACTIVE applies to anyone or anything not in action or in operation or at work; IDLE applies to persons that are not busy or occupied or to their powers or their implements; INERT as applied to things implies powerlessness to move or to affect other things; as applied to persons it suggests an inherent or habitual indisposition to activity; PASSIVE implies immobility or lack of normally expected response to an external force or influence and often suggests deliberate submissiveness or self-control; SUPINE applies only to persons and commonly implies abjectness or indolence.

in·ad·e·qua·cy \(ˈ)in-ˈad-i-kwə-sē\ *n, pl* **-cies** (1787) **1 :** the quality or state of being inadequate **2 :** INSUFFICIENCY, DEFICIENCY

in·ad·e·quate \-kwət\ *adj* (1671) : not adequate : INSUFFICIENT — **in·ad·e·quate·ly** *adv* — **in·ad·e·quate·ness** *n*

in·ad·mis·si·ble \ˌin-əd-ˈmis-ə-bəl\ *adj* (1776) : not admissible — **in·ad·mis·si·bil·i·ty** \-ˌmis-ə-ˈbil-ət-ē\ *n* — **in·ad·mis·si·bly** \-ˈmis-ə-blē\ *adv*

in·ad·ver·tence \ˌin-əd-ˈvərt-ᵊn(t)s\ *n* [ML *inadvertentia,* fr. L *in-* + *advertent-, advertens,* prp. of *advertere* to advert] (15c) **1 :** the fact or action of being inadvertent : INATTENTION **2 :** a result of inattention : OVERSIGHT

in·ad·ver·ten·cy \-ᵊn-sē\ *n, pl* **-cies** (1592) : INADVERTENCE

in·ad·ver·tent \-ᵊnt\ *adj* [back-formation of *inadvertence*] (1653) **1 :** not turning the mind to a matter : INATTENTIVE **2 :** UNINTENTIONAL — **in·ad·ver·tent·ly** *adv*

in·ad·vis·able \ˌin-əd-ˈvī-zə-bəl\ *adj* (1870) : not advisable — **in·ad·vis·abil·i·ty** \-ˌvī-zə-ˈbil-ət-ē\ *n*

-i·nae \ˈī-(ˌ)nē\ *n pl suffix* [NL *-inae,* fr. L, fem. pl. of *-inus*] : members of the subfamily of — in all names of zoological subfamilies in recent classifications ⟨*Felinae*⟩

in·alien·able \(ˈ)in-ˈāl-yə-nə-bəl, -ˈā-lē-ə-nə-\ *adj* [prob. fr. F *inaliénable,* fr. *in-* + *aliénable* alienable] (1645) : incapable of being alienated, surrendered, or transferred ⟨~ rights⟩ — **in·alien·abil·i·ty** \(ˌ)in-ˌāl-yə-nə-ˈbil-ət-ē, -ˌā-lē-ə-nə-\ *n* — **in·alien·ably** \(ˈ)in-ˈāl-yə-nə-blē, -ˈā-lē-ə-nə-\ *adv*

in·al·ter·able \(ˈ)in-ˈȯl-t(ə-)rə-bəl\ *adj* (1541) : not alterable : UNALTERABLE — **in·al·ter·abil·i·ty** \(ˌ)in-ˌȯl-t(ə-)rə-ˈbil-ət-ē\ *n* — **in·al·ter·able·ness** \(ˈ)in-ˈȯl-t(ə-)rə-bəl-nəs\ *n* — **in·al·ter·ably** \-blē\ *adv*

in·amo·ra·ta \in-ˌam-ə-ˈrät-ə\ *n* [It *innamorata,* fr. fem. of *innamorato,* pp. of *innamorare* to inspire with love, fr. *in-* (fr. L) + *amore* love, fr. L *amor* — more at AMOROUS] (1651) : a woman with whom one is in love or has intimate relations

in–and–in \ˌin-ən-ˈ(d)in\ *adv or adj* (1765) : in repeated generations of the same or closely related stock ⟨families . . . of one blood through mating or marrying ~ —F. H. Giddings⟩ ⟨this freak of color in range-bred horses is the result of ~ breeding —Andy Adams⟩

1inane \in-ˈān\ *adj* **inan·er; -est** [L *inanis*] (1662) **1 :** EMPTY, INSUBSTANTIAL **2 :** lacking significance, meaning, or point : SILLY ***syn*** see INSIPID — **inane·ly** *adv* — **inane·ness** \-ˈān-nəs\ *n*

2inane *n* (1677) : void or empty space ⟨a voyage into the limitless ~ —V. G. Childe⟩

in·an·i·mate \(ˈ)in-ˈan-ə-mət\ *adj* [LL *inanimatus,* fr. L *in-* + *animatus,* pp. of *animare* to animate] (15c) **1 :** not animate: **a :** not endowed with life or spirit **b :** lacking consciousness or power of motion **2 :** not animated or lively : DULL — **in·an·i·mate·ly** *adv* — **in·an·i·mate·ness** *n*

in·a·ni·tion \ˌin-ə-ˈnish-ən\ *n* (14c) : the quality or state of being empty: **a :** the loss of vitality that results from lack of food and water **b :** the absence or loss of social, moral, or intellectual vitality or vigor : LETHARGY

inan·i·ty \in-ˈan-ət-ē\ *n, pl* **-ties** (1603) **1 :** the quality or state of being inane: as **a :** lack of substance : EMPTINESS **b :** vapid, pointless, or fatuous character : SHALLOWNESS **2 :** something that is inane

in·ap·par·ent \ˌin-ə-ˈpar-ənt, -ˈper-\ *adj* (1626) : not apparent — **in·ap·par·ent·ly** *adv*

in·ap·peas·able \ˌin-ə-ˈpē-zə-bəl\ *adj* (1803) : UNAPPEASABLE

in·ap·pe·tence \(ˈ)in-ˈap-ət-ən(t)s\ *n* (1691) : loss or lack of appetite

in·ap·pli·ca·ble \(ˈ)in-ˈap-li-kə-bəl *also* ˌin-ə-ˈplik-ə-\ *adj* (1656) : not applicable : IRRELEVANT — **in·ap·pli·ca·bil·i·ty** \(ˌ)in-ˌap-li-kə-ˈbil-ət-ē *also* ˌin-ə-ˌplik-ə-\ *n* — **in·ap·pli·ca·bly** \(ˈ)in-ˈap-li-kə-blē *also* ˌin-ə-ˈplik-ə-\ *adv*

in·ap·po·site \(ˈ)in-ˈap-ə-zət\ *adj* (1661) : not apposite — **in·ap·po·site·ly** *adv* — **in·ap·po·site·ness** *n*

in·ap·pre·cia·ble \ˌin-ə-ˈprē-shə-bəl, -ˈprish(-ē)-ə-bəl\ *adj* [prob. fr. F *inappréciable,* fr. MF *inappreciable,* fr. *in-* + *appreciable*] (1802) : too small to be perceived ⟨an ~ difference in the temperature⟩ — **in·ap·pre·cia·bly** \-blē\ *adv*

in·ap·pre·cia·tive \ˌin-ə-ˈprē-shət-iv, -ˈprish-ət- *also* -ˈprē-shē-ˌāt-\ *adj* (1869) : not appreciative — **in·ap·pre·cia·tive·ly** *adv* — **in·ap·pre·cia·tive·ness** *n*

in·ap·proach·able \ˌin-ə-ˈprō-chə-bəl\ *adj* (ca. 1828) : not approachable : INACCESSIBLE

in·ap·pro·pri·ate \ˌin-ə-ˈprō-prē-ət\ *adj* (1804) : not appropriate : UNSUITABLE — **in·ap·pro·pri·ate·ly** *adv* — **in·ap·pro·pri·ate·ness** *n*

in·apt \(ˈ)in-ˈapt\ *adj* (ca. 1680) : not apt: **a :** not suitable **b :** INEPT — **in·apt·ly** \-ˈap-(t)lē\ *adv* — **in·apt·ness** \-ˈap(t)-nəs\ *n*

in·ap·ti·tude \-ˈap-tə-ˌt(y)üd\ *n* (1620) : lack of aptitude

in·ar·gu·able \(ˈ)in-ˈär-gyə-wə-bəl\ *adj* (1875) : not arguable — **in·ar·gu·ably** \-blē\ *adv*

\ə\ abut \ᵊ\ kitten, F table \ər\ further \a\ ash \ā\ ace \ä\ cot, cart \au̇\ out \ch\ chin \e\ bet \ē\ easy \g\ go \i\ hit \ī\ ice \j\ job \ŋ\ sing \ō\ go \ȯ\ law \ȯi\ boy \th\ thin \t͟h\ the \ü\ loot \u̇\ foot \y\ yet \zh\ vision \à, k̲, ⁿ, œ, œ̄, ue, ue̅, ʸ\ *see* Guide to Pronunciation

in·ar·tic·u·la·cy \ˌin-(ˌ)är-ˈtik-yə-lə-sē\ *n* (1921) : the quality or state of being inarticulate

¹in·ar·tic·u·late \-yə-lət\ *adj* [LL *inarticulatus,* fr. L *in-* + *articulatus,* pp. of *articulare* to utter distinctly — more at ARTICULATE] (1603) **1 a** *of a sound* : uttered or formed without the definite articulations of intelligible speech **b** (1) : incapable of speech esp. under stress of emotion : MUTE (2) : incapable of being expressed by speech ⟨~ fear⟩ (3) : not voiced or expressed : UNSPOKEN ⟨society functions on many ~ premises⟩ **2** : incapable of giving coherent, clear, or effective expression to one's ideas or feelings **3** [NL *inarticulatus,* fr. L *in-* + NL *articulatus* articulate] : relating to, characteristic of, or being an inarticulate or its shell — **in·ar·tic·u·late·ly** *adv* — **in·ar·tic·u·late·ness** *n*

²inarticulate *n* [NL *inarticulata,* fr. L *in-* + *articulus* joint — more at ARTICLE] (1952) : any of a class (Inarticulata) of brachiopods lacking a hinge connecting the two shell valves

in·ar·tis·tic \ˌin-är-ˈtis-tik\ *adj* (1859) **1** : not conforming to the principles of art **2** : not appreciative of art — **in·ar·tis·ti·cal·ly** \-ti-k(ə-)lē\ *adv*

in·as·much as \ˌin-əz-ˌməch-əz\ *conj* (14c) **1** : in the degree that : INSOFAR AS **2** : in view of the fact that : SINCE

in·at·ten·tion \ˌin-ə-ˈten-chən\ *n* (ca. 1680) : failure to pay attention : DISREGARD

in·at·ten·tive \-ˈtent-iv\ *adj* (1692) : not attentive — **in·at·ten·tive·ly** *adv* — **in·at·ten·tive·ness** *n*

in·au·di·ble \(ˈ)in-ˈȯd-ə-bəl\ *adj* [LL *inaudibilis,* fr. L *in-* + LL *audibilis* audible] (1601) : not audible — **in·au·di·bil·i·ty** \(ˌ)in-ˌȯd-ə-ˈbil-ət-ē\ *n* — **in·au·di·bly** \(ˈ)in-ˈȯd-ə-blē\ *adv*

¹in·au·gu·ral \in-ˈȯ-gyə-rəl, -g(ə-)rəl\ *adj* (1689) **1** : of or relating to an inauguration **2** : marking a beginning : first in a projected series

²inaugural *n* (1832) **1** : an inaugural address **2** : INAUGURATION

in·au·gu·rate \in-ˈȯ-g(y)ə-ˌrāt\ *vt* **-rat·ed; -rat·ing** [L *inauguratus,* pp. of *inaugurare,* lit., to practice augury, fr. *in-* + *augurare* to augur; fr. the rites connected with augury] (1606) **1** : to induct into an office with suitable ceremonies **2 a** : to dedicate ceremoniously : observe formally the beginning of **b** : to bring about the beginning of ***syn*** see BEGIN — **in·au·gu·ra·tor** \-ˌrāt-ər\ *n*

in·au·gu·ra·tion \-ˌȯ-g(y)ə-ˈrā-shən\ *n* (1569) : an act of inaugurating; *esp* : a ceremonial induction into office

Inauguration Day *n* (1829) : January 20 following a presidential election on which the president of the U.S. is inaugurated

in·aus·pi·cious \ˌin-ˌȯ-ˈspish-əs\ *adj* (1592) : not auspicious — **in·aus·pi·cious·ly** *adv* — **in·aus·pi·cious·ness** *n*

in·au·then·tic \ˌin-ˌȯ-ˈthent-ik\ *adj* (1860) : not authentic — **in·au·then·tic·i·ty** \ˌin-ˌȯ-ˌthen-ˈtis-ət-ē, -thən-\ *n*

in–be·tween \ˌin-bi-ˈtwēn\ *adj or n* (1927) : INTERMEDIATE

in between *adv or prep* (1917) : BETWEEN

¹in·board \ˈin-ˌbō(ə)rd, -ˌbȯ(ə)rd\ *adv* (1830) **1** : inside the line of a ship's bulwarks or hull : toward the center line of a ship **2** : toward the inside **3** : in a position closer or closest to the longitudinal axis of an aircraft

²inboard *adj* (1847) : located, moving, or being inboard ⟨an ~ engine⟩; *also* : having an inboard engine ⟨~ boats⟩

in·born \ˈin-ˈbȯ(ə)rn\ *adj* (1513) **1** : born in or with one : NATURAL **2** : HEREDITARY, INHERITED

in·bound \ˈin-ˌbau̇nd\ *adj* (1894) : inward bound

in·bounds \ˌin-ˌbau̇n(d)z\ *adj* (1968) : involving putting a basketball in play by passing it onto the court from out of bounds

inbounds line *n* (ca. 1961) : either of two broken lines running the length of a football field at right angles to the yard lines

in·breathe \ˈin-ˈbrēth\ *vt* (14c) : to breathe (something) in : INHALE

in·bred \ˈin-ˈbred\ *adj* (1592) **1** : rooted and ingrained in one's nature as deeply as if implanted by heredity ⟨an ~ love of freedom⟩ **2** [fr. pp. of *inbreed*] : subjected to or produced by inbreeding — **in·bred** \ˈin-ˌbred\ *n*

in·breed \ˈin-ˈbrēd\ *vb* **-bred** \-ˈbred\; **-breed·ing** *vt* (ca. 1879) : to subject to inbreeding ~ *vi* : to engage in inbreeding

in·breed·ing \ˈin-ˌbrēd-iŋ\ *n* (1842) **1** : the interbreeding of closely related individuals esp. to preserve and fix desirable characters of and to eliminate unfavorable characters from a stock **2** : confinement to a narrow range or a local or limited field of choice

in·built \ˈin-ˈbilt\ *adj* (1923) : BUILT-IN

In·ca \ˈiŋ-kə\ *n* [Sp, fr. Quechua *inka* king, prince] (1594) **1 a** : a member of the Quechuan peoples of Peru maintaining an empire until the Spanish conquest **b** : a king or noble of this empire **2** : a member of any people under Inca influence — **In·ca·ic** \in-ˈkā-ik\ *adj* — **In·can** \ˈiŋ-kən\ *adj*

in·cal·cu·la·ble \(ˈ)in-ˈkal-kyə-lə-bəl\ *adj* (1795) : not capable of being calculated: as **a** : very great **b** : not predictable : UNCERTAIN — **in·cal·cu·la·bil·i·ty** \(ˌ)in-ˌkal-kyə-lə-ˈbil-ət-ē\ *n* — **in·cal·cu·la·bly** \(ˈ)in-ˈkal-kyə-lə-blē\ *adv*

in·ca·les·cence \ˌin-kə-ˈles-ᵊn(t)s, ˌiŋ-\ *n* [L *incalescere* to become warm, fr. *in-* + *calescere* to become warm, incho. of *calēre* to be warm — more at LEE] (1646) : a growing warm or ardent — **in·ca·les·cent** \-ᵊnt\ *adj*

in camera *adv* [NL, lit., in a chamber] (1882) : in private : SECRETLY

in·can·desce \ˌin-kən-ˈdes *also* -(ˌ)kan-\ *vb* **-desced; -desc·ing** [L *incandescere*] *vi* (1874) : to be or become incandescent ~ *vt* : to cause to become incandescent

in·can·des·cence \ˌin-kən-ˈdes-ᵊn(t)s *also* -(ˌ)kan-\ *n* (1656) : the quality or state of being incandescent; *esp* : emission by a hot body of radiation that makes it visible

in·can·des·cent \-ᵊnt\ *adj* [prob. fr. F, fr. L *incandescent-, incandescens,* prp. of *incandescere* to become hot, fr. *in-* + *candescere* to become hot, fr. *candēre* to glow — more at CANDID] (1794) **1 a** : white, glowing, or luminous with intense heat **b** : strikingly bright, radiant, or clear **c** : marked by brilliance esp. of expression ⟨~ wit⟩ **d** : characterized by glowing zeal : ARDENT ⟨~ affection⟩ **2 a** : of, relating to, or being light produced by incandescence **b** : producing light by incandescence — **in·can·des·cent·ly** *adv*

incandescent lamp *n* (1881) : an electric lamp in which a filament gives off light when heated to incandescence by an electric current

in·cant \in-ˈkant\ *vi* [L *incantare*] (1945) : RECITE, UTTER

in·can·ta·tion \ˌin-ˌkan-ˈtā-shən\ *n* [ME *incantacioun,* fr. MF *incantation,* fr. LL *incantation-, incantatio,* fr. L *incantatus,* pp. of *incantare* to enchant — more at ENCHANT] (14c) : a use of spells or verbal charms spoken or sung as a part of a ritual of magic; *also* : a written or recited formula of words designed to produce a particular effect — **in·can·ta·tion·al** \-shnəl, -shən-ᵊl\ *adj* — **in·can·ta·to·ry** \in-ˈkant-ə-ˌtōr-ē, -ˌtȯr-\ *adj*

in·ca·pa·ble \(ˈ)in-ˈkā-pə-bəl\ *adj* [MF, fr. *in-* + *capable* capable] (1594) **1** : lacking capacity, ability, or qualification for the purpose or end in view: as **a** *archaic* : not able to take in, hold, or keep **b** *archaic* : not receptive **c** : not being in a state or of a kind to admit : INSUSCEPTIBLE **d** : not able or fit for the doing or performance : INCOMPETENT **2** : lacking legal qualification or power (as by reason of mental incompetence) : DISQUALIFIED — **in·ca·pa·bil·i·ty** \(ˌ)in-ˌkā-pə-ˈbil-ət-ē\ *n* — **in·ca·pa·ble·ness** \(ˈ)in-ˈkā-pə-bəl-nəs\ *n* — **in·ca·pa·bly** \-blē\ *adv*

in·ca·pac·i·tate \ˌin-kə-ˈpas-ə-ˌtāt\ *vt* **-tat·ed; -tat·ing** (1657) **1** : to make legally incapable or ineligible **2** : to deprive of capacity or natural power : DISABLE — **in·ca·pac·i·ta·tion** \-ˌpas-ə-ˈtā-shən\ *n* — **in·ca·pac·i·ta·tor** \-ˈpas-ə-ˌtāt-ər\ *n*

in·ca·pac·i·ty \ˌin-kə-ˈpas-ət-ē, -ˈpas-tē\ *n, pl* **-ties** [F *incapacité,* fr. MF, fr. *in-* + *capacité* capacity] (1611) : the quality or state of being incapable; *esp* : lack of physical or intellectual power or of natural or legal qualifications

in·car·cer·ate \in-ˈkär-sə-ˌrāt\ *vt* **-at·ed; -at·ing** [L *incarceratus,* pp. of *incarcerare,* fr. *in-* + *carcer* prison] (1560) **1** : to put in prison **2** : to subject to confinement — **in·car·cer·a·tion** \(ˌ)in-ˌkär-sə-ˈrā-shən\ *n*

in·car·di·na·tion \(ˌ)in-ˌkärd-ᵊn-ˈā-shən\ *n* [LL *incardination-, incardinatio,* fr. *incardinatus,* pp. of *incardinare* to ordain as chief priest, fr. *in-* ²in- + *cardinalis* principal — more at CARDINAL] (1897) : the formal acceptance by a diocese of a clergyman from another diocese

¹in·car·na·dine \in-ˈkär-nə-ˌdīn, -ˌdēn, -dən\ *adj* [MF *incarnadin,* fr. OIt *incarnadino,* fr. *incarnato* flesh-colored, fr. LL *incarnatus*] (1591) **1** : having the color of flesh **2** : RED; *esp* : BLOODRED

²incarnadine *vt* **-dined; -din·ing** (1605) : to make incarnadine : REDDEN

¹in·car·nate \in-ˈkär-nət, -ˌnāt\ *adj* [ME *incarnat,* fr. LL *incarnatus,* pp. of *incarnare* to incarnate, fr. L *in-* + *carn-, caro* flesh — more at CARNAL] (14c) **1 a** : invested with bodily and esp. human nature and form **b** : made manifest or comprehensible : EMBODIED ⟨a fiend ~⟩ **2** : INCARNADINE ⟨~ clover⟩

²in·car·nate \in-ˈkär-ˌnāt, ˈin-ˌ\ *vt* **-nat·ed; -nat·ing** (1533) : to make incarnate: as **a** : to give bodily form and substance to **b** (1) : to give a concrete or actual form to : ACTUALIZE (2) : to constitute an embodiment or type of ⟨no one culture ~*s* every important human value —Denis Goulet⟩

in·car·na·tion \ˌin-ˌkär-ˈnā-shən\ *n* (13c) **1 a** (1) : the embodiment of a deity or spirit in some earthly form (2) *cap* : the union of divinity with humanity in Jesus Christ **b** : a concrete or actual form of a quality or concept; *esp* : a person showing a trait or typical character to a marked degree ⟨she is the ~ of goodness⟩ **2** : the act of incarnating : the state of being incarnate **3** : time passed in a particular bodily form or state ⟨in another ~ he might be a first vice-president —Walter Teller⟩

incase *var of* ENCASE

in·cau·tion \(ˈ)in-ˈkō-shən\ *n* (1715) : lack of caution : HEEDLESSNESS

in·cau·tious \-shəs\ *adj* (1703) : lacking in caution : CARELESS — **in·cau·tious·ly** *adv* — **in·cau·tious·ness** *n*

in·cen·di·a·rism \in-ˈsen-dē-ə-ˌriz-əm\ *n* (1674) : incendiary action or behavior

¹in·cen·di·ary \in-ˈsen-dē-ˌer-ē, -ˈsen-d(y)ə-rē\ *n, pl* **-ar·ies** [L *incendiarius,* fr. *incendium* conflagration, fr. *incendere*] (15c) **1 a** : a person who deliberately sets fire to a building or other property **b** : an incendiary agent (as a bomb) **2** : a person who excites factions, quarrels, or sedition : AGITATOR

²incendiary *adj* (15c) **1** : of, relating to, or involving a deliberate burning of property **2** : tending to excite or inflame : INFLAMMATORY ⟨~ speeches⟩ **3 a** : igniting combustible materials spontaneously **b** : relating to, being, or involving the use of a missile containing chemicals that ignite on bursting or on contact

¹in·cense \ˈin-ˌsen(t)s\ *n* [ME *encens,* fr. OF, fr. LL *incensum,* fr. L, neut. of *incensus,* pp. of *incendere* to set on fire, fr. *in-* + *-cendere* to burn; akin to L *candēre* to glow — more at CANDID] (13c) **1** : material used to produce a fragrant odor when burned **2** : the perfume exhaled from some spices and gums when burned; *broadly* : a pleasing scent **3** : pleasing attention : FLATTERY ***syn*** see FRAGRANCE

²incense *vt* **in·censed; in·cens·ing** (13c) **1** : to apply or offer incense to **2** : to perfume with incense

³in·cense \in-ˈsen(t)s\ *vt* **in·censed; in·cens·ing** [ME *encensen,* fr. MF *incenser,* fr. L *incensus*] (15c) **1** *archaic* : to cause (a passion or emotion) to become aroused **2** : to arouse the extreme anger or indignation of

in·cen·tive \in-ˈsent-iv\ *n* [ME, fr. LL *incentivum,* fr. neut. of *incentivus* stimulating, fr. L, setting the tune, fr. *incentus,* pp. of *incinere* to set the tune, fr. *in-* + *canere* to sing — more at CHANT] (15c) : something that incites or has a tendency to incite to determination or action ***syn*** see MOTIVE — **incentive** *adj*

in·cept \in-ˈsept\ *vt* [L *in-* + *-ceptus,* fr. *captus,* pp. of *capere* to take — more at HEAVE] (1863) : to take in; *esp* : INGEST — **in·cep·tor** \-ˈsep-tər\ *n*

in·cep·tion \in-ˈsep-shən\ *n* [L *inception-, inceptio,* fr. *inceptus,* pp. of *incipere* to begin, fr. *in-* + *capere* to take — more at HEAVE] (15c) : an act, process, or instance of beginning : COMMENCEMENT ***syn*** see ORIGIN

¹in·cep·tive \in-ˈsep-tiv\ *n* (1612) : an inchoative verb

²inceptive *adj* (1656) **1** : INCHOATIVE 2 **2** : of or relating to a beginning — **in·cep·tive·ly** *adv*

in·cer·ti·tude \(ˈ)in-ˈsərt-ə-ˌt(y)üd\ *n* [ME, fr. MF, fr. LL *incertitudo,* fr. L *in-* + LL *certitudo* certitude] (15c) : UNCERTAINTY: **a** : absence of assurance or confidence : DOUBT **b** : the quality or state of being unstable or insecure

in·ces·san·cy \(ˈ)in-ˈses-ᵊn-sē\ *n* (1615) : the quality or state of being incessant

in·ces·sant \(ˈ)in-ˈses-ᵊnt\ *adj* [ME *incessaunt,* fr. LL *incessant-, incessans,* fr. L *in-* + *cessant-, cessans,* prp. of *cessare* to delay — more at CEASE] (15c) : continuing or following without interruption : UNCEASING ***syn*** see CONTINUAL — **in·ces·sant·ly** *adv*

in·cest \'in-ˌsest\ *n* [ME, fr. L *incestum,* fr. neut. of *incestus* impure, fr. *in-* + *castus* pure — more at CASTE] (13c) **:** sexual intercourse between persons so closely related that they are forbidden by law to marry; *also* **:** the statutory crime of such a relationship ***syn*** see ADULTERY

in·ces·tu·ous \in-'ses(h)-chə-wəs\ *adj* (1532) **1 :** constituting or involving incest **2 :** guilty of incest — **in·ces·tu·ous·ly** *adv* — **in·ces·tu·ous·ness** *n*

[1]**inch** \'inch\ *n* [ME, fr. OE *ynce,* fr. L *uncia* — more at OUNCE] (bef. 12c) **1 :** a unit of length equal to 1/36 yard — see WEIGHT table **2 :** a small amount, distance, or degree ⟨is like cutting a dog's tail off by ~*es* —Milton Friedman⟩ **3** *pl* **:** STATURE, HEIGHT **4 a :** a fall (as of rain or snow) sufficient to cover a surface or to fill a gauge to the depth of one inch **b :** a degree of atmospheric or other pressure sufficient to balance the weight of a column of liquid (as mercury) one inch high in a barometer or manometer **c :** WATER-INCH — **every inch :** to the utmost degree ⟨looks *every inch* a winner⟩ — **within an inch of :** almost to the point of

[2]**inch** *vi* (1599) **:** to move by small degrees ⟨the long line of people ~*ing* up the stairs⟩ ~ *vt* **:** to cause to move slowly ⟨sooner or later they begin ~*ing* prices back up —*Forbes*⟩

[3]**inch** *n* [ME, fr. ScGael *innis*] *chiefly Scot* (15c) **:** ISLAND

inched \'incht\ *adj* (1605) **:** measuring a specified number of inches

-inch·er \'in-chər\ *comb form* **:** one that has a dimension of a specified number of inches

inch·meal \'inch-ˌmēl, -'mē(ə)l\ *adv* [[1]*inch* + *-meal* (as in *piecemeal*)] (ca. 1530) **:** LITTLE BY LITTLE, GRADUALLY

in·cho·ate \in-'kō-ət, 'in-kə-ˌwāt\ *adj* [L *inchoatus,* pp. of *inchoare,* lit., to hitch up, fr. *in-* + *cohum* strap fastening a plow beam to the yoke; akin to L *colum* sieve — more at HEDGE] (1534) **:** being only partly in existence or operation; *esp* **:** imperfectly formed or formulated ⟨misty, ~ suspicions that all is not well with the nation —J. M. Perry⟩ — **in·cho·ate·ly** *adv* — **in·cho·ate·ness** *n*

in·cho·ative \in-'kō-ət-iv\ *adj* (1631) **1 :** INITIAL, FORMATIVE ⟨the ~ stages⟩ **2 :** denoting the beginning of an action, state, or occurrence — used of verbs — **inchoative** *n* — **in·cho·ative·ly** *adv*

inch·worm \'inch-ˌwərm\ *n* (1861) **:** LOOPER 1

in·ci·dence \'in(t)-səd-ən(t)s, -sə-ˌden(t)s\ *n* (1656) **1 a :** an act or the fact or manner of falling upon or affecting **:** OCCURRENCE **b :** rate of occurrence or influence ⟨a high ~ of crime⟩ **2 a :** the arrival of something (as a projectile or a ray of light) at a surface **b :** ANGLE OF INCIDENCE

[1]**in·ci·dent** \'in(t)-səd-ənt, -sə-ˌdent\ *n* [ME, fr. MF, fr. ML *incident-, incidens,* fr. L, prp. of *incidere* to fall into, fr. *in-* + *cadere* to fall — more at CHANCE] (15c) **1 :** something dependent on or subordinate to something else of greater or principal importance **2 a :** an occurrence of an action or situation that is a separate unit of experience **:** HAPPENING **b :** an accompanying minor occurrence or condition **:** CONCOMITANT **3 :** an action likely to lead to grave consequences esp. in diplomatic matters ⟨a serious border ~⟩ ***syn*** see OCCURRENCE

[2]**incident** *adj* (15c) **1 :** occurring or likely to occur esp. as a minor consequence or accompaniment ⟨the confusion ~ to moving day⟩ **2 :** dependent on or relating to another thing in law **3 :** falling or striking on something ⟨~ light rays⟩

[1]**in·ci·den·tal** \ˌin(t)-sə-'dent-ᵊl\ *adj* (1616) **1 :** being likely to ensue as a chance or minor consequence ⟨social obligations ~ to his job⟩ **2 :** occurring merely by chance or without intention or calculation

[2]**incidental** *n* (1707) **1** *pl* **:** minor items (as of expense) that are not particularized **2 :** something that is incidental

in·ci·den·tal·ly \-'dent-ᵊl-ē, *esp for 2* -'dent-lē\ *adv* (1665) **1 :** by chance **:** CASUALLY **2 :** by way of interjection or digression **:** PARENTHETICALLY

incidental music *n* (1864) **:** descriptive music played during a play to project a mood (as for a battle, a storm, or a death scene) or to accompany stage action

in·cin·er·ate \in-'sin-ə-ˌrāt\ *vt* **-at·ed; -at·ing** [ML *incineratus,* pp. of *incinerare,* fr. L *in-* + *ciner-, cinis* ashes; akin to Gk *konis* dust, ashes] (1555) **:** to cause to burn to ashes — **in·cin·er·a·tion** \-ˌsin-ə-'rā-shən\ *n*

in·cin·er·a·tor \in-'sin-ə-ˌrāt-ər\ *n* (1883) **:** one that incinerates; *esp* **:** a furnace or a container for incinerating waste materials

in·cip·i·ence \in-'sip-ē-ən(t)s\ *n* (ca. 1864) **:** INCIPIENCY

in·cip·i·en·cy \-ən-sē\ *n* (1817) **:** the state or fact of being incipient **:** BEGINNING

in·cip·i·ent \-ənt\ *adj* [L *incipient-, incipiens,* prp. of *incipere* to begin — more at INCEPTION] (1669) **:** beginning to come into being or to become apparent **:** COMMENCING ⟨an ~ solar system⟩ ⟨evidence of ~ racial tension⟩ — **in·cip·i·ent·ly** *adv*

in·ci·pit \'in(t)-sə-pət, 'iŋ-kə-ˌpit; in-'sip-ət, -'kip-\ *n* [L, it begins, fr. *incipere*] (1897) **:** the first part **:** BEGINNING; *specif* **:** the opening words of a text of a medieval manuscript or early printed book

in·ci·sal \in-'sī-zəl, -səl\ *adj* (1903) **:** relating to, involving, or being the cutting edge or surface of a tooth (as an incisor)

in·cise \in-'sīz, -'sīs\ *vt* **in·cised; in·cis·ing** [MF or L; MF *inciser,* fr. L *incisus,* pp. of *incidere,* fr. *in-* + *caedere* to cut — more at CONCISE] (1567) **1 :** to cut into **2 a :** to carve figures, letters, or devices into **:** ENGRAVE **b :** to carve (as an inscription) into a surface

in·cised *adj* (15c) **1 :** cut in **:** ENGRAVED; *esp* **:** decorated with incised figures **2 :** having a margin that is deeply and sharply notched ⟨an ~ leaf⟩

in·ci·sion \in-'sizh-ən\ *n* (15c) **1 a :** a marginal notch (as in a leaf) **b :** CUT, GASH; *specif* **:** a wound made esp. in surgery by incising the body **2 :** an act of incising something **3 :** the quality or state of being incisive

in·ci·sive \in-'sī-siv\ *adj* (1850) **:** impressively direct and decisive (as in manner or presentation) ⟨~ writing⟩ — **in·ci·sive·ly** *adv* — **in·ci·sive·ness** *n*

in·ci·sor \in-'sī-zər\ *n* (1666) **:** a tooth adapted for cutting; *esp* **:** one of the cutting teeth in mammals in front of the canines — see TOOTH illustration

in·ci·ta·tion \ˌin-ˌsī-'tā-shən, ˌin(t)-sə-\ *n* (15c) **1 :** an act of inciting **:** STIMULATION **2 :** something that incites to action **:** INCENTIVE

in·cite \in-'sīt\ *vt* **in·cit·ed; in·cit·ing** [MF *inciter,* fr. L *incitare,* fr. *in-* + *citare* to put in motion — more at CITE] (15c) **:** to move to action **:** stir up **:** spur on **:** urge on — **in·cit·ant** \-'sīt-ᵊnt\ *n* — **in·cite·ment** \-mənt\ *n* — **in·cit·er** *n*

syn INCITE, INSTIGATE, ABET, FOMENT mean to spur to action. INCITE stresses a stirring up and urging on, and may or may not imply initiating; INSTIGATE definitely implies responsibility for initiating another's action and often connotes underhandedness or evil intention; ABET implies both assisting and encouraging; FOMENT implies persistence in goading.

in·ci·vil·i·ty \ˌin(t)-sə-'vil-ət-ē\ *n* [MF *incivilité,* fr. LL *incivilitat-, incivilitas,* fr. *incivilis,* fr. L *in-* + *civilis* civil] (1584) **1 :** the quality or state of being uncivil **2 :** a rude or discourteous act

in·clem·en·cy \(')in-'klem-ən-sē\ *n* (1559) **:** the quality or state of being inclement

in·clem·ent \(')in-'klem-ənt\ *adj* [L *inclement-, inclemens,* fr. *in-* + *clement-, clemens* clement] (1621) **:** lacking clemency: as **a :** physically severe **:** STORMY ⟨~ weather⟩ **b** *archaic* **:** severe in temper or action **:** UNMERCIFUL — **in·clem·ent·ly** *adv*

in·clin·able \in-'klī-nə-bəl\ *adj* (15c) **:** having a tendency or inclination; *also* **:** disposed to favor or think well of

in·cli·na·tion \ˌin-klə-'nā-shən, ˌiŋ-\ *n* (14c) **1 a** *obs* **:** natural disposition **:** CHARACTER **b :** a particular disposition of mind or character **:** PROPENSITY; *esp* **:** LIKING ⟨had little ~ for housekeeping⟩ **2 :** an act or the action of bending or inclining: as **a :** BOW, NOD **b :** a tilting of something **3 a :** a deviation from the true vertical or horizontal **:** SLANT; *also* **:** the degree of such deviation **b :** an inclined surface **:** SLOPE **c (1) :** the angle determined by two lines or planes **(2) :** the angle made by a line with the x-axis measured counterclockwise from the positive direction of that axis **4 :** a tendency to a particular aspect, state, character, or action ⟨the clutch has an ~ to slip⟩ — **in·cli·na·tion·al** \-shnəl, -shən-ᵊl\ *adj*

[1]**in·cline** \in-'klīn\ *vb* **in·clined; in·clin·ing** [ME *inclinen,* fr. MF *incliner,* fr. L *inclinare,* fr. *in-* + *clinare* to lean — more at LEAN] *vi* (14c) **1 :** to bend the head or body forward **:** BOW **2 :** to lean, tend, or become drawn toward an opinion or course of conduct **3 :** to deviate from a line, direction, or course; *specif* **:** to deviate from the vertical or horizontal ~ *vt* **1 :** to cause to stoop or bow **:** BEND **2 :** to have influence on **:** PERSUADE ⟨his love of books *inclined* him toward a literary career⟩ **3 :** to give a bend or slant to — **in·clin·er** *n*

syn INCLINE, BIAS, DISPOSE, PREDISPOSE mean to influence one to have or take an attitude toward something. INCLINE implies a tendency to favor one of two or more actions or conclusions; BIAS suggests a settled and predictable leaning in one direction and connotes unfair prejudice; DISPOSE suggests an affecting of one's mood or temper so as to incline one toward something; PREDISPOSE implies the operation of a disposing influence well in advance of the opportunity to manifest itself.

[2]**in·cline** \'in-ˌklīn\ *n* (1846) **:** an inclined plane **:** GRADE, SLOPE

in·clined \in-'klīnd, *2 also* 'in-ˌ\ *adj* (14c) **1 :** having inclination, disposition, or tendency **2 a :** having a leaning or slope **b :** making an angle with a line or plane

inclined plane *n* (1710) **:** a plane surface that makes an oblique angle with the plane of the horizon

in·clin·ing \in-'klī-niŋ\ *n* (14c) **1 :** INCLINATION **2** *archaic* **:** PARTY, FOLLOWING

in·cli·nom·e·ter \ˌin-klə-'näm-ət-ər, ˌiŋ-; ˌin-ˌklī-\ *n* (1842) **1 :** an apparatus for determining the direction of the earth's magnetic field with reference to the plane of the horizon **2 :** a machinist's clinometer **3 :** an instrument for indicating the inclination to the horizontal of an axis of a ship or an airplane

in·clip \in-'klip\ *vt, archaic* (1608) **:** CLASP, ENCLOSE

inclose, inclosure *var of* ENCLOSE, ENCLOSURE

in·clude \in-'klüd\ *vt* **in·clud·ed; in·clud·ing** [ME *includen,* fr. L *includere,* fr. *in-* + *claudere* to close — more at CLOSE] (15c) **1 :** to shut up **:** ENCLOSE **2 :** to take in or comprise as a part of a whole **3 :** to contain between or within ⟨two sides and the *included* angle⟩ — **in·clud·able** *or* **in·clud·ible** \-'klüd-ə-bəl\ *adj*

syn INCLUDE, COMPREHEND, EMBRACE, INVOLVE mean to contain within as part of the whole. INCLUDE suggests the containment of something as a constituent, component, or subordinate part of a larger whole; COMPREHEND implies that something comes within the scope of a statement or definition; EMBRACE implies a gathering of separate items within a whole; INVOLVE suggests inclusion by virtue of the nature of the whole, whether by being its natural or inevitable consequence.

in·clu·sion \in-'klü-zhən\ *n* [L *inclusion-, inclusio,* fr. *inclusus,* pp. of *includere*] (1600) **1 :** the act of including **:** the state of being included **2 :** something that is included: as **a :** a gaseous, liquid, or solid foreign body enclosed in a mass (as of a mineral) **b :** a passive product of cell activity (as a starch grain) within the protoplasm **3 :** a relation between two classes that exists when all members of the first are also members of the second — compare MEMBERSHIP 3

inclusion body *n* (ca. 1923) **:** a rounded or oval intracellular body that consists of elementary bodies in a matrix, is characteristic of some virus diseases, and is believed to represent a stage in the multiplication of the virus

in·clu·sive \in-'klü-siv, -ziv\ *adj* (1515) **1 :** comprehending stated limits or extremes ⟨from Monday to Friday ~⟩ **2 a :** broad in orientation or scope **b :** covering or intended to cover all items, costs, or services — **in·clu·sive·ly** *adv* — **in·clu·sive·ness** *n*

inclusive disjunction *n* (1942) **:** a complex sentence in logic that is true when either or both of its constituent propositions are true — see TRUTH TABLE table

inclusive of *prep* (1709) **:** including or taking into account ⟨the cost of building *inclusive of* materials⟩

in·co·erc·ible \ˌin-kō-'ər-sə-bəl\ *adj* (1710) **:** incapable of being controlled, checked, or confined

in·cog·i·tant \in-'käj-ət-ənt\ *adj* [L *incogitant-, incogitans,* fr. *in-* + *cogitant-, cogitans,* prp. of *cogitare* to cogitate] (1628) **:** THOUGHTLESS, INCONSIDERATE

\ə\ abut \ᵊ\ kitten, F table \ər\ further \a\ ash \ā\ ace \ä\ cot, cart \au̇\ out \ch\ chin \e\ bet \ē\ easy \g\ go \i\ hit \ī\ ice \j\ job \ŋ\ sing \ō\ go \ȯ\ law \ȯi\ boy \th\ thin \t͟h\ the \ü\ loot \u̇\ foot \y\ yet \zh\ vision \á, k̲, ⁿ, œ, œ̄, ue, ue̅, ʸ\ see Guide to Pronunciation

in·cog·ni·ta \ˌin-ˌkäg-ˈnēt-ə, in-ˈkäg-nət-ə\ *adv or adj* [It, fem. of *incognito*] (1668) : INCOGNITO — used only of a woman — **incognita** *n*

¹**in·cog·ni·to** \ˌin-ˌkäg-ˈnēt-(ˌ)ō, in-ˈkäg-nə-ˌtō\ *n, pl* **-tos** (1638) **1** : one appearing or living incognito **2** : the state or disguise of one living incognito or incognita

²**incognito** *adv or adj* [It, fr. L *incognitus* unknown, fr. *in-* + *cognitus,* pp. of *cognoscere* to know — more at COGNITION] (1649) : with one's identity concealed

in·cog·ni·zant \(ˈ)in-ˈkäg-nə-zənt\ *adj* (1837) : lacking awareness or consciousness — **in·cog·ni·zance** \-zən(t)s\ *n*

in·co·her·ence \ˌin-kō-ˈhir-ən(t)s, -ˈher-\ *n* (1611) **1** : the quality or state of being incoherent **2** : something that is incoherent

in·co·her·ent \-ənt\ *adj* (1626) : lacking coherence: as **a** : lacking cohesion : LOOSE **b** : lacking orderly continuity, arrangement, or relevance : INCONSISTENT — **in·co·her·ent·ly** *adv*

in·com·bus·ti·ble \ˌin-kəm-ˈbəs-tə-bəl\ *adj* [ME, prob. fr. MF, fr. *in-* + *combustible* combustible] (15c) : not combustible : incapable of being burned — **in·com·bus·ti·bil·i·ty** \-ˌbəs-tə-ˈbil-ət-ē\ *n* — **incombustible** *n*

in·come \ˈin-ˌkəm *also* ˈin-kəm *or* ˈiŋ-kəm\ *n* (14c) **1** : a coming in : ENTRANCE, INFLUX ⟨fluctuations in the nutrient ~ of a body of water⟩ **2** : a gain or recurrent benefit usu. measured in money that derives from capital or labor; *also* : the amount of such gain received in a period of time ⟨has an ~ of $20,000 a year⟩

income account *n* (1869) : a financial statement of a business showing the details of revenues, costs, expenses, losses, and profits for a given period — called also *income statement*

income bond *n* (ca. 1864) : a bond that pays interest at a rate based on the issuer's earnings

income tax \ˌin-(ˌ)kəm-, ˌiŋ-\ *n* (1799) : a tax on the net income of an individual or a business

¹**in·com·ing** \ˈin-ˌkəm-iŋ\ *n* (14c) **1** : the act of coming in : ARRIVAL **2** : INCOME — usu. used in pl.

²**incoming** *adj* (1753) **1** : coming in : ARRIVING ⟨an ~ ship⟩ ⟨~ mail⟩ **2** : taking a new place or position esp. as part of a succession ⟨the ~ president⟩ **3** : just starting or beginning ⟨the ~ year⟩

in·com·men·su·ra·ble \ˌin-kə-ˈmen(t)s(-ə)-rə-bəl, -ˈmench(-ə)-\ *adj* (1570) : not commensurable; *broadly* : lacking a basis of comparison in respect to a quality normally subject to comparison — **in·com·men·su·ra·bil·i·ty** \-ˌmen(t)s(-ə)-rə-ˈbil-ət-ē, -ˌmench(-ə)-\ *n* — **incommensurable** *n* — **in·com·men·su·ra·bly** \-ˈmen(t)s(-ə)-rə-blē, -ˈmench(-ə)-\ *adv*

in·com·men·su·rate \-ˈmen(t)s(-ə)-rət, -ˈmench(-ə)-\ *adj* (1650) : not commensurate: as **a** : INCOMMENSURABLE **b** : INADEQUATE **c** : DISPROPORTIONATE

in·com·mode \ˌin-kə-ˈmōd\ *vt* **-mod·ed; -mod·ing** [MF *incommoder,* fr. L *incommodare,* fr. *incommodus* inconvenient, fr. *in-* + *commodus* convenient — more at COMMODE] (1598) : to give inconvenience or distress to : DISTURB

in·com·mo·di·ous \ˌin-kə-ˈmōd-ē-əs\ *adj* (1551) : not commodious : INCONVENIENT — **in·com·mo·di·ous·ly** *adv* — **in·com·mo·di·ous·ness** *n*

in·com·mod·i·ty \-ˈmäd-ət-ē\ *n* (15c) : a source of inconvenience : DISADVANTAGE

in·com·mu·ni·ca·ble \ˌin-kə-ˈmyü-ni-kə-bəl\ *adj* [MF or LL; MF, fr. LL *incommunicabilis,* fr. L *in-* + LL *communicabilis* communicable] (1568) : not communicable: as **a** : incapable of being communicated or imparted **b** : UNCOMMUNICATIVE — **in·com·mu·ni·ca·bil·i·ty** \-ˌmyü-ni-kə-ˈbil-ət-ē\ *n* — **in·com·mu·ni·ca·bly** \-ˈmyü-ni-kə-blē\ *adv*

in·com·mu·ni·ca·do \-ˌmyü-nə-ˈkäd-(ˌ)ō\ *adv or adj* [Sp *incomunicado,* fr. pp. of *incomunicar* to deprive of communication, fr. *in-* (fr. L) + *comunicar* to communicate, fr. L *communicare*] (1844) : without means of communication; *also* : in solitary confinement

in·com·mu·ni·ca·tive \-ˈmyü-nə-ˌkāt-iv, -ni-kət-\ *adj* (1670) : UNCOMMUNICATIVE

in·com·mut·able \ˌin-kə-ˈmyüt-ə-bəl\ *adj* [ME, fr. L *incommutabilis,* fr. *in-* + *commutabilis* commutable] (15c) : not commutable: as **a** : not interchangeable **b** : UNCHANGEABLE — **in·com·mut·ably** \-blē\ *adv*

in·com·pa·ra·ble \(ˈ)in-ˈkäm-p(ə-)rə-bəl, ÷ˌin-kəm-ˈpar-ə-\ *adj* [ME, fr. MF, fr. L *incomparabilis,* fr. *in-* + *comparabilis* comparable] (15c) **1** : eminent beyond comparison : MATCHLESS **2** : not suitable for comparison — **in·com·pa·ra·bil·i·ty** \(ˌ)in-ˌkäm-p(ə-)rə-ˈbil-ət-ē, ÷ˌin-kəm-ˌpar-ə-\ *n* — **in·com·pa·ra·bly** \(ˈ)in-ˈkäm-p(ə-)rə-blē, ÷ˌin-kəm-ˈpar-ə-\ *adv*

in·com·pat·i·bil·i·ty \ˌin-kəm-ˌpat-ə-ˈbil-ət-ē\ *n, pl* **-ties** (1611) **1 a** : the quality or state of being incompatible **b** : lack of interfertility between two plants **2** *pl* : mutually antagonistic things or qualities

in·com·pat·i·ble \ˌin-kəm-ˈpat-ə-bəl\ *adj* [MF & ML; MF, fr. ML *incompatibilis,* fr. L *in-* + ML *compatibilis* compatible] (15c) **1** : incapable of being held by one person at one time — used of offices that make conflicting demands on the holder **2 a** : incapable of association because incongruous, discordant, or disagreeing ⟨~ colors⟩ **b** : unsuitable for use together because of undesirable chemical or physiological effects ⟨~ drugs⟩ **c** : not both true ⟨~ propositions⟩ **d** : incapable of blending into a stable homogeneous mixture — **incompatible** *n* — **in·com·pat·i·bly** \-blē\ *adv*

in·com·pe·tence \(ˈ)in-ˈkäm-pət-ən(t)s\ *n* (1663) : the state or fact of being incompetent

in·com·pe·ten·cy \-ən-sē\ *n* (1611) : INCOMPETENCE

in·com·pe·tent \(ˈ)in-ˈkäm-pət-ənt\ *adj* [MF *incompétent,* fr. *in-* + *compétent* competent] (1597) **1** : not legally qualified **2** : inadequate to or unsuitable for a particular purpose **3 a** : lacking the qualities needed for effective action **b** : unable to function properly ⟨~ heart valves⟩ — **incompetent** *n* — **in·com·pe·tent·ly** *adv*

in·com·plete \ˌin-kəm-ˈplēt\ *adj* [ME *incompleet,* fr. LL *incompletus,* fr. L *in-* + *completus* complete] (14c) **1** : not complete : UNFINISHED: as **a** : lacking a part; *esp* : lacking one or more sets of floral organs **b** *of insect metamorphosis* : characterized by the absence of a pupal stage between the immature stages and the adult of an insect in which the young usu. resemble the adult — compare COMPLETE 5 **2** *of a football pass* : not legally caught — **in·com·plete·ly** *adv* — **in·com·plete·ness** *n*

in·com·pli·ant \ˌin-kəm-ˈplī-ənt\ *adj* (1647) : not compliant or pliable

in·com·pre·hen·si·ble \(ˌ)in-ˌkäm-pri-ˈhen(t)-sə-bəl\ *adj* [ME, fr. L *incomprehensibilis,* fr. *in-* + *comprehensibilis* comprehensible] (14c) **1** *archaic* : having or subject to no limits **2** : impossible to comprehend : UNINTELLIGIBLE — **in·com·pre·hen·si·bil·i·ty** \-ˌhen(t)-sə-ˈbil-ət-ē\ *n* — **in·com·pre·hen·si·ble·ness** *n* — **in·com·pre·hen·si·bly** \-ˈhen(t)-sə-blē\ *adv*

in·com·pre·hen·sion \-ˈhen-chən\ *n* (1605) : lack of comprehension or understanding

in·com·press·ible \ˌin-kəm-ˈpres-ə-bəl\ *adj* (1730) : incapable of or resistant to compression — **in·com·press·ibil·i·ty** \-ˌpres-ə-ˈbil-ət-ē\ *n* — **in·com·press·ibly** \-ˈpres-ə-blē\ *adv*

in·com·put·able \ˌin-kəm-ˈpyüt-ə-bəl\ *adj* (1606) : not computable : very great — **in·com·put·ably** \-blē\ *adv*

in·con·ceiv·able \ˌin-kən-ˈsē-və-bəl\ *adj* (1631) : not conceivable: as **a** : impossible to comprehend **b** : UNBELIEVABLE — **in·con·ceiv·abil·i·ty** \-ˌsē-və-ˈbil-ət-ē\ *n* — **in·con·ceiv·able·ness** \-ˈsē-və-bəl-nəs\ *n* — **in·con·ceiv·ably** \-blē\ *adv*

in·con·cin·ni·ty \ˌin-kən-ˈsin-ət-ē\ *n* [L *inconcinnitas,* fr. *in-* + *concinnitas* concinnity] (ca. 1616) : lack of suitability or congruity : INELEGANCE

in·con·clu·sive \ˌin-kən-ˈklü-siv, -ziv\ *adj* (1690) : leading to no conclusion or definite result — **in·con·clu·sive·ly** *adv* — **in·con·clu·sive·ness** *n*

in·con·dens·able \ˌin-kən-ˈden(t)-sə-bəl\ *adj* (1736) : incapable of being condensed

in·con·dite \in-ˈkän-dət, -ˌdīt\ *adj* [L *inconditus,* fr. *in-* + *conditus,* pp. of *condere* to put together, fr. *com-* + *-dere* to put — more at DO] (1539) : badly put together : CRUDE

in·con·for·mi·ty \ˌin-kən-ˈfȯr-mət-ē\ *n* (1594) : NONCONFORMITY

in·con·gru·ence \ˌin-kən-ˈgrü-ən(t)s, (ˈ)in-ˈkäŋ-grə-wən(t)s\ *n* (1610) : INCONGRUITY

in·con·gru·ent \-ənt, -wənt\ *adj* [L *incongruent-, incongruens,* fr. *in-* + *congruent-, congruens* congruent] (15c) : not congruent ⟨~ triangles⟩ — **in·con·gru·ent·ly** *adv*

in·con·gru·i·ty \ˌin-kən-ˈgrü-ət-ē, -ˌkän-\ *n, pl* **-ities** (1532) **1** : the quality or state of being incongruous **2** : something that is incongruous

in·con·gru·ous \(ˈ)in-ˈkäŋ-grə-wəs\ *adj* [LL *incongruus,* fr. L *in-* + *congruus* congruous] (1611) : lacking congruity: as **a** : not harmonious : INCOMPATIBLE ⟨~ colors⟩ **b** : not conforming : DISAGREEING ⟨conduct ~ with his principles⟩ **c** : inconsistent within itself ⟨an ~ story⟩ **d** : lacking propriety : UNSUITABLE ⟨~ manners⟩ — **in·con·gru·ous·ly** *adv* — **in·con·gru·ous·ness** *n*

in·con·scient \(ˈ)in-ˈkän-chənt\ *adj* [prob. fr. F, fr. *in-* + *conscient* mindful, fr. L *conscient-, consciens,* prp. of *conscire* to be conscious — more at CONSCIENCE] (1885) : UNCONSCIOUS, MINDLESS

in·con·sec·u·tive \ˌin-kən-ˈsek-(y)ət-iv\ *adj* (1831) : not consecutive

in·con·se·quence \(ˈ)in-ˈkän(t)-sə-ˌkwen(t)s, -si-kwən(t)s\ *n* (1588) : the quality or state of being inconsequent

in·con·se·quent \-ˌkwent, -kwənt\ *adj* [LL *inconsequent-, inconsequens,* fr. L *in-* + *consequent-, consequens* consequent] (1579) **1 a** : lacking reasonable sequence : ILLOGICAL **b** : INCONSECUTIVE **2** : INCONSEQUENTIAL 2 **3** : IRRELEVANT — **in·con·se·quent·ly** *adv*

in·con·se·quen·tial \(ˌ)in-ˌkän(t)-sə-ˈkwen-chəl\ *adj* (1621) **1 a** : ILLOGICAL **b** : IRRELEVANT **2** : of no significance : UNIMPORTANT — **in·con·se·quen·ti·al·i·ty** \-ˌkwen-chē-ˈal-ət-ē\ *n* — **in·con·se·quen·tial·ly** \-ˈkwench-(ə-)lē\ *adv*

in·con·sid·er·able \ˌin-kən-ˈsid-ər-(ə-)bəl, -ˈsid-rə-bəl\ *adj* [F, fr. *in-* + *considerable* considerable, fr. ML *considerabilis*] (1637) : not considerable : TRIVIAL — **in·con·sid·er·able·ness** *n* — **in·con·sid·er·ably** \-blē\ *adv*

in·con·sid·er·ate \ˌin-kən-ˈsid-(ə-)rət\ *adj* [L *inconsideratus,* fr. *in-* + *consideratus* considerate] (15c) **1** : not adequately considered : ILL-ADVISED **2 a** : HEEDLESS, THOUGHTLESS **b** : careless of the rights or feelings of others — **in·con·sid·er·ate·ly** *adv* — **in·con·sid·er·ate·ness** *n* — **in·con·sid·er·ation** \-ˌsid-ə-ˈrā-shən\ *n*

in·con·sis·tence \ˌin-kən-ˈsis-tən(t)s\ *n* (1643) : INCONSISTENCY

in·con·sis·ten·cy \ˌin-kən-ˈsis-tən-sē\ *n* (1647) **1** : the quality or state of being inconsistent **2** : an instance of being inconsistent

in·con·sis·tent \-tənt\ *adj* (1646) : lacking consistency: as **a** : not compatible with another fact or claim ⟨~ statements⟩ **b** : containing incompatible elements ⟨an ~ argument⟩ **c** : incoherent or illogical in thought or actions : CHANGEABLE **d** : not satisfiable by the same set of values for the unknowns ⟨~ equations⟩ ⟨~ inequalities⟩ — **in·con·sis·tent·ly** *adv*

in·con·sol·able \ˌin-kən-ˈsō-lə-bəl\ *adj* [L *inconsolabilis,* fr. *in-* + *consolabilis* consolable] (1596) : incapable of being consoled : DISCONSOLATE — **in·con·sol·able·ness** *n* — **in·con·sol·ably** \-blē\ *adv*

in·con·so·nance \(ˈ)in-ˈkän(t)-s(ə-)nən(t)s\ *n* (ca. 1811) : lack of consonance or harmony : DISAGREEMENT

in·con·so·nant \-s(ə-)nənt\ *adj* (1658) : not consonant : DISCORDANT

in·con·spic·u·ous \ˌin-kən-ˈspik-yə-wəs\ *adj* [L *inconspicuus,* fr. *in-* + *conspicuus* conspicuous] (1648) : not readily noticeable — **in·con·spic·u·ous·ly** *adv* — **in·con·spic·u·ous·ness** *n*

in·con·stan·cy \(ˈ)in-ˈkän(t)-stən-sē\ *n* (1526) : the quality or state of being inconstant

in·con·stant \-stənt\ *adj* [ME, fr. MF, fr. L *inconstant-, inconstans,* fr. *in-* + *constant-, constans* constant] (15c) : likely to change frequently without apparent or cogent reason — **in·con·stant·ly** *adv*

syn INCONSTANT, FICKLE, CAPRICIOUS, MERCURIAL, UNSTABLE mean lacking firmness or steadiness (as in purpose or devotion). INCONSTANT implies an incapacity for steadiness and an inherent tendency to change; FICKLE suggests unreliability because of perverse changeability and incapacity for steadfastness; CAPRICIOUS suggests motivation by sudden whim or fancy and stresses unpredictability; MERCURIAL implies a rapid changeability in mood; UNSTABLE implies an incapacity for remaining in a fixed position or steady course and applies esp. to a lack of emotional balance.

in·con·sum·able \ˌin-kən-ˈsü-mə-bəl\ *adj* (1646) : not capable of being consumed — **in·con·sum·ably** \-blē\ *adv*

in·con·test·able \ˌin-kən-ˈtes-tə-bəl\ *adj* [F, fr. *in-* + *contestable,* fr. *contester* to contest] (1673) : not contestable : INDISPUTABLE — **in·con·test·abil·i·ty** \-ˌtes-tə-ˈbil-ət-ē\ *n* — **in·con·test·ably** \-ˈtes-tə-blē\ *adv*

in·con·ti·nence \(ˈ)in-ˈkänt-ᵊn-ən(t)s\ *n* (14c) : the quality or state of being incontinent: as **a** : failure to restrain sexual appetite : UNCHASTITY **b** : inability of the body to control the evacuative functions

in·con·ti·nen·cy \-ən-sē\ *n* (15c) : INCONTINENCE

¹**in·con·ti·nent** \(ˈ)in-ˈkänt-ᵊn-ənt\ *adj* [ME, fr. MF or L; MF, fr. L *incontinent-, incontinens,* fr. *in-* + *continent-, continens* continent] (14c) : not continent: as **a (1)** : lacking self-restraint **(2)** : not being under

control ⟨that play . . . is singularly ~ and full of loose ends —*Times Lit. Supp.*⟩ **b :** unable to retain a bodily discharge (as urine) voluntarily

[2]**incontinent** *adv* [ME, fr. MF, fr. LL *in continenti*] (15c) **:** [1]INCONTINENTLY

[1]**in·con·ti·nent·ly** *adv* (15c) **:** without delay **:** IMMEDIATELY

[2]**incontinently** *adv* (ca. 1552) **:** in an incontinent or unrestrained manner: as **a :** without moral restraint **:** LEWDLY **b :** without due or reasonable consideration

in·con·trol·la·ble \ˌin-kən-ˈtrō-lə-bəl\ *adj* (1599) **:** UNCONTROLLABLE

in·con·tro·vert·ible \(ˌ)in-ˌkän-trə-ˈvərt-ə-bəl\ *adj* (1646) **:** not open to question **:** INDISPUTABLE ⟨~ evidence⟩ — **in·con·tro·vert·ibly** \-blē\ *adv*

[1]**in·con·ve·nience** \ˌin-kən-ˈvē-nyən(t)s\ *n* [ME, harm, damage, fr. LL *inconvenientia,* fr. L *inconvenient-, inconveniens*] (1578) **1 :** something that is inconvenient **2 :** the quality or state of being inconvenient

[2]**inconvenience** *vt* (1656) **:** to subject to inconvenience **:** put to trouble

in·con·ve·nien·cy \ˌin-kən-ˈvē-nyən-sē\ *n* (ca. 1552) **:** INCONVENIENCE

in·con·ve·nient \ˌin-kən-ˈvē-nyənt\ *adj* [ME, fr. MF, fr. L *inconvenient-, inconveniens,* fr. *in-* + *convenient-, conveniens* convenient] (1651) **:** not convenient esp. in giving trouble or annoyance **:** INOPPORTUNE — **in·con·ve·nient·ly** *adv*

in·con·vert·ible \-ˈvərt-ə-bəl\ *adj* [prob. fr. LL *inconvertibilis,* fr. L *in-* + *convertibilis* convertible] (1646) **:** not convertible: as **a** *of paper money* **:** not exchangeable for coin **b** *of a currency* **:** not exchangeable for a foreign currency — **in·con·vert·ibil·i·ty** \-ˌvərt-ə-ˈbil-ət-ē\ *n* — **in·con·vert·ibly** \-ˈvərt-ə-blē\ *adv*

in·con·vinc·ible \ˌin-kən-ˈvin(t)-sə-bəl\ *adj* (1674) **:** incapable of being convinced

in·co·or·di·na·tion \-ˌōrd-ᵊn-ˈā-shən\ *n* (1876) **:** lack of coordination esp. of muscular movements resulting from loss of voluntary control

[1]**in·cor·po·rate** \in-ˈkȯr-pə-ˌrāt\ *vb* **-rat·ed; -rat·ing** [ME *incorporaten,* fr. LL *incorporatus,* pp. of *incorporare,* fr. L *in-* + *corpor-, corpus* body — more at MIDRIFF] *vt* (14c) **1 a :** to unite or work into something already existent so as to form an indistinguishable whole **b :** to blend or combine thoroughly **2 a :** to form into a legal corporation **b :** to admit to membership in a corporate body **3 :** to give material form to **:** EMBODY ~ *vi* **1 :** to unite in or as one body **2 :** to form or become a corporation — **in·cor·po·ra·ble** \-p(ə-)rə-bəl\ *adj* — **in·cor·po·ra·tion** \-ˌkȯr-pə-ˈrā-shən\ *n* — **in·cor·po·ra·tive** \-ˈkȯr-pə-ˌrāt-iv, -p(ə-)rət-\ *adj* — **in·cor·po·ra·tor** \-pə-ˌrāt-ər\ *n*

[2]**in·cor·po·rate** \in-ˈkȯr-p(ə-)rət\ *adj* (14c) **:** INCORPORATED

in·cor·po·rat·ed \-pə-ˌrāt-əd\ *adj* (1594) **1 :** united in one body **2 :** formed into a legal corporation

in·cor·po·re·al \ˌin-(ˌ)kȯr-ˈpōr-ē-əl, -ˈpȯr-\ *adj* [L *incorporeus,* fr. *in-* + *corporeus* corporeal] (15c) **1 :** not corporeal **:** having no material body or form **2 :** of, relating to, or constituting a right that is based on property (as bonds or patents) which has no intrinsic value — **in·cor·po·re·al·ly** \-ə-lē\ *adv*

in·cor·po·re·ity \(ˌ)in-ˌkȯr-pə-ˈrē-ət-ē\ *n* (1601) **:** the quality or state of being incorporeal **:** IMMATERIALITY

in·cor·rect \ˌin-kə-ˈrekt\ *adj* [ME, fr. MF or L; MF, fr. L *incorrectus,* fr. *in-* + *correctus* correct] (15c) **1** *obs* **:** not corrected or chastened **2 a :** INACCURATE, FAULTY **b :** not true **:** WRONG **3 :** UNBECOMING, IMPROPER — **in·cor·rect·ly** \-ˈrek-(t)lē\ *adv* — **in·cor·rect·ness** \-ˈrek(t)-nəs\ *n*

in·cor·ri·gi·ble \(ˈ)in-ˈkȯr-ə-jə-bəl, -ˈkär-\ *adj* [ME, fr. LL *incorrigibilis,* fr. L *in-* + *corrigere* to correct — more at CORRECT] (14c) **:** incapable of being corrected or amended: as **a** (1) **:** not reformable **:** DEPRAVED (2) **:** DELINQUENT **b :** not manageable **:** UNRULY **c :** UNALTERABLE, INVETERATE — **in·cor·ri·gi·bil·i·ty** \(ˌ)in-ˌkȯr-ə-jə-ˈbil-ət-ē, -ˌkär-\ *n* — **incorrigible** *n* — **in·cor·ri·gi·ble·ness** \(ˈ)in-ˈkȯr-ə-jə-bəl-nəs, -ˈkär-\ *n* — **in·cor·ri·gi·bly** \-blē\ *adv*

in·cor·rupt \ˌin-kə-ˈrəpt\ *also* **in·cor·rupt·ed** \-ˈrəp-təd\ *adj* [ME, fr. L *incorruptus,* fr. *in-* + *corruptus* corrupt] (14c) **:** free from corruption: as **a** *obs* **:** not affected with decay **b :** not defiled or depraved **:** UPRIGHT **c :** free from error — **in·cor·rupt·ly** \-ˈrəp-(t)lē\ *adv* — **in·cor·rupt·ness** \-ˈrəp(t)-nəs\ *n*

in·cor·rupt·ible \ˌin-kə-ˈrəp-tə-bəl\ *adj* (14c) **:** incapable of corruption: as **a :** not subject to decay or dissolution **b :** incapable of being bribed or morally corrupted — **in·cor·rupt·ibil·i·ty** \-ˌrəp-tə-ˈbil-ət-ē\ *n* — **incorruptible** *n* — **in·cor·rupt·ibly** \-ˈrəp-tə-blē\ *adv*

in·cor·rup·tion \ˌin-kə-ˈrəp-shən\ *n, archaic* (15c) **:** the quality or state of being free from physical decay

[1]**in·crease** \in-ˈkrēs, ˈin-ˌ\ *vb* **in·creased; in·creas·ing** [ME *encresen,* fr. MF *encreistre,* fr. L *increscere,* fr. *in-* + *crescere* to grow — more at CRESCENT] *vi* (14c) **1 :** to become progressively greater (as in size, amount, number, or intensity) **2 :** to multiply by the production of young ~ *vt* **1 :** to make greater **:** AUGMENT **2** *obs* **:** ENRICH — **in·creas·able** \-ˈkrē-sə-bəl, -ˌkrē-\ *adj* — **in·creas·er** *n*

syn INCREASE, ENLARGE, AUGMENT, MULTIPLY mean to make or become greater. INCREASE used intransitively implies progressive growth in size, amount, intensity; used transitively it may imply simple not necessarily progressive addition; ENLARGE implies expansion or extension that makes greater in size or capacity; AUGMENT implies addition to what is already well grown or well developed; MULTIPLY implies increase in number by natural generation or by indefinite repetition of a process.

[2]**in·crease** \ˈin-ˌkrēs, in-ˈ\ *n* (14c) **1 :** the act or process of increasing: as **a :** addition or enlargement in size, extent, quantity **b** *obs* **:** PROPAGATION **2 :** something that is added to an original stock or amount by augmentation or growth (as offspring, produce, profit)

in·creas·ing·ly \in-ˈkrē-siŋ-lē, ˈin-ˌkrē-\ *adv* (14c) **:** to an increasing degree

in·cre·ate \ˌin-krē-ˈāt, in-ˈkrē-ət\ *adj* [ME *increat,* fr. LL *increatus,* fr. L *in-* + *creatus,* pp. of *creare* to create — more at CRESCENT] (15c) **:** UNCREATED

in·cred·i·ble \(ˈ)in-ˈkred-ə-bəl\ *adj* [ME, fr. L *incredibilis,* fr. *in-* + *credibilis* credible] (15c) **:** too extraordinary and improbable to be believed; *also* **:** hard to believe — **in·cred·ibil·i·ty** \(ˌ)in-ˌkred-ə-ˈbil-ət-ē\ *n* — **in·cred·i·ble·ness** \(ˈ)in-ˈkred-ə-bəl-nəs\ *n* — **in·cred·i·bly** \-blē\ *adv*

in·cre·du·li·ty \ˌin-kri-ˈd(y)ü-lət-ē\ *n* (15c) **:** the quality or state of being incredulous **:** DISBELIEF

in·cred·u·lous \(ˈ)in-ˈkrej-ə-ləs\ *adj* [L *incredulus,* fr. *in-* + *credulus* credulous] (1579) **1 :** unwilling to admit or accept what is offered as true **:** not credulous **:** SKEPTICAL **2** *obs* **:** INCREDIBLE **3 :** expressing incredulity — **in·cred·u·lous·ly** *adv*

in·cre·ment \ˈiŋ-krə-mənt, ˈin-\ *n* [ME, fr. L *incrementum,* fr. *increscere* to increase] (15c) **1 :** the action or process of increasing esp. in quantity or value **:** ENLARGEMENT **2 a :** something gained or added **b :** one of a series of regular consecutive additions **c :** a minute increase in quantity **3 :** the amount or degree by which something changes; *esp* **:** the amount of positive or negative change in the value of one or more of a set of variables — **in·cre·men·tal** \ˌiŋ-krə-ˈment-ᵊl, ˌin-\ *adj* — **in·cre·men·tal·ly** \-ᵊl-ē\ *adv*

in·cre·men·tal·ism \ˌiŋ-krə-ˈment-ᵊl-ˌiz-əm\ *n* (1966) **:** a policy or advocacy of a policy of political or social change by degrees **:** GRADUALISM — **in·cre·men·tal·ist** \-ᵊl-əst\ *n*

incremental repetition *n* (1918) **:** repetition in each stanza (as of a ballad) of part of the preceding stanza usu. with a slight change in wording for dramatic effect

in·cres·cent \in-ˈkres-ᵊnt\ *adj* [L *increscent-, increscens,* prp. of *increscere*] (ca. 1658) **:** becoming gradually greater **:** WAXING ⟨the ~ moon⟩

in·crim·i·nate \in-ˈkrim-ə-ˌnāt\ *vt* **-nat·ed; -nat·ing** [LL *incriminatus,* pp. of *incriminare,* fr. L *in-* + *crimin-, crimen* crime] (1730) **:** to charge with or show evidence or proof of involvement in a crime or fault — **in·crim·i·na·tion** \-ˌkrim-ə-ˈnā-shən\ *n* — **in·crim·i·na·to·ry** \-ˈkrim-(ə-)nə-ˌtōr-ē, -ˌtȯr-\ *adj*

incrust *var of* ENCRUST

in·crus·ta·tion \ˌin-ˌkrəs-ˈtā-shən\ *n* [L *incrustation-, incrustatio,* fr. *incrustatus,* pp. of *incrustare* to encrust] (1644) **1 :** the act of encrusting **:** the state of being encrusted **2 a :** a crust or hard coating **b :** a growth or accumulation (as of habits, opinions, or customs) resembling a crust **3 a :** OVERLAY **a b :** INLAY

in·cu·bate \ˈiŋ-kyə-ˌbāt, ˈin-\ *vb* **-bat·ed; -bat·ing** [L *incubatus,* pp. of *incubare,* fr. *in-* + *cubare* to lie — more at HIP] *vt* (ca. 1721) **1 :** to sit on (eggs) so as to hatch by the warmth of the body; *also* **:** to maintain (as an embryo or a chemically active system) under conditions favorable for hatching, development, or reaction **2 :** to cause (as an idea) to develop ~ *vi* **1 :** to sit on eggs **2 :** to undergo incubation — **in·cu·ba·tive** \-ˌbāt-iv\ *adj* — **in·cu·ba·to·ry** \-kyə-bə-ˌtōr-ē, -ˌtȯr-; -ˌbāt-ə-rē\ *adj*

in·cu·ba·tion \ˌiŋ-kyə-ˈbā-shən, ˌin-\ *n* (1646) **1 :** the act or process of incubating **2 :** the period between the infection of an individual by a pathogen and the manifestation of the disease it causes — **in·cu·ba·tion·al** \-shnəl, -shən-ᵊl\ *adj*

in·cu·ba·tor \ˈiŋ-kyə-ˌbāt-ər, ˈin-\ *n* (1857) **:** one that incubates: as **a :** an apparatus by which eggs are hatched artificially **b :** an apparatus with a chamber used to provide controlled environmental conditions esp. for the cultivation of microorganisms or the care and protection of premature or sick babies

in·cu·bus \ˈiŋ-kyə-bəs, ˈin-\ *n, pl* **-bi** \-ˌbī, -ˌbē\ *also* **-bus·es** [ME, fr. LL, fr. L *incubare*] (13c) **1 :** an evil spirit that lies on persons in their sleep; *esp* **:** one that has sexual intercourse with women while they are sleeping — compare SUCCUBUS **2 :** NIGHTMARE 2 **3 :** one that oppresses or burdens like a nightmare

in·cul·cate \in-ˈkəl-ˌkāt, ˈin-(ˌ)\ *vt* **-cat·ed; -cat·ing** [L *inculcatus,* pp. of *inculcare,* lit., to tread on, fr. *in-* + *calcare* to trample, fr. *calc-, calx* heel — more at CALK] (1550) **:** to teach and impress by frequent repetitions or admonitions ***syn*** see IMPLANT — **in·cul·ca·tion** \ˌin-(ˌ)kəl-ˈkā-shən\ *n* — **in·cul·ca·tor** \in-ˈkəl-ˌkāt-ər, ˈin-(ˌ)\ *n*

in·cul·pa·ble \(ˈ)in-ˈkəl-pə-bəl\ *adj* (15c) **:** free from guilt **:** BLAMELESS

in·cul·pate \in-ˈkəl-ˌpāt, ˈin-(ˌ)\ *vt* **pat·ed; -pat·ing** [LL *inculpatus,* fr. L *in-* + *culpatus,* pp. of *culpare* to blame — more at CULPABLE] (1799) **:** INCRIMINATE — **in·cul·pa·tion** \ˌin-(ˌ)kəl-ˈpā-shən\ *n* — **in·cul·pa·to·ry** \in-ˈkəl-pə-ˌtōr-ē, -ˌtȯr-\ *adj*

in·cult \in-ˈkəlt\ *adj* [L *incultus,* fr. *in-* + *cultus,* pp. of *colere* to cultivate — more at WHEEL] (1599) **:** COARSE, UNCULTURED

in·cum·ben·cy \in-ˈkəm-bən-sē\ *n, pl* **-cies** (1608) **1 :** something that is incumbent **:** DUTY **2 :** the quality or state of being incumbent **3 :** the sphere of action or period of office of an incumbent

[1]**in·cum·bent** \in-ˈkəm-bənt\ *n* [ME, fr. L *incumbent-, incumbens,* prp. of *incumbere* to lie down on, fr. *in-* + *-cumbere* to lie down — more at HIP] (15c) **1 :** the holder of an office or ecclesiastical benefice **2 :** OCCUPANT

[2]**incumbent** *adj* (1567) **1 :** imposed as a duty **:** OBLIGATORY **2 :** having the status of an incumbent; *esp* **:** occupying a specified office **3 a :** lying or resting on something else **b** *of a geologic stratum* **:** lying over other material **:** SUPERIMPOSED **4 :** bent over so as to rest on or touch an underlying surface

incumber *var of* ENCUMBER

in·cu·na·ble \in-ˈkyü-nə-bəl\ *n* [F, fr. NL *incunabulum*] (1886) **:** INCUNABULUM

in·cu·nab·u·lum \ˌin-kyə-ˈnab-yə-ləm, ˌiŋ-\ *n, pl* **-la** \-lə\ [NL, fr. L *incunabula,* pl., swaddling clothes, cradle, fr. *in-* + *cunae* cradle — more at CEMETERY] (ca. 1861) **1 :** a book printed before 1501 **2 :** a work of art or of industry of an early period

in·cur \in-ˈkər\ *vt* **in·curred; in·cur·ring** [L *incurrere,* lit., to run into, fr. *in-* + *currere* to run — more at CURRENT] (15c) **:** to become liable or subject to **:** bring down upon oneself ⟨persons who adopt a child ~ great responsibilities⟩

in·cur·able \(ˈ)in-ˈkyůr-ə-bəl\ *adj* [ME, fr. MF or LL; MF, fr. LL *incurabilis,* fr. L *in-* + *curabilis* curable] (14c) **:** not curable ⟨an ~ disease⟩; *broadly* **:** not likely to be changed or corrected ⟨~ optimism⟩ — **incurable** *n* — **in·cur·ably** \-blē\ *adv*

in·cu·ri·ous \(ˈ)in-ˈkyůr-ē-əs\ *adj* [L *incuriosus,* fr. *in-* + *curiosus* curious] (1613) **:** lacking a normal or usual curiosity **:** UNINTERESTED ⟨a blank ~ stare⟩ ***syn*** see INDIFFERENT — **in·cu·ri·os·i·ty** \(ˌ)in-ˌkyůr-ē-ˈäs-ət-ē\ *n* — **in·cu·ri·ous·ly** \(ˈ)in-ˈkyůr-ē-əs-lē\ *adv* — **in·cu·ri·ous·ness** *n*

in·cur·rence \in-'kər-ən(t)s, -'kə-rən(t)s\ *n* (1656) **:** the act or process of incurring
in·cur·rent \-ənt, -rənt\ *adj* [L *incurrent-, incurrens,* prp. of *incurrere*] (1851) **:** giving passage to a current that flows inward
in·cur·sion \in-'kər-zhən\ *n* [ME, fr. MF or L; MF, fr. L *incursion-, incursio,* fr. *incursus,* pp. of *incurrere*] (15c) **1 :** a hostile entrance into a territory **:** RAID **2 :** an entering in or into (as an activity or undertaking) ⟨his only ~ into the arts⟩
in·cur·vate \'in-,kər-,vāt, (')in-'kər-\ *vt* **-vat·ed; -vat·ing** (1578) **:** to cause to curve inward **:** BEND — **in·cur·vate** \'in-,kər-,vāt, (')in-'kər-vət\ *adj* — **in·cur·va·tion** \,in-,kər-'vā-shən\ *n* — **in·cur·va·ture** \(')in-'kər-və-,chu̇(ə)r, -chər, -,t(y)u̇(ə)r\ *n*
in·curve \(')in-'kərv, 'in-,\ *vt* [L *incurvare,* fr. *in-* + *curvare* to curve, fr. *curvus* curved — more at CROWN] (15c) **:** to bend so as to curve inward
in·cus \'iŋ-kəs\ *n, pl* **in·cu·des** \iŋ-'kyüd-(,)ēz, 'iŋ-kyə-,dēz\ [NL, fr. L, anvil, fr. *incudere*] (1669) **:** the middle of a chain of three small bones in the ear of a mammal — called also *anvil;* see EAR illustration
in·cuse \in-'kyüz, -'kyüs\ *adj* [L *incusus,* pp. of *incudere* to stamp, strike, fr. *in-* + *cudere* to beat — more at HEW] (1818) **:** formed by stamping or punching in — used chiefly of old coins or features of their design
Ind \'ind, 'īnd\ *n* (13c) **1** *archaic* **:** India **2** *obs* **:** Indies
ind- *or* **indi-** *or* **indo-** *comb form* [ISV, fr. L *indicum* — more at INDIGO] **1 :** indigo ⟨*ind*oxyl⟩ **2 :** resembling indigo (as in color) ⟨*indo*phenol⟩
in·da·ba \in-'däb-ə\ *n* [Zulu *in-daba* affair] *chiefly So Afr* (1827) **:** CONFERENCE, PARLEY
in·da·gate \'in-də-,gāt\ *vt* **-gat·ed; -gat·ing** [L *indagatus,* pp. of *indagare,* fr. *indago* act of enclosing, investigation, fr. OL *indu* in + L *agere* to drive — more at INDIGENOUS, AGENT] (1623) **:** to search into **:** INVESTIGATE — **in·da·ga·tion** \,in-də-'gā-shən\ *n* — **in·da·ga·tor** \'in-də-,gāt-ər\ *n*
ind·amine \'in-də-,mēn\ *n* [ISV] (1888) **:** any of a series of organic bases of which the simplest has the formula $C_{12}H_{11}N_3$ and which form salts that are unstable blue and green dyes
in·debt·ed \in-'det-əd\ *adj* [ME *indetted,* fr. OF *endeté,* pp. of *endeter* to involve in debt, fr. *en-* + *dete* debt] (13c) **1 :** owing money **2 :** owing gratitude or recognition to another **:** BEHOLDEN
in·debt·ed·ness *n* (1647) **1 :** the condition of being indebted **2 :** something (as an amount of money) that is owed
in·de·cen·cy \(')in-'dēs-ᵊn-sē\ *n* (1589) **1 :** the quality or state of being indecent **2 :** something (as a word or action) that is indecent
in·de·cent \-ᵊnt\ *adj* [MF or L; MF *indécent,* fr. L *indecent-, indecens,* fr. *in-* + *decent-, decens* decent] (1563) **:** not decent; *esp* **:** grossly unseemly or offensive to manners or morals ***syn*** see INDECOROUS — **in·de·cent·ly** *adv*
indecent assault *n* (1861) **:** an immoral act or series of acts exclusive of rape committed against another person without consent
indecent exposure *n* (1851) **:** intentional exposure of part of one's body (as the genitals) in a place where such exposure is likely to be an offense against the generally accepted standards of decency
in·de·ci·pher·able \,in-di-'sī-f(ə-)rə-bəl\ *adj* (1802) **:** incapable of being deciphered
in·de·ci·sion \,in-di-'sizh-ən\ *n* [F *indécision,* fr. *indécis* undecided, fr. LL *indecisus,* fr. L *in-* + *decisus,* pp. of *decidere* to decide] (ca. 1763) **:** a wavering between two or more possible courses of action **:** IRRESOLUTION
in·de·ci·sive \,in-di-'sī-siv\ *adj* (1726) **1 :** not decisive **:** INCONCLUSIVE **2 :** marked by or prone to indecision **:** IRRESOLUTE **3 :** not clearly marked out **:** INDEFINITE — **in·de·ci·sive·ly** *adv* — **in·de·ci·sive·ness** *n*
in·de·clin·able \,in-di-'klī-nə-bəl\ *adj* [MF, fr. LL *indeclinabilis,* fr. L *in-* + LL *declinabilis* capable of being inflected, fr. L *declinare* to inflect — more at DECLINE] (14c) **:** having no grammatical inflections
in·de·com·pos·able \,in-,dē-kəm-'pō-zə-bəl\ *adj* (1807) **:** not capable of being separated into component parts or elements
in·de·co·rous \(')in-'dek-(ə-)rəs; ,in-di-'kōr-əs, -'kȯr-\ *adj* [L *indecorus,* fr. *in-* + *decorus* decorous] (1682) **:** not decorous — **in·de·co·rous·ly** *adv* — **in·de·co·rous·ness** *n*

syn INDECOROUS, IMPROPER, UNSEEMLY, INDECENT, UNBECOMING, INDELICATE mean not conforming to what is accepted as right, fitting, or in good taste. INDECOROUS suggests a violation of accepted standards of good manners; IMPROPER applies to a broader range of transgressions of rules not only of social behavior but of ethical practice or logical procedure or prescribed method; UNSEEMLY adds a suggestion of special inappropriateness to a situation or an offensiveness to good taste; INDECENT implies great unseemliness or gross offensiveness esp. in referring to sexual matters; UNBECOMING suggests behavior or language that does not suit one's character or status; INDELICATE implies a lack of modesty or of tact or of refined perception of feeling.

in·de·co·rum \,in-di-'kōr-əm, -'kȯr-\ *n* [L, neut. of *indecorus*] (1575) **1 :** something that is indecorous **2 :** lack of decorum **:** IMPROPRIETY
in·deed \in-'dēd\ *adv* (14c) **1 :** without any question **:** TRULY, UNDENIABLY — often used interjectionally to express irony or disbelief or surprise **2 :** in reality **3 :** all things considered **:** as a matter of fact
in·de·fat·i·ga·ble \,in-di-'fat-i-gə-bəl\ *adj* [MF, fr. L *indefatigabilis,* fr. *in-* + *defatigare* to fatigue, fr. *de-* down + *fatigare* to fatigue — more at DE-] (1586) **:** incapable of being fatigued **:** UNTIRING — **in·de·fa·ti·ga·bil·i·ty** \-,fat-i-gə-'bil-ət-ē\ *n* — **in·de·fat·i·ga·ble·ness** \-'fat-i-gə-bəl-nəs\ *n* — **in·de·fat·i·ga·bly** \-blē\ *adv*
in·de·fea·si·ble \-'fē-zə-bəl\ *adj* (1548) **:** not capable of being annulled or voided or undone ⟨an ~ right⟩ — **in·de·fea·si·bil·i·ty** \-,fē-zə-'bil-ət-ē\ *n* — **in·de·fea·si·bly** \-'fē-zə-blē\ *adv*
in·de·fec·ti·ble \-'fek-tə-bəl\ *adj* (1659) **1 :** not subject to failure or decay **:** LASTING **2 :** free of faults **:** FLAWLESS — **in·de·fec·ti·bil·i·ty** \-,fek-tə-'bil-ət-ē\ *n* — **in·de·fec·ti·bly** \-'fek-tə-blē\ *adv*
in·de·fen·si·ble \-'fen(t)-sə-bəl\ *adj* (1529) **1 a :** incapable of being maintained as right or valid **:** UNTENABLE **b :** incapable of being justified or excused **:** INEXCUSABLE **2 :** incapable of being protected against physical attack — **in·de·fen·si·bil·i·ty** \-,fen(t)-sə-'bil-ət-ē\ *n* — **in·de·fen·si·bly** \-'fen(t)-sə-blē\ *adv*
in·de·fin·able \-'fī-nə-bəl\ *adj* (1690) **:** incapable of being precisely described or analyzed — **in·de·fin·abil·i·ty** \-,fī-nə-'bil-ət-ē\ *n* — **indefinable** *n* — **in·de·fin·able·ness** \-'fī-nə-bəl-nəs\ *n* — **in·de·fin·ably** \-blē\ *adv*
in·def·i·nite \(')in-'def-(ə-)nət\ *adj* [L *indefinitus,* fr. *in-* + *definitus* definite] (15c) **:** not definite: as **a :** typically designating an unidentified or not immediately identifiable person or thing ⟨the ~ articles *a* and *an*⟩ **b :** not precise **:** VAGUE **c :** having no exact limits **d** *of floral organs* **:** numerous and difficult to ascertain in number — **indefinite** *n* — **in·def·i·nite·ly** *adv* — **in·def·i·nite·ness** *n*
indefinite integral *n* (ca. 1877) **:** any function whose derivative is a given function
in·de·his·cent \,in-di-'his-ᵊnt\ *adj* (1832) **:** remaining closed at maturity ⟨~ fruits⟩ — **in·de·his·cence** \-ᵊn(t)s\ *n*
in·del·i·ble \in-'del-ə-bəl\ *adj* [ML *indelibilis,* alter. of L *indelebilis,* fr. *in-* + *delēre* to delete] (1529) **1 :** that cannot be removed, washed away, or erased **2 :** making marks that cannot easily be removed ⟨an ~ pencil⟩ **3 :** LASTING, UNFORGETTABLE — **in·del·i·bil·i·ty** \(,)in-,del-ə-'bil-ət-ē\ *n* — **in·del·i·bly** \in-'del-ə-blē\ *adv*
in·del·i·ca·cy \-kə-sē\ *n* (1712) **1 :** the quality or state of being indelicate **2 :** something that is indelicate
in·del·i·cate \(')in-'del-i-kət\ *adj* (1742) **:** not delicate: **a** (1) **:** lacking in or offending against propriety **:** IMPROPER (2) **:** verging on the indecent **:** COARSE **b :** marked by a lack of feeling for the sensibilities of others **:** TACTLESS ***syn*** see INDECOROUS — **in·del·i·cate·ly** *adv* — **in·del·i·cate·ness** *n*
in·dem·ni·fi·ca·tion \in-,dem-nə-fə-'kā-shən\ *n* (1732) **1 a :** the action of indemnifying **b :** the condition of being indemnified **2 :** INDEMNITY 2b
in·dem·ni·fy \in-'dem-nə-,fī\ *vt* **-fied; -fy·ing** [L *indemnis* unharmed, fr. *in-* + *damnum* damage] (1611) **1 :** to secure against hurt, loss, or damage **2 :** to make compensation to for incurred hurt, loss, or damage ***syn*** see PAY — **in·dem·ni·fi·er** \-,fī(-ə)r\ *n*
in·dem·ni·ty \in-'dem-nət-ē\ *n, pl* **-ties** (15c) **1 a :** security against hurt, loss, or damage **b :** exemption from incurred penalties or liabilities **2 a :** INDEMNIFICATION 1 **b :** something that indemnifies
in·de·mon·stra·ble \,in-di-'män(t)-strə-bəl, (,)in-'dem-ən-strə-\ *adj* (1570) **:** incapable of being demonstrated **:** not subject to proof — **in·de·mon·stra·bly** \-blē\ *adv*
in·dene \'in-,dēn\ *n* [ISV, fr. *indole*] (1888) **:** a liquid hydrocarbon C_9H_8 obtained from coal tar and used esp. in making resins
[1]in·dent \in-'dent\ *vb* [ME *indenten,* fr. MF *endenter,* fr. OF, fr. *en-* + *dent* tooth, fr. L *dent-, dens* — more at TOOTH] *vt* (14c) **1 a :** to divide (a document) so as to produce sections with irregular edges that can be matched for authentication **b :** to draw up (as a deed) in two or more exactly corresponding copies **2 :** INDENTURE **3 a :** to notch the edge of **:** make jagged **b :** to cut into for the purpose of mortising or dovetailing **4 :** to set (as a line of a paragraph) in from the margin **5 :** to join together by or as if by mortises or dovetails **6** *chiefly Brit* **:** to order by an indent ~ *vi* **1** *obs* **:** to make a formal or express agreement **2 :** to form an indentation **3** *chiefly Brit* **:** to make out an indent for something — **in·dent·er** *n* — **indent on 1** *chiefly Brit* **:** to make a requisition on **2** *chiefly Brit* **:** to draw on
[2]in·dent \in-'dent, 'in-,\ *n* (15c) **1 a :** INDENTURE 1 **b :** a certificate issued by the U.S. at the close of the American Revolution for the principal or interest on the public debt **2** *chiefly Brit* **a :** an official requisition **b :** a purchase order for goods esp. when sent from a foreign country **3 :** INDENTION
[3]in·dent \in-'dent\ *vt* [ME *endenten,* fr. *en-* + *denten* to dent] (15c) **1 :** to force inward so as to form a depression **2 :** to form a dent in — **in·dent·er** *n*
[4]in·dent \in-'dent, 'in-,\ *n* (1596) **:** INDENTATION
in·den·ta·tion \,in-,den-'tā-shən\ *n* (1728) **1 a :** an angular cut in an edge **:** NOTCH **b :** a recess in a surface **2 :** the action of indenting **:** the condition of being indented **3 :** DENT **4 :** INDENTION 2b
in·den·tion \in-'den-chən\ *n* (1763) **1** *archaic* **:** INDENTATION 1 **2 a :** the action of indenting **:** the condition of being indented **b :** the blank space produced by indenting
[1]in·den·ture \in-'den-chər\ *n* [ME *endenture,* fr. MF, fr. *endenter*] (14c) **1 a** (1) **:** a document or a section of a document that is indented (2) **:** a formal or official document usu. executed in two or more copies (3) **:** a contract binding one person to work for another for a given period of time — usu. used in pl. **b :** a formal certificate (as an inventory or voucher) prepared for purposes of control **c :** a document stating the terms under which a security (as a bond) is issued **2 :** INDENTATION 1 **3** [[3]*indent*] **:** DENT
[2]indenture *vt* **in·den·tured; in·den·tur·ing** \-'dench-(ə-)riŋ\ (1676) **:** to bind (as an apprentice) by or as if by indentures
indentured servant *n* (1723) **:** a person who binds himself by indentures to work for another for a specified time esp. in return for payment of his travel expenses and maintenance
in·de·pen·dence \,in-də-'pen-dən(t)s\ *n* (1640) **1 :** the quality or state of being independent **2** *archaic* **:** COMPETENCE 1
Independence Day *n* (1791) **:** a civil holiday for the celebration of the anniversary of the beginnings of national independence; *specif* **:** July 4 observed as a legal holiday in the U.S. in commemoration of the adoption of the Declaration of Independence in 1776
in·de·pen·den·cy \,in-də-'pen-dən-sē\ *n* (1611) **1 :** INDEPENDENCE 1 **2** *cap* **:** the Independent polity or movement **3 :** an independent political unit
[1]in·de·pen·dent \,in-də-'pen-dənt\ *adj* (1611) **1 :** not dependent: as **a** (1) **:** not subject to control by others **:** SELF-GOVERNING (2) **:** not affiliated with a larger controlling unit **b** (1) **:** not requiring or relying on something else **:** not contingent ⟨an ~ conclusion⟩ (2) **:** not looking to others for one's opinions or for guidance in conduct (3) **:** not bound by or committed to a political party **c** (1) **:** not requiring or relying on others (as for care or livelihood) ⟨~ of his parents⟩ (2) **:** being enough to free one from the necessity of working for a living ⟨a man of ~ means⟩ **d :** showing a desire for freedom ⟨an ~ manner⟩ **e** (1) **:** not determined by or capable of being deduced or derived from or expressed in terms of members (as axioms or equations) of the set under consideration; *esp* **:** having linear independence ⟨an ~ set of vectors⟩ (2) **:** having the property that the joint probability (as of events or samples) or the joint probability density function (as of random variables) equals the product of the probabilities or probability density functions of separate occurrence **2** *cap* **:** of or relating to the Independents **3 a :** MAIN 5 ⟨the ~ clause⟩ **b :** neither deducible from nor incompatible with another statement ⟨~ postulates⟩ ***syn*** see FREE — **in·de·pen·dent·ly** *adv*

²independent *n* (1644) **1** *cap* **:** a sectarian of an English religious movement for congregational autonomy originating in the late 16th century, giving rise to Congregationalists, Baptists, and Friends, and forming one of the major political groupings of the period of Cromwell **2 :** one that is independent; *esp, often cap* **:** one that is not bound by or definitively committed to a political party

independent assortment *n* (ca. 1948) **:** formation of random combinations of chromosomes in meiosis and of genes on different pairs of homologous chromosomes by the passage at random of one of each diploid pair of homologous chromosomes into each gamete independently of each other pair

independent variable *n* (1852) **:** a mathematical variable whose value is specified first and determines the value of one or more other values in an expression or function ⟨in $z = x^2 + 3xy + y^2$, *x* and *y* are *independent variables*⟩

in–depth \(ˌ)in-ˈdepth\ *adj* (1965) **:** COMPREHENSIVE, THOROUGH ⟨an ~ study⟩

in·de·scrib·able \ˌin-di-ˈskrī-bə-bəl\ *adj* (1794) **1 :** that cannot be described ⟨an ~ sensation⟩ **2 :** surpassing description ⟨~ joy⟩ — **in·de·scrib·able·ness** *n* — **in·de·scrib·ably** \-blē\ *adv*

in·de·struc·ti·ble \-ˈstrək-tə-bəl\ *adj* [prob. fr. LL *indestructibilis,* fr. L *in-* + *destructus,* pp. of *destruere* to tear down — more at DESTROY] (1667) **:** not destructible — **in·de·struc·ti·bil·i·ty** \-ˌstrək-tə-ˈbil-ət-ē\ *n* — **in·de·struc·ti·ble·ness** \-ˈstrək-tə-bəl-nəs\ *n* — **in·de·struc·ti·bly** \-blē\ *adv*

in·de·ter·min·able \ˌin-di-ˈtərm-(ə-)nə-bəl\ *adj* (15c) **1 :** incapable of being definitely decided or settled **2 :** incapable of being definitely fixed or ascertained — **in·de·ter·min·ably** \-blē\ *adv*

in·de·ter·mi·na·cy \-ˈtərm-(ə-)nə-sē\ *n* (1649) **:** the quality or state of being indeterminate

indeterminacy principle *n* (ca. 1928) **:** UNCERTAINTY PRINCIPLE

in·de·ter·mi·nate \ˌin-di-ˈtərm-(ə-)nət\ *adj* [ME *indeterminat,* fr. LL *indeterminatus,* fr. L *in-* + *determinatus,* pp. of *determinare* to determine] (14c) **1 a :** not definitely or precisely determined or fixed **:** VAGUE **b :** not known in advance **c :** not leading to a definite end or result **2 :** having an infinite number of solutions ⟨a system of ~ equations⟩ **3 :** being one of the seven undefined mathematical expressions

$$\frac{0}{0}, \frac{\infty}{\infty}, \infty \cdot 0, 1^{\infty}, 0^{0}, \infty^{0}, \infty - \infty$$

4 : RACEMOSE — **in·de·ter·mi·nate·ly** *adv* — **in·de·ter·mi·nate·ness** *n* — **in·de·ter·mi·na·tion** \-ˌtər-mə-ˈnā-shən\ *n*

in·de·ter·min·ism \-ˈtər-mə-ˌniz-əm\ *n* (1874) **1 a :** a theory that the will is free and that deliberate choice and actions are not determined by or predictable from antecedent causes **b :** a theory that holds that not every event has a cause **2 :** the quality or state of being indeterminate; *esp* **:** UNPREDICTABILITY — **in·de·ter·min·ist** \-ˈtərm-(ə-)nəst\ *n* — **in·de·ter·min·is·tic** \-ˌtər-mə-ˈnis-tik\ *adj*

¹in·dex \ˈin-ˌdeks\ *n, pl* **in·dex·es** *or* **in·di·ces** \-də-ˌsēz\ [L *indic-, index,* fr. *indicare* to indicate] (1571) **1 a :** a device (as the pointer on a scale or the gnomon of a sundial) that serves to indicate a value or quantity **b :** something (as a physical feature or a mode of expression) that leads one to a particular fact or conclusion **:** INDICATION ⟨the fertility of the land is an ~ of the country's wealth⟩ **2 :** a list (as of bibliographical information or citations to a body of literature) arranged usu. in alphabetical order of some specified datum (as author, subject, or keyword): as **a :** a list of items (as topics or names) treated in a printed work that gives for each item the page number where it may be found **b :** THUMB INDEX **c :** a bibliographical analysis of groups of publications that is usu. published periodically **3 :** a list of restricted or prohibited material; *specif, cap* **:** a list of books the reading of which is prohibited or restricted for Roman Catholics by the church authorities **4** *pl usu indices* **:** a number or symbol or expression (as an exponent) associated with another to indicate a mathematical operation to be performed or to indicate use or position in an arrangement ⟨the *indices* 2 and 3 locate the element a_{23} in the second row and third column of a determinant⟩ **5 :** a character ☞ used to direct attention to a note or paragraph — called also *fist* **6 a :** a number (as a ratio) derived from a series of observations and used as an indicator or measure (as of a condition, property, or phenomenon); *specif* **:** INDEX NUMBER **b :** the ratio of one dimension of a thing (as an anatomical structure) to another dimension — **in·dex·i·cal** \in-ˈdek-si-kəl\ *adj*

²index *vt* (1720) **1 a :** to provide with an index **b :** to list in an index ⟨all persons and places mentioned are carefully *~ed*⟩ **2 :** to serve as an index of **3 :** to regulate (as wages, prices, or interest rates) by indexation **~** *vi* **:** to index something — **in·dex·er** *n*

in·dex·ation \ˌin-dek-ˈsā-shən\ *n* (1960) **:** a system of economic control in which certain variables (as wages and interest) are tied to a cost-of-living index so that both rise or fall at the same rate and the detrimental effect of inflation is theoretically eliminated

index finger *n* (1849) **:** FOREFINGER

index fossil *n* (1900) **:** a fossil usu. with a narrow time range and wide spatial distribution that is used in the identification of related geologic formations

in·dex·ing *n* (ca. 1974) **:** INDEXATION

index number *n* (ca. 1896) **:** a number used to indicate change in magnitude (as of cost or price) as compared with the magnitude at some specified time usu. taken as 100

index of refraction (ca. 1829) **:** the ratio of the speed of radiation (as light) in the first of two media to its speed in the second as it passes from one into the other

indi- — see IND-

In·dia \ˈin-dē-ə\ (ca. 1952) — a communications code word for the letter *i*

india ink *n, often cap 1st I* (1665) **1 :** a solid black pigment (as specially prepared lampblack) used in drawing and lettering **2 :** a fluid ink consisting usu. of a fine suspension of india ink in a liquid

In·dia·man \ˈin-dē-ə-mən\ *n* (1709) **:** a merchant ship formerly used in trade with India; *esp* **:** a large sailing ship used in this trade

In·di·an \ˈin-dē-ən *also* ˈin-din *or chiefly dial* -jən\ *n* (14c) **1 :** a native or inhabitant of the subcontinent of India or of the East Indies **2 a** [fr. the belief held by Columbus that the lands he discovered were part of Asia] **:** AMERICAN INDIAN **b :** one of the native languages of American Indians — **Indian** *adj* — **In·di·an·ness** *n*

Indian agent *n* (1807) **:** an official representative of the U.S. federal government to American Indian tribes esp. on reservations

Indian club *n* (1857) **:** a usu. wooden club shaped like a large bottle or tenpin that is swung for gymnastic exercise

Indian corn *n* (1617) **1 :** a tall widely cultivated American cereal grass (*Zea mays*) bearing seeds on elongated ears **2 :** the ears of Indian corn; *also* **:** its edible seeds

Indian elephant *n* (1607) **:** ELEPHANT 1b

Indian file *n* (1758) **:** SINGLE FILE

Indian giver *n* (ca. 1848) **:** one that gives something to another and then takes it back or expects an equivalent in return — **Indian giving** *n*

Indian hemp *n* (1619) **1 :** an American dogbane (*Apocynum cannabinum*) with milky juice, tough fibrous bark, and an emetic and cathartic root **2 :** HEMP 1

In·di·an·ism \ˈin-dē-ə-ˌniz-əm\ *n* (1651) **1 :** the qualities or culture distinctive of Indians **2 :** policy designed to further the interests or culture of Indians — **In·di·an·ist** \-nəst\ *adj or n*

Indian licorice *n* (ca. 1890) **:** ROSARY PEA 1

Indian meal *n* (1609) **:** CORNMEAL

Indian paintbrush *n* (1892) **1 :** any of a genus (*Castilleja*) of herbaceous plants of the figwort family that have brightly colored bracts — called also *painted cup* **2 :** ORANGE HAWKWEED

Indian pipe *n* (1817) **:** a waxy white leafless saprophytic herb (*Monotropa uniflora* of the family Monotropaceae, the Indian-pipe family) of Asia and the U.S.

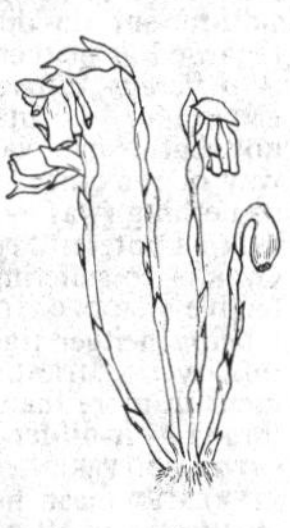

Indian pipe

Indian pudding *n* (1722) **:** a baked pudding made chiefly of cornmeal, milk, and molasses

Indian red *n* (ca. 1753) **1 a :** a yellowish red earth containing hematite and used as a pigment **b :** any of various light red to purplish brown pigments made by calcining iron salts **2 :** a strong or moderate reddish brown

Indian sign *n* (1910) **:** HEX, SPELL

Indian summer *n* (1778) **1 :** a period of warm or mild weather in late autumn or early winter **2 :** a happy or flourishing period occurring toward the end of something ⟨life in the *Indian summer* of Czarist Russia —John Davenport⟩

Indian tobacco *n* (1618) **1 :** an American wild lobelia (*Lobelia inflata*) with small blue flowers **2 :** a wild tobacco (*Nicotiana bigelovii*) found in dry valleys from southern California to southern Oregon

In·di·an–wres·tle \ˈin-dē-ən-ˌres-əl, -ˌras-\ *vi* [back-formation fr. *Indian wrestling*] (1938) **:** to engage in Indian wrestling

Indian wrestling *n* (1913) **1 :** wrestling in which two people lie side by side on their backs in reversed position locking their near arms and raising and locking the corresponding legs and attempt to force each other's leg down and turn the other wrestler on his face **2 :** wrestling in which two people stand face to face gripping usu. their right hands and setting the outsides of the corresponding feet together and attempt to force each other off balance **3 :** ARM WRESTLING

India paper *n* (1768) **1 :** a thin absorbent paper used esp. for proving inked intaglio surfaces (as steel engravings) **2 :** a thin tough opaque printing paper

india rubber *n, often cap I* (1790) **:** ¹RUBBER 2a

In·dic \ˈin-dik\ *adj* (1877) **1 :** of or relating to the subcontinent of India **:** INDIAN **2 :** of, relating to, or constituting the Indian branch of the Indo-European languages — see INDO-EUROPEAN LANGUAGES table — **Indic** *n*

in·di·can \ˈin-də-ˌkan\ *n* [L *indicum* indigo — more at INDIGO] (1859) **1 :** an indigo-forming substance $C_8H_7NO_4S$ found as a salt in urine and other animal fluids; *also* **:** its potassium salt $C_8H_6KNO_4S$ **2 :** a glucoside $C_{14}H_{17}NO_6$ occurring esp. in the indigo plant and being a source of natural indigo

in·di·cant \ˈin-di-kənt\ *n* (1623) **:** something that serves to indicate

in·di·cate \ˈin-də-ˌkāt\ *vt* **-cat·ed; -cat·ing** [L *indicatus,* pp. of *indicare,* fr. *in-* + *dicare* to proclaim, dedicate — more DICTION] (1651) **1 a :** to point out or point to **b :** to be a sign, symptom, or index of ⟨the high fever *~s* a serious condition⟩ **c :** to demonstrate or suggest the necessity or advisability of ⟨*indicated* the need for a new school⟩ **2 :** to state or express briefly **:** SUGGEST ⟨*indicated* his desire to cooperate⟩

in·di·ca·tion \ˌin-də-ˈkā-shən\ *n* (15c) **1 a :** something that serves to indicate **b :** something that is indicated as advisable or necessary **2 :** the action of indicating **3 :** the degree indicated on a graduated instrument **:** READING — **in·di·ca·tion·al** \-shnəl, -shən-ᵊl\ *adj*

¹in·dic·a·tive \in-ˈdik-ət-iv\ *adj* (15c) **1 :** of, relating to, or constituting a verb form or set of verb forms that represents the denoted act or state as an objective fact ⟨the ~ mood⟩ **2 :** serving to indicate ⟨actions ~ of fear⟩ — **in·dic·a·tive·ly** *adv*

²indicative *n* (1530) **1 :** the indicative mood of a language **2 :** a form in the indicative mood

in·di·ca·tor \ˈin-də-ˌkāt-ər\ *n* (1660) **1 :** one that indicates: as **a :** an index hand (as on a dial) **:** POINTER **b** (1) **:** a pressure gauge (2) **:** an instrument for automatically making a diagram that indicates the pressure in and volume of the working fluid of an engine throughout the cycle **c :** a dial that registers something (as the movement of an elevator) **2 a :** a substance (as litmus) used to show visually (as by change of color) the condition of a solution with respect to the presence of a particular material (as a free acid or alkali) **b :** TRACER 4b **3 :** an organism or ecological community so strictly associated with particular environmental conditions that its presence is indicative of the existence of these conditions **4 :** any of a group of statistical values (as level of employment) that taken together give an indication of the health of the economy — **in·dic·a·to·ry** \in-ˈdik-ə-ˌtȯr-ē, -ˌtȯr-\ *adj*

indices *pl of* INDEX

in·di·cia \in-ˈdish-(ē-)ə\ *n pl* [L, pl. of *indicium* sign, fr. *indicare*] (1625) **1 :** distinctive marks **:** INDICATIONS **2 :** postal markings often imprinted on mail or on labels to be affixed to mail

in·dict \in-ˈdīt\ *vt* [alter. of earlier *indite,* fr. ME *inditen,* fr. AF *enditer,* fr. OF, to write down — more at INDITE] (14c) **1 :** to charge with a fault or offense **:** CRITICIZE, ACCUSE **2 :** to charge with a crime by the finding or presentment of a jury (as a grand jury) in due form of law — **in·dict·er** *or* **in·dict·or** \-ˈdīt-ər\ *n*

in·dict·able \-ˈdīt-ə-bəl\ *adj* (1706) **1 :** subject to being indicted **:** liable to indictment **2 :** making one liable to indictment ⟨an ~ offense⟩

in·dic·tion \in-ˈdik-shən\ *n* [ME *indiccioun,* fr. LL *indiction-, indictio,* fr. L, proclamation, fr. *indictus,* pp. of *indicere* to proclaim, fr. *in-* + *dicere* to say — more at DICTION] (14c) **:** a 15-year cycle used as a chronological unit in several ancient and medieval systems

in·dict·ment \in-ˈdīt-mənt\ *n* (14c) **1 a :** the action or the legal process of indicting **b :** the state of being indicted **2 :** a formal written statement framed by a prosecuting authority and found by a jury (as a grand jury) charging a person with an offense

in·dif·fer·ence \in-ˈdif-ərn(t)s, -ˈdif-(ə-)rən(t)s\ *n* (15c) **1 :** the quality, state, or fact of being indifferent **2 a** *archaic* **:** lack of difference or distinction between two or more things **b :** absence of compulsion to or toward one thing or another

in·dif·fer·en·cy \-ərn-sē, -(ə-)rən-sē\ *n, archaic* (15c) **:** INDIFFERENCE

in·dif·fer·ent \in-ˈdif-ərnt, -ˈdif-(ə-)rənt\ *adj* [ME, fr. MF or L; MF, regarded as neither good nor bad, fr. L *indifferent-, indifferens,* fr. *in-* + *different-, differens,* prp. of *differre* to be different — more at DIFFERENT] (14c) **1 :** marked by impartiality **:** UNBIASED **2 a :** that does not matter one way or the other **b :** of no importance or value one way or the other **3 a :** marked by no special liking for or dislike of something ⟨was ~ about which book he was given⟩ **b :** marked by a lack of interest, enthusiasm, or concern for something **:** APATHETIC ⟨was ~ to suffering and poverty⟩ **4 :** being neither excessive nor defective **:** MODERATE **5 a :** being neither good nor bad **:** MEDIOCRE **b :** being neither right nor wrong **6 :** characterized by lack of active quality **:** NEUTRAL **7 a :** not differentiated **b :** capable of development in more than one direction; *esp* **:** not yet embryologically determined — **in·dif·fer·ent·ly** *adv*

syn INDIFFERENT, UNCONCERNED, INCURIOUS, ALOOF, DETACHED, DISINTERESTED mean not showing or feeling interest. INDIFFERENT implies neutrality of attitude from lack of inclination, preference, or prejudice; UNCONCERNED suggests a lack of sensitivity or regard for others' needs or troubles; INCURIOUS implies an inability to take a normal interest due to dullness of mind or to self-centeredness; ALOOF suggests a cool reserve arising from a sense of superiority or disdain for inferiors or from shyness; DETACHED implies an objective attitude achieved through absence of prejudice or selfishness; DISINTERESTED implies a circumstantial freedom from concern for personal or esp. financial advantage that enables one to judge or advise without bias.

in·dif·fer·ent·ism \-ərnt-ˌiz-əm, -(ə-)rənt-\ *n* (1827) **:** INDIFFERENCE; *specif* **:** belief that all religions are equally valid — **in·dif·fer·ent·ist** \-əst\ *n*

in·di·gence \ˈin-di-jən(t)s\ *n* (14c) **:** a level of poverty in which real hardship and deprivation are suffered and comforts of life are wholly lacking ***syn*** see POVERTY

in·di·gene \ˈin-də-ˌjēn\ *also* **in·di·gen** \-di-jən, -də-ˌjen\ *n* [L *indigena*] (1598) **:** NATIVE

in·dig·e·nous \in-ˈdij-ə-nəs\ *adj* [LL *indigenus,* fr. L *indigena,* n., native, fr. OL *indu, endo* in, within (akin to L *in* and to L *de* down) + L *gignere* to beget — more at DE-, KIN] (1646) **1 :** having originated in and being produced, growing, living, or occurring naturally in a particular region or environment **2 :** INNATE, INBORN ***syn*** see NATIVE — **in·dig·e·nous·ly** *adv* — **in·dig·e·nous·ness** *n*

in·di·gent \ˈin-di-jənt\ *adj* [ME, fr. MF, fr. L *indigent-, indigens,* prp. of *indigēre* to need, fr. OL *indu* + L *egēre* to need; akin to OHG *ekrōdi* thin] (15c) **1 :** suffering from indigence **:** IMPOVERISHED **2 a** *archaic* **:** DEFICIENT **b** *archaic* **:** totally lacking in something specified — **indigent** *n*

in·di·gest·ed \ˌin-(ˌ)dī-ˈjes-təd, -də-\ *adj* (1587) **:** not carefully thought out or arranged **:** FORMLESS

in·di·gest·ible \-ˈjes-tə-bəl\ *adj* [LL *indigestibilis,* fr. L *in-* + LL *digestibilis* digestible] (15c) **:** not digestible **:** not easily digested — **in·di·gest·ibil·i·ty** \-ˌjes-tə-ˈbil-ət-ē\ *n* — **indigestible** *n*

in·di·ges·tion \-ˈjes(h)-chən\ *n* (14c) **1 :** inability to digest or difficulty in digesting something **2 :** a case or attack of indigestion

in·dign \in-ˈdīn\ *adj* [ME *indigne,* fr. MF, fr. L *indignus*] (14c) **1** *archaic* **:** UNWORTHY, UNDESERVING **2** *obs* **:** UNBECOMING, DISGRACEFUL

in·dig·nant \in-ˈdig-nənt\ *adj* [L *indignant-, indignans,* prp. of *indignari* to be indignant, fr. *indignus* unworthy, fr. *in-* + *dignus* worthy — more at DECENT] (1590) **:** filled with or marked by indignation ⟨became ~ at the accusation⟩ — **in·dig·nant·ly** *adv*

in·dig·na·tion \ˌin-dig-ˈnā-shən\ *n* (14c) **:** anger aroused by something unjust, unworthy, or mean ***syn*** see ANGER

in·dig·ni·ty \in-ˈdig-nət-ē\ *n, pl* **-ties** [L *indignitat-, indignitas,* fr. *indignus*] (1584) **1 a :** an act that offends against a person's dignity or self-respect **:** INSULT **b :** humiliating treatment **2** *obs* **:** lack or loss of dignity or honor

in·di·go \ˈin-di-ˌgō\ *n, pl* **-gos** *or* **-goes** [It dial., fr. L *indicum,* fr. Gk *indikon,* fr. neut. of *indikos* Indic, fr. *Indos* India] (1555) **1 a :** a blue vat dye obtained from plants (as indigo plants) **b :** the principal coloring matter $C_{16}H_{10}N_2O_2$ of natural indigo usu. synthesized as a blue powder with a coppery luster **c :** any of several blue vat dyes derived from or closely related to indigo **2 :** INDIGO PLANT **3 :** a variable color averaging a dark grayish blue

indigo bunting *n* (1783) **:** a common small finch (*Passerina cyanea*) of the eastern U.S. of which the male is largely indigo-blue

indigo plant *n* (1757) **:** a plant that yields indigo; *esp* **:** any of a genus (*Indigofera*) of leguminous herbs

indigo snake *n* (ca. 1885) **:** a large harmless blue-black snake (*Drymarchon corais couperi*) of the southern U.S. — called also *gopher snake*

in·di·go·tin \in-ˈdig-ət-ən, ˌin-di-ˈgōt-ᵊn\ *n* [ISV *indigo* + connective *-t-* + *-in*] (1838) **:** INDIGO 1b

in·di·rect \ˌin-də-ˈrekt, -(ˌ)dī-\ *adj* [ME, fr. ML *indirectus,* fr. L *in-* + *directus* direct] (14c) **:** not direct: as **a** (1) **:** deviating from a direct line or course **:** ROUNDABOUT (2) **:** not going straight to the point ⟨an ~ accusation⟩ (3) **:** being or involving proof of a proposition or theorem by demonstration that its negation leads to an absurdity or contradiction **b :** not straightforward and open **:** DECEITFUL **c :** not directly aimed at or achieved ⟨~ consequences⟩ **d :** stating what a real or supposed original speaker said with changes in wording that conform the statement grammatically to the sentence in which it is included ⟨~ discourse⟩ **e :** not effected by the action of the people or the electorate ⟨~ government representation⟩ — **in·di·rect·ly** \-ˈrek-(t)lē\ *adv* — **in·di·rect·ness** \-ˈrek(t)-nəs\ *n*

indirect cost *n* (ca. 1909) **:** a cost that is not identifiable with a specific product, function, or activity

indirect evidence *n* (1824) **:** evidence that establishes immediately collateral facts from which the main fact may be inferred **:** CIRCUMSTANTIAL EVIDENCE

in·di·rec·tion \ˌin-də-ˈrek-shən, -(ˌ)dī-\ *n* (1595) **1 a :** lack of straightforwardness and openness **:** DECEITFULNESS **b :** something (as an act or statement) marked by lack of straightforwardness ⟨hated diplomatic ~*s* —*Rev. of Reviews*⟩ **2 a :** indirect action or procedure **b :** lack of direction **:** AIMLESSNESS

indirect lighting *n* (1922) **:** lighting in which the light emitted by a source is diffusely reflected (as by the ceiling)

indirect object *n* (ca. 1879) **:** a grammatical object representing the secondary goal of the action of its verb ⟨*her* in "I gave her the book" is an *indirect object*⟩

in·dis·cern·ible \ˌin-dis-ˈər-nə-bəl, -diz-\ *adj* (1635) **:** incapable of being discerned **:** not recognizable as distinct

in·dis·ci·plin·able \(ˌ)in-ˌdis-ə-ˈplin-ə-bəl; (ˈ)in-ˈdis-ə-plən-\ *adj* (1600) **:** not subject to or capable of being disciplined

in·dis·ci·pline \(ˈ)in-ˈdis-ə-plən\ *n* (1783) **:** lack of discipline — **in·dis·ci·plined** \-plənd, -(ˌ)plind\ *adj*

in·dis·cov·er·able \ˌin-dis-ˈkəv-(ə-)rə-bəl\ *adj* (1640) **:** not discoverable

in·dis·creet \ˌin-dis-ˈkrēt\ *adj* [ME *indiscrete,* fr. MF & LL; MF *indiscret,* fr. LL *indiscretus,* fr. L, indistinguishable, fr. *in-* + *discretus,* pp. of *discernere* to separate — more at DISCERN] (15c) **:** not discreet **:** IMPRUDENT — **in·dis·creet·ly** *adv* — **in·dis·creet·ness** *n*

in·dis·crete \ˌin-dis-ˈkrēt, (ˈ)in-ˈdis-ˌ\ *adj* [L *indiscretus*] (1782) **:** not separated into distinct parts ⟨an ~ mass⟩

in·dis·cre·tion \ˌin-dis-ˈkresh-ən\ *n* (14c) **1 :** lack of discretion **:** IMPRUDENCE **2 :** something (as an act or remark) marked by lack of discretion; *specif* **:** an act at variance with the accepted morality of a society

in·dis·crim·i·nate \ˌin-dis-ˈkrim-(ə-)nət\ *adj* (1649) **1 a :** not marked by careful distinction **:** deficient in discrimination and discernment ⟨~ reading habits⟩ **b :** HAPHAZARD, RANDOM ⟨~ application of a law⟩ **2 a :** PROMISCUOUS, UNRESTRAINED ⟨~ sexual behavior⟩ **b :** HETEROGENEOUS, CONFUSED ⟨clothes tossed in an ~ heap⟩ — **in·dis·crim·i·nate·ly** *adv* — **in·dis·crim·i·nate·ness** *n*

in·dis·crim·i·nat·ing \-ˈkrim-ə-ˌnāt-iŋ\ *adj* (1754) **:** not discriminating — **in·dis·crim·i·nat·ing·ly** \-iŋ-lē\ *adv*

in·dis·crim·i·na·tion \-ˌkrim-ə-ˈnā-shən\ *n* (1649) **:** lack of discrimination

in·dis·cuss·ible \ˌin-dis-ˈkəs-ə-bəl\ *adj* (1893) **:** not capable of being discussed

in·dis·pens·able \ˌin-dis-ˈpen(t)-sə-bəl\ *adj* (1653) **1 :** not subject to being set aside or neglected ⟨an ~ obligation⟩ **2 :** absolutely necessary **:** ESSENTIAL ⟨carbon dioxide is ~ for plants⟩ — **in·dis·pens·abil·i·ty** \-ˌpen(t)-sə-ˈbil-ət-ē\ *n* — **indispensable** *n* — **in·dis·pens·able·ness** \-ˈpen(t)-sə-bəl-nəs\ *n* — **in·dis·pens·ably** \-blē\ *adv*

in·dis·pose \ˌin-dis-ˈpōz\ *vt* **-posed; -pos·ing** [prob. back-formation fr. *indisposed*] (1657) **1 a :** to make unfit **:** DISQUALIFY **b :** to make averse **:** DISINCLINE **2** *archaic* **:** to cause to be in poor physical health

in·dis·posed \-ˈpōzd\ *adj* (15c) **1 :** slightly ill **2 :** AVERSE

in·dis·po·si·tion \(ˌ)in-ˌdis-pə-ˈzish-ən\ *n* (15c) **:** the condition of being indisposed: **a :** DISINCLINATION **b :** a usu. slight illness

in·dis·put·able \ˌin-dis-ˈpyüt-ə-bəl, (ˈ)in-ˈdis-pyət-\ *adj* [LL *indisputabilis,* fr. L *in-* + *disputabilis* disputable] (1551) **:** not disputable **:** UNQUESTIONABLE ⟨~ proof⟩ — **in·dis·put·able·ness** *n* — **in·dis·put·ably** \-blē\ *adv*

in·dis·so·cia·ble \ˌin-dis-ˈō-sh(ē-)ə-bəl, -sē-ə-\ *adj* (1855) **:** not dissociated **:** INSEPARABLE — **in·dis·so·cia·bly** \-blē\ *adv*

in·dis·sol·u·ble \ˌin-dis-ˈäl-yə-bəl\ *adj* (1542) **:** not dissoluble: as **a :** incapable of being annulled, undone, or broken **:** PERMANENT ⟨an ~ contract⟩ **b :** incapable of being separated, dissolved, decomposed, or disintegrated — **in·dis·sol·u·bil·i·ty** \-ˌäl-yə-ˈbil-ət-ē\ *n* — **in·dis·sol·u·ble·ness** \-ˈäl-yə-bəl-nəs\ *n* — **in·dis·sol·u·bly** \-blē\ *adv*

in·dis·tinct \ˌin-dis-ˈtiŋ(k)t\ *adj* [L *indistinctus,* fr. *in-* + *distinctus* distinct] (1526) **:** not distinct: as **a :** not sharply outlined or separable **:** BLURRED ⟨~ figures in the fog⟩ **b :** FAINT, DIM ⟨an ~ light in the distance⟩ **c :** not clearly recognizable or understandable **:** UNCERTAIN — **in·dis·tinct·ly** \-ˈtiŋ(k)-tlē, -ˈtiŋ-klē\ *adv* — **in·dis·tinct·ness** \-ˈtiŋt-nəs, -ˈtiŋk-nəs\ *n*

in·dis·tinc·tive \-ˈtiŋ(k)-tiv\ *adj* (1846) **:** lacking distinctive qualities

in·dis·tin·guish·able \ˌin-dis-ˈtiŋ-(g)wish-ə-bəl\ *adj* (1606) **:** not distinguishable: as **a :** indeterminate in shape or structure **b :** not clearly recognizable or understandable **c :** lacking identifying or individualizing qualities — **in·dis·tin·guish·abil·i·ty** \-ˌtiŋ-(g)wish-ə-ˈbil-ət-ē\ *n* — **in·dis·tin·guish·able·ness** \-ˈtiŋ-(g)wish-ə-bəl-nəs\ *n* — **in·dis·tin·guish·ably** \-blē\ *adv*

in·dite \in-ˈdīt\ *vt* **in·dit·ed; in·dit·ing** [ME *enditen,* fr. OF *enditer* to write down, proclaim, fr. (assumed) VL *indictare* to proclaim, fr. L *indictus,* pp. of *indicere* to proclaim, fr. *in-* + *dicere* to say — more at DICTION] (14c) **1 a :** MAKE UP, COMPOSE ⟨~ a poem⟩ **b :** to give literary or formal expression to **c :** to put down in writing ⟨~ a message⟩ **2** *obs* **:** DICTATE — **in·dit·er** *n*

in·di·um \ˈin-dē-əm\ *n* [ISV *ind-* + NL *-ium*] (1864) **:** a malleable fusible silvery metallic element that is chiefly trivalent, occurs esp. in sphalerite ores, and is used as a plating for bearings, in alloys melting at a low temperature, and in the making of transistors — see ELEMENT table

¹in·di·vid·u·al \ˌin-də-ˈvij-(ə-)wəl, -ˈvij-əl\ *adj* [ML *individualis,* fr. L *individuus* indivisible, fr. *in-* + *dividuus* divided, fr. *dividere* to divide] (15c) **1** *obs* **:** INSEPARABLE **2 a :** of, relating to, or distinctively associated with an individual ⟨an ~ effort⟩ **b :** being an individual or existing as an indivisible whole **c** : intended for one person ⟨an ~ serving⟩ **3** : existing as a distinct entity : SEPARATE **4** : having marked individuality ⟨an ~ style⟩ ***syn*** see SPECIAL, CHARACTERISTIC — **in·di·vid·u·al·ly** \-ē\ *adv*

²individual *n* (1605) **1 a** : a particular being or thing as distinguished from a class, species, or collection: as **(1)** : a single human being as contrasted with a social group or institution ⟨a teacher who works with ~s⟩ **(2)** : a single organism as distinguished from a group **b** : a particular person ⟨are you the ~ I spoke with on the telephone?⟩ **2** : an indivisible entity **3** : the reference of a name or variable of the lowest logical type in a calculus

in·di·vid·u·al·ism \ˌin-də-ˈvij-(ə-)wə-ˌliz-əm, -ˈvij-ə-ˌliz-\ *n* (1827) **1 a (1)** : a doctrine that the interests of the individual are or ought to be ethically paramount; *also* : conduct guided by such a doctrine **(2)** : the conception that all values, rights, and duties originate in individuals **b** : a theory maintaining the political and economic independence of the individual and stressing individual initiative, action, and interests; *also* : conduct or practice guided by such a theory **2 a** : INDIVIDUALITY **b** : an individual peculiarity : IDIOSYNCRASY

in·di·vid·u·al·ist \-ləst\ *n* (1840) **1** : one that pursues a markedly independent course in thought or action **2** : one that advocates or practices individualism — **individualist** *or* **in·di·vid·u·al·is·tic** \-ˌvij-(ə-)wə-ˈlis-tik, -ˌvij-ə-ˈlis-\ *adj* — **in·di·vid·u·al·is·ti·cal·ly** \-ˈlis-ti-k(ə-)lē\ *adv*

in·di·vid·u·al·i·ty \-ˌvij-ə-ˈwal-ət-ē\ *n, pl* **-ties** (1614) **1 a** : total character peculiar to and distinguishing an individual from others **b** : PERSONALITY **2** *archaic* : the quality or state of being indivisible : INSEPARABILITY **3** : separate or distinct existence **4** : INDIVIDUAL, PERSON

in·di·vid·u·al·ize \-ˈvij-(ə-)wə-ˌlīz, -ˈvij-ə-ˌlīz\ *vt* **-ized; -iz·ing** (1637) **1** : to make individual in character **2** : to treat or notice individually : PARTICULARIZE **3** : to adapt to the needs or special circumstances of an individual ⟨efforts to ~ teaching according to student ability and interest⟩ — **in·di·vid·u·al·iza·tion** \-ˌvij-(ə-)wə-lə-ˈzā-shən, -ˌvij-ə-lə-\ *n*

individual medley *n* (ca. 1949) : a swimming race in which each contestant swims each quarter of the course with a different stroke

in·di·vid·u·ate \ˌin-də-ˈvij-ə-ˌwāt\ *vt* **-at·ed; -at·ing** (1614) **1** : to give individuality to **2** : to form into a distinct entity

in·di·vid·u·a·tion \-ˌvij-ə-ˈwā-shən\ *n* (1628) **1** : the act or process of individuating: as **a (1)** : the development of the individual from the universal **(2)** : the determination of the individual in the general **b** : the process by which individuals in society become differentiated from one another **c** : regional differentiation along a primary embryonic axis **2** : the state of being individuated; *specif* : INDIVIDUALITY

in·di·vis·i·ble \ˌin-də-ˈviz-ə-bəl\ *adj* [ME, fr. LL *indivisibilis,* fr. L *in-* + LL *divisibilis* divisible] (14c) : not divisible — **in·di·vis·i·bil·i·ty** \-ˌviz-ə-ˈbil-ət-ē\ *n* — **indivisible** *n* — **in·di·vis·i·bly** \-ˈviz-ə-blē\ *adv*

indo- — see IND-

Indo- *comb form* [Gk, fr. *Indos* India] **1** : India or the East Indies ⟨*Indo*phile⟩ ⟨*Indo*-Briton⟩ ⟨*Indo*-Pakistani⟩ **2** : Indo-European ⟨*Indo*-Hittite⟩

In·do–Ar·y·an \ˌin-dō-ˈar-ē-ən, -ˈer-; -ˈär-yən\ *n* (1881) **1** : a member of one of the peoples of India of Aryan speech and physique **2** : one of the early Indo-European invaders of Persia, Afghanistan, and India **3** : the Indo-European languages of India and Pakistan as a group — **Indo–Aryan** *adj*

In·do–Chi·nese \-ˌchī-ˈnēz, -ˈnēs\ *n* (ca. 1934) **1** : a native or inhabitant of Indochina **2** : SINO-TIBETAN — **Indo–Chinese** *adj*

in·doc·ile \(ˈ)in-ˈdäs-əl *also* -ˌīl, *esp Brit* -ˈdō-ˌsīl\ *adj* [MF, fr. L *indocilis,* fr. *in-* + *docilis* docile] (1603) : unwilling or indisposed to be taught or disciplined : INTRACTABLE — **in·do·cil·i·ty** \ˌin-dä-ˈsil-ət-ē, -dō-\ *n*

in·doc·tri·nate \in-ˈdäk-trə-ˌnāt\ *vt* **-nat·ed; -nat·ing** [prob. fr. ME *endoctrinen,* fr. MF *endoctriner,* fr. OF, fr. *en-* + *doctrine* doctrine] (1626) **1** : to instruct esp. in fundamentals or rudiments : TEACH **2** : to imbue with a usu. partisan or sectarian opinion, point of view, or principle — **in·doc·tri·na·tion** \(ˌ)in-ˌdäk-trə-ˈnā-shən\ *n* — **in·doc·tri·na·tor** \in-ˈdäk-trə-ˌnāt-ər\ *n*

In·do–Eu·ro·pe·an \ˌin-dō-ˌyu̇r-ə-ˈpē-ən\ *adj* (1815) : of, relating to, or constituting the Indo-European languages — **Indo–European** *n*

Indo–European languages *n pl* (ca. 1814) : a family of languages comprising those spoken in most of Europe and in the parts of the world colonized by Europeans since 1500 and also in Persia, the subcontinent of India, and some other parts of Asia

In·do–Ger·man·ic \ˌin-dō-jər-ˈman-ik\ *n* (ca. 1934) : INDO-EUROPEAN — **Indo–Germanic** *adj*

In·do–Hit·tite \-ˈhi-ˌtīt\ *n* (ca. 1930) **1** : a hypothetical parent language of Indo-European and Anatolian **2** : a language family including Indo-European and Anatolian — **Indo–Hittite** *adj*

In·do–Ira·ni·an \-ir-ˈā-nē-ən\ *adj* (1876) : of, relating to, or constituting a subfamily of the Indo-European languages that consists of the Indic and the Iranian branches — see INDO-EUROPEAN LANGUAGES table — **Indo–Iranian** *n*

in·dole \ˈin-ˌdōl\ *n* [ISV *ind-* + *-ole*] (1869) : a crystalline compound C_8H_7N that is a decomposition product of proteins containing tryptophan, often formed by reduction distillation of indigo, and used in perfumes; *also* : a derivative of indole

in·dole·ace·tic acid \ˈin-ˌdōl-ə-ˌsēt-ik-\ *n* (1886) : a crystalline plant hormone $C_{10}H_9NO_2$ that promotes growth and rooting of plants — called also *heteroauxin*

in·dole·bu·tyr·ic acid \-byü-ˌtir-ik-\ *n* (1936) : a crystalline acid $C_{12}H_{13}NO_2$ similar to indoleacetic acid in its effects on plants

in·do·lence \ˈin-də-lən(t)s\ *n* (1656) **1** : a condition of causing little or no pain **2** : inclination to laziness : SLOTH

in·do·lent \-lənt\ *adj* [LL *indolent-, indolens* insensitive to pain, fr. L *in-* + *dolent-, dolens,* prp. of *dolēre* to feel pain — more at CONDOLE] (1663) **1 a** : causing little or no pain **b** : slow to develop or heal **2 a** : averse to activity, effort, or movement : habitually lazy **b** : conducing to or encouraging laziness ⟨~ heat⟩ **c** : exhibiting indolence ⟨an ~ sigh⟩ ***syn*** see LAZY — **in·do·lent·ly** *adv*

In·dol·o·gy \(ˌ)in-ˈdäl-ə-jē\ *n* (1888) : the study of India and its people — **In·dol·o·gist** \-jəst\ *n*

in·do·meth·a·cin \ˌin-dō-ˈmeth-ə-sən\ *n* [*indole* + *meth-* + *acetic acid* + *-in*] (1963) : a nonsteroidal drug $C_{19}H_{16}ClNO_4$ with anti-inflammatory, analgesic, and antipyretic properties used esp. in treating arthritis

in·dom·i·ta·ble \in-ˈdäm-ət-ə-bəl\ *adj* [LL *indomitabilis,* fr. L *in-* + *domitare* to tame — more at DAUNT] (1830) : incapable of being subdued : UNCONQUERABLE ⟨~ courage⟩ — **in·dom·i·ta·bil·i·ty** \(ˌ)in-ˌdäm-ət-ə-ˈbil-ət-ē\ *n* — **in·dom·i·ta·ble·ness** \in-ˈdäm-ət-ə-bəl-nəs\ *n* — **in·dom·i·ta·bly** \-blē\ *adv*

In·do·ne·sian \ˌin-də-ˈnē-zhən, -shən\ *n* (1850) **1** : a native or inhabitant of the Malay archipelago **2 a** : a native or inhabitant of the Republic of Indonesia **b** : the language based on Malay that is the national language of the Republic of Indonesia — **Indonesian** *adj*

in·door \ˌin-ˌdō(ə)r, -ˌdȯ(ə)r\ *adj* (1711) **1** : of or relating to the interior of a building **2** : living, located, or carried on within a building ⟨an ~ sport⟩

in·doors \(ˈ)in-ˈdō(ə)rz, -ˈdȯ(ə)rz\ *adv* (ca. 1890) : in or into a building

in·do·phe·nol \ˌin-dō-ˈfē-ˌnōl, -ˌnȯl, ˌin-(ˌ)dō-fi-ˈ\ *n* [ISV] (ca. 1881) : any of various blue or green dyes

indorse *var of* ENDORSE

in·dox·yl \in-ˈdäk-səl\ *n* [ISV *ind-* + hydr*oxyl*] (ca. 1886) : a crystalline compound C_8H_7NO found in plants and animals or synthesized as a step in indigo manufacture

in·draft \ˈin-ˌdraft, -ˌdräft\ *n* (1594) **1** : an inward flow or current (as of air or water) **2** : a drawing or pulling in

in·drawn \ˈin-ˌdrȯn\ *adj* (1751) **1** : ALOOF, RESERVED **2** : drawn in

in·du·bi·ta·ble \(ˈ)in-ˈd(y)ü-bət-ə-bəl\ *adj* [F or L; F, fr. L *indubitabilis,* fr. *in-* + *dubitabilis* dubitable] (15c) : too evident to be doubted : UNQUESTIONABLE — **in·du·bi·ta·bil·i·ty** \(ˌ)in-ˌdyü-bət-ə-ˈbil-ət-ē\ *n* — **in·du·bi·ta·ble·ness** \(ˈ)in-ˈd(y)ü-bət-ə-bəl-nəs\ *n* — **in·du·bi·ta·bly** \-blē\ *adv*

in·duce \in-ˈd(y)üs\ *vt* **in·duced; in·duc·ing** [ME *inducen,* fr. L *inducere,* fr. *in-* + *ducere* to lead — more at TOW] (14c) **1 a** : to move by persuasion or influence : LEAD ON **b** : to call forth or bring about by influence or stimulation **2 a** : EFFECT, CAUSE **b** : to cause the formation of **c** : to produce (as an electric current) by induction **d** : to arouse by indirect stimulation ⟨~ a contrast color⟩ **3** : to determine by induction; *specif* : to infer from particulars — **in·duc·ibil·i·ty** \-ˌd(y)ü-sə-ˈbil-ət-ē\ *n* — **in·duc·ible** \-ˈd(y)ü-sə-bəl\ *adj*

in·duce·ment \in-ˈd(y)ü-smənt\ *n* (1594) **1** : a motive or consideration that leads one to action or to additional or more effective actions ⟨prizes offered as ~s to students to do better work⟩ **2** : the act or process of inducing **3** : matter presented by way of introduction or background to explain the principal allegations of a legal cause, plea, or defense ***syn*** see MOTIVE

in·duc·er \-ˈd(y)ü-sər\ *n* (1554) : one that induces; *specif* : a substance that is capable of activating a structural gene by combining with and inactivating a genetic repressor

in·duct \in-ˈdəkt\ *vt* [ME *inducten,* fr. ML *inductus,* pp. of *inducere,* fr. L] (14c) **1** : to put in formal possession (as of a benefice or office) : INSTALL ⟨was ~ed as president of the college⟩ **2 a** : to admit as a member ⟨~ed into a scholastic society⟩ **b** : INTRODUCE, INITIATE **c** : to enroll for military training or service (as under a selective service act) **3** : LEAD, CONDUCT

in·duc·tance \in-ˈdək-tən(t)s\ *n* (ca. 1886) **1** : a property of an electric circuit by which an electromotive force is induced in it by a variation of current either in the circuit itself or in a neighboring circuit **2** : a circuit or a device possessing inductance

in·duct·ee \(ˌ)in-ˌdək-ˈtē, in-ˈdək-ˌ\ *n* (1940) : one who is inducted; *esp* : a person inducted into military service

in·duc·tion \in-ˈdək-shən\ *n* (15c) **1 a** : the act or process of inducting (as into office) **b** : an initial experience : INITIATION **c** : the formality by which a civilian is inducted into military service **2 a (1)** : inference of a generalized conclusion from particular instances — compare DEDUCTION 2a **(2)** : a conclusion arrived at by induction **b** : mathematical demonstration of the validity of a law concerning all the positive integers by proving that it holds for the integer 1 and that if it holds for all the integers preceding a given integer it must hold for the next following integer **3** : a preface, prologue, or introductory scene esp. of an early English play **4 a** : the act of bringing forward or adducing (as facts or particulars) **b** : the act of causing or bringing on or about **c** : the process by which an electrical conductor becomes electrified when near a charged body, by which a magnetizable body becomes magnetized when in a magnetic field or in the magnetic flux set up by a magnetomotive force, or by which an electromotive force is produced in a circuit by varying the magnetic field linked with the circuit **d** : the inspiration of the fuel-air charge from the carburetor into the combustion chamber of an internal-combustion engine **e** : the sum of the processes by which the fate of embryonic cells is determined and morphogenetic differentiation brought about

induction coil *n* (1837) : an apparatus for obtaining intermittent high voltage consisting of a primary coil through which the direct current flows, an interrupter, and a secondary coil of a larger number of turns in which the high voltage is induced

induction heating *n* (1919) : heating of material by means of an electric current that is caused to flow through the material or its container by electromagnetic induction

in·duc·tive \in-ˈdək-tiv\ *adj* (15c) **1** : leading on : INDUCING **2** : of, relating to, or employing mathematical or logical induction ⟨~ reasoning⟩ **3** : of or relating to inductance or electrical induction **4** : INTRODUCTORY **5** : involving the action of an embryological inductor : tending to produce induction — **in·duc·tive·ly** *adv*

in·duc·tor \in-ˈdək-tər\ *n* (1652) **1** : one that inducts **2 a** : a part of an electrical apparatus that acts upon another or is itself acted upon by induction **b** : REACTOR 2 **3** : ORGANIZER 2

indue *var of* ENDUE

in·dulge \in-ˈdəlj\ *vb* **in·dulged; in·dulg·ing** [L *indulgēre* to be complaisant] *vt* (1656) **1 a** : to give free rein to **b** : to take unrestrained pleasure in : GRATIFY **2 a** : to yield to the desire of : HUMOR **b** : to treat with excessive leniency, generosity, or consideration ~ *vi* : to indulge oneself — **in·dulg·er** *n*

syn INDULGE, PAMPER, HUMOR, SPOIL, BABY, MOLLYCODDLE mean to show undue favor to a person's desires and feelings. INDULGE implies exces-

INDO-EUROPEAN LANGUAGES

BRANCH	GROUP	LANGUAGES AND MAJOR DIALECTS[1]			PROVENIENCE
		ANCIENT	MEDIEVAL	MODERN	
GERMANIC	East		*Gothic*		eastern Europe
GERMANIC	North		*Old Norse*	Icelandic	Iceland
GERMANIC	North			Faeroese	Faeroe Islands
GERMANIC	North			Norwegian	Norway
GERMANIC	North			Swedish	Sweden
GERMANIC	North			Danish	Denmark
GERMANIC	West		*Old High German*	German	Germany, Switzerland, Austria
GERMANIC	West		*Middle High German*		
GERMANIC	West			Yiddish	Germany, eastern Europe
GERMANIC	West		*Old Saxon*	Low German	northern Germany
GERMANIC	West		*Middle Low German*		
GERMANIC	West		*Middle Dutch*	Dutch	Netherlands
GERMANIC	West			Afrikaans	South Africa
GERMANIC	West		*Middle Flemish*	Flemish	Belgium
GERMANIC	West		*Old Frisian*	Frisian	Netherlands, Germany
GERMANIC	West		*Old English*	English	England
GERMANIC	West		*Middle English*		
CELTIC	Continental	*Gaulish*			Gaul
CELTIC	Goidelic		*Old Irish*	Irish Gaelic	Ireland
CELTIC	Goidelic		*Middle Irish*		
CELTIC	Goidelic			Scottish Gaelic	Scotland
CELTIC	Goidelic			*Manx*	Isle of Man
CELTIC	Brythonic		*Old Welsh*	Welsh	Wales
CELTIC	Brythonic		*Middle Welsh*		
CELTIC	Brythonic		*Old Cornish*	*Cornish*	Cornwall
CELTIC	Brythonic		*Middle Breton*	Breton	Brittany
ITALIC	Osco-Umbrian	*Oscan, Sabellian Umbrian*			ancient Italy
ITALIC	Latinian or Romance[2]	*Venetic, Faliscan, Lanuvian, Praenestine*			ancient Italy
ITALIC	Latinian or Romance[2]	Latin		Portuguese	Portugal
ITALIC	Latinian or Romance[2]			Spanish	Spain
ITALIC	Latinian or Romance[2]			Judeo-Spanish	Mediterranean lands
ITALIC	Latinian or Romance[2]			Catalan	Spain (Catalonia)
ITALIC	Latinian or Romance[2]		*Old Provençal*	Provençal	southern France
ITALIC	Latinian or Romance[2]		*Old French*	French	France, Belgium, Switzerland
ITALIC	Latinian or Romance[2]		*Middle French*		
ITALIC	Latinian or Romance[2]			Haitian Creole	Haiti
ITALIC	Latinian or Romance[2]			Italian	Italy, Switzerland
ITALIC	Latinian or Romance[2]			Rhaeto-Romanic	Switzerland, Italy
ITALIC	Latinian or Romance[2]			Sardinian	Sardinia
ITALIC	Latinian or Romance[2]			*Dalmatian*	Adriatic Coast
ITALIC	Latinian or Romance[2]			Rumanian	Rumania, Balkans
	Scantily recorded and of uncertain affinities within Indo-European	*Ligurian, Messapian, Illyrian, Thracian, Phrygian*			ancient Italy / Balkans / Asia Minor
	Albanian			Albanian	Albania, southern Italy
	Greek or Hellenic	*Greek*	*Greek*	Greek	Greece, the eastern Mediterranean
BALTO-SLAVIC	Baltic		*Old Prussian*		East Prussia
BALTO-SLAVIC	Baltic			Lithuanian	Lithuania
BALTO-SLAVIC	Baltic			Latvian	Latvia
BALTO-SLAVIC	Slavic — South		*Old Church Slavonic*		
BALTO-SLAVIC	Slavic — South			Slovene	Yugoslavia
BALTO-SLAVIC	Slavic — South			Serbo-Croatian	Yugoslavia
BALTO-SLAVIC	Slavic — South			Macedonian	Macedonia
BALTO-SLAVIC	Slavic — South			Bulgarian	Bulgaria
BALTO-SLAVIC	Slavic — West		*Old Czech*	Czech, Slovak	Czechoslovakia
BALTO-SLAVIC	Slavic — West			Polish, Kashubian	Poland
BALTO-SLAVIC	Slavic — West			Wendish, *Polabian*	Germany
BALTO-SLAVIC	Slavic — East		*Old Russian*	Russian	Russia
BALTO-SLAVIC	Slavic — East			Ukrainian	Ukraine
BALTO-SLAVIC	Slavic — East			Belorussian	White Russia
	Armenian		*Armenian*	Armenian	Asia Minor, Caucasus
INDO-IRANIAN	Anatolian	*Hittite, Lydian, Lycian Luwian Palaic Hieroglyphic Hittite*			ancient Asia Minor
INDO-IRANIAN	Iranian — West	*Old Persian*	*Pahlavi*		Persia
INDO-IRANIAN	Iranian — West		*Persian*	Persian	Persia (Iran)
INDO-IRANIAN	Iranian — West			Kurdish	Persia, Iraq, Turkey
INDO-IRANIAN	Iranian — West			Baluchi	Pakistan
INDO-IRANIAN	Iranian — West			Tajiki	central Asia
INDO-IRANIAN	Iranian — East	*Avestan*			ancient Persia
INDO-IRANIAN	Iranian — East		*Sogdian*		central Asia
INDO-IRANIAN	Iranian — East		*Khotanese*		central Asia
INDO-IRANIAN	Iranian — East			Pashto	Afghanistan, Pakistan
INDO-IRANIAN	Iranian — East			Ossetic	Caucasus
INDO-IRANIAN	Dard			Shina, Khowar, Kafiri	upper Indus valley
INDO-IRANIAN	Dard			Kashmiri	Kashmir
INDO-IRANIAN	Sanskritic	*Sanskrit, Pali*			India
INDO-IRANIAN	Sanskritic	*Prakrits*	*Prakrits*		
INDO-IRANIAN	Indic			Lahnda	western Punjab
INDO-IRANIAN	Indic			Sindhi	Sind
INDO-IRANIAN	Indic			Panjabi	Punjab
INDO-IRANIAN	Indic			Rajasthani	Rajasthan
INDO-IRANIAN	Indic			Gujarati	Gujarat
INDO-IRANIAN	Indic			Marathi	western India
INDO-IRANIAN	Indic			Konkani	western India
INDO-IRANIAN	Indic			Oriya	Orissa
INDO-IRANIAN	Indic			Bengali	Bengal
INDO-IRANIAN	Indic			Assamese	Assam
INDO-IRANIAN	Indic			Bihari	Bihar
INDO-IRANIAN	Indic			Hindi	northern India
INDO-IRANIAN	Indic			Urdu	Pakistan, India
INDO-IRANIAN	Indic			Nepali	Nepal
INDO-IRANIAN	Indic			Sinhalese	Ceylon
INDO-IRANIAN	Indic			Romany	uncertain
	Tocharian		*Tocharian A Tocharian B*		central Asia

[1] Italics denote dead languages. Languages listed in roman type in the ancient or medieval column are those which survive only in some special use, as in literary composition or liturgy.

[2] Romance is normally applied only to medieval and modern languages; Latinian is normally applied only to ancient languages.

sive compliance and weakness in gratifying another's or one's own desires; PAMPER implies inordinate gratification of desire for luxury and comfort with consequent enervating effect; HUMOR stresses a yielding to a person's moods or whims; SPOIL stresses the injurious effects on character by indulging or pampering; BABY suggests excessive care, attention, or solicitude; MOLLYCODDLE suggests an excessive degree of care and attention to another's health or welfare.

¹in·dul·gence \in-'dəl-jən(t)s\ *n* (14c) **1 :** remission of part or all of the temporal and esp. purgatorial punishment that according to Roman Catholicism is due for sins whose eternal punishment has been remitted and whose guilt has been pardoned (as through the sacrament of penance) **2 :** the act of indulging : the state of being indulgent 〈treated her moody child with ∼〉 **3 a :** an indulgent act **b :** an extension of time for payment or performance granted as a favor **4 a :** the act of indulging in something : the thing indulged in **b :** SELF-INDULGENCE
²indulgence *vt* **-genced; -genc·ing** (1866) **:** to attach an indulgence to 〈*indulgenced* prayers〉
in·dul·gent \in-'dəl-jənt\ *adj* [L *indulgent-, indulgens,* prp. of *indulgēre*] (1509) **:** indulging or characterized by indulgence : LENIENT — **in·dul·gent·ly** *adv*
in·du·line \'in-d(y)ə-,lēn\ *n* [ISV *ind-* + *-ule* + *-ine*] (ca. 1882) **:** any of numerous blue or violet dyes related to the safranines
in·dult \'in-,dəlt, in-'\ *n* [ME (Sc), fr. ML *indultum,* fr. LL, grant, fr. L, neut. of *indultus,* pp. of *indulgēre*] (15c) **:** a special often temporary dispensation granted in the Roman Catholic Church
¹in·du·rate \'in-d(y)ə-rət, in-'d(y)ur-ət\ *adj* (15c) **:** physically or morally hardened
²in·du·rate \'in-d(y)ə-,rāt\ *vb* **-rat·ed; -rat·ing** [L *induratus,* pp. of *indurare,* fr. *in-* + *durare* to harden, fr. *durus* hard — more at DURING] *vt* (1538) **1 :** to make unfeeling, stubborn, or obdurate **2 :** to make hardy : INURE **3 :** to make hard 〈great heat ∼s clay〉 *vi* **1 :** to grow hard : HARDEN **2 :** to become established — **in·du·ra·tion** \,in-d(y)ə-'rā-shən\ *n* — **in·du·ra·tive** \'in-d(y)ə-,rāt-iv, in-'d(y)ur-ət-\ *adj*
in·du·rat·ed *adj* (1604) **:** having become firm or hard esp. by increase of fibrous elements (∼ tissue)
in·du·si·um \in-'d(y)ü-z(h)ē-əm\ *n, pl* **-sia** \-z(h)ē-ə\ [NL, fr. L, tunic] (1807) **:** an investing outgrowth or membrane: as **a :** an outgrowth of a fern frond that invests the sori **b :** the annulus of a fungus esp. when large and full
¹in·dus·tri·al \in-'dəs-trē-əl\ *adj* (1590) **1 :** of or relating to industry **2 :** derived from human industry 〈∼ wealth〉 **3 :** engaged in industry 〈the ∼ classes〉 **4 :** used in industry 〈∼ diamonds〉 **5 :** characterized by highly developed industries 〈an ∼ nation〉 — **in·dus·tri·al·ly** \-trē-ə-lē\ *adv*
²industrial *n* (1865) **1 a :** one that is employed in industry **b :** a company engaged in industrial production or service **2 :** a stock or bond issued by an industrial corporation or enterprise
industrial action *n, Brit* (ca. 1931) **:** JOB ACTION
industrial archaeology *n* (1951) **:** the study of the buildings, machinery, and equipment of the industrial revolution — **industrial archaeologist** *n*
industrial arts *n pl but sing in constr* (1924) **:** a subject taught in elementary and secondary schools that aims at developing manual skill and familiarity with tools and machines
industrial engineering *n* (1923) **:** engineering that deals with the design, improvement, and installation of integrated systems of people, materials, equipment, and energy — **industrial engineer** *n*
in·dus·tri·al·ism \in-'dəs-trē-ə-,liz-əm\ *n* (1831) **:** social organization in which industries and esp. large-scale industries are dominant
in·dus·tri·al·ist \-ləst\ *n* (1864) **:** one owning or engaged in the management of an industry — **MANUFACTURER**
in·dus·tri·al·ize \in-'dəs-trē-ə-,līz\ *vb* **-ized; -iz·ing** *vt* (1882) **:** to make industrial 〈an agricultural region〉 ∼ *vi* **:** to become industrial — **in·dus·tri·al·iza·tion** \-,dəs-trē-ə-lə-'zā-shən\ *n*
industrial melanism *n* (1943) **:** genetically determined melanism esp. in insect populations that occurs in areas darkened by industrial pollutants
industrial psychology *n* (1917) **:** the application of the findings and methods of experimental, clinical, and social psychology to industrial problems (as personnel selection and training) — **industrial psychologist** *n*
industrial relations *n pl* (1904) **:** the dealings or relationships of a usu. large business or industrial enterprise with its own workers, with labor in general, with governmental agencies, or with the public
industrial revolution *n* (1848) **:** a rapid major change in an economy (as in England in the late 18th century) marked by the general introduction of power-driven machinery or by an important change in the prevailing types and methods of use of such machines
industrial school *n* (1853) **:** a school specializing in the teaching of industrial arts; *specif* **:** a public institution of this kind for juvenile delinquents
industrial sociology *n* (1948) **:** sociological analysis directed at institutions and social relationships within and largely controlled or affected by industry
industrial union *n* (1902) **:** a labor union that admits to membership workers in an industry irrespective of their occupation or craft — compare CRAFT UNION
in·dus·tri·ous \in-'dəs-trē-əs\ *adj* (1523) **1** *obs* **:** SKILLFUL, INGENIOUS **2 :** persistently active : ZEALOUS **3 :** constantly, regularly, or habitually occupied : DILIGENT *syn* see BUSY — **in·dus·tri·ous·ly** *adv* — **in·dus·tri·ous·ness** *n*
in·dus·try \'in-(,)dəs-trē\ *n, pl* **-tries** [ME *industrie* skill, employment involving skill, fr. MF, fr. L *industria* diligence, fr. *industrius* diligent, fr. OL *indostruus,* fr. *indu* in + *-struus* (akin to L *struere* to build) — more at INDIGENOUS, STRUCTURE] (15c) **1 :** diligence in an employment or pursuit **2 a :** systematic labor esp. for some useful purpose or the creation of something of value **b :** a department or branch of a craft, art, business, or manufacture; *esp* **:** one that employs a large personnel and capital esp. in manufacturing **c :** a distinct group of productive or profit-making enterprises 〈the banking ∼〉 **d :** manufacturing activity as a whole 〈the nation's ∼〉 **3 :** work devoted to the study of a particular subject or author 〈the Shakespeare ∼〉 *syn* see BUSINESS

in·dwell \(')in-'dwel\ *vi* (14c) **:** to exist as an inner activating spirit, force, or principle ∼ *vt* **:** to exist within as an activating spirit, force, or principle — **in·dwell·er** *n*
in·dwell·ing \'in-,dwel-iŋ\ *adj* (1932) **:** left within a bodily organ or passage esp. to promote drainage — used of an implanted tube (as a catheter)
¹-ine \,īn, ən, (,)ēn, ,ēn\ *adj suffix* **1** [ME *-in, -ine,* fr. MF&L; MF *-in,* fr. L *-inus* — more at -EN] **:** of or relating to 〈estuar*ine*〉 **2** [ME *-in, -ine,* fr. MF&L; MF *-in,* fr. L *-inus,* fr. Gk *-inos* — more at -EN] **:** made of : like 〈opal*ine*〉
²-ine \,ēn, 'ēn, ən, (,)in, ,īn, 'īn\ *n suffix* [ME *-ine, -in,* fr. MF&L; MF *-ine,* fr. L *-ina,* fr. fem. of *-inus* adj. suffix] **1 :** chemical substance: as **a :** halogen element 〈chlor*ine*〉 **b :** basic or base-containing carbon compound that contains nitrogen 〈quin*ine*〉 〈cyst*ine*〉 **c :** mixture of compounds (as of hydrocarbons) 〈gasol*ine*〉 **d :** hydride 〈ars*ine*〉 **2 :** -IN 1a **3 :** commercial product or material 〈glass*ine*〉
ine·bri·ant \in-'ē-brē-ənt\ *n* (1819) **:** INTOXICANT — **inebriant** *adj*
¹ine·bri·ate \in-'ē-brē-,āt\ *vt* **-at·ed; -at·ing** [L *inebriatus,* pp. of *inebriare,* fr. *in-* + *ebriare* to intoxicate, fr. *ebrius* drunk — more at SOBER] (15c) **1 :** to exhilarate or stupefy as if by liquor **2 :** to make drunk : INTOXICATE — **ine·bri·a·tion** \-,ē-brē-'ā-shən\ *n*
²ine·bri·ate \in-'ē-brē-ət, -,āt\ *adj* (15c) **1 :** affected by alcohol : DRUNK **2 :** addicted to excessive drinking
³ine·bri·ate \-ət\ *n* (1794) **:** one who is drunk; *esp* **:** an habitual drunkard
ine·bri·at·ed \-brē-,āt-əd\ *adj* (1615) **:** exhilarated or confused by or as if by alcohol : INTOXICATED
in·ebri·ety \,in-i-'brī-ət-ē\ *n* [prob. blend of *inebriation* and *ebriety* (drunkenness)] (1801) **:** the state of being inebriated : DRUNKENNESS
in·ed·i·ble \(')in-'ed-ə-bəl\ *adj* (1822) **:** not fit to be eaten
in·ed·u·ca·ble \(')in-'ej-ə-kə-bəl\ *adj* (1884) **:** incapable of being educated — **in·ed·u·ca·bil·i·ty** \(,)in-,ej-ə-kə-'bil-ət-ē\ *n*
in·ef·fa·ble \(')in-'ef-ə-bəl\ *adj* [ME, fr. MF, fr. L *ineffabilis,* fr. *in-* + *effabilis* capable of being expressed, fr. *effari* to speak out, fr. *ex-* + *fari* to speak — more at BAN] (14c) **1 a :** incapable of being expressed in words : INDESCRIBABLE 〈∼ joy〉 **b :** UNSPEAKABLE 〈∼ disgust〉 **2 :** not to be uttered : TABOO 〈the ∼ name of Jehovah〉 — **in·ef·fa·bil·i·ty** \(,)in-,ef-ə-'bil-ət-ē\ *n* — **in·ef·fa·ble·ness** \(')in-'ef-ə-bəl-nəs\ *n* — **in·ef·fa·bly** \-blē\ *adv*
in·ef·face·able \,in-ə-'fā-sə-bəl\ *adj* [prob. fr. F *ineffaçable,* fr. MF, fr. *in-* + *effaçable* effaceable] (1804) **:** not effaceable : INERADICABLE — **in·ef·face·abil·i·ty** \-,fā-sə-'bil-ət-ē\ *n* — **in·ef·face·ably** \-'fā-sə-blē\ *adv*
in·ef·fec·tive \,in-ə-'fek-tiv\ *adj* (1651) **1 :** not producing an intended effect : INEFFECTUAL 〈∼ lighting〉 **2 :** not capable of performing efficiently or as expected : INCAPABLE 〈an ∼ executive〉 — **in·ef·fec·tive·ly** *adv* — **in·ef·fec·tive·ness** *n*
in·ef·fec·tu·al \,in-ə-'fek-chə-(wə)l, -'feksh-wəl\ *adj* (15c) **1 :** not producing the proper or intended effect : FUTILE **2 :** INEFFECTIVE 2 — **in·ef·fec·tu·al·i·ty** \-,fek-chə-'wal-ət-ē\ *n* — **in·ef·fec·tu·al·ly** \-'fek-chə-(wə)lē, -'feksh-wə-\ *adv* — **in·ef·fec·tu·al·ness** *n*
in·ef·fi·ca·cious \(,)in,ef-ə-'kā-shəs\ *adj* (1658) **:** lacking the power to produce a desired effect : INEFFECTIVE — **in·ef·fi·ca·cious·ly** *adv* — **in·ef·fi·ca·cious·ness** *n*
in·ef·fi·ca·cy \(')in-'ef-i-kə-sē\ *n* [LL *inefficacia,* fr. L *inefficac-, inefficax* inefficacious, fr. *in-* + *efficac-, efficax* efficacious] (1612) **:** lack of power to produce a desired effect
in·ef·fi·cien·cy \,in-ə-'fish-ən-sē\ *n, pl* **-cies** (1749) **1 :** the quality or state of being inefficient **2 :** something that is inefficient
in·ef·fi·cient \-'fish-ənt\ *adj* (1750) **:** not efficient: **a :** not producing the effect intended or desired : INEFFICACIOUS 〈the scare technique proved to be ∼〉 **b :** wasteful of time or energy 〈∼ operating procedures〉 **c :** INCAPABLE, INCOMPETENT 〈an ∼ worker〉 — **inefficient** *n* — **in·ef·fi·cient·ly** *adv*
in·e·gal·i·tar·i·an \,in-i-,gal-ə-'ter-ē-ən\ *adj* (1940) **:** marked by disparity in social and economic standing
in·elas·tic \,in-ə-'las-tik\ *adj* (1748) **:** not elastic: **a :** slow to react or respond to changing conditions **b :** INFLEXIBLE, UNYIELDING — **in·elas·tic·i·ty** \,in-i-,las-'tis-ət-ē, (,)in-ē-,las-, -'tis-tē\ *n*
inelastic collision *n* (1937) **:** a collision in which part of the kinetic energy of the colliding particles changes into another form of energy (as radiation)
inelastic scattering *n* (1938) **:** a scattering of particles as the result of inelastic collision in which the total kinetic energy of the colliding particles changes
in·el·e·gance \(')in-'el-i-gən(t)s\ *n* (1726) **:** lack of elegance
in·el·e·gant \-gənt\ *adj* [MF, fr. L *inelegant-, inelegans,* fr. *in-* + *elegant-, elegans* elegant] (ca. 1570) **:** lacking in refinement, grace, or good taste — **in·el·e·gant·ly** *adv*
in·el·i·gi·ble \(')in-'el-ə-jə-bəl\ *adj* [F *inéligible,* fr. *in-* + *éligible* eligible] (1770) **1 :** not qualified to be chosen for an office **2 :** not worthy to be chosen or preferred **3 :** not permitted under football rules to catch a forward pass — **in·el·i·gi·bil·i·ty** \(,)in-,el-ə-jə-'bil-ət-ē\ *n* — **ineligible** *n*
in·el·o·quent \(')in-'el-ə-kwənt\ *adj* (1530) **:** not eloquent — **in·el·o·quent·ly** *adv*
in·eluc·ta·ble \,in-i-'lək-tə-bəl\ *adj* [L *ineluctabilis,* fr. *in-* + *eluctari* to struggle out, fr. *ex-* + *luctari* to struggle — more at LOCK] (ca. 1623) **:** not to be avoided, changed, or resisted : INEVITABLE — **in·eluc·ta·bil·i·ty** \-,lək-tə-'bil-ət-ē\ *n* — **in·eluc·ta·bly** \-'lək-tə-blē\ *adv*
in·elud·i·ble \,in-i-'lüd-ə-bəl\ *adj* (1662) **:** INESCAPABLE
in·enar·ra·ble \,in-i-'nar-ə-bəl\ *adj* [ME, fr. MF, fr. L *inenarrabilis,* fr. *in-* + *enarrare* to explain in detail, fr. *e-* + *narrare* to narrate] (15c) **:** incapable of being narrated : INDESCRIBABLE
in·ept \in-'ept\ *adj* [F *inepte,* fr. L *ineptus,* fr. *in-* + *aptus* apt] (1542) **1 :** lacking in fitness or aptitude : UNFIT **2 :** lacking sense or reason : FOOLISH **3 :** not suitable to the time, place, or occasion : inappropriate often to an absurd degree **4 :** generally incompetent : BUNGLING

\ə\ abut \ᵊ\ kitten, F table \ər\ further \a\ ash \ā\ ace \ä\ cot, cart
\aú\ out \ch\ chin \e\ bet \ē\ easy \g\ go \i\ hit \ī\ ice \j\ job
\ŋ\ sing \ō\ go \ò\ law \òi\ boy \th\ thin \t̷h\ the \ü\ loot \ù\ foot
\y\ yet \zh\ vision \ä, k̲, ⁿ, œ, œ̄, ᵫ, ᵫ̄, �⟩ *see* Guide to Pronunciation

syn see AWKWARD — **in·ep·ti·tude** \-ˈep-tə-ˌt(y)üd\ *n* — **in·ept·ly** \-ˈep-(t)lē\ *adv* — **in·ept·ness** \-ˈep(t)-nəs\ *n*
in·equal·i·ty \ˌin-i-ˈkwäl-ət-ē\ *n* [MF *inequalité*, fr. L *inaequalitat-*, *inaequalitas*, fr. *inaequalis* unequal, fr. *in-* + *aequalis* equal] (15c) **1** : the quality of being unequal or uneven: as **a** : lack of evenness **b** : social disparity **c** : disparity of distribution or opportunity **d** : the condition of being variable : CHANGEABLENESS **2** : an instance of being unequal **3** : a formal statement of inequality between two quantities usu. separated by a sign of inequality (as <, >, or ≠ signifying respectively *is less than, is greater than*, or *is not equal to*) ⟨$a \neq b$, $2 < 3$, and $4 > 1$ are *inequalities*⟩
in·eq·ui·ta·ble \(ˈ)in-ˈek-wət-ə-bəl\ *adj* (1667) : not equitable : UNFAIR — **in·eq·ui·ta·bly** \-blē\ *adv*
in·eq·ui·ty \(ˈ)in-ˈek-wət-ē\ *n* (1556) **1** : INJUSTICE, UNFAIRNESS **2** : an instance of injustice or unfairness
in·equi·valve \(ˈ)in-ˈē-kwə-ˌvalv\ *also* **in·equi·valved** \-ˌvalvd\ *adj* (1776) : having the valves unequal in size and form — used of a bivalve mollusk or shell
in·erad·i·ca·ble \ˌin-i-ˈrad-i-kə-bəl\ *adj* (1818) : incapable of being eradicated — **in·erad·i·ca·bil·i·ty** \-ˌrad-i-kə-ˈbil-ət-ē\ *n* — **in·erad·i·ca·bly** \-ˈrad-i-kə-blē\ *adv*
in·er·ran·cy \(ˈ)in-ˈer-ən-sē\ *n* (1818) : exemption from error : INFALLIBILITY ⟨the concept of the verbal ~ of the Scriptures —George Hedley⟩
in·er·rant \-ənt\ *adj* [L *inerrant-*, *inerrans*, fr. *in-* + *errant-*, *errans*, prp. of *errare* to err] (1837) : free from error : INFALLIBLE
in·ert \in-ˈərt\ *adj* [L *inert-*, *iners* unskilled, idle, fr. *in-* + *art-*, *ars* skill — more at ARM] (1647) **1** : lacking the power to move **2** : very slow to move or act : SLUGGISH **3** : deficient in active properties; *esp* : lacking a usual or anticipated chemical or biological action ***syn*** see INACTIVE — **inert** *n* — **in·ert·ly** *adv* — **in·ert·ness** *n*
inert gas *n* (1902) : NOBLE GAS
in·er·tia \in-ˈər-shə, -shē-ə\ *n* [NL, fr. L, lack of skill, fr. *inert-*, *iners*] (1713) **1 a** : a property of matter by which it remains at rest or in uniform motion in the same straight line unless acted upon by some external force **b** : an analogous property of other physical quantities (as electricity) **2** : indisposition to motion, exertion, or change : INERTNESS ⟨failed to make a needed change in the system through sheer ~⟩ — **in·er·tial** \-shəl\ *adj* — **in·er·tial·ly** \-ˈərsh-(ə-)lē\ *adv*
inertial guidance *n* (ca. 1948) : guidance (as of an aircraft or spacecraft) by means of self-contained automatically controlling devices that respond to inertial forces — called also *inertial navigation*
in·es·cap·able \ˌin-ə-ˈskā-pə-bəl\ *adj* (1792) : incapable of being avoided, ignored, or denied : INEVITABLE — **in·es·cap·ably** \-blē\ *adv*
in·es·sen·tial \ˌin-ə-ˈsen-chəl\ *adj* (1677) **1** : having no essence **2** : not essential : UNESSENTIAL — **inessential** *n*
in·es·ti·ma·ble \(ˈ)in-ˈes-tə-mə-bəl\ *adj* [ME, fr. MF, fr. L *inaestimabilis*, fr. *in-* + *aestimabilis* estimable] (14c) **1** : incapable of being estimated or computed ⟨storms caused ~ damage⟩ **2** : too valuable or excellent to be measured or appreciated ⟨has performed an ~ service for his country⟩ — **in·es·ti·ma·bly** \-blē\ *adv*
in·ev·i·ta·ble \in-ˈev-ət-ə-bəl\ *adj* [ME, fr. L *inevitabilis*, fr. *in-* + *evitabilis* evitable] (14c) : incapable of being avoided or evaded — **in·ev·i·ta·bil·i·ty** \(ˌ)in-ˌev-ət-ə-ˈbil-ət-ē\ *n* — **in·ev·i·ta·ble·ness** \(ˈ)in-ˈev-ət-ə-bəl-nəs\ *n* — **in·ev·i·ta·bly** \-blē\ *adv*
in·ex·act \ˌin-ig-ˈzakt\ *adj* [F, fr. *in-* + *exact* exact] (ca. 1828) **1** : not precisely correct or true : INACCURATE ⟨an ~ translation⟩ **2** : not rigorous and careful ⟨an ~ thinker⟩ — **in·ex·ac·ti·tude** \-ˈzak-tə-ˌt(y)üd\ *n* — **in·ex·act·ly** \-ˈzak-(t)lē\ *adv* — **in·ex·act·ness** \-ˈzak(t)-nəs\ *n*
in ex·cel·sis \ˌin-ik-ˈsel-səs\ *adv* [L] (1602) : in the highest degree
in·ex·cus·able \ˌin-ik-ˈskyü-zə-bəl\ *adj* [L *inexcusabilis*, fr. *in-* + *excusabilis* excusable] (15c) : being without excuse or justification — **in·ex·cus·able·ness** *n* — **in·ex·cus·ably** \-blē\ *adv*
in·ex·haust·ible \ˌin-ig-ˈzȯ-stə-bəl\ *adj* (1601) : not exhaustible: as **a** : incapable of being used up ⟨~ riches⟩ **b** : incapable of being wearied or worn out ⟨an ~ hiker⟩ — **in·ex·haust·ibil·i·ty** \-ˌzȯ-stə-ˈbil-ət-ē\ *n* — **in·ex·haust·ible·ness** \-ˈzȯ-stə-bəl-nəs\ *n* — **in·ex·haust·ibly** \-blē\ *adv*
in·ex·is·tence \ˌin-ig-ˈzis-tən(t)s\ *n* (ca. 1623) : absence of existence : NONEXISTENCE
in·ex·is·tent \-tənt\ *adj* [LL *inexsistent-*, *inexsistens*, fr. L *in-* + *exsistent-*, *exsistens*, prp. of *exsistere* to exist] (1646) : not having existence : NONEXISTENT
in·ex·o·ra·ble \(ˈ)in-ˈeks-(ə-)rə-bəl, -ˈegz-ə-rə-\ *adj* [L *inexorabilis*, fr. *in-* + *exorabilis* pliant, fr. *exorare* to prevail upon, fr. *ex-* + *orare* to speak — more at ORATION] (1553) : not to be persuaded or moved by entreaty : RELENTLESS ***syn*** see INFLEXIBLE — **in·ex·o·ra·bil·i·ty** \(ˌ)in-ˌeks-(ə-)rə-ˈbil-ət-ē, -ˌegz-ə-rə-\ *n* — **in·ex·o·ra·ble·ness** \(ˈ)in-ˈeks-(ə-)rə-bəl-nəs, -ˈegz-ə-rə-\ *n* — **in·ex·o·ra·bly** \-blē\ *adv*
in·ex·pe·di·ence \ˌin-ik-ˈspēd-ē-ən(t)s\ *n* (1608) : INEXPEDIENCY
in·ex·pe·di·en·cy \-ən-sē\ *n* (1641) : the quality or fact of being inexpedient
in·ex·pe·di·ent \-ənt\ *adj* (1608) : not expedient : INADVISABLE — **in·ex·pe·di·ent·ly** *adv*
in·ex·pen·sive \ˌin-ik-ˈspen(t)-siv\ *adj* (1837) : reasonable in price : CHEAP — **in·ex·pen·sive·ly** *adv* — **in·ex·pen·sive·ness** *n*
in·ex·pe·ri·ence \ˌin-ik-ˈspir-ē-ən(t)s\ *n* [MF, fr. LL *inexperientia*, fr. L *in-* + *experientia* experience] (1598) **1** : lack of practical experience **2** : lack of knowledge of the ways of the world — **in·ex·pe·ri·enced** \-ən(t)st\ *adj*
in·ex·pert \(ˈ)in-ˈek-ˌspərt, ˌin-ik-ˈ\ *adj* [ME, fr. MF, fr. L *inexpertus*, fr. *in-* + *expertus* expert] (15c) : not expert : UNSKILLED — **in·ex·pert** \(ˈ)in-ˈek-ˌspərt\ *n* — **in·ex·pert·ly** \(ˈ)in-ˈek-ˌspərt-lē, ˌin-ik-ˈ\ *adv* — **in·ex·pert·ness** *n*
in·ex·pi·a·ble \(ˈ)in-ˈek-spē-ə-bəl\ *adj* [L *inexpiabilis*, fr. *in-* + *expiare* to expiate] (15c) **1** : not capable of being atoned for **2** *obs* : IMPLACABLE, UNAPPEASABLE — **in·ex·pi·a·bly** \-blē\ *adv*
in·ex·plain·able \ˌin-ik-ˈsplā-nə-bəl\ *adj* (ca. 1923) : INEXPLICABLE
in·ex·pli·ca·ble \ˌin-ik-ˈsplik-ə-bəl, (ˈ)in-ˈek-(ˌ)splik-\ *adj* [MF, fr. L *inexplicabilis*, fr. *in-* + *explicabilis* explicable] (15c) : incapable of being explained, interpreted, or accounted for — **in·ex·pli·ca·bil·i·ty** \ˌin-ik-ˌsplik-ə-ˈbil-ət-ē, (ˌ)in-ˌek-(ˌ)splik-\ *n* — **in·ex·pli·ca·ble·ness** \ˌin-ik-ˈsplik-ə-bəl-nəs, (ˈ)in-ˈek-(ˌ)splik-\ *n* — **in·ex·pli·ca·bly** \-blē\ *adv*
in·ex·plic·it \ˌin-ik-ˈsplis-ət\ *adj* (1775) : not explicit
in·ex·press·ible \-ˈspres-ə-bəl\ *adj* (1625) : not capable of being expressed : INDESCRIBABLE — **in·ex·press·ibil·i·ty** \-ˌspres-ə-ˈbil-ət-ē\ *n* — **in·ex·press·ible·ness** \-ˈspres-ə-bəl-nəs\ *n* — **in·ex·press·ibly** \-blē\ *adv*
in·ex·pres·sive \-ˈspres-iv\ *adj* (1652) **1** *archaic* : INEXPRESSIBLE **2** : lacking expression or meaning ⟨an ~ face⟩ — **in·ex·pres·sive·ly** *adv* — **in·ex·pres·sive·ness** *n*
in·ex·pug·na·ble \ˌin-ik-ˈspəg-nə-bəl, -ˈspyü-nə-\ *adj* [MF, fr. L *inexpugnabilis*, fr. *in-* + *expugnare* to take by storm, fr. *ex-* + *pugnare* to fight — more at PUNGENT] (15c) **1** : incapable of being subdued or overthrown : IMPREGNABLE ⟨an ~ position⟩ **2** : STABLE, FIXED ⟨~ hatred⟩ — **in·ex·pug·na·ble·ness** *n* — **in·ex·pug·na·bly** \-blē\ *adv*
in·ex·pung·ible \ˌin-ik-ˈspən-jə-bəl\ *adj* [*in-* + *expunge*] (1888) : incapable of being obliterated
in ex·ten·so \ˌin-ik-ˈsten(t)-(ˌ)sō\ *adv* [ML] (1826) : at full length
in·ex·tin·guish·able \ˌin-ik-ˈstiŋ-(g)wish-ə-bəl\ *adj* (1509) : not extinguishable : UNQUENCHABLE ⟨an ~ flame⟩ ⟨an ~ longing⟩ — **in·ex·tin·guish·ably** \-blē\ *adv*
in ex·tre·mis \ˌin-ik-ˈstrē-məs, -ˈstrā-\ *adv* [L] (1530) : in extreme circumstances; *esp* : at the point of death
in·ex·tri·ca·ble \ˌin-ik-ˈstrik-ə-bəl, (ˈ)in-ˈek-(ˌ)strik-\ *adj* [MF or L; MF, fr. L *inextricabilis*, fr. *in-* + *extricabilis* extricable] (15c) **1** : forming a maze or tangle from which it is impossible to get free **2 a** : incapable of being disentangled or untied ⟨an ~ knot⟩ **b** : not capable of being solved — **in·ex·tri·ca·bil·i·ty** \ˌin-ik-ˌstrik-ə-ˈbil-ət-ē, (ˈ)in-ˌek-(ˌ)strik-\ *n* — **in·ex·tri·ca·bly** \ˌin-ik-ˈstrik-ə-blē, (ˈ)in-ˈek-(ˌ)strik-\ *adv*
in·fal·li·ble \(ˈ)in-ˈfal-ə-bəl\ *adj* [ML *infallibilis*, fr. L *in-* + LL *fallibilis* fallible] (15c) **1** : incapable of error : UNERRING ⟨an ~ memory⟩ **2** : not liable to mislead, deceive, or disappoint : CERTAIN ⟨an ~ remedy⟩ **3** : incapable of error in defining doctrines touching faith or morals — **in·fal·li·bil·i·ty** \(ˌ)in-ˌfal-ə-ˈbil-ət-ē\ *n* — **in·fal·li·bly** \(ˈ)in-ˈfal-ə-blē\ *adv*
in·fa·mous \ˈin-fə-məs\ *adj* [ME, fr. L *infamis*, fr. *in-* + *fama* fame] (14c) **1** : having a reputation of the worst kind **2** : causing or bringing infamy : DISGRACEFUL **3** : convicted of an offense bringing infamy — **in·fa·mous·ly** *adv*
in·fa·my \-mē\ *n, pl* **-mies** (15c) **1** : evil reputation brought about by something grossly criminal, shocking, or brutal **2 a** : an extreme and publicly known criminal or evil act **b** : the state of being infamous ***syn*** see DISGRACE
in·fan·cy \ˈin-fən-sē\ *n, pl* **-cies** (14c) **1** : early childhood **2** : a beginning or early period of existence **3** : the legal status of an infant
[1]**in·fant** \ˈin-fənt\ *n* [ME *enfaunt*, fr. MF *enfant*, fr. L *infant-*, *infans*, fr. *infant-*, *infans*, adj., incapable of speech, young, fr. *in-* + *fant-*, *fans*, prp. of *fari* to speak — more at BAN] (14c) **1** : a child in the first period of life **2** : a person who is not of full age : MINOR
[2]**infant** *adj* (1586) **1** : intended for young children **2** : being in an early stage of development **3** : of, relating to, or being in infancy
in·fan·ta \in-ˈfant-ə, -ˈfänt-\ *n* [Sp & Pg, fem. of *infante*] (1601) : a daughter of a Spanish or Portuguese monarch
in·fan·te \in-ˈfant-ē, -ˈfän-(ˌ)tā\ *n* [Sp & Pg, lit., infant, fr. L *infant-*, *infans*] (1555) : a younger son of a Spanish or Portuguese monarch
in·fan·ti·cide \in-ˈfant-ə-ˌsīd\ *n* [LL *infanticidium*, fr. L *infant-*, *infans* + *-i-* + *-cidium* -cide] (1656) **1** : the killing of an infant **2** : one who kills an infant — **in·fan·ti·ci·dal** \-ˌfant-ə-ˈsīd-ᵊl\ *adj*
in·fan·tile \ˈin-fən-ˌtīl, -tᵊl, -ˌtēl, -(ˌ)til\ *adj* (1696) **1** : of or relating to infants or infancy **2** : suitable to or characteristic of an infant; *esp* : very immature **3** *of topography* : being in a very early stage of development following an uplift or equivalent change — **in·fan·til·i·ty** \ˌin-fən-ˈtil-ət-ē\ *n*
infantile paralysis *n* (1843) : POLIOMYELITIS
in·fan·til·ism \ˈin-fən-ˌtīl-ˌiz-əm, -tə-ˌliz-; in-ˈfan-tᵊl-ˌiz-\ *n* (1895) **1** : retention of childish physical, mental, or emotional qualities in adult life; *esp* : failure to attain sexual maturity **2** : an act or expression that indicates lack of maturity
in·fan·til·ize \ˈin-fən-ˌtī-ˌlīz, -fənt-ᵊl-ˌīz; in-ˈfant-ᵊl-ˌīz\ *vt* **-ized; -iz·ing** (1943) **1** : to make or keep infantile **2** : to treat as if infantile — **in·fan·til·i·za·tion** \ˌin-fən-ˌtī-lə-ˈzā-shən, -fənt-ᵊl-ə-; in-ˌfant-ᵊl-ə-\ *n*
in·fan·tine \ˈin-fən-ˌtīn, -ˌtēn\ *adj* (1603) : INFANTILE, CHILDISH
in·fan·try \ˈin-fən-trē\ *n, pl* **-tries** [MF & OIt; MF *infanterie*, fr. OIt *infanteria*, fr. *infante* boy, foot soldier, fr. L *infant-*, *infans*] (1579) **1 a** : soldiers trained, armed, and equipped to fight on foot **b** : a branch of an army composed of these soldiers **2** : an infantry regiment or division
in·fan·try·man \-trē-mən\ *n* (1883) : an infantry soldier
infant school *n, Brit* (1824) : KINDERGARTEN
in·farct \ˈin-ˌfärkt, in-ˈ\ *n* [L *infarctus*, pp. of *infarcire* to stuff, fr. *in-* + *farcire* to stuff — more at FARCE] (1873) : an area of necrosis in a tissue or organ resulting from obstruction of the local circulation by a thrombus or embolus — **in·farct·ed** \in-ˈfärk-təd\ *adj* — **in·farc·tion** \in-ˈfärk-shən\ *n*
in·fare \ˈin-ˌfa(ə)r, -ˌfe(ə)r\ *n* [ME *infer*, fr. OE *infær* entrance, fr. *in* + *fær* way, fr. *faran* to go — more at FARE] *chiefly dial* (14c) : a reception for a newly married couple
[1]**in·fat·u·ate** \in-ˈfach-ə-wət\ *adj* (15c) : being in an infatuated state or condition
[2]**in·fat·u·ate** \-ˌwāt\ *vt* **-at·ed; -at·ing** [L *infatuatus*, pp. of *infatuare*, fr. *in-* + *fatuus* fatuous] (1533) **1** : to affect with folly **2** : to inspire with a foolish or extravagant love or admiration — **in·fat·u·a·tion** \-ˌfach-ə-ˈwā-shən\ *n*
in·fau·na \ˈin-ˌfȯn-ə, -ˌfän-\ *n* [NL, fr. [2]*in-* + *fauna*] (1914) : benthic fauna living in the substrate and esp. in a soft sea bottom — compare EPIFAUNA — **in·fau·nal** \-ˌfȯn-ᵊl, -ˌfän-\ *adj*
in·fea·si·ble \(ˈ)in-ˈfē-zə-bəl\ *adj* (1533) : not feasible : IMPRACTICABLE — **in·fea·si·bil·i·ty** \(ˌ)in-ˌfē-zə-ˈbil-ət-ē\ *n*
in·fect \in-ˈfekt\ *vt* [ME *infecten*, fr. L *infectus*, pp. of *inficere*, fr. *in-* + *facere* to make, do — more at DO] (14c) **1** : to contaminate with a disease-producing substance or agent (as bacteria) **2 a** : to communicate a pathogen or a disease to **b** *of a pathogenic organism* : to invade (an individual or organ) usu. by penetration **3 a** : CONTAMINATE, CORRUPT ⟨manages to ~ her with a sense of guilt⟩ **b** : to work upon or seize upon so as to induce sympathy, belief, or support ⟨the teacher ~*ed* his pupils with his enthusiasm⟩ — **in·fec·tor** \-ˈfek-tər\ *n*
in·fec·tion \in-ˈfek-shən\ *n* (14c) **1** : the act or result of affecting injuriously **2** : an infective agent or material contaminated with an infective

agent 3 **a :** the state produced by the establishment of an infective agent in or on a suitable host **b :** a disease resulting from infection 4 **:** an act or process of infecting; *also* **:** the establishment of a pathogen in its host after invasion 5 **:** the communication of emotions or qualities through example or contact

in·fec·tious \-shəs\ *adj* (1542) 1 **a :** capable of causing infection **b :** communicable by infection — compare CONTAGIOUS 2 **:** that corrupts or contaminates 3 **:** spreading or capable of spreading rapidly to others ⟨their enthusiasm was ~⟩ ⟨an ~ grin⟩ — **in·fec·tious·ly** *adv* — **in·fec·tious·ness** *n*

infectious hepatitis *n* (ca. 1941) **:** an acute usu. benign hepatitis caused by an RNA virus that does not persist in the blood serum and is transmitted esp. in food and water contaminated with infected fecal matter — called also *hepatitis A;* compare SERUM HEPATITIS

infectious mononucleosis *n* (1920) **:** an acute infectious disease associated with Epstein-Barr virus and characterized by fever, swelling of lymph nodes, and lymphocytosis

in·fec·tive \in-ˈfek-tiv\ *adj* (14c) 1 **:** producing or capable of producing infection 2 **:** affecting others **:** INFECTIOUS — **in·fec·tiv·i·ty** \(ˌ)in-ˌfek-ˈtiv-ət-ē\ *n*

in·fe·lic·i·tous \ˌin-fi-ˈlis-ət-əs\ *adj* (1833) **:** not appropriate in application or expression — **in·fe·lic·i·tous·ly** *adv*

in·fe·lic·i·ty \-ət-ē\ *n, pl* **-ties** [ME *infelicite,* fr. L *infelicitas,* fr. *infelic-, infelix* unhappy, fr. *in-* + *felic-, felix* fruitful — more at FEMININE] (1617) 1 **:** the quality or state of being infelicitous 2 **:** something that is infelicitous

in·fer \in-ˈfər\ *vb* **in·ferred; in·fer·ring** [MF or L; MF *inferer,* fr. L *inferre,* lit., to carry or bring into, fr. *in-* + *ferre* to carry — more at BEAR] *vt* (1528) 1 **:** to derive as a conclusion from facts or premises ⟨we see smoke and ~ fire —L. A. White⟩ — compare IMPLY 2 **:** GUESS, SURMISE ⟨your letter . . . allows me to ~ that you are as well as ever —O. W. Holmes †1935⟩ 3 **a :** to involve as a normal outcome of thought **b :** to point out **:** INDICATE ⟨this doth ~ the zeal I had to see him —Shak.⟩ 4 **:** SUGGEST, HINT ⟨another survey . . . ~*s* that two-thirds of all present computer installations are not paying for themselves —H. R. Chellman⟩ ~ *vi* **:** to draw inferences ⟨men . . . have observed, *inferred,* and reasoned . . . to all kinds of results —John Dewey⟩ — **in·fer·able** *also* **in·fer·ri·ble** \in-ˈfər-ə-bəl\ *adj* — **in·fer·rer** \-ˈfər-ər\ *n*

syn INFER, DEDUCE, CONCLUDE, JUDGE, GATHER mean to arrive at a mental conclusion. INFER implies arriving at a conclusion by reasoning from evidence; if the evidence is slight the term comes close to *surmise;* DEDUCE adds to INFER the special implication of drawing a particular inference from a generalization; CONCLUDE implies arriving at a logically necessary inference at the end of a chain of reasoning; JUDGE stresses critical examination of the evidence on which a conclusion is based; GATHER suggests a direct or intuitive forming of a conclusion from hints or implications.

usage Sir Thomas More is the first writer known to have used both *infer* and *imply* in their approved senses (1528). He is also the first to have used *infer* in a sense close in meaning to *imply* (1533). Both of these uses of *infer* coexisted without comment until some time around the end of World War I. Since then, senses 3 and 4 of *infer* have been frequently condemned as an undesirable blurring of a useful distinction. Their use, esp. with a personal subject, will still incur the wrath of some in spite of the usage of four centuries and the fact that in a given instance the meaning will be clear from the context.

in·fer·ence \ˈin-f(ə-)rən(t)s, -fərn(t)s\ *n* (1594) 1 **:** the act or process of inferring: as **a :** the act of passing from one proposition, statement, or judgment considered as true to another whose truth is believed to follow from that of the former **b :** the act of passing from statistical sample data to generalizations (as of the value of population parameters) usu. with calculated degrees of certainty 2 **:** something that is inferred; *esp* **:** a proposition arrived at by inference 3 **:** the premises and conclusion of a process of inferring

in·fer·en·tial \ˌin-fə-ˈren-chəl\ *adj* [ML *inferentia,* fr. L *inferent-, inferens,* prp. of *inferre*] (1657) 1 **:** relating to, involving, or resembling inference 2 **:** deduced or deducible by inference — **in·fer·en·tial·ly** \-ˈrench-(ə-)lē\ *adv*

in·fe·ri·or \in-ˈfir-ē-ər\ *adj* [ME, fr. L, compar. of *inferus* — more at UNDER] (15c) 1 **:** situated lower down **:** LOWER 2 **a :** of low or lower degree or rank **b :** of poor quality **:** MEDIOCRE 3 **:** of little or less importance, value, or merit ⟨always felt ~ to his older brother⟩ 4 **a :** situated below another and esp. another similar superior part of an upright body **b :** situated in a relatively low posterior or ventral position in a quadrupedal body **c** (1) **:** situated below another plant part or organ (2) **:** ABAXIAL 5 **:** relating to or being a subscript 6 **a :** nearer the sun than the earth is ⟨~ planets⟩ **b :** nearer the earth than the sun is ⟨~ conjunction of Venus⟩ — **inferior** *n* — **in·fe·ri·or·i·ty** \(ˌ)in-ˌfir-ē-ˈȯr-ət-ē, -ˈär-\ *n* — **in·fe·ri·or·ly** \in-ˈfir-ē-ər-lē\ *adv*

inferiority complex *n* (1922) **:** an acute sense of personal inferiority resulting either in timidity or through overcompensation in exaggerated aggressiveness

in·fer·nal \in-ˈfərn-ᵊl\ *adj* [ME, fr. MF, fr. LL *infernalis,* fr. *infernus* hell, fr. L, lower; akin to L *inferus* inferior] (14c) 1 **:** of or relating to a nether world of the dead 2 **a :** of or relating to hell **b :** HELLISH, DIABOLICAL 3 **:** DAMNABLE ⟨an ~ nuisance⟩ — **in·fer·nal·ly** \-ᵊl-ē\ *adv*

infernal machine *n* (1810) **:** a machine or apparatus maliciously designed to explode and destroy life or property; *esp* **:** a concealed or disguised bomb

in·fer·no \in-ˈfər-(ˌ)nō\ *n, pl* **-nos** [It, hell, fr. LL *infernus*] (1834) **:** a place or a state that resembles or suggests hell ⟨the ~ of war⟩; *also* **:** intense heat ⟨the roaring ~ of the blast furnace⟩

in·fero- \ˌin-fə-(ˌ)rō\ *comb form* [L *inferus*] **:** below and ⟨*infero*lateral⟩

in·fer·tile \(ˈ)in-ˈfərt-ᵊl\ *adj* [MF, fr. LL *infertilis,* fr. L *in-* + *fertilis* fertile] (1597) **:** not fertile or productive ⟨~ eggs⟩ ⟨~ fields⟩ — **in·fer·til·i·ty** \ˌin-(ˌ)fər-ˈtil-ət-ē\ *n*

in·fest \in-ˈfest\ *vt* [MF *infester,* fr. L *infestare,* fr. *infestus* hostile] (15c) 1 **:** to spread or swarm in or over in a troublesome manner ⟨a slum ~*ed* with crime⟩ ⟨shark-*infested* waters⟩ 2 **:** to live in or on as a parasite — **in·fes·tant** \-ˈfes-tənt\ *n* — **in·fes·ta·tion** \ˌin-ˌfes-ˈtā-shən\ *n* — **in·fest·er** \in-ˈfes-tər\ *n*

in·fi·del \ˈin-fəd-ᵊl, -fə-ˌdel\ *n* [MF *infidele,* fr. LL *infidelis* unbelieving, fr. L, unfaithful, fr. *in-* + *fidelis* faithful — more at FIDELITY] (15c) 1 **:** one who is not a Christian or who opposes Christianity 2 **a :** an unbeliever with respect to a particular religion **b :** one who acknowledges no religious belief 3 **:** a disbeliever in something specified or understood — **infidel** *adj*

in·fi·del·i·ty \ˌin-fə-ˈdel-ət-ē, -(ˌ)fī-\ *n, pl* **-ties** (15c) 1 **:** lack of belief in a religion 2 **a :** unfaithfulness to a moral obligation **:** DISLOYALTY **b :** marital unfaithfulness or an instance of it

in·field \ˈin-ˌfēld\ *n* (ca. 1867) 1 **a :** the area of a baseball field enclosed by the three bases and home plate **b :** the defensive positions comprising first base, second base, shortstop, and third base; *also* **:** the players who play these positions 2 **:** a field near a farmhouse 3 **:** the area enclosed by a racetrack or running track

in·field·er \-ˌfēl-dər\ *n* (1867) **:** a baseball player who plays in the infield

infield hit *n* (1912) **:** a base hit on a ball that does not leave the infield

infield out *n* (1926) **:** a ground ball on which the batter is put out by an infielder

in·fight·ing \ˈin-ˌfīt-iŋ\ *n* (1816) 1 **:** fighting or boxing at close quarters 2 **:** rough-and-tumble fighting 3 **:** prolonged and often bitter dissension or rivalry among members of a group or organization ⟨bureaucratic ~ and departmental jealousies —H. H. Ransom⟩ — **in·fight** \ˈin-ˌfīt\ *vi* — **in·fight·er** \-ər\ *n*

in·fil·trate \in-ˈfil-ˌtrāt, ˈin-(ˌ)\ *vb* **-trat·ed; -trat·ing** *vt* (1758) 1 **:** to cause (as a liquid) to permeate something by penetrating its pores or interstices 2 **:** to pass into or through (a substance) by filtering or permeating 3 **:** to pass (troops) singly or in small groups through gaps in the enemy line 4 **:** to enter or become established in gradually or unobtrusively usu. for subversive purposes ⟨the intelligence staff had been *infiltrated* by spies⟩ ~ *vi* **:** to enter, permeate, or pass through a substance or area by filtering or by insinuating gradually ⟨police can't ~ into the closely knit organization⟩ — **infiltrate** *n* — **in·fil·tra·tion** \ˌin-(ˌ)fil-ˈtrā-shən\ *n* — **in·fil·tra·tive** \ˈin-(ˌ)fil-ˌtrāt-iv, in-ˈfil-trət-\ *adj* — **in·fil·tra·tor** \in-ˈfil-ˌtrāt-ər, ˈin-(ˌ)\ *n*

¹in·fi·nite \ˈin-fə-nət\ *adj* [ME *infinit,* fr. MF or L; MF, fr. L *infinitus,* fr. *in-* + *finitus* finite] (14c) 1 **:** extending indefinitely **:** ENDLESS ⟨~ space⟩ 2 **:** immeasurably or inconceivably great or extensive **:** INEXHAUSTIBLE ⟨~ patience⟩ 3 **:** subject to no limitation or external determination 4 **a :** extending beyond, lying beyond, or being greater than any preassigned finite value however large ⟨~ number of positive numbers⟩ **b :** extending to infinity ⟨~ plane surface⟩ **c :** characterized by an infinite number of elements or terms ⟨an ~ set⟩ ⟨an ~ series⟩ — **in·fi·nite·ly** *adv* — **in·fi·nite·ness** *n*

²infinite *n* (1535) **:** something that is infinite (as in extent, duration, or number)

¹in·fin·i·tes·i·mal \(ˌ)in-ˌfin-ə-ˈtes-ə-məl, -ˈtez-\ *n* [NL *infinitesimus* infinite in rank, fr. L *infinitus*] (1706) **:** an infinitesimal quantity or variable

²infinitesimal *adj* (1710) 1 **:** taking on values arbitrarily close to but greater than zero 2 **:** immeasurably or incalculably small — **in·fin·i·tes·i·mal·ly** \-mə-lē\ *adv*

infinitesimal calculus *n* (1801) **:** CALCULUS 1b

in·fin·i·ti·val \(ˌ)in-ˌfin-ə-ˈtī-vəl\ *adj* (1869) **:** relating to the infinitive

¹in·fin·i·tive \in-ˈfin-ət-iv\ *adj* [LL *infinitivus,* fr. L *infinitus*] (15c) **:** formed with the infinitive — **in·fin·i·tive·ly** *adv*

²infinitive *n* (1530) **:** a verb form normally identical in English with the first person singular that performs some functions of a noun and at the same time displays some characteristics of a verb and that is used with *to* (as in "I asked him *to go*") except with auxiliary and various other verbs (as in "no one saw him *leave*")

in·fin·i·tude \in-ˈfin-ə-ˌt(y)üd\ *n* (1641) 1 **:** the quality or state of being infinite **:** INFINITENESS 2 **:** something that is infinite esp. in extent 3 **:** an infinite number or quantity

in·fin·i·ty \in-ˈfin-ət-ē\ *n, pl* **-ties** (14c) 1 **a :** the quality of being infinite **b :** unlimited extent of time, space, or quantity **:** BOUNDLESSNESS 2 **:** an indefinitely great number or amount ⟨an ~ of stars⟩ 3 **a :** the limit of the value of a function or variable when it tends to become numerically larger than any preassigned finite number **b :** a part of a geometric magnitude that lies beyond any part whose distance from a given reference position is finite ⟨do parallel lines ever meet if they extend to ~⟩ **c :** a transfinite number (as aleph-null) 4 **:** a distance so great that the rays of light from a point source at that distance may be regarded as parallel

in·firm \in-ˈfərm\ *adj* [ME, fr. L *infirmus,* fr. *in-* + *firmus* firm] (14c) 1 **:** of poor or deteriorated vitality; *esp* **:** feeble from age 2 **:** weak of mind, will, or character **:** IRRESOLUTE, VACILLATING 3 **:** not solid or stable **:** INSECURE ***syn*** see WEAK — **in·firm·ly** *adv*

in·fir·ma·ry \in-ˈfərm-(ə-)rē\ *n, pl* **-ries** (15c) **:** a place where the infirm or sick are lodged for care and treatment

in·fir·mi·ty \in-ˈfər-mət-ē\ *n, pl* **-ties** (14c) 1 **a :** the quality or state of being infirm **b :** the condition of being feeble **:** FRAILTY 2 **:** DISEASE, MALADY 3 **:** a personal failing **:** FOIBLE ⟨one of the besetting *infirmities* of living creatures is egotism —A. J. Toynbee⟩

¹in·fix \ˈin-ˌfiks, in-ˈ\ *vt* [L *infixus,* pp. of *infigere,* fr. *in-* + *figere* to fasten — more at DIKE] (15c) 1 **:** to fasten or fix by piercing or thrusting in 2 **:** INSTILL, INCULCATE 3 **:** to insert (as a sound or letter) as an infix ***syn*** see IMPLANT — **in·fix·ation** \ˌin-(ˌ)fik-ˈsā-shən\ *n*

²in·fix \ˈin-ˌfiks\ *n* (1881) **:** a derivational or inflectional affix appearing in the body of a word ⟨Sanskrit *-n-* is an ~ in *vindami* "I know" as contrasted with *vid* "to know"⟩

in fla·gran·te de·lic·to \ˌin-flə-ˌgrant-ē-di-ˈlik-(ˌ)tō\ *adv* (1772) **:** FLAGRANTE DELICTO

in·flame \in-ˈflām\ *vb* **in·flamed; in·flam·ing** [ME *enflamen,* fr. MF *enflamer,* fr. L *inflammare,* fr. *in-* + *flamma* flame] *vt* (14c) 1 **:** to set on fire **:** KINDLE 2 **a :** to excite to excessive or uncontrollable action or feeling **b :** to make more heated or violent **:** INTENSIFY ⟨insults served only to ~ the feud⟩ 3 **:** to cause to redden or grow hot from anger or excitement 4 **:** to cause inflammation in (bodily tissue) ~ *vi*

\ə\ abut \ᵊ\ kitten, F table \ər\ further \a\ ash \ā\ ace \ä\ cot, cart \au̇\ out \ch\ chin \e\ bet \ē\ easy \g\ go \i\ hit \ī\ ice \j\ job \ŋ\ sing \ō\ go \ȯ\ law \ȯi\ boy \th\ thin \t͟h\ the \ü\ loot \u̇\ foot \y\ yet \zh\ vision \à, k̟, ⁿ, œ, œ̄, ue, ue̅, ʸ\ *see* Guide to Pronunciation

1 : to burst into flame **2 :** to become excited or angered **3 :** to become affected with inflammation — **in·flam·er** *n*

in·flam·ma·ble \in-'flam-ə-bəl\ *adj* [F, fr. ML *inflammabilis,* fr. L *inflammare*] (1605) **1 :** FLAMMABLE **2 :** easily inflamed, excited, or angered : IRASCIBLE — **in·flam·ma·bil·i·ty** \-ˌflam-ə-'bil-ət-ē\ *n* — **inflammable** *n* — **in·flam·ma·ble·ness** \-'flam-ə-bəl-nəs\ *n* — **in·flam·ma·bly** \-blē\ *adv*

in·flam·ma·tion \ˌin-flə-'mā-shən\ *n* (15c) **1 :** a local response to cellular injury that is marked by capillary dilatation, leukocytic infiltration, redness, heat, and pain and that serves as a mechanism initiating the elimination of noxious agents and of damaged tissue **2 :** the act of inflaming : the state of being inflamed

in·flam·ma·to·ry \in-'flam-ə-ˌtōr-ē, -ˌtȯr-\ *adj* (1711) **1 :** tending to excite anger, disorder, or tumult : SEDITIOUS **2 :** tending to inflame or excite the senses **3 :** accompanied by or tending to cause inflammation — **in·flam·ma·to·ri·ly** \-ˌflam-ə-'tōr-ə-lē, -'tȯr-\ *adv*

in·flat·able \in-'flāt-ə-bəl\ *adj* (1878) : capable of being inflated ⟨an ~ boat⟩ — **inflatable** *n*

in·flate \in-'flāt\ *vb* **in·flat·ed; in·flat·ing** [L *inflatus,* pp. of *inflare,* fr. *in-* + *flare* to blow — more at BLOW] *vt* (14c) **1 :** to swell or distend with air or gas **2 :** to puff up : ELATE **3 :** to expand or increase abnormally or imprudently ~ *vi* : to become inflated ***syn*** see EXPAND — **in·fla·tor** *or* **in·flat·er** \-'flāt-ər\ *n*

in·flat·ed *adj* (1652) **1 :** elaborated or heightened by artificial or empty means ⟨an ~ style of writing⟩ **2 :** distended with air or gas **3 :** expanded to an abnormal or unjustifiable volume or level ⟨~ prices⟩ **4 :** being hollow and enlarged or distended

in·fla·tion \in-'flā-shən\ *n* (14c) **1 :** an act of inflating : a state of being inflated: as **a :** DISTENSION **b :** empty pretentiousness : POMPOSITY **2 :** an increase in the volume of money and credit relative to available goods resulting in a substantial and continuing rise in the general price level

in·fla·tion·ary \-shə-ˌner-ē\ *adj* (1920) : of, characterized by, or productive of inflation

inflationary spiral *n* (1931) : a continuous rise in prices that is sustained by the tendency of wage increases and cost increases to react on each other

in·fla·tion·ism \in-'flā-shə-ˌniz-əm\ *n* (1919) : the policy of economic inflation — **in·fla·tion·ist** \-sh(ə-)nəst\ *n or adj*

in·flect \in-'flekt\ *vb* [ME *inflecten,* fr. L *inflectere,* fr. *in-* + *flectere* to bend] *vt* (15c) **1 :** to turn from a direct line or course : CURVE **2 :** to vary (a word) by inflection : DECLINE, CONJUGATE **3 :** to change or vary the pitch of (as the voice) : MODULATE ~ *vi* : to become modified by inflection — **in·flect·able** \-flek-tə-bəl\ *adj* — **in·flec·tive** \-'flek-tiv\ *adj*

in·flec·tion \in-'flek-shən\ *n* (1531) **1 :** the act or result of curving or bending : BEND **2 :** change in pitch or loudness of the voice **3 a :** the change of form that words undergo to mark such distinctions as those of case, gender, number, tense, person, mood, or voice **b :** a form, suffix, or element involved in such variation **c :** ACCIDENCE **4 a :** change in curvature of an arc or curve from concave to convex or conversely **b :** INFLECTION POINT

in·flec·tion·al \-shnəl, -shən-ᵊl\ *adj* (1832) : of, relating to, or characterized by inflection ⟨an ~ suffix⟩ — **in·flec·tion·al·ly** \-ē\ *adv*

inflection point *n* (ca. 1721) : a point on a curve that separates an arc concave upward from one concave downward and vice versa

in·flexed \'in-ˌflekst\ *adj* [L *inflexus,* pp. of *inflectere*] (1661) : bent or turned abruptly inward or downward or toward the axis ⟨~ petals⟩

in·flex·i·ble \(')in-'flek-sə-bəl\ *adj* [ME, fr. L *inflexibilis,* fr. *in-* + *flexibilis* flexible] (14c) **1 :** rigidly firm in will or purpose : UNYIELDING **2 :** not readily bent : lacking or deficient in suppleness **3 :** incapable of change : UNALTERABLE — **in·flex·i·bil·i·ty** \(ˌ)in-ˌflek-sə-'bil-ət-ē\ *n* — **in·flex·i·ble·ness** \(')in-'flek-sə-bəl-nəs\ *n* — **in·flex·i·bly** \-blē\ *adv*

syn INFLEXIBLE, INEXORABLE, OBDURATE, ADAMANT mean unwilling to alter a predetermined course or purpose. INFLEXIBLE implies rigid adherence or even slavish conformity to principle; INEXORABLE implies relentlessness of purpose or, esp. when applied to things, inevitableness; OBDURATE stresses hardness of heart and insensitivity to appeals for mercy or the influence of divine grace; ADAMANT implies utter immovability in the face of all temptation or entreaty. ***syn*** see in addition STIFF

in·flex·ion *chiefly Brit var of* INFLECTION

in·flict \in-'flikt\ *vt* [L *inflictus,* pp. of *infligere,* fr. *in-* + *fligere* to strike — more at PROFLIGATE] (1566) **1 :** AFFLICT **2 a :** to give by striking ⟨~*s* a blow on his opponent's jaw⟩ **b :** to cause (something damaging or painful) to be endured : IMPOSE ⟨~ punishment⟩ — **in·flict·er** *or* **in·flic·tor** \-'flik-tər\ *n* — **in·flic·tive** \-tiv\ *adj*

in·flic·tion \in-'flik-shən\ *n* (1534) **1 :** the act of inflicting **2 :** something (as punishment or suffering) that is inflicted

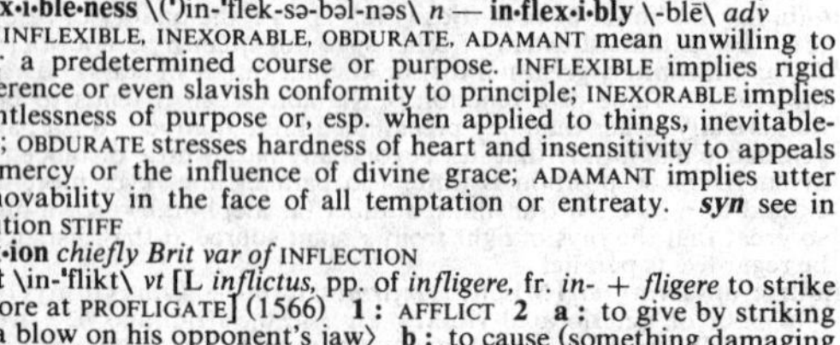

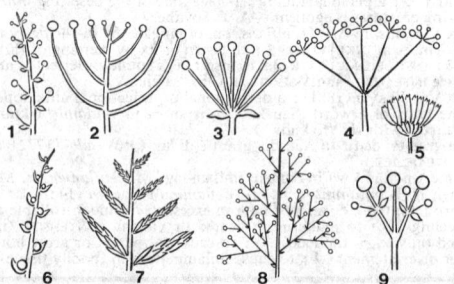

inflorescence 1a (1): *1* raceme, *2* corymb, *3* umbel, *4* compound umbel, *5* capitulum, *6* spike, *7* compound spike, *8* panicle, *9* cyme

in–flight \in-'flīt\ *adj* (1944) : made, carried out, or provided for use or enjoyment while in flight ⟨~ movies⟩

in·flo·res·cence \ˌin-flə-'res-ᵊn(t)s\ *n* [NL *inflorescentia,* fr. LL *inflorescent-, inflorescens,* prp. of *inflorescere* to begin to bloom, fr. L *in-* + *florescere* to begin to bloom — more at FLORESCENCE] (ca. 1760) **1 a** (1) : the mode of development and arrangement of flowers on an axis (2) : a floral axis with its appendages; *also* : a flower cluster or sometimes a solitary flower **b :** a cluster of reproductive organs on a moss usu. subtended by a bract **2 :** the budding and unfolding of blossoms : FLOWERING — **in·flo·res·cent** \-ᵊnt\ *adj*

in·flow \'in-ˌflō\ *n* (1839) : a flowing in ⟨the ~ of air⟩ ⟨an ~ of funds⟩

[1]**in·flu·ence** \'in-ˌflü-ən(t)s, *esp Southern* in-'\ *n* [ME, fr. MF, fr. ML *influentia,* fr. L *influent-, influens,* prp. of *influere* to flow in, fr. *in-* + *fluere* to flow — more at FLUID] (14c) **1 a :** an ethereal fluid held to flow from the stars and to affect the actions of humans **b :** an emanation of occult power held to derive from stars **2 :** an emanation of spiritual or moral force **3 a :** the act or power of producing an effect without apparent exertion of force or direct exercise of command **b :** corrupt interference with authority for personal gain **4 :** the power or capacity of causing an effect in indirect or intangible ways : SWAY **5 :** one that exerts influence

syn INFLUENCE, AUTHORITY, PRESTIGE, WEIGHT, CREDIT mean power exerted over the minds or behavior of others. INFLUENCE may apply to a force exercised and received consciously or unconsciously; AUTHORITY implies the power of winning devotion or allegiance or of compelling acceptance and belief; PRESTIGE implies the ascendancy given by conspicuous excellence or reputation for superiority; WEIGHT implies measurable or decisive influence in determining acts or choices; CREDIT suggests influence that arises from proven merit or favorable reputation.

— **under the influence :** affected by liquor : DRUNK ⟨was arrested for driving *under the influence*⟩

[2]**influence** *vt* **-enced; -enc·ing** (1658) **1 :** to affect or alter by indirect or intangible means : SWAY **2 :** to have an effect on the condition or development of : MODIFY ***syn*** see AFFECT — **in·flu·ence·able** \-ən(t)-sə-bəl\ *adj*

[1]**in·flu·ent** \'in-ˌflü-ənt, in-'\ *adj* (15c) : flowing in

[2]**influent** *n* (1859) **1 :** something that flows in: as **a :** a tributary stream **b :** fluid input into a reservoir or process **2 :** a factor (as a particular animal) modifying the balance and stability of an ecological community

[1]**in·flu·en·tial** \ˌin-(ˌ)flü-'en-chəl\ *adj* (1570) : exerting or possessing influence — **in·flu·en·tial·ly** \-'ench-(ə-)lē\ *adv*

[2]**influential** *n* (1831) : one who has great influence

in·flu·en·za \ˌin-(ˌ)flü-'en-zə\ *n* [It, lit., influence, fr. ML *influentia;* fr. the belief that epidemics were due to the influence of the stars] (1743) **1 :** an acute highly contagious virus disease caused by various strains of a myxovirus and characterized by sudden onset, fever, prostration, severe aches and pains, and progressive inflammation of the respiratory mucous membrane; *broadly* : a human respiratory infection of undetermined cause **2 :** any of numerous febrile usu. virus diseases of domestic animals marked by respiratory symptoms, inflammation of mucous membranes, and often systemic involvement — **in·flu·en·zal** \-zəl\ *adj*

in·flux \'in-ˌfləks\ *n* [LL *influxus,* fr. L, pp. of *influere*] (1626) : a coming in ⟨an ~ of tourists⟩

in·fo \'in-(ˌ)fō\ *n* (1913) : INFORMATION

in·fold \in-'fōld\ *vt* (15c) : ENFOLD, ENVELOP ~ \'in-\ *vi* : to fold inward or toward one another

in·form \in-'fȯ(ə)rm\ *vb* [ME *informen,* fr. MF *enformer,* fr. L *informare,* fr. *in-* + *forma* form] *vt* (14c) **1** *obs* : to give material form to **2 a :** to give character or essence to ⟨the principles which ~ modern teaching⟩ **b :** to be the characteristic quality of : ANIMATE ⟨the compassion that ~*s* his work⟩ **3** *obs* : GUIDE, DIRECT **4** *obs* : to make known **5 :** to communicate knowledge to ⟨~ a prisoner of his rights⟩ ~ *vi* **1 :** to impart information or knowledge **2 :** to give information (as of another's wrongdoing) to an authority

syn INFORM, ACQUAINT, APPRISE, NOTIFY mean to make one aware of something. INFORM implies the imparting of knowledge esp. of facts or occurrences; ACQUAINT lays stress on introducing to or familiarizing with; APPRISE implies communicating something of special interest or importance; NOTIFY implies sending notice of something requiring attention or demanding action.

in·for·mal \(')in-'fȯr-məl\ *adj* (1585) **1 :** marked by the absence of formality or ceremony ⟨an ~ meeting⟩ ⟨an ~ group⟩ **2 :** characteristic of or appropriate to ordinary, casual, or familiar use ⟨~ English⟩ ⟨~ clothes⟩ — **in·for·mal·i·ty** \ˌin-(ˌ)fȯr-'mal-ət-ē, -fər-\ *n* — **in·for·mal·ly** \(')in-'fȯr-mə-lē\ *adv*

in·for·mant \in-'fȯr-mənt\ *n* (1693) : one who gives information: as **a :** INFORMER **b :** one who supplies cultural or linguistic data in response to interrogation by an investigator

in for·ma pau·pe·ris \ˌin-ˌfȯr-mə-'pȯ-pə-rəs, -'pau̇-\ *adj or adv* [L, in the form of a pauper] (1592) : as a poor man

in·for·ma·tion \ˌin-fər-'mā-shən\ *n* (14c) **1 :** the communication or reception of knowledge or intelligence **2 a** (1) : knowledge obtained from investigation, study, or instruction (2) : INTELLIGENCE, NEWS (3) : FACTS, DATA **b :** the attribute inherent in and communicated by one of two or more alternative sequences or arrangements of something (as nucleotides in DNA or binary digits in a computer program) that produce specific effects **c** (1) : a signal or character (as in a communication system or computer) representing data (2) : something (as a message, experimental data, or a picture) which justifies change in a construct (as a plan or theory) that represents physical or mental experience or another construct **d :** a quantitative measure of the content of information; *specif* : a numerical quantity that measures the uncertainty in the outcome of an experiment to be performed **3 :** the act of informing against a person **4 :** a formal accusation of a crime made by a prosecuting officer as distinguished from an indictment presented by a grand jury — **in·for·ma·tion·al** \-shnəl, -shən-ᵊl\ *adj* — **in·for·ma·tion·less** \-shən-ləs\ *adj*

information retrieval *n* (1950) : the techniques of storing and recovering and often disseminating recorded data esp. through the use of a computerized system

information science *n* (1960) : the collection, classification, storage, retrieval, and dissemination of recorded knowledge treated both as a pure and as an applied science

information theory *n* (1950) : a theory that deals statistically with information, the measurement of its content in terms of its distinguishing essential characteristics or by the number of alternatives from which it makes a choice possible, and with the efficiency of processes of communication between humans and machines (as in telecommunication or in computing machines)

in·for·ma·tive \in-ˈfȯr-mət-iv\ *adj* (1655) : imparting knowledge : INSTRUCTIVE — **in·for·ma·tive·ly** *adv* — **in·for·ma·tive·ness** *n*

in·for·ma·to·ry \-mə-ˌtōr-ē, -ˌtȯr-\ *adj* (ca. 1879) : conveying information : INFORMATIVE — **in·for·ma·to·ri·ly** \in-ˌfȯr-mə-ˈtōr-ə-lē, -ˈtȯr-\ *adv*

in·formed \in-ˈfȯ(ə)rmd\ *adj* (1549) **1 a** : having information ⟨~ sources⟩ ⟨~ observers⟩ **b** : based on possession of information ⟨an ~ opinion⟩ **2** : EDUCATED, KNOWLEDGEABLE ⟨what the ~ person should know about psychology⟩ — **in·formed·ly** \-ˈfȯ(ə)rm-dlē, -ˈfȯr-məd-lē\ *adv*

informed consent *n* (ca. 1967) : consent to surgery by a patient or to participation in a medical experiment by a subject after achieving an understanding of what is involved

in·form·er \-ˈfȯr-mər\ *n* (14c) **1** : one that imparts knowledge or news **2** : one that informs against another; *specif* : one who makes a practice esp. for a financial reward of informing against others for violations of penal laws

in·fra \ˈin-frə, -ˌfrä\ *adv* [L] (ca. 1740) : BELOW : later in this writing ⟨for additional examples see ~⟩

infra- *prefix* [L *infra* — more at UNDER] **1** : below ⟨*infra*human⟩ ⟨*infra*sonic⟩ **2** : within ⟨*infra*specific⟩ **3** : below in a scale or series ⟨*infra*red⟩

in·fract \in-ˈfrakt\ *vt* [L *infractus*, pp. of *infringere* to break off — more at INFRINGE] (1727) : INFRINGE, VIOLATE ⟨~ the law⟩ — **in·frac·tion** \-ˈfrak-shən\ *n* — **in·frac·tor** \-ˈfrak-tər\ *n*

in·fra dig \ˌin-frə-ˈdig\ *adj* [short for L *infra dignitatem*] (1824) : being beneath one's dignity : UNDIGNIFIED ⟨while his work . . . was financially profitable, it was just a bit *infra dig* —John McCarten⟩

in·fra·hu·man \ˌin-frə-ˈhyü-mən, -(ˌ)frä-, -ˈyü-\ *adj* (1847) : less or lower than human; *esp* : ANTHROPOID — **infrahuman** *n*

in·fran·gi·bil·i·ty \(ˌ)in-ˌfran-jə-ˈbil-ət-ē\ *n* (ca. 1864) : the quality or state of being infrangible

in·fran·gi·ble \(ˈ)in-ˈfran-jə-bəl\ *adj* [MF, fr. LL *infrangibilis*, fr. L *in-* + *frangere* to break — more at BREAK] (1597) **1** : not capable of being broken or separated into parts **2** : not to be infringed or violated — **in·fran·gi·ble·ness** *n* — **in·fran·gi·bly** \-blē\ *adv*

in·fra·red \ˌin-frə-ˈred, -(ˌ)frä-\ *adj* (1881) **1** : lying outside the visible spectrum at its red end — used of thermal radiation of wavelengths longer than those of visible light **2** : relating to, producing, or employing infrared radiation ⟨~ therapy⟩ **3** : sensitive to infrared radiation ⟨~ photographic film⟩ — **infrared** *n*

in·fra·son·ic \-ˈsän-ik\ *adj* (1927) **1** : having or relating to a frequency below the audibility range of the human ear **2** : utilizing or produced by infrasonic waves or vibrations

in·fra·spe·cif·ic \-spi-ˈsif-ik\ *adj* (1939) : included within a species ⟨~ categories⟩

in·fra·struc·ture \ˈin-frə-ˌstrək-chər, -(ˌ)frä-\ *n* (1927) **1** : the underlying foundation or basic framework (as of a system or organization) **2** : the permanent installations required for military purposes

in·fre·quence \(ˈ)in-ˈfrē-kwən(t)s\ *n* (1644) : INFREQUENCY

in·fre·quen·cy \-kwən-sē\ *n* (1677) : rarity of occurrence

in·fre·quent \(ˈ)in-ˈfrē-kwənt\ *adj* [L *infrequent-, infrequens*, fr. *in-* + *frequent-, frequens* frequent] (1531) **1** : seldom happening or occurring : RARE **2** : placed or occurring at wide intervals in space or time ⟨a slope scattered with ~ pines⟩ ⟨his ~ complaints⟩ — **in·fre·quent·ly** *adv*

syn INFREQUENT, UNCOMMON, SCARCE, RARE, SPORADIC mean not common or abundant. INFREQUENT implies occurrence at wide intervals in space or time; UNCOMMON suggests a frequency below normal expectation; SCARCE implies falling short of a standard or required abundance; RARE suggests extreme scarcity or infrequency and often implies consequent high value; SPORADIC implies occurrence in scattered instances or isolated outbursts.

in·fringe \in-ˈfrinj\ *vb* **in·fringed; in·fring·ing** [L *infringere*, lit., to break off, fr. *in-* + *frangere* to break — more at BREAK] *vt* (1533) **1** : to encroach upon in a way that violates law or the rights of another ⟨~ a patent⟩ **2** *obs* : DEFEAT, FRUSTRATE ~ *vi* : ENCROACH — used with *on* or *upon* ⟨~ on his rights⟩ ***syn*** see TRESPASS — **in·fring·er** *n*

in·fringe·ment \in-ˈfrinj-mənt\ *n* (1628) **1** : the act of infringing : VIOLATION **2** : an encroachment or trespass on a right or privilege

in·fun·dib·u·lar \ˌin-(ˌ)fən-ˈdib-yə-lər\ *adj* (1795) **1** : INFUNDIBULIFORM **2** : of, relating to, or having an infundibulum

in·fun·dib·u·li·form \-lə-ˌfȯrm\ *adj* [NL *infundibulum* + E *-iform*] (1752) : having the form of a funnel or cone

in·fun·dib·u·lum \ˌin-(ˌ)fən-ˈdib-yə-ləm\ *n, pl* **-la** \-lə\ [NL, fr. L, funnel — more at FUNNEL] (ca. 1799) : any of various conical or dilated organs or parts: as **a** : the hollow conical process of gray matter by which the pituitary gland is continuous with the brain **b** : the calyx of a kidney **c** : the abdominal opening of a fallopian tube

[1]**in·fu·ri·ate** \in-ˈfyür-ē-ˌāt\ *vt* **-at·ed; -at·ing** [ML *infuriatus*, pp. of *infuriare*, fr. L *in-* + *furia* fury] (1667) : to make furious : ENRAGE — **in·fu·ri·at·ing·ly** \-ˌāt-iŋ-lē\ *adv* — **in·fu·ri·a·tion** \-ˌfyür-ē-ˈā-shən\ *n*

[2]**in·fu·ri·ate** \in-ˈfyür-ē-ət\ *adj* (1667) : furiously angry

in·fuse \in-ˈfyüz\ *vt* **in·fused; in·fus·ing** [ME *infusen* to pour in, fr. MF & L; MF *infuser*, fr. L *infusus*, pp. of *infundere* to pour in, fr. *in-* + *fundere* to pour — more at FOUND] (1526) **1 a** : to cause to be permeated with something (as a principle or quality) that alters usu. for the better ⟨attributes the fine spirit of the whole project to the self-respect with which men had been *infused* —Dixon Wecter⟩ **b** : INTRODUCE, INSINUATE ⟨a new spirit was *infused* into American art —*Amer. Guide Series: N.Y.*⟩ **2** : INSPIRE, ANIMATE ⟨the sense of purpose that *infuses* scientific research⟩ **3** : to steep in liquid (as water) without boiling so as to extract the soluble properties or constituents — **in·fus·er** *n*

syn INFUSE, SUFFUSE, IMBUE, INGRAIN, INOCULATE, LEAVEN mean to introduce one thing into another so as to affect it throughout. INFUSE implies a pouring in of something that gives new life or significance; SUFFUSE implies a spreading through of something that gives an unusual color or quality; IMBUE implies the introduction of a quality that fills and permeates the whole being; INGRAIN suggests the indelible stamping or deep implanting of a quality or trait; INOCULATE implies an imbuing or implanting with a germinal idea and often suggests surreptitiousness or subtlety; LEAVEN implies introducing something that enlivens, tempers, or markedly alters the total quality.

in·fus·ible \(ˈ)in-ˈfyü-zə-bəl\ *adj* (1555) : incapable of being fused : very difficult to fuse — **in·fus·ibil·i·ty** \(ˌ)in-ˌfyü-zə-ˈbil-ət-ē\ *n* — **in·fus·ible·ness** \(ˈ)in-ˈfyü-zə-bəl-nəs\ *n*

in·fu·sion \in-ˈfyü-zhən\ *n* (15c) **1** : the act or process of infusing **2** : a product obtained by infusing **3** : the continuous slow introduction of a solution esp. into a vein

in·fu·so·ri·al earth \ˌin-fyü-ˌzōr-ē-əl-, -ˌsōr-, -ˌzȯr-, -ˌsȯr-\ *n* (1882) : KIESELGUHR

in·fu·so·ri·an \-ē-ən\ *n* [deriv. of L *infusus*] (1859) : any of a heterogeneous group of minute organisms found esp. in decomposing infusions of organic matter; *esp* : a ciliated protozoan — **infusorian** *adj*

[1]**-ing** \iŋ, ēŋ; *in some dialects usu & in other dialects informally* in, ēn, ən; *also after certain consonants* ᵊn, ᵊm, ᵊŋ\ *vb suffix or adj suffix* [ME, alter. of *-ende*, fr. OE, fr. *-e-*, verb stem vowel + *-nde*, prp. suffix — more at -ANT] — used to form the present participle ⟨sail*ing*⟩ and sometimes to form an adjective resembling a present participle but not derived from a verb ⟨swashbuckl*ing*⟩

usage Though the pronunciation of *-ing* with the consonant \n\, misleadingly referred to as "dropping the g," is often deprecated, this pronunciation is frequently heard. It is not known for certain why the Middle English present participle ending *-ende* changed into *-ing*. Analogy with the earlier noun suffix *-ing* prob. had something to do with it. In early modern English, present participles were regularly formed with *-ing* pronounced \iŋg\ (as can still be heard in a few dialects) and later \iŋ\. Evidence also shows that some speakers used \in\ and by the 18th century this pronunciation became widespread. Though teachers (with some success) campaigned against it, \in\ remained a feature of the speech of many of the best speakers in Britain and the U.S. well into this century. It has by now lost its respectability, at least when attention is drawn to it, but throughout the U.S. it persists largely unnoticed and in some dialects it predominates over \iŋ\. Also largely unremarked, even by linguists, is widespread variation in the vowel of *-ing*. Esp. in Northern and Midland dialects and across the upper Midwest to California \ēn\ and \ēŋ\ are quite frequent, while \in\ and \ən\ show a predominance of Southern usage. To save space this book usu. shows only \iŋ\.

[2]**-ing** *n suffix* [ME, fr. OE *-ing, -ung*; akin to OHG *-ing* one of a (specified) kind] : one of a (specified) kind ⟨sweet*ing*⟩

[3]**-ing** *n suffix* [ME, fr. OE *-ung, -ing*, suffix forming nouns from verbs; akin to OHG *-ung*, suffix forming nouns from verbs] **1** : action or process ⟨runn*ing*⟩ ⟨sleep*ing*⟩ : instance of an action or process ⟨a meet*ing*⟩ **2 a** : product or result of an action or process ⟨an engrav*ing*⟩ — often in pl. ⟨earn*ings*⟩ **b** : something used in an action or process ⟨a bed cover*ing*⟩ ⟨the lin*ing* of a coat⟩ **3** : action or process connected with (a specified thing) ⟨boat*ing*⟩ **4** : something connected with, consisting of, or used in making (a specified thing) ⟨scaffold*ing*⟩ ⟨shirt*ing*⟩ **5** : something related to (a specified concept) ⟨off*ing*⟩

in·gath·er \ˈin-ˌgath-ər, -ˌgeth-\ *vt* (1557) : to gather in ~ *vi* : ASSEMBLE — **in·gath·er·ing** \-ˌgath-(ə-)riŋ, -ˌgeth-\ *n*

in·ge·nious \in-ˈjēn-yəs\ *adj* [ME *ingenyous*, fr. MF *ingenieux*, fr. L *ingeniosus*, fr. *ingenium* natural capacity — more at ENGINE] (15c) **1** *obs* : showing or calling for intelligence, aptitude, or discernment **2** : marked by especial aptitude at discovering, inventing, or contriving **3** : marked by originality, resourcefulness, and cleverness in conception or execution ⟨an ~ contraption⟩ ***syn*** see CLEVER — **in·ge·nious·ly** *adv* — **in·ge·nious·ness** *n*

in·ge·nue *or* **in·gé·nue** \ˈan-jə-ˌnü, ˈän-; ˈaⁿ-zhə-, ˈäⁿ-\ *n* [F *ingénue*, fem. of *ingénu* ingenuous, fr. L *ingenuus*] (1848) **1** : a naive girl or young woman **2** : the stage role of an ingenue; *also* : an actress playing such a role

in·ge·nu·ity \ˌin-jə-ˈn(y)ü-ət-ē\ *n, pl* **-ities** (1614) **1** *obs* : CANDOR, INGENUOUSNESS **2 a** : skill or cleverness in devising or combining : INVENTIVENESS **b** : cleverness or aptness of design or contrivance **3** : an ingenious device or contrivance

[1]**in·gen·u·ous** \in-ˈjen-yə-wəs\ *adj* [by alter.] *obs* (1588) : INGENIOUS

[2]**ingenuous** *adj* [L *ingenuus* native, free born, fr. *in-* + *gignere* to beget — more at KIN] (1598) **1** *obs* : NOBLE, HONORABLE **2 a** : showing innocent or childlike simplicity and candidness **b** : lacking craft or subtlety ***syn*** see NATURAL — **in·gen·u·ous·ly** *adv* — **in·gen·u·ous·ness** *n*

in·gest \in-ˈjest\ *vt* [L *ingestus*, pp. of *ingerere* to carry in, fr. *in-* + *gerere* to bear — more at CAST] (1620) : to take in for or as if for digestion : ABSORB — **in·gest·ible** \-ˈjes-tə-bəl\ *adj* — **in·ges·tion** \-ˈjes(h)-chən\ *n* — **in·ges·tive** \-ˈjes-tiv\ *adj*

in·ges·ta \in-ˈjes-tə\ *n pl* [NL, fr. L, neut. pl. of *ingestus*] (1727) : material taken into the body by way of the digestive tract

in·gle \ˈiŋ-(g)əl\ *n* [ScGael *aingeal*] (1508) **1** : a fire in a fireplace **2** : FIREPLACE **3** : CORNER, ANGLE

in·gle·nook \-ˌnu̇k\ *n* (1772) : a nook by a large open fireplace; *also* : a bench or settle occupying this nook

in·glo·ri·ous \(ˈ)in-ˈglōr-ē-əs, -ˈglȯr-\ *adj* [L *inglorius*, fr. *in-* + *gloria* glory] (1573) **1** : SHAMEFUL, IGNOMINIOUS **2** : not glorious : lacking fame or honor — **in·glo·ri·ous·ly** *adv* — **in·glo·ri·ous·ness** *n*

in·got \ˈiŋ-gət\ *n* [ME, perh. modif. of MF *lingot* ingot of metal, incorrectly divided as *l'ingot*, as if fr. *le* the, fr. L *ille* that] (14c) **1** : a mold in which metal is cast **2** : a mass of metal cast into a convenient shape for storage or transportation to be later processed

ingot iron *n* (ca. 1877) : iron containing only small proportions of impurities (as less than 0.05 percent carbon)

[1]**in·grain** \(ˈ)in-ˈgrān\ *vt* (1641) : to work indelibly into the natural texture or mental or moral constitution ***syn*** see INFUSE

\ə\ abut \ᵊ\ kitten, F table \ər\ further \a\ ash \ā\ ace \ä\ cot, cart \au̇\ out \ch\ chin \e\ bet \ē\ easy \g\ go \i\ hit \ī\ ice \j\ job \ŋ\ sing \ō\ go \ȯ\ law \ȯi\ boy \th\ thin \t͟h\ the \ü\ loot \u̇\ foot \y\ yet \zh\ vision \à, k̲, ⁿ, œ, œ̄, ue, ue̅, ʸ\ see Guide to Pronunciation

2in·grain \ˌin-ˌgrān\ *adj* (1766) **1 a :** made of fiber that is dyed before being spun into yarn **b :** made of yarn that is dyed before being woven or knitted **2 :** thoroughly worked in : INNATE

3in·grain \'in-ˌgrān\ *n* (ca. 1890) **:** innate quality or character

in·grained \'in-ˌgrānd, (ˈ)in-'\ *adj* (1599) **1 :** worked into the grain or fiber **2 :** forming a part of the essence or inmost being : DEEP-SEATED ⟨~ prejudice⟩ — **in·grained·ly** \'in-ˌgrā-nəd-lē, 'in-ˌgrān-dlē, (ˈ)in-'\ *adv*

in·grate \'in-ˌgrāt\ *n* [L *ingratus* ungrateful, fr. *in-* + *gratus* grateful — more at GRACE] (1622) **:** an ungrateful person

in·gra·ti·ate \in-'grā-shē-ˌāt\ *vt* **-at·ed; -at·ing** [*in-* + L *gratia* grace] (1622) **:** to gain favor or favorable acceptance for by deliberate effort — usu. used with *with* ⟨~ themselves with the community leaders — William Attwood⟩ — **in·gra·ti·a·tion** \-ˌgrā-shē-'ā-shən\ *n* — **in·gra·tia·to·ry** \-'grā-sh(ē-)ə-ˌtōr-ē, -ˌtȯr-\ *adj*

in·gra·ti·at·ing *adj* (1655) **1 :** capable of winning favor : PLEASING ⟨an ~ smile⟩ **2 :** intended or adopted in order to gain favor : FLATTERING — **in·gra·ti·at·ing·ly** \-'grā-shē-ˌāt-iŋ-lē\ *adv*

in·grat·i·tude \(ˈ)in-'grat-ə-ˌt(y)üd\ *n* [ME, fr. MF, fr. ML *ingratitudo*, fr. L *in-* + LL *gratitudo* gratitude] (14c) **:** forgetfulness of or poor return for kindness received : UNGRATEFULNESS

in·gre·di·ent \in-'grēd-ē-ənt\ *n* [ME, fr. L *ingredient-, ingrediens*, prp. of *ingredi* to go into, fr. *in-* + *gradi* to go — more at GRADE] (15c) **:** something that enters into a compound or is a component part of any combination or mixture : CONSTITUENT ***syn*** see ELEMENT — **ingredient** *adj*

in·gress \'in-ˌgres\ *n* [ME, fr. L *ingressus*, fr. *ingressus*, pp. of *ingredi*] (15c) **1 :** the act of entering : ENTRANCE; *specif* **:** the entrance of a celestial object into eclipse, occultation, or transit **2 :** the power or liberty of entrance or access — **in·gres·sion** \in-'gresh-ən\ *n*

in·gres·sive \in-'gres-iv\ *adj* (1649) **1 :** of, relating to, or involving ingress ⟨an ~ current of air⟩ **2 :** INCHOATIVE 2 — **ingressive** *n* — **in·gres·sive·ness** *n*

in–group \'in-ˌgrüp\ *n* (1907) **1 :** a group with which one feels a sense of solidarity or community of interests — compare OUT-GROUP **2 :** CLIQUE

in·grow·ing \'in-ˌgrō-iŋ\ *adj* (1869) **:** growing or tending inward

in·grown \-ˌgrōn\ *adj* (1878) **1 :** grown in; *specif* **:** having the free tip or edge embedded in the flesh ⟨an ~ toenail⟩ **2 :** having the direction of growth or activity or interest inward rather than outward : WITHDRAWN — **in·grown·ness** \-'grōn-nəs\ *n*

in·growth \'in-ˌgrōth\ *n* (1870) **1 :** a growing inward (as to fill a void) **2 :** something that grows in or into a space

in·gui·nal \'iŋ-gwən-ᵊl\ *adj* [L *inguinalis*, fr. *inguin-, inguen* groin — more at ADEN-] (15c) **:** of, relating to, or situated in the region of the groin or in either of the lowest lateral regions of the abdomen

in·gur·gi·tate \in-'gər-jə-ˌtāt\ *vt* **-tat·ed; -tat·ing** [L *ingurgitatus*, pp. of *ingurgitare*, fr. *in-* + *gurgit-, gurges* whirlpool — more at VORACIOUS] (ca. 1570) **:** to swallow greedily or in large quantities : GUZZLE — **in·gur·gi·ta·tion** \(ˌ)in-ˌgər-jə-'tā-shən\ *n*

in·hab·it \in-'hab-ət\ *vb* [ME *enhabiten*, fr. MF & L; MF *enhabiter*, fr. L *inhabitare*, fr. *in-* + *habitare* to dwell, fr. *habitus*, pp. of *habēre* to have — more at GIVE] *vt* (14c) **1 :** to occupy as a place of settled residence or habitat : live in ⟨~ a small house⟩ **2 :** to be present in or occupy in any manner or form ⟨the human beings who ~ this tale —Al Newman⟩ ~ *vi, archaic* **:** to have residence in a place : DWELL — **in·hab·it·able** \-ə-bəl\ *adj* — **in·hab·it·er** *n*

in·hab·it·an·cy \in-'hab-ət-ən-sē\ *n* (1681) **:** INHABITATION

in·hab·it·ant \in-'hab-ət-ənt\ *n* (15c) **:** one that occupies a particular place regularly, routinely, or for a period of time ⟨~s of large cities⟩ ⟨the tapeworm is an ~ of the intestine⟩

in·hab·i·ta·tion \in-ˌhab-ə-'tā-shən\ *n* (15c) **:** the act of inhabiting : the state of being inhabited

in·hab·it·ed *adj* (15c) **:** having inhabitants

in·hal·ant \in-'hā-lənt\ *n* (ca. 1890) **:** something (as an allergen or medication) that is inhaled — **inhalant** *adj*

in·ha·la·tion \ˌin-(h)ə-'lā-shən, ˌin-ᵊl-'ā-\ *n* (ca. 1623) **1 :** the act or an instance of inhaling **2 :** material (as medication) to be taken in by inhaling — **in·ha·la·tion·al** \-shnəl, -shən-ᵊl\ *adj*

in·ha·la·tor \'in-(h)ə-ˌlāt-ər, 'in-ᵊl-ˌāt-\ *n* (1925) **:** a device providing a mixture of oxygen and carbon dioxide for breathing that is used esp. in conjunction with artificial respiration

in·hale \in-'hā(ə)l\ *vb* **in·haled; in·hal·ing** [*in-* + *-hale* (as in *exhale*)] *vt* (1725) **1 :** to draw in by breathing **2 :** to take in eagerly or greedily ⟨*inhaled* about four meals at once —Ring Lardner⟩ ~ *vi* **:** to breathe in — **in·hale** \in-', 'in-ˌ\ *n*

in·hal·er \in-'hā-lər\ *n* (1778) **1 :** a device by means of which medicinal material is inhaled **2 :** one that inhales

in·har·mon·ic \ˌin-(ˌ)här-'män-ik\ *adj* (ca. 1828) **:** not harmonic

in·har·mo·ni·ous \-'mō-nē-əs\ *adj* (1711) **1 :** not harmonious : DISCORDANT **2 :** not fitting or congenial : CONFLICTING — **in·har·mo·ni·ous·ly** *adv* — **in·har·mo·ni·ous·ness** *n*

in·har·mo·ny \(ˈ)in-'här-mə-nē\ *n* (1799) **:** DISCORD

in·here \in-'hi(ə)r\ *vi* **in·hered; in·her·ing** [L *inhaerēre*, fr. *in-* + *haerēre* to adhere — more at HESITATE] (15c) **:** to be inherent : BELONG

in·her·ence \in-'hir-ən(t)s, -'her-\ *n* (1577) **:** the quality, state, or fact of inhering

in·her·ent \-ənt\ *adj* [L *inhaerent-, inhaerens*, prp. of *inhaerēre*] (1581) **:** involved in the constitution or essential character of something : belonging by nature or settled habit : INTRINSIC — **in·her·ent·ly** *adv*

in·her·it \in-'her-ət\ *vb* [ME *enheriten* to make one an heir, inherit, fr. MF *enheriter* to make one an heir, fr. LL *inhereditare*, fr. L *in-* + *hereditas* inheritance — more at HEREDITY] *vt* (14c) **1 :** to come into possession of or receive esp. as a right or divine portion ⟨and every one who has left houses or brothers or sisters . . . for my name's sake, will receive a hundredfold, and ~ eternal life —Mt 19:29 (RSV)⟩ **2 a :** to receive as a right or title descendible by law from an ancestor at his death **b :** to receive as a devise or legacy **3 :** to receive from ancestors by genetic transmission ⟨~ a strong constitution⟩ **4 :** to have in turn or receive as if from an ancestor ⟨~*ed* the problem from his predecessor⟩ ~ *vi* **:** to take or hold a possession or rights by inheritance — **in·her·i·tor** \-ət-ər\ *n* — **in·her·i·tress** \-ə-trəs\ *or* **in·her·i·trix** \-ə-(ˌ)triks\ *n*

in·her·it·able \in-'her-ət-ə-bəl\ *adj* (15c) **1 :** capable of being inherited : TRANSMISSIBLE **2 :** capable of taking by inheritance — **in·her·it·abil·i·ty** \-ˌher-ət-ə-'bil-ət-ē\ *n* — **in·her·it·able·ness** \-'her-ət-ə-bəl-nəs\ *n*

in·her·i·tance \in-'her-ət-ən(t)s\ *n* (14c) **1 a :** the act of inheriting property **b :** the reception of genetic qualities by transmission from parent to offspring **c :** the acquisition of a possession, condition, or trait from past generations **2 :** something that is or may be inherited **3 a :** TRADITION **b :** a valuable possession that is a common heritage from nature **4** *obs* **:** POSSESSION

inheritance tax *n* (1841) **1 :** an excise in the form of a percentage of the value of the property received that is levied on the privilege of an heir to receive property as an inheritance **2 :** DEATH TAX; *esp* **:** ESTATE TAX

in·hib·it \in-'hib-ət\ *vb* [ME *inhibiten*, fr. L *inhibitus*, pp. of *inhibēre*, fr. *in-* 2in- + *habēre* to have — more at HABIT] *vt* (15c) **1 :** to prohibit from doing something **2 a :** to hold in check : RESTRAIN **b :** to discourage from free or spontaneous activity esp. through the operation of inner psychological impediments or of social controls ~ *vi* **:** to cause inhibition ***syn*** see FORBID — **in·hib·i·tive** \-ət-iv\ *adj* — **in·hib·i·to·ry** \-ə-ˌtōr-ē, -ˌtȯr-\ *adj*

in·hi·bi·tion \ˌin-(h)ə-'bish-ən\ *n* (14c) **1 a :** the act of inhibiting : the state of being inhibited **b :** something that forbids, debars, or restricts **2 :** an inner impediment to free activity, expression, or functioning: as **a :** a psychical activity imposing restraint upon another activity **b :** a restraining of the function of a bodily organ or an agent (as an enzyme)

in·hib·i·tor \in-'hib-ət-ər\ *n* (ca. 1611) **:** one that inhibits; *esp* **:** an agent that slows or interferes with a chemical action (as rusting)

in·hos·pi·ta·ble \ˌin-(ˌ)häs-'pit-ə-bəl, (ˈ)in-'häs-(ˌ)pit-\ *adj* (ca. 1570) **1 :** not showing hospitality : not friendly or receptive **2 :** providing no shelter or sustenance : BARREN — **in·hos·pi·ta·ble·ness** *n* — **in·hos·pi·ta·bly** \-blē\ *adv*

in·hos·pi·tal·i·ty \(ˌ)in-ˌhäs-pə-'tal-ət-ē\ *n* (1570) **:** the quality or state of being inhospitable

in–house \ˌin-ˌhau̇s, 'in-'\ *adj* (ca. 1956) **:** existing, originating, or carried on within a group or organization or its facilities : not outside ⟨~ training⟩ ⟨an ~ publication⟩ ⟨a company's ~ staff⟩ — **in–house** *adv*

in·hu·man \(ˈ)in-'hyü-mən, -'yü-\ *adj* [MF & L; MF *inhumain*, fr. L *inhumanus*, fr. *in-* + *humanus* human] (15c) **1 a :** lacking pity, kindness, or mercy : SAVAGE ⟨an ~ tyrant⟩ **b :** COLD, IMPERSONAL ⟨his usual quiet, almost ~ courtesy —F. Tennyson Jesse⟩ **c :** not worthy of or conforming to the needs of human beings ⟨~ living conditions⟩ **2 :** of or suggesting a nonhuman class of beings — **in·hu·man·ly** *adv* — **in·hu·man·ness** \-mən-nəs\ *n*

in·hu·mane \ˌin-(ˌ)hyü-'mān, -(ˌ)yü-\ *adj* [MF *inhumain* & L *inhumanus*] (1599) **:** not humane : INHUMAN 1 — **in·hu·mane·ly** *adv*

in·hu·man·i·ty \-'man-ət-ē\ *n, pl* **-ties** (15c) **1 a :** the quality or state of being cruel or barbarous **b :** a cruel or barbarous act **2 :** absence of warmth or geniality : IMPERSONALITY

in·hume \in-'hyüm\ *vt* **in·humed; in·hum·ing** [prob. fr. F *inhumer*, fr. L *inhumare*, fr. *in-* + *humus* earth — more at HUMBLE] (1604) **:** BURY, INTER — **in·hu·ma·tion** \ˌin-hyü-'mā-shən\ *n*

in·im·i·cal \in-'im-i-kəl\ *adj* [LL *inimicalis*, fr. L *inimicus* enemy — more at ENEMY] (1573) **1 :** being adverse often by reason of hostility or malevolence **2 a :** having the disposition of an enemy : HOSTILE **b :** reflecting or indicating hostility : UNFRIENDLY — **in·im·i·cal·ly** \-i-k(ə-)lē\ *adv*

in·im·i·ta·ble \(ˈ)in-'im-ət-ə-bəl\ *adj* [MF or L; MF, fr. L *inimitabilis*, fr. *in-* + *imitabilis* imitable] (15c) **:** not capable of being imitated : MATCHLESS — **in·im·i·ta·ble·ness** *n* — **in·im·i·ta·bly** \-blē\ *adv*

in·i·on \'in-ē-ˌän, -ən\ *n* [NL, fr. Gk, back of the head, dim. of *in-, is* sinew, tendon — more at WITHY] (ca. 1811) **:** the external occipital protuberance of the skull

in·iq·ui·tous \in-'ik-wət-əs\ *adj* (1726) **:** characterized by iniquity ***syn*** see VICIOUS — **in·iq·ui·tous·ly** *adv* — **in·iq·ui·tous·ness** *n*

in·iq·ui·ty \-wət-ē\ *n, pl* **-ties** [ME *iniquite*, fr. MF *iniquité*, fr. L *iniquitat-, iniquitas*, fr. *iniquus* uneven, fr. *in-* + *aequus* equal] (14c) **1 :** gross injustice : WICKEDNESS **2 :** an iniquitous act or thing : SIN

1ini·tial \in-'ish-əl\ *adj* [MF & L; MF, fr. L *initialis*, fr. *initium* beginning, fr. *initus*, pp. of *inire* to go into, fr. *in-* + *ire* to go — more at ISSUE] (1526) **1 :** of or relating to the beginning : INCIPIENT **2 :** placed at the beginning : FIRST — **ini·tial·ly** \-'ish-(ə-)lē\ *adv* — **ini·tial·ness** \-'ish-əl-nəs\ *n*

2initial *n* (1627) **1 a :** the first letter of a name **b** *pl* **:** the first letter of each word in a full name ⟨found that their ~s were identical⟩ **2 :** a large letter beginning a text or a division or paragraph **3 :** ANLAGE, PRECURSOR; *specif* **:** a meristematic cell

3initial *vt* **ini·tialed** *or* **ini·tialled; ini·tial·ing** *or* **ini·tial·ling** \-'ish-(ə-)liŋ\ (ca. 1864) **1 :** to affix an initial to **2 :** to authenticate or give preliminary approval to by affixing the initials of an authorizing representative

ini·tial·ism \in-'ish-ə-ˌliz-əm\ *n* (1899) **:** an acronym formed from initial letters

ini·tial·ize \-ˌlīz\ *vt* **-ized; -iz·ing** (1957) **:** to set (as a computer program counter) to a starting position or value — **ini·tial·iza·tion** \-in-ˌish-(ə-)lə-'zā-shən\ *n*

initial rhyme *n* (1838) **:** ALLITERATION

initial side *n* (ca. 1957) **:** a stationary straight line that contains a point about which another straight line is rotated to form an angle measured in a clockwise or counterclockwise direction — compare TERMINAL SIDE

1ini·ti·ate \in-'ish-ē-ˌāt\ *vt* **-at·ed; -at·ing** [LL *initiatus*, pp. of *initiare*, fr. L, to induct, fr. *initium*] (1569) **1 :** to cause or facilitate the beginning of : set going ⟨~ a program of reform⟩ ⟨enzymes that ~ fermentation⟩ **2 :** to induct into membership by or as if by special rites **3 :** to instruct in the rudiments or principles of something : INTRODUCE ***syn*** see BEGIN — **ini·ti·a·tor** \-ˌāt-ər\ *n*

2ini·tiate \in-'ish-(ē-)ət\ *adj* (1605) **1** *obs* **:** relating to an initiate **2 a :** initiated or properly admitted (as to membership or an office) **b :** instructed in some secret knowledge

3ini·tiate \in-'ish-(ē-)ət\ *n* (1811) **1 :** a person who is undergoing or has undergone an initiation **2 :** a person who is instructed or adept in some special field

ini·ti·a·tion \in-ˌish-ē-'ā-shən\ *n* (1583) **1 a :** the act or an instance of initiating **b :** the process of being initiated **c :** the rites, ceremonies, ordeals, or instructions with which one is made a member of a sect or society or is invested with a particular function or status **2 :** the condition of being initiated into some experience or sphere of activity : KNOWLEDGEABLENESS ⟨clear to a reader of any degree of ~ —J. W. Beach⟩

[1]ini·tia·tive \in-'ish-ət-iv\ *adj* (1642) **:** of or relating to initiation **:** INTRODUCTORY, PRELIMINARY

[2]initiative *n* (1793) **1 :** an introductory step ⟨he took the ~ in attempting to settle the issue⟩ **2 :** energy or aptitude displayed in initiation of action **:** ENTERPRISE ⟨a person of great ~⟩ **3 a :** the right to initiate legislative action **b :** a procedure enabling a specified number of voters by petition to propose a law and secure its submission to the electorate or to the legislature for approval — compare REFERENDUM — **on one's own initiative :** at one's own discretion **:** independently of outside influence or control

ini·tia·to·ry \in-'ish-(ē-)ə-,tōr-ē, -,tȯr-\ *adj* (1612) **1 :** constituting a beginning **2 :** tending or serving to initiate

in·ject \in-'jekt\ *vt* [L *injectus,* pp. of *inicere,* fr. *in-* + *jacere* to throw — more at JET] (1601) **1 a :** to throw, drive, or force into something ⟨~ fuel into an engine⟩ **b :** to force a fluid into (as for medical purposes) **2 :** to introduce as an element or factor in or into some situation or subject ⟨condemning any attempt to ~ religious bigotry into the campaign —*Current Biog.*⟩ — **in·ject·able** \-'jek-tə-bəl\ *adj* — **in·jec·tor** \-'jek-tər\ *n*

in·jec·tant \-'jek-tənt\ *n* (1950) **:** a substance that is injected into something

in·jec·tion \in-'jek-shən\ *n* (15c) **1 a :** an act or instance of injecting **b :** the placing of an artificial satellite or a spacecraft into an orbit or on a trajectory; *also* **:** the time or place at which injection occurs **2 :** something (as a medication) that is injected **3 :** a mathematical function that is a one-to-one mapping — compare BIJECTION, SURJECTION

in·jec·tive \in-'jek-tiv\ *adj* (1952) **:** being a one-to-one mathematical function

in–joke \'in-,jōk, -'jōk\ *n* (1964) **:** a joke for or about a select group of people

in·ju·di·cious \,in-jü-'dish-əs\ *adj* (1649) **:** not judicious **:** INDISCREET, UNWISE — **in·ju·di·cious·ly** *adv* — **in·ju·di·cious·ness** *n*

in·junc·tion \in-'jəŋ(k)-shən\ *n* [MF & LL; MF *injonction,* fr. LL *injunction-, injunctio,* fr. L *injunctus,* pp. of *injungere* to enjoin — more at ENJOIN] (15c) **1 :** the act or an instance of enjoining **:** ORDER, ADMONITION **2 :** a writ granted by a court of equity whereby one is required to do or to refrain from doing a specified act — **in·junc·tive** \-'jəŋ(k)-tiv\ *adj*

in·jure \'in-jər\ *vt* **in·jured; in·jur·ing** \'inj-(ə-)riŋ\ [back-formation fr. *injury*] (15c) **1 a :** to do an injustice to **:** WRONG **b :** to harm, impair, or tarnish the standing of **c :** to give pain to ⟨~ a person's pride⟩ **2 a :** to inflict bodily hurt on **b :** to impair the soundness of **c :** to inflict material damage or loss on — **in·jur·er** \'in-jər-ər\ *n*

syn INJURE, HARM, HURT, DAMAGE, IMPAIR, MAR mean to affect injuriously. INJURE implies the inflicting of anything detrimental to one's looks, comfort, health, or success; HARM often stresses the inflicting of pain, suffering, or loss; HURT implies inflicting a wound to the body or to the feelings; DAMAGE suggests injury that lowers value or impairs usefulness; IMPAIR suggests a making less complete or efficient by deterioration or diminution; MAR applies to injury that spoils perfection (as of a surface) or causes disfigurement.

in·ju·ri·ous \in-'jür-ē-əs\ *adj* (15c) **1 :** inflicting or tending to inflict injury **:** DETRIMENTAL ⟨~ to health⟩ **2 :** ABUSIVE, DEFAMATORY ⟨speak not ~ words —George Washington⟩ — **in·ju·ri·ous·ly** *adv* — **in·ju·ri·ous·ness** *n*

in·ju·ry \'inj-(ə-)rē\ *n, pl* **-ries** [ME *injurie,* fr. L *injuria,* fr. *injurus* injurious, fr. *in-* + *jur-, jus* right — more at JUST] (14c) **1 a :** an act that damages or hurts **:** WRONG **b :** violation of another's rights for which the law allows an action to recover damages **2 :** hurt, damage, or loss sustained ***syn*** see INJUSTICE

in·jus·tice \(')in-'jəs-təs\ *n* [ME, fr. MF, fr. L *injustitia,* fr. *injustus* unjust, fr. *in-* + *justus* just] (14c) **1 :** absence of justice **:** violation of right or of the rights of another **:** UNFAIRNESS **2 :** an unjust act **:** WRONG

syn INJUSTICE, INJURY, WRONG, GRIEVANCE mean an act that inflicts undeserved hurt. INJUSTICE applies to any act that involves unfairness to another or violation of his rights; INJURY applies in law specifically to an injustice for which one may sue to recover compensation; WRONG applies also in law to any act punishable according to the criminal code; it may apply more generally to any flagrant injustice; GRIEVANCE applies to any circumstance or condition that constitutes an injustice to the sufferer and gives him just ground for complaint.

[1]ink \'iŋk\ *n, often attrib* [ME *enke,* fr. OF, fr. LL *encaustum,* fr. neut. of L *encaustus* burned in, fr. Gk *enkaustos,* verbal of *enkaiein* to burn in — more at ENCAUSTIC] (13c) **1 :** a colored usu. liquid material for writing and printing **2 :** the black protective secretion of a cephalopod **3** *slang* **:** PUBLICITY 2d — **ink·i·ness** \'iŋ-kē-nəs\ *n* — **inky** \'iŋ-kē\ *adj*

[2]ink *vt* (1562) **1 :** to put ink on ⟨~ a pen⟩; *also* **:** to draw or write on in ink **2 :** to affix one's signature to **:** SIGN ⟨~*ed* a new contract⟩

ink·ber·ry \'iŋk-,ber-ē\ *n* [fr. the use of the berries for making ink] (1765) **1 a :** a holly (*Ilex glabra*) of eastern No. America with evergreen oblong leathery leaves and small black berries **b :** POKEWEED **2 :** the fruit of an inkberry

ink·blot test \,iŋk-,blät-\ *n* (1928) **:** any of several psychological tests (as a Rorschach test) based on the interpretation of irregular figures (as blots of ink)

[1]ink·horn \'iŋk-,hȯ(ə)rn\ *n* (14c) **:** a small portable bottle (as of horn) for holding ink

[2]inkhorn *adj* (1543) **:** ostentatiously learned **:** PEDANTIC ⟨~ terms⟩

in·kle \'iŋ-kəl\ *n* [origin unknown] (1541) **:** a colored linen tape or braid woven on a very narrow loom and used for trimming; *also* **:** the thread used

in·kling \'iŋ-kliŋ\ *n* [ME *yngkiling,* prob. fr. *inclen* to hint at; perh. akin to OE *inca* suspicion] (1513) **1 :** a slight indication or suggestion **:** HINT, CLUE ⟨there was no path — no ~ even of a track —*New Yorker*⟩ **2 :** a slight knowledge or vague notion ⟨had not the faintest ~ of what it was all about —H. W. Carter⟩

ink·stand \'iŋk-,stand\ *n* (1773) **:** INKWELL; *also* **:** a stand with fittings for holding ink and pens

ink·well \'iŋ-,kwel\ *n* (ca. 1875) **:** a container (as in a school desk) for ink

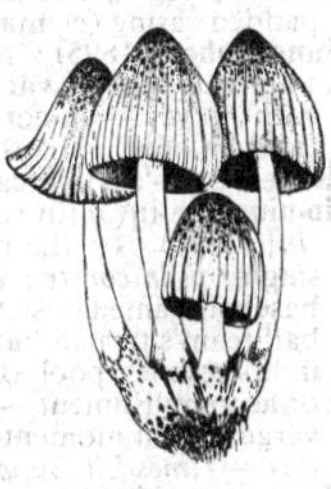
inky cap

inky cap *n* (ca. 1887) **:** a mushroom (genus *Coprinus,* esp. *C. atramentarius*) whose pileus melts into an inky fluid after the spores have matured — called also *ink cap*

in·laid \'in-'lād\ *adj* (1598) **1 a :** set into a surface in a decorative design ⟨tables with ~ marble⟩ **b :** decorated with a design or material set into a surface ⟨a table with an ~ top⟩ **2** *of linoleum* **:** having a design that goes all the way through to the backing

[1]in·land \'in-,land, -lənd\ *adj* (1546) **1** *chiefly Brit* **:** not foreign **:** DOMESTIC **2 :** of or relating to the interior of a country

[2]inland *n* (1573) **:** the interior part of a country

[3]inland *adv* (1600) **:** into or toward the interior

in·land·er \'in-,lan-dər, -lən-\ *n* (1610) **:** one who lives inland

in–law \'in-,lȯ\ *n* [back-formation fr. *mother-in-law,* etc.] (1894) **:** a relative by marriage

[1]in·lay \(')in-'lā, 'in-,\ *vt* **in·laid** \-'lād\; **in·lay·ing** (1596) **1 a :** to set into a surface or ground material **b :** to adorn with insertions **c :** to insert (as a color plate) into a mat or other reinforcement **d :** to reinforce (silver-plated ware) at points of wear with additional silver **2 :** to rub, beat, or fuse (as wire) into an incision in metal, wood, or stone — **in·lay·er** *n*

[2]in·lay \'in-,lā\ *n* (1667) **1 :** inlaid work or a decorative inlaid pattern **2 :** a tooth filling shaped to fit a cavity and then cemented into place

in·let \'in-,let, -lət\ *n* [fr. its letting water in] (1570) **1 a :** a bay or recess in the shore of a sea, lake, or river; *also* **:** CREEK **b :** a narrow water passage between peninsulas or through a barrier island leading to a bay or lagoon **2 :** a way of entering; *esp* **:** an opening for intake ⟨a fuel ~⟩

in·li·er \'in-,lī(-ə)r\ *n* [[3]*in* + *-lier* (as in *outlier*)] (ca. 1859) **1 :** a mass of rock whose outcrop is surrounded by rock of younger age **2 :** a distinct area or formation completely surrounded by another; *also* **:** ENCLAVE

in–line engine \(,)in-,līn-\ *n* (1929) **:** an internal-combustion engine in which the cylinders are arranged in one or more straight lines

[1]in lo·co pa·ren·tis \in-,lō-kō-pə-'rent-əs\ *adv* [L] (1828) **:** in the place of a parent

[2]in loco parentis *n* (1968) **:** regulation or supervision by an administrative body (as at a university) acting in loco parentis

in·ly \'in-lē\ *adv* (bef. 12c) **1 :** INWARDLY **2 :** in a manner suggesting great depth of knowledge or understanding **:** THOROUGHLY

in·mate \'in-,māt\ *n* (1589) **:** one of a group occupying a single place of residence; *esp* **:** a person confined (as in a prison or hospital)

in me·di·as res \in-,med-ē-əs-'rās, -,mēd-ē-əs-'rēz\ *adv* [L, lit., into the midst of things] (1786) **:** in or into the middle of a narrative or plot ⟨the script . . . hops from one thing to another, starting *in medias res* —H. C. Schonberg⟩

in me·mo·ri·am \,in-mə-'mōr-ē-əm, -'mȯr-\ *prep* [L] (1850) **:** in memory of — used esp. in epitaphs

in–mi·grant \'in-,mī-grənt\ *n* (1942) **:** one that in-migrates

in–mi·grate \'in-,mī-,grāt\ *vi* (1942) **:** to move into or come to live in a region or community esp. as part of a large-scale and continuing movement of population — compare OUT-MIGRATE — **in–mi·gra·tion** \-,grā-shən\ *n*

in·most \'in-,mōst\ *adj* [ME, fr. OE *innemest,* superl. of *inne,* adv., in, within, fr. *in,* adv.] (bef. 12c) **:** deepest within **:** farthest from the outside

[1]inn \'in\ *n* [ME, fr. OE; akin to ON *inni* dwelling, inn, OE *in,* adv.] (bef. 12c) **1 a :** an establishment for the lodging and entertaining of travelers **b :** TAVERN **2 :** a residence formerly provided for British students in London and esp. for students of law

[2]inn *vi* (14c) **:** to put up at an inn

in·nards \'in-ərdz\ *n pl* [alter. of *inwards*] (ca. 1825) **1 :** the internal organs of a human being or animal; *esp* **:** VISCERA **2 :** the internal parts esp. of a structure or mechanism

in·nate \in-'āt, 'in-,\ *adj* [ME *innat,* fr. L *innatus,* pp. of *innasci* to be born in, fr. *in-* + *nasci* to be born — more at NATION] (15c) **1 :** existing in, belonging to, or determined by factors present in an individual from birth **:** NATIVE, INBORN ⟨~ behavior⟩ **2 :** belonging to the essential nature of something **:** INHERENT **3 :** originating in or derived from the mind or the constitution of the intellect rather than from experience — **in·nate·ly** *adv* — **in·nate·ness** *n*

in·ner \'in-ər\ *adj* [ME, fr. OE *innera,* compar. of *inne* within — more at INMOST] (bef. 12c) **1 a :** situated farther in ⟨the ~ bark⟩ **b :** being near a center esp. of influence ⟨the ~ circles of political power⟩ **2 :** of or relating to the mind or spirit ⟨the ~ life⟩ — **inner** *n* — **in·ner·ly** *adv*

inner city *n* (1961) **:** the usu. older and more densely populated central section of a city — **inner–city** *adj*

in·ner–di·rect·ed \,in-ər-də-'rek-təd, -(,)dī-\ *adj* (ca. 1950) **:** directed in thought and action by one's own scale of values as opposed to external norms

inner ear *n* (ca. 1923) **:** the essential organ of hearing and equilibrium located in the temporal bone and innervated by the auditory nerve

inner light *n, often cap I&L* (1856) **:** a divine presence held (as in Quaker doctrine) to enlighten and guide the soul

[1]in·ner·most \'in-ər-,mōst\ *adj* (14c) **:** farthest inward **:** INMOST

[2]innermost *n* (14c) **:** the inmost part

inner planet *n* (ca. 1951) **:** any of the planets Mercury, Venus, Earth, and Mars that as a group have orbits nearer the sun than the outer planets

inner product *n* (ca. 1909) **:** SCALAR PRODUCT

in·ner·sole \,in-ər-'sōl\ *n* (ca. 1892) **:** INSOLE

inner space *n* (1958) **1 :** space at or near the earth's surface and esp. under the sea **2 :** one's inner self

\ə\ abut \ᵊ\ kitten, F table \ər\ further \a\ ash \ā\ ace \ä\ cot, cart \au̇\ out \ch\ chin \e\ bet \ē\ easy \g\ go \i\ hit \ī\ ice \j\ job \ŋ\ sing \ō\ go \ȯ\ law \ȯi\ boy \th\ thin \t͟h\ the \ü\ loot \u̇\ foot \y\ yet \zh\ vision \à, k̲, ⁿ, œ, œ̄, ue, u̅e̅, ʸ\ see Guide to Pronunciation

in·ner·spring \ˌin-ər-ˌspriŋ\ *adj* (1928) : having coil springs inside a padded casing ⟨~ mattress⟩

inner tube *n* (1895) : TUBE 3

in·ner·vate \in-ˈər-ˌvāt, ˈin-(ˌ)ər-\ *vt* **-vat·ed; -vat·ing** (1870) : to supply with nerves — **in·ner·va·tion** \ˌin-(ˌ)ər-ˈvā-shən, in-ˌər-\ *n* — **in·ner·va·tion·al** \-shnəl, -shən-ᵊl\ *adj*

in·nerve \in-ˈərv\ *vt* (ca. 1828) : to give nervous energy or power to

in·ning \ˈin-iŋ\ *n* [in sense 1, fr. E dial. *in* to reclaim; in other senses, fr. [2]*in*] (1530) **1** : the reclaiming of land esp. from the sea **2 a** *pl but sing or pl in constr* : a division of a cricket match **b** : a division of a baseball game consisting of a turn at bat for each team; *also* : a baseball team's turn at bat ending with the third out **c** : a player's turn (as in horseshoes, pool, or croquet) **3** : a chance or opportunity for action or accomplishment — usu. used in pl. but sing. or pl. in constr. ⟨on the verge of that momentous ~*s* which was to project him into world politics —*Times Lit. Supp.*⟩

inn·keep·er \ˈin-ˌkē-pər\ *n* (15c) **1** : a proprietor of an inn **2** : HOTELMAN

in·no·cence \ˈin-ə-sən(t)s\ *n* (14c) **1 a** : freedom from guilt or sin through being unacquainted with evil : BLAMELESSNESS **b** : CHASTITY **c** : freedom from legal guilt of a particular crime or offense **d** (1) : freedom from guile or cunning : SIMPLICITY (2) : lack of worldly experience or sophistication **e** : lack of knowledge : IGNORANCE ⟨written in entire ~ of the Italian language —E. R. Bentley⟩ **2** : one that is innocent **3** : BLUET

in·no·cen·cy \-sən-sē\ *n, pl* **-cies** (14c) : INNOCENCE; *also* : an innocent action or quality

in·no·cent \ˈin-ə-sənt\ *adj* [ME, fr. MF, fr. L *innocent-, innocens,* fr. *in-* + *nocent-, nocens* wicked, fr. prp. of *nocēre* to harm — more at NOXIOUS] (14c) **1 a** : free from guilt or sin esp. through lack of knowledge of evil : BLAMELESS ⟨an ~ child⟩ **b** : harmless in effect or intention ⟨searching for a hidden motive in even the most ~ conversation —Leonard Wibberley⟩; *also* : CANDID ⟨gave me an ~ gaze⟩ **c** : free from legal guilt or fault; *also* : LAWFUL ⟨a wholly ~ transaction⟩ **2 a** : lacking or reflecting a lack of sophistication, guile, or self-consciousness : ARTLESS, INGENUOUS **b** : IGNORANT ⟨almost entirely ~ of Latin —C. L. Wrenn⟩; *also* : UNAWARE ⟨perfectly ~ of the confusion he had created —B. R. Haydon⟩ **3** : lacking or deprived of something ⟨her face ~ of cosmetics —Marcia Davenport⟩ — **innocent** *n* — **in·no·cent·ly** *adv*

in·noc·u·ous \in-ˈäk-yə-wəs\ *adj* [L *innocuus,* fr. *in-* + *nocēre*] (1598) **1** : producing no injury : HARMLESS **2** : not likely to give offense or to arouse strong feelings or hostility : INOFFENSIVE, INSIPID — **in·noc·u·ous·ly** *adv* — **in·noc·u·ous·ness** *n*

in·nom·i·nate \in-ˈäm-ə-nət\ *adj* [LL *innominatus,* fr. L *in-* + *nominatus,* pp. of *nominare* to nominate] (1638) : having no name : UNNAMED; *also* : ANONYMOUS

innominate artery *n* (1870) : a short artery that arises from the arch of the aorta and divides into the carotid and subclavian arteries of the right side — called also *brachiocephalic artery, brachiocephalic trunk*

innominate bone *n* (1866) : the large flaring bone that makes a lateral half of the pelvis in mammals and is composed of the ilium, ischium, and pubis which are consolidated into one bone in the adult

innominate vein *n* (1876) : either of two large veins that occur one on each side of the neck, receive blood from the head and neck, and unite to form the superior vena cava — called also *brachiocephalic vein*

in·no·vate \ˈin-ə-ˌvāt\ *vb* **-vat·ed; -vat·ing** [L *innovatus,* pp. of *innovare,* fr. *in-* + *novus* new — more at NEW] *vt* (1548) **1** : to introduce as or as if new **2** *archaic* : to effect a change in ⟨the dictates of my father were ... not to be altered, *innovated,* or even discussed —Sir Walter Scott⟩ ~ *vi* : to make changes : do something in a new way — **in·no·va·tor** \-ˌvāt-ər\ *n* — **in·no·va·to·ry** \ˈin-ə-və-ˌtōr-ē, in-ˈō-və-, -ˌtȯr-; ˈin-ə-ˌvāt-ə-rē\ *adj*

in·no·va·tion \ˌin-ə-ˈvā-shən\ *n* (15c) **1** : the introduction of something new **2** : a new idea, method, or device : NOVELTY — **in·no·va·tion·al** \-shnəl, -shən-ᵊl\ *adj*

in·no·va·tive \ˈin-ə-ˌvāt-iv\ *adj* (1608) : characterized by, tending to, or introducing innovations — **in·no·va·tive·ness** *n*

Inns of Court (15c) **1** : the four sets of buildings in London belonging to four societies of students and practitioners of the law **2** : the four societies that alone admit to practice at the English bar

in·nu·en·do \ˌin-yə-ˈwen-(ˌ)dō\ *n, pl* **-dos** *or* **-does** [L, by hinting, fr. *innuere* to hint, fr. *in-* + *nuere* to nod — more at NUMEN] (1678) **1** : an oblique allusion : HINT, INSINUATION; *esp* : a veiled or equivocal reflection on character or reputation **2** : a parenthetical explanation introduced into the text of a legal document

Innuit *var of* INUIT

in·nu·mer·a·ble \in-ˈ(y)üm(-ə)-rə-bəl\ *adj* [ME, fr. L *innumerabilis,* fr. *in-* + *numerabilis* numerable] (14c) : too many to be numbered : COUNTLESS — **in·nu·mer·a·ble·ness** *n* — **in·nu·mer·a·bly** \-blē\ *adv*

in·nu·mer·ate \in-ˈ(y)üm(-ə)-rət\ *adj, Brit* (1959) : marked by an ignorance of mathematics and the scientific approach — **in·nu·mer·a·cy** \-rə-sē\ *n, Brit* — **innumerate** *n, Brit*

in·nu·mer·ous \-rəs\ *adj* [L *innumerus,* fr. *in-* + *numerus* number — more at NIMBLE] (1531) : INNUMERABLE

in·ob·ser·vance \ˌin-əb-ˈzər-vən(t)s\ *n* [F & L; F, fr. L *inobservantia,* fr. *in-* + *observantia* observance] (1611) **1** : lack of attention : HEEDLESSNESS **2** : failure to fulfill : NONOBSERVANCE — **in·ob·ser·vant** \-vənt\ *adj*

in·oc·u·lant \in-ˈäk-yə-lənt\ *n* (1898) : INOCULUM

in·oc·u·late \in-ˈäk-yə-ˌlāt\ *vt* **-lat·ed; -lat·ing** [ME *inoculaten* to insert a bud in a plant, fr. L *inoculatus,* pp. of *inoculare,* fr. *in-* + *oculus* eye, bud — more at EYE] (1722) **1 a** : to introduce a microorganism into ⟨~ mice with anthrax⟩ ⟨beans *inoculated* with nitrogen-fixing bacteria⟩ **b** : to introduce (as a microorganism) into a suitable situation for growth **c** : to introduce immunologically active material (as an antibody or antigen) into esp. in order to treat or prevent a disease ⟨~ children against diphtheria⟩ **2** : to introduce something into the mind of **3** : to protect as if by inoculation ***syn*** see INFUSE — **in·oc·u·la·tive** \-ˌlāt-iv\ *adj* — **in·oc·u·la·tor** \-ˌlāt-ər\ *n*

in·oc·u·la·tion \in-ˌäk-yə-ˈlā-shən\ *n* (1714) **1** : the act or process or an instance of inoculating; *esp* : the introduction of a pathogen or antigen into a living organism to stimulate the production of antibodies **2** : INOCULUM

in·oc·u·lum \in-ˈäk-yə-ləm\ *n, pl* **-la** \-lə\ [NL, fr. L *inoculare*] (1902) : material used for inoculation

in·of·fen·sive \ˌin-ə-ˈfen(t)-siv\ *adj* (1598) **1** : causing no harm or injury **2 a** : giving no provocation : PEACEABLE **b** : not objectionable to the senses — **in·of·fen·sive·ly** *adv* — **in·of·fen·sive·ness** *n*

in·op·er·a·ble \(ˈ)in-ˈäp-(ə-)rə-bəl\ *adj* [prob. fr. F *inopérable*] (1886) **1** : not suitable for surgery **2** : INOPERATIVE

in·op·er·a·tive \-ˈäp-(ə-)rət-iv, -ˈäp-ə-ˌrāt-\ *adj* (1631) : not functioning : not operable — **in·op·er·a·tive·ness** *n*

in·oper·cu·late \ˌin-ō-ˈpər-kyə-lət\ *adj* (1835) : having no operculum — **inoperculate** *n*

in·op·por·tune \(ˌ)in-ˌäp-ər-ˈt(y)ün\ *adj* [L *inopportunus,* fr. *in-* + *opportunus* opportune] (1531) : INCONVENIENT, UNSEASONABLE — **in·op·por·tune·ly** *adv* — **in·op·por·tune·ness** \-ˈt(y)ün-nəs\ *n*

in order that *conj* (1711) : THAT 2a(1)

in·or·di·nate \in-ˈȯrd-ᵊn-ət, -ˈȯrd-nət\ *adj* [ME *inordinat,* fr. L *inordinatus,* fr. *in-* + *ordinatus,* pp. of *ordinare* to arrange — more at ORDAIN] (14c) **1** : DISORDERLY, UNREGULATED **2** : exceeding reasonable limits : IMMODERATE ***syn*** see EXCESSIVE — **in·or·di·nate·ly** *adv* — **in·or·di·nate·ness** *n*

in·or·gan·ic \ˌin-ˌȯr-ˈgan-ik\ *adj* (1794) **1 a** (1) : being or composed of matter other than plant or animal : MINERAL (2) : forming or belonging to the inanimate world **b** : of, relating to, or dealt with by a branch of chemistry concerned with substances not usu. classed as organic **2** : not arising from natural growth : ARTIFICIAL; *also* : lacking structure, character, or vitality ⟨dull ~ things, without individuality or prestige —John Buchan⟩ — **in·or·gan·i·cal·ly** \-i-k(ə-)lē\ *adv*

in·os·cu·late \in-ˈäs-kyə-ˌlāt\ *vb* **-lat·ed; -lat·ing** [[2]*in-* + *osculate*] (1671) : JOIN, UNITE — **in·os·cu·la·tion** \(ˌ)in-ˌäs-kyə-ˈlā-shən\ *n*

ino·si·tol \in-ˈō-sə-ˌtȯl, ī-ˈnō-, -ˌtōl\ *n* [ISV, fr. *inosite* inositol, fr. Gk *inos,* gen. of *is* sinew — more at WITHY] (1891) : any of several crystalline stereoisomeric cyclic alcohols $C_6H_{12}O_6$; *esp* : MYOINOSITOL

ino·tro·pic \ˌē-nə-ˈtrō-pik, ˌī-nə-, -ˈträp-ik\ *adj* [ISV *ino-* (fr. Gk *in-, is* sinew) + *-tropic*] (1903) : influencing muscular contractility

in·pa·tient \ˈin-ˌpā-shənt\ *n* (1760) : a hospital patient who receives lodging and food as well as treatment — compare OUTPATIENT

in per·so·nam \ˌin-pər-ˈsō-ˌnam, -ˌnäm\ *adv or adj* [LL, against a person] (1885) : against a person for the purpose of imposing a liability or obligation — used esp. of legal actions or judgments; compare IN REM

in pet·to \in-ˈpet-(ˌ)ō\ *adv or adj* [It, lit., in the breast] (ca. 1674) **1** : in private : SECRETLY **2** : in miniature

in·phase \(ˌ)in-ˌfāz\ *adj* [fr. the phrase *in phase*] (1896) : being of the same electrical phase

in·pour \(ˈ)in-ˈpō(ə)r, -ˈpȯ(ə)r\ *vi* (1885) : to pour in ⟨goods and money ~*ed* ... and cheered the population —J. J. Mallon⟩

in–print \(ˌ)in-ˌprint\ *adj* (1950) : being in print

in–pro·cess \(ˌ)in-ˌpräs-ˌes, -ˌprōs-, -əs\ *adj* (1925) : of, relating to, or being goods in manufacture as distinguished from raw materials or from finished products

in pro·pria per·so·na \in-ˌprō-prē-ə-pər-ˈsō-nə\ *adv* [ML] (1654) : in one's own person or character : PERSONALLY; *specif* : without the assistance of an attorney

[1]**in·put** \ˈin-ˌpu̇t\ *n* (1753) **1** : something that is put in: as **a** : an amount put in ⟨increased ~ of fertilizer increases crop yield⟩ **b** : power or energy put into a machine or system for storage, conversion in kind, or conversion of characteristics usu. with the intent of sizable recovery in the form of output **c** : a component of production (as land, labor, or raw materials) **d** : information fed into a data processing system or computer; *also* : ADVICE, OPINION, COMMENT **2** : the means by which or the point at which an input (as of energy, material, or data) is made **3** : the act or process of putting in

[2]**input** *vt* **in·put·ted** *or* **input; in·put·ting** (1946) : to enter (as data) into a computer or data processing system

in·quest \ˈin-ˌkwest\ *n* [ME, fr. OF *enqueste,* fr. (assumed) VL *inquaestus,* pp. of *inquaerere* to inquire] (13c) **1 a** : a judicial or official inquiry or examination esp. before a jury ⟨a coroner's ~⟩ **b** : a body of people (as a jury) assembled to hold such an inquiry **c** : the finding of the jury upon such inquiry or the document recording it **2** : INQUIRY, INVESTIGATION

in·qui·etude \(ˈ)in-ˈkwī-ə-ˌt(y)üd\ *n* [ME, fr. MF or LL; MF, fr. LL *inquietudo,* fr. L *inquietus* disturbed, fr. *in-* + *quietus* quiet] (15c) : disturbed state : DISQUIETUDE

in·qui·line \ˈin-kwə-ˌlīn, ˈiŋ-, -lən\ *n* [L *inquilinus* tenant, lodger, fr. *in-* + *colere* to cultivate, dwell — more at WHEEL] (1879) : an animal that lives habitually in the nest or abode of some other species

in·quire \in-ˈkwī(ə)r\ *vb* **in·quired; in·quir·ing** [ME *enquiren,* fr. OF *enquerre,* fr. (assumed) VL *inquaerere,* alter. of L *inquirere,* fr. *in-* + *quaerere* to seek] *vt* (13c) **1** : to ask about ⟨some kindred spirit shall ~ thy fate —Thomas Gray⟩ **2** : to search into : INVESTIGATE ~ *vi* **1** : to put a question : seek for information by questioning ⟨*inquired* about the horses⟩ **2** : to make investigation or inquiry — often used with *into* ***syn*** see ASK — **in·quir·er** *n* — **in·quir·ing·ly** \-ˈkwī-riŋ-lē\ *adv* — **inquire after** : to ask about the health of

in·qui·ry \in-ˈkwī(ə)r-ē, ˈin-ˌ; ˈin-kwə-rē, ˈiŋ-; ˈin-ˌkwī(ə)r-ē\ *n, pl* **-ries** (15c) **1** : a request for information **2** : a systematic investigation often of a matter of public interest

in·qui·si·tion \ˌin-kwə-ˈzish-ən, ˌiŋ-\ *n* [ME *inquisicioun,* fr. MF *inquisition,* fr. L *inquisition-, inquisitio,* fr. *inquisitus,* pp. of *inquirere*] (14c) **1** : the act of inquiring : EXAMINATION **2** : a judicial or official inquiry or examination usu. before a jury; *also* : the finding of the jury **3 a** *cap* : a former Roman Catholic tribunal for the discovery and punishment of heresy **b** : an investigation conducted with little regard for individual rights **c** : a severe questioning — **in·qui·si·tion·al** \-ˈzish-nəl, -ən-ᵊl\ *adj*

in·quis·i·tive \in-ˈkwiz-ət-iv\ *adj* (14c) **1** : given to examination or investigation **2** : inclined to ask questions; *esp* : inordinately or improperly curious about the affairs of others ***syn*** see CURIOUS — **in·quis·i·tive·ly** *adv* — **in·quis·i·tive·ness** *n*

in·quis·i·tor \in-ˈkwiz-ət-ər\ *n* (1504) : one who inquires or makes inquisition; *esp* : one who is unduly harsh, severe, or hostile in making an inquiry — **in·quis·i·to·ri·al** \-ˌkwiz-ə-ˈtōr-ē-əl, -ˈtȯr-\ *adj* — **in·quis·i·to·ri·al·ly** \-ē-ə-lē\ *adv*

in re \in-ˈrā, -ˈrē\ *prep* [L] (1877) : in the matter of : CONCERNING, RE — often used in the title or name of a law case

in rem \in-ˈrem\ *adv or adj* [LL] (1885) **:** against a thing (as a right, status, or property) — used esp. of legal actions or judgments; compare IN PERSONAM

in–res·i·dence *adj* (1845) **:** being officially associated with an organization in a specified capacity — usu. used in combination ⟨writer-*in-residence* at the university⟩

in·ro \ˈin-(ˌ)rō\ *n, pl* **inro** [Jp *inrō* pillbox] (1617) **:** a small compartmented and usu. ornamented container hung from an obi to hold small objects (as medicines and perfumes) — see NETSUKE illustration

in·road \ˈin-ˌrōd\ *n* (1548) **1 :** a sudden hostile incursion **:** RAID **2 :** an advance or penetration often at the expense of someone or something — usu. used in pl.

in·rush \ˈin-ˌrəsh\ *n* (1817) **:** a crowding or flooding in

in·sa·lu·bri·ous \ˌin(t)-sə-ˈlü-brē-əs\ *adj* [L *insalubris,* fr. *in-* + *salubris* healthful — more at SAFE] (1629) **:** not conducive to health **:** UNWHOLESOME ⟨an ~ climate⟩ — **in·sa·lu·bri·ty** \-brət-ē\ *n*

ins and outs \ˌin-zən-ˈ(d)au̇ts\ *n pl* (1670) **:** characteristic peculiarities or technicalities **:** RAMIFICATIONS

in·sane \(ˈ)in-ˈsān\ *adj* [L *insanus,* fr. *in-* + *sanus* sane] (1550) **1 :** mentally disordered **:** exhibiting insanity **2 :** used by, typical of, or intended for insane persons ⟨an ~ asylum⟩ **3 :** ABSURD ⟨an ~ scheme for making money⟩ — **in·sane·ly** *adv* — **in·sane·ness** \-ˈsān-nəs\ *n*

in·san·i·tary \(ˈ)in-ˈsan-ə-ˌter-ē\ *adj* (1874) **:** unclean enough to endanger health **:** FILTHY, CONTAMINATED — **in·san·i·ta·tion** \in-ˌsan-ə-ˈtā-shən\ *n*

in·san·i·ty \in-ˈsan-ət-ē\ *n, pl* **-ties** (1590) **1 a :** a deranged state of the mind usu. occurring as a specific disorder (as schizophrenia) and usu. excluding such states as mental deficiency, psychoneurosis, and various character disorders **b :** a mental disorder **2 :** such unsoundness of mind or lack of understanding as prevents one from having the mental capacity required by law to enter into a particular relationship, status, or transaction or as removes one from criminal or civil responsibility **3 a :** extreme folly or unreasonableness **b :** something utterly foolish or unreasonable

in·sa·tia·ble \(ˈ)in-ˈsā-shə-bəl\ *adj* [ME *insaciable,* fr. MF, fr. L *insatiabilis,* fr. *in-* + *satiare* to satisfy — more at SATIATE] (15c) **:** incapable of being satisfied **:** QUENCHLESS ⟨had an ~ desire for wealth⟩ — **in·sa·tia·bil·i·ty** \(ˌ)in-ˌsā-shə-ˈbil-ət-ē\ *n* — **in·sa·tia·ble·ness** \(ˈ)in-ˈsā-shə-bəl-nəs\ *n* — **in·sa·tia·bly** \-blē\ *adv*

in·sa·tiate \(ˈ)in-ˈsā-sh(ē-)ət\ *adj* (15c) **:** INSATIABLE — **in·sa·tiate·ly** *adv* — **in·sa·tiate·ness** *n*

in·scribe \in-ˈskrīb\ *vt* [ME *inscriben,* fr. L *inscribere,* fr. *in-* + *scribere* to write — more at SCRIBE] (15c) **1 a :** to write, engrave, or print as a lasting record **b :** to enter on a list **:** ENROLL **c :** to write (characters) in a particular format in cryptography **2 a :** to write, engrave, or print characters upon **b :** to autograph or address as a gift **3 :** to dedicate to someone **4 :** to draw within a figure so as to touch in as many places as possible ⟨a regular polygon *inscribed* in a circle⟩ **5** *Brit* **:** to register the name of the holder of (a security) — **in·scrib·er** *n*

in·scrip·tion \in-ˈskrip-shən\ *n* [ME *inscripcioun,* fr. L *inscription-, inscriptio,* fr. *inscriptus,* pp. of *inscribere*] (14c) **1 a :** something that is inscribed; *also* **:** SUPERSCRIPTION **b :** EPIGRAPH 2 **c :** the wording on a coin, medal, seal, or currency note **2 :** the dedication of a book or work of art **3 a :** the act of inscribing **b :** the entering of a name on or as if on a list **:** ENROLLMENT **4** *Brit* **a :** the act of inscribing securities **b** *pl* **:** inscribed securities — **in·scrip·tion·al** \-shnəl, -shən-ᵊl\ *adj*

in·scrip·tive \in-ˈskrip-tiv\ *adj* (1740) **:** relating to or constituting an inscription — **in·scrip·tive·ly** *adv*

in·scroll \in-ˈskrōl\ *archaic var of* ENSCROLL

in·scru·ta·ble \in-ˈskrüt-ə-bəl\ *adj* [ME, fr. LL *inscrutabilis,* fr. L *in-* + *scrutari* to search — more at SCRUTINY] (15c) **:** not readily investigated, interpreted, or understood **:** MYSTERIOUS ⟨God, thy judgments are ~ —Robert Browning⟩ — **in·scru·ta·bil·i·ty** \-ˌskrüt-ə-ˈbil-ət-ē\ *n* — **in·scru·ta·ble·ness** \-ˈskrüt-ə-bəl-nəs\ *n* — **in·scru·ta·bly** \-blē\ *adv*

in·sculp \in-ˈskəlp\ *vt* [ME *insculpen,* fr. L *insculpere,* fr. *in-* + *sculpere* to carve — more at SHELF] *archaic* (15c) **:** ENGRAVE, SCULPTURE

in·seam \ˈin-ˌsēm\ *n* (ca. 1908) **:** the seam on the inside of the leg of a pair of pants; *also* **:** the length of this seam

in·sect \ˈin-ˌsekt\ *n* [L *insectum,* fr. neut. of *insectus,* pp. of *insecare* to cut into, fr. *in-* + *secare* to cut — more at SAW] (1601) **1 a :** any of numerous small invertebrate animals (as spiders or centipedes) that are more or less obviously segmented **b :** any of a class (Insecta) of arthropods (as bugs or bees) with well-defined head, thorax, and abdomen, only three pairs of legs, and typically one or two pairs of wings **2 :** any of various small animals (as earthworms or turtles) **3 :** a trivial or contemptible person — **insect** *adj*

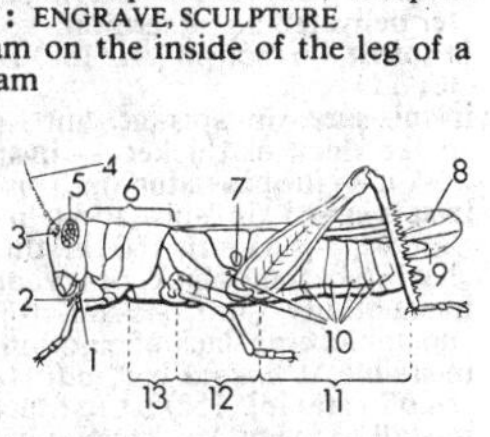

insect 1b: *1* labial palpus, *2* maxillary palpus, *3* simple eye, *4* antenna, *5* compound eye, *6* prothorax, *7* tympanum, *8* wing, *9* ovipositor, 10 spiracles, *11* abdomen, *12* metathorax, *13* mesothorax

in·sec·ta·ry \ˈin-ˌsek-tə-rē, in-ˈ\ *n, pl* **-ries** (1888) **:** a place for the keeping or rearing of living insects

in·sec·ti·cid·al \(ˌ)in-ˌsek-tə-ˈsīd-ᵊl\ *adj* (1857) **1 :** destroying or controlling insects **2 :** of or relating to an insecticide — **in·sec·ti·cid·al·ly** \-ᵊl-ē\ *adv*

in·sec·ti·cide \in-ˈsek-tə-ˌsīd\ *n* [ISV] (1865) **:** an agent that destroys insects

in·sec·ti·vore \in-ˈsek-tə-ˌvō(ə)r, -ˌvȯ(ə)r\ *n* [NL *Insectivora,* fr. L *insectum* + *-vorus* -vorous] (1840) **1 :** any of an order (Insectivora) of mammals comprising forms (as moles, shrews, and hedgehogs) that are mostly small, insectivorous, and nocturnal **2 :** an insectivorous plant or animal

in·sec·tiv·o·rous \ˌin-ˌsek-ˈtiv-(ə-)rəs\ *adj* (ca. 1661) **:** depending on insects as food

in·se·cure \ˌin(t)-si-ˈkyu̇(ə)r\ *adj* [ML *insecurus,* fr. L *in-* + *securus* secure] (1649) **1 :** not confident or sure **:** UNCERTAIN ⟨feeling somewhat ~ of his reception⟩ **2 :** not adequately guarded or sustained **:** UNSAFE ⟨an ~ investment⟩ **3 :** not firmly fastened or fixed **:** SHAKY ⟨the hinge is loose and ~⟩ **4 a :** not highly stable or well-adjusted ⟨an ~ marriage⟩ **b :** deficient in assurance **:** beset by fear and anxiety ⟨always felt ~ in a group of strangers⟩ — **in·se·cure·ly** *adv* — **in·se·cure·ness** *n* — **in·se·cu·ri·ty** \-ˈkyu̇r-ət-ē\ *n*

in·sem·i·nate \in-ˈsem-ə-ˌnāt\ *vt* **-nat·ed; -nat·ing** [L *inseminatus,* pp. of *inseminare,* fr. *in-* + *semin-, semen* seed — more at SEMEN] (ca. 1623) **1 :** SOW **2 :** to introduce semen into the genital tract of (a female) ***syn*** see IMPLANT — **in·sem·i·na·tion** \-ˌsem-ə-ˈnā-shən\ *n*

in·sem·i·na·tor \-ˈsem-ə-ˌnāt-ər\ *n* (1944) **:** one that inseminates cattle artificially

in·sen·sate \(ˈ)in-ˈsen-ˌsāt, -sət\ *adj* [LL *insensatus,* fr. L *in-* + LL *sensatus* having sense, fr. L *sensus* sense] (1508) **1 :** lacking animate awareness or sensation **2 :** lacking sense or understanding; *also* **:** FOOLISH **3 :** lacking humane feeling **:** BRUTAL — **in·sen·sate·ly** *adv* — **in·sen·sate·ness** *n*

in·sen·si·ble \(ˈ)in-ˈsen(t)-sə-bəl\ *adj* [ME, fr. MF & L; MF, fr. L *insensibilis,* fr. *in-* + *sensibilis* sensible] (14c) **1 :** IMPERCEPTIBLE ⟨dampened by an ~ dew⟩; *broadly* **:** SLIGHT, GRADUAL ⟨~ motion⟩ **2 :** incapable or bereft of feeling or sensation: as **a :** not endowed with life or spirit **:** INSENTIENT ⟨~ earth⟩ **b :** UNCONSCIOUS ⟨knocked ~ by a sudden blow⟩ **c :** lacking sensory perception or ability to react ⟨~ to pain⟩ ⟨hands ~ from cold⟩ **3 a :** lacking emotional response **:** APATHETIC, INDIFFERENT ⟨~ to fear⟩ **b :** UNAWARE ⟨~ of their danger⟩ **4** *archaic* **:** STUPID, SENSELESS **5 :** not intelligible **:** MEANINGLESS **6 :** lacking delicacy or refinement — **in·sen·si·bil·i·ty** \(ˌ)in-ˌsen(t)-sə-ˈbil-ət-ē\ *n* — **in·sen·si·ble·ness** \(ˈ)in-ˈsen(t)-sə-bəl-nəs\ *n* — **in·sen·si·bly** \-blē\ *adv*

in·sen·si·tive \(ˈ)in-ˈsen(t)-sət-iv, -ˈsen(t)-stiv\ *adj* (1834) **1 a :** not responsive or susceptible ⟨~ to the demands of the public⟩ **b :** lacking feeling or tact ⟨so ~ as to laugh at someone in pain⟩ **2 :** not physically or chemically sensitive — **in·sen·si·tive·ly** *adv* — **in·sen·si·tive·ness** *n* — **in·sen·si·tiv·i·ty** \(ˌ)in-ˌsen(t)-sə-ˈtiv-ət-ē\ *n*

in·sen·tient \(ˈ)in-ˈsen-ch(ē-)ənt\ *adj* (1764) **:** lacking perception, consciousness, or animation — **in·sen·tience** \-ch(ē-)ən(t)s\ *n*

in·sep·a·ra·ble \(ˈ)in-ˈsep-(ə-)rə-bəl\ *adj* [ME, fr. L *inseparabilis,* fr. *in-* + *separabilis* separable] (14c) **:** incapable of being separated or disjoined — **in·sep·a·ra·bil·i·ty** \(ˌ)in-ˌsep-(ə-)rə-ˈbil-ət-ē\ *n* — **inseparable** *n* — **in·sep·a·ra·ble·ness** \(ˈ)in-ˈsep-(ə-)rə-bəl-nəs\ *n* — **in·sep·a·ra·bly** \-blē\ *adv*

¹in·sert \in-ˈsərt\ *vb* [L *insertus,* pp. of *inserere,* fr. *in-* + *serere* to join — more at SERIES] *vt* (1529) **1 :** to put or thrust in ⟨~ the key in the lock⟩ ⟨~ a spacecraft into orbit⟩ **2 :** to put or introduce into the body of something **:** INTERPOLATE ⟨~ a change in a manuscript⟩ **3 :** to set in and make fast; *esp* **:** to insert by sewing between two cut edges ~ *vi, of a muscle* **:** to be in attachment to the part to be moved ***syn*** see INTRODUCE — **in·sert·er** *n*

²in·sert \ˈin-ˌsərt\ *n* (ca. 1891) **:** something that is inserted or is for insertion; *esp* **:** written or printed material inserted (as between the leaves of a book)

in·ser·tion \in-ˈsər-shən\ *n* (1539) **1 :** something that is inserted: as **a :** the part of a muscle that inserts **b :** the mode or place of attachment of an organ or part **c :** embroidery or needlework inserted as ornament between two pieces of fabric **2 :** the act or process of inserting — **in·ser·tion·al** \-shnəl, -shən-ᵊl\ *adj*

in–ser·vice \(ˌ)in-ˌsər-vəs\ *adj* (1928) **1 :** going on or continuing while one is fully employed ⟨~ teacher education workshops⟩ **2 :** of, relating to, or being one that is fully employed ⟨~ police officers⟩

¹in·set \ˈin-ˌset\ *n* (1559) **1 a :** a place where something flows in **:** CHANNEL **b :** a setting or flowing in **2 :** something that is inset: as **a :** a small graphic representation (as a map or picture) set within a larger one **b :** a piece of cloth set into a garment for decoration **c :** a part or section of a utensil that fits into an outer part

²in·set \ˈin-ˌset, in-ˈ\ *vt* **inset** *or* **in·set·ted; in·set·ting** (1890) **1 :** to set in **:** insert as an inset **2 :** to provide with an inset

¹in·shore \ˈin-ˈshō(ə)r, -ˈshȯ(ə)r\ *adj* (1701) **1 :** situated or carried on near shore **2 :** moving toward shore ⟨an ~ current⟩

²inshore *adv* (1748) **:** to or toward shore ⟨boats driven ~ by the storm⟩

¹in·side \(ˈ)in-ˈsīd, ˈin-ˌ\ *n* (14c) **1 a :** an interior or internal part **:** the part within **b :** inward nature, thoughts, or feeling **c :** VISCERA, ENTRAILS — usu. used in pl. **2 :** an inner side or surface **3 a :** a position of power or confidence ⟨only someone on the ~ could have told⟩ **b :** confidential information ⟨has the ~ on what happened at the convention⟩ **4 :** the area nearest a specified or implied point of reference: as **a :** the side of home plate nearest the batter **b :** the middle portion of a playing area **c :** the area near or underneath the basket in basketball

²inside *adj* (1611) **1 :** of, relating to, or being on or near the inside ⟨an ~ pitch⟩ **2 :** relating or known to a select group ⟨~ information⟩

³inside *prep* (1791) **1 a :** in or into the interior of **b :** on the inner side of **2 :** WITHIN ⟨~ an hour⟩

⁴inside *adv* (1803) **1 :** on the inner side **2 :** in or into the interior **3 :** to or on the inside **4 :** in prison

inside address *n* (ca. 1941) **:** ADDRESS 5c

inside of *prep* (1839) **:** INSIDE

inside out *adv* (1600) **1 :** in such a manner that the inner surface becomes the outer ⟨turned the shirt *inside out*⟩ **2 :** to a thorough degree ⟨knows his subject *inside out*⟩

in·sid·er \(ˈ)in-ˈsīd-ər\ *n* (1848) **:** a person recognized or accepted as a member of a group, category, or organization: as **a :** a person who is in a position of power or has access to confidential information **b :** one (as an officer or director or a holder of 10 percent or more of an equity security) who is in a position to have special knowledge of the affairs of or to influence the decisions of a company

inside track *n* (1857) **:** an advantageous competitive position ⟨the owner's son has the *inside track* for the job⟩

in·sid·i·ous \in-ˈsid-ē-əs\ *adj* [L *insidiosus,* fr. *insidiae* ambush, fr. *insidēre* to sit in, sit on, fr. *in-* + *sedēre* to sit — more at SIT] (1545) **1 a :** awaiting a chance to entrap **:** TREACHEROUS **b :** harmful but enticing **:** SEDUCTIVE ⟨~ drugs that destroy the young⟩ **2 a :** having a gradual and cumulative effect : SUBTLE ⟨the ~ pressures of modern life⟩ **b** *of a disease* : developing so gradually as to be well established before becoming apparent — **in·sid·i·ous·ly** *adv* — **in·sid·i·ous·ness** *n*

in·sight \'in-,sīt\ *n* (13c) **1** : the power or act of seeing into a situation : PENETRATION **2** : the act or result of apprehending the inner nature of things or of seeing intuitively *syn* see DISCERNMENT

in·sight·ful \'in-,sīt-fəl, in-'\ *adj* (1907) : exhibiting or characterized by insight — **in·sight·ful·ly** *adv*

in·sig·nia \in-'sig-nē-ə\ *or* **in·sig·ne** \-(,)nē\ *n, pl* **-nia** *or* **-ni·as** [L *insignia*, pl. of *insigne* mark, badge, fr. neut. of *insignis* marked, distinguished, fr. *in-* + *signum* mark — more at SIGN] (1648) **1** : a badge of authority or honor : EMBLEM **2** : a distinguishing mark or sign

in·sig·nif·i·cance \,in(t)-sig-'nif-i-kən(t)s\ *n* (1699) : the quality or state of being insignificant

in·sig·nif·i·can·cy \-kən-sē\ *n* (1651) **1** : INSIGNIFICANCE **2** : an insignificant thing or person

in·sig·nif·i·cant \-kənt\ *adj* (1627) : not significant: as **a** : lacking meaning or import : INCONSEQUENTIAL **b** : not worth considering : UNIMPORTANT **c** : lacking weight, position, or influence : CONTEMPTIBLE **d** : small in size, quantity, or number — **in·sig·nif·i·cant·ly** *adv*

in·sin·cere \,in(t)-sin-'si(ə)r, -sən-\ *adj* [L *insincerus*, fr. *in-* + *sincerus* sincere] (1634) : not sincere : HYPOCRITICAL — **in·sin·cere·ly** *adv* — **in·sin·cer·i·ty** \-'ser-ət-ē *also* -'sir-\ *n*

in·sin·u·ate \in-'sin-yə-,wāt\ *vb* **-at·ed; -at·ing** [L *insinuatus*, pp. of *insinuare*, fr. *in-* + *sinuare* to bend, curve, fr. *sinus* curve] *vt* (1529) **1 a** : to introduce (as an idea) gradually or in a subtle, indirect, or covert way ⟨~ doubts into a trusting mind⟩ **b** : to impart or communicate with artful or oblique reference ⟨~ an evil one dares not charge openly⟩ **2** : to introduce (as oneself) by stealthy, smooth, or artful means ~ *vi* **1** *archaic* : to enter gently, slowly, or imperceptibly : CREEP **2** *archaic* : to ingratiate oneself *syn* see INTRODUCE, SUGGEST — **in·sin·u·a·tive** \-,wāt-iv\ *adj* — **in·sin·u·a·tor** \-,wāt-ər\ *n*

in·sin·u·at·ing *adj* (1591) **1** : winning favor and confidence by imperceptible degrees : INGRATIATING **2** : tending gradually to cause doubt, distrust, or change of outlook ⟨~ remarks⟩ — **in·sin·u·at·ing·ly** \-,wāt-iŋ-lē\ *adv*

in·sin·u·a·tion \(,)in-,sin-yə-'wā-shən\ *n* (1526) **1** : the act or process of insinuating **2** : something that is insinuated; *esp* : a sly, subtle, and usu. derogatory utterance

in·sip·id \in-'sip-əd\ *adj* [F & LL; F *insipide*, fr. LL *insipidus*, fr. L *in-* + *sapidus* savory, fr. *sapere* to taste — more at SAGE] (1620) **1** : lacking taste or savor : TASTELESS **2** : lacking in qualities that interest, stimulate, or challenge : DULL, FLAT — **in·si·pid·i·ty** \,in(t)-sə-'pid-ət-ē\ *n* — **in·sip·id·ly** \in-'sip-əd-lē\ *adv*

syn INSIPID, VAPID, FLAT, JEJUNE, BANAL, INANE mean devoid of qualities that make for spirit and character. INSIPID implies a lack of sufficient taste or savor to please or interest ⟨*insipid* art and dull prose⟩ VAPID suggests a lack of liveliness, force, or spirit ⟨a potentially exciting story given a *vapid* treatment⟩ FLAT applies to things that have lost their sparkle or zest ⟨although well-regarded in its day, this novel now seems *flat*⟩ JEJUNE suggests a lack of rewarding or satisfying substance ⟨on close reading the poem comes across as *jejune*⟩ BANAL stresses the complete absence of freshness, novelty, or immediacy ⟨a *banal* tale of unrequited love⟩ INANE implies a lack of any significant or convincing quality ⟨an *inane* interpretation of the play⟩

in·sist \in-'sist\ *vb* [MF or L; MF *insister*, fr. L *insistere* to stand upon, persist, fr. *in-* + *sistere* to stand; akin to L *stare* to stand — more at STAND] *vi* (1570) **1** : to be emphatic, firm, or resolute about something intended, demanded, or required ⟨they ~ on going⟩ **2** *archaic* : PERSIST ~ *vt* : to maintain in a persistent or positive manner ⟨~*ed* that his story was true⟩

in·sis·tence \in-'sis-tən(t)s\ *n* (15c) **1** : the act or an instance of insisting **2** : the quality or state of being insistent : URGENCY

in·sis·ten·cy \-tən-sē\ *n, pl* **-cies** (1859) : INSISTENCE

in·sis·tent \in-'sis-tənt\ *adj* [L *insistent-, insistens*, prp. of *insistere*] (1868) : disposed to insist : PERSISTENT — **in·sis·tent·ly** *adv*

in si·tu \(')in-'sī-(,)t(y)ü, -'si- *also* -'sē- *or* -(,)chü\ *adv or adj* [L, in position] (1740) : in the natural or original position

in·so·bri·ety \,in(t)-sə-'brī-ət-ē, -sō-\ *n* (1611) : lack of sobriety or moderation; *esp* : intemperance in drinking

in·so·cia·ble \(')in-'sō-shə-bəl\ *adj* [L *insociabilis*, fr. *in-* + *sociabilis* sociable] (1588) : not sociable — **in·so·cia·bil·i·ty** \(,)in-(,)sō-shə-'bil-ət-ē\ *n* — **in·so·cia·bly** \(')in-'sō-shə-blē\ *adv*

in·so·far \,in(t)-sə-'fär\ *adv* (1596) : to such extent or degree

insofar as \,in(t)-sə-,fär-əz\ *conj* (15c) : to the extent or degree that

in·so·late \'in(t)-(,)sō-,lāt, in-'\ *vt* **-lat·ed; -lat·ing** [L *insolatus*, pp. of *insolare*, fr. *in-* + *sol* sun — more at SOLAR] (1623) : to expose to the sun's rays

in·so·la·tion \,in(t)-(,)sō-'lā-shən, in-,sō-\ *n* (1654) **1** : the act or an instance of insolating **2** : SUNSTROKE **3 a** : solar radiation that has been received **b** : the rate of delivery of direct solar radiation per unit of horizontal surface; *broadly* : that relating to total solar radiation

in·sole \'in-,sōl\ *n* (1851) **1** : an inside sole of a shoe **2** : a loose thin strip placed inside a shoe for warmth or comfort

in·so·lence \'in(t)-s(ə-)lən(t)s\ *n* (14c) **1** : the quality or state of being insolent **2** : an instance of insolent conduct or treatment

in·so·lent \-s(ə-)lənt\ *adj* [ME, fr. L *insolent-, insolens*; akin to L *insolescere* to grow haughty] (14c) **1** : insultingly contemptuous in speech or conduct : OVERBEARING **2** : exhibiting boldness or effrontery : IMPUDENT *syn* see PROUD — **insolent** *n* — **in·so·lent·ly** *adv*

in·sol·u·bi·lize \(')in-'säl-yə-bə-,līz\ *vt* (1897) : to make insoluble — **in·sol·u·bi·li·za·tion** \(,)in-,säl-yə-bə-lə-'zā-shən\ *n*

in·sol·u·ble \(')in-'säl-yə-bəl\ *adj* [ME *insolible*, fr. L *insolubilis*, fr. *in-* + *solvere* to free, dissolve — more at SOLVE] (14c) : not soluble: as **a** *archaic* : INDISSOLUBLE **b** : having or admitting of no solution or explanation **c** : incapable of being dissolved in a liquid; *also* : soluble only with difficulty or to a slight degree — **in·sol·u·bil·i·ty** \(,)in-,säl-yə-'bil-ət-ē\ *n* — **insoluble** *n* — **in·sol·u·ble·ness** \(')in-'säl-yə-bəl-nəs\ *n* — **in·sol·u·bly** \-blē\ *adv*

in·solv·able \(')in-'säl-və-bəl, -'sȯl-\ *adj* (1693) : admitting no solution ⟨an apparently ~ problem⟩ — **in·solv·ably** \-blē\ *adv*

in·sol·vent \(')in-'säl-vənt, -'sȯl-\ *adj* (1591) **1 a** : unable to pay debts as they fall due in the usual course of business; *specif* : having liabilities in excess of a reasonable market value of assets held **b** : insufficient to pay all debts ⟨an ~ estate⟩ **c** : not up to a normal standard or complement : IMPOVERISHED **2** : relating to or for the relief of insolvents — **in·sol·ven·cy** \-vən-sē\ *n* — **insolvent** *n*

in·som·nia \in-'säm-nē-ə\ *n* [L, fr. *insomnis* sleepless, fr. *in-* + *somnus* sleep — more at SOMNOLENT] (ca. 1623) : prolonged and usu. abnormal inability to obtain adequate sleep — **in·som·ni·ac** \-nē-,ak\ *adj or n*

in·so·much as \,in(t)-sə-,məch-əz\ *conj* (14c) : INASMUCH AS

insomuch that *conj* (14c) : SO 1

in·sou·ci·ance \in-'sü-sē-ən(t)s, aⁿ-süs-yäⁿs\ *n* [F, fr. *in-* + *soucier* to trouble, disturb, fr. L *sollicitare* — more at SOLICIT] (1799) : lighthearted unconcern : NONCHALANCE — **in·sou·ci·ant** \in-'sü-sē-ənt, aⁿ-süs-yäⁿ\ *adj* — **in·sou·ci·ant·ly** \in-'sü-sē-ənt-lē\ *adv*

insoul *var of* ENSOUL

in·span \in-'span, 'in-,\ *vb* [Afrik, fr. D *inspannen*] *chiefly So Afr* (1827) : YOKE, HARNESS

in·spect \in-'spekt\ *vb* [L *inspectus*, pp. of *inspicere*, fr. *in-* + *specere* to look — more at SPY] *vt* (ca. 1623) **1** : to view closely in critical appraisal : look over **2** : to examine officially ⟨~s the barracks every Friday⟩ ~ *vi* : to make an inspection *syn* see SCRUTINIZE — **in·spec·tive** \-'spek-tiv\ *adj*

in·spec·tion \in-'spek-shən\ *n* (14c) **1** : the act of inspecting **2** : a checking or testing of an individual against established standards

inspection arms *n* [fr. the command *inspection arms!*] (ca. 1884) : a position in the manual of arms in which the rifle is held at port arms with the chamber open for inspection; *also* : a command to assume this position

in·spec·tor \in-'spek-tər\ *n* (1641) **1** : a person employed to inspect something **2 a** : a police officer who is in charge of several precincts and ranks below a superintendent or deputy superintendent **b** : a person appointed to oversee a polling place — **in·spec·tor·ate** \-t(ə-)rət\ *n* — **in·spec·tor·ship** \-tər-,ship\ *n*

inspector general *n* (1702) : an officer of a military or naval corps of inspectors that investigates and reports on organizational matters

insphere *var of* ENSPHERE

in·spi·ra·tion \,in(t)-spə-'rā-shən, -(,)spir-'ā-\ *n* (14c) **1 a** : a divine influence or action on a person believed to qualify him to receive and communicate sacred revelation **b** : the action or power of moving the intellect or emotions **c** : the act of influencing or suggesting opinions ⟨the ~ of this rumor was traced to a source near the governor⟩ **2** : the act of drawing in; *specif* : the drawing of air into the lungs **3 a** : the quality or state of being inspired **b** : something that is inspired ⟨a scheme that was pure ~⟩ **4** : an inspiring agent or influence — **in·spi·ra·tion·al** \-shnəl, -shən-ᵊl\ *adj* — **in·spi·ra·tion·al·ly** \-ē\ *adv*

in·spi·ra·tor \'in(t)s-pə-,rāt-ər, -(,)pir-,āt-\ *n* (1624) **1** : one that inspires ⟨teachers who are ~s of the young⟩ **2** : a device (as an injector or respirator) by which something (as gas or vapor) is drawn in

in·spi·ra·to·ry \in-'spī-rə-,tōr-ē, 'in(t)-sp(ə-)rə-, -,tȯr-\ *adj* (1773) : of, relating to, used for, or associated with inspiration

in·spire \in-'spī(ə)r\ *vb* **in·spired; in·spir·ing** [ME *inspiren*, fr. MF & L; MF *inspirer*, fr. L *inspirare*, fr. *in-* + *spirare* to breathe — more at SPIRIT] *vt* (14c) **1 a** : to influence, move, or guide by divine or supernatural inspiration **b** : to exert an animating, enlivening, or exalting influence on ⟨was particularly *inspired* by the Romanticists⟩ **c** : to spur on : IMPEL, MOTIVATE ⟨threats don't necessarily ~ people to work⟩ **d** : AFFECT ⟨seeing the old room again *inspired* him with nostalgia⟩ **2 a** *archaic* : to breathe or blow into or upon **b** *archaic* : to infuse (as life) by breathing **3 a** : to communicate to an agent supernaturally **b** : to draw forth or bring out ⟨thoughts *inspired* by his visit to the cathedral⟩ **4** : INHALE 1 **5 a** : BRING ABOUT, OCCASION ⟨the book was *inspired* by his travels in the Far East⟩ **b** : INCITE **6** : to spread (rumor) by indirect means or through the agency of another ~ *vi* : INHALE — **in·spir·er** *n*

in·spired *adj* (15c) : outstanding or brilliant in a way or to a degree suggestive of divine inspiration ⟨gave an ~ performance⟩

in·spir·ing *adj* (1717) : having an animating or exalting effect ⟨the minister delivered an ~ sermon⟩

in·spir·it \in-'spir-ət\ *vt* (15c) : to fill with spirit — **in·spir·it·ing·ly** \-iŋ-lē\ *adv*

in·spis·sate \in-'spis-,āt, 'in(t)-spə-,sāt\ *vt* **-sat·ed; -sat·ing** (1626) : to make thick or thicker — **in·spis·sa·tion** \,in(t)-spə-'sā-shən, (,)in-,spis-'ā-\ *n* — **in·spis·sa·tor** \in-'spis-,āt-ər, 'in(t)-spə-,sāt-\ *n*

in·spis·sat·ed \in-'spis-,āt-əd, 'in(t)-spə-,sāt-\ *also* **in·spis·sate** \in-'spis-ət, 'in(t)-spə-,sāt\ *adj* (1603) : thickened in consistency; *broadly* : made or having become thick, heavy, or intense

in·sta·bil·i·ty \,in(t)-stə-'bil-ət-ē\ *n* (15c) : the quality or state of being unstable; *esp* : lack of emotional or mental stability

in·sta·ble \(')in-'stā-bəl\ *adj* [MF or L; MF, fr. L *instabilis*, fr. *in-* + *stabilis* stable] (15c) : UNSTABLE

in·stall *or* **in·stal** \in-'stȯl\ *vt* **in·stalled; in·stall·ing** [ME *installen*, fr. MF *installer*, fr. ML *installare*, fr. L *in-* + ML *stallum* stall, fr. OHG *stal*] (15c) **1 a** : to place in an office or dignity by seating in a stall or official seat **b** : to induct into an office, rank, or order ⟨~*ed* the new president⟩ **2** : to establish in an indicated place, condition, or status ⟨~*ing* herself in front of the fireplace⟩ **3** : to set up for use or service ⟨had an exhaust fan ~*ed* in the kitchen⟩ — **in·stall·er** *n*

in·stal·la·tion \,in(t)-stə-'lā-shən\ *n* (15c) **1** : the act of installing : the state of being installed **2** : something that is installed for use **3** : a military camp, fort, or base

¹in·stall·ment *or* **in·stal·ment** \in-'stȯl-mənt\ *n* (1589) : INSTALLATION 1

²installment *also* **instalment** *n* [alter. of earlier *estallment* payment by installment, deriv. of OF *estaler* to place, fix, fr. *estal* place, of Gmc origin; akin to OHG *stal* place, stall] (1776) **1** : one of the parts into which a debt is divided when payment is made at intervals **2 a** : one of several parts (as of a publication) presented at intervals **b** : one part of a serial story — **installment** *adj*

installment plan *n* (1876) : a system of paying for goods by installments

¹in·stance \'in(t)-stən(t)s\ *n* (14c) **1 a** *archaic* : urgent or earnest solicitation **b** : INSTIGATION, REQUEST ⟨am writing to you at the ~ of my client⟩ **c** *obs* : an impelling cause or motive **2 a** *archaic* : EXCEPTION **b** : an individual illustrative of a category or brought forward in support or disproof of a generalization **c** *obs* : TOKEN, SIGN **3** : the institution and prosecution of a lawsuit : SUIT **4** : a step, stage, or situation viewed as part of a process or series of events ⟨prefers, in this ~, to remain anonymous —*Times Lit. Supp.*⟩

syn INSTANCE, CASE, ILLUSTRATION, EXAMPLE, SAMPLE, SPECIMEN mean something that exhibits distinguishing characteristics in its category. INSTANCE applies to any individual person, act, or thing that may be offered to illustrate or explain; CASE is used to direct attention to a real or assumed occurrence or situation that is to be considered, studied, or dealt with; ILLUSTRATION applies to an instance offered as a means of clarifying or illuminating a general statement; EXAMPLE applies to a typical, representative, or illustrative instance or case; SAMPLE implies a part or unit taken at random from a larger whole and so presumed to be typical of its qualities; SPECIMEN applies to any example or sample whether representative or merely existent and available.
— **for in·stance** \fə-'rin(t)-stən(t)s, 'frin(t)-\ **:** as an example

2instance *vt* **in·stanced; in·stanc·ing** (1601) **1 :** to illustrate or demonstrate by an instance **2 :** to mention as a case or example **:** CITE

in·stan·cy \'in(t)-stən-sē\ *n, pl* **-cies** (1515) **1 :** URGENCY, INSISTENCE **2 :** nearness of approach **:** IMMINENCE **3 :** immediacy of occurrence or action **:** INSTANTANEOUSNESS

1in·stant \'in(t)-stənt\ *n* [ME, fr. ML *instant-, instans,* fr. *instant-, instans,* adj., instant, fr. L] (14c) **1 :** an infinitesimal space of time; *esp* **:** a point in time separating two states ⟨at the ~ of death⟩ **2 :** the present or current month

2instant *adj* [ME, fr. MF or L; MF, fr. L *instant-, instans,* fr. prp. of *instare* to stand upon, urge, fr. *in-* + *stare* to stand — more at STAND] (15c) **1 :** IMPORTUNATE, URGENT **2 a :** PRESENT, CURRENT ⟨previous felonies not related to the ~ crime⟩ **b :** of or occurring in the present month **3 :** IMMEDIATE, DIRECT ⟨the play was an ~ success⟩ **4 a** (1) **:** premixed or precooked for easy final preparation ⟨~ mashed potatoes⟩ (2) **:** appearing in or as if in ready-to-use form ⟨~ culture⟩ ⟨updating . . . your image with ~ beards, mustaches, and sideburns — *Playboy*⟩ **b :** immediately soluble in water ⟨~ coffee⟩ **5 :** produced or occurring with or as if with extreme rapidity and ease — **in·stant·ness** *n*

in·stan·ta·neous \ˌin(t)-stən-'tā-nē-əs, -nyəs\ *adj* [ML *instantaneus,* fr. *instant-, instans* n.] (1651) **1 :** done, occurring, or acting without any perceptible duration of time ⟨death was ~⟩ **2 :** done without any delay being purposely introduced ⟨took ~ action to correct the abuse⟩ **3 :** occurring or present at a particular instant ⟨~ velocity⟩ — **in·stan·ta·ne·ity** \ˌin-ˌstant-ᵊn-'ē-ət-ē, ˌin(t)-stən-tə-'nē-\ *n* — **in·stan·ta·neous·ly** \ˌin(t)-stən-'tā-nē-ə-slē, -nyə-slē\ *adv* — **in·stan·ta·neous·ness** *n*

in·stan·ter \in-'stant-ər\ *adv* [ML, fr. *instant-, instans*] (1688) **:** at once

in·stan·ti·ate \in-'stan-chē-ˌāt\ *vt* **-at·ed; -at·ing** (1949) **:** to represent (an abstraction) by a concrete instance ⟨heroes ~ ideals — W.J. Bennett⟩ — **in·stan·ti·a·tion** \-ˌstan-chē-'ā-shən\ *n*

1in·stant·ly \'in(t)-stənt-lē\ *adv* (15c) **1 :** with importunity **:** URGENTLY **2 :** without the least delay **:** IMMEDIATELY

2instantly *conj* (1793) **:** as soon as ⟨he ran across the grass ~ he perceived his mother —W. P. Thackeray⟩

instant replay *n* (1966) **:** a videotape recording of an action (as a play in football) that can be played back (as in slow motion) immediately after the action has been completed

in·star \'in-ˌstär\ *n* [NL, fr. L, equivalent, figure; akin to L *instare* to stand upon] (ca. 1895) **:** a stage in the life of an arthropod (as an insect) between two successive molts; *also* **:** an individual in a specified instar

in·state \in-'stāt\ *vt* (1603) **1** *obs* **a :** INVEST, ENDOW **b :** BESTOW, CONFER **2 :** to set or establish in a rank or office **:** INSTALL

in sta·tu quo \in-ˌstā-(ˌ)tü-'kwō, -ˌsta-; -ˌstach-(ˌ)ü-\ *adv* [NL, lit., in the state in which] (1602) **:** in the former or same state

in·stau·ra·tion \ˌin-ˌstȯ-'rā-shən, ˌin(t)-stə-\ *n* [L *instauration-, instauratio,* fr. *instauratus,* pp. of *instaurare* to renew, restore — more at STORE] (1603) **1 :** restoration after decay, lapse, or dilapidation **2 :** an act of instituting or establishing something

in·stead \in-'sted\ *adv* (1667) **1 :** as a substitute or equivalent ⟨was going to write but called ~⟩ **2 :** as an alternative to something expressed or implied **:** RATHER ⟨longed ~ for a quiet country life⟩

instead of \in-ˌsted-ə(v), -ˌstid-\ *prep* [ME *in sted of*] (13c) **:** in place of **:** as a substitute for or alternative to

in·step \'in-ˌstep\ *n* (15c) **1 :** the arched middle portion of the human foot in front of the ankle joint; *esp* **:** its upper surface **2 :** the part of a shoe or stocking over the instep

in·sti·gate \'in(t)-stə-ˌgāt\ *vt* **-gat·ed; -gat·ing** [L *instigatus,* pp. of *instigare* — more at STICK] (1542) **:** to goad or urge forward **:** PROVOKE *syn* see INCITE — **in·sti·ga·tion** \ˌin(t)-stə-'gā-shən\ *n* — **in·sti·ga·tive** \'in(t)-stə-ˌgāt-iv\ *adj* — **in·sti·ga·tor** \-ˌgāt-ər\ *n*

in·still *also* **in·stil** \in-'stil\ *vt* **in·stilled; in·still·ing** [MF & L; MF *instiller,* fr. L *instillare,* fr. *in-* + *stillare* to drip — more at DISTILL] (15c) **1 :** to cause to enter drop by drop ⟨~ medication into the infected eye⟩ **2 :** to impart gradually ⟨~*ing* in children a love of learning⟩ *syn* see IMPLANT — **in·stil·la·tion** \ˌin(t)-stə-'lā-shən, -(ˌ)stil-'ā-\ *n* — **in·still·er** \in-'stil-ər\ *n* — **in·still·ment** \-mənt\ *n*

1in·stinct \'in-ˌstiŋ(k)t\ *n* [ME, fr. L *instinctus* impulse, fr. *instinctus,* pp. of *instinguere* to incite; akin to L *instigare* to instigate] (15c) **1 :** a natural or inherent aptitude, impulse, or capacity ⟨had an ~ for the right word⟩ **2 a :** a largely inheritable and unalterable tendency of an organism to make a complex and specific response to environmental stimuli without involving reason **b :** behavior that is mediated by reactions below the conscious level — **in·stinc·tu·al** \in-'stiŋ(k)-chə(-wə)l, -'stiŋ(k)sh-wəl\ *adj*

2in·stinct \in-'stiŋ(k)t, 'in-ˌ\ *adj* (1667) **1** *obs* **:** impelled by an inner or animating or exciting agency **2 :** profoundly imbued **:** INFUSED ⟨my mood, ~ with romance —S. J. Perelman⟩

in·stinc·tive \in-'stiŋ(k)-tiv\ *adj* (1649) **1 :** of, relating to, or being instinct **2 :** prompted by natural instinct or propensity **:** arising spontaneously and being independent of judgment or will ⟨an ~ fear of innovation —V. L. Parrington⟩ *syn* see SPONTANEOUS — **in·stinc·tive·ly** *adv*

1in·sti·tute \'in(t)-stə-ˌt(y)üt\ *vt* **-tut·ed; -tut·ing** [ME *instituten,* fr. L *institutus,* pp. of *instituere,* fr. *in-* + *statuere* to set up — more at STATUTE] (14c) **1 :** to establish in a position or office **2 a :** to originate and get established **:** ORGANIZE ⟨*instituted* reading clinics⟩ **b :** to set going **:** INAUGURATE ⟨*instituting* an investigation of the charges⟩ — **in·sti·tut·er** *or* **in·sti·tu·tor** \-ˌt(y)üt-ər\ *n*

2institute *n* (1546) **:** something that is instituted: as **a** (1) **:** an elementary principle recognized as authoritative (2) *pl* **:** a collection of such principles and precepts; *esp* **:** a legal compendium **b :** an organization for the promotion of a cause **:** ASSOCIATION ⟨a research ~⟩ ⟨an ~ for the blind⟩ **c :** an educational institution and esp. one devoted to technical fields **d :** a usu. brief intensive course of instruction on selected topics relating to a particular field ⟨an urban studies ~⟩

in·sti·tu·tion \ˌin(t)-stə-'t(y)ü-shən\ *n* (14c) **1 :** an act of instituting **:** ESTABLISHMENT **2 a :** a significant practice, relationship, or organization in a society or culture ⟨the ~ of marriage⟩; *also* **:** something or someone firmly associated with a place or thing ⟨she has become an ~ in the theater⟩ **b :** an established organization or corporation (as a college or university) esp. of a public character; *also* **:** ASYLUM 4 — **in·sti·tu·tion·al** \-shnəl, -shən-ᵊl\ *adj* — **in·sti·tu·tion·al·ly** \-ē\ *adv*

in·sti·tu·tion·al·ism \-shnəl-ˌiz-əm, -shən-ᵊl-\ *n* (1862) **1 :** emphasis on organization (as in religion) at the expense of other factors **2 :** public institutional care of defective, delinquent, or dependent persons **3 :** an economic school of thought that emphasizes the role of social institutions in influencing economic behavior — **in·sti·tu·tion·al·ist** \-əst\ *n*

in·sti·tu·tion·al·ize \-ˌīz\ *vt* **-ized; -iz·ing** (1865) **1 :** to make into or give the character of an institution to ⟨*institutionalized* housing⟩; *esp* **:** to incorporate into a structured and often highly formalized system ⟨*institutionalized* values⟩ **2 :** to put in the care of an institution ⟨~ alcoholics⟩ — **in·sti·tu·tion·al·iza·tion** \-ˌt(y)ü-shnəl-ə-'zā-shən, -shən-ᵊl-\ *n*

in–store \ˌin-ˌstō(ə)r, -ˌstȯ(ə)r\ *adj* (1961) **:** relating to or being an operation or activity located or taking place inside a store ⟨~ consumer survey⟩

in·struct \in-'strəkt\ *vt* [ME *instructen,* fr. L *instructus,* pp. of *instruere,* fr. *in-* + *struere* to build — more at STRUCTURE] (15c) **1 :** to give knowledge to **:** TEACH, TRAIN ⟨she had ~*ed* three generations of village children⟩ **2 :** to provide with authoritative information or advice ⟨the judge ~*ed* the jury⟩ **3 :** to give an order or command to **:** DIRECT *syn* see TEACH, COMMAND

in·struc·tion \in-'strək-shən\ *n* (15c) **1 a :** PRECEPT **b :** a direction calling for compliance **:** ORDER — usu. used in pl. ⟨had ~*s* not to admit strangers⟩ **c** *pl* **:** an outline or manual of technical procedure **:** DIRECTIONS **d :** a code that tells a computer to perform a particular operation **2 :** the action, practice, or profession of teaching — **in·struc·tion·al** \-shnəl, -shən-ᵊl\ *adj*

in·struc·tive \in-'strək-tiv\ *adj* (1611) **:** carrying a lesson **:** ENLIGHTENING — **in·struc·tive·ly** *adv* — **in·struc·tive·ness** *n*

in·struc·tor \in-'strək-tər\ *n* (15c) **:** one that instructs **:** TEACHER; *esp* **:** a college teacher below professorial rank — **in·struc·tor·ship** \-ˌship\ *n*

in·struc·tress \-'strək-trəs\ *n* (1630) **:** a female instructor

1in·stru·ment \'in(t)-strə-mənt\ *n* [ME, fr. L *instrumentum,* fr. *instruere* to arrange, instruct] (13c) **1 :** a device used to produce music **2 a :** a means whereby something is achieved, performed, or furthered **b :** one used by another as a means or aid **:** DUPE, TOOL **3 :** UTENSIL, IMPLEMENT **4 :** a formal legal document (as a deed, bond, or agreement) **5 a :** a measuring device for determining the present value of a quantity under observation **b :** an electrical or mechanical device used in navigating an airplane; *esp* **:** such a device used as the sole means of navigating *syn* see IMPLEMENT

2in·stru·ment \-ˌment\ *vt* (1752) **1 :** to address a legal instrument to **2 :** to score for musical performance **:** ORCHESTRATE **3 :** to equip with instruments

in·stru·men·tal \ˌin(t)-strə-'ment-ᵊl\ *adj* (14c) **1 a :** serving as a means, agent, or tool ⟨was ~ in organizing the strike⟩ **b :** of, relating to, or done with an instrument or tool **2 :** relating to, composed for, or performed on a musical instrument **3 :** of, relating to, or being a grammatical case or form expressing means or agency **4 :** of or relating to instrumentalism **5 :** OPERANT 3 ⟨~ learning⟩ ⟨~ conditioning⟩ — **instrumental** *n* — **in·stru·men·tal·ly** \-ᵊl-ē\ *adv*

in·stru·men·tal·ism \-ˌiz-əm\ *n* (1909) **:** a doctrine that ideas are instruments of action and that their usefulness determines their truth

in·stru·men·tal·ist \-əst\ *n* (1823) **1 :** a player on a musical instrument **2 :** an exponent of instrumentalism — **instrumentalist** *adj*

in·stru·men·tal·i·ty \ˌin(t)-strə-mən-'tal-ət-ē, -ˌmen-\ *n, pl* **-ties** (1651) **1 :** the quality or state of being instrumental **2 :** MEANS, AGENCY

in·stru·men·ta·tion \ˌin(t)-strə-mən-'tā-shən, -ˌmen-\ *n* (1845) **1 :** the arrangement or composition of music for instruments esp. for a band or orchestra **2 a :** the use of instruments **b :** the application of instruments for observation, measurement, or control **3 a :** a science concerned with the development and manufacture of instruments **b :** instruments for a particular purpose; *also* **:** a selection or arrangement of instruments

instrument flying *n* (1928) **:** navigation of an airplane by instruments only

instrument landing *n* (1938) **:** a landing made with little or no external visibility by means of instruments and by ground radio directive devices

instrument panel *n* (1922) **:** a panel on which instruments are mounted; *esp* **:** DASHBOARD 2

in·sub·or·di·nate \ˌin(t)-sə-'bȯrd-ᵊn-ət, -'bȯrd-nət\ *adj* (ca. 1828) **:** disobedient to authority — **insubordinate** *n* — **in·sub·or·di·nate·ly** *adv* — **in·sub·or·di·na·tion** \-ˌbȯrd-ᵊn-'ā-shən\ *n*

in·sub·stan·tial \ˌin(t)-səb-'stan-chəl\ *adj* [prob. fr. F *insubstantiel,* fr. LL *insubstantialis,* fr. L *in-* + LL *substantialis* substantial] (1610) **:** not substantial: as **a :** lacking substance or material nature **b :** lacking firmness or solidity **:** FLIMSY — **in·sub·stan·ti·al·i·ty** \-ˌstan-chē-'al-ət-ē\ *n*

in·suf·fer·able \(ˈ)in-'səf-(ə-)rə-bəl\ *adj* (15c) **:** not to be endured **:** INTOLERABLE ⟨an ~ bore⟩ — **in·suf·fer·able·ness** *n* — **in·suf·fer·ably** \-blē\ *adv*

in·suf·fi·cience \ˌin(t)-sə-'fish-ən(t)s\ *n* (15c) **:** INSUFFICIENCY

in·suf·fi·cien·cy \-ən-sē\ *n, pl* **-cies** (1526) **1 :** the quality or state of being insufficient: as **a :** lack of mental or moral fitness **:** INCOMPETENCE ⟨the ~ of this person for public office⟩ **b :** lack of adequate supply ⟨~ of provisions⟩ **c :** lack of physical power or capacity; *specif* **:** inability of an organ or body part to function normally **2 :** something insufficient ⟨aware of my own *insufficiencies*⟩

in·suf·fi·cient \,in(t)-sə-'fish-ənt\ *adj* [ME, fr. MF, fr. LL *insufficient-, insufficiens,* fr. L *in-* + *sufficient-, sufficiens* sufficient] (14c) **:** not sufficient **:** INADEQUATE; *esp* **:** deficient in power, capacity, or competence — **in·suf·fi·cient·ly** *adv*

in·suf·fla·tion \,in(t)-sə-'flā-shən, in-,səf-'lā-\ *n* [MF, fr. LL *insufflation-, insufflatio,* fr. *insufflatus,* pp. of *insufflare* to blow upon, fr. L *in-* ²in- + *sufflare* to inflate, fr. *sub-* + *flare* to blow — more at BLOW] (15c) **:** an act or the action of blowing on, into, or in: as **a :** a Christian ceremonial rite of exorcism performed by breathing on a person **b :** the act of blowing something (as a gas, powder, or vapor) into a body cavity — **in·suf·flate** \'in(t)-sə-,flāt, in-'səf-,lāt\ *vt* — **in·suf·fla·tor** \-,flāt-ər, -,lāt-ər\ *n*

in·su·lant \'in(t)-sə-lənt\ *n* (ca. 1929) **:** an insulating material **:** INSULATION

in·su·lar \'in(t)s-(y)ə-lər, 'in-shə-lər\ *adj* [LL *insularis,* fr. L *insula* island] (1611) **1 a :** of, relating to, or constituting an island **b :** dwelling or situated on an island ⟨~ residents⟩ **2** *of a plant or animal* **:** having a restricted or isolated natural range or habitat **3 :** characteristic of an isolated people; *esp* **:** being, having, or reflecting a narrow provincial viewpoint **4 :** of or relating to an island of cells or tissue — **in·su·lar·ism** \-lə-,riz-əm\ *n* — **in·su·lar·i·ty** \,in(t)s-(y)ə-'lar-ət-ē, ,in-shə-'lar-\ *n* — **in·su·lar·ly** \'in(t)s-(y)ə-lər-lē, 'in-shə-\ *adv*

in·su·late \'in(t)-sə-,lāt\ *vt* **-lat·ed; -lat·ing** [L *insula*] (ca. 1727) **:** to place in a detached situation **:** ISOLATE; *esp* **:** to separate from conducting bodies by means of nonconductors so as to prevent transfer of electricity, heat, or sound

in·su·la·tion \,in(t)-sə-'lā-shən\ *n* (1798) **1 a :** the action of insulating **b :** the state of being insulated **2 :** material used in insulating

in·su·la·tor \'in(t)-sə-,lāt-ər\ *n* (1801) **:** one that insulates; *esp* **:** a material that is a poor conductor of electricity or a device made of such material and used for separating or supporting conductors to prevent undesired flow of electricity

in·su·lin \'in(t)-s(ə-)lən\ *n* [NL *insula* islet (of Langerhans), fr. L, island] (ca. 1914) **:** a protein pancreatic hormone secreted by the islets of Langerhans that is essential esp. for the metabolism of carbohydrates and is used in the treatment and control of diabetes mellitus

insulin shock *n* (1925) **:** hypoglycemia associated with the presence of excessive insulin in the system and characterized by progressive development of coma

¹in·sult \in-'səlt\ *vb* [MF or L; MF *insulter,* fr. L *insultare,* lit., to spring upon, fr. *in-* + *saltare* to leap — more at SALTATION] *vi, archaic* (1540) **:** to behave with pride or arrogance **:** VAUNT ~ *vt* **:** to treat with insolence, indignity, or contempt **:** AFFRONT; *also* **:** to affect offensively or damagingly ⟨doggerel that ~*s* the reader's intelligence⟩ ***syn*** see OFFEND — **in·sult·er** *n* — **in·sult·ing·ly** \in-'səl-tiŋ-lē\ *adv*

²in·sult \'in-,səlt\ *n* (1603) **1 :** a gross indignity **2 :** injury to the body or one of its parts; *also* **:** something that causes or has a potential for causing such insult ⟨pollution and other environmental ~*s*⟩

in·su·per·a·ble \(')in-'sü-p(ə-)rə-bəl\ *adj* [ME, fr. MF & L; MF, fr. L *insuperabilis;* fr. *in-* + *superare* to surmount, fr. *super* over — more at OVER] (14c) **:** incapable of being surmounted, overcome, or passed over ⟨~ difficulties⟩ — **in·su·per·a·bly** \-blē\ *adv*

in·sup·port·able \,in(t)-sə-'pōrt-ə-bəl, -'pȯrt-\ *adj* [MF or LL; MF, fr. LL *insupportabilis,* fr. L *in-* + *supportare* to support] (1530) **:** not supportable: **a :** more than can be endured ⟨~ pain⟩ **b :** impossible to justify ⟨~ charges⟩ — **in·sup·port·able·ness** *n* — **in·sup·port·ably** \-blē\ *adv*

in·sup·press·ible \,in(t)-sə-'pres-ə-bəl\ *adj* (1610) **:** IRREPRESSIBLE — **in·sup·press·ibly** \-blē\ *adv*

in·sur·able \in-'shu̇r-ə-bəl\ *adj* (1810) **:** that may be insured — **in·sur·abil·i·ty** \-,shu̇r-ə-'bil-ət-ē\ *n*

¹in·sur·ance \in-'shu̇r-ən(t)s, *chiefly Southern* 'in-,\ *n* (1651) **1 a :** the business of insuring persons or property **b :** coverage by contract whereby one party undertakes to indemnify or guarantee another against loss by a specified contingency or peril **c :** the sum for which something is insured **2 :** a means of guaranteeing protection or safety ⟨the contract is your ~ against price changes⟩ ⟨the shelter provides ~ against enemy attack⟩

²insurance *adj* (1954) **:** being a score that adds to a team's lead and makes it impossible for the opposing team to tie the game with its next score ⟨~ run⟩

in·sure \in-'shu̇(ə)r\ *vb* **in·sured; in·sur·ing** [ME *insuren,* prob. alter. of *assuren* to assure] *vt* (1635) **1 :** to provide or obtain insurance on or for **2 :** to make certain esp. by taking necessary measures and precautions ~ *vi* **:** to contract to give or take insurance ***syn*** see ENSURE

in·sured *n* (1681) **:** a person whose life or property is insured

in·sur·er \in-'shu̇r-ər\ *n* (1654) **:** one that insures; *specif* **:** an insurance underwriter

in·sur·gence \in-'sər-jən(t)s\ *n* (1847) **:** an act or the action of being insurgent **:** INSURRECTION

in·sur·gen·cy \-jən-sē\ *n, pl* **-cies** (1803) **1 :** the quality or state of being insurgent; *specif* **:** a condition of revolt against a government that is less than an organized revolution and that is not recognized as belligerency **2 :** INSURGENCE

¹in·sur·gent \-jənt\ *n* [L *insurgent-, insurgens,* prp. of *insurgere* to rise up, fr. *in-* + *surgere* to rise — more at SURGE] (1765) **1 :** a person who revolts against civil authority or an established government; *esp* **:** a rebel not recognized as a belligerent **2 :** one who acts contrary to the policies and decisions of his political party

²insurgent *adj* (1814) **:** rising in opposition to civil authority or established leadership **:** REBELLIOUS — **in·sur·gent·ly** *adv*

in·sur·mount·able \,in(t)-sər-'mau̇nt-ə-bəl\ *adj* (1690) **:** incapable of being surmounted **:** INSUPERABLE ⟨~ problems⟩ — **in·sur·mount·ably** \-blē\ *adv*

in·sur·rec·tion \,in(t)-sə-'rek-shən\ *n* [ME, fr. MF, fr. LL *insurrection-, insurrectio,* fr. *insurrectus,* pp. of *insurgere*] (15c) **:** an act or instance of revolting against civil authority or an established government ***syn*** see REBELLION — **in·sur·rec·tion·al** \-shnəl, -shən-ᵊl\ *adj* — **in·sur·rec·tion·ary** \-shə-,ner-ē\ *adj or n* — **in·sur·rec·tion·ist** \-sh(ə-)nəst\ *n*

in·sus·cep·ti·ble \,in(t)-sə-'sep-tə-bəl\ *adj* (1603) **:** not susceptible ⟨~ to flattery⟩ — **in·sus·cep·ti·bil·i·ty** \-,sep-tə-'bil-ət-ē\ *n* — **in·sus·cep·ti·bly** \,in(t)-sə-'sep-tə-blē\ *adv*

in·tact \in-'takt\ *adj* [ME *intacte,* fr. L *intactus,* fr. *in-* + *tactus,* pp. of *tangere* to touch — more at TANGENT] (15c) **1 :** untouched esp. by anything that harms or diminishes **:** ENTIRE, UNINJURED **2** *of a living body or its parts* **:** having no relevant component removed or destroyed: **a :** physically virginal **b :** not castrated ***syn*** see PERFECT — **in·tact·ness** \-'tak(t)-nəs\ *n*

in·ta·glio \in-'tal-(,)yō, -'täl-; -'tag-lē-,ō, -'täg-\ *n, pl* **-glios** [It, fr. *intagliare* to engrave, cut, fr. ML *intaliare,* fr. L *in-* + LL *taliare* to cut — more at TAILOR] (1644) **1 a :** an engraving or incised figure in stone or other hard material depressed below the surface of the material so that an impression from the design yields an image in relief **b :** the art or process of executing intaglios **c :** printing (as in die stamping and gravure) done from a plate in which the image is sunk below the surface **2 :** something (as a gem) carved in intaglio

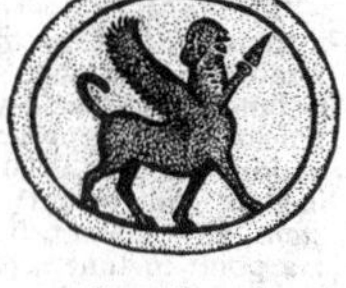

intaglio 1a

in·take \'in-,tāk\ *n* (1690) **1 :** an opening through which fluid enters an enclosure **2 a :** a taking in **b (1) :** the amount taken in **(2) :** something (as energy) taken in **:** INPUT

¹in·tan·gi·ble \(')in-'tan-jə-bəl\ *adj* [F or ML; F, fr. ML *intangibilis,* fr. L *in-* + LL *tangibilis* tangible] (1640) **:** not tangible **:** IMPALPABLE — **in·tan·gi·bil·i·ty** \(,)in-,tan-jə-'bil-ət-ē\ *n* — **in·tan·gi·ble·ness** \(')in-'tan-jə-bəl-nəs\ *n* — **in·tan·gi·bly** \-blē\ *adv*

²intangible *n* (1914) **:** something intangible; *specif* **:** an asset (as goodwill) that is not corporeal

in·tar·sia \in-'tär-sē-ə\ *n* [G, modif. of It *intarsio*] (1867) **:** a mosaic usu. of wood fitted into a support; *also* **:** the art or process of making such a mosaic

in·te·ger \'int-i-jər\ *n* [L, adj., whole, entire — more at ENTIRE] (1571) **1 :** any of the natural numbers, the negatives of these numbers, or zero **2 :** a complete entity

in·te·gra·ble \'int-i-grə-bəl\ *adj* (1727) **:** capable of being integrated ⟨~ functions⟩ — **in·te·gra·bil·i·ty** \,int-i-grə-'bil-ət-ē\ *n*

¹in·te·gral \'int-i-grəl (*usu so in mathematics*); in-'teg-rəl *also* -'tēg-\ *adj* (1551) **1 a :** essential to completeness **:** CONSTITUENT ⟨an ~ part of the curriculum⟩ **b (1) :** being, containing, or relating to one or more mathematical integers **(2) :** relating to or concerned with mathematical integrals or integration **c :** formed as a unit with another part **2 :** composed of integral parts **:** INTEGRATED **3 :** lacking nothing essential **:** ENTIRE — **in·te·gral·i·ty** \,int-ə-'gral-ət-ē\ *n* — **in·te·gral·ly** \'int-i-grə-lē; in-'teg-rə- *also* -'tēg-\ *adv*

²integral *n* (1727) **:** the result of a mathematical integration — compare DEFINITE INTEGRAL, INDEFINITE INTEGRAL

integral calculus *n* (ca. 1727) **:** a branch of mathematics concerned with the theory and applications (as in the determination of lengths, areas, and volumes and in the solution of differential equations) of integrals and integration

integral domain *n* (1937) **:** a mathematical ring in which multiplication is commutative, which has a multiplicative identity element, and which contains no pair of nonzero elements whose product is zero ⟨the integers under the operations of addition and multiplication form an *integral domain*⟩

in·te·grand \'int-ə-,grand\ *n* [L *integrandus,* gerundive of *integrare*] (1897) **:** a mathematical expression to be integrated

in·te·grate \'int-ə-,grāt\ *vb* **-grat·ed; -grat·ing** [L *integratus,* pp. of *integrare,* fr. *integr-, integer*] *vt* (1638) **1 :** to form, coordinate, or blend into a functioning or unified whole **:** UNITE **2 :** to find the integral of (as a function or equation) **3 a :** to unite with something else **b :** to incorporate into a larger unit **4 a :** to end the segregation of and bring into common and equal membership in society or an organization **b :** DESEGREGATE ⟨~ school districts⟩ ~ *vi* **:** to become integrated

integrated circuit *n* (1959) **:** a tiny complex of electronic components and their connections that is produced in or on a small slice of material (as silicon) — **integrated circuitry** *n*

in·te·gra·tion \,int-ə-'grā-shən\ *n* (1620) **1 :** the act or process or an instance of integrating: as **a :** incorporation as equals into society or an organization of individuals of different groups (as races) **b :** coordination of mental processes into a normal effective personality or with the individual's environment **2 a :** the operation of finding a function whose differential is known **b :** the operation of solving a differential equation

in·te·gra·tion·ist \-sh(ə-)nəst\ *n* (1951) **:** a person who believes in, advocates, or practices social integration — **integrationist** *adj*

in·te·gra·tive \'int-ə-,grāt-iv\ *adj* (1862) **:** serving to integrate or favoring integration **:** directed toward integration ⟨~ forces in a fragmented society⟩

in·te·gra·tor \-,grāt-ər\ *n* (1876) **:** one that integrates; *esp* **:** a device or computer unit that totalizes variable quantities in a manner comparable to mathematical integration

in·teg·ri·ty \in-'teg-rət-ē\ *n* (15c) **1 :** an unimpaired condition **:** SOUNDNESS **2 :** firm adherence to a code of esp. moral or artistic values **:** INCORRUPTIBILITY **3 :** the quality or state of being complete or undivided **:** COMPLETENESS ***syn*** see HONESTY

in·teg·u·ment \in-'teg-yə-mənt\ *n* [L *integumentum,* fr. *integere* to cover, fr. *in-* + *tegere* to cover — more at THATCH] (1611) **:** something that covers or encloses; *esp* **:** an enveloping layer (as a skin, membrane, or husk) of an organism or one of its parts — **in·teg·u·men·ta·ry** \-'ment-ə-rē, -'men-trē\ *adj*

in·tel·lect \'int-ᵊl-,ekt\ *n* [ME, fr. MF or L; MF, fr. L *intellectus,* fr. *intellectus,* pp. of *intellegere* to understand — more at INTELLIGENT] (14c) **1 a :** the power of knowing as distinguished from the power to feel and to will **:** the capacity for knowledge **b :** the capacity for rational or intelligent thought esp. when highly developed **2 :** a person with great intellectual powers

in·tel·lec·tion \,int-ᵊl-'ek-shən\ *n* (15c) **1 :** exercise of the intellect **:** REASONING **2 :** an act of the intellect **:** THOUGHT

in·tel·lec·tive \-'ek-tiv\ *adj* (15c) : having, relating to, or belonging to the intellect : RATIONAL — **in·tel·lec·tive·ly** *adv*

¹**in·tel·lec·tu·al** \ˌint-ᵊl-'ek-ch(ə-w)əl, -'eksh-wəl\ *adj* (14c) **1 a** : of or relating to the intellect or its use **b** : developed or chiefly guided by the intellect rather than by emotion or experience : RATIONAL **c** : requiring use of the intellect **2 a** : given to study, reflection, and speculation **b** : engaged in activity requiring the creative use of the intellect — **in·tel·lec·tu·al·i·ty** \-ˌek-chə-'wal-ət-ē\ *n* — **in·tel·lec·tu·al·ly** \-'ek-chə-(wə-)lē, -'eksh-wə-lē\ *adv* — **in·tel·lec·tu·al·ness** \-'ek-chə(-wə)l-nəs, -'eksh-wəl-\ *n*

²**intellectual** *n* (1599) **1** *pl, archaic* : intellectual powers **2** : an intellectual person

in·tel·lec·tu·al·ism \ˌint-ᵊl-'ek-chə(-wə)-ˌliz-əm, -'eksh-wə-\ *n* (1838) : devotion to the exercise of intellect or to intellectual pursuits — **in·tel·lec·tu·al·ist** \-ləst\ *n* — **in·tel·lec·tu·al·is·tic** \-ˌek-chə(-wə)-'lis-tik, -ˌeksh-wə-\ *adj*

in·tel·lec·tu·al·ize \ˌint-ᵊl-'ek-chə(-wə)-ˌlīz, -'eksh-wə-\ *vt* **-ized; -iz·ing** (1819) : to give rational form or content to — **in·tel·lec·tu·al·iza·tion** \-ˌek-chə(-wə)-lə-'zā-shən, -ˌeksh-wə-\ *n* — **in·tel·lec·tu·al·iz·er** \-'ek-chə(-wə)-ˌlī-zər, -'eksh-wə-\ *n*

in·tel·li·gence \in-'tel-ə-jən(t)s\ *n* [ME, fr. MF, fr. L *intelligentia,* fr. *intelligent-, intelligens* intelligent] (14c) **1 a** (1) : the ability to learn or understand or to deal with new or trying situations : REASON; *also* : the skilled use of reason (2) : the ability to apply knowledge to manipulate one's environment or to think abstractly as measured by objective criteria (as tests) **b** *Christian Science* : the basic eternal quality of divine Mind **c** : mental acuteness : SHREWDNESS **2 a** : an intelligent entity; *esp* : ANGEL **b** : intelligent minds or mind ⟨cosmic ~⟩ **3** : the act of understanding : COMPREHENSION **4 a** : INFORMATION, NEWS **b** : information concerning an enemy or possible enemy or an area; *also* : an agency engaged in obtaining such information

intelligence quotient *n* (1916) : a number used to express the apparent relative intelligence of a person determined by dividing his mental age as reported on a standardized test by his chronological age and multiplying by 100

in·tel·li·genc·er \in-'tel-ə-jən-sər; -'tel-ə-ˌjen(t)-, -ˌtel-ə-'\ *n* (1581) **1** : a secret agent : SPY **2** : a bringer of news : REPORTER

intelligence test *n* (1914) : a test designed to determine the relative mental capacity of a person

in·tel·li·gent \in-'tel-ə-jənt\ *adj* [L *intelligent-, intelligens,* prp. of *intelligere, intellegere* to understand, fr. *inter-* + *legere* to gather, select — more at LEGEND] (1509) **1 a** : having or indicating a high or satisfactory degree of intelligence and mental capacity **b** : revealing or reflecting good judgment or sound thought : SKILLFUL **2 a** : possessing intelligence **b** : guided or directed by intellect : RATIONAL **3** : able to perform computer functions ⟨an ~ terminal⟩; *also* : able to convert digital information to hard copy ⟨an ~ copier⟩ — **in·tel·li·gen·tial** \-ˌtel-ə-'jen-chəl\ *adj* — **in·tel·li·gent·ly** \-'tel-ə-jənt-lē\ *adv*

syn INTELLIGENT, CLEVER, ALERT, QUICK-WITTED mean mentally keen or quick. INTELLIGENT stresses success in coping with new situations and solving problems; CLEVER implies native ability or aptness and sometimes suggests a lack of more substantial qualities; ALERT stresses quickness in perceiving and understanding; QUICK-WITTED implies promptness in finding answers in debate or in devising expedients in moments of danger or challenge.

in·tel·li·gen·tsia \in-ˌtel-ə-'jen(t)-sē-ə, -'gen(t)-\ *n* [Russ *intelligentsiya,* fr. L *intelligentia* intelligence] (1907) : intellectuals who form an artistic, social, or political vanguard or elite

in·tel·li·gi·ble \in-'tel-ə-jə-bəl\ *adj* [ME, fr. L *intelligibilis;* fr. *intelligere*] (14c) **1** : apprehensible by the intellect only **2** : capable of being understood or comprehended — **in·tel·li·gi·bil·i·ty** \-ˌtel-ə-jə-'bil-ət-ē\ *n* — **in·tel·li·gi·ble·ness** \-'tel-ə-jə-bəl-nəs\ *n* — **in·tel·li·gi·bly** \-blē\ *adv*

in·tem·per·ance \(ˈ)in-'tem-p(ə-)rən(t)s\ *n* (15c) : lack of moderation; *esp* : habitual or excessive drinking of intoxicants

in·tem·per·ate \-p(ə-)rət\ *adj* [ME *intemperat,* fr. L *intemperatus,* fr. *in-* + *temperatus,* pp. of *temperare* to temper] (14c) : not temperate; *esp* : given to excessive use of intoxicating liquors — **in·tem·per·ate·ly** *adv* — **in·tem·per·ate·ness** *n*

in·tend \in-'tend\ *vb* [ME *entenden, intenden,* fr. MF *entendre* to purpose, fr. L *intendere* to stretch out, to purpose, fr. *in-* + *tendere* to stretch — more at THIN] *vt* (14c) **1 a** : to have in mind as a purpose or goal : PLAN **b** : to design for a specified use or future **2 a** : SIGNIFY, MEAN **b** : to refer to **3** *archaic* : to proceed on (a course) **4** : to direct the mind on ~ *vi, archaic* : SET OUT, START — **in·tend·er** *n*

in·ten·dance \in-'ten-dən(t)s\ *n* (1739) **1** : MANAGEMENT, SUPERINTENDENCE **2** : an administrative department

in·ten·dant \-dənt\ *n* [F, fr. MF, fr. L *intendent-, intendens,* prp. of *intendere* to intend, attend] (1652) : an administrative official (as a governor) esp. under the French, Spanish, or Portuguese monarchies

¹**in·tend·ed** *adj* (1586) **1** : expected to be such in the future ⟨an ~ career⟩ ⟨his ~ bride⟩ **2** : INTENTIONAL — **in·tend·ed·ly** *adv* — **in·tend·ed·ness** *n*

²**intended** *n* (1767) : the person to whom another is engaged : a fiancé or fiancée

in·tend·ing *adj* (1788) : PROSPECTIVE, ASPIRING ⟨an ~ teacher⟩

in·tend·ment \in-'ten(d)-mənt\ *n* (14c) : the true meaning or intention esp. of a law

in·ten·er·ate \in-'ten-ə-ˌrāt\ *vt* **-at·ed; -at·ing** [²*in-* + L *tener* soft, tender — more at TENDER] (1595) : to make tender : SOFTEN — **in·ten·er·a·tion** \-ˌten-ə-'rā-shən\ *n*

in·tense \in-'ten(t)s\ *adj* [ME, fr. MF, fr. L *intensus,* fr. pp. of *intendere* to stretch out] (15c) **1 a** : existing in an extreme degree **b** : having or showing a characteristic in extreme degree **c** : very large : CONSIDERABLE **2** : strained or straining to the utmost **3 a** : feeling deeply esp. by nature or temperament **b** : deeply felt — **in·tense·ly** *adv* — **in·tense·ness** *n*

in·ten·si·fi·er \in-'ten(t)-sə-ˌfī(-ə)r\ *n* (1835) : one that intensifies; *esp* : INTENSIVE

in·ten·si·fy \in-'ten(t)-sə-ˌfī\ *vb* **-fied; -fy·ing** *vt* (1817) **1** : to make intense or more intensive : STRENGTHEN **2 a** : to increase the density and contrast of (a photographic image) by chemical treatment **b** : to make more acute : SHARPEN ~ *vi* : to become intense or more intensive : grow stronger or more acute — **in·ten·si·fi·ca·tion** \-ˌten(t)s-(ə-)fə-'kā-shən\ *n*

syn INTENSIFY, AGGRAVATE, HEIGHTEN, ENHANCE mean to increase markedly in measure or degree. INTENSIFY implies a deepening or strengthening of a thing or of its characteristic quality; AGGRAVATE implies an increasing in gravity or seriousness, esp. the worsening of something already bad or undesirable; HEIGHTEN suggests a lifting above the ordinary or accustomed; ENHANCE implies a raising or strengthening above the normal in desirability, value, or attractiveness.

in·ten·sion \in-'ten-chən\ *n* (1604) **1** : INTENSITY **2** : CONNOTATION 3 — **in·ten·sion·al** \-'tench-nəl, -'ten-chən-ᵊl\ *adj* — **in·ten·sion·al·ly** \-ē\ *adv*

in·ten·si·ty \in-'ten(t)-sət-ē\ *n, pl* **-ties** (1665) **1** : the quality or state of being intense; *esp* : extreme degree of strength, force, energy, or feeling **2** : the magnitude of force or energy per unit (as of surface, charge, mass, or time) **3** : SATURATION 4a

¹**in·ten·sive** \in-'ten(t)-siv\ *adj* (15c) : of, relating to, or marked by intensity or intensification: as **a** : highly concentrated ⟨~ study⟩ **b** : tending to strengthen or increase; *esp* : tending to give force or emphasis ⟨~ adverb⟩ **c** : constituting or relating to a method designed to increase productivity by the expenditure of more capital and labor rather than by increase in scope ⟨~ farming⟩ — **in·ten·sive·ly** *adv* — **in·ten·sive·ness** *n*

²**intensive** *n* (1813) : an intensive linguistic element

intensive care *adj* (1963) : having special medical facilities, services, and monitoring devices to meet the needs of gravely ill patients ⟨an *intensive care* unit⟩ — **intensive care** *n*

¹**in·tent** \in-'tent\ *n* [ME *entent,* fr. OF, fr. LL *intentus,* fr. L, act of stretching out, fr. *intentus,* pp. of *intendere*] (13c) **1 a** : the act or fact of intending : PURPOSE **b** : the state of mind with which an act is done : VOLITION **2** : a usu. clearly formulated or planned intention : AIM **3 a** : MEANING, SIGNIFICANCE **b** : CONNOTATION 3 ***syn*** see INTENTION

²**intent** *adj* [L *intentus,* fr. pp. of *intendere*] (14c) **1** : directed with strained or eager attention : CONCENTRATED **2** : having the mind, attention, or will concentrated on something or some end or purpose ⟨~ on their work⟩ — **in·tent·ly** *adv* — **in·tent·ness** *n*

in·ten·tion \in-'ten-chən\ *n* (14c) **1** : a determination to act in a certain way : RESOLVE **2** : IMPORT, SIGNIFICANCE **3 a** : what one intends to do or bring about **b** : the object for which a prayer, mass, or pious act is offered **4** : a process or manner of healing of incised wounds **5** : CONCEPT; *esp* : a concept considered as the product of attention directed to an object of knowledge **6** *pl* : purpose with respect to marriage

syn INTENTION, INTENT, PURPOSE, DESIGN, AIM, END, OBJECT, OBJECTIVE, GOAL mean what one purposes to accomplish or attain. INTENTION implies little more than what one has in mind to do or bring about; INTENT suggests clearer formulation or greater deliberateness; PURPOSE suggests a more settled determination; DESIGN implies a more carefully calculated plan; AIM adds to these implications of effort directed toward attaining or accomplishing; END stresses the intended effect of action often in distinction or contrast to the action or means as such; OBJECT may equal END but more often applies to a more individually determined wish or need; OBJECTIVE implies something tangible and immediately attainable; GOAL suggests something attained only by prolonged effort and hardship.

in·ten·tion·al \in-'tench-nəl, -'ten-chən-ᵊl\ *adj* (1677) **1** : done by intention or design : INTENDED ⟨~ damage⟩ **2 a** : of or relating to epistemological intention **b** : having external reference ***syn*** see VOLUNTARY — **in·ten·tion·al·i·ty** \-ˌten-chə-'nal-ət-ē\ *n* — **in·ten·tion·al·ly** \in-'tench-nə-lē, -'ten-chən-ᵊl-ē\ *adv*

in·ter \in-'tər\ *vt* **in·terred; in·ter·ring** [ME *enteren,* fr. MF *enterrer,* fr. (assumed) VL *interrare,* fr. *in-* + L *terra* earth — more at TERRACE] (14c) : to deposit (a dead body) in the earth or in a tomb

inter- *prefix* [ME *inter-, enter-,* fr. MF & L; MF *inter-, entre-,* fr. L *inter-,* fr. *inter;* akin to OHG *untar* between, among, Gk *enteron* intestine, OE *in* in] **1** : between : among : in the midst ⟨*inter*crop⟩ ⟨*inter*penetrate⟩ ⟨*inter*stellar⟩ **2** : reciprocal ⟨*inter*relation⟩ : reciprocally ⟨*inter*marry⟩ **3** : located between ⟨*inter*face⟩ **4** : carried on between ⟨*inter*national⟩ **5** : occurring between ⟨*inter*borough⟩ : intervening ⟨*inter*glacial⟩ **6** : shared by or derived from two or more ⟨*inter*faith⟩ **7** : between the limits of : within ⟨*inter*tropical⟩ **8** : existing between ⟨*inter*communal⟩ ⟨*inter*company⟩

in·ter–Af·ri·can
in·ter·age
in·ter·agen·cy
in·ter·al·le·lic
in·ter–Amer·i·can
in·ter·an·i·ma·tion
in·ter·an·nu·al
in·ter·as·so·ci·a·tion
in·ter·avail·abil·i·ty
in·ter·bank
in·ter·ba·sin
in·ter·bed
in·ter·be·hav·ior
in·ter·be·hav·ior·al
in·ter·bor·ough
in·ter·branch
in·ter·cal·i·bra·tion
in·ter·cam·pus
in·ter–Ca·rib·be·an
in·ter·caste
in·ter·cel·e·bra·tion
in·ter·cell
in·ter·cel·lu·lar
in·ter·cel·lu·lar·ly
in·ter·chain
in·ter·chan·nel
in·ter·chro·mo·som·al
in·ter·church
in·ter·city
in·ter·clan
in·ter·class
in·ter·club
in·ter·clus·ter
in·ter·coast·al
in·ter·co·lo·nial
in·ter·com·mu·nal
in·ter·com·mu·ni·ty
in·ter·com·pa·ny
in·ter·com·pare
in·ter·com·par·i·son
in·ter·com·pre·hen·si·bil·i·ty
in·ter·cor·po·rate
in·ter·cor·re·late
in·ter·cor·re·la·tion
in·ter·cor·ti·cal
in·ter·coun·try
in·ter·coun·ty
in·ter·cou·ple
in·ter·cra·ter
in·ter·crys·tal·line
in·ter·cul·tur·al
in·ter·cul·tur·al·ly
in·ter·cul·ture
in·ter·deal·er
in·ter·de·pend
in·ter·de·pen·dence
in·ter·de·pen·den·cy
in·ter·de·pen·dent
in·ter·de·pen·dent·ly
in·ter·di·a·lec·tal
in·ter·dis·trict
in·ter·di·vi·sion·al
in·ter·do·min·ion
in·ter·ec·cle·si·as·ti·cal
in·ter·elec·trode
in·ter·elec·tron
in·ter·elec·tron·ic
in·ter·el·e·ment
in·ter·en·vi·ron·men·tal
in·ter·ep·i·dem·ic
in·ter·eth·nic
in·ter·fac·ul·ty
in·ter·fa·mil·ial
in·ter·fam·i·ly
in·ter·fi·ber
in·ter·firm
in·ter·flow
in·ter·flu·vi·al

in·ter·fold
in·ter·fra·ter·ni·ty
in·ter·gang
in·ter·gen·er·a·tion
in·ter·gen·er·a·tion·al
in·ter·graft
in·ter·gran·u·lar
in·ter·group
in·ter·host
in·ter·in·di·vid·u·al
in·ter·in·dus·try
in·ter·in·flu·ence
in·ter·in·sti·tu·tion·al
in·ter·in·volve
in·ter·is·land
in·ter·la·cus·trine
in·ter·lam·i·nar
in·ter·lam·i·nate
in·ter·lam·i·na·tion
in·ter·lay
in·ter·lay·er
in·ter·lay·er·ing
in·ter·lend
in·ter·lev·el
in·ter·li·brary
in·ter·lin·er
in·ter·lob·u·lar
in·ter·lo·cal
in·ter·male
in·ter·mar·gin·al
in·ter·mas·cu·line
in·ter·mem·brane
in·ter·men·stru·al
in·ter·met·ro·pol·i·tan
in·ter·min·is·te·ri·al
in·ter·mi·tot·ic
in·ter·moun·tain
in·ter·mu·se·um
in·ter·nu·cle·on
in·ter·nu·cle·on·ic
in·ter·nu·cle·o·tide
in·ter·ob·serv·er
in·ter·ocean
in·ter·oce·an·ic
in·ter·of·fice
in·ter·op·er·a·bil·i·ty
in·ter·op·er·a·ble
in·ter·op·er·a·tive
in·ter·or·bit·al
in·ter·or·gan
in·ter·pan·dem·ic
in·ter·par·ish
in·ter·pa·ro·chi·al
in·ter·par·ox·ys·mal
in·ter·par·ti·cle
in·ter·par·ty
in·ter·per·cep·tu·al
in·ter·per·me·ate
in·ter·pha·lan·ge·al
in·ter·plan·e·tary
in·ter·plu·vi·al
in·ter·pop·u·la·tion
in·ter·pro·fes·sion·al
in·ter·pro·vin·cial
in·ter·psy·chic
in·ter·re·gion·al
in·ter·re·li·gious
in·ter·re·nal
in·ter·row
in·ter·sam·ple
in·ter·school
in·ter·sec·tion·al
in·ter·seg·ment
in·ter·seg·men·tal
in·ter·sen·so·ry
in·ter·site
in·ter·so·ci·etal
in·ter·so·ci·ety
in·ter·stage
in·ter·sta·tion
in·ter·stim·u·la·tion
in·ter·stim·u·lus
in·ter·strain
in·ter·strand
in·ter·strat·i·fi·ca·tion
in·ter·strat·i·fy
in·ter·sub·sti·tut·abil·i·ty
in·ter·sub·sti·tut·able
in·ter·sys·tem
in·ter·term
in·ter·ter·mi·nal
in·ter·ter·ri·to·ri·al
in·ter·tex·tu·al
in·ter·trans·lat·able
in·ter·tri·al
in·ter·trib·al
in·ter·troop
in·ter·union
in·ter·unit
in·ter·uni·ver·si·ty
in·ter·val·ley
in·ter·ven·tric·u·lar
in·ter·vil·lage
in·ter·vis·i·bil·i·ty
in·ter·vis·i·ble
in·ter·vis·i·ta·tion
in·ter·war
in·ter·work
in·ter·zon·al
in·ter·zone

in·tera·bang *var of* INTERROBANG
in·ter·act \ˌint-ə-ˈrakt\ *vi* (1839) : to act upon one another
in·ter·ac·tant \-ˈrak-tənt\ *n* (1949) : one that interacts
in·ter·ac·tion \ˌint-ə-ˈrak-shən\ *n* (1832) : mutual or reciprocal action or influence — **in·ter·ac·tion·al** \-shnəl, -shən-ᵊl\ *adj*
in·ter·ac·tive \-ˈrak-tiv\ *adj* (1832) **1** : mutually or reciprocally active **2** : of, relating to, or being a two-way electronic communication system (as a telephone, cable television, or a computer) that involves a user's orders (as for information or merchandise) or responses (as to a poll) — **in·ter·ac·tive·ly** *adv*
in·ter alia \ˌint-ə-ˈrā-lē-ə, -ˈrä-\ *adv* [L *alia*, neut. pl. of *alius* — more at ELSE] (1665) : among other things
in·ter ali·os \-lē-ˌōs\ *adv* [L *alios*, masc. pl. of *alius*] (1670) : among other persons
in·ter·al·lied \ˌint-ə-ˈral-ˌīd, -rə-ˈlīd\ *adj* (1919) : relating to, composed of, or involving allies
in·ter·atom·ic \ˌint-ə-rə-ˈtäm-ik\ *adj* (1863) : existing or acting between atoms
in·ter·breed \ˌint-ər-ˈbrēd\ *vb* **-bred** \-ˈbred\; **-breed·ing** *vi* (1859) : to breed together: as **a** : CROSSBREED **b** : to breed within a closed population ~ *vt* : to cause to breed together
in·ter·ca·la·ry \in-ˈtər-kə-ˌler-ē, ˌint-ər-ˈkal-ə-rē\ *adj* [L *intercalarius*, fr. *intercalare*] (1614) **1 a** : inserted in a calendar ⟨an ~ day⟩ **b** *of a year* : containing an intercalary period (as a day or month) **2** : inserted between other things or parts : INTERPOLATED
in·ter·ca·late \in-ˈtər-kə-ˌlāt\ *vt* **-lat·ed**; **-lat·ing** [L *intercalatus*, pp. of *intercalare*, fr. *inter-* + *calare* to call, summon — more at LOW] (1614) **1** : to insert (as a day) in a calendar **2** : to insert between or among existing elements or layers *syn* see INTRODUCE — **in·ter·ca·la·tion** \-ˌtər-kə-ˈlā-shən\ *n*
in·ter·cede \ˌint-ər-ˈsēd\ *vi* **-ced·ed**; **-ced·ing** [L *intercedere*, fr. *inter-* + *cedere* to go — more at CEDE] (1597) : to intervene between parties with a view to reconciling differences : MEDIATE *syn* see INTERPOSE — **in·ter·ced·er** *n*
in·ter·cen·sal \ˌint-ər-ˈsen(t)-səl\ *adj* [*inter-census* + *-al*] (1887) : occurring between censuses ⟨~ estimates⟩ ⟨~ period⟩
¹in·ter·cept \ˌint-ər-ˈsept\ *vt* [L *interceptus*, pp. of *intercipere*, fr. *inter-* + *capere* to take, seize — more at HEAVE] (15c) **1** *obs* : PREVENT, HINDER **2** : to stop, seize, or interrupt in progress or course or before arrival **3** *obs* : to interrupt communication or connection with **4** : to include (part of a curve, surface, or solid) between two points, curves, or surfaces ⟨the part of a circumference ~*ed* between two radii⟩ **5** : to gain possession of (an opponent's pass)
²in·ter·cept \ˈint-ər-ˌsept\ *n* (1821) **1** : the distance from the origin to a point where a graph crosses a coordinate axis **2** : INTERCEPTION; *esp* : the interception of a missile by an interceptor or of a target by a missile
in·ter·cept·er \ˌint-ər-ˈsep-tər\ *n* (1601) : INTERCEPTOR
in·ter·cep·tion \ˌint-ər-ˈsep-shən\ *n* (15c) **1 a** : the action of intercepting **b** : the state of being intercepted **2** : something that is intercepted; *esp* : an intercepted forward pass
in·ter·cep·tor \-ˈsep-tər\ *n* (1598) : one that intercepts; *specif* : a light high-speed fast-climbing fighter plane or missile designed for defense against raiding bombers or missiles
in·ter·ces·sion \ˌint-ər-ˈsesh-ən\ *n* [MF or L; MF, fr. L *intercession-, intercessio*, fr. *intercessus*, pp. of *intercedere*] (15c) **1** : the act of interceding **2** : prayer, petition, or entreaty in favor of another — **in·ter·ces·sion·al** \-ˈsesh-nəl, -ən-ᵊl\ *adj* — **in·ter·ces·sor** \-ˈses-ər\ *n* — **in·ter·ces·so·ry** \-ˈses-(ə-)rē\ *adj*
¹in·ter·change \ˌint-ər-ˈchānj\ *vb* [ME *entrechaungen*, fr. MF *entrechangier*, fr. OF, fr. *entre-* inter- + *changier* to change] *vt* (14c) **1** : to put each of (two things) in the place of the other **2** : EXCHANGE ~ *vi* : to change places mutually — **in·ter·chang·er** *n*
²in·ter·change \ˈint-ər-ˌchānj\ *n* (15c) **1** : the act, process, or an instance of interchanging : EXCHANGE **2** : a junction of two or more highways by a system of separate levels that permit traffic to pass from one to another without the crossing of traffic streams
in·ter·change·able \ˌint-ər-ˈchān-jə-bəl\ *adj* (14c) : capable of being interchanged; *esp* : permitting mutual substitution ⟨~ parts⟩ — **in·ter·change·abil·i·ty** \-ˌchān-jə-ˈbil-ət-ē\ *n* — **in·ter·change·able·ness** \-ˈchān-jə-bəl-nəs\ *n* — **in·ter·change·ably** \-blē\ *adv*
in·ter·col·le·giate \ˌint-ər-kə-ˈlē-j(ē-)ət\ *adj* (1873) : existing, carried on, or participating in activities between colleges ⟨~ athletics⟩
in·ter·co·lum·ni·a·tion \ˌint-ər-kə-ˌləm-nē-ˈā-shən\ *n* [L *intercolumnium* space between two columns, fr. *inter-* + *columna* column] (1624) **1** : the clear space between the columns of a series **2** : the system of spacing of the columns of a colonnade
in·ter·com \ˈint-ər-ˌkäm\ *n* (1940) : INTERCOMMUNICATION SYSTEM
in·ter·com·mu·ni·cate \ˌint-ər-kə-ˈmyü-nə-ˌkāt\ *vi* (1586) **1** : to exchange communication with one another **2** : to afford passage from one to another — **in·ter·com·mu·ni·ca·tion** \-ˌmyü-nə-ˈkā-shən\ *n*
intercommunication system *n* (1911) : a two-way communication system with microphone and loudspeaker at each station for localized use
in·ter·com·mu·nion \ˌint-ər-kə-ˈmyü-nyən\ *n* (1921) : interdenominational participation in communion
in·ter·con·nect \ˌint-ər-kə-ˈnekt\ *vt* (1865) : to connect with one another ~ *vi* : to be or become mutually connected — **in·ter·con·nec·tion** \-ˈnek-shən\ *n*
in·ter·con·nect·ed *adj* (1865) **1** : mutually joined or related ⟨~ highways⟩ ⟨~ political issues⟩ **2** : having internal connections between the parts or elements ⟨a complex and ~ society⟩ — **in·ter·con·nec·ted·ness** *n*
in·ter·con·ti·nen·tal \ˌint-ər-ˌkänt-ᵊn-ˈent-ᵊl\ *adj* (ca. 1855) **1** : extending among continents or carried on between continents **2** : capable of traveling between continents ⟨~ ballistic missile⟩
in·ter·con·ver·sion \ˌint-ər-kən-ˈvər-zhən, -shən\ *n* (1865) : mutual conversion ⟨~ of chemical compounds⟩ — **in·ter·con·vert** \-ˈvərt\ *vt* — **in·ter·con·vert·ibil·i·ty** \-ˌvərt-ə-ˈbil-ət-ē\ *n* — **in·ter·con·vert·ible** \-ˈvərt-ə-bəl\ *adj*
in·ter·cool·er \ˌint-ər-ˈkü-lər\ *n* (1899) : a device for cooling a fluid (as air) between successive heat-generating processes
in·ter·cos·tal \ˌint-ər-ˈkäs-tᵊl\ *adj* [NL *intercostalis*, fr. L *inter-* + *costa* rib — more at COAST] (1597) : situated or extending between the ribs ⟨~ spaces⟩ ⟨~ muscles⟩ — **intercostal** *n*
in·ter·course \ˈint-ər-ˌkō(ə)rs, -ˌkȯ(ə)rs\ *n* [ME *intercurse*, prob. fr. MF *entrecours*, fr. ML *intercursus*, fr. L, act of running between, fr. *intercursus*, pp. of *intercurrere* to run between, fr. *inter-* + *currere* to run — more at CURRENT] (15c) **1** : connection or dealings between persons or groups **2** : exchange esp. of thoughts or feelings : COMMUNION **3** : physical sexual contact between individuals that involves the genitalia of at least one person ⟨heterosexual ~⟩ ⟨anal ~⟩ ⟨oral ~⟩; *esp* : SEXUAL INTERCOURSE 1
in·ter·crop \ˌint-ər-ˈkräp, ˈint-ər-ˌ\ *vt* (1898) : to grow a crop in between (another) ~ *vi* : to grow two or more crops simultaneously (as in alternate rows) on the same plot — **in·ter·crop** \ˈint-ər-ˌkräp\ *n*
¹in·ter·cross \ˌint-ər-ˈkrȯs\ *vb* (1711) : CROSS
²in·ter·cross \ˈint-ər-ˌkrȯs\ *n* (1859) : an instance or a product of crossbreeding
in·ter·cur·rent \ˌint-ər-ˈkər-ənt, -ˈkə-rənt\ *adj* [L *intercurrent-, intercurrens*, prp. of *intercurrere*] (1611) : occurring during and modifying the course of another disease ⟨an ~ infection⟩
in·ter·cut \ˌint-ər-ˈkət\ *vt* (1938) **1** : to insert (a contrasting camera shot) into a take by cutting **2** : to insert a contrasting camera shot into (a take) by cutting ~ *vi* : to alternate contrasting camera shots by cutting
in·ter·de·nom·i·na·tion·al \ˌint-ər-di-ˌnäm-ə-ˈnā-shnəl, -shən-ᵊl\ *adj* (1893) : involving or occurring between different denominations — **in·ter·de·nom·i·na·tion·al·ism** \-ˌiz-əm\ *n*
in·ter·den·tal \ˌint-ər-ˈdent-ᵊl\ *adj* (1874) **1** : situated or intended for use between the teeth **2** : formed with the tip of the tongue between the upper and lower front teeth — **in·ter·den·tal·ly** \-ᵊl-ē\ *adv*
in·ter·de·part·men·tal \ˌint-ər-di-ˌpärt-ˈment-ᵊl, -ˌdē-\ *adj* (1895) : carried on between or involving departments (as of an educational institution) — **in·ter·de·part·men·tal·ly** \-ᵊl-ē\ *adv*
¹in·ter·dict \ˈint-ər-ˌdikt\ *n* [ME *entredit*, fr. OF, fr. L *interdictum* prohibition, praetorian interdict, fr. neut. of *interdictus*, pp. of *interdicere* to interpose, forbid, fr. *inter-* + *dicere* to say — more at DICTION] (13c) **1** : a Roman Catholic ecclesiastical censure withdrawing most sacraments and Christian burial from a person or district **2** : a prohibitory decree : PROHIBITION
²in·ter·dict \ˌint-ər-ˈdikt\ *vt* (13c) **1** : to lay under or prohibit by an interdict **2** : to forbid in a usu. formal or authoritative manner **3** : to destroy, cut, or damage (as an enemy line of supply) by firepower to stop or hamper an enemy *syn* see FORBID — **in·ter·dic·tion** \-ˈdik-shən\ *n* — **in·ter·dic·tive** \-ˈdik-tiv\ *adj* — **in·ter·dic·tor** \-tər\ *n* — **in·ter·dic·to·ry** \-t(ə-)rē\ *adj*
in·ter·dif·fuse \-dif-ˈyüz\ *vi* (ca. 1860) : to diffuse and mix freely so as to approach a homogeneous mixture — **in·ter·dif·fu·sion** \-ˈyü-zhən\ *n*
in·ter·dig·i·tate \-ˈdij-ə-ˌtāt\ *vi* **-tat·ed**; **-tat·ing** [*inter-* + L *digitus* finger — more at TOE] (1847) : to become interlocked like the fingers of folded hands — **in·ter·dig·i·ta·tion** \-ˌdij-ə-ˈtā-shən\ *n*
in·ter·dis·ci·plin·ary \-ˈdis-ə-plə-ˌner-ē\ *adj* (1937) : involving two or more academic, scientific, or artistic disciplines
¹in·ter·est \ˈin-trəst; ˈint-ə-ˌrest, -ə-rəst, ˈint-ərst; ˈin-ˌtrest\ *n* [ME, prob. alter. of earlier *interesse*, fr. AF & ML; AF, fr. ML, fr. L, to be between, make a difference, concern, fr. *inter-* + *esse* to be — more at IS] (15c) **1 a (1)** : right, title, or legal share in something **(2)** : participation in advantage and responsibility **b** : BUSINESS, COMPANY **2 a** : a charge for borrowed money generally a percentage of the amount borrowed **b** : an excess above what is due **3** : ADVANTAGE, BENEFIT; *also* : SELF-INTEREST **4** : SPECIAL INTEREST **5 a** : a feeling that accompanies or causes special attention to an object or class of objects : CONCERN **b** : something that arouses such attention **c** : a quality in a thing that arouses interest
²interest *vt* (1608) **1** : to induce or persuade to participate or engage **2** : to engage the attention or arouse the interest of
in·ter·est·ed *adj* (1665) **1** : having the attention engaged ⟨~ listeners⟩ **2** : being affected or involved ⟨~ parties⟩ — **in·ter·est·ed·ly** *adv*

interest group *n* (1908) : a group of persons having a common identifying interest that often provides a basis for action

in·ter·est·ing *adj* (1768) : holding the attention : arousing interest — **in·ter·est·ing·ly** *adv* — **in·ter·est·ing·ness** *n*

¹in·ter·face \ˈint-ər-ˌfās\ *n* (1882) **1** : a surface forming a common boundary of two bodies, spaces, or phases ⟨an oil-water ~⟩ **2 a** : the place at which independent systems meet and act on or communicate with each other ⟨the man-machine ~⟩; *broadly* : an area in which diverse things interact ⟨the high school-college ~⟩ **b** : the means by which interaction or communication is effected at an interface — **in·ter·fa·cial** \ˌint-ər-ˈfā-shəl\ *adj*

²interface *vt* (1964) **1** : to connect by means of an interface ⟨~ a machine with a computer⟩ **2** : to serve as an interface for ~ *vi* **1** : to become interfaced **2** : to interact or coordinate harmoniously

in·ter·faith \ˌint-ər-ˈfāth\ *adj* (1932) : involving persons of different religious faiths

in·ter·fere \ˌint-ə(r)-ˈfi(ə)r\ *vi* **-fered; -fer·ing** [MF (*s'*)*entreferir* to strike one another, fr. OF, fr. *entre-* inter- + *ferir* to strike, fr. L *ferire* — more at BORE] (15c) **1** : to interpose in a way that hinders or impedes : come into collision or be in opposition **2** : to strike one foot against the opposite foot or ankle in walking or running — used esp. of horses **3** : to enter into or take a part in the concerns of others **4** : to act reciprocally so as to augment, diminish, or otherwise affect one another — used of waves *syn* see INTERPOSE — **in·ter·fer·er** *n*

in·ter·fer·ence \-ˈfir-ən(t)s\ *n* (1783) **1 a** : the act or process of interfering **b** : something that interferes : OBSTRUCTION **2** : the mutual effect on meeting of two wave trains of the same type so that such light waves produce lines, bands, or fringes either alternately light and dark or variously colored and sound waves produce silence, increased intensity, or beats **3 a** : the legal blocking of an opponent in football to make way for the ballcarrier **b** : the illegal hindering of an opponent in sports **4** : partial or complete inhibition or sometimes facilitation of other genetic crossovers in the vicinity of a chromosomal locus where one occurs **5 a** : confusion of received radio signals due to strays or undesired signals **b** : something that produces such confusion **6** : the disturbing effect of new learning on the performance of previously learned behavior with which it is inconsistent — **in·ter·fer·en·tial** \-fə-ˈren-chəl, -ˌfir-ˈen-\ *adj*

in·ter·fer·o·gram \ˌint-ə(r)-ˈfir-ə-ˌgram\ *n* (1921) : a photographic record made by an apparatus for recording optical interference phenomena

in·ter·fer·om·e·ter \ˌint-ə(r)-fə-ˈräm-ət-ər, -ˌfir-ˈäm-\ *n* [ISV] (1897) : an instrument that utilizes the interference of waves (as of light) for precise determinations of wavelength, spectral fine structure, indices of refraction, and very small linear displacements — **in·ter·fer·o·met·ric** \-ˌfir-ə-ˈme-trik\ *adj* — **in·ter·fer·o·met·ri·cal·ly** \-tri-k(ə-)lē\ *adv* — **in·ter·fer·om·e·try** \-fə-ˈräm-ə-trē, -ˌfir-ˈäm-\ *n*

in·ter·fer·on \ˌint-ə(r)-ˈfi(ə)r-ˌän\ *n* [*interference* + *-on*] (ca. 1957) : a heat-stable soluble basic antiviral glycoprotein of low molecular weight produced usu. by cells exposed to the action of a virus, sometimes to that of another intracellular parasite (as a brucella), or experimentally to that of some chemicals

in·ter·fer·tile \ˌint-ər-ˈfərt-ᵊl\ *adj* (1899) : capable of interbreeding — **in·ter·fer·til·i·ty** \-(ˌ)fər-ˈtil-ət-ē\ *n*

in·ter·file \ˌint-ər-ˈfī(ə)l\ *vt* (1950) : ⁴FILE *vt* 1 ~ *vi* : ⁴FILE *vi* 2; *also* : to fit in with an existing file

in·ter·fluve \ˈint-ər-ˌflüv\ *n* [*inter-* + L *fluvius* river — more at FLUVIAL] (ca. 1895) : the area between adjacent streams flowing in the same direction

in·ter·fuse \ˌint-ər-ˈfyüz\ *vb* [L *interfusus,* pp. of *interfundere* to pour between, fr. *inter-* + *fundere* to pour — more at FOUND] *vt* (1593) **1** : to combine by fusing : BLEND **2** : to cause to pass into or through others : INFUSE ~ *vi* : BLEND, FUSE — **in·ter·fu·sion** \-ˈfyü-zhən\ *n*

in·ter·ga·lac·tic \ˌint-ər-gə-ˈlak-tik\ *adj* (1928) : situated in or relating to the spaces between galaxies

in·ter·ge·ner·ic \-jə-ˈner-ik\ *adj* (1921) : existing or occurring between genera ⟨~ hybridization⟩

in·ter·gla·cial \-ˈglā-shəl\ *adj* (ca. 1867) : occurring or formed between glacial epochs ⟨~ climate⟩ — **interglacial** *n*

in·ter·gov·ern·men·tal \-ˌgəv-ər(n)-ˈment-ᵊl\ *adj* (1927) : existing or occurring between two or more governments or levels of government

in·ter·gra·da·tion \-grā-ˈdā-shən, -grə-\ *n* (1874) : the condition of an individual or population that intergrades — **in·ter·gra·da·tion·al** \-shnəl, -shən-ᵊl\ *adj*

¹in·ter·grade \ˌint-ər-ˈgrād\ *vi* (1874) : to merge gradually one with another through a continuous series of intermediate forms

²in·ter·grade \ˈint-ər-ˌgrād\ *n* (1888) : an intermediate form

in·ter·growth \ˈint-ər-ˌgrōth\ *n* (1844) : a growing between or together; *also* : the product of such growth

in·ter·hemi·spher·ic \ˈint-ər-ˌhem-ə-ˈsfi(ə)r-ik, -ˈsfer-\ *adj* (ca. 1885) : extending or occurring between hemispheres (as of the cerebrum)

¹in·ter·im \ˈint-ə-rəm\ *n* [L, adv., meanwhile, fr. *inter* between — more at INTER-] (1563) : an intervening time : INTERVAL

²interim *adj* (1604) : done, made, or occurring for an interim

in·ter·ion·ic \ˌint-ə-(ˌ)rī-ˈän-ik\ *adj* (1903) : situated or acting between ions

¹in·te·ri·or \in-ˈtir-ē-ər\ *adj* [MF & L; MF, fr. L, compar. of (assumed) OL *interus* inward, on the inside; akin to L *inter*] (15c) **1** : lying, occurring, or functioning within the limiting boundaries : INNER ⟨an ~ point of a triangle⟩ **2** : belonging to mental or spiritual life ⟨a simple ~ piety⟩ **3** : belonging to the inner constitution or concealed nature of something ⟨~ meaning of a poem⟩ **4** : lying away or remote from the border or shore — **in·te·ri·or·i·ty** \(ˌ)in-ˌtir-ē-ˈȯr-ət-ē, -ˈär-\ *n* — **in·te·ri·or·ly** \in-ˈtir-ē-ər-lē\ *adv*

²interior *n* (1596) **1** : the inner or spiritual nature : CHARACTER **2** : the interior part (as of a country or island) **3** : the internal or inner part of a thing : INSIDE **4** : the internal affairs of a state or nation **5** : a representation of the interior of a building

interior angle *n* (1756) **1** : the inner of the two angles formed where two sides of a polygon come together **2** : any of the four angles formed in the area between a pair of parallel lines when a third line cuts them

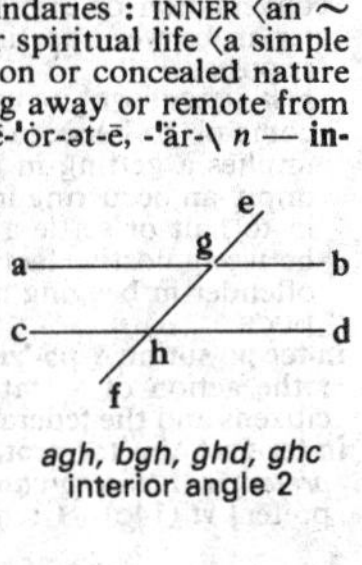

agh, bgh, ghd, ghc
interior angle 2

interior decoration *n* (1807) : INTERIOR DESIGN

interior decorator *n* (1867) **1** : INTERIOR DESIGNER **2** : one who supplies house furnishings **3** : one who paints or wallpapers architectural interiors

interior design *n* (1927) : the art or practice of planning and supervising the design and execution of architectural interiors and their furnishings

interior designer *n* (1938) : one who specializes in interior design

in·te·ri·or·ize \in-ˈtir-ē-ə-ˌrīz\ *vt* **-ized; -iz·ing** (1906) : to make interior; *esp* : to make a part of one's own inner being or mental structure — **in·te·ri·or·iza·tion** \-ˌtir-ē-ə-rə-ˈzā-shən\ *n*

interior monologue *n* (1922) : a usu. extended representation in monologue of a fictional character's thought and feeling

in·ter·ject \ˌint-ər-ˈjekt\ *vt* [L *interjectus,* pp. of *intericere,* fr. *inter-* + *jacere* to throw — more at JET] (1588) : to throw in between or among other things : INTERPOLATE ⟨~ a remark⟩ *syn* see INTRODUCE — **in·ter·jec·tor** \-ˈjek-tər\ *n* — **in·ter·jec·to·ry** \-t(ə-)rē\ *adj*

in·ter·jec·tion \ˌint-ər-ˈjek-shən\ *n* (15c) **1 a** : the act of uttering exclamations : EJACULATION **b** : the act of putting in between : INTERPOSITION **2** : an ejaculatory utterance usu. lacking grammatical connection: as **a** : a word or phrase used in exclamation (as *Heavens! Dear me!*) **b** : a cry or inarticulate utterance (as *Alas! ouch! phooey! ugh!*) expressing an emotion **3** : something that is interjected or that interrupts

in·ter·jec·tion·al \-shnəl, -shən-ᵊl\ *adj* (1761) **1** : of, relating to, or constituting an interjection : EJACULATORY **2** : thrown in between other words : PARENTHETICAL — **in·ter·jec·tion·al·ly** \-ē\ *adv*

in·ter·lace \ˌint-ər-ˈlās\ *vb* [ME *entrelacen,* fr. MF *entrelacer,* fr. OF *entrelacier,* fr. *entre-* inter- + *lacier* to lace] *vt* (14c) **1** : to unite by or as if by lacing together : INTERWEAVE **2** : to vary by alternation or intermixture : INTERSPERSE ⟨narrative *interlaced* with anecdotes⟩ ~ *vi* : to cross one another as if woven together : INTERTWINE — **in·ter·lace·ment** \-ˈlā-smənt\ *n*

in·ter·lard \ˌint-ər-ˈlärd\ *vt* [MF *entrelarder,* fr. OF, fr. *entre* inter- + *larder* to lard, fr. *lard,* n.] (1563) : to intersperse something often foreign or irrelevant into

in·ter·leave \ˌint-ər-ˈlēv\ *vt* **-leaved; -leav·ing** (1668) : to arrange in or as if in alternate layers

¹in·ter·line \ˌint-ər-ˈlīn\ *vt* [ME *enterlinen,* fr. ML *interlineare,* fr. L *inter-* + *linea* line] (15c) : to insert between lines already written or printed — **in·ter·lin·ea·tion** \-ˌlin-ē-ˈā-shən\ *n*

²interline *vt* [ME *interlinen,* fr. *inter-* + *linen* to line] (15c) : to provide (a garment) with an interlining

³interline *adj* (1897) : relating to, involving, or carried by two or more transportation lines

¹in·ter·lin·ear \ˌint-ər-ˈlin-ē-ər\ *adj* [ME *interliniare,* fr. ML *interlinearis,* fr. L *inter-* + *linea* line] (14c) **1** : inserted between lines already written or printed **2** : written or printed in different languages or texts in alternate lines — **in·ter·lin·ear·ly** *adv*

²interlinear *n* (1850) : a book having interlinear matter; *esp* : a book in a foreign language with interlinear translation

in·ter·lin·ing \ˈint-ər-ˌlī-niŋ\ *n* (1881) : a lining (as of a coat) sewn between the ordinary lining and the outside fabric

in·ter·link \ˌint-ər-ˈliŋk\ *vt* (1587) : to link together — **in·ter·link** \ˈint-ər-ˌliŋk\ *n*

¹in·ter·lock \ˌint-ər-ˈläk\ *vi* (1632) : to become engaged or interrelated with one another ~ *vt* **1** : to lock together : UNITE **2** : to connect so that motion of any part is constrained by another; *esp* : to arrange the connections of (as railroad signals) to ensure movement in proper sequence

²in·ter·lock \ˈint-ər-ˌläk\ *n* (1874) **1** : the quality, state, sense, or an instance of being interlocked **2** : an arrangement in which the operation of one part or mechanism automatically brings about or prevents the operation of another **3 a** : a stretchable fabric made on a circular knitting machine and consisting of two ribbed fabrics joined by interlocking **b** : a garment made of interlock

in·ter·loc·u·tor \ˌint-ər-ˈläk-yət-ər\ *n* (1514) **1** : one who takes part in dialogue or conversation **2** : a man in the middle of the line in a minstrel show who questions the end men and acts as leader

in·ter·loc·u·to·ry \-yə-ˌtōr-ē, -ˌtȯr-\ *adj* (15c) : pronounced during the progress of a legal action and having only provisional force ⟨~ decree⟩

in·ter·lope \ˌint-ər-ˈlōp, ˈint-ər-ˌ\ *vi* **-loped; -lop·ing** [prob. back-formation fr. *interloper,* fr. *inter-* + *-loper* (akin to MD *lopen* to run, OE *hlēapan* to leap) — more at LEAP] (1603) **1** : to encroach on the rights (as in trade) of others **2** : INTRUDE, INTERFERE — **in·ter·lop·er** *n*

in·ter·lude \ˈint-ər-ˌlüd\ *n* [ME *enterlude,* fr. ML *interludium,* fr. L *inter-* + *ludus* play — more at LUDICROUS] (14c) **1** : a usu. short simple play or dramatic entertainment **2** : an intervening or interruptive period, space, or event : INTERVAL **3** : a musical composition inserted between the parts of a longer composition, a drama, or a religious service

in·ter·lu·nar \ˌint-ər-ˈlü-nər\ *also* **in·ter·lu·na·ry** \-nə-rē\ *adj* [prob. fr. MF *interlunaire,* fr. L *interlunium* interlunary period, fr. *inter-* + *luna* moon — more at LUNAR] (1598) : relating to the interval between old and new moon when the moon is invisible

in·ter·mar·riage \ˌint-ər-ˈmar-ij\ *n* (1602) **1** : marriage between members of different groups **2** : ENDOGAMY

in·ter·mar·ry \-ˈmar-ē\ *vi* (1574) **1 a** : to marry each other **b** : to marry within a group **2** : to become connected by intermarriage

in·ter·med·dle \ˌint-ər-ˈmed-ᵊl\ *vi* [ME *entermedlen,* fr. MF *entremedler,* fr. OF, fr. *entre-* inter- + *medler* to mix — more at MEDDLE] (15c) : to meddle impertinently and officiously and usu. so as to interfere — **in·ter·med·dler** \-ˈmed-lər, -ᵊl-ər\ *n*

in·ter·me·di·a·cy \ˌint-ər-ˈmēd-ē-ə-sē\ *n* (1713) **1** : the act or action of intermediating **2** : the quality or state of being intermediate

¹in·ter·me·di·ary \ˌint-ər-ˈmēd-ē-ˌer-ē\ *adj* (1788) **1** : INTERMEDIATE **2** : acting as a mediator ⟨an ~ agent⟩

²intermediary *n, pl* **-ar·ies** (1791) **1 a** : MEDIATOR, GO-BETWEEN **b** : MEDIUM, MEANS **2** : an intermediate form, product, or stage

\ə\ abut \ᵊ\ kitten, F table \ər\ further \a\ ash \ā\ ace \ä\ cot, cart \au̇\ out \ch\ chin \e\ bet \ē\ easy \g\ go \i\ hit \ī\ ice \j\ job \ŋ\ sing \ō\ go \ȯ\ law \ȯi\ boy \th\ thin \t͟h\ the \ü\ loot \u̇\ foot \y\ yet \zh\ vision \à, k̟, ⁿ, œ, œ̄, ue, ue̅, ʸ\ *see* Guide to Pronunciation

[1]in·ter·me·di·ate \ˌint-ər-ˈmēd-ē-ət\ *adj* [ML *intermediatus,* fr. L *intermedius,* fr. *inter-* + *medius* mid, middle — more at MID] (15c) **1 :** being or occurring at the middle place, stage, or degree or between extremes **2 :** of or relating to an intermediate school ⟨an ~ curriculum⟩ — **in·ter·me·di·ate·ly** *adv* — **in·ter·me·di·ate·ness** *n*

[2]intermediate *n* (1650) **1 :** one that is intermediate **2 :** MEDIATOR, GO-BETWEEN **3 :** a chemical compound formed as an intermediate step between the starting material and the final product **4 :** an automobile larger than a compact but smaller than a full-sized automobile

[3]in·ter·me·di·ate \-ē-ˌāt\ *vi* [ML *intermediatus,* pp. of *intermediare,* fr. L *inter-* + LL *mediare* to mediate] (1610) **1 :** INTERVENE, INTERPOSE **2 :** to act as an intermediate

intermediate host *n* (1878) **1 :** a host which is normally used by a parasite in the course of its life cycle and in which it may multiply asexually but not sexually **2 a :** RESERVOIR 3 **b :** VECTOR

intermediate school *n* (1842) **1 :** JUNIOR HIGH SCHOOL **2 :** a school usu. comprising grades 4 to 6

in·ter·me·di·a·tion \ˌint-ər-ˌmēd-ē-ˈā-shən\ *n* (1602) **:** the act of coming between **:** INTERVENTION, MEDIATION

in·ter·me·din \ˌint-ər-ˈmēd-ᵊn\ *n* (1932) **:** MELANOCYTE-STIMULATING HORMONE

in·ter·ment \in-ˈtər-mənt\ *n* (14c) **:** the act or ceremony of interring

in·ter·me·tal·lic \ˌint-ər-mə-ˈtal-ik\ *adj* (1900) **:** composed of two or more metals or of a metal and a nonmetal; *esp* **:** being an alloy having a characteristic crystal structure and usu. a definite composition — **intermetallic** *n*

in·ter·mez·zo \ˌint-ər-ˈmets-(ˌ)ō, -ˈmedz-\ *n, pl* **-zi** \-(ˌ)ē\ *or* **-zos** [It, deriv. of L *intermedius* intermediate] (1771) **1 :** a short light entr'acte **2 a :** a movement coming between the major sections of an extended musical work (as an opera) **b :** a short independent instrumental composition

in·ter·mi·na·ble \(ˈ)in-ˈtərm-(ə-)nə-bəl\ *adj* [ME, fr. LL *interminabilis,* fr. L *in-* + *terminare* to terminate] (15c) **:** having or seeming to have no end; *esp* **:** wearisomely protracted ⟨an ~ sermon⟩ — **in·ter·mi·na·ble·ness** *n* — **in·ter·mi·na·bly** \-blē\ *adv*

in·ter·min·gle \ˌint-ər-ˈmiŋ-gəl\ *vb* (15c) **:** INTERMIX

in·ter·mis·sion \ˌint-ər-ˈmish-ən\ *n* [L *intermission-, intermissio,* fr. *intermissus,* pp. of *intermittere*] (15c) **1 :** the act of intermitting **:** the state of being intermitted **2 :** an interval between the parts of an entertainment (as the acts of a play) — **in·ter·mis·sion·less** *adj*

in·ter·mit \-ˈmit\ *vb* **-mit·ted; -mit·ting** [L *intermittere,* fr. *inter-* + *mittere* to send — more at SMITE] *vt* (1542) **:** to cause to cease for a time or at intervals **:** DISCONTINUE ~ *vi* **:** to be intermittent — **in·ter·mit·ter** *n*

in·ter·mit·tent \-ˈmit-ᵊnt\ *adj* [L *intermittent-, intermittens,* prp. of *intermittere*] (1603) **:** coming and going at intervals **:** not continuous ⟨~ rain⟩; *also* **:** OCCASIONAL ⟨~ trips abroad⟩ — **in·ter·mit·tence** \-ᵊn(t)s\ *n* — **in·ter·mit·tent·ly** *adv*

in·ter·mix \ˌint-ər-ˈmiks\ *vb* [back-formation fr. obs. *intermixt* (intermingled), fr. L *intermixtus,* pp. of *intermiscēre* to intermix, fr. *inter-* + *miscēre* to mix — more at MIX] *vt* (1542) **:** to mix together ~ *vi* **:** to become mixed together — **in·ter·mix·ture** \-ˈmiks-chər\ *n*

in·ter·mo·lec·u·lar \ˌint-ər-mə-ˈlek-yə-lər\ *adj* (1843) **:** existing or acting between molecules — **in·ter·mo·lec·u·lar·ly** *adv*

in·ter·mon·tane \ˌint-ər-ˈmän-ˌtān\ *or* **in·ter·mont** \ˈint-ər-ˌmänt\ *adj* (1807) **:** situated between mountains ⟨an ~ basin⟩

[1]in·tern *or* **in·terne** \in-ˈtərn, ˈin-ˌ\ *adj* [MF *interne,* fr. L *internus*] *archaic* (1508) **:** INTERNAL

[2]in·tern \ˈin-ˌtərn, in-ˈ\ *vt* (1866) **:** to confine or impound esp. during a war ⟨~ enemy aliens⟩ — **in·tern·ee** \(ˌ)in-ˌtər-ˈnē\ *n* — **in·tern·ment** \in-ˈtərn-mənt, ˈin-ˌ\ *n*

[3]in·tern *also* **in·terne** \ˈin-ˌtərn\ *n* [F *interne,* fr. *interne,* adj.] (ca. 1879) **:** an advanced student or graduate usu. in a professional field (as medicine or teaching) gaining supervised practical experience (as in a hospital or classroom) — **in·tern·ship** \-ˌship\ *n*

[4]in·tern \ˈin-ˌtərn\ *vi* (ca. 1928) **:** to act as an intern

in·ter·nal \in-ˈtərn-ᵊl\ *adj* [L *internus;* akin to L *inter* between] (15c) **1 :** existing or situated within the limits or surface of something: as **a** (1) **:** situated near the inside of the body (2) **:** situated on the side toward the median plane of the body **b :** of, relating to, or occurring within the confines of an organized structure (as a club, company, or state) ⟨~ affairs⟩ ⟨a country's ~ food production⟩ **2 :** relating or belonging to or existing within the mind **3 :** INTRINSIC, INHERENT ⟨~ evidence of forgery in a document⟩ **4 :** present or arising within an organism or one of its parts ⟨~ stimulus⟩ **5 :** applied or intended for application through the stomach by being swallowed ⟨an ~ remedy⟩ — **in·ter·nal·i·ty** \ˌin-ˌtər-ˈnal-ət-ē\ *n* — **in·ter·nal·ly** \in-ˈtərn-ᵊl-ē\ *adv*

internal–combustion engine *n* (1884) **:** a heat engine in which the combustion that generates the heat takes place inside the engine proper instead of in a furnace

in·ter·nal·ise *Brit var of* INTERNALIZE

in·ter·nal·ize \in-ˈtərn-ᵊl-ˌīz\ *vt* **-ized; -iz·ing** (1884) **:** to give a subjective character to; *specif* **:** to incorporate (as values or patterns of culture) within the self as conscious or subconscious guiding principles through learning or socialization — **in·ter·nal·iza·tion** \-ˌtərn-ᵊl-ə-ˈzā-shən\ *n*

internal medicine *n* (ca. 1904) **:** a branch of medicine that deals with the diagnosis and treatment of nonsurgical diseases

internal respiration *n* (ca. 1890) **:** an exchange of gases between the cells of the body and the blood by way of the fluid bathing the cells — compare EXTERNAL RESPIRATION

internal rhyme *n* (1903) **:** rhyme between a word within a line and another either at the end of the same line or within another line

internal secretion *n* (1895) **:** HORMONE

[1]in·ter·na·tion·al \ˌint-ər-ˈnash-nəl, -ən-ᵊl\ *adj* (1780) **1 :** of, relating to, or affecting two or more nations ⟨~ trade⟩ **2 :** of, relating to, or constituting a group or association having members in two or more nations ⟨~ movement⟩ **3 :** active, known, or reaching beyond national boundaries ⟨the ~ set⟩ ⟨an ~ reputation⟩ — **in·ter·na·tion·al·i·ty** \-ˌnash-ə-ˈnal-ət-ē\ *n* — **in·ter·na·tion·al·ly** \-ˈnash-nə-lē, -ən-ᵊl-ē\ *adv*

[2]international *n* (1871) **:** one that is international; *esp* **:** an organization of international scope

international date line *n* (ca. 1909) **:** DATE LINE

in·ter·na·tion·al·ise *Brit var of* INTERNATIONALIZE

in·ter·na·tion·al·ism \-ˈnash-nəl-ˌiz-əm, -ˈnash-ən-ᵊl-\ *n* (1851) **1 :** international character, principles, interests, or outlook **2 a :** a policy of cooperation among nations **b :** an attitude or belief favoring such a policy — **in·ter·na·tion·al·ist** \-əst\ *n or adj*

in·ter·na·tion·al·ize \ˌint-ər-ˈnash-nəl-ˌīz, -ˈnash-ən-ᵊl-\ *vt* (ca. 1864) **:** to make international; *also* **:** to place under international control ⟨a proposal to ~ the city⟩ — **in·ter·na·tion·al·iza·tion** \-ˌnash-nəl-ə-ˈzā-shən, -ən-ᵊl-\ *n*

international law *n* (ca. 1828) **:** a body of rules that control or affect the rights of nations in their relations with each other

International Phonetic Alphabet *n* (1898) **:** IPA

international pitch *n* (1904) **:** a tuning standard of 440 vibrations per second for A above middle C

international relations *n pl but sing in constr* (1951) **:** a branch of political science concerned with relations between nations and primarily with foreign policies

International Scientific Vocabulary *n* (ca. 1959) **:** a part of the vocabulary of the sciences and other specialized studies that consists of words or other linguistic forms current in two or more languages and differing from New Latin in being adapted to the structure of the individual languages in which they appear

International System *n* (1961) **:** METRIC SYSTEM

international unit *n* (1922) **:** a quantity of a biologic (as a vitamin) that produces a particular biological effect agreed upon as an international standard

international volt *n* (ca. 1926) **:** [2]VOLT 2

in·ter·ne·cine \ˈint-ər-ˈnes-ˌēn, -ˈnēs-ᵊn, -ˈnē-ˌsīn, -nə-ˈsēn; in-ˈtər-nə-ˌsēn\ *adj* [L *internecinus,* fr. *internecare* to destroy, kill, fr. *inter-* + *necare* to kill, fr. *nec-, nex* violent death — more at NOXIOUS] (1663) **1 :** marked by slaughter **:** DEADLY; *esp* **:** mutually destructive **2 :** of, relating to, or involving conflict within a group ⟨bitter ~ feuds⟩

in·ter·neu·ron \ˌint-ər-ˈn(y)ü-ˌrän, -ˈn(y)u̇(ə)r-ˌän\ *n* (ca. 1939) **:** an internuncial neuron — **in·ter·neu·ro·nal** \-ˈn(y)u̇r-ən-ᵊl, -nyu̇-ˈrōn-\ *adj*

in·ter·nist \ˈin-ˌtər-nəst\ *n* (1904) **:** a specialist in internal medicine esp. as distinguished from a surgeon

in·ter·node \ˈint-ər-ˌnōd\ *n* [L *internodium,* fr. *inter-* + *nodus* knot] (1667) **:** an interval or part between two nodes (as of a stem) — **in·ter·nod·al** \ˌint-ər-ˈnōd-ᵊl\ *adj*

in·ter·nu·cle·ar \ˌint-ər-ˈn(y)ü-klē-ər, ÷-kyə-lər\ *adj* (1878) **:** situated or occurring between atomic or biological nuclei

in·ter·nun·ci·al \ˌint-ər-ˈnən(t)-sē-əl, -ˈnu̇n(t)-\ *adj* (1845) **1 :** of or relating to an internuncio **2 :** serving to link sensory and motor neurons

in·ter·nun·cio \ˌint-ər-ˈnən(t)-sē-ˌō, -ˈnu̇n(t)-\ *n* [It *internunzio,* fr. L *internuntius, internuncius,* fr. *inter-* + *nuntius, nuncius* messenger] (1641) **1 :** a messenger between two parties **:** GO-BETWEEN **2 :** a papal legate of lower rank than a nuncio

in·tero·cep·tive \ˌint-ə-rō-ˈsep-tiv\ *adj* [*inter-* (as in *interior*) + *-o-* + *-ceptive* (as in *receptive*)] (1906) **:** of, relating to, or being stimuli arising within the body and esp. in the viscera

in·tero·cep·tor \-tər\ *n* (1906) **:** a sensory receptor excited by interoceptive stimuli

in·ter·pel·late \ˌint-ər-ˈpel-ˌāt, -pə-ˈlāt\ *vt* **-lat·ed; -lat·ing** [L *interpellatus,* pp. of *interpellare* to interrupt, fr. *inter-* + *-pellare* (fr. *pellere* to drive) — more at FELT] (1874) **:** to question (as a foreign minister) formally concerning an official action or policy or personal conduct — **in·ter·pel·la·tion** \-pə-ˈlā-shən\ *n* — **in·ter·pel·la·tor** \-ˈpel-ˌāt-ər, -pə-ˈlāt-\ *n*

in·ter·pen·e·trate \ˌint-ər-ˈpen-ə-ˌtrāt\ *vi* (1809) **:** to penetrate mutually ~ *vt* **:** to penetrate between, within, or throughout **:** PERMEATE — **in·ter·pen·e·tra·tion** \-ˌpen-ə-ˈtrā-shən\ *n*

in·ter·per·son·al \-ˈpərs-nəl, -ᵊn-əl\ *adj* (1842) **:** being, relating to, or involving relations between persons — **in·ter·per·son·al·ly** \-ē\ *adv*

in·ter·phase \ˈint-ər-ˌfāz\ *n* (1925) **:** the interval between the end of one mitotic or meiotic division and the beginning of another

in·ter·plant \ˌint-ər-ˈplant\ *vt* (1911) **:** to plant a crop between (plants of another kind); *also* **:** to set out young trees among (existing growth)

in·ter·play \ˈint-ər-ˌplā\ *n* (1862) **:** INTERACTION ⟨the ~ of opposing forces⟩ — **in·ter·play** \ˌint-ər-ˈ, ˈint-ər-ˌ\ *vi*

in·ter·plead \ˌint-ər-ˈplēd\ *vi* [AF *enterpleder,* fr. *enter-* inter- + *pleder* to plead, fr. OF *plaidier* — more at PLEAD] (1567) **:** to go to trial with each other in order to determine a right on which the action of a third party depends

[1]in·ter·plead·er \-ər\ *n* [AF *enterpleder,* fr. *enterpleder,* v.] (1567) **:** a proceeding to enable a person to compel parties making the same claim against him to litigate the matter between themselves

[2]interpleader *n* (ca. 1846) **:** one that interpleads

in·ter·po·late \in-ˈtər-pə-ˌlāt\ *vb* **-lat·ed; -lat·ing** [L *interpolatus,* pp. of *interpolare* to refurbish, alter, interpolate, fr. *inter-* + *-polare* (fr. *polire* to polish)] *vt* (1612) **1 a :** to alter or corrupt (as a text) by inserting new or foreign matter **b :** to insert (words) into a text or into a conversation **2 :** to insert between other things or parts **:** INTERCALATE **3 :** to estimate values of (a function) between two known values ~ *vi* **:** to make insertions (as of estimated values) ***syn*** see INTRODUCE — **in·ter·po·la·tion** \-ˌtər-pə-ˈlā-shən\ *n* — **in·ter·po·la·tive** \-ˈtər-pə-ˌlāt-iv\ *adj* — **in·ter·po·la·tor** \-ˌlāt-ər\ *n*

in·ter·pose \ˌint-ər-ˈpōz\ *vb* **-posed; -pos·ing** [MF *interposer,* fr. L *interponere* (perf. indic. *interposui*), fr. *inter-* + *ponere* to put — more at POSITION] *vt* (1599) **1 a :** to place in an intervening position **b :** to put (oneself) between **:** INTRUDE **2 :** to put forth by way of interference or intervention **3 :** to introduce or throw in between the parts of a conversation or argument ~ *vi* **1 :** to be or come between **2 :** to step in between parties at variance **:** INTERVENE **3 :** INTERRUPT — **in·ter·pos·er** *n*

syn INTERPOSE, INTERFERE, INTERVENE, MEDIATE, INTERCEDE mean to come or go between. INTERPOSE implies no more than this; INTERFERE implies a getting in the way or otherwise hindering; INTERVENE may imply an occurring in space or time between two things or a stepping in to halt or settle a quarrel or conflict; MEDIATE implies intervening between hostile factions; INTERCEDE implies acting in behalf of an offender in begging mercy or forgiveness. ***syn*** see in addition INTRODUCE

in·ter·po·si·tion \-pə-ˈzish-ən\ *n* (14c) **1 a :** the act of interposing **b :** the action of a state whereby its sovereignty is placed between its citizens and the federal government **2 :** something interposed

in·ter·pret \in-ˈtər-prət, -pət\ *vb* [ME *interpreten,* fr. MF&L; MF *interpreter,* fr. L *interpretari,* fr. *interpret-, interpres* agent, negotiator, interpreter] *vt* (14c) **1 :** to explain or tell the meaning of **:** present in understandable terms 2 : to conceive in the light of individual belief, judgment, or circumstance : CONSTRUE 3 : to represent by means of art : bring to realization by performance ⟨~s a role⟩ ~ *vi* : to act as an interpreter between speakers of different languages ***syn*** see EXPLAIN — **in·ter·pret·abil·i·ty** \-ˌtər-prət-ə-ˈbil-ət-ē, -pət-\ *n* — **in·ter·pret·able** \-ˈtər-prət-ə-bəl, -pət-\ *adj*

in·ter·pre·ta·tion \in-ˌtər-prə-ˈtā-shən, -pə-\ *n* (14c) 1 : the act or the result of interpreting : EXPLANATION 2 : an instance of artistic interpretation in performance or adaptation 3 : a teaching technique that stresses appreciation and understanding by combining factual with stimulating explanatory information ⟨natural history ~ program⟩ — **in·ter·pre·ta·tion·al** \-shnəl, -shən-ᵊl\ *adj* — **in·ter·pre·ta·tive** \in-ˈtər-prə-ˌtāt-iv, -prət-ət-iv\ *adj* — **in·ter·pre·ta·tive·ly** *adv* — **in·ter·pre·tive** \-ˈtər-prət-iv, -pət-\ *adj* — **in·ter·pre·tive·ly** *adv*

in·ter·pret·er \in-ˈtər-prət-ər, -pət-\ *n* (14c) 1 : one that interprets; *esp* : a person who translates orally for parties conversing in different languages 2 **a** : a machine that prints on punch cards the symbols recorded in them by perforations **b** : a computer program that translates an instruction into machine language and executes it before going to the next instruction

in·ter·prox·i·mal \ˌint-ər-ˈpräk-sə-məl\ *adj* (1897) : situated or used in the areas between adjoining teeth ⟨~ space⟩

in·ter·pu·pil·lary \ˌint-ər-ˈpyü-pə-ˌler-ē\ *adj* (ca. 1904) : extending between the pupils of the eyes; *also* : extending between the centers of a pair of spectacle lenses ⟨~ distance⟩

in·ter·ra·cial \-ˈrā-shəl\ *adj* (1888) : of, involving, or designed for members of different races — **in·ter·ra·cial·ly** \-shə-lē\ *adv*

interred *past and past part of* INTER

in·ter·reg·num \ˌint-ə-ˈreg-nəm\ *n, pl* **-nums** *or* **-na** \-nə\ [L, fr. *inter-* + *regnum* reign — more at REIGN] (1590) 1 : the time during which a throne is vacant between two successive reigns or regimes 2 : a period during which the normal functions of government or control are suspended 3 : a lapse or pause in a continuous series

in·ter·re·late \ˌint-ə(r)-ri-ˈlāt\ *vt* (1888) : to bring into mutual relation ~ *vi* : to have mutual relationship — **in·ter·re·la·tion** \-ˈlā-shən\ *n* — **in·ter·re·la·tion·ship** \-ˌship\ *n*

in·ter·re·lat·ed \-ˈlāt-əd\ *adj* (1827) : having a mutual or reciprocal relation or parallelism — **in·ter·re·lat·ed·ly** *adv* — **in·ter·re·lat·ed·ness** *n*

interring *pres part of* INTER

in·ter·ro·bang \in-ˈter-ə-ˌbaŋ\ *n* [*interrogation (point)* + *bang* (printers' slang for *exclamation point*)] (ca. 1967) : a punctuation mark ? designed for use esp. at the end of an exclamatory rhetorical question

in·ter·ro·gate \in-ˈter-ə-ˌgāt\ *vt* **-gat·ed; -gat·ing** [L *interrogatus*, pp. of *interrogare*, fr. *inter-* + *rogare* to ask — more at RIGHT] (15c) 1 : to question formally and systematically 2 : to give or send out a signal to (as a transponder or computer) for triggering an appropriate response ***syn*** see ASK — **in·ter·ro·ga·tee** \-ˌter-ə-(ˌ)gāt-ˈē\ *n* — **in·ter·ro·ga·tion** \-ˌter-ə-ˈgā-shən\ *n* — **in·ter·ro·ga·tion·al** \-shnəl, -shən-ᵊl\ *adj*

interrogation point *n* (ca. 1864) : QUESTION MARK

¹**in·ter·rog·a·tive** \ˌint-ə-ˈräg-ət-iv\ *adj* (1500) 1 **a** : having the form or force of a question **b** : used in a question 2 : INQUISITIVE, QUESTIONING — **in·ter·rog·a·tive·ly** *adv*

²**interrogative** *n* (1522) 1 : a word (as *who, what, which*) or a particle (as Latin *-ne*) used in asking questions 2 : an interrogative utterance

in·ter·ro·ga·tor \in-ˈter-ə-ˌgāt-ər\ *n* (1751) 1 : one that interrogates 2 : a radio transmitter and receiver for sending out a signal that triggers a transponder and for receiving and displaying the reply

¹**in·ter·rog·a·to·ry** \ˌint-ə-ˈräg-ə-ˌtōr-ē, -ˌtȯr-\ *n, pl* **-ries** (1533) : a formal question or inquiry; *esp* : a written question required to be answered under direction of a court

²**interrogatory** *adj* (1576) : INTERROGATIVE

in·ter·ro·gee \in-ˌter-ə-ˈgē\ *n* (1919) : one who is interrogated

¹**in·ter·rupt** \ˌint-ə-ˈrəpt\ *vb* [ME *interrupten*, fr. L *interruptus*, pp. of *interrumpere*, fr. *inter-* + *rumpere* to break — more at REAVE] *vt* (15c) 1 : to stop or hinder by breaking in 2 : to break the uniformity or continuity of ~ *vi* : to break in upon an action; *esp* : to break in with questions or remarks while another is speaking — **in·ter·rupt·ible** \-ˈrəp-tə-bəl\ *adj* — **in·ter·rup·tion** \-ˈrəp-shən\ *n* — **in·ter·rup·tive** \-ˈrəp-tiv\ *adv*

²**in·ter·rupt** \ˌint-ə-ˈrəpt, ˈint-ə-ˌ\ *n* (1957) : a feature of a computer that permits the execution of one program to be interrupted in order to execute another; *also* : the interruption itself

in·ter·rupt·er \ˌint-ə-ˈrəp-tər\ *n* (1511) : one that interrupts; *esp* : a device for periodically and automatically interrupting an electric current

in·ter·scho·las·tic \ˌint-ər-skə-ˈlas-tik\ *adj* (1900) : existing or carried on between schools ⟨~ athletics⟩

in·ter se \ˌint-ər-ˈsā, -ˈsē\ *adv or adj* [L] (1845) : among or between themselves

in·ter·sect \ˌint-ər-ˈsekt\ *vb* [L *intersectus*, pp. of *intersecare*, fr. *inter-* + *secare* to cut — more at SAW] *vt* (1615) : to pierce or divide by passing through or across : CROSS ~ *vi* 1 : to meet and cross at a point 2 : to share a common area : OVERLAP

in·ter·sec·tion \ˌint-ər-ˈsek-shən, *esp in sense 2* ˈint-ər-ˌ\ *n* (1559) 1 : the act or process of intersecting 2 : a place or area where two or more things (as streets) intersect 3 : the set of elements common to two or more sets; *esp* : the set of points common to two geometric configurations

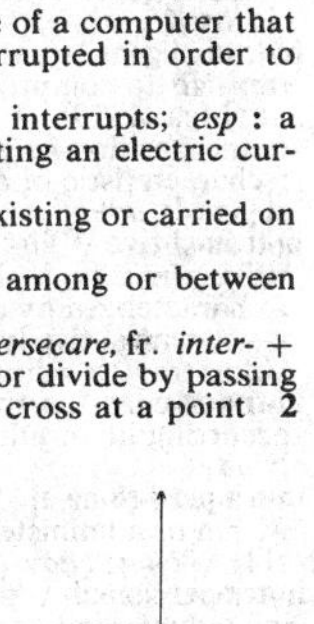

intersection 3

in·ter·ser·vice \ˌint-ər-ˈsər-vəs\ *adj* (1942) : existing between or relating to two or more of the armed services ⟨~ rivalry⟩

in·ter·ses·sion \ˈint-ər-ˌsesh-ən\ *n* (1932) : a period between two academic sessions or terms sometimes utilized for brief concentrated courses

in·ter·sex \ˈint-ər-ˌseks\ *n* [ISV] (1910) : an intersexual individual

in·ter·sex·u·al \ˌint-ər-ˈseksh-(ə-)wəl, -ˈsek-shəl\ *adj* [ISV] (1866) 1 : existing between sexes ⟨~ hostility⟩ 2 : intermediate in sexual characters between a typical male and a typical female — **in·ter·sex·u·al·i·ty** \-ˌsek-shə-ˈwal-ət-ē\ *n* — **in·ter·sex·u·al·ly** \-ˈseksh-(ə-)wə-lē, -(ə-)lē\ *adv*

¹**in·ter·space** \ˈint-ər-ˌspās\ *n* (15c) : an intervening space : INTERVAL

²**in·ter·space** \ˌint-ər-ˈspās\ *vt* (1685) : to occupy or fill the space between

in·ter·spe·cif·ic \ˌint-ər-spi-ˈsif-ik\ *also* **in·ter·spe·cies** \-ˈspē-(ˌ)shēz, -(ˌ)sēz\ *adj* (1889) : existing or arising between species ⟨~ hybrid⟩

in·ter·sperse \ˌint-ər-ˈspərs\ *vt* **-spersed; -spers·ing** [L *interspersus* interspersed, fr. *inter-* + *sparsus*, pp. of *spargere* to scatter — more at SPARK] (1566) 1 : to place something at intervals in or among 2 : to insert at intervals among other things ⟨*interspersing* drawings throughout the text⟩ — **in·ter·sper·sion** \-ˈspər-zhən, -shən\ *n*

in·ter·sta·di·al \ˌint-ər-ˈstād-ē-əl\ *n* [ISV *inter-* + NL *stadium* stage, phase, fr. L — more at STADIUM] (1917) : a subdivision within a glacial stage marking a temporary retreat of the ice

¹**in·ter·state** \ˌint-ər-ˈstāt\ *adj* (1844) : of, connecting, or existing between two or more states esp. of the U.S. ⟨an ~ highway⟩

²**in·ter·state** \ˈint-ər-ˌstāt\ *n* (1968) : an interstate highway

in·ter·stel·lar \-ˈstel-ər\ *adj* (1626) : located or taking place among the stars

in·ter·ster·ile \-ˈster-əl, *chiefly Brit* -ˌīl\ *adj* (1916) : incapable of producing offspring by interbreeding — **in·ter·ste·ril·i·ty** \-stə-ˈril-ət-ē\ *n*

in·ter·stice \in-ˈtər-stəs\ *n, pl* **-stic·es** \-stə-ˌsēz, -stə-səz\ [F, fr. LL *interstitium*, fr. L *interstitus*, pp. of *intersistere* to stand still in the middle, fr. *inter-* + *sistere* to come to a stand; akin to L *stare* to stand] (15c) 1 : a space that intervenes between things : INTERVAL; *esp* : one between closely spaced things 2 : a short space of time between events

in·ter·sti·tial \ˌint-ər-ˈstish-əl\ *adj* (1646) 1 : relating to or situated in the interstices 2 **a** : situated within but not restricted to or characteristic of a particular organ or tissue — used esp. of fibrous tissue **b** : affecting the interstitial tissues of an organ or part 3 : being or relating to a crystalline compound in which usu. small atoms or ions of a nonmetal occupy holes between the larger metal atoms or ions in the crystal lattice — **in·ter·sti·tial·ly** \-ə-lē\ *adv*

in·ter·sub·jec·tive \ˌint-ər-səb-ˈjek-tiv\ *adj* (1899) 1 : involving or occurring between separate conscious minds ⟨~ communication⟩ 2 : accessible to or capable of being established for two or more subjects : OBJECTIVE — **in·ter·sub·jec·tive·ly** *adv* — **in·ter·sub·jec·tiv·i·ty** \-(ˌ)səb-ˌjek-ˈtiv-ət-ē\ *n*

in·ter·tes·ta·men·tal \-ˌtes-tə-ˈment-ᵊl\ *adj* (1929) : of, relating to, or forming the period of two centuries between the composition of the last book of the Old Testament and the first book of the New Testament

in·ter·tid·al \-ˈtīd-ᵊl\ *adj* (1883) : of, relating to, or being the part of the littoral zone above low-tide mark — **in·ter·tid·al·ly** \-ᵊl-ē\ *adv*

in·ter·tie \ˈint-ər-ˌtī\ *n* (1951) : an interconnection permitting passage of current between two or more electric utility systems

in·ter·till \ˌint-ər-ˈtil\ *vt* (1912) : to cultivate between the rows of (a crop) — **in·ter·till·age** \-ˈtil-ij\ *n*

in·ter·trop·i·cal \-ˈträp-i-kəl\ *adj* (1794) 1 : situated between or within the tropics 2 : relating to regions within the tropics : TROPICAL

in·ter·twine \-ˈtwīn\ *vt* (1641) : to unite by twining one with another ~ *vi* : to twine about one another; *also* : to become mutually involved — **in·ter·twine·ment** \-mənt\ *n*

in·ter·twist \-ˈtwist\ *vb* (1659) : INTERTWINE — **in·ter·twist** \ˈint-ər-ˌtwist\ *n*

in·ter·ur·ban \ˌint-ər-ˈər-bən\ *adj* (1883) : going between cities or towns

in·ter·val \ˈint-ər-vəl\ *n* [ME *intervalle*, fr. MF, fr. L *intervallum* space between ramparts, interval, fr. *inter-* + *vallum* rampart — more at WALL] (14c) 1 **a** : a space of time between events or states : PAUSE **b** *Brit* : INTERMISSION 2 **a** : a space between objects, units, or states **b** : difference in pitch between tones 3 : a set of real numbers between two numbers either including or excluding one or both of them — **in·ter·val·lic** \ˌint-ər-ˈval-ik\ *adj*

in·ter·vale \ˈint-ər-vəl, -ˌvāl\ *n* [obs. *intervale* interval] *chiefly NewEng* (1647) : BOTTOM 5

in·ter·val·om·e·ter \ˌint-ər-və-ˈläm-ət-ər\ *n* (1941) : a device that operates a control (as for a camera shutter) at regular intervals

in·ter·vene \ˌint-ər-ˈvēn\ *vi* **-vened; -ven·ing** [L *intervenire* to come between, fr. *inter-* + *venire* to come — more at COME] (1587) 1 : to occur, fall, or come between points of time or events 2 : to enter or appear as an irrelevant or extraneous feature or circumstance 3 : to come in or between by way of hindrance or modification ⟨~ to settle a quarrel⟩ 4 : to occur or lie between two things 5 **a** : to become a third party to a legal proceeding begun by others for the protection of an alleged interest **b** : to interfere usu. by force or threat of force in another nation's internal affairs esp. to compel or prevent an action or to maintain or alter a condition ***syn*** see INTERPOSE — **in·ter·ven·tion** \-ˈven-chən\ *n*

in·ter·ve·nor \-ˈvē-nər, -ˌnȯ(ə)r\ *or* **in·ter·ven·er** \-ˈvē-nər\ *n* (1621) : one who intervenes; *esp* : one who intervenes as a third party in a legal proceeding

in·ter·ven·tion·ism \-ˈven-chə-ˌniz-əm\ *n* (1923) : the theory or practice of intervening; *specif* : governmental interference in economic affairs at home or in political affairs of another country — **in·ter·ven·tion·ist** \-ˈvench-(ə-)nəst\ *n or adj*

in·ter·ver·te·bral \ˌint-ər-ˈvərt-ə-brəl, -(ˌ)vər-ˈtē-\ *adj* (1782) : situated between vertebrae — **in·ter·ver·te·bral·ly** \-brə-lē\ *adv*

intervertebral disk *n* (ca. 1860) : any of the tough elastic disks that are interposed between the centra of adjoining vertebrae and that consist of an outer fibrous ring enclosing an inner pulpy nucleus

in·ter·view \ˈint-ər-ˌvyü\ *n* [MF *entrevue*, fr. (*s'*)*entrevoir* to see one another, meet, fr. *entre-* inter- + *voir* to see — more at VIEW] (1514) 1 : a formal consultation usu. to evaluate qualifications (as of a prospective student or employee) 2 **a** : a meeting at which information is obtained (as by a reporter, television commentator, or pollster) from a person **b** : a report or reproduction of information so obtained 3 : INTERVIEWEE — **interview** *vb* — **in·ter·view·er** *n*

in·ter·view·ee \ˌint-ər-(ˌ)vyü-ˈē\ *n* (1884) : one who is interviewed

in·ter vi·vos \ˌint-ər-ˈvē-ˌvōs, -ˈvī-\ *adv or adj* [LL] (1837) **:** between living persons ⟨transaction *inter vivos*⟩; *esp* **:** from one living person to another ⟨*inter vivos* gifts⟩ ⟨property transferred *inter vivos*⟩

in·ter·vo·cal·ic \ˌint-ər-vō-ˈkal-ik\ *adj* (1887) **:** immediately preceded and immediately followed by a vowel — **in·ter·vo·cal·i·cal·ly** \-i-k(ə-)lē\ *adv*

in·ter·weave \ˌint-ər-ˈwēv\ *vb* **-wove** \-ˈwōv\ *also* **-weaved; -wo·ven** \-ˈwō-vən\ *also* **-weaved; -weav·ing** *vt* (1578) **1 :** to weave together **2 :** to intermingle or blend together ⟨*interweaving* his own insights . . . with letters and memoirs —Phoebe Adams⟩ ~ *vi* **:** INTERTWINE, INTERMINGLE — **in·ter·weave** \ˈint-ər-ˌwēv\ *n* — **in·ter·wo·ven** \ˌint-ər-ˈwō-vən\ *adj*

in·tes·ta·cy \in-ˈtes-tə-sē\ *n* (1767) **:** the quality or state of being or dying intestate

¹in·tes·tate \in-ˈtes-ˌtāt, -tət\ *adj* [ME, fr. L *intestatus,* fr. *in-* + *testatus* testate] (14c) **1 :** having made no valid will ⟨died ~⟩ **2 :** not disposed of by will ⟨an ~ estate⟩

²intestate *n* (1658) **:** one who dies intestate

in·tes·ti·nal \in-ˈtes-tən-ᵊl, -ˈtes(t)-nəl, -ˈtes-ᵊn-əl, *Brit often* ˌin-(ˌ)tes-ˈtīn-ᵊl\ *adj* (15c) **1 :** affecting or occurring in the intestine; *also* **:** living in the intestine **2 :** of, relating to, or being the intestine — **in·tes·ti·nal·ly** \-ē\ *adv*

intestinal fortitude *n* [euphemism for *guts*] (ca. 1937) **:** COURAGE, STAMINA

¹in·tes·tine \in-ˈtes-tən\ *adj* [MF or L; MF *intestin,* fr. L *intestinus,* fr. *intus* within — more at ENT-] (15c) **:** INTERNAL; *specif* **:** of or relating to the internal affairs of a state or country ⟨~ war⟩

²intestine *n* [MF *intestin,* fr. L *intestinum,* fr. neut. of *intestinus*] (15c) **:** the tubular part of the alimentary canal that extends from the stomach to the anus

in·ti \ˈin-tē\ *n* [Quechua, lit., sun] (1985) — see MONEY table

in·ti·ma \ˈint-ə-mə\ *n, pl* **-mae** \-ˌmē, -ˌmī\ *or* **-mas** [NL, fr. L, fem. of *intimus*] (1873) **:** the innermost coat of an organ (as a blood vessel) consisting usu. of an endothelial layer backed by connective tissue and elastic tissue — **in·ti·mal** \-məl\ *adj*

in·ti·ma·cy \ˈint-ə-mə-sē\ *n* (1641) **1 :** the state of being intimate **:** FAMILIARITY **2 :** something of a personal or private nature

¹in·ti·mate \ˈint-ə-ˌmāt\ *vt* **-mat·ed; -mat·ing** [LL *intimatus,* pp. of *intimare* to put in, announce, fr. L *intimus* innermost, superl. of (assumed) OL *interus* inward — more at INTERIOR] (1522) **1 :** to make known esp. publicly or formally **:** ANNOUNCE **2 :** to communicate delicately and indirectly **:** HINT ***syn*** see SUGGEST — **in·ti·mat·er** *n* — **in·ti·ma·tion** \ˌint-ə-ˈmā-shən\ *n*

²in·ti·mate \ˈint-ə-mət\ *adj* [alter. of obs. *intime,* fr. L *intimus*] (1632) **1 a :** INTRINSIC, ESSENTIAL **b :** belonging to or characterizing one's deepest nature **2 :** marked by very close association, contact, or familiarity ⟨~ knowledge of the law⟩ **3 a :** marked by a warm friendship developing through long association **b :** suggesting informal warmth or privacy ⟨~ clubs⟩ **4 :** of a very personal or private nature ***syn*** see FAMILIAR — **in·ti·mate·ly** *adv* — **in·ti·mate·ness** *n*

³in·ti·mate \ˈint-ə-mət\ *n* (1659) **:** an intimate friend or confidant

in·tim·i·date \in-ˈtim-ə-ˌdāt\ *vt* **-dat·ed; -dat·ing** [ML *intimidatus,* pp. of *intimidare,* fr. L *in-* + *timidus* timid] (1646) **:** to make timid or fearful **:** FRIGHTEN; *esp* **:** to compel or deter by or as if by threats — **in·tim·i·dat·ing·ly** \-iŋ-lē\ *adv* — **in·tim·i·da·tion** \-ˌtim-ə-ˈdā-shən\ *n* — **in·tim·i·da·tor** \-ˈtim-ə-ˌdāt-ər\ *n*

in·tim·i·da·to·ry \-ˈtim-ə-də-ˌtōr-ē, -ˌtȯr-\ *adj* (1846) **:** tending to intimidate

in·tinc·tion \in-ˈtiŋ(k)-shən\ *n* [LL *intinction-, intinctio* baptism, fr. L *intinctus,* pp. of *intingere* to dip in, fr. *in-* + *tingere* to dip, moisten — more at TINGE] (1872) **:** the administration of the sacrament of Communion by dipping the bread in the wine and giving both together to the communicant

in·tine \ˈin-ˌtēn\ *n* [prob. fr. G, fr. L *intus* within + NL *in-* fibrous tissue, fr. Gk *in-, is* tendon — more at WITHY] (1835) **:** the inner mostly cellulose wall of a spore (as a pollen grain)

in·ti·tule \in-ˈtich-(ˌ)ü(ə)l\ *vt* **-uled; -ul·ing** [MF *intituler,* fr. LL *intitulare,* fr. L *in-* + *titulus* title] *Brit* (15c) **:** to furnish (as a legislative act) with a title or designation

in·to \ˌin-tə(-w), ˈin-(ˌ)tü\ *prep* [ME, fr. OE *intō,* fr. ²*in* + *tō* to] (bef. 12c) **1** — used as a function word to indicate entry, introduction, insertion, superposition, or inclusion ⟨came ~ the house⟩ ⟨enter ~ an alliance⟩ **2 a :** to the state, condition, or form of ⟨got ~ trouble⟩ **b :** to the occupation, action, or possession of ⟨go ~ farming⟩ **c :** involved with ⟨they were ~ hard drugs⟩ **3** — used as a function word to indicate a period of time or an extent of space part of which is passed or occupied ⟨far ~ the night⟩ **4 :** in the direction of ⟨looking ~ the sun⟩ **5 :** to a position of contact with **:** AGAINST ⟨ran ~ a wall⟩ **6** — used as a function word to indicate the dividend in division ⟨dividing 3 ~ 6 gives 2⟩

in·tol·er·a·ble \(ˈ)in-ˈtäl-(ə-)rə-bəl, -ˈtäl-ər-bəl\ *adj* [ME, fr. L *intolerabilis,* fr. *in-* + *tolerabilis* tolerable] (15c) **1 :** not tolerable **:** UNBEARABLE ⟨~ pain⟩ **2 :** EXCESSIVE — **in·tol·er·a·bil·i·ty** \(ˌ)in-ˌtäl-(ə-)rə-ˈbil-ət-ē\ *n* — **in·tol·er·a·ble·ness** \(ˈ)in-ˈtäl-(ə-)rə-bəl-nəs, -ˈtäl-ər-bəl-\ *n* — **in·tol·er·a·bly** \-blē\ *adv*

in·tol·er·ance \(ˈ)in-ˈtäl(-ə)-rən(t)s\ *n* (1765) **:** the quality or state of being intolerant; *esp* **:** exceptional sensitivity (as to a drug)

in·tol·er·ant \-rənt\ *adj* (1735) **1 :** unable or unwilling to endure ⟨a plant ~ of direct sunlight⟩ ⟨~ of criticism⟩ **2 a :** unwilling to grant equal freedom of expression esp. in religious matters **b :** unwilling to grant or share social, political, or professional rights **:** BIGOTED — **in·tol·er·ant·ly** *adv* — **in·tol·er·ant·ness** *n*

in·to·nate \ˈin-tə-ˌnāt\ *vt* **-nat·ed; -nat·ing** (1795) **:** INTONE, UTTER

in·to·na·tion \ˌin-tə-ˈnā-shən, -(ˌ)tō-\ *n* (1620) **1 :** the act of intoning and esp. of chanting **2 :** something that is intoned; *specif* **:** the opening tones of a Gregorian chant **3 :** the ability to play or sing notes in tune **4 :** manner of utterance; *specif* **:** the rise and fall in pitch of the voice in speech — **in·to·na·tion·al** \-shnəl, -shən-ᵊl\ *adj*

in·tone \in-ˈtōn\ *vb* **in·toned; in·ton·ing** [ME *entonen,* fr. MF *entoner,* fr. ML *intonare,* fr. L *in-* + *tonus* tone] *vt* (15c) **:** to utter in musical or prolonged tones **:** recite in singing tones or in a monotone ~ *vi* **:** to utter something in singing tones or in monotone — **in·ton·er** *n*

in to·to \in-ˈtōt-(ˌ)ō\ *adv* [L, on the whole] (1796) **:** TOTALLY, ENTIRELY

in·tox·i·cant \in-ˈtäk-si-kənt\ *n* (1863) **:** something that intoxicates; *esp* **:** an alcoholic drink — **intoxicant** *adj*

¹in·tox·i·cate \-si-kət\ *adj, archaic* (15c) **:** INTOXICATED

²in·tox·i·cate \-sə-ˌkāt\ *vt* **-cat·ed; -cat·ing** [ML *intoxicatus,* pp. of *intoxicare,* fr. L *in-* + *toxicum* poison — more at TOXIC] (15c) **1 :** POISON **2 a :** to excite or stupefy by alcohol or a drug esp. to the point where physical and mental control is markedly diminished **b :** to excite or elate to the point of enthusiasm or frenzy ⟨*intoxicated* with joy⟩

in·tox·i·cat·ed \-sə-ˌkāt-əd\ *adj* (1576) **:** affected by or as if by alcohol — **in·tox·i·cat·ed·ly** \-ˌkāt-əd-lē\ *adv*

in·tox·i·ca·tion \in-ˌtäk-sə-ˈkā-shən\ *n* (15c) **1 :** an abnormal state that is essentially a poisoning ⟨intestinal ~⟩ **2 a :** the condition of being drunk **:** INEBRIATION **b :** a strong excitement or elation

in·tra- \ˌin-trə, -(ˌ)trä\ *prefix* [LL, fr. L *intra,* fr. (assumed) OL *interus,* adj., inward — more at INTERIOR] **1 a :** within ⟨*intra*continental⟩ **b :** during ⟨*intra*natal⟩ **c :** between layers of ⟨*intra*dermal⟩ **2 :** INTRO- ⟨an *intra*muscular injection⟩

in·tra–ar·te·ri·al \-är-ˈtir-ē-əl\ *adj* (1897) **:** situated or occurring within, administered into, or involving entry by way of an artery — **in·tra–ar·te·ri·al·ly** \-ē-ə-lē\ *adv*

in·tra·car·di·ac \-ˈkärd-ē-ˌak\ *also* **in·tra·car·di·al** \-ē-əl\ *adj* (1876) **:** situated or occurring within or introduced or involving entry into the heart ⟨~ surgery⟩ ⟨an ~ catheter⟩ — **in·tra·car·di·al·ly** \-ē-ə-lē\ *adv*

in·tra·cel·lu·lar \-ˈsel-yə-lər\ *adj* (1876) **:** existing, occurring, or functioning within a protoplasmic cell — **in·tra·cel·lu·lar·ly** *adv*

in·tra·ce·re·bral \-sə-ˈrē-brəl, -ˈser-ə\ *adj* (1881) **:** situated in, introduced into, or made into the cerebrum ⟨~ injections⟩ ⟨~ bleeding⟩ — **in·tra·ce·re·bral·ly** \-brə-lē\ *adv*

in·tra·cra·ni·al \-ˈkrā-nē-əl\ *adj* (1847) **:** existing or occurring within the cranium; *also* **:** affecting or involving intracranial structures — **in·tra·cra·ni·al·ly** \-nē-ə-lē\ *adv*

in·trac·ta·ble \(ˈ)in-ˈtrak-tə-bəl\ *adj* [L *intractabilis,* fr. *in-* + *tractabilis* tractable] (1531) **1 :** not easily governed, managed, or directed **:** OBSTINATE **2 :** not easily manipulated or wrought ⟨~ metal⟩ **3 :** not easily relieved or cured ⟨~ pain⟩ ***syn*** see UNRULY — **in·trac·ta·bil·i·ty** \(ˌ)in-ˌtrak-tə-ˈbil-ət-ē\ *n* — **in·trac·ta·ble·ness** \(ˈ)in-ˈtrak-tə-bəl-nəs\ *n* — **in·trac·ta·bly** \-blē\ *adv*

in·tra·cu·ta·ne·ous \ˌin-trə-kyu̇-ˈtā-nē-əs, -(ˌ)trä-\ *adj* (ca. 1885) **:** INTRADERMAL — **in·tra·cu·ta·ne·ous·ly** *adv*

in·tra·day \ˈin-trə-ˌdā, -(ˌ)trä-\ *adj* (1950) **:** occurring in the course of a single day ⟨the market showed wide ~ fluctuations⟩

in·tra·der·mal \ˌin-trə-ˈdər-məl, -(ˌ)trä-\ *adj* (ca. 1900) **:** situated, occurring, or done within or between the layers of the skin; *also* **:** administered by entering the skin ⟨~ injections⟩ — **in·tra·der·mal·ly** \-mə-lē\ *adv*

intradermal test *n* (1916) **:** a test for immunity or hypersensitivity made by injecting a minute amount of diluted antigen into the skin

in·tra·dos \ˈin-trə-ˌdäs, -ˌdō; in-ˈtrā-ˌdäs\ *n, pl* **-dos** \-ˌdōz, -ˌdäs\ *or* **-dos·es** \-ˌdäs-əz\ [F, fr. L *intra* within + F *dos* back — more at DOSSIER] (1772) **:** the interior curve of an arch — see ARCH illustration

in·tra·ga·lac·tic \ˌin-trə-gə-ˈlak-tik, -(ˌ)trä-\ *adj* (1964) **:** situated or occurring within the confines of a single galaxy

in·tra·gen·ic \-ˈjen-ik\ *adj* [*intra-* + *genic*] (1937) **:** being or occurring within a gene ⟨~ recombination⟩ ⟨~ mutation⟩

in·tra·mo·lec·u·lar \-mə-ˈlek-yə-lər\ *adj* [ISV] (1884) **:** existing or acting within the molecule; *also* **:** formed by reaction between different parts of the same molecule — **in·tra·mo·lec·u·lar·ly** *adv*

in·tra·mu·ral \-ˈmyu̇r-əl\ *adj* (1846) **1 a :** being or occurring within the limits usu. of a community, organization, or institution **b :** competitive only within the student body ⟨~ sports⟩ **2 :** situated or occurring within the substance of the walls of an organ — **in·tra·mu·ral·ly** \-ə-lē\ *adv*

in·tra·mus·cu·lar \-ˈməs-kyə-lər\ *adj* [ISV] (1874) **:** situated in, occurring in, or administered by entering a muscle — **in·tra·mus·cu·lar·ly** *adv*

in·tra·na·sal \-ˈnā-zəl\ *adj* (1886) **:** lying within or administered by way of the nasal structures — **in·tra·na·sal·ly** \-ˈnāz-(ə-)lē\ *adv*

in·tran·si·geance \in-ˈtran(t)s-ə-jən(t)s, -ˈtranz-\ *n* [F, trans. of Sp *intransigente*] (1899) **:** INTRANSIGENCE — **in·tran·si·geant** \-jənt\ *adj or n* — **in·tran·si·geant·ly** *adv*

in·tran·si·gence \-jən(t)s\ *n* (1882) **:** the quality or state of being intransigent

in·tran·si·gent \-jənt\ *adj* [Sp *intransigente,* fr. *in-* + *transigente,* prp. of *transigir* to compromise, fr. L *transigere* to transact — more at TRANSACT] (ca. 1879) **1 a :** refusing to compromise or to abandon an extreme position or attitude **:** UNCOMPROMISING **b :** IRRECONCILABLE **2 :** characteristic of an intransigent person — **intransigent** *n* — **in·tran·si·gent·ly** *adv*

in·tran·si·tive \(ˈ)in-ˈtran(t)s-ət-iv, -ˈtranz-; -ˈtran(t)s-tiv\ *adj* [LL *intransitivus,* fr. L *in-* + LL *transitivus* transitive] (1612) **:** not transitive; *esp* **:** characterized by not having or containing a direct object ⟨an ~ verb⟩ — **in·tran·si·tive·ly** *adv* — **in·tran·si·tive·ness** *n* — **in·tran·si·tiv·i·ty** \(ˌ)in-ˌtran(t)s-ə-ˈtiv-ət-ē, -ˌtranz-\ *n*

in·tra·oc·u·lar \ˌin-trə-ˈäk-yə-lər, -(ˌ)trä-\ *adj* [ISV] (1826) **:** situated in, occurring in, or administered by entering the eyeball — **in·tra·oc·u·lar·ly** *adv*

in·tra·per·i·to·ne·al \ˌin-trə-ˌper-ət-ᵊn-ˈē-əl\ *adj* (ca. 1835) **:** existing within or administered by entering the peritoneum — **in·tra·per·i·to·ne·al·ly** \-ˈē-ə-lē\ *adv*

in·tra·per·son·al \-ˈpərs-nəl, -ᵊn-əl\ *adj* (1909) **:** occurring within the individual mind or self ⟨~ concerns of the aged⟩

in·tra·pop·u·la·tion \ˈin-trə-ˌpäp-yə-ˈlā-shən, -(ˌ)trä-\ *adj* (1959) **:** occurring within or taking place between members of a population

in·tra·pre·neur \ˌin-trə-prə-ˈnər, -ˈn(y)u̇(ə)r\ *n* [*intra-* + entre*preneur*] (1982) **:** a corporate executive who develops new enterprises within the corporation — **in·tra·pre·neur·ial** \-ˈn(y)u̇r-ē-əl, -ˈnər-\ *adj*

in·tra·psy·chic \ˌin-trə-ˈsī-kik, -(ˌ)trä-\ *adj* (1917) **:** being or occurring within the psyche, mind, or personality — **in·tra·psy·chi·cal·ly** \-ki-k(ə-)lē\ *adv*

in·tra·spe·cies \-ˈspē-(ˌ)shēz, -(ˌ)sēz\ *adj* (1927) **:** INTRASPECIFIC

in·tra·spe·cif·ic \-spi-ˈsif-ik\ *adj* (1919) **:** occurring within a species or involving members of one species

in·tra·state \-ˈstāt\ *adj* (1903) **:** existing or occurring within a state

in·tra·tho·rac·ic \-thə-ˈras-ik\ *adj* [ISV] (1862) **:** situated or occurring within the thorax ⟨~ pressure⟩ — **in·tra·tho·rac·i·cal·ly** *adv*

in·tra·uter·ine \-'yüt-ə-rən, -,rīn\ *adj* [ISV] (1835) : situated, used, or occurring within the uterus; *also* : involving the part of development that takes place in the uterus

intrauterine device *n* (1964) : a device inserted and left in the uterus to prevent effective conception — called also *intrauterine contraceptive device, IUD*

in·tra·vas·cu·lar \,in-trə-'vas-kyə-lər, -(,)trä-\ *adj* (1876) : situated in, occurring in, or administered by entry into a blood vessel ⟨~ thrombosis⟩ ⟨an ~ injection⟩ — **in·tra·vas·cu·lar·ly** *adv*

in·tra·ve·nous \,in-trə-'vē-nəs\ *adj* [ISV] (1847) : situated, performed, or occurring within or entering by way of a vein; *also* : used in intravenous procedures — **in·tra·ve·nous·ly** *adv*

in·tra·ven·tric·u·lar \,in-trə-ven-'trik-yə-lər, -(,)trä-\ *adj* (1882) : situated within or administered in or into a ventricle — **in·tra·ven·tric·u·lar·ly** *adv*

in·tra·vi·tal \-'vīt-ᵊl\ *adj* [ISV] (ca. 1890) **1** : performed upon or found in a living subject **2** : having or utilizing the property of staining cells without killing them — compare SUPRAVITAL — **in·tra·vi·tal·ly** \-ᵊl-ē\ *adv*

in·tra·vi·tam \-'vī-,tam, -'wē-,täm\ *adj* [NL *intra vitam* during life] (1881) : INTRAVITAL

in·tra·zon·al \,in-trə-'zōn-ᵊl, -(,)trä-\ *adj* (1927) : of, relating to, or being a soil or a major soil group marked by relatively well-developed characteristics that are determined primarily by essentially local factors (as the parent material) rather than climate and vegetation — compare AZONAL, ZONAL

intreat *archaic var of* ENTREAT

intrench *var of* ENTRENCH

in·trep·id \in-'trep-əd\ *adj* [L *intrepidus,* fr. *in-* + *trepidus* alarmed — more at TREPIDATION] (1697) : characterized by resolute fearlessness, fortitude, and endurance ⟨an ~ explorer⟩ — **in·tre·pid·i·ty** \,in-trə-'pid-ət-ē\ *n* — **in·trep·id·ly** \in-'trep-əd-lē\ *adv* — **in·trep·id·ness** *n*

in·tri·ca·cy \'in-tri-kə-sē\ *n, pl* **-cies** (1602) **1** : the quality or state of being intricate **2** : something intricate ⟨the *intricacies* of a plot⟩

in·tri·cate \'in-tri-kət\ *adj* [ME, fr. L *intricatus,* pp. of *intricare* to entangle, fr. *in-* + *tricae* trifles, impediments] (15c) **1** : having many complexly interrelating parts or elements : COMPLICATED **2** : difficult to resolve or analyze ***syn*** see COMPLEX — **in·tri·cate·ly** *adv* — **in·tri·cate·ness** *n*

in·tri·gant *or* **in·tri·guant** \,in-trē-'gänt, ,an-, -'gäⁿ\ *n* [F *intrigant,* fr. It *intrigante,* prp. of *intrigare*] (1781) : one that intrigues : INTRIGUER

¹in·trigue \in-'trēg\ *vb* **in·trigued; in·trigu·ing** [F *intriguer,* fr. It *intrigare,* fr. L *intricare*] *vt* (1612) **1** : CHEAT, TRICK **2** : to accomplish by intrigue ⟨*intrigued* themselves into office —F. M. Ford⟩ **3** *obs* : ENTANGLE **4** : to arouse the interest, desire, or curiosity of ⟨*intrigued* by the tale⟩ ~ *vi* : to carry on an intrigue; *esp* : PLOT, SCHEME — **in·trigu·er** *n*

²in·trigue \'in-,trēg, in-'\ *n* (1647) **1 a** : a secret scheme : MACHINATION **b** : the practice of engaging in intrigues **2** : a clandestine love affair ***syn*** see PLOT

in·trigu·ing \in-'trē-giŋ\ *adj* (1909) : engaging the interest to a marked degree : FASCINATING — **in·trigu·ing·ly** \-giŋ-lē\ *adv*

in·trin·sic \in-'trin-zik, -'trin(t)-sik\ *adj* [MF *intrinsèque* internal, fr. LL *intrinsecus,* fr. L, adv., inwardly; akin to L *intra* within — more at INTRA-] (1642) **1 a** : belonging to the essential nature or constitution of a thing ⟨the ~ worth of a gem⟩ **b** : being or relating to a semiconductor in which the concentration of charge carriers is characteristic of the material itself instead of the content of any impurities it contains **2** : originating or situated within the body or part acted on — **in·trin·si·cal·ly** \-zi-k(ə-)lē, -si-\ *adv*

in·trin·si·cal \-zi-kəl, -si-\ *adj, archaic* (1548) : INTRINSIC

intrinsic factor *n* (1930) : a substance produced by normal gastrointestinal mucosa that facilitates absorption of vitamin B_{12}

in·tro \'in-(,)trō\ *n* [by shortening] (ca. 1899) : INTRODUCTION

intro- *prefix* [ME, fr. MF, fr. L, fr. *intro* inside, to the inside, fr. (assumed) OL *interus,* adj., inward] **1** : in : into ⟨*intro*jection⟩ **2** : inward : within ⟨*intro*vert⟩ — compare EXTRO-

in·tro·duce \,in-trə-'d(y)üs\ *vt* **-duced; -duc·ing** [L *introducere,* fr. *intro-* + *ducere* to lead — more at TOW] (15c) **1** : to lead or bring in esp. for the first time **2 a** : to bring into play **b** : to bring into practice or use : INSTITUTE **3** : to lead to or make known by a formal act, announcement, or recommendation: as **a** : to cause to be acquainted **b** : to present formally at court or into society **c** : to present or announce formally or officially or by an official reading **d** : to make preliminary explanatory or laudatory remarks about **e** : to bring (as an actor or singer) before the public for the first time **4** : PLACE, INSERT **5** : to bring to a knowledge of something — **in·tro·duc·er** *n*

syn INTRODUCE, INSERT, INSINUATE, INTERPOLATE, INTERCALATE, INTERPOSE, INTERJECT mean to put between or among others. INTRODUCE is a general term for bringing or placing a thing or person into a group or body already in existence; INSERT implies putting into a fixed or open space between or among; INSINUATE implies introducing gradually or by gentle pressure; INTERPOLATE applies to the inserting of something extraneous or spurious; INTERCALATE suggests an intrusive inserting of something in an existing series or sequence; INTERPOSE suggests inserting an obstruction or cause of delay; INTERJECT implies an abrupt or forced introduction.

in·tro·duc·tion \,in-trə-'dək-shən\ *n* [ME *introduccioun* act of introducing, fr. MF *introduction,* fr. L *introduction-, introductio,* fr. *introductus,* pp. of *introducere*] (14c) **1** : something that introduces: as **a** (1) : a part of a book or treatise preliminary to the main portion (2) : a preliminary treatise or course of study **b** : a short introductory musical passage **2** : the act or process of introducing : the state of being introduced **3** : a putting in : INSERTION **4** : something introduced; *specif* : a new or exotic plant or animal

in·tro·duc·to·ry \,in-trə-'dək-t(ə-)rē\ *adj* (1605) : of, relating to, or being a first step that sets something going or in proper perspective ⟨an ~ course in calculus⟩ — **in·tro·duc·to·ri·ly** \-t(ə-)rə-lē\ *adv*

in·tro·gres·sion \,in-trə-'gresh-ən\ *n* [*intro-* + *-gression* (as in *regression*)] (1938) : the entry or introduction of a gene from one gene complex into another — **in·tro·gres·sant** \-'gres-ᵊnt\ *adj or n* — **in·tro·gres·sive** \-'gres-iv\ *adj*

in·troit \'in-,trō-ət, -,trȯit, in-'\ *n* [ME, fr. MF *introite,* fr. ML *introitus,* fr. L, entrance, fr. *introitus,* pp. of *introire* to go in, fr. *intro-* + *ire* to go — more at ISSUE] (15c) **1** *often cap* : the first part of the traditional proper of the Mass consisting of an antiphon, verse from a psalm, and the Gloria Patri **2** : a piece of music sung or played at the beginning of a worship service

in·tro·ject \,in-trə-'jekt\ *vt* [*intro-* + *-ject* (as in *project,* v.)] (1925) : to incorporate (attitudes or ideas) into one's personality unconsciously — **in·tro·jec·tion** \-'jek-shən\ *n*

in·tro·mis·sion \,in-trə-'mish-ən\ *n* [F, fr. MF, fr. L *intromissus,* pp. of *intromittere*] (1601) : the act or process of intromitting; *esp* : the insertion or period of insertion of the penis in the vagina in copulation

in·tro·mit \-'mit\ *vt* **-mit·ted; -mit·ting** [L *intromittere,* fr. *intro-* + *mittere* to send] (1582) : to send or put in : INSERT — **in·tro·mit·tent** \-'mit-ᵊnt\ *adj* — **in·tro·mit·ter** \-ər\ *n*

in·tron \'in-,trän\ *n* [*intervening sequence* + ²*-on*] (ca. 1978) : a polynucleotide sequence in a nucleic acid that does not code information for protein synthesis and is removed before translation of messenger RNA — compare EXON

in·trorse \'in-,trȯ(ə)rs\ *adj* [L *introrsus,* adv., inward, fr. *intro-* + *versus* toward, fr. pp. of *vertere* to turn — more at WORTH] (1842) : facing inward or toward the axis of growth

in·tro·spect \,in-trə-'spekt\ *vb* [L *introspectus,* pp. of *introspicere* to look inside, fr. *intro-* + *specere* to look — more at SPY] *vt* (1683) : to examine (one's own mind or its contents) reflectively ~ *vi* : to engage in an examination of one's thought process and sensory experience — **in·tro·spec·tive** \-'spek-tiv\ *adj* — **in·tro·spec·tive·ly** *adv* — **in·tro·spec·tive·ness** *n*

in·tro·spec·tion \-'spek-shən\ *n* (1677) : the examination of one's own thought and feeling : SELF-EXAMINATION — **in·tro·spec·tion·al** \-shnəl, -shən-ᵊl\ *adj*

in·tro·spec·tion·ism \-shə-,niz-əm\ *n* (1922) : a doctrine that psychology must be based essentially on data derived from introspection — compare BEHAVIORISM — **in·tro·spec·tion·ist** \-sh(ə-)nəst\ *or* **in·tro·spec·tion·is·tic** \-,spek-shə-'nis-tik\ *adj* — **introspectionist** *n*

in·tro·ver·sion \,in-trə-'vər-zhən, -shən\ *n* [*intro-* + *-version* (as in *diversion*)] (1654) **1** : the act of introverting : the state of being introverted **2** : the state or tendency toward being wholly or predominantly concerned with and interested in one's own mental life — **in·tro·ver·sive** \-'vər-siv, -ziv\ *adj* — **in·tro·ver·sive·ly** *adv*

¹in·tro·vert \'in-trə-,vərt\ *vt* [*intro-* + *-vert* (as in *divert*)] (1669) : to turn inward or in upon itself: as **a** : to concentrate or direct upon oneself **b** : to produce psychological introversion in

²introvert *n* (1883) **1** : something (as the retractile proboscis of some worms) that is or can be drawn in esp. by invagination **2** : one whose personality is characterized by introversion

in·trude \in-'trüd\ *vb* **in·trud·ed; in·trud·ing** [L *intrudere* to thrust in, fr. *in-* + *trudere* to thrust — more at THREAT] *vi* (15c) **1** : to thrust oneself in without invitation, permission, or welcome **2** : to enter as a geological intrusion ~ *vt* **1** : to thrust or force in or upon esp. without permission, welcome, or fitness **2** : to cause to enter as if by force — **in·trud·er** *n*

in·tru·sion \in-'trü-zhən\ *n* [ME, fr. MF, fr. ML *intrusion-, intrusio,* fr. L *intrusus,* pp. of *intrudere*] (15c) **1** : the act of intruding or the state of being intruded; *esp* : the act of wrongfully entering upon, seizing, or taking possession of the property of another **2** : the forcible entry of molten rock or magma into or between other rock formations; *also* : the intruded magma

in·tru·sive \in-'trü-siv, -ziv\ *adj* (15c) **1 a** : characterized by intrusion **b** : intruding where one is not welcome or invited **2 a** : projecting inward ⟨an ~ arm of the sea⟩ **b** (1) *of a rock* : having been forced while in a plastic state into cavities or between layers (2) : PLUTONIC **3** : having nothing that corresponds to a sound or letter in orthography or etymon ⟨~ \t\ in \'mints\ for *mince*⟩ — **intrusive** *n* — **in·tru·sive·ly** *adv* — **in·tru·sive·ness** *n*

intrust *var of* ENTRUST

in·tu·ba·tion \,in-(,)t(y)ü-'bā-shən, -tə-\ *n* (1887) : the introduction of a tube into a hollow organ (as the trachea) — **in·tu·bate** \'in-(,)tyü-,bāt, -tə-\ *vt*

in·tu·it \in-'t(y)ü-ət\ *vt* (1858) : to apprehend by intuition — **in·tu·it·able** \-ə-bəl\ *adj*

in·tu·ition \,in-t(y)ù-'ish-ən\ *n* [LL *intuition-, intuitio* act of contemplating, fr. L *intuitus,* pp. of *intueri* to look at, contemplate, fr. *in-* + *tueri* to look at] (15c) **1 a** : immediate apprehension or cognition **b** : knowledge or conviction gained by intuition **c** : the power or faculty of attaining to direct knowledge or cognition without evident rational thought and inference **2** : quick and ready insight — **in·tu·ition·al** \-'ish-nəl, -ən-ᵊl\ *adj*

in·tu·ition·ism \-'ish-ə-,niz-əm\ *n* (1847) **1 a** : a doctrine that there are basic truths intuitively known **b** : a doctrine that objects of perception are intuitively known to be real **2** : a doctrine that right or wrong or fundamental principles about what is right and wrong can be intuited — **in·tu·ition·ist** \-'ish-(ə-)nəst\ *adj or n*

in·tu·itive \in-'t(y)ü-ət-iv\ *adj* (1594) **1 a** : known or perceived by intuition : directly apprehended ⟨had an ~ awareness of his sister's feelings⟩ **b** : knowable by intuition **2** : knowing or perceiving by intuition **3** : possessing or given to intuition or insight ⟨an ~ mind⟩ — **in·tu·itive·ly** *adv* — **in·tu·itive·ness** *n*

in·tu·mes·cence \-'mes-ᵊn(t)s\ *n* (1796) **1 a** : an enlarging, swelling, or bubbling up (as under the action of heat) **b** : the state of being swollen **2** : something swollen or enlarged — **in·tu·mesce** \-'mes\ *vi*

in·tu·mes·cent \-ᵊnt\ *adj* [L *intumescent-, intumescens,* prp. of *intumescere,* fr. *in-* + *tumescere* to swell — more at TUMESCENT] (ca. 1656) **1** : marked by intumescence **2** *of paint* : swelling and charring when exposed to flame

in·tus·sus·cept \,int-ə-sə-'sept\ *vb* [prob. fr. (assumed) NL *intussusceptus,* pp. of *intussuscipere,* fr. L *intus* within + *suscipere* to take up — more at ENT-, SUSCEPTIBLE] *vt* (1870) : to take in by or cause to undergo intussusception; *esp* : INVAGINATE ~ *vi* : to undergo intussusception

\ə\ abut \ᵊ\ kitten, F table \ər\ further \a\ ash \ā\ ace \ä\ cot, cart
\aù\ out \ch\ chin \e\ bet \ē\ easy \g\ go \i\ hit \ī\ ice \j\ job
\ŋ\ sing \ō\ go \ȯ\ law \ȯi\ boy \th\ thin \t͟h\ the \ü\ loot \ù\ foot
\y\ yet \zh\ vision \ȧ, k̲, ⁿ, œ, œ̄, ue, ue̅, ʸ\ see Guide to Pronunciation

in·tus·sus·cep·tion \-'sep-shən\ *n* (1802) **:** a drawing in of something from without: as **a :** INVAGINATION; *esp* **:** the slipping of a length of intestine into an adjacent portion usu. producing obstruction **b :** the assimilation of new material and its dispersal among preexistent matter — **in·tus·sus·cep·tive** \-'sep-tiv\ *adj*

In·u·it \'in-(y)ə-wət\ *n* [Aleut *inuit*, pl. of *inuk* person] (1765) **1** *pl* **Inuit** *or* **Inuits a (1) :** the Eskimo people of America **(2) :** the arctic Eskimo as distinguished from the Aleuts **b :** a member of such people **2 :** the language of the Inuit people

in·u·lin \'in-yə-lən\ *n* [prob. fr. G *inulin*, fr. L *inula* elecampane] (1813) **:** a tasteless white polysaccharide found esp. dissolved in the sap of the roots and rhizomes of composite plants

in·unc·tion \in-'əŋ(k)-shən\ *n* [ME, fr. L *inunction-, inunctio*, fr. *inunctus*, pp. of *inunguere* to anoint — more at ANOINT] (15c) **:** an act of applying oil or ointment **:** ANOINTING

in·un·date \'in-(,)ən-,dāt\ *vt* **-dat·ed; -dat·ing** [L *inundatus*, pp. of *inundare*, fr. *in-* + *unda* wave — more at WATER] (ca. 1623) **1 :** OVERWHELM **2 :** to cover with a flood **:** OVERFLOW — **in·un·da·tion** \,in-(,)ən-'dā-shən\ *n* — **in·un·da·tor** \'in-(,)ən-,dāt-ər\ *n* — **in·un·da·to·ry** \in-'ən-də-,tōr-ē, -,tȯr-\ *adj*

in·ure \in-'(y)u̇(ə)r\ *vb* **in·ured; in·ur·ing** [ME *enuren*, fr. *en-* + *ure*, n., use, custom, fr. MF *uevre* work, practice, fr. L *opera* work — more at OPERA] *vt* (15c) **:** to accustom to accept something undesirable **:** HABITUATE ~ *vi* **:** to become of advantage — **in·ure·ment** \-mənt\ *n*

in·urn \in-'ərn\ *vt* (1602) **1 :** ENTOMB **2 :** to place (as cremated remains) in an urn

in utero \in-'yüt-ə-,rō\ *adv or adj* [L] (1713) **:** in the uterus **:** before birth ⟨a disease acquired *in utero*⟩ ⟨an *in utero* diagnosis⟩

in·utile \(')in-'yüt-ᵊl, -'yü-,tīl\ *adj* [ME, fr. MF, fr. L *inutilis*, fr. *in-* + *utilis* useful — more at UTILITY] (15c) **:** USELESS, UNUSABLE — **in·util·i·ty** \,in-yu̇-'til-ət-ē\ *n*

in vac·uo \in-'vak-yə-,wō\ *adv* [NL] (1660) **:** in a vacuum

in·vade \in-'vād\ *vt* **in·vad·ed; in·vad·ing** [ME *invaden*, fr. L *invadere*, fr. *in-* + *vadere* to go — more at WADE] (15c) **1 :** to enter for conquest or plunder **2 :** to encroach upon **:** INFRINGE **3 a :** to spread over or into as if invading **:** PERMEATE ⟨doubts ~ his mind⟩ **b :** to affect injuriously and progressively ⟨gangrene ~*s* healthy tissue⟩ ***syn*** see TRESPASS — **in·vad·er** *n*

in·vag·i·nate \in-'vaj-ə-,nāt\ *vb* **-nat·ed; -nat·ing** [ML *invaginatus*, pp. of *invaginare*, fr. L *in-* + *vagina* sheath] *vt* (ca. 1656) **1 :** ENCLOSE, SHEATHE **2 :** to fold in so that an outer becomes an inner surface ~ *vi* **:** to undergo invagination

in·vag·i·na·tion \-,vaj-ə-'nā-shən\ *n* (ca. 1658) **1 :** an act or process of invaginating; *esp* **:** the formation of a gastrula by an infolding of part of the wall of the blastula **2 :** an invaginated part

1in·val·id \(')in-'val-əd\ *adj* [L *invalidus* weak, fr. *in-* + *validus* strong — more at VALID] (1542) **:** not valid: **a :** being without foundation or force in fact, truth, or law **b :** logically inconsequent — **in·val·id·ly** \(')in-'val-əd-lē\ *adv*

2in·va·lid \'in-və-ləd, *Brit usu* -,lēd\ *adj* [L & F; F *invalide*, fr. L *invalidus*] (1642) **1 :** suffering from disease or disability **:** SICKLY **2 :** of, relating to, or suited to one that is sick

3invalid *like*²\ *n* (1709) **:** one that is sickly or disabled

4in·va·lid \'in-və-ləd, -,lid, *Brit usu* -,lēd *or* ,in-və-'lēd\ *vt* (1787) **1 :** to remove from active duty by reason of sickness or disability **2 :** to make sickly or disabled

in·val·i·date \(')in-'val-ə-,dāt\ *vt* (1649) **:** to make invalid; *esp* **:** to weaken or destroy the cogency of ***syn*** see NULLIFY — **in·val·i·da·tion** \(,)in-,val-ə-'dā-shən\ *n* — **in·val·i·da·tor** \in-'val-ə-,dāt-ər\ *n*

in·va·lid·ism \'in-və-ləd-,iz-əm\ *n* (1794) **:** a chronic condition of being an invalid

in·va·lid·i·ty \,in-və-'lid-ət-ē, -va-\ *n, pl* **-ties** (1550) **1 :** lack of validity or cogency **2 :** incapacitating bodily disability; *also* **:** INVALIDISM

in·valu·able \(')in-'val-yə(-wə)-bəl\ *adj* [¹*in-* + *value*, v. + *-able*] (1576) **:** valuable beyond estimation **:** PRICELESS — **in·valu·able·ness** *n* — **in·valu·ably** \-blē\ *adv*

In·var \'in-,vär\ *trademark* — used for an iron-nickel alloy that expands little on heating

in·vari·able \(')in-'ver-ē-ə-bəl, -'var-\ *adj* (15c) **:** not changing or capable of change **:** CONSTANT — **in·vari·abil·i·ty** \(,)in-,ver-ē-ə-'bil-ət-ē, -,var-\ *n* — **invariable** *n* — **in·vari·ably** \-blē\ *adv*

in·vari·ance \(')in-'ver-ē-ən(t)s, -'var-\ *n* (1878) **:** the quality or state of being invariant

in·vari·ant \-ənt\ *adj* (1874) **:** CONSTANT, UNCHANGING; *specif* **:** unchanged by specified mathematical or physical operations or transformations ⟨~ factor⟩ — **invariant** *n*

in·va·sion \in-'vā-zhən\ *n* [ME *invasioune*, fr. MF *invasion*, fr. LL *invasion-, invasio*, fr. L *invasus*, pp. of *invadere* to invade] (15c) **1 :** an act of invading; *esp* **:** incursion of an army for conquest or plunder **2 :** the incoming or spread of something usu. hurtful

in·va·sive \-siv, -ziv\ *adj* (15c) **1 :** of, relating to, or characterized by military aggression **2 :** tending to spread; *esp* **:** tending to invade healthy tissue ⟨~ cancer cells⟩ **3 :** tending to infringe **4 :** involving entry into the living body (as by incision or by insertion of an instrument) ⟨~ diagnostic techniques⟩ — **in·va·sive·ness** *n*

1in·vec·tive \in-'vek-tiv\ *adj* [ME *invectif*, fr. MF, fr. L *invectivus*, fr. *invectus*, pp. of *invehere*] (15c) **:** of, relating to, or characterized by insult or abuse — **in·vec·tive·ly** *adv* — **in·vec·tive·ness** *n*

2invective *n* (1523) **1 :** an abusive expression or speech **2 :** insulting or abusive language **:** VITUPERATION ***syn*** see ABUSE

in·veigh \in-'vā\ *vi* [L *invehi* to attack, inveigh, pass. of *invehere* to carry in, fr. *in-* + *vehere* to carry — more at WAY] (1529) **:** to protest or complain bitterly or vehemently **:** RAIL — **in·veigh·er** *n*

in·vei·gle \in-'vā-gəl *sometimes* -'vē-\ *vt* **in·vei·gled; in·vei·gling** \-g(ə-)liŋ\ [modif. of MF *aveugler* to blind, hoodwink, fr. OF *avogler*, fr. *avogle* blind, fr. ML *ab oculis*, lit., lacking eyes] (1540) **1 :** to win over by wiles **:** ENTICE **2 :** to acquire by ingenuity or flattery ***syn*** see LURE — **in·vei·gle·ment** \-gəl-mənt\ *n* — **in·vei·gler** \-g(ə-)lər\ *n*

in·vent \in-'vent\ *vt* [ME *inventen*, fr. L *inventus*, pp. of *invenire* to come upon, find, fr. *in-* + *venire* to come — more at COME] (15c) **1** *archaic* **:** FIND, DISCOVER **2 :** to devise by thinking **:** FABRICATE **3 :** to produce (as something useful) for the first time through the use of the imagination or of ingenious thinking and experiment — **in·ven·tor** \-'vent-ər\ *n* — **in·ven·tress** \-'ven-trəs\ *n*

syn INVENT, CREATE, DISCOVER mean to bring something new into existence. INVENT implies fabricating something useful usu. as a result of ingenious thinking or experiment; CREATE implies an evoking of life out of nothing or producing a thing for the sake of its existence rather than its function or use; DISCOVER presupposes preexistence of something and implies a finding rather than a making.

in·ven·tion \in-'ven-chən\ *n* (14c) **1 :** DISCOVERY, FINDING **2 :** productive imagination **:** INVENTIVENESS **3 a :** something invented: as **(1) :** a product of the imagination; *esp* **:** a false conception **(2) :** a device, contrivance, or process originated after study and experiment **b :** a short keyboard composition featuring two or three part counterpoint **4 :** the act or process of inventing

in·ven·tive \in-'vent-iv\ *adj* (15c) **1 :** adept or prolific at producing inventions **:** CREATIVE **2 :** characterized by invention — **in·ven·tive·ly** *adv* — **in·ven·tive·ness** *n*

1in·ven·to·ry \'in-vən-,tōr-ē, -,tȯr-\ *n, pl* **-ries** (15c) **1 a :** an itemized list of current assets: as **(1) :** a catalog of the property of an individual or estate **(2) :** a list of goods on hand **b :** a survey of natural resources **c :** a list of traits, preferences, attitudes, interests, or abilities used to evaluate personal characteristics or skills **2 :** the quantity of goods or materials on hand **:** STOCK **3 :** the act or process of taking an inventory — **in·ven·to·ri·al** \,in-vən-'tōr-ē-əl\ *adj* — **in·ven·to·ri·al·ly** \-ē-ə-lē\ *adv*

2inventory *vt* **-ried; -ry·ing** (1526) **:** to make an inventory of **:** CATALOG

in·ver·ness \,in-vər-'nes\ *n* [*Inverness*, Scotland] (1863) **:** a loose belted coat having a cape with a close-fitting round collar

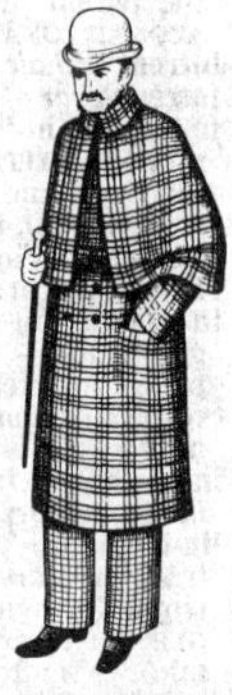
inverness

1in·verse \(')in-'vərs, 'in-,\ *adj* [L *inversus*, fr. pp. of *invertere*] (15c) **1 :** opposite in order, nature, or effect **2 :** being an inverse function ⟨~ sine⟩ — **in·verse·ly** *adv*

2in·verse \'in-,vərs, (')in-'\ *n* (1681) **1 :** something of a contrary nature or quality **:** OPPOSITE, REVERSE **2 :** the result of an inversion; *specif* **:** a proposition which is inferred immediately from another and in which the subject term is the negative of the subject of the given proposition and the predicate term is unchanged **3 a :** an inverse function or operation **b :** a set element that is related to another element in such a way that the result of applying a given binary operation to them is an identity element of the set

inverse function *n* (1816) **:** a function that is equivalent to a given function with the two variables interchanged — compare LOGARITHMIC FUNCTION

inverse square law *n* (1921) **:** a statement in physics: a physical quantity (as illumination) varies with the distance from the source inversely as the square of the distance

in·ver·sion \in-'vər-zhən, -shən\ *n* (1586) **1 :** a reversal of position, order, form, or relationship: as **a (1) :** a change in normal word order; *esp* **:** the placement of a verb before its subject **(2) :** the process or result of changing or reversing the relative positions of the notes of a musical interval, chord, or phrase **b :** the condition of being turned inward or inside out **c :** a breaking off of a chromosome section and its subsequent reattachment in inverted position; *also* **:** a chromosomal section that has undergone this process **2 :** the act or process of inverting **3 a :** a change in the order of the terms of a mathematical proportion effected by inverting each ratio **b :** the operation of forming the inverse of a magnitude, a function, an operation, or an element **4 :** a conversion of a substance showing dextrorotation into one showing levorotation or vice versa ⟨~ of sucrose⟩ **5 :** HOMOSEXUALITY **6 :** an increase of temperature with height through a layer of air **7 :** a conversion of direct current into alternating current

in·ver·sive \-'vər-siv, -ziv\ *adj* (1875) **:** marked by inversion

1in·vert \in-'vərt\ *vt* [L *invertere*, fr. *in-* + *vertere* to turn — more at WORTH] (1533) **1 a :** to reverse in position, order, or relationship **b :** to subject to inversion **2 a :** to turn inside out or upside down **b :** to turn inward ***syn*** see REVERSE

2in·vert \'in-,vərt\ *adj* (ca. 1890) **:** subjected to chemical inversion

3in·vert \'in-,vərt\ *n* (1897) **:** one characterized by inversion; *esp* **:** HOMOSEXUAL

in·ver·tase \in-'vərt-,ās, -,āz; 'in-vər-,tās, -,tāz\ *n* [ISV] (1887) **:** an enzyme capable of inverting sucrose

in·ver·te·brate \(')in-'vərt-ə-brət, -,brāt\ *adj* [NL *invertebratus*, fr. L *in-* + NL *vertebratus* vertebrate] (1838) **1 :** lacking a spinal column; *also* **:** of or relating to invertebrate animals **2 :** lacking in strength or vitality **:** WEAK — **invertebrate** *n*

inverted comma *n, chiefly Brit* (1789) **:** QUOTATION MARK

in·vert·er \in-'vərt-ər\ *n* (1611) **1 :** one that inverts **2 :** a device for converting direct current into alternating current

in·vert·ible \in-'vərt-ə-bəl\ *adj* (ca. 1864) **:** capable of being inverted or subjected to inversion ⟨an ~ matrix⟩

invert sugar *n* (1880) **:** a mixture of dextrose and levulose found in fruits or produced artificially by the inversion of sucrose; *also* **:** dextrose obtained from starch

1in·vest \in-'vest\ *vt* [L *investire* to clothe, surround, fr. *in-* + *vestis* garment — more at WEAR] (1533) **1** [ML *investire*, fr. L, to clothe] **a :** to array in the symbols of office or honor **b :** to furnish with power or authority **c :** to grant someone control or authority over **:** VEST **2 :** to cover completely **:** ENVELOP **3 :** CLOTHE, ADORN **4** [MF *investir*, fr. OIt *investire*, fr. L, to surround] **:** to surround with troops or ships so as to prevent escape or entry **5 :** to endow with a quality **:** INFUSE

2invest *vb* [It *investire* to clothe, invest money, fr. L, to clothe] *vt* (1613) **1 :** to commit (money) in order to earn a financial return **2 :** to make use of for future benefits or advantages ~ *vi* **:** to make an investment — **in·vest·able** \-'ves-tə-bəl\ *adj* — **in·ves·tor** \-tər\ *n*

in·ves·ti·gate \in-'ves-tə-,gāt\ *vb* **-gat·ed; -gat·ing** [L *investigatus*, pp. of *investigare* to track, investigate, fr. *in-* + *vestigium* footprint, track] *vt* (1510) **:** to observe or study by close examination and systematic inquiry ~ *vi* **:** to make a systematic examination; *esp* **:** to conduct an official inquiry — **in·ves·ti·ga·tion** \-,ves-tə-'gā-shən\ *n* — **in·ves·ti·ga·tion·al** \-shnəl, -shən-ᵊl\ *adj* — **in·ves·ti·ga·tive** \-'ves-tə-,gāt-iv\ *adj* — **in·ves·ti·ga·tor** \-,gāt-ər\ *n* — **in·ves·ti·ga·to·ry** \-'ves-ti-gə-,tōr-ē, -,tȯr-\ *adj*

in·ves·ti·ture \in-ˈves-tə-ˌchu̇(ə)r, -chər, -ˌt(y)u̇(ə)r\ *n* [ME, fr. ML *investitura,* fr. *investitus,* pp. of *investire*] (14c) **1 :** the act of establishing in office or ratifying : CONFIRMATION **2 :** something that covers or adorns

[1]**in·vest·ment** \in-ˈves(t)-mənt\ *n* [[1]*invest*] (1597) **1 a** *archaic* : VESTMENT **b :** an outer layer : ENVELOPE **2 :** INVESTITURE 1 **3 :** BLOCKADE, SIEGE

[2]**investment** *n* [[2]*invest*] (1615) **:** the outlay of money usu. for income or profit : capital outlay; *also* **:** the sum invested or the property purchased

investment company *n* (ca. 1917) **:** a company whose primary business is holding securities of other companies purely for investment purposes — compare HOLDING COMPANY

in·vet·er·a·cy \in-ˈvet-ə-rə-sē, -ˈve-trə-sē\ *n* [*inveterate* + *-cy*] (1719) **:** the quality or state of being obstinate or persistent : TENACITY

in·vet·er·ate \in-ˈvet-ə-rət, -ˈve-trət\ *adj* [L *inveteratus,* fr. pp. of *inveterare* to age (v.t.), fr. *in-* + *veter-, vetus* old — more at WETHER] (15c) **1 :** firmly established by long persistence ⟨the ~ tendency to overlook the obvious⟩ **2 :** confirmed in a habit : HABITUAL ⟨an ~ smoker⟩ — **in·vet·er·ate·ly** *adv*

in·vi·a·ble \(ˈ)in-ˈvī-ə-bəl\ *adj* [ISV] (1918) **:** incapable of surviving esp. because of genetic constitution — **in·vi·a·bil·i·ty** \(ˌ)in-ˌvī-ə-ˈbil-ət-ē\ *n*

in·vid·i·ous \in-ˈvid-ē-əs\ *adj* [L *invidiosus* envious, invidious, fr. *invidia* envy — more at ENVY] (1606) **1 :** tending to cause discontent, animosity, or envy **2 :** ENVIOUS **3 a :** of an unpleasant or objectionable nature : OBNOXIOUS ⟨subtle and ~ criticism⟩ **b :** of a kind to cause harm or resentment ⟨a most ~ comparison⟩ ***syn*** see REPUGNANT — **in·vid·i·ous·ly** *adv* — **in·vid·i·ous·ness** *n*

in·vig·o·rate \in-ˈvig-ə-ˌrāt\ *vt* **-rat·ed; -rat·ing** [prob. fr. *in-* + *vigor*] (1646) **:** to give life and energy to : ANIMATE — **in·vig·o·rat·ing·ly** \-ˌrāt-iŋ-lē\ *adv* — **in·vig·o·ra·tion** \-ˌvig-ə-ˈrā-shən\ *n* — **in·vig·o·ra·tor** \-ˈvig-ə-ˌrāt-ər\ *n*

in·vin·ci·ble \(ˈ)in-ˈvin(t)-sə-bəl\ *adj* [ME, fr. MF, fr. LL *invincibilis,* fr. L *in-* + *vincere* to conquer — more at VICTOR] (15c) **:** incapable of being conquered, overcome, or subdued — **in·vin·ci·bil·i·ty** \(ˌ)in-ˌvin(t)-sə-ˈbil-ət-ē\ *n* — **in·vin·ci·ble·ness** \(ˈ)in-ˈvin(t)-sə-bəl-nəs\ *n* — **in·vin·ci·bly** \-blē\ *adv*

in·vi·o·la·ble \(ˈ)in-ˈvī-ə-lə-bəl\ *adj* [MF or L; MF, fr. L *inviolabilis,* fr. *in-* + *violare* to violate] (15c) **1 :** secure from violation or profanation **2 :** secure from assault or trespass : UNASSAILABLE — **in·vi·o·la·bil·i·ty** \(ˌ)in-ˌvī-ə-lə-ˈbil-ət-ē\ *n* — **in·vi·o·la·ble·ness** \(ˈ)in-ˈvī-ə-lə-bəl-nəs\ *n* — **in·vi·o·la·bly** \-blē\ *adv*

in·vi·o·la·cy \(ˈ)in-ˈvī-ə-lə-sē\ *n* (ca. 1846) **:** the quality or state of being inviolate

in·vi·o·late \(ˈ)in-ˈvī-ə-lət\ *adj* (15c) **:** not violated or profaned; *esp* **:** PURE — **in·vi·o·late·ly** *adv* — **in·vi·o·late·ness** *n*

in·vis·cid \(ˈ)in-ˈvis-əd\ *adj* (ca. 1891) **1 :** having zero viscosity **2 :** of or relating to an inviscid fluid ⟨~ flow⟩

in·vis·i·ble \(ˈ)in-ˈviz-ə-bəl\ *adj* [ME, fr. MF, fr. L *invisibilis,* fr. *in-* + *visibilis* visible] (14c) **1 a :** incapable by nature of being seen **b :** inaccessible to view : HIDDEN **2 :** IMPERCEPTIBLE, INCONSPICUOUS **3 a :** not appearing in published financial statements **b :** not reflected in statistics — **in·vis·i·bil·i·ty** \(ˌ)in-ˌviz-ə-ˈbil-ət-ē\ *n* — **invisible** *n* — **in·vis·i·ble·ness** \(ˈ)in-ˈviz-ə-bəl-nəs\ *n* — **in·vis·i·bly** \-blē\ *adv*

in·vi·ta·tion \ˌin-və-ˈtā-shən\ *n* (15c) **1 a :** the act of inviting **b :** an often formal request to be present or participate **2 :** INCENTIVE, INDUCEMENT

in·vi·ta·tion·al \-shnəl, -shən-ᵊl\ *adj* (1922) **1 :** prepared or entered in response to a request ⟨an ~ article⟩ **2 :** limited to invited participants ⟨an ~ tournament⟩

[1]**in·vi·ta·to·ry** \in-ˈvīt-ə-ˌtōr-ē, -ˌtȯr-\ *adj* (14c) **:** containing an invitation

[2]**invitatory** *n, pl* **-ries** (15c) **:** an invitatory psalm or antiphon

[1]**in·vite** \in-ˈvīt\ *vt* **in·vit·ed; in·vit·ing** [MF or L; MF *inviter,* fr. L *invitare;* akin to L *vis* strength — more at VIM] (1533) **1 a :** to offer an incentive or inducement to : ENTICE **b :** to increase the likelihood of **2 a :** to request the presence or participation of **b :** to request formally **c :** to urge politely : WELCOME — **in·vit·er** *n*

[2]**in·vite** \ˈin-ˌvīt\ *n* (1659) **:** INVITATION 1

in·vi·tee \ˌin-və-ˈtē, -ˌvī-\ *n* (1803) **:** an invited person

in·vit·ing \in-ˈvīt-iŋ\ *adj* (1604) **:** ATTRACTIVE, TEMPTING — **in·vit·ing·ly** \-iŋ-lē\ *adv*

in vi·tro \in-ˈvē-(ˌ)trō, -ˈvi-\ *adv or adj* [NL, lit., in glass] (ca. 1894) **:** outside the living body and in an artificial environment

in vi·vo \in-ˈvē-(ˌ)vō\ *adv or adj* [NL, lit., in the living] (1901) **:** in the living body of a plant or animal

in·vo·cate \ˈin-və-ˌkāt\ *vt, archaic* (1526) **:** INVOKE

in·vo·ca·tion \ˌin-və-ˈkā-shən\ *n* [ME *invocacioun,* fr. MF *invocation,* fr. L *invocation-, invocatio,* fr. *invocatus,* pp. of *invocare*] (14c) **1 a :** the act or process of petitioning for help or support; *specif, often cap* **:** a prayer of entreaty (as at the beginning of a service of worship) **b :** a calling upon for authority or justification **2 :** a formula for conjuring : INCANTATION **3 :** an act of legal or moral implementation : ENFORCEMENT — **in·vo·ca·tion·al** \-shnəl, -shən-ᵊl\ *adj* — **in·voc·a·to·ry** \in-ˈväk-ə-ˌtōr-ē, -ˌtȯr-\ *adj*

[1]**in·voice** \ˈin-ˌvȯis\ *n* [modif. of MF *envois,* pl. of *envoi* message — more at ENVOI] (1560) **1 :** an itemized list of goods shipped usu. specifying the price and the terms of sale : BILL **2 :** a consignment of merchandise

[2]**invoice** *vt* **in·voiced; in·voic·ing** (1925) **:** to send an invoice for or to

in·voke \in-ˈvōk\ *vt* **in·voked; in·vok·ing** [ME *invoken,* fr. MF *invoquer,* fr. L *invocare,* fr. *in-* + *vocare* to call — more at VOICE] (15c) **1 a :** to petition for help or support **b :** to appeal to or cite as authority **2 :** to call forth by incantation : CONJURE **3 :** to make an earnest request for : SOLICIT **4 :** to put into effect or operation : IMPLEMENT **5 :** BRING ABOUT, CAUSE — **in·vok·er** *n*

in·vo·lu·cre \ˈin-və-ˌlü-kər\ *n* [F, fr. NL *involucrum*] (ca. 1794) **:** one or more whorls of bracts situated below and close to a flower, flower cluster, or fruit — **in·vo·lu·cral** \ˌin-və-ˈlü-krəl\ *adj* — **in·vo·lu·crate** \-krət, -ˌkrāt\ *adj*

in·vo·lu·crum \ˌin-və-ˈlü-krəm\ *n, pl* **-cra** \-krə\ [NL, sheath, involucre, fr. L, sheath, fr. *involvere* to wrap] (1677) **:** a surrounding envelope or sheath; *esp* **:** INVOLUCRE

in·vol·un·tary \(ˈ)in-ˈväl-ən-ˌter-ē\ *adj* [LL *involuntarius,* fr. L *in-* + *voluntarius* voluntary] (15c) **1 :** done contrary to or without choice **2 :** COMPULSORY **3 :** not subject to control of the will : REFLEX — **in·vol·un·tari·ly** \(ˌ)in-ˌväl-ən-ˈter-ə-lē\ *adv* — **in·vol·un·tari·ness** \(ˈ)in-ˈväl-ən-ˌter-ē-nəs\ *n*

[1]**in·vo·lute** \ˈin-və-ˌlüt\ *adj* [L *involutus* involved, fr. pp. of *involvere*] (15c) **1 a :** curled spirally **b (1) :** curled or curved inward **(2) :** having the edges rolled over the upper surface toward the midrib ⟨an ~ leaf⟩ **c :** having the form of an involute ⟨a gear with ~ teeth⟩ **2 :** INVOLVED, INTRICATE

[2]**involute** *n* (1796) **:** a curve traced by a point on a thread kept taut as it is unwound from another curve

[3]**in·vo·lute** \ˌin-və-ˈlüt\ *vi* **-lut·ed; -lut·ing** (1816) **1 :** to become involute **2 a :** to return to a former condition **b :** to become cleared up : DISAPPEAR

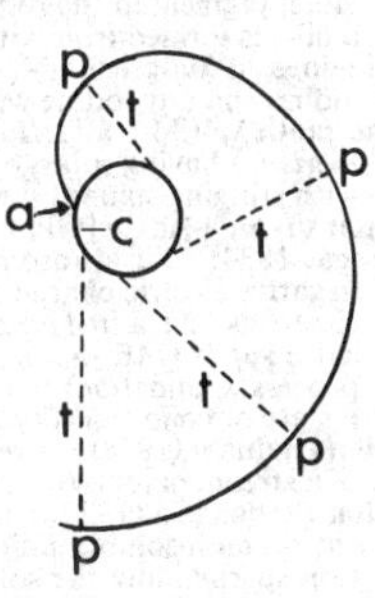

involute *a, p, p, p, p* traced by any point *p* of the thread *t* unwinding from curve *c*

in·vo·lu·tion \ˌin-və-ˈlü-shən\ *n* [L *involution-, involutio,* fr. *involutus,* pp. of *involvere*] (1611) **1 a (1) :** the act or an instance of enfolding or entangling : INVOLVEMENT **(2) :** an involved grammatical construction usu. characterized by the insertion of clauses between the subject and predicate **b :** COMPLEXITY, INTRICACY **2 :** EXPONENTIATION **3 a :** an inward curvature or penetration **b :** the formation of a gastrula by ingrowth of cells formed at the dorsal lip **4 :** a shrinking or return to a former size **5 :** the regressive alterations of a body or its parts characteristic of the aging process; *specif* **:** decline marked by a decrease of bodily vigor and in women by the menopause — **in·vo·lu·tion·al** \-shnəl, -shən-ᵊl\ *adj*

in·volve \in-ˈvälv, -ˈvȯlv *also* -ˈväv *or* -ˈvȯv\ *vt* **in·volved; in·volv·ing** [ME *involven* to roll up, wrap, fr. L *involvere,* fr. *in-* + *volvere* to roll — more at VOLUBLE] (14c) **1** *archaic* **:** to enfold or envelop so as to encumber **2 a :** to engage as a participant ⟨workers *involved* in building a house⟩ **b :** to oblige to take part ⟨right of Congress to ~ the nation in war⟩ **c :** to occupy (as oneself) absorbingly; *esp* **:** to commit (as oneself) emotionally ⟨she became *involved* with a married man⟩ **3 :** to surround as if with a wrapping : ENVELOP **4 a** *archaic* **:** to wind, coil, or wreathe about : ENTWINE **b :** to relate closely : CONNECT **5 a :** to have within or as part of itself : INCLUDE **b :** to require as a necessary accompaniment : ENTAIL **c :** to have an effect on : AFFECT ***syn*** see INCLUDE — **in·volve·ment** \-ˈvälv-mənt, -ˈvȯlv-\ *n* — **in·volv·er** *n*

in·volved \-ˈvälvd, -ˈvȯlvd *also* -ˈvävd *or* -ˈvȯvd\ *adj* (15c) **1 :** INVOLUTE, TWISTED **2 a :** marked by extreme and often needless or excessive complexity **b :** difficult to deal with because of complexity or disorder **3 :** being affected or implicated ***syn*** see COMPLEX — **in·volv·ed·ly** \-ˈväl-vəd-lē, -ˈvȯl- *also* -ˈväv-əd- *or* -ˈvȯv-əd-\ *adv*

in·vul·ner·a·ble \(ˈ)in-ˈvəln-(ə-)rə-bəl, -ˈvəl-nər-bəl\ *adj* [L *invulnerabilis,* fr. *in-* + *vulnerare* to wound — more at VULNERABLE] (1595) **1 :** incapable of being wounded, injured, or harmed **2 :** immune to or proof against attack : IMPREGNABLE — **in·vul·ner·a·bil·i·ty** \(ˌ)in-ˌvəln-(ə-)rə-ˈbil-ət-ē\ *n* — **in·vul·ner·a·ble·ness** \(ˈ)in-ˈvəln-(ə-)rə-bəl-nəs, -ˈvəl-nər-bəl-\ *n* — **in·vul·ner·a·bly** \-blē\ *adv*

[1]**in·ward** \ˈin-wərd\ *adj* [ME, fr. OE *inweard* (akin to OHG *inwert*), fr. *in* + *-weard* ward] (bef. 12c) **1 :** situated on the inside : INNER **2 :** of or relating to the mind or spirit ⟨~ peace⟩ **3 :** marked by close acquaintance : FAMILIAR **4 :** directed toward the interior

[2]**inward** *or* **in·wards** \-wərdz\ *adv* (bef. 12c) **1 :** toward the inside, center, or interior **2 :** toward the inner being

[3]**inward** *n* (bef. 12c) **1 :** something that is inward **2 in·wards** \ˈin-ərdz, -wərdz\ *pl* **:** INNARDS

Inward Light *n* (1706) **:** INNER LIGHT

in·ward·ly \ˈin-wərd-lē\ *adv* (bef. 12c) **1 :** in the innermost being : MENTALLY, SPIRITUALLY **2 a :** beneath the surface : INTERNALLY ⟨bled ~⟩ **b :** to oneself : PRIVATELY ⟨cursed ~⟩

in·ward·ness *n* (14c) **1 :** internal quality or substance **2 :** close acquaintance : FAMILIARITY **3 :** fundamental nature : ESSENCE **4 :** absorption in one's own mental or spiritual life

in·weave \(ˈ)in-ˈwēv\ *vt* **-wove** \-ˈwōv\ *also* **-weaved; -wo·ven** \-ˈwō-vən\ *also* **-weaved; -weav·ing** (15c) **:** INTERWEAVE, INTERLACE

in–wrought \(ˈ)in-ˈrȯt, ˈin-ˌ\ *adj* (1637) **1 :** having decoration worked in : ORNAMENTED; *esp* **:** decorated with embroidery **2 :** worked in esp. as decoration

Io \ˈī-(ˌ)ō\ *n* [L, fr. Gk *Iō*] **:** a maiden loved by Zeus and changed by him into a heifer so that she might escape the jealous rage of Hera

iod- *or* **iodo-** *comb form* [F *iode*] **:** iodine ⟨*iod*ize⟩ ⟨*iodo*form⟩

[1]**io·date** \ˈī-ə-ˌdāt, -əd-ət\ *n* [F, fr. *iode*] (1826) **:** a salt of iodic acid

[2]**io·date** \ˈī-ə-ˌdāt\ *vt* **io·dat·ed; io·dat·ing** [*iod-* + *-ate*] (1853) **:** to impregnate or treat with iodine — **io·da·tion** \ˌī-ə-ˈdā-shən\ *n*

iod·ic acid \ī-ˌäd-ik-\ *n* [F *iodique,* fr. *iode*] (1826) **:** a crystalline oxidizing solid HIO_3 formed by oxidation of iodine

io·dide \ˈī-ə-ˌdīd\ *n* [ISV] (1822) **:** a compound of iodine usu. with a more electropositive element or radical; *esp* **:** a salt or ester of hydriodic acid

io·din·ate \ˈī-ə-də-ˌnāt\ *vt* **-at·ed; -at·ing** (1908) **:** to treat or cause to combine with iodine or a compound of iodine — **io·din·ation** \ˌī-ə-də-ˈnā-shən\ *n*

io·dine *also* **io·din** \ˈī-ə-ˌdīn, -əd-ᵊn, -ə-ˌdēn\ *n, often attrib* [F *iode,* fr. Gk *ioeidēs* violet colored, fr. *ion* violet] (1814) **:** a nonmetallic halogen element obtained usu. as heavy shining blackish gray crystals and used esp. in medicine, photography, and analysis — see ELEMENT table

io·dize \ˈī-ə-ˌdīz\ *vt* **io·dized; io·diz·ing** (1841) **:** to treat with iodine or an iodide ⟨*iodized* salt⟩

io·do·form \ī-ˈōd-ə-ˌfȯrm, -ˈäd-\ *n* [ISV *iod-* + *-form* (as in *chloroform*)] (1838) **:** a yellow crystalline volatile compound CHI_3 with a penetrating persistent odor that is used as an antiseptic dressing

io·do·phor \-ˌfō(ə)r\ *n* [*iod-* + Gk *-phoros* carrier — more at -PHORE] (ca. 1952) **:** a complex of iodine and a surface-active agent that releases iodine gradually and serves as a disinfectant

io·dop·sin \ˌī-ə-ˈdäp-sən\ *n* [*iod-* (fr. Gk *ioeidēs* violet colored) + Gk *opsis* sight, vision + E *-in* — more at OPTIC] (1938) **:** a photosensitive violet pigment in the retinal cones that is similar to rhodopsin but more labile, is formed from vitamin A, and is important in daylight vision

io·dous \ī-ˈōd-əs, ˈī-əd-\ *adj* [ISV] (1826) **:** relating to or containing iodine and esp. iodine with a valence of three

io moth \ˌī-(ˌ)ō-\ *n* [L *Io*] (1870) **:** an American saturniid moth (*Automeris io*) having a large ocellated spot on each hind wing and a larva with stinging spines

ion \ˈī-ən, ˈī-ˌän\ *n* [Gk, neut. of *iōn*, prp. of *ienai* to go — more at ISSUE] (ca. 1834) **1 :** an atom or group of atoms that carries a positive or negative electric charge as a result of having lost or gained one or more electrons **2 :** a free electron or other charged subatomic particle

-ion *n suffix* [ME *-ioun, -ion*, fr. OF *-ion*, fr. L *-ion-, -io*] **1 a :** act or process ⟨validat*ion*⟩ **b :** result of an act or process ⟨regulat*ion*⟩ **2 :** state or condition ⟨hydrat*ion*⟩

ion engine *n* (1958) **:** a reaction engine deriving thrust from the ejection of a stream of ionized particles

ion exchange *n* (1923) **:** a reversible interchange of one kind of ion present on an insoluble solid with another of like charge present in a solution surrounding the solid with the reaction being used esp. for softening or demineralizing water, the purification of chemicals, or the separation of substances — **ion–ex·chang·er** *n*

Io·ni·an \ī-ˈō-nē-ən\ *n* [L *Ionius* + E *-an*] (1563) **1 :** any of an ancient Hellenic race that settled in Attica, on the islands of the Aegean sea, and on the shore of Asia Minor **2 :** a native or inhabitant of Ionia — **Ionian** *adj*

ion·ic \ī-ˈän-ik\ *adj* [ISV] (1890) **1 :** of, relating to, existing as, or characterized by ions ⟨~ gases⟩ ⟨the ~ charge⟩ **2 :** based on or functioning by means of ions ⟨~ conduction⟩ ⟨an ~ lattice⟩ — **ion·ic·i·ty** \ˌī-ə-ˈnis-ət-ē\ *n*

[1]**Ion·ic** \ī-ˈän-ik\ *adj* [L & MF; MF *ionique*, fr. L *ionicus*, fr. Gk *iōnikos*, fr. *Iōnia* Ionia] (1585) **1 :** belonging to or resembling the Ionic order of architecture characterized esp. by the spiral volutes of its capital **2 :** of or relating to Ionia or the Ionians

[2]**Ionic** *n* (1668) **:** a dialect of ancient Greek used in Ionia that is the vehicle of an important body of literature

ionic bond *n* (1939) **:** ELECTROVALENT BOND

io·ni·um \ī-ˈō-nē-əm\ *n* [*ion*; fr. its ionizing action] (ca. 1907) **:** a natural radioactive isotope of thorium having a mass number of 230

ionization chamber *n* (1904) **:** a partially evacuated tube provided with electrodes so that its conductivity due to the ionization of the residual gas reveals the presence of ionizing radiation

ion·ize \ˈī-ə-ˌnīz\ *vb* **ion·ized; ion·iz·ing** [ISV] *vt* (1898) **:** to convert wholly or partly into ions ~ *vi* **:** to become ionized — **ion·iz·able** \-ˌnī-zə-bəl\ *adj* — **ion·iza·tion** \ˌī-ə-nə-ˈzā-shən\ *n* — **ion·iz·er** \ˈī-ə-ˌnī-zər\ *n*

ion·o·phore \ī-ˈän-ə-ˌfō(ə)r, -ˌfȯ(ə)r\ *n* [*ion* + *-o-* + *-phore*] (ca. 1955) **:** a compound that facilitates transmission of an ion (as of calcium) across a lipid barrier (as in a cell membrane) by combining with the ion or by increasing the permeability of the barrier to it

ion·o·sphere \ī-ˈän-ə-ˌsfi(ə)r\ *n* (ca. 1926) **:** the part of the earth's atmosphere beginning at an altitude of about 30 miles (50 kilometers) and extending outward 300 miles (500 kilometers) or more, containing free electrically charged particles by means of which radio waves are transmitted to great distances around the earth, and consisting of several regions within which occur one or more layers that vary in height and ionization with time of day, season, and the solar cycle; *also* **:** a comparable region of charged particles surrounding a celestial body (as Venus or Mars) — **ion·o·spher·ic** \ˌī-ˌän-ə-ˈsfi(ə)r-ik, -ˈsfer-\ *adj* — **ion·o·spher·i·cal·ly** \-i-k(ə-)lē\ *adv*

ion·to·pho·re·sis \(ˌ)ī-ˌänt-ə-fə-ˈrē-səs\ *n, pl* **-re·ses** \-ˌsēz\ (ca. 1909) **:** the introduction of an ionized substance (as a drug) through intact skin by the application of a direct electric current — **ion·to·pho·ret·ic** \-ˈret-ik\ *adj* — **ion·to·pho·ret·i·cal·ly** \-i-k(ə-)lē\ *adv*

io·ta \ī-ˈōt-ə\ *n* [L, fr. Gk *iōta*, of Sem origin; akin to Heb *yōdh* yod] (1607) **1 :** the 9th letter of the Greek alphabet — see ALPHABET table **2 :** an infinitesimal amount **:** JOT

io·ta·cism \ī-ˈōt-ə-ˌsiz-əm\ *n* [LL *iotacismus* repetition of iota, fr. Gk *iōtakismos*, fr. *iōta*] (ca. 1656) **:** excessive use of the letter iota or I or of its sound; *specif* **:** the use in modern Greek of the sound \ē\ of iota in speaking words written with other vowels or diphthongs (as *ē, y, ei, oi*)

IOU \ˌī-(ˌ)ō-ˈyü\ *n* [fr. the pronunciation of *I owe you*] (1618) **1 :** a paper that has on it the letters IOU, a stated sum, and a signature and that is given as an acknowledgment of debt **2 :** DEBT, OBLIGATION

-ious *adj suffix* [ME, partly fr. OF *-ious, -ieux*, fr. L *-iosus*, fr. *-i-* (penultimate vowel of some noun stems) + *-osus* -ous; partly fr. L *-ius*, adj. suffix] **:** -OUS ⟨edac*ious*⟩

IPA \ˌī-ˌpē-ˈā\ *n* [*I*nternational *P*honetic *A*lphabet] (1933) **:** an alphabet designed to represent each human speech sound with a unique symbol

ip·e·cac \ˈip-i-ˌkak\ *or* **ipe·ca·cu·a·nha** *Pg* ē-ˌpek-ə-kü-ˈa-nʸə\ *n* [Pg *ipecacuanha*, fr. Tupi *ipekaaguéne*] (1682) **1 :** the dried rhizome and roots of ipecac valued esp. as a source of emetine; *also* **:** any of several roots similarly used **2 :** a tropical So. American creeping plant (*Cephaelis ipecacuanha*) of the madder family with drooping flowers

Iph·i·ge·nia \ˌif-ə-jə-ˈnī-ə\ *n* [L, fr. Gk *Iphigeneia*] **:** a daughter of Agamemnon nearly sacrificed by him to Artemis but saved by her and made a priestess

ipro·ni·a·zid \ˌī-prə-ˈnī-ə-zəd\ *n* [blend of *isoniazid* and *propyl*] (1952) **:** a derivative $C_9H_{13}N_3O$ of isoniazid that is used as a monoamine oxidase inhibitor and was formerly used in treating tuberculosis

ip·se dix·it \ˌip-sē-ˈdik-sət\ *n* [L, he himself said it] (15c) **:** an assertion made but not proved **:** DICTUM

ip·si·lat·er·al \ˌip-si-ˈlat-ə-rəl, -ˈla-trəl\ *adj* [ISV, fr. L *ipse* self, himself + *later-, latus* side] (1907) **:** situated or appearing on or affecting the same side of the body — **ip·si·lat·er·al·ly** \-ē\ *adv*

ip·sis·si·ma ver·ba \ip-ˌsis-ə-mə-ˈvər-bə\ *n pl* [NL, lit., the selfsame words] (1807) **:** the exact language used by someone quoted

ip·so fac·to \ˌip-(ˌ)sō-ˈfak-(ˌ)tō\ *adv* [NL, lit., by the fact itself] (1548) **:** by the very nature of the case

IQ \ˈī-ˈkyü\ *n* (1920) **:** INTELLIGENCE QUOTIENT

ir- — see IN-

Ira·ni·an \ir-ˈā-nē-ən, -ˈan-ē-, -ˈän-ē-\ *n* (1873) **1 :** a native or inhabitant of Iran **2 :** a branch of the Indo-European family of languages that includes Persian — see INDO-EUROPEAN LANGUAGES table — **Iranian** *adj*

Iraqi \i-ˈräk-ē, -ˈrak-\ *n* [Ar *ʽirāqīy*, fr. *ʽIrāq* Iraq] (1824) **1 :** a native or inhabitant of Iraq **2 :** the dialect of Modern Arabic spoken in Iraq — **Iraqi** *adj*

iras·ci·ble \ir-ˈas-ə-bəl\ *adj* [MF, fr. LL *irascibilis*, fr. L *irasci* to become angry, be angry, fr. *ira*] (ca. 1530) **:** marked by hot temper and easily provoked anger — **iras·ci·bil·i·ty** \-ˌas-ə-ˈbil-ət-ē\ *n* — **iras·ci·ble·ness** \ir-ˈas-ə-bəl-nəs\ *n* — **iras·ci·bly** \-blē\ *adv*

irate \ī-ˈrāt, ˈī-ˌ, i-ˈrāt\ *adj* (1838) **1 :** roused to ire ⟨an ~ taxpayer⟩ **2 :** arising from anger ⟨~ words⟩ — **irate·ly** *adv* — **irate·ness** *n*

ire \ˈī(ə)r\ *n* [ME, fr. MF, fr. L *ira*; akin to OE *ofost* haste, zeal, Gk *hieros* holy, *oistros* gadfly, frenzy] (14c) **:** intense and usu. openly displayed anger ***syn*** see ANGER — **ire** *vt* — **ire·ful** \-fəl\ *adj*

ire·nic \ī-ˈren-ik, -ˈrē-nik\ *adj* [Gk *eirēnikos*, fr. *eirēnē* peace] (ca. 1864) **:** conducive to or operating toward peace or conciliation — **ire·ni·cal·ly** \-ˈren-i-k(ə-)lē, -ˈrē-ni-\ *adv*

irid- *or* **irido-** *comb form* **1** [L *irid-, iris*] **:** rainbow ⟨*irid*escent⟩ **2** [NL *irid-, iris*] **:** iris of the eye ⟨*irid*ectomy⟩ **3** [NL *iridium*] **:** iridium ⟨*irid*ic⟩ **:** iridium and ⟨*irid*osmium⟩

iri·da·ceous \ˌir-ə-ˈdā-shəs, ˌī-rə-\ *adj* (1851) **:** of or relating to the iris family

ir·i·des·cence \ˌir-ə-ˈdes-ᵊn(t)s\ *n* (1804) **1 :** a play of colors producing rainbow effects (as in a soap bubble) **2 :** a display or effect suggestive of iridescence (as in brilliance)

ir·i·des·cent \-ᵊnt\ *adj* (1796) **:** having or exhibiting iridescence — **ir·i·des·cent·ly** *adv*

irid·ic *1 usu* ir-ˈid-ik, *2 usu* ī-ˈrid-\ *adj* (1845) **1 :** of or relating to iridium; *esp* **:** containing tetravalent iridium **2 :** of or relating to the iris of the eye

irid·i·um \ir-ˈid-ē-əm\ *n* [NL, fr. L *irid-, iris*; fr. the colors produced by its dissolving in hydrochloric acid] (ca. 1804) **:** a silver-white hard brittle very heavy metallic element — see ELEMENT table

ir·i·dol·o·gy \ˌī-rə-ˈdäl-ə-jē\ *n, pl* **-gies** (ca. 1923) **:** the study of the iris of the eye for indications of bodily health and disease — **ir·i·dol·o·gist** \-jəst\ *n*

ir·id·os·mine \ˌir-ə-ˈdäz-ˌmēn\ *n* [G, fr. *irid-* + NL *osmium*] (ca. 1827) **:** a mineral that is a native iridium osmium alloy usu. containing some rhodium and platinum

[1]**iris** \ˈī-rəs\ *n, pl* **iris·es** *or* **iri·des** \ˈī-rə-ˌdēz, ˈir-ə-\ [ME, fr. L *irid-, iris* rainbow, iris plant, fr. Gk, rainbow, iris plant, iris of the eye — more at WIRE] (15c) **1 :** RAINBOW **2** [NL *irid-, iris*, fr. Gk] **a :** the opaque contractile diaphragm perforated by the pupil and forming the colored portion of the eye — see EYE illustration **b :** IRIS DIAPHRAGM; *also* **:** a similar device with a circular opening that can be varied in size **3** *or pl* **iris** [NL *Irid-, Iris*, genus name, fr. L] **:** any of a large genus (*Iris* of the family Iridaceae, the iris family) of perennial herbaceous plants with linear usu. basal leaves and large showy flowers

[2]**iris** *vt* (1816) **1 :** to make iridescent **:** give the form or appearance of a rainbow to **2 :** to operate the iris of a motion-picture camera so as to fade (a picture) — used with *in* or *out*

Iris \ˈī-rəs\ *n* [L, fr. Gk] **:** the Greek goddess of the rainbow and a messenger of the gods

iris diaphragm *n* (1867) **:** an adjustable diaphragm of thin opaque plates that can be turned by a ring so as to change the diameter of a central opening usu. to regulate the aperture of a lens

Irish \ˈī(ə)r-ish\ *n* [ME, fr. (assumed) OE *Īrisc*, fr. *Īras* Irishmen, of Celt origin; akin to OIr *Ériu* Ireland] (13c) **1** *pl in constr* **:** natives or inhabitants of Ireland or their descendants esp. when of Celtic speech or culture **2 a :** the Celtic language of Ireland **:** IRISH GAELIC **b :** English spoken by the Irish **3 :** IRISH WHISKEY — **Irish** *adj*

Irish bull *n* (1802) **:** an incongruous statement (as "it was hereditary in his family to have no children")

Irish coffee *n* (1950) **:** hot sugared coffee with Irish whiskey and whipped cream

Irish confetti *n* (1922) **:** a rock or brick used as a missile

Irish Gaelic *n* (1891) **:** the Celtic language of Ireland esp. as used since the end of the medieval period

Irish·ism \ˈī-rish-ˌiz-əm\ *n* (1734) **:** a word, phrase, or expression characteristic of the Irish

Irish·ly \-lē\ *adv* (1571) **:** in a manner characteristic of the Irish

Irish mail *n* (1908) **:** a 3- or 4-wheeled toy vehicle activated by a hand lever

Irish·man \ˈī-rish-mən\ *n* (13c) **1 :** a native or inhabitant of Ireland **2 :** one that is of Irish descent

Irish moss *n* (ca. 1845) **1 :** the dried and bleached plants of two red algae (*Chondrus crispus* and *Gigartina mamillosa*) used as an agent for thickening or emulsifying or as a demulcent **2 :** either of the two red algae that are the source of Irish moss — called also *carrageen*

Irish·ness \ˈī-rish-nəs\ *n* (1804) **:** the fact or quality of being Irish

Irish potato *n* (1664) **:** POTATO 2b

Irish·ry \ˈī-rish-rē\ *n, pl* **-ries** (14c) **1 :** IRISH 1 **2 a :** Irish quality or character **b :** an Irish peculiarity or trait

Irish setter *n* (1885) **:** any of a breed of bird dogs generally comparable to English setters but with a mahogany-red coat

Irish stew *n* (1814) **:** a stew having as its principal ingredients meat (as lamb), potatoes, and onions in a thick gravy

Irish terrier *n* (1891) **:** any of a breed of active medium-sized terriers developed in Ireland and characterized by a dense close usu. reddish wiry coat

Irish water spaniel *n* (1885) **:** any of a breed of large retrievers characterized by a topknot, a heavy curly liver-colored coat, and a short-haired tail

Irish whiskey *n* (1798) **:** whiskey made in Ireland chiefly of barley

Irish wolfhound *n* (ca. 1900) **:** a very tall heavily-built hound having a rough wiry coat

Irish·wom·an \ˈī-rish-ˌwu̇m-ən\ *n* (15c) **:** a woman born in Ireland or of Irish descent

iri·tis \ī-ˈrīt-əs\ *n* (1818) **:** inflammation of the iris of the eye

¹irk \ˈərk\ *vt* [ME *irken*] (15c) **:** to make weary, irritated, or bored ***syn*** see ANNOY

²irk *n* (ca. 1570) **1 :** the fact of being annoying **2 :** a source of annoyance

irk·some \ˈərk-səm\ *adj* (15c) **:** tending to irk **:** TEDIOUS ⟨an ~ task⟩ — **irk·some·ly** *adv* — **irk·some·ness** *n*

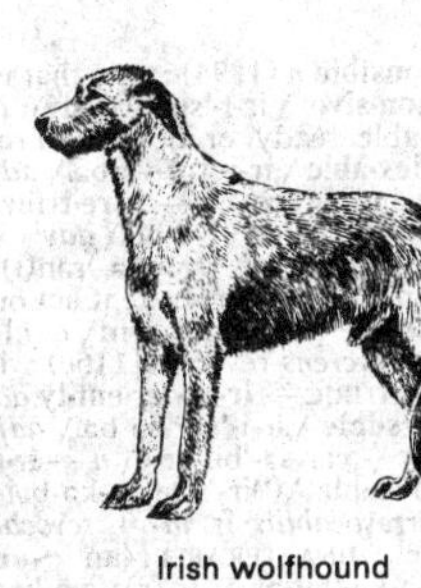

Irish wolfhound

¹iron \ˈī(-ə)rn\ *n* [ME, fr. OE *īsern, īren;* akin to OHG *īsarn* iron] (bef. 12c) **1 :** a heavy malleable ductile magnetic silver-white metallic element that readily rusts in moist air, occurs native in meteorites and combined in most igneous rocks, is the most used of metals, and is vital to biological processes — see ELEMENT table **2 :** something made of iron: as **a** *pl* **:** shackles for the hands or legs **b :** a heated metal implement used for branding or cauterizing **c :** HARPOON **d :** a household device usu. with a flat metal base that is heated to smooth, finish, or press (as cloth) **:** FLATIRON **e :** STIRRUP — usu. used in pl. **f :** any of a series of numbered golf clubs having metal heads **3 :** great strength, hardness, or determination — **iron in the fire 1 :** a matter requiring close attention **2 :** a prospective course of action

²iron *adj* (bef. 12c) **1 :** of, relating to, or made of iron **2 :** resembling iron **3 a :** strong and healthy **:** ROBUST **b :** INFLEXIBLE, UNRELENTING ⟨~ determination⟩ **c :** holding or binding fast ⟨an ~ grip⟩ — **iron·ness** \ˈī(-ə)rn-nəs\ *n*

³iron *vt* (15c) **1 :** to furnish or cover with iron **2 :** to shackle with irons **3 a :** to smooth with or as if with a heated iron ⟨~*ed* his shirt⟩ **b :** to remove (as wrinkles) by ironing ~ *vi* **:** to smooth or press cloth or clothing with a heated iron

Iron Age *n* (ca. 1879) **:** the period of human culture characterized by the smelting of iron and its use in industry beginning somewhat before 1000 B.C. in western Asia and Egypt

iron·bound \ˈī(-ə)rn-ˈbau̇nd\ *adj* (14c) **:** bound with or as if with iron: as **a :** HARSH, RUGGED ⟨~ coast⟩ **b :** STERN, RIGOROUS ⟨~ traditions⟩

¹iron·clad \-ˈklad\ *adj* (ca. 1847) **1 :** sheathed in iron armor — used esp. of naval vessels **2 :** so firm or secure as to be unbreakable: as **a :** BINDING ⟨an ~ oath⟩ **b :** having no obvious weakness ⟨an ~ case against the defendant⟩

²iron·clad \-ˌklad\ *n* (1862) **:** an armored naval vessel

iron curtain *n* (1819) **1 :** an impenetrable barrier ⟨the *iron curtain* between the ego and the unconscious —C. J. Rolo⟩ **2 :** a political, military, and ideological barrier that cuts off and isolates an area; *specif, often cap* **:** one isolating an area under Soviet control

iron·er \ˈī(-ə)r-nər\ *n* (1773) **:** one that irons; *specif* **:** MANGLE

iron·fisted \ˈī(-ə)rn-ˈfis-təd\ *adj* (1852) **1 :** STINGY, MISERLY **2 :** being both harsh and ruthless ⟨~ methods⟩

iron gray *n* (bef. 12c) **:** a slightly greenish dark gray

iron hand *n* (1703) **:** stern or rigorous control ⟨ruled with an *iron hand*⟩ — **iron·hand·ed** \ˌī(-ə)rn-ˈhan-dəd\ *adj* — **iron·hand·ed·ly** *adv* — **iron·hand·ed·ness** *n*

iron·heart·ed \ˌī(-ə)rn-ˈhärt-əd\ *adj* (1600) **:** CRUEL, HARD-HEARTED

iron horse *n* (1840) **:** LOCOMOTIVE 1

iron·ic \ī-ˈrän-ik *also* ir-ˈän-\ *or* **iron·i·cal** \-i-kəl\ *adj* (1576) **1 :** relating to, containing, or constituting irony **2 :** given to irony ***syn*** see SARCASTIC — **iron·i·cal·ly** \-i-k(ə-)lē\ *adv* — **iron·i·cal·ness** \-i-kəl-nəs\ *n*

iron·ing \ˈī(-ə)r-niŋ\ *n* (1710) **1 :** the action or process of smoothing or pressing with or as if with a heated iron **2 :** clothes ironed or to be ironed

ironing board *n* (1843) **:** a flat padded cloth-covered surface on which clothes are ironed

iro·nist \ˈī-rə-nəst\ *n* (1727) **:** one who uses irony esp. in the development of a literary work or theme

iron lung *n* (1932) **:** a device for artificial respiration in which rhythmic alternations in the air pressure in a chamber surrounding a patient's chest force air into and out of the lungs

iron maiden *n* (ca. 1895) **:** a supposed medieval torture device consisting of a hollow iron statue or coffin in the shape of a woman and lined with spikes which impaled the enclosed victim

iron man *n* (1914) **:** a man of unusual physical endurance

iron·mas·ter \ˈī(-ə)rn-ˌmas-tər\ *n* (1674) **:** a manufacturer of iron

iron·mon·ger \-ˌməŋ-gər, -ˌmäŋ-\ *n, Brit* (14c) **:** a dealer in iron and hardware

ironmon·gery \-g(ə-)rē\ *n* (1711) **:** something made of metal; *esp, Brit* **:** HARDWARE 1

iron out *vt* (1905) **1 :** to make smooth or flat by or as if by pressing **2 :** to resolve or work out a solution to ⟨*ironed out* their differences⟩

iron oxide *n* (1885) **:** any of several oxides of iron: as **a :** FERRIC OXIDE **b :** FERROUS OXIDE

iron pyrites *n* (1805) **:** PYRITE — called also *iron pyrite*

iron ration *n* (1876) **:** an emergency ration

iron·side \-ˌsīd\ *n* (13c) **:** a man of great strength or bravery

iron·stone \ˈī(-ə)rn-ˌstōn\ *n* (1522) **1 :** a hard sedimentary rock rich in iron; *esp* **:** a siderite in a coal region **2 :** IRONSTONE CHINA

ironstone china *n* (1825) **:** a hard heavy durable white pottery developed in England early in the 19th century

iron sulfide *n* (1885) **:** any of several sulfides of iron

iron·ware \ˈī(-ə)rn-ˌwa(ə)r, -ˌwe(ə)r\ *n* (15c) **:** articles made of iron

iron·weed \-ˌwēd\ *n* (1819) **:** any of several mostly weedy American composite plants (genus *Vernonia*) with alternate leaves and perfect red or purple tubular flowers in terminal cymose heads

iron·wood \-ˌwu̇d\ *n* (1657) **1 :** any of numerous trees and shrubs (as a hornbeam or hop hornbeam) with exceptionally tough or hard wood **2 :** the wood of an ironwood

iron·work \-ˌwərk\ *n* (15c) **1 :** work in iron; *also* **:** something made of iron **2** *pl but sing or pl in constr* **:** a mill or building where iron or steel is smelted or heavy iron or steel products are made — **iron·work·er** \-ˌwər-kər\ *n*

iro·ny \ˈī-rə-nē *also* ˈī(-ə)r-nē\ *n, pl* **-nies** [L *ironia,* fr. Gk *eirōnia,* fr. *eirōn* dissembler] (1502) **1 :** a pretense of ignorance and of willingness to learn from another assumed in order to make the other's false conceptions conspicuous by adroit questioning — called also *Socratic irony* **2 a :** the use of words to express something other than and esp. the opposite of the literal meaning **b :** a usu. humorous or sardonic literary style or form characterized by irony **c :** an ironic expression or utterance **3 a (1) :** incongruity between the actual result of a sequence of events and the normal or expected result **(2) :** an event or result marked by such incongruity **b :** incongruity between a situation developed in a drama and the accompanying words or actions that is understood by the audience but not by the characters in the play — called also *dramatic irony, tragic irony* ***syn*** see WIT

Ir·o·quoi·an \ˌir-ə-ˈkwȯi-ən\ *n* (1888) **1 :** a language family of eastern No. America including Cayuga, Cherokee, Erie, Mohawk, Onondaga, Oneida, Seneca, and Tuscarora **2 :** a member of any of the peoples constituting the Iroquois — **Iroquoian** *adj*

Ir·o·quois \ˈir-ə-ˌkwȯi *also* -ˌkwä\ *n, pl* **Iroquois** \-ˌkwȯi(z), -ˌkwä(z)\ [F, fr. Algonquin *Irinakhoiw,* lit., real adders] (1666) **1** *pl* **:** an American Indian confederacy of New York that consisted of the Cayuga, Mohawk, Oneida, Onondaga, and Seneca and later included the Tuscarora **2 :** a member of any of the Iroquois peoples

ir·ra·di·ance \ir-ˈād-ē-ən(t)s\ *n* (1667) **1 :** RADIANCE 1 **2 :** radiant flux density on a given surface usu. expressed in watts per square centimeter or square meter

ir·ra·di·ate \ir-ˈād-ē-ˌāt\ *vb* **-at·ed; -at·ing** [L *irradiatus,* pp. of *irradiare,* fr. *in-* + *radius* ray] *vt* (1603) **1 a :** to cast rays of light upon **:** ILLUMINATE **b :** to enlighten intellectually or spiritually **c :** to affect or treat by radiant energy (as heat); *specif* **:** to treat by exposure to radiation **2 :** to emit like rays of light **:** RADIATE ⟨*irradiating* strength and comfort⟩ ~ *vi, archaic* **:** to emit rays **:** SHINE — **ir·ra·di·a·tive** \-ˌāt-iv\ *adj* — **ir·ra·di·a·tor** \-ˌāt-ər\ *n*

ir·ra·di·a·tion \ir-ˌād-ē-ˈā-shən\ *n* (1599) **1 :** emission of radiant energy (as heat or light) **2 :** exposure to radiation (as X rays or alpha rays) **3 :** IRRADIANCE 2

ir·rad·i·ca·ble \ˈi(ə)r-ˈrad-i-kə-bəl\ *adj* [ML *irradicabilis,* fr. L *in-* + *radic-, radix* root — more at ROOT] (1728) **:** impossible to eradicate **:** DEEP-ROOTED — **ir·rad·i·ca·bly** \-blē\ *adv*

¹ir·ra·tio·nal \(ˈ)ir-ˈ(r)ash-nəl, -ən-ᵊl\ *adj* [ME, fr. L *irrationalis,* fr. *in-* + *rationalis* rational] (14c) **:** not rational: as **a (1) :** not endowed with reason or understanding **(2) :** lacking usual or normal mental clarity or coherence **b :** not governed by or according to reason ⟨~ fears⟩ **c** *Greek & Latin prosody* **(1)** *of a syllable* **:** having a quantity other than that required by the meter **(2)** *of a foot* **:** containing such a syllable **d (1) :** being an irrational number ⟨an ~ root of an equation⟩ **(2) :** having a numerical value that is an irrational number ⟨a length that is ~⟩ — **ir·ra·tio·nal·i·ty** \(ˌ)ir-ˌ(r)ash-ə-ˈnal-ət-ē\ *n* — **ir·ra·tio·nal·ly** \(ˈ)ir-ˈ(r)ash-nə-lē, -ən-ᵊl-ē\ *adv*

²irrational *n* (1646) **1 :** an irrational being **2 :** IRRATIONAL NUMBER

ir·ra·tio·nal·ism \(ˈ)ir-ˈ(r)ash-nəl-ˌiz-əm, -ən-ᵊl-\ *n* (1811) **1 :** a system emphasizing intuition, instinct, feeling, or faith rather than reason or holding that the universe is governed by irrational forces **2 :** the quality or state of being irrational — **ir·ra·tio·nal·ist** \-əst\ *n or adj* — **ir·ra·tio·nal·is·tic** \(ˌ)ir-ˌ(r)ash-nəl-ˈis-tik, -ən-ᵊl-\ *adj*

irrational number *n* (1551) **:** a number that can be expressed as an infinite decimal with no set of consecutive digits repeating itself indefinitely and that cannot be expressed as the quotient of two integers

ir·re·al \(ˈ)ir-ˈrē(-ə)l, -ˈri(-ə)l\ *adj* (1944) **:** not real

ir·re·al·i·ty \ˌir-ē-ˈal-ət-ē\ *n* (1803) **:** UNREALITY

ir·re·claim·able \ˌir-i-ˈklā-mə-bəl\ *adj* (1662) **:** incapable of being reclaimed — **ir·re·claim·ably** \-blē\ *adv*

¹ir·rec·on·cil·able \(ˌ)ir-ˌ(r)ek-ən-ˈsī-lə-bəl, (ˈ)ir-ˈ(r)ek-ən-ˌ\ *adj* (1599) **:** impossible to reconcile — **ir·rec·on·cil·abil·i·ty** \(ˌ)ir-ˌ(r)ek-ən-ˌsī-lə-ˈbil-ət-ē\ *n* — **ir·rec·on·cil·able·ness** \(ˌ)ir-ˌ(r)ek-ən-ˈsī-lə-bəl-nəs, (ˈ)ir-ˈ(r)ek-ən-ˌ\ *n* — **ir·rec·on·cil·ably** \-blē\ *adv*

²irreconcilable *n* (1748) **:** one that is irreconcilable; *esp* **:** a member of a group (as a political party) opposing compromise or collaboration

ir·re·cov·er·able \ˌir-i-ˈkəv-(ə-)rə-bəl\ *adj* (15c) **:** not capable of being recovered or rectified **:** IRREPARABLE — **ir·re·cov·er·able·ness** *n* — **ir·re·cov·er·ably** \-blē\ *adv*

ir·re·cu·sa·ble \ˌir-i-ˈkyü-zə-bəl\ *adj* [LL *irrecusabilis,* fr. L *in-* + *recusare* to reject, refuse — more at RECUSANCY] (1776) **:** not subject to exception or rejection — **ir·re·cu·sa·bly** \-blē\ *adv*

ir·re·deem·able \ˌir-i-ˈdē-mə-bəl\ *adj* (1609) **1 :** not redeemable: as **a :** not terminable by payment of the principal ⟨~ bond⟩ **b :** INCONVERTIBLE a **2 :** being beyond remedy **:** HOPELESS ⟨~ mistakes⟩ — **ir·re·deem·ably** \-blē\ *adv*

ir·re·den·ta \ˌir-i-ˈdent-ə\ *n* [It *Italia irredenta,* lit., unredeemed Italy, Italian-speaking territory not incorporated in Italy] (1914) **:** a territory historically or ethnically related to one political unit but under the political control of another

ir·re·den·tism \-ˈden-ˌtiz-əm\ *n* (1883) **:** a political principle or policy directed toward the incorporation of irredentas within the boundaries of their historically or ethnically related political unit — **ir·re·den·tist** \-ˈdent-əst\ *n or adj*

ir·re·duc·ible \ˌir-i-ˈd(y)ü-sə-bəl\ *adj* (1633) **:** impossible to transform into or restore to a desired or simpler condition ⟨an ~ matrix⟩; *specif* **:** incapable of being factored into polynomials of lower degree with coefficients in some given field (as the rational numbers) or integral domain (as the integers) ⟨~ polynomials⟩ ⟨an ~ equation⟩ — **ir·re·duc·ibil·i·ty** \-ˌd(y)ü-sə-ˈbil-ət-ē\ *n* — **ir·re·duc·ibly** \-ˈd(y)ü-sə-blē\ *adv*

ir·re·flex·ive \ˌir-i-ˈflek-siv\ *adj* (ca. 1890) **:** being a relation for which the reflexive property does not hold for any element of a given set

ir·re·form·able \ˌir-i-ˈfȯr-mə-bəl\ *adj* (1609) **1 :** incapable of being reformed **:** INCORRIGIBLE **2 :** not subject to revision or alteration ⟨~ dogma⟩ — **ir·re·form·abil·i·ty** \-ˌfȯr-mə-ˈbil-ət-ē\ *n*

ir·re·fra·ga·ble \(ˈ)ir-ˈ(r)ef-rə-gə-bəl, ˌir-i-ˈfrag-ə-\ *adj* [LL *irrefragabilis,* fr. L *in-* + *refragari* to oppose, fr. *re-* + *-fragari* (as in *suffragari* to vote for); akin to L *suffragium* suffrage] (1533) **1 :** impossible to refute ⟨~ arguments⟩ **2 :** impossible to break or alter ⟨~ rules⟩ — **ir·re·fra·ga·bil·i·ty** \(ˌ)ir-ˌ(r)ef-rə-gə-ˈbil-ət-ē, ˌir-i-ˌfrag-ə-\ *n* — **ir·ref·ra·ga·bly** \(ˈ)ir-ˈ(r)ef-rə-gə-blē, ˌir-i-ˈfrag-ə-\ *adv*

ir·re·fut·able \ˌir-i-ˈfyüt-ə-bəl, (ˈ)ir-ˈ(r)ef-yət-\ *adj* [LL *irrefutabilis,* fr. L *in-* + *refutare* to refute] (1620) **:** impossible to refute **:** INCONTROVERTIBLE ⟨~ proof⟩ — **ir·re·fut·abil·i·ty** \ˌir-i-ˌfyüt-ə-ˈbil-ət-ē, (ˌ)ir-ˌ(r)ef-yət-\ *n* — **ir·re·fut·ably** \ˌir-i-ˈfyüt-ə-blē, (ˈ)ir-ˈ(r)ef-yət-\ *adv*

ir·re·gard·less \ˌir-i-ˈgärd-ləs\ *adv* [prob. blend of *irrespective* and *regardless*] *nonstand* (ca. 1912) **:** REGARDLESS

[1]**ir·reg·u·lar** \(ˈ)ir-ˈ(r)eg-yə-lər\ *adj* [ME *irreguler,* fr. MF, fr. LL *irregularis* not in accordance with rule, fr. L *in-* + *regularis* regular] (14c) **1 a :** not being or acting in accord with laws, rules, or established custom ⟨~ conduct⟩ **b :** not conforming to the usual pattern of inflection ⟨~ verbs⟩; *specif* **:** STRONG 16 **c :** not following a usual or prescribed procedure; *esp, Brit* **:** celebrated without either proclamation of the banns or publication of intention to marry ⟨~ marriage⟩ **2 :** not belonging to or a part of a regular organized group; *specif* **:** not belonging to the regular army organization but raised for a special purpose ⟨~ troops⟩ **3 :** lacking perfect symmetry or evenness ⟨an ~ coastline⟩; *esp* **:** ZYGOMORPHIC ⟨~ flowers⟩ **4 :** lacking continuity or regularity esp. of occurrence or activity ⟨~ employment⟩ — **ir·reg·u·lar·ly** *adv*

syn IRREGULAR, ANOMALOUS, UNNATURAL mean not conforming to rule, law, or custom. IRREGULAR implies not conforming to a law or regulation imposed for the sake of uniformity in method, practice, or conduct ⟨*irregular* behavior⟩ ANOMALOUS implies not conforming to what might be expected because of the class or type to which it belongs or the laws that govern its existence ⟨an *anomalous* situation⟩ UNNATURAL suggests what is contrary to nature or to principles or standards felt to be essential to the well-being of civilized society ⟨*unnatural* cruelty⟩

[2]**irregular** *n* (15c) **:** one that is irregular: as **a :** a soldier who is not a member of a regular military force **b** *pl* **:** merchandise that has minor imperfections or that falls next below the manufacturer's standard for firsts

ir·reg·u·lar·i·ty \(ˌ)ir-ˌ(r)eg-yə-ˈlar-ət-ē\ *n, pl* **-ties** [ME *irregularite,* fr. MF *irregularité,* fr. ML *irregularitat-, irregularitas,* fr. LL *irregularis*] (14c) **1 :** something that is irregular (as improper or dishonest conduct) ⟨alleged *irregularities* in the city government⟩ **2 :** the quality or state of being irregular **3 :** CONSTIPATION

ir·rel·a·tive \(ˈ)ir-ˈ(r)el-ət-iv\ *adj* (1640) **:** not relative: **a :** not related **b :** IRRELEVANT — **ir·rel·a·tive·ly** *adv*

ir·rel·e·vance \(ˈ)ir-ˈ(r)el-ə-vən(t)s\ *n* (1847) **1 :** the quality or state of being irrelevant **2 :** something irrelevant

ir·rel·e·van·cy \-vən-sē\ *n, pl* **-cies** (1802) **:** IRRELEVANCE

ir·rel·e·vant \-vənt\ *adj* (1786) **:** not relevant **:** INAPPLICABLE ⟨that statement is ~ to your argument⟩ — **ir·rel·e·vant·ly** *adv*

ir·re·li·gion \ˌir-i-ˈlij-ən\ *n* [MF or L; MF, fr. L *irreligion-, irreligio,* fr. *in-* + *religion-, religio* religion] (1598) **:** the quality or state of being irreligious — **ir·re·li·gion·ist** \-ˈlij-(ə-)nəst\ *n*

ir·re·li·gious \-ˈlij-əs\ *adj* (15c) **1 :** neglectful of religion **:** lacking religious emotions, doctrines, or practices ⟨so ~ that they exploit popular religion for professional purposes —G. B. Shaw⟩ **2 :** indicating lack of religion — **ir·re·li·gious·ly** *adv*

ir·re·me·able \(ˈ)ir-ˈ(r)ē-mē-ə-bəl\ *adj* [L *irremeabilis,* fr. *in-* + *remeare* to go back, fr. *re-* + *meare* to go — more at PERMEATE] *archaic* (1569) **:** offering no possibility of return

ir·re·me·di·a·ble \ˌir-i-ˈmēd-ē-ə-bəl\ *adj* [L *irremediabilis,* fr. *in-* + *remediabilis* remediable] (15c) **:** not remediable; *specif* **:** INCURABLE — **ir·re·me·di·a·ble·ness** *n* — **ir·re·me·di·a·bly** \-blē\ *adv*

ir·re·mov·able \-ˈmü-və-bəl\ *adj* (1598) **:** not removable — **ir·re·mov·abil·i·ty** \-ˌmü-və-ˈbil-ət-ē\ *n* — **ir·re·mov·ably** \-ˈmü-və-blē\ *adv*

ir·rep·a·ra·ble \(ˈ)ir-ˈ(r)ep-(ə-)rə-bəl *also* ÷ ˌir-(r)ə-ˈpar-ə-bəl\ *adj* [ME, fr. MF, fr. L *irreparabilis,* fr. *in-* + *reparabilis* reparable] (15c) **:** not reparable **:** IRREMEDIABLE ⟨~ damage⟩ — **ir·rep·a·ra·ble·ness** *n* — **ir·rep·a·ra·bly** \-blē\ *adv*

ir·re·peal·able \ˌir-i-ˈpē-lə-bəl\ *adj* (1633) **:** not repealable — **ir·re·peal·abil·i·ty** \-ˌpē-lə-ˈbil-ət-ē\ *n*

ir·re·place·able \-ˈplā-sə-bəl\ *adj* (1807) **:** not replaceable — **ir·re·place·abil·i·ty** \-ˌplā-sə-ˈbil-ət-ē\ *n* — **ir·re·place·able·ness** \-ˈplā-sə-bəl-nəs\ *n* — **ir·re·place·ably** \-blē\ *adv*

ir·re·press·ible \-ˈpres-ə-bəl\ *adj* (1811) **:** impossible to repress, restrain, or control ⟨~ curiosity⟩ — **ir·re·press·ibil·i·ty** \-ˌpres-ə-ˈbil-ət-ē\ *n* — **ir·re·press·ibly** \-ˈpres-ə-blē\ *adv*

ir·re·proach·able \-ˈprō-chə-bəl\ *adj* (1634) **:** not reproachable **:** BLAMELESS, IMPECCABLE ⟨~ conduct⟩ — **ir·re·proach·abil·i·ty** \-ˌprō-chə-ˈbil-ət-ē\ *n* — **ir·re·proach·able·ness** \-ˈprō-chə-bəl-nəs\ *n* — **ir·re·proach·ably** \-blē\ *adv*

ir·re·pro·duc·ible \(ˈ)ir-ˌrē-prə-ˈd(y)ü-sə-bəl\ *adj* (1868) **:** not reproducible — **ir·re·pro·duc·ibil·i·ty** \-ˌd(y)ü-sə-ˈbil-ət-ē\ *n*

ir·re·sist·ible \ˌir-i-ˈzis-tə-bəl\ *adj* (1597) **:** impossible to resist ⟨an ~ attraction⟩ — **ir·re·sist·ibil·i·ty** \-ˌzis-tə-ˈbil-ət-ē\ *n* — **ir·re·sist·ible·ness** \-ˈzis-tə-bəl-nəs\ *n* — **ir·re·sist·ibly** \-blē\ *adv*

ir·re·sol·u·ble \-ˈzäl-yə-bəl\ *adj* [L *irresolubilis,* fr. *in-* + *resolvere* to resolve] (1666) **1** *archaic* **:** INDISSOLUBLE **2 :** having or admitting of no solution or explanation

ir·res·o·lute \(ˈ)ir-ˈ(r)ez-ə-ˌlüt, -lət\ *adj* (1579) **:** uncertain how to act or proceed **:** VACILLATING — **ir·res·o·lute·ly** \-ˌlüt-lē, -lət-; (ˌ)ir-ˌ(r)ez-ə-ˈlüt-\ *adv* — **ir·res·o·lute·ness** \-ˌlüt-nəs, -lət-, -ˈlüt-\ *n* — **ir·res·o·lu·tion** \(ˌ)ir-ˌ(r)ez-ə-ˈlü-shən\ *n*

ir·re·solv·able \ˌir-i-ˈzäl-və-bəl, -ˈzȯl-\ *adj* (1660) **:** incapable of being resolved; *also* **:** not analyzable

ir·re·spec·tive of \ˌir-i-ˈspek-tiv-\ *prep* (1839) **:** regardless of ⟨free public schools open to all *irrespective of* race, color, or creed —J. B. Conant⟩

ir·re·spon·si·bil·i·ty \ˌir-i-ˌspän(t)-sə-ˈbil-ət-ē\ *n* (ca. 1818) **1 :** the quality or state of being irresponsible **2 :** an irresponsible act or individual

[1]**ir·re·spon·si·ble** \-ˈspän(t)-sə-bəl\ *adj* (1648) **:** not responsible: as **a :** not answerable to higher authority ⟨an ~ dictatorship⟩ **b :** said or done with no sense of responsibility ⟨~ accusations⟩ **c :** lacking a sense of responsibility **d :** unable esp. mentally or financially to bear responsibility — **ir·re·spon·si·ble·ness** *n* — **ir·re·spon·si·bly** \-blē\ *adv*

[2]**irresponsible** *n* (1894) **:** one that is irresponsible

ir·re·spon·sive \ˌir-i-ˈspän(t)-siv\ *adj* (ca. 1846) **:** not responsive; *esp* **:** not able, ready, or inclined to respond — **ir·re·spon·sive·ness** *n*

ir·re·triev·able \ˌir-i-ˈtrē-və-bəl\ *adj* (1695) **:** not retrievable **:** impossible to regain or recover — **ir·re·triev·abil·i·ty** \-ˌtrē-və-ˈbil-ət-ē\ *n* — **ir·re·triev·ably** \ˌir-i-ˈtrē-və-blē\ *adv*

ir·rev·er·ence \(ˈ)ir-ˈ(r)ev-(ə-)rən(t)s, -ˈ(r)ev-ərn(t)s\ *n* (14c) **1 :** lack of reverence **2 :** an irreverent act or utterance

ir·rev·er·ent \-(ə-)rənt, -ərnt\ *adj* [L *irreverent-, irreverens,* fr. *in-* + *reverent-, reverens* reverent] (15c) **:** lacking proper respect or seriousness; *also* **:** SATIRIC — **ir·rev·er·ent·ly** *adv*

ir·re·vers·ible \ˌir-i-ˈvər-sə-bəl\ *adj* (1630) **:** not reversible — **ir·re·vers·ibil·i·ty** \-ˌvər-sə-ˈbil-ət-ē\ *n* — **ir·re·vers·ibly** \-ˈvər-sə-blē\ *adv*

ir·re·vo·ca·ble \(ˈ)ir-ˈ(r)ev-ə-kə-bəl *sometimes* ˌir-(r)ə-ˈvō-kə-\ *adj* [ME, fr. L *irrevocabilis,* fr. *in-* + *revocabilis* revocable] (14c) **:** not possible to revoke **:** UNALTERABLE ⟨an ~ decision⟩ — **ir·re·vo·ca·bil·i·ty** \(ˌ)ir-ˌ(r)ev-ə-kə-ˈbil-ət-ē, ˌir-(r)ə-ˌvō-kə-\ *n* — **ir·re·vo·ca·ble·ness** \(ˈ)ir-ˈ(r)ev-ə-kə-bəl-nəs, ˌir-(r)ə-ˈvō-kə-\ *n* — **ir·re·vo·ca·bly** \-blē\ *adv*

irridenta *var of* IRREDENTA

ir·ri·gate \ˈir-ə-ˌgāt\ *vb* **-gat·ed; -gat·ing** [L *irrigatus,* pp. of *irrigare,* fr. *in-* + *rigare* to water; akin to OHG *regan* rain — more at RAIN] *vt* (1615) **1 :** WET, MOISTEN: as **a :** to supply (as land) with water by artificial means **b :** to flush (a body part) with a stream of liquid (as in removing a foreign body or medicating) **2 :** to refresh as if by watering ~ *vi* **:** to practice irrigation — **ir·ri·ga·tion** \ˌir-ə-ˈgā-shən\ *n* — **ir·ri·ga·tor** \ˈir-ə-ˌgāt-ər\ *n*

ir·ri·ta·bil·i·ty \ˌir-ət-ə-ˈbil-ət-ē\ *n, pl* **-ties** (1755) **1 :** the property of protoplasm and of living organisms that permits them to react to stimuli **2 :** the quality or state of being irritable: as **a :** quick excitability to annoyance, impatience, or anger **:** PETULANCE **b :** abnormal or excessive excitability of an organ or part of the body

ir·ri·ta·ble \ˈir-ət-ə-bəl\ *adj* (1662) **:** capable of being irritated: as **a :** easily exasperated or excited **b :** responsive to stimuli — **ir·ri·ta·ble·ness** *n* — **ir·ri·ta·bly** \-blē\ *adv*

[1]**ir·ri·tant** \ˈir-ə-tənt\ *adj* (1636) **:** causing irritation; *specif* **:** tending to produce physical irritation

[2]**irritant** *n* (1802) **:** something that irritates or excites

ir·ri·tate \ˈir-ə-ˌtāt\ *vb* **-tat·ed; -tat·ing** [L *irritatus,* pp. of *irritare*] *vt* (1598) **1 :** to provoke impatience, anger, or displeasure in **:** ANNOY **2 :** to induce irritability in or of ~ *vi* **:** to cause or induce displeasure or irritation — **ir·ri·tat·ing·ly** \-ˌtāt-iŋ-lē\ *adv*

ir·ri·tat·ed *adj* (1595) **:** subjected to irritation; *esp* **:** roughened, reddened, or inflamed by an irritant ⟨~ eyes⟩

ir·ri·ta·tion \ˌir-ə-ˈtā-shən\ *n* (15c) **1 a :** the act of irritating **b :** something that irritates **c :** the state of being irritated **2 :** a condition of irritability, soreness, roughness, or inflammation of a bodily part

ir·ri·ta·tive \ˈir-ə-ˌtāt-iv\ *adj* (1644) **1 :** serving to excite **:** IRRITATING **2 :** accompanied with or produced by irritation ⟨~ coughing⟩

ir·ro·ta·tion·al \ˌir-(r)ō-ˈtā-shnəl, -shən-ᵊl\ *adj* (1875) **1 :** not rotating or involving rotation ⟨an ~ electric field⟩ **2 :** free of vortices ⟨~ flow⟩

ir·rupt \(ˈ)i(ə)r-ˈ(r)əpt\ *vi* [L *irruptus,* pp. of *irrumpere,* lit., to break in, fr. *in-* + *rumpere* to break — more at RUPTURE] (1886) **1 :** to rush in forcibly or violently **2** *of a natural population* **:** to undergo a sudden upsurge in numbers esp. when natural ecological balances and checks are disturbed **3 :** ERUPT 1c ⟨the crowd ~*ed* in a fervor of patriotism —*Time*⟩ — **ir·rup·tion** \-ˈ(r)əp-shən\ *n*

ir·rup·tive \-ˈ(r)əp-tiv\ *adj* (1593) **1 :** irrupting or tending to irrupt **2** *of an igneous rock* **:** INTRUSIVE — **ir·rup·tive·ly** *adv*

is [ME, fr. OE; akin to OHG *ist* is (fr. *sīn* to be), L *est* (fr. *esse* to be), Gk *esti* (fr. *einai* to be)] (bef. 12c) *pres 3d sing of* BE, *dial pres 1st & 2d sing of* BE, *substand pres pl of* BE

is- *or* **iso-** *comb form* [LL, fr. Gk, fr. *isos* equal] **1 :** equal **:** homogeneous **:** uniform ⟨*is*acoustic⟩ **2 :** isomeric ⟨*iso*cyanate⟩ **3 :** for or from different individuals of the same species ⟨*iso*agglutination⟩

Isaac \ˈī-zik, -zək\ *n* [LL, fr. Gk, fr. Heb *Yiṣḥāq*] **:** the son of Abraham and father of Jacob according to the account in Genesis

Isa·iah \ī-ˈzā-ə, *chiefly Brit* -ˈzī-\ *n* [Heb *Yĕshaʽyāhū*] **1 :** a major Hebrew prophet in Judah about 740 to 701 B.C. **2 :** a prophetic book of canonical Jewish and Christian Scripture — see BIBLE table

Isa·ias \-əs\ *n* [LL, fr. Gk *Ēsaias,* fr. Heb *Yĕshaʽyāhū*] **:** ISAIAH

is·al·lo·bar \(ˈ)ī-ˈsal-ə-ˌbär\ *n* [ISV *is-* + *all-* + *-bar* (as in *isobar*)] (1909) **:** an imaginary line or a line on a chart connecting the places of equal change of atmospheric pressure within a specified time — **is·al·lo·bar·ic** \ˌī-ˌsal-ə-ˈbär-ik, -ˈbar-\ *adj*

is·ba \iz-ˈbä\ *n* [Russ *izba*] (ca. 1784) **:** a Russian log hut

isch·emia \is-ˈkē-mē-ə\ *n* [NL *ischaemia,* fr. *ischaemus* styptic, fr. Gk *ischaimos,* fr. *ischein* to restrain (akin to Gk *echein* to hold) + *haima* blood — more at SCHEME] (ca. 1860) **:** localized tissue anemia due to obstruction of the inflow of arterial blood — **isch·emic** \-mik\ *adj*

is·chi·um \ˈis-kē-əm\ *n, pl* **is·chia** \-ə\ [L, hip joint, fr. Gk *ischion*] (1646) **:** the dorsal and posterior of the three principal bones composing either half of the pelvis — **is·chi·al** \-əl\ *adj*

-ise \ˌīz\ *vb suffix, chiefly Brit* **:** -IZE

is·en·tro·pic \ˌīs-ᵊn-ˈtrō-pik, -ˈträp-ik\ *adj* (1873) **:** of or relating to equal or constant entropy; *esp* **:** taking place without change of entropy — **is·en·tro·pi·cal·ly** \-ˈtrō-pi-k(ə-)lē, -ˈträp-i-\ *adv*

Iseult \is-ˈült, iz-\ *n* [OF *Isolt, Iseut*] **:** ISOLDE

-ish \ish\ *adj suffix* [ME, fr. OE *-isc;* akin to OHG *-isc,* -ish, Gk *-iskos,* dim. suffix] **1 :** of, relating to, or being — chiefly in adjectives indicating nationality or ethnic group ⟨Finn*ish*⟩ **2 a :** characteristic of ⟨boy*ish*⟩ ⟨London*ish*⟩ **b :** inclined or liable to ⟨book*ish*⟩ ⟨qualm*ish*⟩ **3 a :** having a touch or trace of ⟨summer*ish*⟩ **:** somewhat ⟨purpl*ish*⟩ **b :** having the approximate age of ⟨forty*ish*⟩ **c :** being or occurring at the approximate time of ⟨eight*ish*⟩

Ish·ma·el \ˈish-(ˌ)mā-əl, -mē-\ *n* [Heb *Yishmāʽēl*] **1 :** the outcast son of Abraham and Hagar according to the account in Genesis **2 :** a social outcast

Ish·ma·el·ite \-ə-ˌlīt\ *n* (14c) **1 :** a descendant of Ishmael **2 :** ISHMAEL 2 — **Ish·ma·el·it·ish** \-ˌlīt-ish\ *adj* — **Ish·ma·el·it·ism** \-ˌlīt-ˌiz-əm\ *n*

isin·glass \ˈīz-ᵊn-ˌglas, ˈī-ziŋ-\ *n* [prob. by folk etymology fr. obs. D *huizenblas,* fr. MD *huusblase,* fr. *huus* sturgeon + *blase* bladder] (1545) **1 :** a semitransparent whitish very pure gelatin prepared from the air bladders of fishes (as sturgeons) and used esp. as a clarifying agent and in jellies and glue **2 :** MICA

Isis \ˈī-səs\ *n* [L *Isid-, Isis,* fr. Gk, fr. Egypt *jst*] **:** an Egyptian nature goddess and wife and sister of Osiris

Is·lam \is-ˈläm, iz-, -ˈlam, ˈis-ˌ, ˈiz-ˌ\ *n* [Ar *islām* submission (to the will of God)] (1817) **1 :** the religious faith of Muslims including belief in Allah as the sole deity and in Muhammad as his prophet **2 a :** the civilization erected upon Islamic faith **b :** the group of modern nations in which Islam is the dominant religion — **Is·lam·ic** \is-ˈläm-ik, iz-, -ˈlam-\ *adj* — **Is·lam·ics** \-iks\ *n pl but sing or pl in constr*

Islamic calendar *n* (1974) **:** a lunar calendar reckoned from the Hegira in A.D. 622 and organized in cycles of 30 years — see MONTH table

Islamic era *n* (1975) **:** the era used in Muslim countries for numbering Islamic calendar years since the Hegira

Is·lam·ism \is-ˈläm-ˌiz-əm, iz-ˈläm-, -ˈlam-; ˈiz-ləm-\ *n* (ca. 1747) **:** the faith, doctrine, or cause of Islam — **Is·lam·ist** \-əst\ *n*

Is·lam·ize \ˈiz-lə-ˌmīz; is-ˈläm-ˌīz, iz-ˈläm-, -ˈlam-\ *vt* **-ized; -iz·ing** (ca. 1846) **:** to make Islamic; *esp* **:** to convert to Islam — **Is·lam·iza·tion** \ˌiz-lə-mə-ˈzā-shən; is-ˌläm-ə-, iz-ˌläm-, -ˌlam-\ *n*

[1]**is·land** \ˈī-lənd\ *n* [alter. (influenced by OF *isle*) of earlier *iland,* fr. ME, fr. OE *igland* (akin to ON *eyland*), fr. *ig* island + *land;* akin to OHG *auwia* island, L *aqua* water, OE *ēa* river] (bef. 12c) **1 :** a tract of land surrounded by water and smaller than a continent **2 :** something resembling an island esp. in its isolated or surrounded position **3 a :** SAFETY ISLAND **b :** SAFETY ZONE **4 :** a superstructure on the deck of a ship **5 :** an isolated group or area; *esp* **:** an isolated ethnological group

[2]**island** *vt* (1661) **1 a :** to make into or as if into an island **b :** to dot with or as if with islands **2 :** ISOLATE

is·land·er \ˈī-lən-dər\ *n* (1550) **:** a native or inhabitant of an island

is·land–hop \ˈī-lənd-ˌhäp\ *vi* (1944) **:** to travel from island to island in a chain

island universe *n* (ca. 1867) **:** a galaxy other than the Milky Way

[1]**isle** \ˈī(ə)l\ *n* [ME, fr. OF, fr. L *insula*] (13c) **:** ISLAND; *esp* **:** ISLET

[2]**isle** *vt* **isled; isl·ing** (1570) **1 :** to make an isle of **2 :** to place on or as if on an isle

is·let \ˈī-lət\ *n* (1538) **:** a little island

islet of Lang·er·hans \-ˈläŋ-ər-ˌhänz, -ˌhän(t)s\ [Paul *Langerhans* †1888 Ger. physician] (1896) **:** any of the groups of small slightly granular endocrine cells that form anastomosing trabeculae among the tubules and alveoli of the pancreas and secrete insulin and glucagon — called also *islet*

ism \ˈiz-əm\ *n* [*-ism*] (1680) **:** a distinctive doctrine, cause, or theory

-ism \ˌiz-əm\ *n suffix* [ME *-isme,* fr. MF & L; MF, partly fr. L *-isma* (fr. Gk) & partly fr. L *-ismus,* fr. Gk *-ismos;* Gk *-isma* & *-ismos,* fr. verbs in *-izein* -ize] **1 a :** act **:** practice **:** process ⟨critic*ism*⟩ ⟨plagiar*ism*⟩ **b :** manner of action or behavior characteristic of a (specified) person or thing ⟨animal*ism*⟩ **2 a :** state **:** condition **:** property ⟨barbarian*ism*⟩ **b :** abnormal state or condition resulting from excess of a (specified) thing ⟨alcohol*ism*⟩ or marked by resemblance to (such) a person or thing ⟨mongol*ism*⟩ **3 a :** doctrine **:** theory **:** cult ⟨Buddh*ism*⟩ **b :** adherence to a system or a class of principles ⟨stoic*ism*⟩ **4 :** characteristic or peculiar feature or trait ⟨colloquial*ism*⟩

isn't \ˈiz-ᵊnt, -ᵊn, *dial also* ˈid-ᵊn(t) *or* (ˈ)in(t)\ **:** is not

iso- — see IS-

iso·ag·glu·ti·na·tion \ˈī-(ˌ)sō-ə-ˌglüt-ᵊn-ˈā-shən\ *n* (1907) **:** agglutination of an agglutinogen of one individual by the serum of another of the same species — **iso·ag·glu·ti·na·tive** \-ˈglüt-ᵊn-ˌāt-iv\ *adj*

iso·ag·glu·ti·nin \ˌī-(ˌ)sō-ə-ˈglüt-ᵊn-ən\ *n* (ca. 1903) **:** an agglutinin from one individual that is specific for the cells of other individuals of the same species

iso·ag·glu·tin·o·gen \ˈī-(ˌ)sō-ˌag-lü-ˈtin-ə-jən\ *n* (1926) **:** a substance capable of provoking formation of or reacting with an isoagglutinin

iso·al·lox·a·zine \ˌī-(ˌ)sō-ə-ˈläk-sə-ˌzēn\ *n* [*iso-* + *all*antoic + *ox*alic + *azine*] (1936) **:** a yellow solid $C_{10}H_6N_4O_2$ that is the parent compound of various flavins (as riboflavin)

iso·an·ti·body \ˌī-(ˌ)sō-ˈant-i-ˌbäd-ē\ *n* (1919) **:** an antibody produced by a member of a species lacking a particular alloantigen when it is introduced into its system — called also *alloantibody*

iso·an·ti·gen \-ˈant-i-jən\ *n* [ISV] (1936) **:** ALLOANTIGEN — **iso·an·ti·gen·ic** \ˈī-(ˌ)sō-ˌant-i-ˈjen-ik\ *adj*

iso·bar \ˈī-sə-ˌbär\ *n* [ISV *is-* + *-bar* (fr. Gk *baros* weight); akin to Gk *barys* heavy — more at GRIEVE] (ca. 1864) **1 :** an imaginary line or a line on a map or chart connecting or marking places on the surface of the earth where the height of the barometer reduced to sea level is the same either at a given time or for a certain period **2 :** one of two or more atoms or elements having the same atomic weights or mass numbers but different atomic numbers — **iso·bar·ic** \ˌī-sə-ˈbär-ik, -ˈbar-\ *adj*

iso·bu·tyl·ene \ˌī-sō-ˈbyüt-ᵊl-ˌēn\ *n* [ISV] (1872) **:** a gaseous butylene C_4H_8 used esp. in making butyl rubber and gasoline components

iso·ca·lo·ric \-kə-ˈlȯr-ik, -ˈlōr-, -ˈlär-; -ˈkal-ə-rik\ *adj* (1922) **:** having similar caloric values ⟨~ diets⟩

iso·car·box·az·id \ˌī-sō-ˌkär-ˈbäk-sə-zəd\ *n* [*iso-* + *carb-* + *ox-* + *az-* + *-id*] (1959) **:** an antidepressant drug $C_{12}H_{13}N_3O_2$

iso·chro·mat·ic \ˌī-sə-krō-ˈmat-ik\ *adj* (1884) **:** ORTHOCHROMATIC

iso·chro·mo·some \-ˈkrō-mə-ˌsōm, -ˌzōm\ *n* (1939) **:** a chromosome with identical arms believed to be derived from a telocentric chromosome by fusion of two daughter chromosomes

iso·chron \ˈī-sə-ˌkrän\ *or* **iso·chrone** \-ˌkrōn\ *n* [ISV *is-* + *-chron* (fr. Gk *chronos* time)] (1881) **:** a line on a chart connecting points at which an event occurs simultaneously or which represents the same time or time difference

iso·chro·nal \ī-ˈsäk-rən-ᵊl, ˌī-sə-ˈkrōn-\ *adj* [Gk *isochronos,* fr. *is-* + *chronos* time] (ca. 1680) **:** uniform in time **:** having equal duration **:** recurring at regular intervals — **iso·chro·nal·ly** \-ᵊl-ē\ *adv* — **iso·chro·nism** \ī-ˈsäk-rə-ˌniz-əm, ˌī-sə-ˈkrō-\ *n*

iso·chro·nous \ī-ˈsäk-rə-nəs, ˌī-sə-ˈkrō-\ *adj* [Gk *isochronos*] (1706) **:** ISOCHRONAL — **iso·chro·nous·ly** *adv*

iso·cit·ric acid \ˌī-sə-ˌsi-trik-\ *n* (1869) **:** a crystalline isomer of citric acid that occurs esp. as an intermediate stage in the Krebs cycle

[1]**iso·cli·nal** \ˌī-sə-ˈklīn-ᵊl\ *adj* [ISV] (1839) **:** relating to, having, or indicating equality of inclination or dip — **iso·cli·nal·ly** \-ᵊl-ē\ *adv*

[2]**isoclinal** *n* (1889) **:** ISOCLINIC LINE

iso·clin·ic \ˌī-sə-ˈklin-ik\ *adj* [ISV] (ca. 1855) **:** ISOCLINAL — **iso·clin·i·cal·ly** \-ˈklin-i-k(ə-)lē\ *adv*

isoclinic line *n* (1892) **:** a line on a map or chart joining points on the earth's surface at which a magnetic needle has the same inclination to the plumb line

iso·cy·a·nate \ˌī-sō-ˈsī-ə-ˌnāt, -nət\ *n* [ISV] (1872) **:** a salt or ester of isomeric cyanic acid used esp. in plastics and adhesives

iso·cy·clic \-ˈsī-klik, -ˈsik-lik\ *adj* [ISV] (1900) **:** having or being a ring composed of atoms of only one element; *esp* **:** CARBOCYCLIC

iso·di·a·met·ric \-ˌdī-ə-ˈme-trik\ *adj* [ISV] (ca. 1879) **:** having equal diameters

iso·dose \ˈī-sə-ˌdōs\ *adj* [ISV] (ca. 1922) **:** of or relating to points or zones in a medium that receive equal doses of radiation

iso·dy·nam·ic \ˌī-sō-dī-ˈnam-ik\ *adj* [ISV] (1837) **1 :** connecting points at which the magnetic intensity is the same ⟨~ line⟩ **2 :** of or relating to equality or uniformity of force

iso·elec·tric \ˌī-sō-i-ˈlek-trik\ *adj* [ISV] (1877) **1 :** having or representing zero difference of electric potential **2 :** being the pH at which the electrolyte will not migrate in an electrical field ⟨the ~ point of a protein⟩

iso·elec·tron·ic \-i-ˌlek-ˈträn-ik\ *adj* [ISV] (1926) **:** having the same number of electrons or valence electrons — **iso·elec·tron·i·cal·ly** \-i-k(ə-)lē\ *adv*

iso·en·zyme \-ˈen-ˌzīm\ *n* (1960) **:** any of two or more chemically distinct but functionally similar enzymes — **iso·en·zy·mat·ic** \ˈī-sō-ˌen-zə-ˈmat-ik, -zī-\ *adj* — **iso·en·zy·mic** \-en-ˈzī-mik\ *adj*

iso·ga·mete \ˌī-sō-gə-ˈmēt, -ˈgam-ˌēt\ *n* [ISV] (1891) **:** a gamete indistinguishable in form or size or behavior from another gamete with which it can unite to form a zygote — **iso·ga·met·ic** \-gə-ˈmet-ik\ *adj*

isog·a·mous \ī-ˈsäg-ə-məs\ *adj* [prob. fr. (assumed) NL *isogamus,* fr. *is-* + *-gamus* -gamous] (1887) **:** having or involving isogametes — compare HETEROGAMOUS — **isog·a·my** \-mē\ *n*

iso·ge·ne·ic \ˌī-sō-jə-ˈnē-ik, -ˈnā-\ *adj* [*is-* + *-geneic* (as in *syngeneic*)] (ca. 1963) **:** SYNGENEIC ⟨an ~ graft⟩

iso·gen·ic \-ˈjen-ik\ *adj* [*is-* + *gene* + *-ic*] (ca. 1931) **:** characterized by essentially identical genes ⟨identical twins are ~⟩

iso·gloss \ˈī-sə-ˌgläs, -ˌglȯs\ *n* [ISV *is-* + Gk *glōssa* language — more at GLOSS] (1925) **1 :** a boundary line between places or regions that differ in a particular linguistic feature **2 :** a line on a map representing an isogloss — **iso·gloss·al** \ˌī-sə-ˈgläs-əl, -ˈglȯ-səl\ *adj* — **iso·gloss·ic** \-ˈgläs-ik, -ˈglȯ-sik\ *adj*

iso·go·nal \ī-ˈsäg-ən-ᵊl, ˌī-sə-ˈgōn-\ *adj* [ISV *is-* + Gk *gōnia* angle — more at -GON] (ca. 1864) **:** of, relating to, or having equal angles

[1]**iso·gon·ic** \ˌī-sə-ˈgän-ik\ *or* **isogonal** *n* (1892) **:** ISOGONIC LINE

[2]**isogonic** *adj* [*isogony,* fr. *is-* + *-gony*] (1924) **:** exhibiting equivalent relative growth of parts such that size relations remain constant — **isog·o·ny** \ī-ˈsäg-ə-nē\ *n*

isogonic line *n* (1851) **:** an imaginary line or a line on a map joining points on the earth's surface at which the magnetic declination is the same

iso·graft \ˈī-sə-ˌgraft\ *n* (1909) **:** HOMOGRAFT — **isograft** *vt*

iso·gram \ˈī-sə-ˌgram\ *n* (ca. 1889) **:** a line on a map or chart along which there is a constant value (as of temperature, pressure, or rainfall)

iso·hel \ˈī-sō-ˌhel\ *n* [*is-* + Gk *hēlios* sun — more at SOLAR] (ca. 1904) **:** a line drawn on a map or chart connecting places of equal duration of sunshine

iso·hy·et \ˌī-sō-ˈhī-ət\ *n* [ISV *is-* + Gk *hyetos* rain — more at HYET-] (1899) **:** a line on a map or chart connecting areas of equal rainfall — **iso·hy·et·al** \-ət-əl\ *adj*

iso·la·ble \ˈī-sə-lə-bəl *also* ˈis-ə-\ *also* **iso·lat·able** \-ˌlāt-ə-bəl\ *adj* (1855) **:** capable of being isolated

[1]**iso·late** \ˈī-sə-ˌlāt *also* ˈis-ə-\ *vt* **-lat·ed; -lat·ing** [back-formation fr. *isolated* set apart, fr. F *isolé,* fr. It *isolato,* fr. *isola* island, fr. L *insula*] (1807) **1 :** to set apart from others; *also* **:** QUARANTINE **2 :** to select from among others; *esp* **:** to separate from another substance so as to obtain pure or in a free state **3 :** INSULATE — **iso·la·tor** \-ˌlāt-ər\ *n*

[2]**iso·late** \-lət, -ˌlāt\ *adj* (1819) **:** being alone **:** SOLITARY, ISOLATED

[3]**iso·late** \-lət, -ˌlāt\ *n* (ca. 1890) **1 :** a product of isolating **:** an individual, population, or kind obtained by or resulting from selection or separation **2 :** an individual socially withdrawn or removed from society

iso·lat·ed *adj* (1763) **1 :** occurring alone or once **:** UNIQUE **2 :** SPORADIC

iso·la·tion \ˌī-sə-ˈlā-shən *also* ˌis-ə-\ *n* (1833) **:** the action of isolating **:** the condition of being isolated ***syn*** see SOLITUDE

iso·la·tion·ism \-shə-ˌniz-əm\ *n* (1922) **:** a policy of national isolation by abstention from alliances and other international political and economic relations — **iso·la·tion·ist** \-sh(ə-)nəst\ *n or adj*

Isol·de \i-ˈzōl-də\ *n* [G, fr. OF *Isolt, Iseut*] **1 :** an Irish princess married to King Mark of Cornwall and loved by Tristram **2 :** the daughter of the King of Brittany and wife of Tristram

iso·leu·cine \ˌī-sō-ˈlü-ˌsēn\ *n* [ISV] (1903) **:** a crystalline essential amino acid $C_6H_{13}NO_2$ isomeric with leucine

iso·line \ˈī-(ˌ)sō-ˌlīn\ *n* (1944) **:** ISOGRAM

isol·o·gous \ī-ˈsäl-ə-gəs\ *adj* [ISV *is-* + *-logous* (as in *homologous*)] (1884) **:** relating to or being any of two or more compounds of related structure and a characteristic difference of composition other than CH_2 or a multiple thereof — **iso·logue** *or* **iso·log** \ˈī-sə-ˌlȯg, -ˌläg\ *n*

iso·mag·net·ic \ˌī-sō-mag-ˈnet-ik\ *adj* [ISV] (1897) **1 :** of or relating to points of equal magnetic intensity or of equal value of a component of such intensity **2 :** connecting isomagnetic points

iso·mer \ˈī-sə-mər\ *n* [ISV, back-formation fr. *isomeric*] (1866) **:** a compound, radical, ion, or nuclide isomeric with one or more others

isom·er·ase \ī-ˈsäm-ə-ˌrās, -ˌrāz\ *n* (1927) **:** an enzyme that catalyzes the conversion of its substrate to an isomeric form

iso·mer·ic \ˌī-sə-ˈmer-ik\ *adj* [ISV, fr. Gk *isomerēs* equally divided, fr. *is-* + *meros* part — more at MERIT] (1838) : of, relating to, or exhibiting isomerism

isom·er·ism \ī-ˈsäm-ə-ˌriz-əm\ *n* (1839) **1** : the relation of two or more compounds, radicals, or ions that contain the same numbers of atoms of the same elements but differ in structural arrangement and properties **2** : the relation of two or more nuclides with the same mass numbers and atomic numbers but different energy states and rates of radioactive decay **3** : the condition of having or being made up of corresponding parts or segments

isom·er·ize \ī-ˈsäm-ə-ˌrīz\ *vb* **-ized; -iz·ing** *vi* (1891) : to become changed into an isomeric form ~ *vt* : to cause to isomerize — **isom·er·iza·tion** \-ˌsäm-ə-rə-ˈzā-shən\ *n*

isom·er·ous \-ə-rəs\ *adj* (1857) : exhibiting isomerism

iso·met·ric \ˌī-sə-ˈme-trik\ *adj* (ca. 1855) **1** : of, relating to, or characterized by equality of measure: as **a** : of, relating to, or being an isometric drawing or projection **b** : relating to or being a crystallographic system characterized by three equal axes at right angles **2** : of, relating to, involving, or being muscular contraction (as in isometrics) against resistance, without significant shortening of muscle fibers, and with marked increase in muscle tone — compare ISOTONIC 2 — **iso·met·ri·cal·ly** \-tri-k(ə-)lē\ *adv*

isometric drawing *n* (ca. 1930) : the representation of an object in isometric projection but with lines parallel to the edges drawn in true length — see ISOMETRIC PROJECTION illustration

isometric line *n* (ca. 1909) **1** : a line representing changes of pressure or temperature under conditions of constant volume **2** : a line (as a contour line) drawn on a map and indicating a true constant value throughout its extent

isometric projection *n* (1840) : axonometric projection in which all three faces are equally inclined to the drawing surface so that all the edges are equally foreshortened

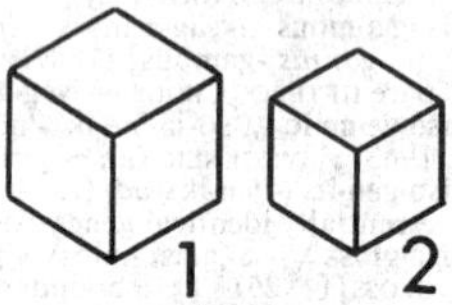

1 isometric drawing, in which the lines of the cube are drawn in their actual length; *2* isometric projection, in which the lines of the cube are foreshortened

iso·met·rics \ˌī-sə-ˈme-triks\ *n pl but sing or pl in constr* (1962) : exercise or a system of exercises in which opposing muscles are so contracted that there is little shortening but great increase in tone of muscle fibers involved

isom·e·try \ī-ˈsäm-ə-trē\ *n, pl* **-tries** (1941) : a mapping of a metric space onto another or onto itself so that the distance between any two points in the original space is the same as the distance between their images in the second space ⟨rotation and translation are *isometries* of the plane⟩

iso·morph \ˈī-sə-ˌmȯrf\ *n* [ISV] (ca. 1864) : something identical with or similar to something else in form or structure; *esp* : one of two or more substances related by isomorphism — **iso·mor·phous** \ˌī-sə-ˈmȯr-fəs\ *adj*

iso·mor·phic \ˌī-sə-ˈmȯr-fik\ *adj* (1862) **1** : being of identical or similar form or shape or structure; *esp* : having sporophytic and gametophytic generations alike in size and shape **2** : related by an isomorphism ⟨~ mathematical rings⟩ — **iso·mor·phi·cal·ly** \-fi-k(ə-)lē\ *adv*

iso·mor·phism \ˌī-sə-ˈmȯr-ˌfiz-əm\ *n* [ISV] (ca. 1828) **1** : the quality or state of being isomorphic: as **a** : similarity in organisms of different ancestry resulting from convergence **b** (1) : similarity of crystalline form between substances of similar composition (2) : similarity of crystalline forms between unlike chemical compounds **2** : a one-to-one correspondence between two mathematical sets; *esp* : a homomorphism that is one-to-one — compare ENDOMORPHISM

iso·ni·a·zid \ˌī-sə-ˈnī-ə-zəd\ *n* [*is-* + *ni*cotinic acid + hydr*azide*] (ca. 1952) : a crystalline compound $C_6H_7N_3O$ used in treating tuberculosis

iso·oc·tane \ˌī-sō-ˈäk-ˌtān\ *n* [ISV] (1909) : an octane of branched-chain structure or a mixture of such octanes; *esp* : a flammable liquid octane used to determine the octane number of fuels

iso·pach \ˈī-sə-ˌpak\ *n* [*is-* + *-pach* (deriv. of Gk *pachys* thick) — more at PACHYDERM] (ca. 1918) : an isogram that connects points of equal thickness of a geological stratum formation or group of formations

iso·phote \ˈī-sə-ˌfōt\ *n* [ISV *is-* + *-phote* (fr. Gk *phōt-, phōs* light) — more at FANCY] (ca. 1909) : a curve on a chart joining points of equal light intensity from a given source — **iso·phot·al** \ˌī-sə-ˈfōt-əl\ *adj*

iso·pi·es·tic \ˌī-sō-pē-ˈes-tik, -pī-\ *adj* [*is-* + Gk *piestos*, verbal of *piezein* to press — more at PIEZO-] (1873) : of, relating to, or marked by equal pressure

iso·pleth \ˈī-sə-ˌpleth\ *n* [ISV *is-* + Gk *plēthos* quantity; akin to Gk *plēthein* to be full — more at FULL] (ca. 1908) **1** : an isogram on a graph showing the occurrence or frequency of a phenomenon as a function of two variables **2** : a line on a map connecting points at which a given variable has a specified constant value — **iso·pleth·ic** \ˌī-sə-ˈpleth-ik\ *adj*

iso·pod \ˈī-sə-ˌpäd\ *n* [deriv. of Gk *is-* + *pod-, pous* foot — more at FOOT] (ca. 1835) : any of a large order (Isopoda) of small sessile-eyed crustaceans with the body composed of seven free thoracic segments each bearing a pair of similar legs — **isopod** *adj*

iso·pren·a·line \ˌī-sə-ˈpren-ᵊl-ən\ *n* [prob. fr. *isopropyl* + *adrenaline*] (1951) : ISOPROTERENOL

iso·prene \ˈī-sə-ˌprēn\ *n* [prob. fr. *is-* + *propyl* + *-ene*] (ca. 1860) : a flammable liquid unsaturated hydrocarbon C_5H_8 used esp. in synthetic rubber

iso·pren·oid \ˌī-sə-ˈprē-ˌnȯid\ *adj* (1940) : relating to, containing, or being a branched-chain grouping characteristic of isoprene

iso·pro·pyl \ˌī-sə-ˈprō-pəl\ *n* [ISV] (1866) : the alkyl radical isomeric with normal propyl

isopropyl alcohol *n* (1872) : a volatile flammable alcohol C_3H_8O used esp. as a solvent and rubbing alcohol

iso·pro·ter·e·nol \ˈī-sə-prō-ˈter-ə-ˌnȯl, -ˌnōl\ *n* [*isopropyl* + *arterenol* (norepinephrine), fr. *Arterenol*, a trademark] (1957) : a drug $C_{11}H_{17}NO_3$ used in the treatment of asthma

iso·pyc·nic \ˌī-sō-ˈpik-nik\ *adj* [*is-* + *pycn-* (fr. Gk *pyknos* dense) + *-ic* — more at PYCNIDIUM] (1890) **1** : of, relating to, or marked by equal or constant density **2** : being or produced by a technique (as centrifugation) in which the components of a mixture are separated on the basis of differences in density

isos·ce·les \ī-ˈsäs-(ə-)ˌlēz-\ *adj* [LL *isosceles* having two equal sides, fr. Gk *isoskelēs*, fr. *is-* + *skelos* leg — more at CYLINDER] (1551) **1** *of a triangle* : having two equal sides — see TRIANGLE illustration **2** *of a trapezoid* : having the two nonparallel sides equal

iso·seis·mal \ˌī-sə-ˈsīz-məl, -ˈsīs-\ *adj* [*is-* + *seism* + *-al*] (1883) : of, relating to, or marked by equal intensity of earthquake shock

is·os·mot·ic \ˌī-ˌsäz-ˈmät-ik, -ˌsäs-\ *adj* [ISV] (1895) : of, relating to, or exhibiting equal osmotic pressure ⟨~ solutions⟩ — **is·os·mot·i·cal·ly** \-ˈmät-i-k(ə-)lē\ *adv*

iso·spin \ˈī-sə-ˌspin\ *n* (1961) : a quantum characteristic of a group of closely related elementary particles (as a proton and a neutron) handled mathematically like ordinary spin with the possible orientations in a hypothetical space specifying the number of particles of different electric charge comprising the group — called also *isotopic spin*

isos·ta·sy \ī-ˈsäs-tə-sē\ *n* [ISV *is-* + Gk *-stasia* condition of standing, fr. *histanai* to cause to stand — more at STAND] (ca. 1889) **1** : general equilibrium in the earth's crust maintained by a yielding flow of rock material beneath the surface under gravitative stress **2** : the quality or state of being subjected to equal pressure from every side — **iso·stat·ic** \ˌī-sə-ˈstat-ik\ *adj* — **iso·stat·i·cal·ly** \-ˈstat-i-k(ə-)lē\ *adv*

iso·tach \ˈī-sə-ˌtak\ *n* [ISV *is-* + *-tach* (fr. Gk *tachys* quick)] (ca. 1947) : a line on a map or chart connecting points of equal wind velocity

iso·tac·tic \ˌī-sə-ˈtak-tik\ *adj* (ca. 1955) : having or relating to a stereochemical regularity of structure in the repeating units of a polymer

iso·therm \ˈī-sə-ˌthərm\ *n* [F *isotherme*, adj.] (1860) **1** : a line on a map or chart of the earth's surface connecting points having the same temperature at a given time or the same mean temperature for a given period **2** : a line on a chart representing changes of volume or pressure under conditions of constant temperature

iso·ther·mal \ˌī-sə-ˈthər-məl\ *adj* [F *isotherme*, fr. *is-* + *-therme* (fr. Gk *thermos* hot) — more at WARM] (1826) **1** : of, relating to, or marked by equality of temperature **2** : of, relating to, or marked by changes of volume or pressure under conditions of constant temperature — **iso·ther·mal·ly** \-mə-lē\ *adv*

iso·ton·ic \ˌī-sə-ˈtän-ik\ *adj* [ISV] (ca. 1890) **1** : ISOSMOTIC — used of solutions **2** : of, relating to, or being muscular contraction in the absence of significant resistance, with marked shortening of muscle fibers, and without great increase in muscle tone — compare ISOMETRIC 2 — **iso·ton·i·cal·ly** \-i-k(ə-)lē\ *adv* — **iso·to·nic·i·ty** \-tō-ˈnis-ət-ē\ *n*

iso·tope \ˈī-sə-ˌtōp\ *n* [*is-* + Gk *topos* place — more at TOPIC] (ca. 1913) **1** : any of two or more species of atoms of a chemical element with the same atomic number and position in the periodic table and nearly identical chemical behavior but with differing atomic mass or mass number and different physical properties **2** : NUCLIDE — **iso·to·pic** \ˌī-sə-ˈtäp-ik, -ˈtō-pik\ *adj* — **iso·to·pi·cal·ly** \-ˈtäp-i-k(ə-)lē, -ˈtō-pi-\ *adv* — **iso·to·py** \ˈī-sə-ˌtō-pē, ī-ˈsät-ə-pē\ *n*

isotopic spin *n* (1937) : ISOSPIN

iso·tro·pic \ˌī-sə-ˈtrō-pik, -ˈträp-ik\ *adj* [ISV] (ca. 1864) : exhibiting properties (as velocity of light transmission) with the same values when measured along axes in all directions ⟨an ~ crystal⟩ — **isot·ro·py** \ī-ˈsä-trə-pē\ *n*

iso·zyme \ˈī-sə-ˌzīm\ *n* (ca. 1959) : ISOENZYME — **iso·zy·mic** \ˌī-sə-ˈzī-mik\ *adj*

Is·ra·el \ˈiz-rē-əl, -(ˌ)rā- *also* ˈis- *or* ˈiz-rəl\ *n* [ME, fr. OE, fr. LL, fr. Gk *Israēl*, fr. Heb *Yiśrāʼēl*] **1** : JACOB 2 **2** : the Jewish people **3** : a people chosen by God — **Israel** *adj*

[1]**Is·rae·li** \iz-ˈrā-lē *also* ˌiz-rə-ˈā-lē\ *adj* [NHeb *yiśrĕʼēlī*, fr. Heb, Israelite, n. & adj., fr. *Yiśrāʼēl*] (1948) : of or relating to the people or the republic of Israel

[2]**Israeli** *n, pl* **Israelis** *also* **Israeli** (ca. 1948) : a native or inhabitant of the republic of Israel

[1]**Is·ra·el·ite** \ˈiz-r(ē-)ə-ˌlīt\ *n* [ME, fr. LL *Israelita*, fr. Gk *Israēlitēs*, fr. *Israēl*] (14c) : a descendant of the Hebrew patriarch Jacob; *specif* : a native or inhabitant of the ancient northern kingdom of Israel

[2]**Israelite** *adj* (14c) : of or relating to Israel

Is·sa \ē-ˈsä\ *n, pl* **Issa** *or* **Is·sas** \-ˈsä(z)\ (1961) : a member of a Somali people of eastern Ethiopia, Somalia, and Djibouti

Is·sa·char \ˈis-ə-ˌkär\ *n* [LL, fr. Gk, fr. Heb *Yiśśākhār*] : a son of Jacob and the traditional eponymous ancestor of one of the tribes of Israel

is·sei \(ˈ)ē-ˈsā, ˈē-ˌsā\ *n* [Jp, lit., first generation] (1937) : a Japanese immigrant esp. to the U.S.

is·su·able \ˈish-ü-ə-bəl\ *adj* (1570) **1** : open to contest, debate, or litigation **2** : authorized for issue ⟨bonds ~ under the merger terms⟩ **3** : possible as a result or consequence — **is·su·ably** \-blē\ *adv*

is·su·ance \ˈish-ə-wən(t)s\ *n* (1863) : ISSUE

is·su·ant \-wənt\ *adj* (1610) **1** *of a heraldic animal* : rising with only the upper part visible **2** *archaic* : coming forth : EMERGING

[1]**is·sue** \ˈish-(ˌ)ü, ˈish-ə(-w), *chiefly Southern* ˈish-ə, *chiefly Brit* ˈis-(ˌ)yü\ *n* [ME, exit, proceeds, fr. MF, fr. OF, fr. *issir* to come out, go out, fr. L *exire* to go out, fr. *ex-* + *ire* to go; akin to Goth *iddja* he went, Gk *ienai* to go, Skt *eti* he goes] (14c) **1** *pl* : proceeds from a source of revenue (as an estate) **2** : the action of going, coming, or flowing out : EGRESS, EMERGENCE **3** : a means or place of going out : EXIT, OUTLET **4** : OFFSPRING, PROGENY ⟨died without ~⟩ **5 a** : a final outcome that usu. constitutes a solution (as of a problem) or resolution (as of a difficulty) **b** *obs* : a final conclusion or decision about something arrived at after consideration **c** *archaic* : TERMINATION, END ⟨hope that his enterprise would have a prosperous ~ —T. B. Macaulay⟩ **6 a** : a matter that is in dispute between two or more parties **b** : the point at which an unsettled matter is ready for a decision ⟨brought the matter to an ~⟩ **7** : a discharge (as of blood) from the body **8 a** : something coming forth from a specified source ⟨~*s* of a disordered imagination⟩ **b** *obs* : DEED **9 a** : the act of publishing or officially giving out or making available ⟨the next ~ of commemorative stamps⟩ ⟨~ of supplies by the quartermaster⟩ **b** : the thing or the whole quantity of things given out at one time ⟨read the latest ~⟩ *syn* see EFFECT — **is·sue·less** \ˈish-ü-ləs\ *adj* — **at issue 1** : in a state of controversy : in disagreement **2** *also* **in issue** : under discussion or in dispute

[2]**issue** *vb* **is·sued; is·su·ing** *vi* (14c) **1 a** : to go, come, or flow out **b** : to come forth : EMERGE **c** : to come to an issue of law or fact in pleading **2** : ACCRUE ⟨profits *issuing* from the sale of the stock⟩ **3** : to

descend from a specified parent or ancestor **4 :** to be a consequence or final outcome : EMANATE, RESULT **5 :** to appear or become available through being officially put forth or distributed **6 :** EVENTUATE, TERMINATE ~ *vt* **1 :** to cause to come forth : DISCHARGE, EMIT **2 a :** to put forth or distribute usu. officially ⟨government *issued* a new airmail stamp⟩ ⟨~ orders⟩ **b :** to send out for sale or circulation : PUBLISH *syn* see SPRING — **is·su·er** *n*

[1]**-ist** \əst\ *n suffix* [ME *-iste,* fr. OF & L; OF *-iste,* fr. L *-ista, -istes,* fr. Gk *-istēs,* fr. verbs in *-izein* -ize] **1 a :** one that performs a (specified) action ⟨cycl*ist*⟩ : one that makes or produces a (specified) thing ⟨novel*ist*⟩ **b :** one that plays a (specified) musical instrument ⟨harp*ist*⟩ **c :** one that operates a (specified) mechanical instrument or contrivance ⟨automobil*ist*⟩ **2 :** one that specializes in a (specified) art or science or skill ⟨geolog*ist*⟩ ⟨ventriloqu*ist*⟩ **3 :** one that adheres to or advocates a (specified) doctrine or system or code of behavior ⟨social*ist*⟩ ⟨royal*ist*⟩ ⟨hedon*ist*⟩ or that of a (specified) individual ⟨Calvin*ist*⟩ ⟨Darwin*ist*⟩

[2]**-ist** *adj suffix* **:** of, relating to, or characteristic of ⟨dilettant*ist*⟩

[1]**isth·mi·an** \ˈis-mē-ən\ *n* (1601) **1 :** a native or inhabitant of an isthmus **2** *cap* **:** a native or inhabitant of the Isthmus of Panama

[2]**isthmian** *adj* (1603) **:** of, relating to, or situated in or near an isthmus: as **a** *often cap* **:** of or relating to the Isthmus of Corinth in Greece or the games held there in ancient times **b** *often cap* **:** of or relating to the Isthmus of Panama connecting the No. American and So. American continents

isth·mic \ˈis-mik\ *adj* (1585) **:** of or relating to an anatomical isthmus

isth·mus \ˈis-məs\ *n* [L, fr. Gk *isthmos*] (1555) **1 :** a narrow strip of land connecting two larger land areas **2 :** a narrow anatomical part or passage connecting two larger structures or cavities

is·tle \ˈist-lē\ *n* [AmerSp *ixtle,* fr. Nahuatl *ichtli*] (1883) **:** a strong fiber (as for cordage or basketry) from various tropical American plants (as of the genus *Agave*)

[1]**it** \(ˈ)it, ət\ *pron* [ME, fr. OE *hit* — more at HE] (bef. 12c) **1 :** that one — used as subject or direct object or indirect object of a verb or object of a preposition usu. in reference to a lifeless thing ⟨took a quick look at the house and noticed ~ was very old⟩, a plant ⟨there is a rosebush near the fence and ~ is now blooming⟩, a person or animal whose sex is unknown or disregarded ⟨don't know who ~ is⟩, a group of individuals or things, or an abstract entity ⟨beauty is everywhere and ~ is a source of joy⟩; compare HE, ITS, SHE, THEY **2 —** used as subject of an impersonal verb that expresses a condition or action without reference to an agent ⟨~ is raining⟩ **3 a —** used as anticipatory subject or object of a verb ⟨~ is necessary to repeat the whole thing⟩; often used to shift emphasis to a part of a statement other than the subject ⟨~ was in this city that the treaty was signed⟩ **b —** used with many verbs as a direct object with little or no meaning ⟨footed ~ back to camp⟩ **4 —** used to refer to an explicit or implicit state of affairs or circumstances ⟨how is ~ going⟩ **5 :** what counts ⟨this is ~⟩

[2]**it** \ˈit\ *n* (1842) **:** the player in a game who performs a function (as trying to catch others in a game of tag) essential to the nature of the game

it·a·col·u·mite \ˌit-ə-ˈkäl-(y)ə-ˌmīt\ *n* [*Itacolumi,* mountain in Brazil] (ca. 1862) **:** a quartzite resembling mica and flexible when split into thin slabs

it·a·con·ic acid \ˌit-ə-ˌkän-ik-\ *n* [ISV, anagram of *aconitic acid,* $C_3H_3(COOH)_3$, fr. *aconite*] (ca. 1865) **:** a crystalline dicarboxylic acid $C_5H_6O_4$ obtained usu. by fermentation of sugars with molds (genus *Aspergillus*) and used as a monomer for vinyl-type polymers and polyesters

[1]**Ital·ian** \ə-ˈtal-yən, i-\ *n* (14c) **1 a :** a native or inhabitant of Italy **b :** a person of Italian descent **2 :** the Romance language of the Italians

[2]**Italian** *adj* (1547) **:** of or relating to the people or the republic of Italy

ital·ian·ate \-yə-ˌnāt\ *vt* **-at·ed; -at·ing** (1553) **:** ITALIANIZE

Ital·ian·ate \-nət, -ˌnāt\ *adj* (1572) **:** Italian in quality or characteristics

Italian dressing *n* (ca. 1902) **:** a salad dressing flavored esp. with garlic and oregano

Italian greyhound *n* (1743) **:** any of a breed of toy dogs resembling the standard greyhound in miniature

Ital·ian·ism \ə-ˈtal-yə-ˌniz-əm, i-\ *n* (1594) **1 a :** a quality characteristic of Italy or the Italian people **b :** a characteristic feature of Italian occurring in another language **2 a :** specialized interest in or emulation of Italian qualities or achievements **b :** promotion or love of Italian policies or ideals

ital·ian·ize \ə-ˈtal-yə-ˌnīz, i-\ *vb* **-ized; -iz·ing** *vi, often cap* (1611) **:** to act Italian; *specif* **:** to follow the style or technique of recognized Italian painters ~ *vt, often cap* **:** to make Italian (as in appearance or behavior) — **Ital·ian·iza·tion** \-ˌtal-yə-nə-ˈzā-shən\ *n*

Italian sandwich *n* (ca. 1949) **:** SUBMARINE 2

Italian sonnet *n* (1879) **:** a sonnet consisting of an octave rhyming *abba abba* and a sestet rhyming in any of various patterns (as *cde cde* or *cdc dcd*) — called also *Petrarchan sonnet*

[1]**ital·ic** \ə-ˈtal-ik, i-, ī-\ *adj* (1612) **1 a :** of or relating to a type style with characters that slant upward to the right (as in "*these words are italic*") — compare ROMAN **b :** of or relating to a style of slanted cursive handwriting developed in the 15th and 16th centuries **2** *cap* **:** of or relating to ancient Italy, its peoples, or their Indo-European languages

[2]**italic** *n* (1676) **1 :** an italic character or type **2** *cap* **:** the Italic branch of the Indo-European language family — see INDO-EUROPEAN LANGUAGES table

ital·i·cize \ə-ˈtal-ə-ˌsīz, i-, ī-\ *vt* **-cized; -ciz·ing** (1795) **1 :** to print in italics or underscore with a single line **2 :** EMPHASIZE ⟨the microphone ~s every curdled top note —P. G. Davis⟩ — **ital·i·ci·za·tion** \-ˌtal-ə-sə-ˈzā-shən\ *n*

Ita·lo- *comb form* **1 :** Italian **2** \ˈit-ᵊl-ō *also* ə-ˈtal-ō *or* i-ˈtal-ō\ **:** Italian and ⟨*Italo*-Austrian⟩

Italo·phile \ə-ˈtal-ə-ˌfīl, i-\ *adj* (1899) **:** friendly to or favoring what is Italian — **Italophile** *n*

[1]**itch** \ˈich\ *vb* [ME *icchen,* fr. OE *giccan;* akin to OHG *jucchen* to itch] *vi* (bef. 12c) **1 a :** to have an itch ⟨her arm ~*ed*⟩ **b :** to produce an itchy sensation ⟨long underwear that ~*es*⟩ **2 :** to have a restless desire or hankering for something ⟨were ~*ing* to go outside⟩ ~ *vt* **1 :** to cause to itch **2 :** VEX, IRRITATE

[2]**itch** *n* (bef. 12c) **1 a :** an uneasy irritating sensation in the upper surface of the skin usu. held to result from mild stimulation of pain receptors **b :** a skin disorder accompanied by such a sensation; *esp* **:** a contagious eruption caused by a mite (*Sarcoptes scabiei*) that burrows in the skin and causes intense itching **2 a :** a restless usu. constant often compulsive desire ⟨an ~ to travel⟩ **b :** LUST, PRURIENCE — **itch·i·ness** \ˈich-ē-nəs\ *n* — **itchy** \-ē\ *adj*

it'd \ˈit-əd, ˌid\ **:** it had **:** it would

[1]**-ite** \ˌīt\ *n suffix* [ME, fr. OF & L; OF, fr. L *-ita, -ites,* fr. Gk *-itēs*] **1 a :** native **:** resident ⟨Brooklyn*ite*⟩ **b :** descendant ⟨Ephraim*ite*⟩ **c :** adherent **:** follower ⟨Jacob*ite*⟩ ⟨Pusey*ite*⟩ **2 a (1) :** product ⟨metabol*ite*⟩ **(2) :** commercially manufactured product ⟨ebon*ite*⟩ **b :** -ITOL ⟨inos*ite*⟩ **3** [NL *-ites,* fr. L] **:** fossil ⟨ammon*ite*⟩ **4 :** mineral ⟨erythr*ite*⟩ **:** rock ⟨anorthos*ite*⟩ **5** [F, fr. L *-ita, -ites*] **:** segment or constituent part of a body or of a bodily part ⟨som*ite*⟩ ⟨dendr*ite*⟩

[2]**-ite** *n suffix* [F, alter. of *-ate* -ate, fr. NL *-atum*] **:** salt or ester of an acid with a name ending in *-ous*

[1]**item** \ˈī-ˌtem, ˈīt-əm\ *adv* [ME, fr. L, fr. *ita* thus] (14c) **:** and in addition **:** ALSO — used to introduce each article in a list or enumeration

[2]**item** \ˈīt-əm\ *n* (1561) **1** *obs* **:** WARNING, HINT **2 :** a separate particular in an enumeration, account, or series **:** ARTICLE **3 :** an object of attention, concern, or interest **4 :** a separate piece of news or information

syn ITEM, DETAIL, PARTICULAR mean one of the distinct parts of a whole. ITEM applies to each thing specified separately in a list or in a group of things that might be listed or enumerated; DETAIL applies to one of the small component parts of a larger whole such as a task, building, painting, narration, or process; PARTICULAR stresses the smallness, singleness, and esp. the concreteness of a detail or item.

[3]**item** \ˈīt-əm\ *vt* (1601) **1** *archaic* **:** COMPUTE, RECKON **2** *archaic* **:** to set down the particular details of

item·iza·tion \ˌīt-ə-mə-ˈzā-shən\ *n* (1894) **:** the act of itemizing; *also* **:** an itemized list

item·ize \ˈīt-ə-ˌmīz\ *vt* **-ized; -iz·ing** (1857) **:** to set down in detail or by particulars **:** LIST ⟨*itemized* all expenses⟩

it·er·ance \ˈit-ə-rən(t)s\ *n* (1604) **:** REPETITION

it·er·ant \-rənt\ *adj* (1626) **:** marked by repetition, reiteration, or recurrence ⟨~ echoes⟩

it·er·ate \ˈit-ə-ˌrāt\ *vt* **-at·ed; -at·ing** [L *iteratus,* pp. of *iterare,* fr. *iterum* again; akin to L *is* he, that, *ita* thus, Skt *itara* the other, *iti* thus] (1533) **:** to say or do again or again and again **:** REITERATE

it·er·a·tion \ˌit-ə-ˈrā-shən\ *n* (15c) **1 :** the action or a process of iterating or repeating: as **a :** a procedure in which repetition of a sequence of operations yields results successively closer to a desired result **b :** the repetition of a sequence of computer instructions a specified number of times or until a condition is met **2 :** one execution of a sequence of operations or instructions in an iteration

it·er·a·tive \ˈit-ə-ˌrāt-iv, -rət-\ *adj* (15c) **:** involving repetition: as **a :** expressing repetition of a verbal action **b :** relating to or being computational iteration — **it·er·a·tive·ly** *adv*

ithy·phal·lic \ˌith-i-ˈfal-ik\ *adj* [LL *ithyphallicus,* fr. Gk *ithyphallikos,* fr. *ithyphallos* erect phallus, fr. *ithys* straight + *phallos* phallus] (1795) **1 :** of or relating to the phallus carried in procession in ancient festivals of Bacchus **2 a :** having an erect penis — usu. used of figures in an art representation **b :** OBSCENE, LEWD

itin·er·a·cy \ī-ˈtin-ə-rə-sē, ə-\ *n* [*itinerate,* adj. (itinerant)] (1827) **:** ITINERANCY

itin·er·an·cy \-rən-sē\ *n* (1789) **1 a :** the act of itinerating **b :** the state of being itinerant **2 :** a system (as in the Methodist Church) of rotating ministers who itinerate

itin·er·ant \-rənt\ *adj* [LL *itinerant-, itinerans,* prp. of *itinerari* to journey, fr. L *itiner-, iter* journey, way, fr. *ire* to go — more at ISSUE] (1570) **:** traveling from place to place; *esp* **:** covering a circuit ⟨~ preacher⟩ — **itinerant** *n* — **itin·er·ant·ly** *adv*

itin·er·ary \ī-ˈtin-ə-ˌrer-ē, ə- *chiefly Brit* -ˈtin-ə-rē\ *n, pl* **-ar·ies** (15c) **1 :** the route of a journey or tour or the proposed outline of one **2 :** a travel diary **3 :** a traveler's guidebook — **itinerary** *adj*

itin·er·ate \ī-ˈtin-ə-ˌrāt, ə-\ *vi* **-at·ed; -at·ing** (1775) **:** to travel a preaching or judicial circuit — **itin·er·a·tion** \-ˌtin-ə-ˈrā-shən, ə-\ *n*

-i·tious \ˈish-əs\ *adj suffix* [L *-icius, -itius*] **:** of, relating to, or having the characteristics of ⟨excrement*itious*⟩

-i·tis \ˈīt-əs *also but not shown at individual entries* ˈēt-\ *n suffix, pl* **-i·tis·es** *also* **-it·i·des** \ˈit-ə-ˌdēz, ˈēt-\ *or* **-i·tes** \ˈīt-(ˌ)ēz, ˈēt-\ [NL, fr. L & Gk; L, fr. Gk, fr. fem. of *-itēs* -ite] **1 :** disease or inflammation ⟨bronch*itis*⟩ **2** *pl usu -itises* **a (1) :** malady arising from ⟨vacation*itis*⟩ **(2) :** forced endurance of ⟨television*itis*⟩ **b (1) :** marked proneness to ⟨accident*itis*⟩ **(2) :** infatuation with ⟨jazz*itis*⟩ **(3) :** excessive advocacy of or reliance on ⟨education*itis*⟩ **c :** excess of the qualities of ⟨big-business*itis*⟩

it'll \ˌit-ᵊl\ **:** it will **:** it shall

-i·tol \ə-ˌtȯl, -ˌtōl\ *n suffix* [ISV [1]*-ite* + *-ol*] **:** polyhydroxy alcohol usu. related to a sugar ⟨mann*itol*⟩

its \(ˌ)its, əts\ *adj* (1598) **:** of or relating to it or itself esp. as possessor, agent, or object of an action ⟨going to ~ kennel⟩ ⟨a child proud of ~ first drawings⟩ ⟨~ final enactment into law⟩

it's \(ˌ)its, əts\ **1 :** it is **2 :** it has

it·self \it-ˈself, ət-, *Southern also* -ˈsef\ *pron* (bef. 12c) **1 :** that identical one — compare [1]IT 1; used reflexively ⟨watched the cat giving ~ a bath⟩, for emphasis ⟨the letter ~ was missing⟩, or in absolute constructions ⟨~ a splendid specimen of classic art, it is sure to be exhibited throughout the world⟩ **2 :** its normal, healthy, or sane condition — **in itself :** in its own nature **:** INTRINSICALLY ⟨was not *in itself* dangerous⟩

it·ty–bit·ty \ˌit-ē-ˈbit-ē\ *or* **it·sy–bit·sy** \ˌit-sē-ˈbit-sē\ *adj* [prob. fr. baby talk for *little bit*] (1938) **:** extremely small **:** TINY

-i·ty \ət-ē\ *n suffix, pl* **-i·ties** [ME *-ite,* fr. OF or L; OF *-ité,* fr. L *-itat-, -itas,* fr. *-i-* (stem vowel of adjs.) + *-tat-, -tas* -ity; akin to Gk *-tēt-, -tēs* -ity] **:** quality **:** state **:** degree ⟨alkalin*ity*⟩ ⟨theatrical*ity*⟩

IUD \ˌī-ˌyü-ˈdē\ *n* (1965) **:** INTRAUTERINE DEVICE

-ium *n suffix* **1** [NL, fr. L, ending of some neut. nouns] **a (1) :** a chemical element ⟨sod*ium*⟩ **(2) :** chemical radical ⟨ammon*ium*⟩ **b**

\ə\ abut \ᵊ\ kitten, F table \ər\ further \a\ ash \ā\ ace \ä\ cot, cart \au̇\ out \ch\ chin \e\ bet \ē\ easy \g\ go \i\ hit \ī\ ice \j\ job \ŋ\ sing \ō\ go \ȯ\ law \ȯi\ boy \th\ thin \t͟h\ the \ü\ loot \u̇\ foot \y\ yet \zh\ vision \à, k̲, ⁿ, œ, œ̄, ue, ue̅, ʸ\ *see* Guide to Pronunciation

: positive ion ⟨imidazol*ium* [C₃H₄N₂H]⁺⟩ **2** *pl* **-iums** *or* **-ia** [NL, fr. L, fr. Gk *-ion*] : small one : mass — esp. in botanical terms ⟨pollin*ium*⟩
-ive \iv\ *adj suffix* [ME *-if*, *-ive*, fr. MF & L; MF *-if*, fr. L *-ivus*] : that performs or tends toward an (indicated) action ⟨amus*ive*⟩
I've \(ˌ)īv\ : I have
ivied \ˈī-vēd\ *adj* (1771) **1** : overgrown with ivy **2** : ACADEMIC
ivo·ry \ˈīv-(ə-)rē\ *n, pl* **-ries** [ME *ivorie*, fr. OF *ivoire*, fr. L *eboreus* of ivory, fr. *ebor-, ebur* ivory, fr. Egypt ; *b, ; bw* elephant, ivory] (13c) **1 a** : the hard creamy-white modified dentine that composes the tusks of a tusked mammal (as an elephant or walrus) **b** : a tusk that yields ivory **2** : a variable color averaging a pale yellow **3** *slang* : TOOTH **4** : something (as dice or piano keys) made of ivory or of a similar substance — **ivory** *adj*
ivo·ry-bill \ˈīv-(ə-)rē-ˌbil\ *n* (1787) : IVORY-BILLED WOODPECKER
ivo·ry–billed woodpecker \ˌīv-(ə-)rē-ˌbild-\ *n* (1811) : a very large, nearly extinct, black-and-white woodpecker (*Campephilus principalis*) of the southeastern U.S. that has a showy red crest in the male
ivory black *n* (1634) : a fine black pigment made by calcining ivory
ivory nut *n* (ca. 1847) : the nutlike seed of a So. American palm (*Phytelephas macrocarpa*) containing a very hard endosperm used for carving and turning — compare VEGETABLE IVORY
ivory tower *n* [trans. of F *tour d'ivoire*] (1911) **1** : an impractical often escapist attitude marked by aloof lack of concern with or interest in practical matters or urgent problems **2** : a secluded place that affords the means of treating practical issues with an impractical often escapist attitude; *esp* : a place of learning — **ivory–tower** *adj* — **ivo·ry-tow·er·ish** \ˌīv-(ə-)rē-ˈtaủ-(ə-)rish\ *adj*
ivo·ry–tow·ered \ˌīv-(ə-)rē-ˈtaủ(-ə)rd\ *adj* (1937) : divorced from reality and practical matters ⟨an ∼ recluse⟩

ivory-billed woodpecker

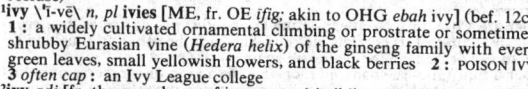

¹ivy \ˈī-vē\ *n, pl* **ivies** [ME, fr. OE *ifig*; akin to OHG *ebah* ivy] (bef. 12c) **1** : a widely cultivated ornamental climbing or prostrate or sometimes shrubby Eurasian vine (*Hedera helix*) of the ginseng family with evergreen leaves, small yellowish flowers, and black berries **2** : POISON IVY **3** *often cap* : an Ivy League college
²ivy *adj* [fr. the prevalence of ivy-covered buildings on the campuses of the older U.S. colleges] (1945) **1** : ACADEMIC **2** : IVY LEAGUE

Ivy League *adj* (1939) **1** : of, relating to, or characteristic of a group of long-established eastern U.S. colleges widely regarded as high in scholastic and social prestige **2** : of, relating to, or characteristic of the students of Ivy League colleges
Ivy Leaguer *n* (1943) : a student at or a graduate of an Ivy League college
iwis \ē-ˈwis, ī-\ *adv* [ME, fr. OE *gewis* certain; akin to OHG *giwisso* certainly, OE *witan* to know — more at WIT] *archaic* (bef. 12c) : SURELY
Ix·i·on \ik-ˈsī-ən\ *n* [L, fr. Gk *Ixiōn*] : a Thessalian king bound by Zeus to a burning wheel in Tartarus for attempting to seduce Hera
ix·o·did \ˈik-sə-ˌdid, ik-ˈsõd-əd\ *adj* [deriv. of Gk *ixōdēs* sticky, fr. *ixos* birdlime] (ca. 1909) : of, relating to, or being a typical tick (family Ixodidae) — **ixodid** *n*
Iyar \ˈē-ˌyär\ *n* [Heb *Iyyār*] (1737) : the 8th month of the civil year or the 2d month of the ecclesiastical year in the Jewish calendar — see MONTH table
-iza·tion \ə-ˈzā-shən *also esp when an unstressed syllable precedes but not shown at individual entries* (ˌ)ī-ˈzā-\ *n suffix* : action, process, or result of making ⟨socialization⟩
-ize \ˌīz\ *vb suffix* [ME *-isen*, fr. OF *-iser*, fr. LL *-izare*, fr. Gk *-izein*] **1 a** (1) : cause to be or conform to or resemble ⟨systemize⟩ ⟨Americanize⟩ : cause to be formed into ⟨unionize⟩ (2) : subject to a (specified) action ⟨plagiarize⟩ (3) : impregnate or treat or combine with ⟨albuminize⟩ **b** : treat like ⟨idolize⟩ **c** : treat according to the method of ⟨bowdlerize⟩ **2 a** : become : become like ⟨crystallize⟩ **b** : be productive in or of ⟨hypothesize⟩ : engage in a (specified) activity ⟨philosophize⟩ **c** : adopt or spread the manner of activity or the teaching of
usage The suffix *-ize* has been productive in English since the time of Thomas Nashe (1567-1601), who claimed credit for introducing it into English to remedy the surplus of monosyllabic words. Almost any noun or adjective can be made into a verb by adding *-ize* ⟨hospitalize⟩ ⟨familiarize⟩; many technical terms are coined this way ⟨oxidize⟩ as well as verbs of ethnic derivation ⟨Americanize⟩ and verbs derived from proper names ⟨bowdlerize⟩ ⟨mesmerize⟩ Nashe noted in 1591 that his coinages in *-ize* were being complained about, and to this day new words in *-ize* ⟨finalize⟩ ⟨prioritize⟩ are sure to draw critical fire.
iz·zard \ˈiz-ərd\ *n* [alter. of earlier *ezod, ezed*, prob. fr. MF *et zede* and Z] *chiefly dial* (1726) : the letter z

---

j \ˈjā\ *n, pl* **j's** *or* **js** \ˈjāz\ *often cap, often attrib* **1 a** : the 10th letter of the English alphabet **b** : a speech counterpart of orthographic *j* **2** : a graphic device for reproducing the letter *j* **b** : a unit vector parallel to the y-axis **3** : one designated *j* esp. as the 10th in order or class **4** : something shaped like the letter J
¹jab \ˈjab\ *vb* **jabbed; jab·bing** [alter. of *job* (to strike)] *vt* (ca. 1825) **1 a** : to pierce with or as if with a sharp object : STAB **b** : to poke quickly or abruptly : THRUST **2** : to strike with a short straight blow ∼ *vi* **1** : to make quick or abrupt thrusts with a sharp object **2** : to strike a person with a short straight blow
²jab *n* (ca. 1825) : an act of jabbing; *esp* : a short straight boxing punch delivered with the leading hand
¹jab·ber \ˈjab-ər\ *vb* **jab·bered; jab·ber·ing** \ˈjab-(ə-)riŋ\ [ME *jaberen*, of imit. origin] *vi* (15c) : to talk rapidly, indistinctly, or unintelligibly ∼ *vt* : to speak rapidly or indistinctly — **jab·ber·er** \ˈjab-ər-ər\ *n*
²jabber *n* (1727) : GIBBERISH, CHATTER
jab·ber·wocky \ˈjab-ər-ˌwäk-ē\ *n* [*Jabberwocky*, nonsense poem by Lewis Carroll] (1908) : meaningless speech or writing
jab·i·ru \ˌzhab-ə-ˈrü\ *n* [Pg, fr. Tupi & Guarani *jabirú*] (1774) : any of several large tropical storks
jab·o·ran·di \ˌzhab-ə-ˌran-dē, -ˈran-dē\ *n* [Pg, fr. Tupi *yaborandí*] (ca. 1875) : the dried leaves of two So. American shrubs (*Pilocarpus jaborandi* and *P. microphyllus*) of the rue family that are a source of pilocarpine
ja·bot \zha-ˈbō, ˈjab-ˌō\ *n* [F] (1823) **1** : a fall of lace or cloth attached to the front of a neckband and worn esp. by men in the 18th century **2** : a pleated frill of cloth or lace attached down the center front of a woman's blouse or dress
ja·bo·ti·ca·ba \zhə-ˌbüt-i-ˈkäb-ə\ *n* [Pg, fr. Tupi] (1824) : a tropical American shrubby tree (*Myrciaria cauliflora*) of the myrtle family cultivated in warm regions for its edible purplish fruit
ja·cal \hə-ˈkäl\ *n, pl* **ja·ca·les** \-ˈkäl-(ˌ)äs\ *also* **ja·cals** [MexSp, fr. Nahuatl *xacalli*] (1838) : a hut in Mexico and southwestern U.S. with a thatched roof and walls made of upright poles or sticks covered and chinked with mud or clay
jac·a·mar \ˈzhak-ə-ˌmär\ *n* [F, fr. Tupi *jacamá-ciri*] (1825) : any of a family (Galbulidae) of usu. iridescent green or bronze insectivorous birds of American tropical forests
ja·ca·na \jə-ˈkän-ə, ˌzhas-²n-ˈaⁿ\ *n* [Pg *jaçanã*, fr. Tupi & Guarani] (ca. 1753) : any of several long-legged and long-toed wading birds (family Jacanidae) that frequent coastal freshwater marshes and ponds in warm regions

jac·a·ran·da \ˌjak-ə-ˈran-də\ *n* [NL, fr. Pg, a tree of this genus] (ca. 1753) : any of a genus (*Jacaranda*) of pinnate-leaved tropical American trees of the trumpet-creeper family with showy blue flowers in panicles
ja·cinth \ˈjās-²n(t)th, ˈjas-\ *n* [ME *iacinct*, fr. OF *jacinthe*, fr. L *hyacinthus*, a flowering plant, a gem] (13c) **1** : HYACINTH **2** : a gem more nearly orange in color than a hyacinth
ja·cinthe \ˈjās-²n(t)th, ˈjas-; zhä-ˈsant\ *n* [F, fr. OF] (1572) : a moderate orange
¹jack \ˈjak\ *n* [ME *jacke*, fr. *Jacke*, nickname for *Johan John*] (14c) **1 a** : MAN — usu. used as an intensive in such phrases as *every man jack* **b** *often cap* : SAILOR **c** (1) : SERVANT, LABORER (2) : LUMBERJACK **2** : any of various mechanical devices: as **a** : a device for turning a spit **b** : any of various portable mechanisms for exerting pressure or lifting a heavy body a short distance **3** : something that supports or holds in position: as **a** : a bar of iron at a topgallant masthead to support a royal mast and spread the royal shrouds **b** : a wooden brace fastened behind a scenic unit in a stage set to prop it up **4 a** : any of several fishes; *esp* : any of various carangids **b** : a male donkey **c** : any of several birds (as a jackdaw) **5 a** : a small white target ball in lawn bowling **b** : a small national flag flown by a ship **c** (1) *pl but sing in constr* : a game played with a set of small objects that are tossed, caught, and moved in various figures (2) : a small 6-pointed metal object used in the game of jacks **6 a** : a playing card carrying the figure of a soldier or servant and ranking usu. below the queen **b** [by shortening] : JACKPOT 1a(2) **7** *slang* : MONEY **8** : a female fitting in an electric circuit used with a plug to make a connection with another circuit **9 a** [by shortening] : APPLEJACK **b** : BRANDY **10** [by shortening] : JACKKNIFE 2
²jack *vi* (1841) : to hunt or fish at night with a jacklight ∼ *vt* **1** : to hunt or fish for at night with a jacklight **2 a** : to move or lift by or as if by a jack **b** : to raise the level or quality of ⟨∼ up the price⟩ **c** : to take to task — **jack·er** *n*
jack·al \ˈjak-ˌol, -ˌól\ *n* [Turk *çakal*, fr. Per *shagāl*, fr. Skt *sṛgāla*] (1603) **1** : any of several Old World wild dogs (genus *Canis aureus*) smaller than the related wolves **2 a** : a person who performs routine or menial tasks for another **b** : a person who serves or collaborates with another esp. in the commission of base acts
Jack–a–Lent \ˈjak-ə-ˌlent\ *n* [¹*jack* + *a* (of) + *Lent*] (1598) **1** : a small stuffed puppet set up to be pelted for fun in Lent **2** : a simple or insignificant person
jack·a·napes \ˈjak-ə-ˌnāps\ *n* [ME *Jack Napis*, nickname for William de la Pole †1450 duke of Suffolk] (1522) **1** : MONKEY, APE **2 a** : an impudent or conceited fellow **b** : a saucy or mischievous child
jack·ass \ˈjak-ˌas\ *n* (1727) **1** : DONKEY; *esp* : a male donkey **2 a** : a stupid person : FOOL

jack·ass·ery \'jak-,as-(ə-)rē\ *n, pl* **-er·ies** (1833) **:** foolish action or behavior

jack bean *n* (1885) **:** a bushy annual tropical American legume (genus *Canavalia*); *esp* **:** a plant (*C. ensiformis*) grown esp. for forage

jack·boot \'jak-,büt\ *n* (1686) **1 :** a heavy military boot made of glossy black leather extending above the knee and worn esp. during the 17th and 18th centuries **2 :** the spirit or policy of militarism or totalitarianism **3 :** a laceless military boot reaching to the calf

jack·boot·ed \-,büt-əd\ *adj* (1846) **1 :** wearing jackboots **2 :** ruthlessly and violently oppressive ⟨~ force⟩

jack crevalle *n* (1948) **:** a carangid fish (*Caranx hippos*) that is an important food fish along the west coast of Florida

jack·daw \'jak-,dȯ\ *n* (1543) **1 :** a common black and gray Eurasian bird (*Corvus monedula*) that is related to but smaller than the common crow **2 :** GRACKLE 2

¹**jack·et** \'jak-ət\ *n* [ME *jaket,* fr. MF *jaquet,* dim. of *jaque* short jacket, fr. *jacque* peasant, fr. the name *Jacques* James] (15c) **1 a :** a garment for the upper body usu. having a front opening, collar, lapels, sleeves, and pockets **b :** something worn or fastened around the body but not for use as clothing **2 a** (1) **:** the natural covering of an animal (2) **:** the fur or wool of a mammal **b :** the skin of a potato **3 :** an outer covering or casing: as **a** (1) **:** a thermally nonconducting cover (2) **:** a covering that encloses an intermediate space through which a temperature-controlling fluid circulates (3) **:** a tough cold-worked metal casing that forms the outer shell of a built-up bullet **b** (1) **:** a wrapper or open envelope for a document (2) **:** an envelope for enclosing registered mail during delivery from one post office to another **c** (1) **:** a detachable protective cover for a book (2) **:** a paper or paperboard envelope for a phonograph record

²**jacket** *vt* (1856) **:** to put a jacket on **:** enclose in or with a jacket

Jack Frost *n* (1826) **:** frost or frosty weather personified

jack·fruit \'jak-,früt\ *n* [Pg *jaca* jackfruit + E *fruit*] (1830) **:** a large widely cultivated tropical tree (*Artocarpus heterophyllus*) related to the breadfruit that yields a fine-grained yellow wood and immense fruits which contain an edible pulp and nutritious seeds; *also* **:** its fruit

jack·ham·mer \'jak-,ham-ər\ *n* (1916) **1 :** a pneumatically operated percussive rock-drilling tool usu. held in the hands **2 :** a device in which a tool (as a chisel for breaking up pavements) is driven percussively by compressed air

jack–in–the–box \'jak-ən-thə-,bäks\ *n, pl* **jack–in–the–box·es** *or* **jacks–in–the–box** (1702) **:** a toy consisting of a small box out of which a figure (as of a clown's head) springs when the lid is raised

jack–in–the–pul·pit \,jak-ən-thə-'pul-,pit, -pət *also* 'pəl-\ *n, pl* **jack–in–the–pulpits** *or* **jacks–in–the–pulpit** (1847) **:** any of several plants (genus *Arisaema*) of the arum family; *esp* **:** an American spring-flowering woodland herb (*A. atrorubens*) having an upright club-shaped spadix arched over by a green and purple spathe

jack-in-the-pulpit

¹**jack·knife** \'jak-,nīf\ *n* (1711) **1 :** a large strong clasp knife for the pocket **2 :** a dive executed headfirst in which the diver bends from the waist and touches his ankles while holding his knees unbent and then straightens out

²**jackknife** *vt* (1806) **1 :** to cut with a jackknife **2 :** to cause to double up like a jackknife ~ *vi* **1 :** to double up like a jackknife **2 :** to turn or rise and form an angle of 90 degrees or less with each other — used esp. of a pair of vehicles (as a tractor and its trailer) that are fastened together

jack·leg \'jak-,leg, -,lāg\ *adj* [¹*jack* + *-leg* (as in *blackleg*)] (1850) **1 a :** lacking skill or training **:** AMATEUR ⟨a ~ carpenter⟩ **b :** characterized by unscrupulousness, dishonesty, or lack of professional standards ⟨a ~ lawyer⟩ **2 :** designed as a temporary expedient **:** MAKESHIFT — **jackleg** *n*

jack·light \-,līt\ *n* (1883) **:** a light used esp. in hunting or fishing at night

jack mackerel *n* (1882) **:** a California market fish (*Trachurus symmetricus*) that is iridescent green or bluish above and silvery below

jack–of–all–trades \,jak-ə-'vȯl-,trādz\ *n, pl* **jacks–of–all–trades** (1618) **:** a person who can do passable work at various tasks **:** a handy versatile person

jack off *vb* [prob. alter. of *jerk off*] (1959) **:** MASTURBATE — usu. considered vulgar

jack–o'–lan·tern \'jak-ə-,lant-ərn\ *n* (1673) **1 a :** IGNIS FATUUS **b :** SAINT ELMO'S FIRE **2 :** a lantern made of a pumpkin cut to look like a human face

jack pine *n* (1883) **:** a slender No. American pine (*Pinus banksiana*) that has two stout twisted leaves in each fascicle and wood used esp. for pulpwood

jack·pot \'jak-,pät\ *n* (1884) **1 a** (1) **:** a hand or game of draw poker in which a pair of jacks or better is required to open (2) **:** a large pot (as in poker) formed by the accumulation of stakes from previous play **b** (1) **:** a combination on a slot machine that wins a top prize or all the coins in the machine (2) **:** the sum so won **c :** a large fund of money or other reward formed by the accumulation of unwon prizes **2 :** an impressive often unexpected success or reward **3** *chiefly West* **:** a tight spot **:** JAM

jack·rab·bit \-,rab-ət\ *n* [¹*jack* (jackass) + *rabbit;* fr. its long ears] (1863) **:** any of several large hares (genus *Lepus*) of western No. America having very long ears and long hind legs

jack salmon *n* (1871) **1 :** WALLEYE 3 **2 :** GRILSE

jack·screw \'jak-,skrü\ *n* (1769) **:** a screw-operated jack for lifting or for exerting pressure

jack·smelt \-,smelt\ *n* (1949) **:** a large silversides (*Atherinopsis californiensis*) of the Pacific coast of No. America that is the chief commercial smelt of the California markets

Jack·son Day \'jak-sən-\ *n* [Andrew *Jackson;* fr. his defense of New Orleans] (1885) **:** January 8 celebrated as a legal holiday in Louisiana to commemorate the successful defense of New Orleans in 1815

Jack·so·ni·an \jak-'sō-nē-ən\ *adj* (1824) **:** of, relating to, or characteristic of Andrew Jackson or his political principles or policies — **Jacksonian** *n*

jack·stay \-,stā\ *n* (1840) **1 :** an iron rod, wooden bar, or wire rope along a yard of a ship to which the sails are fastened **2 :** a support of wood, iron, or rope running up a mast on which the parrel of a yard travels

jack·straw \'jak-,strȯ\ *n* (1801) **1 :** one of the pieces used in the game jackstraws **2** *pl but sing in constr* **:** a game in which a set of straws or thin strips is let fall in a heap with each player in turn trying to remove one at a time without disturbing the rest

jack–tar \-'tär\ *n, often cap* (1781) **:** SAILOR

Ja·cob \'jā-kəb\ *n* [LL, fr. Gk *Iacōb,* fr. Heb *Ya'ăqōbh*] **1 :** a son of Isaac and Rebekah, the twin brother of Esau, and heir of God's promise of blessing to Abraham **2 :** the ancient Hebrew nation

Jac·o·be·an \,jak-ə-'bē-ən\ *adj* [NL *Jacobaeus,* fr. *Jacobus* James] (1844) **:** of, relating to, or characteristic of James I of England or his age — **Jacobean** *n*

jacobean lily *n, often cap J* [LL *Jacobus* (St. James)] (1770) **:** a Mexican bulbous herb (*Sprekelia formosissima*) of the amaryllis family cultivated for its bright red solitary flower

Ja·co·bi·an \jə-'kō-bē-ən, yä-\ *n* [K. G. J. *Jacobi* †1851 Ger. mathematician] (1881) **:** a determinant defined for a finite number of functions of the same number of variables in which each row consists of the first partial derivatives of the same function with respect to each of the variables

Jac·o·bin \'jak-ə-bən\ *n* [ME, fr. MF, fr. ML *Jacobinus,* fr. LL *Jacobus* (St. James); fr. the location of the first Dominican convent in the street of St. James, Paris] (14c) **1 :** DOMINICAN **2** [F, fr. *Jacobin* Dominican; fr. the group's founding in the Dominican convent in Paris] **:** a member of an extremist or radical political group; *esp* **:** a member of such a group advocating egalitarian democracy and engaging in terrorist activities during the French Revolution of 1789 — **Jac·o·bin·ic** \,jak-ə-'bin-ik\ *or* **Jac·o·bin·i·cal** \-i-kəl\ *adj* — **Jac·o·bin·ism** \'jak-ə-bə-,niz-əm\ *n*

¹**Jac·o·bite** \'jak-ə-,bīt\ *n* [ME, fr. ML *Jacobita,* fr. *Jacobus* Baradaeus (Jacob Baradai) †578 Syrian monk] (15c) **:** a member of any of various Monophysite Eastern churches; *esp* **:** a member of the Monophysite Syrian church

²**Jacobite** *n* [*Jacobus* (James II)] (1689) **:** a partisan of James II of England or of the Stuarts after the revolution of 1688 — **Jac·o·bit·i·cal** \,jak-ə-'bit-i-kəl\ *adj* — **Jac·o·bit·ism** \'jak-ə-,bīt-,iz-əm\ *n*

Ja·cob's ladder \,jā-kəbz-\ *n* [fr. the ladder seen in a dream by Jacob in Gen 28:12] (1733) **1 :** any of a genus (*Polemonium*) of herbs of the phlox family that have pinnate leaves, an herbaceous calyx, a bell-shaped corolla with stamens with their filaments bent downward, and a several-seeded capsule; *esp* **:** a perennial (*P. caeruleum*) of European origin with bright blue or white flowers **2 :** a marine ladder of rope or chain with wooden or iron rungs

Ja·co·bus \jə-'kō-bəs\ *n* [*Jacobus* (James I), during whose reign unites were coined] (1612) **:** UNITE

jac·o·net \'jak-ə-,net\ *n* [modif. of Urdu *jagannāthī*] (1769) **:** a lightweight cotton cloth used for clothing and bandages

jac·quard \'jak-,ärd\ *n, often cap* [Joseph *Jacquard*] (1841) **1 a :** a loom apparatus or head for weaving figured fabrics **b :** a loom having a jacquard **2 :** a fabric of intricate variegated weave or pattern

jac·que·rie \,zhäk-ə-'rē, ,zhak-\ *n, often cap* [MF, fr. the French peasant revolt in 1358, fr. *jacque* peasant — more at JACKET] (1523) **:** a peasants' revolt

jac·ti·ta·tion \,jak-tə-'tā-shən\ *n* [LL *jactitation-, jactitatio,* fr. *jactitatus,* pp. of *jactitare,* freq. of *jactare* to throw — more at JET] (1665) **:** a tossing to and fro or jerking and twitching of the body

Ja·cuz·zi \jə-'kü-zē\ *trademark* — used for a whirlpool bath and a recreational bathing tub or pool

¹**jade** \'jād\ *n* [ME] (14c) **1 :** a broken-down, vicious, or worthless horse **2 a :** a disreputable woman **b :** a flirtatious girl

²**jade** *vb* **jad·ed; jad·ing** *vt* (1598) **1 a :** to wear out by overwork or abuse **b :** to tire by severe or tedious tasks **2** *obs* **:** to make ridiculous ~ *vi* **:** to become weary or dulled ***syn*** see TIRE

³**jade** *n* [F, fr. obs. Sp (*piedra de la*) *ijada,* lit., loin stone, fr. L *ilia,* pl. of *ileum* groin, ileum; fr. the belief that jade cures renal colic] (1657) **:** either of two tough compact typically green gemstones that take a high polish: **a :** JADEITE **b :** NEPHRITE

jad·ed *adj* (1693) **1 :** fatigued by overwork **:** EXHAUSTED **2 :** dulled by surfeit or excess — **jad·ed·ly** *adv* — **jad·ed·ness** *n*

jade green *n* (1892) **:** a variable color averaging a light bluish green

jade·ite \'jā-,dīt\ *n* [F] (1864) **:** a monoclinic mineral that is a jade — **ja·dit·ic** \jā-'dit-ik\ *adj*

jade plant *n* (ca. 1944) **:** any of several stonecrops (genus *Crassula*) cultivated as foliage plants

jae·ger \'yā-gər\ *n* [G *jäger*] (1809) **1 a :** HUNTER, HUNTSMAN **b :** one attending a person of rank or wealth and wearing hunter's costume **2 :** any of several large dark-colored birds (genus *Stercorarius* of the family Stercorariidae) of northern seas that are strong fliers and that tend to harass weaker birds until they drop or disgorge their prey

¹**jag** \'jag\ *vb* **jagged; jag·ging** [ME *jaggen*] *vt* (15c) **1** *chiefly dial* **:** PRICK, STAB **2 :** to cut indentations into; *also* **:** to form teeth on (a saw) by cutting indentations ~ *vi* **1 :** PRICK, THRUST **2 :** to move in jerks — **jag·ger** *n*

²**jag** *n* (1578) **:** a sharp projecting part **:** BARB

³**jag** *n* [origin unknown] (1597) **1 :** a small load **2 a :** a state or feeling of exhilaration or intoxication usu. induced by liquor **b :** SPREE ⟨a crying ~⟩

jag·ged \'jag-əd\ *adj* (1577) **1 :** having a sharply uneven edge or surface **2 :** having a harsh, rough, or irregular quality — **jag·ged·ly** *adv* — **jag·ged·ness** *n*

jag·gery \ˈjag-ə-rē\ *n* [Hindi *jāgrī*] (1598) : an unrefined brown sugar made from palm sap

jag·gy \ˈjag-ē\ *adj* (1717) : JAGGED, NOTCHED

jag·uar \ˈjag(-yə)-ˌwär, *esp Brit* ˈjag-yə-wər\ *n* [Sp *yaguar* & Pg *jaguar,* fr. Guarani *yaguara* & Tupi *jaguara*] (1604) : a large cat (*Felis onca*) of tropical America that is larger and stockier than the leopard and is brownish yellow or buff with black spots

jaguar

jag·ua·run·di \ˌzhag-wə-ˈrən-dē\ *also* **jag·ua·ron·di** \-ˈrän-\ *n* [AmerSp & Pg, fr. Tupi *jaguarundi* & Guarani *yaguarundi*] (ca. 1885) : a slender long-tailed short-legged grayish wildcat (*Felis jaguarondi*) of Central and So. America

Jah·veh \ˈyä-(ˌ)vā\ *var of* YAHWEH

jai alai \ˈhī-ˌlī, ˌhī-ə-ˈlī\ *n* [Sp, fr. Basque, fr. *jai* festival + *alai* merry] (1903) : a court game somewhat like handball played by two or four players with a ball and a long curved wicker basket strapped to the wrist

[1]jail \ˈjā(ə)l\ *n* [ME *jaiole,* fr. OF, fr. LL *caveola,* dim. of L *cavea* cage — more at CAGE] (13c) : PRISON; *esp* : a building for the confinement of persons held in lawful custody

[2]jail *vt* (1604) : to confine in or as if in a jail

jail·bait \ˈjā(ə)l-ˌbāt\ *n* (1930) : a girl under the age of consent with whom sexual intercourse is unlawful and constitutes statutory rape

jail·bird \-ˌbərd\ *n* (1618) : a person confined in jail; *specif* : an habitual criminal

jail·break \-ˌbrāk\ *n* (1910) : a forcible escape from jail

jail delivery *n* (15c) **1** : the clearing of a jail by bringing the prisoners to trial **2** : the freeing of prisoners by force

jail·er *or* **jail·or** \ˈjā-lər\ *n* (14c) **1** : a keeper of a jail **2** : one that restricts another's liberty as if by imprisonment

Jain \ˈjīn\ *or* **Jai·na** \ˈjī-nə\ *n* [Hindi *Jain,* fr. Skt *Jaina*] (1805) : an adherent of Jainism

Jain·ism \ˈjī-ˌniz-əm\ *n* (1858) : a religion of India originating in the 6th century B.C. and teaching liberation of the soul by right knowledge, right faith, and right conduct

jake leg \ˈjā-ˌkleg, -ˌklāg\ *n* [*jake* grain alcohol flavored with Jamaica ginger] (1932) : a paralysis caused by drinking improperly distilled or contaminated liquor

jakes \ˈjāks\ *n pl but sing or pl in constr* [perh. fr. F *Jacques* James] (ca. 1530) : PRIVY 2

jal·ap \ˈjal-əp, ˈjäl-\ *n* [F & Sp; F *jalap,* fr. Sp *jalapa,* fr. *Jalapa,* Mexico] (1644) **1 a** : the dried purgative tuberous root of a Mexican plant (*Exogonium purga*) of the morning-glory family; *also* : a powdered drug prepared from it that contains resinous glycosides **b** : the root or derived drug of plants related to the one supplying jalap **2** : a plant yielding jalap

ja·la·pe·ño \ˌhäl-ə-ˈpān-(ˌ)yō\ *n* [MexSp] (ca. 1939) : a Mexican hot pepper — called also *jalapeño pepper*

ja·lopy \jə-ˈläp-ē\ *n, pl* **ja·lop·ies** [origin unknown] (1928) : a dilapidated old automobile or airplane

jal·ou·sie \ˈjal-ə-sē\ *n* [F, lit., jealousy, fr. OF *jelous* jealous] (1783) **1** : a blind with adjustable horizontal slats for admitting light and air while excluding sun and rain **2** : a window made of adjustable glass louvers that control ventilation

[1]jam \ˈjam\ *vb* **jammed; jam·ming** [origin unknown] *vt* (1719) **1 a** : to press into a close or tight position ⟨~ his hat on⟩ **b** (1) : to cause to become wedged so as to be unworkable ⟨~ the typewriter keys⟩ (2) : to make unworkable by jamming **c** : to block passage of : OBSTRUCT **d** : to fill often to excess : PACK ⟨the crowd *jammed* the theater⟩ **2** : to push forcibly; *esp* : to apply (brakes) suddenly and forcibly — used with *on* **3** : CRUSH, BRUISE **4 a** : to make unintelligible by sending out interfering signals or messages **b** : to make (as a radar apparatus) ineffective by jamming signals or by causing reflection of radar waves ~ *vi* **1 a** : to become blocked or wedged **b** : to become unworkable through the jamming of a movable part **2** : to force one's way into a restricted space **3** : to take part in a jam session

[2]jam *n* (1805) **1 a** : an act or instance of jamming **b** : a crowded mass that impedes or blocks ⟨a traffic ~⟩ **2 a** : the quality or state of being jammed **b** : the pressure or congestion of a crowd : CRUSH **3** : a difficult state of affairs : FIX ⟨they get sick and it puts them in a ~ and they end up under a pile of bills —Hamilton Basso⟩ **4** : JAM SESSION **5** : a round in Roller Derby in which a jammer from each team tries to lap members of the opposing team and score points

[3]jam *n* [prob. fr. [1]*jam*] (ca. 1730) : a food made by boiling fruit and sugar to a thick consistency

Ja·mai·ca ginger \jə-ˌmā-kə-\ *n* [*Jamaica,* W. Indies] (1818) **1** : an alcoholic extract of ginger used as a flavoring **2** : the powdered root of ginger used as an intestinal stimulant and carminative

Jamaica rum *n* (1775) : a heavy-bodied rum made by slow fermentation and marked by a pungent bouquet

jamb \ˈjam\ *n* [ME *jambe,* fr. MF, lit., leg, fr. LL *gamba* — more at GAMBIT] (14c) **1** : an upright piece or surface forming the side of an opening (as for a door, window, or fireplace) **2** : a projecting columnar part or mass

jam·ba·laya \ˌjəm-bə-ˈlī-ə\ *n* [LaF, fr. Prov *jambalaia*] (1872) **1** : rice cooked with ham, sausage, chicken, shrimp, or oysters and seasoned with herbs **2** : a mixture of diverse elements ⟨~ of influences that make much contemporary verse unsavory —Babette Deutsch⟩

jam·beau \ˈjam-(ˌ)bō\ *n, pl* **jam·beaux** \-(ˌ)bōz\ [ME, fr. (assumed) AF, fr. MF *jambe*] (14c) : a piece of medieval armor for the leg below the knee — see ARMOR illustration

jam·bo·ree \ˌjam-bə-ˈrē\ *n* [origin unknown] (1864) **1** : a noisy or unrestrained carouse **2 a** : a large festive gathering **b** : a national or international camping assembly of Boy Scouts **3** : a long mixed program of entertainment

James \ˈjāmz\ *n* [F, fr. LL *Jacobus*] **1** : an apostle, son of Zebedee, and brother of the apostle John according to the Gospel accounts **2** : an apostle and son of Alphaeus according to the Gospel accounts — called also *James the Less* **3** : a brother of Jesus traditionally held to be the author of the New Testament Epistle of James **4** : a moral lecture addressed to early Christians and included as a book in the New Testament — see BIBLE table

James·ian \ˈjām-zē-ən\ *adj* (1875) **1** : of, relating to, or characteristic of William James or his teachings **2** : of, relating to, or characteristic of Henry James or his writings

jam·mer \ˈjam-ər\ *n* (1909) **1** : one that jams; *esp* : a usu. modulated transmitter that emits a signal that is intended to interfere with or make unintelligible radio or radar signals **2** : a player on a Roller Derby team who attempts to score during a jam

jam–pack \ˈjam-ˈpak\ *vt* (1924) : to pack tightly or to excess

jam session *n* [[2]*jam*] (1933) : an often impromptu performance by a group esp. of jazz musicians that is characterized by improvisation

Jam·shid *or* **Jam·shyd** \jam-ˈshēd\ *n* [Per *Jamshīd*] : an early legendary king of Persia who reigned for 700 years

jam–up \ˈjam-ˌəp\ *n* (1941) : JAM 1

Jane Doe \ˈjān-ˈdō\ *n* (1936) : a female party to legal proceedings whose true name is unknown

[1]jan·gle \ˈjaŋ-gəl\ *vb* **jan·gled; jan·gling** \-g(ə-)liŋ\ [ME *janglen,* fr. MF *jangler,* of Gmc origin; akin to MD *jangelen* to grumble] *vi* (14c) **1** *archaic* : to talk idly **2** : to quarrel verbally **3** : to make a harsh or discordant often ringing sound ~ *vt* **1** : to utter or sound in a discordant, babbling, or chattering way **2 a** : to cause to sound harshly or inharmoniously **b** : to excite to tense irritation ⟨*jangled* nerves⟩ — **jan·gler** \-g(ə-)lər\ *n*

[2]jangle *n* (14c) **1** : idle talk **2** : noisy quarreling ⟨a degrading ~ between servant and mistress —Jean Stafford⟩ **3** : a discordant often ringing sound : DISCORD

jan·is·sary *or* **jan·i·zary** \ˈjan-ə-ˌser-ē, -ˌzer-\ *n, pl* **-sar·ies** *or* **-zar·ies** [It *gianizzero,* fr. Turk *yeniçeri*] (1529) **1** *often cap* : a soldier of an elite corps of Turkish troops organized in the 14th century and abolished in 1826 **2** : a member of a group of loyal or subservient troops, officials, or supporters

jan·i·tor \ˈjan-ət-ər\ *n* [L, fr. *janua* door, fr. *janus* arch, gate] (1629) **1** : DOORKEEPER **2** : one who keeps the premises of an apartment, office, or other building clean, tends the heating system, and makes minor repairs — **jan·i·to·ri·al** \ˌjan-ə-ˈtōr-ē-əl, -ˈtȯr-\ *adj*

Jan·sen·ism \ˈjan(t)-sə-ˌniz-əm\ *n* [F *jansénisme,* fr. Cornelis *Jansen*] (1656) **1** : a system of doctrine based on moral determinism, defended by various reformist factions among 17th and 18th century western European Roman Catholic clergy, religious, and scholars, and condemned as heretical by papal authority **2** : a puritanical attitude (as toward sex) — **Jan·sen·ist** \-nəst\ *n* — **Jan·sen·is·tic** \ˌjan(t)-sə-ˈnis-tik\ *adj*

Jan·u·ary \ˈjan-yə-ˌwer-ē\ *n* [ME *Januarie,* fr. L *Januarius,* 1st month of the ancient Roman year, fr. *Janus*] (12c) : the 1st month of the Gregorian calendar

Ja·nus \ˈjā-nəs\ *n* [L] : a Roman god that is identified with doors, gates, and all beginnings and that is represented artistically with two opposite faces

Janus–faced \-ˌfāst\ *adj* (1682) : DUPLICITOUS, TWO-FACED

Janus green *n* [prob. fr. *Janus,* a trademark] (1898) : a basic azine dye used esp. as a biological stain (as for mitochondria)

Jap \ˈjap\ *n or adj* (1890) : JAPANESE — usu. used disparagingly

[1]ja·pan \jə-ˈpan\ *adj* (1673) : of, relating to, or originating in Japan : of a kind or style characteristic of Japanese workmanship

[2]japan *n* (1688) **1 a** : any of several varnishes yielding a hard brilliant finish **b** : a hard dark coating containing asphalt and a drier that is used esp. on metal and fixed by heating — called also *japan black* **2** : work (as lacquer ware) finished and decorated in the Japanese manner

[3]japan *vt* **ja·panned; ja·pan·ning** (1688) **1** : to cover with or as if with a coat of japan **2** : to give a high gloss to — **ja·pan·ner** *n*

Japan clover *n* (1868) : an annual lespedeza (*Lespedeza striata*) used as a forage, soil-improving, and pasture crop esp. in the southeastern U.S. — called also *Japanese clover*

Jap·a·nese \ˌjap-ə-ˈnēz, -ˈnēs\ *n, pl* **Japanese** (1604) **1 a** : a native or inhabitant of Japan **b** : a person of Japanese descent **2** : the language of the Japanese — **Japanese** *adj*

Japanese an·drom·e·da \-ˌan-ˈdräm-əd-ə\ *n* [NL *Andromeda* (genus of plants), fr. L *Andromeda,* Ethiopian princess, fr. Gk *Andromedē*] (1948) : a shrubby evergreen Asian heath (*Pieris japonica*) with glossy leaves and drooping clusters of whitish flowers

Japanese barnyard millet *n* (ca. 1905) : JAPANESE MILLET

Japanese beetle *n* (1900) : a small metallic green and brown scarab beetle (*Popillia japonica*) that has been introduced into America from Japan and as a grub feeds on the roots of grasses and decaying vegetation and as an adult eats foliage and fruits

Japanese cedar *n* (ca. 1880) : a large evergreen tree (*Cryptomeria japonica*) grown esp. in China and Japan for its valuable soft wood

Japanese iris *n* (1883) : any of various beardless garden irises with very large showy flowers

Japanese lacquer *n* (1900) : LACQUER 1b

Japanese millet *n* (ca. 1900) : a coarse annual grass (*Echinochloa frumentacea*) cultivated esp. in Asia for its edible seeds

Japanese persimmon *n* (ca. 1909) : an Asian persimmon (*Diospyros kaki*) widely cultivated for its large edible fruits; *also* : its fruit

Japanese plum *n* (1901) **1** : any of numerous large showy usu. yellow to light red cultivated plums **2** : a tree that bears Japanese plums and is derived from a Chinese tree (*Prunus salicina*)

Japanese quail *n* (1966) : any of a subspecies (*Coturnix coturnix japonica*) of Old World quail from China and Japan that are used extensively in laboratory research

Japanese quince *n* (1900) : a hardy Chinese ornamental shrub (*Chaenomeles lagenaria*) of the rose family with scarlet flowers

Japanese spurge *n* (1924) : a low Japanese herb or subshrub (*Pachysandra terminalis*) of the box family often used as a ground cover

jap·a·nize \ˈjap-ə-ˌnīz\ *vt* **-nized; -niz·ing** *often cap* (1890) **1** : to make Japanese **2** : to bring (an area) under the influence of Japan — **jap·a·ni·za·tion** \ˌjap-ə-nə-ˈzā-shən\ *n, often cap*

Japan wax *n* (1859) : a yellowish fat obtained from the berries of several sumacs (as *Rhus verniciflua* and *R. succedanea*) and used chiefly in polishes

[1]**jape** \'jāp\ *vb* **japed; jap·ing** [ME *japen*] *vi* (14c) **:** to say or do something jokingly or mockingly ~ *vt* **:** to make mocking fun of — **jap·er** \'jā-pər\ *n* — **jap·ery** \'jā-p(ə-)rē\ *n*

[2]**jape** *n* (14c) **:** something designed to arouse amusement or laughter: as **a :** an amusing literary or dramatic production **b :** GIBE

Ja·pheth \'jā-fəth\ *n* [L *Japheth* or Gk *Iapheth,* fr. Heb *Yepheth*] **:** a son of Noah held to be the progenitor of the Medes and Greeks

ja·pon·i·ca \jə-'pän-i-kə\ *n* [NL, fr. fem. of *Japonicus* Japanese, fr. *Japonia* Japan] (1819) **:** JAPANESE QUINCE

[1]**jar** \'jär\ *vb* **jarred; jar·ring** [prob. of imit. origin] *vi* (1526) **1 a :** to make a harsh or discordant sound **b :** to have a harshly disagreeable or disconcerting effect **c :** to be out of harmony; *specif* **:** BICKER **2 :** to undergo severe vibration ~ *vt* **:** to cause to jar: as **a :** to affect disagreeably **:** UNSETTLE **b :** to make unstable **:** SHAKE — **jar·ring·ly** \'jär-iŋ-lē\ *adv*

[2]**jar** *n* (1537) **1 a :** a state or manifestation of discord or conflict **b :** a harsh grating sound **2 a :** a sudden or unexpected shake **b :** an unsettling shock **c :** an unpleasant break or conflict in rhythm, flow, or transition

[3]**jar** *n* [MF *jarre,* fr. OProv *jarra,* fr. Ar *jarrah* earthen water vessel] (1592) **1 :** a widemouthed container made typically of earthenware or glass **2 :** as much as a jar will hold — **jar·ful** \-,fu̇l\ *n*

[4]**jar** *n* [alter. of earlier *char* turn, fr. ME — more at CHARE] *archaic* (1674) **:** the position of being ajar — usu. used in the phrase *on the jar*

jar·di·niere \,järd-ᵊn-'i(ə)r, ,zhärd-ᵊn-'(y)e(ə)r\ *n* [F *jardinière,* lit., female gardener] (1841) **1 a :** an ornamental stand for plants or flowers **b :** a large usu. ceramic flowerpot holder **2 :** a garnish for meat consisting of several cooked vegetables cut into pieces

[1]**jar·gon** \'jär-gən, -,gän\ *n* [ME, fr. MF] (14c) **1 a :** confused unintelligible language **b :** a strange, outlandish, or barbarous language or dialect **c :** a hybrid language or dialect simplified in vocabulary and grammar and used for communication between peoples of different speech **2 :** the technical terminology or characteristic idiom of a special activity or group **3 :** obscure and often pretentious language marked by circumlocutions and long words — **jar·gon·is·tic** \,jär-gə-'nis-tik\ *adj*

[2]**jargon** *vi* (14c) **1 :** TWITTER, WARBLE **2 :** JARGONIZE

jar·gon·ize \'jär-gə-,nīz\ *vb* **-ized; -iz·ing** *vi* (1803) **:** to speak or write jargon ~ *vt* **1 :** to express in jargon **2 :** to make into jargon

jar·goon \jär-'gün\ *or* **jar·gon** \-'gän\ *n* [F *jargon* — more at ZIRCON] (1769) **:** a colorless, pale yellow, or smoky zircon

jarl \'yär(-ə)l\ *n* [ON — more at EARL] (1820) **:** a Scandinavian noble ranking immediately below the king

jar·rah \'jar-ə\ *n* [native name in Australia] (ca. 1866) **:** an Australian eucalypt (*Eucalyptus marginata*) with rough bark and ovate leaves; *also* **:** its wood

jas·mine \'jaz-mən\ *n* [F *jasmin,* fr. Ar *yāsamīn,* fr. Per] (1562) **1 a :** any of numerous often climbing shrubs (genus *Jasminum*) of the olive family that usu. have extremely fragrant flowers; *esp* **:** a tall-climbing semievergreen Asian shrub (*J. officinale*) with fragrant white flowers from which a perfume is extracted **b :** any of numerous plants having sweet-scented flowers; *esp* **:** YELLOW JESSAMINE **2 :** a light yellow

Ja·son \'jās-ᵊn\ *n* [L *Iason,* fr. Gk *Iasōn*] **:** a legendary Greek hero distinguished for his successful quest of the Golden Fleece

jas·per \'jas-pər\ *n* [ME *jaspre,* fr. MF, fr. L *jaspis,* fr. Gk *iaspis,* of Sem origin; akin to Heb *yāshĕpheh* jasper] (14c) **1 :** an opaque cryptocrystalline quartz of any of several colors; *esp* **:** green chalcedony **2 :** colored stoneware with raised white decoration **3 :** a blackish green — **jas·pery** \-pə-rē\ *adj*

jas·per·ware \'jas-pər-,wa(ə)r, -,we(ə)r\ *n* (1863) **:** JASPER 2

jas·sid \'jas-əd\ *n* [deriv. of Gk *Iasos,* town in Asia Minor] (1895) **:** any of a large cosmopolitan family (Jassidae) of small leafhoppers that include many economically significant pests of cultivated plants; *broadly* **:** LEAFHOPPER

Jat \'jät\ *n* [Hindi *Jāt*] (1622) **:** a member of an Indo-Aryan people of the Punjab and Uttar Pradesh

ja·to unit \'jāt-(,)ō-\ *n* [*jet-assisted takeoff*] (1947) **:** a unit for assisting the takeoff of an airplane consisting of one or more rocket engines

jaunce \'jȯn(t)s, 'jän(t)s\ *vi* [origin unknown] *archaic* (1593) **:** PRANCE

jaun·dice \'jȯn-dəs, 'jän-\ *n* [ME *jaundis,* fr. MF *jaunisse,* fr. *jaune* yellow, fr. L *galbinus* yellowish green, fr. *galbus* yellow] (14c) **1 :** yellowish pigmentation of the skin, tissues, and body fluids caused by the deposition of bile pigments **2 :** a disease or abnormal condition characterized by jaundice **3 :** a state or attitude characterized by satiety, distaste, or hostility

jaun·diced \-dəst\ *adj* (1640) **1 :** affected with or as if with jaundice **2 :** exhibiting or influenced by envy, distaste, or hostility ⟨a ~ eye⟩

[1]**jaunt** \'jȯnt, 'jänt\ *vi* [origin unknown] (1575) **1** *archaic* **:** to trudge about **2 :** to make a usu. short journey for pleasure

[2]**jaunt** *n* (1801) **1** *archaic* **:** a tiring trip **2 :** an excursion undertaken esp. for pleasure

jaunting car *n* (1801) **:** a light 2-wheeled open horse-drawn vehicle used esp. in Ireland with lengthwise seats placed face-to-face or back to back

jaun·ty \'jȯnt-ē, 'jänt-\ *adj* **jaun·ti·er; -est** [modif. of F *gentil*] (1662) **1** *archaic* **a :** GENTEEL **b :** STYLISH **2 :** sprightly in manner or appearance **:** LIVELY — **jaun·ti·ly** \'jȯnt-ᵊl-ē, 'jänt-\ *adv* — **jaun·ti·ness** \'jȯnt-ē-nəs, 'jänt-\ *n*

ja·va \'jav-ə, 'jäv-, -ē\ *n, often cap* [*Java,* island of Indonesia] (1850) **:** COFFEE

Ja·va man \,jäv-ə-, ,jav-ə-\ *n* (1911) **:** a Pleistocene hominid known from fragmentary skeletons found in Trinil and Djetis, Java and now classified with the pithecanthropines

Ja·va·nese \,jav-ə-'nēz, ,jäv-, -'nēs\ *n, pl* **Javanese** [*Java* + *-nese* (as in *Japanese*)] (1704) **1 :** a member of an Indonesian people inhabiting the island of Java **2 :** an Austronesian language of the Javanese people — **Javanese** *adj*

jav·e·lin \'jav-(ə-)lən\ *n* [MF *javeline,* alter. of *javelot,* of Celt origin; akin to OIr *gabul* forked stick] (15c) **1 :** a light spear thrown as a weapon of war or in hunting **2 :** a slender usu. metal shaft at least 260 centimeters long that is thrown for distance in a field event

ja·ve·li·na \,häv-ə-'lē-nə\ *n* [AmerSp *jabalina,* fr. Sp, fem. of *jabalí* wild boar, fr. Ar *jabalīy*] (1822) **:** PECCARY

Ja·velle water \zha-'vel, zhə-\ *n* [*Javel,* former village in France] (1890) **:** an aqueous solution of sodium hypochlorite used as a disinfectant or a bleaching agent and in photography

[1]**jaw** \'jȯ\ *n* [ME] (14c) **1 a :** either of two complex cartilaginous or bony structures in most vertebrates that border the mouth, support the soft parts enclosing it, usu. bear teeth on their oral margin, and are an upper that is more or less firmly fused with the skull and a lower that is hinged, movable, and articulated with the temporal bone of either side **b :** the parts constituting the walls of the mouth and serving to open and close it — usu. used in pl. **c :** any of various organs of invertebrates that perform the function of the vertebrate jaws **2 :** something resembling the jaw of an animal: as **a :** one of the sides of a narrow pass or channel **b :** either of two or more opposable parts that open and close for holding or crushing something between them **3 :** a friendly chat

[2]**jaw** *vi* (1748) **:** to talk abusively, indignantly, or long-windedly ~ *vt* **:** to talk to in a scolding or boring manner

jaw·bone \'jȯ-'bōn, -,bōn\ *n* (15c) **:** JAW 1a; *esp* **:** MANDIBLE

jaw·bon·ing \-'bō-niŋ, -,bō-\ *n* (1969) **:** the use of usu. public persuasion (as by a president) to influence behavior (as of business or labor leaders) — **jaw·bone** \-'bōn, -,bōn\ *vt*

jaw·break·er \-,brā-kər\ *n* (1839) **1 :** a word difficult to pronounce **2 :** a round hard candy

jawed \'jȯd\ *adj* (1529) **:** having jaws ⟨~ fishes⟩ — usu. used in combination ⟨square-*jawed*⟩ ⟨a 3-*jawed* chuck⟩

jaw·less fish \,jȯ-ləs-\ *n* (1941) **:** any of the taxonomic group (Agnatha) of primitive vertebrates without jaws that is comprised of cyclostomes and extinct related forms

jaw·line \'jȯ-,līn\ *n* (1924) **:** the outline of the lower jaw

[1]**jay** \'jā\ *n* [ME, fr. MF *jai,* fr. LL *gaius*] (14c) **1 a :** a predominantly fawn-colored Old World bird (*Garrulus glandarius*) of the crow family with a black-and-white crest and wings marked with black, white, and blue **b :** any of various usu. crested and largely blue birds that with the common Old World jay constitute a subfamily of the crow family, have roving habits and harsh voices, and are often destructive to the eggs and young of other birds **2 a :** an impertinent chatterer **b :** DANDY 1 **c :** GREENHORN **3 :** a moderate blue

[2]**jay** *n* (ca. 1620) **1 :** the letter *j* **2 :** JOINT 4

jay·bird \'jā-,bərd\ *n* (1661) **:** [1]JAY 1, 2

Jay·cee \'jā-'sē\ *n* [fr. the initials of Junior Citizens, former name of the organization] (1938) **:** a member of a major national and international civic organization

jay·gee \'jā-'jē\ *n* [*junior grade*] (1943) **:** LIEUTENANT JUNIOR GRADE

jay·hawk·er \'jā-,hȯ-kər\ *n* [*jayhawk* (fictitious bird of Kansas)] (1858) **1 a** *often cap* **:** a member of a band of antislavery guerrillas in Kansas and Missouri before and during the Civil War **b :** BANDIT **2** *cap* **:** a native or resident of Kansas — used as a nickname

jay·vee \'jā-'vē\ *n* [*junior varsity*] (1937) **1 :** JUNIOR VARSITY **2 :** a member of a junior varsity team

jay·walk \'jā-,wȯk\ *vi* (1919) **:** to cross a street carelessly or in an illegal manner so as to be endangered by traffic — **jay·walk·er** *n*

[1]**jazz** \'jaz\ *n, often attrib* (1909) **1 a :** American music developed esp. from ragtime and blues and characterized by propulsive syncopated rhythms, polyphonic ensemble playing, varying degrees of improvisation, and often deliberate distortions of pitch and timbre **b :** popular dance music influenced by jazz and played in a loud rhythmic manner **2 :** empty talk **:** HUMBUG ⟨spouted all the scientific ~ —Pete Martin⟩ **3 :** similar but unspecified things **:** STUFF ⟨that wind, and the waves, and all that ~ —John Updike⟩ — **jazz·like** \-,līk\ *adj*

[2]**jazz** *vb* [E slang *jazz* to copulate with, of unknown origin] *vt* (1917) **1 a :** ENLIVEN — usu. used with *up* **b :** ACCELERATE **2 :** to play in the manner of jazz ~ *vi* **1 :** to go here and there **:** GAD **2 :** to dance to or play jazz

jazz·man \'jaz-,man, -mən\ *n* (1926) **:** a jazz musician

jazzy \'jaz-ē\ *adj* **jazz·i·er; -est** (1919) **1 :** having the characteristics of jazz **2 :** marked by unrestraint, animation, or flashiness — **jazz·i·ly** \'jaz-ə-lē\ *adv* — **jazz·i·ness** \'jaz-ē-nəs\ *n*

J–bar lift \'jā-,bär-\ *n* (1954) **:** a ski lift having a series of J-shaped bars each of which pulls one skier

jeal·ous \'jel-əs\ *adj* [ME *jelous,* fr. OF, fr. (assumed) VL *zelosus,* fr. LL *zelus* zeal — more at ZEAL] (13c) **1 a :** intolerant of rivalry or unfaithfulness **b :** disposed to suspect rivalry or unfaithfulness **2 :** hostile toward a rival or one believed to enjoy an advantage **3 :** vigilant in guarding a possession ⟨new colonies were ~ of their new independence — Scott Buchanan⟩ — **jeal·ous·ly** *adv* — **jeal·ous·ness** *n*

jeal·ou·sy \'jel-ə-sē\ *n* (13c) **1 :** a jealous disposition, attitude, or feeling **2 :** zealous vigilance

jean \'jēn\ *n* [short for *jean fustian,* fr. ME *Gene* Genoa, Italy + *fustian*] (1577) **1 :** a durable twilled cotton cloth used esp. for sportswear and work clothes **2 :** close-fitting pants made esp. of jean or denim — usu. used in pl.

[1]**jeep** \'jēp\ *n* [prob. fr. *g. p.* (abbr. of *general purpose*)] (1940) **:** a small general-purpose motor vehicle with 80-inch wheelbase, ¼-ton capacity, and four-wheel drive used by the U.S. army in World War II; *also* **:** a similar but larger and more powerful U.S. army vehicle

[2]**jeep** *vi* (ca. 1942) **:** to travel by jeep

Jeep *trademark* — used for a civilian automotive vehicle

jee·pers \'jē-pərz\ *also* **jee·pers cree·pers** \-'krē-pərz\ *interj* [*jeepers,* euphemism for *Jesus; jeepers creepers,* euphemism for *Jesus Christ*] (1927) — used as a mild oath

jeep·ney \'jēp-nē\ *n* [*jeep* + *jitney*] (ca. 1949) **:** a Philippine jitney bus converted from a jeep

[1]**jeer** \'ji(ə)r\ *vb* [origin unknown] *vi* (1561) **:** to speak or cry out with derision or mockery ~ *vt* **:** to deride with jeers **:** TAUNT *syn* see SCOFF — **jeer·er** *n* — **jeer·ing·ly** \-iŋ-lē\ *adv*

[2]**jeer** *n* (1625) **:** a jeering remark or sound **:** TAUNT

jeez \'jēz\ *interj* [euphemism for *Jesus*] (ca. 1900) — used as a mild oath

Jef·fer·son Da·vis's Birthday \ˌjef-ər-sən-ˌdā-və-səz-\ *n* (1929) **:** the first Monday in June observed as a legal holiday in many Southern states
Jef·fer·son Day \ˈjef-ər-sən-\ *n* (1936) **:** April 13 observed as a holiday in Alabama in commemoration of Thomas Jefferson's birthday
Jef·frey pine \ˌjef-rē-\ *n* [John *Jeffrey*, 19th cent. Scot. botanical explorer] (1858) **:** a pine (*Pinus jeffreyi*) of western No. America with long needles in groups of three
Je·hosh·a·phat \ji-ˈhäs(h)-ə-ˌfat\ *n* [Heb *Yĕhōshāphāth*] **:** a king of Judah who brought Judah into an alliance with the northern kingdom of Israel in the 9th century B.C.
Je·ho·vah \ji-ˈhō-və\ *n* [NL, reading (as *Yĕhōwāh*) of Heb *yhwh* Yahweh with the vowel points of Heb *'adhōnāy* my lord] (1530) **:** GOD 1
Jehovah's Witness *n* (1932) **:** a member of a group that witness by distributing literature and by personal evangelism to beliefs in the theocratic rule of God, the sinfulness of organized religions and governments, and an imminent millennium
je·hu \ˈjē-(ˌ)h(y)ü\ *n* [Heb *Yēhū*] **1** *cap* **:** a king of Israel in the 9th century B.C. who according to the account in II Kings had Jezebel killed in accordance with Elijah's prophecy **2 :** a driver of a coach or cab
jejun- *or* **jejuno-** *comb form* [L *jejunum*] **:** jejunum ⟨*jejun*ectomy⟩
je·ju·nal \ji-ˈjün-ᵊl\ *adj* (ca. 1887) **:** of or relating to the jejunum
je·june \ji-ˈjün\ *adj* [L *jejunus*] (1646) **1 :** lacking nutritive value ⟨~ diets⟩ **2 :** devoid of substance or interest ⟨~ reflections on life and art⟩ ***syn*** see INSIPID — **je·june·ly** *adv* — **je·june·ness** \-ˈjün-nəs\ *n*
je·ju·num \ji-ˈjü-nəm\ *n* [L, fr. neut. of *jejunus*] (14c) **:** the section of the small intestine that comprises the first two fifths beyond the duodenum and that is larger, thicker-walled, and more vascular and has more circular folds than the ileum
Je·kyll and Hyde \ˌjek-ə-lən-ˈhīd, ˌjē-kə-, ˌjā-kə-\ *n* [Dr. *Jekyll* & Mr. *Hyde*, representing the two-sided personality of the protagonist in *The Strange Case of Dr. Jekyll and Mr. Hyde* (1886) by R. L. Stevenson] (ca. 1920) **:** one having a two-sided personality one side of which is good and the other evil
jell \ˈjel\ *vb* [back-formation fr. *jelly*] *vi* (1869) **1 :** to come to the consistency of jelly **2 :** to take shape **:** become cohesive ~ *vt* **:** to cause to jell
jellied gasoline *n* (1944) **:** NAPALM
Jell–O \ˈjel-(ˌ)ō\ *trademark* — used for a gelatin dessert usu. with the flavor and color of fruit
[1]**jel·ly** \ˈjel-ē\ *n, pl* **jellies** [ME *gelly*, fr. MF *gelee*, fr. fem. of *gelé*, pp. of *geler* to freeze, congeal, fr. L *gelare* — more at COLD] (14c) **1 :** a soft somewhat elastic food product made usu. with gelatin or pectin; *esp* **:** a fruit product made by boiling sugar and the juice of fruit **2 :** a substance resembling jelly in consistency **3 :** a state of fear or irresolution **4 :** a shapeless structureless mass **:** PULP — **jel·ly·like** \-ˌlīk\ *adj*
[2]**jelly** *vb* **jel·lied; jel·ly·ing** *vi* (1601) **1 :** JELL **2 :** to make jelly ~ *vt* **:** to bring to the consistency of jelly
jelly bean *n* (1905) **:** a sugar-glazed bean-shaped candy
jel·ly·fish \ˈjel-ē-ˌfish\ *n* (1841) **1 a :** a free-swimming marine coelenterate that is the sexually reproducing form of a hydrozoan or scyphozoan and has a nearly transparent saucer-shaped body and extensile marginal tentacles studded with stinging cells **b :** SIPHONOPHORE **c :** CTENOPHORE **2 :** a person lacking backbone or firmness
jelly roll *n* (1895) **:** a thin sheet of sponge cake spread with jelly and rolled up
jel·u·tong \ˈjel-ə-ˌtȯŋ\ *n* [Malay *jĕlutong*] (ca. 1836) **1 :** any of several trees (genus *Dyera*) of the dogbane family **2 :** the resinous rubbery latex of a jelutong (esp. *Dyera costulata*) used esp. as a chicle substitute
je ne sais quoi \zhə-nə-ˌsā-ˈkwä\ *n* [F, lit., I know not what] (1656) **:** something that cannot be adequately described or expressed
jen·net \ˈjen-ət\ *n* [ME *genett*, fr. MF *genet*, fr. Catal, Zenete (member of a Berber people), horse] (15c) **1 :** a small Spanish horse **2 a :** a female donkey **b :** HINNY
jen·ny \ˈjen-ē\ *n, pl* **jennies** [fr. the name *Jenny*] (1808) **1 a :** a female bird ⟨~ wren⟩ **b :** a female donkey **2 :** SPINNING JENNY
je·on \(ˈ)jā-ˈòn\ *n, pl* **jeon** [native name in Korea] (ca. 1969) **:** the chon of South Korea
jeop·ard \ˈjep-ərd\ *vt* [ME *jeoparden*, back-formation fr. *jeopardie*] (14c) **:** JEOPARDIZE
jeopardise *Brit var of* JEOPARDIZE
jeop·ar·dize \ˈjep-ər-ˌdīz\ *vt* **-dized; -diz·ing** (1646) **:** to expose to danger **:** IMPERIL
jeop·ar·dy \ˈjep-ərd-ē\ *n* [ME *jeopardie*, fr. AF *juparti*, fr. OF *jeu parti* alternative, lit., divided game] (14c) **1 :** exposure to or imminence of death, loss, or injury **:** DANGER **2 :** the danger that an accused person is subjected to when on trial for a criminal offense
je·quir·i·ty bean \jə-ˈkwir-ət-ē-\ *n* [Pg *jequiriti*] (ca. 1900) **1 :** the poisonous scarlet and black seed of the rosary pea often used for beads **2 :** ROSARY PEA 1
jer·boa \jər-ˈbō-ə, jer-\ *n* [Ar *yarbūʿ*] (1662) **:** any of several social nocturnal Old World jumping rodents (family Dipodidae) with long hind legs and long tail

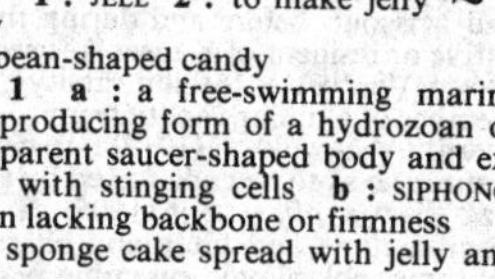
jerboa

jer·e·mi·ad \ˌjer-ə-ˈmī-əd, -ˌad\ *n* [F *jérémiade*, fr. *Jérémie* Jeremiah, fr. LL *Jeremias*] (1780) **:** a prolonged lamentation or complaint
Jer·e·mi·ah \-ˈmī-ə\ *n* [LL *Jeremias*, fr. Gk *Hieremias*, fr. Heb *Yirmĕyāh*] **1 :** a major Hebrew prophet of the 6th and 7th centuries B.C. **2 :** one who is pessimistic about the present and foresees a calamitous future **3 :** a prophetic book of canonical Jewish and Christian Scripture — see BIBLE table
Jer·e·mi·as \-ˈmī-əs\ *n* [LL] **:** JEREMIAH
[1]**jerk** \ˈjərk\ *n* [prob. alter. of *yerk*] (1575) **1 :** a single quick motion of short duration **2 a :** jolting, bouncing, or thrusting motions **b :** a tendency to produce spasmodic motions **3 a :** an involuntary spasmodic muscular movement due to reflex action **b** *pl* **:** involuntary twitchings due to nervous excitement **4 :** a stupid or foolish person **5 :** the pushing of a weight from shoulder height to a position overhead in weight lifting
[2]**jerk** *vt* (1589) **1 :** to give a quick suddenly arrested push, pull, or twist to **2 :** to propel or move with or as if with a quick suddenly arrested motion **3 :** to mix and serve (as sodas) behind a soda fountain ~ *vi* **1 :** to make a sudden spasmodic motion **2 :** to move in short abrupt motions or with frequent jolts — **jerk·er** *n*
[3]**jerk** *vt* [back-formation fr. [1]*jerky*] (1707) **:** to preserve (meat) in long sun-dried slices
jer·kin \ˈjər-kən\ *n* [origin unknown] (1519) **:** a close-fitting hip-length usu. sleeveless jacket
jerk off *vb* (1937) **:** MASTURBATE — usu. considered vulgar
jerk·wa·ter \ˈjər-ˌkwȯt-ər, -ˌkwät-\ *adj* [fr. *jerkwater* (rural train)] (1897) **1 :** remote and unimportant ⟨~ towns⟩ **2 :** TRIVIAL
[1]**jer·ky** \ˈjər-kē\ *n* [Sp *charqui*] (1850) **:** jerked meat
[2]**jerky** \ˈjər-kē\ *adj* **jerk·i·er; -est** (1858) **1 a :** moving along with or marked by fits and starts **b :** characterized by abrupt transitions **2 :** INANE, FOOLISH — **jerk·i·ly** \-kə-lē\ *adv* — **jerk·i·ness** \-kē-nəs\ *n*
jer·o·bo·am \ˌjer-ə-ˈbō-əm\ *n* [*Jeroboam* I †*ab*912 B.C. king of the northern kingdom of Israel] (1889) **:** an oversize wine bottle holding about 3.08 liters
jer·ri·can *or* **jerry can** \ˈjer-ē-ˌkan\ *n* [*Jerry* + *can;* fr. its German design] (1939) **:** a narrow flat-sided 5-gallon liquid container
Jer·ry \ˈjer-ē\ *n, pl* **Jerries** [by shortening & alter.] *chiefly Brit* (1898) **:** GERMAN
jer·ry–build \ˈjer-ē-ˌbild\ *vt* **-built** \-ˌbilt\; **-build·ing** [back-formation fr. *jerry-built*] (1885) **:** to build cheaply and flimsily — **jer·ry–build·er** *n*
jer·ry–built *adj* [origin unknown] (1869) **1 :** built cheaply and unsubstantially **2 :** carelessly or hastily put together
jer·sey \ˈjər-zē\ *n, pl* **jerseys** [*Jersey*, one of the Channel islands] (1587) **1 :** a plain weft-knitted fabric made of wool, cotton, nylon, rayon, or silk and used esp. for clothing **2 :** any of various close-fitting usu. circular-knitted garments esp. for the upper body **3 :** any of a breed of small short-horned predominantly yellowish brown or fawn dairy cattle noted for their rich milk
Jersey pine *n* (1743) **:** VIRGINIA PINE
Je·ru·sa·lem artichoke \jə-ˌrü-s(ə-)ləm-, -ˌrüz-(ə-)ləm-\ *n* [*Jerusalem* by folk etymology fr. It *girasole* girasole] (1641) **:** a perennial American sunflower (*Helianthus tuberosus*) widely cultivated for its tubers that are used as a vegetable, a livestock feed, and a source of levulose
Jerusalem cherry *n* [*Jerusalem*, Palestine] (1788) **:** either of two plants (*Solanum pseudo-capsicum* or *S. capsicastrum*) of the nightshade family cultivated as ornamental houseplants for their orange to red berries
Jerusalem cricket *n* (1947) **:** a large-headed burrowing nocturnal insect (*Stenopelmatus fuscus*) of the southwestern U.S. related to the katydids
Jerusalem thorn *n* (1866) **:** a tropical American leguminous spiny shrub or shrubby tree (*Parkinsonia aculeata*) with pinnate leaves and showy racemose yellow flowers that is used for hedging and as emergency food for livestock
jess \ˈjes\ *n* [ME *ges*, fr. MF *gies*, fr. pl. of *jet* throw, fr. *jeter* to throw — more at JET] (14c) **:** a short strap secured on the leg of a hawk and usu. provided with a ring for attaching a leash — see FALCON illustration — **jessed** \ˈjest\ *adj*
jes·sa·mine \ˈjes-(ə-)mən\ *var of* JASMINE
Jes·se \ˈjes-ē\ *n* [Heb *Yishay*] **:** the father of David, king of Israel, according to the account in I Samuel
jest \ˈjest\ *n* [ME *geste*, fr. OF, fr. L *gesta* deeds, fr. neut. pl. of *gestus*, pp. of *gerere* to bear, wage — more at CAST] (ca. 1548) **1 :** an utterance (as a jeer or a witty quip) intended to be taken as mockery or humor rather than literal truth **2 a :** PRANK **b :** a comic incident **3 a :** a frivolous mood or manner ⟨spoken in ~⟩ **b :** gaiety and merriment **4 :** LAUGHINGSTOCK — **jest** *vb*
syn JEST, JOKE, QUIP, WITTICISM, WISECRACK mean something said for the purpose of evoking laughter. JEST is chiefly literary and applies to any utterance not seriously intended whether sarcastic, ironic, witty, or merely playful; JOKE may apply to an act as well as an utterance and suggests no intent to hurt feelings; QUIP implies lightness and neatness of phrase more definitely than JEST; WITTICISM and WISECRACK both stress cleverness of phrasing and both may suggest flippancy or unfeelingness. ***syn*** see in addition FUN
jest·er \ˈjes-tər\ *n* (14c) **1 :** FOOL 2a **2 :** one given to jests
Je·su·it \ˈjezh-(ə-)wət, ˈjez-\ *n* [NL *Jesuita*, fr. LL *Jesus*] (1559) **1 :** a member of the Roman Catholic Society of Jesus founded by St. Ignatius Loyola in 1534 and devoted to missionary and educational work **2 :** one given to intrigue or equivocation — **je·su·it·ic** \ˌjezh(h)-ə-ˈwit-ik\ *or* **je·su·it·i·cal** \-i-kəl\ *adj, often cap* — **je·su·it·i·cal·ly** \-i-k(ə-)lē\ *adv, often cap* — **je·su·it·ism** \ˈjezh-(ə-)wət-ˌiz-əm, ˈjez-\ *or* **je·su·it·ry** \-(ə-)wə-trē\ *n, often cap*
Je·sus \ˈjē-zəs, -zəz *clerically also* -ˌzəs *and* -ˌzəz\ *n* [LL, fr. Gk *Iēsous*, fr. Heb *Yēshūaʿ*, *Yĕhōshūaʿ* Joshua] **1 :** the Jewish religious teacher whose life, death, and resurrection as reported by the Evangelists are the basis of the Christian message of salvation — called also *Jesus Christ* **2** *Christian Science* **:** the highest human corporeal concept of the divine idea rebuking and destroying error and bringing to light man's immortality
[1]**jet** \ˈjet\ *n* [ME, fr. MF *jaiet*, fr. L *gagates*, fr. Gk *gagatēs*, fr. *Gagas*, town and river in Asia Minor] (14c) **1 :** a compact velvet-black coal that takes a good polish and is often used for jewelry **2 :** an intense black
[2]**jet** *adj* (1607) **:** of the color jet
[3]**jet** *vb* **jet·ted; jet·ting** [MF *jeter*, lit., to throw, fr. L *jactare* to throw, fr. *jactus*, pp. of *jacere* to throw; akin to Gk *hienai* to send] *vi* (1692) **:** to spout forth **:** GUSH ~ *vt* **1 :** to emit in a stream **:** SPOUT **2 :** to place (as a pile) in the ground by means of a jet of water
[4]**jet** *n* (ca. 1696) **1 a :** a usu. forceful stream of fluid (as water or gas) discharged from a narrow opening or a nozzle **b :** a nozzle for a jet of fluid **2 :** something issuing as if in a jet ⟨talk poured from her in a brilliant ~ —*Time*⟩ **3 a :** JET ENGINE **b :** JET AIRPLANE **4 :** JET STREAM
[5]**jet** *vi* **jet·ted; jet·ting** (1949) **:** to travel by jet airplane
jet airplane *n* (1944) **:** an airplane powered by a jet engine that utilizes the surrounding air in the combustion of fuel or by a rocket-type jet engine that carries its fuel and all the oxygen needed for combustion
jet·bead \ˈjet-ˌbēd\ *n* (1930) **:** a shrub (*Rhodotypos scandens*) that has black shining fruit and is used as an ornamental
je·té \zhə-ˈtā\ *n* [F, fr. pp. of *jeter*, fr. MF] (1830) **:** a broad leap in ballet with one leg stretched forward and the other leg backward

jet engine *n* (1943) **:** an engine that produces motion as a result of the rearward discharge of a jet of fluid; *specif* **:** an airplane engine having one or more exhaust nozzles for discharging rearward a jet of heated air and exhaust gases to produce forward propulsion
jet lag *n* (1969) **:** a condition that is characterized by various psychological and physiological effects (as fatigue and irritability), occurs following long flight through several time zones, and prob. results from disruption of circadian rhythms in the human body
jet·lin·er \'jet-ˌlī-nər\ *n* (1949) **:** a jet-propelled airliner
jet·port \'jet-ˌpō(ə)rt, -ˌpȯ(ə)rt\ *n* (1961) **:** an airport designed to handle jet airplanes
jet–pro·pelled \ˌjet-prə-'peld\ *adj* (1877) **1 :** moving by jet propulsion **2 :** suggestive of the speed and force of a jet airplane
jet propulsion *n* (1867) **:** propulsion of a body produced by the forwardly directed forces of the reaction resulting from the rearward discharge of a jet of fluid; *specif* **:** propulsion of an airplane by jet engines
jet·sam \'jet-səm\ *n* [alter. of *jettison*] (1570) **1 :** the part of a ship, its equipment, or cargo that is cast overboard to lighten the load in time of distress and that sinks or is washed ashore **2 :** FLOTSAM 2
jet set *n* (1951) **:** an international social group of wealthy individuals who frequent fashionable resorts — **jet–set·ter** \-ˌset-ər\ *n*
jet stream *n* (1947) **:** a long narrow meandering current of high-speed winds near the tropopause blowing from a generally westerly direction and often exceeding a speed of 250 miles (402 kilometers) per hour
¹**jet·ti·son** \'jet-ə-sən, -ə-zən\ *n* [ME *jetteson,* fr. AF *getteson,* fr. OF *getaison* action of throwing, fr. L *jactation-, jactatio,* fr. *jactatus,* pp. of *jactare* — more at JET] (15c) **:** a voluntary sacrifice of cargo to lighten a ship's load in time of distress
²**jettison** *vt* (1848) **1 :** to make jettison of **2 :** to cast off as superfluous or encumbering **:** DISCARD **3 :** to drop from an airplane or spacecraft in flight — **jet·ti·son·able** \-sə-nə-bəl, -zə-\ *adj*
¹**jet·ty** \'jet-ē\ *n, pl* **jetties** [ME *jette,* fr. MF *jetee,* fr. fem. of *jeté,* pp. of *jeter* to throw — more at JET] (15c) **1 a :** a structure extended into a sea, lake, or river to influence the current or tide or to protect a harbor **b :** a protecting frame of a pier **2 :** a landing wharf
²**jetty** *vi* **jet·tied; jet·ty·ing** (1598) **:** PROJECT, JUT
³**jetty** *adj* (1586) **:** black as jet
jeu d'es·prit \zhœ̄-des-prē\ *n, pl* **jeux d'esprit** *same*\ [F, lit., play of the mind] (1712) **:** a witty comment or composition
jeu·nesse do·rée \zhœ-nes-dȯ-rā\ *n* [F, gilded youth] (1836) **:** young people of wealth and fashion
Jew \'jü\ *n* [ME, fr. OF *gyu,* fr. L *Judaeus,* fr. Gk *Ioudaios,* fr. Heb *Yĕhūdhī,* fr. *Yĕhūdhāh* Judah, Jewish kingdom] (13c) **1 a :** a member of the tribe of Judah **b :** ISRAELITE **2 :** a member of a nation existing in Palestine from the 6th century B.C. to the 1st century A.D. **3 :** a person belonging to a continuation through descent or conversion of the ancient Jewish people **4 :** one whose religion is Judaism
¹**jew·el** \'jü-əl, 'jül *also* 'jü(ə)l\ *n, often attrib* [ME *juel,* fr. OF, prob. dim. of *jeu* game, play, fr. L *jocus* game, joke — more at JOKE] (13c) **1 :** an ornament of precious metal often set with stones or decorated with enamel and worn as an accessory of dress **2 :** one that is highly esteemed **3 :** a precious stone **:** GEM **4 :** a bearing for a pivot (as in a watch or compass) made of crystal, precious stone, or glass — **jew·el-like** \-ˌlīk\ *adj*
²**jewel** *vt* **-eled** *or* **-elled; -el·ing** *or* **-el·ling** (1601) **1 :** to adorn or equip with jewels **2 :** to give beauty to as if with jewels
jew·el·er *or* **jew·el·ler** \'jü-ə-lər, 'jü-lər *also* 'jü(ə)l-ər\ *n* (14c) **1 :** one who makes or repairs jewelry **2 :** one who deals in jewelry, precious stones, watches, and usu. silverware and china
jewellery *chiefly Brit var of* JEWELRY
jew·el·ry \'jü-əl-rē, 'jül-rē, 'jü(ə)l-\ *n* (14c) **:** JEWELS; *esp* **:** objects of precious metal often set with gems and worn for personal adornment
jew·el·weed \-ˌwēd\ *n* (ca. 1817) **:** IMPATIENS
Jew·ess \'jü-əs\ *n* (14c) **:** a Jewish girl or woman — sometimes taken to be offensive
jew·fish \'jü-ˌfish\ *n* (1697) **:** any of various large groupers that are usu. dusky green or blackish, thickheaded, and rough-scaled
Jew·ish \'jü-ish\ *adj* (1546) **:** of, relating to, or characteristic of the Jews; *also* **:** being a Jew — **Jew·ish·ly** *adv* — **Jew·ish·ness** *n*
Jewish calendar *n* (ca. 1888) **:** a calendar in use among Jewish peoples that is reckoned from the year 3761 B.C. and dates in its present form from about A.D. 360 — see MONTH table

JEWISH YEARS 5744–5763

JEWISH YEAR		A.D.	JEWISH YEAR		A.D.
5744	begins	Sept 8, 1983	5754	begins	Sept 16, 1993
5745	begins	Sept 27, 1984	5755	begins	Sept 6, 1994
5746	begins	Sept 16, 1985	5756	begins	Sept 25, 1995
5747	begins	Oct 4, 1986	5757	begins	Sept 14, 1996
5748	begins	Sept 24, 1987	5758	begins	Oct 2, 1997
5749	begins	Sept 12, 1988	5759	begins	Sept 21, 1998
5750	begins	Sept 30, 1989	5760	begins	Sept 11, 1999
5751	begins	Sept 20, 1990	5761	begins	Sept 30, 2000
5752	begins	Sept 9, 1991	5762	begins	Sept 18, 2001
5753	begins	Sept 28, 1992	5763	begins	Sept 7, 2002

Jewish princess *n* (1972) **:** a daughter of a well-to-do American Jewish family — called also *Jewish American princess;* usu. used disparagingly
Jew·ry \'jü(ə)r-ē, 'jü-rē\ *n* (13c) **1** *pl* **Jewries :** a community of Jews **2 :** the Jewish people
Jew's harp *or* **Jews' harp** \'jüz-ˌhärp, 'jüs-\ *n* (1595) **:** a small lyre-shaped instrument that when held between the lips gives tones from a metal tongue struck by the finger
Jez·e·bel \'jez-ə-ˌbel\ *n* [Heb *Izebhel*] **1 :** the Phoenician wife of Ahab who according to the account in I and II Kings pressed the cult of Baal on the Israelite kingdom but was finally killed in accordance with Elijah's prophecy **2** *often not cap* **:** an impudent, shameless, or abandoned woman
JHVH *var of* YHWH

jiao *var of* CHIAO
¹**jib** \'jib\ *n* [origin unknown] (1661) **:** a triangular sail set on a stay extending from the head of the foremast to the bowsprit or the jibboom — see SAIL illustration
²**jib** *vb* **jibbed; jib·bing** *vt* (1691) **:** to cause (as a sail or yard) to swing from one side of a ship to the other ~ *vi* **:** to shift across or swing round from one side of a ship to the other
³**jib** *n* [prob. by shortening & alter. fr. *gibbet*] (1764) **1 :** the projecting arm of a crane **2 :** a derrick boom
⁴**jib** *vi* **jibbed; jib·bing** [prob. fr. ²*jib*] (1811) **:** to refuse to proceed further **:** BALK — **jib·ber** *n*
jib·boom \'jib-'(b)üm\ *n* [¹*jib* + *boom*] (1748) **:** a spar that forms an extension of the bowsprit

Jew's harp

¹**jibe** \'jīb\ *vb* **jibed; jib·ing** [perh. modif. of D *gijben*] *vi* (1693) **1 :** to shift suddenly and forcibly from one side to the other — used of a fore-and-aft sail **2 :** to change a ship's course so that the sail jibes ~ *vt* **:** to cause to jibe
²**jibe** *var of* GIBE
³**jibe** *vi* **jibed; jib·ing** [origin unknown] (1813) **:** to be in accord **:** AGREE
ji·ca·ma \'hē-kə-mə\ *n* [MexSp, fr. Nahuatl *xicama*] (ca. 1903) **:** a tropical twining plant (*Pachyrhizus erosus*) with edible tuberous roots used esp. in salads and with seeds which yield rotenone and oils
jiff \'jif\ *n* [by shortening] (1797) **:** JIFFY
jif·fy \'jif-ē\ *n, pl* **jiffies** [origin unknown] (1785) **:** MOMENT, INSTANT ⟨ready in a ~⟩
¹**jig** \'jig\ *n* [prob. fr. MF *giguer* to dance, fr. *gigue* fiddle, of Gmc origin; akin to OHG *giga* fiddle; akin to ON *geiga* to turn aside — more at GIG] (1560) **1 a :** any of several lively springy dances in triple rhythm **b :** music to which a jig may be danced **2 :** TRICK, GAME — used chiefly in the phrase *the jig is up* **3 a :** any of several fishing devices that are jerked up and down or drawn through the water **b :** a device used to maintain mechanically the correct positional relationship between a piece of work and the tool or between parts of work during assembly **c :** a device in which crushed ore is concentrated or coal is cleaned by agitating in water — **in jig time :** in a short time **:** QUICKLY
²**jig** *vb* **jigged; jig·ging** *vt* (1719) **1 :** to dance in the rapid lively manner of a jig **2 a :** to give a rapid jerky motion to **b :** to separate (a mineral or ore from waste) with a jig **3 :** to catch (a fish) with a jig **4 :** to machine by means of a jig-controlled tool operation ~ *vi* **1 a :** to dance a jig **b :** to move with rapid jerky motions **2 :** to fish with a jig **3 :** to work with the aid of a jig
¹**jig·ger** \'jig-ər\ *n* (1675) **1 :** one that jigs or operates a jig **2 :** any of several sails **3 :** ¹JIG 3a **4 a (1) :** a mechanical device usu. with a jerky reciprocating motion **(2) :** a mold or a machine incorporating a revolving mold on which ceramic items (as plates) are formed **b :** something too complex, tricky, or trivial to designate accurately **:** GADGET **5 :** a measure used in mixing drinks that usu. holds 1 to 1½ ounces
²**jigger** *vb* [freq. of ²*jig*] (1867) *vi* **:** to jerk up and down ~ *vt* **:** to alter or rearrange esp. by manipulating ⟨~ an election district⟩
³**jigger** *n* [of African origin; akin to Wolof *jiga* insect] (1781) **:** CHIGGER
jig·gle \'jig-əl\ *vb* **jig·gled; jig·gling** \-(ə-)liŋ\ [freq. of ²*jig*] *vi* (1836) **:** to move with quick little jerks or oscillating motions ~ *vt* **:** to cause to jiggle — **jiggle** *n* — **jig·gly** \-(ə-)lē\ *adj*
¹**jig·saw** \'jig-ˌsȯ\ *n* (1873) **1 :** a machine saw with a narrow vertically reciprocating blade for cutting curved and irregular lines or ornamental patterns in openwork **2 :** SCROLL SAW 1
²**jigsaw** *vt* (1873) **1 :** to cut or form by or as if by a jigsaw **2 :** to arrange or place in an intricate or interlocking way
³**jigsaw** *adj* (1884) **:** suggesting a jigsaw puzzle or its separate pieces
jigsaw puzzle *n* (1919) **:** a puzzle consisting of small irregularly cut pieces that are to be fitted together to form a picture; *also* **:** something suggesting a jigsaw puzzle
ji·had \ji-'häd, -'had\ *n* [Ar *jihād*] (1869) **1 :** a holy war waged on behalf of Islam as a religious duty **2 :** a crusade for a principle or belief
jil·lion \'jil-yən\ *n* [*j* + *-illion* (as in *million*)] (ca. 1942) **:** an indeterminately large number — **jillion** *adj*
¹**jilt** \'jilt\ *vt* (1673) **:** to drop (a lover) capriciously or unfeelingly — **jilt·er** *n*
²**jilt** *n* [alter. of *jillet* (flirtatious girl)] (ca. 1674) **:** one who capriciously or unfeelingly drops a lover
jim crow \'jim-'krō\ *n, often cap J & C* [*Jim Crow,* stereotype Negro in a 19th cent. song-and-dance act] (1838) **1 :** NEGRO — usu. taken to be offensive **2 :** ethnic discrimination esp. against the Negro by legal enforcement or traditional sanctions — **jim crow** *adj, often cap J & C* — **jim crow·ism** \-ˌiz-əm\ *n, often cap J & C*
jim–dan·dy \'jim-'dan-dē\ *n* [fr. the name *Jim*] (1887) **:** something excellent of its kind
jim·jams \'jim-ˌjamz\ *n pl* [perh. alter. of *delirium tremens*] (1885) **:** JITTERS
jim·mies \'jim-ēz\ *n pl* [origin unknown] (ca. 1947) **:** tiny rod-shaped bits of usu. chocolate-flavored candy often sprinkled on ice cream
¹**jim·my** \'jim-ē\ *n, pl* **jimmies** [fr. the name *Jimmy*] (1811) **:** a short crowbar
²**jimmy** *vt* **jim·mied; jim·my·ing** (1893) **:** to force open with or as if with a jimmy ⟨the burglar *jimmied* a window⟩
jim·son·weed \'jim(p)-sən-ˌwēd\ *n, often cap* [*Jamestown,* Va.] (1832) **:** a poisonous tall coarse annual weed (*Datura stramonium*) of the nightshade family with rank-smelling foliage and large white or violet trumpet-shaped flowers succeeded by globose prickly fruits
¹**jin·gle** \'jiŋ-gəl\ *vb* **jin·gled; jin·gling** \-g(ə-)liŋ\ [ME *ginglen,* of imit. origin] *vi* (14c) **1 :** to make a light clinking or tinkling sound **2 :** to

rhyme or sound in a catchy repetitious manner ~ *vt* : to cause to jingle — **jin·gler** \-g(ə-)lər\ *n*

²**jingle** *n* (1599) **1 a :** a light clinking or tinkling sound **b :** a catchy repetition of sounds in a poem **2 a :** something that jingles **b :** a short verse or song marked by catchy repetition **3 :** a 2-wheeled horse-drawn covered vehicle used esp. in Ireland and Australia as a public conveyance — **jin·gly** \-g(ə-)lē\ *adj*

¹**jin·go** \ˈjiŋ-(ˌ)gō\ *interj* [prob. euphemism for *Jesus*] (1670) — used as a mild oath usu. in the phrase *by jingo*

²**jingo** *n, pl* **jingoes** [fr. the fact that the phrase *by jingo* appeared in the refrain of a chauvinistic song] (1878) **:** one characterized by jingoism — **jin·go·ish** \-ish\ *adj*

jin·go·ism \ˈjiŋ-(ˌ)gō-ˌiz-əm\ *n* (1878) **:** extreme chauvinism or nationalism marked esp. by a belligerent foreign policy — **jin·go·ist** \-əst\ *n* — **jin·go·is·tic** \ˌjiŋ-gō-ˈis-tik\ *adj* — **jin·go·is·ti·cal·ly** \-ti-k(ə-)lē\ *adv*

¹**jink** \ˈjiŋk\ *vi* [origin unknown] (1785) **:** to move quickly or unexpectedly with sudden turns and shifts (as in dodging)

²**jink** *n* (1786) **1 :** a quick evasive turn **:** SLIP **2** *pl* **:** PRANKS, FROLICS; *esp* **:** HIGH JINKS

jin·ni \ˈjē-nē, ˈjin-ē, jə-ˈnē\ *or* **jinn** \ˈjin\ *n, pl* **jinn** *or* **jinns** [Ar *jinnīy* demon] (1684) **1 :** one of a class of spirits that according to Muslim demonology inhabit the earth, assume various forms, and exercise supernatural power **2 :** a supernatural spirit that often takes human form and serves his summoner

jin·rik·i·sha \jin-ˈrik-ˌshȯ\ *n* [Jp] (1874) **:** RICKSHA

¹**jinx** \ˈjiŋ(k)s\ *n* [prob. alter. of *jynx* (wryneck); fr. the use of wrynecks in witchcraft] (1911) **:** one that brings bad luck; *also* **:** the state or spell of bad luck brought on by a jinx

²**jinx** *vt* (1917) **:** to foredoom to failure or misfortune **:** bring bad luck to

ji·pi·ja·pa \ˌhē-pē-ˈhäp-ə\ *n* [Sp, fr. *Jipijapa*, Ecuador] (1858) **1 :** a Central and So. American plant (*Carludovica palmata* of the family Cyclanthaceae) resembling a palm **2 :** PANAMA

jit·ney \ˈjit-nē\ *n, pl* **jitneys** [origin unknown] (1903) **1** *slang* **:** NICKEL 2a(1) **2** [fr. the original 5 cent fare] **:** BUS 1a; *esp* **:** a small bus that carries passengers over a regular route according to a flexible schedule

¹**jit·ter** \ˈjit-ər\ *n* [origin unknown] (1929) **1 :** the state of mind or the movement of one that jitters **2** *pl* **:** a sense of panic or extreme nervousness ⟨had a bad case of the ~*s* before his performance⟩ **3 :** irregular random movement (as of a pointer or an image on a television screen); *also* **:** vibratory motion

²**jitter** *vi* (1931) **1 :** to be nervous or act in a nervous way **2 :** to make continuous fast repetitive movements

¹**jit·ter·bug** \ˈjit-ər-ˌbəg\ *n* (1938) **1 :** a jazz variation of the two-step in which couples swing, balance, and twirl in standardized patterns and often with vigorous acrobatics **2 :** one who dances the jitterbug

²**jitterbug** *vi* (1939) **1 :** to dance the jitterbug **2 :** to move around or back and forth with quick often jerky movements esp. to confuse or disconcert an opponent in sports

jit·tery \ˈjit-ə-rē\ *adj* (1931) **1 :** suffering from the jitters **2 :** marked by jittering movements

jiu·jit·su *or* **jiu·jut·su** *var of* JUJITSU

¹**jive** \ˈjīv\ *n* [origin unknown] (1928) **1 :** swing music or the dancing performed to it **2 a :** glib, deceptive, or foolish talk **b :** the jargon of hipsters **c :** a special jargon of difficult or slang terms

²**jive** *vb* **jived; jiv·ing** *vi* (1928) **1 :** KID **2 :** to dance to or play jive ~ *vt* **1 :** TEASE 3, CAJOLE **2 :** SWING 5

³**jive** *adj, slang* (1953) **:** PHONY

jo \ˈjō\ *n, pl* **joes** [alter. of *joy*] *chiefly Scot* (1529) **:** SWEETHEART, DEAR

¹**job** \ˈjäb\ *n* [perh. fr. obs. E *job* (lump)] (1627) **1 a :** a piece of work; *esp* **:** a small miscellaneous piece of work undertaken on order at a stated rate **b :** the object or material on which work is being done **c :** something produced by or as if by work ⟨do a better ~ next time⟩ **d :** an example of a usu. specified type **:** ITEM ⟨this ~ is round-necked and sleeveless —Lois Long⟩ **2 a :** something done for private advantage ⟨suspected the whole incident was a put-up ~⟩ **b :** a criminal enterprise; *specif* **:** ROBBERY **c :** a damaging or destructive bit of work ⟨did a ~ on him⟩ **3 a** (1) **:** something that has to be done **:** TASK (2) **:** an undertaking requiring unusual exertion ⟨it was a real ~ to talk over that noise⟩ **b :** a specific duty, role, or function **c :** a regular remunerative position **d** *chiefly Brit* **:** state of affairs — used with *bad* or *good* ⟨it was a good ~ you didn't hit the old man —E. L. Thomas⟩ ***syn*** see TASK — **on the job :** on the alert **:** on duty ⟨safety devices that are constantly *on the job*⟩

²**job** *vb* **jobbed; job·bing** *vi* (1694) **1 :** to do odd or occasional pieces of work for hire **2 :** to carry on public business for private gain **3 :** to carry on the business of a middleman or wholesaler ⟨his company ~*s* and doesn't sell to the homeowner⟩ ~ *vt* **1 :** to buy and sell (as stock) for profit **:** SPECULATE **2 :** to hire or let by the job or for a period of service **3 :** to get, deal with, or effect by jobbery **4 :** to do or cause to be done by separate portions or lots **:** SUBCONTRACT **5 :** SWINDLE, TRICK

³**job** *adj* (1710) **1** *Brit* **:** that is for hire for a given service or period **2 :** used in, engaged in, or done as job work ⟨a ~ shop⟩ **3 :** of or relating to a job or to employment ⟨a guarantee of ~ security⟩

Job \ˈjōb\ *n* [L, fr. Gk *Iōb*, fr. Heb *Iyyōbh*] **1 :** the hero of the book of Job who endures afflictions with fortitude and faith **2 :** a narrative and poetic book of canonical Jewish and Christian Scripture — see BIBLE table

job action *n* (ca. 1968) **:** a temporary action (as a slowdown) by workers as a protest and means of enforcing compliance with demands

job·ber \ˈjäb-ər\ *n* (1670) **:** one that jobs: as **a** (1) **:** STOCKJOBBER (2) **:** WHOLESALER; *specif* **:** a wholesaler who operates on a small scale or who sells only to retailers and institutions **b :** one who works by the job or on job work

job·bery \ˈjäb-(ə-)rē\ *n* (1832) **:** the act or practice of jobbing; *esp* **:** corruption in public office

job·hold·er \ˈjäb-ˌhōl-dər\ *n* (1904) **:** one having a regular job

job–hop·ping \-ˌhäp-iŋ\ *n* (ca. 1951) **:** the practice of moving from job to job — **job–hop·per** \-ˌhäp-ər\ *n*

job·less \ˈjäb-ləs\ *adj* (1919) **1 :** having no job **2 :** of or relating to those having no job — **job·less·ness** *n*

job lot *n* (1851) **1 :** a miscellaneous collection of goods for sale as a lot usu. to a retailer **2 :** a miscellaneous and usu. inferior collection or group

Job's comforter \ˈjōbz-\ *n* [fr. the tone of the speeches made to Job by his friends] (1738) **:** one who discourages or depresses while seemingly giving comfort and consolation

Job's tears *n pl* (1597) **1 :** hard pearly white seeds often used as beads **2** *sing in constr* **:** an Asian grass (*Coix lacryma-jobi*) whose seeds are Job's tears

Jo·cas·ta \jō-ˈkas-tə\ *n* [L, fr. Gk *Iokastē*] **:** a queen of Thebes who unknowingly marries her son Oedipus

¹**jock** \ˈjäk\ *n* (1826) **1 :** JOCKEY **2 :** DISC JOCKEY

²**jock** *n* [*jockstrap*] (1922) **1 :** ATHLETIC SUPPORTER **2 :** ATHLETE; *esp* **:** a college athlete

¹**jock·ey** \ˈjäk-ē\ *n, pl* **jockeys** [*Jockey*, Sc nickname for *John*] (1670) **1 :** one who rides a horse esp. as a professional in a race **2 :** one who operates or works with a specified vehicle, device, or object **:** OPERATOR ⟨an accountant, a pencil ~ — with almost no association with the out-of-doors —James Selder⟩

²**jockey** *vb* **jock·eyed; jock·ey·ing** *vt* (1708) **1 :** to deal shrewdly or fraudulently with **2 a :** to ride (a horse) as a jockey **b :** DRIVE, OPERATE **3 a :** to maneuver or manipulate by adroit or devious means ⟨was ~*ed* out of a political job⟩ **b :** to change the position of by a series of movements ⟨~ a truck into position⟩ ~ *vi* **1 :** to act as a jockey **2 :** to maneuver for advantage ⟨~ for a starting position on the team⟩

jockey club *n* (1775) **:** an association for the promotion and regulation of horse racing

jock itch *n* [²*jock*] (1950) **:** ringworm of the crotch **:** TINEA CRURIS

jock·strap \ˈjäk-ˌstrap\ *n* [E slang *jock* (penis) + E *strap*] (1897) **:** ATHLETIC SUPPORTER

jo·cose \jō-ˈkōs, jə-\ *adj* [L *jocosus*, fr. *jocus* joke] (1673) **1 :** given to joking **:** MERRY **2 :** characterized by joking **:** HUMOROUS ***syn*** see WITTY — **jo·cose·ly** *adv* — **jo·cose·ness** *n* — **jo·cos·i·ty** \jō-ˈkäs-ət-ē, jə-\ *n*

joc·u·lar \ˈjäk-yə-lər\ *adj* [L *jocularis*, fr. *joculus*, dim. of *jocus*] (1627) **1 :** given to jesting **:** habitually jolly or jocund **2 :** characterized by jesting **:** PLAYFUL ***syn*** see WITTY — **joc·u·lar·i·ty** \ˌjäk-yə-ˈlar-ət-ē\ *n* — **joc·u·lar·ly** \ˈjäk-yə-lər-lē\ *adv*

jo·cund \ˈjäk-ənd *also* ˈjōk-(ˌ)ənd\ *adj* [ME, fr. LL *jocundus*, alter. of L *jucundus*, fr. *juvare* to help] (14c) **:** marked by or suggestive of high spirits and lively mirthfulness ⟨a poet could not but be gay, in such a ~ company —William Wordsworth⟩ ***syn*** see MERRY — **jo·cun·di·ty** \jō-ˈkən-dət-ē, jä-\ *n* — **jo·cund·ly** \ˈjäk-ən-dlē, ˈjōk-(ˌ)-\ *adv*

jodh·pur \ˈjäd-(ˌ)pər\ *n* [*Jodhpur*, India] (1899) **1** *pl* **:** riding breeches cut full through the hips and close-fitting from knee to ankle **2 :** an ankle-high boot fastened with a strap that is buckled at the side

jodhpur 1

Jo·el \ˈjō-əl\ *n* [L, fr. Gk *Iōēl*, fr. Heb *Yōʼēl*] **1 :** the traditionally assumed author of the book of Joel **2 :** a narrative and apocalyptic book of canonical Jewish and Christian Scripture — see BIBLE table

joe–pye weed \ˌjō-ˈpī-\ *n* [perh. alter. of earlier *eupatory*, fr. NL *Eupatorium*, fr. Gk *eupatorion* hemp agrimony (herb)] (ca. 1817) **:** any of several tall American perennial composite herbs (genus *Eupatorium*) with whorled leaves and corymbose heads of typically purple tubular flowers

jo·ey \ˈjō-ē\ *n* [native name in Australia] *Austral* (1839) **:** a baby animal; *esp* **:** a baby kangaroo

¹**jog** \ˈjäg, ˈjȯg\ *vb* **jogged; jog·ging** [prob. alter. of *shog*] *vt* (1548) **1 :** to give a slight shake or push to **:** NUDGE **2 :** to rouse to alertness ⟨*jogged* his memory⟩ **3 :** to cause (as a horse) to go at a jog **4 :** to align the edges of (piled sheets of paper) by hitting or shaking against a flat surface ~ *vi* **1 :** to move up and down or about with a short heavy motion ⟨his . . . holster *jogging* against his hip —Thomas Williams⟩ **2 a :** to run or ride at a slow trot **b :** to go at a slow, leisurely, or monotonous pace **:** TRUDGE

²**jog** *n* (1635) **1 :** a slight shake **:** PUSH **2 a :** a jogging movement, pace, or trip **b :** a horse's slow measured trot

³**jog** *n* [prob. alter. of ²*jag*] (1715) **1 a :** a projecting or retreating part (as of a line or surface) **b :** the space in the angle of a jog **2 :** a brief abrupt change in direction

⁴**jog** *vi* **jogged; jog·ging** (1953) **:** to make a jog ⟨the road ~*s* to the right⟩

jog·ger \ˈjäg-ər, ˈjȯg-\ *n* (1700) **1 :** one that jogs **2 :** a device for jogging piled sheets of paper

¹**jog·gle** \ˈjäg-əl\ *vb* **jog·gled; jog·gling** \-(ə-)liŋ\ [freq. of ¹*jog*] *vt* (1513) **:** to shake slightly ~ *vi* **:** to move shakily or jerkily — **jog·gler** \-(ə-)lər\ *n*

²**joggle** *n* (ca. 1727) **:** ²JOG 2a

³**joggle** *n* [dim. of ³*jog*] (1793) **1 :** a notch or tooth in a joining surface (as of a piece of building material) to prevent slipping **2 :** a dowel for joining two adjacent blocks of masonry

⁴**joggle** *vt* **jog·gled; jog·gling** \ˈjäg-(ə-)liŋ\ (1820) **:** to join by means of a joggle so as to prevent sliding apart

jog trot *n* (1796) **1 :** ²JOG 2b **2 :** a routine habit or course of action

jo·han·nes \jō-ˈhan-əs\ *n, pl* **johannes** [*Johannes* John V †1750 king of Portugal] (1765) **:** an old Portuguese gold coin worth 6400 reis

Jo·han·nine \jō-ˈhan-ˌīn, -ən\ *adj* [LL *Johannes* John] (1861) **:** of, relating to, or characteristic of the apostle John or the New Testament books ascribed to him

john \ˈjän\ *n* [fr. the name *John*] (ca. 1932) **1 :** TOILET **2 :** a prostitute's client

John \ˈjän\ *n* [LL *Johannes*, fr. Gk *Iōannēs*, fr. Heb *Yōḥānān*] **1 :** a Jewish prophet who according to Gospel accounts foretold Jesus's messianic ministry and baptized him — called also *John the Baptist* **2 :** an apostle who according to various Christian traditions wrote the fourth Gospel, the three Johannine Epistles, and the Book of Revelation **3 :** the fourth Gospel in the New Testament — see BIBLE table **4 :** any of three short didactic letters addressed to early Christians and included in the New Testament — see BIBLE table

John Barleycorn *n* (1620) **:** alcoholic liquor personified

john·boat \ˈjän-ˌbōt\ *n* [fr. the name *John*] (1905) **:** a narrow flat-bottomed square-ended boat usu. propelled by a pole or paddle and used on inland waterways

John Bull \-'bu̇l\ *n* [*John Bull,* character typifying the English nation in *The History of John Bull* (1712) by John Arbuthnot] (1778) **1 :** the English nation personified : the English people **2 :** a typical Englishman — **John Bull·ish** \-ish\ *adj* — **John Bull·ish·ness** *n* — **John Bull·ism** \-ˌiz-əm\ *n*

John Doe \-'dō\ *n* (1768) **1 :** a party to legal proceedings whose true name is unknown **2 :** an average man ⟨brilliant educators and plain *John Does* —K. D. Wells⟩

John Do·ry \-'dōr-ē, -'dȯr-\ *n, pl* **John Dories** [earlier *dory,* fr. ME *dorre,* fr. MF *doree,* lit., gilded one] (1754) **:** a common yellow to olive European food fish (*Zeus faber*) with an oval compressed body, long dorsal spines, and a dark spot on each side; *also* **:** a closely related and possibly identical fish (*Z. capensis*) widely distributed in southern seas

Joh·ne's disease \'yō-nəz-\ *n* [Heinrich A. *Johne* †1910 Ger. bacteriologist] (1907) **:** a chronic often fatal enteritis esp. of cattle that is caused by a bacillus (*Mycobacterium paratuberculosis*) and is characterized by persistent diarrhea and gradual emaciation

John Han·cock \'jän-'han-ˌkäk\ *n* [*John Hancock;* fr. the prominence of his signature on the Declaration of Independence] (1846) **:** an autograph signature

John Hen·ry \-'hen-rē\ *n* [fr. the name *John Henry,* fr. confusion with *John Hancock*] (1914) **:** an autograph signature

John Mark *n* **:** MARK 1a

john·ny \'jän-ē\ *n, pl* **johnnies** [fr. the name *Johnny*] (1673) **1** *often cap* **:** FELLOW, GUY **2 :** a short-sleeved collarless gown with an opening in the back for wear by persons (as hospital patients) undergoing medical examination or treatment

john·ny·cake \'jän-ē-ˌkāk\ *n* [prob. fr. the name *Johnny*] (1739) **:** a bread made with cornmeal

John·ny–come–late·ly \ˌjän-ē-(ˌ)kəm-'lāt-lē\ *n, pl* **Johnny–come–latelies** *or* **Johnnies–come–lately** (1839) **1 :** a late or recent arrival : NEWCOMER **2 :** UPSTART ⟨established families tend to hold themselves above the *Johnny-come-latelies* —William Zeckendorf †1976⟩

John·ny–jump–up \ˌjän-ē-'jəm-ˌpəp\ *n* (1842) **1 :** a common and long-cultivated European viola (*Viola tricolor*) which has short-spurred flowers usu. blue or purple mixed with white and yellow and from which most of the garden pansies are derived; *broadly* **:** any of various small-flowered cultivated pansies **2 :** any of various American violets

John·ny–on–the–spot \ˌjän-ē-ˌȯn-t͟hə-'spät, -ē-ˌän-\ *n* (1896) **:** one who is on hand and ready to perform a service or respond to an emergency

Johnny Reb \-'reb\ *n* [fr. the name *Johnny* + *reb* (rebel)] (1865) **:** a Confederate soldier

John·son·ese \ˌjän(t)-sə-'nēz, -'nēs\ *n* [Samuel *Johnson*] (1843) **:** a literary style characterized by balanced phraseology and Latinate diction

John·son·grass \'jän(t)-sən-\ *n* [William *Johnston* †1859 Am. agriculturist] (1884) **:** a tall perennial sorghum (*Sorghum halepense*) naturalized as a hay and forage grass in warm regions

joie de vi·vre \ˌzhwäd-ə-'vēvrᵊ\ *n* [F, lit., joy of living] (1889) **:** keen or buoyant enjoyment of life

[1]**join** \'jȯin\ *vb* [ME *joinen,* fr. OF *joindre,* fr. L *jungere* — more at YOKE] *vt* (13c) **1 a :** to put or bring together so as to form a unit ⟨~ two blocks of wood with glue⟩ **b :** to connect (as points) by a line **c :** ADJOIN **2 :** to put or bring into close association or relationship ⟨~*ed* in marriage⟩ **3 :** to engage in (battle) **4 a :** to come into the company of ⟨~*ed* us for lunch⟩ **b :** to associate oneself with ⟨~*ed* the church⟩ ~ *vi* **1 a :** to come together so as to be connected ⟨nouns ~ to form compounds⟩ **b :** ADJOIN ⟨the two estates ~⟩ **2 :** to come into close association or relationship: as **a :** to form an alliance ⟨~*ed* to combat crime⟩ **b :** to become a member of a group **c :** to take part in a collective activity ⟨~ in singing⟩ — **join·able** \'jȯi-nə-bəl\ *adj*

syn JOIN, COMBINE, UNITE, CONNECT, LINK, ASSOCIATE, RELATE mean to bring or come together into some manner of union. JOIN implies a bringing into contact or conjunction of any degree of closeness; COMBINE implies some merging or mingling with corresponding loss of identity of each unit; UNITE implies somewhat greater loss of separate identity; CONNECT suggests a loose or external attachment with little or no loss of identity; LINK may imply strong connection or inseparability of elements still retaining identity; ASSOCIATE stresses the mere fact of frequent occurrence or existence together in space or in logical relation; RELATE suggests the existence of a real or presumed logical connection.

[2]**join** *n* (1825) **1 :** JOINT **2 :** UNION 2d

join·der \'jȯin-dər\ *n* [F *joindre* to join, fr. OF] (1601) **1 :** CONJUNCTION 1 **2 a** (1) **:** a joining of parties as plaintiffs or defendants in a suit (2) **:** a joining of causes of action or defense **b :** acceptance of an issue tendered

join·er \'jȯi-nər\ *n* (14c) **:** one that joins: as **a :** a person whose occupation is to construct articles by joining pieces of wood **b :** a gregarious or civic-minded person who joins many organizations

join·ery \'jȯin-(ə-)rē\ *n* (1678) **1 :** the art or trade of a joiner **2 :** work done by a joiner

join·ing \'jȯi-niŋ\ *n* (14c) **1 :** the act or instance of joining one thing to another : JUNCTURE **2 a :** the place or manner of being joined together **b :** something that joins two things together

[1]**joint** \'jȯint\ *n* [ME *jointe,* fr. OF, fr. *joindre*] (13c) **1 a** (1) **:** the point of contact between elements of an animal skeleton with the parts that surround and support it (2) **:** NODE 4b **b :** a part or space included between two articulations, knots, or nodes **c :** a large piece of meat for roasting **2 a :** a place where two things or parts are joined **b :** a space between the adjacent surfaces of two bodies joined and held together (as by cement or mortar) **c :** a fracture or crack in rock not accompanied by dislocation **d :** the flexing part of a cover along either backbone edge of a book **e :** the junction of two or more members of a framed structure **f :** a union formed by two abutting rails in a track including the elements (as bars and bolts) necessary to hold the abutting rails together **g :** an area at which two ends, surfaces, or edges are attached **3 a :** a shabby or disreputable place of entertainment **b :** PLACE, ESTABLISHMENT **4 :** a marijuana cigarette — **joint·ed** \-əd\ *adj* — **joint·ed·ly** *adv* — **joint·ed·ness** *n* — **out of joint 1 a** *of a bone* **:** having the head slipped from its socket **b :** at variance **2 a :** DISORDERED 2a **b :** being out of humor : DISSATISFIED

[2]**joint** *adj* [ME, fr. MF, fr. pp. of *joindre,* fr. OF] (14c) **1 :** UNITED, COMBINED ⟨the ~ influences of culture and climate⟩ **2 :** common to two or more: as **a** (1) **:** involving the united activity of two or more ⟨a ~ effort⟩ (2) **:** constituting an activity, operation, or organization in which elements of more than one armed service participate ⟨~ maneuvers⟩ (3) **:** constituting an action or expression of two or more governments ⟨~ peace talks⟩ **b :** shared by or affecting two or more ⟨a ~ fine⟩ **3 :** united, joined, or sharing with another (as in a right or status) ⟨~ heirs⟩ **4 :** being a function of or involving two or more variables and esp. random variables — **joint·ly** *adv*

[3]**joint** *vb* [[1]*joint*] *vt* (1547) **1 a :** to unite by a joint : fit together **b :** to provide with a joint : ARTICULATE **c :** to prepare (as a board) for joining by planing the edge **2 :** to separate the joints of (as meat) ~ *vi* **1 :** to fit as if by joints ⟨the stones ~ neatly⟩ **2 :** to form joints as a stage in growth — used esp. of small grains

Joint Chiefs of Staff (1946) **:** a military advisory group composed of the chiefs of staff of the army and air force, the chief of naval operations, and sometimes the commandant of the marine corps

joint·er \'jȯint-ər\ *n* (1678) **:** one that joints; *esp* **:** any of various tools used in making joints

joint grass *n* (1835) **:** a coarse creeping grass (*Paspalum distichum*) with jointed stems that is used for fodder and for erosion control

joint resolution *n* (1838) **:** a resolution passed by both houses of a legislative body that has the force of law when signed by or passed over the veto of the executive

join·tress \'jȯin-trəs\ *n* (1602) **:** a woman having a legal jointure

joint–stock company *n* (1776) **:** a company or association consisting of individuals organized to conduct a business for gain and having a joint stock of capital represented by shares owned individually by the members and transferable without the consent of the group

join·ture \'jȯin-chər\ *n* (14c) **1 a :** an act of joining : the state of being joined **b :** JOINT **2 a :** an estate settled on a wife to be taken by her in lieu of dower **b :** a settlement on the wife of a freehold estate for her lifetime

joint·worm \'jȯint-ˌwərm\ *n* (1851) **:** the larva of any of several small chalcid wasps (genus *Harmolita*) that attacks the stems of grain and causes swellings like galls at or just above the first joint

joist \'jȯist\ *n* [ME *giste,* fr. MF, fr. (assumed) VL *jacitum,* fr. L *jacēre* to lie — more at ADJACENT] (14c) **:** any of the small timbers or metal beams ranged parallel from wall to wall in a structure to support a floor or ceiling

jo·jo·ba \hə-'hō-bə\ *n* [MexSp] (1923) **:** a shrub or small tree (*Simmondsia californica*) of the box family of southwestern No. America with edible seeds that yield a valuable liquid wax

[1]**joke** \'jōk\ *n* [L *jocus;* akin to OHG *gehan* to say, Skt *yācati* he implores] (1670) **1 a :** something said or done to provoke laughter; *esp* **:** a brief oral narrative with a climactic humorous twist **b** (1) **:** the humorous or ridiculous element in something (2) **:** an instance of jesting : KIDDING ⟨can't take a ~⟩ **c :** PRACTICAL JOKE **d :** LAUGHINGSTOCK **2 a :** something not to be taken seriously : a trifling matter ⟨consider his skiing a ~ —Harold Callender⟩ — often used in negative construction ⟨it is no ~ to be lost in the desert⟩ **b :** something presenting no difficulty ⟨that exam was a ~⟩ ***syn*** see JEST

[2]**joke** *vb* **joked; jok·ing** *vi* (1670) **:** to make jokes : JEST ~ *vt* **:** to make the object of a joke : KID — **jok·ing·ly** \'jō-kiŋ-lē\ *adv*

jok·er \'jō-kər\ *n* (1729) **1 a :** a person given to joking : WAG **b :** FELLOW, GUY; *esp* **:** an insignificant, obnoxious, or incompetent person ⟨a shame to let a ~ like this win —Harold Robbins⟩ **2 :** a playing card added to a pack as a wild card or as the highest-ranking card **3 a** (1) **:** an ambiguous or apparently immaterial clause inserted in a legislative bill to make it inoperative or uncertain in some respect (2) **:** an unsuspected, misleading, or misunderstood clause, phrase, or word in a document that nullifies or greatly alters it **b :** something (as an expedient or stratagem) held in reserve to gain an end or escape from a predicament **c :** an unsuspected or not readily apparent fact, factor, or condition that thwarts or nullifies a seeming advantage

jok·ey *also* **joky** \'jō-kē\ *adj* **jok·i·er; -est** (ca. 1825) **1 :** given to joking **2 :** HUMOROUS, COMICAL **3 :** amusingly ridiculous : LAUGHABLE — **jok·i·ly** \-kə-lē\ *adv* — **jok·i·ness** \-kē-nəs\ *n*

jol·li·fi·ca·tion \ˌjäl-i-fə-'kā-shən\ *n* (1809) **:** FESTIVITY, MERRYMAKING

jol·li·ty \'jäl-ət-ē\ *n, pl* **-ties** (14c) **1 :** the quality or state of being jolly : MERRIMENT **2** *Brit* **:** a festive gathering ***syn*** see MIRTH

[1]**jol·ly** \'jäl-ē\ *adj* **jol·li·er; -est** [ME *joli,* fr. OF] (14c) **1 a** (1) **:** full of high spirits : JOYOUS (2) **:** given to conviviality : JOVIAL **b :** expressing, suggesting, or inspiring gaiety : CHEERFUL **2 :** extremely pleasant or agreeable : SPLENDID ***syn*** see MERRY

[2]**jolly** *adv* (1549) **:** VERY ⟨would . . . do as they were ~ well told —John Stockbridge⟩

[3]**jolly** *vb* **jol·lied; jol·ly·ing** *vi* (1610) **:** to engage in good-natured banter : KID ~ *vt* **:** to put or try to put in good humor esp. to gain an end

[4]**jolly** *n, pl* **jollies** (1905) **1** *chiefly Brit* **:** a good time : JOLLIFICATION **2** *pl* **:** KICKS ⟨get their *jollies* by reenacting famous murders —H. F. Waters⟩

jol·ly boat \'jäl-ē-\ *n* [origin unknown] (1727) **:** a ship's boat of medium size used for general-purpose work

Jol·ly Rog·er \ˌjäl-ē-'räj-ər\ *n* [prob. fr. [1]*jolly* + the name *Roger*] (ca. 1785) **:** a black flag with a white skull and crossbones formerly used by pirates as their ensign

[1]**jolt** \'jōlt\ *vb* [prob. blend of obs. *joll* (to strike) and *jot* (to bump)] *vt* (1599) **1 :** to cause to move with a sudden jerky motion **2 :** to give a knock or blow to; *specif* **:** to jar with a quick or hard blow **3 a :** to disturb the composure of ⟨crudely ~*ed* out of that mood —Virginia Woolf⟩ **b :** to interfere with roughly, abruptly, and disconcertingly ⟨determination to pursue his own course was ~*ed* badly —F. L. Paxson⟩ ~ *vi* **:** to move with a sudden jerky motion — **jolt·er** *n*

[2]**jolt** *n* (1599) **1 :** an abrupt sharp jerky blow or movement knocking or shaking violently and tending to unsettle or dislodge : JOUNCE **2 a** (1) **:** a sudden feeling of shock, surprise, or disappointment (2) **:** an event or development causing such a feeling ⟨his defeat was quite a ~ to him⟩ **b :** a serious check or reverse ⟨had a severe financial ~⟩ **3**

\ə\ abut \ᵊ\ kitten, F table \ər\ further \a\ ash \ā\ ace \ä\ cot, cart \au̇\ out \ch\ chin \e\ bet \ē\ easy \g\ go \i\ hit \ī\ ice \j\ job \ŋ\ sing \ō\ go \ȯ\ law \ȯi\ boy \th\ thin \t͟h\ the \ü\ loot \u̇\ foot \y\ yet \zh\ vision \à, ḵ, ⁿ, œ, œ̄, ue, ue̅, ʸ\ see Guide to Pronunciation

: a small potent or bracing portion : SHOT ⟨a ~ of fresh air⟩ — **jolty** \'jōl-tē\ *adj*

jolt–wag·on \'jōlt-,wag-ən\ *n, Midland* (1886) : a farm wagon

Jo·nah \'jō-nə, *3 is also* -nər\ *n* [Heb *Yōnāh*] **1** : an Israelite prophet who according to the account in the book of Jonah resisted a divine call to preach repentance to the people of Nineveh, was swallowed and vomited by a great fish, and eventually carried out his mission **2** : a narrative book of canonical Jewish and Christian Scripture — see BIBLE table **3** : one believed to bring bad luck

Jo·nas \'jō-nəs\ *n* [LL, fr. Heb *Yōnāh*] : JONAH

Jon·a·than \'jän-ə-thən\ *n* [Heb *Yōnāthān*] **1** : a son of Saul and friend of David according to the account in I Samuel **2** : AMERICAN; *esp* : a New Englander **3** : any of a variety of red-skinned apples

jon·gleur \zhōⁿ-'glər\ *n* [F, fr. OF *jogleour* — more at JUGGLER] (1779) : an itinerant medieval entertainer proficient in juggling, acrobatics, music, and recitation

jon·quil \'jän-kwəl, 'jäŋ-\ *n* [F *jonquille,* fr. Sp *junquillo,* dim. of *junco* reed, fr. L *juncus;* akin to ON *einir* juniper, L *juniperus*] (1629) : a Mediterranean perennial bulbous herb (*Narcissus jonquilla*) of the amaryllis family with long linear leaves that is widely cultivated for its yellow or white fragrant short-tubed clustered flowers — compare DAFFODIL

Jor·dan almond \,jȯrd-ᵊn-\ *n* [ME *jardin almande,* fr. MF *jardin* garden + ME *almande* almond] (15c) : a large Spanish almond esp. when salted or coated with sugar of various colors

Jor·dan curve \zhȯr-,däⁿ-, ,jȯrd-ᵊn-\ *n* [Camille *Jordan* †1922 Fr. mathematician] (1900) : SIMPLE CLOSED CURVE

Jordan curve theorem *n* (1947) : a fundamental theorem of topology: every simple closed curve divides the plane into two regions for which it is the common boundary

jo·rum \'jȯr-əm, 'jōr-\ *n* [perh. fr. *Joram* in the Bible who "brought with him vessels of silver" —2 Sam 8:10 (AV)] (1730) : a large drinking vessel or its contents

jo·seph \'jō-zəf *also* -səf\ *n* [L, fr. Gk *Iōsēph,* fr. Heb *Yōsēph*] **1** *cap* **a** : a son of Jacob who according to the account in Genesis rose to high political office in Egypt after being sold into slavery by his brothers **b** : the husband of Mary the mother of Jesus according to the Gospel accounts **2** : a long cloak worn esp. by women in the 18th century

Jo·seph·ite \-,īt\ *n* (1890) : a member of St. Joseph's Society of the Sacred Heart founded in 1871 in Baltimore, Md. and devoted to missionary work among black Americans

Joseph of Ar·i·ma·thea \-,ar-ə-mə-'thē-ə\ : a rich councillor of the Sanhedrin who according to the Gospel accounts placed the body of Jesus in his own tomb and according to medieval legend took the Holy Grail to England

Jo·seph·son junction \,jō-zəf-sən- *also* -səf-sən-\ *n* [Brian D. *Josephson*] (ca. 1965) : an electronic fast-switching device consisting of layers of superconducting metal separated by a thin layer of insulator through which low current flows but increased current causes the insulator to block the flow

¹josh \'jäsh\ *vb* [origin unknown] *vt* (1852) : to tease good-naturedly : KID ~ *vi* : to engage in banter : JOKE — **josh·er** *n*

²josh *n* (1878) : a good-humored joke : JEST

Josh·ua \'jäsh-(ə-)wə\ *n* [Heb *Yĕhōshūaʿ*] **1** : the divinely commissioned successor of Moses and military leader of the Israelites during the conquest of Canaan according to the account in the book of Joshua **2** : a mainly narrative book of canonical Jewish and Christian Scripture — see BIBLE table

Joshua tree *n* (1884) : a tall branched arborescent yucca (*Yucca brevifolia*) of the southwestern U.S. that has short leaves and clustered greenish white flowers

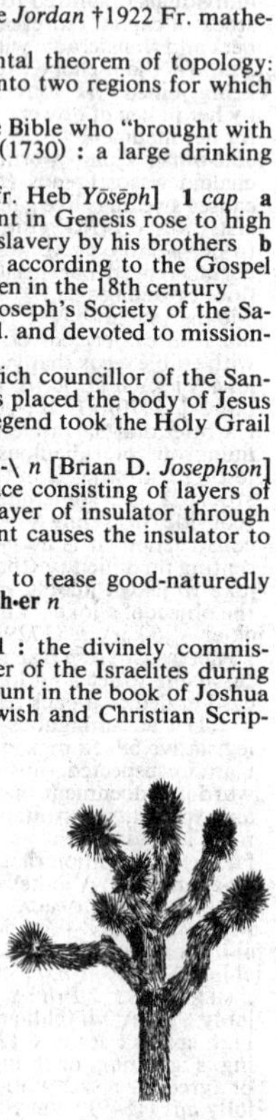

Joshua tree

joss \'jäs, 'jȯs\ *n* [Pidgin E, fr. Pg *deus* god, fr. L — more at DEITY] (1711) : a Chinese idol or cult image

joss house *n* (1771) : a Chinese temple or shrine

joss stick *n* (1845) : a slender stick of incense burned in front of a joss

¹jos·tle \'jäs-əl\ *vb* **jos·tled; jos·tling** \-(ə-)liŋ\ [alter. of *justle,* freq. of *²joust*] *vi* (1546) **1 a** : to come in contact or into collision **b** : to make one's way by pushing and shoving **c** : to exist in close proximity **2** : to vie in gaining an objective : CONTEND ~ *vt* **1 a** : to come in contact or into collision with **b** : to force by pushing : ELBOW **c** : to stir up : AGITATE **d** : to exist in close proximity with **2** : to vie with in attaining an objective

²jostle *n* (1611) **1** : a jostling encounter or experience **2** : the state of being crowded or jostled together

Jos·ue \'jäsh-ə-(,)wē\ *n* [LL, fr. Heb *Yĕhōshūaʿ*] : JOSHUA

¹jot \'jät\ *n* [L *iota, jota* iota] (1500) : the least bit : IOTA

²jot *vt* **jot·ted; jot·ting** (1721) : to write briefly or hurriedly : set down in the form of a note ⟨~ this down⟩

jot·ting \'jät-iŋ\ *n* (ca. 1808) : a brief note : MEMORANDUM

Jo·tun *also* **Jo·tunn** \'yōt-ᵊn, 'yō-,tün\ *n* [ON *jǫtunn;* akin to OE *eoten* giant] (1842) : a member of a race of giants in Norse mythology

Jo·tun·heim *also* **Jo·tunn·heim** \'yōt-ᵊn-,hīm, -,hām\ *n* [ON *Jǫtunheimar,* fr. *jǫtunn* + *heimar,* pl. of *heimr* abode, home; akin to OE *hām* home] (1895) : the home of the Jotuns in Norse mythology

jou·al \zhü-'al, -'äl, -'al\ *n* [CanF, fr. Joual *joual,* lit., horse, fr. F *cheval*] (1962) : a French patois spoken esp. by uneducated French Canadians

joule \'jü(ə)l, 'jaů(ə)l\ *n* [James P. *Joule*] (1882) : the absolute meter-kilogram-second unit of work or energy equal to 10^7 ergs or approximately 0.7375 foot-pounds

¹jounce \'jaůn(t)s\ *vb* **jounced; jounc·ing** [ME *jouncen*] *vi* (15c) : to move in an up-and-down manner : BOUNCE ~ *vt* : to cause to jounce

²jounce *n* (ca. 1787) : JOLT

jouncy \'jaůn(t)-sē\ *adj* **jounc·i·er; -est** (1943) : marked by a jouncing motion or effect

jour·nal \'jərn-ᵊl\ *n* [ME, service book containing the day hours, fr. MF, fr. *journal,* adj., daily, fr. L *diurnalis,* fr. *diurnus* of the day, fr. *dies* day — more at DEITY] (15c) **1 a** : a record of current transactions; *esp* : a book of original entry in double-entry bookkeeping **b** : an account of day-to-day events **c** : a record of experiences, ideas, or reflections kept regularly for private use **d** : a record of transactions kept by a deliberative or legislative body **e** : LOG 3, 4 **2 a** : a daily newspaper **b** : a periodical dealing esp. with matters of current interest **3** : the part of a rotating shaft, axle, roll, or spindle that turns in a bearing

journal box *n* (ca. 1864) : a metal housing to support and protect a journal bearing

jour·nal·ese \,jərn-ᵊl-'ēz, -'ēs\ *n* (1882) : a style of writing held to be characteristic of newspapers

jour·nal·ism \'jərn-ᵊl-,iz-əm\ *n* (1833) **1 a** : the collection and editing of news for presentation through the media **b** : the public press **c** : an academic study concerned with the collection and editing of news or the management of a news medium **2 a** : writing designed for publication in a newspaper or magazine **b** : writing characterized by a direct presentation of facts or description of events without an attempt at interpretation **c** : writing designed to appeal to current popular taste or public interest

jour·nal·ist \-ᵊl-əst\ *n* (1693) **1 a** : one engaged in journalism; *esp* : a writer or editor for a news medium **b** : a writer who aims at a mass audience **2** : one who keeps a journal

jour·nal·is·tic \,jərn-ᵊl-'is-tik\ *adj* (1829) : of, relating to, or characteristic of journalism or journalists — **jour·nal·is·ti·cal·ly** \-ti-k(ə-)lē\ *adv*

jour·nal·ize \'jərn-ᵊl-,īz\ *vb* **-ized; -iz·ing** *vt* (1766) : to record in a journal ~ *vi* **1** : to keep a journal in accounting **2** : to keep a personal journal — **jour·nal·iz·er** *n*

¹jour·ney \'jər-nē\ *n, pl* **journeys** [ME, fr. OF *journee* day's journey, fr. *jour* day, fr. LL *diurnum,* fr. L, neut. of *diurnus*] (13c) **1** : travel or passage from one place to another : TRIP **2** *chiefly dial* : a day's travel **3** : something suggesting travel or passage from one place to another ⟨the . . . ~ from childhood through adolescence to maturity —Peter Marin⟩

²journey *vb* **jour·neyed; jour·ney·ing** *vi* (14c) : to go on a journey : TRAVEL ~ *vt* : to travel over or through : TRAVERSE — **jour·ney·er** *n*

jour·ney·man \-nē-mən\ *n* [ME, fr. *journey* journey, a day's labor + *man*] (15c) **1** : a worker who has learned a trade and works for another person usu. by the day **2** : an experienced reliable worker or performer esp. as distinguished from one who is brilliant or colorful ⟨a good ~ trumpeter —*New Yorker*⟩ ⟨a ~ outfielder⟩

jour·ney·work \-,wərk\ *n* (1601) **1** : work done by a journeyman **2** : HACKWORK

¹joust \'jaůst *sometimes* 'jəst *or* 'jüst\ *n* (13c) **1 a** : a combat on horseback between two knights with lances esp. as part of a tournament **b** *pl* : TOURNAMENT **2** : a personal combat or competition : STRUGGLE

²joust *vi* [ME *jousten,* fr. MF *juster,* fr. (assumed) VL *juxtare,* fr. L *juxta* near; akin to L *jungere* to join — more at YOKE] (14c) **1 a** : to fight on horseback as a knight or man-at-arms **b** : to engage in combat with lances on horseback **2** : to engage in personal combat or competition — **joust·er** *n*

Jove \'jōv\ *n* [L *Jov-, Juppiter*] : JUPITER — often used interjectionally to express surprise or agreement esp. in the phrase *by Jove*

jo·vial \'jō-vē-əl, -vyəl\ *adj* (1604) **1** *cap* : of or relating to Jove **2** : markedly good-humored esp. as evidenced by jollity and conviviality *syn* see MERRY — **jo·vi·al·i·ty** \,jō-vē-'al-ət-ē\ *n* — **jo·vial·ly** \'jō-vē-ə-lē, -vyə-\ *adv*

Jo·vi·an \'jō-vē-ən\ *adj* (1530) : of, relating to, or characteristic of the god or planet Jupiter

jow \'jaů\ *n* [E dial. *jow* (to strike, toll)] *chiefly Scot* (1740) : STROKE, TOLL

jo·war \jə-'wär\ *n* [Hindi *joār, juwār;* akin to Skt *yavaḥ* barley, Gk *zeiai* a kind of wheat] (1800) : DURRA

¹jowl \'jaů(ə)l *sometimes* 'jōl\ *n* [alter. of ME *chavel,* fr. OE *ceafl;* akin to MHG *kivel* jaw, Av *zafar-* mouth] (bef. 12c) **1 a** : JAW; *esp* : MANDIBLE **b** : one of the lateral halves of the mandible **2 a** : CHEEK 1 **b** : the cheek meat of a hog ⟨a dinner of boiled ~*s*⟩ — see PORK illustration

²jowl *n* [ME *cholle*] (14c) : usu. slack flesh (as a dewlap, wattle, or the pendulous part of a double chin) associated with the cheeks, lower jaw, or throat

³jowl *n* [ME *choll*] (15c) : a cut of fish consisting of the head and usu. adjacent parts

jowly \'jaů-lē *sometimes* 'jō-\ *adj* **jowl·i·er; -est** (1873) : having marked jowls : having full or saggy flesh about the lower cheeks and jaw area ⟨elderly man with a disillusioned ~ face —John Dos Passos⟩

¹joy \'jȯi\ *n* [ME, fr. OF *joie,* fr. L *gaudia,* pl. of *gaudium,* fr. *gaudēre* to rejoice; akin to Gk *gēthein* to rejoice] (13c) **1 a** : the emotion evoked by well-being, success, or good fortune or by the prospect of possessing what one desires : DELIGHT **b** : the expression or exhibition of such emotion : GAIETY **2** : a state of happiness or felicity : BLISS **3** : a source or cause of delight — **joy·less** \-ləs\ *adj* — **joy·less·ly** *adv* — **joy·less·ness** *n*

²joy *vi* (14c) : to experience great pleasure or delight : REJOICE ~ *vt* **1** *archaic* : GLADDEN **2** *archaic* : ENJOY

joy·ance \'jȯi-ən(t)s\ *n, archaic* (1586) : DELIGHT, ENJOYMENT

joy·ful \'jȯi-fəl\ *adj* (13c) : experiencing, causing, or showing joy : HAPPY — **joy·ful·ly** \-fə-lē\ *adv* — **joy·ful·ness** *n*

joy·ous \'jȯi-əs\ *adj* (14c) : JOYFUL — **joy·ous·ly** *adv* — **joy·ous·ness** *n*

joy·pop \'jȯi-,päp\ *vi* (1953) : to use habit-forming drugs occasionally or irregularly without becoming addicted — **joy·pop·per** *n*

joy·ride \'jȯi-,rīd\ *n* (1909) **1** : a ride taken for pleasure and often marked by reckless driving **2** : conduct or action resembling a joyride esp. in disregard of cost or consequences — **joyride** *vi* — **joy·rid·er** \-,rīd-ər\ *n* — **joy·rid·ing** *n*

joy·stick \-,stik\ *n* [perh. fr. E slang *joystick* penis] (1910) **1** : a lever in an airplane that operates the elevators by a fore-and-aft motion and the ailerons by a side-to-side motion **2** : a control for any of various devices (as a computer display) that resembles an airplane's joystick esp. in being capable of motion in two or more directions

J particle *n* (ca. 1974) : an unstable neutral fundamental particle of the meson group that has a mass about 6000 times the mass of an electron — called also *J/psi particle, psi particle*

ju·ba \'jü-bə\ *n* [origin unknown] (1834) : a dance of Southern plantation Negroes accompanied by complexly rhythmic hand clapping and slapping of the knees and thighs

Ju·bal \'jü-bəl\ *n* [Heb *Yūbhāl*] : a descendant of Cain who according to the account in Genesis is the father of those who play the harp and organ
ju·bi·lance \'jü-bə-lən(t)s\ *n* (1864) : JUBILATION 1
ju·bi·lant \'jü-bə-lənt\ *adj* (1667) : EXULTANT — **ju·bi·lant·ly** *adv*
ju·bi·lar·i·an \,jü-bə-'ler-ē-ən, -'lar-\ *n* (1782) : one celebrating a jubilee
ju·bi·late \'jü-bə-,lāt\ *vi* **-lat·ed; -lat·ing** [L *jubilatus,* pp. of *jubilare;* akin to MHG *jū* (exclamation of joy), Gk *iygē* shout] (1641) : REJOICE
Ju·bi·la·te \,yü-bə-'lä-,tā, ,jü-\ *n* [L, 2d pers. pl. imper. of *jubilare*] (1549) **1 a :** the 100th Psalm in the Authorized Version **b** *not cap* **:** a joyous song or outburst **2 :** the third Sunday after Easter
ju·bi·la·tion \,jü-bə-'lā-shən\ *n* (14c) **1 :** an act of rejoicing : the state of being jubilant **2 :** an expression of great joy
¹ju·bi·lee \'jü-bə-(,)lē, ,jü-bə-'lē\ *n* [ME, fr. MF & LL; MF *jubilé,* fr. LL *jubilaeus,* modif. of LGk *iōbēlaios,* fr. Heb *yōbhēl* ram's horn, jubilee] (14c) **1** *often cap* **:** a year of emancipation and restoration provided by ancient Hebrew law to be kept every 50 years by the emancipation of Hebrew slaves, restoration of alienated lands to their former owners, and omission of all cultivation of the land **2 a :** a special anniversary; *esp* **:** a 50th anniversary **b :** a celebration of such an anniversary **3 a :** a period of time proclaimed by the Roman Catholic pope ordinarily every 25 years as a time of special solemnity **b :** a special plenary indulgence granted during a year of jubilee to Roman Catholics who perform certain specified works of repentance and piety **4 a :** JUBILATION **b :** a season of celebration **5 :** an Afro-American religious song usu. referring to a time of future happiness
²jubilee *adj, often cap* (ca. 1951) : FLAMBÉ ⟨cherries ~⟩
Ju·dah \'jüd-ə\ *n* [Heb *Yĕhūdhāh*] : a son of Jacob and the traditional eponymous ancestor of one of the tribes of Israel
Ju·da·ic \jü-'dā-ik\ *also* **Ju·da·ical** \-'dā-ə-kəl\ *adj* [L *judaicus,* fr. Gk *ioudaikos,* fr. *Ioudaios* Jew — more at JEW] (15c) : of, relating to, or characteristic of Jews or Judaism
Ju·da·ica \-'dā-ə-kə\ *n pl* [L, neut. pl. of *Judaicus*] (1923) : literary or historical materials relating to Jews or Judaism
Ju·da·ism \'jüd-ə-,iz-əm, 'jüd-ē-,iz-\ *n* (15c) **1 :** a religion developed among the ancient Hebrews and characterized by belief in one transcendent God who has revealed himself to Abraham, Moses, and the Hebrew prophets and by a religious life in accordance with Scriptures and rabbinic traditions **2 :** conformity to Jewish rites, ceremonies, and practices **3 :** the cultural, social, and religious beliefs and practices of the Jews **4 :** the whole body of Jews : the Jewish people
Ju·da·ist \'jüd-ə-əst, 'jüd-ē-, jü-'dā-\ *n* (1846) : one that believes in or practices Judaism — **Ju·da·is·tic** \,jüd-ə-'is-tik, ,jüd-ē-\ *adj*
Ju·da·ize \'jüd-ə-,īz, 'jüd-ē-\ *vb* **-ized; -iz·ing** *vi* (1582) : to adopt the customs, beliefs, or character of a Jew ~ *vt* : to make Jewish — **Ju·da·iza·tion** \,jüd-ə-ə-'zā-shən, ,jüd-ē-ə-\ *n* — **Ju·da·iz·er** \'jüd-ə-,īz-ər, 'jüd-ē-\ *n*
Ju·das \'jüd-əs\ *n* [LL, fr. Gk *Ioudas,* fr. Heb *Yĕhūdhāh*] **1 a :** the apostle who in the Gospel accounts betrayed Jesus **b :** a son of James and one of the twelve apostles **2 :** TRAITOR; *esp* **:** one who betrays under the guise of friendship **3** *not cap* **:** PEEPHOLE — called also *judas hole, judas window*
Judas Is·car·i·ot \-is-'kar-ē-ət\ *n* [LL *Judas Iscariotes,* fr. Gk *Ioudas Iskariōtēs*] : JUDAS 1a
Judas tree *n* [fr. the belief that Judas Iscariot hanged himself from a tree of this kind] (1668) : any of a genus (*Cercis*) of leguminous trees and shrubs (as a redbud) often cultivated for their showy flowers; *esp* **:** a Eurasian tree (*C. siliquastrum*) with purplish rosy flowers
¹jud·der \'jəd-ər\ *vi* [prob. alter. of *shudder*] *chiefly Brit* (1931) : to vibrate with intensity ⟨the engine stalled and kept ~*ing* —Roy Spicer⟩
²judder *n, chiefly Brit* (1935) : the action or sound of juddering
Jude \'jüd\ *n* [LL *Judas*] **1 :** the author of the New Testament Epistle of Jude **2 :** a short hortatory epistle addressed to early Christians and included as a book in the New Testament — see BIBLE table
Ju·deo–Chris·tian \jü-,dā-ō-'kris(h)-chən *also* ,jüd-ē-ō- *or* jü-,dē-ō-\ *adj* [L *Judaeus* Jew — more at JEW] (1899) : having historical roots in both Judaism and Christianity
Ju·deo–Span·ish \-'span-ish\ *n* (1851) : the Romance language of Sephardic Jews in the Balkans and Asia Minor
¹judge \'jəj\ *vb* **judged; judg·ing** [ME *juggen,* fr. OF *jugier,* fr. L *judicare,* fr. *judic-, judex* judge, fr. *jus* right, law + *dicere* to decide, say — more at JUST, DICTION] *vt* (13c) **1 :** to form an opinion about through careful weighing of evidence and testing of premises **2 :** to sit in judgment on **:** TRY **3 :** to determine or pronounce after inquiry and deliberation **4 :** GOVERN, RULE — used of a Hebrew tribal leader **5 :** to form an estimate or evaluation of **6 :** to hold as an opinion : GUESS, THINK ⟨I ~ she knew what she was doing⟩ ~ *vi* **1 :** to form an opinion **2 :** to decide as a judge *syn* see INFER — **judg·er** *n*
²judge *n* [ME *juge,* fr. MF, fr. L *judex*] (14c) : one who judges: as **a :** a public official authorized to decide questions brought before a court **b** *often cap* **:** a tribal hero exercising leadership among the Hebrews after the death of Joshua **c :** one appointed to decide in a contest or competition : UMPIRE **d :** one who gives an authoritative opinion **e :** CRITIC — **judge·ship** \-,ship\ *n*
judge advocate *n* (1748) **1 :** an officer assigned to the judge advocate general's corps or department **2 :** a staff officer serving as legal adviser to a military commander
judge advocate general *n* (1900) : the senior legal officer and chief legal adviser in the army, air force, or navy
Judg·es \'jəj-əz\ *n* : a narrative and historical book of Jewish and Christian Scripture — see BIBLE table
judg·mat·ic \,jəj-'mat-ik\ *or* **judg·mat·i·cal** \-i-kəl\ *adj* [prob. irreg. fr. *judgment*] (1826) : JUDICIOUS — **judg·mat·i·cal·ly** \-i-k(ə-)lē\ *adv*
judg·ment *or* **judge·ment** \'jəj-mənt\ *n* (13c) **1 a :** a formal utterance of an authoritative opinion **b :** an opinion so pronounced **2 a :** a formal decision given by a court **b (1) :** an obligation (as a debt) created by the decree of a court **(2) :** a certificate evidencing such a decree **3 a** *cap* **:** the final judging of mankind by God **b :** a divine sentence or decision; *specif* **:** a calamity held to be sent by God **4 a :** the process of forming an opinion or evaluation by discerning and comparing **b :** an opinion or estimate so formed **5 a :** the capacity for judging : DISCERNMENT **b :** the exercise of this capacity **6 :** a proposition stating something believed or asserted *syn* see SENSE — **judg·men·tal** \,jəj-'ment-ᵊl\ *adj* — **judg·men·tal·ly** \-ē\ *adv*
judgment day *n* (1591) **1** *cap J&D* **:** the day of God's judgment of mankind at the end of the world according to various theologies **2 :** a day of final judgment
ju·di·ca·to·ry \'jüd-i-kə-,tōr-ē, -,tȯr-\ *n, pl* **-ries** (1575) **1 :** JUDICIARY 1a **2 :** JUDICATURE 2
ju·di·ca·ture \'jüd-i-kə-,chu̇(ə)r, -chər, -,t(y)u̇(ə)r\ *n* [MF, fr. ML *judicatura,* fr. L *judicatus,* pp. of *judicare*] (ca. 1530) **1 :** the action of judging : the administration of justice **2 :** a court of justice **3 :** JUDICIARY 1
ju·di·cial \ju̇-'dish-əl\ *adj* [ME, fr. L *judicialis,* fr. *judicium* judgment, fr. *judex*] (14c) **1 a :** of or relating to a judgment, the function of judging, the administration of justice, or the judiciary ⟨~ processes⟩ **b :** belonging to the branch of government that is charged with trying all cases that involve the government and with the administration of justice within its jurisdiction — compare EXECUTIVE, LEGISLATIVE **2 :** ordered or enforced by a court ⟨~ decisions⟩ **3 :** of, characterized by, or expressing judgment : CRITICAL 1c **4 :** arising from a judgment of God **5 :** belonging or appropriate to a judge or the judiciary — **ju·di·cial·ly** \-'dish-(ə-)lē\ *adv*
judicial review *n* (ca. 1924) **1 :** REVIEW 5 **2 :** a constitutional doctrine that gives to a court system the power to annul legislative or executive acts which the judges declare to be unconstitutional
ju·di·cia·ry \ju̇-'dish-ē-,er-ē, -'dish-ə-rē\ *n* [*judiciary,* adj., fr. L *judiciarius* judicial, fr. *judicium*] (1802) **1 a :** a system of courts of law **b :** the judges of these courts **2 :** a branch of government in which judicial power is vested — **judiciary** *adj*
ju·di·cious \ju̇-'dish-əs\ *adj* (1598) : having, exercising, or characterized by sound judgment : DISCREET *syn* see WISE — **ju·di·cious·ly** *adv* — **ju·di·cious·ness** *n*
Ju·dith \'jüd-əth\ *n* [LL, fr. Gk *Ioudith,* fr. Heb *Yĕhūdhīth*] **1 :** the Jewish heroine who saves the city of Bethulia in the book of Judith **2 :** a book of Scripture included in the Roman Catholic canon of the Old Testament and in the Protestant Apocrypha — see BIBLE table
ju·do \'jüd-(,)ō\ *n* [Jp *jūdō,* fr. *jū* weakness, gentleness + *dō* art] (1889) : a sport developed from jujitsu that emphasizes the use of quick movement and leverage to throw an opponent — **judo·ist** \-,ō-əst, -ə-wəst\ *n*
¹jug \'jəg\ *n* [perh. fr. *Jug,* nickname for *Joan*] (1538) **1 a** *chiefly Brit* **:** a small pitcher **b (1) :** a large deep usu. earthenware or glass container with a narrow mouth and a handle **(2) :** the contents of such a container : JUGFUL **2 :** JAIL, PRISON
²jug *vt* **jugged; jug·ging** (1747) **1 :** to stew (as a hare) in an earthenware vessel **2 :** JAIL, IMPRISON
ju·gate \'jü-,gāt, -gət\ *adj* [NL *jugum,* yoke] (ca. 1887) **1 :** having parts arranged in pairs : PAIRED **2 :** having a jugum
jug band *n* (ca. 1933) : a band that uses primitive or improvised instruments (as jugs, washboards, and kazoos) to play blues, jazz, and folk music
jug·ful \'jəg-,fu̇l\ *n* (1831) **1 :** as much as a jug will hold **2 :** a great deal — used in the phrase *not by a jugful*
jug·ger·naut \'jəg-ər-,nȯt, -,nät\ *n* [Hindi *Jagannāth,* lit., lord of the world, title of Vishnu] (1632) **1 :** a massive inexorable force or object that crushes whatever is in its path **2** *chiefly Brit* **:** a large heavy truck
¹jug·gle \'jəg-əl\ *vb* **jug·gled; jug·gling** \-(ə-)liŋ\ [ME *jogelen,* fr. MF *jogler* to joke, fr. L *joculari,* fr. *joculus,* dim. of *jocus* joke] *vi* (14c) **1 :** to perform the tricks of a juggler **2 :** to engage in manipulation esp. in order to achieve a desired end ~ *vt* **1 a :** to practice deceit or trickery on : BEGUILE **b :** to manipulate esp. in order to achieve a desired end ⟨~ an account to hide a loss⟩ **2 a :** to toss in the manner of a juggler **b :** to hold or balance precariously **3 :** to handle or deal with usu. several things (as obligations) at one time so as to satisfy often competing requirements ⟨~ the responsibilities of family life and full-time job —Jane S. Gould⟩
²juggle *n* (1664) : an act or instance of juggling: **a :** a trick of magic **b :** a show of manual dexterity **c :** an act of manipulation esp. to achieve a desired end
jug·gler \'jəg-(ə-)lər\ *n* [ME *jogelour,* fr. OE *geogelere,* fr. OF *jogleour,* fr. L *joculator,* fr. *joculatus,* pp. of *joculari*] (bef. 12c) **1 a :** one who performs tricks or acts of magic or deftness **b :** one skilled in keeping several objects in motion in the air at the same time by alternately tossing and catching them **2 :** one who manipulates esp. in order to achieve a desired end
jug·glery \'jəg-lə-rē\ *n* (14c) **1 :** the art or practice of a juggler **2 :** manipulation or trickery esp. to achieve a desired end
¹jug·u·lar \'jəg-yə-lər *also* 'jüg- *or* -(ə-)lər\ *adj* [LL *jugularis,* fr. L *jugulum* collarbone, throat; akin to L *jungere* to join — more at YOKE] (1597) **1 :** of or relating to the throat or neck **2 :** of or relating to the jugular vein
²jugular *n* (1615) **1 :** JUGULAR VEIN **2 :** the most vital or vulnerable part of something ⟨showed an instinct for the ~ in competition⟩
jugular vein *n* (1597) : any of several veins of each side of the neck that return blood from the head
ju·gum \'jü-gəm\ *n, pl* **ju·ga** \-gə\ *or* **jugums** [NL, fr. L, yoke — more at YOKE] (1857) : the most posterior and basal region of an insect's wing modified in some lepidopterans into a lobe that couples the fore and hind wings during flight
jug wine *n* (1972) : table wine sold in large bottles
¹juice \'jüs\ *n* [ME *jus,* fr. OF, broth, juice, fr. L; akin to ON *ostr* cheese, Gk *zymē* leaven, Skt *yūṣa* broth] (13c) **1 :** the extractable fluid contents of cells or tissues **2 a** *pl* **:** the natural fluids of an animal body **b :** the liquid or moisture contained in something **3 a :** the inherent quality of a thing : ESSENCE **b :** STRENGTH, VIGOR, VITALITY **4 :** a medium (as electricity or gasoline) that supplies power **5** *slang* **:** LIQUOR **6** *slang* **:** exorbitant interest exacted of a borrower under the threat of violence **7** *slang* **:** INFLUENCE, CLOUT **8 :** a motivating, inspiring, or enabling force or factor ⟨creative ~*s*⟩ — **juice·less** \'jü-sləs\ *adj*

2juice *vt* **juiced; juic·ing** (1603) **1** : to add juice to **2** : to extract the juice of
juiced \ˈjüst\ *adj* (1592) **1** : containing juice — usu. used in combination ⟨precious-*juiced* flowers —Shak.⟩ **2** *slang* : DRUNK 1
juice·head \ˈjüs-ˌhed\ *n, slang* (1955) : ALCOHOLIC
juic·er \ˈjü-sər\ *n* (ca. 1928) **1** : an appliance for extracting juice from fruit or vegetables **2** *slang* : a heavy or habitual drinker
juice up *vt* (1955) : to give life, energy, or spirit to
juicy \ˈjü-sē\ *adj* **juic·i·er; -est** (15c) **1** : having much juice : SUCCULENT **2** : rewarding or profitable esp. financially : FAT ⟨~ contract⟩ ⟨a ~ dramatic role⟩ **3 a** : rich in interest : COLORFUL ⟨~ details⟩ **b** : PIQUANT, RACY ⟨a ~ scandal⟩ **c** : full of vitality — **juic·i·ly** \-sə-lē\ *adv* — **juic·i·ness** \-sē-nəs\ *n*
ju·jit·su *or* **ju·jut·su** \jü-ˈjit-(ˌ)sü\ *n* [Jp *jūjutsu*, fr. *jū* weakness, gentleness + *jutsu* art, skill] (1875) : an art of weaponless fighting employing holds, throws, and paralyzing blows to subdue or disable an opponent
ju·ju \ˈjü-(ˌ)jü\ *n* [of W. African origin; akin to Hausa *djudju* fetish] (1894) **1** : a fetish, charm, or amulet of West African peoples **2** : the magic attributed to or associated with jujus
ju·jube \ˈjü-ˌjüb, *esp for 2* ˈjü-jü-ˌbē\ *n* [ME, fr. ML *jujuba*, alter. of L *zizyphum*, fr. Gk *zizyphon*] (15c) **1 a** : an edible drupaceous fruit of any of several trees (genus *Ziziphus*) of the buckthorn family; *esp* : one of an Asian tree (*Z. jujuba*) **b** : a tree producing this fruit **2** : a fruit-flavored gumdrop or lozenge
juke \ˈjük\ *vt* **juked; juk·ing** [prob. alter. of E dial. *jouk* (to cheat, deceive)] (1967) : to fake out of position (as in football)
juke·box \ˈjük-ˌbäks, ˈjüt-\ *n* [Gullah *juke* disorderly, of W. African origin; akin to Bambara *dzugu* wicked] (1939) : a coin-operated phonograph that automatically plays records selected from its list
juke joint \ˈjük-, ˈjüt-\ *n* (1937) : a small inexpensive establishment for eating, drinking, or dancing to the music of a jukebox
ju·lep \ˈjü-ləp\ *n* [ME, fr. MF, fr. Ar *julāb*, fr. Per *gulāb*, fr. *gul* rose + *āb* water] (15c) **1** : a drink consisting of sweet syrup, flavoring, and water **2** : a drink consisting of a liquor (as bourbon or brandy) and sugar poured over crushed ice and garnished with mint
Ju·lian calendar \ˌjül-yən-\ *n* [L *julianus*, fr. Gaius *Julius* Caesar] (ca. 1771) : a calendar introduced in Rome in 46 B.C. establishing the 12-month year of 365 days with each fourth year having 366 days and the months each having 31 or 30 days except for February which has 28 or in leap years 29 days — compare GREGORIAN CALENDAR
ju·li·enne \ˌjü-lē-ˈen, ˌzhü-\ *n* [F] (1841) : food (as meat or vegetables) cut into long thin strips ⟨a ~ of leeks⟩ — **julienne** *adj or vt*
Ju·liet \ˈjül-yət; ˌjü-lē-ˈet, ˈjü-lē-ˌ\ *n* : the heroine of Shakespeare's tragedy *Romeo and Juliet*
Ju·li·ett \ˌjül-ē-ˈet\ [prob. irreg. fr. *Juliet*] (1952) — a communications code word for the letter *j*
Ju·ly \jü-ˈlī\ *n* [ME *Julie*, fr. OE *Julius*, fr. L, fr. Gaius *Julius* Caesar] (bef. 12c) : the 7th month of the Gregorian calendar
Ju·ma·da \jü-ˈmäd-ə\ *n* [Ar *Jumāda*] (ca. 1769) : either of two months of the Islamic year: **a** : the 5th month **b** : the 6th month — see MONTH table
1jum·ble \ˈjəm-bəl\ *vb* **jum·bled; jum·bling** \-b(ə-)liŋ\ [perh. imit.] *vi* (1529) : to move in a confused or disordered manner ~ *vt* : to mix into a confused or disordered mass — often used with *up*
2jumble *n* (1661) **1 a** : a mass of things mingled together without order or plan : HODGEPODGE **b** : a state of confusion **2** *Brit* : articles for a rummage sale
3jumble *n* [origin unknown] (1615) : a small thin usu. ring-shaped sugared cookie or cake
jumble sale *n, Brit* (1898) : RUMMAGE SALE
jum·bo \ˈjəm-(ˌ)bō\ *n, pl* **jumbos** [*Jumbo*, a huge elephant exhibited by P. T. Barnum] (1883) : a very large specimen of its kind — **jumbo** *adj*
1jump \ˈjəmp\ *vb* [prob. akin to LG *gumpen* to jump] *vi* (1530) **1 a** : to spring into the air : LEAP; *esp* : to spring free from the ground or other base by the muscular action of feet and legs **b** : to move suddenly or involuntarily : START **c** : to move over a position occupied by an opponent's man in a board game often thereby capturing the man **d** : to undergo a vertical or lateral displacement owing to improper alignment of the film on a projector mechanism **e** : to start out or forward : BEGIN — usu. used with *off* ⟨~ off to a big lead⟩ **f** : to move energetically : HUSTLE **g** : to go from one sequence of instructions in a computer program to another ⟨~ to a subroutine⟩ **2** : COINCIDE, AGREE **3 a** : to move haphazardly or irregularly ⟨~*ed* from job to job⟩ **b** : to change employment in violation of contract **c** : to rise suddenly in rank or status **d** : to undergo a sudden sharp change in value ⟨prices ~*ed*⟩ **e** : to make a jump in bridge **f** : to make a hurried judgment ⟨~ to conclusions⟩ **g** : to show eagerness ⟨~*ed* at the chance⟩ **h** : to enter eagerly ⟨~ into the new project⟩ ⟨~ on the bandwagon⟩ **4** : to make a sudden physical or verbal attack ⟨~*ed* on him for his criticism⟩ **5** : to bustle with activity ⟨the bar was ~*ing* with young people⟩ ~ *vt* **1 a** : to leap over ⟨~ a hurdle⟩ **b** : to move over (a man) in a board game **c** : BYPASS ⟨~ electrical connections⟩ **d** : to act, move, or begin before (as a signal) ⟨~ the green light⟩ **e** : to leap aboard ⟨~ a freight⟩ **2** *obs* : RISK, HAZARD **3 a** : to escape from or avoid **b** : to leave hastily or in violation of contract ⟨~ town without paying their bills —Hamilton Basso⟩ **c** : to depart from (a normal course) ⟨~ the track⟩ **4 a** : to make a sudden physical or verbal attack on **b** : to occupy illegally ⟨~ a mining claim⟩ **5 a (1)** : to cause to leap **(2)** : to cause (game) to break cover : START, FLUSH **b** : to elevate in rank or status **c** : to raise (a bridge partner's bid) by more than one rank **d** : to increase suddenly and sharply — **jump the gun 1** : to start in a race before the starting signal **2** : to act, move, or begin something before the proper time
2jump *adv, obs* (1539) : EXACTLY, PAT
3jump *n* (ca. 1552) **1 a (1)** : an act of jumping : LEAP **(2)** : any of several sports competitions featuring a leap, spring, or bound **(3)** : a space cleared or covered by a leap **(4)** : an obstacle to be jumped over or from **b** : a sudden involuntary movement : START **c** : a move made in a board game by jumping **d** : a transfer from one sequence of instructions in a computer program to a different sequence ⟨conditional ~⟩ **2** *obs* : VENTURE **3 a (1)** : a sharp sudden increase **(2)** : a bid in bridge of more tricks than are necessary to overcall the preceding bid — compare SHIFT **b** : an abrupt change or transition **c (1)** : a quick short journey **(2)** : one in a series of moves from one place to another **4** : an advantage at the start ⟨desirous of getting the ~ on the competition —Elmer Davis⟩
jump ball *n* (1924) : a method of putting a basketball into play by tossing it into the air between two opponents who jump up and attempt to tap the ball to a teammate
jump boot *n* (1942) : a boot worn esp. by paratroopers
jump cut *n* (1948) : a discontinuity or acceleration in the action of a filmed scene brought about by removal of medial portions of the shot
1jump·er \ˈjəm-pər\ *n* (1611) **1** : a person who jumps **2 a** : any of various devices operating with a jumping motion **b** : any of several sleds **c** : a short wire used to close a break or cut out part of a circuit **3** : any of several jumping animals; *esp* : a saddle horse trained to jump obstacles **4** : JUMP SHOT
2jum·per \ˈjəm-pər\ *n* [prob. fr. E dial. *jump* (jumper)] (1853) **1** : a loose blouse or jacket worn by workmen **2** : a sleeveless one-piece dress worn usu. with a blouse **3** : a child's coverall — usu. used in pl. **4** *chiefly Brit* : SWEATER 2
jumping bean *n* (ca. 1889) : a seed of any of several Mexican shrubs (genera *Sebastiania* and *Sapium*) of the spurge family that tumbles about because of the movements of the larva of a small moth (*Carpocapsa saltitans*) inside it
jumping jack *n* (1883) **1** : a toy figure of a man jointed and made to jump or dance by means of strings or a sliding stick **2** : a conditioning exercise performed from a standing position by jumping to a position with legs spread and hands touching overhead and then to the original position — called also *side-straddle hop*
jumping mouse *n* (1826) : any of several small hibernating No. American rodents (family Zapodidae) with long hind legs and tail and no cheek pouches
jumping–off place \ˌjəm-piŋ-ˈȯf-\ *n* (1826) **1** : a remote or isolated place **2** : a place from which an enterprise is launched — called also *jumping–off point*
jumping plant louse *n* (1901) : any of numerous plant lice (family Psyllidae) with the femurs thickened and adapted for leaping
jumping spider *n* (1813) : any of a family (Salticidae) of small spiders that stalk and leap upon their prey
jump–off \ˈjəm-ˌpȯf\ *n* (1917) **1** : the start of a race or an attack **2** : a jumping competition to break a tie at the end of regular competition (as in a horse show)
jump pass *n* (ca. 1948) : a pass made by a player (as in football or basketball) while jumping
jump rope *n* (1834) : a rope used in a child's game in which a player jumps over a usu. twirling rope each time it reaches its lowest point
jump seat *n* (ca. 1864) **1** : a movable carriage seat **2** : a folding seat between the front and rear seats of a passenger automobile
jump shot *n* (1948) : a shot in basketball made by jumping into the air and releasing the ball with one or both hands at the peak of the jump
jump·suit \ˈjəmp-ˌsüt\ *n* (1944) **1** : a uniform worn by parachutists for jumping **2** : a one-piece garment consisting of a blouse or shirt with attached trousers or shorts
jumpy \ˈjəm-pē\ *adj* **jump·i·er; -est** (1869) **1** : characterized by jumps or sudden variations **2** : NERVOUS, JITTERY — **jump·i·ness** *n*
jun \ˈjən\ *n, pl* **jun** [Korean] (1966) : the chon of North Korea
jun·co \ˈjəŋ-(ˌ)kō\ *n, pl* **juncos** *or* **juncoes** [NL, fr. Sp, reed — more at JONQUIL] (1887) : any of a genus (*Junco*) of small widely distributed American finches usu. having a pink bill, ashy gray head and back, and conspicuous white lateral tail feathers
junc·tion \ˈjəŋ(k)-shən\ *n* [L *junction-, junctio*, fr. *junctus*, pp. of *jungere* to join — more at YOKE] (1711) **1** : an act of joining : the state of being joined **2 a** : a place or point of meeting **b** : an intersection of roads esp. where one terminates **c** : a point (as in a thermocouple) at which dissimilar metals make contact **d** : an interface in a semiconductor device between regions with different electrical characteristics **3** : something that joins — **junc·tion·al** \-shnəl, -shən-ᵊl\ *adj*
junc·tur·al \ˈjəŋ(k)-chə-rəl, ˈjəŋ(k)-shrəl\ *adj* (1942) : of or relating to phonetic juncture
junc·ture \ˈjəŋ(k)-chər\ *n* (14c) **1 a** : JOINT, CONNECTION **b** : the manner of transition or mode of relationship between two consecutive sounds in speech **2** : an instance of joining : UNION, JUNCTION **3** : a point of time; *esp* : one made critical by a concurrence of circumstances
syn JUNCTURE, PASS, EXIGENCY, EMERGENCY, CONTINGENCY, PINCH, STRAITS, CRISIS mean a critical or crucial time or state of affairs. JUNCTURE stresses the significant concurrence or convergence of events; PASS implies a bad or distressing state or situation brought about by a combination of causes; EXIGENCY stresses the pressure of restrictions or urgency of demands created by a special situation; EMERGENCY applies to a sudden unforeseen situation requiring prompt action to avoid disaster; CONTINGENCY implies an emergency or exigency that is regarded as possible but uncertain of occurrence; PINCH implies urgency or pressure for action to a less intense degree than EXIGENCY or EMERGENCY; STRAITS applies to a troublesome situation from which escape is extremely difficult; CRISIS applies to a juncture whose outcome will make a decisive difference.
June \ˈjün\ *n* [ME, fr. MF & L; MF *Juin*, fr. L *Junius*] (bef. 12c) : the 6th month of the Gregorian calendar
June·ber·ry \ˈjün-ˌber-ē\ *n* (ca. 1810) : SERVICEBERRY
june bug *n, often cap J* (1829) : any of numerous rather large leaf-eating beetles (family Melolonthidae) that fly chiefly in late spring and have as larvae white grubs that live in soil and feed chiefly on the roots of grasses and other plants — called also *june beetle*
1Jung·ian \ˈyüŋ-ē-ən\ *n* (1926) : an adherent of the psychological doctrines of C. G. Jung
2Jungian *adj* (1933) : of, relating to, or characteristic of C. G. Jung or his psychological doctrines
jun·gle \ˈjəŋ-gəl\ *n, often attrib* [Hindi *jaṅgal*] (1776) **1 a** : an impenetrable thicket or tangled mass of tropical vegetation **b** : a tract overgrown with thickets or masses of vegetation **2** : a hobo camp **3 a (1)** : a confused or disordered mass of objects : JUMBLE **(2)** : something that baffles or frustrates by its tangled or complex character : MAZE ⟨the ~ of housing laws —Bernard Taper⟩ **b** : a place of ruthless struggle for survival ⟨the city is a ~ where no one is safe after dark —Stuart Chase⟩ — **jun·gly** \-g(ə-)lē\ *adj*

jungle fowl *n* (1824) **:** any of several Asian wild birds (genus *Gallus*); *esp* **:** a bird (*G. gallus*) of southeastern Asia from which domestic fowls have prob. descended
jungle gym *n* [fr. *Junglegym*, a trademark] (1923) **:** a structure of vertical and horizontal bars for use by children at play
¹ju·nior \ˈjün-yər\ *adj* [L, compar. of *juvenis* young — more at YOUNG] (13c) **1 a :** YOUNGER — used chiefly to distinguish a son with the same given name as his father **b** (1) **:** YOUTHFUL (2) **:** designed for young people and esp. adolescents **c :** of more recent date and therefore inferior or subordinate ⟨a ~ lien⟩ **2 :** lower in standing or rank ⟨~ partners⟩ **3 :** of or relating to juniors or the class of juniors at an educational institution ⟨the ~ prom⟩
²junior *n* [L, n. & adj.] (1526) **1 a** (1) **:** a person who is younger than another ⟨a man six years my ~⟩ (2) **:** a male child **:** SON (3) **:** a young person **b :** a clothing size for women and girls with slight figures **2 a :** a person holding a lower position in a hierarchy of ranks **b :** a student in his next-to-the-last year before graduating from an educational institution
ju·nior·ate \ˈjün-yə-ˌrāt, -rət\ *n* (1845) **1 :** a course of high school or college study for candidates for the priesthood, brotherhood, or sisterhood; *specif* **:** one preparatory to the course in philosophy **2 :** a seminary for juniorate training
junior college *n* (1899) **:** an educational institution that offers two years of studies corresponding to those in the first two years of a four-year college and that often offers technical, vocational, and liberal studies to the adults of a community
junior high school *n* (1909) **:** a school usu. including grades 7 to 9
Junior League *n* (1938) **:** a member of a league of young women organized for volunteer service to civic and social organizations
junior miss *n* (1927) **1 :** an adolescent girl **2 :** JUNIOR 1b
junior varsity *n* (1949) **:** a team composed of members lacking the experience or qualification required for the varsity
ju·ni·per \ˈjü-nə-pər\ *n* [ME *junipere*, fr. L *juniperus* — more at JONQUIL] (14c) **1 :** an evergreen shrub or tree (genus *Juniperus*) of the pine family; *esp* **:** one having a prostrate or shrubby habit **2 :** any of several coniferous trees resembling true junipers
juniper oil *n* (ca. 1901) **:** an acrid essential oil obtained from the fruit of the common juniper and used esp. in gin and liqueurs
juniper tar *n* (ca. 1884) **:** a dark tarry liquid used locally in treating skin diseases and obtained by distillation from the wood of a European juniper (*Juniperus oxycedrus*) — called also *cade oil, juniper tar oil*
¹junk \ˈjəŋk\ *n* [ME *jonke*] (14c) **1 :** pieces of old cable or cordage used esp. to make gaskets, mats, swabs, or oakum **2 :** hard salted beef for use on shipboard **3 a** (1) **:** old iron, glass, paper, or other waste that may be used again in some form (2) **:** secondhand, worn, or discarded articles **b :** something of poor quality **:** TRASH **c :** something of little meaning or significance **4** *slang* **:** NARCOTICS; *esp* **:** HEROIN — **junky** \ˈjəŋ-kē\ *adj*
²junk *vt* (1916) **:** to get rid of as worthless **:** SCRAP ***syn*** see DISCARD
³junk *n* [Pg *junco*, fr. Jav *joṅ*] (1555) **:** any of various ships of Chinese waters with bluff lines, a high poop and overhanging stem, little or no keel, high pole masts, and a deep rudder

junk

junk art *n* (1962) **:** three-dimensional art made from discarded material (as metal, mortar, glass, or wood) — **junk artist** *n*
junk bond *n* (1976) **:** a high-risk bond that offers a high yield and is often issued to finance a takeover of a company
junk·er \ˈjəŋ-kər\ *n* [¹*junk* + *-er*] (1944) **:** something (as an automobile) of such age and condition as to be ready for scrapping
Jun·ker \ˈyu̇ŋ-kər\ *n* [G, fr. OHG *junchērro*, lit., young lord] (1554) **:** a member of the Prussian landed aristocracy — **Jun·ker·dom** \-kərd-əm\ *n* — **Jun·ker·ism** \-kə-ˌriz-əm\ *n*
¹jun·ket \ˈjəŋ-kət\ *n* [ME *ioncate*, deriv. of (assumed) VL *juncata*, fr. L *juncus* rush] (15c) **1 :** a dessert of sweetened flavored milk set with rennet **2 a :** a festive social affair **b :** TRIP, JOURNEY; *esp* **:** a trip made by an official at public expense
²junket *vi* (1555) **1 :** FEAST, BANQUET **2 :** to go on a junket — **jun·ke·teer** \ˌjəŋ-kə-ˈti(ə)r\ *or* **jun·ket·er** \ˈjəŋ-kət-ər\ *n*
junk food *n* (1971) **1 :** food that is high in calories but low in nutritional content **2 :** something that is appealing or enjoyable but of little or no real value ⟨the ultimate in *junk food* for young minds — Cleveland Amory⟩
junk·ie *or* **junky** \ˈjəŋ-kē\ *n, pl* **junk·ies** (1940) **1 :** a junk dealer **2** *slang* **:** a narcotics peddler or addict **3 :** one that derives inordinate pleasure from or that is dependent on something ⟨sugar ~⟩ ⟨television news ~⟩
junk mail *n* (1954) **:** third-class mail (as advertising circulars) that is often addressed to "occupant" or "resident"
junk sculpture *n* (1965) **:** JUNK ART
junk·yard \ˈjəŋk-ˌyärd\ *n* (1880) **:** a yard used to store usu. resalable junk
Ju·no \ˈjü-(ˌ)nō\ *n* **:** the wife of Jupiter, queen of heaven, and goddess of light, birth, women, and marriage — compare HERA
Ju·no·esque \ˌjü-(ˌ)nō-ˈesk\ *adj* (1888) **:** marked by stately beauty
jun·ta \ˈhu̇n-tə, ˈjənt-ə, ˈhən-tə\ *n* [Sp, fr. fem. of *junto* joined, fr. L *junctus*, pp. of *jungere* to join — more at YOKE] (1622) **1 :** a council or committee for political or governmental purposes; *esp* **:** a group of persons controlling a government esp. after a revolutionary seizure of power **2 :** JUNTO
jun·to \ˈjənt-(ˌ)ō\ *n, pl* **juntos** [prob. alter. of *junta*] (1623) **:** a group of persons joined for a common purpose
Ju·pi·ter \ˈjü-pət-ər\ *n* [L] **1 :** the chief Roman god, husband of Juno, and god of light, of the sky and weather, and of the state and its welfare and its laws — compare ZEUS **2 :** the largest of the planets and fifth in order from the sun — see PLANET table
Ju·ra \ˈju̇r-ə\ *n* [prob. G, fr. the *Jura* mountain range] (1829) **:** the Jurassic geological period or the rocks belonging to it
ju·ral \ˈju̇r-əl\ *adj* [L *jur-*, *jus* law] (1635) **1 :** of or relating to law **2 :** of or relating to rights or obligations — **ju·ral·ly** \-ə-lē\ *adv*
Ju·ras·sic \ju̇-ˈras-ik\ *adj* [F *jurassique*, fr. *Jura* mountain range] (1831) **:** of, relating to, or being the period of the Mesozoic era between the Cretaceous and the Triassic or the corresponding system of rocks marked by the presence of dinosaurs and the first appearance of birds — **Jurassic** *n*
ju·rat \ˈju̇(ə)r-ˌat\ *n* [short for L *juratum* (*est*) it has been sworn, 3d sing. perf. pass. of *jurare* to swear — more at JURY] (1796) **:** a certificate added to an affidavit stating when, before whom, and where it was made
ju·rel \hü-ˈrel\ *n* [Sp] (1760) **:** any of several food fishes (family Carangidae) of warm seas
ju·rid·i·cal \ju̇-ˈrid-i-kəl\ *or* **ju·rid·ic** \-ik\ *adj* [L *juridicus*, fr. *jur-*, *jus* + *dicere* to say — more at DICTION] (1502) **1 :** of or relating to the administration of justice or the office of a judge **2 :** of or relating to law in general or jurisprudence **:** LEGAL ⟨~ terms⟩ — **ju·rid·i·cal·ly** \-i-k(ə-)lē\ *adv*
ju·ris·con·sult \ˌju̇r-ə-ˈskän-ˌsəlt, -skən-ˈ\ *n* [L *jurisconsultus*, fr. *juris* (gen. of *jus*) + *consultus*, pp. of *consulere* to consult] (1605) **:** JURIST; *esp* **:** one learned in international and public law
ju·ris·dic·tion \ˌju̇r-əs-ˈdik-shən\ *n* [ME *jurisdiccioun*, fr. MF & L; MF *juridiction*, fr. L *jurisdiction-*, *jurisdictio*, fr. *juris* + *diction-*, *dictio* act of saying — more at DICTION] (14c) **1 :** the power, right, or authority to interpret and apply the law **2 :** the authority of a sovereign power to govern or legislate **3 :** the limits or territory within which authority may be exercised **:** CONTROL ***syn*** see POWER — **ju·ris·dic·tion·al** \-shnəl, -shən-ᵊl\ *adj* — **ju·ris·dic·tion·al·ly** \-ē\ *adv*
Ju·ris Doctor \ˌju̇r-əs-\ *n* [L, doctor of law] (ca. 1969) **:** a degree equivalent to bachelor of laws
ju·ris·pru·dence \ˌju̇r-ə-ˈsprüd-ᵊn(t)s\ *n* (ca. 1656) **1 a :** a system or body of law **b :** the course of court decisions **2 :** the science or philosophy of law **3 :** a department of law ⟨medical ~⟩ — **ju·ris·pru·den·tial** \-sprü-ˈden-chəl\ *adj* — **ju·ris·pru·den·tial·ly** \-ˈdench-(ə-)lē\ *adv*
ju·ris·pru·dent \-ˈsprüd-ᵊnt\ *n* [LL *jurisprudent-*, *jurisprudens*, fr. L *juris* + *prudent-*, *prudens* skilled, prudent] (1628) **:** JURIST
ju·rist \ˈju̇(ə)r-əst\ *n* [MF *juriste*, fr. ML *jurista*, fr. L *jur-*, *jus*] (15c) **:** one having a thorough knowledge of law: **a :** LAWYER **b :** JUDGE
ju·ris·tic \ju̇-ˈris-tik\ *adj* (1831) **1 :** of or relating to a jurist or jurisprudence **2 :** of, relating to, or recognized in law — **ju·ris·ti·cal·ly** \-ti-k(ə-)lē\ *adv*
ju·ror \ˈju̇r-ər, ˈju̇(ə)r-ˌȯ(ə)r\ *n* (14c) **1 a :** a member of a jury **b :** a person summoned to serve on a jury **2 :** a person who takes an oath (as of allegiance)
¹ju·ry \ˈju̇(ə)r-ē\ *n, pl* **juries** [ME *jure*, fr. AF *juree*, fr. OF *jurer* to swear, fr. L *jurare*, fr. *jur-*, *jus*] (15c) **1 :** a body of persons sworn to give a verdict on some matter submitted to them; *esp* **:** a body of persons legally selected and sworn to inquire into any matter of fact and to give their verdict according to the evidence **2 :** a committee for judging and awarding prizes at a contest or exhibition
²jury *adj* [origin unknown] (1616) **:** improvised for temporary use esp. in an emergency **:** MAKESHIFT ⟨a ~ mast⟩ ⟨a ~ rig⟩
jury-rig \ˈju̇(ə)r-ē-ˌrig, -ˈrig\ *vt* [²*jury*] (ca. 1788) **:** to erect, construct, or arrange in a makeshift fashion
jus gen·ti·um \ˈyüs-ˈgent-ē-əm\ *n* [L, law of nations] (1548) **:** INTERNATIONAL LAW
jus san·gui·nis \-ˈsäŋ-gwə-nəs\ *n* [L, right of blood] (1902) **:** a rule that a child's citizenship is determined by its parents' citizenship
jus·sive \ˈjəs-iv\ *n* [L *jussus*, pp. of *jubēre* to order; akin to Gk *hysminē* battle] (1846) **:** a word, form, case, or mood expressing command — **jussive** *adj*
jus so·li \ˈyüs-ˈsō-ˌlē\ *n* [L, right of the soil] (1902) **:** a rule that the citizenship of a child is determined by the place of its birth
¹just \ˈjəst, ˈjüst\ *var of* JOUST
²just \ˈjəst\ *adj* [ME, fr. MF & L; MF *juste*, fr. L *justus*, fr. *jus* right, law; akin to Skt *yos* welfare] (14c) **1 a :** having a basis in or conforming to fact or reason **:** REASONABLE ⟨a ~ but not a generous decision⟩ **b** *archaic* **:** faithful to an original **c :** conforming to a standard of correctness **:** PROPER ⟨~ proportions⟩ **2 a** (1) **:** acting or being in conformity with what is morally upright or good **:** RIGHTEOUS ⟨a ~ war⟩ (2) **:** being what is merited **:** DESERVED ⟨a ~ punishment⟩ **b :** legally correct **:** LAWFUL ⟨~ title to an estate⟩ ***syn*** see FAIR, UPRIGHT — **just·ly** *adv* — **just·ness** \ˈjəs(t)-nəs\ *n*
³just \(ˌ)jəst, (ˌ)jist, (ˌ)jest\ *adv* (15c) **1 a :** EXACTLY, PRECISELY ⟨~ right⟩ **b :** very recently ⟨the bell ~ rang⟩ **2 a :** by a very small margin **:** BARELY ⟨~ too late⟩ **b :** IMMEDIATELY, DIRECTLY ⟨~ west of here⟩ **3 a :** ONLY, SIMPLY ⟨~ a note⟩ **b :** QUITE, VERY ⟨~ wonderful⟩ **4 :** PERHAPS, POSSIBLY ⟨it ~ might work⟩ — **just about :** ALMOST ⟨the work is *just about* done⟩ — **just the same :** though that is so **:** NEVERTHELESS
jus·tice \ˈjəs-təs\ *n* [ME, fr. OE & OF; OE *justice*, fr. OF *justice*, fr. L *justitia*, fr. *justus*] (12c) **1 a :** the maintenance or administration of what is just esp. by the impartial adjustment of conflicting claims or the assignment of merited rewards or punishments **b :** JUDGE **c :** the administration of law; *esp* **:** the establishment or determination of rights according to the rules of law or equity **2 a :** the quality of being just, impartial, or fair **b** (1) **:** the principle or ideal of just dealing or right action (2) **:** conformity to this principle or ideal **:** RIGHTEOUSNESS **c :** the quality of conforming to law **3 :** conformity to truth, fact, or reason **:** CORRECTNESS — **do justice 1 a :** to act justly **b :** to treat fairly or adequately **c :** to show due appreciation for **2 :** to acquit in a way worthy of one's powers
justice of the peace (15c) **:** a local magistrate empowered chiefly to administer summary justice in minor cases, to commit for trial, and to administer oaths and perform marriages
jus·ti·cia·ble \ˌjəs-ˈtish-(ē-)ə-bəl\ *adj* (15c) **1 :** liable to trial in a court of justice ⟨a ~ offense⟩ **2 :** capable of being decided by legal princi-

ples or by a court of justice — **jus·ti·cia·bil·i·ty** \jəs-‚tish-(ē-)ə-'bil-ət-ē\ n

jus·ti·ci·ar \jəs-'tish-ē-ər, -ē-‚är\ n [ME, fr. ML justitiarius, fr. L justitia] (1579) : the chief political and judicial officer of the Norman and later kings of England until the 13th century

jus·ti·fi·able \'jəs-tə-‚fī-ə-bəl\ adj (1523) : capable of being justified : EXCUSABLE ⟨~ family pride —Current Biog.⟩ — **jus·ti·fi·abil·i·ty** \‚jəs-tə-‚fī-ə-'bil-ət-ē\ n — **jus·ti·fi·ably** \'jəs-tə-fi-ə-blē\ adv

jus·ti·fi·ca·tion \‚jəs-tə-fə-'kā-shən\ n (14c) 1 : the act, process, or state of being justified by God 2 a : the act or an instance of justifying : VINDICATION b : something that justifies 3 : the process or result of justifying lines of text

jus·ti·fi·ca·tive \'jəs-tə-fə-‚kāt-iv\ adj (ca. 1611) : JUSTIFICATORY

jus·ti·fi·ca·to·ry \jəs-'tif-i-kə-‚tōr-ē, -‚tôr-; 'jəs-tə-fə-‚kāt-ə-rē\ adj (1579) : tending or serving to justify : VINDICATORY

jus·ti·fy \'jəs-tə-‚fī\ vb **-fied; -fy·ing** [ME justifien, fr. MF or LL; MF justifier, fr. LL justificare, fr. L justus] vt (14c) 1 a : to prove or show to be just, right, or reasonable b (1) : to show to have had a sufficient legal reason (2) : to qualify (oneself) as a surety by taking oath to the ownership of sufficient property 2 a archaic : to administer justice to b archaic : ABSOLVE c : to judge, regard, or treat as righteous and worthy of salvation 3 : to space (as lines of text) so that the lines come out even at the margin ~ vi 1 a : to show a sufficient lawful reason for an act done b : to qualify as bail or surety 2 : to justify lines of text **syn** see MAINTAIN — **jus·ti·fi·er** \-‚fī(-ə)r\ n

¹jut \'jət\ vb **jut·ted; jut·ting** [perh. short for ²jutty] vi (1565) : to extend out, up, or forward : PROJECT ⟨mountains jutting into the sky⟩ ⟨a jutting jaw⟩ ~ vt : to cause to project

²jut n (1786) : something that juts : PROJECTION

jute \'jüt\ n [Hindi & Bengali jūt] (1746) : the glossy fiber of either of two East Indian plants (Corchorus olitorius and C. capsularis) of the linden family used chiefly for sacking, burlap, and twine; also : a plant producing jute

Jute \'jüt\ n [ME, fr. ML Jutae Jutes, of Gmc origin; akin to OE Eotenas Jutes] (bef. 12c) : a member of a Germanic people invading England from the Continent and settling in Kent in the 5th century — **Jut·ish** \'jüt-ish\ adj

¹jut·ty \'jət-ē\ n, pl **jutties** [ME] (15c) 1 archaic : JETTY 2 : a projecting part of a building

²jutty vt **jut·tied; jut·ty·ing** obs (15c) : to project beyond

ju·ve·nes·cence \‚jü-və-'nes-ᵊn(t)s\ n (1800) : the state of being youthful or of growing young — **ju·ve·nes·cent** \-ᵊnt\ adj

¹ju·ve·nile \'jü-və-‚nīl, -vən-ᵊl\ adj [F or L; F juvénile, fr. L juvenilis, fr. juvenis young person — more at YOUNG] (1625) 1 a : physiologically immature or undeveloped : YOUNG b : derived from sources within the earth and coming to the surface for the first time — used esp. of water and gas 2 : of, relating to, characteristic of, or suitable for children or young people ⟨~ books⟩ 3 : reflecting psychological or intellectual immaturity : CHILDISH

²juvenile n (1733) 1 a : a young person : YOUTH b : a book for children or young people 2 : a young individual resembling an adult of its kind except in size and reproductive activity: as a : a fledged bird not yet in adult plumage b : a 2-year-old racehorse 3 : an actor or actress who plays youthful parts

juvenile court n (1899) : a court that has special jurisdiction over delinquent and dependent children usu. up to the age of 18

juvenile delinquency n (1816) 1 : conduct by a juvenile characterized by antisocial behavior that is beyond parental control and therefore subject to legal action 2 : a violation of the law committed by a juvenile and not punishable by death or life imprisonment — **juvenile delinquent** n

juvenile hormone n (1940) : an insect hormone that is secreted by the corpora allata, inhibits maturation to the imago, and plays a role in reproduction

juvenile officer n (1954) : a police officer charged with the detection, prosecution, and care of juvenile delinquents

ju·ve·nil·ia \‚jü-və-'nil-ē-ə\ n pl [L, neut. pl. of juvenilis] (1622) 1 : artistic or literary compositions produced in the artist's or author's youth 2 : artistic or literary compositions suited to or designed for the young

ju·ve·nil·i·ty \‚jü-və-'nil-ət-ē\ n, pl **-ties** (ca. 1623) 1 : the quality or state of being juvenile : YOUTHFULNESS 2 a : immaturity of thought or conduct b : an instance of being juvenile

juxta- \‚jək-stə\ comb form [L juxta near] : situated near ⟨juxtaglomerular cells⟩

jux·ta·pose \'jək-stə-‚pōz\ vt **-posed; -pos·ing** [prob. back-formation fr. juxtaposition] (1851) : to place side by side ⟨~ unexpected combinations of colors, shapes and ideas —J. F. T. Bugental⟩

jux·ta·posed adj (1855) : placed side by side : being in juxtaposition **syn** see ADJACENT

jux·ta·po·si·tion \‚jək-stə-pə-'zish-ən\ n [L juxta near + E position — more at JOUST] (1665) : the act or an instance of placing two or more things side by side; also : the state of being so placed — **jux·ta·po·si·tion·al** \-'zish-nəl, -ən-ᵊl\ adj

---

k \'kā\ n, pl **k's** or **ks** \'kāz\ often cap, often attrib 1 a : the 11th letter of the English alphabet b : a graphic representation of this letter c : a speech counterpart of orthographic k 2 a : graphic device for reproducing the letter k 3 : one designated k esp. as the 11th in order or class 4 : something shaped like the letter K 5 : a unit vector parallel to the z-axis 6 [kilo-] : THOUSAND ⟨a salary of $24K⟩ 7 [kilo-] : a unit of computer storage capacity equal to 1024 bytes ⟨a computer memory of 64K⟩

Kaa·ba \'käb-ə\ n [Ar ka'bah, lit., square building] (1734) : a small stone building in the court of the Great Mosque at Mecca that contains a sacred black stone and is the goal of Islamic pilgrimage and the point toward which Muslims turn in praying

kabala or **kabbala** or **kabbalah** var of CABALA

ka·bob \'kä-‚bäb, kə-'\ n [Per, Hindi, Ar & Turk; Per & Hindi kabāb, fr. Ar, fr. Turk kebap] (1673) : cubes of meat (as lamb or beef) marinated and cooked with vegetables (as onions, tomatoes, and green peppers) usu. on a skewer

Ka·bu·ki \kə-'bü-kē, 'käb-ü-(‚)kē\ n [Jp, lit., art of singing and dancing] (1899) : traditional Japanese popular drama with singing and dancing performed in a highly stylized manner

Ka·byle \kə-'bī(ə)l\ n [Ar qabā'il, pl. of qabīlah tribe] (1738) 1 : a Berber of the mountainous coastal area east of Algiers 2 : the Berber language of the Kabyles

ka·chi·na \kə-'chē-nə\ n [Hopi quacina supernatural] (1888) 1 : one of the deified ancestral spirits believed among the Hopi and other Pueblo Indians to visit the pueblos at intervals 2 : one of the elaborately masked kachina impersonators that dance at agricultural ceremonies 3 : a doll representing a kachina

kad·dish \'käd-ish\ n, often cap [Aram qaddīsh holy] (1613) : a Jewish prayer recited in the daily ritual of the synagogue and by mourners at public services after the death of a close relative

kaf·fee·klatsch \'kȯ-fē-‚klach, 'käf-ē-; -‚kläch, -‚klach\ n, often cap [G, fr. kaffee coffee + klatsch gossip] (1888) : an informal social gathering for coffee and conversation

Kaf·fir or **Kaf·ir** \'kaf-ər\ n [Ar kāfir infidel] (1552) 1 archaic : a member of a group of southern African Bantu-speaking peoples 2 often not cap, chiefly SoAfr : an African Negro — usu. used disparagingly

kaf·ir \'kaf-ər\ n (ca. 1785) : a grain sorghum with stout short-jointed somewhat juicy stalks and erect heads

Kafir \'kaf-ər\ n [Ar kāfir] (1759) : a member of a people of the Hindu Kush in northeastern Afghanistan

Kaf·iri \'kaf-ə-rē\ n (1901) : the Dard language of the Kafir people

kaftan var of CAFTAN

ka·hu·na \kə-'hü-nə\ n [Hawaiian] (1886) : a Hawaiian witch doctor

kail·yard school \'kā(ə)l-‚yärd-\ n, often cap K [Sc kailyard (kitchen garden), fr. kail, kale kale + E yard] (1895) : a group of writers whose work is characterized by sentimental description of Scottish life and considerable use of Scots dialect

kai·nite \'kī-‚nīt, 'kā-\ also **kai·nit** \kī-'nēt\ n [G kainit, fr. Gk kainos new — more at RECENT] (1868) : a natural salt KMg(SO₄)Cl·3H₂O consisting of a hydrous sulfate and chloride of magnesium and potassium that is used as a fertilizer and as a source of potassium and magnesium compounds

kai·ser \'kī-zər\ n [ME, fr. ON keisari (akin to OHG keisur emperor), fr. L Caesar, cognomen of the Emperor Augustus] (13c) : the ruler of Germany from 1871 to 1918 — **kai·ser·dom** \-zərd-əm\ n — **kai·ser·ism** \-zə-‚riz-əm\ n

kai·se·rin \'kī-zə-rən\ n [G, fem. of kaiser] (1888) : the wife of a kaiser

ka·ka \'käk-ə\ n [Maori] (1774) : an olive brown New Zealand parrot (Nestor meridionalis) with gray and red markings

ka·ka·po \‚käk-ə-'pō\ n, pl **-pos** [Maori] (1843) : a chiefly nocturnal burrowing New Zealand parrot (Strigops habroptilus) with green and brown barred plumage

ka·ke·mo·no \‚käk-i-'mō-(‚)nō\ n, pl **-nos** [Jp] (1890) : a vertical Japanese ornamental pictorial or calligraphic scroll

kala–azar \‚käl-ə-ə-'zär, ‚kal-; ‚kal-\ n [Hindi kālā-āzar black disease, fr. Hindi kālā black (fr. Skt kāla) + Per āzār disease] (1882) : a severe infectious disease chiefly of Asia marked by fever, progressive anemia, leukopenia, and enlargement of the spleen and liver and caused by a flagellate (Leishmania donovani) transmitted by the bite of sand flies

ka·lan·choe \‚kal-ən-'kō-ē, ‚kal-ə-‚lan-kə-(‚)wē, 'kal-ən-‚chō\ n [NL] (ca. 1900) : any of a genus (Kalanchoe) of chiefly African and Australian tropical herbs or shrubs of the orpine family often cultivated as ornamentals — compare BRYOPHYLLUM

kale \'kā(ə)l\ n [Sc, fr. ME (northern) cal, fr. OE cāl — more at COLE] (14c) 1 a : COLE b : a hardy cabbage (Brassica oleracea acephala) with curled often finely incised leaves that do not form a dense head 2 slang : MONEY

ka·lei·do·scope \kə-'līd-ə-‚skōp\ n [Gk kalos beautiful + eidos form + E -scope — more at CALLIGRAPHY, IDYLL] (1817) 1 : an instrument containing loose bits of colored glass between two flat plates and two plane mirrors so placed that changes of position of the bits of glass are reflected in an endless variety of patterns 2 : something resembling a kaleidoscope: as a : a variegated changing pattern or scene ⟨the lake a ~ of changing colors —Robert Gibbings⟩ b : a succession of changing phases or actions ⟨a . . . ~ of shifting values, information, fashions

—Frank McLaughlin⟩ — **ka·lei·do·scop·ic** \-ˌlīd-ə-ˈskäp-ik\ *adj* — **ka·lei·do·scop·i·cal·ly** \-i-k(ə)lē\ *adv*

kalends *var of* CALENDS

ka·lim·ba \kə-ˈlim-bə\ *n* [of Bantu origin; akin to Bemba *akalimba* zanza, Kimbundu *marimba* xylophone] (1952) : an African musical instrument derived from the zanza

kal·li·din \ˈkal-əd-ən\ *n* [G, fr. *kalli*krein + *-d-* (prob. fr. *deka-*) + *-in*] (1950) : either of two vasodilator kinins formed from blood plasma globulin by the action of kallikrein: **a** : BRADYKININ **b** : one with a terminal lysine amino-acid residue added to bradykinin

kal·li·kre·in \ˌkal-ə-ˈkrē-ən, kə-ˈlik-rē-ən\ *n* [G, fr. *kalli-* beautiful (fr. Gk) + pan*kreas* pancreas + *-in*; prob. fr. its therapeutic use in pancreatic disorders — more at CALLIGRAPHY] (1930) : a hypotensive proteinase that liberates kinins from blood plasma proteins and is used therapeutically for vasodilation

Kal·muck *or* **Kal·muk** \ˈkal-ˌmək, kal-ˈ\ *or* **Kal·myk** \kal-ˈmik\ *n* [Russ *Kalmyk*, fr. Kazan Tatar] (1613) **1** : a member of a Buddhist Mongol people orig. of Dzungaria **2** : the Mongolian language of the Kalmucks

kalsomine *var of* CALCIMINE

Ka·ma \ˈkäm-ə\ *n* [Skt *Kāma*, fr. *kāma* love] : the Hindu god of love

ka·ma·ai·na \ˌkäm-ə-ˈī-nə\ *n* [Hawaiian *kamaʻāina*, fr. *kama* child + *ʻāina* land] (1903) : one who has lived in Hawaii for a long time

ka·ma·la \ˈkäm-ə-lə\ *n* [Skt] (1820) **1** : an East Indian tree (*Mallotus philippinensis*) of the spurge family **2** : an orange red powder from kamala capsules used for dyeing silk and wool or as a vermifuge

kame \ˈkām\ *n* [Sc, kame, comb, fr. ME (northern) *camb* comb, fr. OE] (1795) : a short ridge, hill, or mound of stratified drift deposited by glacial meltwater

Ka·me·ha·me·ha Day \kə-ˌmā-ə-ˈmā-(ˌ)hä-\ *n* (1925) : June 11 observed as a holiday in Hawaii in commemoration of the birthday of Kamehameha I

[1]**ka·mi·ka·ze** \ˌkäm-i-ˈkäz-ē\ *n* [Jp, lit., divine wind] (1945) **1** : a member of a Japanese air attack corps in World War II assigned to make a suicidal crash on a target (as a ship) **2** : an airplane containing explosives to be flown in a suicide crash on a target

[2]**kamikaze** *adj* (1945) : of, relating to, being, or resembling a kamikaze

kam·pong \ˈkäm-ˌpȯŋ, ˈkam-\ *n* [Malay] (1844) : a native hamlet or village in a Malay-speaking country

kana·my·cin \ˌkan-ə-ˈmīs-ᵊn\ *n* [NL *kanamyceticus*, specific epithet of *Streptomyces kanamyceticus*] (1957) : a broad-spectrum antibiotic from a Japanese soil streptomyces (*Streptomyces kanamyceticus*)

Kan·a·rese \ˌkan-ə-ˈrēz, -ˈrēs\ *n, pl* **Kanarese** [*Kanara*, India] (1552) **1** : a member of a Kannada-speaking people of Mysore, southern India **2** : KANNADA

kan·ga·roo \ˌkaŋ-gə-ˈrü\ *n, pl* **-roos** [prob. native name in Australia] (1773) : any of various herbivorous leaping marsupial mammals (family Macropodidae) of Australia, New Guinea, and adjacent islands with a small head, large ears, long powerful hind legs, a long thick tail used as a support and in balancing, and rather small forelegs not used in progression

kangaroo court *n* (1853) **1** : a mock court in which the principles of law and justice are disregarded or perverted **2** : a court characterized by irresponsible, unauthorized, or irregular status or procedures **3** : judgment or punishment given outside of legal procedure

kangaroo rat *n* (1867) : any of numerous pouched nocturnal burrowing rodents (genus *Dipodomys*) of arid parts of the western U.S.

Kan·na·da \ˈkän-əd-ə\ *n* [Kannada *kannaḍa*] (1856) : the major Dravidian language of Mysore, southern India

kan·te·le \ˈkän-tə-lə\ *n* [Finn] (1921) : a traditional Finnish zither orig. having five strings but now having as many as thirty

ka·olin \ˈkā-ə-lən\ *n* [F *kaolin*, fr. *Kao-ling*, hill in China] (1727) : a fine usu. white clay that is used in ceramics and refractories, as a filler or extender, and in medicine esp. as an adsorbent in the treatment of diarrhea

ka·olin·ite \-lə-ˌnīt\ *n* (1867) : a mineral $Al_2Si_2O_5(OH)_4$ consisting of a hydrous silicate of aluminum that constitutes the principal mineral in kaolin — **ka·olin·it·ic** \ˌkā-ə-lə-ˈnit-ik\ *adj*

ka·on \ˈkā-ˌän\ *n* [ISV *ka* kay (fr. *K-meson*, its earlier name) + [2]*-on*] (1958) : an unstable meson produced in high-energy particle collisions with its electrically charged forms and its neutral form being respectively 966.3 and 974.6 times more massive than the electron

ka·pell·mei·ster \kä-ˈpel-ˌmī-stər, kä-\ *n, often cap* [G, fr. *kapelle* choir (fr. ML *cappella* chapel) + *meister* master — more at CHAPEL] (1838) : the director of a choir or orchestra

kaph \ˈkäf, ˈkȯf\ *n* [Heb, lit., palm of the hand] (ca. 1880) : the 11th letter of the Hebrew alphabet — see ALPHABET table

ka·pok \ˈkā-ˌpäk\ *n* [Malay] (1750) : a mass of silky fibers that clothe the seeds of the ceiba tree and are used esp. as a filling for mattresses, life preservers, and sleeping bags and as insulation

Ka·po·si's sarcoma \ˈkap-ə-sēz- *also* -shēz-, kə-ˈpō-sēz-\ *n* [Moritz *Kaposi* †1902 Hung. dermatologist] (ca. 1929) : a disease associated esp. with AIDS, affecting esp. the skin and mucous membranes, and characterized usu. by the formation of pink to reddish-brown or bluish plaques, macules, papules, or nodules

kap·pa \ˈkap-ə\ *n* [Gk, of Sem origin; akin to Heb *kaph*] (15c) : the 10th letter of the Greek alphabet — see ALPHABET table

ka·put *also* **ka·putt** \kə-ˈpu̇t, kä-, -ˈpüt\ *adj* [G *kaputt*, fr. F *capot* not having made a trick at piquet] (1895) **1** : utterly finished, defeated, or destroyed **2** : unable to function : USELESS ⟨my battery went ~ —Henry James Jr.⟩ **3** : hopelessly outmoded

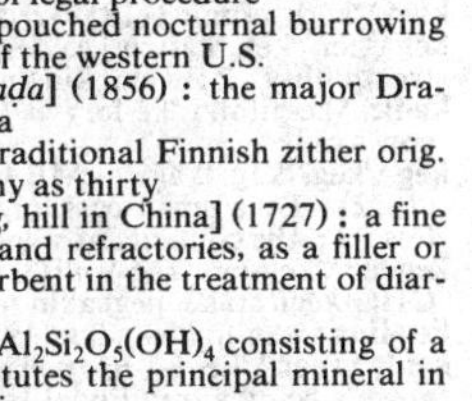

karakul 1

karabiner *var of* CARABINER

Kara·ism \ˈkar-ə-ˌiz-əm\ *n* [LHeb *qĕrāīm* Karaites, fr. Heb *qārā* to read] (1882) : a Jewish doctrine originating in Baghdad in the 8th century that rejects rabbinism and talmudism and bases its tenets on Scripture alone — **Kara·ite** \-ˌīt\ *n*

kar·a·kul \ˈkar-ə-kəl\ *n* [*Karakul*, village in Bukhara] (1853) **1** *often cap* : any of a breed of hardy fat-tailed sheep from Bukhara with a narrow body and coarse wiry fur **2** : the tightly curled glossy coat of the newborn lamb of a karakul valued as fur

kar·at \ˈkar-ət\ *n* [prob. fr. MF *carat*, fr. ML *carratus* unit of weight for precious stones — more at CARAT] (1555) : a unit of fineness for gold equal to $^1/_{24}$ part of pure gold in an alloy

ka·ra·te \kə-ˈrät-ē\ *n* [Jp, lit., empty hand, fr. *kara* emptiness + *te* hand] (1955) : an Oriental art of self-defense in which an attacker is disabled by crippling kicks and punches — **ka·ra·te·ist** \-ē-əst\ *n*

ka·ra·ya gum \kə-ˌrī-ə-\ *n* [Hindi *karāyal* resin] (1893) : any of several vegetable gums similar to tragacanth and often used as substitutes for it that are obtained from tropical Asian trees (genera *Sterculia* of the family Sterculiaceae and *Cochlospermum* of the family Bixaceae); *esp* : one derived from an Indian tree (*S. urens*)

Ka·re·lian \kə-ˈrē-lē-ən, -ˈrēl-yən\ *n* (1855) **1** : a native or inhabitant of Karelia **2** : the Finno-Ugric language of the Karelians — **Karelian** *adj*

Ka·ren \kə-ˈren\ *n, pl* **Karen** *or* **Karens** (1759) **1 a** : a group of peoples of eastern and southern Burma **b** : a member of any of these peoples **2 a** : a group of languages spoken by the Karen peoples **b** : a language of this group

kar·ma \ˈkär-mə, ˈkər-\ *n, often cap* [Skt *karma* fate, work] (1827) **1** : the force generated by a person's actions held in Hinduism and Buddhism to perpetuate transmigration and in its ethical consequences to determine his destiny in his next existence **2** : VIBRATION 4 — **kar·mic** \-mik\ *adj, often cap*

ka·roo *or* **kar·roo** \kə-ˈrü\ *n, pl* **karoos** *or* **karroos** [Afrik *karo*] (1789) : a dry tableland of southern Africa

ka·ross \kə-ˈräs\ *n* [Afrik *karos*] (1731) : a simple garment or rug of skins used esp. by native tribesmen of southern Africa

karst \ˈkärst\ *n* [G] (1902) : an irregular limestone region with sinks, underground streams, and caverns — **karst·ic** \ˈkär-stik\ *adj*

kart \ˈkärt\ *n* [prob. fr. *GoKart*, a trademark] (1959) : a miniature motorcar used esp. in racing — **kart·ing** *n*

kary- *or* **karyo-** *also* **cary-** *or* **caryo-** *comb form* [NL, fr. Gk *karyon* nut — more at CAREEN] **1** : nucleus of a cell ⟨*karyo*kinesis⟩ **2** : nut : kernel ⟨*caryo*psis⟩

kary·og·a·my \ˌkar-ē-ˈäg-ə-mē\ *n, pl* **-mies** (1891) : the fusion of cell nuclei (as in fertilization)

karyo·ki·ne·sis \ˌkar-ē-ō-kə-ˈnē-səs, -kī-\ *n* [NL, fr. *kary-* + Gk *kinēsis* motion — more at KINESIOLOGY] (1882) **1** : the nuclear phenomena characteristic of mitosis **2** : the whole process of mitosis — **karyo·ki·net·ic** \-ˈnet-ik\ *adj*

kary·ol·o·gy \ˌkar-ē-ˈäl-ə-jē\ *n* [ISV] (1895) **1** : the minute cytological characteristics of the cell nucleus esp. with regard to the chromosomes of a single cell or of the cells of an organism or group of organisms **2** : a branch of cytology concerned with the karyology of cell nuclei — **kary·o·log·i·cal** \-ē-ə-ˈläj-i-kəl\ *also* **kary·o·log·ic** \-ik\ *adj*

karyo·lymph \ˈkar-ē-ō-ˌlim(p)f\ *n* [ISV] (1899) : NUCLEAR SAP

karyo·some \ˈkar-ē-ə-ˌsōm\ *n* [ISV] (1889) : a mass of chromatin in a cell nucleus that resembles a nucleolus

karyo·type \ˈkar-ē-ə-ˌtīp\ *n* [ISV] (1929) : the chromosomal characteristics of a cell; *also* : the chromosomes themselves or a representation of them — **karyo·typ·ic** \ˌkar-ē-ə-ˈtip-ik\ *adj* — **karyo·typ·i·cal·ly** \-i-k(ə-)lē\ *adv* — **karyo·typ·ing** \ˈkar-ē-ə-ˌtī-piŋ\ *n*

Kasbah *var of* CASBAH

ka·sha \ˈkäsh-ə, ˈkash-ə\ *n* [Russ; akin to Pol *kasza* kasha] (1808) : a mush made usu. from buckwheat groats

Kash·mir *var of* CASHMERE

Kash·miri \kash-ˈmi(ə)r-ē, kazh-\ *n, pl* **Kashmiris** *or* **Kashmiri** (1885) **1** : a native or inhabitant of Kashmir **2** : the Indic language of Kashmir

kash·ruth *or* **kash·rut** \kä-ˈshrüt(h)\ *n* [Heb *kashrūth*, lit., fitness] (1907) **1** : the state of being kosher **2** : the Jewish dietary laws

Ka·shu·bi·an \kə-ˈshü-bē-ən\ *n* [*Kashube* (a member of a Slavic people)] (1919) : a West Slavic language spoken in the vicinity of Gdansk

kat *var of* KHAT

ka·tchi·na *or* **ka·tci·na** *var of* KACHINA

Ka·tha·re·vu·sa \ˌkäth-ə-ˈrev-ə-ˌsä\ *n* [NGk *kathareuousa*, fr. Gk, fem. of *kathareuōn*, prp. of *kathareuein* to be pure, fr. *katharos* pure] (1936) : modern Greek conforming to classic Greek usage

katharsis *var of* CATHARSIS

ka·ty·did \ˈkāt-ē-ˌdid\ *n* [imit.] (1751) : any of several large green American long-horned grasshoppers usu. having stridulating organs on the forewings of the males that produce a loud shrill sound

kat·zen·jam·mer \ˈkat-sən-ˌjam-ər\ *n* [G, fr. *katzen* cats + *jammer* distress] (1849) **1** : HANGOVER **2** : DISTRESS 2 **3** : a discordant clamor

kau·ri \ˈkau̇(ə)r-ē\ *n* [Maori *kawri*] (1823) **1** : any of various trees (genus *Agathis*) of the pine family; *esp* : a tall timber tree (*A. australis*) of New Zealand having fine white straight-grained wood **2** : a light-colored to brown resin from the kauri tree found as a fossil in the ground or collected from living trees and used esp. in varnishes and linoleum — called also *kauri gum, kauri resin*

ka·va \ˈkäv-ə\ *n* [Tongan & Marquesan, lit., bitter] (1797) **1** : an Australasian shrubby pepper (*Piper methysticum*) from whose crushed root an intoxicating beverage is made **2** : the beverage made from kava

kay \ˈkā\ *n* (14c) : the letter *k*

Kay \ˈkā\ *n* : a boastful overbearing knight of the Round Table who is foster brother and seneschal of King Arthur

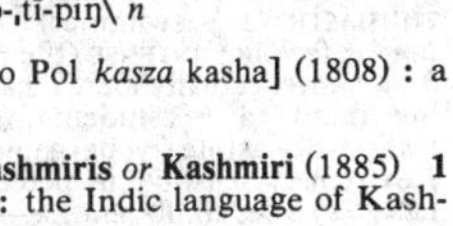

kayak 1

kay·ak \ˈkī-ˌak\ *n* [Esk *qajaq*] (1662) **1** : an Eskimo canoe made of a frame covered with skins except for a small opening in the center and propelled by a double-bladed paddle **2** : a portable boat styled like an Eskimo kayak — **kay·ak·er** \-ˌak-ər\ *n* — **kay·ak·ing** \-iŋ\ *n*

\ə\ abut \ᵊ\ kitten, F table \ər\ further \a\ ash \ā\ ace \ä\ cot, cart \au̇\ out \ch\ chin \e\ bet \ē\ easy \g\ go \i\ hit \ī\ ice \j\ job \ŋ\ sing \ō\ go \ȯ\ law \ȯi\ boy \th\ thin \t͟h\ the \ü\ loot \u̇\ foot \y\ yet \zh\ vision \å, ḵ, ⁿ, œ, œ̄, ue, ue̅, ʸ\ *see* Guide to Pronunciation

[1]kayo \(ˈ)kā-ˈō, ˈkā-(ˌ)ō\ *n* [pronunciation of *KO*, abbr.] (1920) : KNOCKOUT

[2]kayo *vt* **kay·oed; kayo·ing** (1923) : KNOCK OUT

ka·zoo \kə-ˈzü\ *n, pl* **kazoos** [imit.] (1884) : an instrument that imparts a buzzing quality to the human voice and that usu. consists of a small metal or plastic tube with a side hole covered by a thin membrane

kea \ˈkē-ə\ *n* [Maori] (1862) : a large predominantly green New Zealand parrot (*Nestor notabilis*) that is normally insectivorous but sometimes destroys sheep by slashing the back to feed on the kidney fat

ke·bab *or* **ke·bob** \ˈkā-ˌbäb, kə-ˈ\ *var of* KABOB

keb·buck *or* **keb·bock** \ˈkeb-ək\ *n* [ME (Sc dial.) *cabok*, fr. ScGael *ceapag*] *dial Brit* (15c) : a whole cheese

Ke·chu·ma·ran \ˌkech-ə-mə-ˈrän, kə-ˌchü-\ *n* [*Kechua* (Quechua) + *Aymara* + *-an*] (1956) : a language stock comprising Aymara and Quechua

[1]kedge \ˈkej\ *vt* **kedged; kedg·ing** [ME *caggen*] (1627) : to move (a ship) by means of a line attached to a kedge dropped at the distance and in the direction desired

[2]kedge *n* (ca. 1769) : a small anchor used esp. in kedging

ked·ge·ree \ˈkej-ə-rē\ *n* [Hindi *khicaṛī*, fr. Skt *khiccā*] (1662) **1** : an Indian dish of seasoned rice, beans, lentils, and sometimes smoked fish **2** : cooked or smoked fish, rice, hard-boiled eggs, and seasoning heated in cream

[1]keek \ˈkēk\ *vi* [ME *kiken*] *chiefly Scot* (14c) : PEEP, LOOK

[2]keek *n, chiefly Scot* (1721) : PEEP, LOOK

[1]keel \ˈkē(ə)l\ *vb* [ME *kelen*, fr. OE *cēlan*, fr. *cōl* cool] *chiefly dial* (bef. 12c) : COOL

[2]keel *n* [ME *kele*, fr. MD *kiel*; akin to OE *cēol* ship] (14c) **1 a** : a flat-bottomed ship; *esp* : a barge used on the Tyne to carry coal **b** : a barge-load of coal **2** : a British unit of weight for coal equal to 21.2 long tons

[3]keel *n* [ME *kele*, fr. ON *kjǫlr*; akin to OE *ceole* throat, beak of a ship — more at GLUTTON] (14c) **1 a** : a longitudinal timber or plate extending along the center of the bottom of a ship and often projecting from the bottom **b** : SHIP **c** : the assembly of members at the bottom of the hull of a semirigid or rigid airship **2** : a projection suggesting a keel; *esp* : CARINA — **keeled** \ˈkē(ə)ld\ *adj* — **keel·less** \ˈkē(ə)l-ləs\ *adj*

[4]keel *vt* (ca. 1808) : to cause to turn over ~ *vi* **1** : to turn over **2** : to fall in or as if in a faint — usu. used with *over*

[5]keel *n* [ME (Sc dial.) *keyle*] (15c) **1** *chiefly dial* : RED OCHER **2** : a colored crayon used esp. for chalking lines or marking lumber

keel·boat \ˈkē(ə)l-ˌbōt\ *n* (1695) : a shallow covered keeled riverboat that is usu. rowed, poled, or towed and that is used for freight

keel·haul \-ˌhȯl\ *vt* [D *kielhalen*, fr. *kiel* keel + *halen* to haul] (1666) **1** : to haul under the keel of a ship as punishment or torture **2** : to rebuke severely

keel·son \ˈkel-sən, ˈkē(ə)l-\ *n* [prob. of Scand origin; akin to Sw *kölsvin* keelson] (1598) : a longitudinal structure running above and fastened to the keel of a ship in order to stiffen and strengthen its framework

[1]keen \ˈkēn\ *adj* [ME *kene* brave, sharp, fr. OE *cēne* brave; akin to OHG *kuoni* brave, and perh. to OE *cnāwan* to know — more at KNOW] (13c) **1 a** : having a fine edge or point : SHARP ⟨a ~ sword⟩ **b** : affecting one as if by cutting ⟨~ sarcasm⟩ **c** : pungent to the sense ⟨a ~ scent⟩ **2 a** (1) : showing a quick and ardent responsiveness : ENTHUSIASTIC ⟨a ~ swimmer⟩ (2) : EAGER ⟨was ~ to begin⟩ **b** *of emotion or feeling* : INTENSE ⟨the ~ delight in the chase —F. W. Maitland⟩ **3 a** : intellectually alert : having or characteristic of a quick penetrating mind ⟨a ~ student⟩ ⟨a ~ awareness of the problem⟩; *also* : shrewdly astute ⟨~ bargainers⟩ **b** : sharply contested ⟨~ debate⟩ **c** : extremely sensitive in perception ⟨~ eyes⟩ **4** : WONDERFUL, EXCELLENT *syn* see SHARP, EAGER — **keen·ly** *adv* — **keen·ness** \ˈkēn-nəs\ *n*

[2]keen *vb* [IrGael *caoinim* I lament] *vi* (1811) **1 a** : to lament with a keen **b** : to make a sound suggestive of a keen **2** : to lament, mourn, or complain loudly ~ *vt* : to utter by keening — **keen·er** *n*

[3]keen *n* (1830) : a lamentation for the dead uttered in a loud wailing voice or sometimes in a wordless cry

[1]keep \ˈkēp\ *vb* **kept** \ˈkept\; **keep·ing** [ME *kepen*, fr. OE *cēpan*; akin to OHG *chapfēn* to look] *vt* (bef. 12c) **1** : to take notice of by appropriate conduct : FULFILL: as **a** : to be faithful to ⟨~ a promise⟩ **b** : to act fittingly in relation to ⟨~ the Sabbath⟩ **c** : to conform to in habits or conduct ⟨~ late hours⟩ **d** : to stay in accord with (a beat) ⟨~ time⟩ **2** : PRESERVE, MAINTAIN: as **a** : to watch over and defend ⟨~ us from harm⟩ **b** (1) : to take care of : TEND ⟨~ a garden⟩ (2) : SUPPORT ⟨~ a wife⟩ (3) : to maintain in a good, fitting, or orderly condition — usu. used with *up* **c** : to continue to maintain ⟨~ silence⟩ **d** (1) : to cause to remain in a given place, situation, or condition ⟨~ him waiting⟩ (2) : to preserve (food) in an unspoiled condition **e** : to have or maintain in one's service or at one's disposal ⟨~ a mistress⟩ — often used with *on* ⟨*kept* the cook on until he found another job⟩; *also* : to lodge or feed for pay ⟨~ boarders⟩ **f** (1) : to maintain a record in ⟨~ a diary⟩ (2) : to enter in a book ⟨~ records⟩ **g** : to have customarily in stock for sale **3 a** : to restrain from departure or removal : DETAIN ⟨~ children in after school⟩ **b** : HOLD BACK, RESTRAIN ⟨~ him from going⟩ ⟨*kept* him back with difficulty⟩ **c** : SAVE, RESERVE ⟨~ some for later⟩ ⟨*kept* some out for a friend⟩ **d** : to refrain from revealing ⟨~ a secret⟩ **4 a** : to retain in one's possession or power ⟨*kept* the money he found⟩ **b** : to refrain from granting, giving, or allowing ⟨*kept* the news back⟩ **c** : to have in control ⟨~ your temper⟩ **5** : to confine oneself to ⟨~*s* her room⟩ **6 a** : to stay or continue in ⟨~ the path⟩ ⟨~ your seat⟩ **b** : to stay or remain on or in usu. against opposition : HOLD ⟨*kept* his ground⟩ **7** : CONDUCT, MANAGE ⟨~ a tearoom⟩ ~ *vi* **1** *chiefly Brit* : LIVE, LODGE **2 a** : to maintain a course, direction, or progress ⟨~ to the right⟩ **b** : to continue usu. without interruption ⟨~ talking⟩ ⟨~ on smiling⟩ **c** : to persist in a practice ⟨*kept* bothering them⟩ ⟨*kept* on smoking in spite of warnings⟩ **3** : STAY, REMAIN ⟨~ out of the way⟩ ⟨~ off the grass⟩: as **a** : to stay even — usu. used with *up* ⟨~ up with the Joneses⟩ **b** : to remain in good condition ⟨meat will ~ in the freezer⟩ **c** : to remain secret ⟨the secret would ~⟩ **d** : to call for no immediate action ⟨the matter will ~ until morning⟩ **4** : ABSTAIN, REFRAIN ⟨can't ~ from talking⟩ **5** : to be in session ⟨school will ~ through the winter —W. M. Thayer⟩ **6** *of a quarterback* : to retain possession of a football esp. after faking a handoff

syn KEEP, OBSERVE, CELEBRATE, COMMEMORATE mean to notice or honor a day, occasion, or deed. KEEP stresses the idea of not neglecting or violating; OBSERVE suggests marking the occasion by ceremonious performance; CELEBRATE suggests acknowledging an occasion by festivity; COMMEMORATE suggests that an occasion is marked by observances that remind one of the origin and significance of the day.

syn KEEP, RETAIN, DETAIN, WITHHOLD, RESERVE mean to hold in one's possession or under one's control. KEEP may suggest a holding securely in one's possession, custody, or control; RETAIN implies continued keeping, esp. against threatened seizure or forced loss; DETAIN suggests a delay in letting go; WITHHOLD implies restraint in letting go or a refusal to let go; RESERVE suggests a keeping in store for future use.

— **keep at** : to persist in doing or concerning oneself with — **keep company** : to go together as frequent companions or in courtship — **keep house** : to manage a household — **keep one's distance** *or* **keep at a distance** : to stay aloof : maintain a reserved attitude — **keep one's eyes open** *or* **keep one's eyes peeled** : to be on the alert : be watchful — **keep one's hand in** : to keep in practice — **keep pace** : to stay even; *also* : KEEP UP — **keep step** : to keep in step — **keep to 1 a** : to stay in **b** : to limit oneself to **2** : to abide by — **keep to oneself 1** : to keep secret ⟨*kept* the facts *to himself*⟩ **2** : to remain solitary or apart from other people

[2]keep *n* (1579) **1 a** *archaic* : CUSTODY, CHARGE **b** : MAINTENANCE **2** : one that keeps or protects: as **a** : FORTRESS, CASTLE; *specif* : the strongest and securest part of a medieval castle **b** : one whose job is to keep or tend **c** : PRISON, JAIL **3** : the means or provisions by which one is kept ⟨earned his ~⟩ **4** : KEEPER 4 — **for keeps 1 a** : with the provision that one keep what he has won ⟨played marbles *for keeps*⟩ **b** : with deadly seriousness **2** : for an indefinitely long time : PERMANENTLY **3** : with the result of ending the matter

keep back *vi* (1837) : to refrain from approaching or advancing near something ⟨policemen asked the spectators to *keep back*⟩

keep down *vt* (1581) **1** : to keep in control ⟨*keep* expenses *down*⟩ **2** : to prevent from growing, advancing, or succeeding

keep·er \ˈkē-pər\ *n* (14c) **1** : one that keeps: as **a** : PROTECTOR **b** : GAMEKEEPER **c** : WARDEN **d** : CUSTODIAN **e** *chiefly Brit* : CURATOR **2** : any of various devices for keeping something in position **3** : one fit or suitable for keeping; *esp* : a fish large enough to be legally caught **4** : an offensive football play in which the quarterback runs with the ball

keep·ing \ˈkē-piŋ\ *n* (14c) **1** : the act of one that keeps: as **a** : CUSTODY, MAINTENANCE **b** : OBSERVANCE **c** : a reserving or preserving for future use **2 a** : the means by which something is kept : SUPPORT, PROVISION **b** : the state of being kept or the condition in which something is kept ⟨the house is in good ~⟩ **3** : CONFORMITY ⟨in ~ with good taste⟩ ⟨out of ~ with the decor⟩

keep·sake \ˈkēp-ˌsāk\ *n* [[1]*keep* + *-sake* (as in *namesake*)] (1790) : something kept or given to be kept as a memento

keep up *vt* (1513) : to persist or persevere in ⟨*kept up* the good work⟩; *also* : MAINTAIN, SUSTAIN ⟨*keep* standards *up*⟩ ~ *vi* **1** : to keep adequately informed or up-to-date ⟨*keep up* on international affairs⟩ **2** : to continue without interruption ⟨rain *kept up* all night⟩ **3** : to maintain contact or relations with ⟨*keep up* with old friends⟩

kees·hond \ˈkās-ˌhȯnt\ *n, pl* **kees·hon·den** \-ˌhȯn-dən\ [D, prob. fr. *Kees* (nickname for *Cornelis* Cornelius) + *hond* dog, fr. MD; akin to OE *hund* hound] (1926) : any of a Dutch breed of compact medium-sized gray dogs that have a dense heavy coat and a foxy head

keet \ˈkēt\ *n* [imit.] (1859) : GUINEA FOWL; *esp* : a young guinea fowl

kef \ˈkēf, ˈkef, ˈkāf\ *n* [Ar *kayf* pleasure] (1808) **1** : a state of dreamy tranquillity **2** : a smoking material (as marijuana) that produces kef

ke·fir \ke-ˈfi(ə)r, ˈkē-fər\ *n* [Russ] (1884) : a beverage of fermented cow's milk

keg \ˈkeg, ˈkag, ˈkāg\ *n* [ME *kag*, of Scand origin; akin to ON *kaggi* keg] (1632) **1** : a small cask or barrel having a capacity of 30 gallons or less **2** : the contents of a keg

keg·ler \ˈkeg-lər, ˈkāg-\ *n* [G, fr. *kegeln* to bowl, fr. *kegel* bowling pin, fr. OHG *kegil* stake, peg; akin to ON *kaggi*] (1932) : [1]BOWLER

keg·ling \ˈkeg-liŋ, ˈkāg-\ *n* (1938) : BOWLING

kel·ly green \ˈkel-ē-\ *n, often cap K* [fr. the common Irish name *Kelly*; fr. green's being a traditional Irish color] (1935) : a variable color averaging a strong yellowish green

ke·loid \ˈkē-ˌlȯid\ *n* [F *kiloïde*, fr. Gk *chēlē* claw] (1854) : a thick scar resulting from excessive growth of fibrous tissue — **keloid** *adj* — **ke·loi·dal** \kē-ˈlȯid-ᵊl\ *adj*

kelp \ˈkelp\ *n* [ME *culp*] (14c) **1 a** : any of various large brown seaweeds (orders Laminariales and Fucales) **b** : a mass of large seaweeds **2** : the ashes of seaweed used esp. as a source of iodine

kelp bass *n* (1936) : a mottled California sea bass (*Paralabrax clathratus*) that is an important sport fish

[1]kel·pie \ˈkel-pē\ *n* [perh. fr. ScGael *cailpeach, colpach* heifer, colt] (1747) : a water sprite of Scottish folklore that delights in or brings about the drowning of wayfarers

[2]kelpie *n* [*Kelpie*, name of a dog of this breed] (1903) : an Australian sheep dog of a breed developed by crossing the dingo with various British sheepdogs

Kelt \ˈkelt\, **Kelt·ic** \ˈkel-tik\ *var of* CELT, CELTIC

kel·vin \ˈkel-vən\ *n* (1968) : a unit of temperature equal to 1/273.16 of the Kelvin scale temperature of the triple point of water

Kelvin *adj* [William Thomson, Lord *Kelvin*] (1908) : relating to, conforming to, or having a thermometric scale on which the unit of measurement equals the Celsius degree and according to which absolute zero is 0 K, the equivalent of −273.15°C

kempt \ˈkem(p)t\ *adj* [ME, fr. pp. of *kemben* to comb, fr. OE *cemban*; akin to OE *camb* comb] (bef. 12c) : neatly kept : TRIM ⟨old but ~ homes —David Bourdon⟩

[1]ken \ˈken\ *vb* **kenned; ken·ning** [ME *kennen*, fr. OE *cennan* to make known & ON *kenna* to perceive; both akin to OE *can* know — more at CAN] *vt* (13c) **1** *archaic* : SEE **2** *chiefly dial* : RECOGNIZE **3** *chiefly Scot* : KNOW ~ *vi, chiefly Scot* : KNOW

[2]ken *n* (1590) **1 a** : the range of vision **b** : SIGHT, VIEW ⟨'tis double death to drown in ~ of shore —Shak.⟩ **2** : the range of perception, understanding, or knowledge ⟨abstract words that are beyond the ~ of young children —Lois M. Rettie⟩

ke·naf \kə-ˈnaf\ *n* [Per] (1891) : an East Indian hibiscus (*Hibiscus cannabinus*) widely cultivated for its fiber; *also* : the fiber used esp. for cordage

Ken·dal green \ˌken-dᵊl-\ *n* [ME, fr. *Kendal,* England] (1514) **:** a green woolen cloth resembling homespun or tweed

ken·do \ˈken-(ˌ)dō\ *n* [Jp *kendō,* fr. *ken* sword + *dō* art] (1921) **:** a Japanese sport of fencing with bamboo swords

[1]**ken·nel** \ˈken-ᵊl\ *n* [ME *kenel,* deriv. of (assumed) VL *canile,* fr. L *canis* dog — more at HOUND] (14c) **1 a :** a shelter for a dog or cat **b :** an establishment for the breeding or boarding of dogs or cats **2 :** a pack of dogs

[2]**kennel** *vb* **-neled** *or* **-nelled; -nel·ing** *or* **-nel·ling** *vi* (1552) **:** to take shelter in or as if in a kennel ~ *vt* **:** to put or keep in or as if in a kennel

[3]**kennel** *n* [alter. of *cannel* (gutter)] (15c) **:** a gutter in a street

[1]**ken·ning** \ˈken-iŋ\ *n* [ME, sight, view, fr. gerund of *kennen*] *chiefly Scot* (1786) **:** a perceptible but small amount

[2]**kenning** *n* [ON, fr. *kenna*] (1883) **:** a metaphorical compound word or phrase used esp. in Old English and Old Norse poetry ⟨*swan-road* for *ocean* is an example of a ~⟩

ke·no \ˈkē-(ˌ)nō\ *n* [F *quine,* set of five winning numbers in a lottery + E *-o* (as in *lotto*)] (1814) **:** a game resembling bingo

ken·speck·le \ˈken-ˌspek-əl\ *adj* [prob. of Scand origin; akin to Norw *kjennspak* quick to recognize] *chiefly Scot* (1616) **:** CONSPICUOUS

kent·ledge \ˈkent-lij\ *n* [origin unknown] (1607) **:** pig iron or scrap metal used as ballast

Ken·tucky bluegrass \kən-ˌtək-ē-\ *n* [*Kentucky,* state of U.S.] (1849) **:** a valuable pasture and meadow grass (*Poa pratensis*) of both Europe and America — called also *bluegrass*

Kentucky coffee tree *n* (1785) **:** a tall No. American leguminous tree (*Gymnocladus dioica*) with bipinnate leaves and large woody brown pods whose seeds have been used as a substitute for coffee

Kentucky rifle *n* (1832) **:** a muzzle-loading long-barreled flintlock rifle developed in the 18th century in Pennsylvania and used extensively on the American frontier

Ke·ogh plan \ˈkē-(ˌ)ō-\ *n* [Eugene James *Keogh b*1907 Am. politician] (1974) **:** an individual retirement account for the self-employed

ke·pi \ˈkā-pē, ˈkep-ē\ *n* [F *képi,* fr. G dial. (Switzerland) *käppi* cap] (1861) **:** a military cap with a round flat top sloping toward the front and a visor

kept *past and past part of* KEEP

kerat- *or* **kerato-** *comb form* [ISV, fr. Gk *kerato-, keras* horn — more at HORN] **:** cornea ⟨*keratitis*⟩

ker·a·tin \ˈker-ət-ᵊn\ *n* [ISV] (1847) **:** any of various sulfur-containing fibrous proteins that form the chemical basis of horny epidermal tissues — **ke·ra·ti·nous** \kə-ˈrat-ᵊn-əs, ˌker-ə-ˈtī-nəs\ *adj*

ke·ra·ti·ni·za·tion \ˌker-ət-ə-nə-ˈzā-shən, kə-ˌrat-ᵊn-ə-\ *n* (1885) **:** conversion into keratin or keratinous tissue — **ke·ra·ti·nize** \ˈker-ət-ə-ˌnīz, kə-ˈrat-ᵊn-ˌīz\ *vb*

ke·ra·ti·no·phil·ic \ˌker-ət-ə-nə-ˈfil-ik, kə-ˌrat-ᵊn-ə-\ *adj* (1946) **:** exhibiting affinity for keratin (as in hair, skin, feathers, or horns) — used chiefly of fungi capable of growing on such materials

ker·a·ti·tis \ˌker-ə-ˈtīt-əs\ *n, pl* **-tit·i·des** \-ˈtit-ə-ˌdēz\ [NL] (1858) **:** inflammation of the cornea of the eye

ker·a·to·con·junc·ti·vi·tis \ˈker-ə-(ˌ)tō-kən-ˌjəŋ(k)-tə-ˈvīt-əs\ *n* [NL] (1887) **:** combined inflammation of the cornea and conjunctiva

ker·a·to·plas·ty \ˈker-ət-ō-ˌplas-tē\ *n, pl* **-ties** (ca. 1857) **:** plastic surgery on the cornea; *esp* **:** corneal grafting

ker·a·to·sis \ˌker-ə-ˈtō-səs\ *n, pl* **-to·ses** \-ˌsēz\ [NL] (1885) **:** an area of skin marked by overgrowth of horny tissue — **ker·a·tot·ic** \-ˈtät-ik\ *adj*

kerb \ˈkərb\ *n, Brit* (1797) **:** CURB 5

ker·chief \ˈkər-chəf, -ˌchēf\ *n, pl* **kerchiefs** \-chəfs, -ˌchēfs\ *also* **kerchieves** \-ˌchēvz\ [ME *courchef,* fr. OF *cuevrechief,* fr. *covrir* to cover + *chief* head — more at CHIEF] (13c) **1 :** a square of cloth used by women as a head covering or worn as a scarf around the neck **2 :** HANDKERCHIEF 1 — **ker·chiefed** \-chəft, -ˌchēft \ *adj*

kerf \ˈkərf\ *n* [ME, fr. OE *cyrf* action of cutting; akin to OE *ceorfan* to carve — more at CARVE] (1523) **1 :** a slit or notch made by a saw or cutting torch **2 :** the width of cut made by a saw or cutting torch

Ker·man \kər-ˈmän, ke(ə)r-\ *var of* KIRMAN

ker·mes \ˈkər-(ˌ)mēz\ *n* [F *kermès,* fr. Ar *qirmiz*] (1603) **:** the dried bodies of the females of various scale insects (genus *Kermes*) that are found on a Mediterranean oak (*Quercus coccinea*) and constitute a red dyestuff

ker·mis \ˈkər-məs\ *or* **ker·mess** \ˈkər-məs, (ˌ)kər-ˈmes\ *n* [D *kermis,* fr. MD *kercmisse,* fr. *kerc, kerke* church + *misse* mass, church festival] (1577) **1 :** an outdoor festival of the Low Countries **2 :** a fair held usu. for charitable purposes

[1]**kern** *or* **kerne** \ˈkərn, ˈke(ə)rn\ *n* [ME *kerne,* fr. MIr *cethern* band of soldiers] (14c) **1 :** a light-armed foot soldier of medieval Ireland or Scotland **2 :** YOKEL

[2]**kern** \ˈkərn\ *n* [F *carne* corner, fr. L *cardin-, cardo* hinge — more at CARDINAL] (1683) **:** a part of a typeset letter that projects beyond its side bearings

ker·nel \ˈkərn-ᵊl\ *n* [ME, fr. OE *cyrnel,* dim. of *corn*] (bef. 12c) **1** *chiefly dial* **:** a fruit seed **2 :** the inner softer part of a seed, fruit stone, or nut **3 :** a whole seed of a cereal **4 :** a central or essential part ⟨like many stereotypes . . . this one too contains some ~*s* of truth —S. M. Lyman⟩ **5 :** a subset of the elements of one set (as a group) that a function (as a homomorphism) maps onto an identity element of another set

kern·ite \ˈkər-ˌnīt\ *n* [*Kern* co., Calif.] (1927) **:** a mineral $Na_2B_4O_7 \cdot 4H_2O$ that consists of a hydrous borate of sodium and is an important source of borax

ker·o·gen \ˈker-ə-jən\ *n* [Gk *kēros* wax + E *-gen* — more at CERUMEN] (1906) **:** bituminous material occurring in shale and yielding oil when heated

ker·o·sene *or* **ker·o·sine** \ˈker-ə-ˌsēn, ˌker-ə-ˈ, ˈkar-, ˌkar-\ *n* [Gk *kēros* + E *-ene* (as in *camphene*)] (1854) **:** a flammable hydrocarbon oil usu. obtained by distillation of petroleum and used for a fuel and as a solvent and thinner

ker·ria \ˈker-ē-ə\ *n* [NL, fr. William *Kerr* †1814 Eng. gardener] (1823) **:** any of a genus (*Kerria*) of Chinese shrubs of the rose family with solitary yellow and often double flowers

ker·ry \ˈker-ē\ *n, pl* **kerries** *often cap* [County *Kerry,* Ireland] (1829) **:** any of an Irish breed of small hardy long-lived black dairy cattle

Kerry blue terrier *n* (1922) **:** any of an Irish breed of medium-sized terriers with a long head, deep chest, and silky bluish coat

ker·sey \ˈkər-zē\ *n, pl* **kerseys** [ME, fr. *Kersey,* England] (15c) **1 a :** a coarse ribbed woolen cloth for hose and work clothes **b :** a heavy wool or wool and cotton fabric used esp. for uniforms and coats **2 :** a garment of kersey

ker·sey·mere \ˈkər-zē-ˌmi(ə)r\ *n* [alter. of *cassimere*] (1798) **:** a fine woolen fabric with a close nap made in fancy twill weaves

ke·ryg·ma \kə-ˈrig-mə\ *n* [Gk *kērygma,* fr. *kēryssein* to proclaim, fr. *kēryx* herald — more at CADUCEUS] (1889) **:** the apostolic proclamation of salvation through Jesus Christ — **ker·yg·mat·ic** \ˌker-ig-ˈmat-ik\ *adj*

kes·trel \ˈkes-trəl\ *n* [ME *castrel,* fr. MF *crecerelle*] (15c) **:** a small European falcon (*Falco tinnunculus*) that is noted for its habit of hovering in the air against a wind and that is about a foot long, bluish gray above in the male, and reddish brown in the female; *broadly* **:** any of various small Old World falcons

ket- *or* **keto-** *comb form* [ISV] **:** ketone ⟨*ketosis*⟩

ketch \ˈkech\ *n* [ME *cache*] (15c) **:** a fore-and-aft rigged vessel similar to a yawl but with a larger mizzen and with the mizzenmast stepped farther forward

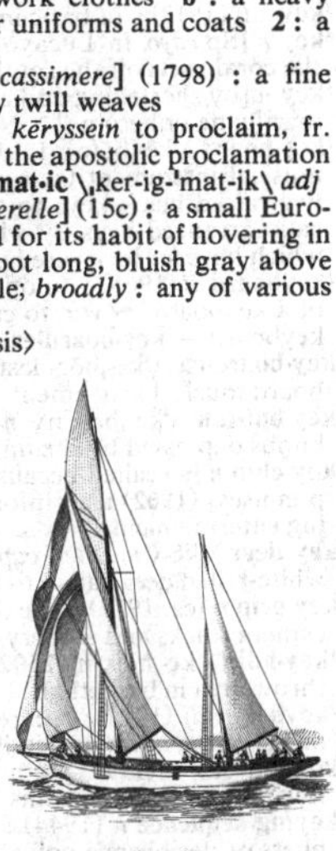
ketch

ketch·up *var of* CATSUP

ke·tene \ˈkē-ˌtēn\ *n* [ISV] (1907) **:** a colorless poisonous gas C_2H_2O of penetrating odor used esp. as an acetylating agent

ke·to \ˈkēt-(ˌ)ō\ *adj* [*ket-*] (1891) **:** of or relating to a ketone; *also* **:** containing a ketone group

ke·to·gen·e·sis \ˌkēt-ō-ˈjen-ə-səs\ *n* [NL] (1915) **:** the production of ketone bodies (as in diabetes) — **ke·to·gen·ic** \-ˈjen-ik\ *adj*

ke·to·glu·tar·ic acid \-glü-ˌtar-ik-\ *n* (1908) **:** either of two crystalline keto derivatives $C_5H_6O_5$ of glutaric acid; *esp* **:** the alpha keto isomer formed in various metabolic processes (as the Krebs cycle)

ke·tone \ˈkē-ˌtōn\ *n* [G *keton,* alter. of *aceton* acetone] (1851) **:** an organic compound (as acetone) with a carbonyl group attached to two carbon atoms — **ke·ton·ic** \kē-ˈtän-ik\ *adj*

ketone body *n* (1915) **:** any of the three compounds acetoacetic acid, acetone, and beta-hydroxybutyric acid which are normal intermediates in lipid metabolism and accumulate in the blood and urine in abnormal amounts in conditions of impaired metabolism (as diabetes mellitus)

ke·tose \ˈkē-ˌtōs, -ˌtōz\ *n* [ISV] (1902) **:** a sugar (as fructose) containing one ketone group per molecule

ke·to·sis \kē-ˈtō-səs\ *n* [NL] (1917) **:** an abnormal increase of ketone bodies in the body — **ke·tot·ic** \-ˈtät-ik\ *adj*

ke·to·ste·roid \ˌkēt-ō-ˈsti(ə)r-ˌȯid *also* -ˈste(ə)r-\ *n* [ISV] (1939) **:** a steroid (as cortisone or estrone) containing a ketone group

ket·tle \ˈket-ᵊl\ *n* [ME *ketel,* fr. ON *ketill* (akin to OE *cietel* kettle), fr. L *catillus,* dim. of *catinus* bowl] (bef. 12c) **1 :** a metallic vessel for boiling liquids; *esp* **:** TEAKETTLE **2 :** KETTLEDRUM **3 a :** POTHOLE **b :** a steep-sided hollow without surface drainage esp. in a deposit of glacial drift

ket·tle·drum \-ˌdrəm\ *n* (1602) **:** a percussion instrument that consists of a hollow brass, copper, or fiberglass hemisphere with a calfskin or plastic head whose tension can be changed to vary the pitch

kettle of fish (1742) **1 :** a bad state of affairs **:** MESS **2 :** something to be considered or reckoned with **:** MATTER ⟨books and discs . . . were two very different *kettles of fish* —Roland Gelatt⟩

Kew·pie \ˈkyü-pē\ *trademark* — used for a small chubby doll with a topknot of hair

[1]**key** \ˈkē\ *n* [ME, fr. OE *cǣg;* akin to MLG *keige* spear] (bef. 12c) **1 a :** a usu. metal instrument by which the bolt of a lock is turned **b :** any of various devices having the form or function of such a key **2 a :** a means of gaining or preventing entrance, possession, or control **b :** an instrumental or deciding factor **3 a :** something that gives an explanation or identification or provides a solution ⟨the ~ to a riddle⟩ **b :** a list of words or phrases giving an explanation of symbols or abbreviations **c :** an aid to interpretation or identification **:** CLUE **d :** an arrangement of the salient characters of a group of plants or animals or of taxa designed to facilitate identification **e :** a map legend **4 a** (1) **:** COTTER PIN (2) **:** [2]COTTER **b :** a keystone in an arch **c :** a small piece of wood or metal used as a wedge or for preventing motion between parts **5 a :** one of the levers of a keyboard musical instrument that actuates the mechanism and produces the tones **b :** a lever that controls a vent in the side of a woodwind instrument or a valve in a brass instrument **c :** a digital that serves as one unit of a keyboard and that works usu. by lever action to set in motion a character or an escapement (as in some typesetting machines) **d :** KEYBUTTON **6 :** SAMARA **7 :** a system of seven tones based on their relationship to a tonic; *specif* **:** the tonality of a scale **8 a :** characteristic style or tone **b :** the tone or pitch of a voice **c :** the predominant tone of a photograph with respect to its lightness or darkness **9 :** a decoration or charm resembling a key **10 :** a small switch for opening or closing an electric circuit **11 :** the set of instructions governing the encipherment and decipherment of messages **12 :** KEYHOLE 2 — **keyed** \ˈkēd\ *adj* — **key·less** \ˈkē-ləs\ *adj*

[2]**key** *vt* (14c) **1 :** to lock with or as if with a key **:** FASTEN: as **a :** to secure (as a pulley on a shaft) by a key **b :** to finish off (an arch) by inserting a keystone **2 :** to regulate the musical pitch of **3 :** to bring into harmony or conformity **:** make appropriate **:** ATTUNE ⟨remarks ~*ed* to a situation⟩ **4 :** to identify (a biological specimen) by a key **5 :** to provide with identifying or explanatory cross-references ⟨instructions ~*ed* to accompanying drawings —John Gartner⟩ **6 :** to make nervous, tense, or excited — usu. used with *up* ⟨was ~*ed* up over her impending operation⟩ **7 :** KEYBOARD ~ *vi* **1 :** to use a key **2 :** to

\ə\ **abut** \ᵊ\ **kitten, F table** \ər\ **further** \a\ **ash** \ā\ **ace** \ä\ **cot, cart** \au̇\ **out** \ch\ **chin** \e\ **bet** \ē\ **easy** \g\ **go** \i\ **hit** \ī\ **ice** \j\ **job** \ŋ\ **sing** \ō\ **go** \ȯ\ **law** \ȯi\ **boy** \th\ **thin** \t͟h\ **the** \ü\ **loot** \u̇\ **foot** \y\ **yet** \zh\ **vision** \à, k̲, ^{n}, œ, œ̄, ue, ue̅, ^{y}\ *see* Guide to Pronunciation

observe the position or movement of an opposing player in football in order to anticipate the play — usu. used with *on* **3 :** KEYBOARD

[3]key *adj* (1913) **:** of basic importance **:** FUNDAMENTAL ⟨~ issues⟩

[4]key *n* [Sp *cayo,* fr. Lucayo] (1697) **:** a low island or reef; *specif* **:** one of the coral islets off the southern coast of Florida

[5]key *n* [by shortening and alter. of *kilo*] *slang* (1968) **:** a kilogram esp. of marijuana or heroin

[1]key·board \'kē-ˌbō(ə)rd, -ˌbȯ(ə)rd\ *n* (1819) **1 :** a bank of keys on a musical instrument (as a piano) that usu. consists of seven white and five raised black keys to the octave **2 :** an assemblage of systematically arranged keys by which a machine is operated **3 :** a board on which keys for locks are hung

[2]keyboard *vi* (1965) **:** to operate a machine (as for typesetting) by means of a keyboard ~ *vt* **:** to capture or set (as data or text) by means of a keyboard — **key·board·er** *n*

key·board·ist \'kē-ˌbōr-dəst, -ˌbȯr-\ *n* (1973) **:** one who plays a keyboard musical instrument

key·but·ton \'kē-ˌbət-ᵊn\ *n* (ca. 1920) **:** any of the small buttons or knobs depressed by the fingers in operating a keyboard machine

key club *n* [so called because each member is provided with a key to the premises] (1962) **:** an informal private club serving liquor and providing entertainment

key deer \ˌkē-\ *n, often cap K* (1950) **:** any of a race of very small rare white-tailed deer native to the Florida Keys

key grip *n* (ca. 1979) **:** the technician in charge of moving and setting up camera tracks and scenery in a motion-picture or television production

[1]key·hole \'kē-ˌhōl\ *n* (1592) **1 :** a hole for receiving a key **2 :** a free-throw area in basketball

[2]keyhole *adj* (1937) **1 :** revealingly intimate ⟨a ~ report⟩ **2 :** intent on revealing intimate details ⟨~ columnists⟩

keyhole saw *n* (1777) **:** a narrow pointed fine-toothed saw used for cutting curves of short radius

keying sequence *n* (1944) **:** a sequence of letters or numbers that enciphers or deciphers a polyalphabetic substitution cipher letter by letter

key light *n* (1937) **:** the main light illuminating a subject in photography

Keynes·ian·ism \'kān-zē-ə-ˌniz-əm\ *n* (1946) **:** the economic theories and programs ascribed to John M. Keynes and his followers; *specif* **:** the advocacy of monetary and fiscal programs by government to increase employment and spending

[1]key·note \'kē-ˌnōt\ *n* (1776) **1 :** the first and harmonically fundamental tone of a scale **2 :** the fundamental or central fact, idea, or mood ⟨sadness is the ~ of this little collection —*Books Abroad*⟩

[2]keynote *vt* (1914) **1 :** to set the keynote of **2 :** to deliver the keynote address at — **key·not·er** *n*

keynote address *n* (1908) **:** an address designed to present the issues of primary interest to an assembly (as a political convention) and often to arouse unity and enthusiasm — called also *keynote speech*

keynote speaker *n* (1950) **:** one who delivers a keynote address

key·pad \'kē-ˌpad\ *n* (ca. 1967) **:** a small often hand-held keyboard

[1]key·punch \'kē-ˌpənch\ *n* (1918) **:** a machine with a keyboard used to cut holes or notches in punch cards

[2]keypunch *vt* (1947) **:** to cut holes or notches in (a punch card) with a keypunch — **key·punch·er** *n*

key signature *n* (ca. 1875) **:** the sharps or flats placed after a clef in music to indicate the key

key·stone \'kē-ˌstōn\ *n* (1637) **1 :** the wedge-shaped piece at the crown of an arch that locks the other pieces in place — see ARCH illustration **2 :** something on which associated things depend for support ⟨collective bargaining — the ~ of industrial democracy —A. E. Stevenson †1965⟩

key·stroke \-ˌstrōk\ *n* (1910) **:** the act or an instance of depressing a key on a keyboard — **keystroke** *vb*

key·way \-ˌwā\ *n* (1870) **1 :** a groove or channel for a key **2 :** the aperture for the key in a lock having a flat metal key

key word *n* (1859) **:** a word that is a key: as **a :** a word exemplifying the meaning or value of a letter or symbol **b** *usu* **key·word** \-ˌwərd\ **:** a significant word from a title or document that is used as an index to content

khad·dar \'käd-ər\ *or* **kha·di** \'käd-ē\ *n* [Hindi *khādar, khādī*] (1885) **:** homespun cotton cloth of India

kha·ki \'kak-ē, 'käk-, *Canad often* 'kärk-\ *n* [Hindi *khākī* dust-colored, fr. *khāk* dust, fr. Per] (1837) **1 :** a light yellowish brown **2 a :** a khaki-colored cloth made usu. of cotton or wool and used esp. for military uniforms **b :** a garment of this cloth; *esp* **:** a military uniform — usu. used in pl. — **khaki** *adj*

Khal·kha \'kal-kə\ *n* (1873) **1 :** a member of a Mongol people of Outer Mongolia **2 :** the language of the Khalkha people used as the official language of the Mongolian People's Republic

kham·sin \kam-'sēn\ *n* [Ar *rīḥ al-khamsīn* the wind of the fifty (days between Easter and Pentecost)] (1685) **:** a hot southerly Egyptian wind

[1]khan \'kän, 'kan\ *n* [ME *caan,* fr. MF, of Turkic origin; akin to Turk *han* prince] (15c) **1 :** a medieval sovereign of China and ruler over the Turkish, Tatar, and Mongol tribes **2 :** a local chieftain or man of rank in some countries of central Asia

[2]khan *n* [Ar *khān*] (15c) **:** a caravansary or rest house in some Asian countries

khan·ate \-ˌāt\ *n* (1799) **:** the state or jurisdiction of a khan

khap·ra beetle \ˌkap-rə-, ˌkäp-\ *n* [Hindi *khaprā,* lit., destroyer] (1896) **:** a dermestid beetle (*Trogoderma granarium*) that is native to the Indian subcontinent and is now a serious pest of stored grain in most parts of the world

khat \'kät\ *n* [Ar *qāt*] (1858) **:** a shrub (*Catha edulis*) cultivated by the Arabs for its leaves and buds that are the source of an habituating stimulant when chewed or used as a tea

khe·dive \kə-'dēv\ *n* [F *khédive,* fr. Turk *hidiv*] (1867) **:** a ruler of Egypt from 1867 to 1914 governing as a viceroy of the sultan of Turkey — **khe·div·ial** \-'dē-vē-əl\ *or* **khe·div·al** \-'dē-vəl\ *adj*

Khmer \kə-'me(ə)r\ *n, pl* **Khmer** *or* **Khmers** (1876) **1 :** a member of an aboriginal people of Cambodia **2 :** the Mon-Khmer language of the Khmer people that is the official language of Cambodia — **Khmer·ian** \-'mer-ē-ən\ *adj*

Khoi·san \'kȯi-ˌsän\ *n* (1936) **1 :** a group of African peoples speaking Khoisan languages **2 :** a subfamily of African languages comprising Hottentot and the several languages known as Bushman

khoum \'küm, 'küm\ *n* [native name in Mauritania] (ca. 1973) — see *ouguiya* at MONEY table

Kho·war \'kō-ˌwär\ *n* (1882) **:** a Dard language of northwest Pakistan

ki·ang \kē-'äŋ\ *n* [Tibetan *rkyaṅ*] (1882) **:** an Asian wild ass (*Equus hemionus*) usu. with reddish back and sides and white underparts, muzzle, and legs

kiaugh \'kyäk\ *n* [prob. fr. ScGael *cabhag*] *Scot* (1786) **:** TROUBLE, ANXIETY

kib·be *or* **kib·beh** \'kib-ə\ *n* [Ar *kubbah*] (ca. 1937) **:** a Near Eastern dish made from ground lamb and bulgur and eaten either cooked or raw

[1]kib·ble \'kib-əl\ *vt* **kib·bled; kib·bling** \-(ə-)liŋ\ [origin unknown] (1790) **:** to grind coarsely ⟨*kibbled* dog biscuit⟩ ⟨*kibbled* grain⟩

[2]kibble *n* (1942) **:** coarsely ground meal or grain

kib·butz \kib-'u̇ts, -'üts\ *n, pl* **kib·but·zim** \-ˌu̇t-'sēm, -ˌüt-\ [NHeb *qibbūṣ*] (1931) **:** a collective farm or settlement in Israel

kib·butz·nik \-'u̇t-snik, -'üt-\ *n* [Yiddish, fr. *kibbutz* (fr. NHeb *qibbūṣ*) + *-nik*] (1947) **:** a member of a kibbutz

kibe \'kīb\ *n* [ME] (14c) **:** an ulcerated chilblain esp. on the heel

ki·bitz \'kib-əts, kə-'bits\ *vb* [Yiddish *kibitsen,* fr. G *kiebitzen,* fr. *kiebitz,* lit., pewit] *vi* (1927) **:** to act as a kibitzer ~ *vt* **:** to observe as a kibitzer; *esp* **:** to be a kibitzer at ⟨~ a card game⟩

ki·bitz·er \'kib-ət-sər, kə-'bit-\ *n* (1925) **:** one who looks on and often offers unwanted advice or comment esp. at a card game

ki·bosh \'kī-ˌbäsh, kī-'; kib-'äsh\ *n* [origin unknown] (1836) **:** something that serves as a check or stop ⟨put the ~ on that⟩ — **kibosh** *vt*

[1]kick \'kik\ *vb* [ME *kiken*] *vi* (14c) **1 a :** to strike out with the foot or feet **b :** to make a kick in football **2 a :** to show opposition **:** RESIST, REBEL **b :** to protest strenuously or urgently **:** express grave discontent; *broadly* **:** COMPLAIN **3** *of a firearm* **:** to recoil when fired **4 :** to go from one place to another as circumstance or whim dictates ~ *vt* **1 a :** to strike, thrust, or hit with the foot **b :** to strike suddenly and forcefully as if with the foot **c :** to remove from a position or status ⟨~*ed* him off the team⟩ **2 :** to score by kicking a ball **3** *slang* **:** to free oneself of (as a drug habit) — **kick·able** \'kik-ə-bəl\ *adj* — **kick over the traces :** to cast off restraint, authority, or control — **kick the bucket :** DIE — **kick up one's heels 1 :** to show sudden delight **2 :** to have a lively time — **kick upstairs :** to promote to a higher but less desirable position

[2]kick *n* (1530) **1 a :** a blow or sudden forceful thrust with the foot; *specif* **:** a sudden propelling of a ball with the foot **b :** the power to kick **c :** a rhythmic motion of the legs used in swimming **d :** a burst of speed in racing **2 :** a sudden forceful jolt or thrust suggesting a kick; *esp* **:** the recoil of a gun **3 a :** a feeling or expression of opposition or objection ⟨a ~ against the administration⟩ **b :** the grounds for objection **4 a :** a stimulating or pleasurable effect or experience **b :** pursuit of an absorbing or obsessive new interest ⟨went on a mystery-reading ~ —*Time*⟩ **5 :** a sudden and striking surprise, revelation, or turn of events

kick around *vt* (1938) **1 :** to treat in an inconsiderate or high-handed fashion **2 :** to consider, examine, or discuss from various angles ~ *vi* **1 :** to wander or pass time aimlessly **2 :** to lie about mostly unnoticed or forgotten

kick·back \'kik-ˌbak\ *n* (1920) **1 :** a sharp violent reaction **2 :** a return of a part of a sum received often because of confidential agreement or coercion ⟨every city contract had been let with a ten percent ~ to city officials —D. K. Shipler⟩

kick·er *n* (ca. 1573) **1 :** one that kicks or kicks something **2 :** KICK 5

kick in *vt* (1908) **:** CONTRIBUTE ~ *vi* **1** *slang* **:** DIE **2 :** to make a contribution

kick·off \'kik-ˌȯf\ *n* (1857) **1 :** a kick that puts the ball into play in a football or soccer game **2 :** COMMENCEMENT 1

kick off *vi* (1857) **1 :** to start or resume play in football by a placekick **2 :** to begin proceedings **3** *slang* **:** DIE ~ *vt* **:** to mark the beginning of

kick out *vt* (1697) **:** to dismiss or eject forcefully or summarily

kick over *vi* (1951) **:** to begin to fire — used of an internal-combustion engine ~ *vt* **:** to cause (an internal-combustion engine) to turn over and usu. begin to fire

kick pleat *n* (1926) **:** a short inverted pleat (as at the bottom of a skirt) used to give breadth

kick·shaw \'kik-ˌshȯ\ *n* [by folk etymology fr. F *quelque chose* something] (1597) **1 :** a fancy dish **:** DELICACY **2 :** TRINKET, GEWGAW

kick·stand \'kik-ˌstand\ *n* [fr. its being put in position by a kick] (1947) **:** a swiveling metal bar or rod for holding up a 2-wheeled vehicle when not in use

kick turn *n* (1910) **:** a standing half turn in skiing made by swinging one ski high with a jerk and planting it in the desired direction and then lifting the other ski into a parallel position

kick·up \'kik-ˌəp\ *n* (1793) **:** a noisy quarrel **:** ROW

kick up \(ˈ)kik-'əp\ *vt* (1756) **1 :** to stir up **:** PROVOKE ⟨*kick up* a fuss⟩ **2 :** to cause to rise upward ⟨clouds of dust *kicked up* by passing cars⟩ ~ *vi* **:** to give evidence of disorder

kicky \'kik-ē\ *adj* (1966) **:** providing a kick or thrill **:** EXCITING

[1]kid \'kid\ *n* [ME *kide,* of Scand origin; akin to ON *kith* kid] (13c) **1 a :** a young goat **b :** a young individual of various animals related to the goat **2 a :** the flesh, fur, or skin of a kid **b :** something made of kid **3 :** a young person **:** CHILD — **kid·dish** \'kid-ish\ *adj*

[2]kid *vi* **kid·ded; kid·ding** (15c) **:** to bring forth young — used of a goat or an antelope

[3]kid *vb* **kid·ded; kid·ding** [prob. fr. [1]*kid*] *vt* (ca. 1811) **1 :** to deceive as a joke ⟨it's the truth; I wouldn't ~ you⟩ **2 :** to make fun of ~ *vi* **:** to engage in good-humored fooling or horseplay — often used with *around* — **kid·der** *n* — **kid·ding·ly** \'kid-iŋ-lē\ *adv*

Kid·der·min·ster \'kid-ər-ˌmin(t)-stər\ *n* [*Kidderminster,* England] (1836) **:** an ingrain carpet

kid·die *or* **kid·dy** \'kid-ē\ *n, pl* **kiddies** [[1]*kid*] (1889) **:** a small child

kid·dush \'kid-əsh, -ish; kid-'üsh\ *n* [LHeb *qiddūsh* sanctification] (1753) **:** a ceremonial blessing pronounced over wine or bread in a Jewish home or synagogue on a sabbath or other holy day

kid glove *n* (1832) **:** a dress glove made of kid leather — **kid-gloved** \'kid-'gləvd\ *adj* — **with kid gloves :** with special consideration

kid leather *n* (1687) **1 :** a soft pliable leather made from kidskin **2 :** a glove leather made from lambskin or goatskin

kid·nap \ˈkid-ˌnap\ *vt* **-napped** *or* **-naped** \-ˌnapt\; **-nap·ping** *or* **-nap·ing** [prob. back-formation fr. *kidnapper,* fr. *kid* + obs. *napper* (thief)] (1682) **:** to seize and detain or carry away by unlawful force or fraud and often with a demand for ransom — **kid·nap·pee** *or* **kid·nap·ee** \ˌkid-ˌnap-ˈē\ *n* — **kid·nap·per** *or* **kid·nap·er** *n*

kid·ney \ˈkid-nē\ *n, pl* **kidneys** [ME] (14c) **1 a :** one of a pair of vertebrate organs situated in the body cavity near the spinal column that excrete waste products of metabolism, in man are bean-shaped organs about $4\frac{1}{2}$ inches long lying behind the peritoneum in a mass of fatty tissue, and consist chiefly of nephrons by which urine is secreted, collected, and discharged into a main cavity whence it is conveyed by the ureter to the bladder **b :** any of various excretory organs of invertebrate animals **2 :** the kidney of an animal eaten as food **3 :** sort or kind esp. with regard to temperament ⟨a nice helpful guy, of a different ~ entirely from the ubiquitous Secret Police —Paula Lecler⟩

kidney bean *n* (1548) **1 :** an edible and nutritious seed of any cultivated bean of the common species (*Phaseolus vulgaris*); *esp* **:** a large dark red bean seed **2 :** a plant bearing kidney beans

kidney stone *n* (1971) **:** a calculus in the kidney

kid·skin \ˈkid-ˌskin\ *n* (14c) **:** the skin of a young or sometimes a mature goat; *also* **:** KID LEATHER

kid stuff *n* (1927) **1 :** something befitting or appropriate only to children **2 :** something extremely simple or easy

kiel·ba·sa \k(y)el-ˈbäs-ə, kil-\ *n, pl* **-basas** *also* **-ba·sy** \-ˈbäs-ē\ [Pol *kiełbasa;* akin to Russ *kolbasa* sausage] (ca. 1923) **:** a smoked sausage of Polish origin

kie·sel·guhr *or* **kie·sel·gur** \ˈkē-zəl-ˌgu̇(ə)r\ *n* [G *kieselgur*] (1875) **:** loose or porous diatomite

kie·ser·ite \ˈkē-zə-ˌrīt\ *n* [G *kieserit,* fr. Dietrich *Kieser* †1862 Ger. physician] (1862) **:** a mineral $MgSO_4H_2O$ that is a white hydrous magnesium sulfate

kif \ˈkif, ˈkēf\ *var of* KEF

kike \ˈkīk\ *n* [prob. alter. of *kiki,* redupl. of *-ki* common ending of names of Jews who lived in Slavic countries] (1904) **:** JEW — usu. taken to be offensive

Ki·ku·yu \ki-ˈkü-(ˌ)yü\ *n, pl* **Kikuyu** *or* **Kikuyus** (1894) **1 :** a member of a Bantu-speaking people of Kenya **2 :** the Bantu language of the Kikuyu people

kil·der·kin \ˈkil-dər-kən\ *n* [ME, fr. MD *kindekijn,* fr. ML *quintale* quintal] (14c) **1 :** an English unit of capacity equal to $\frac{1}{2}$ barrel **2 :** CASK

ki·lim \kē-ˈlēm\ *n* [Turk, fr. Pers *kilīm*] (1881) **:** a pileless tapestry-woven carpet, mat, or spread made in Turkey, Kurdistan, the Caucasus, Iran, and western Turkestan

[1]**kill** \ˈkil\ *vb* [ME *killen*] *vt* (14c) **1 a :** to deprive of life **b** (1) **:** to slaughter (as a hog) for food (2) **:** to convert a food animal into (as pork) by slaughtering **2 a :** to put an end to ⟨~ competition⟩ **b :** DEFEAT, VETO **c :** to mark for omission; *also* **:** DELETE **3 a :** to destroy the vital or essential quality of ⟨~*ed* the pain with drugs⟩ **b :** to cause to stop ⟨~ the motor⟩ **c :** to check the flow of current through **4 :** to make a markedly favorable impression on ⟨she ~*ed* the audience⟩ **5 :** to cause to elapse ⟨~ time⟩ **6 a :** to cause extreme pain to **b :** to tire almost to the point of collapse **7 :** to hit (a ball) so hard in a racket game that a return is impossible **8 :** to consume (as a drink) totally ~ *vi* **:** to deprive one of life

syn KILL, SLAY, MURDER, ASSASSINATE, DISPATCH, EXECUTE mean to deprive of life. KILL merely states the fact of death caused by an agency in any manner; SLAY is a chiefly literary term implying deliberateness and violence but not necessarily motive; MURDER specif. implies stealth and motive and premeditation and therefore full moral responsibility; ASSASSINATE applies to deliberate killing openly or secretly often for political motives; DISPATCH stresses quickness and directness in putting to death; EXECUTE stresses putting to death as a legal penalty.

[2]**kill** *n* (1852) **1 :** an act or instance of killing **2 :** something killed: as **a** (1) **:** an animal shot in a hunt (2) **:** animals killed in a hunt, season, or particular period of time **b :** an enemy airplane, submarine, or ship destroyed by military action **c :** a return shot in a racket game that is too hard for an opponent to handle

[3]**kill** *n, often cap* [D *kil*] (1669) **:** CHANNEL, CREEK — used chiefly in place names in Delaware, Pennsylvania, and New York

kill·deer \ˈkil-ˌdi(ə)r\ *n, pl* **killdeers** *or* **killdeer** [imit.] (1731) **:** a plover (*Charadrius vociferus* syn. *Oxyechus vociferus*) of temperate No. America characterized by a plaintive penetrating cry

kill·er \ˈkil-ər\ *n* (15c) **1 :** one that kills **2 :** KILLER WHALE

killer whale *n* (1884) **:** a carnivorous gregarious largely black whale (*Orcinus orca* syn. *Orca orca*) 20 to 30 feet long

kil·lick \ˈkil-ik\ *n* [origin unknown] (1630) **:** a small anchor; *also* **:** an anchor formed by a stone usu. enclosed by pieces of wood

kil·li·fish \ˈkil-i-ˌfish\ *n* [*killie* (killifish) + *fish*] (1836) **1 :** any of a family (Cyprinodontidae) of numerous small oviparous fishes much used as bait and in mosquito control **2 :** any of a family (Poeciliidae) of live-bearers

[1]**kill·ing** \ˈkil-iŋ\ *n* (15c) **1 :** the act of one that kills **2 :** KILL 2a **3 :** a sudden notable gain or profit

[2]**killing** *adj* (15c) **1 :** that kills or relates to killing **2 :** highly amusing — **kill·ing·ly** \-lē\ *adv*

kill·joy \ˈkil-ˌjȯi\ *n* (1776) **:** one who spoils the pleasure of others

kill off *vt* (1607) **:** to destroy in large numbers or totally

kiln \ˈkiln, ˈkil\ *n* [ME *kilne,* fr. OE *cyln,* fr. L *culina* kitchen, fr. *coquere* to cook — more at COOK] (bef. 12c) **:** an oven, furnace, or heated enclosure used for processing a substance by burning, firing, or drying — **kiln** *vt*

ki·lo \ˈkē-(ˌ)lō\ *n, pl* **kilos** (1870) **1 :** KILOGRAM **2 :** KILOMETER

Kilo (1952) — a communications code word for the letter *k*

kilo- *comb form* [F, modif. of Gk *chilioi*] **:** thousand ⟨*kiloton*⟩

ki·lo·bar \ˈkē-lə-ˌbär, ˈkil-ə-\ *n* [ISV] (1926) **:** a unit of pressure equal to 1000 bars

ki·lo·bit \-ˌbit\ *n* [ISV] (1961) **1 :** 1000 bits **2 :** 1024 bits

ki·lo·byte \-ˌbīt\ *n* [fr. the fact that 1024 (2^{10}) is the power of 2 closest to 1000] (1970) **:** 1024 bytes

ki·lo·cal·o·rie \-ˌkal-(ə-)rē\ *n* [ISV] (1894) **:** CALORIE 1b

ki·lo·cu·rie \-ˌkyu̇(ə)r-(ˌ)ē, -kyu̇-ˌrē\ *n* [ISV] (1946) **:** 1000 curies

kilo·cy·cle \ˈkil-ə-ˌsī-kəl\ *n* [ISV] (1921) **:** 1000 cycles; *esp* **:** KILOHERTZ

ki·lo·gauss \ˈkē-lə-ˌgau̇s, ˈkil-ə-\ *n* [ISV] (1895) **:** 1000 gauss

ki·lo·gram \ˈkē-lə-ˌgram, ˈkil-ə-\ *n* [F *kilogramme,* fr. *kilo-* + *gramme* gram] (1797) **1 :** the basic metric unit of mass equal to the mass of a platinum-iridium cylinder kept at the International Bureau of Weights and Measures near Paris and nearly equal to 1000 cubic centimeters of water at the temperature of its maximum density — see METRIC SYSTEM table **2 :** a unit of force equal to the weight of a kilogram mass under a gravitational attraction of 980.665 centimeters per second per second

kilogram calorie *n* (1900) **:** CALORIE 1b

kilogram-meter *n* (1866) **:** the mks gravitational unit of work and energy equal to the work done by a kilogram force acting through a distance of one meter in the direction of the force **:** about 7.235 foot-pounds

ki·lo·hertz \ˈkil-ə-ˌhərts, ˈkē-lə-, -ˌhe(ə)rts\ *n* [ISV] (1929) **:** 1000 hertz

ki·lo·joule \-ˌjü(ə)l\ *n* [ISV] (ca. 1889) **:** 1000 joules

kilo·li·ter \ˈkil-ə-ˌlēt-ər\ *n* [F *kilolitre,* fr. *kilo-* + *litre* liter] (1810) — see METRIC SYSTEM table

ki·lo·me·ter \÷kə-ˈläm-ət-ər, ÷kil-ˈäm-; ˈkil-ə-ˌmēt-ər\ *n* [F *kilomètre,* fr. *kilo-* + *mètre* meter] (1810) — see METRIC SYSTEM table

usage In No. American speech *kilometer* is most often pronounced with primary stress on the second syllable. This pronunciation is also heard frequently in British speech. Those who object to second syllable stress say that the first syllable should be stressed in accord with the stress patterns of *centimeter, millimeter,* etc. However, the pronunciation of *kilometer* does not parallel that of other metric compounds. From 1828 to 1841 Noah Webster indicated only second syllable stress, and his successor added a first syllable stress variant in the first Merriam-Webster dictionary of 1847. Thus, both pronunciations are venerable. Most scientists use second syllable stress, although first syllable stress seems to occur with a higher rate of frequency among scientists than among nonscientists.

ki·lo·oer·sted \ˈkē-lō-ˌər-stəd, ˈkil-ō-, -ˌȯr-\ *n* [ISV] (1946) **:** 1000 oersteds

ki·lo·par·sec \ˈkil-ə-ˌpär-ˌsek, ˈkē-lə-\ *n* (1922) **:** 1000 parsecs

ki·lo·rad \-ˌrad\ *n* [ISV] (1965) **:** 1000 rads

ki·lo·ton \-ˌtən *also* -ˌtän\ *n* (1950) **1 :** 1000 tons **2 :** an explosive force equivalent to that of 1000 tons of TNT

ki·lo·volt \-ˌvōlt\ *n* [ISV] (ca. 1898) **:** a unit of potential difference equal to 1000 volts

kilo·watt \ˈkil-ə-ˌwät\ *n* [ISV] (ca. 1884) **:** 1000 watts

kilowatt-hour *n* (1892) **:** a unit of work or energy equal to that expended by one kilowatt in one hour or to 3.6 million joules

[1]**kilt** \ˈkilt\ *vb* [ME *kilten,* of Scand origin; akin to ON *kjalta* lap, fold of a gathered skirt] *vt* (14c) **1** *chiefly dial* **:** to tuck up (as a skirt) **2 :** to equip with a kilt ~ *vi* **:** to move nimbly

[2]**kilt** *n* (1730) **1 :** a knee-length pleated skirt usu. of tartan worn by men in Scotland and by Scottish regiments in the British armies **2 :** a garment that resembles a Scottish kilt

kil·ter \ˈkil-tər\ *n* [origin unknown] (1628) **:** proper condition **:** ORDER ⟨out of ~⟩

kilt·ie \ˈkil-tē\ *n* (1842) **1** *or* **kilty :** one who wears a kilt **2 :** a shoe with a long slashed tongue that folds over the instep; *also* **:** such a tongue

Kim·bun·du \kim-ˈbu̇n-(ˌ)dü\ *n* (ca. 1895) **:** a Bantu language of northern Angola

kim·chi *also* **kim·chee** \ˈkim-chē\ *n* [Korean] (1898) **:** a vegetable pickle seasoned with garlic, red pepper, and ginger that is the national dish of Korea

ki·mo·no \kə-ˈmō-nə *also* -(ˌ)nō\ *n, pl* **-nos** [Jp, clothes, fr. *ki* wearing + *mono* thing, apparatus] (1886) **1 :** a long robe with wide sleeves traditionally worn with a broad sash as an outer garment by the Japanese **2 :** a loose dressing gown or jacket — **ki·mo·noed** \-nəd, -(ˌ)nōd\ *adj*

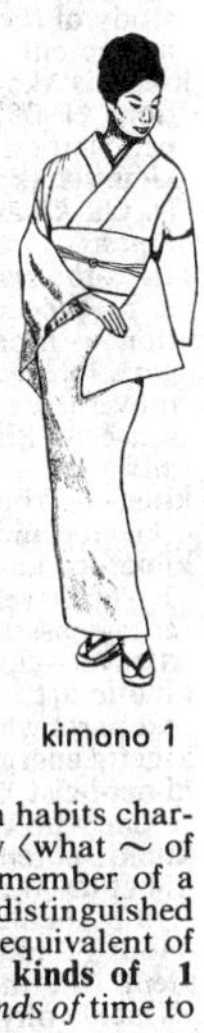

kimono 1

[1]**kin** \ˈkin\ *n* [ME, fr. OE *cyn;* akin to OHG *chunni* race, L *genus* birth, race, kind, Gk *genos,* L *gignere* to beget, Gk *gignesthai* to be born] (bef. 12c) **1 :** a group of persons of common ancestry **:** CLAN **2 a :** one's relatives **:** KINDRED **b :** KINSMAN ⟨he wasn't any ~ to you —Jean Stafford⟩ **3** *archaic* **:** KINSHIP

[2]**kin** *adj* (1597) **:** KINDRED, RELATED

-kin \kən\ *also* **-kins** \kənz\ *n suffix* [ME, fr. MD *-kin;* akin to OHG *-chīn,* dim. suffix] **:** little ⟨cat*kin*⟩ ⟨baby*kins*⟩

ki·na \ˈkē-nə\ *n* [native name in Papua New Guinea] (1975) — see MONEY table

ki·nase \ˈkī-ˌnās, -ˌnāz\ *n* [ISV, fr. *kinetic*] (1953) **:** an enzyme that catalyzes the transfer of phosphate groups from ATP or ADP to a substrate

[1]**kind** \ˈkīnd\ *n* [ME *kinde,* fr. OE *cynd;* akin to OE *cyn* kin] (bef. 12c) **1 a** *archaic* **:** NATURE **b** *archaic* **:** FAMILY, LINEAGE **2** *archaic* **:** MANNER **3 :** fundamental nature or quality **:** ESSENCE **4 a :** a group united by common traits or interests **:** CATEGORY ⟨biting insects with habits characteristic of their ~⟩ **b :** a specific or recognized variety ⟨what ~ of car do you drive⟩ **c :** a doubtful or barely admissible member of a category ⟨a ~ of gray⟩ **5 a :** goods or commodities as distinguished from money ⟨payment in ~ rather than in cash⟩ **b :** the equivalent of what has been offered or received *syn* see TYPE — **all kinds of 1 :** MANY ⟨likes *all kinds of* sports⟩ **2 :** plenty of ⟨has *all kinds of* time to get there⟩

[2]**kind** *adj* (13c) **1** *chiefly dial* **:** AFFECTIONATE, LOVING **2 a :** of a sympathetic nature **:** disposed to be helpful and solicitous **b :** of a forbearing nature **:** GENTLE **c :** arising from or characterized by sympa-

thy or forbearance ⟨a ~ act⟩ **3** : of a kind to give pleasure or relief : AGREEABLE

kin·der·gar·ten \'kin-də(r)-,gärt-ᵊn, -,gärd-\ *n* [G, fr. *kinder* children + *garten* garden] (1852) : a school or class for children usu. from four to six years old

kin·der·gart·ner \-,gärt-nər\ *n* (1919) **1** : a teacher at a kindergarten **2** : a child attending or of an age to attend kindergarten

kind·heart·ed \'kīnd-'härt-əd\ *adj* (1535) : marked by a sympathetic nature — **kind·heart·ed·ly** *adv* — **kind·heart·ed·ness** *n*

¹kin·dle \'kin-dᵊl\ *vb* **kin·dled; kin·dling** \-(d)liŋ, -dᵊl-iŋ\ [ME *kindlen,* prob. modif. of ON *kynda;* akin to OHG *cuntesal* fire] *vt* (13c) **1** : to start (a fire) burning : LIGHT **2** : to stir up : AROUSE ⟨~ interest⟩ **3** : to cause to glow : ILLUMINATE ~ *vi* **1** : to catch fire **2 a** : to flare up **b** : to become animated **3** : to become illuminated — **kin·dler** \-(d)lər, -dᵊl-ər\ *n*

²kindle *vb* **kin·dled; kin·dling** [ME *kindlen,* fr. *kindle,* n., young animal; akin to OE *cynd* ¹kind] *vt* (13c) : BEAR — used esp. of a rabbit ~ *vi* : to bring forth young — used esp. of a rabbit

kind·less \'kīn-(d)ləs\ *adj* (13c) **1** *obs* : INHUMAN **2** : DISAGREEABLE, UNCONGENIAL — **kind·less·ly** *adv*

kind·li·ness \'kīn-(d)lē-nəs\ *n* (15c) **1** : the quality or state of being kindly **2** : a kindly deed

kin·dling \'kin-(d)liŋ, 'kin-lən\ *n* (1513) : easily combustible material for starting a fire

¹kind·ly \'kīn-(d)lē\ *adj* **kind·li·er; -est** [ME, fr. OE *cyndelic,* fr. *cynd*] (bef. 12c) **1 a** *obs* : NATURAL **b** *archaic* : LAWFUL **2** : of an agreeable or beneficial nature : PLEASANT ⟨~ climate⟩ **3** : of a sympathetic or generous nature

²kindly *adv* (bef. 12c) **1 a** : in the normal way : NATURALLY ⟨old wounds which had healed ~ —*Amer. Mercury*⟩ **b** : READILY ⟨did not take ~ to suggestions⟩ **2 a** : in a kind manner : SYMPATHETICALLY **b** : as a gesture of goodwill ⟨would take it ~ if you would put in a good word for the boy⟩ **c** : in a gracious manner : COURTEOUSLY ⟨they ~ invited us along⟩ **d** : as a matter of courtesy : PLEASE ⟨would you ~ order me a cab⟩ **3** *chiefly Southern* : in a way : KIND OF ⟨it's ~ embarrassing —Walter Davis⟩

kind·ness \'kīn(d)-nəs\ *n* (13c) **1** : a kind deed : FAVOR **2 a** : the quality or state of being kind **b** *archaic* : AFFECTION

kind of \,kīn-də(v)\ *adv* (1775) : to a moderate degree : SOMEWHAT ⟨it's *kind of* late to begin⟩

¹kin·dred \'kin-drəd\ *n* [ME, fr. *kin* + OE *rǣden* condition, fr. *rǣdan* to advise, read] (12c) **1 a** : a group of related individuals **b** : one's relatives **2** : family relationship : KINSHIP

²kindred *adj* (14c) **1** : of a similar nature or character : LIKE **2** : of the same ancestry

kine \'kīn\ *archaic pl of* COW

kin·e·ma \'kin-ə-mə\ *Brit var of* CINEMA

ki·ne·mat·ics \,kin-ə-'mat-iks, ,kī-nə-\ *n pl but sing in constr* [F *cinématique,* fr. Gk *kinēmat-, kinēma* motion — more at CINEMATOGRAPH] (1840) : a branch of dynamics that deals with aspects of motion apart from considerations of mass and force — **ki·ne·mat·ic** \-ik\ *or* **ki·ne·mat·i·cal** \-i-kəl\ *adj* — **ki·ne·mat·i·cal·ly** \-i-k(ə-)lē\ *adv*

¹ki·ne·scope \'kin-ə-,skōp, 'kī-nə-\ *n* [fr. *Kinescope,* a trademark] (1933) **1** : PICTURE TUBE **2** : a motion picture made from an image on a picture tube

²kinescope *vt* **-scoped; -scop·ing** (1949) : to make a kinescope of

ki·ne·sics \kə-'nē-siks, kī-, -ziks\ *n pl but sing in constr* [Gk *kinēsis* + E *-ics*] (1952) : a systematic study of the relationship between nonlinguistic body motions (as blushes, shrugs, or eye movement) and communication

ki·ne·si·ol·o·gy \kə-,nē-sē-'äl-ə-jē, kī-, -zē-\ *n* [Gk *kinēsis*] (1894) : the study of the principles of mechanics and anatomy in relation to human movement

ki·ne·sis \kə-'nē-səs, kī-\ *n, pl* **ki·ne·ses** \-,sēz\ [NL, fr. Gk *kinēsis* motion] (1905) : a movement that lacks directional orientation and depends upon the intensity of stimulation

-ki·ne·sis \kə-'nē-səs, (,)kī-\ *n comb form, pl* **-ki·ne·ses** \-'nē-,sēz\ [NL, fr. Gk *kinēsis,* fr. *kinein* to move — more at HIGHT] : division ⟨karyo*kinesis*⟩

kin·es·the·sia \,kin-əs-'thē-zh(ē-)ə, ,kī-nəs-\ *or* **kin·es·the·sis** \-'thē-səs\ *n, pl* **-the·sias** *or* **-the·ses** \-,sēz\ [NL, fr. Gk *kinein* + *aisthēsis* perception — more at ANESTHESIA] (ca. 1902) : a sense mediated by end organs located in muscles, tendons, and joints and stimulated by bodily movements and tensions; *also* : sensory experience derived from this sense — **kin·es·thet·ic** \-'thet-ik\ *adj* — **kin·es·thet·i·cal·ly** \-i-k(ə-)lē\ *adv*

kinet- *or* **kineto-** *comb form* [Gk *kinētos* moving] : movement : motion ⟨*kinetogenic*⟩

ki·net·ic \kə-'net-ik, kī-\ *adj* [Gk *kinētikos,* fr. *kinētos,* fr. *kinein*] (1864) **1** : of or relating to the motion of material bodies and the forces and energy associated therewith **2 a** : ACTIVE, LIVELY **b** : DYNAMIC, ENERGIZING — **ki·net·i·cal·ly** \-i-k(ə-)lē\ *adv*

kinetic art *n* (1961) : art (as sculpture or assemblage) having mechanical parts which can be set in motion — **kinetic artist** *n*

kinetic energy *n* (1870) : energy associated with motion

ki·net·i·cist \kə-'net-ə-səst, kī-\ *n* (1960) **1** : a specialist in kinetics **2** : one who works in kinetic art : KINETIC ARTIST

kinetic potential *n* (1928) : LAGRANGIAN

ki·net·ics \kə-'net-iks, kī-\ *n pl but sing or pl in constr* (ca. 1864) **1 a** : a branch of science that deals with the effects of forces upon the motions of material bodies or with changes in a physical or chemical system **b** : the rate of change in such a system **2** : the mechanism by which a physical or chemical change is effected

kinetic theory *n* (1864) : either of two theories in physics based on the fact that the minute particles of a substance are in vigorous motion: **a** : a theory that the particles of a gas move in straight lines with high average velocity, continually encounter one another and thus change their individual velocities and directions, and cause pressure by their impact against the walls of a container — called also *kinetic theory of gases* **b** : a theory that the temperature of a substance increases with an increase in either the average kinetic energy of the particles or the average potential energy of separation (as in fusion) of the particles or in both when heat is added — called also *kinetic theory of heat*

ki·ne·tin \'kī-nə-tən\ *n* (1955) : a cytokinin $C_{10}H_9N_5O$ that increases mitosis and callus formation

ki·net·o·chore \kə-'net-ə-,kō(ə)r, kī-, -,kȯ(ə)r\ *n* [*kinet-* + Gk *chōros* place] (1934) : CENTROMERE

ki·neto·plast \kə-'net-ə-,plast, kī-\ *n* [ISV] (1925) : an extranuclear cell organelle esp. of trypanosomes that contains DNA and has some mitochondrial characteristics — **ki·neto·plas·tic** \-,net-ə-'plas-tik\ *adj*

ki·neto·scope \kə-'net-ə-,skōp, kī-\ *n* [fr. *Kinetoscope,* a trademark] (1894) : a device for viewing through a magnifying lens a sequence of pictures on an endless band of film moved continuously over a light source and a rapidly rotating shutter that creates an illusion of motion

ki·neto·some \-,sōm\ *n* (1912) : BASAL BODY

kin·folk \'kin-,fōk\ *or* **kinfolks** *n pl* (1873) : RELATIVES

king \'kiŋ\ *n* [ME, fr. OE *cyning;* akin to OHG *kuning* king, OE *cyn* kin] (bef. 12c) **1 a** : a male monarch of a major territorial unit; *esp* : one whose position is hereditary and who rules for life **b** : a paramount chief **2** *cap* : GOD, CHRIST **3** : one that holds a preeminent position; *esp* : a chief among competitors **4** : the principal piece of each color in a set of chessmen having the power to move ordinarily one square in any direction and to capture opposing men but being obliged never to enter or remain in check **5** : a playing card that is marked with a stylized figure of a king **6** : a checker that has been crowned

king·bird \-,bərd\ *n* (1778) : any of various American tyrant flycatchers (genus *Tyrannus*)

king·bolt \-,bōlt\ *n* (1825) : a vertical bolt by which the forward axle and wheels of a vehicle or the trucks of a railroad car are connected with the other parts

king cobra *n* (1894) : a large venomous elapid snake (*Naja hannah*) of southeastern Asia and the Philippines — called also *hamadryad*

king crab *n* (1698) **1** : HORSESHOE CRAB **2** : any of several very large crabs

king·craft \'kiŋ-,kraft\ *n* (1643) : the art of governing as a king

king·cup \-,kəp\ *n* (1538) : any of various buttercups

king·dom \'kiŋ-dəm\ *n* [ME, fr. OE *cyningdōm,* fr. *cyning* king + *-dōm* -dom] (bef. 12c) **1** *archaic* : KINGSHIP **2** : a politically organized community or major territorial unit having a monarchical form of government headed by a king or queen **3** *often cap* **a** : the eternal kingship of God **b** : the realm in which God's will is fulfilled **4 a** : a realm or region in which something is dominant **b** : an area or sphere in which one holds a preeminent position **5** : one of the three primary divisions into which natural objects are commonly classified — compare ANIMAL KINGDOM, MINERAL KINGDOM, PLANT KINGDOM

kingdom come *n* [fr. the expression "Thy *kingdom come*" —Mt 6:10] (1785) : the next world : HEAVEN

king·fish \'kiŋ-,fish\ *n* (1750) **1 a** : any of several marine croakers (family Sciaenidae and esp. genus *Menticirrhus*) **b** : any of various scombroid fishes; *esp* : CERO **c** : any of various marine percoid fishes (as of the family Carangidae) **2** : an undisputed master in an area or group

king·fish·er \-,fish-ər\ *n* (15c) : any of numerous nonpasserine birds (family Alcedinidae) that are usu. crested and bright-colored with a short tail and a long stout sharp bill

King James Version \kiŋ-'jāmz-\ *n* [*James* I of England] (1835) : AUTHORIZED VERSION

king·let \'kiŋ-lət\ *n* (1603) **1** : a weak or petty king **2** : any of several small birds (genus *Regulus*) that resemble warblers but have some of the habits of titmice

king·ly \'kiŋ-lē\ *adj* **king·li·er; -est** (14c) **1** : having royal rank **2** : of, relating to, or befitting a king **3** : MONARCHICAL — **king·li·ness** *n* — **kingly** *adv*

king mackerel *n* (ca. 1930) : a cero (*Scomberomorus cavalla*) that is noted esp. as a fighting sport fish

king·mak·er \'kiŋ-,mā-kər\ *n* (1599) : one having great influence over the choice of candidates for political office

king of arms (15c) : an officer of arms of the highest rank

king·pin \'kiŋ-,pin\ *n* (1801) **1** : any of several bowling pins: as **a** : HEADPIN **b** : the number 5 pin **2** : the chief person in a group or undertaking **3 a** : KINGBOLT **b** : a pin connecting the two parts of a knuckle joint

king post *n* (1776) : a vertical member connecting the apex of a triangular truss (as of a roof) with the base

Kings \'kiŋz\ *n pl but sing in constr* **1** : either of two narrative and historical books of canonical Jewish and Protestant Scripture — see BIBLE table **2** : any of four narrative and historical books in the Roman Catholic canon of the Old Testament — see BIBLE table

king salmon *n* (1881) : CHINOOK SALMON

King's Bench *n* (14c) : a division in the English superior courts system that hears civil and criminal cases

King's Counsel *n* (ca. 1901) : a barrister selected to serve as counsel to the British crown

King's English *n* (1553) : standard, pure, or correct English speech or usage

king's evil *n, often cap K&E* [fr. the former belief that it could be healed by a king's touch] (14c) : SCROFULA

king·ship \'kiŋ-,ship\ *n* (14c) **1** : the position, office, or dignity of a king **2** : the personality of a king : MAJESTY **3** : government by a king

king·side \-,sīd\ *n* (1941) : the side of a chessboard containing the file on which the king sits at the beginning of the game

king–size \-,sīz\ *or* **king–sized** \-,sīzd\ *adj* (1825) **1** : longer than the regular or standard size ⟨a ~ cigarette⟩ **2** : unusually large **3 a** : having dimensions of approximately 76 inches by 80 inches — used of a bed; compare FULL-SIZE, QUEEN-SIZE, TWIN-SIZE **b** : of a size that fits a king-size bed ⟨~ sheets⟩

king snake *n* (1709) : any of numerous brightly marked colubrid snakes (genus *Lampropeltis*) of the southern and central U.S. that are voracious consumers of rodents

king's yellow *n* (1790) : arsenic trisulfide used as a pigment

ki·nin \'kī-nən\ *n* [Gk *kinein* to move, stimulate + E *-in* — more at HIGHT] (1954) **1** : any of various polypeptide hormones that are formed locally in the tissues and have their chief effect on smooth muscle **2** : CYTOKININ kink • kiwi 663

[1]kink \ˈkiŋk\ *n* [D; akin to MLG *kinke* kink] (1678) **1 :** a short tight twist or curl caused by a doubling or winding of something upon itself **2 a :** a mental or physical peculiarity : ECCENTRICITY, QUIRK **b :** WHIM **3 :** a clever unusual way of doing something **4 :** a cramp in some part of the body **5 :** an imperfection likely to cause difficulties in the operation of something

[2]kink *vi* (1697) **:** to form a kink ~ *vt* **:** to make a kink in

kin·ka·jou \ˈkiŋ-kə-ˌjü\ *n* [F, of Algonquian origin; akin to Ojibwa *qwīngwâage* wolverine] (1796) **:** a slender nocturnal arboreal carnivorous mammal (*Potos flavus*, family Procyonidae) of Mexico and Central and So. America that is about three feet long and has a long prehensile tail, large lustrous eyes, and soft woolly yellowish brown fur

kinky \ˈkiŋ-kē\ *adj* **kink·i·er; -est** (1844) **1 :** closely twisted or curled ⟨~ hair⟩ **2 :** relating to, having, or appealing to bizarre or unconventional tastes esp. in sex; *also* **:** sexually deviant **3 :** OUTLANDISH, FAR-OUT — **kink·i·ly** \ˈkiŋ-kə-lē\ *adv* — **kink·i·ness** \ˈkiŋ-kē-nəs\ *n*

kin·ni·kin·nick \ˌkin-i-kə-ˈnik, ˈkin-i-kə-ˌ\ *n* [of Algonquian origin; akin to Natick *kinukkinuk* mixture] (1799) **:** a mixture of dried leaves and bark and sometimes tobacco smoked by the Indians and pioneers esp. in the Ohio valley; *also* **:** a plant (as a sumac or dogwood) used in it

-kins — see -KIN

kins·folk \ˈkinz-ˌfōk\ *n pl* (15c) **:** RELATIVES

kin·ship \ˈkin-ˌship\ *n* (1833) **:** the quality or state of being kin : RELATIONSHIP

kins·man \ˈkinz-mən\ *n* (bef. 12c) **:** RELATIVE; *specif* **:** a male relative

kins·wom·an \-ˌwu̇m-ən\ *n* (14c) **:** a female relative

ki·osk \ˈkē-ˌäsk, kē-ˈ\ *n* [Turk *köşk*, fr. Per *kūshk* portico] (1625) **1 :** an open summerhouse or pavilion **2 :** a small light structure with one or more open sides used esp. as a newsstand or a telephone booth

Ki·o·wa \ˈkī-ə-ˌwȯ, -ˌwä, -ˌwā\ *n, pl* **Kiowa** *or* **Kiowas** (1808) **1 :** a member of an American Indian people of what are now Colorado, Kansas, New Mexico, Oklahoma, and Texas **2 :** the language of the Kiowa people

[1]kip \ˈkip\ *n* [obs. D; akin to MLG *kip* bundle of hides] (1525) **:** a bundle of undressed hides of young or small animals; *also* **:** one of the hides

[2]kip *n* [perh. fr. Dan *kippe* cheap tavern] (ca. 1879) **1 :** BED ⟨ready for the ~ after this screwball day —K. M. Dodson⟩ **2** *chiefly Brit* **:** SLEEP, NAP ⟨roused the indignant family from their ~ —Sylvia Margolis⟩

[3]kip *vi* **kipped; kip·ping** *Brit* (ca. 1889) **:** SLEEP — sometimes used with *down* ⟨~ down on a spare bed —Alice Glenday⟩

[4]kip *n* [*kilo-* + *pound*] (1914) **:** a unit of weight equal to 1000 pounds used to express deadweight load

[5]kip \ˈkip, ˈgip\ *n, pl* **kip** *or* **kips** [Thai] (1955) — see MONEY table

[1]kip·per \ˈkip-ər\ *n* [ME *kypre*, fr. OE *cypera*; akin to OE *coper* copper] (bef. 12c) **1 :** a male salmon or sea trout during or after the spawning season **2 :** a kippered herring or salmon

[2]kipper *vt* **kip·pered; kip·per·ing** \-(ə-)riŋ\ (1773) **:** to cure (split dressed fish) by salting and smoking — **kip·per·er** \-ər-ər\ *n*

Kir·ghiz \ki(ə)r-ˈgēz\ *n, pl* **Kirghiz** *or* **Kir·ghiz·es** [Kirghiz *Kyrghyz*] (1600) **1 :** a member of a people of Mongolian ancestry prob. with some Caucasian intermixture who inhabit chiefly the Central Asian steppes **2 :** the Turkic language of the Kirghiz

kirk \ˈki(ə)rk, ˈkərk\ *n* [ME (northern dial.), fr. ON *kirkja*, fr. OE *cirice* — more at CHURCH] (12c) **1** *chiefly Scot* **:** CHURCH **2** *cap* **:** the national church of Scotland as distinguished from the Church of England or the Episcopal Church in Scotland

Kir·li·an photography \ˌki(ə)r-lē-ən-\ *n* [Semyon D. & Valentina K. *Kirlian* *fl*1939 Soviet inventors] (1972) **:** a process in which an image is obtained by application of a high-frequency electrical field to an object so that it radiates a characteristic pattern of luminescence that is recorded on photographic film

Kir·man \kər-ˈmän, ki(ə)r-\ *n* [*Kirman*, province in Iran] (1876) **:** a Persian carpet or rug characterized by elaborate fluid designs and soft colors

kir·mess \ˈkər-məs, (ˌ)kər-ˈmes\ *var of* KERMIS

kirsch \ˈki(ə)rsh\ *n* [G, short for *kirschwasser*, fr. *kirsche* cherry + *wasser* water] (1869) **:** a dry colorless brandy distilled from the fermented juice of the black morello cherry

Kirt·land's warbler \ˌkərt-lən(d)z-\ *n* [Jared P. *Kirtland* †1877 Am. naturalist] (1858) **:** a rare warbler (*Dendroica kirtlandii*) of northeastern No. America that breeds in Michigan and winters in the Bahamas

kir·tle \ˈkərt-ᵊl\ *n* [ME *kirtel*, fr. OE *cyrtel*, fr. (assumed) OE *curt* short, fr. L *curtus* shortened — more at SHEAR] (bef. 12c) **1 :** a tunic or coat worn by men esp. in the Middle Ages **2 :** a long gown or dress worn by women

kish·ke *also* **kish·ka** \ˈkish-kə\ *n* [Yiddish *kishke* gut, sausage, of Slavic origin; akin to Pol *kiszka* gut, sausage] (ca. 1936) **:** beef or fowl casing stuffed (as with meat, flour, and spices) and cooked

Kis·lev \ˈkis-ləf\ *n* [Heb *Kislēw*] (14c) **:** the 3d month of the civil year or the 9th month of the ecclesiastical year in the Jewish calendar — see MONTH table

kis·met \ˈkiz-ˌmet, -mət\ *n, often cap* [Turk, fr. Ar *qismah* portion, lot] (1849) **:** FATE 1, 2a

[1]kiss \ˈkis\ *vb* [ME *kissen*, fr. OE *cyssan*; akin to OHG *kussen* to kiss] *vt* (bef. 12c) **1 :** to touch with the lips esp. as a mark of affection or greeting **2 :** to touch gently or lightly ⟨wind gently ~*ing* the trees⟩ ~ *vi* **1 :** to salute or caress one another with the lips **2 :** to come in gentle contact — **kiss·able** \-ə-bəl\ *adj* — **kiss ass :** to act obsequiously esp. to gain favor — usu. considered vulgar — **kiss good–bye 1 :** LEAVE **2 :** to resign oneself to the loss of

[2]kiss *n* (bef. 12c) **1 :** a caress with the lips **2 :** a gentle touch or contact **3 a :** a small drop cookie made of meringue **b :** a bite-size piece of candy often wrapped in paper or foil **4 :** an expression of affection ⟨sent him ~*es* in her letter⟩

kiss·er \ˈkis-ər\ *n* (1537) **1 :** one that kisses **2** *slang* **a :** MOUTH **b :** FACE

kissing bug *n* (1899) **:** CONENOSE

kissing cousin *n* (1941) **1 :** a person and esp. a relative whom one knows well enough to kiss more or less formally upon meeting **2 :** one that is closely related in kind to something else

kissing disease *n* [fr. the belief that it is frequently transmitted by kissing] (1962) **:** INFECTIOUS MONONUCLEOSIS

kiss of death [fr. the kiss with which Judas betrayed Jesus in Mk 14:44-46] (1943) **:** something (as an act or association) ultimately causing ruin

kiss off *vt* (1935) **:** to dismiss lightly ⟨*kisses* the other performers *off* as mere amateurs⟩

kiss of life *chiefly Brit* (1961) **:** artificial respiration by the mouth-to-mouth method

kiss of peace (1898) **:** a ceremonial kiss, embrace, or handclasp used in Christian liturgies and esp. the Eucharist as a sign of fraternal unity

kist \ˈkist\ *n* [ME *kiste*, fr. ON *kista* — more at CHEST] *chiefly Scot & So Afr* (12c) **:** CHEST

[1]kit \ˈkit\ *n* [ME] (14c) **1** *dial Brit* **:** a wooden tub **2 a (1) :** a collection of articles usu. for personal use ⟨a travel ~⟩ **(2) :** a set of tools or implements ⟨a carpenter's ~⟩ **(3) :** a set of parts to be assembled or worked up ⟨model-airplane ~⟩ ⟨needlecraft ~⟩ **(4) :** a packaged collection of related material ⟨convention ~⟩ **(5)** *chiefly Brit* **:** GEAR ⟨run over to my billet and get some overnight ~ —Lionel Shapiro⟩ **b :** a container for any of such sets or collections **3 :** a group of persons or things — usu. used in the phrase *the whole kit and caboodle*

[2]kit *vt* **kitted; kit·ting** *chiefly Brit* (1919) **:** EQUIP, OUTFIT — often used with *up* or *out*

[3]kit *n* [origin unknown] (1519) **:** a small narrow violin

[4]kit *n* (1562) **1 :** KITTEN **2 :** a young or undersized fur-bearing animal; *also* **:** its pelt

kit bag *n* [[1]*kit*] (1893) **1 :** KNAPSACK **2 :** a traveling bag with sides that fasten at the top or open to the full width of the bag

kitch·en \ˈkich-ən\ *n* [ME *kichene*, fr. OE *cycene*, fr. LL *coquina*, fr. L *coquere* to cook — more at COOK] (bef. 12c) **1 :** a place (as a room) with cooking facilities **2 :** the personnel that prepares, cooks, and serves food **3 :** CUISINE

kitchen cabinet *n* (1832) **1 :** an informal group of advisers to one in a position of power (as the head of a government) **2 :** a cupboard with drawers and shelves for use in a kitchen

kitch·en·ette \ˌkich-ə-ˈnet\ *n* (1903) **:** a small kitchen or an alcove containing cooking facilities

kitchen garden *n* (1580) **:** a garden in which plants (as vegetables or herbs) for use in the kitchen are cultivated

kitchen midden *n* (1863) **:** a refuse heap; *specif* **:** a mound marking the site of a primitive human habitation

kitchen police *n* (1917) **1 :** KP **2 :** the work of KPs

kitch·en–sink \-ˈsiŋk\ *adj, chiefly Brit* (1941) **:** portraying or emphasizing the squalid aspects of modern life ⟨the ~ realism of contemporary British drama —*Current Biog.*⟩

kitch·en·ware \ˈkich-ən-ˌwa(ə)r, -ˌwe(ə)r\ *n* (1722) **:** utensils and appliances for use in a kitchen

[1]kite \ˈkīt\ *n* [ME, fr. OE *cȳta*; akin to MHG *kūze* owl, Gk *goan* to lament] (bef. 12c) **1 :** any of various hawks (family Accipitridae) with long narrow wings, a deeply forked tail, and feet adapted for taking insects and small reptiles as prey **2 :** a person who preys on others **3 :** a light frame covered usu. with paper or cloth, often provided with a balancing tail, and designed to be flown in the air at the end of a long string **4 :** a check drawn against uncollected funds in a bank account or fraudulently raised before cashing **5 :** a light sail used in a light breeze usu. in addition to the regular working sails; *esp* **:** SPINNAKER — **kite·like** *adj*

[2]kite *vb* **kit·ed; kit·ing** *vt* (1839) **1 :** to use (a bad check) to get credit or money **2 :** to cause to soar ⟨*kited* the prices they charged wealthy clients⟩ ~ *vi* **1 a :** to go in a rapid, carefree, or flighty manner **b :** to rise rapidly **:** SOAR ⟨the prices of necessities continue to ~⟩ **2 :** to get money or credit by a kite

kit fox *n* [[4]*kit*] (1805) **1 a :** a small fox (*Vulpes velox*) of the plains of western No. America **b :** a fox (*Vulpes macrotis*) of the southwestern U.S. and Mexico **2 :** the fur or pelt of a kit fox

kith \ˈkith\ *n* [ME, fr. OE *cȳthth*; akin to *cūth* known — more at UNCOUTH] (bef. 12c) **:** familiar friends, neighbors, or relatives ⟨~ and kin⟩

kith·a·ra \ˈkith-ə-rə\ *n* [Gk] (14c) **:** an ancient Greek stringed instrument similar to but larger than the lyre and having a box-shaped resonator

kithe \ˈkīth\ *vb* **kithed; kith·ing** [ME *kithen*, fr. OE *cȳthan*, fr. *cūth*] *vt, chiefly Scot* (bef. 12c) **:** to make known ~ *vi, chiefly Scot* **:** to become known

kitsch \ˈkich\ *n* [G, kitsch, trash] (1925) **:** something that appeals to popular or low-brow taste and is often of poor quality — **kitschy** \-ē\ *adj*

[1]kit·ten \ˈkit-ᵊn\ *n* [ME *kitoun*, fr. (assumed) ONF *caton*, dim. of *cat*, fr. LL *cattus*] (14c) **:** a young cat; *also* **:** an immature individual of various other small mammals

[2]kitten *vi* **kit·tened; kit·ten·ing** \ˈkit-niŋ, -ᵊn-iŋ\ (15c) **:** to give birth to kittens

kit·ten·ish \ˈkit-nish, -ᵊn-ish\ *adj* (1754) **:** resembling a kitten; *esp* **:** coyly playful — **kit·ten·ish·ly** *adv* — **kit·ten·ish·ness** *n*

kit·ti·wake \ˈkit-ē-ˌwāk\ *n* [imit.] (1661) **:** any of various gulls (genus *Rissa*) having the hind toe short or rudimentary

[1]kit·tle \ˈkit-ᵊl\ *vt* **kit·tled; kit·tling** \ˈkit-liŋ, -ᵊl-iŋ\ [ME (northern dial.) *kytyllen*] (15c) **1** *chiefly Scot* **:** TICKLE **2** *chiefly Scot* **:** PERPLEX

[2]kittle *adj, chiefly Scot* (1568) **:** TICKLISH, TOUCHY

[1]kit·ty \ˈkit-ē\ *n, pl* **kitties** (1719) **:** CAT 1a; *esp* **:** KITTEN

[2]kitty *n, pl* **kitties** [[1]*kit*] (1887) **1 :** a fund in a poker game made up of contributions from each pot **2 :** a sum of money or collection of goods often made up of small contributions **:** POOL

kit·ty–cor·ner *or* **kit·ty–cor·nered** *var of* CATERCORNER

ki·va \ˈkē-və\ *n* [Hopi] (1871) **:** a Pueblo Indian ceremonial structure that is usu. round and partly underground

Ki·wa·ni·an \kə-ˈwän-ē-ən\ *n* [*Kiwanis (club)*] (1921) **:** a member of a major national and international service club

ki·wi \ˈkē-(ˌ)wē\ *n* [Maori] (1835) **1 :** a flightless New Zealand bird (genus *Apteryx*) with rudimentary wings, stout legs, a long bill, and grayish brown hairlike plumage 2 *cap* : a native or resident of New Zealand — used as a nickname

kiwi 1

ki·wi·fruit \-ˌfrüt\ *n* [*kiwi,* nickname for New Zealanders, fr. the fact that it was first established as a commercial crop in New Zealand] (1966) : the fruit of a Chinese gooseberry — called also *kiwi*

Klam·ath weed \ˈklam-əth-\ *n* [*Klamath (river)*] (1922) : a cosmopolitan yellow-flowered perennial Saint-John's-wort (*Hypericum perforatum*) that is often a noxious weed esp. in rangelands

Klan \ˈklan\ *n* [(*Ku Klux*) *Klan*] (1867) : an organization of Ku Kluxers; *also* : a subordinate unit of such an organization — **Klan·ism** \-ˌiz-əm\ *n* — **Klans·man** \ˈklanz-mən\ *n*

klatch *or* **klatsch** \ˈklach, ˈkläch\ *n* [G *klatsch* gossip] (1941) : a gathering characterized usu. by informal conversation

klav·ern \ˈklav-ərn\ *n, often cap* [blend of *klan* & *cavern*] (ca. 1924) : a local unit of the Klan

Klax·on \ˈklak-sən\ *trademark* — used for an electrically operated horn or warning signal

kleb·si·el·la \ˌkleb-zē-ˈel-ə\ *n* [NL, fr. Edwin *Klebs* †1913 Ger. pathologist] (ca. 1925) : any of a genus (*Klebsiella*) of plump nonmotile gram-negative frequently encapsulated bacterial rods

Klee·nex \ˈklē-ˌneks\ *trademark* — used for a cleansing tissue

Klein bottle \ˈklīn-\ *n* [Felix *Klein* †1925 Ger. mathematician] (1941) : a one-sided surface that is formed by passing the narrow end of a tapered tube through the side of the tube and flaring this end out to join the other end

klepht \ˈkleft\ *n, often cap* [NGk *klephtēs,* lit., robber, fr. Gk *kleptēs,* fr. *kleptein*] (1820) : a Greek belonging to any of several independent guerrilla communities formed after the Turkish conquest of Greece — **kleph·tic** \ˈklef-tik\ *adj, often cap*

klept- *or* **klepto-** *comb form* [Gk, fr. *kleptein* to steal; akin to Goth *hlifan* to steal, L *clepere*] : stealing : theft ⟨*kleptomania*⟩

klep·to·ma·nia \ˌklep-tə-ˈmā-nē-ə, -nyə\ *n* [NL] (1830) : a persistent neurotic impulse to steal esp. without economic motive

klep·to·ma·ni·ac \-nē-ˌak\ *n* (1861) : a person evidencing kleptomania

klieg light *or* **kleig light** \ˈklēg-\ *n* [John H. *Kliegl* †1959 & Anton T. *Kliegl* †1927 German-born Am. lighting experts] (1919) : a carbon arc lamp used in taking motion pictures

Kline·fel·ter's syndrome \ˈklīn-ˌfel-tərz-\ *n* [Harry F. *Klinefelter* b1912 Am. physician] (1950) : an abnormal condition in a male characterized by two X and one Y chromosomes, infertility, and smallness of the testicles

klis·ter \ˈklis-tər\ *n* [Norw, lit., paste, fr. MLG *klīster;* akin to OE *clǣg* clay — more at CLAY] (1936) : a soft wax used on skis

kloof \ˈklüf\ *n* [Afrik] *So Afr* (1731) : a deep glen : RAVINE

kludge \ˈklüj\ *or* **kluge** \ˈklüj, ˈklü-jē\ *n* [origin unknown] (1962) : a system and esp. a computer system made up of poorly matched components

klutz \ˈkləts\ *n* [Yiddish *klotz, klutz,* fr. G *klotz,* lit., wooden block, fr. MHG *kloz* lumpy mass — more at CLOUT] (1960) : a clumsy person — **klutz·i·ness** \ˈklət-sē-nəs\ *n* — **klutzy** \-ē\ *adj*

kly·stron \ˈklī-ˌsträn\ *n* [fr. *Klystron,* a trademark] (1939) : an electron tube in which bunching of electrons is produced by electric fields and which is used for the generation and amplification of ultrahigh-frequency current

K–meson \ˈkā-ˈmez-ˌän, -ˈmes-; -ˈmā-ˌzän, -ˈmē-, -ˌsän\ *n* (1951) : KAON

knack \ˈnak\ *n* [ME *knak*] (14c) **1 a** : a clever trick or stratagem **b** : a clever way of doing something **2** : a special ready capacity that is hard to analyze or teach **3** *archaic* : an ingenious device; *broadly* : TOY, KNICKKNACK ***syn*** see GIFT

knack·er \ˈnak-ər\ *n* [prob. fr. E dial., saddlemaker] (1812) **1** *Brit* : a buyer of worn-out domestic animals or their carcasses for use esp. as animal food or fertilizer **2** *Brit* : a buyer of old structures for their constituent materials

knack·wurst *var of* KNOCKWURST

[1]**knap** \ˈnap\ *n* [ME, fr. OE *cnæp;* akin to OE *cnotta* knot] (bef. 12c) **1** *chiefly dial* : a crest of a hill : SUMMIT **2** *chiefly dial* : a small hill

[2]**knap** *vt* **knapped; knap·ping** [ME *knappen,* of imit. origin] (15c) **1** *dial Brit* : [2]RAP **2** : to break with a quick blow; *esp* : to shape (as flints) by breaking off pieces **3** *dial Brit* : SNAP, CROP **4** *dial Brit* : CHATTER — **knap·per** *n*

knap·sack \ˈnap-ˌsak\ *n* [LG *knappsack* or D *knapzak,* fr. LG & D *knappen* to make a snapping noise, eat + LG *sack* or D *zak* sack] (1603) : a bag (as of canvas or nylon) strapped on the back and used (as on a hike) for carrying supplies or personal belongings

knap·weed \-ˌwēd\ *n* [ME *knopwed,* fr. *knop* knop + *wed* weed] (15c) : any of various weedy centaureas; *esp* : a widely naturalized European perennial (*C. nigra*) with tough wiry stems and knobby heads of purple flowers

knave \ˈnāv\ *n* [ME, fr. OE *cnafa;* akin to OHG *knabo* boy] (bef. 12c) **1** *archaic* **a** : a boy servant **b** : a male servant **c** : a man of humble birth or position **2** : a tricky deceitful fellow **3** : JACK 6a

knav·ery \ˈnāv-(ə-)rē\ *n, pl* **-er·ies** (1528) **1 a** : RASCALITY **b** : a roguish or mischievous act **2** *obs* : roguish mischief

knav·ish \ˈnā-vish\ *adj* (14c) : of, relating to, or characteristic of a knave; *esp* : DISHONEST — **knav·ish·ly** *adv*

knead \ˈnēd\ *vt* [ME *kneden,* fr. OE *cnedan;* akin to OHG *knetan* to knead, OE *cnotta* knot] (bef. 12c) **1** : to work and press into a mass with or as if with the hands ⟨~*ing* dough⟩ **2** : to form or shape by or as if by kneading — **knead·able** \-ə-bəl\ *adj* — **knead·er** *n*

[1]**knee** \ˈnē\ *n, often attrib* [ME, fr. OE *cnēow;* akin to OHG *kneo* knee, L *genu,* Gk *gony*] (bef. 12c) **1 a** : a joint in the middle part of the human leg that is the articulation between the femur, tibia, and patella; *also* : the part of the leg that includes this joint **b** (1) : the joint in the hind leg of a four-footed vertebrate that corresponds to the human knee (2) : the carpal joint of the foreleg of a four-footed vertebrate **c** : the tarsal joint of a bird **d** : the joint between the femur and tibia of an insect **2 a** : something resembling the human knee **b** : a rounded or conical process rising from the roots of various swamp-growing trees ⟨cypress ~⟩ **3** : the part of a garment covering the knee **4** : a blow with the bent knee — **kneed** \ˈnēd\ *adj* — **to one's knees** : into a state of submission or defeat

[2]**knee** *vt* **kneed; knee·ing** (bef. 12c) **1** *archaic* : to bend the knee to **2** : to strike with the knee

knee action *n* (ca. 1934) : a front-wheel suspension of an automobile permitting independent vertical movement of each front wheel

knee·cap \ˈnē-ˌkap\ *n* (1869) : PATELLA

knee–deep \-ˈdēp\ *adj* (15c) **1** : KNEE-HIGH **2 a** : sunk to the knees ⟨~ in mud⟩ **b** : deeply engaged or occupied ⟨~ in work⟩

knee–high \-ˈhī\ *adj* (1743) : rising or reaching upward to the knees

knee·hole \-ˌhōl\ *n* (1895) : an open space (as under a desk) for the knees

knee–jerk \ˈnē-ˌjərk, -ˈjərk\ *adj* (1951) : readily predictable : AUTOMATIC ⟨~ reactions⟩; *also* : reacting in a readily predictable way ⟨~ liberals⟩

knee jerk *n* (1876) : an involuntary forward kick produced by a light blow on the tendon below the patella

kneel \ˈnē(ə)l\ *vi* **knelt** \ˈnelt\ *or* **kneeled; kneel·ing** [ME *knelen,* fr. OE *cnēowlian;* akin to OE *cnēow* knee] (bef. 12c) : to bend the knee : fall or rest on the knees — **kneel·er** *n*

knee·pan \ˈnē-ˌpan\ *n* (15c) : PATELLA

[1]**knell** \ˈnel\ *vb* [ME *knellen,* fr. OE *cnyllan;* akin to MHG *erknellen* to toll] *vi* (bef. 12c) **1** : to ring esp. for a death, funeral, or disaster : TOLL **2** : to sound in an ominous manner or with an ominous effect ~ *vt* : to summon or announce by or as if by a knell

[2]**knell** *n* (bef. 12c) **1** : a stroke or sound of a bell esp. when rung slowly (as for a death, funeral, or disaster) **2** : an indication of the end or the failure of something ⟨this decision sounded the death ~ for our hopes⟩

knew *past of* KNOW

knick·er·bock·er \ˈnik-ə(r)-ˌbäk-ər\ *n* [Diedrich *Knickerbocker,* fictitious author of *History of New York* (1809) by Washington Irving] (1848) **1** *cap* : a descendant of the early Dutch settlers of New York; *broadly* : a native or resident of the city or state of New York — used as a nickname **2** *pl* : KNICKERS

knick·ers \ˈnik-ərz\ *n pl* [short for *knickerbockers*] (1881) : loose-fitting short pants gathered at the knee

knick·knack \ˈnik-ˌnak\ *n* [redupl. of *knack*] (1682) : a small trivial article intended for ornament

[1]**knife** \ˈnīf\ *n, pl* **knives** \ˈnīvz\ *often attrib* [ME *knif,* fr. OE *cnīf,* perh. fr. ON *knīfr;* akin to MLG *knīf* knife] (12c) **1 a** : a cutting instrument consisting of a sharp blade fastened to a handle **b** : a weapon resembling a knife **2** : a sharp cutting blade or tool in a machine — **knife·like** \ˈnī-ˌflīk\ *adj* — **under the knife** : undergoing surgery ⟨was *under the knife* for three hours⟩

[2]**knife** *vb* **knifed; knif·ing** *vt* (1865) **1** : to use a knife on; *specif* : to stab, slash, or wound with a knife **2** : to cut, mark, or spread with a knife **3** : to try to defeat by underhanded means **4** : to move like a knife in ⟨birds *knifing* the autumn sky⟩ ~ *vi* : to cut a way with or as if with a knife blade ⟨the cruiser *knifed* through the heavy seas⟩

knife–edge \ˈnī-ˌfej\ *n* (1818) **1** : a sharp wedge of steel or other hard material used as a fulcrum for a lever beam in a precision instrument **2** : a sharp narrow knifelike edge

[1]**knight** \ˈnīt\ *n* [ME, fr. OE *cniht* boy, servant; akin to OHG *kneht* youth, military follower] (12c) **1 a** (1) : a mounted man-at-arms serving a feudal superior; *esp* : a man ceremonially inducted into special military rank usu. after completing service as page and squire (2) : a man honored by a sovereign for merit and in Great Britain ranking below a baronet (3) : a person of antiquity equal to a knight in rank **b** : a man devoted to the service of a lady as her attendant and champion **c** : a member of an order or society **2** : either of two pieces of the same color in a set of chessmen having an L-shaped move of two squares in one row and one square in a perpendicular row over squares that may be occupied

[2]**knight** *vt* (13c) : to make a knight of

knight–er·rant \ˈnīt-ˈer-ənt\ *n, pl* **knights–errant** (14c) : a knight traveling in search of adventures in which to exhibit military skill, prowess, and generosity

knight–er·rant·ry \ˈnīt-ˈer-ən-trē\ *n, pl* **knight–errantries** (1654) **1** : the practice or actions of a knight-errant **2** : quixotic conduct

knight·hood \ˈnīt-ˌhu̇d\ *n* (13c) **1** : the rank, dignity, or profession of a knight **2** : the qualities befitting a knight : CHIVALRY **3** : knights as a class or body

knight·ly \ˈnīt-lē\ *adj* (14c) **1** : of, relating to, or characteristic of a knight **2** : made up of knights — **knight·li·ness** *n* — **knightly** *adv*

Knight of Co·lum·bus \-kə-ˈləm-bəs\ *n, pl* **Knights of Columbus** [Christopher *Columbus*] (1882) : a member of a benevolent and fraternal society of Roman Catholic men

Knight of Pyth·i·as \-ˈpith-ē-əs\ *n, pl* **Knights of Pythias** (1864) : a member of a secret benevolent and fraternal order

Knight of the Mac·ca·bees \-ˈmak-ə-ˌbēz\ *n, pl* **Knights of the Maccabees** (1876) : a member of a secret benevolent society

Knight Templar *n, pl* **Knights Templars** *or* **Knights Templar** (1610) **1** : TEMPLAR 1 **2** : a member of an order of Freemasonry conferring three degrees in the York rite

knish \kə-ˈnish\ *n* [Yiddish, fr. Russ] (1916) : a small round or square of dough stuffed with a filling and baked or fried

[1]**knit** \ˈnit\ *vb* **knit** *or* **knit·ted; knit·ting** [ME *knitten,* fr. OE *cnyttan;* akin to OE *cnotta* knot] *vt* (bef. 12c) **1** *chiefly dial* : to tie together **2 a** : to link firmly or closely ⟨*knitted* my hands⟩ **b** : to cause to grow together ⟨time and rest will ~ a fractured bone⟩ **c** : to contract into wrinkles ⟨*knitted* her brow in thought⟩ **3** : to form by interlacing yarn or thread in a series of connected loops with needles ~ *vi* **1** : to make knitted fabrics or objects **2 a** : to become compact **b** : to grow together **c** : to become drawn together — **knit·ter** *n*

[2]**knit** *n* (1596) : KNIT STITCH; *also* : a knit fabric

knit stitch *n* (ca. 1885) : a basic knitting stitch usu. made with the yarn at the back of the work by inserting the right needle into the front part of a loop on the left needle from the left side, catching the yarn with the point of the right needle, and bringing it through the first loop to form a new loop — compare PURL STITCH

knit·ting *n* (15c) **1** : the action or method of one that knits **2** : work done or being done by one that knits

knit·wear \ˈnit-ˌwa(ə)r, -ˌwe(ə)r\ *n* (1925) : knitted clothing

knob \'näb\ n [ME knobbe; akin to MLG knubbe knob, OE -cnoppa — more at KNOT] (bef. 12c) **1 a :** a rounded protuberance : LUMP **b :** a small rounded ornament or handle **2 :** a rounded usu. isolated hill or mountain — **knobbed** \'näbd\ adj — **knob·by** \'näb-ē\ adj
knob·bly \'näb-(ə)-lē\ adj (ca. 1854) : having very small knobs ⟨a ~ mattress⟩
knob·ker·rie \'näb-,ker-ē\ n [Afrik knopkierie, fr. knop knob + kierie club] (1844) : a short wooden club with a knob at one end used as a missile or in close attack esp. by Zulus of southern Africa
1knock \'näk\ vb [ME knoken, fr. OE cnocian; akin to MHG knochen to press] vi (bef. 12c) **1 :** to strike something with a sharp blow **2 :** to collide with something **3 a :** BUSTLE ⟨heard them ~ing around in the kitchen⟩ **b :** WANDER ⟨~ed about Europe all summer⟩ **4 a :** to make a pounding noise **b :** to have engine knock **5 :** to find fault ~ vt **1 a** (1): to strike sharply (2): to drive, force, or make by or as if by so striking **b :** to set forcibly in motion with a blow **2 :** to cause to collide **3 :** to find fault with ⟨~ing those in authority⟩ — **knock cold :** KNOCK OUT ⟨was knocked cold in the third round⟩ — **knock dead :** to move strongly esp. to admiration or applause ⟨a comedian who really knocks them dead⟩ — **knock for a loop 1 a :** OVERCOME ⟨knocked my opponent for a loop⟩ **b :** DEMOLISH ⟨knocked our faith in human nature for a loop⟩ **2 :** DUMBFOUND, AMAZE ⟨the news knocked them for a loop⟩ — **knock together :** to make or assemble esp. hurriedly or in a makeshift way ⟨knocked together my own bookcase⟩
2knock n (14c) **1 a :** a sharp blow : RAP, HIT **b** (1): a severe misfortune or hardship (2): SETBACK, REVERSAL **2 a :** a pounding noise **b :** a sharp metallic noise caused by abnormal ignition in an automobile engine **3 :** a harsh and often petty criticism ⟨likes praise but can't stand the ~s⟩
knock·about \'näk-ə-,baut\ adj (1880) **1 :** suitable for rough use ⟨~ clothing⟩ **2 a :** being noisy and rough : BOISTEROUS ⟨~ games⟩ **b :** characterized by boisterous antics and often extravagant burlesque ⟨~ comedy⟩ **3** of a sailing vessel : having a simplified rig marked by absence of bowsprit and topmast ⟨a ~ sloop⟩ — **knockabout** n
knock back vt (1931) : SWALLOW; specif : to toss down (an alcoholic beverage)
1knock-down \'näk-,daun\ adj (1690) **1 :** having such force as to strike down or overwhelm ⟨a bewildering assortment of ~ arguments —J. W. Krutch⟩ **2 :** that can easily be assembled or disassembled ⟨a ~ table⟩
2knockdown n (1809) **1 :** the action of knocking down **2 :** something (as a blow) that strikes down or overwhelms **3 :** something (as a piece of furniture) that can be easily assembled or disassembled
knock down \-'daun\ vt (1500) **1 :** to strike to the ground with or as if with a sharp blow : FELL **2 :** to dispose of (an item) to a bidder at an auction sale **3 :** to take apart : DISASSEMBLE **4 :** to receive as income or salary : EARN ⟨positions where they were able to knock down good money —Infantry Jour.⟩ **5 :** REDUCE
knock-down-and-drag-out or **knock-down-drag-out** adj (1834) : marked by extreme violence or bitterness and by the showing of no mercy ⟨~ political debates⟩ — **knock-down-and-drag-out** n
knock·er \'näk-ər\ n (14c) **1 :** one that knocks: as **a :** a metal ring, bar, or hammer hinged to a door for use in knocking **b :** a persistently pessimistic critic **2 :** BREAST — usu. used in pl.; often considered vulgar
knock-knee \'näk-,nē, -,nē\ n (1827) : a condition in which the legs curve inward at the knees — **knock-kneed** \-'nēd\ adj
knock·off \'näk-,òf\ n (1966) : a copy that sells for less than the original
knock off \-'òf\ vi (1646) **1 :** to stop doing something ~ vt **1 :** to do hurriedly or routinely ⟨knocked off one painting after another⟩ **2 :** DISCONTINUE, STOP ⟨they knocked off work at five⟩ **3 :** DEDUCT ⟨knocked off a few cents to make the price more attractive⟩ **4 a :** KILL ⟨knocked off two men . . . on mercenary grounds —Lewis Baker⟩ **b :** OVERCOME, DEFEAT ⟨knocked off each center of rebellion⟩ **5 :** ROB ⟨knocked off a couple of banks⟩ **6 :** to make a knockoff of ⟨knocks off popular dress designs⟩
knock·out \'näk-,aut\ n (1887) **1 a :** the act of knocking out : the condition of being knocked out **b** (1): the termination of a boxing match when one boxer has been knocked down and is unable to rise and resume boxing within a specified time (2): TECHNICAL KNOCKOUT **c :** a blow that knocks out an opponent **2 :** something sensationally striking or attractive — **knockout** adj
knock out \-'aut\ vt (1856) **1 :** to produce roughly or hastily **2 a** (1): to defeat (a boxing opponent) by a knockout (2): to make unconscious ⟨the drug knocked him out⟩ **b :** to make inoperative or useless ⟨telephone communications were knocked out by the storm⟩ **3 :** to tire out : EXHAUST ⟨knocked themselves out with work⟩ **4 :** to cause (an opposing pitcher) to be removed from a baseball game by a batting rally
knockout drops n pl (1895) : drops of a solution of a drug (as chloral hydrate) put into a drink and designed to produce unconsciousness or stupefaction
knock over vt (1814) **1 a** (1): to strike to the ground : FELL (2): OVERWHELM ⟨was knocked over by the news⟩ **b :** ELIMINATE ⟨knocked over every difficulty⟩ **2 a :** STEAL; esp : HIJACK ⟨knocks over a truckload of merchandise —J. B. Martin⟩ **b :** ROB ⟨knocking over a bank⟩
knock up vt (1663) **1** Brit : ROUSE, SUMMON **2 :** to make pregnant
knock·wurst \'näk-(,)wərst, -,vu(ə)rst, -,vüsh(t)\ n [G knackwurst, fr. knacken to crackle (of imit. origin) + wurst wurst] (1929) : a short thick heavily seasoned sausage
1knoll \'nōl\ n [ME knol, fr. OE cnoll; akin to ON knollr mountaintop, OE cnotta knot] (bef. 12c) : a small round hill : MOUND
2knoll vb [ME knollen] archaic (15c) : KNELL
knop \'näp\ n [ME, fr. OE -cnoppa knob] (bef. 12c) : a usu. ornamental knob — **knopped** \'näpt\ adj
1knot \'nät\ n [ME, fr. OE cnotta; akin to OHG knoto knot, OE -cnotta, Lith gniusti to press] (bef. 12c) **1 a :** an interlacement of the parts of one or more flexible bodies forming a lump or knob **b :** the lump or knob so formed **c :** a tight constriction or the sense of constriction ⟨my stomach was all in ~s⟩ **2 :** something hard to solve : PROBLEM ⟨a matter full of legal ~s⟩ **3 :** a bond of union; esp : the marriage bond **4 a :** a protuberant lump or swelling in tissue ⟨a ~ in a gland⟩ **b :** the base of a woody branch enclosed in the stem from which it arises;

also : its section in lumber **5 :** a cluster of persons or things : GROUP **6 :** an ornamental bow of ribbon : COCKADE **7 a :** a division of the log's line serving to measure a ship's speed **b** (1): one nautical mile per hour (2): one nautical mile
2knot vb **knot·ted; knot·ting** vt (1547) **1 :** to tie in or with a knot : form knots in **2 :** to unite closely or intricately : ENTANGLE ~ vi : to form knots — **knot·ter** n
3knot n, pl **knots** or **knot** [ME knott] (15c) : any of several sandpipers (genus Calidris) that breed in the Arctic and winter in temperate or warm parts of the New and Old World
knot·grass \'nät-,gras\ n (1538) **1 :** a cosmopolitan weed (Polygonum aviculare) of the buckwheat family with jointed stems, prominent sheathing stipules, and minute flowers; broadly : any of several congeneric plants **2 :** any of several grasses with markedly jointed stems; esp : JOINT GRASS
knot·hole \-,hōl\ n (1726) : a hole in a board or tree trunk where a knot or branch has come out
knot·ted \'nät-əd\ adj (12c) **1 :** tied in or with a knot **2 :** full of knots : GNARLED **3 :** KNOTTY **4 :** ornamented with knots or knobs
knot·ty \'nät-ē\ adj **knot·ti·er; -est** (13c) **1 :** marked by or full of knots; esp : so full of difficulties and complications as to be likely to defy solution ⟨a ~ problem⟩ syn see COMPLEX — **knot·ti·ness** n
knotty pine n (ca. 1898) : pine wood that has a decorative distribution of knots and is used esp. for interior finish
knot·weed \'nät-,wēd\ n (1884) : any of several herbs (genus Polygonum) of the buckwheat family with leaves and bracts jointed and having a very short petiole; broadly : POLYGONUM
knout \'naut, 'nüt\ n [Russ knut, of Scand origin; akin to ON knūtr knot; akin to OE cnotta] (1716) : a whip used for flogging — **knout** vt
1know \'nō\ vb knew \'n(y)ü\; known \'nōn\; know·ing [ME knowen, fr. OE cnāwan; akin to OHG bichnāan to recognize, L gnoscere, noscere to come to know, Gk gignōskein] vt (bef. 12c) **1 a** (1): to perceive directly : have direct cognition of (2): to have understanding of ⟨importance of ~ing oneself⟩ (3): to recognize the nature of : DISCERN **b** (1): to recognize as being the same as something previously known (2): to be acquainted or familiar with (3): to have experience of **2 a :** to be aware of the truth or factuality of : be convinced or certain of **b :** to have a practical understanding of ⟨~s how to write⟩ **3** archaic : to have sexual intercourse with ~ vi **1 :** to have knowledge **2 :** to be or become cognizant — **know·able** \'nō-ə-bəl\ adj — **know·er** \'nō(-ə)r\ n
2know n (1592) : KNOWLEDGE — **in the know :** in possession of confidential or otherwise exclusive knowledge or information
know-how \'nō-,hau\ n (1838) : knowledge of how to do something smoothly and efficiently : EXPERTISE
1know·ing \'nō-in\ n (14c) : ACQUAINTANCE, COGNIZANCE
2knowing adj (14c) **1 :** having or reflecting knowledge, information, or intelligence **2 :** shrewdly and keenly alert : ASTUTE **3 :** DELIBERATE ⟨~ interference in the affairs of another⟩ — **know·ing·ly** adv — **know·ing·ness** n
know-it-all \'nō-ət-,òl\ n (1895) : one who claims to know everything : one who disdains advice — **know-it-all** adj
knowl·edge \'näl-ij\ n [ME knowlege, fr. knowlechen to acknowledge, irreg. fr. knowen] (14c) **1** obs : COGNIZANCE **2 a** (1): the fact or condition of knowing something with familiarity gained through experience or association (2): acquaintance with or understanding of a science, art, or technique **b** (1): the fact or condition of being aware of something (2): the range of one's information or understanding ⟨answered to the best of my ~⟩ **c :** the circumstance or condition of apprehending truth or fact : COGNITION **d :** the fact or condition of having information or of being learned ⟨a man of unusual ~⟩ **3** archaic : SEXUAL INTERCOURSE **4 a :** the sum of what is known : the body of truth, information, and principles acquired by mankind **b** archaic : a branch of learning
syn KNOWLEDGE, LEARNING, ERUDITION, SCHOLARSHIP mean what is or can be known by an individual or by mankind. KNOWLEDGE applies to facts or ideas acquired by study, investigation, observation, or experience; LEARNING applies to knowledge acquired esp. through formal, often advanced, schooling; ERUDITION strongly implies the acquiring of profound, recondite, or bookish learning; SCHOLARSHIP implies the possession of learning characteristic of the advanced scholar in a specialized field of study or investigation.

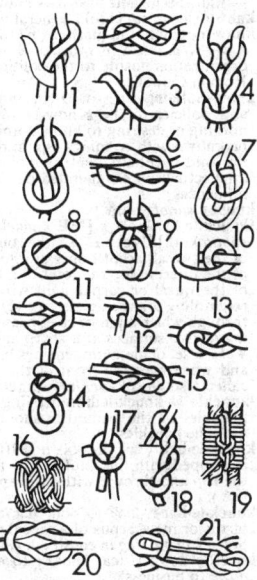

knot 1b: 1 Blackwall hitch, 2 carrick bend, 3 clove hitch, 4 cat's-paw, 5 figure eight, 6 granny knot, 7 bowline, 8 overhand knot, 9 fisherman's bend, 10 half hitch, 11 reef knot, 12 slipknot, 13 stevedore knot, 14 true lover's knot, 15 surgeon's knot, 16 Turk's head, 17 sheet bend, 18 timber hitch, 19 seizing, 20 square knot, 21 sheepshank

knowl·edge·able \ˈnäl-ij-ə-bəl\ *adj* (1829) : having or exhibiting knowledge or intelligence : KEEN — **knowl·edge·abil·i·ty** \ˌnäl-ij-ə-ˈbil-ət-ē\ *n* — **knowl·edge·able·ness** *n* — **knowl·edge·ably** \-blē\ *adv*

known \ˈnōn\ *adj* (13c) : generally recognized ⟨a ~ authority on art⟩

know–noth·ing \ˈnō-ˌnəth-iŋ\ *n* (1827) **1 a** : IGNORAMUS **b** : AGNOSTIC **2** *cap K & N* : a member of a 19th century secret American political organization hostile to the political influence of recent immigrants and Roman Catholics

know–noth·ing·ism \-iŋ-ˌiz-əm\ *n* (1854) **1** *cap K & N* : the principles and policies of the Know-Nothings **2** : the condition of knowing nothing or desiring to know nothing or the conviction that nothing can be known with certainty esp. in religion or morality **3** *often cap K&N* : a mid-twentieth century political attitude characterized by anti-intellectualism, exaggerated patriotism, and fear of foreign subversive influences

knubby *var of* NUBBY

¹knuck·le \ˈnək-əl\ *n* [ME *knokel;* akin to MHG *knöchel* knuckle, OE *cnotta* knot] (14c) **1 a** : the rounded prominence formed by the ends of the two adjacent bones at a joint — used esp. of those at the joints of the fingers **b** : the joint of a knuckle **2** : a cut of meat consisting of the tarsal or carpal joint with the adjoining flesh **3** : something resembling a knuckle: as **a** (1) : one of the joining parts of a hinge through which a pin or rivet passes (2) : KNUCKLE JOINT **b** : the meeting of two surfaces at a sharp angle (as in a roof) **c** : a pivotal point **4** *pl* : a set of metal finger rings or guards attached to a transverse piece and worn over the front of the doubled fist for use as a weapon — called also *brass knuckles* — **knuck·led** *adj*

²knuckle *vb* **knuck·led; knuck·ling** \ˈnək-(ə-)liŋ\ *vi* (1740) : to place the knuckles on the ground in shooting a marble ~ *vt* : to press or rub with the knuckles

knuck·le·ball \ˈnək-əl-ˌbȯl\ *n* (1910) : a baseball pitch in which the ball is gripped with the knuckles or the tips of the fingers pressed against the top and thrown with little speed or spin — **knuck·le·ball·er** \-ˌbȯ-lər\ *n*

knuck·le·bone \ˌnək-əl-ˈbōn, ˈnək-əl-ˌ\ *n* (1577) **1** : a bone (as a metatarsus or metacarpus of a sheep) used in games and formerly in divination **2** *pl but sing in constr* : a game played with knucklebones or jacks

knuckle down *vi* (ca. 1864) : to apply oneself earnestly ⟨let's *knuckle down* to business⟩

knuck·le–dust·er \ˈnək-əl-ˌdəs-tər\ *n* (1858) : KNUCKLE 4

knuck·le·head \-ˌhed\ *n* (1942) : DUMBBELL 2 — **knuck·le·head·ed** \ˌnək-əl-ˈhed-əd\ *adj*

knuckle joint *n* (1863) : a hinge joint in which a projection with an eye on one piece enters a jaw between two corresponding projections with eyes on another piece and is retained by a pin or rivet

knuck·ler \ˈnək-(ə-)lər\ *n* (1928) : KNUCKLEBALL

knuckle under *vi* (1869) : GIVE IN, SUBMIT

knur \ˈnər\ *n* [ME *knorre;* akin to OE *cnotta* knot] (14c) : a hard excrescence (as on a tree trunk) : GNARL

knurl \ˈnər(-ə)l\ *n* [prob. blend of *knur* and *gnarl*] (1608) **1** : a small protuberance, excrescence, or knob **2** : one of a series of small ridges or beads on a metal surface to aid in gripping — **knurled** \ˈnər(-ə)ld\ *adj* — **knurly** \ˈnər-lē\ *adj*

¹KO \(ˈ)kā-ˈō, ˈkā-(ˌ)ō\ *n* [*k*nock *o*ut] (1923) : KNOCKOUT

²KO *vt* **KO'd** \kā-ˈōd, ˈkā-(ˌ)ōd\; **KO'·ing** \-ˈō-iŋ, -(ˌ)ō-\ (1926) : to knock out (as in boxing)

koa \ˈkō-ə\ *n* [Hawaiian] (1850) **1** : a Hawaiian timber tree (*Acacia koa*) with crescent-shaped leaves and white flowers borne in small round heads **2** : the fine-grained red wood of the koa used esp. for furniture

ko·ala \kō-ˈäl-ə, kə-ˈwäl-\ *n* [native name in Australia] (1808) : an Australian arboreal marsupial (*Phascolarctos cinereus*) about two feet long that has large hairy ears, gray fur, and sharp claws and feeds on eucalyptus leaves

ko·an \ˈkō-ˌän\ *n* [Jp *kōan,* fr. *kō* public + *an* proposition] (1945) : a paradox to be meditated upon that is used to train Zen Buddhist monks to abandon ultimate dependence on reason and to force them into gaining sudden intuitive enlightenment

ko·bo \ˈkō-(ˌ)bō\ *n, pl* **kobo** [native name in Nigeria] (1972) — see *naira* at MONEY table

ko·bold \ˈkō-ˌbȯld\ *n* [G — more at COBALT] (1635) **1** : a gnome that in German folklore inhabits underground places **2** : an often mischievous domestic spirit of German folklore

Ko·dak \ˈkō-ˌdak\ *trademark* — used for a small hand camera

kohl \ˈkōl\ *n* [Ar *kuḥl,* fr. or akin to Heb *kuḥla*] (1799) : a preparation used esp. in Arabia and Egypt to darken the edges of the eyelids

kohl·ra·bi \kōl-ˈrab-ē, -ˈräb-\ *n, pl* **-bies** [G, fr. It *cavolo rapa,* fr. *cavolo* cabbage (fr. L *caulis* stalk) + *rapa* turnip, fr. L — more at HOLE, RAPE] (1807) : any of a race of cabbages having a greatly enlarged, fleshy, turnip-shaped edible stem

koi·ne \kȯi-ˈnā, ˈkȯi-ˌ; kē-ˈnē\ *n* [Gk *koinē,* fr. fem. of *koinos* common — more at CO-] (1909) **1** *cap* : the Greek language commonly spoken and written in eastern Mediterranean countries in the Hellenistic and Roman periods **2** : a dialect or language of a region that has become the common or standard language of a larger area

ko·kan·ee \kō-ˈkan-ē\ *n* [prob. fr. *Kokanee* creek, British Columbia] (1875) : a small landlocked sockeye salmon — called also *kokanee salmon*

kok–sa·ghyz *or* **kok–sa·gyz** \ˌkōk-sə-ˈgēz, ˌkäk-, -ˈgiz\ *n* [Russ *kok-sagyz*] (1931) : a perennial Asian dandelion (*Taraxacum kok-saghyz*) cultivated for its fleshy roots that have a high rubber content

kola *var of* COLA

ko·la nut \ˈkō-lə-\ *n* [*kola* of African origin; akin to Mandingo *kolo* kola nut] (1868) : the bitter caffeine-containing chestnut-sized seed of a kola tree used esp. as a masticatory and in beverages

kola tree *n* (1830) : an African tree (genus *Cola,* esp. *C. nitida* of the family Sterculiaceae) cultivated in various tropical areas for its kola nuts

ko·lin·sky \kə-ˈlin(t)-skē\ *n, pl* **-skies** [Russ *kolinskiĭ* of Kola, fr. *Kola,* town and peninsula in U.S.S.R.] (1851) **1** : any of several Asian minks (esp. *Mustela siberica*) **2** : the fur or pelt of a kolinsky

kol·khoz \käl-ˈkȯz, -ˈkȯs\ *n, pl* **kol·kho·zy** \-ˈkȯ-zē\ *or* **kol·khoz·es** \-ˈkȯ-zəz\ [Russ, fr. *kollektivnoe khozyaĭstvo* collective farm] (1921) : a collective farm of the U.S.S.R.

kol·khoz·nik \käl-ˈkȯz-nik\ *n, pl* **-ni·ki** \-ni-kē\ *or* **-niks** [Russ, fr. *kolkhoz* + *-nik* -nik] (1944) : a member of a kolkhoz

Kol Ni·dre \kōl-ˈnid-(ˌ)rā, kȯl-, -rə\ *n* [Aram *kol nidhrē* all the vows; fr. the opening phrase of the prayer] (1881) : a formula for the annulment of private vows chanted in the synagogue on the eve of Yom Kippur

ko·lo \ˈkō-(ˌ)lō\ *n, pl* **kolos** [Serbo-Croatian, fr. OSlav, wheel; akin to Gk *kyklos* circle — more at WHEEL] (1911) : a central European folk dance in which dancers form a circle and progress slowly to right or left while one or more dancers perform elaborate steps in the center of the circle

ko·mat·ik \kō-ˈmat-ik\ *n* [Esk (Labrador dial.)] (1824) : an Eskimo sledge with wooden runners and crossbars lashed with rawhide

kom·man·da·tu·ra \kə-ˌman-də-ˈtu̇r-ə\ *n* [prob. fr. G *kommandantur* command post] (1937) : a military government headquarters

ko·mon·dor \ˈkäm-ən-ˌdȯ(ə)r, ˈkō-mən-\ *n, pl* **-dors** *also* **-dor·ok** \-ˌdȯr-ək\ [Hung] (1931) : any of a Hungarian breed of large powerful shaggy-coated white dogs that are used to guard sheep

Kom·so·mol \ˈkäm-sə-ˌmȯl, -ˌmōl\ *n* [Russ, fr. *Kommunisticheskiĭ Soyuz Molodezhi* Communist Union of Youth] (ca. 1925) : a Russian Communist youth organization

Kon·go \ˈkäŋ-(ˌ)gō\ *n, pl* **Kongo** *or* **Kongos** (ca. 1902) **1** : a member of a Bantu people of the lower Congo river **2** : the Bantu language of the Kongo people

Kon·ka·ni \ˈkäŋ-kə-(ˌ)nē\ *n* [Marathi *Koṅkaṇī*] (1873) : an Indic language of the west coast of India

koo·doo *var of* KUDU

kook \ˈkük\ *n* [by shortening and alter. fr. *cuckoo*] (1960) : one whose ideas or actions are eccentric, fantastic, or insane : SCREWBALL

kook·a·bur·ra \ˈku̇k-ə-ˌbər-ə, -ˌbə-rə\ *n* [native name in Australia] (1890) : a kingfisher (*Dacelo novaeguineae*) of Australia that is about the size of a crow and has a call resembling loud laughter — called also *laughing jackass*

kooky *also* **kook·ie** \ˈkü-kē\ *adj* **kook·i·er; -est** (1959) : having the characteristics of a kook : CRAZY, OFFBEAT — **kook·i·ness** *n*

ko·peck *or* **ko·pek** \ˈkō-ˌpek\ *n* [Russ *kopeĭka*] (1698) — see *ruble* at MONEY table

koph *var of* QOPH

kop·je *or* **kop·pie** \ˈkäp-ē\ *n* [Afrik *koppie,* dim. of D *kop* head; akin to OE *copp* ¹cop] (1848) : a small hill esp. on the African veld

kor \ˈkȯ(ə)r\ *n* [Heb *kōr*] (14c) : an ancient Hebrew and Phoenician unit of measure of capacity

Ko·ran \kə-ˈran, -ˈrän; ˈkō(ə)r-ˌan, ˈkȯ(ə)r-\ *n* [Ar *qur'ān*] (1625) : the book composed of sacred writings accepted by Muslims as revelations made to Muhammad by Allah through the angel Gabriel — **Ko·ran·ic** \kə-ˈran-ik\ *adj*

Ko·rat \kōr-ˈät, kȯr-\ *n* [*Korat* province, Thailand] (ca. 1967) : a breed of shorthaired domestic cat originating in Thailand and having a heart-shaped face, a silver-blue coat, and green eyes

Ko·re·an \kə-ˈrē-ən, *esp Southern* (ˈ)kō-\ *n* (1600) **1** : a native or inhabitant of Korea **2** : the language of the Korean people — **Korean** *adj*

ko·ru·na \ˈkȯr-ə-ˌnä, ˈkär-\ *n, pl* **ko·ru·ny** \-ə-nē\ *or* **korunas** *or* **ko·rum** \ˈkȯr-əm, ˈkär-\ [Czech, lit., crown, fr. L *corona* — more at CROWN] (1930) — see MONEY table

¹ko·sher \ˈkō-shər\ *adj* [Yiddish, fr. Heb *kāshēr* fit, proper] (1851) **1 a** : sanctioned by Jewish law; *esp* : ritually fit for use ⟨~ meat⟩ **b** : selling or serving food ritually fit according to Jewish law ⟨a ~ restaurant⟩ **2** : PROPER ⟨found things going on that were not ~ —Homer Bigart⟩

²kosher *vt* **ko·shered; ko·sher·ing** \-sh(ə-)riŋ\ (1871) : to make kosher

ko·to \ˈkōt-(ˌ)ō\ *n* [Jp] (1795) : a long Japanese zither having 13 silk strings

kou·miss \kü-ˈmis, ˈkü-məs\ *n* [Russ *kumys*] (1598) : a beverage of fermented mare's milk made orig. by the nomadic peoples of central Asia

¹kow·tow \(ˈ)kau̇-ˈtau̇, ˈkau̇-ˌ\ *n* [Chin (Pek) *k'o¹ t'ou²,* fr. *k'o¹* to bump + *t'ou²* head] (1804) : an act of kowtowing

²kowtow *vi* (1826) **1** : to show obsequious deference : FAWN **2** : to kneel and touch the forehead to the ground in token of homage, worship, or deep respect

KP \(ˈ)kā-ˈpē\ *n* [*k*itchen *p*olice] (ca. 1917) **1** : enlisted men detailed to assist the cooks in a military mess **2** : the work of KPs

¹kraal \ˈkrȯl, ˈkräl\ *n* [Afrik, fr. Pg *curral* pen for cattle, enclosure, fr. (assumed) VL *currale* enclosure for vehicles — more at CORRAL] (1731) **1 a** : a village of southern African natives **b** : the native village community **2** : an enclosure for animals esp. in southern Africa

²kraal *vt* (1865) : to pen in a kraal

kraft \ˈkraft\ *n, often attrib* [G, lit., strength, fr. OHG — more at CRAFT] (1906) : a strong paper or paperboard made from wood pulp produced from wood chips boiled in an alkaline solution containing sodium sulfate

krait \ˈkrīt\ *n* [Hindi *karait*] (1874) : any of several brightly banded extremely venomous nocturnal elapid snakes (genus *Bungarus*) of India, eastern Asia, and adjacent islands

kra·ken \ˈkräk-ən\ *n* [Norw dial.] (1755) : a fabulous Scandinavian sea monster

kra·ter \ˈkrāt-ər, krä-ˈte(ə)r\ *n* [Gk *kratēr* — more at CRATER] (ca. 1730) : a jar or vase of classical antiquity having a large round body and a wide mouth and used for mixing wine and water

K ration \ˈkā-\ *n* [A. B. Keys *b*1904 Am. physiologist] (1940) : a lightweight packaged ration of emergency foods developed for the U.S. armed forces in World War II

kraut \ˈkrau̇t\ *n* [G, cabbage, fr. OHG *krūt;* akin to Gk *bryon* moss — more at EMBRYO] (1845) **1** : SAUERKRAUT **2** *often cap* : GERMAN — usu. used disparagingly

Krebs cycle \ˈkrebz-\ *n* [H. A. *Krebs*] (1941) : a sequence of reactions in the living organism in which oxidation of acetic acid or acetyl equivalent provides energy for storage in phosphate bonds — called also *citric acid cycle, tricarboxylic acid cycle*

krem·lin \ˈkrem-lən\ *n* [prob. fr. obs. G *kremelin,* fr. Russ *kreml'*] (1661) **1** : the citadel of a Russian city **2** [the *Kremlin,* citadel of Moscow and governing center of the U.S.S.R.] *cap* : the Russian government

krem·lin·ol·o·gy \ˌkrem-lə-ˈnäl-ə-jē\ *n, often cap* (1958) : the study of the policies and practices of the Soviet government — **krem·lin·ol·o·gist** \-jəst\ *n, often cap*

krep·lach \'krep-lək, -ˌläk\ *n* [Yiddish *kreplech*] (ca. 1892) : square or triangular dumplings filled with ground meat or cheese, boiled or fried, and usu. served in soup

kreu·zer \'kròit-sər\ *n* [G, fr. *kreuz* cross; fr. its markings] (1547) : a small coin formerly used in Austria and Germany

krill \'kril\ *n* [Norw *kril* fry of fish] (1907) : planktonic crustaceans and larvae (order Euphausiacea) that constitute the principal food of whalebone whales

krim·mer \'krim-ər\ *n* [G, fr. *Krim* Crimea] (1834) : a gray fur made from the pelts of young lambs of the Crimean peninsula region

kris \'krēs\ *n* [Malay *kēris*] (ca. 1577) : a Malay or Indonesian dagger with a ridged serpentine blade

Krish·na \'krish-nə\ *n* [Skt *Kṛṣṇa*] : a deity or deified hero of later Hinduism worshiped as an incarnation of Vishnu

Krish·na·ism \-ˌiz-əm\ *n* (1885) : a widespread form of Hindu religion characterized by the worship of Krishna

Kriss Krin·gle \'kris-'krin-gəl\ *n* [G *Christkindl* Christ child, Christmas gift, dim. of *Christkind* Christ child] (1830) : SANTA CLAUS

¹**kro·na** \'krō-nə\ *n*, *pl* **kro·nor** \-ˌnó(ə)r, -nər\ [Sw, lit., crown] (1875) — see MONEY table

²**kro·na** \'krō-nə\ *n*, *pl* **kro·nur** \-nər\ [Icel *króna*, lit., crown] (1886) — see MONEY table

¹**kro·ne** \'krō-nə\ *n*, *pl* **kro·ner** \-nər\ [Dan, lit., crown] (1875) — see MONEY table

²**kro·ne** \'krō-nə\ *n*, *pl* **kro·nen** \-nən\ [G, lit., crown] (1895) **1** : the basic monetary unit of Austria from 1892 to 1925 **2** : a coin representing one krone

Kro·neck·er delta \'krō-ˌnek-ər-\ *n* [Leopold *Kronecker* †1891 Ger. mathematician] (1926) : a function of two variables that is 1 when the variables have the same value and is 0 when they have different values

Kru·ger·rand \'krü-gə(r)-ˌrand, -ˌränd, -ˌränt\ *n* [S.J.P. *Kruger* + *rand*] (1967) : a one-ounce gold coin of the Republic of So. Africa equal in bullion value to 25 rand and having an official price of 31 rand

krumm·holz \'krüm-ˌhōlts\ *n*, *pl* **krummholz** [G, fr. *krumm* crooked + *holz* wood, fr. OHG — more at HOLT] (1903) : stunted forest characteristic of timberline

krumm·horn *also* **krum·horn** \'krəm-ˌhò(ə)rn\ *n* [G *krummhorn*, fr. *krumm* curved fr. OHG *krump*; akin to LG *krampe* hook] + *horn* — more at CRAMP] (1694) : a Renaissance double-reed woodwind instrument consisting of a curved boxwood tube and having a pierced cap covering the reed

kryp·ton \'krip-ˌtän\ *n* [Gk, neut. of *kryptos* hidden — more at CRYPT] (1898) : a colorless relatively inert gaseous element found in air at about one volume per million and used esp. in electric lamps — see ELEMENT table

Ksha·tri·ya \(kə-)'sha-trē-(y)ə, 'cha-\ *n* [Skt *kṣatriya*, fr. *kṣatra* dominion — more at CHECK] (1782) : a Hindu of an upper caste traditionally assigned to governing and military occupations

Ku·che·an \kü-'chē-ən\ *n* [*Kuche, Kucha*, Sinkiang, China] (ca. 1934) : TOCHARIAN B

ku·chen \'kü-kən, -kən\ *n*, *pl* **kuchen** [G, cake, fr. OHG *kuocho* — more at CAKE] (1854) : any of various coffee cakes made from sweet yeast dough

ku·do \'k(y)üd-(ˌ)ō\ *n*, *pl* **kudos** [back-formation fr. *kudos* (taken as a pl.)] (1926) **1** : AWARD, HONOR ⟨a score of honorary degrees and . . . other ~*s* —*Time*⟩ **2** : COMPLIMENT, PRAISE ⟨to all three should go some kind of special ~ for refusing to succumb —Al Hine⟩

usage Some commentators hold that since *kudos* is a singular word it cannot be used as a plural and that the word *kudo* is impossible. But *kudo* does exist; it is simply the most recent example of a word created by back-formation from another word misunderstood as a plural. *Kudos* was introduced into English in the 19th century; it was used in contexts where a reader unfamiliar with Greek could not be sure whether it was singular or plural. By the 1920s it began to appear as a plural, and about 25 years later *kudo* began to appear. It may have begun as a misunderstanding, but then so did *cherry* and *pea.*

ku·dos \'k(y)ü-ˌdäs, -ˌdòs\ *n* [Gk *kydos*; akin to Gk *akouein* to hear — more at HEAR] (1831) : fame and renown resulting from an act or achievement : PRESTIGE

ku·du \'küd-(ˌ)ü\ *n*, *pl* **kudu** *or* **kudus** [Afrik *koedoe*] (1777) : a large grayish brown African antelope (*Tragelaphus strepsiceros*) with large annulated spirally twisted horns; *also* : a related antelope (*T.imberbis*)

kud·zu \'küd-(ˌ)zü, 'kəd-\ *n* [Jp *kuzu*] (1893) : a prostrate Asian leguminous vine (*Pueraria thunbergiana*) used widely for hay and forage and for erosion control

Ku Klux·er \'k(y)ü-ˌklək-sər *also* 'klü-\ *n* (1880) : a member of the Ku Klux Klan — **Ku Klux·ism** \-ˌklək-ˌsiz-əm\ *n*

Ku Klux Klan \ˌk(y)ü-ˌkləks-'klan *also* ˌklü-\ *n* (1868) **1** : a post-Civil War secret society advocating white supremacy **2** : a 20th century secret fraternal group held to confine its membership to American-born white Christians

ku·lak \k(y)ü-'lak, -'läk, 'k(y)ü-ˌ\ *n* [Russ, lit., fist] (1877) **1** : a prosperous or wealthy peasant farmer in 19th century Russia **2** : a farmer characterized by Communists as having excessive wealth

kudu

kul·tur \kủl-'tủ(ə)r\ *n*, *often cap* [G, fr. L *cultura* culture] (1914) **1** : CULTURE 5 **2** : culture emphasizing practical efficiency and individual subordination to the state **3** : German culture held to be superior esp. by militant Nazi and Hohenzollern expansionists

Kul·tur·kampf \-ˌkäm(p)f\ *n* [G, fr. *kultur* + *kampf* conflict] (1879) : conflict between civil government and religious authorities esp. over control of education and church appointments

ku·miss *var of* KOUMISS

küm·mel \'kim-əl\ *n* [G, lit., caraway seed, fr. OHG *kumin* cumin] (1864) : a colorless aromatic liqueur flavored principally with caraway seeds

kum·quat \'kəm-ˌkwät\ *n* [Chin (Cant) *kam kwat*, fr. *kam* gold + *kwat* orange] (1699) : any of several small citrus fruits with sweet spongy rind and somewhat acid pulp that are used chiefly for preserves; *also* : a tree or shrub (genus *Fortunella*) of the rue family that bears kumquats

kung fu \ˌkən-'fü, ˌkuŋ-\ *n* [Chin dial.; akin to Chin (Pek) *ch'üan² fa³* lit., boxing principles] (1966) : a Chinese art of self-defense like karate

kunz·ite \'kůn(t)-ˌsīt\ *n* [G. F. *Kunz* †1932 Am. gem expert] (1903) : a spodumene that occurs in pinkish lilac crystals and is used as a gem

Kurd \'ků(ə)rd, 'kərd\ *n* (1616) : a member of a pastoral and agricultural people who inhabit a plateau region in adjoining parts of Turkey, Iran, Iraq, and Syria and in the Armenian and Azerbaidzhan sectors of the Soviet Caucasus — **Kurd·ish** \-ish\ *adj*

Kurdish *n* (1813) : the Iranian language of the Kurds

Kur·di·stan \ˌkůrd-ə-'stan, ˌkərd-\ *n* [*Kurdistan*, Asia] (1904) : an Oriental rug woven by the Kurds and noted for fine colors and durability

kur·gan \ků(ə)r-'gän, -'gan\ *n* [Russ, of Turkic origin; akin to Turk *kurgan* fortress, castle] (1889) : a burial mound of eastern Europe or Siberia

kur·ra·jong \'kər-ə-ˌjòn, 'kə-rə-, -ˌjän\ *n* [native name in Australia] (1823) : any of several Australian trees or shrubs (family Sterculiaceae) having strong bast fiber used by Australian aborigines; *esp* : a widely planted shelter and forage tree (*Brachychiton populneum*)

kur·to·sis \(ˌ)kər-'tō-səs\ *n* [Gk *kyrtōsis* convexity, fr. *kyrtos* convex; akin to L *curvus* curved — more at CROWN] (1905) : the peakedness or flatness of the graph of a frequency distribution esp. with respect to the concentration of values near the mean as compared with the normal distribution

ku·ru \'ků(ə)r-(ˌ)ü\ *n* [native name in New Guinea, lit., trembling] (1957) : a fatal disease of the nervous system that is caused by a slow virus, resembles scrapie in sheep, and occurs among tribesmen in eastern New Guinea

ku·rus \kə-'rüsh\ *n*, *pl* **kurus** [Turk *kuruş*] (1882) — see lira at MONEY table

kvass \kə-'väs, 'kfäs\ *n* [Russ *kvas*] (1553) : a slightly alcoholic beverage of eastern Europe made from fermented mixed cereals and often flavored

Kwa \'kwä\ *n* (1857) : a branch of the Niger-Congo language family that is spoken along the African coast and a short distance inland from Liberia to Nigeria

kwa·cha \'kwäch-ə\ *n*, *pl* **kwacha** [native name in Zambia, lit., dawn] (1966) — see MONEY table

Kwan·za \'kwän-zə\ *n* [Swahili *kwanza* first] (1972) **1** *or* **Kwan·zaa** \'kwän-zə\ : an African-American festival held in late December **2** *not cap*, *pl* **kwanzas** *or* **kwanza** — see MONEY table

kwash·i·or·kor \ˌkwäsh-ē-'òr-kər, -òr-'kó(ə)r\ *n* [native name in Ghana, lit., red boy] (1935) : severe malnutrition in infants and children that is caused by a diet high in carbohydrate and low in protein

KWIC \'kwik\ *n* [keyword in context] (1965) : a computer-generated index alphabetized on a keyword that appears within a portion of its context

ky·ack \'kī-ˌak\ *n* [origin unknown] (1901) : a packsack to be swung on either side of a packsaddle

ky·a·nite \'kī-ə-ˌnīt\ *n* [G *zyanit*, fr. Gk *kyanos* dark blue enamel, lapis lazuli] (1794) : an aluminum silicate Al₂SiO₅ that occurs usu. in blue thin-bladed triclinic crystals and crystalline aggregates and is sometimes used as a gemstone

kyat \'chät\ *n* [Burmese] (1952) — see MONEY table

ky·mo·gram \'kī-mə-ˌgram\ *n* [ISV] (1923) : a record made by a kymograph

ky·mo·graph \-ˌgraf\ *n* [Gk *kyma* wave + ISV *-graph* — more at CYME] (1867) : a device which graphically records motion or pressure (as of blood) — **ky·mo·graph·ic** \ˌkī-mə-'graf-ik\ *adj* — **ky·mog·ra·phy** \kī-'mäg-rə-fē\ *n*

Kymric *var of* CYMRIC

ky·pho·sis \kī-'fō-səs\ *n* [NL, fr. Gk *kyphōsis*, fr. *kyphos* humbacked; akin to OE *hēah* high] (1847) : abnormal backward curvature of the spine — **ky·phot·ic** \-'fät-ik\ *adj*

ky·rie \'kir-ē-ˌā\ *n*, *often cap* [NL, fr. LL *kyrie eleison*, transliteration of Gk *kyrie eleēson*, Lord, have mercy] (14c) : a short liturgical prayer that begins with or consists of the words "Lord, have mercy"

ky·rie elei·son \ˌkir-ē-ˌā-ə-'lā-(ə-)ˌsän, -(ə-)sən *also* ˌkir-ē-ə-'lā-\ *n*, *often cap* K&E (13c) : KYRIE

kyte \'kit\ *n* [prob. fr. LG *küt* bowel] *chiefly Scot* (1540) : STOMACH, BELLY

kythe *var of* KITHE

L

l \ˈel\ *n, pl* **l's** *or* **ls** \ˈelz\ *often cap, often attrib* **1 a :** the 12th letter of the English alphabet **b :** a graphic representation of this letter **c :** a speech counterpart of orthographic *l* **2 :** fifty — see NUMBER table **3 :** a graphic device for reproducing the letter *l* **4 :** one designated *l* esp. as the 12th in order or class **5 :** something shaped like the letter L; *specif* **:** ELL **6 :** ELEVATED RAILROAD

l- *prefix* [ISV, fr. *lev-*] **1** \ˌlē-(ˌ)vō, ˌel, ˈel\ **:** levorotatory ⟨*l*-tartaric acid⟩ **2** \ˌel, ˈel\ **:** having a similar configuration at a selected carbon atom to the configuration of levorotatory glyceraldehyde — usu. printed as a small capital ⟨L-fructose⟩

[1]**la** \ˈlō, ˈlä\ *interj* [ME (northern dial.), fr. OE *lā*] *chiefly dial* (bef. 12c) — used for emphasis or expressing surprise

[2]**la** \ˈlä\ *n* [ME, fr. ML, fr. the syllable sung to this note in a medieval hymn to St. John the Baptist] (14c) **:** the 6th tone of the diatonic scale in solmization

laa·ger \ˈläg-ər\ *n* [obs. Afrik *lager* (now *laer*), fr. G, fr. OHG *legar* couch — more at LAIR] *SoAfr* (1850) **:** CAMP; *esp* **:** an encampment protected by a circle of wagons or armored vehicles — **laager** *vi*

lab \ˈlab\ *n* (1895) **:** LABORATORY

lab·a·rum \ˈlab-ə-rəm\ *n* [LL] (1606) **:** an imperial standard of the later Roman emperors resembling the vexillum; *esp* **:** the standard adopted by Constantine after his conversion to Christianity

lab·da·num \ˈlab-də-nəm\ *n* [ML *lapdanum*] (14c) **:** a soft dark fragrant bitter oleoresin derived from various rockroses (genus *Cistus*) and used in making perfumes

[1]**la·bel** \ˈlā-bəl\ *n* [ME, fr. MF] (14c) **1** *archaic* **:** BAND, FILLET; *specif* **:** one attached to a document to hold an appended seal **2 :** a heraldic charge that consists of a narrow horizontal band with usu. three pendants **3 a :** a slip (as of paper or cloth) inscribed and affixed to something for identification or description **b :** written or printed matter accompanying an article to furnish identification or other information **c :** a descriptive or identifying word or phrase: as (1) **:** EPITHET (2) **:** a word or phrase used with a dictionary definition to provide additional information **d :** material used in isotopic labeling **4 :** a projecting molding by the sides and over the top of an opening **5 :** an adhesive stamp (as for postage or revenue) **6 a** (1) **:** a brand of commercial recordings issued under a usu. trademarked name (2) **:** a recording so issued (3) **:** a company issuing such recordings **b :** the brand name of a retail store selling clothing, a clothing manufacturer, or a fashion designer

[2]**label** *vt* **la·beled** *or* **la·belled; la·bel·ing** *or* **la·bel·ling** \ˈlā-b(ə-)liŋ\ (1601) **1 a :** to affix a label to **b :** to describe or designate with a label **2 a :** to distinguish (an element or atom) by using a radioactive isotope or an isotope of unusual mass for tracing through chemical reactions or biological processes **b :** to distinguish (as a compound or molecule) by introducing a labeled atom — **la·bel·able** \ˈlā-bə-lə-bəl\ *adj* — **la·bel·er** \ˈlā-b(ə-)lər\ *n*

la·bel·lum \lə-ˈbel-əm\ *n, pl* **la·bel·la** \-ˈbel-ə\ [NL, fr. L, dim. of *labrum* lip — more at LIP] (1830) **1 :** the median member of the corolla of an orchid **2 :** a terminal part of the labium or labrum of various insects

labia *pl of* LABIUM

[1]**la·bi·al** \ˈlā-bē-əl\ *adj* [ML *labialis*, fr. L *labium* lip] (1594) **1 :** of, relating to, or situated near the lips or labia **2 :** uttered with the participation of one or both lips ⟨the ~ sounds \f\, \p\, and \ü\⟩ — **la·bi·al·ly** \-ə-lē\ *adv*

[2]**labial** *n* (1688) **:** a labial consonant

la·bi·al·ize \ˈlā-bē-ə-ˌlīz\ *vt* **-ized; -iz·ing** (1867) **:** to make labial **:** ROUND — **la·bi·al·iza·tion** \ˌlā-bē-ə-lə-ˈzā-shən, -byə-lə-\ *n*

la·bia ma·jo·ra \ˌlā-bē-ə-mə-ˈjōr-ə, -ˈjȯr-\ *n pl* [NL, lit., larger lips] (1838) **:** the outer fatty folds of the vulva bounding the vestibule

labia mi·no·ra \-mə-ˈnōr-ə, -ˈnȯr-\ *n pl* [NL, lit., smaller lips] (1838) **:** the inner highly vascular largely connective-tissue folds of the vulva bounding the vestibule

[1]**la·bi·ate** \ˈlā-bē-ət, -bē-ˌāt\ *adj* [NL *labiatus*, fr. L *labium*] (1706) **1 :** having the limb of a tubular corolla or calyx divided into two unequal parts projecting one over the other like lips ⟨mints and the snapdragon are ~⟩ **2 :** of or relating to the mint family

[2]**labiate** *n* (1845) **:** a plant of the mint family

la·bile \ˈlā-ˌbīl, -bəl\ *adj* [F, fr. MF, prone to err, fr. LL *labilis*, fr. L *labi* to slip — more at SLEEP] (1603) **1 :** readily or continually undergoing chemical, physical, or biological change or breakdown **:** UNSTABLE ⟨a ~ mineral⟩ **2 :** readily open to change **:** PLASTIC — **la·bil·i·ty** \lā-ˈbil-ət-ē\ *n*

labio- *comb form* [L *labium*] **:** labial and ⟨*labio*dental⟩

la·bio·den·tal \ˌlā-bē-ō-ˈdent-ᵊl\ *adj* (1669) **:** uttered with the participation of the lip and teeth ⟨the ~ sounds \f\ and \v\⟩ — **labiodental** *n*

la·bio·ve·lar \-ˈvē-lər\ *adj* [ISV] (1894) **:** both labial and velar ⟨the ~ sound \w\⟩ — **labiovelar** *n*

la·bi·um \ˈlā-bē-əm\ *n, pl* **la·bia** \-ə\ [NL, fr. L, lip — more at LIP] (1634) **1 :** any of the folds at the margin of the vulva — compare LABIA MAJORA, LABIA MINORA **2 :** the lower lip of a labiate corolla **3 a :** a lower mouthpart of an insect that is formed by the second pair of maxillae united in the middle line **b :** a liplike part of various invertebrates

[1]**la·bor** \ˈlā-bər\ *n* [ME, fr. MF, fr. L *labor*; prob. akin to L *labi* to slip — more at SLEEP] (14c) **1 a :** expenditure of physical or mental effort esp. when difficult or compulsory **b** (1) **:** human activity that provides the goods or services in an economy (2) **:** the services performed by workers for wages as distinguished from those rendered by entrepreneurs for profits **c :** the physical activities involved in parturition; *also* **:** the period of such labor **2 :** an act or process requiring labor **:** TASK **3 :** a product of labor **4 a :** an economic group comprising those who do manual labor or work for wages **b** (1) **:** workers employed in an establishment (2) workers available for employment **c :** the organizations or officials representing groups of workers **5** *usu Labour* **:** the Labour party of the United Kingdom or of another nation of the British Commonwealth ***syn*** see WORK

[2]**labor** *vb* **la·bored; la·bor·ing** \-b(ə-)riŋ\ *vi* (14c) **1 :** to exert one's powers of body or mind esp. with painful or strenuous effort **:** WORK **2 :** to move with great effort ⟨a fat person ~*ing* up the stairs⟩ **3 :** to be in the labor of giving birth **4 :** to suffer from some disadvantage or distress ⟨~ under a delusion⟩ **5** *of a ship* **:** to pitch or roll heavily ~ *vt* **1** *archaic* **a :** to spend labor on or produce by labor **b :** to strive to effect or achieve **2 :** to treat or work out in often laborious detail ⟨~ the obvious⟩ **3 :** DISTRESS, BURDEN **4 :** to cause to labor

[3]**labor** *adj* (1549) **1 :** of or relating to labor **2** *cap* **:** of, relating to, or constituting a political party held to represent the interests of workers or characterized by a membership in which organized labor groups predominate

lab·o·ra·to·ry \ˈlab-(ə-)rə-ˌtōr-ē, -ˌtȯr- *sometimes* ˈlab-ə(r)-, *or* lə-ˈbȯr-ə-, *Brit usu* lə-ˈbär-ə-t(ə-)rē\ *n, pl* **-ries** *often attrib* [ML *laboratorium*, fr. L *laboratus*, pp. of *laborare* to labor, fr. *labor*] (1605) **1 :** a place equipped for experimental study in a science or for testing and analysis; *broadly* **:** a place providing opportunity for experimentation, observation, or practice in a field of study **2 :** an academic period set aside for laboratory work

labor camp *n* (1900) **1 :** a penal colony where forced labor is performed **2 :** a camp for migratory laborers

Labor Day *n* (ca. 1882) **:** a day set aside for special recognition of working people: as **a :** the first Monday in September observed in the U.S. and Canada as a legal holiday **b :** May 1 in many countries

la·bored \ˈlā-bərd\ *adj* (15c) **1 :** produced or performed with labor **2 :** bearing marks of labor and effort; *esp* **:** lacking ease of expression ⟨a ~ speech⟩

la·bor·er \-bər-ər\ *n* (14c) **:** one that labors; *specif* **:** a person who does unskilled physical work for wages

labor force *n* (1911) **:** WORK FORCE

la·bor–in·ten·sive \ˈlā-bə-rin-ˌten(t)-siv\ *adj* (1953) **:** having high labor costs per unit of output; *esp* **:** requiring greater expenditure on labor than in capital

la·bo·ri·ous \lə-ˈbōr-ē-əs, -ˈbȯr-\ *adj* (14c) **1 :** devoted to labor **:** INDUSTRIOUS **2 :** involving or characterized by hard or toilsome effort **:** LABORED — **la·bo·ri·ous·ly** *adv* — **la·bo·ri·ous·ness** *n*

la·bor·ite \ˈlā-bə-ˌrīt\ *n* (1889) **1 :** a member of a group favoring the interests of labor **2** *cap* **a :** a member of a political party devoted chiefly to the interests of labor **b** *usu* **La·bour·ite :** a member of the British Labour party

la·bor·sav·ing \ˈlā-bər-ˌsā-viŋ\ *adj* (1775) **:** adapted to replace or decrease human and esp. manual labor

labor union *n* (1866) **:** an organization of workers formed for the purpose of advancing its members' interests in respect to wages, benefits, and working conditions

labour *chiefly Brit var of* LABOR

lab·ra·dor·ite \ˈlab-rə-ˌdȯ(ə)r-ˌīt\ *n* [*Labrador* peninsula, Canada] (1814) **:** a triclinic feldspar showing a play of several colors

Lab·ra·dor retriever \ˌlab-rə-ˌdȯr-\ *n* [*Labrador*, Newfoundland] (1910) **:** a compact, strongly built retriever largely developed in England from stock originating in Newfoundland and having a short dense black, yellow, or chocolate coat — called also *Labrador*

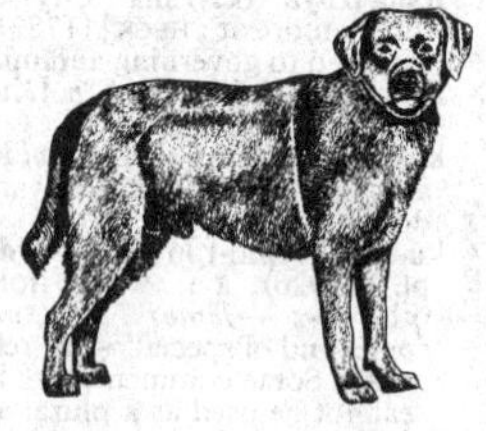

Labrador retriever

labrador tea *n* (1767) **:** a low-growing ericaceous evergreen shrub (*Ledum groenlandicium*) of eastern No. America with white or creamy bell-shaped flowers and leaves sometimes used in making tea; *also* **:** a related Rocky mountain shrub (*L. glandulosum*)

la·bret \ˈlā-brət\ *n* [L *labrum*] (1857) **:** an ornament worn in a perforation of the lip

la·brum \ˈlā-brəm\ *n* [NL, fr. L, lip, edge — more at LIP] (1826) **:** an upper or anterior mouthpart of an arthropod consisting of a single median piece in front of or above the mandibles

la·bur·num \lə-ˈbər-nəm\ *n* [NL, fr. L] (1567) **:** any of a small genus (*Laburnum*) of poisonous Eurasian leguminous shrubs and trees with pendulous racemes of bright yellow flowers; *esp* **:** an ornamental tree (*L. anagyroides*) often cultivated for Easter decoration

lab·y·rinth \ˈlab-ə-ˌrin(t)th, -rən(t)th\ *n* [ME *laborintus*, fr. L *labyrinthus*, fr. Gk *labyrinthos*] (14c) **1 a :** a place constructed of or full of intricate passageways and blind alleys **b :** a maze (as in a garden) formed by paths separated by high hedges **2 :** something extremely complex or tortuous in structure, arrangement, or character **:** INTRICACY, PERPLEXITY ⟨a ~ of swamps and channels⟩ ⟨guided them through the ~*s* of city life —Paul Blanshard⟩ **3 :** a tortuous anatomical structure; *esp* **:** the internal ear or its bony or membranous part

lab·y·rin·thi·an \ˌlab-ə-ˈrin(t)-thē-ən\ *adj* (1588) **:** LABYRINTHINE

lab·y·rin·thine \-ˈrin(t)-thən; -ˈrin-ˌthīn, -ˌthēn\ *adj* (1632) **1 :** of, relating to, or resembling a labyrinth **:** INTRICATE, INVOLVED **2 :** of, relating to, affecting, or originating in the internal ear ⟨human ~ lesions⟩

lab·y·rin·tho·dont \-ˈrin(t)-thə-ˌdänt\ *n* [NL *Labyrinthodontia*, fr. Gk *labyrinthos* + NL *-odontia*] (1847) **:** any of a superorder of extinct amphibians (Labyrinthodontia) typically having bodies resembling salamanders or crocodiles and considered to be the earliest vertebrates with two pairs of limbs — **labyrinthodont** *adj*

[1]**lac** \ˈlak\ *n* [Per *lak* & Hindi *lākh*, fr. Skt *lākṣā*] (15c) **:** a resinous substance secreted by a scale insect (*Laccifer lacca*) and used chiefly in the form of shellac

[2]**lac** *var of* LAKH

lac·co·lith \ˈlak-ə-ˌlith\ *n* [Gk *lakkos* cistern + E *-lith* — more at LAKE] (1879) **:** a mass of igneous rock that is intruded between sedimentary beds and produces a domical bulging of the overlying strata

[1]**lace** \ˈlās\ *vb* **laced; lac·ing** [ME *lacen*, fr. OF *lacier*, fr. L *laqueare* to ensnare, fr. *laqueus*] *vt* (13c) **1 :** to draw together the edges of by or as if by a lace passed through eyelets **2 :** to draw or pass (as a lace) through something (as eyelets) **3 :** to confine or compress by tightening laces esp. of a corset **4 a :** to adorn with or as if with lace **b :** to mark with streaks of color **5 :** BEAT, LASH **6 a :** to add a dash of liquor to **b :** to give savor or zest to ~ *vi* **:** to admit of being tied or fastened with a lace — **lac·er** *n*

[2]**lace** *n* [ME, fr. MF *laz*, fr. L *laqueus* snare; akin to L *lacere* to entice — more at DELIGHT] (14c) **1 :** a cord or string used for drawing together two edges (as of a garment or a shoe) **2 :** an ornamental braid for

trimming coats or uniforms **3 :** an openwork usu. figured fabric made of thread or yarn and used for trimmings, household coverings, and entire garments — **laced** \ˈlāst\ *adj* — **lace·less** \ˈlā-sləs\ *adj* — **lace·like** \ˈlā-ˌslīk\ *adj*

lace–curtain *adj* (1932) **:** copying middle-class attributes **:** aspiring to middle-class standing

[1]**lac·er·ate** \ˈlas-ə-ˌrāt\ *vt* **-at·ed; -at·ing** [L *laceratus,* pp. of *lacerare* to tear; akin to L *lacer* mangled, Gk *lakis* rent] (15c) **1 :** to tear or rend roughly **2 :** to cause sharp mental or emotional pain to **:** DISTRESS — **lac·er·a·tive** \-ˌrāt-iv\ *adj*

[2]**lac·er·ate** \-rət, -ˌrāt\ *or* **lac·er·at·ed** \-ˌrāt-əd\ *adj* (1542) **1 a :** torn jaggedly **:** MANGLED **b :** extremely harrowed or distracted **2 :** having the edges deeply and irregularly cut ⟨a ~ petal⟩

lac·er·a·tion \ˌlas-ə-ˈrā-shən\ *n* (1597) **1 :** the act of lacerating **2 :** a torn and ragged wound

lace·wing \ˈlā-ˌswiŋ\ *n* (1854) **:** any of various neuropterous insects (as genera *Chrysopa* and *Hemerobius*) having delicate lacelike wing venation, long antennae, and brilliant eyes — called also *lacewing fly*

lace·work \ˈlā-ˌswərk\ *n* (1849) **:** objects or patterns consisting of or resembling lace

lac·ey *var of* LACY

la·ches \ˈlach-əz, ˈlā-chəz\ *n, pl* **laches** [ME *lachesse,* fr. MF *laschesse,* fr. OF *lasche* lax, deriv. of L *laxare* to loosen — more at LAXATIVE] (14c) **:** negligence in the observance of duty or opportunity; *specif* **:** undue delay in asserting a legal right or privilege

lach·ry·mal *or* **lac·ri·mal** \ˈlak-rə-məl\ *adj* [MF or ML; MF *lacrymal,* fr. ML *lacrimalis,* fr. L *lacrima* tear, fr. OL *dacruma,* fr. or akin to Gk *dakry* — more at TEAR] (15c) **1** *usu lacrimal* **:** of, relating to, or constituting the glands that produce tears **2 :** of, relating to, or marked by tears

lach·ry·mose \-ˌmōs\ *adj* [L *lacrimosus,* fr. *lacrima*] (1727) **1 :** given to tears or weeping **:** TEARFUL **2 :** tending to cause tears **:** MOURNFUL — **lach·ry·mose·ly** *adv*

lac·ing \ˈlā-siŋ\ *n* (14c) **1 :** the action of one that laces **2 :** something that laces **:** LACE **3 :** a contrasting marginal band of color (as on a feather) **4 a :** a dash of liquor in a food or beverage **b :** a trace or sprinkling that adds spice or flavor **5 :** an act or instance of beating or trouncing

la·cin·i·ate \lə-ˈsin-ē-ət, -ˌāt\ *adj* [L *lacinia* flap; akin to L *lacer*] (ca. 1760) **:** bordered with a fringe; *esp* **:** cut into deep irregular usu. pointed lobes ⟨~ petals⟩ — **la·cin·i·a·tion** \-ˌsin-ē-ˈā-shən\ *n*

[1]**lack** \ˈlak\ *vb* [ME *laken,* fr. MD; akin to ON *leka* to leak] *vi* (12c) **1 :** to be deficient or missing ⟨time ~s for a full explanation⟩ **2 :** to be short or have need of something ⟨he will not ~ for advisers⟩ ~ *vt* **:** to stand in need of **:** suffer from the absence or deficiency of ⟨~ the necessities of life⟩ ⟨he ~s skill in debate⟩

[2]**lack** *n* (14c) **1 :** the fact or state of being wanting or deficient **2 :** something that is lacking or is needed

lack·a·dai·si·cal \ˌlak-ə-ˈdā-zi-kəl\ *adj* [irreg. fr. *lackaday* + *-ical*] (1768) **:** lacking life, spirit, or zest **:** LANGUID — **lack·a·dai·si·cal·ly** \-k(ə-)lē\ *adv*

lack·a·day \ˈlak-ə-ˌdā\ *interj* [by alter. & shortening of *alack the day*] *archaic* (1695) — used to express regret or deprecation

[1]**lack·ey** \ˈlak-ē\ *n, pl* **lackeys** [MF *laquais*] (1523) **1 :** a liveried retainer **:** FOOTMAN **2 :** a servile follower **:** TOADY

[2]**lackey** *vb* **lack·eyed; lack·ey·ing** *vi, obs* (1568) **:** to act as a lackey **:** TOADY ~ *vt* **:** to wait upon or serve obsequiously

lack·lus·ter \ˈlak-ˌləs-tər\ *adj* (1600) **:** lacking in sheen, radiance, or vitality **:** DULL, MEDIOCRE — **lackluster** *n*

la·con·ic \lə-ˈkän-ik\ *adj* [L *laconicus* Spartan, fr. Gk *lakōnikos;* fr. the Spartan reputation for terseness of speech] (1589) **:** using or involving the use of a minimum of words **:** concise to the point of seeming rude or mysterious ***syn*** see CONCISE — **la·con·i·cal·ly** \-i-k(ə-)lē\ *adv*

lac·o·nism \ˈlak-ə-ˌniz-əm\ *n* (1669) **:** brevity or terseness of expression or style

[1]**lac·quer** \ˈlak-ər\ *n* [Pg *lacré* sealing wax, fr. *laca* lac, fr. Ar *lakk,* fr. Per *lak*] (1592) **1 a :** a spirit varnish (as shellac) **b :** any of various durable natural varnishes; *esp* **:** a varnish obtained from an Asian sumac (*Rhus verniciflua*) — called also *Chinese lacquer, Japanese lacquer* **2 :** any of various clear or colored synthetic organic coatings that typically dry to form a film by evaporation of the solvent; *esp* **:** a solution of a cellulose derivative (as nitrocellulose)

[2]**lacquer** *vt* **lac·quered; lac·quer·ing** \-(ə-)riŋ\ (1688) **1 :** to coat with or as if with lacquer **2 :** to give a smooth finish or appearance to **:** make glossy — **lac·quer·er** \-ər-ər\ *n*

lac·ri·ma·tion \ˌlak-rə-ˈmā-shən\ *n* (1572) **:** the secretion of tears esp. when abnormal or excessive

lac·ri·ma·tor *or* **lach·ry·ma·tor** \ˈlak-rə-ˌmāt-ər\ *n* [L *lacrimatus,* pp. of *lacrimare* to weep, fr. *lacrima* tear — more at LACHRYMAL] (1918) **:** a tear-producing substance (as tear gas)

la·crosse \lə-ˈkrȯs\ *n* [CanF *la crosse,* lit., the crosier] (1718) **:** a goal game in which players use a long-handled stick that has a triangular head with a loose mesh pouch for catching, carrying, and throwing the ball

lact- *or* **lacti-** *or* **lacto-** *comb form* [F & L; F, fr. L, fr. *lact-, lac* — more at GALAXY] **1 :** milk ⟨*lacto*flavin⟩ **2 a :** lactic acid ⟨*lact*ate⟩ **b :** lactose ⟨*lact*ase⟩

lact·al·bu·min \ˌlak-ˌtal-ˈbyü-mən\ *n* [ISV] (ca. 1857) **:** an albumin that is obtained from whey and is similar to serum albumin

lac·tase \ˈlak-ˌtās, -ˌtāz\ *n* [ISV] (1891) **:** an enzyme that hydrolyzes beta-galactosides (as lactose) and occurs esp. in the intestines of young mammals and in yeasts

[1]**lac·tate** \ˈlak-ˌtāt\ *n* (1794) **:** a salt or ester of lactic acid

[2]**lactate** *vi* **lac·tat·ed; lac·tat·ing** [L *lactatus,* pp. of *lactare,* fr. *lact-, lac*] (ca. 1889) **:** to secrete milk — **lac·ta·tion** \lak-ˈtā-shən\ *n* — **lac·ta·tion·al** \-shnəl, -shən-ᵊl\ *adj*

[1]**lac·te·al** \ˈlak-tē-əl\ *adj* [L *lacteus* of milk, fr. *lact-, lac*] (1658) **1 :** relating to, consisting of, producing, or resembling milk **2 a :** conveying or containing a milky fluid **b :** of or relating to the lacteals

[2]**lacteal** *n* (1680) **:** any of the lymphatic vessels arising from the villi of the small intestine and conveying chyle to the thoracic duct

lac·tic \ˈlak-tik\ *adj* (1874) **1 a :** of or relating to milk **b :** obtained from sour milk or whey **2 :** involving the production of lactic acid

lactic acid *n* (1790) **:** a hygroscopic organic acid $C_3H_6O_3$ present normally in tissue, produced in carbohydrate matter usu. by bacterial fermentation, and used esp. in food and medicine and in industry

lac·tif·er·ous \lak-ˈtif-(ə-)rəs\ *adj* [F or LL; F *lactifère,* fr. LL *lactifer,* fr. L *lact-, lac* + *-fer*] (1691) **1 :** secreting or conveying milk **2 :** yielding a milky juice ⟨~ plants⟩

lac·to·ba·cil·lus \ˌlak-tō-bə-ˈsil-əs\ *n* [NL] (1924) **:** any of a genus (*Lactobacillus*) of lactic-acid-forming bacteria

lac·to·gen·ic \ˌlak-tə-ˈjen-ik\ *adj* (1937) **:** inducing lactation ⟨~ hormones⟩

lac·to·glob·u·lin \-ˈgläb-yə-lən\ *n* (1885) **:** a crystalline protein fraction that is obtained from the whey of milk

lac·tone \ˈlak-ˌtōn\ *n* [ISV] (1880) **:** any of various cyclic esters formed from hydroxy acids — **lac·ton·ic** \lak-ˈtän-ik\ *adj*

lac·tose \ˈlak-ˌtōs, -ˌtōz\ *n* [ISV] (1858) **:** a disaccharide sugar $C_{12}H_{22}O_{11}$ that is present in milk and yields glucose and galactose upon hydrolysis and yields esp. lactic acid upon fermentation

la·cu·na \lə-ˈk(y)ü-nə\ *n, pl* **la·cu·nae** \-ˈkyü-(ˌ)nē, -ˈkü-ˌnī\ *or* **la·cu·nas** \-ˈk(y)ü-nəz\ [L, pool, pit, gap — more at LAGOON] (1652) **1 :** a blank space or a missing part **:** GAP **2 :** a small cavity, pit, or discontinuity in an anatomical structure — **la·cu·nar** \-ˈk(y)ü-nər\ *also* **la·cu·nate** \lə-ˈk(y)ü-nət, -ˌnāt; ˈlak-yə-ˌnāt\ *adj*

la·cu·nar \lə-ˈk(y)ü-nər\ *n* [L, fr. *lacuna*] (1696) **1 :** a ceiling with recessed panels **2** *pl* **lac·u·nar·ia** \ˌlak-yə-ˈner-ē-ə\ **:** a recessed panel in a patterned ceiling or soffit

la·cus·trine \lə-ˈkəs-trən\ *adj* [prob. fr. F or It *lacustre,* fr. L *lacus* lake] (1830) **:** of, relating to, formed in, or growing in lakes ⟨~ deposits⟩ ⟨~ faunas⟩

lacy \ˈlā-sē\ *adj* **lac·i·er; -est** (1804) **:** resembling or consisting of lace

lad \ˈlad\ *n* [ME *ladde*] (14c) **1 :** a male person of any age between early boyhood and maturity **:** BOY, YOUTH **2 :** FELLOW, CHAP

lad·a·num \ˈlad-ᵊn-əm, ˈlad-nəm\ *var of* LABDANUM

lad·der \ˈlad-ər\ *n, often attrib* [ME, fr. OE *hlǣder;* akin to OHG *leitara* ladder, OE *hlinian* to lean — more at LEAN] (bef. 12c) **1 :** a structure for climbing up or down that consists essentially of two long sidepieces joined at intervals by crosspieces on which one may step **2 :** something that resembles or suggests a ladder in form or use; *esp* **:** RUN 11a **3 :** a series of usu. ascending steps or stages **:** SCALE ⟨climbing up the corporate ~⟩ — **lad·der·like** \-ˌlīk\ *adj*

lad·der–back \-ˌbak\ *adj, of furniture* (1908) **:** having a back consisting of two upright posts connected by horizontal slats

ladder truck *n* (1889) **:** HOOK AND LADDER TRUCK

lad·die \ˈlad-ē\ *n* (1546) **:** a young lad

lade \ˈlād\ *vb* **lad·ed; laded** *or* **lad·en** \ˈlād-ᵊn\; **lad·ing** [ME *laden,* fr. OE *hladan;* akin to OHG *hladan* to load, OSlav *klasti*] *vt* (bef. 12c) **1 a :** to put a load or burden on or in **:** LOAD **b :** to put or place as a load esp. for shipment **:** SHIP **c :** to load heavily or oppressively **2 :** DIP, LADLE ~ *vi* **1 :** to take on cargo **:** LOAD **2 :** to take up or convey a liquid by dipping

[1]**lad·en** \ˈlād-ᵊn\ *vt* **lad·ened; lad·en·ing** \ˈlād-niŋ, -ᵊn-iŋ\ (bef. 12c) **:** LADE

[2]**laden** *adj* (bef. 12c) **:** carrying a load or burden

la–di–da \ˌläd-ē-ˈdä\ *also* **la–de–da** *adj* [perh. alter. of *lardy-dardy* (foppish)] (1861) **:** affectedly refined in manners or tastes **:** PRETENTIOUS, ELEGANT

ladies' man \ˈlād-ēz-\ *also* **lady's man** *n* (1784) **:** a man who shows a marked fondness for the company of women or is esp. attentive to women

ladies' room *n* (1870) **:** a room equipped with lavatories and toilets for the use of women

ladies' tresses *n pl but sing or pl in constr* (1548) **:** any of a widely distributed genus (*Spiranthes*) of terrestrial orchids with slender often twisted spikes of white irregular flowers

La·din \lə-ˈdēn\ *n* [Rhaeto-Romanic, fr. L *Latinum* Latin] (1877) **1 :** ROMANSH **2 :** one speaking Romansh as a mother tongue

lad·ing \ˈlād-iŋ\ *n* (1526) **1 a :** LOADING 1 **b :** an act of bailing, dipping, or ladling **2 :** CARGO, FREIGHT

la·di·no \lə-ˈdē-(ˌ)nō\ *n, pl* **-nos** [Sp, fr. *ladino* cunning, learned, lit., Latin, fr. L *latinus*] (1863) **1 :** JUDEO-SPANISH **2** *often cap* [AmerSp] **:** a westernized Spanish-speaking Latin American; *esp* **:** MESTIZO

la·di·no clover \lə-ˌdī-(ˌ)nō-, -nə-\ *n* [perh. irreg. fr. *Lodi,* Italy + It *-ino,* adj. suffix] (1924) **:** a large nutritious rapidly growing clover that is a variety of white clover and is widely planted for hay or silage — called also *la·di·no* \lə-ˈdī-(ˌ)nō, -nə\

[1]**la·dle** \ˈlād-ᵊl\ *n* [ME *ladel,* fr. OE *hlædel,* fr. *hladan*] (bef. 12c) **1 :** a deep-bowled long-handled spoon used esp. for dipping up and conveying liquids **2 :** an instrument or device resembling a ladle in form or function

[2]**ladle** *vt* **la·dled; la·dling** \ˈlād-liŋ, -ᵊl-iŋ\ (1525) **:** to take up and convey in or as if in a ladle

la dol·ce vi·ta \(ˌ)lä-ˌdōl-(ˌ)chā-ˈvē-(ˌ)tä\ *var of* DOLCE VITA

la·dy \ˈlād-ē\ *n, pl* **ladies** *often attrib* [ME, fr. OE *hlǣfdige,* fr. *hlāf* bread + *-dige* (akin to *dǣge* kneader of bread) — more at LOAF, DAIRY] (bef. 12c) **1 a :** a woman having proprietary rights or authority esp. as a feudal superior **b :** a woman receiving the homage or devotion of a knight or lover **2** *cap* **:** VIRGIN MARY — usu. used with *Our* **3 a :** a woman of superior social position **b :** a woman of refinement and gentle manners **c :** WOMAN, FEMALE — often used in a courteous reference ⟨show the ~ to a seat⟩ or usu. in the pl. in address ⟨*ladies* and gentlemen⟩ **4 a :** WIFE **b :** GIRLFRIEND, MISTRESS **5 a :** any of various titled women in Great Britain — used as the customary title of (1) a marchioness, countess, viscountess, or baroness or (2) the wife of a knight, baronet, member of the peerage, or one having the courtesy title of *lord* and used as a courtesy title for the daughter of a duke, marquess, or earl **b :** a female member of an order of knighthood — compare DAME

lady beetle *n* (ca. 1876) **:** LADYBUG

la·dy·bird \'lād-ē-ˌbərd\ *n* (1704) : LADYBUG

la·dy·bug \-ˌbəg\ *n* [Our *Lady,* the Virgin Mary] (1699) : any of numerous small nearly hemispherical often brightly colored beetles (family Coccinellidae) of temperate and tropical regions that usu. feed both as larvae and adults on other insects

lady chapel *n, often cap L&C* (15c) : a chapel dedicated to the Virgin Mary

Lady Day *n* (13c) : ANNUNCIATION 2

la·dy·fin·ger \'lād-ē-ˌfiŋ-gər\ *n* (1820) : a small finger-shaped sponge cake

la·dy·fish \-ˌfish\ *n* (1712) **1** : BONEFISH 1a **2** : a large silvery food and sport fish (*Elops saurus*) that resembles a herring but is related to the tarpon

la·dy–in–wait·ing \ˌlād-ē-in-'wāt-iŋ\ *n, pl* **ladies–in–waiting** (1862) : a lady of a queen's or a princess's household appointed to wait on her

la·dy–kill·er \'lād-ē-ˌkil-ər\ *n* (ca. 1810) : a man who is extremely attractive to women

la·dy·kin \'lād-ē-kən\ *n* (1853) : a little lady

la·dy·like \-ˌlīk\ *adj* (1586) **1** : becoming or suitable to a lady **2** : resembling a lady in appearance or manners : WELL-BRED **3 a** : feeling or showing too much concern about elegance or propriety ⟨~ embarrassment at not being the wife of a real doctor —Lewis Vogler⟩ **b** : lacking in strength, force, or virility

la·dy·love \'lād-ē-ˌləv, ˌlād-ē-'\ *n* (1733) : SWEETHEART, MISTRESS

lady of the house (1832) : the chief female in a household

Lady of the Lake (15c) : VIVIAN

la·dy·ship \'lād-ē-ˌship\ *n* (13c) : the condition of being a lady : rank of lady — used as a title for a woman having the rank of lady ⟨her *Ladyship* is not at home⟩ ⟨if your *Ladyship* please⟩

lady's slipper \'lād-ē(z)-ˌslip-ər\ *n* (1597) : any of several No. American temperate-zone orchids (as of the genus *Cypripedium*) having flowers whose shape suggests a slipper — called also *lady slipper*

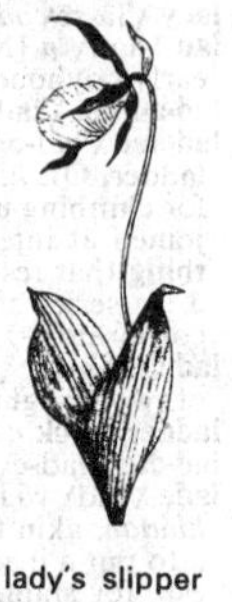

lady's slipper

la·dy's–smock \'lād-ē(z)-ˌsmäk\ *n* (1588) : CUCKOOFLOWER 1

lady's thumb *n* (1837) : a widely distributed weedy annual herb (*Polygonum persicaria*) that has large lanceolate leaves often with a blackish blotch suggesting a thumbprint

La·er·tes \lā-'ərt-ēz\ *n* [L, fr. Gk *Laertēs*] **1** : the father of Odysseus in Greek legend **2** : the son of Polonius and brother of Ophelia in Shakespeare's *Hamlet*

Lae·ta·re Sunday \lā-ˌtär-ē-, -ˌtar-ē-\ *n* [L *laetare,* sing. imper. of *laetari* to rejoice] (ca. 1870) : the fourth Sunday in Lent

la·e·trile \'lā-ə-(ˌ)tril, -trəl\ *n, often cap* [*laev-* (fr. L *laevus* left) prefix used in chemical compounds + *nitrile*] (ca. 1953) : a drug derived from apricot pits that contains amygdalin and has been used in the treatment of cancer although of unproved effectiveness

[1]**lag** \'lag\ *adj* [prob. of Scand origin; akin to Norw dial. *lagga* to go slowly] (15c) : LAST, HINDMOST

[2]**lag** *n* (1514) **1** : one that lags or is last **2 a** : the act or the condition of lagging **b** : comparative slowness or retardation **c** (1) : an amount of lagging or the time during which lagging continues (2) : a space of time esp. between related events or phenomena : INTERVAL **3** : the action of lagging for opening shot (as in marbles or billiards)

[3]**lag** *vb* **lagged; lag·ging** *vi* (1530) **1 a** : to stay or fall behind : LINGER, LOITER **b** : to move, function, or develop with comparative slowness **c** : to become retarded in attaining maximum value **2** : to slacken or weaken gradually : FLAG **3** : to toss or roll a marble toward a line or a cue ball toward the head cushion to determine order of play ~ *vt* **1** : to lag behind ⟨current that ~s the voltage⟩ **2** : to pitch or shoot (as a coin or marble) at a mark ***syn*** see DELAY — **lag·ger** *n*

[4]**lag** *n* [prob. of Scand origin; akin to ON *lögg* rim of a barrel] (1672) **1** : a barrel stave **2** : a stave, slat, or strip (as of wood or asbestos) forming part of a covering for a cylindrical object

[5]**lag** *vt* **lagged; lag·ging** (1870) : to cover or provide with lags

[6]**lag** *vt* **lagged; lag·ging** [origin unknown] (ca. 1812) **1** *slang chiefly Brit* : to transport for crime or send to jail **2** *slang chiefly Brit* : ARREST

[7]**lag** *n* (ca. 1812) **1** *slang chiefly Brit* **a** : a person transported for crime **b** : CONVICT **c** : an ex-convict **2** *slang chiefly Brit* : a jail sentence : STRETCH

lag·an \'lag-ən\ *also* **lag·end** \-ənd\ *n* [MF *lagan* or ML *laganum* debris washed up from the sea] (ca. 1641) : goods thrown into the sea with a buoy attached so that they may be found again

Lag b'Omer \'läg-'bō-mər, ˌläg-bə-'ō-\ *n* [Heb, 33d in Omer] (ca. 1904) : a Jewish holiday falling on the 33d day of the Omer and commemorating the heroism of Bar Kokhba and Akiba ben Joseph

la·ger \'läg-ər\ *n* [G *lagerbier* beer made for storage, fr. *lager* storehouse (fr. OHG *legar* bed) + *bier* beer — more at LAIR] (ca. 1853) : a light beer brewed by slow fermentation and matured under refrigeration

[1]**lag·gard** \'lag-ərd\ *adj* (1702) : lagging or tending to lag : DILATORY — **lag·gard·ly** *adv or adj* — **lag·gard·ness** *n*

[2]**laggard** *n* (1808) : one that lags or lingers

lag·ging \'lag-iŋ\ *n* (1794) : a lag or material used for making lags: as **a** : material for thermal insulation esp. around a cylindrical object **b** : planking used esp. for preventing cave-ins in earthwork or for supporting an arch during construction

la·gniappe \'lan-ˌyap, lan-'\ *n* [AmerF, fr. AmerSp *la ñapa* the lagniappe] (1849) : a small gift given a customer by a merchant at the time of a purchase; *broadly* : something given or obtained gratuitously or by way of good measure

lago·morph \'lag-ə-ˌmȯrf\ *n* [NL *Lagomorpha,* fr. Gk *lagōs* hare + *morphē* form] (1882) : any of an order (Lagomorpha) of gnawing mammals having two pairs of incisors in the upper jaw one behind the other and comprising the rabbits, hares, and pikas

la·goon \lə-'gün\ *n* [F & It; F *lagune,* fr. It *laguna,* fr. L *lacuna* pit, pool, fr. *lacus* lake] (1612) **1** : a shallow sound, channel, or pond near or communicating with a larger body of water **2** : a shallow artificial pool or pond (as for the processing of sewage or storage of a liquid) — **la·goon·al** \-ᵊl\ *adj*

La·grang·ian \lə-'grän-jē-ən, -'grän-zhē-\ *n* [Joseph Louis *Lagrange*] (1938) : a function that describes the state of a dynamic system in terms of position coordinates and their time derivatives and that is equal to the difference between the potential energy and kinetic energy — called also *kinetic potential;* compare HAMILTONIAN

la·gu·na \lə-'gü-nə\ *n* [Sp, fr. L *lacuna*] (1784) : a small lake or pond

la·har \'lä-ˌhär\ *n* [Jav] (1929) : a flowing mass of mingled volcanic debris and water

Lahn·da \'län-də\ *n* (1901) : an Indic language of West Punjab

la·ical \'lā-ə-kəl\ *or* **la·ic** \'lā-ik\ *adj* [LL *laicus,* fr. LGk *laïkos,* fr. Gk, of the people, fr. *laos* people] (ca. 1563) : of or relating to the laity : SECULAR — **laic** *n* — **la·ical·ly** \'lā-ə-k(ə-)lē\ *adv*

la·icism \'lā-ə-ˌsiz-əm\ *n* (ca. 1909) : a political system characterized by the exclusion of ecclesiastical control and influence

la·icize \'lā-ə-ˌsīz\ *vt* **la·icized; la·iciz·ing** (ca. 1865) **1** : to reduce to lay status **2** : to put under the direction of or open to laymen — **la·ici·za·tion** \ˌlā-ə-sə-'zā-shən\ *n*

laid *past and past part of* LAY

laid–back \'lād-'bak\ *adj* (ca. 1969) : having a relaxed style or character ⟨~ music⟩

laid paper \'lād-\ *n* (1839) : paper watermarked with fine lines running across the grain — compare WOVE PAPER

laigh \'lāk\ *Scot var of* LOW

lain *past part of* LIE

[1]**lair** \'la(ə)r, 'le(ə)r\ *n* [ME, fr. OE *leger;* akin to OHG *legar* bed, OE *licgan* to lie — more at LIE] (bef. 12c) **1** *dial Brit* : a resting or sleeping place : BED **2 a** : the resting or living place of a wild animal : DEN **b** : a refuge or place for hiding

[2]**lair** *vb* [Sc *lair* (mire)] *vt, chiefly Scot* (ca. 1560) : to cause to sink in mire ~ *vi, chiefly Scot* : WALLOW

laird \'la(ə)rd, 'le(ə)rd\ *n* [ME (northern dial.) *lord, lard* lord] *Scot* (12c) : a landed proprietor — **laird·ly** \-lē\ *adj*

lais·ser–faire *chiefly Brit var of* LAISSEZ-FAIRE

lais·sez–faire \ˌle-ˌsā-'fa(ə)r, ˌlā-, -ˌzā-, -'fe(ə)r\ *n* [F *laissez faire,* imper. of *laisser faire* to let (people) do (as they choose)] (1825) **1** : a doctrine opposing governmental interference in economic affairs beyond the minimum necessary for the maintenance of peace and property rights **2** : a philosophy or practice characterized by a usu. deliberate abstention from direction or interference esp. with individual freedom of choice and action — **laissez–faire** *adj*

lais·sez–pas·ser \-ˌpa-'sā\ *n* [F, fr. *laissez passer* let (someone) pass] (1914) : PERMIT, PASS

lai·tance \'lāt-ᵊn(t)s\ *n* [F, fr. *lait* milk, fr. L *lact-, lac* — more at GALAXY] (ca. 1902) : an accumulation of fine particles on the surface of fresh concrete due to an upward movement of water (as when excessive mixing water is used)

la·ity \'lā-ət-ē\ *n* [[5]*lay*] (15c) **1** : the people of a religious faith as distinguished from its clergy **2** : the mass of the people as distinguished from those of a particular profession or those specially skilled

La·ius \'lā-(y)əs, 'lī-əs\ *n* [L, fr. Gk *Laïos*] : a king of Thebes slain by his son Oedipus in fulfillment of an oracle

[1]**lake** \'lāk\ *n, often attrib* [ME, fr. OF *lac* lake, fr. L *lacus;* akin to OE *lagu* sea, Gk *lakkos* pond] (13c) : a considerable inland body of standing water; *also* : a pool of other liquid (as lava, oil, or pitch)

[2]**lake** *n* [F *laque* lac, fr. OProv *laca,* fr. Ar *lakk* — more at LACQUER] (1558) **1 a** : a purplish red pigment prepared from lac or cochineal **b** : any of numerous usu. bright translucent organic pigments composed essentially of a soluble dye absorbed on or combined with an inorganic carrier **2** : CARMINE 2 — **laky** \'lā-kē\ *adj*

[3]**lake** *vb* **laked; lak·ing** *vt* (1903) : to cause (blood) to undergo a physiological change in which the hemoglobin becomes dissolved in the plasma ~ *vi, of blood* : to undergo the process by which hemoglobin becomes dissolved in the plasma

lake dwelling *n* (1863) : a dwelling built on piles in a lake; *specif* : one built in prehistoric times — **lake dweller** *n*

lake·front \'lāk-ˌfrənt\ *n* (1880) : an area fronting on a lake

lake herring *n* (1842) : a cisco (*Coregonus artedii*) found from Lake Memphremagog to Lake Superior and northward and important as a commercial food fish; *broadly* : CISCO

Lake·land terrier \ˌlā-ˌklan(d)-, -klən(d)-\ *n* [*Lakeland,* England] (1928) : any of an English breed of rather small harsh-coated straight-legged terriers

lak·er \'lā-kər\ *n* (1823) : one associated with a lake; *esp* : a fish living in or taken from a lake

lake·shore \-ˌshō(ə)r, -ˌshȯ(ə)r\ *n* (1798) : the shore of a lake; *also* : LAKEFRONT

lake·side \-ˌsīd\ *n* (1560) : LAKEFRONT

lake trout *n* (1668) : any of various salmon and trout found in lakes; *esp* : a large dark No. American char (*Salvelinus namaycush*) that is an important commercial food fish in northern lakes

lakh \'läk, 'lak\ *n* [Hindi *lākh*] (1599) **1** : one hundred thousand ⟨50 ~s of rupees⟩ **2** : a great number — **lakh** *adj*

-la·lia \'lā-lē-ə\ *n comb form* [NL, fr. Gk *lalia* chatter, fr. *lalein* to chat; akin to L *latrare* to bark — more at LAMENT] : speech disorder (of a specified type) ⟨echo*lalia*⟩

lal·lan \'lal-ən\ *or* **lal·land** \-ən(d)\ *Scot var of* LOWLAND

Lal·lans \'lal-ənz\ *n* (1785) : Scots as spoken and written in the lowlands of Scotland

Lal·ly \'lal-ē\ *trademark* — used for a concrete-filled cylindrical steel structural column

lal·ly·gag \'läl-\ *var of* LOLLYGAG

[1]**lam** \'lam\ *vb* **lammed; lam·ming** [of Scand origin; akin to ON *lemja* to thrash; akin to OE *lama* lame] *vt* (1596) : to beat soundly : THRASH ~ *vi* **1** : STRIKE, THRASH **2** : to flee hastily : SCRAM

[2]**lam** *n* (1897) : sudden or hurried flight esp. from the law ⟨on the ~⟩

la·ma \'läm-ə\ *n* [Tibetan *blama*] (1654) : a Lamaist monk

La·ma·ism \'läm-ə-ˌiz-əm\ *n* (1817) : the Mahayana Buddhism of Tibet and Mongolia marked by tantric and shamanistic ritual and a dominant monastic hierarchy headed by the Dalai Lama — **La·ma·ist** \-əst\ *n or adj* — **La·ma·is·tic** \ˌläm-ə-'is-tik\ *adj*

La·marck·ian \lə-'mär-kē-ən\ *adj* (1846) : of or relating to Lamarckism

La·marck·ism \lə-'mär-ˌkiz-əm\ *n* [J. B. de Monet *Lamarck*] (1884) : a theory of organic evolution asserting that environmental changes cause structural changes in animals and plants that are transmitted to offspring

la·ma·sery \'läm-ə-,ser-ē\ *n, pl* **-ser·ies** [F *lamaserie,* fr. *lama* + Per *sarāī* palace] (1849) **:** a monastery of lamas

La·maze \lə-'mäz\ *adj* [Fernand *Lamaze* †1957 Fr. obstetrician] (1965) **:** relating to or being a method of childbirth that involves psychological and physical preparation by the mother in order to suppress pain and facilitate delivery without drugs

¹lamb \'lam\ *n* [ME, fr. OE; akin to OHG *lamb* lamb, *elaho* elk — more at ELK] (bef. 12c) **1 a :** a young sheep; *esp* **:** one that is less than one year old or without permanent teeth **b :** the young of various animals (as the smaller antelopes) other than sheep **2 a :** a gentle or weak person **b :** DEAR, PET **c :** a person easily cheated or deceived esp. in trading securities **3 a :** the flesh of a lamb used as food **b :** LAMBSKIN

²lamb *vi* (bef. 12c) **:** to bring forth a lamb ~ *vt* **1 :** to bring forth (a lamb) **2 :** to tend (ewes) at lambing time — **lamb·er** \'lam-ər\ *n*

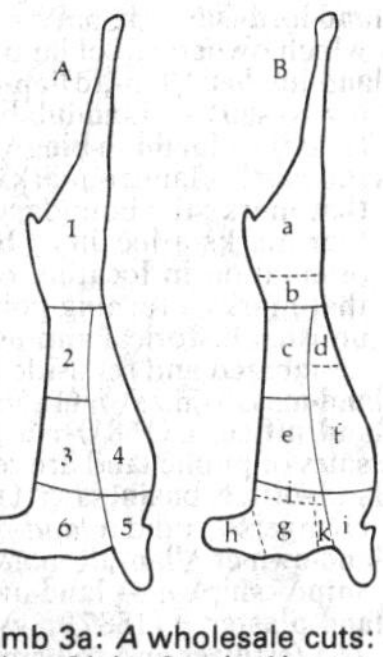

lamb 3a: *A* wholesale cuts: *1* leg, *2* loin, *3* rack, *4* breast, *5* shank, *6* shoulder; *B* retail cuts: *a* leg, *b* sirloin chops and roast, *c* loin chops, rolled loin roast, *d* patties and chopped roast, *e* rib chops, crown roast, *f* riblets, stew, and stuffed or rolled breast, *g* shoulder roast, shoulder chops, *h* neck slices, *i* shanks, *j* blade chops, *k* arm chops

lam·baste *or* **lam·bast** \(')lam-'bāst, -'bast\ *vt* [prob. fr. ¹*lam* + *baste*] (1637) **1 :** to assault violently **:** BEAT, WHIP **2 :** to attack verbally **:** CENSURE

lamb·da \'lam-də\ *n* [Gk, of Sem origin; akin to Heb *lāmedh* lamed] (15c) **1 :** the 11th letter of the Greek alphabet — see ALPHABET table **2 :** one thousandth of a cubic centimeter **3 :** an uncharged unstable elementary particle that has a mass 2183 times that of an electron and that decays typically into a nucleon and a pion

lam·ben·cy \'lam-bən-sē\ *n, pl* **-cies** (1817) **:** the quality, state, or an instance of being lambent

lam·bent \'lam-bənt\ *adj* [L *lambent-, lambens,* prp. of *lambere* to lick — more at LAP] (1647) **1 :** playing lightly on or over a surface **:** FLICKERING **2 :** softly bright or radiant **3 :** marked by lightness or brilliance esp. of expression — **lam·bent·ly** *adv*

lam·bert \'lam-bərt\ *n* [Johann H. *Lambert* †1777 Ger. physicist & philosopher] (1915) **:** the centimeter-gram-second unit of brightness equal to the brightness of a perfectly diffusing surface that radiates or reflects one lumen per square centimeter

lamb·kill \'lam-,kil\ *n* (ca. 1790) **:** SHEEP LAUREL

lam·bre·quin \'lam-bər-kən, -bri-kən\ *n* [F] (1725) **1 :** a scarf used to cover a knight's helmet **2 :** a short decorative drapery for a shelf edge or for the top of a window casing **:** VALANCE

lamb·skin \'lam-,skin\ *n* (14c) **:** a lamb's skin or a small fine-grade sheepskin or the leather made from either; *specif* **:** such a skin dressed with the wool on and used esp. for winter clothing

lamb's-quar·ter \'lamz-,kwȯ(r)t-ər\ *n* (1773) **1 :** a goosefoot (*Chenopodium album*) with glaucous foliage that is sometimes used as a potherb — usu. used in pl. but sing. or pl. in constr. **2 :** any of several oraches — usu. used in pl. but sing. or pl. in constr.

¹lame \'lām\ *adj* **lam·er; lam·est** [ME, fr. OE *lama;* akin to OHG *lam* lame, Lith *limti* to break down] (bef. 12c) **1 a :** having a body part and esp. a limb so disabled as to impair freedom of movement ⟨a ~ old man⟩ **b :** marked by stiffness and soreness ⟨a ~ shoulder⟩ **2 :** lacking needful or desirable substance **:** WEAK ⟨a ~ excuse⟩ **3** *slang* **:** not being in the know **:** SQUARE — **lame·ly** *adv* — **lame·ness** *n*

²lame *vt* **lamed; lam·ing** (14c) **1 :** to make lame **:** CRIPPLE **2 :** to make weak or ineffective **:** DISABLE

³lame *n, slang* (1959) **:** a person who is not in the know **:** SQUARE

⁴lame \'lām, 'lam\ *n* [MF, fr. L *lamina*] (1586) **1 :** a thin plate esp. of metal **:** LAMINA **2** *pl* **:** small overlapping steel plates joined to slide on one another (as in medieval armor)

la·mé \lä-'mā, la-\ *n* [F] (1922) **:** a brocaded clothing fabric made from any of various fibers combined with tinsel filling threads often of gold or silver

lame·brain \'lām-,brān\ *n* (1929) **:** a dull-witted person **:** DOLT — **lamebrain** *or* **lame·brained** \-'brānd\ *adj*

la·med \'läm-,ed\ *n* [Heb *lāmedh,* lit., ox goad] (1665) **:** the 12th letter of the Hebrew alphabet — see ALPHABET table

lame duck *n* (1761) **1 :** one that falls behind in achievement **:** WEAKLING **2 :** an elected official or group continuing to hold political office during a usu. brief interim between the election and the inauguration of a successor — **lame–duck** \lām-,dək\ *adj*

lamell- *or* **lamelli-** *comb form* [NL, fr. *lamella*] **:** lamella ⟨*lamelli*form⟩ ⟨*lamell*ose⟩

la·mel·la \lə-'mel-ə\ *n, pl* **la·mel·lae** \-'mel-(,)ē, -,ī\ *also* **lamellas** [NL, fr. L, dim. of *lamina* thin plate] (1678) **:** a thin flat scale, membrane, or layer: as **a :** one of the thin plates composing the gills of a bivalve mollusk **b :** a gill of a mushroom

la·mel·lar \lə-'mel-ər\ *adj* (1794) **1 :** composed of or arranged in lamellae **2 :** LAMELLIFORM

la·mel·late \lə-'mel-ət, 'lam-ə-,lāt\ *adj* (1826) **1 :** composed of or furnished with lamellae **2 :** LAMELLIFORM — **la·mel·late·ly** *adv*

lam·el·la·tion \,lam-ə-'lā-shən\ *n* (ca. 1903) **1 :** formation or division into lamellae **2 :** LAMELLA

la·mel·li·branch \lə-'mel-ə-,braŋk\ *n, pl* **-branchs** [NL *Lamellibranchia,* fr. *lamell-* + L *branchia* gill — more at BRANCHIA] (1855) **:** any of a class (Lamellibranchia) of bivalve mollusks (as clams, oysters, and mussels) that have the body bilaterally symmetrical, compressed, and enclosed within the mantle and that build up a shell whose right and left parts are connected by a hinge over the animal's back — **lamellibranch** *adj*

la·mel·li·corn \lə-'mel-ə-,kȯrn\ *adj* (1843) **:** of, relating to, or belonging to a taxonomic group (Lamellicornia) of beetles (as a dung beetle and a stag beetle) that are characterized by 5-jointed tarsi and club-shaped antennae — **lamellicorn** *n*

la·mel·li·form \-,fȯrm\ *adj* (1819) **:** having the form of a thin plate

¹la·ment \lə-'ment\ *vb* [MF & L; MF *lamenter,* fr. L *lamentari,* fr. *lamentum,* n., lament; akin to ON *lōmr* loon, L *latrare* to bark, Gk *lēros* nonsense] *vi* (15c) **:** to mourn aloud **:** WAIL ~ *vt* **1 :** to express sorrow or mourning for often demonstratively **:** MOURN **2 :** to regret strongly ***syn*** see DEPLORE

²lament *n* (1591) **1 :** a crying out in grief **:** WAILING **2 :** DIRGE, ELEGY **3 :** COMPLAINT

la·men·ta·ble \'lam-ən-tə-bəl, lə-'ment-ə-\ *adj* (15c) **1 :** that is to be regretted or lamented **:** DEPLORABLE **2 :** expressing grief **:** MOURNFUL — **la·men·ta·ble·ness** *n* — **la·men·ta·bly** \-blē\ *adv*

lam·en·ta·tion \,lam-ən-'tā-shən\ *n* (14c) **:** an act or instance of lamenting

Lam·en·ta·tions \-shənz\ *n pl but sing in constr* **:** a poetic book on the fall of Jerusalem in canonical Jewish and Christian Scripture — see BIBLE table

la·ment·ed \lə-'ment-əd\ *adj* (1611) **:** mourned for — **la·ment·ed·ly** *adv*

la·mia \'lā-mē-ə\ *n* [ME, fr. L, fr. Gk, devouring monster — more at LEMUR] (14c) **:** a female demon **:** VAMPIRE

lamin- *or* **lamini-** *or* **lamino-** *comb form* **:** lamina ⟨*lamin*ar⟩

lam·i·na \'lam-ə-nə\ *n, pl* **-nae** \-,nē, -,nī\ *or* **-nas** [L] (1656) **1 :** a thin plate or scale **:** LAYER **2 :** the expanded part of a foliage leaf **3 :** one of the narrow thin parallel plates of soft vascular sensitive tissue that cover the flesh within the wall of a hoof

lam·i·nal \'lam-ən-ᵊl\ *adj* (1825) **:** LAMINAR

lamina pro·pria \-'prō-prē-ə\ *n, pl* **laminae pro·pri·ae** \-prē-,ē, -,ī\ [NL, lit., lamina proper] (1937) **:** a highly vascular layer of connective tissue under the basement membrane lining a layer of epithelium

lam·i·nar \'lam-ə-nər\ *adj* (1811) **:** arranged in, consisting of, or resembling laminae

laminar flow *n* (1935) **:** streamline flow in a fluid near a solid boundary — compare TURBULENT FLOW

lam·i·nar·ia \,lam-ə-'ner-ē-ə, -'nar-\ *n* [NL] (1848) **:** any of a genus (*Laminaria*) of large chiefly perennial kelps with an unbranched cylindrical or flattened stipe and a smooth or convoluted blade; *broadly* **:** any of various related kelps (order Laminariales) — **lam·i·nar·i·an** \-ē-ən\ *adj or n*

lam·i·nar·in \,lam-ə-'ner-ən, -'nar-\ *n* [ISV *laminar-* (fr. NL *Laminaria*) + *-in*] (ca. 1931) **:** a polysaccharide that is found in various brown algae and yields only glucose on hydrolysis

¹lam·i·nate \'lam-ə-,nāt\ *vb* **-nat·ed; -nat·ing** *vt* (1665) **1 :** to roll or compress into a thin plate **2 :** to separate into laminae **3 a :** to make (as a windshield) by uniting superposed layers of one or more materials **b :** to unite (layers of material) by an adhesive or other means ~ *vi* **:** to divide into laminae — **lam·i·na·tor** \-,nāt-ər\ *n*

²lam·i·nate \-nət, -,nāt\ *adj* (1668) **1 :** consisting of laminae **2 :** bearing or covered with laminae

³lam·i·nate \-nət, -,nāt\ *n* (1939) **:** a product made by laminating

lam·i·nat·ed \-,nāt-əd\ *adj* (1665) **1 :** LAMINATE 1 **2 a :** composed of layers of firmly united material **b :** made by bonding or impregnating superposed layers (as of paper, wood, or fabric) with resin and compressing under heat

lam·i·na·tion \,lam-ə-'nā-shən\ *n* (1676) **1 :** the process of laminating **2 :** the state of being laminated **3 :** a laminate structure **4 :** LAMINA

lam·i·ni·tis \,lam-ə-'nīt-əs\ *n* [NL] (ca. 1843) **:** inflammation of a lamina esp. in the hoof of a horse

Lam·mas \'lam-əs\ *n* [ME *Lammasse,* fr. OE *hlāfmæsse,* fr. *hlāf* loaf, bread + *mæsse* mass; fr. the fact that formerly loaves from the first ripe grain were consecrated on this day] (bef. 12c) **1 :** August 1 orig. celebrated in England as a harvest festival — called also *Lammas Day* **2 :** the time of the year around Lammas Day

Lammastide *n* (14c) **:** LAMMAS 2

lam·mer·gei·er *or* **lam·mer·gey·er** \'lam-ər-,gī(-ə)r\ *n* [G *lämmergeier*] (1817) **:** a large Eurasian vulture (*Gypaetus barbatus aureus*) that occurs in mountain regions from the Pyrenees to northern China and in flight resembles a huge falcon

lamp \'lamp\ *n* [ME, fr. OF *lampe,* fr. L *lampas,* fr. Gk, fr. *lampein* to shine; akin to ON *leiptr* lightning] (13c) **1 a :** a vessel with a wick for burning an inflammable liquid (as oil) to produce artificial light **b :** any of various devices for producing light or heat **2 :** a celestial body **3 :** a source of intellectual or spiritual illumination

lamp·black \-,blak\ *n* (1598) **:** a finely powdered black soot deposited in incomplete combustion of carbonaceous materials and used chiefly as a pigment (as in paints, enamels, and printing inks)

lamp·brush chromosome \,lamp-,brəsh-\ *n* [trans. of G *lampebürstechromosom,* fr. *lampebürste* brush for cleaning oil lamps] (1911) **:** a greatly enlarged pachytene chromosome that has apparently filamentous granular loops extending from the chromomeres and is characteristic of some animal oocytes

lam·per eel \,lam-pər-\ *n* [alter. of *lamprey*] (1709) **:** LAMPREY

lamp·light \'lamp-,plīt\ *n* (14c) **:** the light of a lamp

lamp·light·er \-ər\ *n* (1750) **:** one that lights a lamp

¹lam·poon \lam-'pün\ *n* [F *lampon*] (1645) **:** SATIRE 1; *specif* **:** a harsh satire usu. directed against an individual

²lampoon *vt* (1657) **:** to make the subject of a lampoon **:** RIDICULE — **lam·poon·er** *n* — **lam·poon·ery** \-'pün-(ə-)rē\ *n*

lamp·post \'lam(p)-,pōst\ *n* (1790) **:** a post supporting a usu. outdoor lamp or lantern

lam·prey \'lam-prē, -,prā\ *n, pl* **lampreys** [ME, fr. OF *lampreie,* fr. ML *lampreda*] (12c) **:** any of an order (Hyperoartia) of aquatic vertebrates that are widely distributed in temperate and subarctic regions in both fresh and salt water and resemble eels but have a large suctorial mouth — called also *lamprey eel*

lamp·shell \'lamp-,shel\ *n* [fr. the resemblance of the shell and its protruding peduncle to an ancient oil lamp with the wick protruding] (1854) **:** BRACHIOPOD

lam·ster \'lam(p)-stər\ *also* **lam·is·ter** \'lam-ə-stər\ *n* [²*lam* + *-ster*] (1904) **:** a fugitive esp. from the law

\ə\ abut \ᵊ\ kitten, F table \ər\ further \a\ ash \ā\ ace \ä\ cot, cart \au̇\ out \ch\ chin \e\ bet \ē\ easy \g\ go \i\ hit \ī\ ice \j\ job \ŋ\ sing \ō\ go \ȯ\ law \ȯi\ boy \th\ thin \t͟h\ the \ü\ loot \u̇\ foot \y\ yet \zh\ vision \à, k̲, ⁿ, œ, œ̄, ue, ue̅, ʸ\ see Guide to Pronunciation

LAN \'lan, 'el-'ā-'en\ *n* (1982) : LOCAL AREA NETWORK
la·nai \lə-'nī, lä-\ *n* [Hawaiian] (1823) : PORCH, VERANDA
Lan·ca·shire \'laŋ-kə-,shi(ə)r, -shər\ *n* [*Lancashire*, England] (1896) : a moist crumbly white English cheese that is used esp. in cooking
Lan·cas·tri·an \lan-'kas-trē-ən, laŋ-\ *adj* [John of Gaunt, duke of *Lancaster*] (1612) : of or relating to the English royal house that ruled from 1399 to 1461
[1]**lance** \'lan(t)s\ *n* [ME, fr. OF, fr. L *lancea*] (13c) **1** : a steel-tipped spear carried by mounted knights or light cavalry **2** : any of various sharp objects suggestive of a lance: as **a** : LANCET **b** : a spear used for killing whales or fish **3** : LANCER 1b
[2]**lance** *vb* **lanced; lanc·ing** [ME *launcen*, fr. MF *lancer*, fr. LL *lanceare*, fr. L *lancea*] *vt* (14c) **1 a** : to pierce with or as if with a lance **b** : to open with or as if with a lancet ⟨~ a boil⟩ **2** : to throw forward : HURL ~ *vi* : to move forward quickly
lance corporal *n* [*lance* (as in obs. *lancepesade* lance corporal, fr. MF *lancepessade*)] (1786) : an enlisted man in the marine corps ranking above a private first class and below a corporal
lance·let \'lan(t)-slət\ *n* (1836) : any of various small translucent marine animals (subphylum Cephalochordata) related to the vertebrates — called also *amphioxus*
Lan·ce·lot \'lan(t)-sə-,lät, 'län(t)-, -s(ə-)lət\ *n* [F] : a knight of the Round Table and lover of Queen Guinevere
lan·ceo·late \'lan(t)-sē-ə-,lāt\ *adj* [LL *lanceolatus*, fr. L *lanceola*, dim. of *lancea*] (1760) : shaped like a lance head; *specif* : tapering to a point at the apex and sometimes at the base ⟨~ leaves⟩ ⟨~ prisms⟩
lanc·er \'lan(t)-sər\ *n* (1590) **1 a** : one who carries a lance **b** : a member of a military unit formerly composed of light cavalry armed with lances **2** *pl but sing in constr* **a** : a set of five quadrilles each in a different meter **b** : the music for such dances
lan·cet \'lan(t)-sət\ *n* (15c) **1** : a sharp-pointed and commonly 2-edged surgical instrument used to make small incisions **2 a** : LANCET WINDOW **b** : LANCET ARCH
lancet arch *n* (ca. 1823) : an acutely pointed arch — see ARCH illustration
lan·cet·ed \'lan(t)-sət-əd\ *adj* (1855) : having a lancet arch or lancet windows
lancet window *n* (1781) : a high narrow window with an acutely pointed head and without tracery
lance·wood \'lan(t)-,swu̇d\ *n* (1697) : a tough elastic wood used esp. for shafts, fishing rods, and bows; *also* : a tree (esp. *Oxandra lanceolata*) yielding this wood
lan·ci·nat·ing \'lan(t)-sə-,nāt-iŋ\ *adj* [*lancinate* to pierce, fr. L *lancinatus*, pp. of *lancinare*; akin to L *lacer* mangled — more at LACERATE] (1762) : characterized by piercing or stabbing sensations ⟨~ pain⟩
[1]**land** \'land\ *n, often attrib* [ME, fr. OE; akin to OHG *lant* land, OIr *land* open space] (bef. 12c) **1 a** : the solid part of the surface of the earth; *also* : a corresponding part of a celestial body (as the moon) **b** : ground or soil of a specified situation, nature, or quality ⟨dry ~⟩ **c** : the surface of the earth and all its natural resources **2** : a portion of the earth's solid surface distinguishable by boundaries or ownership ⟨hoping to buy ~ in the country⟩ : as **a** : COUNTRY ⟨campaigned in every corner of the ~⟩ **b** : a rural area characterized by farming or ranching; *also* : farming or ranching as a way of life ⟨modern homesteaders joining the back-to-the-land movement⟩ **3** : REALM, DOMAIN ⟨in the ~ of dreams⟩ **4** : the people of a country ⟨the ~ rose in rebellion⟩ **5** : an area of a partly machined surface that is left without machining — **land·less** \'lan-dləs\ *adj*
[2]**land** *vt* (13c) **1** : to set or put on shore from a ship : DISEMBARK **2 a** : to set down after conveying **b** : to cause to reach or come to rest in a particular place ⟨never ~*ed* a punch⟩ **c** : to bring to a specified condition ⟨his carelessness ~*ed* him in trouble⟩ **d** : to bring (as an airplane) to a landing **3 a** : to catch and bring in (as a fish) **b** : GAIN, SECURE ⟨~ a job⟩ ~ *vi* **1 a** : to go ashore from a ship : DISEMBARK **b** *of a ship or boat* : to touch at a place on shore **2 a** : to come to the end of a course or to a stage in a journey : ARRIVE ⟨took the wrong subway and ~*ed* on the other side of town⟩ **b** : to strike or meet a surface (as after a fall) ⟨~*ed* on my head⟩ **c** *of an airplane or spacecraft* : to alight on a surface
lan·dau \'lan-,dau̇, -,dȯ\ *n* [*Landau*, Bavaria, Germany] (1743) **1** : a four-wheeled carriage with a top divided into two sections that can be let down, thrown back, or removed and with a raised seat outside for the driver **2** : a closed automobile body with a folding top over the rear passenger compartment
lan·dau·let \,lan-dᵊl-'et\ *n* (1794) **1** : a small landau **2** : an automobile body with an open driver's seat and an enclosed rear section having a folding top
land bank *n* (1696) : a bank that provides financing for land development and for farm mortgages
land·ed \'lan-dəd\ *adj* (bef. 12c) **1** : having an estate in land ⟨~ proprietors⟩ **2** : consisting in or derived from land or real estate ⟨~ wealth⟩
land·er \'lan-dər\ *n* (1859) : one that lands; *esp* : a space vehicle that is designed to land on a celestial body (as the moon or a planet)
land·fall \'lan(d)-,fȯl\ *n* (1627) **1** : a sighting or making of land after a voyage or flight **2** : the land first sighted on a voyage or flight
land·fill \-,fil\ *n* (1952) **1** : a system of trash and garbage disposal in which the waste is buried between layers of earth to build up low-lying land — called also *sanitary landfill* **2** : an area built up by landfill
land·form \-,fȯrm\ *n* (1893) : a natural feature of a land surface
land grant *n* (1862) : a grant of land made by the government esp. for roads, railroads, or agricultural colleges
land·hold·er \'land-,hōl-dər\ *n* (15c) : a holder or owner of land — **land·hold·ing** \-diŋ\ *adj or n*
land·ing *n* (15c) **1** : an act or process of one that lands; *esp* : a going or bringing to a surface (as land or shore) after a voyage or flight **2** : a place for discharging and taking on passengers and cargo **3** : a level part of a staircase (as at the end of a flight of stairs)
landing craft *n* (1940) : any of numerous naval craft designed for putting troops and equipment ashore
landing field *n* (ca. 1920) : a field where aircraft may land and take off
landing gear *n* (1911) : the part that supports the weight of an airplane or spacecraft when in contact with the land or water — see AIRPLANE illustration
landing strip *n* (1930) : AIRSTRIP
land·la·dy \'lan-,(d)lād-ē\ *n* (1536) : a woman who is a landlord
land·locked \'lan-,(d)läkt\ *adj* (1622) **1** : enclosed or nearly enclosed by land ⟨a ~ country⟩ **2** : confined to fresh water by some barrier ⟨~ salmon⟩
land·lord \'lan-,(d)lȯ(ə)rd\ *n* (bef. 12c) **1** : the owner of property (as land, houses, or apartments) that is leased or rented to another **2** : the master of an inn or lodging house : INNKEEPER
land·lord·ism \-,iz-əm\ *n* (1844) : an economic system or practice by which ownership of land is vested in one who leases it to cultivators
land·lub·ber \'lan-,(d)ləb-ər\ *n* (1700) : LANDSMAN 2 ⟨clumsy ~*s* learning to sail⟩ — **land·lub·ber·li·ness** \-ər-lē-nəs\ *n* — **land·lub·ber·ly** \-ər-lē\ *adj* — **land·lub·bing** \-iŋ\ *adj*
land·mark \'lan(d)-,märk\ *n* (bef. 12c) **1** : an object (as a stone or tree) that marks the boundary of land **2 a** : a conspicuous object on land that marks a locality **b** : an anatomical structure used as a point of orientation in locating other structures **3** : an event or development that marks a turning point or a stage **4** : a structure (as a building) of unusual historical and usu. aesthetic interest; *esp* : one that is officially designated and set aside for preservation
land·mass \-,mas\ *n* (1856) : a large area of land ⟨continental ~*es*⟩
land office *n* (1681) : a government office in which entries upon and sales of public land are registered
land–office business *n* (1839) : extensive and rapid business ⟨money changers . . . did a *land-office business* on payday —F. J. Haskin⟩
land·own·er \'lan-,dō-nər\ *n* (1733) : an owner of land — **land·own·er·ship** \-,ship\ *n* — **land·own·ing** \-,dō-niŋ\ *adj or n*
land plaster *n* (1887) : gypsum or gypsiferous rock ground fine for use as a fertilizer and soil amendment
land–poor \'lan(d)-,pu̇(ə)r\ *adj* (1873) : owning so much unprofitable or encumbered land as to lack funds to develop the land or pay the charges due on it
Land·ra·ce \'län-,(d)räs-ə\ *n* [Dan, fr. *land* + *race*] (1935) : a swine of any of several breeds locally developed in northern Europe
land rail *n* (1766) : CORNCRAKE
land reform *n* (1846) : measures designed to effect a more equitable distribution of agricultural land esp. by governmental action; *also* : the resulting redistribution
[1]**land·scape** \'lan(d)-,skāp\ *n, often attrib* [D *landschap*, fr. *land* + *-schap* -ship] (1598) **1 a** : a picture representing a view of natural inland scenery **b** : the art of depicting such scenery **2 a** : the landforms of a region in the aggregate **b** : a portion of territory that can be viewed at one time from one place **c** : a particular area of activity : SCENE ⟨political ~⟩ **3** *obs* : VISTA, PROSPECT
[2]**landscape** *vb* **land·scaped; land·scap·ing** *vt* (1914) : to modify or ornament (a natural landscape) by altering the plant cover ~ *vi* : to engage in landscape gardening — **land·scap·er** *n*
landscape architect *n* (1863) : one whose profession is the arrangement of land for human use and enjoyment involving the placement of structures, vehicular and pedestrian ways, and plantings — **landscape architecture** *n*
landscape gardener *n* (1763) : one skilled in the development and decorative planting of gardens and grounds — **landscape gardening** *n*
land·scap·ist \'lan(d)-,skā-pəst\ *n* (1843) : a painter of landscapes
[1]**land·slide** \'lan(d)-,slīd\ *n* (1838) **1** : the usu. rapid downward movement of a mass of rock, earth, or artificial fill on a slope; *also* : the mass that moves down **2 a** : a great majority of votes for one side **b** : an overwhelming victory
[2]**landslide** *vi* **-slid** \-,slid\; **-slid·ing** \-,slīd-iŋ\ (1926) **1** : to win an election by a heavy majority **2** : to produce a landslide
land·slip \-,slip\ *n* (1679) : LANDSLIDE 1
Lands·mål *or* **Lands·maal** \'län(t)s-,mȯl\ *n* [Norw, lit., language of the country] (1886) : NYNORSK
lands·man \'lan(d)z-mən\ *n* (13c) **1** : a fellow countryman **2** : one who lives on the land; *esp* : one who knows little or nothing of the sea or seamanship
land·ward \'lan-dwərd\ *adv or adj* (1610) : to or toward the land
land yacht *n* (1928) : a 3-wheel wind-driven recreation vehicle consisting usu. of a bare-frame structure and a single sail and used esp. on areas of firmly packed sand
[1]**lane** \'lān\ *n* [ME, fr. OE *lanu*; akin to MD *lane* lane] (bef. 12c) **1** : a narrow passageway between fences or hedges **2** : a relatively narrow way or track: as **a** : an ocean route used by or prescribed for ships **b** : a strip of roadway for a single line of vehicles **c** : AIR LANE **d** : any of several parallel courses on a track in which a competitor must stay during a race **e** : a narrow hardwood surface having pins at one end and a shallow channel along each side that is used in bowling **f** : FREE THROW LANE
[2]**lane** *Scot var of* LONE
lang·bein·ite \'laŋ-,bī-,nīt\ *n* [G *langbeinit*, fr. A. *Langbein*, 19th cent. Ger. chemist] (ca. 1897) : a mineral $K_2Mg_2(SO_4)_3$ that is a double sulfate of potassium and magnesium much used in the fertilizer industry
lang·lauf \'läŋ-,lau̇f\ *n* [G, fr. *lang* long + *lauf* race] (1927) : cross-country running or racing on skis — **lang·lauf·er** \-,lau̇-fər\ *n*
lang·ley \'laŋ-lē\ *n, pl* **langleys** [Samuel P. *Langley*] (1947) : a unit of solar radiation equivalent to one gram calorie per square centimeter of irradiated surface
Lan·go·bard \'laŋ-gə-,bärd\ *n* [L *Langobardus*] (1788) : LOMBARD 1a — **Lan·go·bar·dic** \,laŋ-gə-'bär-dik\ *adj*
lan·gouste \läⁿ-'güst\ *n* [F, fr. (assumed) VL *lacusta*, alter. of L *locusta* lobster, locust] (1832) : SPINY LOBSTER
lan·gous·tine \,laŋ-gə-'stēn\ *also* **lan·gos·ti·no** \,laŋ-gə-'stē-(,)nō\ *n, pl* **-tines** *also* **-ti·nos** [*langoustine*, fr. F, dim. of *langouste*; *langostino*, fr. Sp, dim. of *langosta* spiny lobster, locust, fr. (assumed) VL *lacusta*] (ca. 1915) : a large prawn
[1]**lang syne** \(')laŋ-'zīn\ *adv* [ME(Sc), fr. *lang* long + *syne* since] *chiefly Scot* (15c) : at a distant time in the past
[2]**lang syne** *n, chiefly Scot* (1694) : times past ⟨should auld acquaintance be forgot, and days o' auld *lang syne* —Robert Burns⟩
lan·guage \'laŋ-gwij, -wij\ *n* [ME, fr. OF, fr. *langue* tongue, language, fr. L *lingua* — more at TONGUE] (13c) **1 a** : the words, their pronunciation, and the methods of combining them used and understood by a considerable community **b** (1) : audible, articulate, meaningful sound as produced by the action of the vocal organs (2) : a systematic means of communicating ideas or feelings by the use of conventional-

ized signs, sounds, gestures, or marks having understood meanings (3) : the suggestion by objects, actions, or conditions of associated ideas or feelings ⟨body ∼⟩ (4) : the means by which animals communicate (5) : a formal system of signs and symbols (as FORTRAN or a calculus in logic) including rules for the formation and transformation of admissible expressions (6) : MACHINE LANGUAGE **2 a** : form or manner of verbal expression; *specif* : STYLE **b** : the vocabulary and phraseology belonging to an art or a department of knowledge **c** : PROFANITY **3** : the study of language esp. as a school subject

HOME LANGUAGES WITH OVER THIRTY MILLION SPEAKERS[1]

LANGUAGE	MILLIONS	LANGUAGE	MILLIONS
Mandarin Chinese	720[2]	Korean	61
English	305	French	60
Spanish	240	Telugu	57
Arabic	150	Marathi	56
Bengali	150	Tamil	55
Russian	145	Vietnamese	50
Portuguese	140	Eastern Hindi	49
Hindi with Urdu	140	Ukrainian	47
Japanese	120	Bhojpuri	46
German	105	Amoy-Swatow Chinese	46
Wu [Shanghai] Chinese	75	Turkish	42
Javanese	66	Thai with Lao	41
Cantonese	66	Polish	40
Italian	65	Gujarati	34
Panjabi	63		

[1]By permission of the Center for Applied Linguistics, Washington, D.C. Home language used here means the language usually spoken at home.
[2]Figures 100 million or above are given to the nearest 5 million.

language arts *n pl* (1948) : the subjects (as reading, spelling, literature, and composition) that aim at developing the student's comprehension and capacity for use of written and oral language

langue \läⁿg\ *n* [F, lit., language] (1924) : language that is a system of elements or a set of habits common to a community of speakers — compare PAROLE

langue d'oc \läⁿ-ˈdòk, läⁿg-ˈdòk\ *n* [F, fr. OF, lit., language of *oc*; fr. the Provençal use of the word *oc* for "yes"] (1703) : PROVENÇAL 1

langue d'oïl \läⁿ-ˈdòi(ə)l, -ˈdòi; läⁿg-dò-ēl, -dòi\ *n* [F, fr. OF, lit., language of *oïl*; fr. the French use of the word *oïl* for "yes"] (1703) : FRENCH 1

lan·guet \ˈlaⁿ-gwət, laⁿ-ˈgwet\ *n* [ME, fr. MF *languete*, dim. of *langue*] (15c) : something resembling the tongue in form or function

lan·guid \ˈlaⁿ-gwəd\ *adj* [MF *languide*, fr. L *languidus*, fr. *languēre* to languish — more at SLACK] (1597) **1** : drooping or flagging from or as if from exhaustion : WEAK **2** : sluggish in character or disposition : LISTLESS **3** : lacking force or quickness of movement : SLOW — **lan·guid·ly** *adv* — **lan·guid·ness** *n*

lan·guish \ˈlaⁿ-gwish\ *vi* [ME *languishen*, fr. MF *languiss-*, stem of *languir*, fr. (assumed) VL *languire*, fr. L *languēre*] (14c) **1 a** : to be or become feeble, weak, or enervated **b** : to be or live in a state of depression or decreasing vitality **2 a** : to become dispirited : PINE ⟨∼*ing* in prison⟩ **b** : to suffer neglect ⟨the bill ∼*ed* in the Senate for eight months⟩ **3** : to assume an expression of grief or emotion appealing for sympathy — **lan·guish·er** *n* — **lan·guish·ing·ly** \-gwish-iⁿ-lē\ *adv* — **lan·guish·ment** \-gwish-mənt\ *n*

lan·guor \ˈlaⁿ-(g)ər\ *n* [ME, fr. MF, fr. L, fr. *languēre*] (14c) **1** : weakness or weariness of body or mind **2** : SLUGGISHNESS *syn* see LETHARGY

lan·guor·ous \ˈlaⁿ-(g)ə-rəs, -grəs\ *adj* (15c) **1** : producing or tending to produce languor ⟨a ∼ climate⟩ **2** : full of or characterized by languor — **lan·guor·ous·ly** *adv*

lan·gur \läⁿ-ˈgu̇(ə)r\ *n* [Hindi *lāgūr*] (1825) : any of various Asian slender long-tailed monkeys (family Colobidae) with bushy eyebrows and a chin tuft

lank \ˈlaⁿk\ *adj* [(assumed) ME, fr. OE *hlanc*; akin to OHG *hlanca* loin, L *clingere* to girdle] (bef. 12c) **1** : not well filled out : SLENDER, THIN ⟨∼ cattle⟩ **2** : insufficient in quantity, degree, or extent ⟨∼ grass⟩ **3** : hanging straight and limp without spring or curl ⟨∼ hair⟩ *syn* see LEAN — **lank·ly** *adv* — **lank·ness** *n*

lanky \ˈlaⁿ-kē\ *adj* **lank·i·er; -est** (1818) : ungracefully tall and thin *syn* see LEAN — **lank·i·ly** \-kə-lē\ *adv* — **lank·i·ness** \-kē-nəs\ *n*

lan·ner \ˈlan-ər\ *n* [ME *laner*, fr. MF *lanier*] (14c) : a falcon (*Falco biarmicus*) of southern Europe, southwestern Asia, or Africa; *specif* : a female lanner

langur

lan·ner·et \ˌlan-ə-ˈret\ *n* (15c) : a male lanner

lan·o·lin \ˈlan-ᵊl-ən\ *n* [L *lana* wool + ISV *-ol* + *-in*] (1885) : wool grease esp. when refined for use in ointments and cosmetics

lan·ta·na \lan-ˈtän-ə\ *n* [NL, deriv. of It dial., viburnum] (1791) : any of a genus (*Lantana*) of tropical shrubs of the vervain family with showy heads of small bright flowers

lan·tern \ˈlant-ərn\ *n, often attrib* [ME *lanterne*, fr. OF, fr. L *lanterna*, fr. Gk *lamptēr*, fr. *lampein* to shine — more at LAMP] (13c) **1** : a usu. portable protective case for a light with transparent openings — compare CHINESE LANTERN **2 a** *obs* : LIGHTHOUSE **b** : the chamber in a lighthouse containing the light **c** : a structure with glazed or open sides above an opening in a roof for light or ventilation **d** : a small tower or cupola or one stage of a cupola **3** : PROJECTOR 2b

lantern fly *n* (1753) : any of several large brightly marked homopterous insects (family Fulgoridae) having the front of the head prolonged into a hollow structure

lantern jaw *n* (ca. 1690) : an undershot jaw — **lan·tern–jawed** \ˌlant-ərn-ˈjòd\ *adj*

lantern pinion *n* (1884) : a gear pinion having cylindrical bars instead of teeth

lan·tha·nide \ˈlan(t)-thə-ˌnīd\ *n* [ISV] (1926) : any element in a series of elements of increasing atomic numbers beginning with lanthanum (57) or cerium (58) and ending with lutetium (71) — see PERIODIC TABLE table

lan·tha·non \-ˌnän\ *n* (1947) : LANTHANIDE

lan·tha·num \-nəm\ *n* [NL, fr. Gk *lanthanein* to escape notice — more at LATENT] (1841) : a white soft malleable metallic element that occurs in rare-earth minerals — see ELEMENT table

lant·horn \ˈlant-ərn\ *n, chiefly Brit* (1587) : LANTERN

la·nu·gi·nous \lə-ˈn(y)ü-jə-nəs\ *adj* [L *lanuginosus*, fr. *lanugin-, lanugo*] (1575) : covered with down or fine soft hair : DOWNY

la·nu·go \lə-ˈn(y)ü-(ˌ)gō\ *n* [L, down — more at WOOL] (15c) : a dense cottony or downy growth; *specif* : the soft woolly hair that covers the fetus of some mammals

lan·yard \ˈlan-yərd\ *n* [ME *lanyer* thong, strap, fr. MF *laniere*] (1626) **1** : a piece of rope or line for fastening something in a ship; *esp* : one of the pieces passing through deadeyes to extend shrouds or stays **2 a** : a cord or strap to hold something (as a knife or a whistle) and usu. worn around the neck **b** : a cord worn as a symbol of a military citation **3** : a strong line used to activate a system (as in firing a cannon or sounding a whistle)

Lao \ˈlau̇\ *n, pl* **Lao** *or* **Laos** \ˈlau̇z\ (1625) **1** : a member of a Buddhist people living in Laos and adjacent parts of northeastern Thailand and constituting an important branch of the Tai race **2** : the Thai language of the Lao people — **Lao** *adj*

La·oc·o·ön \lā-ˈäk-ə-ˌwän\ *n* [L, fr. Gk *Laokoōn*] : a Trojan priest killed with his sons by two sea serpents after warning the Trojans against the wooden horse

La·od·i·ce·an \(ˌ)lā-ˌäd-ə-ˈsē-ən\ *adj* [fr. the reproach to the church of the Laodiceans in Rev 3:15-16] (1633) : lukewarm or indifferent in religion or politics — **Laodicean** *n*

Lao·tian \lā-ˈō-shən, ˈlau̇-shən\ *n* [prob. fr. F *laotien*, adj. & n., irreg. fr. *Lao*] (1847) : LAO — **Laotian** *adj*

¹lap \ˈlap\ *n* [ME *lappe*, fr. OE *læppa*; akin to OHG *lappa* flap, L *labi* to slide — more at SLEEP] (bef. 12c) **1 a** : a loose overlapping or hanging panel or flap esp. of a garment **b** *archaic* : the skirt of a coat or dress **2 a** : the clothing that lies on the knees, thighs, and lower part of the trunk when one sits **b** : the front part of the lower trunk and thighs of a seated person **3** : responsible custody : CONTROL ⟨going to drop the whole thing in your ∼ —Hamilton Basso⟩ — **lap·ful** \ˈlap-ˌfu̇l\ *n* — **the lap of luxury** : an environment of great ease, comfort, and wealth ⟨was reared in *the lap of luxury*⟩

²lap *vb* **lapped; lap·ping** *vt* (14c) **1 a** : to fold over or around something : WIND **b** : to envelop entirely : SWATHE **2** : to fold over esp. into layers **3** : to hold protectively in or as if in the lap : CUDDLE **4 a** : to place over and cover a part of : OVERLAP ⟨∼ shingles on a roof⟩ **b** : to join (as two boards) by a lap joint **5 a** : to dress, smooth, or polish (as a metal surface) to a high degree of refinement or accuracy **b** : to shape or fit by working two surfaces together with or without abrasives until a very close fit is produced **6 a** : to overtake and thereby lead or increase the lead over (another contestant) by a full circuit of a racecourse **b** : to complete the circuit of (a racecourse) ∼ *vi* **1** : FOLD, WIND **2 a** : to project beyond or spread over something **b** : to lie partly over or alongside of something or of one another : OVERLAP **3** : to traverse a course — **lap·per** *n*

³lap *n* (1800) **1 a** : the amount by which one object overlaps or projects beyond another **b** : the part of an object that overlaps another **2** : a smoothing and polishing tool usu. consisting of a piece of wood, leather, felt, or soft metal in a special shape used with or without an embedded abrasive **3** : a doubling or layering of a flexible substance (as fibers or paper) **4 a** : the act or an instance of traversing a course (as a racing track or swimming pool); *also* : the distance covered **b** : one segment of a larger unit (as a journey) **c** : one complete turn of a rope around a drum

⁴lap *vb* **lapped; lap·ping** [ME *lapen*, fr. OE *lapian*; akin to OHG *laffan* to lick, L *lambere*, Gk *laphyssein* to devour] *vi* (bef. 12c) **1** : to take in food or drink with the tongue **2 a** : to make a gentle intermittent splashing sound **b** : to move in little waves : WASH ∼ *vt* **1** : to take in (food or drink) with the tongue **b** : to take in or absorb eagerly or quickly — used with *up* ⟨the crowd *lapped* up every word he said⟩ **2** : to flow or splash against in little waves — **lap·per** *n*

⁵lap *n* (14c) **1 a** : an act or instance of lapping **b** : the amount that can be carried to the mouth by one lick or scoop of the tongue **2 a** : a thin or weak beverage or food **3** : a gentle splashing sound

lap·a·ro·scope \ˈlap-(ə-)rə-ˌskōp\ *n* [ISV *laparo-* (fr. Gk *lapara* flank) + *-scope*] (ca. 1855) : a long slender optical instrument for insertion through the abdominal wall that is used to visualize the interior of the peritoneal cavity

lap·a·ros·co·py \ˌlap-ə-ˈräs-kə-pē\ *n, pl* **-pies** (ca. 1855) **1** : visual examination of the abdomen by means of a laparoscope **2** : an operation involving laparoscopy; *esp* : one for sterilization of the female or for removal of ova that involves use of a laparoscope to guide surgical procedures within the abdomen — **lap·a·ro·scop·ic** \-rə-ˈskäp-ik\ *adj* — **lap·a·ros·co·pist** \ˌlap-ə-ˈräs-kə-pəst\ *n*

lap·a·rot·o·my \ˌlap-ə-ˈrät-ə-mē\ *n, pl* **-mies** (1878) : surgical section of the abdominal wall

lap belt *n* (1952) : a seat belt that fastens across the lap

lap·board \ˈlap-ˌbō(ə)rd, -ˌbò(ə)rd\ *n* (1804) : a board used on the lap as a table or desk

lap·dog \-ˌdòg\ *n* (1645) : a small dog that may be held in the lap

la·pel \lə-ˈpel\ *n* [dim. of ¹*lap*] (1789) : the part of a garment that is turned back; *specif* : the fold of the front of a coat that is usu. a continuation of the collar — **la·pelled** *or* **la·peled** *adj*

lap·i·dar·i·an \ˌlap-ə-ˈder-ē-ən\ *adj* (1683) : LAPIDARY 1

1**lap·i·dary** \ˈlap-ə-ˌder-ē\ *n, pl* **-dar·ies** (14c) **1** : a cutter, polisher, or engraver of precious stones usu. other than diamonds **2** : the art of cutting gems

2**lapidary** *adj* [L *lapidarius* of stone, fr. *lapid-, lapis* stone; akin to Gk *lepas* crag] (1724) **1** : having the elegance and precision associated with inscriptions on monumental stone ⟨the ~ phrasing . . . and subtle condensations of emotions . . . reward attentive reading —G. A. Cardwell⟩ **2 a** : sculptured in or engraved on stone **b** : of or relating to precious stones or the art of cutting them

la·pil·lus \lə-ˈpil-əs\ *n, pl* **-li** \-ˌī, -(ˌ)ē\ [L, dim. of *lapis*] (1747) : a small stony or glassy fragment of lava thrown out in a volcanic eruption

lap·in \ˈlap-ən\ *n* [F] (ca. 1905) **1** : RABBIT; *specif* : a castrated male rabbit **2** : rabbit fur usu. sheared and dyed

la·pis la·zu·li \ˌlap-ə-ˈslaz(h)-ə-lē\ *n* [ME, fr. ML, fr. L *lapis* + ML *lazuli*, gen. of *lazulum* lapis lazuli, fr. Ar *lāzaward* — more at AZURE] (14c) : a semiprecious stone that is usu. rich azure blue and is essentially a complex silicate often with spangles of iron pyrites — called also *lapis*

lap joint *n* (1823) : a joint made by overlapping two ends or edges and fastening them together — **lap–joint·ed** \ˈlap-ˈjȯint-əd\ *adj*

La·place transform \lə-ˈpläs-, -ˈplas-\ [Pierre Simon de *Laplace*] (ca. 1942) : a transformation of a function $f(x)$ into the function

$$g(t)=\int_0^\infty e^{-xt}f(x)dx$$

that is useful esp. in reducing the solution of an ordinary linear differential equation with constant coefficients to the solution of a polynomial equation

Lapp \ˈlap\ *n* [Sw] (1859) **1** : a member of a people of northern Scandinavia, Finland, and the Kola peninsula of northern Russia who are typically fishermen, nomadic herders of reindeer, and hunters of sea mammals **2** : any or all of the closely related Finno-Ugric languages of the Lapps

lap·pet \ˈlap-ət\ *n* (1573) **1** : a fold or flap on a garment or headdress — see VESTMENT illustration **2** : a flat overlapping or hanging piece (as a roofing tile or the wattle of a bird)

lap robe *n* (ca. 1866) : a covering (as a blanket) for the legs, lap, and feet esp. of a passenger in a car or carriage

Lap·sang souchong \ˌläp-ˌsäŋ-, ˌlap-ˌsaŋ-\ *n* [origin unknown] (ca. 1878) : a souchong tea having a pronounced smoky flavor and aroma

1**lapse** \ˈlaps\ *n* [L *lapsus*, fr. *lapsus*, pp. of *labi* to slip — more at SLEEP] (1526) **1 a** : a slight error typically due to forgetfulness or inattention ⟨a ~ in table manners⟩ **b** : a temporary deviation or fall esp. from a higher to a lower state ⟨a ~ from grace⟩ **2 a** : DROP; *specif* : a decrease of temperature or pressure as the height increases — compare LAPSE RATE **b** : a becoming less : DECLINE **3 a** (1) : the termination of a right or privilege through neglect to exercise it within some limit of time (2) : termination of coverage for nonpayment of premiums **b** : INTERRUPTION, DISCONTINUANCE ⟨returned to college after a ~ of several years⟩ **4** : an abandonment of religious faith : APOSTASY **5** : a passage of time; *also* : INTERVAL ***syn*** see ERROR

2**lapse** *vb* **lapsed; laps·ing** *vi* (1611) **1 a** : to fall from an attained and usu. high level (as of morals or manners) to one much lower; *also* : to depart from an accepted pattern or standard **b** : to sink or slip gradually : SUBSIDE ⟨*lapsed* into unconsciousness⟩ **2** : to go out of existence : CEASE ⟨after a few polite exchanges, the conversation *lapsed*⟩ **3** : to pass from one proprietor to another or from an original owner by omission or negligence ⟨allowed the insurance policy to ~⟩ **4 a** : to glide along : PASS ⟨time ~*s*⟩ ~ *vt* : to let slip : FORFEIT ⟨all of those who have *lapsed* their membership —*AAUP Bull.*⟩ — **laps·er** *n*

lapsed *adj, of a person* (1638) : having given up or allowed the lapse of a former position, relationship, or commitment ⟨a ~ Catholic⟩

lapse rate *n* (ca. 1918) : the adiabatic rate of change of a meteorological element (as temperature) associated with a change in height

lap·strake \ˈlap-ˌstrāk\ *also* **lap·streak** \-ˌstrēk\ *adj* (1771) : CLINKER-BUILT

lap·top \ˈlap-ˌtäp\ *adj* (1985) : of a size and design that makes operation and use on one's lap convenient ⟨a ~ personal computer⟩ — compare DESKTOP — **laptop** *n*

La·pu·tan \lə-ˈpyüt-ᵊn\ *n* : an inhabitant of a flying island in Swift's *Gulliver's Travels* characterized by a neglect of useful occupations and a devotion to visionary projects — **Laputan** *adj*

lap·wing \ˈlap-ˌwiŋ\ *n* [ME, by folk etymology fr. OE *hlēapewince;* akin to OE *hlēapan* to leap and to OE *wincian* to wink] (bef. 12c) : a crested Old World plover (*Vanellus vanellus*) noted for its slow irregular flapping flight and its shrill wailing cry; *also* : any of several related plovers

Lar \ˈlär\ *n, pl* **Lar·es** \ˈla(ə)r-(ˌ)ēz, ˈle(ə)r-\ [L — more at LARVA] : a tutelary god or spirit associated with Vesta and the Penates as a guardian of the household by the ancient Romans

lar·board \ˈlär-bərd\ *n* [ME *ladeborde*] (14c) : PORT — **larboard** *adj*

lar·ce·ner \ˈlärs-nər, -ᵊn-ər\ *n* (1634) : LARCENIST

lar·ce·nist \ˈlärs-nəst, -ᵊn-əst\ *n* (1803) : one who commits larceny

lar·ce·nous \ˈlärs-nəs, -ᵊn-əs\ *adj* (1742) **1** : having the character of or constituting larceny **2** : committing larceny — **lar·ce·nous·ly** *adv*

lar·ce·ny \ˈlärs-nē, -ᵊn-ē\ *n, pl* **-nies** [ME, fr. MF *larcin* theft, fr. L *latrocinium* robbery, fr. *latron-, latro* mercenary soldier; akin to OE *unlǣd* poor, Gk *latron* pay] (15c) : the unlawful taking of personal property with intent to deprive the rightful owner of it permanently

larch \ˈlärch\ *n* [prob. fr. G *lärche*, fr. L *laric-, larix*] (1548) **1** : any of a genus (*Larix*) of trees of the pine family with short fascicled deciduous leaves; *also* : any of several related trees (as of the genus *Abies*) **2** : the wood of a larch

1**lard** \ˈlärd\ *vt* (14c) **1 a** : to dress (meat) for cooking by inserting or covering with something (as strips of fat) **b** : to cover or soil with grease **2** : to decorate or intersperse with something : GARNISH ⟨the book is well ~*ed* with anecdotes⟩ **3** *obs* : to make rich with or as if with fat : ENRICH

2**lard** *n* [ME, fr. MF, fr. L *lardum;* akin to Gk *larinos* fat] (14c) : a soft white solid or semisolid fat obtained by rendering fatty tissue of the hog — **lardy** \ˈlärd-ē\ *adj*

lar·der \ˈlärd-ər\ *n* [ME, fr. MF *lardier*, fr. *lard*] (14c) **1** : a place where food is stored : PANTRY **2** : a supply of food

lar·doon \lär-ˈdün\ *or* **lar·don** \ˈlär-ˌdän\ *n* [ME, fr. MF *lardon* piece of fat pork, fr. *lard*] (14c) : a strip (as of salt pork) with which meat is larded

lares and penates *see* LAR, PENATES\ *n pl* (1775) **1** : household gods **2** : personal or household effects

1**large** \ˈlärj\ *adj* **larg·er; larg·est** [ME, fr. OF, fr. L *largus*] (12c) **1** *obs* : LAVISH **2** *obs* **a** : AMPLE, ABUNDANT **b** : EXTENSIVE, BROAD **3** : having more than usual power, capacity, or scope : COMPREHENSIVE ⟨take the ~ view⟩ ⟨will take a *larger* role in the negotiations⟩ **4 a** : exceeding most other things of like kind esp. in quantity or size : BIG **b** : dealing in great numbers or quantities ⟨a ~ and highly profitable business⟩ **5** *obs* **a** *of language or expression* : COARSE, VULGAR **b** : lax in conduct : LOOSE **6** *of a wind* : FAVORABLE **7** : EXTRAVAGANT, BOASTFUL ⟨~ talk⟩ — **large·ness** *n* — **larg·ish** \ˈlär-jish\ *adj*

2**large** *adv* (14c) **1** *obs* : in abundance : AMPLY, LIBERALLY **2** : with the wind abaft the beam

3**large** *n, obs* (14c) : LIBERALITY, GENEROSITY — **at large** **1** : free of restraint or confinement ⟨the escaped prisoner is still *at large*⟩ **2** : at length **3** : in a general way : at random **4** : as a whole ⟨society *at large*⟩ **5** : as the political representative of or to a whole area rather than of one of its subdivisions — used in combination with a preceding noun ⟨a congressman-*at-large*⟩

large calorie *n* (ca. 1909) : CALORIE 1b

large·heart·ed \ˈlärj-ˈhärt-əd\ *adj* (1645) : having a generous disposition : SYMPATHETIC — **large·heart·ed·ness** *n*

large intestine *n* (1823) : the more terminal division of the vertebrate intestine that is wider and shorter than the small intestine, typically divided into cecum, colon, and rectum, and concerned esp. with the resorption of water and the formation of feces

large·ly \ˈlärj-lē\ *adv* (13c) : to a large extent : MOSTLY, PRIMARILY

large–mind·ed \ˈlärj-ˈmīn-dəd\ *adj* (1725) : generous or comprehensive in outlook, range, or capacity — **large–mind·ed·ly** *adv* — **large–mind·ed·ness** *n*

large·mouth bass \ˌlärj-ˌmau̇th-\ *n* (1878) : a large black bass (*Micropterus salmoides*) that is blackish green above and lighter below and has the maxillary bones of the upper jaw extending behind the eyes — called also *largemouth, largemouth black bass*

large–print \-ˈprint\ *adj* (1968) : being set in a large size of type (as 14 point or larger) esp. for use by the partially sighted ⟨~ books⟩

large–scale integration *n* (1966) : the process of placing a large number of circuits on a small chip

lar·gess *or* **lar·gesse** \lär-ˈzhes, lär-ˈjes *also* ˈlär-ˌjes\ *n* [ME *largesse*, fr. OF, fr. *large*] (13c) **1** : liberal giving (as of money) to or as if to an inferior; *also* : something so given **2** : GENEROSITY

1**lar·ghet·to** \lär-ˈget-(ˌ)ō\ *n, pl* **-tos** (1724) : a movement played larghetto

2**larghetto** *adv or adj* [It, somewhat slow, fr. *largo*] (ca. 1801) : slower than andante but not so slow as largo — used as a direction in music

1**lar·go** \ˈlär-(ˌ)gō\ *adv or adj* [It, slow, broad, fr. L *largus* abundant — more at LARD] (1683) : in a very slow and stately manner — used as a direction in music

2**largo** *n, pl* **largos** (ca. 1724) : a largo movement

lar·i·at \ˈlar-ē-ət, ˈler-\ *n* [AmerSp *la reata* the lasso, fr. Sp *la* the (fem. of *el*, fr. L *ille* that) + AmerSp *reata* lasso, fr. Sp *reatar* to tie again, fr. *re-* + *atar* to tie, fr. L *aptare* to fit — more at ADAPT] (1832) : a long light rope (as of hemp or leather) used with a running noose to catch livestock or with or without the noose to tether grazing animals : LASSO

1**lark** \ˈlärk\ *n* [ME *laveroc, laverke*, fr. OE *lāwerce;* akin to OHG *lērihha* lark] (bef. 12c) **1** : any of numerous singing birds (family Alaudidae) mostly of Europe, Asia, and northern Africa; *esp* : SKYLARK **2** : any of various usu. ground-living birds ⟨meadow*lark*⟩ ⟨tit*lark*⟩

2**lark** *n* (ca. 1811) : something done solely for fun or adventure : ESCAPADE

3**lark** *vi* [prob. alter. of *lake* (to frolic)] (1813) : to engage in harmless fun or mischief — usu. used with *about* — **lark·er** *n*

lark·spur \ˈlärk-ˌspər\ *n* (1578) : any of a genus (*Delphinium*) of plants of the buttercup family; *esp* : a cultivated annual delphinium grown for its showy irregular flowers with spurred calyxes

larky \ˈlär-kē\ *adj* **lark·i·er; -est** (1841) **1** : given to or ready for larking **2** : resulting from a lark

lar·ri·gan \ˈlar-i-gən\ *n* [origin unknown] (1886) : an oil-tanned moccasin with a leg often reaching the knee

lar·ri·kin \ˈlar-i-kən\ *n* [origin unknown] *chiefly Austral* (1868) : HOODLUM, ROWDY — **larrikin** *adj*

1**lar·rup** \ˈlar-əp\ *n* [origin unknown] *dial* (ca. 1820) : BLOW

2**larrup** *vt* (ca. 1823) **1** *dial* : to flog soundly : WHIP **2** *dial* : to defeat decisively : TROUNCE ~ *vi, dial* : to move indolently or clumsily

la·rum \ˈlar-əm, ˈler-\ *n* [short for *alarum*] (15c) : ALARM

lar·va \ˈlär-və\ *n, pl* **lar·vae** \-(ˌ)vē, -ˌvī\ *also* **larvas** [NL, fr. L, specter, mask; akin to L *lar*] (1768) **1** : the immature, wingless, and often vermiform feeding form that hatches from the egg of many insects, alters chiefly in size while passing through several molts, and is finally transformed into a pupa or chrysalis from which the adult emerges **2** : the early form of an animal (as a frog) that at birth or hatching is fundamentally unlike its parent and must metamorphose before assuming the adult characters — **lar·val** \-vəl\ *adj*

larvi- *comb form* [NL, fr. *larva*] : larva ⟨*larvi*cide⟩

lar·vi·cide \ˈlär-və-ˌsīd\ *n* (ca. 1875) : an agent for killing larval pests — **lar·vi·cid·al** \ˌlär-və-ˈsīd-ᵊl\ *adj* — **lar·vi·cid·ing** \ˈlär-və-ˌsīd-iŋ\ *n*

laryng- *or* **laryngo-** *comb form* [NL, fr. Gk, fr. *laryng-, larynx*] **1** : larynx ⟨*laryng*itis⟩ **2** \lə-ˌriŋ-gō, -ˌrin-jō\ : laryngeal and ⟨*laryngo*pharyngeal⟩

1**la·ryn·geal** \lə-ˈrin-j(ē-)əl, ˌlar-ən-ˈjē-əl\ *adj* (1795) **1** : of, relating to, or used on the larynx **2** : produced by or with constriction of the larynx ⟨~ articulation of sounds⟩

2**laryngeal** *n* (ca. 1902) **1** : an anatomical part (as a nerve or artery) that supplies or is associated with the larynx **2 a** : a laryngeal sound **b** : any of a set of several conjectured phonemes reconstructed for Proto-Indo-European chiefly on indirect evidence

lar·yn·gec·to·mee \ˌlar-ən-ˌjek-tə-ˈmē\ *n* (1956) : a person who has undergone laryngectomy

lar·yn·gec·to·my \-ˈjek-tə-mē\ *n, pl* **-mies** (1888) : surgical removal of all or part of the larynx — **lar·yn·gec·to·mized** \-tə-ˌmīzd\ *adj*

lar·yn·gi·tis \ˌlar-ən-ˈjīt-əs\ *n* [NL] (ca. 1822) : inflammation of the larynx — **lar·yn·git·ic** \-ˈjit-ik\ *adj*

lar·yn·gol·o·gy \ˌlar-ən-ˈgäl-ə-jē\ *n* [ISV] (ca. 1842) : a branch of medicine dealing with diseases of the larynx and nasopharynx

la·ryn·go·scope \lə-ˈriŋ-gə-ˌskōp, -ˈrin-jə-\ *n* [ISV] (1860) : an instrument for examining the interior of the larynx — **lar·yn·gos·co·py** \ˌlar-ən-ˈgäs-kə-pē\ *n*

lar·ynx \ˈlar-iŋ(k)s\ *n, pl* **la·ryn·ges** \lə-ˈrin-(ˌ)jēz\ *or* **lar·ynx·es** [NL *laryng-, larynx,* fr. Gk] (1578) : the modified upper part of the trachea of air-breathing vertebrates that in man, most other mammals, and a few lower forms contains the vocal cords

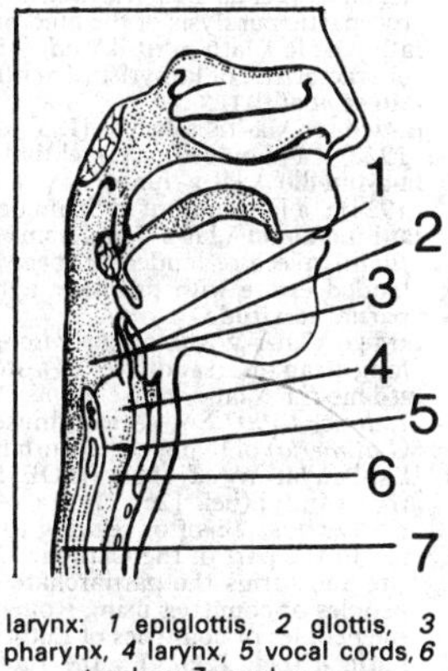

larynx: *1* epiglottis, *2* glottis, *3* pharynx, *4* larynx, *5* vocal cords, *6* trachea, *7* esophagus

la·sa·gna \lə-ˈzän-yə\ *n* [It *lasagna* (pl. *lasagne*), fr. (assumed) VL *lasania,* fr. L *lasanum* cooking pot, fr. Gk *lasanon* chamber pot] (1846) **1** *also* **la·sa·gne** \-yə, -(ˌ)yā\ : broad flat noodles **2** : a baked dish consisting of layers of boiled lasagna noodles, cheese, and a sauce of tomatoes and usu. meat

las·car \ˈlas-kər\ *n* [Hindi *lashkar* army] (1615) : an Indian sailor, army servant, or artilleryman

las·civ·i·ous \lə-ˈsiv-ē-əs\ *adj* [LL *lasciviosus,* fr. L *lascivia* wantonness, fr. *lascivus* wanton — more at LUST] (15c) : LEWD, LUSTFUL — **las·civ·i·ous·ly** *adv* — **las·civ·i·ous·ness** *n*

lase \ˈlāz\ *vi* **lased; las·ing** [back-formation fr. *laser*] (1962) : to emit coherent light

la·ser \ˈlā-zər\ *n, often attrib* [*l*ight *a*mplification by *s*timulated *e*mission of *r*adiation] (1957) : a device that utilizes the natural oscillations of atoms or molecules between energy levels for generating coherent electromagnetic radiation in the ultraviolet, visible, or infrared regions of the spectrum

laser disc *n* (1980) : OPTICAL DISC; *esp* : one on which video images are recorded

laser printer *n* (1979) : a high-resolution printer for computer output that xerographically prints an image formed by a laser

[1]**lash** \ˈlash\ *vb* [ME *lashen*] *vi* (14c) **1** : to move violently or suddenly : DASH **2** : to thrash or beat violently ⟨rain ~*ed* at the windowpanes⟩ **3** : to make a verbal attack or retort — usu. used with *out* ~ *vt* **1 a** : to whip or fling about violently ⟨the big cat ~*ed* its tail about threateningly⟩ **b** : to strike or beat with or as if with a whip ⟨waves ~*ed* the shore⟩ **2 a** : to assail with stinging words **b** : DRIVE, WHIP ⟨~*ed* them into a fury with his fiery speech⟩ — **lash·er** *n*

[2]**lash** *n* (14c) **1 a** (1) : a stroke with or as if with a whip (2) : the flexible part of a whip; *also* : WHIP **b** : punishment by whipping **2** : a beating, whipping, or driving force **3** : a stinging rebuke **4** : EYELASH **5** : the clearance or play between adjacent movable mechanical parts

[3]**lash** *vt* [ME *lasschen* to lace, fr. MF *lacier* — more at LACE] (15c) : to bind with a line (as of rope, cord, or chain) — **lash·er** *n*

lash·ing *n* (15c) : something used for binding, wrapping, or fastening

lash·ings \ˈlash-iŋz, -ənz\ *also* **lash·ins** \-ənz\ *n pl* [fr. gerund of [1]*lash*] *chiefly Brit* (1829) : a great plenty : ABUNDANCE ⟨piles of bread and butter and ~ of tea —Molly Weir⟩

lash–up \ˈlash-ˌəp\ *n* [[3]*lash*] (1898) **1** : something hastily put together or improvised **2** : OUTFIT 3

L–as·par·a·gi·nase \ˈel-as-ˈpar-ə-jə-ˌnās, -ˌnāz\ *n* (1967) : an enzyme that breaks down the physiologically commoner form of asparagine, is obtained esp. from bacteria, and is used esp. to treat leukemia

lass \ˈlas\ *n* [ME *las*] (14c) **1** : a young woman : GIRL **2** : SWEETHEART

Las·sa fever \ˌlas-ə-\ *n* [*Lassa,* village in Nigeria] (1970) : a virus disease esp. of Africa that is characterized by a high fever, headaches, mouth ulcers, muscle aches, small hemorrhages under the skin, heart and kidney failure, and a high mortality rate

lass·ie \ˈlas-ē\ *n* (1725) : LASS 1

las·si·tude \ˈlas-ə-ˌt(y)üd\ *n* [MF, fr. L *lassitudo,* fr. *lassus* weary — more at LET] (15c) **1** : a condition of weariness or debility : FATIGUE **2** : a condition of listlessness : LANGUOR ***syn*** see LETHARGY

[1]**las·so** \ˈlas-(ˌ)ō, la-ˈsü\ *n, pl* **lassos** *or* **lassoes** [Sp *lazo,* fr. L *laqueus* snare; akin to L *lacere* to entice — more at DELIGHT] (ca. 1768) : a rope or long thong of leather with a noose used esp. for catching horses and cattle : LARIAT

[2]**lasso** *vt* (1807) : to catch with or as if with a lasso : ROPE — **las·so·er** *n*

[1]**last** \ˈlast\ *vb* [ME *lasten,* fr. OE *lǣstan* to last, follow; akin to OE *lāst* footprint] *vi* (bef. 12c) **1** : to continue in time **2 a** : to remain fresh or unimpaired : ENDURE **b** : to manage to continue (as in a course of action) **c** : to continue to live ⟨he won't ~ much longer⟩ ~ *vt* **1** : to continue in existence or action as long as or longer than — often used with *out* ⟨couldn't ~ out the training program⟩ **2** : to be enough for the needs of ⟨the supplies will ~ them a week⟩ ***syn*** see CONTINUE — **last·er** *n*

[2]**last** *n* [ME, fr. OE *lǣste,* fr. *lāst* footprint; akin to OHG *leist* shoemaker's last, L *lira* furrow — more at LEARN] (bef. 12c) : a form (as of metal or plastic) which is shaped like the human foot and over which a shoe is shaped or repaired

[3]**last** *vt* (ca. 1859) : to shape with a last — **last·er** *n*

[4]**last** *adj* [ME, fr. OE *latost,* superl. of *læt* late] (bef. 12c) **1 a** : following all the rest ⟨he was the ~ one out⟩ **b** : being the only remaining ⟨our ~ dollar⟩ **2 a** : belonging to the final stage (as of life) ⟨his ~ hours on earth⟩ **b** : administered to the seriously sick or dying ⟨the ~ rites of the church⟩ **3 a** : next before the present : most recent ⟨~ week⟩ ⟨his ~ book was a failure⟩ **b** : most up-to-date : LATEST ⟨it's the ~ thing in fashion⟩ **4 a** : lowest in rank or standing; *also* : WORST **b** : farthest from a specified quality, attitude, or likelihood ⟨would be the ~ person to fall for flattery⟩ **5 a** : CONCLUSIVE ⟨there is no ~ answer to a problem of human relations⟩ **b** : highest in degree : SUPREME, ULTIMATE **c** : DISTINCT, SEPARATE — used as an intensive ⟨ate every ~ piece of food on the plate⟩ — **last·ly** *adv*

syn LAST, FINAL, TERMINAL, EVENTUAL, ULTIMATE mean following all others (as in time, order, or importance). LAST applies to something that comes at the end of a series but does not always imply that the series is completed or stopped ⟨*last* page of a book⟩ ⟨*last* news we had of him⟩ FINAL applies to that which definitely closes a series, process, or progress ⟨*final* day of school⟩ TERMINAL may indicate a limit of extension, growth, or development ⟨*terminal* phase of a disease⟩ EVENTUAL applies to something that is bound to follow sooner or later as the final effect of causes already operating ⟨*eventual* defeat of the enemy⟩ ULTIMATE implies the last degree or stage of a long process beyond which further progress or change is impossible ⟨*ultimate* collapse of civilization⟩

[5]**last** *adv* (bef. 12c) **1** : after all others : at the end ⟨came ~ and left first⟩ **2** : most lately ⟨saw him ~ in New York⟩ **3** : in conclusion ⟨and ~, I'd like to consider the economic aspect⟩

[6]**last** *n* (13c) : something that is last — **at last** *or* **at long last** : at the end of a period of time : FINALLY ⟨*at last* you've come home⟩

last–ditch *adj* (1937) : made as a final effort esp. to avert disaster ⟨a ~ attempt to raise the money⟩

last ditch *n* (1715) : a place of final defense

Las·tex \ˈlas-ˌteks\ *trademark* — used for an elastic yarn consisting of a core of latex thread wound with threads of cotton, rayon, nylon, or silk

last hurrah *n* [fr. *The Last Hurrah* (1956) by Edwin O'Connor †1968 Am. novelist] (1956) : a last effort or attempt ⟨his unsuccessful Senate run was his *last hurrah* —R. W. Daly⟩

last–in first–out *adj* (ca. 1940) : of, relating to, or being a method of inventory accounting that values all stock on hand at the cost of the lot last received

[1]**last·ing** *adj* (12c) : existing or continuing a long while : ENDURING — **last·ing·ly** \ˈlas-tiŋ-lē\ *adv* — **last·ing·ness** *n*

syn LASTING, PERMANENT, DURABLE, STABLE mean enduring for so long as to seem fixed or established. LASTING implies a capacity to continue indefinitely ⟨a book that left a *lasting* impression on me⟩ PERMANENT adds usu. the implication of being designed or planned to stand or continue indefinitely ⟨*permanent* living arrangement⟩ DURABLE implies power to resist destructive agencies ⟨*durable* fabrics⟩ STABLE implies lastingness because of resistance to being overturned or displaced ⟨a *stable* government⟩

[2]**lasting** *n* (15c) **1** *archaic* : long life **2** : a sturdy cotton or worsted cloth used esp. in shoes and luggage

Last Judgment *n* (14c) : the judgment of mankind before God at the end of the world

last minute *n* (1920) : the moment just before some climactic, decisive, or disastrous event

last name *n* (1897) : SURNAME 2

last rites *n* (ca. 1930) : EXTREME UNCTION

last straw *n* [fr. the fable of the last straw that broke the camel's back when added to its burden] (1848) : the last of a series (as of events or indignities) that brings one beyond the point of endurance

Last Supper *n* (14c) : the supper eaten by Jesus and his disciples on the night of his betrayal

Last Things *n pl* [trans. of ML *Novissima*] (1522) : events (as the resurrection and divine judgment of all humankind) marking the end of the world : eschatological happenings

last word *n* (1563) **1** : the final remark in a verbal exchange **2 a** : the power of final decision **b** : a definitive statement or treatment ⟨this study will surely be the *last word* on the subject for many years⟩ **3** : the most advanced, up-to-date, or fashionable exemplar of its kind ⟨the *last word* in sports cars⟩

lat·a·kia \ˌlat-ə-ˈkē-ə\ *n* [*Latakia,* seaport in Syria] (1833) : a highly aromatic Turkish smoking tobacco

[1]**latch** \ˈlach\ *vi* [ME *lachen,* fr. OE *læccan;* akin to Gk *lambanein* to take, seize] (bef. 12c) **1** : to catch or get hold — used with *on* or *onto* **2** : to attach oneself ⟨~*ed* onto a rich widow⟩

[2]**latch** *n* (13c) : any of various devices in which mating mechanical parts engage to fasten but usu. not to lock something: **a** : a fastener (as for a door) consisting essentially of a pivoted bar that falls into a notch **b** : a fastener (as for a door) in which a spring slides a bolt into a hole; *also* : NIGHT LATCH

[3]**latch** *vt* (15c) : to make fast with or as if with a latch

latch·et \ˈlach-ət\ *n* [ME *lachet,* fr. MF, shoestring, fr. *laz* snare, fr. L *laqueus;* akin to L *lacere* to entice — more at DELIGHT] (15c) : a narrow leather strap, thong, or lace that fastens a shoe or sandal on the foot

latch·key \ˈlach-ˌkē\ *n* (1825) : a key to an outside and esp. a front door

latchkey child *n* (1944) : a young child of working parents who must spend part of the day at home unsupervised

latch·string \-ˌ(s)triŋ\ *n* (1791) : a string on a latch that may be left hanging outside the door to permit the raising of the latch from the outside or drawn inside to prevent intrusion

[1]**late** \ˈlāt\ *adj* **lat·er; lat·est** [ME, late, slow, fr. OE *læt;* akin to OHG *laz* slow, OE *lǣtan* to let] (bef. 12c) **1 a** (1) : coming or remaining after the due, usual, or proper time ⟨a ~ spring⟩ (2) : of, relating to, or imposed because of tardiness **b** : of or relating to an advanced stage in point of time or development ⟨the ~ Middle Ages⟩; *esp* : far advanced toward the close of the day or night ⟨~ hours⟩ **2 a** : living comparatively recently — used of persons ⟨the ~ John Doe⟩ and often with reference to a specific relationship or status ⟨his ~ wife⟩ **b** : being something or holding some position or relationship recently but not now ⟨the ~ belligerents⟩ **c** : made, appearing, or happening just previous to the present time esp. as the most recent of a succession ⟨our ~ quarrel⟩ ***syn*** see DEAD — **late·ness** *n*

[2]**late** *adv* **lat·er; lat·est** (bef. 12c) **1 a** : after the usual or proper time ⟨got to work ~⟩ **b** : at or to an advanced point of time ⟨saw her ~ in the day⟩ — often used with *on* ⟨work until noon and relax *later* on⟩ **2** : not long ago : RECENTLY ⟨a man ~ of Chicago⟩ — **of late** : in the

\ə\ **abut** \ᵊ\ **kitten,** F **table** \ər\ **further** \a\ **ash** \ā\ **ace** \ä\ **cot, cart** \au̇\ **out** \ch\ **chin** \e\ **bet** \ē\ **easy** \g\ **go** \i\ **hit** \ī\ **ice** \j\ **job** \ŋ\ **sing** \ō\ **go** \ȯ\ **law** \ȯi\ **boy** \th\ **thin** \t͟h\ **the** \ü\ **loot** \u̇\ **foot** \y\ **yet** \zh\ **vision** \à, k̟, ⁿ, œ, œ̄, ue, ue̅, ʸ\ *see* Guide to Pronunciation

period shortly or immediately preceding : RECENTLY ⟨have not seen him *of late*⟩

late blight *n* (ca. 1900) : a disease of solanaceous plants (as the potato and tomato) that is caused by a fungus (*Phytophthora infestans*) and is characterized by decay of stems, leaves, and in the potato also of tubers

late·com·er \'lāt-,kəm-ər\ *n* (1892) : one that arrives late; *also* : a recent arrival

lat·ed \'lāt-əd\ *adj* (1592) : BELATED

[1]**la·teen** \lə-'tēn\ *adj* [F (*voile*) *latine* lateen sail] (ca. 1727) : being or relating to a rig used esp. on the north coast of Africa and characterized by a triangular sail extended by a long spar slung to a low mast

[2]**lateen** *n* (ca. 1775) **1** *also* **la·teen·er** \-'tē-nər\ : a lateen-rigged ship **2** : a lateen sail

Late Greek *n* (ca. 1902) : the Greek language as used in the 3d to 6th centuries

Late Latin *n* (1888) : the Latin language used by writers in the 3d to 6th centuries

late·ly \'lāt-lē\ *adv* (15c) : of late : RECENTLY ⟨has been friendlier ~⟩

lat·en \'lāt-ᵊn\ *vb* **lat·ened; lat·en·ing** \'lāt-niŋ, -ᵊn-iŋ\ *vi* (1880) : to grow late ~ *vt* : to cause to grow late

la·ten·cy \'lāt-ᵊn-sē\ *n, pl* **-cies** (1638) **1** : the quality or state of being latent : DORMANCY **2** : something latent **3** : a stage of personality development that extends from about the age of five to the beginning of puberty and during which sexual urges often appear to lie dormant **4** : LATENT PERIOD 2

latency period *n* (1910) **1** : LATENCY 3 **2** : LATENT PERIOD 2

La Tène \lä-'ten, -'tān\ *adj* [*La Tène*, shallows of the Lake of Neuchâtel, Switzerland] (ca. 1901) : of or relating to the later period of the Iron Age in Europe assumed to date from 500 B.C. to A.D. 1

la·ten·si·fi·ca·tion \lā-,ten(t)-sə-fə-'kā-shən, lə-\ *n* [blend of [1]*latent* and *intensification*] (1940) : intensification of a latent photographic image by chemical treatment or exposure to light of low intensity — **la·ten·si·fy** \-'ten(t)-sə-,fī\ *vt*

[1]**la·tent** \'lāt-ᵊnt\ *adj* [L *latent-, latens*, fr. prp. of *latēre* to lie hidden; akin to OHG *luog* den, Gk *lanthanein* to escape notice] (15c) : present and capable of becoming though not now visible or active ⟨a ~ infection⟩ ⟨his desire for success remained ~⟩

syn LATENT, DORMANT, QUIESCENT, POTENTIAL, ABEYANT mean not now showing signs of activity or existence. LATENT applies to a power or quality that has not yet come forth but may emerge and develop; DORMANT suggests the inactivity of something (as a feeling or power) as though sleeping; QUIESCENT suggests a usu. temporary cessation of activity; POTENTIAL applies to what does not yet have existence or effect but is likely soon to have; ABEYANT applies to what is for the time being held off or suppressed.

[2]**latent** *n* (1923) : a fingerprint (as at the scene of a crime) that is scarcely visible but can be developed for study

latent heat *n* (1757) : heat given off or absorbed in a process (as fusion or vaporization) other than a change of temperature

latent period *n* (1837) **1** : the incubation period of a disease **2** : the interval between stimulation and response

latent root *n* (ca. 1883) : an eigenvalue of a matrix

-l·a·ter \l-ət-ər\ *n comb form* [ME *-latrer*, fr. MF *-latre*, fr. LL *-latres*, fr. Gk *-latrēs*; akin to Gk *latron* pay — more at LARCENY] : worshiper ⟨icono*later*⟩

lat·er·ad \'lat-ə-,rad\ *adv* [L *later-, latus*] (1814) : toward the side

[1]**lat·er·al** \'lat-ə-rəl, 'la-trəl\ *adj* [L *lateralis*, fr. *later-, latus* side] (15c) : of or relating to the side : situated on, directed toward, or coming from the side — **lat·er·al·ly** \-ē\ *adv*

[2]**lateral** *n* (1887) **1** : a side ditch or conduit (as in a water system) **2** : a mining drift to one side of and parallel to a main drift **3** : a pass in football thrown parallel to the line of scrimmage or in a direction away from the opponent's goal

[3]**lateral** *vi* (1944) : to throw a lateral

lateral bud *n* (ca. 1892) : a bud that develops in the axil between a petiole and a stem

lat·er·al·iza·tion \,lat-ə-rə-lə-'zā-shən, ,la-trə-lə-\ *n* (ca. 1899) : localization of function or activity (as of verbal processes in the brain) on one side of the body in preference to the other — **lat·er·al·ize** \'lat-ə-rə-,līz, 'la-trə-,līz\ *vt*

lateral line *n* (1870) : a canal along the side of a fish containing pores that open into tubes supplied with sense organs sensitive to low vibrations; *also* : one of these tubes or sense organs

lat·er·ite \'lat-ə-,rīt\ *n* [L *later* brick] (ca. 1807) : a residual product of rock decay that is red in color and has a high content in the oxides of iron and hydroxide of aluminum — **lat·er·it·ic** \,lat-ə-'rit-ik\ *adj*

lat·er·i·za·tion \,lat-ə-rə-'zā-shən\ *n* (ca. 1882) : the process of conversion of rock to laterite

lat·est \'lāt-əst\ *n* (1886) **1** : the most recent or currently fashionable style or development ⟨the ~ in diving techniques⟩ **2** : the latest acceptable time — usu. used in the phrase *at the latest* ⟨be home by one *at the latest*⟩

late·wood \'lāt-,wu̇d\ *n* (ca. 1933) : SUMMERWOOD

la·tex \'lā-,teks\ *n, pl* **la·ti·ces** \'lat-ə-,sēz, 'lat-\ *or* **la·tex·es** [NL *latic-, latex*, fr. L, fluid] (1835) **1** : a milky usu. white fluid that is produced by cells of various seed plants (as of the milkweed, spurge, and poppy families) and is the source of rubber, gutta-percha, chicle, and balata **2** : a water emulsion of a synthetic rubber or plastic obtained by polymerization and used esp. in coatings (as paint) and adhesives

[1]**lath** \'lath *also* 'lath\ *n, pl* **laths** *or* **lath** [ME, fr. OE *lætt*; akin to OHG *latta* lath, W *llath* yard] (bef. 12c) **1** : a thin narrow strip of wood nailed to rafters, joists, or studding as a groundwork for slates, tiles, or plaster **2** : a building material in sheets used as a base for plaster **3** : a quantity of laths

[2]**lath** *vt* (15c) : to cover or line with laths

[1]**lathe** \'lāth\ *n* [prob. fr. ME *lath* supporting stand] (14c) : a machine in which work is rotated about a horizontal axis and shaped by a fixed tool

[2]**lathe** *vt* **lathed; lath·ing** (1903) : to cut or shape with a lathe

[1]**lath·er** \'lath-ər\ *n* [(assumed) ME, fr. OE *lēathor*; akin to OE *lēag* lye — more at LYE] (bef. 12c) **1** **a** : a foam or froth formed when a detergent (as soap) is agitated in water **b** : foam or froth from profuse sweating (as on a horse) **2** : an agitated or overwrought state : DITHER — **lath·ery** \-(ə-)rē\ *adj*

[2]**lather** *vb* **lath·ered; lath·er·ing** \-(ə-)riŋ\ *vt* (bef. 12c) **1** : to spread lather over **2** : to beat severely : FLOG ~ *vi* : to form a lather or a froth like lather — **lath·er·er** \-ər-ər\ *n*

lath·ing \'lath-iŋ, 'lath-\ *n* (15c) **1** : the action or process of placing laths **2** : a quantity or an installation of laths

lath·y·rism \'lath-ə-,riz-əm\ *n* [NL *Lathyrus*, fr. Gk *lathyros*, a type of pea] (ca. 1888) : a diseased condition of man, domestic animals, and esp. horses that results from poisoning by a substance found in some legumes (genus *Lathyrus* and esp. *L. sativus*) and is characterized esp. by spastic paralysis of the hind or lower limbs

lath·y·rit·ic \,lath-ə-'rit-ik\ *adj* (1960) : of, relating to, affected with, or characteristic of lathyrism ⟨~ rats⟩ ⟨~ cartilage⟩

latices *pl of* LATEX

la·tic·i·fer \lā-'tis-ə-fər\ *n* [ISV *latici-* (fr. NL *latic-, latex*) + *-fer*] (ca. 1928) : a plant cell or vessel that contains latex

la·ti·fun·dio \,lat-ə-'fün-dē-,ō\ *n, pl* **-di·os** [Sp, fr. L *latifundium*] (ca. 1924) : a latifundium in Spain or Latin America

lat·i·fun·di·um \,lat-ə-'fən-dē-əm\ *n, pl* **-dia** \-dē-ə\ [L, fr. *latus* wide + *fundus* piece of landed property — more at BOTTOM] (1630) : a great landed estate with primitive agriculture and labor often in a state of partial servitude

lat·i·go \'lat-i-,gō\ *n, pl* **-gos** *also* **-goes** [Sp *látigo*] *chiefly West* (1873) : a long strap on a saddletree of a stock saddle to adjust the cinch

lat·i·me·ria \,lat-ə-'mir-ē-ə\ *n* [NL, fr. Marjorie E. D. Courtenay-Latimer *b*1907 So. African museum director] (1939) : any of a genus (*Latimeria*) of living coelacanth fishes of deep seas off southern Africa

[1]**Lat·in** \'lat-ᵊn\ *adj* [ME, fr. OE, fr. L *Latinus*, fr. *Latium*, ancient country of Italy] (bef. 12c) **1** **a** : of, relating to, or composed in Latin **b** : ROMANCE **2** : of or relating to Latium or the Latins **3** : of or relating to the part of the Catholic Church that until recently used a Latin rite and forms the patriarchate of the pope **4** : of or relating to the peoples or countries using Romance languages; *specif* : of or relating to the peoples or countries of Latin America

[2]**Latin** *n* (bef. 12c) **1** : the Italic language of ancient Latium and of Rome and until modern times the dominant language of school, church, and state in western Europe — see INDO-EUROPEAN LANGUAGES table **2** : a member of the people of ancient Latium **3** : a Catholic of the Latin rite **4** : a member of one of the Latin peoples; *specif* : a native or inhabitant of Latin America **5** : LATIN ALPHABET

Latin alphabet *n* (ca. 1867) : an alphabet that was used for writing Latin and that has been modified for writing many modern languages

Lat·in·ate \'lat-ᵊn-,āt\ *adj* (1904) : of, relating to, resembling, or derived from Latin

Latin cross *n* (1797) : a figure of a cross having a long upright shaft and a shorter crossbar traversing it above the middle — see CROSS illustration

La·tin·i·an \la-'tin-ē-ən, lə-\ *n* (1953) : a division of the Italic languages that includes Latin — see INDO-EUROPEAN LANGUAGES table

Lat·in·ism \'lat-ᵊn-,iz-əm\ *n* (ca. 1570) **1** : a characteristic feature of Latin occurring in another language **2** : Latin quality or character

Lat·in·ist \'lat-ᵊn-əst, 'lat-nəst\ *n* (15c) : a specialist in the Latin language or Roman culture

la·tin·i·ty \la-'tin-ət-ē, lə-\ *n, often cap* (1619) **1** : a manner of speaking or writing Latin **2** : LATINISM 2

lat·in·ize \'lat-ᵊn-,īz\ *vb* **-ized; -iz·ing** *often cap, vt* (1589) **1** **a** *obs* : to translate into Latin **b** : to give a Latin form to **c** : to introduce Latinisms into **d** : ROMANIZE 2 **2** : to make Latin or Italian in doctrine, ideas, or traits; *specif* : to cause to resemble the Roman Catholic Church ~ *vi* **1** : to use Latinisms **2** : to exhibit the influence of the Romans or of the Roman Catholic Church — **lat·in·iza·tion** \,lat-ᵊn-ə-'zā-shən, ,lat-nə-\ *n*

La·ti·no \lə-'tē-(,)nō\ *n, pl* **-nos** [AmerSp, fr. Sp *latino* Latin] (1946) **1** : a native or inhabitant of Latin America **2** : a person of Latin-American origin living in the U.S.

Latin Quarter *n* [trans. of F *Quartier Latin*] (1869) : a section of Paris south of the Seine frequented by students and artists

Latin square *n* (1890) : a square array which contains *n* different elements with each element occurring *n* times but with no element occurring twice in the same column or row and which is used esp. in the statistical design of experiments (as in agriculture)

lat·ish \'lāt-ish\ *adj* (1611) : being somewhat late

lat·i·tude \'lat-ə-,t(y)üd\ *n* [ME, fr. L *latitudin-, latitudo*, fr. *latus* wide; akin to Arm *lain* wide] (14c) **1** *archaic* : extent or distance from side to side : WIDTH **2** : angular distance from some specified circle or plane of reference: as **a** : angular distance north or south from the earth's equator measured through 90 degrees **b** : angular distance of a celestial body from the ecliptic **c** : a region or locality as marked by its latitude **3** **a** *archaic* : SCOPE, RANGE **b** : the range of exposures within which a film or plate will produce a negative or positive of satisfactory quality **4** : freedom of action or choice — **lat·i·tu·di·nal** \,lat-ə-'t(y)üd-nəl, -ᵊn-əl\ *adj* — **lat·i·tu·di·nal·ly** \-ē\ *adv*

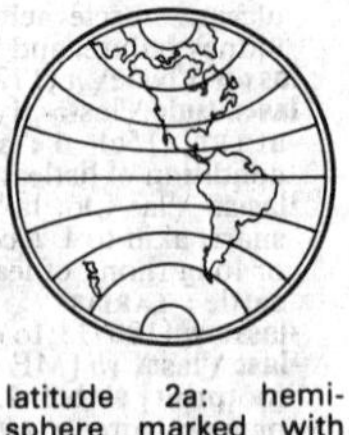

latitude 2a: hemisphere marked with parallels of latitude

lat·i·tu·di·nar·i·an \,lat-ə-,t(y)üd-ᵊn-'er-ē-ən\ *n* (1662) : a person who is broad and liberal in his standards of religious belief and conduct — **latitudinarian** *adj* — **lat·i·tu·di·nar·i·an·ism** \-ē-ə-,niz-əm\ *n*

lat·o·sol \'lat-ə-,sȯl\ *n* [irreg. fr. L *later* brick + E *-sol* (as in *podsol*, var. of *podzol*)] (ca. 1949) : a leached red and yellow tropical soil — **lat·o·sol·ic** \,lat-ə-'sȯ-lik\ *adj*

la·trine \lə-'trēn\ *n* [F, fr. L *latrina*, contr. of *lavatrina*, fr. *lavare* to wash — more at LYE] (1642) **1** : a receptacle (as a pit in the earth) for use as a toilet **2** : TOILET

-l·a·try \l-ə-trē\ *n comb form* [ME *-latrie*, fr. OF, fr. LL *-latria*, fr. Gk, fr. *latreia*] : worship ⟨helio*latry*⟩

lat·ten *or* **lat·tin** \'lat-ᵊn\ *n* [ME *laton*, fr. MF] (14c) **1** : a yellow alloy identical to or resembling brass typically hammered into thin sheets and formerly much used for church utensils **2** **a** : iron plate covered with tin **b** : metal in thin sheets ⟨gold ~⟩

lat·ter \'lat-ər\ *adj* [ME, fr. OE *lætra*, compar. of *læt* late] (bef. 12c) **1** **a** : more recent : LATER ⟨the ~ stages of a process⟩ **b** : of or relating to the end : FINAL **c :** RECENT, PRESENT **2 :** of, relating to, or being the second of two groups or things or the last of several groups or things referred to ⟨of ham and beef the ~ meat is cheaper today⟩

lat·ter–day \ˌlat-ər-ˌdā\ *adj* (1834) **1 :** of present or recent times **2 :** of a later or subsequent time

Latter–day Saint *n* (1834) **:** a member of a religious body tracing its origin to Joseph Smith in 1830 and accepting the Book of Mormon as divine revelation : MORMON

lat·ter·ly *adv* (1734) **1 :** at a subsequent time : LATER **2 :** of late : RECENTLY

lat·tice \ˈlat-əs\ *n* [ME *latis,* fr. MF *lattis*] (14c) **1 a :** a framework or structure of crossed wood or metal strips **b :** a window, door, or gate having a lattice **c :** a network or design resembling a lattice **2 :** a regular geometrical arrangement of points or objects over an area or in space: as **a :** SPACE LATTICE **b :** a geometrical arrangement of fissionable material in a nuclear reactor **c :** a mathematical set that has some elements ordered and that is such that for any two elements there exists a greatest element in the subset of all elements less than or equal to both and a least element in the subset of all elements greater than or equal to both — **lattice** *vt* — **lat·ticed** \-əst\ *adj*

lattice girder *n* (1852) **:** a girder with top and bottom flanges connected by a latticework web

lat·tice·work \ˈlat-ə-ˌswərk\ *n* (15c) **:** a lattice or work made of lattices

la·tus rec·tum \ˌlat-əs-ˈrek-təm\ *n* [NL, lit., straight side] (1702) **:** a chord of a conic section (as an ellipse) that passes through a focus and is parallel to the directrix

Lat·vi·an \ˈlat-vē-ən\ *n* (ca. 1934) **1 :** a native or inhabitant of Latvia **2 :** the Baltic language of the Latvian people — **Latvian** *adj*

lau·an \ˈlü-ˌän, lü-ˈ; lau̇-ˈän\ *n* [Tag *lawaan*] (1894) **:** any of various Philippine timbers (as of the genera *Shorea* and *Parashorea*) that are light yellow to reddish brown or brown, are of moderate strength and durability, and include some which enter commerce as Philippine mahogany

[1]laud \ˈlȯd\ *n* [ME *laudes* (pl.), fr. ML, fr. L, pl. of *laud-, laus* praise; akin to OHG *liod* song] (14c) **1** *pl but sing or pl in constr, often cap* **:** an office of solemn praise to God forming with matins the first of the canonical hours **2 :** PRAISE, ACCLAIM

[2]laud *vt* [L *laudare,* fr. *laud-, laus*] (14c) **:** PRAISE, EXTOL

laud·able \ˈlȯd-ə-bəl\ *adj* (15c) **:** worthy of praise : COMMENDABLE — **laud·abil·i·ty** \ˌlȯd-ə-ˈbil-ət-ē\ *n* — **laud·able·ness** \ˈlȯd-ə-bəl-nəs\ *n* — **laud·ably** \-blē\ *adv*

lau·da·num \ˈlȯd-nəm, -ᵊn-əm\ *n* [NL] (1602) **1 :** any of various formerly used preparations of opium **2 :** a tincture of opium

lau·da·tion \lȯ-ˈdā-shən\ *n* (15c) **:** the act of praising : EULOGY

lau·da·tive \ˈlȯd-ət-iv\ *adj* (15c) **:** LAUDATORY

lau·da·to·ry \ˈlȯd-ə-ˌtōr-ē, -ˌtȯr-\ *adj* (1555) **:** of, relating to, or expressing praise

[1]laugh \ˈlaf, ˈläf\ *vb* [ME *laughen,* fr. OE *hliehhan;* akin to OHG *lachēn* to laugh, OE *hlōwan* to moo — more at LOW] *vi* (bef. 12c) **1 a :** to show mirth, joy, or scorn with a smile and chuckle or explosive sound **b :** to find amusement or pleasure in something ⟨~*ed* at his own clumsiness⟩ **c :** to become amused or derisive ⟨a very skeptical public ~*ed* at our early efforts —Graenum Berger⟩ **2 a :** to produce the sound or appearance of laughter ⟨a ~*ing* brook⟩ **b :** to be of a kind that inspires joy ~ *vt* **1 :** to influence or move by laughter ⟨~*ed* the bad singer off the stage⟩ **2 :** to utter with a laugh — **laugh·er** *n* — **laugh·ing·ly** \-iŋ-lē\ *adv*

[2]laugh *n* (1690) **1 :** the act of laughing **2 a :** a cause for derision or merriment : JOKE ⟨swim in that current? That's a ~⟩ **b :** an expression of scorn or mockery : JEER **3** *pl* **:** DIVERSION, SPORT ⟨play baseball just for ~*s*⟩

laugh·able \ˈlaf-ə-bəl, ˈläf-\ *adj* (1596) **:** of a kind to provoke laughter or sometimes derision : amusingly ridiculous — **laugh·able·ness** *n* — **laugh·ably** \-blē\ *adv*

syn LAUGHABLE, LUDICROUS, RIDICULOUS, COMIC, COMICAL mean provoking laughter or mirth. LAUGHABLE applies to anything occasioning laughter intentionally or unintentionally; LUDICROUS suggests absurdity or preposterousness that excites both laughter and scorn or sometimes pity; RIDICULOUS suggests extreme absurdity, foolishness, or contemptibility; COMIC applies esp. to that which arouses thoughtful amusement; COMICAL applies to that which arouses unrestrained spontaneous hilarity.

laughing gas *n* (ca. 1842) **:** NITROUS OXIDE

laughing jackass *n* (1798) **:** KOOKABURRA

laugh·ing·stock \ˈlaf-iŋ-ˌstäk, ˈläf-\ *n* (1533) **:** an object of ridicule : BUTT

laugh off *vt* (1715) **:** to minimize by treating as amusingly or absurdly trivial

laugh·ter \ˈlaf-tər, ˈläf-\ *n* [ME, fr. OE *hleahtor;* akin to OE *hliehhan*] (bef. 12c) **1 :** a sound of or as if of laughing **2** *archaic* **:** a cause of merriment

launce \ˈlȯn(t)s, ˈlän(t)s\ *n* [prob. fr. [1]*lance*] (1623) **:** SAND LANCE

[1]launch \ˈlȯnch, ˈlänch\ *vb* [ME *launchen,* fr. ONF *lancher,* fr. LL *lanceare* to wield a lance — more at LANCE] *vt* (14c) **1 a :** to throw forward : HURL **b :** to release, catapult, or send off (a self-propelled object) ⟨~ a rocket⟩ **2 a :** to set (a boat or ship) afloat **b :** to give (a person) a start **c** (1) **:** to originate or set in motion : INITIATE (2) **:** to get off to a good start ~ *vi* **1 a :** to spring forward : TAKE OFF **b :** to throw oneself energetically : PLUNGE **2 a** *archaic* **:** to slide down the ways **b :** to make a start

[2]launch *n* (1749) **:** an act or instance of launching

[3]launch *n* [Sp or Pg; Sp *lancha,* fr. Pg] (1697) **1 :** a large boat that operates from a ship **2 :** a small motorboat that is open or that has the forepart of the hull covered

launch·er \ˈlȯn-chər, ˈlän-\ *n* (1911) **:** one that launches: as **a :** a device for firing a grenade from a rifle **b :** a device for launching a rocket or rocket shell **c :** CATAPULT

launch·pad \ˈlȯnch-ˌpad, ˈlänch-\ *n* (1958) **:** a nonflammable platform from which a rocket, launch vehicle, or guided missile can be launched — called also *launching pad*

launch vehicle *n* (ca. 1960) **:** a rocket engine used to send off a spacecraft or satellite or to guide it into an orbit or trajectory

launch window *n* (1962) **:** WINDOW 8

[1]laun·der \ˈlȯn-dər, ˈlän-\ *vb* **laun·dered; laun·der·ing** \-d(ə-)riŋ\ [ME *launder,* n.] *vt* (1664) **1 :** to wash (as clothes) in water **2 :** to make ready for use by washing and ironing ⟨a freshly ~*ed* shirt⟩ **3 :** to cause (illegally obtained funds) to appear legitimate by conversion performed by a third party ~ *vi* **:** to wash or wash and iron clothing or household linens — **laun·der·er** \-dər-ər\ *n*

[2]launder *n* [ME, launderer, fr. MF *lavandier,* fr. ML *lavandarius,* fr. L *lavandus,* gerundive of *lavare* to wash — more at LYE] (1667) **:** TROUGH; *esp* **:** a box conduit conveying particulate material suspended in water in ore dressing

laun·der·ette \ˌlȯn-də-ˈret, ˌlän-\ *n* [fr. *Launderette,* a service mark] (ca. 1946) **:** a self-service laundry

laun·dress \ˈlȯn-drəs, ˈlän-\ *n* (1550) **:** LAUNDRYWOMAN

Laun·dro·mat \ˈlȯn-drə-ˌmat, ˈlän-\ *service mark* — used for a self-service laundry

laun·dry \ˈlȯn-drē, ˈlän-\ *n, pl* **laundries** (14c) **1 a :** a room for doing the family wash **b :** a commercial laundering establishment **2 :** clothes or linens that have been or are to be laundered

laun·dry·man \-mən\ *n* (1708) **:** a male laundry worker

laun·dry·wom·an \-ˌwu̇m-ən\ *n* (1838) **:** a female laundry worker

Laun·fal \ˈlȯn-fəl, ˈlän-\ *n* **:** a knight of the Round Table in late Arthurian legend

lau·ra \ˈläv-rə\ *n* [LGk, fr. Gk, lane] (ca. 1727) **:** a monastery of an Eastern church

[1]lau·re·ate \ˈlȯr-ē-ˌāt, ˈlär-\ *vt* **-at·ed; -at·ing** [L *laureatus* crowned with laurel, fr. *laurea* laurel wreath, deriv. of *laurus*] (15c) **1 :** to crown with or as if with a laurel wreath for excellence or achievement **2 :** to appoint to the office of poet laureate — **lau·re·ation** \ˌlȯr-ē-ˈā-shən, ˌlär-\ *n*

[2]lau·re·ate \ˈlȯr-ē-ət, ˈlär-\ *n* (1529) **:** the recipient of honor for achievement in an art or science; *specif* **:** POET LAUREATE — **laureate** *adj* — **lau·re·ate·ship** \-ˌship\ *n*

[1]lau·rel \ˈlȯr-əl, ˈlär-\ *n* [ME *lorel,* fr. OF *lorier,* fr. *lor* laurel, fr. L *laurus*] (12c) **1 :** any of a genus (*Laurus* of the family Lauraceae, the laurel family) of trees or shrubs that have alternate entire leaves, small tetramerous flowers surrounded by bracts, and fruits that are ovoid berries; *specif* **:** a tree (*L. nobilis*) of southern Europe with foliage used by the ancient Greeks to crown victors in the Pythian games **2 :** a tree or shrub that resembles the true laurel; *esp* **:** MOUNTAIN LAUREL **3 :** a crown of laurel : HONOR — usu. used in pl.

[2]laurel *vt* **-reled** *or* **-relled; -rel·ing** *or* **-rel·ling** (1631) **:** to deck or crown with laurel

lau·ric acid \ˌlȯr-ik-, ˌlär-\ *n* [ISV, fr. L *laurus*] (1873) **:** a crystalline fatty acid $C_{12}H_{24}O_2$ found esp. in coconut oil and used in making soaps, esters, and lauryl alcohol

lau·ryl alcohol \ˌlȯr-əl-, ˌlär-\ *n* (1922) **:** a compound $C_{12}H_{26}O$; *also* **:** a liquid mixture of this and other alcohols used esp. in making detergents

la·va \ˈläv-ə, ˈlav-\ *n* [It, fr. L *labes* fall; akin to L *labi* to slide — more at SLEEP] (1750) **:** fluid rock that issues from a volcano or from a fissure in the earth's surface; *also* **:** such rock solidified — **la·va·like** \-ˌlīk\ *adj*

la·va·bo \lə-ˈväb-(ˌ)ō\ *n, pl* **-bos** [L, I shall wash, fr. *lavare*] (ca. 1858) **1** *often cap* **:** a ceremony at Mass in which the celebrant washes his hands after offering the oblations and says Psalm 25:6–12 **2 a :** a washbasin and a tank with a spigot that are fastened to a wall **b :** this combination used as a planter

la·vage \lə-ˈväzh\ *n* [F, fr. MF, fr. *laver* to wash, fr. L *lavare*] (ca. 1885) **:** WASHING; *esp* **:** the therapeutic washing out of an organ

la·va·la·va \ˌläv-ə-ˈläv-ə\ *n* [Samoan, clothing] (ca. 1891) **:** a rectangular cloth of cotton print worn like a kilt or skirt in Polynesia and esp. in Samoa

la·va·liere *or* **la·val·liere** \ˌläv-ə-ˈli(ə)r, ˌlav-\ *n* [F *lavallière* necktie with a large bow] (1906) **:** a pendant on a fine chain that is worn as a necklace

lavaliere microphone *n* (ca. 1962) **:** a small microphone hung around the neck of the user

la·va·tion \lā-ˈvā-shən\ *n* [L *lavation-, lavatio,* fr. *lavatus*] (15c) **:** the act or an instance of washing or cleansing

lav·a·to·ry \ˈlav-ə-ˌtōr-ē, -ˌtȯr-, *Brit* -ə-t(ə-)rē\ *n, pl* **-ries** [ME *lavatorie,* fr. ML *lavatorium,* fr. L *lavatus,* pp. of *lavare* to wash — more at LYE] (14c) **1 :** a vessel (as a basin) for washing; *esp* **:** a fixed bowl or basin with running water and drainpipe for washing **2 :** a room with conveniences for washing and usu. with one or more toilets **3 :** TOILET — **lavatory** *adj*

[1]lave \ˈlāv\ *n* [ME (northern dial.), fr. OE *lāf;* akin to OE *belīfan* to remain — more at LEAVE] *chiefly dial* (bef. 12c) **:** something that is left : RESIDUE

[2]lave *vb* **laved; lav·ing** [ME *laven,* fr. OE *lafian,* fr. L *lavare*] *vt* (bef. 12c) **1 a :** WASH, BATHE **b :** to flow along or against **2 :** POUR ~ *vi, archaic* **:** to wash oneself : BATHE

la·veer \lə-ˈvi(ə)r\ *vi* [D *laveren*] (1598) **:** to sail against the wind : TACK

[1]lav·en·der \ˈlav-ən-dər\ *n* [ME *lavendre,* fr. AF, fr. ML *lavandula*] (13c) **1 a :** a Mediterranean mint (*Lavandula officinalis*) widely cultivated for its narrow aromatic leaves and spikes of lilac-purple flowers which are dried and used in sachets **b :** any of several plants congeneric with true lavender and used similarly but often considered inferior **2 :** a variable color averaging a pale purple

[2]lavender *vt* **lav·en·dered; lav·en·der·ing** \-d(ə-)riŋ\ (1820) **:** to sprinkle or perfume with lavender

[1]la·ver \ˈlā-vər\ *n* [ME *lavour,* fr. MF *lavoir,* fr. ML *lavatorium*] (1535) **:** a large basin used for ceremonial ablutions in the ancient Jewish Tabernacle and Temple worship

[2]la·ver \ˈlā-vər, ˈläv-ər\ *n* [NL, fr. L, a water plant] (1611) **:** any of several mostly edible seaweeds: as **a :** SEA LETTUCE **b :** any of several common red algae (genus *Porphyra* and esp. *P. laciniata* and *P. vulgaris*) with fronds used for stewing or pickling

la·ver·ock *or* **lav·rock** \ˈlāv-rək, ˈlav-(ə-)rək\ *n* [ME *laverok*] *chiefly Scot* (14c) **:** LARK

\ə\ abut \ᵊ\ kitten, F table \ər\ further \a\ ash \ā\ ace \ä\ cot, cart \au̇\ out \ch\ chin \e\ bet \ē\ easy \g\ go \i\ hit \ī\ ice \j\ job \ŋ\ sing \ō\ go \ȯ\ law \ȯi\ boy \th\ thin \t͟h\ the \ü\ loot \u̇\ foot \y\ yet \zh\ vision \á, k̲, ⁿ, œ, œ̄, ue, ue̅, ʸ\ *see* Guide to Pronunciation

La·vin·ia \lə-ˈvin-ē-ə\ *n* [L] : a daughter of King Latinus in Vergil's *Aeneid* who is betrothed to Turnus but marries Aeneas

¹lav·ish \ˈlav-ish\ *adj* [ME *lavas* abundance, fr. MF *lavasse* downpour of rain, fr. *laver* to wash — more at LAVAGE] (15c) **1** : expending or bestowing profusely : PRODIGAL **2** : expended or produced in abundance ***syn*** see PROFUSE — **lav·ish·ly** *adv* — **lav·ish·ness** *n*

²lavish *vt* (1542) : to expend or bestow with profusion : SQUANDER

¹law \ˈlȯ\ *n* [ME, fr. OE *lagu*, of Scand origin; akin to ON *lǫg* law; akin to OE *licgan* to lie — more at LIE] (bef. 12c) **1 a** (1) : a binding custom or practice of a community : a rule of conduct or action prescribed or formally recognized as binding or enforced by a controlling authority (2) : the whole body of such customs, practices, or rules (3) : COMMON LAW **b** (1) : the control brought about by the existence or enforcement of such law (2) : the action of laws considered as a means of redressing wrongs; *also* : LITIGATION (3) : the agency of or an agent of established law **c** : a rule or order that it is advisable or obligatory to observe **d** : something compatible with or enforceable by established law **e** : CONTROL, AUTHORITY **2 a** *often cap* : the revelation of the will of God set forth in the Old Testament **b** *cap* : the first part of the Jewish scriptures : PENTATEUCH — see BIBLE table **3** : a rule of construction or procedure ⟨the ~s of poetry⟩ **4** : the whole body of laws relating to one subject **5 a** : the legal profession **b** : law as a department of knowledge : JURISPRUDENCE **c** : legal knowledge **6 a** : a statement of an order or relation of phenomena that so far as is known is invariable under the given conditions **b** : a general relation proved or assumed to hold between mathematical or logical expressions

syn LAW, RULE, REGULATION, PRECEPT, STATUTE, ORDINANCE, CANON mean a principle governing action or procedure. LAW implies imposition by a sovereign authority and the obligation of obedience on the part of all subject to that authority; RULE applies to more restricted or specific situations; REGULATION implies prescription by authority in order to control an organization or system; PRECEPT commonly suggests something advisory and not obligatory communicated typically through teaching; STATUTE implies a law enacted by a legislative body; ORDINANCE applies to an order governing some detail of procedure or conduct enforced by a limited authority such as a municipality; CANON suggests in nonreligious use a principle or rule of behavior or procedure commonly accepted as a valid guide. ***syn*** see in addition HYPOTHESIS

— **at law** : under or within the provisions of the law ⟨enforceable *at law*⟩

²law *vi* (ca. 1550) : LITIGATE ~ *vt, chiefly dial* : to sue or prosecute at law

law–abid·ing \ˈlȯ-ə-ˌbīd-iŋ\ *adj* (1834) : abiding by or obedient to the law — **law–abid·ing·ness** *n*

law·break·er \ˈlȯ-ˌbrā-kər\ *n* (bef. 12c) : one who violates the law — **law·break·ing** \-kiŋ\ *adj or n*

law·ful \ˈlȯ-fəl\ *adj* (14c) **1 a** : being in harmony with the law ⟨a ~ judgment⟩ **b** : constituted, authorized, or established by law : RIGHTFUL ⟨~ institutions⟩ **2** : LAW-ABIDING ⟨~ citizens⟩ — **law·ful·ly** \-f(ə-)lē\ *adv* — **law·ful·ness** \-fəl-nəs\ *n*

syn LAWFUL, LEGAL, LEGITIMATE, LICIT mean being in accordance with law. LAWFUL may apply to conformity with law of any sort (as natural, divine, common, or canon) ⟨William desired to reign not as a conqueror but as a *lawful* king —J. R. Green⟩ LEGAL applies to what is sanctioned by law or in conformity with the law, esp. as it is written or administered by the courts ⟨*legal* residents of the state⟩ LEGITIMATE may apply to a legal right or status but also, in extended use, to a right or status supported by tradition, custom, or accepted standards ⟨language is a *legitimate* part of the subject matter or content of English —A. H. Marckwardt⟩ LICIT applies to a strict conformity to the provisions of the law and applies esp. to what is regulated by law ⟨regulatory matters having to do with *licit* commerce in narcotic drugs — *Security World*⟩

law·giv·er \ˈlȯ-ˌgiv-ər\ *n* (14c) **1** : one who gives a code of laws to a people **2** : LEGISLATOR

law·less \ˈlȯ-ləs\ *adj* (13c) **1** : not regulated by or based on law **2 a** : not restrained or controlled by law : UNRULY **b** : ILLEGAL — **law·less·ly** *adv* — **law·less·ness** *n*

law·mak·er \ˈlȯ-ˌmā-kər\ *n* (14c) : one that makes laws : LEGISLATOR — **law·mak·ing** \-kiŋ\ *n*

law·man \ˈlȯ-mən\ *n* (1944) : a law-enforcement officer (as a sheriff or marshal)

law merchant *n, pl* **laws merchant** (15c) : the legal rules formerly applied to cases arising in commercial transactions

¹lawn \ˈlȯn, ˈlän\ *n* [ME *launde*, fr. MF *lande* heath, of Celt origin; akin to OIr *land* open space — more at LAND] (14c) **1** *archaic* : an open space between woods : GLADE **2** : ground (as around a house or in a garden or park) that is covered with grass and is kept mowed — **lawn** *or* **lawny** \-ē\ *adj*

²lawn *n* [ME, fr. *Laon*, France] (15c) : a fine sheer linen or cotton fabric of plain weave that is thinner than cambric — **lawny** \-ē\ *adj*

lawn bowling *n* (ca. 1929) : a bowling game played on a green with wooden balls which are rolled at a jack

lawn mower *n* (1869) : a machine for cutting grass on lawns

lawn tennis *n* (ca. 1874) : TENNIS 2

law of dominance (ca. 1942) : MENDEL'S LAW 3

law of independent assortment (1943) : MENDEL'S LAW 2

law of large numbers (1910) : a theorem in mathematical statistics: the probability that the absolute value of the difference between the mean of a population sample and the mean of the population from which it is drawn is greater than an arbitrarily small amount approaches zero as the size of the sample approaches infinity

Law of Moses (14c) : PENTATEUCH

law of nations (1548) : INTERNATIONAL LAW

law of parsimony (1837) : OCCAM'S RAZOR

law of segregation (ca. 1942) : MENDEL'S LAW 1

law of war (1947) : the code that governs or one of the rules that govern the rights and duties of belligerents in international war

law·ren·ci·um \lȯ-ˈren(t)-sē-əm\ *n* [NL, fr. Ernest O. *Lawrence*] (1961) : a short-lived radioactive element that is produced artificially from californium — see ELEMENT table

law·suit \ˈlȯ-ˌsüt\ *n* (1624) : a suit in law : a case before a court

law·yer \ˈlȯ-yər, ˈlȯi-ər\ *n* (14c) : one whose profession is to conduct lawsuits for clients or to advise as to legal rights and obligations in other matters — **law·yer·like** \-ˌlīk\ *adj* — **law·yer·ly** \-lē-\ *adj*

law·yer·ing \ˈlȯ-yə-riŋ, ˈlȯi-ə-\ *n* (1676) : the profession or work of a lawyer

lax \ˈlaks\ *adj* [ME, fr. L *laxus* loose — more at SLACK] (14c) **1 a** *of the bowels* : LOOSE, OPEN **b** : having loose bowels **2** : deficient in firmness : not stringent ⟨~ control⟩ ⟨a ~ foreman⟩ **3 a** : not tense, firm, or rigid : SLACK ⟨a ~ rope⟩ **b** : having an open or loose texture **c** : having the constituents spread apart ⟨a ~ flower cluster⟩ **4** : articulated with the muscles involved in a relatively relaxed state (as the vowel \i\ in contrast with the vowel \ē\) ***syn*** see NEGLIGENT — **lax·a·tion** \lak-ˈsā-shən\ *n* — **lax·ly** \ˈlak-slē\ *adv* — **lax·ness** *n*

¹lax·a·tive \ˈlak-sət-iv\ *adj* [ME *laxatif*, fr. ML *laxativus*, fr. L *laxatus*, pp. of *laxare* to loosen, fr. *laxus*] (14c) : having a tendency to loosen or relax; *specif* : relieving constipation

²laxative *n* (14c) : a usu. mild laxative drug

lax·ity \ˈlak-sət-ē\ *n* (1528) : the quality or state of being lax

¹lay \ˈlā\ *vb* **laid** \ˈlād\; **lay·ing** [ME *leyen*, fr. OE *lecgan*; akin to OE *licgan* to lie — more at LIE] *vt* (bef. 12c) **1** : to beat or strike down with force **2 a** : to put or set down **b** : to place for rest or sleep; *esp* : BURY **3** : to bring forth and deposit (an egg) **4** : CALM, ALLAY ⟨~ the dust⟩ **5** : BET, WAGER **6** : to press down giving a smooth and even surface **7 a** : to dispose or spread over or on a surface ⟨~ track⟩ ⟨~ plaster⟩ **b** : to set in order or position ⟨~ a table for dinner⟩ ⟨~ brick⟩ **c** : to put (strands) in place and twist to form a rope, hawser, or cable; *also* : to make by so doing ⟨~ up rope⟩ **8 a** : to impose as a duty, burden, or punishment ⟨~ a tax⟩ **b** : to put as a burden of reproach ⟨*laid* the blame on him⟩ **c** : to advance as an accusation : IMPUTE ⟨the disaster was *laid* to faulty inspection⟩ **9** : to place (something immaterial) on something ⟨~ stress on grammar⟩ **10** : PREPARE, CONTRIVE ⟨a well-*laid* plan⟩ **11 a** : to bring against or into contact with something : APPLY ⟨*laid* the watch to his ear⟩ **b** : to prepare or position for action or operation ⟨~ a fire in the fireplace⟩; *also* : to adjust (a gun) to the proper direction and elevation **12** : to bring to a specified condition ⟨~ waste the land⟩ **13 a** : ASSERT, ALLEGE ⟨~ claim to an estate⟩ **b** : to submit for examination and judgment ⟨*laid* his case before the commission⟩ **14** : to copulate with — sometimes considered vulgar ~ *vi* **1** : to produce and deposit eggs **2** *nonstand* : ¹LIE **3** : WAGER, BET **4** *dial* : PLAN, PREPARE **5 a** : to apply oneself vigorously ⟨*laid* to his oars⟩ **b** : to proceed to a specified place or position on a ship ⟨~ aloft⟩ — **lay off** \(ˈ)lā-ˈȯf\ : to leave alone; *also* : QUIT ⟨*lay off* smoking⟩ — **lay on the table 1** : to remove (a parliamentary motion) from consideration indefinitely **2** *Brit* : to put (as legislation) on the agenda

²lay *n* (1594) **1** : COVERT, LAIR **2** : something (as a layer) that lies or is laid **3 a** : line of action : PLAN **b** : line of work : OCCUPATION **4 a** : terms of sale or employment : PRICE **b** : share of profit (as on a whaling voyage) paid in lieu of wages **5 a** : the amount of advance of any point in a rope strand for one turn **b** : the nature of a fiber rope as determined by the amount of twist, the angle of the strands, and the angle of the threads in the strands **6** : the way in which a thing lies or is laid in relation to something else ⟨the ~ of the land⟩ **7** : the state of one that lays eggs ⟨hens coming into ~⟩ **8 a** : a partner in sexual intercourse — usu. considered vulgar **b** : SEXUAL INTERCOURSE — usu. considered vulgar

³lay *past of* LIE

⁴lay *n* [ME, fr. OF *lai*] (13c) **1** : a simple narrative poem : BALLAD **2** : MELODY, SONG

⁵lay *adj* [ME, fr. MF *lai*, fr. LL *laicus*, fr. Gk *laikos* of the people, fr. *laos* people] (15c) **1** : of or relating to the laity : not ecclesiastical **2** : of or relating to members of a religious house occupied with domestic or manual work ⟨a ~ brother⟩ **3** : not of or from a particular profession : UNPROFESSIONAL ⟨the ~ public⟩

lay·about \ˈlā-ə-ˌbau̇t\ *n* (1932) : a lazy shiftless person : IDLER

lay·away \ˈlā-ə-ˌwā\ *n* (1944) : a purchasing agreement by which a retailer agrees to hold merchandise secured by a deposit until the price is paid in full by the customer

lay away *vt* (ca. 1928) : to put aside for future use or delivery

lay–by \ˈlā-ˌbī\ *n* (1939) **1** *Brit* : a branch from or a widening of a road to permit vehicles to stop without obstructing traffic **2** : the final operation (as a last cultivating) in the growing of a field crop

lay by *vt* (15c) **1** : to lay aside : DISCARD **2** : to store for future use : SAVE **3** : to cultivate (as corn) for the last time

lay day *n* (ca. 1845) **1** : one of the days allowed by the charter for loading or unloading a vessel **2** : a day of delay in port

lay down *vt* (13c) **1** : to give up : SURRENDER ⟨*lay down* your arms⟩ **2 a** : ESTABLISH, PRESCRIBE ⟨*lay down* a scale for a map⟩ **b** : to assert or command dogmatically ⟨*lay down* the law⟩ **3** : STORE, PRESERVE **4 a** : to direct toward a target ⟨*lay down* a barrage⟩ **b** : to hit along the ground ⟨*laid down* a sacrifice bunt⟩ ~ *vi, nonstand* : to lie down

¹lay·er \ˈlā-ər, ˈle(-ə)r\ *n* (13c) **1** : one that lays (as a workman who lays brick or a hen that lays eggs) **2 a** : one thickness, course, or fold laid or lying over or under another **b** : STRATUM **c** : HORIZON 2 **3 a** : a branch or shoot of a plant treated to induce rooting while still attached to the parent plant **b** : a plant developed by layering — **lay·ered** \ˈlā-ərd, ˈle-ərd\ *adj*

²layer *vt* (1832) : to propagate (a plant) by means of layers ~ *vi* **1 a** : to separate into layers **b** : to form out of superimposed layers **2** *of a plant* : to form roots where a stem comes in contact with the ground

lay·er·age \ˈlā-ə-rij, ˈle-ə-\ *n* (ca. 1902) : the practice or art of layering plants

lay·ette \lā-ˈet\ *n* [F, fr. MF, dim. of *laye* box, fr. MD *lade*; akin to OE *hladan* to load — more at LADE] (1839) : a complete outfit of clothing and equipment for a newborn infant

lay figure \ˈlā-\ *n* [obs. E *layman* (lay figure), fr. D *leeman*] (1795) **1** : a jointed model of the human body used by artists to show the disposition of drapery **2** : a person likened to a dummy or puppet

lay in *vt* (1625) : LAY BY, SAVE

laying on of hands (15c) : the act of laying hands on a person's head to confer a spiritual blessing (as in Christian ordination, confirmation, or faith healing)

lay·man \'lā-mən\ *n* (15c) **1** : a person who is not a clergyman **2** : a person who does not belong to a particular profession or who is not expert in some field

lay·off \'lā-,ȯf\ *n* (1886) **1** : the act of laying off an employee or a work force; *also* : SHUTDOWN **2** : a period of inactivity or idleness

lay off \(')lā-'ȯf\ *vt* (1748) **1** : to mark or measure off **2** : to cease to employ (a worker) usu. temporarily **3** *of a bookie* : to place all or part of (an accepted bet) with another bookie to reduce the risk **4 a** : to leave undisturbed **b** : AVOID, QUIT ~ *vi* : to stop doing or taking something

lay on *vt* (1853) **1 a** : to apply by or as if by spreading on a surface ⟨*laying* it *on* thick⟩ **b** : PROVIDE, ARRANGE ⟨*lay on* a buffet lunch⟩ **c** : HAND OUT ⟨*laid on* awards⟩ **2** *chiefly Brit* : HIRE ~ *vi* : ATTACK, BEAT

lay·out \'lā-,au̇t\ *n* (1888) **1** : the act or process of planning or laying out in detail **2** : the plan or design or arrangement of something that is laid out: as **a** : DUMMY 6b **b** : final arrangement of matter to be reproduced esp. by printing **3 a** : something that is laid out ⟨a model train ~⟩ **b** : land or structures or rooms used for a particular purpose ⟨a cattle-ranching ~⟩; *also* : PLACE **c** : a set or outfit esp. of tools

lay out \(')lā-'au̇t\ *vt* (1595) **1 a** : to prepare (a corpse) for viewing **b** : to knock flat or unconscious **2** : to plan in detail ⟨*lay out* a campaign⟩ **3** : to mark (work) for drilling, machining, or filing **4** : ARRANGE, DESIGN **5** : DISPLAY, EXHIBIT **6** : SPEND

lay·over \'lā-,ō-vər\ *n* (1873) : STOPOVER

lay over \(')lā-'ō-vər\ *vt* (1862) : POSTPONE ~ *vi* : to make a stopover

lay·per·son \'lā-pərs-ᵊn\ *n* (1972) : LAYMAN

lay reader *n* (1751) : an Anglican or Roman Catholic layman authorized to conduct parts of the church services not requiring a clergyman

lay to \(')lā-'tü\ *vt* (1798) : to bring (a ship) into the wind and hold stationary ~ *vi* : LIE TO

lay–up \'lā-,əp\ *n* (1925) **1** : the action of laying up or the condition of being laid up **2** : a shot in basketball made from near the basket usu. by playing the ball off the backboard

lay up \(')lā-'əp\ *vt* (14c) **1** : to store up : LAY BY **2** : to disable or confine with illness or injury **3** : to take out of active service

lay·wom·an \'lā-,wu̇m-ən\ *n* (1529) : a woman who is a member of the laity

la·zar \'laz-ər, 'lā-zər\ *n* [ME, fr. ML *lazarus,* fr. LL *Lazarus*] (14c) : a person afflicted with a repulsive disease; *specif* : LEPER

laz·a·ret·to \,laz-ə-'ret-(,)ō\ *or* **laz·a·ret** \-'ret, -'rēt\ *n, pl* **-rettos** *or* **-rets** [It *lazzaretto,* alter. (influenced by *Santa Maria di Nazaret,* church in Venice that maintained a hospital) of *lazzaro* leper, fr. ML *lazarus*] (1549) **1** *usu lazaretto* : an institution (as a hospital) for those with contagious diseases **2** : a building or a ship used for detention in quarantine **3** *usu lazaret* : a space in a ship between decks used as a storeroom

La·za·rist \'laz-ə-rəst, lə-'zär-əst\ *n* [College of St. *Lazare,* Paris, former home of the congregation] (1747) : VINCENTIAN

Laz·a·rus \'laz-(ə-)rəs\ *n* [LL, fr. Gk *Lazaros,* fr. Heb *El'āzār*] **1** : a brother of Mary and Martha raised by Jesus from the dead according to the account in John 11 **2** : the diseased beggar in the parable of the rich man and the beggar found in Luke 16

laze \'lāz\ *vb* **lazed; laz·ing** [back-formation fr. *lazy*] *vi* (1592) : to act or lie lazily : IDLE ~ *vt* : to pass (time) in idleness or relaxation — **laze** *n*

la·zu·lite \'laz(h)-ə-,līt\ *n* [G *lazulith,* fr. ML *lazulum* lapis lazuli] (ca. 1807) : an often crystalline azure-blue mineral $(Mg,Fe)Al_2(PO_4)_2(OH)_2$ that is a hydrous phosphate of aluminum, iron, and magnesium — **la·zu·lit·ic** \,laz(h)-ə-'lit-ik\ *adj*

¹**la·zy** \'lā-zē\ *adj* **la·zi·er; -est** [perh. fr. MLG *lasich* feeble; akin to MHG *erleswen* to become weak] (1549) **1 a** : disinclined to activity or exertion : not energetic or vigorous **b** : encouraging inactivity or indolence **2** : moving slowly : SLUGGISH **3** : DROOPY, LAX **4** : placed on its side ⟨~ E livestock brand⟩ — **la·zi·ly** \-zə-lē\ *adv* — **la·zi·ness** \-zē-nəs\ *n* — **la·zy·ish** \-zē-ish\ *adj*

syn LAZY, INDOLENT, SLOTHFUL mean not easily aroused to activity. LAZY suggests a disinclination to work or to take trouble; INDOLENT suggests a love of ease and a settled dislike of movement or activity; SLOTHFUL implies a temperamental inability to act promptly or speedily when action or speed is called for.

²**lazy** *vi* **la·zied; la·zy·ing** (1612) : to move or lie lazily : LAZE

la·zy·bones \'lā-zē-,bōnz\ *n pl but sing or pl in constr* (1592) : a lazy person

lazy eye *n* (1939) : AMBLYOPIA; *also* : an eye affected with amblyopia

lazy Su·san \-'süz-ᵊn\ *n* (1917) : a revolving tray used for serving food, condiments, or relishes

lazy tongs *n pl* (ca. 1836) : a series of jointed and pivoted bars capable of great extension used to pick up or handle something at a distance

LCD \,el-(,)sē-'dē\ *n* [*l*iquid *c*rystal *d*isplay] (1973) : a constantly operating display (as of the time in a digital watch) that consists of segments of a liquid crystal whose reflectivity varies according to the voltage applied to them

LDL \'el-'dē-'el\ *n* [*l*ow-*d*ensity *l*ipoprotein] (1976) : a cholesterol-rich protein-poor lipoprotein of blood plasma correlated with increased risk of atherosclerosis — compare HDL

L–do·pa \'el-'dō-pə\ *n* [*l*evorotatory + *dopa*] (1939) : the levorotatory form of dopa found esp. in broad beans or prepared synthetically and used in treating Parkinson's disease

lea *or* **ley** \'lē, 'lā\ *n* [ME *leye,* fr. OE *lēah;* akin to OHG *lōh* thicket, L *lucus* grove, *lux* light — more at LIGHT] (bef. 12c) **1** : GRASSLAND, PASTURE **2** *usu ley* : arable land used temporarily for hay or grazing

¹**leach** \'lēch\ *var of* LEECH

²**leach** *n* [prob. alter. of *letch* (muddy ditch)] (1673) **1** : a perforated vessel to hold wood ashes through which water is passed to extract the lye **2** : LEACHATE **3** [³*leach*] : the process of leaching

³**leach** *vt* (1796) **1** : to dissolve out by the action of a percolating liquid ⟨~ out alkali from ashes⟩ **2** : to subject to the action of percolating liquid (as water) in order to separate the soluble components ~ *vi* : to pass out or through by percolation — **leach·abil·i·ty** \,lē-chə-'bil-ət-ē\ *n* — **leach·able** \'lē-chə-bəl\ *adj* — **leach·er** *n*

leach·ate \'lē-,chāt\ *n* (1934) : a solution or product obtained by leaching

¹**lead** \'lēd\ *vb* **led** \'led\; **lead·ing** [ME *leden,* fr. OE *lǣdan;* akin to OHG *leiten* to lead, OE *līthan* to go] *vt* (bef. 12c) **1 a** : to guide on a way esp. by going in advance **b** : to direct on a course or in a direction **c** : to serve as a channel for ⟨a pipe ~s water to the house⟩ **2** : to go through : LIVE ⟨~ a quiet life⟩ **3 a** (1) : to direct the operations, activity, or performance of ⟨~ an orchestra⟩ (2) : to have charge of ⟨~ a campaign⟩ **b** (1) : to go at the head of ⟨~ a parade⟩ (2) : to be first in or among ⟨~ the league⟩ (3) : to have a margin over ⟨*led* his opponent⟩ **4** : to bring to some conclusion or condition ⟨I am *led* to conclude that it failed⟩ **5** : to begin play with ⟨~ trumps⟩ **6 a** : to aim in front of (a moving object) ⟨~ a duck⟩ **b** : to pass a ball or puck just in front of (a moving teammate) ~ *vi* **1 a** : to guide someone or something along a way **b** : to lie, run, or open in a specified place or direction ⟨path ~s uphill⟩ **2 a** : to be first **b** (1) : BEGIN, OPEN (2) : to play the first card of a trick, round, or game **3** : to tend toward or have a result ⟨study ~*ing* to a degree⟩ **4** : to direct the first of a series of blows at an opponent in boxing ***syn*** see GUIDE

²**lead** *n* (14c) **1 a** (1) : position at the front : VANGUARD (2) : INITIATIVE (3) : the act or privilege of leading in cards; *also* : the card or suit led **b** (1) : LEADERSHIP (2) : EXAMPLE, PRECEDENT **c** : a margin or measure of advantage or superiority or position in advance **2** : one that leads: as **a** (1) : LODE 2 (2) : an auriferous gravel deposit in an old riverbed; *esp* : one buried under lava **b** : a channel of water esp. through a field of ice **c** : INDICATION, CLUE **d** : a principal role in a dramatic production; *also* : one who plays such a role **e** : LEASH 1 **f** (1) : an introductory section of a news story (2) : a news story of chief importance **3** : an insulated electrical conductor **4** : the length of a rope from end to end **5** : the amount of axial advance of a point accompanying a complete turn of a thread (as of a screw or worm) **6** : a position taken by a base runner off a base toward the next **7** : the first punch of a series or an exchange of punches in boxing

³**lead** *adj* (1843) : acting or serving as a lead or leader ⟨a ~ article⟩

⁴**lead** \'led\ *n, often attrib* [ME *leed,* fr. OE *lēad;* akin to MHG *lōt* lead] (bef. 12c) **1** : a heavy soft malleable ductile plastic but inelastic bluish white metallic element found mostly in combination and used esp. in pipes, cable sheaths, batteries, solder, and shields against radioactivity — see ELEMENT table **2 a** : a plummet for sounding at sea **b** *pl, Brit* : a usu. flat lead roof **c** *pl* : lead framing for panes in windows **d** : a thin strip of metal used to separate lines of type in printing **3 a** : a thin stick of marking substance in or for a pencil **b** : WHITE LEAD **4** : BULLETS, PROJECTILES **5** : TETRAETHYL LEAD — **lead·less** \-ləs\ *adj*

⁵**lead** \'led\ *vt* (14c) **1** : to cover, line, or weight with lead **2** : to fix (window glass) in position with leads **3** : to put space between the lines of (typeset matter) **4** : to treat or mix with lead or a lead compound ⟨~*ed* gasoline⟩

lead acetate *n* (ca. 1897) : an acetate of lead; *esp* : a poisonous soluble salt $PbC_4H_6O_4{\cdot}3H_2O$

lead arsenate *n* (ca. 1903) : an arsenate of lead: as **a** : an acid salt $PbHAsO_4$ used esp. as an insecticide **b** : a neutral salt $Pb_3(AsO_4)_2$ used esp. as an insecticide

lead azide *n* (1918) : a crystalline explosive compound $Pb(N_3)_2$ used as a detonating agent

lead carbonate *n* (1873) : a carbonate of lead; *esp* : a poisonous basic salt $Pb_3(OH)_2(CO_3)_2$ used esp. as a white pigment

lead chromate *n* (ca. 1903) : a chromate of lead; *esp* : CHROME YELLOW

lead dioxide *n* (ca. 1903) : a poisonous compound PbO_2 used esp. as an oxidizing agent and as an electrode in batteries

lead·en \'led-ᵊn\ *adj* (bef. 12c) **1 a** : made of lead **b** : of the color of lead : dull gray **2 a** : oppressively heavy **b** : SLUGGISH **c** : lacking spirit or animation — **lead·en·ly** *adv* — **lead·en·ness** \-ᵊn-(n)əs\ *n*

lead·er \'lēd-ər\ *n* (13c) **1** : something that leads: as **a** : a primary or terminal shoot of a plant **b** : TENDON, SINEW **c** *pl* : dots or hyphens (as in an index) used to lead the eye horizontally : ELLIPSIS 2 **d** *chiefly Brit* : a newspaper editorial **e** (1) : something for guiding fish into a trap (2) : a short length of material for attaching the end of a fishing line to a lure or hook **f** : a pipe for conducting fluid **g** : LOSS LEADER **h** : something that ranks first **i** : a blank section at the beginning of a reel of film or recorded tape **2** : a person that leads: as **a** : GUIDE, CONDUCTOR **b** (1) : a person who directs a military force or unit (2) : a person who has commanding authority or influence **c** (1) : the principal officer of a British political party (2) : a member chosen by his party to manage party activities in a legislative body (3) : such a member presiding over the whole legislative body when his party constitutes a majority **d** (1) : CONDUCTOR c (2) : a first or principal performer of a group **3** : a horse placed in advance of the other horses of a team — **lead·er·less** \-ləs\ *adj*

leader of the opposition (1771) : the principal member of the opposition party in a British legislative body who is given the status of a salaried government official and an important role in organizing the business of the house

lead·er·ship \'lēd-ər-,ship\ *n* (1821) **1** : the office or position of a leader **2** : capacity to lead **3** : LEADERS

lead glass *n* (1830) : glass of high refractive index containing lead oxide

lead–in \'lēd-,in\ *n* (1913) : something that leads in — **lead–in** *adj*

lead·ing \'lēd-iŋ\ *adj* (1597) **1** : coming or ranking first : FOREMOST **2** : exercising leadership **3** : providing direction or guidance ⟨a ~ question⟩ **4** : given most prominent display ⟨the ~ story⟩

leading edge \'lēd-iŋ-\ *n* (1877) **1** : the foremost edge of an airfoil or propeller blade **2** : the forward part of something that moves or seems to move

leading lady *n* (1874) : an actress who plays the leading female role in a play or movie

leading man *n* (1827) : an actor who plays the leading male role in a play or movie

leading tone *n* (ca. 1911) : the seventh tone of a diatonic scale — called also *leading note*

lead line \'led-\ *n* (15c) : SOUNDING LINE

lead·man \'lēd-,man, -mən\ *n* (1939) : a worker in charge of other workers

lead monoxide *n* (ca. 1909) **:** a yellow to brownish red poisonous compound PbO used in rubber manufacture and glassmaking

lead·off \'lēd-,ȯf\ *n* (ca. 1886) **1 :** a beginning or leading action **2 :** one that leads off — **leadoff** *adj*

lead off \(')lēd-'ȯf\ *vt* (1817) **1 :** to make a start on **:** OPEN **2 :** to bat first for a baseball team in (an inning) ~ *vi* **:** BEGIN; *also* **:** to come on or perform first

lead on *vt* (1598) **:** to entice or induce to proceed in a course esp. when unwise or mistaken

lead pencil \'led-\ *n* (1688) **:** a pencil using graphite as the marking material

lead–pipe \,led-,pīp\ *adj* (1898) **:** CERTAIN, GUARANTEED ⟨a ~ cinch⟩

lead·plant \'led-,plant\ *n* (ca. 1833) **:** a leguminous shrub (*Amorpha canescens*) of the western U.S. that has hoary pinnate leaves and bears dull-colored racemose flowers

lead poisoning *n* (ca. 1841) **:** chronic intoxication that is produced by the absorption of lead into the system and is characterized by severe colicky pains, a dark line along the gums, and local muscular paralysis

leads·man \'ledz-mən\ *n* (1857) **:** a man who uses a sounding lead to determine depth of water

lead time \'lēd-\ *n* (1944) **:** the time between the beginning of a process or project and the appearance of its results

lead–up \'lēd-,əp\ *n* (1942) **:** something that leads up to or prepares the way for something else

lead up \(')lēd-'əp\ *vi* (1861) **1 :** to prepare the way **2 :** to make a gradual or indirect approach to a topic

lead·work \'led-,wərk\ *n* (1641) **1 :** something made of lead **2 :** work that is done with lead

leady \'led-ē\ *adj* **lead·i·er; -est** (14c) **:** containing or resembling lead

[1]leaf \'lēf\ *n, pl* **leaves** \'lēvz\ *also* **leafs** \'lēfs\ *often attrib* [ME *leef,* fr. OE *lēaf;* akin to OHG *loub* leaf, L *liber* bast, book] (bef. 12c) **1 a** (1) **:** a lateral outgrowth from a stem that constitutes a unit of the foliage of a plant and functions primarily in food manufacture by photosynthesis (2) **:** a modified leaf primarily engaged in functions other than food manufacture **b** (1) **:** FOLIAGE (2) **:** the leaves of a plant as an article of commerce **2 :** something suggestive of a leaf: as **a :** a part of a book or folded sheet containing a page on each side **b** (1) **:** a part (as of window shutters, folding doors, or gates) that slides or is hinged (2) **:** the movable parts of a table top **c** (1) **:** a thin sheet or plate of any substance **:** LAMINA (2) **:** metal (as gold or silver) in sheets usu. thinner than foil (3) **:** one of the plates of a leaf spring — **leaf·less** \'lē-fləs\ *adj* — **leaf·like** \'lē-,flīk\ *adj*

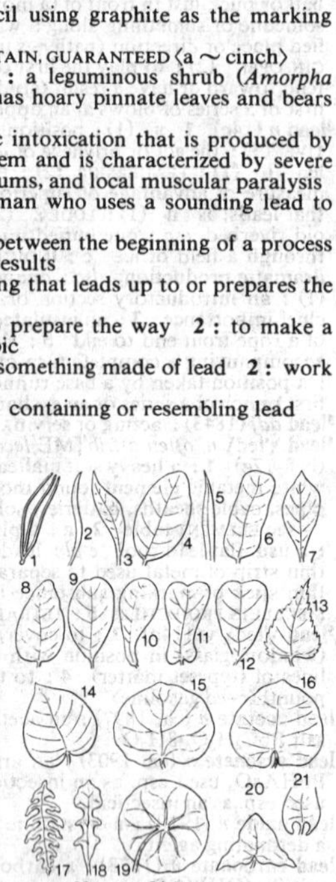

forms of leaf 1a(1): *1* needle-shaped, *2* linear, *3* lanceolate, *4* elliptic, *5* ensiform, *6* oblong, *7* oblanceolate with acuminate tip, *8* ovate with acute tip, *9* obovate, *10* spatulate, *11* fiddle-shaped, *12* cuneate, *13* deltoid, *14* cordate, *15* reniform, *16* orbiculate, *17* runcinate, *18* lyrate, *19* peltate, *20* hastate, *21* sagittate, *22* odd-pinnate, *23* abruptly pinnate, *24* trifoliolate, *25, 26* palmate

[2]leaf *vi* (1611) **1 :** to shoot out or produce leaves **2 :** to turn over pages ⟨~ through a book⟩ ~ *vt* **:** to turn over the pages of

leaf·age \'lē-fij\ *n* (1599) **1 :** FOLIAGE 2 **2 :** the representation of leafage (as in architecture)

leaf bud *n* (1664) **:** a bud that develops into a leafy shoot and does not produce flowers

leaf butterfly *n* (1882) **:** any of a genus (*Kallima*) of nymphalid butterflies of southern Asia and the East Indies that mimic leaves

leaf curl *n* (ca. 1899) **:** a plant disease characterized by curling of leaves; *esp* **:** PEACH LEAF CURL

leafed \'lēft\ *adj* (1552) **:** LEAVED

leaf fat *n* (1725) **:** the fat that lines the abdominal cavity and encloses the kidneys; *esp* **:** that of a hog used in the manufacture of lard

leaf·hop·per \'lēf-,häp-ər\ *n* (ca. 1852) **:** any of numerous small leaping homopterous insects (family Cicadellidae) that suck the juices of plants

leaf lard *n* (ca. 1847) **:** high-quality lard made from leaf fat

[1]leaf·let \'lē-flət\ *n* (1787) **1 a :** one of the divisions of a compound leaf **b :** a small or young foliage leaf **2 :** a leaflike organ or part **3 :** a usu. folded printed sheet intended for free distribution

[2]leaflet *vi* **-let·ed** *or* **-let·ted; -let·ing** *or* **let·ting** (1968) **:** to hand out leaflets — **leaf·le·teer** \,lē-flə-'ti(ə)r\ *n*

leaf miner *n* (1830) **:** any of various small insects (as moths or two-winged flies) that in the larval stages burrow in and eat the parenchyma of leaves

leaf mold *n* (1845) **1 :** a compost or layer composed chiefly of decayed vegetable matter **2 :** a mold or mildew that affects foliage

leaf roll *n* (1916) **:** a virus disease of the potato that is transmitted by aphids and is characterized by an upward rolling of the leaf margins, smaller tubers, and netlike necrotic areas in the phloem

leaf roller *n* (1830) **:** any of various lepidopterans whose larvae make a nest by rolling up plant leaves

leaf rust *n* (1865) **:** a rust disease of plants and esp. of wheat that affects primarily the leaves

leaf scar *n* (1835) **:** the mark left on a stem after a leaf falls

leaf spot *n* (ca. 1895) **:** any of various plant diseases characterized by discolored often circular spots on the leaves

leaf spring *n* (ca. 1893) **:** a spring made of superposed strips, plates, or leaves

leaf·stalk \'lēf-,stȯk\ *n* (ca. 1828) **:** PETIOLE

leaf trace *n* [[3]*trace*] (1875) **:** a trace associated with a leaf

leafy \'lē-fē\ *adj* **leaf·i·er; -est** (15c) **1 a :** furnished with or abounding in leaves ⟨~ woodlands⟩ **b :** having broad-bladed leaves ⟨mosses, grasses, and ~ plants⟩ **c :** consisting chiefly of leaves ⟨~ vegetables⟩ **2 :** resembling a leaf; *specif* **:** LAMINATE

leafy liverwort *n* (ca. 1922) **:** any of an order (Jungermanniales) of usu. epiphytic liverworts with a leafy gametophyte that has one ventral and two dorsal rows of leaves on the stem

leafy spurge *n* (ca. 1911) **:** a tall perennial European herb (*Euphorbia esula*) that is naturalized and troublesome as a weed in the northern U.S. and Canada

[1]league \'lēg\ *n* [ME *leuge, lege,* fr. LL *leuga*] (14c) **1 :** any of various units of distance from about 2.4 to 4.6 statute miles (3.9 to 7.4 kilometers) **2 :** a square league

[2]league *n* [ME (Sc) *ligg,* fr. MF *ligue,* fr. OIt *liga,* fr. *ligare* to bind, fr. L — more at LIGATURE] (15c) **1 a :** an association of nations or other political entities for a common purpose **b** (1) **:** an association of persons or groups united by common interests or goals (2) **:** a group of sports teams that regularly play one another **c :** an informal alliance **2 :** CLASS, CATEGORY

[3]league *vb* **leagued; leagu·ing** *vt* (1604) **:** to unite in a league ~ *vi* **:** to form a league

[1]lea·guer \'lē-gər\ *n* [D *leger;* akin to OHG *legar* bed — more at LAIR] (1577) **1 :** a military camp **2 :** SIEGE

[2]leaguer *vt, archaic* (1715) **:** BESIEGE, BELEAGUER

[3]leagu·er \'lē-gər\ *n* [[2]*league*] (1591) **:** a member of a league

[1]leak \'lēk\ *vb* [ME *leken,* fr. ON *leka;* akin to OE *leccan* to moisten, OIr *legaim* I melt] *vi* (14c) **1 a :** to enter or escape through an opening usu. by a fault or mistake ⟨fumes ~ in⟩ **b :** to let a substance or light in or out through an opening **2 :** to become known despite efforts at concealment ~ *vt* **1 :** to permit to enter or escape through or as if through a leak **2 :** to give out (information) surreptitiously ⟨~*ed* the story to the press⟩ — **leak·er** \'lē-kər\ *n*

[2]leak *n* (15c) **1 a :** a crack or hole that usu. by mistake admits or lets escape **b :** something that permits the admission or escape of something else usu. with prejudicial effect **c :** a loss of electricity due to faulty insulation; *also* **:** the point or the path at which such loss occurs **2 :** the act, process, or an instance of leaking **3 :** an act of urinating — usu. used with *take;* sometimes considered vulgar — **leak·proof** \'lēk-,prüf\ *adj*

leak·age \'lē-kij\ *n* (15c) **1 :** the act or process or an instance of leaking **2 :** something or the amount that leaks

leaky \'lē-kē\ *adj* **leak·i·er; -est** (15c) **:** permitting fluid to leak in or out — **leak·i·ly** \-kə-lē\ *adv* — **leak·i·ness** \-kē-nəs\ *n*

leal \'lē(ə)l\ *adj* [ME *leel,* fr. MF *leial, leel* — more at LOYAL] *chiefly Scot* (14c) **:** LOYAL, TRUE — **leal·ly** \'lē-əl-(l)ē, 'lēl-lē\ *adv*

[1]lean \'lēn\ *vb* **leaned** \'lēnd, *chiefly Brit* 'lent\; **lean·ing** \'lē-niŋ\ [ME *lenen,* fr. OE *hleonian;* akin to OHG *hlinēn* to lean, Gk *klinein,* L *clinare*] *vi* (bef. 12c) **1 a :** to incline, deviate, or bend from a vertical position **b :** to cast one's weight to one side for support **2 :** to rely for support or inspiration **3 :** to incline in opinion, taste, or desire ~ *vt* **:** to cause to lean **:** INCLINE — **lean on :** to apply pressure to

[2]lean *n* (1776) **:** the act or an instance of leaning **:** INCLINATION

[3]lean *adj* [ME *lene,* fr. OE *hlǣne*] (bef. 12c) **1 a :** lacking or deficient in flesh **b :** containing little or no fat **2 :** lacking richness, sufficiency, or productiveness **3 :** deficient in an essential or important quality or ingredient: as **a** *of ore* **:** containing little valuable mineral **b :** low in combustible component — used esp. of fuel mixtures **4 :** characterized by economy (as of style, expression, or operation) — **lean·ly** *adv* — **lean·ness** \'lēn-nəs\ *n*

syn LEAN, SPARE, LANK, LANKY, GAUNT, RAWBONED, SCRAWNY, SKINNY mean thin because of an absence of excess flesh. LEAN stresses lack of fat and of curving contours; SPARE suggests leanness from abstemious living or constant exercise; LANK implies tallness as well as leanness; LANKY suggests awkwardness and loose-jointedness as well as thinness; GAUNT implies marked thinness or emaciation as from overwork or suffering; RAWBONED suggests a large ungainly build without implying undernourishment; SCRAWNY and SKINNY imply an extreme leanness that suggests deficient strength and vitality.

[4]lean *vt* (bef. 12c) **:** to make lean

[5]lean *n* (15c) **:** the part of meat that consists principally of fat-free muscle

Le·an·der \lē-'an-dər\ *n* [L, fr. Gk *Leandros*] **:** a youth in Greek legend who swims the Hellespont nightly to visit Hero and who ultimately drowns in one of the crossings

lean·ing \'lē-niŋ\ *n* (15c) **:** a definite but not decisive attraction or tendency

syn LEANING, PROPENSITY, PROCLIVITY, PENCHANT mean a strong instinct or liking for something. LEANING suggests a liking or attraction not strong enough to be decisive or uncontrollable; PROPENSITY implies a deeply ingrained and usu. irresistible longing; PROCLIVITY suggests a strong natural proneness usu. to something objectionable or evil; PENCHANT implies a strongly marked taste in the person or an irresistible attraction in the object.

leant \'lent\ *chiefly Brit past of* LEAN

[1]lean–to \'lēn-,tü\ *n, pl* **lean–tos** \-,tüz\ (15c) **1 :** a wing or extension of a building having a lean-to roof **2 :** a rough shed or shelter with a lean-to roof

[2]lean–to *adj* (1649) **:** having only one slope or pitch ⟨~ roof⟩ — see ROOF illustration

[1]leap \'lēp\ *vb* **leapt** \'lēpt *also* 'lept\ *or* **leaped; leap·ing** \'lē-piŋ\ [ME *lepen,* fr. OE *hlēapan;* akin to OHG *hlouffan* to run] *vi* (bef. 12c) **1 :** to spring free from or as if from the ground **:** JUMP ⟨~ over a fence⟩ ⟨a fish ~*s* out of the water⟩ **2 a :** to pass abruptly from one state or topic to another **b :** to act precipitately ⟨~*ed* at the chance⟩ ~ *vt* **:** to pass over by leaping — **leap·er** \'lē-pər\ *n*

[2]leap *n* (bef. 12c) **1 a :** an act of leaping **:** SPRING, BOUND **b** (1) **:** a place leaped over or from (2) **:** the distance covered by a leap **2 a :** a sudden passage or transition ⟨a great ~ forward⟩ **b :** a choice made in an area of ultimate concern ⟨a ~ of faith⟩ — **by leaps and bounds :** with extraordinary rapidity

[1]leap·frog \'lēp-,frȯg, -,fräg\ *n* (1599) **:** a game in which one player bends down and another vaults over him

[2]leapfrog *vb* **leap·frogged; leap·frog·ging** *vi* (1872) **:** to leap or progress in or as if in leapfrog ~ *vt* **1 :** to go ahead of (each other) in turn; *specif* **:** to advance (two military units) by keeping one unit in action while moving the other unit past it to a position farther in front **2 :** to evade by or as if by a bypass

leap year *n* (14c) **1 :** a year in the Gregorian calendar containing 366 days with February 29 as the extra day **2 :** an intercalary year in any calendar

Lear \'li(ə)r\ *n* **:** a legendary king of Britain and hero of Shakespeare's tragedy *King Lear*

learn \'lərn\ *vb* **learned** \'lərnd, 'lərnt\; **learning** [ME *lernen,* fr. OE *leornian;* akin to OHG *lernēn* to learn, OE *last* footprint, L *lira* furrow, track] *vt* (bef. 12c) **1 a** (1) **:** to gain knowledge or understanding of or skill in by study, instruction, or experience ⟨~ a trade⟩ (2) **:** MEMORIZE ⟨~ the lines of a play⟩ **b :** to come to be able ⟨~ to dance⟩ **c :** to come to realize ⟨~*ed* that honesty paid⟩ **2 a** *substand* **:** TEACH **b** *obs* **:** to inform of something **3 :** to come to know **:** HEAR ⟨we just ~*ed* that he was ill⟩ ~ *vi* **:** to acquire knowledge or skill or a behavioral tendency ***syn*** see DISCOVER — **learn·able** \'lər-nə-bəl\ *adj* — **learn·er** *n*

learned *adj* (14c) **1** \'lər-nəd\ **:** characterized by or associated with learning **:** ERUDITE **2** \'lərnd, 'lərnt\ **:** acquired by learning ⟨~ versus innate behavior patterns⟩ — **learn·ed·ly** \'lər-nəd-lē\ *adv* — **learn·ed·ness** \-nəd-nəs\ *n*

learn·ing *n* (bef. 12c) **1 :** the act or experience of one that learns **2 :** knowledge or skill acquired by instruction or study **3 :** modification of a behavioral tendency by experience (as exposure to conditioning) ***syn*** see KNOWLEDGE

learnt \'lərnt\ *chiefly Brit past and past part of* LEARN

[1]lease \'lēs\ *n* (14c) **1 :** a contract by which one conveys real estate, equipment, or facilities for a specified term and for a specified rent; *also* **:** the act of such conveyance or the term for which it is made **2 :** a piece of land or property that is leased **3 :** a continuance or opportunity for continuance ⟨a new ~ on life⟩

[2]lease *vt* **leased; leas·ing** [AF *lesser,* fr. OF *laissier* to let go, fr. L *laxare* to loosen, fr. *laxus* slack — more at SLACK] (ca. 1570) **1 :** to grant by lease **2 :** to hold under a lease ***syn*** see HIRE — **leas·able** \'lē-sə-bəl\ *adj*

lease·hold \'lēs-ˌhōld\ *n* (1720) **1 :** a tenure by lease **2 :** property held by lease — **lease·hold·er** *n*

leash \'lēsh\ *n* [ME *lees, leshe,* fr. MF *laisse,* fr. OF *laissier*] (14c) **1 a :** a line for leading or restraining an animal **b :** something that restrains **2 a :** a set of three animals (as greyhounds, foxes, bucks, or hares) **b :** a set of three — **leash** *vt*

leas·ing \'lē-siŋ, -ziŋ\ *n* [ME *lesing,* fr. OE *lēasung,* fr. *lēasian* to lie, fr. *lēas* false] *archaic* (bef. 12c) **:** the act of lying; *also* **:** LIE, FALSEHOOD

[1]least \'lēst\ *adj* [ME *leest,* fr. OE *lǣst* superl. of *lǣssa* less] (bef. 12c) **1 :** lowest in importance or position **2 a :** smallest in size or degree **b :** being a member of a kind distinguished by diminutive size ⟨~ bittern⟩ **c :** smallest possible **:** SLIGHTEST

[2]least *n* (12c) **:** one that is least — **at least 1 :** at the minimum **2 :** in any case

[3]least *adv* (13c) **:** in the smallest or lowest degree — **least of all :** especially not ⟨no one, *least of all* the children, paid attention⟩

least common denominator *n* (ca. 1875) **:** the least common multiple of two or more denominators

least common multiple *n* (1823) **1 :** the smallest common multiple of two or more numbers **2 :** the common multiple of lowest degree of two or more polynomials

least squares *n pl* (ca. 1864) **:** a method of fitting a curve to a set of points representing statistical data in such a way that the sum of the squares of the distances of the points from the curve is a minimum

least·ways \'lēs-ˌtwāz\ *adv, dial* (14c) **:** at least

least·wise \-ˌtwīz\ *adv* (15c) **:** at least

[1]leath·er \'leth-ər\ *n* [ME *lether,* fr. OE *lether-;* akin to OHG *leder* leather] (bef. 12c) **1 :** animal skin dressed for use **2 :** the flap of the ear of a dog — see DOG illustration **3 :** something wholly or partly made of leather — **leath·er·like** \-ˌlīk\ *adj*

[2]leather *vt* **leath·ered; leath·er·ing** \'leth-(ə-)riŋ\ (14c) **1 :** to cover with leather **2 :** to beat with a strap **:** THRASH

leath·er·back \'leth-ər-ˌbak\ *n* (ca. 1855) **:** the largest existing sea turtle (*Dermochelys coriacea*) distinguished by its flexible carapace composed of a mosaic of small bones embedded in a thick leathery skin

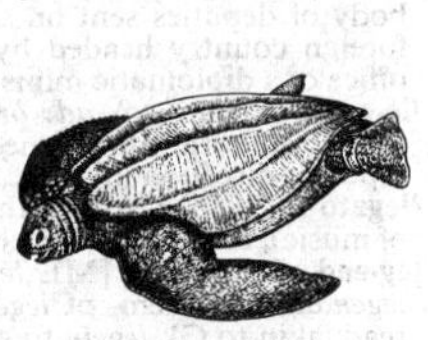
leatherback

Leath·er·ette \ˌleth-ə-'ret\ *trademark* — used for a product colored, finished, and embossed in imitation of leather grains

leath·er·leaf \'leth-ər-ˌlēf\ *n* (ca. 1818) **:** a north temperate ericaceous bog shrub (*Chamaedaphne calyculata*) with evergreen coriaceous leaves and small white cylindrical flowers

leath·ern \'leth-ərn\ *adj* (bef. 12c) **:** made of, consisting of, or resembling leather

leath·er·neck \-ər-ˌnek\ *n* [fr. the leather collar formerly part of the uniform] (ca. 1914) **:** a member of the U.S. Marine Corps

leath·er·wood \'leth-ər-ˌwu̇d\ *n* (ca. 1743) **:** a small tree (*Dirca palustris*) of the mezereon family with pliant stems and yellow flowers

leath·ery \'leth-(ə-)rē\ *adj* (ca. 1552) **:** resembling leather in appearance or consistency

[1]leave \'lēv\ *vb* **left** \'left\; **leav·ing** [ME *leven,* fr. OE *lǣfan;* akin to OHG *verleiben* to leave, OE *belīfan* to be left over, Gk *lipos* fat] *vt* (bef. 12c) **1 a** (1) **:** BEQUEATH, DEVISE ⟨*left* a fortune to his son⟩ (2) **:** to have remaining after one's death ⟨~*s* a widow and two children⟩ **b :** to cause to remain as a trace or aftereffect ⟨oil ~*s* a stain⟩ ⟨the wound *left* an ugly scar⟩ **2 a :** to cause or allow to be or remain in a specified condition ⟨~ the door open⟩ ⟨his manner *left* me cold⟩ **b :** to fail to include or take along ⟨*left* the notes at home⟩ ⟨the movie ~*s* a lot out⟩ **c :** to have as a remainder ⟨4 from 7 ~*s* 3⟩ **d :** to permit to be or remain subject to another's action or control ⟨just ~ everything to me⟩ **e** *substand* **:** LET **f :** to cause or allow to be or remain available ⟨~ room for expansion⟩ ⟨*left* my phone number with the receptionist⟩ ⟨wanted to ~ himself an out⟩ **3 a :** to go away from **:** DEPART ⟨~ the room⟩ **b :** DESERT, ABANDON ⟨*left* his wife⟩ **c :** to terminate association with **:** withdraw from ⟨*left* school before graduation⟩ **4 :** to put, deposit, or deliver before or in the process of departing ⟨the postman *left* a package for you⟩ ~ *vi* **:** SET OUT, DEPART — **leav·er** *n*

usage Although some commentators profess to fear that *let* is falling into disuse, it is not; use of *leave* in senses equivalent to *let* is generally limited to speech and is considered substandard except in the combination *leave alone.*

— **leave alone :** to refrain from bothering or using

[2]leave *n* [ME *leve,* fr. OE *lēaf;* akin to MHG *loube* permission, OE *alȳfan* to allow — more at BELIEVE] (bef. 12c) **1 a :** permission to do something **b :** authorized esp. extended absence from duty or employment **2 :** an act of leaving **:** DEPARTURE

[3]leave *vi* **leaved; leav·ing** [ME *leven,* fr. *leef* leaf] (13c) **:** LEAF

leaved *adj* (13c) **:** having leaves — usu. used in combination ⟨palmate-leaved⟩ ⟨a four-*leaved* clover⟩

[1]leav·en \'lev-ən\ *n* [ME *levain,* fr. MF, fr. (assumed) VL *levamen,* fr. L *levare* to raise — more at LEVER] (14c) **1 a :** a substance (as yeast) used to produce fermentation in dough or a liquid; *esp* **:** SOURDOUGH **b :** a material (as baking powder) used to produce a gas that lightens dough or batter **2 :** something that modifies or lightens a mass or aggregate

[2]leaven *vt* **leav·ened; leav·en·ing** \'lev-(ə-)niŋ\ (15c) **1 :** to raise (as bread) with a leaven **2 :** to mingle or permeate with some modifying, alleviating, or vivifying element ***syn*** see INFUSE

leav·en·ing *n* (1626) **:** a leavening agent **:** LEAVEN

leave of absence (1771) **1 :** permission to be absent from duty or employment **2 :** LEAVE 1b

leave off *vb* (14c) **:** STOP, CEASE

leaves *pl of* LEAF

leave–tak·ing \'lēv-ˌtā-kiŋ\ *n* (14c) **:** DEPARTURE, FAREWELL

leav·ings \'lē-viŋz\ *n pl* (14c) **:** REMNANT, RESIDUE

le·bens·raum \'lā-bənz-ˌrau̇m, -bən(t)s-\ *n, often cap* [G, fr. *leben* living, life (akin to OHG *lebēn* to live) + *raum* space, fr. OHG *rūm* — more at LIVE, ROOM] (1905) **1 :** territory believed esp. by Nazis to be necessary for national existence or economic self-sufficiency **2 :** space required for life, growth, or activity

[1]lech \'lech\ *n* (1830) **1 :** LETCH **2 :** LECHER

[2]lech *vi* (1911) **:** LUST

lech·er \'lech-ər\ *n* [ME *lechour,* fr. OF *lecheor,* fr. *lechier* to lick, live in debauchery, of Gmc origin; akin to OHG *leckōn* to lick — more at LICK] (12c) **:** a man who engages in lechery

lech·er·ous \'lech-(ə-)rəs\ *adj* (14c) **:** given to or suggestive of lechery — **lech·er·ous·ly** *adv* — **lech·er·ous·ness** *n*

lech·ery \'lech-(ə-)rē\ *n* (13c) **:** inordinate indulgence in sexual activity **:** LASCIVIOUSNESS

lec·i·thin \'les-ə-thən\ *n* [ISV, fr. Gk *lekithos* yolk of an egg] (1861) **:** any of several waxy hygroscopic phosphatides that are widely distributed in animals and plants, form colloidal solutions in water, and have emulsifying, wetting, and antioxidant properties; *also* **:** a mixture of or substance rich in lecithins

lec·i·thin·ase \-thə-ˌnās, -ˌnāz\ *n* (1910) **:** PHOSPHOLIPASE

lec·tern \'lek-tərn\ *n* [ME *lettorne,* fr. MF *letrun,* fr. ML *lectorinum,* fr. L *lector* reader, fr. *lectus,* pp. of *legere* to read — more at LEGEND] (14c) **:** READING DESK; *esp* **:** one from which scripture lessons are read in a church service

lec·tion \'lek-shən\ *n* [LL *lection-, lectio,* fr. L, act of reading — more at LESSON] (1608) **1 :** a liturgical lesson for a particular day **2** [NL *lection-, lectio,* fr. L] **:** a variant reading of a text

lec·tion·ary \'lek-shə-ˌner-ē\ *n, pl* **-ar·ies** (1780) **:** a book or list of lections for the church year

lec·tor \'lek-tər, -ˌtȯ(ə)r\ *n* [ME, fr. LL, reader of the lessons in a church service, fr. L, reader, fr. *lectus,* pp.] (14c) **:** one who assists at a worship service chiefly by reading a lesson

lec·to·type \'lek-tə-ˌtīp\ *n* [Gk *lektos* chosen (fr. *legein* to gather, choose) + E *type* — more at LEGEND] (ca. 1905) **:** a specimen chosen as the type of a species or subspecies if the author of the name fails to designate a type

[1]lec·ture \'lek-chər, -shər\ *n* [ME, act of reading, fr. LL *lectura,* fr. L *lectus,* pp.] (15c) **1 :** a discourse given before an audience or class esp. for instruction **2 :** a formal reproof — **lec·ture·ship** \-ˌship\ *n*

[2]lecture *vb* **lec·tured; lec·tur·ing** \'lek-chə-riŋ, 'lek-shriŋ\ *vi* (ca. 1590) **:** to deliver a lecture or a course of lectures ~ *vt* **1 :** to deliver a lecture to **2 :** to reprove formally — **lec·tur·er** \-chər-ər, -shrər\ *n*

led *past and past part of* LEAD

LED \ˌel-(ˌ)ē-'dē\ *n* [*l*ight-*e*mitting *d*iode] (ca. 1970) **:** a semiconductor diode that emits light when subjected to an applied voltage and that is used in an electronic display (as for a digital watch)

Le·da \'lēd-ə\ *n* [L, fr. Gk *Lēda*] **:** the mother of Clytemnestra and Castor by her husband Tyndareus and of Helen and Pollux by Zeus who comes to her in the form of a swan

le·der·ho·sen \'lād-ər-ˌhōz-ᵊn\ *n pl* [G, fr. MHG *lederhose,* fr. *leder* leather + *hose* trousers] (1936) **:** leather shorts often with suspenders worn esp. in Bavaria

ledge \'lej\ *n* [ME *legge* bar of a gate] (1535) **1 :** a raised or projecting edge or molding intended to protect or check ⟨a window ~⟩ **2 :** an underwater ridge or reef esp. near the shore **3 a :** a narrow flat surface or shelf; *esp* **:** one that projects from a wall of rock **b :** rock solid or continuous enough to form ledges ⟨the field was full of ~⟩ **4 :** LODE, VEIN — **ledgy** \'lej-ē\ *adj*

led·ger \'lej-ər\ *n* [ME *legger,* prob. fr. *leyen, leggen* to lay] (1588) **1 :** a book containing accounts to which debits and credits are posted from books of original entry **2 :** a horizontal timber secured to the uprights of scaffolding to support the putlog

ledger board *n* (ca. 1909) **1 :** a horizontal board forming the top rail of a simple fence or the handrail of a balustrade **2 :** RIBBON 2a

ledger line *n* (ca. 1700) **:** a short line added above or below a musical staff to extend its range

\ə\ abut \ᵊ\ kitten, F table \ər\ further \a\ ash \ā\ ace \ä\ cot, cart
\au̇\ out \ch\ chin \e\ bet \ē\ easy \g\ go \i\ hit \ī\ ice \j\ job
\ŋ\ sing \ō\ go \ȯ\ law \ȯi\ boy \th\ thin \th\ the \ü\ loot \u̇\ foot
\y\ yet \zh\ vision \à, k̲, ⁿ, œ, œ̄, ue, ue̅, ʸ\ see Guide to Pronunciation

1lee \'lē\ *n* [ME, fr. OE *hlēo;* akin to OHG *lāo* lukewarm, L *calēre* to be warm] (bef. 12c) **1 :** protecting shelter **2 :** the side (as of a ship) that is sheltered from the wind

2lee *adj* (15c) **1 :** of or relating to the lee — compare WEATHER **2 :** facing in the direction of motion of an overriding glacier — used esp. of a hillside

lee·board \'lē-,bō(ə)rd, -,bȯ(ə)rd\ *n* (1691) **:** either of the wood or metal planes attached outside the hull of a sailboat to prevent leeway

1leech \'lēch\ *n* [ME *leche,* fr. OE *lǣce;* akin to OHG *lāhhi* physician] (bef. 12c) **1** *archaic* **:** PHYSICIAN, SURGEON **2** [fr. its former use by physicians for bleeding patients] **:** any of numerous carnivorous or bloodsucking usu. freshwater annelid worms (class Hirudinea) that have typically a flattened lanceolate segmented body with a sucker at each end **3 :** a hanger-on who seeks advantage or gain ***syn*** see PARASITE — **leech·like** \-,līk\ *adj*

2leech *vt* (1828) **1 :** to bleed by the use of leeches **2 :** to drain the substance of **:** EXHAUST ~ *vi* **:** to attach oneself to a person as a leech

3leech *n* [ME *leche,* fr. MLG *līk* boltrope; akin to MHG *geleich* joint — more at LIGATURE] (15c) **1 :** either vertical edge of a square sail **2 :** the after edge of a fore-and-aft sail

leek \'lēk\ *n* [ME, fr. OE *lēac;* akin to OHG *louh* leek] (bef. 12c) **:** a biennial garden herb (*Allium porrum*) of the lily family grown for its mildly pungent succulent linear leaves and esp. for its thick cylindrical stalk

1leer \'li(ə)r\ *vi* [prob. fr. obs. *leer* (cheek)] (1530) **:** to cast a sidelong glance; *esp* **:** to give a leer — **leer·ing·ly** \-iŋ-lē\ *adv*

2leer *n* (1598) **:** a lascivious, knowing, or wanton look

leery \'li(ə)r-ē\ *adj* (ca. 1718) **:** SUSPICIOUS, WARY

lees \'lēz\ *n pl* [ME *lie,* fr. MF, fr. ML *lia*] (14c) **:** the sediment of a liquor (as wine) during fermentation and aging **:** DREGS

Lee's Birthday \'lēz-\ *n* [Robert E. *Lee*] (ca. 1924) **:** January 19 observed as a legal holiday in many southern states

lee shore *n* (1579) **:** a shore lying off a ship's leeward side and constituting a severe danger in storm

1lee·ward \'lē-wərd, *esp naut* 'lü-ərd\ *n* (1549) **:** the lee side

2leeward *adj* (1666) **:** being in or facing the direction toward which the wind is blowing; *also* **:** being the side opposite the windward

lee·way \'lē-,wā\ *n* (1669) **1 a :** off-course lateral movement of a ship when under way **b :** the angle between the heading and the track of an airplane **2 :** an allowable margin of freedom or variation **:** TOLERANCE

1left \'left\ *adj* [ME, fr. OE, weak; akin to MLG *lucht* left; fr. the left hand's being the weaker in most individuals] (bef. 12c) **1 a :** of, relating to, situated on, or being the side of the body in which the heart is mostly located **b :** located nearer to the left hand than to the right **c (1) :** located on the left of an observer facing in the same direction as the object specified ⟨stage ~⟩ **(2) :** located on the left when facing downstream ⟨the ~ bank of a river⟩ **2** *often cap* **:** of, adhering to, or constituted by the left esp. in politics — **left** *adv*

2left *n* (13c) **1 a :** the left hand **b :** the location or direction of the left side **c :** the part on the left side **2** *often cap* **a :** the part of a legislative chamber located to the left of the presiding officer **b :** the members of a continental European legislative body occupying the left as a result of holding more radical political views than other members **3** *cap* **a :** those professing views usu. characterized by desire to reform or overthrow the established order esp. in politics and usu. advocating change in the name of the greater freedom or well-being of the common man **b :** a radical as distinguished from a conservative position

3left *past and past part of* LEAVE

Left Bank *n* (1893) **:** the bohemian district of Paris situated on the left bank of the Seine river

left field *n* (1857) **1 :** the position of the player defending left field **2 :** the part of the baseball outfield to the left looking out from the plate **3 :** a position far from the mainstream (as of prevailing opinion) — **left fielder** *n*

left–hand \,left-,hand, ,lef-,tand\ *adj* (15c) **1 :** LEFT-HANDED **2 :** situated on the left

left–hand·ed \'left-'han-dəd, 'lef-'tan-\ *adj* (14c) **1 :** using the left hand habitually or more easily than the right; *also* **:** swinging from left to right ⟨a ~ batter⟩ **2 :** relating to, designed for, or done with the left hand **3 :** MORGANATIC **4 a :** CLUMSY, AWKWARD **b :** INSINCERE, BACKHANDED, DUBIOUS ⟨a ~ compliment⟩ **5 a :** having a direction contrary to that of the hands of a watch viewed from in front **:** COUNTERCLOCKWISE **b :** having a spiral structure or form that ascends or advances to the left ⟨a ~ rope⟩ — **left–handed** *adv* — **left–hand·ed·ly** *adv* — **left–hand·ed·ness** *n*

left–hand·er \-'han-dər, -'tan-\ *n* (ca. 1871) **:** a left-handed person

left·ish \'lef-tish\ *adj* (1934) **:** showing leftist tendencies

left·ism \'lef-,tiz-əm\ *n* (1920) **1 :** the principles and views of the Left; *also* **:** the movement embodying these principles **2 :** advocacy of or adherence to the doctrines of the Left — **left·ist** \-təst\ *n or adj*

1left·over \'lef-,tō-vər\ *n* (1891) **:** something that remains unused or unconsumed; *esp* **:** leftover food served at a later meal — usu. used in pl.

2left·over \,lef-,tō-vər\ *adj* (1897) **:** remaining as unused residue

left shoulder arms *n* [fr. the command *left shoulder arms!*] (ca. 1918) **:** a position in the manual of arms in which the butt of the rifle is held in the left hand with the barrel resting on the left shoulder; *also* **:** a command to assume this position

left·ward \'lef-twərd\ *adj or adv* (15c) **:** being toward or on the left

left wing *n* (1919) **1 :** the leftist division of a group **2 :** LEFT 3a — **left–wing** *adj* — **left–wing·er** \'left-'twiŋ-ər\ *n*

lefty \'lef-tē\ *n, pl* **left·ies** (1886) **1 :** LEFT-HANDER **2 :** an advocate of leftism

1leg \'leg, 'lāg\ *n* [ME, fr. ON *leggr;* akin to OE *līra* muscle, calf, L *lacertus* muscle, upper arm] (13c) **1 :** a limb of an animal used esp. for supporting the body and for walking: as **a :** the part of the vertebrate limb between the knee and foot **b :** the back half of a hindquarter of a meat animal **c :** one of the rather generalized segmental appendages of an arthropod used in walking and crawling **2 a :** a pole or bar serving as a support or prop ⟨the ~*s* of a tripod⟩ **b :** a branch of a forked or jointed object ⟨the ~*s* of a compass⟩ **3 a :** the part of an article of clothing that covers the leg **b :** the part of the upper (as of a boot) that extends above the ankle **4 :** OBEISANCE, BOW — used chiefly in the phrase *to make a leg* **5 :** a side of a right triangle that is not the hypotenuse; *also* **:** a side of an isosceles triangle that is not the base **6 a :** the course and distance sailed by a boat on a single tack **b :** a portion of a trip **:** STAGE **c :** one section of a relay race **d :** one of several events or games necessary to be won to decide a competition ⟨won the first two ~*s* of horse racing's Triple Crown⟩ **7 :** a branch or part of an object or system — **leg·less** \-ləs\ *adj* — **a leg to stand on :** SUPPORT; *esp* **:** a basis for one's position in a controversy — **on one's last legs :** at or near the end of one's resources **:** on the verge of failure, exhaustion, or ruin

2leg *vi* **legged; leg·ging** (1601) **:** to use the legs in walking; *esp* **:** RUN

leg·a·cy \'leg-ə-sē\ *n, pl* **-cies** [ME *legacie* office of a legate, bequest, fr. MF or ML; MF, office of a legate, fr. ML *legatia,* fr. L *legatus* — more at LEGATE] (15c) **1 :** a gift by will esp. of money or other personal property **:** BEQUEST **2 :** something received from an ancestor or predecessor or from the past ⟨the ~ of the ancient philosophers⟩

1le·gal \'lē-gəl\ *adj* [MF, fr. L *legalis,* fr. *leg-, lex* law] (1500) **1 :** of or relating to law **2 a :** deriving authority from or founded on law **:** DE JURE **b :** having a formal status derived from law often without a basis in actual fact **:** TITULAR ⟨a corporation is a ~ but not a real person⟩ **c :** established by law; *esp* **:** STATUTORY **3 :** conforming to or permitted by law or established rules **4 :** recognized or made effective by a court of law as distinguished from a court of equity **5 :** of, relating to, or having the characteristics of the profession of law or of one of its members **6 :** created by the constructions of the law ⟨a ~ fiction⟩ ***syn*** see LAWFUL — **le·gal·ly** \-gə-lē\ *adv*

2legal *n* (1526) **:** one that conforms to rules or the law

legal age *n* (ca. 1930) **:** the age at which a person enters into full adult legal rights and responsibilities (as of making contracts or wills)

legal aid *n* (ca. 1929) **:** aid provided by an organization established esp. to serve the legal needs of the poor

le·gal·ese \,lē-gə-'lēz, -'lēs\ *n* (1914) **:** the specialized language of the legal profession ⟨replaced ~ with plain talk —Steve Weinberg⟩

legal holiday *n* (1867) **:** a holiday established by legal authority and characterized by legal restrictions on work and transaction of official business

le·gal·ism \'lē-gə-,liz-əm\ *n* (ca. 1864) **1 :** strict, literal, or excessive conformity to the law or to a religious or moral code ⟨a revolt against formalism and ~ . . . inspired by American pragmatic philosophy —T. I. Cook⟩ **2 :** a legal term or rule

le·gal·ist \-ləst\ *n* (ca. 1864) **1 :** an advocate or adherent of moral legalism **2 :** one that views things from a legal standpoint; *esp* **:** one that places primary emphasis on legal principles or on the formal structure of governmental institutions — **le·gal·is·tic** \,lē-gə-'lis-tik\ *adj* — **le·gal·is·ti·cal·ly** \-ti-k(ə-)lē\ *adv*

le·gal·i·ty \li-'gal-ət-ē\ *n, pl* **-ties** (15c) **1 :** attachment to or observance of law **2 :** the quality or state of being legal **:** LAWFULNESS **3** *pl* **:** obligations imposed by law

le·gal·ize \'lē-gə-,līz\ *vt* **-ized; -iz·ing** (1716) **:** to make legal; *esp* **:** to give legal validity or sanction to — **le·gal·iza·tion** \,lē-gə-lə-'zā-shən\ *n*

legal pad *n* (1967) **:** a writing tablet of ruled yellow paper that is usu. 8.5 by 14 inches (22 by 36 centimeters)

legal reserve *n* (ca. 1923) **:** the minimum amount of bank deposits or life insurance company assets required by law to be kept as reserves

legal tender *n* (1739) **:** money that is legally valid for the payment of debts and that must be accepted for that purpose when offered

1leg·ate \'leg-ət\ *n* [ME, fr. MF & L; MF *legat,* fr. L *legatus* deputy, emissary, fr. pp. of *legare* to depute, send as emissary, bequeath, fr. *leg-, lex*] (14c) **:** a usu. official emissary — **leg·ate·ship** \-,ship\ *n*

2le·gate \li-'gāt\ *vt* **le·gat·ed; le·gat·ing** [*legatus,* pp. of *legare* to bequeath] (1546) **:** BEQUEATH 1 — **le·ga·tor** \-'gāt-ər\ *n*

leg·a·tee \,leg-ə-'tē\ *n* (1679) **:** one to whom a legacy is bequeathed or a devise is given

leg·a·tine \'leg-ə-,tēn, -,tīn\ *adj* (1611) **:** of, headed by, or enacted under the authority of a legate

le·ga·tion \li-'gā-shən\ *n* (15c) **1 :** the sending forth of a legate **2 :** a body of deputies sent on a mission; *specif* **:** a diplomatic mission in a foreign country headed by a minister **3 :** the official residence and office of a diplomatic minister in a foreign country

1le·ga·to \li-'gät-(,)ō\ *adv or adj* [It, lit., tied] (ca. 1811) **:** in a manner that is smooth and connected (as between successive tones) — used esp. as a direction in music

2legato *n* (1885) **:** a smooth and connected manner of performance (as of music); *also* **:** a passage of music so performed

leg·end \'lej-ənd\ *n* [ME *legende,* fr. MF & ML; MF *legende,* fr. ML *legenda,* fr. L, fem. of *legendus,* gerundive of *legere* to gather, select, read; akin to Gk *legein* to gather, say, *logos* speech, word, reason] (14c) **1 a :** a story coming down from the past; *esp* **:** one popularly regarded as historical although not verifiable **b :** a body of such stories ⟨a place in the ~ of the frontier⟩ **c :** a popular myth of recent origin **d :** a person or thing that inspires legends **2 a :** an inscription or title on an object (as a coin) **b :** CAPTION 2b **c :** an explanatory list of the symbols on a map or chart

leg·end·ary \'lej-ən-,der-ē\ *adj* (1563) **1 :** of, relating to, or characteristic of legend or a legend **2 :** WELL-KNOWN, FAMOUS ***syn*** see FICTITIOUS — **leg·en·dari·ly** \,lej-ən-'der-ə-lē\ *adv*

leg·end·ry \'lej-ən-drē\ *n* (1849) **:** a body of legends

leg·er \'lej-ər\ *var of* LEDGER

leg·er·de·main \,lej-ərd-ə-'mān\ *n* [ME, fr. MF *leger de main* light of hand] (15c) **1 :** SLEIGHT OF HAND **2 :** a display of skill or adroitness

le·ger·i·ty \lə-'jer-ət-ē, le-\ *n* [MF *legereté,* fr. OF, lightness, fr. *leger* light, fr. (assumed) VL *leviarius,* fr. L *levis* — more at LIGHT] (1561) **:** alert facile quickness of mind or body

leger line *n* (ca. 1828) **:** LEDGER LINE

leges *pl of* LEX

legged \'leg-əd, 'lāg-, *Brit usu* 'legd\ *adj* (15c) **:** having a leg or legs esp. of a specified kind or number — often used in combination ⟨a four-legged animal⟩

leg·ging *or* **leg·gin** \'leg-ən, 'lāg-, -iŋ\ *n* (1751) **:** a covering (as of leather or cloth) for the leg

leg·gy \'leg-ē, 'lāg-\ *adj* **leg·gi·er; -est** (1787) **1 :** having disproportionately long legs **2 :** having attractive legs **3 :** SPINDLY — used of a plant — **leg·gi·ness** \-ē-nəs\ *n*

leg·horn \'leg-,(h)ȯ(ə)rn, 'leg-ərn\ n [Leghorn, Italy] (1740) **1 a** : a fine plaited straw made from an Italian wheat **b** : a hat of this straw **2** : any of a Mediterranean breed of small hardy fowls noted for their large production of white eggs

leg·i·ble \'lej-ə-bəl\ adj [ME, fr. LL legibilis, fr. L legere to read] (14c) : capable of being read or deciphered : PLAIN — **leg·i·bil·i·ty** \,lej-ə-'bil-ət-ē\ n — **leg·i·bly** \'lej-ə-blē\ adv

¹le·gion \'lē-jən\ n [ME, fr. OF, fr. L legion-, legio, fr. legere to gather — more at LEGEND] (13c) **1** : the principal unit of the Roman army comprising 3000 to 6000 foot soldiers with cavalry **2** : a large military force; esp : ARMY 1a **3** : a very large number : MULTITUDE **4** : a national association of ex-servicemen

²legion adj (1678) : MANY, NUMEROUS ⟨the problems are ∼⟩

¹le·gion·ary \'lē-jə-,ner-ē\ adj [L legionarius, fr. legion-, legio] (1577) : of, relating to, or constituting a legion

²legionary n, pl **-ar·ies** (1598) : LEGIONNAIRE

le·gion·naire \,lē-jə-'na(ə)r, -'ne(ə)r\ n [F légionnaire, fr. L legionarius] (1818) : a member of a legion

Legionnaires' disease \-,na(ə)rz-, -,ne(ə)rz-\ also **Legionnaire's disease** n [so called fr. its first recognized occurrence during the 1976 American Legion convention] (1976) : a lobar pneumonia caused by a bacterium (Legionella pneumophila)

Legion of Honor (1827) : a French order conferred as a reward for civil or military merit

Legion of Merit (ca. 1942) : a U.S. military decoration awarded for exceptionally meritorious conduct in the performance of outstanding services

leg·is·late \'lej-ə-,slāt\ vb **-lat·ed; -lat·ing** [back-formation fr. legislator] vi (1805) : to perform the function of legislation; specif : to make or enact laws ∼ vt : to cause, create, provide, or bring about by legislation

leg·is·la·tion \,lej-ə-'slā-shən\ n (1655) **1** : the action of legislating; specif : the exercise of the power and function of making rules (as laws) that have the force of authority by virtue of their promulgation by an official organ of a state or other organization **2** : the enactments of a legislator or a legislative body **3** : a matter of business for or under consideration by a legislative body

¹leg·is·la·tive \'lej-ə-,slāt-iv, -slət-\ n (1642) : the body or department exercising the power and function of legislating : LEGISLATURE

²legislative adj (1651) **1 a** : having the power or performing the function of legislating **b** : belonging to the branch of government that is charged with such powers as making laws, levying and collecting taxes, and making financial appropriations — compare EXECUTIVE, JUDICIAL **2 a** : of or relating to a legislature ⟨∼ committees⟩ **b** : composed of members of a legislature ⟨∼ caucus⟩ **c** : created by a legislature esp. as distinguished from an executive or judicial body **d** : designed to assist a legislature or its members ⟨a ∼ research agency⟩ **3** : of, concerned with, or created by legislation — **leg·is·la·tive·ly** adv

legislative assembly n, often cap L&A (ca. 1797) **1** : a bicameral legislature (as in an American state) **2** : the lower house of a bicameral legislature **3** : a unicameral legislature; esp : one in a Canadian province

legislative council n, often cap L&C (1787) **1** : a unicameral legislature (as in a British colony) **2** : the upper house of a British bicameral legislature **3** : a permanent committee chosen from both houses that meets between sessions of a state legislature to study problems and plan a legislative program

leg·is·la·tor \'lej-ə-,slā-,tȯ(ə)r, -,slāt-ər also ,lej-ə-'slā-,tȯ(ə)r\ n [L legislator, lit., proposer of a law, fr. legis (gen. of lex law) + lator proposer, fr. latus suppletive pp. of ferre to carry, propose — more at TOLERATE, BEAR] (1603) : one that makes laws esp. for a political unit; esp : a member of a legislative body — **leg·is·la·to·ri·al** \,lej-ə-slə-'tȯr-ē-əl, -'tȯr-\ adj — **leg·is·la·tor·ship** \'lej-ə-,slāt-ər-,ship\ n

leg·is·la·ture n \'lej-ə-,slā-chər also ,lej-ə-\, Brit often 'lej-ə-slə-\ (1676) : a body of persons having the power to legislate; specif : an organized body having the authority to make laws for a political unit

le·gist \'lē-jəst\ n [ME, fr. MF legiste, fr. ML legista, fr. L leg-, lex] (15c) : a specialist in law; esp : one learned in Roman or civil law

le·git \li-'jit\ adj, slang (1908) : LEGITIMATE

le·git·i·ma·cy \li-'jit-ə-mə-sē\ n (1691) : the quality or state of being legitimate

¹le·git·i·mate \li-'jit-ə-mət\ adj [ME legitimat, fr. ML legitimatus, pp. of legitimare to legitimate, fr. L legitimus legitimate, fr. leg-, lex law] (15c) **1 a** : lawfully begotten; specif : born in wedlock **b** : having full filial rights and obligations by birth ⟨a ∼ child⟩ **2** : being exactly as purposed : neither spurious nor false ⟨∼ grievance⟩ **3 a** : accordant with law or with established legal forms and requirements ⟨a ∼ government⟩ **b** : ruling by or based on the strict principle of hereditary right ⟨a ∼ king⟩ **4** : conforming to recognized principles or accepted rules and standards ⟨∼ advertising expenditure⟩ ⟨∼ inference⟩ **5** : relating to plays acted by professional actors but not including revues, burlesque, or some forms of musical comedy ⟨the ∼ theater⟩ syn see LAWFUL — **le·git·i·mate·ly** adv

²le·git·i·mate \-,māt\ vt **-mat·ed; -mat·ing** (1586) : to make legitimate: **a** (1) : to give legal status or authorization to (2) : to show or affirm to be justified **b** : to put (a bastard) in the position of a legitimate child before the law by legal means — **le·git·i·ma·tion** \-,jit-ə-'mā-shən\ n — **le·git·i·ma·tor** \-'jit-ə-,māt-ər\ n

le·git·i·ma·tize \li-'jit-ə-mə-,tīz\ vt **-tized; -tiz·ing** (1791) : LEGITIMATE

le·git·i·mism \li-'jit-ə-,miz-əm\ n, often cap (1877) : adherence to the principles of political legitimacy or to a person claiming legitimacy — **le·git·i·mist** \-məst\ n, often cap — **legitimist** adj

le·git·i·mize \-,mīz\ vt **-mized; -miz·ing** (1848) : LEGITIMATE — **le·git·i·mi·za·tion** \-,jit-ə-mə-'zā-shən\ n — **le·git·i·miz·er** \-'jit-ə-,mī-zər\ n

leg·man \'leg-,man, 'lag-\ n (1923) **1** : a reporter assigned usu. to gather information **2** : an assistant who performs various subordinate tasks (as gathering information or running errands)

leg-of-mut·ton or **leg-o'-mut·ton** \,leg-ə(v)-'mət-ᵊn, ,lag-\ adj (1840) : having the approximately triangular shape or outline of a leg of mutton ⟨∼ sleeve⟩ ⟨∼ sail⟩

leg out vt (1965) : to make (as a base hit) by fast running

leg-pull \'leg-,pu̇l, 'lag-\ n [fr. the phrase to pull one's leg] (1915) : a humorous deception or hoax

leg·room \-,rüm, -,ru̇m\ n (1926) : space in which to extend the legs while seated

le·gume \'leg-,yüm, li-'gyüm\ n [F légume, fr. L legumin-, legumen leguminous plant, fr. legere to gather — more at LEGEND] (1676) **1 a** : the fruit or seed of leguminous plants (as peas or beans) used for food **b** : a vegetable used for food **2** : any of a large family (Leguminosae) of dicotyledonous herbs, shrubs, and trees having fruits that are legumes or loments, bearing nodules on the roots that contain nitrogen-fixing bacteria, and including important food and forage plants (as peas, beans, or clovers) **3** : a dry dehiscent one-celled fruit developed from a simple superior ovary and usu. dehiscing into two valves with the seeds attached to the ventral suture : POD

le·gu·mi·nous \li-'gyü-mə-nəs, le-\ adj (15c) **1** : of, relating to, or consisting of plants that are legumes **2** : resembling a legume

leg up n (1837) **1** : a helping hand : BOOST **2** : HEAD START

leg warmer n (1974) : a usu. knitted covering for the leg

leg·work \'leg-,wərk, 'lag-\ n (ca. 1891) : work (as gathering information) that involves a preponderance of physical activity and that forms the basis of more creative or mentally exacting work (as writing a book)

le·hua \lā-'hü-ə\ n [Hawaiian] (1888) : a common very showy tree (Metrosideros villosa) of the myrtle family of the Pacific islands having bright red corymbose flowers and a hard wood; also : its flower

¹lei \'lā, 'lā-,ē\ n [Hawaiian] (1843) : a wreath or necklace usu. of flowers or leaves

²lei \'lā\ pl of LEU

Leices·ter \'les-tər\ n [Leicester, county in England] (1798) **1** : an individual of either of two English breeds of white-faced long-wool sheep raised esp. for mutton **2** : a hard usu. orange-colored cheese similar to cheddar

leish·man·ia \'lēsh-'man-ē-ə\ n [NL, fr. Sir W. B. Leishman †1926 Brit. medical officer] (1903) : any of a genus (Leishmania) of flagellate protozoans that are parasitic in the tissues of vertebrates; broadly : an organism resembling the leishmanias that is included in the family (Trypanosomatidae) to which they belong — **leish·man·i·al** \-ē-əl\ adj

leish·man·i·a·sis \,lēsh-mə-'nī-ə-səs\ n [NL] (1912) : infection with or disease caused by leishmanias

leis·ter \'lē-stər\ n [of Scand origin; akin to ON ljōstr leister] (1533) : a spear armed with three or more barbed prongs for catching fish

lei·sure \'lēzh-ər, 'lezh-, 'lāzh-\ n [ME leiser, fr. MF leisir, fr. leisir to be permitted, fr. L licēre — more at LICENSE] (14c) **1** : freedom provided by the cessation of activities; esp : time free from work or duties **2** : EASE, LEISURELINESS — **leisure** adj — **at leisure** or **at one's leisure** : in one's leisure time : at one's convenience ⟨read the book at his leisure⟩

lei·sured \-ərd\ adj (1631) : having leisure : characterized by leisureliness

lei·sure·ly \-ər-lē\ adv (15c) : without haste : DELIBERATELY

²leisurely adj (1604) : characterized by leisure : UNHURRIED — **lei·sure·li·ness** n

leisure suit n (ca. 1972) : a suit consisting of a shirt jacket and matching trousers for informal wear

leit·mo·tiv or **leit·mo·tif** \'līt-mō-,tēf\ n [G leitmotiv, fr. leiten to lead + motiv motive] (ca. 1876) **1** : an associated melodic phrase or figure that accompanies the reappearance of an idea, person, or situation esp. in a Wagnerian music drama **2** : a dominant recurring theme

¹lek \'lek\ n [prob. fr. Sw, sport, play] (1871) : an assembly area where animals and esp. black grouse carry on display and courtship behavior

²lek n, pl **leks** or **le·ke** \'lek-ə\ also **lek** or **le·ku** \'lek-(,)ü\ [Alb] (1927) — see MONEY table

lek·var \'lek-,vär\ n [Hung] (ca. 1958) : a prune butter used as a pastry filling

le·man \'lem-ən, 'lē-mən\ n [ME lefman, leman, fr. lef lief] archaic (13c) : SWEETHEART, LOVER; esp : MISTRESS

¹lem·ma \'lem-ə\ n, pl **lemmas** or **lem·ma·ta** \-ət-ə\ [L, fr. Gk lēmma thing taken, assumption, fr. lambanein to take — more at LATCH] (1570) **1** : an auxiliary proposition used in the demonstration of another proposition **2** : the argument or theme of a composition prefixed as a title or introduction; also : the heading or theme of a comment or note on a text **3** : a glossed word or phrase

²lemma n [Gk, husk, fr. lepein to peel — more at LEPER] (ca. 1906) : the lower of the two bracts enclosing the flower in the spikelet of grasses

lem·ming \'lem-iŋ\ n [Norw; akin to ON lōmr loon, L latrare to bark — more at LAMENT] (1607) : any of several small short-tailed furry-footed rodents (genera Lemmus and Dicrostonyx) of circumpolar distribution that are notable for the recurrent mass migrations of a European form (L. lemmus) which often continue into the sea where vast numbers are drowned — **lem·ming·like** \-,līk\ adj

lem·nis·cate \lem-'nis-kət\ n [NL lemniscata, fr. fem. of L lemniscatus with hanging ribbons, fr. lemniscus] (ca. 1781) : a figure-eight shaped curve whose equation in polar coordinates is $\rho^2 = a^2 \cos 2\theta$

lem·nis·cus \lem-'nis-kəs\ n, pl **-nis·ci** \-'nis-,(k)ī, -'nis-,kē\ [NL, fr. L, ribbon, fr. Gk lēmniskos] (ca. 1905) : a band of fibers and esp. nerve fibers — **lem·nis·cal** \-kəl\ adj

¹lem·on \'lem-ən\ n [ME lymon, fr. MF limon, fr. ML limon-, limo, fr. Ar laymūn] (15c) **1 a** : an acid fruit that is botanically a many-seeded pale yellow oblong berry and is produced by a stout thorny tree (Citrus limon) **b** : a tree that bears lemons **2** : one (as an automobile) that is unsatisfactory or defective — **lem·ony** \'lem-ə-nē\ adj

²lemon adj (1736) **1 a** : containing lemon **b** : having the flavor or scent of lemon **2** : of the color lemon yellow

lem·on·ade \,lem-ə-'nād\ n (1604) : a beverage of sweetened lemon juice mixed with water

lemon balm n (ca. 1888) : a bushy perennial Old World mint (Melissa officinalis) often cultivated for its fragrant lemon-flavored leaves

lem·on·grass \'lem-ən-,gras\ n (1801) : a grass (Cymbopogon citratus) of robust habit that grows in tropical regions (as the West Indies) and is the source of an essential oil with an odor of lemon or verbena; also : a similar tropical grass (C. flexuosus)

\ə\ abut \ᵊ\ kitten, F table \ər\ further \a\ ash \ā\ ace \ä\ cot, cart \au̇\ out \ch\ chin \e\ bet \ē\ easy \g\ go \i\ hit \ī\ ice \j\ job \ŋ\ sing \ō\ go \ȯ\ law \ȯi\ boy \th\ thin \t̲h̲\ the \ü\ loot \u̇\ foot \y\ yet \zh\ vision \à, k̲, ⁿ, œ, œ̄, ᵫ, ᵫ̄, �\ ʸ\ see Guide to Pronunciation

lemon yellow *n* (1807) **:** a variable color averaging a brilliant greenish yellow

lem·pi·ra \lem-'pir-ə\ *n* [AmerSp, fr. *Lempira,* 16th cent. Indian chief] (ca. 1934) — see MONEY table

le·mur \'lē-mər\ *n* [L *lemures,* pl., ghosts; akin to Gk *lamia* devouring monster] (1795) **:** any of numerous arboreal chiefly nocturnal mammals that were formerly widespread but are now largely confined to Madagascar, are related to the monkeys but are usu. regarded as constituting a distinct superfamily (Lemuroidea), and usu. have a muzzle like a fox, large eyes, very soft woolly fur, and a long furry tail

le·mu·res \'lem-ə-ˌrās, 'lem-yə-ˌrēz\ *n pl* [L] (ca. 1555) **:** spirits of the unburied dead exorcised from homes in early Roman religious observances

lend \'lend\ *vb* **lent** \'lent\; **lend·ing** [ME *lenen, lenden,* fr. OE *lǣnan,* fr. *lǣn* loan — more at LOAN] *vt* (bef. 12c) **1 a :** to give for temporary use on condition that the same or its equivalent be returned **b :** to let out (money) for temporary use on condition of repayment with interest **2 a :** to give the assistance or support of **:** AFFORD, FURNISH ⟨a dispassionate and scholarly manner which ~*s* great force to his criticisms — *Times Lit. Supp.*⟩ **b :** to adapt or apply (oneself) **:** ACCOMMODATE ⟨a topic that ~*s* itself admirably to class discussion⟩ ~ *vi* **:** to make a loan — **lend·able** \'len-də-bəl\ *adj* — **lend·er** *n*

lending library *n* (1708) **:** RENTAL LIBRARY

lend–lease \'len-'dlēs\ *n* [U.S. *Lend-Lease* Act (1941)] (1941) **:** the transfer of goods and services to an ally to aid in a common cause with payment being made by a return of the original items or their use in the common cause or by a similar transfer of other goods and services — **lend–lease** *vt*

length \'leŋ(k)th, 'len(t)th\ *n, pl* **lengths** \'leŋ(k)ths, 'len(t)ths, 'leŋ(k)s\ [ME *lengthe,* fr. OE *lengthu,* fr. *lang* long] (bef. 12c) **1 a :** the longer or longest dimension of an object **b :** a measured distance or dimension ⟨10-inch ~⟩ — see METRIC SYSTEM table, WEIGHT table **c :** the quality or state of being long **2 a :** duration or extent in time **b :** relative duration or stress of a sound **3 a :** distance or extent in space **b :** the length of something taken as a unit of measure ⟨his horse led by a ~⟩ **4 :** the degree to which something (as a course of action or a line of thought) is carried — often used in pl. ⟨went to great ~*s* to learn the truth⟩ **5 a :** a long expanse or stretch **b :** a piece constituting or usable as part of a whole or of a connected series **:** SECTION ⟨a ~ of pipe⟩ **6 :** a vertical dimension of an article of clothing — **at length 1 :** FULLY, COMPREHENSIVELY **2 :** at last **:** FINALLY

length·en \'leŋ(k)-thən, 'len(t)-\ *vb* **length·ened; length·en·ing** \'leŋ(k)th-(ə-)niŋ, 'len(t)th-\ *vt* (14c) **:** to make longer ~ *vi* **:** to grow longer *syn* see EXTEND — **length·en·er** \'leŋ(k)th-(ə-)nər, 'len(t)th-\ *n*

length·ways \'leŋ(k)th-ˌwāz, 'len(t)th-\ *adv* (1599) **:** LENGTHWISE

length·wise \-ˌwīz\ *adv* (1580) **:** in the direction of the length **:** LONGITUDINALLY — **lengthwise** *adj*

lengthy \'leŋ(k)-thē, 'len(t)-\ *adj* **length·i·er; -est** (1689) **1 :** protracted excessively **:** OVERLONG **2 :** EXTENDED, LONG — **length·i·ly** \-thə-lē\ *adv* — **length·i·ness** \-thē-nəs\ *n*

le·nience \'lē-nyən(t)s, -nē-ən(t)s\ *n* (1796) **:** LENIENCY

le·nien·cy \'lē-nē-ən-sē, -nyən-sē\ *n, pl* **-cies** (1780) **1 :** the quality or state of being lenient **2 :** a lenient disposition or practice

le·nient \'lē-nē-ənt, -nyənt\ *adj* [L *lenient-, leniens,* prp. of *lenire* to soften, soothe, fr. *lenis* soft, mild — more at LET] (1652) **1 :** exerting a soothing or easing influence **:** relieving pain or stress **2 :** of mild and tolerant disposition; *esp* **:** INDULGENT — **le·nient·ly** *adv*

Leni–Le·nape *or* **Len·ni–Le·nape** \ˌlen-ē-lə-'näp-ē, ˌlen-ē-'len-ə-pē, ˌlen-ē-lə-'näp\ *n* [Delaware] (1781) **:** DELAWARE 1

Le·nin·ism \'len-ə-ˌniz-əm\ *n* (1918) **:** the political, economic, and social principles and policies advocated by Lenin; *esp* **:** the theory and practice of communism developed by or associated with Lenin — **Le·nin·ist** \-nəst\ *n or adj* — **Le·nin·ite** \-ˌnīt\ *n or adj*

le·nis \'lē-nəs, 'lā-\ *adj* [NL, fr. L, mild, smooth] (ca. 1897) **:** produced with relatively lax articulation and weak expiration ⟨\d\ in *doe* is ~, \t\ in *toe* is fortis⟩

len·i·tive \'len-ət-iv\ *adj* [ME *lenitif,* fr. MF, fr. ML *lenitivus,* fr. L *lenitus,* pp. of *lenire*] (15c) **:** alleviating pain or harshness **:** SOOTHING — **lenitive** *n* — **len·i·tive·ly** *adv*

len·i·ty \'len-ət-ē\ *n* (1548) **:** the quality or state of being lenient **:** CLEMENCY *syn* see MERCY

le·no \'lē-(ˌ)nō\ *n* [perh. fr. F *linon* linen fabric, lawn, fr. MF *lin* flax, linen, fr. L *linum* flax] (1821) **1 :** an open weave in which pairs of warp yarns cross one another and thereby lock the filling yarn in position **2 :** a fabric made with a leno weave

[1]**lens** *also* **lense** \'lenz\ *n* [NL *lent-, lens,* fr. L, lentil; fr. its shape — more at LENTIL] (1693) **1 a :** a piece of transparent material (as glass) that has two opposite regular surfaces either both curved or one curved and the other plane and that is used either singly or combined in an optical instrument for forming an image by focusing rays of light **b :** a combination of two or more simple lenses **2 :** a device for directing or focusing radiation other than light (as sound waves, radio microwaves, or electrons) **3 :** something shaped like a double-convex optical lens ⟨~ of sandstone⟩ **4 :** a highly transparent biconvex lens-shaped or nearly spherical body in the eye that focuses light rays (as upon the retina) — see EYE illustration — **lensed** \'lenzd\ *adj* — **lens·less** \'lenz-ləs\ *adj*

[2]**lens** *vt* (1942) **:** to make a motion picture of **:** FILM

Lent \'lent\ *n* [ME *lente* springtime, Lent, fr. OE *lencten;* akin to OHG *lenzin* spring] (13c) **:** the 40 weekdays from Ash Wednesday to Easter observed by the Roman Catholic, Eastern, and some Protestant churches as a period of penitence and fasting

len·ta·men·te \ˌlent-ə-'men-(ˌ)tā\ *adv or adj* [It, fr. *lento* slow] (1724) **:** LENTO

len·tan·do \len-'tän-(ˌ)dō\ *adv or adj* [It] (ca. 1847) **:** becoming slower — used as a direction in music

Lent·en \'lent-ᵊn\ *adj* (bef. 12c) **:** of, relating to, or suitable for Lent; *esp* **:** MEAGER ⟨~ fare⟩

len·tic \'lent-ik\ *adj* [L *lentus* sluggish] (ca. 1930) **:** of, relating to, or living in still waters (as lakes, ponds, or swamps) — compare LOTIC

len·ti·cel \'lent-ə-ˌsel\ *n* [NL *lenticella,* dim. of L *lent-, lens* lentil] (ca. 1864) **:** a pore in the stems of woody plants through which gases are exchanged between the atmosphere and the stem tissues

len·tic·u·lar \len-'tik-yə-lər\ *adj* [L *lenticularis* lentil-shaped, fr. *lenticula* lentil] (15c) **1 :** having the shape of a double-convex lens **2 :** of or relating to a lens **3 :** provided with or utilizing lenticules ⟨a ~ screen⟩

len·tic·u·late \-lət\ *vt* **-lat·ed; -lat·ing** (1925) **:** to provide with lenticules (as by embossing, molding, or coating) ⟨*lenticulated* film⟩ — **len·tic·u·la·tion** \-ˌtik-yə-'lā-shən\ *n*

len·ti·cule \'lent-ə-ˌkyü(ə)l\ *n* [L *lenticula*] (1942) **1 :** any of the minute lenses on the base side of a film used in stereoscopic or color photography **2 :** any of the tiny corrugations or grooves molded or embossed into the surface of a projection screen

len·til \'lent-ᵊl\ *n* [ME, fr. OF *lentille,* fr. L *lenticula,* dim. of *lent-, lens;* akin to Gk *lathyros* vetch] (13c) **1 :** a widely cultivated Eurasian annual leguminous plant (*Lens culinaris*) with flattened edible seeds and leafy stalks used as fodder **2 :** the seed of the lentil

len·tis·si·mo \len-'tis-ə-ˌmō\ *adv or adj* [It, superl. of *lento*] (ca. 1903) **:** in a very slow manner — used as a direction in music

len·to \'len-(ˌ)tō\ *adv or adj* [It, fr. *lento,* adj., slow, fr. L *lentus* pliant, sluggish, slow — more at LITHE] (1724) **:** in a slow manner — used as a direction in music

Leo \'lē-(ˌ)ō\ *n* [L (gen. *Leonis*), lit., lion — more at LION] **1 :** a northern constellation east of Cancer **2 a :** the 5th sign of the zodiac in astrology — see ZODIAC table **b :** one born under this sign — **Le·o·nine** \'lē-ə-ˌnīn\ *adj*

le·one \lē-'ōn\ *n, pl* **leones** *or* **leone** [*Sierra Leone*] (ca. 1964) — see MONEY table

Leo·nid \'lē-ə-nəd\ *n, pl* **Leo·nids** *or* **Le·on·i·des** \lē-'än-ə-ˌdēz\ [L *Leon-, Leo;* fr. their appearing to radiate from a point in Leo] (1876) **:** one of the shooting stars constituting the meteoric shower that recurs near the 15th of November

le·o·nine \'lē-ə-ˌnīn\ *adj* [ME, fr. L *leoninus,* fr. *leon-, leo*] (14c) **:** of, relating to, suggestive of, or resembling a lion

leop·ard \'lep-ərd\ *n* [ME, fr. OF *leupart,* fr. LL *leopardus,* fr. Gk *leopardos,* fr. *leōn* lion + *pardos* leopard] (13c) **1 :** a large strong cat (*Felis pardus*) of southern Asia and Africa that is usu. tawny or buff with black spots arranged in broken rings or rosettes — called also *panther* **2 :** a heraldic representation of a lion passant guardant — **leop·ard·ess** \-ərd-əs\ *n*

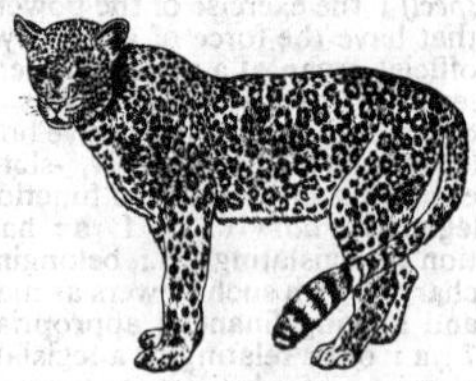

leopard 1

leopard frog *n* (1839) **:** a common American frog (*Rana pipiens*) that is bright green with large black white-margined blotches on the back; *also* **:** a similar frog (*R. sphenocephala*) of the southeastern U.S.

le·o·tard \'lē-ə-ˌtärd\ *n* [Jules *Léotard,* †1870 Fr. aerial gymnast] (1920) **:** a close-fitting one-piece garment worn by dancers, acrobats, and aerialists; *also* **:** TIGHTS

Lep·cha \'lep-chə\ *n, pl* **Lepcha** *or* **Lepchas** (1819) **1 :** a member of a Mongoloid people of Sikkim, India **2 :** the Tibeto-Burman language of the Lepcha people

lep·er \'lep-ər\ *n* [ME, fr. *lepre* leprosy, fr. MF, fr. LL *lepra,* fr. Gk, fr. *lepein* to peel; akin to OE *læfer* reed] (14c) **1 :** a person affected with leprosy **2 :** a person shunned for moral or social reasons

lepid- *or* **lepido-** *comb form* [NL, fr. Gk, fr. *lepid-, lepis* scale, fr. *lepein*] **:** flake **:** scale ⟨*Lepidoptera*⟩

le·pid·o·lite \li-'pid-ᵊl-ˌīt\ *n* [G *lepidolith,* fr. *lepid-* + *-lith*] (ca. 1796) **:** a variable mineral typically $K(Li,Al)_3(Si,Al)_4O_{10}(F,OH_2)$ that consists of a mica containing lithium and is used esp. in glazes and enamels

lep·i·dop·tera \ˌlep-ə-'däp-tə-rə\ *n pl* (1773) **:** insects that are lepidopterans

lep·i·dop·ter·an \-rən\ *n* [NL *Lepidoptera,* fr. *lepid-* + Gk *pteron* wing — more at FEATHER] (ca. 1902) **:** any of a large order (Lepidoptera) of insects comprising the butterflies, moths, and skippers that as adults have four broad or lanceolate wings usu. covered with minute overlapping and often brightly colored scales and that as larvae are caterpillars — **lepidopteran** *adj* — **lep·i·dop·ter·ous** \-tə-rəs\ *adj*

lep·i·dop·ter·ist \-tə-rəst\ *n* (1826) **:** a specialist in lepidopterology

lep·i·dop·ter·ol·o·gy \-ˌdäp-tə-'räl-ə-jē\ *n* (1899) **:** a branch of entomology concerned with lepidopterans — **lep·i·dop·ter·o·log·i·cal** \-tə-rə-'läj-i-kəl\ *adj* — **lep·i·dop·ter·ol·o·gist** \-tə-'räl-ə-jəst\ *n*

lep·i·dote \'lep-ə-ˌdōt\ *adj* [Gk *lepidōtos* scaly, fr. *lepid-, lepis*] (ca. 1836) **:** covered with scurf or scurfy scales ⟨~ rhododendrons⟩

lep·re·chaun \'lep-rə-ˌkän, -ˌkȯn\ *n* [IrGael *leipreachān*] (1604) **:** a mischievous elf of Irish folklore usu. believed to reveal the hiding place of treasure if caught — **lep·re·chaun·ish** \-ish\ *adj*

le·pro·ma·tous \lə-'präm-ət-əs, -'prō-mət-\ *adj* [NL *lepromat-, leproma* leprous lesion, fr. LL *lepra*] (1898) **:** characterized by, exhibiting, or being leprosy with infective superficial granulomatous nodules

lep·ro·sar·i·um \ˌlep-rə-'ser-ē-əm\ *n, pl* **-i·ums** *or* **-ia** \-ē-ə\ [ML, fr. LL *leprosus*] (1846) **:** a hospital for leprosy patients

lep·ro·sy \'lep-rə-sē\ *n* [*leprous* + *-y*] (15c) **1 :** a chronic disease caused by a bacillus (*Mycobacterium leprae*) and characterized by the formation of nodules or of macules that enlarge and spread accompanied by loss of sensation with eventual paralysis, wasting of muscle, and production of deformities and mutilations **2 :** a morally or spiritually harmful influence — **lep·rot·ic** \le-'prät-ik\ *adj*

lep·rous \'lep-rəs\ *adj* [ME, fr. LL *leprosus* leprous, fr. *lepra* leprosy — more at LEPER] (13c) **1 a :** infected with leprosy **b :** of, relating to, or resembling leprosy or a leper **2 :** SCALY, SCURFY — **lep·rous·ly** *adv* — **lep·rous·ness** *n*

-lep·sy \ˌlep-sē\ *n comb form* [MF *-lepsie,* fr. LL *-lepsia,* fr. Gk *-lēpsia,* fr. *lēpsis,* fr. *lambanein* to take, seize — more at LATCH] **:** taking **:** seizure ⟨nympho*lepsy*⟩

lep·to·ceph·a·lus \ˌlep-tə-'sef-ə-ləs\ *n, pl* **-li** \-ˌlī, -ˌlē\ [NL, fr. Gk *leptos* + *kephalē* head — more at CEPHALIC] (1769) **:** a long thin small-headed transparent pelagic first larva of various eels

[1]**lep·ton** \lep-'tän\ *n, pl* **lep·ta** \-'tä\ [NGk, fr. Gk, a small coin, fr. neut. of *leptos* peeled, slender, small, fr. *lepein* to peel — more at LEPER] (ca. 1727) — see *drachma* at MONEY table

[2]**lep·ton** \'lep-ˌtän\ *n* [Gk *leptos* + E [2]*-on*] (ca. 1948) **:** any of a family of particles (as electrons, muons, and neutrinos) that have spin quantum

number ½ and that experience no strong interactions — **lep·ton·ic** \lep-'tän-ik\ *adj*
lep·to·some \'lep-tə-,sōm\ *adj* [G *leptosom,* fr. Gk *leptos* + *sōma* body] (1931) : ECTOMORPHIC — **leptosome** *n*
lep·to·spire \-,spī(ə)r\ *n* [NL *Leptospira,* fr. Gk *leptos* + L *spira* coil — more at SPIRE] (ca. 1952) : any of a genus (*Leptospira*) of slender aerobic spirochetes that are free-living or parasitic in mammals — **lep·to·spir·al** \,lep-tə-'spī-rəl\ *adj*
lep·to·spi·ro·sis \,lep-tə-spī-'rō-səs\ *n, pl* **-ro·ses** \-,sēz\ [NL] (1926) : any of several diseases of man and domestic animals that are caused by infection with leptospires
lep·to·tene \'lep-tə-,tēn\ *n* [ISV] (1912) : a stage of meiotic prophase immediately preceding synapsis in which the chromosomes appear as fine discrete threads — **leptotene** *adj*
[1]**les·bi·an** \'lez-bē-ən\ *adj, often cap* (1703) **1** : of or relating to Lesbos **2** [fr. the reputed homosexual band associated with Sappho of Lesbos] : of or relating to homosexuality between females
[2]**lesbian** *n, often cap* (ca. 1890) : a female homosexual
les·bi·an·ism \'lez-bē-ə-,niz-əm\ *n* (1870) : female homosexuality
lèse–ma·jes·té *or* **lese maj·es·ty** \(')lēz-'maj-ə-stē\ *n* [MF *lese majesté,* fr. L *laesa majestas,* lit., injured majesty] (1536) **1 a** : a crime (as treason) committed against a sovereign power **b** : an offense violating the dignity of a ruler as the representative of a sovereign power **2** : a detraction from or affront to dignity or importance
le·sion \'lē-zhən\ *n* [ME, fr. MF, fr. L *laesion-, laesio,* fr. *laesus,* pp. of *laedere* to injure] (15c) **1** : INJURY, HARM **2** : an abnormal change in structure of an organ or part due to injury or disease; *esp* : one that is circumscribed and well defined — **le·sioned** \-zhənd\ *adj*
les·pe·de·za \,les-pə-'dē-zə\ *n* [NL, irreg. fr. V. M. de *Zespedes fl*1785 Span. governor of East Florida] (ca. 1891) : any of a genus (*Lespedeza*) of herbaceous or shrubby leguminous plants including some widely used for forage, soil improvement, and esp. hay
[1]**less** \'les\ *adj* [ME, partly fr. OE *lǣs,* adv. & n.; partly fr. *lǣssa,* adj.; akin to OFris *lēs* less, Gk *limos* hunger] (bef. 12c) **1** : constituting a more limited number ⟨~ than three⟩ **2** : of lower rank, degree, or importance ⟨no ~ a person than the president himself⟩ **3 a** : of reduced size, extent, or degree **b** : more limited in quantity ⟨in ~ time⟩
usage The traditional view is that *less* applies to matters of degree, value, or amount and modifies collective nouns, mass nouns, or nouns denoting an abstract whole while *fewer* applies to matters of number and modifies plural nouns. *Less* has been used to modify plural nouns since the days of King Alfred and the usage, though roundly decried, appears to be increasing. *Less* is more likely than *fewer* to modify plural nouns when distances, sums of money, and a few fixed phrases are involved ⟨*less* than 100 miles⟩ ⟨an investment of *less* than $2000⟩ ⟨in 25 words or *less*⟩ and as likely as *fewer* to modify periods of time ⟨in *less* (or *fewer*) than four hours⟩
[2]**less** *adv* (bef. 12c) : to a lesser extent or degree — **less and less** : to a progressively smaller size or extent — **less than** : by no means : not at all ⟨was being *less than* honest in his replies⟩
[3]**less** *prep* (bef. 12c) : diminished by : MINUS
[4]**less** *n, pl* **less** (bef. 12c) **1** : a smaller portion or quantity **2** : something of less importance
-less \ləs\ *adj suffix* [ME *-les, -lesse,* fr. OE *-lēas,* fr. *lēas* devoid, false; akin to OHG *lōs* loose, OE *losian* to get lost — more at LOSE] **1** : destitute of : not having ⟨wit*less*⟩ ⟨child*less*⟩ **2** : unable to be acted on or to act (in a specified way) ⟨daunt*less*⟩ ⟨fade*less*⟩
les·see \le-'sē\ *n* [ME, fr. AF, fr. *lessé,* pp. of *lesser* to lease — more at LEASE] (15c) : one that holds real or personal property under a lease
less·en \'les-ᵊn\ *vb* **less·ened; less·en·ing** \'les-niŋ, -ᵊn-iŋ\ *vi* (13c) : to shrink in size, number, or degree : DECREASE ~ *vt* **1** : to reduce in size, extent, or degree **2 a** *archaic* : to represent as of little value : MINIMIZE **b** : to lower in status or dignity : DEGRADE ***syn*** see DECREASE
[1]**less·er** \'les-ər\ *adj* (13c) : of less size, quality, or significance
[2]**lesser** *adv* (1594) : LESS ⟨*lesser*-known⟩
lesser celandine *n* (ca. 1890) : CELANDINE 2
lesser cornstalk borer *n* (ca. 1925) : a pyralid moth (*Elasmopalpus lignosellus*) whose slender greenish larva is a destructive pest that burrows in the stalk esp. of Indian corn near ground level
Lesser Dog *n* : CANIS MINOR
lesser peach tree borer *n* (ca. 1924) : a moth (*Synanthedon pictipes* family Aegeriidae) whose larva is a borer in the forks and crotches of stone-fruit trees and esp. the peach
lesser yellowlegs *n pl but sing or pl in constr* (ca. 1903) : a common American marsh and shore bird (*Tringa flavipes*) that closely resembles the greater yellowlegs in color and markings but is smaller with a shorter more slender bill
[1]**les·son** \'les-ᵊn\ *n* [ME, fr. OF *leçon,* fr. LL *lection-, lectio,* fr. L, act of reading, fr. *lectus,* pp. of *legere* to read — more at LEGEND] (13c) **1** : a passage from sacred writings read in a service of worship **2 a** : a piece of instruction : TEACHING **b** : a reading or exercise to be studied by a pupil **c** : a division of a course of instruction **3 a** : something learned by study or experience ⟨his years of travel had taught him valuable ~*s*⟩ **b** : an instructive example ⟨the ~*s* history has for us⟩ **c** : REPRIMAND
[2]**lesson** *vt* **les·soned; les·son·ing** \'les-ə-niŋ, 'les-niŋ\ (1555) **1** : to give a lesson to : INSTRUCT **2** : LECTURE, REBUKE
les·sor \'les-,ȯ(ə)r, le-'sȯ(ə)r\ *n* [ME *lessour,* fr. AF, fr. *lesser* to lease] (14c) : one that conveys property by lease
lest \(,)lest\ *conj* [ME *les the, leste,* fr. OE *thȳ lǣs the,* fr. *thȳ* (instrumental of *thæt* that) + *lǣs* + *the,* relative particle] (bef. 12c) : for fear that — used after an expression denoting fear or apprehension ⟨worried ~ he should be late⟩ ⟨hesitant to speak out ~ he be branded a troublemaker⟩
[1]**let** \'let\ *vt* **let·ted; letted** *or* **let; let·ting** [ME *letten,* fr. OE *lettan* to delay, hinder; akin to OHG *lezzen* to delay, hurt, OE *lǣt* late] *archaic* (bef. 12c) : HINDER, PREVENT
[2]**let** *n* (12c) **1** : something that impedes : OBSTRUCTION **2** : a shot or point in racket games that does not count and must be replayed
[3]**let** *vb* **let; let·ting** [ME *leten,* fr. OE *lǣtan;* akin to OHG *lāzzan* to permit, L *lassus* weary, *lenis* soft, mild] *vt* (bef. 12c) **1** : to cause to : MAKE ⟨~ it be known⟩ **2 a** : to offer or grant for rent or lease ⟨~ rooms⟩ **b** : to assign esp. after bids ⟨~ a contract⟩ **3 a** : to give opportunity to whether by positive action or by failure to prevent ⟨live and ~ live⟩ ⟨a break in the clouds ~ him see his objective⟩ **b** — used in the imperative to introduce a request or proposal ⟨~ us pray⟩ **c** — used as an auxiliary to express a warning ⟨~ him try⟩ **4** : to free from or as if from confinement : RELEASE ⟨~ the prisoner leave⟩ ⟨she ~ out a scream⟩ **5** : to permit to enter, pass, or leave ⟨~ them through⟩ ~ *vi* **1** : to become rented or leased **2** : to become awarded to a contractor ***usage*** see LEAVE
syn LET, ALLOW, PERMIT mean not to forbid or prevent. LET may imply a positive giving of permission but more often implies failure to prevent either through inadvertence and negligence or through lack of power or effective authority; ALLOW implies little more than a forbearing to prohibit; PERMIT implies willingness or acquiescence. ***syn*** see in addition HIRE
— **let go** : to dismiss from employment ⟨the firm *let* him *go* at the end of the month⟩ — **let it all hang out** : to reveal one's true feelings : act without dissimulation
-let \lət\ *n suffix* [ME, fr. MF *-elet,* fr. *-el,* dim. suffix (fr. L *-ellus*) + *-et*] **1** : small one ⟨book*let*⟩ **2** : article worn on ⟨wrist*let*⟩
let alone *conj* (1812) : to say nothing of : not to mention ⟨lacked the courage, *let alone* the skill, to be effective⟩ ⟨believed that he would never walk again *let alone* play golf —*Sports Illus.*⟩
letch \'lech\ *n* [back-formation fr. *letcher,* alter. of *lecher*] (ca. 1796) : CRAVING; *specif* : sexual desire
let·down \'let-,dau̇n\ *n* (1768) **1 a** : DISCOURAGEMENT, DISAPPOINTMENT **b** : a slackening of effort : RELAXATION **2** : the descent of an aircraft or spacecraft to the point at which a landing approach is begun
let down \(')let-'dau̇n\ *vt* (12c) **1** : to allow to descend gradually **2 a** : to fail to support ⟨felt her parents had *let* her *down*⟩ **b** : to fall short of the expectations of ⟨the plot is good but the end *lets* you *down*⟩
[1]**le·thal** \'lē-thəl\ *adj* [L *letalis, lethalis,* fr. *letum* death] (1613) **1 a** : of, relating to, or causing death ⟨a ~ injury⟩ **b** : capable of causing death ⟨~ chemicals⟩ **2** : gravely damaging or destructive : DEVASTATING ⟨a ~ attack on his reputation⟩ ***syn*** see DEADLY — **le·thal·i·ty** \lē-'thal-ət-ē\ *n* — **le·thal·ly** \'lē-thə-lē\ *adv*
[2]**lethal** *n* (1917) **1** : an abnormality of genetic origin causing the death of the organism possessing it **2** : LETHAL GENE
lethal gene *n* (1939) : a gene that in some (as homozygous) conditions may prevent development or cause the death of an organism or its germ cells — called also *lethal factor, lethal mutant, lethal mutation*
le·thar·gic \lə-'thär-jik, le-\ *adj* (14c) **1** : of, relating to, or characterized by lethargy : SLUGGISH **2** : INDIFFERENT, APATHETIC — **le·thar·gi·cal·ly** \-ji-k(ə-)lē\ *adv*
leth·ar·gy \'leth-ər-jē\ *n* [ME *litargie,* fr. ML *litargia,* fr. LL *lethargia,* fr. Gk *lēthargia,* fr. *lēthargos* forgetful, lethargic, fr. *lēthē* + *argos* lazy — more at ARGON] (14c) **1** : abnormal drowsiness **2** : the quality or state of being lazy, sluggish, or indifferent
syn LETHARGY, LANGUOR, LASSITUDE, STUPOR, TORPOR mean physical or mental inertness. LETHARGY implies such drowsiness or aversion to activity as is induced by disease, injury, drugs; LANGUOR suggests inertia induced by an enervating climate or illness or love; LASSITUDE stresses listlessness or indifference resulting from fatigue or poor health; STUPOR implies a deadening of the mind and senses by shock, narcotics, or intoxicants; TORPOR implies a state of suspended animation as of hibernating animals but may suggest merely extreme sluggishness.
le·the \'lē-thē\ *n* [L, fr. Gk *Lēthē,* fr. *lēthē* forgetfulness; akin to Gk *lanthanein* to escape notice, *lanthanesthai* to forget — more at LATENT] **1** *cap* : a river in Hades whose waters cause drinkers to forget their past **2** : OBLIVION, FORGETFULNESS — **le·the·an** \'lē-thē-ən, li-'thē-\ *adj, often cap*
let on *vi* (1725) **1** : to make acknowledgment : ADMIT ⟨knows more than he *lets on*⟩ **2** : to reveal a secret ⟨nobody *let on* about the surprise party⟩ **3** : PRETEND ⟨*let on* to being a stranger⟩
let out *vi* (1888) : to conclude a session or performance ⟨school *let out* in June⟩
let's \(,)lets, *in rapid speech* (,)les\ : let us
Lett \'let\ *n* [G *Lette,* fr. Latvian *Latvi*] (1589) : a member of a people closely related to the Lithuanians and mainly inhabiting Latvia
[1]**let·ter** \'let-ər\ *n* [ME, fr. OF *lettre,* fr. L *littera* letter of the alphabet, *litterae,* pl., epistle, literature] (13c) **1** : a symbol usu. written or printed representing a speech sound and constituting a unit of an alphabet **2 a** : a direct or personal written or printed message addressed to a person or organization **b** : a written communication containing a grant — usu. used in pl. **3** *pl but sing or pl in constr* **a** : LITERATURE, BELLES LETTRES **b** : LEARNING **4** : the strict or outward sense or significance ⟨the ~ of the law⟩ **5 a** : a single piece of type **b** : a style of type **6** : the initial of a school awarded to a student for achievement usu. in athletics
[2]**letter** *vt* (1668) **1** : to set down in letters : PRINT **2** : to mark with letters ~ *vi* : to win an athletic letter — **let·ter·er** \-ər-ər\ *n*
[3]**let·ter** \'let-ər\ *n* (1552) : one that rents or leases
letter carrier *n* (1552) : a person who delivers mail
let·tered \'let-ərd\ *adj* (14c) **1 a** : LEARNED, EDUCATED **b** : of, relating to, or characterized by learning : CULTURED **2** : inscribed with or as if with letters
let·ter·form \-ər-,fȯrm\ *n* (1908) : the shape of a letter of an alphabet esp. from the standpoint of design or development
let·ter·head \'let-ər-,hed\ *n* (1887) **1** : a sheet of stationery printed or engraved usu. with the name and address of an organization **2** : the heading at the top of a letterhead
let·ter·ing \'let-ə-riŋ\ *n* (1811) : letters used in an inscription
letter missive *n, pl* **letters missive** [ME, fr. MF *lettre missive* letter intended to be sent] (15c) : a letter from a superior authority conveying a command, recommendation, permission, or invitation

\ə\ abut \ᵊ\ kitten, F table \ər\ further \a\ ash \ā\ ace \ä\ cot, cart \au̇\ out \ch\ chin \e\ bet \ē\ easy \g\ go \i\ hit \ī\ ice \j\ job \ŋ\ sing \ō\ go \ȯ\ law \ȯi\ boy \th\ thin \t͟h\ the \ü\ loot \u̇\ foot \y\ yet \zh\ vision \à, k̲, ⁿ, œ, œ̄, ue, uē, ʸ\ see Guide to Pronunciation

letter of credence (14c) : a formal document furnished a diplomatic agent attesting to his power to act for his government — called also *letters of credence*

letter of credit (1645) **1** : a letter addressed by a banker to a correspondent certifying that a person named therein is entitled to draw on him or his credit up to a certain sum **2** : a letter addressed by a banker to a person to whom credit is given authorizing him to draw on the issuing bank or on a bank in his country up to a certain sum and guaranteeing to accept the drafts if duly made

letter of intent (ca. 1942) : a written statement of the intention to enter into a formal agreement

let·ter–per·fect \ˌlet-ər-ˈpər-fikt\ *adj* (1845) : correct to the smallest detail; *esp* : VERBATIM

let·ter·press \ˈlet-ər-ˌpres\ *n* (1758) **1** : the process of printing from an inked raised surface esp. when the paper is impressed directly upon the surface **2** *chiefly Brit* : text (as of a book) distinct from pictorial illustrations

letter sheet *n* (1851) : a sheet of stationery that can be folded and sealed with the message inside to form its own envelope

letters of administration (15c) : a letter evidencing the right of an administrator to administer the goods or estate of a deceased person

letters of marque \-ˈmärk\ (15c) : written authority granted to a private person by a government to seize the subjects of a foreign state or their goods; *specif* : a license granted to a private person to fit out an armed ship to plunder the enemy

let·ter·spac·ing \ˈlet-ər-ˌspā-siŋ\ *n* (ca. 1917) : insertion of space between the letters of a word

letters patent *n pl* (14c) : a writing (as from a sovereign) that confers on a designated person a grant in a form readily open for inspection by all

[1]Lett·ish \ˈlet-ish\ *adj* (1831) : of or relating to the Latvians or their language

[2]Lettish *n* (1841) : LATVIAN 2

let·tre de ca·chet \ˌle-trə-də-ˌka-ˈshā\ *n, pl* **lettres de cachet** \-trə(z)-\ [F, lit., letter with a seal] (1718) : a letter bearing an official seal and usu. authorizing imprisonment without trial of a named person

let·tuce \ˈlet-əs\ *n* [ME *letuse*, fr. MF *laitues*, pl. of *laitue*, fr. L *lactuca*, fr. *lact-, lac* milk; fr. its milky juice — more at GALAXY] (14c) : any of a genus (*Lactuca*) of composite plants; *esp* : a common garden vegetable (*L. sativa*) whose succulent leaves are used esp. in salads

let·up \ˈlet-ˌəp\ *n* (1837) : a lessening of effort or intensity

let up \(ˈ)let-ˈəp\ *vi* (1787) **1 a** : to diminish or slow down : SLACKEN **b** : CEASE, STOP **2** : to become less severe — used with *on*

leu \ˈleü\ *n, pl* **lei** \ˈlā\ [Rom, lit., lion, fr. L *leo* — more at LION] (1879) — see MONEY table

leu·cine \ˈlü-ˌsēn\ *n* [ISV] (1826) : a white crystalline essential amino acid $C_6H_{13}NO_2$ obtained by the hydrolysis of most dietary proteins

leu·cite \ˈlü-ˌsīt\ *n* [G *leuzit*, fr. *leuz-* leuk-] (1799) : a white or gray mineral $KAlSi_2O_6$ consisting of a potassium aluminum silicate and occurring in igneous rocks — **leu·cit·ic** \lü-ˈsit-ik\ *adj*

leu·co·ci·din \ˌlü-kə-ˈsīd-ᵊn\ *n* [ISV *leuc-* + *-cide* + *-in*] (ca. 1894) : a bacterial substance that destroys leukocytes

leu·co·plast \ˈlü-kə-ˌplast\ *also* **leu·co·plas·tid** \ˌlü-kə-ˈplas-təd\ *n* [ISV] (1886) : a colorless plastid esp. in the cytoplasm of interior plant tissues that is potentially capable of developing into a chromoplast

leuk- *or* **leuko-** *also* **leuc-** *or* **leuco-** *comb form* [NL *leuc-, leuco-*, fr. Gk *leuk-, leuko-*, fr. *leukos* — more at LIGHT] **1** : white : colorless : weakly colored ⟨*leuko*cyte⟩ ⟨*leuk*orrhea⟩ **2** : leukocyte ⟨*leuk*emia⟩ **3** : white matter of the brain ⟨*leuko*tomy⟩

leu·kae·mia *chiefly Brit var of* LEUKEMIA

leu·kae·mo·gen·e·sis *chiefly Brit var of* LEUKEMOGENESIS

leu·ke·mia \lü-ˈkē-mē-ə\ *n* [NL] (1855) : an acute or chronic disease in man and other warm-blooded animals characterized by an abnormal increase in the number of leukocytes in the tissues and often in the blood — **leu·ke·mic** \-mik\ *adj or n*

leu·ke·mo·gen·e·sis \lü-ˌkē-mə-ˈjen-ə-səs\ *n* (1942) : induction or production of leukemia — **leu·ke·mo·gen·ic** \-ˈjen-ik\ *adj*

leu·ke·moid \-ˌmȯid\ *adj* (1926) : resembling leukemia but not involving the same changes in the blood-forming organs ⟨a ~ reaction in malaria⟩

leukocyt- *or* **leukocyto-** *also* **leucocyt-** *or* **leucocyto-** *comb form* [ISV] : leukocyte ⟨*leukocyt*osis⟩

leu·ko·cyte *also* **leu·co·cyte** \ˈlü-kə-ˌsīt\ *n* [ISV] (1870) : any of the white or colorless nucleated cells that occur in blood — **leu·ko·cyt·ic** \ˌlü-kə-ˈsit-ik\ *adj*

leu·ko·cy·to·sis \ˌlü-kə-sī-ˈtō-səs, -kə-sə-\ *n* [NL] (1866) : an increase in the number of leukocytes in the circulating blood — **leu·ko·cy·tot·ic** \-ˈtät-ik\ *adj*

leu·ko·dys·tro·phy \ˌlü-kō-ˈdis-trə-fē\ *n, pl* **-phies** (1968) : any of several genetically determined diseases characterized by degeneration of the white matter of the brain

leu·ko·pe·nia \ˌlü-kə-ˈpē-nē-ə\ *n* [NL, fr. *leuc-* + Gk *penia* poverty, lack] (ca. 1898) : a condition in which the number of leukocytes circulating in the blood is abnormally low — **leu·ko·pe·nic** \-nik\ *adj*

leu·ko·pla·kia \ˌlü-kō-ˈplā-kē-ə\ *n* [NL, fr. *leuk-* + Gk *plak-, plax* flat surface + NL *-ia*] (ca. 1885) : an abnormal condition in which thickened white patches of epithelium occur on the mucous membranes (as of the mouth or vulva); *also* : a lesion or lesioned area of leukoplakia — **leu·ko·pla·kic** \-ˈplā-kik\ *adj*

leu·ko·poi·e·sis \-ˌpȯi-ˈē-səs\ *n* [NL] (ca. 1913) : the formation of white blood cells — **leu·ko·poi·et·ic** \-ˈet-ik\ *adj*

leu·kor·rhea \ˌlü-kə-ˈrē-ə\ *n* [NL] (ca. 1797) : a whitish viscid discharge from the vagina resulting from inflammation or congestion of the mucous membrane — **leu·kor·rhe·al** \-ˈrē-əl\ *adj*

leu·ko·sis \lü-ˈkō-səs\ *n, pl* **-ko·ses** \-ˌsēz\ [NL] (ca. 1922) : LEUKEMIA; *esp* : any of various leukemic diseases of poultry — **leu·kot·ic** \-ˈkät-ik\ *adj*

leu·kot·o·my \lü-ˈkät-ə-mē\ *also* **leu·cot·o·my** *n, pl* **-mies** (1937) : LOBOTOMY

lev \ˈlef\ *n, pl* **le·va** \ˈlev-ə\ [Bulg, lit., lion] (ca. 1900) — see MONEY table

lev- *or* **levo-** *comb form* [F *lévo-*, fr. L *laevus* left; akin to Gk *laios* left] **1** : levorotatory ⟨*lev*ulose⟩ **2** : to the left ⟨*levo*rotatory⟩

Le·val·loi·si·an \ˌlev-ə-ˈlȯi-zē-ən, lə-ˌval-ˈwä-zē-\ *adj* [*Levallois*-Perret, suburb of Paris, France] (1932) : of or relating to a middle Paleolithic culture characterized by a technique of manufacturing tools by striking flakes from a flint nodule

le·vant \lə-ˈvant\ *vi* [perh. fr. Sp *levantar* to break camp, deriv. of L *levare*] *chiefly Brit* (1797) : to run away from a debt

le·vant·er \lə-ˈvant-ər\ *n* (1668) **1** *cap* : a native or inhabitant of the Levant **2** : a strong easterly Mediterranean wind

Le·vant storax \lə-ˈvant-\ *n* (1937) : STORAX 1a

le·va·tor \li-ˈvāt-ər\ *n, pl* **lev·a·to·res** \ˌlev-ə-ˈtōr-(ˌ)ēz\ *or* **le·va·tors** \li-ˈvāt-ərz\ [NL, fr. L *levatus*, pp. of *levare* to raise — more at LEVER] (ca. 1615) : a muscle that serves to raise a body part — compare DEPRESSOR

[1]le·vee \ˈlev-ē; lə-ˈvē, -ˈvā\ *n* [F *lever*, fr. MF, act of arising, fr. (*se*) *lever* to rise] (1672) **1** : a reception held by a person of distinction on rising from bed **2** : an afternoon assembly at which the British sovereign or his or her representative receives only men **3** : a reception usu. in honor of a particular person

[2]lev·ee \ˈlev-ē\ *n* [F *levée*, fr. OF, act of raising, fr. *lever* to raise — more at LEVER] (1718) **1 a** : an embankment for preventing flooding **b** : a river landing place : PIER **2** : a continuous dike or ridge (as of earth) for confining the irrigation areas of land to be flooded

[3]lev·ee \ˈlev-ē\ *vt* **lev·eed; lev·ee·ing** (1832) : to provide with a levee

[1]lev·el \ˈlev-əl\ *n* [ME, fr. MF *livel*, fr. (assumed) VL *libellum*, alter. of L *libella*, fr. dim. of *libra* weight, balance] (14c) **1** : a device for establishing a horizontal line or plane by means of a bubble in a liquid that shows adjustment to the horizontal by movement to the center of a slightly bowed glass tube **2** : a measurement of the difference of altitude of two points by means of a level **3** : horizontal condition; *esp* : equilibrium of a fluid marked by a horizontal surface of even altitude ⟨water seeks its own ~⟩ **4 a** : an approximately horizontal line or surface taken as an index of altitude **b** : a practically horizontal surface or area (as of land) **5** : a position in a scale or rank (as of value, significance, importance, or achievement) ⟨of upper ~ management⟩ ⟨politics on the international ~⟩ **6 a** : a line or surface that cuts perpendicularly all plumb lines that it meets and hence would everywhere coincide with a surface of still water **b** : the plane of the horizon or a line in it **7** : a horizontal passage in a mine intended for regular working and transportation **8** : a concentration of a constituent esp. of a body fluid (as blood) **9** : the magnitude of a quantity considered in relation to an arbitrary reference value; *broadly* : MAGNITUDE, INTENSITY ⟨a high ~ of hostility⟩ — **on the level** : BONA FIDE, HONEST

[2]level *vb* **-eled** *or* **-elled; -el·ing** *or* **-el·ling** \ˈlev-(ə-)liŋ\ *vt* (15c) **1** : to make (a line or surface) horizontal : make flat or level ⟨~ a field for planting⟩ ⟨~ off a house lot⟩ **2 a** : to bring to a horizontal aiming position **b** : AIM, DIRECT ⟨~*ed* a charge of fraud at him⟩ **3** : to bring to a common level or plane : EQUALIZE ⟨love ~*s* all ranks —W. S. Gilbert⟩ **4** : to lay level with or as if with the ground : RAZE **5** : to make (as color) even or uniform **6** : to find the heights of different points in (a piece of land) esp. with a surveyor's level ~ *vi* **1** : to attain or come to a level ⟨the plane ~*ed* off at 10,000 feet⟩ **2** : to aim a gun or other weapon horizontally **3** : to bring persons or things to a level **4** : to deal frankly and openly

[3]level *adj* (15c) **1 a** : having no part higher than another : conforming to the curvature of the liquid parts of the earth's surface **b** : parallel with the plane of the horizon : HORIZONTAL **2 a** : even or unvarying in height **b** : equal in advantage, progression, or standing **c** : proceeding monotonously or uneventfully **d** (1) : STEADY, UNWAVERING ⟨gave him a ~ look⟩ (2) : CALM, UNEXCITED ⟨spoke in ~ tones⟩ **3** : REASONABLE, BALANCED ⟨arrive at a justly proportional and ~ judgment on this affair — Sir Winston Churchill⟩ **4** : distributed evenly ⟨~ stress⟩ **5** : being a surface perpendicular to all lines of force in a field of force : EQUIPOTENTIAL **6** : suited to a particular rank or plane of ability or achievement ⟨top-*level* thinking⟩ **7** : of or relating to the spreading out of a cost or charge in even payments over a period of time — **lev·el·ly** \ˈlev-əl-(l)ē\ *adv* — **lev·el·ness** \-əl-nəs\ *n*

syn LEVEL, FLAT, PLANE, EVEN, SMOOTH mean having a surface without bends, curves, or irregularities. LEVEL applies to a horizontal surface that lies on a line parallel with the horizon; FLAT applies to a surface devoid of noticeable curvatures, prominences, or depressions; PLANE applies to any real or imaginary flat surface in which a straight line between any two points on it lies wholly within that surface; EVEN applies to a surface that is noticeably flat or level or to a line that is observably straight; SMOOTH applies esp. to a polished surface free of irregularities.

— **level best** : very best

level crossing *n, Brit* (1841) : GRADE CROSSING

lev·el·er *or* **lev·el·ler** \ˈlev-(ə-)lər\ *n* (1598) **1** : one that levels **2 a** *cap* : one of a group of radicals arising during the English Civil War and advocating equality before the law and religious toleration **b** : one favoring the removal of political, social, or economic social inequalities **c** : something that tends to reduce or eliminate differences among men

lev·el·head·ed \ˌlev-əl-ˈhed-əd\ *adj* (1879) : having sound judgment : SENSIBLE — **lev·el·head·ed·ness** *n*

leveling rod *n* (ca. 1902) : a graduated rod used in measuring the vertical distance between a point on the ground and the line of sight of a surveyor's level

level off *vi* (1917) : to approach or reach a steady rate, volume, or amount : STABILIZE ⟨defense expenditures would eventually *level off* — Eli Ginzberg⟩

level of significance (1925) : the probability of rejecting the null hypothesis in a statistical test when it is true — called also *significance level*

[1]le·ver \ˈlev-ər, ˈlē-vər\ *n* [ME, fr. MF *levier*, fr. *lever* to raise, fr. L *levare*; akin to L *levis* light in weight — more at LIGHT] (14c) **1 a** : a bar used for prying or dislodging something **b** : an inducing or compelling force : TOOL ⟨attempts to use food as a political ~ —*Time*⟩ **2 a** : a rigid piece that transmits and modifies force or motion when forces are applied at two points and it turns about a third; *specif* : a rigid bar used to exert a pressure or sustain a weight at one point of its length by the application of a force at a second and turning at a third on a fulcrum **b** : a projecting piece by which a mechanism is operated or adjusted

[2]lever *vt* **le·vered; le·ver·ing** \ˈlev-(ə-)riŋ, ˈlēv-\ (1876) **1** : to pry, raise, or move with or as if with a lever **2** : to operate (a device) in the manner of a lever

1le·ver·age \ˈlev-(ə-)rij, ˈlēv-\ *n* (1724) **1 :** the action of a lever or the mechanical advantage gained by it **2 :** POWER, EFFECTIVENESS ⟨organizing . . . to gain greater professional, economic, and political ~ —*Change*⟩ **3 :** the use of credit to enhance one's speculative capacity

2leverage *vt* **-aged; -ag·ing** (1937) **:** to provide with leverage

lev·er·aged \ˈlev-(ə-)rijd, ˈlēv-\ *adj* (1953) **1 :** having a high proportion of debt relative to equity **2** *of the purchase of a company* **:** made with borrowed money that is secured by the assets of the company bought ⟨a ~ buyout⟩

lev·er·et \ˈlev-(ə-)rət\ *n* [ME, fr. (assumed) MF *levret,* fr. MF *levre* hare, fr. L *lepor-, lepus*] (15c) **:** a hare in its first year

Le·vi \ˈlē-ˌvī\ *n* [LL, from Heb *Lēwī*] **:** a son of Jacob and the traditional eponymous ancestor of the priestly tribe of Levi

levi·able \ˈlev-ē-ə-bəl\ *adj* (15c) **:** capable of being levied or levied upon

le·vi·a·than \li-ˈvī-ə-thən\ *n* [ME, fr. LL, fr. Heb *liwyāthān*] (14c) **1 a** *often cap* **:** a sea monster defeated by Yahweh in various scriptural accounts **b (1) :** a large sea animal **(2) :** a large oceangoing ship **2** *cap* **:** the political state; *esp* **:** a totalitarian state having a vast bureaucracy **3 :** something large or formidable — **leviathan** *adj*

levi·er \ˈlev-ē-ər\ *n* (15c) **:** one that levies

lev·i·gate \ˈlev-ə-ˌgāt\ *vt* **-gat·ed; -gat·ing** [L *levigatus,* pp. of *levigare,* fr. *levis* smooth + *-igare* (akin to *agere* to drive) — more at LIME, AGENT] (1612) **1 :** POLISH, SMOOTH **2 a :** to grind to a fine smooth powder while in moist condition **b :** to separate (fine powder) from coarser material by suspending in a liquid — **lev·i·ga·tion** \ˌlev-ə-ˈgā-shən\ *n*

lev·in \ˈlev-ən\ *n* [ME *levene*] *archaic* (13c) **:** LIGHTNING

le·vi·rate \ˈlev-ə-rət, ˈlē-və-, -ˌrāt\ *n* [L *levir* husband's brother; akin to OE *tācor* husband's brother, Gk *daēr*] (1725) **:** the sometimes compulsory marriage of a widow by a brother of her deceased husband — **le·vi·rat·ic** \ˌlev-ə-ˈrat-ik, ˌlē-və-\ *adj*

Le·vi's \ˈlē-ˌvīz\ *trademark* — used esp. for blue denim jeans

lev·i·tate \ˈlev-ə-ˌtāt\ *vb* **-tat·ed; -tat·ing** [*levity*] *vi* (1673) **:** to rise or float in the air esp. in seeming defiance of gravitation ~ *vt* **:** to cause to levitate

lev·i·ta·tion \ˌlev-ə-ˈtā-shən\ *n* (1668) **:** the act or process of levitating; *esp* **:** the rising or lifting of a person or thing by means held to be supernatural — **lev·i·ta·tion·al** \-shnəl, -shən-ᵊl\ *adj*

Le·vite \ˈlē-ˌvīt\ *n* (14c) **:** a member of the priestly Hebrew tribe of Levi; *specif* **:** a Levite of non-Aaronic descent assigned to lesser ceremonial offices under the Levitical priests of the family of Aaron

Le·vit·i·cal \li-ˈvit-i-kəl\ *adj* [LL *Leviticus*] (1535) **:** of or relating to the Levites or to Leviticus

Le·vit·i·cus \-kəs\ *n* [LL, lit., of the Levites] **:** the third book of canonical Jewish and Christian Scripture consisting mainly of priestly legislation — see BIBLE table

lev·i·ty \ˈlev-ət-ē\ *n* [L *levitat-, levitas,* fr. *levis* light in weight — more at LIGHT] (1564) **1 a :** excessive or unseemly frivolity **b :** lack of steadiness **:** CHANGEABLENESS **2 :** the quality or state of being light in weight **:** BUOYANCY

le·vo \ˈlē-(ˌ)vō\ *adj* (1938) **:** LEVOROTATORY

levo- — see LEV-

levo·do·pa \ˈlev-ə-ˌdō-pə\ *n* (1969) **:** L-DOPA

le·vo·ro·ta·tion \ˌlē-və-rō-ˈtā-shən\ *n* (1882) **:** left-handed or counterclockwise rotation — used of the plane of polarization of light

le·vo·ro·ta·to·ry \-ˈrōt-ə-ˌtōr-ē, -ˌtȯr-\ *or* **le·vo·ro·ta·ry** \-ˈrōt-ə-rē\ *adj* (1873) **:** turning toward the left or counterclockwise; *esp* **:** rotating the plane of polarization of light to the left — compare DEXTROROTATORY

lev·u·lose \ˈlev-yə-ˌlōs, -ˌlōz\ *n* [ISV, irreg. fr. *lev-* + *-ose*] (1871) **:** FRUCTOSE 2

1levy \ˈlev-ē\ *n, pl* **lev·ies** [ME, fr. OF *levee,* act of raising — more at LEVEE] (13c) **1 a :** the imposition or collection of an assessment **b :** an amount levied **2 a :** the enlistment or conscription of men for military service **b :** troops raised by levy

2levy *vb* **lev·ied; levy·ing** *vt* (14c) **1 a :** to impose or collect by legal authority ⟨~ a tax⟩ **b :** to require by authority **2 :** to enlist or conscript for military service **3 :** to carry on (war) **:** WAGE ~ *vi* **:** to seize property

lewd \ˈlüd\ *adj* [ME *lewed* vulgar, fr. OE *lǣwede* laical, ignorant] (14c) **1** *obs* **:** EVIL, WICKED **2 a :** sexually unchaste or licentious **b :** OBSCENE, SALACIOUS — **lewd·ly** *adv* — **lewd·ness** *n*

lew·is \ˈlü-əs\ *n* [prob. fr. the name *Lewis*] (1743) **:** an iron dovetailed tenon that is made in sections, can be fitted into a dovetail mortise, and is used in hoisting large stones

lew·is·ite \ˈlü-ə-ˌsīt\ *n* [Winford L. *Lewis* †1943 Am. chemist] (1919) **:** a colorless or brown vesicant liquid $C_2H_2AsCl_3$ developed as a poison gas for war use

lew·is·son \ˈlü-ə-sən\ *n* (ca. 1842) **:** LEWIS

lex \ˈleks\ *n, pl* **le·ges** \ˈlā-(ˌ)gās\ [L *leg-, lex*] (15c) **:** LAW

lex·eme \ˈlek-ˌsēm\ *n* [Gk *lexis* word, speech + E *-eme*] (1940) **:** a meaningful linguistic unit that is an item in the vocabulary of a language — **lex·emic** \lek-ˈsē-mik\ *adj*

lex·i·cal \ˈlek-si-kəl\ *adj* (1836) **1 :** of or relating to words or the vocabulary of a language as distinguished from its grammar and construction **2 :** of or relating to a lexicon or to lexicography — **lex·i·cal·i·ty** \ˌlek-sə-ˈkal-ət-ē\ *n* — **lex·i·cal·ly** \ˈlek-si-k(ə-)lē\ *adv*

lexical meaning *n* (1933) **:** the meaning of the base (as the word *play*) in a paradigm (as *plays, played, playing*) — compare GRAMMATICAL MEANING

lex·i·cog·ra·pher \ˌlek-sə-ˈkäg-rə-fər\ *n* [LGk *lexikographos,* fr. *lexikon* + Gk *-graphos* -grapher] (1658) **:** an author or editor of a dictionary

lex·i·co·graph·i·cal \ˌlek-sə-kō-ˈgraf-i-kəl\ *or* **lex·i·co·graph·ic** \-ik\ *adj* (1791) **:** of or relating to lexicography — **lex·i·co·graph·i·cal·ly** \-i-k(ə-)lē\ *adv*

lex·i·cog·ra·phy \ˌlek-sə-ˈkäg-rə-fē\ *n* (1680) **1 :** the editing or making of a dictionary **2 :** the principles and practices of dictionary making

lex·i·col·o·gy \ˌlek-sə-ˈkäl-ə-jē\ *n* [F *lexicologie,* fr. *lexico-* (fr. LGk *lexiko-,* fr. *lexikon*) + *-logie* -logy] (ca. 1828) **:** a branch of linguistics concerned with the signification and application of words — **lex·i·col·o·gist** \-jəst\ *n*

lex·i·con \ˈlek-sə-ˌkän, -si-kən\ *n, pl* **lex·i·ca** \-si-kə\ *or* **lexicons** [LGk *lexikon,* fr. neut. of *lexikos* of words, fr. Gk *lexis* word, speech, fr. *legein* to say — more at LEGEND] (1603) **1 :** a book containing an alphabetical arrangement of the words in a language and their definitions **:** DICTIONARY **2 a :** the vocabulary of a language, an individual speaker or group of speakers, or a subject **b :** the total stock of morphemes in a language **3 :** REPERTOIRE, INVENTORY

lex·is \ˈlek-səs\ *n, pl* **lex·es** \-ˌsēz\ [Gk, speech, word] (1960) **:** LEXICON 2a

ley *var of* LEA

Ley·den jar \ˌlīd-ᵊn-\ *n* [*Leiden, Leyden,* Netherlands] (1825) **:** an electrical condenser consisting of a glass jar coated inside and outside with metal foil and having the inner coating connected to a conducting rod passed through the insulating stopper

L–form \ˈel-ˌfȯrm\ *n* [*L*ister Institute, London, where it was first isolated] (1948) **:** a filterable form of some bacteria that may be a specialized reproductive body appearing chiefly when the environment is unfavorable and resembling typical pleuropneumonia organisms

Lha·sa ap·so \ˌläs-ə-ˈäp-(ˌ)sō, ˌlas-ə-ˈap-\ *n, pl* **Lhasa apsos** [*Lhasa,* Tibet + Tibetan *apso*] *often cap A* (1935) **:** any of a Tibetan breed of small dogs that have a dense coat of long hard straight hair, a heavy fall over the eyes, heavy whiskers and beard, and a well-feathered tail curled over the back — called also *Lhasa* \ˈläs-ə, ˈlas-\

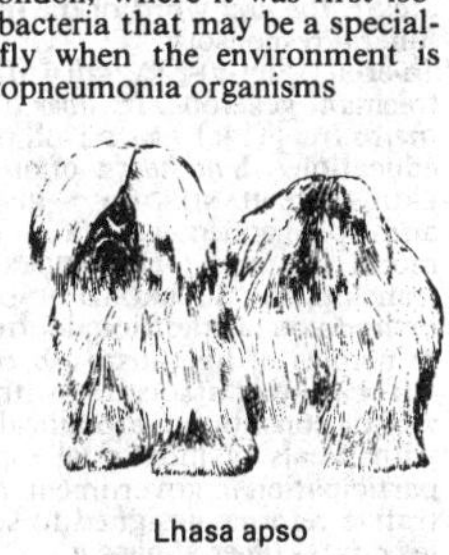

Lhasa apso

li \ˈlē\ *n, pl* **li** *also* **lis** \ˈlēz\ [Chin (Pek) *li*^{3}] (1588) **:** any of various Chinese units of distance; *esp* **:** one equal to about $^1/_3$ mile (0.5 kilometer)

li·a·bil·i·ty \ˌlī-ə-ˈbil-ət-ē\ *n, pl* **-ties** (1794) **1 a :** the quality or state of being liable **b :** PROBABILITY **2 :** something for which one is liable; *esp, pl* **:** pecuniary obligations **:** DEBTS **3 :** one that works as a disadvantage **:** DRAWBACK

li·a·ble \ˈlī-ə-bəl, *esp in sense 2 often* ˈlī-bəl\ *adj* [(assumed) AF, fr. OF *lier* to bind, fr. L *ligare* — more at LIGATURE] (15c) **1 a :** obligated according to law or equity **:** RESPONSIBLE **b :** subject to appropriation or attachment **2 a :** being in a position to incur — used with *to* ⟨~ to diseases⟩ **b :** exposed or subject to some usu. adverse contingency or action ⟨watch out or you're ~ to fall⟩

syn LIABLE, OPEN, EXPOSED, SUBJECT, PRONE, SUSCEPTIBLE, SENSITIVE mean being by nature or through circumstances likely to experience something adverse. LIABLE implies a possibility or probability of incurring something because of position, nature, or particular situation; OPEN stresses a lack of barriers preventing incurrence; EXPOSED suggests lack of protection or powers of resistance against something actually present or threatening; SUBJECT implies an openness for any reason to something that must be suffered or undergone; PRONE stresses natural tendency or propensity to incur something; SUSCEPTIBLE implies conditions existing in one's nature or individual constitution that make incurrence probable; SENSITIVE implies a readiness to respond to or be influenced by forces or stimuli. ***syn*** see in addition RESPONSIBLE

usage Both *liable* and *apt* when followed by an infinitive are used nearly interchangeably with *likely.* Although conflicting advice has been given over the years, most current commentators accept *apt* when so used. They generally recommend limiting *liable* to situations having an undesirable outcome, and our evidence shows that in edited writing it is more often so used than not.

li·aise \lē-ˈāz\ *vi* **li·aised; li·ais·ing** [back-formation fr. *liaison*] *chiefly Brit* (1928) **1 :** to establish liaison **2 :** to act as a liaison officer

li·ai·son \ˈlē-ə-ˌzän, lē-ˈā-, ÷ˈlā-ə-\ *n* [F, fr. MF, fr. *lier,* fr. OF] (1809) **1 a :** a close bond or connection **:** INTERRELATIONSHIP **b :** an illicit sexual relationship **:** AFFAIR 3a **2 :** the pronunciation of an otherwise absent consonant sound at the end of the first of two consecutive words the second of which begins with a vowel sound and follows without pause **3 a :** communication for establishing and maintaining mutual understanding (as between parts of an armed force) **b :** one that establishes and maintains liaison

li·a·na \lē-ˈän-ə, -ˈan-ə\ *also* **li·ane** \-ˈän, -ˈan\ *n* [F *liane*] (1796) **:** any of various usu. woody vines esp. of tropical rain forests that root in the ground — **li·a·noid** \-ˈän-ˌȯid, -ˈan-\ *adj*

li·ang \lē-ˈäŋ\ *n, pl* **liang** *also* **liangs** [Chin (Pek) *liang*^{3}] (1827) **:** an old Chinese unit of weight equal to $^1/_{16}$ catty

li·ar \ˈlī(-ə)r\ *n* [ME, fr. OE *lēogere,* fr. *lēogan* to lie — more at LIE] (bef. 12c) **:** one that tells lies

Li·as \ˈlī-əs\ *adj* [*Lias,* division of the European Jurassic, fr. F, fr. E (a limestone rock)] (1813) **:** LIASSIC

Li·as·sic \lī-ˈas-ik\ *adj* [modif. (influenced by *Jurassic*) of F *liasique,* fr. *Lias*] (1833) **:** of, relating to, or being a subdivision of the European Jurassic

lib \ˈlib\ *n* (1970) **:** LIBERATION 2

li·ba·tion \lī-ˈbā-shən\ *n* [L *libation-, libatio,* fr. *libatus,* pp. of *libare* to pour as an offering; akin to Gk *leibein* to pour] (14c) **1 a :** an act of pouring a liquid as a sacrifice (as to a deity) **b :** a liquid (as wine) used in a libation **2 a :** an act or instance of drinking often ceremoniously **b :** BEVERAGE; *esp* **:** a drink containing alcohol — **li·ba·tion·ary** \-shə-ˌner-ē\ *adj*

li·bec·cio \li-ˈbech-(ē-ˌ)ō\ *or* **li·bec·chio** \-ˈbek-ē-ˌō\ *n* [It] (1667) **:** a southwest wind

1li·bel \ˈlī-bəl\ *n* [ME, written declaration, fr. MF, fr. L *libellus,* dim. of *liber* book — more at LEAF] (14c) **1 a** *archaic* **:** a handbill esp. attacking or defaming someone **b :** a written statement in which a plaintiff in certain courts sets forth his cause of action or the relief he seeks **2 a :** a written or oral defamatory statement or representation that conveys an unjustly unfavorable impression **b (1) :** a statement or representation published without just cause and tending to expose another to public contempt **(2) :** defamation of a person by written or representational means **(3) :** the publication of blasphemous, treasonable, seditious, or obscene writings or pictures **(4) :** the act, tort, or crime of publishing such a libel

\ə\ abut \ᵊ\ kitten, F table \ər\ further \a\ ash \ā\ ace \ä\ cot, cart \au̇\ out \ch\ chin \e\ bet \ē\ easy \g\ go \i\ hit \ī\ ice \j\ job \ŋ\ sing \ō\ go \ȯ\ law \ȯi\ boy \th\ thin \t͟h\ the \ü\ loot \u̇\ foot \y\ yet \zh\ vision \à, k̲, ⁿ, œ, œ̄, ue, ue̅, ʸ\ *see* Guide to Pronunciation

²libel *vb* **-beled** *or* **-belled; -bel·ing** *or* **-bel·ling** \-b(ə-)liŋ\ *vi* (1570) **:** to make libelous statements ~ *vt* **:** to make or publish a libel against — **li·bel·er** \-b(ə-)lər\ *n* — **li·bel·ist** \-bə-ləst\ *n*

li·bel·ant *or* **li·bel·lant** \ˈlī-bə-lənt\ *n* (1726) **:** one that institutes a suit by a libel

li·bel·ee *or* **li·bel·lee** \ˌlī-bə-ˈlē\ *n* (1856) **:** one against whom a libel has been filed in a court

li·bel·ous *or* **li·bel·lous** \ˈlī-b(ə-)ləs\ *adj* (1619) **:** constituting or including a libel **:** DEFAMATORY ⟨a ~ statement⟩

Li·be·ra \ˈlē-bə-ˌrä, ˈlē-brə\ *n* [L, lit., deliver, imper. of *liberare* to liberate; fr. the first word of the responsory] (ca. 1903) **:** a Roman Catholic funeral responsory

¹**lib·er·al** \ˈlib(-ə)-rəl\ *adj* [ME, fr. MF, fr. L *liberalis* suitable for a freeman, generous, fr. *liber* free; akin to OE *lēodan* to grow, Gk *eleutheros* free] (14c) **1 a :** of, relating to, or based on the liberal arts ⟨~ education⟩ **b** *archaic* **:** of or befitting a man of free birth **2 a :** GENEROUS, OPENHANDED ⟨a ~ giver⟩ **b :** given or provided in a generous and openhanded way ⟨a ~ meal⟩ **c :** AMPLE, FULL **3** *obs* **:** lacking moral restraint **:** LICENTIOUS **4 :** not literal or strict **:** LOOSE ⟨a ~ translation⟩ **5 :** BROAD-MINDED; *esp* **:** not bound by authoritarianism, orthodoxy, or traditional forms **6 a :** of, favoring, or based upon the principles of liberalism **b** *cap* **:** of or constituting a political party advocating or associated with the principles of political liberalism; *esp* **:** of or constituting a political party in the United Kingdom associated with ideals of individual esp. economic freedom, greater individual participation in government, and constitutional, political, and administrative reforms designed to secure these objectives — **lib·er·al·ly** \-rə-lē\ *adv* — **lib·er·al·ness** *n*

syn LIBERAL, GENEROUS, BOUNTIFUL, MUNIFICENT mean giving freely and unstintingly. LIBERAL suggests openhandedness in the giver and largeness in the thing or amount given; GENEROUS stresses warmhearted readiness to give more than size or importance of the gift; BOUNTIFUL suggests lavish, unremitting giving or providing; MUNIFICENT suggests a scale of giving appropriate to lords or princes.

²**liberal** *n* (1816) **:** one who is liberal: as **a :** one who is open-minded or not strict in the observance of orthodox, traditional or established forms or ways **b** *cap* **:** a member or supporter of a liberal political party **c :** an advocate or adherent of liberalism esp. in individual rights

liberal arts *n pl* (14c) **1 :** the medieval studies comprising the trivium and quadrivium **2 :** the studies (as language, philosophy, history, literature, abstract science) in a college or university intended to provide chiefly general knowledge and to develop the general intellectual capacities (as reason and judgment) as opposed to professional or vocational skills

lib·er·al·ism \ˈlib(-ə)-rə-ˌliz-əm\ *n* (1819) **1 :** the quality or state of being liberal **2 a** *often cap* **:** a movement in modern Protestantism emphasizing intellectual liberty and the spiritual and ethical content of Christianity **b :** a theory in economics emphasizing individual freedom from restraint and usu. based on free competition, the self-regulating market, and the gold standard **c :** a political philosophy based on belief in progress, the essential goodness of man, and the autonomy of the individual and standing for the protection of political and civil liberties **d** *cap* **:** the principles and policies of a Liberal party — **lib·er·al·ist** \-rə-ləst\ *n or adj* — **lib·er·al·is·tic** \ˌlib(-ə)-rə-ˈlis-tik\ *adj*

lib·er·al·i·ty \ˌlib-ə-ˈral-ət-ē\ *n, pl* **-ties** (14c) **:** the quality or state of being liberal; *also* **:** an instance of this

lib·er·al·ize \ˈlib(-ə)-rə-ˌlīz\ *vb* **-ized; -iz·ing** *vt* (1774) **:** to make liberal or more liberal ~ *vi* **:** to become liberal or more liberal — **lib·er·al·iza·tion** \ˌlib(-ə)-rə-lə-ˈzā-shən\ *n* — **lib·er·al·iz·er** \ˈlib(-ə)-rə-ˌlī-zər\ *n*

lib·er·ate \ˈlib-ə-ˌrāt\ *vt* **-at·ed; -at·ing** [L *liberatus*, pp. of *liberare*, fr. *liber*] (ca. 1623) **1 :** to set at liberty **:** FREE; *specif* **:** to free (as a country) from domination by a foreign power **2 :** to free from combination ⟨~ the gas by adding acid⟩ **3 :** to take or take over illegally or unjustly ⟨a . . . barricade was constructed . . . with material *liberated* from a nearby construction site —Thorne Dreyer⟩ ***syn*** see FREE — **lib·er·a·tor** \-ˌāt-ər\ *n*

lib·er·at·ed *adj* (1946) **:** freed from or opposed to traditional social and sexual attitudes or roles ⟨a ~ woman⟩ ⟨a ~ marriage⟩

lib·er·a·tion \ˌlib-ə-ˈrā-shən\ *n* (15c) **1 :** the act of liberating **:** the state of being liberated **2 :** a movement seeking equal rights and status for a group ⟨women's ~⟩ — **lib·er·a·tion·ist** \-sh(ə-)nəst\ *n*

lib·er·tar·i·an \ˌlib-ər-ˈter-ē-ən\ *n* (1789) **1 :** an advocate of the doctrine of free will **2 :** one who upholds the principles of absolute and unrestricted liberty esp. of thought and action — **libertarian** *adj* — **lib·er·tar·i·an·ism** \-ē-ə-ˌniz-əm\ *n*

lib·er·tin·age \ˈlib-ər-ˌtē-nij\ *n* (1611) **:** LIBERTINISM

¹**lib·er·tine** \ˈlib-ər-ˌtēn\ *n* [ME *libertyn*, freedman, fr. L *libertinus*, fr. *libertinus*, adj., of a freedman, fr. *libertus* freedman, fr. *liber*] (1563) **1 :** a freethinker esp. in religious matters — usu. used disparagingly **2 :** a person who is unrestrained by convention or morality; *specif* **:** one leading a dissolute life

²**libertine** *adj* (1577) **:** of, relating to, or characteristic of a libertine

lib·er·tin·ism \ˈlib-ər-ˌtē-ˌniz-əm, -tə-\ *n* (1611) **:** the quality or state of being libertine **:** the behavior of a libertine

lib·er·ty \ˈlib-ərt-ē\ *n, pl* **-ties** [ME, fr. MF *liberté*, fr. L *libertat-, libertas*, fr. *liber* free — more at LIBERAL] (14c) **1 :** the quality or state of being free: **a :** the power to do as one pleases **b :** freedom from physical restraint **c :** freedom from arbitrary or despotic control **d :** the positive enjoyment of various social, political, or economic rights and privileges **e :** the power of choice **2 a :** a right or immunity enjoyed by prescription or by grant **:** PRIVILEGE **b :** permission esp. to go freely within specified limits **3 :** an action going beyond normal limits: as **a :** a breach of etiquette or propriety **:** FAMILIARITY **b :** RISK, CHANCE ⟨took foolish *liberties* with his health⟩ **c :** a violation of rules or a deviation from standard practice **d :** a distortion of fact **4 :** a short authorized absence from naval duty usu. for less than 48 hours ***syn*** see FREEDOM — **at liberty 1 :** FREE **2 :** at leisure **:** UNOCCUPIED

liberty cap *n* (1803) **:** a close-fitting conical cap used as a symbol of liberty by the French revolutionists and in the U.S. before 1800

liberty pole *n* (1770) **:** a tall flagstaff surmounted by a liberty cap or the flag of a republic and set up as a symbol of liberty

li·bid·i·nal \lə-ˈbid-ᵊn-əl, -ˈbid-nᵊl\ *adj* (1922) **:** of or relating to the libido — **li·bid·i·nal·ly** \-ē\ *adv*

li·bid·i·nous \-ᵊn-əs, -ˈbid-nəs\ *adj* [ME, fr. MF *libidineus*, fr. L *libidinosus*, fr. *libidin-, libido*] (15c) **1 :** having or marked by lustful desires **:** LASCIVIOUS **2 :** LIBIDINAL — **li·bid·i·nous·ly** *adv* — **li·bid·i·nous·ness** *n*

li·bi·do \lə-ˈbēd-(ˌ)ō, ˈlib-ə-ˌdō\ *n, pl* **-dos** [NL *libidin-, libido*, fr. L, desire, lust, fr. *libēre* to please — more at LOVE] (1909) **1 :** emotional or psychic energy that in psychoanalytic theory is derived from primitive biological urges and that is usu. goal-directed **2 :** sexual drive

li·bra *for 1 & 2a* ˈlē-brə *or* ˈlī-brə, *for 2b* ˈlē-brə *or* ˈlēv-rə\ *n* [ME, fr. L (gen. *Librae*), lit., scales, pound] **1** *cap* **a :** a southern zodiacal constellation between Virgo and Scorpio represented by a pair of scales **b** (1) **:** the 7th sign of the zodiac in astrology — see ZODIAC table (2) **:** one born under this sign **2 a** *pl* **li·brae** \ˈlī-ˌbrē, ˈlē-ˌbrī\ [L] **:** an ancient Roman unit of weight equal to 327.45 grams **b** [Sp & Pg, fr. L] **:** any of various Spanish, Portuguese, Colombian, or Venezuelan units of weight

Li·bran \ˈlē-brən, ˈlī-\ *n* (1967) **:** LIBRA 1b(2)

li·brar·i·an \lī-ˈbrer-ē-ən\ *n* (1713) **:** a specialist in the care or management of a library — **li·brar·i·an·ship** \-ˌship\ *n*

li·brary \ˈlī-ˌbrer-ē; *Brit usu & US sometimes* -brər-ē; *US sometimes* -brē, ÷-ˌber-ē\ *n, pl* **-brar·ies** [ME, fr. ML *librarium*, fr. L, neut. of *librarius* of books, fr. *libr-, liber* book — more at LEAF] (14c) **1 a :** a place in which literary, musical, artistic, or reference materials (as books, manuscripts, recordings, or films) are kept for use but not for sale **b :** a collection of such materials **2 a :** a collection resembling or suggesting a library ⟨a ~ of computer programs⟩ ⟨wine ~⟩ **b :** MORGUE 2 **3 a :** a series of related books issued by a publisher **b :** a collection of publications on the same subject

usage While the pronunciation \ˈlī-ˌbrer-ē\ is the most frequent variant in the U.S., the other variants are not uncommon. The contraction \ˈlī-brē\ and the dissimilated form \ˈlī-ˌber-ē\ result from the relative difficulty of repeating \r\ in successive syllables and are heard from educated speakers, including college presidents and professors, as well as with somewhat greater frequency from less educated speakers.

library paste *n* (1953) **:** a thick white adhesive made from starch

library science *n* (1902) **:** the study or the principles and practices of library care and administration

li·bra·tion \lī-ˈbrā-shən\ *n* [L *libration-, libratio*, fr. *libratus*, pp. of *librare* to balance, fr. *libra* scales] (1669) **:** an oscillation in the apparent aspect of a secondary body (as a planet or a satellite) as seen from the primary object around which it revolves — **li·bra·tion·al** \-shnəl, -shən-ᵊl\ *adj* — **li·bra·to·ry** \ˈlī-brə-ˌtōr-ē, -ˌtȯr-\ *adj*

li·bret·tist \lə-ˈbret-əst\ *n* (1862) **:** the writer of a libretto

li·bret·to \lə-ˈbret-(ˌ)ō\ *n, pl* **-tos** *or* **-ti** \-(ˌ)ē\ [It, dim. of *libro* book, fr. L *libr-, liber*] (1742) **1 :** the text of a work (as an opera) for the musical theater **2 :** the book containing a libretto

li·bri·form \ˈlī-brə-ˌfȯrm\ *adj* [L *libr-, liber* + ISV *-iform*] (1877) **:** resembling phloem fibers

Lib·ri·um \ˈlib-rē-əm\ *trademark* — used for a preparation of chlordiazepoxide

Lib·y·an \ˈlib-ē-ən\ *n* (1607) **1 :** a native or inhabitant of Libya **2 :** a Berber language of ancient No. Africa — **Libyan** *adj*

lice *pl of* LOUSE

¹**li·cense** *or* **li·cence** \ˈlīs-ᵊn(t)s\ *n* [ME, fr. MF *licence*, fr. L *licentia*, fr. *licent-, licens*, prp. of *licēre* to be permitted; akin to Latvian *ligt* to come to terms] (14c) **1 a :** permission to act **b :** freedom of action **2 a :** a permission granted by competent authority to engage in a business or occupation or in an activity otherwise unlawful **b :** a document, plate, or tag evidencing a license granted **3 a :** freedom that allows or is used with irresponsibility **b :** disregard for rules of personal conduct **:** LICENTIOUSNESS **4 :** deviation from fact, form, or rule by an artist or writer for the sake of the effect gained ***syn*** see FREEDOM

²**license** *also* **licence** *vt* **li·censed; li·cens·ing** (15c) **1 :** to issue a license to **2 :** to permit or authorize esp. by formal license — **li·cens·able** \-ᵊn-sə-bəl\ *adj* — **li·cens·er** \-sər\ *or* **li·cen·sor** \-sər, ˌlīs-ᵊn-ˈsō(ə)r\ *n*

licensed practical nurse *n* (1951) **:** a person who has undergone training and obtained a license (as from a state) conferring authorization to provide routine care for the sick

li·cens·ee \ˌlīs-ᵊn-ˈsē\ *n* (1864) **:** one that is licensed

license plate *n* (1926) **:** a plate or tag (as of metal) attesting that a license has been secured and usu. bearing a registration number

li·cen·sure \ˈlīs-ᵊn-shər, -ˌshu̇(ə)r\ *n* (ca. 1846) **:** the granting of licenses esp. to practice a profession

li·cen·te \lə-ˈsent-ē\ *n, pl* **licente** *or* **li·cen·ti** \-ē\ [native name in Lesotho] (1966) — see *loti* at MONEY table

li·cen·ti·ate \lī-ˈsen-chē-ət, *esp in sense 2* li-\ *n* [ML *licentiatus*, fr. pp. of *licentiare* to allow, fr. L *licentia*] (14c) **1 :** one who has a license granted esp. by a university to practice a profession **2 :** an academic degree ranking below that of doctor given by some European universities

li·cen·tious \lī-ˈsen-chəs\ *adj* [L *licentiosus*, fr. *licentia*] (1535) **1 :** lacking legal or moral restraints; *esp* **:** disregarding sexual restraints **2 :** marked by disregard for strict rules of correctness — **li·cen·tious·ly** *adv* — **li·cen·tious·ness** *n*

li·chee *var of* LITCHI

li·chen \ˈlī-kən, *Brit also* ˈlich-ən\ *n* [L, fr. Gk *leichēn, lichēn*; akin to Gk *leichein* to lick] (1601) **1 :** any of numerous complex thallophytic plants (group Lichenes) made up of an alga and a fungus growing in symbiotic association on a solid surface (as a rock) **2 :** any of several skin diseases characterized by a papular eruption — **li·chened** \-kənd\ *adj* — **li·chen·ous** \-kə-nəs\ *adj*

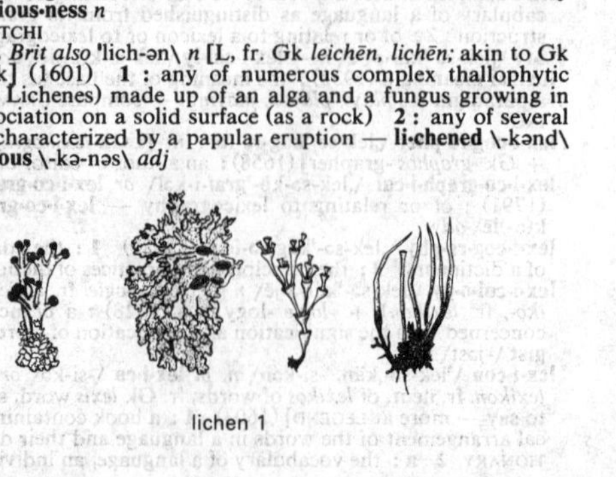

lichen 1

lich–gate *var of* LYCH-GATE

licht \'likt\ *Scot var of* LIGHT

lic•it \'lis-ət\ *adj* [ME, fr. MF *licite,* fr. L *licitus,* fr. pp. of *licēre* to be permitted — more at LICENSE] (15c) : conforming to the requirements of the law : not forbidden by law : PERMISSIBLE ***syn*** see LAWFUL — **lic•it•ly** *adv*

^{1}**lick** \'lik\ *vb* [ME *licken,* fr. OE *liccian;* akin to OHG *leckōn* to lick, L *lingere,* Gk *leichein*] *vt* (bef. 12c) **1 a** (1) : to draw the tongue over ⟨~ a stamp⟩ (2) : to flicker over like a tongue **b** : to take into the mouth with the tongue : LAP **2 a** : to strike repeatedly : THRASH **b** : to get the better of : OVERCOME ⟨has ~*ed* every problem⟩ ~ *vi* **1** : to lap with or as if with the tongue **2** : to dart like a tongue ⟨flames ~*ing* out of windows⟩ — **lick into shape** : to put into proper form or condition — **lick one's wounds** : to recover from defeat or disappointment

^{2}**lick** *n* (1603) **1 a** : an act or instance of licking **b** : a small amount : BIT **c** : a hasty careless effort **2 a** : a sharp hit : BLOW **b** : OPPORTUNITY, TURN — usu. used in pl. **3 a** : a natural salt deposit (as a salt spring) that animals lick **b** : a block of often medicated saline preparation given to livestock to lick **4** : a musical figure; *specif* : an interpolated and usu. improvised figure or flourish **5** : a critical thrust : DIG, BARB — **lick and a promise** : a perfunctory performance of a task

lick•er•ish \'lik-(ə-)rish\ *adj* [alter. of *lickerous,* fr. ME *likerous,* fr. (assumed) ONF, fr. ONF *leckeur* lecher; akin to OF *lecheor* lecher] (14c) **1** : GREEDY, DESIROUS **2** *obs* : tempting to the appetite **3** : LECHEROUS — **lick•er•ish•ly** *adv* — **lick•er•ish•ness** *n*

lick•e•ty–split \ˌlik-ət-ē-'split\ *adv* [prob. irreg. fr. ^{1}*lick* + *split*] (ca. 1859) : at great speed

lick•ing *n* (1756) **1** : a sound thrashing : DRUBBING **2** : a severe setback : DEFEAT

lick•spit•tle \'lik-ˌspit-ᵊl\ *n* (1825) : a fawning subordinate : TOADY

lic•o•rice \'lik(-ə)-rish, -rəs\ *n* [ME *licorice,* fr. OF, fr. LL *liquiritia,* alter. of L *glycyrrhiza,* fr. Gk *glykyrrhiza,* fr. *glykys* sweet + *rhiza* root — more at DULCET, ROOT] (13c) **1 a** : the dried root of a European leguminous plant (*Glycyrrhiza glabra*) with pinnate leaves and spikes of blue flowers; *also* : an extract of this used esp. in medicine, brewing, and confectionery **b** : a candy flavored with licorice **2** : a plant yielding licorice

lic•tor \'lik-tər\ *n* [L] (14c) : an ancient Roman officer who bore the fasces as the insignia of his office and whose duties included accompanying the chief magistrates in public appearances

^{1}**lid** \'lid\ *n* [ME, fr. OE *hlid;* akin to OHG *hlit* cover, OE *hlinian* to lean — more at LEAN] (bef. 12c) **1** : a movable cover for the opening of a hollow container (as a vessel or box) **2** : EYELID **3** : the operculum in mosses **4** *slang* : HAT **5** : a force that confines or represses : CHECK **6** : an ounce of marijuana

^{2}**lid** *vt* **lid•ded; lid•ding** (13c) : to cover or supply with a lid

li•dar \'lī-ˌdär\ *n* [*light* + *radar*] (1963) : a device that is similar in operation to radar but emits pulsed laser light instead of microwaves

lid•ded *adj* (bef. 12c) **1** : having or covered with a lid ⟨a ~ tureen⟩ **2** : having lids esp. of a specified kind — usu. used in combination ⟨heavy-*lidded* eyes⟩

lid•less \'lid-ləs\ *adj* (14c) **1** : having no lid **2** *archaic* : WATCHFUL

li•do \'lēd-(ˌ)ō\ *n, pl* **lidos** [*Lido,* Italy] (1860) : a fashionable beach resort

li•do•caine \'līd-ə-ˌkān\ *n* [acetani*lid* + *-o-* + *-caine*] (1949) : a crystalline compound $C_{14}H_{22}N_2O$ that is used in the form of its hydrochloride as a local anesthetic and as an antiarrhythmic agent

^{1}**lie** \'lī\ *vi* **lay** \'lā\; **lain** \'lān\; **ly•ing** \'lī-iŋ\ [ME *lien,* fr. OE *licgan;* akin to OHG *ligen* to lie, L *lectus* bed, Gk *lechos*] (bef. 12c) **1 a** : to be or to stay at rest in a horizontal position : be prostrate : REST, RECLINE ⟨~ motionless⟩ ⟨~ asleep⟩ **b** : to assume a horizontal position — often used with *down* **c** *archaic* : to reside temporarily : stay for the night : LODGE **d** *archaic* : to have sexual intercourse — used with *with* **e** : to remain inactive (as in concealment) ⟨~ in wait⟩ **2** : to be in a helpless or defenseless state ⟨the town *lay* at the mercy of the invaders⟩ **3** *of an inanimate thing* : to be or remain in a flat or horizontal position upon a broad support ⟨books *lying* on the table⟩ **4** : to have direction : EXTEND ⟨the route *lay* to the west⟩ **5 a** : to occupy a certain relative place or position ⟨hills ~ behind us⟩ **b** : to have a place in relation to something else ⟨the real reason ~*s* deeper⟩ **c** : to have an effect through mere presence, weight, or relative position ⟨remorse *lay* heavily on him⟩ **d** : to be sustainable or admissible **6** : to remain at anchor or becalmed **7 a** : to have place : EXIST ⟨the choice *lay* between fighting or surrendering⟩ **b** : CONSIST, BELONG ⟨the success of the book ~*s* in its direct style⟩ ⟨responsibility *lay* with the adults⟩ **8** : REMAIN; *esp* : to remain unused, unsought, or uncared for — **li•er** \'lī(-ə)r\ *n* — **lie low 1** : to lie prostrate, defeated, or disgraced **2** : to stay in hiding : strive to avoid notice **3** : to bide one's time : remain secretly ready for action

^{2}**lie** *n* (1697) **1** : the position or situation in which something lies **2** *chiefly Brit* : LAY 6 **3** : the haunt of an animal (as a fish) : COVERT **4** *Brit* : an act or instance of lying or resting

^{3}**lie** *vb* **lied; ly•ing** \'lī-iŋ\ [ME *lien,* fr. OE *lēogan;* akin to OHG *liogan* to lie, OSlav *lŭgati*] *vi* (bef. 12c) **1** : to make an untrue statement with intent to deceive **2** : to create a false or misleading impression ~ *vt* : to affect by telling lies ⟨*lied* his way out of trouble⟩

syn LIE, PREVARICATE, EQUIVOCATE, PALTER, FIB mean to tell an untruth. LIE is the blunt term, imputing dishonesty; PREVARICATE softens the bluntness of LIE by implying quibbling or confusing the issue; EQUIVOCATE implies using words having more than one sense so as to seem to say one thing but intend another; PALTER implies making unreliable statements of fact or intention or insincere promises; FIB applies to a telling of a trivial untruth.

^{4}**lie** *n* [ME *lige, lie,* fr. OE *lyge;* akin to OHG *lugi,* OE *lēogan* to lie] (bef. 12c) **1 a** : an assertion of something known or believed by the speaker to be untrue with intent to deceive **b** : an untrue or inaccurate statement that may or may not be believed true by the speaker **2** : something that misleads or deceives **3** : a charge of lying

lieb•frau•milch \'lēp-ˌfraů-ˌmilk\ *n* [G, alter. of *liebfrauenmilch,* fr. *Liebfrauenstift,* religious foundation in Worms, Germany + *milch* milk] (1833) : a dry white Rhine wine

lie by *vi* (1613) : to remain inactive : REST

lied \'lēt\ *n, pl* **lie•der** \'lēd-ər\ [G, song, fr. OHG *liod* — more at LAUD] (1852) : a German art song esp. of the 19th century

Lie•der•kranz \'lēd-ər-ˌkran(t)s, -ˌkrän(t)s\ *trademark* — used for a pungent surface-ripened cheese

lie detector *n* (1909) : an instrument for detecting physical evidences of the tension that accompanies lying

lie down *vi* (1888) **1** : to submit meekly or abjectly to defeat, disappointment, or insult ⟨won't take that criticism *lying down*⟩ **2** : to fail to perform or to neglect one's part deliberately ⟨*lying down* on the job⟩

^{1}**lief** \'lēf, 'lēv\ *adj* [ME *lief, lef,* fr. OE *lēof;* akin to OE *lufu* love] (bef. 12c) **1** *archaic* : DEAR, BELOVED **2** *archaic* : WILLING, GLAD

^{2}**lief** \'lēv, 'lēf\ *adv* (13c) : SOON, GLADLY ⟨I'd as ~ go as not⟩

^{1}**liege** \'lēj\ *adj* [ME, fr. OF, fr. LL *laeticus,* fr. *laetus* serf, of Gmc origin; akin to OFris *let* serf] (13c) **1 a** : having the right to feudal allegiance or service ⟨his ~ lord⟩ **b** : obligated to render feudal allegiance and service **2** : FAITHFUL, LOYAL

^{2}**liege** *n* (14c) **1 a** : a vassal bound to feudal service and allegiance **b** : a loyal subject **2** : a feudal superior to whom allegiance and service are due

liege man *n* (14c) **1** : VASSAL **2** : a devoted follower

lie–in \'lī-ˌin\ *n* (1963) : an act of lying down (as on a public thoroughfare) in organized protest and as a means of forcing compliance with demands

lien \'lēn, 'lē-ən\ *n* [MF, tie, band, fr. L *ligamen,* fr. *ligare* to bind — more at LIGATURE] (1531) **1** : a charge upon real or personal property for the satisfaction of some debt or duty ordinarily arising by operation of law **2** : the security interest created by a mortgage

lie off *vi* (1573) **1** : to hold back in the early part of a race **2** : to keep a little away from the shore or another ship **3** : to cease work for a time

lie over *vi* (ca. 1847) : to await disposal or attention at a later time ⟨several jobs *lying over* from last week⟩

li•erne \lē-'ərn, -'e(ə)rn\ *n* [F, fr. MF, prob. fr. *lier* to bind, fr. L *ligare*] (1842) : a rib in Gothic vaulting that passes from one intersection of the principal ribs to another

lie to \(ˈ)lī-'tü\ *vi, of a ship* (1711) : to stay stationary with head to windward

lieu \'lü\ *n* [ME *liue,* fr. OF *lieu,* fr. L *locus* — more at STALL] *archaic* (13c) : PLACE, STEAD — **in lieu** : INSTEAD — **in lieu of** : in the place of : instead of

lie up *vi* (1868) **1** : to stay in bed or at rest **2** : to go into or remain in a dock

lieu•ten•an•cy \lü-'ten-ən-sē, *Brit* le(f)-'ten-\ *n* (15c) : the office, rank, or commission of a lieutenant

lieu•ten•ant \-'ten-ənt\ *n* [ME, fr. MF, fr. *lieu* + *tenant* holding, fr. *tenir* to hold, fr. L *tenēre* — more at THIN] (14c) **1 a** : an official empowered to act for a higher official **b** : an aide or representative of another in the performance of duty : ASSISTANT **2 a** (1) : FIRST LIEUTENANT (2) : SECOND LIEUTENANT **b** : a commissioned officer in the navy or coast guard ranking above a lieutenant junior grade and below a lieutenant commander **c** : a fire or police department officer ranking below a captain

lieutenant colonel *n* (1598) : a commissioned officer in the army, air force, or marine corps ranking above a major and below a colonel

lieutenant commander *n* (1839) : a commissioned officer in the navy or coast guard ranking above a lieutenant and below a commander

lieutenant general *n* (1589) : a commissioned officer in the army, air force, or marine corps who ranks above a major general and whose insignia is three stars

lieutenant governor *n* (1595) : a deputy or subordinate governor: as **a** : an elected official serving as deputy to the governor of an American state **b** : the formal head of the government of a Canadian province appointed by the federal government as the representative of the crown — **lieutenant governorship** *n*

lieutenant junior grade *n, pl* **lieutenants junior grade** (ca. 1909) : a commissioned officer in the navy or coast guard ranking above an ensign and below a lieutenant

^{1}**life** \'līf\ *n, pl* **lives** \'līvz\ [ME *lif,* fr. OE *līf;* akin to OE *libban* to live — more at LIVE] (bef. 12c) **1 a** : the quality that distinguishes a vital and functional being from a dead body **b** : a principle or force that is considered to underlie the distinctive quality of animate beings — compare VITALISM 1 **c** : an organismic state characterized by capacity for metabolism, growth, reaction to stimuli, and reproduction **2 a** : the sequence of physical and mental experiences that make up the existence of an individual **b** : one or more aspects of the process of living ⟨sex ~ of the frog⟩ **3** : BIOGRAPHY 1 **4** : spiritual existence transcending physical death **5 a** : the period from birth to death **b** : a specific phase of earthly existence ⟨adult ~⟩ **c** : the period from an event until death ⟨a judge appointed for ~⟩ **d** : a sentence of imprisonment for the remainder of a convict's life **6** : a way or manner of living **7** : LIVELIHOOD **8** : a vital or living being; *specif* : PERSON ⟨many *lives* were lost in the disaster⟩ **9** : an animating and shaping force or principle **10** : SPIRIT, ANIMATION ⟨there was no ~ in her dancing⟩ **11** : the form or pattern of something existing in reality ⟨painted from ~⟩ **12** : the period of duration, usefulness, or popularity of something ⟨the expected ~ of flashlight batteries⟩ **13** : the period of existence (as of a subatomic particle) — compare HALF-LIFE **14** : a property (as resilience or elasticity) of an inanimate substance or object resembling the animate quality of a living being **15** : living beings (as of a particular kind or environment) ⟨forest ~⟩ **16 a** : human activities **b** : animate activity and movement ⟨stirrings of ~⟩ **c** : the activities of a given sphere, area, or time ⟨the political ~ of the country⟩ **17** : one providing interest and vigor ⟨~ of the party⟩ **18** : an opportunity for continued viability ⟨gave the patient a new ~⟩ **19** *cap, Christian Science* : GOD 1b **20** : something resembling animate life ⟨a grant saved the project's ~⟩

\ə\ abut \ᵊ\ kitten, F table \ər\ further \a\ ash \ā\ ace \ä\ cot, cart \aů\ out \ch\ chin \e\ bet \ē\ easy \g\ go \i\ hit \ī\ ice \j\ job \ŋ\ sing \ō\ go \ȯ\ law \ȯi\ boy \th\ thin \th\ the \ü\ loot \ů\ foot \y\ yet \zh\ vision \à, k, ⁿ, œ, œ̄, ue, uē, ʸ\ *see* Guide to Pronunciation

[2]**life** *adj* (bef. 12c) **1 :** of or relating to animate being **2 :** LIFELONG ⟨a ~ member⟩ **3 :** using a living model ⟨a ~ class⟩ **4 :** of, relating to, or provided by life insurance ⟨a ~ policy⟩

life–and–death *also* **life–or–death** *adj* (1822) **:** involving or culminating in life or death **:** vitally important as if involving life or death

life belt *n* (ca. 1858) **1 :** a life preserver in the form of a buoyant belt **2 :** SAFETY BELT

life•blood \ˈlīf-ˈbləd, -ˌbləd\ *n* (1590) **1 :** blood regarded as the seat of vitality **2 :** a vital or life-giving force ⟨freedom of inquiry is the ~ of a university⟩

life•boat \-ˌbōt\ *n* (1801) **:** a strong buoyant boat (as one carried by a ship) for use in an emergency and esp. in saving lives at sea

life buoy *n* (1886) **:** a ring-shaped life preserver

life cycle *n* (ca. 1892) **1 :** the series of stages in form and functional activity through which an organism passes between successive recurrences of a specified primary stage **2 :** LIFE HISTORY 1a **3 :** a series of stages through which an individual, group, or culture passes during its lifetime

life–form \ˈlīf-ˈfȯ(ə)rm\ *n* (1899) **:** the body form that characterizes a kind of organism (as a species) at maturity

life•ful \ˈlīf-fəl\ *adj, archaic* (13c) **:** full of or giving vitality

life–giv•ing \-ˌgiv-iŋ\ *adj* (1596) **:** giving or having power to give life and spirit **:** INVIGORATING

life•guard \-ˌgärd\ *n* (1896) **:** a usu. expert swimmer employed (as at a beach or a pool) to safeguard other swimmers — **lifeguard** *vi*

life history *n* (1873) **1 a :** a history of the changes through which an organism passes in its development from the primary stage to its natural death **b :** one series of the changes in a life history **2 :** the history of an individual's development in his social environment

life insurance *n* (1809) **:** insurance providing for payment of a stipulated sum to a designated beneficiary upon death of the insured

life jacket *n* (1883) **:** a life preserver in the form of a buoyant vest

life•less \ˈlī-fləs\ *adj* (bef. 12c) **:** having no life: **a :** DEAD **b :** INANIMATE **c :** lacking qualities expressive of life and vigor **:** INSIPID **d :** destitute of living beings — **life•less•ly** *adv* — **life•less•ness** *n*

life•like \ˈlī-ˌflīk\ *adj* (14c) **:** accurately representing or imitating real life ⟨a ~ portrait⟩ — **life•like•ness** *n*

life•line \ˈlī-ˌflīn\ *n* (1700) **1 a :** a line to which persons may cling to save or protect their lives; *esp* **:** one stretched along the deck or from the yards of a ship **b :** a line attached to a diver's helmet by which he is lowered and raised **c :** a rope line for lowering a person to safety **2 :** something (as a trade route or means of communication) regarded as indispensable for the maintaining or protection of life

life list *n* (1960) **:** a record kept of all birds sighted and identified by a birder

life•long \ˈlī-ˌflȯŋ\ *adj* (1855) **1 :** lasting or continuing through life **2 :** LONG-STANDING

life•man•ship \ˈlīf-mən-ˌship\ *n* (1949) **:** the skill or practice of achieving superiority or an appearance of superiority over others (as in conversation) by perplexing and demoralizing them

life net *n* (1902) **:** a strong net or sheet (as of canvas) used (as by firemen) to catch a person jumping from a burning building

life of Ri•ley \-ˈrī-lē\ [fr. the name *Riley*] (1923) **:** a carefree comfortable way of living

life peer *n* (1869) **:** a British peer whose title is not hereditary — **life peerage** *n* — **life peeress** *n*

life plant *n* (1851) **:** BRYOPHYLLUM

life preserver *n* (1804) **1 :** a device (as a life jacket or life buoy) designed to save a person from drowning by buoying up the body while in the water **2** *chiefly Brit* **:** BLACKJACK 3

lif•er \ˈlī-fər\ *n* (1830) **1 :** a person sentenced to imprisonment for life **2 :** a person who makes a career of one of the armed forces **3 :** a person who has made a lifelong commitment (as to a way of life)

life raft *n* (1819) **:** a raft usu. made of wood or an inflatable material and designed for use by people forced into the water

life ring *n* (ca. 1909) **:** LIFE BUOY

life•sav•er \ˈlīf-ˌsā-vər\ *n* (1887) **1 :** one trained to save lives of drowning persons **2 :** something at once timely and effective in the relief of distress

[1]**life•sav•ing** \-viŋ\ *adj* (1858) **:** designed for or used in saving lives ⟨~ drugs⟩

[2]**lifesaving** *n* (1919) **:** the skill or practice of saving or protecting the lives esp. of drowning persons

life science *n* (1945) **:** a branch of science (as biology, medicine, anthropology, or sociology) that deals with living organisms and life processes — usu. used in pl. — **life scientist** *n*

life–size \ˈlīf-ˈsīz\ *or* **life–sized** \-ˈsīzd\ *adj* (1841) **:** of natural size **:** of the size of the original ⟨a ~ statue⟩

life span *n* (1918) **1 :** the duration of existence of an individual **2 :** the average length of life of a kind of organism or of a material object esp. in a particular environment or under specified circumstances

life–style \ˈlīf-ˈstī(ə)l\ *n* (1946) **:** the typical way of life of an individual, group, or culture

life–support system *n* (1959) **:** an artificial or natural system that provides all or some of the items (as oxygen, food, water, control of temperature and pressure, disposition of carbon dioxide and body wastes) necessary for maintaining life or health

life table *n* (ca. 1859) **:** MORTALITY TABLE

[1]**life•time** \ˈlīf-ˌtīm\ *n* (13c) **1 :** the duration of the existence of a living being or a thing **2 :** the duration of the existence of an ion or subatomic particle **3 :** an amount accumulated or experienced in a lifetime ⟨a ~ of regrets⟩

[2]**lifetime** *adj* (1904) **:** LIFELONG

life vest *n* (1939) **:** LIFE JACKET

life•way \-ˌwā\ *n* (1948) **:** LIFE 6

life•work \-ˈwərk\ *n* (1871) **:** the entire or principal work of one's lifetime; *also* **:** a work extending over a lifetime

life zone *n* (1901) **:** a biogeographic zone

[1]**lift** \ˈlift\ *n* [ME, fr. OE *lyft*] *chiefly Scot* (bef. 12c) **:** HEAVENS, SKY

[2]**lift** *vb* [ME *liften*, fr. ON *lypta*; akin to OE *lyft* air — more at LOFT] *vt* (14c) **1 a :** to raise from a lower to a higher position **:** ELEVATE **b :** to raise in rank or condition **c :** to raise in rate or amount **2 :** to put an end to (a blockade or siege) by withdrawing investing forces **3 :** REVOKE, RESCIND ⟨~ an embargo⟩ **4 a :** STEAL ⟨had her purse ~*ed*⟩ **b :** PLAGIARIZE **c :** to take out of normal setting ⟨~ a word out of context⟩ **5 :** to take up (as a root crop or transplants) from the ground **6 :** to pay off (an obligation) ⟨~ a mortgage⟩ **7 a :** to shift (artillery fire) from one area to another **b :** to withhold (artillery fire) from an area **8 :** to move from one place to another (as by aircraft) **:** TRANSPORT **9 :** to take up (a fingerprint) from a surface ~ *vi* **1 a :** ASCEND, RISE **b :** to appear elevated (as above surrounding objects) **2 a :** to disperse upward ⟨until the fog ~*s*⟩ **b :** to cease temporarily — used of rain — **lift•able** \ˈlif-tə-bəl\ *adj* — **lift•er** *n*

syn LIFT, RAISE, REAR, ELEVATE, HOIST, HEAVE, BOOST mean to move from a lower to a higher place or position. LIFT usu. implies exerting effort to overcome resistance of weight; RAISE carries a stronger implication of bringing up to the vertical or to a high position; REAR may add an element of suddenness to RAISE; ELEVATE may replace LIFT or RAISE esp. when exalting or enhancing is implied; HOIST implies lifting something heavy esp. by mechanical means; HEAVE implies lifting with great effort or strain; BOOST suggests assisting to climb or advance by a push.

[3]**lift** *n* (14c) **1 :** the amount that may be lifted at one time **:** LOAD **2 a :** the action or an instance of lifting **b :** the action or an instance of rising **c :** elevated carriage (as of a body part) **d :** the lifting up (as of a dancer) usu. by a partner **3 :** a device (as a handle or latch) for lifting **4 :** an act of stealing **:** THEFT **5 a :** ASSISTANCE, HELP **b :** a ride along one's way **6 :** a layer in the heel of a shoe **7 :** a rise or advance in position or condition **8 :** a slight rise or elevation **9 :** the distance or extent to which something rises **10 :** an apparatus or machine used for hoisting: as **a :** a set of pumps used in a mine **b** *chiefly Brit* **:** ELEVATOR 1b **c :** an apparatus for raising an automobile (as for repair) **d :** SKI LIFT **11 a :** an elevating influence **b :** an elevation of the spirit **12 :** the component of the total aerodynamic force acting on an airplane or airfoil that is perpendicular to the relative wind and that for an airplane constitutes the upward force that opposes the pull of gravity **13 :** an organized movement of men, equipment, or supplies by some form of transportation; *esp* **:** AIRLIFT

lift•gate \ˈlift-ˌgāt\ *n* (1953) **:** an upper rear panel (as on a station wagon) that opens upward

lift•man \ˈlift-ˌman\ *n, Brit* (1883) **:** an elevator operator

lift•off \ˈlif-ˌtȯf\ *n* (ca. 1956) **:** a vertical takeoff by an aircraft or a rocket vehicle or missile

lift truck *n* (1926) **:** a small truck equipped for lifting and transporting loads

lig•a•ment \ˈlig-ə-mənt\ *n* [ME, fr. ML & L; ML *ligamentum*, fr. L, band, tie, fr. *ligare*] (15c) **1 :** a tough band of tissue connecting the articular extremities of bones or supporting an organ in place **2 :** a connecting or unifying bond ⟨the law of nations, the great ~ of mankind —Edmund Burke⟩ — **lig•a•men•tous** \-ˈment-əs\ *adj*

li•gan \ˈlī-gən, ˈlig-ən\ *var of* LAGAN

li•gand \ˈlig-ənd, ˈlīg-\ *n* [L *ligandus*, gerundive of *ligare*] (ca. 1949) **:** a group, ion, or molecule coordinated to a central atom or molecule in a complex

li•gase \ˈlī-ˌgās, -ˌgāz\ *n* [ISV *lig-* (fr. L *ligare*) + *-ase*] (ca. 1961) **:** SYNTHETASE

li•gate \ˈlī-ˌgāt, lī-ˈ\ *vt* **li•gat•ed; li•gat•ing** [L *ligatus*] (1599) **:** to tie with a ligature

li•ga•tion \lī-ˈgā-shən\ *n* (1597) **1 :** an act of ligating **2 :** something that binds **:** LIGATURE

lig•a•ture \ˈlig-ə-ˌchu̇(ə)r, -chər, -ˌt(y)u̇(ə)r\ *n* [ME, fr. MF, fr. LL *ligatura*, fr. L *ligatus*, pp. of *ligare* to bind, tie; akin to MHG *geleich* joint, Alb *lith* I tie] (15c) **1 a :** something that is used to bind; *specif* **:** a filament (as a thread) used in surgery **b :** something that unites or connects **:** BOND **2 :** the action of binding or tying **3 :** a compound note in mensural notation indicating a group of musical notes to be sung to one syllable **4 :** a printed or written character (as *æ*) consisting of two or more letters or characters joined together

[1]**light** \ˈlīt\ *n* [ME, fr. OE *lēoht*; akin to OHG *lioht* light, L *luc-*, *lux* light, *lucēre* to shine, Gk *leukos* white] (bef. 12c) **1 a :** something that makes vision possible **b :** the sensation aroused by stimulation of the visual receptors **c :** an electromagnetic radiation in the wavelength range including infrared, visible, ultraviolet, and X rays and traveling in a vacuum with a speed of about 186,281 miles (300,000 kilometers) per second; *specif* **:** the part of this range that is visible to the human eye **2 a :** DAYLIGHT **b :** DAWN **3 :** a source of light: as **a :** a celestial body **b :** CANDLE **c :** an electric light **4** *archaic* **:** SIGHT 4a **5 a :** spiritual illumination **b :** INNER LIGHT **c :** ENLIGHTENMENT **d :** TRUTH **6 a :** public knowledge ⟨facts brought to ~⟩ **b :** a particular aspect or appearance presented to view ⟨saw the matter in a different ~⟩ **7 :** a particular illumination **8 :** something that enlightens or informs ⟨he shed some ~ on the problem⟩ **9 :** a medium (as a window) through which light is admitted **10** *pl* **:** a set of principles, standards, or opinions ⟨worship according to one's ~*s* —Adrienne Koch⟩ **11 :** a noteworthy person in a particular place or field **12 :** a particular expression of the eye **13 a :** LIGHTHOUSE, BEACON **b (1) :** TRAFFIC SIGNAL **(2) :** a green traffic light **14 :** the representation of light in art **15 :** a flame for lighting something — **in the light of 1 :** from the point of view of **2** *or* **in light of :** in view of

[2]**light** *adj* (bef. 12c) **1 :** having light **:** BRIGHT ⟨a ~ airy room⟩ **2 a :** not dark, intense, or swarthy in color or coloring **:** PALE **b** *of colors* **:** medium in saturation and high in lightness ⟨~ blue⟩ **3** *of coffee* **:** served with extra milk or cream

[3]**light** *vb* **light•ed** *or* **lit** \ˈlit\; **light•ing** *vi* (bef. 12c) **1 :** to become light **:** BRIGHTEN — usu. used with *up* ⟨her face *lit* up⟩ **2 :** to take fire **3 :** to ignite something (as a cigarette) — often used with *up* ~ *vt* **1 :** to set fire to **2 a :** to conduct with a light **:** GUIDE **b :** ILLUMINATE ⟨rockets ~ up the sky⟩ **c :** ANIMATE, BRIGHTEN ⟨a smile *lit* up her face⟩

[4]**light** *adj* [ME, fr. OE *lēoht*; akin to OHG *lihti* light, L *levis*, Gk *elachys* small] (bef. 12c) **1 a :** having little weight **:** not heavy **b :** designed to carry a comparatively small load ⟨a ~ truck⟩ **c :** having relatively little weight in proportion to bulk ⟨aluminum is a ~ metal⟩ **d :** containing less than the legal, standard, or usual weight ⟨a ~ coin⟩ **2 a :** of little importance **:** TRIVIAL **b :** not abundant **:** SCANTY ⟨~ rain⟩ **3 a :** easily disturbed ⟨a ~ sleeper⟩ **b :** exerting a minimum of force or pressure **:** GENTLE ⟨a ~ touch⟩ **c :** resulting from a very slight pressure **:** FAINT ⟨~ print⟩ **4 a :** easily endurable ⟨a ~ illness⟩ **b :** requiring little effort ⟨~ work⟩ **5 :** capable of moving swiftly or nimbly ⟨~ on his feet⟩ **6 a :** FRIVOLOUS ⟨~ conduct⟩ **b :** lacking in stability

: CHANGEABLE ⟨~ opinions⟩ **c** : sexually promiscuous **7** : free from care : CHEERFUL **8** : intended chiefly to entertain ⟨~ verse⟩ ⟨~ comedy⟩ **9 a** : having a comparatively low alcoholic content ⟨~ wines⟩ **b** : having a relatively mild flavor **10 a** : easily digested ⟨a ~ soup⟩ **b** : well leavened ⟨a ~ crust⟩ **11** : lightly armed or equipped ⟨~ cavalry⟩ **12** : coarse and sandy or easily pulverized ⟨~ soil⟩ **13** : DIZZY, GIDDY ⟨felt ~ in the head⟩ **14 a** : carrying little or no cargo ⟨the ship returned ~⟩ **b** : producing goods for direct consumption by the consumer ⟨~ industry⟩ **15** : not bearing a stress or accent ⟨a ~ syllable⟩ **16** : having a clear soft quality ⟨a ~ voice⟩ **17** : being in debt to the pot in a poker game ⟨three chips ~⟩ ***syn*** see EASY — **light·ish** \-ish\ *adj*

[5]**light** *adv* (bef. 12c) **1** : LIGHTLY **2** : with little baggage ⟨travel ~⟩

[6]**light** *vi* **light·ed** *or* **lit** \'lit\; **light·ing** [ME *lighten,* fr. OE *līhtan;* akin to OE *lēoht* light in weight] (bef. 12c) **1** : DISMOUNT **2** : SETTLE, ALIGHT ⟨a bird *lit* on the lawn⟩ **3** : to fall unexpectedly —usu. used with *on* or *upon* **4** : to arrive by chance : HAPPEN —usu. used with *on* or *upon* ⟨*lit* upon a solution⟩ — **light into** : to attack forcefully ⟨I *lit into* that food until I'd finished off the heel of the loaf —Helen Eustis⟩

light adaptation *n* (1900) : the process including contraction of the pupil and decrease in visual purple by which the eye adapts to conditions of increased illumination

light–adapt·ed \'līt-ə-ˌdap-təd\ *adj* (1900) : adjusted for vision in bright light : having undergone light adaptation

light air *n* (1805) : wind having a speed of 1 to 3 miles (1.6 to 4.8 kilometers) per hour

light bread \'līt-ˌbred\ *n* [[2]*light*] *chiefly Southern & Midland* (1821) : bread in loaves made from white flour leavened with yeast

light breeze *n* (1805) : wind having a speed of 4 to 7 miles (6.4 to 11 kilometers) per hour

light bulb *n* (1884) : INCANDESCENT LAMP

light chain *n* (1964) : either of the two smaller of the four polypeptide chains comprising antibodies — compare HEAVY CHAIN

light–emitting diode *n* (ca. 1970) : LED

[1]**light·en** \'līt-ᵊn\ *vb* **light·ened; light·en·ing** \'līt-niŋ, -ᵊn-iŋ\ [ME *lighten,* fr. *light*] *vt* (14c) **1** : to make light or clear : ILLUMINATE **2** *archaic* : ENLIGHTEN **3** : to make (as a color) lighter ~ *vi* **1 a** : to shine brightly **b** : to grow lighter : BRIGHTEN **2** : to give out flashes of lightning — **light·en·er** \'līt-nər, -ᵊn-ər\ *n*

[2]**lighten** *vb* **light·ened; light·en·ing** \'līt-niŋ, -ᵊn-iŋ\ *vt* (14c) **1 a** : to relieve of a burden in whole or in part ⟨the news ~*ed* his mind⟩ **b** : to reduce in weight or quantity : LESSEN ⟨~ her duties⟩ **c** : to make less wearisome : ALLEVIATE ⟨~ our sorrow⟩ **2** : CHEER, GLADDEN ~ *vi* **1** : to become lighter or less burdensome **2** : to become more cheerful ***syn*** see RELIEVE — **light·en·er** \'līt-nər, -ᵊn-ər\ *n*

[1]**ligh·ter** \'līt-ər\ *n* [ME, fr. (assumed) MD *lichter,* fr. MD *lichten* to unload; akin to OE *lēoht* light in weight] (14c) : a large usu. flat-bottomed barge used esp. in unloading or loading ships

[2]**lighter** *vt* (1840) : to convey by a lighter

[3]**light·er** \'līt-ər\ *n* (1553) **1** : one that lights or sets a fire **2** : a device for lighting a fire; *esp* : a mechanical or electrical device used for lighting cigarettes, cigars, or pipes

ligh·ter·age \'līt-ə-rij\ *n* (15c) **1** : the loading, unloading, or transportation of goods by means of a lighter **2** : a price paid for lightering **3** : boats engaged in lightering

lighter–than–air *adj* (1887) : of less weight than the air displaced

light·face \'līt-ˌfās\ *n* (ca. 1871) : a typeface having comparatively light thin lines; *also* : printing in lightface — **light·faced** \-'fāst\ *adj*

light·fast \-ˌfast\ *adj* (1950) : resistant to light and esp. to sunlight; *esp* : colorfast to light — **light·fast·ness** \-ˌfas(t)-nəs\ *n*

light–fin·gered \-'fiŋ-gərd\ *adj* (1547) **1** : adroit in stealing esp. by picking pockets **2** : having a light and dexterous touch : NIMBLE — **light–fin·gered·ness** *n*

light–foot·ed \-'fu̇t-əd\ *also* **light–foot** \-ˌfu̇t\ *adj* (15c) **1** : having a light and springy step **2** : moving gracefully and nimbly

light guide *n* (1951) : fiber optics used esp. for telecommunication with light waves

light–hand·ed \-'han-dəd\ *adj* (15c) : having a light or delicate touch : FACILE — **light–hand·ed·ness** *n*

light–head·ed \-'hed-əd\ *adj* (1537) **1** : mentally disoriented : DIZZY **2** : lacking in maturity or seriousness : FRIVOLOUS — **light–head·ed·ly** *adv* — **light–head·ed·ness** *n*

light·heart·ed \-'härt-əd\ *adj* (15c) **1** : free from care or anxiety : GAY **2** : cheerfully optimistic and hopeful : EASYGOING — **light·heart·ed·ly** *adv* — **light·heart·ed·ness** *n*

light heavyweight *n* (1903) : a boxer in a weight division having a maximum limit of 175 pounds for professionals and 178 pounds for amateurs — compare HEAVYWEIGHT, MIDDLEWEIGHT

light·house \'līt-ˌhau̇s\ *n* (1622) : a structure (as a tower) with a powerful light that gives a continuous or intermittent signal to navigators

light housekeeping *n* (1904) **1** : domestic work restricted to the less laborious duties **2** : housekeeping in quarters with limited facilities for cooking

light·ing \'līt-iŋ\ *n* (bef. 12c) **1 a** : ILLUMINATION **b** : IGNITION **2** : an artificial supply of light or the apparatus providing it

light·less \'līt-ləs\ *adj* (bef. 12c) **1** : receiving no light : DARK **2** : giving no light

light·ly \'līt-lē\ *adv* (bef. 12c) **1** : with little weight or force : GENTLY **2** : with indifference or carelessness : UNCONCERNEDLY ⟨the problem should not be passed over ~ —Shelly Halpern⟩ **3** : with little difficulty : EASILY **4** : GAILY, CHEERFULLY ⟨offenses not ~ forgiven⟩ **5** : in an agile manner : NIMBLY, SWIFTLY **6** : in a small degree or amount ⟨~ salted food⟩

light machine gun *n* (ca. 1925) : an air-cooled machine gun of not more than .30 caliber

light meter *n* (1921) : a small and often portable device for measuring illumination; *esp* : EXPOSURE METER

light–mind·ed \'līt-'mīn-dəd\ *adj* (1611) : lacking in seriousness : FRIVOLOUS — **light–mind·ed·ly** *adv* — **light–mind·ed·ness** *n*

[1]**light·ness** \-nəs\ *n* (bef. 12c) **1** : the quality or state of being illuminated : ILLUMINATION **2** : the attribute of object colors by which the object appears to reflect or transmit more or less of the incident light

[2]**lightness** *n* (12c) **1** : the quality or state of being light in weight **2** : lack of seriousness and stability of character often accompanied by casual heedlessness **3 a** : the quality or state of being nimble **b** : an ease and gaiety of style or manner **4** : a lack of weightiness or force : DELICACY

[1]**light·ning** \'līt-niŋ\ *n* [ME, fr. gerund of *lightenen* to lighten] (13c) **1** : the flashing of light produced by a discharge of atmospheric electricity from one cloud to another or between a cloud and the earth; *also* : the discharge itself **2** : a sudden stroke of fortune

[2]**lightning** *adj* (1640) : having or moving with or as if with the speed and suddenness of lightning ⟨a ~ assault⟩

[3]**lightning** *vi* **light·ninged; lightning** (1903) : to discharge a flash of lightning

lightning arrester *n* (1860) : a device for protecting an electrical apparatus from injury by lightning

lightning bug *n* (1778) : FIREFLY

lightning rod *n* (1789) : a metallic rod set up on a building or mast and connected with the moist earth or water below to diminish the chances of destructive effect by lightning

light–o'–love \ˌlīt-ᵊl-'əv\ *n, pl* **light–o'–loves** (1589) **1** : PROSTITUTE **2** : LOVER, PARAMOUR

light opera *n* (1882) : OPERETTA

light out *vi* [[6]*light*] (1866) : to leave in a hurry ⟨*lit out* for home at once⟩

light pen *n* (1958) : a pen-shaped device for direct interaction with a computer through a cathode-ray tube display

light pipe *n* (1950) : fiber optics or a solid transparent plastic rod for transmitting light lengthwise

light·plane \'līt-ˌplān\ *n* (1923) : a small and comparatively lightweight airplane; *esp* : a privately owned passenger airplane

light pollution *n* (ca. 1971) : artificial skylight (as from city lights) that interferes with astronomical observations

light·proof \'līt-'prüf\ *adj* (1923) : impenetrable by light

light quantum *n* (1925) : PHOTON; *esp* : one of luminous radiation

light–rail \'līt-ˌrā(ə)l\ *adj* (1975) : of, relating to, or being a means of transportation by trolley cars

light reaction *n* (ca. 1929) : the phase of photosynthesis that requires the presence of light and that involves photophosphorylation

light red *n* (1803) : any of various pale red or reddish orange pigments; *esp* : a calcined yellow ocher

lights \'līts\ *n pl* [ME *lightes,* fr. *light* light in weight] (13c) : the lungs esp. of a slaughtered animal

light·ship \'līt-ˌship\ *n* (1837) : a ship equipped with a brilliant light and moored at a place dangerous to navigation

light show *n* (1966) : a kaleidoscopic display of colored lights, slides, and film loops designed to imitate the effects of psychedelic drugs

[1]**light·some** \'līt-səm\ *adj* (14c) **1** : free from care : LIGHTHEARTED **2** : AIRY, NIMBLE — **light·some·ly** *adv* — **light·some·ness** *n*

[2]**lightsome** *adj* (15c) **1** : well lighted : BRIGHT **2** : giving light

lights–out \'līt-'sau̇t\ *n* (1868) **1** : a command or signal for putting out lights **2** : a prescribed bedtime for persons living under discipline

light–struck \'līt-ˌstrək\ *adj* (1890) : fogged by accidental exposure to light — used of a photographic material

light·tight \'līt-ˌtīt\ *adj* (1884) : LIGHTPROOF

light trap *n* (1906) **1** : a device that allows movement of a sliding part or passage of a person (as into a darkroom) but excludes light **2** : a device for collecting or destroying insects that consists of a bright light in association with a trapping or killing medium

light water *n* (1933) : WATER 1a — compare HEAVY WATER

[1]**light·weight** \'līt-ˌwāt\ *n* (1773) **1** : one of less than average weight; *specif* : a boxer in a weight division having a maximum limit of 135 pounds for professionals and 132 pounds for amateurs — compare FEATHERWEIGHT, WELTERWEIGHT **2** : one of little consequence ⟨shows up its author as a ~ —C. J. Rolo⟩

[2]**lightweight** *adj* (1809) **1** : lacking in earnestness or profundity : INCONSEQUENTIAL **2** : having less than average weight **3** : of, relating to, or characteristic of a lightweight ⟨the ~ championship⟩

light·wood \'līt-ˌwu̇d, 'līt-əd\ *n, chiefly Southern* (1705) : wood used for kindling; *esp* : coniferous wood abounding in pitch

light–year \'līt-ˌyi(ə)r\ *n* (1888) **1** : a unit of length in interstellar astronomy equal to the distance that light travels in one year in a vacuum or about 5,878,000,000,000 miles (9,458,000,000,000 kilometers) **2** : an extremely long distance esp. as a measure of progress ⟨two minutes and yet ~*s* away from the crowded village —Suzanne Patterson⟩

lign- *or* **ligni-** *or* **ligno-** *comb form* [L *lign-, ligni-,* fr. *lignum*] : wood ⟨*lign*in⟩ ⟨*ligno*cellulose⟩

lig·ne·ous \'lig-nē-əs\ *adj* [L *ligneus,* fr. *lignum* wood; perh. akin to L *legere* to gather — more at LEGEND] (1626) : of or resembling wood

lig·ni·fy \'lig-nə-ˌfī\ *vb* **-fied; -fy·ing** [F *lignifier,* fr. L *lignum*] *vt* (ca. 1828) : to convert into wood or woody tissue ~ *vi* : to become wood or woody — **lig·ni·fi·ca·tion** \ˌlig-nə-fə-'kā-shən\ *n*

lig·nin \'lig-nən\ *n* (1822) : an amorphous polymeric substance related to cellulose that together with cellulose forms the woody cell walls of plants and the cementing material between them

lig·nite \'lig-ˌnīt\ *n* [F, fr. L *lignum*] (ca. 1808) : a usu. brownish black coal intermediate between peat and bituminous coal; *esp* : one in which the texture of the original wood is distinct — called also *brown coal* — **lig·nit·ic** \lig-'nit-ik\ *adj*

lig·no·cel·lu·lose \ˌlig-nō-'sel-yə-ˌlōs, -ˌlōz\ *n* [ISV] (ca. 1900) : any of several closely related substances constituting the essential part of woody cell walls and consisting of cellulose intimately associated with lignin — **lig·no·cel·lu·los·ic** \-ˌsel-yə-'lō-sik, -zik\ *adj*

lig·no·sul·fo·nate \-'səl-fə-ˌnāt\ *n* (1908) : any of various compounds that are produced from the spent sulfite liquor in the pulping of softwood in papermaking and that are used esp. for binders and dispersing agents

lig·num vi·tae \ˌlig-nəm-'vīt-ē\ *n, pl* **lignum vitaes** [NL, lit., wood of life] (1594) **1** : the very hard heavy wood of any of several tropical American trees (genus *Guaiacum* of the family Zygophyllaceae) **2** : a tree yielding lignum vitae

lig·ro·in \'lig-rə-wən\ *n* [origin unknown] (1881) : any of several petroleum naphtha fractions that boil usu. in the range 20° to 135°C and are used esp. as solvents

lig·u·la \'lig-yə-lə\ *n, pl* **-lae** \-,lē, -,lī\ *also* **-las** [NL] (ca. 1760) **1** : LIGULE **2** : the distal lobed part of the labium of an insect

lig·u·late \'lig-yə-lət, -,lāt\ *adj* (1760) **1** : furnished with ligules, ligulae, or ligulate corollas **2** [L *ligula*] : shaped like a strap ⟨~ corolla of a ray flower⟩

lig·ule \'lig-(,)yü(ə)l\ *n* [NL *ligula*, fr. L, small tongue, strap; akin to L *lingere* to lick — more at LICK] (ca. 1847) : a scalelike projection esp. on a plant: as **a** : a thin appendage of a foliage leaf and esp. of the sheath of a blade of grass **b** : a ligulate corolla of a ray floret in a composite head

lig·ure \'lig-,yu̇(ə)r, -yər\ *n* [LL *ligurius*, fr. Gk *ligyrion*] (14c) : a traditional precious stone that is prob. the jacinth

lik·able *or* **like·able** \'lī-kə-bəl\ *adj* (1730) : having qualities that bring about a favorable regard : PLEASANT, AGREEABLE — **lik·abil·i·ty** \,lī-kə-'bil-ət-ē\ *n* — **lik·able·ness** *n*

¹**like** \'līk\ *vb* **liked; lik·ing** [ME *liken*, fr. OE *līcian*; akin to OE *gelīc* alike] *vt* (bef. 12c) **1** *chiefly dial* : to be suitable or agreeable to **2 a** : to feel attraction toward or take pleasure in : ENJOY ⟨~*s* baseball⟩ **b** : to feel toward : REGARD ⟨how would you ~ a change⟩ **3** : to wish to have : WANT ⟨would ~ a drink⟩ ~ *vi* **1** *dial* : APPROVE **2** : to feel inclined ⟨leave any time you ~⟩ **3** : to find oneself attracted

²**like** *n* (1851) **1** : a feeling of attraction : PREFERENCE **2** : something that one likes

³**like** *adj* [ME, alter. of *ilich*, fr. OE *gelīc* like, alike, fr. *ge-* (associative prefix) + *līc* body; akin to OHG *gilīh* like, alike, Lith *lygus* like — more at CO-] (bef. 12c) **1** : the same or nearly the same (as in appearance, character, or quantity) ⟨suits of ~ design⟩ **2** : LIKELY ⟨the importance of statistics as the one discipline ~ to give accuracy of mind —H. J. Laski⟩

⁴**like** *prep* (13c) **1 a** : having the characteristics of : similar to ⟨his house is ~ a barn⟩ **b** : typical of ⟨was ~ him to do that⟩ **2** : in the manner of : similarly to ⟨acts ~ a fool⟩ **3** : inclined to ⟨looks ~ rain⟩ **4** : such as ⟨a subject ~ physics⟩ **5** — used to form intensive or ironic phrases ⟨fought ~ hell⟩ ⟨~ fun he did⟩

⁵**like** *n* (13c) **1** : one that is like another : COUNTERPART, EQUAL ⟨have . . . never seen the ~ before —Sir Winston Churchill⟩ ⟨had no use for the ~*s* of him⟩ **2** : KIND 4a ⟨put him and his ~ to some job —J.R.R. Tolkien⟩

⁶**like** *adv* (14c) **1** *archaic* : EQUALLY **2** : LIKELY, PROBABLY ⟨you'll try it, some day, ~ enough —Mark Twain⟩ **3** : to some extent : RATHER ⟨saunter over nonchalantly ~ —Walter Karig⟩ **4** : NEARLY ⟨the actual interest is more ~ 18 percent⟩ — **as like as not** *or* **like as not** : PROBABLY

⁷**like** *conj* (14c) **1 a** : AS IF ⟨middle-aged men who looked ~ they might be out for their one night of the year —Norman Mailer⟩ **b** — used in intensive phrases ⟨drove ~ mad⟩ **2** : in the same way that : AS ⟨they raven down scenery ~ children do sweetmeats —John Keats⟩

usage The use of *like* as a conjunction may have had its origin in a compound conjunction *like as*, which is attested as early as the 14th century and continued into the 19th. But *like* without *as* is also attested as early as the 14th century, and *like* went on being used alone without comment until sometime in the mid-19th century. It has been stigmatized since then, but at first not on the grounds that it could not be used as a conjunction: 19th century grammarians were wrangling over whether *like* should be called a preposition or not. There is no doubt that after more than 500 years of use, *like* is firmly established as a conjunction. It has been used by many prestigious literary figures of the past, though perhaps not in their most elevated works; in modern use it may be found in literature, journalism, and scholarly writing. While the present objection to it is perhaps more heated than rational, someone writing formal prose may want to use *as* or *as if* instead.

⁸**like** *or* **liked** \'līkt\ *verbal auxiliary, chiefly dial* (15c) : came near : was near ⟨so loud I ~ to fell out of bed —Helen Eustis⟩

⁹**like** \(,)līk\ *interj* (1778) — used chiefly in informal speech as a meaningless expletive or intensifier or to lessen the emphasis of a preceding or following word or phrase

-like \,līk\ *adj comb form* : resembling or characteristic of ⟨bell-*like*⟩ ⟨lady*like*⟩

like·li·hood \'lī-klē-,hu̇d\ *n* (14c) : PROBABILITY ⟨a strong ~ that he is correct —T. D. Anderson⟩

¹**like·ly** \'lī-klē\ *adj* **like·li·er; -est** [ME, fr. ON *glikligr*, fr. *glikr* like; akin to OE *gelīc*] (14c) **1** : of such a nature or circumstance as to make something probable ⟨~ of success⟩ **2** : apparently qualified : SUITABLE ⟨a ~ place⟩ **3 a** : RELIABLE, CREDIBLE ⟨a ~ enough story⟩ **b** : having a high probability of occurring or being true : very probable **4** : PROMISING ⟨a ~ candidate⟩ **5** : ATTRACTIVE ⟨a ~ child⟩

²**likely** *adv* (14c) : in all probability : PROBABLY ⟨those who seek power will most ~ wind up exercising it —Halton Arp⟩

like–mind·ed \'līk-'mīn-dəd\ *adj* (1526) : having a like disposition or purpose : of the same mind or habit of thought — **like–mind·ed·ly** *adv* — **like–mind·ed·ness** *n*

lik·en \'lī-kən\ *vt* **lik·ened; lik·en·ing** \'līk-(ə-)niŋ\ (14c) : COMPARE

like·ness \'līk-nəs\ *n* (13c) **1** : COPY, PORTRAIT **2** : APPEARANCE, SEMBLANCE **3** : the quality or state of being like : RESEMBLANCE

syn LIKENESS, SIMILARITY, RESEMBLANCE, SIMILITUDE, ANALOGY, AFFINITY mean agreement or correspondence in details. LIKENESS implies a closer correspondence than SIMILARITY which often implies that things are merely somewhat alike; RESEMBLANCE implies similarity chiefly in appearance or external qualities; SIMILITUDE applies chiefly to correspondence between abstractions; ANALOGY implies likeness or parallelism in relations rather than in appearance or qualities; AFFINITY suggests a cause such as kinship or experiences or influences in common which is accountable for the similarity.

like·wise \'lī-,kwīz\ *adv* (15c) **1** : in like manner : SIMILARLY ⟨go and do ~⟩ **2** : in addition **3** : similarly so with me ⟨answered "~" to "Pleased to meet you"⟩

lik·ing \'lī-kiŋ\ *n* (14c) : favorable regard : FONDNESS, TASTE ⟨had a greater ~ for law —E. M. Coulter⟩ ⟨took a ~ to the newcomer⟩

li·ku·ta \li-'küt-ə\ *n, pl* **ma·ku·ta** \mä-\ [of Niger-Congo origin; prob. akin to obs. Nupe *kuta* stone] (1967) — see *zaire* at MONEY table

li·lac \'lī-lək, -,lak, -,läk\ *n* [obs. F (now *lilas*), fr. Ar *līlak*, fr. Per *nīlak* bluish, fr. *nīl* blue, fr. Skt *nīla* dark blue] (1625) **1 a** : a European shrub (*Syringa vulgaris*) of the olive family that is often an escape in No. America and has cordate ovate leaves and large panicles of fragrant pink-purple or white flowers **b** : a tree or shrub congeneric with the lilac **2** : a variable color averaging a moderate purple

lil·an·ge·ni \,lil-ən-'gen-ē\ *n, pl* **em·a·lan·ge·ni** \,em-ə-lən-'gen-ē\ [native name in Swaziland] (ca. 1976) — see MONEY table

lil·ied \'lil-ēd\ *adj* (1614) **1** *archaic* : resembling a lily in fairness **2** : full of or covered with lilies

Lil·ith \'lil-əth\ *n* [LHeb *līlīth*, fr. Heb, a female demon] **1** : a female figure who in rabbinic legend is Adam's first wife, is supplanted by Eve, and becomes an evil spirit **2** : a famous witch in medieval demonology

Lil·li·put \'lil-i-(,)pət\ *n* : an island in Swift's *Gulliver's Travels* where the inhabitants are six inches tall

lil·li·pu·tian \,lil-ə-'pyü-shən\ *adj, often cap* (1726) **1** : of, relating to, or characteristic of the Lilliputians or the island of Lilliput **2 a** : SMALL, MINIATURE **b** : PETTY

Lilliputian *n* **1** : an inhabitant of Lilliput **2** *often not cap* : one resembling a Lilliputian; *esp* : an undersized individual

¹**lilt** \'lilt\ *vb* [ME *lulten*] *vt* (14c) : to sing or play in a lively cheerful manner ~ *vi* **1** : to sing or speak rhythmically and with fluctuating pitch **2** : to move in a lively springy manner

²**lilt** *n* (1635) **1** : a spirited and usu. cheerful song or tune **2** : a rhythmical swing, flow, or cadence **3** : a springy buoyant movement

lilt·ing \'lil-tiŋ\ *adj* (1800) **1** : characterized by a rhythmical swing or cadence ⟨a ~ stride⟩ **2** : CHEERFUL, BUOYANT ⟨a ~ comedy⟩ — **lilt·ing·ly** \-tiŋ-lē\ *adv* — **lilt·ing·ness** *n*

¹**lily** \'lil-ē\ *n, pl* **lil·ies** [ME *lilie*, fr. OE, fr. L *lilium*] (bef. 12c) **1** : any of a genus (*Lilium* of the family Liliaceae, the lily family) of erect perennial leafy-stemmed bulbous herbs that are native to the northern hemisphere and are widely cultivated for their showy flowers; *broadly* : any of various plants of the lily family or of the related amaryllis or iris families **2** : any of various plants with showy flowers: as **a** : a scarlet anemone (*Anemone coronaria*) that grows wild in Palestine **b** : WATER LILY **c** : CALLA LILY **3** : FLEUR-DE-LIS 2

²**lily** *adj* (1500) : resembling a lily in fairness, purity, or fragility ⟨my lady's ~ hand —John Keats⟩

lily–liv·ered \,lil-ē-'liv-ərd\ *adj* (1605) : lacking courage : COWARDLY

lily of the valley (1563) : a low perennial herb (*Convallaria majalis*) of the lily family that has usu. two large oblong lanceolate leaves and a raceme of fragrant nodding bell-shaped white flowers

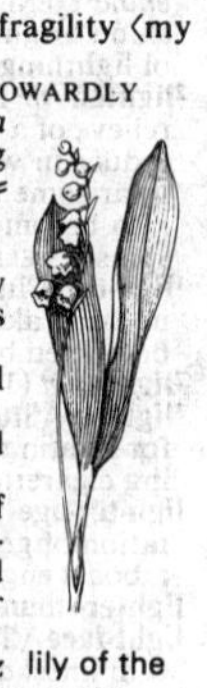

lily of the valley

lily pad *n* (1814) : a floating leaf of a water lily

¹**lily–white** \,lil-ē-'hwīt, -'wīt\ *adj* (14c) **1** : white as a lily **2** : characterized by or favoring the exclusion of blacks esp. from politics **3** : IRREPROACHABLE, PURE

²**lily–white** *n* (ca. 1909) : a member of a lily-white political organization

Li·ma \'lē-mə\ (ca. 1952) — a communications code word for the letter *l*

li·ma bean \,lī-mə-\ *n* [*Lima*, Peru] (1756) **1 a** : any of various bushy or tall-growing beans derived from a perennial tropical American bean (*Phaseolus limensis*) and widely cultivated for their flat edible usu. pale green or whitish seeds **b** : SIEVA BEAN **2** : the seed of a lima bean

li·ma·çon \,lē-mə-'sōⁿ\ *n* [F, lit., snail, fr. OF, dim. of *limaz* slug, snail, fr. L *limax*, fr. Gk *leimax* slug; akin to Gk *leios* smooth — more at LIME] (1874) : a curve that consists of the collection of points obtained by measuring a fixed distance in both directions from the second and variable point of intersection with a circle of a half line that extends from a fixed point on the circle

li·man \li-'män, -'man\ *n* [Russ] (ca. 1858) : a shallow coastal bay or estuary usu. at the mouth of a river : LAGOON

¹**limb** \'lim\ *n* [ME *lim*, fr. OE; akin to ON *limr* limb, L *limes* limit, *limen* threshold, Gk *leimōn* meadow] (bef. 12c) **1** : one of the projecting paired appendages (as wings) of an animal body used esp. for movement and grasping but sometimes modified into sensory or sexual organs; *esp* : a leg or arm of a human being **2** : a large primary branch of a tree **3** : an active member or agent **4** : EXTENSION, BRANCH **5** : a mischievous child — **limb·less** \'lim-ləs\ *adj* — **limby** \'lim-ē\ *adj* — **out on a limb** : in an exposed or dangerous position with little chance of retreat

²**limb** *vt* (1674) **1** : DISMEMBER **2** : to cut off the limbs of (a felled tree)

³**limb** *n* [L *limbus* border — more at LIMP] (14c) **1** : the graduated margin of an arc or circle in an instrument for measuring angles **2** : the outer edge of the apparent disk of a celestial body **3** : the expanded portion of an organ or structure; *esp* : the spreading upper portion of a gamosepalous calyx or a gamopetalous corolla as distinguished from the lower tubular portion

lim·ba \'lim-bə\ *n* [prob. native name in West Africa] (ca. 1937) **1** : a tall whitish-trunked West African tree (*Terminalia superba*) with straight-grained wood **2** : the wood of a limba

lim·beck \'lim-,bek\ *n* [ME *lembike*, fr. ML *alembicum*] (14c) : ALEMBIC

limbed \'limd\ *adj* (14c) : having limbs esp. of a specified kind or number — usu. used in combination ⟨strong-*limbed*⟩

¹**lim·ber** \'lim-bər\ *n* [ME *lymour*] (15c) : a two-wheeled vehicle to which a gun or caisson may be attached

²**limber** *adj* [origin unknown] (1565) **1** : capable of being shaped : FLEXIBLE **2** : having a supple and resilient quality (as of mind or body) : AGILE, NIMBLE — **lim·ber·ly** *adv* — **lim·ber·ness** *n*

³**limber** *vb* **lim·bered; lim·ber·ing** \-b(ə-)riŋ\ *vt* (1748) : to cause to become limber ⟨~ up his fingers⟩ ~ *vi* : to become limber ⟨~ up by running⟩

lim·bers \'lim-bərz\ *n pl* [modif. of F *lumière*, fr. OF, light, opening, fr. L *luminare* window — more at LUMINARY] (1626) : gutters or conduits on each side of the keelson of a ship that provide a passage for water to the pump well

lim·bic \'lim-bik\ *adj* [NL *limbicus* of a border or margin, fr. L *limbus*] (1882) : of, relating to, or being the limbic system of the brain

limbic system *n* (1952) : a group of subcortical structures (as the hypothalamus, the hippocampus, and the amygdala) of the brain that are concerned esp. with emotion and motivation

[1]**lim·bo** \ˈlim-(ˌ)bō\ *n, pl* **limbos** [ME, fr. ML, abl. of *limbus* limbo, fr. L, border — more at LIMP] (14c) **1** *often cap* **:** an abode of souls that are according to Roman Catholic theology barred from heaven because of not having received Christian baptism **2 a :** a place or state of restraint or confinement **b :** a place or state of neglect or oblivion ⟨proposals kept in ~⟩ **c :** an intermediate or transitional place or state

[2]**limbo** *n, pl* **limbos** [native name in West Indies] (ca. 1949) **:** a West Indian acrobatic dance orig. for men that involves bending over backwards and passing under a horizontal pole lowered slightly for each successive pass

Lim·burg·er \ˈlim-ˌbər-gər\ *n* [Flem, one from Limburg, fr. *Limburg*, Belgium] (1817) **:** a pungent semisoft surface-ripened cheese

lim·bus \ˈlim-bəs\ *n* [L, border] (1671) **:** the marginal region of the cornea of the eye by which it is continuous with the sclera

[1]**lime** \ˈlīm\ *n* [ME, fr. OE *līm;* akin to OHG *līm* birdlime, L *linere* to smear, *levis* smooth, Gk *leios*] (bef. 12c) **1 :** BIRDLIME **2 a :** a caustic highly infusible solid that consists of calcium oxide often together with magnesia, that is obtained by calcining forms of calcium carbonate (as shells or limestone), and that is used in building (as in mortar and plaster) and in agriculture — called also *caustic lime* **b :** a dry white powder consisting essentially of calcium hydroxide that is made by treating caustic lime with water **c :** CALCIUM ⟨carbonate of ~⟩

[2]**lime** *vt* **limed; lim·ing** (13c) **1 :** to smear with a sticky substance (as birdlime) **2 :** to entangle with or as if with birdlime **3 :** to treat or cover with lime ⟨~ the lawn in the spring⟩

[3]**lime** *adj* (15c) **:** of, relating to, or containing lime or limestone

[4]**lime** *n* [alter. of ME *lind,* fr. OE; akin to OHG *linta* linden] (bef. 12c) **:** LINDEN 1a

[5]**lime** *n* [F, fr. Prov *limo,* fr. Ar *līm*] (1638) **1 :** the small globose greenish yellow fruit of a lime with an acid juicy pulp used as a flavoring agent and as a source of vitamin C **2 :** a spiny tropical citrus tree (*Citrus aurantifolia*) with elliptic oblong narrowly winged leaves

lime·ade \lī-ˈmād\ *n* (1892) **:** a beverage of sweetened lime juice mixed with plain or carbonated water

lime glass *n* (ca. 1909) **:** glass containing a substantial proportion of lime

lime–juic·er \ˈlīm-ˌjü-sər\ *n* [fr. the use of lime juice on British ships as a beverage to prevent scurvy] (1859) **1** *slang* **a :** a British ship **b :** a British sailor **2** *slang* **:** ENGLISHMAN

lime·kiln \-ˌkil(n)\ *n* (13c) **:** a kiln or furnace for reducing limestone or shells to lime by burning

[1]**lime·light** \-ˌlīt\ *n* (1826) **1 a :** a stage lighting instrument producing illumination by means of an oxyhydrogen flame directed on a cylinder of lime and usu. equipped with a lens to concentrate the light in a beam **b :** the white light produced by such an instrument **c** *Brit* **:** SPOTLIGHT **2 :** the center of public attention

[2]**limelight** *vt* (1909) **:** to center attention on **:** SPOTLIGHT

li·men \ˈlī-mən\ *n* [L *limin-, limen* — more at LIMB] (ca. 1895) **:** THRESHOLD 3a

lim·er·ick \ˈlim-(ə-)rik\ *n* [*Limerick,* Ireland] (1896) **:** a light or humorous verse form of 5 chiefly anapestic verses of which lines 1, 2, and 5 are of 3 feet and lines 3 and 4 are of 2 feet with a rhyme scheme of *aabba*

lime·stone \ˈlīm-ˌstōn\ *n* (14c) **:** a rock that is formed chiefly by accumulation of organic remains (as shells or coral), consists mainly of calcium carbonate, is extensively used in building, and yields lime when burned

lime–twig \ˈlīm-ˌtwig\ *n* (15c) **1 :** a twig covered with birdlime to catch birds **2 :** SNARE

lime·wa·ter \-ˌwȯt-ər, -ˌwät-\ *n* (1500) **1 :** an alkaline water solution of calcium hydroxide used as an antacid **2 :** natural water containing calcium carbonate or calcium sulfate in solution

lim·ey \ˈlī-mē\ *n, pl* **limeys** *often cap* [*lime-*juicer + *-y*] (1918) **1** *slang* **:** a British sailor **2** *slang* **:** ENGLISHMAN

lim·i·nal \ˈlim-ən-ᵊl\ *adj* [L *limin-, limen* threshold] (1884) **1 :** of or relating to a sensory threshold **2 :** barely perceptible

[1]**lim·it** \ˈlim-ət\ *vt* (14c) **1 :** to assign certain limits to **:** PRESCRIBE ⟨reserved the right to ~ use of the land⟩ **2 a :** to restrict to set bounds or limits ⟨the specialist can no longer ~ himself to his specialty⟩ **b :** to curtail or reduce in quantity or extent ⟨we must ~ the power of aggressors⟩ — **lim·it·able** \-ət-ə-bəl\ *adj* — **lim·it·er** *n*

syn LIMIT, RESTRICT, CIRCUMSCRIBE, CONFINE mean to set bounds for. LIMIT implies setting a point or line (as in time, space, speed, or degree) beyond which something cannot or is not permitted to go ⟨visits are *limited* to 30 minutes⟩ RESTRICT suggests a narrowing or tightening or restraining within or as if within an encircling boundary ⟨laws intended to *restrict* the freedom of the press⟩ CIRCUMSCRIBE stresses a restriction on all sides and by clearly defined boundaries ⟨the work of the investigating committee was carefully *circumscribed*⟩ CONFINE suggests severe restraint and a resulting cramping, fettering, or hampering ⟨our freedom of choice was *confined* by finances⟩

[2]**limit** *n* [ME, fr. MF *limite,* fr. L *limit-, limes* boundary — more at LIMB] (15c) **1 a :** a geographical or political boundary **b** *pl* **:** the place enclosed within a boundary **:** BOUNDS **2 a :** something that bounds, restrains, or confines **b :** the utmost extent **3 :** LIMITATION **4 :** a determining feature or differentia in logic **5 :** a prescribed maximum or minimum amount, quantity, or number: as **a :** the maximum quantity of game or fish that may be taken legally in a specified period **b :** a maximum established for a gambling bet, raise, or payoff **6 a :** a number whose numerical difference from a mathematical function is arbitrarily small for all values of the independent variables that are sufficiently close to but not equal to given prescribed numbers or that are sufficiently large positively or negatively **b :** a number that for an infinite sequence of numbers is such that ultimately each of the remaining terms of the sequence differs from this number by less than any given positive amount **7 :** something that is exasperating or intolerable — **lim·it·less** \-ləs\ *adj* — **lim·it·less·ly** *adv* — **lim·it·less·ness** *n*

lim·i·tary \ˈlim-ə-ˌter-ē\ *adj* (1620) **1** *archaic* **:** subject to limits **2 a** *archaic* **:** of or relating to a boundary **b :** LIMITING, ENCLOSING

lim·i·ta·tion \ˌlim-ə-ˈtā-shən\ *n* (14c) **1 :** an act or instance of limiting **2 :** the quality or state of being limited **3 :** something that limits **:** RESTRAINT **4 :** a certain period limited by statute after which actions, suits, or prosecutions cannot be brought in the courts — **lim·i·ta·tion·al** \-shnəl, -shən-ᵊl\ *adj*

lim·i·ta·tive \ˈlim-ə-ˌtāt-iv\ *adj* (1530) **:** LIMITING, RESTRICTIVE

lim·it·ed *adj* (1610) **1 a :** confined within limits **:** RESTRICTED ⟨~ success⟩ **b** *of a train* **(1) :** having a limited number of cars and making a limited number of stops **(2) :** offering superior and faster service and transportation **2 :** characterized by enforceable limitations prescribed (as by a constitution) upon the scope or exercise of powers ⟨a ~ monarchy⟩ **3 :** lacking breadth and originality ⟨a bit ~; a bit thick in the head —Virginia Woolf⟩ — **lim·it·ed·ly** *adv* — **lim·it·ed·ness** *n*

limited–access highway *n* (1944) **:** EXPRESSWAY

limited edition *n* (1903) **:** an issue of something collectible (as books, prints, or medals) that is advertised to be limited to a relatively small number of copies

limited liability *n* (1855) **:** liability (as of a stockholder or shipowner) limited by statute or treaty

limited partner *n* (1907) **:** a partner in a venture who has no management authority and whose liability is restricted to the amount of his investment

limited war *n* (1939) **:** a war whose objective is less than the total defeat of the enemy

lim·it·ing *adj* (1580) **1 :** functioning as a limit **:** RESTRICTIVE ⟨~ factors⟩ **2 :** serving to specify the application of the modified noun ⟨*this* in "this book" is a ~ word⟩ — **lim·it·ing·ly** *adv*

limit point *n* (1905) **:** a point that is related to a set of points in such a way that every neighborhood of the point no matter how small contains another point belonging to the set — called also *point of accumulation*

lim·i·trophe \ˈlim-ə-ˌtrōf, -ˌtrȯf\ *adj* [F, fr. LL *limitrophus* bordering upon, fr. L *limit-, limes* limit + Gk *trophos* feeder, fr. *trephein* to nourish — more at ATROPHY] (1763) **:** situated on a border or frontier **:** ADJACENT

lim·mer \ˈlim-ər\ *n* [ME (Sc)] (15c) **1** *chiefly Scot* **:** SCOUNDREL **2** *chiefly Scot* **:** PROSTITUTE

limn \ˈlim\ *vt* **limned; limn·ing** \lim-(n)iŋ\ [ME *luminen, limnen* to illuminate (a manuscript), fr. MF *enluminer,* fr. L *illuminare* to illuminate] (1592) **1 :** to draw or paint on a surface **2 :** to outline in clear sharp detail **:** DELINEATE **3 :** DESCRIBE — **limn·er** \ˈlim-(n)ər\ *n*

lim·net·ic \lim-ˈnet-ik\ *adj* [ISV, fr. Gk *limnē* pool, marshy lake; akin to L *limen* threshold — more at LIMB] (1899) **:** of, relating to, or inhabiting the open water of a body of fresh water ⟨~ environment⟩

lim·nol·o·gy \lim-ˈnäl-ə-jē\ *n* [Gk *limnē* + ISV *-logy*] (ca. 1875) **:** the scientific study of physical, chemical, meteorological, and biological conditions in fresh waters — **lim·no·log·i·cal** \ˌlim-nə-ˈläj-i-kəl\ *adj* — **lim·nol·o·gist** \lim-ˈnäl-ə-jəst\ *n*

limo \ˈlim-(ˌ)ō\ *n, pl* **lim·os** (1968) **:** LIMOUSINE

Li·moges \li-ˈmōzh\ *n* [*Limoges,* France] (1844) **:** enamelware or porcelain made at Limoges

lim·o·nene \ˈlim-ə-ˌnēn\ *n* [ISV, fr. F *limon* lemon, fr. MF] (1845) **:** a widely distributed terpene hydrocarbon $C_{10}H_{16}$ that occurs in essential oils (as of oranges or lemons) and has a lemon odor

li·mo·nite \ˈlī-mə-ˌnīt\ *n* [G *limonit,* fr. Gk *leimōn* meadow — more at LIMB] (1823) **:** a native hydrous ferric oxide of variable composition that is a major ore of iron — **li·mo·nit·ic** \ˌlī-mə-ˈnit-ik\ *adj*

lim·ou·sine \ˈlim-ə-ˌzēn, ˌlim-ə-ˈ\ *n* [F, lit., cloak, fr. *Limousin,* France] (1902) **1 :** a large luxurious often chauffeur-driven sedan that sometimes has a glass partition separating the driver's seat from the passenger compartment **2 :** a large passenger vehicle with scheduled runs esp. to and from airports

limousine liberal *n* (1969) **:** a wealthy political liberal

[1]**limp** \ˈlimp\ *vi* [prob. fr. ME *lympen* to fall short; akin to OE *limpan* to happen, L *limbus* border, *labi* to slide — more at SLEEP] (ca. 1570) **1 a :** to walk lamely; *esp* **:** to walk favoring one leg **b :** to go unsteadily **:** FALTER **2 :** to proceed slowly or with difficulty ⟨commerce ~*ed* toward a standstill —*Time*⟩ — **limp·er** *n*

[2]**limp** *n* (1818) **:** a limping movement or gait

[3]**limp** *adj* [akin to [1]*limp*] (ca. 1706) **1 a :** lacking firm texture, substance, or structure ⟨~ curtains⟩ ⟨her hair hung ~ about her shoulders⟩ **b :** not stiff or rigid ⟨~ bookbinding⟩ **2 a :** WEARY, EXHAUSTED ⟨~ with fatigue⟩ **b :** lacking in strength, vigor, or firmness **:** SPIRITLESS — **limp·ly** *adv* — **limp·ness** *n*

lim·pa \ˈlim-pə\ *n* [Sw] (1948) **:** rye bread made with molasses or brown sugar

lim·pet \ˈlim-pət\ *n* [ME *lempet,* fr. OE *lempedu,* fr. ML *lampreda* lamprey] (bef. 12c) **1 :** a marine gastropod mollusk (esp. families Acmaeidae and Patellidae) that has a low conical shell broadly open beneath, browses over rocks or timbers in the littoral area, and clings very tightly when disturbed **2 :** one that clings tenaciously to someone or something **3 :** an explosive designed to cling to the hull of a ship

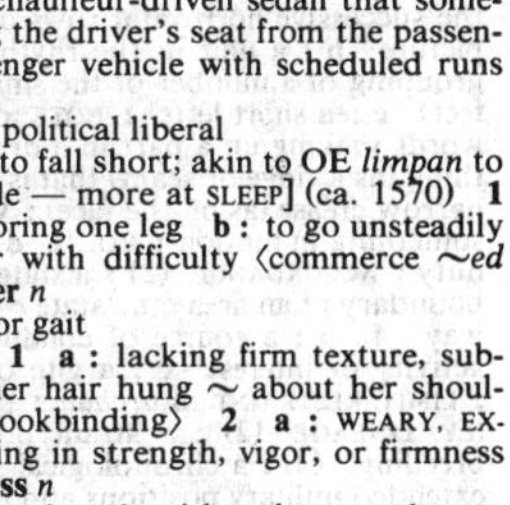

limpet 1

lim·pid \ˈlim-pəd\ *adj* [F or L; F *limpide,* fr. L *limpidus,* fr. *lympha, limpa* water — more at LYMPH] (14c) **1 a :** marked by transparency **:** PELLUCID ⟨~ streams⟩ **b :** clear and simple in style ⟨~ prose⟩ **2 :** absolutely serene and untroubled **syn** see CLEAR — **lim·pid·i·ty** \lim-ˈpid-ət-ē\ *n* — **lim·pid·ly** \ˈlim-pəd-lē\ *adv* — **lim·pid·ness** *n*

limp·kin \ˈlim(p)-kən\ *n* [[1]*limp*] (1883) **:** a large brown wading bird (*Aramus pictus*) of Florida and southern Georgia that resembles a bittern but has a longer slightly curved bill, longer neck and legs, and white stripes on head and neck

\ə\ abut \ᵊ\ kitten, F table \ər\ further \a\ ash \ā\ ace \ä\ cot, cart
\au̇\ out \ch\ chin \e\ bet \ē\ easy \g\ go \i\ hit \ī\ ice \j\ job
\ŋ\ sing \ō\ go \ȯ\ law \ȯi\ boy \th\ thin \t͟h\ the \ü\ loot \u̇\ foot
\y\ yet \zh\ vision \à, k̲, ⁿ, œ, œ̄, ue, ue̅, ʸ\ *see* Guide to Pronunciation

limp–wrist·ed \(ˌ)lim-ˈpris-təd\ *adj* (1966) **1 :** EFFEMINATE **2 :** WEAK

lim·u·lus \ˈlim-yə-ləs\ *n, pl* **-li** \-ˌlī, -ˌlē\ [NL, genus name, fr. L *limus* sidelong] (1837) **:** HORSESHOE CRAB

limy \ˈlī-mē\ *adj* **lim·i·er; -est** (ca. 1552) **1 :** smeared with or consisting of lime **:** VISCOUS **2 :** containing lime or limestone **3 :** resembling or having the qualities of lime

lin·ac \ˈlin-ˌak\ *n* (1950) **:** LINEAR ACCELERATOR

lin·age \ˈlī-nij\ *n* (1884) **:** the number of lines of printed or written matter

lin·alo·ol \lə-ˈnal-ə-ˌwȯl, lī-, -ˌwōl\ *n* [ISV, fr. MexSp *lináloe,* tree yielding perfume, fr. ML *lignum aloes,* lit., wood of the aloe] (1891) **:** a fragrant liquid alcohol $C_{10}H_{18}O$ that occurs both free and in the form of esters in many essential oils and is used in perfumes, soaps, and flavoring materials

linch·pin \ˈlinch-ˌpin\ *n* [ME *lynspin,* fr. *lyns* linchpin (fr. OE *lynis*) + *pin;* akin to OE *eln* ell] (13c) **1 :** a locking pin inserted crosswise (as through the end of an axle or shaft) **2 :** one that serves to hold together the elements of a complex ⟨the ~ in the prosecution's case was a subpoenaed canceled check —Joel Sayre⟩

Lin·coln \ˈliŋ-kən\ *n* [*Lincoln*shire, England] (1837) **:** any of an English breed of long-wool mutton-type sheep

Lin·coln·i·a·na \(ˌ)liŋ-ˌkō-nē-ˈän-ə, -ˈan-ə, -ˈā-nə\ *n pl* (1921) **:** materials relating to Abraham Lincoln

Lincoln's Birthday \ˌliŋ-kənz-\ *n* (1898) **1 :** February 12 observed as a legal holiday in many states of the U.S. **2 :** the first Monday in February observed as a legal holiday by some states of the U.S.

lin·co·my·cin \ˌliŋ-kə-ˈmīs-ᵊn\ *n* [*linco-* (fr. *Streptomyces lincolnensis*) + *-mycin*] (1963) **:** an antibiotic obtained from an actinomycete (*Streptomyces lincolnensis*) and effective esp. against cocci

lin·dane \ˈlin-ˌdān\ *n* [T. van der *Linden,* 20th cent. Du. chemist] (ca. 1949) **:** an insecticide that consists chiefly of the gamma isomer of BHC and is biodegraded very slowly

lin·den \ˈlin-dən\ *n* [ME, made of linden wood, fr. OE, fr. *lind* linden tree; prob. akin to OE *līthe* gentle — more at LITHE] (bef. 12c) **1 :** any of a genus (*Tilia* of the family Tiliaceae, the linden family) of trees that are native in temperate regions, are planted as shade trees, and are distinguished by having cordate leaves and a winglike bract attached to the peduncle of the flower and fruit: as **a :** a European tree (*T. europaea*) much used for ornamental planting **b :** a tall No. American forest tree (*T. americana*) — called also *basswood, whitewood* **2 :** the light fine-grained white wood of a linden; *esp* **:** BASSWOOD

lin·dy \ˈlin-dē\ *n* [prob. fr. *Lindy,* nickname of Charles A. Lindbergh] (1931) **:** a jitterbug dance originating in Harlem and later developing many local variants

¹line \ˈlīn\ *n, often attrib* [ME; partly fr. OF *ligne,* fr. L *linea,* fr. fem. of *lineus* made of flax, fr. *linum* flax; partly fr. OE *līne;* akin to OE *līn*] (bef. 12c) **1 a :** THREAD, STRING, CORD, ROPE: as **(1) :** a comparatively strong slender cord **(2) :** CLOTHESLINE **(3) :** a rope used on shipboard **b (1) :** a device for catching fish consisting of a cord with hooks and other fishing gear **(2) :** scope for activity **c :** a length of material used in measuring and leveling **d :** piping for conveying a fluid (as steam) **e (1) :** a wire or pair of wires connecting one telegraph or telephone station with another or a whole system of such wires; *also* **:** any circuit in an electronic communication system **(2) :** a telephone connection ⟨tried to get a ~⟩; *also* **:** an individual telephone extension ⟨a call on ~ 2⟩ **(3) :** the principal circuits of an electric power system **2 a :** a horizontal row of written or printed characters; *also* **:** any of the successive horizontal rows of elements that constitute a television picture **b :** a unit in the rhythmic structure of verse formed by the grouping of a number of the smallest units of the rhythm (as metrical feet) **c :** a short letter **:** NOTE **d** *pl* **:** a certificate of marriage **e :** the words making up a part in a drama — usu. used in pl. **3 a :** something (as a ridge or seam) that is distinct, elongated, and narrow **b :** a narrow crease (as on the face) **:** WRINKLE **c :** the course or direction of something in motion **:** ROUTE **d (1) :** a state of agreement or conformity **:** ACCORDANCE **(2) :** a state of order, control, or obedience **e :** a boundary of an area ⟨the state ~⟩ **f :** the track and roadbed of a railway **4 a :** a course of conduct, action, or thought **b :** a field of activity or interest **c :** a glib often persuasive way of talking **5 a :** LIMIT, RESTRAINT **b** *archaic* **:** position in life **:** LOT **6 a (1) :** FAMILY, LINEAGE **(2) :** a strain produced and maintained by selective breeding **(3) :** a chronological series **b :** dispositions made to cover extended military positions and presenting a front to the enemy — usu. used in pl. **c :** a military formation in which the different elements are abreast of each other **d :** naval ships arranged in a regular order **e (1) :** the combatant forces of an army distinguished from the staff corps and supply services **(2) :** the force of a regular navy **f (1) :** officers of the navy eligible for command at sea distinguished from officers of the staff **(2) :** officers of the army belonging to a combatant branch **g :** an arrangement or placement of persons or objects of one kind in an orderly series ⟨a ~ of trees⟩ ⟨waiting in ~⟩; *also* **:** the persons or objects so positioned ⟨the ~ moved slowly at the bank⟩ **h (1) :** a group of public conveyances plying regularly under one management over a route **(2) :** a system of transportation together with its equipment, routes, and appurtenances; *also* **:** the company owning or operating it **i :** a succession of musical notes esp. considered in melodic phrases **j (1) :** an arrangement of operations in manufacturing permitting sequential occurrence on various stages of production **(2) :** the personnel of an organization that are responsible for its stated objective **k (1) :** the 7 players including center, 2 guards, 2 tackles, and 2 ends who in offensive football play line up on or within one foot of the line of scrimmage **(2) :** the players who in defensive play line up within one yard of the line of scrimmage **7 :** a narrow elongated mark drawn or projected: as **a (1) :** a circle of latitude or longitude on a map **(2) :** EQUATOR **b :** a mark (as on a map) recording a boundary, division, or contour **c :** any of the horizontal parallel strokes on a music staff on or between which notes are placed — compare SPACE **d :** a mark (as by pencil) that forms part of the formal design of a picture distinguished from the shading or color **e :** a division on a bridge score dividing the score for bonuses from that for tricks **f (1) :** a demarcation of a limit with reference to which the playing of some game or sport is regulated — usu. used in combination **(2) :** a marked or imaginary line across a playing area (as a football field) parallel to the end line **(3) :** LINE OF SCRIMMAGE **8 :** a straight or curved geometric element that is generated by a moving point and that has extension only along the path of the point **:** CURVE **9 a :** a defining outline **:** CONTOUR **b :** a general plan **:** MODEL — usu. used in pl. **10 a** *chiefly Brit* **:** PICA — used to indicate the size of large type **b :** the unit of fineness of halftones expressed as the number of screen lines to the linear inch **11 :** merchandise or services of the same general class for sale or regularly available **12 :** a source of information **:** INSIGHT **13 :** a complete game of 10 frames in bowling — called also *string* **14 :** LINE DRIVE — **liny** *also* **lin·ey** \ˈlī-nē\ *adj* — **between the lines 1 :** by implication **:** in an indirect way **2 :** by way of inference — **down the line :** all the way **:** FULLY — **in line for :** due or in a position to receive — **on line :** in or into operation — **on the line 1 :** in complete commitment and at great risk ⟨puts his future *on the line* by backing that policy⟩ **2 :** on the border between two categories **3 :** IMMEDIATELY ⟨paid cash *on the line*⟩

²line *vb* **lined; lin·ing** *vt* (1530) **1 :** to mark or cover with a line or lines **2 :** to depict with lines **:** DRAW **3 :** to place or form a line along ⟨pedestrians ~ the walks⟩ **4 :** to form into a line or lines **:** ALIGN ⟨~ up troops⟩ **5 :** to hit (as a baseball) hard and in a usu. straight line ~ *vi* **1 :** to hit a line drive in baseball **2 :** to come into the correct relative position **:** ALIGN

³line *vt* **lined; lin·ing** [ME *linen,* fr. *line* flax, fr. OE *līn* — more at LINEN] (14c) **1 :** to cover the inner surface of ⟨~ a cloak with silk⟩ **2 :** to put something in the inside of **:** FILL **3 :** to serve as the lining of ⟨tapestries *lined* the walls⟩ **4** *obs* **:** FORTIFY — **line one's pockets :** to take money freely and esp. dishonestly

¹lin·eage \ˈlin-ē-ij *also* ˈlin-ij\ *n* (14c) **1 a :** descent in a line from a common progenitor **b :** DERIVATION **2 :** a group of individuals tracing descent from a common ancestor; *esp* **:** such a group of persons whose common ancestor is regarded as its founder

²line·age \ˈlī-nij\ *var of* LINAGE

lin·eal \ˈlin-ē-əl\ *adj* (14c) **1 :** LINEAR **2 :** composed of or arranged in lines **3 a :** consisting of or being in a direct male or female line of ancestry **b :** relating to or derived from ancestors **:** HEREDITARY **c :** descended in a direct line **4 a :** belonging to one lineage ⟨~ relatives⟩ **b :** of, relating to, or dealing with a lineage — **lin·eal·i·ty** \ˌlin-ē-ˈal-ət-ē\ *n* — **lin·eal·ly** \ˈlin-ē-ə-lē\ *adv*

lin·ea·ment \ˈlin-ē-ə-mənt\ *n* [ME, fr. L *lineamentum,* fr. *linea*] (15c) **1 a :** an outline, feature, or contour of a body or figure and esp. of a face — usu. used in pl. **b :** a linear topographic feature (as of the earth or a planet) that reveals a characteristic (as a fault or the subsurface structure) **2 :** a distinguishing or characteristic feature — usu. used in pl. — **lin·ea·men·tal** \ˌlin-ē-ə-ˈment-ᵊl\ *adj*

lin·ear \ˈlin-ē-ər\ *adj* (1706) **1 a (1) :** of, relating to, resembling, or having a graph that is a line and esp. a straight line **:** STRAIGHT **(2) :** involving a single dimension **b (1) :** of the first degree with respect to one or more variables **(2) :** of, relating to, based on, or being linear equations, linear differential equations, linear functions, linear transformations, or linear algebra **c (1) :** characterized by an emphasis on line ⟨~ art⟩ **(2) :** composed of simply drawn lines with little attempt at pictorial representation ⟨~ script⟩ **d :** consisting of a straight chain of atoms **2 :** elongated with nearly parallel sides ⟨~ leaf⟩ **3 :** having or being a response or output that is directly proportional to the input **4 :** of, relating to, or based or depending on sequential development ⟨~ thinking⟩ ⟨a ~ narrative⟩ — **lin·ear·i·ty** \ˌlin-ē-ˈar-ət-ē\ *n* — **lin·ear·ly** \ˈlin-ē-ər-lē\ *adv*

Linear A \-ˈā\ *n* (1948) **:** a linear form of writing used in Crete from the 18th to the 15th centuries B.C.

linear accelerator *n* (1945) **:** a device in which charged particles are accelerated in a straight line by successive impulses from a series of electric fields

linear algebra *n* (ca. 1891) **1 :** a branch of mathematics that is concerned with mathematical structures closed under the operations of addition and scalar multiplication and with their applications and that includes the theory of systems of linear equations, matrices, determinants, vector spaces, and linear transformations **2 :** a mathematical ring which is also a vector space with scalars from an associated field and whose multiplicative operation is such that $(aA)(bB) = (ab)(AB)$ where a and b are scalars and A and B are vectors — called also *algebra*

Linear B \-ˈbē\ *n* (1948) **:** a linear form of writing employing syllabic characters and used at Knossos on Crete and on the Greek mainland from the 15th to the 12th centuries B.C. for documents in the Mycenaean language

linear combination *n* (1960) **:** a mathematical entity (as $4x + 5y + 6z$) which is composed of sums and differences of elements (as variables, matrices, or functions) whose coefficients are not all zero

linear dependence *n* (1955) **:** the property of one set (as of matrices or vectors) of having at least one linear combination of its elements equal to zero when the coefficients are taken from another given set and at least one of its coefficients is not equal to zero — **linearly dependent** *adj*

linear differential equation *n* (ca. 1890) **:** a differential equation of the first degree with respect to the dependent variable or variables and their derivatives

linear equation *n* (1816) **:** an equation of the first degree in any number of variables

linear function *n* (ca. 1889) **1 :** a mathematical function in which the variables appear only in the first degree, are multiplied by constants, and are combined only by addition and subtraction **2 :** LINEAR TRANSFORMATION

linear independence *n* (1967) **:** the property of a set (as of matrices or vectors) of having no linear combination of all its elements equal to zero when coefficients are taken from a given set unless the coefficient of each element is zero — **linearly independent** *adj*

lin·ear·ize \ˈlin-ē-ə-ˌrīz\ *vt* **-ized; -iz·ing** (1895) **:** to give a linear form to; *also* **:** to project in linear form — **lin·ear·iza·tion** \ˌlin-ē-ə-rə-ˈzā-shən\ *n*

linear measure *n* (ca. 1890) **1 :** a measure of length **2 :** a system of measures of length

linear motor *n* (1957) **:** a motor that produces thrust in a straight line by direct induction rather than with the use of gears

linear perspective *n* (1656) **:** representation in a drawing or painting of parallel lines as converging in order to give the illusion of depth and distance

linear programming *n* (1949) **:** a mathematical method of solving practical problems (as the allocation of resources) by means of linear functions where the variables involved are subject to constraints
linear space *n* (ca. 1895) **:** VECTOR SPACE
linear transformation *n* (ca. 1890) **1 :** a transformation in which the new variables are linear functions of the old variables **2 :** a function that maps the vectors of one vector space onto the vectors of the same or another vector space with the same field of scalars in such a way that the image of the sum of two vectors equals the sum of their images and the image of the product of a scalar and a vector equals the product of the scalar and the image of the vector
lin·ea·tion \ˌlin-ē-ˈā-shən\ *n* [ME *lineacion* outline, fr. L *lineation-, lineatio,* fr. *lineatus,* pp. of *lineare* to make straight, fr. *linea*] (14c) **1 a :** the action of marking with lines **:** DELINEATION **b :** OUTLINE **2 :** an arrangement of lines
line·back·er \ˈlīn-ˌbak-ər\ *n* (1949) **:** a defensive football player who lines up immediately behind the line of scrimmage to make tackles on running plays through the line or defend against short passes
line·back·ing \-ˌbak-iŋ\ *n* (1953) **:** the action or art of playing linebacker
line·breed·ing \ˈlīn-ˈbrēd-iŋ\ *n* (ca. 1879) **:** the interbreeding of individuals within a particular line of descent usu. to perpetuate desirable characters
line·cast·er \-ˌkas-tər\ *n* (1964) **:** a machine that casts metal type in lines — **line·cast·ing** \-tiŋ\ *n*
line chief *n* (ca. 1944) **:** an air force noncommissioned officer who supervises flight-line upkeep
line·cut \ˈlīn-ˌkət\ *n* (ca. 1902) **:** a photoengraving of a line drawing
line drawing *n* (1891) **:** a drawing made in solid lines
line drive *n* (1912) **:** a batted baseball hit in a nearly straight line usu. not far above the ground
line engraving *n* (1802) **:** an engraving cut by hand directly in the plate
line gauge *n* (ca. 1923) **:** a printer's ruler showing point sizes
line graph *n* (ca. 1924) **:** a graph in which points representing values of a variable for suitable values of an independent variable are connected by a broken line
line–haul \ˈlīn-ˌhȯl\ *n* (ca. 1923) **:** the transporting of items or persons between terminals
line judge *n* (1970) **:** a football linesman whose duties include keeping track of the official time for the game
line·man \ˈlīn-mən\ *n* (1876) **1 :** one who sets up or repairs electric wire communication or power lines — called also *linesman* **2 :** a player in the forward line of a team; *specif* **:** a football player in the line
[1]**lin·en** \ˈlin-ən\ *adj* [ME, fr. OE *līnen,* fr. *līn* flax, fr. L *linum* flax; akin to Gk *linon* flax, thread] (bef. 12c) **1 :** made of flax **2 :** made of or resembling linen
[2]**linen** *n* (14c) **1 a :** cloth made of flax and noted for its strength, coolness, and luster **b :** thread or yarn spun from flax **2 :** clothing or household articles made of linen cloth or similar fabric **3 :** paper made from linen fibers or with a linen finish
line of credit (1917) **:** the maximum credit allowed a buyer or borrower
line of duty (ca. 1918) **:** all that is authorized, required, or normally associated with some field of responsibility
line officer *n* (1850) **:** a commissioned officer assigned to the line of the army or navy — compare STAFF OFFICER
line of force (1873) **:** a line in a field of force (as a magnetic or electric field) whose tangent at any point gives the direction of the field at that point
line of scrimmage (ca. 1909) **:** an imaginary line in football that is parallel to the goal lines and tangent to the nose of the ball laid on the ground and that marks the position of the ball at the start of each down
line of sight (1559) **1 :** a line from an observer's eye to a distant point toward which he is looking **2 :** the straight path between a radio or television transmitting antenna and receiving antenna when unobstructed by the horizon
line out *vt* (1618) **1 :** to indicate with or as if with lines **:** OUTLINE ⟨*line out* a route⟩ **2 a :** to plant (young nursery stock) in rows **b :** to arrange in an extended line **3 :** BELT ⟨*line out* a song⟩ ~ *vi* **1 :** to move rapidly ⟨*lined out* for home⟩ **2 :** to make an out by hitting a baseball in a line drive that is caught
line printer *n* (1955) **:** a high-speed printing device (as for a computer) that prints each line as a unit rather than character by character
[1]**lin·er** \ˈlī-nər\ *n* (15c) **1 :** one that makes, draws, or uses lines **2 a :** a ship belonging to a regular line **b :** an airplane belonging to an airline **3 :** LINE DRIVE **4 :** something with which lines are made
[2]**liner** *n* (1611) **1 :** one that lines or is used to line or back something **2 :** JACKET 3c(2) — **lin·er·less** \-ləs\ *adj*
li·ner·board \ˈlī-nər-ˌbō(ə)rd, -ˌbȯ(ə)rd\ *n* (1948) **:** a thin paperboard used for the flat facings of corrugated containerboard
liner notes *n pl* (1955) **:** comments or explanatory notes about a recording printed on the jacket or an insert
line score *n* (1946) **:** a score of a baseball game giving the runs, hits, and errors made by each team — compare BOX SCORE
lines·man \ˈlīnz-mən\ *n* (1883) **1 :** LINEMAN 1 **2 :** an official who assists a referee in various games (as football or hockey) esp. in determining if a ball, puck, or player is out-of-bounds or offside
line squall *n* (ca. 1887) **:** a squall or thunderstorm occurring along a cold front
line storm *n* (1850) **:** an equinoctial storm
line·up \ˈlī-ˌnəp\ *n* (1889) **1 a :** a list of players taking part in a game (as of baseball) **b :** the players on such a list **2 a :** an alignment of persons or things having a common purpose or interest **b :** LINE 11 **c :** a television programming schedule **3 :** a line of persons arranged esp. for inspection or for identification by police
line up \(ˈ)lī-ˈnəp\ *vi* (1864) **1 :** to assume an orderly linear arrangement ⟨*line up* for inspection⟩ **2 :** to align oneself ⟨he *lined up* with the liberals against the bill⟩ ~ *vt* **1 :** to put into alignment **2 :** to arrange for ⟨*line up* support for a candidate⟩
[1]**ling** \ˈliŋ\ *n* [ME; akin to D *leng* ling, OE *lang* long] (13c) **1 :** any of various fishes (as a hake or burbot) of the cod family (Gadidae) **2 :** LINGCOD
[2]**ling** *n* [ME, fr. ON *lyng;* akin to Lith *lenkti* to bend — more at -LING] (13c) **:** a heath plant; *esp* **:** a common Old World heather (*Calluna vulgaris*)
[1]**-ling** \liŋ\ *n suffix* [ME, fr. OE; akin to OE *-ing*] **1 :** one connected with or having the quality of ⟨hire*ling*⟩ **2 :** young, small, or inferior one ⟨duck*ling*⟩
[2]**-ling** \liŋ\ *or* **-lings** \liŋz\ *adv suffix* [ME *-ling* (fr. OE), *-linges* (fr. *-ling* + *-es* -s); akin to OHG *-lingūn* -ling, Lith *lenkti* to bend] **:** in (such) a direction or manner ⟨side*ling*⟩ ⟨flat*lings*⟩
Lin·ga·la \liŋ-ˈgäl-ə\ *n* (1922) **:** a Bantu language widely used in trade and public affairs in the Congo river area
lin·gam \ˈliŋ-gəm\ *or* **lin·ga** \-gə\ *n* [Skt *liṅga* (nom. *liṅgam*), lit., characteristic] (1719) **:** a stylized phallic symbol of the masculine cosmic principle and of the Hindu god Siva — compare YONI
Lin·ga·yat \liŋ-ˈgä-yət\ *n* [Kannada *lingāyata*] (1673) **:** a member of a Saiva sect of southern India marked by wearing of the lingam and characterized by denial of caste distinctions
ling·cod \ˈliŋ-ˌkäd\ *n* (ca. 1888) **:** a large greenish-fleshed fish (*Ophiodon elongatus*) of the Pacific coast of No. America that is an important food fish and belongs to the same family as the greenlings
lin·ger \ˈliŋ-gər\ *vb* **lin·gered; lin·ger·ing** \-g(ə-)riŋ\ [ME (northern dial.) *lengeren* to dwell, freq. of *lengen* to prolong, fr. OE *lengan;* akin to OE *lang* long] *vi* (14c) **1 :** to be slow in parting or in quitting something **:** TARRY **2 a :** to remain alive although gradually dying **b :** to remain existent although waning in strength, importance, or influence **3 :** to be slow to act **:** PROCRASTINATE **4 :** to move slowly **:** SAUNTER ~ *vt* **1** *obs* **:** DELAY **2 :** to pass (as a period of time) slowly — **lin·ger·er** \-gər-ər\ *n* — **lin·ger·ing·ly** \-g(ə-)riŋ-lē\ *adv*
lin·ge·rie \ˌlän-jə-ˈrā, ˌläⁿ-zhə-, -ˈrē; ˈlaⁿ-zhə-(ˌ)rē, ˈlän-jə-, ˈläⁿ-zhə-, -ˌrā\ *n* [F, fr. MF, fr. *linge* linen, fr. L *lineus* made of linen — more at LINE] (1835) **1** *archaic* **:** linen articles or garments **2 :** women's intimate apparel — **lingerie** *adj*
lin·go \ˈliŋ-(ˌ)gō\ *n, pl* **lingoes** [prob. fr. Prov, tongue, fr. L *lingua* — more at TONGUE] (1660) **:** strange or incomprehensible language or speech: as **a :** a foreign language **b :** the special vocabulary of a particular field of interest **c :** language characteristic of an individual
ling·on·ber·ry \ˈliŋ-ən-ˌber-ē\ *n* [Sw *lingon* mountain cranberry; akin to ON *lyng* ling] (1920) **:** the fruit of the mountain cranberry; *also* **:** MOUNTAIN CRANBERRY
lingu- *or* **lingui-** *or* **linguo-** *comb form* [L *lingu-,* fr. *lingua*] **1 :** language ⟨*lingu*ist⟩ **2 :** tongue ⟨*lingui*form⟩
lin·gua \ˈliŋ-gwə\ *n, pl* **lin·guae** \-ˌgwē, -ˌgwī\ [L — more at TONGUE] (ca. 1826) **:** a tongue or an organ resembling a tongue
lin·gua fran·ca \ˌliŋ-gwə-ˈfraŋ-kə\ *n, pl* **lingua francas** *or* **lin·guae fran·cae** \-gwē-ˈfraŋ-(ˌ)kē\ [It, lit., Frankish language] (1619) **1 :** a common language that consists of Italian mixed with French, Spanish, Greek, and Arabic and is spoken in Mediterranean ports **2 :** any of various languages used as common or commercial tongues among peoples of diverse speech **3 :** something resembling a common language
lin·gual \ˈliŋ-g(yə-)wəl\ *adj* (15c) **1 a :** of, relating to, or resembling the tongue **b :** lying near or next to the tongue; *esp* **:** relating to or being the surface of tooth next to the tongue **c :** produced by the tongue **2 :** LINGUISTIC — **lin·gual·ly** \-ē\ *adv*
lin·gui·ne *or* **lin·gui·ni** \liŋ-ˈgwē-nē\ *n* [It, pl. of *linguina,* dim. of *lingua* tongue, fr. L] (ca. 1948) **:** thin flat pasta
lin·guist \ˈliŋ-gwəst\ *n* (1591) **1 :** a person accomplished in languages; *esp* **:** one who speaks several languages **2 :** one who specializes in linguistics
lin·guis·tic \liŋ-ˈgwis-tik\ *also* **lin·guis·ti·cal** \-ti-kəl\ *adj* (1846) **:** of or relating to language or linguistics — **lin·guis·ti·cal·ly** \-ti-k(ə-)lē\ *adv*
linguistic analysis *n* (1945) **:** PHILOSOPHICAL ANALYSIS
linguistic atlas *n* (1923) **:** a publication containing a set of maps on which speech variations are recorded — called also *dialect atlas*
linguistic form *n* (1921) **:** a meaningful unit of speech (as a morpheme, word, or sentence) — called also *speech form*
linguistic geography *n* (1926) **:** local or regional variations of a language or dialect studied as a field of knowledge — called also *dialect geography* — **linguistic geographer** *n*
lin·guis·ti·cian \ˌliŋ-gwə-ˈstish-ən\ *n* (1895) **:** LINGUIST 2
lin·guis·tics \liŋ-ˈgwis-tiks\ *n pl but sing in constr* (ca. 1847) **:** the study of human speech including the units, nature, structure, and modification of language — compare PHILOLOGY
lin·i·ment \ˈlin-ə-mənt\ *n* [ME, fr. LL *linimentum,* fr. L *linere* to smear — more at LIME] (15c) **:** a liquid or semiliquid preparation that is applied to the skin as an anodyne or a counterirritant
lin·ing \ˈlī-niŋ\ *n* (14c) **1 :** material that lines or that is used to line esp. the inner surface of something (as a garment) **2 :** the act or process of providing something with a lining
[1]**link** \ˈliŋk\ *vt* (14c) **:** to couple or connect by or as if by a link ~ *vi* **:** to become connected by or as if by a link ***syn*** see JOIN — **link·er** *n*
[2]**link** *n* [ME, of Scand origin; akin to ON *hlekkr* chain; akin to OE *hlanc* lank] (15c) **1 :** a connecting structure: as **a** (1) **:** a single ring or division of a chain (2) **:** one of the standardized divisions of a surveyor's chain that is 7.92 inches (20.1 centimeters) long and serves as a measure of length **b :** CUFF LINK **c :** BOND 3c **d :** an intermediate rod or piece for transmitting force or motion; *esp* **:** a short connecting rod with a hole or pin at each end **e :** the fusible member of an electrical fuse **2 :** something analogous to a link of chain: as **a :** a segment of sausage in a chain **b :** a connecting element or factor ⟨sought a ~ between smoking and cancer⟩ **c :** a unit in a communication system **d :** an identifier attached to an element (as an index term) in a system in order to indicate or permit connection with other similarly identified elements
[3]**link** *n* [perh. modif. of ML *linchinus* candle, alter. of L *lychnus,* fr. Gk *lychnos;* akin to Gk *leukos* white — more at LIGHT] (1526) **:** a torch formerly used to light a person's way through the streets
[4]**link** *vi* [origin unknown] *Scot* (1715) **:** to skip smartly along
link·age \ˈliŋ-kij\ *n* (1874) **1 :** the manner or style of being united: as **a :** the manner in which atoms or radicals are linked in a molecule **b**

\ə\ abut \ᵊ\ kitten, F table \ər\ further \a\ ash \ā\ ace \ä\ cot, cart \au̇\ out \ch\ chin \e\ bet \ē\ easy \g\ go \i\ hit \ī\ ice \j\ job \ŋ\ sing \ō\ go \ȯ\ law \ȯi\ boy \th\ thin \t͟h\ the \ü\ loot \u̇\ foot \y\ yet \zh\ vision \à, k̲, ⁿ, œ, œ̄, ue, ue̅, ʸ\ *see* Guide to Pronunciation

: BOND 3c **2** : the quality or state of being linked; *esp* : the relationship between genes on the same chromosome that causes them to be inherited together **3 a** : a system of links; *esp* : a system of links or bars which are jointed together and more or less constrained by having a link or links fixed and by means of which straight or nearly straight lines or other point paths may be traced **b** : the product of the magnetic flux through an electrical coil by its number of turns with the magnetic flux and the coil being connected like two links of a chain **4** : LINK 2b

linkage group *n* (1921) : a set of genes at different loci on the same chromosome that except for crossing-over tend to act as a single pair of genes in meiosis instead of undergoing independent assortment

link·boy \ˈliŋk-ˌbȯi\ *n* (1660) : an attendant formerly employed to bear a light for a person on the streets at night

linked \ˈliŋ(k)t\ *adj* (15c) **1** : marked by linkage and esp. genetic linkage ⟨~ genes⟩ **2** : having or provided with links ⟨a ~ list⟩

linking verb *n* (1923) : a word or expression (as a form of *be, become, feel,* or *seem*) that links a subject with its predicate

link·man \ˈliŋk-mən\ *n* (1716) **1** : LINKBOY **2** *Brit* : a broadcasting moderator or anchorman

links \ˈliŋ(k)s\ *n pl* [ME, fr. OE *hlincas,* pl. of *hlinc* ridge; akin to OE *hlanc* lank] (bef. 12c) **1** *Scot* : sand hills esp. along the seashore **2** : GOLF COURSE

links·man \ˈliŋ(k)-smən\ *n* (1937) : one who plays golf

link–up \ˈliŋ-ˌkəp\ *n* (1945) **1** : establishment of contact : MEETING ⟨the ~ of two spacecraft⟩ **2 a** : something that serves as a linking device or factor **b** : a functional whole resulting from the linking up of separate elements ⟨an instructional TV ~⟩

linn \ˈlin\ *n* [ScGael *linne* pool] (1513) **1** *chiefly Scot* : WATERFALL **2** *chiefly Scot* : PRECIPICE

Lin·nae·an *or* **Lin·ne·an** \lə-ˈnē-ən, -ˈnā-; ˈlin-ē-\ *adj* [NL Carolus *Linnaeus* (Carl von Linné)] (1753) : of, relating to, or following the systematic methods of the Swedish botanist Linné who established the system of binomial nomenclature

lin·net \ˈlin-ət\ *n* [MF *linette,* fr. *lin* flax, fr. L *linum;* fr. its feeding on flax seeds] (1530) : a common small Old World finch (*Carduelis cannabina*) having plumage that varies greatly according to age, sex, and season

li·no \ˈlī-(ˌ)nō\ *n, pl* **linos** *chiefly Brit* (1907) : LINOLEUM

li·no·cut \ˈlī-nō-ˌkət\ *n* (1907) : a print made from a design cut into a mounted piece of linoleum

li·no·le·ate \lə-ˈnō-lē-ˌāt\ *n* (1865) : a salt or ester of linoleic acid

lin·ole·ic acid \ˌlin-ə-ˌlē-ik-, -ˌlā-\ *n* [Gk *linon* flax + ISV *oleic (acid)*] (1857) : a liquid unsaturated fatty acid $C_{18}H_{32}O_2$ found in drying and semidrying oils (as linseed or peanut oil) and essential for the nutrition of some animals

lin·ole·nic acid \-ˌlē-nik-, -ˌlā-\ *n* [ISV, irreg. fr. *linoleic*] (1887) : a liquid unsaturated fatty acid $C_{18}H_{30}O_2$ found esp. in drying oils (as linseed oil) and essential for the nutrition of some animals

li·no·leum \lə-ˈnō-lē-əm, -ˈnōl-yəm\ *n, often attrib* [L *linum* flax + *oleum* oil — more at OIL] (1878) **1** : a floor covering made by laying on a burlap or canvas backing a mixture of solidified linseed oil with gums, cork dust or wood flour or both, and usu. pigments **2** : a material similar to linoleum

Li·no·type \ˈlī-nə-ˌtīp\ *trademark* — used for a keyboard-operated typesetting machine that uses circulating matrices and produces each line of type in the form of a solid metal slug

lin·sang \ˈlin-ˌsaŋ\ *n* [Malay] (1821) : either of two Asian mammals (*Prionodon pardicolor* and *P. linsang*) that resemble long-tailed cats and are related to the civets and genets; *also* : a related mammal (*Poiana richardsoni*) of Africa

lin·seed \ˈlin-ˌsēd\ *n* [ME, fr. OE *līnsǣd,* fr. *līn* flax + *sǣd* seed — more at LINEN] (bef. 12c) : FLAXSEED

linseed oil *n* (15c) : a yellowish drying oil obtained from flaxseed and used esp. in paint, varnish, printing ink, and linoleum

lin·sey–wool·sey \ˌlin-zē-ˈwu̇l-zē\ *n* [ME *lynsy wolsye*] (15c) : a coarse sturdy fabric of wool and linen or cotton

lin·stock \ˈlin-ˌstäk\ *n* [D *lontstok,* fr. *lont* match + *stok* stick] (1575) : a staff having a pointed foot (as for sticking into the ground) and a forked tip and formerly used to hold a lighted match for firing cannon

lint \ˈlint\ *n* [ME] (15c) **1 a** : a soft fleecy material made from linen usu. by scraping **b** : fuzz consisting esp. of fine ravelings and short fibers of yarn and fabric **2** : a fibrous coat of thick convoluted hairs borne by cotton seeds that yields the cotton staple — **linty** \-ē\ *adj*

lin·tel \ˈlint-ᵊl\ *n* [ME, fr. MF, fr. LL *limitaris* threshold, fr. L, constituting a boundary, fr. *limit-, limes* boundary — more at LIMB] (14c) : a horizontal architectural member spanning and usu. carrying the load above an opening

lint·er \ˈlint-ər\ *n* (ca. 1890) **1** : a machine for removing linters **2** *pl* : the fuzz of short fibers that adheres to cottonseed after ginning

lint·white \ˈlint-ˌhwīt, -ˌwīt\ *n* [ME *lynkwhyt,* by folk etymology fr. OE *līnetwige*] (bef. 12c) : LINNET

li·on \ˈlī-ən\ *n, pl* **lions** [ME, fr. OF, fr. L *leon-, leo,* fr. Gk *leōn*] (12c) **1 a** *or pl* **lion** : a large carnivorous chiefly nocturnal cat (*Felis leo*) of open or rocky areas of Africa and esp. formerly southern Asia that has a tawny body with a tufted tail and a shaggy blackish or dark brown mane in the male **b** : any of several large wildcats; *esp* : COUGAR **c** *cap* : LEO **2 a** : a person felt to resemble a lion (as in courage or ferocity) **b** : a person of outstanding interest or importance **3** *cap* [*Lions (club)*] : a member of a major national and international service club — **li·on·like** \-ən-ˌlīk\ *adj*

li·on·ess \ˈlī-ə-nəs\ *n* [ME *liones, leonesse,* fr. MF *lionesse, leonesse,* fr. *lion, leon* lion, fr. OF] (14c) : a female lion

li·on·fish \ˈlī-ən-ˌfish\ *n* (ca. 1907) : any of several scorpion fishes (genus *Pterois*) of the tropical Pacific that are brilliantly striped and barred with elongated fins and venomous dorsal spines

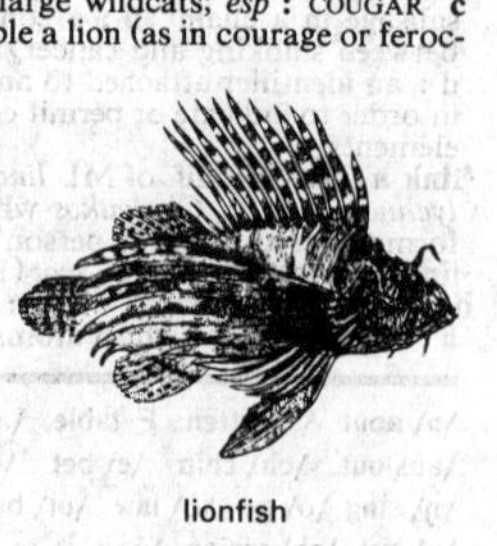

lionfish

li·on·heart·ed \ˌlī-ən-ˈhärt-əd\ *adj* (1708) : COURAGEOUS, BRAVE

li·on·ize \ˈlī-ə-ˌnīz\ *vt* **-ized; -iz·ing** (1809) **1** : to treat as an object of great interest or importance **2** *Brit* : to show the sights of a place to — **li·on·iza·tion** \ˌlī-ə-nə-ˈzā-shən\ *n* — **li·on·iz·er** \ˈlī-ə-ˌnī-zər\ *n*

lion's share *n* (1790) : the largest portion ⟨received the *lion's share* of the research money⟩

¹lip \ˈlip\ *n* [ME, fr. OE *lippa;* akin to OHG *leffur* lip and prob. to L *labium, labrum* lip] (bef. 12c) **1** : either of two fleshy folds that surround the mouth in man and many other vertebrates and in man are organs of speech; *also* : the red or pinkish margin of the human lip **2** *slang* : BACK TALK **3 a** : a fleshy edge or margin (as of a wound) **b** : LABIUM **c** : LABELLUM 1 **d** : a limb of a labiate corolla **4 a** : the edge of a hollow vessel or cavity **b** : a projecting edge: as (1) : the beveled upper edge of the mouth of an organ flue pipe (2) : the sharp cutting edge on the end of an auger or similar tool (3) : a short spout (as on a pitcher) **5** : EMBOUCHURE — **lip·less** \-ləs\ *adj* — **lip·like** \-ˌlīk\ *adj*

²lip *adj* (1558) **1** : spoken with the lips only : INSINCERE ⟨~ praise⟩ **2** : produced with the participation of the lips : LABIAL ⟨~ consonants⟩

³lip *vt* **lipped; lip·ping** (1604) **1** : to touch with the lips; *esp* : KISS **2** : UTTER **3** : to lap against : LICK **4** : to hit (a putt) so that the ball hits the edge of the cup but fails to drop in

lip- *or* **lipo-** *comb form* [NL, fr. Gk, fr. *lipos* — more at LEAVE] : fat : fatty tissue : fatty ⟨*lipoid*⟩ ⟨*lipoprotein*⟩

li·pase \ˈlī-ˌpās, -ˌpāz\ *n* [ISV] (1897) : an enzyme that accelerates the hydrolysis or synthesis of fats or the breakdown of lipoproteins

lip·id \ˈlip-əd\ *also* **lip·ide** \-ˌīd\ *n* [ISV] (1912) : any of various substances that are soluble in nonpolar organic solvents (as chloroform and ether), that with proteins and carbohydrates constitute the principal structural components of living cells, and that include fats, waxes, phosphatides, cerebrosides, and related and derived compounds — **li·pid·ic** \lip-ˈid-ik\ *adj*

li·po·gen·e·sis \ˌlī-pə-ˈjen-ə-səs\ *n* [NL] (1882) : the formation of fatty acids from acetyl coenzyme A in the living body

li·po·ic acid \lī-ˌpō-ik-, lip-ˌō-\ *n* [*lip-, lipo-*] (ca. 1951) : any of several microbial growth factors; *esp* : a crystalline compound $C_8H_{14}O_2S_2$ that is essential for the oxidation of alpha-keto acids (as pyruvic acid) in metabolism

¹li·poid \ˈlī-ˌpȯid, ˈlip-ˌȯid\ *or* **li·poi·dal** \lī-ˈpȯid-ᵊl, lip-ˈȯid-\ *adj* [ISV] (1876) : resembling fat

²lipoid *n* [ISV] (1906) : LIPID

li·pol·y·sis \lī-ˈpäl-ə-səs, lip-ˈäl-\ *n* [NL] (ca. 1903) : the hydrolysis of fat — **li·po·lyt·ic** \ˌlī-pə-ˈlit-ik, ˌlip-ə-\ *adj*

li·po·ma \lī-ˈpō-mə, lip-ˈō-\ *n, pl* **-mas** *or* **-ma·ta** \-mət-ə\ [NL] (1830) : a tumor of fatty tissue — **li·po·ma·tous** \-mət-əs\ *adj*

li·po·phil·ic \ˌlī-pə-ˈfil-ik, ˌlip-ə-\ *adj* (1939) : having an affinity for lipids (as fats) ⟨a ~ metabolite⟩

li·po·poly·sac·cha·ride \ˌlī-pō-ˌpäl-i-ˈsak-ə-ˌrīd, ˌlip-ō-\ *n* (1950) : a large molecule consisting of lipids and sugars joined by chemical bonds

li·po·pro·tein \-ˈprō-ˌtēn, -ˈprōt-ē-ən\ *n* (1909) : a conjugated protein that is a complex of protein and lipid

li·po·some \ˈlī-pə-ˌsōm, ˈlip-ə-\ *n* (1968) : an artificial vesicle composed of one or more concentric phospholipid bilayers — **li·po·so·mal** \ˌlī-pə-ˈsō-məl, ˌlip-ə-\ *adj*

li·po·suc·tion \ˈlip-ə-ˌsək-shən\ *n* (1986) : surgical removal of local fat deposits (as in the thighs) esp. for cosmetic purposes

li·po·tro·pic \ˌlī-pō-ˈtrō-pik, ˌlip-ō-, -ˈträp-ik\ *adj* [ISV] (1935) : promoting the physiological utilization of fat ⟨~ dietary factors⟩

li·po·tro·pin \-ˈtrō-pən\ *n* (1964) : either of two protein hormones of the anterior part of the pituitary gland that function in the mobilization of fat reserves

lipped \ˈlipt\ *adj* (14c) : having a lip or lips esp. of a specified kind or number — often used in combination ⟨tight-*lipped*⟩

lip·pen \ˈlip-ən\ *vb* [ME *lipnien*] *vi, chiefly Scot* (12c) : TRUST, RELY ~ *vt, chiefly Scot* : ENTRUST

Lippes loop \ˌlip-əs-, ˈlips-\ *n* [Jack *Lippes,* 20th cent. Am. physician] (1964) : an S-shaped plastic intrauterine device

lip·ping \ˈlip-iŋ\ *n* (1894) **1** : outgrowth of bone in liplike form at a joint margin **2** : a piece of wood set in an archer's bow where a flaw has been cut out **3** : EMBOUCHURE 1

lip·py \ˈlip-ē\ *adj* **lip·pi·er; -est** (ca. 1875) : given to back talk

lip–read \ˈlip-ˌrēd\ *vb* **-read** \-ˌred\; **-read·ing** \-ˌrēd-iŋ\ *vt* (1892) : to understand by lipreading ~ *vi* : to use lipreading — **lip–read·er** \-ˌrēd-\ *n*

lip·read·ing \-ˌrēd-iŋ\ *n* (1874) : the interpreting of a speaker's words by watching his lip and facial movements without hearing his voice

lip service *n* (1644) : an avowal of advocacy, adherence, or allegiance that goes no further than expression in words

lip·stick \ˈlip-ˌstik\ *n* (1880) : a waxy solid usu. colored cosmetic in stick form for the lips; *also* : a stick of such cosmetic with its case — **lip·sticked** *adj*

lip sync *n* (1949) : the synchronization of recorded speech or song with the movement of the lips of a person mouthing the sounds — **lip–synch** *or* **lip–sync** \ˈlip-ˌsiŋk\ *vb*

li·quate \ˈlī-ˌkwāt\ *vt* **li·quat·ed; li·quat·ing** [L *liquatus,* pp. of *liquare;* akin to L *liquēre*] (ca. 1864) : to cause (a more fusible substance) to separate out of a combination or mixture by the application of heat ⟨~ metallic lead from its ore⟩ — **li·qua·tion** \lī-ˈkwā-shən\ *n*

liq·ue·fac·tion \ˌlik-wə-ˈfak-shən\ *n* [ME, fr. LL *liquefaction-, liquefactio,* fr. L *liquefactus,* pp. of *liquefacere,* fr. *liquēre* to be fluid + *facere* to make — more at DO] (15c) **1** : the process of making or becoming liquid **2** : the state of being liquid

liquefied petroleum gas *n* (ca. 1925) : a compressed gas that consists of flammable hydrocarbons (as propane and butane) and is used esp. as fuel or as raw material for chemical synthesis

liq·ue·fy *also* **liq·ui·fy** \ˈlik-wə-ˌfī\ *vb* **-fied; -fy·ing** [MF *liquefier,* fr. L *liquefacere*] *vt* (15c) : to reduce to a liquid state ~ *vi* : to become liquid — **liq·ue·fi·abil·i·ty** \ˌlik-wə-ˌfī-ə-ˈbil-ət-ē\ *n* — **liq·ue·fi·able** \-ˌfī-ə-bəl\ *adj* — **liq·ue·fi·er** \-ˌfī(-ə)r\ *n*

li·ques·cent \lik-ˈwes-ᵊnt\ *adj* [L *liquescent-, liquescens,* prp. of *liquescere* to become fluid, incho. of *liquēre*] (ca. 1727) : being or tending to become liquid : MELTING

li·queur \li-ˈkər, -ˈk(y)u̇(ə)r\ *n* [F, fr. OF *licour* liquid — more at LIQUOR] (1729) : a usu. sweetened spirituous liquor (as brandy) flavored with fruit, spices, nuts, herbs, or seeds

[1]**liq·uid** \ˈlik-wəd\ *adj* [ME, fr. MF *liquide*, fr. L *liquidus*, fr. *liquēre* to be fluid; akin to L *lixa* water, lye, OIr *fliuch* damp] (14c) **1 :** flowing freely like water **2 :** neither solid nor gaseous **:** characterized by free movement of the constituent molecules among themselves but without the tendency to separate ⟨∼ mercury⟩ **3 a :** shining and clear ⟨large ∼ eyes⟩ **b :** being musical and free of harshness in sound **c :** smooth and unconstrained in movement **d :** articulated without friction and capable of being prolonged like a vowel ⟨a ∼ consonant⟩ **4 :** consisting of or capable of ready conversion into cash ⟨∼ assets⟩ — **li·quid·i·ty** \lik-ˈwid-ət-ē\ *n* — **liq·uid·ly** \ˈlik-wəd-lē\ *adv* — **liq·uid·ness** *n*

[2]**liquid** *n* (1530) **1 :** a liquid consonant **2 :** a liquid substance

liquid air *n* (ca. 1898) **:** air in the liquid state that can be prepared by subjecting it to great pressure and then cooling it by its own expansion to a temperature below the boiling point of its chief constituents and that is used chiefly as a refrigerant

liq·uid·am·bar \ˌlik-wə-ˈdam-bər\ *n* [NL, fr. L *liquidus* + ML *ambar, ambra* amber] (1598) **1 :** any of a genus (*Liquidambar*) of trees of the witch-hazel family with monoecious flowers and a globose fruit of many woody carpels **2 :** an American storax from the sweet gum (*Liquidambar styraciflua*)

liq·ui·date \ˈlik-wə-ˌdāt\ *vb* **-dat·ed; -dat·ing** [LL *liquidatus*, pp. of *liquidare* to melt, fr. L *liquidus*] *vt* (1575) **1 a** (1) **:** to determine by agreement or by litigation the precise amount of (indebtedness, damages, or accounts) (2) **:** to determine the liabilities and apportion assets toward discharging the indebtedness of **b :** to settle (a debt) by payment or other settlement **2** *archaic* **:** to make clear **3 :** to do away with **4 :** to convert (assets) into cash ∼ *vi* **1 :** to liquidate debts or damages or accounts **2 :** to determine liabilities and apportion assets toward discharging indebtedness — **liq·ui·da·tion** \ˌlik-wə-ˈdā-shən\ *n*

liq·ui·da·tor \ˈlik-wə-ˌdāt-ər\ *n* (ca. 1828) **:** one that liquidates; *esp* **:** an individual appointed by law to liquidate assets

liquid crystal *n* (1891) **:** an organic liquid whose physical properties resemble those of a crystal in the formation of loosely ordered molecular arrays similar to a regular crystalline lattice and the anisotropic refraction of light

liquid crystal display *n* (1973) **:** LCD

liq·uid·ize \ˈlik-wə-ˌdīz\ *vt* **-ized; -iz·ing** (1837) **:** to cause to be liquid

liquid measure *n* (ca. 1855) **:** a unit or series of units for measuring liquid capacity — see METRIC SYSTEM table, WEIGHT table

[1]**li·quor** \ˈlik-ər\ *n* [ME *licour*, fr. OF, fr. L *liquor*, fr. *liquēre*] (13c) **:** a liquid substance: as **a :** a usu. distilled rather than fermented alcoholic beverage **b :** a watery solution of a drug **c :** BATH 2b(1)

[2]**liquor** *vb* **li·quored; li·quor·ing** \ˈlik-(ə-)riŋ\ *vt* (1502) **1 :** to dress (as leather) with oil or grease **2 :** to make drunk with alcoholic liquor — usu. used with *up* ∼ *vi* **:** to drink alcoholic liquor esp. to excess — usu. used with *up*

li·quo·rice *chiefly Brit var of* LICORICE

[1]**li·ra** \ˈlir-ə, ˈlē-rə\ *n, pl* **li·re** \ˈlē-(ˌ)rā\ *also* **liras** [It, fr. L *libra*, a unit of weight] (1617) — see MONEY table

[2]**lira** *n, pl* **liras** *also* **lire** [Turk, fr. It] (1871) **:** a Turkish, Syrian, or Maltese pound — see MONEY table

[3]**lira** *n, pl* **li·roth** *or* **li·rot** \lē-ˌrōt(h)\ [NHeb, fr. It] (ca. 1946) **:** the former Israeli pound

lir·i·pipe \ˈlir-ə-ˌpīp\ *n* [ML *liripipium*] (1737) **:** a pendent part of a tippet; *also* **:** TIPPET, SCARF

lisle \ˈlī(ə)l\ *n* [*Lisle* Lille, France] (1851) **:** a smooth tightly twisted thread usu. made of long-staple cotton

[1]**lisp** \ˈlisp\ *vb* [ME *lispen*, fr. OE *-wlyspian*; akin to OHG *lispen* to lisp] *vi* (bef. 12c) **1 :** to pronounce the sibilants \s\ and \z\ imperfectly esp. by giving them the sounds \th\ and \t͟h\ **2 :** to speak falteringly, childishly, or with a lisp ∼ *vt* **:** to utter falteringly or with a lisp — **lisp·er** *n*

[2]**lisp** *n* (1625) **1 :** a speech defect or affectation characterized by lisping **2 :** a sound resembling a lisp

lis·some *also* **lis·som** \ˈlis-əm\ *adj* [alter. of *lithesome*] (ca. 1800) **1 :** easily flexed **:** LITHE **2 :** NIMBLE — **lis·some·ly** *adv* — **lis·some·ness** *n*

[1]**list** \ˈlist\ *vb* [ME *lysten*, fr. OE *lystan*; akin to OE *lust* desire, lust] *vt, archaic* (bef. 12c) **:** PLEASE, SUIT ∼ *vi, archaic* **:** WISH, CHOOSE

[2]**list** *n* [ME, prob. fr. *lysten*] *archaic* (13c) **:** INCLINATION, CRAVING

[3]**list** *vb* [ME *listen*, fr. OE *hlystan*, fr. *hlyst* hearing, fr. *hlysnan* to listen] *vi, archaic* (bef. 12c) **:** LISTEN ∼ *vt, archaic* **:** to listen to **:** HEAR

[4]**list** *n* [ME, fr. OE *līste*; akin to OHG *līsta* edge, Alb *leth*] (bef. 12c) **1 :** a band or strip of material: as **a :** LISTEL **b :** SELVAGE **c :** a narrow strip of wood cut from the edge of a board **2** *pl but sing or pl in constr* **a :** an arena for combat (as jousting) **b :** a field of competition or controversy **3** *obs* **:** LIMIT, BOUNDARY **4 :** STRIPE

[5]**list** *vt* (1635) **1 :** to cut away a narrow strip (as sapwood) from the edge of **2 :** to prepare or plant (land) in ridges and furrows with a lister

[6]**list** *n* [F *liste*, fr. It *lista*, of Gmc origin; akin to OHG *lista* edge] (1602) **1 a :** a simple series of words or numerals (as the names of persons or objects) ⟨a guest ∼⟩ **b :** an official roster **:** ROLL **2 :** CATALOG, CHECKLIST **3 :** the total number to be considered or included ⟨a situation that heads their ∼ of troubles⟩

[7]**list** *vt* (1614) **1 a :** to make a list of **:** ENUMERATE **b :** to include on a list **:** REGISTER **2 :** to place (oneself) in a specified category ⟨∼*s* himself as a political liberal⟩ **3** *archaic* **:** RECRUIT ∼ *vi* **1** *archaic* **:** ENLIST **2 :** to become entered in a catalog with a selling price ⟨a car that ∼*s* for $9000⟩

[8]**list** *vb* [origin unknown] *vi* (1626) **:** to tilt to one side; *esp, of a boat or ship* **:** to tilt to one side in a state of equilibrium (as from an unbalanced load) — compare HEEL ∼ *vt* **:** to cause to list

[9]**list** *n* (1633) **:** a deviation from the vertical **:** TILT; *also* **:** the extent of such a deviation

lis·tel \ˈlis-tᵊl, lis-ˈtel\ *n* [F, fr. It *listello*, dim. of *lista* fillet, roster] (ca. 1598) **:** a narrow band in architecture **:** FILLET

[1]**lis·ten** \ˈlis-ᵊn\ *vb* **lis·tened; lis·ten·ing** \ˈlis-niŋ, -ᵊn-iŋ\ [ME *listnen*, fr. OE *hlysnan*; akin to Skt *śroṣati* he hears, OE *hlūd* loud] *vt, archaic* (bef. 12c) **:** to give ear to **:** HEAR ∼ *vi* **1 :** to pay attention to sound ⟨∼ to music⟩ **2 :** to hear something with thoughtful attention **:** give consideration ⟨∼ to a plea⟩ **3 :** to be alert to catch an expected sound ⟨∼ for his step⟩ — **lis·ten·er** \ˈlis-nər, -ᵊn-ər\ *n*

[2]**listen** *n* (1788) **:** an act of listening

lis·ten·able \ˈlis-nə-bəl, -ᵊn-ə-\ *adj* (ca. 1942) **:** agreeable to listen to

lis·ten·er·ship \ˈlis-nər-ˌship, -ᵊn-ər-\ *n* (1943) **:** the audience for a radio program or record; *also* **:** the number or kind of such an audience

listen in *vi* (1905) **1 :** to tune in to or monitor a broadcast **2 :** to listen to a conversation without participating in it; *esp* **:** EAVESDROP — **lis·ten·er–in** \ˌlis-nə-ˈrin, ˌlis-ᵊn-ə-\ *n*

[1]**list·er** \ˈlis-tər\ *n* (1678) **:** one that lists or catalogs

[2]**lister** *n* [[5]*list*] (1887) **:** a double-moldboard plow often equipped with a subsoiling attachment and used mainly where rainfall is limited

lis·te·ri·osis \lis-ˌtir-ē-ˈō-səs\ *n, pl* **-oses** \-ˌsēz\ [NL, fr. *Listeria*, fr. Joseph *Lister*] (1941) **:** a serious commonly fatal encephalitic disease of a great variety of wild and domestic mammals and birds and occas. man that is caused by a bacterium (*Listeria monocytogenes*)

list·ing *n* (1659) **1 :** an act or instance of making or including in a list **2 :** something that is listed

list·less \ˈlist-ləs\ *adj* [ME *listles*, fr. *list* [2]list] (15c) **:** characterized by lack of interest, energy, or spirit **:** LANGUID ⟨a ∼ melancholy attitude⟩ — **list·less·ly** *adv* — **list·less·ness** *n*

list price *n* (1871) **:** the basic price of an item as published in a catalog, price list, or advertisement but subject to discounts (as trade or quantity discounts)

[1]**lit** \ˈlit\ *past and past part of* LIGHT

[2]**lit** *n* [by shortening] (1850) **:** LITERATURE

[3]**lit** *adj* [pp. of [3]*light*] (1904) **:** affected by alcohol **:** DRUNK

lit·a·ny \ˈlit-ᵊn-ē, ˈlit-nē\ *n, pl* **-nies** [ME *letanie*, fr. OF & LL; OF, fr. LL *litania*, fr. LGk *litaneia*, fr. Gk, entreaty, fr. *litanos* entreating] (13c) **1 :** a prayer consisting of a series of invocations and supplications by the leader with alternate responses by the congregation **2 a :** a resonant or repetitive chant ⟨a ∼ of cheering phrases —Herman Wouk⟩ **b :** a usu. lengthy recitation or enumeration ⟨a familiar ∼ of complaints⟩

li·tchi \ˈlī-(ˌ)chē, ˈlē-\ *n* [Chin (Pek) *li⁴ chih¹*] (1588) **1 :** the oval fruit of a tree (*Litchi chinensis*) of the soapberry family having a hard scaly outer covering, hard, medium-sized seed, and edible flesh that surrounds the seed and is firm, sweetish, and black when dried — called also *litchi nut* **2 :** a tree bearing litchis

-lite \ˌlīt\ *n comb form* [F, alter. of *-lithe*, fr. Gk *lithos* stone] **:** mineral ⟨rhodo*lite*⟩ **:** rock ⟨aero*lite*⟩ **:** fossil ⟨ichno*lite*⟩

li·ter \ˈlēt-ər\ *n* [F *litre*, fr. ML *litra*, a measure, fr. Gk, a weight] (1797) **:** a metric unit of capacity equal to one cubic decimeter — see METRIC SYSTEM table

lit·er·a·cy \ˈlit-ə-rə-sē, ˈli-trə-\ *n* (1883) **:** the quality or state of being literate

[1]**lit·er·al** \ˈlit-ə-rəl, ˈli-trəl\ *adj* [ME, fr. MF, fr. ML *litteralis*, fr. L, of a letter, fr. *littera* letter] (14c) **1 a :** according with the letter of the scriptures **b :** adhering to fact or to the ordinary construction or primary meaning of a term or expression **:** ACTUAL ⟨liberty in the ∼ sense is impossible —B. N. Cardozo⟩ **c :** free from exaggeration or embellishment ⟨the ∼ truth⟩ **d :** characterized by a concern mainly with facts ⟨a very ∼ man⟩ **2 :** of, relating to, or expressed in letters **3 :** reproduced word for word **:** EXACT, VERBATIM ⟨a ∼ translation⟩ — **lit·er·al·i·ty** \ˌlit-ə-ˈral-ət-ē\ *n* — **lit·er·al·ness** \ˈlit-ə-rəl-nəs, ˈli-trəl-\ *n*

[2]**literal** *n* (1622) **:** a small error usu. of a single letter in writing or printing

lit·er·al·ism \ˈlit-ə-rə-ˌliz-əm, ˈli-trə-\ *n* (1644) **1 :** adherence to the explicit substance of an idea or expression ⟨biblical ∼⟩ **2 :** fidelity to observable fact **:** REALISM — **lit·er·al·ist** \-ləst\ *n* — **lit·er·al·is·tic** \ˌlit-ə-rə-ˈlis-tik, ˌli-trə-\ *adj*

lit·er·al·ize \ˈlit-ə-rə-ˌlīz, ˈli-trə-\ *vt* **-ized; -iz·ing** (1826) **:** to make literal — **lit·er·al·iza·tion** \ˌlit-ə-rə-lə-ˈzā-shən, ˌli-trə-lə-\ *n*

lit·er·al·ly \ˈlit-ər-(ə-)lē, ˈli-trə-lē\ *adv* (1533) **1 :** in a literal sense or manner **:** ACTUALLY ⟨took the remark ∼⟩ ⟨was ∼ insane⟩ **2 :** in effect **:** VIRTUALLY ⟨will ∼ turn the world upside down to combat cruelty or injustice —Norman Cousins⟩

usage Since some people take sense 2 to be the opposite of sense 1, it has been frequently criticized as a misuse. Instead, the use is pure hyperbole intended to gain emphasis, but it often appears in contexts where no additional emphasis is necessary.

lit·er·ary \ˈlit-ə-ˌrer-ē\ *adj* (1749) **1 a :** of, relating to, or having the characteristics of humane learning or literature **b :** BOOKISH 2 **c :** of or relating to books **2 a :** WELL-READ **b :** of or relating to authors or scholars or to their professions — **lit·er·ari·ly** \ˌlit-ə-ˈrer-ə-lē\ *adv* — **lit·er·ari·ness** \ˈlit-ə-ˌrer-ē-nəs\ *n*

literary executor *n* (1868) **:** a person entrusted with the management of the papers and unpublished works of a deceased author

[1]**lit·er·ate** \ˈlit-ə-rət, ˈli-trət\ *adj* [ME *literat*, fr. L *litteratus* marked with letters, literate, fr. *litterae* letters, literature, fr. pl. of *littera*] (15c) **1 a :** EDUCATED, CULTURED **b :** able to read and write **2 a :** versed in literature or creative writing **:** LITERARY **b :** LUCID, POLISHED ⟨a ∼ essay⟩ **c :** having knowledge or competence ⟨computer-*literate*⟩ ⟨politically ∼⟩ — **lit·er·ate·ly** *adv* — **lit·er·ate·ness** *n*

[2]**literate** *n* (1550) **1 :** an educated person **2 :** one who can read and write

li·te·ra·ti \ˌlit-ə-ˈrät-(ˌ)ē\ *n pl* [obs. It *litterati*, fr. L, pl. of *litteratus*] (1621) **1 :** the educated class **:** INTELLIGENTSIA **2 :** persons interested in literature or the arts

lit·er·a·tim \ˌlit-ə-ˈrät-əm, -ˈrāt-\ *adv or adj* [ML, fr. L *littera*] (1643) **:** letter for letter ⟨printed ∼ from the manuscript —I. A. Gordon⟩

lit·er·a·tion \ˌlit-ə-ˈrā-shən\ *n* [L *littera* + E *-ation*] (ca. 1890) **:** the representation of sound or words by letters

lit·er·a·tor \ˈlit-ə-ˌrāt-ər, ˌlit-ə-ˈrä-ˌtȯ(ə)r\ *n* (1791) **:** LITTERATEUR

lit·er·a·ture \ˈlit-ə-rə-ˌchu̇(ə)r, ˈli-trə-ˌchu̇(ə)r, ˈlit-ə(r)-ˌchu̇(ə)r, -chər, -ˌt(y)u̇(ə)r\ *n* [ME, fr. L *litteratura* writing, grammar, learning, fr. *litteratus*] (14c) **1** *archaic* **:** literary culture **2 :** the production of literary work esp. as an occupation **3 a :** writings in prose or verse; *esp* **:** writings having excellence of form or expression and expressing ideas of permanent or universal interest **b :** the body of written works produced in a particular language, country, or age **c :** the body of writ-

\ə\ **abut** \ᵊ\ **kitten**, F **table** \ər\ **further** \a\ **ash** \ā\ **ace** \ä\ **cot, cart** \au̇\ **out** \ch\ **chin** \e\ **bet** \ē\ **easy** \g\ **go** \i\ **hit** \ī\ **ice** \j\ **job** \ŋ\ **sing** \ō\ **go** \ȯ\ **law** \ȯi\ **boy** \th\ **thin** \t͟h\ **the** \ü\ **loot** \u̇\ **foot** \y\ **yet** \zh\ **vision** \à, k̲, ⁿ, œ, œ̄, ue, ue̅, ʸ\ *see* Guide to Pronunciation

ings on a particular subject ⟨scientific ~⟩ **d :** printed matter (as leaflets or circulars) ⟨campaign ~⟩ **4 :** the aggregate of musical compositions ⟨Brahms piano ~⟩
lit·er·a·tus \ˌlit-ə-ˈrät-əs\ *n* [NL, back-formation fr. E *literati* (taken as L)] (1704) **:** a member of the literati
lith- *or* **litho-** *comb form* [L, fr. Gk, fr. *lithos*] **1 :** stone ⟨*litho*logy⟩ **2** [NL *lithium*] **:** lithium ⟨*lith*ic⟩
-lith \ˌlith\ *n comb form* [NL *-lithus* & F *-lithe*, fr. Gk *lithos*] **1 a :** structure or implement of stone ⟨mega*lith*⟩ ⟨eo*lith*⟩ **b :** artificial stone ⟨grano*lith*⟩ **2 :** calculus ⟨uro*lith*⟩ **3 :** -LITE ⟨lacco*lith*⟩
li·tharge \ˈlith-ˌärj, lith-ˈ\ *n* [ME, fr. MF, fr. L *lithargyrus*, fr. Gk *lithargyros*, fr. *lithos* + *argyros* silver — more at ARGENT] (14c) **:** a fused lead monoxide; *broadly* **:** LEAD MONOXIDE
lithe \ˈlīth, ˈlīth\ *adj* [ME, fr. OE *līthe* gentle; akin to OHG *lindi* gentle, L *lentus* slow] (14c) **1 :** easily bent or flexed ⟨~ steel⟩ ⟨a ~ vine⟩ **2 :** characterized by easy flexibility and grace ⟨a ~ dancer⟩ ⟨treading with a ~ silent step⟩ — **lithe·ly** *adv* — **lithe·ness** *n*
lithe·some \ˈlīth-səm, ˈlith-\ *adj* (1768) **:** LISSOME
lith·ia \ˈlith-ē-ə\ *n* [NL, fr. Gk *lithos*] (1818) **:** a white crystalline oxide of lithium Li_2O
li·thi·a·sis \lith-ˈī-ə-səs\ *n, pl* **-a·ses** \-ˌsēz\ [NL, fr. Gk, fr. *lithos*] (1657) **:** the formation of stony concretions in the body (as in the gallbladder)
lithia water *n* (1878) **:** a mineral water containing lithium salts
lith·ic \ˈlith-ik\ *adj* [Gk *lithikos*, fr. *lithos*] (1797) **1 :** of, relating to, or made of stone **2 :** of or relating to lithium — **lith·i·cal·ly** \-i-k(ə-)lē\ *adv*
-lith·ic \ˈlith-ik\ *adj comb form* [*lithic*] **:** relating to or characteristic of a (specified) stage in man's use of stone as a cultural tool ⟨Neo*lithic*⟩
lith·i·um \ˈlith-ē-əm\ *n* [NL, fr. *lithia*] (1818) **:** a soft silver-white element of the alkali metal group that is the lightest metal known and that is used esp. in nuclear reactions and metallurgy — see ELEMENT table
lithium carbonate *n* (1873) **:** a crystalline salt Li_2CO_3 used in the glass and ceramic industries and in medicine in the treatment of manic-depressive psychosis
lithium fluoride *n* (ca. 1944) **:** a white compound LiF used esp. in making prisms and ceramics and as a flux
litho \ˈlī-th(ˌ)ō\ *n, pl* **lith·os** (ca. 1890) **1 :** LITHOGRAPH **2 :** LITHOGRAPHY
[1]**litho·graph** \ˈlith-ə-ˌgraf\ *vt* (1825) **:** to produce, copy, or portray by lithography — **li·tho·gra·pher** \lith-ˈäg-rə-fər, ˈlith-ə-ˌgraf-ər\ *n*
[2]**lithograph** *n* (1828) **:** a print made by lithography — **litho·graph·ic** \ˌlith-ə-ˈgraf-ik\ *adj* — **litho·graph·i·cal·ly** \-i-k(ə-)lē\ *adv*
li·thog·ra·phy \lith-ˈäg-rə-fē\ *n* [G *lithographie*, fr. *lith-* + *-graphie* -graphy] (1813) **:** the process of printing from a plane surface (as a smooth stone or metal plate) on which the image to be printed is ink-receptive and the blank area ink-repellent
li·thol·o·gy \lith-ˈäl-ə-jē\ *n, pl* **-gies** (1716) **1 :** the study of rocks **2 :** the character of a rock formation — **lith·o·log·ic** \ˌlith-ə-ˈläj-ik\ *also* **lith·o·log·i·cal** \-i-kəl\ *adj* — **lith·o·log·i·cal·ly** \-i-k(ə-)lē\ *adv*
lith·o·phane \ˈlith-ə-ˌfān\ *n* [prob. fr. G *lithophan*, fr. Gk *lithos* + G *diaphan* diaphanous] (ca. 1890) **:** porcelain impressed with figures that are made distinct by transmitted light; *also* **:** an object of this material
litho·phyte \ˈlith-ə-ˌfīt\ *n* [F, fr. *lith-* + *-phyte*] (1774) **:** a plant that grows on rock
lith·o·pone \ˈlith-ə-ˌpōn\ *n* [ISV *lith-* + Gk *ponos* work] (ca. 1884) **:** a white pigment consisting essentially of zinc sulfide and barium sulfate
litho·sol \ˈlith-ə-ˌsäl, -ˌsȯl\ *n* [*lith-* + L *solum* soil] (ca. 1938) **:** any of a group of azonal shallow soils consisting of imperfectly weathered rock fragments
litho·sphere \ˈlith-ə-ˌsfi(ə)r\ *n* [ISV] (1887) **:** the solid part of a celestial body (as the earth); *specif* **:** the outer part of the solid earth composed of rock essentially like that exposed at the surface and usu. considered to be about 50 miles (80 kilometers) in thickness — **litho·spher·ic** \ˌlith-ə-ˈsfi(ə)r-ik, -ˈsfer-\ *adj*
li·thot·o·my \lith-ˈät-ə-mē\ *n, pl* **-mies** [LL *lithotomia*, fr. Gk, fr. *lithotomein* to perform a lithotomy, fr. *lith-* + *temnein* to cut — more at TOME] (1721) **:** surgical incision of the urinary bladder for removal of a stone
lith·o·trip·sy \ˈlith-ə-ˌtrip-sē\ *n, pl* **-sies** [*lith-* + Gk *tripsis* a rubbing] (1834) **:** the breaking of a stone (as by shock waves or crushing with a surgical instrument) in the urinary system into pieces small enough to be voided or washed out
Lith·u·a·nian \ˌlith-(y)ə-ˈwā-nē-ən, -nyən\ *n* (1607) **1 :** a native or inhabitant of Lithuania **2 :** the Baltic language of the Lithuanian people — **Lithuanian** *adj*
lit·i·gant \ˈlit-i-gənt\ *n* (1659) **:** one engaged in a lawsuit — **litigant** *adj*
lit·i·gate \ˈlit-ə-ˌgāt\ *vb* **-gat·ed; -gat·ing** [L *litigatus*, pp. of *litigare*, fr. *lit-, lis* lawsuit + *agere* to drive — more at AGENT] *vi* (1615) **:** to carry on a legal contest by judicial process ~ *vt* **1** *archaic* **:** DISPUTE **2 :** to contest in law — **lit·i·ga·ble** \ˈlit-i-gə-bəl\ *adj* — **lit·i·ga·tion** \ˌlit-ə-ˈgā-shən\ *n*
li·ti·gious \lə-ˈtij-əs, li-\ *adj* [ME, fr. MF *litigieux*, fr. L *litigiosus*, fr. *litigium* dispute, fr. *litigare*] (14c) **1 a :** DISPUTATIOUS, CONTENTIOUS **b :** prone to engage in lawsuits **2 :** subject to litigation **3 :** of, relating to, or marked by litigation — **li·ti·gious·ly** *adv* — **li·ti·gious·ness** *n*
lit·mus \ˈlit-məs\ *n* [of Scand origin; akin to ON *litmosi* herbs used in dyeing, fr. *litr* color (akin to OE *wlite* brightness) + *mosi* moss; akin to OE *mōs* moss] (1502) **:** a coloring matter from lichens that turns red in acid solutions and blue in alkaline solutions and is used as an acid-base indicator
litmus paper *n* (1803) **:** unsized paper colored with litmus and used as an indicator
litmus test *n* (1952) **:** a test in which a single factor (as an attitude, event, or fact) is decisive
li·to·tes \ˈlīt-ə-ˌtēz, ˈlit-, lī-ˈtōt-ˌēz\ *n, pl* **litotes** [Gk *litotēs*, fr. *litos* simple; akin to Gk *leios* smooth — more at LIME] (1589) **:** understatement in which an affirmative is expressed by the negative of the contrary (as in "not a bad singer")
li·tre \ˈlēt-ər\ *var of* LITER
lit·ten \ˈlit-ᵊn\ *adj* [alter. of *lit*, pp. of *light*] *archaic* (1849) **:** being lighted
[1]**lit·ter** \ˈlit-ər\ *n* [ME, fr. MF *litiere*, fr. *lit* bed, fr. L *lectus* — more at LIE] (14c) **1 a :** a covered and curtained couch provided with shafts and used for carrying a single passenger **b :** a device (as a stretcher) for carrying a sick or injured person **2 a (1) :** material used as bedding for animals **(2) :** material used to absorb the urine and feces of animals **b :** the uppermost slightly decayed layer of organic matter on the forest floor **3 :** the offspring at one birth of a multiparous animal **4 a :** trash, wastepaper, or garbage lying scattered about ⟨trying to clean up the roadside ~⟩ **b :** an untidy accumulation of objects ⟨a shabby writing-desk covered with a ~ of yellowish dusty documents —Joseph Conrad⟩ — **lit·tery** \-ə-rē\ *adj*

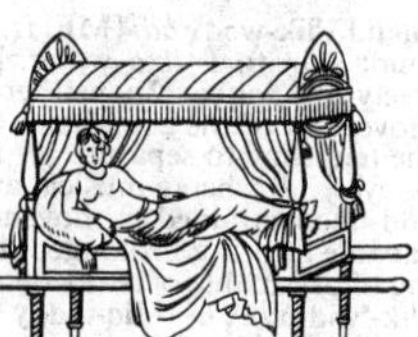
litter 1a

[2]**litter** *vt* (14c) **1 :** BED *vt* 1a **2 :** to give birth to a litter of (young) **3 a :** to strew with scattered articles **b :** to scatter about in disorder **c :** to lie about in disorder ~ *vi* **1 :** to give birth to a litter **2 :** to strew litter
lit·te·rae hu·ma·ni·o·res \ˈlit-ə-ˌrī-hü-ˌmän-ē-ˈō(ə)r-ˌās, -ˈȯ(ə)r-\ *n pl* [ML, lit., more humane letters] (1747) **:** HUMANITIES
lit·ter·a·teur \ˌlit-ə-rə-ˈtər, ˌli-trə-, -ˈtu̇(ə)r\ *n* [F *littérateur*, fr. L *litterator* critic, fr. *litteratus* literate] (1806) **:** a literary person; *esp* **:** a professional writer
lit·ter·bag \ˈlit-ər-ˌbag\ *n* (ca. 1955) **:** a bag used (as in an automobile) for temporary refuse disposal
lit·ter·bug \-ˌbəg\ *n* (1947) **:** one who litters a public area
lit·ter·er \ˈlit-ər-ər\ *n* (1928) **:** LITTERBUG
lit·ter·mate \ˈlit-ər-ˌmāt\ *n* (1921) **:** one of the offspring in a litter in relation to the others
[1]**lit·tle** \ˈlit-ᵊl\ *adj* **lit·tler** \ˈlit-ᵊl-ər, ˈlit-lər\ *or* **less** \ˈles\ *or* **less·er** \ˈles-ər\; **lit·tlest** \ˈlit-ᵊl-əst, ˈlit-ləst\ *or* **least** \ˈlēst\ [ME *littel*, fr. OE *lȳtel*; akin to OHG *luzzil* little, Lith *liūsti* to be sad] (bef. 12c) **1 :** not big: as **a :** small in size or extent **:** TINY ⟨has ~ feet⟩ **b** *of a plant or animal* **:** small in comparison with related forms — used in vernacular names **c :** small in number **d :** small in condition, distinction, or scope ⟨~ men temporarily inflated by big jobs —S. K. Padover⟩ **e :** NARROW, MEAN ⟨the pettiness of ~ minds⟩ **f :** pleasingly small ⟨she's a cute ~ thing⟩ **2 :** not much: as **a :** existing only in a small amount or to a slight degree ⟨he has ~ money⟩ **b :** short in duration **:** BRIEF **c :** existing to an appreciable though not extensive degree or amount —used with *a* ⟨she had a ~ money in the bank⟩ **3 :** small in importance or interest **:** TRIVIAL ***syn*** see SMALL — **lit·tle·ness** \ˈlit-ᵊl-nəs\ *n*
[2]**little** *adv* **less** \ˈles\; **least** \ˈlēst\ (bef. 12c) **1 a :** in only a small quantity or degree **:** SLIGHTLY ⟨facts that were ~ known at the time⟩ **b :** not at all ⟨cared ~ for their neighbors⟩ **2 :** RARELY, INFREQUENTLY
[3]**little** *n* (bef. 12c) **1 :** a small amount, quantity, or degree **2 a :** a short time **b :** a short distance — **a little :** SOMEWHAT, RATHER ⟨found the play *a little* dull⟩ — **in little :** on a small scale; *esp* **:** in miniature
Little Bear *n* **:** URSA MINOR
lit·tle bit·ty \ˌlit-ᵊl-ˈbit-ē\ *adj* (ca. 1904) **:** SMALL, TINY
little bluestem *n* (ca. 1898) **:** a forage grass (*Andropogon scoparius*) of eastern and central No. America
little by little *adv* (15c) **:** by small degrees or amounts **:** GRADUALLY
Little Dipper *n* (1842) **:** DIPPER 3b
little finger *n* (bef. 12c) **:** the fourth and smallest finger of the hand counting the forefinger as the first
Little Hours *n pl* (ca. 1872) **:** the offices of prime, terce, sext, and none forming part of the canonical hours
little leaf \ˈlit-ᵊl-ˌ(l)ēf\ *n* (1916) **:** a plant disorder characterized by small and often chlorotic and distorted foliage: as **a :** a zinc-deficiency disease of deciduous woody plants (as grape, peach, and pecan) **b :** a destructive disease of southern pines (as *Pinus echinata*) of unknown cause — called also *little-leaf disease*
Little League *n* (ca. 1952) **:** a commercially sponsored baseball league for boys and girls from 8 to 12 years old — **Little Leaguer** *n*
little magazine *n* (1900) **:** a literary usu. noncommercial magazine that features works esp. of writers who are not well-known
little man *n* (1933) **:** the ordinary individual
lit·tle·neck \ˈlit-ᵊl-ˌnek\ *n* [*Littleneck Bay, Long Island, N.Y.*] (ca. 1883) **:** a young quahog suitable to be eaten raw — called also *littleneck clam*
Little Office *n* (ca. 1872) **:** an office in honor of the Virgin Mary like but shorter than the Divine Office
little people *n pl* (1726) **1 :** tiny imaginary beings (as fairies, elves, and leprechauns) of folklore **2 :** CHILDREN **3 :** MIDGETS **4 :** common people
little slam *n* (ca. 1897) **:** the winning of all tricks except one in bridge
little theater *n* (1771) **:** a small theater for low-cost dramatic productions designed for a relatively limited audience
little toe *n* (15c) **:** the outermost and smallest digit of the foot
little woman *n* (1795) **:** WIFE
[1]**lit·to·ral** \ˈlit-ə-rəl; ˌlit-ə-ˈral, -ˈräl\ *adj* [L *litoralis*, fr. *litor-, litus* seashore] (1656) **:** of, relating to, or situated or growing on or near a shore esp. of the sea
[2]**littoral** *n* (1815) **:** a coastal region; *esp* **:** the shore zone between high and low watermarks
lit up *adj* (ca. 1914) **:** DRUNK
li·tur·gi·cal \lə-ˈtər-ji-kəl, li-\ *adj* (1641) **1 :** of, relating to, or having the characteristics of liturgy **2 :** using or favoring the use of liturgy ⟨~ churches⟩ — **li·tur·gi·cal·ly** \-k(ə-)lē\ *adv*
li·tur·gics \-jiks\ *n pl but sing or pl in constr* (ca. 1855) **:** the practice or study of formal public worship
li·tur·gi·ol·o·gist \-ˌtər-jē-ˈäl-ə-jəst\ *n* (1866) **:** LITURGIST 2
li·tur·gi·ol·o·gy \-jē\ *n* (1863) **:** LITURGICS
lit·ur·gist \ˈlit-ər-jəst\ *n* (1649) **1 :** one who adheres to, compiles, or leads a liturgy **2 :** a specialist in liturgics
lit·ur·gy \ˈlit-ər-jē\ *n, pl* **-gies** [LL *liturgia*, fr. Gk *leitourgia*, fr. (assumed) Gk (Attic) *leitos* public (fr. Gk *laos* — Attic *leōs* — people) + *-ourgia* -urgy] (1560) **1** *often cap* **:** a eucharistic rite **2 :** a rite or body of rites prescribed for public worship
liv·abil·i·ty *also* **live·abil·i·ty** \ˌliv-ə-ˈbil-ət-ē\ *n* (1914) **1 :** survival expectancy **:** VIABILITY — used esp. of poultry and livestock **2 :** suitability for human living
liv·able *also* **live·able** \ˈliv-ə-bəl\ *adj* (1814) **1 :** suitable for living in or with **2 :** ENDURABLE — **liv·able·ness** *n*

¹**live** \'liv\ *vb* **lived; liv•ing** [ME *liven,* fr. OE *libban;* akin to OHG *lebēn* to live, L *caelebs* unmarried] *vi* (bef. 12c) **1 :** to be alive **:** have the life of an animal or plant **2 :** to continue alive **3 :** to maintain oneself **:** SUBSIST **4 :** to occupy a home **:** DWELL ⟨*living* in a shabby room⟩ ⟨they had always *lived* in the country⟩ **5 :** to attain eternal life ⟨though he die, yet shall he ~ —Jn 11:25 (RSV)⟩ **6 :** to conduct or pass one's life ⟨*lived* only for his work⟩ **7 :** to remain in human memory or record ⟨the past ~*s* in us all —W. R. Inge⟩ **8 :** to have a life rich in experience **9 :** COHABIT ~ *vt* **1 :** to pass through or spend the duration of ⟨*lived* their lives alone⟩ **2 :** ACT OUT, PRACTICE — often used with *out* ⟨to ~ out his fantasies⟩ **3 :** to exhibit vigor, gusto, or enthusiasm in ⟨*lived* life to the fullest⟩ — **live it up :** to live with gusto and usu. fast and loose ⟨*lived it up* with wine and song —*Newsweek*⟩ — **live up to** \liv-'əp-tə, -(,)tü\ **:** to act or be in accordance with ⟨had no intention of *living up to* his promise⟩

²**live** \'līv\ *adj* [short for *alive*] (1542) **1 :** having life **:** LIVING **2 :** exerting force or containing energy: as **a :** AFIRE, GLOWING ⟨a ~ cigar⟩ **b :** connected to electric power **c :** charged with explosives and containing shot or a bullet ⟨~ ammunition⟩; *also* **:** armed but not exploded ⟨a ~ bomb⟩ **d :** imparting or driven by power **e :** charged with fissionable material **3 :** abounding with life **:** VIVID **4 :** being in a pure native state **5 :** of bright vivid color **6 :** of continuing or current interest **:** UNCLOSED ⟨~ issues⟩ **7 a :** not yet printed from or plated ⟨~ type⟩ **b :** not yet typeset ⟨~ copy⟩ **8 a :** of or involving a presentation (as a play or concert) in which both the performers and an audience are physically present ⟨a ~ record album⟩ ⟨a nightclub featuring ~ entertainment⟩ **b :** broadcast directly at the time of production ⟨a ~ radio program⟩ **9 :** being in play ⟨a ~ ball⟩

³**live** \'līv\ *adv* (1946) **:** at the actual time of occurrence **:** during, from, or at a live production ⟨the programming originated ~ from New York City —*Current Biog.*⟩

live–bear•er \'līv-,bar-ər, -,ber-\ *n* (1934) **:** a fish that brings forth living young rather than eggs; *esp* **:** any of a family (Poeciliidae) of numerous small surface-feeding fishes

live–box \-,bäks\ *n* (1862) **:** a box or pen suspended in water to keep aquatic animals alive

-lived \'līvd, 'livd\ *adj comb form* [ME, fr. *lif* life] **:** having a life of a specified kind or length ⟨long-*lived*⟩

lived–in \'liv-,din\ *adj* (1873) **:** of or suggesting long-term human habitation or use **:** COMFORTABLE

live down *vt* (1842) **:** to live so as to wipe out the memory or effects of ⟨made a mistake and couldn't *live it down*⟩

live–for•ev•er \'liv-fə-,rev-ər\ *n* (ca. 1597) **:** SEDUM

live–in \,liv-,in\ *adj* (1953) **1 :** living in one's place of employment ⟨a ~ maid⟩ **2 :** involving or involved with cohabitation ⟨a ~ relationship⟩ ⟨a ~ partner⟩

live in \(')liv-'in\ *vi* (1890) **:** to live in one's place of employment **:** to live in another's home

live•li•hood \'līv-lē-,hůd\ *n* [ME *livelode* course of life, fr. OE *liflād,* fr. *lif* + *lād* course — more at LODE] (bef. 12c) **1 :** means of support or subsistence **2** *obs* **:** the quality or state of being lively

live•long \,liv-,lȯŋ\ *adj* [ME *lef long,* fr. *lef* dear + *long* — more at LIEF] (15c) **:** WHOLE, ENTIRE ⟨the ~ day⟩

live•ly \'līv-lē\ *adj* **live•li•er; -est** [ME, fr. OE *līflīc,* fr. *līf* life] (bef. 12c) **1** *obs* **:** LIVING **2 :** briskly alert and energetic **:** VIGOROUS, ANIMATED ⟨a ~ discussion⟩ ⟨~ children racing for home⟩ **3 :** ACTIVE, INTENSE ⟨takes a ~ interest in the people around her⟩ **4 :** BRILLIANT, FRESH ⟨a ~ flashing wit⟩ **5 :** imparting spirit or vivacity **:** STIMULATING ⟨many a peer of England brews *livelier* liquor than the Muse —A. E. Housman⟩ **6 :** quick to rebound **:** RESILIENT **7 :** responding readily to the helm ⟨a ~ boat⟩ **8 :** full of life, movement, or incident ⟨river . . . was ~ with craft of all descriptions —*Amer. Guide Series: Mich.*⟩ — **live•li•ly** \'līv-lə-lē\ *adv* — **live•li•ness** \'līv-lē-nəs\ *n* — **lively** *adv*

syn LIVELY, ANIMATED, VIVACIOUS, SPRIGHTLY, GAY mean keenly alive and spirited. LIVELY suggests briskness, alertness, or energy; ANIMATED applies to what is spirited, active, and sparkling; VIVACIOUS suggests an activeness of gesture and wit, often playful or alluring; SPRIGHTLY suggests lightness and spirited vigor of manner or of wit; GAY stresses complete freedom from care and overflowing spirits.

liv•en \'lī-vən\ *vb* **liv•ened; liv•en•ing** \'līv-(ə-)niŋ\ *vt* (1897) **:** ENLIVEN — often used with *up* ⟨he . . . ~*ed* up the editorial page —*Current Biog.*⟩ ~ *vi* **:** to become lively

live oak \'lī-,vōk\ *n* (1610) **:** any of several American evergreen oaks: as **a :** a medium-sized oak (*Quercus virginiana*) of southeastern No. America often cultivated as a shelter and shade tree and noted for its extremely hard tough durable wood **b :** any of various western No. American oaks with evergreen foliage and hard durable wood

¹**liv•er** \'liv-ər\ *n* [ME, fr. OE *lifer;* akin to OHG *lebra* liver] (bef. 12c) **1 a :** a large very vascular glandular organ of vertebrates that secretes bile and causes important changes in many of the substances contained in the blood (as by converting sugars into glycogen which it stores up until required and by forming urea) **b :** any of various large compound glands associated with the digestive tract of invertebrate animals and prob. concerned with the secretion of digestive enzymes **2** *archaic* **:** a determinant of the quality or temper of a man **3 :** the liver of an animal (as a calf or chicken) eaten as food **4 :** a grayish reddish brown — called also *liver brown, liver maroon*

²**liv•er** \'liv-ər\ *n* (14c) **1 :** one that lives esp. in a specified way ⟨a fast ~⟩ **2 :** RESIDENT

-liv•ered \'liv-ərd\ *adj comb form* **:** expressing vigor or courage considered suggestive of one with (such) a liver ⟨chicken-*livered*⟩ ⟨lily-*livered*⟩

liver fluke *n* (ca. 1790) **:** any of various trematode worms (as *Fasciola hepatica*) that invade the mammalian liver

liv•er•ied \'liv-(ə-)rēd\ *adj* (1634) **:** wearing a livery ⟨a ~ chauffeur⟩

liv•er•ish \'liv-(ə-)rish\ *adj* (1740) **1 :** resembling liver esp. in color **2 a :** suffering from liver disorder **:** BILIOUS **b :** PEEVISH, IRASCIBLE — **liv•er•ish•ness** *n*

liver sausage *n* (1855) **:** a sausage containing cooked ground liver and pork trimmings — called also *liver pudding*

liv•er•wort \'liv-ər-,wərt, -,wȯ(ə)rt\ *n* [ME, fr. OE *liferwyrt,* fr. *lifer* (trans. of ML *hepatica*) + *wyrt* plant — more at ROOT] (bef. 12c) **1 :** a bryophyte of a class (Hepaticae) related to and resembling the mosses but differing in reproduction, development, and in the structure of the gametophyte **2 :** HEPATICA

liv•er•wurst \'liv-ə(r)-,wərst, -,wů(ə)rst; 'liv-ər-,wůs(h)t\ *n* [part trans. of G *leberwurst,* fr. *leber* liver + *wurst* sausage] (1869) **:** LIVER SAUSAGE

¹**liv•ery** \'liv-(ə-)rē\ *n, pl* **-er•ies** [ME, fr. MF *livree,* lit., delivery, fr. *livrer* to deliver, fr. L *liberare* to free — more at LIBERATE] (14c) **1** *archaic* **:** the apportioning of provisions esp. to servants **:** ALLOWANCE **2 :** the act of delivering legal possession of property **3 a :** the distinctive clothing or badge formerly worn by the retainers of a person of rank **b :** a servant's uniform **c :** distinctive dress **:** GARB **4** *archaic* **a :** one's retainers or retinue **b :** the members of a British livery company **5 a :** the feeding, stabling, and care of horses for pay **b :** LIVERY STABLE **c :** a concern offering vehicles (as boats) for rent

²**livery** *adj* (1778) **1 :** resembling liver **2 :** suggesting liver disorder **:** LIVERISH

livery company *n* (1766) **:** any of various London craft or trade associations that are descended from medieval guilds

liv•ery•man \'liv-(ə-)rē-mən\ *n* (1682) **1 :** a freeman of the City of London entitled to wear the livery of the company to which he belongs **2** *archaic* **:** a liveried retainer **3 :** the keeper of a vehicle-rental service

livery stable *n* (1705) **:** a stable where horses and vehicles are kept for hire and where stabling is provided — called also *livery barn*

lives *pl of* LIFE

live steam *n* (ca. 1875) **:** steam direct from a boiler and under full pressure

live•stock \'līv-,stäk\ *n* (1742) **:** animals kept or raised for use or pleasure; *esp* **:** farm animals kept for use and profit

live•trap \'līv-,trap\ *vt* (1944) **:** to capture (an animal) in a live trap

live trap *n* (ca. 1875) **:** a trap for catching an animal alive and uninjured

live wire *n* (1903) **:** an alert, active, or aggressive person

liv•id \'liv-əd\ *adj* [F *livide,* fr. L *lividus,* fr. *livēre* to be blue; akin to OE *slāh* sloe, Russ *sliva* plum] (1622) **1 :** discolored by bruising **:** BLACK-AND-BLUE ⟨the ~ traces of the sharp scourges —Abraham Cowley⟩ **2 :** ASHEN, PALLID ⟨this cross, thy ~ face, thy pierced hands and feet —Walt Whitman⟩ **3 :** REDDISH ⟨a fan of gladiolas blushed ~ under the electric letters —Truman Capote⟩ **4 :** very angry **:** ENRAGED ⟨was ~ at his son's disobedience⟩ — **li•vid•i•ty** \liv-'id-ət-ē\ *n* — **liv•id•ness** \'liv-əd-nəs\ *n*

¹**liv•ing** \'liv-iŋ\ *adj* (bef. 12c) **1 a :** having life **b :** ACTIVE, FUNCTIONING ⟨~ languages⟩ **2 a :** exhibiting the life or motion of nature **:** NATURAL ⟨the wilderness is a ~ museum . . . of natural history —*NEA Jour.*⟩ **b :** ²LIVE 3a **3 a :** full of life or vigor ⟨made mathematics a ~ subject⟩ **b :** true to life **:** VIVID ⟨the program was televised in ~ color⟩ **c :** suited for living ⟨the ~ area⟩ **4 :** involving living persons **5 :** VERY — used as an intensive ⟨scared the ~ daylights out of him⟩ — **liv•ing•ness** *n*

²**living** *n* (14c) **1 :** the condition of being alive **2 a :** means of subsistence **:** LIVELIHOOD ⟨earning a ~⟩ **b** *archaic* **:** ESTATE, PROPERTY **c** *Brit* **:** BENEFICE 1 **3 :** conduct or manner of life ⟨the collegiate way of ~ —J.B. Conant⟩

living death *n* (1671) **:** life emptied of joys and satisfactions ⟨the *living death* of a concentration camp⟩

living fossil *n* (1922) **:** an organism (as a horseshoe crab or a ginkgo tree) that has remained essentially unchanged from earlier geologic times and whose close relatives are usu. extinct

liv•ing•ly \'liv-iŋ-lē\ *adv* (15c) **:** in a vital manner **:** REALISTICALLY

living room *n* (1857) **1 :** a room in a residence used for the common social activities of the occupants **2 :** LEBENSRAUM — called also *living space*

living standard *n* (1944) **:** STANDARD OF LIVING

living unit *n* (ca. 1937) **:** an apartment or house for use by one family

living wage *n* (1888) **1 :** a subsistence wage **2 :** a wage sufficient to provide the necessities and comforts essential to an acceptable standard of living

li•vre \lēvrᵊ\ *n* [F, fr. L *libra,* a unit of weight] (1553) **1 :** an old French monetary unit equal to 20 sols **2 :** a coin representing one livre

lix•iv•i•ate \lik-'siv-ē-,āt\ *vt* **-at•ed; -at•ing** [LL *lixivium* lye, fr. L *lixivius* made of lye, fr. *lixa* lye — more at LIQUID] (1758) **:** to extract a soluble constituent from (a solid mixture) by washing or percolation — **lix•iv•i•a•tion** \(,)lik-,siv-ē-'ā-shən\ *n*

liz•ard \'liz-ərd\ *n* [ME *liserd,* fr. MF *laisarde,* fr. L *lacerta;* akin to L *lacertus* muscle — more at LEG] (14c) **:** any of a suborder (Lacertilia) of reptiles distinguished from the snakes by a fused inseparable lower jaw, a single temporal opening, two pairs of well differentiated functional limbs which may be lacking in burrowing forms, external ears, and eyes with movable lids; *broadly* **:** any relatively long-bodied reptile (as a crocodile or dinosaur) with legs and tapering tail

lizard's tail *n* (1753) **:** a No. American herbaceous perennial plant (*Saururus cernuus*) with small white apetalous flowers

'll \l, əl, ᵊl\ *vb* **:** WILL ⟨you'*ll* be late⟩

lla•ma \'läm-ə, 'yäm-ə\ *n* [Sp, fr. Quechua] (1600) **:** any of several wild and domesticated So. American ruminants (genus *Lama*) related to the camels but smaller and without a hump; *esp* **:** the domesticated guanaco used in the Andes as a beast of burden and a source of wool

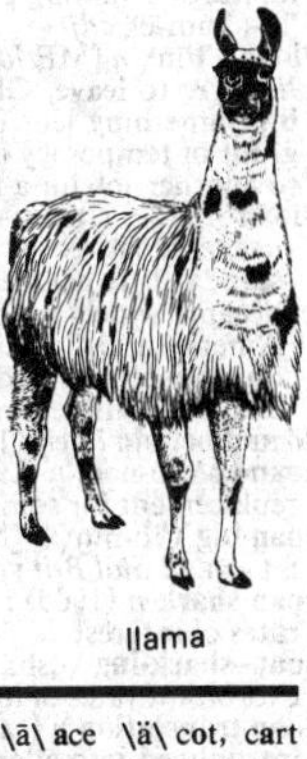

llama

lla•no \'län-(,)ō, 'lan-\ *n, pl* **llanos** [Sp, plain, fr. L *planum* — more at PLAIN] (ca. 1613) **:** an open grassy plain in Spanish America or the southwestern U.S.

Lloyd's \'lȯidz\ *n* (1819) **:** an association of individual underwriters in London specializing in marine insurance and shipping news and insuring for losses of almost every conceivable kind

lo \'lō\ *interj* [ME, fr. OE *lā*] (bef. 12c) — used to call attention or to express wonder or surprise

loach \'lōch\ *n* [ME *loche,* fr. MF] (14c) **:** any of

\ə\ abut \ᵊ\ kitten, F table \ər\ further \a\ ash \ā\ ace \ä\ cot, cart \aů\ out \ch\ chin \e\ bet \ē\ easy \g\ go \i\ hit \ī\ ice \j\ job \ŋ\ sing \ō\ go \ȯ\ law \ȯi\ boy \th\ thin \th\ the \ü\ loot \ů\ foot \y\ yet \zh\ vision \à, k, ⁿ, œ, ᵫ, ue, ᵫ, ʸ\ *see* Guide to Pronunciation

a family (Cobitidae) of small Old World freshwater fishes related to the carps

[1]load \'lōd\ *n* [ME *lod,* fr. OE *lād* support, carrying — more at LODE] (13c) **1 a :** whatever is put on a person or pack animal to be carried **:** PACK **b :** whatever is put in a ship or vehicle or airplane for conveyance **:** CARGO; *esp* **:** a quantity of material assembled or packed as a shipping unit **c :** the quantity that can be carried at one time by a specified means; *esp* **:** a measured quantity of a commodity fixed for each type of carrier — often used in combination ⟨a boat*load* of tourists⟩ **2 a :** a mass or weight supported by something ⟨branches bent low by their ~ of fruit⟩ **b :** the forces to which a structure is subjected due to superposed weight or to wind pressure on the vertical surfaces **3 a :** something that weighs down the mind or spirits ⟨took a ~ off her mind⟩ **b :** a burdensome or laborious responsibility ⟨always carried his share of the ~⟩ **4** *slang* **:** an intoxicating amount of liquor drunk **5 :** a large quantity **:** LOT — usu. used in pl. **6 a :** a charge for a firearm **b :** the quantity of material loaded into a device at one time **7 :** external resistance overcome by a machine or prime mover **8 a :** power output (as of a power plant) or power consumption (as by a device) **b :** a device to which power is delivered **9 a** (1) **:** the amount of work that a person carries or is expected to carry (2) **:** the amount of authorized work to be performed by a machine, a group, a department, or a factory **b :** the demand on the operating resources of a system (as a telephone exchange or a refrigerating apparatus) **10** *slang* **:** EYEFUL — used in the phrase *get a load of* **11 :** an amount added (as to the price of a security or the net premium in insurance) to represent selling expense and profit to the distributor **12 :** the decrease in capacity for survival of the average individual in a population due to the presence of deleterious genes in the gene pool ⟨the mutational ~ is the genetic ~ caused by mutation⟩

[2]load *vt* (15c) **1 a :** to put a load in or on ⟨~ a truck⟩ **b :** to place in or on a means of conveyance ⟨~ freight⟩ **2 a :** to encumber or oppress with something heavy, laborious, or disheartening **:** BURDEN ⟨a company ~*ed* down with debts⟩ **b :** to place as a burden or obligation ⟨~ more work on him⟩ **3 a :** to increase the weight of by adding something heavy **b :** to add a conditioning substance (as a mineral salt) to for body **c :** to add filler to (paper) **d :** to weight or shape (dice) to fall unfairly **e :** to pack with one-sided or prejudicial influences **:** BIAS **f :** to charge with multiple meanings (as emotional associations or hidden implications) **g :** to weight (as a test) with factors influencing validity or outcome **4 a :** to supply in abundance or excess **:** HEAP, PACK **b :** to put runners on (first, second, and third bases) in baseball **5 a :** to put a load or charge in (a device or piece of equipment) ⟨~ a gun⟩ **b :** to place or insert as a load in a device or piece of equipment ⟨~ film in a camera⟩ **6 :** to alter (as an alcoholic drink) by adding an adulterant or drug **7 a :** to add a load to (an insurance premium) **b :** to add a sum to after profits and expenses are accounted for ⟨~*ed* prices⟩ **~** *vi* **1 :** to receive a load **2 :** to put a load on or in a carrier, device, or container; *esp* **:** to insert the charge or cartridge in the chamber of a firearm **3 :** to go or go in as a load ⟨sightseers ~*ing* onto a bus⟩ — **load·er** *n*

load·ed *adj* (ca. 1884) **1** *slang* **:** DRUNK **2 :** having a large amount of money

load factor *n* (1943) **:** the percentage of available seats paid for and occupied in an aircraft

load·ing *n* (15c) **1 :** a cargo, weight, or stress placed on something **2 :** LOAD 11 **3 :** material used to load something **:** FILLER

load line *n* (ca. 1864) **:** the line on a ship indicating the depth to which it sinks in the water when properly loaded — see PLIMSOLL MARK illustration

load·mas·ter \'lōd-,mas-tər\ *n* (1961) **:** a crew member of a transport aircraft who is in charge of the cargo

load·star *var of* LODESTAR

load·stone *var of* LODESTONE

[1]loaf \'lōf\ *n, pl* **loaves** \'lōvz\ [ME *lof,* fr. OE *hlāf;* akin to OHG *hleib* loaf] (bef. 12c) **1 :** a shaped or molded mass of bread **2 :** a shaped or molded often symmetrical mass of food

[2]loaf *vi* [prob. back-formation fr. *loafer*] (1835) **:** to spend time in idleness

loaf·er \'lō-fər\ *n* [perh. short for *landloafer,* fr. G *landläufer* tramp, fr. *land* + *läufer* runner] (1830) **:** one that loafs **:** IDLER

Loafer *trademark* — used for a low step-in shoe

loam \'lōm, *chiefly Northern & Midland* 'lüm, *neNewEng* 'lu̇m\ *n* [ME *lom,* fr. OE *lām;* akin to OE *līm* lime] (bef. 12c) **1 a :** a mixture (as for plastering) composed chiefly of moistened clay **b :** a coarse molding sand used in founding **2 :** SOIL; *specif* **:** a soil consisting of a friable mixture of varying proportions of clay, silt, and sand — **loamy** \'lō-mē, 'lü-; 'lu̇m-ē\ *adj*

[1]loan \'lōn\ *n* [ME *lon,* fr. ON *lān;* akin to OE *lǣn* loan, *lēon* to lend, L *linquere* to leave, Gk *leipein*] (bef. 12c) **1 a :** money lent at interest **b :** something lent usu. for the borrower's temporary use **2 a :** the grant of temporary use **b :** the temporary duty of a person transferred to another job for a limited time **3 :** LOANWORD

[2]loan *vt* (13c) **:** LEND — **loan·able** \'lō-nə-bəl\ *adj*

usage Most recent commentators accept the use of *loan* as a verb as standard. It has been in use at least since the time of Henry VIII but became widely used first in the U.S. About 100 years ago a prominent American critic denounced the use, apparently basing his objections on a misunderstanding of Old English. Even though they are based on a mistake, these same objections may still be heard today

lo and behold *interj* (1808) — used to express wonder or surprise

loan·er \'lō-nər\ *n* (1926) **:** one (as a car or a watch) that is lent esp. as a replacement for something being repaired

loan·ing \'lō-niŋ\ *n* [ME *loning,* fr. *lone,* alter. of *lane*] (14c) **1** *dial Brit* **:** LANE **2** *dial Brit* **:** a milking yard

loan shark *n* (1905) **:** one who lends money to individuals at exorbitant rates of interest

loan–shark·ing \-,shär-kiŋ\ *n* (1914) **:** the practice of lending money at exorbitant rates of interest

loan translation *n* (ca. 1933) **:** a compound, derivative, or phrase that is introduced into a language through translation of the constituents of a term in another language (as *superman* from German *Übermensch*)

loan·word \'lōn-,wərd\ *n* (1874) **:** a word taken from another language and at least partly naturalized

loath \'lōth, 'lōt͟h\ *also* **loathe** \'lōt͟h, 'lōth\ *adj* [ME *loth* loathsome, fr. OE *lāth;* akin to OHG *leid* loathsome, OIr *liuss* aversion] (bef. 12c) **:** unwilling to do something contrary to one's ways of thinking **:** RELUCTANT ***syn*** see DISINCLINED — **loath·ness** *n*

loathe \'lōt͟h\ *vt* **loathed; loath·ing** [ME *lothen,* fr. OE *lāthian,* fr. *lāth*] (bef. 12c) **:** to dislike greatly and often with disgust or intolerance **:** DETEST ***syn*** see HATE — **loath·er** *n*

loath·ing \'lō-t͟hiŋ\ *n* (14c) **:** extreme disgust **:** DETESTATION

[1]loath·ly \'lōt͟h-lē, 'lōth-\ *adj* (bef. 12c) **:** LOATHSOME, REPULSIVE

[2]loath·ly \'lōth-lē, 'lōt͟h-\ *adv* (15c) **:** not willingly **:** RELUCTANTLY

loath·some \'lōth-səm, 'lōt͟h-\ *adj* [ME *lothsum,* fr. *loth* evil, fr. OE *lāth,* fr. *lāth,* adj.] (15c) **:** giving rise to loathing **:** DISGUSTING — **loath·some·ly** *adv* — **loath·some·ness** *n*

[1]lob \'läb\ *n* [prob. of LG origin; akin to LG *lubbe* coarse person] *dial Brit* (14c) **:** a dull heavy person **:** LOUT

[2]lob *vb* **lobbed; lob·bing** [*lob* (a loosely hanging object)] *vt* (1599) **1 :** to let hang heavily **:** DROOP **2 :** to throw, hit, or propel easily or in a high arc **~** *vi* **1 a :** to move slowly and heavily **b :** to move in an arc **2 :** to hit a tennis ball easily in a high arc

[3]lob *n* (1890) **:** a soft high-arching shot, throw, or kick

lob- *or* **lobo-** *comb form* [*lobe*] **:** lobe ⟨*lobar*⟩ ⟨*lobotomy*⟩

lo·bar \'lō-bər, -,bär\ *adj* (1856) **:** of or relating to a lobe

lo·bate \'lō-,bāt\ *also* **lo·bat·ed** \-,bāt-əd\ *adj* [NL *lobatus,* fr. LL *lobus*] (ca. 1760) **1 :** LOBED **2 :** resembling a lobe — **lo·ba·tion** \lō-'bā-shən\ *n*

[1]lob·by \'läb-ē\ *n, pl* **lobbies** [ML *lobium* gallery, of Gmc origin; akin to OHG *louba* porch — more at LODGE] (1593) **1 :** a corridor or hall connected with a larger room or series of rooms and used as a passageway or waiting room: as **a :** an anteroom of a legislative chamber; *esp* **:** one of two anterooms of a British parliamentary chamber to which members go to vote during a division **b :** a large hall serving as a foyer (as of a hotel or theater) **2 :** a group of persons engaged in lobbying esp. as representatives of a particular interest group

[2]lobby *vb* **lob·bied; lob·by·ing** *vi* (1837) **:** to conduct activities aimed at influencing public officials and esp. members of a legislative body on legislation **~** *vt* **1 :** to promote (as a project) or secure the passage of (as legislation) by influencing public officials **2 :** to attempt to influence or sway (as a public official) toward a desired action — **lob·by·er** *n* — **lob·by·ism** \-ē-,iz-əm\ *n* — **lob·by·ist** \-ē-əst\ *n*

lob·by·gow \'läb-ē-,gau̇\ *n* [origin unknown] (1906) **:** an errand boy

lobe \'lōb\ *n* [MF, fr. LL *lobus,* fr. Gk *lobos*] (1525) **:** a curved or rounded projection or division; *specif* **:** a usu. somewhat rounded projection or division of a bodily organ or part

lo·bec·to·my \lō-'bek-tə-mē\ *n, pl* **-mies** [ISV] (ca. 1911) **:** surgical removal of a lobe of an organ (as a lung) or gland (as the thyroid)

lobed \'lōbd\ *adj* (1787) **:** having lobes ⟨palmately ~ leaves⟩

lobe–fin \'lōb-,fin\ *n* (1941) **:** CROSSOPTERYGIAN — **lobe–finned** \-'find\ *adj*

lo·be·lia \lō-'bēl-yə, -'bē-lē-ə\ *n* [NL, fr. Matthias de *Lobel* †1616 Flem. botanist] (1739) **1 :** any of a genus (*Lobelia* of the family Lobeliaceae, the lobelia family) of widely distributed herbaceous plants cultivated for their terminal clusters of showy lipped flowers **2 :** the leaves and tops of Indian tobacco

lo·be·line \'lō-bə-,lēn\ *n* [NL *Lobelia* + E *-ine*] (1844) **:** a crystalline alkaloid $C_{22}H_{27}NO_2$ that is obtained from Indian tobacco and is used chiefly as a respiratory stimulant and as a smoking deterrent

lob·lol·ly \'läb-,läl-ē\ *n, pl* **-lies** [prob. fr. E dial. *lob* (to boil) + obs. E dial. *lolly* broth] (1597) **1** *dial* **a :** a thick gruel **b :** MIRE, MUDHOLE **2** *dial* **:** LOUT

loblolly pine *n* (1760) **:** a pine (*Pinus taeda*) of the southern U.S. with flaky bark, long needles in groups of three, and spiny tipped cones; *also* **:** its coarse-grained wood

lo·bo \'lō-(,)bō\ *n, pl* **lobos** [Sp, wolf, fr. L *lupus* — more at WOLF] (1839) **:** TIMBER WOLF — called also *lobo wolf*

lo·bot·o·mize \lō-'bät-ə-,mīz\ *vt* **-mized; -miz·ing** (1943) **1 :** to sever the frontal lobes of the brain of **2 :** to deprive of sensitivity, vitality, or energy

lo·bot·o·my \lō-'bät-ə-mē\ *n, pl* **-mies** [ISV] (1936) **:** severance of nerve fibers (as of the frontal lobes) by incision into the brain for the relief of some mental disorders and tensions

lob·scouse \'läb-,skau̇s\ *n* [origin unknown] (1706) **:** a sailor's dish of stewed or baked meat with vegetables and hardtack

lob·ster \'läb-stər\ *n* [ME, fr. OE *loppestre,* fr. *loppe* spider] (bef. 12c) **1 :** any of a family (Homaridae and esp. genus *Homarus*) of large edible marine decapod crustaceans that have stalked eyes, a pair of large claws, and a long abdomen and that include species from coasts on both sides of the No. Atlantic and from the Cape of Good Hope **2 :** SPINY LOBSTER

lob·ster·man \-mən\ *n* (1881) **:** one whose business is catching lobsters

lobster pot *n* (1764) **:** an oblong case with slat sides and a funnel-shaped net used as a trap for catching lobsters — called also *lobster trap*

lobster shift *n* (ca. 1933) **:** a work shift (as on a newspaper) that covers the late evening and early morning hours — called also *lobster trick*

lobster ther·mi·dor \-'thər-mə-,dȯ(ə)r\ *n* [*thermidor,* fr. F, fr. *Thermidor,* drama (1891) by Victorien Sardou] (ca. 1930) **:** cooked lobster meat in a rich wine sauce stuffed into a lobster shell and browned

lob·u·lar \'läb-yə-lər\ *adj* (1822) **:** of, relating to, or resembling a lobule

lob·u·lat·ed \'läb-yə-,lāt-əd\ *also* **lob·u·late** \-,lāt\ *adj* (1862) **:** made up of or provided with lobules ⟨the pancreas is a ~ organ⟩ — **lob·u·la·tion** \,läb-yə-'lā-shən\ *n*

lob·ule \'läb-(,)yü(ə)l\ *n* (1682) **:** a small lobe; *also* **:** a subdivision of a lobe

[1]lo·cal \'lō-kəl\ *adj* [ME *localle,* fr. MF *local,* fr. LL *localis,* fr. L *locus* place — more at STALL] (15c) **1 :** characterized by or relating to position in space **:** having a definite spatial form or location **2 :** of or relating to a particular place **:** characteristic of a particular place **:** not general or widespread **3 a :** primarily serving the needs of a particular limited district **b** *of a public conveyance* **:** making all the stops on a route **4 :** involving or affecting only a restricted part of the organism **:** TOPICAL **5 :** of or relating to telephone communication within a specified area — **lo·cal·ly** \-kə-lē\ *adv*

2local *n* (ca. 1824) : a local person or thing: as **a** : a local public conveyance (as a train or an elevator) **b** : a local or particular branch, lodge, or chapter of an organization (as a labor union)
local area network *n* (1982) : a network of personal computers in a small area (as an office) that are linked by cable, can communicate directly with other devices in the network, and can share resources
local color *n* (1884) : the presentation of the features and peculiarities of a particular locality and its inhabitants in writing
lo·cale \lō-ˈkal\ *n* [modif. of F *local,* fr. *local,* adj.] (1772) **1** : a place or locality esp. when viewed in relation to a particular event or characteristic **2** : SITE, SCENE ⟨the ~ of a story⟩
local government *n* (1884) : the government of a specific local area constituting a subdivision of a major political unit (as a nation or state); *also* : the body of persons constituting such a government
lo·cal·ism \ˈlō-kə-ˌliz-əm\ *n* (1823) **1 a** : a local idiom **b** : a local peculiarity of speaking or acting **2** : affection or partiality for a particular place : SECTIONALISM
lo·cal·ite \ˈlō-kə-ˌlīt\ *n* (1951) : a native or resident of the locality under consideration : LOCAL
lo·cal·i·ty \lō-ˈkal-ət-ē\ *n, pl* **-ties** (1628) **1** : the fact or condition of having a location in space or time **2** : a particular place, situation, or location
lo·cal·ize \ˈlō-kə-ˌlīz\ *vb* **-ized; -iz·ing** *vt* (1792) **1** : to make local : orient locally **2** : to assign to or keep within a definite locality ~ *vi* : to accumulate in or be restricted to a specific or limited area ⟨an infection that ~*s* in the ear⟩ — **lo·cal·iz·abil·i·ty** \ˌlō-kə-ˌlī-zə-ˈbil-ət-ē\ *n* — **lo·cal·iz·able** \ˈlō-kə-ˌlī-zə-bəl\ *adj* — **lo·cal·iza·tion** \ˌlō-kə-lə-ˈzā-shən\ *n*
local option *n* (1878) : the power granted by a legislature to a political subdivision to determine by popular vote the local applicability of a law on a controversial issue (as the sale of liquor)
local time *n* (1833) : time based on the meridian through a particular place as contrasted with that of a time zone
lo·cate \ˈlō-ˌkāt, lō-ˈ\ *vb* **lo·cat·ed; lo·cat·ing** [L *locatus,* pp. of *locare* to place, fr. *locus*] *vi* (1652) : to establish oneself or one's business : SETTLE ~ *vt* **1** : to determine or indicate the place, site, or limits of **2** : to set or establish in a particular spot : STATION **3** : to seek out and determine the location of **4** : to find or fix the place of esp. in a sequence : CLASSIFY — **lo·cat·able** \-ˌkāt-ə-bəl, -ˈkāt-\ *adj* — **lo·cat·er** *n*
lo·ca·tion \lō-ˈkā-shən\ *n* (1597) **1 a** : a position or site occupied or available for occupancy or marked by some distinguishing feature : SITUATION **b** (1) : a tract of land designated for a purpose (2) *Austral* : FARM, STATION **c** : a place outside a motion-picture studio where a picture or part of it is filmed — usu. used in the phrase *on location* **2** : the act or process of locating — **lo·ca·tion·al** \-shnəl, -shən-ᵊl\ *adj* — **lo·ca·tion·al·ly** \-ē\ *adv*
1loc·a·tive \ˈläk-ət-iv\ *n* [L *locus* + E *-ative* (as in *vocative*)] (1804) : the locative case; *also* : a word in that case
2locative *adj* (1841) : of or being a grammatical case that denotes place or the place where or wherein
lo·ca·tor \ˈlō-ˌkāt-ər, lō-ˈ\ *n* (1784) : one that locates something (as a mining claim or the course of a road)
loch \ˈläk, ˈläḵ\ *n* [ME (Sc) *louch,* fr. ScGael *loch;* akin to L *lacus* lake] (14c) **1** *Scot* : LAKE **2** *Scot* : a bay or arm of the sea esp. when nearly landlocked
loci *pl of* LOCUS
1lock \ˈläk\ *n* [ME *lok,* fr. OE *locc;* akin to OHG *loc* lock, L *luctari* to struggle, *luxus* dislocated] (bef. 12c) **1 a** : a tuft, tress, or ringlet of hair **b** *pl* : the hair of the head **2** : a cohering bunch (as of wool, cotton, or flax) : TUFT
2lock *n* [ME *lok,* fr. OE *loc;* akin to OHG *loh* enclosure, OE *locc* lock of hair] (bef. 12c) **1 a** : a fastening (as for a door) operated by a key or a combination **b** : the mechanism for exploding the charge or cartridge of a firearm **2 a** : an enclosure (as in a canal) with gates at each end used in raising or lowering boats as they pass from level to level **b** : AIR LOCK **3 a** : a locking or fastening together **b** : an intricate mass of objects impeding each other (as in a traffic jam) **c** : a hold in wrestling secured on one part of the body; *broadly* : a controlling hold ⟨his paper . . . had a ~ on a large part of the state —John Corry⟩ **d** : something assured of success or favorable outcome
3lock *vt* (14c) **1 a** : to fasten the lock of **b** : to make fast with or as if with a lock ⟨~ up the house⟩ **2 a** : to fasten in or out or to make secure or inaccessible by or as if by means of locks ⟨~*ed* himself away from the curious world⟩ ⟨~*ed* her husband out⟩ **b** : to hold fast or inactive : fix in a particular situation or method of operation ⟨a team firmly ~*ed* in last place⟩ **c** : to sight and follow (a target) automatically by means of a radar beam or sensor — used with *on* or *onto* ⟨~ on Canopus for guidance⟩ **3 a** : to make fast by the interlacing or interlocking of parts **b** : to hold in a close embrace **c** : to grapple in combat; *also* : to bind closely ⟨administration and students were ~*ed* in conflict⟩ **4** : to invest (capital) without assurance of easy convertibility into money **5 a** : to move or permit to pass (as a ship) by raising or lowering in a lock **b** : to provide (as a canal) with locks ~ *vi* **1 a** : to become locked **b** : to be capable of being locked **2** : INTERLACE, INTERLOCK **3 a** : to build locks to facilitate navigation **b** : to go or pass by means of a lock (as in a canal) — **lock·able** \ˈläk-ə-bəl\ *adj* — **lock horns** : to come into conflict
lock·age \ˈläk-ij\ *n* (1771) **1** : toll paid for passing through a lock **2** : a system of locks **3** : an act or the process of passing a ship through a lock
lock·box \ˈläk-ˌbäks\ *n* (1872) : a box (as a post-office box, strongbox, or safe-deposit box) that locks
locked–in \ˈläk-ˈtin\ *adj* (1952) **1** : unalterably fixed **2** : unable or unwilling to shift invested funds because of the tax effect of realizing capital gains
lock·er \ˈläk-ər\ *n* (14c) **1 a** : a drawer, cupboard, or compartment that may be closed with a lock; *esp* : one for individual storage use **b** : a chest or compartment on shipboard for compact storage of articles **c** : a compartment for storing quick-frozen foods for long periods usu. at or below 0° F and at 80% relative humidity **2** : one that locks
lock·er–room \ˈläk-ə(r)-ˌrüm\ *adj* (1946) : of, relating to, or suitable for use in a locker room; *esp* : of an earthy or sexual nature ⟨~ language⟩
locker room *n* (1895) : a room for changing clothes and for storing clothing and equipment in lockers; *esp* : one for use by sports participants
lock·et \ˈläk-ət\ *n* [MF *loquet* latch, fr. MD *loke;* akin to OE *loc*] (1679) : a small case usu. of precious metal that has space for a memento and that is worn typically suspended from a chain or necklace
lock·jaw \ˈläk-ˌjō\ *n* (1803) : an early symptom of tetanus characterized by spasm of the jaw muscles and inability to open the jaws; *also* : TETANUS
lock·keep·er \ˈläk-ˌkē-pər\ *n* (1794) : a person in charge of a lock (as on a canal)
lock·nut \-ˌnət, -ˈnət\ *n* (1864) **1** : a nut screwed down hard on another to prevent it from slacking back **2** : a nut so constructed that it locks itself when screwed up tight
lock·out \ˈläk-ˌau̇t\ *n* (1854) : the withholding of employment by an employer and the whole or partial closing of his business establishment in order to gain concessions from or resist demands of employees
lock out \(ˈ)läk-ˈau̇t\ *vt* (1868) : to subject (a body of employees) to a lockout
lock·ram \ˈläk-rəm\ *n* [ME *lokerham,* fr. *Locronan,* town in Brittany] (14c) : a coarse plain-woven linen formerly used in England
lock·smith \ˈläk-ˌsmith\ *n* (13c) : one who makes or repairs locks
lock·smith·ing \-iŋ\ *n* (ca. 1909) : the work or business of a locksmith
lock·step \ˈläk-ˌstep\ *n* (1802) **1** : a mode of marching in step by a body of men going one after another as closely as possible **2** : a standard method or procedure that is mindlessly adhered to or that minimizes individuality
lock·stitch \-ˌstich\ *n* (ca. 1859) : a sewing machine stitch formed by the looping together of two threads one on each side of the material being sewn — **lockstitch** *vb*
lock, stock, and barrel *adv* [fr. the principal parts of a flintlock] (1842) : WHOLLY, COMPLETELY ⟨the only thing which had not been sold *lock, stock, and barrel* with the . . . house was this piano —Marcia Davenport⟩
lock·up \ˈläk-ˌəp\ *n* (1767) **1** : JAIL; *esp* : a local jail where persons are detained prior to court hearing **2** : an act of locking : the state of being locked
1lo·co \ˈlō-(ˌ)kō\ *adv or adj* [It dial, there, fr. L *in loco* in the place] (ca. 1801) : in the register as written — used as a direction in music
2loco *n, pl* **locos** *or* **locoes** [MexSp, fr. Sp, crazy] (1844) **1** : LOCOWEED **2** : LOCOISM
3loco *vt* (1884) **1** : to poison with locoweed **2** : to make frenzied or crazy
4loco *adj* [Sp] *slang* (1887) : mentally disordered : CRAZY, FRENZIED
lo·co·fo·co \ˌlō-kə-ˈfō-(ˌ)kō\ *n, pl* **-focos** [prob. fr. *¹locomotive* + It *fuoco, foco* fire, fr. L *focus* hearth] (ca. 1835) **1** : a match capable of being ignited by friction on a hard dry rough surface **2** *cap* **a** : a member of a radical group of New York Democrats organized in 1835 in opposition to the regular party organization **b** : DEMOCRAT 2
lo·co·ism \ˈlō-(ˌ)kō-ˌiz-əm\ *n* (1900) : a disease of horses, cattle, and sheep caused by chronic poisoning with locoweeds
lo·co·mote \ˌlō-kə-ˈmōt\ *vi* **-mot·ed; -mot·ing** [back-formation fr. *locomotion*] (1834) : to move about
lo·co·mo·tion \ˌlō-kə-ˈmō-shən\ *n* [L *locus* + E *motion*] (1646) **1** : an act or the power of moving from place to place **2** : TRAVEL ⟨interest in free ~ and choice of occupation —Zechariah Chafee, Jr.⟩
1lo·co·mo·tive \ˌlō-kə-ˈmōt-iv\ *adj* (1612) **1** : LOCOMOTORY **2** : of or relating to travel **3** : of, relating to, or being a machine that moves about by operation of its own mechanism
2locomotive *n* (1829) **1** : a self-propelled vehicle that runs on rails, utilizes any of several forms of energy for producing motion, and is used for moving railroad cars **2** : a school or college cheer characterized by a slow beginning and a progressive increase in speed
lo·co·mo·tor \ˌlō-kə-ˈmōt-ər\ *adj* (1870) **1** : of, relating to, or functioning in locomotion **2** : affecting or involving the locomotor organs
locomotor ataxia *n* (1878) : TABES DORSALIS
lo·co·mo·to·ry \ˌlō-kə-ˈmōt-ə-rē\ *adj* (1835) **1** : LOCOMOTOR ⟨~ appendages⟩ **2** : capable of moving independently from place to place ⟨~ animals⟩
lo·co·weed \ˈlō-(ˌ)kō-ˌwēd\ *n* (1879) : any of several leguminous plants (genera *Astragalus* and *Oxytropis*) of western No. America that cause locoism in livestock
loc·u·lar \ˈläk-yə-lər\ *adj* (1847) : having or composed of loculi — often used in combination ⟨multi*locular*⟩
loc·u·lat·ed \ˈläk-yə-ˌlāt-əd\ *adj* (1801) : having, forming, or divided into loculi — **loc·u·la·tion** \ˌläk-yə-ˈlā-shən\ *n*
loc·ule \ˈläk-(ˌ)yü(ə)l\ *n* [F, fr. L *loculus*] (ca. 1888) : LOCULUS; *esp* : any of the cells of a compound ovary of a plant — **loc·uled** \-(ˌ)yü(ə)ld\ *adj*
loc·u·li·ci·dal \ˌläk-yə-lə-ˈsīd-ᵊl\ *adj* [NL *loculus* + L *-cidere* to cut, fr. *caedere* — more at CONCISE] (ca. 1819) : dehiscing longitudinally so as to bisect each loculus ⟨~ fruit⟩
loc·u·lus \ˈläk-yə-ləs\ *n, pl* **-li** \-ˌlī, -ˌlē\ [NL, fr. L, dim. of *locus*] (1861) : a small chamber or cavity esp. in a plant or animal body
lo·cum \ˈlō-kəm\ *n* [by shortening] *chiefly Brit* (1901) : LOCUM TENENS
lo·cum te·nens \ˌlō-kəm-ˈtē-ˌnenz, -nənz\ *n, pl* **locum te·nen·tes** \-ti-ˈnen-ˌtēz\ [ML, lit., (one) holding a place] (1641) : one filling an office for a time or temporarily taking the place of another — used esp. of a doctor or clergyman
lo·cus \ˈlō-kəs\ *n, pl* **lo·ci** \ˈlō-ˌsī, -ˌkī, -ˌkē\ [L — more at STALL] (1715) **1 a** : PLACE, LOCALITY ⟨was the culture of medicine in the beginning dispersed from a single focus or did it arise in several *loci?* —S. C. Harvey⟩ **b** : a center of activity or concentration ⟨in democracy the ~ of power is in the people —H. G. Rickover⟩ **2** : the set of all points whose location is determined by stated conditions **3** : the position in a chromosome of a particular gene or allele
lo·cus clas·si·cus \ˌlō-kəs-ˈklas-i-kəs\ *n, pl* **lo·ci clas·si·ci** \-ˌsī-ˈklas-ə-ˌsī, -ˌkī-ˈklas-ə-ˌkī, -ˌkē-ˈklas-ə-ˌkē\ [NL] (1853) : a passage that has become a standard for the elucidation of a word or subject

\ə\ abut \ᵊ\ kitten, F table \ər\ further \a\ ash \ā\ ace \ä\ cot, cart \au̇\ out \ch\ chin \e\ bet \ē\ easy \g\ go \i\ hit \ī\ ice \j\ job \ŋ\ sing \ō\ go \ó\ law \ói\ boy \th\ thin \t͟h\ the \ü\ loot \u̇\ foot \y\ yet \zh\ vision \à, k̲, ⁿ, œ, œ̄, ue, ue̅, ʸ\ *see* Guide to Pronunciation

locus coe·ru·le·us *also* **locus ce·ru·le·us** \ˌlō-kə(s)-si-ˈrü-lē-əs\ *n* [NL, lit., dark blue place, fr. L *caeruleus, coeruleus* dark blue, prob. fr. *caelum* sky — more at CELESTIAL] (ca. 1895) : a blue area of the brain stem with many norepinephrine-containing neurons

lo·cust \ˈlō-kəst\ *n* [ME, fr. L *locusta*] (14c) **1 :** SHORT-HORNED GRASSHOPPER; *esp* : a migratory grasshopper often traveling in vast swarms and stripping the areas passed of all vegetation **2 :** CICADA **3 a :** any of various hard-wooded leguminous trees: as (1) : CAROB 1 (2) : BLACK LOCUST (3) : HONEY LOCUST **b :** the wood of a locust tree

locust bean *n* (1847) : CAROB

lo·cu·tion \lō-ˈkyü-shən\ *n* [ME *locucioun,* fr. L *locution-, locutio,* fr. *locutus,* pp. of *loqui* to speak] (15c) **1 :** a particular form of expression or a peculiarity of phrasing; *esp* : a word or expression characteristic of a region, group, or cultural level **2 :** style of discourse : PHRASEOLOGY

lode \ˈlōd\ *n* [ME, fr. OE *lād* course, support; akin to OE *līthan* to go — more at LEAD] (bef. 12c) **1** *dial Eng* : WATERWAY **2 :** an ore deposit **3 :** something that resembles a lode : an abundant store

lo·den \ˈlōd-ᵊn\ *n* [G, fr. OHG *lodo* coarse cloth; akin to OE *lotha* mantle] (1911) **1 :** a thick woolen cloth used for outer clothing **2 :** a variable color averaging a dull grayish green

lode·star \ˈlōd-ˌstär\ *n* [ME *lode sterre,* fr. *lode* course, fr. OE *lād*] (14c) **1 :** a star that leads or guides; *esp* : NORTH STAR **2 :** something that serves as a guiding star

lode·stone \-ˌstōn\ *n* [obs. *lode* course, fr. ME] (1515) **1 :** magnetite possessing polarity **2 :** something that strongly attracts

[1]**lodge** \ˈläj\ *vb* **lodged; lodg·ing** *vt* (13c) **1 a** (1) : to provide temporary quarters for (2) : to rent lodgings to **b :** to establish or settle in a place **2 :** to serve as a receptacle for : CONTAIN **3 :** to beat (as a crop) flat to the ground **4 :** to bring to an intended or a fixed position (as by throwing or thrusting) **5 :** to deposit for safeguard or preservation **6 :** to place or vest esp. in a source, means, or agent **7 :** to lay (as a complaint) before a proper authority : FILE ~ *vi* **1 a :** to occupy a place temporarily : SLEEP **b** (1) : to have a residence : DWELL (2) : to be a lodger **2 :** to come to a rest **3 :** to fall or lie down — used esp. of hay or grain crops

[2]**lodge** *n* [ME *loge,* fr. OF, of Gmc origin; akin to OHG *louba* porch, ON *lopt* balcony, upper room] (13c) **1** *chiefly dial* : a rude shelter or abode **2 a :** a house set apart for residence in a particular season (as the hunting season) **b :** a resort hotel : INN **3 a :** a house on an estate orig. for the use of a gamekeeper, caretaker, or porter **b :** a shelter for an employee (as a gatekeeper) **4 :** a den or lair esp. of gregarious animals **5 a :** the meeting place of a branch of an organization and esp. a fraternal organization **b :** the body of members of such a branch **6 a :** WIGWAM **b :** a family of No. American Indians

lodge·pole pine \ˌläj-ˌpōl-\ *n* (1859) : either of two pines of western No. America with needles in pairs and short ovoid usu. asymmetric cones: **a :** a scrubby coastal pine (*Pinus contorta*) with thick deeply furrowed bark and hard strong coarse-grained medium-light wood **b :** a tall straight pine (*P. contorta* var. *latifolia* syn. *P. murrayana*) with thin and little furrowed bark and soft weak fine-grained lightweight wood

lodg·er \ˈläj-ər\ *n* (1511) : ROOMER

lodg·ing *n* (14c) **1 a :** a place to live : DWELLING **b :** LODGMENT 3b **2 a** (1) : sleeping accommodations ⟨found ~ in the barn⟩ (2) : a temporary place to stay ⟨a ~ for the night⟩ **b :** a room in the house of another used as a place of residence — usu. used in pl. **3 :** the act of lodging

lodging house *n* (1766) : ROOMING HOUSE

lodg·ment *or* **lodge·ment** \ˈläj-mənt\ *n* (1598) **1 a :** a lodging place : SHELTER ⟨a hut for temporary ~ of cattlemen⟩ **b :** ACCOMMODATIONS, LODGINGS ⟨found ~ in the city⟩ **2 a :** the act, fact, or manner of lodging **b :** a placing, depositing, or coming to rest **3 a :** an accumulation or collection deposited in a place or remaining at rest **b :** a place of rest or deposit

lod·i·cule \ˈläd-i-ˌkyü(ə)l\ *n* [L *lodicula,* dim. of *lodic-, lodix* cover] (1864) : one of usu. two delicate membranous hyaline scales at the base of the ovary of a grass that by their swelling assist in anthesis

loess \ˈles, ˈlə(r)s, ˈlō-əs\ *n* [G *löss*] (ca. 1833) : an unstratified usu. buff to yellowish brown loamy deposit found in No. America, Europe, and Asia and believed to be chiefly deposited by the wind — **loess·ial** \ˈles-ē-əl, ˈlə(r)s-, lō-ˈes-\ *adj*

[1]**loft** \ˈlȯft\ *n* [ME, fr. OE, fr. ON *lopt* air; akin to OHG *luft* air — more at LODGE] (bef. 12c) **1 :** an upper room or floor : ATTIC **2 a :** a gallery in a church or hall **b :** one of the upper floors of a warehouse or business building esp. when not partitioned **c :** HAYLOFT **3 a :** the backward slant of the face of a golf-club head **b :** the act of lofting **4 :** the thickness of a fabric or insulated garment (as a down-filled sleeping bag)

[2]**loft** *vt* (1518) **1 :** to place, house, or store in a loft **2 :** to propel through the air or into space ⟨~*ed* a long hit to center⟩ ⟨instruments ~*ed* by a powerful rocket⟩ **3 :** to lay out a full-sized working drawing of the lines and contours of (as a ship's hull) ~ *vi* **1 :** to propel a ball high into the air **2 :** to rise high

lofty \ˈlȯf-tē\ *adj* **loft·i·er; -est** (15c) **1 a :** elevated in character and spirit : NOBLE **b :** elevated in position : SUPERIOR **2 :** having a haughty overbearing manner : SUPERCILIOUS **3 a :** rising to a great height : impressively high ⟨~ mountains⟩ **b :** REMOTE, ESOTERIC ***syn*** see HIGH — **loft·i·ly** \-tə-lē\ *adv* — **loft·i·ness** \-tē-nəs\ *n*

[1]**log** \ˈlȯg, ˈläg\ *n, often attrib* [ME *logge,* prob. of Scand origin; akin to ON *lāg* fallen tree; akin to OE *licgan* to lie — more at LIE] (14c) **1 :** a usu. bulky piece or length of unshaped timber; *esp* : a length of a tree trunk ready for sawing and over six feet long **2 :** an apparatus for measuring the rate of a ship's motion through the water that consists of a block fastened to a line and run out from a reel **3 a :** the record of the rate of a ship's speed or of her daily progress; *also* : the full nautical record of a ship's voyage **b :** the full record of a flight by an aircraft **4 :** any of various records of performance ⟨a computer ~⟩

[2]**log** *vb* **logged; log·ging** *vt* (1699) **1 a :** to cut (trees) for lumber **b :** to clear (land) of trees in lumbering — often used with *off* **2 :** to enter details of or about in a log **3 a :** to move (an indicated distance) or attain (an indicated speed) as noted in a log **b** (1) : to sail a ship or fly an airplane for (an indicated distance or period of time) (2) : to have (an indicated record) to one's credit : ACHIEVE ~ *vi* : [3]LUMBER 1

[3]**log** *n, often attrib* [by shortening] (1631) : LOGARITHM

log- *or* **logo-** *comb form* [Gk, fr. *logos* — more at LEGEND] : word : thought : speech : discourse ⟨*logogram*⟩ ⟨*logorrhea*⟩

-log — see -LOGUE

lo·gan·ber·ry \ˈlō-gən-ˌber-ē\ *n* [James H. *Logan* †1928 Am. lawyer + E *berry*] (1893) : a red-fruited upright-growing dewberry regarded as a variety (*Rubus ursinus loganobaccus*) of the western dewberry or as a hybrid of the western dewberry and the red raspberry; *also* : its berry

log·a·oe·dic \ˌläg-ə-ˈēd-ik\ *adj* [LL *logaoedicus,* fr. LGk *logaoidikos,* fr. Gk *log-* + *aeidein* to sing; fr. the resemblance of such rhythm to prose — more at ODE] (1844) : marked by the mixture of several meters; *specif* : having a rhythm that uses both dactyls and trochees or anapests and iambs — **logaoedic** *n*

log·a·rithm \ˈlȯg-ə-ˌrith-əm, ˈläg-\ *n* [NL *logarithmus,* fr. *log-* + Gk *arithmos* number — more at ARITHMETIC] (1615) : the exponent that indicates the power to which a number is raised to produce a given number ⟨the ~ of 100 to the base 10 is 2⟩ — **log·a·rith·mic** \ˌlȯg-ə-ˈrith-mik, ˌläg-\ *adj* — **log·a·rith·mi·cal·ly** \-mi-k(ə-)lē\ *adv*

logarithmic function *n* (ca. 1949) : a function (as $y = \log_a x$ or $y = \ln x$) that is the inverse of an exponential function (as $y = a^x$ or $y = e^x$) so that the independent variable appears in a logarithm

log·book \ˈlȯg-ˌbu̇k, ˈläg-\ *n* (1679) : LOG 3, 4

loge \ˈlōzh\ *n* [F, fr. OF, a shelter — more at LODGE] (1749) **1 a :** a small compartment : BOOTH **b :** a box in a theater **2 a :** a small partitioned area **b :** a separate forward section of a theater mezzanine or balcony

logged \ˈlȯgd, ˈlägd\ *adj* (1820) **1 :** HEAVY, SLUGGISH **2 :** sodden esp. with water

log·ger \ˈlȯg-ər, ˈläg-\ *n* (1732) : one engaged in logging

log·ger·head \ˈlȯg-ər-ˌhed, ˈläg-\ *n* [prob. fr. E dial. *logger* (block of wood) + *head*] (1588) **1** *chiefly dial* **a :** BLOCKHEAD **b :** HEAD; *esp* : a disproportionately large head **2 a :** any of various very large marine turtles (family Cheloniidae); *esp* : a carnivorous turtle (*Caretta caretta*) of the warmer parts of the western Atlantic **b :** ALLIGATOR SNAPPER **3 :** an iron tool consisting of a long handle terminating in a ball or bulb that is heated and used to melt tar or to heat liquids — **at loggerheads :** in or into a state of quarrelsome disagreement

log·gets *or* **log·gats** \ˈlȯg-əts, ˈläg-\ *n pl but sing or pl in constr* [prob. fr. [1]*log* + *-et*] (1581) : a game formerly played in England in which participants throw pieces of wood at a stake

log·gia \ˈlō-jē-ə, ˈlō-(ˌ)jä\ *n, pl* **loggias** \ˈlō-jē-əz, ˈlō-(ˌ)jäz\ *also* **log·gie** \ˈlō-(ˌ)jā\ [It, fr. F *loge* loge] (1742) : a roofed open gallery esp. at an upper story overlooking an open court

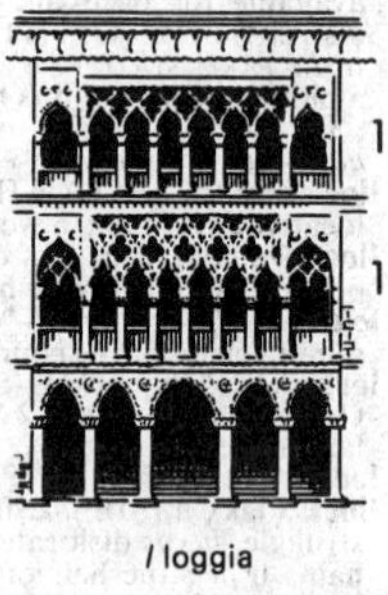

loggia

log·ic \ˈläj-ik\ *n* [ME *logik,* fr. MF *logique,* fr. L *logica,* fr. Gk *logikē,* fr. fem. of *logikos* of reason, fr. *logos* reason — more at LEGEND] (12c) **1 a** (1) : a science that deals with the principles and criteria of validity of inference and demonstration : the science of the formal principles of reasoning (2) : a branch or variety of logic ⟨modal ~⟩ ⟨Boolean ~⟩ (3) : a branch of semiotic; *esp* : SYNTACTICS (4) : the formal principles of a branch of knowledge **b** (1) : a particular mode of reasoning viewed as valid or faulty (2) : RELEVANCE, PROPRIETY **c :** interrelation or sequence of facts or events when seen as inevitable or predictable **d :** the arrangement of circuit elements (as in a computer) needed for computation; *also* : the circuits themselves **2 :** something that forces a decision apart from or in opposition to reason ⟨the ~ of war⟩ — **lo·gi·cian** \lō-ˈjish-ən\ *n*

log·i·cal \ˈläj-i-kəl\ *adj* (15c) **1 a** (1) : of, relating to, involving, or being in accordance with logic (2) : skilled in logic **b :** formally true or valid : ANALYTIC, DEDUCTIVE **2 :** capable of reasoning or of using reason in an orderly cogent fashion ⟨a ~ thinker⟩ — **log·i·cal·i·ty** \ˌläj-ə-ˈkal-ət-ē\ *n* — **log·i·cal·ly** \ˈläj-i-k(ə-)lē\ *adv* — **log·i·cal·ness** \-kəl-nəs\ *n*

logical positivism *n* (1931) : a 20th century philosophical movement that holds characteristically that all meaningful statements are either analytic or conclusively verifiable or at least confirmable by observation and experiment and that metaphysical theories are therefore strictly meaningless — called also *logical empiricism* — **logical positivist** *n*

log·i·co- \ˌläj-i-kō\ *comb form* : logical : logical and ⟨*logico*-mathematical⟩

lo·gi·on \ˈlō-gē-ˌän\ *n, pl* **lo·gia** \-gē-ˌä\ *or* **logions** [Gk, dim. of *logos*] (1875) : SAYING; *esp* : a saying attributed to Jesus

[1]**lo·gis·tic** \lō-ˈjis-tik, lə-\ *or* **lo·gis·ti·cal** \-ti-kəl\ *adj* (1628) **1 a :** of or relating to symbolic logic **b :** of or relating to the philosophical attempt to reduce mathematics to logic **2 :** of or relating to logistics **3** *logistic* : of, represented by, or relating to a logistic curve ⟨a ~ process⟩ — **lo·gis·ti·cal·ly** \-ti-k(ə-)lē\ *adv*

[2]**logistic** *n* (1905) : SYMBOLIC LOGIC

logistic curve *n* (ca. 1903) : an S-shaped curve that represents an exponential function and is used in mathematical models of growth processes

lo·gis·ti·cian \(ˌ)lō-ˌjis-ˈtish-ən, ˌlō-jəs-\ *n* (1943) : a specialist in logistics

lo·gis·tics \lō-ˈjis-tiks, lə-\ *n pl but sing or pl in constr* [F *logistique* art of calculating, logistics, fr. Gk *logistikē* art of calculating, fr. fem. of *logistikos* of calculation, fr. *logizein* to calculate, fr. *logos* reason] (ca. 1861) **1 :** the aspect of military science dealing with the procurement, maintenance, and transportation of military matériel, facilities, and personnel **2 :** the handling of the details of an operation

log·jam \ˈlȯg-ˌjam, ˈläg-\ *n* (1885) **1 :** a jumble of logs jammed together in a watercourse **2 a :** DEADLOCK, IMPASSE ⟨trying to break the ~ in negotiations⟩ **b :** BLOCKAGE

log·nor·mal \(ˈ)lȯg-ˈnȯr-məl, (ˈ)läg-\ *adj* (1945) : relating to or being a normal distribution that is the distribution of the logarithm of a random variable; *also* : relating to or being such a random variable — **log·nor·mal·i·ty** \ˌlȯg-nȯr-ˈmal-ət-ē, ˌläg-\ *n* — **log·nor·mal·ly** \(ˈ)lȯg-ˈnȯr-mə-lē, (ˈ)läg-\ *adv*

logo \ˈlō-(ˌ)gō; ˈlȯg-(ˌ)ō, ˈläg-\ *n, pl* **log·os** \-(ˌ)gōz, -(ˌ)ōz\ (1937) **1 :** LOGOTYPE **2 :** an identifying statement : MOTTO

logo- — see LOG-
logo·gram \'lȯg-ə-ˌgram, 'läg-\ *n* (1840) **:** a letter, symbol, or sign used to represent an entire word — **logo·gram·mat·ic** \ˌlȯg-ə-grə-'mat-ik, ˌläg-\ *adj*
logo·graph \'lȯg-ə-ˌgraf, 'läg-\ *n* (ca. 1888) **:** LOGOGRAM
logo·graph·ic \ˌlȯg-ə-'graf-ik, ˌläg-\ *adj* (1801) **:** of, relating to, or marked by the use of logographs **:** consisting of logographs — **logo·graph·i·cal·ly** \-i-k(ə-)lē\ *adv*
logo·griph \'lȯg-ə-ˌgrif, 'läg-\ *n* [*log-* + Gk *griphos* reed basket, riddle — more at CRIB] (1597) **:** a word puzzle (as an anagram)
lo·gom·a·chy \lō-'gäm-ə-kē\ *n, pl* **-chies** [Gk *logomachia,* fr. *log-* + *machesthai* to fight] (1569) **1 :** a dispute over or about words **2 :** a controversy marked by verbiage
log·or·rhea \ˌlȯg-ə-'rē-ə, ˌläg-\ *n* [NL] (ca. 1892) **:** excessive and often incoherent talkativeness or wordiness — **log·or·rhe·ic** \-'rē-ik\ *adj*
Lo·gos \'lō-ˌgäs, -ˌgōs\ *n, pl* **Lo·goi** \-ˌgȯi\ [Gk, speech, word, reason — more at LEGEND] (1587) **1 :** the divine wisdom manifest in the creation, government, and redemption of the world and often identified with the second person of the Trinity **2 :** reason that in ancient Greek philosophy is the controlling principle in the universe
logo·type \'lȯg-ə-ˌtīp, 'läg-\ *n* (1816) **1 :** a single piece of type or a single plate faced with a term (as the name of a newspaper or a trademark) **2 :** an identifying symbol (as for advertising)
log·roll \'lȯg-ˌrōl, 'läg-\ *vb* [back-formation fr. *logrolling*] *vi* (1835) **:** to take part in logrolling ~ *vt* **:** to promote passage of by logrolling — **log·roll·er** *n*
log·roll·ing \-ˌrō-liŋ\ *n* (1812) **1** [fr. a former American custom of neighbors assisting one another in rolling logs into a pile for burning] **:** the exchanging of assistance or favors; *specif* **:** the trading of votes by legislators to secure favorable action on projects of interest to each one **2 :** the rolling of logs in water by treading; *also* **:** a sport in which contestants treading logs try to dislodge one another
-logue *or* **-log** \ˌlȯg, ˌläg\ *n comb form* [ME *-logue,* fr. OF, fr. L *-logus,* fr. Gk *-logos,* fr. *legein* to speak — more at LEGEND] **1 :** discourse **:** talk ⟨duo*logue*⟩ **2 :** student **:** specialist ⟨sino*logue*⟩
log·wood \'lȯg-ˌwu̇d, 'läg-\ *n* (1581) **1 a :** a Central American and West Indian leguminous tree (*Haematoxylon campechianum*) **b :** the very hard brown or brownish red heartwood of logwood **2 :** a dye extracted from the heartwood of logwood — compare HEMATOXYLIN
lo·gy \'lō-gē\ *also* **log·gy** \'lȯg-ē, 'läg-\ *adj* **lo·gi·er; -est** [perh. fr. D *log* heavy; akin to MLG *luggich* lazy] (1847) **:** marked by sluggishness and lack of vitality **:** GROGGY
-l·o·gy \l-ə-jē\ *n comb form* [ME *-logie,* fr. OF, fr. L *-logia,* fr. Gk, fr. *logos* word] **1 :** oral or written expression ⟨phraseo*logy*⟩ **2 :** doctrine **:** theory **:** science ⟨ethno*logy*⟩
Lo·hen·grin \'lō-ən-ˌgrin\ *n* [G] **:** a son of Parsifal and knight of the Holy Grail in Germanic legend
loin \'lȯin\ *n* [ME *loyne,* fr. MF *loigne,* fr. (assumed) VL *lumbea,* fr. L *lumbus;* akin to OE *lendenu* loins, OSlav *lędvĭję*] (14c) **1 a :** the part of a human being or quadruped on each side of the spinal column between the hipbone and the false ribs **b :** a cut of meat comprising this part of one or both sides of a carcass with the adjoining half of the vertebrae included but without the flank **2** *pl* **a :** the upper and lower abdominal regions and the region about the hips **b (1) :** the pubic region **(2) :** the generative organs
loin·cloth \-ˌklȯth\ *n* (1859) **:** a cloth worn about the loins often as the sole article of clothing in warm climates
loi·ter \'lȯit-ər\ *vi* [ME *loiteren*] (14c) **1 :** to delay an activity with aimless idle stops and pauses **:** DAWDLE **2 a :** to remain in an area for no obvious reason **:** HANG AROUND **b :** to lag behind ***syn*** see DELAY — **loi·ter·er** \-ər-ər\ *n*
Lo·ki \'lō-kē\ *n* [ON] **:** a Norse god who contrives evil and mischief for his fellow gods
Lo·li·ta \lō-'lēt-ə\ *n* [after *Lolita,* character in the novel *Lolita* (1955) by Vladimir Nabokov] (1959) **:** a precociously seductive girl
[1]**loll** \'läl\ *vb* [ME *lollen*] *vi* (14c) **1 :** to hang loosely or laxly **:** DROOP **2 :** to act or move in a lax, lazy, or indolent manner **:** LOUNGE ~ *vt* **:** to let droop or dangle
[2]**loll** *n, archaic* (1709) **:** the act of lolling **:** a relaxed posture
Lol·lard \'läl-ərd\ *n* [ME, fr. MD *lollaert,* fr. *lollen* to mutter] (14c) **:** one of the followers of Wycliffe who traveled in the 14th and 15th centuries as lay preachers throughout England and Scotland — **Lol·lard·ism** \-ər-ˌdiz-əm\ *n* — **Lol·lardy** \-ərd-ē\ *n*
lol·li·pop *or* **lol·ly·pop** \'läl-i-ˌpäp\ *n* [prob. fr. [1]*loll* + *-i-* + *pop*] (1784) **:** a lump of hard candy on the end of a stick
lol·lop \'läl-əp\ *vi* [[1]*loll* + *-op* (as in *gallop*)] (1745) **1** *dial Eng* **:** LOLL **2 :** to proceed with a bounding or bobbing motion
lol·ly \'läl-ē\ *n, pl* **lollies** [short for *lollipop*] (1854) **1** *Brit* **:** a piece of candy; *esp* **:** hard candy **2** *Brit* **:** MONEY
lol·ly·gag \'läl-ē-ˌgag\ *vi* **-gagged; -gag·ging** [origin unknown] (1868) **:** to fool around **:** DAWDLE
Lom·bard \'läm-ˌbärd, -bərd\ *n* [ME *Lumbarde,* fr. MF *lombard,* fr. OIt *lombardo,* fr. L *Langobardus*] (14c) **1 a :** a member of a Teutonic people that invaded Italy in A.D. 568, settled in the Po valley, and established a kingdom **b :** a native or inhabitant of Lombardy **2** [fr. the prominence of Lombards as moneylenders] **:** BANKER, MONEYLENDER — **Lom·bar·di·an** \läm-'bärd-ē-ən\ *adj* — **Lom·bar·dic** \läm-'bärd-ik\ *adj*
Lom·bar·dy poplar \ˌläm-ˌbärd-ē-, -bərd-\ *n* [*Lombardy,* Italy] (1797) **:** a poplar of a staminate variety (*Populus nigra italica*) of a European poplar that is distinguished by its columnar fastigiate shape and strongly ascending branches
lo·ment \'lō-ˌment, -mənt\ *n* [NL *lomentum,* fr. L, wash made fr. bean meal, fr. *lotus,* pp. of *lavare* to wash — more at LYE] (ca. 1836) **:** a dry indehiscent one-celled fruit that is produced from a single superior ovary and breaks transversely into numerous segments at maturity
Lon·don broil \ˌlən-dən-\ *n* (1946) **:** a boneless cut of beef (as from the shoulder or flank) usu. served sliced diagonally across the grain
lone \'lōn\ *adj* [ME, short for *alone*] (14c) **1 a :** having no company **:** SOLITARY **b :** preferring solitude **2 :** ONLY, SOLE **3 :** situated by itself **:** ISOLATED ***syn*** see ALONE — **lone·ness** \'lōn-nəs\ *n*
lone·li·ness \'lōn-lē-nəs\ *n* (1586) **:** the quality or state of being lonely
lone·ly \'lōn-lē\ *adj* **lone·li·er; -est** (1607) **1 a :** being without company **:** LONE **b :** cut off from others **:** SOLITARY **2 :** not frequented by human beings **:** DESOLATE **3 :** sad from being alone **:** LONESOME **4 :** producing a feeling of bleakness or desolation ***syn*** see ALONE — **lone·li·ly** \-lə-lē\ *adv*
lonely hearts *adj* (1949) **:** of or relating to lonely persons who are seeking companions or spouses
lon·er \'lō-nər\ *n* (1947) **:** one that avoids others; *esp* **:** INDIVIDUALIST
[1]**lone·some** \'lōn(t)-səm\ *adj* (1647) **1 a :** sad or dejected as a result of lack of companionship or separation from others ⟨don't be ~ while we are gone⟩ **b :** causing a feeling of loneliness ⟨the empty house seemed so ~⟩ **2 a :** REMOTE, UNFREQUENTED ⟨look down, look down that ~ road —Gene Austin⟩ **b :** LONE ***syn*** see ALONE — **lone·some·ly** *adv* — **lone·some·ness** *n*
[2]**lonesome** *n* (1899) **:** SELF ⟨sat all by his ~⟩
lone wolf *n* (1909) **:** a person who prefers to work, act, or live alone
[1]**long** \'lȯŋ\ *adj* **lon·ger** \'lȯŋ-gər *also* -ər\; **lon·gest** \'lȯŋ-gəst *also* -əst\ [ME *long, lang,* fr. OE; akin to OHG *lang* long, L *longus,* Gk *dolichos*] (bef. 12c) **1 a :** extending for a considerable distance **b :** having greater length than usual **c :** having greater height than usual **:** TALL **d :** having a greater length than breadth **:** ELONGATED **e :** having a greater length than desirable or necessary **f :** FULL-LENGTH ⟨~ pants⟩ **2 a :** having a specified length ⟨six feet ~⟩ **b :** forming the chief linear dimension ⟨the ~ side of the room⟩ **3 a :** extending over a considerable time ⟨a ~ friendship⟩ **b :** having a specified duration ⟨two hours ~⟩ **c :** prolonged beyond the usual time ⟨a ~ look⟩ **4 a :** containing many items in a series ⟨a ~ list⟩ **b :** having a specified number of units ⟨300 pages ~⟩ **c :** consisting of a greater number or amount than usual **:** LARGE **5 a** *of a speech sound* **:** having a relatively long duration **b :** being the member of a pair of similarly spelled vowel or vowel-containing sounds that is descended from a vowel long in duration ⟨~ *a* in *fate*⟩ ⟨~ *i* in *sign*⟩ **c** *of a syllable in prosody* **(1) :** of relatively extended duration **(2) :** bearing a stress or accent **6 a :** having the capacity to reach or extend a considerable distance ⟨a ~ left jab⟩ **b :** hit for a considerable distance ⟨a batter trying for the ~ ball⟩ **7 :** larger or longer than the standard ⟨a ~ count by the referee⟩ **8 a :** extending far into the future ⟨the thoughts of youth are ~, ~ thoughts —H. W. Longfellow⟩ **b :** extending beyond what is known ⟨a ~ guess⟩ **c :** payable after a considerable period ⟨a ~ note⟩ **9 :** possessing a high degree or a great deal of something specified **:** STRONG ⟨~ on common sense⟩ **10 a :** of an unusual degree of difference between the amounts wagered on each side ⟨~ odds⟩ **b :** of or relating to the larger amount wagered ⟨take the ~ end of the bet⟩ **11 :** subject to great odds **12 :** owning or accumulating securities or goods esp. in anticipation of an advance in prices ⟨they are now ~ on wheat⟩ ⟨take a ~ position in steel⟩ — **long·ness** \'lȯŋ-nəs\ *n* — **before long :** in a short time **:** SOON — **long in the tooth :** past one's best days **:** OLD — **not long for :** having little time left to do or enjoy something
[2]**long** *adv* (bef. 12c) **1 :** for or during a long time ⟨~ a popular hangout⟩ **2 :** at or to a long distance **:** FAR ⟨*long*-traveled⟩ **3 :** for the duration of a specified period **4 :** at a point of time far before or after a specified moment or event ⟨was excited ~ before the big day⟩ **5 :** after or beyond a specified or implied time ⟨didn't stay ~*er* than midnight⟩ ⟨said it was no ~*er* possible⟩ **6 :** for a considerable distance ⟨faded back and threw the ball ~⟩ **7 :** in or into a long position (as on a market) — **so long :** GOOD-BYE
[3]**long** *n* (bef. 12c) **1 :** a long period of time **2 :** a long syllable **3 :** one taking a long position esp. in a security or commodity market **4 a** *pl* **:** long trousers **b :** a size in clothing for tall men — **the long and short** *or* **the long and the short :** GIST
[4]**long** *vi* **longed; long·ing** \'lȯŋ-iŋ\ [ME *longen,* fr. OE *langian;* akin to OHG *langēn* to long, OE *lang* long] (bef. 12c) **:** to feel a strong desire or craving esp. for something not likely to be attained ⟨they ~ for peace but are driven to war⟩ — **long·er** \'lȯŋ-ər\ *n*
syn LONG, YEARN, HANKER, PINE, HUNGER, THIRST mean to have a strong desire for something. LONG implies a wishing with one's whole heart and often a striving to attain; YEARN suggests an eager, restless, or painful longing; HANKER suggests the uneasy promptings of unsatisfied appetite or desire; PINE implies a languishing or a fruitless longing for what is impossible; HUNGER and THIRST imply an insistent or impatient craving or a compelling need.
[5]**long** *vi* [ME *longen,* fr. *along* (on) because (of)] *archaic* (13c) **:** to be suitable or fitting
long–ago \ˌlȯŋ-ə-ˌgō\ *adj* (1834) **:** of or relating to the past ⟨~ leaders⟩
long ago *n* (1851) **:** the distant past
lon·gan \'lȯŋ-(g)ən\ *n* [Chin (Pek) *lung*[2] *yen*[3], lit., dragon's eye] (1732) **1 :** a pulpy fruit related to the litchi and produced by an East Indian tree (*Euphoria longana*) **2 :** a tree that bears the longan
lon·ga·nim·i·ty \ˌlȯŋ-gə-'nim-ət-ē\ *n* [LL *longanimitas,* fr. *longanimis* patient, fr. L *longus* long + *animus* soul — more at ANIMATE] (15c) **:** a disposition to bear injuries patiently **:** FORBEARANCE
long·boat \'lȯŋ-ˌbōt\ *n* (15c) **:** the largest boat carried by a merchant sailing ship
long bone *n* (ca. 1860) **:** any of the elongated bones supporting a vertebrate limb and consisting of an essentially cylindrical shaft that contains marrow and ends in enlarged heads for articulation with other bones
long·bow \'lȯŋ-ˌbō\ *n* (14c) **1 :** a wooden bow drawn by hand that is usu. 5½ to 6 feet long **2 :** the medieval English bow sometimes up to 6 feet, 7 inches long
long·bow·man \-'bō-mən\ *n* (1925) **:** an archer who uses a longbow
long–case clock *n* (1892) **:** GRANDFATHER CLOCK
long–chain *adj* (1930) **:** having a relatively long chain of atoms and esp. carbon atoms in the molecule ⟨~ hydrocarbons⟩
long–day *adj* (ca. 1920) **:** responding to a long photoperiod — used esp. of a plant; compare DAY-NEUTRAL, SHORT-DAY
[1]**long–distance** *adj* (1884) **1 :** of or relating to telephone communication with a distant point **2 a :** situated a long distance away **b**

\ə\ abut \ᵊ\ kitten, F table \ər\ further \a\ ash \ā\ ace \ä\ cot, cart \au̇\ out \ch\ chin \e\ bet \ē\ easy \g\ go \i\ hit \ī\ ice \j\ job \ŋ\ sing \ō\ go \ȯ\ law \ȯi\ boy \th\ thin \t͟h\ the \ü\ loot \u̇\ foot \y\ yet \zh\ vision \á, k̲, ⁿ, œ, œ̄, ue, ue̅, ʸ\ *see* Guide to Pronunciation

: covering a long distance **c** : effective over long distance ⟨~ listening devices⟩
[2]**long–distance** *adv* (ca. 1961) : by long-distance telephone
long distance *n* (1904) **1** : communication by long-distance telephone **2** : a telephone operator or exchange that gives long-distance connections
long division *n* (1827) : arithmetical division in which the several steps involved in the division of parts of the dividend by the divisor are indicated in detail
long dozen *n* (ca. 1864) : one more than a dozen : THIRTEEN
long–drawn–out *adj* (1904) : extended to a great length : PROTRACTED
lon·ge·ron \ˈlän-jə-ˌrän\ *n* [F] (1912) : a fore-and-aft framing member of an airplane fuselage
lon·gev·i·ty \län-ˈjev-ət-ē, lȯn-\ *n* [LL *longaevitas,* fr. L *longaevus* long-lived, fr. *longus* long + *aevum* age — more at AYE] (1615) **1 a** : a long duration of individual life **b** : length of life ⟨a study of ~⟩ **2** : long continuance; *esp* : SENIORITY
lon·ge·vous \-ˈjē-vəs\ *adj* (1680) : LONG-LIVED
long face *n* (1786) : a facial expression of sadness or melancholy
long green *n, slang* (ca. 1891) : paper money : CASH
long·hair \ˈlȯŋ-ˌha(ə)r, -ˌhe(ə)r\ *n* [back-formation fr. *long-haired*] (1920) **1** : an impractical intellectual **2** : a person of artistic gifts or interests; *esp* : a lover of classical music **3** : a person with long hair; *specif* : HIPPIE **4** : a domestic cat having long outer fur — **long–hair** *or* **long–haired** \-ˈha(ə)rd, -ˈhe(ə)rd\ *adj*
long·hand \-ˌhand\ *n* (1666) : HANDWRITING: **a** : characters or words written out fully by hand ⟨wrote the essay in ~ before typing it⟩ **b** : cursive writing
long haul *n* (1936) **1** : a long distance **2** : a considerable period of time; *esp* : LONG RUN — **long–haul** *adj*
long·head \ˈlȯŋ-ˌhed\ *n* (1650) : a dolichocephalic person
long·head·ed \-ˈhed-əd\ *adj* (1700) **1** : having unusual foresight or wisdom **2** : DOLICHOCEPHALIC — **long·head·ed·ness** *n*
long·horn \-ˌhȯ(ə)rn\ *n* (1834) **1** : any of the long-horned cattle of Spanish derivation formerly common in southwestern U.S. **2** : a firm-textured cheddar ranging from white to orange in color and from mild to sharp in flavor
long–horned beetle \ˌlȯŋ-ˌhȯrn(d)-\ *n* (1840) : any of various beetles (family Cerambycidae) usu. distinguished by their very long antennae — called also *longhorn beetle*
long–horned grasshopper *n* (1893) : any of various grasshoppers (family Tettigoniidae) distinguished by their very long antennae
long horse *n* (ca. 1934) : VAULTING HORSE
long·house \ˈlȯŋ-ˌhau̇s, -ˈhau̇s\ *n* (1643) : a long communal dwelling esp. of the Iroquois
long hundredweight *n, Brit* (ca. 1934) : HUNDREDWEIGHT 2
longi- *comb form* [ME, fr. L, fr. *longus*] : long ⟨*longi*pennate⟩
lon·gi·corn \ˈlän-jə-ˌkȯ(ə)rn\ *adj* [deriv. of *longi-* + L *cornu* horn — more at HORN] (1848) **1** : of, relating to, or being long-horned beetles **2** : having long antennae — **longicorn** *n*
long·ing \ˈlȯŋ-iŋ\ *n* (bef. 12c) : a strong desire esp. for something unattainable : CRAVING — **long·ing·ly** \-iŋ-lē\ *adv*
long·ish \ˈlȯŋ-ish\ *adj* (1611) : somewhat long : moderately long
lon·gi·tude \ˈlän-jə-ˌt(y)üd, *Brit also* ˈläŋ-gə-\ *n* [ME, fr. L *longitudin-, longitudo,* fr. *longus*] (14c) **1 a** : LENGTH **b** *archaic* : long duration **2 a** : angular distance measured on a great circle of reference from the intersection of the adopted zero meridian with this reference circle to the similar intersection of the meridian passing through the object **b** : the arc or portion of the earth's equator intersected between the meridian of a given place and the prime meridian (as from Greenwich, England) and expressed either in degrees or in time

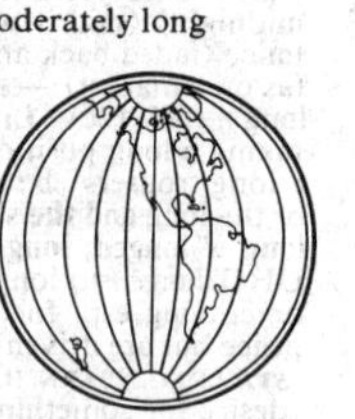

longitude 2a: hemisphere marked with meridians of longitude

lon·gi·tu·di·nal \ˌlän-jə-ˈt(y)üd-nəl, -ᵊn-əl, *Brit also* ˌläŋ-gə-\ *adj* (15c) **1** : placed or running lengthwise **2** : of or relating to length or the lengthwise dimension **3** : dealing with the growth and change of an individual or group over a period of years ⟨~ studies⟩ — **lon·gi·tu·di·nal·ly** \-ē\ *adv*
longitudinal wave *n* (ca. 1931) : a wave (as a sound wave) in which the particles of the medium vibrate in the direction of the line of advance of the wave
long johns \ˈlȯŋ-ˌjänz\ *n pl* (1943) : long underwear
long jump *n* (1882) : a jump for distance in track-and-field athletics usu. from a running start — **long jumper** *n*
long·leaf pine \ˌlȯŋ-ˌlēf-\ *n* (1796) : a large pine (*Pinus palustris*) of the southern U.S. with green leaves and long cones that is a major timber tree; *also* : its tough coarse-grained reddish orange wood
long–leaved pine \-ˌlēv(d)-\ *n* (1765) : LONGLEAF PINE
long·line \ˈlȯŋ-ˌlīn, -ˈlīn\ *n* (1876) : a heavy fishing line that may be several miles long and that has baited hooks in series
long–lin·er \-ˈlī-nər\ *n* (1909) : one that fishes with a longline; *also* : a fishing vessel used in long-lining
long–lin·ing \-ˈlī-niŋ\ *n* (1877) : fishing with a longline
long–lived \ˈlȯŋ-ˈlīvd, -ˈlivd\ *adj* (15c) **1** : having a long life : characterized by long life ⟨a ~ family⟩ **2** : lasting a long time : ENDURING — **long–lived·ness** \-ˈlīv(d)-nəs, -ˈliv(d)-\ *n*
long meter *n* (1718) : a quatrain in iambic tetrameter in which the second and fourth lines and often the first and third lines rhyme — called also *long measure*
Lon·go·bard \ˈlȯŋ-gə-ˌbärd, ˈläŋ-\ *n, pl* **Longobards** *or* **Lon·go·bar·di** \ˌlȯŋ-gə-ˈbär-ˌdī, ˌläŋ-, -ˈbärd-ē\ [L *Langobardus, Longobardus*] (14c) : LOMBARD 1a — **Lon·go·bar·dic** \ˌlȯŋ-gə-ˈbärd-ik, ˌläŋ-\ *adj*
long play *n* (1952) : a long-playing record
long–play·ing \ˈlȯŋ-ˈplā-iŋ\ *adj* (1929) : designed to be played at 33⅓ revolutions per minute — used of a microgroove record
long–range \-ˈrānj\ *adj* (1854) **1** : relating to or fit for long distances ⟨~ rockets⟩ **2** : involving or taking into account a long period of time ⟨~ planning⟩
long run *n* (1627) : a relatively long period of time — usu. used in the phrase *in the long run* — **long–run** \ˌlȯŋ-ˌrən\ *adj*
long·shore·man \ˈlȯŋ-ˈshōr-mən, -ˈshȯr-\ *n* [*longshore,* short for *alongshore*] (1811) : one who loads and unloads ships at a seaport
long·shor·ing \ˈlȯŋ-ˈshōr-iŋ, -ˈshȯr-, ˈlȯŋ-ˌ\ *n* (1926) : the act or occupation of working as a longshoreman
long shot \ˈlȯŋ-ˌshät\ *n* (1867) **1** : a venture involving great risk but promising a great reward if successful; *also* : a venture unlikely to succeed **2** : an entry (as in a horse race) given little chance of winning **3** : a bet in which the chances of winning are slight but the possible winnings great — **by a long shot** : by a great deal
long·sight·ed \-ˈsīt-əd\ *adj* (1790) : FARSIGHTED — **long·sight·ed·ness** *n*
long since *adv* (14c) **1** : long ago ⟨programs which have *long since* ceased to be useful⟩ **2** : for a long time ⟨has *long since* been recognized as a great writer⟩
long·some \ˈlȯŋ(k)-səm\ *adj* (bef. 12c) : tediously long — **long·some·ly** *adv* — **long·some·ness** *n*
long·spur \ˈlȯŋ-ˌspər\ *n* (1831) : any of several long-clawed finches (esp. genus *Calcarius*) of the arctic regions and the Great Plains of No. America
long–stand·ing \-ˈstan-diŋ\ *adj* (1814) : of long duration
long–suf·fer·ing \-ˈsəf(-ə)-riŋ\ *n* (1526) : long and patient endurance of offense — **long–suffering** *adj* — **long–suf·fer·ing·ly** \-riŋ-lē\ *adv*
long suit *n* (1876) **1** : a holding of more than the average number of cards in a suit **2** : the activity or quality in which a person excels
long–term \ˈlȯŋ-ˈtərm\ *adj* (1904) **1** : occurring over or involving a relatively long period of time **2 a** : of, relating to, or constituting a financial operation or obligation based on a considerable term and esp. one of more than 10 years ⟨~ bonds⟩ **b** : generated by assets held for longer than six months ⟨a ~ capital gain⟩
long·time \ˌlȯŋ-ˌtīm\ *adj* (1584) : LONG-STANDING
Long Tom \ˈlȯŋ-ˈtäm\ *n* [fr. the name *Tom*] (1832) **1 a** : a long pivot gun formerly carried on the deck of a warship **b** : a large land gun having a long range **2** : a trough for washing gold-bearing earth
long ton *n* (1829) — see WEIGHT table
lon·gueur \lōⁿ-gœr\ *n, pl* **longueurs** \-gœr(z)\ [F, lit., length] (1791) : a dull and tedious passage or section (as of a book)
long view *n* (1912) : an approach to a problem or situation that emphasizes long-range factors
long–wind·ed \ˈlȯŋ-ˈwin-dəd\ *adj* (1589) **1** : tediously long in speaking or writing **2** : not easily subject to loss of breath — **long–wind·ed·ly** *adv* — **long–wind·ed·ness** *n*
[1]**loo** \ˈlü\ *n* [short for obs. E *lanterloo,* fr. F *lanturelu* piffle] (1675) **1** : an old card game in which the winner of each trick or a majority of tricks takes a portion of the pool while losing players are obligated to contribute to the next pool **2** : money staked at loo
[2]**loo** *vt* (1680) : to obligate to contribute to a new pool at loo for failing to win a trick
[3]**loo** *n* [perh. modif. of F *lieux d'aisances,* lit., places of ease] *chiefly Brit* (1940) : TOILET 3
loo·by \ˈlü-bē\ *n, pl* **loobies** [ME *loby*] (14c) : an awkward clumsy fellow : LUBBER
loo·fah \ˈlü-fə\ *n* [NL *luffa,* fr. Ar *lūf*] (1865) **1** : any of a genus (*Luffa*) of plants of the gourd family with white flowers and large fruits; *also* : its fruit **2** : the fibrous skeleton of the fruit of a loofah used as a sponge
[1]**look** \ˈlu̇k\ *vb* [ME *looken,* fr. OE *lōcian;* akin to OS *lōcōn* to look] *vt* (bef. 12c) **1** : to make sure or take care (that something is done) **2** : to ascertain by the use of one's eyes **3 a** : to exercise the power of vision upon : EXAMINE **b** *archaic* : to search for **4** : to await expectantly or watchfully ⟨we ~ to have immediate success⟩ **5** *archaic* : to bring into a place or condition by the exercise of the power of vision **6** : to express by the eyes or facial expression **7** : to have an appearance that befits or accords with ~ *vi* **1 a** : to exercise the power of vision : SEE **b** : to direct one's attention ⟨~ upon the future with hope⟩ **c** : to direct the eyes **2** : to have the appearance of being : SEEM **3** : to have a specified outlook ⟨the house ~*ed* east⟩ **4** : to gaze in wonder or surprise : STARE **5** : to show a tendency ⟨the evidence ~*s* to acquittal⟩ ***syn*** see EXPECT — **look after** : to take care of — **look down one's nose** : to view something with arrogance, disdain, or disapproval — **look for** : to await with hope or anticipation — **look into** : EXPLORE 1a
[2]**look** *n* (13c) **1 a** : the act of looking **b** : GLANCE **2 a** : the expression of the countenance **b** : physical appearance; *esp* : attractive physical appearance — usu. used in pl. **c** : a combination of design features giving a unified appearance ⟨a new ~ in women's fashions⟩ **3** : the state or form in which something appears
look–alike \ˈlu̇k-ə-ˌlīk\ *n* (1947) : one that looks like another : DOUBLE — **look–alike** *adj*
look·down \ˈlu̇k-ˌdau̇n\ *n* (1882) : any of several fishes (genus *Selene* and esp. *S. vomer*) that are widely distributed in warm seas and have high truncated foreheads
look down \(ˈ)lu̇k-ˈdau̇n\ *vi* (1711) : to regard with contempt : DESPISE — used with *on* or *upon* ⟨snobbishly *looks down* on the poor⟩
look·er \ˈlu̇k-ər\ *n* (14c) **1** : one that looks **2 a** : one having an appearance of a specified kind **b** : one that has an attractive appearance : BEAUTY
look·er–on \ˌlu̇k-ə-ˈrȯn, -ˈrän\ *n, pl* **lookers–on** (1539) : ONLOOKER
look–in \ˈlu̇k-ˌin\ *n* (1870) **1** : a chance of success **2** : a quick pass in football to a receiver running diagonally toward the center of the field
looking glass *n* (1562) : MIRROR
look·out \ˈlu̇k-ˌau̇t\ *n* (1699) **1** : one engaged in keeping watch : WATCHMAN **2** : an elevated place or structure affording a wide view for observation **3** : a careful looking or watching **4** : VIEW, OUTLOOK **5** : a matter of care or concern
look·up \ˈlu̇k-ˌəp\ *n* (1936) : the process or an instance of looking something up; *esp* : the process of matching by computer the words of a text with material stored in memory
look up \(ˈ)lu̇k-ˈəp\ *vi* (14c) **1** : to cheer up ⟨*look up* — things are not all bad⟩ **2** : to improve in prospects or conditions ⟨conditions are *looking up*⟩ ~ *vt* **1** : to search for in or as if in a reference work ⟨*look up* a phone number⟩ **2** : to seek out esp. for a brief visit
[1]**loom** \ˈlüm\ *n* [ME *lome* tool, loom, fr. OE *gelōma* tool; akin to MD *allame* tool] (15c) : a frame or machine for interlacing at right angles two or more sets of threads or yarns to form a cloth
[2]**loom** *vi* [origin unknown] (ca. 1536) **1** : to come into sight in enlarged or distorted and indistinct form often as a result of atmospheric condi-

tions **2 a :** to appear in an impressively great or exaggerated form **b :** to take shape as an impending occurrence

[3]loom *n* (1836) **:** the indistinct and exaggerated appearance of something seen on the horizon or through fog or darkness; *also* **:** a looming shadow or reflection

[1]loon \'lün\ *n* [ME *loun*] (15c) **1 :** LOUT, IDLER **2** *chiefly Scot* **:** BOY **3 a :** a crazy person **b :** SIMPLETON

[2]loon *n* [of Scand origin; akin to ON *lōmr* loon — more at LAMENT] (1634) **:** any of several large fish-eating diving birds (genus *Gavia*) of the northern part of the northern hemisphere that have the legs placed far back under the body and as a result have a clumsy floundering gait on land

loo·ny *or* **loo·ney** \'lü-nē\ *adj* **loo·ni·er; -est** [by shortening & alter. fr. *lunatic*] (1872) **:** CRAZY, FOOLISH — **loo·ni·ness** *n* — **loony** *n*

loony bin *n* (ca. 1890) **:** an insane asylum **:** MADHOUSE

[1]loop \'lüp\ *n* [ME *loupe;* perh. akin to MD *lupen* to watch, peer] *archaic* (14c) **:** LOOPHOLE 1a

[2]loop *n* [ME *loupe,* of unknown origin] (14c) **1 a :** a curving or doubling of a line so as to form a closed or partly open curve within itself through which another line can be passed or into which a hook may be hooked **b :** such a fold of cord or ribbon serving as an ornament **2 a :** something shaped like a loop **b :** a maneuver in which an airplane starting from straight and level flight passes successively through a climb, inverted flight, a dive, and then returns to normal flight **3 :** a ring or curved piece used to form a fastening or a handle **4 a :** the portion of a vibrating body between two nodes **b :** the middle point of such a portion **5 :** a closed electric circuit **6 :** a piece of film or magnetic tape whose ends are spliced together so as to project or play back the same material continuously **7 :** a series of instructions (as for a computer) that is repeated until a terminating condition is reached **8 :** a sports league — **loopy** \'lü-pē\ *adj* — **for a loop :** into a state of amazement, confusion, or distress

[3]loop *vi* (1832) **1 :** to make or form a loop **2 :** to execute a loop in an airplane **3 :** to move in loops or in an arc ~ *vt* **1 a :** to make a loop in, on, or about **b :** to fasten with a loop **2 :** to join (two courses of loops) in knitting **3 :** to connect (electric conductors) so as to complete a loop **4 :** to cause to move in an arc

loop·er \'lü-pər\ *n* (1731) **1 :** any of the usu. rather small hairless caterpillars that are mostly larvae of moths (families Geometridae and Noctuidae) and move with a looping movement in which the anterior legs and the posterior prolegs are alternately made fast and released **2 :** one that loops

[1]loop·hole \'lüp-,hōl\ *n* [[1]*loop*] (1591) **1 a :** a small opening through which small arms may be fired **b :** a similar opening to admit light and air or to permit observation **2 :** a means of escape; *esp* **:** an ambiguity or omission in the text through which the intent of a statute, contract, or obligation may be evaded

[2]loophole *vt* (1664) **:** to make loopholes in

loop of Hen·le \-'hen-lē\ [F. G. J. *Henle* †1885 Ger. pathologist] (1867) **:** a part of the vertebrate nephron that lies between the proximal and distal convoluted tubules and plays a part in water resorption

[1]loose \'lüs\ *adj* **loos·er; loos·est** [ME *lous,* fr. ON *lauss;* akin to OHG *lōs* loose — more at -LESS] (13c) **1 a :** not rigidly fastened or securely attached **b (1) :** having worked partly free from attachments ⟨~ masonry⟩ **(2) :** having relative freedom of movement **c :** produced freely and accompanied by raising of mucus ⟨a ~ cough⟩ **d :** not tight-fitting **2 a :** free from a state of confinement, restraint, or obligation ⟨a lion ~ in the streets⟩ ⟨spend ~ funds wisely⟩ **b :** not brought together in a bundle, container, or binding **c** *archaic* **:** DISCONNECTED, DETACHED **3 :** not dense, close, or compact in structure or arrangement **4 a :** lacking in restraint or power of restraint ⟨a ~ tongue⟩ ⟨~ bowels⟩ **b :** lacking moral restraint **:** UNCHASTE **5 a :** not tightly drawn or stretched **:** SLACK **b :** having a flexible or relaxed character **6 a :** lacking in precision, exactness, or care **b :** permitting freedom of interpretation **7 :** expressed in or characterized by loose sentences ⟨~ style⟩ — **loose·ly** *adv* — **loose·ness** *n*

[2]loose *vb* **loosed; loos·ing** *vt* (13c) **1 a :** to let loose **:** RELEASE **b :** to free from restraint **2 :** to make loose **:** UNTIE ⟨~ a knot⟩ **3 :** to cast loose **:** DETACH **4 :** to let fly **:** DISCHARGE **5 :** to make less rigid, tight, or strict **:** RELAX ~ *vi* **:** to let fly a missile (as an arrow) **:** FIRE

[3]loose *adv* (15c) **:** in a loose manner **:** LOOSELY

loose box *n, Brit* (1849) **:** BOX STALL

loose cannon *n* (1982) **:** a dangerously uncontrollable person or thing

loose end *n* (1546) **1 :** something left hanging loose **2 :** a fragment of unfinished business — usu. used in pl.

loose–joint·ed \'lüs-'jȯint-əd\ *adj* (1859) **1 :** having joints apparently not closely articulated **2 :** characterized by unusually free movements — **loose–joint·ed·ness** *n*

loose–leaf \'lü-'slēf\ *adj* (1902) **1 :** having leaves secured in book form in a cover whose backbone may be opened for the removal, rearrangement, or replacement of leaves ⟨~ notebook⟩ **2 :** of, relating to, or used with a loose-leaf binding ⟨~ paper⟩

loos·en \'lüs-ᵊn\ *vb* **loos·ened; loos·en·ing** \'lüs-niŋ, -ᵊn-iŋ\ *vt* (14c) **1 :** to release from restraint **2 :** to make looser **3 :** to relieve (the bowels) of constipation **4 :** to cause or permit to become less strict — often used with *up* ~ *vi* **:** to become loose or looser

loosen up *vi* (1906) **:** to become less tense **:** RELAX

loose sentence *n* (ca. 1891) **:** a sentence in which the principal clause comes first and the latter part contains subordinate modifiers or trailing elements

loose smut *n* (1890) **:** a smut disease of grains in which the entire head is transformed into a dusty mass of spores

loose·strife \'lü(s)-,strīf\ *n* [intended as trans. of Gk *lysimacheios* loosestrife (as if fr. *lysis* act of loosing + *machesthai* to fight) — more at LYS-] (1548) **1 :** any of a genus (*Lysimachia*) of plants of the primrose family with leafy stems and yellow or white flowers **2 :** any of a genus (*Lythrum,* family Lythraceae, the loosestrife family) of herbs including some with showy spikes of purple flowers; *esp* **:** PURPLE LOOSESTRIFE

[1]loot \'lüt\ *n* [Hindi *lūṭ,* fr. Skt *luṇṭati* he robs] (ca. 1788) **1 :** goods usu. of considerable value taken in war **:** SPOILS **2 :** something held to resemble goods of value seized in war: as **a :** something appropriated illegally often by force or violence **b :** illicit gains by public officials **c :** MONEY **3 :** the action of looting *syn* see SPOIL

[2]loot *vt* (1845) **1 a :** to plunder or sack in war **b :** to rob esp. on a large scale and usu. by violence or corruption **2 :** to seize and carry away by force esp. in war ~ *vi* **:** to engage in robbing or plundering esp. in war — **loot·er** *n*

[1]lop \'läp\ *n* [ME *loppe*] (14c) **:** material cut away from a tree; *esp* **:** parts discarded in lumbering

[2]lop *vt* **lopped; lop·ping** (1519) **1 a (1) :** to cut off branches or twigs from **(2) :** to sever from a woody plant **b (1)** *archaic* **:** to cut off the head or limbs of **(2) :** to cut from a person **2 a :** to remove superfluous parts from **b :** to eliminate as unnecessary or undesirable — usu. used with *off* — **lop·per** *n*

[3]lop *vi* **lopped; lop·ping** [perh. imit.] (1578) **:** to hang downward **:** DROOP

[1]lope \'lōp\ *n* [ME *loup, lope* leap, fr. ON *hlaup;* akin to OE *hlēapan* to leap — more at LEAP] (1809) **1 :** an easy natural gait of a horse resembling a canter **2 :** an easy usu. bounding gait capable of being sustained for a long time

[2]lope *vi* **loped; lop·ing** (1825) **:** to go, move, or ride at a lope — **lop·er** *n*

lop–eared \'läp-'i(ə)rd\ *adj* (1687) **:** having ears that droop

loph·o·phore \'läf-ə-,fō(ə)r, -,fȯ(ə)r\ *n* [Gk *lophos* crest + E *-phore*] (1850) **:** a circular or horseshoe-shaped organ about the mouth esp. of a brachiopod or bryozoan that bears tentacles and functions esp. in food-getting

lop·sid·ed \'läp-'sīd-əd\ *adj* (1711) **1 :** leaning to one side **2 :** lacking in balance, symmetry, or proportion **:** disproportionately heavy on one side ⟨a ~ vote of 99-1⟩ — **lop·sid·ed·ly** *adv* — **lop·sid·ed·ness** *n*

lo·qua·cious \lō-'kwā-shəs\ *adj* [L *loquac-, loquax,* fr. *loqui* to speak] (1667) **a :** given to excessive talking **:** GARRULOUS **b :** full of excessive talk **:** WORDY *syn* see TALKATIVE — **lo·qua·cious·ly** *adv* — **lo·qua·cious·ness** *n*

lo·quac·i·ty \-'kwas-ət-ē\ *n* (13c) **:** the quality or state of being very talkative

lo·quat \'lō-,kwät\ *n* [Chin (Cant) *lō-kwat*] (1820) **:** an Asian evergreen tree (*Eriobotrya japonica*) of the rose family often cultivated for its fruit; *also* **:** its yellow edible fruit used esp. for preserves

lo·ran \'lō(ə)r-,an, 'lȯ(ə)r-\ *n* [*long-range navigation*] (ca. 1932) **:** a system of long-range navigation in which pulsed signals sent out by two pairs of radio stations are used by a navigator to determine the geographical position of a ship or an airplane

[1]lord \'lȯ(ə)rd\ *n* [ME *loverd, lord,* fr. OE *hlāford,* fr. *hlāf* loaf + *weard* keeper — more at LOAF, WARD] (bef. 12c) **1 :** one having power and authority over others: **a :** a ruler by hereditary right or preeminence to whom service and obedience are due **b :** one of whom a fee or estate is held in feudal tenure **c :** an owner of land or other real property **d** *obs* **:** the male head of a household **e :** HUSBAND **f :** one that has achieved mastery or that exercises leadership or great power in some area ⟨vice ~*s*⟩ **2** *cap* **a :** GOD 1 **b :** JESUS **3 :** a man of rank or high position: as **a :** a feudal tenant whose right or title comes directly from the king **b :** a British nobleman: as **(1) :** BARON 2a **(2) :** an hereditary peer of the rank of marquess, earl, or viscount **(3) :** the son of a duke or a marquess or the eldest son of an earl **(4) :** a bishop of the Church of England **c** *pl, cap* **:** HOUSE OF LORDS **4 —** used as a British title: as **a —** used as part of an official title ⟨*Lord* Advocate⟩ **b —** used informally in place of the full title for a marquess, earl, or viscount **c —** used for a baron **d —** used by courtesy before the name and surname of a younger son of a duke or a marquess **5 :** a person chosen to preside over a festival

[2]lord *vi* (14c) **:** to act like a lord; *esp* **:** to put on airs — usu. used with *it* ⟨~*s* it over his friends⟩

lord chancellor *n, pl* **lords chancellor** (15c) **:** a British officer of state who presides over the House of Lords in both its legislative and judicial capacities, serves as the head of the British judiciary, and is usu. a leading member of the cabinet

lord·ing \'lȯrd-iŋ\ *n* (13c) **1** *archaic* **:** LORD **2** *obs* **:** LORDLING

lord·ling \'lȯ(ə)rd-liŋ\ *n* (13c) **:** a little or insignificant lord

lord·ly \-lē\ *adj* **lord·li·er; -est** (bef. 12c) **1 a :** of, relating to, or having the characteristics of a lord **:** DIGNIFIED **b :** GRAND, NOBLE **2 :** exhibiting such pride and assurance as could only be felt as appropriate to one of the highest birth or rank *syn* see PROUD — **lord·li·ness** *n* — **lordly** *adv*

lord of misrule (15c) **:** a master of Christmas revels in England esp. in the 15th and 16th centuries

lor·do·sis \lȯr-'dō-səs\ *n* [NL, fr. Gk *lordōsis,* fr. *lordos* curving forward; akin to OE *belyrtan* to deceive] (1704) **:** abnormal curvature of the spine forward — **lor·dot·ic** \-'dät-ik\ *adj*

Lord Protector of the Commonwealth (ca. 1653) **:** PROTECTOR 2b

Lord's day *n, often cap D* [ME *Lordis day,* trans. of LL *dominica dies,* trans. of Gk *kyriakē hēmera* in Rev. 1:10] (12c) **:** SUNDAY

lord·ship \'lȯ(ə)rd-,ship\ *n* (bef. 12c) **1 a :** the rank or dignity of a lord — used as a title **b :** the authority or power of a lord **:** DOMINION **2 :** the territory under the jurisdiction of a lord **:** SEIGNIORY

Lord's Prayer *n* (1548) **:** the prayer with variant versions in Matthew and Luke that according to the Lucan account Christ taught his disciples

Lord's Supper *n* [ME *Lordis sopere,* trans. of LL *dominica cena,* trans. of Gk *kyriakon deipnon* in I Cor. 11:20] (14c) **:** COMMUNION 2a

Lord's table *n, often cap T* [trans. of Gk *trapeza kyriou* in I Cor. 10:21] (1535) **:** ALTAR 2

Lordy \'lȯrd-ē\ *interj* [[1]*lord* (God) + *-y*] (1853) — used to express surprise or strength of feeling

[1]lore \'lō(ə)r, 'lȯ(ə)r\ *n* [ME, fr. OE *lār;* akin to OHG *lēra* doctrine, OE *leornian* to learn] (bef. 12c) **1** *archaic* **:** something that is taught **:** LESSON **2 :** something that is learned: **a :** knowledge gained through study or experience **b :** traditional knowledge or belief **3 :** a particular body of knowledge or tradition

[2]lore *n* [NL *lorum,* fr. L, thong, rein; akin to Gk *eulēra* reins] (1828) **:** the space between the eye and bill in a bird or the corresponding region in a reptile or fish — **lo·re·al** \'lōr-ē-əl, 'lȯr-\ *adj*

\ə\ abut \ᵊ\ kitten, F table \ər\ further \a\ ash \ā\ ace \ä\ cot, cart \au̇\ out \ch\ chin \e\ bet \ē\ easy \g\ go \i\ hit \ī\ ice \j\ job \ŋ\ sing \ō\ go \ȯ\ law \ȯi\ boy \th\ thin \t͟h\ the \ü\ loot \u̇\ foot \y\ yet \zh\ vision \à, k̲, ⁿ, œ, œ̄, ue, ue̅, ʸ\ *see* Guide to Pronunciation

Lo·re·lei \'lōr-ə-,lī, 'lȯr-\ *n* [G] **:** a siren of Germanic legend whose singing lures Rhine river boatmen to destruction on a reef

lor·gnette \lȯrn-'yet\ *n* [F, fr. *lorgner* to take a sidelong look at, fr. MF, fr. *lorgne* cross-eyed] (ca. 1776) **:** a pair of eyeglasses or opera glasses with a handle

lor·gnon \lȯrn-'yōⁿ\ *n* [F, fr. *lorgner*] (1846) **:** LORGNETTE

lo·ri·ca \lə-'rī-kə\ *n, pl* **-cae** \-kē, -,sē\ [L, fr. *lorum*] (ca. 1706) **1 :** a Roman cuirass of leather or metal **2** [NL, fr. L] **:** a hard protective case or shell (as of a rotifer)

lor·i·keet \'lȯr-ə-,kēt, 'lär-\ *n* [*lory* + *-keet* (as in *parakeet*)] (1772) **:** any of numerous small arboreal parrots mostly of Australasia that usu. have the tongue papillae long and slender forming an organ resembling a brush

lo·ris \'lōr-əs, 'lȯr-\ *n* [F] (ca. 1774) **:** either of two small nocturnal slow-moving lemurs: **a :** a slim-bodied lemur (*Loris gracilis*) of southern India and Ceylon **b :** a stocky relatively heavy-limbed lemur (*Bradicebus tardigradus*) of India and the East Indies

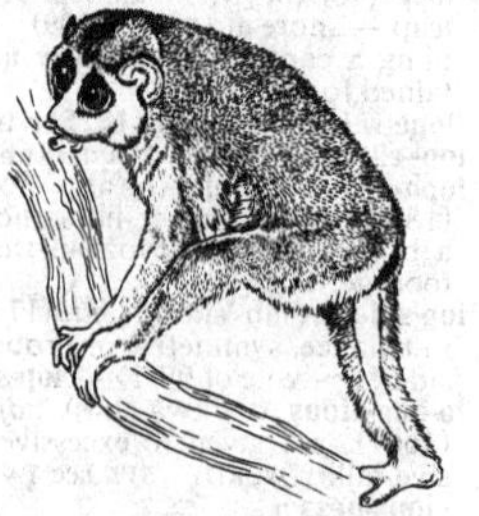

loris a

lorn \'lȯ(ə)rn\ *adj* [ME, fr. *loren,* pp. of *lesen* to lose, fr. OE *lēosan* — more at LOSE] (bef. 12c) **:** DESOLATE, FORSAKEN — **lorn·ness** \'lȯ(ə)rn-nəs\ *n*

Lor·raine cross \lə-,rān-, lȯ-\ *n* (1898) **:** CROSS OF LORRAINE

lor·ry \'lȯr-ē, 'lär-\ *n, pl* **lorries** [origin unknown] (1838) **1 a :** a large low horse-drawn wagon without sides **b** *chiefly Brit* **:** a motortruck esp. if open **2 :** any of various trucks running on rails

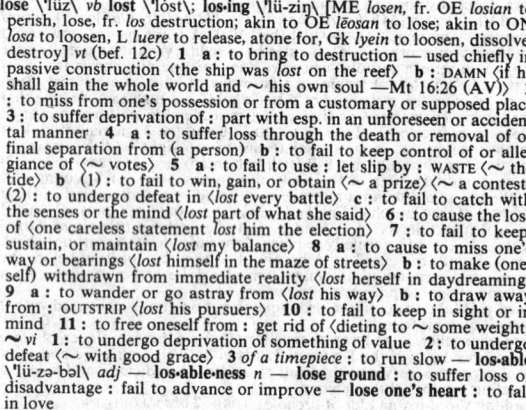

lo·ry \'lōr-ē, 'lȯr-\ *n, pl* **lories** [Malay *nuri, luri*] (1673) **:** any of numerous parrots (esp. of the genera *Domicella, Trichoglossus, Chalcopsitta,* and *Eos*) of Australia, New Guinea, and adjacent islands usu. having the tongue papillose at the tip and the mandibles less toothed than in other parrots

lose \'lüz\ *vb* **lost** \'lȯst\; **los·ing** \'lü-ziŋ\ [ME *losen,* fr. OE *losian* to perish, lose, fr. *los* destruction; akin to OE *lēosan* to lose; akin to ON *losa* to loosen, L *luere* to release, atone for, Gk *lyein* to loosen, dissolve, destroy] *vt* (bef. 12c) **1 a :** to bring to destruction — used chiefly in passive construction ⟨the ship was *lost* on the reef⟩ **b :** DAMN ⟨if he shall gain the whole world and ~ his own soul —Mt 16:26 (AV)⟩ **2 :** to miss from one's possession or from a customary or supposed place **3 :** to suffer deprivation of **:** part with esp. in an unforeseen or accidental manner **4 a :** to suffer loss through the death or removal of or final separation from (a person) **b :** to fail to keep control of or allegiance of ⟨~ votes⟩ **5 a :** to fail to use **:** let slip by **:** WASTE ⟨~ the tide⟩ **b** (1) **:** to fail to win, gain, or obtain ⟨~ a prize⟩ ⟨~ a contest⟩ (2) **:** to undergo defeat in ⟨*lost* every battle⟩ **c :** to fail to catch with the senses or the mind ⟨*lost* part of what she said⟩ **6 :** to cause the loss of ⟨one careless statement *lost* him the election⟩ **7 :** to fail to keep, sustain, or maintain ⟨*lost* my balance⟩ **8 a :** to cause to miss one's way or bearings ⟨*lost* himself in the maze of streets⟩ **b :** to make (oneself) withdrawn from immediate reality ⟨*lost* herself in daydreaming⟩ **9 a :** to wander or go astray from ⟨*lost* his way⟩ **b :** to draw away from **:** OUTSTRIP ⟨*lost* his pursuers⟩ **10 :** to fail to keep in sight or in mind **11 :** to free oneself from **:** get rid of ⟨dieting to ~ some weight⟩ ~ *vi* **1 :** to undergo deprivation of something of value **2 :** to undergo defeat ⟨~ with good grace⟩ **3** *of a timepiece* **:** to run slow — **los·able** \'lü-zə-bəl\ *adj* — **los·able·ness** *n* — **lose ground :** to suffer loss or disadvantage **:** fail to advance or improve — **lose one's heart :** to fall in love

lo·sel \'lō-zəl\ *n* [ME, fr. *losen* (pp. of *lesen* to lose), alter. of *loren* — more at LORN] (14c) **:** a worthless person

lose out *vi* (1858) **:** to fail to win in competition **:** fail to receive an expected reward or gain

los·er \'lü-zər\ *n* (1548) **1 :** one that loses esp. consistently **2 :** one who is incompetent or unable to succeed; *also* **:** something doomed to fail or disappoint

loss \'lȯs\ *n* [ME *los,* prob. back-formation fr. *lost,* pp. of *losen* to lose] (13c) **1 a :** the act of losing possession **b :** the harm or privation resulting from loss or separation **c :** an instance of losing **2 :** a person or thing or an amount that is lost: as **a** *pl* **:** killed, wounded, or captured soldiers **b :** the power diminution of a circuit element corresponding to conversion of electric power into heat by resistance **3 a :** failure to gain, win, obtain, or utilize **b :** an amount by which the cost of an article or service exceeds the selling price **4 :** decrease in amount, magnitude, or degree **5 :** DESTRUCTION, RUIN **6 :** the amount of an insured's financial detriment by death or damage that the insurer becomes liable for — **at a loss :** UNCERTAIN, PUZZLED — **for a loss :** into a state of distress

loss leader *n* (1917) **:** something (as merchandise) sold at a loss in order to draw customers

loss ratio *n* (ca. 1926) **:** the ratio between insurance losses incurred and premiums earned during a given period

lossy \'lȯ-sē\ *adj* (1946) **:** causing attenuation or dissipation of electrical energy ⟨a ~ transmission line⟩ ⟨a ~ dielectric⟩

lost \'lȯst\ *adj* [pp. of *lose*] (1500) **1 :** not made use of, won, or claimed **2 a :** no longer possessed **b :** no longer known **3 :** ruined or destroyed physically or morally **:** DESPERATE **4 a :** taken away or beyond reach or attainment **:** DENIED ⟨regions ~ to the faith⟩ **b :** INSENSIBLE, HARDENED ⟨~ to shame⟩ **5 a :** unable to find the way **b :** no longer visible **c :** lacking assurance or self-confidence **:** HELPLESS **6 :** RAPT, ABSORBED ⟨~ in reverie⟩ — **lost·ness** \'lȯs(t)-nəs\ *n*

[1]**lot** \'lät\ *n* [ME, fr. OE *hlot;* akin to OHG *hlōz* — more at CLOSE] (bef. 12c) **1 :** an object used as a counter in determining a question by chance **2 a :** the use of lots as a means of deciding something **b :** the resulting choice **3 a :** something that comes to one upon whom a lot has fallen **:** SHARE **b :** one's way of life or worldly fate **:** FORTUNE **4 a :** a portion of land **b :** a measured parcel of land having fixed boundaries and designated on a plot or survey **c :** a motion-picture studio and its adjoining property **5 a :** a number of units of an article or a parcel of articles offered as one item (as in an auction sale) **b :** all the members of a present group, kind, or quantity — used with *the* **6 a :** a number of associated persons **:** SET **b :** KIND, SORT **7 :** a considerable quantity or extent ⟨a ~ of money⟩ ⟨~s of friends⟩ — **a lot 1 :** to a considerable degree or extent ⟨this is *a lot* nicer⟩ **2 :** OFTEN, FREQUENTLY ⟨runs *a lot* every day⟩ *syn* see FATE

[2]**lot** *vt* **lot·ted; lot·ting** (15c) **1 :** ALLOT, APPORTION **2 :** to form or divide into lots

Lot \'lät\ *n* [Heb *Lōṭ*] **:** a nephew of Abraham who according to the account in Genesis escaped from the doomed city of Sodom with his wife who turned into a pillar of salt when she looked back

lo·ta *or* **lo·tah** \'lōt-ə\ *n* [Hindi *loṭā*] (1809) **:** a small usu. spherical water vessel of brass or copper used in India

loth \'lōth, 'lōt͟h\ *var of* LOATH

lo·thar·io \lō-'thar-ē-,ō, -'ther-, -'thär-\ *n, pl* **-ios** *often cap* [*Lothario,* seducer in the play *The Fair Penitent* (1703) by Nicholas Rowe] (1756) **:** a man whose chief interest is seducing women

lo·ti \'lō-tē\ *n, pl* **ma·lo·ti** \mə-'lō-tē\ [native name in Lesotho] (1980) — see MONEY table

lo·tic \'lōt-ik\ *adj* [L *lotus,* pp.] (1916) **:** of, relating to, or living in actively moving water ⟨~ biology⟩ — compare LENTIC

lo·tion \'lō-shən\ *n* [L *lotion-, lotio* act of washing, fr. *lotus,* pp. of *lavere* to wash — more at LYE] (15c) **:** a liquid preparation for cosmetic or external medicinal use

lots \'läts\ *adv* [pl. of [1]*lot*] (1891) **:** MUCH ⟨feeling ~ better⟩

lot·tery \'lät-ə-rē, 'lä-trē\ *n, pl* **-ter·ies** *often attrib* [MF *loterie,* fr. MD, fr. *lot* lot; akin to OE *hlot* lot] (1567) **1 a :** a drawing of lots in which prizes are distributed to the winners among persons buying a chance **b :** a drawing of lots used to decide something **2 :** an event or affair whose outcome is or seems to be determined by chance

lot·to \'lät-(,)ō\ *n* [It, lottery, lotto, fr. F *lot* lot, of Gmc origin; akin to OE *hlot* lot] (1778) **:** a game of chance resembling bingo

lo·tus \'lōt-əs\ *n* [L & Gk; L *lotus,* fr. Gk *lōtos,* fr. Heb *lōṭ* myrrh] (1540) **1** *also* **lo·tos** \'lōtəs\ **:** a fruit eaten by the lotus-eaters and considered to cause indolence and dreamy contentment; *also* **:** a tree (as *Zizyphus lotus* of the buckthorn family) reputed to bear this fruit **2 :** any of various water lilies including several represented in ancient Egyptian and Hindu art and religious symbolism **3** [NL, fr. L] **a :** any of a genus (*Lotus*) of widely distributed upright leguminous herbs or subshrubs **b :** SWEET CLOVER

lo·tus–eat·er \'lōt-ə-,sēt-ər\ *n* (1832) **1 :** any of a people in Homer's Odyssey subsisting on the lotus and living in the dreamy indolence it induces **2 :** an indolent person

lo·tus·land \'lōt-ə-,sland\ *n* [fr. the Homeric land of lotus-eaters] (1842) **1 :** a place inducing contentment esp. through offering an idyllic living situation **2 :** a state or an ideal marked by contentment often achieved through self-indulgence

louche \'lüsh\ *adj* [F, lit., cross-eyed, squint-eyed, fr. L *luscus* one-eyed] (1819) **:** not reputable or decent

loud \'lau̇d\ *adj* [ME, fr. OE *hlūd;* akin to OHG *hlūt* loud, L *inclutus* famous, Gk *klytos,* Skt *śṛṇoti* he hears] (bef. 12c) **1 a :** marked by intensity or volume of sound **b :** producing a loud sound **2 :** CLAMOROUS, NOISY **3 :** obtrusive or offensive in appearance or smell **:** OBNOXIOUS — **loud** *adv* — **loud·ly** *adv*

syn LOUD, STENTORIAN, EARSPLITTING, RAUCOUS, STRIDENT mean marked by intensity or volume of sound. LOUD applies to any volume above normal and may suggest undue vehemence or obtrusiveness ⟨a *loud* obnoxious person⟩ STENTORIAN implies great power and range ⟨an actor with a *stentorian* voice⟩ EARSPLITTING implies loudness that is physically discomforting ⟨the *earsplitting* sound of a siren⟩ RAUCOUS implies a loud harsh grating tone, esp. of voice, and may suggest rowdiness ⟨a barroom filled with the *raucous* shouts of drunken revelers⟩ STRIDENT implies a rasping discordant but insistent quality, esp. of voice ⟨talks at the top of a very high and *strident* voice —Rose Macaulay⟩

loud·en \'lau̇d-ᵊn\ *vb* **loud·ened; loud·en·ing** \'lau̇d-niŋ, -ᵊn-iŋ\ *vi* (1848) **:** to become loud ~ *vt* **:** to make loud

loud·mouth \'lau̇d-,mau̇th\ *n* (1914) **:** a loudmouthed person

loud·mouthed \-'mau̇t͟hd, -'mau̇tht\ *adj* (1628) **:** given to loud offensive talk

loud·ness *n* (bef. 12c) **:** the attribute of a sound that determines the magnitude of the auditory sensation produced and that primarily depends on the amplitude of the sound wave involved

loud·speak·er \'lau̇d-'spē-kər\ *n* (1884) **:** a device similar to a telephone receiver in operation but amplifying sound

Lou Geh·rig's disease \,lü-,ge(ə)r-igz-, -,ga(ə)r-\ *n* [*Lou Gehrig* †1941 Am. baseball player who died of this disease] (ca. 1958) **:** AMYOTROPHIC LATERAL SCLEROSIS

lough \'läk, 'läk̲\ *n* [ME, of Celt origin; akin to OIr *loch* lake; akin to L *lacus* lake] (14c) **1** *chiefly Irish* **:** LAKE **2** *chiefly Irish* **:** a bay or inlet of the sea

lou·is d'or \,lü-ē-'dȯ(ə)r\ *n, pl* **louis d'or** [F, fr. *Louis* XIII of France + *d'or* of gold] (1665) **1 :** a French gold coin first struck in 1640 and issued up to the Revolution **2 :** the French 20-franc gold piece issued after the Revolution

Lou·is Qua·torze \,lü-ē-kə-'tȯ(ə)rz\ *adj* [F, Louis XIV] (1848) **:** of, relating to, or characteristic of the architecture or furniture of the reign of Louis XIV of France

Louis Quinze \-'kaⁿz\ *adj* [F, Louis XV] (1855) **:** of, relating to, or characteristic of the architecture or furniture of the reign of Louis XV of France

Louis Seize \-'sāz, -'sez\ *adj* [F, Louis XVI] (1882) **:** of, relating to, or characteristic of the architecture or furniture of the reign of Louis XVI of France

Louis Treize \-'trāz, -'trez\ *adj* [F, Louis XIII] (1883) **:** of, relating to, or characteristic of the furniture or architecture of the reign of Louis XIII of France

[1]**lounge** \'lau̇nj\ *vb* **lounged; loung·ing** [origin unknown] *vi* (1508) **:** to act or move idly or lazily **:** LOAF ~ *vt* **:** to pass (time) idly ⟨~ away the afternoon⟩ — **loung·er** *n*

[2]**lounge** *n* (1775) **1 :** a place for lounging: as **a :** a room in a private home or public building for leisure occupations **:** LIVING ROOM; *also* **:** LOBBY **b :** a room in a usu. public building or vehicle often combining lounging, smoking, and toilet facilities **2 :** a long couch

lounge car *n* (1947) **:** a railroad passenger car with seats for lounging and facilities for serving refreshments — called also *club car*

lounge lizard *n* (1918) **1** LADIES' MAN **2 :** FOP **3 :** a social parasite **:** NE'ER-DO-WELL

lounge·wear \ˈlau̇nj-ˌwa(ə)r, -ˌwe(ə)r\ *n* (ca. 1957) **:** informal clothing designed to be worn at home

loup \ˈlau̇p, ˈlōp\ *vb* [ME *loupen*, fr. ON *hlaupa;* akin to OE *hlēapan* to leap — more at LEAP] *chiefly Scot* (14c) **:** LEAP — **loup** *n*

loupe \ˈlüp\ *n* [F, gem of imperfect brilliancy, loupe] (1886) **:** a small magnifier used esp. by jewelers and watchmakers

loup–ga·rou \ˌlü-gə-ˈrü\ *n, pl* **loups–garous** \ˌlü-gə-ˈrü(z)\ [MF, alter. of OF *leu garoul*, fr. *leu* (fr. L *lupus*) wolf + *garoul* werewolf, of Gmc origin; akin to OHG *werwolf* werewolf] (1579) **:** WEREWOLF

lour \ˈlau̇(-ə)r\, **loury** \ˈlau̇(ə)r-ē\ *var of* LOWER, LOWERY

1louse \ˈlau̇s\ *n* [ME *lous*, fr. OE *lūs;* akin to OHG *lūs* louse, W *llau* lice] (bef. 12c) **1** *pl* **lice** \ˈlīs\ **a :** any of various small wingless usu. flattened insects (orders Anoplura and Mallophaga) parasitic on warm-blooded animals **b :** a small usu. sluggish arthropod that lives on other animals or on plants and sucks their blood or juices — usu. used in combination ⟨plant ~⟩ **c :** any of several small arthropods that are not parasitic — usu. used in combination ⟨book ~⟩ ⟨wood ~⟩ **2** *pl* **lous·es** \ˈlau̇-səz\ **:** a contemptible person **:** HEEL

2louse \ˈlau̇s, ˈlau̇z\ *vt* **loused; lous·ing** (14c) **:** to pick lice from **:** DELOUSE

louse up \(ˈ)lau̇-ˈsəp\ *vt* (1934) **:** FOUL UP, SNARL **~** *vi* **:** to make a mess

louse·wort \ˈlau̇-ˌswərt, -ˌswȯ(ə)rt\ *n* (1597) **:** any of a genus (*Pedicularis*) of plants of the figwort family with pinnate or pinnatifid leaves and variously colored bilabiate flowers in terminal spikes

lousy \ˈlau̇-zē\ *adj* **lous·i·er; -est** (14c) **1 :** infested with lice **2 a :** totally repulsive **:** CONTEMPTIBLE **b :** miserably poor or inferior **c :** amply supplied **:** REPLETE ⟨~ with money⟩ **3** *of silk* **:** fuzzy and specked because of splitting of the fiber — **lous·i·ly** \-zə-lē\ *adv* — **lous·i·ness** \-zē-nəs\ *n*

1lout \ˈlau̇t\ *vi* [ME *louten*, fr. OE *lūtan;* akin to ON *lūta* to bow down, OE *lȳtel* little] (bef. 12c) **1 :** to bow in respect **2 :** SUBMIT, YIELD

2lout *vt* (1530) **:** to treat as a lout **:** SCORN

3lout *n* [perh. fr. ON *lūtr* bent down, fr. *lūta*] (1542) **:** an awkward brutish person

lout·ish \ˈlau̇t-ish\ *adj* (1542) **:** resembling or befitting a lout ***syn*** see BOORISH — **lout·ish·ly** *adv* — **lout·ish·ness** *n*

lou·ver *or* **lou·vre** \ˈlü-vər\ *n* [ME *lover*, fr. MF *lovier*] (14c) **1 :** a roof lantern or turret often with slatted apertures for escape of smoke or admission of light in a medieval building **2 a :** an opening (as in a wall or at the front of an automobile) provided with one or more slanted fixed or movable fins to allow flow of air but to exclude rain or sun or to provide privacy **b :** a finned or vaned device for controlling a flow of air or the radiation of light **c :** a fin or shutter of a louver — **lou·vered** \-vərd\ *adj*

lov·able *also* **love·able** \ˈlə-və-bəl\ *adj* (14c) **:** having qualities that attract affection — **lov·able·ness** *n* — **lov·ably** \-blē\ *adv*

lov·age \ˈlə-vij\ *n* [ME *lovache*, fr. AF, fr. LL *levisticum*, alter. of L *ligusticum*, fr. neut. of *ligusticus* Ligurian, fr. *Ligur-*, *Ligus*, n., Ligurian] (14c) **:** any of several aromatic perennial herbs of the carrot family; *esp* **:** a European herb (*Levisticum officinale*) sometimes cultivated as a domestic remedy, flavoring agent, or potherb

lov·at \ˈlə-vət\ *n* [prob. fr. *Lovat*, locality in Inverness-shire, Scotland; fr. its use in Scottish tweeds] (1907) **:** a predominantly dusty color mixture (as of green) in fabrics

1love \ˈləv\ *n* [ME, fr. OE *lufu;* akin to OHG *luba* love, OE *lēof* dear, L *lubēre*, *libēre* to please] (bef. 12c) **1 a** (1) **:** strong affection for another arising out of kinship or personal ties ⟨maternal ~ for a child⟩ (2) **:** attraction based on sexual desire **:** affection and tenderness felt by lovers (3) **:** affection based on admiration, benevolence, or common interests ⟨~ for his old schoolmates⟩ **b :** an assurance of love ⟨give her my ~⟩ **2 :** warm attachment, enthusiasm, or devotion ⟨~ of the sea⟩ **3 a :** the object of attachment, devotion, or admiration ⟨baseball was his first ~⟩ **b :** a beloved person **:** DARLING — often used as a term of endearment **4 a :** unselfish loyal and benevolent concern for the good of another: (1) **:** the fatherly concern of God for man (2) **:** brotherly concern for others **b :** a person's adoration of God **5 :** a god or personification of love **6 :** an amorous episode **:** LOVE AFFAIR **7 :** the sexual embrace **:** COPULATION **8 :** a score of zero (as in tennis) **9** *cap, Christian Science* **:** GOD — **at love :** holding one's opponent scoreless in tennis ⟨won three games *at love*⟩ — **in love :** inspired by affection

2love *vb* **loved; lov·ing** *vt* (bef. 12c) **1 :** to hold dear **:** CHERISH **2 a :** to feel a lover's passion, devotion, or tenderness for **b** (1) **:** CARESS (2) **:** to fondle amorously (3) **:** to copulate with **3 :** to like or desire actively **:** take pleasure in ⟨*loved* to play the violin⟩ **4 :** to thrive in ⟨the rose *~s* sunlight⟩ **~** *vi* **:** to feel affection or experience desire

love affair *n* (1591) **1 :** a romantic attachment or episode between lovers **2 :** a lively enthusiasm

love apple *n* [prob. trans. of F *pomme d'amour*] (1578) **:** TOMATO

love beads *n pl* (1968) **:** beads worn as a symbol of love and peace

love·bird \ˈləv-ˌbərd\ *n* (1595) **:** any of various small usu. gray or green parrots (as of the genera *Agapornis* of Africa, *Loriculus* of Asia, and *Psittacula* of So. America) that show great affection for their mates

love·bug \-ˌbəg\ *n* [so called fr. the fact that it is usu. seen copulating] (ca. 1966) **:** a small black fly (*Plecia nearctica*) with a red thorax that swarms along highways in states of the U.S. bordering the Gulf of Mexico

love child *n* (1805) **:** an illegitimate child

love feast *n* (1580) **1 :** a meal eaten in common by a Christian congregation in token of brotherly love **2 :** a gathering held to promote reconciliation and good feeling or show someone affectionate honor

love grass *n* (1702) **:** any of a genus (*Eragrostis*) of grasses that resemble the bluegrasses but have flattened spikelets and deciduous lemmas

love–in \ˈləv-ˌin\ *n* [*love* + *2-in*] (1967) **:** a gathering of people esp. for the expression of their mutual love

love–in–a–mist \ˈləv-ə-nə-ˌmist\ *n* (ca. 1760) **:** a European garden plant (*Nigella damascena*) of the buttercup family having the flowers enveloped in numerous finely dissected bracts

love knot *n* (14c) **:** a stylized knot sometimes used as an emblem of love

love·less \ˈləv-ləs\ *adj* (14c) **1 :** having no love **2 :** not loved — **love·less·ly** *adv* — **love·less·ness** *n*

love·lock \-ˌläk\ *n* (1592) **:** a long lock of hair worn over the shoulder by men in the 17th and 18th centuries

love·lorn \-ˌlȯ(ə)rn\ *adj* (1634) **:** bereft of love or of a lover — **love·lorn·ness** \-ˌlȯrn-nəs\ *n*

1love·ly \ˈləv-lē\ *adj* **love·li·er; -est** (bef. 12c) **1** *obs* **:** LOVABLE **2 :** delightful for beauty, harmony, or grace **:** ATTRACTIVE **3 :** GRAND, SWELL **4 :** eliciting love by moral or ideal worth ***syn*** see BEAUTIFUL — **love·li·ly** \ˈləv-lə-lē\ *adv* — **love·li·ness** \ˈləv-lē-nəs\ *n* — **lovely** *adv*

2lovely *n, pl* **lovelies** (1911) **1 :** a beautiful woman **2 :** a lovely object

love·mak·ing \ˈləv-ˌmā-kiŋ\ *n* (15c) **1 :** COURTSHIP **2 :** sexual activity; *esp* **:** COPULATION

lov·er \ˈlə-vər\ *n* (13c) **1 a :** a person in love; *esp* **:** a man in love with a woman **b** *pl* **:** two persons in love with each other **2 :** an affectionate or benevolent friend **3 :** DEVOTEE **4 :** PARAMOUR

lov·er·ly \-lē\ *adj* (1875) **:** resembling or befitting a lover

love seat *n* (1904) **:** a double chair, sofa, or settee for two persons

love·sick \ˈləv-ˌsik\ *adj* (15c) **1 :** languishing with love **:** YEARNING **2 :** expressing a lover's longing — **love·sick·ness** *n*

love·some \-səm\ *adj* (bef. 12c) **1 :** WINSOME, LOVELY **2 :** AFFECTIONATE, AMOROUS

lov·ing \ˈlə-viŋ\ *adj* (bef. 12c) **:** AFFECTIONATE — **lov·ing·ly** \-viŋ-lē\ *adv* — **lov·ing·ness** *n*

loving cup *n* [fr. its former use in ceremonial drinking] (1808) **1 :** a large ornamental drinking vessel with two or more handles **2 :** a loving cup given as a token or trophy

lov·ing–kind·ness \ˌlə-viŋ-ˈkīn(d)-nəs\ *n* (1535) **:** tender and benevolent affection

1low \ˈlō\ *vi* [ME *loowen*, fr. OE *hlōwan;* akin to OHG *hluoen* to moo, L *calare* to call, summon, Gk *kalein*] (bef. 12c) **:** MOO

2low *n* (1549) **:** the deep sustained sound characteristic esp. of a cow

3low *adj* **low·er** \ˈlō(-ə)r\; **low·est** \ˈlō-əst\ [ME *lah, low*, fr. ON *lāgr;* akin to MHG *læge* low, flat] (12c) **1 a :** having a small upward extension or elevation ⟨a ~ wall⟩ **b :** situated or passing little above a reference line, point, or plane ⟨~ bridges⟩ **c** (1) **:** having a low-cut neckline (2) **:** not extending as high as the ankle ⟨~ oxfords⟩ **2 a :** situated or passing below the normal level, surface, or base of measurement, or the mean elevation ⟨~ ground⟩ **b :** marking a nadir or bottom ⟨the ~ point of his career⟩ **3 :** DEAD — used as a predicate adjective **4 a :** not loud **:** SOFT; *also* **:** FLAT **b :** characterized by being toward the bottom of the range of pitch attainable (as by an instrument) **5 a :** being near the equator ⟨~ northern latitudes⟩ **b :** being near the horizon **6 :** socially or economically humble in character or status ⟨~ birth⟩ **7 a :** lacking strength, health, or vitality **:** WEAK, PROSTRATE ⟨very ~ with pneumonia⟩ **b :** lacking spirit or vivacity **:** DEPRESSED ⟨a ~ frame of mind⟩ **8 a :** of lesser degree, size, or amount than average or ordinary ⟨~ pressure⟩ **b** (1) **:** small in number or amount (2) **:** SUBSTANDARD, INADEQUATE ⟨a ~ level of employment⟩ ⟨a ~ income group⟩ (3) **:** CHEAP ⟨~ prices⟩ (4) **:** SHORT, DEPLETED ⟨oil is in ~ supply⟩ **c :** of lesser position, rank, or order ⟨one of the *~est* ranking of the nine assistantships —*Current Biog.*⟩ **9 :** falling short of some standard: as **a :** lacking dignity or elevation ⟨a ~ style of writing⟩ **b :** morally reprehensible **:** BASE ⟨a ~ trick⟩ **c :** COARSE, VULGAR ⟨~ language⟩ **10 a :** not advanced in complexity, development, or elaboration ⟨~ organisms⟩ **b** *often cap* **:** LOW CHURCH **11 :** UNFAVORABLE, DISPARAGING ⟨had a ~ opinion of him⟩ **12 :** designed for slow and usu. the slowest speed ⟨~ gear⟩ **13 :** articulated with a wide opening between the relatively flat tongue and the palate **:** OPEN ⟨\ä\ is a ~ vowel⟩ **14 :** intended to attract little attention ⟨kept a ~ profile⟩ ***syn*** see BASE — **low** *adv* — **low·ness** *n*

4low *n* (12c) **1 :** something that is low: as **a :** DEPTH **b :** a region of low barometric pressure **2 :** the transmission gear of an automotive vehicle giving the lowest ratio of propeller-shaft to engine-shaft speed and the highest amplification of torque

5low *or* **lowe** \ˈlō\ *n* [ME, fr. ON *logi, log;* akin to OE *lēoht* light — more at LIGHT] *chiefly Scot* (13c) **:** FLAME, BLAZE

6low *or* **lowe** *vb* **lowed; low·ing** *Scot* (14c) **:** FLAME, BLAZE

low·ball \ˈlō-ˌbȯl\ *vt* (ca. 1961) **:** to give (a customer) a deceptively low price or cost estimate — **lowball** *n*

low beam *n* (ca. 1948) **:** the short-range focus of a vehicle headlight

low blood pressure *n* (1924) **:** HYPOTENSION

low blow *n* (1952) **:** an unprincipled attack ⟨gossip column that landed one *low blow* after another —James Fallows⟩

low·born \ˈlō-ˈbȯ(ə)rn\ *adj* (13c) **:** born in a low condition or rank

low·boy \-ˌbȯi\ *n* (ca. 1891) **:** a chest or side table about three feet high with drawers and usu. with cabriole legs

low·bred \-ˈbred\ *adj* (1757) **:** RUDE, VULGAR

low·brow \-ˌbrau̇\ *n* (1906) **:** an uncultivated person — **lowbrow** *adj*

Low Church *adj* (1710) **:** tending esp. in Anglican worship to minimize emphasis on the priesthood, sacraments, and ceremonial in worship and often to emphasize evangelical principles — **Low Churchman** *n*

low comedy *n* (1608) **:** comedy bordering on farce and employing burlesque, horseplay, or the representation of low life — compare HIGH COMEDY

low country *n, often cap L&C* (15c) **:** a low-lying country or region; *esp* **:** the part of a southern state extending from the seacoast inland to the fall line — **low–country** *adj, often cap L&C*

low–density lipoprotein *n* (1951) **:** LDL

low·down \ˈlō-ˌdau̇n\ *n* (1915) **:** the inside facts **:** DOPE

low–down \ˈlō-ˈdau̇n\ *adj* (1865) **1 :** CONTEMPTIBLE, BASE **2 :** deeply emotional ⟨~ blues⟩

low–end \ˈlō-ˌend\ *adj* (1926) **:** of, relating to, or being the lowest priced merchandise in a manufacturer's line

1low·er \ˈlau̇(-ə)r, ˈlō(-ə)r\ *vi* [ME *louren;* akin to MHG *lūren* to lie in wait] (13c) **1 :** to look sullen **:** FROWN **2 :** to be or become dark, gloomy, and threatening

²lower n (14c) 1 : FROWN 2 : a gloomy sky or aspect of weather
³low·er \'lō(-ə)r\ adj [³low] (13c) 1 : relatively low in position, rank, or order 2 : SOUTHERN ⟨~ New York State⟩ 3 : less advanced in the scale of evolutionary development 4 a : situated or held to be situated beneath the earth's surface b cap : of, relating to, or constituting an earlier geologic period or formation 5 : constituting the popular and often the larger and more representative branch of a bicameral legislative body
⁴low·er \'lō(-ə)r\ vi (1606) : to move down : DROP; also : DIMINISH ~ vt 1 a : to let descend : let down b : to depress as to direction ⟨~ your aim⟩ c : to reduce the height of 2 a : to reduce in value, number, or amount ⟨~ the price⟩ b (1) : to bring down in quality or character : DEGRADE (2) : ABASE, HUMBLE c : to reduce the objective of
¹low·er·case \,lō(-ə)r-'kās\ adj [fr. the compositor's practice of keeping such types in the lower of a pair of type cases] *of a letter* (1683) : having as its typical form a f g or b n i rather than A F G or *B N I* — lowercase n
²lowercase vt -cased; -cas·ing (ca. 1909) : to print or set in lowercase letters
low·er-class \,lō(-ə)r-'klas\ adj (1892) 1 : of, relating to, or characteristic of the lower class 2 : being an inferior or low-ranking specimen of its kind
lower class n (1772) : a social class occupying a position below the middle class and having the lowest status in a society
lower criticism n (1897) : criticism concerned with the recovery of original texts esp. of Scripture through collation of extant manuscripts — compare HIGHER CRITICISM
lower fungus n (1900) : a fungus with hyphae absent or rudimentary and nonseptate
low·er·ing \'lau̇(-ə-)riŋ, 'lō-\ adj (14c) : dark and threatening : GLOOMY
low·er·most \'lō(-ə)r-,mōst\ adj (1561) : LOWEST
low·ery \'lau̇-(ə-)rē, 'lō-\ adj (1500) : GLOOMY, LOWERING
lowest common denominator n (ca. 1936) 1 : LEAST COMMON DENOMINATOR 2 : something acceptable to the greatest number of people ⟨the networks were battling for prime time supremacy — striving for the *lowest . . . common denominator* —K. E. Meyer⟩
lowest common multiple n (ca. 1924) : LEAST COMMON MULTIPLE
lowest terms n pl (1806) : the form of a fraction in which the numerator and denominator have no factor in common except 1 ⟨reduce a fraction to *lowest terms*⟩
low frequency n (ca. 1868) : a radio frequency between medium frequency and very low frequency — see RADIO FREQUENCY table
Low German n [so called fr. its prevalence in the low-lying areas near the North Sea] (1838) 1 : the German dialects of northern Germany esp. as used since the end of the medieval period : PLATTDEUTSCH 2 : the West Germanic languages other than High German
low-grade \'lō-'grād\ adj (1878) 1 : of inferior grade or quality 2 : being near that extreme of a specified range which is lowest, least intense, or least competent ⟨a ~ fever⟩ ⟨a ~ imbecile⟩
low-key \-'kē\ also low-keyed \-'kēd\ adj (1907) 1 : having or producing dark tones only with little contrast 2 : of low intensity : RESTRAINED
¹low·land \'lō-lənd, -,land\ n (15c) : low or level country
²lowland adj (1500) 1 cap : of or relating to the Lowlands of Scotland 2 : of or relating to a lowland
low·land·er \-lən-dər, -,lan-\ n (1692) 1 cap : an inhabitant of the Lowlands of Scotland 2 : a native or inhabitant of a lowland region
Low Latin n (1872) : postclassical Latin in its later stages
low-lev·el \'lō-'lev-əl\ adj (1881) 1 : occurring, done, or placed at a low level 2 : being of low importance or rank
low·life \'lō-,līf\ n, pl low·lifes \-,līfs\ also low·lives \-,līvz\ (1718) 1 : a person of low social status 2 : a person of low moral character — low-life \,lō-,līf\ adj
low·li·head \'lō-lē-,hed\ n [ME lowliheed, fr. *lowly* + *-hed* -hood; akin to ME *-hod* -hood] *archaic* (15c) : lowly state
low-low \,lō-,lō\ adj, *of tide* (1949) : lower than the normal low
¹low·ly \'lō-lē\ adv (14c) 1 : in a humble or meek manner 2 : in a low position, manner, or degree 3 : not loudly
²lowly adj low·li·er; -est (14c) 1 : humble in manner or spirit : free from self-assertive pride 2 : not lofty or sublime : PROSAIC 3 : ranking low in some hierarchy 4 : of or relating to a low social or economic rank 5 : low in the scale of biological or cultural evolution — low·li·ness n
low-ly·ing \'lō-'lī-iŋ\ adj (1856) 1 : rising relatively little above the base of measurement ⟨~ hills⟩ 2 : lying below the normal level, surface, or the base of measurement or mean elevation ⟨~ clouds⟩
low mass n, *often cap L&M* (1568) : a mass that is recited without singing by the celebrant, without a deacon, subdeacon, or choir assisting the celebrant, and without the use of incense
low-mind·ed \'lō-'mīn-dəd\ adj (1730) : inclined to low or unworthy things — low-mind·ed·ly adv — low-mind·ed·ness n
lown \'lau̇n, 'lün\ adj [ME (Sc) *lowne*] *dial* (15c) : CALM, QUIET
low-pres·sure \'lō-'presh-ər\ adj (1827) 1 : having, exerting, or operating under a relatively small pressure 2 : EASYGOING
low-profile \'lō-'prō-,fīl\ adj (1967) 1 : having little height : LOW 2 : intended to attract little attention
low relief n (1711) : BAS-RELIEF
low-rise \'lō-'rīz\ adj (1957) : being one or two stories and not equipped with elevators ⟨a ~ classroom building⟩
low-spir·it·ed \'lō-'spir-ət-əd\ adj (1693) : DEJECTED, DEPRESSED — low-spir·it·ed·ly adv — low-spir·it·ed·ness n
Low Sunday n (15c) : the Sunday following Easter
low-ten·sion \'lō-'ten-chən\ adj (ca. 1898) 1 : having a low potential or voltage 2 : constructed to be used at low voltage
low-test \-'test\ adj (1926) : having a low volatility ⟨~ gasoline⟩
low tide n (ca. 1864) : the farthest ebb of the tide
low water n (15c) : a low stage of the water in a river or lake; *also* : LOW TIDE
¹lox \'läks\ n [*l*iquid *ox*ygen] (1923) : liquid oxygen
²lox n, pl lox *or* lox·es [Yiddish *laks*, fr. MHG *lahs* salmon, fr. OHG; akin to OE *leax* salmon] (1941) : smoked salmon
loxo·drome \'läk-sə-,drōm\ n [ISV, back-formation fr. *loxodromic*] (1880) : RHUMB LINE
loxo·drom·ic \,läk-sə-'dräm-ik\ adj [prob. fr. (assumed) NL *loxodromicus*, fr. Gk *loxos* oblique (akin to L *ulna* elbow) + *dromos* course — more at ELL, DROMEDARY] (ca. 1702) : relating to a rhumb line or to sailing on rhumb lines — loxo·drom·i·cal·ly \-i-k(ə-)lē\ adv
loy·al \'lȯi(-ə)l\ adj [MF, fr. OF *leial, leel*, fr. L *legalis* legal] (1531) 1 : unswerving in allegiance: as a : faithful in allegiance to one's lawful sovereign or government b : faithful to a private person to whom fidelity is due c : faithful to a cause, ideal, or custom 2 : showing loyalty 3 *obs* : LAWFUL, LEGITIMATE **syn** see FAITHFUL — loy·al·ly \'lȯi-ə-lē\ adv
loy·al·ist \'lȯi-ə-ləst\ n (1647) : one who is or remains loyal esp. to a political cause, party, government, or sovereign
loy·al·ty \'lȯi(-ə)l-tē\ n, pl -ties [ME *loyaltee*, fr. MF *loialté*, fr. OF *leialté*, fr. *leial*] (15c) 1 : the quality or state of being loyal 2 : the tie binding a person to something to which he is loyal **syn** see FIDELITY
loz·enge \'läz-ᵊnj *also* 'läs-\ n [ME *losenge*, fr. MF *losange*] (14c) 1 : a figure with four equal sides and two acute and two obtuse angles : DIAMOND 2 : something shaped like a lozenge 3 : a small often medicated candy
LP \'el-'pē\ n [*long-playing*] (1948) : a microgroove phonograph record designed to be played at 33⅓ revolutions per minute
LPN \,el-,pē-'en\ n (1948) : LICENSED PRACTICAL NURSE
LSD \,el-,es-'dē\ n [*lysergic acid diethylamide*] (1950) : an organic compound $C_{20}H_{25}N_3O$ that induces psychotic symptoms similar to those of schizophrenia — called also *lysergic acid diethylamide*
lu·au \'lü-,au̇\ n [Hawaiian *lu'au*] (1853) : an Hawaiian feast
Lu·ba·vitch·er \'lü-bə-,vich-ər\ n [Yiddish, fr. *Lubavitch*, lit., city of love, Jewish town in Russia + *-er* -er] (1954) : a member of a Hasidic sect founded by Schneour Zalman of Lyady in the late 18th century — Lubavitcher adj
lub·ber \'ləb-ər\ n [ME *lobre, lobur*] (14c) 1 : a big clumsy fellow 2 : a clumsy seaman — lub·ber·li·ness \-lē-nəs\ n — lub·ber·ly \-lē\ adj *or adv*
lubber line n (1858) : a fixed line on the compass of a ship or airplane that is aligned with the longitudinal axis of the vehicle
lubber's hole n (1772) : a hole in a ship's top near the mast through which one may go farther aloft without going over the rim by the futtock shrouds
lube \'lüb\ n [short for *lubricating oil*] (1926) 1 : LUBRICANT 2 : an application of a lubricant : LUBRICATION
lu·bric \'lü-brik\ adj [MF *lubrique*, fr. ML *lubricus*] *archaic* (15c) : LUBRICIOUS — lu·bri·cal \-bri-kəl\ adj
lu·bri·cant \'lü-bri-kənt\ n (ca. 1928) 1 : a substance (as grease) capable of reducing friction, heat, and wear when introduced as a film between solid surfaces 2 : something that lessens or prevents friction or difficulty — lubricant adj
lu·bri·cate \'lü-brə-,kāt\ vb -cat·ed; -cat·ing [L *lubricatus*, pp. of *lubricare* fr. *lubricus* slippery — more at SLEEVE] vt (1623) 1 : to make smooth or slippery 2 : to apply a lubricant to ~ vi : to act as a lubricant — lu·bri·ca·tion \,lü-brə-'kā-shən\ n — lu·bri·ca·tive \'lü-brə-,kāt-iv\ adj — lu·bri·ca·tor \-,kāt-ər\ n
lu·bri·cious \lü-'brish-əs\ *or* lu·bri·cous \'lü-bri-kəs\ adj [ML *lubricus*, fr. L, slippery, easily led astray] (1583) 1 [L *lubricus*] : having a smooth or slippery quality ⟨a ~ skin⟩ 2 : marked by wantonness : LECHEROUS; *also* : SALACIOUS — lu·bri·cious·ly adv
lu·bric·i·ty \lü-'bris-ət-ē\ n, pl -ties (15c) : the property or state of being lubricious; *also* : the capacity for reducing friction
lu·bri·to·ri·um \,lü-brə-'tōr-ē-əm, -'tȯr-\ n [*lubricate* + *-torium* (as in *sanatorium*)] (1930) : a station for lubricating motor vehicles
Lu·can \'lü-kən\ adj [LL *lucanus*, fr. *Lucas* Luke, fr. Gk *Loukas*] (1876) : of or relating to Luke or the Gospel ascribed to him
lu·carne \lü-'kärn\ n [F] (1548) : DORMER
Lu·ca·yo \lü-'kī-(,)ō\ *also* Lu·ca·yan \-,kī-ən\ n (ca. 1934) 1 : an extinct aboriginal Arawakan tribe of the Bahamas 2 : the language of the Lucayo people
lu·cen·cy \'lüs-ᵊn-sē\ n (1656) : the quality or state of being lucent
lu·cent \'lüs-ᵊnt\ adj [L *lucent-, lucens*, prp. of *lucēre* to shine — more at LIGHT] (15c) 1 : glowing with light : LUMINOUS 2 : marked by clarity or translucence : CLEAR — lu·cent·ly adv
lu·cern n [prob. modif. of G *lüchsern* of a lynx, fr. *luchs* lynx] *obs* (1532) : LYNX
lu·cerne *also* lu·cern \lü-'sərn\ n [F *luzerne*, fr. Prov *luserno*] *chiefly Brit* (1626) : ALFALFA
lu·cid \'lü-səd\ adj [L *lucidus*; akin to L *lucēre*] (1591) 1 a : suffused with light : LUMINOUS b : TRANSLUCENT 2 : having full use of one's faculties : SANE 3 : clear to the understanding : INTELLIGIBLE **syn** see CLEAR — lu·cid·ly adv — lu·cid·ness n
lu·cid·i·ty \lü-'sid-ət-ē\ n (1851) 1 : clearness of thought or style 2 : a presumed capacity to perceive the truth directly and instantaneously : CLAIRVOYANCE
Lu·ci·fer \'lü-sə-fər\ n [ME, the morning star, a fallen rebel archangel, the Devil, fr. OE, fr. L, the morning star, fr. *lucifer* light-bearing, fr. *luc-, lux* light + *-fer* -ferous — more at LIGHT] 1 — used as a name of the devil 2 : the planet Venus when appearing as the morning star 3 *not cap* : a friction match having as active substances antimony sulfide and potassium chlorate
lu·cif·er·ase \lü-'sif-ə-,rās, -,rāz\ n [ISV, fr. *luciferin*] (1888) : an enzyme that catalyzes the oxidation of luciferin
lu·cif·er·in \-(ə-)rən\ n [ISV, fr. L *lucifer* light-bearing] (1888) : a pigment in luminescent organisms (as fireflies) that furnishes practically heatless light in undergoing oxidation
lu·cif·er·ous \lü-'sif-(ə-)rəs\ adj [L *lucifer*] (1648) : bringing light or insight : ILLUMINATING
Lu·ci·na \lü-'sī-nə\ n [L, Roman goddess of childbirth] *archaic* (1658) : MIDWIFE
Lu·cite \'lü-,sīt\ *trademark* — used for an acrylic resin or plastic consisting essentially of polymerized methyl methacrylate
¹luck \'lək\ n [ME *lucke*, fr. MD *luc*; akin to MHG *gelücke* luck] (15c) 1 a : a force that brings good fortune or adversity b : the events or circumstances that operate for or against an individual 2 : favoring chance; *also* : SUCCESS — luck·less \-ləs\ adj
²luck vi (1547) 1 : to prosper or succeed esp. through chance or good fortune ⟨things were going bad and then he ~*ed* out⟩ 2 : to come

upon something desirable by chance — usu. used with *out, on, onto,* or *into* ⟨~ onto a vein of gold⟩

lucky \'lək-ē\ *adj* **luck·i·er; -est** (15c) **1 :** having good luck **2 :** happening by chance : FORTUITOUS **3 :** producing or resulting in good by chance : FAVORABLE **4 :** seeming to bring good luck ⟨a ~ rabbit's foot⟩ — **luck·i·ly** \'lək-ə-lē\ *adv* — **luck·i·ness** \'lək-ē-nəs\ *n*

syn LUCKY, FORTUNATE, HAPPY, PROVIDENTIAL mean meeting with unforeseen success. LUCKY stresses the agency of chance in bringing about a favorable result; FORTUNATE suggests being rewarded beyond one's deserts; HAPPY combines the implications of LUCKY and FORTUNATE with stress on being blessed; PROVIDENTIAL more definitely implies the help or intervention of a higher power.

lucky dip *n, Brit* (1925) : GRAB BAG

lu·cra·tive \'lü-krət-iv\ *adj* [ME *lucratif,* fr. MF, fr. L *lucrativus,* fr. *lucratus,* pp. of *lucrari* to gain, fr. *lucrum*] (15c) : producing wealth : PROFITABLE — **lu·cra·tive·ly** *adv* — **lu·cra·tive·ness** *n*

lu·cre \'lü-kər\ *n* [ME, fr. L *lucrum;* akin to OE *lēan* reward, OHG *lōn,* Gk *leia* booty] (14c) : monetary gain : PROFIT; *also* : MONEY

lu·cu·bra·tion \,lü-k(y)ə-'brā-shən\ *n* [L *lucubration-, lucubratio* study by night, work produced at night, fr. *lucubratus,* pp. of *lucubrare* to work by lamplight; akin to L *luc- lux*] (1595) **1 :** laborious study : MEDITATION **2 :** studied or pretentious ideas expressed in speech or writing

lu·cu·lent \'lü-kyə-lənt\ *adj* [ME, fr. L *luculentus,* fr. *luc-, lux* light] (1548) : clear in thought or expression : LUCID — **lu·cu·lent·ly** *adv*

Lu·cul·lan \lü-'kəl-ən\ *or* **Lu·cul·li·an** \-'kəl-ē-ən\ *adj* [L *lucullanus* of Licinius *Lucullus;* fr. his reputation for luxurious banquets] (1861) : LAVISH, LUXURIOUS ⟨a ~ feast⟩

Lud·dite \'lə-,dīt\ *n* [Ned *Ludd* supposed Leicestershire workman who destroyed machinery] (1811) : one of a group of early 19th century English workmen destroying laborsaving machinery as a protest; *broadly* : one who is opposed to esp. technological change

lu·di·crous \'lüd-ə-krəs\ *adj* [L *ludicrus,* fr. *ludus* play, sport; akin to L *ludere* to play, Gk *loidoros* abusive] (1782) **1 :** amusing or laughable through obvious absurdity, incongruity, exaggeration, or eccentricity **2 :** meriting derisive laughter or scorn as absurdly inept, false, or foolish ***syn*** see LAUGHABLE — **lu·di·crous·ly** *adv* — **lu·di·crous·ness** *n*

lu·es \'lü-(,)ēz\ *n, pl* **lues** [NL, fr. L, plague; akin to Gk *lyein* to loosen, destroy — more at LOSE] (1634) : SYPHILIS — **lu·et·ic** \lü-'et-ik\ *adj*

[1]**luff** \'ləf\ *n* [ME, weather side of a ship, luff, fr. MF *lof* weather side of ship] (14c) **1 :** the act of sailing a ship nearer the wind **2 :** the forward edge of a fore-and-aft sail

[2]**luff** *vi* (14c) : to turn the head of a ship toward the wind

luffa *var of* LOOFAH

[1]**lug** \'ləg\ *vb* **lugged; lug·ging** [ME *luggen* to pull by the hair or ear, drag, prob. of Scand origin; akin to Norw *lugga* to pull by the hair] *vt* (14c) **1 :** DRAG, PULL **2 :** to carry laboriously **3 :** to introduce in a forced manner ⟨~ his name into the talk⟩ ~ *vi* **1 :** to pull with effort : TUG **2 :** to move heavily or by jerks ⟨the car ~*s* on hills⟩

[2]**lug** *n* (1616) **1** *archaic* **a :** an act of lugging **b :** something that is lugged **c :** a shipping container for produce **2 :** LUGSAIL **3** *pl* **:** superior airs or affectations ⟨put on ~*s*⟩ **4** *slang* **:** an exaction of money — used in the phrase *put the lug on*

[3]**lug** *n* [ME (Sc) *lugge,* perh. fr. ME *luggen*] (1500) **1** *chiefly dial* : EAR **2 :** something (as a handle) that projects like an ear: as **a :** a leather loop on a harness saddle through which the shaft passes **b :** a fitting of copper or brass to which electrical wires are soldered or connected **c :** a ridge on the rim of a wheel, on a rubber tire, or on the bottom of a shoe to increase traction **d :** a rounded nut that covers the end of a bolt **3 :** BLOCKHEAD, LOUT

luge \'lüzh\ *n* [F] (1905) : a small sled that is ridden in a supine position and used esp. in competition

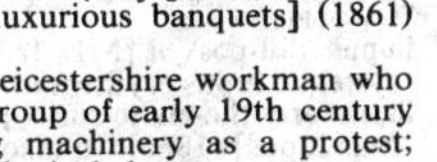

luge

lug·gage \'ləg-ij\ *n* (1596) : something that is lugged; *esp* : suitcases or traveling bags for a traveler's belongings : BAGGAGE

lug·ger \'ləg-ər\ *n* [*lugsail*] (1757) : a small fishing or coasting boat that carries one or more lugsails

lug·gie \'ləg-ē\ *n* [[3]*lug*] *chiefly Scot* (1725) : a small wooden pail or dish with a handle

lug·sail \'ləg-,sāl, -səl\ *n* [perh. fr. [3]*lug*] (1677) : a 4-sided sail bent to an obliquely hanging yard that is hoisted and lowered with the sail

lu·gu·bri·ous \lù-'gü-brē-əs *also* -'gyü-\ *adj* [L *lugubris,* fr. *lugēre* to mourn; akin to Gk *lygros* mournful] (1601) **1 :** MOURNFUL; *esp* : exaggeratedly or affectedly mournful **2 :** DISMAL ⟨at night, the low level of lighting is positively ~ —Mimi Sheraton⟩ — **lu·gu·bri·ous·ly** *adv* — **lu·gu·bri·ous·ness** *n*

lug·worm \'ləg-,wərm\ *n* [origin unknown] (ca. 1802) : any of a genus (*Arenicola*) of marine polychaete worms that have a row of tufted gills along each side of the back and are used for bait

Luk·an \'lü-kən\ *var of* LUCAN

Luke \'lük\ *n* [L *Lucas,* fr. Gk *Loukas*] **1 :** a Gentile physician and companion of the apostle Paul traditionally identified as the author of the third Gospel in the New Testament and of the Book of Acts **2 :** the third Gospel in the New Testament — see BIBLE table

luke·warm \'lü-'kwȯ(ə)rm\ *adj* [ME, fr. *luke* lukewarm + *warm;* akin to OHG *lāo* lukewarm — more at LEE] (14c) **1 :** moderately warm : TEPID **2 :** lacking conviction : HALFHEARTED — **luke·warm·ly** *adv* — **luke·warm·ness** *n*

[1]**lull** \'ləl\ *vt* [ME *lullen;* prob. akin to L *latare* to bark — more at LAMENT] (14c) **1 :** to cause to sleep or rest : SOOTHE **2 :** to cause to relax vigilance

[2]**lull** *n* (1719) **1** *archaic* : something that lulls; *esp* : LULLABY **2 :** a temporary pause or decline in activity ⟨the early morning ~ in urban noise⟩: as **a :** a temporary calm before or during a storm **b :** a temporary drop in business activity

[1]**lul·la·by** \'ləl-ə-,bī\ *n, pl* **-bies** [obs. E *lulla,* interj. used to lull a child (fr. ME) + *bye,* interj. used to lull a child, fr. ME *by*] (1588) : a soothing refrain; *specif* : a song to quiet children or lull them to sleep

[2]**lullaby** *vt* **-bied; -by·ing** (1592) : to quiet with or as if with a lullaby

lu·lu \'lü-(,)lü\ *n* [prob. fr. *Lulu,* nickname fr. *Louise*] *slang* (1857) : one that is remarkable or wonderful

lum \'ləm\ *n* [origin unknown] *chiefly Scot* (1628) : CHIMNEY

lumb- *or* **lumbo-** *comb form* [L *lumbus* loin — more at LOIN] : lumbar and ⟨*lumbo*sacral⟩

lum·ba·go \,ləm-'bā-(,)gō\ *n* [L, fr. *lumbus*] (ca. 1693) : usu. painful muscular rheumatism involving the lumbar region

lum·bar \'ləm-bər, -,bär\ *adj* [NL *lumbaris,* fr. L *lumbus*] (1656) : of, relating to, or constituting the loins or the vertebrae between the thoracic vertebrae and sacrum ⟨~ region⟩

[1]**lum·ber** \'ləm-bər\ *vi* **lum·bered; lum·ber·ing** \-b(ə-)riŋ\ [ME *lomeren*] (14c) **1 :** to move ponderously **2 :** RUMBLE

[2]**lumber** *n* [perh. fr. *Lombard;* fr. the use of pawnshops as storehouses of disused property] (1552) **1 :** surplus or disused articles (as furniture) that are stored away **2 a :** timber or logs esp. when dressed for use **b :** any of various structural materials prepared in a form similar to lumber — **lumber** *adj*

[3]**lumber** *vb* **lum·bered; lum·ber·ing** \-b(ə-)riŋ\ *vt* (1642) **1 :** to clutter with or as if with lumber : ENCUMBER **2 :** to heap together in disorder **3 :** to log and saw the timber of ~ *vi* **1 :** to cut logs for lumber **2 :** to saw logs into lumber for the market — **lum·ber·er** \-bər-ər\ *n*

lum·ber·jack \'ləm-bər-,jak\ *n* (1831) : LOGGER

lum·ber·man \-mən\ *n* (1817) : one who is engaged in or oversees the business of cutting, processing, and marketing lumber

lum·ber·yard \-,yärd\ *n* (1786) : a yard where a stock of lumber is kept for sale

lum·bo·sa·cral \,ləm-bō-'sak-rəl, -'sā-krəl\ *adj* (1840) : relating to the lumbar and sacral regions or parts

lu·men \'lü-mən\ *n, pl* **lu·mi·na** \-mə-nə\ *or* **lumens** [NL *lumin-, lumen,* fr. L, light, air shaft, opening] (1873) **1 :** the cavity of a tubular organ ⟨the ~ of a blood vessel⟩ **2 :** the bore of a tube (as of a hollow needle or catheter) **3 :** a unit of luminous flux equal to the light emitted in a unit solid angle by a uniform point source of one candle intensity — **lu·mi·nal** *also* **lu·men·al** \-mən-ᵊl\ *adj*

lumin- *or* **lumini-** *or* **lumino-** *comb form* [ME *lumin-,* fr. L *lumin-, lumen*] : light ⟨*lumini*ferous⟩

lu·mi·naire \,lü-mə-'na(ə)r, -'ne(ə)r\ *n* [F, lamp, lighting] (1921) : a complete lighting unit

lu·mi·nance \'lü-mə-nən(t)s\ *n* (1880) **1 :** the quality or state of being luminous **2 :** the luminous intensity of a surface in a given direction per unit of projected area

lu·mi·nar·ia \,lü-mə-'ner-ē-ə\ *n, pl* **-nar·ias** [Sp, decorative light, fr. LL] (1949) : a traditional Mexican Christmas lantern consisting of a brown paper bag with a lighted candle inside

lu·mi·nary \'lü-mə-,ner-ē\ *n, pl* **-nar·ies** [ME *luminarye,* fr. MF & LL; MF *luminaire* lamp, fr. LL *luminaria,* pl. of *luminare* lamp, heavenly body, fr. L, window, fr. *lumin-, lumen* light; akin to L *lucēre* to shine — more at LIGHT] (15c) **1 :** a person of prominence or brilliant achievement **2 :** a body that gives light; *esp* : one of the celestial bodies — **luminary** *adj*

lu·mi·nesce \,lü-mə-'nes\ *vi* **-nesced; -nesc·ing** [back-formation fr. *luminescent*] (1896) : to exhibit luminescence

lu·mi·nes·cence \-'nes-ᵊn(t)s\ *n* (1889) **1 :** an emission of light that is not ascribable directly to incandescence and therefore occurs at low temperatures and that is produced by physiological processes (as in the firefly), by chemical action, by friction, or by electrical action **2 :** the light produced by luminescence — **lu·mi·nes·cent** \-ᵊnt\ *adj*

lu·mi·nif·er·ous \,lü-mə-'nif-(ə-)rəs\ *adj* (1801) : transmitting, producing, or yielding light

lu·mi·nist \'lü-mə-nəst\ *n* [F *luministe,* fr. L *lumin-, lumen*] (ca. 1899) : a painter who makes a specialty of the effects of light on colored objects

lu·mi·nos·i·ty \,lü-mə-'näs-ət-ē\ *n, pl* **-ties** (1634) **1 a :** the quality or state of being luminous **b :** something luminous **2 a :** the relative quantity of light **b :** relative brightness of something **3 :** the quantity of radiation emitted by a celestial source (as a star) **4 :** the luminous efficiency of radiant energy

lu·mi·nous \'lü-mə-nəs\ *adj* [ME, fr. L *luminosus,* fr. *lumin-, lumen*] (15c) **1 a :** emitting or reflecting usu. steady, suffused, or glowing light **b :** of or relating to light or to luminous flux **2 :** bathed in or exposed to steady light ⟨a public square ~ with sunlight⟩ **3 :** CLEAR, ENLIGHTENING ***syn*** see BRIGHT — **lu·mi·nous·ly** *adv* — **lu·mi·nous·ness** *n*

luminous energy *n* (ca. 1931) : energy transferred in the form of visible radiation

luminous flux *n* (ca. 1925) : radiant flux in the visible-wavelength range usu. expressed in lumens instead of watts

luminous paint *n* (ca. 1890) : a paint containing a phosphor (as zinc sulfide activated with copper) and so able to glow in the dark

lum·mox \'ləm-əks, -iks\ *n* [origin unknown] (1825) : a clumsy person

[1]**lump** \'ləmp\ *n* [ME] (14c) **1 :** a piece or mass of indefinite size and shape **2 a :** AGGREGATE, TOTALITY ⟨taken in the ~⟩ **b :** MAJORITY **3 :** PROTUBERANCE; *esp* : an abnormal swelling **4 :** a person who is heavy and awkward; *also* : one who is stupid or dull **5** *pl* **a :** BEATING, BRUISE ⟨had taken a lot of ~*s* growing up in the city⟩ **b :** DEFEAT, LOSS ⟨can cheerfully take his ~*s* on losers, because the payout is big on the winners —Martin Mayer⟩ — **lump in one's throat :** a constriction of the throat caused by emotion

[2]**lump** *vt* (1624) **1 :** to group without discrimination **2 :** to make into lumps; *also* : to make lumps on or in **3 :** to move noisily and clumsily ~ *vi* **1 :** to become formed into lumps **2 :** to move oneself noisily and clumsily

[3]**lump** *adj* (1700) : not divided into parts : ENTIRE ⟨~ sum⟩

[4]**lump** *vt* [origin unknown] (1791) : to put up with ⟨like it or ~ it⟩

lump·ec·to·my \,ləm-'pek-tə-mē\ *n, pl* **-mies** (ca. 1972) : excision of a breast tumor with a limited amount of associated tissue

[1]**lum·pen** \'lùm-pən\ *adj* [G *lumpenproletariat* degraded and contemptible section of the proletariat, fr. *lump* contemptible person (fr. *lumpen* rags) + *proletariat*] (1936) : of or relating to dispossessed and

uprooted individuals cut off from the economic and social class with which they might normally be identified ⟨~ proletariat⟩ ⟨~ intellectuals⟩
[2]**lumpen** *n, pl* **lumpen** *also* **lumpens** (1941) : a member of the crude and uneducated lowest class of society
lump·er \'ləm-pər\ *n* (1785) : a laborer employed to handle freight or cargo
lump·ish \'ləm-pish\ *adj* (1528) **1** : DULL, SLUGGISH **2** *obs* : low in spirits : DEJECTED **3** : HEAVY, AWKWARD **4** : LUMPY 1a **5** : tediously slow or dull : BORING; *also* : LUMPY 3 — **lump·ish·ly** *adv* — **lump·ish·ness** *n*
lumpy \'ləm-pē\ *adj* **lump·i·er; -est** (1707) **1 a** : filled or covered with lumps **b** : characterized by choppy waves **2** : having a heavy clumsy appearance **3** : uneven and often crude in style — **lump·i·ly** \-pə-lē\ *adv* — **lump·i·ness** \-pē-nəs\ *n*
lumpy jaw *n* (1890) : ACTINOMYCOSIS; *esp* : actinomycosis of the head in cattle
lu·na·cy \'lü-nə-sē\ *n, pl* **-cies** [*lunatic*] (1541) **1** : any of various forms of insanity: as **a** : intermittent insanity once believed to be related to phases of the moon **b** : insanity amounting to lack of capacity or of responsibility in the eyes of the law **2** : wild foolishness : extravagant folly **3** : a foolish act
lu·na moth \'lü-nə-\ *n* [NL *luna* (specific epithet of *Actias luna*), fr. L, moon] (1869) : a large mostly pale green American saturniid moth (*Actias luna*) with long tails on the hind wings
lu·nar \'lü-nər *also* -,när\ *adj* [L *lunaris*, fr. *luna* moon; akin to L *lucēre* to shine — more at LIGHT] (15c) **1** : CRESCENT, LUNATE **2 a** : of or relating to the moon **b** : designed for use on the moon ⟨~ vehicles⟩ **3** : measured by the moon's revolution ⟨~ month⟩
lunar caustic *n* [obs. *luna* silver, fr. ML, fr. L, moon] (1800) : silver nitrate esp. when fused and molded into sticks for use as a caustic
lunar eclipse *n* (ca. 1890) : an eclipse in which the moon near the full phase passes partially or wholly through the umbra of the earth's shadow
lu·nate \'lü-,nāt\ *adj* [L *lunatus*, pp. of *lunare* to bend in a crescent, fr. *luna*] (ca. 1777) : shaped like a crescent
lu·na·tic \'lü-nə-,tik\ *adj* [ME *lunatik*, fr. OF or LL; OF *lunatique*, fr. LL *lunaticus*, fr. L *luna*; fr. the belief that lunacy fluctuated with the phases of the moon] (13c) **1 a** : affected with lunacy : INSANE **b** : designed for the care of insane persons ⟨~ asylum⟩ **2** : wildly foolish — **lunatic** *n*
lunatic fringe *n* (1913) : the members of a usu. political or social movement espousing extreme, eccentric, or fanatical views
lu·na·tion \lü-'nā-shən\ *n* [ME *lunacioun*, fr. ML *lunation-, lunatio*, fr. L *luna*] (14c) : the period of time averaging 29 days, 12 hours, 44 minutes, and 2.8 seconds elapsing between two successive new moons
[1]**lunch** \'lənch\ *n* [prob. short for *luncheon*] (1812) **1** : a light meal; *esp* : one taken in the middle of the day **2** : the food prepared for a lunch — **out to lunch** *slang* : out of touch with reality
[2]**lunch** *vi* (1823) : to eat lunch ~ *vt* : to treat to lunch — **lunch·er** *n*
lunch counter *n* (1869) **1** : a long counter at which lunches are sold **2** : LUNCHEONETTE
lun·cheon \'lən-chən\ *n* [perh. alter. of *nuncheon* (light snack)] (1652) : LUNCH; *esp* : a formal usu. midday meal as part of a meeting or for entertaining a guest
lun·cheon·ette \,lən-chə-'net\ *n* (1924) : a small restaurant serving light lunches
lunch·room \'lənch-,rüm, -,rům\ *n* (1830) **1** : LUNCHEONETTE **2** : a room (as in a school) where lunches supplied on the premises or brought from home may be eaten
lunch·time \-,tīm\ *n* (1859) : the time at which lunch is usu. eaten : NOON
lune \'lün\ *n* [L *luna* moon — more at LUNAR] (ca. 1704) : the part of a plane surface bounded by two intersecting arcs or of a spherical surface bounded by two great circles
lunes \'lünz\ *n pl* [F, pl. of *lune* crazy whim, fr. MF, moon, crazy whim, fr. L *luna*] (1602) : fits of lunacy
lu·nette \lü-'net\ *n* [F, fr. OF *lunete* small object shaped like the moon, fr. *lune* moon] (1613) **1** : something that has the shape of a crescent or half-moon: as **a** : an opening in a vault esp. for a window **b** : the surface at the upper part of a wall that is partly surrounded by a vault which the wall intersects and that is often filled by windows or by mural painting **c** : a temporary fortification consisting of two faces forming a salient angle and two parallel flanks **d** : a low crescentic mound (as of sand) formed by the wind **2** : the figure or shape of a crescent moon
lung \'ləŋ\ *n* [ME *lunge*, fr. OE *lungen*; akin to OHG *lungun* lung, *līhti* light in weight — more at LIGHT] (bef. 12c) **1 a** : one of the usu. paired compound saccular thoracic organs that constitute the basic respiratory organ of air-breathing vertebrates **b** : any of various respiratory organs of invertebrates **2 a** : a device enabling individuals abandoning a submarine to rise to the surface **b** : a mechanical device for regularly introducing fresh air into and withdrawing stale air from the lung : RESPIRATOR
[1]**lunge** \'lənj\ *n* [modif. of F *allonge* extension, reach, fr. OF *alonge*, fr. *alongier* to lenghten, fr. (assumed) VL *allongare*, fr. L *ad-* ad- + LL *longare*, fr. L *longus* long] (1748) **1** : a quick thrust or jab (as of a sword) usu. made by leaning or striding forward **2** : a sudden forward rush or reach ⟨made a ~ to catch the ball⟩
[2]**lunge** *vb* **lunged; lung·ing** *vi* (1821) : to make a lunge : move with or as if with a lunge ~ *vt* : to thrust or propel (as a blow) in a lunge
lunged \'ləŋd\ *adj* (1693) **1** : having lungs : PULMONATE **2** : having a lung or lungs of a specified kind or number — used in combination ⟨one-*lunged*⟩
[1]**lung·er** \'lən-jər\ *n* (1842) : one that lunges
[2]**lung·er** \'ləŋ-ər\ *n* (1893) : one suffering from a chronic disease of the lungs; *esp* : one that is tubercular
lung·fish \'ləŋ-,fish\ *n* (1883) : any of various fishes (order Dipneusti or Cladistia) that breathe by a modified air bladder as well as gills
lung·worm \-,wərm\ *n* (1882) : any of various nematodes that infest the lungs and air passages of mammals
lung·wort \-,wərt, -,wȯ(ə)rt\ *n* (bef. 12c) : any of several plants (as a mullein) formerly used in the treatment of respiratory disorders; *esp* : a European herb (*Pulmonaria officinalis*) of the borage family with hispid leaves and bluish flowers
lu·ni·so·lar \,lü-ni-'sō-lər *also* -,lär\ *adj* [L *luna* moon + E *-i-* + *solar*] (1691) : relating or attributed to the moon and the sun
lu·ni·tid·al \-'tīd-ᵊl\ *adj* [L *luna* + E *-i-* + *tidal*] (1851) : relating to or being tidal movements dependent on the moon
lun·ker \'ləŋ-kər\ *n* [origin unknown] (ca. 1912) : something large of its kind — used esp. of a game fish
lunk·head \'ləŋk-,hed\ *n* [prob. alter. of *lump* + *head*] (1852) : a stupid person : DOLT — **lunk·head·ed** \-'hed-əd\ *adj*
lunt \'lənt\ *n* [D *lont*] (1525) **1** *chiefly Scot* : SLOW MATCH **2** *chiefly Scot* : SMOKE
lu·nule \'lü-(,)nyü(ə)l\ *n* [NL *lunula*, fr. L, crescent-shaped ornament, fr. dim. of *luna* moon] (1828) : a crescent-shaped body part or marking (as the whitish mark at the base of a fingernail)
lu·ny \'lü-nē\ *var of* LOONY
lu·pa·nar \lü-'pā-nər, -'pän-ər\ *n* [L, fr. *lupa* prostitute, lit., she-wolf, fem. of *lupus*] (1864) : BROTHEL
Lu·per·ca·lia \,lü-pər-'kā-lē-ə, -'kāl-yə\ *n* [L, pl., fr. *Lupercus*, god of flocks] (1600) : an ancient Roman festival celebrated February 15 to ensure fertility for the people, fields, and flocks — **Lu·per·ca·lian** \-'kā-lē-ən, -'kāl-yən\ *adj*
[1]**lu·pine** *also* **lu·pin** \'lü-pən\ *n* [ME, fr. L *lupinus*, *lupinum*, fr. *lupinus*, adj.] (14c) : any of a genus (*Lupinus*) of leguminous herbs some of which are poisonous and others cultivated for green manure, fodder, or their edible seeds; *also* : an edible lupine seed (as of the European *L. albus*)
[2]**lu·pine** \-,pīn\ *adj* [L *lupinus*, fr. *lupus* wolf — more at WOLF] (1660) : WOLFISH
lu·pus \'lü-pəs\ *n* [ML, fr. L, wolf] (15c) : any of several diseases (as systemic lupus erythematosus) characterized by skin lesions
lupus er·y·the·ma·to·sus \-,er-ə-,thē-mə-'tō-səs\ *n* [NL, lit., erythematous lupus] (1860) : a disorder characterized by skin inflammation; *esp* : SYSTEMIC LUPUS ERYTHEMATOSUS
[1]**lurch** \'lərch\ *vb* [ME *lorchen*, prob. alter. of *lurken* to lurk] *vi, dial chiefly Eng* (15c) : to loiter about a place furtively : PROWL ~ *vt* **1** *obs* : STEAL **2** *archaic* : CHEAT
[2]**lurch** *n* [MF *lourche*, adj., defeated by a lurch, deceived] (1598) : a decisive defeat in which an opponent wins a game by more than double the defeated player's score esp. in cribbage — **in the lurch** : in a vulnerable and unsupported position
[3]**lurch** *vt* (1651) **1** *archaic* : to leave in the lurch **2** : to defeat by a lurch (as in cribbage)
[4]**lurch** *n* [origin unknown] (1819) **1** : a sudden roll of a ship to one side **2** : a jerking or swaying movement; *also* : STAGGER 3
[5]**lurch** *vi* (ca. 1828) : to roll or tip abruptly : PITCH; *also* : STAGGER
lurch·er \'lər-chər\ *n* [[3]*lurch*] (1528) **1** *archaic* : a petty thief : PILFERER **2** *Brit* : a crossbred dog; *esp* : one that resembles a greyhound **3** : one who lurks; *also* : SPY
lur·dane \'lərd-ᵊn\ *n* [ME *lurdan*, fr. MF *lourdin* dullard, fr. *lourd* dull, stupid, fr. L *luridus* lurid] *archaic* (14c) : a lazy stupid person — **lurdane** *adj*
[1]**lure** \'lů(ə)r\ *n* [ME, fr. MF *loire*, of Gmc origin; akin to MHG *luoder* bait; akin to OE *lathian* to invite, OHG *ladōn*] (14c) **1** : an object usu. of leather or feathers attached to a long cord and used by a falconer to recall a hawk **2 a** : an inducement to pleasure or gain : ENTICEMENT **b** : APPEAL, ATTRACTION **3** : a decoy for attracting animals to capture: as **a** : artificial bait used for catching fish **b** : an often luminous structure on the head of pediculate fishes that is used to attract prey
[2]**lure** *vt* **lured; lur·ing** (14c) **1** : to recall (a hawk) by means of a lure **2** : to draw with a hint of pleasure or gain : attract actively and strongly — **lur·er** *n*
syn LURE, ENTICE, INVEIGLE, DECOY, TEMPT, SEDUCE mean to lead astray from one's true course. LURE implies a drawing into danger, evil, or difficulty through attracting and deceiving; ENTICE suggests drawing by artful or adroit means; INVEIGLE implies enticing by cajoling or flattering; DECOY implies a luring into entrapment by artifice; TEMPT implies the presenting of an attraction so strong that it overcomes the restraints of conscience or better judgment; SEDUCE implies a leading astray by persuasion or false promises.
lu·rid \'lůr-əd\ *adj* [L *luridus* pale yellow, sallow] (ca. 1656) **1 a** : wan and ghastly pale in appearance **b** : of any of several light or medium grayish colors ranging in hue from yellow to orange **2** : shining with the red glow of fire seen through smoke or cloud **3 a** : causing horror or revulsion : GRUESOME **b** : MELODRAMATIC, SENSATIONAL; *also* : SHOCKING ⟨paperbacks in the usual ~ covers —T. R. Fyvel⟩ ***syn*** see GHASTLY — **lu·rid·ly** *adv* — **lu·rid·ness** *n*
lurk \'lərk\ *vi* [ME *lurken*; akin to MHG *lūren* to lie in wait — more at LOWER] (14c) **1 a** : to lie in wait in a place of concealment esp. for an evil purpose **b** : to move furtively or inconspicuously : SNEAK **c** : to persist in staying **2 a** : to be concealed but capable of being discovered; *specif* : to constitute a latent threat **b** : to lie hidden — **lurk·er** *n*
syn LURK, SKULK, SLINK, SNEAK mean to behave so as to escape attention. LURK implies a lying in wait in a place of concealment and often suggests an evil intent; SKULK suggests more strongly cowardice or fear or sinister intent; SLINK implies moving stealthily often merely to escape attention; SNEAK may add an implication of entering or leaving a place or evading a difficulty by furtive, indirect, or underhanded methods.
lus·cious \'ləsh-əs\ *adj* [ME *lucius*, perh. alter. of *licius*, short for *delicious*] (15c) **1 a** : having a delicious taste or smell : SWEET **b** *archaic* : excessively sweet : CLOYING **2** : sexually attractive : SEDUCTIVE, SEXY **3 a** : richly luxurious or appealing to the senses **b** : excessively ornate — **lus·cious·ly** *adv* — **lus·cious·ness** *n*
[1]**lush** \'ləsh\ *adj* [ME *lusch* soft, tender] (1610) **1 a** : growing vigorously esp. with luxuriant foliage ⟨~ grass⟩ **b** : lavishly productive: as (1) : FERTILE (2) : THRIVING (3) : characterized by abundance : PLENTIFUL (4) : PROSPEROUS, PROFITABLE **2 a** : SAVORY, DELICIOUS **b** : appealing to the senses ⟨the ~ sounds of the orchestra⟩ **c** : OPULENT, SUMPTUOUS ***syn*** see PROFUSE — **lush·ly** *adv* — **lush·ness** *n*
[2]**lush** *n* [origin unknown] (ca. 1790) **1** *slang* : intoxicating liquor : DRINK **2** : an habitual heavy drinker : DRUNKARD
[3]**lush** *vb, slang* (ca. 1810) : DRINK
Luso- *comb form* [Pg, fr. *lusitano* Portuguese, fr. L *lusitanus* of Lusitania (ancient region corresponding approximately to modern

Portugal)] 1 \ˌlü-(ˌ)sō\ : Portuguese and ⟨*Luso*-Brazilian⟩ 2 : of Portugal

[1]**lust** \ˈləst\ *n* [ME, fr. OE; akin to OHG *lust* pleasure, L *lascivus* wanton] (bef. 12c) 1 *obs* **a** : PLEASURE, DELIGHT **b** : personal inclination : WISH 2 : usu. intense or unbridled sexual desire : LASCIVIOUSNESS 3 **a** : an intense longing : CRAVING **b** : ENTHUSIASM, EAGERNESS

[2]**lust** *vi* (12c) : to have an intense desire or need : CRAVE; *specif* : to have a sexual urge

[1]**lus·ter** *or* **lus·tre** \ˈləs-tər\ *n* [ME *lustre,* fr. L *lustrum*] (14c) : a period of five years : LUSTRUM 2

[2]**luster** *or* **lustre** *n* [MF *lustre,* fr. OIt *lustro,* fr. *lustrare* to brighten, fr. L; akin to L *lucēre* to shine — more at LIGHT] (1522) 1 : a glow of reflected light : SHEEN; *specif* : the appearance of the surface of a mineral dependent upon its reflecting qualities 2 **a** : a glow of light from within : LUMINOSITY **b** : an inner beauty : RADIANCE 3 : a superficial attractiveness or appearance of excellence 4 **a** : a glass pendant used esp. to ornament a candlestick or chandelier **b** : a decorative object (as a chandelier) hung with glass pendants 5 *chiefly Brit* : a fabric with cotton warp and a filling of wool, mohair, or alpaca 6 : LUSTERWARE — **lus·ter·less** \-tər-ləs\ *adj*

[3]**luster** *or* **lustre** *vb* **lus·tered** *or* **lus·tred; lus·ter·ing** *or* **lus·tring** \-t(ə-)riŋ\ *vi* (1582) : to have luster : GLEAM ~ *vt* 1 : to give luster or distinction to 2 : to coat or treat with a substance that imparts luster

lus·ter·ware \ˈləs-tər-ˌwa(ə)r, -ˌwe(ə)r\ *n* (1825) : pottery with an iridescent metallic sheen in the glaze

lust·ful \ˈləst-fəl\ *adj* (14c) : excited by lust : LECHEROUS — **lust·ful·ly** \-fə-lē\ *adv* — **lust·ful·ness** *n*

lust·i·hood \ˈləs-tē-ˌhu̇d\ *n* (1599) 1 : vigor of body or spirit : ROBUSTNESS 2 : sexual inclination or capacity

lus·tral \ˈləs-trəl\ *adj* [L *lustralis,* fr. *lustrum*] (1533) : PURIFICATORY

lus·trate \ˈləs-ˌtrāt\ *vt* **lus·trat·ed; lus·trat·ing** [L *lustratus,* pp. of *lustrare* to brighten, purify] (1653) : to purify ceremonially — **lus·tra·tion** \ˌləs-ˈtrā-shən\ *n*

[1]**lus·tring** \ˈləs-triŋ\ *n* [modif. of It *lustrino*] (1697) : LUTESTRING

[2]**lus·tring** \-t(ə-)riŋ\ *n* [*lustring,* gerund of [3]*luster*] (ca. 1891) : a finishing process (as calendering) for giving a gloss to yarns and cloth

lus·trous \ˈləs-trəs\ *adj* (1601) 1 : reflecting light evenly and efficiently without glitter or sparkle ⟨a ~ satin⟩ ⟨the ~ glow of an opal⟩ 2 : radiant in character or reputation : ILLUSTRIOUS ***syn*** see BRIGHT — **lus·trous·ly** *adv* — **lus·trous·ness** *n*

lus·trum \ˈləs-trəm\ *n, pl* **lustrums** *or* **lus·tra** \-trə\ [L; akin to L *lustrare* to brighten, purify] (1590) 1 : a period of five years 2 **a** : a purification of the whole Roman people made in ancient times after the census every five years **b** : the Roman census

lusty \ˈləs-tē\ *adj* **lust·i·er; -est** (13c) 1 *archaic* : MERRY, JOYOUS 2 : LUSTFUL ⟨~ passion⟩ 3 **a** : full of strength and vitality : HEALTHY, VIGOROUS ⟨a young, ~, growing country —Helen Harris⟩ **b** : HEARTY, ROBUST ⟨a ~ beef stew⟩ **c** : ENTHUSIASTIC, ROUSING ⟨a ~ rendition of the song⟩ ***syn*** see VIGOROUS — **lust·i·ly** \-tə-lē\ *adv* — **lust·i·ness** \-tē-nəs\ *n*

lu·sus na·tu·rae \ˌlü-səs-nə-ˈt(y)u̇(ə)r-(ˌ)ē, -ˈtu̇(ə)r-ˌī\ *n* [NL, lit., play of nature] (1661) : a sport or freak of nature

[1]**lute** \ˈlüt\ *n* [ME, fr. MF *lut,* fr. OProv *laut,* fr. Ar *al-ʽūd,* lit., the wood] (13c) : a stringed instrument having a large pear-shaped body, a vaulted back, a fretted fingerboard, and a head with tuning pegs which is often angled backward from the neck

lute

[2]**lute** *vt* **lut·ed; lut·ing** [ME *luten,* fr. L *lutare,* fr. *lutum* mud — more at POLLUTE] (14c) : to seal or cover with lute

[3]**lute** *n* (15c) : a substance (as cement or clay) for packing a joint or coating a porous surface to make it impervious to gas or liquid

lute- *or* **luteo-** *comb form* [NL (*corpus*) *luteum*] : corpus luteum ⟨*lute*al⟩

lu·te·al \ˈlüt-ē-əl\ *adj* (1920) : of, relating to, characterized by, or involving the corpus luteum ⟨the ~ phase of the menstrual cycle⟩

lu·tein \ˈlüt-ē-ən, ˈlü-ˌtēn\ *n* [fr. its occurrence in corpus luteum] (1869) : an orange xanthophyll $C_{40}H_{56}O_2$ occurring in plants usu. with carotenes and chlorophylls and in animal fat, egg yolk, and the corpus luteum

lu·tein·iza·tion \ˌlüt-ē-ən-ə-ˈzā-shən, ˌlü-ˌtēn-\ *n* (1929) : the process of forming corpora lutea — **lu·tein·ize** \ˈlüt-ē-ə-ˌnīz, ˈlü-ˌtē-ˌnīz\ *vb*

luteinizing hormone *n* (1931) : a hormone from the anterior lobe of the pituitary gland that in the female stimulates esp. the development of corpora lutea and in the male the development of interstitial tissue in the testis

luteinizing hormone–releasing hormone *n* (1971) : a hormone secreted by the hypothalamus that stimulates the pituitary gland to release luteinizing hormone — called also *luteinizing hormone-releasing factor*

lu·te·nist *or* **lu·ta·nist** \ˈlüt-ᵊn-əst, ˈlüt-nəst\ *n* [ML *lutanista,* fr. *lutana* lute, prob. fr. MF *lut*] (1600) : a lute player

lu·teo·tro·pic \ˌlüt-ē-ə-ˈtrō-pik, -ˈträp-ik\ *or* **lu·teo·tro·phic** \-ˈtrō-fik, -ˈträf-ik\ *adj* (1941) : acting on the corpora lutea

luteotropic hormone *or* **luteotrophic hormone** *n* (1949) : PROLACTIN

lu·teo·tro·pin \ˌlüt-ē-ə-ˈtrō-pən\ *or* **lu·teo·tro·phin** \-fən\ *n* (1941) : PROLACTIN

lu·te·ous \ˈlüt-ē-əs\ *adj* [L *luteus* yellowish, fr. *lutum,* a plant used for dyeing yellow] (1657) : yellow tinged with green or brown

lute·string \ˈlüt-(ˌ)striŋ\ *n* [by folk etymology fr. It *lustrino* glossy fabric, fr. *lustro* luster] (1661) : a plain glossy silk formerly much used for women's dresses and ribbons

lu·te·tium *also* **lu·te·cium** \lü-ˈtē-sh(ē-)əm\ *n* [NL, fr. L *Lutetia,* ancient name of Paris] (1907) : a metallic element of the rare-earth group — see ELEMENT table

[1]**Lu·ther·an** \ˈlü-th(ə-)rən\ *n* (1521) : a member of a Lutheran church

[2]**Lutheran** *adj* (1530) 1 : of or relating to religious doctrines (as justification by faith alone) developed by Martin Luther or his followers 2 : of or relating to the Protestant churches adhering to Lutheran doctrines, liturgy, and polity — **Lu·ther·an·ism** \-ˌiz-əm\ *n*

lu·thi·er \ˈlüt-ē-ər, ˈlü-thē-ər\ *n* [F, fr. *luth* lute (fr. MF *lut*) + *-ier* -er] (1879) : one who makes stringed musical instruments (as violins or guitars)

lut·ing \ˈlüt-iŋ\ *n* (1527) : [3]LUTE

Lu·wi·an \ˈlü-(w)ē-ən\ *n* [*Luwi* (an ancient people of the southern coast of Asia Minor)] (1924) : an Anatolian language of the Indo-European language family — see INDO-EUROPEAN LANGUAGES table — **Luwian** *adj*

lux \ˈləks\ *n, pl* **lux** *or* **lux·es** [L, light — more at LIGHT] (1889) : a unit of illumination equal to the direct illumination on a surface that is everywhere one meter from a uniform point source of one candle intensity or equal to one lumen per square meter

lux·a·tion \ˌlək-ˈsā-shən\ *n* [LL *luxation-, luxatio,* fr. L *luxatus,* pp. of *luxare* to dislocate, fr. *luxus* dislocated — more at LOCK] (1552) : dislocation of an anatomical part (as a bone at a joint or the lens of the eye)

luxe \ˈlu̇ks, ˈləks, ˈlüks\ *n* [F, fr. L *luxus* — more at LUXURY] (1558) : LUXURY — **luxe** *adj*

lux·u·ri·ance \(ˌ)ləg-ˈzhu̇r-ē-ən(t)s, (ˌ)lək-ˈshu̇r-\ *n* (1728) : the quality or state of being luxuriant

lux·u·ri·ant \-ē-ənt\ *adj* (1540) 1 **a** : yielding abundantly : FERTILE, FRUITFUL **b** : characterized by abundant growth : LUSH 2 : abundantly and often extravagantly rich and varied : PROLIFIC 3 : characterized by luxury : LUXURIOUS ***syn*** see PROFUSE — **lux·u·ri·ant·ly** *adv*

lux·u·ri·ate \-ē-ˌāt\ *vi* **-at·ed; -at·ing** [L *luxuriatus,* pp. of *luxuriare,* fr. *luxuria*] (1621) 1 **a** : to grow profusely : THRIVE **b** : to develop extensively 2 : to indulge oneself luxuriously : REVEL

lux·u·ri·ous \(ˌ)ləg-ˈzhu̇r-ē-əs, (ˌ)lək-ˈshu̇r-\ *adj* (1606) 1 : of, relating to, or marked by luxury ⟨a ~ resort⟩ 2 : marked by or given to self-indulgence ⟨~ tastes⟩ ⟨~ feeling⟩ 3 : exceedingly choice and costly : of the finest and richest kind ⟨~ wines⟩ ***syn*** see SENSUOUS — **lux·u·ri·ous·ly** *adv* — **lux·u·ri·ous·ness** *n*

lux·u·ry \ˈləksh-(ə-)rē, ˈləgzh-\ *n, pl* **-ries** [ME *luxurie,* fr. MF, fr. L *luxuria* rankness, luxury, excess; akin to L *luxus* luxury, excess] (14c) 1 *archaic* : LECHERY, LUST 2 : a condition of abundance or great ease and comfort : sumptuous environment ⟨lived in ~⟩ 3 **a** : something adding to pleasure or comfort but not absolutely necessary **b** : an indulgence in something that provides pleasure, satisfaction, or ease ⟨had the ~ of rejecting a handful of job offers . . . before accepting a choice assignment —Terri Minsky⟩ — **luxury** *adj*

lwei \lə-ˈwā\ *n, pl* **lwei** *also* **lweis** [native name in Angola] (ca. 1979) — see *kwanza* at MONEY table

[1]**-ly** \lē; *in some dialects, esp Brit, Southern, NewEng, often* li *but not shown at individual entries*\ *adj suffix* [ME, fr. OE *-lic, -lic;* akin to OHG *-līh, -lic,* OE *līc* body — more at LIKE] 1 : like in appearance, manner, or nature : having the characteristics of ⟨queen*ly*⟩ ⟨father*ly*⟩ 2 : characterized by regular recurrence in (specified) units of time : every ⟨hour*ly*⟩

[2]**-ly** *adv suffix* [ME, fr. OE *-līce, -lice,* fr. *-līc,* adj. suffix] 1 **a** : in a (specified) manner ⟨slow*ly*⟩ **b** : at a (specified) time interval ⟨annual*ly*⟩ 2 : from a (specified) point of view ⟨eschatological*ly*⟩ 3 : with respect to ⟨part*ly*⟩ 4 : to a (specified) degree ⟨relative*ly*⟩

ly·am–hound \ˈlī-əm-ˌhau̇nd\ *or* **lyme–hound** \ˈlīm-ˌhau̇nd\ *n* [obs. *lyam* (leash)] *archaic* (1527) : BLOODHOUND

ly·art \ˈlī-ərt\ *adj* [ME, fr. MF *liart*] *chiefly Scot* (14c) : streaked with gray : GRAY

ly·ase \ˈlī-ˌās, -ˌāz\ *n* [Gk *lyein* to loosen, release + E *-ase* — more at LOSE] (1965) : an enzyme (as a decarboxylase) that forms double bonds by removing groups from a substrate other than by hydrolysis or that adds groups to double bonds

ly·can·thro·py \lī-ˈkan(t)-thrə-pē\ *n* [NL *lycanthropia,* fr. Gk *lykanthrōpia,* fr. *lykanthrōpos* werewolf, fr. *lykos* wolf + *anthrōpos* man — more at WOLF] (1584) 1 : a delusion that one has become a wolf 2 : the assumption of the form and characteristics of a wolf held to be possible by witchcraft or magic

ly·cée \lē-ˈsā\ *n* [F, fr. MF, lyceum, fr. L *Lyceum*] (1865) : a French public secondary school that prepares students for the university

ly·ce·um \lī-ˈsē-əm, ˈlī-sē-\ *n* [L *Lyceum,* gymnasium near Athens where Aristotle taught, fr. Gk *Lykeion,* fr. neut. of *lykeios,* epithet of Apollo] (1786) 1 : a hall for public lectures or discussions 2 : an association providing public lectures, concerts, and entertainments 3 : LYCÉE

ly·chee *var of* LITCHI

lych–gate \ˈlich-ˌgāt\ *n* [ME *lycheyate,* fr. *lich* body, corpse (fr. OE *līc*) + *gate, yate* gate] (15c) : a roofed gate in a churchyard under which a bier rests during the initial part of the burial service

lych·nis \ˈlik-nəs\ *n* [NL, fr. L, a red flower, fr. Gk; akin to Gk *lychnos* lamp, L *lux* light — more at LIGHT] (1601) : any of a genus (*Lychnis*) of herbs of the pink family with terminal cymes of showy mostly red or white flowers having 5 or rarely 4 styles

Ly·cian \ˈlish-(ē-)ən\ *n* (1598) 1 : a native or inhabitant of Lycia 2 : an Anatolian language of the Indo-European language family — see INDO-EUROPEAN LANGUAGES table — **Lycian** *adj*

ly·co·pene \ˈlī-kə-ˌpēn\ *n* [ISV *lycop-* (fr. NL *Lycopersicon,* genus of herbs) + *-ene*] (ca. 1929) : a carotenoid pigment $C_{40}H_{56}$ that is the red coloring matter of the tomato

ly·co·pod \ˈlī-kə-ˌpäd\ *n* [NL *Lycopodium*] (1861) : LYCOPODIUM 1; *broadly* : CLUB MOSS

ly·co·po·di·um \ˌlī-kə-ˈpōd-ē-əm\ *n* [NL, fr. Gk *lykos* wolf + *podion,* dim. of *pod-, pous* foot — more at FOOT] (1756) 1 : any of a large genus (*Lycopodium*) of erect or creeping club mosses with evergreen one-nerved leaves in four to many ranks 2 : a fine yellowish flammable powder composed of lycopodium spores and used in pharmacy and as a component of fireworks and flashlight powders

lydd·ite \ˈlid-ˌīt\ *n* [*Lydd,* England] (1888) : a high explosive composed chiefly of picric acid

Lyd·i·an \ˈlid-ē-ən\ *n* (15c) 1 : a native or inhabitant of Lydia 2 : an Anatolian language of the Indo-European language family — see INDO-EUROPEAN LANGUAGES table — **Lydian** *adj*

lye \ˈlī\ *n* [ME, fr. OE *lēag;* akin to OHG *louga* lye, L *lavare, lavere* to wash, Gk *louein*] (bef. 12c) 1 : a strong alkaline liquor rich in potassium carbonate leached from wood ashes and used esp. in making soap and washing; *broadly* : a strong alkaline solution (as of sodium hydroxide or potassium hydroxide) **2** : a solid caustic (as sodium hydroxide)

ly·gus bug \ˈlī-gəs-\ *n* [NL *Lygus*] (1940) : any of various small sucking bugs (genus *Lygus*) including some vectors of virus diseases of plants

ly·ing \ˈlī-iŋ\ *adj* [prp. of [3]*lie*] (13c) : marked by or containing falsehoods : FALSE ⟨a ~ account of the accident⟩ ***syn*** see DISHONEST

ly·ing–in \ˌlī-iŋ-ˈin\ *n, pl* **lyings–in** *or* **lying–ins** (15c) : the state attending and consequent to childbirth : CONFINEMENT

Lyme disease \ˈlīm-\ *n* [*Lyme*, Connecticut, where it was first reported] (1980) : an acute inflammatory disease caused by a spirochete (*Borrelia burgdorferi*) transmitted by ticks (genus *Ixodes* and esp. *I. dammini*) and characterized by fever and chills, often by an itching red patch at the site of infection, and by arthritis if untreated

lymph \ˈlim(p)f\ *n* [L *lympha*, water goddess, water, modif. of Gk *nymphē* nymph — more at NUPTIAL] (1630) **1** *archaic* : the sap of plants **2** [NL *lympha*, fr. L, water] : a pale coagulable fluid that bathes the tissues, passes into lymphatic channels and ducts, is discharged into the blood by way of the thoracic duct, and consists of a liquid portion resembling blood plasma and containing white blood cells but normally no red blood cells

lymph- *or* **lympho-** *comb form* [NL *lympha*] : lymph : lymphatic tissue ⟨*lympho*granuloma⟩

lymph·ad·e·ni·tis \ˌlim-ˌfad-ᵊn-ˈīt-əs\ *n* [NL, fr. *lymphaden* lymph gland (fr. *lymph-* + *aden-*) + *-itis*] (1860) : inflammation of lymph nodes

lymph·ade·nop·a·thy \ˌlim-ˌfad-ᵊn-ˈäp-ə-thē\ *n, pl* **-thies** (1920) : abnormal enlargement of the lymph nodes

lymph·an·gi·og·ra·phy \ˌlim-ˌfan-jē-ˈäg-rə-fē\ *n* (ca. 1941) : X-ray depiction of lymph vessels and nodes after use of a radiopaque material — called also *lymphography* — **lymph·an·gio·gram** \(ˌ)lim-ˈfan-jē-ə-ˌgram\ *n* — **lymph·an·gio·graph·ic** \ˌlim-ˌfan-jē-ə-ˈgraf-ik\ *adj*

[1]**lym·phat·ic** \lim-ˈfat-ik\ *adj* (1649) **1 a** : of, relating to, or produced by lymph, lymphoid tissue, or lymphocytes **b** : conveying lymph **2** : lacking physical or mental energy : SLUGGISH — **lym·phat·i·cal·ly** \-i-k(ə-)lē\ *adv*

[2]**lymphatic** *n* (1667) : a vessel that contains or conveys lymph — called also *lymph vessel*

lymph gland *n* (1856) : LYMPH NODE

lymph node *n* (1892) : any of the rounded masses of lymphoid tissue surrounded by a capsule of connective tissue that occur in association with the lymphatic vessels and that consist of a reticulum of connective tissue fibers in the meshes of which are contained numerous small round cells each having a large round deeply staining nucleus and when carried off by the flow of lymph through the node become a lymphocyte

lym·pho·blast \ˈlim(p)-fə-ˌblast\ *n* [ISV] (ca. 1909) : a cell giving rise to lymphocytes — **lym·pho·blas·tic** \ˌlim(p)-fə-ˈblas-tik\ *adj*

lym·pho·cyte \ˈlim(p)-fə-ˌsīt\ *n* [ISV] (1890) : any of the colorless weakly motile cells produced in lymphoid tissue that are the typical cellular elements of lymph, include the cellular mediators of immunity, and constitute 20 to 30 percent of the leukocytes of normal human blood — compare B CELL, T CELL — **lym·pho·cyt·ic** \ˌlim(p)-fə-ˈsit-ik\ *adj*

lymphocytic cho·rio·men·in·gi·tis \-ˌkȯr-ē-ō-ˌmen-ən-ˈjīt-əs\ *n* [NL *choriomeningitis* cerebral meningitis, fr. *chorio-* of a membrane resembling the chorion] (1934) : an acute virus disease that is characterized by fever, nausea and vomiting, headache, stiff neck, and slow pulse, is marked by the presence of numerous lymphocytes in the cerebrospinal fluid, and is transmitted esp. by rodents and bloodsucking insects

lym·pho·cy·to·sis \ˌlim(p)-fə-ˌsī-ˈtō-səs, -fə-sə-\ *n* [NL, fr. ISV *lymphocyte*] (1896) : an increase in the number of lymphocytes in the blood usu. associated with chronic infections or inflammations

lym·pho·gran·u·lo·ma \ˈlim(p)-fō-ˌgran-yə-ˈlō-mə\ *n, pl* **-mas** *or* **-ma·ta** \-mət-ə\ [NL] (1924) : LYMPHOGRANULOMA VENEREUM

lymphogranuloma in·gui·na·le \-ˌiŋ-gwə-ˈnäl-ē, -ˈnal-, -ˈnāl-\ *n* [NL, inguinal lymphogranuloma] (1932) : LYMPHOGRANULOMA VENEREUM

lym·pho·gran·u·lo·ma·to·sis \-ˌlō-mə-ˈtō-səs\ *n, pl* **-to·ses** \-ˌsēz\ [NL *lymphogranulomat-*, *lymphogranuloma* + *-osis*] (1911) : the development of benign or malignant nodular swellings of lymph nodes in various parts of the body; *also* : a condition characterized by these

lymphogranuloma ve·ne·re·um \-və-ˈnir-ē-əm\ *n* [NL, venereal lymphogranuloma] (ca. 1938) : a contagious venereal disease caused by various strains of a rickettsia (*Chlamydia trachomatis*) and marked by swelling and ulceration of lymphatic tissue in the iliac and inguinal regions

lym·phog·ra·phy \lim-ˈfäg-rə-fē\ *n* (1935) : LYMPHANGIOGRAPHY — **lym·pho·gram** \ˈlim(p)-fə-ˌgram\ *n* — **lym·pho·graph·ic** \ˌlim-fə-ˈgraf-ik\ *adj*

lym·phoid \ˈlim-ˌfȯid\ *adj* (1867) **1** : of, relating to, or constituting the tissue characteristic of the lymph nodes **2** : of, relating to, or resembling lymph

lym·pho·kine \ˈlim(p)-fə-ˌkīn\ *n* [*lymph-* + *-kine*, fr. Gk *kinein* to move about — more at HIGHT] (1969) : any of various substances (as interferon) of low molecular weight that are not immunoglobulins, are secreted by T cells in response to stimulation by antigens, and have a role (as the activation of macrophages or the enhancement or inhibition of antibody production) in cell-mediated immunological reactions

lym·pho·ma \lim-ˈfō-mə\ *n, pl* **-mas** *or* **-ma·ta** \-mət-ə\ [NL] (1873) : a tumor of lymphoid tissue — **lym·pho·ma·tous** \-mət-əs\ *adj*

lym·pho·ma·to·sis \(ˌ)lim-ˌfō-mə-ˈtō-səs\ *n, pl* **-to·ses** \-ˌsēz\ [NL *lymphomat-*, *lymphoma* + *-osis*] (ca. 1900) : the presence of multiple lymphomas in the body

lym·pho·sar·co·ma \ˌlim(p)-fə-sär-ˈkō-mə\ *n, pl* **-mas** *or* **-ma·ta** \-mət-ə\ [NL] (ca. 1874) : a malignant lymphoma that tends to metastasize freely esp. along the regional lymphatic drainage

lynch \ˈlinch\ *vt* [*lynch law*] (1836) : to put to death (as by hanging) by mob action without legal sanction — **lynch·er** *n*

lynch law *n* [William *Lynch* †1820 Am. vigilante] (1782) : the punishment of presumed crimes or offenses usu. by death without due process of law

lynchpin *var of* LINCHPIN

lynx \ˈliŋ(k)s\ *n, pl* **lynx** *or* **lynx·es** [L, fr. Gk; akin to OE *lox* lynx, Gk *leukos* white — more at LIGHT] (14c) : any of various wildcats with relatively long legs, a short stubby tail, mottled coat, and often tufted ears: as **a** : the common lynx (*Lynx lynx*) of northern Europe and Asia **b** : BOBCAT **c** : a No. American lynx (*L. canadensis*) distinguished from the bobcat by its larger size, longer tufted ears, large padded claws, and wholly black tail tip — called also *Canadian lynx*

lynx–eyed \ˈliŋ(k)-ˈsīd\ *adj* (1597) : SHARP-SIGHTED

lyo- *comb form* [prob. fr. NL, fr. Gk *lyein* to loosen, dissolve — more at LOSE] : dispersed state : dispersion ⟨*lyo*philic⟩

ly·on·naise \ˌlī-ə-ˈnāz\ *adj* [F (*à la*) *lyonnaise* in the manner of Lyons, fr. fem. of *lyonnais* of Lyons, fr. *Lyon* Lyons, France] (1846) : prepared with onions ⟨~ potatoes⟩

Ly·on·nesse \ˌlī-ə-ˈnes\ *n* : a country that according to Arthurian legend was contiguous to Cornwall before sinking beneath the sea

lyo·phile \ˈlī-ə-ˌfīl\ *adj* [ISV] (ca. 1915) **1** : LYOPHILIC **2 a** : of or relating to freeze-drying **b** *or* **lyo·philed** \-ˌfīld\ : obtained by freeze-drying

lyo·phil·ic \ˌlī-ə-ˈfil-ik\ *adj* (ca. 1911) : marked by strong affinity between a dispersed phase and the liquid in which it is dispersed ⟨a ~ colloid⟩

ly·oph·i·lize \lī-ˈäf-ə-ˌlīz\ *vt* **-lized; -liz·ing** (1938) : FREEZE-DRY — **ly·oph·i·li·za·tion** \-ˌäf-ə-lə-ˈzā-shən\ *n* — **ly·oph·i·liz·er** \-ˈäf-ə-ˌlī-zər\ *n*

lyo·pho·bic \ˌlī-ə-ˈfō-bik\ *adj* (ca. 1911) : marked by lack of strong affinity between a dispersed phase and the liquid in which it is dispersed ⟨a ~ colloid⟩

Ly·ra \ˈlī-rə\ *n* [L (gen. *Lyrae*), lit., lyre] : a northern constellation representing the lyre of Orpheus or Mercury and containing Vega

ly·rate \ˈlī-ˌrāt\ *adj* (ca. 1760) : having or suggesting the shape of a lyre ⟨the ~ horns of the impala⟩

lyre \ˈlī(ə)r\ *n* [ME *lire*, fr. OF, fr. L *lyra*, fr. Gk] (13c) **1** : a stringed instrument of the harp class used by the ancient Greeks esp. to accompany song and recitation **2** *cap* : LYRA

lyre·bird \-ˌbərd\ *n* (1834) : either of two Australian passerine birds (genus *Menura*) distinguished in the male by very long tail feathers displayed in the shape of a lyre during courtship

lyrebird

[1]**lyr·ic** \ˈlir-ik\ *n* (1581) **1** : a lyric composition; *specif* : a lyric poem **2** : the words of a song

[2]**lyric** *adj* [MF or L; MF *lyrique*, fr. L *lyricus*, fr. Gk *lyrikos*, fr. *lyra*] (1589) **1 a** : suitable for singing to the lyre or for being set to music and sung **b** : of, relating to, or being drama set to music; *esp* : OPERATIC ⟨~ stage⟩ **2 a** : expressing direct usu. intense personal emotion esp. in a manner suggestive of song ⟨~ poetry⟩ **b** : EXUBERANT, RHAPSODIC **3** *of an opera singer* : having a light voice and a melodic style — compare DRAMATIC

lyr·i·cal \ˈlir-i-kəl\ *adj* (1581) : LYRIC — **lyr·i·cal·ly** \-i-k(ə-)lē\ *adv* — **lyr·i·cal·ness** \-kəl-nəs\ *n*

lyr·i·cism \ˈlir-ə-ˌsiz-əm\ *n* (1760) **1** : the quality or state of being lyric : SONGFULNESS **2 a** : an intense personal quality expressive of feeling or emotion in an art (as poetry or music) **b** : EXUBERANCE ⟨the sort of author who inspires ~ or invective, not judicious interpretation —*Time*⟩

lyr·i·cist \-səst\ *n* (1881) : a writer of lyrics

lyr·ism \ˈli(ə)r-ˌiz-əm\ *n* (1859) : LYRICISM

lyr·ist *n* (ca. 1656) **1** \ˈlī(ə)r-əst\ : a player on the lyre **2** \ˈlir-əst\ : LYRICIST

lys- *or* **lysi-** *or* **lyso-** *comb form* [NL, fr. Gk *lys-*, *lysi-* loosening, fr. *lysis*] : lysis ⟨*lys*in⟩

ly·sate \ˈlī-ˌsāt\ *n* (1922) : a product of lysis

lyse \ˈlīs, ˈlīz\ *vb* **lysed; lys·ing** [back-formation fr. NL *lysis*] *vt* (1922) : to cause to undergo lysis ~ *vi* : to undergo lysis

Ly·sen·ko·ism \lə-ˈseŋ-kō-ˌiz-əm\ *n* [Trofim *Lysenko*] (1948) : a biological doctrine asserting the fundamental influence of somatic and environmental factors on heredity in contradiction of orthodox genetics

ly·ser·gic acid \lə-ˌsər-jik-, (ˌ)lī-\ *n* [*lys-* + *ergot*] (1934) : a crystalline acid $C_{16}H_{16}N_2O_2$ from ergotic alkaloids; *also* : LSD

lysergic acid di·eth·yl·am·ide \-ˌdī-ˌeth-ə-ˈlam-ˌīd\ *n* (1944) : LSD

ly·sim·e·ter \lī-ˈsim-ət-ər\ *n* (ca. 1879) : a device for measuring the percolation of water through soils and for determining the soluble constituents removed in the drainage — **ly·si·met·ric** \ˌlī-sə-ˈme-trik\ *adj*

ly·sin \ˈlīs-ᵊn\ *n* (1900) : a substance (as an antibody) capable of causing lysis

ly·sine \ˈlī-ˌsēn\ *n* (1892) : a crystalline basic amino acid $C_6H_{14}N_2O_2$ that is essential to animal nutrition

ly·sis \ˈlī-səs\ *n, pl* **ly·ses** \-ˌsēz\ [NL, fr. Gk, act of loosening, dissolution, remission of fever, fr. *lyein* to loosen — more at LOSE] (1822) **1** : the gradual decline of a disease process (as fever) **2** : a process of disintegration or dissolution (as of cells)

-ly·sis \l-ə-səs, ˈlī-səs\ *n comb form, pl* **-ly·ses** \l-ə-ˌsēz\ [NL, fr. L & Gk; L, loosening, fr. Gk, fr. *lysis*] **1** : decomposition ⟨electro*lysis*⟩ **2** : disintegration : breaking down ⟨auto*lysis*⟩

ly·so·gen \ˈlī-sə-jən\ *n* (ca. 1934) : a lysogenic bacterium or bacterial strain

ly·so·gen·ic \ˌlī-sə-ˈjen-ik\ *adj* [fr. the capacity of the prophage to lyse other bacteria] (1899) **1** : harboring a prophage as hereditary material ⟨~ bacteria⟩ **2** : TEMPERATE 3 ⟨~ viruses⟩ — **ly·so·ge·nic·i·ty** \-jə-ˈnis-ət-ē\ *n*

ly·sog·e·nize \lī-ˈsäj-ə-ˌnīz\ *vt* **-nized; -niz·ing** (1953) : to render lysogenic — **ly·sog·e·ni·za·tion** \-ˌsäj-ə-nə-ˈzā-shən\ *n*

ly·sog·e·ny \lī-ˈsäj-ə-nē\ *n* (1956) : the state of being lysogenic

ly·so·lec·i·thin \ˌlī-sə-ˈles-ə-thən\ *n* (1923) : a hydrolytic substance formed by the enzymatic hydrolysis (as by some snake venoms) of a lecithin

ly·so·some \ˈlī-sə-ˌsōm\ *n* [ISV *lys-* + [3]*-some*] (1955) : a saclike cellular organelle that contains various hydrolytic enzymes — see CELL illustration — **ly·so·som·al** \ˌlī-sə-ˈsō-məl\ *adj* — **ly·so·som·al·ly** \-mə-lē\ *adv*

ly·so·zyme \ˈlī-sə-ˌzīm\ *n* (1922) : a basic bacteriolytic protein that is present in egg white and in human tears and saliva and that functions as a mucolytic enzyme

-lyte \ˌlīt\ *n comb form* [Gk *lytos* that may be untied, soluble, fr. *lyein*] : substance capable of undergoing (such) decomposition ⟨hydro*lyte*⟩

lyt·ic \ˈlit-ik\ *adj* [Gk *lytikos* able to loose, fr. *lyein*] (1889) : of or relating to lysis or a lysin; *also* : productive of or effecting lysis (as of cells) — **ly·ti·cal·ly** \-i-k(ə-)lē\ *adv*

-lyt·ic \'lit-ik\ *adj suffix* [Gk *lytikos*] : of, relating to, or effecting (such) decomposition ⟨hydro*lytic*⟩

-lyze \ˌlīz\ *vb comb form* [ISV, prob. irreg. fr. NL *-lysis*] : produce or undergo lytic disintegration or dissolution ⟨electro*lyze*⟩

m \'em\ *n, pl* **m's** *or* **ms** \'emz\ *often cap, often attrib* **1 a** : the 13th letter of the English alphabet **b** : a graphic representation of this letter **c** : a speech counterpart of orthographic *m* **2** : one thousand — see NUMBER table **3** : a graphic device for reproducing the letter *m* **4** : one designated *m* esp. as the 13th in order or class **5** : something shaped like the letter M **6 a** : EM 2 **b** : PICA 2

'm \m\ *vb* : AM ⟨I'*m* going⟩

ma \'mä, 'mȯ\ *n* [short for *mama*] (1829) : MOTHER

ma'am \'mam, *after* "yes" *often* əm\ *n* (1668) : MADAM

ma-and-pa \ˌmä(-ə)n-'pä, ˌmȯ(-ə)n-'pȯ\ *adj* (ca. 1963) : MOM-AND-POP

Mab \'mab\ *n* : a queen of fairies in English literature

mabe \'mäb\ *n* [origin unknown] (1951) : a cultured pearl essentially hemispherical in form — called also *mabe pearl*

mac \'mak\ *n, Brit* (1901) : MACKINTOSH

Mac \'mak\ *n* [*Mac-, Mc-*, common patronymic prefix in Scotch and Irish surnames] (ca. 1937) : FELLOW — used informally to address a man whose name is not known

ma·ca·bre \mə-'käb(-rə), -'käb-ər, -'käbrᵊ\ *adj* [F, fr. (*danse*) *macabre* dance of death, fr. MF (*danse de*) *Macabré*] (15c) **1** : having death as a subject : comprising or including a personalized representation of death **2** : dwelling on the gruesome **3** : tending to produce horror in a beholder *syn* see GHASTLY

mac·ad·am \mə-'kad-əm\ *n* [John L. *McAdam* †1836 Brit. engineer] (1824) : macadamized roadway or pavement esp. with a bituminous binder

mac·a·da·mia nut \ˌmak-ə-'dā-mē-ə-\ *n* [NL *Macadamia*, fr. John *Macadam* †1865 Australian chemist] (1929) : a hard-shelled nut somewhat resembling a filbert and produced by an Australian evergreen tree (*Macadamia ternifolia*) of the protea family that is cultivated extensively in Hawaii

mac·ad·am·ize \mə-'kad-ə-ˌmīz\ *vt* **-ized; -iz·ing** (1826) : to construct or finish (a road) by compacting into a solid mass a layer of small broken stone on a convex well-drained roadbed and using a binder (as cement or asphalt) for the mass

ma·caque \mə-'kak, -'käk\ *n* [F, fr. Pg *macaco*] (1840) : any of numerous short-tailed Old World monkeys (*Macaca* and related genera) chiefly of southern Asia and the East Indies; *esp* : RHESUS MONKEY

mac·a·ro·ni \ˌmak-ə-'rō-nē\ *n* [It *maccheroni*, pl. of *maccherone*, fr. It dial. *maccarone* dumpling, macaroni] (1599) **1** : pasta made from semolina and shaped in the form of slender tubes **2** *pl* **macaronis** *or* **macaronies a** : a member of a class of traveled young Englishmen of the late 18th and early 19th centuries who affected foreign ways **b** : an affected young man : FOP

mac·a·ron·ic \-'rän-ik\ *adj* [NL *macaronicus*, fr. It dial. *maccarone* macaroni] (1638) **1** : characterized by a mixture of vernacular words with Latin words or with non-Latin words having Latin endings **2** : characterized by a mixture of two languages — **macaronic** *n*

mac·a·roon \ˌmak-ə-'rün\ *n* [F *macaron*, fr. It dial. *maccarone*] (ca. 1611) : a small cookie composed chiefly of egg whites, sugar, and ground almonds or coconut

ma·caw \mə-'kȯ\ *n* [Pg *macau*] (1668) : any of numerous parrots (esp. genus *Ara*) of South and Central America including some of the largest and showiest of parrots

Mac·beth \mək-'beth, mak-\ *n* : a Scottish general who is the protagonist of Shakespeare's tragedy *Macbeth*

Mac·ca·bees \'mak-ə-ˌbēz\ *n pl* [Gk *Makkabaioi*, fr. pl. of *Makkabaios*, surname of Judas Maccabaeus 2d cent. B.C. Jewish patriot] **1** : a priestly family leading a Jewish revolt begun in 168 B.C. against Hellenism and Syrian rule and reigning over Palestine from 142 B.C. to 63 B.C. **2** *sing in constr* : either of two narrative and historical books included in the Roman Catholic canon of the Old Testament and in the Protestant Apocrypha — see BIBLE table — **Mac·ca·be·an** \ˌmak-ə-'bē-ən\ *adj*

macaw

mac·ca·boy \'mak-ə-ˌbȯi\ *n* [F *macouba*, fr. *Macouba*, district in Martinique] (1740) : a snuff from Martinique

'mace \'mās\ *n* [ME, fr. OF, fr. (assumed) VL *mattia*; akin to OHG *medela* plow, L *mateola* mallet] (13c) **1 a** : a heavy often spiked staff or club used esp. in the Middle Ages for breaking armor **b** : a club used as a weapon **2 a** : an ornamental staff borne as a symbol of authority before a public official or a legislative body **b** : one who carries a mace

²mace *n* [ME, fr. MF *macis*, fr. L *macir*, an East Indian spice, fr. Gk *makir*] (13c) : an aromatic spice consisting of the dried external fibrous covering of a nutmeg

³mace *vt* **maced; mac·ing** (1968) : to attack with the liquid Mace

Mace \'mās\ *trademark* — used for a temporarily disabling liquid that when sprayed in the face of a person (as a rioter) causes tears, dizziness, immobilization, and sometimes nausea

ma·cé·doine \ˌmas-ə-'dwän\ *n* [F, fr. *Macédoine* Macedonia; perh. fr. the mixture of races in Macedonia] (1846) **1** : a mixture of fruits or vegetables served as a salad or cocktail or in a jellied dessert or used in a sauce or as a garnish **2** : a confused mixture : MEDLEY

Mac·e·do·nian \ˌmas-ə-'dō-nyən, -nē-ən\ *n* (1582) **1** : a native or inhabitant of Macedonia **2** : the Slavic language of modern Macedonia **3** : the language of ancient Macedonia of uncertain affinity but generally assumed to be Indo-European

mac·er·ate \'mas-ə-ˌrāt\ *vb* **-at·ed; -at·ing** [L *maceratus*, pp. of *macerare* to soften, steep] *vt* (1547) **1** : to cause to waste away by or as if by excessive fasting **2** : to cause to become soft or separated into constituent elements by or as if by steeping in fluid; *broadly* : STEEP, SOAK ~ *vi* : to soften and wear away esp. as a result of being wetted or steeped — **mac·er·a·tion** \ˌmas-ə-'rā-shən\ *n* — **mac·er·a·tor** \'mas-ə-ˌrāt-ər\ *n*

Mach \'mäk\ *n* [*Mach number*] (1946) : a usu. high speed expressed by a Mach number ⟨an airplane flying at ~ 2⟩

Mach·a·bees \'mak-ə-(ˌ)bēz\ *n pl but sing in constr* [LL *Machabaei*, modif. of Gk *Makkabaioi*] : MACCABEES

ma·chete \mə-'shet-ē, -'chet-; -'shet\ *n* [Sp] (1598) : a large heavy knife used for cutting sugarcane and underbrush and as a weapon

Ma·chi·a·vel·lian \ˌmak-ē-ə-'vel-ē-ən, -'vel-yən\ *adj* [Niccolo *Machiavelli*] (1579) **1** : of or relating to Machiavelli or Machiavellianism **2** : suggesting the principles of conduct laid down by Machiavelli; *specif* : characterized by cunning, duplicity, or bad faith — **Machiavellian** *n*

Ma·chi·a·vel·lian·ism \-ˌiz-əm\ *n* (1626) : the political theory of Machiavelli; *esp* : the view that politics is amoral and that any means however unscrupulous can justifiably be used in achieving political power

ma·chic·o·late \mə-'chik-ə-ˌlāt\ *vt* **-lat·ed; -lat·ing** [ML *machicolatus*, pp. of *machicolare*, fr. OF *machicoller*, fr. *machicoleis* machicolation, fr. *macher* to crush + *col* neck, fr. L *collum* — more at COLLAR] (1773) : to furnish with machicolations

ma·chic·o·la·tion \mə-ˌchik-ə-'lā-shən\ *n* (1788) **1 a** : an opening between the corbels of a projecting parapet or in the floor of a gallery or roof of a portal for discharging missiles upon assailants below — see BATTLEMENT illustration **b** : a gallery or parapet containing such openings **2** : construction imitating medieval machicolation

mach·i·nate \'mak-ə-ˌnāt, 'mash-ə-\ *vb* **-nat·ed; -nat·ing** [L *machinatus*, pp. of *machinari*, fr. *machina* machine, contrivance] *vi* (1600) : to plan or plot esp. to do harm ~ *vt* : to scheme or contrive to bring about : PLOT — **mach·i·na·tor** \-ˌnāt-ər\ *n*

mach·i·na·tion \ˌmak-ə-'nā-shən, ˌmash-ə-\ *n* (15c) **1** : an act of machinating **2** : a scheming or crafty action or artful design intended to accomplish some usu. evil end ⟨backstage ~s and power plays that have dominated the film industry —Peter Bogdanovich⟩ *syn* see PLOT

¹ma·chine \mə-'shēn\ *n, often attrib* [MF, fr. L *machina* — more at MAY] (1549) **1 a** *archaic* : a constructed thing whether material or immaterial **b** : CONVEYANCE, VEHICLE; *specif* : AUTOMOBILE **c** *archaic* : a military engine **d** : any of various apparatuses formerly used to produce stage effects **e** (1) : an assemblage of parts that transmit forces, motion, and energy one to another in a predetermined manner (2) : an instrument (as a lever) designed to transmit or modify the application of power, force, or motion **f** : a mechanically, electrically, or electronically operated device for performing a task ⟨a calculating ~⟩ ⟨a card-sorting ~⟩ **g** : a coin-operated device ⟨a cigarette ~⟩ **h** : MACHINERY — used with *the* or in pl. ⟨man must not become the servant of the ~⟩ **2 a** : a living organism or one of its functional systems **b** : a person or organization that resembles a machine (as in being methodical, tireless, or unemotional) **c** (1) : a combination of persons acting together for a common end along with the agencies they use (2) : a highly organized political group under the leadership of a boss or small clique **3** : a literary device or contrivance introduced for dramatic effect

²machine *vt* **ma·chined; ma·chin·ing** (ca. 1864) : to process by or as if by machine; *esp* : to reduce or finish by or as if by turning, shaping, planing, or milling by machine-operated tools — **ma·chin·abil·i·ty** \-ˌshē-nə-'bil-ət-ē\ *n* — **ma·chin·able** *also* **ma·chine·able** \-'shē-nə-bəl\ *adj*

ma·chine-gun \mə-'shēn-ˌgən\ *adj* (1906) : characterized by rapidity and sharpness : RAPID-FIRE ⟨a comic's ~ delivery⟩

machine gun *n* (1870) **1** : a gun for continuous rapid firing that uses bullets **2** : SUBMACHINE GUN — **machine-gun** *vb* — **machine gunner** *n*

machine language *n* (ca. 1954) **1** : the set of symbolic instruction codes usu. in binary form that is used to represent operations and data in a machine (as a computer) **2** : ASSEMBLY LANGUAGE

ma·chine·like \mə-ˈshēn-ˌlīk\ *adj* (1698) : resembling a machine esp. in regularity of action or stereotyped uniformity of product
machine–readable *adj* (1961) : directly usable by a computer ⟨~ text⟩
ma·chin·ery \mə-ˈshēn-(ə-)rē\ *n, pl* **-er·ies** (1687) **1 a** : machines in general or as a functioning unit **b** : the working parts of a machine **2** : the means or system by which something is kept in action or a desired result is obtained ⟨the ~ of government⟩ ⟨genetic ~ of cells⟩
machine shop *n* (1827) : a workshop in which work is machined to size and assembled
machine tool *n* (1861) : a machine designed for shaping solid work
ma·chin·ist \mə-ˈshē-nəst\ *n* (ca. 1706) **1 a** : a worker who fabricates, assembles, or repairs machinery **b** : a craftsman skilled in the use of machine tools **c** : one who operates a machine **2** *archaic* : a person in charge of the mechanical aspects of a theatrical production **3** : a warrant officer who supervises machinery and engine operation
ma·chis·mo \mä-ˈchēz-(ˌ)mō, mə-, -ˈkēz-, -ˈkiz-, -ˈchiz-\ *n* [MexSp, fr. Sp *macho* male, fr. L *masculus* — more at MASCULINE] (1947) **1** : a strong sense of masculine pride : an exaggerated masculinity **2** : an exaggerated or exhilarating sense of power or strength
Mach number \ˈmäk-\ *n* [Ernst *Mach* †1916 Austrian physicist] (1937) : a number representing the ratio of the speed of a body to the speed of sound in the surrounding atmosphere ⟨a *Mach number* of 2 indicates a speed that is twice that of sound⟩
[1]**ma·cho** \ˈmä-ˌchō\ *adj* [Sp, male, fr. L *masculus* — more at MASCULINE] (1928) : characterized by machismo : aggressively virile
[2]**macho** *n* (1951) **1** : one who exhibits machismo **2** : MACHISMO
mack *var of* MAC
mack·er·el \ˈmak-(ə-)rəl\ *n, pl* **mackerel** *or* **mackerels** [ME *makerel,* fr. MF] (14c) **1** : a fish (*Scomber scombrus*) of the No. Atlantic that is green above with dark blue bars and silvery below, reaches a length of about 18 inches, and is one of the most important food fishes **2** : a fish of the suborder (Scombroidea) to which the common mackerel belongs; *esp* : a comparatively small member of this group as distinguished from a bonito or tuna
mackerel shark *n* (1819) : any of a family (Lamnidae) of large fierce pelagic sharks; *esp* : PORBEAGLE
mackerel sky *n* (1669) : a sky covered with rows of altocumulus or cirrocumulus clouds resembling the patterns on a mackerel's back
mack·i·naw \ˈmak-ə-ˌnȯ\ *n* [*Mackinaw* City, Michigan, formerly an Indian trading post] (1812) **1** : a flat-bottomed boat with pointed prow and square stern formerly much used on the upper Great Lakes **2** : a heavy woolen blanket formerly distributed by the U.S. government to the Indians **3 a** : a heavy cloth of wool or wool and other fibers often with a plaid design and usu. heavily napped and felted **b** : a short coat of mackinaw or similar heavy fabric
Mackinaw trout *n* (1840) : a No. American lake trout (*Salvelinus namaycush*)
mack·in·tosh *also* **mac·in·tosh** \ˈmak-ən-ˌtäsh\ *n* [Charles *Macintosh* †1843 Scot. chemist & inventor] (1836) **1** *chiefly Brit* : RAINCOAT **2** : a lightweight waterproof fabric orig. of rubberized cotton
Mac·lau·rin's series \mə-ˈklȯr-ən(z)-\ *n* [Colin *Maclaurin* †1746 Scot. mathematician] (ca. 1909) : a Taylor's series of the form

$$f(x) = f(0) + \frac{f'(0)}{1!}x + \frac{f''(0)}{2!}x^2 + \ldots + \frac{f^{[n]}(0)}{n!}x^n + \ldots$$

in which the expansion is about the reference point zero — called also *Maclaurin series*
ma·cle \ˈmak-əl\ *n* [F, wide-meshed net, lozenge voided, macle, fr. OF, mesh, lozenge voided, of Gmc origin; akin to OHG *masca* mesh — more at MESH] (1801) **1 a** : a twin crystal **b** : a flat often triangular diamond that is usu. a twin crystal **2** : a dark or discolored spot (as in a mineral) — **ma·cled** \ˈmak-əld\ *adj*
ma·con \ma-ˈkōⁿ\ *n, often cap* [F *mâcon,* fr. *Mâcon,* France] (1863) : a dry red or white wine produced in the area around Mâcon, France
macr- *or* **macro-** *comb form* [F & L, fr. Gk *makr-, makro-* long, fr. *makros* — more at MEAGER] **1** : long ⟨*macro*diagonal⟩ **2** : large ⟨*macro*spore⟩
mac·ra·mé *also* **mac·ra·me** \ˈmak-rə-ˌmā\ *n* [F or It; F *macramé,* fr. It *macramè,* fr. Turk *makrama* napkin, towel, fr. Ar *miqramah* coverlet] (1869) : a coarse lace or fringe made by knotting threads or cords in a geometrical pattern; *also* : the art of tying knots in patterns
[1]**mac·ro** \ˈmak-(ˌ)rō\ *adj* [*macr-*] (1923) **1** : being large, thick, or exceptionally prominent **2 a** : of, involving, or intended for use with relatively large quantities or on a large scale **b** : of or relating to macroeconomics **3** : GROSS 1c
[2]**macro** *n, pl* **macros** [short for *macroinstruction*] (1959) : a single computer instruction that stands for a sequence of operations
mac·ro·ag·gre·gate \ˌmak-rō-ˈag-ri-gət\ *n* (1926) : a relatively large particle (as of soil or a protein) — **mac·ro·ag·gre·gat·ed** \-ˌgāt-əd\ *adj*
mac·ro·bi·ot·ic \-bī-ˈät-ik, -bē-\ *adj* (1965) : of, relating to, or being an extremely restricted diet (as one containing chiefly whole grains) that is held by its advocates to promote health and well-being although it may actually be deficient in essential nutrients (as fats)
mac·ro·cosm \ˈmak-rə-ˌkäz-əm\ *n* [ME, fr. OF *macrocosme,* fr. ML *macrocosmos,* fr. L *macr-* + Gk *kosmos* order, universe] (1600) **1** : the great world : UNIVERSE **2** : a complex that is a large-scale reproduction of one of its constituents — **mac·ro·cos·mic** \ˌmak-rə-ˈkäz-mik\ *adj* — **mac·ro·cos·mi·cal·ly** \-mi-k(ə-)lē\ *adv*
mac·ro·cy·clic \ˌmak-rō-ˈsīk-lik, -ˈsī-klik\ *adj* (1936) : containing or being a chemical ring that consists usu. of 15 or more atoms
mac·ro·cyte \ˈmak-rə-ˌsīt\ *n* [ISV] (ca. 1889) : an exceptionally large red blood cell occurring chiefly in anemias — **mac·ro·cyt·ic** \ˌmak-rə-ˈsit-ik\ *adj*
mac·ro·cy·to·sis \ˌmak-rə-sī-ˈtō-səs, -rə-sə-\ *n, pl* **-to·ses** \-ˌsēz\ [NL] (1893) : the occurrence of macrocytes in the blood
mac·ro·eco·nom·ics \ˈmak-rō-ˌek-ə-ˈnäm-iks, -ˌē-kə-\ *n pl but usu sing in constr* (1948) : a study of economics in terms of whole systems esp. with reference to general levels of output and income and to the interrelations among sectors of the economy — compare MICROECONOMICS — **mac·ro·eco·nom·ic** \-ik\ *adj*
mac·ro·evo·lu·tion \ˈmak-rō-ˌev-ə-ˈlü-shən *also* -ˌē-və-\ *n* (1939) : evolution that cumulates in relatively large and complex changes (as in species formation) — **mac·ro·evo·lu·tion·ary** \-shə-ˌner-ē\ *adj*
mac·ro·fos·sil \ˈmak-rō-ˌfäs-əl\ *n* (1937) : a fossil large enough to be observed by direct inspection
mac·ro·ga·mete \ˌmak-rō-gə-ˈmēt, -ˈgam-ˌēt\ *n* [ISV] (1899) : the larger and usu. female gamete of a heterogamous organism
mac·ro·glob·u·lin \-ˈgläb-yə-lən\ *n* [ISV] (1952) : a highly polymerized globulin of high molecular weight
mac·ro·glob·u·lin·emia \-ˌgläb-yə-lə-ˈnē-mē-ə\ *n* [NL] (1949) : a disorder characterized by increased blood serum viscosity and the presence of macroglobulins in the serum — **mac·ro·glob·u·lin·emic** \-mik\ *adj*
mac·ro·in·struc·tion \ˌmak-rō-in-ˈstrək-shən\ *n* (1959) : MACRO
macro lens *n* [*macr-,* fr. the fact that the focal length is greater than normal] (1961) : a camera lens designed to focus at very short distances with up to life-size magnification of the image
mac·ro·lep·i·dop·tera \ˈmak-rō-ˌlep-ə-ˈdäp-tə-rə\ *n pl* [NL] (1882) : lepidoptera (as butterflies, skippers, saturniids, noctuids, and geometrids) that include most of the large forms and none of the minute ones
mac·ro·mere \ˈmak-rə-ˌmi(ə)r\ *n* (1877) : a large blastomere — see BLASTULA illustration
mac·ro·mol·e·cule \ˌmak-rō-ˈmäl-i-ˌkyü(ə)l\ *n* [ISV] (ca. 1929) : a large molecule (as of a protein or rubber) built up from smaller chemical structures — **mac·ro·mo·lec·u·lar** \-mə-ˈlek-yə-lər\ *adj*
ma·cron \ˈmā-ˌkrän, ˈmak-, -rən\ *n* [Gk *makron,* neut. of *makros* long] (1851) : a mark ¯ placed over a vowel to indicate that the vowel is long or placed over a syllable or used alone to indicate a stressed or long syllable in a metrical foot
mac·ro·nu·cle·us \ˌmak-rō-ˈn(y)ü-klē-əs\ *n* [NL] (1892) : a relatively large densely staining nucleus that is believed to exert a controlling influence over the trophic activities of most ciliate protozoans — **mac·ro·nu·cle·ar** \ˌmak-rō-ˈn(y)ü-klē-ər, ÷-kyə-lər\ *adj*
mac·ro·nu·tri·ent \-ˈn(y)ü-trē-ənt\ *n* (1942) : a chemical element of which relatively large quantities are essential to the growth and welfare of a plant
mac·ro·phage \ˈmak-rə-ˌfāj, -ˌfäzh\ *n* [F, fr. *macr-* + *-phage*] (1890) : a phagocytic tissue cell of the reticuloendothelial system that may be fixed or freely motile, is derived from a monocyte, and functions in the protection of the body against infection and noxious substances — called also *histiocyte* — **mac·ro·phag·ic** \ˌmak-rə-ˈfaj-ik\ *adj*
mac·ro·pho·tog·ra·phy \ˌmak-rō-fə-ˈtäg-rə-fē\ *n* (1889) : the making of photographs in which the object is either unmagnified or slightly magnified up to a limit often of about 10 diameters
mac·ro·phyte \ˈmak-rə-ˌfīt\ *n* (ca. 1909) : a member of the macroscopic plant life esp. of a body of water — **mac·ro·phyt·ic** \ˌmak-rə-ˈfit-ik\ *adj*
mac·rop·ter·ous \ma-ˈkräp-tə-rəs\ *adj* [Gk *makropteros,* fr. *makr-* + *pteron* wing — more at FEATHER] (1835) : having long or large wings or fins
mac·ro·scale \ˈmak-rō-ˌskāl\ *n* (1931) : a large often macroscopic scale
mac·ro·scop·ic \ˌmak-rə-ˈskäp-ik\ *adj* [ISV *macr-* + *-scopic* (as in *microscopic*)] (1872) **1** : large enough to be observed by the naked eye **2** : considered in terms of large units or elements — **mac·ro·scop·i·cal·ly** \-i-k(ə-)lē\ *adv*
mac·ro·struc·ture \ˈmak-rō-ˌstrək-chər\ *n* (ca. 1899) : the structure (as of metal, a body part, or the soil) revealed by visual examination with little or no magnification — **mac·ro·struc·tur·al** \ˌmak-rō-ˈstrək-chə-rəl, -ˈstrək-shə-rəl\ *adj*
mac·u·la \ˈmak-yə-lə\ *n, pl* **-lae** \-ˌlē, -ˌlī\ *also* **-las** [L] (15c) **1** : SPOT, BLOTCH; *esp* : MACULE **2** : an anatomical structure (as the macula lutea) having the form of a spot differentiated from surrounding tissues — **mac·u·lar** \-lər\ *adj*
macula lu·tea \-ˈlüt-ē-ə\ *n, pl* **maculae lu·te·ae** \-ē-ˌē, -ē-ˌī\ [NL, lit., yellow spot] (1848) : a small yellowish area lying slightly lateral to the center of the retina that constitutes the region of maximum visual acuity — called also *yellow spot*
mac·u·late \ˈmak-yə-lət\ *or* **mac·u·lat·ed** \-ˌlāt-əd\ *adj* [L *maculatus,* pp. of *maculare* to stain, fr. *macula*] (15c) **1** : marked with spots : BLOTCHED **2** : IMPURE, BESMIRCHED
mac·u·la·tion \ˌmak-yə-ˈlā-shən\ *n* (15c) **1** *archaic* : the state of being spotted **2 a** : a blemish in the form of a discrete spot ⟨acne scars and ~*s*⟩ **b** : the arrangement of spots and markings on an animal or plant
mac·ule \ˈmak-(ˌ)yü(ə)l\ *n* [F, fr. L *macula*] (1863) : a patch of skin that is altered in color but usu. not elevated and that is a characteristic feature of various diseases (as smallpox)
[1]**mad** \ˈmad\ *adj* **mad·der; mad·dest** [ME *medd, madd,* fr. OE *gemǣd,* pp. of (assumed) *gemǣdan* to madden, fr. *gemād* silly, mad; akin to OHG *gimeit* foolish, crazy, Skt *methati* he hurts] (bef. 12c) **1** : disordered in mind : INSANE **2 a** : completely unrestrained by reason and judgment : SENSELESS **b** : incapable of being explained or accounted for : ILLOGICAL **3 a** : carried away by intense anger : FURIOUS **b** : keenly displeased : ANGRY **4** : carried away by enthusiasm or desire **5** : affected with rabies : RABID **6** : marked by wild gaiety and merriment : HILARIOUS **7** : intensely excited : FRANTIC **8** : marked by intense and often chaotic activity : WILD ⟨a ~ scramble⟩ — **mad·dish** \ˈmad-ish\ *adj* — **like mad** : to a great degree : at a high rate ⟨selling *like mad*⟩
[2]**mad** *vb* **mad·ded; mad·ding** (14c) : MADDEN
[3]**mad** *n* (1834) **1** : a fit or mood of bad temper **2** : ANGER, FURY
Mad·a·gas·car periwinkle \ˌmad-ə-ˈgas-kər-\ *n* [*Madagascar,* Africa] (1821) : [1]PERIWINKLE b
mad·am \ˈmad-əm\ *n, pl* **madams** [ME, fr. MF *ma dame,* lit., my lady] (14c) **1** *pl* **mes·dames** \mā-ˈdäm, -ˈdam\ : LADY — used without a name as a form of respectful or polite address to a woman **2** : MISTRESS 1 — used as a title formerly with the given name but now with the surname or esp. with a designation of rank or office ⟨*Madam* Chairman⟩ ⟨*Madam* President⟩ **3** : the female head of a house of prostitution **4** : the female head of a household : WIFE
ma·dame \mə-ˈdam, ma-ˈ, *before a surname also* ˌmad-əm\ *n* [F, fr. OF *ma dame*] (14c) **1** *pl* **mes·dames** \mā-ˈdäm, -ˈdam\ — used as a title equivalent to *Mrs.* for a married woman not of English-speaking nationality **2** *pl* **madames** : MADAM 3
mad–brained \ˈmad-ˈbrānd\ *adj* (1562) : RASH, HOTHEADED
mad·cap \ˈmad-ˌkap\ *adj* (1588) : marked by impulsiveness, recklessness, or foolishness — **madcap** *n*
mad·den \ˈmad-ᵊn\ *vb* **mad·dened; mad·den·ing** \ˈmad-niŋ, -ᵊn-iŋ\ *vi* (1735) : to become or act as if mad ~ *vt* **1** : to drive mad : CRAZE **2** : to make intensely angry : ENRAGE

mad·den·ing *adj* (1822) **1 :** tending to craze **2 a :** tending to infuriate **b :** tending to vex : IRRITATING — **mad·den·ing·ly** \ˈmad-niŋ-lē, -ᵊn-iŋ-\ *adv*

mad·der \ˈmad-ər\ *n* [ME, fr. OE *mædere;* akin to OHG *matara* madder] (bef. 12c) **1 :** a Eurasian herb (*Rubia tinctorum* of the family Rubiaceae, the madder family) with verticillate leaves and small yellowish panicled flowers succeeded by berries; *broadly* **:** any of several related herbs (genus *Rubia*) **2 a :** the root of the Eurasian madder used formerly in dyeing; *also* **:** an alizarin dye prepared from it **b :** a moderate to strong red

made \ˈmād\ *adj* [ME, fr. pp. of *maken* to make] (14c) **1 a :** artificially produced **b :** FICTITIOUS, INVENTED ⟨a ~ excuse⟩ **c :** put together of various ingredients ⟨a ~ dish⟩ **2 :** assured of success ⟨a ~ man⟩ — usu. used in the phrase *have it made*

Ma·dei·ra \mə-ˈdir-ə, -ˈder-\ *n* [Pg, fr. *Madeira* islands] (1596) **:** an amber-colored fortified wine from Madeira; *also* **:** a similar wine made elsewhere

mad·e·leine \ˈmad-ᵊl-ən, ˌmad-ᵊl-ˈān\ *n* [F, perh. fr. *Madeleine* Paulmier, 19th cent. Fr. pastry cook] (1845) **:** a small rich shell-shaped cake

ma·de·moi·selle \ˌmad-(ə-)m(w)ə-ˈzel, mam-ˈzel\ *n, pl* **ma·de·moi·selles** \-ˈzelz\ *or* **mes·de·moi·selles** \ˌmād-(ə-)m(w)ə-ˈzel\ [F, fr. OF *ma damoisele,* lit., my (young) lady] (15c) **1 :** an unmarried French girl or woman — used as a title equivalent to *Miss* for an unmarried woman not of English-speaking nationality **2 :** a French governess **3 :** SILVER PERCH a

made–to–order \ˌmād-tə-ˈ(w)ȯrd-ər\ *adj* (ca. 1908) **1 :** produced to supply a special or an individual demand **:** CUSTOM-MADE **2 :** being ideally suited (as to a particular purpose) ⟨a ground ball ~ for a double play⟩

made–up \ˈmā-ˈdəp\ *adj* (1725) **1 :** fully manufactured **2 :** fancifully conceived or falsely devised **3 :** marked by the use of makeup

mad·house \ˈmad-ˌhau̇s\ *n* (1687) **1 :** a place where insane persons are detained and treated **2 :** a place of uproar or confusion

Mad·i·son Avenue \ˌmad-ə-sən-\ *n* [*Madison Avenue,* New York City, center of the American advertising business] (1952) **:** the American advertising industry

mad·ly \ˈmad-lē\ *adv* (13c) **1 :** in a mad manner **2 :** to an extreme or excessive degree ⟨~ in love⟩

mad·man \ˈmad-ˌman, -mən\ *n* (14c) **:** a man who is or acts as if insane

mad·ness \ˈmad-nəs\ *n* (14c) **1 :** the quality or state of being mad: as **a :** INSANITY **b :** extreme folly **c :** RAGE **d :** ECSTASY, ENTHUSIASM **2 :** any of several ailments of animals marked by frenzied behavior; *specif* **:** RABIES

Ma·don·na \mə-ˈdän-ə\ *n* [It, fr. OIt *ma donna,* lit., my lady] (1584) **1** *archaic* **:** LADY — used as a form of respectful address **2** *obs* **:** an Italian lady **3 a :** VIRGIN MARY **b :** an artistic depiction (as a painting or statue) of the Virgin Mary

Madonna lily *n* (1877) **:** a white lily (*Lilium candidum*) with bell-shaped to broad funnel-shaped flowers formerly extensively forced for spring blooming

ma·dras \ˈmad-rəs; mə-ˈdras, -ˈdräs\ *n* [*Madras,* India] (1830) **1 :** a large silk or cotton kerchief usu. of bright colors that is often worn as a turban **2 a :** a fine plain-woven shirting and dress fabric usu. of cotton with varied designs (as plaid) in bright colors or in white **b :** a light open usu. cotton fabric with a heavy design used for curtains

mad·re·pore \ˈmad-rə-ˌpō(ə)r, -ˌpȯ(ə)r\ *n* [F *madrépore,* fr. It *madrepora,* fr. *madre* mother (fr. L *mater*) + *poro* pore (fr. L *porus*) — more at MOTHER] (1751) **:** any of various stony reef-building corals (order Madreporaria) of tropical seas that assume a variety of branching, encrusting, or massive forms — **mad·re·po·ri·an** \ˌmad-rə-ˈpōr-ē-ən, -ˈpȯr-\ *adj or n* — **mad·re·por·ic** \-ˈpōr-ik, -ˈpȯr-\ *adj*

mad·re·por·ite \ˈmad-rə-ˌpōr-ˌīt, -ˌpȯr-\ *n* [ISV *madrepore* + ¹*-ite* (segment); fr. the resemblances of the perforations to those of a madrepore] (1877) **:** a perforated or porous body that is situated at the distal end of the stone canal in echinoderms

mad·ri·gal \ˈmad-ri-gəl\ *n* [It *madrigale,* fr. ML *matricale,* fr. neut. of (assumed) *matricalis* simple, fr. LL, of the womb, fr. L *matric-, matrix* womb, fr. *mater* mother] (1588) **1 :** a medieval short lyrical poem in a strict poetic form **2 a :** a complex polyphonic unaccompanied vocal piece on a secular text developed esp. in the 16th and 17th centuries **b :** PART-SONG; *esp* **:** GLEE — **mad·ri·gal·ian** \ˌmad-rə-ˈgal-ē-ən, -ˈgāl-\ *adj* — **mad·ri·gal·ist** \ˈmad-ri-gə-ləst\ *n*

ma·dri·lene \ˌmad-rə-ˈlen, -ˈlān\ *n* [F (*consommé*) *madrilène,* lit., Madrid consommé] (1907) **:** a consommé flavored with tomato

ma·dro·na *or* **ma·dro·ne** *or* **ma·dro·no** \mə-ˈdrō-nə\ *n* [Sp *madroño*] (1841) **:** an evergreen tree or shrub (*Arbutus menziesii*) of the heath family of the Pacific coast of No. America with smooth bark, thick shining leaves, and edible red berries

ma·du·ro \mə-ˈdu̇(ə)r-(ˌ)ō\ *n, pl* **-ros** [Sp, fr. *maduro* ripe, fr. L *maturus* — more at MATURE] (1850) **:** a dark-colored relatively strong cigar

mad·wom·an \ˈmad-ˌwu̇m-ən\ *n* (15c) **:** a woman who is or acts as if insane

mad·wort \-ˌwərt, -ˌwȯ(ə)rt\ *n* (1597) **1 :** ALYSSUM 1 **2 :** a low hairy annual herb (*Asperugo procumbens*) of the borage family with blue flowers and a root used as a substitute for madder

Mae·ce·nas \mi-ˈsē-nəs\ *n* [L, fr. Gaius *Maecenas* †8 B.C. Roman statesman & patron of literature] (1542) **:** a generous patron esp. of literature or art

mael·strom \ˈmā(ə)l-strəm, -ˌsträm\ *n* [obs. D (now *maalstroom*), fr. *malen* to grind + *strom* stream; akin to OHG *malan* to grind and to OHG *stroum* stream — more at MEAL, STREAM] (1682) **1 :** a powerful often violent whirlpool sucking in objects within a given radius **2 :** something resembling a maelstrom in turbulence

mae·nad \ˈmē-ˌnad\ *n* [L *maenad-, maenas,* fr. Gk *mainad-, mainas,* fr. *mainesthai* to be mad; akin to Gk *menos* spirit — more at MIND] (1579) **1 :** a woman participant in orgiastic Dionysian rites **:** BACCHANTE **2 :** an unnaturally excited or distraught woman — **mae·nad·ic** \mē-ˈnad-ik\ *adj*

mae·sto·so \mī-ˈstō-(ˌ)sō, -(ˌ)zō\ *adj or adv* [It, fr. L *majestosus,* fr. *majestas* majesty] (1724) **:** majestic and stately — used as a direction in music

mae·stro \ˈmī-(ˌ)strō\ *n, pl* **maestros** *or* **mae·stri** \-ˌstrē\ [It, lit., master, fr. L *magister* — more at MASTER] (1724) **:** a master in an art; *esp* **:** an eminent composer, conductor, or teacher of music

Mae West \ˈmā-ˈwest\ *n* [*Mae West* †1980 Am. actress noted for her full figure] (1940) **:** an inflatable life jacket in the form of a collar extending down the chest that was worn by fliers in World War II

maf·fick \ˈmaf-ik\ *vi* [back-formation fr. *Mafeking night,* English celebration of the lifting of the siege of Mafeking, So. Africa, May 17, 1900] (1900) **:** to celebrate with boisterous rejoicing and hilarious behavior

Ma·fia \ˈmäf-ē-ə, ˈmaf-\ *n* [*Mafia, Maffia,* a Sicilian secret criminal society, fr. It] (1875) **1 :** a secret society of political terrorists **2 :** a secret organization composed chiefly of criminal elements and usu. held to control racketeering, peddling of narcotics, gambling, and other illicit activities throughout the world **3** *often not cap* **:** a group of people of similar interests or backgrounds prominent in a particular field or enterprise **:** CLIQUE

maf·ic \ˈmaf-ik\ *adj* [NL *ma*gnesium + L *ferrum* iron + E *-ic*] (1912) **:** of, relating to, or being a group of usu. dark-colored minerals rich in magnesium and iron

ma·fi·o·so \ˌmäf-ē-ˈō-(ˌ)sō, ˌmaf-, -(ˌ)zō\ *n, pl* **-si** \-(ˌ)sē, -(ˌ)zē\ [It, fr. *Mafia*] (1875) **:** a member of the Mafia or a mafia

mag \ˈmag\ *n* (1796) **:** MAGAZINE

mag·a·zine \ˈmag-ə-ˌzēn, ˌmag-ə-ˈ\ *n* [MF, fr. OProv, fr. Ar *makhāzin,* pl. of *makhzan* storehouse] (1583) **1 :** a place where goods or supplies are stored **:** WAREHOUSE **2 :** a room in which powder and other explosives are kept in a fort or a ship **3 :** the contents of a magazine: as **a :** an accumulation of munitions of war **b :** a stock of provisions or goods **4 a :** a periodical containing miscellaneous pieces (as articles, stories, poems) often illustrated **b :** a similar section of a newspaper usu. appearing on Sunday **c :** a radio or television program presenting usu. several short segments on a variety of topics **5 :** a supply chamber: as **a :** a holder in or on a gun for cartridges to be fed into the gun chamber **b :** a lightproof chamber for films or plates on a camera or for film on a motion-picture projector

mag·a·zin·ist \-ˌzē-nəst, -ˈzē-\ *n* (1823) **:** one who writes for or edits a magazine

mag·da·len \ˈmag-də-lən\ *or* **mag·da·lene** \-ˌlēn\ *n, often cap* [Mary *Magdalen* or *Magdalene* woman healed by Jesus of evil spirits in Lk 8:2, considered identical with a reformed prostitute in Lk 7:36–50] (1697) **1 :** a reformed prostitute **2 :** a house of refuge or reformatory for prostitutes

Mag·da·le·ni·an \ˌmag-də-ˈlē-nē-ən\ *adj* [F *magdalénien,* fr. *La Madeleine,* rock shelter in southwest France] (1885) **:** of or relating to an Upper Paleolithic culture characterized by flint, bone, and ivory implements, carving, and paintings

mage \ˈmāj\ *n* [ME, fr. L *magus*] (14c) **:** MAGUS

Mag·el·lan·ic Cloud \ˌmaj-ə-ˌlan-ik-, *chiefly Brit* ˌmag-\ *n* [Ferdinand *Magellan*] (1685) **:** either of the two nearest galaxies to the Milky Way system located within 25 degrees of the south celestial pole and appearing as conspicuous patches of light

Ma·gen Da·vid \ˌmȯ-gən-ˈdȯ-vəd\ *n* [Heb *māghēn Dāwīdh,* lit., shield of David] (1904) **:** a hexagram used as a symbol of Judaism

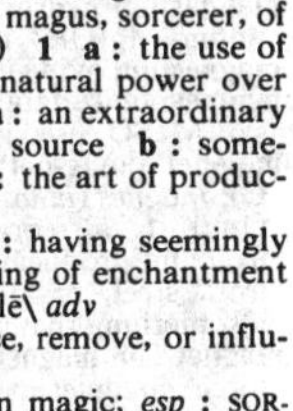
Magen David

ma·gen·ta \mə-ˈjent-ə\ *n* [*Magenta,* Italy] (1860) **1 :** FUCHSINE **2 :** a deep purplish red

mag·got \ˈmag-ət\ *n* [ME *mathek, magotte,* of Scand origin; akin to ON *mathkr* maggot; akin to OE *matha* maggot] (13c) **1 :** a soft-bodied legless grub that is the larva of a dipterous insect (as the housefly) **2 :** a fantastic or eccentric idea **:** WHIM — **mag·goty** \-ē\ *adj*

magi *pl of* MAGUS

¹**Ma·gi·an** \ˈmā-jē-ən\ *n* (1578) **:** MAGUS

²**Ma·gi·an** \-jē-ən, -jī-\ *adj* (1716) **:** of or relating to the Magi — **Ma·gi·an·ism** \-ə-ˌniz-əm\ *n*

¹**mag·ic** \ˈmaj-ik\ *n* [ME *magik,* fr. MF *magique,* fr. L *magice,* fr. Gk *magikē,* fem. of *magikos* Magian, magical, fr. *magos* magus, sorcerer, of Iranian origin; akin to OPer *magush* sorcerer] (14c) **1 a :** the use of means (as charms or spells) believed to have supernatural power over natural forces **b :** magic rites or incantations **2 a :** an extraordinary power or influence seemingly from a supernatural source **b :** something that seems to cast a spell **:** ENCHANTMENT **3 :** the art of producing illusions by sleight of hand

²**magic** *adj* (14c) **1 :** of or relating to magic **2 a :** having seemingly supernatural qualities or powers **b :** giving a feeling of enchantment — **mag·i·cal** \ˈmaj-i-kəl\ *adj* — **mag·i·cal·ly** \-i-k(ə-)lē\ *adv*

³**magic** *vt* **mag·icked; mag·ick·ing** (1906) **:** to produce, remove, or influence by magic

ma·gi·cian \mə-ˈjish-ən\ *n* (14c) **1 :** one skilled in magic; *esp* **:** SORCERER **2 :** one who performs tricks of illusion and sleight of hand

magic lantern *n* (1696) **:** an early form of optical projector of still pictures using a transparent slide

magic realism *n* [trans. of G *magischer realismus*] (ca. 1927) **:** painting in a meticulously realistic style of imaginary or fantastic scenes or images — **magic realist** *n*

magic square *n* (ca. 1704) **:** a square containing a number of integers arranged so that the sum of the numbers in each row, column, and diagonal is the same

Ma·gi·not Line \ˌmazh-ə-ˌnō-, ˌmaj-\ *n* [André *Maginot* †1932 Fr. minister of war] (1936) **:** a line of defensive fortifications built before World War II to protect the eastern border of France but easily outflanked by German invaders

mag·is·te·ri·al \ˌmaj-ə-ˈstir-ē-əl\ *adj* [LL *magisterialis* of authority, fr. *magisterium* office of a master, fr. *magister*] (1632) **1 a (1) :** of, relating to, or having the characteristics of a master or teacher **:** AUTHORITATIVE **(2) :** marked by an overbearingly dignified or assured manner or aspect ⟨a tone of ~ condescension⟩ **b :** of, relating to, or required for a master's degree **2 :** of or relating to a magistrate, his

office, or his duties *syn* see DICTATORIAL — **mag·is·te·ri·al·ly** \-ē-ə-lē\ *adv*

mag·is·te·ri·um \ˌmaj-ə-'stir-ē-əm\ *n* [L] (1866) : teaching authority esp. of the Roman Catholic Church

mag·is·tra·cy \'maj-ə-strə-sē\ *n, pl* **-cies** (1585) **1** : the state of being a magistrate **2** : the office, power, or dignity of a magistrate **3** : a body of magistrates **4** : the district under a magistrate

ma·gis·tral \'maj-ə-strəl, mə-'jis-trəl\ *adj* [LL *magistralis,* fr. L *magistr-, magister*] (1605) : MAGISTERIAL 1a — **ma·gis·tral·ly** \-ē\ *adv*

mag·is·trate \'maj-ə-ˌstrāt, -strət\ *n* [ME *magistrat,* fr. L *magistratus* magistracy, magistrate, fr. *magistr-, magister* master, political superior — more at MASTER] (14c) : an official entrusted with administration of the laws: as **a** : a principal official exercising governmental powers over a major political unit (as a nation) **b** : a local official exercising administrative and often judicial functions **c** : a local judiciary official having limited original jurisdiction esp. in criminal cases — **mag·is·trat·i·cal** \ˌmaj-ə-'strat-i-kəl\ *adj* — **mag·is·trat·i·cal·ly** \-k(ə-)lē\ *adv*

magistrate's court *n* (1867) **1** : POLICE COURT **2** : a court that has minor civil and criminal jurisdiction

mag·is·tra·ture \'maj-ə-ˌstrā-chər, -strə-ˌchu̇(ə)r\ *n* (1672) : MAGISTRACY

mag·ma \'mag-mə\ *n* [L *magmat-, magma,* fr. Gk, thick unguent, fr. *massein* to knead — more at MINGLE] (15c) **1** *archaic* : DREGS, SEDIMENT **2** : a thin pasty suspension (as of a precipitate in water) **3** : molten rock material within the earth from which an igneous rock results by cooling — **mag·mat·ic** \mag-'mat-ik\ *adj*

Mag·na Car·ta *or* **Mag·na Char·ta** \ˌmag-nə-'kärt-ə\ *n* [ML, lit., great charter] (15c) **1** : a charter of liberties to which the English barons forced King John to give his assent in June 1215 at Runnymede **2** : a document constituting a fundamental guarantee of rights and privileges

mag·na cum lau·de \ˌmäg-nə-(ˌ)ku̇m-'lau̇d-ə, -'lau̇d-ē; ˌmag-nə-ˌkəm-'lȯd-ē\ *adv or adj* [L] (1900) : with great distinction ⟨graduated *magna cum laude*⟩ — compare CUM LAUDE, SUMMA CUM LAUDE

mag·na·nim·i·ty \ˌmag-nə-'nim-ət-ē\ *n, pl* **-ties** (14c) **1** : the quality of being magnanimous : loftiness of spirit enabling one to bear trouble calmly, to disdain meanness and revenge, and to make sacrifices for worthy ends **2** : a magnanimous act

mag·nan·i·mous \mag-'nan-ə-məs\ *adj* [L *magnanimus,* fr. *magnus* great + *animus* spirit — more at MUCH, ANIMATE] (1584) **1** : showing or suggesting a lofty and courageous spirit ⟨the irreproachable lives and ~ sufferings of their followers —Joseph Addison⟩ **2** : showing or suggesting nobility of feeling and generosity of mind ⟨too sincere for dissimulation, too ~ for resentment —Ellen Glasgow⟩ — **mag·nan·i·mous·ly** *adv* — **mag·nan·i·mous·ness** *n*

mag·nate \'mag-ˌnāt, -nət\ *n* [ME *magnates,* pl., fr. LL, fr. L *magnus*] (15c) : a person of rank, power, influence, or distinction often in a specified area

mag·ne·sia \mag-'nē-shə, -'nē-zhə\ *n* [NL, fr. *magnes carneus,* a white earth, lit., flesh magnet] (1755) **1** : a white highly infusible oxide of magnesium MgO used esp. in refractories, in cements, insulation, fertilizers, and rubber, and in medicine as an antacid and mild laxative **2** : MAGNESIUM — **mag·ne·sian** \-shən, -zhən\ *adj*

mag·ne·site \'mag-nə-ˌsīt\ *n* (1815) : native magnesium carbonate used esp. in making refractories and magnesia

mag·ne·sium \mag-'nē-zē-əm, -zhəm\ *n* [NL, fr. *magnesia*] (1812) : a silver-white light malleable ductile metallic element that occurs abundantly in nature and is used in metallurgical and chemical processes, in photography, in signaling, and in the manufacture of pyrotechnics because of the intense white light it produces on burning, and in construction esp. in the form of light alloys — see ELEMENT table

magnesium carbonate *n* (ca. 1903) : a carbonate of magnesium; *esp* : a white crystalline salt $MgCO_3$ that occurs naturally as dolomite and magnesite

magnesium chloride *n* (1910) : a bitter deliquescent salt $MgCl_2$ used esp. as a source of magnesium metal

magnesium hydroxide *n* (ca. 1909) : a slightly alkaline crystalline compound $Mg(OH)_2$ used esp. as a laxative and gastric antacid

magnesium oxide *n* (ca. 1909) : MAGNESIA 1

magnesium sulfate *n* (ca. 1890) : a sulfate of magnesium: as **a** : a white salt $MgSO_4$ used in medicine and in industry **b** : EPSOM SALTS

mag·net \'mag-nət\ *n* [ME *magnete,* fr. MF, fr. L *magnet-, magnes,* fr. Gk *magnēs* (*lithos*), lit., stone of Magnesia, ancient city in Asia Minor] (14c) **1 a** : LODESTONE **b** : a body having the property of attracting iron and producing a magnetic field external to itself; *specif* : a mass of iron, steel, or alloy that has this property artificially imparted **2** : something that attracts

magnet- *or* **magneto-** *comb form* [L *magnet-, magnes*] **1** : magnetic force ⟨*magneto*meter⟩ **2** : magnetism : magnetic ⟨*magneto*electric⟩ ⟨*magneton*⟩ **3** : magnetoelectric ⟨*magneto*generator⟩

[1]**mag·net·ic** \mag-'net-ik\ *adj* (1632) **1** : possessing an extraordinary power or ability to attract ⟨a ~ personality⟩ **2 a** : of or relating to a magnet or to magnetism **b** : of, relating to, or characterized by the earth's magnetism **c** : magnetized or capable of being magnetized **d** : actuated by magnetic attraction — **mag·net·i·cal·ly** \-i-k(ə-)lē\ *adv*

[2]**magnetic** *n* (1654) : a magnetic substance

magnetic bubble *n* (1969) : a tiny movable magnetized cylindrical volume in a thin amorphous or crystalline magnetic material that along with other like volumes can be used to represent a bit of information (as in a computer)

magnetic disk *n* (ca. 1960) : DISK 4c

magnetic equator *n* (1832) : ACLINIC LINE

magnetic field *n* (1845) : the portion of space near a magnetic body or a current-carrying body in which the forces due to the body or current can be detected

magnetic flux *n* (1896) : lines of force used to represent magnetic induction

magnetic head *n* (1947) : an electromagnet used in magnetic recording for converting electrical signals into a magnetic record (as on tape), converting a magnetic recording into electrical signals, or erasing a magnetic recording

magnetic moment *n* (1865) : a vector quantity that is a measure of the torque exerted on a magnetic system (as a bar magnet or dipole) when placed in a magnetic field : the product of the distance between the poles of a magnet and the strength of either pole

magnetic needle *n* (ca. 1846) : a slender bar of magnetized steel that when suspended so as to be free to turn indicates the direction of a magnetic field in which it is placed and that constitutes the essential part of a compass

magnetic north *n* (1812) : the northerly direction in the earth's magnetic field indicated by the north-seeking pole of the horizontal magnetic needle

magnetic pole *n* (1701) **1** : either of two small nonstationary regions which are located respectively in the polar areas of the northern and southern hemispheres and toward which the compass needle points from any direction throughout adjacent regions; *also* : either of two comparable regions on a celestial body **2** : either of the poles of a magnet

magnetic quantum number *n* (1923) : an integer that expresses the component of the quantized angular momentum of an electron, atom, or molecule in the direction of an externally applied magnetic field

magnetic recording *n* (1945) : the process of recording sound, data (as for a computer), or a television program by producing varying local magnetization of a moving tape, wire, or disc — **magnetic recorder** *n*

magnetic resonance *n* (1903) : the response of electrons, atoms, molecules, or nuclei to various discrete radiation frequencies as a result of space quantization in a magnetic field

magnetic storm *n* (1860) : a marked temporary disturbance of the earth's magnetic field held to be related to sunspots

magnetic tape *n* (1937) : a thin ribbon (as of plastic) coated with a magnetic material on which information (as sound or television images) may be stored

magnetic wire *n* (1945) : a thin wire used in magnetic recording

magnetise *Brit var of* MAGNETIZE

mag·ne·tism \'mag-nə-ˌtiz-əm\ *n* (1616) **1 a** : a class of physical phenomena that include the attraction for iron observed in lodestone and a magnet, are believed to be inseparably associated with moving electricity, are exhibited by both magnets and electric currents, and are characterized by fields of force **b** : a science that deals with magnetic phenomena **2** : an ability to attract or charm ⟨the large audience attests to the performer's ~⟩

mag·ne·tite \'mag-nə-ˌtīt\ *n* (1851) : a black isometric mineral (Fe_3O_4) of the spinel group that is an oxide of iron and an important iron ore — **mag·ne·tit·ic** \ˌmag-nə-'tit-ik\ *adj*

mag·ne·ti·za·tion \ˌmag-nət-ə-'zā-shən\ *n* (1801) : a magnetizing or state of being magnetized; *also* : degree to which a body is magnetized

mag·ne·tize \'mag-nə-ˌtīz\ *vt* **-tized; -tiz·ing** (1801) **1** : to induce magnetic properties in **2** : to attract like a magnet : CHARM — **mag·ne·tiz·able** \-ˌtī-zə-bəl\ *adj* — **mag·ne·tiz·er** *n*

mag·ne·to \mag-'nēt-(ˌ)ō\ *n, pl* **-tos** (1882) : a magnetoelectric machine; *esp* : an alternator with permanent magnets used to generate current for the ignition in an internal-combustion engine

mag·ne·to·elec·tric \-ˌnēt-ō-ə-'lek-trik\ *adj* (1831) : relating to or characterized by electromotive forces developed by magnetic means ⟨~ induction⟩

mag·ne·to·flu·id·dy·nam·ic \mag-'nēt-ō-ˌflü-əd-dī-'nam-ik, -'net-, -də-\ *adj* (1965) : MAGNETOHYDRODYNAMIC — **mag·ne·to·flu·id·dy·nam·ics** \-iks\ *n pl but sing or pl in constr*

mag·ne·to·gas·dy·nam·ic \-ˌgas-dī-'nam-ik, -də-\ *adj* (1964) : MAGNETOHYDRODYNAMIC — **mag·ne·to·gas·dy·nam·ics** \-iks\ *n pl but sing or pl in constr*

mag·ne·to·graph \-ˌgraf\ *n* (1847) : an automatic instrument for recording measurements of a magnetic field (as of the earth or the sun)

mag·ne·to·hy·dro·dy·nam·ic \mag-'nēt-ō-ˌhī-drə-dī-'nam-ik, -'net-, -də-\ *adj* (1943) : of or relating to phenomena arising from the motion of electrically conducting fluids in the presence of electric and magnetic fields — **mag·ne·to·hy·dro·dy·nam·ics** \-iks\ *n pl but sing or pl in constr*

mag·ne·tom·e·ter \ˌmag-nə-'täm-ət-ər\ *n* (1827) : an instrument used to detect the presence of a metallic object or to measure the intensity of a magnetic field — **mag·ne·to·met·ric** \mag-ˌnēt-ə-'me-trik, -ˌnet-\ *adj* — **mag·ne·tom·e·try** \ˌmag-nə-'täm-ə-trē\ *n*

mag·ne·to·mo·tive force \mag-ˌnēt-ə-ˌmōt-iv-, -ˌnet-\ *n* (1883) : a force that is the cause of a flux of magnetic induction

mag·ne·ton \'mag-nə-ˌtän\ *n* [ISV *magnet-* + [2]*-on*] (1911) : a unit of the quantized magnetic moment of a particle (as an atom)

mag·ne·to–op·tic \mag-ˌnēt-ō-'äp-tik, -ˌnet-\ *also* **mag·ne·to–op·ti·cal** \-ti-kəl\ *adj* (1881) : of or relating to the influence of a magnetic field upon light — **mag·ne·to–op·tics** \-tiks\ *n pl but sing or pl in constr*

mag·ne·to·pause \mag-'nēt-ə-ˌpȯz, -'net-\ *n* [*magneto*sphere + L *pausa* stop — more at PAUSE] (1962) : the outer boundary of a magnetosphere

mag·ne·to·plas·ma·dy·nam·ic \mag-'nēt-ō-ˌplaz-mə-dī-'nam-ik, -'net-, -də-\ *adj* [*magnet-* + *plasma* + *dynamic*] (1962) : MAGNETOHYDRODYNAMIC — **mag·ne·to·plas·ma·dy·nam·ics** \-iks\ *n pl but sing or pl in constr*

mag·ne·to·re·sis·tance \-ˌnēt-ō-ri-'zis-tən(t)s, -ˌnet-\ *n* (1927) : a change in electrical resistance due to the presence of a magnetic field

mag·ne·to·sphere \mag-'nēt-ə-ˌsfi(ə)r, -'net-\ *n* (1959) : a region of space surrounding a celestial object (as the earth or a star) that is dominated by the object's magnetic field so that charged particles are trapped in it — **mag·ne·to·spher·ic** \-ˌnēt-ə-'sfi(ə)r-ik, -'sfer-\ *adj*

mag·ne·to·stat·ic \mag-ˌnēt-ō-'stat-ik, -ˌnet-\ *adj* (1893) : of, relating to, or being a stationary magnetic field

mag·ne·to·stric·tion \-'strik-shən\ *n* [ISV *magnet-* + *-striction* (as in *constriction*)] (1896) : the change in the dimensions of a ferromagnetic body caused by a change in its state of magnetization — **mag·ne·to·stric·tive** \-'strik-tiv\ *adj* — **mag·ne·to·stric·tive·ly** *adv*

mag·ne·tron \'mag-nə-ˌträn\ *n* [blend of *magnet* and *-tron*] (1924) : a diode vacuum tube in which the flow of electrons is controlled by an externally applied magnetic field to generate power at microwave frequencies

magnet school *n* (ca. 1968) : a school with superior facilities and staff designed to attract pupils from all elements of the community

mag·nif·ic \mag-'nif-ik\ *adj* [MF *magnifique,* fr. L *magnificus*] (15c) **1** : MAGNIFICENT 2 **2** : imposing in size or dignity **3 a** : SUBLIME, EXALTED **b** : characterized by grandiloquence : POMPOUS ⟨commenced the conversation in the most ~ style —S.T. Coleridge⟩ — **mag·nif·i·cal** \-i-kəl\ *adj* — **mag·nif·i·cal·ly** \-k(ə-)lē\ *adv*

mag·nif·i·cat \mag-'nif-i-ˌkat, -ˌkät; män-'yif-i-ˌkät\ *n* [ME, fr. L, magnificat, fr. *magnificare* to magnify; fr. the first word of the canticle] (13c) **1** *cap* **a :** the canticle of the Virgin Mary in Luke 1:46–55 **b :** a musical setting for the Magnificat **2 :** an utterance of praise

mag·ni·fi·ca·tion \ˌmag-nə-fə-'kā-shən\ *n* (15c) **1 :** the act of magnifying **2 a :** the state of being magnified **b :** the apparent enlargement of an object by an optical instrument — called also *power*

mag·nif·i·cence \mag-'nif-ə-sən(t)s, məg-\ *n* [ME, fr. MF, fr. L *magnificentia*, fr. *magnificus* noble in character, magnificent, fr. *magnus* great — more at MUCH] (14c) **1 :** the quality or state of being magnificent **2 :** splendor of surroundings

mag·nif·i·cent \-sənt\ *adj* (15c) **1 :** great in deed or exalted in place — used only of former famous rulers ⟨Lorenzo the *Magnificent*⟩ **2 :** marked by stately grandeur and lavishness ⟨a ~ way of life⟩ **3 :** sumptuous in structure and adornment ⟨a ~ cathedral⟩; *broadly* **:** strikingly beautiful or impressive ⟨a ~ physique⟩ **4 :** impressive to the mind or spirit **:** SUBLIME ⟨~ prose⟩ **5 :** exceptionally fine ⟨a ~ day⟩ ***syn*** see GRAND — **mag·nif·i·cent·ly** *adv*

mag·nif·i·co \mag-'nif-i-ˌkō\ *n, pl* **-coes** *or* **-cos** [It, fr. *magnifico*, adj., magnificent, fr. L *magnificus*] (1573) **1 :** a nobleman of Venice **2 :** a person of high position

mag·ni·fi·er \'mag-nə-ˌfī(-ə)r\ *n* (1550) **:** one that magnifies; *esp* **:** a lens or combination of lenses that makes something appear larger

mag·ni·fy \'mag-nə-ˌfī\ *vb* **-fied; -fy·ing** [ME *magnifien*, fr. MF *magnifier*, fr. L *magnificare*, fr. *magnificus*] *vt* (14c) **1 a :** EXTOL, LAUD **b :** to cause to be held in greater esteem or respect **2 a :** to increase in significance **:** INTENSIFY **b :** EXAGGERATE **3 :** to enlarge in fact or in appearance ~ *vi* **:** to have the power of causing objects to appear larger than they are

mag·nil·o·quence \mag-'nil-ə-kwən(t)s\ *n* [L *magniloquentia*, fr. *magniloquus* magniloquent, fr. *magnus* + *loqui* to speak] (1623) **:** the quality or state of being magniloquent

mag·nil·o·quent \-kwənt\ *adj* [back-formation fr. *magniloquence*] (1656) **:** speaking in or characterized by a high-flown often bombastic style or manner — **mag·nil·o·quent·ly** *adv*

mag·ni·tude \'mag-nə-ˌt(y)üd\ *n* [ME, fr. L *magnitudo*, fr. *magnus*] (15c) **1 a :** great size or extent **b (1) :** spatial quality **:** SIZE **(2) :** QUANTITY, NUMBER **2 :** the importance, quality, or caliber of something **3 :** a number representing the intrinsic or apparent brightness of a celestial body on a logarithmic scale in which an increase of one unit corresponds to a reduction in the brightness of light by a factor of 2.512 **4 :** a numerical quantitative measure expressed usu. as a multiple of a standard unit

mag·no·lia \mag-'nōl-yə\ *n* [NL, fr. Pierre *Magnol* †1715 Fr. botanist] (1748) **:** any of a genus (*Magnolia* of the family Magnoliaceae, the magnolia family) of No. American and Asian shrubs and trees with entire evergreen or deciduous leaves and usu. showy white, yellow, rose, or purple flowers appearing in early spring

mag·num \'mag-nəm\ *n* [L, neut. of *magnus* great] (1788) **:** a large wine bottle holding about 1.5 liters

mag·num opus \ˌmag-nə-'mō-pəs\ *n* [L] (1791) **:** a great work; *esp* **:** the greatest achievement of an artist or writer

1mag·pie \'mag-ˌpī\ *n* [*Mag* (nickname for *Margaret*) + *pie*] (1605) **1 :** any of numerous birds (esp. of the genus *Pica*) related to the jays but having a long graduated tail and black-and-white plumage **2 :** a person who chatters noisily

2magpie *adj* (1808) **1 :** collected indiscriminately **:** MISCELLANEOUS ⟨~ compilations of unrelated tidbits —Helen R. Cross⟩ **2 :** given to indiscriminate collecting **:** ACQUISITIVE ⟨what possible ~ instinct had impelled me to retain them —S. J. Perelman⟩

magpie

ma·guey \mə-'gā\ *n* [Sp, fr. Taino] (1555) **1 :** any of various fleshy-leaved agaves; *also* **:** a plant (genus *Furcraea*) related to the agaves **2 :** any of several hard fibers derived from magueys; *esp* **:** CANTALA

ma·gus \'mā-gəs\ *n, pl* **ma·gi** \'mā-ˌjī\ [L, fr. Gk *magos* — more at MAGIC] (1621) **1 a :** a member of a hereditary priestly class among the ancient Medes and Persians **b** *often cap* **:** one of the traditionally three wise men from the East paying homage to the infant Jesus **2 :** MAGICIAN, SORCERER

Mag·yar \'mag-ˌyär, 'mäg-; 'mäj-ˌär\ *n* [Hung] (1797) **1 :** a member of the dominant people of Hungary **2 :** the Finno-Ugric language of the Magyars — **Magyar** *adj*

ma·ha·ra·ja *or* **ma·ha·ra·jah** \ˌmä-hə-'räj-ə, -'räzh-ə\ *n* [Skt *mahārāja*, fr. *mahat* great + *rājan* raja; akin to L *rex* king — more at MUCH, ROYAL] (1698) **:** a Hindu prince ranking above a raja

ma·ha·ra·ni *or* **ma·ha·ra·nee** \-'rän-ē\ *n* [Hindi *mahārānī*, fr. *mahā* great (fr. Skt *mahat*) + *rānī* rani] (1855) **1 :** the wife of a maharaja **2 :** a Hindu princess ranking above a rani

ma·ha·ri·shi \ˌmä-hə-'rē-shē, mə-'här-ə-shē\ *n* [Skt *maharṣi*, fr. *mahat* + *ṛṣi* sage and poet] (1785) **:** a Hindu teacher of mystical knowledge

ma·hat·ma \mə-'hät-mə, -'hat-\ *n* [Skt *mahātman*, fr. *mahātman* great-souled, fr. *mahat* + *ātman* soul — more at ATMAN] (1923) **1 :** a person to be revered for high-mindedness, wisdom, and selflessness **2 :** a person of great prestige in a field of endeavor

Ma·ha·ya·na \ˌmä-hə-'yän-ə\ *n* [Skt *mahāyāna*, lit., great vehicle] (1855) **:** a liberal and theistic branch of Buddhism comprising sects chiefly in China and Japan, recognizing a large body of scripture in addition to the Pali canon, and teaching social concern and universal salvation — compare THERAVADA — **Ma·ha·ya·nist** \-'yän-əst\ *n* — **Ma·ha·ya·nis·tic** \-yä-'nis-tik\ *adj*

Mah·di \'mäd-ē\ *n* [Ar *mahdīy*, lit., one rightly guided] (1800) **1 :** the expected messiah of Muslim tradition **2 :** a Muslim leader who assumes a messianic role — **Mah·dism** \'mäd-ˌiz-əm\ *n* — **Mah·dist** \'mäd-əst\ *n*

Ma·hi·can \mə-'hē-kən\ *n, pl* **Mahican** *or* **Mahicans** [Mahican] (1614) **1 :** a member of an American Indian people of the upper Hudson river valley **2 :** the language of the Mahican people

ma·hi·ma·hi \ˌmä-hē-'mä-(ˌ)hē\ *n* [Hawaiian, Tahitian, & Marquesan] (ca. 1943) **:** the flesh of the dolphin (genus *Coryphaena*) used for food esp. in Hawaii

mah–jongg \(ˈ)mäzh-'äŋ, (ˈ)mäj-, -'ȯŋ, 'mäzh-ˌ, 'mäj-ˌ\ *n* [fr. *Mah-Jongg*, a trademark] (1920) **:** a game of Chinese origin usu. played by four persons with 144 tiles that are drawn and discarded until one player secures a winning hand

mahl·stick \'mȯl-\ *var of* MAULSTICK

ma·hoe \mə-'hō, 'mä-ˌ\ *n* [F *maho*, fr. Taino] (1666) **:** any of various tropical trees with strong bast fibers; *esp* **:** MAJAGUA

ma·hog·a·ny \mə-'häg-ə-nē\ *n, pl* **-nies** [origin unknown] (1671) **1 :** the wood of any of various chiefly tropical trees (family Meliaceae, the mahogany family): **a (1) :** the durable yellowish brown to reddish brown usu. moderately hard and heavy wood of a West Indian tree (*Swietenia mahagoni*) that is widely used for cabinetwork and fine finish work **(2) :** a wood similar to mahogany from a congeneric tree **b (1) :** the rather hard heavy usu. odorless wood of any of several African trees (genus *Khaya*) **(2) :** the rather lightweight cedar-scented wood of any of several African trees (genus *Entandrophragma*) that varies in color from pinkish to deep reddish brown **2 :** any of various woods resembling or substituted for mahogany obtained from trees of the mahogany family **3 :** a tree that yields mahogany **4 :** a moderate reddish brown

ma·ho·nia \mə-'hō-nē-ə\ *n* [NL, fr. Bernard Mc*Mahon* †1816 Am. botanist] (1829) **:** any of a genus (*Mahonia*) of No. American and Asian shrubs (as the Oregon grape) of the barberry family

ma·hout \mə-'hau̇t\ *n* [Hindi *mahāwat, mahāut*] (1662) **:** a keeper and driver of an elephant

Mah·rat·ta *var of* MARATHA

maid \'mād\ *n* [ME *maide*, short for *maiden*] (13c) **1 :** an unmarried girl or woman esp. when young **:** VIRGIN **2 :** a female servant

1maid·en \'mād-ᵊn\ *n* [ME, fr. OE *mægden, mǣden*, dim. of *mægeth*; akin to OHG *magad* maiden, OIr *mug* serf, *macc* son] (bef. 12c) **1 :** an unmarried girl or woman **:** MAID **2 :** a former Scottish beheading device resembling the guillotine **3 :** a horse that has never won a race

2maiden *adj* (14c) **1 a (1) :** not married ⟨~ aunt⟩ **(2) :** VIRGIN **b** *of a female animal* **(1) :** never yet mated **(2) :** never having borne young **2 :** of, relating to, or befitting a maiden **3 :** FIRST, EARLIEST ⟨~ voyage⟩ ⟨~ flight of a spacecraft⟩

maid·en·hair \-ˌha(ə)r, -ˌhe(ə)r\ *n* (14c) **:** any of a genus (*Adiantum*) of ferns with delicate palmately branched fronds — called also *maidenhair fern*

maidenhair tree *n* (1773) **:** GINKGO

maid·en·head \'mād-ᵊn-ˌhed\ *n* [ME *maidenhed*, fr. *maiden* + *-hed* -hood; akin to ME *-hod* -hood] (13c) **1 :** the quality or state of being a maiden **:** VIRGINITY **2 :** HYMEN

maid·en·hood \-ˌhu̇d\ *n* (bef. 12c) **:** the quality, state, or time of being a maiden

maid·en·li·ness \-lē-nəs\ *n* (1555) **:** conduct or traits befitting a maiden

maid·en·ly \-lē\ *adj* (15c) **:** of, resembling, or suitable to a maiden

maiden name *n* (1689) **:** the surname of a woman before she married

maid·hood \'mād-ˌhu̇d\ *n* (bef. 12c) **:** MAIDENHOOD

maid–in–wait·ing \ˌmād-ᵊn-'wāt-iŋ\ *n, pl* **maids–in–wait·ing** \ˌmād-zən-\ (1953) **:** a young woman of a queen's or princess's household appointed to attend her

Maid Mar·i·an \-'mer-ē-ən, -'mar-\ *n* **:** a companion of Robin Hood in some forms of his legend

maid of honor (1586) **1 :** an unmarried lady usu. of noble birth whose duty it is to attend a queen or a princess **2 :** a bride's principal unmarried wedding attendant

maid·ser·vant \'mād-ˌsər-vənt\ *n* (14c) **:** a female servant

ma·ieu·tic \mā-'yüt-ik, mī-\ *adj* [Gk *maieutikos* of midwifery] (1655) **:** relating to or resembling the Socratic method of eliciting new ideas from another

1mail \'mā(ə)l\ *n* [ME *male, maille*, fr. OE *māl* agreement, pay, fr. ON *māl* speech, agreement; akin to OE *mǣl* speech, *mōt* meeting — more at MEET] *chiefly Scot* (bef. 12c) **:** PAYMENT, RENT

2mail *n, often attrib* [ME *male*, fr. OF, of Gmc origin; akin to OHG *malaha* bag] (13c) **1** *chiefly Scot* **:** BAG, WALLET **2 a :** the bags of letters and the other postal matter conveyed under public authority from one post office to another **b :** the postal matter consigned at one time to or from one person or one post office or conveyed by a particular train, airplane, or ship **c :** a conveyance that transports mail **3 a :** a nation's postal system — often used in pl. **b :** postal matter

3mail *vt* (1827) **:** to send by mail **:** POST — **mail·abil·i·ty** \ˌmā-lə-'bil-ət-ē\ *n* — **mail·able** \'mā-lə-bəl\ *adj*

4mail *n* [ME *maille*, fr. MF, fr. L *macula* spot, mesh] (14c) **1 :** armor made of metal links or sometimes plates **2 :** a hard enclosing covering of an animal (as a tortoise) — **mailed** \'mā(ə)ld\ *adj*

5mail *vt* (1795) **:** to arm with mail

mail·bag \'mā(ə)l-ˌbag\ *n* (1812) **1 :** a letter carrier's shoulder bag **2 :** a pouch used in the shipment of mail

mail·box \-ˌbäks\ *n* (1872) **1 :** a public box for deposit of outgoing mail **2 :** a box at or near a dwelling for the occupant's mail

mail drop *n* (1945) **1 :** an address used in transmitting secret communications **2 :** a receptacle or a slot for deposit of mail

mai·le \'mī-lē\ *n* [Hawaiian] (1903) **:** a Pacific island vine (*Alyxia olivaeformis* of the family Apocynaceae) with fragrant leaves and bark that are used for decoration and in Hawaii for leis

mailed fist *n* (1897) **:** a threat of armed force

mail·er \'mā-lər\ *n* (1884) **1 :** one that mails **2 :** a container for mailing something **3 :** something (as an advertisement) sent by mail

mail·ing \'mā-liŋ\ *n* (1946) **:** the mail dispatched at one time by a sender

mail·lot \mī-'ō, mä-'yō\ *n* [F] (1888) **1 :** tights for dancers or gymnasts **2 :** JERSEY 2 **3 :** a woman's one-piece bathing suit

mail·man \'mā(ə)l-ˌman\ *n* (1881) **:** a man who delivers mail — called also *postman*

mail order *n* (1867) : an order for goods that is received and filled by mail
mail–order house *n* (1906) : a retail establishment whose business is conducted by mail
[1]maim \'mām\ *vt* [ME *maynhen, maymen,* fr. OF *maynier*] (14c) **1** : to commit the felony of mayhem upon **2** : to mutilate, disfigure, or wound seriously — **maim·er** *n*
syn MAIM, CRIPPLE, MUTILATE, BATTER, MANGLE mean to injure so severely as to cause lasting damage. MAIM implies the loss or injury of a bodily member through violence; CRIPPLE implies the loss or serious impairment of an arm or leg; MUTILATE implies the cutting off or removal of an essential part of a person or thing thereby impairing its completeness, beauty, or function; BATTER implies a series of blows that bruise deeply, deform, or mutilate; MANGLE implies a tearing or crushing that leaves deep extensive wounds.
[2]maim *n* (14c) **1** *obs* : serious physical injury; *esp* : loss of a member of the body **2** *obs* : a serious loss
[1]main \'mān\ *n* [in sense 1, fr. ME, fr. OE *mægen;* akin to OHG *magan* strength, OE *magan* to be able; in other senses, fr. [2]*main* or by shortening — more at MAY] (bef. 12c) **1** : physical strength : FORCE — used in the phrase *with might and main* **2 a** : MAINLAND **b** : HIGH SEA **3** : the chief part : essential point ⟨they are in the ~ well-trained⟩ **4** : a pipe, duct, or circuit which carries the combined flow of tributary branches of a utility system **5 a** : MAINMAST **b** : MAINSAIL
[2]main *adj* [ME, fr. OE *mægen-,* fr. *mægen* strength] (bef. 12c) **1** : CHIEF, PRINCIPAL ⟨the ~ idea⟩ **2** : fully exerted : SHEER ⟨~ force⟩ ⟨by ~ strength⟩ **3** *obs* : of or relating to a broad expanse (as of sea) **4** : connected with or located near the mainmast or mainsail **5** : expressing the chief predication in a complex sentence ⟨the ~ clause⟩
Maine coon *n* (1935) : any of a breed of large long-haired domestic cats that have a very full tapered tail — called also *coon cat, Maine cat*
main·frame \'mān-,frām\ *n* (1964) : a computer with its cabinet and internal circuits; *also* : a large fast computer that can handle multiple tasks concurrently
main·land \'mān-,land, -lənd\ *n* (14c) : a continent or the main part of a continent as distinguished from an offshore island or sometimes from a cape or peninsula — **main·land·er** \-ər\ *n*
[1]main·line \'mān-'līn\ *vt, slang* (1938) : to take by or as if by mainlining ~ *vi, slang* : to inject a narcotic drug (as heroin) into a principal vein
[2]main·line \'mān-,līn\ *adj* (1941) : being part of an established group; *also* : being in the mainstream
main line *n* (1841) **1** : a principal highway or railroad line **2** *slang* : a principal vein of the circulatory system
main·ly \'mān-lē\ *adv* (13c) **1** *obs* : in a forceful manner **2** : for the most part : CHIEFLY
main·mast \'mān-,mast, -məst\ *n* (15c) : a sailing ship's principal mast usu. second from the bow
main·sail \'mān-,sāl, 'mān(t)-səl\ *n* (15c) : the principal sail on the mainmast — see SAIL illustration
main·sheet \'mān-,shēt\ *n* (15c) : a rope by which the mainsail is trimmed and secured
main·spring \'mān-,spriŋ\ *n* (1591) **1** : the chief spring in a mechanism esp. of a watch or clock **2** : the chief or most powerful motive, agent, or cause
main·stay \-,stā\ *n* (15c) **1** : a ship's stay extending from the maintop forward usu. to the foot of the foremast **2** : a chief support
main stem *n* (1832) : a main trunk or channel: as **a** : the main course of a stream **b** : the main line of a railroad **c** : the main street of a city or town
[1]main·stream \'mān-,strēm\ *n* (1831) : a prevailing current or direction of activity or influence — **mainstream** *adj*
[2]main·stream \'mān-'strēm\ *vt* (1974) : to place (as a handicapped child) in regular school classes
Main Street *n* (1598) **1** : the principal street of a small town **2 a** : the sections of a country centering about its small towns **b** : a place or environment characterized by materialistic self-complacent provincialism — **Main Street·er** \'mān-,strēt-ər\ *n*
main·tain \mān-'tān, mən-\ *vt* [ME *mainteinen,* fr. OF *maintenir,* fr. ML *manutenēre,* fr. L *manu tenēre* to hold in the hand] (14c) **1** : to keep in an existing state (as of repair, efficiency, or validity) : preserve from failure or decline ⟨~ machinery⟩ **2** : to sustain against opposition or danger : uphold and defend ⟨~ a position⟩ **3** : to continue or persevere in : CARRY ON, KEEP UP ⟨couldn't ~ his composure⟩ **4 a** : to support or provide for : bear the expense of ⟨has a family to ~⟩ **b** : SUSTAIN ⟨enough food to ~ life⟩ **5** : to affirm in or as if in argument : ASSERT ⟨~*ed* that all men are not equal⟩ — **main·tain·abil·i·ty** \-,tā-nə-'bil-ət-ē\ *n* — **main·tain·able** \-'tā-nə-bəl\ *adj* — **main·tain·er** *n*
syn MAINTAIN, ASSERT, DEFEND, VINDICATE, JUSTIFY mean to uphold as true, right, just, or reasonable. MAINTAIN stresses firmness of conviction; ASSERT suggests determination to make others accept one's claim; DEFEND implies maintaining in the face of attack or criticism; VINDICATE implies successfully defending; JUSTIFY implies showing to be true, just, or valid by appeal to a standard or to precedent.
main·te·nance \'mānt-nən(t)s, -ᵊn-ən(t)s\ *n* [ME, fr. MF, fr. OF, fr. *maintenir*] (15c) **1** : the act of maintaining : the state of being maintained : SUPPORT **2** : something that maintains **3** : the upkeep of property or equipment **4** : an officious or unlawful intermeddling in a legal suit by assisting either party with means to carry it on
main·top \'mān-,täp\ *n* (15c) : a platform about the head of the mainmast of a square-rigged ship
main–top·mast \mān-'täp-,mast, -məst\ *n* (15c) : a mast next above the mainmast
main yard *n* (15c) : the yard of a mainsail
mair \'mār\ *chiefly Scot var of* MORE
mai·son·ette \,māz-ᵊn-'et, ,mās-\ *n* [F *maisonnette,* fr. OF, dim. of *maison* house, fr. L *mansion-, mansio* dwelling place — more at MANSION] (1793) **1** : a small house **2** : an apartment often on two floors
maî·tre d' *or* **mai·tre d'** \,mā-trə-'dē, ,me-; ,māt-ər-'dē, ,met-\ *n, pl* **maître d's** *or* **maitre d's** \-'dēz\ (1950) : MAÎTRE D'HÔTEL
maî·tre d'hô·tel \,mā-trə-(,)dō-'tel, ,me-; ,māt-dō-, ,met-\ *n, pl* **maîtres d'hôtel** *same*\ [F, lit., master of house] (1540) **1 a** : MAJORDOMO **b** : HEADWAITER **2** : a sauce of butter, parsley, salt, pepper, and lemon juice — called also *maître d'hôtel butter*
maize \'māz\ *n* [Sp *maíz,* fr. Taino *mahiz*] (1555) : INDIAN CORN
ma·ja·gua \mə-'häg-wə\ *n* [AmerSp, fr. Taino] (ca. 1903) : either of two tropical trees of the mallow family that are often considered variant forms of a single species: **a** : an irregularly spreading or shrubby tree (*Hibiscus tilaceus*) that yields a light tough wood and a fibrous bast **b** : an erect forest tree (*H. elatus*) of the West Indian uplands that yields a moderately dense timber with variegated heartwood that is used esp. for cabinetwork and the stocks of guns
ma·jes·tic \mə-'jes-tik\ *adj* (1601) : having or exhibiting majesty : STATELY ***syn*** see GRAND — **ma·jes·ti·cal·ly** \-ti-k(ə-)lē\ *adv*
maj·es·ty \'maj-ə-stē\ *n, pl* **-ties** [ME *maieste,* fr. MF *majesté,* fr. L *majestat-, majestas;* akin to L *major* greater] (14c) **1** : sovereign power, authority, or dignity **2** — used in addressing or referring to reigning sovereigns and their consorts ⟨Your *Majesty*⟩ ⟨Her *Majesty's* Government⟩ **3 a** : royal bearing or aspect : GRANDEUR **b** : greatness or splendor of quality or character
ma·jol·i·ca \mə-'jäl-i-kə\ *also* **ma·iol·i·ca** \-'yäl-\ *n* [It *maiolica,* fr. ML *Majolica* Majorca, fr. LL *Majorca*] (1555) **1** : earthenware covered with an opaque tin glaze and decorated on the glaze before firing; *esp* : an Italian ware of this kind **2** : a 19th century earthenware modeled in naturalistic shapes and glazed in lively colors
[1]ma·jor \'mā-jər\ *adj* [ME *maiour,* fr. L *major,* compar. of *magnus* great, large — more at MUCH] (14c) **1** : greater in dignity, rank, importance, or interest ⟨one of the ~ poets⟩ **2** : greater in number, quantity, or extent ⟨the ~ part of his work⟩ **3** : having attained majority **4** : notable or conspicuous in effect or scope : CONSIDERABLE ⟨a ~ improvement⟩ **5** : involving grave risk : SERIOUS ⟨a ~ illness⟩ **6** : of or relating to a subject of academic study chosen as a field of specialization **7 a** : having half steps between the third and fourth and the seventh and eighth degrees ⟨~ scale⟩ **b** : based on a major scale ⟨~ key⟩ **c** : equivalent to the distance between the keynote and another tone (except the fourth and fifth) of a major scale ⟨~ third⟩ **d** : containing a major third ⟨~ triad⟩
[2]major *n* (1616) **1** : a person who has attained majority **2 a** : one that is superior in rank, importance, size, or performance ⟨economic power of the oil ~*s*⟩ **b** : a major musical interval, scale, key, or mode **3** : a commissioned officer in the army, air force, or marine corps ranking above a captain and below a lieutenant colonel **4 a** : a subject of academic study chosen as a field of specialization **b** : a student specializing in such a field ⟨he is a history ~⟩ **5** *pl* : major league baseball
[3]major *vi* **ma·jored; ma·jor·ing** \'māj-(ə-)riŋ\ (1913) : to pursue an academic major
major axis *n* (1854) : the axis passing through the foci of an ellipse
ma·jor·do·mo \,mā-jər-'dō-(,)mō\ *n, pl* **-mos** [Sp *mayordomo* or obs. It *maiordomo,* fr. ML *major domus,* lit., chief of the house] (1589) **1** : a head steward of a large household (as a palace) **2** : BUTLER, STEWARD **3** : a person who speaks, makes arrangements, or takes charge for another
ma·jor·ette \,mā-jə-'ret\ *n* (1940) : DRUM MAJORETTE 2
major general *n* [F *major général,* fr. *major,* n. + *général,* adj., general] (1642) : a commissioned officer in the army, air force, or marine corps who ranks above a brigadier general and whose insignia is two stars
ma·jor·i·tar·i·an \mə-,jȯr-ə-'ter-ē-ən, -,jär-\ *n* (1942) : one that believes in or advocates majoritarianism — **majoritarian** *adj*
ma·jor·i·tar·i·an·ism \-ē-ə-,niz-əm\ *n* (1942) : the philosophy or practice according to which decisions of an organized group should be made by a numerical majority of its members
ma·jor·i·ty \mə-'jȯr-ət-ē, -'jär-\ *n, pl* **-ties** (1552) **1** *obs* : the quality or state of being greater **2 a** : the age at which full civil rights are accorded **b** : the status of one who has attained this age **3 a** : a number greater than half of a total **b** : the excess of a majority over the remainder of the total : MARGIN **c** : the preponderant quantity or share **4** : the group or political party whose votes preponderate **5** : the military office, rank, or commission of a major — **majority** *adj*
majority leader *n* (1952) : a leader of the majority party in a legislative body (as the U.S. Senate)
majority rule *n* (1893) : a political principle providing that a majority usu. constituted by fifty percent plus one of an organized group will have the power to make decisions binding upon the whole
major league *n* (1906) **1** : a league of highest classification in U.S. professional baseball; *broadly* : a league of major importance in any of various sports **2** : BIG TIME 2
major–medical *adj* (ca. 1955) : of, relating to, or being a form of insurance designed to pay all or part of the medical bills of major illnesses usu. after deduction of a fixed initial sum
major order *n* (ca. 1727) : one of the Roman Catholic or Eastern clerical orders that are sacramentally conferred and have a sacred character that implies major religious obligations (as clerical celibacy) — usu. used in pl.; compare MINOR ORDER
major party *n* (1950) : a political party having electoral strength sufficient to permit it to win control of a government usu. with comparative regularity and when defeated to constitute the principal opposition to the party in power
major penalty *n* (ca. 1936) : a 5-minute suspension of a player in ice hockey
major premise *n* (1860) : the premise of a syllogism containing the major term
major seminary *n* (1945) : a Roman Catholic seminary giving usu. the entire six years of senior college and theological training required for major orders
major suit *n* (1916) : either of two bridge suits of superior scoring value: **a** : SPADES **b** : HEARTS
major term *n* (1860) : the term of a syllogism constituting the predicate of the conclusion
ma·jus·cule \'maj-əs-,kyü(ə)l, mə-'jəs-\ *n* [F, fr. L *majusculus* rather large, dim. of *major*] (1727) : a large letter (as a capital) — **ma·jus·cu·lar** \mə-'jəs-kyə-lər\ *adj* — **majuscule** *adj*
mak·able *or* **make·able** \'mā-kə-bəl\ *adj* (15c) : capable of being made
mak·ar \'mäk-ər, 'mäk-\ *n* [ME *maker*] *chiefly Scot* (14c) : POET
[1]make \'māk\ *vb* **made** \'mād\; **mak·ing** [ME *maken,* fr. OE *macian;* akin to OHG *mahhōn* to prepare, make, OSlav *mazati* to anoint] *vt* (bef. 12c) **1 a** *obs* : BEHAVE, ACT **b** : to seem to begin (an action) ⟨*made* to go⟩ **2 a** : to cause to happen to or be experienced by someone ⟨*made* trouble for us⟩ **b** : to cause to exist, occur, or appear : CREATE ⟨~ a disturbance⟩ **c** : to favor the growth or occurrence of ⟨haste

~s waste〉 **d :** to fit, intend, or destine by or as if by creating 〈was *made* to be an actor〉 **3 a :** to bring into being by forming, shaping, or altering material : FASHION 〈~ a dress〉 **b :** COMPOSE, WRITE 〈~ verses〉 **c :** to lay out and construct 〈~ a road〉 **4 :** to frame or formulate in the mind 〈~ plans〉 **5 :** to put together from components : CONSTITUTE 〈houses *made* of stone〉 **6 a :** to compute or estimate to be **b :** to form and hold in the mind 〈~ no doubt of it〉 **7 a :** to assemble and set alight the materials for (a fire) **b :** to set in order 〈~ beds〉 **c :** PREPARE, FIX 〈~ dinner〉 **d :** to shuffle (a deck of cards) in preparation for dealing **8 :** to prepare (hay) by cutting, drying, and storing **9 a :** to cause to be or become 〈*made* them happy〉 **b :** APPOINT 〈*made* him bishop〉 **10 a :** ENACT, ESTABLISH 〈~ laws〉 **b :** to execute in an appropriate manner 〈~ a will〉 **c :** SET, NAME 〈~ a price〉 **11 a** *chiefly dial* **:** SHUT 〈the doors are *made* against you —Shak.〉 **b :** to cause (an electric circuit) to be completed **12 a :** to conclude as to the nature or meaning of something 〈didn't know what to ~ of his actions〉 **b :** to regard as being 〈not the fool some ~ him〉 **13 a :** to carry out (an action indicated or implied by the object) 〈~ war〉 〈~ a speech〉 **b :** to perform with a bodily movement 〈~ a sweeping gesture〉 **c :** to achieve by traversing 〈~ a detour〉 〈*making* the rounds〉 **14 a :** to produce as a result of action, effort, or behavior with respect to something 〈~ a mess of the job〉 〈tried to ~ a thorough job of it〉 **b** *archaic* **:** to turn into another language by translation **15 :** to cause to act in a certain way : COMPEL 〈~ him give it back〉 **16 :** to cause or assure the success or prosperity of 〈anyone he takes a liking to is *made*〉 **17 a :** to amount to in significance 〈~s a great difference〉 **b :** to form the essential being of 〈clothes ~ the man〉 **c :** to form by an assembling of individuals 〈~ a quorum〉 **d :** to count as 〈that ~s the third time he's said it〉 **18 a :** to be or be capable of being changed or fashioned into 〈rags ~ the best paper〉 **b :** to develop into 〈she will ~ a fine judge〉 **c :** FORM 5b **19 a :** REACH, ATTAIN — often used with *it* 〈you'll never ~ it that far〉 **b :** to gain the rank of 〈~ major〉 **c :** to gain a place on or in 〈~ the team〉 〈the story *made* the papers〉 **20 :** to gain (as money) by working, trading, or dealing 〈~ a living〉 **21 a :** to act so as to win or acquire 〈~s friends easily〉 **b :** to score (points) in a game or sport **c :** to convert (a split) into a spare in bowling **22 a :** to fulfill (a contract) in a card game **b :** to win a trick with (a card) **23 a :** to include in a route or itinerary 〈~ New York on the return trip〉 **b :** CATCH 6b 〈*made* the bus just in time〉 **24 :** to persuade to consent to sexual intercourse : SEDUCE **25 :** to provide the most enjoyable or satisfying experience of 〈meeting the star of the show really *made* our day〉 ~ *vi* **1** *archaic* **:** to compose poetry **2 a :** BEHAVE, ACT **b :** to begin or seem to begin a certain action 〈*made* as though to hand it to me〉 **c :** to act so as to be or to seem to be 〈~ merry〉 **d** *slang* **:** to play a part — usu. used with *like* **3 :** SET OUT, HEAD 〈*made* after the fox〉 〈*made* straight for home〉 **4 :** to increase in height or size 〈the tide is *making* now〉 **5 :** to reach or extend in a certain direction **6 :** to have weight or effect : TELL 〈courtesy ~s for safer driving〉 **7 :** to undergo manufacture or processing 〈the silk ~s up beautifully〉

syn MAKE, FORM, SHAPE, FASHION, FABRICATE, MANUFACTURE, FORGE mean to cause to come into being. MAKE applies to producing or creating whether by an intelligent agency or blind forces and to either material or immaterial existence; FORM implies a definite outline, structure, or design in the thing produced; SHAPE suggests impressing a form upon some material; FASHION suggests the use of inventive power or ingenuity; FABRICATE suggests a uniting of many parts into a whole and often implies an ingenious inventing of something false; MANUFACTURE implies making repeatedly by a fixed process and usu. by machinery; FORGE implies a making or effecting by great physical or mental effort.

— **make a face :** to distort one's features : GRIMACE — **make a mountain out of a molehill :** to treat a trifling matter as of great importance — **make away with 1 :** to carry off **2 :** SPEND, DISSIPATE **3 :** DESTROY, KILL **4 :** CONSUME, EAT — **make believe :** PRETEND, FEIGN — **make bold :** VENTURE, DARE — **make book :** to accept bets at calculated odds on all the entrants in a race or contest — **make do :** to get along or manage with the means at hand — **make ends meet :** to make one's means adequate to one's needs — **make eyes :** OGLE — **make fun of :** to make an object of amusement or laughter : RIDICULE, MOCK — **make good 1 :** to make valid or complete: as **a :** to make up for (a deficiency) **b :** INDEMNIFY 〈*make good* the loss〉 **c :** to carry out successfully 〈*made good* his promise〉 〈*made good* their escape〉 **d :** PROVE 〈*make good* a charge〉 **2 :** to prove to be capable; *also* **:** SUCCEED — **make hay :** to make use of offered opportunity esp. in gaining an early advantage — **make head 1 :** to make progress esp. against resistance **2 :** to rise in armed revolt **3 :** to build up pressure (as in a steam boiler) — **make it 1 :** to be successful 〈trying to *make it* in the big time as a fashion photographer —Joe Kane〉 **2 :** to have sexual intercourse — **make light of :** to treat as of little account — **make love 1 :** WOO, COURT **2 a :** NECK, PET **b :** to engage in sexual intercourse — **make much of 1 :** to treat as of importance **2 :** to treat with obvious affection or special consideration — **make no bones :** to be straightforward, unhesitating, or sure 〈*makes no bones* about giving his opinion on the matter〉 — **make public :** DISCLOSE — **make sail 1 :** to raise or spread sail **2 :** to set out on a voyage — **make sport of :** RIDICULE, MOCK — **make the grade :** to measure up to some standard : be successful — **make the most of :** to show or use to the best advantage — **make the scene** *slang* **:** to be present at or participate in a usu. specified activity or event — **make time 1 :** to travel fast **2 :** to gain time **3 :** to make progress toward winning favor 〈trying to *make time* with the waitress〉 — **make tracks 1 :** to proceed at a walk or run **2 :** to go in a hurry : run away : FLEE — **make use of :** to put to use : EMPLOY — **make water 1** *of a boat* **:** LEAK **2 :** URINATE — **make waves :** to create a stir or disturbance — **make way 1 :** to give room for passing, entering, or occupying **2 :** to make progress — **make with** *slang* **:** PRODUCE, PERFORM — usu. used with *the*

²make *n* (14c) **1 a :** the manner or style in which a thing is constructed **b :** BRAND 4a **2 :** the physical, mental, or moral constitution of a person 〈men of his ~ are rare〉 **3 a :** the action of producing or manufacturing **b :** the actual yield or amount produced over a specified period : OUTPUT **4 :** the declaration of trumps in an early form of bridge **5 :** the closing or completing of an electric circuit **6 :** the act of shuffling cards; *also* **:** turn to shuffle — **on the make 1 :** in the process of forming, growing, or improving **2 :** in quest of a higher social or financial status **3 :** in search of sexual adventure

make·bate \ˈmāk-ˌbāt\ *n* [¹*make* + obs. *bate* (strife)] *archaic* (1529) **:** one that excites contention and quarrels

¹make–be·lieve \ˈmāk-bə-ˌlēv\ *n* (1811) **:** a pretending to believe

²make–believe *adj* (1824) **:** IMAGINARY, PRETENDED

make–do \ˈmāk-ˌdü\ *adj* (1923) **:** MAKESHIFT — **make–do** *n*

make·fast \-ˌfast\ *n* (1898) **:** something (as a post or buoy) to which a boat can be fastened

make off *vi* (1709) **:** to leave in haste — **make off with :** to take away; *esp* **:** GRAB, STEAL

make–or–break \ˌmā-kər-ˌbrāk\ *adj* (1919) **:** allowing no middle ground between success and failure

make out *vt* (15c) **1 :** to complete (as a printed form) by supplying required information 〈*make out* a check〉 **2 :** to find or grasp the meaning of 〈tried to *make out* what had really happened〉 **3 :** to form an opinion or idea about : CONCLUDE 〈how do you *make* that *out*〉 **4 :** to pretend to be true 〈*made out* that he had never heard of me〉 **5 :** to represent or delineate in detail **6 :** to see and identify with difficulty or effort : DISCERN 〈*make out* a ship through the fog〉 ~ *vi* **1 :** GET ALONG, FARE 〈how are you *making out* with the new job〉 **2 :** to engage in sexual intercourse **3 :** NECK 1

make over \(ˈ)mā-ˈkō-vər\ *vt* (1546) **1 :** to transfer the title of (property) **2 :** REMAKE, REMODEL 〈*made* the whole house *over*〉 — **make–over** \ˈmā-ˌkō-vər\ *n*

mak·er \ˈmā-kər\ *n* (14c) **:** one that makes: as **a** *cap* **:** GOD 1 **b** *archaic* **:** POET **c :** a person who borrows money on a promissory note **d :** a declarer in bridge **e :** MANUFACTURER

make·ready \ˈmā-ˌkred-ē\ *n* (1887) **:** final preparation (as of a form on a printing press) for running

make·shift \ˈmāk-ˌshift\ *n* (1802) **:** a usu. crude and temporary expedient : SUBSTITUTE ***syn*** see RESOURCE — **makeshift** *adj*

make·up \ˈmā-ˌkəp\ *n* (1821) **1 a :** the way in which the parts or ingredients of something are put together : COMPOSITION **b :** physical, mental, and moral constitution **2 a :** the operation of making up esp. pages for printing **b :** design or layout of printed matter **3 a (1) :** cosmetics used to color and beautify the face **(2) :** a cosmetic applied to other parts of the body **b :** materials (as wigs and cosmetics) used in making up or in special costuming (as for a play) **4 :** a special examination in which a student may make up for absence or previous failure

make up \(ˈ)mā-ˈkəp\ *vt* (14c) **1 a :** to form by fitting together or assembling 〈*make up* a train of cars〉 **b :** to arrange typeset matter in (as pages) for printing **2 a :** to combine to produce (a sum or whole) **b :** CONSTITUTE, COMPOSE 〈10 chapters *make up* this volume〉 **3 :** to make good (a deficiency) **4 :** SETTLE, DECIDE 〈*made up* his mind to depart〉 **5 :** to wrap or fasten up 〈*make* the books *up* into a parcel〉 **6 a :** to prepare in physical appearance for a role **b :** to apply cosmetics to **7 a :** INVENT, IMPROVISE 〈*make up* a story〉 **b :** to set in order 〈rooms are *made up* daily〉 ~ *vi* **1 :** to become reconciled 〈quarreled but later *made up*〉 **2 a :** to act ingratiatingly and flatteringly 〈*made up* to his aunt for a new bicycle〉 **b :** to make advances : COURT **3 :** COMPENSATE 〈*make up* for lost time〉 **4 a :** to put on costumes or makeup (as for a play) **b :** to apply cosmetics

make·weight \ˈmā-ˌkwāt\ *n* (1695) **1 a :** something thrown into a scale to bring the weight to a desired value **b :** something of little independent value thrown in to fill a gap **2 :** COUNTERWEIGHT, COUNTERPOISE

make–work \ˈmā-ˌkwərk\ *n* (ca. 1909) **:** work assigned chiefly to keep one busy

ma·ki·mo·no \ˌmäk-i-ˈmō-(ˌ)nō\ *n, pl* **-nos** [Jp, scroll, fr. *maki* roll + *mono* thing] (1882) **:** a horizontal Japanese ornamental pictorial or calligraphic scroll

mak·ing \ˈmā-kiŋ\ *n* [ME, fr. OE *macung,* fr. *macian* to make] (12c) **1 :** the act or process of forming, causing, doing, or coming into being 〈spots problems in the ~〉 **2 :** a process or means of advancement or success **3 :** something made; *esp* **:** a quantity produced at one time : BATCH **4 a :** POTENTIALITY — often used in pl. 〈had the ~s of a great artist〉 **b** *pl* **:** the material from which something is to be made; *esp* \usu ˈmā-kənz\ **:** paper and tobacco for rolling cigarettes by hand

ma·ko \ˈmā-(ˌ)kō, ˈmā-\ *n, pl* **makos** [Maori] (1848) **:** either of two mackerel sharks (*Isurus glaucus* and *I. oxyrinchus*) that are notable sport fish and are considered dangerous to man — called also *mako shark;* see SHARK illustration

makuta *pl of* LIKUTA

mal- *comb form* [ME, fr. MF, fr. OF, fr. *mal* bad (fr. L *malus*) & *mal* badly, fr. L *male,* fr. *malus* — more at SMALL] **1 a :** bad 〈*mal*practice〉 **b :** badly 〈*mal*odorous〉 **2 a :** abnormal 〈*mal*formation〉 **b :** abnormally 〈*mal*formed〉 **3 a :** inadequate 〈*mal*adjustment〉 **b :** inadequately 〈*mal*nourished〉

mal·ab·sorp·tion \ˌmal-əb-ˈsȯrp-shən, -ˈzȯrp-\ *n* (ca. 1929) **:** faulty absorption of nutrient materials from the alimentary canal

malac- *or* **malaco-** *comb form* [L, fr. Gk *malak-, malako-,* fr. *malakos;* akin to L *molere* to grind] **:** soft 〈*malac*oid〉 〈*malaco*phyllous〉

ma·lac·ca \mə-ˈlak-ə\ *adj* [*Malacca,* Malaya] (1844) **:** made or comprised of the cane of an Asian rattan palm (*Calamus rotang*) 〈an umbrella with a ~ handle〉 — **malacca** *n*

Mal·a·chi \ˈmal-ə-ˌkī\ *n* [Heb *Mal'ākhī*] **1** — used as the conventional name for the unidentified 5th century B.C. writer of the book of Malachi **2 :** a prophetic book of canonical Jewish and Christian Scripture — see BIBLE table

Mal·a·chi·as \ˌmal-ə-ˈkī-əs\ *n* [LL, fr. Gk, fr. Heb *Mal'ākhī*] **:** MALACHI

mal·a·chite \ˈmal-ə-ˌkīt\ *n* [ME *melochites,* fr. L *molochites,* fr. Gk *molochitēs,* fr. *molochē* mallow] (14c) **:** a mineral $Cu_2CO_3(OH)_2$ that is a green basic carbonate of copper used as an ore and for making ornamental objects

\ə\ **abut** \ᵊ\ **kitten,** F **table** \ər\ **further** \a\ **ash** \ā\ **ace** \ä\ **cot, cart**
\au̇\ **out** \ch\ **chin** \e\ **bet** \ē\ **easy** \g\ **go** \i\ **hit** \ī\ **ice** \j\ **job**
\ŋ\ **sing** \ō\ **go** \ȯ\ **law** \ȯi\ **boy** \th\ **thin** \t͟h\ **the** \ü\ **loot** \u̇\ **foot**
\y\ **yet** \zh\ **vision** \à, k̟, ⁿ, œ, œ̄, ue, uē, ʸ\ *see* Guide to Pronunciation

mal·a·col·o·gy \ˌmal-ə-ˈkäl-ə-jē\ *n* [F *malacologie,* contr. of *malacozoologie,* fr. NL *Malacozoa,* zoological group including soft-bodied animals (fr. *malac-* + *-zoa*) + F *-logie* -logy] (1836) : a branch of zoology dealing with mollusks — **mal·a·co·log·i·cal** \ˌmal-ə-kə-ˈläj-i-kəl\ *adj* — **mal·a·col·o·gist** \ˌmal-ə-ˈkäl-ə-jəst\ *n*

mal·a·cos·tra·can \ˌmal-ə-ˈkäs-tri-kən\ *n* [deriv. of Gk *malakostrakos* soft-shelled, fr. *malak-* + *ostrakon* shell — more at OYSTER] (1835) : any of a major subclass (Malacostraca) of crustaceans including most of the well-known marine, freshwater, and terrestrial members of the group (as crabs and sow bugs) — **malacostracan** *adj*

mal·ad·ap·ta·tion \ˌmal-ˌad-ˌap-ˈtā-shən\ *n* (1877) : poor or inadequate adaptation

mal·adapt·ed \ˌmal-ə-ˈdap-təd\ *adj* (1943) : unsuited or poorly suited (as to a particular use, purpose, or situation)

mal·adap·tive \-tiv\ *adj* (1931) **1** : marked by poor or inadequate adaptation **2** : not conducive to adaptation

mal·ad·just·ed \ˌmal-ə-ˈjəs-təd\ *adj* (1855) : poorly or inadequately adjusted; *specif* : lacking harmony with one's environment from failure to adjust one's desires to the conditions of one's life

mal·ad·jus·tive \-ˈjəs-tiv\ *adj* (1928) : not conducive to adjustment

mal·ad·just·ment \-ˈjəs(t)-mənt\ *n* (1833) : poor, faulty, or inadequate adjustment

mal·ad·min·is·tra·tion \ˌmal-əd-ˌmin-ə-ˈstrā-shən\ *n* (1644) : administration that is corrupt or incompetent (as that of a public office) or incorrect (as that of a drug) — **mal·ad·min·is·ter** \-ˈmin-ə-stər\ *vt*

mal·adroit \ˌmal-ə-ˈdrȯit\ *adj* [F, fr. MF, fr. *mal-* + *adroit*] (1685) : lacking adroitness : INEPT ***syn*** see AWKWARD — **mal·adroit·ly** *adv* — **mal·adroit·ness** *n*

mal·a·dy \ˈmal-əd-ē\ *n, pl* **-dies** [ME *maladie,* fr. OF, fr. *malade* sick, fr. L *male habitus* in bad condition] (13c) **1** : a disease or disorder of the animal body **2** : an unwholesome condition

ma·la fi·de \ˌmal-ə-ˈfīd-ē, -ˈfīd-ə\ *adv or adj* [LL] (1561) : with or in bad faith

Ma·la·ga \ˈmal-ə-gə\ *n* (1608) : a sweet brown fortified wine from Málaga, Spain; *also* : a similar wine made elsewhere

Mal·a·gasy \ˌmal-ə-ˈgas-ē\ *n, pl* **Malagasy** *also* **Mal·a·gas·ies** (1839) **1** : a native or inhabitant of Madagascar or of the Malagasy Republic **2** : the Austronesian language of the Malagasy people — **Malagasy** *adj*

ma·la·gue·na \ˌmal-ə-ˈgān-yə, ˌmäl-\ *n* [Sp *malagueña,* fr. fem. of *malagueño* of Málaga, fr. *Málaga*] (1883) **1** : a folk tune native to Málaga that is similar to a fandango **2** : a Spanish dance for couples that is similar to a fandango

mal·aise \mə-ˈlāz, ma-, -ˈlez\ *n* [F *malaise,* fr. OF, fr. *mal-* + *aise* comfort — more at EASE] (ca. 1768) **1** : an indefinite feeling of debility or lack of health often indicative of or accompanying the onset of an illness **2** : a vague sense of mental or moral ill-being ⟨a ~ of cynicism and despair —Malcolm Boyd⟩

mal·a·mute \ˈmal-ə-ˌmyüt\ *n* [*Malemute,* an Alaskan Eskimo people] (ca. 1874) : a sled dog of northern No. America; *esp* : ALASKAN MALAMUTE

mal·apert \ˌmal-ə-ˈpərt\ *adj* [ME, fr. MF, unskillful, fr. *mal-* + *apert* skillful, modif. of L *expertus* expert] (15c) : impudently bold : SAUCY — **mal·apert·ly** *adv* — **mal·apert·ness** *n*

mal·ap·por·tioned \ˌmal-ə-ˈpōr-shənd, -ˈpȯr-\ *adj* (1965) : characterized by an inequitable or unsuitable apportioning of representatives to a legislative body — **mal·ap·por·tion·ment** \-shən-mənt\ *n*

¹**mal·a·prop** \ˈmal-ə-ˌpräp\ *n* [Mrs. *Malaprop*] (1823) : an example of malapropism ⟨was famed for ~*s*: he always said "polo bears" and "Remember Pearl Island" and "neon stockings" —*Time*⟩

²**malaprop** *or* **mal·a·prop·ian** \ˌmal-ə-ˈpräp-ē-ən\ *adj* (1840) : using or marked by the use of malapropisms

mal·a·prop·ism \ˈmal-ə-ˌpräp-ˌiz-əm\ *n* [Mrs. *Malaprop,* character noted for her misuse of words in R. B. Sheridan's comedy *The Rivals* (1775)] (1834) **1** : a usu. humorous misapplication of a word; *specif* : the use of a word sounding somewhat like the one intended but ludicrously wrong in the context **2** : MALAPROP — **mal·a·prop·ist** \-ˌpräp-əst\ *n*

mal·ap·ro·pos \ˌmal-ˌap-rə-ˈpō, (ˌ)mal-ˈap-rə-ˌ\ *adv* [F *mal à propos*] (1668) : in an inappropriate or inopportune way — **malapropos** *adj*

¹**ma·lar** \ˈmā-lər, -ˌlär\ *adj* [NL *malaris,* fr. L *mala* jawbone, cheek] (1782) : of or relating to the cheek or the side of the head

²**malar** *n* (ca. 1828) : ZYGOMATIC BONE — called also *malar bone*

ma·lar·ia \mə-ˈler-ē-ə\ *n* [It, fr. *mala aria* bad air] (1740) **1** *archaic* : air infected with a noxious substance capable of causing disease; *esp* : MIASMA **2 a** : a human disease that is caused by sporozoan parasites (genus *Plasmodium*) in the red blood cells, is transmitted by the bite of anopheline mosquitoes, and is characterized by periodic attacks of chills and fever **b** : any of various diseases of birds and mammals caused by blood protozoans — **ma·lar·i·al** \-əl\ *adj* — **ma·lar·i·ous** \-əs\ *adj*

ma·lar·i·ol·o·gy \-ˌler-ē-ˈäl-ə-jē\ *n* (ca. 1923) : the scientific study of malaria — **ma·lar·i·ol·o·gist** \-jəst\ *n*

ma·lar·key \mə-ˈlär-kē\ *n* [origin unknown] (1929) : insincere or foolish talk : BUNKUM

ma·late \ˈmal-ˌāt, ˈmā-ˌlāt\ *n* (1794) : a salt or ester of malic acid

mal·a·thi·on \ˌmal-ə-ˈthī-ən, -ˌän\ *n* [fr. *Malathion,* a trademark] (1953) : an insecticide $C_{10}H_{19}O_6PS_2$ with a lower mammalian toxicity than parathion

Ma·lay \mə-ˈlā, ˈmā-(ˌ)lā\ *n* [obs. D *Malayo* (now *Maleier*), fr. Malay *Mĕlayu*] (1598) **1** : a member of a people of the Malay peninsula, eastern Sumatra, parts of Borneo, and some adjacent islands **2** : the Austronesian language of the Malays — **Malay** *adj* — **Ma·lay·an** \mə-ˈlā-ən, ˈmā-ˌlā-\ *n or adj*

Mal·a·ya·lam \ˌmal-ə-ˈyäl-əm\ *n* (1837) : the Dravidian language of Kerala, southwest India, closely related to Tamil

Ma·layo- \mə-ˌlā-(ˌ)ō-, mā-\ *comb form* : Malayan and ⟨*Malayo*-Indonesian⟩

¹**mal·con·tent** \ˌmal-kən-ˈtent\ *n* (1581) : a discontented person: **a** : one who bears a grudge from a sense of grievance or thwarted ambition **b** : one who is in active opposition to an established order or government : REBEL

²**malcontent** *adj* [MF, fr. OF, fr. *mal-* + *content* content] (1586) : dissatisfied with the existing state of affairs : DISCONTENTED

mal·con·tent·ed \-əd\ *adj* (1586) : MALCONTENT — **mal·con·tent·ed·ly** *adv* — **mal·con·tent·ed·ness** *n*

mal de mer \ˌmal-də-ˈme(ə)r\ *n* [F] (1778) : SEASICKNESS

mal·dis·tri·bu·tion \ˌmal-ˌdis-trə-ˈbyü-shən\ *n* (1895) : bad or faulty distribution : undesirable inequality or unevenness of placement or apportionment (as of population, resources, or wealth) over an area or among members of a group

¹**male** \ˈmā(ə)l\ *adj* [ME, fr. MF *masle, male,* adj. & n., fr. L *masculus,* — more at MASCULINE] (14c) **1 a** (1) : of, relating to, or being the sex that begets young by performing the fertilizing function in generation and produces relatively small usu. motile gametes (as sperms, spermatozoids, or spermatozoa) by which the eggs of a female are made fertile ⟨~ organs⟩ (2) : STAMINATE; *esp* : having only staminate flowers and not producing fruit or seeds ⟨a ~ holly⟩ **b** (1) : of, relating to, or characteristic of the male sex ⟨a deep ~ voice⟩ (2) : made up of male individuals and esp. men ⟨a ~ choir⟩ **2** : MASCULINE 3a **3** : designed for fitting into a corresponding female part ⟨~ hose coupling⟩ — **male·ness** \-nəs\ *n*

²**male** *n* (14c) : a plant or animal that is male

male alto *n* (ca. 1879) : COUNTERTENOR

ma·le·ate \ˈmā-lē-ˌāt, -lē-ət\ *n* (1794) : a salt or ester of maleic acid

¹**male·dict** \ˌmal-ə-ˈdikt\ *adj* [LL *maledictus*] *archaic* (1599) : ACCURSED

²**maledict** *vt* (1780) : CURSE, EXECRATE

male·dic·tion \ˌmal-ə-ˈdik-shən\ *n* [ME *malediccioun,* fr. LL *malediction-, maledictio,* fr. *maledictus,* pp. of *maledicere* to curse, fr. L, to speak evil of, fr. *male* badly + *dicere* to speak, say — more at MALDICTION] (14c) : CURSE, EXECRATION — **male·dic·to·ry** \-ˈdik-t(ə-)rē\ *adj*

male·fac·tion \ˌmal-ə-ˈfak-shən\ *n* (15c) : an evil deed : CRIME

male·fac·tor \ˈmal-ə-ˌfak-tər\ *n* [ME, fr. L, fr. *malefactus,* pp. of *malefacere* to do evil, fr. *male* + *facere* to do — more at DO] (15c) **1** : one who commits an offense against the law; *esp* : FELON **2** : one who does ill toward another

male fern *n* (1562) : a fern (*Dryopteris filix-mas*) producing an oleoresin used in expelling tapeworms

ma·lef·ic \mə-ˈlef-ik\ *adj* [L *maleficus* wicked, mischievous, fr. *male*] (1652) **1** : having malignant influence : BALEFUL **2** : MALICIOUS

ma·lef·i·cence \mə-ˈlef-ə-sən(t)s\ *n* [It *maleficenza,* fr. L *maleficentia,* fr. *maleficus*] (1598) **1 a** : the act of committing harm or evil **b** : a harmful or evil act **2** : the quality or state of being maleficent

ma·lef·i·cent \-sənt\ *adj* [back-formation fr. *maleficence*] (1678) : working or productive of harm or evil : BALEFUL

ma·le·ic acid \mə-ˌlē-ik-, -ˌlā-\ *n* [F *acide maléique,* alter. of *acide malique* malic acid; fr. its formation by dehydration of malic acid] (1838) : a crystalline dicarboxylic acid $C_4H_4O_4$ that is isomeric with fumaric acid and used esp. in organic synthesis

maleic anhydride *n* (1857) : a caustic crystalline cyclic anhydride $C_4H_2O_3$ used esp. in making resins

maleic hydrazide *n* (1949) : a crystalline cyclic hydrazide $C_4H_4N_2O_2$ used to retard plant growth

mal·e·mute *var of* MALAMUTE

male–ster·ile \ˈmā(ə)l-ˈster-əl\ *adj* (1921) : having male gametes lacking or nonfunctional

ma·lev·o·lence \mə-ˈlev-ə-lən(t)s\ *n* (15c) **1** : the quality or state of being malevolent **2** : malevolent behavior ***syn*** see MALICE

ma·lev·o·lent \-lənt\ *adj* [L *malevolent-, malevolens,* fr. *male* badly + *volent-, volens,* prp. of *velle* to wish — more at MAL-, WILL] (1509) **1** : having, showing, or arising from intense often vicious ill will, spite, or hatred **2** : productive of harm or evil — **ma·lev·o·lent·ly** *adv*

mal·fea·sance \(ˈ)mal-ˈfēz-ᵊn(t)s\ *n* [*mal-* + obs. *feasance* (doing, execution)] (1696) : wrongdoing or misconduct esp. by a public official

mal·for·ma·tion \ˌmal-fȯr-ˈmā-shən, -fər-\ *n* (1800) : irregular, anomalous, abnormal, or faulty formation or structure

mal·formed \(ˈ)mal-ˈfȯ(ə)rmd\ *adj* (1817) : characterized by malformation : badly or imperfectly formed : MISSHAPEN

mal·func·tion \(ˈ)mal-ˈfəŋ(k)-shən\ *vi* (1928) : to function imperfectly or badly : fail to operate in the normal or usual manner — **malfunction** *n*

mal·gré \mal-ˈgrā, ˈmal-ˌ\ *prep* [F, fr. OF *maugré* — more at MAUGRE] (1608) : DESPITE

ma·lic \ˈmal-ik, ˈmā-lik\ *adj* (ca. 1909) : involved in and esp. catalyzing a reaction in which malic acid participates ⟨~ dehydrogenase⟩ ⟨~ enzyme⟩

malic acid *n* [F *acide malique,* deriv. of L *malum* apple, fr. Gk *mēlon, malon*] (1797) : a crystalline dicarboxylic acid $C_4H_6O_5$; *esp* : the one of three optical isomers of malic acid that is found in various plant juices and is formed as an intermediate in the Krebs cycle

mal·ice \ˈmal-əs\ *n* [ME, fr. MF, fr. L *malitia,* fr. *malus* bad — more at SMALL] (14c) : desire to see another suffer that may be fixed and unreasonable or no more than a passing mischievous impulse; *also* : intent to commit an unlawful act or cause harm without legal justification or excuse

syn MALICE, MALEVOLENCE, ILL WILL, SPITE, MALIGNITY, SPLEEN, GRUDGE mean the desire to see another experience pain, injury, or distress. MALICE implies a deep-seated often unexplainable desire to see another suffer; MALEVOLENCE suggests a bitter persistent hatred that is likely to be expressed in malicious conduct; ILL WILL implies a feeling of antipathy of limited duration; SPITE implies petty feelings of envy and resentment that are often expressed in small harassments; MALIGNITY implies deep passion and relentlessness; SPLEEN suggests the wrathful release of latent spite or persistent malice; GRUDGE implies a harbored feeling of resentment or ill will that seeks satisfaction.

ma·li·cious \mə-ˈlish-əs\ *adj* (13c) : given to, marked by, or arising from malice — **ma·li·cious·ly** *adv* — **ma·li·cious·ness** *n*

malicious mischief *n* (1769) : willful, wanton, or reckless damage to or destruction of another's property

¹**ma·lign** \mə-ˈlīn\ *adj* [ME *maligne,* fr. MF, fr. L *malignus,* fr. *male* badly + *gignere* to beget — more at MAL-, KIN] (14c) **1 a** : evil in nature, influence, or effect : INJURIOUS **b** : MALIGNANT, VIRULENT **2** : having or showing intense often vicious ill will : MALEVOLENT ***syn*** see SINISTER — **ma·lign·ly** *adv*

²**malign** *vt* [ME *malignen,* fr. MF *maligner* to act maliciously, fr. LL *malignari,* fr. L *malignus*] (1647) : to utter injuriously misleading or false reports about : speak evil of

syn MALIGN, TRADUCE, ASPERSE, VILIFY, CALUMNIATE, DEFAME, SLANDER mean to injure by speaking ill of. MALIGN suggests specific and often subtle misrepresentation but may not always imply deliberate lying;

TRADUCE stresses the resulting ignominy and distress to the victim; ASPERSE implies continued attack on a reputation often by indirect or insinuated detraction; VILIFY implies attempting to destroy a reputation by open and direct abuse; CALUMNIATE imputes malice to the speaker and falsity to his assertions; DEFAME and SLANDER stress the effects, DEFAME suggesting actual loss of or injury to one's good name, SLANDER the suffering of the victim.

ma·lig·nance \mə-ˈlig-nən(t)s\ *n* (1603) : MALIGNANCY

ma·lig·nan·cy \-nən-sē\ *n, pl* **-cies** (1601) **1** : the quality or state of being malignant **2** **a** : exhibition (as by a tumor) of malignant qualities : VIRULENCE **b** : a malignant tumor

ma·lig·nant \mə-ˈlig-nənt\ *adj* [LL *malignant-, malignans,* prp. of *malignari*] (14c) **1** **a** *obs* : MALCONTENT, DISAFFECTED **b** : evil in nature, influence, or effect : INJURIOUS **c** : passionately and relentlessly malevolent : aggressively malicious **2** : tending to produce death or deterioration ⟨~ malaria⟩; *esp* : tending to infiltrate, metastasize, and terminate fatally ⟨~ tumor⟩ — **ma·lig·nant·ly** *adv*

ma·lig·ni·ty \mə-ˈlig-nət-ē\ *n* (14c) **1** : MALIGNANCY, MALEVOLENCE **2** : an instance of malignant or malicious behavior or nature ***syn*** see MALICE

ma·li·hi·ni \ˌmäl-i-ˈhē-nē\ *n* [Hawaiian] (1914) : a newcomer or stranger among the people of Hawaii

ma·lines \mə-ˈlēn\ *n, pl* **ma·lines** \-ˈlēn(z)\ [F, fr. *Malines* (Mechelen), Belgium] (1833) **1** : MECHLIN **2** *also* **ma·line** : a fine stiff net with a hexagonal mesh that is usu. made of silk or rayon and that is often used for veils

ma·lin·ger \mə-ˈliŋ-gər\ *vi* **ma·lin·gered; ma·lin·ger·ing** \-g(ə-)riŋ\ [F *malingre* sickly] (1820) : to pretend incapacity (as illness) so as to avoid duty or work — **ma·lin·ger·er** \-gər-ər\ *n*

Ma·lin·ke \mə-ˈliŋ-kē\ *n, pl* **Malinke** *or* **Malinkes** (1883) **1** : a member of a people of Mandingo affiliation widespread in the western part of Africa **2** : the language of the Malinke people

Ma·li·nois \ˌmal-ən-ˈwä\ *n* [F, one from Malines, fr. *Malines* (Mechelen), Belgium] (1929) : BELGIAN MALINOIS

mal·i·son \ˈmal-ə-sən, -zən\ *n* [ME, fr. OF *maleïçon,* fr. LL *malediction-, maledictio*] (13c) : CURSE, MALEDICTION

mal·kin \ˈmȯ(l)-kən, ˈmal-\ *n* [ME *malkyn,* fr. *Malkyn,* dim. of the name *Maud*] (13c) **1** *dial chiefly Brit* : an untidy woman : SLATTERN **2** *dial chiefly Brit* **a** : CAT **b** : HARE

[1]**mall** \ˈmȯl\ *var of* MAUL

[2]**mall** \ˈmȯl, *esp Brit & for 1* ˈmal\ *n* [short for obs. *pall-mall* (mallet used in pall-mall)] (1644) **1** : an alley used for pall-mall **2** [The *Mall,* promenade in London, orig. a pall-mall alley] **a** : a usu. public area often set with shade trees and designed as a promenade or as a pedestrian walk **b** : a usu. paved or grassy strip between two roadways **3** **a** : an urban shopping area featuring a variety of shops surrounding a usu. open-air concourse reserved for pedestrian traffic **b** : a usu. large suburban building or group of buildings containing various shops with associated passageways

mal·lard \ˈmal-ərd\ *n, pl* **mallard** *or* **mallards** [ME, fr. MF *mallart*] (14c) : a common and widely distributed wild duck (*Anas platyrhynchos*) of the northern hemisphere that is the source of the domestic ducks

mal·lea·ble \ˈmal-ē-ə-bəl, ˈmal-(y)ə-bəl\ *adj* [ME *malliable,* fr. MF or ML; MF *malleable,* fr. ML *malleabilis,* fr. *malleare* to hammer, fr. L *malleus* hammer — more at MAUL] (14c) **1** : capable of being extended or shaped by beating with a hammer or by the pressure of rollers **2** **a** : capable of being altered or controlled by outside forces or influences **b** : having a capacity for adaptive change ***syn*** see PLASTIC — **mal·lea·bil·i·ty** \ˌmal-ē-ə-ˈbil-ət-ē, ˌmal-(y)ə-\ *n* — **mal·lea·ble·ness** \ˈmal-ē-ə-bəl-nəs, ˈmal-(y)ə-\ *n*

mal·lee \ˈmal-ē\ *n* [native name in Australia] (1848) **1** : any of several low-growing shrubby Australian eucalypts (as *Eucalyptus dumosa* and *E. oleosa*) **2** : a dense thicket or growth of mallees; *also* : land covered by such growth

mal·let \ˈmal-ət\ *n* [ME *maillet,* fr. MF, fr. OF, dim. of *mail* maul — more at MAUL] (14c) : a hammer with typically a barrel-shaped head of wood: as **a** : a tool with a large head for driving another tool or for striking a surface without marring it **b** : an implement for striking a ball (as in polo or croquet) **c** : a light hammer with a small rounded or spherical usu. padded head used in playing certain musical instruments (as a vibraphone)

mal·le·us \ˈmal-ē-əs\ *n, pl* **mal·lei** \-ē-ˌī, -ē-ˌē\ [NL, fr. L, hammer; akin to L *molere* to grind — more at MEAL] (1669) : the outermost of a chain of three small bones of the mammalian ear — see EAR illustration

mal·low \ˈmal-(ˌ)ō, -ə(-w)\ *n* [ME *malwe,* fr. OE *mealwe,* fr. L *malva*] (bef. 12c) : any of a genus (*Malva* of the family Malvaceae, the mallow family) of herbs with palmately lobed or dissected leaves, usu. showy flowers, and a disk-shaped fruit

malm \ˈmä(l)m, *NewEng also* ˈmȧm\ *n* [ME *malme,* soft chalky rock, fr. OE *mealm-;* akin to OE *melu* meal — more at MEAL] (ca. 1855) : an artificial mixture of clay and chalk used in the manufacture of bricks

malm·sey \ˈmä(l)m-zē, *NewEng also* ˈmȧm-\ *n, often cap* [ME *malmesey,* fr. ML *Malmasia* Monemvasia, village in Greece where it was orig. produced] (15c) : the sweetest variety of Madeira wine

mal·nour·ished \(ˈ)mal-ˈnər-isht, -ˈnə-risht\ *adj* (1927) : UNDERNOURISHED

mal·nu·tri·tion \ˌmal-n(y)u̇-ˈtrish-ən\ *n* (1862) : faulty or inadequate nutrition

mal·oc·clu·sion \ˌmal-ə-ˈklü-zhən\ *n* (1888) : improper occlusion; *esp* : abnormality in the coming together of teeth

mal·odor \(ˈ)mal-ˈōd-ər\ *n* (1825) : an offensive odor

mal·odor·ous \-ˈōd-ə-rəs\ *adj* (1850) **1** : ill-smelling **2** : highly improper ⟨~ practices and chicanery in high financial places —*New Republic*⟩ — **mal·odor·ous·ly** *adv* — **mal·odor·ous·ness** *n*

syn MALODOROUS, STINKING, FETID, NOISOME, PUTRID, RANK, FUSTY, MUSTY mean bad-smelling. MALODOROUS may range from the unpleasant to the strongly offensive; STINKING and FETID suggest the foul or disgusting; NOISOME adds a suggestion of being harmful or unwholesome as well as offensive; PUTRID implies particularly the sickening odor of decaying organic matter; RANK suggests a strong unpleasant smell; FUSTY and MUSTY suggest lack of fresh air and sunlight, FUSTY also implying prolonged uncleanliness, MUSTY stressing the effects of dampness, mildew, or age.

ma·lo·lac·tic \ˌmal-ō-ˈlak-tik, ˌmā-lō-\ *adj* [*malic* + *-o-* + *lactic*] (1965) : relating to or involved in the bacterial conversion of malic acid to lactic acid in wine ⟨~ fermentation⟩

maloti *pl of* LOTI

Mal·pi·ghi·an corpuscle \mal-ˌpig-ē-ən-, -ˌpē-gē-ən-\ *n* [Marcello *Malpighi*] (1848) : the part of a nephron that consists of a glomerulus and its membrane — called also *Malpighian body*

Malpighian layer *n* (1878) : the deeper part of the epidermis consisting of cells whose protoplasm has not yet changed into horny material

Malpighian tubule *n* (1877) : any of a group of long blind vessels opening into the posterior part of the alimentary canal in most insects and some other arthropods and functioning primarily as excretory organs — called also *Malpighian tube*

mal·po·si·tion \ˌmal-pə-ˈzish-ən\ *n* (1836) : wrong or faulty position

mal·prac·tice \(ˈ)mal-ˈprak-təs\ *n* (1671) **1** : a dereliction from professional duty or a failure to exercise an accepted degree of professional skill or learning by one (as a physician) rendering professional services which results in injury, loss, or damage **2** : an injurious, negligent, or improper practice : MALFEASANCE

mal·prac·ti·tio·ner \ˌmal-prak-ˈtish-(ə-)nər\ *n* (1800) : one who engages in or commits malpractice

[1]**malt** \ˈmȯlt\ *n* [ME, fr. OE *mealt;* akin to OHG *malz* malt, OE *meltan* to melt] (bef. 12c) **1** : grain softened by steeping in water, allowed to germinate, and used esp. in brewing and distilling **2** : MALT LIQUOR **3** : MALTED MILK — **malty** \ˈmȯl-tē\ *adj*

[2]**malt** *vt* (15c) **1** : to convert into malt **2** : to make or treat with malt or malt extract ~ *vi* **1** : to become malt **2** : to make grain into malt

malt·ase \ˈmȯl-ˌtās, -ˌtāz\ *n* (1890) : an enzyme that accelerates the hydrolysis of maltose to glucose

malted milk *n* (1887) **1** : a soluble powder prepared from dried milk and malted cereals **2** : a beverage made by dissolving malted milk in milk and usu. adding ice cream and flavoring — called also *malted*

Mal·tese \mȯl-ˈtēz, -ˈtēs\ *n, pl* **Maltese** (1615) **1** : a native or inhabitant of Malta **2** : the Semitic language of the Maltese people **3** : any of a breed of toy dogs with a long white coat, a black nose, and very dark eyes — **Maltese** *adj*

Maltese 3

Maltese cat *n* (1857) : a bluish gray domestic short-haired cat

Maltese cross *n* (1877) **1** **a** : a cross formée **b** : a cross that resembles the cross formée but has the outer face of each arm indented in a V — see CROSS illustration **2** : a Eurasian perennial (*Lychnis chalcedonica*) having scarlet or rarely white flowers in dense terminal heads

Mal·thu·sian \mal-ˈth(y)ü-zhən, mȯl-\ *adj* [Thomas R. *Malthus*] (1812) : of or relating to Malthus or to his theory that population tends to increase at a faster rate than its means of subsistence and that unless it is checked by moral restraint or by disease, famine, war, or other disaster widespread poverty and degradation inevitably result — **Malthusian** *n* — **Mal·thu·sian·ism** \-zhə-ˌniz-əm\ *n*

malt liquor *n* (1693) : a fermented liquor (as beer) made with malt

malt·ose \ˈmȯl-ˌtōs, -ˌtōz\ *n* [F, fr. E [1]*malt*] (1862) : a crystalline dextrorotatory fermentable sugar $C_{12}H_{22}O_{11}$ formed esp. from starch by amylase

mal·treat \(ˈ)mal-ˈtrēt\ *vt* [part. trans. of F *maltraiter,* fr. MF, fr. *mal-* + *traiter* to treat, fr. OF *traitier* — more at TREAT] (1708) : to treat cruelly or roughly : ABUSE — **mal·treat·er** \-ər\ *n* — **mal·treat·ment** \-mənt\ *n*

malt·ster \ˈmȯlt-stər\ *n* (14c) : a maker of malt

malt sugar *n* (1862) : MALTOSE

mal·ver·sa·tion \ˌmal-vər-ˈsā-shən\ *n* [MF, fr. *malverser* to be corrupt, fr. *mal* + *verser* to turn, handle, fr. L *versare,* fr. *versus,* pp. of *vertere* to turn — more at WORTH] (1549) **1** : misbehavior and esp. corruption in an office, trust, or commission **2** : corrupt administration

ma·ma *or* **mam·ma** \ˈmäm-ə, *chiefly Brit* mə-ˈmä\ *n* [baby talk] (1579) **1** : MOTHER **2** *slang* : WIFE, WOMAN

mam·ba \ˈmäm-bə, ˈmam-\ *n* [Zulu *im-amba*] (1862) : any of several tropical and southern African venomous snakes (genus *Dendraspis*) related to the cobras but with no hood; *esp* : an aggressive southern African snake (*D. angusticeps*) that grows to a length of 12 feet, has a light or olive green phase and a black phase, and readily inflicts its often fatal bite

mam·bo \ˈmäm-(ˌ)bō\ *n, pl* **mambos** [AmerSp] (1948) : a ballroom dance of Cuban origin that resembles the rumba and the cha-cha; *also* : the music for this dance — **mambo** *vi*

Mam·luk \ˈmam-ˌlük\ *or* **Mam·e·luke** \ˈmam-ə-ˌlük\ *n* [Ar *mamlūk,* lit., slave] (1506) **1** : a member of a politically powerful Egyptian military class occupying the sultanate from 1250 to 1517 **2** *usu Mameluke, often not cap* : a Caucasian or oriental slave in Muslim countries

mam·ma \ˈmam-ə\ *n, pl* **mam·mae** \ˈmam-ˌē, -ˌī\ [L, mother, breast, of baby-talk origin] (1693) : a mammary gland and its accessory parts — **mam·mate** \ˈmam-ˌāt\ *adj*

mam·mal \ˈmam-əl\ *n* [deriv. of LL *mammalis* of the breast, fr. L *mamma* breast] (ca. 1826) : any of a class (Mammalia) of higher vertebrates comprising man and all other animals that nourish their young with milk secreted by mammary glands and have the skin usu. more or less covered with hair — **mam·ma·li·an** \mə-ˈmā-lē-ən, ma-\ *adj or n*

mam·mal·o·gy \mə-ˈmal-ə-jē, ma-ˈmal-, -ˈmäl-\ *n* [ISV, blend of *mammal* and *-logy*] (1835) : a branch of zoology dealing with mammals — **mam·mal·o·gist** \-jəst\ *n*

mam·ma·ry \ˈmam-ə-rē\ *adj* (1682) : of, relating to, lying near, or affecting the mammae

mammary gland *n* (1831) : any of the large compound modified sebaceous glands that in female mammals are modified to secrete milk, are situated ventrally in pairs, and usu. terminate in a nipple

mam·ma·to·cu·mu·lus \ma-ˌmāt-ō-ˈkyü-myə-ləs\ *n* [NL, fr. L *mammatus* having breasts, (fr. *mamma*) + NL *cumulus* cumulus] (1880) : a cumulus or cumulostratus storm cloud having breast-shaped protuberances below

mammer *vi* [ME *mameren* to stammer, of imit. origin] *obs* (1555) : WAVER, HESITATE

mam·mil·la·ry \ˈmam-ə-ˌler-ē, ma-ˈmil-ə-rē\ *adj* [L *mammilla* breast, nipple, dim. of *mamma*] (1615) **1** : of, relating to, or resembling the breasts **2** : studded with breast-shaped protuberances

mam·mil·lat·ed \ˈmam-ə-ˌlāt-əd\ *adj* [LL *mammillatus*, fr. L *mammilla*] (1741) **1** : having nipples or small protuberances **2** : having the form of a bluntly rounded protuberance

1**mam·mock** \ˈmam-ək\ *n* [origin unknown] *chiefly dial* (1529) : a broken piece : SCRAP

2**mammock** *vt, chiefly dial* (1607) : to tear into fragments : MANGLE

mam·mo·gram \ˈmam-ə-ˌgram\ *n* [L *mamma* + E *-o-* + *-gram*] (ca. 1937) : a photograph of the breasts made by X rays

mam·mog·ra·phy \ma-ˈmäg-rə-fē\ *n* (ca. 1937) : X-ray examination of the breasts (as for early detection of cancer) — **mam·mo·graph·ic** \ˌmam-ə-ˈgraf-ik\ *adj*

mam·mon \ˈmam-ən\ *n, often cap* [LL *mammona*, fr. Gk *mamōna*, fr. Aram *māmōnā* riches] (14c) : material wealth or possessions esp. as having a debasing influence ⟨you cannot serve God and ~ —Mt 6:24 (RSV)⟩ — **mam·mon·ism** \-ə-ˌniz-əm\ *n*

mam·mon·ist \-ə-nəst\ *n, archaic* (1550) : one devoted to the ideal or pursuit of wealth

1**mam·moth** \ˈmam-əth\ *n* [Russ *mamont, mamot*] (1706) **1** : any of numerous extinct Pleistocene elephants distinguished from recent elephants by molars with cementum filling the spaces between the ridges of enamel and by large size, very long tusks that curve upward, and well-developed body hair **2** : something immense of its kind : GIANT ⟨a company that is a ~ of the industry⟩

2**mammoth** *adj* (1802) : of very great size : GIGANTIC **syn** see ENORMOUS

mam·my \ˈmam-ē\ *n, pl* **mammies** [alter. of *mamma*] (1523) **1** : MAMA **2** : a black woman serving as a nurse to white children esp. formerly in the southern U.S.

1**man** \ˈman, *in compounds* ˌman *or* mən\ *n, pl* **men** \ˈmen, *in compounds* ˌmen *or* mən\ [ME, fr. OE; akin to OHG *man* man, Skt *manu*] (bef. 12c) **1 a** (1) : a human being; *esp* : an adult male human (2) : a man belonging to a particular category (as by birth, residence, membership, or occupation) — usu. used in combination ⟨council*man*⟩ (3) : HUSBAND (4) : LOVER **b** : the human race : MANKIND **c** : a bipedal primate mammal (*Homo sapiens*) that is anatomically related to the great apes but distinguished esp. by notable development of the brain with a resultant capacity for articulate speech and abstract reasoning, is usu. considered to form a variable number of freely interbreeding races, and is the sole representative of a natural family (Hominidae); *broadly* : any living or extinct member of this family **d** (1) : one possessing in high degree the qualities considered distinctive of manhood (2) *obs* : the quality or state of being manly : MANLINESS **e** : FELLOW, CHAP ⟨come, come, my good ~⟩ **f** — used interjectionally to express intensity of feeling ⟨~, what a game⟩ **2 a** : a feudal tenant : VASSAL **b** : an adult male servant **c** *pl* : the working force as distinguished from the employer and usu. the management **3** : INDIVIDUAL, PERSON ⟨a ~ could get killed there⟩ **4** : one of the distinctive objects moved by each player in various board games **5** *Christian Science* : the compound idea of infinite Spirit : the spiritual image and likeness of God : the full representation of Mind **6** *often cap* : POLICE ⟨when I heard the siren, I knew it was the *Man* —*Amer. Speech*⟩ **7** *often cap* : the white establishment : white society ⟨surprise that any black . . . should take on so about The *Man* —Peter Goldman⟩ — **man·less** \ˈman-ləs\ *adj* — **man·like** \-ˌlīk\ *adj* — **as one man** : with the agreement and consent of all : UNANIMOUSLY — **one's own man** : free from interference or control : INDEPENDENT — **to a man** : without exception

2**man** *vt* **manned; man·ning** (15c) **1 a** : to supply with men ⟨~ a fleet⟩ **b** : to station members of a ship's crew at ⟨~ the capstan⟩ **c** : to serve in the force or complement of ⟨workers who ~ the production lines⟩ **2** : to accustom (as a hawk) to humans and the human environment **3** : to furnish with strength or powers of resistance : BRACE

ma·na \ˈmän-ə\ *n* [of Melanesian & Polynesian origin; akin to Hawaiian & Maori *mana*] (1843) **1** : the power of the elemental forces of nature embodied in an object or person **2** : moral authority : PRESTIGE

man–about–town \ˌman-ə-ˌbau̇t-ˈtau̇n\ *n, pl* **men–about–town** \ˌmen-\ (ca. 1785) : a worldly and socially active man

1**man·a·cle** \ˈman-i-kəl\ *n* [ME *manicle*, fr. MF, fr. L *manicula*, dim. of *manus* hand — more at MANUAL] (14c) **1** : a shackle for the hand or wrist : HANDCUFF **2** : something used as a restraint

2**manacle** *vt* **man·a·cled; man·a·cling** \-k(ə-)liŋ\ (14c) **1** : to confine (the hands) with manacles **2** : to make fast or secure : BIND; *broadly* : to restrain from movement, progress, or action **syn** see HAMPER

1**man·age** \ˈman-ij\ *vb* **man·aged; man·ag·ing** [It *maneggiare*, fr. *mano* hand, fr. L *manus*] *vt* (1561) **1** : to handle or direct with a degree of skill or address: as **a** : to make and keep submissive ⟨my mother . . . was the only one that ever could ~ him —George Macdonald †1905⟩ **b** : to treat with care : HUSBAND ⟨*managed* his resources carefully⟩ **c** : to exercise executive, administrative, and supervisory direction of ⟨~ a business⟩ ⟨~ a bond issue⟩ **2** : to alter by manipulation **3** : to succeed in accomplishing : CONTRIVE **4** : to direct the professional career of ⟨an agency that ~s entertainers⟩ ~ *vi* **1 a** : to direct or carry on business or affairs **b** : to admit of being carried on **2** : to achieve one's purpose **syn** see CONDUCT

2**manage** *n* [It *maneggio* management, training of a horse, fr. *maneggiare*] (1577) **1 a** *archaic* : the action and paces of a trained riding horse **b** : the schooling or handling of a horse **c** : a riding school : MANEGE **2** *obs* : MANAGEMENT

man·age·able \ˈman-ij-ə-bəl\ *adj* (1598) : capable of being managed : TRACTABLE — **man·age·abil·i·ty** \ˌman-ij-ə-ˈbil-ət-ē\ *n* — **man·age·able·ness** \ˈman-ij-ə-bəl-nəs\ *n* — **man·age·ably** \-blē\ *adv*

man·age·ment \ˈman-ij-mənt\ *n* (1598) **1** : the act or art of managing : the conducting or supervising of something (as a business) **2** : judicious use of means to accomplish an end **3** : capacity for managing : executive skill **4** : the collective body of those who manage or direct an enterprise — **man·age·men·tal** \ˌman-ij-ˈment-ᵊl\ *adj*

man·ag·er \ˈman-ij-ər\ *n* (1588) : one that manages: as **a** : one who conducts business or household affairs **b** : a person whose work or profession is management **c** (1) : a person who directs a team or athlete (2) : a student who in scholastic or collegiate sports supervises equipment and records under the direction of a coach — **man·a·ge·ri·al** \ˌman-ə-ˈjir-ē-əl\ *adj* — **man·a·ge·ri·al·ly** \-ē-ə-lē\ *adv* — **man·ag·er·ship** \ˈman-ij-ər-ˌship\ *n*

man·ag·er·ess \ˈman-ij-ə-rəs\ *n* (1797) : a woman who is a manager

managing editor *n* (1865) : an editor in executive and supervisory charge of all editorial activities of a publication (as a newspaper)

1**ma·ña·na** \mən-ˈyän-ə\ *n* [Sp, lit., tomorrow, fr. earlier *cras mañana* early tomorrow, fr. *cras* tomorrow (fr. L) + *mañana* early, fr. L *mane* early in the morning] (1845) : an indefinite time in the future

2**mañana** *adv* (ca. 1898) : at an indefinite time in the future

man ape *n* (ca. 1864) **1** : GREAT APE **2** : any of various fossil primates intermediate in characters between recent man and the great apes

Ma·nas·seh \mə-ˈnas-ə\ *n* [Heb *Mĕnashsheh*] **1** : a son of Joseph and the traditional eponymous ancestor of one of the tribes of Israel **2** : a king of Judah reigning in the 7th century B.C. and noted for his attempt to establish polytheism

man–at–arms \ˌman-ət-ˈärmz\ *n, pl* **men–at–arms** \ˌmen-\ (1581) : SOLDIER; *esp* : a heavily armed and usu. mounted soldier

man·a·tee \ˈman-ə-ˌtē\ *n* [Sp *manatí*] (1555) : any of several chiefly tropical aquatic herbivorous mammals (genus *Trichechus*) that differ from the related dugong esp. in having the tail broad and rounded

Man·ches·ter terrier \ˌman-ˌches-tər-, -chə-stər-\ *n* [*Manchester*, England] (ca. 1874) : any of an English breed of small short-haired black-and-tan terriers

man–child \ˈman-ˌchīld\ *n, pl* **men–chil·dren** \ˈmen-ˌchil-drən, -dərn\ (15c) : a male child : SON

man·chi·neel \ˌman-chə-ˈnē(ə)l\ *n* [F *mancenille*, fr. Sp *manzanilla*, fr. dim. of *manzana* apple] (1630) : a poisonous tropical American tree (*Hippomane mancinella*) of the spurge family having a blistering milky juice and apple-shaped fruit

Man·chu \ˈman-(ˌ)chü, man-ˈ\ *n, pl* **Manchu** *or* **Manchus** (1697) **1** : a member of the native Mongolian race of Manchuria that is related to the Tungus, was orig. nomadic but conquered China and established a dynasty there in 1644, and has largely assimilated Chinese culture **2** : the Tungusic language of the Manchu people — **Manchu** *adj*

man·ci·ple \ˈman(t)-sə-pəl\ *n* [ME, fr. ML *mancipium* office of steward, fr. L, act of purchase, fr. *mancip-, manceps* purchaser — more at EMANCIPATE] (13c) : a steward or purveyor esp. for a college or monastery

-man·cy \ˌman(t)-sē\ *n comb form* [ME *-mancie*, fr. OF, fr. L *-mantia*, fr. Gk *-manteia*, fr. *manteia*, fr. *mantis* diviner, prophet — more at MANTIS] : divination ⟨oneiro*mancy*⟩

Man·dae·an \man-ˈdē-ən\ *n* [Mandaean *mandayyā* having knowledge] (ca. 1875) **1** : a member of a Gnostic sect of the lower Tigris and Euphrates **2** : a form of Aramaic found in documents written by Mandaeans — **Mandaean** *adj*

man·da·la \ˈmən-də-lə\ *n* [Skt *maṇḍala* circle] (1859) **1** : a Hindu or Buddhist graphic symbol of the universe; *specif* : a circle enclosing a square with a deity on each side **2** : a graphic and often symbolic pattern usu. in the form of a circle divided into four separate sections or bearing a multiple projection of an image — **man·dal·ic** \ˌmən-ˈdal-ik\ *adj*

man·da·mus \man-ˈdā-məs\ *n* [L, we enjoin, fr. *mandare*] (1535) : a writ issued by a superior court commanding the performance of a specified official act or duty

1**man·da·rin** \ˈman-d(ə-)rən\ *n* [Pg *mandarim*, fr. Malay *mĕntĕri*, fr. Skt *mantrin* counselor, fr. *mantra* counsel — more at MANTRA] (1589) **1 a** : a public official in the Chinese Empire of any of nine superior grades **b** (1) : a pedantic official (2) : BUREAUCRAT **c** : a person of position and influence esp. in intellectual or literary circles; *esp* : an elder and often traditionalist or reactionary member of such a circle **2** *cap* **a** : the primarily northern dialect of Chinese used by the court and the official classes of the Empire **b** : the chief dialect of China that is spoken in about four fifths of the country and has a standard variety centering about Peking **3** [F *mandarine*, fr. Sp *mandarina*, prob. fr. *mandarín* mandarin, fr. Pg *mandarim*; prob. fr. the color of a mandarin's robes] **a** : a small spiny Chinese orange tree (*Citrus reticulata*) with yellow to reddish orange loose-skinned fruits; *also* : a derivative of the Chinese mandarin developed in cultivation by artificial selection or hybridization **b** : the fruit of a mandarin — **man·da·rin·ic** \ˌman-də-ˈrin-ik\ *adj* — **man·da·rin·ism** \ˈman-d(ə-)rə-ˌniz-əm\ *n*

2**mandarin** *adj* (1604) **1** : of, relating to, or typical of a mandarin ⟨~ graces⟩ **2** : marked by polished ornate complexity of language ⟨~ prose⟩

man·da·rin·ate \ˈman-d(ə-)rə-ˌnāt\ *n* [prob. fr. F *mandarinat*, fr. *mandarin* mandarin, fr. Pg *mandarim*] (1727) **1** : the office or status of a mandarin **2** : a body of mandarins **3** : rule by mandarins

mandarin collar *n* (1947) : a narrow stand-up collar usu. open in front

mandarin orange *n* (1771) : MANDARIN 3

man·da·tary \ˈman-də-ˌter-ē\ *n, pl* **-tar·ies** (15c) : MANDATORY

1**man·date** \ˈman-ˌdāt\ *n* [MF & L; MF *mandat*, fr. L *mandatum*, fr. neut. of *mandatus*, pp. of *mandare* to entrust, enjoin, prob. irreg. fr. *manus* hand + *-dere* to put — more at MANUAL, DO] (1501) **1** : an authoritative command; *esp* : a formal order from a superior court or official to an inferior one **2** : an authorization to act given to a representative ⟨accepted the ~ of the people⟩ **3 a** : an order or commission granted by the League of Nations to a member nation for the establishment of a responsible government over a former German colony or other conquered territory **b** : a mandated territory

2**mandate** *vt* **man·dat·ed; man·dat·ing** (1919) **1** : to administer or assign (as a territory) under a mandate **2** : to make mandatory : ORDER; *also* : DIRECT, REQUIRE

man·da·tor \ˈman-ˌdāt-ər\ *n* (1681) : one that gives a mandate

1**man·da·to·ry** \ˈman-də-ˌtōr-ē, -ˌtȯr-\ *adj* (1576) **1** : containing or constituting a command : OBLIGATORY ⟨~ retirement age⟩ **2** : of, relating to, or holding a League of Nations mandate

2**mandatory** *n, pl* **-ries** (1661) : one given a mandate; *esp* : a nation holding a mandate from the League of Nations

man–day \ˈman-ˈdā\ *n* (ca. 1934) **1 :** the labor of one man in one normal working day **2 :** a unit consisting of a hypothetical average man-day

Man·de \ˈmän-ˌdā, män-ˈ\ *n* (1883) **1 :** MANDINGO **2 :** a branch of the Niger-Congo language family spoken in French West Africa, Sierra Leone, and Liberia

man·di·ble \ˈman-də-bəl\ *n* [MF, fr. LL *mandibula,* fr. L *mandere* to chew — more at MOUTH] (15c) **1 a :** JAW 1a; *esp* **:** a lower jaw consisting of a single bone or of completely fused bones **b :** the lower jaw with its investing soft parts **c :** either the upper or lower segment of the bill of a bird **2 :** any of various invertebrate mouthparts serving to hold or bite food materials; *esp* **:** either member of the anterior pair of mouth appendages of an arthropod often forming strong biting jaws — **man·dib·u·lar** \man-ˈdib-yə-lər\ *adj* — **man·dib·u·late** \-lət\ *adj*

Man·din·go \man-ˈdiŋ-(ˌ)gō\ *n, pl* **Mandingo** *or* **Mandingoes** *or* **Mandingos** (1623) **1 :** a member of a people of western Africa centering in the area of the upper Niger valley **2 :** the language of the Mandingo people

man·di·o·ca \ˌman-dē-ˈō-kə\ *var of* MANIOC

man·do·la \man-ˈdō-lə\ *n* [It, fr. F *mandore,* modif. of LL *pandura* 3-stringed lute — more at BANDORE] (1758) **:** a 16th and 17th century lute that is the ancestor of the smaller mandolin

man·do·lin \ˌman-də-ˈlin, ˈman-dᵊl-ən\ *also* **man·do·line** \ˌman-də-ˈlēn, ˈman-dᵊl-ən\ *n* [It *mandolino,* dim. of *mandola*] (1707) **1 :** a musical instrument of the lute family that has a usu. pear-shaped body and fretted neck and four to six pairs of strings **2** *usu* *mandoline* [F, fr. It *mandolino* mandolin] **:** a kitchen utensil with a blade for slicing and shredding — **man·do·lin·ist** \ˌman-də-ˈlin-əst\ *n*

man·drag·o·ra \man-ˈdrag-ə-rə\ *n* [ME, fr. OE, fr. L *mandragoras,* fr. Gk] (bef. 12c) **:** MANDRAKE 1

man·drake \ˈman-ˌdrāk\ *n* [ME, prob. alter. of *mandragora*] (14c) **1 a :** a Mediterranean herb (*Mandragora officinarum*) of the nightshade family with ovate leaves, whitish or purple flowers, and a large forked root traditionally credited with human attributes **b :** the root of a mandrake formerly used esp. to promote conception, as a cathartic, or as a narcotic and soporific **2 :** MAYAPPLE

man·drel *also* **man·dril** \ˈman-drəl\ *n* [prob. modif. of F *mandrin*] (1790) **1 a :** a usu. tapered or cylindrical axle, spindle, or arbor inserted into a hole in a piece of work to support it during machining **b :** a metal bar that serves as a core around which material (as metal) may be cast, molded, forged, bent, or otherwise shaped **2 :** the shaft and bearings on which a tool (as a circular saw) is mounted

man·drill \ˈman-drəl\ *n* [prob. fr. ¹*man* + *drill*] (1744) **:** a large fierce gregarious baboon (*Mandrillus sphinx*) of western Africa

mandrill

mane \ˈmān\ *n* [ME, fr. OE *manu;* akin to OHG *mana* mane, L *monile* necklace] (bef. 12c) **1 :** long and heavy hair growing about the neck of some mammals (as a horse or lion) **2 :** long heavy hair on a person's head — **maned** \ˈmānd\ *adj*

man–eat·er \ˈman-ˌēt-ər\ *n* (1600) **:** one that has or is thought to have an appetite for human flesh: as **a :** CANNIBAL **b :** MACKEREL SHARK; *esp* **:** WHITE SHARK **c :** a large feline (as a lion or tiger) that has acquired the habit of feeding on human flesh — **man–eat·ing** \-ˌēt-iŋ\ *adj*

man–eater shark *n* (1882) **:** MACKEREL SHARK; *esp* **:** WHITE SHARK

man–eating shark *n* (ca. 1890) **:** MAN-EATER SHARK

ma·nège *also* **ma·nege** \ma-ˈnezh, mə-, -ˈnāzh\ *n* [F *manège,* fr. It *maneggio* training of a horse — more at MANAGE] (1644) **1 :** a school for teaching horsemanship and for training horses **2 :** the art of horsemanship or of training horses **3 :** the movements or paces of a trained horse

ma·nes \ˈmän-ˌās, ˈmā-ˌnēz\ *n pl* [L] (14c) **1** *often cap* **:** the deified spirits of the ancient Roman dead honored with graveside sacrifices **2 :** the venerated or appeased spirit of a dead person

¹ma·neu·ver \mə-ˈn(y)ü-vər\ *n* [F *manœuvre,* fr. OF *maneuvre* work done by hand, fr. ML *manuopera,* fr. L *manu operare* to work by hand] (1758) **1 a :** a military or naval movement **b :** an armed forces training exercise; *esp* **:** an extended and large-scale training exercise involving military and naval units separately or in combination — often used in pl. **2 :** a procedure or method of working usu. involving expert physical movement **3 a :** evasive movement or shift of tactics **b :** an intended and controlled variation from a straight and level flight path in the operation of an airplane **4 a :** an action taken to gain a tactical end **b :** an adroit and clever management of affairs often using trickery and deception ***syn*** see TRICK

²maneuver *vb* **ma·neu·vered; ma·neu·ver·ing** \-ˈn(y)üv-(ə-)riŋ\ *vi* (1777) **1 a :** to perform a movement in military or naval tactics in order to secure an advantage **b :** to make a series of changes in direction and position for a specific purpose **2 :** to use stratagems **:** SCHEME ~ *vt* **1 :** to cause to execute tactical movements **2 :** to manage into or out of a position or condition **:** MANIPULATE **3 a :** to guide with adroitness and design **b :** to bring about or secure as a result of skillful management — **ma·neu·ver·abil·i·ty** \-ˌn(y)üv-(ə-)rə-ˈbil-ət-ē\ *n* — **ma·neu·ver·able** \-ˈn(y)üv-(ə-)rə-bəl\ *adj* — **ma·neu·ver·er** \-ˈn(y)ü-vər-ər\ *n*

man–for–man \ˌman-fər-ˈman\ *adj* (ca. 1949) **:** MAN-TO-MAN 2

man Fri·day \ˈman-ˈfrīd-ē\ *n* [*Friday,* native servant in *Robinson Crusoe* (1719), novel by Daniel Defoe] (1887) **:** an efficient and devoted aide or employee **:** a right-hand man

man·ful \ˈman-fəl\ *adj* (14c) **:** having or showing courage and resolution — **man·ful·ly** \-fə-lē\ *adv* — **man·ful·ness** *n*

mangan- *or* **mangano-** *comb form* [G *mangan,* fr. F *manganèse*] **:** manganese ⟨*manganous*⟩

man·ga·nate \ˈmaŋ-gə-ˌnāt\ *n* (1839) **1 :** a salt containing manganese in the anion MnO_4 **2 :** MANGANITE

man·ga·nese \ˈmaŋ-gə-ˌnēz, -ˌnēs\ *n* [F *manganèse,* fr. It *manganese* magnesia, manganese, fr. ML *magnesia*] (1783) **:** a grayish white usu. hard and brittle metallic element that resembles iron but is not magnetic — see ELEMENT table — **man·ga·ne·sian** \ˌmaŋ-gə-ˈnē-zhən, -shən\ *adj*

manganese dioxide *n* (1882) **:** a dark insoluble compound MnO_2 used esp. as an oxidizing agent, as a depolarizer of dry cells, and in making glass and ceramics

manganese spar *n* (1821) **:** RHODONITE

man·gan·ic \man-ˈgan-ik, maŋ-\ *adj* (ca. 1828) **:** of, relating to, or derived from manganese; *esp* **:** containing this element with a valence of three or six

man·ga·nite \ˈmaŋ-gə-ˌnīt\ *n* (1827) **1 :** an ore of manganese MnO(OH) that is a hydroxide of manganese usu. in brilliant gray crystals **2 :** any of various unstable salts made by reaction of manganese dioxide with a base

man·ga·nous \-nəs\ *adj* (1823) **:** of, relating to, or derived from manganese; *esp* **:** containing this element with a valence of two

mange \ˈmānj\ *n* [ME *manjewe,* fr. MF *mangene* itching, fr. *mangier* to eat] (15c) **:** any of various persistent contagious skin diseases marked esp. by eczematous inflammation and loss of hair that affect domestic animals or sometimes man; *esp* **:** one caused by a minute parasitic mite

man·gel \ˈmaŋ-gəl\ *n* [short for *mangel-wurzel*] (1856) **:** a large coarse yellow to reddish orange beet extensively grown as food for cattle

man·gel–wur·zel \-ˌwər-zəl\ *n* [G *mangold wurzel,* fr. *mangold* beet + *wurzel* root] (1767) **:** MANGEL

man·ger \ˈmān-jər\ *n* [ME *mangeour, manger,* fr. MF *maingeure,* fr. *mangier* to eat, fr. L *manducare* to chew, devour, fr. *manducus* glutton, fr. *mandere* to chew — more at MOUTH] (14c) **:** a trough or open box in a stable designed to hold feed or fodder for livestock

¹man·gle \ˈmaŋ-gəl\ *vt* **man·gled; man·gling** \-g(ə-)liŋ\ [ME *manglen,* fr. AF *mangler,* freq. of OF *maynier* to maim] (15c) **1 :** to injure with deep disorganizing wounds by cutting, tearing, or crushing ⟨people . . . *mangled* by sharks —V. G. Heiser⟩ **2 :** to spoil or injure in making or performing ***syn*** see MAIM — **man·gler** \-g(ə-)lər\ *n*

²mangle *n* [D *mangel,* fr. G, fr. MHG, dim. of *mange* mangonel, mangle, fr. L *manganum*] (1774) **:** a machine for ironing laundry by passing it between heated rollers

³mangle *vt* **man·gled; man·gling** \-g(ə-)liŋ\ (1775) **:** to press or smooth (as damp linen) with a mangle — **man·gler** \-g(ə-)lər\ *n*

man·go \ˈmaŋ-(ˌ)gō\ *n, pl* **mangoes** *also* **mangos** [Pg *manga,* fr. Tamil *māṅ-kāy*] (1582) **1 :** a yellowish red tropical fruit with a firm skin, hard central stone, and juicy aromatic somewhat pungent pulp; *also* **:** the evergreen tree (*Mangifera indica*) of the sumac family that bears this fruit **2 :** SWEET PEPPER

man·go·nel \ˈmaŋ-gə-ˌnel\ *n* [ME, fr. OF, prob. fr. ML *manganellus,* dim. of LL *manganum* philter, mangonel, fr. Gk *manganon;* akin to MIr *meng* deception] (13c) **:** a military engine formerly used to throw missiles

man·go·steen \ˈmaŋ-gə-ˌstēn\ *n* [Malay *mangustan*] (1598) **:** a dark reddish brown East Indian fruit with thick rind and juicy flesh having a flavor suggestive of both peach and pineapple; *also* **:** a tree (*Garcinia mangostana,* family Guttiferae) that bears this fruit

man·grove \ˈman-ˌgrōv, ˈmaŋ-\ *n* [prob. fr. Pg *mangue* mangrove (fr. Sp *mangle,* fr. Taino) + E *grove*] (1613) **1 :** any of a genus (*Rhizophora,* esp. *R. mangle*) of tropical maritime trees or shrubs that throw out many prop roots and form dense masses important in coastal land building **2 :** a tree (genus *Avicennia*) of the vervain family with growth habits like those of the true mangroves

mangy \ˈmān-jē\ *adj* **mang·i·er; -est** (1540) **1 :** affected with or resulting from mange **2 :** having many worn or bare spots **:** SEEDY, SHABBY — **man·gi·ness** \-jē-nəs\ *n*

man·han·dle \ˈman-ˌhan-dᵊl\ *vt* (1865) **1 :** to handle roughly **2 :** to move or manage by human force ⟨~ their car out of a ditch —*Scots Mag.*⟩

man·hat·tan \man-ˈhat-ᵊn, mən-\ *n, often cap* [*Manhattan,* borough of New York City] (1890) **:** a cocktail consisting of vermouth, whiskey, and sometimes a dash of bitters

man·hole \ˈman-ˌhōl\ *n* (1793) **:** a hole through which a man may go esp. to gain access to an underground or enclosed structure

man·hood \ˈman-ˌhu̇d\ *n* (13c) **1 :** the condition of being a human being **2 :** manly qualities **:** COURAGE **3 :** the condition of being an adult male as distinguished from a child or female **4 :** adult males **:** MEN

man–hour \ˈman-ˈau̇(-ə)r\ *n* (1912) **:** a unit of one hour's work by one man that is used esp. as a basis for cost accounting and wages

man·hunt \ˈman-ˌhənt\ *n* (1846) **:** an organized and usu. intensive hunt for a person and esp. for one charged with a crime

ma·nia \ˈmā-nē-ə, -nyə\ *n* [ME, fr. LL, fr. Gk, fr. *mainesthai* to be mad; akin to Gk *menos* spirit — more at MIND] (14c) **1 :** excitement manifested by mental and physical hyperactivity, disorganization of behavior, and elevation of mood; *specif* **:** the manic phase of manic-depressive psychosis **2 :** excessive or unreasonable enthusiasm **:** CRAZE ⟨had a ~ for saving things⟩

ma·ni·ac \ˈmā-nē-ˌak\ *n* [LL *maniacus* maniacal, fr. Gk *maniakos,* fr. *mania*] (1763) **1 :** MADMAN, LUNATIC **2 :** a person characterized by an inordinate or ungovernable enthusiasm for something

ma·ni·a·cal \mə-ˈnī-ə-kəl\ *also* **ma·ni·ac** \ˈmā-nē-ak\ *adj* (1678) **1 :** affected with or suggestive of madness **2 :** characterized by ungovernable excitement or frenzy **:** FRANTIC — **ma·ni·a·cal·ly** \mə-ˈnī-ə-k(ə-)lē\ *adv*

man·ic \ˈman-ik\ *adj* (1902) **:** affected with, relating to, or resembling mania — **manic** *n* — **man·i·cal·ly** \-i-k(ə-)lē\ *adv*

man·ic–de·pres·sive \ˌman-ik-di-ˈpres-iv\ *adj* (1902) **:** characterized either by mania or by psychotic depression or by alternating mania and depression — **manic–depressive** *n*

Man·i·chae·an *or* **Man·i·che·an** \ˌman-ə-ˈkē-ən\ *or* **Man·i·chee** \ˈman-ə-ˌkē\ *n* [LL *manichaeus,* fr. LGk *manichaios,* fr. *Manichaios* Manes †*ab* 276 A.D. Pers. founder of the sect] (1556) **1 :** a believer in a syncretistic religious dualism originating in Persia in the 3d century A.D. and teaching the release of the spirit from matter through asceticism **2 :** a be-

\ə\ abut \ᵊ\ kitten, F table \ər\ further \a\ ash \ā\ ace \ä\ cot, cart \au̇\ out \ch\ chin \e\ bet \ē\ easy \g\ go \i\ hit \ī\ ice \j\ job \ŋ\ sing \ō\ go \ȯ\ law \ȯi\ boy \th\ thin \t͟h\ the \ü\ loot \u̇\ foot \y\ yet \zh\ vision \à, k̲, ⁿ, œ, œ̄, ue, ue̅, ʸ\ *see* Guide to Pronunciation

liever in religious or philosophical dualism — **Manichaean** *adj* — **Man·i·chae·an·ism** \ˌman-ə-ˈkē-ə-ˌniz-əm\ *n* — **Man·i·chae·ism** \ˈman-ə-(ˌ)kē-ˌiz-əm\ *n*

ma·ni·cot·ti \ˌman-ə-ˈkät-ē\ *n, pl* **manicotti** [It, pl. of *manicotto,* lit., muff, fr. *manica* sleeve, fr. L, fr. *manus* hand] (1948) : tubular pasta shells that may be stuffed with ricotta or a meat mixture; *also* : a dish of stuffed manicotti usu. with tomato sauce

[1]man·i·cure \ˈman-ə-ˌkyu̇(ə)r\ *n* [F, fr. L *manus* hand + F *-icure* (as in *pédicure* pedicure) — more at MANUAL] (1880) **1** : MANICURIST **2** : a treatment for the care of the hands and fingernails

[2]manicure *vt* **-cured; -cur·ing** (1889) **1** : to do manicure work on; *esp* : to trim and polish the fingernails of **2** : to trim closely and evenly ⟨*manicured* lawns⟩

man·i·cur·ist \-ˌkyu̇r-əst\ *n* (1889) : a person who gives manicures

[1]man·i·fest \ˈman-ə-ˌfest\ *adj* [ME, fr. MF or L; MF *manifeste,* fr. L *manifestus,* lit., hit by the hand, fr. *manus* + *-festus* (akin to L *infestus* hostile) — more at DARE] (14c) **1** : readily perceived by the senses and esp. by the sight **2** : easily understood or recognized by the mind : OBVIOUS ***syn*** see EVIDENT — **man·i·fest·ly** *adv*

[2]manifest *vt* (14c) : to make evident or certain by showing or displaying ***syn*** see SHOW — **man·i·fest·er** *n*

[3]manifest *n* (1561) **1** : MANIFESTATION, INDICATION **2** : MANIFESTO **3** : a list of passengers or an invoice of cargo for a ship or plane

man·i·fes·tant \ˌman-ə-ˈfes-tənt\ *n* (1880) : one who makes or participates in a manifestation

man·i·fes·ta·tion \ˌman-ə-fə-ˈstā-shən, -ˌfes-ˈtā-\ *n* (15c) **1 a** : the act, process, or an instance of manifesting **b** : something that manifests or is manifest **c** : one of the forms in which an individual is manifested **d** : an occult phenomenon; *specif* : MATERIALIZATION **2** : a public demonstration of power and purpose

manifest destiny *n, often cap M&D* (1845) : a future event accepted as inevitable ⟨in the mid-19th century expansion to the Pacific was regarded as the *Manifest Destiny* of the United States⟩; *broadly* : an ostensibly benevolent or necessary policy of imperialistic expansion

[1]man·i·fes·to \ˌman-ə-ˈfes-(ˌ)tō\ *n, pl* **-tos** *or* **-toes** [It, denunciation, manifest, fr. *manifestare* to manifest, fr. L, fr. *manifestus*] (1620) : a public declaration of intentions, motives, or views

[2]manifesto *vi* (1748) : to issue a manifesto

[1]man·i·fold \ˈman-ə-ˌfōld\ *adj* [ME, fr. OE *manigfeald,* fr. *manig* many + *-feald* -fold] (bef. 12c) **1 a** : marked by diversity or variety **b** : MANY **2** : comprehending or uniting various features : MULTIFARIOUS **3** : rightfully so-called for many reasons ⟨a ~ liar⟩ **4** : consisting of or operating many of one kind combined ⟨a ~ bellpull⟩ — **man·i·fold·ly** \-ˌfōl-(d)lē\ *adv* — **man·i·fold·ness** \-ˌfōl(d)-nəs\ *n*

[2]manifold *adv* (bef. 12c) : many times : a great deal ⟨will increase your blessings ~⟩

[3]manifold *n* (13c) : something that is manifold: as **a** : a whole that unites or consists of many diverse elements ⟨the ~ of aspirations, passions, frustrations —Harry Slochower⟩ **b** : a pipe fitting with several lateral outlets for connecting one pipe with others; *also* : a fitting on an internal-combustion engine that receives the exhaust gases from several cylinders **c** : SET 21 **d** : a topological space such that every point has a neighborhood which is homeomorphic to the interior of a sphere in Euclidean space of the same number of dimensions

[4]manifold *vt* (ca. 1864) **1** : to make several or many copies of **2** : to make manifold : MULTIPLY ~ *vi* : to make several or many copies

man·i·kin *or* **man·ni·kin** \ˈman-i-kən\ *n* [D *mannekijn* little man, fr. MD, dim. of *man;* akin to OE *man*] (1535) **1** : MANNEQUIN **2** : a little man : DWARF, PYGMY

ma·nila *also* **ma·nil·la** \mə-ˈnil-ə\ *adj* (1834) **1** : made of manila paper **2** *cap* : made from Manila hemp — **manila** *n*

Manila hemp *n* [*Manila,* Philippine islands] (ca. 1847) : ABACA

manila paper *n, often cap M* (1873) : a strong and durable paper of a brownish or buff color and smooth finish made orig. from Manila hemp

ma·nille \mə-ˈnil\ *n* [modif. of Sp *malilla*] (1674) : the second highest trump in various card games (as ombre)

man in the street (1831) : an average or ordinary man

man·i·oc \ˈman-ē-ˌäk\ *n* [F *manioc* & Sp & Pg *mandioca,* of Tupian origin; akin to Tupi *manioca* cassava] (1568) : CASSAVA

man·i·ple \ˈman-ə-pəl\ *n* [ML *manipulus,* fr. L, handful, fr. *manus* hand + *-pulus* (akin to L *plēre* to fill); fr. its having been orig. held in the hand — more at MANUAL, FULL] (14c) **1** : a long narrow strip of silk worn at mass over the left arm by clerics of or above the order of subdeacon — see VESTMENT illustration **2** [L *manipulus,* fr. *manipulus* handful] : a subdivision of the Roman legion consisting of either 120 or 60 men

ma·nip·u·la·ble \mə-ˈnip-yə-lə-bəl\ *adj* (1881) : capable of being manipulated — **ma·nip·u·la·bil·i·ty** \-ˌnip-yə-lə-ˈbil-ət-ē\ *n*

ma·nip·u·lar \mə-ˈnip-yə-lər\ *adj* (1623) **1** : of or relating to the ancient Roman maniple **2** : of, relating to, or performed by manipulation : MANIPULATIVE

ma·nip·u·late \mə-ˈnip-yə-ˌlāt\ *vt* **-lat·ed; -lat·ing** [back-formation fr. *manipulation,* fr. F, fr. *manipule* handful, fr. L *manipulus*] (1831) **1** : to treat or operate with the hands or by mechanical means esp. in a skillful manner **2 a** : to manage or utilize skillfully **b** : to control or play upon by artful, unfair, or insidious means esp. to one's own advantage **3** : to change by artful or unfair means so as to serve one's purpose : DOCTOR ***syn*** see HANDLE — **ma·nip·u·lat·able** \-ˌlāt-ə-bəl\ *adj* — **ma·nip·u·la·tion** \-ˌnip-yə-ˈlā-shən\ *n* — **ma·nip·u·la·tive** \-ˈnip-yə-ˌlāt-iv, -lət-\ *adj* — **ma·nip·u·la·tive·ly** *adv* — **ma·nip·u·la·tive·ness** *n* — **ma·nip·u·la·tor** \-ˌlāt-ər\ *n* — **ma·nip·u·la·to·ry** \-lə-ˌtōr-ē, -ˌtȯr-\ *adj*

man·i·tou *or* **man·i·tu** \ˈman-ə-ˌtü\ *also* **man·i·to** \-ˌtō\ *n* [of Algonquian origin; akin to Ojibwa *manito* spirit, god] (1671) : a supernatural force that according to an Algonquian conception pervades the natural world

man jack \ˈman-ˌjak, -ˈjak\ *n* (1840) : individual man ⟨every *man jack*⟩

man·kind *n sing but sing or pl in constr* (bef. 12c) **1** \ˈman-ˈkīnd, -ˌkīnd\ : the human race : the totality of human beings **2** \-ˌkīnd\ : men as distinguished from women

[1]man·ly \ˈman-lē\ *adj* **man·li·er; -est** (13c) **1** : having qualities generally associated with a man : STRONG, VIRILE **2** : appropriate in character to a man ⟨~ sports⟩ — **man·li·ness** *n*

[2]manly *adv* (13c) : in a manly manner

man–made \ˈman-ˈmād\ *adj* (1718) : manufactured, created, or constructed by man; *specif* : SYNTHETIC ⟨~ fibers⟩

mann- *or* **manno-** *comb form* [ISV, fr. *manna*] : manna ⟨*mannose*⟩

man·na \ˈman-ə\ *n* [ME, fr. OE, fr. LL, fr. Gk, fr. Heb *mān*] (bef. 12c) **1 a** : food miraculously supplied to the Israelites in their journey through the wilderness **b** : divinely supplied spiritual nourishment **c** : a usu. sudden and unexpected source of gratification, pleasure, or gain **2 a** : the sweetish dried exudate of a European ash (esp. *Fraxinus ornus*) that contains mannitol and has been used as a laxative and demulcent **b** : a similar product excreted by a scale insect (*Trabutina mannipara*) feeding on the tamarisk

manna grass *n* (1597) : any of a genus (*Glyceria*) of chiefly No. American perennial paludal or aquatic grasses with 5- to 9- nerved lemmas

man·nan \ˈman-ˌan, -ən\ *n* [ISV *mannose* + [3]*-an*] (1895) : any of several polysaccharides that are polymers of mannose and occur esp. in plant cell walls

manned \ˈmand\ *adj* (1685) : carrying or performed by a man ⟨~ spaceflight⟩

man·ne·quin \ˈman-i-kən\ *n* [F, fr. D *mannekijn* little man — more at MANIKIN] (1730) **1** : an artist's, tailor's, or dressmaker's lay figure; *also* : a form representing the human figure used esp. for displaying clothes **2** : one employed to model clothing

man·ner \ˈman-ər\ *n* [ME *manere,* fr. OF *maniere* way of acting, fr. (assumed) VL *manuaria,* fr. L, fem. of *manuarius* of the hand, fr. *manus* hand — more at MANUAL] (12c) **1 a** : KIND, SORT ⟨what ~ of man is he⟩ **b** : KINDS, SORTS ⟨all ~ of problems⟩ **2 a** (1) : a characteristic or customary mode of acting : CUSTOM (2) : a mode of procedure or way of acting : FASHION (3) : method of artistic execution or mode of presentation : STYLE **b** *pl* : social conduct or rules of conduct as shown in the prevalent customs ⟨Victorian ~*s*⟩ **c** : characteristic or distinctive bearing, air, or deportment ⟨his poised gracious ~⟩ **d** *pl* (1) : habitual conduct or deportment : BEHAVIOR ⟨mind your ~*s*⟩ (2) : good manners **e** : a distinguished or stylish air ***syn*** see BEARING, METHOD — **man·ner·less** \-ləs\ *adj*

man·nered \ˈman-ərd\ *adj* (14c) **1** : having manners of a specified kind ⟨well-*mannered*⟩ **2 a** : having or displaying a particular manner **b** : having an artificial or stilted character ⟨passages . . . so ~ as to be unintelligible —R. G. G. Price⟩

man·ner·ism \ˈman-ə-ˌriz-əm\ *n* (1803) **1 a** : exaggerated or affected adherence to a particular style or manner : ARTIFICIALITY, PRECIOSITY ⟨refined almost to the point of ~ —Winthrop Sargeant⟩ **b** *often cap* : an art style in late 16th century Europe characterized by spatial incongruity and excessive elongation of the human figures **2** : a characteristic and often unconscious mode or peculiarity of action, bearing, or treatment ***syn*** see POSE — **man·ner·ist** \-rəst\ *n* — **man·ner·is·tic** \ˌman-ə-ˈris-tik\ *adj*

man·ner·ly \ˈman-ər-lē\ *adj* (1529) : showing good manners — **man·ner·li·ness** *n* — **mannerly** *adv*

man·nish \ˈman-ish\ *adj* (14c) **1** : resembling or suggesting a man rather than a woman **2** : generally associated with or characteristic of a man rather than a woman ⟨her ~ clothes⟩ — **man·nish·ly** *adv* — **man·nish·ness** *n*

man·nite \ˈman-ˌīt\ *n* [F, fr. *manna,* fr. LL] (1830) : MANNITOL

man·ni·tol \ˈman-ə-ˌtȯl, -ˌtōl\ *n* [ISV] (1879) : a slightly sweet crystalline alcohol $C_6H_{14}O_6$ found in many plants and used esp. as a diuretic and in testing kidney function

man·nose \ˈman-ˌōs, -ˌōz\ *n* [ISV] (1888) : an aldose $C_6H_{12}O_6$ whose dextrorotatory enantiomorph occurs esp. as a structural unit of mannans from which it can be recovered by hydrolysis

ma·no \ˈmän-(ˌ)ō\ *n, pl* **manos** [Sp, lit., hand, fr. L *manus* — more at MANUAL] (ca. 1892) : a stone used as the upper millstone for grinding foods (as Indian corn) by hand in a metate

ma·noeu·vre \mə-ˈn(y)ü-vər\ *chiefly Brit var of* MANEUVER

man of God (14c) : CLERGYMAN

man of letters (1645) **1** : SCHOLAR **2** : AUTHOR

man of straw (1624) : STRAW MAN

man of the house (ca. 1904) : the chief male in a household

man of the world (13c) : a practical or worldly-wise man of wide experience

man–of–war \ˌman-ə(v)-ˈwȯ(ə)r\ *n, pl* **men–of–war** \ˌmen-\ (15c) : a combatant warship of a recognized navy

ma·nom·e·ter \mə-ˈnäm-ət-ər\ *n* [F *manomètre,* fr. Gk *manos* sparse, loose, rare + F *-mètre* — more at MONK] (ca. 1730) **1** : an instrument (as a pressure gauge) for measuring the pressure of gases and vapors **2** : SPHYGMOMANOMETER — **mano·met·ric** \ˌman-ə-ˈme-trik\ *adj* — **mano·met·ri·cal·ly** \-tri-k(ə-)lē\ *adv* — **ma·nom·e·try** \mə-ˈnäm-ə-trē\ *n*

man on horseback [*Man on Horseback,* epithet applied to Georges E. J. M. Boulanger, who frequently appeared in public on horseback] (1860) **1** : a usu. military figure whose ambitions and popularity mark him as a potential dictator **2** : DICTATOR

man·or \ˈman-ər\ *n* [ME *maner,* fr. OF *manoir,* fr. *manoir* to sojourn, dwell, fr. L *manēre* — more at MANSION] (14c) **1 a** : the house or hall of an estate : MANSION **b** : a landed estate **2 a** : a unit of English rural territorial organization; *esp* : such a unit in the Middle Ages consisting of an estate under a lord enjoying a variety of rights over land and tenants including the right to hold court **b** : a tract of land in No. America occupied by tenants who pay a fixed rent in money or kind to the proprietor — **ma·no·ri·al** \mə-ˈnōr-ē-əl, -ˈnȯr-\ *adj* — **ma·no·ri·al·ism** \-ə-ˌliz-əm\ *n*

manor house *n* (1575) : the house of the lord of a manor

man–o'–war bird \ˌman-ə-ˈwȯr-\ *n* (1707) : FRIGATE BIRD

man·pack \ˈman-ˌpak\ *adj* (1965) : designed to be carried by one person

man power *n* (1862) **1** : power available from or supplied by the physical effort of man **2** *usu* **manpower** : the total supply of persons available and fitted for service (as in the armed forces or industry)

man·qué \mäⁿ-ˈkā\ *adj* [F, fr. pp. of *manquer* to lack, fail] (1778) : short of or frustrated in the fulfillment of one's aspirations or talents — used postpositively ⟨a poet ~⟩

man·rope \ˈman-ˌrōp\ *n* (1769) : a side rope (as to a ship's gangway or ladder) used as a handrail

man·sard \ˈman-ˌsärd, -sərd\ *n* [F *mansarde,* fr. François *Mansart* †1666 Fr. architect] (1734) : a roof having two slopes on all sides with the lower slope steeper than the upper one — see ROOF illustration — **man·sard·ed** \-əd\ *adj*

manse \'man(t)s\ *n* [ME *manss*, fr. ML *mansa, mansus, mansum*, fr. L *mansus*, pp. of *manēre*] (15c) **1** *archaic* : the dwelling of a householder **2** : the residence of a clergyman; *esp* : the house of a Presbyterian clergyman **3** : a large imposing residence

man·ser·vant \'man-₁sər-vənt\ *n, pl* **men·ser·vants** \'men-₁sər-vən(t)s\ (14c) : a male servant

-man·ship \-mən-₁ship\ *n suffix* [*sportsmanship*] : the art or practice of maneuvering to gain a tactical advantage ⟨games*manship*⟩

man·sion \'man-chən\ *n* [ME, fr. MF, fr. L *mansion-, mansio*, fr. *mansus*, pp. of *manēre* to remain, dwell; akin to Gk *menein* to remain] (14c) **1 a** *obs* : the act of remaining or dwelling : STAY **b** *archaic* : DWELLING, ABODE **2 a** (1) : the house of the lord of a manor (2) : a large imposing residence **b** : a separate apartment or lodging in a large structure **3 a** : HOUSE 3b **b** : one of the 28 parts into which the moon's monthly course through the heavens is divided

man–size \'man-₁sīz\ *or* **man–sized** \-₁sīzd\ *adj* (1913) **1** : suitable for or requiring a man ⟨a ~ job⟩ **2** : larger than others of its kind ⟨constructed a ~ model⟩

man·slaugh·ter \'man-₁slot-ər\ *n* (15c) : the unlawful killing of a human being without express or implied malice

man·slay·er \-₁slā-ər\ *n* (14c) : one who slays a man

man·sue·tude \'man(t)-swi-₁t(y)üd, man-'sü-ə-\ *n* [ME, fr. L *mansuetudo*, fr. *mansuetus* tame, mild, fr. pp. of *mansuescere* to tame, fr. *manus* hand + *suescere* to accustom; akin to Gk *ēthos* custom — more at MANUAL, ETHICAL] (14c) : the quality or state of being gentle : MEEKNESS, TAMENESS

man·ta \'mant-ə\ *n* [Sp, alter. of *manto* cloak, fr. L *mantus* short cloak; prob. akin to L *mantellum* mantle] (1697) **1** : a square piece of cloth or blanket used in southwestern U.S. and Latin America usu. as a cloak or shawl **2** [AmerSp, fr. Sp; fr. its shape] : DEVILFISH 1

man–tai·lored \'man-₁tā-lərd\ *adj* (1922) : made with the severe simplicity associated with men's coats and suits

manta ray *n* (1936) : DEVILFISH 1

man·teau \'man-₁tō, 'man-₁\ *n* [F, fr. OF *mantel*] (1671) : a loose cloak, coat, or robe

man·tel \'mant-ᵊl\ *n* [ME, fr. MF, fr. OF, mantle] (15c) **1 a** : a beam, stone, or arch serving as a lintel to support the masonry above a fireplace **b** : the finish around a fireplace **2** : a shelf above a fireplace

man·te·let \'mant-lət, -ᵊl-ət, ₁mant-ᵊl-'et\ *n* [ME, fr. MF *mantelet*, dim. of *mantel*] (14c) **1** : a very short cape or cloak **2** *or* **mant·let** \'mant-lət\ : a movable shelter formerly used by besiegers as a protection when attacking

man·tel·piece \'mant-ᵊl-₁pēs\ *n* (1686) **1** : a mantel with its side elements **2** : MANTEL 2

man·tel·shelf \-₁shelf\ *n* (ca. 1828) : MANTEL 2

man·tic \'mant-ik\ *adj* [Gk *mantikos*, fr. *mantis*] (1850) : of or relating to the faculty of divination : PROPHETIC

man·ti·core \'mant-i-₁kō(ə)r, -₁kó(ə)r\ *n* [ME, fr. L *mantichora*, fr. Gk *mantichōras*] (14c) : a legendary animal with the head of a man, the body of a lion, and the tail of a dragon or scorpion

man·tid \'mant-əd\ *n* [NL *Mantidae*, group name, fr. *Mantis*, genus name] (1895) : MANTIS

man·til·la \man-'tē-(y)ə, -'til-ə\ *n* [Sp, dim. of *manta*] (1717) **1** : a light scarf worn over the head and shoulders esp. by Spanish and Latin American women **2** : a short light cape or cloak

man·tis \'mant-əs\ *n, pl* **man·tis·es** *or* **man·tes** \'man-₁tēz\ [NL, fr. Gk, lit., diviner, prophet; akin to Gk *mainesthai* to be mad — more at MANIA] (1658) : an insect (order Manteodea and esp. genus *Mantis*) that feeds on other insects and clasps its prey in forelimbs held up as if in prayer

man·tis·sa \man-'tis-ə\ *n* [L *mantisa, mantissa* makeweight, fr. Etruscan] (ca. 1847) : the decimal part of a logarithm

¹man·tle \'mant-ᵊl\ *n* [ME *mantel*, fr. OF, fr. L *mantellum*] (13c) **1 a** : a loose sleeveless garment worn over other clothes : CLOAK **b** : a mantle regarded as a symbol of preeminence or authority ⟨invested his people with the ~ of universal champions of justice —Denis Goulet⟩ **2 a** : something that covers, enfolds, or envelops **b** (1) : a fold or lobe or pair of lobes of the body wall of a mollusk or brachiopod that lines the shell in shell-bearing forms and bears shell-secreting glands (2) : the soft external body wall that lines the test or shell of a tunicate or barnacle **c** : the outer wall and casing of a blast furnace above the hearth; *broadly* : an insulated support or casing in which something is heated **3** : the back, scapulars, and wings of a bird **4** : a lacy hood or sheath of some refractory material that gives light by incandescence when placed over a flame **5 a** : REGOLITH **b** : the part of the interior of a terrestrial planet and esp. the earth that lies beneath the lithosphere and above the central core **6** : MANTEL

²mantle *vb* **man·tled; man·tling** \'mant-liŋ, -ᵊl-iŋ\ *vt* (13c) : to cover with or as if with a mantle : CLOAK ⟨the encroaching jungle growth that *mantled* the building —Sanka Knox⟩ ~ *vi* **1** : to become covered with a coating **2** : to spread over a surface **3** : BLUSH ⟨her rich face *mantling* with emotion —Benjamin Disraeli⟩

man·tle·rock \'mant-ᵊl-₁räk\ *n* (1895) : REGOLITH

man–to–man \₁man-tə-'man\ *adj* (1925) **1** : characterized by frankness and honesty ⟨a ~ talk⟩ **2** : of, relating to, or being a system of defense (as in football or basketball) in which each defensive player guards a specified opponent

Man·toux test \₁man-₁tü-, ₁män-\ *n* [Charles *Mantoux* †1947 Fr. physician] (ca. 1923) : an intracutaneous test for hypersensitivity to tuberculin that indicates past or present infection with tubercle bacilli

man·tra \'man-trə, 'män-\ *n* [Skt, sacred counsel, formula, fr. *manyate* he thinks; akin to L *mens* mind — more at MIND] (1808) : a mystical formula of invocation or incantation (as in Hinduism) — **man·tric** \-trik\ *adj*

man·trap \'man-₁trap\ *n* (1788) : a trap for catching men : SNARE

man·tua \'manch-(ə-)wə, 'mant-ə-wə\ *n* [modif. of F *manteau* mantle] (1678) : a usu. loose-fitting gown worn esp. in the 17th and 18th centuries

Manu \'man-₁ü\ *n* [Skt] : the progenitor of the human race and giver of the religious laws of Manu according to Hindu mythology

¹man·u·al \'man-yə-(wə)l\ *adj* [ME *manuel*, fr. MF, fr. L *manualis*, fr. *manus* hand; akin to OE *mund* hand, Gk *marē*] (15c) **1 a** : of, relating to, or involving the hands ⟨~ dexterity⟩ **b** : worked or done by hand and not by machine ⟨a ~ choke⟩ ⟨~ computation⟩ ⟨~ indexing⟩ **2** : requiring or using physical skill and energy ⟨~ labor⟩ ⟨~ workers⟩ — **man·u·al·ly** \-ē\ *adv*

²manual *n* (15c) **1** : a book that is conveniently handled; *esp* : HANDBOOK **2** : the prescribed movements in the handling of a weapon or other military item during a drill or ceremony ⟨the ~ of arms⟩ **3 a** : a keyboard for the hands; *specif* : one of the several keyboards of an organ or harpsichord that controls a separate division of the instrument **b** : a device or apparatus intended for manual operation

manual alphabet *n* (ca. 1864) : an alphabet for the deaf in which the letters are represented by finger positions

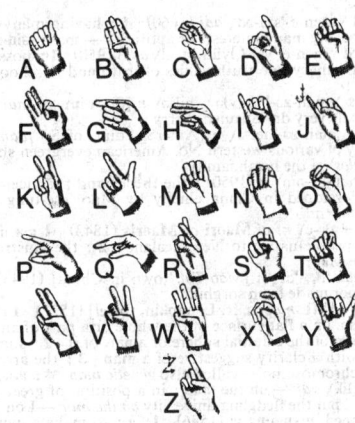

manual alphabet

manual training *n* (1880) : a course of training to develop skill in using the hands and to teach practical arts (as woodworking and metalworking)

ma·nu·bri·um \mə-'n(y)ü-brē-əm\ *n, pl* **-bria** \-brē-ə\ *also* **-bri·ums** [NL, fr. L, handle, fr. *manus*] (ca. 1848) : an anatomical process or part shaped like a handle: as **a** : the cephalic segment of the sternum of man and many other mammals **b** : the process that bears the mouth of a hydrozoan : HYPOSTOME

man·u·fac·to·ry \₁man-(y)ə-'fak-t(ə-)rē\ *n* (1647) : FACTORY 2a

¹man·u·fac·ture \₁man-(y)ə-'fak-chər\ *n* [MF, fr. L *manu factus*, lit., made by hand] (1567) **1** : something made from raw materials by hand or by machinery **2 a** : the process of making wares by hand or by machinery esp. when carried on systematically with division of labor **b** : a productive industry using mechanical power and machinery **3** : the act or process of producing something

²manufacture *vb* **-tured; -tur·ing** \-'fak-chə-riŋ, -'fak-shriŋ\ *vt* (1683) **1** : to make into a product suitable for use **2 a** : to make from raw materials by hand or by machinery **b** : to produce according to an organized plan and with division of labor **3** : INVENT, FABRICATE **4** : to produce as if by manufacturing : CREATE ⟨writers who ~ stories for television⟩ ~ *vi* : to engage in manufacture *syn* see MAKE — **man·ufacturing** *n*

man·u·fac·tur·er \₁man-(y)ə-'fak-chər-ər, -'fak-shrər\ *n* (1719) : one that manufactures; *esp* : an employer of workers in manufacturing

man·u·mis·sion \₁man-yə-'mish-ən\ *n* [ME, fr. MF, fr. L *manumission-, manumissio*, fr. *manumissus*, pp. of *manumittere*] (15c) : the act or process of manumitting; *esp* : formal emancipation from slavery

man·u·mit \₁man-yə-'mit\ *vt* **-mit·ted; -mit·ting** [ME *manumitten*, fr. MF *manumitter*, fr. L *manumittere*, fr. *manus* hand + *mittere* to let go, send] (15c) : to release from slavery *syn* see FREE

¹ma·nure \mə-'n(y)u̇(ə)r\ *vt* **ma·nured; ma·nur·ing** [ME *manouren*, fr. MF *manouvrer*, lit., to do work by hand, fr. L *manu operare* — more at MANEUVER] (15c) **1** *obs* : CULTIVATE **2** : to enrich (land) by the application of manure — **ma·nur·er** *n*

²manure *n* (1549) : material that fertilizes land; *esp* : refuse of stables and barnyards consisting of livestock excreta with or without litter — **ma·nu·ri·al** \-'n(y)u̇r-ē-əl\ *adj*

ma·nus \'mā-nəs, 'mä-\ *n, pl* **ma·nus** \-nəs, -₁nüs\ [NL, fr. L, hand] (ca. 1823) : the distal segment of the vertebrate forelimb including the carpus and forefoot or hand

¹manu·script \'man-yə-₁skript\ *adj* [L *manu scriptus*] (1597) : written by hand or typed ⟨~ letters⟩

²manuscript *n* (1600) **1** : a written or typewritten composition or document as distinguished from a printed copy **2** : writing as opposed to print

---

\ə\ abut \ᵊ\ kitten, F table \ər\ further \a\ ash \ā\ ace \ä\ cot, cart \au̇\ out \ch\ chin \e\ bet \ē\ easy \g\ go \i\ hit \ī\ ice \j\ job \ŋ\ sing \ō\ go \ȯ\ law \ȯi\ boy \th\ thin \t͟h\ the \ü\ loot \u̇\ foot \y\ yet \zh\ vision \ə̇, k̲, ⁿ, œ, œ̄, ᵫ, ᵭᵉ, ᶢ\ see Guide to Pronunciation

(mantis illustration, captioned "mantis", appears in left column)

[1]**Manx** \'maŋ(k)s\ *adj* [alter. of earlier *Maniske*, fr. (assumed) ON *manskr*, fr. *Mana* Isle of Man] (1572) : of, relating to, or characteristic of the Isle of Man, its people, or the Manx language

[2]**Manx** *n* (1672) **1** : the Celtic language of the Manx people almost completely displaced by English **2** *pl in constr* : the people of the Isle of Man

Manx cat *n* (1859) : a short-haired domestic cat with no external tail — called also *Manx;* see CAT illustration

[1]**many** \'men-ē\ *adj* **more** \'mō(ə)r, 'mȯ(ə)r\; **most** \'mōst\ [ME, fr. OE *manig;* akin to OHG *manag* many, OSlav *mŭnogŭ* much] (bef. 12c) **1** : consisting of or amounting to a large but indefinite number ⟨worked for ~ years⟩ **2** : being one of a large but indefinite number ⟨~ a man⟩ ⟨~ another student⟩ — **as many** : the same in number ⟨saw three plays in *as many* days⟩

[2]**many** *pron, pl in constr* (bef. 12c) : a large number of persons or things ⟨~ are called⟩

[3]**many** *n, pl in constr* (12c) **1** : a large but indefinite number ⟨a good ~ of them⟩ **2** : the great majority of people ⟨the ~⟩

man–year \'man-'yi(ə)r\ *n* (1916) : the work of one man in a year composed of a standard number of working days

many·fold \ˌmen-ē-'fōld\ *adv* (14c) : by many times ⟨aid to research has increased ~⟩

many–sid·ed \ˌmen-ē-'sīd-əd\ *adj* (1660) **1** : having many sides or aspects **2** : having many interests or aptitudes — **many–sid·ed·ness** *n*

many–val·ued \ˌmen-ē-'val-(ˌ)yüd, -yəd\ *adj* (1950) **1** : possessing more than the customary two truth-values of truth and falsehood **2** : MULTIPLE-VALUED

Man·za·nil·la \ˌman-zə-'nē-(y)ə, -'nil-ə\ *n* [Sp, dim. of *manzana* apple] (1843) : a pale very dry Spanish sherry

man·za·ni·ta \ˌman-zə-'nēt-ə\ *n* [AmerSp, dim. of Sp *manzana* apple] (1846) : any of various western No. American evergreen shrubs (genus *Arctostaphylos*) of the heath family

Mao·ism \'mau̇-ˌiz-əm\ *n* (1950) : the theory and practice of Marxism=Leninism developed in China chiefly by Mao Tse-tung — **Mao·ist** \'mau̇-əst\ *n or adj*

Mao·ri \'mau̇(ə)r-ē\ *n, pl* **Maori** *or* **Maoris** (1843) **1** : a member of a Polynesian people native to New Zealand **2** : the Austronesian language of the Maori

mao–tai \'mau̇-'tī, -'dī\ *n* [*Mao-Tai*, town in China] (1943) : a strong Chinese liquor made from sorghum

[1]**map** \'map\ *n* [ML *mappa*, fr. L, napkin, towel] (1527) **1 a** : a representation usu. on a flat surface of the whole or a part of an area **b** : a representation of the celestial sphere or a part of it **2** : something that represents with a clarity suggestive of a map **3** : the arrangement of genes on a chromosome — called also *genetic map* **4** : FUNCTION 5a — **map·like** \-ˌlīk\ *adj* — **on the map** : in a position of great prominence or fame ⟨had put the fledgling university *on the map* —Lon Tinkle⟩

[2]**map** *vb* **mapped; map·ping** *vt* (1586) **1 a** : to make a map of ⟨~ the surface of the moon⟩ **b** : to delineate as if on a map ⟨sorrow was *mapped* on her face⟩ **c** : to make a survey of for the purpose of making a map **d** : to assign (a set or element) in a mathematical correspondence ⟨~ a set onto itself⟩ **2** : to plan in detail — often used with *out* ⟨~ out a program⟩ ~ *vi, of a gene* : to be located ⟨a repressor ~*s* near the corresponding structural gene⟩ — **map·pa·ble** \'map-ə-bəl\ *adj* — **map·per** *n*

ma·ple \'mā-pəl\ *n* [ME, fr. OE *mapul-;* akin to ON *möpurr* maple] (bef. 12c) : any of a genus (*Acer* of the family Aceraceae, the maple family) of trees or shrubs with opposite leaves and a fruit of two united samaras; *also* : the hard light-colored close-grained wood of a maple used esp. for flooring and furniture

maple sugar *n* (1720) : sugar made by boiling maple syrup

maple syrup *n* (1849) : syrup made by concentrating the sap of maple trees and esp. the sugar maple

map·mak·er \'map-ˌmā-kər\ *n* (1775) : CARTOGRAPHER — **map·mak·ing** \-kiŋ\ *n*

map·ping \'map-iŋ\ *n* (ca. 1775) **1** : the act or process of making a map **2** : FUNCTION 5a ⟨a one-to-one continuous ~⟩

ma·quette \ma-'ket\ *n* [F, fr. It *macchietta* sketch, dim. of *macchia*, deriv. of L *macula* spot] (1903) : a usu. small preliminary model (as of a sculpture or a building)

ma·quil·lage \ˌmak-ē-'(y)äzh\ *n* [F] (1892) : MAKEUP 3

ma·quis \ma-'kē, mä-\ *n, pl* **ma·quis** \-'kē(z)\ [F, fr. It *macchie*, pl. of *macchia* thicket, sketch, spot] (1858) **1** : thick scrubby underbrush of Mediterranean shores and esp. of the island of Corsica; *also* : an area of such underbrush **2** *often cap* **a** : a guerrilla fighter in the French underground during World War II **b** : a band of maquis

[1]**mar** \'mär\ *vt* **marred; mar·ring** [ME *marren*, fr. OE *mierran* to obstruct, waste; akin to OHG *merren* to obstruct] (bef. 12c) **1** : to detract from the perfection or wholeness of : SPOIL **2** *archaic* **a** : to inflict serious bodily harm on **b** : DESTROY ***syn*** see INJURE

[2]**mar** *n* (14c) : something that mars : BLEMISH

mar·a·bou *also* **mar·a·bout** \'mar-ə-ˌbü\ *n* [F *marabout*, lit., marabout] (1823) **1 a** : a soft feathery fluffy material prepared from the long coverts of marabous or usu. from turkey feathers and used esp. for trimming women's hats or clothes **b** : a large African stork (*Leptoptilos crumeniferus*) that has a distensible pouch of pink skin at the front of the neck and feeds esp. on refuse and carrion — called also *marabou stork* **2 a** : a thrown silk usu. dyed in the gum **b** : a fabric made of this silk

mar·a·bout \'mar-ə-bü\ *n, often cap* [F, fr. Pg *marabuto*, fr. Ar *murābiṭ*] (1621) : a dervish in Muslim Africa believed to have supernatural power

ma·ra·ca \mə-'räk-ə, -'rak-\ *n* [Pg *maracá*] (ca. 1824) : a rattle usu. made from a gourd that is used as a percussion instrument

mar·ag·ing steel \ˌmär-ˌā-jiŋ-\ *n* [*mar*tensite + *aging*] (1962) : a strong tough low-carbon martensitic steel which contains up to 25 percent nickel and in which hardening precipitates are formed by aging

mar·a·schi·no \ˌmar-ə-'skē-(ˌ)nō, -'shē-\ *n, pl* **-nos** *often cap* [It, fr. *marasca* bitter wild cherry, alter. of *amarasca*, fr. *amaro* bitter — more at AMARETTO] (1791) **1** : a sweet liqueur distilled from the fermented juice of a bitter wild cherry **2** : a usu. large cherry preserved in true or imitation maraschino

ma·ras·mus \mə-'raz-məs\ *n* [LL, fr. Gk *marasmos*, fr. *marainein* to waste away — more at SMART] (1656) : progressive emaciation esp. in children undernourished because of a diet deficient in calories and proteins — **ma·ras·mic** \-'raz-mik\ *adj*

Ma·ra·tha \mə-'rät-ə\ *n* [Marathi *Marāṭhā* & Hindi *Marhaṭṭā*, fr. Skt *Mahārāṣṭra* Maharashtra] (1748) : a member of a people of the south central part of the subcontinent of India

Ma·ra·thi \mə-'rät-ē\ *n* [Marathi *marāṭhī*] (1673) : the chief Indic language of the state of Maharashtra in India

mar·a·thon \'mar-ə-ˌthän\ *n* [*Marathon*, Greece, site of a victory of Greeks over Persians in 490 B.C., the news of which was carried to Athens by a long-distance runner] (1896) **1** : a long-distance race: **a** : a footrace run on an open course usu. of 26 miles 385 yards (42.2 kilometers) **b** : a race other than a footrace marked esp. by great length **2 a** : an endurance contest ⟨a dance ~⟩ **b** : something (as an event or activity) characterized by great length or concentrated effort

mar·a·thon·er \-ˌthän-ər\ *n* (1923) : one (as a runner) who takes part in a marathon — **mar·a·thon·ing** \-iŋ\ *n*

ma·raud \mə-'rȯd\ *vb* [F *marauder*] *vi* (1711) : to roam about and raid in search of plunder ~ *vt* : RAID, PILLAGE — **ma·raud·er** *n*

[1]**mar·ble** \'mär-bəl\ *n* [ME, fr. OF *marbre*, fr. L *marmor*, fr. Gk *marmaros*] (13c) **1 a** : limestone that is more or less crystallized by metamorphism, that ranges from granular to compact in texture, that is capable of taking a high polish, and that is used esp. in architecture and sculpture **b** : something (as a piece of sculpture) composed of or made from marble **c** : something suggesting marble (as in hardness, coldness, or smoothness) ⟨she has a heart of ~⟩ **2 a** : a little ball made of a hard substance (as glass) and used in various games **b** *pl but sing in constr* : any of several games played with these little balls with the object being to hit a mark or hole, hit another player's marble, or knock as many marbles as possible out of a ring **3** : MARBLING **4** *pl* : elements of common sense; *esp* : SANITY ⟨persons who are born without all their ~*s* —Arthur Miller⟩

[2]**marble** *adj* (13c) : resembling, composed of, or suggestive of marble ⟨~ floors⟩

[3]**marble** *vt* **mar·bled; mar·bling** \-b(ə-)liŋ\ (1683) : to give a veined or mottled appearance to ⟨~ the edges of a book⟩

marble cake *n* (1871) : a cake made with light and dark batter so as to have a mottled appearance

mar·bled \'mär-bəld\ *adj* (1599) **1** [[1]*marble*] **a** : done in or covered with marble **b** : marked by an extensive use of marble as an architectural or decorative feature ⟨ancient ~ cities⟩ **2** [[3]*marble*] : marked by an intermixture of fat and lean ⟨a well-*marbled* cut of beef⟩

mar·ble·ize \'mär-bə-ˌlīz\ *vt* **-ized; -iz·ing** (ca. 1864) : MARBLE

mar·bling \-b(ə-)liŋ\ *n* (1727) **1** : coloration or markings resembling or suggestive of marble **2** : an intermixture of fat and lean in a cut of meat esp. when evenly distributed

mar·bly \-b(ə-)lē\ *adj* (15c) : resembling or suggestive of marble

marc \'märk\ *n* [F, fr. MF, fr. *marchier* to trample, march] (1601) **1** : the residue remaining after a fruit has been pressed; *broadly* : the organic residue from an extraction process ⟨the protein-rich cottonseed ~⟩ **2** : brandy made from the residue of wine grapes after pressing

mar·ca·site \'mär-kə-ˌsīt, -ˌzīt; ˌmär-kə-'zēt\ *n* [ME *marchasite*, fr. ML *marcasita*] (15c) **1 a** : crystallized iron pyrites **b** : a mineral of the same composition and appearance as iron pyrites but of different crystalline organization and lower specific gravity **2** : a piece of marcasite used for ornaments — **mar·ca·sit·i·cal** \ˌmär-kə-'sit-i-kəl, -'zit-\ *adj*

mar·ca·to \mär-'kät-(ˌ)ō\ *adv or adj* [It, pp. of *marcare* to mark, accent, of Gmc origin; akin to OHG *marcōn* to determine the boundaries — more at MARK] (ca. 1840) : with strong accentuation — used as a direction in music

[1]**mar·cel** \mär-'sel\ *n* [*Marcel* Grateau †1936 Fr. hairdresser] (1895) : a deep soft wave made in the hair by the use of a heated curling iron

[2]**marcel** *vb* **mar·celled; mar·cel·ling** *vt* (1906) : to make a marcel in ~ *vi* : to make a marcel

[1]**march** \'märch\ *n* [ME *marche*, fr. OF, of Gmc origin; akin to OHG *marha* boundary — more at MARK] (13c) : a border region : FRONTIER; *esp* : a district orig. set up to defend a boundary — usu. used in pl. ⟨the Welsh ~*es*⟩

[2]**march** *vi* (14c) : to have common borders or frontiers ⟨a region that ~*es* with Canada in the north and the Pacific in the west⟩

[3]**march** \'märch, *imperatively often* 'härch *in the military*\ *vb* [MF *marchier* to trample, march, fr. OF, to trample, prob. of Gmc origin; akin to OHG *marcōn* to mark] *vi* (15c) **1** : to move along steadily usu. with a rhythmic stride and in step with others **2 a** : to move in a direct purposeful manner : PROCEED **b** : to make steady progress : ADVANCE ⟨time ~*es* on⟩ **3** : to stand in orderly array suggestive of marching ⟨pine trees ~*ing* up the mountainside⟩ ~ *vt* **1** : to cause to march ⟨~*ed* the children off to bed⟩ **2** : to cover by marching : TRAVERSE ⟨~*ed* 10 miles⟩

[4]**march** \'märch\ *n* (15c) **1 a** (1) : the action of marching (2) : the distance covered within a specific period of time by marching (3) : a regular measured stride or rhythmic step used in marching **b** : forward movement : PROGRESS ⟨the ~ of a movie toward the climax⟩ **2** : a musical composition that is usu. in duple or quadruple time with a strongly accentuated beat and that is designed or suitable to accompany marching **3** : an organized procession of demonstrators who are supporting or protesting something — **march·like** \-ˌlīk\ *adj* — **on the march** : moving steadily : ADVANCING

March \'märch\ *n* [ME, fr. OF, fr. L *martius*, fr. *martius* of Mars, fr. *Mart-, Mars*] (bef. 12c) : the 3d month of the Gregorian calendar

mär·chen \'me(ə)r-kən\ *n, pl* **märchen** [G] (1871) : TALE; *esp* : FOLKTALE

[1]**march·er** \'mär-chər\ *n* (14c) : one who inhabits a border region

[2]**marcher** *n* (1611) : one that marches; *esp* : one that marches for a specific cause ⟨a peace ~⟩

mar·che·sa \mär-'kā-zə\ *n, pl* **-se** \-(ˌ)zā\ [It, fem. of *marchese*] (1797) : an Italian woman holding the rank of a marchese : MARCHIONESS

mar·che·se \-(ˌ)zā\ *n, pl* **-si** \-(ˌ)zē\ [It, fr. ML *marcensis*, fr. *marca* border region, of Gmc origin; akin to OHG *marha*] (1517) : an Italian nobleman next in rank above a count : MARQUIS

mar·chio·ness \'mär-sh(ə-)nəs\ *n* [ML *marchionissa*, fr. *marchion-, marchio* marquess, fr. *marca*] (16c) **1** : the wife or widow of a marquess **2** : a woman who holds the rank of marquess in her own right

march·pane \'märch-ˌpān\ *n* [It *marzapane*] (15c) : MARZIPAN

march–past \'märch-ˌpast\ *n* (ca. 1881) : a filing by : PROCESSION

Mar·cion·ism \'mär-shə-,niz-əm, -s(h)ē-ə-\ *n* [*Marcion* 2d cent. A.D. Christian Gnostic] (1882) **:** the doctrinal system of a sect of the 2d and 3d centuries A.D. accepting some parts of the New Testament but denying Christ's corporality and humanity and condemning the Creator God of the Old Testament — **Mar·cion·ite** \-,nīt\ *n*

Mar·co·ni \mär-'kō-nē\ *adj* [prob. fr. the resemblance of the complex arrangement of stays and struts to that used to support the antennae used in wireless telegraphy, invented by Guglielmo Marconi] (1912) **:** of, relating to, or marked by a Bermuda rig

mar·co·ni·gram \mär-'kō-nē-,gram\ *n* [Guglielmo *Marconi*] (1902) **:** RADIOGRAM

Marconi rig *n* (1916) **:** BERMUDA RIG

Mar·di Gras \'märd-ē-,grä, *in New Orleans commonly* -,grȯ\ *n* [F, lit., fat Tuesday] (1699) **1 a :** Shrove Tuesday often observed (as in New Orleans) with parades and festivities **b :** a carnival period climaxing on Shrove Tuesday **2 :** a festive occasion resembling a pre-Lenten Mardi Gras

[1]**mare** *n* [ME, fr. OE; akin to OHG *mara* incubus, Croatian *mora*] *obs* (bef. 12c) **:** an evil preternatural being causing nightmares

[2]**mare** \'ma(ə)r, 'me(ə)r\ *n* [ME, fr. OE *mere;* akin to OHG *merha* mare, OE *mearh* horse, W *march*] (bef. 12c) **:** a female horse or other equine animal esp. when fully mature or of breeding age

[3]**ma·re** \'mär-(,)ā\ *n, pl* **ma·ria** \'mär-ē-ə\ [NL, fr. L, sea — more at MARINE] (1765) **:** one of several dark areas of considerable extent on the surface of the moon or Mars

ma·re clau·sum \,mär-(,)ā-'klau̇-səm, -'klȯ-\ *n* [NL, lit., closed sea] (ca. 1652) **:** a navigable body of water (as a sea) that is under the jurisdiction of one nation and is closed to other nations

Mar·ek's disease \'mar-iks-, 'mer-\ *n* [*J. Marek* †1952 Ger. veterinarian] (1947) **:** a cancerous disease of poultry that is characterized esp. by proliferation of lymphoid cells and is caused by a virus resembling a herpesvirus

ma·re li·be·rum \'mär-(,)ā-'lē-bə-,ru̇m\ *n* [NL, lit., free sea] (1652) **1 :** a navigable body of water (as a sea) that is open to all nations **2 :** FREEDOM OF THE SEAS

ma·ren·go \mə-'reŋ-(,)gō\ *adj, often cap* [F, fr. *Marengo,* village in northwest Italy] (ca. 1924) **:** of, consisting of, or served with a sauce of mushrooms, tomatoes, olives, oil, and wine ⟨veal ~⟩

ma·re no·strum \,mär-(,)ā-'nō-strəm\ *n* [NL, lit., our sea] (1941) **:** a navigable body of water (as a sea) that belongs to a single nation or is mutually shared by two or more nations

mare's nest *n, pl* **mare's nests** *or* **mares' nests** (1619) **1 :** a false discovery, illusion, or deliberate hoax **2 :** a place, condition, or situation of great disorder or confusion ⟨a *mare's nest* of spurious ambiguities to bewilder the simpleminded —J. H. Sledd⟩

mare's tail *n, pl* **mare's tails** *or* **mares' tails** (ca. 1762) **1 a :** a common aquatic plant (*Hippuris vulgaris*) with elongated shoots clothed with dense whorls of subulate leaves **b :** HORSEWEED 1 **2 :** a cirrus cloud that has a long slender flowing appearance

mar·ga·rine \'märj-(ə-)rən, -ə-,rēn\ *n* [F, fr. Gk *margaron* pearl] (1873) **:** a food product made usu. from vegetable oils churned with ripened skim milk to a smooth emulsion, often fortified with vitamins A and D, and used as a substitute for butter

mar·ga·ri·ta \,mär-gə-'rēt-ə\ *n* [MexSp, prob. fr. the name *Margarita* Margaret] (1963) **:** a cocktail consisting of tequila, lime or lemon juice, and an orange-flavored liqueur

mar·ga·rite \'mär-gə-,rīt\ *n* [ME, fr. MF, fr. L *margarita,* fr. Gk *margaritēs,* fr. *margaron*] *archaic* (13c) **:** PEARL

mar·gay \'mär-,gā, mär-'\ *n* [F, fr. Tupi *maracaja*] (1781) **:** a small American spotted cat (*Felis tigrina*) resembling the ocelot and ranging from southernmost Texas to Brazil

marge \'märj\ *n* [MF, fr. L *margo*] *archaic* (1551) **:** MARGIN

mar·gent \'mär-jənt\ *n, archaic* (15c) **:** MARGIN

[1]**mar·gin** \'mär-jən\ *n* [ME, fr. L *margin-, margo* border — more at MARK] (14c) **1 :** the part of a page or sheet outside the main body of printed or written matter **2 :** the outside limit and adjoining surface of something **:** EDGE ⟨at the ~ of the woods⟩ **3 a :** a spare amount or measure or degree allowed or given for contingencies or special situations ⟨left no ~ for error in his calculations⟩ **b (1) :** a bare minimum below which or an extreme limit beyond which something becomes impossible or is no longer desirable ⟨a joke that was on the ~ of good taste⟩ **(2) :** the limit below which economic activity cannot be continued under normal conditions **4 a :** the difference which exists between net sales and the cost of merchandise sold and from which expenses are usu. met or profit derived **b :** the excess market value of collateral over the face of a loan **c (1) :** cash or collateral that is deposited by a client with a commodity or securities broker to protect the broker from loss on a contract **(2) :** the client's equity in securities bought with the aid of credit obtained specif. (as from a broker) for that purpose **d :** a range about a specified figure within which a purchase is to be made **5 :** measure or degree of difference ⟨the bill passed by a one-vote ~⟩ — **mar·gined** \-jənd\ *adj*

[2]**margin** *vt* (1715) **1 a :** to provide with an edging or border **b :** to form a margin to **:** BORDER **2 a :** to add margin to ⟨~ up an account in a falling market⟩ **b (1) :** to use as margin ⟨~ bonds to buy stock⟩ **(2) :** to provide margin for ⟨~ a transaction⟩ **c :** to buy (securities) on margin

mar·gin·al \'märj-nəl, -ən-ᵊl\ *adj* [ML *marginalis,* fr. L *margin-, margo*] (1573) **1 :** written or printed in the margin of a page or sheet ⟨~ notes⟩ **2 a :** of, relating to, or situated at a margin or border ⟨regards violence as a ~ rather than a central problem⟩ **b (1) :** occupying the borderland of a relatively stable territorial or cultural area ⟨~ tribes⟩ **(2) :** characterized by the incorporation of habits and values from two divergent cultures and by incomplete assimilation in either ⟨the ~ cultural habits of new immigrant groups⟩ **3 :** located at the fringe of consciousness ⟨~ sensations⟩ **4 a :** close to the lower limit of qualification, acceptability, or function ⟨a semiliterate person of ~ ability⟩ **b (1) :** having a character or capacity fitted to yield a supply of goods which when marketed at existing price levels will barely cover the cost of production ⟨~ land⟩ **(2) :** of, relating to, or derived from goods produced and marketed with such result ⟨~ profits⟩ **5 :** relating to or being a function of a random variable that is obtained from a function of several random variables by integrating or summing over all possible values of the other variables ⟨a ~ probability function⟩ — **mar·gin·al·i·ty** \,mär-jə-'nal-ət-ē\ *n* — **mar·gin·al·ly** \'märj-nə-lē, -ən-ᵊl-ē\ *adv*

mar·gi·na·lia \,mär-jə-'nā-lē-ə\ *n pl* [NL, fr. ML, neut. pl. of *marginalis*] (1832) **1 :** marginal notes (as in a book) **2 :** nonessential items ⟨the meat and ~ of American politics —*Saturday Rev.*⟩

mar·gin·al·ize \'märj-nəl-,īz, -ən-ᵊl-\ *vt* **-ized; -iz·ing** (1970) **:** to relegate to an unimportant position within a society or group — **mar·gin·al·iza·tion** \,märj-nəl-ə-'zā-shən, -ən-ᵊl-ə-\ *n*

marginal utility *n* (ca. 1890) **:** the amount of additional utility provided by an additional unit of an economic good or service

mar·gin·ate \'mär-jə-,nāt\ *vt* **-at·ed; -at·ing** (1623) **:** MARGIN 1, 2a — **mar·gin·ation** \,mär-jə-'nā-shən\ *n*

mar·gin·at·ed \-,nāt-əd\ *adj* (ca. 1727) **:** having a distinct margin

mar·gra·vate \'mär-grə-,vāt\ *or* **mar·gra·vi·ate** \mär-'grā-vē-ət, -,āt\ *n* (1802) **:** the territory of a margrave

mar·grave \'mär-,grāv\ *n* [D *markgraaf,* fr. MD *marcgrave*] (1551) **1 :** the military governor esp. of a German border province **2 :** a member of the German nobility corresponding in rank to a British marquess — **mar·gra·vi·al** \mär-'grā-vē-əl\ *adj*

mar·gra·vine \'mär-grə-,vēn, ,mär-grə-'\ *n* (1692) **:** the wife of a margrave

mar·gue·rite \,mär-g(y)ə-'rēt\ *n* [F, fr. MF *margarite* pearl, daisy — more at MARGARITE] (ca. 1866) **1 :** DAISY 1b **2 :** any of various single-flowered chrysanthemums; *esp* **:** a chrysanthemum (*Chrysanthemum frutescens*) of the Canary islands

maria *pl of* MARE

ma·ri·a·chi \,mär-ē-'äch-ē\ *n* [MexSp, perh. modif. of F *mariage* marriage] (1927) **1 :** a Mexican street band; *also* **:** a musician belonging to such a band **2 :** the music performed by a mariachi

Mar·i·an \'mer-ē-ən, 'mar-ē-, 'mā-rē-\ *adj* (1608) **1 :** of or relating to Mary Tudor or her reign (1553-58) **2 :** of or relating to the Virgin Mary

Mar·i·an·ist \-ə-nəst\ *n* (ca. 1899) **:** a member of the Roman Catholic Society of Mary of Paris founded by William Joseph Chaminade in France in 1817 and devoted esp. to education

Ma·ria The·re·sa dollar \mə-,rē-ə-tə-,rā-sə-, -,rā-zə-\ *n* (ca. 1883) **:** a 1780 silver trade coin used in the Middle East

mari·cul·ture \'mar-ə-,kəl-chər\ *n* [L *mare* sea + E *-culture* (as in *agriculture*)] (ca. 1909) **:** the cultivation of marine organisms by exploiting their natural environment — **mari·cul·tur·ist** \,mar-ə-'kəlch(-ə)-rəst\ *n*

mari·gold \'mar-ə-,gōld, 'mer-\ *n* [ME, fr. *Mary,* mother of Jesus + ME *gold*] (14c) **1 :** POT MARIGOLD **2 :** any of a genus (*Tagetes*) of herbaceous composite plants with showy yellow or red and yellow flower heads

mar·i·jua·na *also* **mar·i·hua·na** \,mar-ə-'wän-ə *also* -'hwän-\ *n* [MexSp *mariguana, marihuana*] (1894) **1 :** HEMP 1a, 1c **2 :** the dried leaves and flowering tops of the pistillate hemp plant that yield THC and are sometimes smoked in cigarettes for their intoxicating effect — compare BHANG, CANNABIS, HASHISH

ma·rim·ba \mə-'rim-bə\ *n* [of African origin; akin to Kimbundu *marimba* xylophone] (ca. 1883) **:** a primitive xylophone of southern Africa and Central America with resonators beneath each bar; *also* **:** a modern improved form of this instrument

ma·ri·na \mə-'rē-nə\ *n* [It & Sp, seashore, fr. fem. of *marino,* adj., marine, fr. L *marinus*] (1924) **:** a dock or basin providing secure moorings for motorboats and yachts and often offering supply, repair, and other facilities

[1]**mar·i·nade** \,mar-ə-'nād\ *n* [alter. of *marinate*] (1704) **:** a savory usu. acidic sauce in which meat, fish, or a vegetable is soaked to enrich its flavor or to tenderize it

[2]**marinade** *vt* **-nad·ed; -nad·ing** (1727) **:** MARINATE

mar·i·na·ra \,mar-ə-'nar-ə, ,mer-ə-'ner-, -'när-\ *adj* [It (*alla*) *marinara,* lit., in sailor style] (ca. 1948) **:** made with tomatoes, onions, garlic, and spices ⟨~ sauce⟩; *also* **:** served with marinara sauce ⟨spaghetti ~⟩

mar·i·nate \'mar-ə-,nāt\ *vb* **-nat·ed; -nat·ing** [prob. fr. It *marinato,* pp. of *marinare* to marinate, fr. *marino*] *vt* (1645) **:** to steep (meat, fish, or vegetables) in a marinade ~ *vi* **:** to become marinated

[1]**ma·rine** \mə-'rēn\ *adj* [ME, fr. L *marinus,* fr. *mare* sea; akin to OE *mere* sea, pool, OHG *meri* sea, OSlav *morje*] (15c) **1 a :** of or relating to the sea ⟨~ life⟩ **b :** of or relating to the navigation of the sea **:** NAUTICAL ⟨a ~ chart⟩ **c :** of or relating to the commerce of the sea **:** MARITIME ⟨~ law⟩ **d :** depicting the sea, seashore, or ships ⟨a ~ painter⟩ **2 :** of or relating to marines ⟨~ barracks⟩

[2]**marine** *n* (1669) **1 a :** the mercantile and naval shipping of a country **b :** seagoing ships esp. in relation to nationality or class **2 :** one of a class of soldiers serving on shipboard or in close association with a naval force; *specif* **:** a member of the U.S. Marine Corps **3 :** an executive department (as in France) having charge of naval affairs **4 :** a marine picture **:** SEASCAPE

marine architect *n* (1949) **:** NAVAL ARCHITECT — **marine architecture** *n*

marine glue *n* (ca. 1846) **:** a water-insoluble adhesive

mar·i·ner \'mar-ə-nər\ *n* [ME, fr. AF *marinier,* fr. ML *marinarius,* fr. *marinus*] (13c) **:** one who navigates or assists in navigating a ship **:** SEAMAN, SAILOR

mariner's compass *n* (1627) **:** a compass used in navigation that consists of parallel magnetic needles or bundles of needles permanently attached to a card marked to indicate direction and degrees of a circle

Mar·i·ol·a·try \,mer-ē-'äl-ə-trē, ,mar-ē-, ,mā-rē-\ *n* (1612) **:** excessive veneration of the Virgin Mary — **Mar·i·ol·a·ter** \-'äl-ət-ər\ *n*

Mar·i·ol·o·gy \-'äl-ə-jē\ *n* (1857) **:** study or doctrine relating to the Virgin Mary — **Mar·i·o·log·i·cal** \-ə-'läj-i-kəl\ *adj*

mar·i·o·nette \,mar-ē-ə-'net, ,mer-\ *n* [F *marionnette,* fr. MF *maryonete,* fr. *Marion,* dim. of *Marie* Mary] (1620) **:** a small-scale usu. wooden figure (as of a person) with jointed limbs that is moved from above by manipulation of the attached strings or wires — called also *puppet*

mar·i·po·sa lily \,mar-ə-,pō-zə-, -sə-\ *n* [prob. fr. AmerSp *mariposa,* fr. Sp, butterfly] (1882) **:** any of a genus (*Calochortus*) of western No.

American plants of the lily family usu. with showily blotched flowers — called also *mariposa tulip;* compare SEGO LILY
mar·ish \'mar-ish\ *n, archaic* (14c) : MARSH
Mar·ist \'mar-əst, 'mer-\ *n* [F *mariste,* fr. *Marie* Mary] (ca. 1872) : a member of the Roman Catholic Society of Mary founded by Jean Claude Colin in France in 1816 and devoted to education
mar·i·tal \'mar-ət-ᵊl, *Brit also* mə-'rīt-\ *adj* [L *maritalis,* fr. *maritus* married] (1603) **1** : of or relating to marriage or the married state ⟨~ vows⟩ **2** : of or relating to a husband and his role in marriage — **mar·i·tal·ly** \-ᵊl-ē\ *adv*
mar·i·time \'mar-ə-,tīm\ *adj* [L *maritimus,* fr. *mare*] (1550) **1** : of, relating to, or bordering on the sea ⟨a ~ province⟩ **2** : of or relating to navigation or commerce on the sea **3** : having the characteristics of a mariner
mar·jo·ram \'märj-(ə-)rəm\ *n* [alter. of ME *majorane,* fr. MF, fr. ML *majorana*] (14c) : any of various usu. fragrant and aromatic mints (genera *Origanum* and *Majorana*) often used in cookery
[1]**mark** \'märk\ *n* [ME, fr. OE *mearc* boundary, march, sign; akin to OHG *marha* boundary, L *margo,* OHG *marcōn* to determine the boundaries of] (bef. 12c) **1** : a boundary land **2 a** (1) : a conspicuous object serving as a guide for travelers (2) : something (as a line, notch, or fixed object) designed to record position **b** : one of the bits of leather or colored bunting placed on a sounding line at intervals **c** : TARGET **d** : the starting line or position in a track event **e** (1) : GOAL, OBJECT (2) : an object of attack, ridicule, or abuse; *specif* : a victim of a swindle (3) : the point under discussion **f** : a standard of performance, quality, or condition : NORM ⟨hadn't been feeling up to the ~ lately⟩ **3 a** (1) : SIGN, INDICATION ⟨gave her the necklace as a ~ of his esteem⟩ (2) : an impression (as a scratch, scar, or stain) made on something (3) : a distinguishing trait or quality : CHARACTERISTIC ⟨the ~*s* of an educated person⟩ **b** : a symbol used for identification or indication of ownership **c** : a cross made in place of a signature **d** (1) : TRADEMARK (2) *cap* — used with a numeral to designate a particular model of a weapon or machine ⟨*Mark* II⟩ **e** : a written or printed symbol (as a comma or colon) **f** : POSTMARK **g** : a symbol used to represent a teacher's estimate of a student's work or conduct; *esp* : GRADE **h** : a figure registering a point or level reached or achieved ⟨the halfway ~ in the first period of play⟩; *esp* : RECORD **4 a** : ATTENTION, NOTICE ⟨nothing worthy of ~⟩ **b** : IMPORTANCE, DISTINCTION ⟨stands out as a person of ~⟩ **c** : a lasting or strong impression ⟨worked at several jobs but didn't make much of a ~⟩ **d** : an assessment of merits : RATING ⟨got high ~*s* for honesty⟩ ***syn*** see SIGN
[2]**mark** *vt* (bef. 12c) **1 a** (1) : to fix or trace out the bounds or limits of (2) : to plot the course of : CHART **b** : to set apart by or as if by a line or boundary — usu. used with *off* **2 a** (1) : to designate as if by a mark ⟨~*ed* for greatness⟩ (2) : to make or leave a mark on (3) : to furnish with natural marks ⟨wings ~*ed* with white⟩ (4) : to label so as to indicate price or quality (5) : to make notations in or on **b** (1) : to make note of in writing : JOT ⟨~*ing* the date in his journal⟩ (2) : to indicate by a mark or symbol ⟨~ an accent⟩ (3) : REGISTER, RECORD (4) : to determine the value of by means of marks or symbols : GRADE ⟨~ term papers⟩ **c** (1) : CHARACTERIZE, DISTINGUISH ⟨the flamboyance that ~*s* her stage appearance⟩ (2) : SIGNALIZE ⟨this year ~*s* the 50th anniversary of the organization⟩ **3** : to take notice of : OBSERVE ⟨~ my words⟩ **4** : to pick up (one's golf ball) from a putting green and substitute a marker ~ *vi* : to take careful notice — **mark time 1** : to keep the time of a marching step by moving the feet alternately without advancing **2** : to function or operate in a listless or unproductive manner
[3]**mark** *n* [ME, fr. OE *marc,* prob. of Scand origin; akin to ON *mǫrk* mark; akin to OE *mearc* sign] (bef. 12c) **1** : any of various old European units of weight used esp. for gold and silver; *esp* : a unit equal to about 8 ounces (0.2 kilogram) **2** : a unit of value: **a** : an old English unit equal to 13*s* 4*d* **b** : any one of various old Scandinavian or German units of value; *specif* : a unit and corresponding silver coin of the 16th century worth ½ taler **c** (1) : DEUTSCHE MARK (2) : the former basic monetary unit of East Germany replaced in 1990 by the West German deutsche mark **d** : MARKKA
Mark \'märk\ *n* [L *Marcus*] **1 a** : an early Jewish Christian traditionally identified as the writer of the Gospel of Mark — called also *John Mark* **b** : the second Gospel in the New Testament — see BIBLE table **2** : a king of Cornwall, uncle of Tristram, and husband of Isolde
mark·down \'märk-,daůn\ *n* (1880) **1** : a lowering of price **2** : the amount by which an original selling price is reduced
mark down \(')märk-'daůn\ *vt* (1859) : to put a lower price on
marked \'märkt\ *adj* (bef. 12c) **1** : having an identifying mark ⟨a ~ card⟩ **2** : having a distinctive or emphasized character : NOTICEABLE ⟨has a ~ drawl⟩ **3 a** : enjoying fame or notoriety **b** : being an object of attack, suspicion, or vengeance ⟨a ~ man⟩ **4** : overtly signaled by a linguistic feature ⟨with most English nouns the plural is the ~ number⟩ — **mark·ed·ly** \'mär-kəd-lē\ *adv*
mark·er \'mär-kər\ *n* (15c) **1** : one that marks **2** : something used for marking **3** : SCORE 7; *specif* : RUN **4** : GENETIC MARKER
[1]**mar·ket** \'mär-kət\ *n* [ME, fr. ONF, fr. L *mercatus* trade, marketplace, fr. *mercatus,* pp. of *mercari* to trade, fr. *merc-, merx* merchandise] (12c) **1 a** (1) : a meeting together of people for the purpose of trade by private purchase and sale and usu. not by auction (2) : the people assembled at such a meeting **b** (1) : a public place where a market is held; *esp* : a place where provisions are sold at wholesale (2) : a retail establishment usu. of a specified kind ⟨a fish ~⟩ **2** *archaic* : the act or an instance of buying and selling **3** : the rate or price offered for a commodity or security **4 a** (1) : a geographical area of demand for commodities or services ⟨the foreign ~ for consulting firms⟩ (2) : a specified category of potential buyers ⟨the youth ~⟩ **b** : the course of commercial activity by which the exchange of commodities is effected : extent of demand ⟨the ~ is dull⟩ **c** (1) : an opportunity for selling ⟨a good ~ for used cars⟩ (2) : the available supply of or potential demand for specified goods or services ⟨the labor ~⟩ **d** : the area of economic activity in which buyers and sellers come together and the forces of supply and demand affect prices ⟨producing goods for ~ rather than for consumption⟩ — **in the market** : interested in buying ⟨*in the market* for a house⟩ — **on the market** : available for purchase ⟨a good selection of fresh produce *on the market*⟩; *also* : up for sale ⟨put their house *on the market*⟩
[2]**market** *vi* (1635) : to deal in a market ~ *vt* **1** : to expose for sale in a market **2** : SELL
mar·ket·able \'mär-kət-ə-bəl\ *adj* (1600) **1 a** : fit to be offered for sale in a market ⟨contaminated food that is not ~⟩ **b** : wanted by purchasers or employers : SALABLE ⟨~ securities⟩ ⟨~ skills⟩ **2** : of or relating to buying or selling — **mar·ket·abil·i·ty** \,mär-kət-ə-'bil-ət-ē\ *n*
mar·ket·er \'mär-kət-ər\ *n* (1787) : one that deals in a market; *esp* : one that markets a specified commodity ⟨the company is a big gasoline ~⟩
market garden *n* (1811) : a plot in which vegetables are raised for market — **market gardener** *n* — **market gardening** *n*
mar·ket·ing *n* (1561) **1** : the act or process of selling or purchasing in a market **2** : an aggregate of functions involved in moving goods from producer to consumer
marketing research *n* (ca. 1937) : research conducted to establish the extent and location of the market for a product or to analyze the cost of products and processes as compared with that of alternative or competitive products or processes
market order *n* (ca. 1920) : an order to buy or sell securities or commodities immediately at the best price obtainable in the market
mar·ket·place \'mär-kət-,plās\ *n* (14c) **1 a** : an open square or place in a town where markets or public sales are held **b** : MARKET ⟨the ~ is the interpreter of supply and demand⟩ **2** : the world of trade or economic activity : the everyday world ⟨a conviction that religion belongs in the ~ —*Current Biog.*⟩ **3** : a sphere in which intangible values compete for acceptance ⟨the ~ of ideas⟩
market price *n* (15c) : a price actually given in current market dealings
market research *n* (1926) : the gathering of factual information as to consumer preferences for goods and services
market value *n* (1691) : a price at which both buyers and sellers are willing to do business
mark·ing *n* (14c) **1** : the act, process, or an instance of making or giving a mark **2 a** : a mark made **b** : arrangement, pattern, or disposition of marks
mark·ka \'mär-,kä\ *n, pl* **mark·kaa** \'mär-,kä\ *also* **mark·kas** \-,käz\ [Finn, fr. Sw *mark,* a unit of value; akin to ON *mǫrk* [3]mark] (ca. 1896) — see MONEY table
Mar·kov chain \,mär-,kóf-, -,kóv-\ *n* [A. A. *Markov* †1922 Russ. mathematician] (1942) : a usu. discrete stochastic process (as a random walk) in which the probabilities of occurrence of various future states depend only on the present state of the system or on the immediately preceding state and not on the path by which the present state was achieved — called also *Markoff chain*
Mar·kov·ian \mär-'kō-vē-ən, -'kó-\ *or* **Mar·kov** \'mär-,kóf, -,kóv\ *also* **Mar·koff** \'mär-,kóf\ *adj* (1950) : of, relating to, or resembling a Markov process or Markov chain esp. by having probabilities defined in terms of transition from the possible existing states to other states
Markov process *also* **Markoff process** *n* (1939) : a stochastic process (as Brownian movement) that resembles a Markov chain except that the states are continuous; *also* : MARKOV CHAIN
marks·man \'märk-smən\ *n* (1577) : one that shoots at a mark; *esp* : a person skillful or practiced at hitting a mark or target — **marks·man·ship** \-,ship\ *n*
marks·wom·an \'märk-,swům-ən\ *n* (1802) : a woman skilled in shooting at a mark
mark·up \'mär-,kəp\ *n* (1916) **1** : a raise in the price of an article **2** : an amount added to the cost price to determine the selling price **3** : a U.S. Congressional committee session at which a bill is put into final form before it is reported out
mark up \(')mär-'kəp\ *vt* (1869) : to set a higher price on
[1]**marl** \'mär(-ə)l\ *vt* [ME *marlen,* fr. OF *marler,* fr. ML *marlare,* prob. fr. *margila*] (13c) : to dress (land) with marl
[2]**marl** *n* [ME, fr. MF *marle,* fr. ML *margila,* dim. of L *marga* marl, fr. Gaulish] (14c) : a loose or crumbling earthy deposit (as of sand, silt, or clay) that contains a substantial amount of calcium carbonate and is used esp. as a fertilizer for soils deficient in lime — **marly** \'mär-lē\ *adj*
[3]**marl** *vt* [D *marlen,* back-formation fr. *marling*] (1704) : to cover or fasten with marline
mar·lin \'mär-lən\ *n* [short for *marlinspike;* fr. the appearance of its beak] (1917) : any of several large oceanic sport fishes (genera *Makaira* and *Tetrapturus*) related to sailfishes and spearfishes
mar·line *also* **mar·lin** \'mär-lən\ *n* [D *marlijn,* alter. of *marling,* fr. *meren, marren* to tie, moor, fr. MD *meren, maren* — more at MOOR] (15c) : a small usu. tarred line of two strands twisted loosely left-handed that is used esp. for seizing and as a covering for wire rope
mar·line·spike *also* **mar·lin·spike** \'mär-lən-,spīk\ *n* (1626) : a tool (as of wood or iron) that tapers to a point and is used to separate strands of rope or wire (as in splicing)
marl·stone \'mär(-ə)l-,stōn\ *n* (ca. 1839) : a rock that consists of a mixture of clay materials and calcium carbonate and often contains kerogen
mar·ma·lade \'mär-mə-,lād\ *n* [Pg *marmelada* quince conserve, fr. *marmelo* quince, fr. L *melimelum,* a sweet apple, fr. Gk *melimēlon,* fr. *meli* honey + *mēlon* apple — more at MELLIFLUOUS] (1524) : a clear sweetened jelly in which pieces of fruit and fruit rind are suspended
mar·mo·re·al \mär-'mōr-ē-əl, -'mór-\ *or* **mar·mo·re·an** \-ē-ən\ *adj* [L *marmoreus,* fr. *marmor* marble] (1798) : of, relating to, or resembling marble or a marble statue — **mar·mo·re·al·ly** \-ē-ə-lē\ *adv*
mar·mo·set \'mär-mə-,set, -,zet\ *n* [ME *marmusette,* fr. MF *marmoset* grotesque figure, fr. *marmouser* to mumble, of imit. origin] (14c) : any of numerous soft-furred So. and Central American monkeys (family Callithricidae) with claws instead of nails on all the digits except the great toe
mar·mot \'mär-mət\ *n* [F *marmotte*] (1607) : a stout-bodied short-legged burrowing rodent (genus *Marmota*) with coarse fur, a short bushy tail, and very small ears — compare WOODCHUCK
Mar·o·nite \'mar-ə-,nīt\ *n* [ML *maronita,* fr. *Maron-, Maro* 5th cent. A.D. Syrian

marmoset

monk] (1511) : a member of a Uniate church chiefly in Lebanon having a Syriac liturgy and married clergy
1**ma·roon** \mə-'rün\ *n* [modif. of AmerSp *cimarrón*, fr. *cimarrón* wild, savage] (1666) **1** *cap* : a fugitive Negro slave of the West Indies and Guiana in the 17th and 18th centuries; *also* : a descendant of such a slave **2** : a person who is marooned
2**maroon** *vt* (ca. 1709) **1** : to put ashore on a desolate island or coast and leave to one's fate **2** : to place or leave in isolation or without hope of ready escape
3**maroon** *n* [F *marron* Spanish chestnut] (1791) : a variable color averaging a dark red
mar·plot \'mär-,plät\ *n* (1764) : one who frustrates or ruins a plan or undertaking by his meddling
1**marque** \'märk\ *n* [ME, fr. MF, fr. OProv *marca*, fr. *marcar* to mark, seize as pledge, of Gmc origin; akin to OHG *marcōn* to mark] (15c) **1** *obs* : REPRISAL, RETALIATION **2** : LETTERS OF MARQUE
2**marque** *n* [F, mark, brand, fr. MF, fr. *marquer* to mark, of Gmc origin; akin to OHG *marcōn* to mark] (1906) : a brand or make of a product (as a sports car)
mar·quee \mär-'kē\ *n* [modif. of F *marquise*, lit., marchioness] (1690) **1** : a large tent set up for an outdoor party, reception, or exhibition **2** : a permanent canopy often of metal and glass projecting over an entrance (as of a hotel or theater)
Mar·que·san \mär-'kā-z^{ə}n, -'kā-s-\ *n* (1799) **1** : a native or inhabitant of the Marquesas islands **2** : the Austronesian language of the Marquesans — **Marquesan** *adj*
mar·quess \'mär-kwəs\ *or* **mar·quis** \'mär-kwəs, mär-'kē\ *n, pl* **mar·quess·es** *or* **mar·quis·es** \-kwə-səz\ *or* **mar·quis** \-'kē(z)\ [ME *marquis, markis*, fr. MF *marquis*, alter. of *marchis*, fr. *marche* march] (14c) **1** : a nobleman of hereditary rank in Europe and Japan **2** : a member of the British peerage ranking below a duke and above an earl — **mar·quess·ate** \'mär-kwə-sət\ *or* **mar·quis·ate** \'mär-kwə-zət, -sət\ *n*
mar·que·try *also* **mar·que·terie** \'mär-kə-trē\ *n* [MF *marqueterie*, fr. *marqueter* to checker, inlay, fr. *marque* mark] (1563) : decorative work in which elaborate patterns are formed by the insertion of pieces of material (as wood, shell, or ivory) into a wood veneer that is then applied to a surface (as of a piece of furniture)
mar·quise \mär-'kēz\ *n, pl* **mar·quises** \-'kēz(-əz)\ [F, fem. of *marquis*] (14c) **1** : MARCHIONESS **2** : MARQUEE **3** : a gem or a ring setting or bezel usu. elliptical in shape but with pointed ends — see BRILLIANT illustration
mar·qui·sette \,mär-k(w)ə-'zet\ *n* [*marquise* + *-ette*] (1908) : a sheer meshed fabric used for clothing, curtains, and mosquito nets
mar·ram grass \'mar-əm-\ *n* [of Scand origin; akin to ON *maralmr*, a beach grass] (1834) : any of several beach grasses (genus *Ammophila* and esp. *A. arenaria*)
Mar·ra·no \mə-'rän-(,)ō\ *n, pl* **-nos** [Sp, lit., pig] (1583) : a Christianized Jew of medieval Spain
mar·riage \'mar-ij *also* 'mer-\ *n* [ME *mariage*, fr. OF, fr. *marier* to marry] (13c) **1 a** : the state of being married **b** : the mutual relation of husband and wife : WEDLOCK **c** : the institution whereby men and women are joined in a special kind of social and legal dependence for the purpose of founding and maintaining a family **2** : an act of marrying or the rite by which the married status is effected; *esp* : the wedding ceremony and attendant festivities or formalities **3** : an intimate or close union ⟨the ~ of painting and poetry —J. T. Shawcross⟩ — **mar·riage·able** \-ə-bəl\ *adj*
marriage of convenience (1711) : a marriage contracted for social, political, or economic advantage rather than for mutual affection
1**mar·ried** \'mar-ēd *also* 'mer-\ *adj* (14c) **1 a** : being in the state of matrimony : WEDDED **b** : of or relating to marriage : CONNUBIAL **2** : UNITED, JOINED
2**married** *n, pl* **marrieds** *or* **married** (1890) : a married person ⟨young ~s are paid undue . . . attention —Paul Goodman⟩
mar·ron \ma-'rō^{n}\ *n* [F] (1594) **1** : a large Mediterranean chestnut (*Castanea sativa*) or its sweet edible nut — called also *Spanish chestnut* **2 mar·rons** \-'rō^{n}(z)\ *pl* : chestnuts preserved in vanilla-flavored syrup
Mar·ron \ma-'rō^{n}\ *n* [F, fr. AmerSp *cimarrón*] (1666) : MAROON 1
mar·rons gla·cés \ma-,rō^{n}-gla-'sā\ *n pl* [F, lit., glazed marrons] (1871) : MARRON 2
1**mar·row** \'mar-(,)ō, -ə(-w)\ *n* [ME *marowe*, fr. OE *mearg*; akin to OHG *marag* marrow, Skt *majjan*] (bef. 12c) **1 a** : a soft highly vascular modified connective tissue that occupies the cavities and cancellous part of most bones **b** : the substance of the spinal cord **2 a** : the choicest of food **b** : the seat of animal vigor **c** : the inmost, best, or essential part : CORE ⟨personal liberty is the ~ of the American tradition —Clinton Rossiter⟩ **3** *chiefly Brit* : VEGETABLE MARROW — **mar·rowy** \'mar-ə-wē\ *adj*
2**marrow** *n* [ME *marwe, marrow*] *chiefly Scot* (15c) : one of a pair
mar·row·bone \'mar-ə-,bōn, -ō-,bōn\ *n* (14c) **1** : a bone (as a shinbone) rich in marrow **2** *pl* : KNEES
mar·row·fat \-ō-,fat, -ə-,fat\ *n* (1733) : any of several wrinkled-seeded garden peas
1**mar·ry** \'mar-ē *also* 'mer-\ *vb* **mar·ried; mar·ry·ing** [ME *marien*, fr. OF *marier*, fr. L *maritare*, fr. *maritus* married] *vt* (13c) **1 a** : to join as husband and wife according to law or custom ⟨were *married* yesterday⟩ **b** : to give in marriage ⟨*married* his daughter to his partner's son⟩ **c** : to take as spouse : WED ⟨*married* the girl next door⟩ **d** : to perform the ceremony of marriage for ⟨*married* the couple⟩ **e** : to obtain by marriage ⟨~ wealth⟩ **2** : to unite in close and usu. permanent relation ~ *vi* **1** : to take a spouse : WED **2** : to enter into a close or intimate union ⟨these wines ~ well⟩ — **marry into** : to become a member of by marriage ⟨*married into* a prominent family⟩
2**marry** *interj* [ME *marie*, fr. *Marie*, the Virgin Mary] *archaic* (14c) — used for emphasis and esp. to express amused or surprised agreement
Mars \'märz\ *n* [L *Mart-, Mars*] **1** : the Roman god of war — compare ARES **2** : the planet fourth in order from the sun and conspicuous for the redness of its light — see PLANET table
mar·sa·la \mär-'säl-ə\ *n, often cap* [*Marsala*, town in Sicily] (1806) : a fortified Sicilian wine that varies from dry to sweet
marse \'märs\ *n* [by shortening and alter.] *Southern* (1869) : MASTER ⟨was called ~, approached with fear, and addressed hat in hand —A. W. Tourgee⟩
Mar·seilles \mär-'sā(ə)lz\ *n* [*Marseilles*, France] (1762) : a firm cotton fabric that is similar to piqué
marsh \'märsh\ *n, often attrib* [ME *mersh*, fr. OE *merisc, mersc*; akin to MD *mersch* marsh, OE *mere* sea, pool — more at MARINE] (bef. 12c) : a tract of soft wet land usu. characterized by monocotyledons (as grasses or cattails)
1**mar·shal** *also* **mar·shall** \'mär-shəl\ *n* [ME, fr. OF *mareschal*, of Gmc origin; akin to OHG *marahscalc* marshal, fr. *marah* horse + *scalc* servant] (13c) **1 a** : a high official in the household of a medieval king, prince, or noble orig. having charge of the cavalry but later usu. in command of the military forces **b** : a person who arranges and directs the ceremonial aspects of a gathering **2 a** : FIELD MARSHAL **b** : a general officer of the highest military rank **3 a** : an officer having charge of prisoners **b** (1) : a ministerial officer appointed for a judicial district (as of the U.S.) to execute the process of the courts and perform various duties similar to those of a sheriff (2) : a city law officer entrusted with particular duties **c** : the administrative head of a city police department or fire department — **mar·shal·cy** \-sē\ *n* — **mar·shal·ship** \-,ship\ *n*
2**marshal** *vb* **-shaled** *or* **-shalled; -shal·ing** *or* **-shal·ling** \'märsh-(ə-)liŋ\ *vt* (15c) **1** : to place in proper rank or position ⟨~*ing* the troops⟩ **2** : to bring together and order in an appropriate or effective way ⟨~ arguments⟩ **3** : to lead ceremoniously or solicitously : USHER ⟨~*ing* her little group of children down the street⟩ ~ *vi* : to take form or order ⟨ideas ~*ing* neatly⟩ ***syn*** see ORDER
marshal of the Royal Air Force (1947) : the highest ranking officer in the British air force
marsh elder *n* (ca. 1755) : any of various coarse shrubby composite plants (genus *Iva*) of moist areas in eastern and central No. America
marsh gas *n* (1848) : METHANE
marsh hawk *n* (1772) : a widely distributed No. American hawk (*Circus cyaneus hudsonius*) with a conspicuous white patch on the rump

marsh hawk

marsh hen *n* (1709) **1** : any of various American rails **2** : BITTERN
marsh·land \'märsh-,land\ *n* (12c) : a marshy district : MARSH
marsh·mal·low \'märsh-,mel-ō, -,mel-ə(-w), -,mal-\ *n* [ME *mershmalwe*, fr. OE *merscmealwe*, fr. *mersc* marsh + *mealwe* mallow] (bef. 12c) **1** : a pink-flowered European perennial herb (*Althaea officinalis*) of the mallow family that is naturalized in the eastern U.S. and has a mucilaginous root sometimes used in confectionery and in medicine **2** : a confection made from the root of the marshmallow or from corn syrup, sugar, albumen, and gelatin beaten to a light spongy consistency; *also* : a piece of partially dried marshmallow ⟨a bag of ~s⟩ — **marsh·mal·lowy** \-,mel-ə-wē, -,mal-\ *adj*
marsh marigold *n* (1578) : a swamp herb (*Caltha palustris*) of the buttercup family that occurs in Europe and No. America and has bright yellow flowers — called also *cowslip*
marshy \'mär-shē\ *adj* **marsh·i·er; -est** (14c) **1** : resembling or constituting a marsh : BOGGY ⟨~ ground⟩ **2** : relating to or occurring in marshes ⟨~ vegetation⟩ — **marsh·i·ness** *n*
Mars·quake \'märz-,kwāk\ *n* (1974) : an agitation of the surface of Mars comparable to an earthquake
1**mar·su·pi·al** \mär-'sü-pē-əl\ *adj* (1696) **1** : of, relating to, or being a marsupial **2** : of, relating to, or forming a marsupium
2**marsupial** *n* [deriv. of NL *marsupium*] (ca. 1835) : any of an order (Marsupialia) of lowly mammals comprising kangaroos, wombats, bandicoots, opossums, and related animals that with few exceptions develop no placenta and have a pouch on the abdomen of the female containing the teats and serving for carrying the young
mar·su·pi·um \mär-'sü-pē-əm\ *n, pl* **-pia** \-pē-ə\ [NL, fr. L, purse, pouch, fr. Gk *marsypion*] (1698) **1** : an abdominal pouch formed by a fold of the skin and enclosing the mammary glands of most marsupials **2** : any of several structures in various invertebrates (as a bryozoan or mollusk) for enclosing or carrying eggs or young
1**mart** \'märt\ *n* [ME, fr. MD *marct, mart*, prob. fr. ONF *market*] (15c) **1** *archaic* : a coming together of people to buy and sell : 5FAIR 1 **2** *obs* : the activity of buying and selling; *also* : BARGAIN **3** : MARKET
2**mart** *vt* (1553) : to deal in : SELL
mar·tel·lo tower \mär-'tel-ō-\ *n, often cap M* [Cape *Mortella*, Corsica] (1803) : a circular masonry fort or blockhouse
mar·ten \'märt-^{ə}n\ *n, pl* **marten** *or* **martens** [ME *martryn*, fr. MF *martrine* marten fur, fr. OF, fr. *martre* marten, of Gmc origin; akin to OE *mearth* marten] (13c) **1** : any of several semiarboreal slender-bodied carnivorous mammals (genus *Martes*) larger than the related weasels **2** : the fur or pelt of a marten
mar·tens·ite \'märt-^{ə}n-,zīt\ *n* [Adolf *Martens* †1914 Ger. metallurgist] (1898) : the hard constituent of which quenched steel is chiefly composed — **mar·tens·it·ic** \,mart-^{ə}n-'zit-ik, -'sit-\ *adj* — **mar·tens·it·i·cal·ly** \-i-k(ə-)lē\ *adv*
Mar·tha \'mär-thə\ *n* [LL, fr. Gk] : a sister of Lazarus and Mary and friend of Jesus
mar·tial \'mär-shəl\ *adj* [ME, fr. L *martialis* of Mars, fr. *Mart-, Mars*] (14c) **1** : of, relating to, or suited for war or a warrior **2** : relating to an army or to military life **3** : experienced in or inclined to war : WARLIKE — **mar·tial·ly** \-shə-lē\ *adv*
martial law *n* (1533) **1** : the law applied in occupied territory by the military authority of the occupying power **2** : the law administered by military forces that is invoked by a government in an emergency when the civilian law enforcement agencies are unable to maintain public order and safety

mar·tian \'mär-shən\ *adj, often cap* (14c) **:** of or relating to the planet Mars or its hypothetical inhabitants — **martian** *n, often cap*
mar·tin \'märt-ᵊn\ *n* [MF, fr. St. *Martin*] (15c) **1 :** a small European swallow (*Delichon urbica*) with a forked tail, bluish black head and back, and white rump and underparts **2 :** any of various swallows and flycatchers other than the martin
mar·ti·net \,märt-ᵊn-'et\ *n* [Jean *Martinet*, 17th cent. Fr. army officer] (1779) **1 :** a strict disciplinarian **2 :** one who stresses a rigid adherence to the details of forms and methods
mar·tin·gale \'märt-ᵊn-,gāl, -iŋ-\ *n* [MF] (1589) **1 :** a device for steadying a horse's head or checking its upward movement that typically consists of a strap fastened to the girth, passing between the forelegs, and bifurcating to end in two rings through which the reins pass **2 a :** a lower stay of rope or chain for the jibboom used to sustain the strain of the forestays and fastened to or rove through the dolphin striker **b :** DOLPHIN STRIKER **3 :** any of several systems of betting in which a player increases his stake usu. by doubling each time he loses a bet
mar·ti·ni \mär-'tē-nē\ *n* [prob. fr. the name *Martini*] (1894) **:** a cocktail made of gin and dry vermouth
Mar·tin Lu·ther King Day \,märt-ᵊn-,lü-thər-'kiŋ-\ *n* (1977) **:** the third Monday in January observed as a legal holiday in some states of the U.S.
Mar·tin·mas \'märt-ᵊn-məs, -,mas\ *n* [ME *martinmasse*, fr. St. *Martin* + ME *masse* mass] (13c) **:** November 11 celebrated as the feast of Saint Martin
mart·let \'märt-lət\ *n* [MF, prob. alter. of *martinet*, dim. of *martin*] (1538) **:** MARTIN 1
[1]**mar·tyr** \'märt-ər\ *n* [ME, fr. OE, fr. LL, fr. Gk *martyr-, martys*, lit., witness; akin to L *memor* mindful] (bef. 12c) **1 :** one who voluntarily suffers death as the penalty of witnessing to and refusing to renounce his religion **2 :** one who sacrifices his life or something of great value for the sake of principle **3 :** VICTIM; *esp* **:** a great or constant sufferer ⟨a ~ to asthma all his life —A. J. Cronin⟩ — **mar·tyr·iza·tion** \,märt-ə-rə-'zā-shən\ *n* — **mar·tyr·ize** \'märt-ə-,rīz\ *vt*
[2]**martyr** *vt* (bef. 12c) **1 :** to put to death for adhering to a belief, faith, or profession **2 :** to inflict agonizing pain on **:** TORTURE
mar·tyr·dom \'märt-ərd-əm\ *n* (bef. 12c) **1 :** the suffering of death on account of adherence to a cause and esp. to one's religious faith **2 :** AFFLICTION, TORTURE
mar·tyr·ol·o·gist \,märt-ə-'räl-ə-jəst\ *n* (1676) **:** a writer of or a specialist in martyrology
mar·tyr·ol·o·gy \-jē\ *n* (14c) **1 :** a catalog of Roman Catholic martyrs and saints arranged by the dates of their feasts **2 :** ecclesiastical history treating the lives and sufferings of martyrs
mar·tyry \'märt-ə-rē\ *n, pl* **-tyr·ies** [LL *martyrium*, fr. LGk *martyrion*, fr. Gk *martyr-, martys*] (1708) **:** a shrine erected in honor of a martyr
[1]**mar·vel** \'mär-vəl\ *n* [ME *mervel*, fr. OF *merveille*, fr. LL *mirabilia* marvels, fr. L, neut. pl. of *mirabilis* wonderful, fr. *mirari* to wonder — more at SMILE] (14c) **1 :** something that causes wonder or astonishment **2 :** intense surprise or interest **:** ASTONISHMENT
[2]**marvel** *vb* **mar·veled** *or* **mar·velled; mar·vel·ing** *or* **mar·vel·ling** \'märv-(ə-)liŋ\ *vi* (14c) **:** to become filled with surprise, wonder, or amazed curiosity ⟨~*ed* at the magician's skill⟩ ~ *vt* **:** to feel astonishment or perplexity at or about ⟨~*ed* that they had escaped⟩
mar·vel·ous *or* **mar·vel·lous** \'märv-(ə-)ləs\ *adj* (14c) **1 :** causing wonder **:** ASTONISHING **2 :** MIRACULOUS, SUPERNATURAL ⟨Gothic tales of the ~ and the bizarre⟩ **3 :** of the highest kind or quality **:** notably superior ⟨has a ~ way with children⟩ — **mar·vel·ous·ly** *adv* — **mar·vel·ous·ness** *n*
Marx·ism \'märk-,siz-əm\ *n* (1897) **:** the political, economic, and social principles and policies advocated by Marx; *esp* **:** a theory and practice of socialism including the labor theory of value, dialectical materialism, the class struggle, and dictatorship of the proletariat until the establishment of a classless society — **Marx·ist** \-səst\ *n or adj*
Marx·ism–Le·nin·ism \'märk-,siz-əm-'len-ə-,niz-əm, -'lān-\ *n* (1932) **:** a theory and practice of communism developed by Lenin from the doctrines of Marx — **Marx·ist–Len·in·ist** \'märk-səst-'len-ə-nəst\ *n or adj*
Mary \'me(ə)r-ē, 'ma(ə)r-ē, 'mā-rē\ *n* [LL *Maria*, fr. Gk *Mariam, Maria*, fr. Heb *Miryām* Miriam] **1 :** the mother of Jesus **2 :** a sister of Lazarus and Martha and a friend of Jesus
Mary Jane \-'jān\ *n* [by folk etymology (influenced by Sp *Juana* Jane)] *slang* (1928) **:** MARIJUANA
Mary·knoll·er \-,nō-lər\ *n* (1943) **:** a member of the Catholic Foreign Mission Society of America founded by T. F. Price and J. A. Walsh at Maryknoll, N.Y. in 1911
Mary Mag·da·lene \-'mag-də-lən, -,lēn; -,mag-də-'lē-nē\ *n* [LL *Magdalene*, fr. Gk *Magdalēnē*] **:** a woman who was healed of evil spirits by Jesus and who saw the risen Christ near his sepulcher
mar·zi·pan \'märt-sə-,pän, -,pan; 'mär-zə-,pan\ *n* [G, fr. It *marzapane*] (1542) **:** a confection of crushed almonds or almond paste, sugar, and egg whites that is often shaped into various forms
Ma·sai \mä-'sī, 'mä-,\ *n, pl* **Masai** *or* **Masais** (1857) **1 :** a member of a pastoral and hunting people of Kenya and Tanganyika **2 :** a Nilotic language of the Masai people
mas·cara \ma-'skar-ə\ *n* [It *maschera* mask, fr. OIt, fr. *masca* witch, fr. ML] (ca. 1890) **:** a cosmetic for coloring the eyelashes and eyebrows
mas·con \'mas-,kän\ *n* [[2]*mass* + *concentration*] (1968) **:** one of the concentrations of large mass under the surface of the moon in the maria held to cause perturbations of the paths of spacecraft orbiting the moon
mas·cot \'mas-,kät *also* -kət\ *n* [F *mascotte*, fr. Prov *mascoto*, fr. *masco* witch, fr. ML *masca*] (1881) **:** a person, animal, or object adopted by a group as a symbolic figure esp. to bring them good luck ⟨the team had a mountain lion as their ~⟩
[1]**mas·cu·line** \'mas-kyə-lən\ *adj* [ME *masculin*, fr. MF, fr. L *masculinus*, fr. *masculus*, n., male, dim. of *mas* male] (14c) **1 a :** MALE **b :** having qualities appropriate to a man **2 :** of, relating to, or constituting the gender that ordinarily includes most words or grammatical forms referring to males **3 a :** having or occurring in a stressed final syllable ⟨~ rhyme⟩ **b :** having the final chord occurring on a strong beat ⟨~ cadence⟩ **4 :** of or forming the formal, active, or generative principle of the cosmos — **mas·cu·line·ly** *adv* — **mas·cu·lin·i·ty** \,mas-kyə-'lin-ət-ē\ *n*
[2]**masculine** *n* (14c) **1 :** the masculine gender **2 :** a noun, pronoun, adjective, or inflectional form or class of the masculine gender **3 :** a male person
mas·cu·lin·ize \'mas-kyə-lə-,nīz\ *vt* **-ized; -iz·ing** (1912) **:** to give a preponderantly masculine character to; *esp* **:** to cause (a female) to take on male characteristics — **mas·cu·lin·iza·tion** \,mas-kyə-lə-nə-'zā-shən\ *n*
ma·ser \'mā-zər\ *n* [*m*icrowave *a*mplification by *s*timulated *e*mission of *r*adiation] (1955) **:** a device or object that utilizes the natural oscillations of atoms or molecules between energy levels for generating electromagnetic radiation in the microwave region of the spectrum
[1]**mash** \'mash\ *n* [ME, fr. OE *māx-*; akin to MHG *meisch* mash] (bef. 12c) **1 :** crushed malt or grain meal steeped and stirred in hot water to ferment (as for the production of beer or whiskey) **2 :** a mixture of ground feeds for livestock **3 :** a soft pulpy mass
[2]**mash** *vt* (13c) **1 a :** to reduce to a soft pulpy state by beating or pressure **b :** CRUSH, SMASH ⟨~ a finger⟩ **2 :** to subject (as crushed malt) to the action of water with heating and stirring in preparing wort
[3]**mash** *vt* [prob. fr. [2]*mash*] (1879) **:** to flirt with or seek to gain the affection of
[4]**mash** *n* (1880) **:** CRUSH 3
[1]**mash·er** \'mash-ər\ *n* (1500) **:** one that mashes ⟨a potato ~⟩
[2]**masher** *n* (1875) **:** a man who makes passes at women
[1]**mask** \'mask\ *n* [MF *masque*, fr. OIt *maschera*] (1534) **1 a** (1) **:** a cover or partial cover for the face used for disguise (2) **:** a person wearing a mask **:** MASKER **b** (1) **:** a figure of a head worn on the stage in antiquity to identify the character and project the voice (2) **:** a grotesque false face worn at carnivals or in rituals **c :** an often grotesque carved head or face used as an ornament (as on a keystone) **d :** a sculptured face or a copy of a face made by means of a mold **2 a :** something that serves to conceal or disguise **:** PRETENSE, CLOAK ⟨aware of the ~*s*, facades and defenses people erect to protect themselves —Kenneth Keniston⟩ **b :** something that conceals from view **c :** a translucent or opaque screen to cover part of the sensitive surface in taking or printing a photograph; *also* **:** an opaque material used to shield selected parts of a photosensitive surface for deposition or etching (as in producing an integrated circuit) **3 a :** a protective covering for the face **b :** GAS MASK **c :** a device covering the mouth and nose to facilitate inhalation **d :** a comparable device to prevent exhalation of infective material **e :** a cosmetic preparation for the skin of the face that produces a tightening effect as it dries **4 :** the head or face of an animal (as a fox or dog)
[2]**mask** *vi* (1562) **1 :** to take part in a masquerade **2 a :** to assume a mask **b :** to disguise one's true character or intentions ~ *vt* **1 :** to provide or conceal with a mask: as **a :** to conceal from view ⟨~ a gun battery⟩ **b :** to make indistinct or imperceptible ⟨~*s* undesirable flavors⟩ **c :** to cover up ⟨~*ed* his real purpose⟩ **2 :** to cover for protection **3 :** to modify the size or shape of (as a photograph) by means of an opaque border ***syn*** see DISGUISE — **mask·able** \'mas-kə-bəl\ *adj*
masked \'maskt\ *adj* (1585) **1 :** marked by the use of masks ⟨a ~ ball⟩ **2 :** failing to present or produce the usual symptoms **:** LATENT ⟨~ infection⟩ ⟨a ~ virus⟩
mask·er \'mas-kər\ *n* (1548) **:** a person who wears a mask; *esp* **:** a participant in a masquerade
mas·och·ism \'mas-ə-,kiz-əm, 'maz-\ *n* [ISV, fr. Leopold von Sacher-Masoch †1895 Ger. novelist] (ca. 1893) **1 :** a sexual perversion characterized by pleasure in being subjected to pain or humiliation esp. by a love object — compare SADISM **2 :** pleasure in being abused or dominated **:** a taste for suffering — **mas·och·ist** \-kəst\ *n* — **mas·och·is·tic** \,mas-ə-'kis-tik, ,maz-\ *adj* — **mas·och·is·ti·cal·ly** \,mas-ə-'kis-ti-k(ə-)lē, ,maz-\ *adv*
[1]**ma·son** \'mās-ᵊn\ *n* [ME, fr. OF *maçon*] (13c) **1 :** a skilled worker who builds by laying units of substantial material (as stone or brick) **2** *cap* **:** FREEMASON
[2]**mason** *vt* **ma·soned; ma·son·ing** \'mās-niŋ, -ᵊn-iŋ\ (15c) **1 :** to construct of or repair with masonry **2 :** to build stonework or brickwork about, under, in, or over
Ma·son·ic \mə-'sän-ik\ *adj* (1797) **:** of, relating to, or characteristic of Freemasons or Freemasonry
Ma·son·ite \'mās-ᵊn-,īt\ *trademark* — used for fiberboard made from steam-exploded wood fiber
ma·son jar \,mās-ᵊn-\ *n* [John L. *Mason*, 19th cent. Am. inventor] (1888) **:** a widemouthed jar used esp. for home canning
ma·son·ry \'mās-ᵊn-rē\ *n, pl* **-ries** (13c) **1 a :** something constructed of materials used by masons **b :** the art, trade, or occupation of a mason **c :** work done by a mason **2** *cap* **:** FREEMASONRY
mason wasp *n* (1792) **:** any of various solitary wasps that construct nests of hardened mud
Ma·so·ra *or* **Ma·so·rah** \mə-'sōr-ə, -'sȯr-\ *n* [NHeb *mĕsōrāh*, fr. LHeb *māsōreth* tradition, fr. Heb, bond] (1613) **:** a body of notes on the textual traditions of the Hebrew Old Testament compiled by scribes during the 1st millennium of the Christian era
Mas·o·rete *or* **Mas·so·rete** \'mas-ə-,rēt\ *n* [MF *massoreth*, fr. LHeb *māsōreth*] (1587) **:** one of the scribes who compiled the Masora — **Mas·o·ret·ic** \,mas-ə-'ret-ik\ *adj*
masque *also* **mask** \'mask\ *n* [MF *masque* — more at MASK] (1514) **1 :** MASQUERADE **2 :** a short allegorical dramatic entertainment of the 16th and 17th centuries performed by masked actors
masqu·er \'mas-kər\ *var of* MASKER
[1]**mas·quer·ade** \,mas-kə-'rād\ *n* [MF, fr. OIt dial. *mascarada*, fr. OIt *maschera* mask] (1587) **1 a :** a social gathering of persons wearing masks and often fantastic costumes **b :** a costume for wear at such a gathering **2 :** an action or appearance that is mere disguise or outward show
[2]**masquerade** *vi* **-ad·ed; -ad·ing** (1692) **1 a :** to disguise oneself; *also* **:** to go about disguised **b :** to take part in a masquerade **2 :** to assume the appearance of something that one is not — **mas·quer·ad·er** *n*
[1]**mass** \'mas\ *n* [ME, fr. OE *mæsse*, modif. of (assumed) VL *messa*, lit., dismissal at the end of a religious service, fr. LL *missa*, fr. L, fem. of *missus*, pp. of *mittere* to send — more at SMITE] (bef. 12c) **1** *cap* **:** the liturgy of the Eucharist esp. in accordance with the traditional Latin rite **2** *often cap* **:** a celebration of the Eucharist ⟨Sunday ~*es* held at three different hours⟩ **3 :** a musical setting for the ordinary of the Mass

²**mass** *n* [ME *masse,* fr. MF, fr. L *massa,* fr. Gk *maza;* akin to Gk *massein* to knead — more at MINGLE] (14c) **1 a :** a quantity or aggregate of matter usu. of considerable size **b** (1) **:** EXPANSE, BULK (2) **:** massive quality or effect ⟨impressed me with such ~ and such vividness —F. M. Ford⟩ (3) **:** the principal part or main body ⟨the great ~ of the continent is buried under an ice cap —Walter Sullivan⟩ (4) **:** AGGREGATE, WHOLE ⟨men in the ~⟩ **c :** the property of a body that is a measure of its inertia, that is commonly taken as a measure of the amount of material it contains and causes it to have weight in a gravitational field, and that along with length and time constitutes one of the fundamental quantities on which all physical measurements are based **2 :** a large quantity, amount, or number ⟨a great ~ of material⟩ **3 a :** a large body of persons in a compact group **:** a body of persons regarded as an aggregate **b :** the body of people as contrasted with the elite — often used in pl. ⟨a better future for the underprivileged and disadvantaged ~*es* —C. A. Buss⟩ ***syn*** see BULK

³**mass** *vt* (14c) **:** to form or collect into a mass ~ *vi* **:** to assemble in a mass ⟨three thousand students had ~*ed* in the plaza —A. E. Neville⟩

⁴**mass** *adj* (1733) **1 a :** of or relating to the mass of the people ⟨~ market⟩ ⟨~ education⟩; *also* **:** being one of or at one with the mass **:** AVERAGE, COMMONPLACE ⟨~ man⟩ **b :** participated in by or affecting a large number of individuals ⟨~ destruction⟩ ⟨~ demonstrations⟩ **c :** having a large-scale character **:** WHOLESALE ⟨~ production⟩ **2 :** viewed as a whole **:** TOTAL ⟨the ~ effect of a design⟩

mas·sa \ˈmas-ə\ *n, Southern* (1774) **:** MASTER ⟨this Louisiana sugar planter was called ~ by a hundred Negroes —Katharine L. Bates⟩

Mas·sa·chu·set \ˌmas-(ə-)ˈchü-sət, -zət\ *n, pl* **Massachuset** *or* **Massachusets** *also* **Massachusetts** [Massachuset *Massa-adchu-es-et,* a locality, lit., about the big hill] (1616) **1 :** a member of an American Indian people of Massachusetts **2 :** the Algonquian language of the Massachuset people

¹**mas·sa·cre** \ˈmas-i-kər\ *n* [MF] (1578) **1 :** the act or an instance of killing a number of usu. helpless or unresisting human beings under circumstances of atrocity or cruelty **2 :** a cruel or wanton murder **3 :** a wholesale slaughter of animals **4 :** an act of complete destruction ⟨the author's ~ of traditional federalist presuppositions —R. G. McCloskey⟩

²**massacre** *vt* **mas·sa·cred; mas·sa·cring** \-k(ə-)riŋ\ (1581) **1 :** to kill by massacre **:** SLAUGHTER **2 :** MANGLE ⟨words were misspelled and syntax *massacred* —Bice Clemow⟩ — **mas·sa·crer** \-kər-ər, -krər\ *n*

¹**mas·sage** \mə-ˈsäzh, -ˈsäj\ *n* [F, fr. *masser* to massage, fr. Ar *massa* to stroke] (ca. 1860) **:** manipulation of tissues (as by rubbing, stroking, kneading, or tapping) with the hand or an instrument for remedial or hygienic purposes

²**massage** *vt* **mas·saged; mas·sag·ing** (1887) **1 :** to subject to massage **2 a :** to treat flatteringly **:** BLANDISH **b :** MANIPULATE 3, DOCTOR 2b ⟨researchers *massaged* the data to support their thesis⟩ — **mas·sag·er** *n*

massage parlor *n* (1913) **:** an establishment that provides massage treatments; *also* **:** one offering sexual services in addition to or in lieu of massage

mas·sa·sau·ga \ˌmas-ə-ˈsȯ-gə\ *n* [*Missisauga* river, Ontario, Canada] (1835) **:** any of several small rattlesnakes (genus *Sistrurus*)

mass card *n* (1948) **:** a card notifying the recipient (as a bereaved family) that a mass is to be offered for the repose of the soul of a specified deceased person

mass defect *n* (ca. 1923) **:** the difference between the mass of an isotope and its mass number

mas·sé \ma-ˈsā\ *n* [F, fr. pp. of *masser* to make a massé shot, fr. *masse* sledgehammer, fr. MF *mace* mace] (1873) **:** a shot in billiards or pool made by hitting the cue ball vertically or nearly vertically on the side to drive it around one ball in order to strike another

mass–energy equation *n* (ca. 1942) **:** an equation for the interconversion of mass and energy: $E = MC^2$ where E is energy in ergs, M is mass in grams, and C is the velocity of light in centimeters per second

mas·se·ter \mə-ˈsēt-ər, ma-\ *n* [NL, fr. Gk *masētēr,* fr. *masasthai* to chew] (1666) **:** a large muscle that raises the lower jaw and assists in mastication — **mas·se·ter·ic** \ˌmas-ə-ˈter-ik\ *adj*

mas·seur \ma-ˈsər, mə-\ *n* [F, fr. *masser*] (ca. 1876) **:** a man who practices massage and physiotherapy

mas·seuse \-ˈsə(r)z, -ˈsüz\ *n* [F, fem. of *masseur*] (ca. 1876) **:** a woman who practices massage and physiotherapy

mas·si·cot \ˈmas-ə-ˌkät, -ˌkō(t)\ *n* [ME *masticot,* fr. MF *massicot, masticot,* fr. OIt *massicotto* pottery glaze] (15c) **:** a yellow unfused lead monoxide PbO used esp. as a pigment

mas·sif \ma-ˈsēf\ *n* [F, fr. *massif,* adj., fr. MF] (1885) **1 :** a principal mountain mass **2 :** a block of the earth's crust bounded by faults or flexures and displaced as a unit without internal change

mas·sive \ˈmas-iv\ *adj* [ME *massiffe,* fr. MF *massif,* fr. *masse* mass] (15c) **1 :** forming or consisting of a large mass: **a :** BULKY **b :** WEIGHTY, HEAVY ⟨~ walls⟩ ⟨a ~ volume⟩ **c :** impressively large or ponderous **d :** having no regular form but not necessarily lacking crystalline structure ⟨~ sandstone⟩ **2 a :** large, solid, or heavy in structure ⟨~ jaw⟩ **b :** large in scope or degree ⟨the feeling of frustration, of being ineffectual, is ~ —David Halberstam⟩ **c** (1) **:** large in comparison to what is typical ⟨~ dose of penicillin⟩ (2) **:** being extensive and severe ⟨~ hemorrhage⟩ ⟨~ collapse of a lung⟩ (3) **:** imposing in excellence or grandeur **:** MONUMENTAL ⟨~ simplicity⟩ — **mas·sive·ly** *adv* — **mas·sive·ness** *n*

mass·less \ˈmas-ləs\ *adj* (1879) **:** having no mass ⟨a ~ particle⟩

mass medium *n, pl* **mass media** (1923) **:** a medium of communication (as newspapers, radio, or television) that is designed to reach the mass of the people — usu. used in pl.

mass noun *n* (1933) **:** a noun (as *sand* or *water*) that characteristically denotes in many languages a homogeneous substance or a concept without subdivisions and that in English is preceded in indefinite singular constructions by *some* rather than *a* or *an* — compare COUNT NOUN

mass number *n* (1923) **:** an integer that expresses the mass of an isotope and designates the number of nucleons in the nucleus

mass–pro·duce \ˌmas-prə-ˈd(y)üs\ *vt* [back-formation fr. *mass production*] (1923) **:** to produce in quantity usu. by machinery — **mass production** *n*

mass spectrometry *n* (1943) **:** an instrumental method for identifying the chemical constitution of a substance by means of the separation of gaseous ions according to their differing mass and charge — **mass spectrometric** *adj* — **mass spectrometer** *n*

mass spectrum *n* (1920) **:** the spectrum of a stream of gaseous ions separated according to their mass and charge

massy \ˈmas-ē\ *adj* (14c) **:** MASSIVE

¹**mast** \ˈmast\ *n* [ME, fr. OE *mæst;* akin to OHG *mast,* mast, L *malus*] (bef. 12c) **1 :** a long pole or spar rising from the keel or deck of a ship and supporting the yards, booms, and rigging **2 :** a vertical or nearly vertical pole (as an upright post in various cranes) **3 :** a disciplinary proceeding at which the commanding officer of a naval unit hears and disposes of cases against his enlisted men — called also *captain's mast* — **mast·ed** \ˈmas-təd\ *adj* — **before the mast 1 :** forward of the foremast **2 :** as a common sailor

²**mast** *vt* (1627) **:** to furnish with a mast

³**mast** *n* [ME, fr. OE *mæst;* akin to OHG *mast* food, mast, OE *mete* food — more at MEAT] (bef. 12c) **:** nuts (as beechnuts and acorns) accumulated on the forest floor and often serving as food for animals (as hogs)

mast- *or* **masto-** *comb form* [NL, fr. Gk, fr. *mastos*] **:** breast **:** nipple **:** mammary gland ⟨*mast*itis⟩

mas·ta·ba \ˈmas-tə-bə\ *n* [Ar *maṣṭabah* stone bench] (1882) **:** an Egyptian tomb of the time of the Memphite dynasties that is oblong in shape with sloping sides and a flat roof

mast cell \ˈmast-\ *n* [part trans. of G *mast zelle,* fr. *mast* food, mast (fr. OHG) + *zelle* cell] (ca. 1890) **:** a large cell with numerous heparin-containing basophilic granules that occurs esp. in connective tissue

mas·tec·to·my \ma-ˈstek-tə-mē\ *n, pl* **-mies** (1923) **:** excision or amputation of the breast

¹**mas·ter** \ˈmas-tər\ *n* [ME, fr. OE *magister* & OF *maistre,* both fr. L *magister;* akin to L *magnus* great — more at MUCH] (bef. 12c) **1 a** (1) **:** a male teacher (2) **:** a person holding an academic degree higher than a bachelor's but lower than a doctor's **b** *often cap* **:** a revered religious leader **c :** a workman qualified to teach apprentices **d** (1) **:** an artist, performer, or player of consummate skill (2) **:** a great figure of the past (as in science or art) whose work serves as a model or ideal **2 a :** one having authority over another **:** RULER, GOVERNOR **b :** one that conquers or masters **:** VICTOR, SUPERIOR ⟨in this young, obscure challenger the champion found his ~⟩ **c :** a person licensed to command a merchant ship **d** (1) **:** one having control (2) **:** an owner esp. of a slave or animal **e :** the employer esp. of a servant **f** (1) *dial* **:** HUSBAND (2) **:** the male head of a household **3 a** (1) *archaic* **:** MR. (2) **:** a youth or boy too young to be called *mister* — used as a title **b :** the eldest son of a Scottish viscount or baron **4 a :** a presiding officer in an institution or society (as a college) **b :** any of several officers of court appointed to assist (as by hearing and reporting) a judge **5 a :** a master mechanism or device **b :** an original from which copies can be made; *esp* **:** a master phonograph record or magnetic tape — **mas·ter·ship** \-ˌship\ *n*

²**master** *adj* (12c) **:** being or relating to a master: as **a :** having chief authority **:** DOMINANT **b :** SKILLED, PROFICIENT ⟨a prosperous ~ builder —*Current Biog.*⟩ **c :** PRINCIPAL, PREDOMINANT **d :** SUPERLATIVE — often used in combination ⟨a *master*-liar⟩ **e :** being a device or mechanism that controls the operation of another mechanism or that establishes a standard (as a dimension or weight) **f :** being or relating to a master from which duplicates are made

³**master** *vt* **mas·tered; mas·ter·ing** \-t(ə-)riŋ\ (13c) **1 :** to become master of **:** OVERCOME **2 a :** to become skilled or proficient in the use of ⟨~ a foreign language⟩ **b :** to gain a thorough understanding of ⟨had ~*ed* every aspect of publishing — *Current Biog.*⟩ **3 :** to produce a master phonograph record or magnetic tape of (as a musical rendition)

master–at–arms *n, pl* **masters–at–arms** (1748) **:** a petty officer charged with maintaining discipline aboard ship

master bedroom *n* (1925) **:** a large or principal bedroom

master chief petty officer *n* (1958) **:** an enlisted man in the navy or coast guard ranking above a senior chief petty officer

master chief petty officer of the coast guard (1966) **:** the ranking petty officer in the coast guard serving as adviser to the commandant

master chief petty officer of the navy (1966) **:** the ranking petty officer in the navy serving as adviser to the chief of naval operations

master class *n* (1952) **:** a seminar for advanced music students conducted by a master musician

mas·ter·ful \ˈmas-tər-fəl\ *adj* (15c) **1 a :** inclined and usu. competent to play the master **b :** suggestive of a masterful nature **2 :** having or reflecting the power and skill of a master — **mas·ter·ful·ly** \-fə-lē\ *adv* — **mas·ter·ful·ness** *n*

syn MASTERFUL, DOMINEERING, IMPERIOUS, PEREMPTORY, IMPERATIVE mean tending to impose one's will on others. MASTERFUL implies a strong personality and ability to act authoritatively ⟨she was ever a *masterful* woman, better fitted to command than to obey —H. O. Taylor⟩ DOMINEERING suggests an overbearing or arbitrary manner and an obstinate determination to enforce one's will ⟨like *domineering* mothers, the states refuse cities the right to run their own lives —T. C. Desmond⟩ IMPERIOUS implies a commanding nature or manner and often suggests arrogant assurance ⟨she is the cynical, *imperious* guide for the politician's early steps, seething with impotent and suppressed rage as she watches him grow out of her control —Alton Cook⟩ PEREMPTORY implies an abrupt dictatorial manner coupled with an unwillingness to brook disobedience or dissent ⟨his *peremptory* command that she decide at once about his proposal —James Purdy⟩ IMPERATIVE implies peremptoriness arising more from the urgency of the situation than from an inherent will to dominate ⟨he heard her *imperative* voice at the telephone; he heard her summon the doctor —Ellen Glasgow⟩

usage Some commentators insist that use of *masterful* should be limited to sense 1 in order to preserve a distinction between it and *masterly.* The distinction is a modern one, excogitated by a 20th century pundit in disregard of the history of the word. Both words developed in a parallel manner but the earlier sense of *masterly,* equivalent to *masterful* 1, dropped out of use. Since *masterly* had but one sense, the pundit opined that it would be tidy if *masterful* were likewise limited to one sense and he forthwith condemned use of *masterful* 2 as an error. Sense 2 of *masterful,* which is slightly older than the sense of *masterly* intended to replace it, has continued in reputable use all along; it cannot rationally be called an error.

master gunnery sergeant *n* (1958) **:** a noncommissioned officer in the marine corps ranking above a master sergeant

master key *n* (1576) **:** a key designed to open several different locks

mas·ter·ly \'mas-tər-lē\ *adj* (15c) **:** suitable to or resembling that of a master; *esp* **:** indicating thorough knowledge or superior skill and power ⟨~ performance⟩ *usage* see MASTERFUL — **mas·ter·li·ness** *n* — **masterly** *adv*

[1]**mas·ter·mind** \'mas-tər-,mīnd, ,mas-tər-'\ *n* (1720) **:** a person who supplies the directing or creative intelligence for a project

[2]**mastermind** *vt* (1940) **:** to be the mastermind of

master of arts *often cap M&A* (15c) **1 :** the recipient of a master's degree that usu. signifies that the recipient has passed an integrated course of study in one or more of the humanities and sometimes has completed a thesis involving research or a creative project and that typically requires two years of work beyond a bachelor's degree **2 :** the degree making one a master of arts — abbr. *M.A., A.M.*

master of ceremonies (1662) **1 :** a person who determines the forms to be observed on a public occasion **2 :** a person who acts as host at a formal event **3 :** a person who acts as host for a program of entertainment (as on television)

master of science *often cap M&S* (ca. 1904) **1 :** the recipient of a master's degree that usu. signifies that the recipient has passed an integrated course of study in one or more of the sciences and sometimes has completed a thesis involving research and that typically requires two years of work beyond a bachelor's degree **2 :** the degree making one a master of science — abbr. *M.S., M.Sc.*

mas·ter·piece \'mas-tər-,pēs\ *n* (1605) **1 :** a piece of work presented to a medieval guild as evidence of qualification for the rank of master **2 :** a work done with extraordinary skill; *esp* **:** a supreme intellectual or artistic achievement

master plan *n* (1929) **:** a plan giving overall guidance

master race *n* (1937) **:** a people held to be racially preeminent and hence fitted to rule or enslave other peoples

master sergeant *n* (ca. 1934) **:** a noncommissioned officer ranking in the army above a sergeant first class and below a staff sergeant major, in the air force above a technical sergeant and below a senior master sergeant, and in the marine corps above a gunnery sergeant and below a master gunnery sergeant

mas·ter·sing·er \'mas-tər-,siŋ-ər\ *n* (1810) **:** MEISTERSINGER

mas·ter·stroke \-,strōk\ *n* (1679) **:** a masterly performance or move

mas·ter·work \-,wərk\ *n* (1617) **:** MASTERPIECE

mas·tery \'mas-t(ə-)rē\ *n* [ME *maistrie,* fr. OF, fr. *maistre* master] (13c) **1 a :** the authority of a master **:** DOMINION **b :** the upper hand in a contest or competition **:** SUPERIORITY, ASCENDANCY **2 a :** possession or display of great skill or technique **b :** skill or knowledge that makes one master of a subject **:** COMMAND

mast·head \'mast-,hed\ *n* (1748) **1 :** the top of a mast **2 a :** the printed matter in a newspaper or periodical that gives the title and pertinent details of ownership, advertising rates, and subscription rates **b :** the name of a publication (as a newspaper) displayed on the top of the first page

mas·tic \'mas-tik\ *n* [ME *mastik,* fr. L *mastiche,* fr. Gk *mastichē;* akin to Gk *mastichan*] (14c) **1 :** an aromatic resinous exudate from mastic trees used chiefly in varnishes **2 :** any of various pasty materials used as protective coatings or cements

mas·ti·cate \'mas-tə-,kāt\ *vb* **-cat·ed; -cat·ing** [LL *masticatus,* pp. of *masticare,* fr. Gk *mastichan* to gnash the teeth; akin to Gk *masasthai* to chew — more at MOUTH] *vt* (1649) **1 :** to grind or crush (food) with or as if with the teeth in preparation for swallowing **:** CHEW **2 :** to soften or reduce to pulp by crushing or kneading ~ *vi* **:** CHEW — **mas·ti·ca·tion** \,mas-tə-'kā-shən\ *n* — **mas·ti·ca·tor** \'mas-tə-,kāt-ər\ *n*

[1]**mas·ti·ca·to·ry** \'mas-ti-kə-,tōr-ē, -,tȯr-\ *adj* (1611) **1 :** used for or adapted to chewing ⟨~ limbs of an arthropod⟩ **2 :** of, relating to, or involving the organs of mastication ⟨~ paralysis⟩

[2]**masticatory** *n, pl* **-ries** (1611) **:** a substance chewed to increase saliva

mastic tree *n* (15c) **:** a small southern European tree (*Pistacia lentiscus*) of the sumac family that yields mastic

mas·tiff \'mas-təf\ *n* [ME *mastif,* modif. of MF *mastin,* fr. (assumed) VL *mansuetinus,* fr. L *mansuetus* tame — more at MANSUETUDE] (14c) **:** any of a breed of very large powerful deep-chested smooth-coated dogs used chiefly as watchdogs and guard dogs

mastiff

mas·ti·goph·o·ran \,mas-tə-'gäf-ə-rən\ *n* [deriv. of Gk *mastig-, mastix* whip + *pherein* to carry — more at BEAR] (ca. 1909) **:** any of a class (Mastigophora) of protozoans comprising forms with flagella and including many often treated as algae — **mastigophoran** *adj*

mas·ti·tis \ma-'stīt-əs\ *n, pl* **-tit·i·des** \-'tit-ə-,dēz\ [NL] (ca. 1842) **:** inflammation of the breast or udder usu. caused by infection — **mas·tit·ic** \-'tit-ik\ *adj*

masto- — see MAST-

mast·odon \'mas-tə-,dän, -dən\ *n* [NL *mastodont-, mastodon,* fr. Gk *mast-* + *odont-, odōn, odous* tooth — more at TOOTH] (1813) **1 :** any of numerous extinct mammals (esp. genus *Mammut*) that differ from the related mammoths and existing elephants chiefly in the form of the molar teeth **2 :** one that is unusually large — **mast·odon·ic** \,mas-tə-'dän-ik\ *adj* — **mast·odont** \'mas-tə-,dänt\ *adj or n*

[1]**mas·toid** \'mas-,tȯid\ *adj* [NL *mastoides* resembling a nipple, mastoid, fr. Gk *mastoeidēs,* fr. *mastos* breast] (1732) **1 :** being the process of the temporal bone behind the ear; *also* **:** being any of several bony elements that occupy a similar position in the skull of lower vertebrates **2 :** of, relating to, or occurring in the region of the mastoid process

[2]**mastoid** *n* (1842) **:** a mastoid bone or process

mastoid cell *n* (1800) **:** one of the small cavities in the mastoid process that develop after birth and are filled with air

mas·toid·ec·to·my \,mas-,tȯid-'ek-tə-mē\ *n, pl* **-mies** [ISV] (1898) **:** surgical removal of the mastoid cells or of the mastoid process of the temporal bone

mas·toid·itis \,mas-,tȯid-'īt-əs\ *n* [NL] (ca. 1890) **:** inflammation of the mastoid and esp. of the mastoid cells

mas·tur·bate \'mas-tər-,bāt\ *vb* **-bat·ed; -bat·ing** [L *masturbatus,* pp. of *masturbari*] *vi* (1623) **:** to practice masturbation ~ *vt* **:** to practice masturbation on — **mas·tur·ba·tor** \-,bāt-ər\ *n*

mas·tur·ba·tion \,mas-tər-'bā-shən\ *n* (1621) **:** erotic stimulation of the genital organs commonly resulting in orgasm and achieved by manual or other bodily contact exclusive of sexual intercourse, by instrumental manipulation, occas. by sexual fantasies, or by various combinations of these agencies

mas·tur·ba·tory \'mas-tər-bə-,tōr-ē, -,tȯr-\ *adj* (1864) **:** of, relating to, or involving masturbation ⟨~ fantasies⟩

[1]**mat** \'mat\ *n* [ME, fr. OE *meatte,* fr. LL *matta,* of Sem origin; akin to Heb *miṭṭāh* bed] (bef. 12c) **1 a** (1) **:** a piece of coarse, woven, plaited, or felted fabric used esp. as a floor covering or a support (2) **:** a piece of material placed at a door for wiping soiled shoe soles **b :** a decorative piece of material used under a small item (as a dish) esp. for support or protection **c :** a large thick pad or cushion used as a surface for wrestling, tumbling, and gymnastics **2 :** something made up of many intertwined or tangled strands **3 :** a large slab usu. of reinforced concrete used as the supporting base of a building

[2]**mat** *vb* **mat·ted; mat·ting** *vt* (1549) **1 :** to provide with a mat or matting **2 a :** to form into a tangled mass **b :** to pack down so as to form a dense mass ~ *vi* **:** to become matted

[3]**mat** *or* **matt** *or* **matte** \'mat\ *vt* **mat·ted; mat·ting** (1602) **1 :** to make (as a metal, glass, or color) mat **2 :** to provide (a picture) with a mat

[4]**mat** *or* **matt** *or* **matte** *adj* [F, fr. OF, defeated, fr. L *mattus* drunk; akin to L *madēre* to be wet — more at MEAT] (1648) **:** lacking or deprived of luster or gloss: as **a :** having a usu. smooth even surface free from shine or highlights ⟨~ metals⟩ ⟨a ~ white face⟩ **b** *usu matte* **:** having a rough or granular surface

[5]**mat** *or* **matt** *or* **matte** *n* [F *mat* dull color, unpolished surface, fr. *mat,* adj.] (1845) **1 :** a border going around a picture between picture and frame or serving as the frame **2 :** a dead or dull finish or a roughened surface (as of gilt or paint)

[6]**mat** *n* (1904) **:** MATRIX 2a

mat·a·dor \'mat-ə-,dȯ(ə)r\ *n* [Sp, fr. *matar* to kill] (1681) **:** a bullfighter who has the principal role and who kills the bull in a bullfight

[1]**match** \'mach\ *n* [ME *macche,* fr. OE *mæcca;* akin to OE *macian* to make — more at MAKE] (bef. 12c) **1 a :** a person or thing equal or similar to another **b :** one able to cope with another **c :** an exact counterpart **2 :** a pair suitably associated ⟨carpet and curtains are a ~⟩ **3 a :** a contest between two or more parties ⟨a golf ~⟩ ⟨a soccer ~⟩ ⟨a shouting ~⟩ **b :** a tennis contest completed when one player or side wins a specified number of sets **4 a :** a marriage union **b :** a prospective partner in marriage

[2]**match** *vt* (14c) **1 a :** to encounter successfully as an antagonist **b** (1) **:** to set in competition or opposition (2) **:** to provide with a worthy competitor **c :** to set in comparison **2 :** to join or give in marriage **3 a** (1) **:** to put in a set possessing equal or harmonizing attributes (2) **:** to cause to correspond **:** SUIT **b** (1) **:** to be the counterpart of; *also* **:** to compare favorably with (2) **:** to harmonize with **c :** to provide with a counterpart **d :** to provide funds complementary to **4 :** to fit together or make suitable for fitting together **5 a :** to flip or toss (coins) and compare exposed faces **b :** to toss coins with ~ *vi* **:** to be a counterpart — **match·able** \'mach-ə-bəl\ *adj* — **match·er** *n*

[3]**match** *n* [ME *macche,* fr. MF *meiche*] (1549) **1 :** a chemically prepared wick or cord formerly used in firing firearms or powder **2 :** a short slender piece of flammable material (as wood) tipped with a combustible mixture that bursts into flame when slightly heated through friction (as by being scratched against a rough surface)

match·board \'mach-,bō(ə)rd, -,bȯ(ə)rd\ *n* (1858) **:** a board with a groove cut along one edge and a tongue along the other so as to fit snugly with the edges of similarly cut boards — called also *matched board*

match·book \-,bu̇k\ *n* (1944) **:** a small folder containing rows of paper matches

match·box \-,bäks\ *n* (1850) **:** a box for matches

match·less \-ləs\ *adj* (1530) **:** having no equal **:** PEERLESS — **match·less·ly** *adv*

match·lock \-,läk\ *n* (1637) **1 :** a slow-burning match lowered over a hole in the breech of a musket to ignite the charge **2 :** a musket equipped with a matchlock

match·mak·er \-,mā-kər\ *n* (1639) **:** one that arranges a match; *esp* **:** one who tries to bring two unmarried individuals together in an attempt to promote a marriage — **match·mak·ing** \-kiŋ\ *n*

match play *n* (1893) **:** a golf competition in which the winner is the person or team winning the greater number of holes — compare STROKE PLAY

match point *n* (1921) **:** a situation (as in tennis) in which one player will win the match by winning the next point; *also* **:** the point itself

match·stick \'mach-,stik\ *n* (1791) **1 :** a slender piece esp. of wood from which a match is made **2 :** something resembling a matchstick esp. in slenderness

match·up \-,əp\ *n* (1964) **:** [1]MATCH

match·wood \-,wu̇d\ *n* (1838) **:** small pieces of wood **:** SPLINTERS

[1]**mate** \'māt\ *vt* **mat·ed; mat·ing** [ME *maten,* fr. MF *mater,* fr. OF *mat,* n., checkmate, fr. Ar *māt* (in *shāh māt*)] (14c) **:** CHECKMATE 2

[2]**mate** *n* (14c) **:** CHECKMATE 1

[3]**mate** *n* [ME, prob. fr. MLG *māt;* akin to OE *gemetta* guest at one's table, *mete* food — more at MEAT] (14c) **1 a** (1) **:** ASSOCIATE, COMPANION (2) **:** an assistant to a more skilled worker **:** HELPER ⟨plumber's ~⟩ **b** *archaic* **:** MATCH, PEER **2 :** a deck officer on a merchant ship ranking below the captain **3 :** one of a pair: as **a :** either member of a couple and esp. a married couple **b :** either member of a breeding pair of animals **c :** either of two matched objects

4mate *vb* **mat·ed; mat·ing** *vt* (1509) **1** *archaic* **:** EQUAL, MATCH **2 :** to join or fit together **:** COUPLE **3 a :** to join together as mates **b :** to provide a mate for ~ *vi* **1 :** to become mated ⟨gears that ~ well⟩ **2 :** COPULATE

ma·té *or* **ma·te** \ˈmä-ˌtā\ *n* [F & AmerSp; F *maté,* fr. AmerSp *mate,* fr. Quechua] (1758) **1 :** a tealike beverage drunk esp. in So. America **2 :** a So. American shrub or tree (*Ilex paraguayensis*) of the holly family whose leaves and shoots are used in making maté; *also* **:** these leaves and shoots

ma·te·lote \ˌmat-ᵊl-ˈōt, mat-ˈlōt\ *n* [F, lit., sailor's wife, fr. *matelot* sailor, fr. MD *mattenoot,* lit., bed-companion] (ca. 1730) **:** a stew made usu. of fish in a seasoned wine sauce

ma·ter \ˈmāt-ər\ *n* [L — more at MOTHER] (ca. 1859) *chiefly Brit* **:** MOTHER

ma·ter·fa·mil·i·as \ˌmāt-ər-fə-ˈmil-ē-əs, ˌmät-\ *n* [L, fr. *mater* + *familias,* archaic gen. of *familia* household — more at FAMILY] (1756) **:** a woman who is head of a household

1ma·te·ri·al \mə-ˈtir-ē-əl\ *adj* [ME *materiel,* fr. MF & LL; MF, fr. LL *materialis,* fr. L *materia* matter — more at MATTER] (14c) **1 a** (1) **:** relating to, derived from, or consisting of matter; *esp* **:** PHYSICAL ⟨the ~ world⟩ (2) **:** BODILY ⟨~ needs⟩ **b** (1) **:** of or relating to matter rather than form ⟨~ cause⟩ (2) **:** of or relating to the subject matter of reasoning; *esp* **:** EMPIRICAL ⟨~ knowledge⟩ **2 :** having real importance or great consequences ⟨facts ~ to the investigation⟩ ⟨had no ~ effect on net income⟩ **3 a :** being of a physical or worldly nature **b :** relating to or concerned with physical rather than spiritual or intellectual things ⟨~ progress⟩ — **ma·te·ri·al·ly** \-ē-ə-lē\ *adv* — **ma·te·ri·al·ness** *n*

syn MATERIAL, PHYSICAL, CORPOREAL, PHENOMENAL, SENSIBLE, OBJECTIVE mean of or belonging to actuality. MATERIAL implies formation out of tangible matter; used in contrast with *spiritual* or *ideal* it may connote the mundane, crass, or grasping; PHYSICAL applies to what is perceived directly by the senses and may contrast with *mental, spiritual,* or *imaginary;* CORPOREAL implies having the tangible qualities of a body such as shape, size, or resistance to force; PHENOMENAL applies to what is known or perceived through the senses rather than by intuition or rational deduction; SENSIBLE stresses the capability of readily or forcibly impressing the senses; OBJECTIVE may stress material or independent existence apart from a subject perceiving it. ***syn*** see in addition RELEVANT

2material *n* (14c) **1 a** (1) **:** the elements, constituents, or substances of which something is composed or can be made (2) **:** matter that has qualities which give it individuality and by which it may be categorized ⟨sticky ~⟩ ⟨explosive ~*s*⟩ **b** (1) **:** something (as data) that may be worked into a more finished form ⟨~ for a biography⟩ (2) **:** something used for or made the object of study ⟨~ for the next semester⟩ (3) **:** a performer's repertoire ⟨a comedian's ~⟩ **c :** MATTER 3b **d :** CLOTH **e :** a person potentially suited to some pursuit ⟨varsity ~⟩ ⟨leadership ~⟩ **2 a :** apparatus necessary for doing or making something ⟨writing ~*s*⟩ **b :** MATÉRIEL

materialise *Brit var of* MATERIALIZE

ma·te·ri·al·ism \mə-ˈtir-ē-ə-ˌliz-əm\ *n* (1748) **1 a :** a theory that physical matter is the only or fundamental reality and that all being and processes and phenomena can be explained as manifestations or results of matter **b :** a doctrine that the only or the highest values or objectives lie in material well-being and in the furtherance of material progress **c :** a doctrine that economic or social change is materially caused — compare HISTORICAL MATERIALISM **2 :** a preoccupation with or stress upon material rather than intellectual or spiritual things — **ma·te·ri·al·ist** \-ləst\ *n or adj* — **ma·te·ri·al·is·tic** \-ˌtir-ē-ə-ˈlis-tik\ *adj* — **ma·te·ri·al·is·ti·cal·ly** \-ti-k(ə-)lē\ *adv*

ma·te·ri·al·i·ty \mə-ˌtir-ē-ˈal-ət-ē\ *n, pl* **-ties** (1570) **1 :** the quality or state of being material **2 :** something that is material

ma·te·ri·al·iza·tion \mə-ˌtir-ē-ə-lə-ˈzā-shən\ *n* (1843) **1 :** the action of materializing or becoming materialized **2 :** something that has been materialized; *esp* **:** APPARITION

ma·te·ri·al·ize \mə-ˈtir-ē-ə-ˌlīz\ *vb* **-ized; -iz·ing** *vt* (1710) **1 a :** to make material **:** OBJECTIFY ⟨*materializing* an idea in words⟩ **b :** to cause to appear in bodily form ⟨~ the spirits of the dead⟩ **2 :** to cause to be materialistic ~ *vi* **1 :** to assume bodily form **2 a :** to come into existence **b :** to put in an appearance; *esp* **:** to appear suddenly — **ma·te·ri·al·iz·er** *n*

ma·te·ria med·i·ca \mə-ˌtir-ē-ə-ˈmed-i-kə\ *n* [NL, lit., medical matter] (1699) **1 :** substances used in the composition of medical remedies **:** DRUGS, MEDICINE **2 a :** a branch of medical science that deals with the sources, nature, properties, and preparation of drugs **b :** a treatise on materia medica

ma·té·ri·el *or* **ma·te·ri·el** \mə-ˌtir-ē-ˈel\ *n* [F *matériel,* fr. *matériel,* adj.] (1814) **:** equipment, apparatus, and supplies used by an organization or institution

ma·ter·nal \mə-ˈtərn-ᵊl\ *adj* [ME, fr. MF *maternel,* fr. L *maternus,* fr. *mater* mother — more at MOTHER] (15c) **1 :** of, relating to, belonging to, or characteristic of a mother **:** MOTHERLY **2 a :** related through a mother ⟨his ~ aunt⟩ **b :** inherited or derived from the female parent ⟨~ genes⟩ — **ma·ter·nal·ly** \-ᵊl-ē\ *adv*

1ma·ter·ni·ty \mə-ˈtər-nət-ē\ *n, pl* **-ties** (1611) **1 a :** the quality or state of being a mother **:** MOTHERHOOD **b :** the qualities of a mother **:** MOTHERLINESS **2 :** a hospital facility designed for the care of women before and during childbirth and for the care of newborn babies

2maternity *adj* (1893) **1 :** designed for wear during pregnancy ⟨a ~ dress⟩ **2 :** effective for the period close to and including childbirth ⟨~ leave⟩

mat·ey \ˈmāt-ē\ *adj, chiefly Brit* (1915) **:** COMPANIONABLE

math \ˈmath\ *n* (ca. 1890) **:** MATHEMATICS

math·e·mat·i·cal \ˌmath-ə-ˈmat-i-kəl, math-ˈmat-\ *also* **math·e·mat·ic** \-ik\ *adj* [L *mathematicus,* fr. Gk *mathēmatikos,* fr. *mathēmat-, mathēma* mathematics, fr. *manthanein* to learn; akin to Goth *mundon* to pay attention, Skt *medhā* intelligence] (15c) **1 :** of, relating to, or according with mathematics **2 a :** rigorously exact **:** PRECISE **b :** CERTAIN **3 :** possible but highly improbable ⟨only a ~ chance⟩ — **math·e·mat·i·cal·ly** \-i-k(ə-)lē\ *adv*

mathematical expectation *n* (1838) **:** EXPECTED VALUE

mathematical induction *n* (1838) **:** INDUCTION 2b

mathematical logic *n* (1858) **:** SYMBOLIC LOGIC

math·e·ma·ti·cian \ˌmath-(ə-)mə-ˈtish-ən\ *n* (15c) **:** a specialist or expert in mathematics

math·e·mat·ics \ˌmath-ə-ˈmat-iks, math-ˈmat-\ *n pl but usu sing in constr* (1581) **1 :** the science of numbers and their operations, interrelations, combinations, generalizations, and abstractions and of space configurations and their structure, measurement, transformations, and generalizations **2 :** a branch of, operation in, or use of mathematics ⟨the ~ of physical chemistry⟩

math·e·ma·ti·za·tion \ˌmath(-ə)-mət-ə-ˈzā-shən\ *n* (1928) **:** reduction to mathematical form

maths \ˈmaths\ *n pl, chiefly Brit* (1911) **:** MATHEMATICS

mat·in \ˈmat-ᵊn\ *adj* [ME, fr. OF] (14c) **:** of or relating to matins or to early morning

mat·in·al \ˈmat-ᵊn-əl\ *adj* (1803) **1 :** of or relating to matins **2 :** EARLY

mat·i·nee *or* **mat·i·née** \ˌmat-ᵊn-ˈā\ *n* [F *matinée,* lit., morning, fr. OF, fr. *matin* morning, fr. L *matutinum,* fr. neut. of *matutinus* of the morning, fr. *Matuta,* goddess of morning; akin to L *maturus* ripe — more at MATURE] (1850) **:** a musical or dramatic performance or social or public event held in the daytime and esp. the afternoon

matinee idol *n* (1902) **:** a handsome male performer

mat·ins \ˈmat-ᵊnz\ *n pl but sing or pl in constr, often cap* [ME *matines,* fr. OF, fr. LL *matutinae,* fr. L, fem. pl. of *matutinus*] (13c) **1 :** the night office forming with lauds the first of the canonical hours **2 :** MORNING PRAYER

matr- *or* **matri-** *or* **matro-** *comb form* [L *matr-, matri-,* fr. *matr-, mater*] **:** mother ⟨*matri*arch⟩ ⟨*matro*nymic⟩

ma·tri·arch \ˈmā-trē-ˌärk\ *n* (1606) **:** a female who rules or dominates a family, group, or state; *specif* **:** a mother who is head and ruler of her family and descendants — **ma·tri·ar·chal** \ˌmā-trē-ˈär-kəl\ *adj*

ma·tri·ar·chate \ˈmā-trē-ˌär-kət, -ˌkāt\ *n* (1885) **:** MATRIARCHY 1

ma·tri·ar·chy \ˈmā-trē-ˌär-kē\ *n, pl* **-chies** (1885) **1 :** a family, group, or state governed by a matriarch **2 :** a system of social organization in which descent and inheritance are traced through the female line

ma·tri·cide \ˈma-trə-ˌsīd, ˈmā-\ *n* (1594) **1** [L *matricidium,* fr. *matr-* + *-cidium* -cide] **:** murder of a mother by her son or daughter **2** [L *matricida,* fr. *matr-* + *-cida* -cide] **:** one that murders his mother — **ma·tri·cid·al** \ˌma-trə-ˈsīd-ᵊl, ˌmā-\ *adj*

ma·tric·u·late \mə-ˈtrik-yə-ˌlāt\ *vb* **-lat·ed; -lat·ing** [ML *matriculatus,* pp. of *matriculare,* fr. LL *matricula* public roll, dim. of *matric-, matrix* list, fr. L, womb] *vt* (1577) **:** to enroll as a member of a body and esp. of a college or university ~ *vi* **:** to become matriculated — **ma·tric·u·lant** \-lənt\ *n* — **ma·tric·u·la·tion** \-ˌtrik-yə-ˈlā-shən\ *n*

ma·tri·lin·eal \ˌma-trə-ˈlin-ē-əl, ˌmā-\ *adj* (1904) **:** relating to, based on, or tracing descent through the maternal line ⟨~ society⟩ — **ma·tri·lin·eal·ly** \-ē-ə-lē\ *adv*

mat·ri·mo·nial \ˌma-trə-ˈmō-nē-əl, -nyəl\ *adj* (15c) **:** of or relating to marriage, the married state, or married persons — **mat·ri·mo·nial·ly** \-ē\ *adv*

mat·ri·mo·ny \ˈma-trə-ˌmō-nē\ *n* [ME, fr. MF *matremoine,* fr. L *matrimonium,* fr. *matr-, mater* mother, matron — more at MOTHER] (14c) **:** the union of man and woman as husband and wife **:** MARRIAGE

matrimony vine *n* (1817) **:** a shrub or vine (genus *Lycium*) of the nightshade family with often showy flowers and bright berries

ma·trix \ˈmā-triks\ *n, pl* **ma·tri·ces** \ˈmā-trə-ˌsēz, ˈma-\ *or* **ma·trix·es** \ˈmā-trik-səz\ [L, womb, fr. *matr-, mater*] (15c) **1 :** something within which something else originates or develops **2 a :** a mold from which a relief surface (as a piece of type) is made **b :** DIE 4a(1) **c :** an engraved or inscribed die or stamp **d :** an electroformed impression of a phonograph record used for mass-producing duplicates of the original **3 a :** the natural material in which a fossil, metal, gem, crystal, or pebble is embedded **b :** material in which something is enclosed or embedded (as for protection or study) **4 a :** the intercellular substance in which tissue cells (as of connective tissue) are embedded **b :** the thickened epithelium at the base of a fingernail or toenail from which new nail substance develops **5 a :** a rectangular array of mathematical elements (as the coefficients of simultaneous linear equations) that can be combined to form sums and products with similar arrays having an appropriate number of rows and columns **b :** something resembling a mathematical matrix esp. in rectangular arrangement of elements into rows and columns; *also* **:** an array of circuit elements (as diodes and transistors) for performing a specific function as interconnected

matrix sentence *n* (1964) **:** that one of a pair of transformationally joined sentences that maintains its essential external structure ⟨in "the book that I want is gone", "the book is gone" is a *matrix sentence*⟩

ma·tron \ˈmā-trən\ *n* [ME *matrone,* fr. MF, fr. L *matrona,* fr. *matr-, mater*] (14c) **1 a :** a married woman usu. marked by dignified maturity or social distinction **b :** a woman who supervises women or children (as in a school or police station) **c :** the chief officer in a women's organization **2 :** a brood female

ma·tron·ly \ˈmā-trən-lē\ *adj* (1656) **:** having the character of or suitable to a matron

matron of honor (1903) **:** a bride's principal married wedding attendant

mat·ro·nym·ic \ˌma-trə-ˈnim-ik\ *n* [*matr-* + *-onymic* (as in *patronymic*)] (1874) **:** a name derived from that of the mother or a maternal ancestor

matt *or* **matte** \ˈmat\ *var of* MAT

matte \ˈmat\ *n* [F] (1839) **:** a crude mixture of sulfides formed in smelting sulfide ores of metals (as copper, lead, or nickel)

1mat·ter \ˈmat-ər\ *n* [ME *matere,* fr. OF, fr. L *materia* matter, physical substance, fr. *mater*] (13c) **1 a :** a subject under consideration **b :** a subject of disagreement or litigation **c** *pl* **:** the events or circumstances of a particular situation **d :** the subject or substance of a discourse or writing **e :** something of an indicated kind or having to do with an indicated field or situation ⟨this is a serious ~⟩ ⟨as a ~ of policy⟩ ⟨~*s* of faith⟩ **f :** something to be proved in law **g** *obs* **:** sensible or serious material as distinguished from nonsense or drollery **h** (1) *obs* **:** REASON, CAUSE (2) **:** a source esp. of feeling or emotion **i :** PROBLEM, DIFFI-

CULTY **2 a :** the substance of which a physical object is composed **b :** material substance that occupies space and has weight, that constitutes the observable universe, and that together with energy forms the basis of objective phenomena **c :** a material substance of a particular kind or for a particular purpose ⟨vegetable ~⟩ **d** (1) **:** material (as feces or urine) discharged from the living body (2) **:** material discharged by suppuration **:** PUS **3 a :** the indeterminate subject of reality; *esp* **:** the element in the universe that undergoes formation and alteration **b :** the formless substratum of all things which exists only potentially and upon which form acts to produce realities **4 :** a more or less definite amount or quantity ⟨cooks in a ~ of minutes⟩ **5 :** something written or printed **6 :** MAIL **7** *Christian Science* **:** the illusion that the objects perceived by the physical senses have the reality of substance — **for that matter :** so far as that is concerned — **no matter :** without regard to **:** irrespective of ⟨points in the same direction *no matter* how it is tilted⟩ — **the matter :** WRONG ⟨nothing's *the matter* with me⟩

[2]**matter** *vi* (1530) **1 :** to form or discharge pus **:** SUPPURATE ⟨~*ing* wound⟩ **2 :** to be of importance **:** SIGNIFY

matter of course (1739) **:** something that is to be expected as a natural or logical consequence

mat·ter–of–fact \ˌmat-ə-rə(v)-ˈfakt\ *adj* (1712) **:** adhering to the unembellished facts; *also* **:** being plain, straightforward, or unemotional — **mat·ter–of–fact·ly** \-ˈfak-(t)lē\ *adv* — **mat·ter–of–fact·ness** \-ˈfak(t)-nəs\ *n*

mat·tery \ˈmat-ə-rē\ *adj* (14c) **:** producing or containing pus or material resembling pus ⟨eyes all ~⟩

Mat·the·an *or* **Mat·thae·an** \ma-ˈthē-ən, mə-\ *adj* [LL *Matthaeus*] (1897) **:** of, relating to, or characteristic of the evangelist Matthew or the gospel ascribed to him

Mat·thew \ˈmath-(ˌ)yü *also* ˈmath-(ˌ)ü\ *n* [F *Mathieu,* fr. LL *Matthaeus,* fr. Gk *Matthaios,* fr. Heb *Mattithyāh*] **1 :** an apostle traditionally identified as the author of the first Gospel in the New Testament **2 :** the first Gospel in the New Testament — see BIBLE table

[1]**mat·ting** \ˈmat-iŋ\ *n* (ca. 1847) **1 :** material for mats **2 :** MATS

[2]**matting** *n* [fr. gerund of [3]*mat*] (1854) **:** a dull lusterless surface (as on gilding, metalwork, or satin)

mat·tins *often cap, chiefly Brit var of* MATINS

mat·tock \ˈmat-ək\ *n* [ME *mattok,* fr. OE *mattuc*] (bef. 12c) **:** a digging and grubbing tool with features of an adz and an ax or pick

mat·tress \ˈma-trəs\ *n* [ME *materas,* fr. OF, fr. Ar *matrah* place where something is thrown] (14c) **1 a :** a fabric case filled with resilient material (as cotton, hair, feathers, foam rubber, or an arrangement of coiled springs) used either alone as a bed or on a bedstead **b :** an inflatable airtight sack for use as a mattress **2 :** a mass of interwoven brush and poles to protect a bank from erosion; *also* **:** a similar mass serving as a foundation in soft ground

mat·u·rate \ˈmach-ə-ˌrāt\ *vb* **-rat·ed; -rat·ing** (1628) **:** MATURE

mat·u·ra·tion \ˌmach-ə-ˈrā-shən\ *n* (1541) **1 a :** the process of becoming mature **b :** the emergence of personal and behavioral characteristics through growth processes **c :** the final stages of differentiation of cells, tissues, or organs **2 a :** the entire process by which diploid gonocytes are transformed into haploid gametes that includes both meiosis and physiological and structural changes fitting the gamete for its future role **b :** SPERMIOGENESIS 2 — **mat·u·ra·tion·al** \-shnəl, -shən-ᵊl\ *adj*

[1]**ma·ture** \mə-ˈt(y)u̇(ə)r *also* -ˈchu̇(ə)r\ *adj* **ma·tur·er; -est** [ME, fr. L *maturus* ripe; akin to L *mane* in the morning, *manus* good] (15c) **1 :** based on slow careful consideration ⟨a ~ judgment⟩ **2 a** (1) **:** having completed natural growth and development **:** RIPE (2) **:** having undergone maturation **b :** having attained a final or desired state ⟨~ wine⟩ **c :** having achieved a low but stable growth rate ⟨paper is a ~ industry⟩ **3 a :** of or relating to a condition of full development **b :** characteristic of or suitable to a mature individual ⟨~ outlook⟩ **4 :** due for payment ⟨a ~ loan⟩ **5 a :** well dissected by the erosion of running water so that slopes predominate greatly over flats **b :** belonging to the middle portion of a cycle of erosion — **ma·ture·ly** *adv*

[2]**mature** *vb* **matured; ma·tur·ing** *vt* (15c) **:** to bring to maturity or completion ~ *vi* **1 :** to become fully developed or ripe **2 :** to become due

ma·tu·ri·ty \mə-ˈt(y)u̇r-ət-ē *also* -ˈchu̇r-\ *n* (15c) **1 :** the quality or state of being mature; *esp* **:** full development **2 :** termination of the period that an obligation has to run **3 :** the second of the three principal stages in a cycle of geologic change (as erosion)

ma·tu·ti·nal \ˌmach-u̇-ˈtīn-ᵊl; mə-ˈt(y)üt-nəl, -ᵊn-əl\ *adj* [LL *matutinalis,* fr. L *matutinus* — more at MATINEE] (1656) **:** of, relating to, or occurring in the morning **:** EARLY — **ma·tu·ti·nal·ly** \-ē\ *adv*

mat·zo *or* **mat·zoh** \ˈmät-sə, -(ˌ)sō\ *n, pl* **mat·zoth** \-ˌsōt(h), -sōs\ *or* **mat·zos** *or* **mat·zohs** \-səz, -səs, -ˌsōz\ [Yiddish *matse,* fr. Heb *maṣṣāh*] (1846) **1 :** unleavened bread eaten esp. at the Passover **2 :** a wafer of matzo

matzo ball *n* (1952) **:** a small ball-shaped dumpling made from matzo meal

maud·lin \ˈmȯd-lən\ *adj* [alter. of Mary *Magdalene;* fr. her depiction as a weeping penitent] (1616) **1 :** drunk enough to be emotionally silly **2 :** weakly and effusively sentimental

mau·gre \ˌmȯ-gər\ *prep* [ME, fr. MF *maugré,* fr. *maugré* displeasure, fr. *mau, mal* evil + *gré* pleasure] (13c) *archaic* **:** in spite of

[1]**maul** \ˈmȯl\ *n* [ME *malle* mace, maul, fr. OF *mail,* fr. L *malleus;* akin to L *molere* to grind — more at MEAL] (13c) **:** a heavy often wooden-headed hammer used esp. for driving wedges; *also* **:** a tool like a sledgehammer with one wedge-shaped end that is used to split wood

[2]**maul** *vt* (13c) **1 :** BEAT, BRUISE **2 :** to injure by beating **:** MANGLE **3 :** to handle roughly — **maul·er** *n*

maul·stick \ˈmȯl-stik\ *n* [part trans. of D *maalstok,* fr. obs. D *malen* to paint + D *stok* stick, stock] (1658) **:** a stick used by painters as a rest for the hand while working

maun \(ˈ)mȯn, (ˈ)män, mən\ *verbal auxiliary* [ME *man,* fr. ON, pres. of *munu* shall, will; akin to L *monēre* to remind — more at MIND] (13c) *chiefly Scot* **:** MUST

maund \ˈmȯnd\ *n* [Hindi *man*] (1584) **:** any of various Indian units of weight; *esp* **:** a unit equal to 82.28 pounds (37.32 kilograms)

maun·der \ˈmȯn-dər, ˈmän-\ *vi* **maun·dered; maun·der·ing** \-d(ə-)riŋ\ [prob. imit.] (1621) **1** *dial Brit* **:** GRUMBLE **2 :** to wander slowly and idly **3 :** to speak indistinctly or disconnectedly — **maun·der·er** \-dər-ər\ *n*

Maun·dy Thursday \ˌmȯn-dē-, ˌmän-\ *n* [ME *maunde* ceremony of washing the feet of the poor on Maundy Thursday, fr. OF *mandé,* fr. L *mandatum* command; fr. Jesus' words in John 13:34 — more at MANDATE] (15c) **:** the Thursday before Easter observed in commemoration of the institution of the Eucharist

mau·so·le·um \ˌmȯ-sə-ˈlē-əm, ˌmȯ-zə-\ *n, pl* **-leums** *or* **-lea** \-ˈlē-ə\ [L, fr. Gk *mausōleion,* fr. *Mausōlos* Mausolus †*ab* 353 B.C., ruler of Caria] (15c) **1 :** a large tomb; *esp* **:** a usu. stone building with places for entombment of the dead above ground **2 :** a large gloomy building or room

mauve \ˈmōv, ˈmȯv\ *n* [F, mallow, fr. L *malva*] (1859) **1 a :** a moderate purple, violet, or lilac color **b :** a strong purple **2 :** a dyestuff that produces a mauve color — **mauve** *adj*

ma·ven *or* **ma·vin** \ˈmā-vən\ *n* [Yiddish *meyvn,* fr. LHeb *mēbhīn,* fr. Heb *l'havin* to understand] (1952) **:** one who is experienced or knowledgeable

[1]**mav·er·ick** \ˈmav-(ə-)rik\ *n* [perh. fr. Samuel A. *Maverick* †1870 Am. pioneer who did not brand his calves] (1867) **1 :** an unbranded range animal; *esp* **:** a motherless calf **2 :** an independent individual who does not go along with a group or party

[2]**maverick** *adj* (1886) **:** characteristic of, suggestive of, or inclined to be a maverick

ma·vis \ˈmā-vəs\ *n* [ME, fr. MF *mauvis*] (14c) **1 :** SONG THRUSH **2 :** a European thrush (*Turdus viscivorus*) with spotted underparts that feeds on mistletoe berries — called also *mistle thrush*

maw \ˈmȯ\ *n* [ME, fr. OE *maga;* akin to OHG *mago* stomach, Lith *makas* purse] (bef. 12c) **1 :** the receptacle into which food is taken by swallowing: **a :** STOMACH **b :** CROP **2 a :** the throat, gullet, or jaws esp. of a voracious carnivore **b :** something like a gaping maw

mawk·ish \ˈmȯ-kish\ *adj* [ME *mawke* maggot, fr. ON *mathkr* — more at MAGGOT] (1697) **1 :** having an insipid often unpleasant taste **2 :** sickly or puerilely sentimental — **mawk·ish·ly** *adv* — **mawk·ish·ness** *n*

maxi \ˈmak-sē\ *n, pl* **max·is** [*maxi-*] (1967) **:** a long skirt, dress, or coat

maxi- *comb form* [*maximum,* after E *minimum: mini-*] **1 :** extra long ⟨*maxi*-kilt⟩ **2 :** extra large ⟨*maxi*-problems⟩

max·il·la \mak-ˈsil-ə\ *n, pl* **max·il·lae** \-ˈsil-(ˌ)ē, -ˌī\ *or* **maxillas** [L, dim. of *mala* jaw] (15c) **1 a :** JAW 1a **b** (1) **:** an upper jaw esp. of man or other mammals in which the bony elements are closely fused (2) **:** either of two membrane bone elements of the upper jaw that lie lateral to the premaxillae and that in higher vertebrates including man bear most of the teeth **2 :** one of the first or second pair of mouthparts posterior to the mandibles in insects, myriapods, crustaceans, and closely related arthropods — **max·il·lary** \ˈmak-sə-ˌler-ē, *chiefly Brit* mak-ˈsil-ə-rē\ *adj or n*

max·il·li·ped \mak-ˈsil-ə-ˌped\ *n* [ISV, fr. *maxilli-* (fr. L *maxilla*) + *-ped*] (1846) **:** any of the crustacean appendages that comprise the first pair or first three pairs situated next behind the maxillae

max·il·lo- \mak-ˌsil-(ˌ)ō, ˌmak-sə-(ˌ)lō\ *comb form* [L *maxilla*] **:** maxillary and ⟨*maxillo*facial⟩

max·il·lo·fa·cial \-ˈfā-shəl\ *adj* (ca. 1923) **:** of, relating to, or treating the maxilla and the face ⟨~ surgeons⟩

max·im \ˈmak-səm\ *n* [ME *maxime,* fr. MF, fr. ML *maxima,* fr. L, fem. of *maximus,* superl. of *magnus* great — more at MUCH] (15c) **1 :** a general truth, fundamental principle, or rule of conduct **2 :** a saying of proverbial nature

max·i·mal \ˈmak-s(ə-)məl\ *adj* (1882) **1 :** most comprehensive **:** COMPLETE **2 :** being an upper limit **:** HIGHEST — **max·i·mal·ly** \-ē\ *adv*

max·i·mal·ist \-s(ə-)mə-ləst\ *n* (1907) **:** one who advocates immediate and direct action to secure the whole of a program

maxi·min \ˈmak-sə-ˌmin\ *n* [*maxi*mum + *mini*mum] (1951) **:** the maximum of a set of minima; *esp* **:** the largest of a set of minimum possible gains each of which occurs in the least advantageous outcome of a strategy followed by a participant in a situation governed by the theory of games — compare MINIMAX

maximise *Brit var of* MAXIMIZE

max·i·mize \ˈmak-sə-ˌmīz\ *vt* **-mized; -miz·ing** (1802) **1 :** to increase to a maximum **2 :** to make the most of **3 :** to find a maximum value of — **max·i·mi·za·tion** \ˌmak-sə-mə-ˈzā-shən\ *n* — **max·i·miz·er** \ˈmak-sə-ˌmī-zər\ *n*

max·i·mum \ˈmak-s(ə-)məm\ *n, pl* **max·i·ma** \-sə-mə\ *or* **maximums** \-s(ə-)məmz\ [L, neut. of *maximus*] (1740) **1 a :** the greatest quantity or value attainable or attained **b :** the period of highest, greatest, or utmost development **2 :** an upper limit allowed (as by a legal authority) or allowable (as by the circumstances of a particular case) **3 :** the largest of a set of numbers; *specif* **:** the largest value assumed by a real-valued continuous function defined on a closed interval — **maximum** *adj*

maximum likelihood *n* (1959) **:** a statistical method for estimating population parameters (as the mean and variance) from sample data that selects as estimates those parameter values maximizing the probability of obtaining the observed data

ma·xixe \mə-ˈshēsh(-ə)\ *n, pl* **ma·xi·xes** \-ˈshē-shəz\ [Pg] (1914) **:** a ballroom dance of Brazilian origin that resembles the two-step

max·well \ˈmak-ˌswel, -swəl\ *n* [James Clerk *Maxwell*] (ca. 1900) **:** the centimeter-gram-second electromagnetic unit of magnetic flux equal to the flux per square centimeter of normal cross section in a region where the magnetic induction is one gauss

[1]**may** \(ˈ)mā\ *verbal auxiliary, past* **might** \(ˈ)mīt\; *pres sing & pl* **may** [ME (1st & 3d sing. pres. indic.), fr. OE *mæg;* akin to OHG *mag* (1st & 3d sing. pres. indic.) have power, am able (infin. *magan*), Gk *mēchos* means, expedient] (bef. 12c) **1 a** *archaic* **:** have the ability to **b :** have permission to ⟨you ~ go now⟩ **:** be free to ⟨a rug on which children ~ sprawl —C. E. Silberman⟩ — used nearly interchangeably with *can* **c** — used to indicate possibility or probability ⟨you ~ be right⟩ ⟨things you ~ need⟩; sometimes used interchangeably with *can* ⟨need not be accompanied by dictatorship . . . but ~ be achieved within a democratic framework — *Current Biog.*⟩ ⟨one of those slipups that ~ happen from time to time —Jessica Mitford⟩ ⟨copula ~ optionally be deleted —J. D. McCawley⟩ **2** — used in auxiliary function to express a wish or desire esp. in prayer, imprecation, or benediction ⟨long ~ he reign⟩ **3** — used in auxiliary function expressing purpose or expectation ⟨I laugh that I ~ not weep⟩ or contingency ⟨he'll do his duty come what ~⟩ or concession ⟨he ~ be slow but he is thorough⟩ or

choice ⟨the angler ~ catch them with a dip net, or he ~ cast a large, bare treble hook —Nelson Bryant⟩ **4 :** SHALL, MUST — used in law where the sense, purpose, or policy requires this interpretation ***usage*** see CAN

²may \'mā\ *n* [ME, fr. OE *mǣg* kinsman, kinswoman, maiden] *archaic* (bef. 12c) **:** MAIDEN

May \'mā\ *n* [ME, fr. OF & L; OF *mai,* fr. L *Maius,* fr. *Maia,* Roman goddess] (bef. 12c) **1 :** the 5th month of the Gregorian calendar **2** *often not cap* **:** the early vigorous blooming part of human life **:** PRIME **3 :** the festivities of May Day **4** *not cap* **a :** green or flowering branches used for May Day decorations **b :** a plant that yields may: as (1) **:** HAWTHORN (2) **:** a spring-flowering spirea

ma·ya \'mä-yə, 'mī-ə\ *n* [Skt *māyā*] (1788) **:** the sense-world of manifold phenomena held in Vedanta to conceal the unity of absolute being; *broadly* **:** ILLUSION

Ma·ya \'mī-ə\ *n, pl* **Maya** *or* **Mayas** [Sp] (1825) **1 a :** a Mayan language of the ancient Maya peoples recorded in inscriptions **b :** YUCATEC; *esp* **:** the older form of that language known from documents of the Spanish period **2 :** a member of a group of Indian peoples chiefly of Yucatán, British Honduras, Guatemala, and the state of Tabasco, Mexico, whose languages are Mayan

Ma·yan \'mī-ən\ *n* (1900) **1 a :** the peoples speaking Mayan languages **b :** a member of these peoples **2 :** an extensive language stock of Central America and Mexico — **Mayan** *adj*

may·ap·ple \'mā-ˌap-əl\ *n* [*May*] (1733) **:** a No. American herb (*Podophyllum peltatum*) of the barberry family with a poisonous rootstock, one or two large-lobed peltate leaves, and a single large white flower followed by a yellow egg-shaped edible fruit; *also* **:** its fruit

¹may·be \'mā-bē, 'meb-ē\ *adv* (15c) **:** PERHAPS

²maybe *n* (1586) **:** UNCERTAINTY

May·day \mā-'dā, 'mā-ˌ\ [F *m'aider* help me] (1927) — an international radio-telephone signal word used as a distress call

May Day \'mā-ˌdā\ *n* (13c) **:** May 1 celebrated as a springtime festival and in some countries as Labor Day

may·est *or* **mayst** \'mā-əst, (ˈ)māst\ *archaic pres 2d sing of* MAY

may·flow·er \'mā-ˌflau̇(-ə)r\ *n* (1570) **:** any of various spring-blooming plants; *esp* **:** ARBUTUS 2

may·fly \'mā-ˌflī\ *n* (1651) **:** any of an order (Ephemeroptera) of insects with an aquatic nymph and a short-lived fragile adult having membranous wings and two or three long caudal styles — called also *ephemerid*

may·hap \'mā-ˌhap, mā-'\ *adv* [fr. the phrase *may hap*] (1536) **:** PERHAPS

may·hem \'mā-ˌhem, 'mā-əm\ *n* [ME *mayme,* fr. AF *mahaim,* fr. OF, loss of a limb, fr. *maynier* to maim] (15c) **1 a :** willful and permanent deprivation of a bodily member resulting in the impairment of a person's fighting ability **b :** willful and permanent crippling, mutilation, or disfigurement of any part of the body **2 :** needless or willful damage or violence

may·ing \'mā-iŋ\ *n, often cap* (14c) **:** the celebrating of May Day

mayn't \'mā-ənt, (ˈ)mānt\ **:** may not

may·on·naise \'mā-ə-ˌnāz, ˌmā-ə-'\ *n* [F] (1841) **:** a dressing made of egg yolks, vegetable oils, and vinegar or lemon juice

may·or \'mā-ər, 'me(-)ər, *esp before names* (ˌ)mer\ *n* [ME *maire,* fr. OF, fr. L *major* greater — more at MAJOR] (13c) **:** an official elected or appointed to act as chief executive or nominal head of a city or borough — **may·or·al** \'mā-ə-rəl, 'me-ə-\ *adj*

may·or·al·ty \'mā-ə-rəl-tē, 'me-; 'mer-əl-\ *n* [ME *mairaltee,* fr. MF *mairalté,* fr. OF, fr. *maire*] (14c) **:** the office or term of office of a mayor

may·or·ess \'mā-ə-rəs, 'me-\ *n* (15c) **1 :** the wife of a mayor **2 :** a woman holding the office of mayor

mayor's court *n* (1806) **:** a court in some cities that has jurisdiction over violations of city ordinances and petty criminal or civil matters and that is presided over by the mayor

may·pole \'mā-ˌpōl\ *n, often cap* (1554) **:** a tall flower-wreathed pole forming a center for May Day sports and dances

may·pop \'mā-ˌpäp\ *n* [modif. of *maracock* (in some Algonquian language of Virginia)] (1851) **:** a climbing perennial passionflower (*Passiflora incarnata*) of the southern U.S. with a large ovoid yellow edible but insipid berry; *also* **:** its fruit

May·time \'mā-ˌtīm\ *n* (1804) **:** the month of May

maz·ard \'maz-ərd\ *n* [obs. E *mazard* mazer, alter. of E *mazer*] *chiefly dial* (1602) **:** HEAD, FACE

¹maze \'māz\ *vt* **mazed; maz·ing** [ME *mazen*] (14c) **1** *chiefly dial* **:** STUPEFY, DAZE **2 :** BEWILDER, PERPLEX

²maze *n* (14c) **1 a :** a confusing intricate network of passages **b :** something intricately or confusingly elaborate or complicated ⟨a ~ of regulations⟩ **2** *chiefly dial* **:** a state of bewilderment

ma·zer \'mā-zər\ *n* [ME, fr. MF *mazere,* of Gmc origin; akin to OHG *masar* gnarled excrescence on a tree] (14c) **:** a large drinking bowl orig. of a hard wood

ma·zur·ka \mə-'zər-kə, -'zu̇(ə)r-\ *also* **ma·zour·ka** \-'zu̇(ə)r-\ *n* [Pol, acc. of *mazurek,* lit., of Masuria, region of NE Poland] (1818) **1 :** a Polish folk dance in moderate triple measure **2 :** music for the mazurka or in its rhythm usu. in moderate $^3/_4$ or $^3/_8$ time

mazy \'mā-zē\ *adj* (1579) **:** resembling a maze

¹maz·zard \'maz-ərd\ *n* [origin unknown] (1578) **:** SWEET CHERRY; *esp* **:** wild or seedling sweet cherry used as a rootstock for grafting

²mazzard *var of* MAZARD

mbi·ra \em-'bir-ə\ *n* [of Bantu origin] (ca. 1909) **:** an African musical instrument that consists of a wooden or gourd resonator and a varying number of tuned metal or wooden strips that vibrate when plucked with the thumbs or fingers

MC \(ˈ)em-'sē\ *n* (1790) **:** MASTER OF CEREMONIES

Mc·Car·thy·ism \mə-'kär-thē-ˌiz-əm *also* -'kärt-ē-\ *n* [Joseph R. *McCarthy*] (1950) **:** a mid-20th century political attitude characterized chiefly by opposition to elements held to be subversive and by the use of tactics involving personal attacks on individuals by means of widely publicized indiscriminate allegations esp. on the basis of unsubstantiated charges — **Mc·Car·thy·ite** \-ˌīt\ *n or adj*

Mc·Coy \mə-'kȯi\ *n* [alter. of *Mackay* (in the phrase *the real Mackay* the true chief of the Mackay clan, a position often disputed)] (1883) **:** something that is neither imitation nor substitute — often used in the phrase *the real McCoy*

Mc·In·tosh \'mak-ən-ˌtäsh\ *n* [John McIntosh, *fl* 1796 Canad. settler] (1878) **:** a juicy bright red eating apple with a thin skin, white flesh, and aromatic flavor

M–day \'em-ˌdā\ *n* [mobilization *day*] (1924) **:** a day on which a military mobilization is to begin

me \(ˈ)mē\ *pron* [ME, fr. OE *mē;* akin to OHG *mih* me, L *me,* Gk *me,* Skt *mā*] *objective case of* I

usage *Me* is used in many constructions where strict grammarians prescribe *I.* This usage is not so much ungrammatical as indicative of the shrinking range of the nominative form: *me* began to replace *I* sometime around the 16th century largely because of the pressure of word order. *I* is now chiefly used as the subject of an immediately following verb. *Me* occurs in every other position: absolutely ⟨who, *me*?⟩, emphatically ⟨*me* too⟩, and after prepositions, conjunctions, and verbs, including *be* ⟨come with *me*⟩ ⟨you're as big as *me*⟩ ⟨it's *me*⟩ Almost all usage books recognize the legitimacy of *me* in these positions, esp. in speech; some recommend *I* in formal and esp. written contexts after *be* and after *as* and *than* when the first term of the comparison is the subject of a verb.

mea cul·pa \ˌmā-ə-'ku̇l-pə, ˌmā-ä-, -'ku̇l-pä\ *n* [L, through my fault] (14c) **:** a formal acknowledgment of personal fault or error

¹mead \'mēd\ *n* [ME *mede,* fr. OE *medu;* akin to OHG *metu* mead, Gk *methy* wine] (bef. 12c) **:** a fermented beverage made of water and honey, malt, and yeast

²mead *n* [ME *mede,* fr. OE *mǣd*] *archaic* (bef. 12c) **:** MEADOW

mead·ow \'med-(ˌ)ō, -ə(-w)\ *n, often attrib* [ME *medwe,* fr. OE *mǣdwe,* oblique case form of *mǣd;* akin to OE *māwan* to mow — more at MOW] (bef. 12c) **:** land in or predominantly in grass; *esp* **:** a tract of moist low-lying usu. level grassland

meadow beauty *n* (1840) **:** any of a genus (*Rhexia*) of low perennial American herbs (family Melastomaceae, the meadow-beauty family) with showy cymose flowers

meadow fescue *n* (1794) **:** a tall vigorous perennial European fescue grass (*Festuca elatior*) with broad flat leaves widely cultivated for permanent pasture and hay — compare TALL FESCUE

meadow grass *n* (13c) **:** any of various grasses (as of the genus *Poa*) that thrive in the presence of abundant moisture; *esp* **:** KENTUCKY BLUEGRASS

mead·ow·land \'med-ō-ˌland, -ə-\ *n* (1530) **:** land that is or is used for meadow

mead·ow·lark \'med-ō-ˌlärk, -ə-\ *n* (1611) **:** any of several No. American songbirds (genus *Sturnella*) that are largely brown and buff above and have a yellow breast marked with a black crescent

meadow mouse *n* (1801) **:** any of various voles (esp. genus *Microtus*) that frequent open fields

meadow mushroom *n* (1884) **:** a common edible agaric (*Agaricus campestris*) that occurs naturally in moist open organically rich soil and is the cultivated edible mushroom of commerce

meadow nematode *n* (1946) **:** any of numerous plant-parasitic nematode worms (esp. genus *Pratylenchus*) that were formerly classified as a single variable species (*P. pratensis*) and that destructively invade the roots of plants

meadow rue *n* (1668) **:** any of a genus (*Thalictrum*) of plants of the buttercup family with leaves resembling those of rue

meadowlark

meadow saffron *n* (1578) **:** COLCHICUM 1

meadow spittlebug *n* (1942) **:** a No. American spittlebug (*Philaenus spumarius*) that does severe damage esp. to grasses

mead·ow·sweet \'med-ō-ˌswēt, -ə-\ *n* (1530) **1 :** SPIREA 1; *esp* **:** a No. American native or naturalized spirea (as *Spiraea alba* or *S. tomentosa*) **2 :** a plant of a genus (*Filipendula*) closely related to the spireas

mea·ger *or* **mea·gre** \'mē-gər\ *adj* [ME *megre,* fr. MF *maigre,* fr. L *macr-, macer* lean; akin to OE *mæger* lean, Gk *makros* long] (14c) **1 :** having little flesh **:** THIN **2 a :** lacking desirable qualities (as richness or strength) ⟨leading a ~ life⟩ **b :** deficient in quality or quantity ⟨a ~ diet⟩ — **mea·ger·ly** *adv* — **mea·ger·ness** *n*

syn MEAGER, SCANTY, SCANT, SKIMPY, SPARE, SPARSE mean falling short of what is normal, necessary, or desirable. MEAGER implies the absence of elements, qualities, or numbers necessary to a thing's richness, substance, or potency ⟨a *meager* portion of meat⟩ SCANTY stresses insufficiency in amount, quantity, or extent ⟨supplies too *scanty* to last the winter⟩ SCANT suggests a falling short of what is desired or desirable rather than of what is essential ⟨in January the daylight hours are *scant*⟩ SKIMPY usu. suggests niggardliness or penury as the cause of the deficiency ⟨tacky housing developments on *skimpy* lots⟩ SPARE may suggest a slight falling short of adequacy or merely an absence of superfluity ⟨a *spare,* concise style of writing⟩ SPARSE implies a thin scattering of units ⟨a *sparse* population⟩

¹meal \'mē(ə)l\ *n* [ME *meel* appointed time, meal, fr. OE *mǣl;* akin to OHG *māl* time, L *metiri* to measure — more at MEASURE] (bef. 12c) **1 :** the portion of food taken at one time to satisfy appetite **2 :** an act or the time of eating a meal

²meal *n* [ME *mele,* fr. OE *melu;* akin to OHG *melo* meal, L *molere* to grind, Gk *mylē* mill] (12c) **1 :** the usu. coarsely ground and unbolted seeds of a cereal grass or pulse; *esp* **:** CORNMEAL **2 :** a product resembling seed meal esp. in particle size or texture

-meal \ˌmēl, 'mē(ə)l\ *adv comb form* [ME *-mele,* fr. OE *-mǣlum,* fr. *mǣlum,* dat. pl. of *mǣl*] **:** by a (specified) portion or measure at a time ⟨piecemeal⟩

mea·lie \'mē-lē\ *n* [Afrik *mielie*] *So Afr* (1853) **:** INDIAN CORN; *also* **:** an ear of Indian corn

meal ticket *n* (ca. 1899) **:** one that serves as the ultimate source of one's income ⟨an advanced degree was his *meal ticket*⟩

meal·time \'mē(ə)l-ˌtīm\ *n* (12c) **:** the usual time for serving a meal

meal·worm \-ˌwərm\ *n* (1658) : the larva of various beetles (family Tenebrionidae) that infests and pollutes grain products but is often raised as food for insectivorous animals, for laboratory use, or as bait for fishing

mealy \ˈmē-lē\ *adj* **meal·i·er; -est** (1533) **1** : soft, dry, and friable **2** : containing meal : FARINACEOUS **3 a** : covered with meal or with fine granules **b** : flecked with another color **c** : SPOTTY, UNEVEN **d** : PALLID, BLANCHED ⟨a ~ complexion⟩ **4** : MEALYMOUTHED

mealy·bug \ˈmē-lē-ˌbəg\ *n* (1824) : any of numerous scale insects (family Pseudococcidae) that have a white powdery covering and are destructive pests esp. of fruit trees

mealy·mouthed \ˌmē-lē-ˈmau̇thd, -ˈmau̇tht\ *adj* (1572) : not plain and straightforward : DEVIOUS ⟨a ~ orator⟩

[1]mean \ˈmēn\ *adj* [ME *mene,* fr. *imene,* fr. OE *gemǣne;* akin to OHG *gimeini* common, L *communis* common, *munus* service, gift] (bef. 12c) **1** : lacking distinction or eminence : HUMBLE **2** : lacking in mental discrimination : DULL **3 a** : of poor shabby inferior quality or status ⟨~*er* quarters of the city⟩ **b** : worthy of little regard : CONTEMPTIBLE — often used in negative constructions as a term of praise ⟨no ~ achievement⟩ **4** : lacking dignity or honor : BASE **5 a** : PENURIOUS, STINGY **b** : characterized by petty selfishness or malice **c** : causing trouble or bother : VEXATIOUS **d** : EXCELLENT, EFFECTIVE ⟨plays a ~ trumpet⟩ **6** : ASHAMED 1b — **mean·ness** \ˈmēn-nəs\ *n*

syn MEAN, IGNOBLE, ABJECT, SORDID mean being below the normal standards of human decency and dignity. MEAN suggests having repellent characteristics (as small-mindedness, ill temper, or cupidity); IGNOBLE suggests a loss or lack of some essential high quality of mind or spirit; ABJECT may imply degradation, debasement, or servility; SORDID is stronger than all of these in stressing physical or spiritual degradation and abjectness.

[2]mean \ˈmēn\ *vb* **meant** \ˈment\; **mean·ing** \ˈmē-niŋ\ [ME *menen,* fr. OE *mǣnan;* akin to OHG *meinen* to have in mind, OSlav *mēniti* to mention] *vt* (bef. 12c) **1** : to have in the mind as a purpose : INTEND **2** : to serve or intend to convey, show, or indicate : SIGNIFY **3** : to have importance to the degree of ⟨health ~*s* everything⟩ **4** : to direct to a particular individual ~ *vi* : to have an intended purpose ⟨he ~*s* well⟩ — **mean·er** \ˈmē-nər\ *n* — **mean business** : to be in earnest

[3]mean *adj* [ME *mene,* fr. MF *meien,* fr. L *medianus* — more at MEDIAN] (14c) **1** : occupying a middle position : intermediate in space, order, time, kind, or degree **2** : occupying a position about midway between extremes; *esp* : being the mean of a set of values : AVERAGE ⟨~ temperature⟩ **3** : serving as a means : INTERMEDIARY ***syn*** see AVERAGE

[4]mean *n* (14c) **1 a (1)** : something intervening or intermediate **(2)** : a middle point between extremes **b** : a value that lies within a range of values and is computed according to a prescribed law: as **(1)** : ARITHMETIC MEAN **(2)** : EXPECTED VALUE **c** : either of the middle two terms of a proportion **2** *pl but sing or pl in constr* : something useful or helpful to a desired end **3** *pl* : resources available for disposal; *esp* : material resources affording a secure life

[1]me·an·der \mē-ˈan-dər\ *n* [L *maeander,* fr. Gk *maiandros,* fr. *Maiandros* (now *Menderes*), river in Asia Minor] (1576) **1** : a winding path or course; *esp* : LABYRINTH **2** : a turn or winding of a stream — **me·an·drous** \-drəs\ *adj*

[2]meander *vi* **-dered; -der·ing** \-d(ə-)riŋ\ (1616) **1** : to follow a winding or intricate course **2** : to wander aimlessly or casually without urgent destination : RAMBLE ***syn*** see WANDER

mean deviation *n* (1894) : the mean of the absolute values of the numerical differences between the numbers of a set (as statistical data) and their mean or median

mean distance *n* (ca. 1890) : the arithmetical mean of the maximum and minimum distances of a planet, satellite, or secondary star from its primary

mean·ing \ˈmē-niŋ\ *n* (14c) **1 a** : the thing one intends to convey esp. by language : PURPORT **b** : the thing that is conveyed esp. by language : IMPORT **2** : something meant or intended : AIM ⟨a mischievous ~ was apparent⟩ **3** : significant quality; *esp* : implication of a hidden or special significance ⟨a glance full of ~⟩ **4 a** : the logical connotation of a word or phrase **b** : the logical denotation or extension of a word or phrase — **meaning** *adj*

mean·ing·ful \-fəl\ *adj* (1852) **1 a** : having a meaning or purpose **b** : full of meaning : SIGNIFICANT ⟨a ~ life⟩ **2** : having an assigned function in a language system ⟨~ propositions⟩ — **mean·ing·ful·ly** \-fə-lē\ *adv* — **mean·ing·ful·ness** *n*

mean·ing·less \ˈmē-niŋ-ləs\ *adj* (1797) **1** : having no meaning **2** : having no assigned function in a language system ⟨a ~ metaphysical statement⟩ — **mean·ing·less·ly** *adv* — **mean·ing·less·ness** *n*

[1]mean·ly \ˈmēn-lē\ *adv, obs* (14c) : fairly well : MODERATELY

[2]meanly *adv* (14c) : in a mean manner: as **a** : in a lowly manner : HUMBLY **b** : in an inferior manner : BADLY **c** : in a base or ungenerous manner

mean proportional *n* (1571) : GEOMETRIC MEAN; *esp* : the square root (as *x*) of the product of two numbers (as *a* and *b*) when expressed as the means of a proportion (as $a/x = x/b$)

mean solar day *n* (ca. 1816) : the interval between successive transits of the lower meridian by the mean sun

mean square *n* (1845) : the mean of the squares of a set of values

mean square deviation *n* (1894) **1** : VARIANCE 5 **2** : STANDARD DEVIATION

means test \ˈmēnz-\ *n* (1930) : an examination into the financial state of a person to determine his eligibility for public assistance

mean sun *n* (ca. 1890) : a fictitious sun used for timekeeping that moves uniformly along the celestial equator and maintains a constant rate of apparent motion

[1]mean·time \ˈmēn-ˌtīm\ *n* (14c) : the intervening time

[2]meantime *adv* (1588) : MEANWHILE

mean time *n* (ca. 1864) : time that is based on the motion of the mean sun and that has the mean solar second as its unit — called also *mean solar time*

mean value theorem *n* (1902) **1** : a theorem in differential calculus: if a function of one variable is continuous on a closed interval and differentiable on the interval minus its endpoints there is at least one point where the derivative of the function is equal to the slope of the line joining the endpoints of the curve representing the function on the interval **2** : a theorem in integral calculus: if a function of one variable is continuous on a closed interval and differentiable on the interval minus its endpoints, there is at least one point in the interval where the product of the value of the function and the length of the interval is equal to the integral of the function over the interval

[1]mean·while \ˈmēn-ˌhwīl, -ˌwīl\ *n* (14c) : MEANTIME

[2]meanwhile *adv* (14c) **1** : during the intervening time **2** : at the same time

mea·sle \ˈmē-zəl\ *n* [sing. of *measles*] (1863) : a tapeworm cysticercus larva; *specif* : one found in the muscles of a domesticated mammal — **mea·sled** \-zəld\ *adj*

mea·sles \ˈmē-zəlz\ *n pl but sing or pl in constr* [ME *meseles,* pl. of *mesel* measles, spot characteristic of measles; akin to MD *masel* spot characteristic of measles] (14c) **1 a** : an acute contagious viral disease marked by an eruption of distinct red circular spots **b** : any of various eruptive diseases (as German measles) **2** [ME *mesel* infested with tapeworms, lit., leprous, fr. OF, fr. ML *misellus* leper, fr. L, wretch, fr. *misellus,* dim. of *miser* miserable] : infestation with or disease caused by larval tapeworms in the muscles and tissues

mea·sly \ˈmēz-(ə-)lē\ *adj* **mea·sli·er; -est** (1687) **1** : infected with measles **2 a** : containing larval tapeworms **b** : infested with trichinae **3** : contemptibly small

[1]mea·sure \ˈmezh-ər, ˈmāzh-\ *n* [ME *mesure,* fr. OF, fr. L *mensura,* fr. *mensus,* pp. of *metiri* to measure; akin to OE *mǣth* measure, Gk *metron*] (13c) **1 a (1)** : an adequate or due portion **(2)** : a moderate degree; *also* : MODERATION, TEMPERANCE **(3)** : a fixed or suitable limit : BOUNDS **b** : the dimensions, capacity, or amount of something ascertained by measuring **c** : an estimate of what is to be expected (as of a person or situation) **d (1)** : a measured quantity **(2)** : AMOUNT, DEGREE **2 a** : an instrument or utensil for measuring **b (1)** : a standard or unit of measurement — see WEIGHT table **(2)** : a system of standard units of measure ⟨metric ~⟩ **3** : the act or process of measuring **4 a (1)** : MELODY, TUNE **(2)** : DANCE; *esp* : a slow and stately dance **b** : rhythmic structure or movement : CADENCE: as **(1)** : poetic rhythm measured by temporal quantity or accent; *specif* : METER **(2)** : musical time **c (1)** : a grouping of musical beats made by the regular recurrence of primary accents and located on the staff immediately following a vertical bar **(2)** : a metrical unit : FOOT **5** : an exact divisor of a number **6** : a basis or standard of comparison ⟨wealth is not a ~ of happiness⟩ **7** : a step planned or taken as a means to an end; *specif* : a proposed legislative act — **for good measure** : in addition to the minimum required

[2]measure *vb* **mea·sured; mea·sur·ing** \ˈmezh-(ə-)riŋ, ˈmāzh-\ *vt* (14c) **1 a** : to choose or control with cautious restraint : REGULATE ⟨~ his acts⟩ **b** : to regulate by a standard : GOVERN **2** : to allot or apportion in measured amounts ⟨~ out 3 cups⟩ **3** : to lay off by making measurements **4** : to ascertain the measurements of **5** : to estimate or appraise by a criterion ⟨~*s* his skill against his rival⟩ **6** *archaic* : to travel over : TRAVERSE **7** : to serve as a means of measuring ⟨a thermometer ~*s* temperature⟩ ~ *vi* **1** : to take or make a measurement **2** : to have a specified measurement — **mea·sur·abil·i·ty** \ˌmezh-(ə-)rə-ˈbil-ət-ē, ˌmāzh-\ *n* — **mea·sur·able** \ˈmezh-(ə-)rə-bəl, ˈmāzh-\ *adj* — **mea·sur·ably** \-blē\ *adv* — **mea·sur·er** \-ər-ər\ *n*

mea·sured \ˈmezh-ərd, ˈmāzh-\ *adj* (15c) **1** : marked by due proportion **2 a** : marked by rhythm : regularly recurrent **b** : METRICAL **3** : DELIBERATE, CALCULATED — **mea·sured·ly** *adv*

mea·sure·less \-ər-ləs\ *adj* (14c) **1** : having no observable limit : IMMEASURABLE ⟨the ~ universe⟩ **2** : very great ⟨treated them with ~ contempt⟩

mea·sure·ment \ˈmezh-ər-mənt, ˈmāzh-\ *n* (1751) **1** : the act or process of measuring **2** : a figure, extent, or amount obtained by measuring : DIMENSION **3** : MEASURE 2b

measurement ton *n* (ca. 1934) : TON 1c

measure up *vi* (1910) **1** : to have necessary or fitting qualifications **2** : to be the equal (as in ability) — used with *to*

measuring worm *n* (1843) : LOOPER 1

meat \ˈmēt\ *n* [ME *mete,* fr. OE; akin to OHG *maz* food and prob. to L *madēre* to be wet, Gk *madaros* wet] (bef. 12c) **1 a** : FOOD; *esp* : solid food as distinguished from drink **b** : the edible part of something as distinguished from its covering (as a husk or shell) **2** : animal tissue considered esp. as food: **a** : FLESH 2b **b** : FLESH 1a; *specif* : flesh of domesticated animals **3** *archaic* : [1]MEAL 2; *esp* : DINNER **4 a** : the core of something : HEART **b** : PITH 2b ⟨a novel with ~⟩ **5** : favorite pursuit or interest — **meat·less** *adj*

meat–and–po·ta·toes \ˌmēt-ᵊn-pə-ˈtāt-(ˌ)ōz, -pət-ˈāt-, -əz\ *adj* (1949) **1** : of fundamental importance : BASIC **2** : PRACTICAL, EVERYDAY

meat and potatoes *n pl but sing or pl in constr* (1951) : a main object of interest : MEAT 4

meat–ax \ˈmēt-ˌaks\ *n* (1834) **1** : CLEAVER 1 **2** : an extreme or heavy-handed method of cutting or altering something ⟨used the ~ to reduce the budget⟩

meat·ball \-ˌbȯl\ *n* (1838) : a small ball of chopped or ground meat often mixed with bread crumbs and spices

meat loaf *n* (1899) : a dish of ground meat seasoned and baked in the form of a loaf

me·atus \mē-ˈāt-əs\ *n, pl* **me·atus·es** \-ə-səz\ *or* **me·atus** \-ˈāt-əs, -ˈā-ˌtüs\ [LL, fr. L, going, passage, fr. *meatus,* pp. of *meare* to go — more at PERMEATE] (1665) : a natural body passage

meaty \ˈmēt-ē\ *adj* **meat·i·er; -est** (ca. 1787) **1** : full of meat **2** : rich esp. in matter for thought : SUBSTANTIAL — **meat·i·ness** *n*

mec·a·myl·amine \ˌmek-ə-ˈmil-ə-ˌmēn\ *n* [fr. *Mecamylamine,* a trademark] (1955) : a drug that in the hydrochloride $C_{11}H_{21}N{\cdot}HCl$ is used orally as a ganglionic blocking agent to effect a rapid lowering of severely elevated blood pressure

mec·ca \ˈmek-ə\ *n, often cap* [*Mecca,* Saudi Arabia, birthplace of Muhammad and holy city of Islam] (1850) : a center of activity sought as a goal by people sharing a common interest

mechan- *or* **mechano-** *comb form* [ME *mechan-,* fr. MF or L; MF, fr. L, fr. Gk *mēchan-,* fr. *mēchanē* machine — more at MACHINE] : machine ⟨*mechano*morphic⟩ : mechanical ⟨*mechan*ize⟩

[1]me·chan·ic \mi-ˈkan-ik\ *adj* [prob. fr. MF *mechanique,* adj. & n., fr. L *mechanicus,* fr. Gk *mēchanikos,* fr. *mēchanē*] (14c) **1** : of or relating to manual work or skill **2** : suggestive of a machine esp. in routine or automatic performance

²**mechanic** *n* (1562) **1** : a manual worker : ARTISAN **2** : MACHINIST; *esp* : one who repairs machines

¹**me·chan·i·cal** \mi-ˈkan-i-kəl\ *adj* (15c) **1 a** (1) : of or relating to machinery or tools ⟨~ applications of science⟩ ⟨a ~ genius⟩ ⟨~ aptitude⟩ (2) : produced or operated by a machine or tool ⟨~ power⟩ ⟨a ~ refrigerator⟩ ⟨a ~ saw⟩ **b** : of or relating to manual operations **2** : of or relating to artisans or machinists ⟨the ~ trades⟩ **3 a** : done as if by machine : seemingly uninfluenced by the mind or emotions : AUTOMATIC ⟨her singing was cold and ~⟩ **b** : of or relating to technicalities or petty matters **4 a** : relating to, governed by, or in accordance with the principles of mechanics ⟨~ work⟩ ⟨~ energy⟩ **b** : relating to the quantitative relations of force and matter ⟨~ pressure of wind on a tower⟩ **5** : caused by, resulting from, or relating to a process that involves a purely physical as opposed to a chemical change ⟨~ erosion of rock⟩ ***syn*** see SPONTANEOUS — **me·chan·i·cal·ly** \-i-k(ə-)lē\ *adv*

²**mechanical** *n* (1590) **1** *obs* : MECHANIC 1 **2** : a piece of finished copy consisting typically of type proofs and artwork positioned and mounted for photomechanical reproduction

mechanical advantage *n* (1894) : the advantage gained by the use of a mechanism in transmitting force; *specif* : the ratio of the force that performs the useful work of a machine to the force that is applied to the machine

mechanical drawing *n* (ca. 1890) **1** : drawing done with the aid of instruments **2** : a drawing made with instruments

mech·a·ni·cian \ˌmek-ə-ˈnish-ən\ *n* (1570) : MECHANIC, MACHINIST

me·chan·ics \mi-ˈkan-iks\ *n pl but sing or pl in constr* (1648) **1** : a branch of physical science that deals with energy and forces and their effect on bodies **2** : the practical application of mechanics to the design, construction, or operation of machines or tools **3** : mechanical or functional details or procedure

mech·a·nism \ˈmek-ə-ˌniz-əm\ *n* (1662) **1 a** : a piece of machinery **b** : a process or technique for achieving a result **2** : mechanical operation or action : WORKING 2 **3** : a doctrine that holds natural processes (as of life) to be mechanically determined and capable of complete explanation by the laws of physics and chemistry **4** : the fundamental physical or chemical processes involved in or responsible for an action, reaction, or other natural phenomenon (as organic evolution)

mech·a·nist \-nəst\ *n* (1606) **1** *archaic* : MECHANIC **2** : an adherent of the doctrine of mechanism

mech·a·nis·tic \ˌmek-ə-ˈnis-tik\ *adj* (1884) **1** : mechanically determined ⟨~ universe⟩ **2** : of or relating to the doctrine of mechanism **3** : MECHANICAL — **mech·a·nis·ti·cal·ly** \-ti-k(ə-)lē\ *adv*

mech·a·nize \ˈmek-ə-ˌnīz\ *vt* **-nized; -niz·ing** (1678) **1** : to make mechanical; *esp* : to make automatic or routine **2 a** : to equip with machinery esp. to replace human or animal labor **b** : to equip with armed and armored motor vehicles **c** : to provide with mechanical power **3** : to produce by or as if by machine — **mech·a·niz·able** \-ˌnī-zə-bəl\ *adj* — **mech·a·ni·za·tion** \ˌmek-ə-nə-ˈzā-shən\ *n* — **mech·a·niz·er** \ˈmek-ə-ˌnī-zər\ *n*

mech·a·no·chem·is·try \ˌmek-ə-nō-ˈkem-ə-strē\ *n* (ca. 1928) : chemistry that deals with the conversion of chemical energy into mechanical work (as in the contraction of a muscle) — **mech·a·no·chem·i·cal** \-ˈkem-i-kəl\ *adj*

mech·a·no·re·cep·tor \-ri-ˈsep-tər\ *n* (1927) : a neural end organ (as a tactile receptor) that responds to a mechanical stimulus (as a change in pressure) — **mech·a·no·re·cep·tion** \-ˈsep-shən\ *n* — **mech·a·no·re·cep·tive** \-ˈsep-tiv\ *adj*

Mech·lin \ˈmek-lən\ *n* [*Mechlin*, Belgium] (1699) : a delicate bobbin lace used for dresses and millinery

mec·li·zine \ˈmek-lə-ˌzēn\ *n* [*methyl* + *chlor-* + *-izine* (alter. of *azine*)] (1954) : a drug $C_{25}H_{27}ClN_2$ used usu. in the form of its hydrochloride to treat nausea and vertigo

me·co·ni·um \mi-ˈkō-nē-əm\ *n* [L, lit., poppy juice, fr. Gk *mēkōnion*, fr. *mēkōn* poppy; akin to OHG *mago* poppy] (1706) : a dark greenish mass that accumulates in the bowel during fetal life and is discharged shortly after birth

me·cop·ter·ous \mi-ˈkäp-tə-rəs\ *adj* [NL *Mecoptera*, fr. *meco-* long (fr. Gk *mēkos* length) + Gk *pteron* wing; akin to Gk *makros* long — more at MEAGER, FEATHER] (1901) : of, relating to, or being any of an order (Mecoptera) of primitive carnivorous insects (as scorpion flies) usu. with membranous wings and a long beak with biting mouthparts at the tip

med \ˈmed\ *adj* (ca. 1891) : MEDICAL ⟨~ school⟩

me·da·ka \mə-ˈdäk-ə\ *n* [Jp] (1933) : a small Japanese freshwater fish (*Oryzias latipes*) usu. silvery brown in the wild but from pale yellow to deep red in aquarium strains

med·al \ˈmed-ᵊl\ *n* [MF *medaille*, fr. OIt *medaglia* coin worth half a denarius, medal, fr. (assumed) VL *medalis* half, fr. LL *medialis* middle, fr. L *medius* — more at MID] (1578) **1** : a small usu. metal object bearing a religious emblem or picture **2** : a piece of metal often resembling a coin and having a stamped design that is issued to commemorate a person or event or awarded for excellence or achievement

Medal for Merit (1942) : a U.S. decoration awarded to civilians for exceptionally meritorious conduct in the performance of outstanding services

med·al·ist *or* **med·al·list** \ˈmed-ᵊl-əst\ *n* (1756) **1** : a designer, engraver, or maker of medals **2** : a recipient of a medal as an award

me·dal·lic \mə-ˈdal-ik\ *adj* (1702) : of, relating to, or shown on a medal

me·dal·lion \mə-ˈdal-yən\ *n* [F *médaillon*, fr. It *medaglione*, aug. of *medaglia*] (1658) **1** : a large medal **2** : something resembling a large medal; *esp* : a tablet or panel in a wall or window bearing a figure in relief, a portrait, or an ornament **3** *also* **me·dail·lon** \mā-dȧ-yōⁿ\ : a small round or oval serving (as of meat)

Medal of Freedom (1945) : a U.S. decoration awarded to civilians for meritorious achievement in any of various fields

Medal of Honor (1862) : a U.S. military decoration awarded in the name of the Congress for conspicuous intrepidity at the risk of life in action with an enemy

medal play *n* (1899) : STROKE PLAY

med·dle \ˈmed-ᵊl\ *vi* **med·dled; med·dling** \ˈmed-liŋ, -ᵊl-iŋ\ [ME *medlen*, fr. MF *mesler*, *medler*, fr. (assumed) VL *misculare*, fr. L *miscēre* to mix — more at MIX] (14c) : to interest oneself in what is not one's concern : interfere without right or propriety — **med·dler** \ˈmed-lər, -ᵊl-ər\ *n*

med·dle·some \ˈmed-ᵊl-səm\ *adj* (1615) : given to meddling ***syn*** see IMPERTINENT — **med·dle·some·ness** *n*

Mede \ˈmēd\ *n* [ME, fr. L *Medus*, fr. Gk *Mēdos*] (14c) : a native or inhabitant of ancient Media in Persia

Me·dea \mə-ˈdē-ə\ *n* [L, fr. Gk *Mēdeia*] : an enchantress noted in Greek myth for helping Jason gain the Golden Fleece and for repeatedly resorting to murder to gain her ends

med·fly \ˈmed-ˌflī\ *n, often cap* (ca. 1935) : MEDITERRANEAN FRUIT FLY

medi- *or* **medio-** *comb form* [L, fr. *medius*] : middle ⟨*medio*dorsal⟩

¹**me·dia** \ˈmēd-ē-ə\ *n, pl* **me·di·ae** \-ē-ˌē\ (1841) **1** [LL, fr. L, fem. of *medius*; fr. the voiced stops' being regarded as intermediate between the tenues and the aspirates] : a voiced stop **2** [NL, fr. L] : the middle coat of the wall of a blood or lymph vessel consisting chiefly of circular muscle fibers

²**media** *n, pl* **me·di·as** *often attrib* [pl. of *medium*] (1923) : MEDIUM 2b

usage The singular *media* and its plural *medias* seem to have originated in the field of advertising over 50 years ago; they are apparently still so used without stigma in that specialized field. In most other applications *media* is used as a plural of *medium*. The great popularity of the word in references to the agencies of mass communication is leading to the formation of a mass noun, construed as a singular ⟨there's no basis for it. You know, the news *media* gets on to something —Edwin Meese 3d⟩ but this use is not as well established as the mass-noun use of *data* and is likely to incur criticism esp. in writing.

me·di·ad \ˈmēd-ē-ˌad\ *adv* (1878) : toward the median line or plane of a body or part

media event *n* (1972) : a publicity event staged for coverage by the news media

me·di·al \ˈmēd-ē-əl\ *adj* [LL *medialis*, fr. *medius*] (1570) **1** : MEAN, AVERAGE **2 a** : being or occurring in the middle : MEDIAN **b** : extending toward the middle **3** : situated between the extremes of initial and final in a word or morpheme — **medial** *n* — **me·di·al·ly** \-ə-lē\ *adv*

¹**me·di·an** \ˈmēd-ē-ən\ *n* (15c) **1** : a medial part (as a vein or nerve) **2 a** : a value in an ordered set of values below and above which there is an equal number of values or which is the arithmetic mean of the two middle values if there is no one middle number **b** : a vertical line that divides the histogram of a frequency distribution into two parts of equal area **c** : a value of a random variable for which all greater values make the distribution function greater than one half and all lesser values make it less than one half **3 a** : a line from a vertex of a triangle to the midpoint of the opposite side **b** : a line joining the midpoints of the nonparallel sides of a trapezoid ***syn*** see AVERAGE

²**median** *adj* [MF or L; MF, fr. L *medianus*, fr. *medius* middle — more at MID] (1645) **1** : being in the middle or in an intermediate position : MEDIAL **2** : relating to or constituting a statistical median **3** : lying in the plane dividing a bilateral animal into right and left halves **4** : produced without occlusion along the lengthwise middle line of the tongue — **me·di·an·ly** *adv*

median strip *n* (1948) : a paved or planted strip dividing a highway into lanes according to direction of travel

me·di·ant \ˈmēd-ē-ənt\ *n* [It *mediante*, fr. LL *mediant-*, *medians*, prp. of *mediare* to be in the middle] (ca. 1727) : the third tone of a diatonic scale midway between the tonic and the dominant

me·di·as·ti·num \ˌmēd-ē-ə-ˈstī-nəm\ *n, pl* **-na** \-nə\ [NL, fr. L, neut. of *mediastinus* medial, fr. *medius*] (1541) : the space in the chest between the pleural sacs of the lungs that contains all the viscera of the chest except the lungs and pleurae; *also* : this space with its contents — **me·di·as·ti·nal** \-ˈstīn-ᵊl\ *adj*

¹**me·di·ate** \ˈmēd-ē-ət\ *adj* [ME, fr. LL *mediatus* intermediate, fr. pp. of *mediare*] (15c) **1** : occupying a middle position **2 a** : acting through an intervening agency **b** : exhibiting indirect causation, connection, or relation — **me·di·a·cy** \-ē-ə-sē\ *n* — **me·di·ate·ly** *adv* — **me·di·ate·ness** *n*

²**me·di·ate** \ˈmēd-ē-ˌāt\ *vb* **-at·ed; -at·ing** [ML *mediatus*, pp. of *mediare*, fr. LL, to be in the middle, fr. L *medius* middle] *vt* (1568) **1 a** : to effect by action as an intermediary **b** : to bring accord out of by action as an intermediary **2 a** : to act as intermediary agent in bringing, effecting, or communicating : CONVEY **b** : to transmit as intermediate mechanism or agency ~ *vi* **1** : to interpose between parties in order to reconcile them **2** : to reconcile differences ***syn*** see INTERPOSE — **me·di·a·tive** \-ˌāt-iv\ *adj* — **me·di·a·to·ry** \-ə-ˌtōr-ē, -ˌtȯr-\ *adj*

me·di·a·tion \ˌmēd-ē-ˈā-shən\ *n* (14c) : the act or process of mediating; *esp* : intervention between conflicting parties to promote reconciliation, settlement, or compromise — **me·di·a·tion·al** \-shnəl, -shən-ᵊl\ *adj*

me·di·a·tor \ˈmēd-ē-ˌāt-ər\ *n* [LL, fr. *mediatus*, pp.] (14c) **1** : one that mediates; *esp* : one that mediates between parties at variance **2** : a mediating agent in a chemical or biological process

me·di·a·trix \-ˈā-triks\ *n* [ME, fr. LL, fem. of *mediator*] (15c) : a female mediator

¹**med·ic** \ˈmed-ik\ *n* [ME *medike*, fr. L *medica*, fr. Gk *mēdikē*, fr. fem. of *mēdikos* of Media, fr. *Mēdia* Media] (15c) : any of a genus (*Medicago*) of leguminous herbs (as alfalfa)

²**medic** *n* [L *medicus*] (1659) : one engaged in medical work or study; *esp* : CORPSMAN

med·i·ca·ble \ˈmed-i-kə-bəl\ *adj* (ca. 1616) : CURABLE, REMEDIABLE

med·ic·aid \ˈmed-i-ˌkād\ *n, often cap* [*medical aid*] (1966) : a program of medical aid designed for those unable to afford regular medical service and financed by the state and federal governments

med·i·cal \ˈmed-i-kəl\ *adj* [F or LL; F *médical*, fr. LL *medicalis*, fr. L *medicus* physician, fr. *mederi* to heal; akin to Av vī-*mad-* healer, L *meditari* to meditate] (1646) **1** : of, relating to, or concerned with physicians or the practice of medicine **2** : requiring or devoted to medical treatment — **med·i·cal·ly** \-k(ə-)lē\ *adv*

medical examiner *n* (1877) : a public officer who makes postmortem examinations of bodies to find the cause of death

me·di·ca·ment \mi-ˈdik-ə-mənt, ˈmed-i-kə-\ *n* (1541) : a substance used in therapy — **me·di·ca·men·tous** \mi-ˌdik-ə-ˈment-əs, ˌmed-i-kə-\ *adj*

medi·care \ˈmed-i-ˌke(ə)r, -ˌka(ə)r\ *n, often cap* [blend of *medical* and *care*] (1955) : a government program of medical care esp. for the aged

med·i·cate \ˈmed-ə-ˌkāt\ *vt* **-cat·ed; -cat·ing** [L *medicatus,* pp. of *medicare* to heal, fr. *medicus*] (ca. 1623) **1** : to treat medicinally **2** : to impregnate with a medicinal substance ⟨*medicated* soap⟩

med·i·ca·tion \ˌmed-ə-ˈkā-shən\ *n* (15c) **1** : the act or process of medicating **2** : a medicinal substance : MEDICAMENT

me·dic·i·na·ble \mi-ˈdis-nə-bəl, -ᵊn-ə-; *in Shak* ˈmed-sə-nə-\ *adj* (14c) : MEDICINAL

me·dic·i·nal \mə-ˈdis-nəl, -ᵊn-əl; *in Shak & Milton* ˌmed-i-ˈsīn-ᵊl & ˈmed-sə-nəl\ *adj* (14c) **1** : tending or used to cure disease or relieve pain **2** : SALUTARY — **medicinal** *n* — **me·dic·i·nal·ly** \-ē\ *adv*

medicinal leech *n* (ca. 1890) : a large European freshwater leech (*Hirudo medicinalis*) formerly used by physicians for bleeding patients

med·i·cine \ˈmed-ə-sən, *Brit usu* ˈmed-sən\ *n* [ME, fr. OF, fr. L *medicina,* fr. fem. of *medicinus* of a physician, fr. *medicus*] (13c) **1 a** : a substance or preparation used in treating disease **b** : something that affects well-being **2 a** : the science and art dealing with the maintenance of health and the prevention, alleviation, or cure of disease **b** : the branch of medicine concerned with the nonsurgical treatment of disease **3** : a substance (as a drug or potion) used to treat something other than disease **4** : an object held by the American Indians to give control over natural or magical forces; *also* : magical power or a magical rite — **medicine** *vt*

medicine ball *n* (1895) : a heavy stuffed leather-covered ball used for conditioning exercises

medicine dropper *n* (1898) : DROPPER 2

medicine man *n* (1801) : a priestly healer or sorcerer esp. among the American Indians : SHAMAN

medicine show *n* (ca. 1906) : a traveling show using entertainers to attract a crowd among which remedies or nostrums are sold

med·i·co \ˈmed-i-ˌkō\ *n, pl* **-cos** [It *medico* or Sp *médico,* both fr. L *medicus*] (1689) : a medical practitioner : PHYSICIAN; *also* : a medical student

medico- *comb form* [NL, fr. L *medicus*] **1** : medical ⟨*medico*psychology⟩ **2** : medical and ⟨*medico*legal⟩

med·i·co·le·gal \ˌmed-i-kō-ˈlē-gəl\ *adj* [NL *medicolegalis,* fr. L *medicus* medical + *-o-* + *legalis* legal] (1835) : of or relating to both medicine and law

1me·di·eval *or* **me·di·ae·val** \ˌmēd-ē-ˈē-vəl, ˌmed-, ˌmid-; mē-ˈdē-vəl, mid-ˈē-, med-ˈē-\ *adj* [*medi-* + L *aevum* age — more at AYE] (1827) : of, relating to, or characteristic of the Middle Ages — **me·di·eval·ly** \-ē\ *adv*

2medieval *or* **mediaeval** *n* (1856) : a person of the Middle Ages

me·di·eval·ism \-ˌiz-əm\ *n* (1853) **1** : medieval quality, character, or state **2** : devotion to the institutions, arts, and practices of the Middle Ages

me·di·eval·ist \-ˈēv-(ə-)ləst, -ˈdēv-\ *n* (1874) **1** : a specialist in medieval history and culture **2** : a connoisseur or devotee of medieval arts and culture

Medieval Latin *n* (ca. 1881) : the Latin used esp. for liturgical and literary purposes from the 7th to the 15th centuries inclusive

medio- — see MEDI-

me·di·o·cre \ˌmēd-ē-ˈō-kər\ *adj* [ME, fr. MF, fr. L *mediocris,* lit., halfway up a mountain, fr. *medi-* + *ocris* stony mountain; akin to L *acer* sharp — more at EDGE] (1586) : of moderate or low quality : ORDINARY

me·di·oc·ri·ty \ˌmēd-ē-ˈäk-rət-ē\ *n, pl* **-ties** [ME, fr. MF *mediocrité,* fr. L *mediocritat-, mediocritas,* fr. *mediocris*] (15c) **1 a** : the quality or state of being mediocre **b** : moderate ability or value **2** : a mediocre person

med·i·tate \ˈmed-ə-ˌtāt\ *vb* **-tat·ed; -tat·ing** [L *meditatus,* pp. of *meditari* — more at METE] *vi* (1560) : to engage in contemplation or reflection ~ *vt* **1** : to focus one's thoughts on : reflect on or ponder over **2** : to plan or project in the mind : INTEND, PURPOSE ***syn*** see PONDER — **med·i·ta·tor** \-ˌtāt-ər\ *n*

med·i·ta·tion \ˌmed-ə-ˈtā-shən\ *n* (13c) **1** : a discourse intended to express its author's reflections or to guide others in contemplation **2** : the act or process of meditating

med·i·ta·tive \ˈmed-ə-ˌtāt-iv\ *adj* (ca. 1656) **1** : disposed or given to meditation **2** : marked by or conducive to meditation — **med·i·ta·tive·ly** *adv* — **med·i·ta·tive·ness** *n*

Med·i·ter·ra·nean \ˌmed-ə-tə-ˈrā-nē-ən, -nyən\ *adj* (15c) **1** : of or relating to the Mediterranean sea **2** *not cap* [L *mediterraneus,* fr. *medi-* + *terra* land — more at TERRACE] : enclosed or nearly enclosed with land **3** : of or relating to a group or physical type of the Caucasian race characterized by medium or short stature, slender build, dolichocephaly, and dark complexion

Mediterranean flour moth *n* (1895) : a small largely gray and black nearly cosmopolitan moth (*Anagasta kuehniella*) whose larva destroys processed grain products

Mediterranean fruit fly *n* (1907) : a widely distributed two-winged fly (*Ceratitis capitata*) with black and white markings whose larva lives and feeds in ripening fruit

1me·di·um \ˈmēd-ē-əm\ *n, pl* **mediums** *or* **me·dia** \-ē-ə\ [L, fr. neuter of *medius* middle — more at MID] (1593) **1 a** : something in a middle position **b** : a middle condition or degree : MEAN **2** : a means of effecting or conveying something: as **a** (1) : a substance regarded as the means of transmission of a force or effect (2) : a surrounding or enveloping substance **b** *pl usu media* (1) : a channel or system of communication, information, or entertainment — compare MASS MEDIUM (2) : a publication or broadcast that carries advertising (3) : a mode of artistic expression or communication **c** : GO-BETWEEN, INTERMEDIARY **d** *pl mediums* : an individual held to be a channel of communication between the earthly world and a world of spirits **e** : material or technical means of artistic expression **3 a** : a condition or environment in which something may function or flourish **b** *pl media* (1) : a nutrient system for the artificial cultivation of cells or organisms and esp. bacteria (2) : a fluid or solid in which organic structures are placed (as for preservation or mounting) **c** : a liquid with which pigment is mixed by a painter ***usage*** see MEDIA

2medium *adj* (1670) : intermediate in amount, quality, position, or degree

medium frequency *n* (1920) : a radio frequency between high frequency and low frequency — see RADIO FREQUENCY table

me·di·um·is·tic \ˌmēd-ē-ə-ˈmis-tik\ *adj* (1868) : of, relating to, or having the qualities of a spiritualistic medium

medium of exchange (1740) : something commonly accepted in exchange for goods and services and recognized as representing a standard of value

me·di·um·ship \ˈmēd-ē-əm-ˌship\ *n* (1868) : the capacity, function, or profession of a spiritualistic medium

med·lar \ˈmed-lər\ *n* [ME *medeler,* fr. MF *medlier,* fr. *medle* medlar fruit, fr. L *mespilum,* fr. Gk *mespilon*] (14c) : a small Eurasian tree (*Mespilus germanica*) of the rose family whose fruit resembles a crab apple and is used in preserves; *also* : its fruit

1med·ley \ˈmed-lē\ *n, pl* **medleys** [ME *medle,* fr. MF *medlee,* fr. fem. of *medlé,* pp. of *medler* to mix — more at MEDDLE] (14c) **1** *archaic* : MELEE **2** : MIXTURE; *esp* : HODGEPODGE **3** : a musical composition made up of a series of songs or short musical pieces

2medley *adj* (14c) : MIXED, MOTLEY

medley relay *n* (1949) : a relay race in swimming in which each member of a team uses a different stroke

me·dul·la \mə-ˈdəl-ə\ *n, pl* **-las** *or* **-lae** \-(ˌ)ē, -ˌī\ [L] (15c) **1** *pl medullae* **a** : MARROW 1 **b** : MEDULLA OBLONGATA **2 a** : the inner or deep part of an animal or plant structure ⟨the adrenal ~⟩ **b** : MYELIN SHEATH

medulla ob·lon·ga·ta \-ˌäb-ˌlȯŋ-ˈgät-ə\ *n, pl* **medulla oblongatas** *or* **medullae ob·lon·ga·tae** \-ˈgät-ē, -ˈgä-ˌtī\ [NL, lit., oblong medulla] (1676) : the somewhat pyramidal last part of the vertebrate brain continuous posteriorly with the spinal cord — see BRAIN illustration

med·ul·lary \ˈmed-ᵊl-ˌer-ē, ˈmej-ə-ˌler-; mə-ˈdəl-ə-rē\ *adj* (1620) **1** : of or relating to the pith of a plant **2** : of or relating to a medulla and esp. the medulla oblongata

medullary ray *n* (1830) **1** : a primary tissue composed of radiating bands of parenchyma cells extending between the vascular bundles of herbaceous dicotyledonous stems and connecting the pith with the cortex **2** : VASCULAR RAY

medullary sheath *n* (1849) : MYELIN SHEATH

med·ul·lat·ed \ˈmed-ᵊl-ˌāt-əd, ˈmej-ə-ˌlāt-\ *adj* (1867) **1** : MYELINATED **2** : having a medulla — used of fibers other than nerve fibers

me·dul·lo·blas·to·ma \mə-ˌdəl-ō-ˌblas-ˈtō-mə\ *n, pl* **-to·mas** *also* **-to·ma·ta** \-ˈtō-mət-ə\ [NL, fr. *medulla* + *-o-* + *blast-* + *-oma*] (ca. 1925) : a malignant tumor of the central nervous system arising in the cerebellum esp. in children

me·du·sa \mi-ˈd(y)ü-sə, -zə\ *n* **1** *cap* [L, fr. Gk *Medousa*] : a mortal Gorgon who is slain when decapitated by Perseus **2** *pl* **me·du·sae** \-ˌsē, -ˌzē, -ˌsī, -ˌzī\ [NL, fr. L] : JELLYFISH; *esp* : a small hydrozoan jellyfish — **me·du·san** \-ˈd(y)üs-ᵊn, -ˈd(y)üz-\ *adj or n* — **me·du·soid** \-ˈd(y)ü-ˌsȯid, -ˌzȯid\ *adj or n*

meed \ˈmēd\ *n* [ME, fr. OE *mēd;* akin to OHG *miata* reward, Gk *misthos*] (bef. 12c) **1** *archaic* : an earned reward or wage **2** : a fitting return or recompense

meek \ˈmēk\ *adj* [ME, of Scand origin; akin to ON *mjūkr* gentle; akin to L *mucus* mucus] (13c) **1** : enduring injury with patience and without resentment : MILD **2** : deficient in spirit and courage : SUBMISSIVE **3** : not violent or strong : MODERATE — **meek·ly** *adv* — **meek·ness** *n*

meer·schaum \ˈmi(ə)r-shəm, -ˌshȯm\ *n* [G, fr. *meer* sea (fr. OHG *meri*) + *schaum* foam, fr. OHG *scūm* — more at MARINE, SCUM] (ca. 1784) **1** : a fine light white clayey mineral that is a hydrous magnesium silicate $H_4Mg_2Si_3O_{10}$ found chiefly in Asia Minor and used esp. for tobacco pipes **2** : a tobacco pipe of meerschaum

1meet \ˈmēt\ *vb* **met** \ˈmet\; **meet·ing** [ME *meten,* fr. OE *mētan;* akin to OHG *muoz* meeting, Arm *matčim* I approach] *vt* (bef. 12c) **1 a** : to come into the presence of : FIND **b** : to come together with esp. at a particular time or place ⟨I'll ~ you at the station⟩ **c** : to come into contact or conjunction with : JOIN **d** : to appear to the perception of **2** : to encounter as antagonist or foe : OPPOSE **3** : to enter into conference, argument, or personal dealings with **4** : to conform to esp. with exactitude and precision ⟨a concept to ~ all requirements⟩ **5** : to pay fully : SETTLE **6** : to cope with : MATCH ⟨was able to ~ every social situation⟩ **7** : to provide for ⟨had enough money to ~ the needs of the moment⟩ **8** : to become acquainted with **9** : ENCOUNTER, EXPERIENCE **10** : to receive or greet in an official capacity ~ *vi* **1 a** : to come face-to-face **b** : to come together for a common purpose : ASSEMBLE **c** : to come together as contestants, opponents, or enemies **2** : to form a junction or confluence ⟨the lines ~ in a point⟩ **3** : to occur together — **meet·er** *n* — **meet halfway** : to compromise with — **meet with** : to be subjected to : ENCOUNTER ⟨the proposal *met with* opposition⟩

2meet *n* (1831) **1** : the act of assembling for a hunt or for competitive sports **2** : a competition in which individuals (as athletes) match skills

3meet *adj* [ME *mete,* fr. OE *gemǣte;* akin to OE *metan* to mete] (bef. 12c) : precisely adapted to a particular situation, need, or circumstance : very proper ***syn*** see FIT — **meet·ly** *adv*

meet·ing \ˈmēt-iŋ\ *n* (14c) **1** : an act or process of coming together: as **a** : an assembly for a common purpose (as worship) **b** : a session of horse or dog racing **2** : a permanent organizational unit of the Society of Friends **3** : INTERSECTION, JUNCTION

meet·ing·house \-ˌhau̇s\ *n* (1632) : a building used for public assembly and esp. for Protestant worship

meeting of minds (1939) : AGREEMENT, CONCORD

mef·e·nam·ic acid \ˌmef-ə-ˌnam-ik-\ *n* [dimethyl- + *fen-* (by shortening & alter. fr. *phenyl*) + *aminobenzoic acid*] (ca. 1964) : a drug $C_{15}H_{15}NO_2$ used as an anti-inflammatory

mega- *or* **meg-** *comb form* [Gk, fr. *megas* large — more at MUCH] **1 a** : great : large ⟨*mega*spore⟩ **b** : having a (specified) part of large size ⟨*mega*cephalic⟩ **2** : million : multiplied by one million ⟨*meg*ohm⟩ ⟨*mega*cycle⟩

mega·bar \ˈmeg-ə-ˌbär\ *n* [ISV] (ca. 1903) : a unit of pressure equal to 1,000,000 bars

mega·bit \-ˌbit\ *n* (1956) : 1,000,000 bits

mega·buck \-ˌbək\ *n* (1946) : 1,000,000 dollars

mega·byte \-ˌbīt\ *n* (1970) : 1,048,576 bytes

mega·cy·cle \-ˌsī-kəl\ *n* (1926) : 1,000,000 cycles; *esp* : MEGAHERTZ

mega·death \-ˌdeth\ *n* (1953) : 1,000,000 deaths — usu. used as a unit in reference to atomic warfare

mega·dose \-ˌdōs\ *n* (ca. 1972) : a large dose (as of a vitamin)

mega·ga·mete \ˌmeg-ə-gə-'mēt, -'gam-ˌēt\ *n* (1891) : MACROGAMETE
mega·ga·me·to·phyte \-gə-'mēt-ə-ˌfīt\ *n* (1933) : the female gametophyte produced by a megaspore
mega·hertz \'meg-ə-ˌhərts, -ˌhe(ə)rts\ *n* [ISV] (1941) : a unit of frequency equal to 1,000,000 hertz — abbr. *MHz*
mega·kary·o·cyte \ˌmeg-ə-'kar-ē-ō-ˌsīt\ *n* [*mega-* + *kary-* + *-cyte*] (1890) : a large cell that has a lobulated nucleus, is found esp. in the bone marrow, and is considered to be the source of blood platelets — **mega·kary·o·cyt·ic** \-ō-ˌsit-ik\ *adj*
megal- *or* **megalo-** *comb form* [NL, fr. Gk, fr. *megal-, megas* — more at MUCH] : large : of giant size ⟨*megalo*polis⟩ : grandiose ⟨*megalo*mania⟩
mega·lith \'meg-ə-ˌlith\ *n* (1853) : a very large usu. rough stone used as a monument or in construction — **mega·lith·ic** \ˌmeg-ə-'lith-ik\ *adj*

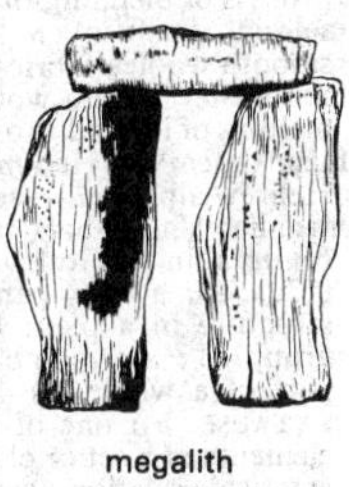
megalith

meg·a·lo·blast \'meg-ə-lō-ˌblast\ *n* (1899) : a large erythroblast that appears in the blood esp. in pernicious anemia — **meg·a·lo·blas·tic** \ˌmeg-ə-lō-'blas-tik\ *adj*
meg·a·lo·ma·nia \ˌmeg-ə-lō-'mā-nē-ə, -nyə\ *n* [NL] (ca. 1890) **1** : a mania for great or grandiose performance **2** : a delusional mental disorder that is marked by infantile feelings of personal omnipotence and grandeur — **meg·a·lo·ma·ni·ac** \-'mā-nē-ˌak\ *adj or n* — **meg·a·lo·ma·ni·a·cal** \-mə-'nī-ə-kəl\ *also* **meg·a·lo·man·ic** \-'man-ik\ *adj* — **meg·a·lo·ma·ni·a·cal·ly** \-mə-'nī-ə-k(ə-)lē\ *adv*
meg·a·lop·o·lis \ˌmeg-ə-'läp-ə-ləs\ *n* (ca. 1828) **1** : a very large city **2** : a thickly populated region centering in a metropolis or embracing several metropolises — **meg·a·lo·pol·i·tan** \-lō-'päl-ət-ᵊn\ *n or adj* — **meg·a·lo·pol·i·tan·ism** \-ˌiz-əm\ *n*
meg·a·lop·ter·an \ˌmeg-ə-'läp-tə-rən\ *n* [NL *Megaloptera*, fr. *megal-* + Gk *pteron* wing — more at FEATHER] (1946) : any of a small order (Megaloptera) of usu. large insects (as a dobsonfly) that are often classified as neuropterans, have wings with a folded anal area in the hind pair, and develop from aquatic predacious larvae (as a hellgrammite) — **meg·a·lop·ter·ous** \-tə-rəs\ *adj*
mega·par·sec \ˌmeg-ə-'pär-ˌsek\ *n* [ISV] (1933) : a unit of measure for distances in interstellar space equal to 1,000,000 parsecs
[1]**mega·phone** \'meg-ə-ˌfōn\ *n* (1878) : a cone-shaped device used to intensify or direct the voice — **mega·phon·ic** \ˌmeg-ə-'fän-ik\ *adj*
[2]**megaphone** *vt* (1901) : to transmit or address through or as if through a megaphone ~ *vi* : to speak through or as if through a megaphone
me·gap·o·lis \mə-'gap-ə-ləs, me-\ *n* (1638) : MEGALOPOLIS — **meg·a·pol·i·tan** \ˌmeg-ə-'päl-ət-ᵊn\ *adj*
Me·gar·i·an \mə-'gar-ē-ən, me-\ *adj* (1603) : of or relating to a Socratic school of philosophy founded by Euclid of Megara and noted for its subtle attention to logic — **Megarian** *n*
Me·gar·ic \-'gar-ik\ *adj* (1656) : MEGARIAN — **Megaric** *n*
mega·scop·ic \ˌmeg-ə-'skäp-ik\ *adj* [*mega-* + *-scopic* (as in *microscopic*)] (1879) **1** : MACROSCOPIC 1 ⟨~ features of leaves⟩ **2** : based on or relating to observations made with the unaided eye — **mega·scop·i·cal·ly** \-i-k(ə-)lē\ *adv*
mega·spo·ran·gi·um \ˌmeg-ə-spə-'ran-jē-əm\ *n* [NL] (1886) : a sporangium that develops only megaspores
mega·spore \'meg-ə-ˌspō(ə)r, -ˌspȯ(ə)r\ *n* [ISV] (1858) : a spore in heterosporous plants that gives rise to female gametophytes and is generally larger than a microspore — **mega·spor·ic** \ˌmeg-ə-'spōr-ik, -'spȯr-\ *adj*
mega·spo·ro·gen·e·sis \ˌmeg-ə-ˌspōr-ə-'jen-ə-səs, -ˌspȯr-\ *n* [NL] (ca. 1928) : the formation and maturation of a megaspore
mega·spo·ro·phyll \ˌmeg-ə-'spōr-ə-ˌfil, -'spȯr-\ *n* (ca. 1899) : a sporophyll that develops only megasporangia
mega·ton \'meg-ə-ˌtən\ *n* (1952) : an explosive force equivalent to that of 1,000,000 tons of TNT
mega·vi·ta·min \-ˌvīt-ə-mən, *Brit usu* -ˌvit-\ *adj* (1970) : relating to or consisting of very large doses of vitamins ⟨~ therapy⟩
mega·vi·ta·mins \-mənz\ *n pl* (1974) : a large quantity of vitamins
mega·watt \'meg-ə-ˌwät\ *n* [ISV] (ca. 1900) : 1,000,000 watts
me·gil·lah \mə-'gil-ə\ *n* [Yiddish, fr. Heb *mĕgillāh* scroll, volume (used esp. of the Book of Esther, read aloud at the Purim celebration)] *slang* (ca. 1952) : a long involved story or account ⟨the whole ~⟩
me·gilp \mə-'gilp\ *n* [origin unknown] (1768) : a gelatinous preparation commonly of linseed oil and mastic varnish that is used by artists as a vehicle for oil colors
meg·ohm \'meg-ˌōm\ *n* [ISV] (ca. 1868) : 1,000,000 ohms
me·grim \'mē-grəm\ *n* [ME *migreime*, fr. MF *migraine*] (15c) **1** **a** : MIGRAINE **b** : VERTIGO, DIZZINESS **2** **a** : FANCY, WHIM **b** *pl* : low spirits
Mei·ji \'mā-(ˌ)jē\ *n* [Jp, lit., enlightened rule] (1873) : the period of the reign (1868–1912) of Emperor Mutsuhito of Japan
mei·kle \'mē-kəl\ *var of* MICKLE
mei·ny *n, pl* **meinies** [ME *meynie* — more at MENIAL] (13c) **1** \'mā-nē\ *archaic* : RETINUE, COMPANY **2** \'men-yē\ *chiefly Scot* : MULTITUDE
mei·o·sis \mī-'ō-səs\ *n* [NL, fr. Gk *meiōsis* diminution, fr. *meioun* to diminish, fr. *meiōn* less — more at MINOR] (1586) **1** : the representation of a thing as less than it actually is in order to compel greater esteem for it : UNDERSTATEMENT **2** : the cellular process that results in the number of chromosomes in gamete-producing cells being reduced to one half and that involves a reduction division in which one of each pair of homologous chromosomes passes to each daughter cell and a mitotic division — compare MITOSIS — **mei·ot·ic** \mī-'ät-ik\ *adj* — **mei·ot·i·cal·ly** \-i-k(ə-)lē\ *adv*
Meis·sen \'mīs-ᵊn\ *n* [*Meissen*, Saxony, Germany] (1863) : a ceramic ware made at Meissen near Dresden; *esp* : a European porcelain developed under the patronage of the king of Saxony about 1715 and used for both ornamental and table wares — called also *Meissen china, Meissen ware*
Mei·ster·sing·er \'mī-stər-ˌsiŋ-ər, -ˌziŋ-\ *n, pl* **Meistersinger** *or* **Meistersingers** [G, fr. MHG, fr. *meister* master + *singer* singer] (1845) : a member of any of various German guilds formed chiefly in the 15th and 16th centuries by workingmen and craftsmen for the cultivation of poetry and music
mel·a·mine \'mel-ə-ˌmēn\ *n* [G *melamin*] (ca. 1835) **1** : a white crystalline organic base $C_3H_6N_6$ with a high melting point that is used esp. in melamine resins **2** : a melamine resin or a plastic made from such a resin
melamine resin *n* (1939) : a thermosetting resin made from melamine and an aldehyde and used esp. in molded or laminated products, adhesives, and coatings
melan- *or* **melano-** *comb form* [ME, fr. MF, fr. LL, fr. Gk, fr. *melan-, melas* — more at MULLET] **1** : black : dark ⟨*melan*ic⟩ ⟨*melan*in⟩ **2** : melanin ⟨*melan*oid⟩
mel·an·cho·lia \ˌmel-ən-'kō-lē-ə\ *n* [NL, fr. LL, melancholy] (14c) : a mental condition characterized by extreme depression, bodily complaints, and often hallucinations and delusions; *esp* : a manic-depressive psychosis — **mel·an·cho·li·ac** \-lē-ˌak\ *n*
mel·an·chol·ic \ˌmel-ən-'käl-ik\ *adj* (14c) **1** : of, relating to, or subject to melancholy : DEPRESSED **2** : of or relating to melancholia **3** : tending to depress the spirits : SADDENING — **melancholic** *n*
[1]**mel·an·choly** \'mel-ən-ˌkäl-ē\ *n, pl* **-chol·ies** [ME *malencolie*, fr. MF *melancolie*, fr. LL *melancholia*, fr. Gk, fr. *melan-* + *cholē* bile — more at GALL] (14c) **1** **a** : an abnormal state attributed to an excess of black bile and characterized by irascibility or depression **b** : BLACK BILE **c** : MELANCHOLIA **2** **a** : depression of spirits : DEJECTION **b** : a pensive mood
[2]**melancholy** *adj* (14c) **1** **a** : suggestive or expressive of melancholy ⟨sang in a ~ voice⟩ **b** : causing or tending to cause sadness or depression of mind or spirit : DISMAL ⟨a ~ thought⟩ **2** **a** : depressed in spirits : DEJECTED, SAD **b** : PENSIVE
Mel·a·ne·sian \ˌmel-ə-'nē-zhən, -shən\ *n* (1849) **1** : a language group consisting of the Austronesian languages of Melanesia **2** : a member of the dominant native group of Melanesia — **Melanesian** *adj*
mé·lange \mā-'läⁿzh, -'länj\ *n* [F, fr. MF, fr. *mesler, meler* to mix — more at MEDDLE] (1653) : a mixture often of incongruous elements
[1]**me·lan·ic** \mə-'lan-ik\ *adj* (1826) **1** : MELANOTIC **2** : affected with or characterized by melanism
[2]**melanic** *n* (1952) : a melanic individual
mel·a·nin \'mel-ə-nən\ *n* (1843) : a dark brown or black animal or plant pigment
mel·a·nism \'mel-ə-ˌniz-əm\ *n* (1843) **1** : an increased amount of black or nearly black pigmentation (as of skin, feathers, or hair) of an individual or kind of organism **2** : intense pigmentation in man in skin, eyes, and hair — **mel·a·nis·tic** \ˌmel-ə-'nis-tik\ *adj*
mel·a·nite \'mel-ə-ˌnīt\ *n* [G *melanit*, fr. *melan-*] (ca. 1807) : a black andradite garnet — **mel·a·nit·ic** \ˌmel-ə-'nit-ik\ *adj*
mel·a·nize \'mel-ə-ˌnīz\ *vt* **-nized; -niz·ing** (1885) **1** : to convert into or infiltrate with melanin **2** : to make dark or black — **mel·a·ni·za·tion** \ˌmel-ə-nə-'zā-shən\ *n*
me·la·no·blast \mə-'lan-ə-ˌblast, 'mel-ə-nō-\ *n* [ISV] (1901) : a cell that is a precursor of a melanocyte or melanophore
me·la·no·cyte \mə-'lan-ə-ˌsīt, 'mel-ə-nō-\ *n* [ISV] (ca. 1890) : an epidermal cell that produces melanin
melanocyte–stimulating hormone *n* (1953) : a vertebrate hormone of the pituitary gland that darkens the skin by stimulating melanin dispersion in pigment-containing cells — called also *melanophore-stimulating hormone*
me·la·no·gen·e·sis \mə-ˌlan-ə-'jen-ə-səs, ˌmel-ə-nō-\ *n* [NL] (ca. 1928) : the formation of melanin
mel·a·noid \'mel-ə-ˌnȯid\ *n* [ISV] (1854) : a pigment (as one contributing esp. to the yellow color of the skin) that is a disintegration product of a melanin
mel·a·no·ma \ˌmel-ə-'nō-mə\ *n, pl* **-mas** *also* **-ma·ta** \-mət-ə\ [NL] (1830) : a usu. malignant tumor containing dark pigment
me·la·no·phore \mə-'lan-ə-ˌfō(ə)r, 'mel-ə-nə-, -ˌfȯ(ə)r\ *n* (1903) : a melanin-containing cell esp. of fishes, amphibians, and reptiles
me·la·no·some \-ˌsōm\ *n* [NL] (1940) : a melanin-producing granule in a melanocyte
mel·a·not·ic \ˌmel-ə-'nät-ik\ *adj* (1829) : having or characterized by black pigmentation
mela·phyre \'mel-ə-ˌfī(ə)r\ *n* [F *mélaphyre*, fr. Gk *melas* black + F *-phyre* (as in *porphyre* porphyry) — more at MULLET] (ca. 1841) : a porphyritic igneous rock with dark-colored aphanitic groundmass and phenocrysts of various kinds
mel·a·to·nin \ˌmel-ə-'tō-nən\ *n* [prob. fr. *mela*nocyte + sero*tonin*] (1958) : a vertebrate hormone of the pineal gland that produces lightening of the skin by causing concentration of melanin in pigment-containing cells
mel·ba toast \ˌmel-bə-\ *n* [Nellie *Melba*] (ca. 1925) : very thin crisp toast
Mel·chite *or* **Mel·kite** \'mel-ˌkīt\ *n* [ML *Melchita*, fr. MGk *Melchitēs*, lit., royalist, fr. Syr *malkā* king] (1619) **1** : an Eastern Christian chiefly of Syria and Egypt adhering to Chalcedonian orthodoxy in preference to Monophysitism **2** : a member of a Uniate body derived from the Melchites
[1]**Mel·chiz·e·dek** \mel-'kiz-ə-ˌdek\ *n* [Gk *Melchisedek*, fr. Heb *Malkī-ṣedheq*] : a priest-king of Jerusalem who prepared a ritual meal for Abraham and received tithes from him
[2]**Melchizedek** *adj* (1842) : of or relating to the higher order of the Mormon priesthood
[1]**meld** \'meld\ *vb* [G *melden* to announce, fr. OHG *meldōn*; akin to OE *meldian* to announce, OSlav *moliti* to ask for] *vt* (1897) : to declare or announce (a card or combination of cards) for a score in a card game esp. by placing face up on the table ~ *vi* : to declare a card or combination of cards as a meld
[2]**meld** *n* (1897) : a card or combination of cards that is or can be melded in a card game
[3]**meld** *vb* [blend of *melt* and *weld*] (1936) : MERGE, BLEND
[4]**meld** *n* (1954) : BLEND, MIXTURE

\ə\ abut \ᵊ\ kitten, F table \ər\ further \a\ ash \ā\ ace \ä\ cot, cart \au̇\ out \ch\ chin \e\ bet \ē\ easy \g\ go \i\ hit \ī\ ice \j\ job \ŋ\ sing \ō\ go \ȯ\ law \ȯi\ boy \th\ thin \t͟h\ the \ü\ loot \u̇\ foot \y\ yet \zh\ vision \å, k̲, ⁿ, œ, œ̄, ue, ue̅, ʸ\ *see* Guide to Pronunciation

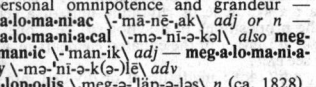

me·lee *also* **mê·lée** \'mā-,lā, mā-'\ *n* [F *mêlée,* fr. OF *meslee,* fr. *mesler* to mix — more at MEDDLE] (1648) : a confused struggle; *esp* : a hand-to-hand fight among several people

mel·ic \'mel-ik\ *adj* [L *melicus,* fr. Gk *melikos,* fr. *melos* song — more at MELODY] (1699) : of or relating to song : LYRIC; *esp* : of or relating to Greek lyric poetry of the 7th and 6th centuries B.C.

mel·i·lot \'mel-ə-,lät\ *n* [ME *mellilot,* fr. OF *melilot,* fr. L *melilotos,* fr. Gk *melilōtos,* fr. *meli* honey + *lōtos* clover, lotus — more at MELLIFLUOUS] (12c) : SWEET CLOVER; *esp* : a yellow-flowered sweet clover (*Melilotus officinalis*)

me·lio·rate \'mēl-yə-,rāt, 'mē-lē-ə-\ *vb* **-rat·ed; -rat·ing** [LL *melioratus,* pp. of *meliorare,* fr. L *melior* better; akin to L *multus* much, Gk *mala* very] (1542) : AMELIORATE — **me·lio·ra·tion** \,mēl-yə-'rā-shən, ,mē-lē-ə-\ *n* — **me·lio·ra·tive** \'mēl-yə-,rāt-iv, 'mē-lē-ə-\ *adj* — **me·lio·ra·tor** \-,rāt-ər\ *n*

me·lio·rism \'mēl-yə-,riz-əm, 'mē-lē-ə-\ *n* (1877) : the belief that the world tends to become better and that man can aid its betterment — **me·lio·rist** \-rəst\ *adj or n* — **me·lio·ris·tic** \,mēl-yə-'ris-tik, ,mē-lē-ə-\ *adj*

me·lis·ma \mi-'liz-mə\ *n, pl* **-ma·ta** \-mət-ə\ [NL, fr. Gk, song, melody, fr. *melizein* to sing, fr. *melos* song] (1880) **1** : a group of notes or tones sung on one syllable in plainsong **2** : melodic embellishment or ornamentation **3** : CADENZA — **mel·is·mat·ic** \,mel-əz-'mat-ik\ *adj*

mell \'mel\ *vb* [ME *mellen,* fr. MF *mesler*] *archaic* (14c) : MIX

mel·lif·lu·ent \me-'lif-lə-wənt\ *adj* [LL *mellifluent-, mellifluens,* fr. L *mell-, mel* + *fluent-, fluens,* prp. of *fluere*] (1601) : MELLIFLUOUS — **mel·lif·lu·ent·ly** *adv*

mel·lif·lu·ous \me-'lif-lə-wəs, mə-\ *adj* [ME *mellyfluous,* fr. LL *mellifluus,* fr. L *mell-, mel* honey + *fluere* to flow; akin to Goth *milith* honey, Gk *melit-, meli*] (15c) **1** : filled with something (as honey) that sweetens **2** : having a smooth rich flow ⟨a ~ voice⟩ — **mel·lif·lu·ous·ly** *adv* — **mel·lif·lu·ous·ness** *n*

mel·lo·phone \'mel-ə-,fōn\ *n* [[1]*mellow* + *-phone*] (1926) : a valved brass instrument similar in form and range to the French horn and used chiefly in marching bands

Mel·lo·tron \'mel-ə-,trän\ *trademark* — used for an electronic keyboard instrument programmed to produce the tape-recorded sounds usu. of orchestral instruments

[1]**mel·low** \'mel-(,)ō, -ə(-w)\ *adj* [ME *melowe*] (15c) **1 a** *of a fruit* : tender and sweet because of ripeness **b** *of a wine* : well aged and pleasingly mild **2 a** : made gentle by age or experience **b** : rich and full but free from garishness or stridency **c** : warmed and relaxed by or as if by liquor **d** : PLEASANT, AGREEABLE ⟨in a ~ mood⟩ **3** *of soil* : having a soft and loamy consistency — **mel·low·ly** *adv* — **mel·low·ness** *n*

[2]**mellow** *vt* (1572) : to make mellow ~ *vi* : to become mellow

me·lo·de·on \mə-'lōd-ē-ən\ *n* [G *melodion,* fr. *melodie* melody, fr. OF] (1847) : a small reed organ in which a suction bellows draws air inward through the reeds

me·lod·ic \mə-'läd-ik\ *adj* (1823) : of or relating to melody : MELODIOUS — **me·lod·i·cal·ly** \-i-k(ə-)lē\ *adv*

me·lo·di·ous \mə-'lōd-ē-əs\ *adj* (14c) **1** : having a pleasing melody **2** : of, relating to, or producing melody — **me·lo·di·ous·ly** *adv* — **me·lo·di·ous·ness** *n*

mel·o·dist \'mel-əd-əst\ *n* (1789) **1** : SINGER **2** : a composer of melodies

mel·o·dize \'mel-ə-,dīz\ *vb* **-dized; -diz·ing** *vi* (1662) : to compose a melody ~ *vt* : to make melodious : set to melody — **mel·o·diz·er** *n*

melo·dra·ma \'mel-ə-,dräm-ə, -,dram-\ *n* [modif. of F *mélodrame,* fr. Gk *melos* song + F *drame* drama, fr. LL *drama*] (1809) **1 a** : a work (as a movie or play) characterized by extravagant theatricality and by the predominance of plot and physical action over characterization **b** : the genre of dramatic literature constituted by such works **2** : melodramatic events or behavior — **melo·dra·ma·tist** \,mel-ə-'dram-ət-əst, -'dräm-\ *n*

melo·dra·mat·ic \,mel-ə-drə-'mat-ik\ *adj* (1816) **1** : of, relating to, or characteristic of melodrama **2** : appealing to the emotions : SENSATIONAL ***syn*** see DRAMATIC — **melo·dra·mat·i·cal·ly** \-i-k(ə-)lē\ *adv*

melo·dra·mat·ics \-iks\ *n pl but sing or pl in constr* (1915) : melodramatic conduct or writing

melo·dra·ma·tize \,mel-ə-'dram-ə-,tīz, -'dräm-\ *vt* (1820) **1** : to make melodramatic ⟨~ a situation⟩ **2** : to make a melodrama of (as a novel) — **melo·dra·ma·ti·za·tion** \-,dram-ət-ə-'zā-shən, -,dräm-\ *n*

mel·o·dy \'mel-əd-ē\ *n, pl* **-dies** [ME *melodie,* fr. OF, fr. LL *melodia,* fr. Gk *melōidia* chanting, music, fr. *melos* limb, musical phrase, song (akin to Bret *mell* joint) + *aeidein* to sing — more at ODE] (13c) **1** : a sweet or agreeable succession or arrangement of sounds : TUNEFULNESS **2** : a rhythmic succession of single tones organized as an aesthetic whole

mel·on \'mel-ən\ *n, often attrib* [ME, fr. MF, fr. LL *melon-, melo,* short for L *melopepon-, melopepo,* fr. Gk *mēlopepōn,* fr. *mēlon* apple + *pepōn,* an edible gourd — more at PUMPKIN] (14c) **1** : any of various gourds (as a muskmelon or watermelon) usu. eaten raw as fruits **2** : something rounded like a melon; *also* : a protruding abdomen **3 a** : a surplus of profits available for distribution to stockholders **b** : a financial windfall

mel·pha·lan \'mel-fə-,lan\ *n* [prob. fr. *methanol* + *phenylalanine*] (ca. 1964) : an antineoplastic drug $C_{13}H_{18}Cl_2N_2O_2$

Mel·pom·e·ne \mel-'päm-ə-(,)nē\ *n* [L, fr. Gk *Melpomenē*] : the Greek Muse of tragedy

[1]**melt** \'melt\ *vb* [ME *melten,* fr. OE *meltan;* akin to L *mollis* soft, *molere* to grind — more at MEAL] *vi* (bef. 12c) **1** : to become altered from a solid to a liquid state usu. by heat **2 a** : DISSOLVE, DISINTEGRATE ⟨the sugar ~*ed* in the coffee⟩ **b** : to disappear as if by dissolving ⟨her anger ~*ed* at his kind words⟩ **3** *obs* : to become subdued or crushed (as by sorrow) **4** : to become mild, tender, or gentle **5** : to lose distinct outline : BLEND ~ *vt* **1** : to reduce from a solid to a liquid state usu. by heat **2** : to cause to disappear or disperse **3** : to make tender or gentle : SOFTEN — **melt·abil·i·ty** \,mel-tə-'bil-ət-ē\ *n* — **melt·able** \'mel-tə-bəl\ *adj* — **melt·er** *n*

[2]**melt** *n* (1854) **1 a** : material in the molten state **b** : the mass melted at a single operation or the quantity melted during a specified period **2 a** : the action or process of melting or the period during which it occurs ⟨roads softened during the spring ~⟩ **b** : the condition of being melted

[3]**melt** *n* [ME *milte,* fr. OE; akin to OHG *miltzi* spleen] (bef. 12c) : SPLEEN; *esp* : spleen of slaughtered animals for use as feed or food

melt·down \'melt-,daun\ *n* (1963) : the melting of the core of a nuclear reactor

melt·ing \'mel-tiŋ\ *adj* (1593) : TENDER, DELICATE ⟨a love song's ~ lyric⟩ — **melt·ing·ly** *adv*

melting point *n* (1842) : the temperature at which a solid melts

melting pot *n* (15c) **1** : a vessel for melting something : CRUCIBLE **2 a** : a place where racial amalgamation and social and cultural assimilation are going on ⟨long cherished the myth of the public school as the *melting pot* —M. R. Berube⟩ **b** : the population of such a place **3** : a process of blending that often results in invigoration or novelty

mel·ton \'melt-ᵊn\ *n* [*Melton* Mowbray, England] (1823) : a heavy smooth woolen fabric with short nap

melt·wa·ter \'melt-,wȯt-ər, -,wät-\ *n* (1923) : water derived from the melting of ice and snow

mem \'mem\ *n* [Heb *mēm,* lit., water] (ca. 1899) : the 13th letter of the Hebrew alphabet — see ALPHABET table

mem·ber \'mem-bər\ *n, often attrib* [ME *membre,* fr. OF, fr. L *membrum;* akin to Goth *mimz* flesh, Gk *mēros* thigh, *mēninx* membrane] (13c) **1** : a body part or organ: as **a** : LIMB **b** : PENIS **c** : a unit of structure in a plant body **2** : one of the individuals composing a group **3** : a person baptized or enrolled in a church **4** : a constituent part of a whole: as **a** : a syntactic or rhythmic unit of a sentence : CLAUSE **b** : one of the propositions of a syllogism **c** : one of the elements of a set or class **d** : either of the equated elements in a mathematical equation ***syn*** see PART

mem·bered \'mem-bərd\ *adj* (14c) : made up of or divided into members

mem·ber·ship \'mem-bər-,ship\ *n* (1647) **1** : the state or status of being a member **2** : the body of members ⟨an organization with a large ~⟩ **3** : the relation between an element of a set or class and the set or class — compare INCLUSION 3

mem·brane \'mem-,brān\ *n* [L *membrana* skin, parchment, fr. *membrum*] (15c) **1** : a thin soft pliable sheet or layer esp. of animal or plant origin **2** : a piece of parchment forming part of a roll — **mem·braned** \'mem-,brānd\ *adj*

membrane bone *n* (1880) : a bone that ossifies directly in connective tissue without previous existence as cartilage

mem·bra·nous \'mem-brə-nəs\ *adj* (1597) **1** : of, relating to, or resembling membrane **2** : thin, pliable, and often somewhat transparent ⟨~ leaves⟩ **3** : characterized or accompanied by the formation of a usu. abnormal membrane or membranous layer ⟨~ croup⟩ — **mem·bra·nous·ly** *adv*

membranous labyrinth *n* (1840) : the sensory structures of the inner ear

me·men·to \mi-'ment-(,)ō\ *n, pl* **-tos** *or* **-toes** [ME, fr. L, remember, imper. of *meminisse* to remember — more at MENTAL] (1580) : something that serves to warn or remind; *also* : SOUVENIR

me·men·to mo·ri \mi-,ment-ō-'mōr-ē, -'mȯr-ē\ *n, pl* **memento mori** [L, remember that you must die] (1596) **1** : a reminder of mortality; *esp* : DEATH'S-HEAD **2** : a reminder of man's failures or mistakes

Mem·non \'mem-,nän\ *n* [Gk *Memnōn*] : an Ethiopian king slain by Achilles at a late stage of the Trojan War

memo \'mem-(,)ō\ *n, pl* **mem·os** (1889) : MEMORANDUM

mem·oir \'mem-,wär, -,wȯ(ə)r\ *n* [F *mémoire,* lit., memory, fr. L *memoria*] (15c) **1** : an official note or report : MEMORANDUM **2 a** : a narrative composed from personal experience **b** : AUTOBIOGRAPHY — usu. used in pl. **c** : BIOGRAPHY **3 a** : an account of something noteworthy : REPORT **b** *pl* : the record of the proceedings of a learned society — **mem·oir·ist** \-əst\ *n*

mem·o·ra·bil·ia \,mem-ə-rə-'bil-ē-ə, -'bil-yə\ *n pl* [L, fr. neut. pl. of *memorabilis*] (1806) : things that are remarkable and worthy of remembrance; *also* : things that stir recollection : MEMENTOS

mem·o·ra·bil·i·ty \-'bil-ət-ē\ *n* (1661) **1** : the quality or state of being memorable **2** : the quality or state of being rememberable

mem·o·ra·ble \'mem-(ə-)rə-bəl, 'mem-ər-bəl\ *adj* [ME, fr. L *memorabilis,* fr. *memorare* to remind, mention, fr. *memor* mindful] (15c) : worth remembering : NOTABLE — **mem·o·ra·ble·ness** *n* — **mem·o·ra·bly** \-blē\ *adv*

mem·o·ran·dum \,mem-ə-'ran-dəm\ *n, pl* **-dums** *or* **-da** \-də\ [ME, fr. L, neut. of *memorandus* to be remembered, gerundive of *memorare*] (1542) **1** : an informal record; *also* : a written reminder **2** : an informal written note of a transaction or proposed instrument **3 a** : an informal diplomatic communication **b** : a usu. brief communication written for interoffice circulation **c** : a communication that contains directive, advisory, or informative matter

usage Although some commentators warn against the use of *memoranda* as a singular and condemn the plural *memorandas,* our evidence indicates that these forms are rarely encountered in print. We have a little evidence of the confusion of forms, including use of *memorandum* as a plural, in speech (as at congressional hearings). As plurals *memoranda* and *memorandums* are about equally frequent.

[1]**me·mo·ri·al** \mə-'mōr-ē-əl, -'mȯr-\ *adj* (14c) **1** : serving to preserve remembrance : COMMEMORATIVE **2** : of or relating to memory — **me·mo·ri·al·ly** \-ə-lē\ *adv*

[2]**memorial** *n* (14c) **1** : something that keeps remembrance alive: as **a** : MONUMENT **b** : something (as a speech or ceremony) that commemorates **c** : KEEPSAKE, MEMENTO **2 a** : RECORD, MEMOIR ⟨language and literature . . . the ~*s* of another age —J. H. Fisher⟩ **b** : MEMORANDUM, NOTE; *specif* : a legal abstract **c** : a statement of facts addressed to a government and often accompanied by a petition or remonstrance

Memorial Day *n* (1869) **1** : May 30 formerly observed as a legal holiday in most states of the U.S. in remembrance of war dead **2** : the last Monday in May observed as a legal holiday in most states of the U.S. **3** : CONFEDERATE MEMORIAL DAY

me·mo·ri·al·ist \mə-'mōr-ē-ə-ləst, -'mȯr-\ *n* (1706) **1** : a person who writes or signs a memorial **2** : a person who writes a memoir

me·mo·ri·al·ize \-,līz\ *vt* **-ized; -iz·ing** (1798) **1** : to address or petition by a memorial **2** : COMMEMORATE

memorial park *n* (ca. 1928) : CEMETERY

me·mo·ri·ter \mə-'mȯr-ə-,te(ə)r, -'mär-\ *adj* [L, adv., by memory, fr. *memor*] (1802) : marked by emphasis on memorization

mem·o·rize \'mem-ə-,rīz\ *vt* **-rized; -riz·ing** (ca. 1838) : to commit to memory : learn by heart — **mem·o·riz·able** \-,rī-zə-bəl\ *adj* — **mem·o·ri·za·tion** \,mem-(ə-)rə-'zā-shən\ *n* — **mem·o·riz·er** *n*

mem·o·ry \'mem-(ə-)rē\ *n, pl* **-ries** [ME *memorie,* fr. MF *memoire,* fr. L *memoria,* fr. *memor* mindful; akin to OE *mimorian* to remember, L *mora* delay, Gk *mermēra* care, Skt *smarati* he remembers] (14c) **1 a** : the power or process of reproducing or recalling what has been learned and retained esp. through associative mechanisms **b** : the store of things learned and retained from an organism's activity or experience as evidenced by modification of structure or behavior or by recall and recognition **2 a** : commemorative remembrance ⟨erected a statue in ~ of the hero⟩ **b** : the fact or condition of being remembered ⟨days of recent ~⟩ **3 a** : a particular act of recall or recollection **b** : an image or impression of one that is remembered ⟨fond *memories* of her youth⟩ **c** : the time within which past events can be or are remembered ⟨within the ~ of living men⟩ **4 a** : a device in which information esp. for a computer can be inserted and stored and from which it may be extracted when wanted **b** : capacity for storing information ⟨a computer with 16K words of ~⟩ **5** : a capacity for showing effects as the result of past treatment or for returning to a former condition — used esp. of a material (as metal or plastic)

memory lane *n* (1954) : an imaginary path through the nostalgically remembered past — usu. used in such phrases as *a walk down memory lane*

memory trace *n* (1923) : ENGRAM

mem·sa·hib \'mem-,sä-,(h)ib, -,säb\ *n* [Hindi *memṣāhib,* fr. E *ma'am* + Hindi *ṣāhib* sahib] (1857) : a white foreign woman of high social status living in India; *esp* : the wife of a British official

men *pl of* MAN

men- *or* **meno-** *comb form* [NL, fr. Gk *mēn* month — more at MOON] : menstruation ⟨*menorrhagia*⟩

1**men·ace** \'men-əs\ *n* [ME, fr. MF, fr. L *minacia,* fr. *minac-, minax* threatening, fr. *minari* to threaten — more at MOUNT] (14c) **1** : a show of intention to inflict harm : THREAT **2 a** : one that represents a threat : DANGER **b** : a person who causes annoyance

2**menace** *vb* **men·aced; men·ac·ing** *vt* (14c) **1** : to make a show of intention to harm **2** : to represent or pose a threat to : ENDANGER ~ *vi* : to act in a threatening manner — **men·ac·ing·ly** \-ə-siŋ-lē\ *adv*

me·nad *var of* MAENAD

men·a·di·one \,men-ə-'dī-,ōn, -dī-'\ *n* [*methyl* + *naphthoquinone* + *di-* + *ketone*] (1941) : a yellow crystalline compound $C_{11}H_8O_2$ with the biological activity of natural vitamin K

mé·nage \mā-'näzh\ *n* [F, fr. OF *mesnage* dwelling, fr. (assumed) VL *mansionaticum,* fr. L *mansion-, mansio* mansion] (13c) : a domestic establishment : HOUSEHOLD; *also* : HOUSEKEEPING

mé·nage à trois \-ä-'trwä\ *n* [F, lit., household for three] (1891) : an arrangement in which three persons (as a married pair and the lover of one of the pair) share sexual relations esp. while living together

me·nag·er·ie \mə-'naj-(ə-)rē *also* -'nazh-\ *n* [F *ménagerie,* fr. MF, management of a household or farm, fr. *menage*] (1676) **1 a** : a place where animals are kept and trained esp. for exhibition **b** : a collection of wild or foreign animals kept esp. for exhibition **2** : a varied mixture ⟨a wonderful ~ of royal hangers-on —V. S. Pritchett⟩

men·ar·che \'men-,är-kē\ *n* [NL, fr. *men-* + Gk *archē* beginning] (1900) : the beginning of the menstrual function; *esp* : the first menstrual period of an individual — **men·ar·che·al** \,men-är-'kē-əl\ *adj*

1**mend** \'mend\ *vb* [ME *menden,* short for *amenden* — more at AMEND] *vt* (13c) **1** : to free from faults or defects: as **a** : to improve in manners or morals : REFORM **b** : to set right : CORRECT **c** : to put into good shape or working order again : patch up : REPAIR **d** : to restore to health : CURE **2** : to make amends or atonement for ⟨least said, soonest ~*ed*⟩ ~ *vi* **1** : to improve morally : REFORM **2** : to become corrected or improved **3** : to improve in health; *also* : HEAL — **mend·able** \'men-də-bəl\ *adj* — **mend·er** *n*

syn MEND, REPAIR, PATCH, REBUILD mean to put into good order something that has been injured, damaged, or defective. MEND implies making whole or sound something broken, torn, or injured; REPAIR applies to the mending of more extensive damage or dilapidation; PATCH implies an often temporary mending of a rent or breach with new material; REBUILD suggests making like new without completely replacing.

2**mend** *n* (14c) **1** : an act of mending : REPAIR **2** : a mended place — **on the mend** : getting better : IMPROVING

men·da·cious \men-'dā-shəs\ *adj* [L *mendac-, mendax* — more at AMEND] (1616) : given to or characterized by deception or falsehood which often is not intended to genuinely mislead or delude ⟨spinning ~ tales of his adventures⟩ ***syn*** see DISHONEST — **men·da·cious·ly** *adv* — **men·da·cious·ness** *n*

men·dac·i·ty \men-'das-ət-ē\ *n, pl* **-ties** (1646) **1** : the quality or state of being mendacious **2** : LIE

men·de·le·vi·um \,men-də-'lē-vē-əm, -'lā-\ *n* [NL, fr. Dmitry *Mendeleyev*] (1955) : a radioactive element that is artificially produced — see ELEMENT table

Men·de·lian \men-'dē-lē-ən, -'dēl-yən\ *adj* (1901) : of, relating to, or according with Mendel's laws or Mendelism — **Mendelian** *n*

Mendelian factor *n* (ca. 1927) : GENE

Mendelian inheritance *n* (ca. 1923) : PARTICULATE INHERITANCE

Men·del·ism \'men-dᵊl-,iz-əm\ *n* (1903) : the principles or the operations of Mendel's laws; *also* : PARTICULATE INHERITANCE — **Men·del·ist** \-dᵊl-əst\ *adj or n*

Men·del's law \,men-dᵊlz-\ *n* [Gregor *Mendel*] (1903) **1** : a principle in genetics: hereditary units occur in pairs that separate during gamete formation so that every gamete receives but one member of a pair — called also *law of segregation* **2** : a principle in genetics limited and modified by the subsequent discovery of the phenomenon of linkage: the different pairs of hereditary units are distributed to the gametes independently of each other, the gametes combine at random, and the various combinations of hereditary pairs occur in the zygotes according to the laws of chance — called also *law of independent assortment* **3** : a principle in genetics proved subsequently to be subject to many limitations: because one of each pair of hereditary units dominates the other in expression, characters are inherited alternatively on an all or nothing basis — called also *law of dominance*

men·di·can·cy \'men-di-kən-sē\ *n* (1790) **1** : the condition of being a beggar **2** : the practice of begging

men·di·cant \'men-di-kənt\ *n* [L *mendicant-, mendicans,* prp. of *mendicare* to beg, fr. *mendicus* beggar — more at AMEND] (14c) **1** : BEGGAR 1 **2** *often cap* : a member of a religious order (as the Franciscans) combining monastic life and outside religious activity and orig. owning neither personal nor community property : FRIAR — **mendicant** *adj*

men·dic·i·ty \men-'dis-ət-ē\ *n* [ME *mendicite,* fr. MF *mendicité,* fr. L *mendicitat-, mendicitas,* fr. *mendicus*] (15c) : MENDICANCY

Men·e·la·us \,men-ᵊl-'ā-əs\ *n* [L, fr. Gk *Menelaos*] : a king of Sparta, brother of Agamemnon, and husband of the abducted Helen of Troy

men·folk \'men-,fōk\ *or* **men·folks** \-,fōks\ *n pl* (1802) **1** : men in general **2** : the men of a family or community

men·ha·den \men-'hād-ᵊn, mən-\ *n, pl* **-den** *also* **-dens** [of Algonquian origin; prob. akin to Narraganset *munnawhatteaûg* menhaden] (1643) : a marine fish (*Brevoortia tyrannus*) of the herring family abundant along the Atlantic coast of the U.S. where it is used for bait or converted into oil and fertilizer

men·hir \'men-,hi(ə)r\ *n* [F, fr. Bret, fr. *men* stone + *hir* long] (1840) : a single upright rude monolith usu. of prehistoric origin

1**me·nial** \'mē-nē-əl, -nyəl\ *n* (14c) : a person doing menial work; *specif* : a domestic servant or retainer

2**menial** *adj* [ME *meynial,* fr. *meynie* household, retinue, fr. OF *mesnie,* fr. (assumed) VL *mansionata,* fr. L *mansion-, mansio* dwelling — more at MANSION] (15c) **1** : of or relating to servants : LOWLY **2 a** : appropriate to a servant : HUMBLE, SERVILE ⟨answered in ~ tones⟩ **b** : lacking interest or dignity ⟨a ~ task⟩ — **me·nial·ly** \-ē\ *adv*

Mé·nière's disease \mən-'ye(ə)rz-, 'men-yərz-\ *n* [Prosper *Ménière* †1862 Fr. physician] (1876) : a disorder of the membranous labyrinth of the inner ear that is marked by recurrent attacks of dizziness, tinnitus, and deafness — called also *Ménière's syndrome*

mening- *or* **meningo-** *also* **meningi-** *comb form* [NL, fr. *mening-, meninx*] **1** : meninges ⟨*meningococcus*⟩ ⟨*meningitis*⟩ **2** : meninges and ⟨*meningoencephalitis*⟩

men·in·ge·al \,men-ən-'jē-əl\ *adj* (1829) : of, relating to, or affecting the meninges

meninges *pl of* MENINX

me·nin·gi·o·ma \mə-,nin-jē-'ō-mə\ *n, pl* **-omas** *or* **-o·ma·ta** \-'ō-mət-ə\ [NL] (1922) : a slow-growing encapsulated tumor arising from the meninges and often causing damage by pressing upon the brain and adjacent parts

men·in·gi·tis \,men-ən-'jīt-əs\ *n, pl* **-git·i·des** \-'jit-ə-,dēz\ [NL] (1828) **1** : inflammation of the meninges and esp. of the pia mater and the arachnoid **2** : a usu. bacterial disease in which inflammation of the meninges occurs — **men·in·git·ic** \-'jit-ik\ *adj*

me·nin·go·coc·cus \mə-,niŋ-gə-'käk-əs, -,nin-jə-\ *n, pl* **-coc·ci** \-'käk-,(s)ī, -(,)(s)ē\ [NL] (ca. 1893) : the bacterium (*Neisseria meningitidis*) that causes cerebrospinal meningitis — **me·nin·go·coc·cal** \-'käk-əl\ *also* **me·nin·go·coc·cic** \-'käk-(s)ik\ *adj*

me·nin·go·en·ceph·a·li·tis \-gō-ən-,sef-ə-'līt-əs\ *n, pl* **-lit·i·des** \-'lit-ə-,dēz\ [NL] (ca. 1860) : inflammation of the brain and meninges — **me·nin·go·en·ceph·a·lit·ic** \-'lit-ik\ *adj*

me·ninx \'mē-niŋ(k)s, 'men-iŋ(k)s\ *n, pl* **me·nin·ges** \mə-'nin-(,)jēz\ [NL, fr. Gk *mēning-, mēninx* membrane; akin to L *membrana* membrane] (1666) : any of the three membranes that envelop the brain and spinal cord

me·nis·cus \mə-'nis-kəs\ *n, pl* **me·nis·ci** \-'nis-,(k)ī, -,kē\ *also* **me·nis·cus·es** [NL, fr. Gk *mēniskos,* fr. dim. of *mēnē* moon, crescent — more at MOON] (1693) **1** : a concavo-convex lens **2** : a crescent or crescent-shaped body **3** : the curved upper surface of a liquid column that is concave when the containing walls are wetted by the liquid and convex when not **4** : a fibrous cartilage within a joint esp. of the knee

Men·no·nite \'men-ə-,nīt\ *n* [G *Mennonit,* fr. *Menno* Simons] (1565) : a member of any of various Protestant groups derived from the Anabaptist movement in Holland and characterized by congregational autonomy and rejection of military service

meno- — see MEN-

me·no mos·so \,mā-nō-'mò(s)-(,)sō\ *adv* [It] (ca. 1854) : less rapid — used as a direction in music

meno·pause \'men-ə-,pòz, 'mēn-\ *n* [F *ménopause,* fr. *méno-* men- + *pause* stop, pause] (1872) : the period of natural cessation of menstruation occurring usu. between the ages of 45 and 50 — **meno·paus·al** \,men-ə-'pò-zəl, ,mēn-\ *adj*

me·no·rah \mə-'nōr-ə, -'nòr-\ *n* [Heb *mĕnōrāh* candlestick] (1888) : a candelabrum used in Jewish worship

menorah

men·or·rha·gia \,men-ə-'rā-j(ē-)ə, -'rā-zhə; -'räj-ə, -'räzh-\ *n* [NL] (1776) : abnormally profuse menstrual flow

men·sal \'men(t)-səl\ *adj* [LL *mensalis,* fr. L *mensa* table] (15c) : of, relating to, or done at the table

mensch \'mench\ *n* [Yiddish, fr. G, man, human being, fr OHG *mennisco;* akin to ON *mennska* humanity] (1953) : a person of integrity and honor

1**mense** \'men(t)s\ *n* [ME *menske,* fr. ON *mennska* humanity; akin to OE *man* man] *chiefly Scot* (15c) : PROPRIETY — **mense·ful** \-fəl\ *adj* — **mense·less** \-ləs\ *adj*

2**mense** *vt* **mensed; mens·ing** *chiefly Scot* (1540) : to do honor to : GRACE

men·ses \'men-,sēz\ *n pl but sing or pl in constr* [L, lit., months, pl. of *mensis* month — more at MOON] (1597) : the menstrual flow

Men·she·vik \'men-chə-,vik, -,vēk\ *n, pl* **Mensheviks** *or* **Men·she·vi·ki** \,men-chə-'vik-ē, -'vē-kē\ [Russ *men'shevik,* fr. *men'she* less; fr. their forming the minority group of the party] (1907) : a member of a wing of the Russian Social Democratic party before and during the Russian Revolution believing in the gradual achievement of socialism by parlia-

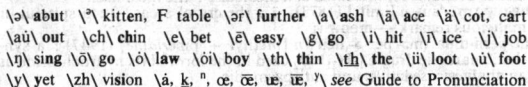

\ə\ abut \ᵊ\ kitten, F table \ər\ further \a\ ash \ā\ ace \ä\ cot, cart \aů\ out \ch\ chin \e\ bet \ē\ easy \g\ go \i\ hit \ī\ ice \j\ job \ŋ\ sing \ō\ go \ò\ law \òi\ boy \th\ thin \t͟h\ the \ü\ loot \ů\ foot \y\ yet \zh\ vision \à, k̟, ⁿ, œ, œ̄, ue, ue̅, ʸ\ see Guide to Pronunciation

mentary methods in opposition to the Bolsheviks — **Men·she·vism** \'men-chə-ˌviz-əm\ n — **Men·she·vist** \-vəst\ n or adj

mens rea \(ˌ)menz-'rē-ə\ n [NL, lit., guilty mind] (1861) : criminal intent

men's room n (1929) : a room equipped with lavatories, toilets, and usu. urinals for the use of men

men·stru·al \'men(t)-strə(-wə)l\ adj (14c) : of or relating to menstruation

men·stru·ate \'men(t)-strə-ˌwāt, 'men-ˌstrāt\ vi **-at·ed; -at·ing** [LL menstruatus, pp. of menstruari, fr. L menstrua menses, fr. neut. pl. of menstruus monthly, fr. mensis] (1800) : to undergo menstruation

men·stru·a·tion \ˌmen(t)-strə-'wā-shən, men-'strā-\ n (1776) : a discharging of blood, secretions, and tissue debris from the uterus that recurs in nonpregnant breeding-age primate females at approximately monthly intervals and that is considered to represent a readjustment of the uterus to the nonpregnant state following proliferative changes accompanying the preceding ovulation; also : PERIOD 6c

men·stru·um \'men(t)-strə(-wə)m\ n, pl **-stru·ums** or **-strua** \-str(ə-w)ə\ [ML, lit., menses, alter. of L menstrua] (1612) : a substance that dissolves a solid or holds it in suspension : SOLVENT

men·su·ra·ble \'men(t)s-(ə-)rə-bəl, 'mench-(ə-)rə-\ adj [LL mensurabilis, fr. mensurare to measure, fr. L mensura measure — more at MEASURE] (1604) 1 : capable of being measured : MEASURABLE 2 : MENSURAL 1

men·su·ral \'men(t)s-(ə-)rəl, 'mench-(ə-)rəl\ adj [LL mensuralis measurable, fr. L mensura] (1609) 1 : of, relating to, or being polyphonic music originating in the 13th century with each note having a definite and exact time value 2 : of or relating to measure

men·su·ra·tion \ˌmen(t)-sə-'rā-shən; ˌmen-chə-\ n (1571) 1 : the act of measuring : MEASUREMENT 2 : geometry applied to the computation of lengths, areas, or volumes from given dimensions or angles

mens·wear \'menz-ˌwa(ə)r, -ˌwe(ə)r\ n (1908) : clothing for men

-ment \mənt; homographic verbs are ˌment also mənt, the latter less often before a syllable-increasing suffix\ n suffix [ME, fr. OF, fr. L -mentum; akin to L -men, suffix denoting concrete result, Gk -mat-, -ma] 1 a : concrete result, object, or agent of a (specified) action ⟨embankment⟩ ⟨entanglement⟩ b : concrete means or instrument of a (specified) action ⟨entertainment⟩ 2 a : action : process ⟨encirclement⟩ ⟨development⟩ b : place of a (specified) action ⟨encampment⟩ 3 : state or condition resulting from a (specified action)

¹**men·tal** \'ment-ᵊl\ adj [ME, fr. MF, fr. LL mentalis, fr. L ment-, mens mind; akin to L monēre to remind, warn, meminisse to remember, Gk mnasthai, mimnēskesthai, to remember, menos spirit, OE gemynd mind, memory] (15c) 1 a : of or relating to the mind; specif : of or relating to the total emotional and intellectual response of an individual to his environment ⟨~ health⟩ b : of or relating to intellectual as contrasted with emotional activity c : of, relating to, or being intellectual as contrasted with overt physical activity d : occurring or experienced in the mind : INNER ⟨~ anguish⟩ e : relating to the mind, its activity, or its products as an object of study : IDEOLOGICAL f : relating to spirit or idea as opposed to matter 2 a (1) : of, relating to, or affected by a psychiatric disorder ⟨a ~ patient⟩ ⟨~ illness⟩ (2) : mentally disordered : MAD, CRAZY b : intended for the care or treatment of persons affected by psychiatric disorders ⟨~ hospitals⟩ 3 : of or relating to telepathic or mind-reading powers — **men·tal·ly** \-ᵊl-ē\ adv

²**mental** adj [L mentum chin; akin to L mont-, mons mountain — more at MOUNT] (ca. 1727) : of or relating to the chin : GENIAL

mental age n (1912) : a measure used in psychological testing that expresses an individual's mental attainment in terms of the number of years it takes an average child to reach the same level

mental deficiency n (1856) : failure in intellectual development that results in social incompetence and is considered to be the result of a defective central nervous system and to be incurable : FEEBLEMINDEDNESS

men·tal·ist \'ment-ᵊl-əst\ n (1930) : MIND READER

men·tal·is·tic \ˌment-ᵊl-'is-tik\ adj (1917) 1 : of or relating to any school of psychology or psychiatry that in contrast to behaviorism values subjective data (as those gained by introspection) in the study and explanation of behavior 2 : of or relating to mental phenomena — **men·tal·ism** \'ment-ᵊl-ˌiz-əm\ n

men·tal·i·ty \men-'tal-ət-ē\ n, pl **-ties** (1691) 1 : mental power or capacity : INTELLIGENCE 2 : mode or way of thought : OUTLOOK

men·ta·tion \men-'tā-shən\ n [L ment-, mens + E -ation] (1850) : mental activity

men·thol \'men-ˌthȯl, -ˌthōl\ n [G, deriv. of L mentha mint] (1876) : a crystalline alcohol C₁₀H₂₀O that occurs esp. in mint oils and has the odor and cooling properties of peppermint

men·tho·lat·ed \'men(t)-thə-ˌlāt-əd\ adj (1922) : containing or impregnated with menthol ⟨a ~ salve⟩

¹**men·tion** \'men-chən\ n [ME mencioun, fr. MF mention, fr. L mention-, mentio, fr. ment-, mens] (14c) 1 : the act or an instance of citing or calling attention to someone or something esp. in a casual or incidental manner 2 : formal citation for outstanding achievement

²**mention** vt **men·tioned; men·tion·ing** \'mench-(ə-)niŋ\ (1530) : to make mention of : refer to; also : to cite for outstanding achievement — **men·tion·a·ble** \'mench-(ə-)nə-bəl\ adj — **men·tion·er** \-(ə-)nər\ n — **not to mention** : AS WELL AS

men·tor \'men-ˌtȯ(ə)r, 'ment-ər\ n [L, fr. Gk Mentōr] 1 cap : a friend of Odysseus entrusted with the education of Odysseus' son Telemachus 2 a : a trusted counselor or guide b : TUTOR, COACH — **men·tor·ship** \-ˌship\ n

men·tum \'ment-əm\ n, pl **men·ta** \-ə\ [L — more at MENTAL] (ca. 1693) 1 : CHIN 2 : a median plate of the labium of an insect

menu \'men-(ˌ)yü, 'mān-\ n, pl **menus** [F, fr. menu small, detailed, fr. OF — more at MINUET] (1837) 1 a : a list of the dishes that may be ordered (as in a restaurant) or that are to be served (as at a banquet) b (1) : a comparable list or assortment of offerings ⟨a ~ of television programs⟩ (2) : a list shown on the display of a computer from which a user can select the operation the computer is to perform 2 : the dishes available for or served at a meal; also : the meal itself

me·ow \mē-'aù\ n [imit.] (1873) 1 : the cry of a cat 2 : a spiteful or malicious remark — **meow** vi

me·per·i·dine \mə-'per-ə-ˌdēn\ n [methyl + piperidine] (1947) : a synthetic narcotic drug C₁₅H₂₁NO₂ used in the form of its hydrochloride as an analgesic, sedative, and antispasmodic

Meph·is·toph·e·les \ˌmef-ə-'stäf-ə-ˌlēz\ n [G] : a chief devil in the Faust legend — **Me·phis·to·phe·lian** \ˌmef-ə-stə-'fēl-yən, mə-ˌfis-tə-\ or **Me·phis·to·phe·lean** \same, or ˌmef-ə-ˌstäf-ə-'lē-ən\ adj

me·phit·ic \mə-'fit-ik\ adj (ca. 1623) : of, relating to, or resembling mephitis : foul-smelling

me·phi·tis \mə-'fit-əs\ n [L, fr. Oscan] (ca. 1706) : a noxious, pestilential, or foul exhalation from the earth; also : STENCH

mep·ro·bam·ate \ˌmep-rō-'bam-ˌāt\ n [methyl + propyl + dicarbamate] (1955) : a bitter carbamate C₉H₁₈N₂O₄ used as a tranquilizer

-mer \mər\ n comb form [ISV, fr. Gk meros part — more at MERIT] : member of a (specified) class ⟨monomer⟩

mer·bro·min \mər-'brō-mən\ n [mercuric acetate + dibrom- + fluorescein] (1945) : a green crystalline mercurial compound C₂₀H₈Br₂HgNa₂O₆ used as a local antiseptic and germicide in the form of its red solution — compare MERCUROCHROME

Mer·cal·li scale \mer-ˌkäl-ē-, (ˌ)mər-\ n [Giuseppe Mercalli †1914 Ital. priest and geologist] (1921) : a scale of earthquake intensity ranging from I for an earthquake detected only by seismographs to XII for one causing total destruction of all buildings

mer·can·tile \'mər-kən-ˌtēl, -ˌtil\ adj [F, fr. It. fr. mercante merchant, fr. L mercant-, mercans, fr. prp. of mercari to trade — more at MERCHANT] (1642) 1 : of or relating to merchants or trading 2 : of, relating to, or having the characteristics of mercantilism ⟨~ system⟩

mer·can·til·ism \ˌ-ˌtē-ˌliz-əm, -ˌti-\ n (1873) 1 : the theory or practice of mercantile pursuits : COMMERCIALISM 2 : an economic system developing during the decay of feudalism to unify and increase the power and esp. the monetary wealth of a nation by a strict governmental regulation of the entire national economy usu. through policies designed to secure an accumulation of bullion, a favorable balance of trade, the development of agriculture and manufactures, and the establishment of foreign trading monopolies — **mer·can·til·ist** \-ləst\ n or adj — **mer·can·til·is·tic** \ˌmər-kən-ˌtē-'lis-tik, -ˌti-\ adj

mercapt- or **mercapto-** comb form : derived from or related to a mercaptan ⟨mercaptopurine⟩

mer·cap·tan \(ˌ)mər-'kap-ˌtan\ n [G, fr. Dan. fr. ML mercurium captans, lit., seizing mercury] (1835) : any of various compounds with the general formula RSH that are analogous to the alcohols and phenols but contain sulfur in place of oxygen and often have disagreeable odors

mer·cap·to·pu·rine \(ˌ)mər-ˌkap-tə-'pyü(ə)r-ˌēn\ n (ca. 1953) : an antimetabolite C₅H₄N₄S that interferes esp. with the metabolism of purine bases and the biosynthesis of nucleic acids and that is sometimes useful in the treatment of acute leukemia

Mer·ca·tor \(ˌ)mər-'kāt-ər\ adj (ca. 1876) : of, relating to, or drawn on the Mercator projection

Mer·ca·tor projection \(ˌ)mər-ˌkāt-ər-\ n [Gerhardus Mercator] (1669) : a conformal map projection in the usual case of which the meridians are drawn parallel to each other and the parallels of latitude are straight lines whose distance from each other increases with their distance from the equator

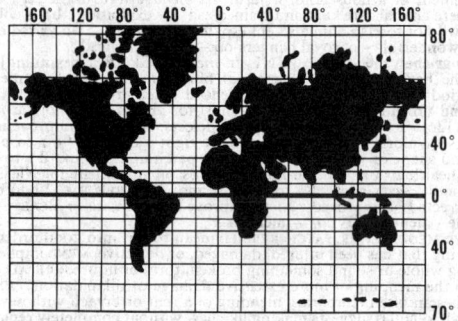

Mercator projection

¹**mer·ce·nary** \'mərs-ᵊn-ˌer-ē\ n, pl **-nar·ies** [ME, fr. L mercenarius, fr. merced-, merces wages — more at MERCY] (14c) : one that serves merely for wages; esp : a soldier hired into foreign service

²**mercenary** adj (1532) 1 : serving merely for pay or sordid advantage : VENAL; also : GREEDY 2 : hired for service in the army of a foreign country — **mer·ce·nari·ly** \ˌmərs-ᵊn-'er-ə-lē\ adv — **mer·ce·nari·ness** \'mərs-ᵊn-ˌer-ē-nəs\ n

mer·cer \'mər-sər\ n [ME, fr. OF mercier merchant, fr. mers merchandise, fr. L merc-, merx — more at MARKET] Brit (12c) : a dealer in usu. expensive fabrics

mer·cer·ize \'mər-sə-ˌrīz\ vt **-ized; -iz·ing** [John Mercer †1866 Eng. calico printer] (1859) : to give (as cotton yarn) luster, strength, and receptiveness to dyes by treatment under tension with caustic soda — **mer·cer·iza·tion** \ˌmər-s(ə-)rə-'zā-shən\ n

mer·cery \'mərs-(ə-)rē\ n, pl **-cer·ies** Brit (13c) : a mercer's wares, shop, or occupation

¹**mer·chan·dise** \'mər-chən-ˌdīz, -ˌdīs\ n [ME marchaundise, fr. OF marcheandise, fr. marchéant] (13c) 1 : the commodities or goods that are bought and sold in business : WARES 2 archaic : the occupation of a merchant : TRADE

²**mer·chan·dise** also **mer·chan·dize** \-ˌdīz\ vb **-dised** also **-dized; -dis·ing** also **-diz·ing** vi, archaic (14c) : to carry on commerce : TRADE ~ vt 1 : to buy and sell in business 2 : to promote or for as if for sale ⟨~ a movie star⟩ — **mer·chan·dis·er** n

mer·chan·dis·ing \-ˌdī-ziŋ\ n (1932) : sales promotion as a comprehensive function including market research, development of new products, coordination of manufacture and marketing, and effective advertising and selling

¹**mer·chant** \'mər-chənt\ n [ME marchant, fr. OF marcheant, fr. (assumed) VL mercatant-, mercatans, fr. prp. of mercatare to trade, fr. L mercatus, pp. of mercari — more at MARKET] (13c) 1 : a buyer and

seller of commodities for profit : TRADER 2 : the operator of a retail business : STOREKEEPER 3 : one that is noted for a particular quality or activity : SPECIALIST ⟨a speed ~⟩ — **merchant** *adj*

²merchant *vi, archaic* (14c) : to deal or trade as a merchant ~ *vt* : to deal or trade in

mer·chant·able \'mər-chənt-ə-bəl\ *adj* (15c) : of commercially acceptable quality : SALABLE — **mer·chant·abil·i·ty** \,mər-chənt-ə-'bil-ət-ē\ *n*

merchant bank *n, chiefly Brit* (1930) : a bank that specializes in bankers' acceptances and in underwriting or syndicating equity or bond issues

mer·chant·man \'mər-chənt-mən\ *n* (15c) 1 *archaic* : MERCHANT 2 : a ship used in commerce

merchant marine *n* (1855) 1 : the privately or publicly owned commercial ships of a nation 2 : the personnel of a merchant marine

merchant ship *n* (15c) : MERCHANTMAN 2

Mer·cian \'mər-sh(ē-)ən\ *n* (1612) 1 : a native or inhabitant of Mercia 2 : the Old English dialect of Mercia — **Mercian** *adj*

mer·ci·ful \'mər-si-fəl\ *adj* (14c) : full of mercy : COMPASSIONATE — **mer·ci·ful·ly** \-f(ə-)lē\ *adv* — **mer·ci·ful·ness** \-fəl-nəs\ *n*

mer·ci·less \'mər-si-ləs\ *adj* (14c) : having no mercy : PITILESS — **mer·ci·less·ly** *adv* — **mer·ci·less·ness** *n*

mercur- *or* **mercuro-** *comb form* [ISV, fr. *mercury*] : mercury ⟨*mercurous*⟩

mer·cu·rate \'mər-kyə-,rāt\ *vt* **-rat·ed; -rat·ing** (1923) : to combine or treat with mercury or a mercury salt — **mer·cu·ra·tion** \,mər-kyə-'rā-shən\ *n*

¹mer·cu·ri·al \(,)mər-'kyůr-ē-əl\ *adj* (14c) 1 : of, relating to, or born under the planet Mercury 2 : having qualities of eloquence, ingenuity, or thievishness attributed to the god Mercury or to the influence of the planet Mercury 3 : characterized by rapid and unpredictable changeableness of mood 4 : of, relating to, containing, or caused by mercury ***syn*** see INCONSTANT — **mer·cu·ri·al·ly** \-ē-ə-lē\ *adv* — **mer·cu·ri·al·ness** *n*

²mercurial *n* (1676) : a pharmaceutical or chemical containing mercury

mer·cu·ric \(,)mər-'kyů(ə)r-ik\ *adj* (ca. 1828) : of, relating to, or containing mercury; *esp* : containing mercury with a valence of two

mercuric chloride *n* (1874) : a heavy crystalline poisonous compound $HgCl_2$ used as a disinfectant and fungicide and in photography — called also *corrosive sublimate*

Mer·cu·ro·chrome \(,)mər-'kyůr-ə-,krōm\ *trademark* — used for merbromin

mer·cu·rous \(,)mər-'kyůr-əs, 'mər-kyə-rəs\ *adj* (ca. 1865) : of, relating to, or containing mercury; *esp* : containing mercury with a valence of one

mercurous chloride *n* (ca. 1885) : CALOMEL

mer·cu·ry \'mər-kyə-rē, -k(ə-)rē\ *n, pl* **-ries** [L *Mercurius*, Roman god and the planet] 1 a *cap* : a Roman god of commerce, eloquence, travel, cunning, and theft who serves as messenger to the other gods — compare HERMES b *often cap, archaic* : a bearer of messages or news or a conductor of travelers 2 [ME *mercurie*, fr. ML *mercurius*, fr. L, the god] a : a heavy silver-white poisonous metallic element that is liquid at ordinary temperatures and used esp. in scientific instruments — called also *quicksilver;* see ELEMENT table b : the mercury in a thermometer or barometer 3 *cap* : the planet nearest the sun — see PLANET table

mercury chloride *n* (ca. 1885) : a chloride of mercury: as a : CALOMEL b : MERCURIC CHLORIDE

mercury–vapor lamp *n* (1901) : an electric lamp in which the discharge takes place through mercury vapor — called also *mercury lamp*

mer·cy \'mər-sē\ *n, pl* **mercies** [ME, fr. OF *merci*, fr. ML *merced-, merces*, fr. L, price paid, wages, fr. *merc-, merx* merchandise — more at MARKET] (13c) 1 a : compassion or forbearance shown esp. to an offender or to one subject to one's power b : imprisonment rather than death imposed as penalty for first-degree murder 2 a : a blessing that is an act of divine favor or compassion b : a fortunate circumstance ⟨it was a ~ they found her before she froze⟩ 3 : compassionate treatment of those in distress ⟨ works of ~ among the poor⟩ — **mercy** *adj*

syn MERCY, CHARITY, CLEMENCY, GRACE, LENITY mean a disposition to show kindness or compassion. MERCY implies compassion that forbears punishing even when justice demands it; CHARITY stresses benevolence and goodwill shown in broad understanding and tolerance of others; CLEMENCY implies a mild or merciful disposition in one having the power or duty of punishing; GRACE implies a benign attitude and a willingness to grant favors or make concessions; LENITY implies lack of severity in punishing.

— **at the mercy of** : wholly in the power of : with no way to protect oneself against

mercy killing *n* (1935) : EUTHANASIA

merde \'me(ə)rd, 'ma(ə)rd\ *n* [F, lit., shit, dung, fr. L *merda;* prob. akin to L *mordēre* to bite — more at SMART] (15c) : CRAP 1a, 2 — sometimes considered vulgar

¹mere \'mi(ə)r\ *n* [ME, fr. OE — more at MARINE] (bef. 12c) : an expanse of standing water : LAKE, POOL

²mere *n* [ME, fr. OE *mǣre* — more at MUNITION] (bef. 12c) : BOUNDARY; *also* : LANDMARK

³mere \'mi(ə)r\ *adj, superlative* **mer·est** [ME, fr. L *merus* pure, unmixed — more at MORN] (1536) 1 *obs* : being nothing less than : ABSOLUTE 2 : being nothing more than : BARE ⟨a ~ mortal⟩ 3 : having no admixture : PURE — **mere·ly** *adv*

-mere \,mi(ə)r\ *n comb form* [F *-mère*, fr. Gk *meros* part — more at MERIT] : part : segment ⟨arthro*mere*⟩

me·ren·gue \mə-'reŋ-(,)gā\ *n* [AmerSp *merengue* & Haitian Creole *méringue*] (1936) : a ballroom dance of Haitian and Dominican origin in which one foot is dragged on every step; *also* : the music for a merengue

mer·e·tri·cious \,mer-ə-'trish-əs\ *adj* [L *meretricius*, fr. *meretric-, meretrix* prostitute, fr. *merēre* to earn — more at MERIT] (1626) 1 : of or relating to a prostitute : having the nature of prostitution ⟨~ relationship⟩ 2 a : tawdrily and falsely attractive ⟨the paradise they found was a piece of ~ trash —Carolyn See⟩ b : superficially significant : PRETENTIOUS ⟨scholarly names to provide fig-leaves of respectability for ~ but stylish books — *Times Lit. Supp.*⟩ ***syn*** see GAUDY — **mer·e·tri·cious·ly** *adv* — **mer·e·tri·cious·ness** *n*

mer·gan·ser \(,)mər-'gan(t)-sər\ *n* [NL, fr. L *mergus*, a waterfowl (fr. *mergere*) + *anser* goose — more at GOOSE] (1752) : any of various fish-eating diving ducks (esp. genus *Mergus*) with a slender bill hooked at the end and serrated along the margins and usu. a crested head

merge \'mərj\ *vb* **merged; merg·ing** [L *mergere;* akin to Skt *majjati* he dives] *vt* (1636) 1 *archaic* : to plunge or engulf in something : IMMERSE 2 : to cause to combine, unite, or coalesce 3 : to blend gradually by stages that blur distinctions ⟨as cultures are *merged* and traditions lost⟩ ~ *vi* 1 : to become combined into one 2 : to blend or come together without abrupt change ⟨*merging* traffic⟩ ***syn*** see MIX — **mer·gence** \'mər-jən(t)s\ *n*

merg·er \'mər-jər\ *n* [*merge* + *-er* (as in *waiver*)] (1728) 1 *law* : the absorption of an estate, a contract, or an interest in another, of a minor offense in a greater, or of an obligation into a judgment 2 a : the act or process of merging b : absorption by a corporation of one or more others; *also* : any of various methods of combining two or more organizations (as business concerns)

me·rid·i·an \mə-'rid-ē-ən\ *n* [ME, fr. MF *meridien*, fr. *meridien* of noon, fr. L *meridianus*, fr. *meridies* noon, south, irreg. fr. *medius* mid + *dies* day — more at MID, DEITY] (14c) 1 *archaic* : the hour of noon : MIDDAY 2 : a great circle of the celestial sphere passing through its poles and the zenith of a given place 3 : a high point 4 a (1) : a great circle on the surface of the earth passing through the poles (2) : the half of such a circle included between the poles b : a representation of such a circle or half circle numbered for longitude on a map or globe — see LONGITUDE illustration 5 : a line or circle (as on a projection of a planet or a lens) comparable to a meridian of longitude — **meridian** *adj*

¹me·rid·i·o·nal \mə-'rid-ē-ən-ᵊl\ *adj* [ME, fr. MF *meridionel*, fr. LL *meridionalis*, irreg. fr. L *meridies*] (14c) 1 : of, relating to, or situated in the south : SOUTHERN 2 : of, relating to, or characteristic of people living in the south esp. of France 3 : of, relating to, or situated on or along a meridian — **me·rid·i·o·nal·ly** \-ᵊl-ē\ *adv*

²meridional *n* (1591) : a native or inhabitant of southern Europe and esp. southern France

me·ringue \mə-'raŋ\ *n* [F] (1706) 1 : a dessert topping baked from a mixture of stiffly beaten egg whites and sugar 2 : a shell made of meringue and filled with fruit or ice cream

me·ri·no \mə-'rē-(,)nō\ *n, pl* **-nos** [Sp] (1781) 1 : any of a breed of fine-wooled white sheep originating in Spain and producing a heavy fleece of exceptional quality 2 : a soft wool or wool and cotton clothing fabric resembling cashmere 3 : a fine wool and cotton yarn used for hosiery and knitwear — **merino** *adj*

-m·er·ism \m-ə-,riz-əm\ *n comb form* [ISV, fr. Gk *meros* part — more at MERIT] 1 : possession of (such) an arrangement of or relation among constituent chemical units ⟨tauto*merism*⟩ 2 : possession of (such or so many) parts ⟨penta*merism*⟩

mer·i·stem \'mer-ə-,stem\ *n* [Gk *meristos* divided (fr. *merizein* to divide, fr. *meros*) + E *-em* (as in *system*)] (1874) : a formative plant tissue usu. made up of small cells capable of dividing indefinitely and giving rise to similar cells or to cells that differentiate to produce the definitive tissues and organs — **mer·i·ste·mat·ic** \,mer-ə-stə-'mat-ik\ *adj* — **mer·i·ste·mat·i·cal·ly** \-i-k(ə-)lē\ *adv*

me·ris·tic \mə-'ris-tik\ *adj* [Gk *meristos*] (1894) 1 : SEGMENTAL 2 : involving modification in number or in geometrical relation of body parts ⟨~ variation in flower petals⟩ — **me·ris·ti·cal·ly** \-ti-k(ə-)lē\ *adv*

¹mer·it \'mer-ət\ *n* [ME, fr. MF *merite*, fr. L *meritum*, fr. neut. of *meritus*, pp. of *merēre* to deserve, earn; akin to Gk *meros* part, L *memor* mindful — more at MEMORY] (14c) 1 a *obs* : reward or punishment due b : the qualities or actions that constitute the basis of one's deserts c : a praiseworthy quality : VIRTUE d : character or conduct deserving reward, honor, or esteem; *also* : ACHIEVEMENT 2 : spiritual credit held to be earned by performance of righteous acts and to ensure future benefits 3 a *pl* : the intrinsic nature of a legal case apart from considerations of circumstance, jurisdiction, or procedure b : individual significance or justification

²merit *vt* (1526) : to be worthy of or entitled or liable to : EARN ~ *vi* 1 *obs* : to be entitled to reward or honor 2 : DESERVE

mer·i·toc·ra·cy \,mer-ə-'täk-rə-sē\ *n, pl* **-cies** [¹*merit* + *-o-* + *-cracy*] (1958) 1 : a system (as an educational system) whereby the talented are chosen and moved ahead on the basis of their achievement 2 : leadership selected on the basis of intellectual criteria — **mer·it·ocrat·ic** \,mer-ət-ə-'krat-ik\ *adj*

mer·i·to·ri·ous \,mer-ə-'tōr-ē-əs, -'tòr-\ *adj* (15c) : deserving of honor or esteem — **mer·i·to·ri·ous·ly** *adv* — **mer·i·to·ri·ous·ness** *n*

merit system *n* (1879) : a system by which appointments and promotions in the civil service are based on competence rather than political favoritism

¹merle *also* **merl** \'mər(-ə)l\ *n* [ME, fr. MF, fr. L *merulus;* akin to OE *ōsle* blackbird, OHG *amsla*] (15c) : BLACKBIRD 1a

²merle *n* [origin unknown] (1905) : a bluish gray mixed with splotches of black that is the color of the coats of some dogs

mer·lin \'mər-lən\ *n* [ME *meriloun*, fr. AF *merilun*, fr. OF *esmerillon*, aug. of *esmeril*, of Gmc origin; akin to OHG *smiril* merlin] (14c) : a small compact Holarctic falcon (*Falco columbarius*) which has a broad dark terminal band on the tail and of which the upperparts are slate blue in males and dark brown in females — compare PIGEON HAWK 1

Mer·lin \'mər-lən\ *n* [ML *Merlinus*, fr. MW *Myrddin*] : a prophet and magician in Arthurian legend

mer·lon \'mər-lən\ *n* [F, fr. It *merlone*, aug. of *merlo* battlement, fr. ML *merulus*, fr. L, merle] (ca. 1704) : one of the solid intervals between crenels of a battlement — see BATTLEMENT illustration

mer·lot \me(ə)r-'lō\ *n* [F] (ca. 1941) : a dry red wine made from a grape widely grown in Bordeaux and California

mer·maid \'mər-,mād\ *n* [ME *mermayde*, fr. *mere* sea (fr. OE) + *mayde* maid — more at MARINE] (14c) : a fabled marine creature with the head and upper body of a woman and the tail of a fish

\ə\ abut \ᵊ\ kitten, F table \ər\ further \a\ ash \ā\ ace \ä\ cot, cart \aů\ out \ch\ chin \e\ bet \ē\ easy \g\ go \i\ hit \ī\ ice \j\ job \ŋ\ sing \ō\ go \ò\ law \òi\ boy \th\ thin \t͟h\ the \ü\ loot \ů\ foot \y\ yet \zh\ vision \á, k̲, ⁿ, œ, œ̄, ue, ue̅, ʸ\ see Guide to Pronunciation

mer·man \ˈ-ˌman, -mən\ *n* (1601) **:** a fabled marine creature with the head and upper body of a man and the tail of a fish

mero- *comb form* [ISV, fr. Gk, fr. *meros* part — more at MERIT] **:** part **:** partial ⟨*mero*myein⟩

mero·blas·tic \ˌmer-ə-ˈblas-tik\ *adj* (1870) **:** characterized by incomplete cleavage as a result of the presence of an impeding mass of yolk material — compare HOLOBLASTIC — **mero·blas·ti·cal·ly** \-ti-k(ə-)lē\ *adv*

mero·crine \ˈmer-ə-krən, -ˌkrīn, -ˌkrēn\ *adj* [ISV, fr *mero-* + Gk *krinein* to separate — more at CERTAIN] (1905) **:** producing a secretion that is discharged without major damage to the secreting cells; *also* **:** produced by a merocrine gland

mero·mor·phic \ˌmer-ə-ˈmȯr-fik\ *adj* (ca. 1890) **:** relating to or being a function of a complex variable that is analytic everywhere in a region except for singularities at each of which infinity is the limit and each of which is contained in a neighborhood where the function is analytic except for the singular point itself

mero·my·o·sin \ˌmer-ə-ˈmī-ə-sən\ *n* (1952) **:** either of two structural subunits of myosin that are obtained esp. by tryptic digestion

-m·er·ous \m-ə-rəs\ *adj comb form* [NL *-merus*, fr. Gk *-merēs*, fr. *meros* — more at MERIT] **:** having (such or so many) parts ⟨*dimerous*⟩

Mer·o·vin·gian \ˌmer-ə-ˈvin-j(ē-)ən\ *adj* [F *mérovingien*, fr. ML *Merovingi* Merovingians, fr. *Merovaeus* Merowig †458 Frankish founder of the dynasty] (1694) **:** of or relating to the first Frankish dynasty reigning from about A.D. 500 to 751 — **Merovingian** *n*

mero·zo·ite \ˌmer-ə-ˈzō-ˌīt\ *n* [ISV, fr. *mero-* + *zo-* + *ite*] (1900) **:** a small ameboid sporozoan trophozoite produced by schizogony that is capable of initiating a new sexual or asexual cycle of development

mer·ri·ment \ˈmer-i-mənt\ *n* (1576) **1 :** lighthearted gaiety or fun-making **:** HILARITY **2 :** a lively celebration or party **:** FESTIVITY

mer·ry \ˈmer-ē\ *adj* **mer·ri·er; -est** [ME *mery*, fr. OE *myrge*, *merge*; akin to OHG *murg* short — more at BRIEF] (bef. 12c) **1** *archaic* **:** giving pleasure **:** DELIGHTFUL **2 :** full of gaiety or high spirits **:** MIRTHFUL **3 :** marked by festivity or gaiety **4 :** QUICK, BRISK ⟨a ~ pace⟩ — **mer·ri·ly** \ˈmer-ə-lē\ *adv* — **mer·ri·ness** \ˈmer-ē-nəs\ *n*

syn MERRY, BLITHE, JOCUND, JOVIAL, JOLLY mean showing high spirits or lightheartedness. MERRY suggests cheerful, joyous, uninhibited enjoyment of frolic or festivity; BLITHE suggests carefree, innocent, or even heedless gaiety; JOCUND stresses elation and exhilaration of spirits; JOVIAL suggests the stimulation of conviviality and good fellowship; JOLLY suggests high spirits expressed in laughing, bantering, and jesting.

mer·ry–an·drew \ˌmer-ē-ˈan-(ˌ)drü\ *n, often cap M&A* [*merry* + *Andrew*, proper name] (1673) **:** one that clowns publicly **:** BUFFOON

mer·ry–go–round \ˈmer-ē-gō-ˌrau̇nd, -gə-\ *n* (1729) **1 :** an amusement park ride with seats often in the form of animals (as horses) revolving about a fixed center **2 :** a busy round of activity **:** WHIRL

mer·ry·mak·er \ˈmer-ē-ˌmā-kər\ *n* (1827) **:** REVELER

mer·ry·mak·ing \-kiŋ\ *n* (1714) **1 :** gay or festive activity **:** CONVIVIALITY **2 :** a convivial occasion **:** FESTIVITY

mer·ry·thought \ˈmer-ē-ˌthȯt\ *n, chiefly Brit* (1607) **:** WISHBONE

Mer·thi·o·late \(ˌ)mər-ˈthī-ə-ˌlāt, -lət\ *trademark* — used for thimerosal

mes- *or* **meso-** *comb form* [L, fr. Gk, fr. *mesos* — more at MID] **1 :** mid **:** in the middle ⟨*meso*carp⟩ **2 :** intermediate (as in size or type) ⟨*meso*morph⟩ ⟨*meson*⟩

me·sa \ˈmā-sə\ *n* [Sp, lit., table, fr. L *mensa*] (1759) **:** an isolated relatively flat-topped natural elevation usu. more extensive than a butte and less extensive than a plateau; *also* **:** a broad terrace with an abrupt slope on one side **:** BENCH

més·al·liance \ˌmā-ˌzal-ˈyäns, ˌmā-zə-ˈlī-ən(t)s\ *n, pl* **més·alliances** \-ˈyäns(-əz), -ˈlī-ən-səz\ [F, fr. *més-* mis- + *alliance*] (1782) **:** a marriage with a person of inferior social position

mes·arch \ˈmez-ˌärk, ˈmēz-, ˈmēs-, ˈmes-\ *adj* (1891) **1 :** having metaxylem developed both internal and external to the protoxylem **2 :** originating in a mesic habitat — used of an ecological succession

mes·cal \me-ˈskal, mə-\ *n* [Sp *mezcal*, *mescal*, fr. Nahuatl *mexcalli* mescal liquor] (1702) **1 :** a small cactus (*Lophophora williamsii*) with rounded stems covered with jointed tubercles that are used as a stimulant and antispasmodic esp. among the Mexican Indians **2 a :** a usu. colorless Mexican liquor distilled esp. from the central leaves of maguey plants **b :** a plant from which mescal is produced; *esp* **:** MAGUEY

mescal button *n* (1888) **:** one of the dried discoid tops of the mescal

Mes·ca·le·ro \ˌmes-kə-ˈle(ə)r-(ˌ)ō\ *n, pl* **Mescalero** *or* **Mescaleros** [AmerSp, fr. *mezcal*, *mescal*] (1844) **:** a member of an Apache people of Texas and New Mexico

mes·ca·line \ˈmes-kə-lən, -ˌlēn\ *n* (1896) **:** a hallucinatory crystalline alkaloid $C_{11}H_{17}NO_3$ that is the chief active principle in mescal buttons

mesdames *pl of* MADAM *or of* MADAME *or of* MRS.

mesdemoiselles *pl of* MADEMOISELLE

me·seems \mi-ˈsēmz\ *vb impersonal, past* **me·seemed** \-ˈsēmd\ *archaic* (15c) **:** it seems to me

me·sem·bry·an·the·mum \mə-ˌzem-brē-ˈan(t)-thə-məm\ *n* [NL, fr. Gk *mesēmbria* midday (fr. *mes-* + *hēmera* day) + *anthemon* flower, fr. *anthos* — more at ANTHOLOGY] (1753) **:** any of a genus (*Mesembryanthemum*) of chiefly southern African fleshy-leaved herbs or subshrubs of the carpetweed family

mes·en·ceph·a·lon \ˌmez-ˌen-ˈsef-ə-ˌlän, ˌmez-ən-, ˌmēz-, ˌmēs-, ˌmes-, -lən\ *n* [NL] (1846) **:** MIDBRAIN — **mes·en·ce·phal·ic** \-ˌen(t)-sə-ˈfal-ik, -ən-sə-\ *adj*

mes·en·chy·mal \mə-ˈzeŋ-kə-məl, -ˈseŋ-; ˌmez-ən-ˈkī-məl, ˌmēz-, ˌmēs-, ˌmes-\ *adj* [ISV] (1886) **:** of, resembling, or being mesenchyme

mes·en·chyme \ˈmez-ən-ˌkīm, ˈmēz-, ˈmēs-, ˈmes-\ *n* [G *mesenchym*, fr. *mes-* + NL *-enchyma*] (1888) **:** loosely organized undifferentiated mostly mesodermal cells that give rise to such structures as connective tissues, blood, lymphatics, bone, and cartilage

mes·en·ter·on \(ˈ)mez-ˈent-ə-ˌrän, (ˈ)mēz-, (ˈ)mēs-, (ˈ)mes-, -rən\ *n, pl* **-tera** \-ə-rə\ [NL] (1877) **:** the part of the alimentary canal that is developed from the archenteron and is lined with hypoblast

mes·en·tery \ˈmez-ən-ˌter-ē, ˈmes-\ *n, pl* **-ter·ies** [NL *mesenterium*, fr. MF & Gk; MF *mesentere*, fr. Gk *mesenterion*, fr. *mes-* + *enteron* intestine — more at INTER-] (15c) **1 a :** one or more vertebrate membranes that consist of a double fold of the peritoneum and invest the intestines and their appendages and connect them with the dorsal wall of the abdominal cavity **b :** a fold of membrane comparable to a mesentery and supporting a viscus (as the heart) that is not a part of the digestive tract **2 :** a support or partition in an invertebrate like the vertebrate mesentery — **mes·en·ter·ic** \ˌmez-ən-ˈter-ik, ˌmes-\ *adj*

1mesh \ˈmesh\ *n* [prob. fr. obs. D *maesche*; akin to OHG *masca* mesh, Lith *mazgos* knot] (14c) **1 :** one of the openings between the threads or cords of a net; *also* **:** one of the similar spaces in a network — often used to designate screen size as the number of openings per linear inch **2 a :** the fabric of a net **b :** a woven, knit, or knotted material of open texture with evenly spaced holes **c :** an arrangement of interlocking metal links used esp. for jewelry **3 a :** an interlocking or intertwining arrangement or construction **:** NETWORK **b :** WEB, SNARE — usu. used in pl. **4 :** working contact (as of the teeth of gears) ⟨in ~⟩ — **meshed** \ˈmesht\ *adj*

2mesh *vt* (1547) **1 a :** to catch in the openings of a net **b :** ENMESH, ENTANGLE **2 :** to cause to resemble network **3 a :** to cause (as gears) to engage **b :** to coordinate closely **:** INTERLOCK ~ *vi* **1 :** to become entangled in or as if in meshes **2 :** to be in or come into mesh — used esp. of gears **3 :** to fit or work together properly **:** COORDINATE

me·shuga *or* **me·shug·ge** *also* **me·shug·ah** *or* **me·shug·gah** \mə-ˈshu̇g-ə\ *adj* [Yiddish or Heb; Yiddish *meshuge*, fr. Heb *mĕshuggā*ʿ] (1892) **:** CRAZY, FOOLISH

me·shug·gen·er \-ˈshu̇g-ə-nər\ *n* [Yiddish, fr. *meshuge*] (1900) **:** a foolish or crazy person

mesh·work \ˈmesh-ˌwərk\ *n* (1830) **:** NETWORK ⟨a vascular ~⟩

me·si·al \ˈmē-zē-əl, -sē-\ *adj* [*mes-* + *-ial*] (1803) **1 :** MIDDLE, MEDIAN **2 :** of, relating to, or being the surface of a tooth that is next to the tooth in front of it or that is closest to the middle of the front of the jaw — compare DISTAL 2 — **me·si·al·ly** \-ə-lē\ *adv*

1me·sic \ˈmez-ik, ˈmēz-, ˈmēs-, ˈmes-\ *adj* [*mes-* + *-ic*] (1926) **:** characterized by, relating to, or requiring a moderate amount of moisture ⟨a ~ habitat⟩ ⟨a ~ plant⟩ — compare HYDRIC, XERIC

2mesic *adj* [*meson* + *-ic*] (1939) **:** of or relating to a meson

me·sio- \ˌmē-zē-ō, -sē-\ *comb form* **:** mesial and ⟨*mesio*distal⟩ ⟨*mesio*buccal⟩

me·sit·y·lene \mə-ˈsit-əl-ˌēn\ *n* [*mesityl* (the radical C_3H_5)] (1838) **:** an oily hydrocarbon C_9H_{12} that is found in coal tar and petroleum or made synthetically and is a powerful solvent

mes·i·tyl oxide \ˌmes-ə-ˌtil-, -ət-əl-\ *n* [*mesityl* (the radical C_3H_5)] (1873) **:** a fragrant liquid ketone $C_6H_{10}O$ used esp. as a solvent

mes·mer·ic \mez-ˈmer-ik *also* mes-\ *adj* (1829) **1 :** of, relating to, or induced by mesmerism **2 :** FASCINATING, IRRESISTIBLE — **mes·mer·i·cal·ly** \-i-k(ə-)lē\ *adv*

mes·mer·ism \ˈmez-mə-ˌriz-əm *also* ˈmes-\ *n* [F. A. *Mesmer*] (1784) **1 :** hypnotic induction held to involve animal magnetism; *broadly* **:** HYPNOTISM **2 :** hypnotic appeal — **mes·mer·ist** \-rəst\ *n*

mes·mer·ize \-mə-ˌrīz\ *vt* **-ized; -iz·ing** (1829) **1 :** to subject to mesmerism; *also* **:** HYPNOTIZE **2 :** SPELLBIND, FASCINATE — **mes·mer·iz·er** *n*

mesne \ˈmēn\ *adj* [AF, alter. of MF *meien* — more at MEAN] (15c) **:** INTERMEDIATE, INTERVENING — used in law

mesne lord *n* (1614) **:** a feudal lord who holds land as tenant of a superior (as a king) but who is lord to his own tenant

meso- — see MES-

me·so·carp \ˈmez-ə-ˌkärp, ˈmēz-, ˈmēs-, ˈmes-\ *n* (1849) **:** the middle layer of a pericarp — see ENDOCARP illustration

me·so·derm \-ˌdərm\ *n* [ISV] (1873) **:** the middle of the three primary germ layers of an embryo that is the source of bone, muscle, connective tissue, inner layer of the skin, and other adult structures; *broadly* **:** tissue derived from this germ layer — **me·so·der·mal** \ˌmez-ə-ˈdər-məl, ˌmēz-, ˌmēs-, ˌmes-\ *adj*

me·so·glea *or* **me·so·gloea** \ˌmez-ə-ˈglē-ə, ˌmēz-, ˌmēs-, ˌmes-\ *n* [NL, fr. *mes-* + LGk *gloia*, *glia* glue — more at CLAY] (1886) **:** a gelatinous substance between the endoderm and ectoderm of sponges or coelenterates

Me·so·lith·ic \-ˈlith-ik\ *adj* [ISV] (1888) **:** of, relating to, or being a transitional period of the Stone Age between the Paleolithic and the Neolithic

me·so·mere \ˈmez-ə-ˌmi(ə)r, ˈmēz-, ˈmēs-, ˈmes-\ *n* (ca. 1909) **:** a blastomere of medium size; *also* **:** an intermediate part of the mesoderm

me·som·er·ism \mə-ˈsäm-ə-ˌriz-əm, -ˈzäm-\ *n* [*mes-* + *-merism*] (1928) **:** RESONANCE 4

me·so·morph \ˈmez-ə-ˌmȯrf, ˈmēz-, ˈmēs-, ˈmes-\ *n* [*meso*derm + *-morph*] (1940) **:** a mesomorphic body or person

me·so·mor·phic \ˌmez-ə-ˈmȯr-fik, ˌmēz-, ˌmēs-, ˌmes-\ *adj* [*meso*derm + *-morphic*; fr. the predominance in such types of structures developed from the mesoderm] (1940) **1 :** of or relating to the component in W. H. Sheldon's classification of body types that measures esp. the degree of muscularity and bone development **2 :** having a husky muscular body build — **me·so·mor·phism** \-ˌfiz-əm\ *n* — **me·so·mor·phy** \ˈmez-ə-ˌmȯr-fē, ˈmes-\ *n*

me·son \ˈmez-ˌän, ˈmes-; ˈmā-ˌzän, ˈmē-, -ˌsän\ *n* [ISV *mes-* + 2*-on*] (1939) **:** any of a group of fundamental particles (as the pion and kaon) that are strongly interacting and have zero or an integer number of quantum units of spin — **me·son·ic** \me-ˈzän-ik, mē-, -ˈsän-\ *adj*

me·so·neph·ros \ˌmez-ə-ˈnef-rəs, ˌmēz-, ˌmēs-, ˌmes-, -ˌräs\ *n, pl* **-neph·roi** \-ˌrȯi\ [NL, fr. *mes-* + Gk *nephros* kidney — more at NEPHRITIS] (1877) **:** either member of the second and midmost of the three paired vertebrate renal organs that functions in adult fishes and amphibians but functions only in the embryo of reptiles, birds, and mammals in which it is replaced by a metanephros in the adult — compare PRONEPHROS — **me·so·neph·ric** \-rik\ *adj*

me·so·pause \ˈmez-ə-ˌpȯz, ˈmēz-, ˈmēs-, ˈmes-\ *n* [*meso*sphere + *pause*] (1950) **:** the upper boundary of the mesosphere where the temperature of the atmosphere reaches its lowest point

me·so·pe·lag·ic \ˌmez-ə-pə-ˈlaj-ik, ˌmēz-, ˌmēs-, ˌmes-\ *adj* (1947) **:** of or relating to oceanic depths from about 600 feet to 3000 feet

me·so·phyll \ˈmez-ə-ˌfil, ˈmēz-, ˈmēs-, ˈmes-\ *n* [NL *mesophyllum*, fr. *mes-* + Gk *phyllon* leaf — more at BLADE] (1839) **:** the parenchyma between the epidermal layers of a foliage leaf — **me·so·phyl·lic** \ˌmez-ə-ˈfil-ik, ˌmes-\ *or* **me·so·phyl·lous** \ˌmez-ə-ˈfil-əs, ˌmēz-, ˌmēs-, ˌmes-\ *adj*

me·so·phyte \ˈmez-ə-ˌfīt, ˈmēz-, ˈmēs-, ˈmes-\ *n* [ISV] (1899) **:** a plant that grows under medium conditions of moisture — **me·so·phyt·ic** \ˌmez-ə-ˈfit-ik, ˌmēz-, ˌmēs-, ˌmes-\ *adj*

me·so·scale \ˈmez-ə-ˌskāl, ˈmēz-, ˈmēs-, ˈmes-\ *adj* (1956) **:** of or relating to a meteorological phenomenon approximately 1 to 100 kilometers in horizontal extent ⟨~ cloud pattern⟩ ⟨~ wind circulation⟩

me·so·some \-ˌsōm\ *n* (1960) : an organelle of bacteria that appears in electron micrographs as an invagination of the plasma membrane and is a site of localization of respiratory enzymes

me·so·sphere \-ˌsfi(ə)r\ *n* (1950) : a layer of the atmosphere extending from the top of the stratosphere to an altitude of about 50 miles (80 kilometers) — **me·so·spher·ic** \ˌmez-ə-'sfi(ə)r-ik, ˌmēz-, ˌmēs-, ˌmes-, -'sfer-\ *adj*

me·so·the·li·o·ma \ˌmez-ə-ˌthē-lē-'ō-mə, ˌmēz-, ˌmēs-, ˌmes-\ *n, pl* **-mas** *or* **-ma·ta** \-mət-ə\ [NL, fr. *mesothelium* + *-oma*] (1899) : a tumor derived from mesothelial tissue (as that lining the peritoneum or pleura)

me·so·the·li·um \-'thē-lē-əm\ *n, pl* **-lia** \-lē-ə\ [NL, fr. *mes-* + *epithelium*] (1886) : epithelium derived from mesoderm that lines the body cavity of a vertebrate embryo and gives rise to epithelia (as of the peritoneum, pericardium, and pleurae), striated muscle, heart muscle, and several minor structures — **me·so·the·li·al** \-lē-əl\ *adj*

me·so·tho·rac·ic \-thə-'ras-ik\ *adj* (1839) : of or relating to the mesothorax

me·so·tho·rax \-'thō(ə)r-ˌaks, -'thō(ə)r-\ *n* [NL] (1826) : the middle of the three segments of the thorax of an insect — see INSECT illustration

me·so·tho·ri·um \-'thōr-ē-əm, -'thȯr-\ *n* [NL] (1907) : either of two radioactive products intermediate between thorium and radiothorium: **a** : an isotope of radium — called also *mesothorium 1* **b** : an isotope of actinium — called also *mesothorium 2*

me·so·tron \'mez-ə-ˌträn, 'mēz-, 'mēs-, 'mes-\ *n* [*mes-* + *electron*] (1938) : MESON — **me·so·tron·ic** \ˌmez-ə-'trän-ik, ˌmēz-, ˌmēs-, ˌmes-\ *adj*

me·so·tro·phic \ˌmez-ə-'trō-fik, ˌmēz-, ˌmēs-, ˌmes-, -'träf-ik\ *adj, of a body of water* (ca. 1940) : having a moderate amount of dissolved nutrients — compare EUTROPHIC, OLIGOTROPHIC

Me·so·zo·ic \-'zō-ik\ *adj* (1840) : of, relating to, or being an era of geological history including the interval between the Permian and the Tertiary and marked by the dinosaurs, marine and flying reptiles, ganoid fishes, cycads, and evergreen trees; *also* : relating to the system of rocks formed in this era — see GEOLOGIC TIME table — **Mesozoic** *n*

mes·quite \mə-'skēt, me-\ *n* [Sp, fr. Nahuatl *mizquitl*] (1759) : a spiny deep-rooted leguminous tree or shrub (*Prosopis fuliflora*) that forms extensive thickets in the southwestern U.S. and Mexico, bears pods rich in sugar, and is important as a livestock feed

¹mess \'mes\ *n* [ME *mes*, fr. MF, fr. LL *missus* course at a meal, fr. *missus*, pp. of *mittere* to put, fr. L, to send — more at SMITE] (14c) **1 a** : a quantity of food: **a** *archaic* : food set on a table at one time **b** : a prepared dish of soft food; *also* : a mixture of ingredients cooked or eaten together **c** : enough food of a specified kind for a dish or a meal ⟨picked a ~ of peas for dinner⟩ **2 a** : a group of persons who regularly take their meals together; *also* : a meal so taken **b** : a place where meals are regularly served to a group : MESS HALL **3 a** : a disordered, untidy, or unpleasant state or condition ⟨your room is in a ~⟩ **b** : one that is disordered, untidy, or unpleasant ⟨the movie⟩ is a ~, as sloppy in concept as it is in execution —Judith Crist⟩

²mess *vt* (14c) **1** : to provide with meals at a mess **2 a** : to make dirty or untidy : DISARRANGE ⟨warned not to ~ up your room⟩ **b** : to mix up : BUNGLE ⟨really ~ed up my life⟩ **3** : to interfere with ⟨magnetic storms that ~ up communications —*Time*⟩ **4** : to rough up : MANHANDLE ⟨~ him up good so he won't double-cross us again⟩ ~ *vi* **1** : to take meals with a mess **2** : to make a mess **3 a** : PUTTER, TRIFLE ⟨small boys and girls who like to ~ around with paints⟩ **b** : to handle or play with something esp. carelessly ⟨don't ~ with my camera⟩ — often used with *around* **c** : to take an active interest in something or someone ⟨~*ing* around with new video techniques⟩; *also* : INTERFERE, MEDDLE ⟨~*ing* in other people's affairs⟩ ⟨you'd better not ~ with me⟩ **4** : to become confused or make an error — usu. used with *up* ⟨got another chance and didn't want to ~ up again⟩

¹mes·sage \'mes-ij\ *n* [ME, fr. OF, fr. ML *missaticum*, fr. L *missus*, pp. of *mittere*] (13c) **1** : a communication in writing, in speech, or by signals **2** : a messenger's errand or function **3** : an underlying theme or idea

²message *vb* **mes·saged; mes·sag·ing** *vt* (1583) **1** : to send as a message or by messenger **2** : to send a message to ~ *vi* : to communicate by message

mes·sa·line \ˌmes-ə-'lēn\ *n* [F] (ca. 1891) : a soft lightweight silk dress fabric with a satin weave

mes·san \'mes-ᵊn\ *n* [ScGael *measan*] *chiefly Scot* (1500) : LAPDOG

mess around *vi* (ca. 1932) **1** : to waste time : DAWDLE, IDLE **2 a** : ASSOCIATE ⟨don't *mess around* with admirals much —K. M. Dodson⟩ **b** : FLIRT, PHILANDER ⟨caught him *messing around* with my wife⟩

messeigneurs *pl of* MONSEIGNEUR

mes·sen·ger \'mes-ᵊn-jər\ *n* [ME *messangere*, fr. OF *messagier*, fr. *message*] (13c) **1** : one who bears a message or does an errand: as **a** *archaic* : FORERUNNER, HERALD **b** : a dispatch bearer in government or military service **c** : an employee who carries messages **2** : a light line used in hauling a heavier line (as between ships) **3** : MESSENGER RNA

messenger RNA *n* (1961) : an RNA that carries the code for a particular protein from the nuclear DNA to a ribosome in the cytoplasm and acts as a template for the formation of that protein — compare TRANSFER RNA

mess hall *n* (1862) : a hall or building (as on an army post) in which mess is served

mes·si·ah \mə-'sī-ə\ *n* [Heb *māshīaḥ* & Aram *mĕshīḥā*, lit., anointed] **1** *cap* **a** : the expected king and deliverer of the Jews **b** : JESUS 1 **2** : a professed or accepted leader of some hope or cause — **mes·si·ah·ship** \-ˌship\ *n*

mes·si·an·ic \ˌmes-ē-'an-ik\ *adj* [(assumed) NL *messianicus*, fr. LL *Messias* + L *-anicus* (as in *romanicus* Romanic)] (1834) **1** : of or relating to a messiah **2** : marked by idealism and an aggressive crusading spirit ⟨a ~ sense of historic mission —Edmond Taylor⟩

mes·si·a·nism \'mes-ē-ə-ˌniz-əm; mə-'sī-ə-, me-\ *n* (1876) **1** : belief in a messiah as the savior of mankind **2** : religious devotion to an ideal or cause

Mes·si·as \mə-'sī-əs\ *n* [ME, fr. LL, fr. Gk, fr. Aram *mĕshīḥā*] : MESSIAH 1

messieurs *pl of* MONSIEUR

mess jacket *n* (1891) : a fitted waist-length man's jacket worn esp. as part of a dress uniform

mess kit *n* (ca. 1877) : a compact kit of nested cooking and eating utensils for use by soldiers and campers

mess·mate \'mes-ˌmāt\ *n* (1746) : a person with whom one regularly takes mess (as on a ship)

mess over *vt, slang* (1965) : to treat harshly or unfairly : ABUSE

Messrs. \ˌmes-ərz\ *pl of* MR. ⟨~ Jones, Brown, and Robinson⟩

mes·suage \'mes-wij\ *n* [ME, fr. AF, prob. alter. of OF *mesnage* — more at MÉNAGE] (14c) : PREMISE 3b

messy \'mes-ē\ *adj* **mess·i·er; -est** (1843) **1** : marked by confusion, disorder, or dirt : UNTIDY ⟨a ~ room⟩ **2** : lacking neatness or precision : CARELESS, SLOVENLY ⟨~ thinking⟩ **3** : extremely unpleasant or trying ⟨~ lawsuits⟩ — **mess·i·ly** \'mes-ə-lē\ *adv* — **mess·i·ness** \'mes-ē-nəs\ *n*

mes·ti·za \me-'stē-zə\ *n* [Sp, fem. of *mestizo*] (1582) : a woman who is a mestizo

mes·ti·zo \-(ˌ)zō\ *n, pl* **-zos** [Sp, fr. *mestizo*, adj., mixed, fr. LL *mixticius*, fr. L *mixtus*, pp. of *miscēre* to mix — more at MIX] (1582) : a person of mixed blood; *specif* : a person of mixed European and American Indian ancestry

mes·tra·nol \'mes-tra-ˌnȯl, -ˌnōl\ *n* [*meth-* + *estrogen* + *pregnane* ($C_{21}H_{36}$) + *-ol*] (ca. 1962) : a synthetic estrogen $C_{21}H_{26}O_2$ used in oral contraceptives

met *past and past part of* MEET

meta- *or* **met-** *prefix* [NL & ML, fr. L or Gk; L, change, fr. Gk, among, with, after, change, fr. *meta* among, with, after; akin to OE *mid, mith* with, OHG *mit*] **1 a** : occurring later than or in succession to : after ⟨*metestrus*⟩ **b** : situated behind or beyond ⟨*met*encephalon⟩ ⟨*meta*carpus⟩ **c** : later or more highly organized or specialized form of ⟨*meta*xylem⟩ **2** : change : transformation **3** : more comprehensive : transcending ⟨*meta*psychology⟩ — used with the name of a discipline to designate a new but related discipline designed to deal critically with the original one ⟨*meta*mathematics⟩ **4 a** : isomeric with or otherwise closely related to ⟨*met*aldehyde⟩ **b** : involving substitution at or characterized by two positions in the benzene ring that are separated by one carbon atom ⟨*meta*phosphoric acid⟩

met·a·bol·ic \ˌmet-ə-'bäl-ik\ *adj* (1845) : of, relating to, or based on metabolism — **met·a·bol·i·cal·ly** \-i-k(ə-)lē\ *adv*

me·tab·o·lism \mə-'tab-ə-ˌliz-əm\ *n* [ISV, fr. Gk *metabolē* change, fr. *metaballein* to change, fr. *meta-* + *ballein* to throw — more at DEVIL] (1872) **1 a** : the sum of the processes in the buildup and destruction of protoplasm; *specif* : the chemical changes in living cells by which energy is provided for vital processes and activities and new material is assimilated **b** : the sum of the processes by which a particular substance is handled in the living body **c** : the sum of the metabolic activities taking place in a particular environment ⟨the ~ of a lake⟩ **2** : METAMORPHOSIS 2 — usu. used in combination ⟨holo*metabolism*⟩

me·tab·o·lite \-ˌlīt\ *n* (1884) **1** : a product of metabolism **2** : a substance essential to the metabolism of a particular organism or to a particular metabolic process

me·tab·o·lize \-ˌlīz\ *vb* **-lized; -liz·ing** *vt* (1887) : to subject to metabolism ~ *vi* : to perform metabolism — **me·tab·o·liz·able** \-ˌlī-zə-bəl\ *adj*

¹meta·car·pal \ˌmet-ə-'kär-pəl\ *adj* (1739) : of, relating to, or being the metacarpus or a metacarpal

²metacarpal *n* (1854) : a bone of the part of the hand or forefoot between the carpus and the phalanges that typically contains five more or less elongated bones when all the digits are present

meta·car·pus \ˌmet-ə-'kär-pəs\ *n* [NL] (1676) : the part of the hand or forefoot that contains the metacarpals

meta·cen·ter \'met-ə-ˌsent-ər\ *n* [F *métacentre*, fr. *méta-* meta- + *centre* center] (1794) : the point of intersection of the vertical through the center of buoyancy of a floating body with the vertical through the new center of buoyancy when the body is displaced

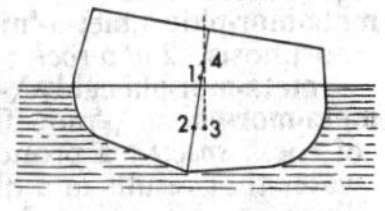

metacenter: *1* center of gravity, *2* center of buoyancy, *3* new center of buoyancy when floating body is displaced, *4* point of intersection

meta·cen·tric \ˌmet-ə-'sen-trik\ *adj* (1798) **1** : of or relating to a metacenter **2** : having two equal arms because of the median position of the centromere ⟨a ~ chromosome⟩ — **metacentric** *n*

meta·cer·car·ia \ˌmet-ə-(ˌ)sər-'kar-ē-ə, -'ker-\ *n* [NL] (1928) : a tailless encysted late larva of a digenetic trematode that is usu. the form which is infective for the definitive host — **meta·cer·car·i·al** \-ē-əl\ *adj*

meta·chro·mat·ic \-krō-'mat-ik\ *adj* (1876) **1** : staining or characterized by staining in a different color or shade from what is typical ⟨~ granules in a bacterium⟩ **2** : having the capacity to stain different elements of a cell or tissue in different colors or shades ⟨~ stains⟩

meta·eth·ics \ˌmet-ə-'eth-iks\ *n pl but usu sing in constr* (1949) : the study of the meanings of ethical terms, the nature of ethical judgments, and the types of ethical arguments — **meta·eth·i·cal** \-i-kəl\ *adj*

meta·gal·axy \-'gal-ək-sē\ *n* [ISV] (1930) : the entire system of galaxies : UNIVERSE — **meta·ga·lac·tic** \-gə-'lak-tik\ *adj*

meta·gen·e·sis \-'jen-ə-səs\ *n* [NL] (ca. 1849) : ALTERNATION OF GENERATIONS; *esp* : regular alteration of a sexual and an asexual generation — **meta·ge·net·ic** \-jə-'net-ik\ *adj*

¹met·al \'met-ᵊl\ *n, often attrib* [ME, fr. OF, fr. L *metallum* mine, metal, fr. Gk *metallon*] (13c) **1** : any of various opaque, fusible, ductile, and typically lustrous substances that are good conductors of electricity and heat, form cations by loss of electrons, and yield basic oxides and hydroxides; *esp* : one that is a chemical element as distinguished from an alloy **2 a** : METTLE 2a **b** : the material or substance out of which a person or thing is made **3** : glass in its molten state **4 a** : printing type metal **b** : matter set in metal type **5** : ROAD METAL

²metal *vt* **-aled** *or* **-alled; -al·ing** *or* **-al·ling** (1610) : to cover or furnish with metal

meta·lan·guage \'met-ə-ˌlaŋ-gwij\ *n* (ca. 1936) : a language used to talk about another language

meta·lin·guis·tic \ˌmet-ə-liŋ-ˈgwis-tik, ˈmet-ᵊl-iŋ-\ *adj* (1944) **:** of or relating to a metalanguage or to metalinguistics

meta·lin·guis·tics \-tiks\ *n pl but sing in constr* (1949) **:** a branch of linguistics that deals with the relation between language and other cultural factors in a society

¹**me·tal·lic** \mə-ˈtal-ik\ *adj* (15c) **1 a :** of, relating to, or being a metal **b :** made of or containing a metal **c :** having properties of a metal **2 :** yielding metal **3 :** resembling metal: as **a :** having iridescent and reflective properties ⟨~ blond hair⟩ **b :** having an acrid quality like that of metal ⟨the tea has a ~ taste⟩ **4 a :** having a harsh resonance **:** GRATING ⟨a ~ voice⟩ **b :** having an impersonal or mechanical quality ⟨a ~ smile⟩ — **me·tal·li·cal·ly** \-i-k(ə-)lē\ *adv*

²**metallic** *n* (1952) **:** a fiber or yarn made of or coated with metal; *also* **:** a fabric made with this

met·al·lif·er·ous \ˌmet-ᵊl-ˈif-(ə-)rəs\ *adj* [L *metallifer,* fr. *metallum* + *-fer* -ferous] (ca. 1656) **:** yielding or containing metal

met·al·lize *also* **met·al·ize** \ˈmet-ᵊl-ˌīz\ *vt* **met·al·lized** *also* **met·al·ized; met·al·liz·ing** *also* **met·al·iz·ing** (1594) **:** to coat, treat, or combine with a metal — **met·al·li·za·tion** \ˌmet-ᵊl-ə-ˈzā-shən\ *n*

met·al·log·ra·phy \ˌmet-ᵊl-ˈäg-rə-fē\ *n* [F *métallographie,* fr. L *metallum* + F *-graphie* -graphy] (1871) **:** a study of the structure of metals esp. with the microscope — **met·al·log·ra·pher** \ˌmet-ᵊl-ˈäg-rə-fər\ *n* — **me·tal·lo·graph·ic** \mə-ˌtal-ə-ˈgraf-ik\ *adj* — **me·tal·lo·graph·i·cal·ly** \-ˈgraf-i-k(ə-)lē\ *adv*

¹**met·al·loid** \ˈmet-ᵊl-ˌȯid\ *n* [L *metallum*] (ca. 1828) **1 :** a nonmetal that can combine with a metal to form an alloy **2 :** an element intermediate in properties between the typical metals and nonmetals

²**metalloid** *also* **met·al·loi·dal** \ˌmet-ᵊl-ˈȯid-ᵊl\ *adj* (1836) **1 :** resembling a metal **2 :** of, relating to, or being a metalloid

me·tal·lo·phone \mə-ˈtal-ə-ˌfōn\ *n* [*metallo-* (fr. L *metallum* or Gk *metallon*) + *-phone*] (ca. 1883) **:** a percussion musical instrument consisting of a series of metal bars of varying pitch struck with hammers

met·al·lur·gy \ˈmet-ᵊl-ˌər-jē, *esp Brit* mə-ˈtal-ər-\ *n* [NL *metallurgia,* fr. Gk *metallon* + NL *-urgia* -urgy] (ca. 1704) **:** the science and technology of metals — **met·al·lur·gi·cal** \ˌmet-ᵊl-ˈər-ji-kəl\ *adj* — **met·al·lur·gi·cal·ly** \-k(ə-)lē\ *adv* — **met·al·lur·gist** \ˈmet-ᵊl-ˌər-jəst, *esp Brit* mə-ˈtal-ər-\ *n*

met·al·mark \ˈmet-ᵊl-ˌmärk\ *n* (ca. 1909) **:** any of a family (Riodinidae) of small or medium-sized usu. brightly colored butterflies that have metallic coloration on the wings

met·al·ware \-ˌwa(ə)r, -ˌwe(ə)r\ *n* (ca. 1896) **:** ware made of metal; *esp* **:** metal utensils for household use

met·al·work \-ˌwərk\ *n* (ca. 1850) **:** the product of metalworking — **met·al·work·er** \-ˌwər-kər\ *n*

met·al·work·ing \-ˌwər-kiŋ\ *n* (1882) **:** the act or process of shaping things out of metal

meta·math·e·mat·ics \ˈmet-ə-ˌmath-ə-ˈmat-iks, -math-ˈmat-\ *n pl but usu sing in constr* (ca. 1890) **:** a field of study concerned with the formal structure and properties (as the consistency and completeness of axioms) of mathematical systems — **meta·math·e·mat·i·cal** \-i-kəl\ *adj*

meta·mere \ˈmet-ə-ˌmi(ə)r\ *n* [ISV] (1877) **:** any of a linear series of primitively similar segments into which the body of a higher invertebrate or vertebrate is divisible — **meta·mer·ic** \ˌmet-ə-ˈmer-ik, -ˈmi(ə)r-\ *adj* — **meta·mer·i·cal·ly** \-i-k(ə-)lē\ *adv*

me·tam·er·ism \mə-ˈtam-ə-ˌriz-əm\ *n* (1877) **:** the condition of having or the stage of evolutionary development characterized by a body made up of metameres

meta·mor·phic \ˌmet-ə-ˈmȯr-fik\ *adj* (1816) **1 :** of or relating to metamorphosis **2** *of a rock* **:** of, relating to, or produced by metamorphism — **meta·mor·phi·cal·ly** \-fi-k(ə-)lē\ *adv*

meta·mor·phism \-ˈmȯr-ˌfiz-əm\ *n* (1845) **:** a change in the constitution of rock; *specif* **:** a pronounced change effected by pressure, heat, and water that results in a more compact and more highly crystalline condition

meta·mor·phose \-ˌfōz, -ˌfōs\ *vb* **-phosed; -phos·ing** [prob. fr. MF *metamorphoser,* fr. *metamorphose* metamorphosis, fr. L *metamorphosis*] *vt* (1576) **1 a :** to change into a different physical form esp. by supernatural means **b :** to change strikingly the appearance or character of **:** TRANSFORM ⟨you are so *metamorphosed* I can hardly think you my master —Shak.⟩ **2 :** to cause (rock) to undergo metamorphism ~ *vi* **1 :** to undergo metamorphosis **2 :** to become transformed ***syn*** see TRANSFORM

meta·mor·pho·sis \ˌmet-ə-ˈmȯr-fə-səs\ *n, pl* **-pho·ses** \-ˌsēz\ [L, fr. Gk *metamorphōsis,* fr. *metamorphoun* to transform, fr. *meta-* + *morphē* form] (1533) **1 a :** change of physical form, structure, or substance esp. by supernatural means **b :** a striking alteration in appearance, character, or circumstances **2 :** a marked and more or less abrupt developmental change in the form or structure of an animal (as a butterfly or a frog) occurring subsequent to birth or hatching

meta·neph·ros \-ˈnef-rəs, -ˌräs\ *n, pl* **-roi** \-ˌrȯi\ [NL, fr. *meta-* + Gk *nephros* kidney — more at NEPHRITIS] (1884) **:** either member of the final and most caudal pair of the three successive pairs of vertebrate renal organs that functions as a permanent adult kidney in reptiles, birds, and mammals but is not present at all in lower forms — compare MESONEPHROS, PRONEPHROS — **meta·neph·ric** \-rik\ *adj*

meta·phase \ˈmet-ə-ˌfāz\ *n* [ISV] (1887) **:** the stage of mitosis and meiosis in which the chromosomes become arranged in the equatorial plane of the spindle

metaphase plate *n* (1939) **:** a plane cell section in the equatorial plane of the metaphase spindle with the chromosomes oriented upon it

met·a·phor \ˈmet-ə-ˌfȯ(ə)r *also* -fər\ *n* [MF or L; MF *metaphore,* fr. L *metaphora,* fr. Gk, fr. *metapherein* to transfer, fr. *meta-* + *pherein* to bear — more at BEAR] (1533) **1 :** a figure of speech in which a word or phrase literally denoting one kind of object or idea is used in place of another to suggest a likeness or analogy between them (as in *drowning in money*) ⟨using ~, we say that computers have senses and a memory —William Jovanovich⟩; *broadly* **:** figurative language — compare SIMILE **2 :** an object, activity, or idea treated as a metaphor — **met·a·phor·ic** \ˌmet-ə-ˈfȯr-ik, -ˈfär-\ *or* **met·a·phor·i·cal** \-i-kəl\ *adj* — **met·a·phor·i·cal·ly** \-i-k(ə-)lē\ *adv*

meta·phos·phate \ˌmet-ə-ˈfäs-ˌfāt\ *n* [ISV] (1833) **:** a salt or ester of a metaphosphoric acid

meta·phos·pho·ric acid \-ˌfäs-ˌfȯr-ik-, -ˌfär-; -ˌfäs-f(ə-)rik-\ *n* (1833) **:** a glassy solid acid HPO_3 or $(HPO_3)_n$ formed by heating orthophosphoric acid

meta·phys·ic \ˌmet-ə-ˈfiz-ik\ *n* [ME *metaphesyk,* fr. ML *metaphysica*] (14c) **1 a :** METAPHYSICS **b :** a particular system of metaphysics **2 :** the system of principles underlying a particular study or subject **:** PHILOSOPHY 3b — **metaphysic** *adj*

meta·phys·i·cal \ˌmet-ə-ˈfiz-i-kəl\ *adj* (15c) **1 :** of or relating to metaphysics **2 a :** of or relating to the transcendent or to a reality beyond what is perceptible to the senses **b :** SUPERNATURAL **3 :** highly abstract or abstruse; *also* **:** THEORETICAL **4** *often cap* **:** of or relating to poetry esp. of the early 17th century that is highly intellectual and philosophical and marked by unconventional imagery — **meta·phys·i·cal·ly** \-i-k(ə-)lē\ *adv*

Metaphysical *n* (1898) **:** a metaphysical poet of the 17th century

meta·phy·si·cian \ˌmet-ə-fə-ˈzish-ən\ *n* (15c) **:** a student of or specialist in metaphysics

meta·phys·ics \ˌmet-ə-ˈfiz-iks\ *n pl but sing in constr* [ML *Metaphysica,* title of Aristotle's treatise on the subject, fr. Gk *(ta) meta (ta) physika,* lit., the (works) after the physical (works); fr. its position in his collected works] (14c) **1 a (1) :** a division of philosophy that is concerned with the fundamental nature of reality and being and that includes ontology, cosmology, and often epistemology **(2) :** ONTOLOGY 2 **b :** abstract philosophical studies **:** a study of what is outside objective experience **2 :** METAPHYSIC 2

meta·pla·sia \ˌmet-ə-ˈplā-zh(ē-)ə\ *n* [NL] (1890) **1 :** transformation of one tissue into another **2 :** abnormal replacement of cells of one type by cells of another — **meta·plas·tic** \-ˈplas-tik\ *adj*

meta·psy·chol·o·gy \ˌmet-ə-sī-ˈkäl-ə-jē\ *n* [ISV] (ca. 1909) **:** speculative psychology concerned with postulating the structure (as the ego and id) and processes (as cathexis) of the mind which usu. cannot be demonstrated objectively — **meta·psy·cho·log·i·cal** \-ˌsī-kə-ˈläj-i-kəl\ *adj*

meta·se·quoia \-si-ˈkwȯi-ə\ *n* [NL, fr. *meta-* + *Sequoia sequoia*] (1948) **:** any of a genus (*Metasequoia*) of fossil and living deciduous coniferous trees of the pine family that have leaves, buds, and branches arranged oppositely and flat leaves resembling needles

meta·so·ma·tism \ˌmet-ə-ˈsō-mə-ˌtiz-əm\ *n* (1886) **:** metamorphism that involves changes in the chemical composition as well as in the texture of rock — **meta·so·mat·ic** \-sō-ˈmat-ik\ *adj* — **meta·so·mat·i·cal·ly** \-i-k(ə-)lē\ *adv*

meta·sta·ble \ˌmet-ə-ˈstā-bəl\ *adj* [ISV] (1897) **:** having or characterized by only a slight margin of stability ⟨a ~ compound⟩ — **meta·sta·bil·i·ty** \-stə-ˈbil-ət-ē\ *n* — **meta·sta·bly** \-ˈstā-b(ə-)lē\ *adv*

me·tas·ta·sis \mə-ˈtas-tə-səs\ *n, pl* **-ta·ses** \-ˌsēz\ [NL, fr. LL, transition, fr. Gk, fr. *methistanai* to change, fr. *meta-* + *histanai* to set — more at STAND] (1663) **:** change of position, state, or form: as **a :** transfer of a disease-producing agency from the site of disease to another part of the body **b :** a secondary metastatic growth of a malignant tumor — **met·a·stat·ic** \ˌmet-ə-ˈstat-ik\ *adj* — **met·a·stat·i·cal·ly** \-i-k(ə-)lē\ *adv*

me·tas·ta·size \mə-ˈtas-tə-ˌsīz\ *vi* **-sized; -siz·ing** (1907) **:** to spread by metastasis

¹**meta·tar·sal** \ˌmet-ə-ˈtär-səl\ *adj* (1739) **:** of, relating to, or being the part of the foot in man or of the hind foot in quadrupeds between the tarsus and the phalanges

²**metatarsal** *n* (1854) **:** a metatarsal bone

meta·tar·sus \ˌmet-ə-ˈtär-səs\ *n* [NL] (1676) **:** the metatarsal part of a foot in man or of a hind foot in quadrupeds

me·ta·te \mə-ˈtät-ē\ *n* [Sp, fr. Nahuatl *metatl*] (1834) **:** a stone with a concave upper surface used as the lower millstone for grinding grains and esp. maize

me·tath·e·sis \mə-ˈtath-ə-səs\ *n, pl* **-e·ses** \-ˌsēz\ [Gk, fr. *metatithenai* to transpose, fr. *meta-* + *tithenai* to place — more at DO] (1608) **:** a change of place or condition: as **a :** transposition of two phonemes in a word (as in the development of *crud* from *curd* or the pronunciation \ˈpu̇rt-ē\ for *pretty*) **b :** a chemical reaction in which different kinds of molecules exchange parts to form other kinds of molecules — called also *double decomposition* — **met·a·thet·i·cal** \ˌmet-ə-ˈthet-i-kəl\ *or* **met·a·thet·ic** \-ik\ *adj* — **met·a·thet·i·cal·ly** \-i-k(ə-)lē\ *adv*

meta·tho·rac·ic \ˌmet-ə-thə-ˈras-ik\ *adj* (1836) **:** of, relating to, or situated in or on the metathorax ⟨~ legs⟩

meta·tho·rax \-ˈthō(ə)r-ˌaks, -ˈthȯ(ə)r-\ *n* [NL] (1816) **:** the posterior segment of the thorax of an insect — see INSECT illustration

meta·xy·lem \-ˈzī-ləm, -ˌlem\ *n* (ca. 1872) **:** the part of the primary xylem that differentiates after the protoxylem and that is distinguished typically by broader tracheids and vessels with pitted or reticulate walls

meta·zo·al \ˌmet-ə-ˈzō-əl\ *adj* [NL *Metazoa*] (1928) **:** of or relating to the metazoans

meta·zo·an \-ˈzō-ən\ *n* [NL *Metazoa,* fr. *meta-* + *-zoa*] (1884) **:** any of a group (*Metazoa*) that comprises all animals having the body composed of cells differentiated into tissues and organs and usu. a digestive cavity lined with specialized cells — **metazoan** *adj*

¹**mete** \ˈmēt\ *vt* **met·ed; met·ing** [ME *meten,* fr. OE *metan;* akin to OHG *mezzan* to measure, L *modus* measure, *meditari* to meditate] (bef. 12c) **1** *archaic* **:** MEASURE **2 :** to give out by measure **:** DOLE — usu. used with *out* ⟨~ out punishment⟩

²**mete** *n* [AF, fr. L *meta*] (15c) **:** BOUNDARY ⟨~*s* and bounds⟩

me·tem·psy·cho·sis \mə-ˌtem(p)-si-ˈkō-səs, ˌmet-əm-ˌsī-\ *n* [LL, fr. Gk *metempsychōsis,* fr. *metempsychousthai* to undergo metempsychosis, fr. *meta-* + *empsychos* animate, fr. *en-* + *psychē* soul — more at PSYCHE] (1590) **:** the passing of the soul at death into another body either human or animal

met·en·ceph·a·lon \ˌmet-ˌen-ˈsef-ə-ˌlän, -lən\ *n* [NL] (ca. 1871) **1 :** the anterior segment of the rhombencephalon **2 :** the cerebellum and pons that evolve from this segment — **met·en·ce·phal·ic** \-ˌen(t)-sə-ˈfal-ik\ *adj*

me·te·or \ˈmēt-ē-ər, -ē-ˌȯ(ə)r\ *n* [ME, fr. MF *meteore,* fr. ML *meteorum,* fr. Gk *meteōron* phenomenon in the sky, fr. neut. of *meteōros* high in air, fr. *meta-* + *-eōros* (akin to Gk *aeirein* to lift)] (15c) **1 :** a phenomenon or appearance in the atmosphere (as lightning, a rainbow, or a snowfall) **2 a :** one of the small particles of matter in the solar system observable directly only when it falls into the earth's atmosphere where friction may cause its temporary incandescence **b :** the streak of light produced by the passage of a meteor

me·te·or·ic \ˌmēt-ē-'ȯr-ik, -'är-\ *adj* (1789) **1 :** of, relating to, or derived from the earth's atmosphere **2 a :** of or relating to a meteor **b :** resembling a meteor in speed or in sudden and temporary brilliance ⟨a ~ rise to fame⟩ — **me·te·or·i·cal·ly** \-i-k(ə-)lē\ *adv*

me·te·or·ite \'mēt-ē-ə-ˌrīt\ *n* (1824) **:** a meteor that reaches the surface of the earth without being completely vaporized — **me·te·or·it·ic** \ˌmēt-ē-ə-'rit-ik\ *or* **me·te·or·it·i·cal** \-i-kəl\ *adj*

me·te·or·it·ics \ˌmēt-ē-ə-'rit-iks\ *n pl but sing in constr* (ca. 1930) **:** a science that deals with meteors — **me·te·or·it·i·cist** \-'rit-ə-səst\ *n*

me·te·or·o·graph \-'ȯr-ə-ˌgraf, -'är-\ *n* (1780) **:** an apparatus for recording automatically and simultaneously several meteorologic elements — **me·te·or·o·graph·ic** \-ˌȯr-ə-'graf-ik, -ˌär-\ *adj*

me·te·or·oid \'mēt-ē-ə-ˌrȯid\ *n* (1865) **1 :** a meteor revolving around the sun **2 :** a meteor particle itself without relation to the phenomena it produces when entering the earth's atmosphere — **me·te·or·oi·dal** \ˌmēt-ē-ə-'rȯid-ᵊl\ *adj*

me·te·o·rol·o·gy \ˌmēt-ē-ə-'räl-ə-jē\ *n* [F or Gk; F *météorologie,* fr. MF, fr. Gk *meteōrologia,* fr. *meteōron* + *-logia* -logy] (1620) **1 :** a science that deals with the atmosphere and its phenomena and esp. with weather and weather forecasting **2 :** the atmospheric phenomena and weather of a region — **me·te·o·ro·log·ic** \-rə-'läj-ik\ *or* **me·te·o·ro·log·i·cal** \-i-kəl\ *adj* — **me·te·o·ro·log·i·cal·ly** \-i-k(ə-)lē\ *adv* — **me·te·o·rol·o·gist** \-'räl-ə-jəst\ *n*

meteor shower *n* (1877) **:** the phenomenon observed when members of a group of meteors encounter the earth's atmosphere and their luminous paths appear to diverge from a single point

¹me·ter \'mēt-ər\ *n* [ME, fr. OE & MF; OE *mēter,* fr. L *metrum,* fr. Gk *metron* measure, meter; MF *metre,* fr. OF, fr. L *metrum* — more at MEASURE] (bef. 12c) **1 a :** systematically arranged and measured rhythm in verse: (1) **:** rhythm that continuously repeats a single basic pattern ⟨iambic ~⟩ (2) **:** rhythm characterized by regular recurrence of a systematic arrangement of basic patterns in larger figures ⟨ballad ~⟩ **b :** a measure or unit of metrical verse — usu. used in combination and pronounced \m-ət-ər\ ⟨penta*meter*⟩; compare FOOT 4 **c :** a fixed metrical pattern **:** verse form **2 :** the basic recurrent rhythmical pattern of note values, accents, and beats per measure in music

²met·er \'mēt-ər\ *n* [ME, fr. *meten* to mete] (14c) **:** one that measures; *esp* **:** an official measurer of commodities

³me·ter \'mēt-ər\ *n* [F *mètre,* fr. Gk *metron* measure] (1797) **:** the basic metric unit of length — see METRIC SYSTEM table

⁴me·ter \'mēt-ər\ *n* [*-meter*] (1815) **1 :** an instrument for measuring and sometimes recording the time or amount of something ⟨a parking ~⟩ ⟨a gas ~⟩ **2 :** POSTAGE METER; *also* **:** a postal marking printed by a postage meter

⁵me·ter *vt* (1884) **1 :** to measure by means of a meter **2 :** to supply in a measured or regulated amount **3 :** to print postal indicia on by means of a postage meter

-me·ter \m-ət-ər, *in some words* ˌmēt-\ *n comb form* [F *-mètre,* fr. Gk *metron* measure] **:** instrument or means for measuring ⟨baro*meter*⟩

meter–kilogram–second *adj* (1940) **:** of, relating to, or being a system of units based on the meter as the unit of length, the kilogram as the unit of mass, and the mean solar second as the unit of time — abbr. *mks*

meter maid *n* (ca. 1957) **:** a female member of a police department who is assigned to write tickets for parking violations

me·ter·stick \'mēt-ər-ˌstik\ *n* (ca. 1903) **:** a measuring stick one meter long that is marked off in centimeters and usu. millimeters

met·es·trus \(ˈ)met-'es-trəs\ *n* [NL] (1900) **:** the period of regression that follows estrus

meth- *or* **metho-** *comb form* [ISV, fr. *methyl*] **:** methyl ⟨*meth*acrylic⟩

meth·ac·ry·late \(ˈ)meth-'ak-rə-ˌlāt\ *n* [ISV] (1865) **1 :** a salt or ester of methacrylic acid **2 :** an acrylic resin or plastic made from a derivative of methacrylic acid

meth·acryl·ic acid \ˌmeth-ə-ˌkril-ik-\ *n* [ISV] (1865) **:** an acid $C_4H_6O_2$ used esp. in making acrylic resins or plastics

meth·a·done \'meth-ə-ˌdōn\ *also* **meth·a·don** \-ˌdän\ *n* [6-di*meth*ylamino-4, 4-diphenyl-3-heptan*one*] (1947) **:** a synthetic addictive narcotic drug $C_{21}H_{27}NO$ used esp. in the form of its hydrochloride for the relief of pain and as a substitute narcotic in the treatment of heroin addiction

meth·am·phet·amine \ˌmeth-am-'fet-ə-ˌmēn, ˌmeth-əm-, -mən\ *n* (1949) **:** an amine $C_{10}H_{15}N$ used in the form of its crystalline hydrochloride as a stimulant for the central nervous system and in the treatment of obesity — compare METHEDRINE

metha·na·tion \ˌmeth-ə-'nē-shən\ *n* (ca. 1926) **:** the production of methane esp. from carbon monoxide and hydrogen

meth·ane \'meth-ˌān, *Brit usu* 'mē-ˌthān\ *n* [ISV] (ca. 1868) **:** a colorless odorless flammable gaseous hydrocarbon CH_4 that is a product of decomposition of organic matter in marshes and mines or of the carbonization of coal and is used as a fuel and raw material in chemical synthesis

methane series *n* (ca. 1890) **:** a homologous series of saturated open-chain hydrocarbons C_nH_{2n+2} of which methane is the first and lowest member — compare ALKANE

meth·a·nol \'meth-ə-ˌnȯl, -ˌnōl\ *n* [ISV] (ca. 1892) **:** a light volatile flammable poisonous liquid alcohol CH_3OH formed in the destructive distillation of wood or made synthetically and used esp. as a solvent, antifreeze, or denaturant for ethyl alcohol and in the synthesis of other chemicals

meth·aqua·lone \me-'thak-wə-ˌlōn\ *n* [prob. fr. *meth-* + *-a-* (arbitrary infix) + *quin-* + *azole* + *-one*] (1961) **:** a sedative and hypnotic drug $C_{16}H_{14}N_2O$ that is not a barbiturate but is habit-forming and subject to abuse — compare QUAALUDE

Meth·e·drine \'meth-ə-ˌdrēn, -drən\ *trademark* — used for methamphetamine

me·theg·lin \mə-'theg-lən\ *n* [W *meddyglyn*] (1533) **:** ¹MEAD

met·he·mo·glo·bin \(ˈ)met-'hē-mə-ˌglō-bən\ *n* [ISV] (1870) **:** a soluble brown crystalline basic blood pigment that differs from hemoglobin in containing ferric iron and in being unable to combine reversibly with molecular oxygen

met·he·mo·glo·bi·ne·mia \ˌmet-ˌhē-mə-ˌglō-bə-'nē-mē-ə\ *n* [NL] (1888) **:** the presence of methemoglobin in the blood

me·the·na·mine \mə-'thē-nə-ˌmēn, -mən\ *n* [*methene* (methylene) + *amine*] (1926) **:** HEXAMETHYLENETETRAMINE

meth·i·cil·lin \ˌmeth-ə-'sil-ən\ *n* [*meth-* + *penicillin*] (1961) **:** a semisynthetic penicillin $C_{17}H_{19}N_2O_6NaS$ that is esp. effective against penicillinase-producing staphylococci

me·thinks \mi-'thiŋ(k)s\ *vb impersonal, past* **me·thought** \-'thȯt\ [ME *me thinketh,* fr. OE *mē thincth,* fr. *mē* (dat. of *ic* I) + *thincth* seems, fr. *thyncan* to seem — more at I, THINK] *archaic* (bef. 12c) **:** it seems to me

me·thi·o·nine \mə-'thī-ə-ˌnēn\ *n* [ISV, fr. *methyl* + *thion-* + *-ine*] (ca. 1927) **:** a crystalline sulfur-containing essential amino acid $C_5H_{11}NO_2S$

meth·od \'meth-əd\ *n* [MF or L; MF *methode,* fr. L *methodus,* fr. Gk *methodos,* fr. *meta-* + *hodos* way — more at CEDE] (1541) **1 :** a procedure or process for attaining an object: as **a** (1) **:** a systematic procedure, technique, or mode of inquiry employed by or proper to a particular discipline or art (2) **:** a systematic plan followed in presenting material for instruction **b** (1) **:** a way, technique, or process of or for doing something (2) **:** a body of skills or techniques **2 :** a discipline that deals with the principles and techniques of scientific inquiry **3 a :** orderly arrangement, development, or classification **:** PLAN **b :** the habitual practice of orderliness and regularity **4** *cap* **:** a dramatic technique by which an actor seeks to gain complete identification with the inner personality of the character being portrayed

syn METHOD, MODE, MANNER, WAY, FASHION, SYSTEM mean the means taken or procedure followed in achieving an end. METHOD implies an orderly logical effective arrangement usu. in steps; MODE implies an order or course followed by custom, tradition, or personal preference; MANNER is close to MODE but may imply a procedure or method that is individual or distinctive; WAY is very general and may be used for any of the preceding words; FASHION may suggest a peculiar or characteristic way of doing something; SYSTEM suggests a fully developed or carefully formulated method often emphasizing the idea of rational orderliness.

me·thod·i·cal \mə-'thäd-i-kəl\ *also* **me·thod·ic** \-ik\ *adj* (1570) **1 :** arranged, characterized by, or performed with method or order ⟨a ~ treatment of the subject⟩ **2 :** habitually proceeding according to method **:** SYSTEMATIC ⟨~ in his daily routine⟩ — **me·thod·i·cal·ly** \-i-k(ə-)lē\ *adv* — **me·thod·i·cal·ness** \-i-kəl-nəs\ *n*

meth·od·ism \'meth-ə-ˌdiz-əm\ *n* (1739) **1** *cap* **a :** the doctrines and practice of Methodists **b :** the Methodist churches **2 :** methodical procedure

meth·od·ist \-əd-əst\ *n* (1593) **1 :** a person devoted to or laying great stress on method **2** *cap* **:** a member of one of the denominations deriving from the Wesleyan revival in the Church of England, having Arminian doctrine and in the U.S. modified episcopal polity, and stressing personal and social morality — **methodist** *adj, often cap* — **meth·od·is·tic** \ˌmeth-ə-'dis-tik\ *adj*

meth·od·ize \'meth-ə-ˌdīz\ *vt* **-ized; -iz·ing** (1589) **:** to reduce to method **:** SYSTEMATIZE ***syn*** see ORDER

method of fluxions : DIFFERENTIAL CALCULUS

meth·od·olog·i·cal \ˌmeth-əd-ᵊl-'äj-i-kəl\ *adj* (1849) **:** of or relating to method or methodology — **meth·od·olog·i·cal·ly** \-k(ə-)lē\ *adv*

meth·od·ol·o·gist \-ə-'däl-ə-jəst\ *n* (1865) **:** a student of methodology

meth·od·ol·o·gy \ˌmeth-ə-'däl-ə-jē\ *n, pl* **-gies** [NL *methodologia,* fr. L *methodus* + *-logia* -logy] (1800) **1 :** a body of methods, rules, and postulates employed by a discipline **:** a particular procedure or set of procedures **2 :** the analysis of the principles or procedures of inquiry in a particular field

meth·o·trex·ate \ˌmeth-ə-'trek-ˌsāt\ *n* [*meth-* + *-trexate,* of unknown origin] (1955) **:** a toxic anticancer drug $C_{20}H_{22}N_8O_5$ that is an analogue of folic acid and an antimetabolite

me·thoxy·chlor \me-'thäk-si-ˌklō(ə)r, -ˌklȯ(ə)r\ *n* [*meth-* + *oxy-* + *tri-chlor*ethane] (1947) **:** a chlorinated hydrocarbon insecticide $C_{16}H_{15}Cl_3O_2$

me·thoxy·flu·rane \me-ˌthäk-sē-'flu̇(ə)r-ˌān\ *n* [*meth-* + *oxy-* + *fluor-* + *ethane*] (1962) **:** a potent nonexplosive inhalational general anesthetic $C_3H_4Cl_2F_2O$ administered as a vapor

Me·thu·se·lah \mə-'th(y)üz-(ə-)lə\ *n* [Heb *Měthūshā'ēl*] **1 :** an ancestor of Noah held to have lived 969 years **2 :** an oversize wine bottle holding about 6.15 liters

meth·yl \'meth-əl\ *n* [ISV, back-formation fr. *methylene*] (ca. 1844) **:** an alkyl radical CH_3 derived from methane by removal of one hydrogen atom — **me·thyl·ic** \mə-'thil-ik\ *adj*

methyl acetate *n* (ca. 1901) **:** a flammable fragrant liquid $C_3H_6O_2$ used esp. as a solvent and paint remover

meth·yl·al \'meth-ə-ˌlal\ *n* [ISV] (1838) **:** a volatile flammable liquid $C_3H_8O_2$ of pleasant ethereal odor used esp. as a solvent, in perfumery, and in making adhesives

methyl alcohol *n* (ca. 1847) **:** METHANOL

me·thyl·amine \ˌmeth-ə-lə-'mēn, -'lam-ən; mə-'thil-ə-ˌmēn\ *n* [ISV] (ca. 1850) **:** a flammable explosive gas CH_5N with a strong ammoniacal odor used esp. in organic synthesis (as of dyes and insecticides)

meth·yl·ase \'meth-ə-ˌlās, -ˌlāz\ *n* (ca. 1952) **:** an enzyme that catalyzes methylation (as of RNA or DNA)

meth·yl·ate \'meth-ə-ˌlāt\ *vt* **-at·ed; -at·ing** (1861) **1 :** to introduce the methyl group into **2 :** to impregnate or mix with methanol — **meth·yl·ation** \ˌmeth-ə-'lā-shən\ *n* — **meth·yl·ator** \'meth-ə-ˌlāt-ər\ *n*

methyl bromide *n* (1903) **:** a poisonous gaseous compound CH_3Br used chiefly as a fumigant against rodents, worms, and insects

meth·yl·cel·lu·lose \ˌmeth-əl-'sel-yə-ˌlōs, -ˌlōz\ *n* (1921) **:** any of various gummy products of cellulose methylation that swell in water and are used esp. as emulsifiers, adhesives, thickeners and bulk laxatives

meth·yl·cho·lan·threne \-kə-'lan-ˌthrēn\ *n* [*methyl* + *cholic* acid + *anthracene*] (ca. 1933) **:** a potent carcinogenic hydrocarbon $C_{21}H_{16}$

meth·yl·do·pa \ˌmeth-əl-'dō-pə\ *n* (1954) **:** a drug $C_{10}H_{13}NO_4$ used to lower blood pressure

meth·y·lene \'meth-ə-ˌlēn, -lən\ *n* [F *méthylène,* fr. Gk *methy* wine + *hylē* wood — more at MEAD] (1835) **:** a bivalent hydrocarbon radical CH_2 derived from methane by removal of two hydrogen atoms

methylene blue *n* (ca. 1890) : a basic thiazine dye $C_{16}H_{18}ClN_3S·3H_2O$ used esp. as a biological stain, an antidote in cyanide poisoning, and an oxidation-reduction indicator

methylene chloride *n* (1880) : a nonflammable liquid CH_2Cl_2 used esp. as a solvent, paint remover, and aerosol propellant

meth·yl·mer·cury \,meth-əl-'mər-kyə-rē, -'mər-k(ə-)rē\ *n* (ca. 1919) : any of various toxic compounds of mercury containing the complex CH_3Hg– that tend to accumulate in living organisms (as fish) esp. in food chains

methyl methacrylate *n* (1933) : a volatile flammable liquid $C_5H_8O_2$ that polymerizes readily and is used esp. as a monomer for resins

meth·yl·naph·tha·lene \,meth-əl-'naf-thə-,lēn, -'nap-\ *n* (ca. 1885) : either of two isomeric hydrocarbons $C_{11}H_{10}$; *esp* : an oily liquid used in determining cetane numbers

methyl orange *n* (1881) : an alkaline dye used as a chemical indicator that in dilute solution is yellow when neutral and pink when acid

methyl parathion *n* (1957) : a potent synthetic organophosphate insecticide $C_8H_{10}NO_5PS$ that is more toxic than parathion

meth·yl·phe·ni·date \,meth-əl-'fen-ə-,dāt, -'fē-nə-\ *n* [*methyl* + *phenyl* + *piperidine* + *acetate*] (1958) : a mild stimulant $C_{14}H_{19}NO_2$ of the central nervous system used in the form of its hydrochloride to treat narcolepsy and hyperkinetic behavior disorders in children — compare RITALIN

meth·yl·pred·nis·o·lone \-pred-'nis-ə-,lōn\ *n* (1957) : a glucocorticoid $C_{22}H_{30}O_5$ that is a derivative of prednisolone and is used as an anti-inflammatory agent; *also* : any of several of its salts (as an acetate) used similarly

meth·y·ser·gide \,meth-ə-'sər-,jid\ *n* [*methyl* + *lysergic* acid + *amide*] (1962) : a serotonin antagonist $C_{21}H_{27}N_3O_2$ used in the form of its maleate esp. in the treatment and prevention of migraine headaches

met·i·cal \'met-i-kəl\ *n* [Ar *mithqāl*] (1980) — see MONEY TABLE

me·tic·u·lous \mə-'tik-yə-ləs\ *adj* [L *meticulosus* timid, fr. *metus* fear] (1827) : marked by extreme or excessive care in the consideration or treatment of details   *syn* see CAREFUL   *syn* see WORK — **me·tic·u·los·i·ty** \-,tik-yə-'läs-ət-ē\ *n* — **me·tic·u·lous·ly** \-'tik-yə-lə-slē\ *adv* — **me·tic·u·lous·ness** \-lə-snəs\ *n*

mé·tier *also* **me·tier** \'me-,tyā, me-'\ *n* [F, fr. VL *misterium*, alter. of L *ministerium* work, ministry] (1792) **1** : VOCATION, TRADE **2** : an area of activity in which one excels : FORTE   *syn* see WORK

mé·tis \mā-'tē(s)\ *n, pl* **mé·tis** \-'tē(s), -'tēz\ [F, fr. LL *mixticius* mixed — more at MESTIZO] (1816) : one of mixed blood; *esp, often cap* : HALF-BREED

Me·tol \'mē-,tȯl, -,tōl\ *trademark* — used for a photographic developer

met·onym \'met-ə-,nim\ *n* [back-formation fr. *metonymy*] (1837) : a word used in metonymy

me·ton·y·my \mə-'tän-ə-mē\ *n, pl* **-mies** [L *metonymia*, fr. Gk *metōnymia*, fr. *meta-* + *-ōnymon* -onym + *-ia* -y] (1547) : a figure of speech consisting of the use of the name of one thing for that of another of which it is an attribute or with which it is associated (as in "lands belonging to the *crown*") — **met·onym·ic** \,met-ə-'nim-ik\ *or* **met·onym·i·cal** \-i-kəl\ *adj*

me·too \'mē-'tü\ *adj* (1926) **1** : marked by similarity to or acceptance of the successful or persuasive policies or practices of someone else **2** : similar or identical to an established product (as a drug) with no significant advantage over it — **me·too·er** \-ər\ *n* — **me·too·ism** \-,iz-əm\ *n*

met·o·pe \'met-ə-(,)pē\ *n* [Gk *metopē*, fr. *meta-* + *opē* opening; akin to Gk *ōps* eye, face — more at EYE] (1563) : the space between two triglyphs of a Doric frieze often adorned with carved work

met·o·pon \'met-ə-,pän\ *n* [*meth-* + *hydro* + *morphine* + *-one*] (1941) : a narcotic drug $C_{18}H_{21}NO_3$ that is derived from morphine and is used in the form of the hydrochloride to relieve pain

metr- *or* **metro-** *comb form* [NL, fr. Gk *mētr-*, fr. *mētra*, fr. *mētr-*, *mētēr* mother — more at MOTHER] : uterus 〈*metr*itis〉 〈*metro*rrhagia〉

me·tre \'mēt-ər\ *chiefly Brit var of* METER

¹met·ric \'me-trik\ *n* (1760) **1** *pl* : a part of prosody that deals with metrical structure **2** : a standard of measurement 〈no ~ exists that can be applied directly to happiness —*Scientific Monthly*〉 **3** : a mathematical function that associates with each pair of elements of a set a real nonnegative number constituting their distance and satisfying the conditions that the number is zero only if the two elements are identical, the number is the same regardless of the order in which the two elements are taken, and the number associated with one pair of elements plus that associated with one member of the pair and a third element is equal to or greater than the number associated with the other member of the pair and the third element

²metric *or* **met·ri·cal** \'me-tri-kəl\ *adj* (1797) **1** : based on the meter as a standard of measurement 〈the ~ system〉 **2** : of, relating to, or using the metric system 〈a ~ study〉 — **met·ri·cal·ly** \-tri-k(ə-)lē\ *adv*

-met·ric \'me-trik\ *or* **-met·ri·cal** \-tri-kəl\ *adj comb form* **1** : of, employing, or obtained by (such) a meter 〈galvano*metric*〉 **2** : of or relating to (such) an art, process, or science of measuring 〈baro*metrical*〉

met·ri·cal \'me-tri-kəl\ *or* **met·ric** \-'trik\ *adj* (15c) **1** : of, relating to, or composed in meter **2** : of or relating to measurement — **met·ri·cal·ly** \-tri-k(ə-)lē\ *adv*

met·ri·ca·tion \,me-tri-'kā-shən\ *n* (1965) : the act or process of metricizing; *specif* : conversion of an existent system of units into the metric system

met·ri·cize \'me-trə-,sīz\ *vt* **-cized; -ciz·ing** (1873) : to change into or express in the metric system

metric space *n* (1927) : a mathematical set for which a metric is defined for any pair of elements

metric system *n* (1864) : a decimal system of weights and measures based on the meter and on the kilogram

metric ton *n* (ca. 1900) — see METRIC SYSTEM table

me·trist \'me-trəst, 'mē-\ *n* (1535) **1** : a maker of verses **2** : one skillful in handling meter **3** : a student of meter or metrics

METRIC SYSTEM[1]

LENGTH

unit	abbreviation	number of meters	approximate U.S. equivalent
kilometer	km	1,000	0.62 mile
hectometer	hm	100	109.36 yards
dekameter	dam	10	32.81 feet
meter	m	1	39.37 inches
decimeter	dm	0.1	3.94 inches
centimeter	cm	0.01	0.39 inch
millimeter	mm	0.001	0.039 inch

AREA

unit	abbreviation	number of square meters	approximate U.S. equivalent
square kilometer	sq km *or* km²	1,000,000	0.3861 square mile
hectare	ha	10,000	2.47 acres
are	a	100	119.60 square yards
square centimeter	sq cm *or* cm²	0.0001	0.155 square inch

VOLUME

unit	abbreviation	number of cubic meters	approximate U.S. equivalent
cubic centimeter	cu cm *or* cm³ *also* cc	0.000001	0.061 cubic inch
cubic decimeter	dm³	0.001	61.023 cubic inches
cubic meter	m³	1	1.307 cubic yards

CAPACITY

unit	abbreviation	number of liters	approximate U.S. equivalent		
			cubic	dry	liquid
kiloliter	kl	1,000	1.31 cubic yards		
hectoliter	hl	100	3.53 cubic feet	2.84 bushels	
dekaliter	dal	10	0.35 cubic foot	1.14 pecks	2.64 gallons
liter	l	1	61.02 cubic inches	0.908 quart	1.057 quarts
cubic decimeter	dm³	1	61.02 cubic inches	0.908 quart	1.057 quarts
deciliter	dl	0.10	6.1 cubic inches	0.18 pint	0.21 pint
centiliter	cl	0.01	0.61 cubic inch		0.338 fluidounce
milliliter	ml	0.001	0.061 cubic inch		0.27 fluidram

MASS AND WEIGHT

unit	abbreviation	number of grams	approximate U.S. equivalent
metric ton	t	1,000,000	1.102 short tons
kilogram	kg	1,000	2.2046 pounds
hectogram	hg	100	3.527 ounces
dekagram	dag	10	0.353 ounce
gram	g	1	0.035 ounce
decigram	dg	0.10	1.543 grains
centigram	cg	0.01	0.154 grain
milligram	mg	0.001	0.015 grain

[1]For metric equivalents of U.S. units see Weights and Measures table

[1]met·ro \'me-(,)trō, *in French context also* mā-'\ *n, pl* **metros** [F *métro,* short for (*chemin de fer*) *métropolitain* metropolitan railroad] (1904) : SUBWAY b

[2]met·ro \'me-(,)trō\ *adj* (1957) : METROPOLITAN 2

me·trol·o·gy \me-'träl-ə-jē\ *n* [F *métrologie,* fr. Gk *metrologia* theory of ratios, fr. *metron* measure — more at MEASURE] (ca. 1816) **1 :** the science of weights and measures or of measurement **2 :** a system of weights and measures — **met·ro·log·i·cal** \,me-trə-'läj-i-kəl\ *adj* — **met·ro·log·i·cal·ly** \-k(ə-)lē\ *adv* — **me·trol·o·gist** \me-'träl-ə-jəst\ *n*

met·ro·ni·da·zole \,me-trə-'nīd-ə-,zōl\ *n* [*methyl* + *-tron-* (prob. fr. *nitro*) + *imide* + *azole*] (1962) : a drug $C_6H_9N_3O_3$ used in treating vaginal trichomoniasis

met·ro·nome \'me-trə-,nōm\ *n* [Gk *metron* + *-nomos* controlling, fr. *nomos* law — more at NIMBLE] (1816) : an instrument designed to mark exact time by a regularly repeated tick

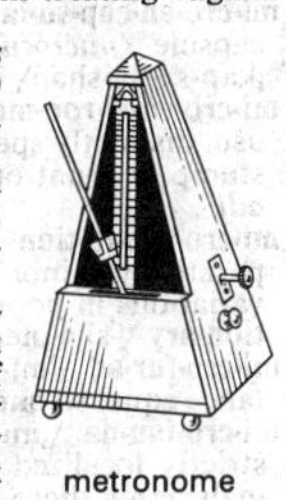

metronome

met·ro·nom·ic \,me-trə-'näm-ik\ *also* **met·ro·nom·i·cal** \-i-kəl\ *adj* (1881) : mechanically regular (as in action or tempo) — **met·ro·nom·i·cal·ly** \-i-k(ə-)lē\ *adv*

me·trop·o·lis \mə-'träp-(ə-)ləs\ *n* [LL, fr. Gk *mētropolis,* fr. *mētr-, mētēr* mother + *polis* city — more at MOTHER, POLICE] (14c) **1 :** the chief or capital city of a country, state, or region **2 :** the mother city or state of a colony (as of ancient Greece) **3 a :** a city regarded as a center of a specified activity ⟨a great business ~⟩ **b :** a large important city ⟨the world's great ~*es* —P. E. James⟩

[1]met·ro·pol·i·tan \,me-trə-'päl-ət-ᵊn\ *n* (15c) **1 :** the primate of an ecclesiastical province **2 :** one who lives in a metropolis or displays metropolitan manners or customs

[2]metropolitan *adj* [LL *metropolitanus* of the see of a metropolitan, fr. *metropolita,* n., metropolitan, fr. LGk *mētropolitēs,* fr. *mētropolis* see of a metropolitan, fr. Gk, capital] (15c) **1 :** of or constituting a metropolitan or his see **2 :** of, relating to, or characteristic of a metropolis and sometimes including its suburbs **3 :** of, relating to, or constituting a mother country

me·tror·rha·gia \,mē-trə-'rā-j(ē-)ə, -'rā-zhə; -'räj-ə, -'räzh-\ *n* [NL] (ca. 1776) : profuse bleeding from the uterus esp. between menstrual periods

-m·e·try \m-ə-trē\ *n comb form* [ME *-metrie,* fr. MF, fr. L *-metria,* fr. Gk, fr. *metrein* to measure, fr. *metron* — more at MEASURE] : art, process, or science of measuring (something specified) ⟨chrono*metry*⟩ ⟨photo*metry*⟩

met·tle \'met-ᵊl\ *n* [alter. of *metal*] (1581) **1 :** quality of temperament or disposition ⟨gentlemen of brave ~ —Shak.⟩ **2 a :** vigor and strength of spirit or temperament ⟨suspected to have more tongue in his head than ~ in his bosom —Sir Walter Scott⟩ **b :** staying quality : STAMINA ⟨trucks had proved their ~ in army transport —*Pioneer & Pacemaker*⟩ ***syn*** see COURAGE — **met·tled** \-ᵊld\ *adj* — **on one's mettle** : aroused to do one's best

met·tle·some \'met-ᵊl-səm\ *adj* (1662) : full of mettle : SPIRITED

meu·nière \(,)mə(r)n-'ye(ə)r, mœn-\ *adj* [F (*à la*) *meunière,* lit., in the manner of a miller's wife; F *meunière* miller's wife, fem. of *meunier* miller, fr. L *molinarius,* fr. *molina* mill — more at MILL] (1903) : rolled lightly in flour and sautéed in butter ⟨sole ~⟩

[1]mew \'myü\ *n* [ME, fr. OE *mǣw;* akin to ON *mār* gull] (bef. 12c) : GULL; *esp* : the common European gull (*Larus canus*)

[2]mew *vb* [ME *mewen,* of imit. origin] *vi* (14c) : to utter a mew or similar sound ⟨gulls ~*ed* over the bay⟩ ~ *vt* : to utter by mewing : MEOW

[3]mew *n* (1596) : MEOW

[4]mew *n* [ME *mewe,* fr. MF *mue,* fr. *muer* to molt, fr. L *mutare* to change — more at MISS] (14c) **1 :** an enclosure for trained hawks — usu. used in pl. **2 :** a place for hiding or retirement **3** *pl but sing or pl in constr, chiefly Brit* **a** (1) : stables usu. with living quarters built around a court (2) : living quarters adapted from such stables **b :** back street : ALLEY

[5]mew *vt* (15c) : to shut up : CONFINE — often used with *up*

mewl \'myü(ə)l\ *vi* [imit.] (1600) : to cry weakly : WHIMPER

Mex·i·can \'mek-si-kən\ *n* (1604) **1 a :** a native or inhabitant of Mexico **b :** a person of Mexican descent **c** *Southwest* : a person of mixed Spanish and Indian descent **2 :** NAHUATL 2 — **Mexican** *adj*

Mexican bean beetle *n* (1921) : a spotted ladybug (*Epilachna varivestis*) that feeds on the leaves of beans

Mexican Spanish *n* (1945) : the Spanish used in Mexico

Mexican standoff *n* (1891) : a situation in which no one emerges a clear winner

me·ze·re·on \mə-'zir-ē-ən\ *n* [ME *mizerion,* fr. ML *mezereon,* fr. Ar *māzariyūn,* fr. Per] (15c) : a small European shrub (*Daphne mezereum* of the family Thymelaeaceae, the mezereon family) with fragrant lilac purple flowers and poisonous emetic leaves, fruit, and bark

me·zu·zah *or* **me·zu·za** \mə-'züz-ə\ *n, pl* **-zahs** *or* **-zas** *or* **zot** \-'züz-,ōt\ [Heb *mĕzūzāh* doorpost] (1650) : a small parchment scroll inscribed with Deut 6:4–9 and 11:13–21 and the name Shaddai and placed in a case fixed to the doorpost by some Jewish families as a sign and reminder of their faith

mez·za·nine \'mez-ᵊn-,ēn, ,mez-ᵊn-'\ *n* [F, fr. It *mezzanino,* fr. *mezzano* middle, fr. L *medianus* middle, median] (1711) **1 :** a low-ceilinged story between two main stories of a building; *esp* : an intermediate story that projects in the form of a balcony **2 a :** the lowest balcony in a theater **b :** the first few rows of such a balcony

mez·za vo·ce \,met-sä-'vō-(,)chā, ,med-zä-\ *adv or adj* [It, half voice] (1775) : with medium or half volume of tone — used as a direction in music

mez·zo \'met-(,)sō, 'med-(,)zō\ *n, pl* **mezzos** [It, lit., middle, moderate, half, fr. L *medius* — more at MIDDLE] (1832) : MEZZO-SOPRANO

mez·zo for·te \,met-(,)sō-'fōr-,tā, ,med-(,)zō-, -'fōrt-ē\ *adj or adv* [It] (ca. 1811) : moderately loud — used as a direction in music

mez·zo pia·no \-pē-'än-(,)ō\ *adj or adv* [It] (ca. 1811) : moderately soft — used as a direction in music

mez·zo–re·lie·vo *or* **mez·zo–ri·lie·vo** \-ri-'lē-(,)vō, -rēl-'yā-(,)vō\ *n, pl* **–vos** [It *mezzorilievo,* fr. *mezzo* + *rilievo* relief] (ca. 1598) : sculptural relief intermediate between bas-relief and high relief

mez·zo–so·pra·no \-sə-'pran-(,)ō, -'prän-\ *n* [It *mezzosoprano,* fr. *mezzo* + *soprano* soprano] (ca. 1753) **1 :** a woman's voice with a range between that of the soprano and contralto **2 :** a singer having a mezzo-soprano voice

mez·zo·tint \'met-sō-,tint, 'med-zō-\ *n* [modif. of It *mezzatinta,* fr. *mezza* (fem. of *mezzo*) + *tinta* tint] (1660) **1 :** a manner of engraving on copper or steel by scraping or burnishing a roughened surface to produce light and shade **2 :** an engraving produced by mezzotint

mho \'mō\ *n, pl* **mhos** [backward spelling of *ohm*] (ca. 1883) : the practical unit of conductance equal to the reciprocal of the ohm

mi \'mē\ *n* [ML, fr. the syllable sung to this note in a medieval hymn to St. John the Baptist] (15c) : the 3d tone of the diatonic scale in solmization

mi- *or* **mio-** *comb form* [prob. fr. NL *meio-,* fr. Gk, fr. *meiōn* — more at MINOR] : less ⟨*Mio*cene⟩

MIA \,em-(,)ī-'ā\ *n* [*m*issing *i*n *a*ction] (ca. 1944) : a member of the armed forces whose whereabouts following a combat mission are unknown and whose death cannot be established beyond reasonable doubt

Mi·ami \mī-'am-ē, -'am-ə\ *n, pl* **Mi·ami** *or* **Mi·am·is** (1808) : a member of an American Indian people orig. of Wisconsin and Indiana

mi·aow \mē-'aủ\ *var of* MEOW

mi·as·ma \mī-'az-mə, mē-\ *n, pl* **-mas** *also* **-ma·ta** \-mət-ə\ [NL, fr. Gk, defilement, fr. *miainein* to pollute; akin to OE *māl* mole] (ca. 1665) **1 :** a vaporous exhalation formerly believed to cause disease; *also* : a heavy vaporous emanation or atmosphere ⟨a ~ of tobacco smoke⟩ **2 :** an influence or atmosphere that tends to deplete or corrupt ⟨freed from the ~ of poverty —Sir Arthur Bryant⟩; *also* : an atmosphere that obscures : FOG ⟨retreated into an asexual mental ~ —*Times Lit. Supp.*⟩ — **mi·as·mal** \-məl\ *adj* — **mi·as·mat·ic** \,mī-əz-'mat-ik\ *adj* — **mi·as·mic** \mī-'az-mik, mē-\ *adj* — **mi·as·mi·cal·ly** \-mi-k(ə-)lē\ *adv*

mi·ca \'mī-kə\ *n* [NL, fr. L, grain, crumb; akin to Gk *mikros* small] (1777) : any of various colored or transparent mineral silicates crystallizing in monoclinic forms that readily separate into very thin leaves — **mi·ca·ceous** \mī-'kā-shəs\ *adj*

Mi·cah \'mī-kə\ *n* [Heb *Mīkhāh,* short for *Mīkhāyāh*] **1 :** a Hebrew prophet of the 8th century B.C. **2 :** a prophetic book of canonical Jewish and Christian Scripture — see BIBLE table

Mi·caw·ber \mi-'kȯb-ər, -'käb-\ *n* [Wilkins *Micawber,* character in the novel *David Copperfield* (1849–50) by Charles Dickens] (1852) : one who is poor but lives in optimistic expectation of better fortune — **Mi·caw·ber·ish** \-ə-rish\ *adj*

mice *pl of* MOUSE

mi·celle \mī-'sel\ *n* [NL *micella,* fr. L *mica*] (1881) : a unit of structure built up from polymeric molecules or ions: as **a :** an ordered region in a fiber (as of cellulose or rayon) **b :** a molecular aggregate that constitutes a colloidal particle — **mi·cel·lar** \-'sel-ər\ *adj*

Mi·chael \'mī-kəl\ *n* [Heb *Mīkhā'ēl*] : one of the four archangels named in Hebrew tradition

Mi·chae·lis constant \mī-,kā-ləs-, mə-\ *n* [Leonor *Michaelis* †1949 Am. biochemist] (1949) : a constant that is a measure of the kinetics of an enzyme reaction and that is equivalent to the concentration of substrate at which the reaction takes place at one half its maximum rate

Mich·ael·mas \'mik-əl-məs\ *n* [ME *mychelmesse,* fr. OE *Michaeles mæsse* Michael's mass] (bef. 12c) : September 29 celebrated as the feast of St. Michael the Archangel

Michaelmas daisy *n* (1785) : a wild aster; *esp* : one blooming about Michaelmas

Mi·che·as \'mī-kē-əs, mī-'\ *n* [LL *Michaeas,* fr. Gk *Michaias,* fr. Heb *Mīkhāyāh*] : MICAH

mick \'mik\ *n, often cap* [*Mick,* nickname for *Michael,* common Irish given name] (1856) : IRISHMAN — often taken to be offensive

Mick·ey Finn \,mik-ē-'fin\ *n* [prob. fr. the name *Mickey Finn*] (1928) : a drink of liquor doctored with a purgative or a drug

Mickey Mouse \'mik-ē-'maủs\ *adj* [*Mickey Mouse,* cartoon character created by Walt Disney] (1938) **1** *often not cap* : being or performing insipid or corny popular music **2 :** lacking importance : INSIGNIFICANT ⟨*Mickey Mouse* courses, where you don't work too hard —Willie Cager⟩ **3 :** annoyingly petty ⟨*Mickey Mouse* regulations⟩

mick·le \'mik-əl\ *adj* [ME *mikel,* fr. OE *micel* — more at MUCH] *chiefly Scot* (bef. 12c) : GREAT, MUCH — **mickle** *adv, chiefly Scot*

Mic·mac \'mik-,mak\ *n, pl* **Micmac** *or* **Micmacs** [Micmac *Migmac,* lit., allies] (1830) **1 :** a member of an Indian people of eastern Canada **2 :** the Algonquian language of the Micmac people

micr- *or* **micro-** *comb form* [ME *micro-,* fr. L, fr. Gk *mikr-, mikro-,* fr. *mikros, smikros* small, short; akin to OE *smēalīc* careful, exquisite] **1 a :** small : minute ⟨*micro*film⟩ **b :** used for or involving minute quantities or variations ⟨*micro*barograph⟩ **c :** minutely ⟨*micro*level⟩ **2 :** one millionth part of a (specified) unit ⟨*micro*gram⟩ ⟨*micro*hm⟩ **3 a :** using microscopy ⟨*micro*dissection⟩ : used in microscopy **b :** revealed by or having the structure discernible only by microscopic examination ⟨*micro*organism⟩ **4 :** abnormally small ⟨*micro*cyte⟩ **5 :** of or relating to a small area ⟨*micro*climate⟩ **6 :** employed in or connected with microphotographing or microfilming ⟨*micro*copy⟩

micra *pl of* MICRON

[1]mi·cro \'mī-(,)krō\ *adj* [*micr-*] (1923) **1 :** very small; *esp* : MICROSCOPIC **2 :** involving minute quantities or variations

[2]micro *n, pl* **micros** [by shortening] (1972) **1 :** MICROCOMPUTER **2 :** MICROPROCESSOR

mi·cro·am·pere \'mī-krō-,am-,pi(ə)r\ *n* (ca. 1890) : a unit of current equal to one millionth of an ampere

mi·cro·anal·y·sis \,mī-krō-ə-'nal-ə-səs\ *n* (ca. 1856) : chemical analysis on a small or minute scale that usu. requires special, very sensitive, or small-scale apparatus — **mi·cro·an·a·lyst** \-'an-ᵊl-əst\ *n* — **mi·cro·an·a·lyt·ic** \-,an-ᵊl-'it-ik\ *or* **mi·cro·an·a·lyt·i·cal** \-'it-i-kəl\ *adj*

mi·cro·anat·o·my \-ə-'nat-ə-mē\ *n* (ca. 1899) : HISTOLOGY — **mi·cro·an·a·tom·i·cal** \-,an-ə-'täm-i-kəl\ *adj*

---

mi·cro·bal·ance \'mī-krō-,bal-ən(t)s\ *n* (1903) : a balance designed to measure very small weights
mi·cro·baro·graph \,mī-krō-'bar-ə-,graf\ *n* [ISV] (1904) : a barograph for recording small and rapid changes
mi·crobe \'mī-,krōb\ *n* [ISV *micr-* + Gk *bios* life — more at QUICK] (1881) : MICROORGANISM, GERM — **mi·cro·bi·al** \mī-'krō-bē-əl\ *also* **mi·cro·bic** \-bik\ *adj*
mi·cro·beam \'mī-krō-,bēm\ *n* (1951) : a beam of radiation of small cross section ⟨a focused laser ~⟩ ⟨a ~ of electrons⟩
mi·cro·bi·ol·o·gy \,mī-krō-bī-'äl-ə-jē\ *n* [ISV] (1888) : a branch of biology dealing esp. with microscopic forms of life — **mi·cro·bi·o·log·i·cal** \'mī-krō-,bī-ə-'läj-i-kəl\ *also* **mi·cro·bi·o·log·ic** \-'läj-ik\ *adj* — **mi·cro·bi·o·log·i·cal·ly** \-i-k(ə-)lē\ *adv* — **mi·cro·bi·ol·o·gist** \,mī-krō-bī-'äl-ə-jəst\ *n*
mi·cro·bus \'mī-krō-,bəs\ *n* (1945) : a station wagon shaped like a bus
mi·cro·cal·o·rim·e·ter \,mī-krō-,kal-ə-'rim-ət-ər\ *n* (1911) : an instrument for measuring very small quantities of heat — **mi·cro·ca·lo·ri·met·ric** \-,kal-ə-rə-'me-trik; -kə-,lȯr-ə-, -,lȯr-, -,lär-\ *adj* — **mi·cro·cal·o·rim·e·try** \-,kal-ə-'rim-ə-trē\ *n*
mi·cro·cap·sule \'mī-krō-,kap-səl, -(,)sül\ *n* (1961) : a tiny capsule containing material (as an adhesive or a medicine) that is released when the capsule is broken, melted, or dissolved
Mi·cro·card \-,kärd\ *trademark* — used for a card bearing microcopies of printed matter
¹**mi·cro·ce·phal·ic** \,mī-krō-sə-'fal-ik\ *adj* (ca. 1856) : having a small head; *specif* : having an abnormally small head
²**microcephalic** *n* (ca. 1873) : one that is microcephalic
mi·cro·ceph·a·ly \-'sef-ə-lē\ *n* [NL *microcephalia,* fr. *microcephalus* microcephalic, fr. *micr-* + Gk *kephalē* head — more at CEPHALIC] (1863) : a condition of abnormal smallness of the head usu. associated with mental defects
mi·cro·chip \'mī-krō-,chip\ *n* (1969) : INTEGRATED CIRCUIT
mi·cro·cir·cuit \-,sər-kət\ *n* (1959) : a compact electronic circuit : INTEGRATED CIRCUIT — **mi·cro·cir·cuit·ry** \-kə-trē\ *n*
mi·cro·cir·cu·la·tion \'mī-krō-,sər-kyə-'lā-shən\ *n* (1959) : the part of the circulatory system made up of very fine channels (as capillaries and venules); *also* : circulation through such a system — **mi·cro·cir·cu·la·to·ry** \,mī-krō-'sər-kyə-lə-,tōr-ē, -,tȯr-\ *adj*
mi·cro·cli·mate \'mī-krō-,klī-mət\ *n* [ISV] (1925) : the essentially uniform local climate of a usu. small site or habitat — **mi·cro·cli·mat·ic** \,mī-krō-klī-'mat-ik\ *adj*
mi·cro·cli·ma·tol·o·gy \'mī-krō-,klī-mə-'täl-ə-jē\ *n* (1934) : the study of microclimates : climatology of restricted areas — **mi·cro·cli·ma·to·log·i·cal** \-mət-ᵊl-'äj-i-kəl\ *adj* — **mi·cro·cli·ma·tol·o·gist** \-mə-'täl-ə-jəst\ *n*
mi·cro·cline \'mī-krō-,klīn\ *n* [G *mikroklin,* fr. *mikr-* micr- + Gk *klinein* to lean — more at LEAN] (1849) : a triclinic white to pale yellow, red, or green mineral $KAlSi_3O_8$ of the feldspar group that is like orthoclase in composition
mi·cro·coc·cus \,mī-krō-'käk-əs\ *n, pl* **-coc·ci** \-'käk-,(s)ī, -'käk-(,)(s)ē\ [NL] (1870) : a small spherical bacterium; *esp* : one of a genus (*Micrococcus*) in which growth forms irregular groups — **mi·cro·coc·cal** \-'käk-əl\ *adj*
mi·cro·code \'mī-krə-,kōd\ *n* (ca. 1962) : the microinstructions esp. of a microprocessor
mi·cro·com·put·er \'mī-krō-kəm-,pyüt-ər\ *n* (1971) **1** : a very small computer that uses a microprocessor to handle information **2** : MICROPROCESSOR
¹**mi·cro·copy** \'mī-krō-,käp-ē\ *n* [ISV] (ca. 1934) : a photographic copy in which graphic matter is reduced in size (as on microfilm)
²**microcopy** *vt* (1935) : to prepare a microcopy of ~ *vi* : to make microcopies
mi·cro·cosm \'mī-krə-,käz-əm\ *n* [ME, fr. ML *microcosmus,* modif. of Gk *mikros kosmos*] (13c) **1** : a little world; *esp* : man or human nature that is an epitome of the world or the universe **2** : a community or other unity that is an epitome of a larger unity — **mi·cro·cos·mic** \,mī-krə-'käz-mik\ *adj* — **mi·cro·cos·mi·cal·ly** \-mi-k(ə-)lē\ *adv* — **in microcosm** : in a greatly diminished size, form, or scale
microcosmic salt *n* (1783) : a white crystalline salt $NaNH_5PO_4·4H_2O$ used as a flux in testing for metallic oxides and salts
mi·cro·cos·mos \'mī-krə-,käz-məs, -,mōs, -,mäs\ *n* [ME *mycrocossmos,* fr. ML *microcosmus*] (13c) **1** : MICROCOSM **2** : the microscopic or submicroscopic world
mi·cro·crys·tal \'mī-krō-,kris-tᵊl\ *n* (1886) : a crystal visible only under the microscope — **mi·cro·crys·tal·line** \,mī-krō-'kris-tə-lən *also* -,līn *or* -,lēn\ *adj* — **mi·cro·crys·tal·lin·i·ty** \-,kris-tə-'lin-ət-ē\ *n*
mi·cro·cul·ture \'mī-krō-,kəl-chər\ *n* (1944) **1** : the culture of a small group of human beings with limited perspective **2** : a microscopic culture of cells or organisms — **mi·cro·cul·tur·al** \,mī-krō-'kəlch-(ə-)rəl\ *adj*
mi·cro·cu·rie \'mī-krō-,kyu̇(ə)r-ē, ,mī-krō-kyu̇-'rē\ *n* (1911) : a unit of quantity or of radioactivity equal to one millionth of a curie
mi·cro·cyte \'mī-krə-,sīt\ *n* [ISV] (1876) : a small red blood cell present esp. in some anemias — **mi·cro·cyt·ic** \,mī-krə-'sit-ik\ *adj*
mi·cro·den·si·tom·e·ter \'mī-krō-,den(t)-sə-'täm-ət-ər\ *n* (1935) : a densitometer for measuring the densities of very small areas of a photographic film or plate (as for detecting invisible spectrographic lines) — **mi·cro·den·si·to·met·ric** \-sət-ə-'me-trik\ *adj* — **mi·cro·den·si·tom·e·try** \-sə-'täm-ə-trē\ *n*
mi·cro·dis·sec·tion \,mī-krō-dis-'ek-shən, -dī-'sek-\ *n* (1915) : dissection under the microscope; *specif* : dissection of cells and tissues by means of fine needles that are precisely manipulated by levers
mi·cro·dot \'mī-krə-,dät, -krō-\ *n* (1946) : a photographic reproduction of printed matter reduced to the size of a dot for ease or security of transmittal
mi·cro·earth·quake \'mī-krō-,ərth-,kwāk\ *n* (1965) : an earthquake of low intensity
mi·cro·eco·nom·ics \-,ek-ə-'näm-iks, -,ē-kə-\ *n pl but usu sing in constr* (1947) : a study of economics in terms of individual areas of activity (as a firm, household, or prices) — compare MACROECONOMICS — **mi·cro·eco·nom·ic** \-'näm-ik\ *adj*
mi·cro·elec·trode \,mī-krō-i-'lek-,trōd\ *n* (1917) : a minute electrode; *esp* : one that is inserted in a living biological cell or tissue in studying its electrical characteristics
mi·cro·elec·tron·ics \i-,lek-'trän-iks\ *n pl* (1958) **1** *sing in constr* : a branch of electronics that deals with the miniaturization of electronic circuits and components **2** : devices, equipment, or circuits produced using the methods of microelectronics — **mi·cro·elec·tron·ic** \-ik\ *adj* — **mi·cro·elec·tron·i·cal·ly** \-i-k(ə-)lē\ *adv*
mi·cro·elec·tro·pho·re·sis \-,lek-trə-fə-'rē-səs\ *n* [NL] (1936) : electrophoresis in which the movement of single particles is observed in a microscope; *also* : electrophoresis in which micromethods are used — **mi·cro·elec·tro·pho·ret·ic** \-'ret-ik\ *adj* — **mi·cro·elec·tro·pho·ret·i·cal·ly** \-i-k(ə-)lē\ *adv*
mi·cro·el·e·ment \,mī-krō-'el-ə-mənt\ *n* (1936) : TRACE ELEMENT
mi·cro·en·cap·su·late \-in-'kap-sə-,lāt\ *vt* (1963) : to enclose in a microcapsule ⟨*microencapsulated* aspirin⟩ — **mi·cro·en·cap·su·la·tion** \-in-,kap-sə-'lā-shən\ *n*
mi·cro·en·vi·ron·ment \-in-'vī-rən-mənt, -'vī(-ə)rn-\ *n* (1938) : a small usu. distinctly specialized and effectively isolated habitat (as a decaying stump or a pat of dung) — **mi·cro·en·vi·ron·men·tal** \-,vī-rən-'ment-ᵊl\ *adj*
mi·cro·evo·lu·tion \'mī-krō-,ev-ə-'lü-shən *also* -,ē-və-\ *n* (1940) : comparatively minor evolutionary change involving the accumulation of variations in populations usu. below the species level — **mi·cro·evo·lu·tion·ary** \-shə-,ner-ē\ *adj*
mi·cro·far·ad \'mī-krō-,fa(ə)r-,ad, -,far-əd\ *n* (1873) : a unit of capacitance equal to one millionth of a farad
mi·cro·fau·na \,mī-krō-'fȯn-ə, -'fän-\ *n* [NL] (1902) **1** : a small or strictly localized fauna (as of a microenvironment) **2** : minute animals; *esp* : those invisible to the naked eye ⟨the soil ~⟩ — **mi·cro·fau·nal** \-'fȯn-ᵊl, -'fän-\ *adj*
mi·cro·fi·bril \-'fīb-rəl, -'fib-\ *n* (1938) : a fine fibril; *esp* : one of the submicroscopic elongated bundles of cellulose of a plant cell wall — **mi·cro·fi·bril·lar** \-rə-lər\ *adj*
mi·cro·fiche \'mī-krō-,fēsh, -,fish\ *n, pl* **-fiche** *or* **-fiches** \-,fēsh(-əz), -,fish(-əz)\ [F, fr. *micr-* micr- + *fiche* fiche] (ca. 1948) : a sheet of microfilm containing rows of microimages of pages of printed matter
mi·cro·fil·a·ment \,mī-krō-'fil-ə-mənt\ *n* (1963) : any of the minute protein filaments that are widely distributed in the cytoplasm of eukaryotic cells
mi·cro·fi·lar·ia \,mī-krō-fə-'lar-ē-ə, -'ler-\ *n* [NL] (1878) : a minute larval filaria — **mi·cro·fi·lar·i·al** \-ē-əl\ *adj*
¹**mi·cro·film** \'mī-krə-,film\ *n* [ISV] (1927) : a film bearing a photographic record on a reduced scale of printed or other graphic matter
²**microfilm** *vt* (1937) : to reproduce on microfilm ~ *vi* : to make microfilms — **mi·cro·film·able** \-,fil-mə-bəl\ *adj* — **mi·cro·film·er** *n*
mi·cro·flo·ra \,mī-krə-'flōr-ə, -'flȯr-\ *n* [NL] (ca. 1904) **1** : a small or strictly localized flora (as of a microenvironment) **2** : minute plants; *esp* : those invisible to the naked eye — **mi·cro·flo·ral** \-əl\ *adj*
mi·cro·form \'mī-krə-,fȯrm\ *n* (1958) **1** : a process for reproducing printed matter in a much reduced size ⟨documents in ~⟩ **2 a** : matter reproduced by microform **b** : MICROCOPY
mi·cro·fos·sil \,mī-krō-'fäs-əl\ *n* (1924) : a fossil that can be studied only microscopically and that may be either a fragment of a larger organism or an entire minute organism
mi·cro·fun·gus \-'fəŋ-gəs\ *n* [NL] (1874) : a fungus (as a mold) with a microscopic fruiting body
mi·cro·ga·mete \,mī-krō-gə-'mēt, -'gam-,ēt\ *n* [ISV] (ca. 1891) : the smaller and usu. male gamete of a heterogamous organism
mi·cro·ga·me·to·cyte \-gə-'mēt-ə-,sīt\ *n* [ISV] (1902) : a gametocyte producing microgametes
mi·cro·gram \'mī-krə-,gram\ *n* [ISV] (ca. 1890) : one millionth of a gram
mi·cro·graph \-,graf\ *n* [ISV] (1904) : a graphic reproduction of the image of an object formed by a microscope — **micrograph** *vt*
mi·cro·graph·ics \,mī-krə-'graf-iks\ *n pl but sing in constr* (1969) : the industry concerned with the manufacture and sale of graphic material in microform; *also* : the production of such material — **mi·cro·graph·ic** \-ik\ *adj* — **mi·cro·graph·i·cal·ly** \-i-k(ə-)lē\ *adv*
mi·cro·groove \'mī-krō-,grüv\ *n* (1948) : a narrow continuous V-shaped spiral track that has closely spaced turns and that is used on long-playing records
mi·cro·hab·i·tat \,mī-krō-'hab-ə-,tat\ *n* (1933) : MICROENVIRONMENT
mi·cro·im·age \-'im-ij\ *n* (1950) : an image (as on a microfilm) that is greatly reduced in size
mi·cro·inch \-'inch\ *n* (1941) : one millionth of an inch
mi·cro·in·jec·tion \,mī-krō-in-'jek-shən\ *n* (1921) : injection under the microscope; *specif* : injection into tissues by means of a fine mechanically controlled capillary tube — **mi·cro·in·ject** \-'jekt\ *vt*
mi·cro·in·struc·tion \-'strək-shən\ *n* (1959) : a computer instruction that activates the circuits necessary to perform a single machine operation usu. as part of the execution of a machine-language instruction
mi·cro·lep·i·dop·tera \'mī-krō-,lep-ə-'däp-tə-rə\ *n pl* [NL] (1852) : lepidopterous insects (as tortricids) that belong to families of minute or medium-sized moths — **mi·cro·lep·i·dop·ter·ous** \-tə-rəs\ *adj*
mi·cro·li·ter \,mī-krō-'lēt-ər\ *n* [ISV] (ca. 1890) : a unit of capacity equal to one millionth of a liter
mi·cro·lith \'mī-krə-,lith\ *n* [ISV] (1908) : a tiny blade tool esp. of the Mesolithic usu. in the form of a geometric figure (as a triangle) and often set in a bone or wooden haft — **mi·cro·lith·ic** \,mī-krə-'lith-ik\ *adj*
mi·cro·ma·nip·u·la·tion \'mī-krō-mə-,nip-yə-'lā-shən\ *n* (1921) : the technique or practice of microdissection and microinjection
mi·cro·ma·nip·u·la·tor \-'nip-yə-,lāt-ər\ *n* (1921) : an instrument for micromanipulation
mi·cro·mere \'mī-krō-,mi(ə)r\ *n* [ISV] (1877) : a small blastomere — see BLASTULA illustration
mi·cro·me·te·or·ite \,mī-krō-'mēt-ē-ə-,rīt\ *n* (ca. 1949) **1** : a meteorite so small that it can pass through the earth's atmosphere without becoming intensely heated **2** : a very small particle in interplanetary space — **mi·cro·me·te·or·it·ic** \-,mēt-ē-ə-'rit-ik\ *adj*
mi·cro·me·te·or·oid \-'mēt-ē-ə-,rȯid\ *n* (1954) : MICROMETEORITE 2
mi·cro·me·te·o·rol·o·gy \-,mēt-ē-ə-'räl-ə-jē\ *n* (ca. 1930) : meteorology that deals with small-scale weather systems ranging up to several kilometers in diameter and confined to the lower troposphere — **mi·cro·me·te·o·ro·log·i·cal** \-,mēt-ē-,ȯr-ə-'läj-i-kəl, -,är-ə-, -ə-rə-\ *adj* — **mi·cro·me·te·o·rol·o·gist** \-,mēt-ē-ə-'räl-ə-jəst\ *n*

[1]**mi·crom·e·ter** \mī-ˈkräm-ət-ər\ *n* [F *micromètre,* fr. *micr-* + *-mètre* -meter] (1670) : an instrument used with a telescope or microscope for measuring minute distances

[2]**mi·cro·me·ter** \ˈmī-krō-ˌmēt-ər\ *n* [ISV *micr-* + [3]*meter*] (1880) : a unit of length equal to one millionth of a meter — called also *micron*

mi·crom·e·ter caliper \mī-ˌkräm-ət-ər-\ *n* (ca. 1890) : a caliper having a spindle moved by a finely threaded screw for making precise measurements

mi·cro·meth·od \ˈmī-krō-ˌmeth-əd\ *n* (1919) : a method (as of microanalysis) that requires only very small quantities of material or that involves the use of the microscope

mi·crom·e·try \mī-ˈkräm-ə-trē\ *n* [ISV] (1853) : measurement with a micrometer

mi·cro·mi·cron \ˌmī-krō-ˈmī-ˌkrän\ *n* (ca. 1923) : one millionth of a micrometer

mi·cro·min·ia·ture \-ˈmin-ē-ə-ˌchu̇(ə)r, -ˈmin-i-ˌchu̇(ə)r, -ˈmin-yə-, -chər, -ˌt(y)u̇(ə)r\ *adj* (1958) **1** : MICROMINIATURIZED **2** : suitable for use with microminiaturized parts

mi·cro·min·ia·tur·iza·tion \-ˌmin-ē-ə-ˌchu̇r-ə-ˈzā-shən, -ˌmin-i-ˌchu̇r-, -ˌmin-yə-ˌchu̇r-, -chər-, -ˌt(y)u̇r-\ *n* (1955) : the process of producing microminiaturized things

mi·cro·min·ia·tur·ized *adj* \-ˈmin-ē-ə-chə-ˌrīzd, -ˈmin-i-chə-, -ˈmin-yə-chə-, -ˌtyu̇-ˌrīzd\ (1959) : reduced to or produced in a very small size and esp. in a size smaller than one considered miniature

mi·cro·mole \ˈmī-krə-ˌmōl\ *n* [ISV] (1936) : one millionth of a mole — **mi·cro·mo·lar** \ˌmī-krə-ˈmō-lər\ *adj*

mi·cron \ˈmī-ˌkrän\ *n, pl* **microns** *also* **mi·cra** \-krə\ [NL, fr. Gk *mikron,* neut. of *mikros* small — more at MICR-] (1892) : [2]MICROMETER

Mi·cro·ne·sian \ˌmī-krə-ˈnē-zhən, -shən\ *n* (1847) **1** : a native or inhabitant of Micronesia **2** : a group of Austronesian languages spoken in the Micronesian islands — **Micronesian** *adj*

mi·cron·ize \ˈmī-krə-ˌnīz\ *vt* **-ized; -iz·ing** [*micron*] (1940) : to pulverize esp. into particles a few micrometers in diameter

mi·cro·nu·cle·us \ˌmī-krō-ˈn(y)ü-klē-əs\ *n* [NL] (1892) : a minute nucleus; *specif* : one regarded as primarily concerned with reproductive and genetic functions in most ciliated protozoans

mi·cro·nu·tri·ent \-ˈn(y)ü-trē-ənt\ *n* (1939) **1** : TRACE ELEMENT **2** : an organic compound (as a vitamin) essential in minute amounts to the growth and welfare of an animal

mi·cro·or·gan·ism \-ˈȯr-gə-ˌniz-əm\ *n* [ISV] (1880) : an organism of microscopic or ultramicroscopic size

mi·cro·pa·le·on·tol·o·gy \-ˌpā-lē-ˌän-ˈtäl-ə-jē, -ən-, *esp Brit* -ˌpal-ē-\ *n* [ISV] (1883) : the study of microscopic fossils — **mi·cro·pa·le·on·to·log·i·cal** \-ˌänt-ᵊl-ˈäj-i-kəl\ *also* **mi·cro·pa·le·on·to·log·ic** \-ik\ *adj* — **mi·cro·pa·le·on·tol·o·gist** \-ˌän-ˈtäl-ə-jəst, -ən-\ *n*

mi·cro·phage \ˈmī-krə-ˌfāj, -ˌfäzh\ *n* [ISV] (1890) : a small phagocyte

mi·cro·phone \ˈmī-krə-ˌfōn\ *n* [ISV] (ca. 1875) : an instrument whereby sound waves are caused to generate or modulate an electric current usu. for the purpose of transmitting or recording sound (as speech or music) — **mi·cro·phon·ic** \ˌmī-krə-ˈfän-ik\ *adj*

mi·cro·phon·ics \ˌmī-krə-ˈfän-iks\ *n pl* (1929) : noises in a loudspeaker caused by mechanical shock or vibration of the electronic components

mi·cro·pho·to·graph \-ˈfōt-ə-ˌgraf\ *n* [ISV] (1858) **1** : a small photograph that is normally magnified for viewing : MICROCOPY **2** : PHOTOMICROGRAPH — **microphotograph** *vt* — **mi·cro·pho·tog·ra·pher** \-fə-ˈtäg-rə-fər\ *n* — **mi·cro·pho·to·graph·ic** \-ˌfōt-ə-ˈgraf-ik\ *adj* — **mi·cro·pho·tog·ra·phy** \-fə-ˈtäg-rə-fē\ *n*

mi·cro·pho·tom·e·ter \-fō-ˈtäm-ət-ər\ *n* [ISV] (1899) : an instrument for measuring the amount of light transmitted or reflected by small areas or for measuring the relative densities of spectral lines on a photographic film or plate — **mi·cro·pho·to·met·ric** \-ˌfōt-ə-ˈme-trik\ *adj* — **mi·cro·pho·to·met·ri·cal·ly** \-tri-k(ə-)lē\ *adv* — **mi·cro·pho·tom·e·try** \-fō-ˈtäm-ə-trē\ *n*

mi·cro·phyll \ˈmī-krə-ˌfil\ *n* [ISV] (1935) **1** : a small leaf **2** : a leaf (as of a club moss) that has single unbranched veins and no demonstrable leaf gap — **mi·cro·phyl·lous** \ˌmī-krə-ˈfil-əs\ *adj*

mi·cro·phys·ics \ˌmī-krō-ˈfiz-iks\ *n* (1885) : the physics of molecules, atoms, and elementary particles — **mi·cro·phys·i·cal** \-ˈfiz-i-kəl\ *adj* — **mi·cro·phys·i·cal·ly** \-k(ə-)lē\ *adv*

mi·cro·pi·pette *or* **mi·cro·pi·pet** \-pī-ˈpet\ *n* (1918) **1** : a pipette for the measurement of minute volumes **2** : a small and extremely fine-pointed pipette used in making microinjections

mi·cro·plank·ton \-ˈplaŋ(k)-tən, -ˌtän\ *n* [ISV] (1903) : microscopic plankton

mi·cro·pore \ˈmī-krə-ˌpō(ə)r, -ˌpȯ(ə)r\ *n* [ISV] (1940) : a very fine pore — **mi·cro·po·ros·i·ty** \-pə-ˈräs-ət-ē, -pōr-ˈäs-, -pȯ-ˈräs-\ *n* — **mi·cro·po·rous** \ˌmī-krə-ˈpōr-əs, -ˈpȯr-\ *adj*

mi·cro·prism \ˈmī-krə-ˌpriz-əm\ *n* (ca. 1965) : a usu. circular area on the focusing screen of a camera that is made up of tiny prisms and that causes the image in the viewfinder to blur if the subject is not in focus

mi·cro·probe \-ˌprōb\ *n* (1944) : a device for microanalysis that operates by exciting radiation in a minute area of material so that the composition may be determined from the emission spectrum

mi·cro·pro·ces·sor \ˈmī-krō-ˈpräs-ˌes-ər, -ˈprōs-\ *n* (1970) : a computer processor contained on an integrated-circuit chip; *also* : such a processor with memory and associated circuits

mi·cro·pro·gram \ˌmī-krə-ˈprō-ˌgram, -grəm\ *n* (1953) : a routine composed of microinstructions used in microprogramming

mi·cro·pro·gram·ming \-ˌgram-iŋ\ *n* (1953) : the use of routines stored in memory rather than specialized circuits to control a device (as a computer)

mi·cro·pro·jec·tor \ˌmī-krō-prə-ˈjek-tər\ *n* (1927) : a projector utilizing a compound microscope for projecting on a screen a greatly enlarged image of a microscopic object — **mi·cro·pro·jec·tion** \-ˈjek-shən\ *n*

mi·cro·pub·lish·ing \-ˈpəb-lish-iŋ\ *n* (1966) : publishing in microform — **mi·cro·pub·lish·er** \-lish-ər\ *n*

mi·cro·pul·sa·tion \-ˌpəl-ˈsā-shən\ *n* (1949) : a pulsation having a short period ⟨a ~ of the earth's magnetic field with a period in the range from a fraction of a second to several hundred seconds⟩

mi·cro·punc·ture \-ˈpəŋ(k)-chər\ *n* (1948) : an extremely small puncture ⟨a ~ of the nephron⟩

mi·cro·pyle \ˈmī-krə-ˌpīl\ *n* [ISV *micr-* + Gk *pylē* gate] (1821) **1** : a minute opening in the integument of an ovule of a seed plant through which the pollen tube penetrates to the embryo sac **2** : a differentiated area of surface in an egg through which a sperm enters — **mi·cro·py·lar** \ˌmī-krə-ˈpī-lər\ *adj*

mi·cro·quake \ˈmī-krō-ˌkwāk\ *n* (1967) : MICROEARTHQUAKE

mi·cro·ra·di·og·ra·phy \ˌmī-krō-ˌrād-ē-ˈäg-rə-fē\ *n* (1913) : radiography in which an X-ray photograph is prepared showing minute internal structure — **mi·cro·ra·dio·graph** \-ˈrād-ē-ə-ˌgraf\ *n* — **mi·cro·ra·dio·graph·ic** \-ˌrād-ē-ə-ˈgraf-ik\ *adj*

mi·cro·read·er \ˈmī-krō-ˌrēd-ər\ *n* (1949) : an apparatus that gives an enlarged image of a microphotograph esp. for reading

mi·cro·re·pro·duc·tion \ˈmī-krō-ˌrē-prə-ˈdək-shən\ *n* (1938) : the reproduction of written or printed matter in microform; *also* : an item so reproduced

mi·cro·scale \ˈmī-krō-ˌskāl\ *n* (1931) : a very small scale

mi·cro·scope \ˈmī-krə-ˌskōp\ *n* [NL *microscopium,* fr. *micr-* + *-scopium* -scope] (1654) **1** : an optical instrument consisting of a lens or combination of lenses for making enlarged images of minute objects; *esp* : COMPOUND MICROSCOPE **2** : an instrument using radiations other than light or using vibrations for making enlarged images of minute objects ⟨acoustic ~⟩

mi·cro·scop·ic \ˌmī-krə-ˈskäp-ik\ *or* **mi·cro·scop·i·cal** \-i-kəl\ *adj* (1732) **1** : resembling a microscope esp. in perception **2 a** : invisible or indistinguishable without the use of a microscope **b** : very small or fine or precise **3** : of, relating to, or conducted with the microscope or microscopy — **mi·cro·scop·i·cal·ly** \-i-k(ə-)lē\ *adv*

mi·cros·co·py \mī-ˈkräs-kə-pē\ *n* (ca. 1664) : the use of or investigation with the microscope — **mi·cros·co·pist** \-pəst\ *n*

mi·cro·sec·ond \ˈmī-krō-ˌsek-ənd, -ənt\ *n* [ISV] (1906) : one millionth of a second

mi·cro·seism \ˈmī-krə-ˌsī-zəm\ *n* [ISV] (1887) : a feeble rhythmically and persistently recurring earth tremor — **mi·cro·seis·mic** \ˌmī-krə-ˈsīz-mik, -ˈsīs-\ *adj* — **mi·cro·seis·mic·i·ty** \-sīz-ˈmis-ət-ē, -sīs-\ *n*

mi·cro·some \ˈmī-krə-ˌsōm\ *n* [G *mikrosom,* fr. *mikr-* micr- + *-som* -some] (1885) **1** : any of various minute cellular structures (as a ribosome) **2** : a particle in a particulate fraction that is obtained by heavy centrifugation of broken cells and consists of various amounts of ribosomes, fragmented endoplasmic reticulum, and mitochondrial cristae — **mi·cro·som·al** \ˌmī-krə-ˈsō-məl\ *adj*

mi·cro·spec·tro·pho·tom·e·ter \ˌmī-krə-ˌspek-trə-fō-ˈtäm-ət-ər\ *n* (1949) : a spectrophotometer adapted to the examination of light transmitted by a very small specimen (as a single organic cell) — **mi·cro·spec·tro·pho·to·met·ric** \-ˌfōt-ə-ˈme-trik\ *adj* — **mi·cro·spec·tro·pho·tom·e·try** \-fō-ˈtäm-ə-trē\ *n*

mi·cro·sphere \ˈmī-krə-ˌsfi(ə)r\ *n* (1950) : a minute sphere — **mi·cro·spher·i·cal** \ˌmī-krə-ˈsfir-i-kəl, -ˈsfer-\ *adj*

mi·cro·spo·ran·gi·um \ˌmī-krō-spə-ˈran-jē-əm\ *n* [NL] (1881) : a sporangium that develops only microspores — **mi·cro·spo·ran·gi·ate** \-jē-ət\ *adj*

mi·cro·spore \ˈmī-krə-ˌspō(ə)r, -ˌspȯ(ə)r\ *n* [ISV] (1858) : any of the spores in heterosporous plants that give rise to male gametophytes and are generally smaller than the megaspore — **mi·cro·spo·rous** \ˌmī-krə-ˈspōr-əs, -ˈspȯr-; mī-ˈkräs-pə-rəs\ *adj*

mi·cro·spo·ro·cyte \-ˈspōr-ə-ˌsīt, -ˈspȯr-\ *n* (1940) : a microspore mother cell

mi·cro·spo·ro·gen·e·sis \ˌmī-krə-ˌspōr-ə-ˈjen-ə-səs, -ˌspȯr-\ *n* [NL] (1921) : the formation and maturation of microspores

mi·cro·spo·ro·phyll \-ˌfil\ *n* (ca. 1890) : a sporophyll that develops only microsporangia

mi·cro·state \ˈmī-krō-ˌstāt\ *n* (1967) : a nation that is extremely small in area and population

mi·cro·struc·ture \ˈmī-krō-ˌstrək-chər\ *n* [ISV] (1885) : the microscopic structure of a material (as a mineral or a biological cell) — **mi·cro·struc·tur·al** \ˌmī-krō-ˈstrək-chə-rəl, -ˈstrək-shrəl\ *adj*

mi·cro·sur·gery \ˌmī-krō-ˈsərj-(ə-)rē\ *n* (1926) : minute dissection or manipulation (as by a micromanipulator or laser beam) of living structures (as cells) for surgical or experimental purposes — **mi·cro·sur·gi·cal** \-ˈsər-ji-kəl\ *adj*

mi·cro·tech·nique \ˌmī-krō-tek-ˈnēk\ *also* **mi·cro·tech·nic** \ˈmī-krō-ˌtek-nik, ˌmī-krō-tek-ˈnēk\ *n* [ISV] (1892) : any of various methods of handling and preparing material for microscopic observation and study

mi·cro·tome \ˈmī-krə-ˌtōm\ *n* [ISV] (1856) : an instrument for cutting sections (as of organic tissues) for microscopic examination

mi·cro·tone \ˈmī-krə-ˌtōn\ *n* (1920) : a musical interval smaller than a halftone — **mi·cro·ton·al** \ˌmī-krə-ˈtōn-ᵊl\ *adj* — **mi·cro·to·nal·i·ty** \-tō-ˈnal-ət-ē\ *n* — **mi·cro·ton·al·ly** \-ˈtōn-ᵊl-ē\ *adv*

mi·cro·tu·bule \ˌmī-krō-ˈt(y)ü-(ˌ)byü(ə)l\ *n* (1961) : any of the minute cylindrical structures in cells that are widely distributed in protoplasm and are made up of protein subunits — **mi·cro·tu·bu·lar** \-byə-lər\ *adj*

mi·cro·vas·cu·lar \-ˈvas-kyə-lər\ *adj* (1959) : of, relating to, or constituting the part of the circulatory system made up of minute vessels (as venules or capillaries) that average less than 0.3 millimeters in diameter — **mi·cro·vas·cu·la·ture** \-lə-ˌchu̇(ə)r, -ˌt(y)u̇(ə)r\ *n*

mi·cro·vil·lus \-ˈvil-əs\ *n* [NL] (1953) : a microscopic projection of a tissue, cell, or cell organelle; *esp* : any of the fingerlike outward projections of some cell surfaces — **mi·cro·vil·lar** \-ˈvil-ər\ *adj* — **mi·cro·vil·lous** \-ˈvil-əs\ *adj*

mi·cro·volt \ˈmī-krə-ˌvōlt\ *n* (1868) : one millionth of a volt

mi·cro·watt \-ˌwät\ *n* (ca. 1909) : one millionth of a watt

[1]**mi·cro·wave** \-ˌwāv\ *n, often attrib* (1931) : a comparatively short electromagnetic wave; *esp* : one between about 1 millimeter and 1 meter in wavelength

[2]**microwave** *vt* (1973) : to cook or heat in a microwave oven — **mi·cro·wav·able** *or* **mi·cro·wave·able** \ˌmī-krō-ˈwā-və-bəl\ *adj*

microwave oven *n* (1963) : an oven in which food is cooked by the heat produced as a result of microwave penetration of the food

mic·tu·rate \ˈmik-chə-ˌrāt, ˈmik-tə-\ *vi* **-rat·ed; -rat·ing** [L *micturire,* fr. *mictus,* pp. of *mingere;* akin to OE *mīgan* to urinate, Gk *omeichein*] (1842) : URINATE — **mic·tu·ri·tion** \ˌmik-chə-ˈrish-ən, ˌmik-tə-\ *n*

¹mid \ˈmid\ *adj* [ME, fr. OE *midde;* akin to OHG *mitti* middle, L *medius,* Gk *mesos*] (bef. 12c) **1 :** being the part in the middle or midst ⟨in ~ ocean⟩ — often used in combination ⟨*mid*-August⟩ **2 :** occupying a middle position ⟨the ~ finger⟩ **3** *of a vowel* **:** articulated with the arch of the tongue midway between its highest and its lowest elevation — **mid** *adv*

²mid \(ˌ)mid\ *prep* (1808) **:** AMID

mid·air \ˈmid-ˈa(ə)r, -ˈe(ə)r\ *n* (1667) **:** a point or region in the air not immediately adjacent to the ground ⟨planes collided in ~⟩

Mi·das \ˈmī-dəs\ *n* [L, fr. Gk] **:** a legendary Phrygian king who is given the power of turning everything he touches to gold

mid·brain \ˈmid-ˌbrān\ *n* (1875) **:** the middle division of the three primary divisions of the embryonic vertebrate brain; *also* **:** the parts of the definitive brain developed from it — see BRAIN illustration

mid·day \ˈmid-ˌdā, -ˈdā\ *n, often attrib* [ME, fr. OE *middæg,* fr. *midde* + *dæg* day] (bef. 12c) **:** the middle of the day

mid·den \ˈmid-ᵊn\ *n* [ME *midding,* of Scand origin; akin to ON *myki* dung & ON *dyngja* manure pile — more at MUCUS, DUNG] (14c) **1 :** DUNGHILL **2 :** a refuse heap; *esp* **:** KITCHEN MIDDEN

¹mid·dle \ˈmid-ᵊl\ *adj* [ME *middel,* fr. OE; akin to L *medius*] (bef. 12c) **1 :** equally distant from the extremes **:** MEDIAL, CENTRAL ⟨the ~ house in the row⟩ **2 :** being at neither extreme **:** INTERMEDIATE **3** *cap* **a :** constituting a division intermediate between those prior and later or upper and lower ⟨*Middle* Paleozoic⟩ **b :** constituting a period of a language or literature intermediate between one called *Old* and one called *New* or *Modern* ⟨*Middle* Dutch⟩ **4** *of a verb form or voice* **:** typically asserting that a person or thing both performs and is affected by the action represented

²middle *n* (bef. 12c) **1 :** a middle part, point, or position **2 :** the central portion of the human body **:** WAIST **3 :** the position of being among or in the midst of something **4 :** something intermediate between extremes **:** MEAN **5 :** the center of an offensive or defensive formation; *esp* **:** the area between the second baseman and the shortstop

middle age *n* (14c) **:** the period of life from about 40 to about 60 — **mid·dle–aged** \ˌmid-ᵊl-ˈājd\ *adj* — **middle–ag·er** \-ˈā-jər\ *n*

Middle Ages *n pl* (1722) **:** the period of European history from about A.D. 500 to about 1500

Middle America *n* (1898) **1 :** the region of the western hemisphere including Mexico, Central America, often the West Indies, and sometimes Colombia and Venezuela **2 :** the midwestern section of the U.S. **3 :** the middle-class segment of the U.S. population; *esp* **:** the traditional or conservative element of the middle class — **Middle American** *n* — **middle–American** *adj*

mid·dle·brow \ˈmid-ᵊl-ˌbrau̇\ *n* (1925) **:** a person who is moderately but not highly cultivated — **middlebrow** *adj*

middle C *n* (1840) **:** the note designated by the first ledger line below the treble staff and the first above the bass staff

mid·dle–class \ˌmid-ᵊl-ˈklas\ *adj* (1836) **:** of or relating to the middle class; *esp* **:** characterized by a high material standard of living, sexual morality, and respect for property — **mid·dle–class·ness** \-nəs\ *n*

middle class *n* (1812) **:** a class occupying a position between the upper class and the lower class; *esp* **:** a fluid heterogeneous socioeconomic grouping composed principally of business and professional people, bureaucrats, and some farmers and skilled workers sharing common social characteristics and values

middle distance *n* (1813) **1 :** a part of a pictorial representation or scene between the foreground and the background **2 :** any footrace distance usu. from 800 meters or 880 yards to 1500 meters or one mile

middle ear *n* (ca. 1860) **:** a small membrane-lined cavity that is separated from the outer ear by the eardrum and that transmits sound waves from the eardrum to the partition between the middle and inner ears through a chain of tiny bones

Middle English *n* (1830) **:** the English in use from the 12th to 15th centuries — see INDO-EUROPEAN LANGUAGES table

middle finger *n* (bef. 12c) **:** the midmost of the five digits of the hand

Middle French *n* (ca. 1890) **:** the French in use from the 14th to 16th centuries — see INDO-EUROPEAN LANGUAGES table

middle game *n* (1938) **:** the middle phase of a board game; *specif* **:** the part of a chess game after the pieces have been developed when players attempt to gain and exploit positional and material superiority — compare ENDGAME, OPENING

Middle Greek *n* (ca. 1890) **:** the Greek language used in the 7th to 15th centuries

middle ground *n* (ca. 1850) **1 :** MIDDLE DISTANCE 1 **2 :** a standpoint midway between extremes

Middle High German *n* (ca. 1890) **:** the High German in use from about 1100 to 1500 — see INDO-EUROPEAN LANGUAGES table

Middle Irish *n* (ca. 1952) **:** the Irish in use between the 11th and 15th centuries — see INDO-EUROPEAN LANGUAGES table

middle lamella *n* (ca. 1886) **:** a layer of pectinaceous intercellular material that as seen by conventional staining and microscopic techniques lies between the walls of adjacent plant cells — see CELL illustration

Middle Low German *n* (ca. 1890) **:** the Low German in use from about 1100 to 1500 — see INDO-EUROPEAN LANGUAGES table

mid·dle·man \ˈmid-ᵊl-ˌman\ *n* (1795) **:** an intermediary or agent between two parties; *esp* **:** a dealer or agent intermediate between the producer of goods and the retailer or consumer

middle management *n* (ca. 1948) **:** management personnel intermediate between operational supervisors and policy-making administrators — **middle manager** *n*

middle name *n* (1835) **:** a name between one's first name and surname

middle–of–the–road *adj* (1894) **:** standing for or following a course of action midway between extremes; *esp* **:** being neither liberal nor conservative in politics — **mid·dle–of–the–road·er** \-ˈrōd-ər\ *n* — **mid·dle–of–the–road·ism** \-ˈrōd-ˌiz-əm\ *n*

middle of the road (1777) **:** a course of action or a standpoint midway between extremes

mid·dler \ˈmid-lər, -ᵊl-ər\ *n* (1882) **:** one belonging to an intermediate group, division, or class: as **a :** a student in the second-year class of a three-year program (as at a seminary or law school) **b :** a student in the second- or third-year class in some private secondary schools having a four-year course **c :** a student in a division in some private schools that corresponds approximately to junior high school

middle school *n* (1945) **:** a school including grades 5 to 8 or 6 to 8

Middle Scots *n* (ca. 1903) **:** the Scots language in use between the latter half of the 15th and the early decades of the 17th centuries

middle term *n* (1685) **:** the term of a syllogism that occurs in both premises

mid·dle·weight \ˈmid-ᵊl-ˌwāt\ *n* (1889) **:** one of average weight; *specif* **:** a boxer in a weight division having a maximum limit of 160 pounds for professionals and 165 pounds for amateurs — compare LIGHT HEAVYWEIGHT, WELTERWEIGHT

Middle Welsh *n* (ca. 1922) **:** the Welsh in use from about 1150 to 1500 — see INDO-EUROPEAN LANGUAGES table

¹mid·dling \ˈmid-liŋ, -lən\ *n* (1543) **1 :** any of various commodities of intermediate size, quality, or position **2** *pl but sing or pl in constr* **:** a granular product of grain milling; *esp* **:** a wheat milling by-product used in animal feeds

²middling *adj* (1596) **1 :** of middle, medium, or moderate size, degree, or quality **2 :** MEDIOCRE, SECOND-RATE — **mid·dling** *adv* — **mid·dling·ly** \-liŋ-lē, -lən-\ *adv*

mid·dor·sal \(ˈ)mid-ˈdȯr-səl\ *adj* (1879) **:** situated in the middle part or median line of the back

mid·dy \ˈmid-ē\ *n, pl* **middies** [by shortening & alter.] (1818) **1 :** MIDSHIPMAN **2 :** a loosely fitting blouse with a sailor collar worn by women and children

mid·field \ˈmid-ˌfēld, (ˈ)mid-ˈ\ *n* (15c) **1 :** the middle portion of a field; *esp* **:** the portion of a playing field (as in football) that is midway between goals **2 :** the players on a team (as in lacrosse) that normally play in midfield

mid·field·er \-ər\ *n* (ca. 1938) **:** a member of a midfield (as in lacrosse)

Mid·gard \ˈmid-ˌgärd\ *n* [ON *mithgarthr*] **:** the abode of human beings in Norse mythology

midge \ˈmij\ *n* [ME *migge,* fr. OE *mycg;* akin to OHG *mucka* midge, Gk *myia* fly, L *musca*] (bef. 12c) **:** a tiny two-winged fly (as a chironomid)

midg·et \ˈmij-ət\ *n* [*midge*] (1865) **1 :** a very small person; *specif* **:** a person of unusually small size who is physically well-proportioned **2 :** something (as an animal) much smaller than usual **3 :** a front-engine, single-seat, open-wheel racing car smaller and of less engine displacement than standard cars of the type — **midget** *adj*

mid·gut \ˈmid-ˌgət\ *n* (1875) **:** the middle part of an alimentary canal

midi \ˈmid-ē\ *n* [ˈ*mid* + *-i* (as in *mini*)] (1967) **:** a dress, skirt, or coat that usu. extends to the mid-calf

Mid·i·an·ite \ˈmid-ē-ə-ˌnīt\ *n* [*Midian,* son of Abraham] (14c) **:** a member of an ancient northern Arabian people

mid·land \ˈmid-lənd, -ˌland\ *n* (1555) **1 :** the interior or central region of a country **2** *cap* **a :** the dialect of English spoken in the midland counties of England **b :** the dialect of English spoken in an area of the east central U.S. often divided into north Midland extending westward from an area including southern New Jersey; northern Delaware and Maryland; central and southern Pennsylvania; and central Ohio, Indiana, and Illinois and south Midland extending westward and southwestward from an area including the Appalachian regions of Virginia, No. Carolina, So. Carolina, and Georgia; Tennessee, Kentucky, West Virginia; and southern Ohio, Indiana, and Illinois — **midland** *adj, often cap*

mid–life \(ˈ)mid-ˈlīf\ *n* (1898) **:** MIDDLE AGE

mid·line \-ˌlīn, -ˈlīn\ *n* (1868) **:** a median line; *esp* **:** the median line or median plane of the body or some part of the body

mid·most \-ˌmōst\ *adj* (bef. 12c) **1 :** being in or near the exact middle **2 :** most intimate **:** INNERMOST — **midmost** *adv or n*

mid·night \ˈmid-ˌnīt\ *n* (bef. 12c) **1 :** the middle of the night; *specif* **:** 12 o'clock at night **2 :** deep or extended darkness or gloom — **midnight** *adj* — **mid·night·ly** *adv or adj*

midnight sun *n* (1857) **:** the sun above the horizon at midnight in the arctic or antarctic summer

mid·point \ˈmid-ˌpȯint, -ˈpȯint\ *n* (14c) **:** a point at or near the center or middle

mid·rash \ˈmid-ˌräsh\ *n, pl* **mid·rash·im** \mid-ˈräsh-əm\ [Heb *midhrāsh* exposition, explanation] (1613) **1 :** a haggadic or halakic exposition of the underlying significance of a Bible text **2 :** a collection of midrashim **3** *cap* **:** the midrashic literature written during the first Christian millennium — **mid·rash·ic** \mid-ˈräsh-ik\ *adj, often cap*

mid·rib \ˈmid-ˌrib\ *n* (ca. 1776) **:** the central vein of a leaf

mid·riff \ˈmid-ˌrif\ *n* [ME *midrif,* fr. OE *midhrif,* fr. *midde* mid + *hrif* belly; akin to OHG *href* body, L *corpus*] (bef. 12c) **1 :** DIAPHRAGM 1 **2 :** the mid-region of the human torso **3 a :** a section of a woman's garment that covers the midriff **b :** a woman's garment that exposes the midriff

mid–rise \ˈmid-ˌrīz, -ˈrīz\ *adj* (1967) **:** being approximately 5 to 10 stories high ⟨~ condominiums⟩

mid·sag·it·tal \(ˈ)mid-ˈsaj-ət-ᵊl\ *adj* (1947) **:** median and sagittal

mid·sec·tion \ˈmid-ˌsek-shən\ *n* (1936) **:** a section midway between the extremes; *esp* **:** MIDRIFF 2

mid·ship·man \ˈmid-ˌship-mən, (ˈ)mid-ˈ\ *n* (1626) **:** one in training for a naval commission; *esp* **:** a student in a naval academy

mid·ships \ˈmid-ˌships\ *adv* (ca. 1828) **:** AMIDSHIPS

mid·size \ˈmid-ˌsīz\ *adj* (1970) **:** of intermediate size ⟨~ car⟩

midst \ˈmidst, ˈmitst\ *n* [ME *middest,* alter. of *middes,* back-formation fr. *amiddes* amid] (15c) **1 :** the interior or central part or point **:** MIDDLE, INTERIOR ⟨in the ~ of the forest⟩ **2 :** a position of proximity to the members of a group or company ⟨a visitor in our ~⟩ **3 :** the condition of being surrounded or beset ⟨in the ~ of his troubles⟩ **4 :** a period of time about the middle of a continuing act or condition ⟨in the ~ of a long reign⟩ — **midst** *prep*

mid·stream \ˈmid-ˈstrēm, -ˌstrēm\ *n* (1669) **1 :** the portion of a stream away from both sides ⟨keep the boat in ~⟩ **2 :** the portion of a course away from both the beginning and the end ⟨in the ~ of his career — Arthur Berger⟩

mid·sum·mer \ˈmid-ˈsəm-ər, -ˌsəm-\ *n* (bef. 12c) **1 :** the middle of summer **2 :** the summer solstice — **midsummer** *adj*

Midsummer Day *n* (bef. 12c) **:** June 24 celebrated as the feast of the nativity of John the Baptist

mid·term \ˈmid-ˌtərm (*usual for 1b*), -ˈtərm\ *n* (1906) **1 a :** the middle of an academic term **b :** an examination at midterm **2 :** the approximate middle of a term of office

mid·town \ˈmid-ˌtau̇n, -ˈtau̇n\ *n* (1926) **:** a central section of a city; *esp* **:** one situated between sections conventionally called *downtown* and *uptown* — **midtown** *adj*

1**mid·way** \ˈmid-ˌwā, -ˈwā\ *adv* (13c) **:** in the middle of the way or distance **:** HALFWAY

2**mid·way** \-ˌwā\ *n* [*Midway (Plaisance)*, Chicago, site of the amusement section of the Columbian Exposition 1893] (1893) **:** an avenue at a fair, carnival, or amusement park for concessions and amusements

mid·week \-ˌwēk\ *n* (1707) **:** the middle of the week — **midweek** *adj* — **mid·week·ly** \-ˌwē-klē, -ˈwē-\ *adj or adv*

1**mid·wife** \ˈmid-ˌwīf\ *n* [ME *midwif*, fr. *mid* with (fr. OE) + *wif* woman] (14c) **1 :** one who assists women in childbirth **2 :** one that helps to produce or bring forth something

2**midwife** *vt* **mid·wifed** \-ˌwīft\ *or* **mid·wived** \-ˌwīvd\; **mid·wif·ing** *or* **mid·wiv·ing** (1638) **:** to assist in producing, bringing forth, or bringing about

mid·wife·ry \ˌmid-ˈwif-(ə-)rē, -ˈwīf-; ˈmid-ˌwīf-\ *n* (15c) **1 :** the art or act of assisting at childbirth; *also* **:** OBSTETRICS **2 :** the art, act, or process of producing, bringing forth, or bringing about

mid·win·ter \ˈmid-ˈwint-ər, -ˌwint-\ *n* (bef. 12c) **1 :** the middle of winter **2 :** the winter solstice — **midwinter** *adj*

mid·year \-ˌyi(ə)r\ *n* (1897) **1 a :** an examination at the middle of an academic year **b** *pl* **:** the set of examinations at the middle of an academic year; *also* **:** the period of such examinations **2 a :** the middle or middle portion of a calendar year **b :** the middle of an academic year — **midyear** *adj*

mien \ˈmēn\ *n* [by shortening & alter. of 1*demean*] (1513) **1 :** air or bearing esp. as expressive of mood or personality **:** DEMEANOR ⟨beneath that ~ of a commercial traveller who has been everywhere . . . he was very nervous —Arnold Bennett⟩ **2 :** APPEARANCE, ASPECT ⟨the inherent dangers of government encroachment . . . presented such a distasteful ~ —H. W. Baldwin⟩ ***syn*** see BEARING

1**miff** \ˈmif\ *n* [origin unknown] (1623) **1 :** a fit of ill humor **2 :** a trivial quarrel

2**miff** *vt* (1811) **:** to put into an ill humor **:** OFFEND

1**might** \(ˈ)mīt\ [ME, fr. OE *meahte, mihte;* akin to OHG *mahta, mohta* could] *past of* MAY (bef. 12c) — used in auxiliary function to express permission, liberty, probability, possibility in the past ⟨the president ~ do nothing without the board's consent⟩ or a present condition contrary to fact ⟨if you were older you ~ understand⟩ or less probability or possibility than *may* ⟨~ get there before it rains⟩ or as a polite alternative to *may* ⟨~ I ask who is calling⟩ or to *ought* or *should* ⟨you ~ at least apologize⟩

2**might** \ˈmīt\ *n* [ME, fr. OE *miht;* akin to OHG *maht* might, *magan* to be able — more at MAY] (bef. 12c) **1 a :** the power, authority, or resources wielded (as by an individual or group) ⟨the growing ~ of the middle class⟩ **b** (1) **:** bodily strength (2) **:** the power, energy, or intensity of which one is capable ⟨striving with ~ and main⟩ **2** *dial* **:** a great deal ***syn*** see POWER

might·i·ly \ˈmīt-ᵊl-ē\ *adv* (bef. 12c) **1 :** in a mighty manner **:** VIGOROUSLY ⟨applauded ~⟩ **2 :** very much ⟨depressed me ~⟩

might·i·ness \ˈmīt-ē-nəs\ *n* (14c) **:** the quality or state of being mighty

mightn't \ˈmīt-ᵊnt\ **:** might not

1**mighty** \ˈmīt-ē\ *adj* **might·i·er; -est** (bef. 12c) **1 :** possessing might **:** POWERFUL **2 :** accomplished or characterized by might ⟨a ~ thrust⟩ **3 :** great or imposing in size or extent **:** EXTRAORDINARY

2**mighty** *adv* (14c) **:** EXTREMELY, VERY ⟨a ~ handy gadget⟩

usage The use of *mighty* as an intensive usu. conveys a folksy down-home feeling ⟨plain and simple fare . . . but *mighty* filling and *mighty* satisfying —*Asheville (N.C.) Citizen-Times*⟩ It is used esp. to create a chatty style ⟨turnip greens, corn bread and biscuits. That sounds *mighty* good to me — Julia Child⟩ or to stress a rural atmosphere ⟨a man must be *mighty* serious about his squirrel hunting —Stuart Williams, *Field & Stream*⟩ In a more formal context, *mighty* is used to create additional emphasis by drawing attention to itself ⟨the chairman made sure that there were *mighty* few of them —Mollie Panter-Downes⟩

mi·gnon \mēn-ˈyōⁿ\ *n* (ca. 1950) **:** FILET MIGNON

mi·gnon·ette \ˌmin-yə-ˈnet\ *n* [F *mignonnette*, fr. obs. F, fem. of *mignonnet* dainty, fr. MF, fr. *mignon* darling] (1752) **:** any of a genus (*Reseda* of the family Resedaceae, the mignonette family) of herbs; *esp* **:** a garden annual (*R. odorata*) bearing racemes of fragrant greenish yellow flowers

mi·graine \ˈmī-ˌgrān, *Brit often* ˈmē-\ *n* [F, fr. LL *hemicrania* pain in one side of the head, fr. Gk *hēmikrania*, fr. *hēmi-* hemi- + *kranion* cranium] (15c) **:** a condition marked by recurrent severe headache often with nausea and vomiting — **mi·grain·ous** \-ˈgrā-nəs\ *adj*

mi·grant \ˈmī-grənt\ *n* [L *migrant-, migrans*, prp. of *migrare*] (1768) **:** one that migrates: as **a :** a person who moves regularly in order to find work esp. in harvesting crops **b :** an animal that shifts from one habitat to another — **migrant** *adj*

mi·grate \ˈmī-ˌgrāt, mī-ˈ\ *vi* **mi·grat·ed; mi·grat·ing** [L *migratus*, pp. of *migrare;* akin to Gk *ameibein* to change] (1697) **1 :** to move from one country, place, or locality to another **2 :** to pass usu. periodically from one region or climate to another for feeding or breeding **3 :** to change position in an organism or substance ⟨filarial worms ~ within the human body⟩ — **mi·gra·tion** \mī-ˈgrā-shən\ *n* — **mi·gra·tion·al** \-shnəl, -shən-ᵊl\ *adj* — **mi·gra·tor** \ˈmī-ˌgrāt-ər, mī-ˈ\ *n*

mi·gra·to·ry \ˈmī-grə-ˌtōr-ē, -ˌtȯr-\ *adj* (ca. 1753) **1 :** of, relating to, or characterized by migration **2 :** WANDERING, ROVING

mih·rab \ˈmē-rəb\ *n* [Ar *miḥrāb*] (1816) **:** a niche or chamber in a mosque indicating the direction of Mecca

mi·ka·do \mə-ˈkäd-(ˌ)ō\ *n, pl* **-dos** [Jp] (1727) **:** an emperor of Japan

mike \ˈmīk\ *n* [by shortening & alter.] (1925) **:** MICROPHONE

Mike \ˈmīk\ (1943) — a communications code word for the letter *m*

mil \ˈmil\ *n* [L *mille* thousand] (1721) **1 :** THOUSAND ⟨found a salinity of 38.4 per ~⟩ **2 :** a monetary unit formerly used in Cyprus equal to 1/1000 pound **3 :** a unit of length equal to 1/1000 inch used esp. for the diameter of wire **4 :** a unit of angular measurement equal to 1/6400 of 360 degrees and used esp. in artillery

mi·la·dy \mil-ˈād-ē, *US also* mi-ˈlād-\ *n* [F, fr. E *my lady*] (1839) **1 :** an Englishwoman of noble or gentle birth **2 :** a woman of fashion

milch \ˈmilk, ˈmilch, ˈmilks\ *adj* [ME *milche*, fr. OE *-milce;* akin to OE *melcan* to milk — more at EMULSION] (13c) **:** MILK

mil·chig \ˈmilk̲-ik\ *adj* [Yiddish, fr. *milch* milk, fr. MHG, fr. OHG *miluh* — more at MILK] (ca. 1928) **:** made of or derived from milk or dairy products — compare FLEISHIG, PAREVE

mild \ˈmī(ə)ld\ *adj* [ME, fr. OE *milde;* akin to Gk *malthakos* soft, OE *melu* meal — more at MEAL] (bef. 12c) **1 :** gentle in nature or behavior ⟨has a ~ disposition⟩ **2 a :** moderate in action or effect ⟨a ~ cigar⟩ **b :** not being or involving what is extreme ⟨an analysis under ~ conditions⟩ ⟨a ~ slope⟩ **3 :** not severe **:** TEMPERATE ⟨a ~ climate⟩ ⟨~ symptoms of disease⟩ **4 :** comparatively soft and easily worked **:** MALLEABLE ⟨~ steel⟩ — **mild·ly** \ˈmī(ə)l-(d)lē\ *adv* — **mild·ness** \ˈmī(ə)l(d)-nəs\ *n*

1**mil·dew** \ˈmil-ˌd(y)ü\ *n* [ME, fr. OE *meledēaw;* akin to OHG *militou* honeydew] (14c) **1 a :** a superficial usu. whitish growth produced on organic matter or living plants by fungi (as of the families Erysiphaceae and Peronosporaceae) **b :** a fungus producing mildew **2 :** a discoloration caused by fungi — **mil·dewy** \-ē\ *adj*

2**mildew** *vt* (1552) **:** to affect with or as if with mildew ~ *vi* **:** to become affected with mildew

mile \ˈmī(ə)l\ *n* [ME, fr. OE *mīl*, fr. L *milia* miles, fr. *milia passuum*, lit., thousands of paces, fr. *milia*, pl. of *mille* thousand] (bef. 12c) **1 :** any of various units of distance: as **a :** a unit equal to 5280 feet — see WEIGHT table **b :** NAUTICAL MILE **2 :** a race of a mile **3 :** a relatively great distance

mile·age \ˈmī-lij\ *n* (1754) **1 :** an allowance for traveling expenses at a certain rate per mile **2 :** aggregate length or distance in miles: as **a :** the total miles traveled in a day or other period of time **b :** the amount of service that something will yield esp. as expressed in terms of miles of travel **c :** the average number of miles a car will travel on a gallon of gas ⟨gets good ~⟩ **3 :** USEFULNESS, PROFIT

mile·post \ˈmī(ə)l-ˌpōst\ *n* (1768) **:** a post indicating the distance in miles from or to a given point; *also* **:** a post placed a mile from a similar post

mil·er \ˈmī-lər\ *n* (1889) **:** one that competes in mile races

-mil·er \ˈmī-lər\ *n comb form* **1 :** one that competes in a race of a specified number of miles ⟨the best quarter-*miler* in our school⟩ **2 :** one that is a specified number of miles in length ⟨the ski run was a two-*miler*⟩

mi·les glo·ri·o·sus \ˈmē-ˌlās-ˌglōr-ə-ˈō-səs, -ˌglȯr-\ *n, pl* **mi·li·tes glo·ri·o·si** \ˈmē-lə-ˌtās-ˌglōr-ē-ˈō-(ˌ)sē, -ˌglȯr-\ [L] (ca. 1902) **:** a boastful soldier; *esp* **:** a stock character of this type in comedy

mi·le·si·mo \mi-ˈles-ə-ˌmō, -ˈlās-\ *n, pl* **-mos** [Sp, fr. *milésimo* one thousandth] (ca. 1916) **:** a former Chilean monetary unit equal to 1/1000 escudo

mile·stone \ˈmī(ə)l-ˌstōn\ *n* (1746) **1 :** a stone serving as a milepost **2 :** a significant point in development

mil·foil \ˈmil-ˌfȯil\ *n* [ME, fr. OF, fr. L *millefolium*, fr. *mille* + *folium* leaf — more at BLADE] (13c) **1 :** YARROW **2 :** WATER MILFOIL

mil·i·ar·ia \ˌmil-ē-ˈar-ē-ə, -ˈer-\ *n* [NL, fr. L, fem. of *miliarius*] (1807) **:** an inflammatory disorder of the skin characterized by redness, eruption, burning or itching, and the release of sweat in abnormal ways (as by the eruption of vesicles) due to blockage of the ducts of the sweat glands; *esp* **:** PRICKLY HEAT — **mil·i·ar·i·al** \-əl\ *adj*

mil·i·ary \ˈmil-ē-ˌer-ē\ *adj* [L *miliarius* of millet, fr. *milium* millet — more at MILLET] (1760) **:** having or made up of many small projections or lesions ⟨~ tubercles⟩

mi·lieu \mēl-ˈyə(r), -ˈyü; ˈmēl-ˌyü, mē-lyœ̄\ *n, pl* **milieus** *or* **mi·lieux** \-ˈyə(r)(z), -ˈyüz; -ˌyü(z), -lyœ̄(z)\ [F, fr. OF, midst, fr. *mi* middle (fr. L *medius*) + *lieu* place, fr. L *locus* — more at MID, STALL] (1854) **:** ENVIRONMENT, SETTING

mil·i·tance \ˈmil-ə-tən(t)s\ *n* (1946) **:** MILITANCY

mil·i·tan·cy \-tən-sē\ *n* (1648) **:** the quality or state of being militant

mil·i·tant \-tənt\ *adj* (15c) **1 :** engaged in warfare or combat **:** FIGHTING **2 :** aggressively active (as in a cause) **:** COMBATIVE ⟨~ conservationists⟩ ⟨a ~ attitude⟩ ***syn*** see AGGRESSIVE — **militant** *n* — **mil·i·tant·ly** *adv* — **mil·i·tant·ness** *n*

mil·i·tar·ia \ˌmil-ə-ˈter-ē-ə\ *n pl* (1964) **:** military objects (as firearms and uniforms) of historical value or interest

mil·i·tari·ly \ˌmil-ə-ˈter-ə-lē\ *adv* (1660) **1 :** in a military manner **2 :** from a military standpoint

mil·i·ta·rism \ˈmil-ə-tə-ˌriz-əm\ *n* (1864) **1 a :** predominance of the military class or its ideals **b :** exaltation of military virtues and ideals **2 :** a policy of aggressive military preparedness — **mil·i·ta·rist** \-rəst\ *n* — **mil·i·ta·ris·tic** \ˌmil-ə-tə-ˈris-tik\ *adj* — **mil·i·ta·ris·ti·cal·ly** \-ti-k(ə-)lē\ *adv*

mil·i·ta·rize \ˈmil-ə-tə-ˌrīz\ *vt* **-rized; -riz·ing** (1880) **1 :** to equip with military forces and defenses **2 :** to give a military character to **3 :** to adapt for military use — **mil·i·ta·ri·za·tion** \ˌmil-ə-t(ə-)rə-ˈzā-shən\ *n*

1**mil·i·tary** \ˈmil-ə-ˌter-ē\ *adj* [MF *militaire*, fr. L *militaris*, fr. *milit-, miles* soldier] (15c) **1 a :** of or relating to soldiers, arms, or war **b :** of or relating to armed forces; *esp* **:** of or relating to ground or sometimes ground and air forces as opposed to naval forces **2 a :** performed or made by armed forces **b :** supported by armed force **3 :** of or relating to the army

2**military** *n, pl* **military** *also* **mil·i·tar·ies** (15c) **1 :** ARMED FORCES **2 :** military persons; *esp* **:** army officers

military police *n* (1827) **:** a branch of an army that exercises guard and police functions

military science *n* (ca. 1830) **:** the principles of military conflict

mil·i·tate \ˈmil-ə-ˌtāt\ *vi* **-tat·ed; -tat·ing** [L *militatus*, pp. of *militare* to engage in warfare, fr. *milit-, miles*] (1642) **:** to have weight or effect ⟨his boyish appearance *militated* against his getting an early promotion⟩ ***usage*** see MITIGATE

mi·li·tia \mə-ˈlish-ə\ *n* [L, military service, fr. *milit-, miles*] (ca. 1659) **1 :** a part of the organized armed forces of a country liable to call only in emergency **2 :** the whole body of able-bodied male citizens declared by law as being subject to call to military service — **mi·li·tia·man** \-mən\ *n*

mil·i·um \'mil-ē-əm\ *n, pl* **mil·ia** \-ē-ə\ [NL, fr. L, millet — more at MILLET] (1856) : a small whitish lump in the skin due to retention of secretion in an oil gland duct

[1]**milk** \'milk\ *n* [ME, fr. OE *meolc, milc;* akin to OHG *miluh* milk] (bef. 12c) **1 a :** a fluid secreted by the mammary glands of females for the nourishment of their young; *esp* **:** cow's milk used as a food by humans **b :** LACTATION ⟨cows in ~⟩ **2 :** a liquid resembling milk in appearance: as **a :** the latex of a plant **b :** the juice of a coconut **c :** the contents of an unripe kernel of grain

[2]**milk** *vt* [ME *milken,* fr. OE *melcan;* akin to OE *meolc* milk — more at EMULSION] (bef. 12c) **1 a** (1) **:** to draw milk from the breasts or udder of (2) *obs* **:** SUCKLE 2 **b :** to draw (milk) from the breast or udder **c :** SUCKLE 1 — used of lower mammals **2 :** to draw something from as if by milking: as **a :** to induce (a snake) to eject venom **b :** to compel or persuade to yield profit or advantage illicitly or to an unreasonable degree **:** EXPLOIT ~ *vi* **:** to draw or yield milk — **milk·er** *n*

[3]**milk** *adj* (14c) **:** giving milk; *specif* **:** bred or suitable primarily for milk production ⟨~ cows⟩

milk–and–wa·ter \,mil-kən-'(d)wȯt-ər, -'(d)wät-\ *adj* (1783) **:** WEAK, INSIPID

milk fever *n* (1758) **1 :** a febrile disorder following parturition **2 :** a disease of fresh cows, sheep, or goats that is caused by excessive drain on the body mineral reserves during the establishment of the milk flow

milk·fish \'milk-,fish\ *n* (ca. 1900) **:** a large active silvery herbivorous food fish (*Chanos chanos*) that is widely distributed in the warm parts of the Pacific and Indian oceans and is the sole living representative of its family (Chanidae)

milk glass *n* (1874) **:** an opaque and typically milk white glass used esp. for novelty and ornamental objects

milk house *n* (1589) **:** a building for the cooling, handling, or bottling of milk

milk leg *n* (ca. 1860) **:** a painful swelling of the leg at childbirth caused by inflammation and clotting in the veins

milk–liv·ered \'mil-'kliv-ərd\ *adj, archaic* (1605) **:** COWARDLY, TIMOROUS

milk·maid \'milk-,mād\ *n* (1552) **:** DAIRYMAID

milk·man \-,man, -mən\ *n* (1589) **:** one who sells or delivers milk and milk products

milk of magnesia (1880) **:** a milk-white suspension of magnesium hydroxide in water used as an antacid and laxative

milk punch *n* (1704) **:** a mixed drink of alcoholic liquor, milk, and sugar

milk shake *n* (1889) **:** a thoroughly shaken or blended drink made of milk, a flavoring syrup, and often ice cream

milk sickness *n* (1823) **1 :** an acute disease characterized by weakness, vomiting, and constipation and caused by eating dairy products or meat from cattle poisoned by various plants **2 :** TREMBLE 2

milk snake *n* (1800) **:** a common harmless grayish or tan snake (*Lampropeltis triangulum*) with black-bordered brown blotches and an arrow-shaped occipital spot; *broadly* **:** KING SNAKE

milk·sop \'milk-,säp\ *n* [ME, lit., bread soaked in milk] (14c) **:** an unmanly man **:** MOLLYCODDLE

milk sugar *n* (1846) **:** LACTOSE

milk tooth *n* (ca. 1727) **:** a temporary deciduous tooth of a mammal; *esp* **:** one of man's set consisting of four incisors, two canines, and four molars in each jaw

milk vetch *n* [fr. the popular belief that it increases the milk yield of goats] (1597) **:** a perennial Old World leguminous herb (*Astragalus glycyphyllos*) that has sulfur yellow flowers in dense spikes; *also* **:** any of various related plants

milk·weed \'mil-,kwēd\ *n* (ca. 1598) **:** any of various plants that secrete latex; *esp* **:** any of a genus (*Asclepias* of the family Asclepiadaceae, the milkweed family) of erect perennial herbs with milky juice and umbellate flowers

milkweed bug *n* (1905) **:** a large black red-marked bug (*Oncopeltus fasciatus*) now cultured widely as a research organism

milk·wort \'mil-,kwərt, -,kwȯ(ə)rt\ *n* (1578) **:** any of a genus (*Polygala* of the family Polygalaceae, the milkwort family) of herbs and shrubs that have many-colored often showy flowers with the three sometimes crested petals united below into a tube and an irregular calyx with two petaloid sepals

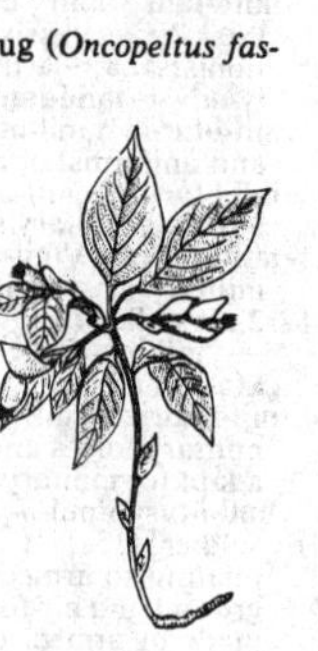

milkwort

milky \'mil-kē\ *adj* **milk·i·er; -est** (14c) **1 :** resembling milk in color or consistency **2 :** MILD, TIMOROUS **3 a :** consisting of, containing, or abounding in milk **b :** yielding milk; *specif* **:** having the characteristics of a good milk producer — **milk·i·ness** *n*

milky disease *n* (ca. 1940) **:** a destructive bacterial disease of Japanese beetle larvae and other scarabaeid grubs

Milky Way *n* (14c) **1 :** a broad luminous irregular band of light that stretches completely around the celestial sphere and is caused by the light of myriads of faint stars **2 :** MILKY WAY GALAXY

Milky Way galaxy *n* (1948) **:** the galaxy of which the sun and the solar system are a part and which contains the myriads of stars that comprise the Milky Way together with all the individual stars, clusters, and bright and dark nebulosities in the sky

[1]**mill** \'mil\ *n* [ME *mille,* fr. OE *mylen,* fr. LL *molina, molinum,* fr. fem. and neut. of *molinus* of a mill, of a millstone, fr. L *mola* mill, millstone; akin to L *molere* to grind — more at MEAL] (bef. 12c) **1 :** a building provided with machinery for grinding grain into flour **2 a :** a machine or apparatus (as a quern) for grinding grain **b :** a machine for crushing or comminuting **3 :** a machine that manufactures by the continuous repetition of some simple action **4 :** a building or collection of buildings with machinery for manufacturing **5 a :** a machine formerly used for stamping coins **b :** a machine for expelling juice from vegetable tissues by pressure or grinding **c :** a machine for polishing **6 :** MILLING MACHINE, MILLING CUTTER **7 a :** a slow, laborious, or mechanical process or routine **b :** a place that processes people or things mechanically ⟨a diploma ~⟩ ⟨medicaid ~⟩ **8** *slang* **:** the engine of an automobile or boat

[2]**mill** *vt* (1570) **1 :** to subject to an operation or process in a mill: as **a :** to grind into flour, meal, or powder **b :** to shape or dress by means of a rotary cutter **c :** to mix and condition (as rubber) by passing between rotating rolls **2 :** to give a raised rim or a ridged or corrugated edge to (a coin) **3 :** to cut grooves in the metal surface of (as a knob) ~ *vi* **1 :** to hit out with the fists **2 :** to move in a circle or in an eddying mass **3 :** to undergo milling

[3]**mill** *n* [L *mille* thousand] (1791) **:** a money of account equal to $^{1}/_{10}$ cent

mill·age \'mil-ij\ *n* (1891) **:** a rate (as of taxation) expressed in mills per dollar

mill·dam \-,dam\ *n* (14c) **:** a dam to make a millpond; *also* **:** MILLPOND

mille \'mil\ *n* [L] (1894) **:** THOUSAND

mil·le·fi·o·ri \,mil-ə-fē-'ōr-ē, -'ȯr-\ *n* [It, fr. *mille* thousand (fr. L) + *fiori* flowers, pl. of *fiore,* fr. L *flor-, flos* — more at BLOW] (1849) **:** ornamental glass produced by cutting cross sections of fused bundles of glass rods of various colors and sizes

[1]**mil·le·nar·i·an** \,mil-ə-'ner-ē-ən\ *adj* (1631) **1 :** of or relating to belief in the millennium **2 :** of or relating to 1000 years

[2]**millenarian** *n* (1674) **:** one that believes in a millennium

mil·le·nar·i·an·ism \-ē-ə-,niz-əm\ *n* (ca. 1847) **1 :** belief in the millennium of Christian prophecy **2 :** belief in a coming ideal society and esp. one created by revolutionary action

[1]**mil·le·na·ry** \'mil-ə-,ner-ē, mə-'len-ə-rē\ *n, pl* **-ries** [LL *millenarium,* fr. neut. of *millenarius* of a thousand, fr. L *milleni* one thousand each, fr. *mille*] (1550) **1 a :** a group of 1000 units or things **b :** 1000 years **:** MILLENNIUM **2 :** MILLENARIAN

[2]**millenary** *adj* [L *millenarius*] (1641) **1 :** relating to or consisting of 1000 **2 :** suggesting a millennium

mil·len·ni·al \mə-'len-ē-əl\ *adj* (1807) **:** of or relating to a millennium

mil·len·ni·al·ism \-ē-ə-,liz-əm\ *n* (1906) **:** MILLENARIANISM

mil·len·ni·um \mə-'len-ē-əm\ *n, pl* **-nia** \-ē-ə\ *or* **-niums** [NL, fr. L *mille* thousand + NL *-ennium* (as in *biennium*)] (1638) **1 a :** the thousand years mentioned in Revelation 20 during which holiness is to prevail and Christ is to reign on earth **b :** a period of great happiness or human perfection **2 a :** a period of 1000 years **b :** a 1000th anniversary or its celebration

mil·le·pore \'mil-ə-,pō(ə)r, -,pȯ(ə)r\ *n* [deriv. of L *mille* thousand + *porus* pore] (1751) **:** any of an order (Milleporina) of often large stony hydrozoan reef-building corals of encrusting, branching, or massive form that differ from the madrepores in passing through a free-swimming medusoid stage

mill·er \'mil-ər\ *n* (14c) **1 :** one that operates a mill; *specif* **:** one that grinds grain into flour **2 :** any of various moths having powdery wings **3 a :** MILLING MACHINE **b :** a tool for use in a milling machine

mil·ler·ite \'mil-ə-,rīt\ *n* [G *millerit,* fr. William H. *Miller* †1880 Eng. mineralogist] (1854) **:** sulfide of nickel NiS usu. occurring as a mineral in capillary yellow crystals

mill·er's–thumb \,mil-ərz-'thəm\ *n* (15c) **:** any of several small freshwater spiny-finned sculpins (genus *Cottus*) of Europe and No. America

mil·les·i·mal \mə-'les-ə-məl\ *n* [L *millesimus,* adj., thousandth, fr. *mille*] (1719) **:** the quotient of a unit divided by 1000 **:** one of 1000 equal parts — **millesimal** *adj* — **mil·les·i·mal·ly** \-ə-mə-lē\ *adv*

mil·let \'mil-ət\ *n* [ME *milet,* fr. MF, dim. of *mil,* fr. L *milium;* akin to Gk *melinē* millet] (15c) **1 :** any of various small-seeded annual cereal and forage grasses: **a :** a grass (*Panicum miliaceum*) cultivated for its grain which is used for food **b :** any of several grasses related to common millet **2 :** the seed of a millet

milli- *comb form* [F, fr. L *milli-* thousand, fr. *mille*] **:** thousandth ⟨*milliampere*⟩

mil·li·am·pere \,mil-ē-'am-,pi(ə)r\ *n* [ISV] (1885) **:** one thousandth of an ampere

mil·liard \'mil-,yärd, 'mil-ē-,ärd\ *n* [F, fr. MF *miliart,* fr. *mili-,* (fr. *milion* million)] *Brit* (1793) **:** a thousand millions — see NUMBER table

mil·li·ary \'mil-ē-,er-ē\ *adj* [L *milliarius, miliarius* consisting of a thousand, one mile long, fr. *mille* thousand, mile] (1644) **:** marking the distance of a Roman mile

mil·li·bar \'mil-ə-,bär\ *n* [ISV] (1910) **:** a unit of atmospheric pressure equal to $^{1}/_{1000}$ bar or 1000 dynes per square centimeter

mil·li·cu·rie \,mil-ə-'kyu̇(ə)r-(,)ē, -kyu̇-'rē\ *n* [ISV] (1910) **:** one thousandth of a curie

mil·li·de·gree \-di-'grē\ *n* (1942) **:** one thousandth of a degree

mil·lieme \mē(l)-'yem\ *n, pl* **milliemes** \-'yem(z)\ [F *millième* thousandth, fr. MF, fr. *mille* thousand, fr. L] (1902) **:** a unit of value of Egypt and Sudan equal to $^{1}/_{1000}$ pound

mil·li·far·ad \,mil-ə-'far-,ad, -əd\ *n* [ISV] (ca. 1961) **:** one thousandth of a farad

mil·li·gal \'mil-ə-,gal\ *n* [ISV] (1914) **:** a unit of acceleration equivalent to $^{1}/_{1000}$ gal

mil·li·gram \-,gram\ *n* [F *milligramme,* fr. *milli-* + *gramme* gram] (ca. 1810) — see METRIC SYSTEM table

mil·li·hen·ry \-,hen-rē\ *n* [ISV] (ca. 1897) **:** one thousandth of a henry

mil·li·lam·bert \-'lam-bərt\ *n* (1916) **:** one thousandth of a lambert

mil·li·li·ter \'mil-ə-,lēt-ər\ *n* [F *millilitre,* fr. *milli-* + *litre* liter] (ca. 1810) — see METRIC SYSTEM table

mil·lime \mə-'lēm\ *n* [modif. of Ar *mallim,* fr. F *millième*] (1902) — see *dinar* at MONEY table

mil·li·me·ter \'mil-ə-,mēt-ər\ *n* [F *millimètre,* fr. *milli-* + *mètre* meter] (1807) — see METRIC SYSTEM table

mil·li·mi·cro- \,mil-ə-'mī-krə, -krō\ *comb form* **:** billionth ⟨*millimicrosecond*⟩

mil·li·mi·cron \,mil-ə-'mī-,krän\ *n* [ISV] (1904) **:** a unit of length equal to one thousandth of a micrometer **:** NANOMETER

mil·li·mole \'mil-ə-,mōl\ *n* [ISV *milli-* + [5]*mole*] (1904) **:** one thousandth of a gram molecule — **mil·li·mo·lar** \-,mō-lər\ *adj*

mil·li·ner \'mil-ə-nər\ *n* [irreg. fr. *Milan,* Italy; fr. the importation of women's finery from Italy in the 16th century] (1530) **:** one who designs, makes, trims, or sells women's hats

mil·li·nery \'mil-ə-,ner-ē\ *n* (ca. 1679) **1 :** women's apparel for the head **2 :** the business or work of a milliner

mill·ing \'mil-iŋ\ *n* (1817) **:** a corrugated edge on a coin

milling cutter *n* (1884) **:** a rotary tool-steel cutter used in a milling machine for shaping and dressing metal surfaces

milling machine *n* (1876) **:** a machine tool on which work usu. of metal secured to a carriage is shaped by rotating milling cutters

mil·lion \'mil-yən\ *n, pl* **millions** *or* **million** [ME *milioun,* fr. MF *million,* fr. OIt *milione,* aug. of *mille* thousand, fr. L] (14c) **1** — see NUMBER table **2** : a very large number ⟨~s of cars on the road⟩ **3** : the mass of common people ⟨someone who writes for the ~s — Bergen Evans⟩ — **million** *adj* — **mil·lion·fold** \-,fōld\ *adv or adj* — **mil·lionth** \'mil-yən(t)th\ *adj or n*

mil·lion·aire \,mil(l)-yə-'na(ə)r, -'ne(ə)r, 'mil(l)-yə-,\ *n* [F *millionnaire,* fr. *million,* fr. MF *milion*] (1826) : one whose wealth is estimated at a million or more (as of dollars or pounds)

mil·lion·air·ess \-'ar-əs, -'er-, -,er-, -,er-\ *n* (1881) : a woman who is a millionaire or the wife of a millionaire

mil·li·os·mol \,mil-ē-'äz-,mōl, -'äs-\ *n* (ca. 1939) : one thousandth of an osmol

mil·li·pede \'mil-ə-,pēd\ *n* [L *millepeda,* a small crawling animal, fr. *mille* thousand + *ped-, pes* foot — more at FOOT] (1601) : any of numerous myriapods (class Diplopoda) having usu. a cylindrical segmented body covered with hard integument, two pairs of legs on most apparent segments, and no poison fangs

mil·li·ra·di·an \,mil-ə-'rād-ē-ən\ *n* [ISV] (1954) : one thousandth of a radian

mil·li·rem \'mil-ə-,rem\ *n* (1947) : one thousandth of a rem

mil·li·roent·gen \,mil-ə-'rent-gən, -'rənt-, -jən; -'ren-chən, -'rən-\ *n* [ISV] (1948) : one thousandth of a roentgen

mil·li·sec·ond \'mil-ə-,sek-ənd, -ənt\ *n* [ISV] (1909) : one thousandth of a second

mil·li·volt \-,vōlt\ *n* [ISV] (1861) : one thousandth of a volt

mil·li·watt \-,wät\ *n* [ISV] (ca. 1914) : one thousandth of a watt

mill·pond \'mil-,pänd\ *n* (15c) : a pond produced by damming a stream to produce a head of water for operating a mill

mill·race \-,rās\ *n* (15c) : a canal in which water flows to and from a mill wheel; *also* : the current that drives the wheel

mill·stone \'mil-,stōn\ *n* (bef. 12c) **1** : either of two circular stones used for grinding (as grain) **2 a** : something that grinds or crushes **b** : a heavy burden

mill·stream \-,strēm\ *n* (bef. 12c) **1** : a stream whose flow is utilized to run a mill **2** : MILLRACE

mill wheel *n* (bef. 12c) : a waterwheel that drives a mill

mill·wright \'mil-,rīt\ *n* (14c) **1** : one whose occupation is planning and building mills or setting up their machinery **2** : one who maintains and cares for mechanical equipment (as of a mill or factory)

mi·lo \'mī-(,)lō\ *n, pl* **milos** [Sotho *maili*] (1882) : a small usu. early and drought-resistant grain sorghum with compact bearded heads of large yellow or whitish seeds

mi·lord \mil-'ó(ə)r(d)\ *n* [F, fr. E *my lord*] (1596) : an Englishman of noble or gentle birth

mil·pa \'mil-pə\ *n* [MexSp, fr. Nahuatl] (1844) **1 a** : a small field in Mexico or Central America that is cleared from the jungle, cropped for a few seasons, and abandoned for a fresh clearing **b** : a maize field in Mexico or Central America **2** : the maize plant

Milque·toast \'milk-,tōst\ *n* [Caspar *Milquetoast,* comic strip character created by H. T. Webster †1952 Am. cartoonist] (1935) : a timid, meek, or unassertive person

mil·reis \mil-'rās(h)\ *n, pl* **mil·reis** \-'rās(h), -'rāz(h)\ [Pg *milréis*] (1589) **1** : a Portuguese unit of value equal before 1911 to 1000 reis **2** : the basic monetary unit of Brazil until 1942 **3** : a coin representing one milreis

milt \'milt\ *n* [prob. fr. MD *milte* milt of fish, spleen; akin to OE *milte* spleen — more at MELT] (15c) : the male reproductive glands of fishes when filled with secretion; *also* : the secretion itself — **milty** \-tē\ *adj*

milt·er \'mil-tər\ *n* (1601) : a male fish in breeding condition

mim \'mim\ *adj* [imit. of the act of pursing the lips] *dial* (1641) : affectedly shy or modest

¹mime \'mīm, 'mēm\ *vb* **mimed; mim·ing** *vi* (1616) : to act a part with mimic gesture and action usu. without words ~ *vt* **1** : MIMIC **2** : to act out in the manner of a mime — **mim·er** *n*

²mime *n* [L *mimus,* fr. Gk *mimos;* akin to Gk *mimeisthai* to imitate] (1616) **1 a** : an actor in a mime **b** : one that practices mime **2** : MIMIC **3** : an ancient dramatic entertainment representing scenes from life usu. in a ridiculous manner **4 a** : the art of portraying a character or narration by body movement **b** : a performance of mime

mim·eo·graph \'mim-ē-ə-,graf\ *n* [fr. *Mimeograph,* a trademark] (1889) : a duplicator for making many copies that utilizes a stencil through which ink is pressed — **mimeograph** *vt*

mi·me·sis \mə-'mē-səs, mī-\ *n* [LL, fr. Gk *mimēsis,* fr. *mimeisthai*] (1550) : IMITATION, MIMICRY

mi·met·ic \-'met-ik\ *adj* [LL *mimeticus,* fr. Gk *mimētikos,* fr. *mimeisthai*] (1637) **1** : IMITATIVE **2** : relating to, characterized by, or exhibiting mimicry ⟨~ coloring of a butterfly⟩ — **mi·met·i·cal·ly** \-i-k(ə-)lē\ *adv*

¹mim·ic \'mim-ik\ *n* (1590) **1** : MIME 1 **2** : one that mimics

²mimic *adj* [L *mimicus,* fr. Gk *mimikos,* fr. *mimos* mime] (1598) **1 a** : IMITATIVE **b** : IMITATION, MOCK ⟨a ~ battle⟩ **2** : of or relating to mime or mimicry

³mimic *vt* **mim·icked** \-ikt\; **mim·ick·ing** (1697) **1** : to imitate closely : APE **2** : to ridicule by imitation **3** : SIMULATE **4** : to resemble by biological mimicry *syn* see COPY

mim·ic·ry \'mim-i-krē\ *n, pl* **-ries** (1709) **1 a** : an instance of mimicking **b** : the action, practice, or art of mimicking **2** : a superficial resemblance of one organism to another or to natural objects among which it lives that secures it a selective advantage (as protection from predation)

mi·mo·sa \mə-'mō-sə, mī-, -zə\ *n* [NL, fr. L *mimus* mime] (1751) **1** : any of a genus (*Mimosa*) of leguminous trees, shrubs, and herbs of tropical and warm regions with usu. bipinnate often prickly leaves and globular heads of small white or pink flowers **2** : SILK TREE

mi·na \'mī-nə\ *n* [L, fr. Gk *mna,* of Sem origin; akin to Heb *māneh* mina] (1579) : an ancient unit of weight and value equal to $\frac{1}{60}$ talent

min·able *or* **mine·able** \'mī-nə-bəl\ *adj* (ca. 1570) : capable of being mined

min·a·ret \,min-ə-'ret, 'min-ə-,\ *n* [F, fr. Turk *minare,* fr. Ar *manārah* lighthouse] (1682) : a slender lofty tower attached to a mosque and surrounded by one or more projecting balconies from which the summons to prayer is cried by the muezzin

mi·na·to·ry \'min-ə-,tōr-ē, 'mī-nə-, -,tōr-\ *adj* [LL *minatorius,* fr. L *minatus,* pp. of *minari* to threaten — more at MOUNT] (1532) : having a menacing quality : THREATENING

min·au·dière \,mē-nōd-'ye(ə)r\ *n* [F, lit., affected person, fr. *minaudière,* adj., coquettish, affected] (1940) : a small decorative case for cosmetics or jewelry often designed as a woman's fashion accessory

¹mince \'min(t)s\ *vb* **minced; minc·ing** [ME *mincen,* fr. MF *mincer,* fr. (assumed) VL *minutiare,* fr. L *minutia* smallness — more at MINUTIA] *vt* (14c) **1 a** : to cut or chop into very small pieces **b** : to subdivide minutely; *esp* : to damage by cutting up **2** : to utter or pronounce with affectation **3 a** *archaic* : MINIMIZE **b** : to restrain (words) within the bounds of decorum ~ *vi* : to walk with short steps in a prim affected manner — **minc·er** *n*

minaret

²mince *n* (1850) : small chopped bits (as of food); *specif* : MINCEMEAT

mince·meat \'min(t)-,smēt\ *n* (1747) **1** : minced meat **2** : a finely chopped mixture (as of raisins, apples, and spices) with or without meat **3** : a state of destruction or annihilation — used in the phrase **make mincemeat of**

mince pie *n* (1600) : a pie filled with mincemeat

minc·ing \'min(t)-siŋ\ *adj* (1530) : affectedly dainty or delicate — **minc·ing·ly** \-siŋ-lē\ *adv*

¹mind \'mīnd\ *n* [ME, fr. OE *gemynd* — more at MENTAL] (bef. 12c) **1** : RECOLLECTION, MEMORY ⟨keep that in ~⟩ ⟨time out of ~⟩ **2 a** : the element or complex of elements in an individual that feels, perceives, thinks, wills, and esp. reasons **b** : the conscious mental events and capabilities in an organism **c** : the organized conscious and unconscious adaptive mental activity of an organism **3** : INTENTION, DESIRE ⟨I changed my ~⟩ **4** : the normal or healthy condition of the mental faculties **5** : OPINION, VIEW **6** : DISPOSITION, MOOD **7 a** : a person or group embodying mental qualities ⟨the public ~⟩ **b** : intellectual ability **8** *cap, Christian Science* : GOD 1b **9** : a conscious substratum or factor in the universe

²mind *vt* (14c) **1** *chiefly dial* : REMIND **2** *chiefly dial* : REMEMBER **3** : to attend to closely **4 a** : to become aware of : NOTICE **b** *chiefly dial* : INTEND, PURPOSE **5 a** : to give heed to attentively in order to obey **b** : to follow the orders or instructions of **6 a** : to be concerned about **b** : DISLIKE ⟨I don't ~ going⟩ **7 a** : to be careful : SEE ⟨~ you finish it⟩ **b** : to be cautious about ⟨~ the broken rung⟩ **8** : to give protective care to : TEND ~ *vi* **1** : to be attentive or wary **2** : to become concerned : CARE **3** : to pay obedient heed or attention — **mind·er** *n*

mind–bend·ing \'mīn(d)-,ben-diŋ\ *adj* (1965) : MIND-BLOWING

mind–blow·ing \-,blō-iŋ\ *adj* (1967) **1** : PSYCHEDELIC 1a **2** : MIND-BOGGLING — **mind–blow·er** \-,blō-(ə)r\ *n*

mind–bog·gling \-,bäg-(ə-)liŋ\ *adj* (1964) : mentally or emotionally exciting : OVERWHELMING

mind·ed \'mīn-dəd\ *adj* (1503) **1** : having a mind esp. of a specified kind — usu. used in combination ⟨narrow-*minded*⟩ **2** : INCLINED, DISPOSED — **mind·ed·ness** \-dəd-nəs\ *n*

mind–ex·pand·ing \'mīn-dik-,span-diŋ\ *adj* (1963) : PSYCHEDELIC 1a

mind·ful \'mīn(d)-fəl\ *adj* (14c) **1** : bearing in mind : AWARE **2** : inclined to be aware — **mind·ful·ly** \-fə-lē\ *adv* — **mind·ful·ness** *n*

mind·less \'mīn-(d)ləs\ *adj* (bef. 12c) **1** : destitute of mind or consciousness; *esp* : UNINTELLIGENT **2** : INATTENTIVE, HEEDLESS — **mind·less·ly** *adv* — **mind·less·ness** *n*

mind reader *n* (1887) : one that professes or is held to be able to perceive another's thought without normal means of communication — **mind reading** *n*

mind–set \'mīn(d)-,set\ *n* (ca. 1926) **1** : a mental inclination, tendency, or habit **2** : a fixed state of mind

mind's eye *n* (14c) : the mental faculty of conceiving imaginary or recollected scenes

¹mine \(')mīn\ *adj* [ME *min* — more at MY] *archaic* (bef. 12c) : MY — used before a word beginning with a vowel or *h* ⟨this treasure in ~ arms —Shak.⟩ or sometimes as a modifier of a preceding noun

²mine \'mīn\ *pron, sing or pl in constr* (bef. 12c) : that which belongs to me — used without a following noun as a pronoun equivalent in meaning to the adjective *my*

³mine \'mīn\ *n* [ME, fr. MF, fr. OF] (14c) **1 a** : a pit or excavation in the earth from which mineral substances are taken **b** : an ore deposit **2** : a subterranean passage under an enemy position **3** : an encased explosive designed to destroy enemy personnel, vehicles, or ships **4** : a rich source of supply **5** : a pyrotechnic piece comprising various small fireworks that are scattered into the air with a loud report

⁴mine \'mīn\ *vb* **mined; min·ing** *vt* (14c) **1 a** : to dig under to gain access or cause the collapse of (an enemy position) **b** : UNDERMINE **2** : to get (as ore) from the earth **3** : to burrow beneath the surface of ⟨larva that ~s leaves⟩ **4** : to place military mines in, on, or under ⟨~ a harbor⟩ **5 a** : to dig into for ore or metal **b** : to process for obtaining a natural constituent ⟨~ the air for nitrogen⟩ **c** : to seek valuable material in ~ *vi* : to dig a mine — **min·er** *n*

mine·lay·er \'mīn-,lā-ər, -,le(ə)r\ *n* (1909) : a naval vessel for laying underwater mines

¹min·er·al \'min-(ə-)rəl\ *n* [ME, fr. ML *minerale,* fr. neut. of *mineralis*] (15c) **1** : ORE **2** : an inorganic substance (as in the ash of calcined tissue) **3** *obs* : MINE **4** : something neither animal nor vegetable **5 a** : a solid homogeneous crystalline chemical element or compound that results from the inorganic processes of nature; *broadly* : any of various naturally occurring homogeneous substances (as stone, coal, salt, sulfur, sand, petroleum, water, or natural gas) obtained for man's use usu.

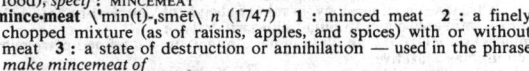

\ə\ abut \ᵊ\ kitten, F table \ər\ further \a\ ash \ā\ ace \ä\ cot, cart \aù\ out \ch\ chin \e\ bet \ē\ easy \g\ go \i\ hit \ī\ ice \j\ job \ŋ\ sing \ō\ go \ò\ law \òi\ boy \th\ thin \th\ the \ü\ loot \ù\ foot \y\ yet \zh\ vision \ȧ, k̠, ⁿ, œ, œ̄, ᵫ, ᵿ, �) *see* Guide to Pronunciation

from the ground **b** : a synthetic substance having the chemical composition and crystalline form and properties of a naturally occurring mineral **6** *pl, Brit* : MINERAL WATER

[2]**mineral** *adj* [ME, fr. ML *mineralis,* fr. *minera* mine, ore, fr. OF *miniere,* fr. *mine*] (1599) **1** : of or relating to minerals; *also* : INORGANIC **2** : impregnated with mineral substances

min·er·al·ize \'min-(ə-)rə-,līz\ *vt* **-ized; -iz·ing** (1655) **1** : to transform (a metal) into an ore **2** **a** : to impregnate or supply with minerals or an inorganic compound **b** : to convert into mineral or inorganic form **3** : PETRIFY — **min·er·al·iz·able** \-rə-,lī-zə-bəl\ *adj* — **min·er·al·iza·tion** \,min(-ə)-rə-lə-'zā-shən\ *n* — **min·er·al·iz·er** \'min(-ə)-rə-,lī-zər\ *n*

mineral kingdom *n* (1691) : the one of the three basic groups of natural objects that includes inorganic objects — compare ANIMAL KINGDOM, PLANT KINGDOM

min·er·al·o·cor·ti·coid \,min(-ə)-rə-lō-'kȯrt-ə-,kȯid\ *n* (1946) : a corticoid (as aldosterone) that affects chiefly the electrolyte and fluid balance in the body — compare GLUCOCORTICOID

min·er·al·o·gy \,min-ə-'räl-ə-jē, -'ral-\ *n* [prob. fr. (assumed) NL *mineralogia,* irreg. fr. ML *minerale* + L *-logia* -logy] (1690) **1** : a science dealing with minerals, their crystallography, properties, classification, and the ways of distinguishing them **2** : the materials of mineralogy **3** : a treatise on mineralogy — **min·er·al·og·i·cal** \,min(-ə)-rə-'läj-i-kəl\ *adj* — **min·er·al·o·gist** \,min-ə-'räl-ə-jəst, -'ral-\ *n*

mineral oil *n* (1805) : an oil of mineral origin; *esp* : a refined petroleum oil used as a laxative

mineral spirits *n pl but sing or pl in constr* (ca. 1890) : a petroleum distillate that is used esp. as a paint or varnish thinner

mineral water *n* (1562) : water naturally or artificially infused with mineral salts or gases (as carbon dioxide)

mineral wax *n* (ca. 1864) : a wax of mineral origin; *esp* : OZOKERITE

mineral wool *n* (1881) : any of various lightweight vitreous fibrous materials used esp. in heat and sound insulation

Mi·ner·va \mə-'nər-və\ *n* [L] : the Roman goddess of wisdom — compare ATHENA

min·e·stro·ne \,min-ə-'strō-nē, -'strōn\ *n* [It, aug. of *minestra,* fr. *minestrare* to serve, dish up, fr. L *ministrare,* fr. *minister* servant — more at MINISTER] (1891) : a rich thick vegetable soup usu. with dried beans and pasta (as macaroni or vermicelli)

mine·sweep·er \'mīn-,swē-pər\ *n* (1905) : a warship designed for removing or neutralizing mines by dragging — **mine·sweep·ing** \-piŋ\ *n*

Ming \'miŋ\ *n* [Chin (Pek) *ming*[2] luminous] (1671) : a Chinese dynasty dated 1368–1644 and marked by restoration of earlier traditions and in the arts by perfection of established techniques

min·gle \'miŋ-gəl\ *vb* **min·gled; min·gling** \-g(ə-)liŋ\ [ME *menglen,* freq. of *mengen* to mix, fr. OE *mengan;* akin to MHG *mengen* to mix, Gk *massein* to knead] *vt* (15c) **1** : to bring or mix together or with something else usu. without fundamental loss of identity : INTERMIX **2** : to prepare by mixing : CONCOCT ~ *vi* **1** : to become mingled **2** **a** : to come in contact : ASSOCIATE ⟨encouraged both races to ~⟩ **b** : to move about (as in a group) ⟨*mingled* with the guests⟩ *syn* see MIX

ming tree \'miŋ-\ *n* [perh. fr. *Ming*] (1948) : a dwarfed evergreen conifer grown as bonsai; *also* : an artificial plant resembling this

min·gy \'min-jē\ *adj* **min·gi·er; -est** [perh. blend of [1]*mean* and *stingy*] (1911) : MEAN, STINGY

[1]**mini** \'min-ē\ *adj* [*mini-*] (1954) **1** : very small : MINIATURE **2** : of short length or duration : BRIEF

[2]**mini** *n, pl* **min·is** [*mini-*] (1961) : something small of its kind: as **a** : MINICAR **b** : MINISKIRT **c** : MINICOMPUTER

mini- *comb form* [*miniature*] : miniature : very small ⟨*mini*bus⟩

[1]**min·ia·ture** \'min-ē-ə-,chu̇(ə)r, 'min-i-,chu̇(ə)r, 'min-yə-, -chər, -,t(y)u̇(ə)r\ *n* [It *miniatura* art of illuminating a manuscript, fr. ML, fr. L *miniatus,* pp. of *miniare* to color with minium, fr. *minium*] (ca. 1586) **1** **a** : a copy on a much reduced scale **b** : something small of its kind **2** : a painting in an illuminated book or manuscript **3** : the art of painting miniatures **4** : a very small portrait or other painting (as on ivory or metal) — **min·ia·tur·ist** \-,chu̇r-əst, -chər-, -,t(y)u̇r-\ *n* — **min·ia·tur·is·tic** \,min-ē-ə-chə-'ris-tik, ,min-i-, ,min-yə-, -,tyü-\ *adj*

[2]**miniature** *adj* (1714) **1** : being or represented on a small scale **2** : of or relating to still photography using film 35 millimeters wide or smaller *syn* see SMALL

miniature golf *n* (1915) : a novelty golf game played with a putter on a miniature course having tunnels, bridges, sharp corners, and obstacles

miniature pin·scher \-'pin-chər\ *n* (ca. 1929) : a toy dog that suggests a small Doberman pinscher and is 10 to $12^{1}/_{2}$ inches high at the withers

miniature schnauzer *n* (ca. 1929) : a schnauzer of a breed that is 12 to 14 inches in height and is classified as a terrier

min·ia·tur·ize \'min-ē-ə-chə-,rīz, 'min-i-chə-, 'min-yə-chə-, -,tyü-,rīz\ *vt* **-ized; -iz·ing** (1946) : to design or construct in small size — **min·ia·tur·iza·tion** \,min-ē-ə-,chu̇r-ə-'zā-shən, ,min-i-, ,min-yə-, -chər-, -,tyu̇r-\ *n*

mini·bike \'min-i-,bīk\ *n* (1964) : a small one-passenger motorcycle with a low frame and raised handlebars — **mini·bik·er** *n*

mini·bus \-,bəs\ *n* (ca. 1957) : a small bus for comparatively short trips

Mini·cam \'min-ē-,kam\ *trademark* — used for a portable television camera

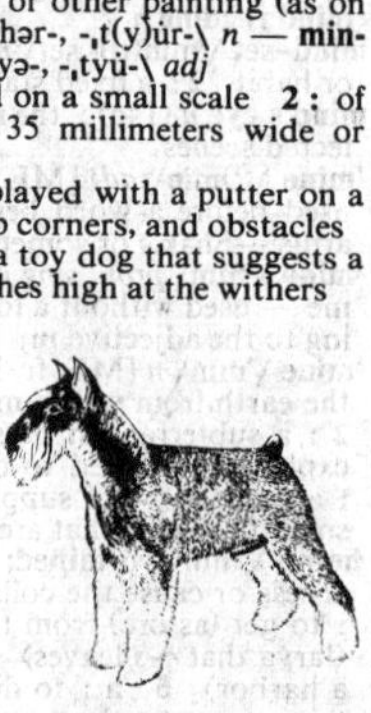

miniature schnauzer

mini·car \-,kär\ *n* (1949) : a very small automobile; *esp* : SUBCOMPACT

mini·com·put·er \,min-i-kəm-'pyüt-ər\ *n* (1968) : a small computer that is intermediate between a microcomputer and a mainframe in size, speed, and capacity, that can support time-sharing, and that is often dedicated to a single application

mini·course \'min-ē-,kō(ə)rs, -,kȯ(ə)rs\ *n* (1970) : a brief course of study usu. lasting less than a semester

min·ié ball \'min-ē-,bȯl, ,min-ē-,ā-'bȯl\ *n* [Claude Étienne *Minié* †1879 Fr. army officer] (1859) : a rifle bullet with a conical head used in muzzle-loading firearms

min·i·fy \'min-ə-,fī\ *vt* **-fied; -fy·ing** [L *minimus* smallest + E *-fy*] (1676) : LESSEN

min·i·kin \'min-i-kən\ *n* [obs. D *minneken* darling, deriv. of MD *minne* love, beloved; akin to OE *gemynd* mind, memory — more at MENTAL] *archaic* (1761) : a small or dainty creature — **minikin** *adj*

min·im \'min-əm\ *n* [L *minimus* least] (15c) **1** : HALF NOTE **2** : something very minute **3** — see WEIGHT table — **minim** *adj*

min·i·mal \'min-ə-məl\ *adj* (1810) **1** : relating to or being a minimum **2** *often cap* : of, relating to, or being minimal art or minimalism — **min·i·mal·ly** \-mə-lē\ *adv*

minimal art *n* (1965) : abstract art consisting primarily of simple geometric forms executed in an impersonal style

min·i·mal·ism \'min-ə-mə-,liz-əm\ *n* (1969) **1** : MINIMAL ART **2** : a style or technique (as in music or design) that is characterized by the use of few and simple elements

[1]**min·i·mal·ist** \-ləst\ *n* (1967) **1** : one who favors restricting the functions and powers of a political organization or the achievement of a set of goals to a minimum **2** **a** : a minimal artist **b** : an adherent of minimalism

[2]**minimalist** *adj* (1967) : of, relating to, or done in the style of minimalism

mini·max \'min-i-,maks\ *n* [*mini*mum + *max*imum] (1918) : the minimum of a set of maxima; *esp* : the smallest of a set of maximum possible losses each of which occurs in the most unfavorable outcome of a strategy followed by a participant in a situation governed by the theory of games — compare MAXIMIN

min·i·mize \'min-ə-,mīz\ *vt* **-mized; -miz·ing** (1802) **1** : to reduce to a minimum **2** : to estimate at a minimum often as a measure of disparagement or self-defense ⟨the habit of *minimizing* losses in our own forces while maximizing those of the enemy⟩ *syn* see DECRY — **min·i·mi·za·tion** \,min-ə-mə-'zā-shən\ *n* — **min·i·miz·er** \'min-ə-,mī-zər\ *n*

min·i·mum \'min-ə-məm\ *n, pl* **-i·ma** \-ə-mə\ *or* **-i·mums** [L, neut. of *minimus* smallest; akin to L *minor* smaller] (1674) **1** : the least quantity assignable, admissible, or possible **2** : the least of a set of numbers; *specif* : the smallest value assumed by a continuous function defined on a closed interval **3** **a** : the lowest degree or amount of variation (as of temperature) reached or recorded **b** : the lowest speed allowed on a highway — **minimum** *adj*

minimum wage *n* (1860) **1** : LIVING WAGE **2** : the lowest wage paid or permitted to be paid; *specif* : a wage fixed by legal authority or by contract as the least that may be paid either to employed persons generally or to a particular category of employed persons

min·ing \'mī-niŋ\ *n* (1523) : the process or business of working mines

min·ion \'min-yən\ *n* [MF *mignon* darling] (ca. 1548) **1** : a servile dependent **2** : one highly favored : IDOL **3** : a subordinate official

mini·park \'min-ē-,pärk\ *n* (1967) : a small city park

mini·school \-,skül\ *n* (1968) : an experimental school offering specialized or individual instruction to its students

min·is·cule \'min-əs-,kyü(ə)l\ *var of* MINUSCULE

mini·se·ries \'min-ē-,si(ə)r-(,)ēz\ *n* (1973) : a motion picture made for television and presented in several parts

mini·skirt \'min-i-,skərt\ *n* (1965) : a woman's short skirt with the hemline several inches above the knee — **mini·skirt·ed** *adj*

mini·state \-,stāt\ *n* (1966) : a small independent nation

[1]**min·is·ter** \'min-ə-stər\ *n* [ME *ministre,* fr. OF, fr. L *minister* servant; akin to L *minor* smaller] (13c) **1** : AGENT **2** **a** : one officiating or assisting the officiant in church worship **b** : a clergyman esp. of a Protestant communion **3** **a** : the superior of one of several religious orders — called also *minister-general* **b** : the assistant to the rector or the bursar of a Jesuit house **4** : a high officer of state entrusted with the management of a division of governmental activities **5** **a** : a diplomatic representative (as an ambassador) accredited to the court or seat of government of a foreign state **b** : a diplomatic representative ranking below an ambassador

[2]**minister** *vi* **-tered; -ter·ing** \-st(ə-)riŋ\ (14c) **1** : to perform the functions of a minister of religion **2** : to give aid or service ⟨~ to the sick⟩

min·is·te·ri·al \,min-ə-'stir-ē-əl\ *adj* (1561) **1** : of or relating to a minister or the ministry **2** **a** : being or having the characteristics of an act or duty prescribed by law as part of the duties of an administrative office **b** : relating to or being an act done after ascertaining the existence of a specified state of facts in obedience to a legal order without exercise of personal judgment or discretion **3** : acting or active as an agent : INSTRUMENTAL — **min·is·te·ri·al·ly** \-ē-ə-lē\ *adv*

minister plenipotentiary *n, pl* **ministers plenipotentiary** (ca. 1645) : a diplomatic agent ranking below an ambassador but possessing full power and authority

minister resident *n, pl* **ministers resident** (1848) : a diplomatic agent resident at a foreign court or seat of government and ranking below a minister plenipotentiary

[1]**min·is·trant** \'min-ə-strənt\ *adj, archaic* (1667) : performing service in attendance on someone

[2]**ministrant** *n* (1818) : one that ministers

min·is·tra·tion \,min-ə-'strā-shən\ *n* (14c) : the act or process of ministering

min·is·try \'min-ə-strē\ *n, pl* **-tries** (14c) **1** : MINISTRATION **2** : the office, duties, or functions of a minister **3** : the body of ministers of religion : CLERGY **4** : AGENCY 2, INSTRUMENTALITY **5** : the period of service or office of a minister or ministry **6** *often cap* **a** : the body of ministers governing a nation or state from which a smaller cabinet is sometimes selected **b** : the group of ministers constituting a cabinet **7** **a** : a government department presided over by a minister **b** : the building in which the business of a ministry is transacted

mini·track \'min-i-,trak\ *n* (1956) : an electronic system for tracking an earth satellite by radio waves transmitted from it to a chain of ground stations

min·i·um \'min-ē-əm\ *n* [ME, fr. L, cinnabar, red lead, of Iberian origin; akin to Basque *arminea* cinnabar] (1650) : RED LEAD

mini·van \'min-ē-,van\ *n* (1960) : a small van

min·i·ver \'min-ə-vər\ *n* [ME *meniver,* fr. MF *menu vair* small vair] (14c) : a white fur worn orig. by medieval nobles and used chiefly for robes of state

mink \'miŋk\ *n, pl* **mink** *or* **minks** [ME] (15c) **1** : soft fur or pelt of the mink varying in color from white to dark brown **2** : any of several slender-bodied semiaquatic carnivorous mammals (genus *Mustela*) that resemble and are closely related to the weasels and have partially webbed feet, a rather short bushy tail, and a soft thick coat

min·ke whale \,miŋ-kə-\ *n* [Norw *minkehval,* fr. *minke* lesser, smaller (fr. ON *minni* less, akin to OHG *minniro*) + *hval* whale — more at

MINOR] (1939) : a small whalebone whale (*Balaenoptera acutorostrata*) — called also *min·ke* \'miŋ-kə\

min·ne·sing·er \'min-i-,siŋ-ər, 'min-ə-,ziŋ-\ *n* [G, fr. MHG, fr. *minne* love (akin to MD) + *singer* singer — more at MINIKIN] (1825) : one of a class of German poets and musicians of the 12th to the 14th centuries

Min·ne·so·ta Multiphasic Personality Inventory \,min-ə-'sōt-ə-,məl-ti-'fā-zik-, -,məl-,tī-\ *n* [University of *Minnesota*] (1943) : a test of personal and social adjustment based on a complex scaling of the answers to an elaborate true or false test

min·now \'min-(,)ō, -ə(-w)\ *n, pl* **minnows** *also* **minnow** [ME *menawe;* akin to OE *myne* minnow, Russ *men'* eelpout] (14c) **1 a :** a small cyprinid, killifish, or topminnow **b :** any of various small fish that are less than a designated size and are not game fish **2 :** a live or artificial minnow used as bait

1Mi·no·an \mə-'nō-ən, mī-\ *adj* [L *minous* of Minos, fr. Gk *minōios,* fr. *Minōs* Minos] (1894) : of or relating to a Bronze Age culture of Crete (3000 B.C.–1100 B.C.)

2Minoan *n* (1902) : a native or inhabitant of ancient Crete

1mi·nor \'mī-nər\ *adj* [ME, fr. L, smaller, inferior; akin to OHG *minniro* smaller, L *minuere* to lessen, Gk *meiōn* less] (13c) **1 :** inferior in importance, size, or degree : comparatively unimportant **2 :** not having reached majority **3 a :** having half steps between the second and third, the fifth and sixth, and sometimes the seventh and eighth degrees ⟨~ scale⟩ **b :** based on a minor scale ⟨~ key⟩ **c :** less by a semitone than the corresponding major interval ⟨~ third⟩ **d :** containing a minor third ⟨~ triad⟩ **4 :** not serious or involving risk to life ⟨~ illness⟩ **5 :** of or relating to an academic subject requiring fewer courses than a major

2minor *n* (1612) **1 :** a person who has not attained majority **2 :** a minor musical interval, scale, key, or mode **3 a :** a minor academic subject **b :** a student taking a specified minor **4 :** a determinant or matrix obtained from a given determinant or matrix by eliminating the row and column in which a given element lies **5** *pl* **:** minor league baseball

3minor *vi* (ca. 1926) : to take courses in a minor subject

minor axis *n* (1862) : the chord of an ellipse passing through the center and perpendicular to the major axis

mi·nor·ca \mə-'nȯr-kə\ *n* [*Minorca,* one of the Balearic islands] (1848) : any of a breed of domestic fowls that resemble leghorns but are larger

minor element *n* (ca. 1945) : TRACE ELEMENT

Mi·nor·ite \'mī-nə-,rīt\ *n* [fr. *Friar Minor* (Franciscan)] (ca. 1577) : FRANCISCAN

mi·nor·i·ty \mə-'nȯr-ət-ē, mī-, -'när-\ *n, pl* **-ties** *often attrib* (1547) **1 a :** the period before attainment of majority **b :** the state of being a legal minor **2 :** the smaller in number of two groups constituting a whole; *specif* **:** a group having less than the number of votes necessary for control **3 a :** a part of a population differing from others in some characteristics and often subjected to differential treatment **b :** a member of a minority group ⟨an effort to hire more *minorities*⟩

minority leader *n* (1949) : the leader of the minority party in a legislative body

minor league *n* (1889) : a league of professional clubs in a sport other than the recognized major leagues

minor order *n* (1844) : one of the Roman Catholic or Eastern clerical orders that are lower in rank and less sacred in character than major orders — usu. used in pl.

minor party *n* (1949) : a political party whose electoral strength is so small as to prevent its gaining control of a government except in rare and exceptional circumstances

minor penalty *n* (1936) : a two-minute suspension of a player in ice hockey with no substitute allowed

minor planet *n* (1861) : ASTEROID

minor premise *n* (ca. 1727) : the premise of a syllogism that contains the minor term

minor seminary *n* (ca. 1947) : a Roman Catholic seminary giving all or part of high school and junior college training with emphasis on preparing candidates for a major seminary

minor suit *n* (1926) : either of two bridge suits of inferior scoring value: **a :** DIAMONDS **b :** CLUBS

minor term *n* (1843) : the term of a syllogism that forms the subject of the conclusion

Mi·nos \'mī-nəs\ *n* [L, fr. Gk *Minōs*] : a son of Zeus and Europa and king of Crete who for his just rule is made supreme judge in the underworld after his death

Mi·no·taur \'min-ə-,tȯ(ə)r, 'mī-nə-\ *n* [ME, fr. MF, fr. L *Minotaurus,* fr. Gk *Minōtauros,* fr. *Minōs* + *tauros* bull] : a monster shaped half like a man and half like a bull, confined in the labyrinth built by Daedalus for Minos, and given a periodical tribute of youths and maidens as food until slain by Theseus

min·ster \'min(t)-stər\ *n* [ME, monastery, church attached to a monastery, fr. OE *mynster,* fr. LL *monasterium* monastery] (bef. 12c) : a large or important church often having cathedral status

min·strel \'min(t)-strəl\ *n* [ME *menestrel,* fr. OF, official, servant, minstrel, fr. LL *ministerialis* imperial household officer, fr. L *ministerium* service, fr. *minister* servant — more at MINISTER] (13c) **1 :** one of a class of medieval musical entertainers; *esp* **:** a singer of verses to the accompaniment of a harp **2 a :** MUSICIAN **b :** POET **3 a :** one of a troupe of performers typically giving a program of Negro melodies, jokes, and impersonations and usu. blacked in imitation of Negroes **b :** a performance by a troupe of minstrels

min·strel·sy \-sē\ *n* [ME *minstralcie,* fr. MF *menestralsie,* fr. *menestrel*] (14c) **1 :** the singing and playing of a minstrel **2 :** a body of minstrels **3 :** a group of songs or verse

1mint \'mint\ *n* [ME *minte,* fr. OE, fr. L *mentha, menta*] (bef. 12c) **1 :** any of a family (Labiatae, the mint family) of aromatic plants with a 4-lobed ovary which produces four one-seeded nutlets in fruit; *esp* **:** any of a genus (*Mentha*) of mints which have white or pink verticillate flowers with a nearly regular corolla and four equal stamens and some of which are used in flavoring and cookery **2 :** a confection flavored with mint

2mint *n* [ME *mynt* coin, money, fr. OE *mynet,* fr. L *moneta* mint, coin, fr. *Moneta,* epithet of Juno; fr. the fact that the Romans coined money in the temple of Juno Moneta] (15c) **1 :** a place where coins, medals, or tokens are made **2 :** a place where something is manufactured **3 :** a vast sum or amount

3mint *vt* (1546) **1 :** to make (as coins) out of metal : COIN **2 :** CREATE, PRODUCE — **mint·er** *n*

4mint *adj* (1902) : unmarred as if fresh from a mint ⟨~ coins⟩

mint·age \'mint-ij\ *n* (1570) **1 :** the action or process of minting coins **2 :** an impression placed upon a coin **3 :** coins produced by minting or in a single period of minting **4 :** the cost of minting

mint julep *n* (1809) : JULEP 2

min·u·end \'min-yə-,wend\ *n* [L *minuendum,* neut. of *minuendus,* gerundive of *minuere* to lessen — more at MINOR] (1706) : a number from which the subtrahend is to be subtracted

min·u·et \,min-yə-'wet\ *n* [F *menuet,* fr. obs. F, tiny, fr. OF, fr. *menu* small, fr. L *minutus*] (1673) **1 :** a slow graceful dance in 3/4 time characterized by forward balancing, bowing, and toe pointing **2 :** music for or in the rhythm of a minuet

1mi·nus \'mī-nəs\ *prep* [ME, fr. L *minus,* adv., less, fr. neut. of *minor* smaller — more at MINOR] (15c) **1 :** diminished by : LESS ⟨seven ~ four is three⟩ **2 :** deprived of : WITHOUT ⟨~ his hat⟩

2minus *n* (1654) **1 :** a negative quantity **2 :** DEFICIENCY, DEFECT

3minus *adj* (1800) **1 :** algebraically negative ⟨a ~ quantity⟩ **2 :** having negative qualities **3 :** relating to or being a particular one of the two mating types that are required for successful fertilization in sexual reproduction in some lower plants (as a fungus) **4 :** falling low in a specified range ⟨B ~⟩

1mi·nus·cule \'min-əs-,kyü(ə)l, min-'əs-, 'min-yəs-, mī-'nəs-\ *n* [F, fr. L *minusculus* rather small, dim. of *minor* smaller] (1705) **1 a :** one of several ancient and medieval writing styles developed from cursive and having simplified and small forms **b :** a letter in this style **2 :** a lowercase letter

2minuscule *adj* (ca. 1727) **1 :** written in or in the size or style of minuscules **2 :** very small

minus sign *n* (1668) : a sign — used in mathematics to indicate subtraction (as in 8−6=2) or a negative quantity (as in −10°)

1min·ute \'min-ət\ *n* [ME, fr. MF, fr. LL *minuta,* fr. L *minutus* small, fr. pp. of *minuere* to lessen — more at MINOR] (14c) **1 :** the 60th part of an hour of time or of a degree **2 :** the distance one can traverse in a minute **3 :** a short space of time : MOMENT **4 a :** MEMORANDUM, DRAFT **b** *pl* **:** the official record of the proceedings of a meeting

2minute *vt* **min·ut·ed; min·ut·ing** (1648) : to make notes or a brief summary of

3mi·nute \mī-'n(y)üt, mə-\ *adj* **mi·nut·er; -est** [L *minutus*] (ca. 1626) **1 :** very small : INFINITESIMAL **2 :** of small importance : TRIFLING **3 :** marked by close attention to details ***syn*** see SMALL, CIRCUMSTANTIAL — **mi·nute·ness** *n*

minute hand *n* (1726) : the long hand that marks the minutes on the face of a watch or clock

1mi·nute·ly \mī-'n(y)üt-lē, mə-\ *adv* (1599) **1 :** into very small pieces **2 :** in a minute manner or degree

2min·ute·ly \'min-ət-lē\ *adj, archaic* (1605) : minute by minute

min·ute·man \'min-ət-,man\ *n* (1774) : a member of a group of armed men pledged to take the field at a minute's notice during and immediately before the American Revolution

min·ute steak \,min-ət-\ *n* (1921) : a small thin steak that can be quickly cooked

mi·nu·tia \mə-'n(y)ü-sh(ē-)ə, mī-\ *n, pl* **-ti·ae** \-shē-,ē, -,ī\ [L *minutiae* trifles, details, fr. pl. of *minutia* smallness, fr. *minutus*] (1751) : a minute or minor detail — usu. used in pl.

minx \'miŋ(k)s\ *n* [origin unknown] (1592) **1 :** a pert girl **2** *obs* **:** a wanton woman

min·yan \'min-yən\ *n, pl* **-ya·nim** \,min-yə-'nēm\ *or* **-yans** [Heb *minyān,* lit., number, count] (1753) : the quorum of 10 adult Jews required for communal worship

mio- — see MI-

Mio·cene \'mī-ə-,sēn\ *adj* (1831) : of, relating to, or being an epoch of the Tertiary between the Pliocene and the Oligocene or the corresponding system of rocks — **Miocene** *n*

mi·o·sis \mī-'ō-səs, mē-\ *n, pl* **mi·o·ses** \-,sēz\ [NL, fr. Gk *myein* to be closed (of the eyes) + NL *-osis*] (1819) : excessive smallness or contraction of the pupil of the eye

1mi·ot·ic \-'ät-ik\ *n* (1864) : an agent that causes miosis

2miotic *adj* (1864) : relating to or characterized by miosis

mi·que·let \,mik-ə-'let, ,mēk-\ *n* [Sp *miquelete*] (1827) : a Spanish or French irregular soldier during the Peninsular War

mir \'mi(ə)r\ *n* [Russ] (1877) : a village community in czarist Russia characterized by joint ownership of the land and cultivation by individual families

mi·ra·bi·le dic·tu \mə-,räb-ə-lē-'dik-(,)tü\ [L] (1831) : wonderful to relate

mi·ra·cid·i·um \,mir-ə-'sid-ē-əm, ,mī-rə-\ *n, pl* **-cid·ia** \-ē-ə\ [NL, fr. Gk *meirak-, meirax* youth, stripling + NL *-idium*] (1898) : the free-swimming ciliated first larva of a digenetic trematode that seeks out and penetrates a suitable snail intermediate host in which it develops into a sporocyst — **mi·ra·cid·i·al** \-ē-əl\ *adj*

mir·a·cle \'mir-i-kəl\ *n* [ME, fr. OF, fr. LL *miraculum,* fr. L, a wonder, marvel, fr. *mirari* to wonder at — more at SMILE] (12c) **1 :** an extraordinary event manifesting divine intervention in human affairs **2 :** an extremely outstanding or unusual event, thing, or accomplishment **3** *Christian Science* **:** a divinely natural phenomenon experienced humanly as the fulfillment of spiritual law

miracle drug *n* (1950) : a drug usu. newly discovered that elicits a dramatic response in a patient's condition — called also *wonder drug*

miracle fruit *n* (ca. 1964) : a small shrubby tropical African tree (*Synsepalum dulcificum* of the family Sapotaceae) whose fruit contains a glycoprotein that when applied to the tongue causes sour substances to taste sweet; *also* **:** its fruit

miracle play *n* (ca. 1852) **1 :** a medieval drama based on episodes from the life of a saint or martyr **2 :** MYSTERY PLAY

mi·rac·u·lous \mə-ˈrak-yə-ləs\ *adj* [MF *miraculeux,* fr. ML *miraculosus,* fr. L *miraculum*] (15c) **1 :** of the nature of a miracle : SUPERNATURAL ⟨a ~ event⟩ **2 :** suggesting a miracle : MARVELOUS ⟨gave proof of a ~ memory —*Time*⟩ **3 :** working or able to work miracles ⟨~ power⟩ — **mi·rac·u·lous·ly** *adv* — **mi·rac·u·lous·ness** *n*

mir·a·dor \ˈmir-ə-ˌdȯ(ə)r, ˌmir-ə-ˈ\ *n* [Sp, fr. Catal, fr. *mirar* to look at, fr. L *mirari*] (ca. 1797) **:** a turret, window, or balcony designed to command an extensive outlook

mi·rage \mə-ˈräzh\ *n* [F, fr. *mirer* to look at, fr. L *mirari*] (1837) **1 :** an optical effect that is sometimes seen at sea, in the desert, or over a hot pavement, that may have the appearance of a pool of water or a mirror in which distant objects are seen inverted, and that is caused by the bending or reflection of rays of light by a layer of heated air of varying density **2 :** something illusory and unattainable like a mirage

[1]**mire** \ˈmī(ə)r\ *n* [ME, fr. ON *mȳrr;* akin to OE *mōs* marsh — more at MOSS] (14c) **1 :** wet spongy earth : MARSH, BOG **2 :** heavy often deep mud or slush **3 :** a troublesome or intractable situation ⟨found themselves in a ~ of debt⟩ — **miry** \ˈmī(ə)r-ē\ *adj*

[2]**mire** *vb* **mired; mir·ing** *vt* (1559) **1 a :** to cause to stick fast in or as if in mire **b :** to hamper or hold back as if by mire : ENTANGLE **2 :** to cover or soil with mire ~ *vi* **:** to stick or sink in mire

mi·rex \ˈmī-ˌreks\ *n* [perh. fr. pis*mire* + *ex*terminator] (1962) **:** an organochlorine insecticide $C_{10}Cl_{12}$ used esp. against ants

mirk, mirky *var of* MURK, MURKY

mir·li·ton \ˌmir-ə-ˈtōn\ *n* [F] (ca. 1909) **:** CHAYOTE

[1]**mir·ror** \ˈmir-ər\ *n* [ME *mirour,* fr. OF, fr. *mirer* to look at, fr. L *mirari* to wonder at — more at SMILE] (13c) **1 :** a polished or smooth surface (as of glass) that forms images by reflection **2 a :** something that gives a true representation **b :** an exemplary model — **mir·rored** \-ə(r)d\ *adj* — **mir·ror·like** \-ˌlīk\ *adj*

[2]**mirror** *vt* (1820) **:** to reflect in or as if in a mirror

mirror image *n* (1885) **:** something that has its parts reversely arranged in comparison with another similar thing or that is reversed with reference to an intervening axis or plane

mirth \ˈmərth\ *n* [ME, fr. OE *myrgth,* fr. *myrge* merry — more at MERRY] (13c) **:** gladness or gaiety as shown by or accompanied with laughter — **mirth·ful** \-fəl\ *adj* — **mirth·ful·ly** \-fə-lē\ *adv* — **mirth·ful·ness** *n* — **mirth·less** \-ləs\ *adj*

syn MIRTH, GLEE, JOLLITY, HILARITY mean a feeling of high spirits that is expressed in laughter, play, or merrymaking. MIRTH implies generally lightness of heart and love of gaiety; GLEE stresses exultation shown in laughter, cries of joy, or sometimes malicious delight; JOLLITY suggests exuberance or lack of restraint in mirth or glee; HILARITY suggests loud or irrepressible laughter or high-spirited boisterousness.

[1]**MIRV** \ˈmərv\ *n* [*m*ultiple *i*ndependently targeted *r*eentry *v*ehicle] (1967) **:** a missile with two or more warheads designed to reenter the atmosphere on the way to separate enemy targets; *also* **:** any of the warheads of such a missile

[2]**MIRV** *vb* **MIRVed; MIRV·ing** *vt* (1969) **:** to equip with MIRV warheads ⟨both sides would ~ their submarine-borne missiles —Stewart Alsop⟩ ~ *vi* **:** to arm one's forces with MIRVs

[1]**mis-** *prefix* [partly fr. ME, fr. OE; partly fr. ME *mes-, mis-,* fr. OF *mes-,* of Gmc origin; akin to OE *mis-;* akin to OE *missan* to miss] **1 a :** badly : wrongly ⟨*mis*judge⟩ **b :** unfavorably ⟨*mis*esteem⟩ **c :** in a suspicious manner ⟨*mis*doubt⟩ **2 :** bad : wrong ⟨*mis*deed⟩ **3 :** opposite or lack of ⟨*mis*trust⟩ **4 :** not ⟨*mis*know⟩

mis·act
mis·ad·dress
mis·ad·just
mis·ad·min·is·tra·tion
mis·ad·vise
mis·aim
mis·align
mis·align·ment
mis·al·lo·cate
mis·al·lo·ca·tion
mis·anal·y·sis
mis·an·a·lyze
mis·ap·pli·ca·tion
mis·ap·ply
mis·ap·prais·al
mis·ar·tic·u·late
mis·ar·tic·u·la·tion
mis·as·sem·ble
mis·as·sump·tion
mis·at·trib·ute
mis·at·tri·bu·tion
mis·bal·ance
mis·be·have
mis·be·hav·er
mis·be·hav·ior
mis·bound
mis·but·ton
mis·cal·cu·late
mis·cal·cu·la·tion
mis·cap·tion
mis·cat·a·log
mis·chan·nel
mis·charge
mis·choice
mis·ci·ta·tion
mis·clas·si·fi·ca·tion
mis·clas·si·fy
mis·code
mis·com·pre·hen·sion
mis·com·pu·ta·tion
mis·com·pute
mis·con·nect
mis·con·nec·tion
mis·con·struc·tion
mis·con·strue
mis·copy
mis·cor·re·la·tion
mis·cut
mis·date
mis·de·clare
mis·deem
mis·de·fine
mis·de·scribe
mis·de·scrip·tion
mis·de·vel·op
mis·di·ag·nose
mis·di·ag·no·sis
mis·dial
mis·dis·tri·bu·tion
mis·di·vi·sion
mis·draw
mis·ed·u·cate
mis·ed·u·ca·tion
mis·ed·u·ca·tor
mis·em·pha·sis
mis·em·pha·size
mis·em·ploy
mis·em·ploy·ment
mis·es·ti·mate
mis·es·ti·ma·tion
mis·eval·u·ate
mis·eval·u·a·tion
mis·field
mis·file
mis·fo·cus
mis·func·tion
mis·gauge
mis·gov·ern
mis·gov·ern·ment
mis·grade
mis·iden·ti·fi·ca·tion
mis·iden·ti·fy
mis·in·form
mis·in·for·ma·tion
mis·kick
mis·la·bel
mis·learn
mis·lo·cate
mis·lo·ca·tion
mis·make
mis·man·age
mis·man·age·ment
mis·mark
mis·mar·riage
mis·match
mis·mate
mis·mo·ti·vate
mis·or·der
mis·ori·ent
mis·ori·en·ta·tion
mis·pack·age
mis·per·ceive
mis·per·cep·tion
mis·pic·ture
mis·plan
mis·po·si·tion
mis·pre·scribe
mis·print
mis·quo·ta·tion
mis·quote
mis·rec·ol·lec·tion
mis·re·demp·tion
mis·ref·er·ence
mis·reg·is·ter
mis·reg·is·tra·tion
mis·re·late
mis·re·mem·ber
mis·ren·der
mis·re·port
mis·route
mis·set
mis·shape
mis·shap·en
mis·shap·en·ly
mis·sort
mis·strike
mis·throw
mis·time
mis·ti·tle
mis·train
mis·tran·scribe
mis·tran·scrip·tion
mis·trans·late
mis·trans·la·tion
mis·truth
mis·tune
mis·type
mis·uti·li·za·tion
mis·vo·cal·iza·tion

[2]**mis-** *or* **miso-** *comb form* [Gk, fr. *misein* to hate] **:** hatred ⟨*miso*gamy⟩

mis·ad·ven·ture \ˌmis-əd-ˈven-chər\ *n* [ME *mesaventure,* fr. OF, fr. *mesavenir* to chance badly, fr. *mes-* [1]mis- + *avenir* to chance, happen, fr. L *advenire* — more at ADVENTURE] (13c) **:** MISFORTUNE, MISHAP

mis·al·li·ance \ˌmis-ə-ˈlī-ən(t)s\ *n* [modif. of F *mésalliance*] (1738) **1 :** an improper alliance **2 a :** MÉSALLIANCE **b :** a marriage between persons unsuited to each other

mis·an·thrope \ˈmis-ᵊn-ˌthrōp\ *n* [Gk *misanthrōpos* hating mankind, fr. [2]*mis-* + *anthrōpos* man] (1563) **:** one who hates or distrusts mankind

mis·an·throp·ic \ˌmis-ᵊn-ˈthräp-ik\ *adj* (ca. 1762) **1 :** of, relating to, or characteristic of a misanthrope **2 :** marked by a hatred or contempt for mankind ***syn*** see CYNICAL — **mis·an·throp·i·cal·ly** \-i-k(ə-)lē\ *adv*

mis·an·thro·py \mis-ˈan(t)-thrə-pē\ *n* (1656) **:** a hatred or distrust of mankind

mis·ap·pre·hend \(ˌ)mis-ˌap-ri-ˈhend\ *vt* (1653) **:** to apprehend wrongly : MISUNDERSTAND — **mis·ap·pre·hen·sion** \-ˈhen-chən\ *n*

mis·ap·pro·pri·ate \ˌmis-ə-ˈprō-prē-ˌāt\ *vt* (1857) **:** to appropriate wrongly (as by theft or embezzlement) — **mis·ap·pro·pri·a·tion** \-ˌprō-prē-ˈā-shən\ *n*

mis·be·come \ˌmis-bi-ˈkəm\ *vt* **-came** \-ˈkām\; **-come; -com·ing** (1530) **:** to be inappropriate or unbecoming to

mis·be·got·ten \-ˈgät-ᵊn\ *adj* (14c) **1 :** unlawfully conceived : ILLEGITIMATE ⟨a ~ child⟩ **2 a :** having a disreputable or improper origin : ill-conceived ⟨antiquated and ~ tax laws —R. M. Blough⟩ **b :** CONTEMPTIBLE, DEFORMED ⟨a ~ scoundrel⟩

mis·be·lief \ˌmis-bə-ˈlēf\ *n* (13c) **:** erroneous or false belief

mis·be·lieve \-ˈlēv\ *vi, obs* (14c) **:** to hold a false or unorthodox belief

mis·be·liev·er \-ˈlē-vər\ *n* (15c) **:** HERETIC, INFIDEL

mis·brand \(ˈ)mis-ˈbrand\ *vt* (1903) **:** to brand falsely or in a misleading way; *also* **:** to label in violation of statutory requirements

mis·call \(ˈ)mis-ˈkȯl\ *vt* (14c) **:** to call by a wrong name : MISNAME

mis·car·riage \mis-ˈkar-ij\ *n* (ca. 1651) **1 :** corrupt or incompetent management; *esp* **:** a failure in the administration of justice **2 :** expulsion of a human fetus before it is viable and esp. between the 12th and 28th weeks of gestation

mis·car·ry \(ˈ)mis-ˈkar-ē\ *vi* (14c) **1** *obs* **:** to come to harm **2 :** to suffer miscarriage of a fetus **3 :** to fail of the intended purpose : go wrong or amiss ⟨the plan *miscarried*⟩

mis·cast \(ˈ)mis-ˈkast\ *vt* **-cast; -cast·ing** (1925) **:** to cast in an unsuitable role ⟨life had ~ her in the role of wife and mother —Edna Ferber⟩

mis·ce·ge·na·tion \(ˌ)mis-ˌej-ə-ˈnā-shən, ˌmis-i-jə-ˈnā-\ *n* [irreg. fr. L *miscēre* to mix + *genus* race — more at MIX, KIN] (1864) **:** a mixture of races; *esp* **:** marriage or cohabitation between a white person and a member of another race — **mis·ce·ge·na·tion·al** \-shnəl, -shən-ᵊl\ *adj*

mis·cel·la·nea \ˌmis-ə-ˈlā-nē-ə, -nyə\ *n pl* [L, fr. neut. pl. of *miscellaneus*] (1571) **:** a collection of miscellaneous objects or writings

mis·cel·la·neous \ˌmis-ə-ˈlā-nē-əs, -nyəs\ *adj* [L *miscellaneus,* fr. *miscellus* mixed, prob. fr. *miscēre*] (1637) **1 :** consisting of diverse things or members : HETEROGENEOUS **2 a :** having various traits **b :** dealing with or interested in diverse subjects ⟨as a writer I was too ~ —George Santayana⟩ — **mis·cel·la·neous·ly** *adv* — **mis·cel·la·neous·ness** *n*

mis·cel·la·nist \ˈmis-ə-ˌlā-nəst, *chiefly Brit* mis-ˈel-ə-nist\ *n* (1810) **:** a writer of miscellanies

mis·cel·la·ny \-nē\ *n, pl* **-nies** [prob. modif. of F *miscellanées,* pl., fr. L *miscellanea*] (1615) **1 a** *pl* **:** separate writings collected in one volume **b :** a collection of writings on various subjects **2 :** a mixture of various things

mis·chance \(ˈ)mis(h)-ˈchan(t)s\ *n* [ME *mischaunce,* fr. OF *meschance,* fr. *mes-* [1]mis- + *chance* chance] (13c) **1 :** bad luck **2 :** a piece of bad luck : MISHAP ***syn*** see MISFORTUNE

mis·chief \ˈmis(h)-chəf\ *n* [ME *meschief,* fr. OF, calamity, fr. *mes-* + *chief* head, end — more at CHIEF] (14c) **1 :** a specific injury or damage attributed to a particular agent **2 :** a cause or source of harm, evil, or irritation; *esp* **:** a person who causes mischief **3 a :** action that annoys or irritates **b :** the quality or state of being mischievous : MISCHIEVOUSNESS ⟨had ~ in his eyes⟩

mis·chie·vous \ˈmis(h)-chə-vəs\ *adj* (14c) **1 :** HARMFUL, INJURIOUS ⟨~ gossip⟩ **2 a :** able or tending to cause annoyance, trouble, or minor injury **b :** irresponsibly playful ⟨~ behavior⟩ — **mis·chie·vous·ly** *adv* — **mis·chie·vous·ness** *n*

misch metal \ˈmish-\ *n* [G *mischmetall,* fr. *mischen* to mix (fr. OHG *miskan,* fr. L *miscēre*) + *metall* metal] (1916) **:** a complex alloy of rare earth metals used esp. in tracer bullets and as a flint in lighters

mis·ci·ble \ˈmis-ə-bəl\ *adj* [ML *miscibilis,* fr. L *miscēre* to mix — more at MIX] (1570) **:** capable of being mixed; *specif* **:** capable of mixing in any ratio without separation of two phases ⟨~ liquids⟩ — **mis·ci·bil·i·ty** \ˌmis-ə-ˈbil-ət-ē\ *n*

mis·com·mu·ni·ca·tion \ˌmis-kə-ˌmyü-nə-ˈkā-shən\ *n* (1964) **:** failure to communicate clearly

mis·con·ceive \ˌmis-kən-ˈsēv\ *vt* (14c) **:** to interpret incorrectly — **mis·con·ceiv·er** *n* — **mis·con·cep·tion** \-ˈsep-shən\ *n*

mis·con·duct \(ˈ)mis-ˈkän-(ˌ)dəkt\ *n* (1710) **1 :** mismanagement esp. of governmental or military responsibilities **2 :** intentional wrongdoing; *specif* **:** deliberate violation of a law or standard esp. by a government official : MALFEASANCE **3 a :** improper behavior **b :** ADULTERY — **mis·con·duct** \ˌmis-kən-ˈdəkt\ *vt*

mis·count \(ˈ)mis-ˈkau̇nt\ *vb* [ME *misconten,* fr. MF *mesconter,* fr. *mes-* + *conter* to count] *vt* (14c) **:** to count wrongly : MISCALCULATE ~ *vi* **:** to make a wrong count — **miscount** \(ˈ)mis-ˈkau̇nt, ˈmis-ˌ\ *n*

[1]**mis·cre·ant** \ˈmis-krē-ənt\ *adj* [ME *miscreaunt,* fr. MF *mescreant,* prp. of *mescroire* to disbelieve, fr. *mes-* [1]mis- + *croire* to believe, fr. L *credere* — more at CREED] (14c) **1 :** UNBELIEVING, HERETICAL **2 :** DEPRAVED, VILLAINOUS

[2]**miscreant** *n* (14c) **1 :** INFIDEL, HERETIC **2 :** one who behaves criminally or viciously

mis·cre·ate \ˌmis-krē-ˈāt\ *vt* (1603) **:** to create badly or wrongly — **mis·cre·ate** \ˈmis-krē-ət, ˌmis-krē-ˈāt\ *adj* — **mis·cre·ation** \ˌmis-krē-ˈā-shən\ *n*

[1]**mis·cue** \(ˈ)mis-ˈkyü\ *n* (1873) **1 :** a faulty stroke in billiards in which the cue slips **2 :** MISTAKE, SLIP

[2]**miscue** *vi* (1894) **1 :** to make a miscue **2 a :** to miss a stage cue **b :** to answer a wrong cue
mis·deal \(ˈ)mis-ˈdē(ə)l\ *vb* **-dealt** \-ˈdelt\; **-deal·ing** *vi* (1746) **:** to deal cards incorrectly ~ *vt* **:** to deal incorrectly — **misdeal** *n*
mis·deed \(ˈ)mis-ˈdēd\ *n* (bef. 12c) **:** a wrong deed **:** OFFENSE
mis·de·mean·ant \ˌmis-di-ˈmē-nənt\ *n* (1819) **:** a person convicted of a misdemeanor
mis·de·mean·or \ˌmis-di-ˈmē-nər\ *n* (15c) **1 :** a crime less serious than a felony **2 :** MISDEED
mis·di·rect \ˌmis-də-ˈrekt, -(ˌ)dī-\ *vt* (1603) **:** to give a wrong direction to
mis·di·rec·tion \-ˈrek-shən\ *n* (1768) **1 a :** the act or an instance of misdirecting **b :** the state of being misdirected **2 :** a wrong direction
mis·do \(ˈ)mis-ˈdü\ *vt* **-did** \-ˈdid\; **-done** \-ˈdən\; **-do·ing** \-ˈdü-iŋ\; **-does** \-ˈdəz\ (1840) **:** to do wrongly or improperly — **mis·do·er** *n* — **mis·do·ing** *n*
mis·doubt \(ˈ)mis-ˈdau̇t\ *vt* (ca. 1540) **1 :** to doubt the reality or truth of **2 :** SUSPECT, FEAR — **misdoubt** *n*
mise–en–scène \ˌmē-ˌzäⁿ-ˈsen, -ˈsān\ *n, pl* **mise–en–scènes** \-ˈsen(z), -ˈsān(z)\ [F *mise en scène*] (1833) **1 a :** the arrangement of actors and scenery on a stage for a theatrical production **b :** stage setting **2 a :** the physical setting of an action **b :** ENVIRONMENT, MILIEU
mi·ser \ˈmī-zər\ *n* [L *miser* miserable] (ca. 1560) **:** a mean grasping person; *esp* **:** one who lives miserably in order to hoard his wealth
mis·er·a·ble \ˈmiz-ər-bəl, ˈmiz-(ə-)rə-bəl\ *adj* [ME, fr. MF, fr. L *miserabilis* wretched, pitiable, fr. *miserari* to pity, fr. *miser*] (15c) **1 a :** wretchedly inadequate or meager ⟨a ~ hovel⟩ **b :** causing extreme discomfort or unhappiness ⟨a ~ situation⟩ **2 :** being in a pitiable state of distress or unhappiness (as from want or shame) ⟨~ refugees⟩ **3 :** being likely to discredit or shame ⟨his ~ neglect of his wife⟩ ⟨it was ~ of you to make fun of him⟩ — **miserable** *n* — **mis·er·a·ble·ness** *n* — **mis·er·a·bly** \-blē\ *adv*
mi·se·re·re \ˌmiz-ə-ˈri(ə)r-ē, -ˈre(ə)r-; ˌmē-zə-ˈrā-(ˌ)rā\ *n* [L, be merciful, fr. *misereri* to be merciful, fr. *miser* wretched; fr. the first word of the Psalm] (13c) **1** *cap* **:** the 50th Psalm in the Vulgate **2 :** MISERICORD **3 :** a vocal complaint or lament
mi·seri·cord *or* **mi·seri·corde** \mə-ˈzer-ə-ˌkȯ(ə)rd, -ˈser-\ *n* [ML *misericordia* seat in church, fr. L, mercy, fr. *misericord-, misericors* merciful, fr. *misereri* + *cord-, cor* heart — more at HEART] (1515) **:** a small projection on the bottom of a hinged church seat that gives support to a standing worshiper when the seat is turned up
mi·ser·ly \ˈmī-zər-lē\ *adj* (1593) **:** of, relating to, or characteristic of a miser; *esp* **:** marked by sordid grasping meanness and penuriousness *syn* see STINGY — **mi·ser·li·ness** *n*
mis·ery \ˈmiz-(ə-)rē\ *n, pl* **-er·ies** (14c) **1 :** a state of suffering and want that is the result of poverty or affliction **2 :** a circumstance, thing, or place that causes suffering or discomfort **3 :** a state of great unhappiness and emotional distress *syn* see DISTRESS
mis·es·teem \ˌmis-ə-ˈstēm\ *vt* (1611) **:** to esteem wrongly; *esp* **:** to hold in too little regard
mis·fea·sance \mis-ˈfēz-ᵊn(t)s\ *n* [MF *mesfaisance*, fr. *mesfaire* to do wrong, fr. *mes-* [1]mis- + *faire* to make, do, fr. L *facere* — more at DO] (1596) **:** TRESPASS; *specif* **:** the performance of a lawful action in an illegal or improper manner — **mis·fea·sor** \-ˈfē-zər, -ˌzȯ(ə)r\ *n*
[1]**mis·fire** \(ˈ)mis-ˈfī(ə)r\ *vi* (1752) **1 :** to have the explosive or propulsive charge fail to ignite at the proper time ⟨the engine *misfired*⟩ **2 :** to fail to fire ⟨the gun *misfired*⟩ **3 :** to miss an intended effect or objective
[2]**mis·fire** \(ˈ)mis-ˈfī(ə)r, ˈmis-ˌ\ *n* (1839) **1 :** a failure (as of a cartridge or firearm) to fire **2 :** something that misfires
mis·fit \ˈmis-ˌfit, (ˈ)mis-ˈfit\ *n* (ca. 1823) **1 :** something that fits badly **2 :** a person poorly adjusted to his environment ⟨social ~*s*⟩
mis·for·tune \(ˈ)mis-ˈfȯr-chən\ *n* (15c) **1 a :** an event or conjunction of events that causes an unfortunate or distressing result **:** bad fortune ⟨by ~ he fell into bad company⟩ ⟨had the ~ to break his leg⟩ **b :** the ensuing unhappy situation ⟨always ready to help people in ~⟩ **2 :** a distressing or unfortunate incident or event ⟨~*s* never come singly⟩
syn MISFORTUNE, MISCHANCE, ADVERSITY, MISHAP mean adverse fortune or an instance of this. MISFORTUNE may apply to either the incident or conjunction of events that is the cause of an unhappy change of fortune or to the ensuing state of distress; MISCHANCE applies esp. to a situation involving no more than slight inconvenience or minor annoyance; ADVERSITY applies to a state of grave or persistent misfortune; MISHAP applies to a trivial instance of bad luck.
mis·give \(ˈ)mis-ˈgiv\ *vb* **-gave** \-ˈgāv\; **-giv·en** \-ˈgiv-ən\; **-giv·ing** *vt* (1513) **:** to suggest doubt or fear to ~ *vi* **:** to be fearful or apprehensive
mis·giv·ing \-ˈgiv-iŋ\ *n* (1601) **:** a feeling of doubt or suspicion esp. concerning a future event
mis·guid·ance \(ˈ)mis-ˈgīd-ᵊn(t)s\ *n* (1640) **:** MISDIRECTION
mis·guide \-ˈgīd\ *vt* (14c) **:** to lead astray **:** MISDIRECT ⟨well-meaning but *misguided* benefactors⟩ ⟨prejudice ~*s* our minds⟩ — **mis·guid·ed·ly** *adv* — **mis·guid·ed·ness** *n* — **mis·guid·er** *n*
mis·han·dle \-ˈhan-dᵊl\ *vt* (1530) **1 :** to treat roughly **:** MALTREAT **2 :** to manage wrongly or ignorantly
mi·shan·ter \mish-ˈänt-ər\ *n* [ME *misaunter*, alter. of *mesaventure*] *chiefly Scot* (1742) **:** MISADVENTURE
mis·hap \ˈmis-ˌhap, mis-ˈ\ *n* (14c) **1 :** bad luck **:** MISFORTUNE **2 :** an unfortunate accident *syn* see MISFORTUNE
mis·hear \(ˈ)mis-ˈhi(ə)r\ *vb* **-heard** \-ˈhərd\; **-hear·ing** \-ˈhi(ə)r-iŋ\ *vt* (bef. 12c) **:** to hear wrongly ~ *vi* **:** to misunderstand what is heard
mis·hit \(ˈ)mis-ˈhit\ *vt* **-hit; -hit·ting** (1904) **:** to hit in a faulty manner — **mis·hit** \(ˈ)mis-ˈhit, ˈmis-ˌ\ *n*
mish·mash \ˈmish-ˌmäsh, -ˌmash\ *n* [partly fr. MHG *mischmasch*, redupl. of *mischen* to mix; partly fr. Yiddish *mishmash*, fr. MHG *mischmasch*] (15c) **:** HODGEPODGE, JUMBLE
Mish·mi \ˈmish-mē\ *n* (1893) **:** a Tibeto-Burman language of northeastern India
Mish·nah *or* **Mish·na** \ˈmish-nə\ *n* [Heb *mishnāh* instruction, oral law] (1610) **:** the collection of mostly halakic Jewish traditions compiled about A.D. 200 and made the basic part of the Talmud — **Mish·na·ic** \mish-ˈnā-ik\ *adj*
mis·im·pres·sion \ˌmis-im-ˈpresh-ən\ *n* (1670) **:** a mistaken impression
mis·in·ter·pret \ˌmis-ᵊn-ˈtər-prət, -pət\ *vt* (1589) **1 :** to understand wrongly **2 :** to explain wrongly — **mis·in·ter·pre·ta·tion** \-ˌtər-prə-ˈtā-shən, -pə-\ *n*
mis·join·der \(ˈ)mis-ˈjȯin-dər\ *n* (ca. 1847) **:** an improper union of parties or of causes of action in a single legal proceeding
mis·judge \(ˈ)mis-ˈjəj\ *vt* (15c) **1 :** to estimate wrongly **2 :** to have an unjust opinion of ~ *vi* **:** to be mistaken in judgment — **mis·judg·ment** \-ˈjəj-mənt\ *n*
Mi·ski·to \mis-ˈkēt-(ˌ)ō\ *n, pl* **Miskito** *or* **Miskitos** (1699) **1 :** a member of a people of the Atlantic coast of Nicaragua and Honduras **2 :** a language of the Miskito people
mis·know \-ˈnō\ *vt* **-knew** \-ˈn(y)ü\; **-known** \-ˈnōn\; **-know·ing** (1535) **:** MISUNDERSTAND — **mis·knowl·edge** \-ˈnäl-ij\ *n*
mis·lay \(ˈ)mis-ˈlā\ *vt* **-laid** \-ˈlād\; **-lay·ing** (1614) **:** to put in an unremembered place **:** LOSE
mis·lead \(ˈ)mis-ˈlēd\ *vt* **-led** \-ˈled\; **-lead·ing** (bef. 12c) **:** to lead in a wrong direction or into a mistaken action or belief often by deliberate deceit *syn* see DECEIVE — **mis·lead·er** *n* — **mis·lead·ing·ly** \-iŋ-lē\ *adv*
mis·leared \-ˈli(ə)rd, -ˈle(ə)rd\ *adj* [[1]*mis-* + *lear* (to learn)] *chiefly Scot* (1560) **:** UNMANNERLY, ILL-BRED
mis·like \-ˈlīk\ *vt* (bef. 12c) **1** *archaic* **:** DISPLEASE **2 :** DISLIKE — **mislike** *n*
mis·name \-ˈnām\ *vt* (1537) **:** to name incorrectly **:** MISCALL
mis·no·mer \(ˈ)mis-ˈnō-mər\ *n* [ME *misnoumer*, fr. MF *mesnommer* to misname, fr. *mes-* [1]mis- + *nommer* to name, fr. L *nominare* — more at NOMINATE] (15c) **1 :** the misnaming of a person in a legal instrument **2 a :** a use of a wrong name **b :** a wrong name or designation — **mis·no·mered** \-mərd\ *adj*
mi·so \ˈmē-(ˌ)sō\ *n* [Jp] (1727) **:** a high-protein food paste consisting chiefly of soybeans, salt, and usu. fermented grain (as barley or rice) and ranging in taste from very salty to very sweet
miso- — see MIS-
miso·gy·nic \ˌmis-ə-ˈjin-ik, -ˈgīn-\ *adj* [*misogyny*, fr. Gk *misogynia*, fr. [2]*mis-* + *gynē* woman — more at QUEEN] (1825) **:** MISOGYNISTIC
mi·sog·y·nist \mə-ˈsäj-ə-nəst\ *n* (1620) **:** one who hates women — **misogynist** *adj* — **mi·sog·y·ny** \mə-ˈsäj-ə-nē\ *n*
mi·sog·y·nis·tic \mə-ˌsäj-ə-ˈnis-tik\ *adj* (1821) **:** having or showing a hatred and distrust of women *syn* see CYNICAL
mi·sol·o·gy \mə-ˈsäl-ə-jē\ *n* [Gk *misologia*, fr. [2]*mis-* + *-logia* -logy] (1833) **:** a hatred of argument, reasoning, or enlightenment
miso·ne·ism \ˌmis-ə-ˈnē-ˌiz-əm\ *n* [It *misoneismo*, fr. [2]*mis-* + Gk *neos* new + It *-ismo* -ism — more at NEW] (1886) **:** a hatred, fear, or intolerance of innovation or change
mis·place \(ˈ)mis-ˈplās\ *vt* (1594) **1 a :** to put in a wrong place ⟨~ a comma⟩ **b :** MISLAY ⟨*misplaced* the keys⟩ **2 :** to set on a wrong object or eventuality ⟨his trust had been *misplaced*⟩ — **mis·place·ment** \-ˈplās-mənt\ *n*
mis·play \(ˈ)mis-ˈplā\ *n* (1867) **:** a wrong or unskillful play **:** ERROR — **mis·play** \(ˈ)mis-ˈplā, ˈmis-ˌ\ *vt*
[1]**mis·pri·sion** \mis-ˈprizh-ən\ *n* [ME, fr. MF *mesprison* error, wrongdoing, fr. OF, fr. *mespris*, pp. of *mesprendre* to make a mistake, fr. *mes-* [1]*mis-* + *prendre* to take, fr. L *prehendere* to seize — more at PREHENSILE] (15c) **1 a :** neglect or wrong performance of official duty **b :** concealment of treason or felony by one who is not a participant in the treason or felony **c :** seditious conduct against the government or the courts **2 :** MISUNDERSTANDING, MISTAKE
[2]**misprision** *n* [*misprize*] (1586) **:** CONTEMPT, SCORN
mis·prize \(ˈ)mis-ˈprīz\ *vt* [MF *mesprisier*, fr. *mes-* mis- + *prisier* to appraise — more at PRIZE] (14c) **1 :** to hold in contempt **:** DESPISE **2 :** UNDERVALUE
mis·pro·nounce \ˌmis-prə-ˈnau̇n(t)s\ *vt* (1593) **:** to pronounce incorrectly or in a way regarded as incorrect
mis·pro·nun·ci·a·tion \-ˌnən(t)-sē-ˈā-shən\ *n* (1530) **:** the act or an instance of mispronouncing
mis·read \(ˈ)mis-ˈrēd\ *vt* **-read** \-ˈred\; **-read·ing** \-ˈrēd-iŋ\ (1809) **1 :** to read incorrectly **2 :** to misinterpret in or as if in reading ⟨totally ~ the lesson of history —Christopher Hollis⟩
mis·reck·on \-ˈrek-ən\ *vb* (ca. 1524) **:** MISCOUNT, MISCALCULATE
mis·rep·re·sent \(ˌ)mis-ˌrep-ri-ˈzent\ *vt* (1647) **1 :** to give a false or misleading representation of usu. with an intent to deceive or be unfair ⟨~*ed* the facts to suit his purpose⟩ **2 :** to serve badly or improperly as a representative of — **mis·rep·re·sen·ta·tion** \(ˌ)mis-ˌrep-ri-ˌzen-ˈtā-shən, -zən-\ *n* — **mis·rep·re·sen·ta·tive** \-ˈzent-ət-iv\ *adj*
[1]**mis·rule** \(ˈ)mis-ˈrül\ *vt* (14c) **:** to rule incompetently **:** MISGOVERN
[2]**misrule** *n* (14c) **1 :** the action of misruling **:** the condition of being misruled **2 :** DISORDER, ANARCHY
[1]**miss** \ˈmis\ *vb* [ME *missen*, fr. OE *missan*; akin to OHG *missan* to miss and prob. to L *mutare* to change] *vt* (bef. 12c) **1 :** to fail to hit, reach, or contact **2 :** to discover or feel the absence of **3 :** to fail to obtain **4 :** ESCAPE, AVOID ⟨just ~*ed* hitting the other car⟩ **5 :** to leave out **:** OMIT **6 :** to fail to comprehend, sense, or experience ⟨he ~*ed* the point of the speech⟩ **7 :** to fail to perform or attend ⟨had to ~ school for a week⟩ ~ *vi* **1** *archaic* **:** to fail to get, reach, or do something **2 :** to fail to hit something **3 a :** to be unsuccessful **b :** MISFIRE ⟨the engine ~*ed*⟩ — **miss out on :** to lose a good opportunity for ⟨*missed out on* a better job⟩ — **miss the boat :** to fail to take advantage of an opportunity
[2]**miss** *n* (13c) **1** *chiefly dial* **:** disadvantage or regret resulting from loss ⟨we know the ~ of you, and even hunger . . . to see you —Samuel Richardson⟩ **2 a :** a failure to hit **b :** a failure to attain a desired result **3 :** MISFIRE
[3]**miss** *1 is* (ˌ)mis, məs; *2 & 3 are* ˈmis\ *n* [short for *mistress*] (1606) **1** *cap* **a —** used as a title prefixed to the name of an unmarried woman or girl **b —** used before the name of a place or of a line of activity or before some epithet to form a title for a usu. young unmarried female who is representative of the thing indicated ⟨*Miss* America⟩ **2 :** young

lady — used without a name as a conventional term of address to a young woman **3 :** a young unmarried woman or girl

mis·sa can·ta·ta \ˌmis-ə-kən-ˈtät-ə\ *n* [NL, sung mass] (ca. 1903) **:** HIGH MASS

mis·sal \ˈmis-əl\ *n* [ME *messel,* fr. MF & ML; MF, fr. ML *missale,* fr. neut. of *missalis* of the mass, fr. LL *missa* mass — more at MASS] (14c) **:** a book containing all that is said or sung at mass during the entire year

mis·send \(ˌ)mis-ˈsend\ *vt* **-sent** \-ˈsent\; **-send·ing** (15c) **:** to send incorrectly ⟨*missent* mail⟩

mis·sense \ˈmis-ˌsen(t)s\ *n* [¹*mis-* + *-sense* (as in *nonsense*)] (1962) **:** genetic mutation involving alteration of one or more codons so that different amino acids are determined — compare NONSENSE 3

¹mis·sile \ˈmis-əl, *chiefly Brit* -ˌīl\ *adj* [L *missilis,* fr. *missus,* pp. of *mittere* to throw, send — more at SMITE] (1611) **1 :** capable of being thrown or projected to strike a distant object **2 :** adapted for throwing or hurling missiles **3 :** of or relating to missiles ⟨a ~ crisis⟩

²missile *n* (1656) **:** an object (as a weapon) thrown or projected usu. so as to strike something at a distance ⟨stones, artillery shells, bullets, and rockets are ~*s*⟩: as **a :** GUIDED MISSILE **b :** BALLISTIC MISSILE

mis·sil·eer \ˌmis-ə-ˈli(ə)r\ *n* (1958) **:** MISSILEMAN

mis·sile·man \ˈmis-əl-mən\ *n* (1951) **:** one engaged in designing, building, or operating guided missiles

mis·sile·ry *also* **mis·sil·ry** \ˈmis-əl-rē\ *n* (1880) **1 :** MISSILES; *esp* **:** GUIDED MISSILES **2 :** the science dealing with the design, manufacture, and use of guided missiles

miss·ing \ˈmis-iŋ\ *adj* (14c) **:** ABSENT; *also* **:** LOST ⟨~ in action⟩

missing link *n* (1851) **1 :** an absent member needed to complete a series **2 :** a hypothetical intermediate form between man and his presumed simian progenitors

mis·si·ol·o·gy \ˌmis-ē-ˈäl-ə-jē\ *n* [*mission* + *-logy*] (1924) **:** the study of the church's mission esp. with respect to missionary activity

¹mis·sion \ˈmish-ən\ *n* [NL, ML, & L; NL *mission-, missio* religious mission, fr. ML, task assigned, fr. L, act of sending, fr. *missus,* pp. of *mittere*] (1606) **1** *obs* **:** the act or an instance of sending **2 a :** a ministry commissioned by a religious organization to propagate its faith or carry on humanitarian work **b :** assignment to or work in a field of missionary enterprise **c (1) :** a mission establishment **(2) :** a local church or parish dependent on a larger religious organization for direction or financial support **d** *pl* **:** organized missionary work **e :** a course of sermons and services given to convert the unchurched or quicken Christian faith **3 :** a body of persons sent to perform a service or carry on an activity: as **a :** a group sent to a foreign country to conduct diplomatic or political negotiations **b :** a permanent embassy or legation **c :** a team of specialists or cultural leaders sent to a foreign country **4 a :** a specific task with which a person or a group is charged **b (1) :** a definite military, naval, or aerospace task ⟨a bombing ~⟩ ⟨a space ~⟩ **(2) :** a flight operation of an aircraft or spacecraft in the performance of a mission ⟨a ~ to Mars⟩ **5 :** CALLING, VOCATION

²mission *vt* **mis·sioned; mis·sion·ing** \ˈmish-(ə-)niŋ\ (1692) **1 :** to send on or entrust with a mission **2 :** to carry on a religious mission among or in

³mission *adj* (1904) **1 :** of or relating to a style used in the early Spanish missions of the southwestern U.S. ⟨~ architecture⟩ **2 :** of, relating to, of having the characteristics of a style of plain heavy usu. oak furniture originating in the U.S. in the early part of the 20th century

¹mis·sion·ary \ˈmish-ə-ˌner-ē\ *adj* (1644) **1 :** relating to, engaged in, or devoted to missions **2 :** characteristic of a missionary

²missionary *n, pl* **-ar·ies** (1656) **:** a person undertaking a mission and esp. a religious mission

missionary position *n* [perh. so called fr. the notion that missionaries insisted that this coital position is the only acceptable one] (ca. 1948) **:** a coital position in which the female lies on her back with the male on top and with his face opposite hers

mis·sion·er \ˈmish-(ə-)nər\ *n* (1654) **:** MISSIONARY

mis·sion·ize \ˈmish-ə-ˌnīz\ *vb* **-ized; -iz·ing** *vi* (1826) **:** to carry on missionary work ~ *vt* **:** to do missionary work among — **mis·sion·iza·tion** \ˌmish-ə-nə-ˈzā-shən\ *n* — **mis·sion·iz·er** \ˈmish-ə-ˌnī-zər\ *n*

Mis·sis·sip·pi·an \ˌmis-(ə-)ˈsip-ē-ən\ *adj* [*Mississippi* river] (1835) **1 :** of or relating to Mississippi, its people, or the Mississippi river **2 :** of, relating to, or being the period of the Paleozoic era in No. America following the Devonian and preceding the Pennsylvanian or the corresponding system of rocks — **Mississippian** *n*

mis·sive \ˈmis-iv\ *n* [MF *lettre missive,* lit., letter intended to be sent] (1501) **:** a written communication **:** LETTER

miss·out \ˈmis-ˌau̇t\ *n* (1945) **:** a throw of dice that loses the main bet

mis·spell \(ˌ)mis-ˈspel\ *vt* (1655) **:** to spell incorrectly

mis·spell·ing \-iŋ\ *n* (ca. 1695) **:** an incorrect spelling

mis·spend \(ˌ)mis-ˈspend\ *vt* **-spent** \-ˈspent\; **-spend·ing** (14c) **:** to spend wrongly **:** SQUANDER ⟨a *misspent* life⟩

mis·state \(ˌ)mis-ˈstāt\ *vt* (1650) **:** to state incorrectly **:** give a false account of — **mis·state·ment** \-mənt\ *n*

mis·step \-ˈstep\ *n* (1800) **1 :** a wrong step **2 :** a mistake in judgment or action **:** BLUNDER

mis·sus *or* **mis·sis** \ˈmis-əz, -əs, *esp Southern* ˈmiz-\ *n* [alter. of *mistress*] (1833) **1 :** WIFE ⟨men spend money on themselves, but argue over every dime the ~ wants —W. A. Lydgate⟩ **2** *dial* **:** MISTRESS 1a

missy \ˈmis-ē\ *n* (1676) **:** a young girl **:** MISS

¹mist \ˈmist\ *n* [ME, fr. OE; akin to MD *mist* mist, Gk *omichlē*] (bef. 12c) **1 :** water in the form of particles floating or falling in the atmosphere at or near the surface of the earth and approaching the form of rain **2 :** something that dims or obscures **3 :** a film before the eyes **4 a :** a cloud of small particles or objects suggestive of a mist **b :** a suspension of a finely divided liquid in a gas **c :** a fine spray **5 :** a drink of liquor served over cracked ice

²mist *vi* (bef. 12c) **1 :** to be or become misty **2 :** to become dim or blurred ~ *vt* **:** to cover with or convert to mist

mis·tak·able \mə-ˈstā-kə-bəl\ *adj* (1646) **:** capable of being misunderstood or mistaken

¹mis·take \mə-ˈstāk\ *vb* **mis·took** \-ˈstu̇k\; **mis·tak·en** \-ˈstā-kən\; **mis·tak·ing** [ME *mistaken,* fr. ON *mistaka* to take by mistake, fr. *mis-* + *taka* to take — more at TAKE] *vt* (14c) **1 :** to blunder in the choice of ⟨*mistook* her way in the dark⟩ **2 a :** to misunderstand the meaning or intention of **:** MISINTERPRET ⟨don't ~ me, I mean exactly what I said⟩ **b :** to make a wrong judgment of the character or ability of **3 :** to identify wrongly **:** confuse with another ⟨I *mistook* him for his brother⟩ ~ *vi* **:** to be wrong ⟨you *mistook* when you thought I laughed at you —Thomas Hardy⟩ — **mis·tak·en·ly** *adv* — **mis·tak·er** *n*

²mistake *n* (1638) **1 :** a misunderstanding of the meaning or implication of something **2 :** a wrong action or statement proceeding from faulty judgment, inadequate knowledge, or inattention ***syn*** see ERROR

mis·ter \ˈmis-tər, *for 1* ˌmis-tər *or in rapid speech* (ˌ)mis(t)\ *n* [alter. of ¹*master*] (1551) **1 —** used sometimes in writing instead of the usual *Mr.* **2 :** SIR — used without a name as a generalized term of direct address of a man who is a stranger ⟨hey, ~, do you want to buy a paper⟩ **3 :** a man not entitled to a title of rank or an honorific or professional title ⟨though he was only a ~, he was a greater scholar in his field than any Ph.D.⟩ **4 :** HUSBAND

mis·think \(ˌ)mis-ˈthiŋk\ *vb* **-thought** \-ˈthȯt\; **-think·ing** *vi, archaic* (ca. 1530) **:** to think mistakenly or unfavorably ~ *vt, archaic* **:** to think badly or unfavorably of

mis·tle thrush \ˈmis-əl-\ *n* [obs. E *mistle* mistletoe, fr. ME *mistel,* fr. OE] (1774) **:** MAVIS 2

mis·tle·toe \ˈmis-əl-ˌtō, *chiefly Brit* ˈmiz-\ *n* [ME *mistilto* basil, fr. OE *misteltān,* fr. *mistel* mistletoe, basil + *tān* twig; akin to OHG & OS *mistil* mistletoe and to OHG *zein* twig] (bef. 12c) **:** a European semiparasitic green shrub (*Viscum album* of the family Loranthaceae, the mistletoe family) with thick leaves, small yellowish flowers, and waxy-white glutinous berries; *broadly* **:** any of various plants of the mistletoe family (as of an American genus *Phoradendron*) resembling the true mistletoe

mis·tral \ˈmis-trəl, mi-ˈsträl\ *n* [F, fr. Prov, fr. *mistral* masterful, fr. L *magistralis* — more at MAGISTRAL] (1604) **:** a strong cold dry northerly wind of southern France

mis·treat \(ˌ)mis-ˈtrēt\ *vt* [ME *mistreten,* prob. fr. MF *mestraitier,* fr. OF, fr. *mes-* ¹mis- + *traitier* to treat — more at TREAT] (15c) **:** to treat badly **:** ABUSE — **mis·treat·ment** \-mənt\ *n*

mis·tress \ˈmis-trəs\ *n* [ME *maistresse,* fr. MF, fr. OF, fem. of *maistre* master — more at MASTER] (15c) **1 :** a woman who has power, authority, or ownership: as **a :** the female head of a household **b :** a woman who employs or supervises servants **c :** a woman who possesses or controls something **d :** a woman who is in charge of a school or other establishment **e :** a woman of the Scottish nobility having a status comparable to that of a master **2 a** *chiefly Brit* **:** a female teacher or tutor **b :** a woman who has achieved mastery in some field **3 :** a country or state having supremacy over others **4 :** something personified as female that rules or directs **5 a :** a woman with whom a man habitually fornicates **b** *archaic* **:** SWEETHEART **6 a —** used archaically as a title prefixed to the name of a married or unmarried woman **b** \ˈmiz-əz, ˈmis-, -əs\ *chiefly Southern & Midland* **:** MRS. 1a

mistress of ceremonies (1952) **:** a woman who presides at a public ceremony or who acts as hostess of a stage, radio, or television show

mis·tri·al \(ˌ)mis-ˈtrī(-ə)l\ *n* (1628) **:** a trial that has no legal effect by reason of some error or serious prejudicial misconduct in the proceedings

¹mis·trust \(ˌ)mis-ˈtrəst\ *n* (14c) **:** a lack of confidence **:** DISTRUST ***syn*** see UNCERTAINTY — **mis·trust·ful** \-fəl\ *adj* — **mis·trust·ful·ly** \-fə-lē\ *adv* — **mis·trust·ful·ness** *n*

²mistrust *vt* (14c) **1 :** to have no trust or confidence in **:** SUSPECT ⟨~*ed* his neighbors⟩ **2 :** to doubt the truth, validity, or effectiveness of ⟨~*ed* his own judgment⟩ **3 :** SURMISE ⟨your mind ~*ed* there was something wrong —Robert Frost⟩ ~ *vi* **:** to be suspicious

misty \ˈmis-tē\ *adj* **mist·i·er; -est** [ME, fr. OE *mistig,* fr. *mist* mist] (bef. 12c) **1 a :** obscured by mist **b :** consisting of or marked by mist **2 a :** INDISTINCT ⟨a ~ recollection of the event⟩ **b :** VAGUE, CONFUSED ⟨avoided the large, vague, ~ issues —Reuben Abel⟩ — **mist·i·ly** \-tə-lē\ *adv* — **mist·i·ness** \-tē-nəs\ *n*

misty–eyed \ˌmis-tē-ˈīd\ *adj* (1928) **1 :** having eyes covered with mist **2 :** DREAMY, SENTIMENTAL ⟨~ recollections⟩

mis·un·der·stand \(ˌ)mis-ˌən-dər-ˈstand\ *vt* **-stood** \-ˈstu̇d\; **-stand·ing** (13c) **1 :** to fail to understand **2 :** to interpret incorrectly

mis·un·der·stand·ing *n* (15c) **1 :** a failure to understand **:** MISINTERPRETATION **2 :** QUARREL, DISAGREEMENT

mis·us·age \mish-ˈü-sij, (ˌ)mis(h)-ˈyü-, -zij\ *n* [MF *mesusage,* fr. *mes-* ¹mis- + *usage* usage] (ca. 1554) **1 :** bad treatment **:** ABUSE **2 :** wrong or improper use (as of words)

¹mis·use \mish-ˈüz, (ˌ)mis(h)-ˈyüz\ *vt* [ME *misusen,* partly fr. *mis-* + *usen* to use; partly fr. MF *mesuser* to abuse, fr. OF, fr. *mes-* ¹mis- + *user* to use] (14c) **1 :** to use incorrectly **:** MISAPPLY ⟨*misused* his talents⟩ **2 :** ABUSE, MISTREAT ⟨*misused* his servants⟩

²mis·use \mish-ˈüs, (ˌ)mis(h)-ˈyüs\ *n* (14c) **:** incorrect or improper use **:** MISAPPLICATION

mis·val·ue \(ˌ)mis-ˈval-(ˌ)yü, -yə(-w)\ *vt* (1626) **:** UNDERVALUE

mis·ven·ture \(ˌ)mis-ˈven-chər\ *n* (1563) **:** MISADVENTURE

mis·write \(ˌ)mis-ˈrīt\ *vt* **-wrote** \-ˈrōt\; **-writ·ten** \-ˈrit-ᵊn\; **-writ·ing** \-ˈrīt-iŋ\ (bef. 12c) **:** to write incorrectly

¹mite \ˈmīt\ *n* [ME, fr. OE *mīte;* akin to MD *mite* mite, small copper coin, OHG *meizan* to cut, OE *gemād* silly — more at MAD] (bef. 12c) **:** any of numerous small to very minute arachnids (order Acarina) that often infest animals, plants, and stored foods and include important disease vectors

²mite *n* [ME, fr. MF or MD; MF, small Flemish copper coin, fr. MD] (14c) **1 :** a small coin or sum of money **2 a :** a very little **:** BIT **b :** a very small object or creature — **a mite :** SOMEWHAT, RATHER ⟨could be that I am *a mite* prejudiced —John Fischer⟩

¹mi·ter *or* **mi·tre** \ˈmīt-ər\ *n* [ME *mitre,* fr. MF, fr. L *mitra* headband, turban, fr. Gk; akin to Skt *mitra* friend] (14c) **1 :** a liturgical headdress worn by bishops and abbots — see VESTMENT illustration **2 a :** a surface forming the beveled end or edge of a piece where a joint is made by cutting two pieces at an angle and fitting them together **b :** MITER SQUARE

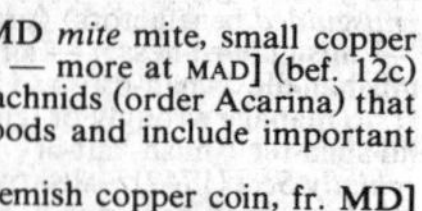

miter 2a: *1* plain, *2* milled, *3* rabbeted

²miter *or* **mitre** *vt* **mi·tered** *or* **mi·tred; mi·ter·ing** *or* **mi·tring** \ˈmīt-ə-riŋ\ (14c) **1 :** to confer a miter on **2 a :** to match or fit together in a miter joint **b :** to bevel the ends of for making a miter joint — **mi·ter·er** \ˈmīt-ər-ər\ *n*

miter box *n* (ca. 1846) **:** a device for guiding a handsaw at the proper angle in making a miter joint in wood

miter gear *n* (ca. 1908) **:** one of a pair of interchangeable bevel gears with axes at right angles

miter square *n* (ca. 1678) **:** a bevel with an immovable arm at an angle of 45 degrees for striking miter lines; *also* **:** a square with an arm adjustable to any angle

Mith·ra·ic \mith-'rā-ik\ *adj* [LGk *mithraikos* of Mithras, ancient Persian god of light, fr. Gk *Mithras,* fr. OPer *Mithra*] (1678) **:** of or relating to an oriental mystery cult for men flourishing in the late Roman empire — **Mith·ra·ism** \'mith-rə-ˌiz-əm, -(ˌ)rā-\ *n* — **Mith·ra·ist** \mith-'rā-əst\ *n or adj*

mith·ri·date \'mith-rə-ˌdāt\ *n* [ML *mithridatum,* fr. LL *mithridatium,* fr. L, dogtooth violet (used as an antidote), fr. Gk *mithridation,* fr. *Mithridatēs* Mithridates VI] (1528) **:** an antidote against poison; *esp* **:** an electuary held to be effective against poison

mi·ti·cide \'mīt-ə-ˌsīd\ *n* [*mite*] (ca. 1946) **:** an agent used to kill mites — **mi·ti·cid·al** \ˌmīt-ə-'sīd-ᵊl\ *adj*

mit·i·gate \'mit-ə-ˌgāt\ *vt* **-gat·ed; -gat·ing** [ME *mitigaten,* fr. L *mitigatus,* pp. of *mitigare* to soften, fr. *mitis* soft + *-igare* (akin to L *agere* to drive); akin to OIr *mōith* soft — more at AGENT] (15c) **1 :** to cause to become less harsh or hostile **:** MOLLIFY ⟨aggressiveness may be *mitigated* or . . . channeled —Ashley Montagu⟩ **2 a :** to make less severe or painful **:** ALLEVIATE **b :** EXTENUATE ***syn*** see RELIEVE — **mit·i·ga·tion** \ˌmit-ə-'gā-shən\ *n* — **mit·i·ga·tive** \'mit-ə-ˌgāt-iv\ *adj* — **mit·i·ga·tor** \-ˌgāt-ər\ *n* — **mit·i·ga·to·ry** \'mit-i-gə-ˌtōr-ē, -ˌtȯr-\ *adj*

usage *Mitigate* is sometimes used as an intransitive (followed by *against*) where *militate* might be expected. Although this usage is at least 40 years old and has been found in the works of William Faulkner, it is generally considered a mistake.

mi·to·chon·dri·on \ˌmīt-ə-'kän-drē-ən\ *n, pl* **-dria** \-drē-ə\ [NL, fr. Gk *mitos* thread + *chondrion,* dim. of *chondros* grain — more at GRIND] (1901) **:** any of various round or long cellular organelles that are found outside the nucleus, produce energy for the cell through cellular respiration, and are rich in fats, proteins, and enzymes — see CELL illustration — **mi·to·chon·dri·al** \-drē-əl\ *adj*

mi·to·gen \'mīt-ə-jən\ *n* [*mitosis* + *-gen*] (1951) **:** a substance that induces mitosis — **mi·to·gen·ic** \ˌmīt-ə-'jen-ik\ *adj* — **mi·to·ge·nic·i·ty** \-jə-'nis-ət-ē\ *n*

mi·to·my·cin \ˌmīt-ə-'mīs-ᵊn\ *n* [ISV *mito-* (prob. fr. NL *mitosis*) + *-mycin*] (1956) **:** a complex of antibiotic substances which is produced by a Japanese streptomyces (*Streptomyces caespitosus*) and one form of which acts directly on DNA and shows promise as an anticancer agent

mi·to·sis \mī-'tō-səs\ *n, pl* **-to·ses** \-ˌsēz\ [NL, fr. Gk *mitos* thread] (1887) **1 :** a process that takes place in the nucleus of a dividing cell, involves typically a series of steps consisting of prophase, metaphase, anaphase, and telophase, and results in the formation of two new nuclei each having the same number of chromosomes as the parent nucleus — compare MEIOSIS **2 :** cell division in which mitosis occurs — **mi·tot·ic** \-'tät-ik\ *adj* — **mi·tot·i·cal·ly** \-i-k(ə-)lē\ *adv*

mi·trail·leuse \ˌmē-trə-'yə(r)z\ *n* [F, fr. *mitrailler* to fire grapeshot, fr. *mitraille* grapeshot, fr. MF old iron, small coin — more at MITE] (1870) **1 :** a breech-loading machine gun with a number of barrels **2 :** MACHINE GUN

mi·tral \'mī-trəl\ *adj* (1610) **1 :** resembling a miter **2 :** of, relating to, being, or adjoining a mitral valve or orifice

mitral valve *n* (1705) **:** BICUSPID VALVE

mi·tre·wort *also* **mi·ter·wort** \'mīt-ər-ˌwərt, -ˌwȯ(ə)rt\ *n* (1817) **:** any of a genus (*Mitella*) of rhizomatous perennial herbs of the saxifrage family that bear a capsule resembling a bishop's miter

mitt \'mit\ *n* [short for *mitten*] (1765) **1 a :** a woman's glove that leaves the fingers uncovered **b :** MITTEN 1 **c :** a baseball catcher's or first baseman's glove made in the style of a mitten **2** *slang* **:** HAND

mit·ten \'mit-ᵊn\ *n* [ME *mitain,* fr. MF *mitaine,* fr. OF, fr. *mite* mitten] (14c) **1 :** a covering for the hand and wrist having a separate section for the thumb only **2 :** MITT 1a

mit·ti·mus \'mit-ə-məs\ *n* [L, we send, fr. *mittere* to send — more at SMITE] (1591) **:** a warrant of commitment to prison

mitz·vah \'mits-və\ *n, pl* **mitz·voth** \-ˌvōt(h), -ˌvōs\ *or* **mitz·vahs** [Heb *miṣwāh*] (1650) **1 :** a commandment of the Jewish law **2 :** a meritorious or charitable act

[1]**mix** \'miks\ *vb* [ME *mixen,* back-formation fr. *mixte* mixed, fr. MF, fr. L *mixtus,* pp. of *miscēre* to mix; akin to Gk *mignynai* to mix] *vt* (15c) **1 a** (1) **:** to combine or blend into one mass (2) **:** to combine with another **b :** to bring into close association ⟨~ business with pleasure⟩ **2 a :** to form by mixing components ⟨~ a drink at the bar⟩ **b :** to produce (a phonograph record) by electronically combining or adjusting sounds from more than one source **3 :** CONFUSE — often used with *up* ⟨~*es* things up in his eagerness to speak out —Irving Howe⟩ ~ *vi* **1 a :** to become mixed **b :** to be capable of mixing **2 :** to enter into relations **:** ASSOCIATE **3 :** CROSSBREED **4 :** to become involved **:** PARTICIPATE ⟨decided not to ~ in politics⟩ — **mix·able** \'mik-sə-bəl\ *adj*

syn MIX, MINGLE, COMMINGLE, BLEND, MERGE, COALESCE, AMALGAMATE, FUSE mean to combine into a more or less uniform whole. MIX may or may not imply loss of each element's identity; MINGLE usu. suggests that the elements are still somewhat distinguishable or separately active; COMMINGLE implies a closer or more thorough mingling; BLEND implies that the elements as such disappear in the resulting mixture; MERGE suggests a combining in which one or more elements are lost in the whole; COALESCE implies an affinity in the merging elements and usu. a resulting organic unity; AMALGAMATE implies the forming of a close union without complete loss of individual identities; FUSE stresses oneness and indissolubility of the resulting product.

[2]**mix** *n* (ca. 1586) **1 :** an act or process of mixing **2 :** a product of mixing; *specif* **:** a commercially prepared mixture of food ingredients ⟨a cake ~⟩ **3 :** MIXER 2b

mixed \'mikst\ *adj* [ME *mixte*] (15c) **1 :** combining characteristics of more than one kind; *specif* **:** combining features of two or more systems of government ⟨a ~ constitution⟩ **2 :** made up of or involving individuals or items of more than one kind: as **a :** made up of or involving persons differing in race, national origin, religion, or class **b :** made up of or involving individuals of both sexes ⟨~ company⟩ **3 :** including or accompanied by inconsistent or incompatible elements ⟨~ emotions⟩ **4 :** deriving from two or more races or breeds ⟨a person of ~ blood⟩

mixed alphabet *n* (1931) **:** an alphabet (as in a cryptographic system) that has been rearranged or disordered systematically or randomly

mixed bag *n* (1926) **:** a miscellaneous collection **:** ASSORTMENT

mixed bud *n* (ca. 1900) **:** a bud that produces a branch and leaves as well as flowers

mixed drink *n* (1943) **:** an alcoholic beverage prepared from two or more ingredients

mixed farming *n* (1872) **:** the growing of food or cash crops, feed crops, and livestock on the same farm

mixed grill *n* (1913) **:** meats (as lamb chop, kidney, and bacon) and vegetables broiled together and served on one plate

mixed marriage *n* (1829) **:** a marriage between persons of different races or religions

mixed–media *adj* (1962) **:** MULTIMEDIA

mixed nerve *n* (1878) **:** a nerve containing both sensory and motor fibers

mixed number *n* (1542) **:** a number (as $5^2/_3$) composed of an integer and a fraction

mixed–up \'mik-'stəp\ *adj* (1862) **:** marked by bewilderment, perplexity, or disorder **:** CONFUSED ⟨an abandoner of husband and child, and a totally ~ kid —Hollis Alpert⟩

mix·er \'mik-sər\ *n* (ca. 1611) **1 :** one that mixes: as **a** (1) **:** one whose work is mixing the ingredients of a product (2) **:** one who balances and controls the dialogue, music, and sound effects to be recorded for or with a motion picture or television **b :** a container, device, or machine for mixing **c :** a game, stunt, or dance used at a get-together to give members of the group an opportunity to meet one another in a friendly and informal atmosphere **2 :** one that mixes with others: as **a :** a person considered as to his casual sociability ⟨was shy and a poor ~⟩ **b :** a nonalcoholic beverage (as ginger ale) used in a mixed drink

mix·ol·o·gy \mik-'säl-ə-jē\ *n* (1948) **:** the art or skill of preparing mixed drinks — **mix·ol·o·gist** \-jəst\ *n*

Mix·tec \'mēs(h)-'tek, mis(h)-\ *n, pl* **Mixtec** *or* **Mixtecs** [AmerSp *mixteco*] (1850) **1 :** the language of the Mixtec people **2 :** a member of an Indian people of Mexico

mix·ture \'miks-chər\ *n* [MF, fr. OF *misture,* fr. L *mixtura,* fr. *mixtus*] (15c) **1 a :** the act, the process, or an instance of mixing **b** (1) **:** the state of being mixed (2) **:** the relative proportions of constituents; *specif* **:** the proportion of fuel to air produced in a carburetor **2 :** a product of mixing **:** COMBINATION: as **a :** a portion of matter consisting of two or more components in varying proportions that retain their own properties **b :** a fabric woven of variously colored threads **c :** a combination of several different kinds

mix–up \'mik-ˌsəp\ *n* (1841) **1 :** a state or instance of confusion **2 :** MIXTURE **3 :** CONFLICT, FIGHT

Mi·zar \'mī-ˌzär\ *n* [Ar *Mi'zar,* lit., veil, cloak] **:** a star of the second magnitude in the handle of the Big Dipper

[1]**miz·zen** *or* **miz·en** \'miz-ᵊn\ *n* [ME *meson,* prob. fr. MF *misaine,* deriv. of It *mezzana,* prob. fr. L *medianus* of the middle — more at MEDIAN] (15c) **1 :** a fore-and-aft sail set on the mizzenmast **2 :** MIZZENMAST

[2]**mizzen** *or* **mizen** *adj* (15c) **:** of or relating to the mizzenmast

miz·zen·mast \-ˌmast, -məst\ *n* (15c) **:** the mast aft or next aft of the mainmast in a ship

[1]**miz·zle** \'miz-əl\ *vi* **miz·zled; miz·zling** \-(ə-)liŋ\ [ME *misellen;* akin to Flem *mizzelen* to drizzle, MD *mist* fog, mist] (15c) **:** to rain in very fine drops **:** DRIZZLE ⟨standing up hatless in the *mizzling* rain —Helen Eustis⟩ — **mizzle** *n* — **miz·zly** \-(ə-)lē\ *adj*

[2]**mizzle** *vi* **miz·zled; miz·zling** \-(ə-)liŋ\ [origin unknown] *chiefly Brit* (1781) **:** to depart suddenly

[1]**mne·mon·ic** \ni-'män-ik\ *adj* [Gk *mnēmonikos,* fr. *mnēmōn* mindful, fr. *mimnēskesthai* to remember — more at MENTAL] (1753) **1 :** assisting or intended to assist memory; *also* **:** of or relating to mnemonics **2 :** of or relating to memory — **mne·mon·i·cal·ly** \-i-k(ə-)lē\ *adv*

[2]**mnemonic** *n* (1858) **:** a mnemonic device or code

mne·mon·ics \ni-'män-iks\ *n pl but sing in constr* (1721) **:** a technique of improving the memory

Mne·mos·y·ne \ni-'mäs-ᵊn-ē, -'mäz-\ *n* [L, fr. Gk *Mnēmosynē*] **:** the Greek goddess of memory and mother of the Muses by Zeus

-mo \(ˌ)mō\ *n suffix* [duodecimo] — after numerals or their names to indicate the number of leaves made by folding a sheet of paper ⟨sixteen*mo*⟩ ⟨16*mo*⟩

moa \'mō-ə\ *n* [Maori] (1842) **:** any of various usu. very large extinct flightless ratite birds of New Zealand (family Dinornithidae) including one (*Dinornis giganteus*) about 12 feet in height

Mo·ab·ite \'mō-ə-ˌbīt\ *n* [ME, fr. LL *Moabita, Moabites,* fr. Gk *Mōabitēs,* fr. *Mōab* Moab, ancient kingdom in Syria] (14c) **:** a member of an ancient Semitic people related to the Hebrews — **Moabite** *or* **Mo·ab·it·ish** \-ˌbīt-ish\ *adj*

[1]**moan** \'mōn\ *n* [ME *mone,* fr. (assumed) OE *mān*] (13c) **1 :** LAMENTATION, COMPLAINT **2 :** a low prolonged sound of pain or of grief

[2]**moan** *vt* (14c) **1 :** to bewail audibly **:** LAMENT **2 :** to utter with moans ~ *vi* **1 :** LAMENT, COMPLAIN **2 a :** to make a moan **:** GROAN **b :** to emit a sound resembling a moan ⟨the wind ~*ed* in the trees⟩

[1]**moat** \'mōt\ *n* [ME *mote,* prob. fr. MF *motte* hill, mound] (14c) **1 :** a deep and wide trench around the rampart of a fortified place (as a castle) that is usu. filled with water **2 :** a channel resembling a moat (as about a seamount or for confinement of animals in a zoo) — **moat·like** \-ˌlīk\ *adj*

[2]**moat** *vt* (15c) **:** to surround with or as if with a moat

[1]**mob** \'mäb\ *n* [L *mobile vulgus* vacillating crowd] (1688) **1 :** a large or disorderly crowd; *esp* **:** one bent on riotous or destructive action **2 :** the lower classes of a community **:** MASSES, RABBLE **3** *chiefly Austral* **:** a flock, drove, or herd of animals **4 :** a criminal set **:** GANG ***syn*** see CROWD — **mob·bish** \'mäb-ish\ *adj*

\ə\ abut \ᵊ\ kitten, F table \ər\ further \a\ ash \ā\ ace \ä\ cot, cart \au̇\ out \ch\ chin \e\ bet \ē\ easy \g\ go \i\ hit \ī\ ice \j\ job \ŋ\ sing \ō\ go \ȯ\ law \ȯi\ boy \th\ thin \t͟h\ the \ü\ loot \u̇\ foot \y\ yet \zh\ vision \à, k̲, ⁿ, œ, œ̄, ue, ue̅, ʸ\ *see* Guide to Pronunciation

[2]mob *vt* **mobbed; mob·bing** (1709) **1 :** to crowd about and attack or annoy ⟨*mobbed* by autograph hunters before he could enter the theater⟩ **2 :** to crowd into or around ⟨customers ~ the stores on sale days⟩

mob·cap \'mäb-,kap\ *n* [*mob* (woman's cap) + *cap*] (1795) **:** a woman's fancy indoor cap made with a high full crown and often tied under the chin

[1]mo·bile \'mō-bəl, -,bēl, -,bīl\ *adj* [MF, fr. L *mobilis*, fr. *movēre* to move] (15c) **1 :** capable of moving or being moved **:** MOVABLE ⟨a ~ missile launcher⟩ **2 a :** changeable in appearance, mood, or purpose ⟨~ face⟩ **b :** ADAPTABLE, VERSATILE **3 :** MIGRATORY **4 a :** characterized by the mixing of social groups **b :** having the opportunity for or undergoing a shift in status within the hierarchical social levels of a society ⟨upwardly ~ workers⟩ **5 :** marked by the use of vehicles for transportation ⟨~ warfare⟩ **6 :** of or relating to a mobile — **mo·bil·i·ty** \mō-'bil-ət-ē\ *n*

[2]mo·bile \'mō-,bēl\ *n* (1936) **:** a construction or sculpture frequently of wire and sheet metal shapes with parts that can be set in motion by air currents; *also* **:** a similar structure (as of paper or plastic) suspended so that it moves in a current of air

mobile home *n* (1949) **:** a trailer that is used as a permanent dwelling, is usu. connected to utilities, and is designed without a permanent foundation — compare MOTOR HOME

mo·bi·li·za·tion \,mō-bə-lə-'zā-shən\ *n* (1799) **1 :** the act of mobilizing **2 :** the state of being mobilized

mo·bi·lize \'mō-bə-,līz\ *vb* **-lized; -liz·ing** *vt* (1838) **1 a :** to put into movement or circulation ⟨~ financial assets⟩ **b :** to release (something stored in the organism) for bodily use **2 a :** to assemble and make ready for war duty **b :** to marshal (as resources) for action ⟨~ support for a proposal⟩ ~ *vi* **:** to undergo mobilization

Mö·bi·us strip \,mœ-bē-əs-, ,mə(r)-, ,mō-\ *n* [August F. *Möbius* †1868 Ger. mathematician] (1904) **:** a one-sided surface that is constructed from a rectangle by holding one end fixed, rotating the opposite end through 180 degrees, and applying it to the first end

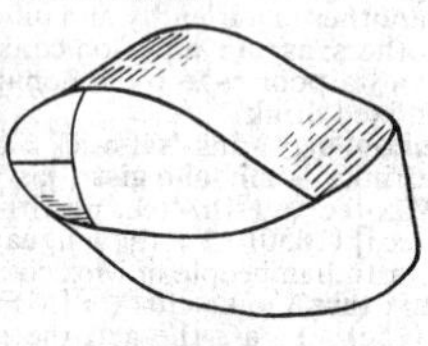
Möbius strip

mob·oc·ra·cy \mä-'bäk-rə-sē\ *n* (1754) **1 :** rule by the mob **2 :** the mob as a ruling class — **mob·ocrat** \'mäb-ə-,krat\ *n* — **mob·ocrat·ic** \,mäb-ə-'krat-ik\ *adj*

mob·ster \'mäb-stər\ *n* (1917) **:** a member of a criminal gang

moc·ca·sin \'mäk-ə-sən\ *n* [of Algonquian origin; akin to Natick *mokkussin* shoe] (1612) **1 a :** a soft leather heelless shoe or boot with the sole brought up the sides of the foot and over the toes where it is joined with a puckered seam to a U-shaped piece lying on top of the foot **b :** a regular shoe having a seam on the forepart of the vamp imitating the seam of a moccasin **2 a :** WATER MOCCASIN **b :** a snake (as of the genus *Natrix*) resembling a water moccasin

moccasin flower *n* (1680) **:** any of several lady's slippers (genus *Cypripedium*); *esp* **:** a once common woodland orchid (*C. acaule*) of eastern No. America with pink or white moccasin-shaped flowers

mo·cha \'mō-kə\ *n* [*Mocha*, Arabia] (1773) **1 a (1) :** a superior Arabian coffee consisting of small green or yellowish beans **(2) :** a coffee of superior quality **b :** a flavoring made of a strong coffee infusion or of a mixture of cocoa or chocolate with coffee **2 :** a pliable suede-finished glove leather from African sheepskins

[1]mock \'mäk, 'mȯk\ *vb* [ME *mocken*, fr. MF *mocquer*] *vt* (15c) **1 :** to treat with contempt or ridicule **:** DERIDE **2 :** to disappoint the hopes of **:** DELUDE **3 :** DEFY, CHALLENGE **4 a :** to imitate (as a sound or mannerism) closely **:** MIMIC **b :** to mimic in sport or derision ~ *vi* **:** JEER, SCOFF ***syn*** see RIDICULE, COPY — **mock·er** *n* — **mock·ing·ly** \-iŋ-lē\ *adv*

[2]mock *n* (15c) **1 :** an act of ridicule or derision **:** JEER **2 :** one that is an object of derision or scorn **3 :** MOCKERY **4 a :** an act of imitation **b :** something made as an imitation

[3]mock *adj* (1548) **:** of, relating to, or having the character of an imitation **:** SIMULATED, FEIGNED ⟨the ~ solemnity of the parody⟩

[4]mock *adv* (1619) **:** in an insincere or counterfeit manner — usu. used in combination ⟨*mock*-serious⟩

mock·ery \'mäk-(ə-)rē, 'mȯk-\ *n, pl* **-er·ies** (15c) **1 :** insulting or contemptuous action or speech **:** DERISION **2 :** a subject of laughter, derision, or sport **3 a :** a counterfeit appearance **:** IMITATION **b :** an insincere, contemptible, or impertinent imitation ⟨arbitrary methods that make a ~ of justice⟩ **4 :** something ridiculously or impudently unsuitable

[1]mock–he·ro·ic \,mäk-hi-'rō-ik, ,mȯk-\ *adj* (ca. 1711) **:** ridiculing or burlesquing heroic style, character, or action ⟨a ~ poem⟩ — **mock–he·ro·ical·ly** \-i-k(ə-)lē\ *adv*

[2]mock–heroic *n* (1728) **:** a mock-heroic composition — called also *mock-epic*

mock·ing·bird \'mäk-iŋ-,bərd, 'mȯk-\ *n* (1676) **:** a common bird (*Mimus polyglottos*) esp. of the southern U.S. that is remarkable for its exact imitations of the notes of other birds

mock orange *n* (1731) **:** any of various usu. shrubby plants considered to resemble the orange; *esp* **:** PHILADELPHUS

mock turtle soup *n* (1783) **:** a soup made of meat (as calf's head or veal), wine, and spices in imitation of green turtle soup

mock–up \'mäk-,əp, 'mȯk-\ *n* (1920) **:** a full-sized structural model built accurately to scale chiefly for study, testing, or display

[1]mod \'mäd\ *adj* (1964) **:** MODERN; *esp* **:** bold and free in style, behavior, or dress

[2]mod *n* (1965) **:** one who wears mod clothes

mod·acryl·ic fiber \,mäd-ə-,kril-ik-\ *n* [*modified acrylic*] (1960) **:** any of various synthetic textile fibers that are long-chain polymers composed of 35 to 85 percent by weight of acrylonitrile units

mod·al \'mōd-ᵊl\ *adj* [ML *modalis*, fr. L *modus*] (1569) **1 :** of or relating to modality in logic **2 :** containing provisions as to the mode of procedure or the manner of taking effect — used of a contract or legacy **3 :** of or relating to a musical mode **4 :** of or relating to structure as opposed to substance **5 :** of, relating to, or constituting a grammatical form or category characteristically indicating predication of an action or state in some manner other than as a simple fact **6 :** of or relating to a statistical mode — **mod·al·ly** \-ᵊl-ē\ *adv*

modal auxiliary *n* (ca. 1904) **:** an auxiliary verb (as *can, must, might, may*) that is characteristically used with a verb of predication and expresses a modal modification and that in English differs formally from other verbs in lacking *-s* and *-ing* forms

mo·dal·i·ty \mō-'dal-ət-ē\ *n, pl* **-ties** (1617) **1 a :** the quality or state of being modal **b :** a modal quality or attribute **:** FORM **2 :** the classification of logical propositions according to their asserting or denying the possibility, impossibility, contingency, or necessity of their content **3 :** one of the main avenues of sensation (as vision) **4 :** a usu. physical therapeutic agency

[1]mode \'mōd\ *n* [ME *moede*, fr. L *modus* measure, manner, musical mode — more at METE] (14c) **1 a :** an arrangement of the eight diatonic notes or tones of an octave according to one of several fixed schemes of their intervals **b :** a rhythmical scheme (as in 13th and 14th century music) **2 :** [2]MOOD 2 **3** [LL *modus*, fr. L] **a :** [2]MOOD 1 **b :** the modal form of the assertion or denial of a logical proposition **4 a :** a particular form or variety of something **b :** a form or manner of expression **:** STYLE **5 :** a possible, customary, or preferred way of doing something ⟨explained in the usual solemn ~⟩ **6 a :** a manifestation, form, or arrangement of being; *specif* **:** a particular form or manifestation of an underlying substance **b :** a particular functioning arrangement or condition **:** STATUS ⟨a spacecraft in reentry ~⟩ ⟨a computer operating in parallel ~⟩ **7 a :** the most frequent value of a set of data **b :** a value of a random variable for which a function of probabilities defined on it achieves a relative maximum **8 :** any of various stationary vibration patterns of which an elastic body or oscillatory system is capable ⟨the vibration ~ of an airplane propeller blade⟩ ⟨the ~*s* of electromagnetic radiation in a waveguide⟩ **9 :** the actual mineral composition of a rock ***syn*** see METHOD

[2]mode *n* [F, fr. L *modus*] (1645) **:** a prevailing fashion or style (as of dress or behavior) ***syn*** see FASHION

[1]mod·el \'mäd-ᵊl\ *n* [MF *modelle*, fr. OIt *modello*, fr. (assumed) VL *modellus*, fr. L *modulus* small measure, fr. *modus*] (1575) **1** *obs* **:** a set of plans for a building **2** *dial Brit* **:** COPY, IMAGE **3 :** structural design ⟨a home on the ~ of an old farmhouse⟩ **4 :** a miniature representation of something; *also* **:** a pattern of something to be made **5 :** an example for imitation or emulation **6 :** a person or thing that serves as a pattern for an artist; *esp* **:** one who poses for an artist **7 :** ARCHETYPE **8 :** an organism whose appearance a mimic imitates **9 :** one who is employed to display clothes or other merchandise **:** MANNEQUIN **10 a :** a type or design of clothing **b :** a type or design of product (as a car) **11 :** a description or analogy used to help visualize something (as an atom) that cannot be directly observed **12 :** a system of postulates, data, and inferences presented as a mathematical description of an entity or state of affairs **13 :** VERSION

syn MODEL, EXAMPLE, PATTERN, EXEMPLAR, IDEAL mean someone or something set before one for guidance or imitation. MODEL applies to something taken or proposed as worthy of imitation; EXAMPLE applies to a person to be imitated or in some contexts on no account to be imitated but to be regarded as a warning; PATTERN suggests a clear and detailed archetype or prototype; EXEMPLAR suggests either a faultless example to be emulated or a perfect typification; IDEAL implies the best possible exemplification either in reality or in conception.

[2]model *vb* **mod·eled** *or* **mod·elled; mod·el·ing** *or* **mod·el·ling** \'mäd-liŋ, -ᵊl-iŋ\ *vt* (1730) **1 :** to plan or form after a pattern **:** SHAPE **2** *archaic* **:** to make into an organization (as an army, government, or parish) **3 a :** to shape or fashion in a plastic material **b :** to produce a representation or simulation of ⟨using a computer to ~ a problem⟩ **4 :** to construct or fashion in imitation of a particular model ⟨~*ed* its constitution on that of the U.S.⟩ **5 :** to display by wearing, using, or posing with ⟨~*ed* gowns⟩ ~ *vi* **1 :** to design or imitate forms **:** make a pattern ⟨enjoys ~*ing* in clay⟩ **2 :** to work or act as a fashion model — **mod·el·er** \'mäd-lər, -ᵊl-ər\ *n*

[3]model *adj* (1844) **1 :** serving as or capable of serving as a pattern ⟨a ~ student⟩ **2 :** being a miniature representation of something ⟨a ~ airplane⟩

mo·dem \'mō-,dem\ *n* [*mo*dulator + *dem*odulator] (ca. 1952) **:** a device that converts signals from one form to a form compatible with another kind of equipment ⟨a ~ for transmitting computer data over telephone lines⟩

[1]mod·er·ate \'mäd-(ə-)rət\ *adj* [ME, fr. L *moderatus*, fr. pp. of *moderare* to moderate; akin to L *modus* measure] (15c) **1 a :** avoiding extremes of behavior or expression **:** observing reasonable limits ⟨a ~ drinker⟩ **b :** CALM, TEMPERATE **2 a :** tending toward the mean or average amount or dimension **b :** having average or less than average quality **:** MEDIOCRE **3 :** avoiding extreme political or social measures ⟨a ~ candidate⟩ **4 :** limited in scope or effect **5 :** not expensive **:** reasonable or low in price **6** *of a color* **:** of medium lightness and medium chroma — **mod·er·ate·ly** *adv* — **mod·er·ate·ness** *n*

[2]mod·er·ate \'mäd-ə-,rāt\ *vb* **-at·ed; -at·ing** *vt* (15c) **1 :** to lessen the intensity or extremeness of ⟨the sun *moderated* the chill⟩ **2 :** to preside over or act as chairman of ~ *vi* **1 :** to act as a moderator **2 :** to become less violent, severe, or intense — **mod·er·a·tion** \,mäd-ə-'rā-shən\ *n*

[3]mod·er·ate \'mäd-(ə-)rət\ *n* (1794) **:** one who holds moderate views or who belongs to a group favoring a moderate course or program (as in politics or religion)

moderate breeze *n* (ca. 1805) **:** wind having a speed of 13 to 18 miles per hour

moderate gale *n* (ca. 1805) **:** wind having a speed of 32 to 38 miles per hour

mo·der·a·to \,mäd-ə-'rät-(,)ō\ *adv or adj* [It, fr. L *moderatus*] (ca. 1724) **:** MODERATE — used as a direction in music to indicate tempo

mod·er·a·tor \'mäd-ə-,rāt-ər\ *n* (1560) **1 :** one who arbitrates **:** MEDIATOR **2 :** one who presides over an assembly, meeting, or discussion: as **a :** the presiding officer of a Presbyterian governing body **b :** the nonpartisan presiding officer of a town meeting **c :** the chairman of a discussion group **3 :** a substance (as graphite) used for slowing down neutrons in a nuclear reactor — **mod·er·a·tor·ship** \-,ship\ *n*

[1]mod·ern \'mäd-ərn, ÷'mäd-(ə-)rən\ *adj* [LL *modernus*, fr. L *modo* just now, fr. *modus* measure — more at METE] (1585) **1 a :** of, relating to, or characteristic of a period extending from a relevant remote past to the present time **b :** of, relating to, or characteristic of the present or the immediate past **:** CONTEMPORARY **2 :** involving recent techniques, methods, or ideas : UP-TO-DATE **3** *cap* : of, relating to, or having the characteristics of the present or most recent period of development of a language *syn* see NEW — **mod·er·ni·ty** \mə-ˈdər-nət-ē, mä- *also* -ˈder-\ *n* — **mod·ern·ly** \ˈmäd-ərn-lē\ *adv* — **mod·ern·ness** \-ərn-nəs\ *n*

²modern *n* (1585) **1** : a person of modern times or views **2** : a style of printing type distinguished by regularity of shape, precise curves, straight hairline serifs, and heavy downstrokes

Modern Hebrew *n* (1949) : Hebrew as used in present-day Israel

mod·ern·ism \ˈmäd-ər-ˌniz-əm\ *n* (1737) **1** : a practice, usage, or expression peculiar to modern times **2** *often cap* : a tendency in theology to accommodate traditional religious teaching to contemporary thought and esp. to devalue traditional supernatural elements **3** : modern artistic or literary philosophy and practice; *esp* : a self-conscious break with the past and a search for new forms of expression — **mod·ern·ist** \-nəst\ *n or adj* — **mod·ern·is·tic** \ˌmäd-ər-ˈnis-tik\ *adj*

mod·ern·iza·tion \ˌmäd-ər-nə-ˈzā-shən\ *n* (1770) **1** : the act of modernizing : the state of being modernized **2** : something modernized : a modernized version

mod·ern·ize \ˈmäd-ər-ˌnīz\ *vb* **-ized; -iz·ing** *vt* (1748) : to make modern in taste, style, or usage ~ *vi* : to adopt modern ways — **mod·ern·iz·er** *n*

modern pentathlon *n* (1943) : a composite contest in which all contestants compete in a 300-meter freestyle swim, a 4000-meter cross-country run, a 5000-meter 30-jump equestrian steeplechase, épée fencing, and target shooting at 25 meters

mod·est \ˈmäd-əst\ *adj* [L *modestus* moderate; akin to L *modus* measure] (1565) **1 a** : placing a moderate estimate on one's abilities or worth **b** : neither bold nor self-assertive : tending toward diffidence **2** : arising from or characteristic of a modest nature **3** : observing the proprieties of dress and behavior : DECENT **4 a** : limited in size, amount, or scope **b** : UNPRETENTIOUS ⟨a ~ cottage⟩ *syn* see SHY, CHASTE — **mod·est·ly** *adv*

mod·es·ty \ˈmäd-ə-stē\ *n* (15c) **1** : freedom from conceit or vanity **2** : propriety in dress, speech, or conduct

mo·di·cum \ˈmäd-i-kəm, ˈmōd-\ *n* [ME, fr. L, neut. of *modicus* moderate, fr. *modus* measure] (15c) : a small portion : a limited quantity

mod·i·fi·ca·tion \ˌmäd-ə-fə-ˈkā-shən\ *n* (1603) **1** : the limiting of a statement : QUALIFICATION **2** : ¹MODE 6a **3 a** : the making of a limited change in something; *also* : the result of such a change **b** : a change in an organism caused by environmental factors

mod·i·fi·er \ˈmäd-ə-ˌfī(-ə)r\ *n* (1583) **1** : one that modifies **2** : a grammatical qualifier **3** : a gene that modifies the effect of another

mod·i·fy \ˈmäd-ə-ˌfī\ *vb* **-fied; -fy·ing** [ME *modifien*, fr. MF *modifier*, fr. L *modificare* to measure, moderate, fr. *modus*] *vt* (14c) **1** : to make less extreme : MODERATE **2 a** : to limit or restrict the meaning of esp. in a grammatical construction : QUALIFY **b** : to change (a vowel) by umlaut **3 a** : to make minor changes in **b** : to make basic or fundamental changes in often to give a new orientation to or to serve a new end ⟨the wing of a bird is an arm *modified* for flying⟩ ~ *vi* : to undergo change *syn* see CHANGE — **mod·i·fi·abil·i·ty** \ˌmäd-ə-ˌfī-ə-ˈbil-ət-ē\ *n* — **mod·i·fi·able** \ˈmäd-ə-ˌfī-ə-bəl\ *adj*

mo·dil·lion \mō-ˈdil-yən\ *n* [It *modiglione*] (1563) : an ornamental block or bracket under the corona of the cornice (as in the Corinthian order)

mod·ish \ˈmōd-ish\ *adj* (1660) : FASHIONABLE, STYLISH ⟨a ~ hat⟩ ⟨a ~ writer⟩ — **mod·ish·ly** *adv* — **mod·ish·ness** *n*

mo·diste \mō-ˈdēst\ *n* [F, fr. *mode* style, mode] (1840) : one who makes and sells fashionable dresses and hats for women

mod·u·la·bil·i·ty \ˌmäj-ə-lə-ˈbil-ət-ē\ *n* (1928) : the capability of being modulated

mod·u·lar \ˈmäj-ə-lər\ *adj* (1798) **1** : of, relating to, or based on a module or a modulus **2** : constructed with standardized units or dimensions for flexibility and variety in use — **mod·u·lar·i·ty** \ˌmäj-ə-ˈlar-ət-ē\ *n* — **mod·u·lar·ly** \ˈmäj-ə-lər-lē\ *adv*

modular arithmetic *n* (1959) : arithmetic that deals with whole numbers where the numbers are replaced by their remainders after division by a fixed number ⟨in a *modular arithmetic* with modulus 5, 3 multiplied by 4 would be 2⟩ ⟨5 hours after 10 o'clock is 3 o'clock because clocks follow a *modular arithmetic* with modulus 12⟩

mod·u·lar·ized \ˈmäj-ə-lə-ˌrīzd\ *adj* (1959) **1** : containing or consisting of modules ⟨~ electronic equipment⟩ **2** : produced in the form of modules

mod·u·late \ˈmäj-ə-ˌlāt\ *vb* **-lat·ed; -lat·ing** [L *modulatus*, pp. of *modulari* to play, sing, fr. *modulus* small measure, rhythm, dim. of *modus* measure — more at METE] *vt* (1615) **1** : to tune to a key or pitch **2** : to adjust to or keep in proper measure or proportion : TEMPER **3** : to vary the amplitude, frequency, or phase of (a carrier wave or a light wave) for the transmission of intelligence (as by radio); *also* : to vary the velocity of electrons in an electron beam ~ *vi* **1** : to play or sing with modulation **2** : to pass from one musical key into another by means of intermediary chords or notes that have some relation to both keys **3** : to pass gradually from one state to another — **mod·u·la·tor** \-ˌlāt-ər\ *n* — **mod·u·la·to·ry** \-lə-ˌtōr-ē, -ˌtȯr-\ *adj*

mod·u·la·tion \ˌmäj-ə-ˈlā-shən\ *n* (1531) **1** : a regulating according to measure or proportion : TEMPERING **2** : an inflection of the tone or pitch of the voice; *specif* : the use of stress or pitch to convey meaning **3** : a change from one musical key to another by modulating **4** : the process of modulating a carrier or signal (as in radio); *also* : the result of this process

mod·ule \ˈmäj-(ˌ)ü(ə)l\ *n* [L *modulus*] (1586) **1** : a standard or unit of measurement **2** : the size of some one part taken as a unit of measure by which the proportions of an architectural composition are regulated **3 a** : any in a series of standardized units for use together: as (1) : a unit of furniture or architecture (2) : an educational unit which covers a single subject or topic **b** : a usu. packaged functional assembly of electronic components for use with other such assemblies **4** : an independently-operable unit that is a part of the total structure of a space vehicle **5 a** : a subset of an additive group that is also a group under addition **b** : a mathematical set that is a commutative group under addition and that is closed under multiplication which is distributive from the left or right or both by elements of a ring and for which $a(bx) = (ab)x$ or $(xb)a = x(ba)$ or both where a and b are elements of the ring and x belongs to the set

mod·u·lo \ˈmäj-ə-ˌlō\ *prep* [NL, abl. of *modulus*] (1897) : with respect to a modulus of ⟨19 and 54 are congruent ~ 7⟩

mod·u·lus \ˈmäj-ə-ləs\ *n, pl* **-li** \-ˌlī, -ˌlē\ [NL, fr. L, small measure] (1753) **1 a** : the factor by which a logarithm of a number to one base is multiplied to obtain the logarithm of the number to a new base **b** : ABSOLUTE VALUE 2 **c** (1) : the number (as a positive integer) or other mathematical entity (as a polynomial) in a congruence that divides the difference of the two congruent members without leaving a remainder — compare RESIDUE b (2) : the number of different numbers used in a system of modular arithmetic **2** : a constant or coefficient that expresses usu. numerically the degree in which a property (as elasticity) is possessed by a substance or body

mo·dus ope·ran·di \ˌmōd-ə-ˌsäp-ə-ˈran-dē, -ˌdī\ *n, pl* **mo·di operandi** \ˈmō-ˌdē-ˌäp-, ˈmō-ˌdī-\ [NL] (1654) : a method of procedure

mo·dus vi·ven·di \ˌmōd-əs-vi-ˈven-dē, -ˌdī\ *n, pl* **mo·di vivendi** \ˈmō-ˌdē-, ˈmō-ˌdī-\ [NL, manner of living] (1879) **1** : a feasible arrangement or practical compromise; *esp* : one that bypasses difficulties **2** : a manner of living : a way of life

Mogen David *var of* MAGEN DAVID

¹mo·gul \ˈmō-(ˌ)gəl, mō-ˈ\ *n* [Per *Mughul*, fr. Mongolian *Mongol*] (1588) **1** *or* **mo·ghul** *cap* : an Indian Muslim of or descended from one of several conquering groups of Mongol, Turkish, and Persian origin; *esp* : GREAT MOGUL **2** : a great personage : MAGNATE — **mogul** *adj, often cap*

²mo·gul \ˈmō-gəl\ *n* [prob. of Scand origin; akin to Norw dial. *muge* heap, fr. ON *mūgi* — more at MOW] (ca. 1959) : a bump in a ski run

mo·hair \ˈmō-ˌha(ə)r, -ˌhe(ə)r\ *n* [modif. of obs. It *mocaiarro*, fr. Ar *mukhayyar*, lit., choice] (1570) : a fabric or yarn made wholly or in part of the long silky hair of the Angora goat; *also* : this hair

Mo·ham·med·an *var of* MUHAMMADAN

Mo·hawk \ˈmō-ˌhȯk\ *n, pl* **Mohawk** *or* **Mohawks** [of Algonquian origin; akin to Narraganset *Mohowaùuck*] (1634) **1 a** : an American Indian people of the Mohawk river valley, New York **b** : a member of this people **2** : the language of the Mohawk people

Mo·he·gan \mō-ˈhē-gən, mə-\ *or* **Mo·hi·can** \-ˈhē-kən\ *n, pl* **Mohegan** *or* **Mohegans** *or* **Mohican** *or* **Mohicans** (1614) : a member of an American Indian people of southeastern Connecticut

Mo·hi·can \mō-ˈhē-kən, mə-\ *var of* MAHICAN

Mo·ho \ˈmō-ˌhō\ *n* [short for *Mohorovicic discontinuity*, fr. Andrija *Mohorovičić* †1936 Yugoslavian geologist] (ca. 1952) : a point ranging from about 3 miles (5 kilometers) beneath the ocean basin floor to about 25 miles (40 kilometers) beneath the continental surface at which seismological studies indicate a transition in earth materials from those of the earth's crust to those of the subjacent mantle

Mo·hock \ˈmō-ˌhäk\ *n* [alter. of *Mohawk*] (1711) : one of a gang of aristocratic ruffians who assaulted and otherwise maltreated people in London streets in the early 18th century — **Mo·hock·ism** \-ˌiz-əm\ *n*

Mo·ho·ro·vi·cic discontinuity \ˌmō-hə-ˈrō-və-ˌchich-\ *n* (1936) : MOHO

Mohs' scale \ˈmōz-, ˈmōs-, ˈmō-səz-\ *n* [Friedrich *Mohs* †1839 Ger. mineralogist] (1879) **1** : a scale of hardness for minerals in which 1 represents the hardness of talc; 2, gypsum; 3, calcite; 4, fluorite; 5, apatite; 6, orthoclase; 7, quartz; 8, topaz; 9, corundum; and 10, diamond **2** : a revised and expanded version of the original Mohs' scale in which 1 represents the hardness of talc; 2, gypsum; 3, calcite; 4, fluorite; 5, apatite; 6, orthoclase; 7, vitreous pure silica; 8, quartz; 9, topaz; 10, garnet; 11, fused zirconium oxide; 12, fused alumina; 13, silicon carbide; 14, boron carbide; and 15, diamond

mo·hur \ˈmō(-ə)r, mə-ˈhù(ə)r\ *n* [Hindi *muhr* gold coin, seal, fr. Per; akin to Skt *mudrā* seal] (1690) : a former gold coin of India and Persia equal to 15 rupees

moi·ety \ˈmȯi-ət-ē\ *n, pl* **-eties** [ME *moite*, fr. MF *moité*, fr. LL *medietat-, medietas*, fr. L *medius* middle — more at MID] (15c) **1 a** : one of two equal parts : HALF **b** : one of two approximately equal parts **2** : one of the portions into which something is divided : COMPONENT, PART **3** : one of two basic complementary tribal subdivisions

¹moil \ˈmȯi(ə)l\ *vb* [ME *moillen*, fr. MF *moillier*, fr. (assumed) VL *molliare*, fr. L *mollis* soft — more at MELT] *vt, chiefly dial* (15c) : to make wet or dirty ~ *vi* **1** : to work hard : DRUDGE **2** : to be in continuous agitation : CHURN, SWIRL — **moil·er** *n*

²moil *n* (ca. 1612) **1** : hard work : DRUDGERY **2** : CONFUSION, TURMOIL

moil·ing \ˈmȯi-liŋ\ *adj* (1603) **1 a** : requiring hard work **b** : INDUSTRIOUS ⟨~ workers⟩ **2** : violently agitated : TURBULENT — **moil·ing·ly** \-liŋ-lē\ *adv*

Moi·rai \ˈmȯi-ˌrī\ *n pl* [Gk, fr. pl. of *moira* lot, fate; akin to Gk *meros* part — more at MERIT] : FATE 4

moire \ˈmȯi(-ə)r, ˈmȯ(ə)r, ˈmwär\ *n* [F, fr. E *mohair*] *archaic* (1660) : a watered mohair

moi·ré \mȯ-ˈrā, mwä-\ *or* **moire** *same, or* ˈmȯi(-ə)r, ˈmȯ(ə)r, ˈmwär\ *n* [F *moiré*, fr. *moiré* like moire, fr. *moire*] (1818) **1 a** : an irregular wavy finish on a fabric **b** : a ripple pattern on a stamp **2** : a fabric having a wavy watered appearance **3** : an independent usu. shimmering pattern seen when two geometrically regular patterns (as two sets of parallel lines or two halftone screens) are superimposed esp. at an acute angle — **moiré** *adj*

moist \ˈmȯist\ *adj* [ME *moiste*, fr. MF, fr. (assumed) VL *muscidus*, alter. of L *mucidus* slimy, fr. *mucus* nasal mucus] (14c) **1** : slightly or moderately wet : DAMP **2** : TEARFUL **3** : characterized by high humidity *syn* see WET — **moist·ly** *adv* — **moist·ness** \ˈmȯis(t)-nəs\ *n*

moist·en \ˈmȯis-ᵊn\ *vb* **moist·ened; moist·en·ing** \ˈmȯis-niŋ, -ᵊn-iŋ\ *vt* (14c) : to make moist ~ *vi* : to become moist — **moist·en·er** \ˈmȯis-nər, -ᵊn-ər\ *n*

mois·ture \ˈmȯis(h)-chər\ *n* [ME, modif. of MF *moistour*, fr. *moiste*] (14c) : liquid diffused or condensed in relatively small quantity

mois·tur·ize \-chə-ˌrīz\ *vt* **-ized; -iz·ing** (1945) : to add moisture to ⟨~ the air⟩ — **mois·tur·iz·er** *n*

moke \ˈmōk\ *n* [origin unknown] (1848) **1** *slang Brit* : DONKEY **2** *slang Austral* : ¹NAG

mol·al \ˈmō-ləl\ *adj* [⁵*mole*] (1905) : of, relating to, or containing a mole of solute per 1000 grams of solvent — **mo·lal·i·ty** \mō-ˈlal-ət-ē\ *n*

\ə\ abut \ᵊ\ kitten, F table \ər\ further \a\ ash \ā\ ace \ä\ cot, cart \au̇\ out \ch\ chin \e\ bet \ē\ easy \g\ go \i\ hit \ī\ ice \j\ job \ŋ\ sing \ō\ go \ȯ\ law \ȯi\ boy \th\ thin \th\ the \ü\ loot \u̇\ foot \y\ yet \zh\ vision \à, k, ⁿ, œ, œ̄, ue, ue̅, ʸ\ *see* Guide to Pronunciation

[1]**mo·lar** \ˈmō-lər\ *n* [L *molaris,* fr. *molaris* of a mill, fr. *mola* millstone — more at MILL] (14c) **:** a tooth with a rounded or flattened surface adapted for grinding; *specif* **:** one of the cheek teeth in mammals behind the incisors and canines — see TOOTH illustration

[2]**molar** *adj* (1626) **1 :** pulverizing by friction **:** GRINDING **2 :** of, relating to, or located near the molar teeth

[3]**molar** *adj* [L *moles* mass — more at MOLE] (1862) **:** of or relating to a mass of matter as distinguished from the properties or motions of molecules or atoms

[4]**molar** *adj* [[5]*mole*] (1902) **:** of, relating to, or containing a mole of solute in one liter of solution — **mo·lar·i·ty** \mō-ˈlar-ət-ē\ *n*

mo·las·ses \mə-ˈlas-əz\ *n* [modif. of Pg *melaço,* fr. LL *mellaceum* grape juice, fr. L *mell-, mel* honey — more at MELLIFLUOUS] (1582) **1 :** the thick dark to light brown syrup that is separated from raw sugar in sugar manufacture **2 :** a syrup made from boiling down sweet vegetable or fruit juice ⟨citrus ~⟩

[1]**mold** \ˈmōld\ *n* [ME, fr. OE *molde;* akin to OHG *molta* soil, L *molere* to grind — more at MEAL] (bef. 12c) **1 :** crumbling soft friable earth suited to plant growth **:** SOIL; *esp* **:** soil rich in humus — compare LEAF MOLD **2** *dial Brit* **a :** the surface of the earth **:** GROUND **b :** the earth of the burying ground **3** *archaic* **:** earth that is the substance of the human body ⟨be merciful great Duke to men of ~ —Shak.⟩

[2]**mold** *n* [ME, modif. of OF *modle,* fr. L *modulus,* dim. of *modus* measure — more at METE] (13c) **1 :** distinctive nature or character **:** TYPE **2 :** the frame on or around which an object is constructed **3 a :** a cavity in which a substance is shaped: as **(1) :** a matrix for casting metal **(2) :** a form in which food is given a decorative shape **b :** a molded object **4 :** MOLDING **5 a** *obs* **:** an example to be followed **b :** PROTOTYPE **c :** a fixed pattern **:** DESIGN

[3]**mold** *vt* (14c) **1** *archaic* **:** to knead (dough) into a desired consistency or shape **2 :** to give shape to ⟨the wind ~*s* the waves⟩ **3 :** to form in a mold ⟨~ candles⟩ **4 :** to determine or influence the quality or nature of ⟨~ public opinion⟩ **5 :** to fit the contours of **6 :** to ornament with molding or carving ⟨~*ed* picture frames⟩ — **mold·able** \ˈmōl-də-bəl\ *adj* — **mold·er** *n*

[4]**mold** *vi* [alter. of ME *moulen*] (13c) **:** to become moldy

[5]**mold** *n* (15c) **1 :** a superficial often woolly growth produced on damp or decaying organic matter or on living organisms **2 :** a fungus (as of the order Mucorales) that produces mold

mold·board \ˈmōl(d)-ˌbō(ə)rd, -ˌbȯ(ə)rd\ *n* (1508) **1 a :** a curved iron plate attached above a plowshare to lift and turn the soil **b :** the flat or curved blade (as of a bulldozer) that pushes material to one side as the machine advances **2 :** one of the boards forming a mold for concrete

mold·er \ˈmōl-dər\ *vi* **mold·ered; mold·er·ing** \-d(ə-)riŋ\ [freq. of [4]*mold*] (1531) **:** to crumble into particles **:** DISINTEGRATE, DECAY

mold·ing \ˈmōl-diŋ\ *n* (14c) **1 a :** the art or occupation of a molder **b :** an object produced by molding **2 a :** a decorative recessed or relieved surface **b :** a decorative plane or curved strip used for ornamentation or finishing

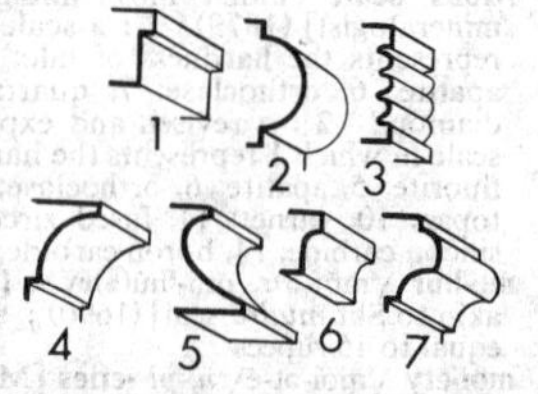

molding 2a: *1* fillet and fascia, *2* torus, *3* reeding, *4* cavetto, *5* scotia, *6* congé, *7* beak

moldy \ˈmōl-dē\ *adj* **mold·i·er; -est** (14c) **1 :** of, resembling, or covered with a mold-producing fungus **2 a :** being old and moldering **:** CRUMBLING **b :** ANTIQUATED, FUSTY ⟨~ tradition⟩ — **mold·i·ness** *n*

[1]**mole** \ˈmōl\ *n* [ME, fr. OE *māl;* akin to OHG *meil* spot] (bef. 12c) **:** a pigmented spot, mark, or small permanent protuberance on the human body; *esp* **:** NEVUS

[2]**mole** *n* [ME; akin to MLG *mol*] (14c) **1 :** any of numerous burrowing insectivores (esp. family Talpidae) with minute eyes, concealed ears, and soft fur **2 :** one who works in the dark **3 :** a machine for tunneling **4 :** a spy (as a double agent) who establishes a cover long before beginning espionage

[3]**mole** *n* [L *mola* mole, lit., mill, millstone — more at MILL] (14c) **:** an abnormal mass in the uterus esp. when containing fetal tissues

[4]**mole** *n* [MF, fr. OIt *molo,* fr. LGk *mōlos,* fr. L *moles,* lit., mass, exertion; akin to OHG *muodi* weary, Gk *mōlos* exertion] (1548) **1 :** a massive work formed of masonry and large stones or earth laid in the sea as a pier or breakwater **2 :** the harbor formed by a mole

[5]**mole** *also* **mol** \ˈmōl\ *n* [G *mol,* short for *molekulargewicht* molecular weight, fr. *molekular* molecular + *gewicht* weight] (1902) **:** the amount of pure substance that contains the same number of elementary entities as there are atoms in exactly 12 grams of the isotope carbon 12

[6]**mo·le** \ˈmō-lē\ *n* [MexSp, fr. Nahuatl *mulli, molli* sauce, stew] (1927) **:** a spicy sauce made with chilies and usu. chocolate and served with meat

mo·lec·u·lar \mə-ˈlek-yə-lər\ *adj* (1823) **1 :** of, relating to, or produced by molecules ⟨~ oxygen⟩ **2 :** of or relating to simple or elementary organization — **mo·lec·u·lar·ly** \mə-ˈlek-yə-lər-lē\ *adv*

molecular biology *n* (1938) **:** a branch of biology dealing with the ultimate physicochemical organization of living matter and esp. with the molecular basis of inheritance and protein synthesis — **molecular biologist** *n*

molecular formula *n* (ca. 1903) **:** a chemical formula that is based on both analysis and molecular weight and gives the total number of atoms of each element in a molecule — compare STRUCTURAL FORMULA

molecular mass *n* (1970) **:** the mass of a molecule that is equal to the sum of the masses of all the atoms contained in the molecule

molecular weight *n* (1880) **:** the average mass of a molecule of a compound compared to $^1/_{12}$ the mass of carbon 12 and calculated as the sum of the atomic weights of the constituent atoms — compare FORMULA WEIGHT

mol·e·cule \ˈmäl-i-ˌkyü(ə)l\ *n* [F *molécule,* fr. NL *molecula,* dim. of L *moles* mass] (1678) **1 :** the smallest particle of a substance that retains all the properties of the substance and is composed of one or more atoms **2 :** a tiny bit **:** PARTICLE

mole·hill \ˈmōl-ˌhil\ *n* (15c) **:** a little mound or ridge of earth pushed up by a mole

mole·skin \-ˌskin\ *n* (1668) **1 :** the skin of the mole used as fur **2 a :** a heavy durable cotton fabric with a short thick velvety nap on one side **b :** a garment made of moleskin — usu. used in pl.

mo·lest \mə-ˈlest\ *vt* [ME *molesten,* fr. MF *molester,* fr. L *molestare,* fr. *molestus* burdensome, annoying, fr. *moles* mass] (14c) **1 :** to annoy, disturb, or persecute esp. with hostile intent or injurious effect **2 :** to make annoying sexual advances to — **mo·les·ta·tion** \ˌmō-ˌles-ˈtā-shən, ˌmōl-əs-, ˌmäl-\ *n* — **mo·lest·er** \mə-ˈles-tər\ *n*

mo·line \mə-ˈlēn, -ˈlīn\ *adj* [(assumed) AF *moliné,* fr. OF *molin* mill, fr. LL *molinum* — more at MILL] *of a heraldic cross* (1562) **:** having the end of each arm forked and recurved — see CROSS illustration

moll \ˈmäl, ˈmȯl\ *n* [prob. fr. *Moll,* nickname for *Mary*] (1604) **1 :** PROSTITUTE **2 a :** DOLL 2 **b :** a gangster's girlfriend

mol·li·fy \ˈmäl-ə-ˌfī\ *vb* **-fied; -fy·ing** [ME *mollifien,* fr. MF *mollifier,* fr. LL *mollificare,* fr. L *mollis* soft — more at MELT] *vt* (15c) **1 :** to soothe in temper or disposition **:** APPEASE ⟨*mollified* her by flattery⟩ **2 :** to reduce the rigidity of **:** SOFTEN **3 :** to reduce in intensity **:** ASSUAGE, TEMPER ~ *vi, archaic* **:** SOFTEN, RELENT ***syn*** see PACIFY — **mol·li·fi·ca·tion** \ˌmäl-ə-fə-ˈkā-shən\ *n*

mol·lus·ci·cide \mə-ˈləs-(k)ə-ˌsīd\ *n* [NL *Mollusca* + E *-i-* + *-cide*] (1947) **:** an agent for destroying mollusks (as snails) — **mol·lus·ci·cid·al** \-ˌləs-(k)ə-ˈsīd-ᵊl\ *adj*

mol·lusk *or* **mol·lusc** \ˈmäl-əsk\ *n* [F *mollusque,* fr. NL *Mollusca,* fr. L, neut. pl. of *molluscus* soft, fr. *mollis*] (1783) **:** any of a large phylum (Mollusca) of invertebrate animals (as snails or clams) with a soft unsegmented body usu. enclosed in a calcareous shell; *broadly* **:** SHELLFISH — **mol·lus·can** *also* **mol·lus·kan** \mə-ˈləs-kən, mä-\ *adj*

Moll·wei·de projection \ˌmȯl-ˌvīd-ə-, mōl-ˌwīd-ə-\ *n* [Karl B. *Mollweide* †1825 Ger. mathematician and astronomer] (1937) **:** an equal-area map projection capable of showing the entire surface of the earth in the form of an ellipse with all parallels as straight lines more widely spaced at the equator than at the poles, with the central meridian as one half the length of the equator, and with all other meridians as ellipses equally spaced

mol·ly *or* **mol·lie** \ˈmäl-ē\ *n* [by shortening fr. NL *Mollienisia,* former genus name, fr. Comte François N. *Mollien* †1850 Fr. statesman] (ca. 1933) **:** any of several brightly colored live-bearers (genus *Poecilia* of the family Poeciliidae) highly valued as aquarium fishes

[1]**mol·ly·cod·dle** \ˈmäl-ē-ˌkäd-ᵊl\ *n* [*Molly,* nickname for *Mary*] (1833) **:** a pampered or effeminate man or boy

[2]**mollycoddle** *vt* **mol·ly·cod·dled; mol·ly·cod·dling** \-ˌkäd-liŋ, -ᵊl-iŋ\ (1864) **:** to surround with an excessive or absurd degree of indulgence and attention ***syn*** see INDULGE — **mol·ly·cod·dler** \-ˌkäd-lər, -ᵊl-ər\ *n*

Mo·loch \ˈmäl-ək, ˈmō-ˌläk\ *n* [LL, fr. Gk, fr. Heb *Mōlekh*] **:** a Semitic god to whom children were sacrificed

Mo·lo·tov cocktail \ˌmäl-ə-ˌtȯf-, ˌmȯl-, ˌmōl-, -ˌtȯv-\ *n* [Vyacheslav M. *Molotov*] (1939) **:** a crude bomb made of a bottle filled with a flammable liquid (as gasoline) and usu. fitted with a wick (as a saturated rag) that is ignited just before the bottle is hurled

[1]**molt** \ˈmōlt\ *vb* [alter. of ME *mouten,* fr. OE *-mūtian* to change, fr. L *mutare* — more at MISS] *vi* (15c) **:** to shed hair, feathers, shell, horns, or an outer layer periodically ~ *vt* **:** to cast off (an outer covering) periodically; *specif* **:** to throw off (the old cuticle) — used of arthropods — **molt·er** *n*

[2]**molt** *n* (1815) **:** the act or process of molting; *specif* **:** ECDYSIS

mol·ten \ˈmōlt-ᵊn\ *adj* [ME, fr. pp. of *melten* to melt] (13c) **1** *obs* **:** made by melting and casting **2 :** fused or liquefied by heat **:** MELTED ⟨~ lava⟩ **3 :** having warmth or brilliance **:** GLOWING ⟨the ~ sunlight of warm skies —T.B. Costain⟩

mol·to \ˈmōl-(ˌ)tō, ˈmȯl-\ *adv* [It, fr. L *multum,* fr. neut. of *multus* much] (ca. 1801) **:** MUCH, VERY — used in music directions ⟨~ vivace⟩

mo·ly \ˈmō-lē\ *n* [L, fr. Gk *mōly;* akin to Skt *mūla* root] (1567) **:** a mythical herb with a black root, white blossoms, and magical powers

mo·lyb·date \mə-ˈlib-ˌdāt\ *n* (1794) **:** a salt of molybdenum containing the group MoO_4 or Mo_2O_7

molybdate orange *n* (ca. 1944) **:** a brilliant orange pigment consisting of the chromate, molybdate, and usu. sulfate of lead

mo·lyb·de·nite \mə-ˈlib-də-ˌnīt\ *n* [NL *molybdena*] (1796) **:** a blue usu. foliated mineral MoS_2 that is molybdenum disulfide and a source of molybdenum

mo·lyb·de·num \-nəm\ *n* [NL, fr. *molybdena,* a lead ore, molybdenite, molybdenum, fr. L *molybdaena* galena, fr. Gk *molybdaina,* fr. *molybdos* lead] (1816) **:** a metallic element that resembles chromium and tungsten in many properties, is used esp. in strengthening and hardening steel, and is a trace element in plant and animal metabolism — see ELEMENT table

molybdenum disulfide *n* (ca. 1931) **:** a compound MoS_2 used esp. as a lubricant in grease

mo·lyb·dic \mə-ˈlib-dik\ *adj* [NL *molybdenum*] (1796) **:** of, relating to, or containing molybdenum esp. with one of its higher valences

mom \ˈmäm, ˈməm\ *n* [short for *momma*] (ca. 1894) **:** MOTHER

mom–and–pop \ˌmäm-ən(d)-ˌpäp\ *adj* (1951) **:** being a small owner-operated business

mome \ˈmōm\ *n, archaic* [origin unknown] (1553) **:** BLOCKHEAD, FOOL

mo·ment \ˈmō-mənt\ *n* [ME, fr. MF, fr. L *momentum* movement, particle sufficient to turn the scales, moment, fr. *movēre* to move] (14c) **1 :** a minute portion or point of time **:** INSTANT **2 a :** present time ⟨at the ~ she is working on a novel⟩ **b :** a time of excellence or conspicuousness ⟨he has his ~*s*⟩ **3 :** importance in influence or effect **:** notable or conspicuous consequence **4** *obs* **:** a cause or motive of action **5 :** a stage in historical or logical development **6 a :** tendency or measure of tendency to produce motion esp. about a point or axis **b :** the product of quantity (as a force) and the distance to a particular axis or point **7 a :** the mean of the *n*th powers of the deviations of the observed values in a set of statistical data from a fixed value **b :** the expected value of a power of the deviation of a random variable from a fixed value ***syn*** see IMPORTANCE

mo·men·tari·ly \ˌmō-mən-ˈter-ə-lē\ *adv* (1654) **1 :** for a moment **2 :** INSTANTLY **3 :** at any moment

mo·men·tary \ˈmō-mən-ˌter-ē\ *adj* (15c) **1 a :** continuing only a moment **:** TRANSITORY **b :** having a very brief life **2 :** operative or recurring at every moment ***syn*** see TRANSIENT — **mo·men·tari·ness** *n*

mo·ment·ly \ˈmō-mənt-lē\ *adv* (1676) **1 :** from moment to moment **2 :** at any moment **3 :** for a moment

mo·men·to \mə-'ment-(,)ō\ *var of* MEMENTO
moment of inertia (ca. 1830) : the ratio of the torque applied to a rigid body free to rotate about a given axis to the angular acceleration thus produced about that axis
moment of truth (1932) **1** : the final sword thrust in a bullfight **2** : a moment of crisis on whose outcome much or everything depends
mo·men·tous \mō-'ment-əs, mə-'ment-\ *adj* (1652) : IMPORTANT, CONSEQUENTIAL — **mo·men·tous·ly** *adv* — **mo·men·tous·ness** *n*
mo·men·tum \mō-'ment-əm, mə-'ment-\ *n, pl* **mo·men·ta** \-'ment-ə\ *or* **momentums** [NL, fr. L, movement] (1610) : a property of a moving body that determines the length of time required to bring it to rest when under the action of a constant force or moment; *broadly* : IMPETUS
mom·ma \'mäm-ə, 'məm-\ *var of* MAMA
mom·my \'mäm-ē, 'məm-\ *n, pl* **mom·mies** [alter. of *mammy*] (1899) : MOTHER
Mo·mus \'mō-məs\ *n* [L, fr. Gk *Mōmos*] : the Greek god of censure and mockery
mon \'män\ *dial chiefly Brit var of* MAN
Mon \'mōn\ *n, pl* **Mon** *or* **Mons** (1798) **1** : a member of the dominant native people of Pegu (a division in Burma) **2** : the Mon-Khmer language of the Mon people
mon- *or* **mono-** *under stress the (1st) "o" is sometimes* ō *although not shown at individual entries*\ *comb form* [ME, fr. MF & L; MF, fr. L, fr. Gk, fr. *monos* alone, single — more at MONK] **1** : one : single : alone ⟨*mono*plane⟩ ⟨*mono*drama⟩ ⟨*mono*phobia⟩ **2** : containing one (usu. specified) atom, radical, or group ⟨*mono*hydrate⟩ ⟨*mono*xide⟩ **b** : monomolecular ⟨*mono*film⟩ ⟨*mono*layer⟩
mon·a·chal \'män-i-kəl\ *adj* [MF or LL; MF, fr. LL *monachalis*, fr. *monachus* monk — more at MONK] (1587) : MONASTIC — **mon·a·chism** \-ə-,kiz-əm\ *n*
mo·nad \'mō-,nad\ *n* [LL *monad-, monas*, fr. Gk, fr. *monos*] (1615) **1 a** : UNIT, ONE **b** : ATOM 1 **c** : an elementary individual spiritual substance from which material properties are derived **2** : a flagellated protozoan (as of the genus *Monas*) — **mo·nad·ic** \mō-'nad-ik, mə-\ *adj* — **mo·nad·ism** \'mō-,nad-,iz-əm\ *n*
mon·a·del·phous \,män-ə-'del-fəs\ *adj, of stamens* (1806) : united by the filaments into one group usu. forming a tube around the gynoecium
mo·nad·nock \mə-'nad-,näk\ *n* [Mt. *Monadnock*, N.H.] (1893) : a hill or mountain of resistant rock surmounting a peneplain
mon·an·dry \'män-,an-drē\ *n, pl* **-dries** [*mon-* + *-andry* (as in *polyandry*)] (1855) : a marriage form or custom in which a woman has only one husband at a time
mon·arch \'män-ərk, -,ärk\ *n* [LL *monarcha*, fr. Gk *monarchos*, fr. *mon-* + *-archos* -arch] (15c) **1** : a person who reigns over a kingdom or empire: as **a** : a sovereign ruler **b** : a constitutional king or queen **2** : one that holds preeminent position or power — **mo·nar·chal** \mə-'när-kəl, mä-\ *or* **mo·nar·chi·al** \-kē-əl\ *adj*
monarch butterfly *n* (1890) : a large migratory American butterfly (*Danaus plexippus*) that has orange-brown wings with black veins and borders and a larva that feeds on milkweed — called also *monarch*
Mo·nar·chi·an \mə-'när-kē-ən, mä-\ *n* (1765) : an adherent of one of two anti-Trinitarian groups of the 2d and 3d centuries A.D. teaching that God is one person as well as one being — **Mo·nar·chi·an·ism** \-,iz-əm\ *n*

monarch butterfly

mo·nar·chi·cal \mə-'när-ki-kəl, mä-\ *also* **mo·nar·chic** \-kik\ *adj* (1576) : of, relating to, suggestive of, or characteristic of a monarch or monarchy — **mo·nar·chi·cal·ly** \-ki-k(ə-)lē\ *adv*
mon·ar·chism \'män-ər-,kiz-əm, -,är-\ *n* (1838) : monarchical government or principles — **mon·ar·chist** \-kəst\ *n or adj*
mon·ar·chy \'män-ər-kē *also* -,är-\ *n, pl* **-chies** (14c) **1** : undivided rule or absolute sovereignty by a single person **2** : a nation or state having a monarchical government **3** : a government having an hereditary chief of state with life tenure and powers varying from nominal to absolute
mo·nar·da \mə-'närd-ə\ *n* [NL, fr. Nicolás *Monardes* †1588 Span. botanist] (1712) : any of a genus (*Monarda*) of coarse No. American mints with a tubular many-nerved calyx and whorls of showy flowers
mon·as·tery \'män-ə-,ster-ē\ *n, pl* **-ter·ies** [ME *monasterie*, fr. LL *monasterium*, fr. LGk *monastērion*, fr. Gk, hermit's cell, fr. *monazein* to live alone, fr. *monos* single — more at MONK] (15c) : a house for persons under religious vows; *esp* : an establishment for monks
mo·nas·tic \mə-'nas-tik\ *adj* (15c) **1** : of or relating to monasteries or to monks or nuns **2** : resembling (as in seclusion or ascetic simplicity) life in a monastery — **monastic** *n* — **mo·nas·ti·cal·ly** \-ti-k(ə-)lē\ *adv* — **mo·nas·ti·cism** \-tə-,siz-əm\ *n*
mon·atom·ic \,män-ə-'täm-ik\ *adj* (1848) **1 a** : consisting of one atom; *esp* : having but one atom in the molecule **b** : having a thickness equal to the diameter of a constituent atom **2** : UNIVALENT 1 **3** : having one replaceable atom or radical ⟨~ alcohols⟩ — **mon·a·tom·i·cal·ly** \-i-k(ə-)lē\ *adv*
mon·au·ral \(')mä-'nȯr-əl\ *adj* (1931) : MONOPHONIC 2 — **mon·au·ral·ly** \-ə-lē\ *adv*
mon·a·zite \'män-ə-,zīt\ *n* [G *monazit*, fr. Gk *monazein*] (1836) : a mineral (Ce,La,Nd,Pr,Th)PO_4 that is a yellow, red, or brown phosphate of the cerium metals and thorium found often in sand and gravel deposits
Mon·day \'mən-dē, -(,)dā\ *n* [ME, fr. OE *mōnandæg*; akin to OHG *mānatag* Monday; akin to OE *mōna* moon and to OE *dæg* day] (bef. 12c) : the second day of the week — **Mon·days** \-dēz\ *adv*
Monday–morning quarterback *n* [fr. a fan's usu. critical rehashing of the weekend football game strategy] (1941) : one who second-guesses — **Monday–morning quarterbacking** *n*
mon·e·cious *var of* MONOECIOUS
M1 rifle \'em-'wən-\ *n* (1938) : a .30 caliber gas-operated clip-fed semi-automatic rifle used by U.S. troops in World War II
mon·es·trous \(')mä-'nes-trəs\ *adj* (1900) : experiencing estrus once each year : having a single annual breeding period

mon·e·tar·ism \'män-ə-tə-,riz-əm *also* 'mən-\ *n* (1969) : a theory in economics: stable economic growth can be assured only by control of the rate of money supply increase to match the capacity for growth of real productivity — **mon·e·tar·ist** \-rəst\ *n or adj*
mon·e·tary \'män-ə-,ter-ē *also* 'mən-\ *adj* [LL *monetarius* of a mint, of money, fr. L *moneta*] (1802) : of or relating to money or to the mechanisms by which it is supplied to and circulates in the economy — **mon·e·tari·ly** \,män-ə-'ter-ə-lē *also* ,mən-\ *adv*
monetary unit *n* (ca. 1864) : the standard unit of value of a currency
mon·e·tize \'män-ə-,tīz *also* 'mən-\ *vt* **-tized; -tiz·ing** [L *moneta*] (ca. 1879) : to coin into money; *also* : to establish as legal tender — **mon·e·ti·za·tion** \,män-ət-ə-'zā-shən *also* ,mən-\ *n*
mon·ey \'mən-ē\ *n, pl* **moneys** *or* **mon·ies** \'mən-ēz\ *often attrib* [ME *moneye*, fr. MF *moneie*, fr. L *moneta* mint, money — more at MINT] (13c) **1** : something generally accepted as a medium of exchange, a measure of value, or a means of payment: as **a** : officially coined or stamped metal currency **b** : MONEY OF ACCOUNT **c** : PAPER MONEY **2** : wealth reckoned in terms of money **3** : a form or denomination of coin or paper money **4 a** : the first, second, and third place winners in a horse or dog race — usu. used in the phrases *in the money* or *out of the money* **b** : prize money ⟨his horse took third ~⟩ **5** : persons or interests possessing or controlling great wealth — **for one's money** : according to one's preference or opinion

MONEY

NAME	SYMBOL	SUBDIVISIONS	COUNTRY
afghani	Af	100 puls	Afghanistan
austral		100 centavos	Argentina
baht *or* tical	B	100 satang	Thailand
balboa	B *or* B/	100 centesimos	Panama
birr	E$ *or* EB	100 cents	Ethiopia
bolivar	B	100 centimos	Venezuela
boliviano		100 centavos	Bolivia
cedi	¢	100 pesewas	Ghana
colon	¢	100 centimos	Costa Rica
colon	¢	100 centavos	El Salvador
cordoba	C$	100 centavos	Nicaragua
cruzado	Cz$		Brazil
dalasi	D	100 bututs	Gambia
deutsche mark	DM	100 pfennigs	East Germany[1]
deutsche mark	DM	100 pfennigs	West Germany
dinar	DA	100 centimes	Algeria
dinar	BD	1000 fils	Bahrain
dinar	ID	1000 fils	Iraq
dinar	JD	1000 fils	Jordan
dinar	KD	1000 fils	Kuwait
dinar	LD	1000 dirhams	Libya
dinar	£SY	1000 fils	Southern Yemen
dinar	D	1000 millimes	Tunisia
dinar	Din	100 paras	Yugoslavia
dirham	DH	100 centimes	Morocco
dirham	UD	10 dinar 1000 fils	United Arab Emirates
dobra	Db	100 centimos	Sao Tome and Principe
dollar	$A	100 cents	Australia
dollar	B$	100 cents	Bahamas
dollar	Bds$	100 cents	Barbados
dollar	$	100 cents	Belize
dollar	$	100 cents	Bermuda
dollar	B$	100 sen	Brunei
dollar	$	100 cents	Canada
dollar *or* yuan	NT$	100 cents	China (Taiwan)
dollar	$F	100 cents	Fiji
dollar	$	100 cents	Grenada
dollar	G$	100 cents	Guyana
dollar	HK$	100 cents	Hong Kong
dollar	$ *or* J$	100 cents	Jamaica
dollar	$	100 cents	Liberia
dollar	NZ$	100 cents	New Zealand
dollar	$	100 cents	St. Vincent and the Grenadines
dollar	S$	100 cents	Singapore
dollar	TT$	100 cents	Trinidad and Tobago
dollar	$	100 cents	United States
dollar	Z$	100 cents	Zimbabwe
dong	D	100 xu	Vietnam
drachma	Dr	100 lepta	Greece
escudo	Esc	100 centavos	Cape Verde
escudo	$ *or* Esc	100 centavos	Portugal
escudo—see PESO, below			
florin—see GULDEN, below			
forint	F *or* Ft	100 filler	Hungary
franc	BF	100 centimes	Belgium
franc	Fr *or* F	100 centimes	Benin

\ə\ abut \ᵊ\ kitten, F table \ər\ further \a\ ash \ā\ ace \ä\ cot, cart
\au̇\ out \ch\ chin \e\ bet \ē\ easy \g\ go \i\ hit \ī\ ice \j\ job
\ŋ\ sing \ō\ go \ȯ\ law \ȯi\ boy \th\ thin \t͟h\ the \ü\ loot \u̇\ foot
\y\ yet \zh\ vision \ȧ, k̟, ⁿ, œ, œ̄, ue, u̅e, ᶦ\ see Guide to Pronunciation

NAME	SYMBOL	SUBDIVISIONS	COUNTRY
franc	Fr *or* F	100 centimes	Burkina Faso
franc	FBu	100 centimes	Burundi
franc	Fr *or* F	100 centimes	Cameroon
franc	Fr *or* F	100 centimes	Central African Republic
franc	Fr *or* F	100 centimes	Chad
franc	Fr *or* F	100 centimes	Congo
franc	DjFr	100 centimes	Djibouti
franc		100 centimes	Equatorial Guinea
franc	Fr *or* F	100 centimes	France
franc	Fr *or* F	100 centimes	Gabon
franc	GF	100 centimes	Guinea
franc	Fr *or* F	100 centimes	Ivory Coast
franc	Fr *or* F	100 centimes	Luxembourg
franc	FMG	100 centimes	Madagascar
franc	MF	100 centimes	Mali
franc	Fr *or* F	100 centimes	Niger
franc	Fr *or* F	100 centimes	Rwanda
franc	Fr *or* F	100 centimes	Senegal
franc	SFr	100 centimes *or* rappen	Switzerland
franc	Fr *or* F	100 centimes	Togo
gourde	G *or* Gde	100 centimes	Haiti
guarani	G *or* G̵	100 centimos	Paraguay
gulden *or* guilder *or* florin	F *or* Fl *or* G	100 cents	Netherlands
gulden *or* guilder *or* florin	F *or* Fl *or* G	100 cents	Suriname
inti			Peru
kina	K	100 toea	Papua New Guinea
kip	K	100 at	Laos
koruna	Kčs	100 haleru	Czechoslovakia
krona	IKr *or* Kr	100 aurar (*sing* eyrir)	Iceland
krona	Skr *or* Kr	100 ore	Sweden
krone	Kr *or* DKr	100 ore	Denmark
krone	Kr *or* NKr	100 ore	Norway
kwacha	K	100 tambala	Malawi
kwacha	K	100 ngwee	Zambia
kwanza	K	100 lwei	Angola
kyat	K	100 pyas	Myanmar
lek	L	100 qindarka	Albania
lempira	L	100 centavos	Honduras
leone	Le	100 cents	Sierra Leone
leu	L	100 bani	Romania
lev	Lv	100 stotinki	Bulgaria
lilangeni (*pl* emalangeni)	E	100 cents	Swaziland
lira	L *or* Lit	100 centesimi[2]	Italy
lira *or* pound	£ *or* Lm	100 pence	Malta
lira *or* pound	£T *or* Lt	100 kurus *or* piastres	Turkey
loti (*pl* maloti)		100 licente	Lesotho
mark—see DEUTSCHE MARK, above			
markka	Mk *or* Fmk	100 pennia	Finland
metical		100 centavos	Mozambique
naira	₦	100 kobo	Nigeria
ngultrum	N	100 chetrums	Bhutan
ouguiya		5 khoums	Mauritania
pa'anga	T$	100 seniti	Tonga
pataca	P *or* $	100 avos	Macao
peseta	Pta *or* P	100 centimos	Spain
peso		100 centavos	Chile
peso	$ *or* P	100 centavos	Colombia
peso	$	100 centavos	Cuba
peso	RD$	100 centavos	Dominican Republic
peso *or* escudo	Esc	100 centavos	Guinea-Bissau
peso	$	100 centavos	Mexico
peso	P	100 sentimos *or* centavos	Philippines
peso	$	100 centesimos	Uruguay
pound	£	100 cents	Cyprus
pound	£E	100 piastres	Egypt
pound	£	100 pence	Ireland
pound	L£ *or* LL	100 piastres	Lebanon
pound	£S *or* LSd	100 piastres	Sudan
pound	£S *or* LS	100 piastres	Syria
pound	£	100 pence	United Kingdom
pound—see LIRA, above			
pula	P	100 thebe	Botswana
quetzal	Q	100 centavos	Guatemala
rand	R	100 cents	South Africa
rial	R *or* Rl	100 dinars	Iran
rial	RO	1000 baiza	Oman
rial *or* riyal	YR	100 fils	Yemen Arab Republic
riel	J *or* CR	100 sen	Cambodia
ringgit	$	100 sen	Malaysia
riyal	QR	100 dirhams	Qatar
riyal	R *or* SR	100 halala	Saudi Arabia
riyal—see RIAL, above			

NAME	SYMBOL	SUBDIVISIONS	COUNTRY
ruble	R *or* Rub	100 kopecks	USSR
rupee	Re (*pl* Rs)	100 paise	India
rupee	Re (*pl* Rs)	100 cents	Mauritius
rupee	Re (*pl* Rs)	100 paisa	Nepal
rupee	Re (*pl* Rs) *or* PRe (*pl* PRs)	100 paisa	Pakistan
rupee	Re (*pl* Rs)	100 cents	Seychelles
rupee	Re (*pl* Rs)	100 cents	Sri Lanka
rupiah	Rp	100 sen	Indonesia
schilling	S *or* Sch	100 groschen	Austria
shekel	IS	100 agorot	Israel
shilingi—see SHILLING, below			
shilling	Sh	100 cents	Kenya
shilling	Sh *or* SoSh	100 cents	Somalia
shilling *or* shilingi	Sh *or* TSh	100 senti *or* cents	Tanzania
shilling	Sh	100 cents	Uganda
sucre	S/	100 centavos	Ecuador
taka	Tk	100 paisa	Bangladesh
tala	WS$	100 sene	Western Samoa
tical—see BAHT, above			
tugrik	Tug	100 mongo	Mongolia
vatu	V		Vanuatu
won	W	100 chon	North Korea
won	W	100 chon	South Korea
yen	¥ *or* Y	100 sen	Japan
yuan	Y	100 fen	China (mainland)
yuan—see DOLLAR, above			
zaire	Z	100 makuta (*sing* likuta), 10,000 sengi	Zaire
zloty	Zl	100 groszy	Poland

[1]Adopted West German currency July 1, 1990.
[2]The It. centesimo is now a subdivision in name only.

mon·ey·bags \'mən-ē-ˌbagz\ *n pl but sing or pl in constr* (1596) **1** : WEALTH **2** : a wealthy person

money changer *n* (14c) **1** : one whose business is the exchanging of kinds or denominations of currency **2** : a device for holding and dispensing sorted change

mon·eyed *also* **mon·ied** \'mən-ēd\ *adj* (15c) **1** : having money : WEALTHY **2** : consisting in or derived from money

mon·ey·er \'mən-ē-ər\ *n* [ME, fr. OF *monier*, fr. LL *monetarius* master of a mint, coiner, fr. *monetarius* of a mint] (15c) : an authorized coiner of money : MINTER

mon·ey·lend·er \'mən-ē-ˌlen-dər\ *n* (ca. 1780) : one whose business is lending money; *specif* : PAWNBROKER

mon·ey·mak·er \'mən-ē-ˌmā-kər\ *n* (1834) **1** : one that accumulates wealth **2** : one (as a plan or product) that produces profit — **mon·ey·mak·ing** \-kiŋ\ *adj or n*

money market *n* (ca. 1927) : the trade in short-term negotiable instruments (as certificates of deposit or U.S. Treasury securities)

money of account (1691) : a denominator of value or basis of exchange which is used in keeping accounts and for which there may or may not be an equivalent coin or denomination of paper money

money order *n* (1802) : an order issued by a post office, bank, or telegraph office for payment of a specified sum of money usu. at any branch of the organization

mon·ey·spin·ner \'mən-ē-ˌspin-ər\ *n, chiefly Brit* (1859) : MONEY-MAKER

mon·ey·wort \'mən-ē-ˌwərt, -ˌwo͝o(ə)rt\ *n* (1578) : a trailing perennial herb (*Lysimachia nummularia*) with rounded opposite leaves and solitary yellow flowers in their axils

[1]**mon·ger** \'məŋ-gər, 'mäŋ-\ *n* [ME *mongere*, fr. OE *mangere*, fr. L *mangon-, mango*, of Gk origin; akin to OE *mangon* charm, philter — more at MANGONEL] (bef. 12c) **1** : BROKER, DEALER — usu. used in combination ⟨ale*monger*⟩ **2** : one who attempts to stir up or spread something that is usu. petty or discreditable — usu. used in combination ⟨gossip*monger*⟩ ⟨war*monger*⟩

[2]**monger** *vt* **mon·gered; mon·ger·ing** \-g(ə-)riŋ\ (ca. 1864) : to deal in : PEDDLE

mon·go \'mäŋ-(ˌ)gō\ *n, pl* **mongo** [Mongolian] (1935) — see *tugrik* at MONEY table

Mon·gol \'mäŋ-gəl; 'män-ˌgōl, 'mäŋ-\ *n* [Mongolian *Moṅgol*] (1698) **1** : MONGOLIAN 2 **2** : a member of one of the chiefly pastoral Mongoloid peoples of Mongolia **3** : a person of Mongoloid racial stock **4** *often not cap* : one affected with Down's syndrome — **Mongol** *adj*

[1]**Mon·go·lian** \män-'gōl-yən, mäŋ-, -'gō-lē-ən\ *adj* (1706) **1** : of, relating to, or constituting Mongolia, the Mongolian People's Republic, the Mongols, or Mongolian **2** : MONGOLOID

[2]**Mongolian** *n* (1846) **1 a** : a person of Mongol racial stock **b** : a native or inhabitant of Mongolia **2** : the Mongolic language of the Mongol people **3** *often not cap* : MONGOL 4

Mongolian fold *n* [fr. its being characteristic of Mongoloid peoples] (1913) : EPICANTHIC FOLD

Mongolian gerbil *n* (ca. 1948) : a gerbil (*Meriones unguiculatus*) of Mongolia and northern China that has an external resemblance to a rat, has a high capacity for temperature regulation, and is used as an experimental laboratory animal

mon·go·lian·ism \män-'gōl-yə-ˌniz-əm, mäŋ-, -'gō-lē-ə-\ *n* (ca. 1924) : DOWN'S SYNDROME

[1]**Mon·gol·ic** \män-'gäl-ik, mäŋ-\ *adj* (1834) : MONGOLOID 1

[2]**Mongolic** *n* (1888) : a group of Altaic languages including Mongolian and Kalmuck

mon·gol·ism \'mäŋ-gə-ˌliz-əm\ *n* (1900) : DOWN'S SYNDROME

Mon·gol·oid \'mäŋ-gə-ˌlȯid\ *adj* (1868) **1** : of, constituting, or characteristic of a major racial stock native to Asia as classified according to physical features (as the presence of an epicanthic fold) that includes peoples of northern and eastern Asia, Malaysians, Eskimos, and often American Indians **2** *often not cap* **:** of, relating to, or affected with Down's syndrome — **Mongoloid** *n*

mon·goose \'män-ˌgüs, 'mäŋ-\ *n, pl* **mon·goos·es** *also* **mon·geese** \-ˌgēs\ [Hindi *māgūs,* fr. Prakrit *maṅguso*] (1698) **:** an agile grizzled ferret-sized mammal (*Herpestes nyula*) of India that feeds on snakes and rodents and that is related to the civets and genets; *broadly* **:** any of various related Asian and African mammals

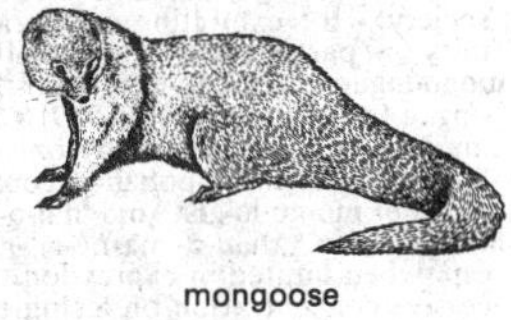
mongoose

mon·grel \'məŋ-grəl, 'mäŋ-\ *n* [prob. fr. ME *mong* mixture, short for *ymong,* fr. OE *gemong* crowd — more at AMONG] (15c) **1 :** an individual resulting from the interbreeding of diverse breeds or strains; *esp* **:** one of unknown ancestry **2 :** a cross between types of persons or things — **mongrel** *adj* — **mon·grel·iza·tion** \ˌməŋ-grə-lə-'zā-shən, ˌmäŋ-\ *n* — **mon·grel·ize** \'məŋ-grə-ˌlīz, 'mäŋ-\ *vt*

monies *pl of* MONEY

mon·i·ker *or* **mon·ick·er** \'män-i-kər\ *n* [origin unknown] *slang* (1851) **:** NAME, NICKNAME

mo·nil·i·a·sis \ˌmō-nə-'lī-ə-səs, ˌmän-ə-\ *n, pl* **-a·ses** \-ˌsēz\ [NL, fr. *Monilia,* genus of fungi, fr. L *monile* necklace] (1920) **:** CANDIDIASIS

mo·nil·i·form \mə-'nil-ə-ˌfȯrm\ *adj* [L *monile* necklace — more at MANE] (1802) **:** jointed or constricted at regular intervals so as to resemble a string of beads ⟨a ~ root⟩ ⟨~ insect antennae⟩

mon·ish \'män-ish\ *vt* [ME *monesen,* alter. of *monesten,* fr. OF *monester,* fr. (assumed) VL *monestare,* fr. L *monēre* to warn] (14c) **:** WARN

mo·nism \'mō-ˌniz-əm, 'män-ˌiz-\ *n* [G *monismus,* fr. *mon-* + *-ismus* -ism] (1862) **1 a :** a view that there is only one kind of ultimate substance **b :** the view that reality is one unitary organic whole with no independent parts **2 :** MONOGENESIS **3 :** a viewpoint or theory that reduces all phenomena to one principle — **mo·nist** \'mō-nəst, 'män-əst\ *n* — **mo·nis·tic** \mō-'nis-tik, mä-\ *or* **mo·nis·ti·cal** \-ti-kəl\ *adj*

mo·ni·tion \mō-'nish-ən, mə-\ *n* [ME *monicioun,* fr. MF *monition,* fr. L *monition-, monitio,* fr. *monitus,* pp. of *monēre*] (14c) **1 :** WARNING, CAUTION **2 :** an intimation of danger

¹**mon·i·tor** \'män-ət-ər\ *n* [L, one that warns, overseer, fr. *monitus,* pp. of *monēre* to warn — more at MENTAL] (1546) **1 a :** a student appointed to assist a teacher **b :** one that warns or instructs **c :** one that monitors or is used in monitoring: as (1) **:** a receiver used to view the picture being picked up by a television camera (2) **:** a device for observing a biological condition or function ⟨a heart ~⟩ (3) **:** software or hardware that monitors the operation of a system and esp. a computer system **2 :** any of various large tropical Old World pleurodont lizards (genus *Varanus* and family Varanidae) closely related to the iguanas **3** [*Monitor,* first ship of the type] **a :** a heavily armored warship formerly used in coastal operations having a very low freeboard and one or more revolving gun turrets **b :** a small modern warship with shallow draft for coastal bombardment **4 :** a raised central portion of a roof having low windows or louvers for providing light and air — **mon·i·to·ri·al** \ˌmän-ə-'tōr-ē-əl, -'tȯr-\ *adj* — **mon·i·tor·ship** \'män-ət-ər-ˌship\ *n*

²**monitor** *vt* **mon·i·tored; mon·i·tor·ing** \'män-ət-ə-riŋ, 'män-ə-triŋ\ (1818) **1 :** to watch, observe, or check esp. for a special purpose **2 :** to check or regulate the volume or quality of (sound) in recording **3 :** to check (as a radio or television signal or program) by means of a receiver for quality or fidelity to a band or for military, political, or criminal significance **4 :** to keep track of, regulate, or control the operation of (as a machine or process) **5 :** to test for intensity of radiations esp. if due to radioactivity

¹**mon·i·to·ry** \'män-ə-ˌtōr-ē, -ˌtȯr-\ *adj* [ME, fr. L *monitorius,* fr. *monitus*] (15c) **:** giving admonition **:** WARNING

²**monitory** *n, pl* **-ries** (15c) **:** a letter containing an admonition or warning

¹**monk** \'məŋk\ *n* [ME, fr. OE *munuc,* fr. LL *monachus,* fr. LGk *monachos,* fr. Gk, adj., single, fr. *monos* single, alone; akin to OHG *mengen* to lack, Gk *manos* sparse] (bef. 12c) **:** a man who is a member of a religious order and lives in a monastery; *also* **:** FRIAR

²**monk** *n* (1843) **:** MONKEY

monk·ery \'məŋ-kə-rē\ *n, pl* **-er·ies** (1536) **1 :** monastic life or practice **:** MONASTICISM **2 :** a monastic house **:** MONASTERY

¹**mon·key** \'məŋ-kē\ *n, pl* **monkeys** [prob. of LG origin; akin to *Moneke,* name of an ape, prob. of Romance origin; akin to OSp *mona* monkey] (ca. 1530) **1 :** a primate mammal with the exception of man and usu. the lemurs and tarsiers; *esp* **:** any of the smaller longer-tailed primates as contrasted with the apes **2 a :** a person resembling a monkey **b :** a ludicrous figure **:** DUPE **3 :** any of various machines, implements, or vessels; *esp* **:** the falling weight of a pile driver **4 :** a desperate desire for or addiction to drugs — often used in the phrase *monkey on one's back; broadly* **:** a persistent or annoying encumbrance or problem

²**monkey** *vb* **mon·keyed; mon·key·ing** *vt* (1859) **:** MIMIC, MOCK ~ *vi* **1 :** to act in a grotesque or mischievous manner **2 a :** FOOL, TRIFLE **b :** TAMPER

monkey bars *n pl* (1955) **:** a three-dimensional framework of horizontal and vertical bars from which children can hang and swing

monkey business *n* (1883) **:** SHENANIGAN

monkey jacket *n* (1830) **:** MESS JACKET

mon·key·pod \'məŋ-kē-ˌpäd\ *n* (1888) **1 :** an ornamental tropical tree (*Pithecolobium saman*) that has bipinnate leaves, globose clusters of flowers with crimson stamens, sweet-pulp pods eaten by cattle, and wood used in carving — called also *rain tree* **2 :** the wood of a monkeypod

mon·key·shine \-ˌshīn\ *n* (1828) **:** PRANK — usu. used in pl.

monkey wrench *n* (1858) **1 :** a wrench with one fixed and one adjustable jaw at right angles to a straight handle **2 :** something that disrupts ⟨threw a *monkey wrench* into the peace negotiations⟩

monk·fish \'məŋk-ˌfish\ *n* (1610) **:** either of two anglerfishes (*Lophius americanus* and *L. piscatorius*)

Mon–Khmer \ˌmōn-kə-'me(ə)r\ *n* (1887) **:** a language family containing Mon, Khmer, and several other languages of southeast Asia

monk·hood \'məŋk-ˌhu̇d\ *n* (bef. 12c) **1 :** the character, condition, or profession of a monk **:** MONASTICISM **2 :** monks as a class

monk·ish \'məŋ-kish\ *adj* (1546) **1 :** of or relating to monks **2 :** inclined to disciplinary self-denial

monk's cloth *n* (ca. 1847) **:** a coarse heavy fabric in basket weave made orig. of worsted and used for monk's habits but now chiefly of cotton or linen and used for draperies

monks·hood \'məŋ(k)s-ˌhu̇d\ *n* (1578) **:** any of a genus (*Aconitum*) of usu. bluish flowered poisonous herbs of the buttercup family; *esp* **:** a poisonous Eurasian herb (*A. napellus*) often cultivated for its showy terminal racemes of white or purplish flowers — compare WOLFSBANE

¹**mono** \'män-(ˌ)ō\ *n, pl* **monos** [by shortening] (1959) **1 :** a monophonic phonograph record **2 :** monophonic reproduction

²**mono** *adj* (1961) **:** MONOPHONIC 2

³**mono** *n* (1962) **:** INFECTIOUS MONONUCLEOSIS

mono- — see MON-

mono·ac·id \ˌmän-ō-'as-əd\ *n* (ca. 1919) **:** an acid having only one acid hydrogen atom

mono·acid·ic \-ə-'sid-ik\ *adj* (ca. 1929) **:** having a single hydroxyl group and able to react with only one molecule of a monobasic acid to form a salt or ester — used of bases and alcohols

mono·al·pha·bet·ic substitution \'män-ō-ˌal-fə-ˌbet-ik-\ *n* (ca. 1936) **:** substitution in cryptography that uses a single cipher alphabet so that each plaintext letter always has the same cipher equivalent — compare POLYALPHABETIC SUBSTITUTION

mono·amine \ˌmän-ō-ə-'mēn\ *n* [ISV] (1859) **:** an amine RNH_2 that has one organic substituent attached to the nitrogen atom; *esp* **:** one (as serotonin) that is functionally important in neural transmission

monoamine oxidase *n* (1943) **:** an enzyme that deaminates monoamines oxidatively and that functions in the nervous system by breaking down monoamine neurotransmitters oxidatively

mono·am·in·er·gic \ˌmän-ō-ˌam-ə-'nər-jik\ *adj* (1966) **:** liberating or involving monoamines (as serotonin or norepinephrine) in neural transmission ⟨~ neurons⟩ ⟨~ mechanisms⟩

mono·ba·sic \ˌmän-ə-'bā-sik\ *adj* [ISV] (1842) **:** having only one acid and replaceable hydrogen atom

mono·car·box·yl·ic \-ˌkär-(ˌ)bäk-'sil-ik\ *adj* (ca. 1909) **:** containing one carboxyl group ⟨acetic acid is a ~ acid⟩

mono·car·pic \-'kär-pik\ *adj* [prob. fr. (assumed) NL *monocarpicus,* fr. NL *mon-* + *-carpicus* -carpic] (1846) **:** bearing fruit but once and then dying

mono·cha·si·um \-'kā-z(h)ē-əm\ *n, pl* **-sia** \-z(h)ē-ə\ [NL, fr. *mon-* + *-chasium* (as in *dichasium*)] (ca. 1890) **:** a cymose inflorescence that produces only one main axis — **mono·cha·sial** \-zh(ē-)əl, -zē-əl\ *adj*

mono·chord \'män-ə-ˌkȯ(ə)rd\ *n* [ME *monocorde,* fr. MF, fr. ML *monochordum,* fr. Gk *monochordon,* fr. *mon-* + *chordē* string — more at YARN] (15c) **:** an instrument of ancient origin for measuring and demonstrating the mathematical relations of musical tones and that consists of a single string stretched over a sound box and a movable bridge set on a graduated scale

mono·chro·mat \'män-ə-krō-ˌmat, ˌmän-ə-'\ *n* [*mon-* + Gk *chrōmat-, chrōma*] (1902) **:** a completely color-blind individual

mono·chro·mat·ic \ˌmän-ə-krō-'mat-ik\ *adj* [L *monochromatos,* fr. Gk *monochrōmatos,* fr. *mon-* + *chrōmat-, chrōma* color — more at CHROMATIC] (1822) **1 a :** having or consisting of one color or hue **b :** MONOCHROME 2 **2 :** consisting of radiation of a single wavelength or of a very small range of wavelengths **3 :** of, relating to, or exhibiting monochromatism — **mono·chro·mat·i·cal·ly** \-i-k(ə-)lē\ *adv* — **mono·chro·ma·tic·i·ty** \-ˌkrō-mə-'tis-ət-ē\ *n*

mono·chro·ma·tism \-'krō-mə-ˌtiz-əm\ *n* (1865) **:** complete color blindness in which all colors appear as shades of gray

mono·chro·ma·tor \ˌmän-ə-'krō-ˌmāt-ər\ *n* [*monochromatic* + *illuminator*] (1909) **:** a device for isolating a narrow portion of a spectrum

¹**mono·chrome** \'män-ə-ˌkrōm\ *n* [ML *monochroma,* fr. L, fem. of *monochromos* of one color, fr. Gk *monochrōmos,* fr. *mon-* + *-chrōmos* -chrome] (1662) **:** a painting, drawing, or photograph in a single hue — **mono·chro·mic** \ˌmän-ə-'krō-mik\ *adj* — **mono·chrom·ist** \'män-ə-ˌkrō-məst\ *n*

²**monochrome** *adj* (1849) **1 :** of, relating to, or made with a single color or hue **2 :** characterized by the reproduction of visual images in tones of gray ⟨~ television⟩

mon·o·cle \'män-i-kəl\ *n* [F, fr. LL *monoculus* having one eye, fr. L *mon-* + *oculus* eye — more at EYE] (ca. 1858) **:** an eyeglass for one eye — **mon·o·cled** \-kəld\ *adj*

mono·cli·nal \ˌmän-ə-'klīn-ᵊl\ *adj* (1843) **:** having or relating to a single oblique inclination ⟨~ folding of rock layers⟩ — **monoclinal** *n*

mono·cline \'män-ə-ˌklīn\ *n* (1879) **:** a monoclinal geologic fold

mono·clin·ic \ˌmän-ə-'klin-ik\ *adj* [ISV] (ca. 1864) **:** having one oblique intersection of the crystallographic axes

monoclinic system *n* (1869) **:** a crystal system characterized by three unequal axes with one oblique intersection

mono·cli·nous \-'klī-nəs\ *adj* [NL *monoclinus,* fr. *mon-* + *-clinus* -clinous] (1828) **:** having both stamens and pistils in the same flower

mono·clo·nal \ˌmän-ə-'klōn-ᵊl\ *adj* (ca. 1914) **:** produced by, being, or composed of cells derived from a single cell ⟨~ antibodies⟩ ⟨a ~ tumor⟩

mono·coque \'män-ə-ˌkōk, -ˌkäk\ *n* [F, fr. *mon-* + *coque* shell, fr. L *coccum* excrescence on a tree, fr. Gk *kokkos* berry] (1913) **1 :** a type of construction (as of a fuselage or a rocket body) in which the outer skin carries all or a major part of the stresses **2 :** a type of vehicle construction (as of a motortruck or railroad car) in which the body is integral with the chassis

mono·cot \-ˌkät\ *n* (1890) **:** MONOCOTYLEDON

mono·cot·yl \-ˌkät-ᵊl\ *n* (1877) **:** MONOCOTYLEDON

mono·cot·y·le·don \ˌmän-ə-ˌkät-ᵊl-'ēd-ᵊn\ *n* [deriv. of NL *mon-* + *cotyledon* cotyledon] (1727) **:** any of a subclass (Monocotyledoneae) of seed

plants having an embryo with a single cotyledon and usu. parallel-veined leaves — **mono·cot·y·le·don·ous** \-ᵊn-əs\ *adj*
mo·noc·ra·cy \mä-ˈnäk-rə-sē, mə-\ *n* (1651) : government by a single person — **mono·crat** \ˈmän-ə-ˌkrat\ *n* — **mono·crat·ic** \ˌmän-ə-ˈkrat-ik\ *adj*
mono·crys·tal \ˈmän-ə-ˌkris-tᵊl\ *n* (ca. 1926) : a single crystal — **mono·crystal** *adj* — **mono·crys·tal·line** \ˌmän-ə-ˈkris-tə-lən *also* -ˌlīn, -ˌlēn\ *adj*
¹**mon·oc·u·lar** \mä-ˈnäk-yə-lər, mə-\ *adj* [LL *monoculus* having one eye] (1640) **1** : of, involving, or affecting a single eye **2** : suitable for use with only one eye — **mon·oc·u·lar·ly** *adv*
²**monocular** *n* (1936) : a monocular device
mono·cul·ture \ˈmän-ə-ˌkəl-chər\ *n* (1915) **1** : the cultivation or growth of a single crop or organism esp. on agricultural or forest land **2** : a crop or a population of a single kind of organism grown on land in monoculture — **mono·cul·tur·al** \ˌmän-ə-ˈkəlch-(ə-)rəl\ *adj*
mono·cy·clic \ˌmän-ə-ˈsī-klik, -ˈsik-lik\ *adj* [ISV] (1910) **1** : containing one ring in the molecular structure **2** : having a single annual maximum of population ⟨a population of ~ water fleas in a lake⟩ — **mono·cy·cly** \ˈmän-ə-ˌsī-klē\ *n*
mono·cyte \ˈmän-ə-ˌsīt\ *n* [ISV] (ca. 1913) : a large phagocytic leukocyte with basophilic cytoplasm containing faint eosinophilic granulations — **mono·cyt·ic** \ˌmän-ə-ˈsit-ik\ *adj*
mono·dis·perse \ˌmän-ō-dis-ˈpərs\ *adj* [*mono-* + *disperse*, adj., fr. *dispersed*, pp. of *disperse*] (1925) : characterized by particles of uniform size in a dispersed phase
mon·o·dist \ˈmän-əd-əst\ *n* (1751) : a writer, singer, or composer of monody
mono·dra·ma \ˈmän-ə-ˌdräm-ə, -ˌdram-\ *n* (1793) : a drama acted or designed to be acted by a single person — **mono·dra·mat·ic** \ˌmän-ə-drə-ˈmat-ik\ *adj*
mon·o·dy \ˈmän-əd-ē\ *n, pl* **-dies** [ML *monodia*, fr. Gk *monōidia*, fr. *monōidos* singing alone, fr. *mon-* + *aidein* to sing — more at ODE] (1589) **1** : an ode sung by one voice (as in a Greek tragedy) **2** : an elegy or dirge performed by one person **3 a** : a monophonic vocal piece **b** : the monophonic style of 17th century opera — **mo·nod·ic** \mə-ˈnäd-ik\ *or* **mo·nod·i·cal** \-i-kəl\ *adj* — **mo·nod·i·cal·ly** \-i-k(ə-)lē\ *adv*
mon·oe·cious \mə-ˈnē-shəs, (ˈ)mä-\ *adj* [deriv. of Gk *mon-* + *oikos* house — more at VICINITY] (1753) **1** : having male and female sex organs in the same individual : HERMAPHRODITIC **2** : having pistillate and staminate flowers on the same plant
mon·oe·cism \-ˈnē-ˌsiz-əm\ *n* (ca. 1875) : the condition of being monoecious
mono·es·ter \ˈmän-ō-ˌes-tər\ *n* (ca. 1927) : an ester (as of a dibasic acid) that contains only one ester group
mono·fil·a·ment \ˌmän-ə-ˈfil-ə-mənt\ *n* (ca. 1940) : a single untwisted synthetic filament (as of nylon)
mo·nog·a·mist \mə-ˈnäg-ə-məst\ *n* (1651) : one who practices or upholds monogamy
mo·nog·a·my \-mē\ *n* [F *monogamie*, fr. LL *monogamia*, fr. Gk, fr. *monogamos* monogamous, fr. *mon-* + *gamos* marriage — more at BIGAMY] (1612) **1** *archaic* : the practice of marrying only once during a lifetime **2** : the state or custom of being married to one person at a time — **mo·nog·a·mous** \mə-ˈnäg-ə-məs\ *also* **mono·gam·ic** \ˌmän-ə-ˈgam-ik\ *adj* — **mo·nog·a·mous·ly** *adv*
mono·gas·tric \ˌmän-ə-ˈgas-trik\ *adj* (1814) : having a stomach with only a single compartment ⟨swine, chicks, and human beings are ~⟩
mono·ge·ne·an \-ˈjē-nē-ən\ *n* [NL *Monogenea*, group name] (ca. 1899) : a monogenetic trematode — **monogenean** *adj*
mono·gen·e·sis \-ˈjen-ə-səs\ *n* [NL] (ca. 1859) : origin of diverse individuals or kinds (as of language) by descent from a single ancestral individual or kind
mono·ge·net·ic \-jə-ˈnet-ik\ *adj* (1873) **1** : relating to or involving monogenesis **2** : of, relating to, or being any of a subclass (Monogenea) of trematode worms that ordinarily live as ectoparasites on a single fish host throughout their entire life cycle
mono·gen·ic \-ˈjen-ik\ *adj* [ISV] (1939) : of, relating to, or controlled by a single gene and esp. by either of an allelic pair — **mono·gen·i·cal·ly** \-i-k(ə-)lē\ *adv*
mono·germ \ˈmän-ə-ˌjərm\ *adj* [*mon-* + *germinate*] (1950) : producing or being a fruit that gives rise to a single plant ⟨a ~ variety of sugar beet⟩
¹**mono·gram** \ˈmän-ə-ˌgram\ *n* [LL *monogramma*, fr. Gk *mon-* + *gramma* letter — more at GRAM] (ca. 1696) : a sign of identity usu. formed of the combined initials of a name — **mono·gram·mat·ic** \ˌmän-ə-grə-ˈmat-ik\ *adj*
²**monogram** *vt* **-grammed; -gram·ming** (1868) : to mark with a monogram — **mono·gram·mer** \-ˌgram-ər\ *n*
¹**mono·graph** \ˈmän-ə-ˌgraf\ *n* (ca. 1821) : a learned treatise on a small area of learning; *also* : a written account of a single thing — **mono·graph·ic** \ˌmän-ə-ˈgraf-ik\ *adj*
²**monograph** *vt* (1876) : to write a monograph on
mo·nog·y·nous \mə-ˈnäj-ə-nəs, mä-\ *adj* (ca. 1890) : of, relating to, or living in monogyny
mo·nog·y·ny \-nē\ *n* [ISV] (1876) : the state or custom of having only one wife at a time
mono·hy·brid \ˌmän-ō-ˈhī-brəd\ *n* (1903) : an individual or strain heterozygous for one specified gene — **monohybrid** *adj*
mono·hy·dric \-ˈhī-drik\ *adj* (ca. 1856) **1** : containing one atom of acid hydrogen **2** : MONOHYDROXY
mono·hy·droxy \-(ˌ)hī-ˈdräk-sē\ *adj* [ISV *monohydroxy-*, fr. *mon-* + *hydroxy-*] (ca. 1945) : containing one hydroxyl group in the molecule
mono·lay·er \ˈmän-ō-ˌlā-ər, -ˌle(-ə)r\ *n* (1926) : a single continuous layer or film that is one cell or molecule in thickness
mono·lin·gual \ˌmän-ə-ˈliŋ-g(yə-)wəl, ˌmō-nə-\ *adj* (1926) : knowing or using only one language — **monolingual** *n*
mono·lith \ˈmän-ᵊl-ˌith\ *n* [F *monolithe*, fr. *monolithe* consisting of a single stone, fr. L *monolithus*, fr. Gk *monolithos*, fr. *mon-* + *lithos* stone] (ca. 1827) **1** : a single great stone often in the form of an obelisk or column **2** : a massive structure **3** : an organized whole that acts as a single unified powerful or influential force
mono·lith·ic \ˌmän-ᵊl-ˈith-ik\ *adj* (1825) **1 a** : of, relating to, or resembling a monolith : HUGE, MASSIVE **b** (1) : formed from a single crystal ⟨a ~ silicon chip⟩ (2) : produced in or on a monolithic chip ⟨a ~ circuit⟩ **2 a** : cast as a single piece ⟨a ~ concrete wall⟩ **b** : formed or composed of material without joints or seams ⟨a ~ floor covering⟩ ⟨a ~ furnace lining⟩ **c** : consisting of or constituting a single unit **3 a** : constituting a massive undifferentiated and often rigid whole ⟨a ~ society⟩ **b** : exhibiting or characterized by often rigidly fixed uniformity ⟨~ party unity⟩ — **mono·lith·i·cal·ly** \-i-k(ə-)lē\ *adv*
mono·logue *also* **mono·log** \ˈmän-ᵊl-ˌȯg, -ˌäg\ *n* [F *monologue*, fr. *mon-* + *-logue* (as in *dialogue*)] (1549) **1** : a dramatic soliloquy; *also* : a dramatic sketch performed by one actor **2** : a literary soliloquy **3** : a long speech monopolizing conversation — **mono·logu·ist** \-ˌȯg-əst, -ˌäg-\ *or* **mo·no·lo·gist** \mə-ˈnäl-ə-jəst; ˈmän-ᵊl-ˌȯg-əst, -ˌäg-\ *n*
mono·ma·nia \ˌmän-ə-ˈmā-nē-ə, -nyə\ *n* [NL] (1823) **1** : mental illness esp. when limited in expression to one idea or area of thought **2** : excessive concentration on a single object or idea — **mono·ma·ni·ac** \-nē-ˌak\ *n or adj* — **mono·ma·ni·a·cal** \-mə-ˈnī-ə-kəl\ *adj*
mono·mer \ˈmän-ə-mər\ *n* [ISV *mon-* + *-mer* (as in *polymer*)] (1914) : a chemical compound that can undergo polymerization — **mo·no·mer·ic** \ˌmän-ə-ˈmer-ik, ˌmō-nə-\ *adj*
mono·me·tal·lic \ˌmän-ō-mə-ˈtal-ik\ *adj* (1877) **1** : of or relating to monometallism **2** : consisting of or employing one metal
mono·met·al·lism \-ˈmet-ᵊl-ˌiz-əm\ *n* [ISV *mon-* + *-metallism* (as in *bimetallism*)] (1879) : the adoption of one metal only in a currency — **mono·met·al·list** \-ᵊl-əst\ *n*
mo·nom·e·ter \mə-ˈnäm-ət-ər, mä-\ *n* [LL, fr. Gk *monometros*, fr. *mon-* + *metron* measure — more at MEASURE] (ca. 1847) : a line of verse consisting of a single metrical foot or dipody
mo·no·mi·al \mä-ˈnō-mē-əl, mə-\ *n* [blend of *mon-* + *-nomial* (as in *binomial*)] (ca. 1706) **1** : a mathematical expression consisting of a single term **2** : a taxonomic name consisting of a single word or term — **monomial** *adj*
mono·mo·lec·u·lar \ˌmän-ō-mə-ˈlek-yə-lər\ *adj* (1917) : being only one molecule thick ⟨a ~ film⟩ — **mono·mo·lec·u·lar·ly** *adv*
mono·mor·phe·mic \-mȯr-ˈfē-mik\ *adj* (1936) : consisting of only one morpheme ⟨the word *talk* is ~ but *talked* is not⟩
mono·mor·phic \-ˈmȯr-fik\ *adj* (ca. 1879) : having but a single form, structural pattern, or genotype ⟨a ~ species of insect⟩ — **mono·mor·phism** \-ˌfiz-əm\ *n*
mono·nu·cle·ar \ˌmän-ō-ˈn(y)ü-klē-ər, ÷-kyə-lər\ *adj* [ISV] (1886) **1** : having only one nucleus ⟨a ~ cell⟩ **2** : MONOCYCLIC 1 — **mononuclear** *n*
mono·nu·cle·at·ed \-ˈn(y)ü-klē-ˌāt-əd\ *also* **mono·nu·cle·ate** \-klē-ət, -ˌāt\ *adj* (1890) : MONONUCLEAR 1
mono·nu·cle·o·sis \-ˌn(y)ü-klē-ˈō-səs\ *n* [NL, fr. ISV *mononuclear* + NL *-osis*] (1920) : an abnormal increase of mononuclear leukocytes in the blood; *specif* : INFECTIOUS MONONUCLEOSIS
mono·nu·cle·o·tide \-ˈn(y)ü-klē-ə-ˌtīd\ *n* (1908) : a nucleotide that is derived from one molecule each of a nitrogenous base, a sugar, and a phosphoric acid
mo·noph·a·gous \mə-ˈnäf-ə-gəs, mä-\ *adj* (ca. 1868) : feeding on or utilizing a single kind of food; *esp* : feeding on a single kind of plant or animal — **mo·noph·a·gy** \-ə-jē\ *n*
mono·pho·nic \ˌmän-ə-ˈfän-ik, -ˈfō-nik\ *adj* (ca. 1864) **1** : having a single unaccompanied melodic line **2** : of or relating to sound transmission, recording, or reproduction involving a single transmission path — **mono·pho·ni·cal·ly** \-i-k(ə-)lē, -ni-\ *adv*
mo·noph·o·ny \mə-ˈnäf-ə-nē, mä-\ *n* (ca. 1890) : monophonic music
mon·oph·thong \ˈmän-ə(f)-ˌthȯŋ\ *n* [LGk *monophthongos* single vowel, fr. Gk *mon-* + *phthongos* sound] (1620) : a vowel sound that throughout its duration has a single constant articulatory position — **mon·oph·thon·gal** \ˌmän-ə(f)-ˈthȯŋ-(g)əl\ *adj*
mono·phy·let·ic \ˌmän-ō-fī-ˈlet-ik\ *adj* [ISV] (1874) : of or relating to a single stock; *specif* : developed from a single common ancestral form — **mono·phy·ly** \ˈmän-ə-ˌfī-lē\ *n*
Mo·noph·y·site \mə-ˈnäf-ə-ˌsīt\ *n* [ML *Monophysita*, fr. MGk *Monophysitēs*, fr. Gk *mon-* + *physis* nature — more at PHYSICS] (1698) : one holding the anti-Chalcedonian doctrine that Christ's nature remains altogether divine and not human even though he has taken on an earthly and human body with its cycle of birth, life, and death — **Monophysite** *or* **Mo·noph·y·sit·ic** \-ˌnäf-ə-ˈsit-ik\ *adj* — **Mo·noph·y·sit·ism** \-ˈnäf-ə-ˌsīt-ˌiz-əm\ *n*
mono·plane \ˈmän-ə-ˌplān\ *n* (1907) : an airplane with only one main supporting surface
¹**mono·ploid** \ˈmän-ə-ˌplȯid\ *n* [ISV] (1928) : a monoploid individual or organism
²**monoploid** *adj* (1941) **1** : having or being a haploid chromosome set **2** : having or being the basic haploid number of chromosomes in a polyploid series of organisms
mono·po·di·al \ˌmän-ə-ˈpōd-ē-əl\ *adj* [NL *monopodium*, fr. *mon-* + *-podium* -podium] (1876) : having or involving the formation of offshoots from a main axis — **mono·po·di·al·ly** \-ē-ə-lē\ *adv*
mono·pole \ˈmän-ə-ˌpōl\ *n* (1937) **1** : a hypothetical single concentrated electric charge or magnetic pole; *also* : a hypothetical unpolarized particle having such a pole **2** : a radio antenna consisting of a single often straight element
mo·nop·o·list \mə-ˈnäp-ə-ləst\ *n* (1601) : one who monopolizes — **mo·nop·o·lis·tic** \-ˌnäp-ə-ˈlis-tik\ *adj* — **mo·nop·o·lis·ti·cal·ly** \-ti-k(ə-)lē\ *adv*
mo·nop·o·lize \mə-ˈnäp-ə-ˌlīz\ *vt* **-lized; -liz·ing** (ca. 1611) : to get a monopoly of : assume complete possession or control of ⟨~ a conversation⟩ — **mo·nop·o·li·za·tion** \-ˌnäp-ə-lə-ˈzā-shən\ *n* — **mo·nop·o·liz·er** \-ˈnäp-ə-ˌlī-zər\ *n*
mo·nop·o·ly \mə-ˈnäp-(ə-)lē\ *n, pl* **-lies** [L *monopolium*, fr. Gk *monopōlion*, fr. *mon-* + *pōlein* to sell] (1534) **1** : exclusive ownership through legal privilege, command of supply, or concerted action **2** : exclusive possession or control **3** : a commodity controlled by one party **4** : one that has a monopoly
mono·pro·pel·lant \ˌmän-ō-prə-ˈpel-ənt\ *n* (ca. 1945) : a rocket propellant containing both the fuel and the oxidizer in a single substance
mo·nop·so·ny \mə-ˈnäp-sə-nē\ *n, pl* **-nies** [*mon-* + *-opsony* (as in *oligopsony*)] (1933) : an oligopsony limited to one buyer
mono·rail \ˈmän-ə-ˌrāl\ *n* (1897) : a single rail serving as a track for a wheeled vehicle; *also* : a vehicle traveling on such a track
mon·or·chid \mä-ˈnȯr-kəd\ *n* [irreg. fr Gk *monorchis*, fr. *mon-* + *orchis* testicle — more at ORCHIS] (ca. 1874) : an individual who has only one

testis or only one descended into the scrotum — **monorchid** *adj* — **mon·or·chi·dism** \-kə-ˌdiz-əm\ *n*

mono·rhyme \'män-ə-ˌrīm\ *n* (1731) **:** a strophe or poem in which all the lines have the same end rhyme — **mono·rhymed** \-ˌrīmd\ *adj*

mono·sac·cha·ride \ˌmän-ə-'sak-ə-ˌrīd\ *n* [ISV] (1896) **:** a sugar not decomposable to simpler sugars by hydrolysis

mono·so·di·um glu·ta·mate \ˌmän-ə-ˌsōd-ē-əm-'glüt-ə-ˌmāt\ *n* (1929) **:** a crystalline salt $C_5H_8O_4NaN$ used for seasoning foods — abbr. *MSG*

mono·some \'män-ə-ˌsōm\ *n* (ca. 1909) **1 :** a chromosome lacking a synaptic mate; *esp* **:** an unpaired X chromosome **2 :** a single ribosome

mono·so·mic \ˌmän-ə-'sō-mik\ *adj* (1926) **:** having one less than the diploid number of chromosomes — **monosomic** *n* — **mono·so·my** \'män-ə-ˌsō-mē\ *n*

mono·spe·cif·ic \ˌmän-ō-spə-'sif-ik\ *adj* (1947) **:** specific for a single antigen or receptor site on an antigen — **mono·spec·i·fic·i·ty** \-ˌspes-ə-'fis-ət-ē\ *n*

mono·stele \'män-ə-ˌstēl, ˌmän-ə-'stē-lē\ *n* (ca. 1900) **:** PROTOSTELE — **mono·ste·lic** \ˌmän-ə-'stē-lik\ *adj* — **mono·ste·ly** \'män-ə-ˌstē-lē\ *n*

mono·syl·lab·ic \ˌmän-ə-sə-'lab-ik\ *adj* [prob. fr. F *monosyllabique,* fr. *monosyllabe*] (1768) **1 :** consisting of one syllable or of monosyllables **2 :** using or speaking only monosyllables **3 :** conspicuously brief in answering or commenting **:** TERSE — **mono·syl·lab·i·cal·ly** \-i-k(ə-)lē\ *adv* — **mono·syl·la·bic·i·ty** \-ˌsil-ə-'bis-ət-ē\ *n*

mono·syl·la·ble \'män-ə-ˌsil-ə-bəl, ˌmän-ə-'\ *n* [modif. of MF or LL; MF *monosyllabe,* fr. LL *monosyllabon,* fr. Gk, fr. neut. of *monosyllabos* having one syllable, fr. *mon-* + *syllabē* syllable] (1533) **:** a word of one syllable

mono·sym·met·ric \ˌmän-ə-sə-'me-trik\ *adj* (ca. 1879) **:** MONOCLINIC

mono·syn·ap·tic \ˌmän-ō-sə-'nap-tik\ *adj* (1942) **:** having or involving a single neural synapse — **mono·syn·ap·ti·cal·ly** \-ti-k(ə-)lē\ *adv*

mono·ter·pene \ˌmän-ə-'tər-ˌpēn\ *n* (ca. 1959) **:** any of a class of terpenes $C_{10}H_{16}$ containing two isoprene units per molecule; *also* **:** one of their derivatives

mono·the·ism \'män-ə-(ˌ)thē-ˌiz-əm\ *n* (1660) **:** the doctrine or belief that there is but one God — **mono·the·ist** \-ˌthē-əst\ *n* — **mono·the·is·tic** \ˌmän-ə-thē-'is-tik\ *also* **mono·the·is·ti·cal** \-ti-kəl\ *adj* — **mono·the·is·ti·cal·ly** \-ti-k(ə-)lē\ *adv*

mono·tint \'män-ə-ˌtint\ *n* (1886) **:** MONOCHROME

¹mono·tone \'män-ə-ˌtōn\ *n* [Gk *monotonos* monotonous] (1644) **1 :** a succession of syllables, words, or sentences in one unvaried key or pitch **2 :** a single unvaried musical tone **3 :** a tedious sameness or reiteration **4 :** a person unable to produce or to distinguish between musical intervals

²monotone *adj* (1769) **1 :** MONOTONIC 2 **2 :** having a uniform color

mono·ton·ic \ˌmän-ə-'tän-ik\ *adj* (1797) **1 :** of, relating to, or uttered in a monotone **2 :** having the property either of never increasing or of never decreasing as the values of the independent variable or the subscripts of the terms increase ⟨~ functions⟩ ⟨a ~ sequence⟩ — **mono·ton·i·cal·ly** \-i-k(ə-)lē\ *adv* — **mono·to·nic·i·ty** \ˌmän-ō-tō-'nis-ət-ē\ *n*

mo·not·o·nous \mə-'nät-ᵊn-əs, -'nät-nəs\ *adj* [Gk *monotonos,* fr. *mon-* + *tonos* tone] (1778) **1 :** uttered or sounded in one unvarying tone **2 :** tediously uniform or unvarying — **mo·not·o·nous·ly** *adv* — **mo·not·o·nous·ness** *n*

mo·not·o·ny \mə-'nät-ᵊn-ē, -'nät-nē\ *n* (1706) **1 :** tedious sameness **2 :** sameness of tone or sound

mono·treme \'män-ə-ˌtrēm\ *n* [NL *Monotremata,* fr. Gk *mon-* + *trēmat-, trēma* hole — more at TREMATODE] (1835) **:** any of an order (Monotremata) of lower mammals comprising the duckbills and echidnas

mono·type \'män-ə-ˌtīp\ *n* (1882) **:** an impression on paper of a design painted usu. with the finger or a brush on a surface (as glass)

Monotype *trademark* — used for a keyboard typesetting machine that casts and sets type in separate characters

mono·typ·ic \ˌmän-ə-'tip-ik\ *adj* [*mon-* + *type* + *-ic*] (ca. 1859) **:** including a single representative — used esp. of a genus with only one species

mono·un·sat·u·rat·ed \'män-ō-ˌən-'sach-ə-ˌrāt-əd\ *adj, of an oil or fatty acid* (1939) **:** containing one double or triple bond per molecule

mono·va·lent \ˌmän-ə-'vā-lənt\ *adj* [ISV] (1869) **1 :** UNIVALENT 1 **2 :** containing antibodies specific for or antigens of a single strain of an organism

mon·ovu·lar \(')mä-'näv-yə-lər, -'nōv-\ *adj* (1929) **:** MONOZYGOTIC

mon·ox·ide \mə-'näk-ˌsīd\ *n* [ISV] (1869) **:** an oxide containing one atom of oxygen in a molecule

mono·zy·got·ic \ˌmän-ə-zī-'gät-ik\ *adj* (1916) **:** derived from a single egg ⟨~ twins⟩

Mon·roe Doctrine \mən-ˌrō- *also* ˌmən- *or* ˌmän-\ *n* [James *Monroe*] (1853) **:** a statement of U.S. foreign policy expressing opposition to extension of European control or influence in the western hemisphere

mon·sei·gneur \ˌmōⁿ-ˌsān-'yər\ *n, pl* **mes·sei·gneurs** \ˌmā-ˌsān-'yər(z)\ [F, lit., my lord] (1602) **:** a French dignitary (as a prince or prelate) — used as a title preceding a title of office or rank

mon·sieur \məs(h)-(')yə(r), mə-'si(ə)r\ *n, pl* **mes·sieurs** \məs(h)-(')yə(r)(z), mās-; mə-'si(ə)r(z)\ [MF, lit., my lord] (ca. 1500) **:** a Frenchman of high rank or station — used as a title equivalent to *Mister* and prefixed to the name of a Frenchman

mon·si·gnor \män-'sē-nyər, män-\ *n, pl* **monsignors** *or* **mon·si·gno·ri** \ˌmän-ˌsēn-'yōr-ē, -'yȯr-\ [It *monsignore,* fr. F *monseigneur*] (1641) **:** a Roman Catholic prelate having a dignity or titular distinction (as of domestic prelate or protonotary apostolic) usu. conferred by the pope — used as a title prefixed to the surname or to the given name and surname — **mon·si·gno·ri·al** \ˌmän-ˌsēn-'yōr-ē-əl, -'yȯr-\ *adj*

mon·soon \män-'sün, 'män-ˌ\ *n* [obs. D *monssoen,* fr. Pg *monção,* fr. Ar *mawsim* time, season] (ca. 1584) **1 :** a periodic wind esp. in the Indian ocean and southern Asia **2 :** the season of the southwest monsoon in India and adjacent areas that is characterized by very heavy rainfall **3 :** rainfall that is associated with the monsoon — **mon·soon·al** \-ᵊl\ *adj*

mons pu·bis \'mänz-'pyü-bəs\ *n, pl* **mon·tes pubis** \'män-tēz-\ [NL, pubic eminence] (ca. 1903) **:** a rounded eminence of fatty tissue upon the pubic symphysis esp. of the human female

¹mon·ster \'män(t)-stər\ *n* [ME *monstre,* fr. MF, fr. L *monstrum* omen, monster, fr. *monēre* to warn — more at MENTAL] (14c) **1 a :** an animal or plant of abnormal form or structure **b :** one who deviates from normal or acceptable behavior or character **2 :** a threatening force **3 a :** an animal of strange or terrifying shape **b :** one unusually large for its kind **4 :** something monstrous; *esp* **:** a person of unnatural or extreme ugliness, deformity, wickedness, or cruelty

²monster *adj* (1837) **:** enormous in size, extent, or numbers

mon·strance \'män(t)-strən(t)s\ *n* [MF, fr. ML *monstrantia,* fr. L *monstrant-, monstrans,* prp. of *monstrare* to show, fr. *monēre*] (15c) **:** a vessel in which the consecrated Host is exposed for the adoration of the faithful

mon·stros·i·ty \män-'sträs-ət-ē\ *n, pl* **-ties** (15c) **1 a :** a malformation of a plant or animal **b :** something deviating from the normal **:** FREAK **2 :** the quality or state of being monstrous **3 a :** an object of great and often frightening size, force, or complexity **b :** an excessively bad or shocking example

mon·strous \'män(t)-strəs\ *adj* (15c) **1** *obs* **:** STRANGE, UNNATURAL **2 :** having extraordinary often overwhelming size **:** GIGANTIC **3 a :** having the qualities or appearance of a monster **b** *obs* **:** teeming with monsters **4 a :** extraordinarily ugly or vicious **:** HORRIBLE **b :** shockingly wrong or ridiculous **5 :** deviating greatly from the natural form or character **:** ABNORMAL **6 :** very great — used as an intensive — **mon·strous·ly** *adv* — **mon·strous·ness** *n*

syn MONSTROUS, PRODIGIOUS, TREMENDOUS, STUPENDOUS mean extremely impressive. MONSTROUS implies a departure from the normal (as in size, form, or character) and often carries suggestions of deformity, ugliness, or fabulousness ⟨the imagination turbid with *monstrous* fancies and misshapen dreams —Oscar Wilde⟩ PRODIGIOUS suggests a marvelousness exceeding belief, usu. in something felt as going far beyond a previous maximum (as of goodness, greatness, intensity, or size) ⟨made a *prodigious* effort and rolled the stone aside⟩ ⟨men have always reverenced *prodigious* inborn gifts —C. W. Eliot⟩ TREMENDOUS may imply a power to terrify or inspire awe ⟨the spell and *tremendous* incantation of the thought of death —L. P. Smith⟩ but in more general and weakened use it means only very large or great or intense ⟨success gave him *tremendous* satisfaction⟩ STUPENDOUS implies a power to stun or astound, usu. because of size, numbers, complexity, or greatness beyond description ⟨all are but parts of one *stupendous* whole, whose body Nature is, and God the soul —Alexander Pope⟩

mons ve·ne·ris \'mänz-'ven-ə-rəs\ *n, pl* **mon·tes veneris** \'män-ˌtēz-'ven-\ [NL, lit., eminence of Venus or of venery] (1621) **:** the mons pubis of the human female

mon·ta·dale \'mänt-ə-ˌdāl\ *n* [*Montana* state + *dale*] (1949) **:** any of an American breed of white-faced hornless sheep noted for heavy fleece and good meat conformation

¹mon·tage \män-'täzh, mōⁿ(n)-, -'tȧzh\ *n* [F, fr. *monter* to mount] (1929) **1 :** the production of a rapid succession of images in a motion picture to illustrate an association of ideas **2 a :** a literary, musical, or artistic composite of juxtaposed more or less heterogeneous elements **b :** a composite picture made by combining several separate pictures **3 :** a heterogeneous mixture **:** JUMBLE

²montage *vt* **mon·taged; mon·tag·ing** (1944) **:** to combine into or depict in a montage

mon·ta·gnard \ˌmōⁿ-ˌtän-'yär(d)\ *n, often cap* [F, mountaineer, fr. *montagne* mountain, fr. OF *montaigne*] (1842) **:** a member of a people inhabiting a highland region chiefly in southern Vietnam bordering on Cambodia — **montagnard** *adj, often cap*

Mon·ta·gue \'mänt-ə-ˌgyü\ *n* **:** the family of Romeo in Shakespeare's *Romeo and Juliet*

mon·tane \(')män-'tān, 'män-ˌ\ *adj* [L *montanus* of a mountain — more at MOUNTAIN] (1863) **1 :** of, relating to, growing in, or being the biogeographic zone of relatively moist cool upland slopes below timberline dominated by large evergreen trees **2 :** of, relating to, or made up of montane plants or animals

Mon·ta·nist \'mänt-ᵊn-əst\ *n* [*Montanus,* 2d cent. A.D. Phrygian schismatic] (1577) **:** an adherent of a Christian sect arising in the late second century and stressing apocalyptic expectations, the continuing prophetic gifts of the Spirit, and strict ascetic discipline — **Mon·ta·nism** \-ᵊn-ˌiz-əm\ *n*

mon·tan wax \'mänt-ᵊn-\ *n* [L *montanus* of a mountain] (1908) **:** a hard brittle mineral wax obtained usu. from lignites by extraction and used esp. in polishes, carbon paper, and insulating compositions

mon·te \'mänt-ē\ *n* [Sp, bank, mountain, heap, fr. It, fr. L *mont-, mons* mountain] (1824) **1 :** a card game in which players select any two of four cards turned face up in a layout and bet that one of them will be matched before the other as cards are dealt one at a time from the pack — called also *monte bank* **2 :** THREE-CARD MONTE

Mon·te Car·lo \ˌmänt-i-'kär-(ˌ)lō\ *adj* [*Monte Carlo,* Monaco, famous for its gambling casino] (1949) **:** of, relating to, or involving the use of random sampling techniques and often the use of computer simulation to obtain approximate solutions to mathematical or physical problems esp. in terms of a range of values each of which has a calculated probability of being the solution ⟨*Monte Carlo* calculations⟩

mon·teith \män-'tēth\ *n* [*Monteith,* 17th cent. Scot. eccentric who wore a cloak with a scalloped hem] (ca. 1683) **:** a large silver punch bowl with scalloped rim

Mon·te·rey Jack \ˌmänt-ə-ˌrā-'jak\ *n* [*Monterey,* California] (ca. 1947) **:** a semisoft whole-milk cheese with high moisture content

mon·te·ro \män-'te(ə)r-(ˌ)ō\ *n, pl* **-ros** [Sp, hunter, fr. *monte* mountain] (1593) **:** a round hunter's cap with ear flaps

Mon·te·zu·ma's revenge \ˌmänt-ə-ˌzü-məz-\ *n* [*Montezuma* II] (1962) **:** diarrhea contracted in Mexico esp. by tourists

month \'mən(t)th\ *n, pl* **months** \'mən(t)s, 'mən(t)ths\ [ME, fr. OE *mōnath;* akin to OHG *mānōd* month, OE *mōna* moon] (bef. 12c) **1 :** a measure of time corresponding nearly to the period of the moon's revolution and amounting to approximately 4 weeks or 30 days or $^1/_{12}$ of a year **2** *pl* **:** an indefinite usu. extended period of time ⟨he has been gone for ~*s*⟩ **3 :** one ninth of the typical duration of human pregnancy ⟨she was in her eighth ~⟩

month·long \'mən(t)th-'lȯŋ\ *adj* (1965) **:** lasting a month

¹month·ly \'mən(t)th-lē\ *adv* (1533) **:** once a month **:** by the month

[2]**monthly** *adj* (1572)　**1 a** : of or relating to a month　**b** : payable or reckoned by the month　**2** : lasting a month　**3** : occurring or appearing every month

[3]**monthly** *n, pl* **monthlies** (1833)　**1** : a monthly periodical　**2** *pl* : a menstrual period

Monthly Meeting *n* (ca. 1772) : a district unit of an organization of Friends

month's mind *n* (15c) : a Roman Catholic requiem mass for a person a month after his death

mon·ti·cule \'mänt-i-ˌkyü(ə)l\ *n* [F, fr. LL *monticulus*, dim. of L *mont-, mons* mountain — more at MOUNT] (1799) : a small elevation or prominence; *esp* : a subordinate cone of a volcano

Mont·mo·ren·cy \ˌmänt-mə-'ren(t)-sē\ *n* [F, fr. *Montmorency*, France] (1925) : a cherry that is grown commercially for its bright red sour fruit

mont·mo·ril·lon·ite \ˌmänt-mə-'ril-ə-ˌnīt, -'rē-ə-\ *n* [F, fr. *Montmorillon*, commune in western France] (1854) : a soft clayey mineral that is a hydrous aluminum silicate with considerable capacity for exchanging part of the aluminum for magnesium and bases — **mont·mo·ril·lon·it·ic** \-ˌril-ə-'nit-ik, -ˌrē-ə-\ *adj*

Mon·tra·chet \ˌmōⁿ-trä-'she\ *n* [F, fr. *Montrachet*, vineyard in Dept. Côte-d'Or, France] (1833) : a superior dry white Burgundy wine

mon·u·ment \'män-yə-mənt\ *n* [ME, fr. L *monumentum*, lit., memorial, fr. *monēre* to remind — more at MENTAL] (13c)　**1** *obs* : a burial vault : SEPULCHER　**2** : a written legal document or record : TREATISE　**3 a** (1) : a lasting evidence, reminder, or example of someone or something notable or great　(2) : a distinguished person　**b** : a memorial stone or a building erected in remembrance of a person or event　**4** *archaic* : an identifying mark : EVIDENCE; *also* : PORTENT, SIGN　**5** *obs* : a carved statue : EFFIGY　**6** : a boundary or position marker (as a stone)　**7** : NATIONAL MONUMENT　**8** : a written tribute

mon·u·men·tal \ˌmän-yə-'ment-ᵊl\ *adj* (1604)　**1** : of or relating to a monument　**2** : serving as or resembling a monument : MASSIVE; *also* : OUTSTANDING　**3** : very great — **mon·u·men·tal·i·ty** \-mən-'tal-ət-ē, -ˌmen-\ *n* — **mon·u·men·tal·ly** \-'ment-ᵊl-ē\ *adv*

mon·u·men·tal·ize \-'ment-ᵊl-ˌīz\ *vt* **-ized; -iz·ing** (1857) : to record or memorialize lastingly by a monument

mon·u·ron \'män-yə-ˌrän\ *n* [*mon-* + *urea* + [1]*-on*] (ca. 1957) : a persistent herbicide C₉H₁₁ClN₂O used esp. to control mixed broad-leaved weeds

mon·zo·nite \män-'zō-ˌnīt, 'män-zə-\ *n* [F, fr. Mt. *Monzoni*, Italy] (1882) : a granular igneous rock composed of plagioclase and orthoclase in about equal quantities together with augite and a little biotite — **mon·zo·nit·ic** \ˌmän-zə-'nit-ik\ *adj*

moo \'mü\ *vi* [imit.] (1549) : to make the throat noise of a cow — **moo** *n*

mooch \'müch\ *vb* [prob. fr. F dial. *muchier* to hide, lurk] *vi* (1851)　**1** : to wander aimlessly : AMBLE; *also* : SNEAK　**2** : SPONGE, CADGE ∼ *vt*　**1** : to take surreptitiously : STEAL　**2** : BEG, CADGE — **mooch·er** *n*

[1]**mood** \'müd\ *n* [ME, fr. OE *mōd*; akin to OHG *muot* mood, L *mos* will, custom] (bef. 12c)　**1** : a conscious state of mind or predominant emotion : FEELING; *also* : the expression of mood esp. in art or literature　**2** *archaic* : a fit of anger : RAGE　**3 a** : a prevailing attitude : DISPOSITION　**b** : a receptive state of mind predisposing to action　**c** : a distinctive atmosphere or context : AURA

[2]**mood** *n* [alter. of [1]*mode*] (1532)　**1** : the form of a syllogism as determined by the quantity and quality of its constituent propositions　**2** : distinction of form or a particular set of inflectional forms of a verb to express whether the action or state it denotes is conceived as fact or in some other manner (as command, possibility, or wish)　**3** : MODE 1b

moody \'müd-ē\ *adj* **mood·i·er; -est** (1593)　**1** : subject to depression : GLOOMY　**2** : subject to moods : TEMPERAMENTAL　**3** : expressive of a

mood — **mood·i·ly** \'müd-ᵊl-ē\ *adv* — **mood·i·ness** \'müd-ē-nəs\ *n*

moo·la *or* **moo·lah** \'mü-lə\ *n* [origin unknown] *slang* (1939) : MONEY

[1]**moon** \'mün\ *n* [ME *mone*, fr. OE *mōna*; akin to OHG *māno* moon, L *mensis* month, Gk *mēn* month, *mēnē* moon] (bef. 12c)　**1 a** : the earth's only known natural satellite shining by the sun's reflected light, revolving about the earth from west to east in about 29¹/₂ days with reference to the sun or about 27¹/₃ days with reference to the stars and having a diameter of 2160 miles (3475 kilometers) and a mean distance from the earth of about 238,700 miles (384,068 kilometers), a mass about one eightieth that of the earth, and a volume about one forty-ninth　**b** : one complete moon cycle consisting of four phases　**c** : SATELLITE　**2** : SYNODIC MONTH　**3** : MOONLIGHT　**4** : something that resembles a moon: as　**a** : a highly translucent spot on old porcelain　**b** : LUNULE　**5** : something impossible or inaccessible ⟨reach for the ∼⟩　**6** *slang* : naked buttocks — **moon·like** \-ˌlīk\ *adj*

[2]**moon** *vt* (1836) : to spend in idle reverie : DREAM — used with *away* ∼ *vi* : to spend time in idle reverie

moon·beam \'mün-ˌbēm\ *n* (1590) : a ray of light from the moon

moon·blind \-ˌblīnd\ *adj* (1668) : afflicted with moon blindness

moon blindness *n* (1720) : a recurrent inflammation of the eye of the horse

moon·calf \'mün-ˌkaf, -ˌkáf\ *n* (1620) : a foolish or absentminded person : SIMPLETON

moon·eye \'mü-ˌnī\ *n* (1842) : any of a genus (*Hiodon*) of silvery No. American freshwater fishes that resemble shad

moon-eyed \'mü-ˌnīd\ *adj* (1790) : having the eyes wide open

moon·fish \'mün-ˌfish\ *n, pl* **moonfish** *or* **moon·fish·es** (1646) : any of various deep-bodied often short deep-bodied silvery or yellowish marine fishes: as　**a** : OPAH　**b** : PLATY

moon·flow·er \-ˌflaú(-ə)r\ *n* (ca. 1909) : a tropical American morning glory (*Calonyction aculeatum*) with fragrant flowers; *also* : any of several related plants

Moon·ie \'mü-nē\ *n* [*Sun Myung Moon* b1920 Korean evangelist] (1974) : a member of the Unification Church founded by Sun Myung Moon

moon·ish \'mü-nish\ *adj* (15c) : influenced by the moon; *also* : CAPRICIOUS — **moon·ish·ly** *adv*

moon·less \'mün-ləs\ *adj* (1508) : lacking the light of the moon

moon·let \'mün-lət\ *n* (1832) : a small natural or artificial satellite

[1]**moon·light** \-ˌlīt\ *n* (14c) : the light of the moon

[2]**moonlight** *vi* **moon·light·ed; moon·light·ing** [back-formation fr. *moon-lighter* (1957) : to hold a second job in addition to a regular one — **moon·light·er** *n*

moon·lit \'mün-ˌlit\ *adj* (1830) : lighted by the moon

moon·quake \-ˌkwāk\ *n* (1946) : a seismic event on the moon

moon·rise \-ˌrīz\ *n* (1728)　**1** : the rising of the moon above the horizon　**2** : the time of the moon's rising

moon·scape \-ˌskāp\ *n* (1916) : the surface of the moon as seen or as depicted; *also* : a landscape resembling this surface

moon·seed \-ˌsēd\ *n* (1739) : any of a genus (*Menispermum* of the family Menispermaceae, the moonseed family) of twining plants with crescent-shaped seeds and black fruits

moon·set \-ˌset\ *n* (1845)　**1** : the descent of the moon below the horizon　**2** : the time of the moon's setting

moon shell *n* (1936) : any of a family (Naticidae) of globose smooth-shelled carnivorous marine snails

moon·shine \'mün-ˌshīn\ *n* (1500)　**1** : MOONLIGHT　**2** : empty talk : NONSENSE　**3** : intoxicating liquor; *esp* : illegally distilled corn whiskey

moon·shin·er \-ˌshī-nər\ *n* (1860) : a maker or seller of illicit whiskey

moon shot *also* **moon shoot** *n* (1958) : the launching of a spacecraft to the moon or its vicinity

---

MONTHS OF THE PRINCIPAL CALENDARS

GREGORIAN[1]		JEWISH		ISLAMIC	
name	days	name	days	name	days
January begins 10 days after the winter solstice	31	Tishri	30	Muharram[4] in A.H. 1403 began Oct. 19, 1982	30
February in leap years	28 29	Heshvan	29 *or* 30	Safar	29
March	31	Kislev	29 *or* 30	Rabi I	30
April	30	Tebet	29	Rabi II	29
May	31	Shebat	30	Jumada I	30
June	30	Adar[2]	29 *or* 30	Jumada II	29
July	31	Nisan[3]	30	Rajab	30
August	31	Iyar	29	Sha'ban	29
September	30	Sivan	30	Ramadan	30
October	31	Tammuz	29	Shawwal	29
November	30	Ab	30	Dhu'l-Qa'dah	30
December	31	Elul	29	Dhu'l-Hijja in leap years	29 30

[1]The equinoxes occur about March 21 and September 23, the solstices about June 22 and December 22.

[2]In leap years Adar is followed by Veadar or Adar Sheni, an intercalary month of 29 days.

[3]The first month of the ecclesiastical year; anciently called Abib.

[4]Retrogresses through the season; the Islamic year is lunar and each month begins at the approximate new moon; the year 1 A.H. began on Friday, July 16, A.D. 622.

moon·stone \'mün-,stōn\ *n* (1632) **:** a transparent or translucent feldspar of pearly or opaline luster used as a gem
moon·struck \-,strək\ *adj* (1674) **:** affected by or as if by the moon: as **a :** mentally unbalanced **b :** romantically sentimental **c :** lost in fantasy or reverie
moon·ward \'mün-wərd\ *adv* (1855) **:** toward the moon
moony \'mü-nē\ *adj* (1586) **1 :** of or relating to the moon **2 a :** crescent-shaped **b :** resembling the full moon **:** ROUND **3 :** MOONLIT **4 :** DREAMY, MOONSTRUCK
[1]**moor** \'mu̇(ə)r\ *n* [ME *mor,* fr. OE *mōr;* akin to OHG *meri* sea — more at MARINE] (bef. 12c) **1** *chiefly Brit* **:** an expanse of open rolling infertile land **2 :** a boggy area of wasteland usu. peaty and dominated by grasses and sedges
[2]**moor** *vb* [ME *moren;* akin to MD *meren, maren* to tie, moor] *vt* (15c) **:** to make fast with or as if with cables, lines, or anchors ~ *vi* **1 :** to secure a boat by mooring **:** ANCHOR **2 :** to be made fast
Moor \'mu̇(ə)r\ *n* [ME *More,* fr. MF, fr. L *Maurus* inhabitant of Mauretania] (14c) **1 :** one of the mixed Arab and Berber conquerors of Spain in the 8th century A.D. **2 :** BERBER — **Moor·ish** \-ish\ *adj*
moor·age \'mu̇(ə)r-ij\ *n* (1648) **1 :** an act of mooring **2 :** a place to moor
moor·hen \-,hen\ *n* (14c) **:** the common gallinule (*Gallinula chloropus*) of the New World, Eurasia, and Africa
moor·ing \-iŋ\ *n* (15c) **1 :** an act of making fast a boat or aircraft with lines or anchors **2 a :** a place where or an object to which something (as a craft) can be moored **b :** a device (as a line or chain) by which an object is secured in place **3 :** an established practice or stabilizing influence **:** ANCHORAGE 2 — usu. used in pl.
moor·land \-lənd, -,land\ *n* (bef. 12c) **:** land consisting of moors **:** a stretch of moor
moose \'müs\ *n, pl* **moose** [of Algonquian origin; akin to Natick *moos* moose] (1603) **1 :** a large ruminant mammal (*Alces americana*) of the deer family inhabiting forested parts of Canada and the northern U.S. **2 :** ELK 1a **3** *cap* [Loyal Order of *Moose*] **:** a member of a major benevolent and fraternal order

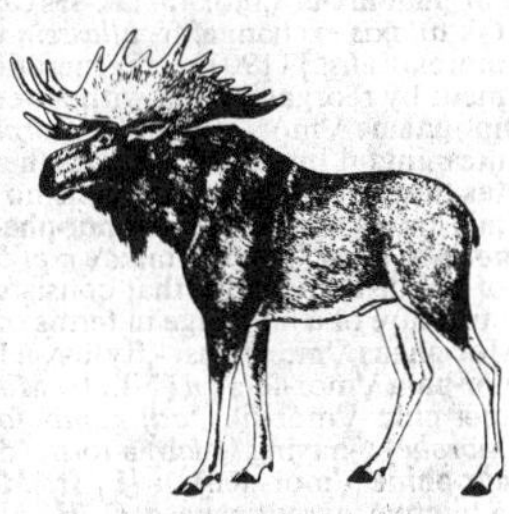
moose 1

[1]**moot** \'müt\ *n* [ME, fr. OE *mōt;* akin to OE *mētan* to meet — more at MEET] (bef. 12c) **1 :** a deliberative assembly primarily for the administration of justice; *esp* **:** one held by the freemen of an Anglo-Saxon community **2** *obs* **:** ARGUMENT, DISCUSSION
[2]**moot** *vt* (bef. 12c) **1** *archaic* **:** to discuss from a legal standpoint **:** ARGUE **2 a :** to bring up for discussion **:** BROACH **b :** DEBATE
[3]**moot** *adj* (1577) **1 a :** open to question **:** DEBATABLE **b :** subjected to discussion **:** DISPUTED **2 :** deprived of practical significance **:** made abstract or purely academic
moot court *n* (1788) **:** a mock court in which law students argue hypothetical cases for practice
[1]**mop** \'mäp\ *n* [ME *mappe*] (15c) **1 :** an implement made of absorbent material fastened to a handle and used esp. for cleaning floors **2 :** something that resembles a mop; *esp* **:** a thick mass of hair
[2]**mop** *vb* **mopped; mop·ping** *vt* (1755) **1 :** to use a mop on: as **a :** to clean or clear away by mopping ⟨~ the floors⟩ — often used with *up* ⟨~ up the spillage⟩ **b :** to wipe as if with a mop ⟨*mopped* his brow with a handkerchief⟩ **2** *Brit* **:** to consume eagerly — usu. used with *up* **3 :** to overcome decisively **:** TROUNCE — often used with *up* ~ *vi* **:** to clean a surface (as a floor) with a mop — **mop·per** *n*
mop·board \'mäp-,bō(ə)rd, -,bȯ(ə)rd\ *n* (1853) **:** BASEBOARD
[1]**mope** \'mōp\ *vi* **moped; mop·ing** [prob. fr. obs. *mop, mope* fool] (1568) **1** *archaic* **:** to act in a dazed or stupid manner **2 :** to give oneself up to brooding **:** become listless or dejected **3 :** to move slowly or aimlessly **:** DAWDLE — **mop·er** *n* — **mop·ey** \'mō-pē\ *adj*
[2]**mope** *n* (1693) **1 :** one that mopes **2** *pl* **:** BLUES 1
mo·ped \'mō-,ped\ *n* [Sw, fr. *motor* motor + *pedal* pedal] (ca. 1955) **:** a lightweight low-powered motorbike that can be pedaled
mop·pet \'mäp-ət\ *n* [obs. E *mop* fool, child] (1601) **1** *archaic* **:** BABY, DARLING **2 :** CHILD
mop–up \'mäp-,əp\ *n* (1900) **:** a concluding action
mop up \(')mäp-'əp\ *vt* (1901) **1 :** to follow in the wake of an attacking military force and clear (an area) of remaining pockets of resistance **2 :** to gather as if by absorbing **:** GARNER ⟨*mopped up* 18 of the 20 first-prize awards⟩ ~ *vi* **:** to complete a project or transaction
mo·quette \mō-'ket\ *n* [F] (1762) **:** a carpet or upholstery fabric having a velvety pile
mor \'mȯ(ə)r\ *n* [Dan, lit., humus; akin to OE *mearu* soft, friable, L *mortarium* mortar] (1931) **:** forest humus that forms a layer of largely organic matter abruptly distinct from the mineral soil beneath
mo·ra \'mōr-ə, 'mȯr-\ *n, pl* **mo·rae** \'mō(ə)r-(,)ē, 'mȯ(ə)r-, -,ī\ *or* **moras** [L, delay — more at MEMORY] (1832) **:** the minimal unit of measure in quantitative verse equivalent to the time of an average short syllable
mo·raine \mə-'rān\ *n* [F] (1789) **:** an accumulation of earth and stones carried and finally deposited by a glacier — **mo·rain·al** \-'rān-ᵊl\ *adj* — **mo·rain·ic** \-'rā-nik\ *adj*
[1]**mor·al** \'mȯr-əl, 'mär-\ *adj* [ME, fr. MF, fr. L *moralis,* fr. *mor-, mos* custom — more at MOOD] (14c) **1 a :** of or relating to principles of right and wrong in behavior **:** ETHICAL ⟨~ judgments⟩ **b :** expressing or teaching a conception of right behavior ⟨a ~ poem⟩ **c :** conforming to a standard of right behavior **d :** sanctioned by or operative on one's conscience or ethical judgment ⟨a ~ obligation⟩ **e :** capable of right and wrong action ⟨a ~ agent⟩ **2 :** probable though not proved **:** VIRTUAL ⟨a ~ certainty⟩ **3 :** having the effects of such on the mind, confidence, or will ⟨a ~ victory⟩ ⟨~ support⟩ — **mor·al·ly** \-ə-lē\ *adv*
syn MORAL, ETHICAL, VIRTUOUS, RIGHTEOUS, NOBLE mean conforming to a standard of what is right and good. MORAL implies conformity to established sanctioned codes or accepted notions of right and wrong; ETHICAL may suggest the involvement of more difficult or subtle questions of rightness, fairness, or equity; VIRTUOUS implies the possession or manifestation of moral excellence in character; RIGHTEOUS stresses guiltlessness or blamelessness and often suggests the sanctimonious; NOBLE implies moral eminence and freedom from anything petty, mean, or dubious in conduct and character.
[2]**mor·al** \'mȯr-əl, 'mär-; *3 is* mə-'ral\ *n* (ca. 1500) **1 a :** the moral significance or practical lesson (as of a story) **b :** a passage pointing out usu. in conclusion the lesson to be drawn from a story **2** *pl* **a :** moral practices or teachings **:** modes of conduct **b :** ETHICS **3 :** MORALE
mo·rale \mə-'ral\ *n* [in sense 1, fr. F, fr. fem. of *moral,* adj.; in other senses, modif. of F *moral* morale, fr. *moral,* adj.] (1752) **1 :** moral principles, teachings, or conduct **2 a :** the mental and emotional condition (as of enthusiasm, confidence, or loyalty) of an individual or group with regard to the function or tasks at hand **b :** a sense of common purpose with respect to a group **:** ESPRIT DE CORPS **3 :** the level of individual psychological well-being based on such factors as a sense of purpose and confidence in the future
moral hazard *n* (ca. 1917) **:** the possibility of loss to an insurance company arising from the character or circumstances of the insured
mor·al·ism \'mȯr-ə-,liz-əm, 'mär-\ *n* (1828) **1 a :** the habit or practice of moralizing **b :** a conventional moral attitude or saying **2 :** an often exaggerated emphasis on morality (as in politics)
mor·al·ist \-ləst\ *n* (1621) **1 :** one who leads a moral life **2 :** a teacher or student of morals **:** a philosopher or writer concerned with moral principles and problems **3 :** one concerned with regulating the morals of others
mor·al·is·tic \,mȯr-ə-'lis-tik, ,mär-\ *adj* (1865) **1 :** characterized by or expressive of a concern with morality **2 :** characterized by or expressive of a narrow and conventional moral attitude — **mor·al·is·ti·cal·ly** \-ti-k(ə-)lē\ *adv*
mo·ral·i·ty \mə-'ral-ət-ē, mȯ-\ *n, pl* **-ties** (14c) **1 a :** a moral discourse, statement, or lesson **b :** a literary or other imaginative work teaching a moral lesson **2 a :** a doctrine or system of moral conduct **b** *pl* **:** particular moral principles or rules of conduct **3 :** conformity to ideals of right human conduct **4 :** moral conduct **:** VIRTUE
morality play *n* (ca. 1929) **:** an allegorical play popular esp. in the 15th and 16th centuries in which the characters personify abstract qualities or concepts (as virtues, vices, or death)
mor·al·ize \'mȯr-ə-,līz, 'mär-\ *vb* **-ized; -iz·ing** *vt* (15c) **1 :** to explain or interpret morally **2 a :** to give a moral quality or direction to **b :** to improve the morals of ~ *vi* **:** to make moral reflections — **mor·al·iza·tion** \,mȯr-ə-lə-'zā-shən, ,mär-\ *n* — **mor·al·iz·er** \'mȯr-ə-,lī-zər, 'mär-\ *n*
moral philosophy *n* (14c) **:** ETHICS; *also* **:** the study of human conduct and values
mo·rass \mə-'ras, mȯ-\ *n* [D *moeras,* modif. of OF *maresc,* of Gmc origin; akin to OE *mersc* marsh — more at MARSH] (1655) **1 :** MARSH, SWAMP **2 :** something that traps, confuses, or impedes ⟨a ~ of troubles⟩ — **mo·rassy** \-'ras-ē\ *adj*
mor·a·to·ri·um \,mȯr-ə-'tōr-ē-əm, ,mär-, -'tȯr-\ *n, pl* **-ri·ums** *or* **-ria** \-ē-ə\ [NL, fr. LL, neut. of *moratorius* dilatory, fr. L *moratus,* pp. of *morari* to delay, fr. *mora* delay] (1875) **1 a :** a legally authorized period of delay in the performance of a legal obligation or the payment of a debt **b :** a waiting period set by an authority **2 :** a suspension of activity
Mo·ra·vi·an \mə-'rā-vē-ən\ *n* (1555) **1 :** a member of a Protestant denomination arising from a 15th century religious reform movement in Bohemia and Moravia **2 a :** a native or inhabitant of Moravia **b :** the group of Czech dialects spoken by the Moravian people and transitional between Slovak and Bohemian — **Moravian** *adj*
mo·ray \mə-'rā, 'mȯr-(,)ā\ *n* [Pg *moréia,* fr. L *muraena,* fr. Gk *myraina*] (1624) **:** any of numerous often brightly colored eels (family Muraenidae) that have sharp teeth capable of inflicting a savage bite, that occur in warm seas, and that include a Mediterranean eel (*Muraena helena*) valued for food — called also *moray eel*
mor·bid \'mȯr-bəd\ *adj* [L *morbidus* diseased, fr. *morbus* disease; akin to Gk *marainein* to waste away — more at SMART] (1656) **1 a :** of, relating to, or characteristic of disease ⟨~ anatomy⟩ **b :** affected with or induced by disease ⟨a ~ condition⟩ **c :** productive of disease ⟨~ substances⟩ **2 :** abnormally susceptible to or characterized by gloomy or unwholesome feelings **3 :** GRISLY, GRUESOME ⟨~ details⟩ ⟨~ curiosity⟩ — **mor·bid·ly** *adv* — **mor·bid·ness** *n*
mor·bid·i·ty \mȯr-'bid-ət-ē\ *n* (1721) **1 :** the quality or state of being morbid **2 :** the relative incidence of disease
mor·ceau \mȯr-'sō\ *n, pl* **mor·ceaux** \-'sō(z)\ [F, fr. OF *morsel* morsel] (1751) **:** a short literary or musical piece
mor·da·cious \mȯr-'dā-shəs\ *adj* [L *mordac-, mordax* biting, fr. *mordēre* to bite — more at SMART] (1650) **1 :** biting in style or manner **:** CAUSTIC **2 :** given to biting — **mor·dac·i·ty** \-'das-ət-ē\ *n*
mor·dan·cy \'mȯrd-ᵊn-sē\ *n* (1656) **1 :** a biting and caustic quality of style **:** INCISIVENESS **2 :** a sharply critical or bitter quality of thought or feeling **:** HARSHNESS
[1]**mor·dant** \'mȯrd-ᵊnt\ *adj* [ME, fr. MF, prp. of *mordre* to bite, fr. L *mordēre*] (15c) **1 :** biting and caustic in thought, manner, or style **:** INCISIVE ⟨a ~ wit⟩ **2 :** acting as a mordant **3 :** BURNING, PUNGENT ***syn*** see CAUSTIC — **mor·dant·ly** *adv*
[2]**mordant** *n* (1791) **1 :** a chemical that fixes a dye in or on a substance by combining with the dye to form an insoluble compound **2 :** a corroding substance used in etching
[3]**mordant** *vt* (1836) **:** to treat with a mordant
Mor·de·cai \'mȯrd-i-,kī\ *n* [Heb *Mordĕkhai*] **:** a relative of Esther who gives advice on saving the Jews from the destruction planned by Haman
mor·dent \'mȯrd-ᵊnt, mȯr-'dent\ *n* [It *mordente,* fr. L *mordent-, mordens,* prp. of *mordēre*] (1806) **:** a musical ornament made by a quick alternation of a principal tone with the tone immediately below it

\ə\ abut \ᵊ\ kitten, F table \ər\ further \a\ ash \ā\ ace \ä\ cot, cart \au̇\ out \ch\ chin \e\ bet \ē\ easy \g\ go \i\ hit \ī\ ice \j\ job \ŋ\ sing \ō\ go \ȯ\ law \ȯi\ boy \th\ thin \t͟h\ the \ü\ loot \u̇\ foot \y\ yet \zh\ vision \à, k̲, ⁿ, œ, œ̄, ue, ue̅, ʸ\ *see* Guide to Pronunciation

[1]**more** \'mō(ə)r, 'mȯ(ə)r\ *adj* [ME, fr. OE *māra;* akin to OE *mā*, adv., more, OHG *mēr*, OIr *mōr* large] (bef. 12c) **1 :** GREATER ⟨something ~ than she expected⟩ **2 :** ADDITIONAL, FURTHER ⟨~ guests arrived⟩
[2]**more** *adv* (bef. 12c) **1 a :** in addition ⟨a couple of times ~⟩ **b :** MOREOVER **2 :** to a greater or higher degree — often used with an adjective or adverb to form the comparative ⟨~ evenly matched⟩
[3]**more** *pron, pl in constr* (bef. 12c) **:** additional persons or things ⟨~ were found as the search continued⟩
[4]**more** *n* (12c) **1 :** a greater quantity, number, or amount ⟨the ~ the merrier⟩ **2 :** something additional **:** an additional amount **3** *obs* **:** persons of higher rank
more and more *adv* (13c) **:** to a progressively increasing extent
mo·reen \mə-'rēn, mȯ-\ *n* [prob. irregular fr. *moire*] (1691) **:** a strong fabric of wool, wool and cotton, or cotton with a plain glossy or moiré finish
mo·rel \mə-'rel, mȯ-\ *n* [F *morille*, of Gmc origin; akin to OHG *morhila* morel] (1672) **:** any of several large pitted edible fungi (genus *Morchella*, esp. *M. esculenta*)

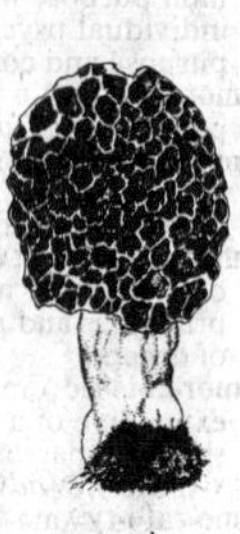
morel

mo·rel·lo \mə-'rel-(,)ō\ *n, pl* **-los** [prob. modif. of Flem *amarelle, marelle*, fr. ML *amarellum*, a sour cherry, fr. L *amarus* bitter, sour] (1598) **:** a cultivated sour cherry (as the Montmorency) having a dark-colored skin and juice
more or less *adv* (13c) **1 :** to a varying or undetermined extent or degree **:** SOMEWHAT ⟨they were *more or less* willing to help⟩ **2 :** with small variations **:** APPROXIMATELY ⟨contains 16 acres *more or less*⟩
more·over \mōr-'ō-vər, mȯr-, 'mōr-,, 'mȯr-,\ *adv* (14c) **:** in addition to what has been said **:** BESIDES
mo·res \'mȯ(ə)r-,āz, 'mō(ə)r- *also* -(,)ēz\ *n pl* [L, pl. of *mor-, mos* custom — more at MOOD] (1898) **1 :** the fixed morally binding customs of a particular group **2 :** moral attitudes **3 :** HABITS, MANNERS
[1]**mo·resque** \mȯ-'resk, mə-\ *adj, often cap* [F, fr. Sp *morisco*, fr. *moro* Moor, fr. L *Maurus*] (ca. 1611) **:** having the characteristics of Moorish art or architecture
[2]**moresque** *n, often cap* (ca. 1727) **:** an ornament or decorative motif in Moorish style
Mor·gan \'mȯr-gən\ *n* [Justin *Morgan* †1798 Am. teacher] (1841) **:** any of an American breed of light strong horses originated in Vermont from the progeny of one prepotent stallion of uncertain ancestry
mor·ga·nat·ic \,mȯr-gə-'nat-ik\ *adj* [NL *matrimonium ad morganaticam*, lit., perh., marriage with morning gift] (ca. 1727) **:** of, relating to, or being a marriage between a member of a royal or noble family and a person of inferior rank in which the rank of the inferior partner remains unchanged and the children of the marriage do not succeed to the titles, fiefs, or entailed property of the parent of higher rank — **mor·ga·nat·i·cal·ly** \-i-k(ə-)lē\ *adv*
mor·gan·ite \'mȯr-gə-,nīt\ *n* [J. P. *Morgan* †1913] (1911) **:** a rose-colored gem variety of beryl
Morgan le Fay \-lə-'fā\ *n* [OF *Morgain la fee* Morgan the fairy] **:** a sorceress and sister of King Arthur
mor·gen \'mȯr-gə(n)\ *n, pl* **morgen** [D, lit., morning] (1674) **:** a Dutch and southern African unit of land area equal to 2.116 acres
morgue \'mȯ(ə)rg\ *n* [F] (1821) **1 :** a place where the bodies of persons found dead are kept until identified and claimed by relatives or are released for burial **2 :** a collection of reference works and files of reference material in a newspaper or news periodical office
mor·i·bund \'mȯr-ə-(,)bənd, 'mär-\ *adj* [L *moribundus*, fr. *mori* to die — more at MURDER] (1721) **:** being in the state of dying **:** approaching death — **mor·i·bun·di·ty** \,mȯr-ə-'bən-dət-ē, ,mär-\ *n*
[1]**mo·ri·on** \'mōr-ē-,än, 'mȯr-\ *n* [MF] (1563) **:** a high-crested helmet with no visor
[2]**morion** *n* [modif. of L *mormorion*] (1748) **:** a nearly black variety of smoky quartz
Mo·ris·co \mə-'ris-(,)kō, mȯ-\ *n, pl* **-cos** *or* **-coes** [Sp, fr. *morisco*, adj., fr. *moro* Moor] (1629) **:** MOOR; *esp* **:** a Spanish Moor — **Morisco** *adj*
Mor·mon \'mȯr-mən\ *n* **1 :** the ancient redactor and compiler of the Book of Mormon presented as divine revelation by Joseph Smith **2 :** LATTER-DAY SAINT; *esp* **:** a member of the Church of Jesus Christ of Latter-day Saints — **Mor·mon·ism** \-mə-,niz-əm\ *n*
Mormon cricket *n* (1896) **:** a large dark wingless katydid (*Anabrus simplex*) that resembles a cricket and is found in the arid parts of the western U.S. where it is occas. an abundant pest of crops
morn \'mȯ(ə)rn\ *n* [ME, fr. OE *morgen;* akin to OHG *morgan* morning, L *merus* pure, unmixed] (bef. 12c) **1 :** DAWN **2 :** MORNING
Mor·nay sauce \mȯr-,nā-\ *n* [Philippe de *Mornay*] (ca. 1924) **:** a cheese-flavored cream sauce
morn·ing \'mȯr-niŋ\ *n* [ME, fr. *morn* + *-ing* (as in *evening*)] (13c) **1 a :** DAWN **b :** the time from sunrise to noon **c :** the time from midnight to noon **2 :** a period of first development **:** BEGINNING
morning-after pill \,mȯr-niŋ-'af-tər-\ *n* [so called fr. its being taken after rather than before intercourse] (1966) **:** an oral drug that interferes with pregnancy by blocking implantation of a fertilized egg in the human uterus
morning glory *n* (1814) **:** any of various usu. twining plants (genus *Ipomoea* of the family Convolvulaceae, the morning-glory family) with showy trumpet-shaped flowers; *broadly* **:** a plant of the morning-glory family including herbs, vines, shrubs, or trees with alternate leaves and regular pentamerous flowers
morning line *n* (1935) **:** a bookmaker's list of entries for a race meet and the probable odds on each that is printed or posted before the betting begins
Morning Prayer *n* (1552) **:** a service of liturgical prayer used for regular morning worship in churches of the Anglican communion
morn·ings \'mȯr-niŋz\ *adv* (1913) **:** in the morning repeatedly **:** on any morning
morning sickness *n* (1879) **:** nausea and vomiting that occur on rising in the morning esp. during the earlier months of pregnancy
morning star *n* (1535) **:** a bright planet (as Venus) seen in the eastern sky before or at sunrise
Mo·ro \'mō(ə)r-(,)ō, 'mȯ(ə)r-\ *n, pl* **Moro** *or* **Moros** [Sp, lit., Moor, fr. L *Maurus*] (1886) **1 :** a member of any of several Muslim peoples of the southern Philippines **2 :** any of the Austronesian languages of the Moro peoples
mo·roc·co \mə-'räk-(,)ō\ *n* [*Morocco*, Africa] (1634) **:** a fine leather from goatskin tanned with sumac
mo·ron \'mō(ə)r-,än, 'mȯ(ə)r-\ *n* [irreg. fr. Gk *mōros* foolish, stupid; akin to Skt *mūra* foolish] (1910) **1 :** a feebleminded person or mental defective who has a potential mental age of between 8 and 12 years and is capable of doing routine work under supervision **2 :** a very stupid person — **mo·ron·ic** \mə-'rän-ik, mȯ-\ *adj* — **mo·ron·i·cal·ly** \-i-k(ə-)lē\ *adv* — **mo·ron·ism** \'mōr-,än-,iz-əm, 'mȯr-\ *n* — **mo·ron·i·ty** \mə-'rän-ət-ē, mȯ-\ *n*
mo·rose \mə-'rōs, mȯ-\ *adj* [L *morosus*, lit., capricious, fr. *mor-, mos* will — more at MOOD] (1565) **1 :** having a sullen and gloomy disposition **2 :** marked by or expressive of gloom ***syn*** see SULLEN — **mo·rose·ly** *adv* — **mo·rose·ness** *n* — **mo·ros·i·ty** \-'räs-ət-ē\ *n*
morph \'mȯrf\ *n* [back-formation fr. *morpheme*] (1947) **1 :** [2]ALLOMORPH **2 :** a phoneme or sequence of phonemes that is presumably an allomorph but that is not considered as assigned to any particular morpheme **3 a :** a local population of a species that consists of interbreeding organisms and is distinguishable from other populations by morphology or behavior though capable of interbreeding with them **b :** a phenotypic variant of a species
morph- *or* **morpho-** *comb form* [G, fr. Gk, fr. *morphē*] **1 :** form ⟨*morpho*genesis⟩ **2 :** relating to form and ⟨*morpho*functional⟩
-morph \,mȯrf\ *n comb form* [ISV, fr. *-morphous*] **:** one having (such) a form ⟨iso*morph*⟩
mor·phac·tin \mȯr-'fak-tən\ *n* [prob. fr. *morph-* + L *actus*, pp. of *agere* to drive, do + E *-in* — more at AGENT] (1966) **:** any of several synthetic fluorine-containing compounds that tend to produce morphological changes and suppress growth in plants
mor·phal·lax·is \,mȯr-fə-'lak-səs\ *n, pl* **-lax·es** \-,sēz\ [NL, fr. *morph-* + Gk *allaxis* exchange, fr. *allassein* to change, exchange, fr. *allos* other — more at ELSE] (1901) **:** regeneration of a part or organism from a fragment by reorganization without cell proliferation
mor·pheme \'mȯr-,fēm\ *n* [F *morphème*, fr. Gk *morphē* form] (1926) **:** a meaningful linguistic unit whether a free form (as *pin*) or a bound form (as the *-s* of *pins*) that contains no smaller meaningful parts — **mor·phe·mic** \mȯr-'fē-mik\ *adj* — **mor·phe·mi·cal·ly** \-mi-k(ə-)lē\ *adv*
mor·phe·mics \mȯr-'fē-miks\ *n pl but sing in constr* (1947) **1 :** a branch of linguistic analysis that consists of the study of morphemes **2 :** the structure of a language in terms of morphemes
Mor·pheus \'mȯr-fē-əs, -,f(y)üs\ *n* [L, fr. Gk] **:** the Greek god of dreams
mor·phia \'mȯr-fē-ə\ *n* [NL, fr. L *Morpheus*] (1818) **:** MORPHINE
-mor·phic \'mȯr-fik\ *adj comb form* [prob. fr. F *-morphique*, fr. Gk *morphē*] **:** having (such) a form ⟨dolicho*morphic*⟩
mor·phine \'mȯr-,fēn\ *n* [F, fr. *Morpheus*] (1828) **:** a bitter crystalline addictive narcotic base $C_{17}H_{19}NO_3$ that is the principal alkaloid of opium and is used in the form of a soluble salt (as a hydrochloride or a sulfate) as an analgesic and sedative — **mor·phin·ic** \mȯr-'fē-nik, -'fin-ik\ *adj*
mor·phin·ism \'mȯr-,fē-,niz-əm, -fə-\ *n* (1882) **:** a disordered condition of health produced by habitual use of morphine
-mor·phism \'mȯr-,fiz-əm\ *n comb form* [LL *-morphus* -morphous fr. Gk *-morphos*] **1 :** quality or state of having (such) a form ⟨hetero*morphism*⟩ **2 :** conceptualization in (such) a form ⟨zoo*morphism*⟩
mor·pho \'mȯr-(,)fō\ *n, pl* **morphos** [NL, fr. Gk *Morphō*, epithet of Aphrodite] (1853) **:** any of a genus (*Morpho*) of large showy tropical American butterflies that typically have a brilliant blue metallic luster on the upper surface of the wings
mor·pho·gen·e·sis \,mȯr-fə-'jen-ə-səs\ *n* [NL] (1884) **:** the formation and differentiation of tissues and organs — compare ORGANOGENESIS
mor·pho·ge·net·ic \-jə-'net-ik\ *adj* (ca. 1890) **:** relating to or concerned with the development of normal organic form ⟨~ movements of early embryonic cells⟩ — **mor·pho·ge·net·i·cal·ly** \-i-k(ə-)lē\ *adv*
mor·pho·gen·ic \-'jen-ik\ *adj* (ca. 1890) **:** MORPHOGENETIC
mor·phol·o·gy \mȯr-'fäl-ə-jē\ *n* [G *morphologie*, fr. *morph-* + *-logie* -logy] (1830) **1 a :** a branch of biology that deals with the form and structure of animals and plants **b :** the form and structure of an organism or any of its parts **2 a :** a study and description of word formation in a language including inflection, derivation, and compounding **b :** the system of word-forming elements and processes in a language **3 a :** a study of structure or form **b :** STRUCTURE, FORM **4 :** the external structure of rocks in relation to the development of erosional forms or topographic features — **mor·pho·log·i·cal** \,mȯr-fə-'läj-i-kəl\ *adj* — **mor·pho·log·i·cal·ly** \-k(ə-)lē\ *adv* — **mor·phol·o·gist** \mȯr-'fäl-ə-jəst\ *n*
mor·phom·e·try \mȯr-'fäm-ə-trē\ *n* (1856) **1 :** measurement of external form **2 :** a branch of limnology that deals with the morphological measurements of a lake and its basin — **mor·pho·met·ric** \,mȯr-fə-'me-trik\ *adj* — **mor·pho·met·ri·cal·ly** \-tri-k(ə-)lē\ *adv*
mor·pho·pho·ne·mics \,mȯr-fō-fə-'nē-miks\ *n pl but sing in constr* [*morpheme* + *-o-* + *phonemics*] (1939) **1 :** a study of the phonemic differences between allomorphs of the same morpheme **2 :** the distribution of allomorphs in one morpheme **3 :** the structure of a language in terms of morphophonemics
-mor·pho·sis \'mȯr-fə-səs *also* mȯr-'fō-\ *n comb form, pl* **-mor·pho·ses** \-,sēz\ [L, fr. Gk *morphōsis* process of forming, fr. *morphoun* to form, fr. *morphē* form] **:** development or change of form of a (specified) thing or in a (specified) manner ⟨geronto*morphosis*⟩
-mor·phous \'mȯr-fəs\ *adj comb form* [Gk *-morphos*, fr. *morphē*] **:** having (such) a form ⟨iso*morphous*⟩
-mor·phy \,mȯr-fē\ *n comb form* [ISV, fr. *-morphous*] **:** quality or state of having (such) a form ⟨homo*morphy*⟩
mor·ris \'mȯr-əs, 'mär-\ *n* [ME *moreys daunce*, fr. *moreys* Moorish (fr. *More* Moor) + *daunce* dance] (1512) **:** a vigorous English dance performed by men wearing costumes and bells
mor·ris chair \,mȯr-əs-, ,mär-\ *n* [William *Morris*] (1900) **:** an easy chair with adjustable back and removable cushions
mor·row \'mär-(,)ō, 'mȯr-, -ə(-w)\ *n* [ME *morn, morwen* morn] (13c) **1** *archaic* **:** MORNING **2 :** the next day **3 :** the time immediately after a specified event
Morse code \'mȯrs-\ *n* [Samuel F. B. *Morse*] (1867) **:** either of two codes consisting of variously spaced dots and dashes or long and short sounds used for transmitting messages by audible or visual signals

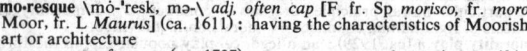

INTERNATIONAL MORSE CODE

A	·—	N	—·	Á	·——·—	8	———··
B	—···	O	———	Ä	·—·—	9	————·
C	—·—·	P	·——·	É	··—··	0	—————
D	—··	Q	——·—	Ñ	——·——	(comma)	——··——
E	·	R	·—·	Ö	———·		
F	··—·	S	···	Ü	··——	?	··——··
G	——·	T	—	1	·————		
H	····	U	··—	2	··———		
I	··	V	···—	3	···——	(apostrophe)	·————·
J	·———	W	·——	4	····—	(hyphen)	—····—
K	—·—	X	—··—	5	·····	/	—··—·
L	·—··	Y	—·——	6	—····	parenthesis	—·——·—
M	——	Z	——··	7	——···	underline	··——·—

¹mor·sel \'mȯr-səl\ *n* [ME, fr. OF, dim. of *mors* bite, fr. L *morsus*, fr. *morsus*, pp. of *mordēre* to bite — more at SMART] (13c) **1 : a** small piece of food : BITE **2 :** a small quantity : FRAGMENT **3 a :** a tasty dish **b :** something delectable and pleasing **4 :** a negligible person
²morsel *vt* **-seled** *or* **-selled; -sel·ing** *or* **-sel·ling** (1598) : to divide into or distribute in small pieces
¹mort \'mō(ə)rt\ *n* [prob. alter. of ME *mot* horn note, fr. MF *word*, horn note — more at MOT] (ca. 1500) **1 :** a note sounded on a hunting horn when a deer is killed **2 :** KILLING 1
²mort *n* [prob. back-formation fr. ¹*mortal*] (1694) : a great quantity or number
mor·ta·del·la \ˌmȯrt-ə-'del-ə\ *n* [It, irreg. fr. L *murtatum* sausage seasoned with myrtle berries, fr. *murtus* myrtle] (1613) : a large smoked sausage made of beef, pork, and pork fat and seasoned with pepper and garlic
¹mor·tal \'mȯrt-ᵊl\ *adj* [ME, fr. MF, fr. L *mortalis*, fr. *mort-, mors* death — more at MURDER] (14c) **1 :** having caused or being about to cause death : FATAL ⟨a ~ injury⟩ **2 :** subject to death ⟨~ man⟩ **3 :** POSSIBLE, CONCEIVABLE ⟨every ~ thing⟩ **c :** very tedious or prolonged ⟨waited three ~ hours⟩ **3 :** marked by unrelenting hostility : IMPLACABLE ⟨a ~ enemy⟩ **4 a :** marked by great intensity or severity : EXTREME ⟨~ fear⟩ **b :** very great : AWFUL ⟨a ~ shame⟩ **5 :** HUMAN ⟨~ limitations⟩ **6 :** of, relating to, or connected with death ⟨~ agony⟩
syn see DEADLY
²mortal *adv, chiefly dial* (15c) : MORTALLY
³mortal *n* (1567) : a human being
mor·tal·i·ty \mȯr-'tal-ət-ē\ *n* (14c) **1 :** the quality or state of being mortal **2 :** the death of large numbers (as of people or animals) **3** *archaic* : DEATH **4 :** the human race : MANKIND **5 a :** the number of deaths in a given time or place **b :** the proportion of deaths to population **c :** the number lost or the rate of loss or failure
mortality table *n* (1880) : an actuarial table based on mortality statistics over a number of years
mor·tal·ly \'mȯrt-ᵊl-ē\ *adv* (14c) **1 :** in a deadly or fatal manner : to death ⟨~ wounded⟩ **2 :** to an extreme degree : INTENSELY ⟨~ afraid⟩
mortal mind *n, Christian Science* (1875) : a belief that life, substance, and intelligence are in and of matter : ILLUSION
mortal sin *n* (15c) : a sin (as murder) that is deliberately committed and is of such serious consequence according to Thomist theology that it deprives the soul of sanctifying grace — compare VENIAL SIN
¹mor·tar \'mȯrt-ər\ *n* [ME *morter*, fr. OE *mortere* & MF *mortier*, fr. L *mortarium*; akin to Gk *marainein* to waste away — more at SMART] (bef. 12c) **1 a :** a strong vessel in which material is pounded or rubbed with a pestle — see PESTLE illustration **b :** a large cast-iron receptacle in which ore is crushed in a stamp mill **2** [MF *mortier*] **a :** a muzzle-loading cannon having a tube short in relation to its caliber that is used to throw projectiles with low muzzle velocities at high angles **b :** any of several similar firing devices
²mortar *n* [ME *morter*, fr. OF *mortier*, fr. L *mortarium*] (13c) : a plastic building material (as a mixture of cement, lime, or gypsum plaster with sand and water) that hardens and is used in masonry or plastering — **mor·tar·less** *adj*
³mortar *vt* (14c) : to plaster or make fast with mortar
mor·tar·board \'mȯrt-ər-ˌbō(ə)rd, -ˌbȯ(ə)rd\ *n* (1854) **1 a :** HAWK 2 **b :** a board or platform about three feet (one meter) square for holding mortar **2 :** an academic cap consisting of a closely fitting headpiece with a broad flat projecting square top
¹mort·gage \'mȯr-gij\ *n* [ME *morgage*, fr. MF, fr. OF, fr. *mort* dead (fr. L *mortuus*, fr. pp. of *mori* to die) + *gage* gage — more at MURDER] (15c) **1 :** a conveyance of property (as for security on a loan) on condition that the conveyance becomes void on payment or performance according to stipulated terms **2 a :** the instrument by which a mortgage conveyance is made **b :** the state of the property so conveyed **c :** the interest of the mortgagee in such property

mortarboard 2

²mortgage *vt* **mort·gaged; mort·gag·ing** (15c) **1 :** to grant or convey by a mortgage **2 :** to subject to a claim or obligation : PLEDGE
mort·gag·ee \ˌmȯr-gi-'jē\ *n* (1584) : a person to whom property is mortgaged
mort·gag·or \ˌmȯr-gi-'jȯ(ə)r\ *also* **mort·gag·er** \'mȯr-gi-jər\ *n* (1584) : a person who mortgages his property
mor·ti·cian \mȯr-'tish-ən\ *n* [L *mort-, mors* death] (1895) : UNDERTAKER 2

mor·ti·fi·ca·tion \ˌmȯrt-ə-fə-'kā-shən\ *n* (14c) **1 :** the subjection and denial of bodily passions and appetites by abstinence or self-inflicted pain or discomfort **2 :** NECROSIS, GANGRENE **3 a :** a sense of humiliation and shame caused by something that wounds one's pride or self-respect **b :** the cause of such humiliation or shame
mor·ti·fy \'mȯrt-ə-ˌfī\ *vb* **-fied; -fy·ing** [ME *mortifien*, fr. MF *mortifier*, fr. LL *mortificare*, fr. L *mort-, mors*] *vt* (14c) **1** *obs* : to destroy the strength, vitality, or functioning of **2 :** to subdue or deaden (as the body or bodily appetites) esp. by abstinence or self-inflicted pain or discomfort **3 :** to subject to severe and vexing embarrassment : SHAME ~ *vi* **1 :** to practice mortification **2 :** to become necrotic or gangrenous
¹mor·tise *also* **mor·tice** \'mȯrt-əs\ *n* [ME *mortays*, fr. MF *mortaise*] (15c) : a hole, groove, or slot into or through which some other part of an arrangement of parts fits or passes; *esp* : a usu. rectangular cavity cut into a piece of timber or other material to receive a tenon — see DOVETAIL illustration
²mortise *also* **mortice** *vt* **mor·tised** *also* **mor·ticed; mor·tis·ing** *also* **mor·tic·ing** (15c) **1 :** to join or fasten securely; *specif* : to join or fasten by a tenon and mortise **2 :** to cut or make a mortise in
mort·main \'mȯrt-ˌmān\ *n* [ME *morte-mayne*, fr. MF *mortemain*, fr. OF, fr. *morte* (fem. of *mort* dead) + *main* hand, fr. L *manus* — more at MANUAL] (15c) **1 a :** an inalienable possession of lands or buildings by an ecclesiastical or other corporation **b :** the condition of property or other gifts left to a corporation in perpetuity esp. for religious, charitable, or public purposes **2 :** the influence of the past regarded as controlling the present
¹mor·tu·ary \'mȯr-chə-ˌwer-ē\ *adj* [L *mortuarius* of the dead, fr. *mortuus* dead, fr. *mortuus*, pp.] (1514) **1 :** of or relating to the burial of the dead **2 :** of, relating to, or characteristic of death
²mortuary *n, pl* **-ar·ies** (1865) : a place in which dead bodies are kept until burial; *esp* : FUNERAL HOME
mor·u·la \'mȯr-(y)ə-lə, 'mär-\ *n, pl* **-lae** \-ˌlē, -ˌlī\ [NL, fr. L *morum* mulberry] (1874) : a globular solid mass of blastomeres formed by cleavage of a zygote that typically precedes the blastula — **mor·u·lar** \-lər\ *adj* — **mor·u·la·tion** \ˌmȯr-(y)ə-'lā-shən, ˌmär-\ *n*
¹mo·sa·ic \mō-'zā-ik\ *n* [ME *musycke*, fr. MF *mosaique*, fr. OIt *mosaico*, fr. ML *musaicum*, alter. of LL *musivum*, fr. neut. of *musivus* of a muse, artistic, fr. L *Musa* muse] (15c) **1 :** a surface decoration made by inlaying small pieces of variously colored material to form pictures or patterns; *also* : the process of making it **2 :** a picture or design made in mosaic **3 :** something resembling a mosaic ⟨a ~ of visions and daydreams and memories —Lawrence Shainberg⟩ **4 a :** an organism or one of its parts composed of cells of more than one genotype : CHIMERA 3 **b :** a virus disease of plants characterized by diffuse light and dark green or yellow and green mottling of the foliage **5 :** a composite map made of photographs taken by an aircraft or spacecraft **6 :** the part of a television camera tube consisting of many minute photoelectric particles that convert light to an electric charge — **mo·sa·ic·like** \-ˈzā-i-ˌklīk\ *adj*
²mosaic *adj* (1585) **1 :** of, relating to, produced by, or resembling a mosaic **2 :** exhibiting mosaicism **3 :** DETERMINATE 5 — **mo·sa·i·cal·ly** \-ˈzā-ə-k(ə-)lē\ *adv*
³mosaic *vt* **-icked; -ick·ing** (1839) **1 :** to decorate with mosaics **2 :** to form into a mosaic
Mo·sa·ic \mō-'zā-ik\ *adj* [NL *Mosaicus*, fr. *Moses* Moses] (1662) : of or relating to Moses or the institutions or writings attributed to him
mosaic gold *n* (1746) **1 :** a yellow scaly crystalline substance that is essentially a yellow sulfide SnS₂ of tin and is used as a pigment and in gilding and bronzing
mo·sa·icism \mō-ˈzā-ə-ˌsiz-əm\ *n* (1926) : a condition in which patches of tissue of unlike genetic constitution are mingled in an organism
mo·sa·icist \-səst\ *n* (1847) **1 a :** a designer of mosaics **b :** a worker who makes mosaics **2 :** a dealer in mosaics
Mos·an \'mōs-ᵊn\ *n* [*mōs* four (in various Mosan languages)] (1929) : an American Indian language phylum of British Columbia and Washington including the Salishan, Wakashan, and Chemakuan stocks
mo·sa·saur \'mō-zə-ˌsȯ(ə)r\ *n* [NL *Mosasaurus*, fr. L *Mosa* the river Meuse + NL *-saurus*, fr. Gk *sauros* lizard — more at SAURIAN] (1841) : any of a genus (*Mosasaurus*) of large extinct aquatic fish-eating lizards with limbs modified into paddles that are related to the recent monitors
Mo·selle \mō-'zel\ *n* [G *moselwein*, fr. *Mosel* Moselle, river in Germany + G *wein* wine] (1687) : a white wine from the Moselle valley
Mo·ses \'mō-zəz *also* -zəs\ *n* [L, fr. Gk *Mōsēs*, fr. Heb *Mōsheh*] : a Hebrew prophet who led the Israelites out of Egyptian slavery and at Mt. Sinai delivered to them the Law establishing God's covenant with them
mo·sey \'mō-zē\ *vi* **mo·seyed; mo·sey·ing** [origin unknown] (1829) **1 :** to hurry away **2 :** to move in a leisurely or aimless manner : SAUNTER ⟨~ed around the general store, testing the cheese straight off the round —Eric Sevareid⟩
mo·shav \mō-'shäv\ *n, pl* **mo·sha·vim** \ˌmō-shə-'vēm\ [NHeb *mōshābh*, fr. Heb, dwelling] (1931) : a cooperative settlement of small individual farms in Israel — compare KIBBUTZ
Mos·lem \'maz-ləm *also* 'mäs-\ *var of* MUSLIM
mosque \'mäsk\ *n* [MF *mosquee*, fr. OIt *moschea*, fr. OSp *mezquita*, fr. Ar *masjid* temple, fr. *sajada* to prostrate oneself, worship] (15c) : a building used for public worship by Muslims
mos·qui·to \mə-'skēt-(ˌ)ō, -ə(-w)ō\ *n, pl* **-toes** *also* **-tos** [Sp, dim. of *mosca* fly, fr. L *musca* — more at MIDGE] (1583) : any of numerous two-winged flies (family Culicidae) with females that have a set of slender organs in the proboscis adapted to puncture the skin of animals and to suck their blood and that are in some cases vectors of serious diseases — **mos·qui·to·ey** \-ˈskēt-ə-wē\ *adj*
mosquito boat *n* (1906) : PT BOAT

mosquito fish *n* (1928) : either of two No. American live-bearers (*Gambusia affinis* and *Heterandria formosa* of the family Poeciliidae) used esp. to exterminate mosquito larvae
mosquito hawk *n* (1737) : DRAGONFLY
mosquito net *n* (1745) : a net or screen for keeping out mosquitoes
[1]**moss** \'mȯs\ *n* [ME, fr. OE *mos;* akin to OHG *mos* moss, L *muscus*] (bef. 12c) **1** *chiefly Scot* : BOG, SWAMP; *esp* : a peat bog **2 a** : any of a class (Musci) of bryophytic plants having a small leafy often tufted stem bearing sex organs at its tip; *also* : a clump or sward of these plants **b** : any of various plants resembling moss in appearance or habit of growth **3** : a mossy covering — **moss·like** \-,līk\ *adj*
[2]**moss** *vt* (15c) : to cover or overgrow with moss
moss agate *n* (1798) : an agate mineral containing brown, black, or green mosslike or dendritic markings
moss animal *n* (1881) : BRYOZOAN
moss·back \'mȯs-,bak\ *n* (1872) **1** : a large sluggish fish **2** : an extremely old-fashioned or reactionary person : FOGY — **moss·backed** \-,bakt\ *adj*
moss green *n* (1884) : a variable color averaging a moderate yellow-green
moss–grown \'mȯs-,grōn\ *adj* (14c) **1** : overgrown with moss **2** : ANTIQUATED
moss pink *n* (ca. 1856) : a low tufted perennial phlox (*Phlox subulata*) widely cultivated for its abundant usu. pink or white flowers
moss rose *n* (1776) : an old-fashioned garden rose that has a glandular mossy calyx and flower stalk
moss–troop·er \'mȯs-,trü-pər\ *n* (1645) **1** : one of a class of 17th century raiders in the marshy border country between England and Scotland **2** : PIRATE — **moss–troop·ing** \-piŋ\ *adj*
mossy \'mȯ-sē\ *adj* **moss·i·er; -est** (15c) **1** : resembling moss **2** : covered with moss or something like moss **3** : ANTIQUATED ⟨the ~ precepts of the . . . prescriptive grammarians —Thomas Pyles⟩
mossy zinc *n* (1910) : a granulated form of zinc made by pouring melted zinc into water
[1]**most** \'mōst\ *adj* [ME, fr. OE *mǣst;* akin to OHG *meist* most, OE *māra* more — more at MORE] (bef. 12c) **1** : greatest in quantity, extent, or degree ⟨the ~ ability⟩ **2** : the majority of ⟨~ people⟩
[2]**most** *adv* (bef. 12c) **1** : to the greatest or highest degree — often used with an adjective or adverb to form the superlative ⟨the ~ challenging job he ever had⟩ **2** : to a very great degree ⟨was ~ persuasive⟩
[3]**most** *n* (12c) : the greatest amount ⟨it's the ~ I can do⟩ — **at most** *or* **at the most** : as an extreme limit ⟨took him an hour *at most* to finish the job⟩
[4]**most** *pron, sing or pl in constr* (13c) : the greatest number or part ⟨~ become discouraged and quit⟩
[5]**most** *adv* [by shortening] (1584) : ALMOST ⟨we'll be crossing the river ~ any time now —Hamilton Basso⟩
usage Although considered by some to be unacceptable in all cases, *most* is often used to mean "almost" in both spoken and, to a lesser extent, written English to modify the adjectives *all, every,* and *any;* the pronouns *all, everyone, everything, everybody, anyone, anything,* and *anybody;* and the adverbs *everywhere, anywhere,* and *always.* Other uses of this sense of *most* are dialectal.
-most \,mōst, *Brit also* məst\ *adj suffix* [ME, alter. of *-mest* (as in *formest* foremost)] : most ⟨inner*most*⟩ : most toward ⟨head*most*⟩
most·ly \'mōst-lē\ *adv* (1594) : for the greatest part : MAINLY
Most Reverend (15c) — used as a title for an archbishop or a Roman Catholic bishop
mot \'mō\ *n, pl* **mots** \'mō(z)\ [F, word, saying, fr. L *muttum* grunt — more at MOTTO] (1586) : a pithy or witty saying
[1]**mote** \(')mōt\ *verbal auxiliary* [ME *moten,* fr. OE *mōtan* to be allowed to — more at MUST] *archaic* (bef. 12c) : MAY, MIGHT
[2]**mote** \'mōt\ *n* [ME *mot,* fr. OE; akin to MD & Fris *mot* sand] (bef. 12c) : a small particle : SPECK
mo·tel \mō-'tel\ *n* [blend of *motor* and *hotel*] (1925) : an establishment which provides lodging and parking and in which the rooms are usu. accessible from an outdoor parking area
mo·tet \mō-'tet\ *n* [ME, fr. MF, dim. of *mot*] (14c) : a polyphonic choral composition on a sacred text usu. without instrumental accompaniment
moth \'mȯth\ *n, pl* **moths** \'mȯt͟hz, 'mȯths\ [ME *mothe,* fr. OE *moththe;* akin to MHG *motte* moth] (bef. 12c) **1** : CLOTHES MOTH **2** : a usu. nocturnal insect (order Lepidoptera) with antennae that are often feathery, with a stouter body, duller coloring, and proportionately smaller wings than the butterflies, and with larvae that are plant-eating caterpillars — **moth·like** \-,līk\ *adj* — **mothy** \-ē\ *adj*
[1]**moth·ball** \'mȯth-,bȯl\ *n* (1906) **1** : a ball made formerly of camphor but now often of naphthalene and used to keep moths from clothing **2** *pl* : a condition of protective storage ⟨put the ships in ~*s* after the war⟩; *also* : a state of having been rejected for further use or dismissed from further consideration ⟨put that idea in ~*s*⟩
[2]**mothball** *vt* (1943) **1** : to deactivate (as a ship) and prevent deterioration chiefly by dehumidification **2** : to withdraw from use or service and keep in reserve
moth bean \'mȯth-\ *n* [prob. by folk etymology fr. Marathi *maṭh* moth bean] (1884) : a bean (*Phaseolus aconitifolius*) that is cultivated esp. in India for forage and soil conditioning, for its cylindrical pods, and for its small yellowish brown seeds; *also* : its seed
moth–eat·en \'mȯ-,thēt-ᵊn\ *adj* (14c) **1** : eaten into by moth larvae ⟨~ clothes⟩ **2 a** : DILAPIDATED **b** : ANTIQUATED, OUTMODED
[1]**moth·er** \'mət͟h-ər\ *n* [ME *moder,* fr. OE *mōdor;* akin to OHG *muoter* mother, L *mater,* Gk *mētēr,* Skt *mātṛ*] (bef. 12c) **1 a** : a female parent **b** (1) : a woman in authority; *specif* : the superior of a religious community of women (2) : an old or elderly woman **2** : SOURCE, ORIGIN ⟨necessity is the ~ of invention⟩ **3** : maternal tenderness or affection **4** [short for *motherfucker*] : one that is particularly impressive or contemptible — sometimes considered vulgar — **moth·er·hood** \-,hu̇d\ *n* — **moth·er·less** \-ləs\ *adj* — **moth·er·less·ness** *n*
[2]**mother** *adj* (13c) **1 a** : of, relating to, or being a mother **b** : bearing the relation of a mother **2** : derived from or as if from one's mother **3** : acting as or providing parental stock — used without reference to sex
[3]**mother** *vt* **moth·ered; moth·er·ing** \'mət͟h-(ə-)riŋ\ (1548) **1 a** : to give birth to **b** : to give rise to : PRODUCE **2** : to care for or protect like a mother
Mother Car·ey's chicken \-,kar-ēz-, -,ker-\ *n* [origin unknown] (1767) : any of several small petrels; *esp* : STORM PETREL
mother cell *n* (1845) : a cell that gives rise to other cells usu. of a different sort
mother country *n* (1587) **1** : the country of one's parents or ancestors **2** : the country from which the people of a colony derive their origin **3** : a country that is the origin of something
moth·er·fuck·er \'mət͟h-ər-,fək-ər\ *n* (1959) : one that is formidable, contemptible, or offensive — usu. considered obscene; usu. used as a generalized term of abuse — **moth·er·fuck·ing** \-iŋ\ *adj*
Mother Goose *n* : the legendary author of a collection of nursery rhymes first published in London about 1760
mother hen *n* (1954) : a person who assumes an overly protective maternal attitude
moth·er·house \-,hau̇s\ *n* (1661) **1** : the convent in which the superior of a religious community resides **2** : the original convent of a religious community
Mother Hub·bard \,mət͟h-ər-'həb-ərd\ *n* [prob. fr. *Mother Hubbard,* character in a nursery rhyme] (1884) : a loose usu. shapeless dress
moth·er–in–law \'mət͟h-(ə-)rən-,lȯ, 'mət͟h-ərn-,lȯ\ *n, pl* **moth·ers–in–law** \'mət͟h-ər-zən-\ (14c) **1** : the mother of one's spouse **2** *archaic* : STEPMOTHER
moth·er·land \'mət͟h-ər-,land\ *n* (1711) **1** : a country regarded as a place of origin (as of an idea or a movement) **2** : FATHERLAND
mother lode *n* (1874) **1** : the principal vein or lode of a region **2** : a principal source or supply
moth·er·ly \-lē\ *adj* (13c) **1** : of, proper to, or characteristic of a mother ⟨~ advice⟩ **2** : resembling a mother : MATERNAL — **moth·er·li·ness** *n*
moth·er–na·ked \,mət͟h-ər-'nā-kəd, *esp Southern* -'nek-əd\ *adj* (14c) : stark naked
Mother Nature *n* (1601) : nature personified as a woman considered as the source and guiding force of creation
moth·er–of–pearl \,mət͟h-ə-rə(v)-'pər(-ə)l\ *n* (1510) : the hard pearly iridescent substance forming the inner layer of a mollusk shell
mother of vinegar (1601) : a slimy membrane composed of yeast and bacterial cells that develops on the surface of alcoholic liquids undergoing acetous fermentation and is added to wine or cider to produce vinegar — called also *mother*
Mother's Day *n* (1908) : the 2d Sunday in May appointed for the honoring of mothers
mother tongue *n* (14c) **1** : one's native language **2** : a language from which another language derives
mother wit *n* (15c) : natural wit or intelligence
[1]**moth·proof** \'mȯth-'prüf\ *adj* (1893) : impervious to penetration by moths ⟨~ wool⟩
[2]**mothproof** *vt* (1925) : to make mothproof — **moth·proof·er** *n*
mo·tif \mō-'tēf\ *n* [F, motive, motif, fr. MF] (1848) **1** : a usu. recurring salient thematic element in a work of art; *esp* : a dominant idea or central theme **2** : a single or repeated design or color — **mo·tif·ic** \-'tē-fik, -'tif-ik\ *adj*
[1]**mo·tile** \'mōt-ᵊl, 'mō-,tīl\ *adj* [L *motus,* pp.] (1864) : exhibiting or capable of movement — **mo·til·i·ty** \mō-'til-ət-ē\ *n*
[2]**motile** *n* (1886) : a person whose prevailing mental imagery takes the form of inner feelings of action
[1]**mo·tion** \'mō-shən\ *n* [ME *mocioun,* fr. MF *motion,* fr. L *motion-, motio* movement, fr. *motus,* pp. of *movēre* to move] (14c) **1 a** : an act, process, or instance of changing place : MOVEMENT **b** : an active or functioning state or condition ⟨set the divorce proceedings in ~⟩ **2** : an impulse or inclination of the mind or will **3 a** : a proposal for action; *esp* : a formal proposal made in a deliberative assembly **b** : an application made to a court or judge to obtain an order, ruling, or direction **4** *obs* **a** : a puppet show **b** : PUPPET **5** : MECHANISM **6 a** : an act or instance of moving the body or its parts : GESTURE **b** *pl* : ACTIVITIES, MOVEMENTS **7** : melodic change of pitch — **mo·tion·al** \'mō-shnəl, -shən-ᵊl\ *adj* — **mo·tion·less** \'mō-shən-ləs\ *adj* — **mo·tion·less·ly** *adv* — **mo·tion·less·ness** *n* — **in motion** *of an offensive football player* : running parallel to the line of scrimmage before the snap
[2]**motion** *vb* **mo·tioned; mo·tion·ing** \'mō-sh(ə-)niŋ\ *vt* (1787) : to direct by a motion ⟨~*ed* me to the seat⟩ ~ *vi* : to signal by a movement or gesture ⟨the pitcher ~*ed* to the catcher⟩
motion picture *n* (1896) **1** : a series of pictures projected on a screen in rapid succession with objects shown in successive positions slightly changed so as to produce the optical effect of a continuous picture in which the objects move **2** : a representation (as of a story) by means of motion pictures : MOVIE
motion sickness *n* (1941) : sickness induced by motion (as in travel by air, car, or ship) and characterized by nausea
mo·ti·vate \'mōt-ə-,vāt\ *vt* **-vat·ed; -vat·ing** (1885) : to provide with a motive : IMPEL ⟨questions that excite and ~ youth⟩ — **mo·ti·va·tive** \-,vāt-iv\ *adj* — **mo·ti·va·tor** \-,vāt-ər\ *n*
mo·ti·va·tion \,mōt-ə-'vā-shən\ *n* (1873) **1 a** : the act or process of motivating **b** : the condition of being motivated **2** : a motivating force, stimulus, or influence : INCENTIVE, DRIVE — **mo·ti·va·tion·al** \-shnəl, -shən-ᵊl\ *adj* — **mo·ti·va·tion·al·ly** \-ē\ *adv*
[1]**mo·tive** \'mōt-iv, *2 is also* mō-'tēv\ *n* [ME, fr. MF *motif,* fr. *motif,* adj., moving, fr. ML *motivus,* fr. L *motus,* pp. of *movēre* to move] (15c) **1** : something (as a need or desire) that causes a person to act **2** : a recurrent phrase or figure that is developed through the course of a musical composition **3** : MOTIF — **mo·tive·less** \-ləs\ *adj* — **mo·tive·less·ly** *adv* — **mo·ti·vic** \mō-'tē-vik\ *adj*
syn MOTIVE, IMPULSE, INCENTIVE, INDUCEMENT, SPUR, GOAD mean a stimulus to action. MOTIVE implies an emotion or desire operating on the will and causing it to act; IMPULSE suggests a driving power arising from personal temperament or constitution; INCENTIVE applies to an external influence (as an expected reward) inciting to action; INDUCEMENT suggests a motive prompted by the deliberate enticements or allurements of another; SPUR applies to a motive that stimulates the faculties or increases energy or ardor; GOAD suggests a motive that keeps one going against one's will or desire.

2mo·tive \'mōt-iv\ *adj* [MF or ML; MF *motif,* fr. ML *motivus*] (1502) **1** : moving or tending to move to action **2** : of or relating to motion or the causing of motion ⟨~ energy⟩
3mo·tive \'mōt-iv\ *vt* **mo·tived; mo·tiv·ing** (1650) : MOTIVATE
motive power *n* (1889) **1** : an agency (as water or steam) used to impart motion to machinery **2** : something (as a locomotive or a motor) that provides motive power to a system
mo·tiv·i·ty \mō-'tiv-ət-ē\ *n* (ca. 1687) : the power of moving or producing motion
mot juste \mō-zhüest\ *n, pl* **mots justes** *same*\ [F] (1912) : the exactly right word or phrasing
1mot·ley \'mät-lē\ *adj* [ME, perh. fr. *mot* mote, speck] (14c) **1** : variegated in color ⟨a ~ coat⟩ **2** : composed of diverse often incongruous elements ⟨a ~ crowd⟩
2motley *n* [ME, prob. fr. *1motley*] (14c) **1** : a woolen fabric of mixed colors made in England between the 14th and 17th centuries **2** : a garment made of motley; *esp* : the characteristic dress of the professional fool **3** : JESTER, FOOL **4** : a mixture esp. of incongruous elements
mot·mot \'mät-,mät\ *n* [AmerSp *mot-mot,* of imit. origin] (1837) : any of numerous long-tailed mostly green nonpasserine birds (family Momotidae) of tropical forests from Mexico to Brazil
mo·to·cross \'mōt-ō-,kròs\ *n* [*motor* + *cross*-country] (1951) : a motorcycle race on a tight closed course over natural terrain that includes steep hills, sharp turns, and often mud
mo·to·neu·ron \,mōt-ə-'n(y)ü-,rän, -'n(y)ü(ə)r-,än\ *n* [*motor* + *neuron*] (1908) : a motor nerve cell with its processes — **mo·to·neu·ro·nal** \-'n(y)ür-ən-ᵊl, -n(y)ü-'rōn-ᵊl\ *adj*
1mo·tor \'mōt-ər\ *n* [L, fr. *motus,* pp. of *movēre* to move] (1586) **1** : one that imparts motion; *specif* : PRIME MOVER **2** : any of various power units that develop energy or impart motion: as **a** : a small compact engine **b** : INTERNAL-COMBUSTION ENGINE; *esp* : a gasoline engine **c** : a rotating machine that transforms electrical energy into mechanical energy **3** : MOTOR VEHICLE; *esp* : AUTOMOBILE — **mo·tor·dom** \-dəm\ *n* — **mo·tor·less** \-ləs\ *adj*
2motor *adj* (1840) **1 a** : causing or imparting motion **b** : of, relating to, or being a nerve or nerve fiber that passes from the central nervous system or a ganglion toward or to a muscle and conducts an impulse that causes movement ⟨~ neurons⟩ **c** : of, relating to, concerned with, or involving muscular movement ⟨~ areas of the brain⟩ **2 a** : equipped with or driven by a motor **b** : of, relating to, or involving an automobile **c** : designed for motor vehicles or motorists
3motor *vi* (1896) : to travel by automobile : DRIVE ~ *vt* : to transport by automobile
mo·tor·bike \'mōt-ər-,bīk\ *n* (1894) : a small usu. lightweight motorcycle — **motorbike** *vi*
mo·tor·boat \-,bōt\ *n* (1902) : a boat propelled by an internal-combustion engine or an electric motor — **mo·tor·boat·er** \-ər\ *n* — **mo·tor·boat·ing** \-iŋ\ *n*
motor bus *n* (1901) : BUS 1a — called also *motor coach*
mo·tor·cade \'mōt-ər-,kād\ *n* (1913) : a procession of motor vehicles — **motorcade** *vi*
mo·tor·car \-,kär\ *n* (ca. 1890) **1** : AUTOMOBILE **2** *usu* **motor car** : a railroad car containing motors for propulsion
motor court *n* (1936) : MOTEL
mo·tor·cy·cle \'mōt-ər-,sī-kəl\ *n* [*motor bicycle*] (1896) : a 2-wheeled automotive vehicle having one or two saddles and sometimes a sidecar with a third supporting wheel — **motorcycle** *vi* — **mo·tor·cy·clist** \-k(ə-)ləst\ *n*
mo·tor·drome \'mōt-ər-,drōm\ *n* (1908) : a track or course with seats for spectators that is used for races or tests of automobiles or motorcycles
motor home *n* (1965) : an automotive vehicle built on a truck or bus chassis and equipped as a self-contained traveling home — compare MOBILE HOME
mo·tor·ic \mō-'tòr-ik, -'tär-\ *adj* (1930) : MOTOR 1c — **mo·tor·i·cal·ly** \-i-k(ə-)lē\ *adv*
motor inn *n* (1951) : a usu. multistory urban motel — called also *motor hotel*
mo·tor·ist \'mōt-ə-rəst\ *n* (1896) : a person who travels by automobile
mo·tor·ize \'mōt-ə-,rīz\ *vt* **-ized; -iz·ing** (ca. 1913) : to equip with a motor: as **a** : to provide with motor-driven equipment (as for transportation) **b** : to equip with automobiles — **mo·tor·iza·tion** \,mōt-ə-rə-'zā-shən\ *n*
motor lodge *n* (1949) : MOTEL
mo·tor·man \'mōt-ər-mən\ *n* (1890) : an operator of a motor-driven vehicle (as a streetcar or subway train)
motor pool *n* (1942) : a group of motor vehicles centrally controlled (as by a governmental agency) and dispatched for use as needed
motor scooter *n* (1919) : a low 2- or 3-wheeled automotive vehicle resembling a child's scooter and having a seat so that the rider does not straddle the engine
motor ship *n* (1915) : a seagoing ship propelled by an internal-combustion engine
motor torpedo boat *n* (1940) : PT BOAT
mo·tor·truck \'mōt-ər-,trək\ *n* (1930) : an automotive truck for transporting freight
motor unit *n* (1950) : a motoneuron together with the muscle fibers on which it acts
motor vehicle *n* (1902) : an automotive vehicle not operated on rails; *esp* : one with rubber tires for use on highways
mo·tor·way \'mōt-ər-,wā\ *n, Brit* (1903) : a motor highway; *esp* : SUPERHIGHWAY
motte \'mät\ *n* [ME, fr. OF *mote, motte,* fr. Prov *mota*] (13c) : MOUND, HILL; *esp* : a hill serving as a site for a Norman castle in Britain
1mot·tle \'mät-ᵊl\ *n* [prob. back-formation fr. *motley*] (1676) **1** : a colored spot **2 a** : a surface having colored spots or blotches **b** : the arrangement of such spots or blotches on a surface **3** : MOSAIC 4b — **mot·tled** \-ᵊld\ *adj*
2mottle *vt* **mot·tled; mot·tling** \'mät-liŋ, -ᵊl-iŋ\ (1676) : to mark with spots or blotches of different color or shades of color as if stained — **mot·tler** \'mät-lər, -ᵊl-ər\ *n*
mottled enamel *n* (1928) : spotted tooth enamel caused by drinking water containing excessive fluorides during the time the teeth are calcifying
mot·to \'mät-(,)ō\ *n, pl* **mottoes** *also* **mottos** [It, fr. L *muttum* grunt, fr. *muttire* to mutter] (1588) **1** : a sentence, phrase, or word inscribed on something as appropriate to or indicative of its character or use **2** : a short expression of a guiding principle
moue \'mü\ *n* [F, fr. MF — more at MOW] (1850) : a little grimace : POUT
mou·flon *also* **mouf·flon** \mü-'flō^{n}\ *n* [F *mouflon,* fr. It dial. *muvrone,* fr. LL *mufron-, mufro*] (1774) : a wild sheep (*Ovis musimon*) of the mountains of Sardinia and Corsica with large curling horns in the male; *broadly* : a wild sheep with large horns

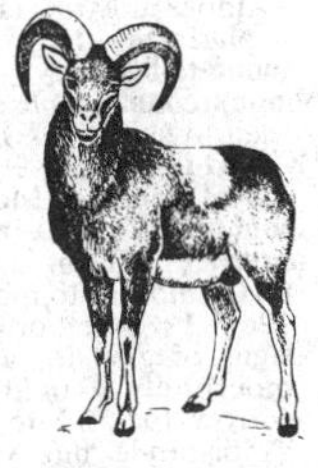
mouflon

mou·jik \mü-'zhēk, -'zhik\ *var of* MUZHIK
mou·lage \mü-'läzh\ *n* [F, molding, fr. MF, fr. *mouler* to mold, fr. OF *modle* mold — more at MOLD] (1902) **1** : an impression or cast made for use esp. as evidence in a criminal investigation **2** : the taking of an impression for use as evidence in a criminal investigation
mould \'mōld\ *var of* MOLD
mould·ing \'mōl-diŋ\ *var of* MOLDING
mou·lin \mü-'la^{n}\ *n* [F, lit., mill, fr. LL *molinum* — more at MILL] (1860) : a nearly cylindrical vertical shaft in a glacier scoured out by water from melting snow and ice and by rock debris
moult \'mōlt\ *var of* MOLT
1mound \'maùnd\ *vt* [origin unknown] (1515) **1** *archaic* : to enclose or fortify with a fence or a ridge of earth **2** : to form into a mound
2mound *n, often attrib* [origin unknown] (1551) **1** *archaic* : HEDGE, FENCE **2 a** (1) : an artificial bank or hill of earth or stones (2) : the slightly elevated ground on which a baseball pitcher stands **b** : KNOLL, HILL **3** : HEAP, PILE
Mound Builder *n* (1838) : a member of a prehistoric American Indian people whose extensive earthworks are found from the Great Lakes down the Mississippi valley to the Gulf of Mexico
1mount \'maùnt\ *n* [ME, fr. OE *munt* & OF *mont,* both fr. L *mont-, mons;* akin to ON *mœna* to project, L *minari* to project, threaten] (bef. 12c) **1** : a high hill : MOUNTAIN — used esp. before an identifying name ⟨*Mount* Everest⟩ **2** *archaic* : a protective earthwork **3** : MOUND 2a(1) **4** *cap* : a small area of raised flesh on the palm of the hand esp. at the base of a finger that is held by palmists to indicate temperament or traits of character
2mount *vb* [ME *mounten,* fr. MF *monter,* fr. (assumed) VL *montare,* fr. L *mont-, mons*] *vi* (14c) **1** : to increase in amount or extent ⟨expenses began to ~⟩ **2** : RISE, ASCEND **3** : to get up on something above the level of the ground; *esp* : to seat oneself (as on a horse) for riding ~ *vt* **1 a** : to go up : CLIMB **b** (1) : to seat or place oneself on (2) : COVER 6a **2 a** : to lift up : RAISE **b** (1) : to put or have (as artillery) in position (2) : to have as equipment **c** (1) : to organize and equip (an attacking force) ⟨~ an army⟩ (2) : to launch and carry out (as an assault or a campaign) **3** : to set on something that elevates **4 a** : to cause to get on a means of conveyance **b** : to furnish with animals for riding **5** : to post or set up for defense or observation ⟨~*ed* some guards⟩ **6 a** : to attach to a support **b** : to arrange or assemble for use or display **7 a** : to prepare (as a specimen) for examination or display **b** : to prepare and supply with the materials necessary for performance or execution : PRODUCE ⟨~ an opera⟩ — **mount·able** \-ə-bəl\ *adj* — **mount·er** *n*
3mount *n* (15c) **1** : an act or instance of mounting; *specif* : an opportunity to ride a horse in a race **2** : FRAME, SUPPORT: as **a** : the material (as cardboard) on which a picture is mounted **b** : a jewelry setting **c** (1) : an undercarriage or part on which a device (as a motor or an artillery piece) rests in service (2) : an attachment for an accessory **d** : a hinge, card, or acetate envelope for mounting a stamp **e** : a glass slide with its accessories on which objects are placed for examination with a microscope **3** : a means of conveyance; *esp* : SADDLE HORSE
moun·tain \'maùnt-ᵊn\ *n, often attrib* [ME, fr. OF *montaigne,* fr. (assumed) VL *montanea,* fr. fem. of *montaneus* of a mountain, alter. of L *montanus,* fr. *mont-, mons*] (13c) **1 a** : a landmass that projects conspicuously above its surroundings and is higher than a hill **b** : an elongated ridge **2 a** : a great mass **b** : a vast number or quantity ⟨had ~s of work to do⟩
mountain ash *n* (1597) : any of various trees (genus *Sorbus*) of the rose family with pinnate leaves and red or orange-red fruits
mountain cranberry *n* (1848) : a low evergreen shrub (*Vaccinium vitis-idaea*) of north temperate uplands with red edible berries — called also *lingonberry*
mountain dew *n* (1878) : MOONSHINE 3
moun·tain·eer \,maùnt-ᵊn-'i(ə)r\ *n* (1610) **1** : a native or inhabitant of a mountainous region **2** : one who climbs mountains for sport
moun·tain·eer·ing *n* (1803) : the sport or technique of scaling mountains
mountain goat *n* (1833) : an antelope (*Oreamnos americanus*) of mountainous northwestern No. America that has a thick white coat and slightly curved black horns and resembles a goat
mountain laurel *n* (1759) : a No. American evergreen shrub (*Kalmia latifolia*) of the heath family with glossy leaves and umbels of rose-colored or white flowers
mountain lion *n* (1859) : COUGAR
mountain mahogany *n* (1810) : any of several western No. American shrubs or small shrubby trees (genus *Cercocarpus*) of the rose family that are often important as browse or forage plants
moun·tain·ous \'maùnt-ᵊn-əs, 'maùnt-nəs\ *adj* (14c) **1** : containing many mountains **2** : resembling a mountain : HUGE — **moun·tain·ous·ly** *adv* — **moun·tain·ous·ness** *n*
mountain sickness *n* (1848) : altitude sickness experienced esp. above 10,000 feet and caused by insufficient oxygen in the air
moun·tain·side \'maùnt-ᵊn-,sīd\ *n* (14c) : the side of a mountain

mountain time *n, often cap M* (1883) **:** the time of the 7th time zone west of Greenwich that includes the Rocky mountain states of the U.S. — see TIME ZONE illustration

moun·tain·top \'maůnt-ᵊn-,täp\ *n* (1593) **:** the summit of a mountain

moun·tainy \'maůnt-ᵊn-ē, 'maůnt-nē\ *adj* (1613) **1 :** MOUNTAINOUS **2 :** of, relating to, or living in mountains

[1]**moun·te·bank** \'maůnt-i-,baŋk\ *n* [It *montimbanco,* fr. *montare* to mount (fr.—assumed—VL) + *in* in, on (fr. L) + *banco, banca* bench — more at BANK] (1586) **1 :** a person who sells quack medicines from a platform **2 :** a boastful unscrupulous pretender **:** CHARLATAN — **moun·te·bank·ery** \-,baŋ-k(ə-)rē\ *n*

[2]**mountebank** *vt, obs* (1607) **:** to beguile or transform by trickery ⟨I'll ~ their loves —Shak.⟩ ~ *vi* **:** to play the mountebank

Mount·ie \'maůnt-ē\ *n* [*mounted* policeman] (1914) **:** a member of the Royal Canadian Mounted Police

mount·ing \'maůnt-iŋ\ *n* (1563) **:** [3]MOUNT 2

mourn \'mō(ə)rn, 'mȯ(ə)rn\ *vb* [ME *mournen,* fr. OE *murnan;* akin to OHG *mornēn* to mourn, Gk *mermēra* care — more at MEMORY] *vi* (bef. 12c) **1 :** to feel or express grief or sorrow **2 :** to show the customary signs of grief for a death; *esp* **:** to wear mourning **3 :** to murmur mournfully — used esp. of doves ~ *vt* **1 :** to feel or express grief or sorrow for **2 :** to utter mournfully — **mourn·er** *n* — **mourn·ing·ly** \'mōr-niŋ-lē, 'mȯr-\ *adv*

mourn·ful \'mō(ə)rn-fəl, 'mȯ(ə)rn-\ *adj* (15c) **1 :** expressing sorrow **:** SORROWFUL **2 :** full of sorrow **:** SAD **3 :** causing sorrow **:** SADDENING — **mourn·ful·ly** \-fə-lē\ *adv* — **mourn·ful·ness** *n*

mourn·ing \'mōr-niŋ, 'mȯr-\ *n* (13c) **1 :** the act of sorrowing **2 a :** an outward sign (as black clothes or an armband) of grief for a person's death ⟨is wearing ~⟩ **b :** a period of time during which signs of grief are shown

mourning cloak *n* (1898) **:** a blackish brown butterfly (*Nymphalis antiopa*) with a broad yellow border on the wings found in temperate parts of Europe, Asia, and No. America

mourning dove *n* (1833) **:** a wild dove (*Zenaidura macroura carolinensis*) of the U.S. with a plaintive call

[1]**mouse** \'maůs\ *n, pl* **mice** \'mīs\ [ME, fr. OE *mūs;* akin to OHG *mūs* mouse, L *mus,* Gk *mys* mouse, muscle] (bef. 12c) **1 :** any of numerous small rodents (as of the genus *Mus*) with pointed snout, rather small ears, elongated body, and slender tail **2 a** *slang* **:** WOMAN **b :** a timid person **3 :** a dark-colored swelling caused by a blow; *specif* **:** BLACK EYE **4 :** a small mobile manual device that controls movement of the cursor on a computer display

[2]**mouse** \'maůz\ *vb* **moused; mous·ing** *vi* (13c) **1 :** to hunt for mice **2 :** to search or move stealthily or slowly ~ *vt* **1** *obs* **a :** BITE, GNAW **b :** to toy with roughly **2 :** to search for carefully — usu. used with *out*

mouse–ear \'maů-,si(ə)r\ *n* (13c) **1 :** a European hawkweed (*Hieracium pilosella*) that has soft hairy leaves and has been introduced into No. America **2 :** any of several plants other than mouse-ear that have soft hairy leaves

mouse–ear chickweed *n* (1731) **:** any of several hairy chickweeds (esp. *Cerastium vulgatum* and *C. viscosum*)

mous·er \'maů-zər\ *n* (15c) **:** a catcher of mice and rats; *esp* **:** a cat proficient at mousing

[1]**mouse·trap** \'maů-,strap\ *n* (14c) **1 :** a trap for mice **2 :** a stratagem that lures one to defeat or destruction **3 :** TRAP 2b

[2]**mousetrap** *vt* (ca. 1890) **:** to snare in or as if in a mousetrap

Mous·que·taire \,mü-skə-'ta(ə)r, -'te(ə)r\ *n* [F — more at MUSKETEER] (1705) **:** a French musketeer; *esp* **:** one of the royal musketeers of the 17th and 18th centuries conspicuous for their daring and their dandified dress

mous·sa·ka \,mü-sə-'kä\ *n* [NGk *mousakas*] (1931) **:** a Middle Eastern dish of ground meat (as lamb or beef) and sliced eggplant often topped with a seasoned sauce

mousse \'müs\ *n* [F, lit., froth, fr. LL *mulsa* hydromel; akin to L *mel* honey — more at MELLIFLUOUS] (1892) **1 :** a light spongy food usu. containing cream or gelatin **2 :** a molded chilled dessert made with sweetened and flavored whipped cream or egg whites and gelatin ⟨chocolate ~⟩ **3 :** a foamy preparation used in styling hair

mous·se·line \,müs-(ə-)'lēn\ *n* [F, lit., muslin — more at MUSLIN] (1696) **1 :** a fine sheer fabric (as of rayon) that resembles muslin **2 a :** a sauce (as hollandaise) to which whipped cream or beaten egg whites have been added **b :** MOUSSE 1 ⟨salmon ~⟩

mousseline de soie \-də-'swä\ *n, pl* **mousselines de soie** *same*\ [F, lit., silk muslin] (1850) **:** a silk muslin having a crisp finish

mous·tache \'məs-,tash, (,)məs-'\ *var of* MUSTACHE

mous·ta·chio \(,)məs-\ *var of* MUSTACHIO

Mous·te·ri·an \mü-'stir-ē-ən\ *adj* [F *moustérien,* fr. Le *Moustier,* cave in Dordogne, France] (1890) **:** of or relating to a middle Paleolithic culture that is characterized by well-made flake tools often considered the work of Neanderthal man

mousy *or* **mous·ey** \'maů-sē, -zē\ *adj* **mous·i·er; -est** (1853) **:** of, relating to, or resembling a mouse: as **a :** QUIET, STEALTHY **b :** TIMID, RETIRING **c :** grayish brown — **mous·i·ly** \-sə-lē, -zə-\ *adv* — **mous·i·ness** \-sē-nəs, -zē-\ *n*

[1]**mouth** \'maůth\ *n, pl* **mouths** \'maůt͟hz *also* 'maůz, 'maůths; *in synecdochic compounds like "blabbermouths"* ths *more frequently*\ *often attrib* [ME, fr. OE *mūth;* akin to OHG *mund* mouth, L *mandere* to chew, Gk *masasthai* to chew, *mastax* mouth, jaws] (bef. 12c) **1 a** (1) **:** the opening through which food passes into the body of an animal (2) **:** the cavity bounded externally by the lips and internally by the pharynx that encloses in the typical vertebrate the tongue, gums, and teeth **b :** GRIMACE ⟨made a ~⟩ **c :** an individual requiring food ⟨had too many ~s to feed⟩ **2 a :** VOICE, SPEECH ⟨finally gave ~ to her feelings⟩ **b :** MOUTHPIECE 3a **c** (1) **:** a tendency to excessive talk (2) **:** saucy or disrespectful language **:** IMPUDENCE **3 :** something that resembles a mouth esp. in affording entrance or exit: as **a :** the place where a stream enters a larger body of water **b :** the surface opening of an underground cavity **c :** the opening of a container **d :** an opening in the side of an organ flue pipe — **mouth·like** \'maůth-,līk\ *adj* — **down in the mouth :** DEJECTED, SULKY

[2]**mouth** \'maůt͟h *also* 'maůth\ *vt* (14c) **1 a :** SPEAK, PRONOUNCE **b :** to utter bombastically **:** DECLAIM **c :** to repeat without comprehension or sincerity ⟨always ~*ing* platitudes⟩ **d :** to form soundlessly with the lips ⟨the librarian ~*ed* the word "quiet"⟩ **e :** to utter indistinctly **:** MUMBLE ⟨~*ed* his words⟩ **2 :** to take into the mouth; *esp* **:** EAT ~ *vi* **1 a :** to talk pompously **:** RANT — often used with *off* **b :** to talk insolently or impudently — usu. used with *off* **2 :** to move the mouth esp. so as to make faces — **mouth·er** *n*

mouth·breed·er \'maůth-,brēd-ər\ *n* (1927) **:** any of several fishes that carry their eggs and young in the mouth; *esp* **:** a No. African cichlid fish (*Haplochromis multicolor*) often kept in aquariums

mouthed \'maůt͟hd, 'maůtht\ *adj* (14c) **:** having a mouth esp. of a specified kind — often used in combination ⟨a soft-*mouthed* fish⟩

mouth·ful \'maůth-,fůl\ *n* (15c) **1 a :** as much as a mouth will hold **b :** the quantity usu. taken into the mouth at one time **2 :** a small quantity **3 a :** a very long word or phrase **b :** a comment or a statement rich in meaning or substance

mouth hook *n* (1937) **:** one of a pair of hooked larval mouthparts of some two-winged flies that function as jaws

mouth organ *n* (1866) **:** HARMONICA 2

mouth·part \'maůth-,pärt\ *n* (1799) **:** a structure or appendage near the mouth (as of an insect) esp. when adapted for use in gathering or eating food

mouth·piece \-,pēs\ *n* (1607) **1 :** something placed at or forming a mouth **2 :** a part (as of an instrument) that goes in the mouth or to which the mouth is applied **3 a :** one that expresses or interprets another's views **:** SPOKESMAN **b** *slang* **:** a criminal lawyer

mouth–to–mouth *adj* (1909) **:** of, relating to, or being a method of artificial respiration in which the rescuer's mouth is placed tightly over the victim's mouth in order to force air into his lungs by blowing forcefully enough every few seconds to inflate them

mouth·wash \'maůth-,wȯsh, -,wäsh\ *n* (1840) **:** a usu. antiseptic liquid preparation for cleaning the mouth and teeth or freshening the breath

mouthy \'maů-t͟hē, -thē\ *adj* **mouth·i·er; -est** (1589) **1 :** excessively talkative **:** GARRULOUS **2 :** marked by or given to bombast

mou·ton \'mü-,tän, mü-'\ *n* [F, sheep, sheepskin, fr. MF, ram — more at MUTTON] (1944) **:** processed sheepskin that has been sheared and dyed to resemble beaver or seal

[1]**mov·able** *or* **move·able** \'mü-və-bəl\ *adj* (14c) **1 :** capable of being moved **2 :** changing date from year to year ⟨~ holidays⟩ — **mov·abil·i·ty** \,mü-və-'bil-ət-ē\ *n* — **mov·able·ness** \'mü-və-bəl-nəs\ *n* — **mov·ably** \-blē\ *adv*

[2]**movable** *or* **moveable** *n* (14c) **:** something (as an article of furniture) that can be removed or displaced

[1]**move** \'müv\ *vb* **moved; mov·ing** [ME *moven,* fr. MF *movoir,* fr. L *movēre*] *vi* (13c) **1 a** (1) **:** to go or pass from one place to another with a continuous motion ⟨*moved* into the shade⟩ (2) **:** to proceed in a certain direction or toward a certain state or condition ⟨*moving* up the executive ladder⟩ ⟨*moved* into second place in the tournament⟩; *also* **:** to become transferred during play ⟨checkers ~ along diagonally adjacent squares⟩ (3) **:** to keep pace ⟨*moving* with the times⟩ **b :** to start away from some point or place **:** DEPART **c :** to change one's residence or location **2 :** to carry on one's life or activities in a specified environment ⟨~*s* in the best circles⟩ **3 :** to change position or posture **:** STIR ⟨told him to be quiet and not to ~⟩ **4 :** to take action **:** ACT **5 a :** to begin operating or functioning or working in a usual way **b :** to show marked activity ⟨after a brief lull things really began to ~⟩ **c :** to move a piece (as in chess or checkers) during one's turn **6 :** to make a formal request, application, or appeal **7 :** to change hands by being sold or rented ⟨goods that were *moving* slowly⟩ **8** *of the bowels* **:** EVACUATE ~ *vt* **1 a** (1) **:** to change the place or position of (2) **:** to dislodge or displace from a fixed position **:** BUDGE **b :** to transfer (as a piece in chess) from one position to another **2 a** (1) **:** to cause to go or pass from one place to another with a continuous motion ⟨*moved* the flag slowly up and down⟩ (2) **:** to cause to advance **b :** to cause to operate or function **:** ACTUATE ⟨this button ~*s* the whole machine⟩ **c :** to put into activity or rouse up from inactivity **3 :** to cause to change position or posture **4 :** to prompt or rouse to the doing of something **:** PERSUADE ⟨the report *moved* the faculty to take action⟩ **5 a :** to stir the emotions, feelings, or passions of ⟨was deeply *moved* by such kindness⟩ **b :** to affect in such a way as to lead to an indicated show of emotion ⟨the story *moved* her to tears⟩ **6 a** *obs* **:** BEG **b :** to make a formal application to **7 :** to propose formally in a deliberative assembly ⟨*moved* adjournment⟩ **8 :** to cause (the bowels) to void **9 :** to cause to change hands through sale or rent

syn MOVE, ACTUATE, DRIVE, IMPEL mean to set or keep in motion. MOVE is very general and implies no more than the fact of changing position; ACTUATE stresses transmission of power so as to work or set in motion; DRIVE implies imparting forward and continuous motion and often stresses the effect rather than the impetus; IMPEL suggests a greater impetus producing more headlong action.

[2]**move** *n* (1656) **1 a :** the act of moving a piece (as in chess) **b :** the turn of a player to move **2 a :** a step taken so as to gain an objective **:** MANEUVER ⟨a ~ to end the dispute⟩ **b :** the action of moving from a motionless position **c :** a change of residence or location — **on the move 1 :** in a state of moving about from place to place ⟨a salesman is constantly *on the move*⟩ **2 :** in a state of moving ahead or making progress ⟨said that civilization is always *on the move*⟩

move in *vi* (1898) **:** to occupy a dwelling or place of work — **move in on :** to make advances or aggressive movements toward

move·less \'müv-ləs\ *adj* (1578) **:** being without movement **:** FIXED, IMMOBILE — **move·less·ly** *adv* — **move·less·ness** *n*

move·ment \'müv-mənt\ *n* (14c) **1 a** (1) **:** the act or process of moving; *esp* **:** change of place or position or posture (2) **:** a particular instance or manner of moving **b** (1) **:** a tactical or strategic shifting of a military unit **:** MANEUVER (2) **:** the advance of a military unit **c :** ACTION, ACTIVITY — usu. used in pl. **2 a :** TENDENCY, TREND ⟨detected a ~ toward fairer pricing⟩ **b :** a series of organized activities working toward an objective; *also* **:** an organized effort to promote or attain an end ⟨the civil rights ~⟩ **3 :** the moving parts of a mechanism that transmit a definite motion **4 a :** MOTION 7 **b :** the rhythmic character or quality of a musical composition **c :** a distinct structural unit or division having its own key, rhythmic structure, and themes and forming part of an extended musical composition **d :** particular rhythmic flow of language **:** CADENCE **5 a :** the quality (as in a painting or sculpture) of representing or suggesting motion **b :** the quality in literature of having a quickly moving plot or an abundance of incident **6** **a** : an act of voiding the bowels **b** : matter expelled from the bowels at one passage

mov·er \'mü-vər\ *n* (14c) : one that moves or sets something in motion; *esp* : one whose business or occupation is the moving of household goods from one residence to another

mov·ie \'mü-vē\ *n* [*moving picture*] (1912) **1** : MOTION PICTURE **2** *pl* : a showing of a motion picture **3** *pl* : the motion-picture medium or industry

mov·ie·dom \'mü-vēd-əm\ *n* (1916) : FILMDOM

mov·ie·go·er \'mü-vē-ˌgō(-ə)r\ *n* (1923) : one who frequently attends the movies — **mov·ie·going** \-ˌgō-iŋ, -ˌgō(-)iŋ\ *n*

mov·ie·mak·er \-ˌmā-kər\ *n* (1915) : one who makes movies — **mov·ie·mak·ing** \-ˌmā-kiŋ\ *n*

mov·ing *adj* (14c) **1** **a** : marked by or capable of movement **b** : of or relating to a change of residence ⟨~ expenses⟩ **c** : used for transferring furnishings from one residence to another ⟨a ~ van⟩ **d** : involving a motor vehicle that is in motion ⟨a ~ violation⟩ **2** **a** : producing or transferring motion or action **b** : stirring deeply in a way that evokes a strong emotional response ⟨a ~ story of a faithful dog⟩ — **mov·ing·ly** \'mü-viŋ-lē\ *adv*

syn MOVING, IMPRESSIVE, POIGNANT, AFFECTING, TOUCHING, PATHETIC mean having the power to produce deep emotion. MOVING may apply to any strong emotional effect including thrilling, agitating, saddening, or calling forth pity or sympathy; IMPRESSIVE implies compelling attention, admiration, wonder, or conviction; POIGNANT applies to what keenly or sharply affects one's sensitivities; AFFECTING is close to MOVING but most often suggests pathos; TOUCHING implies arousing tenderness or compassion; PATHETIC implies moving to pity or sometimes contempt.

moving picture *n* (1896) : MOTION PICTURE

mov·i·ola \ˌmü-vē-'ō-lə\ *n* [fr. *Moviola*, a trademark] (ca. 1922) : a device for editing motion-picture film and synchronizing the sound

1mow \'mau̇\ *n* [ME, heap, stack, fr. OE *mūga;* akin to ON *mūgi* heap, Gk *mykōn*] (bef. 12c) **1** : a piled-up stack (as of hay or fodder); *also* : a pile of hay or grain in a barn **2** : the part of a barn where hay or straw is stored

2mow \'mō\ *vb* **mowed; mowed** *or* **mown** \'mōn\; **mow·ing** [ME *mowen*, fr. OE *māwan;* akin to OHG *māen* to mow, L *metere* to reap, mow, Gk *aman*] *vt* (bef. 12c) **1** **a** : to cut down with a scythe or sickle or machine **b** : to cut the standing herbage (as grass) of **2** **a** (1) : to kill or destroy in great numbers or mercilessly ⟨machine guns ~*ed* down the attackers⟩ (2) : to cause to fall : KNOCK DOWN **b** : to overcome swiftly and decisively : ROUT ⟨~*ed* down the opposing team⟩ ~ *vi* : to cut down standing herbage (as grass) — **mow·er** \'mō(-ə)r\ *n*

3mow \'mau̇, 'mō\ *n* [ME *mowe*, fr. MF *moue*, of Gmc origin; akin to MD *mouwe* protruding lip] (14c) : GRIMACE

4mow \'mau̇, 'mō\ *vi* (15c) : to make grimaces

mox·ie \'mäk-sē\ *n* [fr. *Moxie*, a trademark for a soft drink] (1930) **1** : ENERGY, PEP **2** : COURAGE, DETERMINATION **3** : KNOW-HOW, EXPERTISE

moyen–âge \mwä-ye-näzh\ *adj* [F *moyen âge* Middle Ages] (1849) : of or relating to medieval times

moz·za·rel·la \ˌmät-sə-'rel-ə\ *n* [It] (1911) : a moist white unsalted unripened cheese of mild flavor and a smooth rubbery texture

moz·zet·ta \mōt-'set-ə\ *n* [It, short for *almozzetta*, irreg. fr. ML *almutia* amice, var. of *amictus* — more at AMICE] (1774) : a short cape with a small ornamental hood worn over the rochet by Roman Catholic prelates

M phase *n* [mitosis] (1945) : the period in the cell cycle during which cell division takes place — called also *D phase;* compare G_1 PHASE, G_2 PHASE, S PHASE

Mr. \ˌmis-tər, *in rapid speech esp in sense 2* (ˌ)mis(t)\ *n, pl* **Messrs.** \ˌmes-ərz\ [*Mr.* fr. ME, abbr. of *maister* master; *Messrs.* abbr. of *Messieurs*, fr. F, pl. of *Monsieur*] (15c) **1** — used as a conventional title of courtesy except when usage requires the substitution of a title of rank or an honorific or professional title before a man's surname ⟨spoke to *Mr.* Doe⟩ **2** — used in direct address as a conventional title of respect before a man's title of office ⟨may I ask one more question, *Mr.* President⟩ **3** — used before the name of a place (as a country or city) or of a profession or activity (as a sport) or before some epithet (as *clever*) to form a title applied to a male viewed or recognized as representative of the thing indicated ⟨*Mr.* Baseball⟩

Mr. Char·lie \-'chär-lē\ *n* [*Charlie*, fr. *Charles*, proper name] (ca. 1941) : a white man : white people — usu. used disparagingly

mri·dan·ga \mri-'däŋ-gə, ˌmər-i-\ *or* **mri·dan·gam** \-gəm\ *n* [Skt *mṛdaṅga*] (1888) : a drum of India that is shaped like an elongated barrel and has tuned heads of different diameters

Mrs. \ˌmis-əz, -əs, *esp Southern* ˌmiz-əz, -əs, *or* (*for sense 1*) (ˌ)miz, *or before given names* (ˌ)mis\ *n, pl* **Mes·dames** \mā-'däm, -'dam\ [*Mrs.* abbr. of *mistress; Mesdames* fr. F, pl. of *Madame*] (1612) **1** **a** — used as a conventional title of courtesy except when usage requires the substitution of a title of rank or an honorific or professional title before a married woman's surname ⟨spoke to *Mrs.* Doe⟩ **b** — used before the name of a place (as a country or city) or of a profession or activity (as a sport) or before some epithet (as *clever*) to form a title applied to a married female viewed or recognized as representative of the thing indicated ⟨*Mrs.* Homemaker⟩ **2** : WIFE ⟨took the *Mrs.* to dinner⟩

Mrs. Grun·dy \-'grən-dē\ *n* [fr. a character alluded to in Thomas Morton's *Speed the Plough* (1798)] (1813) : one marked by prudish conventionality in personal conduct

Ms. \(ˌ)miz\ *n* [prob. blend of *Miss* and *Mrs.*] (ca. 1923) — used instead of *Miss* or *Mrs.* (as when the marital status of a woman is unknown or irrelevant) ⟨*Ms.* Mary Smith⟩

M16 \ˌem-(ˌ)sik-'stēn\ *n* [*model 16*] (1967) : a .223 caliber (5.56 mm.) gas-operated magazine-fed rifle for semiautomatic or automatic operation used by U.S. troops since the mid 1960s — called also *M16 rifle*

mu \'myü, 'mü\ *n* [Gk *my*] (1823) **1** : the 12th letter of the Greek alphabet — see ALPHABET table **2** [μ (*mu*), symbol for *micron*] : 2MICROMETER

muc- *or* **muci-** *or* **muco-** *comb form* [L *muc-*, fr. *mucus*] **1** : mucus ⟨*muco*protein⟩ **2** : mucous and ⟨*muco*purulent⟩

1much \'məch\ *adj* **more** \'mō(ə)r, 'mȯ(ə)r\; **most** \'mōst\ [ME *muche* large, much, fr. *michel, muchel*, fr. OE *micel, mycel;* akin to OHG *mihhil* great, large, L *magnus*, Gk *megas*, Skt *mahat*] (bef. 12c) **1** : great in quantity, amount, extent, or degree ⟨there is ~ truth in what you say⟩ ⟨taken too ~ time⟩ **2** *obs* : many in number — **too much** **1** : WONDERFUL, EXCITING **2** : TERRIBLE, AWFUL

2much *adv* **more; most** (bef. 12c) **1** **a** (1) : to a great degree or extent : CONSIDERABLY ⟨~ happier⟩ (2) : VERY **b** (1) : FREQUENTLY, OFTEN (2) : by or for a long time ⟨didn't get to work ~ before noon⟩ **c** : by far ⟨was ~ the brightest student⟩ **2** : NEARLY, APPROXIMATELY ⟨looks ~ the way his father did⟩ — **as much** : the same in quantity — **much less** : and certainly not ⟨data that has never been organized, *much less* analyzed⟩

3much *n* (13c) **1** : a great quantity, amount, extent, or degree ⟨gave away ~⟩ **2** : something considerable or impressive ⟨was not ~ to look at⟩

mu·cha·cho \mü-'chäch-(ˌ)ō\ *n* [Sp, fr. obs. Sp *mochacho*, fr. *mocho* cropped, shorn] (1591) **1** *chiefly Southwest* : a male servant **2** *chiefly Southwest* : a young man

much as *conj* (14c) : however much : even though

much·ness \'məch-nəs\ *n* (14c) : the quality or state of being great : GREATNESS — **much of a muchness** : very much the same

mu·cic acid \ˌmyü-sik-\ *n* [ISV *muc-*] (ca. 1828) : an optically inactive crystalline acid $C_6H_{10}O_8$ obtained from galactose or lactose by oxidation with nitric acid

mu·ci·lage \'myü-s(ə-)lij\ *n* [ME *muscilage*, fr. LL *mucilago* mucus, musty juice, fr. L *mucus*] (15c) **1** : a gelatinous substance esp. from seaweeds that contains protein and polysaccharides and is similar to plant gums **2** : an aqueous usu. viscid solution (as of a gum) used esp. as an adhesive

mu·ci·lag·i·nous \ˌmyü-sə-'laj-ə-nəs\ *adj* [LL *mucilaginosus*, fr. *mucilagin-*, *mucilago*] (15c) **1** : STICKY, VISCID **2** : of, relating to, full of, or secreting mucilage — **mu·ci·lag·i·nous·ly** *adv*

mu·cin \'myüs-ᵊn\ *n* [ISV *muc-*] (1905) : any of various mucoproteins that occur esp. in secretions of mucous membranes — **mu·cin·ous** \-ᵊn-əs, 'myü-snəs\ *adj*

1muck \'mək\ *n* [ME *muk*, perh. fr. OE *-moc;* akin to ON *myki* dung — more at MUCUS] (13c) **1** : soft moist farmyard manure **2** : slimy dirt or filth **3** : defamatory remarks or writings **4** **a** (1) : dark highly organic soil (2) : MIRE, MUD **b** : something resembling muck : GUNK **5** : material removed in the process of excavating or mining — **mucky** \'mək-ē\ *adj*

2muck *vt* (14c) **1** **a** : to clean up; *esp* : to clear of manure or filth — usu. used with *out* **b** : to clear of muck **2** : to dress (as soil) with muck **3** : to dirty with or as if with muck : SOIL ~ *vi* **1** : to move or load muck (as in a mine) **2** : to engage in aimless activity — usu. used with *about* or *around* — **muck·er** *n*

muck·a·muck \'mək-ə-ˌmək\ *n* (1856) : HIGH-MUCK-A-MUCK

muck·luck *var of* MUKLUK

muck·rake \'mək-ˌrāk\ *vi* [obs. *muckrake*, n. (rake for dung)] (1910) : to search out and expose publicly real or apparent misconduct of prominent individuals — **muck·rak·er** *n*

muck up *vt* (1896) : to make a mess of : BUNGLE, SPOIL

mu·co·cu·ta·ne·ous \ˌmyü-kō-kyü-'tā-nē-əs\ *adj* (1898) : made up of or involving both typical skin and mucous membrane

1mu·coid \'myü-ˌkȯid\ *adj* [ISV *muc-*] (1849) : resembling mucus

2mucoid *n* [ISV] (1900) : MUCOPROTEIN

mu·co·lyt·ic \ˌmyü-kə-'lit-ik\ *adj* (ca. 1923) : hydrolyzing mucopolysaccharides : tending to break down or lower the viscosity of mucin-containing body secretions or components ⟨~ enzymes⟩

mu·co·pep·tide \ˌmyü-kō-'pep-ˌtīd\ *n* (1959) : PEPTIDOGLYCAN

mu·co·poly·sac·cha·ride \'myü-kō-ˌpäl-i-'sak-ə-ˌrīd\ *n* [ISV] (1938) : any of various polysaccharides derived from a hexosamine that are constituents of mucoproteins, glycoproteins, and blood-group substances

mu·co·pro·tein \ˌmyü-kə-'prō-ˌtēn, -'prōt-ē-ən\ *n* (1925) : any of various complex conjugated proteins (as mucins) that contain polysaccharides and occur in body fluids and tissues

mu·co·sa \myü-'kō-zə\ *n, pl* **-sae** \-(ˌ)zē, -ˌzī\ *or* **-sas** [NL, fr. L, fem. of *mucosus* mucous] (1880) : MUCOUS MEMBRANE — **mu·co·sal** \-zəl\ *adj*

mu·cous \'myü-kəs\ *adj* [L *mucosus*, fr. *mucus*] (1646) **1** : covered with or as if with mucus : SLIMY **2** : of, relating to, or resembling mucus **3** : secreting or containing mucus

mucous membrane *n* (1812) : a membrane rich in mucous glands; *specif* : one that lines body passages and cavities which communicate directly or indirectly with the exterior

mu·cro \'myü-ˌkrō\ *n, pl* **mu·cro·nes** \myü-'krō-(ˌ)nēz\ [NL *mucron-*, *mucro*, fr. L, point, edge; akin to Gk *amyssein* to scratch, sting] (1646) : an abrupt sharp terminal point or tip or process (as of a leaf) — **mu·cro·nate** \'myü-krə-ˌnāt\ *adj*

mu·cus \'myü-kəs\ *n* [L, nasal mucus; akin to ON *myki* dung, Gk *myxa* mucus] (1661) : a viscid slippery secretion that is usu. rich in mucins and is produced by mucous membranes which it moistens and protects

1mud \'məd\ *n* [ME *mudde*, prob. fr. MLG; akin to OE *mōs* bog — more at MOSS] (14c) **1** : a slimy sticky mixture of solid material with a liquid and esp. water; *esp* : soft wet earth **2** : abusive and malicious remarks or charges

2mud *vt* **mud·ded; mud·ding** (1593) **1** : to make muddy or turbid **2** : to treat or plaster with mud

mud dauber *n* (1856) : any of various wasps (esp. family Sphecidae) that construct mud cells in which the female places an egg with spiders or insects paralyzed by a sting to serve as food for the larva

1mud·dle \'məd-ᵊl\ *vb* **mud·dled; mud·dling** \'məd-liŋ, -ᵊl-iŋ\ [prob. fr. obs. D *moddelen*, fr. MD, fr. *modde* mud; akin to MLG *mudde*] *vt* (1676) **1** : to make turbid or muddy **2** : to befog or stupefy esp. with liquor **3** : to mix confusedly **4** : to make a mess of : BUNGLE ~ *vi* : to think or act in a confused aimless way — **mud·dler** \'məd-lər, -ᵊl-ər\ *n*

2muddle *n* (1818) **1** : a state of esp. mental confusion **2** : a confused mess — **mud·dly** \'məd-lē, -ᵊl-ē\ *adj*

mud·dle·head·ed \ˌməd-ᵊl-'hed-əd\ *adj* (1759) **1** : mentally confused **2** : INEPT, BUNGLING — **mud·dle·head·ed·ly** *adv* — **mud·dle·head·ed·ness** *n*

\ə\ abut \ᵊ\ kitten, F table \ər\ further \a\ ash \ā\ ace \ä\ cot, cart \au̇\ out \ch\ chin \e\ bet \ē\ easy \g\ go \i\ hit \ī\ ice \j\ job \ŋ\ sing \ō\ go \ȯ\ law \ȯi\ boy \th\ thin \t͟h\ the \ü\ loot \u̇\ foot \y\ yet \zh\ vision \à, k̲, ⁿ, œ, œ̄, ue, ue̅, ʸ\ *see* Guide to Pronunciation

mud·dle through *vi* (1864) **:** to achieve a degree of success without much planning or effort

[1]**mud·dy** \'mə-dē\ *adj* **mud·di·er; -est** (15c) **1 :** morally impure **:** BASE **2 a :** full of or covered with mud **b :** characteristic or suggestive of mud ⟨a ~ flavor⟩ ⟨~ colors⟩ **c :** turbid with sediment **3 a :** lacking in clarity or brightness **:** CLOUDY, DULL ⟨retained only a distorted ~ image of the event⟩ ⟨eyes ~ with sleep⟩ **b :** obscure in meaning **:** MUDDLED, CONFUSED ⟨~ thinking⟩ ⟨a ~ style⟩ — **mud·di·ly** \'mə-dᵊl-ē\ *adv* — **mud·di·ness** \'mə-dē-nəs\ *n*

[2]**muddy** *vt* **mud·died; mud·dy·ing** (1601) **1 :** to soil or stain with or as if with mud **2 :** to make turbid **3 :** to make cloudy or dull **4 :** CONFUSE

Mu·de·jar \mü-'the-ˌhär, -ˌkär\ *n, pl* **-ja·res** \-'the-hä-ˌräs, -kä-\ [Sp *mudéjar,* fr. Ar *mudajjan,* lit., allowed to remain] (1865) **:** a Muslim living under a Christian king esp. during the 8th to 11th centuries — **Mudejar** *adj*

mud·flow \'məd-ˌflō\ *n* (ca. 1900) **:** a moving mass of soil made fluid by rain or melting snow

mud·guard \-ˌgärd\ *n* (1886) **1 a :** FENDER d **b :** SPLASH GUARD **2 :** a strip of material applied to a shoe upper just above the sole for protection against dampness or as an ornament

mud puppy *n* (1882) **:** any of several large American salamanders; *esp* **:** one (*Necturus maculosus*) that has external gills and is gray to rusty brown usu. with bluish black spots

mu·dra \mə-'drä\ *n* [Skt *mudrā*] (1811) **:** symbolic hand gestures used in religious ceremonies and dances of India

mud·room \'məd-ˌrüm, -ˌru̇m\ *n* (ca. 1950) **:** a room in a house designed for the shedding of dirty or wet footwear and clothing and located typically off the kitchen or in the basement

mud·sill \'məd-ˌsil\ *n* (1685) **1 :** a supporting sill (as of a building or bridge) resting directly on a base and esp. the earth **2 :** a person of the lowest social level

mud·sling·er \-ˌsliŋ-ər\ *n* (ca. 1890) **:** one that uses offensive epithets and invective esp. against a political opponent — **mud·sling·ing** \-ˌsliŋ-iŋ\ *n*

mud·stone \'məd-ˌstōn\ *n* (ca. 1736) **:** an indurated shale produced by the consolidation of mud

mud turtle *n* (1785) **:** a bottom-dwelling freshwater turtle: as **a :** any of a genus (*Kinosternon*) of musk turtles with two transverse hinges on the plastron **b :** SOFT-SHELLED TURTLE

Muen·ster \'mən(t)-stər, 'm(y)ün(t)-, 'mu̇n(t)-\ *n* [*Münster, Munster,* France] (1902) **:** a semisoft cheese that may be bland or sharp in flavor

mues·li \'myüs-lē, 'myüz-\ *n* [G *müsli, muesli,* fr. *mus* soft food, mush, fr. OHG *muos;* akin to OE *mōs* food] (1939) **:** a breakfast cereal of Swiss origin consisting of rolled oats, nuts, and fruit

mu·ez·zin \m(y)ü-'ez-ᵊn, 'mwez-ᵊn\ *n* [Ar *mu'adhdhin*] (1585) **:** a Muslim crier who calls the hour of daily prayers

[1]**muff** \'məf\ *n* [D *mof,* fr. MF *moufle* mitten, fr. ML *muffula*] (1599) **1 :** a warm tubular covering for the hands **2 :** a cluster of feathers on the side of the face of some domestic fowls

[2]**muff** *vb* [origin unknown] *vt* (1827) **1 :** to handle awkwardly **:** BUNGLE **2 :** to fail to hold (a ball) when attempting a catch **~** *vi* **1 :** to act or do something stupidly or clumsily **2 :** to muff a ball — compare FUMBLE

[3]**muff** *n* (1871) **1 :** a bungling performance **2 :** a failure to hold a ball in attempting a catch

muf·fin \'mə-fən\ *n* [prob. fr. LG *muffen,* pl. of *muffe* cake] (1703) **:** a quick bread made of batter containing egg and baked in a muffin pan

muffin pan *n* (1896) **:** a baking pan formed of a group of connected cups and used esp. for baking muffins or cupcakes

muf·fle \'mə-fəl\ *vt* **muf·fled; muf·fling** \'mə-f(ə-)liŋ\ [ME *muflen*] (15c) **1 :** to wrap up so as to conceal or protect **:** ENVELOP **2** *obs* **:** BLINDFOLD **3 a :** to wrap or pad with something to dull the sound ⟨~ the oarlocks⟩ **b :** to deaden the sound of **4 :** KEEP DOWN, SUPPRESS

muf·fler \'məf-lər\ *n* (1535) **1 a :** a scarf worn around the neck **b :** something that hides or disguises **2 :** a device to deaden noise; *esp* **:** one forming part of the exhaust system of an automotive vehicle — **muf·flered** *adj*

[1]**muf·ti** \'məf-tē, 'mu̇f-\ *n* [Ar *mufti*] (1586) **:** a professional jurist who interprets Muslim law

[2]**muf·ti** \'məf-tē\ *n* [prob. fr. [1]*mufti*] (1816) **:** civilian clothes

[1]**mug** \'məg\ *n* [origin unknown] (1664) **1 :** a cylindrical drinking cup **2 a :** the face or mouth of a person **b :** GRIMACE **c :** a photograph of a suspect's face **3 a** *Brit* **:** a person easily deceived **b :** PUNK, THUG — **mug·ful** *n*

[2]**mug** *vb* **mugged; mug·ging** *vi* (1855) **:** to make faces esp. to attract attention **~** *vt* **:** PHOTOGRAPH

[3]**mug** *vt* **mugged; mug·ging** [prob. fr. earlier *mug* to strike in the face, perh. fr. [1]*mug*] (ca. 1864) **:** to assault usu. with intent to rob — **mug·gee** \ˌmə-'gē\ *n*

[1]**mug·ger** \'mə-gər\ *n* [Hindi *magar,* fr. Skt *makara* water monster] (1844) **:** a common usu. harmless freshwater crocodile (*Crocodylus palustris*) of southeastern Asia

[2]**mugger** *n* [[3]*mug*] (1863) **:** one who attacks with intent to rob

[3]**mugger** *n* [[2]*mug*] (1892) **:** one that grimaces esp. before an audience

mug·gy \'mə-gē\ *adj* **mug·gi·er; -est** [E dial. *mug* (drizzle)] (1746) **:** being warm, damp, and close — **mug·gi·ly** \'mə-gə-lē\ *adv* — **mug·gi·ness** \'mə-gē-nəs\ *n*

Mu·ghal *var of* MOGUL

mu·gho pine \ˌm(y)ü-(ˌ)gō-\ *n* [prob. fr. F *mugho* mugho pine, fr. It *mugo*] (ca. 1756) **:** a shrubby spreading pine (*Pinus mugo mughus*) widely cultivated as an ornamental

mug up \(ˈ)məg-'əp\ *vt, chiefly Brit* (1889) **:** to work up by study

mug·wump \'məg-ˌwəmp\ *n* [obs. slang *mugwump* (kingpin), fr. Natick *mugwomp* captain] (1884) **1 :** a bolter from the Republican party in 1884 **2 :** an independent in politics

Mu·ham·mad·an \mō-'ham-əd-ən, -'häm- *also* mü-\ *adj* (1681) **:** of or relating to Muhammad or Islam — **Muhammadan** *n* — **Mu·ham·mad·an·ism** \-ˌiz-əm\ *n*

Muhammadan calendar *n* (ca. 1889) **:** ISLAMIC CALENDAR

Muhammadan era *n* (ca. 1889) **:** ISLAMIC ERA

Mu·har·ram \mü-'har-əm\ *n* [Ar *Muḥarram*] (ca. 1615) **1 :** the 1st month of the Islamic year — see MONTH table **2 :** a Muslim festival held during Muharram

mu·jik \mü-'zhēk, -'zhik\ *var of* MUZHIK

muk·luk \'mək-ˌlək\ *n* [Esk *muklok* large seal] (1868) **1 :** a sealskin or reindeer-skin boot worn by Eskimos **2 :** a boot often of duck with a soft leather sole and worn over several pairs of socks

muk·tuk \'mək-ˌtək\ *n* [Esk] (ca. 1835) **:** whale skin used for food

mu·lat·to \m(y)u̇-'lat-(ˌ)ō, -'lät-, -ə(-w)\ *n, pl* **-toes** *or* **-tos** [Sp *mulato,* fr. *mulo* mule, fr. L *mulus*] (1593) **1 :** the first-generation offspring of a Negro and a white **2 :** a person of mixed Caucasian and Negro ancestry

mul·ber·ry \'məl-ˌber-ē, -b(ə-)rē\ *n* [ME *murberie, mulberie,* fr. MF *moure* mulberry (fr. L *morum,* fr. Gk *moron*) + ME *berie* berry] (14c) **1 :** any of a genus (*Morus* of the family Moraceae, the mulberry family) of trees with an edible usu. purple multiple fruit that is an aggregate of juicy one-seeded drupes; *also* **:** the fruit **2 :** a dark purple or purplish black

mulch \'məlch\ *n* [perh. irreg. fr. E dial. *melch* (soft, mild)] (1657) **:** a protective covering (as of sawdust, compost, or paper) spread or left on the ground esp. to reduce evaporation, maintain even soil temperature, prevent erosion, control weeds, or enrich the soil — **mulch** *vt*

[1]**mulct** \'məlkt\ *vt* (15c) **1 :** to punish by a fine **2 a :** to defraud esp. of money **:** SWINDLE **b :** to obtain by fraud, duress, or theft

[2]**mulct** *n* [L *multa, mulcta*] (1591) **:** FINE, PENALTY

[1]**mule** \'myü(ə)l\ *n* [ME, fr. OF *mul,* fr. L *mulus*] (13c) **1 a :** a hybrid between a horse and a donkey; *esp* **:** the offspring of a male donkey and a mare **b :** a self-sterile plant whether hybrid or not **c :** a usu. sterile hybrid **2 :** a very stubborn person **3 :** a machine for simultaneously drawing and twisting fiber into yarn or thread and winding it into cops **4 :** a coin or token struck from dies belonging to two different issues

[2]**mule** *vt* **muled; mul·ing** (1914) **1 :** to combine (dies that do not match) to make a mule **2 :** to strike (a coin or token) with nonmatching dies making a mule

[3]**mule** *n* [MF, a kind of slipper, fr. L *mulleus* shoe worn by magistrates] (1562) **:** a shoe or slipper without quarter or heel strap — compare SCUFF

mule deer *n* (1805) **:** a long-eared deer (*Odocoileus hemionus* syn. *Cariacus macrotis*) of western N. America that is larger and more heavily built than the common whitetail

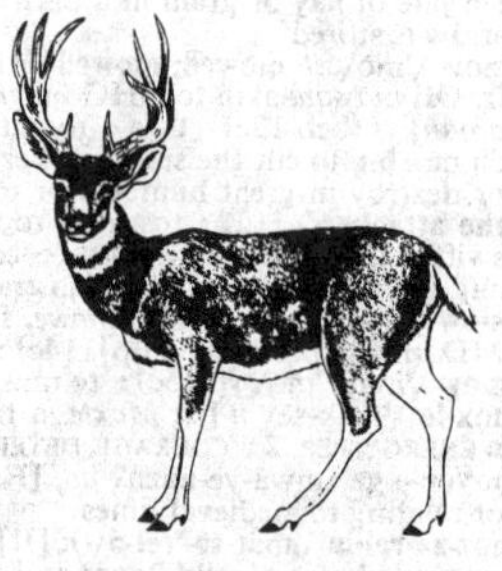

mule deer

mule skinner *n* (1870) **:** MULETEER

mu·le·ta \m(y)ü-'lāt-ə\ *n* [Sp, crutch, muleta, dim. of *mula* she-mule, fr. L, fem. of *mulus* mule] (1838) **:** a small cloth attached to a short tapered stick and used by a matador in place of the large cape during the final stage of a bullfight

mu·le·teer \ˌmyü-lə-'ti(ə)r\ *n* [F *muletier,* fr. *mulet,* fr. OF, dim. of *mul* mule] (1538) **:** one who drives mules

mu·ley \'myü-lē, 'mu̇l-ē, 'mü-lē\ *adj* [of Celtic origin; akin to IrGael & ScGael *maol* bald, hornless, W *moel*] (1885) **:** POLLED, HORNLESS; *esp* **:** naturally hornless

mu·li·eb·ri·ty \ˌmyü-lē-'eb-rət-ē\ *n* [LL *muliebritat-, muliebritas,* fr. L *muliebris* of a woman, fr. *mulier* woman; akin to L *molere* to grind — more at MEAL] (1592) **:** FEMININITY

mul·ish \'myü-lish\ *adj* [[1]*mule*] (1751) **:** unreasonably and inflexibly obstinate ***syn*** see OBSTINATE — **mul·ish·ly** *adv* — **mul·ish·ness** *n*

[1]**mull** \'məl\ *vb* [ME *mullen,* fr. *mul, mol* dust, prob. fr. MD; akin to OE *melu* meal — more at MEAL] *vt* (15c) **1 :** to grind or mix thoroughly **:** PULVERIZE **2 :** to consider at length **:** PONDER — usu. used with *over* **~** *vi* **:** MEDITATE, PONDER

[2]**mull** *vt* [origin unknown] (1618) **:** to heat, sweeten, and flavor (as wine or cider) with spices

[3]**mull** *n* [by shortening & alter. fr. *mulmul* (muslin)] (1798) **:** a soft fine sheer fabric of cotton, silk, or rayon

[4]**mull** *n* [G, fr. Dan *muld,* fr. ON *mold* dust, soil; akin to OHG *molta* dust, soil — more at MOLD] (1928) **1 :** friable forest humus that forms a layer of mixed organic matter and mineral soil and merges gradually into the mineral soil beneath **2 :** a finely powdered solid esp. in a suspension

mul·lah \'məl-ə, 'mu̇l-ə\ *n* [Turk *molla* & Per & Hindi *mulla,* fr. Ar *mawlā*] (1613) **:** a Muslim of a quasi-clerical class trained in traditional law and doctrine — **mul·lah·ism** \-ə-ˌiz-əm\ *n*

mul·lein *also* **mul·len** \'məl-ən\ *n* [ME *moleyne,* fr. AF *moleine*] (15c) **:** any of a genus (*Verbascum*) of usu. woolly-leaved herbs of the figwort family

mullein pink *n* (1846) **:** a European herb (*Lychnis coronaria*) cultivated for its white woolly herbage and showy crimson flowers

mull·er \'məl-ər\ *n* [alter. of ME *molour,* prob. fr. *mullen* to grind] (15c) **:** a stone or piece of wood, metal, or glass used as a pestle

Mül·ler·i·an \myül-'ir-ē-ən, mil-, ˌməl-\ *adj* [Fritz *Müller* †1897 Ger. zoologist] (1899) **:** of, relating to, or being mimicry that exists between two or more inedible or dangerous species (as of butterflies) and that is considered in evolutionary theory to be a mechanism reducing loss to predation by simplification of the recognition process

mul·let \'məl-ət\ *n, pl* **mullet** *or* **mullets** [ME *molet,* fr. MF *mulet,* fr. L *mullus* red mullet, fr. Gk *myllos;* akin to Gk *melas* black, Skt *malina* dirty, black] (14c) **1 :** any of a family (Mugilidae) of valuable food fishes with an elongate rather stout body **2 :** any of a family (Mullidae) of moderate-sized usu. red or golden fishes with two barbels on the chin — called also *red mullet*

mul·li·gan stew \ˌməl-i-gən-\ *n* [prob. fr. the name *Mulligan*] (1904) **:** a stew made from whatever ingredients are available — called also *mulligan*

mul·li·ga·taw·ny \ˌməl-i-gə-'tō-nē, -'tän-ē\ *n* [Tamil *milakutanni,* a strongly seasoned soup, fr. *milaku* pepper + *tanni* water] (1784) **:** a rich soup usu. of chicken stock seasoned with curry

mul·lion \'məl-yən\ *n* [prob. alter. of *monial* (mullion)] (1567) **:** a slender vertical member that forms a division between units of a window, door, or screen or is used decoratively — **mullion** *vt*

mull·ite \ˈməl-ˌīt\ *n* [*Mull,* island of the Inner Hebrides] (1924) **:** a mineral $Al_6Si_2O_{13}$ or $3Al_2O_3{\cdot}2SiO_2$ that is an orthorhombic silicate of aluminum resistant to corrosion and heat and used as a refractory

multi- *comb form* [ME, fr. MF or L; MF, fr. L, fr. *multus* much, many — more at MELIORATE] **1 a :** many **:** multiple **:** much ⟨*multi*valent⟩ **b :** more than two ⟨*multi*lateral⟩ **c :** more than one ⟨*multi*para⟩ **2 :** many times over ⟨*multi*millionaire⟩

mul·ti·age
mul·ti·agen·cy
mul·ti·ap·er·ture
mul·ti·ap·proach
mul·ti·armed
mul·ti·at·om
mul·ti·au·thor
mul·ti·au·thored
mul·ti·ax·i·al
mul·ti·band
mul·ti·bar·rel
mul·ti·bar·reled
mul·ti·bil·lion
mul·ti·bil·lion·aire
mul·ti·blad·ed
mul·ti·branched
mul·ti·build·ing
mul·ti·cam·pus
mul·ti·car
mul·ti·car·bon
mul·ti·caus·al
mul·ti·cell
mul·ti·celled
mul·ti·cel·lu·lar
mul·ti·cel·lu·lar·i·ty
mul·ti·cen·ter
mul·ti·chain
mul·ti·cham·bered
mul·ti·chan·nel
mul·ti·char·ac·ter
mul·ti·city
mul·ti·coat·ed
mul·ti·col·or
mul·ti·col·ored
mul·ti·col·umn
mul·ti·com·po·nent
mul·ti·con·duc·tor
mul·ti·copy
mul·ti·coun·ty
mul·ti·crest·ed
mul·ti·cul·tur·al
mul·ti·cul·tur·al·ism
mul·ti·cu·rie
mul·ti·cur·ren·cy
mul·ti·de·nom·i·na·tion·al
mul·ti·di·a·lec·tal
mul·ti·di·men·sion·al
mul·ti·di·men·sion·al·i·ty
mul·ti·di·rec·tion·al
mul·ti·dis·ci·plin·ary
mul·ti·dis·ci·pline
mul·ti·di·vi·sion·al
mul·ti·do·main
mul·ti·dwell·ing
mul·ti·elec·trode
mul·ti·elec·tron·ic
mul·ti·el·e·ment
mul·ti·en·gine
mul·ti·eth·nic
mul·ti·fac·et·ed
mul·ti·fac·tion·al
mul·ti·fam·i·ly
mul·ti·fil·a·ment
mul·ti·flash
mul·ti·flu·id
mul·ti·fo·cal
mul·ti·fre·quen·cy
mul·ti·fu·el
mul·ti·func·tion
mul·ti·func·tion·al
mul·ti·gen·er·a·tion·al
mul·ti·gen·ic
mul·ti·grade
mul·ti·grid
mul·ti·group
mul·ti·hand·i·capped
mul·ti·head·ed
mul·ti·hos·pi·tal
mul·ti·hued
mul·ti·hull
mul·ti–in·dus·try
mul·ti–in·sti·tu·tion·al
mul·ti·lane
mul·ti·laned
mul·ti·lev·el
mul·ti·lev·eled
mul·ti·lobed
mul·ti·manned
mul·ti·mega·ton
mul·ti·mega·watt
mul·ti·mem·ber
mul·ti·me·tal·lic
mul·ti·me·ter
mul·ti·mil·len·ni·al
mul·ti·mil·lion
mul·ti·mil·lion·aire
mul·ti·mode
mul·ti·mo·lec·u·lar
mul·ti·mo·tor
mul·ti·na·tion
mul·ti·nu·cle·ar
mul·ti·nu·cle·ate
mul·ti·nu·cle·at·ed
mul·ti·or·gas·mic
mul·ti·pa·ram·e·ter
mul·ti·part
mul·ti·par·ti·cle
mul·ti·par·ty
mul·ti·path
mul·ti·pho·ton
mul·ti·pi·on
mul·ti·pis·ton
mul·ti·plane
mul·ti·plant
mul·ti·plot
mul·ti·pole
mul·ti·pow·er
mul·ti·prob·lem
mul·ti·prod·uct
mul·ti·pur·pose
mul·ti·ra·cial
mul·ti·ra·cial·ism
mul·ti·range
mul·ti·roomed
mul·ti·sea·son
mul·ti·ser·vice
mul·ti·sid·ed
mul·ti·site
mul·ti·size
mul·ti·skilled
mul·ti·source
mul·ti·spec·tral
mul·ti·speed
mul·ti·step
mul·ti·sto·ried
mul·ti·sto·ry
mul·ti·syl·lab·ic
mul·ti·sys·tem
mul·ti·tal·ent·ed
mul·ti·tiered
mul·ti·ton
mul·ti·tone
mul·ti·tow·ered
mul·ti·track
mul·ti·union
mul·ti·unit
mul·ti·use
mul·ti·vi·ta·min
mul·ti·vol·ume
mul·ti·vol·umed
mul·ti·wall
mul·ti·war·head
mul·ti·wave·length
mul·ti·year

mul·ti·en·zyme \ˌməl-tē-ˈen-ˌzīm, -ˌtī-\ *adj* (1961) **:** composed of or involving two or more enzymes or subunits similar to enzymes esp. when they have related functions in a biosynthetic pathway ⟨~ complex⟩

mul·ti·fac·to·ri·al \-fak-ˈtōr-ē-əl, -ˈtȯr-\ *adj* (1920) **1 :** having characters or a mode of inheritance dependent on a number of genes at different loci **2** *or* **mul·ti·fac·tor** \-ˈfak-tər\ **:** having, involving, or produced by a variety of elements or causes — **mul·ti·fac·to·ri·al·ly** \-ē-ə-lē\ *adv*

mul·ti·far·i·ous \ˌməl-tə-ˈfar-ē-əs, -ˈfer-\ *adj* [L *multifarius,* fr. *multi-* + *-farius* (akin to *facere* to make, do) — more at DO] (1593) **:** having or occurring in great variety **:** DIVERSE — **mul·ti·far·i·ous·ness** *n*

mul·ti·flo·ra rose \ˌməl-tə-ˌflōr-ə-, -ˌflȯr-\ *n* [NL *multiflora,* lit., having many flowers] (1829) **:** a vigorous thorny rose (*Rosa multiflora*) with clusters of small flowers

mul·ti·fold \ˈməl-ti-ˌfōld\ *adj* (1806) **:** MANY, NUMEROUS

mul·ti·form \ˈməl-ti-ˌfȯrm\ *adj* [F *multiforme,* fr. L *multiformis,* fr. *multi-* + *-formis* -form] (1603) **:** having many forms or appearances — **mul·ti·for·mi·ty** \ˌməl-ti-ˈfȯr-mət-ē\ *n*

mul·ti·germ \ˌməl-ti-ˈjərm, -ˌtī-\ *adj* [prob. fr. *multi-* + *germinate*] (1950) **:** producing or being a fruit cluster capable of giving rise to several plants ⟨a ~ variety of sugar beet⟩

mul·ti·lat·er·al \ˌməl-ti-ˈlat-ə-rəl, -ˌtī-, -ˈla-trəl\ *adj* (1696) **1 :** having many sides **2 :** involving or participated in by more than two nations or parties ⟨~ agreements⟩ — **mul·ti·lat·er·al·ly** \-ē\ *adv*

mul·ti·lay·ered \-ˈlā-ərd, -ˈle(-ə)rd\ *or* **mul·ti·lay·er** \-ˈlā-ər, -ˈle(-ə)r\ *adj* (1931) **:** having or involving several distinct layers, strata, or levels

mul·ti·lin·gual \-ˈliŋ-g(yə-)wəl\ *adj* (1838) **1 :** of, containing, or expressed in several languages ⟨a ~ sign⟩ ⟨~ dictionaries⟩ **2 :** using or able to use several languages ⟨~ translators⟩ — **mul·ti·lin·gual·ism** \-g(yə-)wə-ˌliz-əm\ *n* — **mul·ti·lin·gual·ly** \-g(yə-)wə-lē\ *adv*

mul·ti·me·dia \-ˈmēd-ē-ə\ *adj* (1962) **:** using, involving, or encompassing several media ⟨a ~ approach to learning⟩

mul·ti·mod·al \-ˈmōd-ᵊl\ *adj* (1902) **:** having or involving several modes, modalities, or maxima ⟨~ distributions⟩ ⟨~ responses⟩

mul·ti·na·tion·al \-ˈnash-nəl, -ən-ᵊl\ *adj* (1926) **1 :** of or relating to more than two nationalities ⟨a ~ society⟩ **2 a :** of, relating to, or involving more than two nations ⟨a ~ alliance⟩ **b :** having divisions in more than two countries ⟨a ~ corporation⟩ — **multinational** *n*

mul·ti·no·mi·al \-ˈnō-mē-əl\ *n* [*multi-* + *-nomial* (as in *binomial*)] (1674) **:** a mathematical expression that consists of the sum of several terms **:** POLYNOMIAL — **multinomial** *adj*

mul·tip·a·rous \ˌməl-ˈtip-ə-rəs\ *adj* [NL *multiparus,* fr. *multi-* + L *-parus* -parous] (1646) **1 :** producing many or more than one at a birth **2 :** having experienced one or more previous parturitions

mul·ti·par·tite \ˌməl-ti-ˈpär-ˌtīt\ *adj* [L *multipartitus,* fr. *multi-* + *partitus,* pp. of *partire* to divide, fr. *part-, pars* part] (ca. 1721) **1 :** divided into several or many parts **2 :** having numerous members or signatories ⟨a ~ treaty⟩

mul·ti·phase \ˈməl-ti-ˌfāz\ *adj* (ca. 1890) **:** having various phases; *esp* **:** POLYPHASE

mul·ti·pha·sic \ˌməl-ti-ˈfā-zik, -ˌtī-\ *adj* (1940) **:** having various phases or elements ⟨a ~ test⟩

¹mul·ti·ple \ˈməl-tə-pəl\ *adj* [F, fr. L *multiplex,* fr. *multi-* + *-plex* -fold — more at -FOLD] (1647) **1 :** consisting of, including, or involving more than one ⟨~ births⟩ **2 :** MANY, MANIFOLD ⟨~ achievements⟩ **3 :** shared by many ⟨~ ownership⟩ **4 :** having numerous aspects or functions **:** VARIOUS **5 a :** being a circuit with a number of conductors in parallel **b :** being a group of terminals which make a circuit available at a number of points **6 :** formed by coalescence of the ripening ovaries of several flowers ⟨a ~ fruit⟩

²multiple *n* (1685) **1 a :** the product of a quantity by an integer ⟨35 is a ~ of 7⟩ **b :** something in units of more than one or two **2 :** PARALLEL 4b

multiple allele *n* (1938) **:** any of more than two allelic factors located at one chromosomal locus

multiple–choice *adj* (1927) **1 :** having several answers from which one is to be chosen ⟨a ~ question⟩ **2 :** composed of multiple-choice questions ⟨a ~ test⟩

multiple factor *n* (1915) **:** one of a group of nonallelic genes that according to the multiple-factor hypothesis control various quantitative hereditary characters

multiple myeloma *n* (1897) **:** a disease of bone marrow that is characterized by the presence of numerous myelomas in various bones of the body

multiple personality *n* (1901) **:** an hysterical neurosis in which the personality becomes dissociated into two or more distinct but complex and socially and behaviorally integrated parts each of which becomes dominant and controls behavior from time to time to the exclusion of the others — compare SPLIT PERSONALITY

multiple regression *n* (1924) **:** regression in which one variable is estimated by the use of more than one other variable

multiple sclerosis *n* (1885) **:** a diseased condition marked by patches of hardened tissue in the brain or the spinal cord and associated esp. with partial or complete paralysis and jerking muscle tremor

multiple star *n* (1850) **:** several stars in close proximity that appear to form a single system

multiple store *n, chiefly Brit* (1929) **:** CHAIN STORE

mul·ti·plet \ˈməl-tə-plət\ *n* (1922) **1 :** a spectrum line having several components **2 :** a group of elementary particles that are different in charge but similar in other properties (as mass)

mul·ti·ple–val·ued \ˌməl-tə-pəl-ˈval-(ˌ)yüd\ *adj* (1882) **:** having at least one and sometimes more of the values of the range associated with each value of the domain ⟨a ~ function⟩ — compare SINGLE-VALUED

multiple voting *n* (ca. 1902) **:** illegal voting by one person in two or more constituencies

¹mul·ti·plex \ˈməl-tə-ˌpleks\ *adj* [L] (1557) **1 :** MANY, MULTIPLE **2 :** being or relating to a system of transmitting several messages simultaneously on the same circuit or channel

²multiplex *vt* (1907) **:** to send (messages or signals) by a multiplex system **~** *vi* **:** to multiplex messages or signals — **mul·ti·plex·er** *or* **mul·ti·plex·or** \-ər\ *n*

mul·ti·pli·cand \ˌməl-tə-pli-ˈkand\ *n* [L *multiplicandus,* gerundive of *multiplicare*] (1594) **:** the number that is to be multiplied by another

mul·ti·pli·ca·tion \ˌməl-tə-plə-ˈkā-shən\ *n* [ME *multiplicacioun,* fr. MF *multiplication,* fr. L *multiplication-, multiplicatio,* fr. *multiplicatus,* pp. of *multiplicare* to multiply] (14c) **1 :** the act or process of multiplying **:** the state of being multiplied **2 a :** a mathematical operation that at its simplest is an abbreviated process of adding an integer to itself a specified number of times and that is extended to other numbers in accordance with laws that are valid for integers **b :** any of various mathematical operations that are analogous in some way to multiplication of the real numbers but are defined for other or larger sets of elements (as complex numbers, vectors, matrices, or functions)

multiplication sign *n* (1907) **:** a symbol used to indicate multiplication: **a :** TIMES SIGN **b :** DOT 2b

mul·ti·pli·ca·tive \ˌməl-tə-ˈplik-ət-iv, ˈməl-tə-plə-ˌkāt-\ *adj* (1653) **1 :** tending or having the power to multiply **2 :** of, relating to, or associated with a mathematical operation of multiplication ⟨the ~ property of 0 requires that $a{\cdot}0 = 0$ and $0{\cdot}a = 0$⟩ — **mul·ti·pli·ca·tive·ly** *adv*

multiplicative identity *n* (1958) **:** an identity element (as 1 in the group of rational numbers without 0) that in a given mathematical system leaves unchanged any element by which it is multiplied

multiplicative inverse *n* (1958) **:** an element of a mathematical set that when multiplied by a given element yields the identity element — called also *reciprocal*

mul·ti·plic·i·ty \ˌməl-tə-ˈplis-ət-ē\ *n, pl* **-ties** [ME, fr. MF *multiplicité,* fr. LL *multiplicitat-, multiplicitas,* fr. L *multiplic-, multiplex*] (15c) **1 :** the quality or state of being multiple or various **2 :** a great number **3 :** the number of times a root of an equation or zero of a function occurs when there is more than one root or zero ⟨the ~ of $x = 2$ for the equation $(x - 2)^3 = 0$ is 3⟩ **4 :** the number of components in a system (as a multiplet or a group of energy levels)

mul·ti·pli·er \ˈməl-tə-ˌplī(-ə)r\ *n* (15c) **:** one that multiplies: as **a :** a number by which another number is multiplied **b :** an instrument or device for multiplying or intensifying some effect **c :** a key-operated machine or mechanism or circuit on a machine that multiplies figures and records the products

¹mul·ti·ply \ˈməl-tə-ˌplī\ *vb* **-plied; -ply·ing** [ME *multiplien,* fr. OF *multiplier,* fr. L *multiplicare,* fr. *multiplic-, multiplex* multiple] *vt* (13c) **1 :** to increase in number esp. greatly or in multiples **:** AUGMENT **2 a :** to find the product of by multiplication ⟨~ 7 and 8⟩ **b :** to use as a multiplicand in multiplication with another number ⟨~ 7 by 8⟩ ~ *vi* 1 **a :** to become greater in number : SPREAD **b :** BREED, PROPAGATE **2** : to perform multiplication *syn* see INCREASE

²mul·ti·ply \-plē\ *adv* (1881) : in a multiple manner : in several ways ⟨~ handicapped children⟩

mul·ti·ply \ˌməl-ti-ˈplī\ *adj* (1926) : composed of several plies

mul·ti·po·lar \ˌməl-ti-ˈpō-lər, -ˌtī-\ *adj* [ISV] (1859) **1 :** having several poles ⟨a ~ generator⟩ **2 :** having several dendrites ⟨~ nerve cells⟩ **3** : characterized by more than two centers of power or interest ⟨a ~ world⟩ — **mul·ti·po·lar·i·ty** \-pō-ˈlar-ət-ē\ *n*

mul·ti·po·ten·tial \-pə-ˈten-chəl\ *adj* (1913) : having the potential of becoming any of several mature cell types ⟨~ stem cell⟩

mul·ti·pro·cess·ing \-ˈpräs-ˌes-iŋ, -ˈpräs-əs-, -ˈprōs-\ *n* (1961) : the processing of several computer programs at the same time esp. by a computer system with two or more processors sharing a single memory — **mul·ti·pro·ces·sor** \-ˌes-ər, -əs-\ *n*

mul·ti·pro·gram·ming \-ˈprō-ˌgram-iŋ, -grəm-\ *n* (1959) : the technique of utilizing several interleaved programs concurrently in a single computer system

mul·ti·pronged \-ˈprȯŋd\ *adj* (1957) **1 :** having several prongs ⟨~ fishing spears⟩ **2 :** having several distinct aspects or elements ⟨a ~ attack on the problem⟩

mul·ti·sense \ˈməl-ti-ˌsen(t)s\ *adj* (1957) : having several meanings ⟨~ words⟩

mul·ti·sen·so·ry \ˌməl-ti-ˈsen(t)s-(ə-)rē\ *adj* (1949) : relating to or involving several physiological senses ⟨~ teaching methods⟩ ⟨~ experience⟩

mul·ti·stage \ˈməl-ti-ˌstāj\ *adj* (1904) **1 :** having successive operating stages; *esp* : having propulsion units that operate in turn ⟨~ rockets⟩ **2 :** conducted by stages ⟨a ~ investigation⟩

mul·ti·state \-ˈstāt\ *adj* (1944) **1 :** having divisions in several states ⟨~ enterprises⟩ **2 :** of, relating to, or involving several states ⟨a ~ attack on environmental pollution⟩

mul·ti·tude \ˈməl-tə-ˌt(y)üd\ *n* [ME, fr. MF or L; MF, fr. L *multitudin-, multitudo,* fr. *multus* much — more at MELIORATE] (14c) **1 :** the state of being many **2 :** a great number : HOST **3 :** a great number of people **4 :** POPULACE, PUBLIC

mul·ti·tu·di·nous \ˌməl-tə-ˈt(y)üd-nəs, -ᵊn-əs\ *adj* (1604) **1 :** including a multitude of individuals : POPULOUS ⟨the ~ city⟩ **2 :** existing in a great multitude ⟨~ opportunities⟩ **3 :** existing in or consisting of innumerable elements or aspects ⟨~ applause⟩ — **mul·ti·tu·di·nous·ly** *adv* — **mul·ti·tu·di·nous·ness** *n*

mul·tiv·a·lence \ˌməl-ˈtiv-ə-lən(t)s\ *n* (1933) : the quality or state of having many values, meanings, or appeals

mul·ti·va·lent \ˌməl-ti-ˈvā-lənt, -ˌtī-, *esp in sense 3* ˌməl-ˈtiv-ə-\ *adj* [ISV] (1874) **1 :** POLYVALENT **2 :** represented more than twice in the somatic chromosome number ⟨~ chromosomes⟩ **3 :** having many values, meanings, or appeals — **multivalent** *n*

mul·ti·vari·able \ˌməl-ti-ˈver-ē-ə-bəl, -ˈvar-\ *adj* (1963) : MULTIVARIATE

mul·ti·var·i·ate \-ˈver-ē-ət, -ē-ˌāt\ *adj* [*multi-* + *variable* + ³*-ate*] (1951) : having or involving a number of independent mathematical or statistical variables ⟨~ calculus⟩ ⟨~ data analysis⟩

mul·ti·ver·si·ty \-ˈvər-sət-ē, -stē\ *n, pl* **-ties** [*multi-* + *-versity* (as in *university*)] (1963) : a very large university with many component schools, colleges, or divisions, with widely diverse functions, and with a large staff engaged in activities other than instruction

mul·ti·vol·tine \-ˈvōl-ˌtēn, -ˈvȯl-\ *adj* (1874) : having several broods in a season ⟨~ insects⟩

mul·ture \ˈməl-chər, *Scot usu* ˈmüt-ər\ *n,* [ME *multyr,* fr. MF *molture,* lit., grinding, fr. (assumed) VL *molitura,* fr. L *molitus,* pp. of *molere* to grind — more at MEAL] *chiefly Scot* (14c) : a fee for grinding grain at a mill

¹mum \ˈməm\ *adj* [prob. imit. of a sound made with closed lips] (14c) : SILENT ⟨keep ~⟩ — often used interjectionally

²mum *vi* **mummed; mum·ming** [ME *mommen,* fr. MF *momer* to go masked] (1530) **1 :** to perform in a pantomime **2 :** to go about merrymaking in disguise during festivals

³mum *n* [G *mumme*] (1640) : a strong ale or beer

⁴mum *chiefly Brit var of* MOM

⁵mum *n* (1917) : CHRYSANTHEMUM

mum·ble \ˈməm-bəl\ *vb* **mum·bled; mum·bling** \-b(ə-)liŋ\ [ME *momelen,* of imit. origin] *vi* (14c) : to utter words in a low confused indistinct manner : MUTTER ~ *vt* **1 :** to utter with a low inarticulate voice **2** : to chew or bite with or as if with toothless gums — **mumble** *n* — **mum·bler** \-b(ə-)lər\ *n* — **mum·bly** \-b(ə-)lē\ *adj*

mum·ble·ty-peg *or* **mum·ble–the–peg** \ˈməm-bəl-ˌpeg, -(b)lē-ˌpeg, -(b)əl-tē-, -(b)əl-t͟hə-\ *n* [fr. the phrase *mumble the peg;* fr. the loser's orig. having to pull out with his teeth a peg driven into the ground] (1627) : a game in which the players try to flip a knife from various positions so that the blade will stick into the ground

mum·bo jum·bo \ˌməm-bō-ˈjəm-(ˌ)bō\ *n* [*Mumbo Jumbo,* an idol or deity held to have been worshiped in Africa] (1738) **1 :** an object of superstitious homage and fear **2 a :** a complicated often ritualistic observance with elaborate trappings **b :** complicated activity intended to obscure and confuse **3 :** unnecessarily involved and incomprehensible language : GIBBERISH

mum·mer \ˈməm-ər\ *n* [MF *momeur,* fr. *momer* to go masked] (1502) **1** : a performer in a pantomime; *broadly* : ACTOR **2 :** one who goes merrymaking in disguise during festivals

mum·mery \ˈməm-ə-rē\ *n, pl* **-mer·ies** (1530) **1 :** a performance by mummers **2 :** a ridiculous, hypocritical, or pretentious ceremony or performance

mum·mi·chog \ˈməm-i-ˌchȯg, -ˌchäg\ *n* [Narraganset *moamitteaúg,* lit., they go in great numbers] (1787) : a common American killifish (*Fundulus heteroclitus* of the family Cyprinodontidae)

mum·mi·fy \ˈməm-i-ˌfī\ *vb* **-fied; -fy·ing** *vt* (1628) **1 :** to embalm and dry as or as if a mummy **2 a :** to make into or like a mummy **b :** to cause to dry up and shrivel ~ *vi* : to dry up and shrivel like a mummy — **mum·mi·fi·ca·tion** \ˌməm-i-fə-ˈkā-shən\ *n*

mum·my \ˈməm-ē\ *n, pl* **mummies** [ME *mummie* powdered parts of a mummified body used as a drug, fr. MF *momie,* fr. ML *mumia* mummy, powdered mummy, fr. Ar *mūmiyah* bitumen, mummy, fr. Per *mūm* wax] (1615) **1 a :** a body embalmed or treated for burial with preservatives in the manner of the ancient Egyptians **b :** a body unusually well preserved **2 :** one resembling a mummy

mump \ˈməmp\ *vi* [obs. D *mompen*] *archaic* (1685) : BEG, SPONGE

mumps \ˈməm(p)s\ *n pl but sing or pl in constr* [fr. pl. of obs. *mump* (grimace)] (1598) : an acute contagious virus disease marked by fever and by swelling esp. of the parotid gland

munch \ˈmənch\ *vb* [ME *monchen,* perh. influenced by MF *mangier* to eat — more at MANGER] *vt* (14c) : to chew with a crunching sound : eat with relish ~ *vi* : to chew food with a crunching sound : eat food with relish — **munch·er** *n*

munch·ies \ˈmən-chēz\ *n pl* [*munch* + *-ie* + *-s*] (ca. 1971) **1 :** hunger pangs **2 :** light snack foods

mun·dane \ˌmən-ˈdān, ˈmən-ˌ\ *adj* [ME *mondeyne,* fr. MF *mondain,* fr. LL *mundanus,* fr. L *mundus* world] (15c) **1 :** of, relating to, or characteristic of the world **2 :** characterized by the practical, transitory, and ordinary : COMMONPLACE ⟨the ~ concerns of day-to-day life⟩ *syn* see EARTHLY — **mun·dane·ly** *adv* — **mun·dane·ness** \-ˈdān-nəs, -ˌdān-\ *n* — **mun·dan·ity** \ˌmən-ˈdā-nət-ē\ *n*

mun·dun·gus \ˌmən-ˈdəŋ-(g)əs\ *n* [modif. of Sp *mondongo* tripe] *archaic* (1637) : foul-smelling tobacco

mung bean \ˈməŋ-\ *n* [Hindi *mūg,* fr. Skt *mudga*] (1910) : an erect bushy annual bean (*Phaseolus aureus*) that is widely cultivated in warm regions for its edible usu. green or yellow seeds, for forage, and as the chief source of bean sprouts

mun·go \ˈməŋ-(ˌ)gō\ *n, pl* **mungos** [origin unknown] (1857) : reclaimed wool of poor quality and very short staple

¹mu·nic·i·pal \myu̇-ˈnis-(ə-)pəl *also* m(y)ə-, -ˈnis-ə-bəl, ÷ˌmyü-nə-ˈsip-əl\ *adj* [L *municipalis* of a municipality, fr. *municip-, municeps* inhabitant of a municipality, lit., undertaker of duties, fr. *munus* duty, service + *capere* to take — more at MEAN, HEAVE] (ca. 1540) **1 :** of or relating to the internal affairs of a major political unit (as a nation) **2 a :** of, relating to, or characteristic of a municipality **b :** having local self-government **3 :** restricted to one locality

²municipal *n* (1727) : a security issued by a state or local government or by an authority set up by such a government — usu. used in pl.

municipal court *n* (1828) **1 :** a court that sits in some cities and larger towns and that usu. has civil and criminal jurisdiction over cases arising within the municipality **2 :** POLICE COURT

mu·nic·i·pal·i·ty \myu̇-ˌnis-ə-ˈpal-ət-ē\ *n, pl* **-ties** (1790) **1 :** a primarily urban political unit having corporate status and usu. powers of self-government **2 :** the governing body of a municipality

mu·nic·i·pal·ize \myu̇-ˈnis-ə-pə-ˌlīz\ *vt* **-ized; -iz·ing** (1880) : to bring under municipal ownership or supervision — **mu·nic·i·pal·iza·tion** \-ˌnis-(ə-)pə-lə-ˈzā-shən\ *n*

mu·nic·i·pal·ly \myu̇-ˈnis-ə-p(ə-)lē\ *adv* (1842) : by or in terms of a municipality

mu·nif·i·cent \myu̇-ˈnif-ə-sənt\ *adj* [back-formation fr. *munificence,* fr. L *munificentia,* fr. *munificus* generous, fr. *munus* service, gift] (1583) **1** : very liberal in giving or bestowing : LAVISH **2 :** characterized by great liberality or generosity *syn* see LIBERAL — **mu·nif·i·cence** \-sən(t)s\ *n* — **mu·nif·i·cent·ly** *adv*

mu·ni·ment \ˈmyü-nə-mənt\ *n* [ME, fr. AF, fr. MF, defense, fr. L *munimentum,* fr. *munire* to fortify] (15c) **1 :** the evidence (as documents) that enables one to defend the title to an estate or a claim to rights and privileges — usu. used in pl. **2** *archaic* : a means of defense

mu·ni·tion \myu̇-ˈnish-ən\ *n* [MF, fr. L *munition-, munitio,* fr. *munitus,* pp. of *munire* to fortify, fr. *moenia* walls; akin to OE *mǣre* boundary, L *murus* wall] (1533) **1** *archaic* : RAMPART, DEFENSE **2 :** ARMAMENT, AMMUNITION — **munition** *vt*

Munster *var of* MUENSTER

mun·tin \ˈmənt-ᵊn\ *also* **mun·ting** \-ᵊn, -iŋ\ *n* [alter. of *montant* vertical dividing bar, fr. F, fr. prp. of *monter* to rise — more at MOUNT] (1774) : a strip separating panes of glass in a sash

munt·jac \ˈmən(t)-ˌjak, ˈmən-ˌchak\ *n* [prob. modif. of Jav *mindjangan* deer] (ca. 1798) : any of several small deer (genus *Muntiacus*) of southeastern Asia and the East Indies

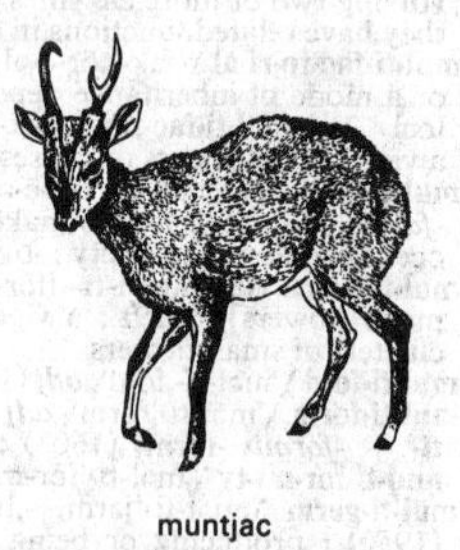
muntjac

mu·on \ˈmyü-ˌän\ *n* [contr. of earlier *mu-meson,* fr. *mu*] (1952) : an unstable lepton that is common in the cosmic radiation near the earth's surface, has a mass about 207 times the mass of the electron, and exists in negative and positive forms — **mu·on·ic** \myü-ˈän-ik\ *adj*

mu·on·ium \myü-ˈō-nē-əm, -ˈän-ē-əm\ *n* [*muon* + *-ium*] (1957) : a short-lived quasi-atom consisting of an electron and a positive muon

¹mu·ral \ˈmyu̇r-əl\ *adj* [L *muralis,* fr. *murus* wall — more at MUNITION] (1586) **1 :** of, relating to, or resembling a wall **2 :** applied to and made integral with a wall or ceiling surface

²mural *n* (1916) : a mural work of art (as a painting) — **mu·ral·ist** \-ə-ləst\ *n*

mu·ram·ic acid \myu̇-ˌram-ik-\ *n* [*mur-* (fr. L *murus* wall) + *glucosamine* + *-ic*] (1957) : an amino sugar $C_9H_{17}NO_7$ that is a lactic acid derivative of glucosamine and is found esp. in bacterial cell walls and in blue-green algae

¹mur·der \ˈmərd-ər\ *n* [partly fr. ME *murther,* fr. OE *morthor;* partly fr. ME *murdre,* fr. OF, of Gmc origin; akin to OE *morthor;* akin to OHG *mord* murder, L *mort-, mors* death, *mori* to die, Gk *brotos* mortal] (bef. 12c) **1 :** the crime of unlawfully killing a person esp. with malice aforethought **2 a :** something very difficult or dangerous ⟨the traffic was ~⟩ **b :** something outrageous or blameworthy ⟨getting away with ~⟩

²murder *vb* **mur·dered; mur·der·ing** \ˈmərd-(ə-)riŋ\ *vt* (13c) **1 :** to kill (a human being) unlawfully and with premeditated malice **2 :** to slaughter wantonly : SLAY **3 a :** to put an end to **b :** TEASE, TORMENT **c** : MUTILATE, MANGLE ⟨~s French⟩ **d :** to defeat badly ~ *vi* : to commit murder *syn* see KILL

mur·der·ee \ˌmər-də-ˈrē\ *n* (1920) : an actual or potential victim of a murder

mur·der·er \'mərd-ər-ər\ *n* (14c) : one who murders; *esp* : one who commits the crime of murder

mur·der·ess \'mərd-ə-rəs\ *n* (14c) : a woman who murders

mur·der·ous \'mərd-(ə-)rəs\ *adj* (1535) **1 a** : having the purpose or capability of murder **b** : characterized by or causing murder or bloodshed **2** : having the ability or power to overwhelm : DEVASTATING ⟨~ heat⟩ — **mur·der·ous·ly** *adv* — **mur·der·ous·ness** *n*

mu·rein \'myu̇r-ē-ən, 'myu̇(ə)r-,ēn\ *n* [*muramic* acid + *-ein*] (1964) : PEPTIDOGLYCAN

mu·rex \'myu̇(ə)r-,eks\ *n, pl* **mu·ri·ces** \'myu̇r-ə-,sēz\ *or* **mu·rex·es** [NL, fr. L, mollusk yielding a purple dye; akin to Gk *myak-, myax* sea-mussel] (1589) : any of a genus (*Murex*) of marine gastropod mollusks having a rough and often spinose shell, abounding in tropical seas, and yielding a purple dye

mu·ri·ate \'myu̇r-ē-,āt\ *n* [F, back-formation fr. (*acide*) *muriatique* muriatic acid] (1790) : CHLORIDE

mu·ri·at·ic acid \,myu̇r-ē-,at-ik-\ *n* [F *muriatique*, fr. L *muriaticus* pickled in brine, fr. *muria* brine; akin to OHG *mos* moss] (1790) : HYDROCHLORIC ACID

mu·rid \'myu̇r-əd\ *adj* [deriv. of L *mur-, mus* mouse — more at MOUSE] (ca. 1909) : of or relating to a family (Muridae) comprising the typical mice and rats — **murid** *n*

mu·rine \'myu̇(ə)r-,īn\ *adj* [deriv. of L *mur-, mus*] (1607) : of or relating to a genus (*Mus*) or the subfamily to which it belongs and which includes the common household rats and mice; *also* : of, relating to, or involving these rodents and esp. the house mouse — **murine** *n*

murine typhus *n* (1933) : a mild febrile disease that is marked by headache and rash, is caused by a rickettsia (*Rickettsia mooseri*), is widespread in nature in rodents, and is transmitted to man by a flea

murk \'mərk\ *n* [ME *mirke*, fr. OE *mirce*; akin to ON *myrkr* darkness] (bef. 12c) : GLOOM, DARKNESS; *also* : FOG — **murk** *adj, archaic*

murky \'mər-kē\ *adj* **murk·i·er; -est** (14c) **1** : characterized by a heavy dimness or obscurity caused by or like that caused by overhanging fog or smoke **2** : characterized by thickness and heaviness of air : FOGGY, MISTY **3** : darkly vague or obscure ⟨~ official rhetoric⟩ — **murk·i·ly** \-kə-lē\ *adv* — **murk·i·ness** \-kē-nəs\ *n*

[1]**mur·mur** \'mər-mər\ *n* [ME *murmure*, fr. MF, fr. L *murmur* murmur, roar, of imit. origin] (14c) **1** : a half-suppressed or muttered complaint : GRUMBLING **2 a** : a low indistinct but often continuous sound **b** : a soft or gentle utterance **3** : an atypical sound of the heart indicating a functional or structural abnormality

[2]**murmur** *vi* (14c) **1** : to make a murmur ⟨the breeze ~*ed* in the pines⟩ **2** : COMPLAIN, GRUMBLE ~ *vt* : to say in a murmur — **mur·mur·er** *n*

mur·mur·ous \'mərm-(ə-)rəs\ *adj* (1582) : filled with or characterized by murmurs : low and indistinct — **mur·mur·ous·ly** *adv*

Mur·phy \'mər-fē\ *n* [fr. the name *Murphy*] (1959) : any of various confidence games; *esp* : one in which the victim believes he is paying for sex

Mur·phy bed \,mər-fē-\ *n* [William L. *Murphy* †1959 Am. inventor] (1925) : a bed that may be folded or swung into a closet

Mur·phy's Law \,mər-fēz-\ *n* [fr. the name *Murphy*] (1958) : an observation: anything that can go wrong will go wrong

mur·rain \'mər-ən, 'mə-rən\ *n* [ME *moreyne*, fr. MF *morine*, fr. *morir* to die, fr. L *mori* — more at MURDER] (15c) : a pestilence or plague affecting domestic animals or plants

murre \'mər\ *n* [origin unknown] (1602) : any of several guillemots (genus *Uria*); *esp* : a common bird (*U. aalge*) of northern seas

mur·rey \'mər-ē, 'mə-rē\ *n* [ME, fr. MF *moré*, fr. ML *moratum*, fr. neut. of *moratus* mulberry colored, fr. L *morum* mulberry — more at MULBERRY] (14c) : a purplish black : MULBERRY

mur·ther \'mər-t͟hər\ *chiefly dial var of* MURDER

mus·ca·det \,məs-kə-'dā, -'de\ *n, often cap* [F, fr. Prov, muscadet grape, fr. *musc* musk scent] (ca. 1899) : a dry white wine from the Loire valley of France

mus·ca·dine \'məs-kə-,dīn\ *n* [prob. alter. of *muscatel*] (ca. 1785) : a grape (*Vitis rotundifolia*) of the southern U.S. with musky fruits borne in small clusters

mus·cae vo·li·tan·tes \'məs-,(k)ē-,väl-ə-'tan-,tēz\ *n pl* [NL, lit., flying flies] (ca. 1753) : spots before the eyes due to cells and cell fragments in the vitreous humor and lens

mus·ca·rine \'məs-kə-,rēn\ *n* [G *muskarin*, fr. NL (*Amanita*) *muscaria* fly agaric] (1872) : an ammonium base $C_9H_{20}NO_2$ that is chemically related to choline, was first found in the fly agaric, and acts directly on smooth muscle — **mus·ca·rin·ic** \,məs-kə-'rin-ik\ *adj*

mus·cat \'məs-,kat, -kət\ *n* [F, fr. Prov, fr. *muscat* musky, fr. *musc* musk, fr. LL *muscus*] (1548) **1** : MUSCATEL **2** : any of several cultivated grapes used in making wine and raisins

mus·ca·tel \,məs-kə-'tel\ *n* [ME *muskadelle*, fr. MF *muscadel*, fr. OProv, fr. *muscadel* resembling musk, fr. *muscat*] (15c) **1** : a sweet fortified wine from muscat grapes **2** : a raisin from muscat grapes

[1]**mus·cle** \'məs-əl\ *n, often attrib* [ME, fr. MF, fr. L *musculus*, fr. dim. of *mus* mouse — more at MOUSE] (14c) **1 a** : a body tissue consisting of long cells that contract when stimulated and produce motion **b** : an organ that is essentially a mass of muscle tissue attached at either end to a fixed point and that by contracting moves or checks the movement of a body part **2 a** : muscular strength : BRAWN **b** : effective strength : POWER ⟨political ~⟩

[2]**muscle** *vb* **mus·cled; mus·cling** \'məs-(ə-)liŋ\ *vt* (1913) : to move or force by or as if by muscular effort ⟨*muscled* him out of office⟩ ~ *vi* : to make one's way by brute strength or by force

mus·cle–bound \'məs-əl-,bau̇nd\ *adj* (1879) **1** : having some of the muscles tense and enlarged and of impaired elasticity sometimes as a result of excessive exercise **2** : lacking in flexibility : RIGID

muscle car \-,kär\ *n* (ca. 1968) : any of a group of American-made 2-door sports coupes with powerful engines designed for high-performance driving

mus·cled \'məs-əld\ *adj* (1644) : having muscles esp. of a specified kind — often used in combination ⟨hard-*muscled* arms⟩

muscle spindle *n* (1894) : a sensory end organ in a muscle that is sensitive to stretch in the muscle, consists of small striated muscle fibers richly supplied with nerve fibers, and is enclosed in a connective tissue sheath — called also *stretch receptor*

mus·co·vite \'məs-kə-,vīt\ *n* [ML or NL *Muscovia, Moscovia* Moscow] (1555) **1** *cap* **a** : a native or resident of the ancient principality of Moscow or of the city of Moscow **b** : RUSSIAN **2** [*muscovy* (*glass*)] : a mineral essentially $KAl_3Si_3O_{10}(OH)_2$ that is a colorless to pale brown potassium mica — **Muscovite** *adj*

Mus·co·vy duck \,məs-,kō-vē-\ *n* [*Muscovy*, principality of Moscow, Russia] (1657) : a large crested duck (*Cairina moschata*) native from Mexico to southern Brazil but widely kept in domestication

muscul- *or* **musculo-** *comb form* [LL *muscul-*, fr. L *musculus*] **1** : muscle ⟨*muscul*ar⟩ **2** : muscular and ⟨*musculo*skeletal⟩

mus·cu·lar \'məs-kyə-lər\ *adj* (1681) **1 a** : of, relating to, or constituting muscle **b** : of, relating to, or performed by the muscles **2** : having well-developed musculature **3 a** : of or relating to physical strength : BRAWNY **b** : having strength of expression or character : VIGOROUS ⟨~ prose⟩ — **mus·cu·lar·i·ty** \,məs-kyə-'lar-ət-ē\ *n* — **mus·cu·lar·ly** \'məs-kyə-lər-lē\ *adv*

muscular dystrophy *n* (1886) : a hereditary disease characterized by progressive wasting of muscles

mus·cu·la·ture \'məs-kyə-lə-,chu̇(ə)r, -chər, -,t(y)u̇(ə)r\ *n* [F, fr. L *musculus*] (1875) : the muscles of all or a part of the animal body

mus·cu·lo·skel·e·tal \,məs-kyə-lō-'skel-ət-ᵊl\ *adj* (ca. 1944) : of, relating to, or involving both musculature and skeleton

[1]**muse** \'myüz\ *vb* **mused; mus·ing** [ME *musen*, fr. MF *muser* to gape, idle, muse, fr. *muse* mouth of an animal, fr. ML *musus*] *vi* (14c) **1** : to become absorbed in thought; *esp* : to turn something over in the mind meditatively and often inconclusively **2** *archaic* : WONDER, MARVEL ~ *vt* : to think or say reflectively **syn** see PONDER — **mus·er** *n*

[2]**muse** *n* (15c) : a state of deep thought or dreamy abstraction

[3]**muse** *n* [ME, fr. MF, fr. L *Musa*, fr. Gk *Mousa*] (14c) **1** *cap* : any of the nine sister goddesses in Greek mythology presiding over song and poetry and the arts and sciences **2** : a source of inspiration; *esp* : a guiding genius **3** : POET

mu·sette \myü-'zet\ *n* [F, fr. MF, dim. of *muse* bagpipe, fr. *muser* to muse, play the bagpipe] (14c) **1** : a French bellows-blown bagpipe popular in court circles in the 17th and 18th centuries **2** : a small knapsack; *also* : a similar bag with one shoulder strap — called also *musette bag*

mu·se·um \myu̇-'zē-əm\ *n* [L *Museum* place for learned occupation, fr. Gk *Mouseion*, fr. neut. of *Mouseios* of the Muses, fr. *Mousa*] (1672) : an institution devoted to the procurement, care, study, and display of objects of lasting interest or value; *also* : a place where objects are exhibited

museum piece *n* (1901) **1** : something preserved in or suitable for a museum **2** : one that is out-of-date : a thing of the past

[1]**mush** \'məsh, *esp 3 also* 'mu̇sh\ *n* [prob. alter. of *mash*] (1671) **1** : a thick porridge made with cornmeal boiled in water or milk **2** : something soft and spongy or shapeless **3 a** : weak sentimentality : DRIVEL **b** : mawkish amorousness

[2]**mush** *vt, chiefly dial* (ca. 1781) : to reduce to a crumbly mass ~ *vi, of an airplane* : to fly in a partly stalled condition with controls ineffective; *also* : to fail to gain altitude — **mush·er** *n*

[3]**mush** *vi* [prob. fr. AmerF *moucher* to go fast, fr. F *mouche* fly, fr. L *musca* — more at MIDGE] (1862) : to travel esp. over snow with a sled drawn by dogs — often used as a command to a dog team — **mush·er** *n*

[4]**mush** *n* (1910) : a trip esp. across snow with a dog team

[1]**mush·room** \'məsh-,rüm, -,ru̇m; *chiefly Northern & Midland* -,rün; *chiefly substand* -ə-,rüm, -ə-,ru̇m, -ə-,rün\ *n* [ME *musseroun*, fr. MF *mousseron*, fr. LL *mussirion-, mussirio*] (14c) **1 a** : an enlarged complex aerial fleshy fruiting body of a fungus (as of the class Basidiomycetes) that consists typically of a stem bearing a flattened cap; *esp* : one that is edible **b** : FUNGUS 1 **2** : UPSTART **3** : something resembling a mushroom

[2]**mushroom** *vi* (1747) **1 a** *of a bullet* : to expand and flatten at the nose upon impact **b** : to well up and spread out laterally from a central source **2** : to spring up suddenly or multiply rapidly

mushroom cloud *n* (ca. 1909) : a mushroom-shaped cloud; *specif* : one caused by the explosion of a nuclear weapon

mushy \'məsh-ē, *esp 2 also* 'mu̇sh-ē\ *adj* **mush·i·er; -est** (1839) **1** : having the consistency of mush : SOFT **2** : excessively tender or emotional; *esp* : mawkishly amorous — **mush·i·ly** \'məsh-ə-lē, 'mu̇sh-\ *adv* — **mush·i·ness** \'məsh-ē-nəs, 'mu̇sh-\ *n*

mu·sic \'myü-zik\ *n, often attrib* [ME *musik*, fr. OF *musique*, fr. L *musica*, fr. Gk *mousikē* any art presided over by the Muses, esp. music, fr. fem. of *mousikos* of the Muses, fr. *Mousa* Muse] (13c) **1 a** : the science or art of ordering tones or sounds in succession, in combination, and in temporal relationships to produce a composition having unity and continuity **b** : vocal, instrumental, or mechanical sounds having rhythm, melody, or harmony **2 a** : an agreeable sound : EUPHONY ⟨her voice was ~ to my ears⟩ **b** : musical quality ⟨the ~ of verse⟩ **3** : a musical accompaniment ⟨a play set to ~⟩ **4** : the score of a musical composition set down on paper **5** : a distinctive type or category of music ⟨there is a ~ for everybody —Eric Salzman⟩

[1]**mu·si·cal** \'myü-zi-kəl\ *adj* [ME, fr. MF, fr. ML *musicalis*, fr. *musica*] (15c) **1 a** : of or relating to music **b** : having the pleasing harmonious qualities of music : MELODIOUS **2** : having an interest in or talent for music **3** : set to or accompanied by music **4** : of or relating to musicians or music lovers — **mu·si·cal·ly** \-k(ə-)lē\ *adv*

[2]**musical** *n* (1823) **1** *archaic* : MUSICALE **2** : a film or theatrical production typically of a sentimental or humorous nature that consists of musical numbers and dialogue based on a unifying plot

musical box *n, chiefly Brit* (1829) : MUSIC BOX

musical chairs *n pl but sing in constr* (1877) : a game in which players march to music around a row of chairs numbering one less than the players and scramble for seats when the music stops; *also* : a situation or series of events suggesting the game of musical chairs (as in rapid change or confusing activity)

musical comedy *n* (1765) : MUSICAL 2

\ə\ abut \ᵊ\ kitten, F table \ər\ further \a\ ash \ā\ ace \ä\ cot, cart \au̇\ out \ch\ chin \e\ bet \ē\ easy \g\ go \i\ hit \ī\ ice \j\ job \ŋ\ sing \ō\ go \ȯ\ law \ȯi\ boy \th\ thin \t͟h\ the \ü\ loot \u̇\ foot \y\ yet \zh\ vision \à, k̲, ⁿ, œ, œ̄, ue, ue̅, ʸ\ see Guide to Pronunciation

mu·si·cale \ˌmyü-zi-ˈkal\ *n* [F *soirée musicale,* lit., musical evening] (1872) **:** a social entertainment with music as the leading feature

mu·si·cal·i·ty \ˌmyü-zi-ˈkal-ət-ē\ *n* (1853) **1 :** sensitivity to, knowledge of, or talent for music **2 :** the quality or state of being musical **:** MELODIOUSNESS

mu·si·cal·ize \ˈmyü-zi-kə-ˌlīz\ *vt* **-ized; -iz·ing** (1919) **:** to set to music — **mu·si·cal·iza·tion** \ˌmyü-zi-kə-lə-ˈzā-shən\ *n*

musical saw *n* (1927) **:** a handsaw made to produce melody by bending the blade with varying tension while sounding it with a hammer or violin bow

music box *n* (1844) **:** a container enclosing an apparatus that reproduces music mechanically when activated by a clockwork

music drama *n* (1877) **:** an opera in which the action is not interrupted by formal song divisions (as recitatives or arias) and the music is determined solely by dramatic appropriateness

music hall *n* (1842) **:** a vaudeville theater; *also* **:** VAUDEVILLE

mu·si·cian \myu̇-ˈzish-ən\ *n* (14c) **:** a composer, conductor, or performer of music; *esp* **:** INSTRUMENTALIST — **mu·si·cian·ly** \-lē\ *adj* — **mu·si·cian·ship** \-ˌship\ *n*

music of the spheres (1609) **:** an ethereal harmony thought by the Pythagoreans to be produced by the vibration of the celestial spheres

mu·si·col·o·gy \ˌmyü-zi-ˈkäl-ə-jē\ *n* [It *musicologia,* fr. L *musica* music + *-logia* -logy] (1909) **:** a study of music as a branch of knowledge or field of research as distinct from composition or performance — **mu·si·co·log·i·cal** \-kə-ˈläj-i-kəl\ *adj* — **mu·si·col·o·gist** \-ˈkäl-ə-jəst\ *n*

[1]**mus·ing** \ˈmyü-ziŋ\ *n* (14c) **:** MEDITATION

[2]**musing** *adj* (15c) **:** thoughtfully abstracted **:** MEDITATIVE — **mus·ing·ly** \-ziŋ-lē\ *adv*

mu·sique con·crète \myü-ˌzēk-kōⁿ-ˈkret, mᵫ-\ *n* [F, lit., concrete music] (1952) **:** a recorded montage of natural sounds often electronically modified and presented as a musical composition

musk \ˈməsk\ *n* [ME *muske,* fr. MF *musc,* fr. LL *muscus,* fr. Gk *moschos,* fr. Per *mushk,* fr. Skt *muṣka* testicle, fr. dim. of *mūṣ* mouse; akin to OE *mūs* mouse] (14c) **1 a :** a substance with a penetrating persistent odor obtained from a sac beneath the abdominal skin of the male musk deer and used as a perfume fixative; *also* **:** a similar substance from another animal or a synthetic substitute **b :** the odor of musk; *also* **:** an odor resembling musk esp. in heaviness or persistence **2 :** any of various plants with musky odors; *esp* **:** MUSK PLANT

musk deer *n* (1681) **:** a small heavy-limbed hornless deer (*Moschus moschiferus*) of central Asian uplands that produces musk in the male

mus·keg \ˈməs-ˌkeg, -ˌkāg\ *n* [of Algonquian origin; akin to Ojibwa *mūskeg* grassy bog] (1806) **1 :** BOG; *esp* **:** a sphagnum bog of northern No. America often with tussocks **2 :** a usu. thick deposit of partially decayed vegetable matter of wet boreal regions

mus·kel·lunge \ˈməs-kə-ˌlənj\ *n, pl* **muskellunge** [of Algonquian origin; akin to Cree *maskinonge* muskellunge] (1789) **:** a large No. American pike (*Esox masquinongy*) that may weigh 60 to 80 pounds (27 to 36 kilograms) and is a valuable sport fish

mus·ket \ˈməs-kət\ *n* [MF *mousquet,* fr. OIt *moschetto* arrow for a crossbow, musket, fr. dim. of *mosca* fly, fr. L *musca* — more at MIDGE] (ca. 1587) **:** a heavy large-caliber smoothbore shoulder firearm (as a flintlock or matchlock); *broadly* **:** a shoulder gun carried by infantry

mus·ke·teer \ˌməs-kə-ˈti(ə)r\ *n* [modif. of MF *mousquetaire,* fr. *mousquet*] (1590) **:** a soldier armed with a musket

mus·ket·ry \ˈməs-kə-trē\ *n* (1646) **1 :** MUSKETS **2 :** MUSKETEERS **3 a :** musket fire **b :** the art or science of using small arms esp. in battle

mus·kie *or* **mus·ky** \ˈməs-kē\ *n, pl* **muskies** (1894) **:** MUSKELLUNGE

musk·mel·on \ˈməsk-ˌmel-ən\ *n* (1573) **:** a usu. sweet musky-odored edible melon that is the fruit of a trailing or climbing Asian herbaceous vine (*Cucumis melo*): as **a :** any of various melons of small or moderate size with netted skin that include most of the muskmelons cultivated in No. America **b :** CANTALOUPE 1 **c :** WINTER MELON

Mus·ko·ge·an *or* **Mus·kho·ge·an** \(ˌ)məs-ˈkō-gē-ən\ *n* (1891) **:** a language family of southeastern U.S. that includes Muskogee

Mus·ko·gee *n, pl* **Muskogee** *or* **Muskogees** (1775) **1 :** a member of an American Indian people of Georgia and eastern Alabama constituting the nucleus of the Creek confederacy **2 :** the language of the Muskogees and of some of the Seminoles

musk–ox \ˈməs-ˌkäks\ *n* (1744) **:** a heavyset shaggy-coated wild ox (*Ovibos moschatus*) now confined to Greenland and the barren northern lands of No. America

musk plant *n* (ca. 1852) **:** a yellow-flowered No. American herb (*Mimulus moschatus*) of the figwort family that has hairy foliage and sometimes a musky odor

musk·rat \ˈməs-ˌkrat\ *n, pl* **muskrat** *or* **muskrats** [prob. by folk etymology fr. a word of Algonquian origin; akin to Natick *musquash* muskrat] (1607) **:** an aquatic rodent (*Ondatra zibethica*) of the U.S. and Canada with a long scaly laterally compressed tail, webbed hind feet, and dark glossy brown fur; *also* **:** its fur or pelt

musk rose *n* (1577) **:** a rose (*Rosa moschata*) of the Mediterranean region with flowers having a musky odor

musk thistle *n* (1731) **:** a Eurasian thistle (*Carduus nutans*) that has nodding musky flower heads and is naturalized in eastern No. America

musk turtle *n* (1868) **:** a small American freshwater turtle (genera *Sternotherus* and *Kinosternon*); *esp* **:** a turtle (*S. odoratus*) having a strong musky odor

musky \ˈməs-kē\ *adj* **musk·i·er; -est** (1613) **:** having an odor of or resembling musk — **musk·i·ness** *n*

Mus·lim \ˈməz-ləm, ˈmu̇s-, ˈmu̇z-\ *n* [Ar *muslim,* lit., one who surrenders (to God)] (1615) **1 :** an adherent of Islam **2 :** BLACK MUSLIM — **Muslim** *adj*

Muslim era *n* (1948) **:** ISLAMIC ERA

mus·lin \ˈməz-lən\ *n* [F *mousseline,* fr. It *mussolina,* fr. Ar *mawṣilīy* of Mosul, fr. al-*Mawṣil* Mosul, Iraq] (1609) **:** a plain-woven sheer to coarse cotton fabric

mus·quash \ˈməs-ˌkwäsh, -ˌkwo̊sh\ *n* [of Algonquian origin; akin to Natick *musquash* muskrat] (ca. 1588) **:** MUSKRAT

[1]**muss** \ˈməs\ *n* [origin unknown] (1591) **1** *obs* **a :** a game in which players scramble for small objects thrown to the ground **b :** SCRAMBLE **2** *slang* **:** a confused conflict **:** ROW **3 :** a state of disorder **:** MESS

[2]**muss** *vt* (1837) **:** to make untidy **:** DISARRANGE

mus·sel \ˈməs-əl\ *n* [ME *muscle,* fr. OE *muscelle,* fr. (assumed) VL *muscula,* fr. L *musculus* muscle, mussel] (bef. 12c) **1 :** a marine bivalve mollusk (esp. genus *Mytilus*) usu. having a dark elongated shell **2 :** a freshwater bivalve mollusk (as of *Unio, Anodonta,* or related genera) that is esp. abundant in rivers of the central U.S. and has a shell with a lustrous nacreous lining

Mus·sul·man *also* **Mus·sal·man** \ˈməs-əl-mən\ *n, pl* **Mus·sul·men** \-mən\ *or* **Mussulmans** [Turk *müslüman* & Per *musulmān,* modif. of Ar *muslim*] (ca. 1563) **:** MUSLIM

mussy \ˈməs-ē\ *adj* **muss·i·er; -est** (ca. 1859) **:** characterized by clutter or muss **:** MESSY — **muss·i·ly** \ˈməs-ə-lē\ *adv* — **muss·i·ness** \ˈməs-ē-nəs\ *n*

[1]**must** \məs(t), ˈməst\ *vb, pres & past all persons* **must** [ME *moste,* fr. OE *mōste,* past indic. & subj. of *mōtan* to be allowed to, have to; akin to OHG *muozan* to be allowed to, have to, OE *metan* to measure — more at METE] *verbal auxiliary* (bef. 12c) **1 a :** be commanded or requested to ⟨you ~ stop⟩ **b :** be urged to **:** ought by all means to ⟨you ~ read that book⟩ **2 :** be compelled by physical necessity to ⟨man ~ eat to live⟩ **:** be required by immediate or future need or purpose to ⟨we ~ hurry to catch the bus⟩ **3 a :** be obliged to **:** be compelled by social considerations to ⟨I ~ say you're looking well⟩ **b :** be required by law, custom, or moral conscience to ⟨we ~ obey the rules⟩ **c :** be determined to ⟨if you ~ go at least wait for me⟩ **d :** be unreasonably or perversely compelled to ⟨why ~ you be so stubborn⟩ **4 :** be logically inferred or supposed to ⟨it ~ be time⟩ **5 :** be compelled by fate or by natural law to ⟨what ~ be will be⟩ **6 :** was or were presumably certain to **:** was or were bound to ⟨if he had really been there I ~ have seen him⟩ **7** *dial* **:** MAY, SHALL — used chiefly in questions **~** *vi, archaic* **:** to be obliged to go ⟨I ~ to Coventry —Shak.⟩

[2]**must** \ˈməst\ *n* (1616) **1 :** an imperative need or duty **:** REQUIREMENT **2 :** an indispensable item **:** ESSENTIAL ⟨exercise is a ~⟩

[3]**must** \ˈməst\ *n* [ME, fr. OE, fr. L *mustum*] (bef. 12c) **:** the expressed juice of fruit and esp. grapes before and during fermentation; *also* **:** the pulp and skins of the crushed grapes

[4]**must** \ˈməst\ *n* [MF, alter. of *musc* musk] (15c) **1 :** MUSK **2 :** MOLD, MUSTINESS

mus·tache \ˈməs-ˌtash, (ˌ)məs-ˈ\ *n* [MF *moustache,* fr. OIt *mustaccio,* fr. MGk *moustaki,* dim. of Gk *mystak-, mystax* upper lip, mustache] (1560) **1 :** the hair growing on the human upper lip; *esp* **:** such hair grown and often trimmed in a particular style ⟨doesn't like men with ~*s*⟩ **2 :** hair or bristles about the mouth of a mammal — **mus·tached** *adj*

mus·ta·chio \(ˌ)məs-ˈtash-(ē-ˌ)ō, -ˈtäsh-\ *n, pl* **-chios** [Sp & It; Sp *mostacho,* fr. It *mustaccio,* fr. OIt] (1551) **:** MUSTACHE; *esp* **:** a large mustache — **mus·ta·chioed** \-(ē-)ˌōd\ *adj*

mus·tang \ˈməs-ˌtaŋ\ *n* [MexSp *mestengo,* fr. Sp, stray, fr. *mesteño* strayed, fr. *mesta* annual roundup of cattle that disposed of strays, fr. ML (*animalia*) *mixta* mixed animals] (1808) **:** the small hardy naturalized horse of the western plains directly descended from horses brought in by the Spaniards; *also* **:** BRONCO

mus·tard \ˈməs-tərd\ *n* [ME, fr. OF *mostarde,* fr. *moust* must, fr. L *mustum*] (13c) **1 a :** a pungent yellow powder of the seeds of any of several common mustards (*Brassica hirta, B. nigra,* or *B. juncea*) used as a condiment or in medicine as a stimulant and diuretic, an emetic, or a counterirritant **b** *slang* **:** ZEST **2 :** any of several herbs (genus *Brassica* of the family Cruciferae, the mustard family) with lobed leaves, yellow flowers, and linear beaked pods — **mus·tardy** \-ē\ *adj*

mustard gas *n* (1917) **:** an irritant vesicant oily liquid $C_4H_8Cl_2S$ used as a war gas

mustard plaster *n* (1810) **:** a counterirritant and rubefacient plaster containing powdered mustard

[1]**mus·ter** \ˈməs-tər\ *vb* **mus·tered; mus·ter·ing** \-t(ə-)riŋ\ [ME *mustren* to show, muster, fr. MF *monstrer,* fr. L *monstrare* to show, fr. *monstrum* evil omen, monster — more at MONSTER] *vt* (15c) **1 a :** to cause to gather **:** CONVENE **b :** to enroll formally — usu. used with *in* or *into* ⟨was ~*ed* into the army⟩ **c :** to call the roll of **2 a :** to bring together **:** COLLECT **b :** to call forth **:** ROUSE **3 :** to amount to **:** COMPRISE **~** *vi* **:** to come together **:** CONGREGATE ***syn*** see SUMMON

[2]**muster** *n* (15c) **1 :** a representative specimen **:** SAMPLE **2 a :** an act of assembling; *specif* **:** formal military inspection **b :** critical examination **c :** an assembled group **:** COLLECTION **d :** INVENTORY

muster out *vt* (1834) **:** to discharge from service

muster roll *n* (1605) **:** INVENTORY, ROSTER; *specif* **:** a register of the officers and men in a military unit or ship's company

musth *or* **must** \ˈməst\ *n* [Hindi *mast* intoxicated, fr. Per; akin to OE *mete* meat] (1878) **:** a periodic state of frenzy of the bull elephant usu. connected with the rutting season

mustn't \ˈməs-ᵊnt\ **:** must not

musty \ˈməs-tē\ *adj* **must·i·er; -est** (1530) **1 a :** impaired by damp or mildew **:** MOLDY **b :** tasting of mold **c :** smelling of damp and decay **:** FUSTY **2 a :** TRITE, STALE **b** (1) **:** ANTIQUATED (2) **:** SUPERANNUATED ***syn*** see MALODOROUS — **must·i·ly** \ˈməs-tə-lē\ *adv* — **must·i·ness** \-tē-nəs\ *n*

mu·ta·ble \ˈmyüt-ə-bəl\ *adj* [L *mutabilis,* fr. *mutare* to change — more at MISS] (14c) **1 :** prone to change **:** INCONSTANT **2 a :** capable of change or of being changed in form, quality, or nature **b :** capable of or liable to mutation — **mu·ta·bil·i·ty** \ˌmyüt-ə-ˈbil-ət-ē\ *n* — **mu·ta·bly** \ˈmyüt-ə-blē\ *adv*

mu·ta·gen \ˈmyüt-ə-jən\ *n* [ISV *mutation* + *-gen*] (1933) **:** an agent (as mustard gas or various radiations) that tends to increase the frequency or extent of mutation — **mu·ta·gen·ic** \ˌmyüt-ə-ˈjen-ik\ *adj* — **mu·ta·gen·i·cal·ly** \-i-k(ə-)lē\ *adv*

mu·ta·gen·e·sis \ˌmyüt-ə-ˈjen-ə-səs\ *n* [NL] (1948) **:** the occurrence or induction of mutation

mu·ta·ge·nic·i·ty \-jə-ˈnis-ət-ē\ *n* (1956) **:** the capacity to induce mutations

mu·tant \ˈmyüt-ᵊnt\ *adj* [L *mutant-, mutans,* prp. of *mutare*] (1903) **:** of, relating to, or produced by mutation — **mutant** *n*

mu·tase \ˈmyü-ˌtās, -ˌtāz\ *n* [ISV *mut-* (fr. L *mutare*) + *-ase*] (1938) **:** any of various enzymes that catalyze molecular rearrangements and esp. those involving the transfer of phosphate from one hydroxyl group to another in the same molecule

mu·tate \ˈmyü-ˌtāt, myü-ˈ\ *vb* **mu·tat·ed; mu·tat·ing** [L *mutatus,* pp. of *mutare*] *vi* (1818) **:** to undergo mutation **~** *vt* **:** to cause to undergo mutation — **mu·ta·tive** \ˈmyü-ˌtāt-iv, ˈmyüt-ət-\ *adj*

mu·ta·tion \myü-'tā-shən\ *n* (14c) **1 :** a significant and basic alteration **:** CHANGE **2 :** UMLAUT **3 a :** a relatively permanent change in hereditary material involving either a physical change in chromosome relations or a biochemical change in the codons that make up genes; *also* **:** the process of producing a mutation **b :** an individual strain or trait resulting from mutation — **mu·ta·tion·al** \-shnəl, -shən-ᵊl\ *adj* — **mu·ta·tion·al·ly** \-ē\ *adv*
mu·ta·tis mu·tan·dis \mü-ˌtät-ə-smü-'tän-dəs\ *adv* [NL] (15c) **1 :** with the necessary changes having been made **2 :** with the respective differences having been considered
mutch·kin \'məch-kən\ *n* [ME (Sc) *muchekyn*] (15c) **:** a Scotch unit of liquid capacity equal to 0.90 pint (0.42 liter)
¹**mute** \'myüt\ *adj* **mut·er; mut·est** [ME *muet,* fr. MF, fr. OF *mu,* fr. L *mutus;* akin to OHG *māwen* to cry out, Gk *mytēs* mute, *myein* to be closed] (14c) **1 :** unable to speak **:** DUMB **2 :** characterized by absence of speech: as **a :** felt or experienced but not expressed ⟨touched her hand in ~ sympathy⟩ **b :** refusing to plead directly or stand trial ⟨the prisoner stands ~⟩ **3 a :** contributing nothing to the pronunciation of a word ⟨the *b* in *plumb* is ~⟩ **b :** contributing to the pronunciation of a word but not representing the nucleus of a syllable ⟨the *e* in *mate* is ~⟩ — **mute·ly** *adv* — **mute·ness** *n*
²**mute** *n* (1530) **1 :** STOP 9 **2 :** a person who cannot or does not speak **3 :** a device attached to a musical instrument to reduce, soften, or muffle its tone

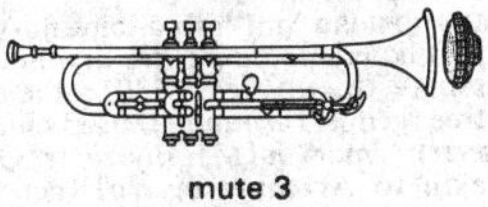
mute 3

³**mute** *vt* **mut·ed; mut·ing** (1883) **1 :** to muffle or reduce the sound of **2 :** to tone down **:** SOFTEN, SUBDUE ⟨~ a color⟩
⁴**mute** *vi* **mut·ed; mut·ing** [ME *muten,* fr. MF *meutir*] *of a bird* (15c) **:** to evacuate the cloaca
mut·ed \'myüt-əd\ *adj* (1861) **1 :** provided with or produced or modified by the use of a mute **2 a :** being mute **:** SILENT **b :** LOW-KEY, SUBDUED — **mut·ed·ly** *adv*
mute swan *n* (1785) **:** the common white swan (*Cygnus olor*) of Europe and western Asia that produces no loud notes
mu·ti·late \'myüt-ᵊl-ˌāt\ *vt* **-lat·ed; -lat·ing** [L *mutilatus,* pp. of *mutilare,* fr. *mutilus* truncated, maimed] (1532) **1 :** to cut off or permanently destroy a limb or essential part of **:** CRIPPLE **2 :** to cut up or alter radically so as to make imperfect ⟨the child *mutilated* the book with his scissors⟩ ***syn*** see MAIM — **mu·ti·la·tion** \ˌmyüt-ᵊl-'ā-shən\ *n* — **mu·ti·la·tor** \'myüt-ᵊl-ˌāt-ər\ *n*
mu·tine \'myüt-ᵊn\ *vi* **mu·tined; mu·tin·ing** [MF (*se*) *mutiner*] *obs* (1555) **:** REBEL, MUTINY
mu·ti·neer \ˌmyüt-ᵊn-'i(ə)r\ *n* (1610) **:** one that mutinies
mu·ti·nous \'myüt-ᵊn-əs, 'myüt-nəs\ *adj* (1578) **1 a :** disposed to or in a state of mutiny **:** REBELLIOUS **b :** TURBULENT, UNRULY **2 :** of, relating to, or constituting mutiny — **mu·ti·nous·ly** *adv* — **mu·ti·nous·ness** *n*
mu·ti·ny \'myüt-ᵊn-ē, 'myüt-nē\ *n, pl* **-nies** [*mutine* to rebel, fr. MF (*se*) *mutiner,* fr. *mutin* mutinous, fr. *meute* revolt, fr. (assumed) VL *movita,* fr. fem. of *movitus,* alter. of L *motus,* pp. of *movēre* to move] (1567) **1** *obs* **:** TUMULT, STRIFE **2 :** forcible or passive resistance to lawful authority; *esp* **:** concerted revolt (as of a naval crew) against discipline or a superior officer ***syn*** see REBELLION — **mutiny** *vi*
mut·ism \'myüt-ˌiz-əm\ *n* [F *mutisme,* fr. L *mutus* mute] (1824) **:** the condition of being mute
mutt \'mət\ *n* [short for *muttonhead* (dull-witted person)] (1901) **1 :** a stupid or insignificant person **:** FOOL **2 :** a mongrel dog **:** CUR
mut·ter \'mət-ər\ *vb* [ME *muteren;* akin to L *muttire* to mutter, *mutus* mute] *vi* (14c) **1 :** to utter sounds or words indistinctly or with a low voice and with the lips partly closed **2 :** to murmur complainingly or angrily **:** GRUMBLE ~ *vt* **:** to utter esp. in a low or imperfectly articulated manner — **mutter** *n* — **mut·ter·er** \-ər-ər\ *n*
mut·ton \'mət-ᵊn\ *n* [ME *motoun,* fr. OF *moton* ram, wether, of Celt origin; akin to MBret *mout* wether] (13c) **:** the flesh of a mature sheep used for food — **mut·tony** \'mət-ᵊn-ē, -nē\ *adj*
mut·ton·chops \'mət-ᵊn-ˌchäps\ *n pl* (1865) **:** side-whiskers that are narrow at the temple and broad and round by the lower jaws — called also *muttonchop whiskers*
mut·ton·fish \-ˌfish\ *n* [fr. its flavor] (1735) **:** a common snapper (*Lutjanus analis*) of the warmer parts of the western Atlantic that is usu. olive green and sometimes nearly white or tinged with rosy red and that is a commercially important food and sport fish — called also *mutton snapper*
mu·tu·al \'myüch-(ə-)wəl, 'myü-chəl\ *adj* [ME, fr. MF *mutuel,* fr. L *mutuus* lent, borrowed, mutual; akin to L *mutare* to change — more at MISS] (15c) **1 a :** directed by each toward the other or the others ⟨~ affection⟩ **b :** having the same feelings one for the other ⟨they had long been ~ enemies⟩ **c :** shared in common ⟨enjoying their ~ hobby⟩ **d :** JOINT **2 :** characterized by intimacy **3 :** of or relating to a plan whereby the members of an organization share in the profits and expenses; *specif* **:** of, relating to, or taking the form of an insurance method in which the policyholders constitute the members of the insuring company — **mu·tu·al·ly** \-ē\ *adv*
mutual fund *n* (1950) **:** an open-end investment company that invests money of its shareholders in a usu. diversified group of securities of other corporations
mu·tu·al·ism \'myüch-(ə-)wə-ˌliz-əm, 'myü-chə-ˌliz-\ *n* (1849) **1 :** the doctrine or practice of mutual dependence as the condition of individual and social welfare **2 :** mutually beneficial association between different kinds of organisms — **mu·tu·al·ist** \-ləst\ *n* — **mu·tu·al·is·tic** \ˌmyüch-(ə-)wə-'lis-tik, ˌmyü-chə-'lis-\ *adj*
mu·tu·al·i·ty \ˌmyü-chə-'wal-ət-ē\ *n* (ca. 1586) **1 :** the quality or state of being mutual **2 :** a sharing of sentiments **:** INTIMACY
mu·tu·al·ize \'myüch-(ə-)wə-ˌlīz, 'myü-chə-ˌlīz\ *vt* **-ized; -iz·ing** (1812) **:** to make mutual — **mu·tu·al·iza·tion** \ˌmyüch-(ə-)wə-lə-'zā-shən, ˌmyü-chə-lə-\ *n*
mutually exclusive *adj* (1874) **:** being related such that each excludes or precludes the other ⟨*mutually exclusive* events⟩; *also* **:** INCOMPATIBLE ⟨their outlooks were not *mutually exclusive*⟩
mutuel *n* (1908) **:** PARI-MUTUEL
muu·muu \'mü-ˌmü\ *n* [Hawaiian *mu'umu'u,* fr. *mu'umu'u* cut off] (1923) **:** a loose often long dress having bright colors and patterns and adapted from the dresses orig. distributed by missionaries to the native women of Hawaii
Mu·zak \'myü-ˌzak\ *trademark* — used for recorded background music that is transmitted by wire to the loudspeaker of a subscriber (as an office or restaurant)
mu·zhik \mü-'zhēk, -'zhik\ *n* [Russ] (1568) **:** a Russian peasant
¹**muz·zle** \'məz-əl\ *n* [ME *musell,* fr. MF *musel,* fr. dim. of *muse* mouth of an animal, fr. ML *musus*] (15c) **1 :** the projecting jaws and nose of an animal **:** SNOUT — see DOG illustration **2 a :** a fastening or covering for the mouth of an animal used to prevent eating or biting **b :** something (as censorship) that restrains normal expression **3 :** the open end of an implement; *esp* **:** the discharging end of a weapon
²**muzzle** *vt* **muz·zled; muz·zling** \-(ə-)liŋ\ (15c) **1 :** to fit with a muzzle **2 :** to restrain from expression **:** GAG — **muz·zler** \-(ə-)lər\ *n*
muz·zy \'məz-ē\ *adj* **muz·zi·er; -est** [perh. blend of *muddled* and *fuzzy*] (1728) **1 :** muddled or confused in mind **2 a :** lacking in clarity and precision ⟨his conclusions can be ~ and naive —*Times Lit. Supp.*⟩ **b :** deficient in brightness **:** DULL, GLOOMY ⟨a ~ day⟩ — **muz·zi·ly** \'məz-ə-lē\ *adv* — **muz·zi·ness** \'məz-ē-nəs\ *n*
MX \ˌem-'eks\ *n* [missile, experimental] (1976) **:** an experimental mobile ICBM having up to 10 independently targeted nuclear warheads
my \(ˈ)mī, mə\ *adj* [ME, fr. OE *mīn,* fr. *mīn,* suppletive gen. of *ic* I; akin to OE *mē* me] (12c) **1 :** of or relating to me or myself esp. as possessor, agent, or object of an action ⟨~ car⟩ ⟨~ promise⟩ ⟨~ injuries⟩ **2** — used interjectionally to express surprise and sometimes reduplicated ⟨~ oh ~⟩; used also interjectionally with names of various parts of the body to express doubt or disapproval ⟨~ foot⟩
my- *or* **myo-** *comb form* [NL, fr. Gk, fr. *mys* mouse, muscle — more at MOUSE] **:** muscle ⟨*myo*graph⟩ **:** muscle and ⟨*myo*neural⟩
my·al·gia \mī-'al-j(ē-)ə\ *n* [NL] (1860) **:** pain in one or more muscles — **my·al·gic** \-jik\ *adj*
my·as·the·nia \ˌmī-əs-'thē-nē-ə\ *n* [NL] (ca. 1856) **:** muscular debility — **my·as·then·ic** \-'then-ik\ *adj or n*
myasthenia gra·vis \-'grav-əs, -'gräv-\ *n* [NL, lit., grave myasthenia] (1900) **:** a disease characterized by progressive weakness and exhaustibility of voluntary muscles without atrophy or sensory disturbance and caused by a defect in the neuromuscular junction
myc- *or* **myco-** *comb form* [NL, fr. Gk *mykēt-, mykēs* fungus; akin to Gk *myxa* nasal mucus] **:** fungus ⟨*myco*logy⟩ ⟨*myc*osis⟩
my·ce·li·um \mī-'sē-lē-əm\ *n, pl* **-lia** \-lē-ə\ [NL, fr. *myc-* + Gk *hēlos* nail, wart, callus] (1836) **:** the mass of interwoven filamentous hyphae that forms esp. the vegetative portion of the thallus of a fungus and is often submerged in another body (as of soil or organic matter or the tissues of a host); *also* **:** a similar mass of filaments formed by a higher bacterium — **my·ce·li·al** \-əl\ *adj*
My·ce·nae·an \ˌmī-sə-'nē-ən\ *also* **My·ce·ni·an** \mī-'sē-nē-ən\ *adj* (1598) **1 :** of, relating to, or characteristic of Mycenae, its people, or the period (1400 to 1100 B.C.) of Mycenae's political ascendancy **2 :** characteristic of the Bronze Age Mycenaean culture of the eastern Mediterranean area — **Mycenaean** *n*
my·ce·to·ma \ˌmī-sə-'tō-mə\ *n, pl* **-mas** *or* **-ma·ta** \-mət-ə\ [NL, fr. Gk *mykēt-, mykēs*] (1874) **:** a condition marked by invasion of the deep subcutaneous tissues with fungi or actinomycetes; *also* **:** a tumorous mass occurring in such a condition — **my·ce·to·ma·tous** \-mət-əs\ *adj*
my·ce·toph·a·gous \ˌmī-sə-'täf-ə-gəs\ *adj* [Gk *mykēt-, mykēs* + E *-phagous*] (ca. 18[illegible]) **:** feeding on fungi
my·ce·to·zo·an \mī-ˌsēt-ə-'zō-ən\ *n* [NL *Mycetozoa,* order of protozoans, fr. Gk *mykēt-, mykēs* + NL *-zoa*] (1881) **:** SLIME MOLD — **mycetozoan** *adj*
-my·cin \'mīs-ᵊn\ *n comb form* [*streptomycin*] **:** substance obtained from a fungus-like bacterium ⟨erythro*mycin*⟩
my·co·bac·te·ri·um \ˌmī-kō-bak-'tir-ē-əm\ *n* [NL] (1909) **:** any of a genus (*Mycobacterium*) of nonmotile aerobic bacteria that are difficult to stain and include numerous saprophytes and the organisms causing tuberculosis and leprosy — **my·co·bac·te·ri·al** \-ē-əl\ *adj*
my·co·flo·ra \ˌmī-kə-'flōr-ə, -'flȯr-\ *n* [NL] (1945) **:** the fungi characteristic of a region or special environment
my·col·o·gy \mī-'käl-ə-jē\ *n* [NL *mycologia,* fr. *myc-* + L *-logia* -logy] (1836) **1 :** a branch of botany dealing with fungi **2 :** fungal life — **my·co·log·i·cal** \ˌmī-kə-'läj-i-kəl\ *adj* — **my·co·log·i·cal·ly** \ˌmī-kə-'läj-i-k(ə-)lē\ *adv* — **my·col·o·gist** \mī-'käl-ə-jəst\ *n*
my·coph·a·gist \mī-'käf-ə-jəst\ *n* [*mycophagy,* fr. *myc-* + *-phagy*] (1861) **:** one that eats fungi (as mushrooms) — **my·coph·a·gy** \-jē\ *n*
my·coph·a·gous \-ə-gəs\ *adj* (ca. 1909) **:** feeding on fungi
my·co·phile \'mī-kō-ˌfīl\ *n* (1953) **:** a person whose hobby is hunting wild edible mushrooms
my·co·plas·ma \ˌmī-kō-'plaz-mə\ *n, pl* **-mas** *or* **-ma·ta** \-mət-ə\ [NL] (1955) **:** any of a genus (*Mycoplasma*) of minute pleomorphic gram-negative nonmotile microorganisms without cell walls that are intermediate in some respects between viruses and bacteria and are mostly parasitic usu. in mammals — called also *pleuropneumonia-like organism* — **my·co·plas·mal** \-məl\ *adj*
my·cor·rhi·za \ˌmī-kə-'rī-zə\ *n, pl* **-zae** \-ˌzē\ *or* **-zas** [NL, fr. *myc-* + Gk *rhiza* root — more at ROOT] (1895) **:** the symbiotic association of the mycelium of a fungus with the roots of a seed plant — **my·cor·rhi·zal** \-zəl\ *adj*
my·co·sis \mī-'kō-səs\ *n, pl* **my·co·ses** \-ˌsēz\ [NL] (1876) **:** infection with or disease caused by a fungus — **my·cot·ic** \-'kät-ik\ *adj*
my·co·tox·in \ˌmī-kə-'täk-sən\ *n* (1962) **:** a toxic substance produced by a fungus and esp. a mold
my·dri·a·sis \mə-'drī-ə-səs\ *n* [L, fr. Gk] (ca. 1657) **:** a long-continued or excessive dilatation of the pupil of the eye — **myd·ri·at·ic** \ˌmid-rē-'at-ik\ *adj or n*
myel- *or* **myelo-** *comb form* [NL, fr. Gk, fr. *myelos,* fr. *mys* mouse, muscle — more at MOUSE] **:** marrow **:** spinal cord ⟨*myel*encephalon⟩
my·el·en·ceph·a·lon \ˌmī-ə-len-'sef-ə-ˌlän, -lən\ *n* [NL] (1871) **:** the posterior portion of the rhombencephalon: **a :** MEDULLA OBLONGATA **b**

: the posterior part of the medulla oblongata that is continuous with the spinal cord — **my·el·en·ce·phal·ic** \-ˌlen(t)-sə-ˈfal-ik\ *adj*

my·elin \ˈmī-ə-lən\ *n* [ISV] (1873) : a soft white somewhat fatty material that forms a thick myelin sheath about the protoplasmic core of a myelinated nerve fiber — **my·elin·ic** \ˌmī-ə-ˈlin-ik\ *adj*

my·elin·at·ed \ˈmī-ə-lə-ˌnāt-əd\ *adj* (1899) : having a myelin sheath ⟨~ nerve fibers⟩

myelin sheath *n* (1896) : a layer of myelin surrounding some nerve fibers — called also *medullary sheath*

my·eli·tis \ˌmī-ə-ˈlīt-əs\ *n, pl* **-elit·i·des** \-ə-ˈlit-ə-ˌdēz\ [NL] (1835) : inflammation of the spinal cord or of the bone marrow

my·elo·blast \ˈmī-ə-lə-ˌblast\ *n* [ISV] (ca. 1904) : a large mononuclear nongranular bone-marrow cell; *esp* : one that is a precursor of a myelocyte — **my·elo·blas·tic** \ˌmī-ə-lə-ˈblas-tik\ *adj*

my·elo·cyte \ˈmī-ə-lə-ˌsīt\ *n* [ISV] (1891) : a bone-marrow cell; *esp* : a motile cell with cytoplasmic granules that gives rise to the granulocytes of the blood and occurs abnormally in the circulating blood — **my·elo·cyt·ic** \ˌmī-ə-lə-ˈsit-ik\ *adj*

my·elo·fi·bro·sis \ˌmī-ə-lō-fī-ˈbrō-səs\ *n* [NL] (1947) : an anemic condition in which bone marrow becomes fibrotic and the liver and spleen usu. exhibit a development of blood-cell precursors — **my·elo·fi·brot·ic** \-ˈbrät-ik\ *adj*

my·elog·e·nous \ˌmī-ə-ˈläj-ə-nəs\ *adj* [ISV] (1876) : of, relating to, originating in, or produced by the bone marrow ⟨~ sarcoma⟩

myelogenous leukemia *n* (1904) : leukemia characterized by proliferation of myeloid tissue (as of the bone marrow and spleen) and an abnormal increase in the number of granulocytes, myelocytes, and myeloblasts in the circulating blood — called also *myelocytic leukemia, myeloid leukemia*

my·eloid \ˈmī-ə-ˌlȯid\ *adj* [ISV] (1857) : of, relating to, or resembling bone marrow

my·elo·ma \ˌmī-ə-ˈlō-mə\ *n* [NL] (ca. 1857) : a primary tumor of the bone marrow — **my·elo·ma·tous** \-mət-əs\ *adj*

my·elop·a·thy \-ˈläp-ə-thē\ *n* [ISV] (ca. 1891) : a disease or disorder of the spinal cord or bone marrow — **my·elo·path·ic** \ˌmī-ə-lō-ˈpath-ik\ *adj*

my·elo·pro·lif·er·a·tive \ˈmī-ə-lō-prə-ˈlif-ə-ˌrāt-iv, -rət-\ *adj* (1951) : of, relating to, or being a disorder (as leukemia) marked by excessive proliferation of bone marrow elements and esp. blood cell precursors

my·ia·sis \mī-ˈī-ə-səs, mē-\ *n, pl* **my·ia·ses** \-ˌsēz\ [NL, fr. Gk *myia* fly — more at MIDGE] (1837) : infestation with fly maggots

my·nah *or* **my·na** \ˈmī-nə\ *n* [Hindi *mainā*, fr. Skt *madana*] (1769) : any of various Asian starlings (esp. genera *Acridotheres, Gracula,* and *Sturnus*); *esp* : a dark brown slightly crested bird (*A. tristis*) of southeastern Asia with a white tail tip and wing markings and bright yellow bill and feet

myn·heer \mə-ˈne(ə)r\ *n* [D *mijnheer*, fr. *mijn* my + *heer* master, sir] (1652) : a male Netherlander — used as a title equivalent to *Mr.*

myo- — see MY-

myo·blast \ˈmī-ə-ˌblast\ *n* [ISV] (1884) : an undifferentiated cell capable of giving rise to muscle cells

myo·car·di·tis \ˌmī-ə-(ˌ)kär-ˈdīt-əs\ *n* [NL] (1866) : inflammation of the myocardium

myo·car·di·um \ˌmī-ə-ˈkärd-ē-əm\ *n* [NL, fr. *my-* + Gk *kardia* heart — more at HEART] (1879) : the middle muscular layer of the heart wall — **myo·car·di·al** \-ē-əl\ *adj*

myo·elec·tric \ˌmī-ō-i-ˈlek-trik\ *also* **myo·elec·tri·cal** \-tri-kəl\ *adj* (ca. 1919) : of, relating to, or utilizing electricity generated by muscle

myo·fi·bril \ˌmī-ō-ˈfīb-rəl, -ˈfib-\ *n* [NL *myofibrilla*, fr. *my-* + *fibrilla* fibril] (1898) : any of the longitudinal parallel contractile elements of a muscle cell that are composed of myosin and actin — **myo·fi·bril·lar** \-rə-lər\ *adj*

myo·fil·a·ment \-ˈfil-ə-mənt\ *n* (1949) : one of the individual filaments of actin or myosin that make up a myofibril

myo·gen·ic \ˌmī-ə-ˈjen-ik\ *adj* [ISV] (1904) : taking place or functioning in ordered rhythmic fashion because of inherent properties of cardiac muscle rather than by reason of specific neural stimuli ⟨a ~ heartbeat⟩

myo·glo·bin \-ˈglō-bən, ˈmī-ə-ˌ\ *n* [ISV] (1925) : a red iron-containing protein pigment in muscles that is similar to hemoglobin

myo·ino·si·tol \ˌmī-ō-in-ˈō-sə-ˌtȯl, -ˌtōl\ *n* (1951) : an optically inactive inositol that is a component of the vitamin B complex and a lipotropic agent and that occurs widely in plants, microorganisms, and higher animals including man

my·ol·o·gy \mī-ˈäl-ə-jē\ *n* [F or NL; F *myologie*, fr. NL *myologia*, fr. *my-* + L *-logia* -logy] (1649) : a scientific study of muscles

my·o·ma \mī-ˈō-mə\ *n, pl* **-mas** *or* **-ma·ta** \-mət-ə\ [NL] (1875) : a tumor consisting of muscle tissue — **my·o·ma·tous** \-mət-əs\ *adj*

myo·neu·ral \ˌmī-ə-ˈn(y)u̇r-əl\ *adj* (1905) : of, relating to, or connecting muscles and nerves ⟨~ junctions⟩

my·op·a·thy \mī-ˈäp-ə-thē\ *n* [ISV] (ca. 1849) : a disorder of muscle tissue or muscles — **myo·path·ic** \ˌmī-ə-ˈpath-ik\ *adj*

my·ope \ˈmī-ˌōp\ *n* [F, fr. LL *myops* myopic, fr. Gk *myōps*, fr. *myein* to be closed + *ōps* eye, face — more at MUTE, EYE] (1728) : a myopic person

my·o·pia \mī-ˈō-pē-ə\ *n* [NL, fr. Gk *myōpia*, fr. *myōp-, myōps*] (ca. 1693) **1** : a condition in which the visual images come to a focus in front of the retina of the eye resulting esp. in defective vision of distant objects **2** : a lack of foresight or discernment : a narrow view of something — **my·o·pic** \-ˈō-pik, -ˈäp-ik\ *adj* — **my·o·pi·cal·ly** \-(ə-)lē\ *adv*

my·o·sin \ˈmī-ə-sən\ *n* [ISV *myos-* (fr. Gk *myos*, gen. of *mys* mouse, muscle)] (1869) **1** : ACTOMYOSIN **2** : a fibrous globulin of muscle that can split ATP and that reacts with actin to form actomyosin

my·o·sis, my·ot·ic *var of* MIOSIS, MIOTIC

myo·si·tis \ˌmī-ə-ˈsīt-əs\ *n* [ISV *myos-* + *-itis*] (ca. 1819) : muscular discomfort or pain from infection or an unknown cause

myo·tome \ˈmī-ə-ˌtōm\ *n* [ISV] (1894) : the portion of an embryonic somite from which skeletal musculature is produced

myo·to·nia \ˌmī-ə-ˈtō-nē-ə\ *n* [NL] (1896) : tonic spasm of one or more muscles; *also* : a condition characterized by such spasms — **myo·ton·ic** \-ˈtän-ik\ *adj*

[1]**myr·i·ad** \ˈmir-ē-əd\ *n* [Gk *myriad-, myrias*, fr. *myrioi* countless, ten thousand] (1555) **1** : ten thousand **2** : a great number

[2]**myriad** *adj* (ca. 1800) **1** : INNUMERABLE **2** : having innumerable aspects or elements ⟨the ~ activity of the new land —Meridel Le Sueur⟩

myr·ia·pod *also* **myr·io·pod** \ˈmir-ē-ə-ˌpäd\ *n* [deriv. of Gk *myrioi* + *pod-, pous* foot — more at FOOT] (1826) : any of a group (Myriapoda) of arthropods having the body made up of numerous similar segments nearly all of which bear true jointed legs and including the millipedes and centipedes — **myriapod** *also* **myriopod** *adj*

my·ris·tic acid \mə-ˌris-tik-, mī-\ *n* [ISV, fr. NL *Myristica*, genus of trees] (1848) : a crystalline fatty acid $C_{14}H_{28}O_2$ occurring esp. in the form of glycerides in most fats

myrmec- *or* **myrmeco-** *comb form* [Gk *myrmēk-, myrmēko-*, fr. *myrmēk-, myrmēx* — more at PISMIRE] : ant ⟨*myrmec*ophagous⟩

myr·me·col·o·gy \ˌmər-mə-ˈkäl-ə-jē\ *n* [ISV] (ca. 1902) : the scientific study of ants — **myr·me·co·log·i·cal** \-kə-ˈläj-i-kəl\ *adj* — **myr·me·col·o·gist** \-ˈkäl-ə-jəst\ *n*

myr·meco·phile \ˈmər-mi-kə-ˌfīl\ *n* [ISV] (1898) : an organism that habitually shares an ant nest

myr·me·coph·i·lous \ˌmər-mə-ˈkäf-ə-ləs\ *adj* (1866) : fond of, associated with, or benefited by ants

myr·mi·don \ˈmər-mə-ˌdän, -məd-ən\ *n* [L *Myrmidon-, Myrmido*, fr. Gk *Myrmidōn*] (15c) **1** *cap* : a member of a legendary Thessalian people who accompanied their king Achilles in the Trojan War **2** : a loyal follower; *esp* : a subordinate who executes orders unquestioningly or unscrupulously

my·rob·a·lan \mī-ˈräb-ə-lən, mə-\ *n* [MF *mirobolan*, fr. L *myrobalanus*, fr. Gk *myrobalanos*, fr. *myron* unguent + *balanos* acorn — more at SMEAR, GLAND] (ca. 1530) : the dried astringent fruit of an East Indian tree (genus *Terminalia*) used chiefly in tanning and in inks

myrrh \ˈmər\ *n* [ME *myrre*, fr. OE, fr. L *myrrha*, fr. Gk, of Sem origin; akin to Ar *murr* myrrh] (bef. 12c) : a yellowish brown to reddish brown aromatic gum resin with a bitter slightly pungent taste obtained from a tree (esp. *Commiphora abyssinica*) of east Africa and Arabia; *also* : a mixture of myrrh and labdanum

myr·tle \ˈmərt-ᵊl\ *n, often attrib* [ME *mirtille*, fr. MF, fr. ML *myrtillus*, fr. L *myrtus*, fr. Gk *myrtos*] (15c) **1 a** : a common evergreen bushy shrub (*Myrtus communis*) of southern Europe with oval to lance-shaped shiny leaves, fragrant white or rosy flowers, and black berries **b** : any of a family (Myrtaceae, the myrtle family) of chiefly tropical shrubs or trees to which the common myrtle belongs **2 a** : [1]PERIWINKLE a **b** : CALIFORNIA LAUREL

my·self \mī-ˈself, mə-, *Southern also* -ˈsef\ *pron* (bef. 12c) **1** : that identical one that is I — used reflexively ⟨I'm going to get ~ a new suit⟩, for emphasis ⟨I ~ will go⟩, or in absolute constructions ⟨~ a tourist, I nevertheless avoided other tourists⟩ **2** : my normal, healthy, or sane condition ⟨didn't feel ~ yesterday⟩

usage *Myself* is often used where *I* or *me* might be expected: as subject ⟨to wonder what *myself* will say —Emily Dickinson⟩ ⟨others and *myself* continued to press for the legislation⟩, after *as* or *than* ⟨an aversion to paying such people as *myself* to tutor⟩ ⟨was enough to make a better man than *myself* quail⟩, and as object ⟨now here you see *myself* with the diver⟩ ⟨for my wife and *myself* it was a happy time⟩ These uses have been frowned on by various critics since about the turn of the century. What is wrong with them is not clear; commentators have labeled them snobbish, unstylish, self-indulgent, self-conscious, old-fashioned, colloquial, informal, formal, nonstandard, literary, and unacceptable in formal written English. The least questioned uses seem to be after *as* or *than* and as part of a compound object of a verb or preposition. Still, if you use any of these constructions you may incur disapproval on some grounds or other. At least you will be in good company. Many admirable writers of the past — including Shakespeare, Milton, Washington, Jefferson, Franklin, Johnson, Boswell, Tennyson, Poe, Lamb, and Stevenson — have used *myself* in these ways.

mys·ta·gogue \ˈmis-tə-ˌgäg\ *n* [L *mystagogus*, fr. Gk *mystagōgos*, fr. *mystēs* initiate (akin to Gk *myein* to be closed) + *agein* to lead — more at MUTE, AGENT] (ca. 1550) **1** : one who initiates another into a mystery cult **2** : one who understands or teaches mystical doctrines — **mys·ta·go·gy** \-ˌgäj-ē, -ˌgō-jē\ *n*

mys·te·ri·ous \mis-ˈtir-ē-əs\ *adj* (ca. 1616) **1 a** : of, relating to, or constituting mystery ⟨the ~ ways of God⟩ **b** : exciting wonder, curiosity, or surprise while baffling efforts to comprehend or identify : MYSTIFYING ⟨heard a ~ noise⟩ ⟨a ~ stranger⟩ **2** : stirred by or attracted to the inexplicable — **mys·te·ri·ous·ly** *adv* — **mys·te·ri·ous·ness** *n*

[1]**mys·tery** \ˈmis-t(ə-)rē\ *n, pl* **-ter·ies** [ME *mysterie*, fr. L *mysterium*, fr. Gk *mystērion*, fr. (assumed) *mystos* keeping silence, fr. Gk *myein* to be closed (of the eyes or lips) — more at MUTE] (14c) **1 a** : a religious truth that one can know only by revelation and cannot fully understand **b** (1) : any of the 15 events (as the Nativity, the Crucifixion, or the Assumption) serving as a subject for meditation during the saying of the rosary (2) *cap* : a Christian sacrament; *specif* : EUCHARIST **c** (1) : a secret religious rite believed (as in Eleusinian and Mithraic cults) to impart enduring bliss to the initiate (2) : a cult devoted to such rites **2 a** : something not understood or beyond understanding : ENIGMA **b** *obs* : a private secret **c** : the secret or specialized practices or ritual peculiar to an occupation or a body of people ⟨the *mysteries* of the tailor's craft⟩ **d** : a piece of fiction dealing usu. with the solution of a mysterious crime **3** : profound, inexplicable, or secretive quality or character ⟨the ~ of her smile⟩

syn MYSTERY, PROBLEM, ENIGMA, RIDDLE, PUZZLE, CONUNDRUM mean something which baffles or perplexes. MYSTERY applies to what cannot be fully understood by human reason or less strictly to whatever resists or defies explanation; PROBLEM applies to any question or difficulty calling for a solution or causing concern; ENIGMA applies to utterance or behavior that is very difficult to interpret; RIDDLE suggests an enigma or problem involving paradox or apparent contradiction; PUZZLE applies to an enigma or problem that challenges ingenuity for its solution; CONUNDRUM applies to a question whose answer involves a pun or less often to a problem whose solution can only be speculative.

[2]**mystery** *n, pl* **-ter·ies** [ME, fr. LL *misterium, mysterium*, alter. of *ministerium* service, occupation, fr. *minister* servant — more at MINISTER] (14c) **1** *archaic* : TRADE, CRAFT **2** *archaic* : a body of persons engaged in a particular trade, business, or profession : GUILD **3** : MYSTERY PLAY

mystery play *n* [²*mystery*] (1852) : a medieval drama based on scriptural incidents (as the creation of the world, the Flood, or the life, death, and resurrection of Christ) — compare MIRACLE PLAY

¹**mys·tic** \'mis-tik\ *adj* [ME mistik, fr. L *mysticus* of mysteries, fr. Gk *mystikos*, fr. (assumed) *mystos*] (14c) **1** : MYSTICAL **1a 2** : of or relating to mysteries or esoteric rites : OCCULT **3** : of or relating to mysticism or mystics **4 a** : MYSTERIOUS **b** : OBSCURE, ENIGMATIC **c** : inducing a feeling of awe or wonder **d** : having magical properties

²**mystic** *n* (1679) **1** : a follower of a mystical way of life **2** : an advocate of a theory of mysticism

mys·ti·cal \'mis-ti-kəl\ *adj* (15c) **1 a** : having a spiritual meaning or reality that is neither apparent to the senses nor obvious to the intelligence ⟨the ∼ food of the sacrament⟩ **b** : involving or having the nature of an individual's direct subjective communion with God or ultimate reality ⟨the ∼ experience of the Inner Light⟩ **2** : MYSTERIOUS, UNINTELLIGIBLE **3** : MYSTIC 2, 3 — **mys·ti·cal·ly** \-k(ə-)lē\ *adv*

mys·ti·cism \'mis-tə-ˌsiz-əm\ *n* (1736) **1** : the experience of mystical union or direct communion with ultimate reality reported by mystics **2** : the belief that direct knowledge of God, spiritual truth, or ultimate reality can be attained through subjective experience (as intuition or insight) **3 a** : vague speculation : a belief without sound basis **b** : a theory postulating the possibility of direct and intuitive acquisition of ineffable knowledge or power

mys·ti·fi·ca·tion \ˌmis-tə-fə-'kā-shən\ *n* (1815) **1** : an act or instance of mystifying **2** : the quality or state of being mystified **3** : something designed to mystify

mys·ti·fy \'mis-tə-ˌfī\ *vt* **-fied; -fy·ing** [F *mistifier*, fr. *mystère* mystery, fr. L *mysterium*] (ca. 1734) **1** : to perplex the mind of : BEWILDER **2** : to make mysterious or obscure ⟨∼ an interpretation of a prophecy⟩ — **mys·ti·fi·er** \-ˌfī(-ə)r\ *n* — **mys·ti·fy·ing·ly** \-ˌfī-iŋ-lē\ *adv*

mys·tique \mis-'tēk\ *n* [F, fr. *mystique*, adj., mystic, fr. L *mysticus*] (1891) : an air or attitude of mystery and reverence developing around something

myth \'mith\ *n* [Gk *mythos*] (1830) **1 a** : a usu. traditional story of ostensibly historical events that serves to unfold part of the world view of a people or explain a practice, belief, or natural phenomenon **b** : PARABLE, ALLEGORY **2 a** : a popular belief or tradition that has grown up around something or someone; *esp* : one embodying the ideals and institutions of a society or segment of society ⟨seduced by the American ∼ of individualism —Orde Coombs⟩ **b** : an unfounded or false notion **3** : a person or thing having only an imaginary or unverifiable existence **4** : the whole body of myths

myth·i·cal \'mith-i-kəl\ *or* **myth·ic** \-ik\ *adj* (1678) **1** : based on or described in a myth esp. as contrasted with history **2** *usu* **mythical** : existing only in the imagination : FICTITIOUS, IMAGINARY ⟨sportswriters picked a ∼ all-star team⟩ **3** *usu* **mythic** : having qualities suitable to myth : LEGENDARY ⟨the twilight of a *mythic* professional career —Clayton Riley⟩ *syn* see FICTITIOUS — **myth·i·cal·ly** \-i-k(ə-)lē\ *adv*

myth·i·cize \'mith-ə-ˌsiz\ *vt* **-cized; -ciz·ing** (1840) **1** : to turn into or envelop in myth **2** : to treat as myth — **myth·i·ciz·er** *n*

myth·mak·er \'mith-ˌmā-kər\ *n* (1871) : a creator of myths or of mythical situations or lore — **myth·mak·ing** \-kiŋ\ *n*

my·thog·ra·phy \mith-'äg-rə-fē\ *n* [Gk *mythographia*, fr. *mythos* + *-graphia* -graphy] (1851) **1** : the representation of mythical subjects in art **2** : a critical compilation of myths — **my·thog·ra·pher** \-fər\ *n*

myth·o·log·i·cal \ˌmith-ə-'läj-i-kəl\ *also* **myth·o·log·ic** \-ik\ *adj* (1614) **1** : of or relating to mythology or myths : dealt with in mythology **2** : lacking factual basis or historical validity : MYTHICAL, FABULOUS — **myth·o·log·i·cal·ly** \-i-k(ə-)lē\ *adv*

my·thol·o·gize \mith-'äl-ə-ˌjīz\ *vb* **-gized; -giz·ing** *vt* (1603) **1** *obs* : to explain the mythological significance of **2** : to build a myth around : MYTHICIZE ∼ *vi* **1** : to relate, classify, and explain myths **2** : to create or perpetuate myths — **my·thol·o·giz·er** *n*

my·thol·o·gy \mith-'äl-ə-jē\ *n, pl* **-gies** [F or LL; F *mythologie*, fr. LL *mythologia* interpretation of myths, fr. Gk, legend, myth, fr. *mythologein* to relate myths, fr. *mythos* + *logos* speech — more at LEGEND] (1603) **1** : an allegorical narrative **2** : a body of myths: as **a** : the myths dealing with the gods, demigods, and legendary heroes of a particular people **b** : MYTHOS 2 ⟨cold war ∼⟩ **3** : a branch of knowledge that deals with myth — **my·thol·o·ger** \-jər\ *n* — **my·thol·o·gist** \-jəst\ *n*

mytho·ma·nia \ˌmith-ə-'mā-nē-ə, -nyə\ *n* [NL, fr. Gk *mythos* + LL *mania* mania] (ca. 1909) : an excessive or abnormal propensity for lying and exaggerating — **mytho·ma·ni·ac** \-nē-ˌak\ *n or adj*

mytho·poe·ia \ˌmith-ə-'pē-(y)ə\ *n* [LL, fr. Gk *mythopoiia*, fr. *mythopoiein* to make a myth, fr. *mythos* + *poiein* to make — more at POEM] (1846) : a creating of myth : a giving rise to myths — **mytho·poe·ic** \-'pē-ik\ *also* **mytho·po·et·ic** \-pō-'et-ik\ *or* **mytho·po·et·i·cal** \-i-kəl\ *adj*

my·thos \'mith-ˌōs, -ˌäs\ *n, pl* **my·thoi** \-ˌȯi\ [Gk] (1753) **1 a** : MYTH 1a **b** : MYTHOLOGY 2a **2** : a pattern of beliefs expressing often symbolically the characteristic or prevalent attitudes in a group or culture **3** : THEME, PLOT

my word *interj* (1857) — used to express surprise or astonishment

myx·ede·ma \ˌmik-sə-'dē-mə\ *n* [NL, fr. Gk *myxa* lamp wick, nasal mucus + NL *edema* edema — more at MUCUS] (1877) : severe hypothyroidism characterized by firm inelastic edema, dry skin and hair, and loss of mental and physical vigor — **myx·ede·ma·tous** \-'dem-ət-əs, -'dē-mət-\ *adj*

myx·o·ma \mik-'sō-mə\ *n, pl* **-mas** *or* **-ma·ta** \-mət-ə\ [NL, fr. Gk *myxa*] (1870) : a soft tumor made up of gelatinous connective tissue resembling that found in the umbilical cord — **myx·o·ma·tous** \-mət-əs\ *adj*

myx·o·ma·to·sis \ˌmik-sō-mə-'tō-səs\ *n* [NL, fr. *myxomat-, myxoma*] (1927) : a condition characterized by the presence of myxomas in the body; *specif* : a severe virus disease of rabbits that is transmitted by mosquitoes and has been used in the biological control of rabbits in plague areas

myxo·my·cete \ˌmik-sō-'mī-ˌsēt, ˌmik-sō-(ˌ)mī-'\ *n* [deriv. of Gk *myxa* + *mykēt-, mykēs* fungus — more at MYC-] (1877) : SLIME MOLD — **myxo·my·ce·tous** \-(ˌ)mī-'sēt-əs\ *adj*

myxo·vi·rus \'mik-sə-ˌvī-rəs\ *n* [NL, fr. Gk *myxa* + NL *virus* virus; fr. its affinity for certain mucins] (1955) : any of a group of rather large RNA-containing viruses that includes the influenza viruses — **myxo·vi·ral** \ˌmik-sə-'vī-rəl\ *adj*

N

n \'en\ *n, pl* **n's** *or* **ns** \'enz\ *often cap, often attrib* **1 a** : the 14th letter of the English alphabet **b** : a graphic representation of this letter **c** : a speech counterpart of orthographic *n* **2** : a graphic device for reproducing the letter *n* **3 a** : one designated *n* esp. as the 14th in order or class **b** : an indefinite number; *esp* : a constant integer or a variable taking on integral values **4** : something shaped like the letter N **5** : the haploid or gametic number of chromosomes **6** : EN 2

-n — see -EN

'n \ən, ᵊn\ *conj* [by shortening] : THAN

'n' *also* **'n** \ən, ᵊn\ *conj* : AND ⟨fish 'n' chips⟩

nab \'nab\ *vt* **nabbed; nab·bing** [perh. alter. of E dial. *nap*] (1686) **1** : to catch or seize in arrest : APPREHEND **2** : to seize suddenly

nabe \'nāb\ *n* [by shortening & alter. fr. *neighborhood*] (1935) : a neighborhood theater — usu. used in pl. with *the*

na·bob \'nā-ˌbäb\ *n* [Hindi & Urdu *nawwāb*, fr. Ar *nuwwāb*, pl. of *nā'ib* governor] (1612) **1** : a provincial governor of the Mogul empire in India **2** : a person of great wealth or prominence

Na·both \'nā-ˌbäth\ *n* [Heb *Nābhōth*] : the owner of a vineyard coveted and seized by Ahab king of Israel

na·celle \nə-'sel\ *n* [F, lit., small boat, fr. LL *navicella*, dim. of L *navis* ship — more at NAVE] (ca. 1901) : an enclosed shelter on an aircraft for an engine or sometimes for the crew

na·cho \'näch-(ˌ)ō\ *n, pl* **nachos** [perh. fr. Sp *nacho* flat-nosed] (1969) : a tortilla chip topped with cheese and a savory substance (as hot peppers) and broiled

na·cre \'nā-kər\ *n* [MF, fr. OIt *naccara* drum, nacre, fr. Ar *naqqārah* drum] (1598) : MOTHER-OF-PEARL — **na·cre·ous** \-krē-əs, -k(ə-)rəs\ *adj*

NAD \ˌen-ˌā-'dē\ *n* [*nicotinamide adenine dinucleotide*] (ca. 1962) : a coenzyme $C_{21}H_{27}N_7O_{14}P_2$ of numerous dehydrogenases that occurs in most cells and plays an important role in all phases of intermediary metabolism as an oxidizing agent or when in the reduced form as a reducing agent for various metabolites — called also *nicotinamide adenine dinucleotide, diphosphopyridine nucleotide, DPN*

Na–dene *also* **Na–dé·né** \nä-'den-ē\ *n, often cap D* [*na-* (fr. an Athapaskan word stem akin to Haida *na* to dwell) + *Déné*] (1915) : a group of related American Indian languages spoken in parts of western No. America from Alaska to northern Mexico

NADH \ˌen-ˌā-ˌdē-'āch\ *n* [*NAD + H* (symbol for hydrogen)] (1966) : the reduced form of NAD

na·dir \'nā-ˌdi(ə)r, 'nād-ər\ *n* [ME, fr. MF, fr. Ar *nazīr* opposite] (15c) **1** : the point of the celestial sphere that is directly opposite the zenith and vertically downward from the observer **2** : the lowest point

NADP \ˌen-ˌā-ˌdē-'pē\ *n* [*nicotinamide adenine dinucleotide phosphate*] (ca. 1962) : a coenzyme $C_{21}H_{28}N_7O_{17}P_3$ of numerous dehydrogenases (as that acting on glucose-6-phosphate) that occurs esp. in red blood cells and plays a role in intermediary metabolism similar to NAD but acting often on different metabolites — called also *nicotinamide adenine dinucleotide phosphate, TPN, triphosphopyridine nucleotide*

NADPH \ˌen-ˌā-ˌdē-(ˌ)pē-'āch\ *n* [*NADP + H* (symbol for hydrogen)] (ca. 1966) : the reduced form of NADP

¹**nag** \'nag\ *n* [ME *nagge*; akin to D *negge* small horse] (15c) : HORSE; *esp* : one that is old or in poor condition

²**nag** *vb* **nagged; nag·ging** [prob. of Scand origin; akin to ON *gnaga* to gnaw; akin to OE *gnagan* to gnaw] *vi* (ca. 1828) **1** : to find fault incessantly : COMPLAIN **2** : to be a continuing source of annoyance ∼ *vt* **1** : to irritate by constant scolding or urging **2** : BADGER, WORRY — **nag·ger** *n* — **nagging** *adj* — **nag·ging·ly** \-iŋ-lē\ *adv*

³**nag** *n* (1925) : one who nags habitually

---

na·ga·na \nə-'gän-ə\ *n* [Zulu *u-nakane, ulu-nakane*] (1895) : trypanosomiasis (esp. when caused by *Trypanosoma brucei*) of domestic animals

nah \'na, 'nä, 'nȧ\ *var of* NO

Na·huatl \'nä-,wät-ᵊl\ *n, pl* **Nahuatl** *or* **Nahuatls** [Sp *nahuatle,* fr. Nahuatl *Nahuatl*] (1822) **1 :** a group of Indian peoples of southern Mexico and Central America **2 :** the Uto-Aztecan language of the Nahuatl peoples — **Na·huat·lan** \nä-'wät-lən\ *adj or n*

Na·hum \'nā-(h)əm\ *n* [Heb *Naḥūm*] **1 :** a Hebrew prophet of the 7th century B.C. **2 :** a prophetic book of canonical Jewish and Christian Scripture — see BIBLE table

na·iad \'nā-əd, 'nī-, -,ad\ *n, pl* **na·iads** *or* **na·ia·des** \-ə-,dēz\ [ME, fr. MF or L; MF *naïade,* fr. L *naiad-, naias,* fr. Gk, fr. *nan* to flow — more at NOURISH] (14c) **1 :** any of the nymphs in classical mythology living in and giving life to lakes, rivers, springs, and fountains **2 :** any of the aquatic young of a mayfly, dragonfly, damselfly, or stone fly — compare NYMPH 3 **3 :** any of a genus (*Naias*) of submerged aquatic plants

na·ïf *or* **na·if** \nä-'ēf\ *adj* [F] (1598) : NAIVE — **naïf** *n*

[1]nail \'nā(ə)l\ *n* [ME, fr. OE *nægl;* akin to OHG *nagal* nail, fingernail, L *unguis* fingernail, toenail, claw, Gk *onyx*] (bef. 12c) **1 a :** a horny sheath protecting the upper end of each finger and toe of man and most other primates **b :** a structure (as a claw) that terminates a digit and corresponds to a nail **2 :** a slender usu. pointed and headed fastener designed to be pounded in **3 :** an English unit of length equal to $^1/_{16}$ yard

[2]nail *vt* (bef. 12c) **1 :** to fasten with or as if with a nail **2 :** to fix in steady attention ⟨~*ed* his eye on the crack⟩ **3 :** CATCH, TRAP; *esp* : to detect and expose usu. so as to discredit **4 a :** STRIKE, HIT **b :** to put out (a runner) in baseball — **nail·er** *n*

nail·brush \'nā(ə)l-,brəsh\ *n* (1802) : a small firm-bristled brush for cleaning the hands and esp. the fingernails

nail down *vt* (1947) **1 :** to settle or establish clearly and unmistakably **2 :** to gain or win decisively ⟨*nail down* his consent⟩

nail file *n* (1875) : a small narrow instrument (as of metal or cardboard) with a rough or emery surface that is used for shaping fingernails

nain·sook \'nān-,sůk\ *n* [Hindi *nainsukh,* fr. *nain* eye + *sukh* delight] (1790) : a soft lightweight muslin

nai·ra \'nī-rə\ *n* [alter. of *Nigeria*] (1972) — see MONEY table

na·ive *or* **na·ïve** \nä-'ēv\ *adj* **na·iv·er; -est** [F *naïve,* fem. of *naïf,* fr. OF, inborn, natural, fr. L *nativus* native] (1650) **1 :** marked by unaffected simplicity : ARTLESS, INGENUOUS **2 a :** deficient in worldly wisdom or informed judgment; *esp* : CREDULOUS **b :** not previously subjected to experimentation or a particular experimental situation ⟨made the test with ~ rats⟩; *also* : not having previously used a particular drug (as marijuana) **3 :** PRIMITIVE 3d ***syn*** see NATURAL — **na·ive·ly** *adv* — **na·ive·ness** *n*

na·ive·té *also* **na·ive·té** *or* **na·ive·te** \(,)nä-,ēv(-ə)-'tā, nä-'ēv(-ə)-,tā\ *n* [F *naïveté,* fr. OF, inborn character, fr. *naif*] (1673) **1 :** a naive remark or action **2 :** the quality or state of being naive

na·ive·ty *also* **na·ïve·ty** \nä-'ē-vət-ē, -'ēv-tē\ *n, pl* **-ties** *chiefly Brit* (1708) : NAÏVETÉ

na·ked \'nā-kəd, *esp Southern* 'nek-əd\ *adj* [ME, fr. OE *nacod;* akin to OHG *nackot* naked, L *nudus,* Gk *gymnos*] (bef. 12c) **1 :** not covered by clothing : NUDE **2 :** devoid of customary or natural covering : BARE: as **a :** not enclosed in a sheath or scabbard **b :** not provided with a shade **c** *of a plant or one of its parts* : lacking pubescence or enveloping or subtending parts **d :** lacking foliage or vegetation **e** *of an animal or one of its parts* : lacking an external covering (as of hair, feathers, or shell) **3 a :** scantily supplied or furnished **b :** lacking embellishment : UNADORNED **4 :** UNARMED, DEFENSELESS **5 :** lacking confirmation or support **6 :** devoid of concealment or disguise **7 :** unaided by any optical device or instrument ⟨visible to the ~ eye⟩ **8 :** not backed by the writer's ownership of the commodity contract or security ***syn*** see BARE — **na·ked·ly** *adv* — **na·ked·ness** *n*

na·led \'nā-,led\ *n* [origin unknown] (ca. 1962) : a short-lived insecticide of relatively low toxicity to warm-blooded animals that is used esp. to control crop pests and mosquitoes

na·li·dix·ic acid \,nā-lə-,dik-sik-\ *n* [perh. fr. *naphthyridine* ($C_8H_6N_2$ — fr. *naphth-* + *pyridine*) + carbox*ylic acid*] (1964) : an antibacterial agent $C_{12}H_{12}N_2O_3$ that is used esp. in the treatment of genitourinary infections

na·lor·phine \nal-'ȯr-,fēn\ *n* [*N-allyl* + *morphine*] (ca. 1953) : a white crystalline compound $C_{19}H_{21}NO_3$ that is derived from morphine and is used in the form of its hydrochloride as a respiratory stimulant to counteract poisoning by morphine and similar narcotic drugs

nal·ox·one \nal-'äk-,sōn\ *n* [*N-allyl* + hydroxy- + *-one*] (1964) : a potent antagonist $C_{19}H_{21}NO_4$ of narcotic drugs and esp. morphine that is administered esp. as the hydrochloride

nal·trex·one \nal-'trek-,sōn\ *n* [*nal-* (designation of nonmorphine narcotic antagonist) + *trex-* (as in *methotrexate*) + *-one*] (1973) : a narcotic antagonist $C_{20}H_{23}NO_4$

nam·by-pam·by \,nam-bē-'pam-bē\ *adj* [*Namby Pamby,* nickname given to Ambrose Philips] (1726) **1 :** lacking in character or substance : INSIPID **2 :** WEAK, INDECISIVE — **namby-pamby** *n*

[1]name \'nām\ *n* [ME, fr. OE *nama;* akin to OHG *namo* name, L *nomen,* Gk *onoma, onyma*] (bef. 12c) **1 a :** a word or phrase that constitutes the distinctive designation of a person or thing **b :** a word or symbol used in logic to designate an entity **2 :** a descriptive often disparaging epithet ⟨called him ~*s*⟩ **3 a :** REPUTATION ⟨gave the town a bad ~⟩ **b :** an illustrious record : FAME ⟨made a ~ for himself in golf⟩ **c :** a person or thing with a reputation **4 :** FAMILY, CLAN **5 :** appearance as opposed to reality ⟨a friend in ~ only⟩ **6 :** one referred to by a name ⟨praise his holy ~⟩ — **in the name of 1 :** by authority of ⟨open *in the name of* the law⟩ **2 :** for the reason of : using the excuse of ⟨called for reforms *in the name of* progress⟩

[2]name *vt* **named; nam·ing** (bef. 12c) **1 :** to give a name to : CALL **2 a :** to mention or identify by name **b :** to accuse by name **3 :** to nominate for office : APPOINT **4 :** to decide on : CHOOSE ⟨~ the day for the wedding⟩ **5 :** to mention explicitly : SPECIFY ⟨unwilling to ~ a price⟩ — **nam·er** *n*

[3]name *adj* (1610) **1 :** of, relating to, or bearing a name ⟨~ tags⟩ **2 :** appearing in the name of a literary or theatrical production **3 a :** having an established reputation **b :** featuring celebrities

name·able *also* **nam·able** \'nā-mə-bəl\ *adj* (1780) **1 :** worthy of being named : MEMORABLE **2 :** capable of being named : IDENTIFIABLE

name–call·ing \'nām-,kȯ-liŋ\ *n* (1853) : the use of offensive names esp. to win an argument or to induce rejection or condemnation (as of a person or project) without objective consideration of the facts

name day *n* (1721) : the church feast day of the saint after whom one is named

name–drop·ping \-,dräp-iŋ\ *n* (1950) : the practice of seeking to impress others by studied but apparently casual mention of prominent persons as associates — **name–drop·per** \-ər\ *n*

name·less \'nām-ləs\ *adj* (14c) **1 :** OBSCURE, UNDISTINGUISHED **2 :** not known by name : ANONYMOUS **3 :** having no legal right to a name : ILLEGITIMATE **4 :** not having been given a name : UNNAMED **5 :** not marked with a name ⟨a ~ grave⟩ **6 a :** incapable of precise description : INDEFINABLE **b :** too repulsive or distressing to describe — **name·less·ly** *adv* — **name·less·ness** *n*

name·ly \'nām-lē\ *adv* (14c) : that is to say : TO WIT

name of the game (1966) **1 :** the essential quality or matter ⟨patience is the *name of the game* in coastal duck hunting —Dick Beals⟩ **2 :** the fundamental goal of an activity

name·plate \-,plāt\ *n* (ca. 1864) : something (as a plate or plaque) bearing a name (as of a resident or manufacturer)

name·sake \-,sāk\ *n* [prob. fr. *name's sake*] (1646) : one that has the same name as another; *esp* : one named after another

nana \'nan-ə\ *n* [baby-talk for *grandma*] (1844) : GRANDMOTHER

nance \'nan(t)s\ *n* [short for *nancy,* fr. the name *Nancy*] (1920) **1 :** an effeminate male — often used disparagingly **2 :** HOMOSEXUAL — often used disparagingly

NAND \'nand\ *n* [*not AND*] (1958) : a computer logic circuit that produces an output which is the inverse of that of an AND circuit

nan·keen \(ˈ)nan-'kēn\ *n* [*Nanking,* China] (1755) **1 :** a durable brownish yellow cotton fabric orig. loomed by hand in China **2** *pl* : trousers made of nankeen

Nan·kin \'nan-'kin, 'nän-\ *or* **Nan·king** \-'kiŋ\ *n* [*Nanking,* China] (1781) : Chinese porcelain decorated in blue on a white ground

nan·no·plank·ton \,nan-ō-'plaŋ(k)-tən, -,tän\ *n* [NL, fr. Gk *nanos, nannos* dwarf + NL *plankton* plankton] (1912) : the smallest plankton that consists of those organisms (as bacteria) that passing through nets of very fine mesh silk cloth

nan·ny *also* **nan·nie** \'nan-ē\ *n, pl* **nannies** [prob. of baby-talk origin] *chiefly Brit* (1795) : a child's nurse : NURSEMAID

nan·ny goat \'nan-ē-\ *n* [*Nanny,* nickname for *Anne*] (1788) : a female domestic goat

nano- \'nan-(,)ō, -ə\ *comb form* [ISV, fr. Gk *nanos* dwarf] : one billionth (10^{-9}) part of ⟨*nanosecond*⟩

nano·gram \'nan-ə-,gram\ *n* [ISV] (1951) : one billionth of a gram

nano·me·ter \'nan-ə-,mēt-ər\ *n* [ISV] (1963) : one billionth of a meter

nano·sec·ond \-,sek-ənd, -ənt\ *n* [ISV] (1959) : one billionth of a second

Nan·tua sauce \nänⁿ(n)-,twä-\ *n* [*Nantua,* France] (ca. 1961) : a cream sauce flavored with shellfish (as lobster)

Na·o·mi \nā-'ō-mē\ *n* [Heb *Nā'ŏmī*] : the mother-in-law of the Old Testament heroine Ruth

[1]nap \'nap\ *vi* **napped; nap·ping** [ME *nappen,* fr. OE *hnappian;* akin to OHG *hnaffezen* to doze] (bef. 12c) **1 :** to sleep briefly esp. during the day : DOZE **2 :** to be off guard

[2]nap *n* (14c) : a short sleep esp. during the day : SNOOZE

[3]nap *n* [ME *noppe,* fr. MD, flock of wool, nap; akin to OE *hnoppian* to pluck, Gk *konis* ashes — more at INCINERATE] (15c) : a hairy or downy surface (as on a woven fabric) — **nap·less** \-ləs\ *adj* — **napped** \'napt\ *adj*

[4]nap *vt* **napped; nap·ping** (1620) : to raise a nap on (fabric or leather)

[5]nap *n* [fr. to go *nap* (to make all the points in the card game Napoleon)] *Brit* (1895) : a pick or recommendation as a good bet to win a contest (as a horse race); *also* : one named in a nap

[6]nap *vt* **napped; nap·ping** *Brit* (1927) : to pick or single out (as a racehorse) in a nap

[1]na·palm \'nā-,päm *also* 'na-, -,pälm; nə-'pä(l)m\ *n* [*naphthene* + *palmitate*] (1942) **1 :** a thickener consisting of a mixture of aluminum soaps used in jelling gasoline (as for incendiary bombs) **2 :** fuel jelled with napalm

[2]napalm *vt* (1950) : to assault with napalm

nape \'nāp, 'nap\ *n* [ME] (14c) : the back of the neck

na·pery \'nā-p(ə-)rē\ *n* [ME, fr. MF *naperie,* fr. *nappe, nape* tablecloth — more at NAPKIN] (14c) : household linen; *esp* : TABLE LINEN

Naph·ta·li \'naf-tə-,lī\ *n* [Heb *Naphtālī*] : a son of Jacob and the traditional eponymous ancestor of one of the tribes of Israel

naphth- *or* **naphtho-** *comb form* [ISV, fr. *naphtha & naphthalene*] **1 :** naphtha ⟨*naphth*ene⟩ **2 :** naphthalene ⟨*naphtho*quinone⟩

naph·tha \'naf-thə, 'nap-\ *n* [L, fr. Gk, of Iranian origin; akin to Per *neft* naphtha] (1572) **1 :** any of various volatile often flammable liquid hydrocarbon mixtures used chiefly as solvents and diluents **2 :** PETROLEUM

naph·tha·lene \-,lēn\ *n* [alter. of earlier *naphthaline,* irreg. fr. *naphtha*] (1821) : a crystalline aromatic hydrocarbon $C_{10}H_8$ usu. obtained by distillation of coal tar and used esp. in organic synthesis — **naph·tha·len·ic** \,naf-thə-'lēn-ik, ,nap-, -'len-\ *adj*

naph·thol \'naf-,thȯl, 'nap-, -,thōl\ *n* [ISV] (1849) **1 :** either of two isomeric derivatives $C_{10}H_8O$ of naphthalene found in coal tar or made synthetically and used as antiseptics and in manufacture of dyes **2 :** any of various hydroxy derivatives of naphthalene that resemble the simpler phenols

naph·thyl·amine \naf-'thil-ə-,mēn, nap-\ *n* [ISV] (1857) : either of two isomeric crystalline bases $C_{10}H_9N$ used esp. as dye intermediates

na·pi·er grass \'nā-pē-ər-\ *n* [*Napier,* town in So. Africa] (1914) : a tall stout perennial grass (*Pennisetum purpureum*) that resembles sugarcane and is widely grown for forage — called also *elephant grass*

Na·pier·ian logarithm \nə-,pir-ē-ən-, nā-\ *n* [John *Napier*] (1816) : NATURAL LOGARITHM

Na·pi·er's bones \,nā-pē-ərz-\ *n* [fr. the short rods by which it was operated] (1658) : a set of graduated rods (as of wood or bone) invented by John Napier and used for multiplication and division based on the principles of logarithms

na·pi·form \ˈnā-pə-ˌfȯrm\ *adj* [L *napus* turnip (fr. Gk *napy* mustard) + ISV *-iform;* akin to Gk *sinapy* mustard] (ca. 1846) **:** globular at the top and tapering off abruptly — used esp. of roots

nap·kin \ˈnap-kən\ *n* [ME *nappekin,* fr. *nappe* tablecloth, fr. MF, fr. L *mappa* napkin] (14c) **1 :** a piece of material (as cloth or paper) used at table to wipe the lips or fingers and protect the clothes **2 :** a small cloth or towel: as **a** *dial Brit* **:** HANDKERCHIEF **b** *chiefly Scot* **:** KERCHIEF **c** *chiefly Brit* **:** DIAPER 3 **3 :** SANITARY NAPKIN

na·po·leon \nə-ˈpōl-yən, -ˈpō-lē-ən\ *n* [F *napoléon,* fr. *Napoléon* Napoleon I] (1814) **1 :** a former French 20-franc gold coin **2 :** an oblong pastry with a filling of cream, custard, or jelly **3** *cap* **:** one like Napoleon I (as in ambition)

nappe \ˈnap\ *n* [F, tablecloth, sheet, nappe — more at NAPKIN] (1904) **1 :** SHEET 6 **2 :** a large mass thrust over other rocks **3 :** one of the two sheets that lie on opposite sides of the vertex and together make up a cone

¹nap·py \ˈnap-ē\ *n* [obs. *nappy,* adj. (foaming)] *chiefly Scot* (1700) **:** LIQUOR; *specif* **:** ALE

²nappy *n, pl* **nappies** [E dial. *nap* bowl, fr. ME, fr. OE *hnæpp;* akin to OHG *hnapf* bowl] (1864) **:** a rimless shallow open serving dish

³nappy *n, pl* **nappies** [*napkin* + *-y*] *chiefly Brit* (1927) **:** DIAPER 3

⁴nappy *adj* **nap·pi·er; -est** [³*nap*] (1928) **:** KINKY 1

na·prap·a·thy \nə-ˈprap-ə-thē\ *n* [Czech *naprava* correction + E *-pathy*] (1916) **:** a system of treatment by manipulation of connective tissue and adjoining structures (as ligaments, joints, and muscles) and by dietary measures that is held to facilitate the recuperative and regenerative processes of the body

narc \ˈnärk\ *n* [short for *narcotics agent*] *slang* (1967) **:** one (as a government agent) who investigates narcotics violations

nar·cis·sism \ˈnär-sə-ˌsiz-əm\ *n* [G *narzissismus,* fr. *Narziss* Narcissus, fr. L *Narcissus*] (1822) **1 :** EGOISM, EGOCENTRISM **2 :** love of or sexual desire for one's own body — **nar·cis·sist** \ˈnär-sə-səst\ *n or adj* — **nar·cis·sis·tic** \ˌnär-sə-ˈsis-tik\ *adj*

nar·cis·sus \när-ˈsis-əs\ *n* [L, fr. Gk *Narkissos*] **1** *cap* **:** a beautiful youth in Greek mythology who pines away for love of his own reflection and is then turned into the narcissus flower **2** *pl* **nar·cis·si** \-ˈsis-ˌī, -(ˌ)ē\ *or* **nar·cis·sus·es** *or* **narcissus** [NL, genus name, fr. L, narcissus, fr. Gk *narkissos*] **:** DAFFODIL; *esp* **:** one whose flowers have a short corona and are usu. borne separately

nar·co \ˈnär-(ˌ)kō\ *n, pl* **narcos** [short for *narcotics agent*] *slang* (1955) **:** NARC

nar·co·lep·sy \ˈnär-kə-ˌlep-sē\ *n, pl* **-sies** [ISV, fr. Gk *narkē*] (1880) **:** a condition characterized by brief attacks of deep sleep — **nar·co·lep·tic** \ˌnär-kə-ˈlep-tik\ *adj*

nar·co·lep·tic \när-kə-ˈlep-tik\ *n* (1928) **:** one who is subject to attacks of narcolepsy

nar·co·sis \när-ˈkō-səs\ *n, pl* **-co·ses** \-ˌsēz\ [NL, fr. Gk *narkōsis,* action of benumbing, fr. *narkoun*] (1693) **:** a state of stupor, unconsciousness, or arrested activity produced by the influence of narcotics or other chemicals

¹nar·cot·ic \när-ˈkät-ik\ *n* [ME *narkotik,* fr. MF *narcotique,* fr. *narcotique,* adj., fr. ML *narcoticus,* fr. Gk *narkōtikos,* fr. *narkoun* to benumb, fr. *narkē* numbness — more at SNARE] (14c) **1 a :** a drug (as opium) that in moderate doses dulls the senses, relieves pain, and induces profound sleep but in excessive doses causes stupor, coma, or convulsions **b :** a drug (as marijuana or LSD) subject to restriction similar to that of addictive narcotics whether in fact physiologically addictive and narcotic or not **2 :** something that soothes, relieves, or lulls

²narcotic *adj* (1601) **1 a :** having the properties of or yielding a narcotic **b :** inducing mental lethargy **:** SOPORIFEROUS **2 :** of, induced by, or concerned with narcotics **3 :** of, involving, or intended for narcotic addicts — **nar·cot·i·cal·ly** \-i-k(ə-)lē\ *adv*

nar·co·tize \ˈnär-kə-ˌtīz\ *vb* **-tized; -tiz·ing** [ISV] *vt* (1843) **1 a :** to treat with or subject to a narcotic **b :** to put into a state of narcosis **2 :** to soothe to unconsciousness or unawareness ~ *vi* **:** to act as a narcotizing agent

nard \ˈnärd\ *n* [ME *narde,* fr. OE, fr. L *nardus,* fr. Gk *nardos,* of Sem origin; akin to Heb *nērd* nard] (bef. 12c) **:** SPIKENARD 1b

na·res \ˈna(ə)r-(ˌ)ēz, ˈne(ə)r-\ *n pl* [L, pl. of *naris;* akin to L *nasus* nose — more at NOSE] (14c) **:** the pair of openings of the nose or nasal cavity of a vertebrate

nar·ghi·le \ˈnär-gə-lē\ *or* **nar·gi·leh** \-ˌle\ *n* [Per *nārgīla,* fr. *nārgīl* coconut, of Indic origin; akin to Skt *nārikela* coconut; fr. the original material used in making its bowl] (1758) **:** a water pipe that originated in the Near East

¹nark \ˈnärk\ *n* [perh. fr. Romany *nak* nose] *Brit* (1859) **:** STOOL PIGEON

²nark *var of* NARC

Nar·ra·gan·set \ˌnar-ə-ˈgan(t)-sət\ *n, pl* **Narraganset** *or* **Narragansets** (1622) **1 :** a member of an American Indian people of Rhode Island **2 :** an Algonquian language of the Narraganset people

nar·rate \ˈna(ə)r-ˌāt, na-ˈrāt\ *vt* **nar·rat·ed; nar·rat·ing** [L *narratus,* pp. of *narrare,* fr. L *gnarus* knowing; akin to L *gnoscere, noscere* to know — more at KNOW] (1656) **:** to tell (as a story) in detail; *also* **:** to provide spoken commentary for (as a movie or television show) — **nar·ra·tor** \ˈna(ə)r-ˌāt-ər; na-ˈrāt-, nə-; ˈnar-ət-\ *n*

nar·ra·tion \na-ˈrā-shən, nə-\ *n* (15c) **1 :** the act or process or an instance of narrating **2 :** STORY, NARRATIVE — **nar·ra·tion·al** \-shnəl, -shən-ᵊl\ *adj*

nar·ra·tive \ˈnar-ət-iv\ *n* (15c) **1 :** something that is narrated **:** STORY **2 :** the art or practice of narration **3 :** the representation in art of an event or story; *also* **:** an example of such a representation — **narrative** *adj* — **nar·ra·tive·ly** *adv*

¹nar·row \ˈnar-(ˌ)ō, -ə(-w)\ *adj* [ME *narowe,* fr. OE *nearu;* akin to OHG *narwa* scar, *snuor* cord, Gk *narnax* box] (bef. 12c) **1 a :** of slender width **b :** of less than standard width **c** *of a textile* **:** woven in widths less than 18 inches **2 :** limited in size or scope **:** RESTRICTED **3 a :** illiberal in views or disposition **:** PREJUDICED **b** *chiefly dial* **:** STINGY, NIGGARDLY **4 a :** barely sufficient **:** CLOSE **b :** barely successful **5 :** minutely precise **:** METICULOUS **6** *of a ration* **:** relatively rich in protein as compared with carbohydrate and fat **7 :** TENSE 3 — **nar·row·ly** *adv* — **nar·row·ness** *n*

²narrow *vt* (bef. 12c) **1 :** to decrease the breadth or extent of **:** CONTRACT — often used with *down* **2 :** to decrease the scope or sphere of **:** LIMIT — often used with *down* ~ *vi* **:** to lessen in width or extent **:** CONTRACT — often used with *down*

³narrow *n* (14c) **:** a narrow part or passage; *specif* **:** a strait connecting two bodies of water — usu. used in pl. but sing. or pl. in constr.

nar·row·cast \ˈnar-ō-ˌkast, ˈnar-ə-\ *vi* **-cast; -cast·ing** [¹*narrow* + *-cast* (as in *broadcast*)] (ca. 1955) **:** to aim a broadcast at a narrowly defined area or audience

nar·row–mind·ed \ˌnar-ō-ˈmīn-dəd, ˌnar-ə-\ *adj* (1625) **:** lacking in tolerance or breadth of vision **:** PETTY — **nar·row–mind·ed·ly** *adv* — **nar·row–mind·ed·ness** *n*

nar·thex \ˈnär-ˌtheks\ *n* [LGk *narthēx,* fr. Gk, giant fennel, cane, casket] (ca. 1673) **1 :** the portico of an ancient church **2 :** a vestibule leading to the nave of a church

nar·whal \ˈnär-ˌ(h)wäl, -wəl\ *also* **nar·whale** \-ˌ(h)wāl\ *n* [Norw & Dan *narhval* & Sw *narval,* prob. modif. of Icel *náhvalur,* fr. ON *nāhvalr,* fr. *nār* corpse + *hvalr* whale; fr. its color] (1646) **:** an arctic cetacean (*Monodon monoceros*) about 20 feet long with the male having a long twisted ivory tusk of commercial value

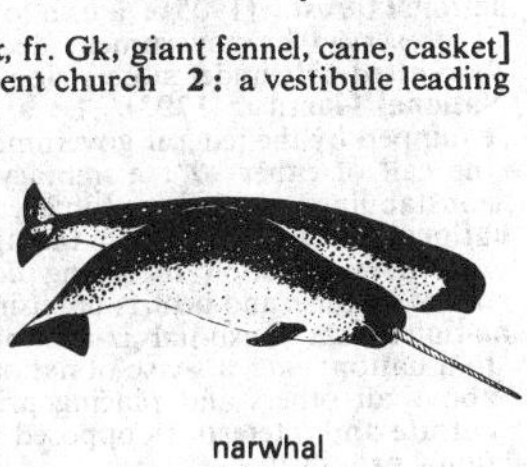

narwhal

nary \ˈna(ə)r-ē, ˈne(ə)r-\ *adj* [alter. of *ne'er a*] (1746) **:** not one ⟨~ a person wanted to go⟩

nas- *or* **naso-** *also* **nasi-** *comb form* [L *nasus* nose — more at NOSE] **1 :** nose **:** nasal ⟨*naso*scope⟩ ⟨*naso*sinusitis⟩ **2 :** nasal and ⟨*naso*labial⟩

¹na·sal \ˈnā-zəl\ *n* [ME, fr. MF, fr. OF, fr. *nes* nose, fr. L *nasus*] (14c) **1 :** the nosepiece of a helmet **2 :** a nasal part **3 :** a nasal consonant or vowel

²nasal *adj* (1656) **1 :** of or relating to the nose **2 a :** uttered through the nose with the mouth passage occluded (as with English *m, n, ng*) **b :** uttered with the mouth open, the soft palate lowered, and the nose passage producing a phonemically essential resonance (as of a vowel in French) or a phonemically nonessential resonance (as of a vowel in English) **c :** characterized by resonance produced through the nose **3** *of a musical tone* **:** SHARP, PENETRATING — **na·sal·i·ty** \nā-ˈzal-ət-ē\ *n* — **na·sal·ly** \ˈnāz-(ə-)lē\ *adv*

na·sal·ize \ˈnā-zə-ˌlīz\ *vb* **-ized; -iz·ing** *vt* (1817) **:** to make nasal ~ *vi* **:** to speak in a nasal manner — **na·sal·iza·tion** \ˌnā-zə-lə-ˈzā-shən\ *n*

na·scence \ˈnas-ᵊn(t)s, ˈnās-\ *n* (1570) **:** NASCENCY

na·scen·cy \-ᵊn-sē\ *n, pl* **-cies** (1682) **:** BIRTH, ORIGIN

na·scent \ˈnas-ᵊnt, ˈnās-\ *adj* [L *nascent-, nascens,* prp. of *nasci* to be born] (1624) **:** coming or having recently come into existence

na·so·pha·ryn·geal \ˌnā-zō-fə-ˈrin-j(ē-)əl, -ˌfar-ən-ˈjē-əl\ *adj* (1872) **:** of, relating to, or affecting the nose and pharynx or the nasopharynx

na·so·phar·ynx \-ˈfar-iŋ(k)s\ *n* [NL] (1877) **:** the upper part of the pharynx continuous with the nasal passages

nas·tic \ˈnas-tik\ *adj* [Gk *nastos* close-pressed, fr. *nassein* to press] (ca. 1908) **:** of, relating to, or constituting a movement of a plant part caused by disproportionate growth or increase of turgor in one surface

nas·tur·tium \nə-ˈstər-shəm, na-\ *n* [L, a cress] (1570) **:** any of a genus (*Tropaeolum* of the family Tropaeolaceae, the nasturtium family) of herbs with showy spurred flowers and pungent seeds; *esp* **:** either of two widely cultivated ornamentals (*T. majus* and *T. minus*)

nas·ty \ˈnas-tē\ *adj* **nas·ti·er; -est** [ME] (14c) **1 a :** disgustingly filthy **b :** physically repugnant **2 :** INDECENT, OBSCENE **3 :** MEAN, TAWDRY **4 a :** extremely hazardous or harmful ⟨had a ~ climb to reach the summit⟩ **b :** sharply unpleasant **:** DISAGREEABLE ⟨~ weather⟩ **5 a :** difficult to understand or deal with **:** VEXATIOUS ⟨ ~ problem⟩ **b :** psychologically unsettling **:** TRYING ⟨faced with a ~ fear that she was lost⟩ **6 :** lacking in courtesy or sportsmanship **:** SPITEFUL ***syn*** see DIRTY — **nas·ti·ly** \-tə-lē\ *adv* — **nas·ti·ness** \-tē-nəs\ *n* — **nasty** *n*

na·tal \ˈnāt-ᵊl\ *adj* [ME, fr. L *natalis,* fr. *natus,* pp. of *nasci* to be born — more at NATION] (15c) **1 :** NATIVE **2 :** of, relating to, or present at birth; *esp* **:** associated with one's birth ⟨a ~ star⟩

na·tal·i·ty \nā-ˈtal-ət-ē, nə-\ *n, pl* **-ties** (1888) **:** BIRTHRATE

na·tant \ˈnāt-ᵊnt\ *adj* [ME, fr. L *natant-, natans,* prp. of *natare* to swim; akin to L *nare* to swim — more at NOURISH] (15c) **:** swimming or floating in water ⟨~ decapods⟩

na·ta·tion \nā-ˈtā-shən, na-\ *n* (1542) **:** the action or art of swimming

na·ta·to·ri·al \ˌnāt-ə-ˈtōr-ē-əl, ˌnat-, -ˈtȯr-\ *or* **na·ta·to·ry** \ˈnāt-ə-ˌtōr-ē, ˈnat-, -ˌtȯr-\ *adj* (1816) **1 :** of or relating to swimming **2 :** adapted to or characterized by swimming ⟨a ~ leg of an aquatic insect⟩

na·ta·to·ri·um \ˌnāt-ə-ˈtōr-ē-əm, ˌnat-, -ˈtȯr-\ *n* [LL, fr. L *natatus,* pp. of *natare*] (ca. 1890) **:** an indoor swimming pool

natch \ˈnach\ *adv* [by shortening & alter. of *naturally*] *slang* (ca. 1945) **:** of course **:** NATURALLY

na·tes \ˈnā-ˌtēz\ *n pl* [L, pl. of *natis* buttock; akin to Gk *nōtos, nōton* back] (1706) **:** BUTTOCKS

nathe·less \ˈnāth-ləs\ *or* **nath·less** \ˈnath-\ *adv* [ME, fr. OE *nā thē lǣs* not the less] *archaic* (bef. 12c) **:** NEVERTHELESS, NOTWITHSTANDING

Na·tick \ˈnāt-ik\ *n* (1829) **:** a dialect of Massachuset

na·tion \ˈnā-shən\ *n* [ME *nacioun,* fr. MF *nation,* fr. L *nation-, natio* birth, race, nation, fr. *natus,* pp. of *nasci* to be born; akin to L *gignere* to beget — more at KIN] (14c) **1 a (1) :** NATIONALITY 5a **(2) :** a politically organized nationality **(3) :** a non-Jewish nationality ⟨why do the ~s conspire —Ps 2:1 (RSV)⟩ **b :** a community of people composed of one or more nationalities and possessing a more or less defined territory and government **c :** a territorial division containing a body of people of one or more nationalities and usu. characterized by relatively large size and independent status **2** *archaic* **:** GROUP, AGGREGATION **3 :** a tribe or federation of tribes (as of American Indians)

¹na·tion·al \ˈnash-nəl, -ən-ᵊl\ *adj* (1597) **1 :** of or relating to a nation **2 :** NATIONALIST **3 :** comprising or characteristic of a nationality **4**

\ə\ abut \ᵊ\ kitten, F table \ər\ further \a\ ash \ā\ ace \ä\ cot, cart \au̇\ out \ch\ chin \e\ bet \ē\ easy \g\ go \i\ hit \ī\ ice \j\ job \ŋ\ sing \ō\ go \ȯ\ law \ȯi\ boy \th\ thin \th̲\ the \ü\ loot \u̇\ foot \y\ yet \zh\ vision \à, k̲, ⁿ, œ, œ̄, ue, ue̅, ʸ\ *see* Guide to Pronunciation

: belonging to or maintained by the federal government **5** : of, relating to, or being a coalition government formed by most or all major political parties usu. in a crisis — **na·tion·al·ly** \-ē\ *adv*

²**national** *n* (1887) **1** : one that owes allegiance to or is under the protection of a nation without regard to the more formal status of citizen or subject **2** : a competition that is national in scope — usu. used in pl. ***syn*** see CITIZEN

national bank *n* (1790) **1** : CENTRAL BANK **2** : a bank operating under federal charter and supervision

national forest *n* (1905) : a usu. forested area of considerable extent that is preserved by government decree from private exploitation and is harvested only under supervision

National Guard *n* (1793) **1** : a militia force recruited by each state, equipped by the federal government, and jointly maintained subject to the call of either **2** : a military establishment serving as a national constabulary and defense force

national income *n* (1878) : the aggregate of earnings from a nation's current production including compensation of employees, interest, rental income, and profits of business after taxes

na·tion·al·ism \'nash-nəl-,iz-əm, -ən-ᵊl-\ *n* (1844) : loyalty and devotion to a nation; *esp* : a sense of national consciousness exalting one nation above all others and placing primary emphasis on promotion of its culture and interests as opposed to those of other nations or supranational groups

¹**na·tion·al·ist** \-əst\ *n* (1715) **1** : an advocate of or believer in nationalism **2** *cap* : a member of a political party or group advocating national independence or strong national government

²**nationalist** *adj* (1889) **1** : of, relating to, or advocating nationalism **2** *cap* : of, relating to, or being a political group advocating or associated with nationalism

na·tion·al·is·tic \,nash-nəl-'is-tik, -ən-ᵊl-\ *adj* (1866) **1** : of, favoring, or characterized by nationalism ⟨~ election speeches⟩ **2** : NATIONAL 1 — **na·tion·al·is·ti·cal·ly** \-ti-k(ə-)lē\ *adv*

na·tion·al·i·ty \,nash-(ə-)'nal-ət-ē\ *n, pl* **-ties** (1691) **1** : national character **2** : NATIONALISM **3** **a** : national status; *specif* : a legal relationship involving allegiance on the part of an individual and usu. protection on the part of the state **b** : membership in a particular nation **4** : political independence or existence as a separate nation **5** **a** : a people having a common origin, tradition, and language and capable of forming or actually constituting a nation-state **b** : an ethnic group constituting one element of a larger unit (as a nation)

na·tion·al·ize \'nash-nəl-,īz, -ən-ᵊl-\ *vt* **-ized; -iz·ing** (1800) **1** : to give a national character to **2** : to invest control or ownership of in the national government — **na·tion·al·iza·tion** \,nash-nəl-ə-'zā-shən, -ən-ᵊl-\ *n* — **na·tion·al·iz·er** \'nash-nəl-,ī-zər, -ən-ᵊl-\ *n*

national monument *n* (1916) : a place of historic, scenic, or scientific interest set aside for preservation usu. by presidential proclamation

national park *n* (1841) : an area of special scenic, historical, or scientific importance set aside and maintained by a national government and in the U.S. by an act of Congress

national seashore *n* (1962) : a recreational area adjacent to a seacoast and maintained by the federal government

national socialism *n* (1931) : NAZISM — **national socialist** *adj*

na·tion·hood \'nā-shən-,hu̇d\ *n* (1850) : NATIONALITY 1, 3a, 4

na·tion-state \'nā-shən-'stāt, -,stāt\ *n* (1918) : a form of political organization under which a relatively homogeneous people inhabits a sovereign state; *esp* : a state containing one as opposed to several nationalities

na·tion·wide \,nā-shən-'wīd\ *adj* (1912) : extending throughout a nation

¹**na·tive** \'nāt-iv\ *adj* [ME *natif,* fr. MF, fr. L *nativus,* fr. *natus,* pp. of *nasci* to be born — more at NATION] (14c) **1** : INBORN, INNATE ⟨~ talents⟩ **2** : belonging to a particular place by birth ⟨~ to Wisconsin⟩ **3** *archaic* : closely related **4** : belonging to or associated with one by birth **5** : NATURAL, NORMAL **6** **a** : grown, produced, or originating in a particular place or in the vicinity : LOCAL **b** : living or growing naturally in a particular region : INDIGENOUS **7** : SIMPLE, UNAFFECTED **8** **a** : constituting the original substance or source **b** : found in nature esp. in an unadulterated form ⟨mining ~ silver⟩ **9** *chiefly Austral* : having a usu. superficial resemblance to a specified English plant or animal — **na·tive·ly** *adv* — **na·tive·ness** *n*

syn NATIVE, INDIGENOUS, ENDEMIC, ABORIGINAL mean belonging to a locality. NATIVE implies birth or origin in a place or region and may suggest compatibility with it ⟨*native* tribal customs⟩ INDIGENOUS applies to species or races and adds to NATIVE the implication of not having been introduced from elsewhere ⟨maize is *indigenous* to America⟩ ENDEMIC implies being peculiar to a region ⟨edelweiss is *endemic* in the Alps⟩ ABORIGINAL implies having no known race preceding in occupancy of the region ⟨the *aboriginal* peoples of Australia⟩

²**native** *n* (1535) **1** : one born or reared in a particular place **2** **a** : an original or indigenous inhabitant **b** : something indigenous to a particular locality **3** : a local resident; *esp* : a person who has always lived in a place as distinguished from a visitor or a temporary resident

Native American *n* (1925) : AMERICAN INDIAN — **Native American** *adj*

na·tiv·ism \'nāt-iv-,iz-əm\ *n* (1844) **1** : a policy of favoring native inhabitants as opposed to immigrants **2** : the revival or perpetuation of an indigenous culture esp. in opposition to acculturation — **na·tiv·ist** \-əst\ *n or adj* — **na·tiv·is·tic** \,nāt-iv-'is-tik\ *adj*

na·tiv·i·ty \nə-'tiv-ət-ē, nā-\ *n, pl* **-ties** [ME *nativite,* fr. MF *nativité,* fr. ML *nativitat-, nativitas,* fr. LL, birth, fr. L *nativus*] (14c) **1** : the process or circumstances of being born : BIRTH; *esp, cap* : the birth of Jesus **2** : a horoscope at or of the time of one's birth **3** : the place of origin

na·tri·ure·sis \,nā-trē-yu̇-'rē-səs\ *n* [NL, fr. *natrium* sodium (fr. ISV *natron*) + *uresis* urination, fr. Gk *ourēsis,* fr. *ourein* to urinate — more at URINE] (1957) : excessive loss of cations and esp. sodium in the urine — **na·tri·uret·ic** \-'ret-ik\ *adj*

na·tro·lite \'nā-trə-,līt\ *n* [G *natrolith,* fr. *natron* (fr. F) + *-lith* -lite] (ca. 1805) : a hydrous sodium aluminum silicate $Na_2Al_2Si_3O_{10}·2H_2O$ related to zeolite

na·tron \'nā-,trän, -trən\ *n* [F, fr. Sp *natrón,* fr. Ar *natrūn,* fr. Gk *nitron*] (1684) : a hydrated native sodium carbonate $Na_2CO_3·10H_2O$ used in ancient times in embalming, in ceramic pastes, and as a cleansing agent

nat·ter \'nat-ər\ *vi* [prob. imit.] (1942) : CHATTER

nat·ty \'nat-ē\ *adj* **nat·ti·er; -est** [perh. alter. of earlier *netty,* fr. obs. *net* neat, clean] (1557) : trimly neat and tidy : SMART — **nat·ti·ly** \'nat-ᵊl-ē\ *adv* — **nat·ti·ness** \'nat-ē-nəs\ *n*

¹**nat·u·ral** \'nach-(ə-)rəl\ *adj* [ME, fr. MF, fr. L *naturalis* of nature, fr. *natura* nature] (14c) **1** : based on an inherent sense of right and wrong ⟨~ justice⟩ **2** **a** : being in accordance with or determined by nature **b** : having or constituting a classification based on features existing in nature **3** **a** (1) : begotten as distinguished from adopted; *also* : LEGITIMATE (2) : being a relation by actual consanguinity as distinguished from adoption ⟨~ parents⟩ **b** : ILLEGITIMATE ⟨a ~ child⟩ **4** : having an essential relation with someone or something : following from the nature of the one in question ⟨his guilt is a ~ deduction from the evidence⟩ **5** : implanted or being as if implanted by nature : seemingly inborn ⟨a ~ talent for art⟩ **6** : of or relating to nature as an object of study and research **7** : having a specified character by nature ⟨a ~ athlete⟩ **8** **a** : occurring in conformity with the ordinary course of nature : not marvelous or supernatural ⟨~ causes⟩ **b** : formulated by human reason alone rather than revelation ⟨~ religion⟩ ⟨~ rights⟩ **c** : having a normal or usual character ⟨events followed their ~ course⟩ **9** : possessing or exhibiting the higher qualities (as kindliness and affection) of human nature ⟨a noble . . . brother . . . ever most kind and ~ —Shak.⟩ **10** **a** : growing without human care; *also* : not cultivated ⟨~ prairie unbroken by the plow⟩ **b** : existing in or produced by nature : not artificial ⟨~ scenery⟩ ⟨~ curiosities⟩ **c** : relating to or being natural food **11** **a** : being in a state of nature without spiritual enlightenment : UNREGENERATE ⟨~ man⟩ **b** : living in or as if in a state of nature untouched by the influences of civilization and society **12** **a** : having a physical or real existence as contrasted with one that is spiritual, intellectual, or fictitious ⟨a corporation is a legal but not a ~ person⟩ **b** : of, relating to, or operating in the physical as opposed to the spiritual world ⟨~ laws describe phenomena of the physical universe⟩ **13** **a** : closely resembling an original : true to nature **b** : marked by easy simplicity and freedom from artificiality, affectation, or constraint **c** : having a form or appearance found in nature **14** **a** : having neither flats nor sharps ⟨the ~ scale of C major⟩ **b** : being neither sharp nor flat **c** : having the pitch modified by the natural sign — **nat·u·ral·ness** \-(ə-)rəl-nəs\ *n*

syn NATURAL, INGENUOUS, NAIVE, UNSOPHISTICATED, ARTLESS mean free from pretension or calculation. NATURAL implies lacking artificiality and self-consciousness and having a spontaneousness suggesting the natural rather than the man-made world; INGENUOUS implies inability to disguise or conceal one's feelings or intentions; NAIVE suggests lack of worldly wisdom often connoting credulousness and unchecked innocence; UNSOPHISTICATED implies a lack of experience and training necessary for social ease and adroitness; ARTLESS suggests a naturalness resulting from unawareness of the effect one is producing on others. ***syn*** see in addition REGULAR

²**natural** *n* (1533) **1** : one born without the usual powers of reason and understanding **2** **a** : a sign placed on any degree of the musical staff to nullify the effect of a preceding sharp or flat **b** : a note or tone affected by the natural sign **3** : a result or combination that immediately wins the stake in a game; *specif* : a throw of 7 or 11 on the first cast in craps **4** **a** : one having natural skills, talents, or abilities **b** : something that is likely to become an immediate success **c** : one that is obviously suitable for a specific purpose **5** : AFRO

natural childbirth *n* (1933) : a system of managing childbirth in which the mother receives preparatory education in order to remain conscious during and assist in delivery with minimal or no use of drugs or anesthetics

natural food *n* (ca. 1917) : food that has undergone minimal processing and contains no preservatives or artificial additives (as synthetic flavorings)

natural gas *n* (1825) **1** : gas issuing from the earth's crust through natural openings or bored wells; *esp* : a combustible mixture of methane and higher hydrocarbons used chiefly as a fuel and raw material **2** : gas manufactured from organic matter (as coal)

natural history *n* (1567) **1** : a treatise on some aspect of nature **2** : the natural development of something (as an organism or disease) over a period of time **3** : the study of natural objects esp. in the field from an amateur or popular point of view

nat·u·ral·ism \'nach-(ə-)rə-,liz-əm\ *n* (1641) **1** : action, inclination, or thought based only on natural desires and instincts **2** : a theory denying that an event or object has a supernatural significance; *specif* : the doctrine that scientific laws are adequate to account for all phenomena **3** : realism in art or literature; *specif* : a theory in literature emphasizing scientific observation of life without idealization or the avoidance of the ugly

nat·u·ral·ist \-ləst\ *n* (1587) **1** : one that advocates or practices naturalism **2** : a student of natural history; *esp* : a field biologist

nat·u·ral·is·tic \,nach-(ə-)rə-'lis-tik\ *also* **nat·u·ral·ist** \'nach-(ə-)rə-ləst\ *adj* (1840) : of, characterized by, or according with naturalism — **nat·u·ral·is·ti·cal·ly** \,nach-(ə-)rə-'lis-ti-k(ə-)lē\ *adv*

nat·u·ral·ize \'nach-(ə-)rə-,līz\ *vb* **-ized; -iz·ing** *vt* (1593) **1** : to introduce into common use or into the vernacular **2** : to bring into conformity with nature **3** : to confer the rights of a national on; *esp* : to admit to citizenship **4** : to cause (as a plant) to become established as if native ~ *vi* : to become established as if native — **nat·u·ral·iza·tion** \,nach-(ə-)rə-lə-'zā-shən\ *n*

natural law *n* (14c) : a body of law or a specific principle held to be derived from nature and binding upon human society in the absence of or in addition to positive law

natural logarithm *n* (1816) : a logarithm with *e* as a base

nat·u·ral·ly \'nach-(ə-)rə-lē, 'nach-ər-lē\ *adv* (14c) **1** : by nature : by natural character or ability ⟨~ timid⟩ **2** : according to the usual course of things : as might be expected ⟨we ~ dislike being hurt⟩ **3** **a** : without artificial aid ⟨hair that curls ~⟩ **b** : without affectation ⟨speak ~⟩ **4** : with truth to nature : REALISTICALLY

natural number *n* (1763) : the number 1 or any number (as 3, 12, 432) obtained by adding 1 to this number one or more times

natural philosophy *n* (14c) : NATURAL SCIENCE; *esp* : PHYSICAL SCIENCE — **natural philosopher** *n*

natural resource *n* (1870) **1** *pl* : industrial materials and capacities (as mineral deposits and waterpower) supplied by nature **2** : RESOURCE 1b

natural science *n* (14c) : any of the sciences (as physics, chemistry, or biology) that deal with matter, energy, and their interrelations and transformations or with objectively measurable phenomena — **natural scientist** *n*

natural selection *n* (1857) : a natural process that results in the survival of individuals or groups best adjusted to the conditions under which they live and that is equally important for the perpetuation of desirable genetic qualities and for the elimination of undesirable ones as these are produced by genic recombination or mutation

natural theology *n* (1677) : theology deriving its knowledge of God from the study of nature independent of special revelation

na·ture \'nā-chər\ *n* [ME, fr. MF, fr. L *natura,* fr. *natus,* pp. of *nasci* to be born — more at NATION] (14c) **1** **a** : the inherent character or basic constitution of a person or thing : ESSENCE **b** : DISPOSITION, TEMPERAMENT **2** **a** : a creative and controlling force in the universe **b** : an inner force or the sum of such forces in an individual **3** : a kind or class usu. distinguished by fundamental or essential characteristics ⟨documents of a confidential ~⟩ ⟨acts of a ceremonial ~⟩ **4** : the physical constitution or drives of an organism; *esp* : an excretory organ or function — usu. used in the phrase *call of nature* **5** : a spontaneous attitude (as of generosity) **6** : the external world in its entirety **7** **a** : man's original or natural condition **b** : a simplified mode of life resembling this condition **8** : natural scenery ***syn*** see TYPE

na·tur·ism \'nā-chə-,riz-əm\ *n* (1847) **1** : NATURALISM 1,2 **2** : the worship of the forces of nature **3** : NUDISM — **na·tur·ist** \-rəst\ *n*

na·tu·ro·path \'nā-chə-rə-,path, nə-'t(y)u̇r-ə-\ *n* [back-formation fr. *naturopathy*] (1901) : a practitioner of naturopathy

na·tu·rop·a·thy \,nā-chə-'räp-ə-thē\ *n* [*nature* + *-o-* + *-pathy*] (1901) : a system of treatment of disease that avoids drugs and surgery and emphasizes the use of natural agents (as air, water, and sunshine) and physical means (as manipulation and electrical treatment) — **na·tu·ro·path·ic** \,nā-chə-rə-'path-ik, nə-,t(y)u̇r-ə-\ *adj*

Nau·ga·hyde \'nȯg-ə-,hīd, 'näg-\ *trademark* — used for vinyl-coated fabrics

[1]**naught** \'nȯt, 'nät\ *pron* [ME, fr. OE *nāwiht,* fr. *nā* no + *wiht* creature, thing — more at NO, WIGHT] (bef. 12c) : NOTHING

[2]**naught** *n* (bef. 12c) **1** : NOTHINGNESS, NONEXISTENCE **2** : the arithmetical symbol 0 : ZERO, CIPHER

naugh·ty \'nȯt-ē, 'nät-\ *adj* **naugh·ti·er; -est** [[2]*naught*] (14c) **1** **a** *archaic* : vicious in moral character : WICKED **b** : guilty of disobedience or misbehavior **2** : lacking in taste or propriety ***syn*** see BAD — **naugh·ti·ly** \'nȯt-ᵊl-ē, 'nät-\ *adv* — **naugh·ti·ness** \'nȯt-ē-nəs, 'nät-\ *n*

nau·ma·chia \nȯ-'māk-ē-ə, -'mak-\ *n, pl* **-chi·ae** \-ē-,ē, -ē-,ī\ *or* **-chi·as** [L, fr. Gk, naval battle, fr. *naus* ship + *machesthai* to fight — more at NAVE] (1596) **1** : an ancient Roman spectacle representing a naval battle **2** : a place for naumachiae

nau·pli·us \'nȯ-plē-əs\ *n, pl* **-plii** \-plē-,ī, -,ē\ [NL, fr. L, a shellfish, fr. Gk *nauplios*] (1836) : a crustacean larva in usu. the first stage after leaving the egg and with three pairs of appendages, a median eye, and little or no segmentation

nau·sea \'nȯ-zē-ə, -sē-ə; 'nȯ-zhə, -shə\ *n* [L, seasickness, nausea, fr. Gk *nautia, nausia,* fr. *nautēs* sailor] (1569) **1** : a stomach distress with distaste for food and an urge to vomit **2** : extreme disgust — **nau·se·ant** \-z(h)ē-ənt, -s(h)ē-\ *n or adj*

nau·se·ate \'nȯ-z(h)ē-,āt, -s(h)ē-\ *vb* **-at·ed; -at·ing** *vi* (1640) **1** : to become affected with nausea **2** : to feel disgust ~ *vt* : to affect with nausea or disgust

nau·se·at·ing \-,āt-iŋ\ *adj* (1645) : causing nausea or esp. disgust ***usage*** see NAUSEOUS — **nau·se·at·ing·ly** *adv*

nau·seous \'nȯ-shəs, 'nȯ-zē-əs\ *adj* (1612) **1** : causing nausea or disgust : NAUSEATING **2** : affected with nausea or disgust — **nau·seous·ly** *adv* — **nau·seous·ness** *n*

usage Those who insist that *nauseous* can properly be used only in sense 1 are in error. Current evidence shows these facts: *nauseous* is most frequently used to mean physically affected with nausea; extended use is quite a bit less frequent. Use of *nauseous* in sense 1 is much more often figurative than literal, but this use appears to be losing ground to *nauseating.* There seems to be little use of *nauseated* except by those who prescribe it in place of *nauseous.*

nautch \'nȯch\ *n* [Hindi *nāc,* fr. Skt *nṛtya,* fr. *nṛtyati* he dances] (1809) : an entertainment in India consisting chiefly of dancing by professional dancing girls

nau·ti·cal \'nȯt-i-kəl, 'nät-\ *adj* [L *nauticus,* fr. Gk *nautikos,* fr. *nautēs* sailor, fr. *naus* ship — more at NAVE] (1552) : of, relating to, or associated with seamen, navigation, or ships — **nau·ti·cal·ly** \-k(ə-)lē\ *adv*

nautical mile *n* (1632) : any of various units of distance used for sea and air navigation based on the length of a minute of arc of a great circle of the earth and differing because the earth is not a perfect sphere: as **a** : a British unit equal to 6080 feet (1853.2 meters) — called also *Admiralty mile* **b** : a U.S. unit no longer in official use equal to 6080.20 feet (1853.248 meters) **c** : an international unit equal to 6076.115 feet (1852 meters) used officially in the U.S. since July 1, 1959

nau·ti·loid \'nȯt-ᵊl-,ȯid, 'nät-\ *n* (ca. 1847) : any of a group (Nautiloidea) of cephalopods that were important in the Ordovician and esp. the Silurian but are represented in the recent fauna only by the nautiluses — **nautiloid** *adj*

nau·ti·lus \'nȯt-ᵊl-əs, 'nät-\ *n, pl* **-lus·es** *or* **-li** \-ᵊl-,ī, -,ē\ [NL, fr. L, paper nautilus, fr. Gk *nautilos,* lit., sailor, fr. *naus* ship] (1601) **1** : any of a genus (*Nautilus*) of cephalopod mollusks of the So. Pacific and Indian oceans with a spiral chambered shell that is pearly on the inside — called also *chambered nautilus* **2** : PAPER NAUTILUS

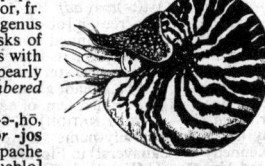

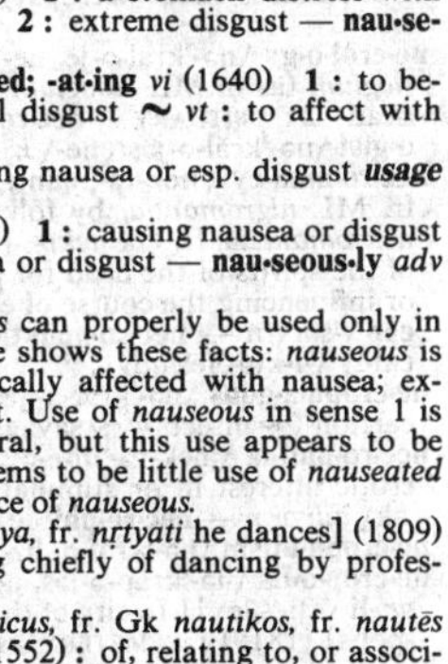
nautilus 1

Na·va·ho *or* **Na·va·jo** \'nav-ə-,hō, 'näv-\ *n, pl* **-ho** *or* **-hos** *or* **-jo** *or* **-jos** [Sp (*Apache de*) *Navajó,* lit., Apache of Navajó, fr. *Navajó,* a pueblo] (1780) **1** : a member of an American Indian people of northern New Mexico and Arizona **2** : the language of the Navaho people

nav·aid \'nav-,ād\ *n* [*navigation aid*] (1956) : a device or system (as a radar beacon) that provides a navigator with navigational data

na·val \'nā-vəl\ *adj* [L *navalis,* fr. *navis* ship] (15c) **1** *obs* : of or relating to ships or shipping **2** **a** : of or relating to a navy **b** : consisting of or involving warships

naval architect *n* (ca. 1846) : one who designs ships

naval stores *n pl* [fr. their former use in the construction and maintenance of wooden sailing vessels] (1678) : products (as turpentine, pitch, and rosin) obtained from resinous conifers and esp. pines

[1]**nave** \'nāv\ *n* [ME, fr. OE *nafu;* akin to OE *nafela* navel] (bef. 12c) : the hub of a wheel

[2]**nave** *n* [ML *navis,* fr. L, ship; akin to OE *nōwend* sailor, Gk *naus* ship, Skt *nau*] (1673) : the main part of the interior of a church; *esp* : the long narrow central hall in a cruciform church that rises higher than the aisles flanking it to form a clerestory

na·vel \'nā-vəl\ *n* [ME, fr. OE *nafela;* akin to OHG *nabalo* navel, L *umbilicus,* Gk *omphalos*] (bef. 12c) **1** : a depression in the middle of the abdomen that marks the point of former attachment of the umbilical cord or yolk stalk **2** : the central point : MIDDLE

navel orange *n* (1846) : a seedless orange having a pit at the apex where the fruit encloses a small secondary fruit — called also *navel*

[1]**na·vic·u·lar** \nə-'vik-yə-lər\ *n* [NL (*os*) *naviculare* navicular bone] (15c) : a navicular bone; *esp* : one situated at the medial side of the tarsus

[2]**navicular** *adj* [L *navicula* boat, dim. of *navis*] (1541) : shaped like a boat ⟨a ~ bone⟩

nav·i·ga·ble \'nav-i-gə-bəl\ *adj* (15c) **1** : deep enough and wide enough to afford passage to ships **2** : capable of being steered — **nav·i·ga·bil·i·ty** \,nav-i-gə-'bil-ət-ē\ *n* — **nav·i·ga·bly** \'nav-i-gə-blē\ *adv*

nav·i·gate \'nav-ə-,gāt\ *vb* **-gat·ed; -gat·ing** [L *navigatus,* pp. of *navigare,* fr. *navis* ship + *-igare* (fr. *agere* to drive) — more at AGENT] *vi* (1588) **1** : to travel by water : SAIL **2** : to steer a course through a medium; *specif* : to operate an airplane **3** : to get about : WALK ~ *vt* **1** **a** : to sail over, on, or through **b** : to make one's way over or through : TRAVERSE **2** **a** : to steer or manage (a boat) in sailing **b** : to operate or control the course of (as an airplane)

nav·i·ga·tion \,nav-ə-'gā-shən\ *n* (1547) **1** : the act or practice of navigating **2** : the science of getting ships, aircraft, or spacecraft from place to place; *esp* : the method of determining position, course, and distance traveled **3** : ship traffic or commerce — **nav·i·ga·tion·al** \-shnəl, -shən-ᵊl\ *adj* — **nav·i·ga·tion·al·ly** \-ē\ *adv*

nav·i·ga·tor \'nav-ə-,gāt-ər\ *n* (1590) : one that navigates or is qualified to navigate

nav·vy \'nav-ē\ *n, pl* **navvies** [by shortening & alter. fr. *navigator* (construction worker on a canal, navvy)] *chiefly Brit* (1832) : an unskilled laborer

na·vy \'nā-vē\ *n, pl* **navies** [ME *navie,* fr. MF, fr. L *navigia* ships, fr. *navigare*] (14c) **1** : a group of ships : FLEET **2** : a nation's ships of war and of logistic support **3** *often cap* : the complete naval establishment of a nation including yards, stations, ships, and personnel **4** : a variable color averaging a dark grayish purplish blue

navy bean *n* (1856) : a white-seeded kidney bean grown esp. for its nutritious seeds

Navy Cross *n* (1919) : a U.S. Navy decoration awarded for extraordinary heroism in operations against an armed enemy

navy exchange *n* (1955) : a post exchange at a naval installation

navy yard *n* (1771) : a yard where naval vessels are built or repaired

na·wab \nə-'wäb\ *n* [Hindi & Urdu *nawwāb*] (1614) : NABOB 1

[1]**nay** \'nā\ *adv* [ME, fr. ON *nei,* fr. *ne* not + *ei* ever — more at AYE] (12c) **1** : NO **2** : not merely this but also : not only so but ⟨the letter made him happy, ~, ecstatic⟩

[2]**nay** *n* (14c) **1** : DENIAL, REFUSAL **2** **a** : a negative reply or vote **b** : one who votes no

nay·say·er \'nā-,sā-ər, -,se(-ə)r\ *n* (1721) : one who denies, refuses, or opposes something

Naz·a·rene \,naz-ə-'rēn\ *n* [ME *Nazaren,* fr. LL *Nazarenus,* fr. Gk *Nazarēnos,* fr. *Nazareth* Nazareth, Palestine] (13c) **1** : a native or resident of Nazareth **2** **a** : CHRISTIAN 1a **b** : a member of the Church of the Nazarene that is a Protestant denomination deriving from the merging of three holiness groups, stressing sanctification, and following Methodist polity

Na·zi \'nät-sē, 'nat-\ *n* [G, by shortening & alter. fr. *nationalsozialist,* fr. *national* national + *sozialist* socialist] (1930) **1** : a member of a German fascist party controlling Germany from 1933 to 1945 under Adolf Hitler **2** *often not cap* : one who resembles a German Nazi — **nazi** *adj, often cap* — **na·zi·fi·ca·tion** \,nät-si-fə-'kā-shən, ,nat-\ *n, often cap* — **na·zi·fy** \'nät-si-,fī, 'nat-\ *vt, often cap*

Naz·i·rite *or* **Naz·a·rite** \'naz-ə-,rīt\ *n* [LL *nazaraeus,* fr. Gk *naziraios, nazaraios,* fr. Heb *nāzīr,* lit., consecrated] (1560) : a Jew of biblical times consecrated to God by a vow to avoid drinking wine, cutting the hair, and being defiled by the presence of a corpse — **Naz·i·rit·ism** \-,rīt-,iz-əm\ *n*

Na·zism \'nät-,siz-əm, 'nat-\ *or* **Na·zi·ism** \-sē-,iz-əm\ *n* [*Nazi* + *-ism*] (1934) : the body of political and economic doctrines held and put into effect by the National Socialist German Workers' party in the Third German Reich including the totalitarian principle of government, state control of all industry, predominance of groups assumed to be racially superior, and supremacy of the führer

NCO \,en-,sē-'ō\ *n* (1905) : NONCOMMISSIONED OFFICER

-nd *symbol* — used after the figure 2 to indicate the ordinal number *second* ⟨2nd⟩ ⟨72nd⟩

né \'nā\ *adj* [F, lit., born — more at NÉE] (1905) **1** — used to indicate the original, former, or legal name of a man ⟨Robert Roe, ~ John Doe⟩ **2** : originally or formerly called

ne- *or* **neo-** *comb form* [Gk, fr. *neos* new — more at NEW] **1** **a** : new : recent ⟨*Neo*cene⟩ **b** : new and different period or form of ⟨*Neo*platonism⟩ : in a new and different form or manner ⟨*Neo*platonic⟩ **c** : New World ⟨*Neo*tropical⟩ **d** : new and abnormal ⟨*neo*plasm⟩ **2** : new chemical compound isomeric with or otherwise related to (such) a compound ⟨*neo*arsphenamine⟩

Ne·an·der·thal \nē-ˈan-dər-ˌt(h)ȯl, nā-ˈän-dər-ˌtäl\ *adj* (1861) **1 :** being, relating to, or resembling Neanderthal man **2 :** suggesting a caveman in appearance or behavior — **Neanderthal** *n*

Neanderthal man *n* [*Neanderthal,* valley in western Germany] (1863) **:** a Middle Paleolithic man (*Homo neanderthalensis*) known from skeletal remains in Europe, northern Africa, and western Asia — **Ne·an·der·thal·oid** \-ˌȯid\ *adj or n*

[1]**neap** \ˈnēp\ *adj* [ME *neep,* fr. OE *nēp* being at the stage of neap tide] (bef. 12c) **:** of, relating to, or constituting a neap tide

[2]**neap** *n* (1584) **:** NEAP TIDE

Ne·a·pol·i·tan \ˌnē-ə-ˈpäl-ət-ᵊn\ *n* [L *neapolitanus* of Naples, fr. Gk *neapolitēs* citizen of Naples, fr. *Neapolis* Naples] (15c) **:** a native or inhabitant of Naples, Italy — **Neapolitan** *adj*

Neapolitan ice cream *n* (ca. 1876) **:** a brick of from two to four layers of ice cream of different flavors

neap tide *n* (1548) **:** a tide of minimum range occurring at the first and the third quarters of the moon

[1]**near** \ˈni(ə)r\ *adv* [ME *ner,* partly fr. *ner* nearer, fr. OE *nēar,* comparative of *nēah* nigh; partly fr. ON *nær* nearer, compar. of *nā-* nigh — more at NIGH] (bef. 12c) **1 :** at, within, or to a short distance or time **2 :** ALMOST, NEARLY ⟨~ dead⟩ **3 :** in a close or intimate manner ⟨~ related⟩ **4** *archaic* **:** in a frugal manner

[2]**near** \(ˈ)ni(ə)r\ *prep* (bef. 12c) **:** close to

[3]**near** \ˈni(ə)r\ *adj* (bef. 12c) **1 :** closely related or intimately associated **2 a :** not far distant in time, place, or degree ⟨in the ~ future⟩ **b :** barely avoided ⟨the bomb's ~ hit rattled but did not harm the troops⟩ **c :** barely occurring **:** nearly not happening ⟨a ~ miss by the torpedo⟩ **3 a :** being the closer of two ⟨the ~ side⟩ **b :** being the left-hand one of a pair ⟨the ~ wheel of a cart⟩ **4 :** DIRECT, SHORT ⟨the ~*est* road⟩ **5 :** STINGY, CLOSEFISTED **6 a :** closely resembling a prototype **b :** approximating the genuine ⟨~ silk⟩ — **near·ness** *n*

[4]**near** \ˈni(ə)r\ *vb* (bef. 12c) **:** APPROACH

near beer *n* (1909) **:** any of various malt liquors considered nonalcoholic because they contain less than a specified percentage of alcohol

near·by \ni(ə)r-ˈbī, ˈni(ə)r-ˌ\ *adv or adj* (14c) **:** close at hand

Ne·arc·tic \(ˈ)nē-ˈärk-tik, -ˈärt-ik\ *adj* (1858) **:** of, relating to, or being the biogeographic subregion that includes Greenland, arctic America, and the parts of No. America north of tropical Mexico

near gale *n* (ca. 1805) **:** MODERATE GALE — see BEAUFORT SCALE table

near·ly \ˈni(ə)r-lē\ *adv* (1540) **1 :** in a close manner or relationship ⟨~ related⟩ **2 :** almost but not quite ⟨~ identical⟩ ⟨~ a year later⟩

near money *n* (ca. 1942) **:** assets (as savings accounts or government bonds) quickly and easily converted to cash

near point *n* (1876) **:** the point nearest the eye at which an object is accurately focused on the retina at full accommodation

near·sight·ed \ˈni(ə)r-ˈsīt-əd\ *adj* (1686) **:** able to see near things more clearly than distant ones **:** MYOPIC — **near·sight·ed·ly** *adv* — **near·sight·ed·ness** *n*

[1]**neat** \ˈnēt\ *n, pl* **neat** *or* **neats** [ME *neet,* fr. OE *nēat;* akin to OHG *nōz* head of cattle, OE *nēotan* to make use of] (bef. 12c) **:** the common domestic bovine (*Bos taurus*)

[2]**neat** *adj* [MF *net,* fr. L *nitidus* bright, neat, fr. *nitēre* to shine; akin to OPer *naiba-* beautiful] (1579) **1 :** free from dirt and disorder **:** habitually clean and orderly **2 a :** free from admixture or dilution **:** STRAIGHT ⟨~ brandy⟩ ⟨~ cement⟩ **b :** free from irregularity **:** SMOOTH ⟨~ silk⟩ **3 :** marked by tasteful simplicity ⟨a ~ outfit⟩ **4 a :** PRECISE, SYSTEMATIC **b :** marked by skill or ingenuity **:** ADROIT **5 :** NET ⟨~ profit⟩ **6 :** FINE, ADMIRABLE — **neat·ly** *adv* — **neat·ness** *n*

[3]**neat** *adv* (1579) **:** without admixture or dilution **:** STRAIGHT

neat·en \ˈnēt-ᵊn\ *vt* **neat·ened; neat·en·ing** \ˈnēt-niŋ, -ᵊn-iŋ\ (1574) **1 :** to set in order **:** make neat **2 :** to finish (as a piece of sewing) carefully

neath \(ˈ)nēth\ *prep, dial* (1685) **:** BENEATH

neat·herd \ˈnēt-ˌhərd\ *n* (14c) **:** HERDSMAN

neat's–foot oil \ˈnēts-ˌfu̇t-\ *n* (1579) **:** a pale yellow fatty oil made esp. from the bones of cattle and used chiefly as a leather dressing

neb \ˈneb\ *n* [ME, fr. OE; akin to ON *nef* beak] (bef. 12c) **1 a :** the beak of a bird or tortoise **:** BILL **b** *chiefly dial* **:** a person's mouth **c :** NOSE 1, SNOUT **2 :** NIB, TIP

neb·bish \ˈneb-ish\ *n* [Yiddish *nebach, nebech* poor thing (used interjectionally), of Slav origin; akin to Polish *niebożę* poor thing] (1892) **:** a timid, meek, or ineffectual person

ne·ben·kern \ˈnā-bən-ˌkərn, -ˌke(ə)rn\ *n* [G, lit., subsidiary nucleus] (1898) **:** a 2-stranded helical structure of the proximal tail region of spermatozoa that is derived from mitochondria

neb·u·la \ˈneb-yə-lə\ *n, pl* **-las** *or* **-lae** \-ˌlē, -ˌlī\ [NL, fr. L, mist, cloud; akin to OHG *nebul* fog, Gk *nephelē, nephos* cloud] (1661) **1 :** a slight cloudy opacity of the cornea **2 a :** any of many immense bodies of highly rarefied gas or dust in interstellar space **b :** GALAXY; *esp* **:** a galaxy other than the Milky Way galaxy — **neb·u·lar** \-lər\ *adj*

nebular hypothesis *n* (1837) **:** a hypothesis in astronomy: the solar system has evolved from a hot gaseous nebula

neb·u·lize \ˈneb-yə-ˌlīz\ *vt* **-lized; -liz·ing** [L *nebula*] (1872) **:** to reduce to a fine spray — **neb·u·li·za·tion** \ˌneb-yə-lə-ˈzā-shən\ *n* — **neb·u·liz·er** \ˈneb-yə-ˌlī-zər\ *n*

neb·u·los·i·ty \ˌneb-yə-ˈläs-ət-ē\ *n, pl* **-ties** (1761) **1 :** the quality or state of being nebulous **2 :** nebulous matter; *also* **:** NEBULA 2a

neb·u·lous \ˈneb-yə-ləs\ *adj* [L *nebulosus* misty, fr. *nebula*] (1679) **1 :** of, relating to, or resembling a nebula **:** NEBULAR **2 :** INDISTINCT, VAGUE — **neb·u·lous·ly** *adv* — **neb·u·lous·ness** *n*

nec·es·sar·i·ly \ˌnes-ə-ˈser-ə-lē\ *adv* (15c) **1 :** of necessity **:** UNAVOIDABLY **2 :** as a logical result or consequence

[1]**nec·es·sary** \ˈnes-ə-ˌser-ē\ *n, pl* **-saries** (14c) **:** an indispensable item **:** ESSENTIAL

[2]**necessary** *adj* [ME *necessarie,* fr. L *necessarius,* fr. *necesse* necessary, fr. *ne-* not + *cedere* to withdraw — more at NO, CEDE] (14c) **1 a :** of an inevitable nature **:** INESCAPABLE **b (1) :** logically unavoidable **(2) :** that cannot be denied without contradiction **c :** determined or produced by the previous condition of things **d :** COMPULSORY **2 :** absolutely needed **:** REQUIRED

necessary condition *n* (1817) **1 :** a proposition whose falsity assures the falsity of another **2 :** a state of affairs that must prevail if another is to occur **:** PREREQUISITE

ne·ces·si·tar·i·an·ism \ni-ˌses-ə-ˈter-ē-ə-ˌniz-əm, -ˌiz-əm\ *n* (1854) **:** the theory that results follow by invariable sequence from causes — **ne·ces·si·tar·i·an** \-ē-ən\ *adj or n*

ne·ces·si·tate \ni-ˈses-ə-ˌtāt\ *vt* **-tat·ed; -tat·ing** (1628) **1 :** to make necessary **:** REQUIRE **2 :** FORCE, COMPEL — **ne·ces·si·ta·tion** \-ˌses-ə-ˈtā-shən\ *n*

ne·ces·si·tous \ni-ˈses-ət-əs\ *adj* (1611) **1 :** NEEDY, IMPOVERISHED **2 :** URGENT, PRESSING **3 :** NECESSARY — **ne·ces·si·tous·ly** *adv* — **ne·ces·si·tous·ness** *n*

ne·ces·si·ty \ni-ˈses-ət-ē, -ˈses-tē\ *n, pl* **-ties** [ME *necessite,* fr. MF *necessité,* fr. L *necessitat-, necessitas,* fr. *necesse*] (14c) **1 :** the quality or state of being necessary **2 a :** pressure of circumstance **b :** physical or moral compulsion **c :** impossibility of a contrary order or condition **3 :** the quality or state of being in need; *esp* **:** POVERTY **4 a :** something that is necessary **:** REQUIREMENT **b :** an urgent need or desire — **of necessity :** in such a way that it cannot be otherwise; *also* **:** as a necessary consequence

[1]**neck** \ˈnek\ *n* [ME *nekke,* fr. OE *hnecca;* akin to OHG *hnac* nape, OE *hnutu* nut — more at NUT] (bef. 12c) **1 a (1) :** the part of an animal that connects the head with the body **(2) :** the siphon of a bivalve mollusk (as a clam) **b :** the part of a garment that covers or is next to the neck **2 :** a relatively narrow part suggestive of a neck: as **a (1) :** the constricted end of a bottle **(2) :** the slender proximal end of a fruit **b :** CERVIX 2 **c :** the part of a stringed musical instrument extending from the body and supporting the fingerboard and strings **d :** a narrow stretch of land **e :** STRAIT 1b **f :** the part of a tooth between the crown and the root **g :** a column of solidified magma of a volcanic pipe or laccolith **3 :** a narrow margin ⟨won by a ~⟩ **4 :** REGION, PART ⟨my ~ of the woods⟩

[2]**neck** *vt* (1784) **1 :** to reduce in diameter **2 :** to kiss and caress amorously ~ *vi* **1 :** to engage in amorous kissing and caressing **2 :** to become constricted **:** NARROW

neck and neck *adv or adj* (1799) **:** very close (as in a race)

necked \ˈnekt\ *adj* (14c) **:** having a neck esp. of a specified kind — often used in combination ⟨long-*necked*⟩

neck·er·chief \ˈnek-ər-chəf, -(ˌ)chif, -ˌchēf\ *n, pl* **-chiefs** *also* **-chieves** *see* HANDKERCHIEF *pl* \ [ME *nekkerchef,* fr. *nekke* + *kerchef* kerchief] (14c) **:** a kerchief for the neck

neck·ing \ˈnek-iŋ\ *n* (1804) **1 :** a small molding near the top of a column or pilaster **2 :** the act or practice of kissing and caressing amorously

neck·lace \ˈnek-ləs\ *n* (1590) **:** an ornament worn around the neck

neck·line \-ˌlīn\ *n* (1909) **:** the line of the neck opening of a garment

neck–rein \-ˌrān\ *vi, of a saddle horse* (1926) **:** to respond to the pressure of a rein on one side of the neck by turning in the opposite direction ~ *vt* **:** to direct (a horse) by pressures of the rein on the neck

neck·tie \-ˌtī\ *n* (1838) **:** a narrow length of material worn about the neck and tied in front; *esp* **:** FOUR-IN-HAND

necr- *or* **necro-** *comb form* [LL, fr. Gk *nekr-, nekro-,* fr. *nekros* dead body — more at NOXIOUS] **1 a :** those that are dead ⟨*necro*philia⟩ **b :** one that is dead ⟨*necro*psy⟩ **2 :** conversion to dead tissue ⟨*necro*biosis⟩

ne·crol·o·gy \nə-ˈkräl-ə-jē, ne-\ *n, pl* **-gies** [NL *necrologium,* fr. *necr-* + *-logium* (as in ML *eulogium* eulogy)] (1854) **1 :** a list of the recently dead **2 :** OBITUARY — **nec·ro·log·i·cal** \ˌnek-rə-ˈläj-i-kəl\ *adj* — **ne·crol·o·gist** \nə-ˈkräl-ə-jəst, ne-\ *n*

nec·ro·man·cy \ˈnek-rə-ˌman(t)-sē\ *n* [alter. of ME *nigromancie,* fr. MF, fr. ML *nigromantia,* by folk etymology fr. LL *necromantia,* fr. LGk *nekromanteia,* fr. Gk *nekr-* + *-manteia* -mancy] (14c) **1 :** conjuration of the spirits of the dead for purposes of magically revealing the future or influencing the course of events **2 :** MAGIC, SORCERY — **nec·ro·man·cer** \-sər\ *n* — **nec·ro·man·tic** \ˌnek-rə-ˈmant-ik\ *adj* — **nec·ro·man·ti·cal·ly** \-i-k(ə-)lē\ *adv*

ne·croph·a·gous \nə-ˈkräf-ə-gəs, ne-\ *adj* (1835) **:** feeding on corpses or carrion ⟨~ insects⟩ ⟨~ savages⟩

nec·ro·phil·ia \ˌnek-rə-ˈfil-ē-ə\ *n* [NL] (1892) **:** obsession with and usu. erotic interest in or stimulation by corpses — **nec·ro·phil·i·ac** \-ˈfil-ē-ˌak\ *adj or n* — **nec·ro·phil·ic** \-ˈfil-ik\ *adj*

ne·croph·i·lism \nə-ˈkräf-ə-ˌliz-əm, ne-\ *n* (1889) **:** NECROPHILIA

ne·crop·o·lis \nə-ˈkräp-ə-ləs, ne-\ *n, pl* **-lis·es** *or* **-les** \-ˌlēz\ *or* **-leis** \-ˌlās\ *or* **-li** \-ˌlī, -ˌlē\ [LL, city of the dead, fr. Gk *nekropolis,* fr. *nekr-* + *-polis* -polis] (1819) **:** CEMETERY; *esp* **:** a large elaborate cemetery of an ancient city

[1]**nec·rop·sy** \ˈnek-ˌräp-sē\ *n, pl* **-sies** (1856) **:** POSTMORTEM EXAMINATION

[2]**necropsy** *vt* **-sied; -sy·ing** (1927) **:** to perform a postmortem examination upon

ne·cro·sis \nə-ˈkrō-səs, ne-\ *n, pl* **ne·cro·ses** \-ˌsēz\ [LL, fr. Gk *nekrōsis,* fr. *nekroun* to make dead, fr. *nekros* — more at NOXIOUS] (1665) **:** usu. localized death of living tissue — **ne·crot·ic** \-ˈkrät-ik\ *adj*

nec·ro·tiz·ing \ˈnek-rə-ˌtī-ziŋ\ *adj* [Gk *nekrōtikos* necrotic, fr. *nekroun*] (1873) **:** causing, associated with, or undergoing necrosis ⟨~ infections⟩ ⟨~ tissue⟩

nec·tar \ˈnek-tər\ *n* [L, fr. Gk *nektar*] (1555) **1 a :** the drink of the Greek and Roman gods **b :** something delicious to drink **c :** a beverage of fruit juice and pulp ⟨apricot ~⟩ **2 :** a sweet liquid that is secreted by the nectaries of a plant and is the chief raw material of honey — **nec·tar·ous** \-t(ə-)rəs\ *adj*

nec·tar·ine \ˌnek-tə-ˈrēn\ *n* [obs. *nectarine,* adj. (like nectar)] (1611) **:** a peach with a smooth-skinned fruit that is a frequent somatic mutation of the normal peach; *also* **:** its fruit

nec·tary \ˈnek-t(ə-)rē\ *n, pl* **-tar·ies** [NL *nectarium,* irreg. fr. L *nectar* + *-arium* -ary] (1759) **:** a plant gland that secretes nectar

née *or* **nee** \ˈnā\ *adj* [F *née,* fem. of *né,* lit., born, pp. of *naître* to be born, fr. L *nasci* — more at NATION] (1758) **1 —** used to identify a woman by her maiden family name **2 :** originally or formerly called ⟨Cape Kennedy (~ Canaveral) in Florida —John Lear⟩

[1]**need** \ˈnēd\ *n* [ME *ned,* fr. OE *nīed, nēd;* akin to OHG *nōt* distress, need] (bef. 12c) **1 :** necessary duty **:** OBLIGATION **2 a :** a lack of something requisite, desirable, or useful **b :** a physiological or psychological requirement for the well-being of an organism **3 :** a condition requiring supply or relief **4 :** lack of the means of subsistence **:** POVERTY

[2]need *vi* (bef. 12c) **1 :** to be in want **2 :** to be needful or necessary ~ *vt* **:** to be in need of **:** REQUIRE ~ *verbal auxiliary* **:** be under necessity or obligation to ⟨you ~ not answer⟩

[1]need·ful \ˈnēd-fəl\ *adj* (bef. 12c) **1 :** being in need **2 :** NECESSARY, REQUISITE — **need·ful·ly** \-fə-lē\ *adv* — **need·ful·ness** *n*

[2]needful *n* (1709) **1 :** something needed or requisite **2 :** MONEY

[1]nee·dle \ˈnēd-ᵊl\ *n* [ME *nedle,* fr. OE *nǣdl;* akin to OHG *nādala* needle, *nājan* to sew, L *nēre* to spin, Gk *nēn*] (bef. 12c) **1 a :** a small slender usu. steel instrument that has an eye for thread at one end and that is used for sewing **b :** any of various devices for carrying thread and making stitches (as in crocheting or knitting) **c** (1) **:** a needle designed to carry sutures when sewing tissues in surgery (2) **:** a slender hollow instrument for introducing material into or removing material from the body parenterally (3) **:** a hollow device designed to contain radioactive material **2 :** a slender usu. sharp-pointed indicator on a dial; *esp* **:** MAGNETIC NEEDLE **3 a :** a slender pointed object resembling a needle: as (1) **:** a pointed crystal (2) **:** a sharp rock (3) **:** OBELISK **b :** a needle-shaped leaf (as of a conifer) **c :** a slender piece of jewel, steel, wood, or fiber with a rounded tip used in a phonograph to transmit vibrations from the record **:** STYLUS **d :** a slender pointed rod controlling a fine inlet or outlet (as in a valve) **4 :** a teasing or gibing remark — **nee·dle·like** \ˈnēd-ᵊl-ˌ(l)īk\ *adj*

[2]needle *vb* **nee·dled; nee·dling** \ˈnēd-liŋ, -ᵊl-iŋ\ *vt* (1715) **1 :** to sew or pierce with or as if with a needle **2 a :** TEASE, TORMENT **b :** to incite to action by repeated gibes ⟨*needled* the boy into a fight⟩ ~ *vi* **:** SEW, EMBROIDER — **nee·dler** \ˈnēd-lər, -ᵊl-ər\ *n*

nee·dle·fish \ˈnēd-ᵊl-ˌfish\ *n* (1601) **1 :** any of a family (Belonidae) of voracious elongate green and silvery teleost fishes with long slender jaws **2 :** PIPEFISH

nee·dle·point \-ˌpȯint\ *n* (ca. 1865) **1 :** lace worked with a needle over a paper pattern **2 :** embroidery done on canvas usu. in simple even stitches across counted threads — **needlepoint** *adj*

need·less \ˈnēd-ləs\ *adj* (bef. 12c) **:** not needed **:** UNNECESSARY ⟨~ waste⟩ — **need·less·ly** *adv* — **need·less·ness** *n*

nee·dle·wom·an \ˈnēd-ᵊl-ˌwu̇m-ən\ *n* (1611) **:** a woman who does needlework; *esp* **:** SEAMSTRESS

nee·dle·work \-ˌwərk\ *n* (14c) **1 :** work done with a needle; *esp* **:** work (as embroidery) other than plain sewing **2 :** the occupation of one who does needlework — **nee·dle·work·er** \-ˌwər-kər\ *n*

needn't \ˈnēd-ᵊnt\ **:** need not

needs \ˈnēdz\ *adv* [ME *nedes,* fr. OE *nēdes,* fr. gen. of *nēd* need] (bef. 12c) **:** of necessity **:** NECESSARILY ⟨must ~ be recognized⟩

needy \ˈnēd-ē\ *adj* **need·i·er; -est** (14c) **:** being in want **:** POVERTY-STRICKEN ⟨~ families⟩ — **need·i·ness** *n*

neem \ˈnēm\ *n* [Hindi *nīm,* fr. Skt *nimba*] (1813) **:** a large East Indian tree (*Azadirachta indica*) whose trunk exudes a tenacious gum and has a bitter bark used as a tonic and whose fruit and seeds yield a medicinal aromatic oil — called also *neem tree*

ne'er \(ˈ)ne(ə)r, (ˈ)na(ə)r\ *adv* (13c) **:** NEVER

ne'er–do–well \ˈne(ə)r-du̇-ˌwel, ˈna(ə)r-\ *n* (1736) **:** an idle worthless person — **ne'er–do–well** *adj*

ne·far·i·ous \ni-ˈfar-ē-əs, -ˈfer-\ *adj* [L *nefarius,* fr. *nefas* crime, fr. *ne-* not + *fas* right, divine law; akin to L *fari* to speak — more at BAN] (ca. 1604) **:** flagrantly wicked or impious **:** EVIL ***syn*** see VICIOUS — **ne·far·i·ous·ly** *adv*

ne·gate \ni-ˈgāt\ *vt* **ne·gat·ed; ne·gat·ing** [L *negatus,* pp. of *negare* to say no, deny, fr. *neg-* no, not (akin to *ne-* not) — more at NO] (ca. 1623) **1 :** to deny the existence or truth of **2 :** to cause to be ineffective or invalid ***syn*** see NULLIFY — **negate** *n* — **ne·ga·tor** *or* **ne·gat·er** \-ˈgāt-ər\ *n*

ne·ga·tion \ni-ˈgā-shən\ *n* (15c) **1 a :** the action or logical operation of negating or making negative **b :** a negative statement, judgment, or doctrine; *esp* **:** a logical proposition formed by asserting the falsity of a given proposition **2 a :** something that is the absence of something actual **:** NONENTITY **b :** something considered the opposite of something regarded as positive — **ne·ga·tion·al** \-shnəl, -shən-ᵊl\ *adj*

[1]neg·a·tive \ˈneg-ət-iv\ *adj* (15c) **1 a :** marked by denial, prohibition, or refusal ⟨received a ~ answer⟩; *also* **:** marked by absence, withholding, or removal of something positive ⟨the ~ motivation of shame — Garrett Hardin⟩ **b** (1) **:** denying a predicate of a subject or a part of a subject ⟨"no A is B" is a ~ proposition⟩ (2) **:** denoting the absence or the contradictory of something ⟨*nontoxic* is a ~ term⟩ (3) **:** expressing negation ⟨~ particles such as *no* and *not*⟩ **c :** ADVERSE, UNFAVORABLE ⟨the reviews were mostly ~⟩ **2 a :** lacking positive qualities; *esp* **:** DISAGREEABLE **b :** marked by features (as hostility or withdrawal) opposing constructive treatment or development ⟨had a ~ outlook on life⟩ **3 a** (1) **:** less than zero and opposite in sign to a positive number that when added to the given number yields zero ⟨−2 is a ~ number⟩ (2) **:** having more outgo than income **:** constituting a loss ⟨~ cash flow⟩ ⟨~ worth⟩ **b :** extending or generated in a direction opposite to an arbitrarily chosen regular direction or position ⟨~ angle⟩ **4 a :** being, relating to, or charged with electricity of which the electron is the elementary unit **b :** gaining electrons **c** (1) **:** having lower electric potential and constituting the part toward which the current flows from the external circuit ⟨the ~ pole⟩ (2) **:** constituting an electrode through which a stream of electrons enters the space between electrodes in an electron tube **5 a :** not affirming the presence of the organism or condition in question ⟨a ~ TB test⟩ **b :** directed or moving away from a source of stimulation ⟨~ tropism⟩ **c :** less than the pressure of the atmosphere ⟨~ pressure⟩ **6 :** having the light and dark parts in approximately inverse order to those of the original photographic subject **7** *of a lens* **:** diverging light rays and forming a virtual inverted image — **neg·a·tive·ly** *adv* — **neg·a·tive·ness** *n* — **neg·a·tiv·i·ty** \ˌneg-ə-ˈtiv-ət-ē\ *n*

[2]negative *n* (1571) **1 a :** a proposition which denies or contradicts another; *esp* **:** the one of a pair of propositions in which negation is expressed **b** (1) **:** a reply that indicates the withholding of assent **:** REFUSAL (2) *archaic* **:** a right of veto (3) *obs* **:** an adverse vote **:** VETO **2 a :** something that is the opposite or negation of something else **b :** DRAWBACK, LIABILITY **3 a :** an expression (as the word *no*) of negation or denial **b :** a negative number **4 :** the side that upholds the contradictory proposition in a debate **5 :** the plate of a voltaic or electrolytic cell that is at the lower potential **6 :** a negative photographic image on transparent material used for printing positive pictures; *also* **:** the material that carries such an image **7 :** a reverse impression taken from a piece of sculpture or ceramics

[3]negative *vt* **-tived; -tiv·ing** (1706) **1 a :** to refuse assent to **b :** to reject by or as if by a vote **2 :** to demonstrate the falsity of **3 :** to deny the truth, reality, or validity of **4 :** NEUTRALIZE, COUNTERACT

negative feedback *n* (1934) **:** feedback that tends to stabilize a process by reducing its rate or output when its effects are too great

negative income tax *n* (1966) **:** a system of federal subsidy payments to families with incomes below a stipulated level

negative staining *n* (1944) **:** a method of demonstrating the form of small objects (as bacteria) by surrounding them with a stain that they do not take up so that they appear as sharply outlined unstained bright bodies on a colored ground

negative transfer *n* (1921) **:** the impeding of learning or performance in a situation by the carry-over of learned responses from another situation

neg·a·tiv·ism \ˈneg-ət-iv-ˌiz-əm\ *n* (1824) **1 :** an attitude of mind marked by skepticism about nearly everything affirmed by others **2 :** a tendency to refuse to do, to do the opposite of, or to do something at variance with what is asked — **neg·a·tiv·ist** \-əst\ *n or adj* — **neg·a·tiv·is·tic** \ˌneg-ət-iv-ˈis-tik\ *adj*

neg·a·tron \ˈneg-ə-ˌträn\ *also* **neg·a·ton** \-ˌtän\ *n* [*negatron,* fr. *negative* + *electron; negaton,* fr. *negative* + [2]*-on*] (1934) **:** ELECTRON

[1]ne·glect \ni-ˈglekt\ *vt* [L *neglectus,* pp. of *neglegere, neclegere,* fr. *nec-* not (akin to *ne-* not) + *legere* to gather — more at NO, LEGEND] (1529) **1 :** to give little attention or respect to **:** DISREGARD **2 :** to leave undone or unattended to esp. through carelessness — **ne·glect·er** *n*
syn NEGLECT, OMIT, DISREGARD, IGNORE, OVERLOOK, SLIGHT, FORGET mean to pass over without giving due attention. NEGLECT implies giving insufficient attention to something that has a claim to one's attention; OMIT implies absence of all attention; DISREGARD suggests voluntary inattention; IGNORE implies a failure to regard something obvious; OVERLOOK suggests disregarding or ignoring through haste or lack of care; SLIGHT implies contemptuous or disdainful disregarding or omitting; FORGET may suggest either a willful ignoring or a failure to impress something on one's mind.

[2]neglect *n* (1588) **1 :** an act or instance of neglecting something **2 :** the condition of being neglected

ne·glect·ful \ni-ˈglek(t)-fəl\ *adj* (1644) **:** given to neglecting **:** CARELESS, HEEDLESS ***syn*** see NEGLIGENT — **ne·glect·ful·ly** \-fə-lē\ *adv* — **ne·glect·ful·ness** *n*

neg·li·gee *also* **neg·li·gé** \ˌneg-lə-ˈzhā, ˈneg-lə-ˌ\ *n* [F *négligé,* fr. pp. of *négliger* to neglect, fr. L *neglegere*] (1756) **1 :** a woman's long flowing usu. sheer dressing gown **2 :** carelessly informal or incomplete attire

neg·li·gence \ˈneg-li-jən(t)s\ *n* (14c) **1 a :** the quality or state of being negligent **b :** failure to exercise the care that a prudent person usu. exercises **2 :** an act or instance of negligence

neg·li·gent \-jənt\ *adj* [ME, fr. MF & L; MF, fr. L *neglegent-, neglegens,* prp. of *neglegere*] (14c) **1 :** marked by or given to neglect esp. habitually or culpably **:** not taking prudent care **2 :** marked by a carelessly easy manner — **neg·li·gent·ly** *adv*
syn NEGLIGENT, NEGLECTFUL, LAX, SLACK, REMISS mean culpably careless or indicative of such carelessness. NEGLIGENT implies inattention to one's duty or business; NEGLECTFUL adds a more disapproving implication of laziness or deliberate inattention; LAX implies a blameworthy lack of strictness, severity, or precision; SLACK implies want of due or necessary diligence or care; REMISS implies blameworthy carelessness shown in slackness, forgetfulness, or neglect.

neg·li·gi·ble \ˈneg-li-jə-bəl\ *adj* [L *neglegere, negligere*] (1829) **:** so small or unimportant or of so little consequence as to warrant little or no attention **:** TRIFLING — **neg·li·gi·bil·i·ty** \ˌneg-li-jə-ˈbil-ət-ē\ *n* — **neg·li·gi·bly** \ˈneg-li-jə-blē\ *adv*

ne·go·tia·ble \ni-ˈgō-sh(ē-)ə-bəl\ *adj* (1758) **:** capable of being negotiated: as **a :** transferable from one person to another by being delivered with or without endorsement so that the title passes to the transferee ⟨~ securities⟩ **b :** capable of being traversed, dealt with, or accomplished ⟨a difficult but ~ road⟩ ⟨~ demands⟩ — **ne·go·tia·bil·i·ty** \-ˌgō-sh(ē-)ə-ˈbil-ət-ē\ *n*

ne·go·tiant \-ˈgō-sh(ē-)ənt\ *n* (1611) **:** one that negotiates

ne·go·ti·ate \ni-ˈgō-shē-ˌāt\ *vb* **-at·ed; -at·ing** [L *negotiatus,* pp. of *negotiari* to carry on business, fr. *negotium* business, fr. *neg-* not + *otium* leisure — more at NEGATE] *vi* (1599) **:** to confer with another so as to arrive at the settlement of some matter ~ *vt* **1 a :** to deal with (some matter or affair that requires ability for its successful handling) **:** MANAGE **b :** to arrange for or bring about through conference, discussion, and compromise ⟨~ a treaty⟩ **2 a :** to transfer (as a bill of exchange) to another by delivery or endorsement **b :** to convert into cash or the equivalent value ⟨~ a check⟩ **3 a :** to successfully travel along or over ⟨~ a turn⟩ **b :** COMPLETE, ACCOMPLISH ⟨~ the trip in two hours⟩ — **ne·go·ti·a·tor** \-ˌāt-ər\ *n* — **ne·go·tia·to·ry** \-sh(ē-)ə-ˌtōr-ē, -ˌtȯr-\ *adj*

ne·go·ti·a·tion \ni-ˌgō-s(h)ē-ˈā-shən\ *n* (15c) **:** the action or process of negotiating or being negotiated — often used in pl.

Ne·gress \ˈnē-grəs\ *n* (1786) **:** a female Negro — sometimes taken to be offensive

Ne·gril·lo \ni-ˈgril-(ˌ)ō, -ˈgrē-(ˌ)(y)ō\ *n, pl* **-los** *or* **-loes** [Sp, dim. of *negro*] (1853) **:** a member of a people (as Pygmies) belonging to a group of Negroid peoples of small stature that live in Africa

Ne·gri·to \nə-ˈgrēt-(ˌ)ō\ *n, pl* **-tos** *or* **-toes** [Sp, dim. of *negro*] (1812) **:** a member of a people (as the Andamanese) belonging to a group of Negroid peoples of small stature that live in Oceania and the southeastern part of Asia

ne·gri·tude \ˈneg-rə-ˌtüd, ˈnē-grə-, -ˌtyüd\ *n* [F *négritude,* fr. *nègre* Negro + *-i-* + *-tude*] (1950) **:** a consciousness of and pride in the cultural and physical aspects of the African heritage

Ne·gro \ˈnē-(ˌ)grō\ *n, pl* **Negroes** [Sp or Pg, fr. *negro* black, fr. L *nigr-, niger*] (1555) **1 :** a member of the black race of mankind distinguished from members of other races by usu. inherited physical and physiological characteristics without regard to language or culture; *esp* : a member of a people belonging to the African branch of the black race **2** : a person of Negro descent — **Negro** *adj* — **Ne·groid** \'nē-ˌgrȯid\ *n or adj, often not cap* — **Ne·gro·ness** \-grō-nəs\ *n*

ne·gro·phile \'nē-grō-ˌfīl\ *n, often cap* (1803) : one who is esp. friendly to Negroes and their interests — **ne·gro·phi·lism** \-ˌfī-ˌliz-əm, ni-'gräf-ə-ˌliz-\ *n, often cap*

ne·gro·phobe \'nē-grə-ˌfōb\ *n, often cap* (1833) : one who strongly dislikes or fears Negroes — **ne·gro·pho·bia** \ˌnē-grə-'fō-bē-ə\ *n, often cap*

[1]**ne·gus** \'nē-gəs, ni-'güs\ *n* [Amharic *negūs*, fr. Eth *nĕgūša nagašt* king of kings] (1594) : KING — used as a title of the sovereign of Ethiopia

[2]**ne·gus** \'nē-gəs\ *n* [Francis *Negus* †1732 Eng. colonel] (1743) : a beverage of wine, hot water, sugar, lemon juice, and spices

Ne·he·mi·ah \ˌnē-(h)ə-'mī-ə\ *n* [Heb *Nĕḥemyāh*] **1** : a Jewish leader of the 5th century B.C. who supervised the rebuilding of the Jerusalem city walls and instituted religious reforms in the city **2** : a narrative and historical book of canonical Jewish and Christian Scripture — see BIBLE table

Ne·he·mi·as \-'mī-əs\ *n* [LL, fr. Heb *Nĕḥemyāh*] : NEHEMIAH

neigh \'nā\ *vi* [ME *neyen*, fr. OE *hnǣgan*; akin to MHG *nēgen* to neigh] (bef. 12c) : to make the loud prolonged cry of a horse — **neigh** *n*

[1]**neigh·bor** \'nā-bər\ *n* [ME, fr. OE *nēahgebūr* (akin to OHG *nāhgibūr*); akin to OE *nēah* near and OE *gebūr* dweller — more at NIGH, BOOR] (bef. 12c) **1** : one living or located near another **2** : FELLOWMAN

[2]**neighbor** *adj* (1530) : being immediately adjoining or relatively near

[3]**neighbor** *vb* **neigh·bored; neigh·bor·ing** \-b(ə-)riŋ\ *vt* (1586) : to adjoin immediately or lie relatively near to ~ *vi* **1** : to live or be located as a neighbor **2** : to associate in a neighborly way

neigh·bor·hood \'nā-bər-ˌhu̇d\ *n* (15c) **1** : neighborly relationship **2** : the quality or state of being neighbors : PROXIMITY **3 a** : a place or region near : VICINITY **b** : an approximate amount, extent, or degree ⟨cost in the ~ of $10⟩ **4 a** : the people living near one another **b** : a section lived in by neighbors and usu. having distinguishing characteristics **5** : the set of all points belonging to a given set whose distances from a given point are less than a given positive number; *broadly* : any set that contains such a set

neigh·bor·ly \-lē\ *adj* (1558) : of, relating to, or characteristic of congenial neighbors; *esp* : FRIENDLY *syn* see AMICABLE — **neigh·bor·li·ness** *n*

neigh·bour \-bər\ *chiefly Brit var of* NEIGHBOR

[1]**nei·ther** \'nē-t͟hər *also* 'nī-\ *pron* [ME, alter. (influenced by *either*) of *nauther, nother*, fr. OE *nāhwæther, nōther*, fr. *nā, nō* not + *hwæther* which of two, whether] (bef. 12c) : not the one or the other of two or more

usage *Neither* is usu. used with a singular verb. But when a prepositional phrase intervenes between *neither* and the verb, use of a plural verb is quite common ⟨*neither* of those ideal solutions are in sight —C.P. Snow⟩ Some commentators consider the plural verb wrong under any circumstances in spite of its use by such writers as Shakespeare and Samuel Johnson.

[2]**neither** *conj* (bef. 12c) **1** : not either ⟨~ black nor white⟩ **2** : also not ⟨~ did I⟩

usage Although use with *or* is neither archaic nor wrong, *neither* is usu. followed by *nor*. Some commentators think that *neither* must be limited in reference to two. While reference to two is certainly the most common, reference to more than two is not wrong and has been used upon occasion since the 17th century.

[3]**neither** *adj* (13c) : not either ⟨~ hand⟩

[4]**neither** *adv* (1551) **1** *chiefly dial* : EITHER ⟨are not to be understood ~ —Earl of Chesterfield⟩ **2** : similarly not : also not ⟨just as the serf was not permitted to leave the land, so ~ was his offspring —G. G. Coulton⟩

nek·ton \'nek-tən, -ˌtän\ *n* [G *nekton*, fr. Gk *nēkton*, neut. of *nēktos* swimming, fr. *nēchein* to swim; akin to L *nare* to swim — more at NOURISH] (1893) : free-swimming aquatic animals (as whales or squid) essentially independent of wave and current action — **nek·ton·ic** \nek-'tän-ik\ *adj*

nel·son \'nel-sən\ *n* [prob. fr. the name *Nelson*] (1889) : a wrestling hold marked by the application of leverage against an opponent's arm, neck, and head — compare FULL NELSON, HALF NELSON

ne·ma \'nē-mə, 'nem-ə\ *n* [by shortening] (ca. 1909) : NEMATODE

nemat- *or* **nemato-** *comb form* [NL, fr. Gk *nēmat-*, fr. *nēmat-, nēma*, fr. *nēn* to spin — more at NEEDLE] **1** : thread ⟨*nemato*cyst⟩ **2** : nematode ⟨*nemato*logy⟩

ne·ma·thel·minth \ˌnem-ə-'thel-ˌmin(t)th, ˌnē-mə-\ *n* [deriv. of Gk *nēma* + *helmis* worm — more at HELMINTH] (ca. 1890) : any of a phylum (Nemathelminthes) of wormlike animals with a cylindrical unsegmented body covered by an ectoderm without cilia that secretes an external cuticle

ne·mat·ic \ni-'mat-ik\ *adj* [ISV *nemat-* + *-ic*] (1923) : of, relating to, or being the phase of a liquid crystal characterized by arrangement of the long axes of the molecules in parallel lines but not layers — compare CHOLESTERIC, SMECTIC

ne·ma·to·cid·al *also* **ne·ma·ti·cid·al** \ˌnem-ət-ə-'sīd-ᵊl, ni-ˌmat-ə-\ *adj* (1943) : capable of destroying nematodes

ne·ma·to·cide *also* **ne·ma·ti·cide** \'nem-ət-ə-ˌsīd, ni-'mat-ə-\ *n* (1898) : a substance or preparation used to destroy nematodes

ne·ma·to·cyst \'nem-ət-ə-ˌsist, ni-'mat-ə-\ *n* [ISV] (1875) : one of the minute stinging organs of various coelenterates

nem·a·tode \'nem-ə-ˌtōd\ *n* [deriv. of Gk *nēmat-, nēma*] (1865) : any of a class or phylum (Nematoda) of elongated cylindrical worms parasitic in animals or plants or free-living in soil or water

nem·a·tol·o·gy \ˌnem-ə-'täl-ə-jē\ *n* (ca. 1916) : a branch of zoology that deals with nematodes — **nem·a·to·log·i·cal** \ˌnem-ət-ᵊl-'äj-i-kəl\ *adj* — **nem·a·tol·o·gist** \ˌnem-ə-'täl-ə-jəst\ *n*

Nem·bu·tal \'nem-byə-ˌtȯl\ *trademark* — used for the sodium salt of pentobarbital

ne·mer·te·an \ni-'mərt-ē-ən\ *n* [deriv. of Gk *Nēmertēs* Nemertes, one of the Nereids] (1861) : any of a class (Nemertea or Nemertinea) of often vividly colored marine worms most of which burrow in the mud or sand along seacoasts — called also *ribbon worm* — **nem·er·tine** \'nem-ər-ˌtīn\ *adj or n*

nem·e·sis \'nem-ə-səs\ *n* [L, fr. Gk] **1** *cap* : the Greek goddess of retributive justice **2** *pl* **-e·ses** \-ˌsēz\ **a** : one that inflicts retribution or vengeance **b** : a formidable and usu. victorious rival or opponent **3** *pl* **-eses a** : an act or effect of retribution **b** : BANE 2

ne·moph·i·la \ni-'mäf-ə-lə\ *n* [NL, fr. Gk *nemos* wooded pasture + *philos* loving] (1838) : any of a genus (*Nemophila*) of American annual herbs of the waterleaf family cultivated for their showy blue or white usu. spotted flowers

ne·ne \'nā-(ˌ)nā\ *n* [Hawaiian *nēnē*] (1902) : a nearly extinct goose (*Nesochen sandvicensis*) of the Hawaiian islands that inhabits waterless uplands and feeds on berries and vegetation

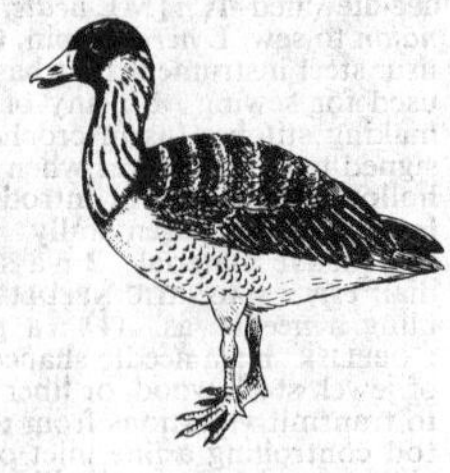
nene

neo- — see NE-

neo·clas·sic \ˌnē-ō-'klas-ik\ *or* **neo·clas·si·cal** \-i-kəl\ *adj* (1877) : of, relating to, or constituting a revival or adaptation of the classical esp. in literature, music, art, or architecture — **neo·clas·si·cism** \-'klas-ə-ˌsiz-əm\ *n* — **neo·clas·si·cist** \-səst\ *n or adj*

neo·co·lo·nial·ism \ˌnē-ō-kə-'lōn-yə-ˌliz-əm, -'lō-nē-ə-ˌliz-\ *n* (1961) : the economic and political policies by which a great power indirectly maintains or extends its influence over other areas or people — **neo·co·lo·nial** \-'lōn-yəl, -'lō-nē-əl\ *adj* — **neo·co·lo·nial·ist** \-əst\ *n or adj*

neo·con·ser·va·tive \-kən-'sər-vət-iv\ *n* (1955) : a former liberal espousing political conservatism — **neo·con·ser·va·tism** \-və-ˌtiz-əm\ *n* — **neoconservative** *adj*

neo·cor·tex \ˌnē-ō-'kȯr-ˌteks\ *n* [NL; fr. its being the cortex of the phylogenetically most recently developed part of the brain] (1909) : the dorsal region of the cerebral cortex that is unique to mammals

neo·cor·ti·cal \-'kȯrt-i-kəl\ *adj* (1909) : of or relating to the neocortex

neo–Dar·win·ian \-där-'win-ē-ən\ *adj, often cap N* (1895) : of or relating to neo-Darwinism

neo–Dar·win·ism \-'där-wə-ˌniz-əm\ *n, often cap N* (ca. 1900) : a theory of evolution that is a synthesis of Darwin's theory in terms of natural selection and modern population genetics — **neo–Dar·win·ist** \-nəst\ *n, often cap N*

neo·dym·i·um \ˌnē-ō-'dim-ē-əm\ *n* [NL, fr. *ne-* + *-dymium* (fr. *didymium*)] (1885) : a yellow metallic element of the rare-earth group — see ELEMENT table

neo–Freud·ian \-'frȯid-ē-ən\ *adj, often cap N* (1945) : of or relating to a school of psychoanalysis that differs from Freudian orthodoxy in emphasizing the importance of social and cultural factors in the development of an individual's personality — **neo–Freudian** *n, often cap N*

Neo·gene \'nē-ə-ˌjēn\ *adj* [ISV] (1878) : of, relating to, or being the later portion of the Tertiary including the Miocene and Pliocene or the corresponding system of rocks — **Neogene** *n*

neo–im·pres·sion·ism \ˌnē-ō-im-'presh-ə-ˌniz-əm\ *n, often cap N&I* [F *néo-impressionisme*, fr. *né-* ne- + *impressionisme* impressionism] (1892) : a late 19th century French art theory and practice characterized by an attempt to make impressionism more precise in form and the use of a pointillist painting technique — **neo–im·pres·sion·ist** \-'presh-(ə-)nəst\ *adj or n, often cap N&I*

Neo–Lat·in \-'lat-ᵊn\ *n* [ISV] (1850) **1** : NEW LATIN **2** : ROMANCE 5

neo·lith \'nē-ə-ˌlith\ *n* [back-formation fr. *neolithic*] (1882) : a Neolithic stone implement

neo·lith·ic \ˌnē-ə-'lith-ik\ *adj* (1865) **1** *cap* : of or relating to the latest period of the Stone Age characterized by polished stone implements **2** : belonging to an earlier age and now outmoded

ne·ol·o·gism \nē-'äl-ə-ˌjiz-əm\ *n* (1800) **1** : a word, usage, or expression that is often disapproved because of its newness or barbarousness **2** : a meaningless word coined by a psychotic — **ne·ol·o·gis·tic** \-ˌäl-ə-'jis-tik\ *adj*

neo–Mal·thu·sian \ˌnē-ō-mal-'th(y)ü-zhən, -mȯl-\ *adj* (1911) : advocating control of population growth (as by contraception) — **neo–Malthusian** *n* — **neo–Mal·thu·sian·ism** \-zhə-ˌniz-əm\ *n*

neo·my·cin \ˌnē-ə-'mīs-ᵊn\ *n* [*ne-* + *myc-* + *-in*] (1949) : a broad-spectrum highly toxic antibiotic or mixture of antibiotics produced by streptomyces (esp. *Streptomyces fradiae*) and used esp. in a variety of local infections

ne·on \'nē-ˌän\ *n* [Gk, neut. of *neos* new — more at NEW] (1898) **1** : a colorless odorless primarily inert gaseous element found in minute amounts in air and used in electric lamps — see ELEMENT table **2 a** : a discharge lamp in which the gas contains a large proportion of neon **b** : a sign composed of such lamps **c** : the illumination provided by such lamps or signs — **neon** *adj* — **ne·oned** \-ˌänd\ *adj*

neo·na·tal \ˌnē-ō-'nāt-ᵊl\ *adj* (1902) : of, relating to, or affecting the newborn and esp. the human infant during the first month after birth ⟨~ mortality⟩ — **neo·na·tal·ly** \-ᵊl-ē\ *adv*

ne·o·nate \'nē-ə-ˌnāt\ *n* [NL *neonatus*, fr. *ne-* + L *natus*, pp. of *nasci* to be born — more at NATION] (1932) : a newborn child; *esp* : a child less than a month old

neo·na·tol·o·gy \ˌnē-ə-nā-'täl-ə-jē\ *n* (1960) : a branch of medicine concerned with the care, development, and diseases of newborn infants — **neo·na·tol·o·gist** \-jəst\ *n*

neo–Na·zi \ˌnē-ō-'nät-sē, -'nat-\ *n* (1938) : a member of a group espousing the programs and policies of Hitler's Nazis — **neo–Nazi** *adj* — **neo–Na·zism** \-'nät-ˌsiz-əm, -'nat-\ *n*

neo·or·tho·dox \ˌnē-ō-'ȯr-thə-ˌdäks\ *adj* (1946) : of or relating to a 20th century movement in Protestant theology characterized by a reaction against liberalism and emphasis on various scripturally based Reformation doctrines — **neo·or·tho·doxy** \-ˌdäk-sē\ *n*

neo·phil·ia \ˌnē-ə-'fil-ē-ə\ *n* (ca. 1947) : love of or enthusiasm for what is new or novel — **neo·phil·i·ac** \-ē-ˌak\ *n*

neo·phyte \'nē-ə-ˌfīt\ *n* [ME, fr. LL *neophytus*, fr. Gk *neophytos*, fr. *neophytos* newly planted, newly converted, fr. *ne-* + *phyein* to bring forth — more at BE] (15c) **1** : a new convert : PROSELYTE **2** : NOVICE 1 **3** : TYRO, BEGINNER

neo·pla·sia \ˌnē-ə-'plā-zh(ē-)ə\ *n* [NL] (1890) **1** : the formation of tumors **2** : a tumorous condition

neo·plasm \'nē-ə-ˌplaz-əm\ *n* [ISV] (1864) : a new growth of tissue serving no physiological function : TUMOR

neo·plas·tic \ˌnē-ə-ˈplas-tik\ *adj* [ISV] (ca. 1890) **1 :** of, relating to, or constituting a neoplasm or neoplasia **2 :** of or relating to neoplasticism

neo·plas·ti·cism \-tə-ˌsiz-əm\ *n* [*ne-* + *plastic* + *-ism*] (1933) **:** the de Stijl art principle in painting — **neo·plas·ti·cist** \-səst\ *n*

Neo·pla·to·nism \ˌnē-ō-ˈplāt-ᵊn-ˌiz-əm\ *n* [ISV] (ca. 1841) **1 :** Platonism modified in later antiquity to accord with Aristotelian, post-Aristotelian, and oriental conceptions that conceives of the world as an emanation from an ultimate indivisible being with whom the soul is capable of being reunited in trance or ecstasy **2 :** doctrines similar to ancient Neoplatonism — **Neo·pla·ton·ic** \-plə-ˈtän-ik, -plā-\ *adj* — **Neo·pla·to·nist** \-ˈplāt-ᵊn-əst\ *n*

neo·prene \ˈnē-ə-ˌprēn\ *n* [*ne-* + chloro*prene*] (1937) **:** a synthetic rubber made by the polymerization of chloroprene and characterized by superior resistance (as to oils)

neo·re·al·ism \ˌnē-ō-ˈrē-ə-ˌliz-əm, -ˈri-ə-\ *n* (1950) **:** a movement esp. in Italian filmmaking characterized by the simple direct depiction of lower-class life — **neo·re·al·ist** \-ləst\ *n* — **neo·re·al·is·tic** \-ˌrē-ə-ˈlis-tik, -ˌri-ə-\ *adj*

Neo·ri·can \ˌnē-ō-ˈrē-kən\ *n* [*ne-* + Puerto *Rican*] (1969) **:** a Puerto Rican who lives on the U.S. mainland or has lived there but has returned to Puerto Rico

neo–scho·las·ti·cism \ˌnē-ō-skə-ˈlas-tə-ˌsiz-əm\ *n* (ca. 1909) **:** a movement among Catholic scholars aiming to restate medieval Scholasticism in a manner suited to present intellectual needs

neo·stig·mine \ˌnē-ə-ˈstig-ˌmēn\ *n* [*ne-* + *-stigmine* (as in *physostigmine*)] (1941) **:** a cholinergic drug used in the form of its bromide $C_{12}H_{19}BrN_2O_2$ or a methyl sulfate derivative $C_{13}H_{22}N_2O_6S$ esp. in the treatment of some ophthalmic conditions and in the diagnosis and treatment of myasthenia gravis

ne·o·te·ny \nē-ˈä-tᵊn-ē, ˌnē-ə-ˈtē-nē\ *n* [NL *neotenia*, fr. *ne-* + Gk *teinein* to stretch — more at THIN] (1901) **1 :** retention of some larval or immature characters in adulthood **2 :** attainment of sexual maturity during the larval stage — **ne·o·ten·ic** \ˌnē-ə-ˈten-ik\ *adj*

ne·o·ter·ic \ˌnē-ə-ˈter-ik\ *adj* [LL *neotericus*, fr. LGk *neōterikos*, fr. Gk, youthful, fr. *neōteros*, compar. of *neos* new, young — more at NEW] (1596) **:** recent in origin **:** MODERN

Neo·trop·i·cal \ˌnē-ō-ˈträp-i-kəl\ *also* **Neo·trop·ic** \-ik\ *adj* [ISV] (1858) **:** of, relating to, or constituting the biogeographic region that includes So. America, the West Indies, and tropical No. America

neo·type \ˈnē-ə-ˌtīp\ *n* (1895) **:** a type specimen that is selected subsequent to the description of a species to replace a preexisting type that has been lost or destroyed

Ne·pali \nə-ˈpȯl-ē, -ˈpäl-, -ˈpal-\ *n, pl* **Nepali** *also* **Nepal·is** [Hindi *naipālī* of Nepal, fr. Skt *naipālīya*, fr. *Nepāla* Nepal] (ca. 1885) **1 :** a native or inhabitant of Nepal **2 :** the Indic language of Nepal — **Nepali** *adj*

ne·pen·the \nə-ˈpen(t)-thē\ *n* [L *nepenthes*, fr. Gk *nēpenthes*, neut. of *nēpenthēs* banishing pain and sorrow, fr. *nē-* not + *penthos* grief, sorrow; akin to Gk *pathos* suffering — more at NO, PATHOS] (1580) **1 :** a potion used by the ancients to induce forgetfulness of pain or sorrow **2 :** something capable of causing oblivion of grief or suffering — **ne·pen·the·an** \-thē-ən\ *adj*

neph·anal·y·sis \ˌnef-ə-ˈnal-ə-səs\ *n* [NL, fr. Gk *nephos* cloud + *analysis* — more at NEBULA] (1945) **:** the analysis of the clouds and related phenomena over a large area of the earth on a chart used esp. in weather forecasting; *also* **:** the chart itself

neph·e·line \ˈnef-ə-ˌlēn\ *also* **neph·e·lite** \-ˌlīt\ *n* [F *néphéline*, fr. Gk *nephelē* cloud — more at NEBULA] (1814) **:** a hexagonal mineral that is a usu. glassy crystalline silicate of sodium, potassium, and aluminum common in igneous rocks — **neph·e·lin·ic** \ˌnef-ə-ˈlin-ik\ *adj*

neph·e·lin·ite \ˈnef-ə-lə-ˌnīt\ *n* [ISV] (1863) **:** a silica-deficient igneous rock having nepheline as the predominant mineral — **neph·e·lin·it·ic** \ˌnef-ə-lə-ˈnit-ik\ *adj*

neph·e·lom·e·ter \ˌnef-ə-ˈläm-ət-ər\ *n* [Gk *nephelē* cloud + ISV *-meter*] (1875) **1 :** an instrument for measuring the extent or degree of cloudiness **2 :** an instrument for determining the concentration or particle size of suspensions by means of transmitted or reflected light — **neph·e·lo·met·ric** \ˌnef-ə-lō-ˈme-trik\ *adj* — **neph·e·lom·e·try** \-ˈläm-ə-trē\ *n*

neph·ew \ˈnef-(ˌ)yü, *chiefly Brit* ˈnev-\ *n* [ME *nevew*, fr. OF *neveu*, fr. L *nepot-, nepos* grandson, nephew; akin to OE *nefa* grandson, nephew, Skt *napāt* grandson] (13c) **1 a :** a son of one's brother or sister or of one's brother-in-law or sister-in-law **b :** an illegitimate son of an ecclesiastic **2** *obs* **:** a lineal descendant; *esp* **:** GRANDSON

ne·phom·e·ter \ne-ˈfäm-ət-ər\ *n* [Gk *nephos* cloud — more at NEBULA] (1910) **:** NEPHELOMETER 1

nepho·scope \ˈnef-ə-ˌskōp\ *n* [Gk *nephos* + ISV *-scope*] (1881) **:** an instrument for observing the direction and velocity of clouds

nephr- *or* **nephro-** *comb form* [NL, fr. Gk, fr. *nephros* — more at NEPHRITIS] **:** kidney ⟨*nephr*ic⟩ ⟨*nephro*logy⟩

ne·phrec·to·my \ni-ˈfrek-tə-mē\ *n, pl* **-mies** [ISV] (1880) **:** the surgical removal of a kidney — **ne·phrec·to·mize** \-ˌmīz\ *vt*

neph·ric \ˈnef-rik\ *adj* [*nephr-* + *-ic*] (1887) **:** RENAL

ne·phrid·i·um \ni-ˈfrid-ē-əm\ *n, pl* **-ia** \-ē-ə\ [NL] (1877) **1 :** a tubular glandular excretory organ characteristic of various coelomate invertebrates **2 :** a primarily excretory structure; *esp* **:** NEPHRON — **ne·phrid·i·al** \-ē-əl\ *adj*

neph·rite \ˈnef-ˌrīt\ *n* [G *nephrit*, fr. Gk *nephros*; fr. its formerly being worn as a remedy for kidney diseases] (1794) **:** a compact tremolite or actinolite that is the commoner and less valuable kind of jade and that varies in color from white to dark green or black

ne·phrit·ic \ni-ˈfrit-ik\ *adj* (1580) **1 :** RENAL **2 :** of, relating to, or affected with nephritis

ne·phri·tis \ni-ˈfrīt-əs\ *n, pl* **ne·phrit·i·des** \-ˈfrit-ə-ˌdēz\ [LL, fr. Gk, fr. *nephros* kidney; akin to ME *nere* kidney] (1580) **:** acute or chronic inflammation of the kidney caused by infection, degenerative process, or vascular disease

ne·phrol·o·gy \ni-ˈfräl-ə-jē\ *n* (1842) **:** a branch of medicine concerned with the kidneys — **ne·phrol·o·gist** \-jəst\ *n*

neph·ron \ˈnef-ˌrän\ *n* [G, fr. Gk *nephros*] (1932) **:** a single excretory unit esp. of the vertebrate kidney

ne·phrop·a·thy \ni-ˈfräp-ə-thē\ *n, pl* **-thies** [ISV] (1856) **:** an abnormal state of the kidney; *esp* **:** one associated with or secondary to some other pathological process — **neph·ro·path·ic** \ˌnef-rə-ˈpath-ik\ *adj*

ne·phro·sis \ni-ˈfrō-səs\ *n* [NL] (1916) **:** a noninflammatory disease of the kidneys chiefly affecting function of the nephrons; *esp* **:** NEPHROTIC SYNDROME — **ne·phrot·ic** \-ˈfrät-ik\ *adj or n*

neph·ro·stome \ˈnef-rə-ˌstōm\ *n* [NL *nephrostoma*, fr. *nephr-* + *stoma* stoma] (1888) **:** the ciliated funnel-shaped coelomic opening of a typical nephridium

nephrotic syndrome *n* [fr. *nephrosis*, after such pairs as E *narcosis*: *narcotic*] (1932) **:** an abnormal condition that is marked by deficiency of albumin in the blood and its excretion in the urine due to altered permeability of the glomerular basement membranes (as by a toxic chemical agent)

neph·ro·tox·ic \ˌnef-rə-ˈtäk-sik\ *adj* (1902) **:** poisonous to the kidney ⟨~ drugs⟩; *also* **:** resulting from or marked by poisoning of the kidney ⟨~ effects⟩ — **neph·ro·tox·i·ci·ty** \-täk-ˈsis-ət-ē\ *n*

ne plus ul·tra \ˌnā-ˌpləs-ˈəl-trə, ˌnē-\ *n* [NL, (go) no more beyond] (1638) **1 :** the highest point capable of being attained **:** ACME **2 :** the most profound degree of a quality or state

nep·o·tism \ˈnep-ə-ˌtiz-əm\ *n* [F *népotisme*, fr. It *nepotismo*, fr. *nepote* nephew, fr. L *nepot-, nepos* grandson, nephew — more at NEPHEW] (1670) **:** favoritism shown to a relative (as by giving an appointive job) on a basis of relationship — **nep·o·tis·tic** \ˌnep-ə-ˈtis-tik\ *adj*

Nep·tune \ˈnep-ˌt(y)ün\ *n* [L *Neptunus*] **1 a :** the Roman god of the sea — compare POSEIDON **b :** OCEAN **2 :** the planet 8th in order from the sun — see PLANET table — **Nep·tu·ni·an** \nep-ˈt(y)ü-nē-ən\ *adj*

nep·tu·ni·um \nep-ˈt(y)ü-nē-əm\ *n* [NL, fr. ISV *Neptune*] (1941) **:** a radioactive metallic element that is chemically similar to uranium and is obtained in nuclear reactors as a by-product in the production of plutonium — see ELEMENT table

nerd \ˈnərd\ *n* [origin unknown] *slang* (1965) **:** an unpleasant, unattractive, or insignificant person

Ne·re·id \ˈnir-ē-əd\ *n* [L *Nereid-, Nereis*, fr. Gk *Nēreid-, Nēreis*, fr. *Nēreus* Nereus] (1680) **:** any of the sea nymphs fathered by Nereus

ne·re·is \ˈnir-ē-əs\ *n, pl* **ne·re·ides** \nə-ˈrē-ə-ˌdēz\ [NL, fr. L, Nereid] (1797) **:** any of a genus (*Nereis*) of usu. large often dimorphic and greenish marine polychaete worms

Ne·re·us \ˈnir-ē-əs\ *n* [L, fr. Gk *Nēreus*] **:** a sea-god in Greek mythology

ne·rit·ic \nə-ˈrit-ik\ *adj* [perh. fr. NL *Nerita*, genus of marine snails] (1891) **:** of, relating to, inhabiting, or constituting the belt or region of shallow water adjoining the seacoast

ne·rol \ˈne(ə)r-ˌȯl, ˈni(ə)r-\ *n* [ISV *ner-* (fr. *neroli oil*) + *-ol*] (1869) **:** a liquid alcohol $C_{10}H_{18}O$ that has a rose scent and is used esp. in perfumery

ner·o·li oil \ˈner-ə-lē-\ *n* [F *néroli*, fr. It *neroli*, fr. Anna Maria de La Trémoille, princess of *Nerole fl* 1670] (1676) **:** a fragrant pale yellow essential oil obtained from orange flowers and used esp. in cologne and as a flavoring

nerts \ˈnərts\ *n pl* [alter. of *nuts*] *slang* (ca. 1925) **:** NONSENSE, NUTS — often used interjectionally

nerv- *or* **nervi-** *or* **nervo-** *comb form* [ME *nerv-*, fr. L, fr. *nervus*] **:** NEUR- ⟨*nerv*ine⟩

ner·va·tion \ˌnər-ˈvā-shən\ *n* (1849) **:** an arrangement or system of nerves; *also* **:** VENATION

[1]**nerve** \ˈnərv\ *n* [L *nervus* sinew, nerve; akin to Gk *neuron* sinew, nerve, *nēn* to spin — more at NEEDLE] (15c) **1 :** SINEW, TENDON ⟨strain every ~⟩ **2 :** any of the filamentous bands of nervous tissue that connect parts of the nervous system with the other organs, conduct nervous impulses, and are made up of axons and dendrites together with protective and supportive structures **3 a :** power of endurance or control **:** FORTITUDE, STRENGTH **b :** ASSURANCE, BOLDNESS; *also* **:** presumptuous audacity **:** GALL **4 a :** a sore or sensitive point **b** *pl* **:** nervous disorganization or collapse **:** NERVOUSNESS **5 :** VEIN 3 **6 :** the sensitive pulp of a tooth ***syn*** see TEMERITY

[2]**nerve** *vt* **nerved; nerv·ing** (1749) **:** to give strength or courage to **:** supply with physical or moral force

nerve cell *n* (1858) **:** NEURON; *also* **:** CELL BODY

nerve center *n* (1868) **1 :** CENTER 2c **2 :** a source of leadership, control, or energy ⟨the financial *nerve center* of the nation⟩

nerve cord *n* (1877) **1 :** the pair of closely united ventral longitudinal nerves with their segmental ganglia that is characteristic of many elongate invertebrates (as earthworms) **2 :** the dorsal tubular cord of nervous tissue above the notochord of a chordate that comprises or develops into the central nervous system

nerved \ˈnərvd\ *adj* (1800) **1 a :** VEINED ⟨a ~ wing⟩ **b :** having veins or nerves esp. of a specified kind or number — used in combination ⟨fan-*nerved* leaves⟩ **2 :** showing courage or strength

nerve fiber *n* (ca. 1839) **:** any of the processes of a neuron including axons with their myelin sheaths when present and dendrites

nerve gas *n* (1940) **:** an organophosphate war gas that interferes with normal nerve transmission and induces intense bronchial spasm with resulting inhibition of respiration

nerve growth factor *n* (ca. 1966) **:** a protein that promotes development of the sensory and sympathetic nervous systems and is required for maintenance of sympathetic neurons

nerve impulse *n* (1900) **:** the progressive physicochemical change in the membrane of a nerve fiber that follows stimulation and serves to transmit a record of sensation from a receptor or an instruction to act to an effector — called also *nervous impulse*

nerve·less \ˈnərv-ləs\ *adj* (1742) **1 :** lacking strength or courage **:** FEEBLE **2 :** exhibiting control or balance **:** POISED, COOL — **nerve·less·ly** *adv* — **nerve·less·ness** *n*

nerve net *n* (1904) **:** a network of nerve cells apparently continuous with one another and conducting impulses in all directions; *also* **:** a primitive nervous system (as in a jellyfish) consisting of such a network

nerve–rack·ing *or* **nerve–wrack·ing** \ˈnərv-ˌrak-iŋ\ *adj* (1812) **:** extremely trying on the nerves ⟨a ~ ordeal⟩

nerve trunk *n* (1851) **:** a bundle of nerve fibers enclosed in a connective tissue sheath

ner·vos·i·ty \ˌnər-'väs-ət-ē\ *n* (1787) **:** the quality or state of being nervous

ner·vous \'nər-vəs\ *adj* (15c) **1** *archaic* **:** SINEWY, STRONG **2 :** marked by strength of thought, feeling, or style **:** SPIRITED ⟨a vibrant tight-packed ~ style of writing⟩ **3 :** of, relating to, or composed of neurons **4 a :** of or relating to the nerves; *also* **:** originating in or affected by the nerves ⟨~ energy⟩ **b :** easily excited or irritated **:** JUMPY **c :** TIMID, APPREHENSIVE ⟨a ~ smile⟩ **5 a :** tending to produce nervousness or agitation **:** UNEASY ⟨a ~ situation⟩ **b :** appearing or acting unsteady, erratic, or irregular — used of inanimate things ***syn*** see VIGOROUS — **ner·vous·ly** *adv* — **ner·vous·ness** *n*

nervous breakdown *n* (1905) **:** an attack of mental or emotional disorder of sufficient severity to be incapacitating esp. when requiring hospitalization

nervous Nel·lie *or* **nervous Nel·ly** \-'nel-ē\ *n, pl* **nervous Nellies** *often cap 1st N* [fr. the name *Nellie*] (1926) **:** a timid or worrisome person

nervous system *n* (1740) **:** the bodily system that in vertebrates is made up of the brain and spinal cord, nerves, ganglia, and parts of the receptor organs and that receives and interprets stimuli and transmits impulses to the effector organs — compare CENTRAL NERVOUS SYSTEM; AUTONOMIC NERVOUS SYSTEM, PERIPHERAL NERVOUS SYSTEM

ner·vure \'nər-vyər\ *n* [F, fr. *nerf* sinew, fr. L *nervus*] (1816) **:** VEIN 3

nervy \'nər-vē\ *adj* **nerv·i·er; -est** (1607) **1** *archaic* **:** SINEWY, STRONG **2 a :** showing calm courage **:** BOLD **b :** marked by effrontery or presumption **:** BRASH **3 :** EXCITABLE, NERVOUS — **nerv·i·ly** \-və-lē\ *adv* — **nerv·i·ness** \-vē-nəs\ *n*

ne·science \'nesh-(ē-)ən(t)s, 'nēsh-; 'nes-ē-ən(t)s, 'nēs-\ *n* [LL *nescientia,* fr. L *nescient-, nesciens,* prp. of *nescire* not to know, fr. *ne-* not + *scire* to know — more at NO, SCIENCE] (1612) **:** lack of knowledge or awareness **:** IGNORANCE — **ne·scient** \-(ē-)ənt, -ē-ənt\ *adj*

ness \'nes\ *n* [ME *nasse,* fr. OE *næss;* akin to OE *nasu* nose — more at NOSE] (bef. 12c) **:** CAPE, PROMONTORY

-ness \nəs\ *n suffix* [ME *-nes,* fr. OE; akin to OHG *-nissa* -ness] **:** state **:** condition **:** quality **:** degree ⟨good*ness*⟩

Nes·sel·rode \'nes-əl-ˌrōd\ *n* [Count Karl R. *Nesselrode* †1862 Russ. statesman] (1845) **:** a mixture of candied fruits, nuts, and maraschino used in puddings, pies, and ice cream

Nes·sus \'nes-əs\ *n* [L, fr. Gk *Nessos*] **:** a centaur slain by Hercules for trying to carry away Hercules' wife but avenged by means of a poisoned garment that causes Hercules to die in torment

[1]nest \'nest\ *n* [ME, fr. OE; akin to OHG *nest* nest, L *nidus*] (bef. 12c) **1 a :** a bed or receptacle prepared by a bird for its eggs and young **b :** a place or specially modified structure serving as an abode of animals and esp. of their immature stages ⟨an ants' ~⟩ **c :** a receptacle resembling a bird's nest **2 a :** a place of rest, retreat, or lodging **:** HOME ⟨grown children who have left the ~⟩ **b :** DEN, HANGOUT **3 :** the occupants or frequenters of a nest **4 a :** a group of similar things **:** AGGREGATION ⟨a ~ of giant mountains —Helen MacInnes⟩ **b :** HOTBED 2 ⟨a ~ of rebellion⟩ **5 :** a group of objects made to fit close together or one within another **6 :** an emplaced group of weapons

[2]nest *vi* (bef. 12c) **1 :** to build or occupy a nest **:** settle in or as if in a nest **2 :** to fit compactly together or within one another **:** EMBED ~ *vt* **1 :** to form a nest for **2 :** to pack compactly together

nest·ed \'nes-təd\ *adj* (1903) **:** forming a sequence or hierarchy with each member contained in or containing the next ⟨~ sequence of closed intervals on a line⟩ ⟨~ subroutines in computer programming⟩

nest egg *n* (14c) **1 :** a natural or artificial egg left in a nest to induce a fowl to continue to lay there **2 :** a fund of money accumulated as a reserve

nest·er \'nes-tər\ *n* (1887) **1 :** one that nests **2** *West* **:** a homesteader or squatter who takes up land on open range for a farm

nes·tle \'nes-əl\ *vb* **nes·tled; nes·tling** \-(ə-)liŋ\ [ME *nestlen,* fr. OE *nestlian,* fr. *nest*] *vi* (bef. 12c) **1** *archaic* **:** NEST 1 **2 :** to settle snugly or comfortably **3 :** to lie in an inconspicuous or sheltered manner ~ *vt* **1 :** to settle, shelter, or house in or as if in a nest ⟨the children were *nestled* all snug in their beds —Clement Moore⟩ **2 :** to press closely and affectionately ⟨~*s* a kitten in her arms⟩ — **nes·tler** \-(ə-)lər\ *n*

nest·ling \'nest-liŋ\ *n* (14c) **:** a young bird that has not abandoned the nest

Nes·tor \'nes-tər, -ˌtȯ(ə)r\ *n* [L, fr. Gk *Nestōr*] **1 :** a king of Pylos who serves in his old age as a counselor to the Greeks at Troy **2** *often not cap* **:** one who is a patriarch or leader in his field

Nes·to·ri·an \ne-'stōr-ē-ən, -'stȯr-\ *adj* (1500) **1 :** of or relating to the doctrine ascribed to Nestorius and ecclesiastically condemned in 431 that divine and human persons remained separate in the incarnate Christ **2 :** of or relating to a church separating from Byzantine Christianity after 431, centering in Persia, and surviving chiefly in Asia Minor — **Nestorian** *n* — **Nes·to·ri·an·ism** \-ˌiz-əm\ *n*

[1]net \'net\ *n* [ME *nett,* fr. OE; akin to OHG *nezzi* net, L ***nodus*** knot] (bef. 12c) **1 a :** an open-meshed fabric twisted, knotted, or woven together at regular intervals **b :** something made of net: as (1) **:** a device for catching fish, birds, or insects (2) **:** a fabric barricade which divides a court in half (as in tennis or volleyball) and over which a ball or shuttlecock must be hit to be in play (3) **:** the fabric that encloses the sides and back of the goal in various games (as soccer or hockey) **2 :** an entrapping device or situation ⟨caught in the ~ of suspicious circumstances⟩ **3 :** something resembling a net in reticulation (as of lines, fibers, or figures) **4 a :** a group of communications stations operating under unified control **b :** NETWORK 4 — **net·less** \-ləs\ *adj* — **net·like** \-ˌlīk\ *adj* — **net·ty** \'net-ē\ *adj*

[2]net *vt* **net·ted; net·ting** (1593) **1 :** to cover or enclose with or as if with a net **2 :** to catch in or as if in a net **3 :** to cover with or as if with a network **4 a :** to hit (a ball) into the net for the loss of a point in a racket game **b :** to hit (a ball) into the goal for a score (as in hockey or soccer) — **net·ter** *n*

[3]net *adj* [ME, clean, bright, fr. MF] (15c) **1 :** free from all charges or deductions: as **a :** remaining after the deduction of all charges, outlay, or loss ⟨~ earnings⟩ ⟨~ worth⟩ — compare GROSS **b :** excluding all tare ⟨~ weight⟩ **2 :** excluding all nonessential considerations **:** BASIC, FINAL ⟨the ~ result⟩ ⟨~ effect⟩

[4]net *vt* **net·ted; net·ting** (1758) **1 a :** to receive by way of profit **:** CLEAR **b :** to produce by way of profit **:** YIELD **2 :** to get possession of **:** GAIN

[5]net *n* (ca. 1904) **1 :** a net amount, profit, weight, or price **2 :** the score of a golfer in a handicap match after deducting his handicap from his gross **3 :** ESSENCE, GIST

neth·er \'neth-ər\ *adj* [ME, fr. OE *nithera,* fr. *nither* down; akin to OHG *nidar* down, Skt *ni,* Gk *en, eni* in — more at IN] (bef. 12c) **1 :** situated down or below **:** LOWER ⟨the ~ side⟩ **2 :** situated or believed to be situated beneath the earth's surface ⟨the ~ regions⟩

neth·er·most \-ˌmōst\ *adj* (14c) **:** farthest down **:** LOWEST

neth·er·world \-ˌwərld\ *n* (1638) **1 :** the world of the dead **2 :** UNDERWORLD 4 ⟨the ~ of deceit, subversion, and espionage —R. M. Nixon⟩

net·su·ke \'net-s(ə-)kē\ *n, pl* **netsuke** *or* **netsukes** [Jp] (1883) **:** a small and often intricately carved toggle (as of wood, ivory, or metal) used to fasten a small container to a kimono sash

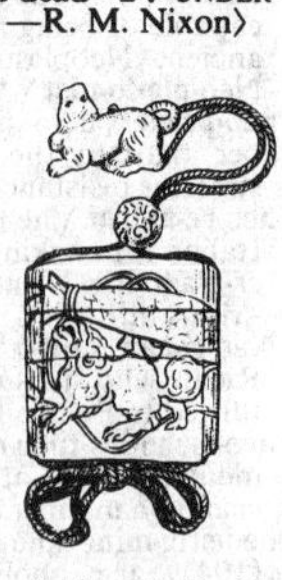
netsuke attached to inro

nett *Brit var of* NET

net·ting \'net-iŋ\ *n* (1567) **1 :** NETWORK **2 :** the act or process of making a net or network **3 :** the act, process, or right of fishing with a net

[1]net·tle \'net-ᵊl\ *n* [ME, fr. OE *netel;* akin to OHG *nazza* nettle, Gk *adikē*] (bef. 12c) **1 :** any of a genus (*Urtica* of the family Urticaceae, the nettle family) of chiefly coarse herbs armed with stinging hairs **2 :** any of various prickly or stinging plants other than the true nettles (genus *Urtica*)

[2]nettle *vt* **net·tled; net·tling** \'net-liŋ, -ᵊl-iŋ\ (15c) **1 :** to strike or sting with or as if with nettles **2 :** to arouse to sharp but transitory annoyance or anger

nettle rash *n* (1740) **:** URTICARIA

net·tle·some \'net-ᵊl-səm\ *adj* (1766) **:** causing vexation **:** IRRITATING

net–veined \-'vānd\ *adj* (1861) **:** having veins arranged in a fine network ⟨a ~ leaf⟩ ⟨a ~ wing⟩ — compare PARALLEL-VEINED — **net venation** *n*

net–winged \'net-'wiŋd\ *adj* (ca. 1890) **:** having wings with a fine network of veins

[1]net·work \'net-ˌwərk\ *n* (1560) **1 :** a fabric or structure of cords or wires that cross at regular intervals and are knotted or secured at the crossings **2 :** a system of lines or channels resembling a network **3 a :** an interconnected or interrelated chain, group, or system ⟨a ~ of hotels⟩ **b :** a system of computers, terminals, and data bases connected by communications lines **4 a :** a group of radio or television stations linked by wire or radio relay **b :** a radio or television company that produces programs for broadcast over such a network

[2]network *vt* (1887) **1 :** to cover with or as if with a network ⟨a continent . . . so ~*ed* with navigable rivers and canals —*Lamp*⟩ **2 :** to present on or integrate into a radio or television network

net·work·ing *n* (1966) **1 :** the exchange of information or services among individuals, groups, or institutions **2 :** the process of establishing or using a computer network

Neuf·châ·tel \ˌn(y)ü-shə-'tel, ˌnə(r)sh-ə-\ *n* [F, fr. *Neufchâtel,* France] (1865) **:** a soft unripened cheese similar to cream cheese but containing less fat and more moisture

neume \'n(y)üm\ *n* [ME, fr. ML *pneuma, neuma,* fr. Gk *pneuma* breath — more at PNEUMATIC] (14c) **:** any of various symbols used in the notation of Gregorian chant — **neu·mat·ic** \n(y)ü-'mat-ik\ *adj*

neur- *or* **neuro-** *comb form* [NL, fr. Gk, nerve, sinew, fr. *neuron* — more at NERVE] **1 :** nerve ⟨*neur*al⟩ ⟨*neuro*logy⟩ **2 :** neural **:** neural and ⟨*neuro*muscular⟩

neu·ral \'n(y)u̇r-əl\ *adj* (1839) **1 :** of, relating to, or affecting a nerve or the nervous system **2 :** situated in the region of or on the same side of the body as the brain and spinal cord **:** DORSAL — **neu·ral·ly** \-ə-lē\ *adv*

neural arch *n* (ca. 1860) **:** the cartilaginous or bony arch enclosing the spinal cord on the dorsal side of a vertebra — see VERTEBRA illustration

neural crest *n* (ca. 1885) **:** the ridge of one of the folds forming the neural tube that gives rise to the spinal ganglia and various structures of the autonomic nervous system

neu·ral·gia \n(y)u̇-'ral-jə\ *n* [NL] (ca. 1822) **:** acute paroxysmal pain radiating along the course of one or more nerves usu. without demonstrable changes in the nerve structure — **neu·ral·gic** \-jik\ *adj*

neural plate *n* (1888) **:** a thickened plate of ectoderm along the dorsal midline of the early vertebrate embryo that gives rise to the neural tube and crests

neural tube *n* (1888) **:** the hollow longitudinal dorsal tube formed by infolding and subsequent fusion of the opposite ectodermal folds in the vertebrate embryo

neur·amin·i·dase \ˌn(y)u̇r-ə-'min-ə-ˌdās, -ˌdāz\ *n* [*neuramin*ic acid (an amino acid) + *-ide* + *-ase*] (1956) **:** a hydrolytic enzyme that is found esp. in microorganisms of the respiratory or intestinal tract and that splits mucoproteins by breaking a glucoside link

neur·as·the·nia \ˌn(y)u̇r-əs-'thē-nē-ə\ *n* [NL] (1856) **:** an emotional and psychic disorder that is characterized esp. by easy fatigability and often by lack of motivation, feelings of inadequacy, and psychosomatic symptoms — **neur·as·then·ic** \-'then-ik\ *adj or n* — **neur·as·then·i·cal·ly** \-i-k(ə-)lē\ *adv*

neu·ri·lem·ma \ˌn(y)u̇r-ə-'lem-ə\ *n* [NL, fr. *neur-* + Gk *eilēma* covering, coil, fr. *eilein* to wind; akin to Gk *eilyein* to wrap — more at VOLUBLE] (1825) **:** the plasma membrane surrounding a Schwann cell of a myelinated nerve fiber and separating layers of myelin — **neu·ri·lem·mal** \-'lem-əl\ *adj*

neu·ris·tor \n(y)u̇-'ris-tər\ *n* [*neur*on + tran*sistor;* fr. its functioning like a neuron and not requiring the use of transistors] (1960) **:** a usu. electronic device along which a signal propagates with uniform velocity and without attenuation

neu·ri·tis \n(y)u̇-'rīt-əs\ *n, pl* **-rit·i·des** \-'rit-ə-ˌdēz\ *or* **-ri·tis·es** [NL] (1840) **:** an inflammatory or degenerative lesion of a nerve marked esp. by pain, sensory disturbances, and impaired or lost reflexes — **neu·rit·ic** \-'rit-ik\ *adj or n*

neu·ro·ac·tive \ˌn(y)u̇r-ō-'ak-tiv\ *adj* (1961) **:** stimulating neural tissue

neu·ro·anat·o·my \-ə-'nat-ə-mē\ *n* (ca. 1899) **:** the anatomy of nervous tissue and the nervous sytem — **neu·ro·anat·om·i·cal** \-ˌan-ə-'täm-i-kəl\ *also* **neu·ro·ana·tom·ic** \-ik\ *adj* — **neu·ro·anat·o·mist** \-ə-'nat-ə-məst\ *n*

neu·ro·bi·ol·o·gy \-bī-'äl-ə-jē\ *n* (1906) **:** a branch of the life sciences that deals with the anatomy, physiology, and pathology of the nervous system — **neu·ro·bi·o·log·i·cal** \-ˌbī-ə-'läj-i-kəl\ *adj* — **neu·ro·bi·ol·o·gist** \-bī-'äl-ə-jəst\ *n*

neu·ro·blas·to·ma \-blas-'tō-mə\ *n, pl* **-mas** *or* **-ma·ta** \-mət-ə\ [NL, fr. ISV *neuroblast* (embryonic ganglion cell), fr. *neur-* + *-blast* -blast] (1910) : a malignant tumor formed of embryonic ganglion cells
neu·ro·chem·is·try \-'kem-ə-strē\ *n* (1924) : the study of the chemical makeup and activities of nervous tissue — **neu·ro·chem·i·cal** \-'kem-i-kəl\ *adj or n* — **neu·ro·chem·ist** \-'kem-əst\ *n*
neu·ro·en·do·crine \-'en-də-krən, -ˌkrīn, -ˌkrēn\ *adj* (1922) **1 :** of, relating to, or being a hormonal substance that influences the activity of nerves **2 :** of, relating to, or functioning in neurosecretion
neu·ro·en·do·cri·nol·o·gy \-ˌen-də-kri-'näl-ə-jē, -(ˌ)krī-\ *n* (ca. 1922) : a branch of the life sciences dealing with neurosecretion and the physiological interaction between the central nervous system and the endocrine system — **neu·ro·en·do·cri·no·log·i·cal** \-ˌkrin-ᵊl-'äj-i-kəl, -ˌkrīn-, -ˌkrēn-\ *adj* — **neu·ro·en·do·cri·nol·o·gist** \-kri-'näl-ə-jəst, -(ˌ)krī-\ *n*
neu·ro·fi·bril \ˌn(y)u̇r-ō-'fīb-rəl, -'fib-\ *n* [NL *neurofibrilla,* fr. *neur-* + *fibrilla* fibril] (1898) : a fine proteinaceous fibril that is found in cytoplasm (as of a neuron or a paramecium) and is capable of conducting excitation — **neu·ro·fi·bril·lary** \-rə-ˌler-ē\ *adj*
neu·ro·gen·ic \ˌn(y)u̇r-ə-'jen-ik\ *adj* (1901) **1 :** originating in or controlled by nervous tissue ⟨~ heartbeat⟩ **2 :** induced or modified by nervous factors; *esp* **:** disordered because of abnormally altered neural relations — **neu·ro·gen·i·cal·ly** \-i-k(ə-)lē\ *adv*
neu·ro·glia \n(y)u̇-'rō-glē-ə, -'räg-lē-ə; ˌn(y)u̇r-ə-'glē-ə, -'glī-\ *n* [NL, fr. *neur-* + MGk *glia* glue] (1873) : supporting tissue intermingled with the essential elements of nervous tissue esp. in the brain, spinal cord, and ganglia — **neu·ro·gli·al** \-əl\ *adj*
neu·ro·hor·mon·al \ˌn(y)u̇r-ō-hȯr-'mōn-ᵊl\ *adj* (ca. 1935) **1 :** involving both neural and hormonal mechanisms **2 :** of, relating to, or being a neurohormone
neu·ro·hor·mone \-'hȯr-ˌmōn\ *n* [ISV] (1935) : a hormone (as acetylcholine or norepinephrine) produced by or acting on nervous tissue
neu·ro·hu·mor \ˌn(y)u̇r-ō-'hyü-mər, -'yü-\ *n* (1932) : NEUROHORMONE; *esp* : NEUROTRANSMITTER — **neu·ro·hu·mor·al** \-mə-rəl\ *adj*
neu·ro·hy·poph·y·sis \-hī-'päf-ə-səs\ *n* [NL] (1912) : the portion of the pituitary gland that is composed of the infundibulum and posterior lobe and is concerned with the secretion of various hormones — **neu·ro·hy·po·phy·se·al** *or* **neu·ro·hy·po·phy·si·al** \-(ˌ)hī-ˌpäf-ə-'sē-əl, -ˌhī-pə-fə-, -'zē-, ˌhī-pə-'fiz-ē-\ *adj*
neu·ro·lep·tic \ˌn(y)u̇r-ə-'lep-tik\ *n* [F *neuroleptique,* fr. *neur-* + *-leptique* affecting, fr. Gk *lēptikos* seizing, fr. *lambanein* to take, seize — more at LATCH] (1958) : TRANQUILIZER 2 — **neuroleptic** *adj*
neu·rol·o·gist \n(y)u̇-'räl-ə-jəst\ *n* (1832) : one specializing in neurology; *esp* : a physician skilled in the diagnosis and treatment of disease of the nervous system
neu·rol·o·gy \-jē\ *n* [NL *neurologia,* fr. *neur-* + *-logia* -logy] (1681) : the scientific study of the nervous system — **neu·ro·log·i·cal** \ˌn(y)u̇r-ə-'läj-i-kəl\ *or* **neu·ro·log·ic** \-ik\ *adj* — **neu·ro·log·i·cal·ly** \-i-k(ə)-lē\ *adv*
neu·ro·ma \n(y)u̇-'rō-mə\ *n, pl* **-mas** *or* **-ma·ta** \-mət-ə\ [NL] (ca. 1839) : a tumor or mass growing from a nerve and usu. consisting of nerve fibers
neu·ro·mus·cu·lar \ˌn(y)u̇r-ō-'məs-kyə-lər\ *adj* [ISV] (1864) : of or relating to nerves and muscles; *esp* : jointly involving nervous and muscular elements ⟨a ~ junction⟩
neu·ron \'n(y)ü-ˌrän, 'n(y)u̇(ə)r-ˌän\ *also* **neu·rone** \-ˌrōn, -ˌōn\ *n* [NL *neuron,* fr. Gk, nerve, sinew — more at NERVE] (1891) : a grayish or reddish granular cell with specialized processes that is the fundamental functional unit of nervous tissue — **neu·ro·nal** \'n(y)u̇r-ən-ᵊl, n(y)u̇-'rōn-ᵊl\ *also* **neu·ron·ic** \n(y)u̇-'rän-ik\ *adj*
neu·ro·pa·thol·o·gy \ˌn(y)u̇r-ō-pə-'thäl-ə-jē, -pa-\ *n* [ISV] (1853) : pathology of the nervous system — **neu·ro·path·o·log·ic** \-ˌpath-ə-'läj-ik\ *or* **neu·ro·path·o·log·i·cal** \-i-kəl\ *adj* — **neu·ro·pa·thol·o·gist** \-pə-'thäl-ə-jəst, -pa-\ *n*
neu·rop·a·thy \n(y)u̇-'räp-ə-thē\ *n, pl* **-thies** [ISV] (1857) : an abnormal and usu. degenerative state of the nervous system or nerves; *also* : a systemic condition that stems from a neuropathy — **neu·ro·path·ic** \ˌn(y)u̇r-ə-'path-ik\ *adj* — **neu·ro·path·i·cal·ly** \-i-k(ə-)lē\ *adv*
neu·ro·pep·tide \ˌn(y)u̇r-ə-'pep-ˌtīd\ *n* (1975) : an endogenous peptide that influences neural activity or functioning
neu·ro·phar·ma·col·o·gy \'n(y)u̇r-ō-ˌfär-mə-'käl-ə-jē\ *n* (1950) **1 :** a branch of medical science dealing with the action of drugs on and in the nervous system **2 :** the properties and reactions of a drug on and in the nervous system — **neu·ro·phar·ma·co·log·i·cal** \-kə-'läj-i-kəl\ *also* **neu·ro·phar·ma·co·log·ic** \-ik\ *adj* — **neu·ro·phar·ma·col·o·gist** \-'käl-ə-jəst\ *n*
neu·ro·phys·i·ol·o·gy \ˌn(y)u̇r-ō-ˌfiz-ē-'äl-ə-jē\ *n* (1868) : physiology of the nervous system — **neu·ro·phys·i·o·log·i·cal** \-ē-ə-'läj-i-kəl\ *also* **neu·ro·phys·i·o·log·ic** \-ik\ *adj* — **neu·ro·phys·i·o·log·i·cal·ly** \-i-k(ə-)lē\ *adv* — **neu·ro·phys·i·ol·o·gist** \-ē-'äl-ə-jəst\ *n*
neu·ro·psy·chi·a·try \-sə-'kī-ə-trē, -sī-\ *n* (1918) : a branch of medicine concerned with both neurology and psychiatry — **neu·ro·psy·chi·at·ric** \-ˌsī-kē-'a-trik\ *adj* — **neu·ro·psy·chi·at·ri·cal·ly** \-tri-k(ə-)lē\ *adv* — **neu·ro·psy·chi·a·trist** \-sə-'kī-ə-trəst, -sī-\ *n*
neu·ro·psy·chol·o·gy \-sī-'käl-ə-jē\ *n* (ca. 1893) : a science that seeks to integrate psychological observations on behavior and the mind with neurological observations on the brain and nervous system — **neu·ro·psy·cho·log·i·cal** \-ˌsī-kə-'läj-i-kəl\ *adj* — **neu·ro·psy·chol·o·gist** \-sī-'käl-ə-jəst\ *n*
neu·rop·ter·an \n(y)u̇-'räp-tə-rən\ *n* [deriv. of Gk *neur-* + *pteron* wing — more at FEATHER] (1842) : any of an order (Neuroptera) of usu. net-winged insects that include the lacewings and ant lions — **neuropteran** *adj* — **neu·rop·ter·ous** \-rəs\ *adj*
neu·ro·ra·di·ol·o·gy \-ˌrād-ē-'äl-ə-jē\ *n* (ca. 1947) : radiology of the nervous system — **neu·ro·ra·dio·log·i·cal** \-ē-ə-'läj-i-kəl\ *adj* — **neu·ro·ra·di·ol·o·gist** \-ē-'äl-ə-jəst\ *n*
neu·ro·sci·ence \ˌn(y)u̇r-ō-'sī-ən(t)s\ *n* (1963) : a branch (as neurophysiology) of the life sciences that deals with the anatomy, physiology, biochemistry, or molecular biology of nerves and nervous tissue and esp. with their relation to behavior and learning — **neu·ro·sci·en·tist** \-ənt-əst\ *n*
neu·ro·se·cre·tion \-si-'krē-shən\ *n* (1941) **1 :** the process of producing a secretion by nerve cells **2 :** a secretion produced by neurosecretion — **neu·ro·se·cre·to·ry** \-'krēt-ə-rē\ *adj*
neu·ro·sen·so·ry \-'sen(t)s-(ə-)rē\ *adj* (1928) : of or relating to afferent nerves
neu·ro·sis \n(y)u̇-'rō-səs\ *n, pl* **-ro·ses** \-ˌsēz\ [NL] (ca. 1776) : a mental and emotional disorder that affects only part of the personality, is accompanied by a less distorted perception of reality than in a psychosis, does not result in disturbance of the use of language, and is accompanied by various physical, physiological, and mental disturbances (as visceral symptoms, anxieties, or phobias)
neu·ros·po·ra \n(y)u̇-'räs-pə-rə\ *n* [NL, fr. *neur-* + *spora* spore] (1928) : any of a genus (*Neurospora* of the family Sphaeriaceae) of ascomycetous fungi which are used extensively in genetic research and have black perithecia and persistent asci and some of which have salmon-pink or orange spore masses and are severe pests in bakeries
neu·ro·sur·gery \-'sərj-(ə-)rē\ *n* (1904) : surgery of nervous structures (as nerves, the brain, or the spinal cord) — **neu·ro·sur·geon** \-'sər-jən\ *n* — **neu·ro·sur·gi·cal** \-'sər-ji-kəl\ *adj*
[1]**neu·rot·ic** \n(y)u̇-'rät-ik\ *adj* (1873) : of, relating to, constituting, or affected with neurosis — **neu·rot·i·cal·ly** \-i-k(ə-)lē\ *adv*
[2]**neurotic** *n* (1896) **1 :** one affected with a neurosis **2 :** an emotionally unstable individual
neu·rot·i·cism \n(y)u̇-'rät-ə-ˌsiz-əm\ *n* (1900) : a neurotic character, condition, or trait
neu·ro·tox·ic \ˌn(y)u̇r-ə-'täk-sik\ *adj* (ca. 1903) : toxic to the nerves or nervous tissue — **neu·ro·tox·ic·i·ty** \-ˌtäk-'sis-ət-ē\ *n*
neu·ro·tox·in \-'täk-sən\ *n* [ISV] (1902) : a poisonous protein complex that acts on the nervous system
neu·ro·trans·mis·sion \-tran(t)s-'mish-ən, -tranz-\ *n* (1961) : the transmission of nerve impulses across a synapse
neu·ro·trans·mit·ter \ˌn(y)u̇r-ō-tran(t)s-'mit-ər, -tranz-\ *n* (1961) : a substance (as norepinephrine or acetylcholine) that transmits nerve impulses across a synapse
neu·ro·trop·ic \ˌn(y)u̇r-ə-'träp-ik\ *adj* [ISV] (1903) : having an affinity for or localizing selectively in nerve tissue
neu·ru·la \'n(y)u̇r-(y)ə-lə\ *n, pl* **-lae** \-ˌlē\ *or* **-las** [NL, fr. *neur-* + L *-ula* -ule] (ca. 1890) : an early vertebrate embryo which follows the gastrula and in which nervous tissue begins to differentiate and the basic pattern of the vertebrate begins to emerge — **neu·ru·la·tion** \ˌn(y)u̇r-(y)ə-'lā-shən\ *n*
neus·ton \'n(y)ü-ˌstän\ *n* [G, fr. Gk, neut. of *neustos* swimming, fr. *nein* to swim — more at NOURISH] (1928) : minute organisms that float in the surface film of water
[1]**neu·ter** \'n(y)üt-ər\ *adj* [ME *neutre,* fr. MF & L; MF *neutre,* fr. L *neuter,* lit., neither, fr. *ne-* not + *uter* which of two — more at NO, WHETHER] (14c) **1 a :** of, relating to, or constituting the gender that ordinarily includes most words or grammatical forms referring to things classed as neither masculine nor feminine **b :** neither active nor passive : INTRANSITIVE **2 :** taking no side : NEUTRAL **3 :** lacking or having imperfectly developed or nonfunctional generative organs ⟨the worker bee is ~⟩
[2]**neuter** *n* (15c) **1 a :** a noun, pronoun, adjective, or inflectional form or class of the neuter gender **b :** the neuter gender **2 :** one that is neutral **3 a :** WORKER 2 **b :** a spayed or castrated animal
[3]**neuter** *vt* (1903) : CASTRATE, ALTER
neu·ter·cane \-ˌkān\ *n* [L *neuter* neither + E *-cane* (as in *hurricane*); from the difficulty of classifying it as either hurricane or frontal storm] (1972) : a subtropical cyclone that is usu. less than 100 miles in diameter and that draws energy from sources common to both the hurricane and the frontal cyclone
[1]**neu·tral** \'n(y)ü-trəl\ *n* (15c) **1 :** one that is neutral **2 :** a neutral color **3 :** a position of disengagement (as of gears)
[2]**neutral** *adj* [MF, fr. (assumed) ML *neutralis,* fr. L, of neuter gender, fr. *neutr-, neuter*] (1549) **1 :** not engaged on either side; *specif* : not aligned with a political or ideological grouping ⟨a ~ nation⟩ **2 :** of or relating to a neutral state or power ⟨~ territory⟩ **3 a :** not decided or pronounced as to characteristics : INDIFFERENT **b (1) :** ACHROMATIC **(2) :** nearly achromatic **c (1) :** NEUTER 3 **(2) :** lacking stamens or pistils **d :** neither acid nor basic **e :** not electrically charged **4 :** produced with the tongue in the position it has when at rest ⟨the ~ vowels of \ə-'bəv\ *above*⟩ — **neu·tral·ly** \-trə-lē\ *adv* — **neu·tral·ness** *n*
neu·tral·ism \'n(y)ü-trə-ˌliz-əm\ *n* (1579) **1 :** NEUTRALITY **2 :** a policy or the advocacy of neutrality esp. in international affairs — **neu·tral·ist** \-ləst\ *n* — **neu·tral·is·tic** \ˌn(y)ü-trə-'lis-tik\ *adj*
neu·tral·i·ty \n(y)ü-'tral-ət-ē\ *n* (15c) : the quality or state of being neutral; *esp* : refusal to take part in a war between other powers
neu·tral·iza·tion \ˌn(y)ü-trə-lə-'zā-shən\ *n* (1808) **1 :** an act or process of neutralizing **2 :** the quality or state of being neutralized
neu·tral·ize \'n(y)ü-trə-ˌlīz\ *vb* **-ized; -iz·ing** *vt* (1759) **1 :** to make chemically neutral **2 :** to counteract the activity or effect of : make ineffective ⟨propaganda that is difficult to ~⟩ **3 :** to make electrically inert by combining equal positive and negative quantities **4 :** to invest (as a territory or a nation) with conventional or obligatory neutrality conferring inviolability during a war **5 :** to make neutral by blending with the complementary color ~ *vi* : to undergo neutralization — **neu·tral·iz·er** *n*
neutral red *n* (1890) : a basic phenazine dye used chiefly as a biological stain and acid-base indicator
neutral spirits *n pl but sing or pl in constr* (1919) : ethyl alcohol of 190 or higher proof used esp. for blending other alcoholic liquors
neu·tri·no \n(y)ü-'trē-(ˌ)nō\ *n, pl* **-nos** [It, dim. of *neutrone* neutron] (1934) : an uncharged elementary particle that has at least two forms, that is believed to be massless, and that interacts very weakly after being created as a result of particle decay
neu·tron \'n(y)ü-ˌträn\ *n* [prob. fr. *neutral*] (ca. 1920) : an uncharged elementary particle that has a mass nearly equal to that of the proton and is present in all known atomic nuclei except the hydrogen nucleus — **neu·tron·ic** \n(y)ü-'trän-ik\ *adj*
neutron bomb *n* (1959) : a nuclear bomb designed to produce lethal neutrons but less blast and fire damage than other nuclear bombs

---

\ə\ abut \ᵊ\ kitten, F table \ər\ further \a\ ash \ā\ ace \ä\ cot, cart \au̇\ out \ch\ chin \e\ bet \ē\ easy \g\ go \i\ hit \ī\ ice \j\ job \ŋ\ sing \ō\ go \ȯ\ law \ȯi\ boy \th\ thin \th\ the \ü\ loot \u̇\ foot \y\ yet \zh\ vision \å, k̲, ⁿ, œ, œ̄, ue, ue̅, ʸ\ *see* Guide to Pronunciation

neutron star *n* [fr. the hypothesis that the cores of such stars are composed entirely of neutrons] (1934) : a hypothetical dense celestial object that consists primarily of closely packed neutrons and that results from the collapse of a much larger stellar body

1neu·tro·phil \'n(y)ü-trə-ˌfil\ *or* **neu·tro·phil·ic** \ˌn(y)ü-trə-'fil-ik\ *adj* [ISV *neutro-* (fr. L *neutr-, neuter* neither) + *-phil*] (ca. 1890) : staining to the same degree with acid or basic dyes ⟨~ granulocytes⟩

2neutrophil *n* (1893) : a finely granular cell that is the chief phagocytic leukocyte of the blood

né·vé \nā-'vā\ *n* [F (Swiss dial.), fr. L *niv-, nix* snow — more at SNOW] (1843) : the partially compacted granular snow that forms the surface part of the upper end of a glacier; *broadly* : a field of granular snow

nev·er \'nev-ər\ *adv* [ME, fr. OE *nǣfre,* fr. *ne* not + *ǣfre* ever — more at NO] (bef. 12c) **1** : not ever : at no time ⟨~ saw him before⟩ **2** : not in any degree : not under any condition ⟨~ the wiser for his experience⟩

nev·er·more \ˌnev-ər-'mō(ə)r, -'mȯ(ə)r\ *adv* (12c) : never again

nev·er–nev·er land \ˌnev-ər-'nev-ər-\ *n* (1900) : an ideal or imaginary place

nev·er·the·less \ˌnev-ər-t͟hə-'les\ *adv* (14c) : in spite of that : HOWEVER ⟨her childish but ~ real delight —Richard Corbin⟩

ne·vus \'nē-vəs\ *n, pl* **ne·vi** \-ˌvī\ [NL, fr. L *naevus*] (1693) : a congenital pigmented area on the skin : BIRTHMARK

1new \'n(y)ü, *before a stress in geographical names also* n(y)u̇ *or* n(y)ə(-w)\ *adj* [ME, fr. OE *nīwe;* akin to OHG *niuwi* new, L *novus,* Gk *neos*] (bef. 12c) **1** : having existed or having been made but a short time : RECENT, MODERN **2 a** (1) : having been seen, used, or known for a short time : NOVEL ⟨rice was a ~ crop for the area⟩ (2) : UNFAMILIAR ⟨visit ~ places⟩ **b** : being other than the former or old ⟨a steady flow of ~ money⟩ **3** : having been in a relationship or condition but a short time ⟨~ to the job⟩ **4 a** : beginning as the resumption or repetition of a previous act or thing ⟨a ~ day⟩ ⟨the ~ edition⟩ **b** : made or become fresh ⟨awoke a ~ man⟩ **5** : different from one of the same category that has existed previously ⟨~ realism⟩ **6** : of dissimilar origin and usu. of superior quality ⟨introducing ~ blood⟩ **7** *cap* : MODERN 3; *esp* : having been in use after medieval times — **new·ish** \'n(y)ü-ish\ *adj* — **new·ness** *n*

syn NEW, NOVEL, MODERN, ORIGINAL, FRESH mean having recently come into existence or use. NEW may apply to what is freshly made and unused ⟨*new* brick⟩ or has not been known before ⟨*new* design⟩ or not experienced before ⟨starts his *new* job⟩ NOVEL applies to what is not only new but strange or unprecedented ⟨a *novel* approach to the problem⟩ MODERN applies to what belongs to or is characteristic of the present time or the present era ⟨the lifestyle of the *modern* woman⟩ ORIGINAL applies to what is the first of its kind to exist ⟨a man without one *original* idea⟩ FRESH applies to what has not lost its qualities of newness such as liveliness, energy, brightness ⟨*fresh* towels⟩ ⟨a *fresh* start⟩

2new \'n(y)ü\ *adv* (bef. 12c) : NEWLY, RECENTLY — usu. used in combination

1new·born \-'bȯ(ə)rn\ *adj* (14c) **1** : recently born **2** : born anew

2newborn *n, pl* **newborn** *or* **newborns** (1768) : a newborn individual : NEONATE

New·burg *or* **New·burgh** \'n(y)ü-ˌbərg\ *adj* [origin unknown] (1901) : served with a sauce made of cream, butter, sherry, and egg yolks ⟨lobster ~⟩ ⟨shrimp ~⟩

new candle *n* (1938) : CANDLE 3

New·cas·tle disease \'n(y)ü-ˌkas-əl-, n(y)ü-'\ *n* [*Newcastle* upon Tyne, England] (1927) : a destructive virus disease of birds and esp. domestic fowl that involves respiratory and nervous symptoms

new·com·er \'n(y)ü-ˌkəm-ər\ *n* (15c) **1** : one recently arrived **2** : BEGINNER

New Criticism *n* (1941) : an analytic literary criticism that is marked by concentration on the language, imagery, and emotional or intellectual tensions in literary works — **New Critic** *n* — **New Critical** *adj*

new deal *n* [fr. the supposed resemblance to the situation of freshness and equality of opportunity afforded by a fresh deal in a card game] (1932) **1** *cap N&D* **a** : the legislative and administrative program of President F. D. Roosevelt designed to promote economic recovery and social reform during the 1930s **b** : the period of this program **2** : a governmental program resembling the Roosevelt New Deal in objectives or techniques — **new deal·er** \-'dē-lər\ *n, often cap N&D* — **new deal·ish** \-'dē-lish\ *adj, often cap N&D* — **new deal·ism** \-'dē(ə)l-ˌiz-əm\ *n, often cap N&D*

new drug *n* (ca. 1951) : a drug that has not been declared safe and effective by qualified experts under the conditions prescribed, recommended, or suggested in the label and that may be a new chemical formula or an established drug prescribed for use in a new way

new economics *n pl but usu sing in constr* (1928) : an economic concept that is a logical extension of Keynesianism and that holds that appropriate fiscal and monetary maneuvering can maintain healthy economic growth and prosperity indefinitely

new·el \'n(y)ü-əl\ *n* [ME *nowell,* fr. MF *nouel* stone of a fruit, fr. LL *nucalis* like a nut, fr. L *nuc-, nux* nut — more at NUT] (14c) **1** : an upright post about which the steps of a circular staircase wind **2** : a post at the foot of a straight stairway or one at a landing

New English Bible *n* (1957) : a translation of the Bible by a British interdenominational committee first published in its entirety in 1970

new·fan·gled \n(y)ü-'faŋ-gəld\ *adj* [ME, fr. *newefangel,* fr. *new* + OE *fangen,* pp. of *fōn* to take, seize — more at PACT] (13c) **1** : attracted to novelty **2** : of the newest style or kind ⟨had many ~ gadgets in the kitchen⟩ — **new·fan·gled·ness** *n*

new–fash·ioned \-'fash-ənd\ *adj* (1611) **1** : made in a new fashion or form **2** : UP-TO-DATE

new·found \-'fau̇nd\ *adj* (15c) : newly found ⟨a ~ friend⟩

New·found·land \'n(y)ü-fən-(d)lənd, -ˌ(d)land, n(y)ü-'fau̇n-(d)lənd\ *n* [*Newfoundland,* Canada] (1773) : any of a breed of very large heavy highly intelligent usu. black dogs developed in Newfoundland

New·gate \'n(y)ü-ˌgāt, -gət\ *n* (14c) : a London prison razed in 1902

New Greek *n* (ca. 1958) : Greek as used by the Greeks since the end of the medieval period

New Hebrew *n* (ca. 1959) : the Hebrew language in use in present-day Israel

new·ie \'n(y)ü-ē\ *n* (ca. 1945) : something new

New Jer·sey tea \n(y)ü-ˌjər-zē-\ *n* [*New Jersey,* state of U.S.; fr. the use of its leaves as a substitute for tea during the American Revolution] (1785) : a low deciduous shrub (*Ceanothus americanus*) of the buckthorn family that is found in the eastern U.S. and has dull green leaves and small white flowers borne in large terminal panicles

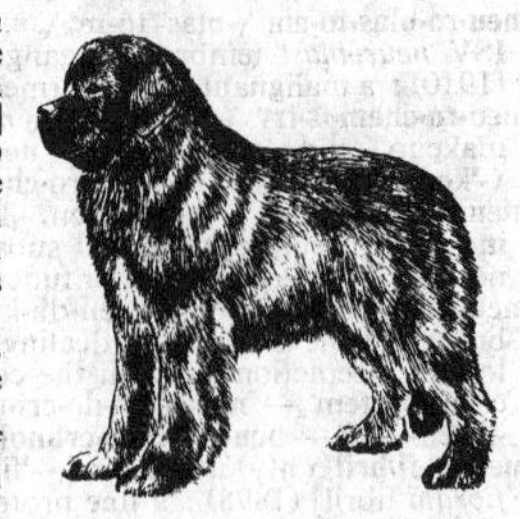
Newfoundland

New Je·ru·sa·lem \-jə-'rü-s(ə-)ləm, -'rüz-(ə-)ləm\ *n* [fr. the phrase "the holy city, *New Jerusalem*" —Rev. 21:2] (1535) **1** : the final abode of souls redeemed by Christ **2** : an ideal earthly community

New Journalism *n* (1967) : journalism that features the author's subjective responses to people and events and that often includes fictional elements meant to illuminate and dramatize those responses

New Latin *n* (ca. 1890) : Latin as used since the end of the medieval period esp. in scientific description and classification

New Left *n* (1960) : a political movement originating in the U.S. in the 1960s that actively advocates (as by demonstrations) radical changes in prevailing political, social, and educational practices — **new leftist** *n, often cap N&L*

new·ly \'n(y)ü-lē\ *adv* (bef. 12c) **1** : LATELY, RECENTLY ⟨a ~ married couple⟩ **2** : ANEW, AFRESH

new·ly·wed \-ˌwed\ *n* (1918) : one recently married

new·mar·ket \'n(y)ü-ˌmär-kət\ *n* [*Newmarket,* England] (1837) : a long close-fitting coat worn in the 19th century

new math *n* (1958) : mathematics that is based on set theory esp. as taught in elementary and secondary school — called also *new mathematics*

new moon *n* (bef. 12c) **1** : the moon's phase when it is in conjunction with the sun so that its dark side is toward the earth; *also* : the thin crescent moon seen shortly after sunset for a few days after the actual occurrence of the new moon phase **2** : the first day of each Jewish month marked by a special liturgy

news \'n(y)üz\ *n pl but sing in constr, often attrib* (15c) **1** : a report of recent events **2 a** : material reported in a newspaper or news periodical or on a newscast **b** : matter that is newsworthy **3** : NEWSCAST — **news·less** \-ləs\ *adj*

news agency *n* (1873) : an organization that supplies news to subscribing newspapers, periodicals, and newscasters

news·agent \'n(y)ü-ˌzā-jənt\ *n, chiefly Brit* (1851) : NEWSDEALER

news·boy \'n(y)üz-ˌbȯi\ *n* (1764) : one who delivers or sells newspapers

news·break \-ˌbrāk\ *n* (1944) : a newsworthy event

news·cast \-ˌkast\ *n* [*news* + broad*cast*] (1930) : a radio or television broadcast of news — **news·cast·er** \-ˌkas-tər\ *n* — **news·cast·ing** \-tiŋ\ *n*

news conference *n* (1946) : PRESS CONFERENCE

news·deal·er \-ˌdē-lər\ *n* (1861) : a dealer in newspapers, magazines, and often paperback books

news·let·ter \'n(y)üz-ˌlet-ər\ *n* (ca. 1903) : a printed sheet, pamphlet, or small newspaper containing news or information of interest chiefly to a special group

news·mag·a·zine \'n(y)üz-ˌmag-ə-ˌzēn, -'zēn\ *n* (1923) **1** : a usu. weekly magazine devoted chiefly to summarizing and analyzing news **2** : MAGAZINE 4c

news·man \-mən, -ˌman\ *n* (1596) : one who gathers, reports, or comments on the news : REPORTER, CORRESPONDENT

news·mon·ger \-ˌməŋ-gər, -ˌmäŋ-\ *n* (1596) : one who is active in gathering and repeating news; *esp* : GOSSIP

1news·pa·per \'n(y)üz-ˌpā-pər, 'n(y)üs-\ *n* (1670) **1** : a paper that is printed and distributed usu. daily or weekly and that contains news, articles of opinion, features, and advertising **2** : an organization that publishes a newspaper **3** : the paper making up a newspaper

2newspaper *vi* (1940) : to do newspaper work

news·pa·per·man \-ˌman\ *n* (1806) : one who owns or is employed by a newspaper

news·pa·per·wom·an \-ˌwu̇mən\ *n* (1881) : a woman who owns or is employed by a newspaper

new·speak \'n(y)ü-ˌspēk\ *n, often cap* [*Newspeak,* a language "designed to diminish the range of thought," in the novel *Nineteen Eighty-Four* (1949) by George Orwell] (1949) : propagandistic language marked by ambiguity and contradictions : DOUBLE-TALK 2

news·peo·ple \'n(y)üz-ˌpē-pəl\ *n pl* (1972) : REPORTERS

news·per·son \-ˌpərs-ᵊn\ *n* (1972) : REPORTER

news·print \-ˌprint\ *n* (1909) : a cheap paper made chiefly from groundwood pulp and used mostly for newspapers

news·read·er \-ˌrēd-ər\ *n, chiefly Brit* (1925) : one who broadcasts the news

news·reel \-ˌrēl\ *n* (1916) : a short movie dealing with current events

news·room \'n(y)üz-ˌrüm, -ˌru̇m\ *n* (1817) **1** : NEWSSTAND **2** : a place (as an office) where news is prepared for publication or broadcast

news·stand \'n(y)üz-ˌstand\ *n* (1871) : a place (as an outdoor stall) where newspapers and periodicals are sold

New Style *adj* (1615) : using or according to the Gregorian calendar

news·week·ly \'n(y)üz-ˌwē-klē\ *n* (1947) : a weekly newspaper or newsmagazine

news·wom·an \-ˌwu̇m-ən\ *n* (1928) : a female reporter

news·wor·thy \-ˌwər-t͟hē\ *adj* (1932) : sufficiently interesting to the general public to warrant reporting (as in a newspaper) — **news·wor·thi·ness** \-t͟hē-nəs\ *n*

news·writ·ing \-ˌrīt-iŋ\ *n* (1916) : JOURNALISM 1a

newsy \'n(y)ü-zē\ *adj* **news·i·er; -est** (1832) **1** : containing or filled with news ⟨~ letters⟩ **2** : NEWSWORTHY — **news·i·ness** *n*

newt \'n(y)üt\ *n* [ME, alter. (resulting from incorrect division of *an ewte*) of *ewte* — more at EFT] (15c) : any of various small semiaquatic salamanders (as of the genus *Triturus*)

New Testament *n* (14c) : the second part of the Christian Bible comprising the canonical Gospels and Epistles and also the book of Acts and book of Revelation — see BIBLE table

New Thought *n* (1887) : a mental healing movement embracing small groups devoted to spiritual healing and the creative power of constructive thinking

new·ton \'n(y)üt-ᵊn\ *n* [Sir Isaac *Newton*] (1904) : the unit of force in the mks system of physical units that is of such size that under its influence a body whose mass is one kilogram would experience an acceleration of one meter per second per second

new town *n* (1918) : an urban development comprising a small to medium-sized city with a broad range of housing and planned industrial, commercial, and recreational facilities

new wave *n, often cap N&W* [trans. of F *nouvelle vague*] (1960) **1** : a cinematic movement that is characterized by improvisation, abstraction, and subjective symbolism and that often makes use of experimental photographic techniques **2** : a new movement in a particular field **3** : rock music characterized by cohesive ensemble playing and usu. lyrics which express anger and social discontent

New World *n* (1555) : WESTERN HEMISPHERE; *esp* : the continental landmass of No. and So. America

New Year *n* (13c) **1** : the calendar year about to start or recently started **2 a** : NEW YEAR'S DAY **b** : the first days of a calendar year **3** : ROSH HASHANAH

New Year's Day *n* (13c) : the first day of the calendar year observed as a legal holiday in many countries

¹next \'nekst\ *adj* [ME, fr. OE *nīehst,* superl. of *nēah* nigh — more at NIGH] (bef. 12c) **1** : immediately preceding or following (as in place, rank, or time) **2** : any other considered hypothetically ⟨knew it as well as the ~ man⟩

²next \(ˌ)nekst\ *prep* (bef. 12c) : nearest or adjacent to

³next \'nekst\ *adv* (14c) **1** : in the time, place, or order nearest or immediately succeeding ⟨~ we drove home⟩ ⟨the ~ closest school⟩ **2** : on the first occasion to come ⟨when ~ we meet⟩

next–door *adj* (15c) : located or living in the next building, house, apartment, or room; *broadly* : NEARBY, ADJACENT

next door *adv* (1579) : in or to the next building, house, apartment, or room ⟨lives *next door*⟩; *broadly* : in or at an adjacent place — **next door to** : NEXT TO

next friend *n* (1579) : a person admitted to or appointed by a court to act for the benefit of a person (as an infant) lacking full legal capacity to act for himself

next of kin (14c) : one or more persons in the nearest degree of relationship to another person

¹next to *prep* (1633) : immediately following or adjacent to

²next to *adv* (1667) : very nearly : ALMOST ⟨it was *next to* impossible to see in the fog⟩

nex·us \'nek-səs\ *n, pl* **nex·us·es** \-sə-səz\ *or* **nex·us** \-səs, -ˌsüs\ [L, fr. *nexus,* pp. of *nectere* to bind; akin to L *nodus* knot — more at NET] (1663) **1** : CONNECTION, LINK **2** : a connected group or series **3** : CENTER, CORE

Nez Percé \'nez-'pərs, 'nes-'pe(ə)rs, *F* nā-per-sā\ *n* [F, lit., pierced nose] (1812) **1** : a member of an American Indian people of Idaho, Washington, and Oregon **2** : a language of the Nez Percé people

ngul·trum \eŋ-'gu̇l-trəm, en-\ *n* [native name in Bhutan] (1973) — see MONEY table

ngwee \eŋ-'gwē, en-\ *n, pl* **ngwee** [native name in Zambia, lit., bright] (1966) — see *kwacha* at MONEY table

ni·a·cin \'nī-ə-sən\ *n* [*ni*cotinic *ac*id + *-in*] (1942) : NICOTINIC ACID; *also* : NICOTINAMIDE

ni·a·cin·amide \ˌnī-ə-'sin-ə-ˌmīd\ *n* (1942) : NICOTINAMIDE

Ni·ag·a·ra \nī-'ag-(ə-)rə\ *n* [*Niagara* Falls] (1841) : an overwhelming flood : TORRENT ⟨a ~ of protests⟩

ni·al·amide \nī-'al-ə-ˌmīd\ *n* [*ni*cotinic acid + *amyl* + *amide*] (1959) : a synthetic antidepressant drug $C_{16}H_{18}N_4O_2$ that is an inhibitor of monoamine oxidase

nib \'nib\ *n* [prob. alter. of *neb*] (1585) **1** : BILL, BEAK **2 a** : the sharpened point of a quill pen **b** : PEN POINT; *also* : each of the two divisions of a pen point **3** : a small pointed or projecting part

¹nib·ble \'nib-əl\ *vb* **nib·bled; nib·bling** \-(ə-)liŋ\ [origin unknown] *vt* (ca. 1500) **1 a** : to bite gently **b** : to eat or chew in small bits **2** : to take away bit by bit ⟨waves *nibbling* the shore⟩ ~ *vi* **1** : to take gentle, small, or cautious bites **2** : to deal with something as if by nibbling — **nib·bler** \-(ə-)lər\ *n*

²nibble *n* (1658) **1** : an act of nibbling **2** : a very small quantity or portion (as of food)

Ni·be·lung \'nē-bə-ˌlu̇ŋ\ *n, pl* **-lungs** *also* **-lung·en** \-ˌlu̇ŋ-ən\ [G] (1861) **1** : a member of a race of dwarfs in Germanic legend **2** : any of the followers of Siegfried **3** : any of the Burgundian kings in the medieval German *Nibelungenlied*

nibs \'nibz\ *n pl but sing in constr* [origin unknown] (1821) : an important or self-important person — usu. used in the phrases *his nibs* or *her nibs*

nic·co·lite \'nik-ə-ˌlīt\ *n* [NL *niccolum* nickel, prob. fr. Sw *nickel*] (1868) : a pale copper-red usu. massive mineral NiAs of metallic luster that is essentially a nickel arsenide

nice \'nīs\ *adj* **nic·er; nic·est** [ME, foolish, wanton, fr. OF, fr. L *nescius* ignorant, fr. *nescire* not to know — more at NESCIENCE] (14c) **1** *obs* **a** : WANTON, DISSOLUTE **b** : COY, RETICENT **2 a** : showing fastidious or finicky tastes : PARTICULAR **b** : exacting in requirements or standards : PUNCTILIOUS **3** : possessing, marked by, or demanding great or excessive precision and delicacy **4** *obs* : TRIVIAL **5 a** : PLEASING, AGREEABLE ⟨a ~ time⟩ ⟨a ~ person⟩ **b** : well-executed ⟨~ shot⟩ **c** : APPROPRIATE, FITTING **6** : most inappropriate : BAD ⟨a ~ one to talk⟩ **7 a** : socially acceptable : WELL-BRED **b** : VIRTUOUS, RESPECTABLE ***syn*** see CORRECT — **nice** *adv* — **nice·ly** *adv* — **nice·ness** *n*

Ni·cene \'nī-ˌsēn, nī-'\ *adj* [ME, fr. LL *nicaenus,* fr. L *Nicaea* Nicaea, fr. Gk *Nikaia*] (14c) **1** : of or relating to Nicaea or the Nicaeans **2** : of or relating to a church council held in Nicaea in A.D. 325 or to the Nicene Creed

Nicene Creed *n* (ca. 1567) : a Christian creed expanded from a creed issued by the first Nicene Council, beginning "I believe in one God," and used in liturgical worship

nice–nel·ly \'nī-'snel-ē\ *adj, often cap 2d N* [fr. the name *Nelly*] (1925) **1** : PRUDISH **2** : marked by euphemism — **nice nelly** *n, often cap 2d N* — **nice–nel·ly·ism** \-ˌiz-əm\ *n, often cap 2d N*

nice·ty \'nī-sət-ē, -stē\ *n, pl* **-ties** [ME *nicete,* fr. MF *niceté* foolishness, fr. *nice,* adj.] (14c) **1** : the quality or state of being nice **2** : an elegant, delicate, or civilized feature ⟨enjoy the *niceties* of life⟩ **3** : a fine point or distinction : SUBTLETY ⟨the *niceties* of table manners⟩ **4** : careful attention to details : delicate exactness : PRECISION **5** : delicacy of taste or feeling : FASTIDIOUSNESS

¹niche \'nich\ *n* [F, fr. MF, fr. *nicher* to nest, fr. (assumed) VL *nidicare,* fr. L *nidus* nest — more at NEST] (1611) **1 a** : a recess in a wall esp. for a statue **b** : something that resembles a niche **2 a** : a place, employment, or activity for which a person or thing is best fitted **b** : a habitat supplying the factors necessary for the existence of an organism or species **c** : the ecological role of an organism in a community esp. in regard to food consumption

²niche *vt* **niched; nich·ing** (1757) : to place in or as if in a niche

¹nick \'nik\ *n* [ME *nyke,* prob. alter. of *nocke* nock] (15c) **1** : a small notch or groove **2** : a final critical moment ⟨in the ~ of time⟩ **3** : a break in a strand of DNA or RNA

²nick *vt* (1530) **1 a** : to make a nick in : NOTCH, CHIP **b** : to cut into or wound slightly ⟨a bullet ~*ed* his leg⟩ **2** : to jot down : RECORD **3** : to cut short ⟨cold weather, which ~*ed* steel and automobile output —*Time*⟩ **4** : to catch at the right point or time **5** : CHEAT, OVERCHARGE ~ *vi* **1** : to make petty attacks : SNIPE **2** : to complement one another genetically and produce superior offspring

¹nick·el *also* **nick·le** \'nik-əl\ *n* [prob. fr. Sw *nickel,* fr. G *kupfernickel* niccolite, prob. fr. *kupfer* copper + *nickel* goblin; fr. the deceptive copper color of niccolite] (1755) **1** : a silver-white hard malleable ductile metallic element capable of a high polish and resistant to corrosion that is used chiefly in alloys and as a catalyst — see ELEMENT table **2 a (1)** : the U.S. 5-cent piece regularly containing 25 percent nickel and 75 percent copper **(2)** : the Canadian 5-cent piece **b** : five cents

²nick·el *vt* **-eled** *or* **-elled; -el·ing** *or* **-el·ling** \'nik-(ə-)liŋ\ (ca. 1875) : to plate with nickel

nick·el–and–dime \ˌnik-ə-lən-'dīm\ *adj* (1950) **1** : involving or offering only a small amount of money **2** : SMALL-TIME

nickel and dime *vt* **nick·eled and dimed** \ˌnik-əl-dən-'dīmd\ *also* **nick·el and dimed** \-ən-'dīmd\; **nickeling and dim·ing** \-'dī-miŋ\ *also* **nickel and diming** (1961) : to impair, weaken, or defeat gradually (as through a series of small incursions or excessive attention to detail)

nick·el·if·er·ous \ˌnik-ə-'lif-(ə-)rəs\ *adj* (1821) : containing nickel

nick·el·ode·on \ˌnik-ə-'lōd-ē-ən\ *n* [prob. fr. ¹*nickel* + *-odeon* (as in archaic *melodeon* music hall)] (1888) **1** : an early movie theater to which admission usu. cost five cents **2** : JUKEBOX

nickel silver *n* (1860) : a silver-white alloy of copper, zinc, and nickel

nick·er \'nik-ər\ *vi* **nick·ered; nick·er·ing** \-(ə-)riŋ\ [perh. alter. of *neigh*] (1641) : NEIGH, WHINNY — **nicker** *n*

nick·nack *var of* KNICKKNACK

¹nick·name \'nik-ˌnām\ *n* [ME *nekename* additional name, alter. (resulting from incorrect division of *an ekename*) of *ekename,* fr. *eke* eke, also + *name* name] (14c) **1** : a usu. descriptive name given instead of or in addition to the one belonging to a person, place, or thing **2** : a familiar form of a proper name (as of a person or a city)

²nickname *vt* (1536) **1** : MISNAME, MISCALL **2** : to give a nickname to — **nick·nam·er** *n*

ni·co·ti·ana \nik-ˌō-shē-'an-ə, -'än-ə, -'ā-nə\ *n* [NL, fr. *herba nicotiana,* lit., Nicot's herb, fr. Jean *Nicot* †1600 Fr. diplomat and scholar] (ca. 1600) : any of several tobaccos (as *Nicotiana alata*) grown for their showy flowers

nic·o·tin·amide \ˌnik-ə-'tē-nə-ˌmīd, -'tin-ə-\ *n* [ISV] (1895) : a compound $C_6H_6N_2O$ of the vitamin B complex found esp. as a constituent of coenzymes and used similarly to nicotinic acid

nicotinamide adenine dinucleotide *n* (1961) : NAD

nicotinamide adenine dinucleotide phosphate *n* (1962) : NADP

nic·o·tine \'nik-ə-ˌtēn\ *n* [F, fr. NL *nicotiana*] (1819) : a poisonous alkaloid $C_{10}H_{14}N_2$ that is the chief active principle of tobacco and is used as an insecticide

nic·o·tin·ic \ˌnik-ə-'tē-nik, -'tin-ik\ *adj* [ISV] (1873) : of or relating to nicotine or nicotinic acid

nicotinic acid *n* (1873) : an acid $C_6H_5NO_2$ of the vitamin B complex found widely in animals and plants and used esp. against pellagra — called also *niacin*

nic·ti·tate \'nik-tə-ˌtāt\ *vi* **-tat·ed; -tat·ing** [alter. of *nictate* (to wink), fr. L *nictatus,* pp. of *nictare* — more at CONNIVE] (ca. 1822) : WINK

nictitating membrane *n* (1713) : a thin membrane found in many animals at the inner angle or beneath the lower lid of the eye and capable of extending across the eyeball

ni·dic·o·lous \nī-'dik-ə-ləs\ *adj* [L *nidus* nest + E *-colous*] (ca. 1902) **1** : reared for a time in a nest **2** : sharing the nest of another kind of animal

ni·di·fi·ca·tion \ˌnid-ə-fə-'kā-shən, ˌnīd-\ *n* [ML *nidification-, nidificatio,* fr. L *nidificatus,* pp. of *nidificare* to build a nest, fr. *nidus* nest] (1658) : the act, process, or technique of building a nest

ni·dif·u·gous \nī-'dif-yə-gəs\ *adj* [L *nidus* nest + *fugere* to flee — more at FUGITIVE] (1896) : leaving the nest soon after hatching

ni·dus \'nīd-əs\ *n, pl* **ni·di** \'nī-ˌdī\ *or* **ni·dus·es** [NL, fr. L] (1742) **1** : a nest or breeding place; *esp* : a place or substance in an animal or plant where bacteria or other organisms lodge and multiply **2** : a place where something originates, develops, or is located

niece \'nēs\ *n* [ME *nece,* granddaughter, niece, fr. OF *niece,* fr. LL *neptia,* fr. L *neptis;* akin to L *nepot-, nepos* grandson, nephew — more at NEPHEW] (13c) **1** : a daughter of one's brother, sister, brother-in-law, or sister-in-law **2** : an illegitimate daughter of an ecclesiastic

¹ni·el·lo \nē-'el-(ˌ)ō\ *n, pl* **ni·el·li** \-'el-(ˌ)ē\ *or* **niellos** [It, fr. ML *nigellum,* fr. neut. of L *nigellus* blackish, dim. of *niger* black] (1816) **1** : any of several black enamel-like alloys usu. of sulfur with silver, copper, and

\ə\ abut \ᵊ\ kitten, F table \ər\ further \a\ ash \ā\ ace \ä\ cot, cart \au̇\ out \ch\ chin \e\ bet \ē\ easy \g\ go \i\ hit \ī\ ice \j\ job \ŋ\ sing \ō\ go \ȯ\ law \ȯi\ boy \th\ thin \t͟h\ the \ü\ loot \u̇\ foot \y\ yet \zh\ vision \à, k̲, ⁿ, œ, œ̄, ue, u̅e, ʸ\ *see* Guide to Pronunciation

lead **2 :** the art or process of decorating metal with incised designs filled with niello **3 :** a piece of metal or an object decorated with niello

2niello *vt* (1866) **:** to inlay or ornament with niello

Nif·lheim \'niv-əl-,hām\ *n* [ON *Niflheimr*] **:** the abode of the dead in Norse mythology

1nif·ty \'nif-tē\ *adj* **nif·ti·er; -est** [origin unknown] (1865) **:** very good **:** very attractive **:** FINE ⟨~ clothes⟩

2nifty *n, pl* **nifties** (1925) **:** something that is nifty; *esp* **:** a clever or neatly turned phrase or joke

Ni·ger–Con·go \,nī-jər-'käŋ-(,)gō\ *n* [*Niger* (river) + *Congo* (river)] (ca. 1949) **:** a language family that includes the Mande and Kwa branches and that is spoken by most of the indigenous peoples of west, central, and south Africa

1nig·gard \'nig-ərd\ *n* [ME, of Scand origin; akin to ON *hnøggr* niggardly; akin to L *cinis* ashes — more at INCINERATE] (14c) **:** a meanly covetous and stingy person **:** MISER — **niggard** *adj*

2niggard *vi, obs* (1600) **:** to act niggardly **~** *vt, obs* **:** to treat in a niggardly manner

nig·gard·ly \-lē\ *adj* (1571) **1 :** grudgingly mean about spending or granting **:** BEGRUDGING **2 :** provided in meanly limited supply ***syn*** see STINGY — **nig·gard·li·ness** *n* — **niggardly** *adv*

nig·ger \'nig-ər\ *n* [alter. of earlier *neger,* fr. MF *negre,* fr. Sp or Pg *negro,* fr. *negro* black, fr. L *niger*] (1700) **1 :** NEGRO — usu. taken to be offensive **2 :** a member of any dark-skinned race — usu. taken to be offensive **3 :** a member of a socially disadvantaged class of persons ⟨it's time for somebody to lead all of America's ~*s* . . . all the people who feel left out of the political process —Ron Dellums⟩

nig·gle \'nig-əl\ *vb* **nig·gled; nig·gling** \-(ə-)liŋ\ [origin unknown] *vi* (1616) **1 a :** TRIFLE **b :** to spend too much effort on minor details **2 :** to find fault constantly in a petty way **:** CARP ⟨she haggles, she ~*s,* she wears out our patience —Virginia Woolf⟩ **3 :** GNAW **~** *vt* **:** to give stingily or in tiny portions — **nig·gler** \-(ə-)lər\ *n*

nig·gling \'nig-(ə-)liŋ\ *adj* (1599) **:** PETTY; *also* **:** bothersome or persistent esp. in a petty or tiresome way — **niggling** *n* — **nig·gling·ly** \-(ə-)liŋ-lē\ *adv*

1nigh \'nī\ *adv* [ME, fr. OE *nēah;* akin to OHG *nāh,* adv., nigh, prep., nigh, after, ON *nā-* nigh] (bef. 12c) **1 :** near in place, time, or relationship — often used with *on, onto,* or *unto* **2 :** NEARLY, ALMOST

2nigh *adj* (bef. 12c) **1 :** CLOSE, NEAR **2** *chiefly dial* **:** DIRECT, SHORT **3 :** being on the left side ⟨the ~ horse⟩

3nigh \(,)nī\ *prep* (bef. 12c) **:** NEAR

4nigh \'nī\ *vt* (13c) **:** to draw or come near to **:** APPROACH **~** *vi* **:** to draw near

1night \'nīt\ *n* [ME, fr. OE *niht;* akin to OHG *naht* night, L *noct-, nox,* Gk *nykt-, nyx*] (bef. 12c) **1 :** the time from dusk to dawn when no sunlight is visible **2 a :** an evening or night taken as an occasion or point of time ⟨the opening ~⟩ **b :** an evening set aside for a particular purpose **3 a :** the quality or state of being dark **b :** a condition or period felt to resemble the darkness of night: as (1) **:** a period of dreary inactivity or affliction (2) **:** absence of moral values **c :** the beginning of darkness **:** NIGHTFALL

2night *adj* (15c) **1 :** of, relating to, or associated with the night ⟨~ air⟩ **2 :** intended for use at night ⟨a ~ lamp⟩ **3 a :** existing, occurring, or functioning at night ⟨~ baseball⟩ ⟨a ~ nurse⟩ **b :** active or functioning best at night ⟨~ people⟩

night and day *adv* (bef. 12c) **:** all the time **:** CONTINUALLY

night blindness *n* (1754) **:** reduced visual capacity in faint light (as at night) — **night–blind** \'nīt-,blīnd\ *adj*

night–blooming cereus *n* (1832) **:** any of several night-blooming cacti; *esp* **:** a slender sprawling or climbing cactus (*Selenicereus grandiflorus*) often cultivated for its large showy fragrant white flowers

night·cap \'nīt-,kap\ *n* (14c) **1 :** a cloth cap worn with nightclothes **2 :** a usu. alcoholic drink taken at the end of the day **3 :** the final race or contest of a day's sports; *esp* **:** the final game of a baseball doubleheader

night·clothes \-,klō(th)z\ *n pl* (1602) **:** garments worn in bed

1night·club \-,kləb\ *n* (1894) **:** a place of entertainment open at night usu. serving food and liquor, having a floor show, and providing music and space for dancing

2nightclub *vi* (1936) **:** to patronize nightclubs — **night·club·ber** *n*

night court *n* (1934) **:** a criminal court in a large city that sits at night (as for the summary disposition of criminal charges and the granting of bail)

night crawler *n* (1924) **:** EARTHWORM; *esp* **:** a large earthworm found on the soil surface at night

night·dress \'nīt-,dres\ *n* (1712) **1 :** NIGHTGOWN **2 :** NIGHTCLOTHES

night·fall \'nīt-,fōl\ *n* (1700) **:** the close of the day **:** DUSK

night·glow \-,glō\ *n* (1951) **:** airglow seen during the night

night·gown \-,gaůn\ *n* (15c) **1** *archaic* **:** DRESSING GOWN **2 :** a loose garment worn in bed

night·hawk \-,hȯk\ *n* (1611) **1 a :** any of several No. American goatsuckers (genus *Chordeiles*) related to the whippoorwill **b :** the European nightjar **2 :** a person who habitually is active late at night

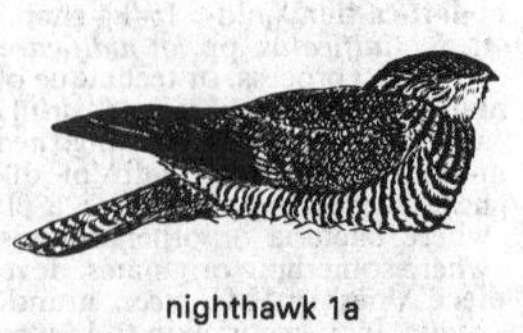

nighthawk 1a

night heron *n* (1784) **:** any of various widely distributed nocturnal or crepuscular herons (as of the genus *Nycticorax*); *esp* **:** one (*N. nycticorax*) widely distributed in the Old World

night·ie \'nīt-ē\ *or* **nighty** *n, pl* **night·ies** [*night*gown + *-ie* or *-y*] (1871) **:** a nightgown for a woman or child

night·in·gale \'nīt-ᵊn-,gāl, -iŋ-\ *n* [ME, fr. OE *nihtegale,* fr. *niht* + *galan* to sing — more at YELL] (bef. 12c) **:** any of several Old World thrushes (genus *Luscinia*) noted for the sweet usu. nocturnal song of the male; *also* **:** any of various other birds that sing at night

night·jar \'nīt-,jär\ *n* [fr. its harsh sound] (1630) **:** a common grayish brown European goatsucker (*Caprimulgus europaeus*); *broadly* **:** GOATSUCKER

night latch *n* (1854) **:** a door lock having a spring bolt operated from the outside by a key and from the inside by a knob

night letter *n* (1910) **:** a telegram sent at night at a reduced rate for delivery the following morning

night·life \'nīt-,līf\ *n* (1852) **:** the activity of pleasure-seekers at night (as in nightclubs)

night–light \-,līt\ *n* (1839) **:** a light kept burning throughout the night

1night·long \-,lȯŋ\ *adj* (1850) **:** lasting the whole night ⟨~ festivities⟩

2night·long \-'lȯŋ\ *adv* (1870) **:** through the whole night

1night·ly \'nīt-lē\ *adj* (bef. 12c) **1 :** happening, done, or used by night or every night **2 :** of or relating to the night or every night

2nightly *adv* (15c) **:** every night; *also* **:** at or by night

night·mare \'nīt-,ma(ə)r, -,me(ə)r\ *n* [ME, fr. 1*night* + 1*mare*] (13c) **1 :** an evil spirit formerly thought to oppress people during sleep **2 :** a frightening dream that usu. awakens the sleeper **3 :** something (as an experience, situation, or object) having the monstrous character of a nightmare or producing a feeling of anxiety or terror — **nightmare** *adj* — **night·mar·ish** \-,ma(ə)r-ish, -,me(ə)r-\ *adj* — **night·mar·ish·ly** *adv*

night owl *n* (1846) **:** a person who keeps late hours at night **:** NIGHTHAWK

night rail \-,rāl\ *n* [*night* + *rail* (garment)] *archaic* (1554) **:** NIGHTGOWN

night raven *n* (bef. 12c) **:** a bird that cries at night

night rider *n* (1877) **:** a member of a secret band who ride masked at night doing acts of violence for the purpose of punishing or terrorizing

nights \'nīts\ *adv* (bef. 12c) **:** in the nighttime repeatedly **:** on any night ⟨works ~⟩

night·shade \'nīt-,shād\ *n* (bef. 12c) **1 :** any of a genus (*Solanum* of the family Solanaceae, the nightshade family) which comprises herbs, shrubs, and trees with alternate leaves, cymose flowers, and fruits that are berries and includes some poisonous weeds, various ornamentals, and important crop plants (as the potato and eggplant) **2 :** BELLADONNA 1

night·shirt \-,shərt\ *n* (1857) **:** a nightgown resembling a shirt

night·side \-,sīd\ *n* (1848) **:** the side of a celestial body (as the earth, the moon, or a planet) not in daylight

night soil *n* (1770) **:** human excrement collected for fertilizing the soil

night·stand \'nīt-,stand\ *n* (1892) **:** NIGHT TABLE

night·stick \-,stik\ *n* (1887) **:** a policeman's club

night table *n* (1788) **:** a small bedside table or stand

night·time \-,tīm\ *n* (14c) **:** the time from dusk to dawn — **nighttime** *adj*

night·walk·er \-,wȯ-kər\ *n* (15c) **:** a person who roams about at night esp. to commit some criminal or immoral act

ni·gro·sine \'nī-grə-,sēn\ *also* **ni·gro·sin** \-sən\ *n, often cap* [L *nigr-, niger* + E *-ose* + 2*-ine*] (ca. 1890) **:** any of several azine dyes closely related to the indulines

ni·hil·ism \'nī-(h)ə-,liz-əm, 'nē-\ *n* [G *nihilismus,* fr. L *nihil* nothing — more at NIL] (1817) **1 a :** a viewpoint that traditional values and beliefs are unfounded and that existence is senseless and useless **b :** a doctrine that denies any objective ground of truth and esp. of moral truths **2 a** (1) **:** a doctrine or belief that conditions in the social organization are so bad as to make destruction desirable for its own sake independent of any constructive program or possibility (2) *cap* **:** the program of a 19th century Russian party advocating revolutionary reform and using terrorism and assassination **b :** TERRORISM — **ni·hil·ist** \-ləst\ *n or adj* — **ni·hil·is·tic** \,nī-(h)ə-'lis-tik, ,nē-\ *adj*

-nik \nik\ *n suffix* [Yiddish, fr. Russ & Pol] **:** one connected with or characterized by being ⟨beat*nik*⟩

Ni·ke \'nī-kē\ *n* [Gk *Nikē*] **:** the Greek goddess of victory

nil \'nil\ *n* [L, nothing, contr. of *nihil,* fr. OL *nihilum,* fr. *ne-* not + *hilum* trifle — more at NO] (1833) **:** NOTHING, ZERO — **nil** *adj*

nile green *n, often cap N* [*Nile* river, Africa] (1871) **:** a variable color averaging a pale yellow green

Nile perch *n* (1926) **:** a large predaceous food fish (*Lates niloticus*) of the rivers and lakes of northern and central Africa that may exceed 200 pounds in weight

nill \'nil\ *vb* [ME *nilen,* fr. OE *nyllan,* fr. *ne* not + *wyllan* to wish — more at NO, WILL] *vi, archaic* (bef. 12c) **:** to be unwilling **:** will not ⟨will you ~ you, I will marry you —Shak.⟩ **~** *vt, archaic* **:** REFUSE

Ni·lot·ic \nī-'lät-ik\ *adj* [L *Niloticus,* fr. Gk *Neilōtēs,* fr. *Neilos* Nile] (1653) **:** of or relating to the Nile or the peoples of the Nile basin

nil·po·tent \'nil-,pōt-ᵊnt\ *adj* [L *nil* nothing + *potent-, potens* having power — more at POTENT] (ca. 1864) **:** equal to zero when raised to some power ⟨~ matrices⟩

1nim \'nim\ *vb* **nimmed; nim·ming** [earlier *nim* to take, fr. ME *nimen,* fr. OE *niman*] *vt, archaic* (bef. 12c) **:** STEAL, FILCH **~** *vi, archaic* **:** THIEVE

2nim *n* [prob. fr. 1*nim*] (1901) **:** any of various games in which counters are laid out in one or more piles and each player in turn draws one or more counters with the object of taking the last counter, forcing the opponent to take it, or taking the most or fewest counters

nim·ble \'nim-bəl\ *adj* **nim·bler** \-b(ə-)lər\; **nim·blest** \-b(ə-)ləst\ [ME *nimel,* fr. OE *numol* holding much, fr. *niman* to take; akin to OHG *neman* to take, L *numerus* number, Gk *nemein* to distribute, manage, *nomos* pasture, *nomos* usage, custom, law] (14c) **1 :** marked by quick light movement **:** LIVELY ⟨~ fingers⟩ **2 a :** marked by quick, alert, clever conception, comprehension, or resourcefulness ⟨a ~ mind⟩ **b :** SENSITIVE, RESPONSIVE ⟨a ~ listener⟩ — **nim·ble·ness** \-bəl-nəs\ *n* — **nim·bly** \-blē\ *adv*

nim·bo·stra·tus \,nim-bō-'strāt-əs, -'strat-\ *n* [NL, fr. L *nimbus* + NL *stratus* stratus] (ca. 1909) **:** a low dark gray rainy cloud layer — see CLOUD illustration

nim·bus \'nim-bəs\ *n, pl* **nim·bi** \-,bī, -,bē\ *or* **nim·bus·es** [L, rainstorm, cloud; akin to Pahlavi *namb* mist] (1616) **1 a :** a luminous vapor, cloud, or atmosphere about a god or goddess when on earth **b :** a cloud or atmosphere (as of romance) about a person or thing **2 :** an indication (as a circle) of radiant light or glory about the head of a drawn or sculptured divinity, saint, or sovereign **3 a :** a rain cloud that is of uniform grayness and extends over the entire sky **b :** a cloud from which rain is falling

ni·mi·ety \nim-'ī-ət-ē\ *n, pl* **-eties** [LL *nimietas,* fr. L *nimius* too much, adj., fr. *nimis,* adv.] (1564) **:** EXCESS, REDUNDANCY

nim·i·ny–pim·i·ny \,nim-ə-nē-'pim-ə-nē\ *adj* [prob. alter. of *namby-pamby*] (1786) **:** affectedly refined **:** FINICKY

Nim·rod \'nim-,räd\ *n* [Heb *Nimrōdh*] **1 :** a descendant of Ham represented in Genesis as a mighty hunter and a king of Shinar **2** *not cap* **:** HUNTER

nin·com·poop \'nin-kəm-,püp, 'niŋ-\ *n* [origin unknown] (1676) : FOOL, SIMPLETON — **nin·com·poop·ery** \-ə-rē\ *n*
nine \'nīn\ *n* [ME, fr. *nyne,* adj., fr. OE *nigon;* akin to OHG *niun* nine, L *novem,* Gk *ennea*] (bef. 12c) **1** — see NUMBER table **2** : the ninth in a set or series ⟨wears a ~⟩ **3** : something having nine units or members: as **a** *cap* : the nine Muses **b** : a baseball team **c** : the first or last nine holes of an 18-hole golf course — **nine** *adj or pron* — **to the nines** : to the highest degree
nine days' wonder *n* (14c) : something that creates a short-lived sensation
nine·fold \'nīn-,fōld, -'fōld\ *adj* (bef. 12c) **1** : being nine times as great or as many **2** : having nine units or members — **nine·fold** \-'fōld\ *adv*
nine·pin \-,pin\ *n* (1580) **1** *pl but sing in constr* : a bowling game resembling tenpins played without the headpin **2** : a pin used in ninepins
nine·teen \(')nīn(t)-'tēn\ *n* [ME *nynetene,* adj., fr. OE *nigontēne,* fr. *nigon* + *-tīene* (akin to OE *tien* ten) — more at TEN] (bef. 12c) — see NUMBER table — **nineteen** *adj or pron* — **nine·teenth** \-'tēn(t)th\ *adj or n*
nine·ty \'nīnt-ē\ *n, pl* **nineties** [ME *ninety,* adj., fr. OE *nigontig,* short for *hundnigontig,* fr. *hundnigontig,* n., group of 90, fr. *hund-* group of 10 (akin to Goth *taihun* 10) + *nigon* nine + *-tig* group of 10 — more at TEN] (bef. 12c) **1** — see NUMBER table **2** *pl* : the numbers 90 to 99; *specif* : the years 90 to 99 in a lifetime or century — **nine·ti·eth** \-ē-əth\ *adj or n* — **ninety** *adj or pron*
nin·hy·drin \nin-'hī-drən\ *n* [fr. *Ninhydrin,* a trademark] (1913) : a poisonous crystalline oxidizing agent $C_9H_6O_4$ used esp. as an analytical reagent
nin·ny \'nin-ē\ *n, pl* **ninnies** [perh. by shortening and alter. fr. *an innocent*] (1593) : FOOL, SIMPLETON
nin·ny·ham·mer \'nin-ē-,ham-ər\ *n* (1592) : NINNY
ni·non \'nē-,nän\ *n* [prob. fr. F *Ninon,* nickname for *Anne*] (1911) : a smooth sheer fabric
ninth \'nīn(t)th\ *n, pl* **ninths** \'nīn(t)s, 'nīn(t)ths\ (bef. 12c) **1** — see NUMBER table **2 a** : a musical interval embracing an octave and a second **b** : the tone at this interval **c** : a chord containing a ninth — **ninth** *adj or adv*
ninth cranial nerve *n* (ca. 1961) : GLOSSOPHARYNGEAL NERVE
Ni·o·be \'nī-ə-bē\ *n* [L, fr. Gk *Niobē*] : a daughter of Tantalus and wife of Amphion who while weeping for her slain children is turned into a stone from which her tears continue to flow
ni·o·bi·um \nī-'ō-bē-əm\ *n* [NL, fr. L *Niobe;* fr. its occurrence in tantalite] (1845) : a lustrous platinum-gray ductile metallic element that resembles tantalum chemically and is used in alloys — see ELEMENT table
¹nip \'nip\ *vb* **nipped; nip·ping** [ME *nippen;* akin to ON *hnippa* to prod] *vt* (14c) **1** : to catch hold of and squeeze tightly between two surfaces, edges, or points : PINCH ⟨the dog *nipped* his ankle⟩ **2 a** : to sever by or as if by pinching sharply **b** : to destroy the growth, progress, maturing, or fulfillment of ⟨*nipped* in the bud⟩ **3** : to injure or make numb with cold : CHILL **4** : SNATCH, STEAL ~ *vi* : to move briskly, nimbly, or quickly
²nip *n* (1549) **1** : something that nips: as **a** *archaic* : a sharp biting comment **b** : a sharp stinging cold ⟨the ~ of the winter air⟩ **c** : a biting or pungent flavor : TANG ⟨cheese with a ~⟩ **2** : the act of nipping : PINCH, BITE **3** : the region of a squeezing or crushing device (as a calender) where the rolls or jaws are closest together **4** : a small portion : BIT
³nip *n* [prob. fr. *nipperkin* (a liquor container)] (1796) : a small quantity of liquor : SIP; *also* : a very small bottle of liquor
⁴nip *vi* **nipped; nip·ping** (1887) : to take liquor in nips : TIPPLE
ni·pa \'nē-pə\ *n* [prob. fr. It, fr. Malay *nipah* nipa palm] (1588) : thatch made of leaves of the nipa palm
nip and tuck \,nip-ən-'tək\ *adj or adv* (1832) : being so close that the lead or advantage shifts rapidly from one opponent to another
nipa palm *n* (1882) : an Australasian semiaquatic creeping palm (*Nipa fruticans*)
nip·per \'nip-ər\ *n* (1541) **1** : any of various devices (as pincers) for nipping — usu. used in pl. **2 a** *chiefly Brit* : a boy employed as a helper (as of a carter or hawker) **b** : CHILD; *esp* : a small boy
nip·ping \'nip-iŋ\ *adj* (1547) : SHARP, CHILLING — **nip·ping·ly** \-iŋ-lē\ *adv*
nip·ple \'nip-əl\ *n* [earlier *neble, nible,* prob. dim. of *neb, nib*] (1530) **1** : the protuberance of a mammary gland upon which the ducts open and from which milk is drawn **2 a** : an artificial teat through which a bottle-fed infant nurses **b** : a device with an orifice through which the discharge of a liquid can be regulated **3 a** : a protuberance resembling or suggesting the nipple of a breast **b** : a small projection through which oil or grease is injected into machinery **4** : a pipe coupling consisting of a short piece of threaded tubing
Nip·pon·ese \,nip-ə-'nēz, -'nēs\ *adj* [*Nippon* (Japan)] (1859) : JAPANESE — **Nipponese** *n*
nip·py \'nip-ē\ *adj* **nip·pi·er; -est** (1575) **1** : marked by a tendency to nip ⟨a ~ dog⟩ **2** : brisk, quick, or nimble in movement : SNAPPY **3** : PUNGENT, SHARP **4** : CHILLY, CHILLING ⟨a ~ day⟩ — **nip·pi·ly** \'nip-ə-lē\ *adv* — **nip·pi·ness** \'nip-ē-nəs\ *n*
nip–up \'nip-,əp\ *n* (1938) : a spring from a supine position to a standing position
nir·va·na \ni(ə)r-'vän-ə, (,)nər-\ *n, often cap* [Skt *nirvāṇa,* lit., act of extinguishing, fr. *nis-* out + *vāti* it blows — more at WIND] (1801) **1** : the final beatitude that transcends suffering, karma, and samsara and is sought esp. in Buddhism through the extinction of desire and individual consciousness **2 a** : a place or state of oblivion to care, pain, or external reality; *also* : BLISS, HEAVEN **b** : a goal hoped for but apparently unattainable : DREAM
Ni·san \'nis-ᵊn, nē-'sän\ *n* [Heb *Nīsān*] (14c) : the 7th month of the civil year or the 1st month of the ecclesiastical year in the Jewish calendar — see MONTH table
ni·sei \(')nē-'sā, 'nē-,\ *n, pl* **nisei** *also* **niseis** [Jp, lit., second generation, fr. *ni* second + *sei* generation] (1940) : a son or daughter of Japanese immigrants who is born and educated in America and esp. in the U.S.
ni·si \'nī-,sī\ *adj* [L, unless, fr. *ne-* not + *si* if] (1836) : taking effect at a specified time unless previously modified or avoided by cause shown, further proceedings, or a condition fulfilled ⟨decree ~⟩
Nis·roch \'nis-,räk, -,rōk\ *n* [Heb *Nisrōkh*] : an Assyrian deity honored with a temple at Nineveh
Nis·sen hut \,nis-ᵊn-\ *n* [Peter N. *Nissen* †1930 Brit. mining engineer] (1932) : a prefabricated shelter built of a semicircular arching roof of corrugated iron with a concrete floor
ni·sus \'nī-səs\ *n, pl* **ni·sus** \-səs, -,süs\ [L, fr. *nisus,* pp. of *niti* to bear down, strive; akin to L *nictare* to wink — more at CONNIVE] (1699) : a mental or physical effort to attain an end : a perfective urge or endeavor
¹nit \'nit\ *n* [ME *nite,* fr. OE *hnitu;* akin to OHG *hniz* nit, Gk *konid-, konis*] (bef. 12c) : the egg of a louse or other parasitic insect; *also* : the insect itself when young
²nit *n, chiefly Brit* (1941) : NITWIT
ni·ter \'nīt-ər\ *n* [ME *nitre* natron, fr. MF, fr. L *nitrum,* fr. Gk *nitron,* fr. Egypt *ntry*] (1684) **1** : POTASSIUM NITRATE **2** : SODIUM NITRATE; *esp* : CHILE SALTPETER
nit·id \'nit-əd\ *adj* [L *nitidus* — more at NEAT] (1656) : BRIGHT, LUSTROUS
ni·ti·nol \'nīt-ᵊn-,ól, -,ōl\ *n* [*ni*ckel + *ti*tanium + *-nol* (fr. *N*aval *O*rdnance *L*aboratory, where it was created)] (1968) : a nonmagnetic alloy of titanium and nickel that after being deformed returns to its original shape upon being reheated
nit·pick \'nit-,pik\ *vb* [back-formation fr. *nit-picking*] *vi* (1966) : to engage in nit-picking ~ *vt* : to criticize by nit-picking — **nit·pick·er** *n*
nit–pick·ing \'nit-,pik-iŋ\ *n* [¹*nit*] (1956) : minute and usu. unjustified criticism
nitr- *or* **nitro-** *comb form* [*niter*] **1** : niter : nitrate ⟨*nitro*bacteria⟩ **2 a** : nitrogen ⟨*nitr*ide⟩ ⟨*nitro*meter⟩ **b** *usu* *nitro-* : containing the univalent group NO_2 composed of one nitrogen and two oxygen atoms ⟨*nitro*benzene⟩
¹ni·trate \'nī-,trāt, -trət\ *n* [F, fr. *nitrique*] (1794) **1** : a salt or ester of nitric acid **2** : sodium nitrate or potassium nitrate used as a fertilizer
²ni·trate \-,trāt\ *vt* **ni·trat·ed; ni·trat·ing** (1872) : to treat or combine with nitric acid or a nitrate; *esp* : to convert (an organic compound) into a nitro compound or a nitrate — **ni·tra·tion** \nī-'trā-shən\ *n* — **ni·tra·tor** \'nī-,trāt-ər\ *n*
nitrate bacterium *n* (1904) : a bacterium that converts nitrites to nitrates in the nitrogen cycle
ni·tre *chiefly Brit var of* NITER
ni·tric \'nī-trik\ *adj* [F *nitrique,* fr. *nitr-*] (1794) : of, relating to, or containing nitrogen esp. with a higher valence than in corresponding nitrous compounds
nitric acid *n* (1794) : a corrosive liquid inorganic acid HNO_3 used esp. as an oxidizing agent, in nitrations, and in making organic compounds (as fertilizers, explosives, and dyes)
nitric oxide *n* (1807) : a colorless poisonous gas NO obtained by oxidation of nitrogen or ammonia
¹ni·tride \'nī-,trīd\ *n* [ISV] (1850) : a binary compound of nitrogen with a more electropositive element
²nitride *vt* **ni·trid·ed; ni·trid·ing** (1928) : to convert into a nitride; *esp* : to case harden (steel) by causing the surface to absorb nitrogen
ni·tri·fi·ca·tion \,nī-trə-fə-'kā-shən\ *n* (1827) : the process of nitrifying; *specif* : the oxidation (as by bacteria) of ammonium salts to nitrites and the further oxidation of nitrites to nitrates
ni·tri·fy \'nī-trə-,fī\ *vt* **-fied; -fy·ing** [F *nitrifier,* fr. *nitr-*] (1827) **1** : to combine or impregnate with nitrogen or a nitrogen compound **2** : to subject to or produce by nitrification — **ni·tri·fi·er** *n*
ni·trile \'nī-trəl, -,trīl\ *n* [ISV *nitr-* + *-il, -ile* (fr. L *-ilis* ¹-ile)] (1848) : an organic cyanide containing the group CN which on hydrolysis yields an acid with elimination of ammonia
ni·trite \'nī-,trīt\ *n* (1800) : a salt or ester of nitrous acid
nitrite bacterium *n* (1955) : a bacterium that oxidizes ammonium to nitrites
¹ni·tro \'nī-(,)trō\ *adj* [*nitr-*] (1857) : containing or being the univalent group NO_2 united through nitrogen
²nitro *n, pl* **nitros** (1903) : any of various nitrated products; *esp* : NITROGLYCERIN
ni·tro·ben·zene \,nī-trō-'ben-,zēn, -ben-'\ *n* [ISV] (1868) : a poisonous yellow insoluble oil $C_6H_5NO_2$ with an almond odor that is used esp. as a solvent, mild oxidizing agent, and in making aniline
ni·tro·cel·lu·lose \-'sel-yə-,lōs, -,lōz\ *n* [ISV] (1882) : CELLULOSE NITRATE — **ni·tro·cel·lu·los·ic** \-,sel-yə-'lō-sik, -zik\ *adj*
ni·tro·fu·ran \,nī-trō-'fyù(ə)r-,an, -fyù-'ran\ *n* (1930) : any of several derivatives of furan that contain a nitro group and are used as bacteria-inhibiting agents
ni·tro·gen \'nī-trə-jən\ *n, often attrib* [F *nitrogène,* fr. *nitr-* + *-gène* -gen] (1794) : a colorless tasteless odorless gaseous element that constitutes 78 percent of the atmosphere by volume and occurs as a constituent of all living tissues in combined form — see ELEMENT table — **ni·trog·e·nous** \nī-'träj-ə-nəs\ *adj*
ni·tro·ge·nase \nī-'träj-ə-,nās, 'nī-trə-jə-, -,nāz\ *n* (ca. 1934) : an enzyme of various nitrogen-fixing bacteria that catalyzes the reduction of molecular nitrogen to ammonia
nitrogen balance *n* (1944) : the difference between nitrogen intake and nitrogen loss in the body or the soil
nitrogen cycle *n* (1908) : a continuous series of natural processes by which nitrogen passes through successive stations in air, soil, and organisms involving principally nitrogen fixation, nitrification, decay, and denitrification
nitrogen fixation *n* (1895) **1** : the industrial conversion of free nitrogen into combined forms useful esp. as starting materials for fertilizers or explosives **2** : the metabolic assimilation of atmospheric nitrogen by soil microorganisms and esp. rhizobia and its release for plant use by nitrification in the soil on the death of the microorganisms
nitrogen–fixer *n* (1912) : any of various soil organisms that are involved in nitrogen fixation
nitrogen–fixing *adj* (1899) : capable of nitrogen fixation ⟨~ bacteria⟩
nitrogen mustard *n* (1943) : any of various toxic blistering compounds analogous to mustard gas but containing nitrogen instead of sulfur

nitrogen narcosis *n* (1937) : a state of euphoria and exhilaration that occurs when nitrogen in normal air enters the bloodstream at approximately seven times atmospheric pressure (as in deep-water diving) — called also *rapture of the deep*
nitrogen trichloride *n* (1924) : a volatile explosive yellow oil NCl_3 formerly used in bleaching and aging flour
ni·tro·glyc·er·in *or* **ni·tro·glyc·er·ine** \ˌnī-trə-ˈglis-(ə-)rən\ *n* [ISV] (1857) : a heavy oily explosive poisonous liquid $C_3H_5N_3O_9$ used chiefly in making dynamites and in medicine as a vasodilator
ni·tro·par·af·fin \ˌnī-trō-ˈpar-ə-fən\ *n* [ISV] (1892) : a nitro derivative of any member of the methane series
nitros- *or* **nitroso-** *comb form* [NL *nitrosus* nitrous] : containing the group NO composed of one nitrogen and one oxygen atom ⟨*nitroso*benzene C_6H_5NO⟩ ⟨*nitros*amines⟩
ni·tro·sa·mine \nī-ˈtrō-sə-ˌmēn\ *also* **ni·tro·so·amine** \-sō-ə-ˌmēn\ *n* (1878) : any of various neutral compounds which are characterized by the grouping NNO and some of which are powerful carcinogens
ni·trous \ˈnī-trəs\ *adj* [NL *nitrosus*, fr. L, full of natron, fr. *nitrum* natron — more at NITER] (1601) **1** : of, relating to, or containing niter **2** : of, relating to, or containing nitrogen esp. with a lower valence than in corresponding nitric compounds
nitrous acid *n* (1676) : an unstable acid HNO_2 known only in solution or in the form of its salts
nitrous oxide *n* (1800) : a colorless gas N_2O that when inhaled produces loss of sensibility to pain preceded by exhilaration and sometimes laughter and is used esp. as an anesthetic in dentistry — called also *laughing gas*
nit·ty–grit·ty \ˈnit-ē-ˌgrit-ē, ˌnit-ē-ˈ\ *n* [origin unknown] (1963) : what is essential and basic : specific practical details ⟨the book gets down to the ~ of economic problems⟩ — **nitty–gritty** *adj*
nit·wit \ˈnit-ˌwit\ *n* [prob. fr. G dial. *nit* not + E *wit*] (1922) : a scatterbrained or stupid person
¹**nix** \ˈniks\ *n* [G *nichts* nothing] (1789) : NOTHING
²**nix** *n* [G, fr. OHG *nihhus;* akin to OE *nicor* water monster, Gk *nizein* to wash] (1833) : a water sprite of Germanic folklore
³**nix** *vt* (1903) : VETO, REJECT ⟨the court ~*ed* the merger⟩
⁴**nix** *adv* (1909) : NO — used to express disagreement or the withholding of permission; often used with *on* ⟨father said ~ on our plan⟩
¹**nix·ie** \ˈnik-sē\ *n* [G *nixe* female nix, fr. OHG *nichessa*, fem. of *nihhus* nix] (1816) : ²NIX
²**nix·ie** *also* **nixy** \ˈnik-sē\ *n, pl* **nix·ies** [¹*nix* + *-ie* or *-y*] (1885) : a piece of mail that is undeliverable because illegibly or incorrectly addressed
Nix·ie \ˈnik-sē\ *trademark* — used for an electronic indicator tube
ni·zam \ni-ˈzäm, ˈnī-ˌzam, nī-ˈ\ *n* [Hindi *nizām* order, governor, fr. Ar *niẓām*] (1768) : one of a line of sovereigns of Hyderabad, India, reigning from 1713 to 1950 — **ni·zam·ate** \ni-ˈzäm-ˌāt, nī-ˈzam-\ *n*
¹**no** \(ˈ)nō\ *adv* [ME, fr. OE *nā*, fr. *ne* not + *ā* always; akin to ON & OHG *ne* not, L *ne-*, Gk *nē-* — more at AYE] (bef. 12c) **1 a** *chiefly Scot* : NOT **b** — used as a function word to express the negative of an alternative choice or possibility ⟨shall we go out to dinner or ~⟩ **2** : in no respect or degree — used in comparisons **3** : not so — used to express negation, dissent, denial, or refusal ⟨~, I'm not going⟩ **4** — used with a following adjective to imply a meaning expressed by the opposite positive statement ⟨~ uncertain terms⟩ **5** — used as a function word to emphasize a following negative or to introduce a more emphatic, explicit, or comprehensive statement **6** — used as an interjection to express surprise, doubt, or incredulity **7** — used in combination with a verb to form a compound adjective ⟨*no*-bake pie⟩
²**no** *adj* (bef. 12c) **1 a** : not any ⟨~ parking⟩ **b** : hardly any : very little ⟨finished in ~ time⟩ **2** : not a : quite other than a ⟨he's ~ expert⟩ **3** — used in combination with a noun to form a compound adjective ⟨a *no*-nonsense realist⟩
³**no** \ˈnō\ *n, pl* **noes** *or* **nos** \ˈnōz\ (1588) **1** : an act or instance of refusing or denying by the use of the word *no* : DENIAL **2 a** : a negative vote or decision **b** *pl* : persons voting in the negative
No *or* **Noh** \ˈnō\ *n, pl* **No** *or* **Noh** [Jp *nō*, lit., talent] (1871) : classic Japanese dance-drama having a heroic theme, a chorus, and highly stylized action, costuming, and scenery
no–account *adj* (1845) : of no account : TRIFLING ⟨his ~ relatives⟩
No·a·chi·an \nō-ˈā-kē-ən\ *adj* [Heb *Nōaḥ* Noah] (1678) **1** : of or relating to the patriarch Noah or his time **2** : ANCIENT, ANTIQUATED
No·ah \ˈnō-ə\ *n* [Heb *Nōaḥ*] : an Old Testament patriarch who built the ark in which he, his family, and living creatures of every kind survived the Flood
¹**nob** \ˈnäb\ *n* [prob. alter. of *knob*] (1700) **1** : HEAD 1 **2** : a jack of the same suit as the starter in cribbage that scores one point for the holder — usu. used in the phrases *his nob* or *his nobs*
²**nob** *n* [perh. fr. ¹*nob*] *chiefly Brit* (1703) : one in a superior position in life
nob·ble \ˈnäb-əl\ *vt* **nob·bled; nob·bling** \-(ə-)liŋ\ [perh. irreg. freq. of *nab*] (1847) **1** *Brit* : to incapacitate (a racehorse) esp. by drugging **2** *slang Brit* **a** : to win over to one's side **b** : STEAL **c** : SWINDLE, CHEAT — **nob·bler** \-(ə-)lər\ *n*
nob·by \ˈnäb-ē\ *adj* **nob·bi·er; -est** (1788) : CHIC, SMART
No·bel·ist \nō-ˈbel-əst\ *n* (1938) : a winner of a Nobel prize
no·bel·i·um \nō-ˈbel-ē-əm\ *n* [NL, fr. Alfred B. *Nobel*] (1957) : a radioactive element produced artificially — see ELEMENT table
No·bel prize \(ˌ)nō-ˌbel-\ *n* (1900) : any of various annual prizes (as in peace, literature, medicine) established by the will of Alfred Nobel for the encouragement of persons who work for the interests of humanity
no·bil·i·ty \nō-ˈbil-ət-ē\ *n* [ME *nobilite*, fr. MF *nobilité*, fr. L *nobilitat-, nobilitas*, fr. *nobilis*] (14c) **1** : the quality or state of being noble in character, quality, or rank **2** : the body of persons forming the noble class in a country or state : ARISTOCRACY
¹**no·ble** \ˈnō-bəl\ *adj* **no·bler** \-b(ə-)lər\; **no·blest** \-b(ə-)ləst\ [ME, fr. OF, fr. L *nobilis* knowable, well-known, noble, fr. *noscere* to come to know — more at KNOW] (13c) **1 a** : possessing outstanding qualities : ILLUSTRIOUS **b** : FAMOUS, NOTABLE ⟨~ deeds⟩ **2** : of high birth or exalted rank : ARISTOCRATIC **3 a** : possessing very high or excellent qualities or properties ⟨~ hawk⟩ **b** : very good or excellent **4** : grand or impressive esp. in appearance ⟨~ edifice⟩ **5** : possessing, characterized by, or arising from superiority of mind or character or of ideals or morals : LOFTY ⟨a ~ ambition⟩ **6** : chemically inert or inactive esp. toward oxygen ⟨a ~ metal such as platinum⟩ — compare BASE 6a **syn** see MORAL — **no·ble·ness** \-bəl-nəs\ *n* — **no·bly** \-blē *also* -bə-lē\ *adv*
²**noble** *n* (14c) **1** : a person of noble rank or birth **2** : an old English gold coin equivalent to 6s 8d
noble gas *n* (1902) : any of a group of rare gases that include helium, neon, argon, krypton, xenon, and sometimes radon and that exhibit great stability and extremely low reaction rates — called also *inert gas*
no·ble·man \ˈnō-bəl-mən\ *n* (13c) : a man of noble rank : PEER
no·blesse \nō-ˈbles\ *n* [ME, fr. OF *noblesce*, fr. *noble*] (13c) **1** : noble birth or condition : NOBILITY **2** : the members esp. of the French nobility
no·blesse oblige \nō-ˌbles-ə-ˈblēzh\ *n* [F, lit., nobility obligates] (1837) : the obligation of honorable, generous, and responsible behavior associated with high rank or birth
no·ble·wom·an \ˈnō-bəl-ˌwu̇m-ən\ *n* (13c) : a woman of noble rank : PEERESS
¹**no·body** \ˈnō-bəd-ē, -ˌbäd-ē\ *pron* (14c) : no person : not anybody
²**nobody** *n, pl* **no·bod·ies** (1581) : a person of no influence or consequence
no·cent \ˈnōs-ᵊnt\ *adj* [ME, fr. L *nocent-, nocens*, fr. prp. of *nocēre* to harm, hurt — more at NOXIOUS] (15c) : HARMFUL
no·ci·cep·tive \ˌnō-si-ˈsep-tiv\ *adj* [L *nocēre* + E *-i-* + *receptive*] (1904) **1** *of a stimulus* : PAINFUL, INJURIOUS **2** : of, induced by, or responding to a nociceptive stimulus — used esp. of receptors or protective reflexes
¹**nock** \ˈnäk\ *n* [ME *nocke* notched tip on the end of a bow; akin to MD *nocke* summit, tip, L *nux* nut — more at NUT] (14c) **1** : one of the notches cut in either of two tips of horn fastened on the ends of a bow or in the bow itself for holding the string **2 a** : the part of an arrow having a notch for the bowstring **b** : the notch itself
²**nock** *vt* (14c) **1** : to make a nock in (a bow or arrow) **2** : to fit (an arrow) against the bowstring
noct·am·bu·list \näk-ˈtam-byə-ləst\ *n* [L *noct-, nox* night + *-ambulist* (as in *somnabulist* — more at NIGHT] (1731) : SLEEPWALKER
noc·ti·lu·cent cloud \ˌnäk-tə-ˌlüs-ᵊnt-\ *n* [*noctilucent* deriv. of L *noct-* & *lucent-, lucens* lucent] (1910) : a luminous thin usu. colored cloud seen at night at a height of about 50 miles
noc·tu·id \ˈnäk-chə-wəd, ˈnäk-tə-\ *n* [NL *Noctuidae*, fr. *Noctua*, genus of moths, fr. L, night owl; akin to L *nox* night] (1880) : any of a large family (Noctuidae) of medium-sized often dull-colored moths with larvae (as cutworms and armyworms) that are often destructive agricultural pests — **noctuid** *adj*
noc·turn \ˈnäk-ˌtərn\ *n* [ME *nocturne*, fr. MF, fr. ML *nocturna*, fr. L, fem. of *nocturnus*] (13c) : a principal division of the office of matins
noc·tur·nal \näk-ˈtərn-ᵊl\ *adj* [MF or LL; MF, fr. LL *nocturnalis*, fr. L *nocturnus* of night, nocturnal, fr. *noct-, nox* night] (15c) **1** : of, relating to, or occurring in the night ⟨a ~ journey⟩ **2** : active at night ⟨a ~ predator⟩ — **noc·tur·nal·ly** \-ᵊl-ē\ *adv*
noc·turne \ˈnäk-ˌtərn\ *n* [F, adj., nocturnal, fr. L *nocturnus*] (1862) : a work of art dealing with evening or night; *esp* : a dreamy pensive composition for the piano — compare AUBADE 3
noc·u·ous \ˈnäk-yə-wəs\ *adj* [L *nocuus*, fr. *nocēre* to harm — more at NOXIOUS] (1635) : HARMFUL — **noc·u·ous·ly** *adv*
¹**nod** \ˈnäd\ *vb* **nod·ded; nod·ding** [ME *nodden;* akin to OHG *hnotōn* to shake, L *cinis* ashes — more at INCINERATE] *vi* (14c) **1** : to make a quick downward motion of the head whether deliberately (as in expressing assent, salutation, or command) or involuntarily (as from drowsiness) **2** : to incline or sway from the vertical as though ready to fall **3** : to bend or sway the upper part gently downward or forward : bob gently **4** : to make a slip or error in a moment of abstraction ~ *vt* **1** : to incline (as the head) downward or forward **2** : to bring, invite, or send by a nod ⟨*nodded* them into the room⟩ **3** : to signify by a nod ⟨*nodded* their approval⟩ — **nod·der** *n*
²**nod** *n* (1540) **1** : the act or an instance of nodding ⟨gave a ~ of greeting⟩ **2** : an indication esp. of approval or recognition ⟨received the party's ~ as candidate for governor⟩
nod·al \ˈnōd-ᵊl\ *adj* (1831) : being, relating to, or located at or near a node — **no·dal·i·ty** \nō-ˈdal-ət-ē\ *n* — **nod·al·ly** \ˈnōd-ᵊl-ē\ *adv*
nod·ding *adj* (1590) **1** : bending downward or forward : PENDULOUS, DROOPING ⟨a plant with ~ flowers⟩ **2** : SLIGHT, SUPERFICIAL ⟨a ~ acquaintance⟩
nod·dle \ˈnäd-ᵊl\ *n* [ME *nodle* back of the head or neck] (15c) : HEAD, PATE
nod·dy \ˈnäd-ē\ *n, pl* **noddies** [prob. short for obs. *noddypoll*, alter. of *hoddypoll* (fumbling inept person)] (1530) **1** : a stupid person **2** : any of several stout-bodied terns (genera *Anous* and *Micranous*) of warm seas
node \ˈnōd\ *n* [L *nodus* knot, node — more at NET] (1572) **1** : an entangling complication (as in a drama) : PREDICAMENT **2 a** : a thickened or swollen enlargement (as of a rheumatic joint) **b** : a discrete mass of one kind of tissue enclosed in tissue of a different kind **3** : either of the two points where the orbit of a planet or comet intersects the ecliptic; *also* : either of the points at which the orbit of an earth satellite crosses the plane of the equator **4 a** : a point at which subsidiary parts originate or center **b** : a point on a stem at which a leaf or leaves are inserted **c** : a point at which a curve intersects itself in such a manner that the branches have different tangents **d** : VERTEX 1a(2) **5** : a point, line, or surface of a vibrating body that is free or relatively free from vibratory motion
node of Ran·vier \-ˈräⁿ-vē-ˌā\ [Louis A. *Ranvier* †1922 Fr. histologist] (ca. 1885) : a constriction in the myelin sheath of a myelinated nerve fiber
no·di·cal \ˈnōd-i-kəl, ˈnäd-\ *adj* (1839) : of or relating to astronomical nodes
nod off *vi* (1914) : to fall asleep
no·dose \ˈnō-ˌdōs\ *adj* [L *nodosus*, fr. *nodus*] (ca. 1721) : having numerous or conspicuous protuberances ⟨~ antennae⟩ — **no·dos·i·ty** \nō-ˈdäs-ət-ē\ *n*
nod·u·lar \ˈnäj-ə-lər\ *adj* (1794) : of, relating to, characterized by, or occurring in the form of nodules ⟨~ lesions⟩
nod·u·la·tion \ˌnäj-ə-ˈlā-shən\ *n* (1872) **1** : the process of forming nodules and esp. root nodules containing symbiotic bacteria **2** : NODULE
nod·ule \ˈnäj-(ˌ)ü(ə)l\ *n* [L *nodulus*, dim. of *nodus*] (15c) : a small mass of rounded or irregular shape: as **a** : a small rounded lump of a min-

eral or mineral aggregate **b :** a swelling on a leguminous root that contains symbiotic bacteria **c :** a small abnormal knobby bodily protuberance (as a tumorous growth or a calcification near an arthritic joint)

no·dus \'nōd-əs\ *n, pl* **no·di** \'nō-,dī, -,dē\ [L, knot, node] (15c) **:** COMPLICATION, DIFFICULTY

no·el \nō-'el\ *n* [F *noël* Christmas, carol, fr. L *natalis* birthday, fr. *natalis* natal] (1811) **1 :** a Christmas carol **2** *cap* **:** CHRISTMAS

noes *pl of* NO

no·et·ic \nō-'et-ik\ *adj* [Gk *noētikos* intellectual, fr. *noein* to think, fr. *nous* mind] (1653) **:** of, relating to, or based on the intellect

no–fault *adj* (1967) **1 :** of, relating to, or being a motor vehicle insurance plan under which an accident victim is compensated usu. up to a stipulated limit for actual losses (as for property damage, medical bills, and lost wages) by his own insurance company regardless of who is responsible for the accident **2 :** of, relating to, or being a divorce law according to which neither party is held responsible for the breakup of the marriage **3 :** characterized by the absence of a general sense of individual responsibility (as for behavior) ⟨a ~ society⟩

1nog \'näg\ *n* [origin unknown] (1611) **1 :** a strong ale formerly brewed in Norfolk, England **2** [by shortening] **:** EGGNOG

2nog *n* [origin unknown] (1693) **:** a wooden peg, pin, or block of the size of a brick; *esp* **:** one built into a wall for nails to be driven into

nog·gin \'näg-ən\ *n* [origin unknown] (1630) **1 :** a small mug or cup **2 :** a small quantity (as a gill) of drink **3 :** a person's head

nog·ging \'näg-ən, -iŋ\ *n* [2*nog*] (1825) **:** rough brick masonry used to fill in the open spaces of a wooden frame

1no–good \,nō-,gu̇d\ *adj* (1908) **:** having no worth, virtue, use, or chance of success

2no–good \'nō-,gu̇d\ *n* (1924) **:** a no-good person or thing

Noh *var of* NO

no–hit *adj* (1916) **:** of, relating to, or being a baseball game or a part of a game in which a pitcher allows the opposition no base hits

no–hit·ter \(')nō-'hit-ər\ *n* (1947) **:** a no-hit game in baseball

no–holds–barred \,nō-,hōl(d)z-'bärd\ *adj* [fr. the (wrestling) expression *no holds barred*] (1942) **:** free of restrictions or hampering conventions

no·how \'nō-,hau̇\ *adv* (1775) **1 :** in no manner or way **:** not at all ⟨was ~ equal to the task⟩ **2** *dial* **:** ANYHOW

noil \'nȯi(ə)l\ *n* [origin unknown] (ca. 1623) **:** short fiber removed during the combing of a textile fiber and often separately spun into yarn

1noise \'nȯiz\ *n* [ME, fr. OF, strife, quarrel, noise, fr. L *nausea* nausea] (13c) **1 :** loud, confused, or senseless shouting or outcry **2 a :** SOUND; *esp* **:** one that lacks agreeable musical quality or is noticeably unpleasant **b :** any sound that is undesired or interferes with one's hearing of something **c :** an unwanted signal or a disturbance (as static or a variation of voltage) in an electronic device or instrument (as radio or television); *broadly* **:** a disturbance interfering with the operation of a usu. mechanical device or system **d :** electromagnetic radiation (as light or radio waves) that is composed of several frequencies and that involves random changes in frequency or amplitude **e :** irrelevant or meaningless bits or words occurring along with desired information (as in a computer output) **3 :** common talk **:** RUMOR; *esp* **:** SLANDER **4 :** something that attracts attention ⟨the play . . . will make little ~ in the world —Brendan Gill⟩ **5 :** something spoken or uttered — **noise·less** \-ləs\ *adj* — **noise·less·ly** *adv*

2noise *vb* **noised; nois·ing** *vi* (14c) **1 :** to talk much or loudly **2 :** to make a noise ~ *vt* **:** to spread by rumor or report — usu. used with *about* or *abroad* ⟨the scandal was quickly *noised* about⟩

noise·mak·er \'nȯiz-,mā-kər\ *n* (1574) **:** one that makes noise; *esp* **:** a device (as a horn or rattle) used to make noise at parties — **noise·mak·ing** \-kiŋ\ *n or adj*

noise pollution *n* (1966) **:** environmental pollution consisting of annoying or harmful noise (as of automobiles or jet airplanes)

noi·sette \nwə-'zet, n(ə-)wä-\ *n* [F, lit., hazelnut, fr. OF, dim. of *nois* nut, fr. L *nux* — more at NUT] (1891) **:** a small piece of lean meat

noi·some \'nȯi-səm\ *adj* [ME *noysome*, fr. *noy* annoyance, fr. OF *enui, anoi* — more at ENNUI] (14c) **1 :** NOXIOUS, UNWHOLESOME **2 :** offensive to the senses and esp. to the sense of smell ***syn*** see MALODOROUS — **noi·some·ly** *adv* — **noi·some·ness** *n*

noisy \'nȯi-zē\ *adj* **nois·i·er; -est** (1693) **1 :** making noise **2 :** full of or characterized by noise **3 :** vocal or active in expression of opinion — **nois·i·ly** \'nȯi-zə-lē\ *adv* — **nois·i·ness** \-zē-nəs\ *n*

no·li me tan·ge·re \,nō-lē-(,)mē-'tan-jə-rē, -,lī-mē-\ *n* [L, do not touch me; fr. Jesus' words to Mary Magdalene in Jn 20:17] (1591) **:** a warning against touching or interference

nol·le pro·se·qui \,näl-ē-'präs-ə-,kwī\ *n* [L, to be unwilling to pursue] (1681) **:** an entry on the record of a legal action denoting that the prosecutor or plaintiff will proceed no further in his action or suit either as a whole or as to some count or as to one or more of several defendants

no·lo \'nō-(,)lō\ *n* (1914) **:** NOLO CONTENDERE

no–load \,nō-,lōd\ *adj* (1963) **:** charging no sales commission ⟨a ~ mutual fund⟩ — **no–load** \'nō-,lōd\ *n*

no·lo con·ten·de·re \,nō-(,)lō-kən-'ten-də-rē\ *n* [L, I do not wish to contend] (1872) **:** a plea by the defendant in a criminal prosecution that without admitting guilt subjects him to conviction but does not preclude him from denying the truth of the charges in a collateral proceeding

nol–pros \'näl-'präs\ *vt* **nol–prossed; nol–pros·sing** [*nol*le *pros*equi] (ca. 1878) **:** to discontinue by entering a nolle prosequi

no·ma \'nō-mə\ *n* [NL, fr. Gk *nomē*, fr. *nemein* to spread (of an ulcer), lit., to graze, pasture — more at NIMBLE] (1834) **:** a spreading invasive gangrene chiefly of the lining of the cheek and lips that is usu. fatal and occurs most often in persons severely debilitated by disease or profound nutritional deficiency

no·mad \'nō-,mad, *Brit also* 'näm-,ad\ *n* [L *nomad-, nomas* member of a wandering pastoral people, fr. Gk, fr. *nemein*] (1579) **1 :** a member of a people with no fixed residence but wandering from place to place usu. seasonally and within a well-defined territory in order to secure a food supply **2 :** an individual who roams about aimlessly — **nomad** *adj* — **no·mad·ism** \'nō-,mad-,iz-əm\ *n*

no·mad·ic \nō-'mad-ik\ *adj* (1818) **1 :** of, relating to, or characteristic of nomads ⟨a ~ tribe⟩ **2 :** roaming about from place to place aimlessly, frequently, or without a fixed pattern of movement

no–man's–land \'nō-,manz-,land\ *n* (14c) **1 a :** an area of unowned, unclaimed, or uninhabited land **b :** an unoccupied area between opposing armies **2 :** an anomalous, ambiguous, or indefinite area esp. of operation, application, or jurisdiction ⟨the ~ between art and science⟩

nom·bril \'näm-brəl\ *n* [MF, lit., navel, deriv. of L *umbilicus*] (1562) **:** the center point of the lower half of an armorial escutcheon

nom de guerre \,näm-di-'ge(ə)r\ *n, pl* **noms de guerre** \,näm(z)-di-\ [F, lit., war name] (ca. 1675) **:** PSEUDONYM

nom de plume \-'plüm\ *n, pl* **noms de plume** \,näm(z)-di-\ [F, fr. *nom* name + *de* of + *plume* pen] (1823) **:** PSEUDONYM, PEN NAME

nome \'nōm\ *n* [Gk *nomos* district — more at NIMBLE] (1727) **:** a province of ancient Egypt

no·men \'nō-mən\ *n, pl* **no·mi·na** \'näm-ə-nə, 'nō-mə-\ [L *nomin-, nomen* name — more at NAME] (ca. 1889) **:** the second of the three usual names of an ancient Roman

no·men·cla·tor \'nō-mən-,klāt-ər\ *n* [L, slave whose duty was to announce the names of persons met during a political campaign, fr. *nomen* + *calatus*, pp. of *calare* to call — more at LOW] (1585) **1 :** a book containing collections or lists of words **2** *archaic* **:** one who announces the names of guests or of persons generally **3 :** one who gives names to or invents names for things

no·men·cla·to·ri·al \,nō-mən-klə-'tōr-ē-əl, -'tȯr-\ *adj* (1885) **:** relating to or connected with nomenclature

no·men·cla·ture \'nō-mən-,klā-chər *also* nō-'men-klə-,chu̇(ə)r, -'meŋ-, -klə-chər, -klə-,t(y)u̇(ə)r\ *n* [L *nomenclatura* calling by name, list of names, fr. *nomen* + *calatus*, pp.] (1610) **1 :** NAME, DESIGNATION **2 :** the act or process or an instance of naming **3 a :** a system or set of terms or symbols **b :** a system of terms used in a particular science, discipline, or art; *esp* **:** an international system of standardized New Latin names used in biology for kinds and groups of kinds of animals and plants — **no·men·cla·tur·al** \,nō-mən-'klāch-(ə-)rəl\ *adj*

no·men con·ser·van·dum \'nō-mən-,kän(t)-sər-'van-dəm\ *n, pl* **no·mi·na con·ser·van·da** \'näm-ə-nə-,kän(t)-sər-'van-də, 'nō-mə-\ [NL, name to be kept] (ca. 1925) **:** a biological taxonomic name (as of a genus) that is preserved by special sanction in exception to the usual rules (as of priority)

nomen du·bi·um \-'d(y)ü-bē-əm\ *n, pl* **nomina du·bia** \-bē-ə\ [NL, doubtful name] (ca. 1937) **:** a taxonomic name that cannot be assigned with certainty to any taxonomic group because the description is insufficient for identification and the original specimens no longer exist

nomen nu·dum \-'n(y)üd-əm\ *n, pl* **nomina nu·da** \-ə\ [NL, bare name] (ca. 1900) **:** a proposed taxonomic name that is invalid because the group designated is not described or illustrated sufficiently for recognition, that has no nomenclatural status, and that consequently can be used as though never previously proposed

1nom·i·nal \'näm-ən-ᵊl, 'näm-nəl\ *adj* [ME *nominalle*, fr. ML *nominalis*, fr. L, of a name, fr. *nomin-, nomen* name — more at NAME] (15c) **1 :** of, relating to, or being a noun or a word or expression taking a noun construction **2 a :** of, relating to, or constituting a name **b :** bearing the name of a person **3 a :** existing or being something in name or form only ⟨~ head of his party⟩ **b :** of, being, or relating to a designated or theoretical size that may vary from the actual **:** APPROXIMATE **c :** TRIFLING, INSIGNIFICANT **4** *of a rate of interest* **:** equal to the annual rate of simple interest that would obtain if interest were not compounded when in fact it is compounded and paid for periods of less than a year ⟨if ~ 3% interest is paid for each quarter, the ~ rate per year is 12% while the annual effective rate is about 12.55%⟩ **5 :** being according to plan **:** SATISFACTORY ⟨everything was ~ during the spacecraft launch⟩ — **nom·i·nal·ly** \-ē\ *adv*

2nominal *n* (1904) **:** a word or word group functioning as a noun

nom·i·nal·ism \-,iz-əm\ *n* (1844) **1 :** a theory that there are no universal essences in reality and that the mind can frame no single concept or image corresponding to any universal or general term **2 :** the theory that only individuals and no abstract entities (as essences, classes, or propositions) exist — compare ESSENTIALISM, REALISM — **nom·i·nal·ist** \-əst\ *n* — **nominalist** *or* **nom·i·nal·is·tic** \,näm-ən-ᵊl-'is-tik, ,näm-nəl-\ *adj*

nominal value *n* (1901) **:** PAR 1b

nominal wages *n pl* (1898) **:** wages measured in money as distinct from actual purchasing power

nom·i·nate \'näm-ə-,nāt\ *vt* **-nat·ed; -nat·ing** [L *nominatus*, pp. of *nominare*, fr. *nomin-, nomen* name] (1545) **1 :** DESIGNATE, NAME **2 a :** to appoint or propose for appointment to an office or place **b :** to propose as a candidate for election to office **c :** to propose for an honor ⟨~ him for player of the year⟩ **3 :** to enter (a horse) in a race — **nom·i·na·tor** \-,nāt-ər\ *n*

nom·i·na·tion \,näm-ə-'nā-shən\ *n* (15c) **1 :** the act, process, or an instance of nominating **2 :** the state of being nominated

nom·i·na·tive \'näm-(ə-)nət-iv; *2 & 3 are also* 'näm-ə-,nāt-\ *adj* [ME *nominatyf*, fr. MF or L; MF *nomiatif*, fr. L *(casus) nominativus* nominative case, fr. *nominare;* fr. the traditional use of the nominative form in naming a noun] (14c) **1 a :** marking typically the subject of a verb esp. in languages that have relatively full inflection ⟨~ case⟩ **b :** of or relating to the nominative case ⟨a ~ ending⟩ **2 :** nominated or appointed by nomination **3 :** bearing a person's name — **nominative** *n*

nom·i·nee \,näm-ə-'nē\ *n* [*nominate*] (1688) **:** a person who has been nominated

no·mo·gram \'näm-ə-,gram, 'nō-mə-\ *n* [Gk *nomos* law + ISV *-gram* — more at NIMBLE] (1908) **:** a graphic representation that consists of several lines marked off to scale and arranged in such a way that by using a straightedge to connect known values on two lines an unknown value can be read at the point of intersection with another line

no·mo·graph \-,graf\ *n* (ca. 1909) **:** NOMOGRAM — **no·mo·graph·ic** \,näm-ə-'graf-ik, ,nō-mə-\ *adj* — **no·mog·ra·phy** \nō-'mäg-rə-fē\ *n*

no·mo·log·i·cal \,näm-ə-'läj-i-kəl, ,nō-mə-\ *adj* [*nomology* (science of physical and logical laws), fr. Gk *nomos* + E *-logy*] (1845) **:** relating to or expressing basic physical laws or rules of reasoning ⟨~ universals⟩

\ə\ abut \ᵊ\ kitten, F table \ər\ further \a\ ash \ā\ ace \ä\ cot, cart \au̇\ out \ch\ chin \e\ bet \ē\ easy \g\ go \i\ hit \ī\ ice \j\ job \ŋ\ sing \ō\ go \ȯ\ law \ȯi\ boy \th\ thin \t͟h\ the \ü\ loot \u̇\ foot \y\ yet \zh\ vision \à, k̲, ⁿ, œ, œ̄, ue, ue̅, ʸ\ *see* Guide to Pronunciation

no·mo·thet·ic \-'thet-ik\ *adj* [Gk *nomothetikos* of legislation, fr. *nomo-thetēs* lawgiver, fr. *nomos* law + *-thetēs* one who establishes, fr. *tithenai* to put — more at DO] (1658) : relating to, involving, or dealing with abstract, general, or universal statements or laws

-no·my \n-ə-mē\ *n comb form* [ME *-nomie*, fr. OF, fr. L *-nomia*, fr. Gk, fr. *nemein* to distribute — more at NIMBLE] : system of laws governing or sum of knowledge regarding a (specified) field ⟨agro*nomy*⟩

non- \(')nän *also* ˌnən *or* 'nən *before* '-*stressed syllable*, ˌnän *also* ˌnən *before* ˌ-*stressed or unstressed syllable; the variant with ə is also to be understood at pronounced entries, where it is not shown* \ *prefix* [ME, fr. MF, fr. L *non* not, fr. OL *noenum*, fr. *ne-* not + *oinom*, neut. of *oinos* one — more at NO, ONE] **1** : not : other than : reverse of : absence of **2** : of little or no consequence : unimportant : worthless ⟨*non*issues⟩ ⟨*non*system⟩ **3** : lacking the usual esp. positive characteristics of the thing specified ⟨*non*celebration⟩ ⟨*non*theater⟩

non-abra·sive
non-abrupt
non-ab·sorb·able
non-ab·sor·bent
non-ab·sorp·tive
non-ab·stract
non-ac·a·dem·ic
non-ac·cept·able
non-ac·ces·si·ble
non-ac·count·able
non-ac·cred·it·ed
non-ac·cru·al
non-achieve·ment
non-ac·id
non-ac·id·ic
non-ac·quis·i·tive
non-act·ing
non-ac·tion
non-ac·ti·vat·ed
non-ac·tor
non-adap·tive
non-ad·dict
non-ad·dict·ing
non-ad·he·sive
non-adi·a·bat·ic
non-ad·ja·cent
non-ad·just·able
non-ad·mir·er
non-ad·mis·sion
non-ad·o·les·cent
non-aes·thet·ic
non-af·fil·i·at·ed
non-af·flu·ent
non–Af·ri·can
non-ag·gres·sion
non-ag·gres·sive
non-ag·ri·cul·tur·al
non-al·co·hol·ic
non-al·ler·gen·ic
non-al·ler·gic
non-al·pha·bet·ic
non-am·big·u·ous
non-an·a·lyt·ic
non-an·a·tom·ic
non-an·i·mal
non-an·swer
non-an·tag·o·nis·tic
non-an·thro·po·log·i·cal
non-an·thro·po·log·ist
non-an·ti·bi·ot·ic
non-an·ti·gen
non-an·ti·gen·ic
non-ap·pear·ance
non-aquat·ic
non-aque·ous
non-ar·a·ble
non-ar·bi·trari·ness
non-ar·bi·trary
non-ar·chi·tect
non-ar·chi·tec·ture
non-ar·gu·ment
non-aris·to·crat·ic
non-ar·o·mat·ic
non-art
non-art·ist
non-ar·tis·tic
non-as·cet·ic
non-as·ser·tive
non-as·so·ci·at·ed
non-as·tro·nom·i·cal
non-ath·lete
non-ath·let·ic
non-atom·ic
non-at·tached
non-at·tach·ment
non-at·ten·dance
non-at·tend·er
non-at·ten·tive
non-au·di·to·ry
non-au·thor
non-au·thor·i·tar·i·an
non-au·thor·i·ta·tive
non-au·to·mat·ed
non-au·to·mat·ic
non-au·to·mo·tive
non-au·ton·o·mous
non-avail·abil·i·ty

non-bac·te·ri·al
non-bal·lis·tic
non-bar·bi·tu·rate
non-ba·sic
non-bear·ing
non-be·hav·ior·al
non-be·ing
non-be·lief
non-be·liev·er
non-bel·lig·er·en·cy
non-bel·lig·er·ent
non-bet·ting
non-bib·lio·graph·ic
non-bi·na·ry
non-bind·ing
non-bio·de·grad·able
non-bio·graph·i·cal
non-bio·log·i·cal
non-bi·ol·o·gist
non-bit·ing
non-black
non-body
non-bond·ed
non-bond·ing
non-bot·a·nist
non-brand
non-break·able
non-breed·er
non-breed·ing
non-broad·cast
non-build·ing
non-burn·able
non-buy·ing
non-cab·i·net
non-cak·ing
non-call·able
non-cam·pus
non-can·cel·able
non-can·cer·ous
non-can·ni·bal·is·tic
non-cap·i·tal
non-cap·i·tal·ist
non-car·cin·o·gen
non-car·ci·no·gen·ic
non-car·di·ac
non-ca·reer
non-car·ri·er
non-cash
non-ca·su·al
non–Cath·o·lic
non-caus·al
non-cel·e·bra·tion
non-cel·lu·lar
non-cel·lu·los·ic
non–Celt·ic
non-cen·tral
non-cer·ti·fi·cat·ed
non-cer·ti·fied
non-chal·leng·ing
non-char·ac·ter
non-char·is·mat·ic
non-chau·vin·ist
non-chem·i·cal
non-cho·sen
non–Chris·tian
non-chro·no·log·i·cal
non-church
non-church·go·er
non-cir·cu·lar
non-cir·cu·lat·ing
non-cit·i·zen
non-clan·des·tine
non-class
non-clas·si·cal
non-clas·si·fied
non-class·room
non-cler·i·cal
non-cling
non-clin·i·cal
non-clog·ging
non-co·er·cive
non-cog·ni·tive
non-co·her·ent
non-co·in·ci·dence
non-co·ital
non-cok·ing
non-col·lec·tor
non-col·lege

non-col·le·giate
non-col·lin·ear
non-col·or
non-col·ored
non-col·or·fast
non-com·bat
non-com·bus·ti·ble
non-com·mer·cial
non-com·mit·ment
non-com·mit·ted
non-com·mu·ni·cat·ing
non-com·mu·ni·ca·tion
non-com·mu·ni·ty
non-com·mu·ta·tive
non-com·mu·ta·tiv·i·ty
non-com·pa·ra·bil·i·ty
non-com·pa·ra·ble
non-com·pat·i·ble
non-com·pe·ti·tion
non-com·pet·i·tive
non-com·pet·i·tor
non-com·ple·men·ta·ry
non-com·plex
non-com·pli·ance
non-com·pli·cat·ed
non-com·ply·ing
non-com·pos·er
non-com·pound
non-com·pre·hen·sion
non-com·press·ible
non-com·put·er
non-con·cep·tu·al
non-con·cern
non-con·clu·sion
non-con·clu·sive
non-con·cur·rent
non-con·dens·able
non-con·di·tioned
non-con·duct·ing
non-con·duc·tion
non-con·duc·tive
non-con·fer·ence
non-con·fi·dence
non-con·fi·den·tial
non-con·flict·ing
non-con·fron·ta·tion
non-con·fron·ta·tion·al
non-con·gru·ent
non-con·ju·gat·ed
non-con·nec·tion
non-con·scious
non-con·sec·u·tive
non-con·sen·su·al
non-con·ser·va·tion
non-con·ser·va·tive
non-con·sol·i·dat·ed
non-con·stant
non-con·sti·tu·tion·al
non-con·struc·tion
non-con·struc·tive
non-con·sum·er
non-con·sum·ing
non-con·sump·tion
non-con·sump·tive
non-con·tact
non-con·ta·gious
non-con·tem·po·rary
non-con·tig·u·ous
non-con·tin·u·ous
non-con·tract
non-con·trac·tu·al
non-con·tra·dic·tion
non-con·tra·dic·to·ry
non-con·trib·ut·ing
non-con·trib·u·to·ry
non-con·trol·la·ble
non-con·trolled
non-con·trol·ling
non-con·tro·ver·sial
non-con·ven·tion·al
non-con·vert·ible
non-co·pla·nar
non-cor·po·rate
non-cor·re·la·tion
non-cor·rod·ing
non-cor·ro·sive
non-coun·ty

non-cov·er·age
non-cre·ative
non-cre·ativ·i·ty
non-crime
non-crim·i·nal
non-cri·sis
non-crit·i·cal
non-crush·able
non-crys·tal·line
non-cul·ti·vat·ed
non-cul·ti·va·tion
non-cul·tur·al
non-cu·mu·la·tive
non-cur·rent
non-cus·tom·er
non-cy·clic
non-cy·cli·cal
non-dance
non-danc·er
non–Eu·ro·pe·an
non-de·cep·tive
non-de·ci·sion
non-de·creas·ing
non-de·duc·tive
non-de·fer·ra·ble
non-de·form·ing
non-de·gen·er·ate
non-de·grad·able
non-de·gree
non-del·e·gate
non-de·lib·er·ate
non-de·lin·quent
non-de·liv·ery
non-de·mand·ing
non-dem·o·crat·ic
non-de·nom·i·na·tion·al
non-de·nom·i·na·tion·al·ism
non-de·part·men·tal
non-de·plet·able
non-de·plet·ing
non-de·po·si·tion
non-de·riv·a·tive
non-de·script·ive
non-de·sert
non-de·ter·min·is·tic
non-de·vel·op·ment
non-de·vi·ant
non-di·a·bet·ic
non-di·a·lyz·able
non-di·dac·tic
non-dif·fus·ible
non-di·men·sion·al
non-dip·lo·mat·ic
non-di·rect·ed
non-di·rec·tion·al
non-dis·abled
non-dis·clo·sure
non-dis·count
non-dis·count·able
non-dis·cre·tion·ary
non-dis·crim·i·na·tion
non-dis·crim·i·na·to·ry
non-dis·cur·sive
non-dis·per·sive
non-dis·rup·tive
non-di·ver·si·fied
non-doc·tor
non-doc·tri·naire
non-doc·u·men·ta·ry
non-dog·mat·ic
non-dol·lar
non-do·mes·tic
non-dom·i·nant
non-dra·mat·ic
non-driv·er
non-drug
non-du·ra·ble
non-earn·ing
non-ec·cle·si·as·ti·cal
non-econ·o·mist
non-ed·i·ble
non-ed·i·to·ri·al
non-ed·u·ca·tion
non-ed·u·ca·tion·al
non-ef·fec·tive
non-elas·tic
non-elect·ed
non-elec·tion
non-elec·tive
non-elec·tric
non-elec·tri·cal
non-elec·tron·ic
non-el·e·men·ta·ry
non-el·i·gi·ble
non-elite
non-emer·gen·cy
non-emo·tion·al
non-em·pir·i·cal
non-em·ploy·ee
non-em·ploy·ment
non-emp·ty
non-en·cap·su·lat·ed
non-end·ing

non-en·force·abil·i·ty
non-en·force·able
non-en·force·ment
non-en·gage·ment
non-en·gi·neer·ing
non-en·ter·tain·ment
non-en·zy·mat·ic
non-en·zy·mic
non-equi·lib·ri·um
non-equiv·a·lence
non-equiv·a·lent
non-erot·ic
non-es·sen·tial
non-es·tab·lished
non-es·tab·lish·ment
non-es·ter·i·fied
non-eth·i·cal
non-eth·nic
non–Eu·ro·pe·an
non-ev·i·dence
non-ex·change·able
non-ex·ec·u·tive
non-ex·empt
non-ex·is·ten·tial
non-ex·pend·able
non-ex·per·i·men·tal
non-ex·pert
non-ex·plan·a·to·ry
non-ex·ploi·ta·tion
non-ex·ploi·ta·tive
non-ex·ploi·tive
non-ex·plo·sive
non-ex·posed
non-ex·tant
non-fact
non-fac·tu·al
non-fac·ul·ty
non-fad·ing
non-fam·i·ly
non-fan
non-farm
non-farm·er
non-fa·tal
non-fat·ten·ing
non-fat·ty
non-fed·er·al
non-fed·er·at·ed
non-fil·a·men·tous
non-fil·ter·able
non-fi·nal
non-fi·nan·cial
non-fi·nite
non-fis·sion·able
non-fluo·res·cent
non-fluo·ri·dat·ed
non-fly·ing
non-food
non-for·feit·able
non-for·fei·ture
non-for·mal
non-fos·sil
non-frat·er·ni·za·tion
non-freez·ing
non-fuel
non-ful·fill·ment
non-func·tion·al
non-func·tion·ing
non-game
non-gas·eous
non-gay
non-gen·er·ic
non-ge·net·ic
non-gen·i·tal
non-geo·met·ri·cal
non-ghet·to
non-glam·or·ous
non-glare
non-gov·ern·ment
non-gov·ern·men·tal
non-grad·ed
non-grad·u·ate
non-gram·mat·i·cal
non-gran·u·lar
non-greasy
non-gre·gar·i·ous
non-grow·ing
non-growth
non-ha·lo·ge·nat·ed
non-hand·i·capped
non-hap·pen·ing
non-har·dy
non-har·mon·ic
non-haz·ard·ous
non-heme
non-he·mo·lyt·ic
non-he·red·i·tary
non-hi·er·ar·chi·cal
non–His·pan·ic
non-his·tor·i·cal
non-home
non-ho·mo·ge·neous
non-ho·mol·o·gous
non-ho·mo·sex·u·al
non-hor·mon·al

non-hos·pi·tal
non-hos·pi·tal·ized
non-hos·tile
non-hu·man
non-hys·ter·i·cal
non-ide·al
non-iden·ti·ty
non-ideo·log·i·cal
non-im·age
non-im·i·ta·tive
non-im·mi·grant
non-im·mune
non-im·pact
non-im·pli·cat·ed
non-im·por·ta·tion
non-in·clu·sion
non-in·creas·ing
non-in·cum·bent
non-in·de·pen·dence
non–In·di·an
non-in·dig·e·nous
non-in·di·vid·u·al
non–In·do–Eu·ro·pe·an
non-in·dus·tri·al
non-in·dus·tri·al·iza·tion
non-in·dus·tri·al·ized
non-in·dus·try
non-in·fect·ed
non-in·fec·tious
non-in·fec·tive
non-in·fest·ed
non-in·flam·ma·ble
non-in·flam·ma·to·ry
non-in·fla·tion·ary
non-in·flec·tion·al
non-in·flu·ence
non-in·for·ma·tion
non-ini·tial
non-ini·ti·ate
non-in·ju·ry
non-in·sec·ti·cid·al
non-in·stall·ment
non-in·sti·tu·tion·al
non-in·sti·tu·tion·al·ized
non-in·struc·tion·al
non-in·sured
non-in·te·gral
non-in·te·grat·ed
non-in·tel·lec·tu·al
non-in·ter·act·ing
non-in·ter·course
non-in·ter·fer·ence
non-in·ter·sect·ing
non-in·tox·i·cant
non-in·tox·i·cat·ing
non-in·tru·sive
non-ion·iz·ing
non-iron
non-ir·ra·di·at·ed
non-ir·ri·gat·ed
non-ir·ri·tant
non-ir·ri·tat·ing
non-is·sue
non–Jew
non–Jew·ish
non-join·er
non-ju·di·cial
non-ju·ry
non-ko·sher
non-lan·guage
non-law·yer
non-lead·ed
non-league
non-le·gal
non-le·gume
non-le·gu·mi·nous
non-le·thal
non-lex·i·cal
non-li·brar·i·an
non-li·brary
non-life
non-lin·e·al
non-lin·ear
non-lin·ear·i·ty
non-liq·uid
non-lit·er·ary
non-liv·ing
non-lo·cal
non-log·i·cal
non-lu·mi·nous
non-mag·net·ic
non-ma·jor
non-ma·lig·nant
non-mal·lea·ble
non-man·age·ment
non-man·a·ge·ri·al
non-man·u·al
non-man·u·fac·tur·ing
non-mar·i·tal
non-mar·ket
non–Marx·ist
non-ma·te·ri·al·is·tic
non-math·e·mat·i·cal

non·mea·sur·able
non·meat
non·me·chan·i·cal
non·mech·a·nis·tic
non·med·i·cal
non·meet·ing
non·mem·ber
non·mem·ber·ship
non·men·tal
non·mer·cu·ri·al
non·meta·mer·ic
non·met·ric
non·met·ri·cal
non·met·ro·pol·i·tan
non·mi·cro·bi·al
non·mi·grant
non·mi·gra·to·ry
non·mil·i·tant
non·mil·i·tary
non·mi·met·ic
non·mi·nor·i·ty
non·mo·lec·u·lar
non·mon·e·tary
non·mon·ey
non·mor·phine
non·mo·tile
non·mo·til·i·ty
non·mo·tor·ist
non·mo·tor·ized
non·mov·ing
non·mu·nic·i·pal
non·mu·sic
non·mu·si·cal
non·mu·tant
non·my·elin·at·ed
non·mys·ti·cal
non·na·tion·al
non·na·tive
non·nat·u·ral
non·ne·ces·si·ty
non·ne·go·tia·ble
non·news
non–New·to·ni·an
non·ni·trog·e·nous
non·nor·ma·tive
non·nov·el
non·nu·cle·at·ed
non·nu·mer·i·cal
non·nu·tri·tious
non·nu·tri·tive
non·ob·ser·vance
non·ob·ser·vant
non·ob·vi·ous
non·oc·cu·pa·tion·al
non·oc·cur·rence
non·of·fi·cial
non·ohm·ic
non·op·er·at·ic
non·op·er·at·ing
non·op·er·a·tion·al
non·or·gan·ic
non·or·tho·dox
non·over·lap·ping
non·own·er
non·ox·i·diz·ing
non·par·al·lel
non·par·a·sit·ic
non·par·tic·i·pant
non·par·tic·i·pat·ing
non·par·tic·i·pa·tion
non·par·tic·i·pa·to·ry
non·par·ty
non·pas·sive
non·past
non·pay·ing
non·pay·ment
non·per·for·mance
non·per·ish·able
non·per·mis·sive
non·per·son·al
non·pe·tro·leum
non·phi·los·o·pher
non·phil·o·soph·i·cal
non·pho·ne·mic
non·pho·net·ic
non·phos·phate
non·pho·to·graph·ic
non·phys·i·cal
non·phy·si·cian
non·pla·nar
non·plas·tic
non·play
non·play·ing
non·po·et·ic
non·poi·son·ous
non·po·lar·iz·able
non·po·lice
non·po·lit·i·cal
non·po·lit·i·cal·ly
non·pol·i·ti·cian
non·pol·lut·ing

non·poor
non·po·rous
non·pos·ses·sion
non·prac·ti·cal
non·prac·tic·ing
non·preg·nant
non·print
non·prob·lem
non·pro·duc·ing
non·pro·fes·sion·al
non·pro·fes·sion·al·ly
non·pro·fes·so·ri·al
non·pro·gram
non·pro·gres·sive
non·pro·pri·etary
non·psy·chi·at·ric
non·psy·chi·a·trist
non·psy·cho·log·i·cal
non·psy·chot·ic
non·pub·lic
non·pu·ni·tive
non·pur·po·sive
non·quan·ti·ta·tive
non·ra·cial
non·ra·cial·ly
non·ra·dio·ac·tive
non·rail·road
non·ran·dom
non·ran·dom·ness
non·rat·ed
non·ra·tio·nal
non·re·ac·tive
non·re·ac·tor
non·re·al·is·tic
non·re·ap·point·ment
non·re·ceipt
non·re·cip·ro·cal
non·rec·og·ni·tion
non·re·course
non·re·duc·ing
non·re·dun·dant
non·re·fill·able
non·re·flect·ing
non·reg·u·lat·ed
non·reg·u·la·tion
non·rel·a·tive
non·rel·e·vant
non·re·li·gious
non·re·new·able
non·re·new·al
non·re·pay·able
non·rep·re·sen·ta·tive
non·res·i·den·tial
non·res·o·nant
non·re·spon·dent
non·re·spond·er
non·re·sponse
non·re·spon·sive
non·re·strict·ed
non·re·trac·tile
non·ret·ro·ac·tive
non·re·us·able
non·rev·e·nue
non·re·vers·ible
non·rev·o·lu·tion·ary
non·ri·ot·er
non·ri·ot·ing
non·ro·tat·ing
non·rou·tine
non·rub·ber
non·ru·mi·nant
non–Rus·sian
non·sal·able
non·sa·line
non·sa·pon·i·fi·able
non·schizo·phren·ic
non·school
non·sci·en·tif·ic
non·sci·en·tist
non·sea·son·al
non·sec·re·tory
non·se·cure
non·seg·re·gat·ed
non·seg·re·ga·tion
non·se·lect·ed
non·se·lec·tive
non–self–gov·ern·ing
non·sen·sa·tion·al
non·sen·si·tive
non·sen·su·ous
non·sen·tence
non·sep·tate
non·se·quen·tial
non·se·ri·ous
non·sex·ist
non·sex·u·al
non·shrink
non·shrink·able
non·sign·er
non·si·mul·ta·neous

non·sink·able
non·skat·er
non·skel·e·tal
non·skep·ti·cal
non·ski·er
non·smok·er
non·smok·ing
non·so·cial·ist
non·so·lar
non·so·lu·tion
non·spa·tial
non·speak·er
non·speak·ing
non·spe·cial·ist
non·spe·cif·ic
non·spe·cif·i·cal·ly
non·spec·tac·u·lar
non·spec·u·la·tive
non·speech
non·spher·i·cal
non·sta·tion·ary
non·sta·tis·ti·cal
non·steady
non·sto·ry
non·stra·te·gic
non·struc·tur·al
non·struc·tured
non·stu·dent
non·sub·jec·tive
non·sub·si·dized
non·suc·cess
non·sug·ar
non·su·per·im·pos·able
non·su·per·vi·so·ry
non·sur·gi·cal
non·swim·mer
non·sym·bol·ic
non·sym·met·ric
non·sym·met·ri·cal
non·syn·chro·nous
non·sys·tem·at·ic
non·sys·tem·ic
non·tar·iff
non·tax·able
non·teach·ing
non·tech·ni·cal
non·tem·po·ral
non·ten·ured
non·ter·mi·nal
non·the·at·ri·cal
non·the·ist
non·the·is·tic
non·the·mat·ic
non·theo·ret·i·cal
non·ther·a·peu·tic
non·think·ing
non·threat·en·ing
non·tid·al
non·to·bac·co
non·ton·al
non·to·tal·i·tar·i·an
non·tox·ic
non·tra·di·tion·al
non·trans·fer·able
non·trop·i·cal
non·tur·bu·lent
non·typ·i·cal
non·unan·i·mous
non·uni·form
non·uni·for·mi·ty
non·unique
non·unique·ness
non·uni·ver·sal
non·uni·ver·si·ty
non·ur·ban
non·ur·gent
non·util·i·tar·i·an
non·util·i·ty
non·uto·pi·an
non·val·id
non·va·lid·i·ty
non·vas·cu·lar
non·ven·om·ous
non·vet·er·an
non·vi·a·ble
non·view·er
non·vi·ral
non·vis·cous
non·vi·su·al
non·vo·cal
non·vo·ca·tion·al
non·vol·ca·nic
non·vol·un·tary
non·vot·er
non·vot·ing
non·win·ning
non·woody
non·work·er
non·work·ing
non·writ·er
non·yel·low·ing

non·ad·di·tive \(')nän-'ad-ət-iv\ adj (1926) 1 : not having a numerical value equal to the sum of values for the component parts 2 : of, relat-

ing to, or being a genic effect that is not additive — **non·ad·di·tiv·i·ty** \,nän-,ad-ə-'tiv-ət-ē\ n

non·age \'nän-ij, 'nō-nij\ n [ME, fr. MF, fr. non- + age age] (14c) 1 : MINORITY 1 2 a : a period of youth b : lack of maturity

no·na·ge·nar·i·an \,nō-nə-jə-'ner-ē-ən, ,nän-ə-\ n [L nonagenarius containing ninety, fr. nonageni ninety each, fr. nonaginta ninety, fr. nona- (akin to novem nine) + -ginta (akin to viginti twenty) — more at NINE, VIGESIMAL] (1804) : a person whose age is in the nineties — **nonagenarian** adj

no·na·gon \'nō-nə-,gän\ n [L nonus ninth + E -gon — more at NOON] (1688) : a polygon of nine angles and nine sides

non·aligned \,nän-ə-'līnd\ adj (1960) : not allied with other nations and esp. with either the Communist or the non-Communist blocs — **non·align·ment** \-'īn-mənt\ n

non·al·le·lic \,nän-ə-'lē-lik, -'lel-ik\ adj (1945) : not behaving as alleles toward one another ⟨~ genes⟩

non·bank \'nän-'baŋk\ adj (1946) : done by or being something other than a bank

¹**non·book** \'nän-'bůk\ adj (1949) : being something other than a book; esp : being a library holding (as a microfilm) that is not a book

²**non·book** \-,bůk\ n (1966) : a book of little literary merit which is often a compilation (as of pictures, press clippings, or speeches)

non·busi·ness \-'biz-nəs, -nəz\ adj (1927) : not related to business; esp : not related to one's primary business

non·ca·lo·ric \,nän-kə-'lȯr-ik, -'lōr-, -'lär-; (')nän-'kal-ə-rik\ adj (1950) : free from or very low in calories

non·can·di·date \(')nän-'kan-d(ə-),dāt, -(d)əd-ət\ n (1944) : one who is not a candidate; esp : one who has declared himself not a candidate for a particular political office — **non·can·di·da·cy** \-(d)ə-sē\ n

¹**nonce** \'nän(t)s\ n [ME nanes, alter. (fr. incorrect division of then anes in such phrases as to then anes for the one purpose) of anes one purpose, irreg. fr. an, on one — more at ONE] (13c) 1 : the one, particular, or present occasion, purpose, or use ⟨for the ~⟩ 2 : the time being

²**nonce** adj (1928) : occurring, used, or made only once or for a special occasion ⟨~ word⟩

non·cha·lance \,nän-shə-'län(t)s; 'nän-shə-,län(t)s, -lən(t)s\ n (1678) : the quality or state of being nonchalant

non·cha·lant \-'länt, -,länt, -lənt\ adj [F, fr. OF, fr. prp. of nonchaloir to disregard, fr. non- + chaloir to concern, fr. L calēre to be warm — more at LEE] (1734) : having an air of easy unconcern or indifference syn see COOL — **non·cha·lant·ly** adv

non·chro·mo·som·al \,nän-,krō-mə-'sō-məl\ adj (1960) 1 : not situated on a chromosome 2 : not involving chromosomes

non·com \'nän-,käm\ n (1747) : NONCOMMISSIONED OFFICER

non·com·bat·ant \,nän-kəm-'bat-ᵊnt also (')nän-'käm-bət-ənt\ n (1811) : one that does not engage in combat: as a : a member (as a chaplain) of the armed forces whose duties do not include fighting b : CIVILIAN — **noncombatant** adj

non·com·mis·sioned officer \,nän-kə-,mish-ənd-\ n (1703) : a subordinate officer (as a sergeant) in the army, air force, or marine corps appointed from among the enlisted men

non·com·mit·tal \,nän-kə-'mit-ᵊl\ adj (1829) 1 : giving no clear indication of attitude or feeling 2 : having no clear or distinctive character — **non·com·mit·tal·ly** \-ᵊl-ē\ adv

non–Com·mu·nist \,nän-'käm-yə-nəst\ adj (1920) : not Communist : being other than Communist

non com·pos men·tis \,nän-,käm-pə-'sment-əs, ,nōn-\ adj [L, lit., not having mastery of one's mind] (1607) : not of sound mind

non·con·cur \,nän-kən-'kər\ vi (1703) : to refuse or fail to concur — **non·con·cur·rence** \-'kər-ən(t)s, -'kə-rən(t)s\ n

non·con·duc·tor \,nän-kən-'dək-tər\ n (1759) : a substance that conducts heat, electricity, or sound only in very small degree

non·con·form \-'fȯ(ə)rm\ vi [back-formation fr. nonconformist] (1681) : to fail to conform — **non·con·form·er** n

non·con·for·mance \-'fȯr-mən(t)s\ n (1843) : failure to conform

non·con·form·ism \-'fȯr-,miz-əm\ n (1844) : NONCONFORMITY

non·con·form·ist \-'fȯr-məst\ n (1619) 1 often cap : a person who does not conform to an established church; esp : one who does not conform to the Church of England 2 : a person who does not conform to a generally accepted pattern of thought or action — **nonconformist** adj, often cap

non·con·for·mi·ty \-'fȯr-mət-ē\ n (1618) 1 a : failure or refusal to conform to an established church b often cap : the movement or principles of English Protestant dissent c often cap : the body of English Nonconformists 2 : refusal to conform to an established or conventional creed, rule, or practice 3 : absence of agreement or correspondence

non·co·op·er·a·tion \,nän-kō-,äp-ə-'rā-shən\ n (1795) : failure or refusal to cooperate; specif : refusal through civil disobedience of a people to cooperate with the government of a country — **non·co·op·er·a·tion·ist** \-sh(ə-)nəst\ n — **non·co·op·er·a·tor** \-'äp-ə-,rāt-ər\ n

non·co·op·er·a·tive \-'äp-(ə-)rət-iv, -ə-,rāt-\ adj (1922) : of, relating to, or characterized by noncooperation

non·cred·it \(')nän-'kred-ət\ adj (1965) : not offering credit toward a degree ⟨~ courses⟩

non·cross·over \(')nän-'krȯ-sō-vər\ adj (1919) : having or being chromosomes that have not participated in genetic crossing-over ⟨~ offspring⟩

non·dairy \'nän-'de(ə)r-ē\ adj (1968) : containing no milk or milk products ⟨~ whipped topping⟩

non·de·duct·ible \,nän-di-'dək-tə-bəl\ adj (1943) : not deductible; esp : not deductible for income tax purposes — **non·de·duct·ibil·i·ty** \-,dək-tə-'bil-ət-ē\ n

non·de·fense \,nän-di-'fen(t)s\ adj (1961) : not used or intended for or associated with the military ⟨~ spending⟩

non·de·script \,nän-di-'skript\ adj [non- + L descriptus, pp. of describere to describe] (ca. 1806) 1 : belonging or appearing to belong to no

\ə\ abut \ᵊ\ kitten, F table \ər\ further \a\ ash \ā\ ace \ä\ cot, cart
\au̇\ out \ch\ chin \e\ bet \ē\ easy \g\ go \i\ hit \ī\ ice \j\ job
\ŋ\ sing \ō\ go \ȯ\ law \ȯi\ boy \th\ thin \th̲\ the \ü\ loot \ů\ foot
\y\ yet \zh\ vision \ə, k, ⁿ, œ, œ̄, ü, œ̄, ᵞ\ see Guide to Pronunciation

particular class or kind : not easily described **2 :** lacking distinctive or interesting qualities : DULL, DRAB — **nondescript** *n*

non·de·struc·tive \-ˈstrək-tiv\ *adj* (1926) **:** not destructive; *specif* **:** not causing destruction of material being investigated or treated ⟨~ testing of metal⟩ — **non·de·struc·tive·ly** *adv* — **non·de·struc·tive·ness** *n*

non·dia·paus·ing \ˌnän-ˌdī-ə-ˈpȯ-ziŋ\ *adj* (1963) **1 :** not having a diapause **2 :** not being in a state of diapause

non·di·rec·tive \ˌnän-də-ˈrek-tiv, -(ˌ)dī-\ *adj* (1931) **:** of, relating to, or being psychotherapy, counseling, or interviewing in which the counselor refrains from interpretation or explanation but encourages the client (as by repeating phrases) to express himself freely

non·dis·junc·tion \ˌnän-dis-ˈjəŋ(k)-shən\ *n* [ISV] (1913) **:** failure of two chromosomes to separate subsequent to metaphase in meiosis or mitosis so that one daughter cell has both and the other neither of the chromosomes — **non·dis·junc·tion·al** \-shnəl, -shən-ᵊl\ *adj*

non·dis·tinc·tive \-ˈtiŋ(k)-tiv\ *adj, of a speech sound* (1916) **:** having no signaling value

non·di·vid·ing \ˌnän-də-ˈvīd-iŋ\ *adj* (1945) **:** not undergoing cell division

non·dor·mant \(ˈ)nän-ˈdȯr-mənt\ *adj* (1940) **1 :** being in such a condition that germination is possible ⟨~ seeds⟩ **2 :** being in active vegetative growth ⟨~ plants⟩

non·drink·er \-ˈdriŋ-kər\ *n* (ca. 1909) **:** one who abstains from alcoholic beverages — **non·drink·ing** \-kiŋ\ *adj*

non·dry·ing oil \ˌnän-ˌdrī-iŋ-\ *n* (1905) **:** a highly saturated oil (as olive oil) that is unable to solidify when exposed in a thin film to air

[1]**none** \ˈnən\ *pron, sing or pl in constr* [ME, fr. OE *nān,* fr. *ne* not + *ān* one — more at NO, ONE] (bef. 12c) **1 :** not any **2 :** not one : NOBODY **3 :** not any such thing or person **4 :** no part : NOTHING

[2]**none** *adj, archaic* (bef. 12c) **:** not any : NO

[3]**none** *adv* (1651) **1 :** by no means : not at all ⟨~ too soon to begin⟩ **2 :** in no way : to no extent ⟨~ the worse for wear⟩

[4]**none** \ˈnōn\ *n, often cap* [LL *nona,* fr. L, 9th hour of the day from sunrise — more at NOON] (1845) **:** the fifth of the canonical hours

non·eco·nom·ic \ˌnän-ˌek-ə-ˈnäm-ik, -ˌē-kə-\ *adj* (1920) **:** not economic; *esp* **:** having no economic importance or implication

non·elec·tro·lyte \ˌnän-ə-ˈlek-trə-ˌlīt\ *n* (1891) **:** a substance (as sugar or benzene) that is not appreciably ionized

non·en·ti·ty \nä-ˈnen(t)-ət-ē\ *n* (1600) **1 :** something that does not exist or exists only in the imagination **2 :** NONEXISTENCE **3 :** one of no consequence or significance

nones \ˈnōnz\ *n pl but sing or pl in constr* [ME *nonys,* fr. L *nonae,* fr. fem. pl. of *nonus* ninth] (14c) **1 :** the ninth day before the ides according to ancient Roman reckoning **2** *often cap* **:** [4]NONE

none·such \ˈnən-ˌsəch\ *n* (1590) **:** a person or thing without an equal — **nonesuch** *adj*

no·net \nō-ˈnet\ *n* [It *nonetto,* fr. *nono* ninth (fr. L *nonus*) + *-etto* (as in *duetto* duet) — more at NOON] (1865) **:** a combination of nine instruments or voices; *also* **:** a musical composition for such a combination

none·the·less \ˌnən-thə-ˈles\ *adv* (1847) **:** NEVERTHELESS

non–eu·clid·e·an \ˌnän-yü-ˈklid-ē-ən\ *adj, often cap E* (ca. 1864) **:** not assuming or in accordance with all the postulates of Euclid's *Elements* ⟨~ geometry⟩

non·event \ˈnän-i-ˌvent, ˌnän-i-ˈ\ *n* (1962) **1 :** an expected event that fails to take place or to satisfy expectations **2 :** a highly publicized event of little intrinsic interest

non·ex·is·tence \ˌnän-ig-ˈzis-tən(t)s\ *n* (1646) **:** absence of existence **:** the negation of being — **non·ex·is·tent** \-tənt\ *adj*

non·fat \ˈnän-ˈfat\ *adj* (1926) **:** lacking fat solids **:** having fat solids removed ⟨~ milk⟩

non·fea·sance \(ˈ)nän-ˈfēz-ᵊn(t)s\ *n* [*non-* + obs. E *feasance* (doing, execution)] (1596) **:** failure to act; *esp* **:** failure to do what ought to be done

non·fer·rous \(ˈ)nän-ˈfer-əs\ *adj* (1887) **1 :** not containing, including, or relating to iron **2 :** of or relating to metals other than iron

non·fic·tion \ˈnän-ˈfik-shən\ *n* (1909) **:** literature that is not fictional — **non·fic·tion·al** \(ˈ)nän-ˈfik-shnəl, -shən-ᵊl\ *adj*

non·fig·u·ra·tive \(ˈ)nän-ˈfig-(y)ə-rət-iv\ *adj* (1927) **:** NONOBJECTIVE 2

non·flam·ma·ble \-ˈflam-ə-bəl\ *adj* (1915) **:** not flammable; *specif* **:** not easily ignited and not burning rapidly if ignited — **non·flam·ma·bil·i·ty** \ˌnän-ˌflam-ə-ˈbil-ət-ē\ *n*

non·flow·er·ing \-ˈflau̇-(ə-)riŋ\ *adj* (ca. 1934) **:** producing no flowers; *specif* **:** lacking a flowering stage in the life cycle

non·flu·en·cy \-ˈflü-ən-sē\ *n, pl* **-cies** (ca. 1944) **1 :** lack of fluency **2 :** an instance of nonfluency

non·gono·coc·cal \ˌnän-ˌgän-ə-ˈkäk-əl\ *adj* (1961) **:** not caused by the gonococcus ⟨~ urethritis⟩

non gra·ta \ˌnän-ˈgrat-ə, -ˈgrät-\ *adj* [*persona non grata*] (1925) **:** not approved : UNWELCOME

non·green \ˈnän-ˈgrēn\ *adj* (1897) **:** not green; *specif* **:** containing no chlorophyll ⟨~ saprophytes⟩

non·he·ro \ˈnän-ˈhē-(ˌ)rō, -ˈhi(ə)r-(ˌ)ō\ *n* (1940) **:** ANTI-HERO

non·his·tone \(ˈ)nän-ˈhis-ˌtōn\ *adj* (ca. 1965) **:** rich in aromatic amino acids and esp. tryptophan ⟨~ proteins⟩

non·iden·ti·cal \ˌnän-(ˌ)ī-ˈdent-i-kəl, ˌnän-ə-ˈdent-\ *adj* (1890) **1 :** DIFFERENT **2 :** FRATERNAL 2

no·nil·lion \nō-ˈnil-yən\ *n, often attrib* [F, fr. L *nonus* ninth + F *-illion* (as in *million*) — more at NOON] (1690) — see NUMBER table

non·in·duc·tive \ˌnän-in-ˈdək-tiv\ *adj* (1896) **:** not inductive; *esp* **:** having negligible inductance

non·in·ter·ven·tion \ˌnän-ˌint-ər-ˈven-chən\ *n* (1831) **:** the state or policy of not intervening ⟨~ in the affairs of other countries⟩ — **non·in·ter·ven·tion·ist** \-ˈvench-(ə-)nəst\ *n or adj*

non·in·va·sive \ˌnän-in-ˈvā-siv, -ziv\ *adj* (ca. 1972) **:** not involving penetration (as by surgery or hypodermic needle) of the skin of the intact organism ⟨~ diagnostic techniques⟩

non·in·volve·ment \ˌnän-in-ˈvälv-mənt, -ˈvȯlv- *also* -ˈväv-, -ˈvȯv-\ *n* (1936) **:** absence of involvement or emotional attachment — **non·in·volved** \-ˈvä(l)vd, -ˈvȯ(l)vd\ *adj*

non·ion·ic \ˌnän-(ˌ)ī-ˈän-ik\ *adj* (1929) **:** not ionic; *esp* **:** not dependent on a surface-active anion for effect ⟨~ surfactants⟩

nonionic detergent *n* (1948) **:** a synthetic detergent that produces electrically neutral colloidal particles in solution

non·join·der \(ˈ)nän-ˈjȯin-dər\ *n* (1833) **:** failure to include a necessary party to a suit at law

non·judg·men·tal \ˌnän-ˌjəj-ˈment-ᵊl\ *adj* (1952) **:** avoiding judgments based on one's personal and esp. moral standards

non·jur·ing \(ˈ)nän-ˈju̇(ə)r-iŋ\ *adj* [*non-* + L *jurare* to swear — more at JURY] (1691) **:** not swearing allegiance — used esp. of a member of a party in Great Britain that would not swear allegiance to William and Mary or to their successors

non·ju·ror \(ˈ)nän-ˈju̇r-ər, -ˈju̇(ə)r-ˌȯ(ə)r\ *n* (1691) **:** a person refusing to take an oath esp. of allegiance, supremacy, or abjuration; *specif* **:** one of the beneficed clergy in England and Scotland refusing to take an oath of allegiance to William and Mary or to their successors after the revolution of 1688

non·lin·guis·tic \ˌnän-liŋ-ˈgwis-tik\ *adj* (1927) **:** not consisting of or relating to language

non·lit·er·ate \(ˈ)nän-ˈlit-ə-rət, -ˈli-trət\ *adj* (1946) **:** having no written language — **nonliterate** *n*

non·match·ing \-ˈmach-iŋ\ *adj* (ca. 1961) **1 :** not matching **2 :** not requiring a matching contribution ⟨~ grants⟩

non·met·al \(ˈ)nän-ˈmet-ᵊl\ *n* (ca. 1864) **:** a chemical element (as boron, carbon, or nitrogen) that lacks typical metallic properties and is able to form anions, acidic oxides and acids, and stable compounds with hydrogen

non·me·tal·lic \ˌnän-mə-ˈtal-ik\ *adj* (1815) **1 :** not metallic **2 :** of, relating to, or being a nonmetal

non·mor·al \-ˈmȯr-əl, -ˈmär-\ *adj* (1866) **:** not falling into or existing in the sphere of morals or ethics

non·neg·a·tive \ˈnän-ˈneg-ət-iv\ *adj* (1885) **:** not negative: **a :** being either positive or zero **b :** taking on nonnegative values ⟨a ~ function⟩

non·nu·cle·ar \(ˈ)nän-ˈn(y)ü-klē-ər, ÷-kyə-lər\ *adj* (1953) **1 :** not producing or involving a nuclear explosion ⟨a ~ bomb⟩ **2 :** not operated by or involving atomic energy ⟨a ~ propulsion system⟩ **3 :** not having the atom bomb ⟨a ~ country⟩ **4 :** not involving the use of atom bombs ⟨a ~ war⟩

no–no \ˈnō-ˌnō\ *n, pl* **no–no's** *or* **no–nos** (1942) **:** something unacceptable or forbidden

non·ob·jec·tive \ˌnän-əb-ˈjek-tiv\ *adj* (1905) **1 :** not objective **2 :** representing or intended to represent no natural or actual object, figure, or scene ⟨~ art⟩ — **non·ob·jec·tiv·ism** \-tiv-ˌiz-əm\ *n* — **non·ob·jec·tiv·ist** \-əst\ *n* — **non·ob·jec·tiv·i·ty** \ˌnän-ˌäb-ˌjek-ˈtiv-ət-ē, ˌnän-əb-\ *n*

non ob·stan·te \ˌnän-əb-ˈstant-ē, ˌnōn-\ *prep* [L] (15c) **:** NOTWITHSTANDING

non–oil \ˈnän-ˈȯi(ə)l\ *adj* (1979) **:** being a net importer of petroleum or petroleum products ⟨~ nations⟩

no–nonsense *adj* (1928) **:** tolerating no nonsense : SERIOUS, BUSINESSLIKE

non·or·gas·mic \ˌnän-ȯr-ˈgaz-mik\ *adj* (1973) **:** not capable of experiencing orgasm

non·para·met·ric \ˌnän-ˌpar-ə-ˈme-trik\ *adj* (1942) **:** not involving the estimation of parameters of a statistical function ⟨~ statistical tests⟩

[1]**non·pa·reil** \ˌnän-pə-ˈrel\ *adj* [MF, fr. *non-* + *pareil* equal, fr. (assumed) VL *pariculus,* fr. L *par* equal] (15c) **:** having no equal

[2]**nonpareil** *n* (1593) **1 :** an individual of unequaled excellence : PARAGON **2 a :** a small flat disk of chocolate covered with white sugar pellets **b :** small sugar pellets of various colors

non·par·ti·san \(ˈ)nän-ˈpärt-ə-zən, -sən\ *adj* (1885) **:** not partisan; *esp* **:** free from party affiliation, bias, or designation ⟨~ ballot⟩ ⟨a ~ board⟩ — **non·par·ti·san·ship** \-ˌship\ *n*

non·pas·ser·ine \(ˈ)nän-ˈpas-ə-ˌrīn\ *adj* (ca. 1909) **:** not passerine; *esp* **:** of or relating to an order (Coraciiformes) of arboreal birds including the rollers, kingfishers, and hornbills

non·patho·gen·ic \ˌnän-ˌpath-ə-ˈjen-ik\ *adj* (1884) **:** not capable of inducing disease — compare AVIRULENT

non·peak \(ˈ)nän-ˈpēk\ *adj* (ca. 1914) **:** OFF-PEAK

non·per·sis·tent \ˌnän-pər-ˈsis-tənt, -ˈzis-\ *adj* (1900) **:** not persistent: as **a :** decomposed rapidly by environmental action ⟨~ insecticides⟩ **b :** capable of being transmitted by a vector for only a relatively short time ⟨~ viruses⟩

non·per·son \ˈnän-ˈpərs-ᵊn, -ˌpərs-\ *n* (ca. 1909) **:** a person who is regarded as nonexistent: as **a :** UNPERSON **b :** one having no social or legal status

non pla·cet \ˈnän-ˈplā-sət, ˈnōn-\ *n* [L, it does not please] (1589) **:** a negative vote

[1]**non·plus** \ˈnän-ˈpləs\ *n* [L *non plus* no more] (1582) **:** a state of bafflement or perplexity : QUANDARY

[2]**nonplus** *vt* **-plussed** *also* **-plused** \-ˈpləst\; **-plus·sing** *also* **-plus·ing** (1591) **:** to cause to be at a loss as to what to say, think, or do : PERPLEX ***syn*** see PUZZLE

non·po·lar \(ˈ)nän-ˈpō-lər\ *adj* (1892) **:** not polar; *esp* **:** not having or requiring the presence of electrical poles ⟨a ~ solvent⟩

non pos·su·mus \ˈnän-ˈpäs-ə-məs, ˈnōn-\ *n* [L, we cannot] (1883) **:** a statement expressing inability to do something

non·pre·scrip·tion \ˌnän-pri-ˈskrip-shən\ *adj* (1958) **:** capable of being bought without a doctor's prescription ⟨~ drugs⟩

non·pro·duc·tive \ˌnän-prə-ˈdək-tiv\ *adj* (1901) **:** not productive: as **a :** failing to produce or yield : UNPRODUCTIVE ⟨a ~ oil well⟩ **b :** not directly concerned with production ⟨the ~ labor of clerks and inspectors⟩ **c** *of a cough* **:** DRY — **non·pro·duc·tive·ness** *n*

non·prof·it \ˈnän-ˈpräf-ət\ *adj* (1903) **:** not conducted or maintained for the purpose of making a profit

non·pro·lif·er·a·tion \ˌnän-prə-ˌlif-ə-ˈrā-shən\ *adj* (1964) **:** providing for the stoppage of proliferation (as of nuclear arms) ⟨~ treaty⟩ — **nonproliferation** *n*

non·pros \ˈnän-ˈpräs\ *vt* **non·prossed; non·pros·sing** [*non prosequitur*] (1755) **:** to enter a non prosequitur against

non pro·se·qui·tur \ˌnän-prə-ˈsek-wət-ər, ˌnōn-\ *n* [LL, he does not prosecute] (1768) **:** a judgment entered against the plaintiff in a suit in which he does not appear to prosecute

non·pro·tein \ˈnän-ˈprō-ˌtēn, -ˈprōt-ē-ən\ *adj* (1926) **:** not being or derived from protein ⟨the ~ part of an enzyme⟩ ⟨~ nitrogen⟩

non·read·er \ˈnän-ˈrēd-ər\ *n* (1924) **:** one who does not or cannot read; *esp* **:** a child who is very slow in learning to read — **non·read·ing** \-iŋ\ *adj*

non·re·com·bi·nant \ˌnän-(ˌ)rē-ˈkäm-bə-nənt\ *adj* (1962) **:** not exhibiting the results of genetic recombination — **nonrecombinant** *n*

non·re·cur·rent \ˌnän-ri-ˈkər-ənt, -ˈkə-rənt\ *adj* (ca. 1925) **:** not recurring

non·re·cur·ring \-ˈkər-iŋ, -ˈkə-riŋ\ *adj* (1967) **:** NONRECURRENT; *specif* **:** unlikely to happen again — used of financial transactions that affect a profit and loss statement abnormally ⟨sale of the factory, a ~ profit, inflated the company's earnings⟩
non·re·fund·able \ˌnän-ri-ˈfən-də-bəl\ *adj* (1963) **:** not subject to refunding ⟨a ~ bond⟩
non·rel·a·tiv·is·tic \ˌnän-ˌrel-ət-iv-ˈis-tik\ *adj* (1930) **1 :** not based on or involving the theory of relativity ⟨~ equations⟩ ⟨~ kinematics⟩ **2 a :** moving at less than a relativistic velocity **b :** of or relating to a body moving at such a velocity — **non·rel·a·tiv·is·ti·cal·ly** \-ˈis-ti-k(ə-)lē\ *adv*
non·rep·re·sen·ta·tion·al \ˌnän-ˌrep-ri-ˌzen-ˈtā-shnəl, -zən-, -shən-ᵊl\ *adj* (1923) **:** NONOBJECTIVE 2 — **non·rep·re·sen·ta·tion·al·ism** \-ˌiz-əm\ *n*
non·res·i·dence \(ˈ)nän-ˈrez-əd-ən(t)s, -ˈrez-dən(t)s, -ˈrez-ə-ˌden(t)s\ *n* (1585) **:** the state or fact of being nonresident
non·res·i·den·cy \-ˈrez-əd-ən-sē, -ˈrez-dən-, -ˈrez-ə-ˌden-\ *n* (1545) **:** NONRESIDENCE
non·res·i·dent \-ˈrez-əd-ənt, -ˈrez-dənt, -ˈrez-ə-ˌdent\ *adj* (1540) **:** not residing in a particular place — **nonresident** *n*
non·re·sis·tance \ˌnän-ri-ˈzis-tən(t)s\ *n* (15c) **:** the principles or practice of passive submission to constituted authority even when unjust or oppressive; *also* **:** the principle or practice of not resisting violence by force
non·re·sis·tant \-tənt\ *adj* (1702) **:** not resistant; *specif* **:** susceptible to the effects of a deleterious agent (as an insecticide, a pathogen, or an extreme environmental condition) — **nonresistant** *n*
non·re·stric·tive \ˌnän-ri-ˈstrik-tiv\ *adj* (1916) **:** not restrictive; *specif* **:** not limiting the reference of a modified word or phrase
nonrestrictive clause *n* (1916) **:** a descriptive clause that is not essential to the definiteness of the meaning of the word it modifies (as *who is retired* in "my father, who is retired, does volunteer work")
non·re·turn·able \ˌnän-ri-ˈtər-nə-bəl\ *adj* (1903) **:** not returnable; *specif* **:** not returnable to a dealer in exchange for a deposit ⟨~ bottles⟩ — **nonreturnable** *n*
non·rig·id \(ˈ)nän-ˈrij-əd\ *adj* (1909) **:** not rigid; *esp* **:** maintaining form by pressure of contained gas ⟨a ~ airship⟩ — **non·ri·gid·i·ty** \ˌnän-rə-ˈjid-ət-ē\ *n*
non·sched·uled \(ˈ)nän-ˈskej-(ˌ)ü(ə)ld, -ˈskej-əld\ *adj* (1947) **:** licensed to carry passengers or freight by air without a regular schedule ⟨~ airlines⟩
[1]**non·sci·ence** \(ˈ)nän-ˈsī-ən(t)s\ *n* (1855) **:** one (as a discipline) that is not a science
[2]**nonscience** *adj* (1944) **:** of or relating to fields other than science
non·se·cre·tor \ˌnän(t)-si-ˈkrēt-ər\ *n* (1944) **:** an individual of blood group A, B, or AB who does not secrete the antigens characteristic of these blood groups in bodily fluids (as saliva)
non·sec·tar·i·an \ˌnän-(ˌ)sek-ˈter-ē-ən\ *adj* (1831) **:** not having a sectarian character **:** not affiliated with or restricted to a particular religious group
non·self \ˈnän-ˈself, *Southern also* -ˈsef\ *n* (1963) **:** material that is foreign to the body of an organism
[1]**non·sense** \ˈnän-ˌsen(t)s, ˈnän(t)-sən(t)s\ *n* (1614) **1 a :** words or language having no meaning or conveying no intelligible ideas **b (1) :** language, conduct, or an idea that is absurd or contrary to good sense **(2) :** an instance of absurd action **2 a :** things of no importance or value **:** TRIFLES **b :** affected or impudent conduct ⟨took no ~ from subordinates⟩ **3 :** genetic information consisting of one or more codons that do not code for any amino acid and usu. cause termination of the molecular chain in protein synthesis — compare MISSENSE — **non·sen·si·cal** \(ˈ)nän-ˈsen(t)-si-kəl\ *adj* — **non·sen·si·cal·ly** \-k(ə-)lē\ *adv* — **non·sen·si·cal·ness** \-kəl-nəs\ *n*
[2]**nonsense** *adj* (1778) **1 :** consisting of an arbitrary grouping of speech sounds or symbols ⟨\ˈshrög-ˌthī-əmpth\ is a ~ word⟩ ⟨a ~ syllable⟩ **2 :** consisting of one or more codons that are genetic nonsense
nonsense verse *n* (1799) **:** humorous or whimsical verse that features unique characters and actions and often contains evocative but meaningless nonce words
non se·qui·tur \(ˈ)nän-ˈsek-wət-ər *also* -ˌtü(ə)r\ *n* [L, it does not follow] (1540) **1 :** an inference that does not follow from the premises; *specif* **:** a fallacy resulting from a simple conversion of a universal affirmative proposition or from the transposition of a condition and its consequent **2 :** a statement (as a response) that does not follow logically from anything previously said
non·sig·nif·i·cant \ˌnän(t)-sig-ˈnif-i-kənt\ *adj* (1902) **:** not significant: as **a :** INSIGNIFICANT **b :** MEANINGLESS **c :** having or yielding a value lying within limits between which variation is attributed to chance ⟨a ~ statistical test⟩ — **non·sig·nif·i·cant·ly** *adv*
non·sked \ˈnän-ˈsked\ *n* [by shortening & alter. fr. *nonscheduled*] (1946) **:** a nonscheduled airline or transport plane
non·skid \-ˈskid\ *adj* (1904) **:** designed or equipped to prevent skidding
non·slip \-ˈslip\ *adj* (1903) **:** designed to reduce or prevent slipping
non·so·cial \(ˈ)nän-ˈsō-shəl\ *adj* (1902) **:** not socially oriented **:** lacking a social component
non·sport·ing \-ˈspōrt-iŋ, -ˈspȯrt-\ *adj* (1852) **:** lacking the qualities characteristic of a hunting dog
non·stan·dard \-ˈstan-dərd\ *adj* (1923) **1 :** not standard **2 :** not conforming in pronunciation, grammatical construction, idiom, or word choice to the usage generally characteristic of educated native speakers of a language — compare SUBSTANDARD
non·start·er \-ˈstärt-ər\ *n* (1902) **1 :** one that does not start **2 :** someone or something that is not productive or effective ⟨his son has been, in politics a ~ —Anthony Lejeune⟩
non·ste·roi·dal \ˌnän-stə-ˈrȯid-ᵊl\ *also* **non·ste·roid** \(ˈ)nän-ˈsti(ə)r-ˌȯid *also* -ˈste(ə)r-\ *adj* (1964) **:** of, relating to, or being a compound and esp. a drug that is not a steroid — **nonsteroid** *n*
non·stick \ˈnän-ˈstik\ *adj* [[3]*stick*] (1958) **:** allowing of easy removal of cooked food particles ⟨a ~ coating in a frying pan⟩
non·stop \ˈnän-ˈstäp\ *adj* (1902) **:** done, made, or held without a stop **:** not easing or letting up — **nonstop** *adv*
non·such \ˈnən-ˌsəch *also* ˈnän-\ *var of* NONESUCH
non·suit \ˈnän-ˈsüt\ *n* [ME, fr. AF *nounsuyte*, fr. *noun-* non- + OF *siute* following, pursuit — more at SUIT] (14c) **:** a judgment against a plaintiff for his failure to prosecute his case or inability to establish a prima facie case — **nonsuit** *vt*
non·sup·port \ˌnän(t)-sə-ˈpō(ə)rt, -ˈpȯ(ə)rt\ *n* (1909) **:** failure to support; *specif* **:** failure (as of a parent) to honor a statutory or contractual obligation to provide maintenance
non·syl·lab·ic \ˌnän(t)-sə-ˈlab-ik\ *adj* (ca. 1909) **:** not constituting a syllable or the nucleus of a syllable ⟨\n\ is syllabic in \ˈbät-ᵊn-ē\ *botany*, ~ in \ˈbät-nē\⟩ ⟨the second vowel of a falling diphthong is ~ (as \i\ in \ȯi\)⟩
non·sys·tem \ˈnän-ˈsis-təm\ *n* (1964) **:** a system that lacks effective organization
non·tar·get \-ˈtär-gət\ *adj* (1945) **:** not being the intended object of action by a particular agent ⟨effect of insecticides on ~ organisms⟩
non·ter·mi·nat·ing \(ˈ)nän-ˈtər-mə-ˌnāt-iŋ\ *adj* (ca. 1908) **:** not terminating or ending; *esp* **:** being a decimal for which there is no place to the right of the decimal point such that all places farther to the right contain the entry 0 ⟨1/3 gives the ~ decimal .33333 . . .⟩
non·ti·tle \ˈnän-ˈtīt-ᵊl\ *adj* (1968) **:** of, relating to, or being an athletic contest in which a title is not at stake
non·triv·i·al \(ˈ)nän-ˈtriv-ē-əl\ *adj* (1915) **1 :** not trivial **2 :** having the value of at least one variable or term not equal to zero ⟨~ solutions to linear equations⟩
non trop·po \(ˈ)nän-ˈtrō-(ˌ)pō, ˈnōn-\ *adv or adj* [It, lit., not too much] (ca. 1854) **:** without excess — used to qualify a direction in music
non–U \(ˈ)nän-ˈyü\ *adj* (1954) **:** not characteristic of the upper classes
non·union \(ˈ)nän-ˈyün-yən\ *adj* (1863) **1 :** not belonging to or connected with a trade union ⟨~ carpenters⟩ **2 :** not recognizing or favoring trade unions or their members **3 :** not produced or worked on by members of a trade union ⟨~ lettuce⟩
non·use \ˈnän-ˈyüs\ *n* (1542) **1 :** failure to use ⟨~ of available material⟩ **2 :** the fact or condition of not being used
non·us·er \-ˈyü-zər\ *n* (1650) **:** one who does not make use of something (as an available public facility or a harmful drug)
non·van·ish·ing \-ˈvan-ish-iŋ\ *adj* (1907) **:** not zero or becoming zero
non·vec·tor \(ˈ)nän-ˈvek-tər\ *n* (1956) **:** an organism (as an insect) that does not transmit a particular pathogen (as a virus)
non·ver·bal \-ˈvər-bəl\ *adj* (1924) **:** not verbal: as **a :** being other than verbal ⟨~ factors⟩ **b :** involving minimal use of language ⟨~ tests⟩ **c :** ranking low in verbal skill — **non·ver·bal·ly** \-bə-lē\ *adv*
non·vin·tage \-ˈvint-ij\ *adj* (1924) **:** undated and usu. blended to approximate a standard ⟨a ~ wine⟩
non·vi·o·lence \-ˈvī-ə-lən(t)s\ *n* (1920) **1 :** abstention from violence as a matter of principle; *also* **:** the principle of such abstention **2 a :** the quality or state of being nonviolent **:** avoidance of violence **b :** nonviolent demonstrations for the purpose of securing political ends ⟨studied the history and techniques of ~⟩
non·vi·o·lent \-lənt\ *adj* (1920) **:** abstaining or free from violence — **non·vi·o·lent·ly** *adv*
non·vol·a·tile \-ˈväl-ət-ᵊl\ *adj* (1866) **:** not volatile; *esp* **:** not volatilizing readily
non–West·ern \(ˈ)nän-ˈwes-tərn\ *adj* (1902) **1 :** not being part of the western tradition ⟨~ countries⟩ **2 :** of or relating to non-Western societies ⟨~ values⟩
non·white \-ˈhwīt, -ˈwīt\ *n* (1927) **:** a person whose features and esp. whose skin color are distinctively different from those of Caucasians of northwestern Europe; *esp* **:** one who has African ancestors of the black race — **nonwhite** *adj*
non·word \ˈnän-ˈwərd\ *n* (1961) **:** a word that has no meaning, is not known to exist, or is disapproved
non·woven \(ˈ)nän-ˈwō-vən\ *adj* (1945) **1 :** made of fibers held together by interlocking or bonding (as by chemical or thermal means) **:** not woven, knitted, or felted ⟨~ fabric⟩ **2 :** made of nonwoven fabric ⟨a ~ dress⟩ — **nonwoven** *n*
non·ze·ro \-ˈzē-(ˌ)rō, -ˈzi(ə)r-(ˌ)ō\ *adj* (1905) **:** being, having, or involving a value other than zero
[1]**noo·dle** \ˈnüd-ᵊl\ *n* [perh. alter. of *noddle*] (1753) **1 :** a stupid person **:** SIMPLETON **2 :** HEAD
[2]**noodle** *n* [G *nudel*] (1799) **:** a food paste made with egg and shaped typically in ribbon form
[3]**noodle** *vi* **noo·dled; noo·dling** \ˈnüd-liŋ, -ᵊl-iŋ\ [imit.] (1937) **:** to improvise on an instrument in an informal or desultory manner
nook \ˈnu̇k\ *n* [ME *noke, nok*] (14c) **1** *chiefly Scot* **:** a right-angled corner **2 a :** an interior angle formed by two meeting walls **:** RECESS **b :** a secluded or sheltered place or part ⟨searched every ~ and cranny⟩
nooky \ˈnu̇k-ē\ *n* [prob. fr. *nook* + *-y*, n. suffix forming diminutives] (1928) **1 :** SEXUAL INTERCOURSE — often considered vulgar **2 :** the female partner in sexual intercourse — often considered vulgar
noon \ˈnün\ *n* [ME, fr. OE *nōn* ninth hour from sunrise, fr. L *nona*, fr. fem. of *nonus* ninth; akin to L *novem* nine — more at NINE] (13c) **1 :** MIDDAY; *specif* **:** 12 o'clock at midday **2** *archaic* **:** MIDNIGHT — used chiefly in the phrase *noon of night* **3 :** the highest point
noon·day \-ˌdā\ *n* (1535) **:** MIDDAY
no one *pron* (bef. 12c) **:** no person **:** NOBODY
noon·ing \ˈnü-niŋ, -nən\ *n* (ca. 1652) **1** *chiefly dial* **:** a meal eaten at noon **2** *chiefly dial* **:** a period at noon for eating or resting
noon·tide \ˈnün-ˌtīd\ *n* (12c) **1 :** NOONTIME **2 :** the culminating point
noon·time \-ˌtīm\ *n* (14c) **:** the time of noon **:** MIDDAY
[1]**noose** \ˈnüs, *Brit also* ˈnüz\ *n* [ME, prob. fr. Prov *nous* knot, fr. L *nodus* — more at NET] (15c) **1 :** a loop with a running knot that binds closer the more it is drawn **2 :** something that snares like a noose
[2]**noose** *vt* **noosed; noos·ing** (1600) **1 :** to secure by a noose **2 :** to make a noose in or of
noo·sphere \ˈnō-ə-ˌsfi(ə)r\ *n* [ISV *noo-* mind (fr. Gk *noos, nous*) + *sphere*] (1945) **:** the sphere of human consciousness and mental activity esp. in regard to its influence on the biosphere and in relation to evolution
Noot·ka \ˈnu̇t-kə\ *n, pl* **Nootka** *or* **Nootkas** (1841) **1 :** a member of a Wakashan people of Vancouver Island and the Cape Flattery region in northwestern Washington **2 :** the language of the Nootka people

no·pal \nō-ˈpäl, -ˈpal; ˈnō-pəl\ *n* [Sp, fr. Nahuatl *nopalli*] (1730) **:** any of a genus (*Nopalea*) of cacti that differ from the prickly pears in having erect petals and scarlet flowers with the stamens much longer than the petals; *broadly* **:** PRICKLY PEAR

no–par *or* **no–par–val·ue** *adj* (1922) **:** having no nominal value ⟨~ stocks⟩

nope \ˈnōp, *or with glottal stop instead of* p\ *adv* [by alter.] (1888) **:** NO

1**nor** \nər, (ˈ)nȯ(ə)r, *Southern also* (ˈ)när\ *conj* [ME, contr. of *nother* neither, nor, fr. *nother,* pron. & adj., neither — more at NEITHER] (14c) **1** — used as a function word to introduce the second or last member or the second and each following member of a series of items each of which is negated ⟨neither here ~ there⟩ ⟨not done by you ~ me ~ anyone⟩ **2** — used as a function word to introduce and negate a following clause or phrase **3** *chiefly Brit* **:** NEITHER

2**nor** \nər\ *conj* [ME, perh. fr. 1*nor*] *dial* (15c) **:** THAN

NOR \ˈnȯ(ə)r\ *n* [*not OR*] (1957) **:** a computer logic circuit that produces an output that is the inverse of that of an OR circuit

nor·adren·a·line *also* **nor·adren·a·lin** \ˌnȯr-ə-ˈdren-ᵊl-ən\ *n* [*nor*mal + *adrenaline*] (1932) **:** NOREPINEPHRINE

nor·ad·ren·er·gic \ˌnȯr-ˌad-rə-ˈnər-jik\ *adj* [*noradren*aline + *-ergic*] (1963) **:** liberating, activated by, or involving norepinephrine in the transmission of nerve impulses ⟨~ nerve endings⟩ ⟨~ nerve fibers⟩

1**Nor·dic** \ˈnȯrd-ik\ *adj* [F *nordique,* fr. *nord* north, fr. OE *north*] (1898) **1 :** of or relating to the Germanic peoples of northern Europe and esp. of Scandinavia **2 :** of or relating to a physical type characterized by tall stature, long head, light skin and hair, and blue eyes **3 :** of or relating to competitive ski events consisting of ski jumping and cross-country racing — compare ALPINE

2**Nordic** *n* (1901) **1 :** a native of northern Europe **2 :** a person of Nordic physical type or of a hypothetical Nordic division of the Caucasian race **3 :** a member of the peoples of Scandinavia

nor·epi·neph·rine \ˈnȯ(ə)r-ˌep-ə-ˈnef-rən\ *n* [*nor*mal + *epinephrine*] (1945) **:** a catecholamine $C_8H_{11}NO_3$ that is the chemical means of transmission across synapses in postganglionic neurons of the sympathetic nervous system and in some parts of the central nervous system, is a vasopressor hormone of the adrenal medulla, and is a precursor of epinephrine in its major biosynthetic pathway

Nor·folk jacket \ˌnȯr-fək-, -ˌfȯk-\ *n* [*Norfolk,* England] (1866) **:** a loose-fitting belted single-breasted jacket with box pleats

Norfolk terrier *n* (1964) **:** a dog of an English breed that resembles the Norwich terrier but has folded-over ears

no·ria \ˈnōr-ē-ə, ˈnȯr-\ *n* [Sp, fr. Ar *nā'ūrah*] (1792) **:** an undershot waterwheel of the bucket type used esp. in primitive irrigation systems

nor·land \ˈnȯ(ə)r-lənd\ *n, chiefly dial* (1578) **:** NORTHLAND

norm \ˈnȯ(ə)rm\ *n* [L *norma,* lit., carpenter's square] (1821) **1 :** an authoritative standard **:** MODEL **2 :** a principle of right action binding upon the members of a group and serving to guide, control or regulate proper and acceptable behavior **3 :** AVERAGE: as **a :** a set standard of development or achievemnt usu. derived from the average or median achievement of a large group **b :** a pattern or trait taken to be typical in the behavior of a social group **4 a :** a real-valued nonnegative function defined on a vector space and satisfying the conditions that the function is zero if and only if the vector is zero, the function of the product of a scalar and a vector is equal to the product of the absolute value of the scalar and the function of the vector, and the function of the sum of two vectors is less than or equal to the sum of the functions of the two vectors; *specif* **:** the square root of the sum of the squares of the absolute values of the elements of a matrix or of the components of a vector **b :** the greatest distance between two successive points of a set of points that partition an interval into smaller intervals ***syn*** see AVERAGE

1**nor·mal** \ˈnȯr-məl\ *adj* [L *normalis,* fr. *norma*] (1696) **1 :** PERPENDICULAR; *esp* **:** perpendicular to a tangent at a point of tangency **2 a :** according with, constituting, or not deviating from a norm, rule, or principle **b :** conforming to a type, standard, or regular pattern **3 :** occurring naturally ⟨~ immunity⟩ **4 a :** of, relating to, or characterized by average intelligence or development **b :** free from mental disorder **:** SANE **5 a** *of a solution* **:** having a concentration of one gram equivalent of solute per liter **b :** containing neither basic hydroxyl nor acid hydrogen ⟨~ silver phosphate⟩ **c :** not associated ⟨~ molecules⟩ **d :** having a straight-chain structure ⟨~ pentane⟩ ⟨~ butyl alcohol⟩ **6** *of a subgroup* **:** having the property that every coset produced by operating on the left by a given element is equal to the coset produced by operating on the right by the same element **7 :** relating to, involving, or being a normal curve or normal distribution ⟨~ approximation to the binomial distribution⟩ **8** *of a matrix* **:** having the property of commutativity under multiplication by the transpose of the matrix each of whose elements is a conjugate complex number with respect to the corresponding element of the given matrix ***syn*** see REGULAR — **nor·mal·i·ty** \nȯr-ˈmal-ət-ē\ *n* — **nor·mal·ly** \ˈnȯr-mə-lē\ *adv*

2**normal** *n* (ca. 1727) **1 a :** a normal line **b :** the portion of a normal line to a plane curve between the curve and the x-axis **2 :** one that is normal **3 :** a form or state regarded as the norm **:** STANDARD

normal curve *n* (1893) **:** the symmetrical bell-shaped curve of a normal distribution

nor·mal·cy \ˈnȯr-məl-sē\ *n* (1857) **:** the state or fact of being normal

normal distribution *n* (1897) **:** a probability density function that approximates the distribution of many random variables (as the proportion of outcomes of a particular sort in a large number of independent repetitions of an experiment in which the probabilities remain constant from trial to trial) and that has the form

$$f(x) = \frac{1}{\sigma\sqrt{2\pi}}\, e^{-\frac{1}{2}\left(\frac{x-\mu}{\sigma}\right)^2}$$

where μ is the mean and σ is the standard deviation — compare NORMAL CURVE

nor·mal·ize \ˈnȯr-mə-ˌlīz\ *vt* **-ized; -iz·ing** (1865) **1 :** to make conform to or reduce to a norm or standard **2 :** to make normal (as by a transformation of variables) **3 :** to bring or restore (as relations between countries) to a normal condition — **nor·mal·iz·able** \-ˌlī-zə-bəl\ *adj* — **nor·mal·iza·tion** \ˌnȯr-mə-lə-ˈzā-shən\ *n*

nor·mal·iz·er \ˈnȯr-mə-ˌlī-zər\ *n* (1926) **1 :** one that normalizes **2 a :** a subgroup consisting of those elements of a group for which the group operation with regard to a given element is commutative **b :** the set of elements of a group for which the group operation with regard to every element of a given subgroup is commutative

normal school *n* [trans. of F *école normale;* fr. the fact that the first French school so named was intended to serve as a model] (1834) **:** a usu. 2-year school for training chiefly elementary teachers

Nor·man \ˈnȯr-mən\ *n* [ME, fr. OF *Normant,* fr. ON *Northmann-, Northmathr* Norseman, fr. *northr* north + *mann-, mathr* man; akin to OE *north* north, and to OE *man* man] (13c) **1 :** a native or inhabitant of Normandy: **a :** one of the Scandinavian conquerors of Normandy in the 10th century **b :** one of the Norman-French conquerors of England in 1066 **2 :** NORMAN-FRENCH — **Norman** *adj*

Norman architecture *n* (1797) **:** a Romanesque style first appearing in and near Normandy about A.D. 950; *also* **:** architecture resembling or imitating this style

Norman–French *n* (1605) **1 :** the French language of the medieval Normans **2 :** the modern dialect of Normandy

nor·ma·tive \ˈnȯr-mət-iv\ *adj* [F *normatif,* fr. *norme* norm, fr. L *norma*] (1878) **:** of, relating to or conforming to, or prescribing norms or standards — **nor·ma·tive·ly** *adv* — **nor·ma·tive·ness** *n*

normed \ˈnȯ(ə)rmd\ *adj* (1935) **:** being a mathematical entity upon which a norm is defined ⟨a ~ vector space⟩

nor·mo·ten·sive \ˌnȯr-mō-ˈten(t)-siv\ *adj* [*normal* + *-o-* + *tension* + *-ive*] (1941) **:** having blood pressure typical of the group to which one belongs — **normotensive** *n*

nor·mo·ther·mia \-ˈthər-mē-ə\ *n* [NL, fr. *normalis* normal + *-o-* + *-thermia* -thermy] (1959) **:** normal body temperature — **nor·mo·ther·mic** \-mik\ *adj*

Norn \ˈnȯ(ə)rn\ *n* [ON] **:** any of the three Norse goddesses of fate

1**Norse** \ˈnȯ(ə)rs\ *n, pl* **Norse** [prob. fr. obs. D *noorsch,* adj., Norwegian, Scandinavian, alter. of obs. D *noordsch* northern, fr. D *noord* north; akin to OE *north* north] (1598) **1** *pl* **a :** SCANDINAVIANS **b :** NORWEGIANS **2 a :** NORWEGIAN 2 **b :** any of the western Scandinavian dialects or languages **c :** the Scandinavian group of Germanic languages

2**Norse** *adj* (1768) **1 :** of or relating to ancient Scandinavia or the language of its inhabitants **2 :** NORWEGIAN

Norse·man \ˈnȯr-smən\ *n* (1864) **:** any of the ancient Scandinavians

1**north** \ˈnȯ(ə)rth\ *adv* [ME, fr. OE; akin to OHG *nord* north, Gk *nerteros* lower, infernal] (bef. 12c) **:** to, toward, or in the north

2**north** *adj* (bef. 12c) **1 :** situated toward or at the north ⟨the ~ entrance⟩ **2 :** coming from the north ⟨a ~ wind⟩

3**north** *n* (bef. 12c) **1 a :** the direction of the north terrestrial pole **:** the direction to the left of one facing east **b :** the compass point directly opposite to south **2** *cap* **:** regions or countries lying to the north of a specified or implied point of orientation **3** *often cap* **a :** the one of four positions at 90-degree intervals that lies to the north or at the top of a diagram **b :** a person occupying this position in the course of a specified activity (as the game of bridge)

north·bound \ˈnȯrth-ˌbau̇nd\ *adj* (1903) **:** traveling or headed north

north by east (ca. 1682) **:** a compass point that is one point east of due north **:** N11°15′E

north by west (ca. 1682) **:** a compass point that is one point west of due north **:** N11°15′W

1**north·east** \nȯr-ˈthēst, *naut* nȯ-ˈrēst\ *adv* (bef. 12c) **:** to, toward, or in the northeast

2**northeast** *n* (bef. 12c) **1 a :** the general direction between north and east **b :** the point midway between the north and east compass points **2** *cap* **:** regions or countries lying to the northeast of a specified or implied point of orientation

3**northeast** *adj* (bef. 12c) **1 :** coming from the northeast ⟨a ~ wind⟩ **2 :** situated toward or at the northeast ⟨the ~ corner⟩

northeast by east (ca. 1682) **:** a compass point that is one point east of due northeast **:** N56°15′E

northeast by north (ca. 1682) **:** a compass point that is one point north of due northeast **:** N33°45′E

north·east·er \nȯr-ˈthē-stər, nȯ-ˈrē-\ *n* (1774) **1 :** a strong northeast wind **2 :** a storm with northeast winds

north·east·er·ly \-stər-lē\ *adv or adj* [2*northeast* + *-erly* (as in *easterly*)] (1743) **1 :** from the northeast **2 :** toward the northeast

north·east·ern \-stərn\ *adj* (14c) **1** *often cap* **:** of, relating to, or characteristic of a region conventionally designated Northeast **2 :** lying toward or coming from the northeast — **north·east·ern·most** \-stərn-ˌmōst\ *adj*

North·east·ern·er \-stə(r)-nər\ *n* (1961) **:** a native or inhabitant of a northeastern region (as of the U.S.)

1**north·east·ward** \nȯr-ˈthēs-twərd, nȯ-ˈrēs-\ *adv or adj* (1553) **:** toward the northeast — **north·east·wards** \-wərdz\ *adv*

2**northeastward** *n* (1890) **:** NORTHEAST

north·er \ˈnȯr-t͟hər\ *n* (1827) **1 :** a strong north wind **2 :** a storm with north winds

1**north·er·ly** \-lē\ *adj or adv* [3*north* + *-erly* (as in *easterly*)] (1551) **1 :** situated toward or belonging to the north ⟨the ~ border⟩ **2 :** coming from the north ⟨a ~ wind⟩

2**northerly** *n, pl* **-lies** (1955) **:** a wind from the north

1**north·ern** \ˈnȯr-t͟hə(r)n\ *adj* [ME *northerne,* fr. OE; akin to OHG *nordrōni* northern, OE *north* north] (bef. 12c) **1** *cap* **a :** of, relating to, or characteristic of a region conventionally designated North **b :** of, relating to, or constituting the northern dialect **2 a :** lying toward the north **b :** coming from the north ⟨a ~ storm⟩ — **north·ern·most** \-ˌmōst\ *adj*

2**northern** *n* (1950) **1** *cap* **:** the dialect of English spoken in the part of the U.S. north of a line running northwest through central New Jersey, below the northern tier of counties in Pennsylvania, through northern Ohio, Indiana, and Illinois, across central Iowa, and through the Northwest corner of So. Dakota **2 :** 3PIKE 1a

northern corn rootworm *n* (1961) **:** a corn rootworm (*Diabrotica longicornis*) often destructive to maize in the northern parts of the central and eastern U.S.

Northern Cross *n* (ca. 1909) **:** a cross formed by six stars in Cygnus

Northern Crown *n* (1594) **:** CORONA BOREALIS

North·ern·er \ˈnȯr-t͟hə(r)-nər\ *n* (1831) **:** a native or inhabitant of the North; *esp* **:** a native or resident of the northern part of the U.S.

northern hemisphere *n, often cap N&H* (ca. 1771) **:** the half of the earth that lies north of the equator
northern lights *n pl* (14c) **:** AURORA BOREALIS
northern pike *n* (1856) **:** [3]PIKE 1a
northern white cedar *n* (1926) **:** an arborvitae (*Thuja occidentalis*) of eastern No. America that has branchlets in horizontal planes; *also* **:** its wood — called also *white cedar*
North Germanic *n* (ca. 1930) **:** a subdivision of the Germanic languages including Icelandic, Norwegian, Swedish, and Danish — see INDO-EUROPEAN LANGUAGES table
north·ing \'nȯr-thiŋ, -t͟hiŋ\ *n* (1669) **1 :** difference in latitude to the north from the last preceding point of reckoning **2 :** northerly progress
north·land \'nȯrth-ˌland, -lənd\ *n, often cap* (bef. 12c) **:** land in the north **:** the north of a country
North·man \'nȯrth-mən\ *n* (bef. 12c) **:** NORSEMAN
north–north·east \'nȯrth-ˌnȯr-'thēst, -ˌnȯ-'rēst\ *n* (14c) **:** a compass point that is two points east of due north **:** N22°30′E
north–north·west \'nȯrth-ˌnȯr(th)-'west\ *n* (14c) **:** a compass point that is two points west of due north **:** N22°30′W
north pole *n* (14c) **1 a** *often cap N&P* **:** the northernmost point of the earth; *broadly* **:** the corresponding point of a celestial body (as a planet) **b :** the zenith of the heavens as viewed from the north terrestrial pole **2** *of a magnet* **:** the pole that points toward the north
north–seek·ing pole *n* (ca. 1920) **:** NORTH POLE 2
North Star *n* **:** the star of the northern hemisphere toward which the axis of the earth points — called also *polestar*
[1]**North·um·bri·an** \nȯr-'thəm-brē-ən\ *adj* (1622) **1 :** of, relating to, or characteristic of ancient Northumbria, its people, or its language **2 :** of, relating to, or characteristic of Northumberland, its people, or its language
[2]**Northumbrian** *n* (1752) **1 :** a native or inhabitant of ancient Northumbria **2 :** a native or inhabitant of Northumberland **3 a :** the Old English dialect of Northumbria **b :** the Modern English dialect of Northumberland
[1]**north·ward** \'nȯrth-wərd\ *adv or adj* (bef. 12c) **:** toward the north — **north·wards** \-wərdz\ *adv*
[2]**northward** *n* (14c) **:** northward direction or part ⟨sail to the ∼⟩
[1]**north·west** \nȯrth-'west, *naut* nȯr-'west\ *adv* (bef. 12c) **:** to, toward, or in the northwest
[2]**northwest** *n* (bef. 12c) **1 a :** the general direction between north and west **b :** the point midway between the north and west compass points **2** *cap* **:** regions or countries lying to the northwest of a specified or implied point of orientation
[3]**northwest** *adj* (bef. 12c) **1 :** coming from the northwest ⟨a ∼ wind⟩ **2 :** situated toward or at the northwest ⟨the ∼ corner⟩
northwest by north (ca. 1682) **:** a compass point that is one point north of due northwest **:** N33°45′W
northwest by west (ca. 1682) **:** a compass point that is one point west of due northwest **:** N56°15′W
north·west·er \nȯr(th)-'wes-tər\ *n* (1737) **:** a strong northwest wind
north·west·er·ly \-lē\ *adv or adj* [[2]*northwest* + *-erly* (as in *westerly*)] (ca. 1611) **1 :** from the northwest **2 :** toward the northwest
north·west·ern \-'wes-tərn\ *adj* [[2]*northwest* + *-ern* (as in *western*)] (1612) **1** *often cap* **:** of, relating to, or characteristic of a region conventionally designated Northwest **2 :** lying toward or coming from the northwest — **north·west·ern·most** \-ˌmōst\ *adj*
North·west·ern·er \-'wes-tə(r)-nər\ *n* (1955) **:** a native or inhabitant of the Northwest and esp. of the northwestern part of the U.S.
[1]**north·west·ward** \-'wes-twərd\ *adv or adj* (14c) **:** toward the northwest — **north·west·wards** \-twərdz\ *adv*
[2]**northwestward** *n* (14c) **:** NORTHWEST
nor·trip·ty·line \nȯr-'trip-tə-ˌlēn\ *n* [*normal* + *tript-* (alter. of *trypt-* — as in *tryptophan*) + *-yl* + [2]*-ine*] (1964) **:** a tricyclic antidepressant $C_{19}H_{21}N$
Nor·way maple \ˌnȯ(ə)r-ˌwā-\ *n* (1797) **:** a European maple (*Acer platanoides*) with dark green or often reddish or red veined leaves that is much planted for shade in the U.S.
Norway rat *n* (1753) **:** BROWN RAT
Norway spruce *n* (1797) **:** a widely cultivated spruce (*Picea abies*) that is native to northern Europe and has a pyramidal shape, spreading branches and pendulous branchlets, dark foliage, and long pendulous cones
Nor·we·gian \nȯr-'wē-jən\ *n* [ML *Norwegia* Norway] (1605) **1 a :** a native or inhabitant of Norway **b :** a person of Norwegian descent **2 :** the Germanic language of the Norwegian people — **Norwegian** *adj*
Norwegian elkhound *n* (1930) **:** any of a Norwegian breed of short-bodied medium-sized dogs with a very heavy gray coat and erect ears
Nor·wich terrier \ˌnȯr(ˌ)wich-, *Brit* ˌnär-ich- *or* ˌnär-ij-\ *n* [*Norwich*, England] (1931) **:** any of an English breed of small active low-set terriers that have a long straight wiry coat and erect ears
nos- *or* **noso-** *comb form* [Gk, fr. *nosos*] **:** disease ⟨*nosology*⟩
[1]**nose** \'nōz\ *n* [ME, fr. OE *nosu;* akin to OHG *nasa* nose, L *nasus*] (bef. 12c) **1 a :** the part of the face that bears the nostrils and covers the anterior part of the nasal cavity; *broadly* **:** this part together with the nasal cavity **b :** the anterior part of the head above or projecting beyond the muzzle **:** SNOUT, PROBOSCIS, MUZZLE **2 a :** the sense of smell **:** OLFACTION **b :** AROMA, BOUQUET **3 :** the vertebrate olfactory organ **4 a :** the forward end or projection of something **b :** the projecting or working end of a tool **5 :** the stem of a boat or its protective metal covering **6 a :** the nose as a symbol of prying or meddling curiosity or interference **b :** a knack for discovery or understanding ⟨a keen ∼ for absurdity⟩ — **on the nose 1 a :** at or to a target point ⟨the bombs landed right *on the nose*⟩ **b** (1) **:** on target

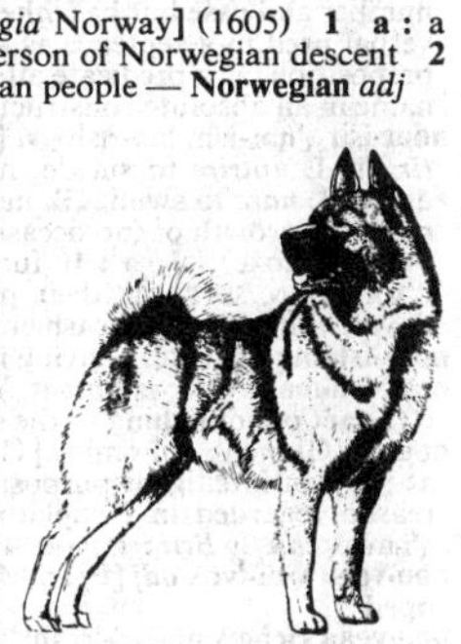
Norwegian elkhound

: ACCURATE (2) **:** ACCURATELY **2 :** to win — used of horse or dog racing bets
[2]**nose** *vb* **nosed; nos·ing** *vt* (ca. 1577) **1 :** to detect by or as if by smell **:** SCENT **2 a :** to push or move with the nose **b :** to advance the nose into or through **3 :** to touch or rub with the nose **:** NUZZLE ∼ *vi* **1 :** to use the nose in examining, smelling, or showing affection **2 :** to search impertinently **:** PRY **3 :** to move ahead slowly or cautiously ⟨the boat *nosed* around the bend⟩
nose·band \'nōz-ˌband\ *n* (1611) **:** the part of a headstall that passes over a horse's nose
nose·bleed \-ˌblēd\ *n* (1848) **:** an attack of bleeding from the nose
nose cone *n* (1949) **:** a protective cone constituting the forward end of a rocket or missile
nosed \'nōzd\ *adj* (15c) **:** having a nose esp. of a specified kind — usu. used in combination ⟨snub-*nosed*⟩
nose·dive \'nōz-ˌdīv\ *n* (1912) **1 :** the downward nose-first plunge of a flying object (as an airplane) or of an automobile **2 :** a sudden extreme drop — **nose–dive** *vi*
no–see–um \nō-'sē-əm\ *n* [fr. the words (as supposedly spoken by American Indians) *no see um* you don't see them] (1847) **:** BITING MIDGE
nose·gay \'nōz-ˌgā\ *n* [[1]*nose* + E dial. *gay* (ornament)] (15c) **:** a small bunch of flowers **:** POSY
nose job *n* (1966) **:** RHINOPLASTY
nose out *vt* (1630) **1 :** to discover often by prying **2 :** to defeat by a narrow margin
nose·piece \-ˌpēs\ *n* (1611) **1 :** a piece of armor for protecting the nose **2 :** the end piece of a microscope body to which an objective is attached **3 :** the bridge of a pair of eyeglasses
nose·wheel \-ˌhwēl, -ˌwēl\ *n* (1934) **:** a landing-gear wheel under the nose of an airplane
nos·ey par·ker \'nō-zē-'pär-kər\ *n, often cap P* [prob. fr. the name *Parker*] *chiefly Brit* (1907) **:** BUSYBODY
[1]**nosh** \'näsh\ *n* (1952) **:** a light snack
[2]**nosh** *vb* [Yiddish *nashn*, fr. MHG *naschen* to eat on the sly] *vi* (1956) **:** to eat a snack ∼ *vt* **:** CHEW, MUNCH — **nosh·er** *n*
no–show \(ˈ)nō-'shō\ *n* [[1]*no* + *show*, v. (as in *show up*)] (1941) **1 :** a person who reserves space (as on an airplane) but neither uses nor cancels the reservation **2 :** a person who buys a ticket (as to a sporting event) but does not attend; *broadly* **:** a person who is expected but who does not attend an event
nos·ing \'nō-ziŋ\ *n* (1775) **:** the usu. rounded edge of a stair tread that projects over the riser; *also* **:** any of various similar rounded projections
no·sol·o·gy \nō-'säl-ə-jē, -'zäl-\ *n* [prob. fr. NL *nosologia*, fr. *nos-* + *-logia* -logy] (1721) **1 :** a classification or list of diseases **2 :** a branch of medical science that deals with classification of diseases — **no·so·log·i·cal** \ˌnō-sə-'läj-i-kəl\ *or* **no·so·log·ic** \-ik\ *adj* — **no·so·log·i·cal·ly** \-i-k(ə-)lē\ *adv*
nos·tal·gia \nä-'stal-jə, nə- *also* nȯ-, nō-; nə-'stäl-\ *n* [NL, fr. Gk *nostos* return home + NL *-algia;* akin to OE *genesan* to survive, Skt *nasate* he approaches] (1770) **1 :** the state of being homesick **:** HOMESICKNESS **2 :** a wistful or excessively sentimental sometimes abnormal yearning for return to or of some past period or irrecoverable condition; *also* **:** something that evokes nostalgia — **nos·tal·gic** \-jik\ *adj or n* — **nos·tal·gi·cal·ly** \-ji-k(ə-)lē\ *adv*
nos·tal·gist \-jəst\ *n* [*nostalgia* + *-ist*] (1953) **:** a person fond of the objects and style of the past
nos·toc \'näs-ˌtäk\ *n* [NL] (1650) **:** any of a genus (*Nostoc*) of blue-green algae that are able to use atmospheric nitrogen
nos·tril \'näs-trəl\ *n* [ME *nosethirl*, fr. OE *nosthyrl*, fr. *nosu* nose + *thyrel* hole; akin to OE *thurh* through] (bef. 12c) **1 :** an external naris; *broadly* **:** a naris with the adjoining passage on the same side of the nasal septum **2 :** either fleshy lateral wall of the nose
nos·trum \'näs-trəm\ *n* [L, neut. of *noster* our, ours, fr. *nos* we — more at US] (1602) **1 :** a medicine of secret composition recommended by its preparer but usu. without scientific proof of its effectiveness **2 :** a usu. questionable remedy or scheme **:** PANACEA
nosy *or* **nos·ey** \'nō-zē\ *adj* **nos·i·er; -est** [[1]*nose*] (1882) **:** of prying or inquisitive disposition or quality **:** INTRUSIVE — **nos·i·ly** \'nō-zə-lē\ *adv* — **nos·i·ness** \-zē-nəs\ *n*
not \(ˈ)nät\ *adv* [ME, alter. of *nought*, fr. *nought*, pron. — more at NAUGHT] (13c) **1** — used as a function word to make negative a group of words or a word **2** — used as a function word to stand for the negative of a preceding group of words ⟨is sometimes hard to see and sometimes ∼⟩
NOT \'nät\ *n* [*not*] (1960) **:** a logical operator that produces a statement that is the inverse of an input statement
not- *or* **noto-** *comb form* [NL, fr. Gk *nōt-*, *nōto-*, fr. *nōton*, *nōtos* back — more at NATES] **:** back **:** back part ⟨*notochord*⟩
nota *pl of* NOTUM
no·ta be·ne \ˌnōt-ə-'bē-nē, -'ben-ē\ [L, mark well] (ca. 1673) — used to call attention to something important
no·ta·bil·i·ty \ˌnōt-ə-'bil-ət-ē\ *n, pl* **-ties** (1832) **:** a notable or prominent person
[1]**no·ta·ble** \'nōt-ə-bəl, *for 2 also* 'nät-\ *adj* (14c) **1 a :** worthy of note **:** REMARKABLE **b :** DISTINGUISHED, PROMINENT **2** *archaic* **:** efficient or capable in performance of housewifely duties — **no·ta·ble·ness** *n*
[2]**no·ta·ble** \'nōt-ə-bəl\ *n* (1815) **1 :** a person of note **:** NOTABILITY **2** *pl, often cap* **:** a group of persons summoned esp. in monarchical France to act as a deliberative body
no·ta·bly \'nōt-ə-blē\ *adv* (14c) **1 :** in a notable manner **:** to a high degree ⟨was ∼ impressed⟩ **2 :** ESPECIALLY, PARTICULARLY ⟨other powers, ∼ Britain and the United States —C. A. Fisher⟩
no·tar·i·al \nō-'ter-ē-əl\ *adj* (15c) **1 :** of, relating to, or characteristic of a notary public **2 :** done or executed by a notary public — **no·tar·i·al·ly** \-ə-lē\ *adv*

no·ta·ri·za·tion \ˌnōt-ə-rə-ˈzā-shən\ *n* (1940) **1 :** the act, process, or an instance of notarizing **2 :** the notarial certificate appended to a document

no·ta·rize \ˈnōt-ə-ˌrīz\ *vt* **-rized; -riz·ing** (1926) **:** to acknowledge or attest as a notary public

no·ta·ry public \ˌnōt-ə-rē-\ *n, pl* **notaries public** *or* **notary publics** [ME *notary* clerk, notary public, fr. L *notarius* clerk, secretary, fr. *notarius* of shorthand, fr. *nota* note, shorthand character] (15c) **:** a public officer who attests or certifies writings (as a deed) to make them authentic and takes affidavits, depositions, and protests of negotiable paper — called also *no·ta·ry* \ˈnōt-ə-rē\

no·tate \ˈnō-ˌtāt\ *vt* **no·tat·ed; no·tat·ing** [back-formation fr. *notation*] (1903) **:** to put into notation

no·ta·tion \nō-ˈtā-shən\ *n* [L *notation-, notatio,* fr. *notatus,* pp. of *notare* to note] (1584) **1 :** ANNOTATION, NOTE **2 a :** the act, process, method, or an instance of representing by a system or set of marks, signs, figures, or characters **b :** a system of characters, symbols, or abbreviated expressions used in an art or science or in mathematics or logic to express technical facts or quantities — **no·ta·tion·al** \-shnəl, -shən-ᵊl\ *adj*

1notch \ˈnäch\ *n* [perh. alter. (fr. incorrect division of *an otch*) of (assumed) *otch,* fr. MF *oche*] (1577) **1 a :** a V-shaped indentation **b :** a slit made to serve as a record **c :** a rounded indentation cut on the fore edge of a book **2 :** a deep close pass **:** GAP **3 :** DEGREE, STEP — **notched** \ˈnächt\ *adj*

2notch *vt* (1600) **1 :** to cut or make a notch in **2 a :** to mark or record by a notch **b :** SCORE, ACHIEVE

notch·back \ˈnäch-ˌbak\ *n* (1965) **1 :** a back on a closed passenger automobile having a distinct deck as distinguished from a fastback **2 :** an automobile having a notchback

1note \ˈnōt\ *vt* **not·ed; not·ing** [ME *noten,* fr. OF *noter,* fr. L *notare* to mark, note, fr. *nota*] (13c) **1 a :** to notice or observe with care **b :** to record or preserve in writing **2 a :** to make special mention of **:** REMARK **b :** INDICATE, SHOW — **not·er** *n*

2note *n* [L *nota* mark, character, written note] (13c) **1 a** (1) *obs* **:** MELODY, SONG (2) **:** TONE 2a (3) **:** CALL, SOUND; *esp* **:** the musical call of a bird **b :** a written symbol used to indicate duration and pitch of a tone by its shape and position on the staff **2 a :** a characteristic feature (as of odor or flavor) **b :** prevailing quality **:** MOOD **c :** an element that reveals an emotion ⟨a ~ of sadness in her voice⟩ **3 a** (1) **:** MEMORANDUM (2) **:** a condensed or informal record **b** (1) **:** a brief comment or explanation (2) **:** a printed comment or reference set apart from the text **c** (1) **:** a written promise to pay a debt (2) **:** a piece of paper money **d** (1) **:** a short informal letter (2) **:** a formal diplomatic communication **e :** a scholarly or technical essay shorter than an article and restricted in scope **f :** a sheet of notepaper **4 a :** DISTINCTION, REPUTATION ⟨a figure of international ~⟩ **b :** OBSERVATION, NOTICE ⟨took full ~ of the proceedings⟩ **c :** KNOWLEDGE, INFORMATION ***syn*** see SIGN

note·book \ˈnōt-ˌbu̇k\ *n* (1579) **:** a book for notes or memoranda

note·case \-ˌkās\ *n, Brit* (1838) **:** WALLET 2a

not·ed \ˈnōt-əd\ *adj* (14c) **:** well-known by reputation **:** EMINENT, CELEBRATED ***syn*** see FAMOUS — **not·ed·ly** *adv* — **not·ed·ness** *n*

note·less \ˈnōt-ləs\ *adj* (1616) **:** not noticed **:** UNDISTINGUISHED

note of hand (1766) **:** PROMISSORY NOTE

note·pad \ˈnōt-ˌpad\ *n* (1922) **:** PAD 4

note·pa·per \-ˌpā-pər\ *n* (1849) **:** writing paper suitable for notes

note·wor·thy \-ˌwər-t͟hē\ *adj* (1552) **:** worthy of or attracting attention esp. because of some special excellence — **note·wor·thi·ly** \-t͟hə-lē\ *adv* — **note·wor·thi·ness** \-t͟hē-nəs\ *n*

not–for–prof·it \ˌnät-fər-ˈpräf-ət\ *adj* (ca. 1966) **:** NONPROFIT

1noth·ing \ˈnəth-iŋ\ *pron* [ME, fr. OE *nān thing, nāthing,* fr. *nān* no + *thing* thing — more at NONE] (bef. 12c) **1 :** not any thing **:** no thing ⟨leaves ~ to the imagination⟩ **2 :** no part **3 :** one of no interest, value, or consequence ⟨they mean ~ to me⟩ — **nothing doing :** by no means **:** definitely no — **nothing for it :** no alternative ⟨*nothing for it* but to start over⟩

2nothing *adv* (12c) **:** not at all **:** in no degree

3nothing *n* (1535) **1 a :** something that does not exist **b :** the absence of all magnitude or quantity; *also* **:** ZERO 1a **c :** NOTHINGNESS 3b **2 :** someone or something of no or slight value or size

4nothing *adj* (1611) **:** of no account **:** WORTHLESS

noth·ing·ness \-nəs\ *n* (1631) **1 :** the quality or state of being nothing: as **a :** NONEXISTENCE **b :** utter insignificance **c :** DEATH **2 :** something insignificant or valueless **3 a :** VOID, EMPTINESS **b :** a metaphysical entity opposed to and devoid of being and regarded by some existentialists as the ground of anxiety

1no·tice \ˈnōt-əs\ *n* [ME, fr. MF, acquaintance, fr. L *notitia* knowledge, acquaintance, fr. *notus* known, fr. pp. of *noscere* to come to know — more at KNOW] (15c) **1 a** (1) **:** warning or intimation of something **:** ANNOUNCEMENT (2) **:** notification by one of the parties to an agreement or relation of intention of terminating it at a specified time (3) **:** the condition of being warned or notified — usu. used in the phrase *on notice* **b :** INFORMATION, INTELLIGENCE **2 a :** ATTENTION, HEED **b :** polite or favorable attention **:** CIVILITY **3 :** a written or printed announcement **4 :** a short critical account or examination

2notice *vt* **no·ticed; no·tic·ing** (15c) **1 :** to give notice of **2 a :** to comment upon **b :** REVIEW **3 a :** to treat with attention or civility **b :** to take notice of **:** MARK **4 :** to give a formal notice to

no·tice·able \ˈnōt-ə-sə-bəl\ *adj* (1796) **1 :** worthy of notice **2 :** capable of being noticed — **no·tice·ably** \-blē\ *adv*

syn NOTICEABLE, REMARKABLE, PROMINENT, OUTSTANDING, CONSPICUOUS, SALIENT, STRIKING mean attracting notice or attention. NOTICEABLE applies to something unlikely to escape observation; REMARKABLE applies to something so extraordinary or exceptional as to invite comment; PROMINENT applies to something commanding notice by standing out from its surroundings or background; OUTSTANDING applies to something that rises above and excels others of the same kind; CONSPICUOUS applies to something that is obvious and unavoidable to the sight or mind; SALIENT applies to something of significance that merits the attention given it; STRIKING applies to something that impresses itself powerfully and deeply upon the observer's mind or vision.

no·ti·fi·able \ˈnōt-ə-ˌfī-ə-bəl, ˌnōt-ə-ˈ\ *adj* (1889) **:** required by law to be reported to official health authorities ⟨a ~ disease⟩

no·ti·fi·ca·tion \ˌnōt-ə-fə-ˈkā-shən\ *n* (14c) **1 :** the act or an instance of notifying **2 :** a written or printed matter that gives notice

no·ti·fy \ˈnōt-ə-ˌfī\ *vt* **-fied; -fy·ing** [ME *notifien,* fr. MF *notifier* to make known, fr. LL *notificare,* fr. L *notus* known] (14c) **1** *obs* **:** to point out **2 :** to give notice of or report the occurrence of ⟨he *notified* his intention to sue⟩ **3 :** to give formal notice to ⟨~ a family of the death of a relation⟩ ***syn*** see INFORM — **no·ti·fi·er** \-ˌfī(-ə)r\ *n*

no–till \(ˌ)nō-ˈtil\ *n* (1968) **:** NO-TILLAGE

no–till·age \-ij\ *n* (1969) **:** a system of farming that consists of planting a narrow slit trench without tillage and with the use of herbicides to suppress weeds

no·tion \ˈnō-shən\ *n* [L *notion-, notio,* fr. *notus,* pp. of *noscere*] (1537) **1 a** (1) **:** an individual's conception or impression of something known, experienced, or imagined (2) **:** an inclusive general concept (3) **:** a theory or belief held by a person or group **b :** a personal inclination **:** WHIM **2** *obs* **:** MIND, INTELLECT **3** *pl* **:** small useful items **:** SUNDRIES ***syn*** see IDEA

no·tion·al \ˈnō-shnəl, -shən-ᵊl\ *adj* (1597) **1 :** THEORETICAL, SPECULATIVE **2 :** existing in the mind only **:** IMAGINARY **3 :** given to foolish or fanciful moods or ideas **4 a :** of, relating to, or being a notion or idea **:** CONCEPTUAL **b** (1) **:** presenting an idea of a thing, action, or quality ⟨*has* is ~ in *he has luck,* relational in *he has gone*⟩ (2) **:** of or representing what exists or occurs in the world of things as distinguished from syntactic categories — **no·tion·al·i·ty** \ˌnō-shə-ˈnal-ət-ē\ *n* — **no·tion·al·ly** \ˈnō-shnə-lē, -shən-ᵊl-ē\ *adv*

noto- — see NOT-

no·to·chord \ˈnōt-ə-ˌkȯ(ə)rd\ *n* [*not-* + L *chorda* cord — more at CORD] (1848) **:** a longitudinal flexible rod of cells that in the lowest chordates (as a lancelet or a lamprey) and in the embryos of the higher vertebrates forms the supporting axis of the body — **no·to·chord·al** \ˌnōt-ə-ˈkȯrd-ᵊl\ *adj*

no·to·ri·ety \ˌnōt-ə-ˈrī-ət-ē\ *n, pl* **-eties** [MF or ML; MF *notorieté,* fr. ML *notorietat-, notorietas,* fr. *notorius*] (ca. 1637) **1 :** the quality or state of being notorious **2 :** a notorious person

no·to·ri·ous \nō-ˈtōr-ē-əs, nə-, -ˈtȯr-\ *adj* [ML *notorius,* fr. LL *notorium* information, indictment, fr. neut. of (assumed) LL *notorius* making known, fr. L *notus,* pp. of *noscere* to come to know — more at KNOW] (1555) **:** generally known and talked of; *esp* **:** widely and unfavorably known ***syn*** see FAMOUS — **no·to·ri·ous·ly** *adv* — **no·to·ri·ous·ness** *n*

not·or·nis \nō-ˈtȯr-nəs\ *n, pl* **notornis** [NL, fr. Gk *notos* south + *ornis* bird; akin to Gk *noteros* damp — more at NOURISH, ERNE] (1848) **:** a flightless New Zealand bird (*Notornis mantelli*) that is related to the gallinules

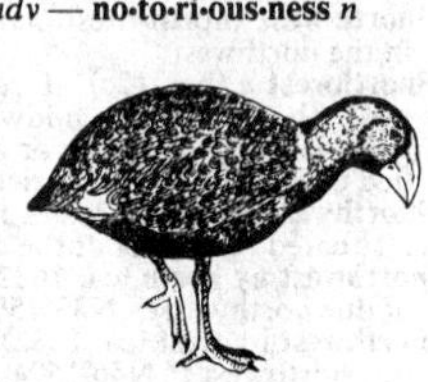

notornis

no–trump \(ˌ)nō-ˈtrəmp\ *adj* (1899) **:** being a bid, contract, or hand suitable to play without any suit being trumps — **no–trump** *n*

no·tum \ˈnōt-əm\ *n, pl* **no·ta** \ˈnōt-ə\ [NL, fr. Gk *nōton* back — more at NATES] (1877) **:** the dorsal surface of a thoracic segment of an insect

1not·with·stand·ing \ˌnät-with-ˈstan-diŋ, -wit͟h-\ *prep* [ME *notwithstonding,* fr. *not* + *withstonding,* prp. of *withstonden* to withstand] (14c) **:** DESPITE ⟨~ their lack of experience, they were an immediate success⟩ — often used after its object ⟨the motion passed, our objection ~⟩

2notwithstanding *adv* (15c) **:** NEVERTHELESS, HOWEVER

3notwithstanding *conj* (15c) **:** ALTHOUGH

nou·gat \ˈnü-gət, *esp Brit* -ˌgä\ *n* [F, fr. Prov, fr. OProv *nogat,* fr. *noga* nut, fr. L *nuc-, nux* — more at NUT] (1827) **:** a confection of nuts or fruit pieces in a sugar paste

nought \ˈnȯt, ˈnät\ *var of* NAUGHT

nou·me·non \ˈnü-mə-ˌnän\ *n, pl* **-na** \-nə, -ˌnä\ [G, fr. Gk *nooumenon* that which is apprehended by thought, fr. neut. of pres. pass. part. of *noein* to think, conceive, fr. *nous* mind] (1798) **:** an object or concept which according to Kant can be known to exist but cannot be experienced and to which no properties can be intelligibly ascribed — **nou·men·al** \-mən-ᵊl\ *adj*

noun \ˈnau̇n\ *n* [ME *nowne,* fr. AF *noun* name, noun, fr. OF *nom,* fr. L *nomen* — more at NAME] (14c) **:** a word that is the name of something (as a person, animal, place, thing, quality, idea, or action) and that in languages with grammatical number, case, and gender is inflected for number and case but has inherent gender **:** a word except a pronoun or verbal used in a sentence as subject or object of a verb, as object of a preposition, as a predicate after a copula, as an appositive name, or as a name in an absolute construction

nour·ish \ˈnər-ish, ˈnə-rish\ *vt* [ME *nurishen,* fr. OF *noriss-,* stem of *norrir,* fr. L *nutrire* to suckle, nourish; akin to Gk *nan* to flow, *noteros* damp, L *nare* to swim, Gk *nein*] (13c) **1 :** NURTURE, REAR **2 :** to promote the growth of ⟨no occasions to exercise the feelings nor ~ passion —L. O. Coxe⟩ **3 a :** to furnish or sustain with nutriment **:** FEED **b :** MAINTAIN, SUPPORT ⟨their profits . . . ~ other criminal activities —Beverly Smith⟩ — **nour·ish·er** *n*

nour·ish·ing *adj* (14c) **:** giving nourishment **:** NUTRITIOUS

nour·ish·ment \ˈnər-ish-mənt, ˈnə-rish-\ *n* (15c) **1 :** FOOD, NUTRIMENT **2 :** the act of nourishing or the state of being nourished

nous *n* [Gk *noos, nous* mind] (1678) **1** \ˈnüs *also* ˈnau̇s\ **:** MIND, REASON: as **a :** an intelligent purposive principle of the world **b :** the divine reason regarded in Neoplatonism as the first emanation of God **2** \ˈnau̇s\ *chiefly Brit* **:** COMMON SENSE, ALERTNESS

nou·veau \nü-ˈvō\ *adj* [F, fr. MF *novel*] (1813) **:** newly arrived or developed

nou·veau riche \ˌnü-ˌvō-ˈrēsh\ *n, pl* **nou·veaux riches** *same*\ [F, lit., new rich] (1813) **:** a person newly rich **:** PARVENU

nou·velle cui·sine \ˌnü-ˌvel-kwi-ˈzēn\ *n* [F, lit., new cuisine] (1977) **:** a form of French cuisine that uses little flour or fat and stresses light sauces and the use of fresh seasonal produce

nou·velle vague \-ˈväg, -ˈväg\ *n* [F] (1959) **:** NEW WAVE 1, 2

no·va \ˈnō-və\ *n, pl* **novas** *or* **no·vae** \-(ˌ)vē, -ˌvī\ [NL, fem. of L *novus* new] (1927) **:** a star that suddenly increases its light output tremendously and then fades away to its former obscurity in a few months or years — **no·va·like** \-və-ˌlīk\ *adj*

no•vac•u•lite \nō-ˈvak-yə-ˌlīt\ *n* [L *novacula* razor] (1796) **:** a very hard fine-grained siliceous rock used for whetstones and possibly of sedimentary origin

no•va•tion \nō-ˈvā-shən\ *n* [LL *novation-, novatio* renewal, legal novation, fr. L *novatus,* pp. of *novare* to make new, fr. *novus*] (1682) **:** the substitution of a new legal obligation for an old one

[1]**nov•el** \ˈnäv-əl\ *adj* [ME, fr. MF, new, fr. L *novellus,* fr. dim. of *novus* new — more at NEW] (15c) **1 :** new and not resembling something formerly known or used **2 :** original or striking esp. in conception or style ⟨a ~ scheme to collect money⟩ ***syn*** see NEW

[2]**novel** *n* [It *novella*] (1639) **1 :** an invented prose narrative that is usu. long and complex and deals esp. with human experience through a usu. connected sequence of events **2 :** the literary genre consisting of novels — **nov•el•is•tic** \ˌnäv-ə-ˈlis-tik\ *adj* — **nov•el•is•ti•cal•ly** \-ti-k(ə-)lē\ *adv*

nov•el•ette \ˌnäv-ə-ˈlet\ *n* (1814) **1 :** a brief novel **2 :** a long short story

nov•el•ett•ish \-ˈet-ish\ *adj* (1904) **:** of, relating to, or characteristic of a novelette; *esp* **:** SENTIMENTAL

nov•el•ist \ˈnäv-(ə-)ləst\ *n* (1728) **:** a writer of novels

nov•el•ize \ˈnäv-ə-ˌlīz\ *vt* **-ized; -iz•ing** (1828) **:** to convert into the form of a novel ⟨~ a play⟩ — **nov•el•iza•tion** \ˌnäv-ə-lə-ˈzā-shən\ *n*

no•vel•la \nō-ˈvel-ə\ *n, pl* **novellas** *or* **no•vel•le** \-ˈvel-ē\ [It, fr. fem. of *novello* new, fr. L *novellus*] (1891) **1** *pl novelle* **:** a story with a compact and pointed plot **2** *pl usu novellas* **:** NOVELETTE 1

nov•el•ty \ˈnäv-əl-tē\ *n, pl* **-ties** [ME *novelte,* fr. MF *noveleté,* fr. *novel*] (14c) **1 :** something new or unusual **2 :** the quality or state of being novel **:** NEWNESS **3 :** a small manufactured article intended mainly for personal or household adornment — usu. used in pl.

[1]**No•vem•ber** \nō-ˈvem-bər, nə-\ *n* [ME *Novembre,* fr. OF, fr. L *November* (ninth month), fr. *novem* nine — more at NINE] (13c) **:** the 11th month of the Gregorian calendar

[2]**November** (1956) — a communications code word for the letter *n*

no•vem•de•cil•lion \ˌnō-ˌvem-di-ˈsil-yən\ *n, often attrib* [L *novemdecim* nineteen (fr. *novem* + *decem* ten) + E *-illion* (as in *million*) — more at TEN] (ca. 1938) — see NUMBER table

no•ve•na \nō-ˈvē-nə\ *n* [ML, fr. L, fem. of *novenus* nine each, fr. *novem*] (1853) **:** a Roman Catholic nine days' devotion

nov•ice \ˈnäv-əs\ *n* [ME, fr. MF, fr. ML *novicius,* fr. L, new, inexperienced, fr. *novus* — more at NEW] (14c) **1 :** a person admitted to probationary membership in a religious community **2 :** BEGINNER, TYRO

no•vi•lle•ro \ˌnō-vē-ˈ(ə)r-(ˌ)ō, -vəl-ˈye(ə)r-\ *n, pl* **-ros** [Sp, fr. *novillo* young bull, fr. L *novellus* new — more at NOVEL] (1921) **:** an aspiring bullfighter who has not yet attained the rank of matador

no•vi•tiate \nō-ˈvish-ət, nə-\ *n* [F *noviciat,* fr. ML *noviciatus,* fr. *novicius*] (1600) **1 :** the period or state of being a novice **2 :** NOVICE **3 :** a house where novices are trained

no•vo•bi•o•cin \ˌnō-və-ˈbī-ə-sən\ *n* [prob. fr. *novo-* (fr. L *novus* new) + E anti*biotic* + streptomy*cin*] (1956) **:** a weak dibasic acid $C_{31}H_{36}N_2O_{11}$ that is highly toxic to man and is used as an antimicrobial drug in some serious cases of staphylococcic and urinary tract infection

No•vo•cain \ˈnō-və-ˌkān\ *trademark* — used for a preparation containing the hydrochloride of procaine

no•vo•caine \-ˌkān\ *n* [ISV *novo-* (fr. L *novus* new) + *cocaine*] (1910) **:** PROCAINE; *also* **:** its hydrochloride

[1]**now** \(ˈ)nau̇\ *adv* [ME, fr. OE *nū;* akin to OHG *nū* now, L *nunc,* Gk *nyn*] (bef. 12c) **1 a :** at the present time or moment **b :** in the time immediately before the present ⟨thought of them just ~⟩ **c :** in the time immediately to follow **:** FORTHWITH ⟨come in ~⟩ **2** — used with the sense of present time weakened or lost to express command, request, or admonition ⟨~ hear this⟩ ⟨~ you be sure to write⟩ **3** — used with the sense of present time weakened or lost to introduce an important point or indicate a transition (as of ideas) **4 :** SOMETIMES ⟨~ one and ~ another⟩ **5 :** under the present circumstances **6 :** at the time referred to ⟨~ the trouble began⟩

[2]**now** *conj* (bef. 12c) **:** in view of the fact that **:** SINCE — often followed by *that* ⟨~ that we are here⟩

[3]**now** \ˈnau̇\ *n* (12c) **:** the present time or moment ⟨been ill up to ~⟩

[4]**now** \ˈnau̇\ *adj* (14c) **1 :** of or relating to the present time **:** EXISTING ⟨the ~ president⟩ **2 a :** excitingly new ⟨~ clothes⟩ **b :** constantly aware of what is new ⟨~ people⟩ ⟨the ~ generation⟩

now•a•days \ˈnau̇-(ə-)ˌdāz\ *adv* [ME *now a dayes,* fr. [1]*now* + *a dayes* during the day] (14c) **:** at the present time

now and then *adv* (15c) **:** from time to time **:** OCCASIONALLY ⟨*now and then* we go off to the country⟩

no•way *adv* (13c) **1** \ˈnō-ˌwā\ *or* **no•ways** \-ˌwāz\ **:** NOWISE **2** *usu* **no way** \-ˈwā**:** NO — used emphatically

[1]**no•where** \ˈnō-ˌ(h)we(ə)r, -ˌ(h)wa(ə)r, -(h)wər\ *adv* (bef. 12c) **1 :** not in or at any place **2 :** to no place

[2]**nowhere** *n* (1831) **1 :** a nonexistent place **2 :** an unknown, distant, or obscure place or state ⟨rose to fame out of ~⟩ — **miles from nowhere :** in an extremely remote place

nowhere near *adv* (14c) **:** not nearly

no•wheres \ˈnō-ˌ(h)we(ə)rz, -ˌ(h)wa(ə)rz, -(ˌ)(h)wərz\ *adv, chiefly dial* (ca. 1846) **:** NOWHERE

no•whith•er \nō-ˈ(h)with-ər, ˈnō-ˌ\ *adv* (bef. 12c) **:** to or toward no place

no–win \ˈnō-ˌwin\ *adj* (1962) **:** not likely to give victory, success, or satisfaction **:** that cannot be won ⟨a ~ situation⟩ ⟨a ~ war⟩

no•wise \ˈnō-ˌwīz\ *adv* (14c) **:** not at all

now•ness \ˈnau̇-nəs\ *n* (1674) **:** the quality or state of existing or occurring in or belonging to the present time

nox•ious \ˈnäk-shəs\ *adj* [L *noxius,* fr. *noxa* harm; akin to L *nocēre* to harm, *nec-, nex* violent death, Gk *nekros* dead body] (1500) **1 a :** physically harmful or destructive to living beings ⟨~ wastes that turn our streams into sewers⟩ **b :** constituting a harmful influence on mind or behavior **:** morally corrupting ⟨~ doctrines⟩ **2 :** DISTASTEFUL, OBNOXIOUS ***syn*** see PERNICIOUS — **nox•ious•ly** *adv* — **nox•ious•ness** *n*

noz•zle \ˈnäz-əl\ *n* [dim. of *nose*] (1608) **1 a :** a projecting vent of something **b :** a short tube with a taper or constriction used (as on a hose) to speed up or direct a flow of fluid **c :** a part in a rocket engine that accelerates the exhaust gases from the combustion chamber to a high velocity **2** *slang* **:** NOSE

-n't \(ᵊ)nt, ənt\ *vb comb form* **:** not ⟨is*n't*⟩

nth \ˈen(t)th\ *adj* [*n* (indefinite number) + *-th*] (1852) **1 :** numbered with an unspecified or indefinitely large ordinal number ⟨for the ~ time⟩ **2 :** EXTREME, UTMOST ⟨to the ~ degree⟩

nu \ˈn(y)ü\ *n* [Gk *ny,* of Sem origin; akin to Heb *nūn* nun] (1823) **:** the 13th letter of the Greek alphabet — see ALPHABET table

nu•ance \ˈn(y)ü-ˌän(t)s, -ˌäⁿs, n(y)ü-ˈ\ *n* [F, fr. MF, shade of color, fr. *nuer* to make shades of color, fr. *nue* cloud, fr. L *nubes;* akin to Gk *nythos* dark] (1781) **1 :** a subtle distinction or variation **2 :** a subtle quality **:** NICETY **3 :** sensibility to, awareness of, or ability to express delicate shadings (as of meaning, feeling, or value) — **nu•anced** \-ˌän(t)st, -ˈän(t)st\ *adj*

nub \ˈnəb\ *n* [alter. of E dial. *knub,* prob. fr. LG *knubbe*] (1727) **1 :** KNOB, LUMP **2 :** NUBBIN **3 :** GIST, POINT

nub•bin \ˈnəb-ən\ *n* [perh. dim. of *nub*] (1692) **1 :** something (as an ear of Indian corn) that is small for its kind, stunted, undeveloped, or imperfect **2 :** a small usu. projecting part or bit **3 :** NUB 3

nub•ble \ˈnəb-əl\ *n* [dim. of *nub*] (1818) **:** a small knob or lump — **nub•bly** \-(ə-)lē\ *adj*

nub•by \ˈnəb-ē\ *adj* **nub•bi•er; -est** [*nub* + *-y*] (1876) **1 :** having or being like nubbles **2 :** having nubs ⟨a ~ knit fabric⟩

Nu•bi•an \ˈn(y)ü-bē-ən\ *n* (15c) **1 a :** a native or inhabitant of Nubia **b :** a member of one of the group of Negroid tribes that formed a powerful empire between Egypt and Ethiopia from the 6th to the 14th centuries **2 :** any of several languages spoken in central and northern Sudan — **Nubian** *adj*

nu•bile \ˈn(y)ü-bəl, -ˌbīl\ *adj* [F, fr. L *nubilis,* fr. *nubere* to marry — more at NUPTIAL] (1642) **1 :** of marriageable condition or age **2 :** sexually attractive — used of a young woman — **nu•bil•i•ty** \n(y)ü-ˈbil-ət-ē\ *n*

nu•cel•lus \n(y)ü-ˈsel-əs\ *n, pl* **nu•cel•li** \-ˈsel-ˌī\ [NL, fr. L *nucella* small nut, fr. *nuc-, nux* nut — more at NUT] (1882) **:** the central and chief part of a plant ovule that contains the embryo sac — **nu•cel•lar** \-ˈsel-ər\ *adj*

nu•chal \ˈn(y)ü-kəl\ *adj* [ML *nucha* nape, fr. Ar *nukhā'* spinal marrow] (1835) **:** of, relating to, or lying in the region of the nape

nucle- *or* **nucleo-** *comb form* [F *nuclé-, nucléo-,* fr. NL *nucleus*] **1 :** nucleus ⟨*nucle*on⟩ **2 :** nucleic acid ⟨*nucleo*protein⟩

nu•cle•ar \ˈn(y)ü-klē-ər, ÷-kyə-lər\ *adj* (1846) **1 :** of, relating to, or constituting a nucleus **2 :** of, relating to, or utilizing the atomic nucleus, atomic energy, the atom bomb, or atomic power

usage Though disapproved of by many, pronunciations ending in \-kyə-lər\ have been found in widespread use among educated speakers including scientists, lawyers, professors, congressmen, U.S. cabinet members and at least one U.S. president and one vice president. While most common in the U.S., these pronunciations have also been heard from British and Canadian speakers.

nuclear family *n* (1947) **:** a family group that consists only of father, mother, and children

nuclear magnetic resonance *n* (1942) **:** the magnetic resonance of an atomic nucleus

nuclear membrane *n* (1888) **:** the boundary of a cell nucleus — see CELL illustration

nuclear–powered *adj* (1948) **:** utilizing atomic power (as for propulsion)

nuclear resonance *n* (1940) **:** the resonance absorption of a gamma ray by a nucleus identical to the nucleus that emitted the gamma ray

nuclear sap *n* (1897) **:** the clear homogeneous ground substance of a cell nucleus — called also *karyolymph*

nuclear winter *n* (1983) **:** the chilling of climate that is hypothesized to be a consequence of nuclear war and to result from the prolonged blockage of sunlight by high-altitude dust clouds produced by nuclear explosions

nu•cle•ase \ˈn(y)ü-klē-ˌās, -ˌāz\ *n* (1903) **:** any of various enzymes that promote hydrolysis of nucleic acids

nu•cle•ate \ˈn(y)ü-klē-ˌāt\ *vb* **-at•ed; -at•ing** [LL *nucleatus,* pp. of *nucleare* to become stony, fr. L *nucleus*] *vt* (ca. 1864) **1 :** to form into a nucleus **:** CLUSTER **2 :** to act as a nucleus for **3 :** to supply nuclei to ~ *vi* **1 :** to form a nucleus **2 :** to act as a nucleus **3 :** to begin to form — **nu•cle•ation** \ˌn(y)ü-klē-ˈā-shən\ *n* — **nu•cle•a•tor** \ˈn(y)ü-klē-ˌāt-ər\ *n*

nu•cle•at•ed \ˈn(y)ü-klē-ˌāt-əd\ *or* **nu•cle•ate** \-klē-ət\ *adj* [L *nucleatus,* fr. *nucleus* kernel] (1845) **1 :** having a nucleus or nuclei ⟨~ cells⟩ **2** *usu nucleate* **:** originating or occurring at nuclei ⟨*nucleate* boiling⟩

nu•cle•ic acid \n(y)ü-ˌklē-ik-, -ˌklā-\ *n* (1892) **:** any of various acids (as an RNA or a DNA) composed of a sugar or derivative of a sugar, phosphoric acid, and a base and found esp. in cell nuclei

nu•cle•in \ˈn(y)ü-klē-ən\ *n* (1878) **1 :** NUCLEOPROTEIN **2 :** NUCLEIC ACID

nu•cleo•cap•sid \ˌn(y)ü-klē-ō-ˈkap-səd\ *n* (1963) **:** the nucleic acid and surrounding protein coat in a virus

nu•cle•oid \ˈn(y)ü-klē-ˌȯid\ *n* (1938) **:** the DNA-containing area of a prokaryote cell (as a bacterium)

nu•cle•o•lus \n(y)ü-ˈklē-ə-ləs\ *n, pl* **-li** \-ˌlī\ [NL, fr. L, dim. of *nucleus*] (1845) **:** a spherical body of the nucleus that becomes enlarged during protein synthesis, is associated with a specific part of a chromosome, and contains the DNA templates for ribosomal RNA — see CELL illustration — **nu•cle•o•lar** \-lər\ *adj*

nucleolus organizer *n* (1939) **:** the specific part of a chromosome with which a nucleolus is associated esp. during its reorganization after nuclear division — called also *nucleolar organizer*

nu•cle•on \ˈn(y)ü-klē-ˌän\ *n* [ISV] (1937) **1 :** a proton or neutron esp. in the atomic nucleus **2 :** a hypothetical single entity with one-half unit of isospin capable of manifesting itself as either a proton or a neutron and of making transitions between these two states — **nu•cle•on•ic** \ˌn(y)ü-klē-ˈän-ik\ *adj*

nu•cle•on•ics \ˌn(y)ü-klē-ˈän-iks\ *n pl but sing or pl in constr* (1937) **:** a branch of physical science that deals with nucleons or with all phenomena of the atomic nucleus

nu•cleo•phile \ˈn(y)ü-klē-ə-ˌfīl\ *n* (1943) **:** a nucleophilic substance (as an electron-donating reagent)

TABLE OF NUMBERS

CARDINAL NUMBERS[1]

NAME[2]	SYMBOL Arabic	Roman[3]
zero or naught or cipher	0	
one	1	I
two	2	II
three	3	III
four	4	IV
five	5	V
six	6	VI
seven	7	VII
eight	8	VIII
nine	9	IX
ten	10	X
eleven	11	XI
twelve	12	XII
thirteen	13	XIII
fourteen	14	XIV
fifteen	15	XV
sixteen	16	XVI
seventeen	17	XVII
eighteen	18	XVIII
nineteen	19	XIX
twenty	20	XX
twenty-one	21	XXI
twenty-two	22	XXII
twenty-three	23	XXIII
twenty-four	24	XXIV
twenty-five	25	XXV
twenty-six	26	XXVI
twenty-seven	27	XXVII
twenty-eight	28	XXVIII
twenty-nine	29	XXIX
thirty	30	XXX
thirty-one	31	XXXI
thirty-two etc	32	XXXII
forty	40	XL
forty-one etc	41	XLI
fifty	50	L
sixty	60	LX
seventy	70	LXX
eighty	80	LXXX
ninety	90	XC
one hundred	100	C
one hundred and one or one hundred one	101	CI
one hundred and two etc	102	CII
two hundred	200	CC
three hundred	300	CCC
four hundred	400	CD
five hundred	500	D
six hundred	600	DC
seven hundred	700	DCC
eight hundred	800	DCCC
nine hundred	900	CM
one thousand or ten hundred etc	1,000	M
two thousand etc	2,000	MM
five thousand	5,000	V̄
ten thousand	10,000	X̄
one hundred thousand	100,000	C̄
one million	1,000,000	M̄

ORDINAL NUMBERS[4]

NAME[5]	SYMBOL[6]
first	1st
second	2d or 2nd
third	3d or 3rd
fourth	4th
fifth	5th
sixth	6th
seventh	7th
eighth	8th
ninth	9th
tenth	10th
eleventh	11th
twelfth	12th
thirteenth	13th
fourteenth	14th
fifteenth	15th
sixteenth	16th
seventeenth	17th
eighteenth	18th
nineteenth	19th
twentieth	20th
twenty-first	21st
twenty-second	22d or 22nd
twenty-third	23d or 23rd
twenty-fourth	24th
twenty-fifth	25th
twenty-sixth	26th
twenty-seventh	27th
twenty-eighth	28th
twenty-ninth	29th
thirtieth	30th
thirty-first	31st
thirty-second etc	32d or 32nd
fortieth	40th
forty-first	41st
forty-second etc	42d or 42nd
fiftieth	50th
sixtieth	60th
seventieth	70th
eightieth	80th
ninetieth	90th
hundredth or one hundredth	100th
hundred and first or one hundred and first	101st
hundred and second etc	102d or 102nd
two hundredth	200th
three hundredth	300th
four hundredth	400th
five hundredth	500th
six hundredth	600th
seven hundredth	700th
eight hundredth	800th
nine hundredth	900th
thousandth or one thousandth	1,000th
two thousandth etc	2,000th
ten thousandth	10,000th
hundred thousandth or one hundred thousandth	100,000th
millionth or one millionth	1,000,000th

[1] The cardinal numbers are used in simple counting or in answer to "how many?" The words for these numbers may be used as nouns (he counted to *twelve*), as pronouns (*twelve* were found), or as adjectives (*twelve* boys).
[2] In formal contexts the numbers one to one hundred and in less formal contexts the numbers one to nine are commonly written out, while larger numbers are given in numerals. In nearly all contexts a number occurring at the beginning of a sentence is usually written out. Except in very formal contexts numerals are invariably used for dates. Arabic numerals from 1,000 to 9,999 are often written without commas (1000, 9999). Year numbers are always written without commas (1783).
[3] The Roman numerals are written either in capitals or in lowercase letters.
[4] The ordinal numbers are used to show the order or succession in which such items as names, objects, and periods of time are considered (the *twelfth* month; the *fourth* row of seats; the *18th* century).
[5] Each of the terms for the ordinal numbers excepting *first* and *second* is used in designating one of a number of parts into which a whole may be divided (a *fourth*; a *sixth*; a *tenth*) and as the denominator in fractions designating the number of such parts constituting a certain portion of a whole (*one fourth*; *three fifths*). When used as nouns the fractions are usually written as two words, although they are regularly hyphenated as adjectives (a *two-thirds* majority). When fractions are written in numerals, the cardinal symbols are used ($\frac{1}{4}$, $\frac{7}{8}$, $\frac{5}{6}$).
[6] The Arabic symbols for the cardinal numbers may be read as ordinals in certain contexts (January 1 = January first; 2 Samuel = Second Samuel). The Roman numerals are sometimes read as ordinals (Henry IV = Henry the Fourth); sometimes they are written with the ordinal suffixes (XIXth Dynasty).

DENOMINATIONS ABOVE ONE MILLION

NAME	American system[1] VALUE IN POWERS OF TEN	NUMBER OF ZEROS[2]	NUMBER OF GROUPS OF THREE 0's AFTER 1,000	NAME	British system[1] VALUE IN POWERS OF TEN	NUMBER OF ZEROS[2]	POWERS OF 1,000,000
billion	10^9	9	2	milliard	10^9	9	—
trillion	10^{12}	12	3	billion	10^{12}	12	2
quadrillion	10^{15}	15	4	trillion	10^{18}	18	3
quintillion	10^{18}	18	5	quadrillion	10^{24}	24	4
sextillion	10^{21}	21	6	quintillion	10^{30}	30	5
septillion	10^{24}	24	7	sextillion	10^{36}	36	6
octillion	10^{27}	27	8	septillion	10^{42}	42	7
nonillion	10^{30}	30	9	octillion	10^{48}	48	8
decillion	10^{33}	33	10	nonillion	10^{54}	54	9
undecillion	10^{36}	36	11	decillion	10^{60}	60	10
duodecillion	10^{39}	39	12	undecillion	10^{66}	66	11
tredecillion	10^{42}	42	13	duodecillion	10^{72}	72	12
quattuordecillion	10^{45}	45	14	tredecillion	10^{78}	78	13
quindecillion	10^{48}	48	15	quattuordecillion	10^{84}	84	14
sexdecillion	10^{51}	51	16	quindecillion	10^{90}	90	15
septendecillion	10^{54}	54	17	sexdecillion	10^{96}	96	16
octodecillion	10^{57}	57	18	septendecillion	10^{102}	102	17
novemdecillion	10^{60}	60	19	octodecillion	10^{108}	108	18
vigintillion	10^{63}	63	20	novemdecillion	10^{114}	114	19
centillion	10^{303}	303	100	vigintillion	10^{120}	120	20
				centillion	10^{600}	600	100

[1] The American system of numeration for denominations above one million was modeled on the French system but more recently the French system has been changed to correspond to the German and British systems. In the American system each of the denominations above 1,000 millions (the American *billion*) is 1,000 times the one preceding (one trillion=1,000 billions; one quadrillion=1,000 trillions). In the British system the first denomination above 1,000 millions (the British *milliard*) is 1,000 times the preceding one, but each of the denominations above 1,000 milliards (the British *billion*) is 1,000,000 times the preceding one (one trillion=1,000,000 billions; one quadrillion=1,000,000 trillions).
[2] For convenience in reading large numerals the thousands, millions, etc., are usually separated by commas (21,530; 1,155,465) or by half spaces (1 155 465). Serial numbers (as a social security number or the engine number of a car) are often written with hyphens (583-695-20).

nu·cleo·phil·ic \ˌn(y)ü-klē-ə-ˈfil-ik\ *adj* (1933) **:** having an affinity for atomic nuclei **:** electron-donating — **nu·cleo·phil·i·cal·ly** \-i-k(ə-)lē\ *adv* — **nu·cleo·phi·lic·i·ty** \-klē-ō-fil-ˈis-ət-ē\ *n*

nu·cleo·plasm \ˈn(y)ü-klē-ə-ˌplaz-əm\ *n* [ISV] (1888) **:** the protoplasm of a nucleus; *esp* **:** NUCLEAR SAP — **nu·cleo·plas·mic** \-klē-ə-ˈplaz-mik\ *adj*

nu·cleo·pro·tein \ˌn(y)ü-klē-ō-ˈprō-ˌtēn, -ˈprōt-ē-ən\ *n* [ISV] (1907) **:** a compound that consists of a protein (as a histone) conjugated with a nucleic acid (as a DNA) and that is the principal constituent of the hereditary material in chromosomes

nu·cle·o·side \ˈn(y)ü-klē-ə-ˌsīd\ *n* [ISV *nucle-* + *-ose* + *-ide*] (1911) **:** a compound (as guanosine or adenosine) that consists of a purine or pyrimidine base combined with deoxyribose or ribose and is found esp. in DNA or RNA

nu·cleo·some \-ˌsōm\ *n* (1962) **:** any of the repeating globular subunits of chromatin that consist of a complex of DNA and histone and are thought to be present only during interphase — **nu·cleo·so·mal** \ˌn(y)ü-klē-ə-ˈsō-məl\ *adj*

nu·cleo·syn·the·sis \ˌn(y)ü-klē-ō-ˈsin(t)-thə-səs\ *n* [NL] (1960) **:** the production of a chemical element from hydrogen nuclei (as in stellar evolution) — **nu·cleo·syn·thet·ic** \-sin-ˈthet-ik\ *adj*

nu·cle·o·tid·ase \ˌn(y)ü-klē-ə-ˈtīd-ˌās, -ˌāz\ *n* (1911) **:** a phosphatase that promotes hydrolysis of a nucleotide (as into a nucleoside and phosphoric acid)

nu·cle·o·tide \ˈn(y)ü-klē-ə-ˌtīd\ *n* [ISV, irreg. fr. *nucle-* + *-ide*] (1908) **:** any of several compounds that consist of a ribose or deoxyribose sugar joined to a purine or pyrimidine base and to a phosphate group and that are the basic structural units of RNA and DNA — compare NUCLEOSIDE

nu·cle·us \ˈn(y)ü-klē-əs\ *n, pl* **nu·clei** \-klē-ˌī\ *also* **nu·cle·us·es** [NL, fr. L, kernel, dim. of *nuc-, nux* nut — more at NUT] (1704) **1 :** the small brighter and denser portion of a galaxy or of the head of a comet **2 :** a central point, group, or mass about which gathering, concentration, or accretion takes place: as **a :** a cellular organelle that is essential to cell functions (as reproduction and protein synthesis), is composed of nuclear sap and a nucleoprotein-rich network from which chromosomes and nucleoli arise, and is enclosed in a definite membrane — see CELL illustration **b :** a mass of gray matter or group of nerve cells in the central nervous system **c :** a characteristic and stable complex of atoms or groups in a molecule; *esp* **:** RING ⟨the naphthalene ~⟩ **d :** the positively charged central portion of an atom that comprises nearly all of the atomic mass and that consists of protons and neutrons except in hydrogen which consists of one proton only **3 :** the peak of energy in the utterance of a syllable

nu·clide \ˈn(y)ü-ˌklīd\ *n* [*nucleus* + Gk *eidos* form, species — more at IDOL] (1947) **:** a species of atom characterized by the constitution of its nucleus and hence by the number of protons, the number of neutrons, and the energy content — **nu·clid·ic** \n(y)ü-ˈklid-ik\ *adj*

[1]**nude** \ˈn(y)üd\ *adj* **nud·er; nud·est** [L *nudus* naked — more at NAKED] (1531) **1 :** lacking something essential esp. to legal validity ⟨a ~ contract⟩ **2 a :** devoid of a natural or conventional covering; *esp* **:** not covered by clothing or a drape **b (1) :** of the color of Caucasian flesh **(2) :** giving the appearance of nudity ⟨a ~ dress⟩ **c :** featuring nudes ⟨a ~ movie⟩ ***syn*** see BARE — **nude** *adv* — **nude·ly** *adv* — **nude·ness** *n* — **nu·di·ty** \ˈn(y)üd-ət-ē\ *n*

[2]**nude** *n* (1708) **1 a :** a representation of a nude human figure **b :** a nude person **2 :** the condition of being nude ⟨in the ~⟩

nudge \ˈnəj\ *vt* **nudged; nudg·ing** [perh. of Scand origin; akin to ON *gnaga* to gnaw; akin to OE *gnagan* to gnaw] (1675) **1 :** to touch or push gently; *esp* **:** to seek the attention of by a push of the elbow **2 :** to prod lightly **:** urge into action **3 :** APPROACH ⟨its circulation is *nudging* the four million mark —Bennett Cerf⟩ ~ *vi* **:** to give a nudge — **nudge** *n* — **nudg·er** *n*

nu·di·branch \ˈn(y)üd-ə-ˌbraŋk\ *n, pl* **-branchs** [NL *Nudibranchia,* fr. L *nudus* + *branchia* gill — more at BRANCHIA] (1841) **:** any of a suborder (Nudibranchia) of marine gastropod mollusks without a shell in the adult state and without true gills — **nudibranch** *adj*

nud·ism \ˈn(y)üd-ˌiz-əm\ *n* (1929) **:** the practice of going nude esp. in sexually mixed groups and during periods of time spent at specially secluded places — **nud·ist** \ˈn(y)üd-əst\ *adj or n*

nud·nick *or* **nud·nik** \ˈnüd-nik\ *n* [Yiddish *nudnik,* fr. Russ *nudnyi* tiresome (fr. *nuda* need, boredom) + Yiddish *-nik* -nik; akin to OE *nied* need] (1947) **:** a person who is a bore or nuisance

nu·ga·to·ry \ˈn(y)ü-gə-ˌtōr-ē, -ˌtȯr-\ *adj* [L *nugatorius,* fr. *nugatus,* pp. of *nugari* to trifle, fr. *nugae* trifles] (1603) **1 :** of little or no consequence **:** TRIFLING, INCONSEQUENTIAL **2 :** having no force **:** INOPERATIVE ***syn*** see VAIN

nug·get \ˈnəg-ət\ *n* [origin unknown] (1852) **1 :** a solid lump; *esp* **:** a native lump of precious metal **2 :** something suggestive of a gold nugget esp. in worth or importance ⟨~*s* of wisdom⟩

nui·sance \ˈn(y)üs-ᵊn(t)s\ *n* [ME *nusaunce,* fr. AF, fr. OF *nuisir* to harm, fr. L *nocēre* — more at NOXIOUS] (15c) **1 :** HARM, INJURY **2 :** one that is annoying, unpleasant, or obnoxious **:** PEST

nuisance tax *n* (1924) **:** an excise tax collected in small amounts on a wide range of commodities directly from the consumer

[1]**nuke** \ˈn(y)ük\ *n* [by shortening] (1959) **1 :** a nuclear weapon **2 :** a nuclear-powered electric generating station

[2]**nuke** *vt* **nuked; nuk·ing** (1967) **:** to attack or destroy with nuclear bombs

[1]**null** \ˈnəl\ *adj* [MF *nul,* lit., not any, fr. L *nullus,* fr. *ne-* not + *ullus* any; akin to L *unus* one — more at NO, ONE] (ca. 1563) **1 :** having no legal or binding force **:** INVALID **2 :** amounting to nothing **:** NIL **3 :** having no value **:** INSIGNIFICANT **4 a :** having no elements ⟨~ set⟩ **b :** having zero as a limit ⟨~ sequence⟩ **c** *of a matrix* **:** having all elements equal to zero **5 a :** indicating usu. by a zero reading on a scale when current or voltage is zero — used of an instrument **b :** being or relating to a method of measurement in which an unknown quantity (as of electric current) is compared with a known quantity of the same kind and found equal by a null detector **6 :** of, being, or relating to zero

[2]**null** *n* (1605) **1 :** ZERO 3a(1) **2 a :** a condition of a radio receiver when minimum or zero signal is received **b :** a minimum or zero value of an electric current or of a radio signal **3 :** a meaningless letter or code group included in a cryptogram to impede cryptanalysis

[3]**null** *vt* (1643) **:** to make null

nul·lah \ˈnəl-ə\ *n* [Hindi *nālā*] (1776) **:** GULLY, RAVINE

null and void *adj* (1669) **:** having no force, binding power, or validity

null hypothesis *n* (1935) **:** a statistical hypothesis to be tested and accepted or rejected in favor of an alternative; *specif* **:** the hypothesis that an observed difference (as between the means of two samples) is due to chance alone and not due to a systematic cause

nul·li·fi·ca·tion \ˌnəl-ə-fə-ˈkā-shən\ *n* (1798) **1 :** the act of nullifying **:** the state of being nullified **2 :** the action of a state impeding or attempting to prevent the operation and enforcement within its territory of a law of the U.S. — **nul·li·fi·ca·tion·ist** \-sh(ə-)nəst\ *n*

nul·li·fi·er \ˈnəl-ə-ˌfī(-ə)r\ *n* (1832) **:** one that nullifies; *specif* **:** one maintaining the right of nullification against the U.S. government

nul·li·fy \ˈnəl-ə-ˌfī\ *vt* **-fied; -fy·ing** [LL *nullificare,* fr. L *nullus*] (1535) **1 :** to make null; *esp* **:** to make legally null and void **2 :** to make of no value or consequence

syn NULLIFY, NEGATE, ANNUL, ABROGATE, INVALIDATE mean to deprive of effective or continued existence. NULLIFY implies counteracting completely the force, effectiveness, or value of something; NEGATE implies the destruction or canceling out of each of two things by the other; ANNUL suggests making ineffective or nonexistent often by legal or official action; ABROGATE is like ANNUL but more definitely implies a legal or official purposeful act; INVALIDATE implies making something powerless or unacceptable by declaration of its logical or moral or legal unsoundness.

nul·lip·a·rous \ˌnə-ˈlip-ə-rəs\ *adj* [NL *nullipara* one who has never borne an offspring, fr. L *nullus* not any + *-para* -para] (1859) **:** of, relating to, or being a female that has not borne offspring

nul·li·ty \ˈnəl-ət-ē\ *n, pl* **-ties** (1570) **1 :** the quality or state of being null; *esp* **:** legal invalidity **2 :** one that is null; *specif* **:** an act void of legal effect **3 :** the number of elements in a basis of a null-space

null–space \ˈnəl-ˌspās\ *n* (1884) **:** a subspace of a vector space consisting of vectors that under a given linear transformation are equal to zero

numb \ˈnəm\ *adj* [ME *nomen,* fr. pp. of *nimen* to take — more at NIM] (15c) **1 :** devoid of sensation esp. as a result of cold or anesthesia **2 :** devoid of emotion **:** INDIFFERENT — **numb** *vt* — **numb·ing·ly** \ˈnəm-iŋ-lē\ *adv* — **numb·ly** \ˈnəm-lē\ *adv* — **numb·ness** *n*

[1]**num·ber** \ˈnəm-bər\ *n* [ME *nombre,* fr. OF, fr. L *numerus* — more at NIMBLE] (13c) **1 a (1) :** a sum of units **:** TOTAL **(2) :** COMPLEMENT 1b **(3) :** an indefinite usu. large total ⟨a ~ of members were absent⟩ **(4)** *pl* **:** a numerous group **:** MANY; *also* **:** a numerical preponderance **b :** the characteristic of an individual by which it is treated as a unit or of a collection by which it is treated in terms of units **:** the aspect of something that can be counted **c (1) :** a unit belonging to an abstract mathematical system and subject to specified laws of succession, addition, and multiplication; *esp* **:** NATURAL NUMBER **(2) :** an element (as π) of any of many mathematical systems obtained by extension of or analogy with the natural number system **(3)** *pl* **:** ARITHMETIC **2 :** a distinction of word form to denote reference to one or more than one; *also* **:** a form or group of forms so distinguished **3** *pl* **a (1) :** metrical structure **:** METER **(2) :** metrical lines **:** VERSES **b** *archaic* **:** musical sounds **:** NOTES **4 a :** a word, symbol, letter, or combination of symbols representing a number **b :** a numeral or combination of numerals or other symbols used to identify or designate **c (1) :** a member of a sequence or collection designated by esp. consecutive numbers (as an issue of a periodical) **(2) :** a position in a numbered sequence **d :** a group of one kind ⟨not of their ~⟩ **5 :** one singled out from a group **:** INDIVIDUAL: as **a :** GIRL, WOMAN ⟨met an attractive ~ at the dance⟩ **b :** a musical, theatrical, or literary selection **c :** an item of merchandise and esp. clothing **6 :** insight into a person's ability or character ⟨had my ~⟩ **7** *pl but sing or pl in constr* **a :** a form of lottery in which an individual wagers on the appearance of a certain combination of digits (as in regularly published numbers) — called also *numbers game* **b :** [2]POLICY 2a ***usage*** see AMOUNT — **by the numbers 1 :** in unison to a specific count or cadence **2 :** in a systematic, routine, or mechanical manner

[2]**number** *vb* **num·bered; num·ber·ing** \-b(ə-)riŋ\ *vt* (13c) **1 :** COUNT, ENUMERATE **2 :** to claim as part of a total **:** INCLUDE **3 :** to restrict to a definite number **4 :** to assign a number to **5 :** to amount to in number **:** TOTAL ~ *vi* **1 :** to reach a total number **2 :** to call off numbers in sequence — **num·ber·able** \-b(ə-)rə-bəl\ *adj* — **num·ber·er** \-bər-ər\ *n*

num·ber·less \ˈnəm-bər-ləs\ *adj* (1573) **:** INNUMERABLE, COUNTLESS

number line *n* (1960) **:** a line of infinite extent whose points correspond to the real numbers according to their distance in a positive or negative direction from a point arbitrarily taken as zero

[1]**number one** *n* (1704) **:** one's own interests or welfare **:** ONESELF ⟨has to look out for *number one*⟩

[2]**number one** *adj* (1839) **1 :** first in rank, importance, or influence **:** FOREMOST ⟨America's *number one* hit⟩ **2 :** of highest or of high quality ⟨a real *number one* dinner⟩

Num·bers \ˈnəm-bərz\ *n pl but sing in constr* **:** the mainly narrative fourth book of canonical Jewish and Christian Scripture — see BIBLE table

number theory *n* (1912) **:** the study of the properties of integers — **number theoretic** *adj*

numb·skull \ˈnəm-ˌskəl\ *var of* NUMSKULL

nu·men \ˈn(y)ü-mən\ *n, pl* **nu·mi·na** \-mə-nə\ [L, nod, divine will, numen; akin to L *nuere* to nod, Gk *neuein*] (1628) **:** a spiritual force or influence often identified with a natural object, phenomenon, or locality

nu·mer·a·ble \ˈn(y)üm-(ə-)rə-bəl\ *adj* [L *numerabilis,* fr. *numerare* to count] (1570) **:** capable of being counted

[1]**nu·mer·al** \ˈn(y)üm-(ə-)rəl\ *adj* [MF, fr. LL *numeralis,* fr. L *numerus*] (14c) **1 :** of, relating to, or expressing numbers **2 :** consisting of numbers or numerals — **nu·mer·al·ly** \-ē\ *adv*

2numeral *n* (1686) **1 :** a conventional symbol that represents a number **2** *pl* **:** numbers that designate by year a school or college class and that are awarded for distinction in an extracurricular activity

1nu·mer·ate \'n(y)ü-mə-,rāt\ *vt* **-at·ed; -at·ing** [L *numeratus,* pp. of *numerare* to count, fr. *numerus*] (1721) **:** ENUMERATE

2nu·mer·ate \'n(y)üm-(ə-)rət\ *adj* [L *numerus* number + E *-ate* (as in *literate*)] (1959) **:** marked by the capacity for quantitative thought and expression — **nu·mer·acy** \-(ə-)rə-sē\ *n*

nu·mer·a·tion \,n(y)ü-mə-'rā-shən\ *n* (15c) **1 a :** the act or process or an instance of counting or numbering; *also* **:** a system of counting or numbering **b :** an act or instance of designating by a number **2 :** the art of reading in words numbers expressed by numerals

nu·mer·a·tor \'n(y)ü-mə-,rāt-ər\ *n* (1575) **1 :** the part of a fraction that is above the line and signifies the number of parts of the denominator taken **2 :** one that numbers

1nu·mer·ic \n(y)ù-'mer-ik\ *n* (ca. 1879) **:** NUMBER, NUMERAL

2numeric *adj* (ca. 1909) **:** NUMERICAL; *esp* **:** denoting a number or a system of numbers ⟨~ code⟩ ⟨a ~ sign⟩

nu·mer·i·cal \n(y)ù-'mer-i-kəl\ *adj* [L *numerus*] (1628) **1 :** of or relating to numbers ⟨the ~ superiority of the enemy⟩ **2 :** expressed in or involving numbers or a number system ⟨~ standing in a class⟩ ⟨a ~ code⟩ — **nu·mer·i·cal·ly** \-k(ə-)lē\ *adv*

numerical analysis *n* (1930) **:** the study of quantitative approximations to the solutions of mathematical problems including consideration of the errors and bounds to the errors involved

numerical taxonomy *n* (1963) **:** taxonomy that applies the quantitative measurement of many characters to the determination of taxa and to the construction of diagrams indicating systematic relationships — **numerical taxonomic** *adj* — **numerical taxonomist** *n*

nu·mer·ol·o·gy \,n(y)ü-mə-'räl-ə-jē\ *n* [L *numerus* + E *-o-* + *-logy*] (1911) **:** the study of the occult significance of numbers — **nu·mer·o·log·i·cal** \-mə-rə-'läj-i-kəl\ *adj* — **nu·mer·ol·o·gist** \-mə-'räl-ə-jəst\ *n*

nu·me·ro uno \,n(y)ü-mə-rō-'ü-(,)nō\ *n or adj* [It or Sp] (ca. 1963) **:** NUMBER ONE

nu·mer·ous \'n(y)üm-(ə-)rəs\ *adj* [ME, fr. MF *numereux,* fr. L *numerosus,* fr. *numerus*] (15c) **:** consisting of great numbers of units or individuals — **nu·mer·ous·ly** *adv* — **nu·mer·ous·ness** *n*

nu·mi·nous \'n(y)ü-mə-nəs\ *adj* [L *numin-, numen* numen] (1647) **1 :** SUPERNATURAL, MYSTERIOUS **2 :** filled with a sense of the presence of divinity **:** HOLY **3 :** appealing to the higher emotions or to the aesthetic sense **:** SPIRITUAL

nu·mis·mat·ic \,n(y)ü-məz-'mat-ik, -məs-\ *adj* [F *numismatique,* fr. L *nomismat-, nomisma* coin, fr. Gk, custom, coin; akin to Gk *nomos* custom, law — more at NIMBLE] (1792) **1 :** of or relating to numismatics **2 :** of or relating to currency **:** MONETARY — **nu·mis·mat·i·cal·ly** \-i-k(ə-)lē\ *adv*

nu·mis·mat·ics \-iks\ *n pl but sing in constr* (1878) **:** the study or collection of coins, tokens, and paper money and sometimes related objects (as medals) — **nu·mis·ma·tist** \n(y)ü-'miz-mət-əst\ *n*

num·mu·lar \'nəm-yə-lər\ *adj* [F *nummulaire,* fr. L *nummulus,* dim. of *nummus* coin, fr. Gk *nomimos* customary; akin to Gk *nomos*] (1846) **:** characterized by circular or oval lesions or drops ⟨~ dermatitis⟩ ⟨~ sputum⟩

num·mu·lit·ic limestone \,nəm-yə-,lit-ik-\ *n* [NL *Nummulites,* genus of foraminifers, fr. L *nummulus*] (1833) **:** the most widely distributed and distinctive formation of the Eocene in Europe, Asia, and northern Africa

num·skull \'nəm-,skəl\ *n* [*numb* + *skull*] (1724) **1 :** a dull or stupid person **:** DUNCE **2 :** a thick or muddled head

1nun \'nən\ *n* [ME, fr. OE *nunne,* fr. LL *nonna*] (bef. 12c) **:** a woman belonging to a religious order; *esp* **:** one under solemn vows of poverty, chastity, and obedience

2nun \'nùn\ *n* [Heb *nūn*] (1823) **:** the 14th letter of the Hebrew alphabet — see ALPHABET table

nun·a·tak \'nən-ə-,tak\ *n* [Esk] (1877) **:** a hill or mountain completely surrounded by glacial ice

Nunc Di·mit·tis \,nəŋk-də-'mit-əs, ,nùŋk-\ *n* [L, now lettest thou depart; fr. the first words of the canticle] (1552) **:** the prayer of Simeon in Luke 2:29-32 used as a canticle

nun·cha·ku \'nən-,chək, ,nən-'chäk-ü\ *n* [Jp] (1970) **:** a weapon of Japanese origin that consists of two hardwood sticks joined at their ends by a short length of rawhide, cord, or chain

nun·ci·a·ture \'nən(t)-sē-ə-,chù(ə)r, 'nùn(t)-, -chər, -,t(y)ù(ə)r\ *n* [It *nunciatura,* fr. *nuncio*] (1652) **1 :** a papal diplomatic mission headed by a nuncio **2 :** the office or period of office of a nuncio

nun·cio \'nən(t)-sē-,ō, 'nùn(t)-\ *n, pl* **-ci·os** [It, fr. L *nuntius* messenger, message] (1528) **:** a papal legate of the highest rank permanently accredited to a civil government

nun·cle \'nəŋ-kəl\ *n* [by alter. (resulting fr. incorrect division of *an uncle*)] *chiefly dial* (1589) **:** UNCLE

nun·cu·pa·tive \'nən-kyù-,pāt-iv, 'nəŋ-; ,nən-'kyü-pət-\ *adj* [ML *nuncupativus,* fr. LL, so-called, fr. L *nuncupatus,* pp. of *nuncupare* to name, contr. of *nomen capere,* fr. *nomen* name + *capere* to take — more at NAME, HEAVE] (1546) **:** not written **:** ORAL ⟨a ~ will⟩

nun·nery \'nən-(ə-)rē\ *n, pl* **-ner·ies** (13c) **:** a convent of nuns

Nu·pe \'nü-(,)pā\ *n, pl* **Nupe** *or* **Nupes** (1829) **1 :** a member of a Negro people of west central Nigeria **2 :** a Kwa language of the Nupe people

1nup·tial \'nəp-shəl, -chəl, ÷-shə-wəl, ÷-chə-wəl\ *adj* [L *nuptialis,* fr. *nuptiae,* pl., wedding, fr. *nuptus,* pp. of *nubere* to marry; akin to Gk *nymphē* bride, nymph] (15c) **1 :** of or relating to marriage or the marriage ceremony **2 :** characteristic of or occurring in the breeding season ⟨~ flight⟩

2nuptial *n* (1555) **:** MARRIAGE, WEDDING — usu. used in pl.

nup·tial·i·ty \,nəp-shē-'al-ət-ē, -chē-\ *n* **-ties** (1899) **:** the marriage rate

nuptial plumage *n* (1840) **:** the brilliantly colored plumage assumed by the males of many birds prior to the start of the annual breeding period — compare ECLIPSE PLUMAGE

1nurse \'nərs\ *n* [ME, fr. OF *nurice,* fr. LL *nutricia,* fr. L, fem. of *nutricius* nourishing — more at NUTRITIOUS] (13c) **1 a :** a woman who suckles an infant not her own **b :** a woman who takes care of a young child **2 :** one that looks after, fosters, or advises **3 :** a person who is skilled or trained in caring for the sick or infirm esp. under the supervision of a physician **4 a :** a member of an insect society that belongs to the worker cast and cares for the young **b :** a female mammal used to suckle the young of another

2nurse *vb* **nursed; nurs·ing** [ME *nurshen* to nourish, contr. of *nurishen*] *vt* (14c) **1 a :** to nourish at the breast **:** SUCKLE **b :** to take nourishment from the breast of **2 :** REAR, EDUCATE **3 a :** to promote the development or progress of **b :** to manage with care or economy ⟨*nursed* the business through hard times⟩ **c :** to take charge of and watch over **4 a :** to care for and wait on (as a sick person) **b :** to attempt to cure by care and treatment **5 :** to hold in one's memory or consideration ⟨~ a grievance⟩ **6 a :** to use, handle, or operate carefully so as to conserve energy or avoid injury or pain ⟨~ a sprained ankle⟩ **b :** to use sparingly **c :** to consume slowly or over a long period ⟨~ a cup of coffee⟩ ~ *vi* **1 a :** to feed an offspring from the breast **b :** to feed at the breast **:** SUCK **2 :** to act or serve as a nurse — **nurs·er** *n*

nurse·maid \'nər-,smād\ *n* (1657) **:** a girl or woman who is regularly employed to look after children

nurs·ery \'nərs-(ə-)rē\ *n, pl* **-er·ies** (15c) **1** *obs* **:** attentive care **:** FOSTERAGE **2 a :** a child's bedroom **b :** a place where children are temporarily cared for in their parents' absence **c :** DAY NURSERY **3 a :** something that fosters, develops, or promotes **b :** a place in which persons are trained or educated **4 :** an area where plants (as trees and shrubs) are grown for transplanting, for use as stocks for budding and grafting, or for sale **5 :** a place where young animals (as fish) grow or are cared for

nurs·ery·man \-mən\ *n* (1672) **:** one whose occupation is the cultivation of plants (as trees and shrubs) esp. for sale

nursery rhyme *n* (1832) **:** a short rhyme for children that often tells a story

nursery school *n* (1835) **:** a school for children usu. under five years

nurse's aide *n* (1943) **:** a worker who assists trained nurses in a hospital by performing unspecialized services (as giving baths)

nurse shark *n* [alter. of ME *nusse*] (1851) **:** any of various sharks of a widely distributed family (Orectolobidae); *esp* **:** a shark (*Ginglymostoma cirratum*) of the warmer parts of the Atlantic ocean

nurs·ing *n* (1860) **1 :** the profession of a nurse ⟨schools of ~⟩ **2 :** the duties of a nurse ⟨proper ~ is difficult work⟩

nursing home *n* (1896) **:** a privately operated establishment where maintenance and personal or nursing care are provided for persons (as the aged or the chronically ill) who are unable to care for themselves properly

nurs·ling \'nər-sliŋ\ *n* (1557) **1 :** one that is solicitously cared for **2 :** a nursing child

nur·tur·ance \'nər-chə-rən(t)s\ *n* [2*nurture* + *-ance*] (1938) **:** affectionate care and attention — **nur·tur·ant** \-rənt\ *adj*

1nur·ture \'nər-chər\ *n* [ME, fr. MF *norriture,* fr. LL *nutritura* act of nursing, fr. L *nutritus,* pp. of *nutrire* to suckle, nourish — more at NOURISH] (14c) **1 :** TRAINING, UPBRINGING **2 :** something that nourishes **:** FOOD **3 :** the sum of the influences modifying the expression of the genetic potentialities of an organism

2nurture *vt* **nur·tured; nur·tur·ing** \'nərch-(ə-)riŋ\ (15c) **1 :** to supply with nourishment **2 :** EDUCATE **3 :** to further the development of **:** FOSTER — **nur·tur·er** \'nər-chər-ər\ *n*

1nut \'nət\ *n* [ME *nute, note,* fr. OE *hnutu;* akin to OHG *nuz* nut, L *nux*] (bef. 12c) **1 a** (1) **:** a hard-shelled dry fruit or seed with a separable rind or shell and interior kernel (2) **:** the kernel of a nut **b :** a dry indehiscent one-seeded fruit with a woody pericarp **2 :** a hard problem or undertaking **3 :** a perforated block usu. of metal that has an internal screw thread and is used on a bolt or screw for tightening or holding something **4 :** the ridge in a stringed instrument (as a violin) over which the strings pass on the upper end of the fingerboard **5** *pl* **:** NONSENSE — often used interjectionally **6** *pl* **:** TESTES — usu. considered vulgar **7** *slang* **:** a person's head **8 a :** a foolish, eccentric, or crazy person **b :** ENTHUSIAST ⟨movie ~⟩ **9 :** the complete expense involved **10 :** EN 2 — **nut·like** \-,lik\ *adj*

2nut *vi* **nut·ted; nut·ting** (1604) **:** to gather or seek nuts

nu·tate \'n(y)ü-,tāt\ *vi* **nu·tat·ed; nu·tat·ing** (1880) **:** to exhibit or undergo nutation

nu·ta·tion \n(y)ü-'tā-shən\ *n* [L *nutation-, nutatio,* fr. *nutatus,* pp. of *nutare* to nod, rock, freq. of *nuere* to nod — more at NUMEN] (1612) **1 :** the act of nodding the head **2 a :** a libratory motion of the earth's axis like the nodding of a top **b :** oscillatory movement of the axis of a rotating body **:** WOBBLE **3 :** a spontaneous usu. spiral movement of a growing plant part — **nu·ta·tion·al** \-shnəl, -shən-ᵊl\ *adj*

nut–brown \'nət-'braùn\ *adj* (14c) **:** of the color of a brown nut

nut·crack·er \-,krak-ər\ *n* (1548) **:** an implement for cracking nuts

nut·gall \-,gȯl\ *n* (15c) **:** a gall that resembles a nut; *esp* **:** a gall produced on oak

nut grass *n* (1775) **:** a perennial sedge (*Cyperus rotundus*) of wide distribution that has slender rootstocks bearing small edible tubers resembling nuts; *also* **:** a related sedge (*C. esculentus*)

nut·hatch \'nət-,hach\ *n* [ME *notehache,* fr. *note* nut + *hache* ax, fr. OF, battle-ax — more at HASH] (14c) **:** any of various small tree-climbing birds (family Sittidae) that have a compact body, a long bill, a short tail, and sometimes a black cap and a ring around the eye

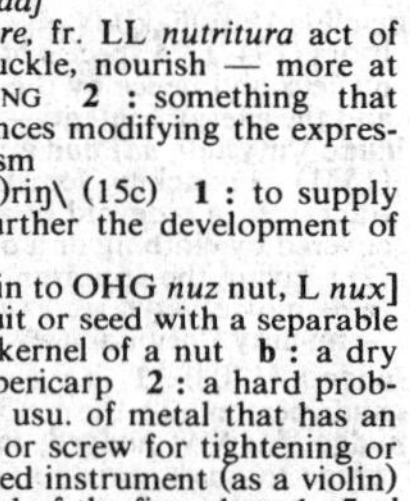

nuthatch

nut·house \'nət-,haùs\ *n, slang* (1900) **:** an insane asylum

nut·let \'nət-lət\ *n* (1856) **1 a :** a small nut **b :** a small fruit similar to a nut **2 :** the stone of a drupelet

nut·meg \'nət-,meg, -,māg\ *n* [ME *notemuge,* deriv. of OProv *noz muscada,* fr. *noz* nut (fr. L *nuc-, nux*) + *muscada,* fem. of *muscat* musky — more at MUSCAT] (14c) **:** an aromatic seed that is used as a spice and is produced by a tree (*Myristica fragrans* of the family Myristicaceae, the nutmeg family) native to the Moluccas; *also* **:** this tree

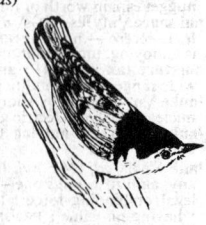

nut·pick \'nət-,pik\ *n* (1889) **:** a small sharp-pointed implement for extracting the kernels from nuts

nu·tria \'n(y)ü-trē-ə\ *n* [Sp, modif. of L *lutra* otter; akin to OE *oter* otter] (1820) **1 :** the durable usu. light brown fur of a nutria **2 :** a So.

American aquatic rodent (*Myocastor coypus*) with webbed feet and dorsal mammae that has been introduced into the U.S. on the Gulf coast and in the Pacific Northwest

¹nu·tri·ent \'n(y)ü-trē-ənt\ *adj* [L *nutrient-, nutriens,* prp. of *nutrire* to nourish — more at NOURISH] (1650) : furnishing nourishment

²nutrient *n* (1828) : a nutritive substance or ingredient

nu·tri·ment \'n(y)ü-trə-mənt\ *n* [L *nutrimentum,* fr. *nutrire*] (15c) : something that nourishes or promotes growth and repairs the natural wastage of organic life

nu·tri·tion \n(y)ü-'trish-ən\ *n* [MF, fr. LL *nutrition-, nutritio,* fr. L *nutritus,* pp. of *nutrire*] (15c) : the act or process of nourishing or being nourished; *specif* : the sum of the processes by which an animal or plant takes in and utilizes food substances — nu·tri·tion·al \-'trish-nəl, -ən-ᵊl\ *adj* — nu·tri·tion·al·ly \-ē\ *adv*

nu·tri·tion·ist \-'trish-(ə-)nəst\ *n* (1926) : a specialist in the study of nutrition

nu·tri·tious \n(y)ü-'trish-əs\ *adj* [L *nutricius,* fr. *nutric-, nutrix* nurse; akin to L *nutrire* to nourish — more at NOURISH] (1665) : NOURISHING — nu·tri·tious·ly *adv* — nu·tri·tious·ness *n*

nu·tri·tive \'n(y)ü-trət-iv\ *adj* (14c) 1 : of or relating to nutrition 2 : NOURISHING — nu·tri·tive·ly *adv*

nutritive ratio *n* (1897) : the ratio of digestible protein to other nutrients in a foodstuff or ration

nuts \'nəts\ *adj* (1785) 1 : ENTHUSIASTIC, KEEN ⟨everyone seems ~ about it —Lois Long⟩ 2 : INSANE, CRAZY ⟨thought I would go ~ waiting around —Polly Adler⟩

nuts and bolts *n* (1960) 1 : the working parts or elements 2 : the practical workings of a machine or enterprise as opposed to theoretical considerations or speculative possibilities — nuts–and–bolts *adj*

nut·sedge \'nət-ˌsej\ *n* (1909) : NUT GRASS

nut·shell \'nət-ˌshel\ *n* (13c) 1 : the hard external covering in which the kernel of a nut is enclosed 2 : something of small size, amount, or scope — in a nutshell : in a very brief statement

nut·ty \'nət-ē\ *adj* nut·ti·er; -est (15c) 1 : having or producing nuts 2 : having a flavor like that of nuts 3 : ECCENTRIC, SILLY; *also* : mentally unbalanced — nut·ti·ness *n*

nux vom·i·ca \'nəks-'väm-i-kə\ *n, pl* nux vomica [NL, lit., emetic nut] (14c) : the poisonous seed of an Asian tree (*Strychnos nux-vomica* of the family Loganiaceae) that contains several alkaloids and esp. strychnine and brucine; *also* : the tree yielding nux vomica

nuz·zle \'nəz-əl\ *vb* nuz·zled; nuz·zling \-(ə-)liŋ\ [ME *noselen,* to bring the nose towards the ground, fr. *nose*] *vi* (15c) 1 : to work with or as if with the nose; *esp* : to root, rub, or snuff something 2 : to lie close or snug : NESTLE ~ *vt* : to root, rub, or touch with or as if with the nose : NUDGE

ny·a·la \nē-'äl-ə\ *n, pl* nyalas *or* nyala [of Bantu origin; akin to Venda *nyala,* Zulu *inxala*] (1894) : an antelope (*Tragelaphus angasi*) of southeastern Africa with vertical white stripes on the sides of the body and with shaggy black hair along the male underside; *also* : a related antelope (*T. buxtoni*)

nyc·ta·lo·pia \ˌnik-tə-'lō-pē-ə\ *n* [LL] (1684) : NIGHT BLINDNESS

ny·lon \'nī-ˌlän\ *n* [coined word] (1938) 1 : any of numerous strong tough elastic synthetic polyamide materials that are fashioned into fibers, filaments, bristles, or sheets, and used esp. in textiles and plastics 2 *pl* : stockings made of nylon

nymph \'nim(p)f\ *n* [ME *nimphe,* fr. MF, fr. L *nympha* bride, nymph, fr. Gk *nymphē* — more at NUPTIAL] (14c) 1 : any of the minor divinities of nature in classical mythology represented as beautiful maidens dwelling in the mountains, forests, trees, and waters 2 : GIRL 3 : any of various immature insects; *esp* : a larva of an insect (as a grasshopper, true bug, or mayfly) with incomplete metamorphosis that differs from the imago esp. in size and in its incompletely developed wings and genitalia — compare NAIAD 2 — nymph·al \'nim(p)-fəl\ *adj*

nym·pha·lid \'nim-'fal-əd, 'nim-fə-ləd\ *n* [NL *Nymphalidae,* deriv. of L *nympha* nymph] (1897) : any of a family (Nymphalidae) of butterflies (as a mourning cloak or fritillary) with the first pair of legs reduced in size in both sexes and useless for walking — nymphalid *adj*

nym·phet *also* nym·phette \nim-'fet, 'nim(p)-fət\ *n* [obs. *nymphet* young nymph, fr. MF *nymphette,* dim. of *nymphe* nymph] (1955) : a sexually precocious girl barely in her teens

nym·pho \'nim(p)-(ˌ)fō\ *n, pl* nymphos [by shortening] (ca. 1910) : one affected by nymphomania

nym·pho·lep·sy \'nim(p)-fə-ˌlep-sē\ *n* [*nympholept,* fr. Gk *nympholēptos* frenzied, lit., caught by nymphs, fr. *nymphē* + *lambanein* to seize — more at CATCH] (1775) 1 : a demoniac enthusiasm held by the ancients to seize one bewitched by a nymph 2 : a frenzy of emotion — nym·pho·lept \-ˌlept\ *n* — nym·pho·lep·tic \ˌnim(p)-fə-'lep-tik\ *adj*

nym·pho·ma·nia \ˌnim(p)-fə-'mā-nē-ə, -nyə\ *n* [NL, fr. *nymphae* inner lips of the vulva (fr. L, pl. of *nympha*) + LL *mania* mania] (1775) : excessive sexual desire by a female — nym·pho·ma·ni·ac \-nē-ˌak\ *n or adj* — nym·pho·ma·ni·a·cal \-mə-'nī-ə-kəl\ *adj*

Ny·norsk \n(y)ü-'nȯ(ə)rsk, nüȯ-\ *n* [Norw, lit., new Norwegian] (1931) : a literary form of Norwegian based on the spoken dialects of Norway — compare BOKMÅL

nys·tag·mus \nis-'tag-məs\ *n* [NL, fr. Gk *nystagmos* drowsiness, fr. *nystazein* to doze; akin to Lith *snusti* to doze] (1822) : a rapid involuntary oscillation of the eyeballs (as from dizziness) — nys·tag·mic \-mik\ *adj*

nys·ta·tin \'nis-tət-ən\ *n* [*New York State* (where it was developed) + *-in*] (1952) : an antibiotic that is derived from a soil actinomycete (*Streptomyces noursei*) and is used esp. in the treatment of candidiasis

o \'ō\ *n, pl* o's *or* os \'ōz\ *often cap, often attrib* 1 a : the 15th letter of the English alphabet b : a graphic representation of this letter c : a speech counterpart of orthographic *o* 2 : a graphic device for reproducing the letter *o* 3 : one designated *o* esp. as the 15th in order or class 4 : something shaped like the letter O; *esp* : ZERO

O \'ō\ *var of* OH

o- *or* oo- *comb form* [Gk *ōi-, ōio-,* fr. *ōion* — more at EGG] : egg ⟨oology⟩; *specif* : ovum ⟨oogonium⟩

-o- [ME, fr. OF, fr. L, fr. Gk, thematic vowel of many nouns and adjectives in combination] — used as a connective vowel orig. to join word elements of Greek origin and now also to join word elements of Latin or other origin ⟨drunkometer⟩ ⟨elastomer⟩

¹-o \(ˌ)ō\ *n suffix* [perh. fr. ¹*oh*] : one that is, has the qualities of, or is associated with ⟨bucko⟩

²-o \(ˌ)ō, 'ō\ *interj suffix* [prob. fr. ¹*oh*] — in interjections formed from other parts of speech ⟨cheerio⟩ ⟨righto⟩

o' *also* o \ə\ *prep* [ME *o, o-,* contr. of *on* & *of*] (14c) 1 *chiefly dial* : ON 2 : OF ⟨one o'clock⟩

oaf \'ōf\ *n* [of Scand origin; akin to ON *alfr* elf — more at ELF] (1625) 1 : a stupid person : BOOB 2 : a big clumsy slow-witted person — oaf·ish \'ō-fish\ *adj* — oaf·ish·ly *adv* — oaf·ish·ness *n*

oak \'ōk\ *n, pl* oaks *or* oak *often attrib* [ME *ook,* fr. OE *āc;* akin to OHG *eih* oak, Gk *aigilōps,* a kind of oak] (bef. 12c) 1 a : a tree or shrub (genera *Quercus* or *Lithocarpus*) of the beech family that produces a rounded one-seeded thin-shelled nut surrounded at the base by an indurated cup b : the tough hard durable wood of an oak tree 2 : the leaves of an oak used as decoration — oak·en \'ō-kən\ *adj*

oak apple *n* (15c) : a large round gall produced on oak leaves by a gall wasp (esp. *Amphibolips confluenta* or *Andricus californicus*)

oak–leaf cluster *n* (1918) : a bronze or silver cluster of oak leaves and acorns added to various military decorations to signify a second or subsequent award of the basic decoration

oak·moss \'ōk-ˌmȯs\ *n* (1921) : any of several lichens that grow on oak trees and yield a resin used in perfumery

oa·kum \'ō-kəm\ *n* [ME *okum,* fr. OE *ācumba* tow, fr. *ā-* (separative & perfective prefix) + *-cumba* (akin to OE *camb* comb) — more at ABIDE] (12c) : loosely twisted hemp or jute fiber impregnated with tar or a tar derivative and used in caulking seams (as of wooden ships) and packing joints (as of pipes)

oak wilt *n* (1942) : a destructive disease of oak trees that is caused by a fungus (*Ceratocystis fagacearum*) and is characterized by wilting, discoloration, and defoliation

¹oar \'ō(ə)r, 'ȯ(ə)r\ *n* [ME *oor,* fr. OE *ār;* akin to ON *ār* oar] (bef. 12c) 1 : a long pole with a broad blade at one end used for propelling or steering a boat 2 : OARSMAN — oared \'ō(ə)rd, 'ȯ(ə)rd\ *adj*

²oar *vt* (1610) : to propel with or as if with oars : ROW ~ *vi* : to progress by or as if by using oars

oar·fish \'ō(ə)r-ˌfish, 'ȯ(ə)r-\ *n* (1860) : any of several sea fishes (genus *Regalecus*) with narrow soft bodies from 20 to 30 feet (6.1 to 9.1 meters) long, a dorsal fin running the entire length of the body, and red-tipped anterior rays rising above the head

oar·lock \-ˌläk\ *n* (bef. 12c) : a U-shaped device for holding an oar in place

oars·man \'ō(ə)rz-mən, 'ȯ(ə)r-\ *n* (1701) : one who rows esp. in a racing crew — oars·man·ship \-ˌship\ *n*

oa·sis \ō-'ā-səs\ *n, pl* oa·ses \-ˌsēz\ [LL, fr. Gk] (1613) 1 : a fertile or green area in an arid region 2 : something providing relief from boring or dreary routine : REFUGE

oast \'ōst\ *n* [ME *ost,* fr. OE *āst;* akin to MD *eest* kiln, L *aestus* heat, *aestas* summer—more at EDIFY] (bef. 12c) : a usu. conical kiln used for drying hops, malt, or tobacco — called also oast·house \-ˌhaus\

oat \'ōt\ *n, often attrib* [ME *ote,* fr. OE *āte*] (bef. 12c) 1 a : any of several grasses (genus *Avena*); *esp* : a widely cultivated cereal grass (*A. sativa*) b : a crop or plot of the oat; *also* : oat seed — usu. used in pl. but sing. or pl. in constr. 2 *archaic* : a reed instrument made of an oat straw

oat·cake \'ōt-ˌkāk\ *n* (14c) : a thin flat oatmeal cake

oat·en \'ōt-ᵊn\ *adj* (14c) : of or relating to oats, oat straw, or oatmeal

oat·er \'ōt-ər\ *n* (1946) : WESTERN 2

oat grass *n* (1578) : WILD OAT 1a; *broadly* : one of several grasses resembling the oat

oath \'ōth\ *n, pl* oaths \'ō*th*z, 'ōths\ [ME *ooth,* fr. OE *āth;* akin to OHG *eid* oath] (bef. 12c) 1 a (1) : a solemn usu. formal calling upon God or a god to witness to the truth of what one says or to witness that one

\ə\ abut \ᵊ\ kitten, F table \ər\ further \a\ ash \ā\ ace \ä\ cot, cart
\au\ out \ch\ chin \e\ bet \ē\ easy \g\ go \i\ hit \ī\ ice \j\ job
\ŋ\ sing \ō\ go \o\ law \oi\ boy \th\ thin *th*\ the \ü\ loot \u\ foot
\y\ yet \zh\ vision \ä, k, ⁿ, œ, œ̄, ue, ūe, ʸ\ *see* Guide to Pronunciation

sincerely intends to do what one says (2) : a solemn attestation of the truth or inviolability of one's words **b** : something (as a promise) corroborated by an oath **c** : a form of expression used in taking an oath **2** : an irreverent or careless use of a sacred name; *broadly* : SWEARWORD

oat·meal \'ōt-ˌmēl, ōt-'mē(ə)l\ *n* (14c) **1 a** : meal made from oats **b** : rolled oats **2** : porridge made from ground or rolled oats

ob- *prefix* [NL, fr. L, in the way, against, toward, fr. *ob* in the way of, on account of; akin to Gk *epi* on, at — more at EPI-] : inversely ⟨*ob*ovate⟩

Oba·di·ah \ˌō-bə-'dī-ə\ *n* [Heb *'Ōbhadhyāh*] **1** : a minor Hebrew prophet **2** : a prophetic book of canonical Jewish and Christian Scripture — see BIBLE table

¹ob·bli·ga·to \ˌäb-lə-'gät-(ˌ)ō\ *adj* [It, obligatory, fr. pp. of *obbligare* to oblige, fr. L *obligare*] (1724) : not to be omitted : OBLIGATORY — used as a direction in music; compare AD LIBITUM

²obbligato *n, pl* **-tos** *also* **-ti** \-'gät-ē\ (1845) **1** : an elaborate esp. melodic part accompanying a solo or principal melody and usu. played by a single instrument ⟨a song with violin ~⟩ **2** : a persistent background sound

ob·cor·date \(')äb-'kȯ(ə)r-ˌdāt\ *adj* (1775) : heart-shaped with the notch apical ⟨~ leaf⟩

ob·du·ra·cy \'äb-d(y)ə-rə-sē; äb-'d(y)u̇r-ə-, əb-\ *n, pl* **-cies** (1597) : the quality or state of being obdurate

ob·du·rate \'äb-d(y)ə-rət; äb-'d(y)u̇r-ət, əb-\ *adj* [ME, fr. L *obduratus*, pp. of *obdurare* to harden, fr. *ob-* against + *durus* hard — more at DURING] (15c) **1 a** : hardened in feelings **b** : stubbornly persistent in wrongdoing **2** : resistant to persuasion or softening influences : UNYIELDING ***syn*** see INFLEXIBLE — **ob·du·rate·ly** *adv* — **ob·du·rate·ness** *n*

obe·ah \'ō-bē-ə\ *also* **obi** \'ō-bē\ *n, often cap* [of African origin; akin to Twi $a^{1}bi^{2}a^{3}$, a creeper used in making charms] (ca. 1760) : a system of belief among Negroes chiefly of the British West Indies, the Guianas, and the southeastern U.S. that is characterized by the use of sorcery and magic ritual

obe·di·ence \ō-'bēd-ē-ən(t)s, ə-\ *n* (13c) **1 a** : an act or instance of obeying **b** : the quality or state of being obedient **2** : a sphere of jurisdiction; *esp* : an ecclesiastical or sometimes secular dominion

obe·di·ent \-ənt\ *adj* [ME, fr. OF, fr. L *oboedient-, oboediens*, fr. prp. of *oboedire* to obey] (13c) : submissive to the restraint or command of authority : willing to obey — **obe·di·ent·ly** *adv*

syn OBEDIENT, DOCILE, TRACTABLE, AMENABLE mean submissive to the will of another. OBEDIENT implies compliance with the demands or requests of one in authority; DOCILE implies a predisposition to submit readily to control or guidance; TRACTABLE suggests having a character that permits easy handling or managing; AMENABLE suggests a willingness to yield or to cooperate either because of a desire to be agreeable or because of a natural open-mindedness.

obei·sance \ō-'bēs-ᵊn(t)s, ə-, -'bās-\ *n* [ME *obeisaunce* obedience, obeisance, fr. MF *obeissance*, fr. *obeissant*, prp. of *obeir* to obey] (14c) **1** : a movement of the body made in token of respect or submission : BOW **2** : DEFERENCE, HOMAGE — **obei·sant** \-ᵊnt\ *adj* — **obei·sant·ly** *adv*

obe·lia \ō-'bēl-yə\ *n* [NL] (ca. 1890) : any of a genus (*Obelia*) of small colonial marine hydroids with colonies branched like trees

obe·lisk \'äb-ə-ˌlisk *also* 'ō-bə-\ *n* [MF *obelisque*, fr. L *obeliscus*, fr. Gk *obeliskos*, fr. dim. of *obelos*] (1549) **1** : an upright 4-sided usu. monolithic pillar that gradually tapers as it rises and terminates in a pyramid **2 a** : OBELUS **b** : DAGGER 2b

obe·lize \-ˌlīz\ *vt* **-lized; -liz·ing** (1656) : to designate or annotate with an obelus

obe·lus \-ləs\ *n, pl* **ob·e·li** \-ˌlī, -ˌlē\ [LL, fr. Gk *obelos* spit, pointed pillar, obelus] (14c) : a symbol — or ÷ used in ancient manuscripts to mark a questionable passage

Ober·on \'ō-bə-ˌrän, -rən\ *n* [F, fr. OF *Auberon*] : the king of the fairies in medieval folklore

obese \ō-'bēs\ *adj* [L *obesus*, fr. pp. of *obedere* to eat up, fr. *ob-* against + *edere* to eat — more at OB-, EAT] (1651) : excessively fat

obe·si·ty \ō-'bē-sət-ē\ *n* (1611) : a condition characterized by excessive bodily fat

obey \ō-'bā, ə-\ *vb* **obeyed; obey·ing** [ME *obeien*, fr. OF *obeir*, fr. L *oboedire*, fr. *ob-* toward + *-oedire* (akin to *audire* to hear) — more at OB-, AUDIBLE] *vt* (13c) **1** : to follow the commands or guidance of **2** : to conform to or comply with ⟨~ an order⟩ ⟨falling objects ~ the laws of physics⟩ ~ *vi* : to behave obediently — **obey·er** *n*

ob·fus·cate \'äb-fə-ˌskāt; äb-'fəs-ˌkāt, əb-\ *vt* **-cat·ed; -cat·ing** [LL *obfuscatus*, pp. of *obfuscare*, fr. L *ob-* in the way + *fuscus* dark brown — more at OB-, DUSK] (1650) **1 a** : DARKEN **b** : to make obscure **2** : CONFUSE — **ob·fus·ca·tion** \ˌäb-(ˌ)fəs-'kā-shən\ *n* — **ob·fus·ca·to·ry** \äb-'fəs-kə-ˌtōr-ē, əb-, -ˌtȯr-\ *adj*

obi \'ō-bē\ *n* [Jp] (1878) : a broad sash worn with a Japanese kimono

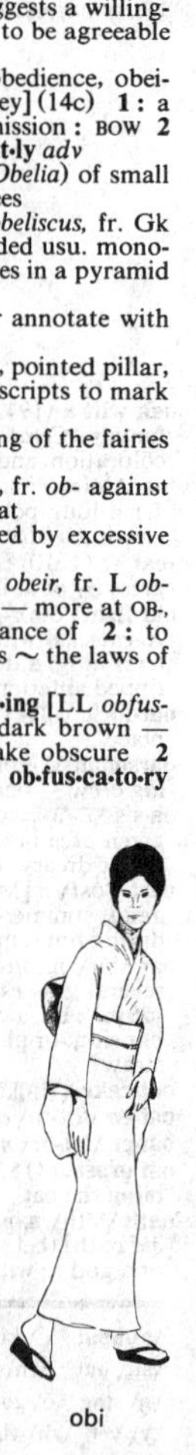

obi

Obie \'ō-bē\ *n* [*O.B.*, abbr. for *off Broadway*] (1965) : an award presented annually by a professional organization for notable achievement in plays performed off-Broadway

obit \ō-'bit, 'ō-bət, *esp Brit* 'äb-it\ *n* [ME, fr. MF, fr. L *obitus* decease, fr. *obitus*, pp. of *obire* to go to meet, die, fr. *ob-* in the way + *ire* to go — more at ISSUE] (15c) : OBITUARY

obi·ter dic·tum \ˌō-bət-ər-'dik-təm, ˌäb-ət-\ *n, pl* **obiter dic·ta** \-tə\ [LL, lit., something said in passing] (1812) **1** : an incidental and collateral opinion that is uttered by a judge but is not binding **2** : an incidental remark or observation

obit·u·ary \ə-'bich-ə-ˌwer-ē, ō-, -'bich-ə-rē\ *n, pl* **-ar·ies** [ML *obituarium*, fr. L *obitus* decease] (1706) : a notice of a person's death usu. with a short biographical account — **obit·u·ar·ist** \-'bich-ə-ˌwər-əst, -'bich-ə-rəst\ *n* — **obituary** *adj*

¹ob·ject \'äb-jikt, -(ˌ)jekt\ *n* [ME, fr. ML *objectum*, fr. L, neut. of *obicere* to throw in the way, present, hinder, fr. *ob-* in the way + *jacere* to throw — more at OB-, JET] (14c) **1 a** : something material that may be perceived by the senses ⟨I see an ~ in the distance⟩ **b** : something that when viewed stirs a particular emotion (as pity) ⟨look to the tragic loading of this bed . . . the ~ poisons sight; let it be hid —Shak.⟩ **2** : something mental or physical toward which thought, feeling, or action is directed ⟨an ~ for study⟩ ⟨the ~ of my affection⟩ ⟨delicately carved art ~*s*⟩ **3** : the goal or end of an effort or activity : PURPOSE, OBJECTIVE ⟨their ~ is to investigate the matter thoroughly⟩ **4** : a thing that forms an element of or constitutes the subject matter of an investigation or science **5 a** : a noun or noun equivalent (as a pronoun, gerund, or clause) denoting the goal or result of the action of a verb **b** : a noun or noun equivalent in a prepositional phrase ***syn*** see INTENTION — **ob·ject·less** \-jik-tləs, -(ˌ)jek-\ *adj* — **ob·ject·less·ness** *n*

²ob·ject \əb-'jekt\ *vb* [ME *objecten*, fr. L *objectus*, pp. of *obicere* to throw in the way, object] *vt* (15c) : to put forth in opposition or as an objection ⟨~*ed* that the statement was misleading⟩ ~ *vi* **1** : to oppose something firmly and usu. with words or arguments **2** : to feel distaste for something — **ob·jec·tor** \-'jek-tər\ *n*

object ball \'äb-jik(t)-, -(ˌ)jek(t)-\ *n* (1856) : the ball first struck by the cue ball in pool or billiards; *also* : a ball hit by the cue ball

ob·jec·ti·fy \əb-'jek-tə-ˌfī\ *vt* **-fied; -fy·ing** (ca. 1836) : to treat as or cause to have objective reality; *esp* : to give expression to (as an abstract notion, feeling, or ideal) in a form that can be experienced by others ⟨it is the essence of the fairy tale to ~ differing facets of the child's emotional experience —John Updike⟩ — **ob·jec·ti·fi·ca·tion** \-ˌjek-tə-fə-'kā-shən\ *n*

ob·jec·tion \əb-'jek-shən\ *n* (14c) **1** : an act of objecting **2 a** : a reason or argument presented in opposition **b** : a feeling or expression of disapproval

ob·jec·tion·able \-sh(ə-)nə-bəl\ *adj* (1781) : UNDESIRABLE, OFFENSIVE — **ob·jec·tion·able·ness** *n* — **ob·jec·tion·ably** \-blē\ *adv*

¹ob·jec·tive \əb-'jek-tiv, äb-\ *adj* (1620) **1 a** : relating to or existing as an object of thought without consideration of independent existence — used chiefly in medieval philosophy **b** : of, relating to, or being an object, phenomenon, or condition in the realm of sensible experience independent of individual thought and perceptible by all observers : having reality independent of the mind ⟨~ reality⟩ ⟨our reveries . . . are significantly and repeatedly shaped by our transactions with the ~ world —Marvin Reznikoff⟩ — compare SUBJECTIVE 3b **c** *of a symptom of disease* : perceptible to persons other than the affected individual — compare SUBJECTIVE 4c **d** : involving or deriving from sense perception or experience with actual objects, conditions, or phenomena ⟨~ awareness⟩ ⟨~ data⟩ **2** : relating to, characteristic of, or constituting the case of words that follow prepositions or transitive verbs **3 a** : expressing or dealing with facts or conditions as perceived without distortion by personal feelings, prejudices, or interpretations ⟨~ art⟩ ⟨an ~ history of the war⟩ ⟨an ~ judgment⟩ **b** *of a test* : limited to choices of fixed alternatives and reducing subjective factors to a minimum ***syn*** see MATERIAL, FAIR — **ob·jec·tive·ly** *adv* — **ob·jec·tive·ness** *n* — **ob·jec·tiv·i·ty** \(ˌ)äb-ˌjek-'tiv-ət-ē, əb-\ *n*

²objective *n* (1835) **1** : a lens or system of lenses that forms an image of an object **2 a** : something toward which effort is directed : an aim, goal, or end of action **b** : a strategic position to be attained or a purpose to be achieved by a military operation ***syn*** see INTENTION

objective complement *n* (1870) : a noun, adjective, or pronoun used in the predicate as complement to a verb and as qualifier of its direct object ⟨*chairman* in "we elected him chairman" is an *objective complement*⟩

objective correlative *n* (1919) : a situation or chain of events that symbolizes or objectifies a particular emotion and that may be used in creative writing to evoke a desired emotional response in the reader

ob·jec·tiv·ism \əb-'jek-tiv-ˌiz-əm, äb-\ *n* (1854) **1** : any of various theories asserting the validity of objective phenomena over subjective experience; *esp* : REALISM 2a **2** : an ethical theory that moral good is objectively real or that moral precepts are objectively valid **3** : a 20th century movement in poetry growing out of imagism and putting stress on form — **ob·jec·tiv·ist** \-əst\ *n* — **ob·jec·tiv·is·tic** \-ˌjek-tiv-'is-tik\ *adj*

object language \'äb-jikt-, -(ˌ)jekt-\ *n* (1937) : TARGET LANGUAGE

object lesson \'äb-jikt-, -(ˌ)jekt-\ *n* (1831) : something that serves as a practical example of a principle or abstract idea

ob·jet d'art \ˌȯb-ˌzhā-'där\ *n, pl* **ob·jets d'art** *same*\ [F, lit., art object] (1865) **1** : an article of some artistic value **2** : CURIO

ob·jet trou·vé \'ȯb-ˌzhā-trü-'vā\ *n, pl* **objets trouvés** *same*\ [F, lit., found object] (1937) : a natural object (as a piece of driftwood) found by chance and held to have aesthetic value esp. through the working of natural forces on it; *also* : an artifact not orig. intended as art but held to have aesthetic value esp. when displayed as a work of art

ob·jur·gate \'äb-jər-ˌgāt\ *vt* **-gat·ed; -gat·ing** [L *objurgatus*, pp. of *objurgare*, fr. *ob-* against + *jurgare* to quarrel, lit., to take to law, fr. *jur-, jus* law + *-igare* (fr. *agere* to lead) — more at OB-, JUST, AGENT] (1616) : to denounce harshly : CASTIGATE — **ob·jur·ga·tion** \ˌäb-jər-'gā-shən\ *n* — **ob·jur·ga·to·ry** \əb-'jər-gə-ˌtōr-ē, -ˌtȯr-\ *adj*

ob·lan·ceo·late \(')äb-'lan(t)-sē-ə-ˌlāt\ *adj* (1850) : inversely lanceolate ⟨an ~ leaf⟩

ob·last \'äb-ˌlast, 'ȯb-ləst\ *n, pl* **oblasts** *also* **ob·las·ti** \-ˌlas-tē, -ləs-\ [Russ *oblast'*] (ca. 1886) : a political subdivision of a republic in the U.S.S.R.

¹ob·late \äb-'lāt, 'äb-ˌ\ *adj* [prob. fr. NL *oblatus*, fr. *ob-* + *-latus* (as in *prolatus* prolate)] (1705) : flattened or depressed at the poles ⟨an ~ spheroid⟩ — **ob·late·ness** *n*

²ob·late \'äb-ˌlāt\ *n* [ML *oblatus*, lit., one offered up, fr. L, pp. of *offerre* — more at OFFER] (1864) **1** : a layman living in a monastery under a modified rule and without vows **2** : a member of one of several Roman Catholic communities of men or women

ob·la·tion \ə-'blā-shən, ō-\ *n* [ME *oblacioun*, fr. MF *oblation*, fr. LL *oblation-, oblatio*, fr. L *oblatus*, pp.] (15c) **1** : the act of making a religious offering; *specif, cap* : the act of offering the eucharistic elements to God **2** : something offered in worship or devotion : a holy gift offered usu. at an altar or shrine

¹ob·li·gate \'äb-lə-ˌgāt\ *vt* **-gat·ed; -gat·ing** [L *obligatus*, pp. of *obligare*] (1668) **1 a** : to bind legally or morally : CONSTRAIN **b** : OBLIGE 2a **2** : to commit (as funds) to meet an obligation

²ob·li·gate \'äb-li-gət, -lə-ˌgāt\ *adj* (1887) **1** : restricted to one particularly characteristic mode of life ⟨an ~ parasite⟩ **2** : biologically essential for survival ⟨~ parasitism⟩ — **ob·li·gate·ly** *adv*

ob·li·ga·tion \ˌäb-lə-ˈgā-shən\ *n* [ME *obligacioun,* fr. OF *obligation,* fr. L *obligation-, obligatio,* fr. *obligatus,* pp. of *obligare*] (13c) **1 :** the action of obligating oneself to a course of action (as by a promise or vow) **2 a :** something (as a formal contract, a promise, or the demands of conscience or custom) that obligates one to a course of action **b :** a debt security (as a mortgage or corporate bond) **c :** a commitment (as by a government) to pay a particular sum of money; *also* **:** an amount owed under such an obligation ⟨unable to meet its ~*s,* the company went into bankruptcy⟩ **3 a :** a condition or feeling of being obligated **b :** a debt of gratitude **4 :** something one is bound to do **:** DUTY, RESPONSIBILITY

oblig·a·to·ry \ə-ˈblig-ə-ˌtōr-ē, ä-, -ˌtȯr- *also* ˈäb-li-gə-\ *adj* (15c) **1 :** binding in law or conscience **2 :** relating to or enforcing an obligation ⟨a writ ~⟩ **3 :** MANDATORY, REQUIRED ⟨~ military service⟩; *also* **:** so commonplace as to be a convention, fashion, or cliché ⟨the ~ death scene in opera⟩ **4 :** OBLIGATE 1 — **oblig·a·to·ri·ly** \ə-ˌblig-ə-ˈtōr-ə-lē, ä-, -ˈtȯr- *also* ˌäb-li-gə-\ *adv*

oblige \ə-ˈblīj\ *vb* **obliged; oblig·ing** [ME *obligen,* fr. OF *obliger,* fr. L *obligare,* lit., to bind to, fr. *ob-* toward + *ligare* to bind — more at LIGATURE] *vt* (13c) **1 :** to constrain by physical, moral, or legal force or by the exigencies of circumstance ⟨*obliged* to find money for taxes⟩ **2 a :** to put in one's debt by a favor or service ⟨we are much *obliged* for your help⟩ **b :** to do a favor for ⟨always ready to ~ a friend⟩ ~ *vi* **:** to do something as a favor — **oblig·er** *n*

ob·li·gee \ˌäb-lə-ˈjē\ *n* (1574) **:** one to whom another is obligated (as by a contract); *specif* **:** one who is protected by a surety bond

oblig·ing \ə-ˈblī-jiŋ\ *adj* (1632) **:** willing to do favors **:** ACCOMMODATING *syn* see AMIABLE — **oblig·ing·ly** \-jiŋ-lē\ *adv* — **oblig·ing·ness** *n*

ob·li·gor \ˌäb-lə-ˈgȯ(ə)r, -ˈjȯ(ə)r\ *n* (1544) **:** one who is bound by a legal obligation

¹oblique \ō-ˈblēk, ə-, -ˈblīk; *military usu* ī\ *adj* [ME *oblike,* fr. L *obliquus,* fr. *ob-* toward + *-liquus* (akin to *ulna* elbow) — more at ELL] (15c) **1 a :** neither perpendicular nor parallel **:** INCLINED **b :** having the axis not perpendicular to the base ⟨an ~ cone⟩ **c :** having no right angle ⟨an ~ triangle⟩ **2 a :** not straightforward **:** INDIRECT; *also* **:** OBSCURE **b :** DEVIOUS, UNDERHAND **3 :** situated obliquely and having one end not inserted on bone ⟨~ muscles⟩ **4 :** taken from an airplane with the camera directed horizontally or diagonally downward ⟨an ~ photograph⟩ — **oblique·ly** *adv* — **oblique·ness** *n*

²oblique *n* (1571) **1 :** something (as a line) that is oblique **2 :** any of several oblique muscles; *esp* **:** any of the thin flat muscles forming the middle and outer layers of the lateral walls of the abdomen

³oblique *adv* (1667) **:** at a 45 degree angle ⟨to the right ~, march⟩

oblique angle *n* (1695) **:** an acute or obtuse angle

oblique case *n* (15c) **:** a grammatical case other than the nominative or vocative

obliq·ui·ty \ō-ˈblik-wət-ē, ə-\ *n, pl* **-ties** (15c) **1 :** deviation from moral rectitude or sound thinking **2 a :** deviation from parallelism or perpendicularity; *also* **:** the amount of such deviation **b :** the angle between the planes of the earth's equator and orbit having a value of about 23°27′ ⟨~ of the ecliptic⟩ **3 a :** indirectness or deliberate obscurity of speech or conduct **b :** an obscure or confusing statement

oblit·er·ate \ə-ˈblit-ə-ˌrāt, ō-\ *vt* **-at·ed; -at·ing** [L *oblitteratus,* pp. of *oblitterare,* fr. *ob-* ob- + *littera* letter] (1611) **1 :** to make undecipherable or imperceptible by obscuring or wearing away **2 a :** to remove utterly from recognition or memory **b :** to remove from existence **:** destroy utterly all trace, indication, or significance of **c :** to cause to disappear (as a bodily part or a scar) or collapse (as a duct conveying body fluid) **:** REMOVE 4 ⟨a blood vessel *obliterated* by inflammation⟩ **3 :** CANCEL 4 — **oblit·er·a·tion** \-ˌblit-ə-ˈrā-shən\ *n* — **oblit·er·a·tor** \-ˈblit-ə-ˌrāt-ər\ *n*

oblit·er·a·tive \ə-ˈblit-ə-ˌrāt-iv, ō-, -ə-rət-\ *adj* (ca. 1802) **:** inducing or characterized by obliteration: as **a :** causing or accompanied by closure or collapse of a lumen ⟨~ arterial disease⟩ **b :** tending to make inconspicuous ⟨~ behavior⟩

obliv·i·on \ə-ˈbliv-ē-ən, ō-, ä-\ *n* [ME, fr. MF, fr. L *oblivion-, oblivio,* fr. *oblivisci* to forget, perh. fr. *ob-* in the way + *levis* smooth — more at OB-, LIME] (14c) **1 :** the fact or condition of forgetting or having forgotten; *esp* **:** the condition of being oblivious **2 :** the condition or state of being forgotten or unknown

obliv·i·ous \-ē-əs\ *adj* (15c) **1 :** lacking remembrance, memory, or mindful attention **2 :** lacking active conscious knowledge or awareness — usu. used with *of* or *to* — **obliv·i·ous·ly** *adv* — **obliv·i·ous·ness** *n*

ob·long \ˈäb-ˌlȯŋ\ *adj* [ME, fr. L *oblongus,* fr. *ob-* toward + *longus* long] (15c) **:** deviating from a square, circular, or spherical form by elongation in one dimension ⟨an ~ piece of paper⟩ ⟨an ~ melon⟩ — **oblong** *n*

ob·lo·quy \ˈäb-lə-kwē\ *n, pl* **-quies** [LL *obloquium,* fr. *obloqui* to speak against, fr. *ob-* against + *loqui* to speak] (15c) **1 :** a strongly condemnatory utterance **:** abusive language **2 :** the condition of one that is discredited **:** bad repute *syn* see ABUSE

ob·nox·ious \äb-ˈnäk-shəs, əb-\ *adj* [L *obnoxius,* fr. *ob* in the way of, exposed to + *noxa* harm — more at NOXIOUS] (1597) **1 :** exposed to something unpleasant or harmful — used with *to* **2** *archaic* **:** deserving of censure **3 :** odiously or disgustingly objectionable **:** highly offensive *syn* see REPUGNANT — **ob·nox·ious·ly** *adv* — **ob·nox·ious·ness** *n*

ob·nu·bi·late \äb-ˈn(y)ü-bə-ˌlāt\ *vt* **-lat·ed; -lat·ing** [L *obnubilatus,* pp. of *obnubilare,* fr. *ob-* in the way + *nubilare* to be cloudy, fr. *nubilus* cloudy, fr. *nubes* cloud — more at OB-, NUANCE] (1583) **:** BECLOUD — **ob·nu·bi·la·tion** \-ˌn(y)ü-bə-ˈlā-shən\ *n*

oboe \ˈō-(ˌ)bō\ *n* [It, fr. F *hautbois* — more at HAUTBOIS] (1724) **:** a double-reed woodwind instrument having a conical tube, a brilliant penetrating tone, and a usual range from B flat below middle C upward for over 2½ octaves — **obo·ist** \ˈō-ˌbō-əst\ *n*

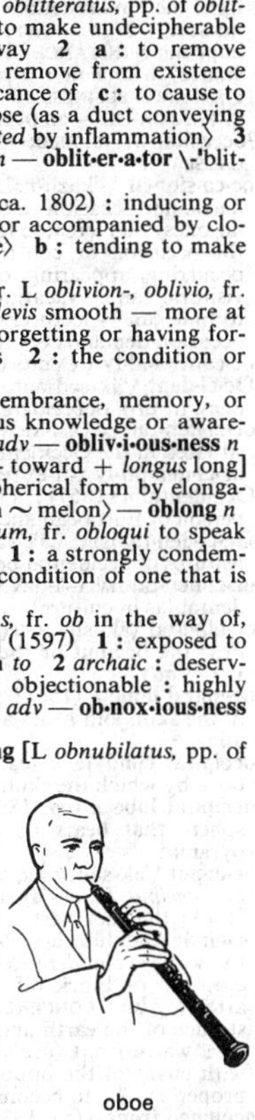

oboe

obol \ˈäb-əl, ˈō-bəl\ *n* [L *obolus,* fr. Gk *obolos*] (1579) **:** an ancient Greek coin or weight equal to ⅙ drachma

ob·ovate \(ˈ)äb-ˈō-ˌvāt\ *adj* (1785) **:** ovate with the narrower end basal ⟨~ leaves⟩

ob·ovoid \-ˌvȯid\ *adj* (1819) **:** ovoid with the broad end toward the apex ⟨an ~ fruit⟩

ob·scene \äb-ˈsēn, əb-\ *adj* [MF, fr. L *obscenus, obscaenus*] (1593) **1 :** disgusting to the senses **:** REPULSIVE **2 :** abhorrent to morality or virtue; *specif* **:** designed to incite to lust or depravity *syn* see COARSE — **ob·scene·ly** *adv*

ob·scen·i·ty \-ˈsen-ət-ē *also* -ˈsēn-\ *n, pl* **-ties** (1608) **1 :** the quality or state of being obscene **2 :** something (as an utterance or act) that is obscene

ob·scur·ant \äb-ˈskyu̇r-ənt, əb-\ *or* **ob·scu·ran·tic** \ˌäb-skyə-ˈrant-ik\ *adj* (1878) **:** tending to make obscure — **obscurant** *n*

ob·scu·ran·tism \äb-ˈskyu̇r-ən-ˌtiz-əm, əb-; ˌäb-skyu̇-ˈran-\ *n* (1834) **1 :** opposition to the spread of knowledge **:** a policy of withholding knowledge from the general public **2 a :** a style (as in literature or art) characterized by deliberate vagueness or abstruseness **b :** an act or instance of obscurantism — **ob·scu·ran·tist** \-ən-təst, -ˈrant-əst\ *n or adj*

¹ob·scure \äb-ˈskyu̇(ə)r, əb-\ *adj* [ME, fr. MF *obscur,* fr. L *obscurus,* fr. *ob-* in the way + *-scurus* (akin to Gk *keuthein* to conceal) — more at HIDE] (15c) **1 a :** DARK, DIM **b :** shrouded in or hidden by darkness **c :** not clearly seen or easily distinguished **:** FAINT **2 :** not readily understood or clearly expressed **:** VAGUE, ABSTRUSE; *also* **:** MYSTERIOUS **3 :** relatively unknown: as **a :** REMOTE, SECLUDED **b :** not prominent or famous ⟨an ~ poet⟩ **4 :** constituting the unstressed vowel \ə\ or having unstressed \ə\ as its value — **ob·scure·ly** *adv* — **ob·scure·ness** *n*

syn OBSCURE, DARK, VAGUE, ENIGMATIC, CRYPTIC, AMBIGUOUS, EQUIVOCAL mean not clearly understandable. OBSCURE implies a hiding or veiling of meaning through some inadequacy of expression or withholding of full knowledge; DARK implies an imperfect or clouded revelation often with ominous or sinister suggestion; VAGUE implies a lack of clear formulation due to inadequate conception or consideration; ENIGMATIC stresses a puzzling, mystifying quality; CRYPTIC implies a purposely concealed meaning; AMBIGUOUS applies to a difficulty of understanding arising from the use of a word or words of multiple meanings; EQUIVOCAL applies to the deliberate use of language open to differing interpretations with the intention of deceiving or evading.

²obscure *vt* **ob·scured; ob·scur·ing** (15c) **1 :** to make dark, dim, or indistinct **2 :** to conceal or hide by or as if by covering **3 :** to reduce (a vowel) to the value \ə\ — **ob·scu·ra·tion** \ˌäb-skyu̇-ˈrā-shən\ *n*

³obscure *n* (1667) **:** OBSCURITY

ob·scu·ri·ty \äb-ˈskyu̇r-ət-ē, əb-\ *n, pl* **-ties** (14c) **1 :** one that is obscure **2 :** the quality or state of being obscure

ob·se·qui·ous \əb-ˈsē-kwē-əs, äb-\ *adj* [ME, fr. L *obsequiosus* compliant, fr. *obsequium* compliance, fr. *obsequi* to comply, fr. *ob-* toward + *sequi* to follow — more at OB-, SUE] (15c) **:** marked by or exhibiting a fawning attentiveness *syn* see SUBSERVIENT — **ob·se·qui·ous·ly** *adv* — **ob·se·qui·ous·ness** *n*

ob·se·quy \ˈäb-sə-kwē\ *n, pl* **-quies** [ME *obsequie,* fr. MF, fr. ML *obsequiae* (pl.), alter. of L *exsequiae,* fr. *exsequi* to follow out, execute] (15c) **:** a funeral or burial rite — usu. used in pl.

ob·serv·able \əb-ˈzər-və-bəl\ *adj* (1609) **1 :** NOTEWORTHY **2 :** capable of being observed **:** DISCERNIBLE — **observable** *n* — **ob·serv·ably** \-blē\ *adv*

ob·ser·vance \əb-ˈzər-vən(t)s\ *n* (14c) **1 a :** a customary practice, rite, or ceremony ⟨Sabbath ~*s*⟩ **b :** a rule governing members of a religious order **2 :** an act or instance of following a custom, rule, or law ⟨~ of the speed limits⟩ **3 :** an act or instance of watching

¹ob·ser·vant \-vənt\ *n, obs* (1605) **:** an assiduous or obsequious servant or attendant

²observant *adj* (1608) **1 a :** paying strict attention **:** WATCHFUL ⟨~ spectators⟩ **b :** KEEN, PERCEPTIVE **2 :** careful in observing (as rites, laws, or customs) **:** MINDFUL ⟨pious and religiously ~ families —Sidney Hook⟩ ⟨always ~ of the amenities⟩ — **ob·ser·vant·ly** *adv*

ob·ser·va·tion \ˌäb-sər-ˈvā-shən, -zər-\ *n* [MF, fr. L *observation-, observatio,* fr. *observatus,* pp. of *observare*] (1557) **1 :** an act or the faculty of observing **2 a :** an act of recognizing and noting a fact or occurrence often involving measurement with instruments ⟨weather ~*s*⟩ **b :** a record so obtained **3 :** a judgment on or inference from what one has observed; *broadly* **:** REMARK, STATEMENT **4** *obs* **:** HEED **5 :** the condition of one that is observed ⟨under ~ at the hospital⟩ — **ob·ser·va·tion·al** \-shnəl, -shən-ᵊl\ *adj*

ob·ser·va·to·ry \əb-ˈzər-və-ˌtōr-ē, -ˌtȯr-\ *n, pl* **-ries** [prob. fr. NL *observatorium,* fr. L *observatus,* pp.] (1676) **1 :** a building or place given over to or equipped for observation of natural phenomena (as in astronomy); *also* **:** an institution whose primary purpose is making such observations **2 :** a situation or structure commanding a wide view **:** LOOKOUT

ob·serve \əb-ˈzərv\ *vb* **ob·served; ob·serv·ing** [ME *observen,* fr. MF *observer,* fr. L *observare* to guard, watch, observe, fr. *ob-* in the way, toward + *servare* to keep — more at CONSERVE] *vt* (14c) **1 :** to conform one's action or practice to (as a law, rite, or condition) **:** comply with **2 :** to inspect or take note of as an augury, omen, or presage **3 :** to celebrate or solemnize (as a ceremony or festival) in a customary or accepted way **4 a :** to watch carefully esp. with attention to details or behavior for the purpose of arriving at a judgment **b :** to make a scientific observation on or of **5 :** to come to realize or know esp. through consideration of noted facts **6 :** to utter as a remark ~ *vi* **1 a :** to take notice **b :** to make observations **:** WATCH **2 :** REMARK, COMMENT *syn* see KEEP — **ob·serv·ing·ly** \-ˈzər-viŋ-lē\ *adv*

ob·serv·er \əb-ˈzər-vər\ *n* (ca. 1550) **:** one that observes: as **a :** a representative sent to observe but not participate officially in an activity (as a meeting or war) **b :** an expert analyst and commentator in a particular field ⟨political ~*s*⟩

ob·sess \əb-ˈses, äb-\ *vt* [L *obsessus,* pp. of *obsidēre* to besiege, beset, fr. *ob-* against + *sedēre* to sit — more at OB-, SIT] (1531) **:** to haunt or excessively preoccupy the mind of ⟨was ~*ed* with a fear of dying⟩

ob·ses·sion \äb-ˈsesh-ən, əb-\ *n* (1680) **1 :** a persistent disturbing preoccupation with an often unreasonable idea or feeling; *broadly* **:** compelling motivation ⟨an ~ with profits⟩ **2 :** something that causes an

obsession — **ob·ses·sion·al** \-ˈsesh-nəl, -ən-ᵊl\ *adj* — **ob·ses·sion·al·ly** \-ē\ *adv*
ob·ses·sive \äb-ˈses-iv, əb-\ *adj* (1901) **1 a :** tending to cause obsession **b :** excessive often to an unreasonable degree **2 :** of, relating to, or characterized by obsession : deriving from obsession — **obsessive** *n* — **ob·ses·sive·ly** *adv* — **ob·ses·sive·ness** *n*
obsessive–compulsive *adj* (ca. 1927) : relating to or characterized by recurring obsessions and compulsions esp. as symptoms of a neurotic state — **obsessive–compulsive** *n*
ob·sid·i·an \əb-ˈsid-ē-ən\ *n* [NL *obsidianus*, fr. L *obsidianus lapis*, false MS reading for *obsianus lapis*, lit., stone of Obsius, fr. *Obsius*, its supposed discoverer] (1601) : volcanic glass that is generally black, banded, or spherulitic and has a marked conchoidal fracture and a composition similar to rhyolite
ob·so·lesce \ˌäb-sə-ˈles\ *vi* **-lesced; -lesc·ing** [L *obsolescere*] (1873) : to be or become obsolescent
ob·so·les·cence \-ˈles-ᵊn(t)s\ *n* (ca. 1847) : the process of becoming obsolete or the condition of being nearly obsolete ⟨the gradual ~ of machinery⟩ ⟨reduced to ~⟩
ob·so·les·cent \-ᵊnt\ *adj* (1755) : going out of use : becoming obsolete — **ob·so·les·cent·ly** *adv*
¹**ob·so·lete** \ˌäb-sə-ˈlēt, ˈäb-sə-ˌ\ *adj* [L *obsoletus*, fr. pp. of *obsolescere* to grow old, become disused] (1579) **1 a :** no longer in use or no longer useful **b :** of a kind or style no longer current : OLD-FASHIONED **2** *of a plant or animal part* : indistinct or imperfect as compared with a corresponding part in related organisms : VESTIGIAL ***syn*** see OLD — **ob·so·lete·ly** *adv* — **ob·so·lete·ness** *n*
²**obsolete** *vt* **-let·ed; -let·ing** (1640) : to make obsolete
ob·sta·cle \ˈäb-sti-kəl, -ˌstik-əl\ *n* [ME, fr. MF, fr. L *obstaculum*, fr. *obstare* to stand in front of, fr. *ob-* in the way + *stare* to stand — more at OB-, STAND] (14c) : something that impedes progress or achievement
obstacle course *n* (1943) : a military training course filled with obstacles (as hurdles, fences, walls, and ditches) that must be negotiated; *broadly* : a series of obstacles that must be overcome
ob·stet·ric \əb-ˈste-trik, äb-\ *or* **ob·stet·ri·cal** \-tri-kəl\ *adj* [prob. fr. (assumed) NL *obstetricus*, fr. L *obstetric-*, *obstetrix* midwife, fr. *obstare*] (1742) : of, relating to, or associated with childbirth or obstetrics — **ob·stet·ri·cal·ly** \-tri-k(ə-)lē\ *adv*
ob·ste·tri·cian \ˌäb-stə-ˈtrish-ən\ *n* (ca. 1828) : a physician specializing in obstetrics
ob·stet·rics \əb-ˈste-triks, äb-\ *n pl but sing or pl in constr* (1819) : a branch of medical science that deals with birth and with its antecedents and sequels
ob·sti·na·cy \ˈäb-stə-nə-sē\ *n, pl* **-cies** (14c) **1 a :** the quality or state of being obstinate : STUBBORNNESS **b :** the quality or state of being difficult to remedy, relieve, or subdue ⟨the ~ of tuberculosis⟩ **2 :** an instance of being obstinate
ob·sti·nate \ˈäb-stə-nət\ *adj* [ME, fr. L *obstinatus*, pp. of *obstinare* to be resolved, fr. *ob-* in the way + *-stinare* (akin to *stare* to stand)] (14c) **1 :** perversely adhering to an opinion, purpose, or course in spite of reason, arguments, or persuasion **2 :** not easily subdued, remedied, or removed ⟨~ fever⟩ — **ob·sti·nate·ly** *adv* — **ob·sti·nate·ness** *n*
syn OBSTINATE, DOGGED, STUBBORN, PERTINACIOUS, MULISH mean fixed and unyielding in course or purpose. OBSTINATE implies usu. a perverse or unreasonable persistence; DOGGED suggests a tenacious unwavering persistence; STUBBORN implies sturdiness in resisting attempts to change or abandon a course or opinion; PERTINACIOUS suggests an annoying or irksome persistence; MULISH implies a thoroughly unreasonable obstinacy.
ob·strep·er·ous \əb-ˈstrep-(ə-)rəs, äb-\ *adj* [L *obstreperus*, fr. *obstrepere* to clamor against, fr. *ob-* against + *strepere* to make a noise; akin to OE *thrǽft* discord] (1600) **1 :** marked by unruly or aggressive noisiness : CLAMOROUS ⟨~ merriment⟩ **2 :** stubbornly resistant to control : UNRULY ***syn*** see VOCIFEROUS — **ob·strep·er·ous·ly** *adv* — **ob·strep·er·ous·ness** *n*
ob·struct \əb-ˈstrəkt, äb-\ *vt* [L *obstructus*, pp. of *obstruere*, fr. *ob-* in the way + *struere* to build — more at OB-, STRUCTURE] (1611) **1 :** to block or close up by an obstacle **2 :** to hinder from passage, action, or operation : IMPEDE **3 :** to cut off from sight ⟨a wall ~s the view⟩ ***syn*** see HINDER — **ob·struc·tive** \-ˈstrək-tiv\ *adj or n* — **ob·struc·tive·ness** *n* — **ob·struc·tor** \-tər\ *n*
ob·struc·tion \əb-ˈstrək-shən, äb-\ *n* (1533) **1 a :** an act of obstructing **b :** the state of being obstructed; *esp* : a condition of being clogged or blocked **2 :** something that obstructs
ob·struc·tion·ism \-shə-ˌniz-əm\ *n* (1879) : deliberate interference with the progress or business esp. of a legislative body — **ob·struc·tion·ist** \-sh(ə-)nəst\ *n or adj* — **ob·struc·tion·is·tic** \-ˌstrək-shə-ˈnis-tik\ *adj*
ob·tain \əb-ˈtān, äb-\ *vb* [ME *obteinen*, fr. MF & L; MF *obtenir*, fr. L *obtinēre* to hold on to, possess, obtain, fr. *ob-* in the way + *tenēre* to hold — more at THIN] *vt* (15c) : to gain or attain usu. by planned action or effort ~ *vi* **1** *archaic* : SUCCEED **2 :** to be generally recognized or established : PREVAIL — **ob·tain·abil·i·ty** \-ˌtā-nə-ˈbil-ət-ē\ *n* — **ob·tain·able** \-ˈtā-nə-bəl\ *adj* — **ob·tain·er** *n* — **ob·tain·ment** \-ˈtān-mənt\ *n*
ob·tect \əb-ˈtekt, äb-\ *also* **ob·tect·ed** \-ˈtek-təd\ *adj* [L *obtectus*, pp. of *obtegere* to cover over, fr. *ob-* in the way + *tegere* to cover — more at THATCH] (ca. 1905) : enclosed in or characterized by enclosure in a firm chitinous case or covering ⟨an ~ pupa⟩
ob·trude \əb-ˈtrüd, äb-\ *vb* **ob·trud·ed; ob·trud·ing** [L *obtrudere* to thrust at, fr. *ob-* in the way + *trudere* to thrust — more at OB-, THREAT] *vt* (ca. 1613) **1 :** to thrust out : EXTRUDE **2 :** to force or impose (as oneself or one's ideas) without warrant or request ~ *vi* : to become unduly prominent or interfering : INTRUDE — **ob·trud·er** *n* — **ob·tru·sion** \-ˈtrü-zhən\ *n*
ob·tru·sive \-ˈtrü-siv, -ziv\ *adj* [L *obtrusus*, pp. of *obtrudere*] (1667) **1 a :** forward in manner or conduct ⟨~ behavior⟩ **b :** undesirably prominent **2 :** thrust out : PROTRUDING ***syn*** see IMPERTINENT — **ob·tru·sive·ly** *adv* — **ob·tru·sive·ness** *n*
ob·tund \äb-ˈtənd\ *vt* [ME *obtunden*, fr. L *obtundere*] (15c) : to reduce the edge or violence of : DULL ⟨~*ed* reflexes⟩
ob·tu·ra·tion \ˌäb-t(y)ə-ˈrā-shən\ *n* [L *obturation-*, *obturatio*, fr. *obturatus*, pp. of *obturare* to obstruct, fr. *ob-* in the way + *-turare* (akin to *tumēre* to swell) — more at THUMB] (1610) : OBSTRUCTION, CLOSURE — **ob·tu·rate** \ˈäb-t(y)ə-ˌrāt\ *vt*
ob·tu·ra·tor \ˈäb-t(y)ə-ˌrāt-ər\ *n* [NL, fr. L *obturatus*, pp.] (ca. 1727) : one that closes: as **a :** one (as a prosthetic device) that closes or blocks up an opening (as a fissure in the palate) **b :** a hooded swelling of the placenta that fits over the nucellus in some plants
ob·tuse \äb-ˈt(y)üs, əb-\ *adj* **ob·tus·er; -est** [L *obtusus* blunt, dull, fr. pp. of *obtundere* to beat against, blunt, fr. *ob-* against + *tundere* to beat — more at OB-, STINT] (15c) **1 a :** lacking sharpness or quickness of sensibility or intellect : INSENSITIVE, STUPID **b :** difficult to comprehend : not clear or precise in thought or expression ⟨~ language⟩ **2 a** (1) *of an angle* : exceeding 90 degrees but less than 180 degrees (2) : having an obtuse angle — see TRIANGLE illustration **b :** not pointed or acute : BLUNT **c** *of a leaf* : rounded at the free end ***syn*** see DULL — **ob·tuse·ly** *adv* — **ob·tuse·ness** *n*
¹**ob·verse** \äb-ˈvərs, əb-, ˈäb-ˌ\ *adj* [L *obversus*, fr. pp. of *obvertere* to turn toward, fr. *ob-* toward + *vertere* to turn — more at OB-, WORTH] (ca. 1656) **1 :** facing the observer or opponent **2 :** having the base narrower than the top ⟨an ~ leaf⟩ **3 :** constituting the obverse of something : OPPOSITE — **ob·verse·ly** *adv*
²**ob·verse** \ˈäb-ˌvərs, äb-ˈ, əb-ˈ\ *n* (1658) **1 :** the side of a coin or currency note that bears the principal device and lettering; *broadly* : a front or principal surface **2 :** a similar but contrasting element or condition : COUNTERPOINT ⟨their rise was merely the ~ of the Empire's fall —A.J. Toynbee⟩ **3 :** a proposition inferred immediately from another by denying the opposite of that which the given proposition affirms ⟨the ~ of "all *A* is *B*" is "no *A* is not *B*"⟩
ob·vi·ate \ˈäb-vē-ˌāt\ *vt* **-at·ed; -at·ing** [LL *obviatus*, pp. of *obviare* to meet, withstand, fr. L *obviam*] (1598) : to anticipate and prevent (as a situation) or make unnecessary (as an action) — **ob·vi·a·tion** \ˌäb-vē-ˈā-shən\ *n*
ob·vi·ous \ˈäb-vē-əs\ *adj* [L *obvius*, fr. *obviam* in the way, fr. *ob* in the way of + *viam*, acc. of *via* way — more at VIA] (1603) **1** *archaic* : being in the way or in front : OPPOSITE **2 :** easily discovered, seen, or understood ***syn*** see EVIDENT — **ob·vi·ous·ly** *adv* — **ob·vi·ous·ness** *n*
oca \ˈō-kə\ *n* [Sp, fr. Quechua *ókka*] (1604) : either of two So. American wood sorrels (*Oxalis crenata* and *O. tuberosa*) cultivated for their edible tubers
oc·a·ri·na \ˌäk-ə-ˈrē-nə\ *n* [It, dim. of *oca* goose, fr. LL *auca*, deriv. of L *avis* bird — more at AVIARY] (ca. 1876) : a simple wind instrument typically having an oval body with finger holes and a projecting mouthpiece
Oc·cam's razor \ˌäk-əmz-\ *n* [William of *Occam*] (1836) : a scientific and philosophic rule that entities should not be multiplied unnecessarily which is interpreted as requiring that the simplest of competing theories be preferred to the more complex or that explanations of unknown phenomena be sought first in terms of known quantities
¹**oc·ca·sion** \ə-ˈkā-zhən\ *n* [ME, fr. MF or L; MF, fr. L *occasion-*, *occasio*, fr. *occasus*, pp. of *occidere* to fall, fall down, fr. *ob-* toward + *cadere* to fall — more at OB-, CHANCE] (14c) **1 :** a favorable opportunity or circumstance ⟨did not have ~ to talk with them⟩ **2 a :** a state of affairs that provides a ground or reason ⟨the ~ of the discord was their mutual intolerance⟩ **b :** an occurrence or condition that brings something about; *esp* : the immediate inciting circumstance as distinguished from the fundamental cause ⟨his insulting remark was the ~ of a bitter quarrel⟩ **3 a :** HAPPENING, INCIDENT **b :** a time at which something happens : INSTANCE **4 a :** a need arising from a particular circumstance **b** *archaic* : a personal want or need — usu. used in pl. **5** *pl* : AFFAIRS, BUSINESS **6 :** a special event or ceremony : CELEBRATION ***syn*** see CAUSE — **on occasion** : from time to time
²**occasion** *vt* **-sioned; -sion·ing** \-ˈkāzh-(ə-)niŋ\ (14c) : BRING ABOUT, CAUSE
oc·ca·sion·al \-ˈkāzh-nəl, -ən-ᵊl\ *adj* (1631) **1 a :** of or relating to a particular occasion ⟨a budget able to meet ~ demands as well as regular ones⟩ **b :** created for a particular occasion ⟨~ verse⟩ **2 :** acting as the occasion or contributing cause of something **3 :** encountered, occurring, appearing, or taken at irregular or infrequent intervals ⟨~ visitors⟩ ⟨an ~ vacation⟩ **4 :** acting in a specified capacity from time to time ⟨an ~ lecturer⟩ **5 :** designed or constructed to be used as the occasion demands ⟨~ furniture⟩
oc·ca·sion·al·ly \-ē\ *adv* (1630) : now and then : on occasion
Oc·ci·dent \ˈäk-səd-ənt, -sə-ˌdent\ *n* [ME, fr. MF, fr. L *occident-*, *occidens*, fr. prp. of *occidere* to fall, set (of the sun)] (14c) : WEST 2a
oc·ci·den·tal \ˌäk-sə-ˈdent-ᵊl\ *adj, often cap* (14c) **1 :** of, relating to, or situated in the Occident : WESTERN **2 :** of or relating to Occidentals — **oc·ci·den·tal·ly** \-ᵊl-ē\ *adv*
Occidental *n* (1857) : a member of one of the occidental peoples; *esp* : a person of European ancestry
Oc·ci·den·tal·ism \ˌäk-sə-ˈdent-ᵊl-ˌiz-əm\ *n* (1839) : the characteristic features of occidental peoples or culture
oc·ci·den·tal·ize \-ᵊl-ˌīz\ *vt* **-ized; -iz·ing** *often cap* (1870) : to make occidental (as in culture)
oc·cip·i·tal \äk-ˈsip-ət-ᵊl\ *adj* (1541) : of, relating to, or located within or near the occiput or the occipital bone — **occipital** *n* — **oc·cip·i·tal·ly** \-ᵊl-ē\ *adv*
occipital bone *n* (15c) : a compound bone that forms the posterior part of the skull and bears a condyle by which the skull articulates with the atlas
occipital condyle *n* (ca. 1860) : an articular surface on the occipital bone by which the skull articulates with the atlas
occipital lobe *n* (ca. 1890) : the posterior lobe of each cerebral hemisphere that bears the visual areas and has the form of a 3-sided pyramid
oc·ci·put \ˈäk-sə-(ˌ)pət\ *n, pl* **occiputs** *or* **oc·cip·i·ta** \äk-ˈsip-ət-ə\ [L *occipit-*, *occiput*, fr. *ob-* against + *capit-*, *caput* head — more at OB-, HEAD] (14c) : the back part of the head or skull — see DOG illustration
oc·clude \ə-ˈklüd, ä-\ *vb* **oc·clud·ed; oc·clud·ing** [L *occludere*, fr. *ob-* in the way + *claudere* to shut, close — more at CLOSE] *vt* (1597) **1 :** to close up or block off : OBSTRUCT ⟨a thrombus *occluding* a coronary artery⟩; *also* : CONCEAL **2 :** SORB **3 :** to cut off from contact with the surface of the earth and force aloft by the convergence of a cold front on a warm front ⟨*occluded* warm air⟩ ~ *vi* **1 :** to come into contact with cusps of the opposing teeth fitting together ⟨his teeth do not ~ properly⟩ **2 :** to become occluded — **oc·clu·sive** \-ˈklü-siv, -ziv\ *adj*
occluded front *n* (ca. 1938) : OCCLUSION 2

oc·clu·sal \ə-ˈklü-səl, ä-, -zəl\ *adj* (1897) **:** of or relating to the grinding or biting surface of a tooth or to occlusion of the teeth

oc·clu·sion \ə-ˈklü-zhən\ *n* [prob. fr. (assumed) NL *occlusion-, occlusio,* fr. L *occlusus,* pp. of *occludere*] (1645) **1 :** the act of occluding **:** the state of being occluded: as **a :** the complete obstruction of the breath passage in the articulation of a speech sound **b :** the bringing of the opposing surfaces of the teeth of the two jaws into contact; *also* **:** the relation between the surfaces when in contact **c :** the inclusion or sorption of gas trapped during solidification of a material **2 :** the front formed by a cold front overtaking a warm front and lifting the warm air above the earth's surface

1**oc·cult** \ə-ˈkəlt, ä-\ *vb* [L *occultare,* fr. *occultus,* pp.] *vt* (1500) **:** to shut off from view or exposure **:** COVER, ECLIPSE ~ *vi* **:** to become concealed briefly at regular intervals — used of the beam from a lighthouse — **oc·cult·er** *n*

2**oc·cult** \ə-ˈkəlt, ä-; ˈäk-ˌəlt\ *adj* [L *occultus,* fr. pp. of *occulere* to cover up, fr. *ob-* in the way + *-culere* (akin to *celare* to conceal) — more at OB-, HELL] (1567) **1 :** not revealed **:** SECRET **2 :** not easily apprehended or understood **:** ABSTRUSE, MYSTERIOUS **3 :** hidden from view **:** CONCEALED **4 :** of or relating to the occult **5 :** not manifest or detectable by clinical methods alone ⟨~ carcinoma⟩; *also* **:** not present in macroscopic amounts ⟨~ blood in a stool specimen⟩ — **oc·cult·ly** *adv*

3**occult** *like*[2]\ *n* (1923) **:** matters regarded as involving the action or influence of supernatural or supernormal powers or some secret knowledge of them — used with *the*

oc·cul·ta·tion \ˌäk-(ˌ)əl-ˈtā-shən\ *n* (15c) **1 :** the state of being hidden from view or lost to notice **2 :** the interruption of the light from a celestial body or of the signals from a spacecraft by the intervention of a celestial body; *esp* **:** an eclipse of a star or planet by the moon

oc·cult·ism \ə-ˈkəl-ˌtiz-əm, ä-; ˈäk-ˌəl-\ *n* (1881) **:** occult theory or practice **:** belief in or study of the action or influence of supernatural or supernormal powers — **oc·cult·ist** \-təst\ *n*

oc·cu·pan·cy \ˈäk-yə-pən-sē\ *n, pl* **-cies** (1596) **1 :** the fact or condition of holding, possessing, or residing in or on something ⟨~ of the estate⟩ ⟨has maintained ~ of a seat in the legislature⟩ **2 :** the act or fact of taking or having possession (as of unowned land) to acquire ownership **3 :** the fact or condition of being occupied ⟨~ by more than 400 persons is unlawful⟩ **4 :** the use to which a property is put ⟨industrial ~⟩ **5 :** a building or part of a building intended to be occupied (as by a tenant) ⟨multiple ~ buildings⟩

oc·cu·pant \-pənt\ *n* (1622) **1 :** one who acquires title by occupancy **2 :** one who occupies a particular place; *esp* **:** RESIDENT

oc·cu·pa·tion \ˌäk-yə-ˈpā-shən\ *n* [ME *occupacioun,* fr. MF *occupation,* fr. L *occupation-, occupatio,* fr. *occupatus,* pp. of *occupare*] (14c) **1 a :** an activity in which one engages ⟨in the first three grades learning to read is perhaps the major ~ of the pupil —J. B. Conant⟩ **b :** the principal business of one's life **:** VOCATION **2 a :** the possession, use, or settlement of land **:** OCCUPANCY **b :** the holding of an office or position **3 a :** the act or process of taking possession of a place or area **:** SEIZURE **b :** the holding and control of an area by a foreign military force **c :** the military force occupying a country or the policies carried out by it ***syn*** see WORK — **oc·cu·pa·tion·al** \-shnəl, -shən-ᵊl\ *adj* — **oc·cu·pa·tion·al·ly** \-ē\ *adv*

occupational therapy *n* (ca. 1915) **:** therapy by means of activity; *esp* **:** creative activity prescribed for its effect in promoting recovery or rehabilitation — **occupational therapist** *n*

oc·cu·py \ˈäk-yə-ˌpī\ *vt* **-pied; -py·ing** [ME *occupien* to take possession of, occupy, modif. of MF *occuper,* fr. L *occupare,* fr. *ob-* toward + *-cupare* (akin to *capere* to seize) — more at OB-, HEAVE] (14c) **1 :** to engage the attention or energies of **2 a :** to take up (a place or extent in space) ⟨this chair is *occupied*⟩ ⟨the fireplace will ~ this corner of the room⟩ **b :** to take or fill (an extent in time) ⟨the hobby *occupies* all of my free time⟩ **3 a :** to take or hold possession or control of ⟨enemy troops *occupied* the ridge⟩ **b :** to fill or perform the functions of (an office or position) **4 :** to reside in as an owner or tenant — **oc·cu·pi·er** \-ˌpī(-ə)r\ *n*

oc·cur \ə-ˈkər\ *vi* **oc·curred; oc·cur·ring** \-ˈkər-iŋ\ [L *occurrere,* fr. *ob-* in the way + *currere* to run — more at OB-, CURRENT] (1536) **1 :** to be found or met with **:** APPEAR **2 :** to come into existence **:** HAPPEN **3 :** to come to mind

oc·cur·rence \ə-ˈkər-ən(t)s, -ˈkə-rən(t)s\ *n* (1539) **1 :** something that occurs ⟨a startling ~⟩ **2 :** the action or instance of occurring ⟨the repeated ~ of petty theft in the locker room⟩

syn OCCURRENCE, EVENT, INCIDENT, EPISODE, CIRCUMSTANCE mean something that happens or takes place. OCCURRENCE may apply to a happening without intent, volition, or plan; EVENT usu. implies an occurrence of some importance and frequently one having antecedent cause; INCIDENT suggests an occurrence of brief duration or secondary importance; EPISODE stresses the distinctiveness or apartness of an incident; CIRCUMSTANCE implies a specific detail attending an action or event as part of its setting or background.

1**oc·cur·rent** \ə-ˈkər-ənt, -ˈkə-rənt\ *adj* [ME, fr. MF, fr. L *occurrent-, occurrens,* prp. of *occurrere*] (15c) **1 :** occurring at a particular time or place **:** CURRENT **2 :** INCIDENTAL

2**occurrent** *n* (1538) **:** something that occurs as distinguished from something that continues to exist

ocean \ˈō-shən\ *n, often attrib* [ME *occean,* fr. L *oceanus,* fr. Gk *Ōkeanos,* a river thought of as encircling the earth, ocean] (13c) **1 :** the whole body of salt water that covers nearly three fourths of the surface of the globe **2 :** one of the large bodies of water into which the great ocean is divided **3 :** an unlimited space or quantity

ocean·ar·i·um \ˌō-shə-ˈnar-ē-əm, -ˈner-\ *n, pl* **-iums** *or* **-ia** \-ē-ə\ (1938) **:** a large marine aquarium

ocean·front \ˈō-shən-ˌfrənt\ *n* (1919) **:** a shore area on the ocean

ocean·go·ing \-ˌgō-iŋ\ *adj* (1885) **:** of, relating to, or designed for travel on the ocean

oce·an·ic \ˌō-shē-ˈan-ik\ *adj* (1656) **1 a :** of or relating to the ocean **b :** occurring in or frequenting the ocean and esp. the open sea as distinguished from littoral or neritic waters **2 :** VAST, GREAT

Oce·anid \ō-ˈsē-ə-nəd\ *n* [Gk *ōkeanid-, ōkeanis,* fr. *Ōkeanos* Oceanus] (1869) **:** any of the ocean nymphs that are daughters of Oceanus and Tethys in Greek mythology

ocean·og·ra·phy \ˌō-shə-ˈnäg-rə-fē\ *n* [ISV] (1859) **:** a science that deals with the oceans and includes the delimitation of their extent and depth, the physics and chemistry of their waters, marine biology, and the exploitation of their resources — **ocean·og·ra·pher** \-fər\ *n* — **ocean·o·graph·ic** \-nə-ˈgraf-ik\ *also* **ocean·o·graph·i·cal** \-i-kəl\ *adj* — **ocean·o·graph·i·cal·ly** \-i-k(ə-)lē\ *adv*

ocean·ol·o·gy \ˌō-shə-ˈnäl-ə-jē\ *n* (ca. 1864) **:** OCEANOGRAPHY; *specif* **:** the science of marine resources and technology — **ocean·ol·o·gist** \-ˈnäl-ə-jəst\ *n*

ocean sunfish *n* (1629) **:** SUNFISH 1

Oce·anus \ō-ˈsē-ə-nəs\ *n* [L, fr. Gk *Ōkeanos*] **:** a Titan who rules over a great river encircling the earth in Greek mythology

ocel·lus \ō-ˈsel-əs\ *n, pl* **ocel·li** \-ˈsel-ˌī, -(ˌ)ē\ [NL, fr. L, dim. of *oculus* eye — more at EYE] (1819) **1 :** a minute simple eye or eyespot of an invertebrate **2 :** an eyelike colored spot (as on a peacock feather or the wings of some butterflies) — **ocel·lar** \ō-ˈsel-ər\ *adj*

oce·lot \ˈäs-ə-ˌlät, ˈō-sə-\ *n* [F, fr. Nahuatl *ocelotl* jaguar] (1774) **:** a medium-sized American wildcat (*Felis pardalis*) that ranges from Texas to Patagonia and has a tawny yellow or grayish coat dotted and striped with black

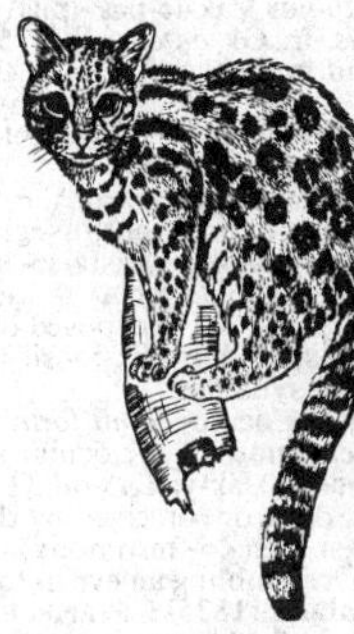

ocelot

ocher *or* **ochre** \ˈō-kər\ *n* [ME *oker,* fr. MF *ocre,* fr. L *ochra,* fr. Gk *ōchra,* fem. of *ōchros* yellow] (14c) **1 :** an earthy usu. red or yellow and often impure iron ore used as a pigment **2 :** the color of ocher; *esp* **:** the color of yellow ocher — **ocher·ous** \ˈō-k(ə-)rəs\ *or* **ochre·ous** \ˈō-k(ə-)rəs, -krē-əs\ *adj*

och·loc·ra·cy \ä-ˈkläk-rə-sē\ *n* [Gk & MF; MF *ochlocratie,* fr. Gk *ochlokratia,* fr. *ochlos* mob + *-kratia* -cracy] (1584) **:** government by the mob **:** mob rule ⟨warned that ~ would lead to anarchy⟩ — **och·lo·crat** \ˈäk-lə-ˌkrat\ *n* — **och·lo·crat·ic** \ˌäk-lə-ˈkrat-ik\ *or* **och·lo·crat·i·cal** \-i-kəl\ *adj*

-ock \ək, ik, ˌäk\ *n suffix* [ME *-oc,* fr. OE] **:** small one ⟨hill*ock*⟩

Ock·ham's razor \ˌäk-əmz-\ *var of* OCCAM'S RAZOR

o'·clock \ə-ˈkläk\ *adv* [contr. of *of the clock*] (ca. 1720) **1 :** according to the clock ⟨the time is three ~⟩ **2 —** used for indicating position or direction as if on a clock dial that is oriented vertically or horizontally ⟨an airplane approaching at six ~⟩

oco·ti·llo \ˌō-kə-ˈtē-(ˌ)(y)ō\ *n, pl* **-llos** [MexSp] (1856) **:** a thorny scarlet-flowered candlewood (*Fouquieria splendens*) of the southwestern U.S. and Mexico

octa- *or* **octo-** *also* **oct-** *comb form* [Gk *okta-, oktō-, okt-* (fr. *oktō*) & L *octo-, oct-,* fr. *octo* — more at EIGHT] **:** eight ⟨*oct*amerous⟩ ⟨*oct*ane⟩ ⟨*oct*oroon⟩

oc·ta·gon \ˈäk-tə-ˌgän\ *n* [L *octagonum,* fr. Gk *oktagōnon,* fr. *okta-* + *-gōnon* -gon] (ca. 1656) **:** a polygon of eight angles and eight sides — **oc·tag·o·nal** \äk-ˈtag-ən-ᵊl\ *adj* — **oc·tag·o·nal·ly** \-ᵊl-ē\ *adv*

oc·ta·he·dral \ˌäk-tə-ˈhē-drəl\ *adj* (1758) **1 :** having eight plane faces **2 :** of, relating to, or formed in octahedrons — **oc·ta·he·dral·ly** \-drə-lē\ *adv*

oc·ta·he·dron \-drən\ *n, pl* **-drons** *or* **-dra** \-drə\ [Gk *oktaedron,* fr. *okta-* + *-edron* -hedron] (1570) **:** a solid bounded by eight plane faces

oc·tal \ˈäk-tᵊl\ *adj* (1948) **:** of, relating to, or being a number system with a base of eight

oc·tam·e·ter \äk-ˈtam-ət-ər\ *n* [LL, having eight feet, fr. LGk *oktametros,* fr. *okta-* + *metron* measure — more at MEASURE] (1889) **:** a line of verse consisting of eight metrical feet

oc·tane \ˈäk-ˌtān\ *n* [ISV] (ca. 1872) **1 :** any of several isomeric liquid paraffin hydrocarbons C_8H_{18} **2 :** OCTANE NUMBER

octane number *n* (1931) **:** a number that is used to measure the antiknock properties of a liquid motor fuel and that represents the percentage by volume of isooctane in a reference fuel consisting of a mixture of isooctane and normal heptane and matching in knocking properties the fuel being tested — called also *octane rating;* compare CETANE NUMBER

oc·tant \ˈäk-tənt\ *n* [L *octant-, octans* eighth of a circle, fr. *octo*] (1690) **1 a :** the position or aspect of a celestial body when distant from another body by 45 degrees **b :** an instrument for observing altitudes of a celestial body from a moving ship or aircraft **2 :** any of the eight parts into which a space is divided by three coordinate planes

oc·ta·pep·tide \ˌäk-tə-ˈpep-ˌtīd\ *n* (1961) **:** a protein fragment or molecule (as oxytocin or vasopressin) that consists of eight amino acids linked in a polypeptide chain

oc·tave \ˈäk-tiv, -təv, -ˌtāv\ *n* [ME, fr. ML *octava,* fr. L, fem. of *octavus* eighth, fr. *octo* eight — more at EIGHT] (13c) **1 :** an 8-day period of observances beginning with a festival day **2 a :** a stanza of eight lines **:** OTTAVA RIMA **b :** the first eight lines of an Italian sonnet **3 a :** a musical interval embracing eight diatonic degrees **b :** a tone or note at this interval **c :** the harmonic combination of two tones an octave apart **d :** the whole series of notes, tones, or digitals comprised within this interval and forming the unit of the modern scale **e :** an organ stop giving tones an octave above those corresponding to the digitals **4 :** the interval between two frequencies (as in an electromagnetic spectrum) having a ratio of 2 to 1 **5 :** a group of eight

oc·ta·vo \äk-ˈtā-(ˌ)vō, -ˈtäv-(ˌ)ō\ *n, pl* **-vos** [L, abl. of *octavus* eighth] (1582) **:** the size of a piece of paper cut eight from a sheet; *also* **:** a book, a page, or paper of this size

oc·tet \äk-ˈtet\ *n* (ca. 1864) **1 :** a musical composition for eight instruments or voices **2 :** a group or set of eight: as **a :** the performers of an octet **b :** OCTAVE 2b

oc·til·lion \äk-'til-yən\ *n* [F, fr. MF, fr. *oct-* octa- + *-illion* (as in *million*)] (1690) — see NUMBER table

Oc·to·ber \äk-'tō-bər\ *n* [ME *Octobre,* fr. OE & OF; OE *October,* fr. L, 8th month, fr. *octo;* OF, fr. L *October*] (bef. 12c) : the 10th month of the Gregorian calendar

oc·to·de·cil·lion \,äk-tō-di-'sil-yən\ *n* [L *octodecim* eighteen + E *-illion* (as in *million*)] (1939) — see NUMBER table

oc·to·ge·nar·i·an \,äk-tə-jə-'ner-ē-ən\ *n* [L *octogenarius* containing eighty, fr. *octogeni* eighty each, fr. *octoginta* eighty, fr. *octo* eight + *-ginta* (akin to *viginti* twenty) — more at VIGESIMAL] (1815) : a person whose age is in the eighties — **octogenarian** *adj*

oc·to·ploid \'äk-tə-,plȯid\ *adj* [ISV] (1925) : having a chromosome number eight times the basic haploid chromosome number — **octoploid** *n*

oc·to·pod \'äk-tə-,päd\ *n* [deriv. of Gk *oktōpod-, oktōpous* scorpion, fr. *oktō-* octa- + *pod-, pous* foot — more at FOOT] (ca. 1835) : any of an order (Octopoda) of cephalopod mollusks (as an octopus or argonaut) that have eight arms bearing sessile suckers — **octopod** *adj*

oc·to·pus \'äk-tə-pəs -,pu̇s\ *n, pl* **-pus·es** *or* **-pi** \-,pī\ [NL *Octopod-, Octopus,* fr. Gk *oktōpous*] (1758) **1 :** any of a genus (*Octopus*) of cephalopod mollusks that have eight muscular arms equipped with two rows of suckers; *broadly* **:** any octopod excepting the paper nautilus **2 :** something that resembles an octopus esp. in having many centrally directed branches

oc·to·roon \,äk-tə-'rün\ *n* [*octa-* + *-roon* (as in *quadroon*)] (1861) : a person of one-eighth Negro ancestry

oc·to·syl·lab·ic \,äk-tə-sə-'lab-ik\ *adj* [LL *octosyllabus,* fr. Gk *oktasyllabos,* fr. *okta-* octa- + *syllabē* syllable] (1771) **1 :** consisting of eight syllables **2 :** composed of verses of eight syllables — **octosyllabic** *n*

oc·to·syl·la·ble \'äk-tə-,sil-ə-bəl, ,äk-tə-'\ *n* (1842) : a word or line of eight syllables

ocul- *or* **oculo-** *comb form* [L *ocul-,* fr. *oculus* — more at EYE] **1 :** eye ⟨*oculomotor*⟩ **2 :** ocular and ⟨*oculocardiac*⟩

[1]**oc·u·lar** \'äk-yə-lər\ *adj* [LL *ocularis* of eyes, fr. L *oculus* eye] (1597) **1 a :** done or perceived by the eye ⟨~ inspection⟩ **b :** based on what has been seen ⟨~ testimony⟩ **2 a :** of or relating to the eye ⟨~ muscles⟩ **b :** resembling an eye in form or function

[2]**ocular** *n* (1835) : EYEPIECE

oc·u·lar·ist \'äk-yə-lə-rəst\ *n* (1866) : a person who makes and fits artificial eyes

oc·u·list \'äk-yə-ləst\ *n* [F *oculiste,* fr. L *oculus*] (ca. 1615) **1 :** OPHTHALMOLOGIST **2 :** OPTOMETRIST

oc·u·lo·mo·tor \,äk-yə-lə-'mōt-ər\ *adj* (1881) **1 :** moving or tending to move the eyeball **2 :** of or relating to the oculomotor nerve

oculomotor nerve *n* (1881) : either of the pair of chiefly motor nerves that comprise the 3d pair of cranial nerves, arise from the midbrain, and supply four muscles of the eye

od *or* **odd** \'äd\ *interj, often cap* [euphemism for *God*] *archaic* (1695) — used as a mild oath

[1]**OD** \(')ō-'dē\ *n* [overdose] (ca. 1960) **1 :** an overdose of a narcotic **2 :** one who has taken an OD

[2]**OD** *vi* **OD'd** *or* **ODed; OD'·ing; OD's** (1966) **1 :** to become ill or die of an OD **2 :** to have or experience too much of something — used with *on* ⟨~ on television⟩

oda·lisque \'ōd-ᵊl-,isk\ *n* [F, fr. Turk *odalık*] (ca. 1681) : a female slave or concubine in a harem

odd \'äd\ *adj* [ME *odde,* fr. ON *oddi* point of land, triangle, odd number; akin to OE *ord* point of a weapon] (14c) **1 a :** being without a corresponding mate ⟨an ~ shoe⟩ **b** (1) **:** left over after others are paired or grouped (2) **:** separated from a set or series **2 a :** somewhat more than the indicated approximate quantity, extent, or degree — usu. used in combination ⟨300-*odd* pages⟩ **b** (1) **:** left over as a remainder ⟨had a few ~ dollars for entertainment after paying his bills⟩ (2) **:** constituting a small amount ⟨had some ~ change in her pocket⟩ **3 a :** being one of the sequence of natural numbers beginning with one and counting by twos that are not divisible by two **b :** marked by an odd number of units **c :** being a function such that $f(-x) = -f(x)$ where the sign is reversed but the absolute value remains the same if the sign of the independent variable is reversed **4 a :** not regular, expected, or planned ⟨worked at ~ jobs⟩ **b :** encountered or experienced from time to time **:** OCCASIONAL **5 :** having an out-of-the-way location **:** REMOTE **6 :** differing markedly from the usual or ordinary or accepted **:** PECULIAR ***syn*** see STRANGE — **odd·ly** *adv* — **odd·ness** *n*

odd·ball \'äd-,bȯl\ *n* (ca. 1945) : one that is eccentric — **oddball** *adj*

Odd Fellow *n* [Independent Order of *Odd Fellows*] (1795) : a member of a major benevolent and fraternal order

odd·i·ty \'äd-ət-ē\ *n, pl* **-ties** (1750) **1 :** an odd person, thing, event, or trait **2 :** the quality or state of being odd

odd lot *n* (1913) : a number or quantity other than the usual unit in transactions; *esp* **:** a quantity of less than 100 shares of stock

odd man out *n* (1889) : one that is eccentric or unorthodox

odd·ment \'äd-mənt\ *n* (1796) **1 a :** something left over **:** REMNANT **b** *pl* **:** ODDS AND ENDS **2 :** something odd **:** ODDITY

odd permutation *n* (1929) : a permutation that is produced by the successive application of an odd number of interchanges of pairs of elements

odd–pin·nate \'äd-'pin-,āt\ *adj* (ca. 1890) : having leaflets on each side of the petiole and having a single leaflet at the tip of the petiole — **odd–pin·nate·ly** *adv*

odds \'ädz\ *n pl but sing or pl in constr* (1500) **1 a** *archaic* **:** INEQUALITIES **b** *obs* **:** degree of unlikeness **2 a :** an amount by which one thing exceeds or falls short of another ⟨won the election by considerable ~⟩ **b** (1) **:** a difference favoring one of two opposed things ⟨the overwhelming ~ it affords the sportsman over bird and animal —Richard Jefferies⟩ (2) **:** a difference in terms of advantage or disadvantage ⟨what's the ~, if thinking so makes them happy —Flora Thompson⟩ **c** (1) **:** the probability that one thing is so or will happen rather than another **:** CHANCES ⟨the ~ are against it⟩ (2) **:** the ratio of the probability of one event to that of an alternative event **3 :** DISAGREEMENT, VARIANCE — usu. used with *at* ⟨faculty and administration often are at ~ on everything —W. E. Brock *b*1930⟩ **4 a :** special favor **:** PARTIALITY **b :** an allowance granted by one making a bet to one accepting the bet and designed to equalize the chances favoring one of the bettors **c :** the ratio between the amount to be paid off for a winning bet and the amount of the bet — **by all odds :** in every way **:** without question ⟨*by all odds* the best book of the year⟩

odds and ends *n pl* (ca. 1746) **1 a :** miscellaneous articles **b :** miscellaneous small matters (as of business) to be attended to **2 :** miscellaneous remnants or leftovers ⟨*odds and ends* of food⟩

odds–on \(')äd-'zȯn, -'zän\ *adj* (1890) **1 :** having or viewed as having a better than even chance to win ⟨the ~ favorite⟩ **2 :** not involving much risk **:** pretty sure ⟨an ~ bet⟩

odd trick *n* (1710) : each trick in excess of six won by declarer's side at bridge — compare BOOK 9

ode \'ōd\ *n* [MF or LL; MF, fr. LL, fr. Gk *ōidē,* lit., song, fr. *aeidein, aidein* to sing; akin to Gk *audē* voice, OHG *farwāzan* to deny] (1588) : a lyric poem usu. marked by exaltation of feeling and style, varying length of line, and complexity of stanza forms — **od·ist** \-əst\ *n*

-ode \,ōd\ *n comb form* [Gk *-odos,* fr. *hodos* — more at CEDE] **1 :** way **:** path ⟨electr*ode*⟩ **2 :** electrode ⟨di*ode*⟩

ode·um \ō-'dē-əm, 'ōd-ē-\ *n, pl* **odea** \-ə\ [L & Gk; L, fr. Gk *ōideion,* fr. *ōidē* song] (1603) **1 :** a small roofed theater of ancient Greece and Rome used chiefly for competitions in music and poetry **2 :** a theater or concert hall

od·ic \'ōd-ik\ *adj* (1863) : of, relating to, or forming an ode

Odin \'ōd-ᵊn\ *n* [Dan, fr. ON *Ōthinn;* akin to OE *Wōden* Odin] : the supreme god and creator in Norse mythology

odi·ous \'ōd-ē-əs\ *adj* [ME, fr. MF *odieus,* fr. L *odiosus,* fr. *odium*] (14c) : exciting or deserving hatred or repugnance ⟨~ associates⟩ ⟨an ~ business⟩ — **odi·ous·ly** *adv* — **odi·ous·ness** *n*

odi·um \'ōd-ē-əm\ *n* [L, hatred, fr. *odisse* to hate; akin to OE *atol* terrible, Gk *odyssasthai* to be angry] (1654) **1 :** the state or fact of being subjected to hatred and contempt as a result of a despicable act or blameworthy situation **2 :** hatred and condemnation accompanied by loathing or contempt **:** DETESTATION **3 :** disrepute or infamy attached to something **:** OPPROBRIUM

odo·graph \'ōd-ə-,graf, 'äd-\ *n* [*odo-* (as in *odometer*) + *-graph*] (1883) : an instrument for automatically plotting (as on a map) the course and distance traveled by a vehicle

odom·e·ter \ō-'däm-ət-ər\ *n* [F *odomètre,* fr. Gk *hodometron,* fr. *hodos* way, road + *metron* measure — more at CEDE, MEASURE] (1791) : an instrument for measuring the distance traveled (as by a vehicle)

odo·nate \'ōd-ᵊn-,āt, ō-'dän-\ *n* [irreg. deriv. of Gk *odous, odōn* tooth] (1947) : any of an order (Odonata) of predacious insects comprising the dragonflies and damselflies — **odonate** *adj*

odont- *or* **odonto-** *comb form* [F, fr. Gk, *odont-, odous* — more at TOOTH] : tooth ⟨*odont*itis⟩ ⟨*odonto*blast⟩

-odont \ə-,dänt\ *adj comb form* [Gk *odont-, odous* tooth] : having teeth of a (specified) nature ⟨mes*odont*⟩

-odon·tia \ə-'dän-ch(ē-)ə\ *n comb form* [NL, fr. Gk *odont-, odous*] : form, condition, or mode of treatment of the teeth ⟨orth*odontia*⟩

odon·to·blast \ō-'dänt-ə-,blast\ *n* [ISV] (1878) : one of the elongated radially arranged outer cells of the dental pulp that secrete dentin — **odon·to·blas·tic** \-,dänt-ə-'blas-tik\ *adj*

odon·to·glos·sum \ō-,dänt-ə-'gläs-əm\ *n* [NL, fr. *odont-* + Gk *glōssa* tongue — more at GLOSS] (1879) : any of a genus (*Odontoglossum*) of widely cultivated tropical American epiphytic orchids

odon·toid process \ō-,dän-,tȯid-\ *n* (1706) : a toothlike process projecting from the anterior end of the centrum of the axis vertebra on which the atlas vertebra rotates

odor \'ōd-ər\ *n* [ME *odour,* fr. MF, fr. L *odor;* akin to L *olēre* to smell, Gk *ozein* to smell, *osmē* smell, odor] (14c) **1 a :** a quality of something that stimulates the olfactory organ **b :** a sensation resulting from adequate stimulation of the olfactory organ **:** SMELL **2 a :** a characteristic or predominant quality **:** FLAVOR ⟨the ~ of sanctity⟩ **b :** REPUTE, ESTIMATION ⟨in bad ~⟩ **3** *archaic* **:** something that emits a sweet or pleasing scent **:** PERFUME ***syn*** see SMELL — **odored** \'ōd-ərd\ *adj* — **odor·less** \-ər-ləs\ *adj*

odor·ant \'ōd-ə-rənt\ *n* (1935) : an odorous substance; *esp* **:** one added to a dangerous odorless substance to warn of its presence

odor·if·er·ous \,ōd-ə-'rif-(ə-)rəs\ *adj* (15c) **1 :** yielding an odor **:** ODOROUS **2 :** morally offensive — **odor·if·er·ous·ly** *adv* — **odor·if·er·ous·ness** *n*

odor·ize \,ōd-ə-,rīz\ *vt* **-ized; -iz·ing** (1884) : to make odorous **:** SCENT

odor·ous \'ōd-ə-rəs\ *adj* (15c) : having an odor: as **a :** FRAGRANT **b :** MALODOROUS — **odor·ous·ly** *adv* — **odor·ous·ness** *n*

syn ODOROUS, FRAGRANT, REDOLENT, AROMATIC mean emitting and diffusing scent. ODOROUS applies to whatever has a strong distinctive smell whether pleasant or unpleasant ⟨*odorous* cheeses should be tightly wrapped⟩ FRAGRANT applies to things (as flowers or spices) with sweet or agreeable odors ⟨roses that were especially *fragrant*⟩ REDOLENT applies usu. to a place or thing impregnated with odors ⟨the kitchen was often *redolent* of garlic and tomatoes⟩ AROMATIC applies to things emitting pungent often fresh odors ⟨an *aromatic* blend of rare tobaccos⟩

odour *chiefly Brit var of* ODOR

Odys·se·an \ō-'dis-ē-ən ("*Odysseus*"), ,äd-ə-'sē-ən ("*journey*")\ *adj* (1711) : of, relating to, or characteristic of Odysseus or his journey

Odys·seus \ō-'dis-ē-əs, -'dis-yəs, -'dish-əs, -'dish-,üs\ *n* [Gk] : a king of Ithaca and Greek leader in the Trojan War who after the war wanders 10 years before reaching home

od·ys·sey \'äd-ə-sē\ *n, pl* **-seys** [the *Odyssey,* epic poem attributed to Homer recounting the long wanderings of Odysseus] (1889) **1 :** a long wandering or voyage usu. marked by many changes of fortune **2 :** an intellectual or spiritual wandering or quest

oe·cu·men·i·cal *esp Brit* ,ēk-\ *var of* ECUMENICAL

oe·de·ma *chiefly Brit var of* EDEMA

oe·di·pal \'ed-ə-pəl, 'ēd-\ *adj, often cap* (1939) : of, relating to, or resulting from the Oedipus complex — **oe·di·pal·ly** \-pə-lē\ *adv, often cap*

[1]**Oe·di·pus** \-pəs\ *n* [L, fr. Gk *Oidipous*] : the son of Laius and Jocasta who in fulfillment of an oracle unknowingly kills his father and marries his mother

[2]**Oedipus** *adj* (1910) : OEDIPAL

Oedipus complex *n* (1910) : the positive libidinal feelings that a child develops toward the parent of the opposite sex and that may be a source of adult personality disorder when unresolved

oeil–de–boeuf \ˌə(r)d-ə-ˈbəf, ˌəid-\ *n, pl* **oeils–de–boeuf** *same*\ [F *œil-de-bœuf,* lit., ox's eye] (1849) **:** a circular or oval window

oeil·lade \ˌə(r)-ˈyäd, œ-yȧd\ *n* [F *œillade,* fr. MF, fr. *oeil* eye, fr. L *oculus* — more at EYE] (1592) **:** a glance of the eye; *esp* **:** OGLE

OEM \ˌō-(ˌ)ē-ˈem\ *n* [original equipment manufacturer] (1968) **:** one that produces complex equipment (as a computer system) from components usu. bought from other manufacturers

oe·nol·o·gy *var of* ENOLOGY

Oe·no·ne \ē-ˈnō-nē\ *n* [L, fr. Gk *Oinōnē*] **:** a nymph who is abandoned by her husband Paris for Helen of Troy

oe·no·phile \ˈē-nə-ˌfīl\ *n* [F *œnophile,* fr. *œno-* (fr. Gk *oinos* wine) + *-phile* -phile — more at WINE] (1930) **:** a lover or connoisseur of wine

[1]o'er \ˈō(ə)r, ˈȯ(ə)r\ *adv* (1592) **:** OVER

[2]o'er \(ˈ)ō(ə)r, (ˈ)ȯ(ə)r\ *prep* (1601) **:** OVER

Oer·li·kon \ˈər-li-ˌkän\ *n* [*Oerlikon,* Switzerland] (1941) **:** any of several 20 mm. automatic aircraft or antiaircraft cannon

oer·sted \ˈər-stəd\ *n* [Hans Christian *Oersted*] (ca. 1889) **:** the centimeter-gram-second electromagnetic unit of magnetic intensity equal to the intensity of a magnetic field in a vacuum in which a unit magnetic pole experiences a mechanical force of one dyne in the direction of the field

oe·soph·a·gus *chiefly Brit var of* ESOPHAGUS

oestr- *or* **oestro-** — see ESTR-

oeu·vre \œvrᵊ\ *n, pl* **oeuvres** *same*\ [F *œuvre,* lit., work, fr. L *opera* — more at OPERA] (1875) **:** a substantial body of work constituting the lifework of a writer, an artist, or a composer

of \əv, *before consonants also* ə; ˈəv, ˈäv\ *prep* [ME, off, of, fr. OE, adv. & prep.; akin to OHG *aba* off, away, L *ab* from, away, Gk *apo*] (bef. 12c) **1** — used as a function word to indicate a point of reckoning ⟨north ~ the lake⟩ **2 a** — used as a function word to indicate origin or derivation ⟨a man ~ noble birth⟩ **b** — used as a function word to indicate the cause, motive, or reason ⟨died ~ flu⟩ **c :** BY ⟨plays ~ Shakespeare⟩ **d :** on the part of ⟨very kind ~ him⟩ **3** — used as a function word to indicate the component material, parts, or elements or the contents ⟨throne ~ gold⟩ ⟨cup ~ water⟩ **4 a** — used as a function word to indicate the whole that includes the part denoted by the preceding word ⟨most ~ the army⟩ **b** — used as a function word to indicate a whole or quantity from which a part is removed or expended ⟨gave ~ his time⟩ **5 a :** relating to **:** ABOUT ⟨stories ~ his travels⟩ **b :** in respect to ⟨slow ~ speech⟩ **6 a** — used as a function word to indicate belonging or a possessive relationship ⟨king ~ England⟩ **b** — used as a function word to indicate relationship between a result determined by a function or operation and a basic entity (as an independent variable) ⟨a function ~ *x*⟩ ⟨the product ~ two numbers⟩ **7** — used as a function word to indicate separation ⟨eased ~ pain⟩ **8 a** — used as a function word to indicate a particular example belonging to the class denoted by the preceding noun ⟨the city ~ Rome⟩ **b** — used as a function word to indicate apposition ⟨that fool ~ a husband⟩ **9 a** — used as a function word to indicate the object of an action denoted or implied by the preceding noun ⟨love ~ nature⟩ **b** — used as a function word to indicate the application of a verb ⟨cheats him ~ a dollar⟩ or of an adjective ⟨fond ~ candy⟩ **10** — used as a function word to indicate a characteristic or distinctive quality or possession ⟨a man ~ courage⟩ **11 a** — used as a function word to indicate the position in time of an action or occurrence ⟨died ~ a Monday⟩ **b :** BEFORE ⟨quarter ~ ten⟩ **12** *archaic* **:** ON ⟨a plague ~ all cowards —Shak.⟩

ofay \ˈō-ˌfā, ō-ˈ\ *n* [origin unknown] (1917) **:** a white person — usu. used disparagingly

[1]off \ˈȯf\ *adv* [ME *of,* fr. OE — more at OF] (bef. 12c) **1 a** (1) **:** from a place or position ⟨march ~⟩; *specif* **:** away from land ⟨ship stood ~ to sea⟩ (2) **:** at a distance in space or time ⟨stood 10 paces ~⟩ ⟨a long way ~⟩ **b :** from a course **:** ASIDE ⟨turned ~ into a bypath⟩; *specif* **:** away from the wind **c :** into an unconscious state ⟨dozed ~⟩ **2 a :** so as to be separated from support ⟨rolled to the edge of the table and ~⟩ or close contact ⟨blew the lid ~⟩ ⟨the handle came ~⟩ **b :** so as to be divided ⟨surface marked ~ into squares⟩ **3 a :** to a state of discontinuance or suspension ⟨shut ~ an engine⟩ **b** — used as an intensifier ⟨drink ~ a glass⟩ ⟨finish it ~⟩ **4 :** in absence from or suspension of regular work or service ⟨take time ~ for lunch⟩ **5 :** OFFSTAGE

[2]off \(ˈ)ȯf\ *prep* (bef. 12c) **1 a** — used as a function word to indicate physical separation or distance from a position of rest, attachment, or union ⟨take it ~ the table⟩ ⟨a path ~ the main walk⟩ ⟨a shop just ~ the main street⟩ **b :** to seaward of ⟨two miles ~ shore⟩ **2** — used as a function word to indicate the object of an action ⟨borrowed a dollar ~ him⟩ ⟨dined ~ oysters⟩ **3 a** — used as a function word to indicate the suspension of an occupation or activity ⟨~ duty⟩ ⟨~ liquor⟩ **b :** below the usual standard or level of ⟨~ his game⟩

[3]off \ˈȯf\ *vi* (1642) **:** to go away **:** DEPART — used chiefly as an imperative ⟨~, or I'll shoot⟩ **~** *vt, slang* **:** KILL, MURDER

[4]off \(ˈ)ȯf\ *adj* (1666) **1 a :** more removed or distant ⟨the ~ side of the building⟩ **b :** SEAWARD **c :** RIGHT **2 a :** started on the way ⟨~ on a spree⟩ **b :** not taking place or staying in effect **:** CANCELED ⟨the deal was ~⟩ **c :** not operating **d :** not placed so as to permit operation **3 a :** not corresponding to fact **:** INCORRECT ⟨~ in his reckoning⟩ **b :** POOR, SUBNORMAL **c :** not entirely sane **:** ECCENTRIC **d :** REMOTE, SLIGHT ⟨an ~ chance⟩ **4 a :** spent off duty ⟨reading on his ~ days⟩ **b :** SLACK ⟨~ season⟩ **5 a :** OFF-COLOR **b :** INFERIOR ⟨~ grade of oil⟩; *also* **:** affected with putrefaction **c :** DOWN ⟨stocks were ~⟩ **6 :** CIRCUMSTANCED ⟨worse ~⟩

of·fal \ˈȯ-fəl, ˈäf-əl\ *n* [ME, fr. *of* off + *fall*] (14c) **1 :** the waste or by-product of a process: as **a :** trimmings of a hide **b :** the by-products of milling used esp. for stock feeds **c :** the viscera and trimmings of a butchered animal removed in dressing **2 :** RUBBISH

off and on *adv* (1535) **:** with periodic cessation **:** INTERMITTENTLY ⟨rained *off and on* all day⟩

[1]off·beat \ˈȯf-ˌbēt\ *n* (ca. 1928) **:** the unaccented beat of a musical measure

[2]offbeat *adj* (ca. 1935) **:** ECCENTRIC, UNCONVENTIONAL

off Broadway *n, often cap O* [fr. its usu. being produced in smaller theaters outside of the Broadway theatrical district] (1952) **:** a part of the New York professional theater stressing fundamental and artistic values and formerly engaging in experimentation — **off–Broadway** *adj or adv, often cap O*

off·cast \ˈȯf-ˌkast\ *adj* (1571) **:** cast off **:** DISCARDED — **offcast** *n*

off–col·or \ˈȯf-ˈkəl-ər\ *or* **off–col·ored** \-ərd\ *adj* (1860) **1 a :** not having the right or standard color **b :** being out of sorts **2 a :** of doubtful propriety **:** DUBIOUS **b :** verging on the indecent

of·fend \ə-ˈfend\ *vb* [ME *offenden,* fr. MF *offendre,* fr. L *offendere* to strike against, offend, fr. *ob-* against + *-fendere* to strike — more at OB-, DEFEND] *vi* (14c) **1 a :** to transgress the moral or divine law **:** SIN ⟨if it be a sin to covet honor, I am the most ~*ing* soul alive —Shak.⟩ **b :** to violate a law or rule **:** do wrong ⟨~ against the law⟩ **2 a :** to cause difficulty, discomfort, or injury ⟨took off his shoe and removed the ~*ing* pebble⟩ **b :** to cause dislike, anger, or vexation ⟨thoughtless words that ~ needlessly⟩ **~** *vt* **1 a :** VIOLATE, TRANSGRESS **b :** to cause pain to **:** HURT **2** *obs* **:** to cause to sin or fall **3 :** to cause to feel vexation or resentment usu. by violation of what is proper or fitting ⟨she was ~*ed* by their failure to introduce her to their new friend⟩ — **of·fend·er** *n*

syn OFFEND, OUTRAGE, AFFRONT, INSULT mean to cause hurt feelings or deep resentment. OFFEND need not imply an intentional hurting but it may indicate merely a violation of the victim's sense of what is proper or fitting; OUTRAGE implies offending beyond endurance and calling forth extreme feelings; AFFRONT implies treating with deliberate rudeness or contemptuous indifference to courtesy; INSULT suggests deliberately causing humiliation, hurt pride, or shame.

of·fense *or* **of·fence** \ə-ˈfen(t)s, *esp for 3* ˈäf-ˌen(t)s, ˈȯf-\ *n* [ME, fr. MF, fr. L *offensa,* fr. *offensus,* pp. of *offendere*] (14c) **1 a** *obs* **:** an act of stumbling **b** *archaic* **:** a cause or occasion of sin **:** STUMBLING BLOCK **2 :** something that outrages the moral or physical senses ⟨corruption in high places that was an ~ to the public conscience⟩ **3 a :** the act of attacking **:** ASSAULT **b :** the means or method of attacking or of attempting to score **c :** the offensive team or members of a team playing offensive positions **d :** scoring ability **4 a :** the act of displeasing or affronting **b :** the state of being insulted or morally outraged ⟨he takes ~ at the slightest criticism⟩ **5 a :** a breach of a moral or social code **:** SIN, MISDEED **b :** an infraction of law; *esp* **:** MISDEMEANOR — **of·fense·less** \-ləs\ *adj*

syn OFFENSE, RESENTMENT, UMBRAGE, PIQUE, DUDGEON, HUFF mean an emotional response to a slight or indignity. OFFENSE implies hurt displeasure; RESENTMENT suggests a longer lasting indignation or smoldering ill will; UMBRAGE implies a feeling of being snubbed or ignored; PIQUE applies to a transient feeling of wounded vanity; DUDGEON suggests an angry fit of indignation; HUFF implies a peevish short-lived spell of anger usu. at a petty cause.

syn OFFENSE, SIN, VICE, CRIME, SCANDAL mean a transgression of law. OFFENSE applies to the infraction of any law, rule, or code; SIN implies an offense against the moral law; VICE applies to a habit or practice that degrades or corrupts; CRIME implies a serious offense punishable by the law of the state; SCANDAL applies to an offense that outrages the public conscience.

[1]of·fen·sive \ə-ˈfen(t)-siv *esp for 1* ˈäf-ˌen(t)-, ˈȯf-\ *adj* (ca. 1548) **1 a :** making attack **:** AGGRESSIVE **b :** of, relating to, or designed for attack ⟨~ weapons⟩ **c :** of or relating to an attempt to score in a game or contest; *also* **:** of or relating to a team in possession of the ball or puck **2 :** giving painful or unpleasant sensations **:** NAUSEOUS, OBNOXIOUS ⟨~ odor of garbage⟩ **3 :** causing displeasure or resentment — **of·fen·sive·ly** *adv* — **of·fen·sive·ness** *n*

[2]offensive *n* (1720) **1 :** the act of an attacking party **2 :** ATTACK

[1]of·fer \ˈȯf-ər, ˈäf-\ *vb* **of·fered; of·fer·ing** \-(ə-)riŋ\ [ME *offren,* in sense 1, fr. OE *offrian,* fr. LL *offerre,* fr. L, to present, tender, fr. *ob-* toward + *ferre* to carry; in other senses, fr. OF *offrir,* fr. L *offerre* — more at BEAR] *vt* (bef. 12c) **1 a :** to present as an act of worship or devotion **:** SACRIFICE **b :** to utter (as a prayer) in devotion **2 a :** to present for acceptance or rejection **:** TENDER ⟨was ~*ed* a job⟩ **b :** to present in order to satisfy a requirement ⟨candidates for degrees may ~ French as one of their foreign languages⟩ **3 a :** PROPOSE, SUGGEST ⟨~ a solution to a problem⟩ **b :** to declare one's readiness or willingness ⟨~*ed* to help me⟩ **4 a :** to try or begin to exert **:** PUT UP ⟨~*ed* stubborn resistance⟩ **b :** THREATEN ⟨~*ed* to strike him with his cane⟩ **5 :** to make available **:** AFFORD; *esp* **:** to place (merchandise) on sale **6 :** to present in performance or exhibition **7 :** to propose as payment **:** BID **~** *vi* **1 :** to present something as an act of worship or devotion **:** SACRIFICE **2** *archaic* **:** to make an attempt **3 :** to present itself **4 :** to make a proposal (as of marriage)

[2]offer *n* (15c) **1 a :** a presenting of something for acceptance ⟨considering job ~*s* from several firms⟩ ⟨an ~ of marriage⟩ **b :** an undertaking to do an act or give something on condition that the party to whom the proposal is made do some specified act or make a return promise **2** *obs* **:** OFFERING **3 :** a price named by one proposing to buy **:** BID **4 a :** ATTEMPT, TRY **b :** an action or movement indicating a purpose or intention — **on offer** *chiefly Brit* **:** being offered esp. for sale

of·fer·ing \ˈȯf-(ə-)riŋ, ˈäf-\ *n* (bef. 12c) **1 a :** the act of one who offers **b :** something offered; *esp* **:** a sacrifice ceremonially offered as a part of worship **c :** a contribution to the support of a church **2 :** something offered for sale or patronage ⟨latest ~*s* of the leading novelists⟩ **3 :** a course of instruction or study

of·fer·to·ry \ˈȯf-ə(r)-ˌtōr-ē, ˈäf-, -ˌtȯr-\ *n, pl* **-ries** [ML *offertorium,* fr. *offertus,* pp. of LL *offerre*] (1539) **1** *often cap* **a :** the eucharistic offering of bread and wine to God before they are consecrated at Communion **b :** a verse from a Psalm said or sung at the beginning of the offertory **2 a :** the period of collection and presentation of the offerings of the congregation at public worship **b :** a musical composition played or sung during an offertory

[1]off·hand \ˈȯf-ˈhand\ *adv* (1694) **:** without premeditation or preparation **:** EXTEMPORE ⟨couldn't give the figures ~⟩

[2]offhand *adj* (1708) **1 :** CASUAL, INFORMAL ⟨a relaxed, ~ manner⟩ **2 :** done or made offhand ⟨~ excuses⟩

off·hand·ed \-ˈhan-dəd\ *adj* (1835) **:** OFFHAND — **off·hand·ed·ly** *adv* — **off·hand·ed·ness** *n*

\ə\ abut \ᵊ\ kitten, F table \ər\ further \a\ ash \ā\ ace \ä\ cot, cart \au̇\ out \ch\ chin \e\ bet \ē\ easy \g\ go \i\ hit \ī\ ice \j\ job \ŋ\ sing \ō\ go \ȯ\ law \ȯi\ boy \th\ thin \t͟h\ the \ü\ loot \u̇\ foot \y\ yet \zh\ vision \ȧ, k̟, ⁿ, œ, œ̄, ue, ue̅, ʸ\ *see* Guide to Pronunciation

off–hour \'ȯf-ˌau̇(-ə)r\ *n* (1932) **1 :** a period of time other than a rush hour **2 :** a period of time other than regular business hours

of·fice \'äf-əs, 'ȯf-\ *n* [ME, fr. MF, fr. L *officium* service, duty, office, fr. *opus* work + *facere* to make, do — more at OPERATE, DO] (14c) **1 a :** a special duty, charge, or position conferred by an exercise of governmental authority and for a public purpose : a position of authority to exercise a public function and to receive whatever emoluments may belong to it **b :** a position of responsibility or some degree of executive authority **2** [ME, fr. OF, fr. LL *officium,* fr. L] **:** a prescribed form or service of worship; *specif, cap* **:** DIVINE OFFICE **3 :** a religious or social ceremonial observance **:** RITE **4 a :** something that one ought to do or must do **:** an assigned or assumed duty, task, or role **b :** the proper or customary action of something **:** FUNCTION **c :** something done for another **:** SERVICE **5 :** a place where a particular kind of business is transacted or a service is supplied: as **a :** a place in which the functions (as consulting, record keeping, clerical work) of a public officer are performed **b :** the directing headquarters of an enterprise or organization **c :** the place in which a professional person conducts his or her professional business **6** *pl, chiefly Brit* **:** the apartments, attached buildings, or outhouses in which the activities attached to the service of a house are carried on **7 a :** a major administrative unit in some governments ⟨British Foreign *Office*⟩ **b :** a subdivision of some government departments ⟨Patent *Office*⟩ ***syn*** see FUNCTION

office boy *n* (1846) **:** a boy or man employed for odd jobs in a business office

of·fice·hold·er \-ˌhōl-dər\ *n* (1818) **:** one holding a public office esp. in the civil service

[1]of·fi·cer \'äf-ə-sər, 'ȯf-\ *n* [ME, fr. MF *officier,* fr. ML *officiarius,* fr. L *officium*] (14c) **1 a** *obs* **:** AGENT **b :** one charged with police duties **2 :** one who holds an office of trust, authority, or command ⟨the ~s of the bank⟩ **3 a :** one who holds a position of authority or command in the armed forces; *specif* **:** COMMISSIONED OFFICER **b :** the master or any of the mates of a merchant or passenger ship

[2]officer *vt* (1670) **1 :** to furnish with officers **2 :** to command or direct as an officer

officer of arms (1500) **:** any of the officers (as king of arms, herald, or pursuivant) of a monarch or government responsible for devising and granting armorial bearings

[1]of·fi·cial \ə-'fish-əl *also* ō-\ *n* (1555) **1 :** one who holds or is invested with an office **:** OFFICER ⟨government ~s⟩ **2 :** one who administers the rules of a game or sport esp. as a referee or umpire

[2]official *adj* (1588) **1 :** of or relating to an office, position, or trust ⟨~ duties⟩ **2 :** holding an office **3 a :** AUTHORITATIVE, AUTHORIZED ⟨~ statement⟩ **b :** prescribed or recognized as authorized; *specif* **:** described by the U.S. Pharmacopeia or the National Formulary **4 :** befitting or characteristic of a person in office ⟨was extended an ~ greeting⟩ — **of·fi·cial·ly** \-'fish-(ə-)lē\ *adv*

of·fi·cial·dom \-'fish-əl-dəm\ *n* (1863) **:** officials as a class

of·fi·cial·ese \-ˌfish-ə-'lēz, -'lēs\ *n* (1884) **:** the characteristic language of official statements **:** wordy, pompous, or obscure language

official family *n* (1903) **:** a group of top officials (as a cabinet) in an organization or government **:** STAFF

of·fi·cial·ism \-'fish-ə-ˌliz-əm\ *n* (1857) **:** lack of flexibility and initiative combined with excessive adherence to regulations in the behavior of usu. government officials

of·fi·ci·ant \ə-'fish-ē-ənt\ *n* (1844) **:** one (as a priest) that officiates at a religious rite

[1]of·fi·ci·ary \ə-'fish-ē-ˌer-ē, ō-, ä-\ *n, pl* **-ar·ies** [ML *officiarius*] (1611) **1 :** OFFICER, OFFICIAL **2 :** a body of officers or officials

[2]officiary *adj* (1612) **:** connected with, derived from, or having a title or rank by virtue of holding an office ⟨~ earl⟩

of·fi·ci·ate \ə-'fish-ē-ˌāt\ *vb* **-at·ed; -at·ing** *vi* (1631) **1 :** to perform a ceremony, function, or duty ⟨~ at a wedding⟩ **2 :** to act in an official capacity **:** act as an official (as at a sports contest) ~ *vt* **1 :** to carry out (an official duty or function) **2 :** to serve as a leader or celebrant of (a ceremony) **3 :** to administer the rules of (a game or sport) esp. as a referee or umpire — **of·fi·ci·a·tion** \-ˌfish-ē-'ā-shən\ *n*

of·fi·ci·nal \ə-'fis-ᵊn-əl, ō-, ä-; ˌȯf-ə-'sin-ᵊl, ˌäf-\ *adj* [ML *officinalis* of a storeroom, fr. *officina* storeroom, fr. L, workshop, fr. *opific-, opifex* workman, fr. *opus* work + *facere* to do] (1720) **1 :** available without special preparation or compounding ⟨~ medicine⟩; *also* **:** OFFICIAL 3b **2 :** MEDICINAL ⟨~ herbs⟩ — **officinal** *n* — **of·fi·ci·nal·ly** \-ē\ *adv*

of·fi·cious \ə-'fish-əs\ *adj* [L *officiosus,* fr. *officium* service, office] (1565) **1** *archaic* **a :** KIND, OBLIGING **b :** DUTIFUL **2 :** volunteering one's services where they are neither asked nor needed **:** MEDDLESOME **3 :** INFORMAL, UNOFFICIAL ***syn*** see IMPERTINENT — **of·fi·cious·ly** *adv* — **of·fi·cious·ness** *n*

off·ing \'ȯf-iŋ, 'äf-\ *n* [[1]*off*] (ca. 1627) **1 :** the part of the deep sea seen from the shore **2 :** the near or foreseeable future ⟨in the ~⟩

off·ish \'ȯf-ish\ *adj* [[1]*off*] (1831) **:** STANDOFFISH — **off·ish·ness** *n*

off–key \'ȯf-'kē\ *adj or adv* (1927) **1 :** varying in pitch from the proper tone of a melody **2 :** IRREGULAR, ANOMALOUS

off–lim·its \'ȯ-'flim-əts\ *adj* (ca. 1945) **:** not to be entered or patronized by a designated class (as military personnel, students, or athletes in training)

off–line \'ȯ-'flīn\ *adj* (1950) **:** not connected to or served by a system and esp. a computer or telecommunications system; *also* **:** done independently of a system ⟨~ computer storage⟩ — **off–line** *adv*

off–load \ȯ-'flōd\ *vb* (1850) **:** UNLOAD

off of *prep* (1593) **:** OFF

usage The *of* is often criticized as superfluous, a comment that is irrelevant because *off of* is an idiom. It is much more common in speech than in edited writing.

off–off–Broadway *n, often cap both Os* [fr. its relation to off Broadway being analogous to the relation of off Broadway to Broadway] (1965) **:** an avant-garde theatrical movement in New York that stresses untraditional techniques and radical experimentation — **off–off–Broadway** *adj or adv, often cap both Os*

off–peak \'ȯf-'pēk\ *adj* (1920) **:** not being in the period of maximum use **:** not peak ⟨telephone rates during ~ hours⟩

off–price \'ȯf-'prīs\ *adj* (1952) **:** of, relating to, selling, or being discounted merchandise ⟨an ~ store⟩ ⟨~ apparel⟩

off·print \'ȯf-ˌprint\ *n* (1885) **:** a separately printed excerpt (as a magazine article) — **offprint** *vt*

off–put·ting \-ˌpu̇t-iŋ\ *adj* (1828) **:** that puts one off **:** REPELLENT, DISAGREEABLE

off–road \'ȯf-'rōd\ *adj* (1961) **:** of, relating to, or being a vehicle designed esp. to operate away from public roads

off·scour·ing \-ˌskau̇(ə)r-iŋ\ *n* (1526) **1 :** something that is scoured off **:** REFUSE **2 :** someone rejected by society **:** OUTCAST

off·screen \'ȯf-'skrēn\ *adv or adj* (1935) **1 :** out of sight of the motion picture or television viewer **2 :** in private life

off–sea·son \'ȯf-ˌsēz-ᵊn\ *n* (1848) **:** a time of suspended or reduced activity

[1]off·set \'ȯf-ˌset\ *n* (1555) **1 a** *archaic* **:** OUTSET, START **b :** CESSATION **2 a (1) :** a short prostrate lateral shoot arising from the base of a plant **(2) :** a small bulb arising from the base of another bulb **b :** a lateral or collateral branch (as of a family or race) **:** OFFSHOOT **c :** a spur from a range of hills **3 a :** a horizontal ledge on the face of a wall formed by a diminution of its thickness above **b :** DISPLACEMENT **c :** an abrupt change in the dimension or profile of an object or the part set off by such change **4 :** something that sets off to advantage or embellishes something else **:** FOIL **5 :** an abrupt bend in an object by which one part is turned aside out of line **6 :** something that serves to counterbalance or to compensate for something else; *specif* **:** either of two balancing ledger items **7 a :** unintentional transfer of ink (as from a freshly printed sheet) **b :** a printing process in which an inked impression from a plate is first made on a rubber-blanketed cylinder and then transferred to the paper being printed — **offset** *adj or adv*

[2]off·set \'ȯf-ˌset, *vt senses are also* ȯf-'\ *vb* **-set; -set·ting** *vt* (1792) **1 a :** to place over against something **:** BALANCE ⟨credits ~ debits⟩ **b :** to serve as a counterbalance for **:** COMPENSATE ⟨his speed ~ his opponent's greater weight⟩ **2 :** to form an offset in ⟨~ a wall⟩ ~ *vi* **:** to become marked by offset

off·shoot \'ȯf-ˌshüt\ *n* (1710) **1 a :** a lateral branch (as of a mountain range) **b :** a collateral or derived branch, descendant, or member **:** OUTGROWTH **2 :** a branch of a main stem esp. of a plant

[1]off·shore \'ȯf-'shō(ə)r, -'shȯ(ə)r\ *adv* (1720) **:** from the shore **:** SEAWARD; *also* **:** at a distance from the shore

[2]off·shore \'ȯf-ˌ\ *adj* (1845) **1 :** coming or moving away from the shore toward the water ⟨an ~ breeze⟩ **2 a :** situated off the shore but within waters under a country's control ⟨~ fisheries⟩ **b :** distant from the shore — compare INSHORE **3 :** situated or operating in a foreign country ⟨~ mutual funds⟩ ⟨~ banking⟩

[3]off·shore \'ȯf-ˌ\ *prep* (1965) **:** off the shore of

off·side \'ȯf-'sīd\ *adv or adj* (1867) **:** illegally in advance of the ball or puck

off–speed \-'spēd\ *adj* (1965) **:** being slower than usual or expected ⟨throwing ~ pitches⟩

off·spring \'ȯf-ˌspriŋ\ *n, pl* **offspring** *also* **offsprings** [ME *ofspring,* fr. OE, fr. *of* off + *springan* to spring] (bef. 12c) **1 a :** the progeny of an animal or plant **:** YOUNG **b :** CHILD **2 :** PRODUCT, RESULT ⟨scholarly manuscripts — the labored ~s of PhDs —Donna Martin⟩

off·stage \'ȯf-'stāj, -ˌstāj\ *adv or adj* (1921) **1 :** on a part of the stage not visible to the audience **2 :** in private life ⟨known ~ as a kindly man⟩ **3 :** behind the scenes **:** out of the public view ⟨much of the important work of the conference was done ~⟩

off–the–cuff *adj* (1941) **:** not prepared in advance **:** SPONTANEOUS, INFORMAL ⟨~ remarks⟩

off–the–record *adj* (1933) **:** given or made in confidence and not for publication ⟨~ comments⟩

off–the–shelf *adj* (1950) **:** available as a stock item **:** not specially designed or custom-made

off–the–wall *adj* (ca. 1971) **:** highly unusual **:** BIZARRE ⟨an ~ sense of humor⟩

off·track \'ȯf-'trak\ *adv or adj* (1944) **:** away from a racetrack ⟨betting ~⟩ ⟨~ bookies⟩

off–white \'ȯf-'hwīt, -'wīt\ *n* (1908) **:** a yellowish or grayish white

off year *n* (1873) **1 :** a year in which no major election is held **2 :** a year of diminished activity or production ⟨an *off year* for auto sales⟩

oft \'ȯft\ *adv* [ME, fr. OE; akin to OHG *ofto* often] (bef. 12c) **:** OFTEN

of·ten \'ȯf-(t)ən\ *adv* [ME, alter. of *oft*] (14c) **:** many times **:** FREQUENTLY

of·ten·times \-ˌtīmz\ *or* **oft·times** \'ȯf(t)-ˌtīmz\ *adv* (14c) **:** OFTEN, REPEATEDLY

ogee *also* **OG** \'ō-ˌjē\ *n* [obs. E *ogee* (ogive); fr. the use of such moldings in ogives] (1677) **1 :** a molding with an S-shaped profile **2 :** a pointed arch having on each side a reversed curve near the apex — see ARCH illustration

ogham *or* **ogam** \'ō(-ə)m; 'äg-əm, 'ōg-\ *n* [IrGael *ogham,* fr. MIr *ogom, ogum*] (1729) **:** the alphabetic system of 5th and 6th century Old Irish in which an alphabet of 20 letters is represented by notches for vowels and lines for consonants and which is known principally from inscriptions cut on the edges of rough standing tombstones — **ogham·ic** \'ō-(ə-)mik; ä-'gäm-ik, ō-\ *adj* — **ogham·ist** \'ō-(ə-)məst; 'äg-ə-məst, 'ōg-\ *n*

ogi·val \ō-'jī-vəl\ *adj* (1841) **:** of, relating to, or having the form of an ogive or an ogee

ogive \'ō-ˌjīv\ *n* [F] (1611) **1 a :** a diagonal arch or rib across a Gothic vault **b :** a pointed arch **2 :** a graph each of whose ordinates represents the sum of all the frequencies up to and including a corresponding frequency in a frequency distribution **3 :** OGEE 1

[1]ogle \'ōg-əl *also* 'äg-\ *vb* **ogled; ogling** \-(ə-)liŋ\ [prob. fr. LG *oegeln,* fr. *oog* eye; akin to OHG *ouga* eye — more at EYE] *vi* (1682) **:** to glance with amorous invitation or challenge ~ *vt* **:** to eye amorously or provocatively — **ogler** \-(ə-)lər\ *n*

[2]ogle *n* (1711) **:** an amorous or coquettish glance

ogre \'ō-gər\ *n* [F, prob. deriv. of L *Orcus,* god of the underworld] (1713) **1 :** a hideous giant of fairy tales and folklore that feeds on human beings **:** MONSTER **2 :** a dreaded person or object — **ogre·ish** \'ō-g(ə-)rish\ *adj* — **ogress** \'ō-g(ə-)rəs\ *n*

[1]oh \(')ō\ *interj* [ME *o*] (12c) **1 —** used to express an emotion (as astonishment or desire) or in response to physical stimuli **2 —** used in direct address ⟨*Oh,* porter! Will you come here, please?⟩ **3 —** used to express acknowledgment or understanding of a statement

[2]oh \'ō\ *n* [*o;* fr. the similarity of the symbol for zero (0) to the letter *O*] (1936) **:** ZERO

ohia \ō-'hē-ə\ *n* [Hawaiian *'ōhi'a*] (1824) **:** LEHUA

ohia lehua *n* [Hawaiian *'ōhi'a-lehua*] (1888) **:** LEHUA

ohm \'ōm\ *n* [Georg Simon *Ohm*] (1870) **:** the practical meter-kilogram-second unit of electric resistance equal to the resistance of a circuit in which a potential difference of one volt produces a current of one ampere — **ohm·ic** \'ō-mik\ *adj* — **ohm·i·cal·ly** \-mi-k(ə-)lē\ *adv*
ohm·age \'ō-mij\ *n* (ca. 1898) **:** the ohmic resistance of a conductor
ohm·me·ter \'ō(m)-,mēt-ər\ *n* [ISV] (ca. 1889) **:** an instrument for indicating resistance in ohms directly
Ohm's law \'ōmz-\ *n* (1863) **:** a law in electricity: the strength of a direct current is directly proportional to the potential difference and inversely proportional to the resistance of the circuit
-o·ic \'ō-ik\ *adj suffix* [*-o-* + *-ic*] **:** containing carboxyl or a derivative ⟨decan*oic* acid⟩
1-oid \,ȯid\ *n suffix* **:** something resembling a (specified) object or having a (specified) quality ⟨glob*oid*⟩
2-oid *adj suffix* [MF & L; MF *-oïde,* fr. L *-oïdes,* fr. Gk *-oeidēs,* fr. *-o-* + *eidos* appearance, form — more at WISE] **:** resembling **:** having the form or appearance of ⟨petal*oid*⟩
oid·i·um \ō-'id-ē-əm\ *n, pl* **-ia** \-ē-ə\ [NL, fr. *o-* + *-idium*] (1857) **1 a :** any of a genus (*Oidium* of the family Moniliaceae) of imperfect fungi many of which are now considered to be conidial stages of various powdery mildews **b :** one of the small conidia borne in chains by various fungi (as an oidium) — called also *arthrospore* **2 :** a powdery mildew caused by an oidium esp. in the grape
1oil \'ȯi(ə)l\ *n, often attrib* [ME *oile,* fr. OF, fr. L *oleum* olive oil, fr. Gk *elaion,* fr. *elaia* olive] (12c) **1 a :** any of numerous unctuous combustible substances that are liquid or at least easily liquefiable on warming, are soluble in ether but not in water, and leave a greasy stain on paper or cloth **b :** PETROLEUM **2 :** a substance (as a cosmetic preparation) of oily consistency ⟨bath ~⟩ **3 a :** an oil color used by an artist **b :** a painting done in oil colors **4 :** unctuous or flattering speech
2oil *vt* (15c) **:** to smear, rub over, furnish, or lubricate with oil ~ *vi* **:** to take on fuel oil — **oil the hand** *or* **oil the palm :** BRIBE, TIP
oil beetle *n* (1658) **:** a blister beetle (*Meloe* or a related genus) that emits a yellowish liquid from the leg joints when disturbed
oil·bird \'ȯi(ə)l-,bərd\ *n* (ca. 1890) **:** a nocturnal bird (*Steatornis caripensis*) of northern So. America and Trinidad that is related to the goatsuckers, feeds chiefly on the fatty fruits of various palms, and has fatty young from which oil is extracted for use instead of butter — called also *guacharo*
oil cake *n* (1743) **:** the solid residue after extracting the oil from seeds (as of cotton)
oil·can \'ȯi(ə)l-,kan\ *n* (1799) **:** a can for oil; *esp* **:** a spouted can designed to release oil drop by drop (as for lubricating machinery)
oil·cloth \-,klȯth\ *n* (1697) **:** cloth treated with oil or paint and used for table and shelf coverings
oil color *n* (1539) **1 :** a pigment used for oil paint **2 :** OIL PAINT
oiled \'ȯi(ə)ld\ *adj* (1550) **1 :** lubricated or treated with or as if with oil ⟨~ paper⟩ **2** *slang* **:** DRUNK
oil·er \'ȯi-lər\ *n* (ca. 1846) **1 :** one (as a workman) that oils something **2 :** a receptacle or device for applying oil **3 :** a producing oil well **4 a :** a ship using oil as fuel **b :** an oil-cargo ship **5** *pl* **:** OILSKIN 3
oil field *n* (1894) **:** a region rich in petroleum deposits; *esp* **:** one that has been brought into production
oil gland *n* (1835) **:** a gland (as of the skin) that produces an oily secretion; *specif* **:** UROPYGIAL GLAND
oil·man \'ȯi(ə)l-mən, -,man\ *n* (1865) **1 :** an oil company executive **2 :** an oil field worker
oil of turpentine (1597) **:** TURPENTINE 2a
oil of vitriol (1580) **:** concentrated sulfuric acid
oil of wintergreen (1845) **:** the methyl ester of salicylic acid that is used as a flavoring and as a counterirritant
oil paint *n* (1790) **:** paint in which a drying oil is the vehicle
oil painting *n* (1782) **1 a :** the act or art of painting in oil colors **b :** a picture painted in oils **2 :** painting that uses pigments orig. ground in oil
oil palm *n* (ca. 1864) **:** an African pinnate-leaved palm (*Elaeis guineensis*) cultivated for its clustered fruit whose flesh and seeds yield oil
oil pan *n* (1908) **:** the lower section of the crankcase used as a lubricating-oil reservoir on an internal-combustion engine
oil·seed \'ȯi(ə)l-,sēd\ *n* (1562) **:** a seed or crop (as flaxseed) grown mainly for oil
oil shale *n* (1873) **:** a rock (as shale) from which oil can be recovered by distillation
oil·skin \'ȯi(ə)l-,skin\ *n* (1816) **1 :** an oiled waterproof cloth used for coverings and garments **2 :** an oilskin raincoat **3** *pl* **:** an oilskin suit of cloth and trousers
oil slick *n* (1889) **:** a film of oil floating on water
oil·stone \'ȯi(ə)l-,stōn\ *n* (1585) **:** a whetstone for use with oil
oil well *n* (1847) **:** a well from which petroleum is obtained
oily \'ȯi-lē\ *adj* **oil·i·er; -est** (14c) **1 :** of, relating to, or consisting of oil **2 :** covered or impregnated with oil ⟨~ rags⟩ **3 :** excessively smooth or suave in manner — **oil·i·ly** \'ȯi-lə-lē\ *adv* — **oil·i·ness** \-lē-nəs\ *n*
oink \'ȯiŋk\ *n* [imit.] (1941) **:** the natural noise of a hog — **oink** *vi*
oint·ment \'ȯint-mənt\ *n* [ME, alter. of *oignement,* fr. OF, modif. of L *unguentum,* fr. *unguere* to anoint; akin to OHG *ancho* butter, Skt *añjati* he salves] (13c) **:** a salve or unguent for application to the skin
oi·ti·ci·ca \,ȯit-ə-'sē-kə\ *n* [Pg, fr. Tupi] (1901) **:** any of several So. American trees; *esp* **:** a Brazilian tree (*Licania rigida*) with seeds that yield a drying oil similar to tung oil
Ojib·wa *or* **Ojib·way** \ō-'jib-(,)wā\ *n, pl* **Ojibwa** *or* **Ojibwas** *or* **Ojibway** *or* **Ojibways** [Ojibwa *ojib-ubway,* a kind of moccasin worn by the Ojibwa] (1700) **1 :** a member of an American Indian people orig. of Michigan **2 :** an Algonquian language of the Ojibwa people
1OK *or* **okay** \ō-'kā, *in assenting or agreeing also* 'ō-,kā *or* 'ō-,kā\ *adv or adj* [abbr. of *oll korrect,* facetious alter. of *all correct*] (1839) **:** all right
2OK *or* **okay** \ō-'kā\ *n* (1840) **:** APPROVAL, ENDORSEMENT
3OK *or* **okay** \ō-'kā\ *vt* **OK'd** *or* **okayed; OK'·ing** *or* **okay·ing** (1888) **:** APPROVE, AUTHORIZE
oka *var of* OCA
oka·pi \ō-'käp-ē\ *n* [native name in Africa] (1900) **:** an African mammal (*Okapia johnstoni*) that is closely related to the giraffe but has a relatively short neck, a coat of solid reddish chestnut on the trunk, yellowish white on the cheeks, and purplish black and cream rings on the upper parts of the legs
oke \'ōk, 'ȯk\ *or* **oka** \ō-'kä\ *n* [F, NGk & Turk; F *ocque,* fr. NGk & Turk; NGk *oka,* fr. Turk *okka,* fr. Ar *ūqīyah*] (1625) **:** any of three units of weight varying around 2.8 pounds (1.3 kilograms) and used respectively in Greece, Turkey, and Egypt

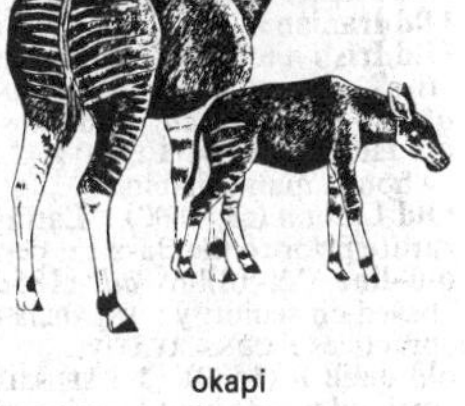
okapi

okey·doke \,ō-kē-'dōk\ *or* **okey·do·key** \-'dō-kē\ *adv* [redupl. of *OK*] (ca. 1930) — used as a function word to express assent
Okie \'ō-kē\ *n* [*Ok*lahoma + *-ie*] (1938) **:** a migrant agricultural worker; *esp* **:** one from Oklahoma in the 1930s
okra \'ō-krə, *Southern also* -krē\ *n* [of African origin; akin to Twi ŋ'ku'rū'mā' okra] (1679) **1 :** a tall annual (*Hibiscus esculentus*) of the mallow family that is cultivated for its mucilaginous green pods used esp. in soups or stews; *also* **:** the pods of this plant **2 :** GUMBO 2
1-ol \,ȯl *also* ,ōl\ *n suffix* [ISV, fr. *alcohol*] **:** chemical compound (as an alcohol or phenol) containing hydroxyl ⟨glycer*ol*⟩ ⟨cres*ol*⟩
2-ol — see -OLE
3-ol *n comb form* [ISV, fr. L *oleum* oil — more at OIL] **:** hydrocarbon chemically related to benzene ⟨xyl*ol*⟩
1old \'ōld\ *adj* [ME, fr. OE *eald;* akin to OHG *alt* old, L *alere* to nourish, *alescere* to grow, *altus* high, deep] (bef. 12c) **1 a :** dating from the remote past **:** ANCIENT ⟨~ traditions⟩ **b :** persisting from an earlier time ⟨an ~ ailment⟩ ⟨they brought up the same ~ argument⟩ **c :** of long standing ⟨an ~ friend⟩ **2 a :** distinguished from an object of the same kind by being of an earlier date ⟨many still used the ~ name⟩ **b** *cap* **:** belonging to an early period in the development of a language or literature ⟨*Old* Persian⟩ **3 :** having existed for a specified period of time ⟨a girl three years ~⟩ **4 :** of, relating to, or originating in a past era ⟨~ chronicles record the event⟩ **5 a :** advanced in years or age ⟨an ~ man⟩ **b :** showing the characteristics of age ⟨looked ~ at 20⟩ **6 :** EXPERIENCED ⟨an ~ trooper speaking of the last war⟩ **7 :** FORMER ⟨his ~ students⟩ **8 a :** showing the effects of time or use **:** WORN, AGED ⟨~ shoes⟩ **b :** well advanced toward reduction to base-level — used of topographic features **c :** no longer in use **:** DISCARDED ⟨~ rags⟩ **d :** of a grayish or dusty color ⟨~ mauve⟩ **9 a :** long familiar ⟨same ~ story⟩ ⟨good ~ Joe⟩ **b** — used as an intensive ⟨a high ~ time⟩ ⟨any ~ time⟩
syn OLD, ANCIENT, VENERABLE, ANTIQUE, ANTIQUATED, ARCHAIC, OBSOLETE mean having come into existence or use in the more or less distant past. OLD may apply to either actual or merely relative length of existence ⟨*old* houses⟩ ⟨an *old* sweater of mine⟩ ANCIENT applies to occurrence, existence, or use in or survival from the distant past ⟨*ancient* accounts of dragons⟩ VENERABLE stresses the impressiveness and dignity of great age ⟨the family's *venerable* patriarch⟩ ANTIQUE applies to what has come down from a former or ancient time ⟨collected *antique* Chippendale furniture⟩ ANTIQUATED implies being discredited or outmoded or otherwise inappropriate to the present time ⟨*antiquated* teaching methods⟩ ARCHAIC implies having the character or characteristics of a much earlier time ⟨the play used *archaic* language to convey a sense of period⟩ OBSOLETE implies having gone out of currency or habitual practice ⟨this nuclear missile will make all others *obsolete*⟩
2old *n* (13c) **1 :** old or earlier time — used in the phrase *of old* ⟨mighty men of ~⟩ **2 :** one of a specified age — usu. used in combination ⟨a 3-year-*old*⟩
Old Bulgarian *n* (1861) **:** OLD CHURCH SLAVONIC
Old Catholic *n* (1846) **:** a member of one of various hierarchical and liturgical churches separating from the Roman Catholic Church at various times since the 18th century
Old Christmas *n, chiefly Midland* (1863) **:** EPIPHANY 1
Old Church Slavonic *n* (1876) **:** the Slavic language used in the Bible translation of Cyril and Methodius and as the liturgical language of several Eastern churches — called also *Old Church Slavic;* see INDO-EUROPEAN LANGUAGES table
old country *n, often cap O & C* (1782) **:** an emigrant's country of origin; *esp* **:** one in Europe — usu. used with *the*
old·en \'ōl-dən\ *adj* (15c) **:** of or relating to a bygone era
Old English *n* (13c) **1 a :** the language of the English people from the time of the earliest documents in the 7th century to about 1100 — see INDO-EUROPEAN LANGUAGES table **b :** English of any period before Modern English **2 :** BLACK LETTER
Old English sheepdog *n* (1885) **:** any of a breed of tailless dogs with a profuse blue-gray and white coat that was developed in England to drive sheep and cattle
old·fan·gled \'ōl(d)-'faŋ-gəld\ *adj* [*old* + *-fangled* (as in *newfangled*)] (1842) **:** OLD-FASHIONED
1old–fash·ioned \-'fash-ənd\ *adj* (1653) **1 a :** of, relating to, or characteristic of a past era ⟨wears an ~ black bow tie —Green Peyton⟩ **b :** adhering to customs of a past era **2 :** OUTMODED — **old–fash·ioned·ly** \-ən-dlē\ *adv*
2old–fashioned *n* (1901) **:** a cocktail usu. made with whiskey, bitters, sugar, a twist of lemon peel, and a small amount of water or soda
Old French *n* (ca. 1890) **:** the French language from the 9th to the 16th century; *esp* **:** French from the 9th to the 13th century — see INDO-EUROPEAN LANGUAGES table
Old Glory *n* (1862) **:** the flag of the U.S.
old gold *n* (1879) **:** a variable color averaging a dark yellow
old guard *n, often cap O & G* (1852) **:** the conservative members (as of a political party) who are unwilling to accept new ideas, practices, or conditions

old hand *n* (ca. 1785) **:** VETERAN

old hat *adj* (1911) **1 :** OLD-FASHIONED **2 :** lacking in freshness **:** TRITE

Old High German *n* (ca. 1890) **:** High German exemplified in documents prior to the 12th century — see INDO-EUROPEAN LANGUAGES table

old·ie \ˈōl-dē\ *n* (1940) **:** something that is old; *esp* **:** a popular song of an earlier day

Old Ionic *n* (ca. 1890) **:** the Greek dialect of the Homeric epics

Old Iranian *n* (1939) **:** any Iranian language in use in the period B.C.

Old Irish *n* (ca. 1890) **:** the Irish in use between the 7th and 11th centuries — see INDO-EUROPEAN LANGUAGES table

old·ish \ˈōl-dish\ *adj* (1668) **:** somewhat old or elderly

old lady *n* (1871) **1 :** WIFE **2 :** MOTHER **3 :** GIRLFRIEND; *esp* **:** one with whom a man cohabits

Old Latin *n* (ca. 1890) **:** Latin used in the early inscriptions and in literature prior to the classical period

old–line \ˈōl-ˈ(d)līn\ *adj* (1856) **1 :** having a reputation or authority based on seniority **:** ESTABLISHED **2 :** adhering to traditional policies or practices **:** CONSERVATIVE

old maid *n* (1530) **1 :** SPINSTER 3 **2 :** a prim fussy person ⟨he was a real *old maid* about burning rubbish —R. C. Ruark⟩ **3 :** a simple card game in which cards are matched in pairs and the player holding the extra card at the end loses — **old–maid·ish** \(ˈ)ōl(d)-ˈmād-ish\ *adj*

old man *n* (1768) **1 a :** HUSBAND **b :** FATHER **2** *cap* **:** one in authority; *esp* **:** COMMANDING OFFICER **3 :** BOYFRIEND; *esp* **:** one with whom a woman cohabits

old–man's beard \ˌōl(d)-ˌmanz-\ *n* (1742) **1 :** any of several clematises (esp. *Clematis vitalba* in England and *C. virginiana* in the U.S.) having plumose styles **2 :** a greenish gray pendulous lichen (*Usnea barbata*) growing on trees

old master *n* (1840) **1 :** a superior artist or craftsman of established reputation; *esp* **:** a distinguished painter of the 16th, 17th, or early 18th century **2 :** a work by an old master

Old Nick \(ˈ)ōl(d)-ˈnik\ *n* (1746) — used as a name of the devil

Old Norse *n* (1844) **:** the North Germanic language of the Scandinavian peoples prior to about 1350 — see INDO-EUROPEAN LANGUAGES table

Old North French *n* (1930) **:** the northern dialects of Old French including esp. those of Normandy and Picardy

Old Prussian *n* (1872) **:** a Baltic language used in East Prussia until the 17th century — see INDO-EUROPEAN LANGUAGES table

old rose *n* (1893) **:** a variable color averaging a grayish red

Old Saxon *n* (bef. 12c) **:** the language of the Saxons of northwest Germany until about the 12th century — see INDO-EUROPEAN LANGUAGES table

old school *n* (1798) **:** adherents of traditional policies and practices

old school tie *n* (1932) **1 a :** a necktie displaying the colors of an English public school **b :** an attitude of conservatism, aplomb, and upper-class solidarity associated with English public school graduates **2 :** clannishness among members of an established clique

old sledge *n* (1830) **:** SEVEN-UP

old–squaw \ˈōl(d)-ˈskwȯ\ *n* (ca. 1838) **:** a common sea duck (*Clangula hyemalis*) of the more northern parts of the northern hemisphere

old·ster \ˈōl(d)-stər\ *n* (1848) **:** an old or elderly person

old style *n* (1617) **1** *cap O&S* **:** a style of reckoning time used before the adoption of the Gregorian calendar **2 :** a style of type distinguished by graceful irregularity among individual letters, bracketed serifs, and but slight contrast between light and heavy strokes

Old Style *adj* (1678) **:** using or according to the Julian calendar

Old Testament *n* (14c) **:** the first part of the Christian Bible containing the books of the Jewish canon of Scripture — see BIBLE table

old–time \ˌōl(d)-ˌtīm\ *adj* (1824) **1 :** of, relating to, or characteristic of an earlier period **2 :** of long standing

old–tim·er \ōl(d)-ˈtī-mər\ *n* (1866) **1 a :** VETERAN **b :** OLDSTER **2 :** something that is old-fashioned **:** ANTIQUE

Old Welsh *n* (1882) **:** the Welsh language exemplified in documents prior to about 1150 — see INDO-EUROPEAN LANGUAGES table

old·wife \ˈōl-ˌ(d)wīf\ *n* (1588) **1 :** any of several marine fishes (as an alewife, menhaden, or triggerfish) **2 :** OLD-SQUAW

old wives' tale *n* (1656) **:** an often traditional belief that is not based on fact **:** SUPERSTITION

old–world \ˈōl-ˈ(d)wər(-ə)ld\ *adj* (1712) **:** of, relating to, or characteristic of the Old World; *esp* **:** having the charm or picturesque qualities of the Old World ⟨narrow ~ streets⟩

Old World *n* (1596) **:** EASTERN HEMISPHERE; *specif* **:** Europe

ole- *or* **oleo-** *comb form* [F *olé-, oléo-,* fr. L *ole-,* fr. *oleum* — more at OIL] **:** oil ⟨*ole*ic⟩ ⟨*oleo*graph⟩

-ole \ˌōl\ *also* **-ol** \ˌōl, ˌōl\ *n comb form* [ISV, fr. L *oleum*] **1 :** chemical compound containing a 5-membered usu. heterocyclic ring ⟨diaz*ole*⟩ ⟨pyrr*ole*⟩ **2 :** chemical compound not containing hydroxyl ⟨eucalypt*ol*⟩ — esp. in names of ethers ⟨phenet*ole*⟩

olé \ō-ˈlā\ *n* [Sp] (1922) **:** [3]BRAVO

ole·ag·i·nous \ˌō-lē-ˈaj-ə-nəs\ *adj* [ME, fr. MF *oleagineux,* fr. L *oleaginus* of an olive tree, fr. *olea* olive tree, fr. Gk *elaia*] (15c) **1 :** resembling or having the properties of oil **:** OILY; *also* **:** containing or producing oil **2 :** UNCTUOUS — **ole·ag·i·nous·ly** *adv* — **ole·ag·i·nous·ness** *n*

ole·an·der \ˈō-lē-ˌan-dər, ˌō-lē-ˈ\ *n* [ME, fr. ML] (15c) **:** a poisonous evergreen shrub (*Nerium oleander*) of the dogbane family with fragrant white to red flowers

ole·an·do·my·cin \ˌō-lē-ˌan-də-ˈmīs-ᵊn\ *n* [prob. fr. *oleander* + *-o-* + *-mycin*] (1956) **:** an antibiotic $C_{35}H_{61}NO_{12}$ produced by a streptomyces (*Streptomyces antibioticus*)

ole·as·ter \ˈō-lē-ˌas-tər, ˌō-lē-ˈ\ *n* [ME, fr. L, fr. *olea*] (14c) **:** any of several plants (genus *Elaeagnus* of the family Elaeagnaceae, the oleaster family) having alternate leaves and perfect flowers with four stamens; *esp* **:** RUSSIAN OLIVE

ole·ate \ˈō-lē-ˌāt\ *n* (ca. 1828) **:** a salt or ester of oleic acid

olec·ra·non \ō-ˈlek-rə-ˌnän\ *n* [NL, fr. Gk *ōlekranon,* fr. *ōlenē* elbow + *kranion* skull — more at ELL, CRANIUM] (ca. 1727) **:** the process of the ulna projecting behind the elbow joint

ole·fin \ˈō-lə-fən\ *n* [ISV, fr. F *(gaz) oléfiant* ethylene, fr. L *oleum*] (1860) **:** an unsaturated open-chain hydrocarbon containing at least one double bond; *esp* **:** any of various long-chain synthetic polymers (as of ethylene or propylene) used esp. as textile fibers and in cordage — **ole·fin·ic** \ˌō-lə-ˈfin-ik\ *adj*

ole·ic \ō-ˈlē-ik, -ˈlā-\ *adj* (1819) **1 :** relating to, derived from, or contained in oil **2 :** of or relating to oleic acid

oleic acid *n* (1819) **:** an unsaturated fatty acid $C_{18}H_{34}O_2$ found as glycerides in natural fats and oils

ole·in \ˈō-lē-ən\ *n* [F *oléine,* fr. L *oleum*] (1838) **1 :** an ester of glycerol and oleic acid **2** *also* **ole·ine** \-ən, -ˌēn\ **:** the liquid portion of a fat

oleo \ˈō-lē-ˌō\ *n, pl* **ole·os** (1884) **1** [short for *oleomargarine*] **:** MARGARINE **2 :** OLEOGRAPH

oleo·graph \ˈō-lē-ə-ˌgraf\ *n* [ISV *ole-* + *-graph*] (1873) **:** a chromolithograph printed on cloth to imitate an oil painting — **oleo·graph·ic** \ˌō-lē-ə-ˈgraf-ik\ *adj* — **ole·og·ra·phy** \ˌō-lē-ˈäg-rə-fē\ *n*

oleo·mar·ga·rine \ˌō-lē-ō-ˈmärj-(ə-)rən, -ˈmärj-ə-ˌrēn\ *n* [F *oléomargarine,* fr. *olé-* + *margarine* margarine] (1871) **:** MARGARINE

oleo·res·in \ˌō-lē-ō-ˈrez-ᵊn\ *n* [ISV] (ca. 1847) **1 :** a natural plant product (as copaiba) containing chiefly essential oil and resin; *esp* **:** TURPENTINE 1b **2 :** a preparation consisting essentially of oil holding resin in solution — **oleo·res·in·ous** \-ˈrez-ᵊn-əs, -ˈrez-nəs\ *adj*

ole·um \ˈō-lē-əm\ *n* [L — more at OIL] (1905) **1** *pl* **olea** \-lē-ə\ **:** OIL **2** *pl* **oleums :** a heavy oily strongly corrosive solution of sulfur trioxide in anhydrous sulfuric acid

O level *n* (1949) **:** the earlier of two standardized British examinations in a secondary school subject; *also* **:** the level of education required to pass such an examination — called also *Ordinary level;* compare A LEVEL

ol·fac·tion \äl-ˈfak-shən, ōl-\ *n* (ca. 1846) **1 :** the sense of smell **2 :** the act or process of smelling

ol·fac·tom·e·ter \ˌäl-ˌfak-ˈtäm-ət-ər, ˌōl-\ *n* (1889) **:** an instrument for measuring the sensitivity of the sense of smell

ol·fac·to·ry \äl-ˈfak-t(ə-)rē, ōl-\ *adj* [L *olfactorius,* fr. *olfactus,* pp. of *olfacere* to smell, fr. *olēre* to smell + *facere* to do — more at ODOR, DO] (ca. 1658) **:** of, relating to, or connected with the sense of smell

olfactory bulb *n* (1870) **:** a bulbous anterior projection of the olfactory lobe that is the place of termination of the olfactory nerves and is esp. well developed in lower vertebrates (as fishes)

olfactory lobe *n* (ca. 1860) **:** an anterior projection of each cerebral hemisphere that is continuous anteriorly with the olfactory nerve

olfactory nerve *n* (1670) **:** either of the pair of nerves that are the first cranial nerves and that arise in the olfactory neurosensory cells of the nasal mucous membrane and pass to the anterior part of the cerebrum

olig- *or* **oligo-** *comb form* [ML, fr. Gk, fr. *oligos;* akin to Arm *ałkat* scant] **:** few ⟨*oligo*phagous⟩

oli·garch \ˈäl-ə-ˌgärk, ˈō-lə-\ *n* [Gk *oligarchēs,* fr. *olig-* + *-archēs* -arch] (1610) **:** a member or supporter of an oligarchy

oli·gar·chic \ˌäl-ə-ˈgär-kik, ˌō-lə-\ *or* **oli·gar·chi·cal** \-ki-kəl\ *adj* (1649) **:** of, relating to, or based on an oligarchy

oli·gar·chy \ˈäl-ə-ˌgär-kē, ˈō-lə-\ *n, pl* **-chies** (1500) **1 :** government by the few **2 :** a government in which a small group exercises control esp. for corrupt and selfish purposes; *also* **:** a group exercising such control **3 :** an organization under oligarchic control

Oli·go·cene \ˈäl-i-gō-ˌsēn, ˈō-li-; ə-ˈlig-ə-\ *adj* [ISV] (1859) **:** of, relating to, or being an epoch of the Tertiary between the Eocene and Miocene or the corresponding system of rocks — **Oligocene** *n*

oli·go·chaete \-ˌkēt\ *n* [NL *Oligochaeta,* deriv. of Gk *olig-* + *chaitē* long hair] (1876) **:** any of a class or order (Oligochaeta) of hermaphroditic terrestrial or aquatic annelids (as an earthworm) that lack a specialized head — **oligochaete** *adj*

oli·go·clase \ˈäl-i-gō-ˌklās, ˈō-li-, -ˌklāz; ə-ˈlig-ə-\ *n* [G *oligoklas,* fr. *olig-* olig- + Gk *klasis* breaking, fr. *klan* to break — more at HALT] (1832) **:** a mineral of the plagioclase series

oli·go·den·dro·cyte \ˈäl-i-gō-ˈden-drə-ˌsīt, ə-ˌlig-ə-\ *n* [ISV, fr. *olig-* + *dendr-* + *-cyte*] (1932) **:** a neuroglial cell resembling an astrocyte but smaller with few and slender processes having few branches

oli·go·den·drog·lia \-den-ˈdräg-lē-ə, -ˈdrōg-\ *n* [NL, fr. *oligodendro*cyte + *-glia* (form of neuroglia)] (1924) **:** neuroglia made up of oligodendrocytes that is held to function in myelin formation in the central nervous system — **oli·go·den·drog·li·al** \-lē-əl\ *adj*

oligo·mer \ə-ˈlig-ə-mər\ *n* (1952) **:** a polymer or polymer intermediate containing relatively few structural units — **oligo·mer·ic** \-ˌlig-ə-ˈmer-ik\ *adj* — **oligo·mer·iza·tion** \-mə-rə-ˈzā-shən\ *n*

oli·go·nu·cle·o·tide \-ˈn(y)ü-klē-ə-ˌtīd\ *n* (1942) **:** a chain of usu. from 2 to 10 nucleotides

oli·goph·a·gous \ˌäl-ə-ˈgäf-ə-gəs, ˌō-lə-\ *adj* (1920) **:** eating only a few specific kinds of food — **oli·goph·a·gy** \-ˈgäf-ə-jē\ *n*

oli·gop·o·ly \-ˈgäp-ə-lē\ *n* [*olig-* + *monopoly*] (1895) **:** a market situation in which each of a few producers affects but does not control the market — **oli·gop·o·lis·tic** \-ˌgäp-ə-ˈlis-tik\ *adj*

oli·gop·so·ny \-ˈgäp-sə-nē\ *n* [*olig-* + Gk *opsōnia* purchase of victuals, fr. *opsōnein* to purchase victuals, fr. *opson* food + *ōneisthai* to buy — more at VENAL] (1942) **:** a market situation in which each of a few buyers exerts a disproportionate influence on the market

oli·go·sac·cha·ride \ˌäl-i-gō-ˈsak-ə-ˌrīd, ˌō-li-\ *n* [ISV] (1930) **:** a saccharide (as a disaccharide) that contains a known small number of monosaccharide units

oli·go·tro·phic \-ˈtrō-fik\ *adj* [ISV] (1928) **:** deficient in plant nutrients ⟨~ boggy acid soils⟩; *esp* **:** having abundant dissolved oxygen with no marked stratification ⟨an ~ body of water⟩ — compare EUTROPHIC, MESOTROPHIC

olio \ˈō-lē-ˌō\ *n, pl* **oli·os** [modif. of Sp *olla*] (1643) **1 :** OLLA PODRIDA 1 **2 a :** a miscellaneous mixture **:** HODGEPODGE **b :** a miscellaneous collection (as of literary or musical selections)

ol·i·va·ceous \ˌäl-ə-ˈvā-shəs\ *adj* (1776) **:** OLIVE 1

[1]**ol·ive** \ˈäl-iv, -əv\ *n* [ME, fr. OF, fr. L *oliva,* fr. Gk *elaia*] (13c) **1 a :** an Old World evergreen tree (*Olea europaea* of the family Oleaceae, the olive family) cultivated for its drupaceous fruit that is an important food and source of oil; *also* **:** the fruit **b :** any of various shrubs and trees resembling the olive **2 :** any of several colors resembling that of the unripe fruit of the olive tree that are yellow to yellow green in hue, of medium to low lightness, and of moderate to low saturation

[2]**olive** *adj* (1657) **1 :** of the color olive or olive green **2 :** approaching olive in color or complexion

olive branch *n* (14c) **1 :** a branch of the olive tree esp. when used as a symbol of peace **2 :** an offer or gesture of conciliation or goodwill

olive drab *n* (1897) **1 :** a variable color averaging a grayish olive **2 a :** a wool or cotton fabric of an olive drab color **b :** a uniform of this fabric
olive green *n* (1756) **:** a variable color that is greener, lighter, and stronger than average olive color
oliv•enite \ō-ˈliv-ə-ˌnīt\ *n* [G *olivenit,* fr. *oliven-, olive* olive] (1820) **:** a mineral $Cu_2(AsO_4)(OH)$ that is a basic olive green, dull brown, or yellowish arsenate of copper
Ol•i•ver \ˈäl-ə-vər\ *n* [F *Olivier*] **:** the close friend of Roland in the Charlemagne legends
ol•iv•ine \ˈäl-ə-ˌvēn\ *n* [G *olivin,* fr. L *oliva*] (1794) **:** a usu. greenish mineral $(Mg,Fe)_2SiO_4$ that is a complex silicate of magnesium and iron used esp. in refractories — compare PERIDOT — **ol•iv•in•ic** \ˌäl-ə-ˈvin-ik\ *or* **ol•iv•in•it•ic** \-və-ˈnit-ik\ *adj*
ol•la \ˈäl-ə, ˈȯi-ə\ *n* [Sp, fr. L, pot — more at OVEN] (1622) **:** a large bulging widemouthed earthenware vessel often with looped handles used (as in Latin America) esp. as a pot for stewing or as a container for water
ol•la po•dri•da \ˌäl-ə-pə-ˈdrēd-ə, ˌȯi-ə-\ *n, pl* **olla podridas** \-ˈdrēd-əz\ *also* **ollas podridas** \ˌäl-ə(z)-, ˌȯi-ə(z)-\ [Sp, lit., rotten pot] (1599) **1 :** a rich highly seasoned stew of meat and vegetables usu. including sausage and chick-peas that is slowly simmered and is a traditional Spanish and Latin-American dish **2 :** HODGEPODGE
olo•li•u•qui \ˌō-ˌlō-lē-ˈü-kē\ *n* [Sp *ololiuque,* fr. Nahuatl *ololiuhqui,* lit., one that covers] (1915) **:** a woody stemmed Mexican vine (*Rivea corymbosa*) of the morning glory family having small fleshy fruits with single seeds that are used esp. by the Indians for medicinal, narcotic, and religious purposes
olym•pi•ad \ə-ˈlim-pē-ˌad, ō-\ *n, often cap* [ME, fr. MF *Olympiade,* fr. L *Olympiad-, Olympias,* fr. Gk, fr. *Olympia,* site of ancient Olympic Games] (14c) **1 :** one of the 4-year intervals between Olympic Games by which time was reckoned in ancient Greece **2 :** a quadrennial celebration of the modern Olympic Games
[1]**Olym•pi•an** \-pē-ən\ *adj* (15c) **1 :** of or relating to Mount Olympus in Thessaly **2 :** befitting or characteristic of an Olympian; *esp* **:** LOFTY ⟨his . . . formula of glib simplicity and ~ arrogance —Richard Pollak⟩
[2]**Olympian** *adj* (1593) **1 :** of or relating to the ancient Greek region of Olympia **2 :** of, relating to, or constituting the Olympic Games
[3]**Olympian** *n* (1606) **:** a participant in Olympic Games
[4]**Olympian** *n* (1843) **1 :** one of the ancient Greek deities dwelling on Olympus **2 :** a being of lofty detachment or superior attainments
Olympian Games *n pl* (1593) **:** OLYMPIC GAMES 1
Olym•pia oyster \ə-ˌlim-pē-ə-, ō-\ *n* [*Olympia,* Washington] (1908) **:** a small flavorful native oyster (*Ostrea lurida*) of the Puget Sound area of the Pacific coast of No. America
Olym•pic \ə-ˈlim-pik, ō-\ *adj* (1600) **1 :** [1]OLYMPIAN **2 :** of or relating to the Olympic Games
Olympic Games *n pl* (1662) **1 :** an ancient Panhellenic festival held every fourth year and made up of contests of sports, music, and literature with the victor's prize a crown of wild olive **2 :** a modified revival of the ancient Olympic Games held once every four years and made up of international athletic contests — called also *Olympics*
Olym•pus \ə-ˈlim-pəs, ō-\ *n* [L, fr. Gk *Olympos*] (1580) **:** a mountain in Thessaly that in Greek mythology is the abode of the gods
om \ˈōm\ *n* [Skt] (1788) **:** a mantra consisting of the sound \ˈōm\ and used in contemplation of ultimate reality
-o•ma \ˈō-mə\ *n suffix, pl* **-o•mas** \-məz\ *or* **-o•ma•ta** \-mət-ə\ [L *-omat-, -oma,* fr. Gk *-ōmat-, -ōma,* fr. *-ō-* (stem vowel of causative verbs in *-oun*) + *-mat-, -ma,* suffix denoting result — more at -MENT] **:** tumor ⟨adeno*ma*⟩ ⟨fibro*ma*⟩
Oma•ha \ˈō-mə-ˌhȯ, -ˌhä\ *n, pl* **Omaha** *or* **Omahas** [Omaha, lit., those going upstream or against the wind] (1804) **:** a member of an American Indian people of northeastern Nebraska
oma•sum \ō-ˈmā-səm\ *n, pl* **oma•sa** \-sə\ [NL, fr. L, tripe of a bullock] (1706) **:** the third chamber of the ruminant stomach that is situated between the reticulum and the abomasum
om•bre \ˈäm-bər; ˈəm-brē, ˈəm-, -ˌbrā\ *n* [F or Sp; F *hombre,* fr. Sp, lit., man] (1660) **:** an old three-handed card game popular in Europe esp. in the 17th and 18th centuries
om•bré \ˈäm-ˌbrā\ *adj* [F, pp. of *ombrer* to shade, fr. It *ombrare,* fr. *ombra* shade, fr. L *umbra* — more at UMBRAGE] (ca. 1896) **:** having colors or tones that shade into each other — used esp. of fabrics in which the color is graduated from light to dark — **ombré** *n*
om•buds•man \ˈäm-ˌbu̇dz-mən, ˈȯm-, -bədz-, -ˌman; äm-ˈbu̇dz-, ȯm-\ *n, pl* **-men** \-mən\ [Sw, lit., representative, fr. ON *umbothsmathr,* fr. *umboth* commission + *mathr* man] (1959) **1 :** a government official (as in Sweden or New Zealand) appointed to receive and investigate complaints made by individuals against abuses or capricious acts of public officials **2 :** one that investigates reported complaints (as from students or consumers), reports findings, and helps to achieve equitable settlements
-ome \ˌōm\ *n suffix* [NL *-oma,* fr. L, -oma] **:** mass ⟨phyll*ome*⟩
ome•ga \ō-ˈmeg-ə, -ˈmē-gə, -ˈmā-gə\ *n* [Gk *ō mega,* lit., large o] (15c) **1 :** the 24th and last letter of the Greek alphabet — see ALPHABET table **2 :** LAST, ENDING **3 a :** a negatively charged elementary particle that has a mass 3270 times the mass of an electron and that decays into a xi and a pion — called also *omega minus* **b :** a very short-lived unstable meson with mass 1532 times the mass of an electron — called also *omega meson*
om•elet *or* **om•elette** \ˈäm-(ə-)lət\ *n* [F *omelette,* alter. of MF *alumelle,* lit., knife blade, modif. of L *lamella,* dim. of *lamina* thin plate] (1611) **:** beaten eggs cooked without stirring until set and served folded in half
omen \ˈō-mən\ *n* [L *omin-, omen*] (1582) **:** an occurrence or phenomenon believed to portend a future event **:** AUGURY
omen•tum \ō-ˈment-əm\ *n, pl* **-ta** \-ə\ *or* **-tums** [L] (1545) **:** a fold of peritoneum connecting or supporting abdominal structures (as the viscera); *also* **:** a fold of peritoneum free at one end — **omen•tal** \-ˈment-ᵊl\ *adj*
omer \ˈō-mər\ *n* [Heb *ʿōmer*] (1611) **1 :** an ancient Hebrew unit of dry capacity equal to $^1/_{10}$ ephah **2 a** *often cap* **:** the sheaf of barley traditionally offered in Jewish Temple worship on the second day of the Passover **b** *cap* **:** a 7-week liturgical period of expectancy between the second day of the Passover and Shabuoth
omi•cron \ˈäm-ə-ˌkrän, ˈōm-, *Brit* ō-ˈmī-krən\ *n* [Gk *o mikron,* lit., small o] (15c) **:** the 15th letter of the Greek alphabet — see ALPHABET table
om•i•nous \ˈäm-ə-nəs\ *adj* (1587) **:** being or exhibiting an omen **:** PORTENTOUS; *esp* **:** foreboding or foreshowing evil **:** INAUSPICIOUS — **om•i•nous•ly** *adv* — **om•i•nous•ness** *n*
syn OMINOUS, PORTENTOUS, FATEFUL mean having a menacing or threatening aspect. OMINOUS implies having a menacing, alarming character foreshadowing evil or disaster; PORTENTOUS suggests being frighteningly big or impressive but now seldom definitely connotes forewarning of calamity; FATEFUL suggests being of momentous or decisive importance.
omis•si•ble \ō-ˈmis-ə-bəl\ *adj* (1816) **:** that may be omitted
omis•sion \ō-ˈmish-ən, ə-\ *n* [ME *omissioun,* fr. LL *omission-, omissio,* fr. L *omissus,* pp. of *omittere*] (15c) **1 a :** apathy toward or neglect of duty **b :** something neglected or left undone **2 :** the act of omitting **:** the state of being omitted
omit \ō-ˈmit, ə-\ *vt* **omit•ted; omit•ting** [ME *omitten,* fr. L *omittere,* fr. *ob-* toward + *mittere* to let go, send — more at OB-, SMITE] (15c) **1 :** to leave out or leave unmentioned **2 :** to fail to perform or make use of **:** FORBEAR **3** *obs* **:** DISREGARD **4** *obs* **:** GIVE UP ***syn*** see NEGLECT
om•ma•tid•i•um \ˌäm-ə-ˈtid-ē-əm\ *n, pl* **-tid•ia** \-ē-ə\ [NL, fr. Gk *ommat-, omma* eye] (1884) **:** one of the elements corresponding to a small simple eye that make up the compound eye of an arthropod — **om•ma•tid•i•al** \-ē-əl\ *adj*
omni- *comb form* [L, fr. *omnis*] **:** all **:** universally ⟨*omni*directional⟩
[1]**om•ni•bus** \ˈäm-ni-(ˌ)bəs\ *n* [F, fr. L, for all, dat. pl. of *omnis*] (1829) **1 :** a usu. automotive public vehicle designed to carry a comparatively large number of passengers **:** BUS **2 :** a book containing reprints of a number of works
[2]**omnibus** *adj* (1842) **1 :** of, relating to, or providing for many things at once **2 :** containing or including many items
om•ni•di•rec•tion•al \ˌäm-ni-də-ˈrek-shnəl, -ˌnī-də-, -ni-(ˌ)dī-, -shən-ᵊl\ *adj* (1927) **:** being in or involving all directions; *esp* **:** receiving or sending radio waves equally well in all directions ⟨~ antenna⟩
om•ni•far•i•ous \ˌäm-nə-ˈfar-ē-əs, -ˈfer-\ *adj* [LL *omnifarius,* fr. L *omni-* + *-farius* (as in *multifarius* having great diversity) — more at MULTIFARIOUS] (1653) **:** of all varieties, forms, or kinds
om•nif•i•cent \äm-ˈnif-ə-sənt\ *adj* [L *omni-* + E *-ficent* (as in *magnificent*)] (1677) **:** unlimited in creative power
om•nip•o•tence \äm-ˈnip-ət-ən(t)s\ *n* (15c) **1 :** the quality or state of being omnipotent **2 :** an agency or force of unlimited power
[1]**om•nip•o•tent** \-ət-ənt\ *adj* [ME, fr. MF, fr. L *omnipotent-, omnipotens,* fr. *omni-* + *potent-, potens* potent] (14c) **1** *often cap* **:** ALMIGHTY 1 **2 :** having virtually unlimited authority or influence **3** *obs* **:** ARRANT — **om•nip•o•tent•ly** *adv*
[2]**omnipotent** *n* (1601) **1 :** one who is omnipotent **2** *cap* **:** GOD 1
om•ni•pres•ence \ˌäm-ni-ˈprez-ᵊn(t)s\ *n* (1601) **:** the quality or state of being omnipresent **:** UBIQUITY
om•ni•pres•ent \-ᵊnt\ *adj* (1610) **:** present in all places at all times
om•ni•range \ˈäm-ni-ˌrānj\ *n* (1946) **:** a system of radio navigation in which any bearing relative to a special radio transmitter on the ground may be chosen and flown by an airplane pilot — called also *omnidirectional range*
om•ni•science \äm-ˈnish-ən(t)s\ *n* [ML *omniscientia,* fr. L *omni-* + *scientia* knowledge — more at SCIENCE] (1612) **:** the quality or state of being omniscient
om•ni•scient \-ənt\ *adj* [NL *omniscient-, omnisciens,* back-formation fr. ML *omniscientia*] (1604) **1 :** having infinite awareness, understanding, and insight **2 :** possessed of universal or complete knowledge — **om•ni•scient•ly** *adv*
om•ni•um–gath•er•um \ˌäm-nē-əm-ˈga<u>th</u>-ə-rəm\ *n, pl* **omnium–gatherums** [L *omnium* (gen. pl. of *omnis*) + E *gather* + L *-um,* noun ending] (1530) **:** a miscellaneous collection (as of things or persons)
om•ni•vore \ˈäm-ni-ˌvō(ə)r, -ˌvȯ(ə)r\ *n* [NL *omnivora,* neut. pl. of *omnivorus*] (1890) **:** one that is omnivorous
om•niv•o•rous \äm-ˈniv-(ə-)rəs\ *adj* [L *omnivorus,* fr. *omni-* + *-vorus* -vorous] (1656) **1 :** feeding on both animal and vegetable substances **2 :** avidly taking in everything as if devouring or consuming — **om•niv•o•rous•ly** *adv*
[1]**on** \(ˈ)ȯn, (ˈ)än\ *prep* [ME *an, on,* prep. & adv., fr. OE; akin to OHG *ana* on, Gk *ana* up, on] (bef. 12c) **1 a —** used as a function word to indicate position in contact with and supported by the top surface of ⟨the book is lying ~ the table⟩ **b —** used as a function word to indicate position in or in contact with an outer surface ⟨the fly landed ~ the ceiling⟩ ⟨I have a cut ~ my finger⟩ ⟨paint ~ the wall⟩ **c —** used as a function word to indicate position in close proximity with ⟨a village ~ the sea⟩ ⟨stay ~ your opponent⟩ **d —** used as a function word to indicate direction or location with respect to something ⟨~ the south⟩ ⟨the garden is ~ the side of the house⟩ **2 a —** used as a function word to indicate a source of attachment or support ⟨~ a string⟩ ⟨stand ~ one foot⟩ ⟨hang it ~ a nail⟩ **b —** used as a function word to indicate a source of dependence ⟨you can rely ~ me⟩ ⟨feeds ~ insects⟩ ⟨lives ~ a pension⟩ **c —** used as a function word to indicate means of conveyance ⟨~ the bus⟩ or presence within the confines or in possession of ⟨had a knife ~ him⟩ **3 —** used as a function word to indicate a time frame during which something takes place ⟨a parade ~ Sunday⟩ or an instant, action, or occurrence when something begins or is done ⟨~ cue⟩ ⟨~ arriving home, I found your letter⟩ ⟨news ~ the hour⟩ ⟨cash ~ delivery⟩ **4** *archaic* **:** OF **5 a —** used as a function word to indicate manner of doing something; often used with *the* ⟨~ the sly⟩ ⟨keep everything ~ the up-and-up⟩ **b —** used as a function word to indicate means or agency ⟨cut myself ~ a knife⟩ ⟨talk ~ the telephone⟩ **c —** used as a function word to indicate a medium of expression; used orig. to refer to physical position ⟨acting ~ the stage⟩ ⟨best show ~ television⟩ **6 a** (1) **—** used as a function word to indicate active involvement in a condition or status ⟨~ fire⟩ ⟨~ the increase⟩ ⟨~ the lookout⟩ (2) **:** regularly using or showing the effects of using ⟨~

drugs⟩ **b** — used as a function word to indicate involvement with the activity, work, or function of ⟨~ tour⟩ ⟨~ the jury⟩ ⟨~ duty⟩ **c** — used as a function word to indicate position or status in proper relationship with a standard or objective ⟨~ schedule⟩ **7 a** — used as a function word to indicate reason, ground, or basis (as for an action, opinion, or computation) ⟨I have it ~ good authority⟩ ⟨~ one condition⟩ ⟨the interest will be 10 cents ~ the dollar⟩ **b** — used as a function word to indicate the cause or source ⟨profited ~ the sale of stock⟩ ⟨the win came ~ a last-second goal⟩ **c** — used as a function word to indicate the focus of obligation or responsibility ⟨drinks are ~ the house⟩ ⟨put the blame ~ my actions⟩ **8 a** — used as a function word to indicate the object of collision, opposition, or hostile action ⟨bumped my head ~ a limb⟩ ⟨an attack ~ religion⟩ ⟨pulled a gun ~ me⟩ **b** — used as a function word to indicate the object with respect to some disadvantage, handicap, or detriment ⟨has three inches in height ~ me⟩ ⟨a 3-game lead ~ the second-place team⟩ ⟨the joke's ~ me⟩ ⟨it's no use denying it, we've got the goods ~ you⟩ **9 a** — used as a function word to indicate destination or the focus of some action, movement, or directed effort ⟨crept up ~ him⟩ ⟨feast your eyes ~ this⟩ ⟨working ~ my skiing⟩ ⟨made a payment ~ the loan⟩ **b** — used as a function word to indicate the focus of feelings, determination, or will ⟨have pity ~ me⟩ ⟨keen ~ sports⟩ ⟨a curse ~ you⟩ **c** — used as a function word to indicate the subject of study, discussion, or consideration ⟨a book ~ insects⟩ ⟨reflect ~ that a moment⟩ ⟨agree ~ price⟩ **10** — used as a function word to indicate reduplication or succession in a series ⟨loss ~ loss⟩

²on \ˈȯn, ˈän\ *adv* (bef. 12c) **1 a :** in or into a position of contact with an upper surface esp. so as to be positioned for use or operation ⟨put the plates ~⟩ **b :** in or into a position of being attached to or covering a surface; *esp* **:** in or into the condition of being worn ⟨put his new shoes ~⟩ **2 a :** forward in space or time ⟨went ~ home⟩ **b :** in continuance or succession ⟨rambled ~⟩ ⟨and so ~⟩ **3 :** into operation or a position permitting operation ⟨switched the light ~⟩

³on \ˈȯn, ˈän\ *adj* (1541) **1 :** engaged in an activity or function (as a dramatic role) **2 a** (1) **:** being in operation ⟨the radio is ~⟩ (2) **:** placed so as to permit operation ⟨the switch is ~⟩ **b :** taking place ⟨the game is ~⟩ **3 :** INTENDED, PLANNED ⟨has nothing ~ for tonight⟩

¹-on \ˌän, ən\ *n suffix* [ISV, alter. of *-one*] **:** chemical compound not a ketone or other oxo compound ⟨parathi*on*⟩

²-on \ˌän\ *n suffix* [fr. *-on* (in *ion*)] **1 :** subatomic particle ⟨nucle*on*⟩ **2 a :** unit **:** quantum ⟨phot*on*⟩ ⟨magnet*on*⟩ **b :** basic hereditary component ⟨cistr*on*⟩ ⟨oper*on*⟩

³-on \ˌän\ *n suffix* [NL, fr. *-on* (in *argon*)] **:** noble gas ⟨rad*on*⟩

on–again, off–again *adj* (1948) **:** existing briefly and then disappearing in an intermittent unpredictable way ⟨*on-again, off-again* fads⟩

on·a·ger \ˈän-i-jər\ *n* [ME, wild ass, fr. L, fr. Gk *onagros*, fr. *onos* ass + *agros* field — more at ACRE] (14c) **1 :** a small pale-colored kiang with a broad dorsal stripe **2** [LL, fr. L] **:** a heavy catapult used in ancient and medieval times

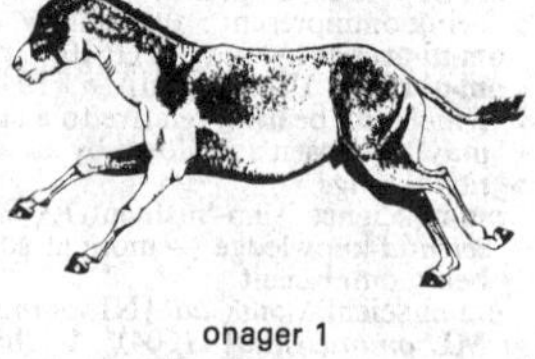
onager 1

on and off *adv* (1855) **:** OFF AND ON

onan·ism \ˈō-nə-ˌniz-əm\ *n* [prob. fr. NL *onanismus*, fr. *Onan*, son of Judah whose disobedient act is described in Gen 38:9] (ca. 1727) **1 :** MASTURBATION **2 :** COITUS INTERRUPTUS **3 :** SELF-GRATIFICATION — **onan·is·tic** \ˌō-nə-ˈnis-tik\ *adj*

¹once \ˈwən(t)s\ *adv* [ME *ones*, fr. gen. of *on* one] (12c) **1 :** one time and no more **2 :** at any one time **:** under any circumstances **:** EVER **3 :** at some indefinite time in the past **:** FORMERLY **4 :** by one degree of relationship

²once *n* (13c) **:** one single time **:** one time at least — **at once 1 :** at the same time **:** SIMULTANEOUSLY **2 :** IMMEDIATELY **3 :** ³BOTH

³once *adj* (1691) **:** that once was **:** FORMER

⁴once *conj* (1761) **:** at the moment when **:** AS SOON AS

once–over \ˈwən(t)-ˌsō-vər\ *n* (1914) **:** a swift examination or survey; *esp* **:** a swift comprehensive appraising glance

once that *conj* (1874) **:** ONCE

on·cho·cer·ci·a·sis \ˌäŋ-kō-ˌsər-ˈkī-ə-səs\ *n, pl* **-a·ses** \-ˌsēz\ [NL, fr. *Onchocerca*, genus of worms] (1911) **:** infestation with or disease caused by filarial worms (genus *Onchocerca*); *esp* **:** a disease of man caused by a worm (*O. volvulus*) that is native to Africa but now present in parts of tropical America and is transmitted by several biting flies

on·cid·i·um \än-ˈsid-ē-əm, äŋ-ˈkid-\ *n* [NL, fr. Gk *onkos* barbed hook — more at ANGLE] (ca. 1868) **:** any of a genus (*Oncidium*) of showy tropical American epiphytic or terrestrial orchids

onco- *comb form* [NL, fr. Gk *onkos* bulk, mass; akin to Gk *enenkein* to carry — more at ENOUGH] **:** tumor ⟨*onco*logy⟩

on·co·gene \ˈäŋ-kō-ˌjēn\ *n* [*onco-* + *gene*] (1969) **:** a gene having the potential to cause a normal cell to become cancerous

on·co·gen·e·sis \ˌäŋ-kō-ˈjen-ə-səs\ *n* [NL] (ca. 1932) **:** the induction or formation of tumors

on·co·gen·ic \-ˈjen-ik\ *adj* (1936) **1 :** relating to tumor formation **2 :** tending to cause tumors

on·co·ge·nic·i·ty \-jə-ˈnis-ət-ē\ *n* (1944) **:** the capacity to induce or form tumors

on·col·o·gy \än-ˈkäl-ə-jē, äŋ-\ *n* (1857) **:** the study of tumors — **on·co·log·i·cal** \ˌäŋ-kə-ˈläj-i-kəl\ *also* **on·co·log·ic** \-ik\ *adj* — **on·col·o·gist** \än-ˈkäl-ə-jəst, äŋ-\ *n*

on·com·ing \ˈȯn-ˌkəm-iŋ, ˈän-\ *adj* (1844) **1 a :** coming nearer in time or space ⟨the ~ year⟩ ⟨an ~ car⟩ **b :** FUTURE ⟨looked forward to his ~ visit⟩ **2 :** EMERGENT, RISING ⟨the ~ generation⟩

on·cor·na·vi·rus \ˌäŋ-ˌkȯ(ə)r-nə-ˈvī-rəs\ *n* [*onco-* + *RNA* + *virus*] (1970) **:** any of a group of RNA-containing viruses that produce tumors

¹one \ˈwən, ˌwən\ *adj* [ME *on*, *an*, fr. OE *ān*; akin to OHG *ein* one, L *unus* (OL *oinos*), Skt *eka*] (bef. 12c) **1 :** being a single unit or thing ⟨~ day at a time⟩ **2 a :** being one in particular ⟨early ~ morning⟩ **b :** being preeminently what is indicated ⟨~ fine person⟩ **3 a :** being the same in kind or quality ⟨both of ~ species⟩ **b** (1) **:** constituting a unified entity of two or more components ⟨the combined elements form ~ substance⟩ (2) **:** UNITED **4 :** existing or occurring as something not definitely fixed or placed ⟨will see you again ~ day⟩ **5 :** being the only individual of an indicated or implied kind ⟨the ~ person she wanted to marry⟩ — **at one :** at harmony **:** in a state of agreement

²one \ˈwən\ *n* (bef. 12c) **1** — see NUMBER table **2 :** the number denoting unity **3 :** the first in a set or series; *esp* **:** an article of clothing of a size designated *one* ⟨wears a ~⟩ **4 :** a single person or thing ⟨has the ~ but needs the other⟩ **5 :** a one-dollar bill

³one \ˈwən, ˌwən\ *pron* (13c) **1 :** a certain indefinitely indicated person or thing ⟨saw ~ of his friends⟩ **2 a :** an individual of a vaguely indicated group **:** anyone at all ⟨~ never knows⟩ **b** — sometimes used as a third person substitute for a first person pronoun ⟨I'd like to read more but ~ doesn't have the time⟩

usage Senses 2a and 2b are usu. signs of a formal style. A formal style excludes the participation of the reader or hearer; thus *one* is used where a less formal style might address the reader directly ⟨for the consequences of such choices, *one* has only oneself to thank —Walker Gibson⟩ Use of *one* to replace a first-person pronoun — criticized by some commentators — appears to be more common in British English than American English. It may be resorted to in order to avoid repetition of *I* ⟨I'm watching this pretty carefully and I hope that the issue will come up in the Lords and *one* may be able to speak about it — Donald Coggan, Archbishop of Canterbury⟩

-one \ˌōn\ *n suffix* [ISV, alter. of *-ene*] **:** ketone or related or analogous compound or class of compounds ⟨lact*one*⟩ ⟨quin*one*⟩

one another *pron* (13c) **:** EACH OTHER ***usage*** see EACH OTHER

one–armed bandit \ˌwən-ˌärm(d)-\ *also* **one–arm bandit** *n* (1934) **:** SLOT MACHINE 2

one–bag·ger \ˈwən-ˈbag-ər\ *n* (1952) **:** SINGLE 2

one–dimensional *adj* (1883) **1 :** having one dimension **2 :** lacking depth **:** SUPERFICIAL ⟨~ characters⟩ — **one–dimensionality** *n*

one–egg *adj* (1948) **:** MONOZYGOTIC

one·fold \ˈwən-ˌfōld, -ˈfōld\ *adj* [ME, fr. OE *ānfeald*, fr. *ān* one + *-feald* -fold] (bef. 12c) **:** constituting a single undivided whole

one–hand·ed \-ˈhan-dəd\ *adj* (15c) **1 :** having or using only one hand ⟨could beat him up ~⟩ **2 a :** designed for or requiring the use of only one hand **b :** effected by the use of only one hand

one–horse *adj* (1750) **1 :** drawn or operated by one horse **2 :** of little real importance or consequence ⟨a ~ town⟩

Onei·da \ō-ˈnīd-ə\ *n, pl* **Oneida** *or* **Oneidas** [Iroquois *Onẽyóde'*, lit., standing rock] (1666) **1 a :** an American Indian people orig. of New York **b :** a member of this people **2 :** the language of the Oneida people

onei·ric \ō-ˈnī-rik\ *adj* [Gk *oneiros* dream; akin to Arm *anurǰ* dream] (1859) **:** of or relating to dreams **:** DREAMY — **onei·ri·cal·ly** \-ri-k(ə-)lē\ *adv*

onei·ro·man·cy \ō-ˈnī-rə-ˌman(t)-sē\ *n* [Gk *oneiros* + E *-mancy*] (1652) **:** divination by means of dreams

one–line octave *n* (1931) **:** the musical octave that begins on middle C — see PITCH illustration

one–lin·er \ˌwən-ˈlī-nər\ *n* (1967) **:** a very succinct joke or witticism

one–man *adj* (1842) **:** of or relating to just one individual: as **a :** consisting of only one individual ⟨a ~ committee⟩ **b** (1) **:** done, presented, or produced by only one individual ⟨a ~ stage play⟩ (2) **:** featuring the work of a single artist (as a painter) ⟨a ~ show of oils⟩ **c :** designed for or limited to one individual

one·ness \ˈwən-nəs\ *n* (1594) **:** the quality or state or fact of being one: as **a :** SINGLENESS **b :** INTEGRITY, WHOLENESS **c :** HARMONY **d :** SAMENESS, IDENTITY **e :** UNITY, UNION

one–night·er \ˌwən-ˈnīt-ər\ *n* (ca. 1937) **:** ONE-NIGHT STAND

one–night stand *n* (1880) **1 :** a performance (as of a play or concert) given (as by a traveling group of actors or musicians) only once in each of a series of localities **2 a :** a locality used for one-night stands **b :** a stopover for a one-night stand **3 :** a sexual encounter limited to a single occasion

one–off \ˌwən-ˈȯf\ *adj, Brit* (1934) **:** limited to a single time, occasion, or instance **:** ONE-SHOT — **one–off** *n*

one–on–one \ˌwən-ȯn-ˈwən, ˌwən-än-\ *adj or adv* (1967) **1 :** playing directly against a single opposing player **2 :** involving a direct encounter between one person and another

one–piece *adj* (1880) **:** consisting of or made in a single undivided piece ⟨a ~ bathing suit⟩ — **one–piec·er** \ˈwən-ˈpē-sər\ *n*

oner·ous \ˈän-ə-rəs, ˈō-nə-\ *adj* [ME, fr. MF *onereus*, fr. L *onerosus*, fr. *oner-*, *onus* burden; akin to Skt *anas* cart] (14c) **1 :** involving, imposing, or constituting a burden **:** TROUBLESOME ⟨an ~ task⟩ **2 :** having legal obligations that outweigh the advantages ⟨~ contract⟩ — **oner·ous·ly** *adv* — **oner·ous·ness** *n*

syn ONEROUS, BURDENSOME, OPPRESSIVE, EXACTING mean imposing hardship. ONEROUS stresses being laborious and heavy esp. because distasteful; BURDENSOME suggests causing mental as well as physical strain; OPPRESSIVE implies extreme harshness or severity in what is imposed; EXACTING implies rigor or sternness rather than tyranny or injustice in the demands made or in the one demanding.

one·self \(ˌ)wən-ˈself, *Southern also* -ˈsef\ *also* **one's self** \(ˌ)wən-, ˌwənz-\ *pron* (1621) **1 :** a person's self **:** one's own self — used reflexively as object of a preposition or verb or for emphasis in various constructions **2 :** one's normal, healthy, or sane condition or self — **be oneself :** to conduct oneself in a usual or fitting manner

one–shot \ˈwən-ˌshät\ *adj* (1927) **1 :** that is complete or effective through being done or used or applied only once ⟨there is no easy ~ answer to the problem⟩ **2 :** that is not followed by something else of the same kind ⟨a ~ tax cut⟩ — **one–shot** *n*

one–sid·ed \ˈwən-ˈsīd-əd\ *adj* (1813) **1 a** (1) **:** having one side prominent or more developed (2) **:** having or occurring on one side only **b :** limited to one side **:** PARTIAL ⟨a ~ interpretation⟩ **2 :** UNILATERAL ⟨a ~ decision⟩ — **one–sid·ed·ly** *adv* — **one–sid·ed·ness** *n*

one–step \ˈwən-ˌstep\ *n* (1911) **1 :** a ballroom dance in $^{2}/_{4}$ time marked by quick walking steps backward and forward **2 :** music used for the one-step — **one–step** *vi*

one–tailed \ˌwən-ˌtāl(d)\ *also* **one–tail** \-ˌtāl\ *adj* (1947) **:** being a statistical test for which the critical region consists of all values of the test statistic greater than a given value or less than a given value but not both — compare TWO-TAILED

¹one·time \ˌwən-ˌtīm\ *adj* (1840) **1 :** FORMER, SOMETIME ⟨a ~ actor⟩ **2 :** occurring only once **:** ONE-SHOT

2**onetime** *adv* (1886) : FORMERLY
one–to–one \ˌwən-tə-ˈwən, -də-\ *adj* (1873) **1** : pairing each element of a set uniquely with an element of another set **2** : ONE-ON-ONE 2
one–track *adj* (1926) : marked by often narrowly restricted attention to or absorption in just one thing ⟨a ~ mind⟩
one–two \ˈwən-ˈtü, -ˌtü\ *n* (1811) **1** : a combination of two quick blows in rapid succession in boxing; *esp* : a left jab followed at once by a hard blow with the right hand **2** *or* **one–two punch** : a combination of two forces acting against something
one–up \ˌwən-ˈəp, ˈwən-\ *vt* [back-formation fr. *one-upmanship*] (1963) : to practice one-upmanship on
one up *adj* (1919) : being in a position of advantage — usu. used with *on*
one–up·man·ship \ˌwən-ˈəp-mən-ˌship\ *also* **one–ups·man·ship** \-ˈəp-smən-\ *n* (1952) : the art or practice of going a friend or competitor one better or keeping one jump ahead of him
one–way *adj* (1824) **1** : that moves in or allows movement in only one direction ⟨~ traffic⟩ **2** : ONE-SIDED, UNILATERAL ⟨a ~ conversation⟩ **3** : that functions in only one of two or more ways
on·go·ing \ˈȯn-ˌgō-iŋ, ˈän-, -ˌgȯ(-)iŋ\ *adj* (1877) **1** : being actually in process **2** : continuously moving forward : GROWING — **on·go·ing·ness** \-nəs\ *n*
on·ion \ˈən-yən\ *n* [ME, fr. MF *oignon*, fr. L *union-, unio*] (14c) **1** : a widely cultivated Asian herb (*Allium cepa*) of the lily family with pungent edible bulbs; *also* : its bulb **2** : any of various plants of the same genus as the onion
onion dome *n* (1941) : a dome (as of a church) having the general shape of an onion — **onion–domed** *adj*
on·ion·skin \-ˌskin\ *n* (1879) : a thin strong translucent paper of very light weight
oni·um \ˈō-nē-əm\ *adj* [*-onium*] (1905) : being or characterized by a usu. complex cation
-o·ni·um \ˈō-nē-əm\ *n suffix* [NL, fr. *ammonium*] : an ion having a positive charge ⟨oxonium⟩ — compare -IUM 1b
on–line *adj or adv* (1950) : connected to, served by, or available through a system and esp. a computer or telecommunications system ⟨an ~ data base⟩; *also* : done while connected to a system ⟨~ computer storage⟩
on·look·er \ˈȯn-ˌlu̇k-ər, ˈän-\ *n* (1606) : one that looks on; *esp* : a passive spectator — **on·look·ing** \-iŋ\ *adj*
1**on·ly** \ˈōn-lē\ *adj* [ME, fr. OE *ānlic*, fr. *ān* one — more at ONE] (bef. 12c) **1** : unquestionably the best : PEERLESS **2** : alone in its class or kind : SOLE ⟨an ~ child⟩
2**only** *adv* (13c) **1 a** : as a single fact or instance and nothing more or different : MERELY ⟨has ~ lost one election —George Orwell⟩ **b** : SOLELY, EXCLUSIVELY ⟨known ~ to him⟩ **2** : at the very least ⟨it was ~ too true⟩ **3 a** : in the final outcome ⟨will ~ make you sick⟩ **b** : with nevertheless the final result ⟨won the battles, ~ to lose the war⟩ **4 a** : as recently as ⟨~ last week⟩ **b** : in the immediate past ⟨~ just talked to her⟩
usage The placement of *only* in a sentence has been a source of studious commentary since the 18th century, most of it intended to prove by force of argument that prevailing standard usage is wrong. After 200 years of preachment the following two observations may be made: the position of *only* in standard spoken English is not fixed, since ambiguity is avoided through sentence stress; and in print *only* tends to be placed immediately before the word or words it modifies.
3**only** *conj* (14c) **1 a** : with the restriction that : BUT ⟨you may go, ~ come back early⟩ **b** : and yet : HOWEVER ⟨they look very nice, ~ we can't use them⟩ **2** : were it not that : EXCEPT
on·o·mas·tic \ˌän-ə-ˈmas-tik\ *adj* [Gk *onomastikos*, fr. *onomazein* to name, fr. *onoma* name — more at NAME] (1716) : of, relating to, or consisting of a name or names — **on·o·mas·ti·cal·ly** \-ti-k(ə-)lē\ *adv*
on·o·mas·tics \-tiks\ *n pl but sing or pl in constr* (1930) **1 a** : the science or study of the origins and forms of words esp. as used in a specialized field **b** : the science or study of the origin and forms of proper names of persons or places **2** : the system underlying the formation and use of words esp. for proper names or of words used in a specialized field — **on·o·mas·ti·cian** \ˌän-ə-mas-ˈtish-ən\ *n*
on·o·ma·tol·o·gy \ˌän-ə-mə-ˈtäl-ə-jē\ *n* [F *onomatologie*, fr. Gk *onomat-, onoma* name + F *-logie* -logy] (ca. 1847) : ONOMASTICS — **on·o·ma·tol·o·gist** \-jəst\ *n*
on·o·mato·poe·ia \ˌän-ə-ˌmat-ə-ˈpē-(y)ə, -ˌmät-\ *n* [LL, fr. Gk *onomatopoiia*, fr. *onomat-, onoma* name + *poiein* to make — more at POET] (ca. 1577) **1** : the naming of a thing or action by a vocal imitation of the sound associated with it (as *buzz, hiss*) **2** : the use of words whose sound suggests the sense — **on·o·mato·poe·ic** \-ˈpē-ik\ *or* **on·o·mato·po·et·ic** \-pō-ˈet-ik\ *adj* — **on·o·mato·poe·i·cal·ly** \-ˈpē-ə-k(ə-)lē\ *or* **on·o·mato·po·et·i·cal·ly** \-pō-ˈet-i-k(ə-)lē\ *adv*
On·on·da·ga \ˌän-ə(n)-ˈdȯ-gə\ *n, pl* **-ga** *or* **-gas** [Iroquois *Onõtáge*, village of the Onondaga people] (1684) **1 a** : an American Indian people of New York and Canada **b** : a member of this people **2** : the language of the Onondaga people
on·rush \ˈȯn-ˌrəsh, ˈän-\ *n* (1844) **1** : a rushing forward or onward **2** : ONSET — **on·rush·ing** \-iŋ\ *adj*
on–screen \ˈȯn-ˈskrēn, ˈän-\ *adv or adj* (1955) : in a motion picture or a television program
on·set \-ˌset\ *n* (1535) **1** : ATTACK, ASSAULT ⟨withstand the ~ of the army⟩ **2** : BEGINNING, COMMENCEMENT ⟨the ~ of winter⟩ — **on·set·ting** \-ˌset-iŋ\ *adj*
on·shore \ˈȯn-ˌshō(ə)r, ˈän-, -ˌshȯ(ə)r\ *adj* (1875) **1** : coming or moving from the water toward or onto the shore ⟨an ~ wind⟩ **2** : situated on or near the shore as distinguished from being in deep or open water **3** : DOMESTIC 2 ⟨~ markets⟩ — **on·shore** \ˈȯn-ˈ, ˈän-ˈ\ *adv*
on·side \-ˈsīd\ *adv or adj* (1871) : not offside : in a position legally to play or receive the ball or puck
onside kick *n* (1926) : a kickoff in football in which the ball travels just far enough to be legally recoverable by the kicking team
on–site \-ˈsīt\ *adj or adv* (1946) : carried out or located at the place connected with a particular activity ⟨~ training in construction skills⟩
on·slaught \ˈän-ˌslȯt, ˈȯn-\ *n* [modif. of D *aanslag* act of striking; akin to OE *an* on and to OE *slēan* to strike — more at SLAY] (1625) : an esp. fierce attack; *also* : something resembling such an attack ⟨an ~ of technological changes⟩
on·stage \ˈȯn-ˈstāj, ˈän-, -ˌstāj\ *adv or adj* (1925) : on a part of the stage visible to the audience
ont- *or* **onto-** *comb form* [NL, fr. LGk, fr. Gk *ont-, ōn*, prp. of *einai* to be — more at IS] **1** : being : existence ⟨ontology⟩ **2** : organism ⟨ontogeny⟩
-ont \ˌänt\ *n comb form* [Gk *ont-, ōn*, prp.] : cell : organism ⟨diplont⟩
on–the–job *adj* (1946) : of, relating to, or being something (as training or experience) learned, gained, or done while working at a job and often under supervision
on·tic \ˈänt-ik\ *adj* (1942) : of, relating to, or having real being — **on·ti·cal·ly** \-i-k(ə-)lē\ *adv*
1**on·to** \ˌȯn-tə(-w), ˌän-; ˈȯn-(ˌ)tü, ˈän-\ *prep* (1581) **1** : to a position on **2** : in or into a state of awareness about ⟨put me ~ your methods⟩ **3** — used as a function word to indicate a set each element of which is the image of at least one element of another set ⟨a function mapping the set *S* ~ the set *T*⟩
2**on·to** \ˈȯn-(ˌ)tü, ˈän-\ *adj* (1942) : mapping elements in such a way that every element in one set is the image of at least one element in another set ⟨a function that is one-to-one and ~⟩ — compare SURJECTION
on·to·gen·e·sis \ˌänt-ə-ˈjen-ə-səs\ *n* [NL] (1875) : ONTOGENY
on·to·ge·net·ic \-jə-ˈnet-ik\ *adj* [ISV] (1878) **1** : of, relating to, or appearing in the course of ontogeny **2** : based on visible morphological characters — **on·to·ge·net·i·cal·ly** \-i-k(ə-)lē\ *adv*
on·tog·e·ny \än-ˈtäj-ə-nē\ *n* [ISV] (1872) : the development or course of development of an individual organism
on·to·log·i·cal \ˌänt-ᵊl-ˈäj-i-kəl\ *adj* (1782) **1** : of or relating to ontology **2** : relating to or based upon being or existence — **on·to·log·i·cal·ly** \-k(ə-)lē\ *adv*
ontological argument *n* (1877) : an argument for the existence of God based upon the meaning of the term *God*
on·tol·o·gy \än-ˈtäl-ə-jē\ *n* [NL *ontologia*, fr. *ont-* + *-logia* -logy] (1721) **1** : a branch of metaphysics concerned with the nature and relations of being **2** : a particular theory about the nature of being or the kinds of existents — **on·tol·o·gist** \-jəst\ *n*
onus \ˈō-nəs\ *n* (1640) **1** [L — more at ONEROUS] **a** : BURDEN **b** : a disagreeable necessity : OBLIGATION **c** : BLAME **d** : STIGMA **2** [NL *onus* (*probandi*), lit., burden of proving] : BURDEN OF PROOF
1**on·ward** \ˈȯn-wərd, ˈän-\ *also* **on·wards** \-wərdz\ *adv* (1532) : toward or at a point lying ahead in space or time : FORWARD
2**onward** *adj* (1674) : directed or moving onward : FORWARD
on·y·choph·o·ran \ˌän-i-ˈkäf-ə-rən\ *n* [NL *Onychophora*, group name, fr. Gk *onych-, onyx* claw + *-phoros* -phore] (ca. 1890) : PERIPATUS — **onychophoran** *adj*
-onym \ə-ˌnim\ *n comb form* [ME, fr. L *-onymum*, fr. Gk *-ōnymon*, fr. *onyma* — more at NAME] : name : word ⟨ant*onym*⟩
on·yx \ˈän-iks\ *n* [ME *onix*, fr. MF & L; MF, fr. L *onych-, onyx*, fr. Gk, lit., claw, nail — more at NAIL] (14c) : a translucent chalcedony in parallel layers of different colors
oo- — see O-
oo·cyst \ˈō-ə-ˌsist\ *n* [ISV] (1875) : ZYGOTE; *specif* : a sporozoan zygote undergoing sporogenous development
oo·cyte \ˈō-ə-ˌsīt\ *n* [ISV] (1895) : an egg before maturation : a female gametocyte
oo·dles \ˈüd-ᵊlz\ *also* **ood·lins** \ˈüd-lənz\ *n pl but sing or pl in constr* [perh. alter. of 2*huddle*] (1869) : a great quantity : LOT
oo·gamete \ˌō-ə-gə-ˈmēt, -ˈgam-ˌēt\ *n* (1891) : a female gamete; *specif* : a relatively large nonmotile gamete containing reserve material
oog·a·mous \ō-ˈäg-ə-məs\ *adj* (1888) : having or involving a small motile male gamete and a large immobile female gamete — **oog·a·my** \-mē\ *n*
oo·gen·e·sis \ˌō-ə-ˈjen-ə-səs\ *n* [NL] (ca. 1879) : formation and maturation of the egg — **oo·ge·net·ic** \-jə-ˈnet-ik\ *adj*
oo·go·ni·um \ˌō-ə-ˈgō-nē-əm\ *n, pl* **-nia** \-nē-ə\ [NL] (1867) **1** : a female sexual organ in various algae and fungi that corresponds to the archegonium of ferns and mosses **2** : a descendant of a primordial germ cell that gives rise to oocytes — **oo·go·ni·al** \-nē-əl\ *adj*
1**ooh** \ˈü\ *interj* (1939) — used to express amazement, joy, or surprise
2**ooh** *vi* (1951) : to exclaim in amazement, joy, or surprise ⟨~ing and aahing over the new automobiles⟩ — **ooh** *n*
oo·lite \ˈō-ə-ˌlīt\ *n* [prob. fr. F *oolithe*, fr. *oo-* o- + *-lithe* -lite] (1785) : a rock consisting of small round grains usu. of calcium carbonate cemented together — **oo·lit·ic** \ˌō-ə-ˈlit-ik\ *adj*
ool·o·gist \ō-ˈäl-ə-jəst\ *n* (1863) **1** : one specializing in the study of birds' eggs **2** : a collector of birds' eggs — **ool·o·gy** \-jē\ *n*
oo·long \ˈü-ˌlȯŋ\ *n* [Chin (Pek) *wu*[1] *lung*[2], lit., black dragon] (1850) : tea made from leaves that have been partially fermented before firing
oo·mi·ak *also* **oo·mi·ack** *var of* UMIAK
oom·pah \ˈüm-(ˌ)pä, ˈum-\ *also* **oom·pah–pah** \ˌüm-(ˌ)pä-ˈpä, ˌu̇m-\ *n* [imit.] (1877) : a repeated rhythmic bass accompaniment esp. in a band — **oompah** *vb*
oomph \ˈu̇m(p)f\ *n* [imit. of a sound made under exertion] (1936) **1** : personal charm or magnetism : GLAMOUR **2** : SEX APPEAL **3** : VITALITY
oo·pho·rec·to·my \ˌō-ə-fə-ˈrek-tə-mē\ *n, pl* **-mies** [NL, fr. *oophoron* ovary + *-ectomy*] (1872) : OVARIECTOMY
oops \ˈ(w)u̇(ə)ps\ *interj* (1933) — used typically to express mild apology, surprise, or dismay
oo·spore \ˈō-ə-ˌspō(ə)r, -ˌspȯ(ə)r\ *n* [ISV] (1865) : ZYGOTE; *esp* : a spore produced by heterogamous fertilization that yields a sporophyte
oo·the·ca \ˌō-ə-ˈthē-kə\ *n, pl* **oo·the·cae** \-ˈthē-(ˌ)kē, -(ˌ)sē\ [NL] (1851) : a firm-walled and distinctive egg case (as of a cockroach) — **oo·the·cal** \-ˈthē-kəl\ *adj*
oo·tid \ˈō-ə-ˌtid\ *n* [irreg. fr. *o-* + *-id*] (1904) : an egg cell after meiosis
1**ooze** \ˈüz\ *n* [ME *wose*, fr. OE *wāse* mire; akin to L *virus* slime — more at VIRUS] (bef. 12c) **1** : a soft deposit (as of mud, slime, or shells) on

the bottom of a body of water **2 :** a piece of soft wet plastic ground

[2]ooze *n* [ME *wose* sap, juice, fr. OE *wōs;* akin to OHG *waso* damp, Gk *hearon* ewer] (bef. 12c) **1 :** a decoction of vegetable material used for tanning leather **2 :** the act of oozing **3 :** something that oozes

[3]ooze *vb* **oozed; ooz·ing** *vi* (14c) **1 :** to pass or flow slowly through or as if through small openings or interstices **2 :** to move slowly or imperceptibly ⟨the crowd began to ~ forward —Bruce Marshall⟩ **3 a :** to exude moisture **b :** to exude something in a way suggestive of the emitting of moisture ⟨a woman *oozing* with charm⟩ ~ *vt* **1 :** to emit slowly **2 :** to exude in a way suggestive of the emitting of moisture

oozy \ˈü-zē\ *adj* **ooz·i·er; -est** (14c) **1 :** containing or composed of ooze **:** resembling ooze **2 :** exuding moisture **:** SLIMY

op \ˈäp\ *n* (1964) **:** OPTICAL ART

opac·i·ty \ō-ˈpas-ət-ē\ *n, pl* **-ties** [F *opacité* shadiness, fr. L *opacitat-, opacitas,* fr. *opacus* shaded, dark] (1611) **1 :** the quality or state of a body that makes it impervious to the rays of light; *broadly* **:** the relative capacity of matter to obstruct the transmission of radiant energy **2 a :** obscurity of sense **:** UNINTELLIGIBLENESS ⟨was put off by the ~ of much philosophical writing⟩ **b :** the quality or state of being mentally obtuse **:** DULLNESS **3 :** an opaque spot in a normally transparent structure (as the lens of the eye)

opah \ˈō-pə, -ˌpä\ *n* [Ibo *úbà*] (1750) **:** a large elliptical marine fish (*Lampris regius*) with brilliant colors and rich oily red flesh

opal \ˈō-pəl\ *n* [L *opalus,* fr. Skt *upala* stone, jewel] (14c) **:** a mineral $SiO_2 \cdot nH_2O$ that is a hydrated amorphous silica softer and less dense than quartz and typically with definite and often marked iridescent play of colors

opal·es·cent \ˌō-pə-ˈles-ᵊnt\ *adj* (1813) **:** reflecting an iridescent light — **opal·es·cence** \-ᵊn(t)s\ *n* — **opal·es·cent·ly** \-ᵊnt-lē\ *adv*

opal·ine \ˈō-pə-ˌlīn, -ˌlēn\ *adj* (1784) **:** resembling opal

[1]opaque \ō-ˈpāk\ *adj* [L *opacus*] (1641) **1 :** exhibiting opacity **:** not pervious to radiant energy and esp. light **2 a :** hard to understand or explain **b :** OBTUSE, THICKHEADED — **opaque·ly** *adv* — **opaque·ness** *n*

[2]opaque *n* (1742) **:** something that is opaque; *esp* **:** an opaque paint for blocking out portions of a photographic negative or print

opaque projector *n* (1951) **:** a projector using reflected light for projecting an image of an opaque object or matter on an opaque support (as a photograph)

op art \ˈäp-\ *n* (1964) **:** OPTICAL ART — **op artist** *n*

ope \ˈōp\ *vb* **oped; op·ing** *archaic* (15c) **:** OPEN

op–ed page \ˈäp-ˈed-\ *n* [short for *opposite editorial*] (1970) **:** a page of special features usu. opposite the editorial page of a newspaper

[1]open \ˈō-pən, ˈōp-ᵊm\ *adj* **open·er** \ˈōp-(ə-)nər\; **open·est** \ˈōp-(ə-)nəst\ [ME, fr. OE; akin to OHG *offan* open, OE *ūp* up] (bef. 12c) **1 :** having no enclosing or confining barrier **:** accessible on all or nearly all sides ⟨cattle grazing on an ~ range⟩ **2 a (1) :** being in a position or adjustment to permit passage **:** not shut or locked ⟨an ~ door⟩ **(2) :** having a barrier (as a door) so adjusted as to allow passage ⟨the house was ~⟩ **b :** having the lips parted ⟨stood there with his mouth wide ~⟩ **3 a :** completely free from concealment **:** exposed to general view or knowledge ⟨their hostilities eventually erupted with ~ war⟩ **b :** exposed or vulnerable to attack or question **:** SUBJECT ⟨~ to doubt⟩ **4 a :** not covered with a top, roof, or lid ⟨an ~ car⟩ ⟨her eyes were ~⟩ **b :** having no protective covering ⟨~ wiring⟩ ⟨an ~ wound⟩ **5 :** not restricted to a particular group or category of participants ⟨~ to the public⟩ ⟨~ housing⟩: as **a :** enterable by both amateur and professional contestants **b :** enterable by a registered voter regardless of political affiliation ⟨an ~ primary⟩ **6 :** fit to be traveled over **:** presenting no obstacle to passage or view ⟨the ~ road⟩ ⟨~ country⟩ **7 :** having the parts or surfaces laid out in an expanded position **:** spread out **:** UNFOLDED ⟨an ~ book⟩ **8 a (1) :** LOW 13 **(2) :** formed with the tongue in a lower position ⟨Italian has an ~ and a close *e*⟩ **b (1) :** having clarity and resonance unimpaired by undue tension or constriction of the throat ⟨an ~ vocal tone⟩ **(2)** *of a tone* **:** produced by an open string or on a wind instrument by the lip without the use of slides, valves, or keys **9 a :** available to follow or make use of ⟨the only course ~ to us⟩ **b :** not taken up with duties or engagements ⟨keep an hour ~ on Friday⟩ **c :** not finally decided **:** subject to further consideration ⟨leave the matter ~⟩ ⟨an ~ question⟩ **d :** available for a qualified applicant **:** VACANT ⟨the job is still ~⟩ **e :** remaining available for use or filling until canceled ⟨an ~ order for more items⟩ **f :** available for future purchase ⟨these items are in ~ stock⟩ ⟨an ~ pattern⟩ **10 a :** characterized by ready accessibility and usu. generous attitude: as **(1) :** generous in giving **(2) :** willing to hear and consider or to accept and deal with **:** RESPONSIVE **(3) :** free from reserve or pretense **:** FRANK **b :** accessible to the influx of new factors (as foreign goods) ⟨an ~ market⟩ **11 a :** having openings, interruptions, or spaces: as **(1) :** being porous and friable ⟨~ soil⟩ **(2) :** sparsely distributed **:** SCATTERED ⟨~ population⟩ **(3)** *of a compound* **:** having components separated by a space in writing or printing ⟨*Spanish mackerel* is an ~ compound⟩ **b :** not made up of a continuous closed circuit of channels ⟨the insect circulatory system is ~⟩ **12 a** *of an organ pipe* **:** not stopped at the top **b** *of a string on a musical instrument* **:** not stopped by the finger **13 :** being in operation ⟨the microphone is ~⟩; *esp* **:** ready for business, patronage, or use ⟨the store is ~ from 9 to 5⟩ ⟨the new highway will be ~ next week⟩ **14 a (1) :** characterized by lack of effective regulation of various commercial enterprises ⟨notorious as an ~ town⟩ **(2) :** not repressed by legal controls ⟨~ gambling⟩ **b :** free from checking or hampering restraints ⟨an ~ economy⟩ ⟨faced with ~ inflation⟩ **c :** relatively unguarded by opponents ⟨passed to an ~ teammate⟩ **15 :** having been opened by a first ante, bet, or bid ⟨the bidding is ~⟩ **16** *of punctuation* **:** characterized by sparing use esp. of the comma **17 a :** containing none of its endpoints ⟨an ~ interval⟩ **b :** being a set each point of which has a neighborhood all of whose points are contained in the set ⟨the interior of a sphere is an ~ set⟩ **18 a :** being an incomplete electrical circuit **b :** not allowing the flow of electricity ⟨an ~ switch⟩ ***syn*** see FRANK, LIABLE — **open** *adv* — **open·ly** \ˈō-pən-lē\ *adv* — **open·ness** \-pən-nəs\ *n*

[2]open \ˈō-pən, ˈōp-ᵊm\ *vb* **opened** \ˈō-pənd, ˈōp-ᵊmd\; **open·ing** \ˈōp-(ə-)niŋ\ *vt* (bef. 12c) **1 a :** to move (as a door) from closed position **b :** to make available for entry or passage by turning back (as a barrier), removing (as a cover), or clearing away (as an obstruction) **2 a :** to make available for or active in a regular function ⟨~ a new store⟩ **b :** to make accessible for a particular purpose ⟨~*ed* new land for settlement⟩ **3 a :** to disclose or expose to view **:** REVEAL **b :** to make more discerning or responsive **:** ENLIGHTEN ⟨must ~ our minds to the needs of minorities⟩ **c :** to bring into view or come in sight of by changing position **4 a :** to make one or more openings in ⟨~*ed* the boil⟩ **b :** to loosen and make less compact ⟨~ the soil⟩ **5 :** to spread out **:** UNFOLD ⟨~*ed* the book⟩ **6 a :** to enter upon **:** BEGIN ⟨~*ed* the meeting⟩ **b :** to commence action in a card game by making (a first bid), putting a first bet in (the pot), or playing (a card or suit) as first lead **7 :** to restore or recall (as an order) from a finally determined state to a state in which the parties are free to prosecute or oppose ~ *vi* **1 :** to become open ⟨the office ~*ed* early⟩ **2 a :** to spread out **:** EXPAND ⟨the wound ~*ed* under the strain⟩ **b :** to become disclosed ⟨a beautiful vista ~*ed* before us⟩ **3 :** to become enlightened or responsive **4 :** to give access ⟨the rooms ~ onto a hall⟩ **5 :** SPEAK OUT 2 ⟨finally he ~*ed* freely on the subject⟩ **6 a :** to begin a course or activity ⟨the play ~*s* on Tuesday⟩ **b :** to make a bet, bid, or lead in commencing a round or hand of a card game — **open·abil·i·ty** \ˌōp-(ə-)nə-ˈbil-ət-ē\ *n* — **open·able** \ˈōp-(ə-)nə-bəl\ *adj*

[3]open *n* (13c) **1 :** OPENING **2 :** open and unobstructed space: as **a :** OPEN AIR **b :** open water **3 :** an open contest, competition, or tournament **4 :** a public or unconcealed state or position

open admission *n* (1969) **:** OPEN ENROLLMENT 2

open–air *adj* (1830) **:** OUTDOOR

open air *n* (15c) **:** the space where air is unconfined; *esp* **:** OUTDOORS

open–and–shut \ˌōp-(ə-)nən-ˈshət\ *adj* (1841) **1 :** perfectly simple **:** OBVIOUS **2 :** easily settled ⟨an ~ case⟩

open bar *n* (1973) **:** a bar (as at a wedding reception) at which drinks are served free — compare CASH BAR

open chain *n* (1884) **:** an arrangement of atoms represented in a structural formula by a chain whose ends are not joined so as to form a ring

open city *n* (1914) **:** a city that is not occupied or defended by military forces and that is immune from enemy bombardment under international law

open dating *n* (1971) **:** the marking of perishable food products with a clearly readable date indicating when the food was packaged or the last date on which it should be sold or used

open door *n* (1526) **1 :** a recognized right of admittance **:** freedom of access **2 :** a policy giving opportunity for commercial relations with a country to all nations on equal terms — **open–door** *adj*

open–end *adj* (1917) **:** organized to allow for contingencies: as **a :** permitting additional debt to be incurred under the original indenture subject to specified conditions ⟨an ~ mortgage⟩ **b :** having a fluctuating capitalization of shares that are issued or redeemed at the current net asset value or at a figure in fixed ratio to this ⟨an ~ investment company⟩ — compare CLOSED-END

open–end·ed \ˌō-pə-ˈnen-dəd\ *adj* (1825) **:** not rigorously fixed: as **a :** adaptable to the developing needs of a situation **b :** permitting or designed to permit spontaneous and unguided responses — **open–end·ed·ness** *n*

open enrollment *n* (1964) **1 :** the voluntary enrollment of a student in a public school other than the one assigned on the basis of residence **2 :** enrollment on demand as a student in an institution of higher learning irrespective of formal qualifications

open·er \ˈōp-(ə-)nər\ *n* (15c) **:** one that opens ⟨a bottle ~⟩: as **a** *pl* **:** cards of sufficient value for a player to open the betting in a poker game **b :** the first item, contest, or event of a series — **for openers :** to begin with

open–eyed \ˌō-pə-ˈnīd\ *adj* (1601) **1 :** having the eyes open **2 :** carefully observant **:** DISCERNING

open·hand·ed \ˌō-pən-ˈhan-dəd\ *adj* (1601) **:** GENEROUS, MUNIFICENT — **open·hand·ed·ly** *adv* — **open·hand·ed·ness** *n*

open–heart *adj* (1960) **:** of, relating to, or performed on a heart temporarily relieved of circulatory function and surgically opened for inspection and treatment ⟨~ surgery⟩

open·heart·ed \ˌō-pən-ˈhärt-əd\ *adj* (1611) **1 :** candidly straightforward **:** FRANK **2 :** responsive to emotional appeal — **open·heart·ed·ly** *adv* — **open·heart·ed·ness** *n*

open–hearth *adj* (1885) **:** of, relating to, involving, or produced by an open hearth ⟨~ steel⟩

open–hearth process *n* (ca. 1890) **:** a process of making steel from pig iron in a furnace of the regenerative reverberatory type

open house *n* (15c) **1 :** ready and usu. informal hospitality or entertainment for all comers **2 :** a house or apartment open for inspection esp. by prospective buyers or tenants

open·ing \ˈōp-(ə-)niŋ\ *n* (12c) **1 a :** an act or instance of making or becoming open **b :** an act or instance of beginning **:** COMMENCEMENT; *esp* **:** a formal and usu. public event by which something new is put officially into operation **2 :** something that is open: as **a (1) :** BREACH, APERTURE **(2) :** an open width **:** SPAN **b :** an area without trees or with scattered usu. mature trees that occurs as a break in a forest **c :** two pages that face one another in a book **3 :** something that constitutes a beginning: as **a :** a planned series of moves made at the beginning of a game of chess or checkers — compare ENDGAME, MIDDLE GAME **b :** a first performance **4 a :** OCCASION, CHANCE **b :** an opportunity for employment

open letter *n* (1878) **:** a published letter of protest or appeal usu. addressed to an individual but intended for the general public

open loop *n* (1947) **:** a control system for an operation or process in which there is no self-correcting action as there is in a closed loop

open marriage *n* (1971) **:** a marriage in which the partners agree to let each other have sexual partners outside the marriage

open–mind·ed \ˌō-pən-ˈmīn-dəd\ *adj* (1828) **:** receptive to arguments or ideas **:** IMPARTIAL — **open–mind·ed·ly** *adv* — **open–mind·ed·ness** *n*

open·mouthed \ˌō-pən-ˈmau̇t͟hd, -ˈmau̇tht\ *adj* (1532) **1 :** having the mouth widely open **2 :** struck with amazement or wonder **3 :** CLAMOROUS, VOCIFEROUS — **open·mouth·ed·ly** \-ˈmau̇-t͟həd-lē, -thəd-\ *adv* — **open·mouth·ed·ness** \-ˈmau̇-t͟həd-nəs, -thəd-\ *n*

open–pol·li·nat·ed \ˌō-pən-ˈpäl-ə-ˌnāt-əd\ *adj* (1925) **:** pollinated by natural agencies without human intervention

open season *n* (ca. 1890) **:** a period during which it is legal to kill or catch game or fish protected at other times by law

open secret *n* (1879) **:** a supposedly secret but generally known matter

open sentence *n* (1937) **:** a statement (as in mathematics) that contains at least one blank or unknown and that becomes true or false when the blank is filled or a quantity is substituted for the unknown
open ses·a·me \-ˈses-ə-mē\ *n* [fr. *open sesame,* the magical command used by Ali Baba to open the door of the robbers' den in *Ali Baba and the Forty Thieves*] (1793) **:** something that unfailingly brings about a desired end
open shop *n* (1903) **:** an establishment in which eligibility for employment and retention on the payroll are not determined by membership or nonmembership in a labor union though there may be an agreement by which a union is recognized as sole bargaining agent
open sight *n* (1591) **:** a firearm rear sight having an open notch
open stance *n* (1948) **:** a preparatory position (as in baseball batting or golf) in which the forward foot (as the left foot of a right-handed person) is farther from the line of play than the back foot — compare CLOSED STANCE
open syllable *n* (1845) **:** a syllable ended by a vowel or diphthong
open up *vt* (1582) **1 :** to make available **2 :** to make plain or visible **:** DISCLOSE **3 :** to open by cutting into ~ *vi* **1 :** to spread out or come into view ⟨the road *opens up* ahead⟩ **2 :** to commence firing **3 :** to become communicative ⟨tried to get the patient to *open up*⟩
open·work \ˈō-pən-ˌwərk\ *n* (1598) **:** work constructed so as to show openings through its substance **:** work that is perforated or pierced ⟨wrought-iron ~⟩ — **open–worked** \-ˌwərkt\ *adj*
¹**opera** *pl of* OPUS
²**op·era** \ˈäp-(ə-)rə, *Southern also* ˈäp-rē\ *n* [It, work, opera, fr. L, work, pains; akin to L *oper-, opus*] (1644) **1 :** a drama set to music and made up of vocal pieces with orchestral accompaniment and orchestral overtures and interludes; *specif* **:** GRAND OPERA **2 :** the score of a musical drama **3 :** the performance of an opera; *also* **:** a house where operas are performed — **op·er·at·ic** \ˌäp-ə-ˈrat-ik\ *adj* — **op·er·at·i·cal·ly** \-i-k(ə-)lē\ *adv*
op·er·a·ble \ˈäp-(ə-)rə-bəl\ *adj* (1646) **1 :** fit, possible, or desirable to use **:** PRACTICABLE **2 :** likely to result in a favorable outcome upon surgical treatment ⟨an ~ cancer⟩ — **op·er·a·bil·i·ty** \ˌäp-(ə-)rə-ˈbil-ət-ē\ *n* — **op·er·a·bly** \ˈäp-ə-rə-blē\ *adv*
opé·ra bouffe \ˌäp-(ə-)rə-ˈbüf\ *n* [F, fr. It *opera buffa*] (1870) **:** satirical comic opera
op·era buf·fa \ˌäp-(ə-)rə-ˈbü-fə\ *n* [It, lit., comic opera] (1801) **:** an 18th century farcical comic opera with dialogue in recitative
opé·ra co·mique \ˌäp-(ə-)rə-käm-ˈēk, -kō-ˈmēk\ *n* [F] (1744) **:** COMIC OPERA
opera glass *n* (1738) **:** a small low-power binocular without prisms for use at the opera or theater — often used in pl.

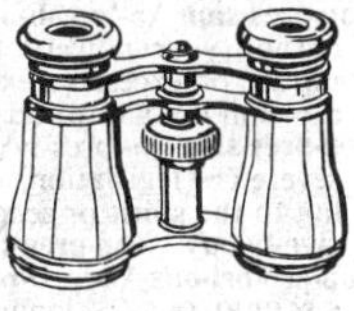
opera glass

op·era·go·er \ˈäp-(ə-)rə-ˌgō(-ə)r\ *n* (1850) **:** a person who frequently goes to operas — **op·era·go·ing** \-ˌgō-iŋ, -ˌgō(-)iŋ\ *n*
opera hat *n* (1810) **:** a man's collapsible top hat consisting usu. of a dull silky fabric stretched over a steel frame
opera house *n* (1720) **:** a theater devoted principally to the performance of operas; *broadly* **:** THEATER
op·er·and \ˌäp-ə-ˈrand\ *n* [L *operandum,* neut. of gerundive of *operari*] (1886) **:** something (as a quantity or data) that is operated on (as in a mathematical operation); *also* **:** the address in a computer instruction of data to be operated on
¹**op·er·ant** \ˈäp-ə-rənt\ *adj* (15c) **1 :** functioning or tending to produce effects **:** EFFECTIVE ⟨an ~ conscience⟩ **2 :** of or relating to the observable or measurable **3 :** of, relating to, or being an operant or operant conditioning ⟨~ behavior⟩ — **op·er·ant·ly** *adv*
²**operant** *n* (1937) **:** behavior (as bar pressing by a rat to obtain food) that operates on the environment to produce rewarding and reinforcing effects
operant conditioning *n* (1941) **:** conditioning in which the desired behavior or increasingly closer approximations to it are followed by a rewarding or reinforcing stimulus — compare CLASSICAL CONDITIONING
op·era se·ria \ˌäp-ə-rə-ˈser-ē-ə, -ˈsir-\ *n* [It, lit., serious opera] (ca. 1854) **:** an 18th century opera with a heroic or legendary subject
op·er·ate \ˈäp-(ə-)ˌrāt\ *vb* **-at·ed; -at·ing** [L *operatus,* pp. of *operari* to work, fr. *oper-, opus* work; akin to OE *efnan* to perform, Skt *apas* work] *vi* (1606) **1 :** to perform a function **:** exert power or influence ⟨factors *operating* against our success⟩ **2 :** to produce an appropriate effect ⟨the drug *operated* quickly⟩ **3 a :** to perform an operation or a series of operations **b :** to perform surgery **c :** to carry on a military or naval action or mission **4 :** to follow a course of conduct that is often irregular ⟨crooked gamblers *operating* in the club⟩ ~ *vt* **1 :** BRING ABOUT, EFFECT **2 a :** to cause to function **:** WORK **b :** to put or keep in operation **3 :** to perform an operation on; *esp* **:** to perform surgery on
op·er·at·ing \ˈäp-(ə-)ˌrāt-iŋ\ *adj* (1808) **:** of, relating to, or used for or in operations ⟨~ expenses⟩ ⟨a hospital ~ room⟩
operating system *n* (1961) **:** software that supports or complements the hardware of a computer system (as by keeping track of the different programs in multiprogramming)
op·er·a·tion \ˌäp-ə-ˈrā-shən\ *n* [ME *operacioun,* fr. MF *operation,* fr. L *operation-, operatio,* fr. *operatus,* pp.] (14c) **1 :** performance of a practical work or of something involving the practical application of principles or processes **2 a :** an exertion of power or influence ⟨the ~ of a drug⟩ **b :** the quality or state of being functional or operative ⟨the plant is now in ~⟩ **c :** a method or manner of functioning ⟨a machine of very simple ~⟩ **3 :** EFFICACY, POTENCY — archaic except in legal usage **4 :** a procedure carried out on a living body usu. with instruments esp. for the repair of damage or the restoration of health **5 :** any of various mathematical or logical processes (as addition) of deriving one entity from others according to a rule **6 a :** a usu. military action, mission, or maneuver including its planning and execution **b** *pl* **:** the office on the flight line of an airfield where pilots file clearance for flights and where flying from the field is controlled **c** *pl* **:** the agency of an organization charged with carrying on the principal planning and operating functions of a headquarters and its subordinate units **7 :** a business transaction esp. when speculative **8 :** a single step performed by a computer in the execution of a program
op·er·a·tion·al \-shnəl, -shən-ᵊl\ *adj* (ca. 1909) **1 :** of or relating to operation or to an operation ⟨the ~ gap between planning and production⟩ **2 :** of, relating to, or based on operations **3 a :** of, engaged in, or connected with execution of military or naval operations in campaign or battle **b :** ready for or in condition to undertake a destined function — **op·er·a·tion·al·ly** \-ē\ *adv*
op·er·a·tion·al·ism \-ˌiz-əm\ *n* (1931) **:** a view that the concepts or terms used in nonanalytic scientific statements must be definable in terms of identifiable and repeatable operations — **op·er·a·tion·al·ist** \-əst\ *n* — **op·er·a·tion·al·is·tic** \-ˌrā-shnəl-ˈis-tik, -shən-ᵊl-\ *adj*
op·er·a·tion·ism \ˌäp-ə-ˈrā-shə-ˌniz-əm\ *n* (1935) **:** OPERATIONALISM — **op·er·a·tion·ist** \-sh(ə-)nəst\ *n*
operations research *n* (ca. 1945) **:** the application of scientific and esp. mathematical methods to the study and analysis of problems involving complex systems (as firm management, economic planning, and the waging of war)
¹**op·er·a·tive** \ˈäp-(ə-)rət-iv, ˈäp-ə-ˌrāt-\ *adj* (15c) **1 :** producing an appropriate effect **:** EFFICACIOUS **2 :** exerting force or influence **:** OPERATING **3 a :** having to do with physical operations (as of machines) **b :** WORKING ⟨an ~ craftsman⟩ **4 :** based on or consisting of an operation ⟨~ dentistry⟩ — **op·er·a·tive·ly** *adv* — **op·er·a·tive·ness** *n*
²**operative** *n* (ca. 1809) **:** OPERATOR: as **a :** ARTISAN, MECHANIC **b :** a secret agent **c :** PRIVATE DETECTIVE
op·er·a·tor \ˈäp-(ə-)ˌrāt-ər\ *n* (1611) **1 :** one that operates: as **a :** one that operates a machine or device **b :** one that operates a business **c :** one that performs surgical operations **d :** one that deals in stocks or commodities **2 a :** MOUNTEBANK, FRAUD **b :** a shrewd and skillful person who knows how to circumvent restrictions or difficulties **3 a :** a mathematical or logical symbol denoting an operation to be performed **b :** a mathematical function **4 :** a chromosomal region that triggers formation of messenger RNA by one or more nearby structural genes and is itself subject to inhibition by a genetic repressor — called also *operator gene;* compare OPERON — **op·er·a·tor·less** *adj*
¹**oper·cu·lar** \ō-ˈpər-kyə-lər\ *adj* (1830) **:** of, relating to, or constituting an operculum
²**opercular** *n* (ca. 1890) **:** an opercular part (as a bone or scale)
oper·cu·late \ō-ˈpər-kyə-lət\ *also* **oper·cu·lat·ed** \-ˌlāt-əd\ *adj* (1775) **:** having an operculum
oper·cu·lum \ō-ˈpər-kyə-ləm\ *n, pl* **-la** \-lə\ *also* **-lums** [NL, fr. L, cover, fr. *operire* to shut, cover] (1788) **1 :** a lid or covering flap (as of a moss capsule or a pyxidium in a seed plant) **2 :** a body process or part that suggests a lid: as **a :** a horny or shelly plate on the posterior dorsal surface of the foot in many gastropod mollusks that closes the shell when the animal is retracted **b :** the covering of the gills of a fish — see FISH illustration
op·er·et·ta \ˌäp-ə-ˈret-ə\ *n* [It, dim. of *opera*] (1770) **:** a usu. romantic comic opera that includes songs and dancing — **op·er·et·tist** \-ˈret-əst\ *n*
op·er·on \ˈäp-ə-ˌrän\ *n* [*oper*ator + ²*-on*] (1961) **:** the closely linked combination of an operator and the structural genes it regulates
op·er·ose \ˈäp-ə-ˌrōs\ *adj* [L *operosus,* fr. *oper-, opus* work — more at OPERATE] (1678) **:** TEDIOUS, WEARISOME — **op·er·ose·ly** *adv* — **op·er·ose·ness** *n*
Ophe·lia \ō-ˈfēl-yə\ *n* **:** the daughter of Polonius in Shakespeare's *Hamlet*
ophid·i·an \ō-ˈfid-ē-ən\ *adj* [deriv. of Gk *ophis*] (1883) **:** of, relating to, or resembling snakes — **ophidian** *n*
ophi·oph·a·gous \ˌō-fē-ˈäf-ə-gəs, ˌäf-ē-\ *adj* [Gk *ophiophagos,* fr. *ophis* + *-phagos* -phagous] (1650) **:** feeding on snakes
Ophir \ˈō-fər\ *n* [Heb *Ōphīr*] **:** a biblical land of uncertain location but reputedly rich in gold
ophite \ˈäf-ˌīt, ˈō-ˌfīt\ *n* [ME, fr. L, fr. Gk *ophitēs* (*lithos*), lit., serpentine (stone), fr. *ophitēs* snakelike, fr. *ophis* snake; akin to L *anguis* snake, *anguilla* eel, Gk *enchelys* eel, *echidna* viper, *echinos* hedgehog, OE *igil*] (14c) **:** any of various usu. green and often mottled or blotched rocks
ophit·ic \ä-ˈfit-ik, ō-\ *adj* (1875) **:** having or being a rock fabric in which lath-shaped plagioclase crystals are enclosed in later formed augite
ophi·u·roid \ˌō-fē-ˈyü(ə)r-ˌȯid, ˌäf-ē-\ *n* [NL *Ophiuroidea,* group name, fr. *Ophiura,* genus name, fr. Gk *ophis* + *oura* tail — more at ASS] (ca. 1879) **:** BRITTLE STAR — **ophiuroid** *adj*
ophthalm- *or* **ophthalmo-** *comb form* [Gk, fr. *ophthalmos*] **:** eye ⟨*ophthalmology*⟩ **:** eyeball ⟨*ophthalmitis*⟩
oph·thal·mia \äf-ˈthal-mē-ə, äp-\ *n* [ME *obtalmia,* fr. LL *ophthalmia,* fr. Gk, fr. *ophthalmos* eye; akin to Gk *ōps* eye — more at EYE] (14c) **:** inflammation of the conjunctiva or the eyeball
oph·thal·mic \-mik\ *adj* (1727) **1 :** of, relating to, or situated near the eye **2 :** supplying or draining the eye or structures in the region of the eye ⟨~ artery⟩
oph·thal·mol·o·gist \ˌäf-thə(l)-ˈmäl-ə-jəst, ˌäp-, -ˌthal-\ *n* (1834) **:** a physician that specializes in ophthalmology — compare OPTICIAN, OPTOMETRIST
oph·thal·mol·o·gy \-ˈmäl-ə-jē\ *n* (1842) **:** a branch of medical science dealing with the structure, functions, and diseases of the eye — **oph·thal·mo·log·ic** \-mə-ˈläj-ik\ *or* **oph·thal·mo·log·i·cal** \-i-kəl\ *adj* — **oph·thal·mo·log·i·cal·ly** \-i-k(ə-)lē\ *adv*
oph·thal·mo·scope \äf-ˈthal-mə-ˌskōp, äp-\ *n* [ISV] (ca. 1857) **:** an instrument with a mirror centrally perforated for use in viewing the interior of the eye and esp. the retina — **oph·thal·mo·scop·ic** \(ˌ)äf-ˌthal-mə-ˈskäp-ik, (ˌ)äp-\ *adj* — **oph·thal·mos·co·py** \ˌäf-ˌthal-ˈmäs-kə-pē, ˌäp-\ *n*
-opia \ˈō-pē-ə\ *n comb form* [NL, fr. Gk *-ōpia,* fr. *ōps*] **1 :** condition of having (such) vision ⟨diplo*pia*⟩ **2 :** condition of having (such) a visual defect ⟨hyper*opia*⟩
¹**opi·ate** \ˈō-pē-ət, -ˌāt\ *n* (15c) **1 :** a preparation or derivative of opium; *broadly* **:** NARCOTIC 1a **2 :** something that induces rest or inaction or quiets uneasiness
²**opiate** *adj* (1543) **1 :** containing or mixed with opium **2 a :** inducing sleep **:** NARCOTIC **b :** causing dullness or inaction

opine \ō-ˈpīn\ *vb* **opined; opin·ing** [ME *opinen,* fr. MF *opiner,* fr. L *opinari* to have an opinion] *vt* (15c) **:** to state as an opinion ~ *vi* **:** to express opinions

opin·ion \ə-ˈpin-yən\ *n* [ME, fr. MF, fr. L *opinion-, opinio;* akin to L *opinari*] (14c) **1 a :** a view, judgment, or appraisal formed in the mind about a particular matter **b :** APPROVAL, ESTEEM **2 a :** belief stronger than impression and less strong than positive knowledge **b :** a generally held view **3 a :** a formal expression of judgment or advice by an expert **b :** the formal expression (as by a judge, court, or referee) of the legal reasons and principles upon which a legal decision is based — **opin·ioned** \-yənd\ *adj*

syn OPINION, VIEW, BELIEF, CONVICTION, PERSUASION, SENTIMENT mean a judgment one holds as true. OPINION implies a conclusion thought out yet open to dispute; VIEW suggests a subjective opinion; BELIEF implies often deliberate acceptance and intellectual assent; CONVICTION applies to a firmly and seriously held belief; PERSUASION suggests a belief grounded on assurance (as by evidence) of its truth; SENTIMENT suggests a settled opinion reflective of one's feelings.

opin·ion·at·ed \-yə-ˌnāt-əd\ *adj* (1601) **:** unduly adhering to one's own opinion or to preconceived notions — **opin·ion·at·ed·ly** *adv* — **opin·ion·at·ed·ness** *n*

opin·ion·ative \-ˌnāt-iv\ *adj* (1536) **1 :** of, relating to, or consisting of opinion **:** DOCTRINAL **2 :** OPINIONATED — **opin·ion·ative·ly** *adv* — **opin·ion·ative·ness** *n*

opi·oid \ˈō-pē-ˌȯid\ *adj* [[1]*opiate* + *-oid*] (1957) **1 :** possessing some properties characteristic of opiate narcotics but not derived from opium **2 :** of, involving, or induced by an opioid substance or an opioid peptide

opioid peptide *n* (1977) **:** any of a group of endogenous neural polypeptides (as an endorphin or enkephalin) that bind esp. to opiate receptors and mimic some of the pharmacological properties of opiates — called also *opioid*

opis·tho·branch \ə-ˈpis-thə-ˌbraŋk\ *n, pl* **-branchs** [NL *Opisthobranchia,* fr. Gk *opisthen* behind + *branchion* gill — more at BRANCHIA] (1851) **:** any of a large order (Opisthobranchia) of marine gastropod mollusks that have the gills when present posterior to the heart and have no operculum — **opisthobranch** *adj*

op·is·thog·na·thous \ˌäp-əs-ˈthäg-nə-thəs\ *adj* [Gk *opisthen* + E *-gnathous;* akin to Gk *epi-* on — more at EPI-] (1864) **1 :** having retreating jaws **2 :** having the mouthparts ventral and posterior to the cranium — used esp. of insects

opi·um \ˈō-pē-əm\ *n* [ME, fr. L, fr. Gk *opion,* fr. dim. of *opos* sap] (14c) **1 :** a bitter brownish addictive narcotic drug that consists of the dried juice of the opium poppy **2 :** something having an effect like that of opium

opium poppy *n* (1863) **:** an annual Eurasian poppy (*Papaver somniferum*) cultivated since antiquity as the source of opium, for its edible oily seeds, or for its showy flowers

opos·sum \(ə-)ˈpäs-əm\ *n, pl* **opossums** *also* **opossum** [fr. *âpäsûm,* lit., white animal (in some Algonquian language of Virginia)] (1610) **1 :** any of various American marsupials (family Didelphidae); *esp* **:** a common omnivorous largely nocturnal and arboreal mammal (*Didelphis virginiana*) of the eastern U.S. **2 :** any of several Australian phalangers

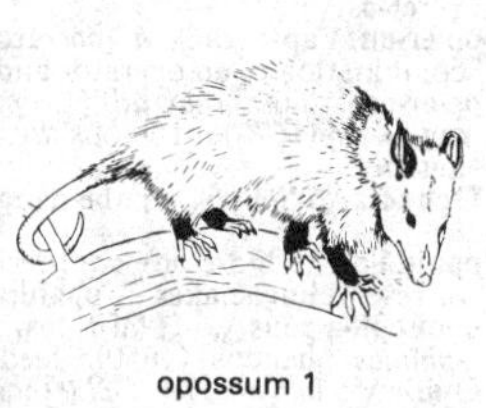

opossum 1

[1]**op·po·nent** \ə-ˈpō-nənt\ *n* [L *opponent-, opponens,* prp. of *opponere*] (1588) **1 :** one that takes an opposite position (as in a debate, contest, or conflict) **2 :** a muscle that opposes or counteracts and limits the action of another

[2]**opponent** *adj* (1647) **1 :** ANTAGONISTIC, OPPOSING **2 :** situated in front

op·por·tune \ˌäp-ər-ˈt(y)ün\ *adj* [ME, fr. MF *opportun,* fr. L *opportunus,* fr. *ob-* toward + *portus* port, harbor — more at OB-] (15c) **1 :** suitable or convenient for a particular occurrence ⟨an ~ moment⟩ **2 :** occurring at an appropriate time ⟨an ~ offer of assistance⟩ — **op·por·tune·ly** *adv* — **op·por·tune·ness** \-ˈt(y)ün-nəs\ *n*

op·por·tun·ism \-ˈt(y)ü-ˌniz-əm\ *n* (1870) **:** the art, policy, or practice of taking advantage of opportunities or circumstances esp. with little regard for principles or consequences — **op·por·tun·ist** \-nəst\ *n or adj* — **op·por·tu·nis·tic** \-t(y)ü-ˈnis-tik\ *adj* — **op·por·tu·nis·ti·cal·ly** \-ti-k(ə-)lē\ *adv*

op·por·tu·ni·ty \ˌäp-ər-ˈt(y)ü-nət-ē\ *n, pl* **-ties** (14c) **1 :** a favorable juncture of circumstances ⟨the halt provided an ~ for rest and refreshment⟩ **2 :** a good chance for advancement or progress

opportunity cost *n* (1911) **:** the cost of making an investment that is the difference between the return on one investment and the return on an alternative

op·pos·able \ə-ˈpō-zə-bəl\ *adj* (1667) **1 :** capable of being opposed or resisted **2 :** capable of being placed against one or more of the remaining digits of a hand or foot ⟨man's ~ thumb⟩ — **op·pos·abil·i·ty** \-ˌpō-zə-ˈbil-ət-ē\ *n*

op·pose \ə-ˈpōz\ *vt* **op·posed; op·pos·ing** [F *opposer,* deriv. of L *opponere,* fr. *ob-* against + *ponere* to place — more at OB-, POSITION] (1579) **1 :** to place opposite or against something **2 :** to place over against something so as to provide resistance, counterbalance, or contrast **3 :** to offer resistance to — **op·pos·er** *n*

syn OPPOSE, COMBAT, RESIST, WITHSTAND, ANTAGONIZE mean to set oneself against someone or something. OPPOSE can apply to any conflict, from mere objection to bitter hostility or warfare; COMBAT stresses the forceful or urgent countering of something; RESIST implies an overt recognition of a hostile or threatening force and a positive effort to counteract or repel it; WITHSTAND suggests a more passive resistance; ANTAGONIZE implies an arousing of resistance or hostility in another.

op·posed \-ˈpōzd\ *adj* (1597) **:** set or placed in opposition **:** CONTRARY

op·pose·less \ə-ˈpōz-ləs\ *adj, archaic* (1605) **:** IRRESISTIBLE

[1]**op·po·site** \ˈäp-ə-zət, ˈäp-sət\ *adj* [ME, fr. MF, fr. L *oppositus,* pp. of *opponere*] (14c) **1 a :** set over against something that is at the other end or side of an intervening line or space ⟨~ interior angles⟩ ⟨~ ends of a diameter⟩ **b :** situated in pairs on an axis with each member being separated from the other by half the circumference of the axis ⟨~ leaves⟩ — compare ALTERNATE **2 a :** occupying an opposing and often antagonistic position ⟨~ sides of the question⟩ **b :** diametrically different (as in nature or character) ⟨~ meanings⟩ **3 :** contrary to one another or to a thing specified **:** REVERSE ⟨gave them ~ directions⟩ **4 :** being the other of a pair that are corresponding or complementary in position, function, or nature ⟨members of the ~ sex⟩ **5 :** of, relating to, or being the side of a baseball field that is near the first base line for a right-handed batter and near the third base line for a left-handed batter — **op·po·site·ly** *adv* — **op·po·site·ness** *n*

syn OPPOSITE, CONTRADICTORY, CONTRARY, ANTITHETICAL mean being so far apart as to be or seem irreconcilable. OPPOSITE applies to things in sharp contrast or in conflict; CONTRADICTORY applies to two things that completely negate each other so that if one is true or valid the other must be untrue or invalid; CONTRARY implies extreme divergence or diametrical opposition; ANTITHETICAL stresses clear and unequivocal diametrical opposition.

[2]**opposite** *n* (15c) **1 :** something that is opposed or contrary **2 :** ANTONYM **3 :** ADDITIVE INVERSE; *esp* **:** the additive inverse of a real number

[3]**opposite** *adv* (1667) **:** on or to an opposite side

[4]**opposite** *prep* (1758) **1 :** across from and usu. facing or on the same level with ⟨sat ~ each other⟩ **2 :** in a role complementary to ⟨played ~ the leading man in the comedy⟩

opposite number *n* (1906) **:** a member of a system or class who holds relatively the same position as a particular member in a corresponding system or class **:** COUNTERPART ⟨union executives met with their *opposite numbers* in industry⟩

op·po·si·tion \ˌäp-ə-ˈzish-ən\ *n* (14c) **1 :** a configuration in which one celestial body is opposite another in the sky or in which the elongation is near or equal to 180 degrees **2 :** the relation between two propositions having the same subject and predicate but differing in quantity or quality or both **3 :** an act of setting opposite or over against **:** the condition of being so set **4 :** hostile or contrary action or condition **5 a :** something that opposes; *specif* **:** a body of persons opposing something **b** *often cap* **:** a political party opposing and prepared to replace the party in power — **op·po·si·tion·al** \-ˈzish-nəl, -ən-ᵊl\ *adj*

op·po·si·tion·ist \-ˈzish(-ə)-nəst\ *n* (1773) **:** a member of an opposition — **oppositionist** *adj*

op·press \ə-ˈpres\ *vt* [ME *oppressen,* fr. MF *oppresser,* fr. L *oppressus,* pp. of *opprimere,* fr. *ob-* against + *premere* to press — more at OB-, PRESS] (14c) **1 a** *archaic* **:** SUPPRESS **b :** to crush or burden by abuse of power or authority **2 :** to burden spiritually or mentally **:** weigh heavily upon *syn* see WRONG — **op·pres·sor** \-ˈpres-ər\ *n*

op·pres·sion \ə-ˈpresh-ən\ *n* (14c) **1 a :** unjust or cruel exercise of authority or power **b :** something that oppresses esp. in being an unjust or excessive exercise of power **2 :** a sense of being weighed down in body or mind **:** DEPRESSION

op·pres·sive \ə-ˈpres-iv\ *adj* (1627) **1 :** unreasonably burdensome or severe ⟨~ legislation⟩ **2 :** TYRANNICAL **3 :** overwhelming or depressing to the spirit or senses ⟨an ~ climate⟩ *syn* see ONEROUS — **op·pres·sive·ly** *adv* — **op·pres·sive·ness** *n*

op·pro·bri·ous \ə-ˈprō-brē-əs\ *adj* (14c) **1 :** expressive of opprobrium **:** SCURRILOUS ⟨~ language⟩ **2 :** deserving of opprobrium **:** INFAMOUS — **op·pro·bri·ous·ly** *adv* — **op·pro·bri·ous·ness** *n*

op·pro·bri·um \-brē-əm\ *n* [L, fr. *opprobrare* to reproach, fr. *ob* in the way of + *probrum* reproach; akin to L *pro* forward and to L *ferre* to carry, bring — more at FOR, BEAR] (1683) **1 :** something that brings disgrace **2 a :** public disgrace or ill fame that follows from conduct considered grossly wrong or vicious **b :** CONTEMPT, REPROACH

op·pugn \ə-ˈpyün, ä-\ *vt* [ME *oppugnen,* fr. L *oppugnare,* fr. *ob-* against + *pugnare* to fight — more at OB-, PUNGENT] (15c) **1 :** to fight against **:** ASSAIL **2 :** to call in question — **op·pugn·er** *n*

Ops \ˈäps\ *n* [L] **:** the Roman goddess of abundance and the wife of Saturn

op·sin \ˈäp-sən\ *n* [prob. back-formation fr. *rhodopsin*] (ca. 1951) **:** any of various colorless proteins that are formed with retinal by the action of light on a visual pigment (as rhodopsin)

-op·sis \ˈäp-səs\ *n comb form, pl* **-op·ses** \-ˌsēz\ *or* **-op·si·des** \-sə-ˌdēz\ [NL, fr. Gk, fr. *opsis* appearance, vision] **:** structure resembling a (specified) thing ⟨cary*opsis*⟩

op·son·ic \äp-ˈsän-ik\ *adj* (1903) **:** of, relating to, or involving opsonin

op·so·nin \ˈäp-sə-nən\ *n* [L *opsonium* relish (fr. Gk *opsōnion* victuals, fr. *opsōnein* to purchase victuals) + E *-in* — more at OLIGOPSONY] (1903) **:** an antibody of blood serum that makes foreign cells more susceptible to the action of the phagocytes

-op·sy \ˌäp-sē, əp-\ *n comb form* [Gk *-opsia,* fr. *opsis*] **:** examination ⟨necr*opsy*⟩

opt \ˈäpt\ *vi* [F *opter,* fr. L *optare* — more at OPTION] (1877) **:** to make a choice; *esp* **:** to decide in favor of something ⟨~*ed* for a tax increase — Tom Wicker⟩

op·ta·tive \ˈäp-tət-iv\ *adj* (15c) **1 a :** of, relating to, or constituting a verbal mood that is expressive of wish or desire **b :** of, relating to, or constituting a sentence that is expressive of wish or hope **2 :** expressing desire or wish — **optative** *n* — **op·ta·tive·ly** *adv*

[1]**op·tic** \ˈäp-tik\ *adj* [ME, fr. MF *optique,* fr. ML *opticus,* fr. Gk *optikos,* fr. *opsesthai* to be going to see; akin to Gk *opsis* appearance, *ōps* eye — more at EYE] (14c) **:** of or relating to vision or the eye

[2]**optic** *n* (1600) **1 :** EYE **2 :** any of the lenses, prisms, or mirrors of an optical instrument; *also* **:** an optical instrument

op·ti·cal \ˈäp-ti-kəl\ *adj* (1570) **1 :** of or relating to the science of optics **2 a :** of or relating to vision **:** VISUAL **b :** of, relating to, or being objects that emit light in the visible range of frequencies ⟨an ~ galaxy⟩ **c :** designed to aid vision ⟨an ~ instrument⟩ **3 a :** of, relating to, or utilizing light ⟨an ~ emission⟩ ⟨an ~ telescope⟩ ⟨~ microscopy⟩ **b :** involving the use of light-sensitive devices to acquire information for a computer ⟨~ character recognition⟩ **4 :** of or relating to optical art — **op·ti·cal·ly** \-k(ə-)lē\ *adv*

optical activity *n* (1877) **:** ability to rotate the plane of vibration of polarized light to the right or left

optical art *n* (1964) **:** nonobjective art characterized by the use of straight or curved lines or geometric patterns often for an illusory effect (as of motion)

optical bench *n* (1883) **:** an apparatus that is fitted for the convenient location and adjustment of light sources and optical devices and that is used for the observation and measurement of optical phenomena
optical disc *n* (1980) **:** a disc with a plastic coating on which information (as music or visual images) is recorded digitally as tiny pits and which is read by using a laser
optical fiber *n* (1962) **:** a single fiber-optic strand
optical glass *n* (1840) **:** flint or crown glass of well-defined characteristics used esp. for making lenses
optical illusion *n* (1794) **:** ILLUSION 2a(1)
optical rotation *n* (1895) **:** the angle through which the plane of vibration of polarized light that traverses an optically active substance is rotated
optic axis *n* (1664) **:** a line in a doubly refracting medium that is parallel to the direction in which all components of plane-polarized light travel with the same speed
optic chiasma *n* [NL *chiasma* X-shaped configuration — more at CHIASMA] (1872) **:** the X-shaped partial decussation on the undersurface of the hypothalamus through which the optic nerves are continuous with the brain — called also *optic chiasm*
optic cup *n* (ca. 1885) **:** the optic vesicle after invaginating to form a 2-layered cup from which the retina and pigmented layer of the eye will develop — called also *eyecup*
optic disk *n* (ca. 1890) **:** BLIND SPOT 1a
op·ti·cian \äp-ˈtish-ən\ *n* (1687) **1 :** a maker of or dealer in optical items and instruments **2 :** one that grinds lenses to prescription and dispenses spectacles — compare OPHTHALMOLOGIST, OPTOMETRIST
optic lobe *n* (1854) **:** either of two prominences of the midbrain concerned with vision
optic nerve *n* (15c) **:** either of the pair of nerves that comprise the 2d pair of cranial nerves, arise from the ventral part of the diencephalon, supply the retina, and conduct visual stimuli to the brain — see EYE illustration
op·tics \ˈäp-tiks\ *n pl but sing or pl in constr* (1579) **1 :** a science that deals with the genesis and propagation of light, the changes that it undergoes and produces, and other phenomena closely associated with it **2 :** optical properties
optic vesicle *n* (ca. 1885) **:** an evagination of each lateral wall of the embryonic vertebrate forebrain from which the nervous structures of the eye develop
op·ti·mal \ˈäp-tə-məl\ *adj* (1890) **:** most desirable or satisfactory **:** OPTIMUM — **op·ti·mal·i·ty** \ˌäp-tə-ˈmal-ət-ē\ *n* — **op·ti·mal·ly** \-mə-lē\ *adv*
op·ti·mism \ˈäp-tə-ˌmiz-əm\ *n* [F *optimisme,* fr. L *optimum,* n., best, fr. neut. of *optimus* best; akin to L *ops* power — more at OPULENT] (1759) **1 :** a doctrine that this world is the best possible world **2 :** an inclination to put the most favorable construction upon actions and events or to anticipate the best possible outcome — **op·ti·mist** \-məst\ *n* — **op·ti·mis·tic** \ˌäp-tə-ˈmis-tik\ *adj* — **op·ti·mis·ti·cal·ly** \-ti-k(ə-)lē\ *adv*
Op·ti·mist \ˈäp-tə-məst\ *n* [*Optimist (club)*] (1911) **:** a member of a major international service club
op·ti·mi·za·tion \ˌäp-tə-mə-ˈzā-shən\ *n* (1857) **:** an act, process, or methodology of making something (as a design, system, or decision) as fully perfect, functional, or effective as possible; *specif* **:** the mathematical procedures (as finding the maximum of a function) involved in this
op·ti·mize \ˈäp-tə-ˌmīz\ *vt* **-mized; -miz·ing** (1857) **:** to make as perfect, effective, or functional as possible — **op·ti·miz·er** \-ˌmī-zər\ *n*
op·ti·mum \ˈäp-tə-məm\ *n, pl* **-ma** \-mə\ *also* **-mums** [L] (1879) **1 :** the amount or degree of something that is most favorable to some end; *esp* **:** the most favorable condition for the growth and reproduction of an organism **2 :** greatest degree attained or attainable under implied or specified conditions — **optimum** *adj*
1op·tion \ˈäp-shən\ *n* [F, fr. L *option-, optio* free choice; akin to L *optare* to choose, Gk epi*opsesthai* to be going to choose] (ca. 1604) **1 :** an act of choosing **2 a :** the power or right to choose **:** freedom of choice **b :** a privilege of demanding fulfillment of a contract on any day within a specified time **c :** a contract conveying a right to buy or sell designated securities or commodities at a specified price during a stipulated period; *also* **:** the right conveyed by an option **d :** a right of an insured person to choose the form in which payments due him on a policy shall be made or applied **3 :** something that may be chosen: as **a :** an alternative course of action ⟨didn't have many ~*s* open⟩ **b :** an item that is offered in addition to or in place of standard equipment ⟨a car that includes air-conditioning among its ~*s*⟩ **4 :** an offensive football play in which a back may choose whether to pass or run with the ball — called also *option pass, option play* ***syn*** see CHOICE
2option *vt* (1926) **:** to grant or take an option on
op·tion·al \ˈäp-shnəl, -shən-ᵊl\ *adj* (1792) **:** involving an option **:** not compulsory — **op·tion·al·ly** \-ē\ *adv*
op·to·elec·tron·ics \ˌäp-(ˌ)tō-i-lek-ˈträn-iks\ *n pl but sing in constr* (1959) **:** a branch of electronics that deals with electronic devices for emitting, modulating, transmitting, and sensing light — **op·to·elec·tron·ic** \-ik\ *adj*
op·to·ki·net·ic \ˌäp-tō-kə-ˈnet-ik, -kī-\ *adj* [Gk *optos* + *kinetic*] (1925) **:** of, relating to, or involving movements of the eyes
op·tom·e·trist \äp-ˈtäm-ə-trəst\ *n* (1903) **:** a specialist licensed to practice optometry — compare OPHTHALMOLOGIST, OPTICIAN
op·tom·e·try \-trē\ *n* [Gk *optos* (verbal of *opsesthai* to be going to see) + ISV *-metry* — more at OPTIC] (1886) **:** the art or profession of examining the eye for defects and faults of refraction and prescribing correctional lenses or exercises but not drugs or surgery — **op·to·met·ric** \ˌäp-tə-ˈme-trik\ *adj*
opt out *vi* (1951) **:** to choose not to participate in something — often used with *of* ⟨*opted out* of the project⟩
op·u·lence \ˈäp-yə-lən(t)s\ *n* (1510) **1 :** WEALTH, AFFLUENCE **2 :** ABUNDANCE, PROFUSION
op·u·lent \-lənt\ *adj* [L *opulentus,* fr. *ops* power, help; akin to L *opus* work] (1601) **:** exhibiting or characterized by opulence: as **a :** having a large estate or property **:** WEALTHY ⟨hoping to marry an ~ widow⟩ **b :** amply or plentifully provided or fashioned often to the point of ostentation ⟨living in ~ comfort⟩ ***syn*** see RICH — **op·u·lent·ly** *adv*
opun·tia \ō-ˈpən-ch(ē-)ə\ *n* [L, a plant, fr. fem. of *opuntius* of Opus, fr. *Opunt-, Opus* Opus, ancient city in Greece] (ca. 1601) **:** PRICKLY PEAR
opus \ˈō-pəs\ *n, pl* **opera** \ˈō-pə-rə, ˈäp-ə-\ *also* **opus·es** \ˈō-pə-səz\ [L *oper-, opus* — more at OPERATE] (1809) **:** WORK; *esp* **:** a musical composition or set of compositions usu. numbered in the order of its issue
opus·cule \ō-ˈpəs-(ˌ)kyü(ə)l\ *n* [F, fr. L *opusculum,* dim. of *opus*] (ca. 1656) **:** a small or petty work **:** OPUSCULUM
opus·cu·lum \ō-ˈpəs-kyə-ləm\ *n, pl* **-la** \-lə\ [L] (1654) **:** a minor work (as of literature) — usu. used in pl.
1or \ər, (ˌ)ȯ(ə)r, *Southern also* (ˌ)är\ *conj* [ME *other, or,* fr. OE *oththe;* akin to OHG *eddo* or] (bef. 12c) **1 —** used as a function word to indicate an alternative ⟨coffee ~ tea⟩ ⟨sink ~ swim⟩, the equivalent or substitutive character of two words or phrases ⟨lessen ~ abate⟩, or approximation or uncertainty ⟨in five ~ six days⟩ **2** *archaic* **:** EITHER **3** *archaic* **:** WHETHER **4 —** used in logic as a sentential connective that forms a complex sentence which is true when at least one of its constituent sentences is true — compare DISJUNCTION
2or *prep* [ME, fr. *or,* adv., early, before, fr. ON *ār;* akin to OE *ǣr* early — more at ERE] *archaic* (13c) **:** BEFORE
3or *conj, archaic* (13c) **:** BEFORE
4or \ˈȯ(ə)r\ *n* [ME, fr. MF, gold, fr. L *aurum* — more at ORIOLE] (15c) **:** the heraldic color gold or yellow
OR \ˈȯ(ə)r\ *n* [*1or*] (1947) **:** a logical operator equivalent to the sentential connective *or* ⟨~ gate in a computer⟩
1-or \ər, ˌȯ(ə)r, ˈȯ(ə)r\ *n suffix* [ME, fr. OF *-eur, -eor* & L *-or;* OF *-eur,* fr. L *-or;* OF *-eor,* fr. L *-ator* -or, fr. *-atus,* pp. suffix + *-or* — more at -ATE] **:** one that does a (specified) thing ⟨grant*or*⟩
2-or \ər\ *n suffix* [ME, fr. OF *-eur,* fr. L *-or*] **:** condition **:** activity ⟨deme*anor*⟩
ora *pl of* OS
or·ache *or* **or·ach** \ˈȯr-ich, ˈär-\ *n* [ME *orage,* fr. MF *arrache,* fr. (assumed) VL *atripic-, atrapex,* fr. Gk *atraphaxys*] (14c) **:** any of a genus (*Atriplex*) of herbs of the goosefoot family that have small diclinous flowers and a utricular fruit enclosed in two bracts
or·a·cle \ˈȯr-ə-kəl, ˈär-\ *n* [ME, fr. MF, fr. L *oraculum,* fr. *orare* to speak — more at ORATION] (15c) **1 a :** a person (as a priestess of ancient Greece) through whom a deity is believed to speak **b :** a shrine in which a deity reveals hidden knowledge or the divine purpose through such a person **c :** an answer or decision given by an oracle **2 a :** a person giving wise or authoritative decisions or opinions **b :** an authoritative or wise expression or answer
orac·u·lar \ȯ-ˈrak-yə-lər, ə-\ *adj* [L *oraculum*] (1678) **1 :** of, relating to, or being an oracle **2 :** resembling an oracle (as in solemnity of delivery) ***syn*** see DICTATORIAL — **orac·u·lar·i·ty** \-ˌrak-yə-ˈlar-ət-ē\ *n* — **orac·u·lar·ly** \-ˈrak-yə-lər-lē\ *adv*
1oral \ˈōr-əl, ˈȯr-, ˈär-\ *adj* [L *or-, os* mouth; akin to OE *ōra* border, L *ora*] (1628) **1 a :** uttered by the mouth or in words **:** SPOKEN **b :** using speech or the lips esp. in teaching the deaf **2 a :** of, given through, or involving the mouth **b :** being on or relating to the same surface as the mouth **3 a :** of, relating to, or characterized by the first stage of psychosexual development in which libidinal gratification is derived from intake (as of food), by sucking, and later by biting **b :** of, relating to, or characterized by personality traits of passive dependency and aggressiveness — **oral·i·ty** \ȯ-ˈral-ət-ē, ō-\ *n* — **oral·ly** \ˈōr-ə-lē, ˈȯr-, ˈär-\ *adv*
2oral *n* (1876) **:** an oral examination — usu. used in pl.
oral history *n* (1955) **:** historical information that is obtained in interviews with persons who have led significant lives and that is usu. tape-recorded — **oral historian** *n*
oral·ism \ˈōr-ə-ˌliz-əm, ˈȯr-, ˈär-\ *n* (1883) **:** advocacy or use of the oral method of teaching the deaf — **oral·ist** \-ləst\ *n*
orang \ə-ˈraŋ\ *n* [by shortening] (1778) **:** ORANGUTAN
1or·ange \ˈär-inj, ˈär(-ə)nj; *chiefly Northern & Midland* ˈȯr-inj, ˈȯr(-ə)nj\ *n* [ME, fr. MF, fr. OProv *auranja,* fr. Ar *nāranj,* fr. Per *nārang,* fr. Skt *nāraṅga* orange tree, of Dravidian origin; akin to Tamil *naṟu* fragrant] (14c) **1 a :** a globose berry with a reddish yellow rind and a sweet edible pulp **b :** any of various rather small evergreen trees (genus *Citrus*) with ovate unifoliolate leaves, hard yellow wood, fragrant white flowers, and fruits that are oranges **2 :** any of several trees or fruits resembling the orange **3 :** any of a group of colors that lie midway between red and yellow in hue and are of medium lightness and moderate to high saturation
2orange *adj* (1542) **1 :** of or relating to the orange **2 :** of the color orange
Orange *adj* (1795) **:** of, relating to, or sympathizing with Orangemen — **Or·ange·ism** \-ˌiz-əm\ *n*
or·ange·ade \ˌär-in-ˈjād, ˌär(-ə)n-, ˌȯr-in-, ˌȯr(-ə)n-\ *n* [F, fr. *orange* + *-ade*] (1706) **:** a beverage of sweetened orange juice mixed with water
orange chromide *n* [*chromide,* deriv. of Gk *chromis,* a sea fish] (1933) **:** a brilliant orange or yellow red-spotted fish (*Etroplus maculatus*) often kept in tropical aquariums
orange hawkweed *n* (ca. 1900) **:** a European hawkweed (*Hieracium aurantiacum*) that has flower heads with bright orange-red rays and is a troublesome weed esp. in northeastern No. America
Or·ange·man \ˈär-inj-mən, ˈär(-ə)nj-, ˈȯr-inj-, ˈȯr(-ə)nj-\ *n* [William III of England, prince of *Orange*] (1796) **1 :** a member of a secret society organized in the north of Ireland in 1795 to defend the British sovereign and to support the Protestant religion **2 :** a Protestant Irishman esp. of Ulster
orange peel *n* (ca. 1909) **:** a rough surface (as on porcelain) like that of an orange
orange pekoe *n* (1877) **:** tea made from the tiny leaf and end bud of the shoot
or·ange·ry \ˈär-inj-(ə-)rē, ˈär(-ə)nj-, ˈȯr-inj-, ˈȯr(-ə)nj-\ *n, pl* **-ries** (1664) **:** a protected place and esp. a greenhouse for raising oranges in cool climates
or·ange·wood \ˈär-inj-ˌwu̇d, ˈär(-ə)nj-, ˈȯr-inj-, ˈȯr(-ə)nj-\ *n* (1884) **:** the wood of the orange tree used esp. in turnery and carving

\ə\ abut \ᵊ\ kitten, F table \ər\ further \a\ ash \ā\ ace \ä\ cot, cart \au̇\ out \ch\ chin \e\ bet \ē\ easy \g\ go \i\ hit \ī\ ice \j\ job \ŋ\ sing \ō\ go \ȯ\ law \ȯi\ boy \th\ thin \t͟h\ the \ü\ loot \u̇\ foot \y\ yet \zh\ vision \ȧ, k̲, ⁿ, œ, œ̄, ue, u̅e, ʸ\ *see* Guide to Pronunciation

or·ang·ish \ˈär-in-jish, ˈar(-ə)n-, ˈȯr-in-, ˈȯr(-ə)n-\ *adj* (1967) **:** somewhat orange

orang·utan \ə-ˈraŋ-ə-ˌtaŋ, -ˌtan\ *n* [Malay *orang hutan,* fr. *orang* man + *hutan* forest] (1691) **:** a largely herbivorous arboreal anthropoid ape (*Pongo pygmaeus*) of Borneo and Sumatra that is about two thirds as large as the gorilla and has brown skin, long sparse reddish brown hair, and very long arms

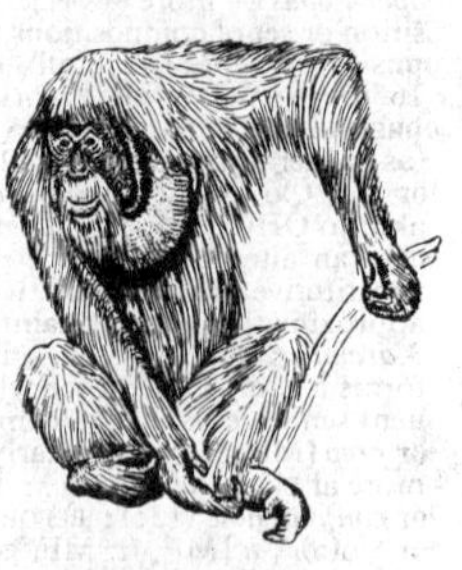

orangutan

or·angy *or* **or·ang·ey** \ˈär-in-jē, ˈar(-ə)n-, ˈȯr-in-, ˈȯr(-ə)n-\ *adj* (1778) **:** having an orange color or tinge

orate \ȯ-ˈrāt\ *vi* **orat·ed; orat·ing** [back-formation fr. *oration*] (1600) **:** to speak in an elevated and often pompous manner

ora·tion \ə-ˈrā-shən, ȯ-\ *n* [L *oration-, oratio* speech, oration, fr. *oratus,* pp. of *orare* to plead, speak, pray; akin to Russ *orat'* to yell] (1502) **:** an elaborate discourse delivered in a formal and dignified manner

or·a·tor \ˈȯr-ət-ər, ˈär-\ *n* (15c) **1 :** one who delivers an oration **2 :** one distinguished for skill and power as a public speaker

Or·a·to·ri·an \ˌȯr-ə-ˈtōr-ē-ən, ˌär-, -ˈtȯr-\ *n* (1656) **:** a member of the Congregation of the Oratory of St. Philip Neri founded in Rome in 1575 and comprising independent communities of secular priests under obedience but without vows — **Oratorian** *adj*

or·a·tor·i·cal \ˌȯr-ə-ˈtȯr-i-kəl, ˌär-ə-ˈtär-\ *adj* (1634) **:** of, relating to, or characteristic of an orator or oratory — **or·a·tor·i·cal·ly** \-k(ə-)lē\ *adv*

or·a·to·rio \ˌȯr-ə-ˈtōr-ē-ˌō, ˌär-, -ˈtȯr-\ *n, pl* **-ri·os** [It, fr. the *Oratorio* di San Filippo Neri (Oratory of St. Philip Neri) in Rome] (ca. 1727) **:** a lengthy choral work usu. of a religious nature consisting chiefly of recitatives, arias, and choruses without action or scenery

¹or·a·to·ry \ˈȯr-ə-ˌtōr-ē, ˈär-, -ˌtȯr-\ *n, pl* **-ries** [ME *oratorie,* fr. LL *oratorium,* fr. L *oratus,* pp.] (14c) **1 :** a place of prayer; *esp* **:** a private or institutional chapel **2** *cap* **:** an Oratorian congregation, house, or church

²oratory *n* [L *oratoria,* fr. fem. of *oratorius* oratorical, fr. *oratus,* pp.] (1593) **1 :** the art of speaking in public eloquently or effectively ⟨a student of ~⟩ **2 a :** public speaking that employs oratory **b :** public speaking that is characterized by the use of stock phrases and that appeals chiefly to the emotions

¹orb \ˈȯ(ə)rb\ *n* [ME, fr. MF *orbe,* fr. L *orbis* circle, disk, orb; akin to L *orbita* track, rut] (14c) **1 :** any of the concentric spheres in old astronomy surrounding the earth and carrying the celestial bodies in their revolutions **2** *archaic* **:** something circular **:** CIRCLE, ORBIT **3 :** a spherical body; *esp* **:** a celestial sphere **4 :** EYE **5 :** a sphere surmounted by a cross symbolizing kingly power and justice

²orb *vt* (1600) **1 :** to form into a disk or circle **2** *archaic* **:** ENCIRCLE, SURROUND, ENCLOSE ~ *vi, archaic* **:** to move in an orbit

or·bic·u·lar \ȯr-ˈbik-yə-lər\ *adj* [ME *orbiculer,* fr. MF or LL; MF *orbiculaire,* fr. LL *orbicularis,* fr. L *orbiculus,* dim. of *orbis*] (15c) **:** SPHERICAL, CIRCULAR — **or·bic·u·lar·ly** \-ˈbik-yə-lər-lē\ *adv*

or·bic·u·late \ȯr-ˈbik-yə-lət\ *adj* (1760) **:** circular or nearly circular in outline ⟨an ~ leaf⟩

¹or·bit \ˈȯr-bət\ *n* [ME, fr. ML *orbita,* fr. L, rut, track] (15c) **:** the bony socket of the eye

²orbit *n* [L *orbita* path, rut, orbit; akin to L *orbis* circle] (1696) **1 a :** a path described by one body in its revolution about another (as by the earth about the sun or by an electron about an atomic nucleus); *also* **:** one complete revolution of a body describing such a path **b :** a circular path **2 :** a range or sphere of activity or influence ⟨countries that are in the communist ~⟩ ***syn*** see RANGE — **or·bit·al** \-ᵊl\ *adj*

³orbit *vt* (1943) **1 :** to revolve in an orbit around **:** CIRCLE **2 :** to send up and make revolve in an orbit ⟨~ a satellite⟩ ~ *vi* **:** to travel in circles

or·bit·al \ˈȯr-bət-ᵊl\ *n* [*orbital,* adj.] (1932) **:** a subdivision of a nuclear shell containing one or two electrons or none

or·bit·er \-bət-ər\ *n* (1951) **:** one that orbits; *esp* **:** a spacecraft designed to orbit a celestial body without landing on its surface

Or·ca·di·an \ȯr-ˈkād-ē-ən\ *n* [L *Orcades* Orkney islands] (1661) **:** a native or inhabitant of the Orkney islands — **Orcadian** *adj*

or·chard \ˈȯr-chərd\ *n* [ME, fr. OE *ortgeard,* fr. *ort-* (fr. L *hortus* garden) + *geard* yard — more at YARD] (bef. 12c) **:** a planting of fruit trees or nut trees; *also* **:** the trees of such a planting

orchard grass *n* (1765) **:** a widely grown tall stout hay and pasture grass (*Dactylis glomerata*) that grows in tufts with loose open panicles

or·chard·ist \ˈȯr-chərd-əst\ *n* (1794) **:** an owner or supervisor of orchards

or·ches·tra \ˈȯr-kə-strə, -ˌkes-trə\ *n* [L, fr. Gk *orchēstra,* fr. *orcheisthai* to dance — more at EERIE] (1606) **1 a :** the circular space used by the chorus in front of the proscenium in an ancient Greek theater **b :** a corresponding semicircular space in a Roman theater used for seating important persons **2 a :** the space in front of the stage in a modern theater that is used by an orchestra **b :** the forward section of seats on the main floor of a theater **c :** the main floor of a theater **3 :** a group of musicians including esp. string players organized to perform ensemble music — compare BAND

or·ches·tral \ȯr-ˈkes-trəl\ *adj* (ca. 1811) **1 :** of, relating to, or composed for an orchestra **2 :** suggestive of an orchestra or its musical qualities — **or·ches·tral·ly** \-trə-lē\ *adv*

or·ches·trate \ˈȯr-kə-ˌstrāt\ *vt* **-trat·ed; -trat·ing** (1880) **1 a :** to compose or arrange (music) for an orchestra **b :** to provide with orchestration ⟨~ a ballet⟩ **2 :** to arrange or combine so as to achieve a maximum effect ⟨~s the elements of his art⟩ — **or·ches·tra·tor** *also* **or·ches·trat·er** \-ˌstrāt-ər\ *n*

or·ches·tra·tion \ˌȯr-kə-ˈstrā-shən\ *n* (ca. 1864) **1 :** the arrangement of a musical composition for performance by an orchestra; *also* **:** orchestral treatment of a musical composition **2 :** harmonious organization ⟨develop a world community through ~ of cultural diversities —L. K. Frank⟩ — **or·ches·tra·tion·al** \-shnəl, -shən-ᵊl\ *adj*

or·chid \ˈȯr-kəd\ *n* [irreg. fr. NL *Orchis*] (1845) **1 :** any plant or flower of a large family (Orchidaceae, the orchid family) of perennial epiphytic or terrestrial plants that usu. have showy 3-petaled flowers with the middle petal enlarged into a lip and differing from the others in shape and color **2 :** a variable color averaging a light purple

or·chi·da·ceous \ˌȯr-kə-ˈdā-shəs\ *adj* [NL *Orchidaceae,* taxonomic name of the orchid family, fr. *Orchis*] (1838) **1 :** of, relating to, or resembling the orchids **2 :** SHOWY, OSTENTATIOUS

or·chis \ˈȯr-kəs\ *n* [NL, fr. L, orchid, fr. Gk, testicle, orchid; akin to MIr *uirgge* testicle] (1562) **:** ORCHID; *esp* **:** one of a genus (*Orchis*) with fleshy roots and a spurred lip

or·dain \ȯr-ˈdān\ *vb* [ME *ordeinen,* fr. OF *ordener,* fr. LL *ordinare,* fr. L, to put in order, appoint, fr. *ordin-, ordo* order] *vt* (13c) **1 :** to invest officially (as by the laying on of hands) with ministerial or priestly authority **2 a :** to establish or order by appointment, decree, or law **:** ENACT **b :** DESTINE, FOREORDAIN ~ *vi* **:** to issue an order — **or·dain·er** *n* — **or·dain·ment** \-ˈdān-mənt\ *n*

or·deal \ȯr-ˈdē(-ə)l, ˈȯr-ˌ\ *n* [ME *ordal,* fr. OE *ordāl;* akin to OHG *urteil* judgment, OE *dāl* division — more at ABIDE, DEAL] (bef. 12c) **1 :** a primitive means used to determine guilt or innocence by submitting the accused to dangerous or painful tests believed to be under supernatural control ⟨~ by fire⟩ **2 :** a severe trial or experience

¹or·der \ˈȯrd-ər\ *vb* **or·dered; or·der·ing** \ˈȯrd-(ə-)riŋ\ *vt* (13c) **1 :** to put in order **:** ARRANGE **2 a :** to give an order to **:** COMMAND **b :** DESTINE, ORDAIN **c :** to command to go or come to a specified place **d :** to give an order for ⟨~ a meal⟩ ~ *vi* **1 :** to bring about order **:** REGULATE **2 a :** to issue orders **:** COMMAND **b :** to give or place an order — **or·der·er** \-ər-ər\ *n*

syn ORDER, ARRANGE, MARSHAL, ORGANIZE, SYSTEMATIZE, METHODIZE mean to put persons or things into their proper places in relation to each other. ORDER suggests a straightening out so as to eliminate confusion; ARRANGE implies a setting in sequence, relationship, or adjustment; MARSHAL suggests gathering and arranging in preparation for a particular operation or effective use; ORGANIZE implies arranging so that the whole aggregate works as a unit with each element having a proper function; SYSTEMATIZE implies arranging according to a predetermined scheme; METHODIZE suggests imposing an orderly procedure rather than a fixed scheme. ***syn*** see in addition COMMAND

²order *n* [MF *ordre,* fr. ML & L; ML *ordin-, ordo* ecclesiastical order, fr. L, arrangement, group, class; akin to L *ordiri* to lay the warp, begin] (14c) **1 a :** a group of people united in a formal way: as **(1) :** a fraternal society ⟨the Masonic *Order*⟩ **(2) :** a community under a religious rule; *esp* **:** one requiring members to take solemn vows **b :** a badge or medal of such a society; *also* **:** a military decoration **2 a :** any of the several grades of the Christian ministry **b** *pl* **:** the office of a person in the Christian ministry **c** *pl* **:** ORDINATION **3 a :** a rank, class, or special group in a community or society **b :** a class of persons or things grouped according to quality, value, or natural characteristics: as **(1) :** a category of taxonomic classification ranking above the family and below the class **(2) :** the broadest category in soil classification **4 a (1) :** RANK, LEVEL ⟨a statesman of the first ~⟩ **(2) :** CATEGORY, CLASS ⟨in emergencies of this ~ —R. B. Westerfield⟩ **b (1) :** the arrangement or sequence of objects or of events in time ⟨listed the items in ~ of importance⟩ **(2) :** a sequential arrangement of mathematical elements **c :** DEGREE 11a, 11b **d (1) :** the number of times differentiation is applied successively ⟨derivatives of higher ~⟩ **(2)** *of a differential equation* **:** the order of the derivative of highest order **e :** the number of columns or rows or columns and rows in a magic square, determinant, or matrix ⟨the ~ of a matrix with 2 rows and 3 columns is 2 by 3⟩ **f :** the number of elements in a finite mathematical group **5 a (1) :** a sociopolitical system ⟨was opposed to changes in the established ~⟩ **(2) :** a particular sphere or aspect of a sociopolitical system ⟨the present economic ~⟩ **b :** a regular or harmonious arrangement ⟨the ~ of nature⟩ **6 a :** a prescribed form of a religious service **:** RITE **b :** the customary mode of procedure esp. in debate ⟨point of ~⟩ **7 a :** the state of peace, freedom from confused or unruly behavior, and respect for law or proper authority ⟨promised to restore law and ~⟩ **b :** a specific rule, regulation, or authoritative direction **:** COMMAND **8 a :** a style of building **b :** a type of column and entablature forming the unit of a style **9 a :** state or condition esp. with regard to functioning or repair ⟨things were in terrible ~⟩ **b :** a proper or orderly condition ⟨their passports were in ~⟩ ⟨the room is now in ~⟩ **10 a :** a written direction to pay money to someone **b :** a commission to purchase, sell, or supply goods or to perform work **c :** goods or items bought or sold **d :** an assigned or requested undertaking ⟨landing men on the moon was a large ~⟩ **11 :** ORDER OF THE DAY ⟨flat roofs were the ~ in the small villages⟩ — **or·der·less** \-ləs\ *adj* — **in order :** APPROPRIATE, DESIRABLE ⟨an apology is *in order*⟩ — **in order that :** SO THAT — **in order to :** for the purpose of — **on order :** in the process of being ordered — **on the order of 1 :** after the fashion of **:** LIKE ⟨much *on the order of* Great Lakes bulk carriers —*Ships and the Sea*⟩ **2 :** ABOUT, APPROXIMATELY ⟨spent *on the order of* two million dollars⟩ — **to order :** according to the specifications of an order ⟨shoes made *to order*⟩

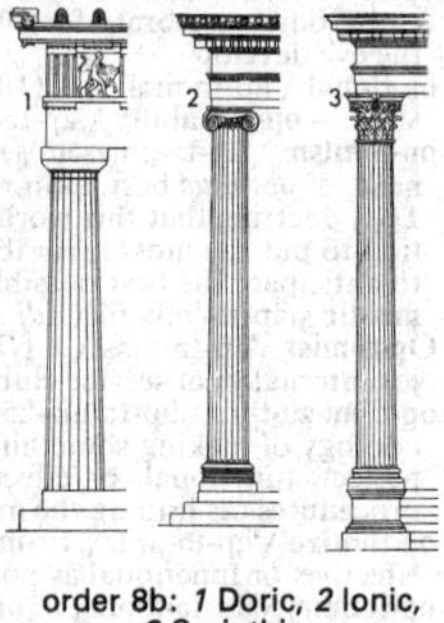

order 8b: *1* Doric, *2* Ionic, *3* Corinthian

order arms *n* [fr. the command *order arms!*] (1844) **1 :** a position in the manual of arms in which the rifle is held vertically beside the right leg with the butt resting on the ground **2 :** a command to return the rifle to order arms from present arms or to drop the hand from a hand salute

or·dered \ˈȯrd-ərd\ *adj* (1579) **:** characterized by order: as **a :** marked by regularity or discipline ⟨led an ~ life⟩ **b :** marked by regular or harmonious arrangement or disposition ⟨an ~ landscape⟩ ⟨the ~ crystal structure⟩ **c :** having elements arranged or identified according to a rule: as **(1) :** having the property that every pair of different elements is related by a transitive relationship that is not symmetric (2) : having elements labeled by ordinal numbers ⟨an ~ triple has a first, second, and third element⟩

or·der·li·ness \ˈȯrd-ər-lē-nəs\ *n* (1571) : the quality or state of being orderly

[1]or·der·ly \-lē\ *adj* (1577) **1 a** (1) : arranged or disposed in some order or pattern : REGULAR ⟨~ rows of houses⟩ (2) : not marked by disorder : TIDY ⟨keeps an ~ desk⟩ **b** : governed by law : REGULATED ⟨an ~ universe⟩ **c** : METHODICAL ⟨an ~ mind⟩ **2** : well behaved : PEACEFUL ⟨an ~ crowd⟩ — **orderly** *adv*

[2]orderly *n, pl* **-lies** (1800) **1** : a soldier assigned to perform various services (as carrying messages) for a superior officer **2** : a hospital attendant who does routine or heavy work (as cleaning, carrying supplies, or moving patients)

order of business [*order of business* (predetermined sequence of matters to be dealt with by an assembly)] (ca. 1903) : a matter which must be dealt with : TASK ⟨the discipline problem was the first *order of business* at the meeting of the school board⟩

order of magnitude (1875) : a range of magnitude extending from some value to ten times that value

order of the day (1698) **1** : the business or tasks appointed for an assembly for a given day **2** : the characteristic or dominant feature or activity ⟨growth and change are the *order of the day* in every field — Ruth G. Strickland⟩

[1]or·di·nal \ˈȯrd-nəl, -ᵊn-əl\ *n* (14c) **1** *cap* [ME, fr. ML *ordinale,* fr. LL, neut. of *ordinalis*] : a collection of forms to be used in ordination **2** [LL *ordinalis,* fr. *ordinalis,* adj.] : ORDINAL NUMBER

[2]ordinal *adj* [LL *ordinalis,* fr. L *ordin-, ordo*] (1599) **1** : of a specified order or rank in a series **2** : of or relating to an order (as of fishes)

ordinal number *n* (1607) **1** : a number designating the place (as first, second, or third) occupied by an item in an ordered sequence — see NUMBER table **2** : a number assigned to an ordered set that designates both the order of its elements and its cardinal number

or·di·nance \ˈȯrd-nən(t)s, ˈȯrd-ᵊn-ən(t)s\ *n* [ME, fr. MF & ML; MF *ordenance,* lit., act of arranging, fr. ML *ordinantia,* fr. L *ordinant-, ordinans,* prp. of *ordinare* to put in order — more at ORDAIN] (14c) **1 a** : an authoritative decree or direction : ORDER **b** : a law set forth by a governmental authority; *specif* : a municipal regulation **2** : something ordained or decreed by fate or a deity **3** : a prescribed usage, practice, or ceremony ***syn*** see LAW

or·di·nand \ˌȯrd-ᵊn-ˈand\ *n* [LL *ordinandus,* gerundive of *ordinare* to ordain] (ca. 1842) : a candidate for ordination

[1]or·di·nary \ˈȯrd-ᵊn-ˌer-ē\ *n, pl* **-nar·ies** [ME *ordinarie,* fr. AF & ML; AF, fr. ML *ordinarius,* fr. L *ordinarius,* adj.] (14c) **1 a** (1) : a prelate exercising original jurisdiction over a specified territory or group (2) : a clergyman appointed formerly in England to attend condemned criminals **b** : a judge of probate in some states of the U.S. **2** *often cap* : the parts of the Mass that do not vary from day to day **3** : the regular or customary condition or course of things — usu. used in the phrase *out of the ordinary* **4 a** *Brit* : a meal served to all comers at a fixed price **b** *chiefly Brit* : a tavern or eating house serving regular meals **5** : a common heraldic charge (as the bend or chevron) of simple form

[2]ordinary *adj* [ME *ordinarie,* fr. L *ordinarius,* fr. *ordin-, ordo* order] (15c) **1** : of a kind to be expected in the normal order of events : ROUTINE, USUAL **2** : having or constituting immediate or original jurisdiction; *also* : belonging to such jurisdiction **3 a** : of common quality, rank, or ability **b** : deficient in quality : POOR, INFERIOR ***syn*** see COMMON — **or·di·nari·ly** \ˌȯrd-ᵊn-ˈer-ə-lē\ *adv* — **or·di·nari·ness** \ˈȯrd-ᵊn-ˌer-ē-nəs\ *n*

ordinary–language philosophy *n* (1964) : a trend in philosophical analysis that seeks to resolve philosophical perplexity by revealing sources of puzzlement in the misunderstanding of ordinary language

Ordinary level *n* (1947) : O LEVEL

ordinary seaman *n* (1702) : a seaman of some experience but not as skilled as an able seaman

or·di·nate \ˈȯrd-nət, -ᵊn-ət, -ᵊn-ˌāt\ *n* [NL (*linea*) *ordinate* (*applicata*), lit., line applied in an orderly manner] (1706) : the Cartesian coordinate obtained by measuring parallel to the y-axis — compare ABSCISSA

or·di·na·tion \ˌȯrd-ᵊn-ˈā-shən\ *n* (15c) : the act or an instance of ordaining : the state of being ordained

ord·nance \ˈȯrd-nən(t)s\ *n* [ME *ordinaunce,* fr. MF *ordenance,* lit., act of arranging] (14c) **1 a** : military supplies including weapons, ammunition, combat vehicles, and maintenance tools and equipment **b** : a service of the army charged with the procuring, distributing, and safekeeping of ordnance **2** : CANNON, ARTILLERY

or·do \ˈȯ(ə)rd-(ˌ)ō\ *n, pl* **ordos** *or* **or·di·nes** \ˈȯrd-ᵊn-ˌēz\ [ML, fr. L, order] (ca. 1849) : a list of offices and feasts of the Roman Catholic Church for each day of the year

or·don·nance \ˌȯrd-ᵊn-ˈäⁿs\ *n* [F, alter. of MF *ordenance*] (1644) : disposition of the parts (as of a literary composition) with regard to one another and the whole : ARRANGEMENT

Or·do·vi·cian \ˌȯrd-ə-ˈvish-ən\ *adj* [L *Ordovices,* ancient people in northern Wales] (1879) : of, relating to, or being the period between the Cambrian and the Silurian or the corresponding system of rocks — **Ordovician** *n*

or·dure \ˈȯr-jər\ *n* [ME, fr. MF, fr. *ord* filthy, fr. L *horridus* horrid] (14c) **1** : EXCREMENT **2** : something that is morally degrading

[1]ore \ˈō(ə)r, ˈȯ(ə)r\ *n, often attrib* [ME *or,* fr. OE *ār;* akin to OHG *ēr* bronze, L *aes* copper, bronze] (bef. 12c) **1** : a mineral containing a valuable constituent (as metal) for which it is mined and worked **2** : a source from which valuable matter is extracted

[2]ore \ˈər-ə\ *n, pl* **ore** [Sw *öre* & Dan & Norw *øre*] (1716) — see *krona, krone* at MONEY table

ore·ad \ˈōr-ē-ˌad, ˈȯr-, -ē-əd\ *n* [L *oread-, oreas,* fr. Gk *oreiad-, oreias,* fr. *oreios* of a mountain, fr. *oros* mountain — more at RISE] (14c) : any of the nymphs of mountains and hills in Greek mythology

ore dressing *n* (1862) : mechanical preparation (as by crushing) and concentration (as by flotation) of ore

oreg·a·no \ə-ˈreg-ə-ˌnō\ *n* [AmerSp *orégano,* fr. Sp, wild marjoram, fr. L *origanum* — more at ORIGANUM] (1771) **1** : a bushy perennial mint (*Origanum vulgare*) that is used as a seasoning and a source of aromatic oil — called also *origanum, wild marjoram* **2** : any of several plants (genera *Lippia* and *Coleus*) other than oregano of the vervain or mint families

Or·e·gon grape \ˌȯr-i-gən-, ˌär-, -ˌgän-\ *n* [*Oregon,* state of the U.S.] (1851) : an evergreen shrub (*Mahonia aquifolium*) of the barberry family that has yellow flowers, bears bluish black berries, and is native to the Pacific coast

Ores·tes \ə-ˈres-(ˌ)tēz, ȯ-\ *n* [L, fr. Gk *Orestēs*] : the son of Agamemnon and Clytemnestra who with his sister Electra avenges his father by killing his mother and her lover Aegisthus

or·gan \ˈȯr-gən\ *n* [ME, partly fr. OE *organa,* fr. L *organum,* fr. Gk *organon,* lit., tool, instrument; partly fr. OF *organe,* fr. L *organum;* akin to Gk *ergon* work — more at WORK] (bef. 12c) **1 a** *archaic* : any of various musical instruments; *esp* : WIND INSTRUMENT **b** (1) : a wind instrument consisting of sets of pipes made to sound by compressed air and controlled by keyboards and producing a variety of musical effects — called also *pipe organ* (2) : REED ORGAN (3) : an instrument in which the sound and resources of the pipe organ are approximated by means of electronic devices (4) : any of various similar cruder instruments **2 a** : a differentiated structure (as a heart, kidney, leaf, or stem) consisting of cells and tissues and performing some specific function in an organism **b** : bodily parts performing a function or cooperating in an activity ⟨the eyes and related structures that make up the visual ~*s*⟩ **3** : a subordinate group or organization that performs specialized functions ⟨the various ~*s* of government⟩ **4** : PERIODICAL

organ- *or* **organo-** *comb form* [ME, fr. ML, fr. L *organum*] **1** : organ ⟨*organo*genesis⟩ **2** : organic ⟨*organo*mercurial⟩

or·gan·dy *also* **or·gan·die** \ˈȯr-gən-dē\ *n, pl* **-dies** [F *organdi*] (1835) : a very fine transparent muslin with a stiff finish

or·gan·elle \ˌȯr-gə-ˈnel\ *n* [NL *organella,* fr. L *organum*] (1909) : a specialized cellular part (as a mitochondrion, lysosome, or ribosome) that is analogous to an organ

or·gan–grind·er \ˈȯr-gən-ˌgrīn-dər\ *n* (ca. 1806) : one that cranks a hand organ; *esp* : an itinerant street musician who operates a barrel organ

[1]or·gan·ic \ȯr-ˈgan-ik\ *adj* (1517) **1** *archaic* : INSTRUMENTAL **2 a** : of, relating to, or arising in a bodily organ **b** : affecting the structure of the organism **3 a** (1) : of, relating to, or derived from living organisms (2) : relating to, yielding, dealing in, or involving the use of food produced with the use of feed or fertilizer of plant or animal origin without employment of chemically formulated fertilizers, growth stimulants, antibiotics, or pesticides ⟨~ farming⟩ ⟨~ stores⟩ **b** (1) : of, relating to, or containing carbon compounds (2) : relating to, being, or dealt with by a branch of chemistry concerned with the carbon compounds of living beings and most other carbon compounds **4 a** : forming an integral element of a whole : FUNDAMENTAL ⟨incidental music rather than ~ parts of the action —Francis Fergusson⟩ **b** : having systematic coordination of parts : ORGANIZED ⟨an ~ whole⟩ **c** : having the characteristics of an organism : developing in the manner of a living plant or animal ⟨society is ~⟩ **5** : of, relating to, or constituting the law by which a government or organization exists — **or·gan·i·cal·ly** \-i-k(ə-)lē\ *adv* — **or·ga·nic·i·ty** \ˌȯr-gə-ˈnis-ət-ē\ *n*

[2]organic *n* (1942) : an organic substance: as **a** : a fertilizer of plant or animal origin **b** : a pesticide whose active component is an organic compound or a mixture of organic compounds

or·gan·i·cism \ȯr-ˈgan-ə-ˌsiz-əm\ *n* [ISV] (1883) **1 a** : the explanation of life and living processes in terms of the levels of organization of living systems rather than in terms of the properties of their smallest components **b** : VITALISM **2** : any of various theories that attribute to society or the universe as a whole an existence or characteristics analogous to those of a biological organism — **or·gan·i·cist** \-səst\ *n*

or·gan·ism \ˈȯr-gə-ˌniz-əm\ *n* (1768) **1** : a complex structure of interdependent and subordinate elements whose relations and properties are largely determined by their function in the whole **2** : an individual constituted to carry on the activities of life by means of organs separate in function but mutually dependent : a living being — **or·gan·is·mic** \ˌȯr-gə-ˈniz-mik\ *also* **or·gan·is·mal** \-məl\ *adj* — **or·gan·is·mi·cal·ly** \-mi-k(ə-)lē\ *adv*

or·gan·ist \ˈȯr-gə-nəst\ *n* (1591) : one who plays the organ

[1]or·ga·ni·za·tion \ˌȯrg-(ə-)nə-ˈzā-shən\ *n* (15c) **1 a** : the act or process of organizing or of being organized **b** : the condition or manner of being organized ⟨a high degree of ~⟩ **2 a** : ASSOCIATION, SOCIETY ⟨tax exemptions for charitable ~*s*⟩ **b** : an administrative and functional structure (as a business or a political party); *also* : the personnel of such a structure

[2]organization *adj* (1949) : characterized by complete conformity to the standards and requirements of an organization ⟨an ~ man⟩

or·ga·ni·za·tion·al \-shnəl, -shən-ᵊl\ *adj* (1881) **1** : of or relating to an organization : involving organization ⟨the ~ state of a crystal⟩ **2** : ORGANIZATION — **or·ga·ni·za·tion·al·ly** \-ē\ *adv*

or·ga·nize \ˈȯr-gə-ˌnīz\ *vb* **-nized; -niz·ing** *vt* (15c) **1** : to cause to develop an organic structure **2** : to arrange or form into a coherent unity or functioning whole : INTEGRATE ⟨trying to ~ her thoughts⟩ **3 a** : to set up an administrative structure for **b** : to persuade to associate in an organization; *esp* : UNIONIZE **4** : to arrange by systematic planning and united effort ~ *vi* **1** : to undergo physical or organic organization **2** : to arrange elements into a whole of interdependent parts **3** : to form an organization; *specif* : to form or persuade workers to join a union ***syn*** see ORDER — **or·gan·iz·able** \-ˌnī-zə-bəl\ *adj*

or·ga·nized *adj* (1817) **1** : having a formal organization to coordinate and carry out activities ⟨~ baseball⟩ ⟨~ crime⟩ **2** : affiliated by membership in an organization (as a union) ⟨~ steelworkers⟩

or·ga·niz·er \-ˌnī-zər\ *n* (1849) **1** : one that organizes **2** : a region of a developing embryo or a substance produced by such a region that is capable of inducing a specific type of development in undifferentiated tissue — called also *inductor*

or·gano·chlo·rine \ȯr-ˌgan-ə-ˈklō(ə)r-ˌēn, -ˈklȯ(ə)r-, -ən\ *adj* (1961) : of, relating to, or belonging to the chlorinated hydrocarbon pesticides (as aldrin, DDT, or dieldrin) — **organochlorine** *n*

organ of Cor·ti \-ˈkȯrt-ē\ [Alfonso *Corti* †1876 Ital. anatomist] (1882) : a complex epithelial structure in the cochlea that rests on the internal surface of the basilar membrane and in mammals is the chief part of the ear by which sound is directly perceived

or·gan·o·gen·e·sis \ˌȯr-gə-nō-ˈjen-ə-səs, ȯr-ˌgan-ə-\ *n* [NL] (ca. 1860) : the origin and development of bodily organs — compare MORPHOGENESIS — **or·gan·o·ge·net·ic** \-jə-ˈnet-ik\ *adj* — **or·gan·o·ge·net·i·cal·ly** \-i-k(ə-)lē\ *adv*

or·gan·o·lep·tic \ˌȯr-gə-nō-ˈlep-tik, ȯr-ˌgan-ə-\ *adj* [F *organoleptique,* fr. *organ-* + Gk *lēptikos* disposed to take, fr. *lambanein* to take — more at LATCH] (1852) **1 :** being, affecting, or relating to qualities (as taste, color, odor, and feel) of a substance (as a food or drug) that stimulate the sense organs **2 :** involving use of the sense organs ⟨~ evaluation of foods⟩ — **or·gan·o·lep·ti·cal·ly** \-ti-k(ə-)lē\ *adv*

or·gan·ol·o·gy \ˌȯr-gə-ˈnäl-ə-jē\ *n* [ISV] (ca. 1842) : the study of the organs of plants and animals

or·gano·mer·cu·ri·al \ȯr-ˌgan-ō-(ˌ)mər-ˈkyu̇r-ē-əl\ *n* (1938) : an organic compound or a pharmaceutical preparation containing mercury

or·gano·me·tal·lic \-mə-ˈtal-ik\ *adj* [ISV] (1852) : of, relating to, or being an organic compound that usu. contains a metal or metalloid bonded directly to carbon — **organometallic** *n*

or·ga·non \ˈȯr-gə-ˌnän\ *n* [Gk, lit., tool — more at ORGAN] (1543) : an instrument for acquiring knowledge; *specif* : a body of principles of scientific or philosophic investigation

or·gano·phos·phate \ȯr-ˌgan-ə-ˈfäs-ˌfāt\ *n* (1949) : an organophosphorus pesticide — **organophosphate** *adj*

or·gano·phos·pho·rus \-ˈfäs-f(ə-)rəs\ *also* **or·gano·phos·pho·rous** \-fäs-ˈfōr-əs, -ˈfȯr-\ *adj* (1950) : of, relating to, or being a phosphorus-containing organic pesticide (as malathion) that acts by inhibiting cholinesterase — **organophosphorus** *n*

organ–pipe cactus *n* (1908) : any of several tall upright cacti of the southwestern U.S. and adjacent Mexico: as **a :** SAGUARO **b :** a cactus (*Lemnaireocereus marginatus* or *Pachycereus marginatus*) that branches at the base to form several ridged upright stems and bears 2-inch red and greenish white flowers

or·ga·num \ˈȯr-gə-nəm\ *n* [ML, fr. L, organ] (1614) **1 :** ORGANON **2 :** early polyphony of the late Middle Ages that consists of one or more voice parts accompanying the cantus firmus in parallel motion usu. at a fourth, fifth, or octave above or below; *also* : a composition in this style

or·gan·za \ȯr-ˈgan-zə\ *n* [prob. alter. of *Lorganza,* a trademark] (1820) : a sheer dress fabric resembling organdy and usu. made of silk, rayon, or nylon

or·gan·zine \ˈȯr-gən-ˌzēn\ *n* [F or It; F *organsin,* fr. It *organzino*] (1699) : a raw silk yarn used for warp threads in fine fabrics

or·gasm \ˈȯr-ˌgaz-əm\ *n* [NL *orgasmus,* fr. Gk *orgasmos,* fr. *organ* to grow ripe, be lustful; akin to Skt *ūrjā* sap, strength] (1763) : intense or paroxysmal emotional excitement; *esp* : the climax of sexual excitement typically occurring toward the end of coitus — **or·gas·mic** \ȯr-ˈgaz-mik\ *also* **or·gas·tic** \-ˈgas-tik\ *adj*

or·geat \ˈȯ(ə)r-ˌzhä(t)\ *n* [F, fr. MF, fr. *orge* barley, fr. L *hordeum;* akin to OHG *gersta* barley, Gk *kri*] (1754) : a sweet almond-flavored nonalcoholic syrup used as a cocktail ingredient or food flavoring

or·gi·as·tic \ˌȯr-jē-ˈas-tik\ *adj* [Gk *orgiastikos,* fr. *orgiazein* to celebrate orgies, fr. *orgia*] (1698) **1 :** of, relating to, or marked by orgies **2 :** characterized by unrestrained emotion — **or·gi·as·ti·cal·ly** \-ti-k(ə-)lē\ *adv*

or·gone \ˈȯ(ə)r-ˌgōn\ *n* [prob. fr. *orgasm* + *-one* (as in *hormone*)] (1942) : a vital energy held to pervade nature and to be made available for use by the human body by sitting in a specially designed box

or·gu·lous \ˈȯr-g(y)ə-ləs\ *adj* [ME, fr. OF *orgueilleus,* fr. *orgueil* pride, of Gmc origin; akin to OHG *urguol* distinguished] (13c) : PROUD

or·gy \ˈȯr-jē\ *n, pl* **orgies** [MF *orgie,* fr. L *orgia,* pl., fr. Gk; akin to Gk *ergon* work — more at WORK] (1589) **1 :** secret ceremonial rites held in honor of an ancient Greek or Roman deity and usu. characterized by ecstatic singing and dancing **2 a :** drunken revelry **b :** an excessive sexual indulgence (as at a wild party) **3 :** something that resembles an orgy in lack of control or moderation ⟨soldiers engaging in an ~ of destruction⟩

-oria *pl of* -ORIUM

-o·ri·al \ˈōr-ē-əl, ˈȯr-\ *adj suffix* [ME, fr. L *-orius* -ory + ME *-al*] : of, belonging to, or connected with ⟨combinat*orial*⟩

orib·a·tid \ō-ˈrib-ət-əd, ˌȯr-ə-ˈbat-əd\ *n* [NL *Oribatidae* (coextensive with *Oribatoidea*), fr. *Oribata,* genus name, fr. Gk *oribatēs* walking the mountains, fr. *oros* mountain + *-batēs,* fr *bainein* to go — more at RISE, COME] (1948) : any of a superfamily (Oribatoidea) of small oval eyeless nonparasitic mites having a heavily sclerotized integument with a leathery appearance — **oribatid** *adj*

ori·el \ˈōr-ē-əl, ˈȯr-\ *n* [ME, porch, oriel, fr. MF *oriol* porch] (14c) : a large bay window projecting from a wall and supported by a corbel or bracket

¹ori·ent \ˈōr-ē-ənt, ˈȯr-, -ē-ˌent\ *n* [ME, fr. MF, fr. L *orient-, oriens,* fr. prp. of *oriri* to rise — more at RISE] (14c) **1** *archaic* **:** EAST 1b **2** *cap* **:** EAST 2 **3 a :** a pearl of great luster **b :** the luster of a pearl

²orient *adj* (15c) **1** *archaic* **:** ORIENTAL 1 **2 a :** LUSTROUS, SPARKLING ⟨~ gems⟩ **b** *archaic* **:** RADIANT, GLOWING **3** *archaic* **:** rising in the sky

³ori·ent \ˈōr-ē-ˌent, ˈȯr-\ *vt* [F *orienter,* fr. MF, fr. *orient*] (1727) **1 a :** to cause to face or point toward the east; *specif* : to build (a church or temple) with the longitudinal axis pointing eastward and the chief altar at the eastern end **b :** to set or arrange in any determinate position esp. in relation to the points of the compass **c :** to ascertain the bearings of **2 a :** to set right by adjusting to facts or principles **b :** to acquaint with the existing situation or environment **3 :** to direct (as a book or film) toward the interests of a particular group **4 :** to cause the axes of the molecules of to assume the same direction

ori·en·tal \ˌōr-ē-ˈent-ᵊl, ˌȯr-\ *adj* (14c) **1** *often cap* **:** of, relating to, or situated in the Orient **2 a :** of superior grade, luster, or value **b :** being corundum or sapphire but simulating another gem in color **3** *often cap* **:** of, relating to, or having the characteristics of Orientals **4** *cap* **:** of, relating to, or constituting the biogeographic region that includes Asia south and southeast of the Himalayas and the Malay archipelago west of Wallace's line — **ori·en·tal·ly** \-ᵊl-ē\ *adv*

Oriental *n* (15c) : a member of one of the indigenous peoples of the Orient

oriental fruit moth *n* (1921) : a small nearly cosmopolitan moth (*Grapholita molesta*) prob. of Japanese origin whose larva is injurious to the twigs and fruit of orchard trees and esp. the peach — called also *oriental peach moth*

ori·en·tal·ism \ˌōr-ē-ˈent-ᵊl-ˌiz-əm\ *n, often cap* (1769) **1 :** a trait, custom, or habit of expression characteristic of oriental peoples **2 :** scholarship or learning in oriental subjects — **ori·en·tal·ist** \-ᵊl-əst\ *n, often cap*

ori·en·tal·ize \-ᵊl-ˌīz\ *vb* **-ized; -iz·ing** *vt, often cap* (1823) **:** to make oriental ~ *vi, often cap* **:** to become oriental

Oriental poppy *n* (1731) : an Asian perennial poppy (*Papaver orientale*) that is commonly cultivated for its large showy flowers

Oriental rug *n* (1881) : a handwoven or hand-knotted one-piece rug or carpet made in the Orient — called also *Oriental carpet*

ori·en·tate \ˈōr-ē-ən-ˌtāt, ˈȯr-, -ˌen-\ *vb* **-tat·ed; -tat·ing** *vt* (1849) : ORIENT ~ *vi* **:** to face or turn to the east

ori·en·ta·tion \ˌōr-ē-ən-ˈtā-shən, ˌȯr-, -ˌen-\ *n* (1849) **1 a :** the act or process of orienting or of being oriented **b :** the state of being oriented; *broadly* : ARRANGEMENT, ALIGNMENT **2 :** a usu. general or lasting direction of thought, inclination, or interest **3 :** change of position by organs, organelles, or organisms in response to external stimulus — **ori·en·ta·tion·al** \-shnəl, -shən-ᵊl\ *adj* — **ori·en·ta·tion·al·ly** \-ē\ *adv*

ori·ent·ed \ˈōr-ē-ˌent-əd, ˈȯr-\ *adj* (1944) : intellectually or emotionally directed ⟨humanistically ~ scholars⟩

ori·en·teer·ing \ˌōr-ē-ən-ˈti(ə)r-iŋ, ˌȯr-, -ˌen-\ *n* [modif. (influenced by *-eer*) of Sw *orientering,* fr. *orientera* to orient] (1948) : a cross-country race in which each participant uses a map and compass to navigate his way between checkpoints along an unfamiliar course

or·i·fice \ˈȯr-ə-fəs, ˈär-\ *n* [ME, fr. MF, fr. LL *orificium,* fr. L *or-, os* mouth — more at ORAL] (15c) : an opening (as a vent, mouth, or hole) through which something may pass — **or·i·fi·cial** \ˌȯr-ə-ˈfish-əl, ˌär-\ *adj*

ori·flamme \ˈȯr-ə-ˌflam, ˈär-\ *n* [ME *oriflamble,* the banner of St. Denis, fr. MF, fr. ML *aurea flamma,* lit., golden flame] (1600) : a banner, symbol, or ideal inspiring devotion or courage

ori·ga·mi \ˌȯr-ə-ˈgäm-ē\ *n* [Jp, folded paper, fr. *ori* folding] (1956) : the art or process of Japanese paper folding

orig·a·num \ə-ˈrig-ə-nəm\ *n* [ME, fr. L, wild marjoram, fr. Gk *origanon*] (12c) : any of various fragrant aromatic plants of the mint or vervain families used as seasonings; *esp* : OREGANO 1

or·i·gin \ˈȯr-ə-jən, ˈär-\ *n* [ME *origine,* prob. fr. MF, fr. L *origin-, origo,* fr. *oriri* to rise — more at RISE] (15c) **1 :** ANCESTRY, PARENTAGE **2 a :** rise, beginning, or derivation from a source **b :** the point at which something begins or rises or from which it derives ⟨the ~ of the custom is lost in the mist of time⟩; *also* : something that creates, causes, or gives rise to another ⟨this spring is the ~ of the brook⟩ **3 :** the more fixed, central, or larger attachment of a muscle **4 :** the intersection of coordinate axes

syn ORIGIN, SOURCE, INCEPTION, ROOT mean the point at which something begins its course or existence. ORIGIN applies to the things or persons from which something is ultimately derived and often to the causes operating before the thing itself comes into being; SOURCE applies more often to the point where something springs into being; INCEPTION stresses the beginning of something without implying causes; ROOT suggests a first, ultimate, or fundamental source often not easily discerned.

¹orig·i·nal \ə-ˈrij-ən-ᵊl, -ˈrij-nəl\ *n* (14c) **1** *archaic* **:** the source or cause from which something arises; *specif* : ORIGINATOR **2 a :** that from which a copy, reproduction, or translation is made **b :** a work composed firsthand **3 a :** a person of fresh initiative or inventive capacity **b :** an eccentric person

²original *adj* (14c) **1 :** of, relating to, or constituting an origin or beginning : INITIAL ⟨the ~ part of the house⟩ **2 a :** not secondary, derivative, or imitative **b :** being the first instance or source from which a copy, reproduction, or translation is or can be made **3 :** independent and creative in thought or action : INVENTIVE ***syn*** see NEW — **orig·i·nal·ly** \-ē\ *adv*

orig·i·nal·i·ty \ə-ˌrij-ə-ˈnal-ət-ē\ *n* (1742) **1 :** the quality or state of being original **2 :** freshness of aspect, design, or style **3 :** the power of independent thought or constructive imagination

original sin *n* (14c) : the state of sin that according to Christian theology characterizes all human beings as a result of Adam's fall

orig·i·nate \ə-ˈrij-ə-ˌnāt\ *vb* **-nat·ed; -nat·ing** *vt* (1657) : to give rise to : INITIATE ~ *vi* : to take or have origin : BEGIN ***syn*** see SPRING — **orig·i·na·tion** \-ˌrij-ə-ˈnā-shən\ *n* — **orig·i·na·tor** \-ˈrij-ə-ˌnāt-ər\ *n*

orig·i·na·tive \ə-ˈrij-ə-ˌnāt-iv, -nət-\ *adj* (1827) : having ability to originate : CREATIVE — **orig·i·na·tive·ly** *adv*

O–ring \ˈō-ˌriŋ\ *n* (1946) : a ring (as of synthetic rubber) used as a gasket

ori·ole \ˈōr-ē-ˌōl, ˈȯr-, -ē-əl\ *n* [F *oriol,* fr. L *aureolus,* dim. of *aureus* golden, fr. *aurum* gold; akin to Lith *auksas* gold] (1776) **1 :** any of a family (Oriolidae) of usu. brightly colored Old World passerine birds related to the crows **2 :** any of a family (Icteridae) of New World passerine birds of which the males are usu. bright black and yellow or orange and the females are chiefly greenish or yellowish

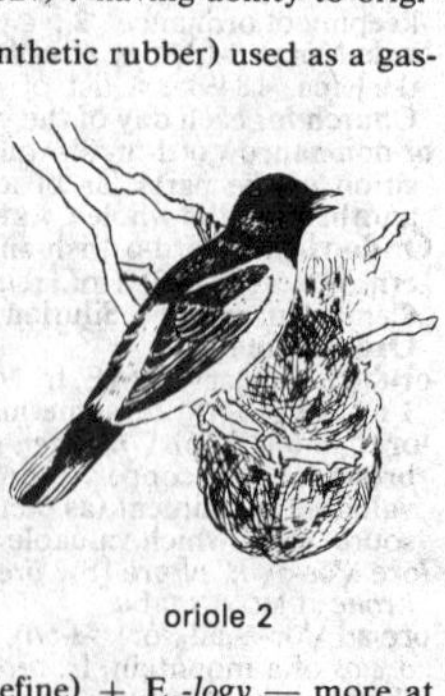

oriole 2

Ori·on \ə-ˈrī-ən, ō-\ *n* [L, fr. Gk *Ōriōn*] **1 :** a giant hunter slain by Artemis in Greek mythology **2** [L (gen. *Orionis*)] **:** a constellation on the equator east of Taurus represented on charts by the figure of a hunter with belt and sword

or·is·mol·o·gy \ˌȯr-əz-ˈmäl-ə-jē, ˌär-\ *n* [Gk *horismos* definition (fr. *horizein* to define) + E *-logy* — more at HORIZON] (1816) : the science of defining technical terms : TERMINOLOGY — **or·is·mo·log·i·cal** \ˌȯr-əz-mə-ˈläj-i-kəl, ˌär-; ō-ˌriz-\ *adj*

or·i·son \ˈȯr-ə-sən, ˈär-, -zən\ *n* [ME, fr. OF, fr. LL *oration-, oratio,* fr. L, oration] (12c) : PRAYER

-o·ri·um \ˈōr-ē-əm, ˈȯr-\ *n suffix, pl* **-oriums** *or* **-o·ria** \-ē-ə\ [L, fr. neut. of *-orius* -ory] : ¹-ORY ⟨haust*orium*⟩

Ori·ya \ó-'rē-(y)ə\ *n* (1801) : the Indic language of Orissa, India

Or·lean·ist \'òr-lē-ə-nəst, òr-'lē-(ə-)nəst\ *n* (1834) : a supporter of the Orleans family in its claim to the throne of France by descent from a younger brother of Louis XIV

Or·lon \'ò(ə)r-,län\ *trademark* — used for an acrylic fiber

or·lop deck \,òr-,läp-\ *n* [ME *overlop* deck of a single decker, fr. MLG *overlōp*, lit., something that overleaps] (1758) : the lowest deck in a ship having four or more decks

Or·mazd \'ò(ə)r-(,)məzd, -,mazd\ *n* [Per *Urmazd*, fr. OPer *Auramazdāh-*, fr. Av *Ahuramazdāh-*] : AHURA MAZDA

or·mo·lu \'òr-mə-,lü\ *n, often attrib* [F *or moulu*, lit., ground gold] (1765) : golden or gilded brass or bronze used for decorative purposes (as in mounts for furniture)

1or·na·ment \'òr-nə-mənt\ *n* [ME, fr. OF *ornement*, fr. L *ornamentum*, fr. *ornare*] (13c) **1** *archaic* : a useful accessory **2 a** : something that lends grace or beauty **b** : a manner or quality that adorns **3** : one whose virtues or graces add luster to his place or society **4** : the act of adorning or being adorned **5** : an embellishing note not belonging to the essential harmony or melody — called also *embellishment, fioritura*

2or·na·ment \-,ment\ *vt* (1720) : to provide with ornament : EMBELLISH *syn* see ADORN

1or·na·men·tal \,òr-nə-'ment-ᵊl\ *adj* (1646) : of, relating to, or serving as ornament; *specif* : grown as an ornamental — **or·na·men·tal·ly** \-ᵊl-ē\ *adv*

2ornamental *n* (1650) : a decorative object; *esp* : a plant cultivated for its beauty rather than for use

or·na·men·ta·tion \,òr-nə-mən-'tā-shən, -,men-\ *n* (1860) **1** : the act or process of ornamenting : the state of being ornamented **2** : something that ornaments : EMBELLISHMENT

or·nate \òr-'nāt\ *adj* [ME *ornat*, fr. L *ornatus*, pp. of *ornare* to furnish, embellish; akin to L *ordinare* to order — more at ORDAIN] (15c) **1** : marked by elaborate rhetoric or florid style **2** : elaborately or excessively decorated — **or·nate·ly** *adv* — **or·nate·ness** *n*

or·nery \'òrn-(ə-)rē, 'än-\ *adj* **or·neri·er; -est** [alter. of *ordinary*] (1816) : having an irritable disposition : CANTANKEROUS — **or·neri·ness** *n*

ornith- *or* **ornitho-** *comb form* [L, fr. Gk, fr. *ornith-, ornis* — more at ERNE] : bird ⟨*ornith*ology⟩

or·nith·ic \òr-'nith-ik\ *adj* [Gk *ornithikos*, fr. *ornith-, ornis*] (1854) : of, relating to, or characteristic of birds

or·ni·thine \'òr-nə-,thēn\ *n* [ISV *ornith*uric acid (an acid of which it is a component, found in the urine of birds) + *-ine*] (1881) : a crystalline amino acid $C_5H_{12}N_2O_2$ that functions esp. in urea production as a carrier by undergoing conversion to citrulline and then arginine in reaction with ammonia and carbon dioxide followed by recovery along with urea by enzymatic hydrolysis of arginine

or·nith·is·chi·an \,òr-nə-'this-kē-ən\ *n* [NL *Ornithischia*, fr. *ornith-* + *ischium*] (1901) : any of an order (Ornithischia) of herbivorous dinosaurs (as a stegosaurus) that have a pelvis with four axes of symmetry — **ornithischian** *adj*

or·ni·thol·o·gy \,òr-nə-'thäl-ə-jē\ *n, pl* **-gies** [NL *ornithologia*, fr. *ornith-* + *-logia* -logy] (1678) **1** : a branch of zoology dealing with birds **2** : a treatise on ornithology — **or·ni·tho·log·i·cal** \-thə-'läj-i-kəl\ *also* **or·ni·tho·log·ic** \-ik\ *adj* — **or·ni·tho·log·i·cal·ly** \-i-k(ə-)lē\ *adv* — **or·ni·thol·o·gist** \-'thäl-ə-jəst\ *n*

or·ni·thop·ter \'òr-nə-,thäp-tər\ *n* [ISV *ornith-* + *-pter* (as in *helicopter*)] (ca. 1908) : an aircraft designed to derive its chief support and propulsion from flapping wings

or·ni·tho·sis \,òr-nə-'thō-səs\ *n, pl* **-tho·ses** \-,sēz\ [NL] (1939) : PSITTACOSIS

1oro- *comb form* [Gk *oros* — more at RISE] : mountain ⟨*oro*logy⟩

2oro- *comb form* [L *or-, os* — more at ORAL] : mouth ⟨*oro*pharynx⟩ : oral and ⟨*oro*facial⟩

oro·gen·e·sis \,ōr-ə-'jen-ə-səs, ,òr-\ *n* [NL] (1886) : OROGENY — **oro·ge·net·ic** \-jə-'net-ik\ *adj*

orog·e·ny \ò-'räj-ə-nē\ *n* [ISV] (1890) : the process of mountain formation esp. by folding of the earth's crust — **oro·gen·ic** \,ōr-ə-'jen-ik, ,òr-\ *adj*

oro·graph·ic \,ōr-ə-'graf-ik, ,òr-\ *also* **oro·graph·i·cal** \-i-kəl\ *adj* (1846) : of or relating to mountains; *esp* : associated with or induced by the presence of mountains ⟨~ rainfall⟩ — **oro·graph·i·cal·ly** \-k(ə-)lē\ *adv*

orog·ra·phy \ò-'räg-rə-fē\ *n* [ISV ¹*oro-* + *geography*] (1846) : a branch of physical geography that deals with mountains

oro·pha·ryn·geal \,ōr-ə-,far-ən-'jē-əl, ,òr-, -fə-'rin-j(ē-)əl\ *adj* (1885) **1** : of or relating to the oropharynx **2** : of or relating to the mouth and pharynx

oro·phar·ynx \-'far-iŋ(k)s\ *n* (1887) : the part of the pharynx that is below the soft palate and above the epiglottis and is continuous with the mouth

oro·tund \'ōr-ə-,tənd, 'är-, 'òr-\ *adj* [modif. of L *ore rotundo*, lit., with round mouth] (1792) **1** : marked by fullness, strength, and clarity of sound : SONOROUS **2** : POMPOUS, BOMBASTIC — **oro·tun·di·ty** \,ōr-ə-'tən-dət-ē, ,är-, ,òr-\ *n*

1or·phan \'òr-fən\ *n* [LL *orphanus*, fr. Gk *orphanos*; akin to OHG *erbi* inheritance, L *orbus* orphaned] (14c) **1** : a child deprived by death of one or usu. both parents **2** : a young animal that has lost its mother — **orphan** *adj* — **or·phan·hood** \-,hu̇d\ *n*

2orphan *vt* **or·phaned; or·phan·ing** \'òrf-(ə-)niŋ\ (1814) : to cause to become an orphan

or·phan·age \'òrf-(ə-)nij\ *n* (1579) **1** : the state of being an orphan **2** : an institution for the care of orphans

orphan's court *n* (1713) : a probate court which in some states has jurisdiction over the affairs of minors and the administration of estates

Or·pheus \'òr-,fyüs, -fē-əs\ *n* [L, fr. Gk] : a poet and musician in Greek mythology who almost rescues his wife Eurydice from Hades by charming Pluto and Persephone with his lyre

or·phic \'òr-fik\ *adj* (1678) **1** *cap* : of or relating to Orpheus or the rites or doctrines ascribed to him **2** : MYSTIC, ORACULAR **3** : FASCINATING, ENTRANCING — **or·phi·cal·ly** \-fi-k(ə-)lē\ *adv*

Or·phism \'òr-,fiz-əm\ *n* [*Orpheus*, its reputed founder] (1880) : a mystic Greek religion offering initiates purification of the soul from innate evil and release from the cycle of reincarnation

or·phrey \'òr-frē\ *n, pl* **orphreys** [ME *orfrey*, fr. MF *orfreis*, fr. ML *aurifrigium*, fr. L *aurum* gold + *Phrygius* Phrygian — more at ORIOLE] (13c) **1 a** : elaborate embroidery **b** : a piece of such embroidery **2** : an ornamental border or band esp. on an ecclesiastical vestment

or·pi·ment \'òr-pə-mənt\ *n* [ME, fr. MF, fr. L *auripigmentum*, fr. *aurum* + *pigmentum* pigment] (14c) : native orange to lemon-yellow arsenic trisulfide

or·pine \'òr-pən\ *n* [ME *orpin*, fr. MF, fr. *orpiment*] (14c) : an herb (*Sedum telephium* of the family Crassulaceae, the orpine family) that has fleshy leaves and pink or purple flowers and was formerly used in folk medicine; *broadly* : SEDUM

Or·ping·ton \'òr-piŋ-tən\ *n* [*Orpington*, England] (1886) : any of an English breed of large deep-chested domestic fowls

or·rery \'òr-ər-ē, 'är-\ *n, pl* **or·rer·ies** [Charles Boyle †1731 4th Earl of *Orrery*] (1713) : an apparatus showing the relative positions and motions of bodies in the solar system by balls moved by wheelwork

or·ris \'òr-əs, 'är-\ *n* [prob. alter. of ME *ireos*, fr. ML, alter. of L *iris*] (1626) : a European iris (*Iris florentina*) with a fragrant rootstock that is used esp. in perfume and sachet powder; *also* : its rootstock

or·ris·root \-,rüt, -,ru̇t\ *n* (1598) : the fragrant rootstock of any of several European irises used esp. in perfume

ort \'ò(ə)rt\ *n* [ME] (15c) : a morsel left at a meal : SCRAP

orth- *or* **ortho-** *comb form* [ME, fr. MF, straight, right, true, fr. L, fr. Gk, fr. *orthos*] **1** : straight : upright : vertical ⟨*ortho*tropic⟩ **2** : perpendicular ⟨*ortho*rhombic⟩ **3** : correct : corrective ⟨*ortho*dontia⟩ **4 a** : hydrated or hydroxylated to the highest degree ⟨*ortho*phosphoric acid⟩ **b** : involving substitution at or characterized by or having the relationship of two neighboring positions in the benzene ring ⟨*ortho*-xylene⟩

or·thi·con \'òr-thi-,kän\ *n* [ISV *orth-* + *iconoscope*] (1939) : a camera tube similar to but more sensitive than an iconoscope in which the charges are scanned by a low-velocity beam

or·tho \'òr-(,)thō\ *adj* (1904) : ORTHOCHROMATIC

or·tho·cen·ter \'òr-thə-,sent-ər\ *n* [ISV] (1869) : the common intersection of the three altitudes of a triangle or their extensions or of the several altitudes of a polyhedron provided these latter exist and meet in a point

or·tho·chro·mat·ic \,òr-thə-krō-'mat-ik\ *adj* [ISV] (1887) **1** : of, relating to, or producing tone values of light and shade in a photograph that correspond to the tones in nature **2** : sensitive to all colors except red

or·tho·clase \'òr-thə-,klās, -,klāz\ *n* [G *orthoklas*, fr. *orth-* + Gk *klasis* breaking, fr. *klan* to break — more at HALT] (1849) : a mineral $KAlSi_3O_8$ consisting of a monoclinic polymorph of common potassic feldspar often with sodium in place of some of the potassium

orth·odon·tia \,òr-thə-'dän-ch(ē-)ə\ *n* [NL] (1849) : ORTHODONTICS

orth·odon·tics \-'dänt-iks\ *n pl but sing in constr* (1909) : a branch of dentistry dealing with irregularities of the teeth and their correction (as by means of braces) — **orth·odon·tic** \-ik\ *adj* — **orth·odon·tist** \-'dänt-əst\ *n*

1or·tho·dox \'òr-thə-,däks\ *adj* [MF or LL; MF *orthodoxe*, fr. LL *orthodoxus*, fr. LGk *orthodoxos*, fr. Gk *orth-* + *doxa* opinion — more at DOXOLOGY] (15c) **1 a** : conforming to established doctrine esp. in religion **b** : CONVENTIONAL **2** *cap* : of, relating to, or constituting any of various conservative religious or political groups: as **a** : EASTERN ORTHODOX **b** : of or relating to Orthodox Judaism — **or·tho·dox·ly** *adv*

2orthodox *n, pl* **orthodox** *also* **or·tho·dox·es** (1587) **1** : one that is orthodox **2** *cap* : a member of an Eastern Orthodox church

Orthodox Judaism *n* (ca. 1904) : Judaism that adheres to the Torah and Talmud as interpreted in an authoritative rabbinic law code and applies their principles and regulations to modern living — compare CONSERVATIVE JUDAISM

or·tho·doxy \'òr-thə-,däk-sē\ *n, pl* **-dox·ies** (1630) **1** : the quality or state of being orthodox **2** : an orthodox belief or practice **3** *cap* **a** : Eastern Orthodox Christianity **b** : ORTHODOX JUDAISM

or·tho·epy \'òr-thə-,wep-ē, òr-'thō-ə-pē\ *n* [NL *orthoepia*, fr. Gk *orthoepeia*, fr. *orth-* + *epos* word — more at VOICE] (1668) **1** : the customary pronunciation of a language **2** : the study of the pronunciation of a language — **or·tho·ep·ic** \,òr-thə-'wep-ik\ *adj* — **or·tho·ep·i·cal·ly** \-i-k(ə-)lē\ *adv* — **or·tho·epist** \'òr-thə-,wep-əst, òr-'thō-ə-pəst\ *n*

or·tho·gen·e·sis \,òr-thə-'jen-ə-səs\ *n* [NL] (1895) : variation of organisms in successive generations that in some evolutionary theories takes place in some predestined direction and results in progressive evolutionary trends independent of external factors — **or·tho·ge·net·ic** \-jə-'net-ik\ *adj* — **or·tho·ge·net·i·cal·ly** \-i-k(ə-)lē\ *adv*

or·thog·o·nal \òr-'thäg-ən-ᵊl\ *adj* [MF, fr. L *orthogonius*, fr. Gk *orthogōnios*, fr. *orth-* + *gōnia* angle — more at -GON] (1612) **1 a** : intersecting or lying at right angles **b** : having perpendicular slopes or tangents at the point of intersection ⟨~ curves⟩ **2** : having a sum of products or an integral that is zero or sometimes one under specified conditions: as **a** *of real-valued functions* : having the integral of the product of each pair of functions over a specific interval equal to zero **b** *of vectors* : having the scalar product equal to zero **c** *of a square matrix* : having the sum of products of corresponding elements in any two rows or any two columns equal to one if the rows or columns are the same and equal to zero otherwise : having a transpose with which the product equals the identity matrix **3** *of a linear transformation* : having a matrix that is orthogonal : preserving length and distance **4** : composed of mutually orthogonal elements ⟨an ~ basis of a vector space⟩ **5** : statistically independent — **or·thog·o·nal·i·ty** \-,thäg-ə-'nal-ət-ē\ *n* — **or·thog·o·nal·ly** \-'thäg-ən-ᵊl-ē\ *adv*

or·thog·o·nal·ize \òr-'thäg-ən-ᵊl-,īz\ *vt* **-ized; -iz·ing** (1937) : to make orthogonal — **or·thog·o·nal·iza·tion** \-,thäg-ən-ᵊl-ə-'zā-shən\ *n*

or·tho·grade \'òr-thə-,grād\ *adj* (1902) : walking with the body upright or vertical

or·tho·graph·ic \,òr-thə-'graf-ik\ *also* **or·tho·graph·i·cal** \-i-kəl\ *adj* (1866) **1** : of, relating to, being, or prepared by orthographic projection ⟨an ~ map⟩ **2 a** : of or relating to orthography **b** : correct in spelling — **or·tho·graph·i·cal·ly** \-i-k(ə-)lē\ *adv*

orthographic projection *n* (1668) **1 :** projection of a single view of an object (as a view of the front) on a drawing surface that is perpendicular to both the view and the lines of projection **2 :** the representation of related views of an object as if they were all in the same plane and projected by orthographic projection

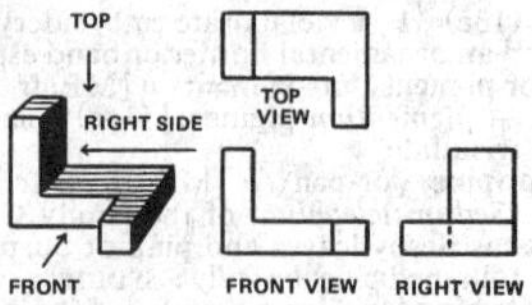

A

object *A* with top view, front view, and right view in orthographic projection

or·thog·ra·phy \ȯr-'thäg-rə-fē\ *n* [ME *ortografie,* fr. MF, fr. L *orthographia,* fr. Gk, fr. *orth-* + *graphein* to write — more at CARVE] (15c) **1 a :** the art of writing words with the proper letters according to standard usage **b :** the representation of the sounds of a language by written or printed symbols **2 :** a part of language study that deals with letters and spelling

or·tho·mo·lec·u·lar \ˌȯr-thə-mə-'lek-yə-lər\ *adj* (1968) **:** relating to, based on, using, or being a theory according to which disease and esp. mental illness may be cured by restoring the optimum amounts of substances normally present in the body ⟨~ therapy⟩ ⟨an ~ psychiatrist⟩

or·tho·nor·mal \ˌȯr-thə-'nȯr-məl\ *adj* (1939) **1** *of real-valued functions* **:** orthogonal with the integral of the square of each function over a specified interval equal to one **2 :** being or composed of orthogonal elements of unit length ⟨~ basis of a vector space⟩

or·tho·pe·dic *also* **or·tho·pae·dic** \ˌȯr-thə-'pē-dik\ *adj* [F *orthopédique,* fr. *orthopédie* orthopedics, fr. *orth-* + Gk *paid-, pais* child — more at FEW] (1840) **1 :** of, relating to, or employed in orthopedics **2 :** marked by deformities or crippling — **or·tho·pe·di·cal·ly** \-'pē-di-k(ə-)lē\ *adv*

or·tho·pe·dics *also* **or·tho·pae·dics** \-'pē-diks\ *n pl but sing or pl in constr* (1853) **:** the correction or prevention of skeletal deformities — **or·tho·pe·dist** \-'pē-dəst\ *n*

or·tho·phos·phate \ˌȯr-thə-'fäs-ˌfāt\ *n* (1859) **:** a salt or ester of orthophosphoric acid

or·tho·phos·pho·ric acid \ˌȯr-thə-ˌfäs-ˌfȯr-ik-, -ˌfär-; -ˌfäs-f(ə-)rik-\ *n* [ISV] (1885) **:** PHOSPHORIC ACID 1

or·tho·psy·chi·a·try \-sə-'kī-ə-trē, -(ˌ)sī-\ *n* (ca. 1927) **:** prophylactic psychiatry concerned esp. with incipient mental and behavioral disorders in youth — **or·tho·psy·chi·at·ric** \-ˌsī-kē-'a-trik\ *adj* — **or·tho·psy·chi·a·trist** \-sə-'kī-ə-trəst, -(ˌ)sī-\ *n*

or·thop·ter·an \ȯr-'thäp-tə-rən\ *n* [NL *Orthoptera*] (1842) **:** any of an order (Orthoptera) of insects (as crickets, grasshoppers, and sometimes mantises) that are characterized by biting mouthparts, two pairs of wings or none, and an incomplete metamorphosis — **orthopteran** *adj* — **or·thop·ter·ist** \-rəst\ *n* — **or·thop·ter·oid** \-ˌrȯid\ *n or adj*

or·thop·ter·on \ȯr-'thäp-tə-rən, -ˌrän\ *n, pl* **-tera** \-tə-rə\ [NL, sing. of *Orthoptera,* fr. *orth-* + Gk *pteron* wing — more at FEATHER] (1880) **:** ORTHOPTERAN

or·tho·rhom·bic \ˌȯr-thə-'räm-bik\ *adj* [ISV] (1864) **:** of, relating to, or constituting a system of crystallization characterized by three unequal axes at right angles to each other

or·tho·scop·ic \-'skäp-ik\ *adj* [ISV *orth-* + *-scopic* (as in *microscopic*)] (1853) **:** giving an image in correct and normal proportions

or·tho·stat·ic \ˌȯr-thə-'stat-ik\ *adj* (1902) **:** of, relating to, or caused by erect posture ⟨~ hypotension⟩

or·thot·ic \ȯr-'thät-ik\ *n* (1962) **:** a support or brace for weak or ineffective joints or muscles

or·thot·ics \-iks\ *n pl but sing in constr* [NL *orthosis* straightening (fr. Gk *orthōsis,* fr. *orthoun* to straighten, fr. *orthos*), after such pairs as NL *prosthesis:* E *prosthetics*] (1962) **:** a branch of mechanical and medical science that deals with the support and bracing of weak or ineffective joints or muscles — **or·thot·ic** \-ik\ *adj* — **or·tho·tist** \ȯr-'thät-əst, 'ȯr-thət-əst\ *n*

or·thot·ro·pous \ȯr-'thä-trə-pəs\ *adj* [ISV] (1830) **:** having the ovule straight so that the chalaza, hilum, and micropyle are in the same axial line

or·to·lan \'ȯrt-ᵊl-ən\ *n* [F or It; F, fr. It *ortolano,* lit., gardener, fr. L *hortulanus,* fr. *hortulus,* dim. of *hortus* garden — more at YARD] (1656) **:** a European bunting (*Emberiza hortulana*) that is about six inches long and is valued as a table delicacy

Or·vie·to \ȯr-'vyāt-(ˌ)ō\ *n* [*Orvieto,* city in central Italy] (1673) **:** a usu. dry Italian white wine

1-o·ry \ˌōr-ē, ˌȯr-ē, (ə-)rē\ *n suffix* [ME *-orie,* fr. L *-orium,* fr. neut. of *-orius,* adj. suffix] **1 :** place of or for ⟨observat*ory*⟩ **2 :** something that serves for ⟨cremat*ory*⟩

2-ory *adj suffix* [ME *-orie,* fr. MF & L; MF, fr. L *-orius*] **1 :** of, relating to, or characterized by ⟨gustat*ory*⟩ **2 :** serving for, producing, or maintaining ⟨justificat*ory*⟩

oryx \'ōr-iks, 'ȯr-, 'är-\ *n, pl* **oryx** *or* **oryx·es** [NL, fr. L, a gazelle, fr. Gk, pickax, antelope, fr. *oryssein* to dig — more at ROUGH] (14c) **:** any of a genus (*Oryx*) of large straight-horned African antelopes

or·zo \'ȯrd-(ˌ)zō\ *n* [It, perh. fr. *orzo* barley] (ca. 1929) **:** rice-shaped pasta

1os \'äs\ *n, pl* **os·sa** \'äs-ə\ [L *oss-, os* — more at OSSEOUS] (15c) **:** BONE

2os \'ōs\ *n, pl* **ora** \'ōr-ə, 'ȯr-ə\ [L *or-, os* — more at ORAL] (1737) **:** MOUTH, ORIFICE

Osage \ō-'sāj, 'ō-\ *n, pl* **Osag·es** *or* **Osage** (1698) **1 :** a member of an American Indian people orig. of Missouri **2 :** the language of the Osage people

Osage orange *n* (1817) **:** an ornamental American tree (*Maclura pomifera*) of the mulberry family with shiny ovate leaves and hard bright orange wood; *also* **:** its yellowish fruit

Os·can \'äs-kən\ *n* [L *Oscus*] (1753) **1 :** a member of a people of ancient Italy occupying Campania **2 :** the language of the Oscan people — see INDO-EUROPEAN LANGUAGES table

1Os·car \'äs-kər\ *trademark* — used esp. for any of a number of golden statuettes awarded annually by a professional organization for notable achievement in motion pictures

2Oscar (1952) — a communications code word for the letter *o*

os·cil·late \'äs-ə-ˌlāt\ *vi* **-lat·ed; -lat·ing** [L *oscillatus,* pp. of *oscillare* to swing, fr. *oscillum* swing] (1726) **1 a :** to swing backward and forward like a pendulum **b :** to move or travel back and forth between two points **2 :** to vary between opposing beliefs, feelings, or theories **3 :** to vary above and below a mean value ***syn*** see SWING — **os·cil·la·to·ry** \'äs-ə-lə-ˌtōr-ē, -ˌtȯr-\ *adj*

os·cil·la·tion \ˌäs-ə-'lā-shən\ *n* (1658) **1 :** the action or state of oscillating **2 :** VARIATION, FLUCTUATION **3 :** a flow of electricity changing periodically from a maximum to a minimum; *esp* **:** a flow periodically changing direction **4 :** a single swing (as of an oscillating body) from one extreme limit to the other — **os·cil·la·tion·al** \-shnəl, -shən-ᵊl\ *adj*

os·cil·la·tor \'äs-ə-ˌlāt-ər\ *n* (1835) **1 :** one that oscillates **2 :** a device for producing alternating current; *esp* **:** a radio-frequency or audio-frequency generator

os·cil·lo·gram \ä-'sil-ə-ˌgram, ə-\ *n* [L *oscillare* + ISV *-gram*] (1903) **:** a record made by an oscillograph or oscilloscope

os·cil·lo·graph \-ˌgraf\ *n* [F *oscillographe,* fr. L *oscillare* + F *-graphe* -graph] (1893) **:** an instrument for recording alternating current wave forms or other electrical oscillations — **os·cil·lo·graph·ic** \ä-ˌsil-ə-'graf-ik, ˌäs-ə-lə-\ *adj* — **os·cil·lo·graph·i·cal·ly** \-i-k(ə-)lē\ *adv* — **os·cil·log·ra·phy** \ˌäs-ə-'läg-rə-fē\ *n*

os·cil·lo·scope \ä-'sil-ə-ˌskōp, ə-\ *n* [L *oscillare* + ISV *-scope*] (1906) **:** an instrument in which the variations in a fluctuating electrical quantity appear temporarily as a visible wave form on the fluorescent screen of a cathode-ray tube; *broadly* **:** OSCILLOGRAPH — **os·cil·lo·scop·ic** \ä-ˌsil-ə-'skäp-ik, ˌäs-ə-lə-\ *adj* — **os·cil·lo·scop·i·cal·ly** \-i-k(ə-)lē\ *adv*

os·cine \'äs-ˌīn\ *adj* [deriv. of L *oscin-, oscen* bird used in divination, fr. *obs-* in front of + *canere* to sing — more at OSTENSIBLE, CHANT] (1883) **:** PASSERINE 2 — **oscine** *n*

Os·co–Um·bri·an \ˌäs-kō-'əm-brē-ən\ *n* [L *Oscus* + E *Umbrian*] (1894) **:** a subdivision of the Italic branch of the Indo-European language family containing Oscan and Umbrian — see INDO-EUROPEAN LANGUAGES table

os·cu·late \'äs-kyə-ˌlāt\ *vt* **-lat·ed; -lat·ing** [L *osculatus,* pp. of *osculari,* fr. *osculum* kiss, fr. dim. of *os* mouth — more at ORAL] (ca. 1656) **:** KISS

os·cu·la·tion \ˌäs-kyə-'lā-shən\ *n* (ca. 1658) **:** the act of kissing; *also* **:** KISS — **os·cu·la·to·ry** \'äs-kyə-lə-ˌtōr-ē, -ˌtȯr-\ *adj*

os·cu·lum \'äs-kyə-ləm\ *n* [NL, fr. L, dim. of *os* mouth] (1887) **:** an excurrent opening of a sponge

1-ose \ˌōs, 'ōs *sometimes* ˌōz, 'ōz\ *adj suffix* [ME, fr. L *-osus*] **:** full of **:** having **:** possessing the qualities of ⟨cym*ose*⟩

2-ose \ˌōs, ˌōz\ *n suffix* [F, fr. *glucose*] **1 :** carbohydrate ⟨amyl*ose*⟩; *esp* **:** sugar ⟨pent*ose*⟩ **2 :** primary hydrolysis product ⟨prote*ose*⟩

Osee \'ō-ˌzē, ō-'zā-ə\ *n* [LL, fr. Heb *Hōshēaʽ*] **:** HOSEA

osier \'ō-zhər\ *n* [ME, fr. MF, fr. ML *auseria* osier bed] (14c) **1 :** any of various willows (esp. *Salix viminalis*) whose pliable twigs are used for furniture and basketry **2 :** a willow rod used in basketry **3 :** any of several American dogwoods

Osi·ris \ō-'sī-rəs\ *n* [L, fr. Gk, fr. Egypt *Ws'r*] **:** the Egyptian god of the underworld and husband and brother of Isis

-o·sis \'ō-səs\ *n suffix, pl* **-o·ses** \-ˌsēz\ *or* **-o·sis·es** [ME, fr. L, fr. Gk *-ōsis,* fr. *-ō-* (stem of causative verbs in *-oun*) + *-sis*] **1 a :** action **:** process **:** condition ⟨hypn*osis*⟩ **b :** abnormal or diseased condition ⟨leuk*osis*⟩ **2 :** increase **:** formation ⟨leukocyt*osis*⟩

Os·man·li \äz-'man-lē\ *n* [Turk *osmanlı,* fr. *Osman,* founder of the Ottoman Empire] (1741) **1 :** a Turk of the western branch of the Turkish peoples **2 :** TURKISH

os·me·te·ri·um \ˌäz-mə-'tir-ē-əm\ *n, pl* **-ria** \-ē-ə\ [NL, fr. Gk *osmē* odor + *-tērion,* suffix denoting an instrument] (1816) **:** a protrusible forked process that emits a disagreeable odor, is borne on the first thoracic segment of the larvae of many swallowtail butterflies and their relatives, and is prob. a defensive organ

osmic acid *n* (1842) **:** OSMIUM TETROXIDE

os·mi·rid·i·um \ˌäz-mə-'rid-ē-əm\ *n* [Gk *osmē* + NL *iridium*] (1880) **:** IRIDOSMINE

os·mi·um \'äz-mē-əm\ *n* [NL, fr. Gk *osmē* odor] (ca. 1804) **:** a hard brittle blue-gray or blue-black polyvalent metallic element of the platinum group with a high melting point that is the heaviest metal known and that is used esp. as a catalyst and in hard alloys — see ELEMENT table

osmium tetroxide *n* (1876) **:** a crystalline compound OsO_4 that is an oxide of osmium, has a poisonous irritating vapor, and is used as a catalyst, oxidizing agent, and biological fixative and stain

os·mol *or* **os·mole** \'äz-ˌmōl, 'äs-\ *n* [blend of *osmosis* and *mol* (5mole)] (1942) **:** a standard unit of osmotic pressure based on a one molal concentration of an ion in a solution

os·mo·lal·i·ty \ˌäz-mō-'lal-ət-ē, ˌäs-\ *n, pl* **-ties** [*osmol* + *-al* + *-ity*] (ca. 1944) **:** the concentration of an osmotic solution esp. when measured in osmols or milliosmols per 1000 grams of solvent — **os·mo·lal** \äz-'mō-ləl, äs-\ *adj*

os·mo·lar·i·ty \ˌäz-mō-'lar-ət-ē, ˌäs-\ *n, pl* **-ties** [*osmol* + *-ar* + *-ity*] (1948) **:** the concentration of an osmotic solution esp. when measured in osmols or milliosmols per liter of solution — **os·mo·lar** \äz-'mō-lər, äs-\ *adj*

os·mom·e·ter \äz-'mäm-ət-ər, äs-\ *n* [*osmosis* + *-meter*] (1854) **:** an apparatus for measuring osmotic pressure — **os·mo·met·ric** \ˌäz-mə-'me-trik, ˌäs-\ *adj* — **os·mom·e·try** \äz-'mäm-ə-trē\ *n*

os·mo·reg·u·la·tion \'äz-mō-ˌreg-yə-'lā-shən, 'äs-\ *n* [*osmosis* + *regulation*] (1927) **:** regulation of osmotic pressure esp. in the body of a living organism

os·mo·reg·u·la·to·ry \-'reg-yə-lə-ˌtōr-ē, -ˌtȯr-\ *adj* (ca. 1911) **:** of, relating to, or concerned with the maintenance of constant osmotic pressure

os·mo·sis \äz-'mō-səs, äs-\ *n* [NL, short for *endosmosis*] (1867) **1 :** movement of a solvent through a semipermeable membrane (as of a living cell) into a solution of higher solute concentration that tends to equalize the concentrations of solute on the two sides of the membrane **2 :** a process of absorption or diffusion suggestive of the flow of osmotic action ⟨were thrown into classes where they were expected to learn English by ~ —Susan Jacoby⟩

os·mot·ic \-'mät-ik\ *adj* (1854) **:** of, relating to, or having the properties of osmosis — **os·mot·i·cal·ly** \-i-k(ə-)lē\ *adv*

osmotic pressure *n* (1888) **:** the pressure produced by or associated with osmosis and dependent on molar concentration and absolute temperature: as **a :** the maximum pressure that develops in a solution separated from a solvent by a membrane permeable only to the solvent **b**

: the pressure that must be applied to a solution to just prevent osmosis

osmotic shock *n* (1950) : a rapid change in the osmotic pressure (as by transfer to a medium of different concentration) affecting a living system

os·mun·da \äz-'mən-də\ *n* [NL, fr. ML, fr. OF *osmonde*] (1578) : any of a genus (*Osmunda*) of rather large ferns with fibrous creeping rhizomes

os·prey \'äs-prē, -ˌprā\ *n, pl* **ospreys** [ME *ospray*, fr. (assumed) MF *osfraie*, fr. L *ossifraga* ossifrage] (15c) **1** : a large fish-eating hawk (*Pandion haliaetus*) that is a dark brown color above and mostly pure white below **2** : a feather trimming used for millinery

ossa *pl of* OS

os·se·in \'äs-ē-ən\ *n* [ISV, fr. L *oss-*, *os*] (1857) : the collagen of bones

os·se·ous \'äs-ē-əs\ *adj* [L *osseus*, fr. *oss-*, *os* bone; akin to Gk *osteon* bone] (1707) : BONY 1

Os·set \'äs-ət, -ˌet\ *or* **Os·sete** \'äs-ˌēt\ *n* [Russ *Osetin*] (1814) : a member of an Aryan people of central Caucasia — **Os·se·tian** \ä-'sē-shən\ *adj or n*

Os·set·ic \ä-'set-ik\ *n* (ca. 1890) : the Iranian language of the Ossets

Os·si·an·ic \ˌäs(h)-ē-'an-ik\ *adj* (1808) : of, relating to, or resembling the legendary Irish bard Ossian, the poems ascribed to him, or the rhythmic prose style used by James Macpherson in his alleged translations

os·si·cle \'äs-i-kəl\ *n* [L *ossiculum*, dim. of *oss-*, *os*] (1578) : a small bone or bony structure (as the malleus, incus, or stapes) — **os·sic·u·lar** \ä-'sik-yə-lər\ *adj*

os·si·fi·ca·tion \ˌäs-ə-fə-'kā-shən\ *n* (1697) **1 a** : the natural process of bone formation **b** : the hardening (as of muscular tissue) into a bony substance **2** : a mass or particle of ossified tissue **3** : a tendency toward or state of being molded into a rigid, conventional, sterile, or unimaginative condition

os·si·frage \'äs-ə-frij, -ˌfrāj\ *n* [L *ossifraga* sea eagle, fr. fem. of *ossifragus* bone-breaking, fr. *oss-*, *os* + *frangere* to break — more at BREAK] (1601) : LAMMERGEIER

os·si·fy \'äs-ə-ˌfī\ *vb* **-fied; -fy·ing** [prob. fr. (assumed) NL *ossificare*, fr. L *oss-*, *os*] *vi* (1713) **1** : to change into bone **2** : to become callous or conventional ~ *vt* **1** : to change (as cartilage) into bone **2** : to make rigidly conventional and opposed to change

os·so bu·co \ˌō-sō-'bü-(ˌ)kō\ *n* [It *ossobuco* marrowbone] (1935) : braised veal shanks

os·su·ary \'äsh-ə-ˌwer-ē, 'äs-(y)ə-\ *n, pl* **-ar·ies** [LL *ossuarium*, fr. L, neut. of *ossuarius* of bones, fr. OL *ossua*, pl. of *oss-*, *os*] (1658) : a depository for the bones of the dead

oste- *or* **osteo-** *comb form* [NL, fr. Gk, fr. *osteon* — more at OSSEOUS] : bone ⟨*oste*al⟩ ⟨*osteo*myelitis⟩

os·te·al \'äs-tē-əl\ *adj* [ISV] (1877) : of, relating to, or resembling bone; *also* : affecting or involving bone or the skeleton

os·te·itis \ˌäs-tē-'īt-əs\ *n* [NL] (ca. 1839) : inflammation of bone

os·ten·si·ble \ä-'sten(t)-sə-bəl, ə-\ *adj* [F, fr. L *ostensus*, pp. of *ostendere* to show, fr. *obs-* in front of (akin to *ob-* in the way) + *tendere* to stretch — more at OB-, THIN] (1762) **1** : intended for display : open to view **2** : being such in appearance : plausible rather than demonstrably true or real ⟨the ~ purpose for the trip⟩ ***syn*** see APPARENT — **os·ten·si·bly** \-blē\ *adv*

os·ten·sive \ä-'sten(t)-siv\ *adj* (1605) **1** : OSTENSIBLE 2 **2** : of, relating to, or constituting definition by exhibiting the thing or quality being defined — **os·ten·sive·ly** *adv*

os·ten·so·ri·um \ˌäs-tən-'sōr-ē-əm, -ˌten-, -'sòr-\ *n, pl* **-ria** \-ē-ə\ [ML, fr. L *ostensus*] (1760) : MONSTRANCE

os·ten·ta·tion \ˌäs-tən-'tā-shən\ *n* [ME *ostentacion*, fr. MF *ostentation*, fr. L *ostentation-*, *ostentatio*, fr. *ostentatus*, pp. of *ostentare* to display ostentatiously, fr. *ostentus*, pp. of *ostendere*] (15c) **1** : excessive display : PRETENTIOUSNESS **2** *archaic* : an act of displaying

os·ten·ta·tious \-shəs\ *adj* (1673) : marked by or indulging in conspicuous or vainglorious and sometimes pretentious display ***syn*** see SHOWY — **os·ten·ta·tious·ly** *adv* — **os·ten·ta·tious·ness** *n*

os·teo·ar·thri·tis \ˌäs-tē-ō-är-'thrīt-əs\ *n* [NL] (1878) : arthritis marked by degeneration of the cartilage and bone of joints — **os·teo·ar·thrit·ic** \-'thrit-ik\ *adj*

os·teo·blast \'äs-tē-ə-ˌblast\ *n* [ISV] (1875) : a bone-forming cell — **os·teo·blas·tic** \ˌäs-tē-ə-'blas-tik\ *adj*

os·teo·clast \'äs-tē-ə-ˌklast\ *n* [ISV *oste-* + Gk *klastos* broken — more at CLASTIC] (1872) : any of the large multinucleate cells in developing bone that are associated with the dissolution of unwanted bone — **os·teo·clas·tic** \ˌäs-tē-ə-'klas-tik\ *adj*

os·teo·cyte \'äs-tē-ə-ˌsīt\ *n* (1942) : a cell that is characteristic of adult bone and is isolated in a lacuna of the bone substance

os·teo·gen·e·sis \ˌäs-tē-ə-'jen-ə-səs\ *n* (1830) : development and formation of bone

osteogenesis im·per·fec·ta \-ˌim-(ˌ)pər-'fek-tə\ *n* [NL, imperfect osteogenesis] (ca. 1901) : a familial disease marked esp. by extreme brittleness of the long bones

os·teo·gen·ic \ˌäs-tē-ə-'jen-ik\ *adj* (1867) **1** : producing bone **2** : originating in bone

osteogenic sarcoma *n* (ca. 1923) : OSTEOSARCOMA

¹os·te·oid \'äs-tē-ˌȯid\ *adj* [ISV] (1840) : resembling bone

²osteoid *n* (1934) : uncalcified bone matrix

os·te·ol·o·gy \ˌäs-tē-'äl-ə-jē\ *n* [NL *osteologia*, fr. Gk, description of bones, fr. *oste-* + *-logia* -logy] (1670) **1** : a branch of anatomy dealing with the bones **2** : the bony structure of an organism — **os·te·o·log·i·cal** \-tē-ə-'läj-i-kəl\ *adj* — **os·te·o·log·i·cal·ly** \-k(ə-)lē\ *adv* — **os·te·ol·o·gist** \-tē-'äl-ə-jəst\ *n*

os·te·o·ma \ˌäs-tē-'ō-mə\ *n, pl* **-mas** *or* **-ma·ta** \-mət-ə\ [NL] (1847) : a benign tumor composed of bone tissue

os·teo·ma·la·cia \ˌäs-tē-ō-mə-'lā-sh(ē-)ə\ *n* [NL, fr. *oste-* + Gk *malakia* softness, fr. *malakos* soft — more at MALAC-] (1822) : a disease characterized by softening of the bones in the adult and equivalent to rickets in the immature

os·teo·my·eli·tis \-ˌmī-ə-'līt-əs\ *n* [NL] (ca. 1854) : an infectious inflammatory disease of bone marked by local death and separation of tissue

os·teo·path \'äs-tē-ə-ˌpath\ *n* (1897) : a practitioner of osteopathy

os·te·op·a·thy \ˌäs-tē-'äp-ə-thē\ *n* [NL *osteopathia*, fr. *oste-* + L *-pathia* -pathy] (1857) : a system of medical practice based on a theory that diseases are due chiefly to loss of structural integrity which can be restored by manipulation of the parts supplemented by therapeutic measures (as use of medicine or surgery) — **os·teo·path·ic** \ˌäs-tē-ə-'path-ik\ *adj* — **os·teo·path·i·cal·ly** \-i-k(ə-)lē\ *adv*

os·teo·plas·tic \ˌäs-tē-ə-'plas-tik\ *adj* (1863) : of or relating to the surgical replacement of bone — **os·teo·plas·ty** \'äs-tē-ə-ˌplas-tē\ *n*

os·teo·po·ro·sis \ˌäs-tē-ō-pə-'rō-səs\ *n, pl* **-ro·ses** \-ˌsēz\ [NL, fr. *oste-* + *porosis* rarefaction, fr. *porus* pore + *-osis*] (1846) : a condition that is characterized by decrease in bone mass with decreased density and enlargement of bone spaces producing porosity and fragility and that results from disturbance of nutrition and mineral metabolism — **os·teo·po·rot·ic** \-'rät-ik\ *adj*

os·teo·sar·co·ma \-sär-'kō-mə\ *n, pl* **-mas** *or* **-ma·ta** \-mət-ə\ [NL] (1807) : a sarcoma derived from bone or containing bone tissue

osti·na·to \ˌäs-tə-'nät-(ˌ)ō, ˌȯ-stə-\ *n, pl* **-tos** [It, obstinate, fr. L *obstinatus*] (1876) : a musical figure repeated persistently at the same pitch throughout a composition — compare IMITATION, SEQUENCE

os·ti·ole \'äs-tē-ˌōl\ *n* [NL *ostiolum*, fr. L, dim. of *ostium*] (1835) : a small bodily aperture, orifice, or pore

os·ti·um \'äs-tē-əm\ *n, pl* **os·tia** \-tē-ə\ [NL, fr. L, door, mouth of a river; akin to L *os* mouth — more at ORAL] (1828) : a mouthlike opening in a bodily organ

ostler *var of* HOSTLER

ost·mark \'ōst-ˌmärk, 'ȯst-\ *n* [G, lit., East mark] (1948) : the former East German mark

os·to·my \'äs-tə-mē\ *n, pl* **-mies** [*colostomy*] (1957) : an operation (as a colostomy) to create an artificial passage for bodily elimination

-os·to·sis \äs-'tō-səs\ *n comb form, pl* **-os·to·ses** \-ˌsēz\ *or* **-os·to·sis·es** \-'tō-sə-səz\ [NL, fr. Gk *-ostōsis*, fr. *osteon* bone — more at OSSEOUS] : ossification of a (specified) part or to a (specified) degree ⟨hyper*ostosis*⟩ ⟨ect*ostosis*⟩

os·tra·cism \'äs-trə-ˌsiz-əm\ *n* (1579) **1** : a method of temporary banishment by popular vote without trial or special accusation practiced in ancient Greece **2** : exclusion by general consent from common privileges or social acceptance

os·tra·cize \-ˌsīz\ *vt* **-cized; -ciz·ing** [Gk *ostrakizein* to banish by voting with potsherds, fr. *ostrakon* shell, potsherd — more at OYSTER] (ca. 1828) **1** : to exile by ostracism **2** : to exclude from a group by common consent

os·tra·cod \'äs-trə-ˌkäd\ *also* **os·tra·code** \-ˌkōd\ *n* [deriv. of Gk *ostrakon*] (1865) : any of a subclass (Ostracoda) of small active mostly freshwater crustaceans that have the body enclosed in a bivalve shell, the body segmentation obscured, the abdomen rudimentary, and only seven pairs of appendages

os·tra·co·derm \'äs-trə-kō-ˌdərm, äs-'trak-ə-\ *n* [deriv. of Gk *ostrakon* + *derma* skin — more at DERM-] (1891) : any of an order (Ostracodermi) of primitive fossil armored fishes — **ostracoderm** *adj*

os·tra·con \'äs-trə-ˌkän\ *n, pl* **-tra·ca** \-trə-kə\ [Gk *ostrakon*, potsherd, shell] (1883) : a fragment (as of pottery) containing an inscription — usu. used in pl.

os·trich \'äs-trich, 'ȯs- *also* -trij\ *n* [ME, fr. OF *ostrusce*, fr. (assumed) VL *avis struthio*, fr. L *avis* bird + LL *struthio* ostrich — more at STRUTHIOUS] (13c) **1 a** : a swift-footed 2-toed flightless ratite bird (genus *Struthio*, esp. *S. camelus* of northern Africa) that has valuable wing and tail plumes, is the largest of existing birds, and often weighs 300 pounds **b** : RHEA **2** [fr. the belief that the ostrich when pursued hides its head in the sand and believes itself to be unseen] : one who attempts to avoid danger by refusing to face it — **os·trich·like** \-ˌlīk\ *adj*

Os·tro·goth \'äs-trə-ˌgäth\ *n* [LL *Ostrogothi*, pl.] (14c) : a member of the eastern division of the Goths — **Os·tro·goth·ic** \ˌäs-trə-'gäth-ik\ *adj*

Os·we·go tea \ä-ˌswē-gō-\ *n* [*Oswego* river, N. Y.] (1752) : a No. American mint (*Monarda didyma*) with showy scarlet irregular flowers

ot- *or* **oto-** *comb form* [Gk *ōt-*, *ōto-*, fr. *ōt-*, *ous* — more at EAR] : ear ⟨*oti*tis⟩ : ear and ⟨*oto*laryngology⟩

Othel·lo \ə-'thel-(ˌ)ō, ō-\ *n* : a Moor in the military service of Venice, husband of Desdemona, and protagonist of Shakespeare's tragedy *Othello*

¹oth·er \'əth-ər\ *adj* [ME, fr. OE *ōther*; akin to OHG *andar* other, Skt *antara*] (bef. 12c) **1 a** : being the one (as of two or more) remaining or not included ⟨held on with one hand and waved with the ~ one⟩ **b** : being the one or ones distinct from that or those first mentioned or implied ⟨taller than the ~ boys⟩ **c** : SECOND ⟨every ~ day⟩ **2** : not the same : DIFFERENT ⟨any ~ color would have been better⟩ ⟨something ~ than it seems to be⟩ **3** : ADDITIONAL ⟨sold in the U.S. and 14 ~ countries⟩ **4 a** : recently past ⟨the ~ evening⟩ **b** : FORMER ⟨in ~ times⟩

²other *n* (bef. 12c) **1 a** : one that remains of two or more **b** : a thing opposite to or excluded by something else ⟨went from one side to the ~⟩ **2** : a different or additional one ⟨the ~s came later⟩

³other *pron, sometimes pl in constr* (bef. 12c) **1** *obs* **a** : one of two that remains **b** : each preceding one **2** : a different or additional one ⟨something or ~⟩

⁴other *adv* (bef. 12c) : OTHERWISE — used with *than* ⟨was unable to see them ~ than by going to their home⟩

oth·er–di·rect·ed \ˌəth-ər-də-'rek-təd, -dī-\ *adj* (1950) : directed in thought and action primarily by external norms rather than by one's own scale of values — **oth·er–di·rect·ed·ness** *n*

oth·er·guess \'əth-ər-ˌges\ *adj* [alter. of E dial. *othergates*] *archaic* (1632) : DIFFERENT

oth·er·ness \'əth-ər-nəs\ *n* (1587) **1** : the quality or state of being other or different **2** : something that is other or different

oth·er·where \-ˌ(h)we(ə)r, -ˌ(h)wa(ə)r\ *adv* (15c) : ELSEWHERE

oth·er·while \-ˌhwīl, -ˌwīl\ *also* **oth·er·whiles** \-ˌhwīlz, -ˌwīlz\ *adv, chiefly dial* (12c) : at another time

¹oth·er·wise \-ˌwīz\ *adv* [ME, fr. OE (*on*) *ōthre wīsan* in another manner] (bef. 12c) **1** : in a different way or manner ⟨glossed over or ~ handled —*Playboy*⟩ **2** : in different circumstances ⟨might ~ have left⟩ **3** : in other respects ⟨an ~ flimsy farce —*Current Biog.*⟩ **4** : if not ⟨do what I tell you, ~ you'll be sorry⟩ **5** : NOT — paired with an adjective or

adverb to indicate its contrary ⟨people whose deeds, admirable or ~ —John Fischer⟩
²**otherwise** *pron* (bef. 12c) : something or anything else : something to the contrary ⟨the statistics show ~⟩ ⟨do very little to enforce competition — and have never intended ~ —Milton Viorst⟩ ⟨his opinion as to the success or ~ of it — *Austral. Dict. of Biog.*⟩
³**otherwise** *adj* (13c) : DIFFERENT
other woman *n* (1855) : a woman with whom a married man has an affair — usu. used with *the* ⟨in the . . . film . . . she played a straight acting role, that of Kitty, the *other woman* — *Current Biog.*⟩
oth·er·world \ˈəth-ər-ˌwərld\ *n* (13c) : a world beyond death or beyond present reality
oth·er·world·ly \-ˌwərl-(d)lē\ *adj* (1879) **1 a :** of, relating to, or resembling that of a world other than the actual world **b :** devoted to preparing for a world to come **2 :** devoted to intellectual or imaginative pursuits — **oth·er·world·li·ness** *n*
¹**-ot·ic** \ˈät-ik\ *adj suffix* [Gk *-ōtikos*, fr. *-ōtos*, ending of verbals, fr. *-o-* (stem of causative verbs in *-oun*) + *-tos*, suffix forming verbals — more at -ED] **1 a :** of, relating to, or characterized by a (specified) action, process, or condition ⟨symbi*otic*⟩ **b :** having an abnormal or diseased condition of a (specified) kind ⟨epizo*otic*⟩ **2 :** showing an increase or a formation of ⟨leukocyt*otic*⟩
²**-otic** \ˈōt-ik\ *adj comb form* [Gk *ōtikos*] : having (such) a relationship to the ear ⟨peri*otic*⟩
oti·ose \ˈō-shē-ˌōs, ˈōt-ē-\ *adj* [L *otiosus*, fr. *otium* leisure] (1850) **1 :** being at leisure : IDLE **2 :** producing no useful result : FUTILE **3 :** lacking use or effect : FUNCTIONLESS ***syn*** see VAIN — **oti·ose·ly** *adv* — **oti·ose·ness** *n* — **oti·os·i·ty** \ˌō-shē-ˈäs-ət-ē, ˌōt-ē-\ *n*
oti·tis \ō-ˈtīt-əs\ *n* [NL] (ca. 1799) : inflammation of the ear
otitis me·dia \-ˈmēd-ē-ə\ *n* [NL] (1874) : inflammation of the middle ear marked by pain, fever, dizziness, and abnormalities of hearing
oto·cyst \ˈōt-ə-ˌsist\ *n* [ISV, fr. its probable auditory function] (1877) : a fluid-containing organ of many invertebrates that contains an otolith : STATOCYST — **oto·cys·tic** \ˌōt-ə-ˈsis-tik\ *adj*
oto·lar·yn·gol·o·gist \ˌōt-ō-ˌlar-ən-ˈgäl-ə-jəst\ *n* (1911) : a specialist in otorhinolaryngology — **oto·lar·yn·gol·o·gy** \-ə-jē\ *n* — **oto·lar·yn·go·log·i·cal** \-gə-ˈläj-i-kəl\ *adj*
oto·lith \ˈōt-ᵊl-ˌith\ *n* [F *otolithe*, fr. *ot-* + *-lithe* -lith] (ca. 1835) : a calcareous concretion in the internal ear of a vertebrate or in the otocyst of an invertebrate — **oto·lith·ic** \ˌōt-ᵊl-ˈith-ik\ *adj*
Oto·mac \ˌōt-ə-ˈmäk, -ˈmak\ *n* (ca. 1908) **1 :** a member of an extinct aboriginal people of southern Venezuela **2 :** the language of the Otomac people
oto·rhi·no·lar·yn·gol·o·gy \ˈōt-ō-ˌrī-nō-ˌlar-ən-ˈgäl-ə-jē\ *n* [*ot-* + *rhin-* + *laryng-* + *-logy*] (ca. 1900) : a medical specialty concerned esp. with the ear, nose, and throat — **oto·rhi·no·lar·yn·go·log·i·cal** \-gə-ˈläj-i-kəl\ *adj* — **oto·rhi·no·lar·yn·gol·o·gist** \-ˈgäl-ə-jəst\ *n*
oto·scle·ro·sis \ˌōt-ō-sklə-ˈrō-səs\ *n* (1901) : growth of spongy bone in the inner ear where it gradually obstructs the vestibular or cochlear window or both and causes progressively increasing deafness
oto·tox·ic \ˌōt-ə-ˈtäk-sik\ *adj* (1951) : producing, involving, or being adverse effects on organs or nerves involved in hearing or balance — **oto·tox·ic·i·ty** \-täk-ˈsis-ət-ē\ *n*
ot·ta·va \ō-ˈtäv-ə\ *adv or adj* [It, octave, fr. ML *octava*] (1848) : at an octave higher or lower than written — used as a direction in music
ot·ta·va ri·ma \ō-ˌtäv-ə-ˈrē-mə\ *n, pl* **ottava rimas** [It, lit., eighth rhyme] (1820) : a stanza of eight lines of heroic verse with a rhyme scheme of *abababcc*
Ot·ta·wa \ˈät-ə-wə, -ˌwä, -ˌwȯ\ *n, pl* **-was** *or* **-wa** (1687) : a member of an American Indian people of Michigan and southern Ontario
ot·ter \ˈät-ər\ *n, pl* **otters** *also* **otter** [ME *oter*, fr. OE *otor*; akin to OHG *ottar* otter, Gk *hydōr* water — more at WATER] (bef. 12c) **1 :** any of several aquatic fish-eating mammals (genus *Lutra*) that are related to the weasels and minks and have webbed and clawed feet and dark brown fur **2 :** the fur or pelt of an otter

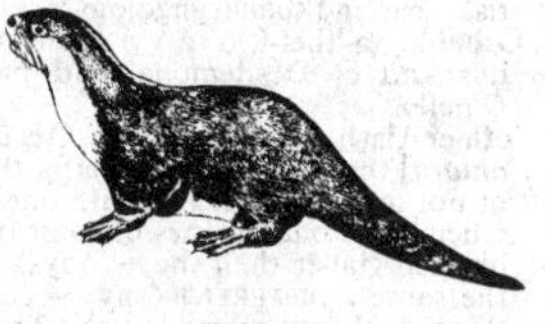
otter 1

otter hound *n* [fr. its use in hunting otters] (1607) : any of a British breed of large hounds that have a wiry water-resistant coat and a keen scent
ot·to \ˈät-(ˌ)ō\ *var of* ATTAR
ot·to·man \ˈät-ə-mən\ *n* (1562) **1** *cap* : TURK **2** [F *ottomane*, fr. fem. of *ottoman*, adj.] **a :** an upholstered often overstuffed seat or couch usu. without a back **b :** an overstuffed footstool
Ot·to·man \ˈät-ə-mən\ *adj* [F, adj. & n., prob. fr. It *ottomano*, fr. Ar *ʿothmānī*, fr. *ʿOthmān* Othman, founder of the Ottoman Empire] (1603) : of or relating to the Turks or Turkey : TURKISH
oua·bain \wä-ˈbā-ən, ˈwä-ˌbān\ *n* [ISV, fr. F *ouabaïo*, an African tree, fr. Somali *waba yo*] (1893) : a poisonous glycoside $C_{29}H_{44}O_{12}$ obtained from several African shrubs or trees of the dogbane family and used medically like digitalis and in Africa as an arrow poison
ou·bli·ette \ˌü-blē-ˈet\ *n* [F, fr. MF, fr. *oublier* to forget, fr. L *oblitus*, pp. of *oblivisci* — more at OBLIVION] (1819) : a dungeon with an opening only at the top
¹**ouch** \ˈau̇ch\ *n* [ME, alter. (resulting fr. incorrect division of *a nouche*) of *nouche*, fr. MF, of Gmc origin; akin to OHG *nusca* clasp; akin to OE *nett* net] (14c) **1** *obs* : CLASP, BROOCH **2 a :** a setting for a precious stone **b :** JEWEL, ORNAMENT; *esp* : a buckle or brooch set with precious stones
²**ouch** *interj* [origin unknown] (1837) — used esp. to express sudden pain
oud \ˈüd\ *n* [Ar *ʿūd*, lit., wood] (1738) : a musical instrument of the lute family used in southwest Asia and northern Africa
¹**ought** \ˈȯ(k)t\ *vt* [ME *oughte*, 1st & 3d sing. past indic. of *owen*] (bef. 12c) **1** *chiefly Scot* : OWE **2** *chiefly Scot* : POSSESS
²**ought** \ˈȯt\ *verbal auxiliary* [ME *oughte* (1st & 3d sing. pres. indic.), fr. *oughte*, 1st & 3d sing. past indic. & subj. of *owen* to own, owe — more at OWE] (12c) — used to express obligation ⟨~ to pay our debts⟩, advisability ⟨~ to take care of yourself⟩, natural expectation ⟨~ to be here by now⟩, or logical consequence ⟨the result ~ to be infinity⟩
³**ought** \ˈȯt\ *n* (1678) : moral obligation : DUTY
⁴**ought** \ˈȯt, ˈät\ *var of* AUGHT
oughtn't \ˈȯt-ᵊnt\ : ought not
ou·gui·ya \ü-ˈg(w)ē-(y)ə\ *n, pl* **ouguiya** [native name in Mauritania] (1973) — see MONEY table
Oui·ja \ˈwē-jə, -jē\ *trademark* — used for a board with the alphabet and other signs on it that is used with a planchette to seek spiritualistic or telepathic messages
¹**ounce** \ˈau̇n(t)s\ *n* [ME, fr. MF *unce*, fr. L *uncia* 12th part, ounce, fr. *unus* one — more at ONE] (14c) **1 a :** any of various units of weight based on the ancient Roman unit equal to $^1/_{12}$ Roman pound — see WEIGHT table **b :** a small portion ⟨an ~ of common sense⟩ **2 :** FLUIDOUNCE
²**ounce** *n* [ME *once*, fr. MF, alter. (by incorrect division, as if *l'once* the ounce) of *lonce*, fr. (assumed) VL *lyncea*, fr. L *lync-*, *lynx* lynx] (14c) : SNOW LEOPARD
our \är, (ˈ)au̇(ə)r\ *adj* [ME *oure*, fr. OE *ūre*; akin to OHG *unsēr* our, OE *ūs* us] (bef. 12c) : of or relating to us or ourselves or ourself esp. as possessors or possessor, agents or agent, or objects or object of an action ⟨~ throne⟩ ⟨~ actions⟩ ⟨~ being chosen⟩
Our Father *n* [fr. the opening words] (1882) : LORD'S PRAYER
ours \(ˈ)au̇(ə)rz, ärz\ *pron, sing or pl in constr* (14c) : that which belongs to us — used without a following noun as a pronoun equivalent in meaning to the adjective *our*
our·self \är-ˈself, au̇(ə)r-\ *pron* (15c) : MYSELF — used to refer to the single-person subject when *we* is used instead of *I* (as by a sovereign) ⟨will keep ~ till supper time alone —Shak.⟩
our·selves \-ˈselvz\ *pron pl* (1591) **1 :** those identical ones that are we — compare WE 1; used reflexively ⟨we're doing it solely for ~⟩, for emphasis ⟨we ~ will never go ⟩, or in absolute constructions ⟨~ no longer young, we can sympathize with those who are old⟩ **2 :** our normal, healthy, or sane condition ⟨just not ~ today⟩
-ous \əs\ *adj suffix* [ME, partly fr. OF *-ous*, *-eus*, *-eux*, fr. L *-osus*; partly fr. L *-us*, nom. sing. masc. ending of many adjectives] **1 :** full of : abounding in : having : possessing the qualities of ⟨clamor*ous*⟩ ⟨poison*ous*⟩ **2 :** having a valence lower than in compounds or ions named with an adjective ending in *-ic* ⟨mercur*ous*⟩
ou·sel \ˈü-zəl\ *var of* OUZEL
oust \ˈau̇st\ *vt* [ME, fr. AF *ouster*, fr. OF *oster*, fr. LL *obstare* to ward off, fr. L, to stand against, fr. *ob-* against + *stare* to stand — more at OB-, STAND] (15c) **1 a :** to remove from or dispossess of property or position by legal action, by force, or by the compulsion of necessity **b :** to take away (as a right or authority) : BAR, REMOVE **2 :** to take the place of : SUPPLANT ***syn*** see EJECT
oust·er \ˈau̇s-tər\ *n* [AF, to oust] (1531) **1 a :** a wrongful dispossession **b :** a judgment removing an officer or depriving a corporation of a franchise **2 :** EXPULSION
¹**out** \ˈau̇t\ *adv* [ME, fr. OE *ūt*; akin to OHG *ūz* out, Gk *hysteros* later, *hybris* arrogance, Skt *ud* up, out] (bef. 12c) **1 a (1) :** in a direction away from the inside or center ⟨went ~ into the garden⟩ **(2) :** OUTSIDE ⟨it's raining ~⟩ **b :** from among others **c :** away from the shore **d :** away from home or work ⟨~ to lunch⟩ **2 a :** so as to be missing or displaced from the usual or proper place ⟨left a word ~⟩ ⟨threw his shoulder ~⟩ **b :** into the possession or control of another ⟨lend ~ money⟩ **c :** into a state of loss or defeat ⟨was voted ~⟩ **d :** into a state of vexation ⟨they do not mark me, and that brings me ~ —Shak.⟩ **e :** into groups or shares ⟨sorted ~ her notes⟩ ⟨parceled ~ the farm⟩ **3 a :** to the point of depletion, extinction, or exhaustion ⟨the food ran ~⟩ ⟨turn the light ~⟩ ⟨all tuckered ~⟩ **b :** to completion or satisfaction ⟨hear me ~⟩ ⟨work the problem ~⟩ **c :** to the fullest extent or degree ⟨all decked ~⟩ **4 a :** in or into the open ⟨the sun came ~⟩ **b :** OUT LOUD ⟨cried ~⟩ **c :** in or into public circulation ⟨the evening paper isn't ~ yet⟩ ⟨hand ~ pamphlets⟩ ⟨the library book is still ~⟩ **5 :** so as to put someone out or to be put out in baseball **6** — used on a two-way radio circuit to indicate that a message is complete and no reply is expected
²**out** *vt* (bef. 12c) : EJECT, OUST ~ *vi* : to become publicly known ⟨the truth will ~⟩
³**out** \(ˌ)au̇t\ *prep* (bef. 12c) — used as a function word to indicate an outward movement ⟨ran ~ the door⟩ ⟨looked ~ the window⟩
⁴**out** \ˈau̇t\ *adj* (13c) **1 a :** situated outside : EXTERNAL **b :** OUT-OF-BOUNDS **2 :** situated at a distance : OUTLYING ⟨the ~ islands⟩ **3 :** not being in power **4 :** ABSENT **5 :** not allowed to continue batting, to occupy a base, or to score in baseball **6 :** not being in vogue or fashion **7 :** not to be considered **8 :** DETERMINED 1 ⟨was ~ to get revenge⟩
⁵**out** *n* (1717) **1 :** OUTSIDE **2 :** one who is out of office or power or on the outside ⟨a matter of ~s versus ins⟩ **3 a :** an act or instance of putting a player out or of being put out in baseball **b :** a player that is put out **4 :** a way of escaping from an embarrassing or difficult situation — **on the outs :** on unfriendly terms : at variance
out- *prefix* [¹*out*] : in a manner that goes beyond, surpasses, or excels ⟨*out*maneuver⟩

out·achieve	**out·drag**	**out·in·trigue**
out·act	**out·dress**	**out·jump**
out·bar·gain	**out·drink**	**out·kick**
out·bid	**out·drive**	**out·kill**
out·bitch	**out·du·el**	**out·last**
out·bluff	**out·earn**	**out·leap**
out·box	**out·eat**	**out·learn**
out·brag	**out·fight**	**out·man**
out·brawl	**out·fig·ure**	**out·ma·nip·u·late**
out·bulk	**out·fish**	**out·march**
out·catch	**out·fly**	**out·mus·cle**
out·charge	**out·fum·ble**	**out·or·ga·nize**
out·climb	**out·gain**	**out·pass**
out·coach	**out·glit·ter**	**out·per·form**
out·com·pete	**out·gross**	**out·pitch**
out·count	**out·hear**	**out·play**
out·dance	**out·hit**	**out·plot**
out·daz·zle	**out·ho·mer**	**out·pol·i·tick**
out·de·bate	**out·hunt**	**out·poll**
out·de·liv·er	**out·hus·tle**	**out·pop·u·late**
out·de·sign	**out·in·flu·ence**	**out·pray**

out·price	**out·score**	**out·throw**
out·pro·duce	**out·shout**	**out·trade**
out·prom·ise	**out·sing**	**out·vie**
out·punch	**out·sit**	**out·vote**
out·rate	**out·skate**	**out·wait**
out·ri·val	**out·spar·kle**	**out·walk**
out·roar	**out·speed**	**out·watch**
out·row	**out·sprint**	**out·wres·tle**
out·rush	**out·stride**	**out·write**
out·sail	**out·swear**	**out·yell**
out·scheme	**out·swim**	**out·yield**
out·scoop		

out·age \'au̇t-ij\ *n* (1899) **1 :** a quantity or bulk of something lost in transportation or storage **2 a :** a failure or interruption in use or functioning **b :** a period of interruption esp. of electric current

out–and–out \ˌau̇t-ᵊn-'(d)au̇t\ *adj* (1813) **:** being completely as described at all times, in every part, or from every point of view ⟨this is an ~ fraud⟩

out–and–out·er \-ər\ *n* (1812) **:** one who goes to extremes

out·back \'au̇t-'bak, -ˌbak\ *n* (1907) **:** isolated rural country esp. of Australia

out·bal·ance \(ˈ)au̇t-'bal-ən(t)s\ *vt* (1644) **:** OUTWEIGH

[1]**out·board** \'au̇t-ˌbō(ə)rd, -ˌbȯ(ə)rd\ *adj* (ca. 1823) **1 :** situated outboard **2 :** being a machine bearing, center, or other support used in conjunction with and outside of a main bearing **3 :** having, using, or limited to the use of an outboard motor

[2]**outboard** *adv* (1836) **1 :** outside a ship's bulwarks **:** in a lateral direction from the hull **2 :** in a position closer or closest to either of the wing tips of an airplane or to the sides of an automobile

[3]**outboard** *n* (1935) **1 :** OUTBOARD MOTOR **2 :** a boat with an outboard motor

outboard motor *n* (1909) **:** a small internal-combustion engine with propeller integrally attached for mounting at the stern of a small boat

out·bound \'au̇t-ˌbau̇nd\ *adj* (1598) **:** outward bound ⟨~ traffic⟩

out·brave \(ˈ)au̇t-'brāv\ *vt* (1589) **1 :** to face or resist defiantly **2 :** to exceed in courage

out·break \'au̇t-ˌbrāk\ *n* (15c) **1 a :** a sudden or violent increase in activity or currency ⟨the ~ of war⟩ **b :** a sudden rise in the incidence of a disease ⟨an ~ of measles⟩ **c :** a sudden increase in numbers of a harmful organism and esp. an insect within a particular area ⟨an ~ of locusts⟩ **2 :** INSURRECTION, REVOLT

out·breed *vt* **-bred** \-ˌbred, -'bred\; **-breed·ing** (ca. 1909) **1** \'au̇t-ˌbrēd\ **:** to subject to outbreeding **2** \(ˈ)au̇t-'\ **:** to breed faster than

out·breed·ing \'au̇t-ˌbrēd-iŋ\ *n* (1901) **:** the interbreeding of individuals or stocks that are relatively unrelated

out·build·ing \'au̇t-ˌbil-diŋ\ *n* (1626) **:** a building (as a stable or a woodshed) separate from but accessory to a main house

out·burst \-ˌbərst\ *n* (1657) **1 :** a violent expression of feeling ⟨an ~ of anger⟩ **2 :** a surge of activity or growth ⟨new ~*s* of creative power —C. E. Montague⟩ **3 :** ERUPTION ⟨volcanic ~*s*⟩

out·bye *or* **out·by** \üt-'bī\ *adv* [ME (Sc) *out-by,* fr. *out* + *by*] *chiefly Scot* (15c) **:** a short distance away; *also* **:** OUTDOORS

out·cast \'au̇t-ˌkast\ *n* (14c) **1 :** one who is cast out by society **:** PARIAH **2** [Sc *cast out* to quarrel] *Scot* **:** QUARREL — **outcast** *adj*

out·caste \-ˌkast\ *n* (1876) **1 :** a Hindu who has been ejected from his caste for violation of its customs or rules **2 :** one who has no caste

out·class \(ˈ)au̇t-'klas\ *vt* (1870) **:** to excel or surpass so decisively as to appear of a higher class

out·come \'au̇t-ˌkəm\ *n* (1788) **:** something that follows as a result or consequence ***syn*** see EFFECT

[1]**out·crop** \'au̇t-ˌkräp\ *n* (1805) **1 :** a coming out of bedrock or of an unconsolidated deposit to the surface of the ground **2 :** the part of a rock formation that appears at the surface of the ground

[2]**out·crop** \'au̇t-ˌkräp, (ˈ)au̇t-'\ *vi* (ca. 1847) **1 :** to project from the surrounding soil ⟨ledges *outcropping* from the eroded slope⟩ **2 :** to come to the surface **:** APPEAR

[1]**out·cross** \'au̇t-ˌkrȯs\ *n* (1890) **1 :** a cross between relatively unrelated individuals **2 :** the progeny of an outcross

[2]**outcross** *vt* (1918) **:** to cross with a relatively unrelated individual or strain

out·cry \'au̇t-ˌkrī\ *n* (14c) **1 a :** a loud cry **:** CLAMOR **b :** a vehement protest **2 :** AUCTION

out·dat·ed \(ˈ)au̇t-'dāt-əd\ *adj* (1616) **:** no longer current **:** OUTMODED — **out·dat·ed·ly** *adv* — **out·dat·ed·ness** *n*

out·dis·tance \(ˈ)au̇t-'dis-tən(t)s\ *vt* (1857) **:** to go far ahead of (as in a race) **:** OUTSTRIP

out·do \-'dü\ *vt* **-did** \-'did\; **-done** \-'dən\; **-do·ing** \-'dü-iŋ\; **-does** \-'dəz\ (1607) **1 :** to go beyond in action or performance **2 :** DEFEAT, OVERCOME ***syn*** see EXCEED

out·door \ˌau̇t-ˌdō(ə)r, -ˌdȯ(ə)r\ *also* **out·doors** \-ˌdō(ə)rz, -ˌdȯ(ə)rz\ *adj* [*out* (*of*) *door, out* (*of*) *doors*] (1748) **1 :** of or relating to the outdoors **2 a :** performed outdoors ⟨~ sports⟩ **b :** OUTDOORSY ⟨an ~ girl⟩ **3 :** not enclosed **:** having no roof ⟨an ~ restaurant⟩

[1]**out·doors** \(ˈ)au̇t-'dō(ə)rz, -'dȯ(ə)rz\ *adv* (1817) **:** outside a building **:** in or into the open air

[2]**outdoors** *n pl but sing in constr* (1844) **1 :** a place or location away from the confines of a building **2 :** the world away from human habitations

out·doors·man \-mən\ *n* (1918) **:** one who spends much time in the outdoors or in outdoor activities — **out·doors·man·ship** \-ˌship\ *n*

out·doorsy \(ˈ)au̇t-'dōr-zē, -'dȯr-\ *adj* (1936) **1 :** relating to, characteristic of, or appropriate for the outdoors ⟨an ~ dress⟩ **2 :** fond of outdoor activities ⟨sounded rugged and ~ —*N.Y. Times*⟩

out·draw \(ˈ)au̇t-'drȯ\ *vt* **-drew** \-'drü\; **-drawn** \-'drȯn\; **-draw·ing** (ca. 1909) **1 :** to attract a larger audience or following than **2 :** to draw a handgun more quickly than

out·er \'au̇t-ər\ *adj* [ME, fr. [4]*out* + *-er,* compar. suffix] (13c) **1 :** existing independent of mind **:** OBJECTIVE **2 a :** situated farther out ⟨the ~ limits⟩ **b :** being away from a center **c :** situated or belonging on the outside ⟨the ~ covering⟩

out·er·coat \'au̇t-ər-ˌkōt\ *n* (1948) **:** COAT 1a

outer ear *n* (1935) **:** the outer visible portion of the ear that collects and directs sound waves toward the eardrum by way of a canal which extends inward through the temporal bone

out·er·most \'au̇t-ər-ˌmōst\ *adj* (14c) **:** farthest out

outer planet *n* (1941) **:** any of the planets Jupiter, Saturn, Uranus, Neptune, and Pluto that as a group have orbits farther from the sun than the inner planets

outer space *n* (1901) **:** space immediately outside the earth's atmosphere; *broadly* **:** interplanetary or interstellar space

out·er·wear \'au̇t-ər-ˌwa(ə)r, -ˌwe(ə)r\ *n* (1921) **:** clothing for outdoor wear

out·face \(ˈ)au̇t-'fās\ *vt* (1529) **1 :** to cause to waver or submit by or as if by staring **2 :** to confront unflinchingly **:** DEFY

out·fall \'au̇t-ˌfȯl\ *n* (1629) **:** the outlet of a body of water (as a river or lake); *esp* **:** the mouth of a drain or sewer

out·field \-ˌfēld\ *n* (1868) **1 :** the part of a baseball field beyond the infield and between the foul lines **2 :** the baseball defensive positions comprising right field, center field, and left field; *also* **:** the players who occupy these positions — **out·field·er** \-ˌfēl-dər\ *n*

[1]**out·fit** \'au̇t-ˌfit\ *n* (1769) **1 :** the act of fitting out or equipping (as for a voyage or expedition) **2 a :** the tools or equipment for the practice of a trade **b :** wearing apparel with accessories usu. for a special occasion or activity **c :** physical, mental, or moral endowments or resources **3 :** a group that works as a team **:** ORGANIZATION; *esp* **:** a military unit

[2]**outfit** *vb* **out·fit·ted; out·fit·ting** *vt* (1847) **1 :** to furnish with an outfit **2 :** SUPPLY ⟨*outfitting* every family with shoes —*Amer. Guide Series: Vt.*⟩ ~ *vi* **:** to acquire an outfit ***syn*** see FURNISH

out·fit·ter \-ˌfit-ər\ *n* (1846) **:** one who outfits: as **a :** HABERDASHER **b :** a dealer in equipment and supplies (as for camping trips)

out·flank \(ˈ)au̇t-'flaŋk\ *vt* (1765) **1 :** to get around the flank of (an opposing force) **2 :** to get around **:** CIRCUMVENT

[1]**out·flow** \'au̇t-ˌflō, (ˈ)au̇t-'\ *vi* (1580) **:** to flow out

[2]**out·flow** \'au̇t-ˌflō\ *n* (ca. 1864) **1 :** a flowing out ⟨the ~ of dollars⟩ **2 :** something that flows out ⟨~ of a sewage treatment plant⟩

out·foot \(ˈ)au̇t-'fu̇t\ *vt* (1737) **:** to outdo in speed **:** OUTSTRIP

out·fox \-'fäks\ *vt* (1924) **:** OUTSMART

out–front \-'frənt\ *adj* (1968) **:** FRANK, OPEN

out·gas \'au̇t-ˌgas, (ˈ)au̇t-'\ *vt* (1925) **1 :** to remove occluded gases from usu. by heating; *broadly* **:** to remove gases from **2 :** to remove (gases) from a material or a space ~ *vi* **:** to lose gases

out·gen·er·al \(ˈ)au̇t-'jen-(ə-)rəl\ *vt* (1767) **:** to surpass in generalship **:** OUTMANEUVER

[1]**out·giv·ing** \'au̇t-ˌgiv-iŋ\ *n* (1663) **:** something that is given out; *esp* **:** a public statement or utterance

[2]**outgiving** *adj* (1942) **:** socially responsive and demonstrative

[1]**out·go** \(ˈ)au̇t-'gō\ *vt* (1530) **:** to go beyond **:** OUTDO

[2]**out·go** \'au̇t-ˌgō\ *n, pl* **outgoes** (1640) **1 :** something that goes out; *specif* **:** EXPENDITURE **2 a :** the act of going out **b :** DEPARTURE **3 :** OUTLET

out·go·ing \'au̇t-ˌgō-iŋ, -ˌgȯ(-)iŋ\ *adj* (14c) **1 a :** going away **:** DEPARTING ⟨an ~ ship⟩ **b :** retiring or withdrawing from a place or position ⟨the ~ president⟩ **c :** directed to an intended recipient ⟨~ mail⟩ **2 :** FRIENDLY, RESPONSIVE ⟨an ~ person⟩ — **out·go·ing·ness** *n*

out–group \'au̇t-ˌgrüp\ *n* (ca. 1907) **:** a group that is distinct from one's own and so usu. an object of hostility or dislike — compare IN-GROUP

out·grow \(ˈ)au̇t-'grō\ *vt* **-grew** \-'grü\; **-grown** \-'grōn\; **-grow·ing** (1594) **1 :** to grow or increase faster than ⟨mankind is ~*ing* food supplies —R. C. Murphy⟩ **2 :** to grow too large or too mature for ⟨the need to ~ the habit of war —Norman Cousins⟩

out·growth \'au̇t-ˌgrōth\ *n* (1837) **1 :** a process or product of growing out ⟨an ~ of hair⟩ **2 :** CONSEQUENCE, BY-PRODUCT ⟨crime is often an ~ of poverty⟩

out·guess \(ˈ)au̇t-'ges\ *vt* (1911) **:** to anticipate the expectations, intentions, or actions of **:** OUTWIT

out·gun \-'gən\ *vt* (1691) **:** to surpass in firepower; *broadly* **:** DEFEAT

out·haul \'au̇t-ˌhȯl\ *n* (1840) **:** a rope used to haul a sail taut along a spar

out–Her·od \(ˈ)au̇t-'her-əd\ *vt* [*out-* + *Herod* the Great, depicted in medieval mystery plays as a blustering tyrant] (1602) **:** to exceed in violence or extravagance — usu. used in the phrase *out-Herod Herod*

out·house \'au̇t-ˌhau̇s\ *n* (14c) **:** OUTBUILDING; *esp* **:** PRIVY 2a

out·ing \'au̇t-iŋ\ *n* (1821) **:** a brief usu. outdoor pleasure trip

outing flannel *n* (1890) **:** a flannelette sometimes having an admixture of wool

out·land \'au̇t-ˌland, -lənd\ *n* (bef. 12c) **1 :** a foreign land **2** *pl* **:** the outlying regions of a country **:** PROVINCES — **outland** *adj*

out·land·er \-ˌlan-dər, -lən-\ *n* (1598) **:** FOREIGNER, STRANGER

out·land·ish \(ˈ)au̇t-'lan-dish\ *adj* (bef. 12c) **1 :** of or relating to another country **:** FOREIGN **2 :** strikingly out of the ordinary **:** BIZARRE ⟨an ~ costume⟩ **3 :** remote from civilization ***syn*** see STRANGE — **out·land·ish·ly** *adv* — **out·land·ish·ness** *n*

[1]**out·law** \'au̇t-ˌlȯ\ *n* [ME *outlawe,* fr. OE *ūtlaga,* fr. ON *ūtlagi,* fr. *ūt* out (akin to OE *ūt* out) + *lag-, lög* law — more at OUT, LAW] (bef. 12c) **1 :** a person excluded from the benefit or protection of the law **2 a :** a lawless person or a fugitive from the law **b :** a person or organization under a ban or restriction **c :** one that is unconventional or rebellious **3 :** an animal (as a horse) that is wild and unmanageable — **outlaw** *adj*

[2]**outlaw** *vt* (bef. 12c) **1 a :** to deprive of the benefit and protection of law **:** declare to be an outlaw **b :** to make illegal ⟨the type of legislation which ~*ed* dueling —Margaret Mead⟩ **2 :** to place under a ban or restriction **3 :** to remove from legal jurisdiction or enforcement — **out·law·ry** \'au̇t-ˌlȯ(ə)r-ē\ *n*

[1]**out·lay** \'au̇t-ˌlā, (ˈ)au̇t-'\ *vt* **-laid** \-ˌlād, -'lād\; **-lay·ing** (1555) **:** to lay out (money) **:** EXPEND

[2]**out·lay** \'au̇t-ˌlā\ *n* (1798) **1 :** the act of expending **2 :** EXPENDITURE, PAYMENT ⟨~*s* for national defense⟩

\ə\ abut \ᵊ\ kitten, F table \ər\ further \a\ ash \ā\ ace \ä\ cot, cart \au̇\ out \ch\ chin \e\ bet \ē\ easy \g\ go \i\ hit \ī\ ice \j\ job \ŋ\ sing \ō\ go \ȯ\ law \ȯi\ boy \th\ thin \th\ the \ü\ loot \u̇\ foot \y\ yet \zh\ vision \à, k̲, ⁿ, œ, œ̄, ue, ue̅, ʸ\ *see* Guide to Pronunciation

out·let \ˈau̇t-ˌlet, -lət\ *n* [1*out* + *let*, v.] (13c) **1 a :** a place or opening through which something is let out : EXIT, VENT **b :** a means of release or satisfaction for an emotion or impulse ⟨sexual ~*s*⟩ **2 :** a stream flowing out of a lake or pond **3 a :** a market for a commodity **b :** an agency (as a store or dealer) through which a product is marketed ⟨retail ~*s*⟩ **4 :** an electrical receptacle into which appliances may be plugged

out·li·er \-ˌlī(-ə)r\ *n* (1676) **1 :** one that does not live where his office, business, or estate is **2 :** something (as a geological feature) that lies or is situated away from or classed differently from a main or related body

1**out·line** \ˈau̇t-ˌlīn\ *n* (1662) **1 a :** a line that marks the outer limits of an object or figure : BOUNDARY **b :** SHAPE **2 a :** a style of drawing in which contours are marked without shading **b :** a sketch in outline **3 a :** a condensed treatment of a particular subject ⟨an ~ of world history⟩ **b :** a summary of a written work : SYNOPSIS **4 :** a preliminary account of a project : PLAN **5 :** a fishing line set out overnight : TROTLINE

syn OUTLINE, CONTOUR, PROFILE, SILHOUETTE mean the line that bounds and gives form to something. OUTLINE applies to a line marking the outer limits or edges of a body or mass; CONTOUR stresses the quality of an outline or a bounding surface as being smooth, jagged, curving, or sharply angled; PROFILE suggests a varied and sharply defined outline against a lighter background; SILHOUETTE suggests a shape esp. of a head or figure with all detail blacked out in shadow leaving only the outline clearly defined.

2**outline** *vt* (1790) **1 :** to draw the outline of **2 :** to indicate the principal features or different parts of ⟨*outlined* their responsibilities⟩

out·live \(ˈ)au̇t-ˈliv\ *vt* (15c) **1 :** to live beyond or longer than ⟨*outlived* most of his friends⟩ ⟨~ its usefulness⟩ **2 :** to survive the effects of ⟨universities . . . ~ many political and social changes —J. B. Conant⟩

out·look \ˈau̇t-ˌlu̇k\ *n* (1667) **1 a :** a place offering a view **b :** a view from a particular place **2 :** POINT OF VIEW ⟨an ~ on life⟩ **3 :** the act of looking out **4 :** the prospect for the future ⟨the ~ for steel demand in the U.S. —*Wall Street Jour.*⟩ ***syn*** see PROSPECT

out loud *adv* (1821) : loudly enough to be heard : ALOUD

out·ly·ing \ˈau̇t-ˌlī-iŋ\ *adj* (1689) : remote from a center or main body ⟨~ areas⟩

out·ma·neu·ver \ˌau̇t-mə-ˈn(y)ü-vər\ *vt* (1799) **1 :** to defeat by more skillful maneuvering **2 :** to surpass in maneuverability

out·match \(ˈ)au̇t-ˈmach\ *vt* (1603) : to prove superior to : OUTDO

out–mi·grant \ˈau̇t-ˌmī-grənt\ *n* (1945) : one that out-migrates

out–mi·grate \-ˌgrāt\ *vi* (1953) : to leave one region or community in order to settle in another esp. as part of a large-scale and continuing movement of population — compare IN-MIGRATE — **out–mi·gra·tion** \ˌau̇t-mī-ˈgrā-shən\ *n*

out·mode \(ˈ)au̇t-ˈmōd\ *vt* **out·mod·ed; out·mod·ing** [*out* (*of*) *mode*] (1906) : to make unfashionable or obsolete

out·mod·ed \-ˈmōd-əd\ *adj* (1903) **1 :** not being in style **2 :** no longer acceptable or usable ⟨~ beliefs⟩

out·most \ˈau̇t-ˌmōst\ *adj* (bef. 12c) : farthest out : OUTERMOST

out·num·ber \(ˈ)au̇t-ˈnəm-bər\ *vt* (1670) : to exceed in number

out of *prep* (bef. 12c) **1 a** (1) — used as a function word to indicate direction or movement from within to the outside of ⟨walked *out of* the room⟩ (2) — used as a function word to indicate a change in quality, state, or form ⟨woke up *out of* a deep sleep⟩ **b** (1) — used as a function word to indicate a position or situation beyond the range, limits, or sphere of ⟨*out of* sight⟩ (2) — used as a function word to indicate a position or state away from the usual or expected ⟨*out of* practice⟩ **2** — used as a function word to indicate origin, source, or cause ⟨a colt *out of* an ordinary mare⟩ ⟨built *out of* old lumber⟩ ⟨came *out of* fear⟩ **3** — used as a function word to indicate exclusion from or deprivation of ⟨cheated him *out of* his savings⟩ **4** — used as a function word to indicate choice or selection from a group ⟨one *out of* four survived⟩ — **out of it :** not part of a group, activity, or fashion

out–of–bounds \ˌau̇t-ə(v)-ˈbau̇n(d)z\ *adv or adj* (1857) : outside the prescribed boundaries or limits

out–of–date \-ˈdāt\ *adj* (1628) : OUTMODED, OBSOLETE

out–of–door \-ˈdō(ə)r, -ˈdȯ(ə)r\ *or* **out–of–doors** \-ˈdō(ə)rz, -ˈdȯ(ə)rz\ *adj* (1800) : OUTDOOR

out–of–doors *n pl but sing in constr* (1819) : OUTDOORS

out–of–pock·et \-ˈpäk-ət\ *adj* (1885) : requiring an outlay of cash ⟨~ expenses⟩

out–of–the–way \-t͟hə-ˈwā\ *adj* (1797) **1 :** being off the beaten track ⟨an ~ restaurant⟩ **2 :** UNUSUAL ⟨~ information⟩

out·pace \(ˈ)au̇t-ˈpās\ *vt* (1611) **1 :** to surpass in speed **2 :** OUTDO

out·pa·tient \ˈau̇t-ˌpā-shənt\ *n* (1715) : a patient who is not an inmate of a hospital but who visits a clinic or dispensary connected with it for diagnosis or treatment — compare INPATIENT

out·place·ment \(ˈ)au̇t-ˈplā-smənt\ *n* (1970) : the process of easing unwanted or unneeded executives out of a company by providing company-paid assistance in finding them new jobs (as through professional counseling and job searches)

out·point \-ˈpȯint\ *vt* (1883) **1 :** to sail closer to the wind than **2 :** to win more points than

out·port \ˈau̇t-ˌpō(ə)rt, -ˌpȯ(ə)rt\ *n* (1642) **1 :** a port other than the main port of a country **2 :** a port of export or departure **3 :** a small fishing village in Newfoundland

out·post \ˈau̇t-ˌpōst\ *n* (1757) **1 a :** a security detachment thrown out by a main body of troops to protect it from enemy surprise **b :** a military base established by treaty or agreement in another country **2 a :** an outlying or frontier settlement **b :** an outlying branch or position of a main organization or group

1**out·pour** \au̇t-ˈpō(ə)r, -ˈpȯ(ə)r, ˈau̇t-ˌ\ *vt* (1671) : to pour out

2**out·pour** \ˈau̇t-ˌpō(ə)r, -ˌpȯ(ə)r\ *n* (1864) : OUTPOURING

out·pour·ing \ˈau̇t-ˌpōr-iŋ, -ˌpȯr-\ *n* (15c) **1 :** the act of pouring out **2 :** something that pours out or is poured out : OUTFLOW

out·pull \(ˈ)au̇t-ˈpu̇l\ *vt* (1926) : OUTDRAW 1

1**out·put** \ˈau̇t-ˌpu̇t\ *n* (1858) **1 :** something produced: as **a :** mineral, agricultural, or industrial production ⟨steel ~⟩ **b :** mental or artistic production ⟨literary ~⟩ **c :** the amount produced by a person in a given time **d :** power or energy produced or delivered by a machine or system (as for storage or for conversion in kind or in characteristics) ⟨solar X-ray ~⟩ **e :** the information fed out by a computer or accounting machine **2 :** the act, process, or an instance of producing **3 :** the terminal for the output on an electrical device

2**output** *vt* **out·put·ted** *or* **output; out·put·ting** (1858) : to produce as output

out·race \(ˈ)au̇t-ˈrās\ *vt* (1657) : OUTPACE

1**out·rage** \ˈau̇t-ˌrāj\ *n* [ME, fr. MF, excess, outrage, fr. *outre* beyond, in excess, fr. L *ultra* — more at ULTRA-] (14c) **1 :** an act of violence or brutality **2 a :** INJURY, INSULT ⟨do no ~*s* on silly women or poor passengers —Shak.⟩ **b :** an act that violates accepted standards of behavior or taste ⟨an ~ alike against decency and dignity —John Buchan⟩ **3 :** the anger and resentment aroused by injury or insult

2**outrage** *vt* **out·raged; out·rag·ing** (1590) **1 a :** RAPE **b :** to violate the standards or principles of ⟨he has *outraged* respectability past endurance —John Braine⟩ **2 :** to arouse anger or resentment in usu. by some grave offense ***syn*** see OFFEND

out·ra·geous \au̇t-ˈrā-jəs\ *adj* (14c) **1 a :** exceeding the limits of what is usual **b :** not conventional or matter-of-fact : FANTASTIC **2 :** VIOLENT, UNRESTRAINED **3 a :** going beyond all standards of what is right or decent ⟨an ~ disregard of human rights⟩ **b :** deficient in propriety or good taste ⟨~ language⟩ ⟨~ manners⟩ — **out·ra·geous·ly** *adv* — **out·ra·geous·ness** *n*

ou·trance \ü-ˈträⁿs\ *n* [ME, fr. MF, fr. *outrer* to pass beyond, carry to excess, fr. *outre*] (15c) : the last extremity

out·range \(ˈ)au̇t-ˈrānj\ *vt* (1858) : to surpass in range

out·rank \-ˈraŋk\ *vt* (1842) **1 :** to rank higher than **2 :** to exceed in importance

ou·tré \ü-ˈtrā\ *adj* [F, fr. pp. of *outrer* to carry to excess] (1722) : violating convention or propriety : BIZARRE

1**out·reach** \(ˈ)au̇t-ˈrēch\ *vt* (1568) **1 a :** to surpass in reach **b :** EXCEED ⟨the demand ~*es* the supply⟩ **2 :** to get the better of by trickery ~ *vi* **1 :** to go too far **2 :** to reach out

2**out·reach** \ˈau̇t-ˌrēch\ *n* (1870) **1 :** the act of reaching out **2 :** the extent or limit of reach ⟨the ~ of the Ohio floods —Clifton Johnson⟩ **3 :** the extending of services or activities beyond current or usual limits; *also* : the extent of such services or activities

1**out·ride** \(ˈ)au̇t-ˈrīd\ *vt* **-rode** \-ˈrōd\; **-rid·den** \-ˈrid-ᵊn\; **-rid·ing** \-ˈrīd-iŋ\ (1530) **1 :** to ride better, faster, or farther than : OUTSTRIP **2 :** to ride out (a storm)

2**out·ride** \ˈau̇t-ˌrīd\ *n* (1880) : an unstressed syllable or group of syllables added to a foot in sprung rhythm but not counted in the scansion

out·rid·er \-ˌrīd-ər\ *n* (1530) **1 :** a mounted attendant **2 :** FORERUNNER, HARBINGER

out·rig·ger \ˈau̇t-ˌrig-ər\ *n* (1748) **1 a :** a projecting spar with a shaped log at the end attached to a canoe to prevent upsetting **b :** a spar or projecting beam run out from a ship's side to help secure the masts or from a mast to extend a rope or sail **c :** a projecting support for an oarlock; *also* : a boat so equipped **2 :** a projecting member run out from a main structure to provide additional stability or to support something; *esp* : a projecting frame to support the elevator or tail planes of an airplane or the rotor of a helicopter

1**out·right** \(ˈ)au̇t-ˈrīt\ *adv* (14c) **1** *archaic* : straight ahead : DIRECTLY **2 :** in entirety : COMPLETELY ⟨rejected the proposal ~⟩ **3 :** on the spot : INSTANTANEOUSLY ⟨was killed ~⟩ **4 :** without lien or encumbrance ⟨purchased the property ~ for cash⟩

2**out·right** \ˈau̇t-ˌrīt\ *adj* (1532) **1 a :** being completely or exactly what is stated ⟨an ~ lie⟩ **b :** given without reservation ⟨~ grants for research⟩ **c :** made without encumbrance or lien ⟨~ sale⟩ **2** *archaic* : proceeding directly onward **3 :** COMPLETE, ENTIRE — **out·right·ly** *adv*

out·run \(ˈ)au̇t-ˈrən\ *vt* **-ran** \-ˈran\; **-run; -run·ning** (1526) **1 :** to run faster than **2 :** EXCEED, SURPASS ⟨his ambitions ~ his abilities⟩

out·sell \-ˈsel\ *vt* **-sold** \-ˈsōld\; **-sell·ing** (1609) **1** *archaic* : to exceed in value **2 :** to exceed in number of items sold **3 :** to surpass in selling or salesmanship

out·set \ˈau̇t-ˌset\ *n* (1759) : BEGINNING, START

out·shine \(ˈ)au̇t-ˈshīn\ *vb* **-shone** \-ˈshōn, *esp Brit* -ˈshän\ *or* **-shined; -shin·ing** *vt* (1596) **1 a :** to shine brighter than **b :** to excel in splendor or showiness **2 :** OUTDO, SURPASS ⟨*outshone* most of the other films in quality —Kathleen Karr⟩ ~ *vi* : to shine out

1**out·shoot** \(ˈ)au̇t-ˈshüt\ *vt* **-shot** \-ˈshät\; **-shoot·ing** (1530) **1 :** to surpass in shooting or making shots **2 :** to shoot or go beyond

2**out·shoot** \ˈau̇t-ˌshüt\ *n* (1613) : something that shoots out

1**out·side** \(ˈ)au̇t-ˈsīd, ˈau̇t-ˌ\ *n* (1505) **1 a :** a place or region beyond an enclosure or boundary **b :** the area farthest from a specified point of reference: as (1) : the side of home plate farthest from the batter (2) : the section of a playing area toward the sidelines; *also* : CORNER **2 :** an outer side or surface **3 :** an outer manifestation : APPEARANCE **4 :** the extreme limit of a guess : MAXIMUM ⟨the crowd numbered 10,000 at the ~⟩

2**outside** *adj* (1634) **1 a :** of, relating to, or being on or toward the outer side or surface ⟨the ~ edge⟩ **b :** of, relating to, or being on or toward the outer side of a curve or turn **c :** of, relating to, or being on or near the outside ⟨an ~ pitch⟩ **2 a :** situated or performed outside a particular place **b :** connected with or giving access to the outside ⟨~ telephone line⟩ **3 :** MAXIMUM **4 a :** not included or originating in a particular group or organization ⟨blamed the riot on ~ agitators⟩ **b :** not belonging to one's regular occupation or duties ⟨~ interests⟩ **5 :** barely possible : REMOTE ⟨an ~ chance⟩ **6 :** made or done from the outside or from a distance ⟨borrowed a basketball and practiced his ~ shot⟩

3**outside** *adv* (1813) **1 :** on or to the outside **2 :** OUTDOORS

4**outside** *prep* (1826) **1** — used as a function word to indicate movement to or position on the outer side of **2 :** beyond the limits of ⟨~ the scope of this report⟩ ⟨~ the law⟩ **3 :** EXCEPT

outside of *prep* (1839) : OUTSIDE

out·sid·er \(ˈ)au̇t-ˈsīd-ər\ *n* (1800) **1 :** a person who does not belong to a particular group **2** *chiefly Brit* : a contender not expected to win — **out·sid·er·ness** *n*

out·sight \ˈau̇t-ˌsīt\ *n* (1605) : the power or act of perceiving external things ⟨the clear-eyed insight and ~ of the born writer —*New Yorker*⟩

1**out·size** \ˈau̇t-ˌsīz\ *n* (1845) : an unusual size; *esp* : a size larger than the standard

2**outsize** *also* **out·sized** \-ˌsīzd\ *adj* (1890) : unusually large or heavy

out·skirt \ˈau̇t-ˌskərt\ *n* (1596) : a part remote from the center : BORDER — usu. used in pl. ⟨on the ~*s* of town⟩

out·smart \(ˈ)au̇t-ˈsmärt\ *vt* (1924) **:** to get the better of; *esp* **:** OUTWIT
out·soar \-ˈsō(ə)r, -ˈsȯ(ə)r\ *vt* (1674) **:** to soar beyond or above
out·sole \ˈau̇t-ˌsōl\ *n* (1884) **:** the outside sole of a boot or shoe
out·speak \(ˈ)au̇t-ˈspēk\ *vt* **-spoke** \-ˈspōk\; **-spo·ken** \-ˈspō-kən\; **-speak·ing** (1603) **1 :** to excel in speaking **2 :** to declare openly or boldly
out·spend \-ˈspend\ *vt* (1586) **1 :** to exceed the limits of in spending ⟨~*s* his income⟩ **2 :** to outdo in spending ⟨he *outspent* the other candidates⟩
out·spent \-ˈspent\ *adj* (1652) **:** completely worn out **:** EXHAUSTED ⟨spurred him, like an ~ horse, to death —P. B. Shelley⟩
out·spo·ken \au̇t-ˈspō-kən\ *adj* (ca. 1808) **1 :** direct and open in speech or expression **:** FRANK ⟨candidly ~ in his criticism —*Current Biog.*⟩ **2 :** spoken or expressed without reserve ⟨his ~ advocacy of gun control⟩ — **out·spo·ken·ly** *adv* — **out·spo·ken·ness** \-kən-nəs\ *n*
out·spread \au̇t-ˈspred\ *vt* **-spread; -spread·ing** (14c) **:** to spread out **:** EXTEND
out·stand \(ˈ)au̇t-ˈstand\ *vb* **-stood; -stand·ing** *vt* (1571) **:** to endure beyond ⟨I have *outstood* my time —Shak.⟩ ~ *vi* **:** STAND OUT
out·stand·ing \au̇t-ˈstan-diŋ, ˈau̇t-ˌ\ *adj* (1611) **1 :** standing out **:** PROJECTING **2 a :** UNPAID ⟨left several bills ~⟩ **b :** CONTINUING, UNRESOLVED ⟨a long ~ problem⟩ **c** *of securities* **:** publicly issued and sold **3 a :** standing out from a group **:** CONSPICUOUS **b :** marked by eminence and distinction ***syn*** see NOTICEABLE — **out·stand·ing·ly** \-diŋ-lē\ *adv*
out·stare \(ˈ)au̇t-ˈsta(ə)r, -ˈste(ə)r\ *vt* (1596) **:** OUTFACE 1
out·sta·tion \ˈau̇t-ˌstā-shən\ *n* (1844) **:** a remote or outlying station
out·stay \(ˈ)au̇t-ˈstā\ *vt* (1600) **1 :** OVERSTAY 1 ⟨~*ed* their welcome⟩ **2 :** to surpass in staying power ⟨~*ed* his competitors⟩
out·stretch \au̇t-ˈstrech\ *vt* (14c) **:** to stretch out **:** EXTEND
out·strip \au̇t-ˈstrip\ *vt* [*out-* + obs. *strip* (to move fast)] (1580) **1 :** to go faster or farther than **2 :** to get ahead of **:** leave behind ⟨has civilization *outstripped* the ability of its users to use it? —Margaret Mead⟩ ***syn*** see EXCEED
out·take \ˈau̇t-ˌtāk\ *n* (1902) **1 :** a passage outward **:** FLUE, VENT **2 :** something that is taken out: as **a :** a take that is not used in an edited version of a film or video tape **b :** a recorded musical selection not included in a record album
out·talk \(ˈ)au̇t-ˈtȯk\ *vt* (1596) **1 :** to surpass in talking **2 :** to get the better of by talking
out·think \-ˈthiŋk\ *vt* **-thought** \-ˈthȯt\; **-think·ing** (1704) **1 :** to surpass in thinking **2 :** to get the better of by thinking
out·turn \ˈau̇t-ˌtərn\ *n* (1800) **:** a quantity produced **:** OUTPUT
¹out·ward \ˈau̇t-wərd\ *adj* (bef. 12c) **1 :** moving, directed, or turned toward the outside or away from a center ⟨an ~ flow⟩ **2 :** situated on the outside **:** EXTERIOR **3 :** of or relating to the body or to appearances rather than to the mind or the inner life ⟨~ beauty⟩ **4 :** EXTERNAL
²outward *or* **out·wards** \-wərdz\ *adv* (bef. 12c) **1 :** toward the outside **2** *obs* **:** on the outside **:** EXTERNALLY
³outward *n* (1627) **:** external form, appearance, or reality
out·ward–bound \ˌau̇t-wərd-ˈbau̇nd\ *adj* (1602) **:** bound in an outward direction or to foreign parts ⟨an ~ ship⟩
out·ward·ly \ˈau̇t-wərd-lē\ *adv* (14c) **1 a :** on the outside **:** EXTERNALLY **b :** toward the outside **2 :** in outward state, behavior, or appearance ⟨was ~ friendly⟩
out·ward·ness \-nəs\ *n* (1580) **1 :** the quality or state of being external **2 :** concern with or responsiveness to outward things
out·wear \(ˈ)au̇t-ˈwa(ə)r, -ˈwe(ə)r\ *vt* **-wore** \-ˈwō(ə)r, -ˈwȯ(ə)r\; **-worn** \-ˈwō(ə)rn, -ˈwȯ(ə)rn\; **-wear·ing** (1541) **1 :** WEAR OUT, EXHAUST **2 :** to last longer than ⟨a fabric that ~*s* others⟩
out·weigh \-ˈwā\ *vt* (1597) **:** to exceed in weight, value, or importance ⟨the advantages ~ the disadvantages⟩
out·wit \au̇t-ˈwit\ *vt* **-wit·ted; -wit·ting** (1652) **1 :** to get the better of by superior cleverness **:** OUTSMART **2** *archaic* **:** to surpass in wisdom ***syn*** see FRUSTRATE
¹out·work *vt* (13c) **1** \au̇t-ˈwərk\ **:** WORK OUT, COMPLETE **2** \(ˈ)au̇t-\ **:** to work harder, faster, or better than
²out·work \ˈau̇t-ˌwərk\ *n* (1639) **:** a minor defensive position constructed outside a fortified area
out·worn \au̇t-ˈwō(ə)rn, -ˈwȯ(ə)rn\ *adj* (1565) **:** no longer useful or acceptable **:** OUTMODED ⟨an ~ social system⟩
ou·zel \ˈü-zəl\ *n* [ME *ousel*, fr. OE *ōsle* — more at MERL] (bef. 12c) **1 :** BLACKBIRD 1a; *also* **:** a related bird **2 :** DIPPER 1
ou·zo \ˈü-(ˌ)zō, -(ˌ)zō\ *n* [NGk *ouzon, ouzo*] (1898) **:** a colorless anise-flavored unsweetened Greek liqueur
ov- *or* **ovi-** *or* **ovo-** *comb form* [L *ov-*, *ovi-*, fr. *ovum* — more at EGG] **:** egg ⟨*ovi*form⟩ **:** ovum ⟨*ovi*duct⟩ ⟨*ovo*cyte⟩ ⟨*ovo*genesis⟩
ova *pl of* OVUM
¹oval \ˈō-vəl\ *n* (1570) **1 :** an oval figure or object **2 :** a racetrack in the shape of an oval or a rectangle having rounded corners
²oval *adj* [ML *ovalis*, fr. LL, of an egg, fr. L *ovum*] (1577) **:** having the shape of an egg; *also* **:** broadly elliptical — **oval·ly** \-və-lē\ *adv* — **oval·ness** *n*
ov·al·bu·min \ˌäv-al-ˈbyü-mən, ˌōv-\ *n* (1835) **1 :** the principal albumin of white of egg; *esp* **:** the crystalline part of egg albumins **2 :** dried whites of eggs
oval window *n* (1683) **:** FENESTRA 1a
ovar·i·an \ō-ˈvar-ē-ən, -ˈver-\ *also* **ovar·i·al** \-ē-əl\ *adj* (1840) **:** of, relating to, or involving an ovary
ovari·ec·to·my \ō-ˌvar-ē-ˈek-tə-mē, -ˌver-\ *n, pl* **-mies** (1889) **:** the surgical removal of an ovary — **ovari·ec·to·mized** \-ˌmīzd\ *adj*
ovar·i·ole \ō-ˈvar-ē-ˌōl, -ˈver-\ *n* [(assumed) NL *ovariolum*, dim. of *ovarium*] (1877) **:** one of the tubes of which the ovaries of most insects are composed
ovar·i·ot·o·my \ō-ˌvar-ē-ˈät-ə-mē, -ˌver-\ *n, pl* **-mies** (1844) **1 :** surgical incision of an ovary **2 :** OVARIECTOMY
ova·ry \ˈōv-(ə-)rē\ *n, pl* **-ries** [NL *ovarium*, fr. L *ovum* egg] (1658) **1 :** the typically paired essential female reproductive organ that produces eggs and in vertebrates female sex hormones **2 :** the enlarged rounded usu. basal portion of the pistil or gynoecium of an angiospermous plant that bears the ovules and consists of one or more carpels — see FLOWER illustration
ovate \ˈō-ˌvāt\ *adj* (1775) **1 :** shaped like an egg **2 :** having an outline like a longitudinal section of an egg with the basal end broader ⟨~ leaves⟩
ova·tion \ō-ˈvā-shən\ *n* [L *ovation-*, *ovatio*, fr. *ovatus*, pp. of *ovare* to exult; akin to Gk *euoi*, interjection used in bacchic revels] (1533) **1 :** a ceremony attending the entering of Rome by a general who had won a victory of less importance than that for which a triumph was granted **2 :** an expression or demonstration of popular acclaim esp. by enthusiastic applause ⟨received a standing ~⟩
ov·en \ˈəv-ən\ *n* [ME, fr. OE *ofen*; akin to OHG *ofan* oven, Gk *ipnos*, L *aulla, olla* pot] (bef. 12c) **:** a chamber used for baking, heating, or drying
ov·en·bird \-ˌbərd\ *n* [fr. the shape of its nest] (1825) **1 :** any of various So. American small brown passerine birds (genus *Furnarius*) **2 :** an American warbler (*Seiurus aurocapillus*) that builds a dome-shaped nest on the ground

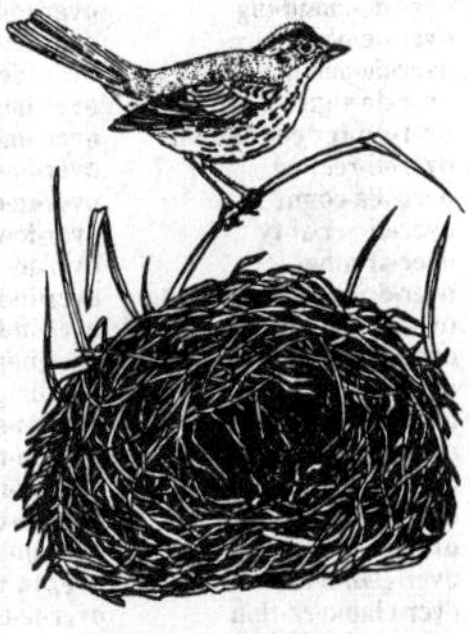
ovenbird 2

ov·en·proof \-ˌprüf\ *adj* (1939) **:** capable of withstanding the temperature range of a kitchen oven ⟨~ dishes⟩
¹over \ˈō-vər\ *adv* [ME, adv. & prep., fr. OE *ofer*; akin to OHG *ubar* (prep.) above, beyond, over, L *super*, Gk *hyper*] (bef. 12c) **1 a :** across a barrier or intervening space; *esp* **:** across the goal line in football **b :** forward beyond an edge or brink and often down ⟨wandered too near the cliff and fell ~⟩ **c :** across the brim ⟨soup boiled ~⟩ **d :** so as to bring the underside up ⟨turned his cards ~⟩ **e :** from a vertical to a prone or inclined position ⟨knocked the lamp ~⟩ **f :** from one person or side to another ⟨hand it ~⟩ **g :** ACROSS ⟨got his point ~⟩ **h :** to agreement or concord ⟨won them ~⟩ **2 a (1) :** beyond some quantity, limit, or norm often by a specified amount or to a specified degree ⟨show ran a minute ~⟩ **(2) :** in an excessive manner **:** INORDINATELY — often used in combination ⟨an *over*optimistic view⟩ **b :** till a later time (as the next day) ⟨stay ~⟩ ⟨sleep ~⟩ **3 a :** ABOVE **b :** so as to cover the whole surface ⟨windows boarded ~⟩ **4 a :** at an end ⟨the day is ~⟩ **b** — used on a two-way radio circuit to indicate that a message is complete and a reply is expected **5 a :** THROUGH ⟨read it ~⟩; *also* **:** in an intensive or comprehensive manner **b :** once more **:** AGAIN ⟨do it ~⟩
²over \ˌō-vər, ˈō-\ *prep* (bef. 12c) **1** — used as a function word to indicate motion or situation in a position higher than or above another ⟨towered ~ his mother⟩ ⟨flew ~ the lake⟩ ⟨rode ~ the old Roman road⟩ **2 a** — used as a function word to indicate the possession of authority, power, or jurisdiction in regard to some thing or person ⟨respected those ~ him⟩ **b** — used as a function word to indicate superiority, advantage, or preference ⟨a big lead ~ the others⟩ **3 :** more than ⟨cost ~ $5⟩ **4 a** — used as a function word to indicate position upon or movement down upon ⟨laid a blanket ~ the child⟩ ⟨hit him ~ the head⟩ **b :** all through or throughout ⟨showed me ~ the house⟩ ⟨went ~ his notes⟩ **c** — used as a function word to indicate a particular medium or channel of communication ⟨~ the radio⟩ **5** — used as a function word to indicate position on the other side or beyond ⟨lives ~ the way⟩ **6 a :** THROUGHOUT, DURING ⟨~ the past 25 years⟩ **b :** until the end of ⟨stay ~ Sunday⟩ **7 a** — used as a function word to indicate an object of solicitude, interest, consideration, or reference ⟨the Lord watches ~ his own⟩ **b** — used as a function word to indicate the object of an expressed or implied occupation, activity, or concern ⟨spent an hour ~ cards⟩ ⟨trouble ~ money⟩
³over \ˈō-vər, ˌō-\ *adj* (bef. 12c) **1 a :** UPPER, HIGHER **b :** OUTER, COVERING **c :** EXCESSIVE ⟨~ imagination⟩ **2 a :** not used up **:** REMAINING ⟨something ~ to provide for unusual requirements —J. A. Todd⟩ **b :** having or showing an excess or surplus **3 :** fried on both sides ⟨ordered two eggs ~⟩
⁴over \ˈō-vər\ *vt* **overed; over·ing** \ˈōv-(ə-)riŋ\ (1837) **:** to leap over
over- *prefix* **1 :** so as to exceed or surpass **2 :** EXCESSIVE **3 :** to an excessive degree

over·ab·stract
over·abun·dance
over·abun·dant
over·ac·cen·tu·ate
over·ad·just·ment
over·ad·ver·tise
over·ag·gres·sive
over·alert
over·am·bi·tious
over·am·bi·tious·ness
over·am·pli·fy
over·anal·y·sis
over·an·a·lyt·i·cal
over·an·a·lyze
over·anx·i·ety
over·anx·ious
over·ap·pli·ca·tion
over·arous·al
over·ar·range
over·ar·tic·u·late
over·as·sert
over·as·ser·tion
over·as·ser·tive
over·as·sess·ment
over·as·sist
over·at·ten·tion
over·bake
over·beat
over·bed
over·be·jeweled
over·bill
over·bleach
over·boil
over·bold
over·bor·row
over·breath·ing
over·bright
over·broad
over·browse
over·bru·tal
over·burn
over·busy
over·busy·ness
over·care·ful
over·cau·tion
over·cau·tious
over·cen·tral·iza·tion
over·cen·tral·ize
over·chill
over·civ·i·lized
over·claim
over·clas·si·fi·ca·tion
over·clas·si·fy
over·clean
over·clear
over·coach
over·com·mer·cial·iza·tion
over·com·mer·cial·ize
over·com·mu·ni·cate
over·com·mu·ni·ca·tion
over·com·plex
over·com·pli·ance
over·com·pli·cate
over·com·pli·cat·ed
over·com·press
over·com·pres·sion
over·con·cen·trate
over·con·cen·tra·tion
over·con·cern
over·con·fi·dence
over·con·fi·dent
over·con·fi·dent·ly
over·con·sci·en·tious
over·con·scious
over·con·ser·va·tive
over·con·struct
over·con·sume
over·con·sump·tion

\ə\ abut \ᵊ\ kitten, F table \ər\ further \a\ ash \ā\ ace \ä\ cot, cart \au̇\ out \ch\ chin \e\ bet \ē\ easy \g\ go \i\ hit \ī\ ice \j\ job \ŋ\ sing \ō\ go \ȯ\ law \ȯi\ boy \th\ thin \th\ the \ü\ loot \u̇\ foot \y\ yet \zh\ vision \à, k, ⁿ, œ, œ̄, ue, ue̅, ʸ\ *see* Guide to Pronunciation

over·con·trol
over·cook
over·cool
over·count
over·crit·i·cal
over·cul·ti·va·tion
over·cure
over·dec·o·rate
over·dec·o·ra·tion
over·de·lib·er·ate
over·de·mand·ing
over·de·pen·dence
over·de·pen·dent
over·de·sign
over·dif·fer·en·ti·a·tion
over·di·rect·ed
over·dis·count
over·di·ver·si·ty
over·dra·mat·ic
over·dra·ma·tize
over·drink
over·dry
over·ea·ger
over·ea·ger·ness
over·ear·nest
over·ed·it
over·ed·u·cate
over·ed·u·ca·tion
over·elab·o·rate
over·elab·o·ra·tion
over·em·bel·lish
over·emote
over·emo·tion·al
over·em·pha·sis
over·em·pha·size
over·em·phat·ic
over·en·am·ored
over·en·cour·age
over·en·er·get·ic
over·en·gi·neer
over·en·rolled
over·en·ter·tained
over·en·thu·si·asm
over·en·thu·si·as·tic
over·equipped
over·es·ti·mate
over·es·ti·ma·tion
over·eval·u·a·tion
over·ex·ag·ger·ate
over·ex·ag·ger·a·tion
over·ex·cite
over·ex·er·cise
over·ex·ert
over·ex·er·tion
over·ex·pand
over·ex·pan·sion
over·ex·pec·ta·tion
over·ex·plain
over·ex·plic·it
over·ex·ploit
over·ex·ploi·ta·tion
over·ex·tract
over·ex·trac·tion
over·ex·trap·o·la·tion
over·ex·trav·a·gant
over·ex·u·ber·ant
over·fac·ile
over·fa·mil·iar
over·fa·mil·iar·i·ty
over·fas·tid·i·ous
over·fa·vor
over·fer·til·iza·tion
over·fer·til·ize
over·fo·cus
over·fond
over·ful·fill
over·fund
over·fussy
over·gen·er·al·iza·tion
over·gen·er·al·ize

over·gen·er·os·i·ty
over·gen·er·ous
over·gen·er·ous·ly
over·glam·or·ize
over·gov·ern
over·hasty
over·ho·mog·e·nize
over·hunt
over·hype
over·ide·al·is·tic
over·ide·al·ize
over·iden·ti·fi·ca·tion
over·iden·ti·fy
over·imag·i·na·tive
over·im·press
over·in·debt·ed·ness
over·in·dus·tri·al·iza·tion
over·in·dus·tri·al·ize
over·in·flate
over·in·fla·tion
over·in·form
over·in·ge·nious
over·in·ge·nu·ity
over·in·sis·tent
over·in·tel·lec·tu·al·iza·tion
over·in·tel·lec·tu·al·ize
over·in·tense
over·in·ten·si·ty
over·in·vest·ment
over·la·bor
over·lad·en
over·large
over·lav·ish
over·lend
over·length
over·length·en
over·light
over·lit·er·al
over·lit·er·ary
over·load
over·long
over·loud
over·lush
over·man·age
over·man·nered
over·ma·ture
over·ma·tu·ri·ty
over·med·i·cate
over·med·i·ca·tion
over·milk
over·mine
over·mix
over·mod·est
over·mod·est·ly
over·mus·cled
over·nice
over·nour·ish
over·nu·tri·tion
over·ob·vi·ous
over·op·er·ate
over·opin·ion·at·ed
over·op·ti·mism
over·op·ti·mist
over·op·ti·mis·tic
over·op·ti·mis·ti·cal·ly
over·or·ga·nize
over·or·na·ment
over·par·tic·u·lar
over·pay
over·pay·ment
over·ped·al
over·peo·ple
over·plan
over·plant
over·plot
over·po·tent
over·praise
over·pre·cise

over·pre·scribe
over·pre·scrip·tion
over·prize
over·pro·cess
over·pro·duce
over·pro·duc·tion
over·prom·ise
over·pro·tect
over·pro·tec·tion
over·pro·tec·tive
over·pump
over·rate
over·re·act
over·re·ac·tion
over·re·fined
over·re·fine·ment
over·reg·u·late
over·reg·u·la·tion
over·re·li·ance
over·re·port
over·re·spond
over·rich
over·rig·id
over·rouge
over·salt
over·san·guine
over·sat·u·rate
over·sat·u·ra·tion
over·sauce
over·scru·pu·lous
over·se·cre·tion
over·se·ri·ous
over·se·ri·ous·ly
over·ser·vice
over·ship·ment
over·smoke
over·so·lic·i·tous
over·so·phis·ti·cat·ed
over·spe·cial·iza·tion
over·spe·cial·ize
over·spec·u·late
over·spec·u·la·tion
over·sta·bil·i·ty
over·staff
over·stim·u·late
over·stim·u·la·tion
over·stock
over·strain
over·stretch
over·struc·tured
over·sub·tle
over·suds
over·sup·ply
over·sus·pi·cious
over·sweet
over·sweet·en
over·sweet·ness
over·swing
over·talk
over·talk·ative
over·thin
over·think
over·tight
over·tight·en
over·tip
over·tired
over·train
over·treat
over·treat·ment
over·use
over·uti·li·za·tion
over·uti·lize
over·vi·o·lent
over·viv·id
over·wa·ter
over·wind
over·with·hold
over·zeal·ous
over·zeal·ous·ness

over·achiev·er \ˌō-və-rə-'chē-vər\ *n* (1952) : one who achieves success over and above the standard or expected level esp. at an early age

over·act \ˌō-və-'rakt\ *vt* (1631) : to exaggerate in acting ~ *vi* **1** : to act more than is necessary **2** : to overact a part — **over·ac·tion** \-'rak-shən\ *n*

over·ac·tive \-'rak-tiv\ *adj* (1854) : excessively or abnormally active — **over·ac·tiv·i·ty** \-ˌrak-'tiv-ət-ē\ *n*

over against *prep* (1611) : as opposed to : in contrast with

¹**over·age** \ˌō-və-'rāj\ *adj* [²*over* + *age*] (1886) **1** : too old to be useful **2** : older than is normal for one's position, function, or grade

²**over·age** \'ōv-(ə-)rij\ *n* [³*over* + *-age*] (1909) : SURPLUS, EXCESS

¹**over·all** \ˌō-və-'rȯl\ *adv* (13c) **1** : as a whole : GENERALLY ⟨~, prices are still rising —*Forbes*⟩ **2** : from the extreme forward point to the extreme after point of a ship's deck including overhangs

²**over·all** \'ō-vər-ˌrȯl\ *n* (1815) **1** *pl* **a** *archaic* : loose protective trousers worn over regular clothes **b** : trousers of strong material usu. with a bib and shoulder straps **2** *chiefly Brit* : a loose-fitting protective smock worn over regular clothing

³**over·all** \'ō-vər-ˌrȯl, ˌō-vər-'\ *adj* (1876) **1** : including everything **2** : viewed as a whole : GENERAL

over·alled \'ō-və-ˌrȯld\ *adj* (1908) : wearing overalls

over and above *prep* (15c) : in addition to : BESIDES

over and over *adv* (15c) : REPEATEDLY

over·arch·ing \ˌō-və-'rär-chiŋ\ *adj* (1720) **1** : forming an arch overhead **2** : dominating or embracing all else

over·arm \ˌō-və-ˌrärm\ *adj* (1864) **1** : OVERHAND **2** *of a swimming stroke* : made with the arm lifted out of the water and stretched forward over the shoulder to begin the stroke

over·awe \ˌō-və-'rȯ\ *vt* (1579) : to restrain or subdue by awe

¹**over·bal·ance** \ˌō-vər-'bal-ən(t)s\ *vt* (1608) **1** : OUTWEIGH **2** : to cause to lose balance

²**over·bal·ance** \'ō-vər-\ *n* (1659) : something more than an equivalent

over·bear \ˌō-vər-'ba(ə)r, -'be(ə)r\ *vt* -**bore** \-'bō(ə)r, -'bȯ(ə)r\; -**borne** \-'bō(ə)rn, -'bȯ(ə)rn\ *also* -**born** \-'bō(ə)rn\ -**bear·ing** (1535) **1** : to bring down by superior weight or force : OVERWHELM **2 a** : to domineer over **b** : to surpass in importance or cogency : OUTWEIGH

over·bear·ing *adj* (1677) **1 a** : tending to overwhelm : OVERPOWERING **b** : decisively important : DOMINANT **2** : harshly and haughtily arrogant *syn* see PROUD — **over·bear·ing·ly** \-iŋ-lē\ *adv*

over·bid \ˌō-vər-'bid\ *vb* -**bid**; -**bid·ding** *vi* (1616) **1** : to bid in excess of value **2 a** : to bid more than the scoring capacity of a hand at cards **b** *Brit* : to make a higher bid than the preceding one ~ *vt* : to bid beyond or in excess of; *esp* : to bid more than the value of (one's hand at cards) — **over·bid** \'ō-vər-ˌbid\ *n*

over·bite \'ō-vər-ˌbīt\ *n* (1887) : the projection of the upper anterior teeth over the lower in the normal occlusal position of the jaws

¹**over·blown** \ˌō-vər-'blōn\ *adj* [³*blow*] (1616) : past the prime of bloom ⟨~ roses⟩

²**overblown** *adj* [¹*blow*] (1864) **1** : excessively large in girth : PORTLY **2** : INFLATED, PRETENTIOUS

over·board \'ō-vər-ˌbō(ə)rd, -ˌbȯ(ə)rd\ *adv* (bef. 12c) **1** : over the side of a ship or boat into the water **2** : to extremes of enthusiasm **3** : into discard : ASIDE

over·book \ˌō-vər-'bùk\ *vt* (1903) : to issue reservations for (as an airplane flight) in excess of the space available ~ *vi* : to issue reservations in excess of the space available

over·bought \-'bȯt\ *adj* (1929) : not likely to show an immediate rise in price because of prior heavy buying and accompanying price rises ⟨an ~ market⟩

over·build \-'bild\ *vb* -**built** \-'bilt\; -**build·ing** *vt* (1601) : to build beyond the actual demand of ~ *vi* : to build houses or commercial developments in excess of demand

¹**over·bur·den** \-'bərd-ᵊn\ *vt* (1532) : to place an excessive burden on

²**over·bur·den** \'ō-vər-ˌbərd-ᵊn\ *n* (1855) : material overlying a deposit of useful geological materials or bedrock

over·buy \ˌō-vər-'bī\ *vb* -**bought** \-'bȯt\; -**buy·ing** *vt* (1745) : to buy in excess of needs or demand ~ *vi* : to make purchases beyond one's needs or in excess of one's ability to pay

over·call \-'kȯl\ *vt* (ca. 1903) : to make a higher bid than (the previous bid or player) in a card game ~ *vi* : to bid over an opponent's bid in bridge when one's partner has not bid or doubled — **over·call** \'ō-vər-ˌkȯl\ *n*

over·ca·pac·i·ty \ˌō-vər-kə-'pas-ət-ē, -'pas-tē\ *n* (1928) : excessive capacity for production or services in relation to demand

over·cap·i·tal·ize \ˌō-vər-'kap-ət-ᵊl-ˌīz, -'kap-t-ᵊl-\ *vt* (1890) **1** : to put a nominal value on the capital of (a corporation) higher than actual cost or fair market value **2** : to capitalize beyond what the business or the profit-making prospects warrant — **over·cap·i·tal·iza·tion** \-ˌkap-ət-ᵊl-ə-'zā-shən, -ˌkap-t-ᵊl-\ *n*

¹**over·cast** *vt* -**cast**; -**cast·ing** (13c) **1** \ˌō-vər-'kast, 'ō-vər-ˌ\ : DARKEN, OVERSHADOW **2** \'ō-vər-ˌ\ : to sew (raw edges of a seam) with long slanting widely spaced stitches to prevent raveling

²**over·cast** \'ō-vər-ˌkast, ˌō-vər-'\ *adj* (1625) : clouded over ⟨an ~ day⟩

³**over·cast** \'ō-vər-ˌkast\ *n* (1686) : COVERING; *esp* : a covering of clouds over the sky

over·cast·ing \'ō-vər-ˌkas-tiŋ\ *n* (1885) : the act of stitching raw edges of fabric to prevent raveling; *also* : the stitching so done

overcast stitch *n* (1891) : a small close embroidery stitch sometimes done over a foundation thread and used to form outlines

over·charge \ˌō-vər-'chärj\ *vt* (14c) **1** : to charge too much or too fully **2** : to fill too full **3** : EXAGGERATE, OVERDRAW ~ *vi* : to make an excessive charge — **over·charge** \'ō-vər-ˌ\ *n*

over·cloud \ˌō-vər-'klaud\ *vt* (1592) : to overspread with clouds

over·coat \'ō-vər-ˌkōt\ *n* (1802) **1** : a warm coat worn over indoor clothing **2** : a protective coating (as of paint)

over·coat·ing \-iŋ\ *n* (1950) : OVERCOAT 2

over·come \ˌō-vər-'kəm\ *vb* -**came** \-'kām\; -**come**; -**com·ing** [ME *overcomen*, fr. OE *ofercuman*, fr. *ofer* over + *cuman* to come] *vt* (bef. 12c) **1** : to get the better of : SURMOUNT ⟨~ difficulties⟩ **2** : OVERWHELM ~ *vi* : to gain the superiority : WIN *syn* see CONQUER — **over·com·er** *n*

over·com·mit \-kə-'mit\ *vt* (1951) : to commit excessively: as **a** : to obligate (as oneself) beyond the ability for fulfillment **b** : to allocate (resources) in excess of the capacity for replenishment — **over·com·mit·ment** \-mənt\ *n*

over·com·pen·sa·tion \-ˌkäm-pən-'sā-shən, -ˌpen-\ *n* (1912) : excessive compensation; *specif* : excessive reaction to a feeling of inferiority, guilt, or inadequacy leading to an exaggerated attempt to overcome the feeling — **over·com·pen·sate** \-'käm-pən-ˌsāt\ *vb* — **over·com·pen·sa·to·ry** \-kəm-'pen(t)-sə-ˌtōr-ē, -ˌtȯr-\ *adj*

over·crowd \ˌō-vər-'kraud\ *vt* (1766) : to cause to be too crowded ~ *vi* : to crowd together too much

over·de·ter·mined \-di-'tər-mənd\ *adj* (1915) **1** : excessively determined **2** : having more than one determining psychological factor

over·de·vel·op \-di-'vel-əp\ *vt* (1869) **1** : to develop excessively; *esp* : to subject (exposed photographic material) to a developing solution for excessive time or at excessive temperature, agitation, or concentration — **over·de·vel·op·ment** \-mənt\ *n*

over·do \ˌō-vər-'dü\ *vb* -**did** \-'did\; -**done** \-'dən\; -**do·ing** \-'dü-iŋ\; -**does** \-'dəz\ *vt* (bef. 12c) **1 a** : to do in excess **b** : to use to excess **c** : EXAGGERATE **2** : to cook too long **3** : EXHAUST ~ *vi* : to go to extremes

over·dom·i·nance \-'däm(-ə)-nən(t)s\ *n* (1947) : the property of having a heterozygote that produces a phenotype more extreme or better adapted than that of the homozygote — **over·dom·i·nant** \-nənt\ *adj*

¹**over·dose** \'ō-vər-ˌdōs\ *n* (1700) : too great a dose (as of a therapeutic agent); *also* : a lethal or toxic amount (as of a drug)

²**over·dose** \ˌō-vər-ˈdōs\ *vt* (1727) **:** to give an overdose or too many doses to ~ *vi* **:** to take an overdose

over·draft \ˈō-vər-ˌdraft\ *n* (1878) **1 a :** an act of overdrawing at a bank **:** the state of being overdrawn; *also* **:** the sum overdrawn **b :** LINE OF CREDIT **2 :** a draft or current of air passing over a fire in a furnace

over·draw \ˌō-vər-ˈdrȯ\ *vb* **-drew** \-ˈdrü\; **-drawn** \-ˈdrȯn\; **-draw·ing** *vt* (1734) **1 :** to draw checks on (a bank account) for more than the balance ⟨his account was *overdrawn*⟩ **2 :** EXAGGERATE, OVERSTATE ~ *vi* **:** to make an overdraft

over·drawn *adj* (1866) **:** having an overdrawn account ⟨the bank informed him that he was ~⟩

¹**over·dress** \ˌō-vər-ˈdres\ *vt* (1706) **:** to dress or adorn to excess ~ *vi* **:** to dress oneself to excess

²**over·dress** \ˈō-vər-ˌdres\ *n* (1812) **:** a dress worn over another

over·drive \ˈō-vər-ˌdrīv\ *n* (1926) **:** an automotive transmission gear that transmits to the drive shaft a speed greater than engine speed

¹**over·dub** \ˈō-vər-ˌdəb\ *n* (ca. 1965) **1 :** the act or an instance of overdubbing **2 :** recorded sound that is overdubbed ⟨vocal ~*s*⟩

²**over·dub** \ˌō-vər-ˈdəb\ *vt* (1967) **:** to transfer (recorded sound) onto a recording that bears sound recorded earlier in order to produce a combined effect

over·due \ˌō-vər-ˈd(y)ü\ *adj* (1845) **1 a :** unpaid when due **b :** delayed beyond an appointed time **2 :** too great **:** EXCESSIVE **3 :** more than ready

over·eat \ˌō-və-ˈrēt\ *vi* **over·ate** \-ˈrāt\; **over·eat·en** \-ˈrēt-ᵊn\; **over·eat·ing** (1599) **:** to eat to excess — **over·eat·er** *n*

over·ex·pose \ˌō-və-rik-ˈspōz\ *vt* (1869) **:** to expose excessively; *esp* **:** to expose (as film) to excessive radiation (as light) — **over·ex·po·sure** \-ˈspō-zhər\ *n*

over·ex·tend \ˌō-və-rik-ˈstend\ *vt* (1937) **:** to extend or expand beyond a safe or reasonable point; *esp* **:** to commit (oneself) financially beyond what can be paid — **over·ex·ten·sion** \-ˈsten-chən\ *n*

over·fa·tigue \ˌō-vər-fə-ˈtēg\ *n* (1727) **:** excessive fatigue esp. when carried beyond the recuperative capacity of the individual — **over·fa·tigued** \-ˈtēgd\ *adj*

over·feed \ˌō-vər-ˈfēd\ *vb* **-fed** \-ˈfed\; **-feed·ing** *vt* (1608) **:** to feed to excess ~ *vi* **:** to eat to excess

over·fill \ˌō-vər-ˈfil\ *vt* (13c) **:** to fill to overflowing ~ *vi* **:** to become full to overflowing

over·fish \-ˈfish\ *vt* (1867) **:** to fish to the detriment of (a fishing ground) or to the depletion of (a kind of organism)

over·flight \ˈō-vər-ˌflīt\ *n* (1950) **:** a passage over an area in an airplane

¹**over·flow** \ˌō-vər-ˈflō\ *vt* (bef. 12c) **1 :** to cover with or as if with water **:** INUNDATE **2 :** to flow over the brim of **3 :** to cause to overflow ~ *vi* **:** to flow over bounds

²**over·flow** \ˈō-vər-ˌflō\ *n* (1589) **1 :** a flowing over **:** INUNDATION **2 :** something that flows over **:** SURPLUS **3 :** an outlet or receptacle for surplus liquid

over·fly \ˌō-vər-ˈflī\ *vt* **-flew** \-ˈflü\; **-flown** \-ˈflōn\; **-fly·ing** (14c) **:** to fly over; *esp* **:** to pass over in an airplane or spacecraft

over·gar·ment \ˈō-vər-ˌgär-mənt\ *n* (15c) **:** an outer garment

over·glaze \-ˌglāz\ *adj* (1879) **:** applied or suitable for applying on top of a fired glaze ⟨~ enamels⟩ — **overglaze** *n*

over·graze \ˌō-vər-ˈgrāz\ *vt* (1919) **:** to allow animals to graze to the point of damaging vegetational cover

over·grow \ˌō-vər-ˈgrō\ *vb* **-grew** \-ˈgrü\; **-grown** \-ˈgrōn\; **-grow·ing** *vt* (14c) **1 :** to grow over so as to cover with herbage **2 :** to grow beyond or rise above **:** OUTGROW ~ *vi* **1 :** to grow excessively **2 :** to become grown over — **over·growth** \ˈō-vər-ˌgrōth\ *n*

¹**over·hand** \ˈō-vər-ˌhand\ *adj* (1656) **:** made with the hand brought forward and down from above shoulder level — **overhand** *adv* — **over·hand·ed** \ˌō-vər-ˈhan-dəd\ *adv or adj*

²**overhand** *vt* (1871) **:** to sew with short vertical stitches

³**overhand** *n* (ca. 1934) **:** an overhand stroke (as in handball)

overhand knot \ˌō-vər-ˌhan(d)-\ *n* (1840) **:** a small knot often used to prevent the end of a cord from fraying — see KNOT illustration

¹**over·hang** \ˈō-vər-ˌhaŋ, ˌō-vər-ˈ\ *vb* **-hung** \-ˌhəŋ, -ˈhəŋ\; **-hang·ing** *vt* (1599) **1 :** to project over **2 :** to impend over **:** THREATEN ~ *vi* **:** to project so as to be over something

²**over·hang** \ˈō-vər-ˌhaŋ\ *n* (1864) **1 :** something that overhangs; *also* **:** the extent of the overhanging **2 :** the part of the bow or stern of a ship that projects over the water above the waterline **3 :** a projection of the roof or upper story of a building beyond the wall of the lower part **4 :** an excess supply of a commodity that cannot be readily converted or sold ⟨dollar ~⟩ ⟨~ of new car inventories⟩

over·haul \ˌō-vər-ˈhȯl\ *vt* (1705) **1 a :** to examine thoroughly **b** (1) **:** REPAIR (2) **:** to renovate, revise, or renew thoroughly **2 :** to haul or drag over **3 :** OVERTAKE — **over·haul** \ˈō-vər-ˌhȯl\ *n*

¹**over·head** \ˌō-vər-ˈhed\ *adv* (15c) **:** above one's head **:** ALOFT

²**over·head** \ˈō-vər-ˌhed\ *adj* (1874) **1 :** operating, lying, or coming from above **2 :** of or relating to overhead expense

³**over·head** \ˈō-vər-ˌhed\ *n* (1914) **1 :** business expenses (as rent, insurance, or heating) not chargeable to a particular part of the work or product **2 :** CEILING; *esp* **:** the ceiling of a ship's compartment **3 :** a stroke in a racket game made above head height **:** SMASH

overhead projector *n* (1951) **:** a projector for projecting onto a vertical screen magnified images of graphic material on a horizontal transparency illuminated from below — called also *overhead*

over·hear \ˌō-vər-ˈhi(ə)r\ *vb* **-heard** \-ˈhərd\; **-hear·ing** \-ˈhi(ə)r-iŋ\ *vt* (1549) **:** to hear without the speaker's knowledge or intention ~ *vi* **:** to overhear something

over·heat \-ˈhēt\ *vt* (14c) **1 :** to heat to excess **2 :** to stimulate unduly ⟨~*ing* the economy⟩ ~ *vi* **:** to become overheated

over·in·dulge \ˌō-və-rin-ˈdəlj\ *vt* (1741) **1 :** to indulge in to an excessive degree **2 :** to indulge (someone) to an excessive degree ~ *vi* **:** to indulge in something to an excessive degree — **over·in·dul·gence** \-ˈdəl-jən(t)s\ *n* — **over·in·dul·gent** \-jənt\ *adj*

over·is·sue \ˌō-və-ˈrish-(ˌ)ü, -ˈrish-ə(-w)\ *n* (1803) **:** an issue exceeding the limit of capital, credit, or authority — **over·is·su·ance** \-ˈrish-ə-wən(t)s\ *n* — **overissue** *vt*

over·joy \ˌō-vər-ˈjȯi\ *vt* (1571) **:** to fill with great joy

¹**over·kill** \ˌō-vər-ˈkil\ *vt* (1957) **:** to obliterate (a target) with more nuclear force than required

²**over·kill** \ˈō-vər-ˌkil\ *n* (1958) **1 :** the capability of destroying an enemy or target with a nuclear force larger than is required **2 :** an excess of something (as a quantity or an action) beyond what is required or suitable for a particular purpose ⟨a propaganda ~⟩ ⟨an ~ in weaponry⟩ **3 :** killing in excess of what is intended or required

¹**over·land** \ˈō-vər-ˌland, -lənd\ *adv* (12c) **:** by, on, or across land

²**overland** *adj* (1800) **:** going or accomplished over the land instead of by sea ⟨an ~ route⟩

over·lap \ˌō-vər-ˈlap\ *vt* (1726) **1 :** to extend over and cover a part of **2 :** to have something in common with ~ *vi* **1 :** to lap over **2 :** to have something in common — **over·lap** \ˈō-vər-ˌlap\ *n*

¹**over·lay** \ˌō-vər-ˈlā\ *vt* **-laid** \-ˈlād\; **-lay·ing** (14c) **1 a :** to lay or spread over or across **:** SUPERIMPOSE **b :** to prepare an overlay for **2 :** OVERLIE 2

²**over·lay** \ˈō-vər-ˌlā\ *n* (1794) **:** a covering either permanent or temporary: as **a :** an ornamental veneer **b :** a decorative and contrasting design or article placed on top of a plain one **c :** a transparent sheet containing graphic matter to be superimposed on another sheet

over·leaf \ˈō-vər-ˌlēf, -ˈlēf\ *adv* (1613) **:** on the other side of a leaf (as of a book)

over·leap \ˌō-vər-ˈlēp\ *vt* **-leaped** *or* **-leapt** \-ˈlēpt *also* -ˈlept\; **-leap·ing** \-ˈlē-piŋ\ (bef. 12c) **1 :** to leap over or across **2 :** to defeat (oneself) by going too far

over·learn \-ˈlərn\ *vt* (1874) **:** to continue to study or practice after attaining proficiency

over·lie \-ˈlī\ *vt* **-lay** \-ˈlā\; **-lain** \-ˈlān\; **-ly·ing** \-ˈlī-iŋ\ (12c) **1 :** to lie over or upon **2 :** to cause the death of by lying upon

¹**over·look** \-ˈlu̇k\ *vt* (14c) **1 :** to look over **:** INSPECT **2 a :** to look down upon from above **b :** to rise above or afford a view of **3 a :** to look past **:** MISS **b :** IGNORE **c :** EXCUSE **4 :** SUPERVISE **5 :** to look on with the evil eye **:** BEWITCH ***syn*** see NEGLECT

²**over·look** \ˈō-vər-ˌlu̇k\ *n* (1861) **:** a place from which one may look down on a scene below ⟨plenty of ~*s* and trails —Thelma H. Bell⟩

over·lord \ˈō-vər-ˌlȯ(ə)rd\ *n* (13c) **1 :** a lord who is lord over other lords **:** a lord paramount **2 :** an absolute or supreme ruler — **over·lord·ship** \-ˌship, ˌō-vər-ˈ\ *n*

over·ly \ˈō-vər-lē\ *adv* (bef. 12c) **:** to an excessive degree

¹**over·man** \-mən, -ˌman\ *n* (13c) **1 :** a man in authority over others; *specif* **:** FOREMAN **2** \-ˌman\ [trans. of G *übermensch*] **:** SUPERMAN 1

²**over·man** \ˌō-vər-ˈman\ *vt* (1607) **:** to have or get too many men for the needs of ⟨~ a ship⟩

over·man·tel \ˈō-vər-ˌmant-ᵊl\ *n* (1882) **:** an ornamental structure (as a painting) above a mantelpiece — **overmantel** *adj*

over·mas·ter \ˌō-vər-ˈmas-tər\ *vt* (14c) **:** OVERPOWER, SUBDUE

over·match \-ˈmach\ *vt* (14c) **1 :** to be more than a match for **:** DEFEAT **2 :** to match with a superior opponent

¹**over·much** \-ˈməch\ *adj* (13c) **:** too much

²**overmuch** *adv* (13c) **:** in too great a degree

³**over·much** \ˈō-vər-ˌməch, ˌō-vər-ˈ\ *n* (ca. 1909) **:** too great an amount

¹**over·night** \ˌō-vər-ˈnīt\ *adv* (14c) **1 :** on or during the evening or night ⟨stayed away ~⟩ **2 :** very quickly or suddenly ⟨became famous ~⟩

²**overnight** *adj* (1824) **1 :** of or lasting the night **2 :** SUDDEN, RAPID

³**over·night** \ˈō-vər-ˌnīt\ *n* (1959) **:** an overnight stay

overnight bag *n* (1925) **:** a traveling bag of a size to carry clothing and personal articles for an overnight trip — called also *overnight case*

¹**over·pass** \ˌō-vər-ˈpas\ *vt* (13c) **1 :** to pass across, over, or beyond **:** CROSS; *also* **:** SURPASS **2 :** TRANSGRESS **3 :** DISREGARD, IGNORE

²**over·pass** \ˈō-vər-ˌpas\ *n* (1929) **:** a crossing of two highways or of a highway and pedestrian path or railroad at different levels where clearance to traffic on the lower level is obtained by elevating the higher level; *also* **:** the upper level of such a crossing

over·per·suade \ˌō-vər-pər-ˈswād\ *vt* (1624) **:** to persuade to act contrary to one's conviction or preference — **over·per·sua·sion** \-ˈswā-zhən\ *n*

over·plaid \ˈō-vər-ˌplad\ *n* (1926) **:** a textile design consisting of a plaid pattern superimposed on another plaid or on a textured ground (as of tweed or herringbone); *also* **:** a fabric with such a design — **over·plaid·ed** *adj*

over·play \ˌō-vər-ˈplā\ *vt* (1896) **1 a :** to present (as a dramatic role) extravagantly **:** EXAGGERATE **b :** to place too much emphasis on **2 :** to rely too much on the strength of — usu. used in the phrase *overplay one's hand* **3 :** to strike a golf ball beyond (a putting green) ~ *vi* **:** to exaggerate a part or effect

over·plus \ˈō-vər-ˌpləs\ *n* [ME, part trans. of MF *surplus*] (14c) **:** SURPLUS

over·pop·u·la·tion \ˌō-vər-ˌpäp-yə-ˈlā-shən\ *n* (1823) **:** the condition of having a population so dense as to cause environmental deterioration, an impaired quality of life, or a population crash — **over·pop·u·lat·ed** \-ˈpäp-yə-ˌlāt-əd\ *adj*

over·pow·er \ˌō-vər-ˈpau̇(-ə)r\ *vt* (1593) **1 :** to overcome by superior force **:** SUBDUE **2 :** to affect with overwhelming intensity ⟨the stench ~*ed* us⟩ **3 :** to provide with more power than is needed or desirable ⟨a dangerously ~*ed* car⟩ — **over·pow·er·ing·ly** \-ˈpau̇r-iŋ-lē\ *adv*

over·pres·sure \ˈō-vər-ˌpresh-ər\ *n* (1644) **:** pressure significantly above what is usual or normal

over·price \ˌō-vər-ˈprīs\ *vt* (1605) **:** to price too high

¹**over·print** \ˌō-vər-ˈprint\ *vt* (1863) **:** to print over with something additional

²**over·print** \ˈō-vər-ˌ\ *n* (1876) **:** something added by or as if by overprinting; *esp* **:** a printed marking added to a postage or revenue stamp esp. to alter the original or to commemorate a special event

over·proof \ˌō-vər-ˈprüf\ *adj* (1807) **:** containing more alcohol than proof spirit

over·pro·por·tion \-prə-ˈpōr-shən, -ˈpȯr-\ *vt* (1642) **:** to make disproportionately large — **overproportion** *n* — **over·pro·por·tion·ate** \-sh(ə-)nət\ *adj* — **over·pro·por·tion·ate·ly** *adv*

over·qual·i·fied \-ˈkwäl-ə-ˌfīd\ *adj* (1954) **:** having more education, training, or experience than a job calls for

over·reach \ˌō-və(r)-ˈrēch\ *vt* (14c) **1** : to reach above or beyond : OVERTOP **2** : to defeat (oneself) by seeking to do or gain too much **3** : to get the better of esp. in dealing and bargaining and typically by unscrupulous or crafty methods ~ *vi* **1** *of a horse* : to strike the forefoot with the front part of the hind foot **2 a** : to go to excess **b** : EXAGGERATE **3** : to overreach oneself — **over·reach** \ˈō-və(r)-ˌrēch, ˌō-və(r)-ˈ\ *n* — **over·reach·er** *n*

over·rep·re·sent·ed \ˈō-və(r)-ˌrep-ri-ˈzent-əd\ *adj* (1900) : represented excessively; *esp* : having representatives in a proportion higher than the average — **over·re·pre·sen·ta·tion** \-ˌrep-ri-ˌzen-ˈtā-shən, -zən-\ *n*

1**over·ride** \-ˈrīd\ *vt* **-rode** \-ˈrōd\; **-rid·den** \-ˈrid-ᵊn\; **-rid·ing** \-ˈrīd-iŋ\ (bef. 12c) **1** : to ride over or across : TRAMPLE **2** : to ride (as a horse) too much or too hard **3 a** : to prevail over : DOMINATE **b** : to set aside : ANNUL ⟨~ a veto⟩ **c** : to neutralize the action of (as an automatic control) **4** : to extend or pass over; *esp* : OVERLAP

2**over·ride** \ˈō-və(r)-ˌrīd\ *n* (1931) **1** : a commission paid to managerial personnel on sales made by subordinates **2** : ROYALTY 5a **3** : a device or system used to override a control **4** : an act or an instance of overriding

over·ripe \ˌō-və(r)-ˈrīp\ *adj* (1671) **1** : passed beyond maturity or ripeness toward decay **2** : DECADENT

over·rule \-ˈrül\ *vt* (1581) **1** : to rule over : GOVERN **2** : to prevail over : OVERCOME **3 a** : to rule against **b** : to set aside : REVERSE

1**over·run** \-ˈrən\ *vt* **-ran** \-ˈran\; **-run**; **-run·ning** (bef. 12c) **1 a** : to defeat decisively and occupy the positions of **b** : to swarm over : INFEST **2 a** : to run or go beyond or past ⟨the plane *overran* the runway⟩ **b** : EXCEED **c** (1) : to readjust (set type) by shifting letters or words from one line into another (2) : OVERSET **3** : to flow over

2**over·run** \ˈō-və(r)-ˌrən\ *n* (1898) **1** : an act or instance of overrunning; *esp* : an exceeding of the costs estimated in a contract for development and manufacture of new equipment **2** : the amount by which something overruns **3** : a run in excess of the quantity ordered by a customer

over·sea \ˌo-vər-ˈsē, ˈō-vər-ˌ\ *adj or adv* (12c) : OVERSEAS

over·seas \-ˈsēz, -ˌsēz\ *adv or adj* (1583) : beyond or across the sea

over·see \ˌō-vər-ˈsē\ *vt* **-saw** \-ˈsȯ\; **-seen** \-ˈsēn\; **-see·ing** (bef. 12c) **1** : SURVEY, WATCH **2 a** : INSPECT, EXAMINE **b** : SUPERVISE

over·seer \ˈō-və(r)-ˌsi(ə)r, -ˌsē-ər, ˌō-və(r)-ˈ\ *n* (1523) : SUPERINTENDENT, SUPERVISOR

over·sell \ˌō-vər-ˈsel\ *vt* **-sold** \-ˈsōld\; **-sell·ing** (ca. 1879) **1 a** : to sell too much to **b** : to sell too much of **2** : to make excessive claims for : OVERPRAISE — **over·sell** \ˈō-vər-ˌsel\ *n*

over·sen·si·tive \ˌō-vər-ˈsen(t)-sət-iv, -stiv\ *adj* (1857) : unduly or extremely sensitive — **over·sen·si·tive·ness** *n* — **over·sen·si·tiv·i·ty** \-ˌsen(t)-sə-ˈtiv-ət-ē\ *n*

over·set \-ˈset\ *vt* **-set**; **-set·ting** (1583) **1 a** : to disturb mentally or physically : UPSET **b** : to turn or tip over : OVERTURN **2** : to set too much type matter for — **over·set** \ˈō-vər-ˌset\ *n*

over·sexed \ˌō-vər-ˈsekst\ *adj* (1898) : exhibiting an excessive sexual drive or interest

over·shad·ow \-ˈshad-(ˌ)ō, -ə(-w)\ *vt* (bef. 12c) **1** : to cast a shadow over : DARKEN **2** : to exceed in importance : OUTWEIGH

over·shirt \ˈō-vər-ˌshərt\ *n* (1805) : a shirt usu. worn over another shirt without being tucked in

over·shoe \-ˌshü\ *n* (1848) : an outer shoe; *esp* : GALOSH

over·shoot \ˌō-vər-ˈshüt\ *vt* **-shot** \-ˈshät\; **-shoot·ing** (14c) **1** : to pass swiftly beyond **2** : to shoot or pass over or beyond so as to miss **3** : to excel in shooting — **over·shoot** \ˈō-vər-ˌshüt\ *n*

1**over·shot** \ˈō-vər-ˌshät\ *adj* (1885) **1 a** : having the upper jaw extending beyond the lower **b** : projecting beyond the lower jaw **2** : actuated by the weight of water passing over and flowing from above ⟨an ~ waterwheel⟩

2**overshot** *n* (1945) : a pattern or weave featuring filling threads which pass two or more warp yarns before reentering the fabric

over·sight \ˈō-vər-ˌsīt\ *n* (14c) **1** : watchful and responsible care **2** : an inadvertent omission or error

over·sim·ple \ˌō-vər-ˈsim-pəl\ *adj* (1700) : too simple : not thoroughgoing or exhaustive ⟨~ theories of personality⟩ — **over·sim·ply** \-plē\ *adv*

over·sim·pli·fy \-ˈsim-plə-ˌfī\ *vt* (1923) : to simplify to such an extent as to bring about distortion, misunderstanding, or error ~ *vi* : to engage in undue or extreme simplification — **over·sim·pli·fi·ca·tion** \-ˌsim-plə-fə-ˈkā-shən\ *n*

over·size \ˌō-vər-ˈsīz\ *or* **over·sized** \-ˈsīzd\ *adj* (1853) : being of more than ordinary size ⟨~ pillows⟩

over·skirt \ˈō-vər-ˌskərt\ *n* (1870) : a skirt worn over another skirt

over·slaugh \ˌō-vər-ˈslȯ\ *vt* [D *overslaan* to pass over, omit] (1846) : to pass over for appointment or promotion in favor of another

over·sleep \ˌō-vər-ˈslēp\ *vi* **-slept** \-ˈslept\; **-sleep·ing** (14c) : to sleep beyond the time for waking

over·slip \ˌō-vər-ˈslip\ *vt* (15c) **1** *archaic* : to let pass by unawares : MISS **2** *obs* : ESCAPE

over·sold \ˌō-vər-ˈsōld\ *adj* (ca. 1909) : likely to show a rise in price because of prior heavy selling and accompanying decline in price ⟨an ~ stock⟩

over·soul \ˈō-vər-ˌsōl\ *n* (1841) : the absolute reality and ground of existences conceived as a spiritual being in which the ideal nature manifested in human beings is perfectly realized

over·spend \ˌō-vər-ˈspend\ *vb* **-spent** \-ˈspent\; **-spend·ing** *vt* (1618) **1** : to spend or use to excess : EXHAUST **2** : to exceed in expenditure ~ *vi* : to spend beyond one's means — **over·spend·er** *n*

over·spill \ˈō-vər-ˌspil\ *n, chiefly Brit* (1884) : the movement of excess urban population into less crowded areas

over·spread \ˌō-vər-ˈspred\ *vt* **-spread**; **-spread·ing** (bef. 12c) : to spread over or above — **over·spread** \ˈō-vər-ˌspred\ *n*

over·state \-ˈstāt\ *vt* (1803) : to state in too strong terms : EXAGGERATE — **over·state·ment** \-mənt\ *n*

over·stay \-ˈstā\ *vt* (1646) : to stay beyond the time or the limits of

over·steer \ˈō-vər-ˌsti(ə)r\ *n* (1951) : the tendency of an automobile to steer into a sharper turn than the driver intends sometimes with a thrusting of the rear to the outside; *also* : the action or an instance of oversteer

over·step \ˌō-vər-ˈstep\ *vt* (bef. 12c) : EXCEED, TRANSGRESS

over·sto·ry \ˈō-vər-ˌstōr-ē, -ˌstȯr-\ *n* (1925) **1** : the layer of foliage in a forest canopy **2** : the trees contributing to an overstory

over·strew \ˌō-vər-ˈstrü\ *vt* **-strewed**; **-strewed** *or* **-strewn** \-ˈstrün\; **-strew·ing** (ca. 1570) **1** : to strew or scatter about **2** : to cover here and there

over·stride \-ˈstrīd\ *vt* **-strode** \-ˈstrōd\; **-strid·den** \-ˈstrid-ᵊn\; **-strid·ing** \-ˈstrīd-iŋ\ (13c) **1 a** : to stride over, across, or beyond **b** : BESTRIDE **2** : to stride faster than or beyond

over·strung \-ˈstrəŋ\ *adj* (1810) : too highly strung : too sensitive

over·stuff \-ˈstəf\ *vt* (1937) **1** : to stuff too full **2** : to cover (as a chair or sofa) completely and deeply with upholstery

over·sub·scribe \-səb-ˈskrīb\ *vt* (1891) : to subscribe for more of than is available — **over·sub·scrip·tion** \-ˈskrip-shən\ *n*

overt \ō-ˈvərt, ˈō-(ˌ)vərt\ *adj* [ME, fr. MF *ouvert, overt,* fr. pp. of *ouvrir* to open, fr. (assumed) VL *operire,* alter. of L *aperire*] (14c) : open to view : MANIFEST — **overt·ly** *adv* — **overt·ness** *n*

over·take \ˌō-vər-ˈtāk\ *vt* **-took** \-ˈtu̇k\; **-tak·en** \-ˈtā-kən\; **-tak·ing** [ME *overtaken,* fr. 1*over* + *taken* to take] (13c) **1 a** : to catch up with **b** : to catch up with and pass by **2** : to come upon suddenly

over·tax \ˌō-vər-ˈtaks\ *vt* (1650) **1** : to tax too heavily **2** : to put too great a burden or strain on

over–the–count·er *adj* (ca. 1923) **1** : not traded or effected on an organized securities exchange ⟨~ transactions⟩ ⟨~ securities⟩ **2** : sold lawfully without prescription ⟨~ drugs⟩

over–the–hill *adj* [fr. the phrase *over the hill*] (1946) **1** : past one's prime **2** : advanced in age

over–the–transom *adj* (1952) : offered without prior arrangement esp. for publication : UNSOLICITED ⟨an ~ manuscript⟩

over·throw \ˌō-vər-ˈthrō\ *vt* **-threw** \-ˈthrü\; **-thrown** \-ˈthrōn\; **-throw·ing** (14c) **1** : OVERTURN, UPSET **2** : to cause the downfall of : BRING DOWN, DEFEAT **3** : to throw a baseball over or past (as a base) ***syn*** see CONQUER — **over·throw** \ˈō-vər-ˌthrō\ *n*

over·time \ˈō-vər-ˌtīm\ *n* (1536) **1** : time in excess of a set limit; *esp* : working time in excess of a standard day or week **2** : the wage paid for overtime — **overtime** *adv*

over·tone \-ˌtōn\ *n* (1867) **1 a** : one of the higher tones produced simultaneously with the fundamental and that with the fundamental comprise a complex musical tone : HARMONIC 1a **b** : HARMONIC 2 **2** : the color of the light reflected (as by a paint) **3** : a secondary effect, quality, or meaning : SUGGESTION

over·top \ˌō-vər-ˈtäp\ *vt* (1593) **1** : to rise above the top of **2** : to be superior to **3** : SURPASS

over·trade \-ˈtrād\ *vi* (1734) : to trade beyond one's capital

over·trick \ˈō-vər-ˌtrik\ *n* (1903) : a card trick won in excess of the number bid

over·trump \ˌō-vər-ˈtrəmp\ *vt* (1746) : to trump with a higher trump card than the highest previously played on the same trick ~ *vi* : to play a higher trump card than the highest previously played on the same trick

1**over·ture** \ˈō-və(r)-ˌchu̇(ə)r, -chər, -ˌt(y)u̇(ə)r\ *n* [ME, lit., opening, fr. MF, fr. (assumed) VL *opertura,* alter. of L *apertura* — more at APERTURE] (15c) **1 a** : an initiative toward agreement or action : PROPOSAL **b** : something introductory : PRELUDE **2 a** : the orchestral introduction to a musical dramatic work **b** : an orchestral concert piece written esp. as a single movement in sonata form

2**overture** *vt* **-tured**; **-tur·ing** (1637) **1** : to put forward as an overture **2** : to make or present an overture to

1**over·turn** \ˌō-vər-ˈtərn\ *vt* (14c) **1** : to cause to turn over : UPSET **2** : INVALIDATE, DESTROY ~ *vi* : UPSET, TURN OVER

2**over·turn** \ˈō-vər-ˌtərn\ *n* (1592) **1** : the act of overturning : the state of being overturned **2** : the sinking of surface water and rise of bottom water in a lake or sea that results from changes in temperature that commonly occur in spring and fall wherever lakes are icebound in winter

over·val·ue \ˌō-vər-ˈval-(ˌ)yü, -yə(-w)\ *vt* (1597) : to assign an excessive or fictitious value to — **over·valu·ation** \-ˌval-yə-ˈwā-shən\ *n*

over·view \ˈō-vər-ˌvyü\ *n* (1588) : a general survey : SUMMARY

over·volt·age \ˌō-vər-ˈvōl-tij\ *n* (1907) **1** : the excess potential required for the discharge of an ion at an electrode over and above the equilibrium potential of the electrode **2** : voltage in excess of the normal operating voltage of a device or circuit

over·watch \-ˈwäch\ *vt* (1563) **1** *archaic* : to weary or exhaust by keeping awake **2** : to watch over

over·wear \-ˈwa(ə)r, -ˈwe(ə)r\ *vt* **-wore** \-ˈwō(ə)r, -ˈwȯ(ə)r\; **-worn** \-ˈwō(ə)rn, -ˈwȯ(ə)rn\; **-wear·ing** (1578) : WEAR OUT, EXHAUST

1**over·wea·ry** \-ˈwi(ə)r-ē\ *vt* (1576) : to tire out

2**overweary** *adj* (1591) : wearied to excess

over·ween·ing \-ˈwē-niŋ\ *adj* [ME *overwening,* prp. of *overwenen* to be arrogant, fr. *over* + *wenen* to ween] (14c) **1** : ARROGANT, PRESUMPTUOUS **2** : IMMODERATE, EXAGGERATED

over·weigh \-ˈwā\ *vt* (13c) **1** : to exceed in weight **2** : OPPRESS

1**over·weight** \ˈō-vər-ˌwāt, *2 is usu* ˌō-vər-ˈ\ *n* (1552) **1** : weight over and above what is required or allowed **2** : excessive or burdensome weight

2**over·weight** \ˌō-vər-ˈwāt\ *vt* (1603) **1** : to give too much weight or consideration to **2** : to weight excessively

3**over·weight** \ˌō-vər-ˈwāt\ *adj* (1638) : exceeding expected, normal, or proper weight; *esp* : exceeding the bodily weight normal for one's age, height, and build

over·whelm \ˌō-vər-ˈhwelm, -ˈwelm\ *vt* [ME *overwhelmen,* fr. 1*over* + *whelmen* to turn over, cover up] (14c) **1** : UPSET, OVERTHROW **2 a** : to cover over completely : SUBMERGE **b** : to overcome by superior force or numbers **c** : to overpower in thought or feeling

over·whelm·ing *adj* (1742) : EXTREME, GREAT ⟨~ indifference⟩ — **over·whelm·ing·ly** *adv*

1**over·win·ter** \ˌō-vər-ˈwint-ər\ *vi* (bef. 12c) : to survive the winter

2**overwinter** *adj* (1900) : occurring during the period spanning the winter

over with *adj* (1924) : being at an end : FINISHED, COMPLETED

over·work \ˌō-vər-ˈwərk\ *vt* (1818) **1** : to cause to work too hard, too long, or to exhaustion **2** : to decorate all over **3 a** : to work too much on : OVERDO **b** : to make excessive use of ~ *vi* : to work too much or too long : OVERDO — **overwork** *n*

over·write \ˌō-və(r)-ˈrīt\ *vb* **-wrote** \-ˈrōt\; **-writ·ten** \-ˈrit-ᵊn\; **-writ·ing** \-ˈrīt-iŋ\ *vt* (1699) **1** : to write over the surface of **2** : to write in inflated or overly elaborate style ~ *vi* : to write too much

over·wrought \-ˈrȯt\ *adj* [pp. of *overwork*] (1670) **1 :** extremely excited : AGITATED **2 :** elaborated to excess : OVERDONE

ovi- *or* **ovo-** — see OV-

ovi·cid·al \ˌō-və-ˈsīd-ᵊl\ *adj* (1932) **:** capable of killing eggs

ovi·cide \ˈō-və-ˌsīd\ *n* [ISV] (1913) **:** an agent that kills eggs; *esp* **:** an insecticide effective against the egg stage

ovi·duct \ˈō-və-ˌdəkt\ *n* [NL *oviductus,* fr. *ov-* + *ductus* duct] (1672) **:** a tube that serves exclusively or esp. for the passage of eggs from an ovary — **ovi·duc·tal** \ˌō-və-ˈdək-tᵊl\ *adj*

ovine \ˈō-ˌvīn\ *adj* [LL *ovinus,* fr. L *ovis* sheep — more at EWE] (ca. 1828) **:** of, relating to, or resembling sheep — **ovine** *n*

ovip·a·rous \ō-ˈvip-(ə-)rəs\ *adj* [L *oviparus,* fr. *ov-* + *-parus* -parous] (1646) **:** producing eggs that develop and hatch outside the maternal body; *also* **:** involving the production of such eggs

ovi·pos·it \ˈō-və-ˌpäz-ət, ˌō-və-ˈ\ *vi* [prob. back-formation fr. *ovipositor*] (1816) **:** to lay eggs — used esp. of insects — **ovi·po·si·tion** \ˌō-və-pə-ˈzish-ən\ *n* — **ovi·po·si·tion·al** \-ˈzish-nəl, -ən-ᵊl\ *adj*

ovi·pos·i·tor \ˈō-və-ˌpäz-ət-ər, ˌō-və-ˈ\ *n* [NL, fr. L *ov-* + *positor* one that places, fr. *positus,* pp. of *ponere* to place — more at POSITION] (1816) **:** a specialized organ (as of an insect) for depositing eggs — see INSECT illustration

ovoid \ˈō-ˌvȯid\ *or* **ovoi·dal** \ō-ˈvȯid-ᵊl\ *adj* [F *ovoïde,* fr. L *ovum* egg — more at EGG] (ca. 1828) **:** shaped like an egg : OVATE — **ovoid** *n*

ovo·lo \ˈō-və-ˌlō\ *n, pl* **-los** [It, dim. of *uovo, ovo* egg, fr. L *ovum*] (1663) **:** a rounded convex molding

Ovon·ics \ō-ˈvän-iks\ *n pl but usu sing in constr* [Stanford R. *Ov*shinsky *b*1923 Am. inventor + electr*onics*] (1968) **:** a branch of electronics that deals with applications of the change from an electrically nonconducting state to a semiconducting state shown by glasses of special composition upon application of a certain minimum voltage — **ovon·ic** \-ik\ *adj*

ovo·tes·tis \ˌō-vō-ˈtes-təs\ *n* [NL] (1877) **:** a hermaphrodite gonad (as in some scale insects)

ovo·vi·vip·a·rous \ˈō-vō-ˌvī-ˈvip-(ə-)rəs\ *adj* [prob. fr. (assumed) NL *ovoviviparus,* fr. L *ov-* + *viviparus* viviparous] (1801) **:** producing eggs that develop within the maternal body and hatch within or immediately after extrusion from the parent — **ovo·vi·vip·a·rous·ly** *adv* — **ovo·vi·vip·a·rous·ness** *n*

¹ovu·late \ˈäv-yə-ˌlāt, ˈōv-, -lət\ *adj* (1861) **:** bearing an ovule

²ovu·late \-ˌlāt\ *vi* **-lat·ed; -lat·ing** (1888) **:** to produce eggs or discharge them from an ovary — **ovu·la·tion** \ˌäv-yə-ˈlā-shən, ˌōv-\ *n*

ovu·la·to·ry \ˈäv-yə-lə-ˌtōr-ē, ˈōv-, -ˌtȯr-\ *adj* (1931) **:** of, relating to, or involving ovulation

ovule \ˈäv-(ˌ)yü(ə)l, ˈōv-\ *n* [NL *ovulum,* dim. of L *ovum*] (1830) **1 :** an outgrowth of the ovary of a seed plant that is a megasporangium and encloses an embryo sac within a nucellus **2 :** a small egg; *esp* **:** one in an early stage of growth

ovum \ˈō-vəm\ *n, pl* **ova** \-və\ [NL, fr. L, egg — more at EGG] (ca. 1706) **:** a female gamete : MACROGAMETE

ow \ˈau̇, ˈü\ *interj* [fr. earlier *ow,* interj. expressing surprise, fr. ME] (ca. 1911) — used esp. to express sudden pain

owe \ˈō\ *vb* **owed; ow·ing** [ME *owen* to possess, own, owe, fr. OE *āgan;* akin to OHG *eigun* (1st & 3d pl. pres. indic.) possess, Skt *īśe* he possesses] *vt* (bef. 12c) **1 a** *archaic* **:** POSSESS, OWN **b :** to have or bear (an emotion or attitude) to someone or something ⟨~*s* the boss a grudge⟩ **2 a** (1) **:** to be under obligation to pay or repay in return for something received **:** be indebted in the sum of ⟨~*s* me $5⟩ (2) **:** to be under obligation to render (as duty or service) **b :** to be indebted to ⟨~*s* the grocer for supplies⟩ **3 :** to be indebted for ⟨*owed* his wealth to his father⟩ ⟨~*s* much to good luck⟩ ~ *vi* **:** to be in debt ⟨~*s* for his house⟩

owing to *prep* (1695) **:** BECAUSE OF ⟨delayed *owing to* a crash⟩

owl \ˈau̇(ə)l\ *n* [ME *owle,* fr. OE *ūle;* akin to OHG *uwila* owl] (bef. 12c) **:** any of an order (Strigiformes) of birds of prey with large head and eyes, short hooked bill, strong talons, and more or less nocturnal habits

owl·et \ˈau̇-lət\ *n* (1542) **:** a small or young owl

owl·ish \ˈau̇-lish\ *adj* (1611) **:** resembling or suggesting an owl — **owl·ish·ly** *adv* — **owl·ish·ness** *n*

¹own \ˈōn\ *adj* [ME *owen,* fr. OE *āgen;* akin to OHG *eigan* own, ON *eiginn,* OE *āgan* to possess — more at OWE] (bef. 12c) **:** belonging to oneself or itself — usu. used following a possessive case or possessive adjective ⟨cooked his ~ dinner⟩

²own *vt* (bef. 12c) **1 a :** to have or hold as property **:** POSSESS **b :** to have power over **:** CONTROL ⟨wanted to ~ his own life⟩ **2 :** to acknowledge to be true, valid, or as claimed **:** ADMIT ⟨~ a debt⟩ ~ *vi* **:** to acknowledge something to be true, valid, or as claimed — used with *to* or *up* **syn** see HAVE, ACKNOWLEDGE — **own·er** \ˈō-nər\ *n* — **own·er·ship** \-ˌship\ *n*

³own *pron, sing or pl in constr* (bef. 12c) **:** one or ones belonging to oneself — used after a possessive and without a following noun as a pronoun equivalent in meaning to the adjective *own* ⟨gave out books so that each student had his ~⟩ — **on one's own :** for or by oneself **:** independently of assistance or control

ox \ˈäks\ *n, pl* **ox·en** \ˈäk-sən\ *also* **ox** [ME, fr. OE *oxa;* akin to OHG *ohso* ox, Gk *hygros* wet — more at HUMOR] (bef. 12c) **1 :** a domestic bovine mammal (*Bos taurus*); *broadly* **:** a bovine mammal **2 :** an adult castrated male domestic ox

ox- *or* **oxo-** *comb form* [F, fr. *oxygène*] **:** oxygen ⟨*oxazine*⟩

ox·a·cil·lin \ˌäk-sə-ˈsil-ən\ *n* [*ox-* + azole + peni*cillin*] (1962) **:** a semisynthetic penicillin that is esp. effective in the control of infections caused by penicillin-resistant staphylococci

ox·a·late \ˈäk-sə-ˌlāt\ *n* (1791) **:** a salt or ester of oxalic acid

ox·al·ic acid \(ˌ)äk-ˌsal-ik-\ *n* [F (*acide*) *oxalique,* fr. L *oxalis*] (1791) **:** a poisonous strong acid $(COOH)_2$ or $H_2C_2O_4$ that occurs in various plants as oxalates and is used esp. as a bleaching or cleaning agent and in making dyes

ox·al·is \äk-ˈsal-əs\ *n* [NL, genus name, fr. L, wood sorrel, fr. Gk, fr. *oxys* sharp — more at OXYGEN] (1601) **:** WOOD SORREL

ox·a·lo·ac·e·tate \ˌäk-sə-lō-ˈas-ə-ˌtāt\ *also* **ox·al·ac·e·tate** \ˌäk-sə-ˈlas-\ *n* [*oxaloacetic* acid + *-ate*] (1939) **:** a salt or ester of oxaloacetic acid

ox·a·lo·ace·tic acid \ˌäk-sə-lō-ə-ˌsēt-ik-\ *also* **ox·al·ace·tic acid** \ˌäk-sə-lə-ˌsēt-ik-\ *n* [*oxal*ic + *acetic acid*] (ca. 1929) **:** a crystalline acid $C_4H_4O_5$ that is formed by reversible oxidation of malic acid (as in carbohydrate metabolism via the citric acid cycle) and in reversible transamination reactions (as from aspartic acid)

ox·a·lo·suc·cin·ic acid \ˈäk-sə-lō-sək-ˌsin-ik-, äk-ˈsal-ō-\ *n* [*oxal*ic + *succinic acid*] (1925) **:** a tricarboxylic acid $C_6H_6O_7$ that is formed as an intermediate in the metabolism of fats and carbohydrates

ox·az·e·pam \äk-ˈsaz-ə-ˌpam\ *n* [hydr*oxy-* + di*azepam*] (ca. 1964) **:** a tranquilizing drug $C_{15}H_{11}ClN_2O_2$

ox·a·zine \ˈäk-sə-ˌzēn\ *n* (1900) **:** any of several parent compounds C_4H_5NO containing a ring composed of four carbon atoms, one oxygen atom, and one nitrogen atom

ox·blood \ˈäks-ˌbləd\ *n* (1705) **:** a moderate reddish brown

ox·bow \ˈäks-ˌbō\ *n* (14c) **1 :** a U-shaped frame forming a collar about an ox's neck and supporting the yoke **2 :** something (as a bend in a river) resembling an oxbow — **oxbow** *adj*

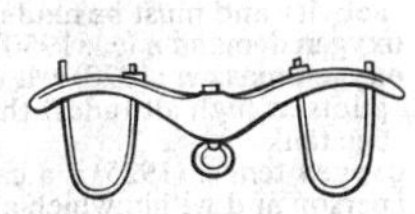

oxbow 1

ox·eye \ˈäk-ˌsī\ *n* (15c) **:** any of several composite plants (as of the genera *Chrysanthemum, Heliopsis,* or *Buphthalmum*) having heads with both disk and ray flowers; *esp* **:** DAISY 1b

oxeye daisy *n* (ca. 1763) **:** DAISY 1b

ox·ford \ˈäks-fərd\ *n* [*Oxford,* England] (1890) **1 :** a low shoe laced or tied over the instep **2 :** a soft durable cotton or synthetic fabric with a silky luster made in plain or basket weaves — called also *oxford cloth*

Oxford down *n, often cap D* [*Oxford*shire, England] (1859) **:** any of a Down breed of large hornless sheep developed by crossing Cotswolds and Hampshires

Oxford movement *n* (1841) **:** a High Church movement within the Church of England begun at Oxford in 1833

ox·heart \ˈäks-ˌhärt\ *n* (1870) **:** any of various large sweet cherries

ox·i·dant \ˈäk-səd-ənt\ *n* (1884) **:** OXIDIZING AGENT — **oxidant** *adj*

ox·i·dase \ˈäk-sə-ˌdās, -ˌdāz\ *n* [ISV] (1896) **:** any of various enzymes that catalyze oxidations; *esp* **:** one able to react directly with molecular oxygen — **ox·i·da·sic** \ˌäk-sə-ˈdā-sik, -zik\ *adj*

ox·i·da·tion \ˌäk-sə-ˈdā-shən\ *n* [F, fr. *oxider, oxyder* to oxidize, fr. *oxide*] (1791) **1 :** the act or process of oxidizing **2 :** the state or result of being oxidized — **ox·i·da·tive** \ˈäk-sə-ˌdāt-iv\ *adj* — **ox·i·da·tive·ly** *adv*

oxidation number *n* (1929) **:** the degree of or potential for oxidation of an element or atom which is usu. expressed as a positive or negative number representing the ionic or effective charge **:** VALENCE — called also *oxidation state*

oxidation–reduction *n* (1909) **:** a chemical reaction in which one or more electrons are transferred from one atom or molecule to another

oxidative phosphorylation *n* (1954) **:** the synthesis of ATP by phosphorylation of ADP for which energy is obtained by electron transport and which takes place in the mitochondria during aerobic respiration

ox·ide \ˈäk-ˌsīd\ *n* [F *oxide, oxyde,* fr. *ox-* (fr. *oxygène* oxygen) + *-ide* (fr. *acide* acid)] (1790) **:** a binary compound of oxygen with an element or radical — **ox·id·ic** \äk-ˈsid-ik\ *adj*

ox·i·dize \ˈäk-sə-ˌdīz\ *vb* **-dized; -diz·ing** [*oxide* + *-ize*] *vt* (1806) **1 :** to combine with oxygen **2 :** to dehydrogenate esp. by the action of oxygen **3 :** to change (a compound) by increasing the proportion of the electronegative part or change (an element or ion) from a lower to a higher positive valence **:** remove one or more electrons from (an atom, ion, or molecule) ~ *vi* **:** to become oxidized — **ox·i·diz·able** \-ˌdī-zə-bəl\ *adj*

ox·i·diz·er \-ˌdī-zər\ *n* (1875) **:** OXIDIZING AGENT; *esp* **:** one used to support the combustion of a rocket propellant

oxidizing agent *n* (ca. 1903) **:** a substance that oxidizes something esp. chemically (as by accepting electrons)

ox·i·do·re·duc·tase \ˈäk-səd-ō-ri-ˈdək-ˌtās, -ˌtāz\ *n* [*oxidation* + *-o-* + *reduction* + *-ase*] (1922) **:** an enzyme that catalyzes an oxidation-reduction reaction

ox·ime \ˈäk-ˌsēm\ *n* [ISV *ox-* + *-ime* (fr. *imide*)] (ca. 1890) **:** any of various compounds obtained chiefly by the action of hydroxylamine on aldehydes and ketones and characterized by the bivalent grouping C=NOH

ox·lip \ˈäk-ˌslip\ *n* [(assumed) ME *oxeslippe,* fr. OE *oxanslyppe,* lit., ox dung, fr. *oxa* ox + *slypa, slyppe* paste — more at SLIP] (bef. 12c) **:** a Eurasian primula (*Primula elatior*) differing from the cowslip chiefly in the flat corolla limb

oxo \ˈäk-(ˌ)sō\ *adj* [*ox-*] (1926) **:** containing oxygen

oxo- — see OX-

Ox·o·ni·an \äk-ˈsō-nē-ən\ *n* [ML *Oxonia* Oxford] (1701) **:** a student or graduate of Oxford University — **Oxonian** *adj*

ox·tail \ˈäk-ˌstāl\ *n* (15c) **:** the tail of a beef animal; *esp* **:** the skinned tail used for food (as in soup)

ox·ter \ˈäk-stər\ *n* [(assumed) ME, alter. of OE *ōxta;* akin to L *axilla* armpit — more at AXIS] (15c) **1** *chiefly Scot & Irish* **:** ARMPIT **2** *chiefly Scot & Irish* **:** ARM

ox·tongue \ˈäk-ˌstəŋ\ *n* (14c) **:** a European hawkweed (*Picris echioides*) that has yellow flowers and is now naturalized in the eastern U.S.

oxy \ˈäk-sē\ *adj* [F, fr. *oxygène* oxygen] (1910) **:** containing oxygen or additional oxygen — often used in combination ⟨*oxy*hemoglobin⟩ ⟨*oxy*hydrogen⟩

oxy·acet·y·lene \ˌäk-sē-ə-ˈset-ᵊl-ən, -ᵊl-ˌēn\ *adj* [ISV] (1909) **:** of, relating to, or utilizing a mixture of oxygen and acetylene ⟨an ~ torch⟩

oxy·ac·id \ˈäk-sē-ˌas-əd\ *n* (1836) **:** an acid (as sulfuric acid) that contains oxygen — called also *oxygen acid*

ox·y·gen \ˈäk-si-jən\ *n, often attrib* [F *oxygène,* fr. Gk *oxys,* adj., acid, lit., sharp + F *-gène* -gen; akin to L *acer* sharp — more at EDGE] (1786) **:** an element that is found free as a colorless tasteless odorless gas in the atmosphere of which it forms about 21 percent or combined in water, in most rocks and minerals, and in numerous organic compounds, that is capable of combining with all elements except the inert gases, is active in physiological processes, and is involved esp. in combustion processes — see ELEMENT table — **ox·y·gen·ic** \ˌäk-si-ˈjen-ik\ *adj* — **ox·y·gen·less** \ˈäk-si-jən-ləs\ *adj*

ox·y·gen·ate \ˈäk-si-jə-ˌnāt, äk-ˈsij-ə-\ *vt* **-at·ed; -at·ing** (1790) : to impregnate, combine, or supply (as blood) with oxygen — **ox·y·gen·ation** \ˌäk-si-jə-ˈnā-shən, äk-ˌsij-ə-\ *n*

ox·y·gen·ator \ˈäk-si-jə-ˌnāt-ər, äk-ˈsij-ə-\ *n* (ca. 1864) : one (as an apparatus for perfusing an organ or tissue) that oxygenates

oxygen cycle *n* (1935) : the cycle whereby atmospheric oxygen is converted to carbon dioxide in animal respiration and regenerated by green plants in photosynthesis

oxygen debt *n* (ca. 1923) : a cumulative deficit of oxygen available to oxidize pyruvic acid that develops during periods of intense bodily activity and must be made good when the body returns to rest

oxygen demand *n* (ca. 1950) : BIOCHEMICAL OXYGEN DEMAND

oxygen mask *n* (1920) : a device worn over the nose and mouth (as by pilots at high altitudes) through which oxygen is supplied from a storage tank

oxygen tent *n* (1925) : a canopy which can be placed over a bedridden person and within which a flow of oxygen can be maintained

oxy·he·mo·glo·bin \ˌäk-si-ˈhē-mə-ˌglō-bən\ *n* [ISV] (1873) : hemoglobin loosely combined with oxygen that it releases to the tissues

oxy·hy·dro·gen \-ˈhī-drə-jən\ *adj* (1827) : of, relating to, or utilizing a mixture of oxygen and hydrogen ⟨~ torch⟩

oxy·mo·ron \ˌäk-si-ˈmō(ə)r-ˌän, -ˈmó(ə)r-\ *n, pl* **-mo·ra** \-ˈmōr-ə, -ˈmòr-\ [LGk *oxymōron*, fr. neut. of *oxymōros* pointedly foolish, fr. Gk *oxys* sharp, keen + *mōros* foolish — more at MORON] (1657) : a combination of contradictory or incongruous words (as *cruel kindness*) — **oxy·mo·ron·ic** \-mə-ˈrän-ik, -mō-\ *adj*

oxy·phen·bu·ta·zone \ˌäk-sē-ˌfen-ˈbyüt-ə-ˌzōn\ *n* [*oxy-* + *phen-* + *butyric* + *az-* + *-one*] (1961) : a phenylbutazone derivative $C_{19}H_{20}N_2O_3$ used for its anti-inflammatory, analgesic, and antipyretic effects

oxy·phil·ic \ˌäk-si-ˈfil-ik\ *adj* [Gk *oxys* acid + E *-phil* — more at OXYGEN] (1901) : ACIDOPHILIC

oxy·sul·fide \ˌäk-si-ˈsəl-ˌfīd\ *n* [ISV] (1854) : a compound of oxygen and sulfur with an element or radical that may be regarded as a sulfide in which part of the sulfur is replaced by oxygen

oxy·tet·ra·cy·cline \-ˌte-trə-ˈsī-ˌklēn\ *n* (1953) : a yellow crystalline broad-spectrum antibiotic $C_{22}H_{24}N_2O_9$ produced by a soil actinomycete (*Streptomyces rimosus*)

oxy·to·cic \ˌäk-si-ˈtō-sik\ *adj* [ISV, fr. Gk *oxys* sharp, quick + *tokos* childbirth, fr. *tiktein* to bear — more at THANE] (ca. 1853) : hastening parturition; *also* : inducing contraction of uterine smooth muscle — **oxytocic** *n*

oxy·to·cin \-ˈtōs-ᵊn\ *n* [ISV, fr. *oxytocic*] (1927) : a postpituitary octapeptide hormone $C_{43}H_{66}N_{12}O_{12}S_2$ that stimulates esp. the contraction of uterine muscle and the secretion of milk

oxy·uri·a·sis \ˌäk-si-ə-yü-ˈrī-ə-səs\ *n* [NL, fr. *Oxyuris*, genus of worms + *-iasis*] (ca. 1909) : infestation with or disease caused by pinworms (family Oxyuridae)

oy·er and ter·mi·ner \ˌói-ə-rən-ˈtər-mə-nər\ *n* [ME, part trans. of AF *oyer et terminer*, lit., to hear and determine] (13c) **1** : a commission

authorizing a British judge to hear and determine a criminal case at the assizes **2** : a high criminal court in some U.S. states

¹oyez \ō-ˈyā, -ˈyes\ *vb imper* [ME, fr. AF, hear ye, imper. pl. of *oir* to hear, fr. L *audire* — more at AUDIBLE] (13c) — used by a court or public crier to gain attention before a proclamation

²oyez *n, pl* **oyes·ses** \-ˈyes-əz\ (15c) : a cry of oyez

oys·ter \ˈói-stər\ *n, often attrib* [ME *oistre*, fr. MF, fr. L *ostrea*, fr. Gk *ostreon*; akin to Gk *ostrakon* shell, *osteon* bone — more at OSSEOUS] (14c) **1 a** : any of various marine bivalve mollusks (family Ostreidae) that have a rough irregular shell closed by a single adductor muscle and include important shellfish **b** : any of various mollusks resembling or related to the oysters **2** : something valuable or deserved and won by skill **3** : a small mass of muscle contained in a concavity of the pelvic bone on each side of the back of a fowl **4** : an extremely taciturn person

oyster bed *n* (1591) : a place where oysters grow or are cultivated

oys·ter·catch·er \-ˌkach-ər, -ˌkech-\ *n* (1731) : any of a genus (*Haematopus*) of wading birds that have stout legs, a heavy wedge-shaped bill, and often black-and-white plumage

oyster crab *n* (1756) : a crab (*Pinnotheres ostreum*) that lives as a commensal in the gill cavity of the oyster

oyster cracker *n* (1873) : a small salted usu. round cracker

oyster drill *n* (1925) : DRILL 4a

oys·ter·ing \ˈói-st(ə-)riŋ\ *n* (1662) : the act or business of taking oysters for the market or for food

oys·ter·man \ˈói-stər-mən\ *n* (1552) : one who gathers, opens, breeds, or sells oysters

oyster plant *n* (1821) : SALSIFY

ozo·ke·rite \ˌō-zō-ˈki(ə)r-ˌīt\ *also* **ozo·ce·rite** \-ˈsi(ə)r-\ *n* [G *ozokerit*, fr. Gk *ozein* to smell + *kēros* wax — more at CERUMEN] (1837) : a waxy mineral mixture of hydrocarbons that is colorless or white when pure and often of unpleasant odor and is used esp. in making candles and in electrotyping

ozon- *or* **ozono-** *comb form* [ISV, fr. *ozone*] : ozone ⟨*ozonize*⟩

ozone \ˈō-ˌzōn\ *n* [G *ozon*, fr. Gk *ozōn*, prp. of *ozein* to smell — more at ODOR] (ca. 1840) **1** : a triatomic form of oxygen that is a bluish irritating gas of pungent odor, is formed naturally in the upper atmosphere by a photochemical reaction with solar ultraviolet radiation or generated commercially by a silent electric discharge in ordinary oxygen or air, is a major agent in the formation of smogs, and is used esp. in disinfection and deodorization and in oxidation and bleaching **2** : pure and refreshing air — **ozon·ic** \ō-ˈzō-nik, -ˈzän-ik\ *adj*

ozon·ide \ˈō-(ˌ)zō-ˌnīd\ *n* (1867) : a compound of ozone; *specif* : a compound formed by the addition of ozone to the double or triple bond of an unsaturated organic compound

ozon·ize \-ˌnīz\ *vt* **-ized; -iz·ing** (1858) **1** : to convert (oxygen) into ozone **2** : to treat, impregnate, or combine with ozone — **ozon·iza·tion** \ˌō-(ˌ)zō-nə-ˈzā-shən\ *n* — **ozon·iz·er** \ˈō-(ˌ)zō-ˌnī-zər\ *n*

ozo·no·sphere \ō-ˈzō-nə-ˌsfi(ə)r\ *n* (1933) : an atmospheric layer at heights of approximately 20 to 30 miles (32 to 48 kilometers) characterized by high ozone content

---

P

p \ˈpē\ *n, pl* **p's** *or* **ps** \ˈpēz\ *often cap, often attrib* **1 a** : the 16th letter of the English alphabet **b** : a graphic representation of this letter **c** : a speech counterpart of orthographic *p* **2** : a graphic device for reproducing the letter *p* **3** : one designated *p* esp. as the 16th in order or class **4** [abbr. for *pass*] **a** : a grade rating a student's work as passing **b** : one graded or rated with a P **5** : something shaped like the letter P

pa \ˈpä, ˈpò\ *n* [short for *papa*] (1811) : FATHER

pa·an·ga \pä-ˈäŋ-(g)ə\ *n* [Tongan, lit., seed] (ca. 1966) — see MONEY table

PABA \ˈpab-ə, ˌpē-ˌä-ˈbē-ˌä\ *n* [*para-aminobenzoic acid*] (ca. 1943) : PARA-AMINOBENZOIC ACID

pab·u·lum \ˈpab-yə-ləm\ *n* [L, food, fodder; akin to L *pascere* to feed — more at FOOD] (1678) **1** : FOOD; *esp* : a suspension or solution of nutrients in a state suitable for absorption **2** : intellectual sustenance **3** : an insipid piece of writing

pa·ca \ˈpäk-ə, ˈpak-\ *n* [Pg & Sp, fr. Tupi *páca*] (1657) : any of a genus (*Cuniculus*) of large So. and Central American rodents; *esp* : a common edible form (*C. paca*) of northern So. America that has a brown coat spotted with white and a hide used locally for leather

paca

¹pace \ˈpās\ *n* [ME *pas*, fr. OF, step, fr. L *passus*, fr. *passus*, pp. of *pandere* to spread — more at FATHOM] (13c) **1 a** : rate of movement; *esp* : an established rate of locomotion **b** : rate of progress; *specif* : parallel rate of growth or development ⟨supplies kept ~ with demand⟩ **c** : an example to be emulated; *specif* : first place in a competition ⟨three strokes off the ~ —*Time*⟩ **d** (1) : rate of performance or delivery : TEMPO; *specif* : SPEED ⟨put ~ on the ball to win the point⟩ (2) : rhythmic

animation : FLUENCY ⟨writes with color, with zest, and with ~ —Amy Loveman⟩ **2** : a manner of walking : TREAD **3 a** : STEP 2a(1) **b** : any of various units of distance based on the length of a human step **4 a** *pl* : an exhibition of skills or capacities ⟨the trainer put the tiger through its ~s⟩ **b** : GAIT; *esp* : a fast 2-beat gait (as of the horse) in which the legs move in lateral pairs and support the animal alternately on the right and left legs

²pace *vb* **paced; pac·ing** *vi* (1513) **1 a** : to walk with often slow or measured tread **b** : to move along : PROCEED **2** : to go at a pace — used esp. of a horse ~ *vt* **1 a** : to measure by pacing — often used with *off* ⟨*paced* off a 10-yard penalty⟩ **b** : to cover at a walk ⟨could hear him *pacing* the floor⟩ **2** : to cover (a course) by pacing — used of a horse **3 a** : to set or regulate the pace of ⟨taught them how to ~ their solos for... impact —Richard Goldstein⟩; *also* : to establish a moderate or steady pace for (oneself) **b** (1) : to go before : PRECEDE (2) : to set an example for : LEAD **c** : to keep pace with

³pa·ce \ˈpä-(ˌ)sē; ˈpä-(ˌ)kā, -(ˌ)chä\ *prep* [L, abl. of *pac-, pax* peace, permission — more at PACT] (1863) : with due respect to ⟨I do not, ~... the correspondents, claim to have made any "discovery" —E. M. Almedingen⟩

pace car *n* (1965) : an automobile that leads the field of competitors through a pace lap but does not participate in the race

pace lap *n* (1971) : a lap of an auto racecourse by the entire field of competitors before the start of a race to allow the engines to warm up and to permit a flying start

pace·mak·er \ˈpā-ˌsmā-kər\ *n* (1884) **1 a** : one that sets the pace for another **b** : one that takes the lead or sets an example **2 a** : a body part (as the sinoatrial node of the heart) that serves to establish and maintain a rhythmic activity **b** : an electrical device for stimulating or steadying the heartbeat or reestablishing the rhythm of an arrested heart — **pace·mak·ing** \-kiŋ\ *n*

pac·er \ˈpā-sər\ *n* (1661) **1** : one that paces; *specif* : a horse whose predominant gait is the pace **2** : PACEMAKER

pace·set·ter \ˈpās-ˌset-ər\ *n* (1895) : PACEMAKER 1

pa·chi·si \pə-ˈchē-zē\ *n* [Hindi *pacīsī*] (1800) **:** an ancient board game played with dice and counters on a cruciform board in which players attempt to be the first to reach the home square

pa·chu·co \pə-ˈchü-(ˌ)kō\ *n, pl* **-cos** [MexSp] (1943) **:** a young Mexican-American having a taste for flashy clothes and a special jargon and usu. belonging to a neighborhood gang

pachy·derm \ˈpak-i-ˌdərm\ *n* [F *pachyderme,* fr. Gk *pachydermos* thick-skinned, fr. *pachys* thick + *derma* skin; akin to ON *bingr* heap, Skt *bahu* dense, much — more at DERM-] (1838) **:** any of various nonruminant hoofed mammals (as an elephant, a rhinoceros, or a pig) most of which have a thick skin

pachy·der·ma·tous \ˌpak-i-ˈdər-mət-əs\ *adj* [deriv. of Gk *pachys* + *dermat-, derma* skin] (1823) **1 :** of or relating to the pachyderms **2 a :** THICK, THICKENED ⟨~ skin⟩ **b :** CALLOUS, INSENSITIVE

pach·ys·an·dra \ˌpak-i-ˈsan-drə\ *n* [NL, fr. Gk *pachys* + NL *-andrus* -androus] (ca. 1900) **:** any of a genus (*Pachysandra*) of the box family of evergreen woody trailing plants often used as a ground cover

pachy·tene \ˈpak-i-ˌtēn\ *n* [ISV *pachy-* (fr. Gk *pachys*) + *-tene*] (1912) **:** the stage of meiotic prophase which immediately follows the zygotene and in which the paired chromosomes are thickened and visibly divided into chromatids — **pachytene** *adj*

pa·cif·ic \pə-ˈsif-ik\ *adj* [ME *pacifique,* fr. L *pacificus,* fr. *pac-, pax* peace + *-i-* + *-ficus* -fic — more at PACT] (1548) **1 a :** tending to lessen conflict **:** CONCILIATORY **b :** rejecting the use of force as an instrument of policy **2 a :** having a soothing appearance or effect ⟨mild ~ breezes⟩ **b :** mild of temper **:** PEACEABLE **3** *cap* **:** of or relating to the Pacific ocean — **pa·cif·i·cal·ly** \-i-k(ə-)lē\ *adv*

pac·i·fi·ca·tion \ˌpas-ə-fə-ˈkā-shən\ *n* (15c) **1 :** the act or process of pacifying **:** the state of being pacified **2 :** a treaty of peace

pa·cif·i·ca·tor \pə-ˈsif-ə-ˌkāt-ər\ *n* (1539) **:** PACIFIER 1

pa·cif·i·cism \pə-ˈsif-ə-ˌsiz-əm\ *n* (1910) **:** PACIFISM — **pa·cif·i·cist** \-səst\ *n*

Pacific time \pə-ˈsif-ik-\ *n* [*Pacific* ocean] (ca. 1883) **:** the time of the 8th time zone west of Greenwich that includes the Pacific coastal region of the U.S. — see TIME ZONE illustration

pac·i·fi·er \ˈpas-ə-ˌfī(-ə)r\ *n* (1533) **1 :** one that pacifies **2 :** a usu. nipple-shaped device for babies to suck or bite on

pac·i·fism \ˈpas-ə-ˌfiz-əm\ *n* [F *pacifisme,* fr. *pacifique* pacific, fr. L *pacificus*] (1902) **1 :** opposition to war or violence as a means of settling disputes; *specif* **:** refusal to bear arms on moral or religious grounds **2 :** an attitude or policy of nonresistance — **pac·i·fist** \-fəst\ *n*

pac·i·fist \ˈpas-ə-fəst\ *or* **pac·i·fis·tic** \ˌpas-ə-ˈfis-tik\ *adj* (1906) **1 :** of, relating to, or characteristic of pacifism or pacifists **2 :** strongly and actively opposed to conflict and esp. war — **pac·i·fis·ti·cal·ly** \ˌpas-ə-ˈfis-ti-k(ə-)lē\ *adv*

pac·i·fy \ˈpas-ə-ˌfī\ *vt* **-fied; -fy·ing** [ME *pacifien,* fr. L *pacificare,* fr. *pac-, pax* peace] (15c) **1 a :** to allay the anger or agitation of **:** SOOTHE ⟨~ a crying child⟩ **b :** APPEASE, PROPITIATE **2 a :** to restore to a tranquil state **:** SETTLE ⟨made an attempt to ~ the commotion⟩ **b :** to reduce to a submissive state **:** SUBDUE ⟨forces moved in to ~ the country⟩ — **pac·i·fi·able** \-ˌfī-ə-bəl\ *adj*

syn PACIFY, APPEASE, PLACATE, MOLLIFY, PROPITIATE, CONCILIATE mean to ease the anger or disturbance of. PACIFY suggests a soothing or calming; APPEASE implies quieting insistent demands by making concessions; PLACATE suggests changing resentment or bitterness to goodwill; MOLLIFY implies soothing hurt feelings or rising anger; PROPITIATE implies averting anger or malevolence esp. of a superior being; CONCILIATE suggests ending an estrangement by persuasion, concession, or settling of differences.

Pa·cin·i·an corpuscle \pə-ˌsin-ē-ən-\ *n* [Filippo *Pacini* †1883 Ital. anatomist] (ca. 1860) **:** an oval capsule that terminates some sensory nerve fibers esp. in the skin of the hands and feet

[1]**pack** \ˈpak\ *n, often attrib* [ME, of LG or D origin; akin to MLG & MD *pak* pack, MFlem *pac*] (13c) **1 a :** a bundle arranged for convenience in carrying esp. on the back **b :** a group or pile of related objects **c (1) :** a number of individual components packaged as a unit **:** PACKET ⟨a ~ of cigarettes⟩ **(2) :** CONTAINER **(3) :** a compact unitized assembly to perform a specific function **(4) :** a stack of magnetic disks in a container for use as a storage device **2 a :** the contents of a bundle **b :** a large amount or number **:** HEAP **c :** a full set of playing cards **3 a :** an act or instance of packing **b :** a method of packing **4 a :** a set of persons with a common interest **:** CLIQUE **b :** an organized troop (as of Cub Scouts) **5 a (1) :** a group of domesticated animals trained to hunt or run together **(2) :** a group of often predatory animals of the same kind ⟨a wolf ~⟩ **(3) :** a large group of individuals massed together (as in a race) **b :** an organized group of combat craft ⟨a submarine ~⟩ **6 :** a concentrated or compacted mass (as of snow) **7 :** wet absorbent material for therapeutic application to the body **8 a :** a cosmetic paste for the face **b :** an application or treatment of oils or creams for conditioning the scalp and hair **9 :** material used in packing

[2]**pack** *vt* (14c) **1 a :** to make into a compact bundle **b :** to fill completely **c :** to fill with packing ⟨~ a joint in a pipe⟩ **d :** to load with a pack ⟨~ a mule⟩ **e :** to put in a protective container ⟨goods ~*ed* for shipment⟩ **2 a :** to crowd together **b :** to increase the density of **:** COMPRESS **3 a :** to cause or command to go without ceremony ⟨~*ed* him off to school⟩ **b :** to bring to an end **:** FINISH — used with *up* or *in* ⟨~ up the assignment⟩ ⟨he's ~*ing* it all in — to lead a life of his own — Peter Oakes⟩ **4 :** to gather into tight formation **:** make a pack of (as hounds) **5 :** to cover or surround with a pack **6 a :** to transport on foot or on the back of an animal ⟨~ a canoe overland⟩ **b :** to wear or carry as equipment ⟨~ a gun⟩ **c :** to be supplied or equipped with **:** POSSESS ⟨a storm ~*ing* hurricane winds⟩ **d :** to cause or be capable of making (an impact) ⟨a book that ~*s* a man-sized punch —C. J. Rolo⟩ ~ *vi* **1 a :** to go away without ceremony **:** DEPART ⟨simply ~*ed* up and left⟩ **b :** QUIT, STOP — used with *up* or *in* ⟨why don't you ~ in, before you kill yourself —Millard Lampell⟩ **2 a :** to stow goods and equipment for transportation **b :** to be suitable for packing ⟨a knit dress ~*s* well⟩ **3 a :** to assemble in a group **:** CONGREGATE **b :** to crowd together **4 :** to become built up or compacted in a layer or mass ⟨the ore ~*ed* into a stony mass⟩ **5 a :** to carry goods or equipment **b :** to travel with one's baggage (as by horse) — **pack·abil·i·ty** \ˌpak-ə-ˈbil-ət-ē\ *n* — **pack·able** \ˈpak-ə-bəl\ *adj*

[3]**pack** *vt* [obs. *pack* (to make a secret agreement)] (1587) **1 :** to influence the composition of (as a political agency) so as to bring about a desired result ⟨~ a jury⟩ **2** *archaic* **:** to arrange (the cards in a pack) so as to cheat

[4]**pack** *adj* [perh. fr. obs. *pack* (to make a secret agreement)] *chiefly Scot* (1701) **:** INTIMATE

[1]**pack·age** \ˈpak-ij\ *n* (ca. 1611) **1** *archaic* **:** the act or process of packing **2 a :** a small or moderate-sized pack **:** PARCEL **b :** a commodity or a unit of a product uniformly wrapped or sealed **c :** a preassembled unit **3 :** a covering wrapper or container **4 :** something that suggests a package: as **a :** PACKAGE DEAL **b :** a radio or television series offered for sale at a lump sum **c :** contract benefits gained through collective bargaining **d (1) :** a ready-made computer program **(2) :** an assembly or apparatus essentially complete and ready for installation or use **e :** a travel arrangement contract that offers for a fixed price transportation, accommodations, and often sightseeing and entertainment **f :** a collection of related items to be considered or acted on together ⟨presented his tax ~ to the nation⟩

[2]**package** *vt* **pack·aged; pack·ag·ing** (1875) **1 :** to make into a package; *esp* **:** to produce as an entertainment package **2 :** to enclose in a package or covering — **pack·ag·er** *n*

package deal *n* (ca. 1948) **1 :** an offer or agreement involving a number of related items or one making acceptance of one item dependent on the acceptance of another **2 :** the items offered in a package deal

package store *n* (ca. 1918) **:** a store that sells bottled or canned alcoholic beverages for consumption off the premises

pack animal *n* (1847) **:** an animal (as a donkey) used for carrying packs

pack·board \ˈpak-ˌbō(ə)rd, -ˌbȯ(ə)rd\ *n* (1939) **:** a usu. canvas-covered light wood or metal frame with shoulder straps used for carrying goods and equipment

packed \ˈpakt\ *adj* (1777) **1 a :** that is crowded or stuffed — often used in combination ⟨an action-*packed* story⟩ **b :** COMPRESSED ⟨hard-*packed* snow⟩ **2 :** filled to capacity ⟨played to a ~ house⟩

pack·er \ˈpak-ər\ *n* (14c) **1 :** one that packs: as **a :** a wholesale dealer **b :** an automotive vehicle with a closed body and a compressing device (as for compacting rubbish) in the rear **2 a :** PORTER 1 **b :** one who conveys goods on pack animals

pack·et \ˈpak-ət\ *n* [MF *pacquet,* of Gmc origin; akin to MD *pak* pack] (1530) **1 a :** a number of letters dispatched at one time **b :** a small group, cluster, or mass **2 :** a passenger boat carrying mail and cargo on a regular schedule **3 a :** a small bundle or parcel **b :** a small thin package **c** *Brit* **:** PAY ENVELOPE **d :** a considerable amount ⟨that trip will cost you a ~⟩

pack·horse \ˈpak-ˌhȯrs\ *n* (15c) **:** a horse used as a pack animal

pack ice *n* (1850) **:** sea ice formed into a mass by the crushing together of pans, floes, and brash

pack·ing \ˈpak-iŋ\ *n* (14c) **1 a :** the action or process of packing something; *also* **:** a method of packing **b :** the processing of food and esp. meat for future sale **2 :** material (as a covering or stuffing) used to protect packed goods (as for shipping); *also* **:** material used for making airtight or watertight ⟨~ for a faucet⟩

pack·ing·house \-ˌhau̇s\ *n* (1834) **:** an establishment for slaughtering, processing, and packing livestock into meat, meat products, and by-products; *also* **:** one for processing and packing other foodstuffs — called also *packing plant*

pack·man \ˈpak-mən\ *n* (1625) **:** PEDDLER

pack rat *n* (ca. 1885) **1 :** WOOD RAT; *esp* **:** a large bushy-tailed rodent (*Neotoma cinerea*) of the Rocky Mountain area that has well-developed cheek pouches and hoards food and miscellaneous objects **2 :** one who collects or hoards esp. unneeded items

pack·sack \ˈpak-ˌsak\ *n* (1851) **:** a case (as of canvas) held on the back by shoulder straps and used to carry gear when traveling on foot

pack·sad·dle \-ˌsad-ᵊl\ *n* (14c) **:** a saddle designed to support loads on the backs of pack animals

pack·thread \-ˌthred\ *n* (14c) **:** strong thread or small twine used for sewing or tying packs or parcels

pact \ˈpakt\ *n* [ME, fr. MF, fr. L *pactum,* fr. neut. of *pactus,* pp. of *pacisci* to agree, contract; akin to OE *fōn* to seize, L *pax* peace, *pangere* to fix, fasten, Gk *pēgnynai*] (15c) **:** [4]COMPACT; *esp* **:** an international treaty

[1]**pad** \ˈpad\ *vb* **pad·ded; pad·ding** [perh. fr. MD *paden* to follow a path, fr. *pad* path — more at PATH] *vt* (1553) **:** to traverse on foot ~ *vi* **1 :** to go on foot **:** WALK **2 :** to move along with a muffled step

[2]**pad** *n* [origin unknown] (1554) **1 a :** a thin flat mat or cushion: as **(1) :** a piece of soft stuffed material used as or under a saddle **(2) :** padding used to shape an article of clothing **(3) :** a guard worn to shield body parts against impact **(4) :** a piece of usu. folded absorbent material (as gauze) used as a surgical dressing or protective covering **(5) :** frictional material that presses against the disks in a disk brake **b :** a piece of material saturated with ink for inking the surface of a rubber stamp **2 a :** the foot of an animal **b :** the cushioned thickening of the underside of the toes of an animal **3 :** a floating leaf of a water plant **4 :** a collection of sheets of paper glued together at one end **5 a :** a section of an airstrip used for warm-ups, takeoffs, or landings **b :** LAUNCHPAD **c :** a horizontal concrete surface (as for parking a mobile home) **6 a :** living quarters **b :** BED

[3]**pad** *vt* **pad·ded; pad·ding** (1827) **1 a :** to furnish with a pad or padding **b :** MUTE, MUFFLE **2 :** to expand or increase with needless, misleading, or fraudulent matter ⟨~ an expense account⟩ — often used with *out* ⟨they ~ out their bibliographies and cut back their footnotes —J.P. Kenyon⟩

[4]**pad** *n* [MD *pad*] (1567) **1** *dial Brit* **:** PATH **2 :** a horse that moves along at an easy pace **3** *archaic* **:** FOOTPAD

[5]**pad** *n* [origin unknown] (1594) **:** a soft muffled or slapping sound

pad·ding \ˈpad-iŋ\ *n* (1828) **:** material with which something is padded

[1]**pad·dle** \ˈpad-ᵊl\ *vi* **pad·dled; pad·dling** \ˈpad-liŋ, -ᵊl-iŋ\ [origin unknown] (1530) **1 :** to move the hands or feet about in shallow water

2 *archaic* **:** to use the hands or fingers in toying or caressing **3 :** TODDLE — **pad·dler** \ˈpad-lər, -ᵊl-ər\ *n*

[2]paddle *n* [ME *padell* spade-shaped tool for cleaning a plow] (1624) **1 a :** a usu. wooden implement that has a long handle and a broad flattened blade and that is used to propel and steer a small craft (as a canoe) **b :** an implement often with a short handle and a broad flat blade that is used for stirring, mixing, or hitting; *esp* **:** one used to hit a ball in any of various games (as table tennis) **2 a :** one of the broad boards at the circumference of a paddle wheel or waterwheel **b :** one of a series of broad blades attached to a shaft (as in an ice cream machine) and used for stirring **3 :** a computer input device with a dial used to control linear movement of a visual cue on a computer display screen

[3]paddle *vb* **pad·dled; pad·dling** \ˈpad-liŋ, -ᵊl-iŋ\ *vi* (1677) **:** to go on or through water by or as if by means of a paddle or paddle wheel ~ *vt* **1 a :** to propel by a paddle **b :** to transport in a paddled craft ⟨*paddled* us to shore in his canoe⟩ **2 a :** to beat or stir with or as if with a paddle (as in washing or dyeing) **b :** to punish by or as if by beating with a paddle — **pad·dler** \ˈpad-lər, -ᵊl-ər\ *n*

pad·dle·ball \ˈpad-ᵊl-ˌbȯl\ *n* (1935) **:** a game for 2, 3, or 4 players played on a 1-, 3-, or 4-walled court with a wood or plastic paddle and a ball similar to a tennis ball; *also* **:** the ball used in this game

pad·dle·board \-ˌbō(ə)rd, -ˌbȯ(ə)rd\ *n* (1938) **:** a long narrow buoyant board used for riding the surf or in rescuing swimmers

pad·dle·boat \-ˌbōt\ *n* (1874) **:** a boat propelled by a wheel that has paddles or boards around its circumference

pad·dle·fish \-ˌfish\ *n* (1807) **:** any of a family (Polyodontidae) of ganoid fishes; *esp* **:** one (*Polyodon spathula*) of the Mississippi valley that is about four feet long and has a spatula-shaped snout

paddle tennis *n* (1925) **:** a game like tennis that is played with a wooden paddle and sponge rubber ball on a small court

paddle wheel *n* (1685) **:** a wheel with paddles, floats, or boards around its circumference used to propel a boat

paddle wheeler *n* (1924) **:** a steamer propelled by a wheel that has paddles or boards around its circumference

pad·dock \ˈpad-ək, -ik\ *n* [alter. of ME *parrok,* fr. OE *pearroc,* fr. VL *parricus*] (bef. 12c) **1 :** a usu. enclosed area used esp. for pasturing or exercising animals; *esp* **:** an enclosure where racehorses are saddled and paraded before a race **2 :** an area at an automobile racecourse where racing cars are parked

pad·dy *also* **padi** \ˈpad-ē\ *n, pl* **paddies** *also* **padis** [Malay *padi*] (ca. 1580) **1 :** RICE; *esp* **:** threshed unmilled rice **2 :** wet land in which rice is grown

pad·dy wagon \ˈpad-ē-\ *n* [prob. fr. E slang *Paddy* (Irishman, policeman), fr. the name *Patrick*] (1930) **:** PATROL WAGON

padi·shah \ˈpäd-(i-)ˌshä, -(i-)ˌshȯ\ *n* [Per *pādshāh,* fr. OPer *pati-* lord + *shāh* king; akin to Skt *pati* master — more at POTENT, CHECK] (1612) **:** a chief ruler **:** SOVEREIGN; *esp* **:** the shah of Iran

pad·lock \ˈpad-ˌläk\ *n* [ME *padlok,* fr. *pad-* (of unknown origin) + *lok* lock] (15c) **:** a removable lock with a shackle that can be passed through a staple or link and then secured — **padlock** *vt*

pa·dre \ˈpäd-(ˌ)rā, -rē\ *n* [Sp or It or Pg, lit., father, fr. L *pater* — more at FATHER] (1584) **1 :** a Christian clergyman; *esp* **:** PRIEST **2 :** a military chaplain

pa·dro·ne \pə-ˈdrō-nē\ *n, pl* **-nes** *or* **-ni** \-nē\ [It, protector, owner, fr. L *patronus* patron] (1670) **1 a :** MASTER **b :** an Italian innkeeper **2 :** one that secures employment for immigrants esp. of Italian extraction

pad·u·a·soy \ˈpaj-(ə-)wə-ˌsȯi\ *n* [alter. of earlier *poudesoy,* fr. F *pou-de-soie*] (1663) **:** a corded silk fabric; *also* **:** a garment made of it

pae·an \ˈpē-ən\ *n* [L, hymn of thanksgiving esp. addressed to Apollo, fr. Gk *paian, paiōn,* fr. *Paian, Paiōn,* epithet of Apollo in the hymn] (1589) **:** a joyous song or hymn of praise, tribute, thanksgiving, or triumph

paed- *or* **paedo-** — see PED-

pae·do·gen·e·sis \ˌpēd-ō-ˈjen-ə-səs\ *n* [NL] (ca. 1871) **:** reproduction by young or larval animals **:** NEOTENY — **pae·do·ge·net·ic** \-jə-ˈnet-ik\ *or* **pae·do·gen·ic** \-ˈjen-ik\ *adj* — **pae·do·ge·net·i·cal·ly** \-jə-ˈnet-i-k(ə-)lē\ *adv*

pae·do·mor·phic \ˌpēd-ə-ˈmȯr-fik\ *adj* (1891) **:** of, relating to, or involving paedomorphosis or paedomorphism

pae·do·mor·phism \-ˌfiz-əm\ *n* (ca. 1891) **:** retention in the adult of infantile or juvenile characters

pae·do·mor·pho·sis \-ˈmȯr-fə-səs\ *n* [NL] (1922) **:** phylogenetic change that involves retention of juvenile characters by the adult

pa·el·la \pä-ˈel-ə, -ˈā(l)-yə\ *n* [Catal, lit., pot, pan, fr. MF *paelle,* fr. L *patella* small pan — more at PATELLA] (ca. 1892) **:** a saffron-flavored dish containing rice, meat, seafood, and vegetables

pae·on \ˈpē-ən, -ˌän\ *n* [L, fr. Gk *paiōn,* fr. *paian, paiōn* paean] (1603) **:** a metrical foot of four syllables with one long and three short syllables (as in classical prosody) or with one stressed and three unstressed syllables (as in English prosody)

pa·gan \ˈpā-gən\ *n* [ME, fr. LL *paganus,* fr. L, country dweller, fr. *pagus* country district; akin to L *pangere* to fix — more at PACT] (14c) **1 :** HEATHEN 1; *esp* **:** a follower of a polytheistic religion (as in ancient Rome) **2 :** one who has little or no religion and who delights in sensual pleasures and material goods **:** an irreligious or hedonistic person — **pagan** *adj* — **pa·gan·ish** \-gə-nish\ *adj*

pa·gan·ism \ˈpā-gə-ˌniz-əm\ *n* [ME *paganysme,* fr. LL *paganismus,* fr. *paganus*] (15c) **1 a :** pagan beliefs or practices **b :** a pagan religion **2 :** the quality or state of being a pagan

pa·gan·ize \-ˌnīz\ *vb* **-ized; -iz·ing** *vt* (1615) **:** to make pagan ~ *vi* **:** to become pagan — **pa·gan·iz·er** *n*

[1]page \ˈpāj\ *n* [ME, fr. MF, fr. It *paggio*] (14c) **1 a** (1) **:** a youth being trained for the medieval rank of knight and in the personal service of a knight (2) **:** a youth attendant on a person of rank esp. in the medieval period **b :** a boy serving as an honorary attendant at a formal function (as a wedding) **2 :** one employed to deliver messages, assist patrons, serve as a guide, or attend to similar duties

[2]page *vt* **paged; pag·ing** (15c) **1 :** to wait on or serve in the capacity of a page **2 :** to summon by repeatedly calling out the name of

[3]page *n* [MF, fr. L *pagina;* akin to L *pangere* to fix, fasten — more at PACT] (1589) **1 :** one of the leaves of a publication or manuscript; *also* **:** a single side of one of these leaves **2 a :** a written record **b :** a noteworthy event or period ⟨one of the brightest ~*s* of my life⟩ **3 :** a sizable subdivision of computer memory; *also* **:** a block of information that fills a page and can be transferred as a unit between the internal and external storage of a computer

[4]page *vb* **paged; pag·ing** *vt* (1628) **:** to number or mark the pages of ~ *vi* **:** to turn the pages (as of a book or magazine) esp. in a steady or haphazard manner — usu. used with *through*

pag·eant \ˈpaj-ənt\ *n* [ME *pagyn, padgeant,* lit., scene of a play, fr. ML *pagina,* fr. L, page] (14c) **1 a :** a mere show **:** PRETENSE **b :** an ostentatious display **2 :** SHOW, EXHIBITION; *esp* **:** an elaborate colorful exhibition or spectacle often with music that consists of a series of tableaux, of a loosely unified drama, or of a procession usu. with floats **3 :** PAGEANTRY 1

pag·eant·ry \ˈpaj-ən-trē\ *n* (1608) **1 :** pageants and the presentation of pageants **2 :** colorful, rich, or splendid display **:** SPECTACLE **3 :** mere show **:** empty display

page boy *n* [[1]*page*] (1874) **1 :** a boy serving as a page **2** *usu* **page·boy :** an often shoulder-length hairdo with the ends of the hair turned under in a smooth roll

pag·er \ˈpā-jər\ *n* (1901) **:** one that pages; *esp* **:** BEEPER

Pag·et's disease \ˌpaj-əts-\ *n* [Sir James *Paget* †1899 Eng. surgeon] (1889) **1 :** an eczematous inflammatory precancerous condition esp. of the nipple and areola **2 :** a chronic disease in which the bones become enlarged, weak, and deformed

pag·i·nal \ˈpaj-ən-ᵊl\ *adj* [LL *paginalis,* fr. L *pagina* page] (1646) **:** of, relating to, or consisting of pages

pag·i·nate \ˈpaj-ə-ˌnāt\ *vt* **-nat·ed; -nat·ing** [L *pagina* page] (1884) **:** [4]PAGE

pag·i·na·tion \ˌpaj-ə-ˈnā-shən\ *n* (1841) **1 :** the action of paging **:** the condition of being paged **2 a :** the numbers or marks used to indicate the sequence of pages (as of a book) **b :** the number and arrangement of pages or an indication of these

pa·go·da \pə-ˈgōd-ə\ *n* [Pg *pagode* oriental idol, temple] (1588) **:** a Far Eastern tower usu. with roofs curving upward at the division of each of several stories and erected as a temple or memorial

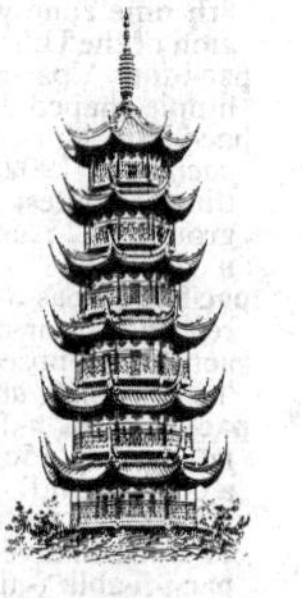

pagoda

pah·la·vi \ˈpal-ə-(ˌ)vē, ˈpäl-\ *n, pl* **pahlavi** *or* **pahlavis** [Per *pahlawī,* fr. Riza Shah *Pahlawī* †1944 Shah of Iran] (1930) **1 :** a monetary unit of Iran equal to 100 rials **2 :** a coin representing one pahlavi

Pah·la·vi \ˈpal-ə-(ˌ)vē, ˈpäl-\ *n* [Per *pahlawī,* fr. *Pahlav* Parthia, fr. OPer *Parthava-*] (1773) **1 :** the Iranian language of Sassanian Persia — see INDO-EUROPEAN LANGUAGES table **2 :** a script used for writing Pahlavi

[1]paid \ˈpād\ *past and past part of* PAY

[2]paid *adj* (1817) **1 :** marked by the receipt of pay ⟨my first ~ job⟩ **2 :** being or having been paid or paid for ⟨a ~ official⟩ ⟨a ~ political announcement⟩

pai–hua \ˈbī-ˈhwä\ *n* [Chin (Pek) *pai*[2] *hua*[4], lit., plain speech] (ca. 1923) **:** a form of written Chinese based on modern colloquial Chinese

pail \ˈpā(ə)l\ *n* [ME *payle, paille*] (14c) **1 :** a usu. cylindrical container with a handle **:** BUCKET **2 :** the quantity that a pail contains — **pail·ful** \-ˌfu̇l\ *n*

pail·lard \pī-ˈ(y)är, pā-ˈyär\ *n* [origin unknown] (1972) **:** a piece of beef or veal usu. pounded thin and grilled

pail·lette \pī-ˈ(y)et, pā-ˈyet, pə-ˈlet\ *n* [F, fr. *paille* straw — more at PALLET] (ca. 1890) **1 :** a small shiny object (as a spangle) applied in clusters as a decorative trimming (as on women's clothing) **2 :** a trimming made of paillettes

[1]pain \ˈpān\ *n* [ME, fr. OF *peine,* fr. L *poena,* fr. Gk *poinē* payment, penalty; akin to Gk *tinein* to pay, *tinesthai* to punish, *timē* price, value, honor] (13c) **1 :** PUNISHMENT **2 a :** usu. localized physical suffering associated with bodily disorder (as a disease or an injury) ⟨the ~ of a boil⟩; *also* **:** a basic bodily sensation induced by a noxious stimulus, received by naked nerve endings, characterized by physical discomfort (as pricking, throbbing, or aching), and typically leading to evasive action **b :** acute mental or emotional distress or suffering **:** GRIEF **3** *pl* **:** the throes of childbirth **4** *pl* **:** trouble, care, or effort taken for the accomplishment of something ⟨was at ~*s* to reassure us⟩ **5 :** one that irks or annoys or is otherwise troublesome — often used in such phrases as *pain in the neck* — **pain·less** \-ləs\ *adj* — **pain·less·ly** *adv* — **pain·less·ness** *n* — **on pain of** *or* **under pain of :** subject to penalty or punishment of ⟨ordered not to leave the country *on pain of* death⟩

[2]pain *vt* (14c) **1 :** to make suffer or cause distress to **:** HURT **2** *archaic* **:** to put (oneself) to trouble or exertion ~ *vi* **1** *archaic* **:** SUFFER **2 :** to give or have a sensation of pain

pained \ˈpānd\ *adj* (14c) **1 :** feeling pain **:** HURT **2 :** showing pain ⟨a ~ expression⟩

pain·ful \ˈpān-fəl\ *adj* **pain·ful·ler** \-fə-lər\; **pain·ful·lest** (14c) **1 a :** feeling or giving pain **b :** IRKSOME, ANNOYING **2 :** requiring effort or exertion ⟨a long ~ trip⟩ **3** *archaic* **:** CAREFUL, DILIGENT — **pain·ful·ly** \-f(ə-)lē\ *adv* — **pain·ful·ness** \-fəl-nəs\ *n*

pain·kill·er \-ˌkil-ər\ *n* (1853) **:** something (as a drug) that relieves pain — **pain·kill·ing** \-iŋ\ *adj*

[1]pains·tak·ing \ˈpān-ˌstā-kiŋ\ *n* (1547) **:** the action of taking pains **:** diligent care and effort

[2]painstaking *adj* (1696) **:** taking pains **:** expending or showing diligent care and effort — **pains·tak·ing·ly** \-kiŋ-lē\ *adv*

[1]paint \ˈpānt\ *vb* [ME *painten,* deriv. of OF *peint,* pp. of *peindre,* fr. L *pingere* to tattoo, embroider, paint; akin to OE *fāh* variegated, Gk *poikilos* variegated, *pikros* sharp, bitter] *vt* (13c) **1 a** (1) **:** to apply color, pigment, or paint to (2) **:** to color with a cosmetic **b** (1) **:** to apply with a movement resembling that used in painting (2) **:** to treat with a liquid by brushing or swabbing ⟨~ the wound with iodine⟩ **2 a** (1) **:** to produce in lines and colors on a surface by applying pigments (2) **:** to depict by such lines and colors **b :** to decorate, adorn, or variegate by applying lines and colors **c :** to produce or evoke as if by painting ⟨~*s* glowing pictures of the farm⟩ **3 :** to touch up or cover over by or as if by painting **4 :** to depict as having specified or implied characteristics ⟨~*s* them whiter than the evidence justifies — Oliver La Farge⟩ ~ *vi* **1 :** to practice the art of painting **2 :** to use cosmetics

2paint *n* (1602) **1 :** the action of painting **:** something produced by painting **2 :** MAKEUP; *esp* **:** a cosmetic to add color **3 a** (1) **:** a mixture of a pigment and a suitable liquid to form a closely adherent coating when spread on a surface in a thin coat (2) **:** the pigment used in this mixture esp. when in the form of a cake ⟨a box of ~*s*⟩ **b :** an applied coating of paint **4 :** PINTO

paint·brush \'pānt-,brəsh\ *n* (1827) **1 :** a brush for applying paint **2 a :** INDIAN PAINTBRUSH 1 **b :** ORANGE HAWKWEED

painted bunting *n* (ca. 1811) **:** a brightly colored finch (*Passerina ciris*) of the southern U.S.

painted cup *n* (1787) **:** INDIAN PAINTBRUSH 1

painted lady *n* (1753) **:** a migratory nymphalid butterfly (*Vanessa cardui*) with wings mottled in brown, orange, red, and white

painted trillium *n* (1855) **:** a trillium (*Trillium undulatum*) of northeastern No. America that has a solitary flower with white petals streaked with purple

1paint·er \'pānt-ər\ *n* (14c) **:** one that paints: as **a :** an artist who paints **b :** one who applies paint (as to a building) esp. as an occupation

2paint·er \'pānt-ər\ *n* [ME *paynter,* prob. fr. MF *pendoir, pentoir* clothesline, fr. *pendre* to hang — more at PENDANT] (15c) **:** a line used for securing or towing a boat

3pain·ter *n* [alter. of *panther*] (ca. 1764) **:** COUGAR

paint·er·ly \'pānt-ər-lē\ *adj* (1586) **:** of, relating to, or typical of a painter **:** ARTISTIC — **paint·er·li·ness** *n*

painter's colic *n* (1822) **:** intestinal colic associated with obstinate constipation due to chronic lead poisoning

paint·ing *n* (13c) **1 :** a product of painting; *esp* **:** a work produced through the art of painting **2 :** the art or occupation of painting

1pair \'pa(ə)r, 'pe(ə)r\ *n, pl* **pairs** *also* **pair** [ME *paire,* fr. OF, fr. L *paria* equal things, fr. neut. pl. of *par* equal] (13c) **1 a** (1) **:** two corresponding things designed for use together ⟨a ~ of shoes⟩ (2) **:** two corresponding bodily parts or members ⟨a ~ of hands⟩ **b :** something made up of two corresponding pieces ⟨a ~ of trousers⟩ **2 a :** two similar or associated things: as (1) **:** two mated animals (2) **:** a couple in love, engaged, or married ⟨were a devoted ~⟩ (3) **:** two playing cards of the same value or denomination ⟨held a ~⟩ (4) **:** two horses harnessed side by side (5) **:** two members of a deliberative body that agree not to vote on a specific issue during a time agreed on; *also* **:** an agreement not to vote made by the two members **b :** a partnership esp. of two players in a contest against another partnership **3** *chiefly dial* **:** a set or series of small objects (as beads)

2pair *vt* (1607) **1 a :** to make a pair of — often used with *off* or *up* ⟨~*ed* off the animals⟩ **b :** to cause to be a member of a pair **c :** to arrange a voting pair between **2 :** to arrange in pairs ~ *vi* **1 :** to constitute a member of a pair ⟨a sock that didn't ~⟩ **2 a :** to become associated with another — often used with *off* or *up* ⟨~*ed* up with an old friend⟩ **b :** to become grouped or separated into pairs — often used with *off* ⟨~*ed* off for the next dance⟩

pair–bond \-'bänd\ *n* (1940) **:** a monogamous relationship — **pair–bond·ing** *n*

paired–associate learning *n* (1967) **:** the learning of syllables, digits, or words in pairs (as in the study of a foreign language) so that one member of the pair evokes recall of the other

pair of compasses (1563) **:** COMPASS 3c

pair of virginals (1542) **:** VIRGINAL

pair production *n* (1934) **:** the simultaneous and complete transformation of a quantum of radiant energy into an electron and a positron when the quantum interacts with the intense electric field near a nucleus

pai·sa \pī-'sä\ *n, pl* **paisa** *or* **pai·se** \-'sā\ [Hindi *paisā*] (ca. 1892) — see *rupee, taka* at MONEY table

pais·ley \'pāz-lē\ *adj, often cap* [*Paisley,* Scotland] (1824) **1 :** made typically of soft wool and woven or printed with colorful curved abstract figures **2 :** marked by designs, patterns, or figures typically used in paisley fabrics ⟨a ~ print⟩ — **paisley** *n*

Pai·ute \'pī-,(y)üt\ *n* (1827) **1 :** a member of an American Indian people orig. of Utah, Arizona, Nevada, and California **2 :** the language of the Paiute people

pa·ja·ma \pə-'jäm-ə, -'jam-\ *n* [Hindi *pājāma,* fr. Per *pā* leg + *jāma* garment] (ca. 1892) **:** PAJAMAS

pa·ja·mas \pə-'jäm-əz, -'jam-\ *n pl* [pl. of *pajama*] (1800) **1 :** loose lightweight trousers formerly much worn in the Near East **2 :** a loose usu. two-piece lightweight suit designed for sleeping or lounging

1pal \'pal\ *n* [Romany *phral, phal* brother, friend, fr. Skt *bhrātṛ* brother; akin to OE *brōthor* brother] (1681) **:** a close friend — **pal·ship** \-,ship\ *n*

2pal *vi* **palled; pal·ling** (1879) **:** to be or become pals **:** associate as pals

1pal·ace \'pal-əs\ *n* [ME *palais,* fr. OF, fr. L *palatium,* fr. *Palatium,* the Palatine Hill in Rome where the emperors' residences were built] (13c) **1 a :** the official residence of a sovereign **b** *chiefly Brit* **:** the official residence of an archbishop or bishop **2 a :** a large stately house **b :** a large public building **c :** a gaudy place for public amusement or refreshment ⟨a movie ~⟩

2palace *adj* (14c) **1 :** of or relating to a palace **2 :** of, relating to, or involving the intimates of a chief executive ⟨a ~ revolution⟩ ⟨~ politics⟩ **3 :** LUXURIOUS, DELUXE

pal·a·din \'pal-əd-ən\ *n* [F, fr. It *paladino,* fr. ML *palatinus* courtier, fr. L, palace official — more at PALATINE] (1592) **1 :** a champion of a medieval prince **2 :** an outstanding protagonist of a cause

pa·laes·tra \pə-'les-trə\ *n, pl* **-trae** \-(,)trē\ [L, fr. Gk *palaistra,* fr. *palaiein* to wrestle; akin to Gk *pallein* to brandish — more at POLEMIC] (15c) **1 :** a school in ancient Greece or Rome for sports (as wrestling) **2 :** GYMNASIUM

pa·lan·quin \,pal-ən-'kēn, -'k(w)in, 'pal-ən-,; pə-'laŋ-kwən\ *n* [Pg *palanquim,* fr. Jav *pĕlaṅki*] (1588) **:** a conveyance formerly used in eastern Asia esp. for one person that consists of an enclosed litter borne on the shoulders of men by means of poles

pal·at·able \'pal-ət-ə-bəl\ *adj* (1669) **1 :** agreeable to the palate or taste **2 :** agreeable or acceptable to the mind — **pal·at·abil·i·ty** \,pal-ət-ə-'bil-ət-ē\ *n* — **pal·at·able·ness** *n* — **pal·at·ably** \-blē\ *adv*

syn PALATABLE, APPETIZING, SAVORY, TASTY, TOOTHSOME mean agreeable or pleasant esp. to the sense of taste. PALATABLE often applies to something that is unexpectedly found to be agreeable; APPETIZING suggests a whetting of the appetite and applies to aroma and appearance as well as taste; SAVORY applies to both taste and aroma and suggests piquancy and often spiciness; TASTY implies a pronounced taste; TOOTHSOME stresses the notion of agreeableness and sometimes implies tenderness or daintiness.

pal·a·tal \'pal-ət-ᵊl\ *adj* (1751) **1 :** of, relating to, forming, or affecting the palate **2 a :** formed with the front of the tongue behind the tip near or touching the hard palate ⟨the \k\ in German \ik\ *ich* and the \y\ in English *yeast* are ~ sounds⟩ **b** (1) **:** formed with the blade of the tongue near the hard palate ⟨the ~ sounds represented by *sh* in *she* and *si* in *vision*⟩ (2) *of a vowel* **:** FRONT 2 — **palatal** *n* — **pal·a·tal·ly** \-ᵊl-ē\ *adv*

pal·a·tal·iza·tion \,pal-ət-ᵊl-ə-'zā-shən\ *n* (1863) **1 :** the quality or state of being palatalized **2 :** an act or instance of palatalizing an utterance

pal·a·tal·ize \'pal-ət-ᵊl-,īz\ *vt* **-ized; -iz·ing** (1867) **:** to pronounce as or change into a palatal sound

pal·ate \'pal-ət\ *n* [ME, fr. L *palatum*] (14c) **1 :** the roof of the mouth separating the mouth from the nasal cavity **2 a :** a usu. intellectual relish **b :** the sense of taste

pa·la·tial \pə-'lā-shəl\ *adj* [L *palatium* palace] (1754) **1 :** of, relating to, or being a palace **2 :** suitable to a palace **:** MAGNIFICENT — **pa·la·tial·ly** \-shə-lē\ *adv* — **pa·la·tial·ness** *n*

pa·lat·i·nate \pə-'lat-ᵊn-ət\ *n* (1580) **:** the territory of a palatine

1pal·a·tine \'pal-ə-,tīn\ *adj* [L *palatinus,* fr. *palatium*] (15c) **1 a :** of or relating to a palace esp. of a Roman or Holy Roman emperor **b :** PALATIAL **2 a :** possessing royal privileges **b :** of or relating to a palatine or a palatinate

2palatine \-,tīn, *3 is also* -,tēn\ *n* [L *palatinus,* fr. *palatinus,* adj.] (1591) **1 a :** a high officer of an imperial palace **b :** a feudal lord having sovereign power within his domains **2** *cap* **:** a native or inhabitant of the Palatinate **3** [F, fr. Elisabeth Charlotte of Bavaria †1722 Princess *Palatine*] **:** a fur cape or stole covering the neck and shoulders

3palatine \-,tīn\ *adj* (ca. 1656) **:** of, relating to, or lying near the palate

4palatine \-,tīn\ *n* (1854) **:** either of a pair of bones that are situated behind and between the maxillae and in man are of extremely irregular form — called also *palatine bone*

1pa·la·ver \pə-'lav-ər, -'läv-\ *n* [Pg *palavra* word, speech, fr. LL *parabola* parable, speech] (1735) **1 a :** a long parley usu. between persons of different levels of culture or sophistication **b :** CONFERENCE, DISCUSSION **2 a :** idle talk **b :** misleading or beguiling speech

2palaver *vb* **pa·la·vered; pa·la·ver·ing** \-(ə-)riŋ\ *vi* (1773) **1 :** to talk profusely or idly **2 :** PARLEY ~ *vt* **:** to use palaver to **:** CAJOLE

pa·laz·zo \pə-'lät-(,)sō\ *n, pl* **pa·laz·zi** \-(,)sē\ [It, fr. L *palatium* palace] (1666) **:** a large imposing building (as a museum or a place of residence) esp. in Italy

1pale \'pā(ə)l\ *adj* **pal·er; pal·est** [ME, fr. MF, fr. L *pallidus,* fr. *pallēre* to be pale — more at FALLOW] (14c) **1 :** deficient in color or intensity of color **:** PALLID ⟨a ~ complexion⟩ **2 :** not bright or brilliant **:** DIM ⟨a ~ sun shining through the fog⟩ **3 :** FEEBLE, FAINT ⟨a ~ imitation⟩ **4 :** deficient in chroma ⟨a ~ pink⟩ — **pale·ly** \'pā(ə)l-lē\ *adv* — **pale·ness** \-nəs\ *n* — **pal·ish** \'pā-lish\ *adj*

2pale *vb* **paled; pal·ing** *vi* (14c) **:** to become pale ~ *vt* **:** to make pale

3pale *vt* **paled; pal·ing** [ME *palen,* fr. MF *paler,* fr. *pal*] (14c) **:** to enclose with pales **:** FENCE

4pale *n* [ME, fr. MF *pal* stake, fr. L *palus* — more at POLE] (14c) **1** *archaic* **:** PALISADE, PALING **2 a :** one of the stakes of a palisade **b :** PICKET **3 a :** a space or field having bounds **:** ENCLOSURE **b :** a territory or district within certain bounds or under a particular jurisdiction **4 :** an area or the limits within which one is privileged or protected (as from censure) ⟨conduct that was beyond the ~⟩ **5 :** a perpendicular stripe on a heraldic shield

pale- *or* **paleo-** *or* **palae-** *or* **palaeo-** *comb form* [Gk *palai-, palaio-* ancient, fr. *palaios,* fr. *palai* long ago; akin to Gk *tēle* far off, Skt *carama* last] **1 :** involving or dealing with ancient forms or conditions ⟨*paleo*botany⟩ **2 :** early **:** primitive **:** archaic ⟨*Paleo*lithic⟩

pa·lea \'pā-lē-ə\ *n, pl* **pa·le·ae** \-lē-,ē\ [NL, fr. L, chaff — more at PALLET] (1753) **1 :** one of the chaffy scales on the receptacle of many composite plants **2 :** the upper bract that with the lemma encloses the flower in grasses — **pa·le·al** \-lē-əl\ *adj*

Pa·le·arc·tic \,pā-lē-'ärk-tik, -'ärt-ik\ *adj* (1858) **:** of, relating to, or being a biogeographic region or subregion that includes Europe, Asia north of the Himalayas, northern Arabia, and Africa north of the Sahara

pale dry *adj* (ca. 1934) **:** dry and light colored ⟨*pale dry* ginger ale⟩

pale·face \'pā(ə)l-,fās\ *n* (1822) **:** a white person **:** CAUCASIAN

pa·leo·an·thro·pol·o·gy \'pā-lē-ō-,an(t)-thrə-'päl-ə-jē, *esp Brit* 'pal-ē-\ *n* (1916) **:** a branch of anthropology dealing with fossil man — **pa·leo·an·thro·po·log·i·cal** \-pə-'läj-i-kəl\ *adj* — **pa·leo·an·thro·pol·o·gist** \-'päl-ə-jəst\ *n*

pa·leo·bot·a·ny \,pā-lē-ō-'bät-ᵊn-ē, -'bät-nē, *esp Brit* ,pal-ē-\ *n* [ISV] (1872) **:** a branch of botany dealing with fossil plants — **pa·leo·bo·tan·i·cal** \-bə-'tan-i-kəl\ *or* **pa·leo·bo·tan·ic** \-'tan-ik\ *adj* — **pa·leo·bo·tan·i·cal·ly** \-i-k(ə-)lē\ *adv*

Pa·leo·cene \'pā-lē-ə-,sēn, *esp Brit* 'pal-ē-\ *adj* [ISV *pale-* + *-cene*] (1877) **:** of, relating to, or being the earliest epoch of the Tertiary or the corresponding system of rocks — **Paleocene** *n*

pa·leo·cli·ma·tol·o·gy \'pā-lē-ō-,klī-mə-'täl-ə-jē, *esp Brit* 'pal-ē-\ *n* [ISV] (ca. 1909) **:** a science dealing with the climate of past ages — **pa·leo·cli·ma·tol·o·gist** \-jəst\ *n*

pa·leo·ecol·o·gy \-i-'käl-ə-jē, -e-'käl-\ *n* (ca. 1898) **:** a branch of ecology that is concerned with the characteristics of ancient environments and with their relationships to ancient plants and animals — **pa·leo·eco·log·i·cal** \-,ē-kə-'läj-i-kəl, -,ek-ə-\ *also* **pa·leo·eco·log·ic** \-ik\ *adj* — **pa·leo·ecol·o·gist** \-i-'käl-ə-jəst, -e-'käl-\ *n*

Pa·leo·gene \'pā-lē-ə-,jēn, *esp Brit* 'pal-ē-\ *adj* [G *paläogen,* fr. *paläo-* pale- + *-gen* -gene] (1882) **:** of, relating to, or being the earlier part of the

\ə\ **abut** \ᵊ\ **kitten,** F **table** \ər\ **further** \a\ **ash** \ā\ **ace** \ä\ **cot, cart** \au̇\ **out** \ch\ **chin** \e\ **bet** \ē\ **easy** \g\ **go** \i\ **hit** \ī\ **ice** \j\ **job** \ŋ\ **sing** \ō\ **go** \ȯ\ **law** \ȯi\ **boy** \th\ **thin** \t͟h\ **the** \ü\ **loot** \u̇\ **foot** \y\ **yet** \zh\ **vision** \à, k̲, ⁿ, œ, œ̄, ue, ue̅, ʸ\ *see* Guide to Pronunciation

Tertiary including the Paleocene, Eocene, and Oligocene or the corresponding system of rocks — **Paleogene** *n*

pa·leo·ge·og·ra·phy \ˌpā-lē-ō-jē-ˈäg-rə-fē, *esp Brit* ˈpal-ē-\ *n* [ISV] (1881) : the geography of ancient times or of a particular past geological epoch — **pa·leo·geo·graph·ic** \-jē-ə-ˈgraf-ik\ *or* **pa·leo·geo·graph·i·cal** \-i-kəl\ *adj* — **pa·leo·geo·graph·i·cal·ly** \-i-k(ə-)lē\ *adv*

pa·le·og·ra·pher \ˌpā-lē-ˈäg-rə-fər, *esp Brit* ˌpal-ē-\ *n* (1847) : a specialist in paleography

pa·leo·graph·ic \-ə-ˈgraf-ik\ *or* **pa·leo·graph·i·cal** \-i-kəl\ *adj* (ca. 1846) : relating to writings of former times — **pa·leo·graph·i·cal·ly** \-i-k(ə-)lē\ *adv*

pa·le·og·ra·phy \ˌpā-lē-ˈäg-rə-fē, *esp Brit* ˌpal-ē-\ *n* [NL *palaeographia*, fr. Gk *palai-* pale- + *-graphia* -graphy] (1822) **1 a :** an ancient manner of writing **b :** ancient writings **2 :** the study of ancient writings and inscriptions

Pa·leo–In·di·an \ˌpā-lē-ō-ˈin-dē-ən, *esp Brit* ˌpal-ē-\ *n* (1940) : one of the early American hunting people extant in the late Pleistocene and later who are thought to be of Asian extraction — **Paleo–Indian** *adj*

pa·leo·lith \ˈpā-lē-ə-ˌlith, *esp Brit* ˈpal-ē-\ *n* (ca. 1879) : a Paleolithic stone implement

Pa·leo·lith·ic \ˌpā-lē-ə-ˈlith-ik, *esp Brit* ˌpal-ē-\ *adj* [ISV] (1865) : of or relating to the second period of the Stone Age characterized by rough or chipped stone implements

pa·leo·mag·ne·tism \ˌpā-lē-ō-ˈmag-nə-ˌtiz-əm, *esp Brit* ˌpal-ē-\ *n* (1854) **1 :** the intensity and direction of residual magnetization in ancient rocks **2 :** a science that deals with paleomagnetism — **pa·leo·mag·net·ic** \-mag-ˈnet-ik\ *adj* — **pa·leo·mag·net·i·cal·ly** \-i-k(ə-)lē\ *adv* — **pa·leo·mag·ne·tist** \-ˈmag-nət-əst\ *n*

pa·le·on·tol·o·gy \ˌpā-lē-ˌän-ˈtäl-ə-jē, -ən-, *esp Brit* ˌpal-ē-\ *n* [F *paléontologie*, fr. *palé-* pale- + Gk *onta* existing things (fr. neut. pl. of *ont-, ōn*, prp. of *einai* to be) + F *-logie* -logy — more at IS] (ca. 1838) : a science dealing with the life of past geological periods as known from fossil remains — **pa·le·on·to·log·i·cal** \-ˌänt-ᵊl-ˈäj-i-kəl\ *or* **pa·le·on·to·log·ic** \-ik\ *adj* — **pa·le·on·tol·o·gist** \-ˌän-ˈtäl-ə-jəst, -ən-\ *n*

Pa·leo·zo·ic \ˌpā-lē-ə-ˈzō-ik, *esp Brit* ˌpal-ē-\ *adj* (1838) : of, relating to, or being an era of geological history which extends from the beginning of the Cambrian to the close of the Permian and is marked by the culmination of nearly all classes of invertebrates except the insects and in the later epochs of which seed-bearing plants, amphibians, and reptiles first appeared; *also* : relating to the system of rocks formed in this era — see GEOLOGIC TIME table — **Paleozoic** *n*

pa·leo·zo·ol·o·gy \-zō-ˈäl-ə-jē, -zə-ˈwäl-\ *n* [F *paléozoologie*, fr. *palé-* pale- + *zoologie* zoology, fr. NL *zoologia*] (1857) : a branch of paleontology dealing with ancient and fossil animals — **pa·leo·zoo·log·i·cal** \-ˌzō-ə-ˈläj-i-kəl\ *adj* — **pa·leo·zo·ol·o·gist** \-jəst\ *n*

pal·et \pā-ˈlet, ˈpā-lət\ *n* [*pale* (palea) + *-et*] (ca. 1880) : PALEA

pal·ette \ˈpal-ət\ *n* [F, fr. MF, dim. of *pale* spade, shovel, fr. L *pala*] (1622) **1 :** a thin oval or rectangular board or tablet which a painter holds and on which he mixes pigments **2 a :** the set of colors put on the palette **b** (1) **:** a particular range, quality, or use of color (2) **:** a comparable range, quality, or use of available elements esp. in another art (as music)

palette knife *n* (1759) : a knife with a flexible steel blade and no cutting edge used to mix colors or to apply colors (as to a painting)

pal·frey \ˈpȯl-frē\ *n, pl* **palfreys** [ME, fr. OF *palefrei*, fr. ML *palafredus*, fr. LL *paraveredus* post-horse for secondary roads, fr. Gk *para-* beside, subsidiary + LL *veredus* post-horse, fr. a Gaulish word akin to W *gorwydd* horse; akin to OIr *rīadaim* I ride — more at PARA-, RIDE] *archaic* (12c) : a saddle horse other than a war-horse; *esp* : a light easy-gaited horse suitable for a woman

Pa·li \ˈpäl-ē\ *n* [Skt *pāli* row, series of Buddhist sacred texts] (1795) : an Indic language used as the liturgical and scholarly language of Theravada Buddhism — see INDO-EUROPEAN LANGUAGES table

pal·i·mo·ny \ˈpal-ə-ˌmō-nē\ *n* [blend of *pal* and *alimony*] (1979) : a court-ordered allowance paid by one member of a couple formerly living together out of wedlock to the other

pa·limp·sest \ˈpal-əm(p)-ˌsest, pə-ˈlim(p)-\ *n* [L *palimpsestus*, fr. Gk *palimpsēstos* scraped again, fr. *palin* + *psēn* to rub, scrape — more at SAND] (1825) : writing material (as a parchment or tablet) used one or more times after earlier writing has been erased

pal·in·drome \ˈpal-ən-ˌdrōm\ *n* [Gk *palindromos* running back again, fr. *palin* back, again + *dramein* to run; akin to Gk *polos* axis, pole — more at POLE, DROMEDARY] (1629) : a word, verse, or sentence (as "Able was I ere I saw Elba") or a number (as 1881) that reads the same backward or forward — **pal·in·drom·ic** \ˌpal-ən-ˈdrō-mik\ *adj* — **pal·in·drom·ist** \ˈpal-ən-ˌdrō-məst\ *n*

pal·ing \ˈpā-liŋ\ *n* (1558) **1 :** a fence of pales or pickets **2 :** wood for making pales **3 :** a pale or picket for a fence

pal·in·gen·e·sis \ˌpal-ən-ˈjen-ə-səs\ *n* [NL, fr. Gk *palin* again + L *genesis* genesis] (1818) : METEMPSYCHOSIS

pal·in·ge·net·ic \-jə-ˈnet-ik\ *adj* (1833) **1 :** of or relating to palingenesis **2 :** of, relating to, or being biological characters (as the gill slits in a human embryo) that are derivations from distant ancestral forms rather than adaptations of recent origin

pal·in·ode \ˈpal-ə-ˌnōd\ *n* [Gk *palinōidia*, fr. *palin* + *aeidein* to sing — more at ODE] (1599) **1 :** an ode or song recanting or retracting something in an earlier poem **2 :** a formal retraction

¹pal·i·sade \ˌpal-ə-ˈsād\ *n* [F *palissade*, deriv. of L *palus* stake — more at POLE] (1596) **1 a :** a fence of stakes esp. for defense **b :** a long strong stake pointed at the top and set close with others as a defense **2 :** a line of bold cliffs

²palisade *vt* **-sad·ed; -sad·ing** (1632) : to surround or fortify with palisades

palisade cell *n* (1875) : a cell of the palisade layer

palisade layer *n* (1897) : a layer of columnar cells rich in chloroplasts found beneath the upper epidermis of foliage leaves — called also *palisade mesophyll, palisade parenchyma, palisade tissue;* compare SPONGY PARENCHYMA

¹pall \ˈpȯl\ *vb* [ME *pallen*, short for *appallen* to become pale — more at APPALL] *vi* (14c) **1 :** to lose strength or effectiveness **2 :** to lose in interest or attraction ⟨his humor began to ~ on us⟩ **3 :** to become tired of something **~** *vt* **1 :** to cause to become insipid **2 :** to deprive of pleasure in something by satiating ***syn*** see SATIATE

²pall *n* [ME, cloak, mantle, fr. OE *pæll*, fr. L *pallium*] (15c) **1 :** PALLIUM 1b **2 a :** a square of linen usu. stiffened with cardboard that is used to cover the chalice **b** (1) **:** a heavy cloth draped over a coffin (2) **:** a coffin esp. when holding a body **3 :** something that covers or conceals; *esp* : an overspreading element that produces an effect of gloom ⟨a ~ of thick black smoke⟩

³pall *vt* (15c) : to cover with a pall : DRAPE

Pal·la·di·an \pə-ˈlād-ē-ən, -ˈläd-\ *adj* (1731) : of or relating to a revived classic style in architecture based on the works of Andrea Palladio — **Pal·la·di·an·ism** \-ˌiz-əm\ *n*

¹pal·la·di·um \pə-ˈlād-ē-əm\ *n* [L, fr. Gk *palladion*, fr. *Pallad-, Pallas*] (14c) **1** *cap* **:** a statue of Pallas whose preservation was believed to ensure the safety of Troy **2** *pl* **pal·la·dia** \-ē-ə\ **:** SAFEGUARD

²palladium *n* [NL, fr. *Pallad-, Pallas*, an asteroid] (1803) : a silver-white ductile malleable metallic element of the platinum group that is used esp. in electrical contacts, as a catalyst, and in alloys — see ELEMENT table — **pal·la·dous** \pə-ˈlād-əs\ *adj*

Pal·las \ˈpal-əs\ *n* [L *Pallad-, Pallas*, fr. Gk] : ATHENA

pall·bear·er \ˈpȯl-ˌbar-ər, -ˌber-\ *n* [²*pall*] (1707) **1 :** a person who helps to carry the coffin at a funeral **2 :** a member of the immediate escort or honor guard of the coffin who does not actually help to carry it

¹pal·let \ˈpal-ət\ *n* [ME *pailet*, fr. (assumed) MF *paillet*, fr. *paille* straw, fr. L *palea* chaff, straw; akin to Skt *palāva* chaff] (14c) **1 :** a straw-filled tick or mattress **2 :** a small, hard, or temporary bed

²pallet *n* [ME *palette*, lit., small shovel — more at PALETTE] (1558) **1 :** a wooden flat-bladed instrument **2 :** a lever or surface in a timepiece that receives an impulse from the escapement wheel and imparts motion to a balance or pendulum **3 :** a portable platform for handling, storing, or moving materials and packages (as in warehouses, factories, or vehicles)

pal·let·ize \ˈpal-ət-ˌīz\ *vt* **-ized; -iz·ing** (1944) : to place on, transport, or store by means of pallets — **pal·let·iza·tion** \ˌpal-ət-ə-ˈzā-shən\ *n* — **pal·let·iz·er** \ˈpal-ət-ˌī-zər\ *n*

pal·lette \pa-ˈlet\ *n* [alter. of *palette*] (1834) : one of the plates at the armpits of a suit of armor — see ARMOR illustration

pal·li·al \ˈpal-ē-əl\ *adj* [NL *pallium*] (1836) **1 :** of or relating to the cerebral cortex **2 :** of, relating to, or produced by a mantle of a mollusk

pal·liasse \pal-ˈyas\ *n* [modif. of F *paillasse*, fr. *paille* straw] (1506) : a thin straw mattress used as a pallet

pal·li·ate \ˈpal-ē-ˌāt\ *vt* **-at·ed; -at·ing** [LL *palliatus*, pp. of *palliare* to cloak, conceal, fr. L *pallium* cloak] (1588) **1 :** to reduce the violence of (a disease) **:** ABATE **2 :** to cover by excuses and apologies **3 :** to moderate the intensity of ⟨trying to ~ the boredom⟩ — **pal·li·a·tion** \ˌpal-ē-ˈā-shən\ *n* — **pal·li·a·tor** \ˈpal-ē-ˌāt-ər\ *n*

¹pal·lia·tive \ˈpal-ē-ˌāt-iv, ˈpal-yət-\ *adj* (1543) : serving to palliate ⟨~ surgery⟩ — **pal·lia·tive·ly** *adv*

²palliative *n* (1724) : something that palliates

pal·lid \ˈpal-əd\ *adj* [L *pallidus* — more at PALE] (1590) **1 :** deficient in color **:** WAN ⟨a ~ countenance⟩ **2 :** lacking sparkle or liveliness **:** DULL ⟨a ~ entertainment⟩ — **pal·lid·ly** *adv* — **pal·lid·ness** *n*

pal·li·um \ˈpal-ē-əm\ *n, pl* **-lia** \-ē-ə\ *or* **-li·ums** [L] (1564) **1 a :** a draped rectangular cloth worn as a cloak by men of ancient Greece and Rome **b :** a white woolen band with pendants in front and back worn over the chasuble by a pope or archbishop as a symbol of full episcopal authority — see VESTMENT illustration **2** [NL, fr. L, cloak] **a :** CEREBRAL CORTEX **b :** the mantle of a mollusk, brachiopod, or bird

pall–mall \ˈpel-ˈmel, ˈpal-ˈmal, *US often* ˈpȯl-ˈmȯl\ *n* [MF *pallemaille*, fr. It *pallamaglio*, fr. *palla* ball (of Gmc origin; akin to OHG *balla* ball) + *maglio* mallet, fr. L *malleus* — more at BALL, MAUL] (1598) : a 17th century game in which each player attempts to drive a wooden ball with a mallet down an alley and through a raised ring in as few strokes as possible; *also* : the alley in which it is played

pal·lor \ˈpal-ər\ *n* [L, fr. *pallēre* to be pale — more at FALLOW] (1656) : deficiency of color esp. of the face : PALENESS

pal·ly \ˈpal-ē\ *adj* (1895) : sharing the relationship of pals : INTIMATE

¹palm \ˈpä(l)m, *NewEng also* ˈpȧm\ *n* [ME, fr. OE, fr. L *palma* palm of the hand, palm tree; fr. the resemblance of the tree's leaves to the outstretched hand; akin to Gk *palamē* palm of the hand, OE *folm*] (bef. 12c) **1 :** any of a family (Palmae, the palm family) of mostly tropical or subtropical monocotyledonous trees, shrubs, or vines with usu. a simple stem and a terminal crown of large pinnate or fan-shaped leaves **2 :** a leaf of the palm as a symbol of victory or rejoicing; *also* : a branch (as of laurel) similarly used **3 :** a symbol of triumph; *also* : VICTORY, TRIUMPH **4 :** an addition to a military decoration in the form of a palm frond esp. to indicate a second award of the basic decoration — **palm·like** \-ˌlīk\ *adj*

²palm *n* [ME *paume*, fr. MF, fr. L *palma*] (14c) **1 :** the somewhat concave part of the human hand between the bases of the fingers and the wrist or the corresponding part of the forefoot of a lower mammal **2 :** a flat expanded part esp. at the end of a base or stalk: as **a :** the blade of an oar or paddle **b** (1) **:** the flat inner face of an anchor fluke (2) **:** ²FLUKE 1 **3** [L *palmus*, fr. *palma*] **:** a unit of length based on the breadth or length of the hand **4 :** something (as a part of a glove) that covers the palm of the hand **5 :** an act of palming (as of cards)

³palm *vt* (1685) **1 :** to touch with the palm: as **a :** to stroke with the palm or hand **b :** to shake hands with **c :** to allow (a basketball) to come to rest momentarily in the hand while dribbling thus committing a violation **2 a :** to conceal in or with the hand ⟨~ a card⟩ **b :** to pick up stealthily ⟨likely to ~ small merchandise in a store⟩ **3 :** to impose by fraud ⟨a second imposter to be ~*ed* upon you —Sir Walter Scott⟩

pal·mar \ˈpal-mər, ˈpä(l)m-ər\ *adj* (1656) : of, relating to, or involving the palm of the hand

pal·ma·ry \ˈpal-mə-rē, ˈpä(l)m-ə-\ *adj* [L *palmarius* deserving the palm, fr. *palma*] (1657) : OUTSTANDING, BEST

pal·mate \ˈpal-ˌmāt, ˈpä(l)m-ˌāt\ *also* **pal·mat·ed** \-ˌmāt-əd, -ˌāt-\ *adj* (ca. 1760) : resembling a hand with the fingers spread: as **a :** having lobes radiating from a common point ⟨a ~ leaf⟩ **b :** having the distal portion broad, flat, and lobed ⟨a ~ antler⟩ — **pal·mate·ly** *adv* — **pal·ma·tion** \pal-ˈmā-shən, pä(l)-ˈmā-\ *n*

-palmed \-ˈpä(l)md\ *adj comb form* : having (such) a palm or palms ⟨leather-*palmed* gloves⟩

palm·er \'päm-ər, 'päl-mər\ *n* (14c) : a person wearing two crossed palm leaves as a sign of his pilgrimage to the Holy Land

palm·er·worm \-,wərm\ *n* (1560) : a caterpillar that suddenly appears in great numbers devouring herbage

pal·met·to \pal-'met-(,)ō *also* pä(l)-\ *n, pl* **-tos** *or* **-toes** [modif. of Sp. *palmito,* fr. *palma* palm, fr. L] (1555) **1** : any of several usu. low-growing fan-leaved palms; *esp* : CABBAGE PALMETTO **2** : strips of the leaf blade of a palmetto used in weaving

palm·ist \'päm-əst, 'päl-məst\ *n* [prob. back-formation fr. *palmistry*] (1886) : one who practices palmistry

palm·ist·ry \'päm-ə-strē, 'päl-mə-\ *n* [ME *pawmestry,* prob. fr. *paume* palm + *maistrie* mastery] (15c) : the art or practice of reading a person's character or future from the markings on his or her palms

pal·mi·tate \'pal-mə-,tāt, 'pä(l)m-ə-\ *n* (1873) : a salt or ester of palmitic acid

pal·mit·ic acid \(,)pal-,mit-ik-, (,)pä(l)-\ *n* [ISV, fr. *palmitin*] (1857) : a waxy crystalline fatty acid $C_{16}H_{32}O_2$ occurring free or in the form of esters (as glycerides) in most fats and fatty oils and in several essential oils and waxes

pal·mi·tin \'pal-mət-ən, 'pä(l)m-ət-\ *n* [F *palmitine,* prob. fr. *palmite* pith of the palm tree, fr. Sp *palmito*] (1857) : an ester of glycerol and palmitic acid; *esp* : a solid ester found with stearin and olein in animal fats

palm off *vt* (1822) **1** : to dispose of usu. by trickery or guile **2** : PASS OFF 2

palm oil *n* (1705) : an edible fat obtained from the flesh of the fruit of several palms and used esp. in soap, candles, and lubricating greases

Palm Sunday *n* [fr. the palm branches strewn in Christ's way] (bef. 12c) : the Sunday before Easter celebrated in commemoration of Christ's triumphal entry into Jerusalem

palmy \'päm-ē, 'päl-mē, *NewEng also* 'pam-ē\ *adj* **palm·i·er; -est** (1602) **1** : marked by prosperity : FLOURISHING **2** : abounding in or bearing palms

pal·my·ra \pal-'mī-rə\ *n* [Pg *palmeira,* fr. *palma* palm, fr. L] (1698) : a tall African fan-leaved palm (*Borassus flabellifer*) cultivated for its hard resistant wood, fiber, and sugar-rich sap — called also *palmyra palm*

pal·o·mi·no \,pal-ə-'mē-(,)nō, -nə(-w)\ *n, pl* **-nos** [AmerSp, fr. Sp, like a dove, fr. L *palumbinus,* fr. *palumbes* ringdove; akin to Gk *peleia* dove, L *pallēre* to be pale — more at FALLOW] (1914) : a horse of a color that varies from pale cream to gold and that has a flaxen or white mane and tail

pa·loo·ka \pə-'lü-kə\ *n* [origin unknown] (1925) **1** : an inexperienced or incompetent boxer **2** : OAF, LOUT

palp \'palp\ *n* [NL *palpus*] (1842) : PALPUS

pal·pa·ble \'pal-pə-bəl\ *adj* [ME, fr. LL *palpabilis,* fr. L *palpare* to stroke, caress — more at FEEL] (14c) **1** : capable of being touched or felt : TANGIBLE **2** : easily perceptible : NOTICEABLE **3** : easily perceptible by the mind : MANIFEST **syn** see PERCEPTIBLE — **pal·pa·bil·i·ty** \,pal-pə-'bil-ət-ē\ *n* — **pal·pa·bly** \'pal-pə-blē\ *adv*

pal·pal \'pal-pəl\ *adj* (1857) : of, relating to, or functioning as a palpus

pal·pate \'pal-,pāt\ *vt* **pal·pat·ed; pal·pat·ing** [prob. back-formation fr. *palpation,* fr. L *palpation- palpatio,* fr. *palpatus,* pp. of *palpare*] (1849) : to examine by touch esp. medically — **pal·pa·tion** \pal-'pā-shən\ *n*

pal·pe·bral \pal-'pē-brəl\ *adj* [LL *palpebralis,* fr. L *palpebra* eyelid; akin to L *palpare*] (1840) : of, relating to, or located on or near the eyelids

pal·pi·tant \'pal-pət-ənt\ *adj* (1837) : marked by trembling or throbbing

pal·pi·tate \'pal-pə-,tāt\ *vi* **-tat·ed; -tat·ing** [L *palpitatus,* pp. of *palpitare,* freq. of *palpare* to stroke] (1623) : to beat rapidly and strongly : THROB — **pal·pi·ta·tion** \,pal-pə-'tā-shən\ *n*

pal·pus \'pal-pəs\ *n, pl* **pal·pi** \-,pī, -(,)pē\ [NL, fr. L, caress, soft palm of the hand; akin to L *palpare*] (1813) : a segmented usu. tactile or gustatory process on an arthropod mouthpart

pals·grave \'pòlz-,grāv\ *n* [D *paltsgrave*] (1548) : COUNT PALATINE 1b

pal·sied \'pòl-zēd\ *adj* (1550) : affected with palsy

1**pal·sy** \'pòl-zē\ *n, pl* **palsies** [ME *parlesie,* fr. MF *paralisie,* fr. L *paralysis*] (14c) **1** : PARALYSIS **2** : a condition marked by uncontrollable tremor of the body or a part

2**palsy** *vt* **pal·sied; pal·sy·ing** (1615) : to affect with or as if with palsy

palsy–walsy \,pal-zē-'wal-zē\ *adj* [redupl. of *palsy* (pally), fr. *pals,* pl. of *pal*] *slang* (1943) : being or appearing to be very intimate

pal·ter \'pòl-tər\ *vi* **pal·tered; pal·ter·ing** \-t(ə-)riŋ\ [origin unknown] (1601) **1** : to act insincerely or deceitfully : EQUIVOCATE **2** : HAGGLE, CHAFFER **syn** see LIE — **pal·ter·er** \-tər-ər\ *n*

pal·try \'pòl-trē\ *adj* **pal·tri·er; -est** [obs. *paltry* (trash)] (1570) **1** : INFERIOR, TRASHY **2** : MEAN, DESPICABLE **3** : TRIVIAL **4** : MEAGER, MEASLY ⟨made a ~ donation⟩ — **pal·tri·ness** *n*

pa·lu·dal \pə-'lüd-ᵊl, 'pal-yəd-ᵊl\ *adj* [L *palud-, palus* marsh; akin to Skt *palvala* pond] (1818) : of or relating to marshes or fens : MARSHY

pal·u·dism \'pal-yə-,diz-əm\ *n* [ISV, fr. L *palud-, palus*] (ca. 1890) : MALARIA

paly \'pā-lē\ *adj, archaic* (1560) : somewhat pale : PALLID

pal·y·nol·o·gy \,pal-ə-'näl-ə-jē\ *n* [Gk *palynein* to sprinkle, fr. *palē* fine meal — more at POLLEN] (1944) : a branch of science dealing with pollen and spores — **pal·y·no·log·i·cal** \-nə-'läj-i-kəl\ *also* **pal·y·no·log·ic** \-ik\ *adj* — **pal·y·no·log·i·cal·ly** \-i-k(ə-)lē\ *adv* — **pal·y·nol·o·gist** \-'näl-ə-jəst\ *n*

pam·pa \'pam-pə, 'päm-\ *n, pl* **pam·pas** \-pəz, -pəs\ [AmerSp, fr. Quechua & Aymara, plain] (1704) : an extensive generally grass-covered plain of temperate So. America east of the Andes : PRAIRIE

pam·pe·an \'pam-pē-ən, 'päm-, pam-', päm-'\ *adj* (1839) : of or relating to the pampas of So. America or their Indian inhabitants

pam·per \'pam-pər\ *vt* **pam·pered; pam·per·ing** \-p(ə-)riŋ\ [ME *pamperen,* prob. of D origin; akin to Flem *pamperen* to pamper] (14c) **1** *archaic* : to cram with rich food : GLUT **2 a** : to treat with extreme or excessive care and attention ⟨~*ed* their guests⟩ **b** : GRATIFY, HUMOR ⟨enabled him to ~ his wanderlust —*New Yorker*⟩ **syn** see INDULGE — **pam·per·er** \-pər-ər\ *n*

pam·pe·ro \pam-'pe(ə)r-(,)ō, päm-\ *n, pl* **-ros** [AmerSp, fr. *pampa*] (1818) : a strong cold wind from the west or southwest that sweeps over the pampas

pam·phlet \'pam(p)-flət\ *n* [ME *pamflet* unbound booklet, fr. *Pamphilus seu De Amore* Pamphilus or On Love, popular Latin love poem of the 12th cent.] (14c) : an unbound printed publication with no cover or with a paper cover

1**pam·phle·teer** \,pam(p)-flə-'ti(ə)r\ *n* (1642) : a writer of pamphlets attacking something or urging a cause

2**pamphleteer** *vi* (1698) **1** : to write and publish pamphlets **2** : to engage in partisan arguments indirectly in writings

1**pan** \'pan\ *n* [ME *panne,* fr. OE, fr. L *patina,* fr. Gk *patanē;* akin to L *patēre* to be open — more at FATHOM] (bef. 12c) **1 a** : a usu. broad, shallow, and open container for domestic use (as for warming, baking, or frying) **b** : any of various similar usu. metal receptacles: as (1) : the hollow part of the lock in a firelock or flintlock gun that receives the priming (2) : either of the receptacles in a pair of scales (3) : a round shallow metal container for separating metal (as gold) from waste by washing **2 a** (1) : a natural basin or depression in land (2) : a similar artificial basin (as for evaporating brine) **b** : a drifting fragment of the flat thin ice that forms in bays or along the shore **3** : HARDPAN 1 **4** *slang* : FACE **5** : a harsh criticism

2**pan** *vb* **panned; pan·ning** *vi* (1839) **1** : to wash earth, gravel, or other materials in a pan in search of metal (as gold) **2** : to yield precious metal in the process of panning ~ *vt* **1 a** : to wash in a pan for the purpose of separating heavy particles **b** : to separate (as gold) by panning **c** : to place in a pan **2** : to criticize severely ⟨the show was *panned*⟩

3**pan** \'pän\ *n* [Hindi *pān,* fr. Skt *parna* wing, leaf — more at FERN] (1616) **1** : a betel leaf **2** : a masticatory of betel nut, lime, and pan

4**pan** \'pan\ *n* [*panorama*] (ca. 1922) : the process of panning a motion-picture or television camera

5**pan** \'pan\ *vb* **panned; pan·ning** *vt* (1930) : to rotate (as a motion-picture camera) so as to keep an object in the picture or secure a panoramic effect ~ *vi* **1** : to pan a motion-picture or television camera **2** *of a camera* : to undergo panning

Pan \'pan\ *n* [L, fr. Gk] : a Greek god of pastures, flocks, and shepherds usu. represented as having the legs, horns, and ears of a goat

pan- *comb form* [Gk, fr. *pan,* neut. of *pant-, pas* all, every; akin to Skt *śaśvat* all, every, *śvayati* he swells] **1** : all : completely ⟨*pan*chromatic⟩ **2 a** : involving all of a (specified) group ⟨*Pan*-American⟩ **b** : advocating or involving the union of a (specified) group ⟨*Pan*-Asian⟩ **3** : whole : general ⟨*pan*leucopenia⟩

pan·a·cea \,pan-ə-'sē-ə\ *n* [L, fr. Gk *panakeia,* fr. *pan-* + *akeisthai* to heal, fr. *akos* remedy] (1548) : a remedy for all ills or difficulties : CURE-ALL — **pan·a·ce·an** \-'sē-ən\ *adj*

pa·nache \pə-'nash, -'näsh\ *n* [MF *pennache,* fr. OIt *pennacchio,* fr. LL *pinnaculum* small wing — more at PINNACLE] (1553) **1** : an ornamental tuft (as of feathers) esp. on a helmet **2** : dash or flamboyance in style and action : VERVE

pa·na·da \pə-'näd-ə\ *n* [Sp, fr. *pan* bread, fr. L *panis* — more at FOOD] (ca. 1598) : a paste of flour or bread crumbs and water or stock used as a base for sauce or a binder for forcemeat or stuffing

pan·a·ma \'pan-ə-,mä, -,mò\ *n, often cap* [AmerSp *panamá,* fr. *Panama,* Central America] (1833) : a lightweight hat of natural-colored straw hand-plaited of narrow strips from the young leaves of the jipijapa; *also* : a machine-made imitation of this

Panama Red *n* (1967) : marijuana of a reddish tint that is of Panamanian origin and is held to be very potent

Pan–Amer·i·can \,pan-ə-'mer-ə-kən\ *adj* (1889) : of, relating to, or involving the independent republics of No. and So. America

Pan–Amer·i·can·ism \-kə-,niz-əm\ *n* (1901) : a movement for greater cooperation among the Pan-American nations

pan·a·tela \,pan-ə-'tel-ə\ *n* [Sp, fr. AmerSp, a long thin biscuit, deriv. of L *panis* bread] (1901) : a long slender straight-sided cigar rounded off at the sealed end

1**pan·cake** \'pan-,kāk\ *n* (15c) : a flat cake made of thin batter and cooked (as on a griddle) on both sides

2**pancake** *vb* **pan·caked; pan·cak·ing** *vi* (1911) : to make a pancake landing ~ *vt* : to cause to pancake

Pan–Cake \'pan-,kāk\ *trademark* — used for a cosmetic in semimoist cake form

pancake landing *n* (ca. 1928) : a landing in which the airplane is leveled off higher than for a normal landing causing it to stall and drop in an approximately horizontal position with little forward motion

pan·chax \'pan-,kaks\ *n* [NL] (1961) : any of numerous small brilliantly colored Old World killifishes (genus *Aplocheilus*) often kept in the tropical aquarium

Pan·chen Lama \,pän-chən-\ *n* [Panchen fr. Chin (Pek) *pan¹ ch'an²*] (1794) : the lama who is the chief spiritual adviser of the Dalai Lama

pan·chro·mat·ic \,pan-krō-'mat-ik\ *adj* [ISV] (1903) : sensitive to light of all colors in the visible spectrum ⟨~ film⟩

pan·cra·ti·um \pan-'krā-shē-əm\ *n* [L, fr. Gk *pankration,* fr. *pan-* + *kratos* strength — more at HARD] (1603) : an ancient Greek athletic contest involving both boxing and wrestling

pan·cre·as \'paŋ-krē-əs, 'pan-\ *n* [NL, fr. Gk *pankreas,* fr. *pan-* + *kreas* flesh, meat — more at RAW] (1578) : a large compound racemose gland of vertebrates that secretes digestive enzymes and the hormone insulin — **pan·cre·at·ic** \,paŋ-krē-'at-ik, ,pan-\ *adj*

pancreat- *or* **pancreato-** *comb form* [NL, fr. Gk *pankreat-, pancreas*] : pancreas ⟨*pancreat*ic⟩

pan·cre·atec·to·my \,paŋ-krē-ə-'tek-tə-mē, ,pan-\ *n* (ca.1900) : surgical removal of all or part of the pancreas — **pan·cre·atec·to·mized** \-,mīzd\ *adj*

pancreatic juice *n* (1665) : a clear alkaline secretion of pancreatic enzymes that is poured into the duodenum and acts on food already acted on by the gastric juice and saliva

pan·cre·atin \pan-'krē-ət-ən; 'paŋ-krē-, 'pan-\ *n* (ca. 1860) : a mixture of enzymes from the pancreatic juice; *also* : a preparation containing such a mixture

pan·cre·ati·tis \,paŋ-krē-ə-'tīt-əs, ,pan-\ *n, pl* **-atit·i·des** \-'tit-ə-,dēz\ [NL] (ca. 1842) : inflammation of the pancreas

pan·creo·zy·min \-krē-ō-'zī-mən\ *n* [*pancreas* + *-o-* + *zym-* + *-in*] (ca. 1943) : CHOLECYSTOKININ

\ə\ abut \ᵊ\ kitten, F table \ər\ further \a\ ash \ā\ ace \ä\ cot, cart \au̇\ out \ch\ chin \e\ bet \ē\ easy \g\ go \i\ hit \ī\ ice \j\ job \ŋ\ sing \ō\ go \ȯ\ law \ȯi\ boy \th\ thin \t͟h\ the \ü\ loot \u̇\ foot \y\ yet \zh\ vision \à, k̲, ⁿ, œ, œ̄, ue, ue̅, ʸ\ *see* Guide to Pronunciation

pan·cy·to·pe·nia \ˌpan-ˌsīt-ə-ˈpē-nē-ə\ *n* [NL, fr. *pan-* + *cyt-* + *-penia* deficiency, fr. Gk *penia* poverty; akin to L *pendere* to hang — more at PENDANT] (ca. 1941) : an abnormal reduction in the number of erythrocytes, leukocytes, and blood platelets in the blood; *also* : a disorder (as aplastic anemia) characterized by such a reduction

pan·da \ˈpan-də\ *n* [F, fr. native name in Nepal] (ca. 1824) **1** : a long-tailed Himalayan carnivore (*Ailurus fulgens*) that is related to and closely resembles the American raccoon, has long fur, and is basically rusty or chestnut in color with mottling and barring of black **2** : a large black-and-white mammal (*Ailuropoda melanoleuca*) of western China that is now usu. classified with the bears (family Ursidae)

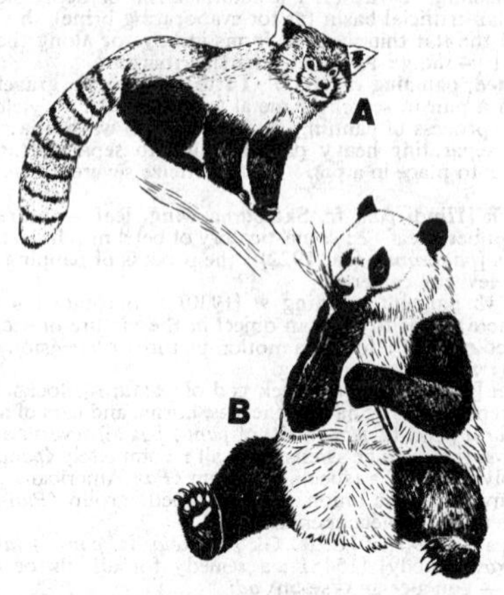

A panda 1; *B* panda 2

pan·da·nus \pan-ˈdān-əs, -ˈdan-əs\ *n, pl* **-ni** \-ˌī\ [NL, genus name, fr. Malay *pandan* screw pine] (1830) : SCREW PINE; *also* : a fiber made from the leaf of this plant and used for woven products (as mats)

Pan·da·rus \ˈpan-də-rəs\ *n* [L, fr. Gk *Pandaros*] : a Lycian archer in the Trojan War who in medieval legend procures Cressida for Troilus

pan·dect \ˈpan-ˌdekt\ *n* [LL *Pandectae*, the Pandects, digest of Roman civil law (6th cent. A.D.), fr. L, pl. of *pandectes* encyclopedic work, fr. Gk *pandektēs* all-receiving, fr. *pan-* + *dechesthai* to receive; akin to Gk *dokein* to seem, seem good — more at DECENT] (ca. 1531) **1** : a complete code of the laws of a country or system of law **2** : a treatise covering an entire subject

¹pan·dem·ic \pan-ˈdem-ik\ *adj* [LL *pandemus*, fr. Gk *pandēmos* of all the people, fr. *pan-* + *dēmos* people — more at DEMAGOGUE] (1666) : occurring over a wide geographic area and affecting an exceptionally high proportion of the population ⟨~ malaria⟩

²pandemic *n* (1853) : a pandemic outbreak of a disease

Pan·de·mo·ni·um \ˌpan-də-ˈmō-nē-əm\ *n* [Gk *pan-* + *daimōn* evil spirit — more at DEMON] **1** : the capital of Hell in Milton's *Paradise Lost* **2** : the infernal regions : HELL **3** *not cap* : a wild uproar : TUMULT

¹pan·der \ˈpan-dər\ *n* [ME *Pandare* Pandarus, fr. L *Pandarus*] (1530) **1 a** : a go-between in love intrigues **b** : PIMP **2** : someone who caters to or exploits the weaknesses of others

²pander *vi* **pan·dered; pan·der·ing** \-d(ə-)riŋ\ (1603) : to act as a pander; *esp* : to provide gratification for others' desires ⟨films that ~ to the basest emotions of moviegoers⟩ — **pan·der·er** \-dər-ər\ *n*

pan·dit \ˈpan-dət, ˈpən-\ *n* [Hindi *paṇḍit*, fr. Skt *paṇḍita*] (ca. 1828) : a wise or learned man in India — often used as an honorary title

pan·do·ra \pan-ˈdōr-ə, -ˈdȯr-\ *n* [It, fr. LL *pandura* 3-stringed lute] (1597) : BANDORE

Pan·do·ra's box \pan-ˌdōr-əz-, -ˌdȯr-\ *n* [fr. the box, sent by the gods to Pandora, which she was forbidden to open and which loosed a swarm of evils upon mankind when she opened it out of curiosity] (1579) : a prolific source of troubles

pan·dow·dy \pan-ˈdau̇d-ē\ *n, pl* **-dies** [origin unknown] (1805) : a deep-dish spiced apple dessert sweetened with sugar, molasses, or maple syrup and covered with a rich crust

pan·dy \ˈpan-dē\ *vt* **pan·died; pan·dy·ing** [prob. fr. L *pande*, imper. sing. of *pandere* to spread out (the hand); command of the schoolmaster to the boy — more at FATHOM] *Brit* (1863) : to punish (a schoolboy) with a blow on the palm of the hand esp. with a ferule

pane \ˈpān\ *n* [ME *pan, pane* strip of cloth, pane, fr. MF *pan*, fr. L *pannus* cloth, rag — more at VANE] (14c) **1** : a piece, section, or side of something: as **a** : a framed sheet of glass in a window or door **b** : one of the sides of a nut or bolt head **2** : one of the sections into which a sheet of postage stamps is cut for distribution — **paned** \ˈpānd\ *adj*

pan·e·gy·ric \ˌpan-ə-ˈjir-ik, -ˈjī-rik\ *n* [L *panegyricus*, fr. Gk *panēgyrikos*, fr. *panēgyrikos* of or for a festival assembly, fr. *panēgyris* festival assembly, fr. *pan-* + *agyris* assembly; akin to Gk *ageirein* to gather — more at GREGARIOUS] (1603) : a eulogistic oration or writing; *also* : formal or elaborate praise *syn* see ENCOMIUM — **pan·e·gy·ri·cal** \-ˈjir-i-kəl, -ˈjī-ri-\ *adj* — **pan·e·gy·ri·cal·ly** \-k(ə-)lē\ *adv*

pan·e·gy·rist \ˌpan-ə-ˈjir-əst, -ˈjī-rəst\ *n* (1605) : EULOGIST

¹pan·el \ˈpan-ᵊl\ *n* [ME, piece of cloth, slip of parchment, jury schedule, fr. MF, piece of cloth, piece, prob. fr. (assumed) VL *pannellus*, dim. of L *pannus*] (14c) **1 a (1)** : a schedule containing names of persons summoned as jurors **(2)** : the group of persons so summoned **(3)** : JURY 1 **b (1)** : a group of persons selected for some service (as investigation or arbitration) ⟨a ~ of experts⟩ **(2)** : a group of persons who discuss before an audience a topic of usu. political or social interest; *also* : PANEL DISCUSSION **(3)** : a group of entertainers or guests engaged as players in a quiz or guessing game on a radio or television program **2** : a separate or distinct part of a surface: as **a** : a fence section : HURDLE **b (1)** : a thin usu. rectangular board set in a frame (as in a door) **(2)** : a usu. sunken or raised section of a surface set off by a margin **(3)** : a flat usu. rectangular piece of construction material (as plywood or precast masonry) made to form part of a surface **c** : a vertical section of fabric (as a gore) **d** : COMIC STRIP; *also* : a frame of a comic strip **e** : any of several units of construction of an airplane wing surface **3** : a thin flat piece of wood on which a picture is painted; *also* : a painting on such a surface **4 a** : a section of a switchboard **b** : a flat often insulating support (as for computer hardware or parts of an electrical device) usu. with control handles on one face **c** : a usu. vertical mount for controls or dials (as of instruments of measurement)

²panel *vt* **-eled** *or* **-elled; -el·ing** *or* **-el·ling** (1508) : to furnish or decorate with panels ⟨*paneled* the living room⟩

panel discussion *n* (ca. 1938) : a formal discussion by a panel of a topic of public interest

panel heating *n* (1928) : space heating by means of wall, floor, baseboard, or ceiling panels with embedded electric conductors or hot-air or hot-water pipes

pan·el·ing *also* **pan·el·ling** *n* (1824) : panels joined in a continuous surface; *esp* : decorative wood panels so joined

pan·el·ist \ˈpan-ᵊl-əst\ *n* (1951) : a member of a discussion or advisory panel or of a radio or television panel

panel truck *n* (1937) : a small motortruck with a fully enclosed body

pan·e·tela *var of* PANATELA

pan·et·to·ne \ˌpän-ə-ˈtō-nē, ˌpan-\ *n* [It, fr. *panetto* small loaf, dim. of *pane* bread, fr. L *panis* — more at FOOD] (1922) : a usu. yeast-leavened bread containing raisins and candied fruit

pan·fish \ˈpan-ˌfish\ *n* (1805) : a small food fish (as a sunfish) usu. taken with hook and line and not available on the market

pan·fry \ˈpan-ˌfrī, pan-ˈfrī\ *vt* (ca. 1929) : SAUTÉ

pan·ful \ˈpan-ˌfu̇l\ *n* (ca. 1864) : as much or as many as a pan will hold

¹pang \ˈpaŋ\ *n* [origin unknown] (15c) **1** : a brief piercing spasm of pain **2** : a sharp attack of mental anguish ⟨~*s* of remorse⟩ ⟨a ~ of jealousy struck me —Graham Greene⟩

²pang *vt* (1502) : to cause to have pangs : TORMENT

pan·gen·e·sis \(ˈ)pan-ˈjen-ə-səs\ *n* [NL] (ca. 1868) : a hypothetical mechanism of heredity in which the cells throw off particles that circulate freely throughout the system, multiply by subdivision, and collect in the reproductive products or in buds so that the egg or bud contains particles from all parts of the parent — **pan·ge·net·ic** \ˌpan-jə-ˈnet-ik\ *adj*

Pan·gloss·ian \pan-ˈgläs-ē-ən, paŋ-, -ˈglȯs-\ *adj* [*Pangloss*, optimistic tutor in Voltaire's *Candide* (1759)] (1831) : marked by the view that all is for the best in this best of possible worlds

pan·go·la grass \pan-ˈgō-lə-, paŋ-\ *n* [*pangola*, fr. native name in So. Africa] (1948) : a rapid-growing perennial grass (*Digitaria decumbens*) of southern Africa that has been introduced into the southern U.S. as a pasture grass

pan·go·lin \ˈpaŋ-gə-lən, ˈpan-\ *n* [Malay *pĕngguling*] (1774) : any of several Asian and African edentate mammals (*Manis* or related genera of the order Pholidota) having the body covered with large imbricated horny scales

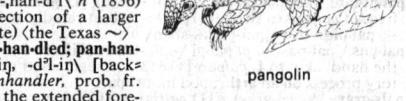

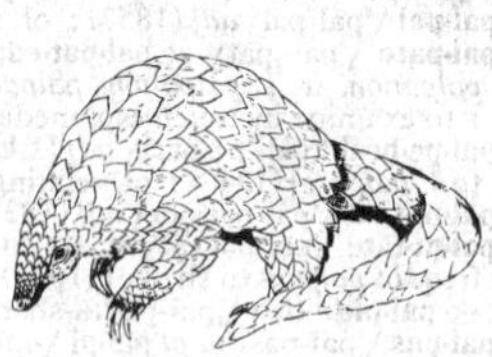
pangolin

¹pan·han·dle \ˈpan-ˌhan-dᵊl\ *n* (1856) : a narrow projection of a larger territory (as a state) ⟨the Texas ~⟩

²panhandle *vb* **pan·han·dled; pan·han·dling** \-ˌhan-(d)liŋ, -dᵊl-iŋ\ [back-formation fr. *panhandler*, prob. fr. *panhandle*, n.; fr. the extended forearm] *vi* (1903) : to stop people on the street and ask for food or money : BEG ~ *vt* **1** : to accost on the street and beg from **2** : to get by panhandling — **pan·han·dler** \-(d)lər, -dᵊl-ər\ *n*

Pan·hel·len·ic \ˌpan-hə-ˈlen-ik\ *adj* (1847) **1** : of or relating to all Greece or all the Greeks **2** : of or relating to the Greek-letter sororities or fraternities in American colleges and universities or to an association representing them

pan·hu·man \(ˈ)pan-ˈhyü-mən, -ˈyü-\ *adj* (ca. 1909) : of or relating to all humanity ⟨the ~ problem of evil —R. K. Merton⟩

¹pan·ic \ˈpan-ik\ *adj* [F *panique*, fr. Gk *panikos*, lit., of Pan, fr. *Pan*] (1603) **1** : of, relating to, or resembling the mental or emotional state believed induced by the god Pan ⟨~ fear⟩ **2** : of, relating to, or arising from a panic ⟨a wave of ~ buying⟩ **3** : of or relating to the god Pan

²panic *n* (1708) **1** : a sudden overpowering fright; *esp* : a sudden unreasoning terror often accompanied by mass flight **2** : a sudden widespread fright concerning financial affairs and resulting in a depression in values caused by violent measures for protection of property (as securities) **3** *slang* : one that is very funny *syn* see FEAR — **pan·icky** \ˈpan-i-kē\ *adj*

³panic *vb* **pan·icked** \-ikt\; **pan·ick·ing** *vt* (1827) **1** : to affect with panic **2** : to produce demonstrative appreciation on the part of ⟨~ an audience with a gag⟩ ~ *vi* : to be affected with panic

panic button *n* (ca. 1950) : something setting off a precipitous emergency response ⟨there was no pushing of *panic buttons* at the White House, no rushing of troops —J. C. Harsch⟩

pan·ic grass \ˈpan-ik-\ *n* [ME *panik*, fr. MF or L; MF *panic* foxtail millet, fr. L *panicum*, fr. *panus* swelling, ear of millet] (1597) : any of various grasses (*Panicum* or related genera) of which some are important forage and cereal grasses

pan·i·cle \ˈpan-i-kəl\ *n* [L *panicula*, fr. dim. of *panus* swelling] (1597) **1** : a compound racemose inflorescence — see INFLORESCENCE illustration **2** : a pyramidal loosely branched flower cluster — **pan·i·cled** \-kəld\ *adj* — **pa·nic·u·late** \pa-ˈnik-yə-lət, pə-\ *adj*

pan·ic–strick·en \ˈpan-ik-ˌstrik-ən\ *adj* (1804) : overcome with panic

pan·i·cum \ˈpan-i-kəm\ *n* [NL, fr. L, panic grass] (ca. 1864) : any of a large and widely distributed genus (*Panicum*) of grasses that have a very diverse habit and 1- to 2-flowered spikelets arranged in a panicle

Pan·ja·bi \ˌpən-ˈjäb-ē, -ˈjab-\ *n* [Hindi *pañjābī*, fr. *pañjābī* of Punjab] (1854) **1** : an Indic language of the Punjab **2** : PUNJABI 2

pan·jan·drum \pan-ˈjan-drəm\ *n, pl* **-drums** *also* **-dra** \-drə\ [Grand *Panjandrum*, burlesque title of an imaginary personage in some nonsense lines by Samuel Foote] (1755) : a powerful personage or pretentious official

pan·leu·ko·pe·nia \ˌpan-ˌlü-kə-ˈpē-nē-ə\ *n* [NL] (1940) : an acute usu. fatal viral epizootic disease esp. of cats characterized by fever, diarrhea and dehydration, and extensive destruction of white blood cells

pan·mic·tic \(ˈ)pan-ˈmik-tik\ *adj* [*pan-* + Gk *miktos,* verbal of *mignynai* to mix] (1943) : of, relating to, or exhibiting panmixia

pan·mix·ia \-ˈmik-sē-ə\ *n* [NL, fr. *pan-* + Gk *mixis* act of mingling, mating, fr. *mignynai* to mix — more at MIX] (ca. 1889) : random mating within a breeding population

panne \ˈpan\ *n* [F, fr. OF *penne, panne* fur used for lining, fr. L *pinna* feather, wing — more at PEN] (ca. 1794) **1 :** a silk or rayon velvet with lustrous pile flattened in one direction **2 :** a heavy silk or rayon satin with high luster and waxy smoothness

pan·nier *also* **pan·ier** \ˈpan-yər, ˈpan-ē-ər\ *n* [ME *panier,* fr. MF, fr. L *panarium,* fr. *panis* bread — more at FOOD] (14c) **1 :** a large container: as **a :** a basket often carried on the back of an animal or the shoulders of a person **b :** one of a pair of packs or baskets hung over the rear wheel of a vehicle (as a bicycle) **2 a :** one of a pair of hoops formerly used to expand women's skirts at the sides **b :** an overskirt draped at the sides of a skirt for an effect of fullness

pan·ni·kin \ˈpan-i-kən\ *n* [¹*pan* + *-nikin* (as in *cannikin*)] *Brit* (1823) : a small pan or cup

pa·no·cha \pə-ˈnō-chə\ *or* **pa·no·che** \-chē\ *var of* PENUCHE

pan·o·plied \ˈpan-ə-plēd\ *adj* (1832) : dressed in or having a panoply

pan·o·ply \ˈpan-ə-plē\ *n, pl* **-plies** [Gk *panoplia,* fr. *pan-* + *hopla* arms, armor, pl. of *hoplon* tool, weapon — more at HOPLITE] (1632) **1 a :** a full suit of armor **b :** ceremonial attire **2 :** something forming a protective covering **3 a :** a magnificent or impressive array ⟨the full ~ of a military funeral⟩ **b :** a display of all appropriate appurtenances ⟨has the ~ of science fiction . . . but it is not true science fiction —Isaac Asimov⟩

pan·ora·ma \ˌpan-ə-ˈram-ə, -ˈräm-\ *n* [*pan-* + Gk *horama* sight, fr. *horan* to see — more at WARY] (1796) **1 a :** CYCLORAMA 1 **b :** a picture exhibited a part at a time by being unrolled before the spectator **2 a :** an unobstructed or complete view of an area in every direction **b :** a comprehensive presentation of a subject ⟨a ~ of American history⟩ **c :** RANGE **3 :** a mental picture of a series of images or events — **pan·oram·ic** \-ˈram-ik\ *adj* — **pan·oram·i·cal·ly** \-i-k(ə-)lē\ *adv*

pan out *vi* [²*pan*] (ca. 1868) : to turn out; *esp* : SUCCEED ⟨the signs revealed that the experiment wasn't *panning out* — Ronald Reagan⟩

pan·pipe \ˈpan-ˌpīp\ *n* [*Pan,* its traditional inventor] (1820) : a primitive wind instrument consisting of a series of short vertical pipes of graduated length bound together with the mouthpieces in an even row — often used in pl.

pan·sex·u·al \(ˈ)pan-ˈseksh-(ə-)wəl, -ˈsek-shəl\ *adj* (1926) : exhibiting or implying many forms of sexual expression — **pan·sex·u·al·i·ty** \ˌpan-ˌsek-shə-ˈwal-ət-ē\ *n*

Pan–Slav·ism \(ˈ)pan-ˈsläv-ˌiz-əm, -ˈslav-\ *n* (1850) : a political and cultural movement orig. emphasizing the cultural ties between the Slavic peoples but later associated with Russian expansionist policies — **Pan–Slav·ic** \-ˈslav-ik, -ˈsläv-\ *adj* — **Pan–Slav·ist** \-ˈsläv-əst, -ˈslav-\ *n*

pan·sy \ˈpan-zē\ *n, pl* **pansies** [MF *pensée,* fr. *pensée* thought, fr. fem. of *pensé,* pp. of *penser* to think, fr. L *pensare* to ponder — more at PENSIVE] (1500) **1 :** a garden plant (*Viola tricolor hortensis*) derived chiefly from the wild pansy of Europe by hybridizing the latter with other wild violets; *also* : its flower **2 a :** an effeminate youth — often used disparagingly **b :** a male homosexual — often used disparagingly

¹pant \ˈpant\ *vb* [ME *panten,* fr. MF *pantaisier,* fr. (assumed) VL *phantasiare* to have hallucinations, fr. Gk *phantasioun,* fr. *phantasia* appearance, imagination — more at FANCY] *vi* (15c) **1 a :** to breathe quickly, spasmodically, or in a labored manner **b :** to run panting ⟨~*ing* along beside the bicycle⟩ **c :** to move with or make a throbbing or puffing sound **2 :** to long eagerly : YEARN **3 :** THROB, PULSATE ~ *vt* : to utter with panting : GASP

²pant *n* (1500) **1 a :** a panting breath **b :** the visible movement of the chest accompanying such a breath **2 :** a throbbing or puffing sound

³pant *n* [short for *pantaloons*] (1840) **1 :** an outer garment covering each leg separately and usu. extending from the waist to the ankle — usu. used in pl. **2** *pl, chiefly Brit* : men's short underpants **3** *pl* : PANTIE — **with one's pants down :** in an embarassing position (as of being unprepared to act)

⁴pant *adj* (1899) : of or relating to pants ⟨a ~ leg⟩

pant- *or* **panto-** *comb form* [MF, fr. L, fr. Gk, fr. *pant-, pas* — more at PAN-] : all ⟨*pant*ology⟩

Pan·ta·gru·el \ˌpant-ə-ˈgrü-əl; pan-ˈtag-rə-wəl, -ˌwel\ *n* [F] : the huge son of Gargantua in Rabelais's *Pantagruel* — **Pan·ta·gru·el·ian** \ˌpant-ə-grü-ˈel-ē-ən, (ˌ)pan-ˌtag-rə-ˈwel-\ *adj* — **Pan·ta·gru·el·ism** \ˌpant-ə-ˈgrü-əl-ˌiz-əm; pan-ˈtag-rə-wəl-ˌiz-əm, -ˌwel-\ *n* — **Pan·ta·gru·el·ist** \-əst\ *n*

pan·ta·lets *or* **pan·ta·lettes** \ˌpant-ᵊl-ˈets\ *n pl* [*pantaloons*] (1834) : long drawers with a ruffle at the bottom of each leg worn esp. by women and children in the first half of the 19th century

pan·ta·loon \ˌpant-ᵊl-ˈün\ *n* [MF & OIt; MF *Pantalon,* fr. OIt *Pantaleone, Pantalone*] (1590) **1 a** *or* **pan·ta·lo·ne** \-ᵊl-ˈō-nē\ *cap* : a character in the commedia dell'arte that is usu. a skinny old dotard who wears spectacles, slippers, and a tight-fitting combination of trousers and stockings **b :** a buffoon in pantomimes **2** *pl* **a :** wide breeches worn esp. in England during the reign of Charles II **b :** close-fitting trousers usu. having straps passing under the instep and worn esp. in the 19th century **3 :** loose-fitting usu. shorter than ankle-length trousers

pant·dress \ˈpant-ˌdres\ *n* (1964) : a dress having a divided skirt

pan·tech·ni·con \pan-ˈtek-ni-kən\ *n* [short for *pantechnicon van,* fr. *pantechnicon* (storage warehouse)] *Brit* (1891) : ³VAN 1

pan·the·ism \ˈpan(t)-thē-ˌiz-əm\ *n* [F *panthéisme,* fr. *panthéiste* pantheist, fr. E *pantheist,* fr. *pan-* + *-theist*] (1732) **1 :** a doctrine that equates God with the forces and laws of the universe **2 :** the worship of all gods of different creeds, cults, or peoples indifferently; *also* : toleration of worship of all gods (as at certain periods of the Roman empire) — **pan·the·ist** \-thē-əst\ *n* — **pan·the·is·tic** \ˌpan(t)-thē-ˈis-tik\ *or* **pan·the·is·ti·cal** \-ti-kəl\ *adj* — **pan·the·is·ti·cal·ly** \-ti-k(ə-)lē\ *adv*

pan·the·on \ˈpan(t)-thē-ˌän, -ən\ *n* [ME *Panteon,* a temple at Rome, fr. L *Pantheon,* fr. Gk *pantheion* temple of all the gods, fr. neut. of *pantheios* of all gods, fr. *pan-* + *theos* god] (14c) **1 :** a temple dedicated to all the gods **2 :** a building serving as the burial place of or containing memorials to the famous dead of a nation **3 :** the gods of a people; *esp* : the officially recognized gods **4 :** a group of illustrious persons

pan·ther \ˈpan(t)-thər\ *n, pl* **panthers** *also* **panther** [ME *pantere,* fr. OF, fr. L *panthera,* fr. Gk *panthēr*] (13c) **1 :** LEOPARD: as **a :** a leopard of a hypothetical exceptionally large fierce variety **b :** a leopard of the black color phase **2 :** COUGAR **3 :** JAGUAR

pant·ie *or* **panty** \ˈpant-ē\ *n, pl* **pant·ies** [*pant*] (1845) : a woman's or child's undergarment covering the lower trunk and made with closed crotch — usu. used in pl.

pantie girdle *n* (1941) : a woman's girdle having a sewed-in or detachable crotch and made with or without garters and bones

pan·tile \ˈpan-ˌtīl\ *n* [¹*pan*] (1640) **1 :** a roofing tile whose cross section is an ogee curve **2 :** a roofing tile of which the cross section is an arc of a circle and which is laid with alternate convex and concave surfaces uppermost — **pan·tiled** \-ˌtīld\ *adj*

pant·isoc·ra·cy \ˌpant-ə-ˈsäk-rə-sē, ˌpant-ˌī-\ *n, pl* **-cies** [*pant-* + *isocracy* (equal rule), fr. Gk *isokratia,* fr. *is-* + *-kratia* -cracy] (1794) : a utopian community in which all rule equally — **pant·iso·crat·ic** \ˌpant-ˌī-sə-ˈkrat-ik\ *or* **pant·iso·crat·i·cal** \-ˈkrat-i-kəl\ *adj* — **pant·isoc·ra·tist** \ˌpant-ə-ˈsäk-rət-əst, ˌpant-ˌī-\ *n*

pan·to·fle \pan-ˈtōf-əl, -ˈtäf-, -ˈtüf-; ˈpant-ə-fəl\ *n* [ME *pantufle,* fr. MF *pantoufle*] (15c) : SLIPPER

pan·to·graph \ˈpant-ə-ˌgraf\ *n* [F *pantographe,* fr. *pant-* + *-graphe* -graph] (1723) **1 :** an instrument for copying (as a map) on a predetermined scale consisting of four light rigid bars jointed in parallelogram form; *also* : any of various extensible devices of similar construction (as for use as brackets or gates) **2 :** an electrical trolley carried by a collapsible and adjustable frame — **pan·to·graph·ic** \ˌpant-ə-ˈgraf-ik\ *adj*

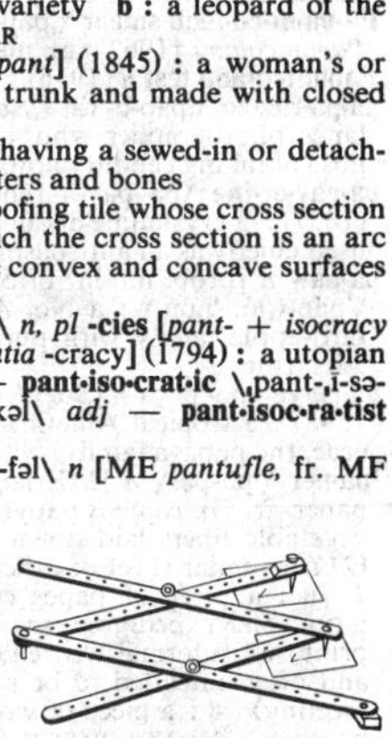

pantograph 1

¹pan·to·mime \ˈpant-ə-ˌmīm\ *n* [L *pantomimus,* fr. *pant-* + *mimus* mime] (1589) **1 :** PANTOMIMIST **2 a :** an ancient Roman dramatic performance featuring a solo dancer and a narrative chorus **b :** any of various dramatic or dancing performances in which a story is told by expressive bodily or facial movements of the performers **c :** a British theatrical entertainment of the Christmas season based on a nursery tale and featuring topical songs, tableaux, and dances **3 :** conveyance of a story by bodily or facial movements esp. in drama or dance **4 :** the art or genre of conveying a story by bodily movements only — **pan·to·mim·ic** \ˌpant-ə-ˈmim-ik\ *adj*

²pantomime *vb* **-mimed; -mim·ing** *vt* (1768) : to represent by pantomime ~ *vi* : to engage in pantomime

pan·to·mim·ist \ˈpant-ə-ˌmim-əst, -ˌmīm-\ *n* (1838) **1 :** an actor or dancer in pantomimes **2 :** a composer of pantomimes

pan·to·the·nate \ˌpant-ə-ˈthen-ˌāt, pan-ˈtäth-ə-ˌnāt\ *n* (ca. 1934) : a salt or ester of pantothenic acid

pan·to·then·ic acid \ˌpant-ə-ˌthen-ik-\ *n* [Gk *pantothen* from all sides, fr. *pant-, pas* all — more at PAN-] (1933) : a viscous oily acid $C_9H_{17}NO_5$ of the vitamin B complex found in all living tissues

pan·trop·ic \(ˈ)pan-ˈträp-ik\ *also* **pan·trop·i·cal** \-i-kəl\ *adj* (1936) : occurring or distributed throughout the tropical regions of the earth

pan·try \ˈpan-trē\ *n, pl* **pantries** [ME *panetrie,* fr. MF *paneterie,* fr. OF, fr. *panetier* servant in charge of the pantry, irreg. fr. *pan* bread, fr. L *panis* — more at FOOD] (14c) **1 :** a room or closet used for storing (as provisions) or from which food is brought to the table **2 :** a room (as in a hotel or hospital) for preparation of foods on order

pan·try·man \-trē-mən\ *n* (1563) : a man in charge of or working in a pantry (as in a hotel or hospital)

pants suit \ˈpan(t)s-ˌsüt, ˈpant-ˌ\ *n* (1966) : PANTSUIT

pant·suit \ˈpant-ˌsüt\ *n* (1964) : a woman's ensemble consisting usu. of a long jacket and tailored pants of the same material — **pant·suit·ed** *adj*

panty hose *n pl* (1963) : a one-piece undergarment for women that consists of hosiery combined with panties

panty raid *n* (ca. 1951) : a raid on a women's dormitory by college men usu. to obtain panties as trophies

panty·waist \ˈpant-ē-ˌwāst\ *n* (ca. 1936) : SISSY — **pantywaist** *adj*

Pan·urge \ˈpan-ˌərj, pa-ˈnu̇(ə)rzh\ *n* [F] : a witty rascal and companion of Pantagruel in Rabelais's *Pantagruel*

¹pan·zer \ˈpan-zər, ˈpän(t)-sər\ *n* [G *panzer,* fr. *panzer* coat of mail, armor, fr. OF *pancière,* fr. *pance* belly — more at PAUNCH] (ca. 1939) : TANK 3

²panzer *adj* (ca. 1940) : of or relating to an armored unit and esp. a panzer division

panzer division *n* (ca. 1939) : a German armored division

¹pap \ˈpap\ *n* [ME *pappe*] (13c) **1** *chiefly dial* : NIPPLE, TEAT **2 :** something shaped like a nipple

²pap *n* [ME] (15c) **1 :** a soft food for infants or invalids **2 :** political patronage **3 :** something lacking solid value or substance

pa·pa \ˈpäp-ə, *chiefly Brit* pə-ˈpä\ *n* [F (baby talk)] (1681) : FATHER

Papa (1952) — a communications code word for the letter *p*

pa·pa·cy \ˈpā-pə-sē\ *n, pl* **-cies** [ME *papacie,* fr. ML *papatia,* fr. LL *papa* pope — more at POPE] (14c) **1 :** the office of pope **2 :** a succession or line of popes **3 :** the term of a pope's reign **4** *cap* : the system of government of the Roman Catholic Church of which the pope is the supreme head

pa·pa·in \pə-ˈpā-ən, -ˈpī-ən\ *n* [ISV, fr. *papaya*] (ca. 1890) : a proteinase in the juice of unripe papaya that is used esp. as a tenderizer for meat and in medicine

pa·pal \ˈpā-pəl\ *adj* [ME, fr. MF, fr. ML *papalis,* fr. LL *papa*] (14c) : of or relating to a pope or to the Roman Catholic Church — **pa·pal·ly** \-pə-lē\ *adv*

papal cross *n* (ca. 1890) **:** a figure of a cross having a long upright shaft and three crossbars with the longest at or somewhat above its middle and the two other successively shorter crossbars above the longest one — see CROSS illustration

papal infallibility *n* (1870) **:** the Roman Catholic doctrine that the pope cannot err when speaking ex cathedra in defining a doctrine of Christian faith or morals

Pa·pa·ni·co·laou smear \ˌpäp-ə-ˈnē-kə-ˌlau̇-, ˌpap-ə-ˈnik-ə-\ *n* [George N. *Papanicolaou* †1962 Am. medical scientist] (1950) **:** PAP SMEAR

Papanicolaou test *n* (1946) **:** PAP SMEAR

pa·pa·raz·zo \ˌpäp-ə-ˈrät-(ˌ)sō\ *n, pl* **-raz·zi** \-(ˌ)sē\ [It] (1966) **:** a free-lance photographer who aggressively pursues celebrities for the purpose of taking candid photographs

pa·pav·er·ine \pə-ˈpav-ə-ˌrēn, -(ə-)rən\ *n* [ISV, fr. L *papaver* poppy] (1857) **:** a crystalline alkaloid $C_{20}H_{21}NO_4$ that is found in opium and is used chiefly as an antispasmodic for its ability to relax smooth muscle

pa·paw *n* [prob. modif. of Sp *papaya*] (1624) **1** \pə-ˈpȯ\ **:** PAPAYA **2** \ˈpäp-(ˌ)ȯ, ˈpȯp-\ **:** a No. American tree (*Asimina triloba*) of the custard-apple family with purple flowers and a yellow edible fruit; *also* **:** its fruit

pa·pa·ya \pə-ˈpī-ə\ *n* [Sp, of AmerInd origin; akin to Otomac *papai*] (ca. 1598) **:** a tropical American tree (*Carica papaya* of the family Caricaceae, the papaya family) with oblong yellow edible fruit; *also* **:** its fruit

¹pa·per \ˈpā-pər\ *n* [ME *papir*, fr. MF *papier*, fr. L *papyrus* papyrus, paper, fr. Gk *papyros* papyrus] (14c) **1 a** (1) **:** a felted sheet of usu. vegetable fibers laid down on a fine screen from a water suspension (2) **:** a similar sheet of other material (as plastic) **b :** a piece of paper **2 a :** a piece of paper containing a written or printed statement **:** DOCUMENT ⟨pedigree ~*s*⟩ **b :** a piece of paper containing writing or print **c :** a formal written composition often designed for publication and often intended to be read aloud ⟨presented a scholarly ~ at the meeting⟩ **d :** a piece of written schoolwork **3 :** a paper container or wrapper **4 :** NEWSPAPER **5 :** the negotiable notes or instruments of commerce **6 :** WALLPAPER **7 :** TICKETS; *esp* **:** free passes **8 :** PAPERBACK — **on paper 1 :** in theory ⟨the plan looks good *on paper*⟩ **2 :** figured at face value ⟨*on paper* he was worth nearly a million dollars⟩

²paper *vb* **pa·pered; pa·per·ing** \ˈpā-p(ə-)riŋ\ *vt* (1594) **1** *archaic* **:** to put down or describe in writing **2 :** to fold or enclose in paper **3 :** to cover or line with paper; *esp* **:** to apply wallpaper to **4 :** to fill by giving out free passes ⟨~ the theater for opening night⟩ **5 :** to cover (an area) with advertising bills, circulars, or posters ~ *vi* **:** to hang wallpaper — **pa·per·er** \-pər-ər\ *n*

³paper *adj* (1596) **1 a :** made of paper, paperboard, or papier-mâché ⟨a ~ bag⟩ **b :** PAPERY **2 :** of or relating to clerical work or written communication **3 :** existing only in theory **:** NOMINAL ⟨a ~ blockade⟩ **4 :** admitted by free passes ⟨a ~ audience⟩ **5 :** finished with a crisp smooth surface similar to that of paper ⟨~ taffeta⟩

pa·per·back \ˈpā-pər-ˌbak\ *n* (1899) **:** a book with a flexible paper binding — **paperback** *also* **pa·per·backed** \-ˌbakt\ *adj*

paper birch *n* (1810) **:** an American birch (*Betula papyrifera*) with peeling white bark that is often worked into fancy articles

pa·per·board \ˈpā-pər-ˌbō(ə)rd, -ˌbȯ(ə)rd\ *n* (1549) **:** a material made from cellulose fiber (as wood pulp) like paper but usu. thicker

pa·per·bound \-ˌbau̇nd\ *n* (1950) **:** PAPERBACK — **paperbound** *adj*

pa·per·boy \-ˌbȯi\ *n* (1876) **:** NEWSBOY

paper clip *n* (1919) **:** a length of wire bent into flat loops that is used to hold papers together

paper cutter *n* (1821) **1 :** PAPER KNIFE **2 :** a machine or device for cutting or trimming sheets of paper to required dimensions

pa·per·hang·er \ˈpā-pər-ˌhaŋ-ər\ *n* (1796) **1 :** one that applies wallpaper **2** *slang* **:** one who passes worthless checks

pa·per·hang·ing \-ˌhaŋ-iŋ\ *n* (1873) **:** the act of applying wallpaper

paper knife *n* (1806) **1 :** a knife for slitting envelopes or uncut pages **2 :** the knife of a paper cutter

pa·per·mak·er \ˈpā-pər-ˌmā-kər\ *n* (ca. 1573) **:** one that makes paper — **pa·per·mak·ing** \-kiŋ\ *n*

paper money *n* (1691) **1 :** money consisting of government notes and bank notes **2 :** BANK MONEY

paper mulberry *n* (1811) **:** an Asian tree (*Broussonetia papyrifera*) of the mulberry family that is widely grown as a shade tree

paper nautilus *n* (1835) **:** a cephalopod (genus *Argonauta*) whose female has a delicate papery shell

paper over *vt* (1955) **1 :** to gloss over, explain away, or patch up (as major differences or disparities) esp. in order to maintain a semblance of unity or agreement **2 :** HIDE, CONCEAL

paper profit *n* (1893) **:** a profit that can be realized only by selling something (as a security) that has appreciated in market value

paper–thin *adj* (1928) **:** extremely thin ⟨~ partitions⟩

paper tiger *n* (1949) **:** one that is outwardly powerful or dangerous but inwardly weak or ineffectual

paper trail *n* (1965) **:** a body of documents (as financial records) collected during an investigation of a course of events

pa·per·weight \ˈpā-pər-ˌwāt\ *n* (ca. 1858) **:** a usu. small heavy object used to hold down loose papers (as on a desk)

pa·per·work \-ˌwərk\ *n* (1889) **:** routine clerical or record-keeping work often incidental to a more important task

pa·pery \ˈpā-p(ə-)rē\ *adj* (1627) **:** resembling paper in thinness or consistency ⟨~ leaves⟩ ⟨~ silk⟩ — **pa·per·i·ness** *n*

pa·pe·terie \ˈpap-ə-trē, ˌpap-ə-ˈ\ *n* [F] (ca. 1847) **:** packaged fancy stationery

¹Pa·phi·an \ˈpā-fē-ən\ *n* [L *paphius*, fr. Gk *paphios*, fr. *Paphos*, ancient city of Cyprus that was the center of worship of Aphrodite] (1598) **1** *often not cap* **:** PROSTITUTE **2 :** a native or inhabitant of Paphos

²Paphian *adj* (1611) **1 :** of or relating to illicit love **:** WANTON **2 :** of or relating to Paphos or its people

pa·pia·men·to \ˌpäp-yə-ˈmen-(ˌ)tō\ *also* **pa·pia·men·tu** \-(ˌ)tü\ *n* [Sp, fr. Papiamento *papia* talk + *-mento* ment] (1923) **:** a Spanish-based creole language of Netherlands Antilles

pa·pier col·lé \ˌpäp-ˌyā-(ˌ)kō-ˈlā, ˌpap-\ *n, pl* **papiers collés** \-ˌyā-(ˌ)kō-ˈlā(z)\ [F, glued paper] (ca. 1934) **:** COLLAGE

¹pa·pier–mâ·ché \ˌpā-pər-mə-ˈshā, ˌpap-ˌyā-mə-, -(ˌ)ma-\ *n* [F, lit., chewed paper] (1753) **:** a light strong molding material of wastepaper pulped with glue and other additives

²papier–mâché *adj* (1753) **1 :** formed of papier-mâché **2 :** UNREAL, ARTIFICIAL

pa·pil·i·o·na·ceous \pə-ˌpil-ē-ə-ˈnā-shəs\ *adj* [L *papilion-*, *papilio* butterfly — more at PAVILION] (1668) **:** having a corolla (as in the bean or pea) with usu. five petals that include a large standard enclosing two lateral wings and a lower carina

pa·pil·la \pə-ˈpil-ə\ *n, pl* **pa·pil·lae** \-ˈpil-(ˌ)ē, -ˌī\ [L, nipple; akin to L *papula* pimple, Lith *papas* nipple] (1713) **:** a small projecting body part similar to a nipple in form: **a :** a vascular process of connective tissue extending into and nourishing the root of a hair, feather, or developing tooth **b :** any of the vascular protuberances of the dermal layer of the skin extending into the epidermal layer and often containing tactile corpuscles **c :** any of the small protuberances on the upper surface of the tongue — **pap·il·lary** \ˈpap-ə-ˌler-ē, *esp Brit* pə-ˈpil-ə-rē\ *adj* — **pa·pil·late** \ˈpap-ə-ˌlāt, pə-ˈpil-ət\ *adj* — **pa·pil·lose** \ˈpap-ə-ˌlōs, pə-ˈpil-ˌōs\ *adj*

pap·il·lo·ma \ˌpap-ə-ˈlō-mə\ *n, pl* **-mas** *or* **-ma·ta** \-mət-ə\ (1866) **1 :** a benign tumor (as a wart) due to overgrowth of epithelial tissue on papillae of vascular connective tissue (as of the skin) **2 :** an epithelial tumor caused by a virus — **pap·il·lo·ma·tous** \-ˈlō-mət-əs\ *adj*

pa·pil·lon \ˌpäp-ē-ˈ(y)ōⁿ, ˌpap-\ *n* [F, lit., butterfly, fr. L *papilion-*, *papilio*] (1907) **:** any of a breed of small slender toy spaniels having large erect heavily fringed ears

pa·pil·lote \ˌpäp-ē-ˈ(y)ōt, ˌpap-\ *n* [F, fr. *papillon* butterfly] (1818) **:** a greased usu. paper wrapper in which food (as meat or fish) is cooked

pa·pist \ˈpā-pəst\ *n, often cap* [MF or NL; MF *papiste*, fr. *pape* pope; NL *papista*, fr. LL *papa* pope] (1534) **:** ROMAN CATHOLIC — usu. used disparagingly — **papist** *adj*

pa·pist·ry \ˈpā-pə-strē\ *n* (1549) **:** the Roman Catholic religion — usu. used disparagingly

pa·poose \pa-ˈpüs, pə-\ *n* [Narraganset *papoòs*] (1634) **:** a young child of American Indian parents

pa·po·va·vi·rus \pə-ˈpō-və-ˌvī-rəs\ *n* [*pa*pilloma + *po*lyoma + *va*cuolation + *virus*] (1962) **:** any of a group of viruses that have a capsid with 42 protuberances resembling knobs and that are associated with or responsible for various neoplasms (as some warts) of mammals

pap·pose \ˈpap-ˌōs\ *adj* (1691) **:** having or being a pappus

pap·pus \ˈpap-əs\ *n, pl* **pap·pi** \ˈpap-ˌī, -ˌē\ [L, fr. Gk *pappos*] (ca. 1704) **:** an appendage or tuft of appendages that crowns the ovary or fruit in various seed plants and functions in dispersal of the fruit

pap·py \ˈpap-ē\ *n, chiefly Southern & Midland* (1763) **:** PAPA

pa·pri·ka \pə-ˈprē-kə, pa-\ *n* [Hung, fr. Serb, fr. *papar* pepper, fr. Gk *peperi*] (ca. 1896) **:** a usu. mild red condiment consisting of the dried finely ground pods of various cultivated sweet peppers; *also* **:** a sweet pepper used for making paprika

Pap smear \ˈpap-\ *n* [George N. *Papanicolaou* †1962 Am. medical scientist] (1952) **:** a method for the early detection of cancer employing exfoliated cells and a special staining technique that differentiates diseased tissue — called also *Papanicolaou smear, Papanicolaou test, Pap test*

Pap·u·an \ˈpap-yə-wən\ *n* (1814) **1 :** a native or inhabitant of Papua **2 :** a member of any of the Negroid native peoples of New Guinea and adjacent areas of Melanesia **3 :** any of a heterogeneous group of languages spoken in New Guinea, New Britain, and the Solomon islands — **Papuan** *adj*

pap·u·lar \ˈpap-yə-lər\ *adj* (1818) **:** consisting of or characterized by papules

pap·ule \ˈpap-(ˌ)yü(ə)l\ *n* [L *papula*] (ca. 1828) **:** a small solid usu. conical elevation of the skin

pap·y·rol·o·gy \ˌpap-ə-ˈräl-ə-jē\ *n* [ISV] (1898) **:** the study of papyrus manuscripts — **pap·y·rol·o·gist** \-jəst\ *n*

pa·py·rus \pə-ˈpī-rəs\ *n, pl* **pa·py·rus·es** *or* **pa·py·ri** \-ˈpī(ə)r-(ˌ)ē, -ˌī\ [ME, fr. L — more at PAPER] (14c) **1 :** a tall sedge (*Cyperus papyrus*) of the Nile valley **2 :** the pith of the papyrus plant esp. when cut in strips and pressed into a material to write on **3 a :** a writing on papyrus **b :** a written scroll made of papyrus

¹par \ˈpär\ *n* [L, one that is equal, fr. *par* equal] (1622) **1 a :** the established value of the monetary unit of one country expressed in terms of the monetary unit of another country using the same metal as the standard of value **b :** the face amount of an instrument of value (as a check or note): as (1) **:** the monetary value assigned to each share of stock in the charter of a corporation (2) **:** the principal of a bond **2 :** common level **:** EQUALITY — usu. used with *on* ⟨judged the recording to be on a ~ with previous ones⟩ **3 a :** an amount taken as an average or norm **b :** an accepted standard; *specif* **:** a usual standard of physical condition or health **4 :** the score standard for each hole of a golf course; *also* **:** a score equal to par — **par** *adj*

²par *vt* **parred; par·ring** (1950) **:** to score par on (a hole)

pa·ra \ˈpär-ə\ *n, pl* **paras** *or* **para** [Turk, fr. Per *pārah*, lit., piece] (1687) **1 a :** any of several monetary units of the Turkish Empire **b :** a coin representing one para **2** — see *dinar* at MONEY table

¹para- \ˌpar-ə, ˈpar-ə\ *or* **par-** *prefix* [ME, fr. MF, fr. L, fr. Gk, fr. *para*; akin to Gk *pro* before — more at FOR] **1 :** beside **:** alongside of **:** beyond **:** aside from ⟨*para*thyroid⟩ ⟨*par*enteral⟩ **2 a :** closely related to ⟨*para*ldehyde⟩ **b :** involving substitution at or characterized by two opposite positions in the benzene ring that are separated by two carbon atoms ⟨*para*dichlorobenzene⟩ **3 a :** faulty **:** abnormal ⟨*par*esthesia⟩ **b :** associated in a subsidiary or accessory capacity ⟨*para*medical⟩ **c :** closely resembling **:** almost ⟨*para*typhoid⟩

²para- \ˈpar-ə\ *comb form* [*parachute*] **1 :** parachute ⟨*para*trooper⟩ **2 :** parachutist ⟨*para*spotter⟩

-p·a·ra \p-ə-rə\ *n comb form, pl* **-p·a·ras** \-ə-rəz\ *or* **-p·a·rae** \-ə-ˌrē, -ˌrī\ [L, fr. *parere* to give birth to — more at PARE] **:** woman delivered of (so many) children ⟨*tri*para⟩

para–ami·no·ben·zo·ic acid \ˈpar-ə-ə-ˌmē-ˌnō-ˌben-ˌzō-ik-, ˈpar-ə-ˌam-ə-(ˌ)nō-\ *n* [ISV] (1906) **:** a colorless para-substituted aminobenzoic acid that is a growth factor of the vitamin B complex

para–ami·no·sal·i·cyl·ic acid \-ˌsal-ə-ˌsil-ik-\ *n* (1946) **:** the white crystalline para-substituted isomer of aminosalicylic acid that is made synthetically and is used in the treatment of tuberculosis

para·bi·o·sis \ˌpar-ə-(ˌ)bī-ˈō-səs, -bē-\ *n* [NL] (ca. 1903) **1 :** reversible suspension of obvious vital activities **2 :** anatomical and physiological union of two organisms — **para·bi·ot·ic** \-ˈät-ik\ *adj* — **para·bi·ot·i·cal·ly** \-i-k(ə-)lē\ *adv*

par·a·ble \'par-ə-bəl\ *n* [ME, fr. MF, fr. LL *parabola*, fr. Gk *parabolē*, fr. *paraballein* to compare, fr. *para-* + *ballein* to throw — more at DEVIL] (14c) : COMPARISON; *specif* : a usu. short fictitious story that illustrates a moral attitude or a religious principle

pa·rab·o·la \pə-'rab-ə-lə\ *n* [NL, fr. Gk *parabolē*, lit., comparison] (1558) **1** : a plane curve generated by a point moving so that its distance from a fixed point is equal to its distance from a fixed line : the intersection of a right circular cone with a plane parallel to an element of the cone **2** : something bowl-shaped (as an antenna or microphone reflector)

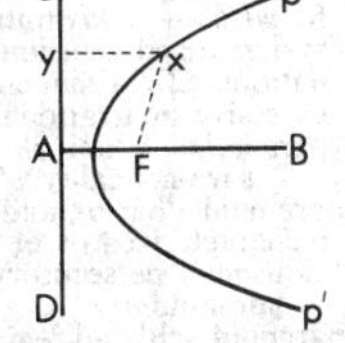

parabola 1: *F* fixed point; *CD* fixed line; *x* moving point; *AB* axis; *xy* distance from *x* to *CD*; *pp'* parabola

par·a·bol·ic \,par-ə-'bäl-ik\ *adj* [in sense 1, fr. LL *parabola* parable; in sense 2, fr. NL *parabola*] (1669) **1** : expressed by or being a parable : ALLEGORICAL **2** : of, having the form of, or relating to a parabola ⟨motion in a ~ curve⟩ — **par·a·bol·i·cal·ly** \-i-k(ə-)lē\ *adv*

pa·rab·o·loid \pə-'rab-ə-,lȯid\ *n* (1702) : a surface all of whose intersections by planes are either parabolas and ellipses or parabolas and hyperbolas — **pa·rab·o·loi·dal** \-,rab-ə-'lȯid-ᵊl\ *adj*

¹para·chute \'par-ə-,shüt\ *n* [F, fr. *para-* (as in *parasol*) + *chute* fall — more at CHUTE] (1785) **1** : a folding umbrella-shaped device of light fabric used esp. for making a safe descent from an aircraft **2** : PATAGIUM **3** : a device or structure suggestive of a parachute in form, use, or operation — **para·chut·ic** \,par-ə-'shüt-ik\ *adj*

²parachute *vb* **-chut·ed; -chut·ing** *vt* (1809) : to convey by means of a parachute ~ *vi* : to descend by means of a parachute

parachute spinnaker *n* (1932) : an exceptionally large spinnaker used esp. on racing yachts

para·chut·ist \'par-ə-,shüt-əst\ *n* (1888) : one that parachutes: as **a** : PARATROOPER **b** : a person who parachutes as a sport

Par·a·clete \'par-ə-,klēt\ *n* [ME *Paraclit*, fr. MF *Paraclet*, fr. LL *Paracletus*, fr. Gk *Paraklētos*, lit., advocate, intercessor, fr. *parakalein* to invoke, fr. *para-* + *kalein* call — more at LOW] (15c) : HOLY SPIRIT

¹pa·rade \pə-'rād\ *n* [F, fr. MF, fr. *parer* to prepare — more at PARE] (ca. 1656) **1** : a pompous show : EXHIBITION **2 a** : the ceremonial formation of a body of troops before a superior officer **b** : a place where troops assemble regularly for parade **3 a** : an informal procession **b** : a public procession **c** : a showy array or succession ⟨a ~ of tycoons' castles —Gail Sheehy⟩ **4 a** : a place for strolling **b** : those who promenade

²parade *vb* **pa·rad·ed; pa·rad·ing** *vt* (1686) **1** : to cause to maneuver or march : MARSHAL **2** : PROMENADE **3** : to exhibit ostentatiously ~ *vi* **1** : to march in or as if in a procession **2** : PROMENADE **3 a** : to show off **b** : MASQUERADE ⟨myths which ~ as modern science —M. R. Cohen⟩ ***syn*** see SHOW — **pa·rad·er** *n*

para·di·chlo·ro·ben·zene \,par-ə-,dī-,klōr-ə-'ben-,zēn, -,klȯr-, -,ben-'\ *n* [ISV] (1876) : a white crystalline compound $C_6H_4Cl_2$ made by chlorinating benzene and used chiefly as a fumigant against clothes moths

par·a·did·dle \'par-ə-,did-ᵊl\ *n* [origin unknown] (1927) : a quick succession of drumbeats slower than a roll and alternating left- and right-hand strokes in a typical L-R-L-L, R-L-R-R pattern

par·a·digm \'par-ə-,dīm, -,dim\ *n* [LL *paradigma*, fr. Gk *paradeigma*, fr. *paradeiknynai* to show side by side, fr. *para-* + *deiknynai* to show — more at DICTION] (15c) **1** : EXAMPLE, PATTERN; *esp* : an outstandingly clear or typical example or archetype **2** : an example of a conjugation or declension showing a word in all its inflectional forms — **par·a·dig·mat·ic** \,par-ə-dig-'mat-ik\ *adj* — **par·a·dig·mat·i·cal·ly** \-i-k(ə-)lē\ *adv*

par·a·di·sa·ic \,par-ə-,dī-'sā-ik, -'zā-\ *adj* [*paradise* + *-aic* (as in *Hebraic*)] (1754) : PARADISIACAL — **par·a·di·sa·ical** \-'sā-ə-kəl, -'zā-\ *adj* — **par·a·di·sa·ical·ly** \-ə-k(ə-)lē\ *adv*

par·a·dis·al \,par-ə-'dī-səl, -'dī-zəl\ *adj* (1560) : PARADISIACAL

par·a·dise \'par-ə-,dīs, -,dīz\ *n* [ME *paradis*, fr. OF, fr. LL *paradisus*, fr. Gk *paradeisos*, lit., enclosed park, of Iranian origin; akin to Av *pairi-daēza-* enclosure; akin to Gk *peri* around and to Gk *teichos* wall — more at PERI-, DOUGH] (12c) **1 a** : the garden of Eden **b** : an intermediate place or state where the righteous departed await resurrection and judgment **c** : HEAVEN **2** : a place or state of bliss, felicity, or delight

par·a·di·si·a·cal \,par-ə-də-'sī-ə-kəl, -,dī-, -'zī-\ *or* **par·a·dis·i·ac** \-'diz-ē-,ak, -'dis-\ *adj* [LL *paradisiacus*, fr. *paradisus*] (1649) : of, relating to, or resembling paradise — **par·a·di·si·a·cal·ly** \-də-'sī-ə-k(ə-)lē, -,dī-, -'zī-\ *adv*

pa·ra·dor \,pä-rä-'t͟hȯr\ *n* [Sp, akin to Sp *parar* to stop, prepare, fr. L *parare* to prepare — more at PARE] (1845) : a usu. government-operated hostelry found esp. in Spain

par·a·dox \'par-ə-,däks\ *n* [L *paradoxum*, fr. Gk *paradoxon*, fr. neut. of *paradoxos* contrary to expectation, fr. *para-* + *dokein* to think — more at DECENT] (1540) **1** : a tenet contrary to received opinion **2 a** : a statement that is seemingly contradictory or opposed to common sense and yet is perhaps true **b** : a self-contradictory statement that at first seems true **c** : an argument that apparently derives self-contradictory conclusions by valid deduction from acceptable premises **3** : something (as a person, condition, or act) with seemingly contradictory qualities or phases

par·a·dox·i·cal \,par-ə-'däk-si-kəl\ *adj* (1581) **1 a** : of the nature of a paradox **b** : inclined to paradoxes **2** : not being the normal or usual kind ⟨~ pulse⟩ — **par·a·dox·i·cal·i·ty** \-,däk-si-'kal-ət-ē\ *n* — **par·a·dox·i·cal·ly** \-'däk-si-k(ə-)lē\ *adv* — **par·a·dox·i·cal·ness** \-kəl-nəs\ *n*

paradoxical sleep *n* (1964) : REM SLEEP

par·aes·the·sia *var of* PARESTHESIA

¹par·af·fin \'par-ə-fən\ *n* [G, fr. L *parum* too little (akin to L *paucus* few) + *affinis* bordering on — more at FEW, AFFINITY] (1838) **1 a** : a waxy crystalline flammable substance obtained esp. from distillates of wood, coal, petroleum, or shale oil that is a complex mixture of hydrocarbons and is used chiefly in coating and sealing, in candles, in rubber compounding, and in pharmaceuticals and cosmetics **b** : any of various mixtures of similar hydrocarbons including mixtures that are semisolid or oily **2** : ALKANE **3** *chiefly Brit* : KEROSENE — **par·af·fin·ic** \,par-ə-'fin-ik\ *adj*

²paraffin *vt* (1876) : to coat or saturate with paraffin

para·for·mal·de·hyde \,par-ə-fȯr-'mal-də-,hīd, -fər-\ *n* (1894) : a white powder $(CH_2O)_x$ that consists of a polymer of formaldehyde and is used esp. as a fungicide

para·gen·e·sis \,par-ə-'jen-ə-səs\ *n* [NL] (1853) : the formation of minerals in contact in such a manner as to affect one another's development — **para·ge·net·ic** \-jə-'net-ik\ *adj* — **para·ge·net·i·cal·ly** \-i-k(ə-)lē\ *adv*

¹par·a·gon \'par-ə-,gän, -gən\ *n* [MF, fr. OIt *paragone*, lit., touchstone, fr. *paragonare* to test on a touchstone, fr. Gk *parakonan* to sharpen, fr. *para-* + *akonē* whetstone, fr. *akē* point; akin to Gk *akmē* point — more at EDGE] (1548) : a model of excellence or perfection

²paragon *vt* (1586) **1** : to compare with : PARALLEL **2** : to put in rivalry : MATCH **3** *obs* : SURPASS

¹para·graph \'par-ə-,graf\ *n* [MF & ML; MF *paragraphe*, fr. ML *paragraphus* sign marking a paragraph, fr. Gk *paragraphos* line used to mark change of persons in a dialogue, fr. *paragraphein* to write alongside, fr. *para-* + *graphein* to write — more at CARVE] (1525) **1 a** : a subdivision of a written composition that consists of one or more sentences, deals with one point or gives the words of one speaker, and begins on a new usu. indented line **b** : a short composition or note that is complete in one paragraph **2** : a character (as ¶) used to indicate the beginning of a paragraph and as a reference mark — **para·graph·ic** \,par-ə-'graf-ik\ *adj*

²paragraph *vt* (1764) **1** : to write paragraphs about **2** : to divide into paragraphs ~ *vi* : to write paragraphs

para·graph·er \'par-ə-,graf-ər\ *n* (1822) : a writer of paragraphs esp. for the editorial page of a newspaper

para·in·flu·en·za virus \'par-ə-,in-flü-,en-zə-\ *n* (1959) : any of several myxoviruses that are associated with or responsible for some respiratory infections in children — called also *parainfluenza*

para·jour·nal·ism \'par-ə-,jərn-ᵊl-,iz-əm\ *n* (1965) : journalism that is heavily colored by the opinions of the reporter

par·a·keet \'par-ə-,kēt\ *n* [Sp & MF; Sp *periquito*, fr. MF *perroquet* parrot] (1581) : any of numerous usu. small slender parrots with a long graduated tail

para·lan·guage \'par-ə-,laŋ-gwij\ *n* (ca. 1958) : optional vocal effects (as tone of voice) that accompany or modify the phonemes of an utterance and that may communicate meaning

par·al·de·hyde \pa-'ral-də-,hīd, pə-\ *n* (1857) : a colorless liquid polymeric modification $C_6H_{12}O_3$ of acetaldehyde used as a hypnotic

para·le·gal \,par-ə-'lē-gəl\ *adj* (1971) : of, relating to, or being a paraprofessional who assists a lawyer — **para·le·gal** \'par-ə-,lē-gəl\ *n*

para·lin·guis·tics \,par-ə-liŋ-'gwis-tiks\ *n* (ca. 1958) : the study of paralanguage — **para·lin·guis·tic** \-tik\ *adj*

Par·a·li·pom·e·non \,par-ə-lə-'päm-ə-,nän, -lī-\ *n* [LL, fr. Gk *Paraleipomenōn*, gen. of *Paraleipomena*, lit. things left out, fr. neut. pl. of prp. passive of *paraleipein* to leave out, fr. *para-* + *leipein* to leave; fr. its forming a supplement to Samuel and Kings — more at LOAN] : CHRONICLES

par·al·lac·tic \,par-ə-'lak-tik\ *adj* [NL *parallacticus*, fr. Gk *parallaktikos*, fr. *parallaxis*] (1630) : of, relating to, or due to parallax

par·al·lax \'par-ə-,laks\ *n* [MF *parallaxe*, fr. Gk *parallaxis*, fr. *parallassein* to change, fr. *para-* + *allassein* to change, fr. *allos* other] (1594) : the apparent displacement or the difference in apparent direction of an object as seen from two different points not on a straight line with the object; *specif* : the difference in direction of a celestial body as measured from two points on the earth

¹par·al·lel \'par-ə-,lel, -ləl\ *adj* [L *parallelus*, fr. Gk *parallēlos*, fr. *para* beside + *allēlōn* of one another, fr. *allos . . . allos* one . . . another, fr. *allos* other — more at ELSE] (1549) **1 a** : extending in the same direction, everywhere equidistant, and not meeting ⟨~ rows of trees⟩ **b** : everywhere equally distant ⟨concentric spheres are ~⟩ **2 a** : having parallel sides ⟨a ~ reamer⟩ **b** : being or relating to an electrical circuit having a number of conductors in parallel **c** : arranged in parallel ⟨a ~ computer⟩ **3 a** : similar, analogous, or interdependent in tendency or development **b** : readily compared : COMPANION **c** : having identical syntactical elements in corresponding positions **d (1)** : having the same tonic — used of major and minor keys and scales **(2)** : keeping the same distance apart in musical pitch **4** : performed while keeping one's skis parallel ⟨~ turns⟩ ***syn*** see SIMILAR

²parallel *n* (1551) **1 a** : a parallel line, curve, or surface **b** : one of the imaginary circles on the surface of the earth paralleling the equator and marking the latitude; *also* : the corresponding line on a globe or map — see LATITUDE illustration **c** : a character ‖ used in printing as a reference mark **2 a** : something equal or similar in all essential particulars : COUNTERPART **b** : SIMILARITY, ANALOGUE **3** : a comparison to show resemblance : a tracing of similarity **4 a** : the state of being physically parallel : PARALLELISM **b** : the arrangement of electrical devices in which all positive poles, electrodes, and terminals are joined to one conductor and all negative ones to another conductor so that each unit is in effect on a parallel branch **c** : an arrangement or state that permits several operations or tasks to be performed simultaneously rather than consecutively

³parallel *vt* (1598) **1** : to indicate analogy of : COMPARE **2 a** : to show something equal to : MATCH **b** : to correspond to **3** : to place so as to be parallel in direction with something **4** : to extend, run, or move in a direction parallel to

⁴parallel *adv* (1787) : in a parallel manner

parallel bars *n pl* (1868) **1** : a pair of wooden bars supported horizontally above the floor at the same height or at different heights usu. by a common base and used in gymnastics **2** : an event in gymnastics competition in which even or uneven parallel bars are used

par·al·lel·epi·ped \,par-ə-,lel-ə-'pī-pəd, -'pip-əd; -,lel-'ep-ə-,ped\ *n* [Gk *parallēlepipedon*, fr. *parallēlos* + *epipedon* plane surface, fr. neut. of *epipedos* flat, fr. *epi-* epi- + *pedon* ground; akin to L *ped-*, *pes* foot — more at FOOT] (1570) : a 6-faced polyhedron all of whose faces are parallelograms lying in pairs of parallel planes

par·al·lel·ism \'par-ə-,lel-,iz-əm, -ləl-\ *n* (1610) **1 :** the quality or state of being parallel **2 :** RESEMBLANCE, CORRESPONDENCE **3 :** recurrent syntactical similarities introduced for rhetorical effect **4 :** a theory that mind and matter accompany one another but are not causally related **5 :** the development of similar new characters by two or more related organisms in response to similarity of environment — called also *parallel evolution*

par·al·lel·o·gram \,par-ə-'lel-ə-,gram\ *n* [LL or Gk; LL *parallelogrammum,* fr. Gk *parallēlogrammon,* fr. neut. of *parallēlogrammos* bounded by parallel lines, fr. *parallēlos* + *grammē* line, fr. *graphein* to write — more at CARVE] (1570) **:** a quadrilateral with opposite sides parallel and equal

par·al·lel–veined \,par-ə-,lel-'vānd, -ləl-\ *adj, of a leaf* (1861) **:** having veins arranged nearly parallel to one another — compare NET-VEINED

pa·ral·o·gism \pə-'ral-ə-,jiz-əm\ *n* [MF *paralogisme,* fr. LL *paralogismus,* fr. Gk *paralogismos,* fr. *paralogos* unreasonable, fr. *para-* + *logos* speech, reason — more at LEGEND] (1565) **:** a fallacious argument

par·a·lyse *Brit var of* PARALYZE

pa·ral·y·sis \pə-'ral-ə-səs\ *n, pl* **-y·ses** \-,sēz\ [L, fr. Gk, fr. *paralyein* to loosen, disable, fr. *para-* + *lyein* to loosen — more at LOSE] (1525) **1 :** complete or partial loss of function esp. when involving the motion or sensation in a part of the body **2 :** loss of the ability to move **3 :** a state of powerlessness or incapacity to act

paralysis agi·tans \-'aj-ə-,tanz\ *n* [NL, lit., shaking palsy] (1817) **:** PARKINSON'S DISEASE

1par·a·lyt·ic \,par-ə-'lit-ik\ *adj* [ME *paralytyk,* fr. MF *paralitike,* fr. L *paralyticus,* fr. Gk *paralytikos,* fr. *paralyein*] (14c) **1 :** affected with or characterized by paralysis **2 :** of, relating to, or resembling paralysis — **par·a·lyt·i·cal·ly** \-i-k(ə-)lē\ *adv*

2paralytic *n* (14c) **:** one affected with paralysis

par·a·lyze \'par-ə-,līz\ *vt* **-lyzed; -lyz·ing** [F *paralyser,* back-formation fr. *paralysie* paralysis, fr. L *paralysis*] (1804) **1 :** to affect with paralysis **2 :** to make powerless or ineffective **3 :** UNNERVE **4 :** STUN, STUPEFY **5 :** to bring to an end **:** PREVENT, DESTROY — **par·a·ly·za·tion** \,par-ə-lə-'zā-shən\ *n* — **par·a·lyz·er** \'par-ə-,lī-zər\ *n* — **par·a·lyz·ing·ly** \-,lī-ziŋ-lē\ *adv*

para·mag·net \'par-ə-,mag-nət\ *n* [back-formation fr. *paramagnetic*] (ca. 1900) **:** a paramagnetic substance

para·mag·net·ic \,par-ə-mag-'net-ik\ *adj* [ISV] (ca. 1850) **:** being or relating to a magnetizable substance that like aluminum and platinum has small but positive susceptibility varying but little with magnetizing force — **para·mag·net·i·cal·ly** \-i-k(ə-)lē\ *adv* — **para·mag·ne·tism** \-'mag-nə-,tiz-əm\ *n*

par·a·mat·ta \,par-ə-'mat-ə\ *n* [*Parramatta,* Australia] (1834) **:** a fine lightweight dress fabric of silk and wool or cotton and wool

par·a·me·cium \,par-ə-'mē-sh(ē-)əm, -sē-əm\ *n, pl* **-cia** \-sh(ē-)ə, -sē-ə\ *also* **-ciums** [NL, fr. Gk *paramēkēs* oblong, fr. *para-* + *mēkos* length; akin to Gk *makros* long — more at MEAGER] (1752) **:** any of a genus (*Paramecium*) of ciliate protozoans that have an elongate body rounded at the anterior end and an oblique funnel-shaped buccal groove bearing the mouth at the extremity

para·med·ic \'par-ə-,med-ik\ *also* **para·med·i·cal** \-i-kəl\ *n* (1967) **:** one who works in a health field in an auxiliary capacity to a physician (as by giving injections and taking X rays)

para·med·i·cal \,par-ə-'med-i-kəl\ *also* **para·med·ic** \-ik\ *adj* (1921) **:** concerned with supplementing the work of highly trained medical professionals ⟨~ aides and technicians⟩

par·a·ment \'par-ə-mənt\ *n* [ME, fr. ML *paramentum,* fr. *parare* to adorn, fr. L, to prepare — more at PARE] (14c) **:** an ornamental ecclesiastical hanging or vestment

pa·ram·e·ter \pə-'ram-ət-ər\ *n* [NL, fr. *para-* + Gk *metron* measure — more at MEASURE] (1656) **1 a :** an arbitrary constant whose value characterizes a member of a system (as a family of curves); *also* **:** a quantity (as a mean or variance) that describes a statistical population **b :** an independent variable used to express the coordinates of a variable point and functions of them — compare PARAMETRIC EQUATION **2 :** any of a set of physical properties whose values determine the characteristics or behavior of something ⟨~*s* of the atmosphere such as temperature, pressure, and density⟩ **3 :** something represented by a parameter **:** a characteristic element; *broadly* **:** CHARACTERISTIC, ELEMENT, FACTOR ⟨political dissent as a ~ of modern life⟩ **4 :** LIMIT, BOUNDARY ⟨the ~*s* of science fiction⟩ — **para·met·ric** \,par-ə-'me-trik\ *adj* — **para·met·ri·cal·ly** \-tri-k(ə-)lē\ *adv*

pa·ram·e·ter·ize \pə-'ram-ət-ə-,rīz\ *or* **pa·ram·e·trize** \-'ram-ə-,trīz\ *vt* **-ter·ized** *or* **-trized; -ter·iz·ing** *or* **-triz·ing** (1940) **:** to express in terms of parameters — **pa·ram·e·ter·iza·tion** \-,ram-ət-ə-rə-'zā-shən, -ə-trə-'zā-\ *or* **pa·ram·e·tri·za·tion** \-ə-trə-'zā-\ *n*

parametric amplifier *n* (1957) **:** a high-frequency amplifier whose operation is based on time variations in a parameter (as reactance) and which converts the energy at the frequency of an alternating current into energy at the input signal frequency in such a way as to amplify the signal

parametric equation *n* (1909) **:** any of a set of equations that express the coordinates of the points of a curve as functions of one parameter or that express the coordinates of the points of a surface as functions of two parameters

para·mil·i·tary \,par-ə-'mil-ə-,ter-ē\ *adj* (1935) **1 :** of or relating to a paramilitary force ⟨~ training⟩ **2 :** formed on a military pattern esp. as a potential auxiliary military force ⟨a ~ border patrol⟩

par·am·ne·sia \,par-,am-'nē-zhə, -əm-\ *n* [NL, fr. *para-* + *-mnesia* (as in *amnesia*)] (1888) **:** a disorder of memory: as **a :** a condition in which the proper meaning of words cannot be remembered **b :** the illusion of remembering scenes and events when experienced for the first time — called also *déjà vu*

1par·a·mount \'par-ə-,maůnt\ *adj* [AF *paramont,* fr. OF *par* by (fr. L *per*) + *amont* above, fr. *a* to (fr. L *ad*) + *mont* mountain — more at FOR, AT, MOUNT] (1579) **:** superior to all others **:** SUPREME ***syn*** see DOMINANT — **par·a·mount·cy** \-,maůn(t)-sē\ *n*

2paramount *n* (1645) **:** a supreme ruler

par·amour \'par-ə-,mů(ə)r\ *n* [ME, fr. *par amour* by way of love, fr. MF] (14c) **:** an illicit lover

par·am·y·lum \(')pa(ə)r-'am-ə-ləm\ *n* [NL, fr. *para-* + L *amylum* starch — more at AMYL-] (1897) **:** a reserve carbohydrate of various protozoans and algae that resembles starch

para·myxo·vi·rus \,par-ə-'mik-sə-,vī-rəs\ *n* (1962) **:** any of a group of RNA-containing viruses (as the mumps and measles viruses) that are larger than the related myxoviruses

pa·rang \'pär-,aŋ\ *n* [Malay] (ca. 1839) **:** a short sword, cleaver, or machete common in Malaysia and Indonesia

para·noia \,par-ə-'nȯi-ə\ *n* [NL, fr. Gk, madness, fr. *paranous* demented, fr. *para-* + *nous* mind] (ca. 1811) **1 :** a psychosis characterized by systematized delusions of persecution or grandeur usu. without hallucinations **2 :** a tendency on the part of an individual or group toward excessive or irrational suspiciousness and distrustfulness of others — **para·noi·ac** \-'nȯi-,ak, -'nȯi-ik\ *also* **para·noic** \-'nȯi(-i)k, -'nō-ik\ *adj or n* — **para·noi·cal·ly** \-'nȯi(-i)-k(ə-)lē, '-nō-i-k(ə-)lē\ *adv*

para·noid \'par-ə-,nȯid\ *also* **para·noi·dal** \,par-ə-'nȯid-ᵊl\ *adj* (1904) **1 :** characterized by or resembling paranoia **2 :** characterized by suspiciousness, persecutory trends, or megalomania **3 :** extremely fearful — **paranoid** *n*

paranoid schizophrenia *n* (1942) **:** schizophrenia characterized esp. by persecutory or grandiose delusions or hallucinations or by delusional jealousy

para·nor·mal \,par-ə-'nȯr-məl\ *adj* (ca. 1920) **:** not scientifically explainable **:** SUPERNATURAL — **para·nor·mal** \'par-ə-,nȯr-məl\ *n* — **para·nor·mal·i·ty** \,par-ə-,nȯr-'mal-ət-ē\ *n* — **para·nor·mal·ly** \-'nȯr-mə-lē\ *adv*

para·nymph \'par-ə-,nim(p)f\ *n* [LL *paranymphus,* fr. Gk *paranymphos,* fr. *para-* + *nymphē* bride — more at NUPTIAL] (1600) **1 :** a friend going with a bridegroom to fetch home the bride in ancient Greece; *also* **:** the bridesmaid conducting the bride to the bridegroom **2 a :** BEST MAN **b :** BRIDESMAID

par·a·pet \'par-ə-pət, -,pet\ *n* [It *parapetto,* fr. *parare* to shield (fr. L, to prepare) + *petto* chest, fr. L *pectus* — more at PARE, PECTORAL] (1590) **1 :** a wall, rampart, or elevation of earth or stone to protect soldiers **:** BREASTWORK **2 :** a low wall or railing to protect the edge of a platform, roof, or bridge — called also *parapet wall* — **par·a·pet·ed** \-,pet-əd\ *adj*

pa·raph \'par-əf, pə-'raf\ *n* [MF, fr. L *paragraphus* paragraph] (1584) **:** a flourish at the end of a signature

par·a·pher·na·lia \,par-ə-fə(r)-'nāl-yə\ *n pl but sing or pl in constr* [ML, deriv. of Gk *parapherna* goods a bride brings over and above the dowry, fr. *para-* + *phernē* dowry, fr. *pherein* to bear — more at BEAR] (1651) **1 :** the separate real or personal property of a married woman that she can dispose of by will and sometimes according to common law during her life **2 :** personal belongings **3 a :** articles of equipment **:** FURNISHINGS **b :** accessory items **:** APPURTENANCES

1para·phrase \'par-ə-,frāz\ *n* [MF, fr. L *paraphrasis,* fr. Gk, fr. *paraphrazein* to paraphrase, fr. *para-* + *phrazein* to point out] (1548) **1 :** a restatement of a text, passage, or work giving the meaning in another form **2 :** the use or process of paraphrasing in studying or teaching composition

2paraphrase *vb* **-phrased; -phras·ing** *vt* (1630) **:** to make a paraphrase of ~ *vi* **:** to make a paraphrase — **para·phras·able** \-,frā-zə-bəl\ *adj* — **para·phras·er** *n*

para·phras·tic \,par-ə-'fras-tik\ *adj* [F *paraphrastique,* fr. Gk *paraphrastikos,* fr. *paraphrazein*] (ca. 1623) **:** explaining or translating more clearly and amply **:** having the nature of a paraphrase — **para·phras·ti·cal·ly** \-ti-k(ə-)lē\ *adv*

pa·raph·y·sis \pə-'raf-ə-səs\ *n, pl* **-y·ses** \-,sēz\ [NL, fr. Gk, sucker, offshoot, fr. *paraphyein* to produce at the side, fr. *para-* + *phyein* to bring forth — more at PHYSICS] (ca. 1857) **:** one of the slender sterile filaments borne among the sporogenous or gametogenous organs in cryptogamic plants

para·ple·gia \,par-ə-'plē-j(ē-)ə\ *n* [NL, fr. Gk *paraplēgiē* hemiplegia, fr. *para-* + *-plēgia* -plegia] (ca. 1657) **:** paralysis of the lower half of the body with involvement of both legs — **para·ple·gic** \-jik\ *adj or n*

para·po·di·um \-'pōd-ē-əm\ *n, pl* **-dia** \-ē-ə\ [NL] (1877) **:** either of a pair of fleshy lateral processes borne by most segments of a polychaete worm — **parapodial** *adj*

para·pro·fes·sion·al \-prə-'fesh-nəl, -ən-ᵊl\ *n* (1965) **:** a trained aide who assists a professional person (as a teacher or doctor) — **paraprofessional** *adj*

para·psy·chol·o·gy \,par-ə-(,)sī-'käl-ə-jē\ *n* [ISV] (1925) **:** a field of study concerned with the investigation of evidence for paranormal psychological phenomena (as telepathy, clairvoyance, and psychokinesis) — **para·psy·cho·log·i·cal** \-,sī-kə-'läj-i-kəl\ *adj* — **para·psy·chol·o·gist** \-(,)sī-'käl-ə-jəst\ *n*

para·quat \'par-ə-,kwät\ *n* [*para-* + *quaternary*] (ca. 1961) **:** an herbicide containing a salt of a cation $C_{12}H_{14}N_2$ that is used esp. as a weed killer

para·ros·an·i·line \,par-ə-,rō-'zan-ᵊl-ən\ *n* [ISV] (ca. 1879) **:** a white crystalline base $C_{19}H_{19}N_3O$ that is the parent compound of many dyes; *also* **:** its red chloride used esp. in coloring paper and as a biological stain

Pa·ra rubber \,par-ə-, pə-,rä-\ *n* [*Pará,* Brazil] (1857) **:** native rubber from So. American rubber trees (genus *Hevea* and esp. *H. brasiliensis*)

Para rubber tree *n* (1930) **:** a So. American rubber tree (*Hevea brasiliensis*)

par·a·sang \'par-ə-,saŋ\ *n* [L *parasanga,* fr. Gk *parasangēs,* of Iranian origin; akin to Per *farsung* parasang] (1594) **:** any of various Persian units of distance; *esp* **:** an ancient unit of about four miles

para·se·le·ne \,par-ə-sə-'lē-nē\ *n, pl* **-nae** \-(,)nē, -,nī\ [NL, fr. *para-* + Gk *selēnē* moon — more at SELENIUM] (1653) **:** a bright spot comparable to a parhelion seen in connection with lunar halos — **para·se·le·nic** \-'lēn-ik, -'len-\ *adj*

para·sex·u·al \-'seksh-(ə-)wəl, -'sek-shəl\ *adj* (1954) **:** relating to or being reproduction that results in recombination of genes from different individuals but does not involve meiosis and formation of a zygote by fertilization as in sexual reproduction ⟨the ~ cycle in some fungi⟩ — **para·sex·u·al·i·ty** \-,sek-shə-'wal-ət-ē\ *n*

pa·ra·shah \'pär-ə-,shä\ *n* [Heb *pārāshāh,* lit., explanation] (1624) **:** a passage in Jewish Scripture dealing with a single topic; *specif* **:** a section of the Torah assigned for weekly reading in synagogue worship

par·a·site \'par-ə-,sīt\ *n* [MF, fr. L *parasitus,* fr. Gk *parasitos,* fr. *para-* + *sitos* grain, food] (1539) **1 :** one frequenting the tables of the rich and earning welcome by flattery **2 :** an organism living in or on another organism in parasitism **3 :** something that resembles a biological parasite in dependence on something else for existence or support without making a useful or adequate return — **par·a·sit·ic** \ˌpar-ə-ˈsit-ik\ *also* **par·a·sit·i·cal** \-i-kəl\ *adj* — **par·a·sit·i·cal·ly** \-i-k(ə-)lē\ *adv*

syn PARASITE, SYCOPHANT, TOADY, LEECH, SPONGE mean an obsequious flatterer or self-seeker. PARASITE applies to one who clings to a person of wealth, power, or influence or is useless to society; SYCOPHANT adds to this a strong suggestion of fawning, flattery, or adulation; TOADY emphasizes the servility and snobbery of the self-seeker; LEECH stresses persistence in clinging to or bleeding another for one's own advantage; SPONGE stresses the parasitic laziness, dependence, and opportunism of the cadger.

par·a·sit·i·cid·al \ˌpar-ə-ˌsit-ə-ˈsīd-ᵊl\ *adj* (1892) **:** destructive to parasites

par·a·sit·i·cide \-ˈsit-ə-ˌsīd\ *n* [L *parasitus* + E *-cide*] (1864) **:** a parasiticidal agent

par·a·sit·ism \ˈpar-ə-sə-ˌtiz-əm, -ˌsīt-ˌiz-\ *n* (1611) **1 :** the behavior of a parasite **2 :** an intimate association between organisms of two or more kinds; *esp* **:** one in which a parasite obtains benefits from a host which it usu. injures **3 :** PARASITOSIS

par·a·sit·ize \-sə-ˌtīz, -ˌsīt-ˌīz\ *vt* **-ized; -iz·ing** (1890) **:** to infest or live on or with as a parasite — **par·a·sit·iza·tion** \ˌpar-ə-sət-ə-ˈzā-shən, -ˌsīt-\ *n*

par·a·sit·oid \ˈpar-ə-sə-ˌtȯid, -ˌsīt-ˌȯid\ *n* (1922) **:** an insect and esp. a wasp that completes its larval development within the body of another insect eventually killing it and is free-living as an adult — **parasitoid** *adj*

par·a·si·tol·o·gy \ˌpar-ə-sə-ˈtäl-ə-jē, -ˌsīt-ˈäl-\ *n* [L *parasitus* + ISV *-logy*] (1882) **:** a branch of biology dealing with parasites and parasitism esp. among animals — **par·a·si·to·log·i·cal** \-ˌsit-ᵊl-ˈäj-i-kəl, -ˌsīt-\ *also* **par·a·si·to·log·ic** \-ik\ *adj* — **par·a·si·to·log·i·cal·ly** \-i-k(ə-)lē\ *adv* — **par·a·si·tol·o·gist** \-sə-ˈtäl-ə-jəst, -ˌsīt-ˈäl-\ *n*

par·a·sit·osis \-sə-ˈtō-səs, -ˌsīt-ˈō-\ *n, pl* **-o·ses** \-ˌsēz\ [NL] (ca. 1899) **:** infestation with or disease caused by parasites

para·sol \ˈpar-ə-ˌsȯl, -ˌsäl\ *n* [F, fr. OIt *parasole,* fr. *parare* to shield + *sole* sun, fr. L *sol* — more at PARAPET, SOLAR] (1660) **:** a lightweight umbrella used as a sunshade esp. by women

[1]**para·sym·pa·thet·ic** \ˌpar-ə-ˌsim-pə-ˈthet-ik\ *adj* [ISV] (1905) **:** of, relating to, being, or acting on the parasympathetic nervous system

[2]**parasympathetic** *n* (1925) **1 :** a parasympathetic nerve **2 :** PARASYMPATHETIC NERVOUS SYSTEM

parasympathetic nervous system *n* (ca. 1934) **:** the part of the autonomic nervous system that contains chiefly cholinergic fibers, that tends to induce secretion, to increase the tone and contractility of smooth muscle, and to cause the dilatation of blood vessels, and that consists of a cranial and a sacral part — compare SYMPATHETIC NERVOUS SYSTEM

para·sym·pa·tho·mi·met·ic \ˌpar-ə-ˈsim-pə-(ˌ)thō-mī-ˈmet-ik, -mə-\ *adj* [ISV] (1942) **:** simulating parasympathetic nervous action in physiological effect

para·syn·the·sis \ˌpar-ə-ˈsin(t)-thə-səs\ *n* [NL] (1862) **:** the formation of words by adding a derivative ending and prefixing a particle (as in *denationalize*) — **para·syn·thet·ic** \-sin-ˈthet-ik\ *adj*

para·tac·tic \ˌpar-ə-ˈtak-tik\ *also* **para·tac·ti·cal** \-ti-kəl\ *adj* (1871) **:** of or relating to parataxis — **para·tac·ti·cal·ly** \-ti-k(ə-)lē\ *adv*

para·tax·is \ˌpar-ə-ˈtak-səs\ *n* [NL, fr. Gk, act of placing side by side, fr. *paratassein* to place side by side, fr. *para-* + *tassein* to arrange — more at TACTICS] (ca. 1842) **:** the placing of clauses or phrases one after another without coordinating or subordinating connectives

para·thi·on \ˌpar-ə-ˈthī-ən, -ˌän\ *n* [*para-* + *thio*phosphate + *-on*] (1947) **:** an extremely toxic insecticide $C_{10}H_{14}NO_5PS$

par·a·thor·mone \ˌpar-ə-ˈthȯr-ˌmōn\ *n* [fr. *Parathormone,* a trademark] (1925) **:** a hormone of the parathyroid gland that is concerned esp. with calcium utilization in the body — called also *parathyroid hormone*

[1]**para·thy·roid** \-ˈthī-ˌrȯid\ *n* (1897) **:** PARATHYROID GLAND

[2]**parathyroid** *adj* [ISV] (1902) **:** of, relating to, or produced by the parathyroid glands

para·thy·roid·ec·to·my \-ˌrȯid-ˈek-tə-mē\ *n, pl* **-mies** (1903) **:** excision of the parathyroid glands — **para·thy·roid·ec·to·mized** \-ˌmīzd\ *adj*

parathyroid gland *n* [ISV] (ca. 1903) **:** any of usu. four small endocrine glands that are adjacent to or embedded in the thyroid gland and produce a hormone concerned with calcium metabolism

para·troop·er \ˈpar-ə-ˌtrü-pər\ *n* (1927) **:** a member of the paratroops

para·troops \-ˌtrüps\ *n pl* [[2]*para-*] (1940) **:** troops trained and equipped to parachute from an airplane — **para·troop** \-ˌtrüp\ *adj*

[1]**para·ty·phoid** \ˌpar-ə-ˈtī-ˌfȯid, -(ˌ)tī-ˈ\ *adj* [ISV] (1903) **1 :** resembling typhoid fever **2 :** of or relating to paratyphoid or its causative organisms ⟨~ infection⟩

[2]**paratyphoid** *n* (1903) **:** a salmonellosis that resembles typhoid fever and is commonly contracted by eating contaminated food — called also *paratyphoid fever*

para·vane \ˈpar-ə-ˌvān\ *n* (1919) **:** a torpedo-shaped protective device with serrate teeth in its forward end used underwater by a ship in mined areas to sever the moorings of mines

par·boil \ˈpär-ˌbȯil\ *vt* [ME *parboilen,* fr. *parboilen* to boil thoroughly, fr. MF *parboillir,* fr. LL *perbullire,* fr. L *per-* thoroughly (fr. *per* through) + *bullire* to boil, fr. *bulla* bubble — more at FOR] (15c) **:** to boil briefly as a preliminary or incomplete cooking procedure

[1]**par·buck·le** \ˈpär-ˌbək-əl\ *n* [origin unknown] (1626) **1 :** a purchase for hoisting or lowering a cylindrical object by making fast the middle of a long rope aloft and looping both ends around the object which rests in the loops and rolls in them as the ends are hauled up or paid out **2 :** a double sling made of a single rope (as for slinging a cask)

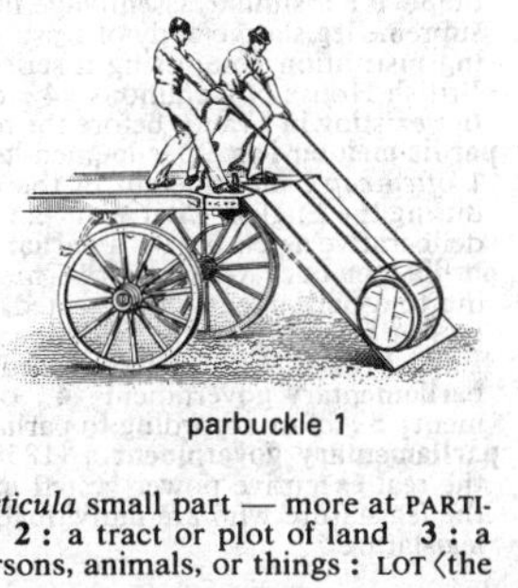

parbuckle 1

[2]**parbuckle** *vt* **-buck·led; -buck·ling** \-ˌbək-(ə-)liŋ\ (1831) **:** to hoist or lower by means of a parbuckle

Par·cae \ˈpär-ˌkī, -ˌsē\ *n pl* [L] (1591) **:** FATE 4

[1]**par·cel** \ˈpär-səl\ *n* [ME, fr. MF, fr. (assumed) VL *particella,* fr. L *particula* small part — more at PARTICLE] (14c) **1 :** FRAGMENT, PORTION **2 :** a tract or plot of land **3 :** a company, collection, or group of persons, animals, or things **:** LOT ⟨the whole story was a ~ of lies⟩ **4 a :** a wrapped bundle **:** PACKAGE **b :** a unit of salable merchandise **5 :** PARCELING 2

[2]**parcel** *adv, archaic* (15c) **:** PARTLY

[3]**parcel** *adj* (15c) **:** PART-TIME, PARTIAL

[4]**parcel** *vt* **-celed** *or* **-celled; -cel·ing** *or* **-cel·ling** \ˈpär-s(ə-)liŋ\ (1584) **1 :** to divide into parts **:** DISTRIBUTE — often used with *out* **2 :** to make up into a parcel **:** WRAP **3 :** to cover (as a rope) with strips of canvas

par·cel·ing *or* **par·cel·ling** *n* (1584) **1 a :** the act of dividing and distributing in portions **b :** the act of wrapping into bundles **2 a :** the act of covering a caulked seam with canvas and then tarring it **b :** tarred strips of canvas wound about a rope to exclude moisture

parcel post *n* (1837) **1 :** a mail service handling parcels **2 :** packages handled by parcel post

parcel post zone *n* (ca. 1923) **:** ZONE 5b

par·ce·nary \ˈpärs-ᵊn-ˌer-ē\ *n* [AF *parcenarie,* fr. OF *parçonerie,* fr. *parçon* portion, fr. L *partition-, partitio* partition] (1544) **:** COPARCENARY 1

par·ce·ner \ˈpärs-nər, -ᵊn-ər\ *n* [AF, fr. OF *parçonier,* fr. *parçon*] (1574) **:** COPARCENER

parch \ˈpärch\ *vb* [ME *parchen*] *vt* (14c) **1 :** to toast under dry heat **2 :** to shrivel with heat **3 :** to dry or shrivel with cold ~ *vi* **:** to become dry or scorched

parched \ˈpärcht\ *adj* (ca. 1552) **:** deprived of natural moisture; *also* **:** THIRSTY

Par·chee·si \pär-ˈchē-zē, pər-, *esp Brit* -sē\ *trademark* — used for a board game adapted from pachisi

parch·ment \ˈpärch-mənt\ *n* [ME *parchemin,* fr. MF, modif. of L *pergamena,* fr. Gk *pergamēnē,* fr. fem. of *Pergamēnos* of Pergamum, fr. *Pergamon* Pergamum] (14c) **1 :** the skin of a sheep or goat prepared for writing on **2 :** strong, tough, and often somewhat translucent paper made to resemble parchment **3 :** a parchment manuscript; *also* **:** an academic diploma

[1]**pard** \ˈpärd\ *n* [ME *parde,* fr. MF, fr. L *pardus,* fr. Gk *pardos*] (14c) **:** LEOPARD

[2]**pard** *n* [short for *pardner*] *chiefly dial* (1850) **:** PARTNER, CHUM

par·die *or* **par·di** *or* **par·dy** \pər-ˈdē, pär-\ *interj* [ME *pardee,* fr. OF *par Dé* by God] *archaic* (13c) — used as a mild oath

pard·ner \ˈpärd-nər\ *n, chiefly dial* (ca. 1795) **:** PARTNER, CHUM

[1]**par·don** \ˈpärd-ᵊn\ *n* (13c) **1 :** INDULGENCE 1 **2 :** the excusing of an offense without exacting a penalty **3 a :** a release from the legal penalties of an offense **b :** an official warrant of remission of penalty **4 :** excuse or forgiveness for a fault, offense, or discourtesy

[2]**pardon** *vt* **par·doned; par·don·ing** \ˈpärd-niŋ, -ᵊn-iŋ\ [ME *pardonen,* fr. MF *pardoner,* fr. LL *perdonare* to grant freely, fr. L *per-* thoroughly + *donare* to give — more at PARBOIL, DONATION] (15c) **1 a :** to absolve from the consequences of a fault or crime **b :** to allow (an offense) to pass without punishment **:** FORGIVE **c :** to relieve of a penalty improperly assessed **2 :** TOLERATE ***syn*** see EXCUSE

par·don·able \ˈpärd-nə-bəl, -ᵊn-ə-bəl\ *adj* (1548) **:** admitting of being pardoned **:** EXCUSABLE ⟨~ offenses⟩ — **par·don·able·ness** *n* — **par·don·ably** \-blē\ *adv*

par·don·er \ˈpärd-nər, -ᵊn-ər\ *n* (14c) **1 :** a medieval preacher delegated to raise money for religious works by soliciting offerings and granting indulgences **2 :** one that pardons

pare \ˈpa(ə)r, ˈpe(ə)r\ *vt* **pared; par·ing** [ME *paren,* fr. MF *parer* to prepare, trim, fr. L *parare* to prepare, acquire; akin to OE *fearr* bull, ox, L *parere* to give birth to, produce] (14c) **1 :** to trim off an outside, excess, or irregular part of ⟨~ apples⟩ ⟨*paring* his nails⟩ **2 :** to diminish or reduce by or as if by paring ⟨~ expenses⟩ — **par·er** *n*

par·e·gor·ic \ˌpar-ə-ˈgȯr-ik, -ˈgōr-, -ˈgär-\ *n* [F *parégorique* mitigating pain, fr. LL *paregoricus,* fr. Gk *parēgorikos,* fr. *parēgorein* to talk over, soothe, fr. *para-* + *agora* assembly — more at GREGARIOUS] (ca. 1847) **:** camphorated tincture of opium used esp. to relieve pain

pa·ren·chy·ma \pə-ˈreŋ-kə-mə\ *n* [NL, fr. Gk, visceral flesh, fr. *parenchein* to pour in beside, fr. *para-* + *en-* en- + *chein* to pour — more at FOUND] (1651) **1 :** a tissue of higher plants that consists of thin-walled living photosynthetic or storage cells capable of division even when mature and that makes up much of the substance of leaves and roots, the pulp of fruits, and parts of stems and supporting structures **2 :** the essential and distinctive tissue of an organ or an abnormal growth as distinguished from its supportive framework — **par·en·chy·ma·tous** \ˌpar-ən-ˈkim-ət-əs, -ˈkīm-\ *or* **pa·ren·chy·mal** \pə-ˈreŋ-kə-məl, ˌpar-ən-ˈkī-\ *adj*

[1]**par·ent** \ˈpar-ənt, ˈper-\ *n* [ME, fr. MF, fr. L *parent-, parens,* fr. prp. of *parere* to give birth to] (15c) **1 :** one that begets or brings forth offspring **2 a :** an animal or plant that is regarded in relation to its offspring **b :** the material or source from which something is derived — **parent** *adj* — **pa·ren·tal** \pə-ˈrent-ᵊl\ *adj* — **pa·ren·tal·ly** \-ᵊl-ē\ *adv*

[2]**parent** *vt* (1663) **:** to be or act as the parent of **:** ORIGINATE, PRODUCE

par·ent·age \ˈpar-ənt-ij, ˈper-\ *n* [ME, fr. MF, fr. *parent*] (15c) **1 a :** descent from parents or ancestors **:** LINEAGE ⟨a person of noble ~⟩ **b :** DERIVATION, ORIGIN ⟨the ballads about them are of common ~ —G. B. Johnson⟩ **2 :** the standing or position of a parent **:** PARENTHOOD

parental generation *n* (ca. 1920) **:** a generation of individuals of distinctively different genotypes that are crossed to produce hybrids

par·en·ter·al \pə-ˈrent-ə-rəl\ *adj* [ISV *para-* + *enteral*] (ca. 1910) **:** situated or occurring outside the intestine; *esp* **:** introduced otherwise than by way of the intestines — **par·en·ter·al·ly** \-rə-lē\ *adv*

pa·ren·the·sis \pə-ˈren(t)-thə-səs\ *n, pl* **-the·ses** \-ˌsēz\ [LL, fr. Gk, lit., act of inserting, fr. *parentithenai* to insert, fr. *para-* + *en-* en- + *tithenai* to place — more at DO] (1568) **1 a :** an amplifying or explanatory word, phrase, or sentence inserted in a passage from which it is usu. set off by punctuation **b :** a remark or passage that departs from the theme of a discourse **:** DIGRESSION **2 :** INTERLUDE, INTERVAL **3 :** one or both of the curved marks ( ) used in writing and printing to enclose a parenthetic expression or to group a symbolic unit in a logical or mathematical expression — **par·en·thet·ic** \ˌpar-ən-ˈthet-ik\ *or* **par·en·thet·i·cal** \-i-kəl\ *adj* — **par·en·thet·i·cal·ly** \-k(ə-)lē\ *adv*

pa·ren·the·size \pə-ˈren(t)-thə-ˌsīz\ *vt* **-sized; -siz·ing** (1837) **:** to make a parenthesis of

par·ent·hood \ˈpar-ənt-ˌhu̇d, ˈper-\ *n* (1856) **:** the position, function, or standing of a parent

par·ent·ing \ˈpar-ənt-iŋ, ˈper-\ *n* (ca. 1959) **:** the raising of a child by its parents

parent–teacher association *n* (1915) **:** an organization of local groups of teachers and the parents of their pupils that works for the improvement of the schools and the benefit of the pupils

pa·re·sis \pə-ˈrē-səs, ˈpar-ə-\ *n, pl* **pa·re·ses** \-ˌsēz\ [NL, fr. Gk, fr. *parienai* to let fall, fr. *para-* + *hienai* to let go, send — more at JET] (1693) **1 :** slight or partial paralysis **2 :** GENERAL PARESIS — **pa·ret·ic** \pə-ˈret-ik\ *adj or n*

par·es·the·sia \ˌpar-əs-ˈthē-zh(ē-)ə\ *n* [NL] (ca. 1860) **:** a sensation of pricking, tingling, or creeping on the skin that has no objective cause — **par·es·thet·ic** \-ˈthet-ik\ *adj*

pa·re·ve \ˈpär-(ə-)və\ *adj* [Yiddish *parev*] (1941) **:** made without milk, meat, or their derivatives ⟨~ margarine⟩ — compare FLEISHIG, MILCHIG

par ex·cel·lence \ˌpär-ˌek-sə-ˈläⁿs\ *adj* [F, lit., by excellence] (1598) **:** being the best of a kind **:** PREEMINENT

par·fait \pär-ˈfā\ *n* [F, lit., something perfect, fr. *parfait* perfect, fr. L *perfectus*] (1894) **1 :** a flavored custard containing whipped cream and syrup frozen without stirring **2 :** a cold dessert made of layers of fruit, syrup, ice cream, and whipped cream

parfait glass *n* (ca. 1951) **:** a tall narrow glass with a short stem used for serving a parfait

par·fleche \ˈpär-ˌflesh\ *n* [CanF *parflèche*] (1827) **1 :** a raw hide soaked in lye to remove the hair and dried **2 :** an article (as a bag or case) made of parfleche

par·fo·cal \(ˈ)pär-ˈfō-kəl\ *adj* [L *par* equal + E *focal*] (1886) **:** being or having lenses or lens sets (as eyepieces) with the corresponding focal points all in the same plane — **par·fo·cal·i·ty** \ˌpär-fō-ˈkal-ət-ē\ *n* — **par·fo·cal·ize** \(ˈ)pär-ˈfō-kə-ˌlīz\ *vt*

parge \ˈpärj\ *vt* **parged; parg·ing** (1701) **:** PARGET

[1]par·get \ˈpär-jət\ *vt* **-get·ed** *or* **-get·ted; -get·ing** *or* **-get·ting** [ME *pargeten*, fr. MF *parjeter* to throw on top of, fr. *par-* thoroughly (fr. L *per-*) + *jeter* to throw — more at JET] (14c) **:** to coat with plaster; *esp* **:** to apply ornamental or waterproofing plaster to

[2]parget *n* (14c) **1 :** plaster, whitewash, or roughcast for coating a wall **2 :** plasterwork esp. in raised ornamental figures on walls

par·gy·line \ˈpär-jə-ˌlēn\ *n* [pro*pargyl* (an alcohol) + *-ine*] (1961) **:** a monoamine oxidase inhibitor $C_{11}H_{13}N$ that is used in the hydrochloride as an antihypertensive and antidepressant agent

parhelic circle *n* (1890) **:** a luminous circle or halo parallel to the horizon at the altitude of the sun — called also *parhelic ring*

par·he·lion \pär-ˈhēl-yən\ *n, pl* **-lia** \-yə\ [L *parelion*, fr. Gk *parēlion*, fr. *para-* + *hēlios* sun — more at SOLAR] (1647) **:** any of several bright spots often tinged with color that often appear on the parhelic circle — **par·he·lic** \-ˈhē-lik\ *adj*

pa·ri·ah \pə-ˈrī-ə\ *n* [Tamil *paraiyan*, lit., drummer] (1613) **1 :** a member of a low caste of southern India and Burma **2 :** OUTCAST

par·i·an \ˈpar-ē-ən, ˈper-\ *n* [*Parian;* fr. its suitability for making statuettes] (1850) **:** a porcelaneous ceramic ware composed essentially of kaolin and feldspar and usu. used unglazed in ornamental articles

Par·i·an \ˈpar-ē-ən, ˈper-\ *adj* (1611) **:** of or relating to the island of Paros noted for its marble used extensively for sculpture in ancient times

Parian ware *n* (1894) **1 :** PARIAN **2 :** articles made of parian

[1]pa·ri·etal \pə-ˈrī-ət-ᵊl\ *adj* [MF, fr. NL *pariet-, paries* wall of a cavity or hollow organ, fr. L, wall; akin to L *sparus* spear — more at SPEAR] (1597) **1 a :** of or relating to the walls of a part or cavity **b :** of, relating to, or forming the upper posterior wall of the head **2 :** attached to the main wall rather than the axis or a cross wall of a plant ovary — used of an ovule or a placenta **3 :** of or relating to college living or its regulation; *esp* **:** of or relating to parietals

[2]parietal *n* (ca. 1706) **1 :** a parietal part (as a bone, scale, or plate) **2** *pl* **:** the regulations governing the visiting privileges of members of the opposite sex in campus dormitories

parietal bone *n* (1704) **:** either of a pair of membrane bones of the roof of the skull between the frontal bones and the occipital bones

parietal cell *n* (1875) **:** any of the large oval cells of the gastric mucous membrane that secrete hydrochloric acid

parietal lobe *n* (ca. 1904) **:** the middle division of each cerebral hemisphere that contains an area concerned with bodily sensations

pari–mu·tu·el \ˌpar-i-ˈmyüch-(ə-)wəl, -ˈmyü-chəl\ *n* [F *pari mutuel*, lit., mutual stake] (1888) **1 :** a betting pool in which those who bet on competitors finishing in the first three places share the total amount bet minus a percentage for the management **2 :** a machine for registering the bets and computing the payoffs in pari-mutuel betting

par·ing \ˈpa(ə)r-iŋ, ˈpe(ə)r-\ *n* (14c) **1 :** the act of cutting away an edge or surface **2 :** something pared off ⟨apple ~s⟩

paring knife *n* (1591) **:** a small short-bladed knife (as for paring fruit)

pa·ri pas·su \ˌpar-i-ˈpas-(ˌ)ü\ *adv or adj* [L, with equal step] (1567) **:** at an equal rate or pace

Par·is \ˈpar-əs\ *n* [L, fr. Gk] **:** a son of Priam whose abduction of Helen leads to the Trojan War

Par·is green \ˌpar-əs-\ *n* [*Paris*, France] (1868) **1 :** a very poisonous bright green powder that is used as an insecticide and pigment **2 :** a variable color averaging a brilliant yellowish green

par·ish \ˈpar-ish\ *n* [ME *parisshe*, fr. MF *parroche*, fr. LL *parochia*, fr. LGk *paroikia*, fr. *paroikos* Christian, fr. Gk, stranger, fr. *para-* + *oikos* house — more at VICINITY] (14c) **1 a (1) :** the ecclesiastical unit of area committed to one pastor **(2) :** the residents of such an area **b** *Brit* **:** a subdivision of a county often coinciding with an original ecclesiastical parish and constituting the unit of local government **2 :** a local church community composed of the members or constituents of a Protestant church **3 :** a civil division of the state of Louisiana corresponding to a county in other states

pa·rish·io·ner \pə-ˈrish-(ə-)nər\ *n* [ME *parisshoner*, prob. modif. of MF *parrochien*, fr. *parroche*] (15c) **:** a member or inhabitant of a parish

[1]par·i·ty \ˈpar-ət-ē\ *n, pl* **-ties** [L *paritas*, fr. *par* equal] (1613) **1 :** the quality or state of being equal or equivalent **2 a :** equivalence of a commodity price expressed in one currency to its price expressed in another **b :** equality of purchasing power established by law between different kinds of money at a given ratio **3 :** an equivalence between farmers' current purchasing power and their purchasing power at a selected base period maintained by government support of agricultural commodity prices **4 a :** the property of an integer with respect to being odd or even ⟨3 and 7 have the same ~⟩ **b :** the property of oddness or evenness of an odd or even function (as certain functions in quantum mechanics) **c (1) :** the state of being odd or even used as the basis of a method of detecting errors in binary-coded data **(2) :** PARITY BIT **5 :** the property of an elementary particle or physical system that indicates whether or not its mirror image occurs in nature

[2]parity *n* [*-parous*] (1874) **:** the state or fact of having borne offspring; *also* **:** the number of children previously borne

parity bit *n* (1957) **:** a bit added to an array of bits (as on magnetic tape) to provide parity

[1]park \ˈpärk\ *n* [ME, fr. OF *parc* enclosure, fr. VL *parricus*] (13c) **1 a :** an enclosed piece of ground stocked with game and held by royal prescription or grant **b :** a tract of land that often includes lawns, woodland, and pasture attached to a country house and is used as a game preserve and for recreation **2 a :** a piece of ground in or near a city or town kept for ornament and recreation **b :** an area maintained in its natural state as a public property **3 a :** a level valley between mountain ranges **b :** an open space and esp. a grassland that is often all or partly surrounded by woodland and is suitable for cultivation or grazing **4 a :** a space occupied by military animals, vehicles, or materials **b :** PARKING LOT **5 :** an enclosed arena or stadium used esp. for ball games **6 :** an area designed for a specified industrial, commercial, or residential use ⟨amusement ~⟩ ⟨industrial ~⟩ ⟨mobile home ~⟩ — **park·like** \ˈpär-ˌklīk\ *adj*

[2]park *vt* (1526) **1 :** to enclose in a park **2 a (1) :** to bring (a vehicle) to a stop and keep standing at the edge of a public way **(2) :** to leave temporarily on a public way or in a parking lot or garage **b :** to land and leave (as an airplane) **c :** to establish (as a satellite) in orbit **3 :** to set and leave temporarily **4 :** to assemble (as equipment or stores) in a military dump or park ~ *vi* **:** to park a vehicle — **park·er** *n*

par·ka \ˈpär-kə\ *n* [Aleut, skin, outer garment, fr. Russ, pelt, fr. Yurak] (1780) **1 :** a hooded fur pullover garment for arctic wear **2 :** a fabric pullover or jacket for sports or military wear

parking lot *n* (1924) **:** an area used for the parking of motor vehicles

parking meter *n* (1935) **:** a coin-operated device which registers the purchase of parking time for a motor vehicle

par·kin·so·nian \ˌpär-kən-ˈsō-nē-ən, -nyən\ *adj* (1906) **1 :** of or similar to that of parkinsonism **2 :** affected with parkinsonism and esp. Parkinson's disease

par·kin·son·ism \ˈpär-kən-sə-ˌniz-əm\ *n* (ca. 1923) **1 :** PARKINSON'S DISEASE **2 :** a chronic nervous disorder that is marked by muscle rigidity but without tremor of resting muscles

Par·kin·son's disease \ˈpär-kən-sənz-\ *n* [James *Parkinson* †1824 Eng. physician] (1877) **:** a chronic progressive nervous disease of later life that is marked by tremor and weakness of resting muscles and by a peculiar gait — called also *paralysis agitans, parkinsonism, Parkinson's syndrome*

Par·kin·son's Law \ˌpär-\ *n* [C. Northcote *Parkinson* b1909 Eng. historian] (1955) **1 :** an observation in office organization: the number of subordinates increases at a fixed rate regardless of the amount of work produced **2 :** an observation in office organization: work expands so as to fill the time available for its completion

park·land \ˈpär-ˌkland\ *n* (1907) **:** land with clumps of trees and shrubs in cultivated condition used as or felt to be suitable for use as a park

park·way \ˈpär-ˌkwā\ *n* (1887) **:** a broad landscaped thoroughfare

par·lance \ˈpär-lən(t)s\ *n* [MF, fr. OF, fr. *parler*] (1579) **1 :** SPEECH; *esp* **:** formal debate or parley **2 :** manner or mode of speech **:** IDIOM

par·lan·do \pär-ˈlän-(ˌ)dō\ *or* **par·lan·te** \-(ˌ)tā\ *adj* [*parlando* fr. It, verbal of *parlare* to speak, fr. ML *parabolare; parlante* fr. It, prp. of *parlare*] (ca. 1854) **:** delivered or performed in a style suggestive of speech — used as a direction in music

[1]par·lay \ˈpär-ˌlā, -lē\ *vt* [F *paroli*, n., parlay, fr. It dial., pl. of *parolo*, fr. *paro* equal, fr. L *par*] (1828) **1 :** to bet in a parlay **2 a :** to exploit successfully **b :** to increase or otherwise transform into something of much greater value

[2]parlay *n* (1904) **:** a series of two or more bets so set up in advance that the original stake plus its winnings are risked on the successive wagers; *broadly* **:** the fresh risking of an original stake together with its winnings

parle \ˈpär(-ə)l\ *vi* **parled; parl·ing** [ME *parlen* to parley, fr. MF *parler*] *archaic* (14c) **:** PARLEY — **parle** *n, archaic*

[1]par·ley \ˈpär-lē\ *vi* [MF *parler* to speak, fr. ML *parabolare*, fr. LL *parabola* speech, parable — more at PARABLE] (1570) **:** to speak with another **:** CONFER; *specif* **:** to discuss terms with an enemy

[2]parley *n, pl* **parleys** (1581) **1 a :** a conference for the discussion of points in dispute **b :** a conference with an enemy **2 :** DISCUSSION

par·lia·ment \ˈpär-lə-mənt *also* ˈpärl-yə-\ *n* [ME, fr. OF *parlement*, fr. *parler*] (13c) **1 :** a formal conference for the discussion of public affairs; *specif* **:** a council of state in early medieval England **2 a :** an assemblage of the nobility, clergy, and commons called together by the British sovereign as the supreme legislative body in the United Kingdom **b :** a similar assemblage in another nation or state **3 a :** the supreme legislative body of a usu. major political unit that is a continuing institution comprising a series of individual assemblages **b :** the British House of Commons **4 :** one of several principal courts of justice existing in France before the revolution of 1789

par·lia·men·tar·i·an \ˌpär-lə-ˌmen-ˈter-ē-ən, -mən- *also* ˌpärl-yə-\ *n* (1644) **1** *often cap* **:** an adherent of the parliament in opposition to the king during the English Civil War **2 :** an expert in the rules and usages of a deliberative assembly (as a parliament)

par·lia·men·ta·ry \-ˈment-ə-rē, -ˈmen-trē\ *adj* (1616) **1 a :** of or relating to a parliament **b :** enacted, done, or ratified by a parliament **2 :** of or adhering to the parliament as opposed to the king during the English Civil War **3 :** of, based on, or having the characteristics of parliamentary government **4 :** of or relating to members of a parliament **5 :** of or according to parliamentary law ⟨~ procedure⟩

parliamentary government *n* (1858) **:** a system of government having the real executive power vested in a cabinet composed of members of the legislature who are individually and collectively responsible to the legislature

parliamentary law *n* (ca. 1909) **:** the rules and precedents governing the proceedings of deliberative assemblies and other organizations

[1]**par·lor** \ˈpär-lər\ *n* [ME *parlour,* fr. OF, fr. *parler*] (13c) **1 :** a room used primarily for conversation or the reception of guests: as **a :** a room in a private dwelling for the entertainment of guests **b :** a conference chamber or private reception room **c :** a room in an inn, hotel, or club for conversation or semiprivate uses **2 :** any of various business places ⟨a funeral ~⟩ ⟨a beauty ~⟩

[2]**parlor** *adj* (1552) **1 :** used in or suitable for a parlor ⟨~ furniture⟩ **2 a :** fostered or advocated in comfortable seclusion without consequent action or application to affairs ⟨~ bolshevism⟩ **b :** given to or characterized by fostering or advocating something (as a doctrine) in such a manner ⟨~ socialist⟩

parlor car *n* (1868) **:** an extra-fare railroad passenger car for day travel equipped with individual chairs

parlor game *n* (1872) **:** a game suitable for playing indoors (as in a parlor)

parlor grand *n* (1856) **:** a grand piano intermediate in length between a concert grand and a baby grand

par·lour \ˈpär-lər\ *chiefly Brit var of* PARLOR

[1]**par·lous** \ˈpär-ləs\ *adj* [ME, alter. of *perilous*] (15c) **1 :** full of danger or risk **:** HAZARDOUS **2** *obs* **:** dangerously shrewd or cunning — **par·lous·ly** *adv*

[2]**parlous** *adv* (15c) **:** to a very great extent **:** EXCEEDINGLY

Par·me·san \ˈpär-mə-ˌzän, -ˌzhän, -zən, -ˌzan\ *n* [*Parmesan* (of Parma), fr. MF *parmesan,* fr. OIt *parmigiano*] (ca. 1556) **:** a very hard dry sharply flavored cheese that is sold grated or in wedges

par·mi·gia·na \ˌpär-mi-ˈjän-ə, ˌpär-mi-ˈzhän, ˈpär-mi-ˌz(h)än\ *or* **par·mi·gia·no** \-ˈjän-(ˌ)ō\ *adj* [It *Parmigiana,* fem. of *Parmigiano* of Parma, fr. *Parma*] (1943) **:** made or covered with Parmesan cheese ⟨veal ~⟩

Par·nas·si·an \pär-ˈnas-ē-ən\ *adj* (1644) **1** [L *parnassius* of Parnassus, fr. Gk *parnasios,* fr. *Parnasos* Parnassus, mountain in Greece sacred to Apollo and the Muses] **:** of or relating to poetry **2** [F *parnassien,* fr. *Parnasse* Parnassus; fr. *Le Parnasse contemporain* (1866) an anthology of poetry] **:** of or relating to a school of French poets of the second half of the 19th century emphasizing metrical form rather than emotion — **Parnassian** *n*

pa·ro·chi·al \pə-ˈrō-kē-əl\ *adj* [ME *parochiall,* fr. MF *parochial,* fr. LL *parochialis,* fr. *parochia* parish — more at PARISH] (14c) **1 :** of or relating to a church parish **2 :** of or relating to a parish as a unit of local government **3 :** confined or restricted as if within the borders of a parish **:** limited in range or scope (as to a narrow area or region) **:** PROVINCIAL, NARROW — **pa·ro·chi·al·ly** \-kē-ə-lē\ *adv*

pa·ro·chi·al·ism \-kē-ə-ˌliz-əm\ *n* (1847) **:** the quality or state of being parochial; *esp* **:** selfish pettiness or narrowness (as of interests, opinions, or views)

parochial school *n* (1755) **:** a private school maintained by a religious body usu. for elementary and secondary instruction

par·o·dist \ˈpar-əd-əst\ *n* (1742) **:** a writer of parodies

[1]**par·o·dy** \ˈpar-əd-ē\ *n, pl* **-dies** [L *parodia,* fr. Gk *parōidia,* fr. *para-* + *aidein* to sing — more at ODE] (1598) **1 :** a literary or musical work in which the style of an author or work is closely imitated for comic effect or in ridicule **2 :** a feeble or ridiculous imitation ***syn*** see CARICATURE — **pa·rod·ic** \pə-ˈräd-ik, pa-\ *adj* — **par·o·dis·tic** \ˌpar-ə-ˈdis-tik\ *adj*

[2]**parody** *vt* **-died; -dy·ing** (1745) **1 :** to compose a parody on ⟨~ a poem⟩ **2 :** to imitate in the manner of a parody

par·ol \ˈpar-əl\ *n* [MF *parole*] (1593) **:** WORD OF MOUTH — **parol** *adj*

[1]**pa·role** \pə-ˈrōl\ *n* [F, speech, parole, fr. MF, fr. LL *parabola* speech — more at PARABLE] (1616) **1 :** a promise made with or confirmed by a pledge of one's honor; *esp* **:** the promise of a prisoner of war to fulfill stated conditions in consideration of his release **2 :** a watchword given only to officers of the guard and of the day **3 :** a conditional release of a prisoner serving an indeterminate or unexpired sentence **4 :** a linguistic act **:** linguistic behavior — compare LANGUE — **parole** *adj*

[2]**parole** *vt* **pa·roled; pa·rol·ing** (1790) **:** to release (a prisoner) on parole

pa·rol·ee \pə-ˌrō-ˈlē, -ˈrō-(ˌ); ˌpar-ə-ˈlē\ *n* (1903) **:** one released on parole

par·ono·ma·sia \ˌpar-ə-nō-ˈmā-zh(ē-)ə, ˌpar-ˌän-ə-ˈmā-\ *n* [L, fr. Gk, fr. *paronomazein* to call with a slight change of name, fr. *para-* + *onoma* name — more at NAME] (1579) **:** a play on words **:** PUN — **par·ono·mas·tic** \-ˈmas-tik\ *adj*

par·onym \ˈpar-ə-ˌnim\ *n* [LL *paronymon,* fr. Gk *parōnymon,* neut. of *parōnymos*] (1846) **:** a paronymous word

par·on·y·mous \pə-ˈrän-ə-məs, pa-\ *adj* [Gk *parōnymos,* fr. *para-* + *-ōnymos* (as in *homōnymos* homonymous)] (1661) **1 :** CONJUGATE 4 **2 a :** formed from a word in another language **b :** having a form similar to that of a cognate foreign word

pa·rot·id \pə-ˈrät-əd\ *adj* [NL *parotid-, parotis* parotid gland, fr. L, tumor near the ear, fr. Gk *parōtid-, parōtis,* fr. *para-* + *ōt-, ous* ear — more at EAR] (1687) **:** of or relating to the parotid gland

parotid gland *n* (1771) **:** either of a pair of large serous salivary glands situated below and in front of the ear

par·oti·tis \ˌpar-ō-ˈtīt-əs\ *n* (1822) **:** inflammation of the parotid glands; *also* **:** MUMPS

par·ous \ˈpar-əs, ˈper-\ *adj* [*-parous*] (ca. 1885) **:** having produced offspring

-p·a·rous \p-(ə-)rəs\ *adj comb form* [L *-parus,* fr. *parere* to give birth to, produce] **:** giving birth to **:** producing ⟨biparous⟩

Par·ou·sia \ˌpär-ü-ˈsē-ə, pə-ˈrü-zē-ə\ *n* [Gk, lit., presence, fr. *paront-, parōn,* prp. of *pareinai* to be present, fr. *para-* + *einai* to be — more at IS] (1875) **:** SECOND COMING

par·ox·ysm \ˈpar-ək-ˌsiz-əm *also* pə-ˈräk-\ *n* [F & ML; F *paroxysme,* fr. ML *paroxysmus,* fr. Gk *paroxysmos,* fr. *paroxynein* to stimulate, fr. *para-* + *oxynein* to provoke, fr. *oxys* sharp — more at OXYGEN] (1604) **1 :** a fit, attack, or sudden increase or recurrence of symptoms (as of a disease) **:** CONVULSION ⟨a ~ of coughing⟩ **2 :** a sudden violent emotion or action ⟨a ~ of rage⟩ — **par·ox·ys·mal** \ˌpar-ək-ˈsiz-məl *also* pə-ˌräk-\ *adj*

[1]**par·quet** \pär-ˈkā\ *vt* **par·queted** \-ˈkād\; **par·quet·ing** \-ˈkā-iŋ\ (1678) **1 :** to furnish with a floor of parquet **2 :** to make of parquetry

[2]**par·quet** \ˈpär-ˌkā, pär-ˈ\ *n* [F, fr. MF, small enclosure, fr. *parc* park] (1816) **1 a :** a patterned flooring; *esp* **:** one made of parquetry **b :** PARQUETRY **2 :** the main floor of a theater; *specif* **:** the part from the front of the stage to the parquet circle

parquet circle *n* (1854) **:** the part of the main floor of a theater that is beneath the galleries

par·que·try \ˈpär-kə-trē\ *n, pl* **-tries** (ca. 1842) **:** work in the form of usu. geometrically patterned wood laid or inlaid esp. for floors

parr \ˈpär\ *n, pl* **parr** *also* **parrs** [origin unknown] (1715) **:** a young salmon actively feeding in fresh water; *also* **:** the young of any of several other fishes

par·ra·keet *var of* PARAKEET

par·rel *or* **par·ral** \ˈpar-əl\ *n* [ME *perell,* fr. alter. of *parail* apparel, short for *apparail,* fr. MF *apareil,* fr. *apareillier* to prepare — more at APPAREL] (15c) **:** a rope loop or sliding collar by which a yard or spar is held to a mast in such a way that it may be hoisted or lowered

par·ri·cid·al \ˌpar-ə-ˈsīd-ᵊl\ *adj* (1627) **:** of, relating to, or guilty of parricide

par·ri·cide \ˈpar-ə-ˌsīd\ *n* (1554) **1** [L *parricida* killer of a close relative, fr. *parri-* (akin to Gk *pēos* kinsman by marriage) + *-cida* -cide] **:** one that murders his father, mother, or a close relative **2** [L *parricidium* murder of a close relative, fr. *parri-* + *-cidium* -cide] **:** the act of a parricide

[1]**par·rot** \ˈpar-ət\ *n* [prob. irreg. fr. MF *perroquet*] (1525) **1 :** any of numerous widely distributed tropical zygodactyl birds (order Psittaciformes) that have a distinctive stout curved hooked bill, are often crested and brightly variegated, and are excellent mimics **2 :** a person who sedulously echoes another's words — **parrot** *adj*

[2]**parrot** *vt* (1596) **:** to repeat by rote

parrot fever *n* (ca. 1930) **:** PSITTACOSIS

parrot fish *n* (1712) **:** any of numerous marine percoid fishes (as of the families Scaridae and Labridae) that have the teeth in each jaw fused into a cutting plate like a beak

par·ry \ˈpar-ē\ *vb* **par·ried; par·ry·ing** [prob. fr. F *parez,* imper. of *parer* to parry, fr. OProv *parar,* fr. L *parare* to prepare — more at PARE] *vi* (1672) **1 :** to ward off a weapon or blow **2 :** to evade or turn aside something ~ *vt* **1 :** to ward off (as a blow) **2 :** to evade esp. by an adroit answer ⟨~ an embarrassing question⟩ — **parry** *n*

[1]**parse** \ˈpärs *also* ˈpärz\ *vb* **parsed; pars·ing** [L *pars orationis* part of speech] *vt* (1553) **1 :** to resolve (as a sentence) into component parts of speech and describe them grammatically **2 :** to describe grammatically by stating the part of speech and explaining the inflection and syntactical relationships ~ *vi* **1 :** to give a grammatical description of a word or a group of words **2 :** to admit of being parsed

[2]**parse** *n* (1963) **:** a product or an instance of parsing

par·sec \ˈpär-ˌsek\ *n* [*par*allax + *sec*ond] (ca. 1913) **:** a unit of measure for interstellar space equal to a distance having a heliocentric parallax of one second or to 206,265 times the radius of the earth's orbit or to 3.26 light-years or to 19.2 trillion miles (30.9 trillion kilometers)

Par·si *also* **Par·see** \ˈpär-(ˌ)sē\ *n* [Per *pārsī,* fr. *Pārs* Persia] (1615) **1 :** a Zoroastrian descended from Persian refugees settled principally at Bombay **2 :** the Iranian dialect of the Parsi religious literature — **Par·si·ism** \-ˌiz-əm\ *n*

par·si·mo·ni·ous \ˌpär-sə-ˈmō-nē-əs\ *adj* (1598) **:** exhibiting or marked by parsimony; *esp* **:** frugal to the point of stinginess ***syn*** see STINGY — **par·si·mo·ni·ous·ly** *adv*

par·si·mo·ny \ˈpär-sə-ˌmō-nē\ *n* [ME *parcimony,* fr. L *parsimonia,* fr. *parsus,* pp. of *parcere* to spare] (15c) **1 a :** the quality of being careful with money or resources **:** THRIFT **b :** the quality or state of being niggardly **:** STINGINESS **2 :** economy in the use of means to an end; *esp* **:** economy of explanation in conformity with Occam's razor

pars·ley \ˈpär-slē\ *n* [ME *persely,* fr. OE *petersilie,* fr. (assumed) VL *petrosilium,* alter. of L *petroselinum,* fr. Gk *petroselinon,* fr. *petros* stone + *selinon* celery] (bef. 12c) **:** an annual or biennial herb (*Petroselinum crispum*) of the carrot family that is native to southern Europe but widely cultivated elsewhere for its leaves which are used as a culinary herb or garnish

pars·nip \ˈpär-snəp\ *n* [ME *pasnepe,* modif. of MF *pasnaie,* fr. L *pastinaca,* fr. *pastinum* 2-pronged dibble] (14c) **:** a biennial herb (*Pastinaca sativa*) of the carrot family with large pinnate leaves and yellow flowers that is native to Europe but cultivated elsewhere; *also* **:** its long tapered root of which some cultivated varieties are used as a vegetable

par·son \ˈpärs-ᵊn\ *n* [ME *persone,* fr. OF, fr. ML *persona,* lit., person, fr. L] (13c) **1 :** RECTOR **2 :** CLERGYMAN; *esp* **:** a Protestant pastor

par·son·age \ˈpär-snij, ˈpärs-ᵊn-ij\ *n* (15c) **:** the house provided by a church for its pastor

Par·sons ta·ble \ˌpärs-ᵊn-ˈstā-bəl, -ᵊnz-ˈtā-\ *n* [prob. fr. the name *Parsons*] (1967) **:** a usu. rectangular table having straight legs that are flush with the edge of the top

[1]**part** \ˈpärt\ *n* [ME, fr. OF & OE, both fr. L *part-, pars;* akin to L *parare* to prepare — more at PARE] (bef. 12c) **1 a** (1) **:** one of the often indefinite or unequal subdivisions into which something is or is regarded as divided and which together constitute the whole (2) **:** an essential portion or integral element **b :** one of several or many equal units of which something is composed or into which it is divisible **:** an amount equal to another amount ⟨mix one ~ of the powder with three ~*s* of water⟩ **c** (1) **:** an exact divisor of a quantity **:** ALIQUOT (2) **:** PARTIAL FRACTION **d :** one of the constituent elements of a plant or animal body: as (1) **:** ORGAN, MEMBER (2) *pl* **:** PRIVATE PARTS **e :** a division of a literary work **f** (1) **:** a vocal or instrumental line or melody in concerted music or in harmony (2) **:** a particular voice or instrument in concerted music; *also* **:** the score for it **g :** a constituent member of a machine or other apparatus; *also* **:** a spare part **2 :** something falling to one in a division or apportionment **:** SHARE **3 :** one's share or allotted task (as in an action) ⟨each must do his ~⟩ **4 :** one of the opposing sides in a conflict or dispute **5 :** a general area of indefinite boundaries — usu. used in pl. ⟨you're not from around these ~*s*⟩ ⟨took off for ~*s* unknown⟩ **6 :** a function or course of action performed **7 a :** an actor's lines in a play **b :** the role of a character in a play **8 :** a constituent of character or capacity **:** TALENT ⟨a man of many ~*s*⟩ **9 :** the line where the hair is parted

syn PART, PORTION, PIECE, MEMBER, DIVISION, SECTION, SEGMENT, FRAGMENT mean something less than the whole. PART is a general term appropriate when indefiniteness is required ⟨they ran only *part* of the way⟩ PORTION implies an assigned or allotted part ⟨cut the pie into six *portions*⟩ PIECE applies to a separate or detached part of a whole ⟨a puzzle with 500 *pieces*⟩ MEMBER suggests one of the functional units composing a body ⟨an arm is a bodily *member*⟩ DIVISION applies to a large or diversified part ⟨the manufacturing *division* of the company⟩ SECTION applies to a relatively small or uniform part ⟨the entertainment *section* of the newspaper⟩ SEGMENT applies to a part separated or marked out by or as if by natural lines of cleavage ⟨the retired *segment* of the population⟩ FRAGMENT applies to a part produced by or as if by breaking off or shattering ⟨only a *fragment* of the play still exists⟩
— **for the most part** : in general : on the whole ⟨*for the most part* the crowd was orderly⟩ — **in part** : in some degree : PARTIALLY — **on the part of** : with regard to the one specified

[2]**part** *vb* [ME *parten*, fr. OF *partir*, fr. L *partire* to divide, fr. *part-, pars*] *vi* (13c) **1 a** : to separate from or take leave of someone **b** : to take leave of one another **2** : to become separated into parts **3 a** : to go away : DEPART **b** : DIE **4** : to become separated, detached, or broken **5** : to relinquish possession or control ⟨hated to ~ with that money⟩ ~ *vt* **1 a** : to divide into parts **b** : to separate by combing on each side of a line **c** : to break or suffer the breaking of (as a rope or anchor chain) **2** : to divide into shares and distribute : APPORTION **3 a** : to remove from contact or association ⟨if aught but death ~ thee and me —Ruth 1:17(AV)⟩ **b** : to keep separate ⟨the narrow channel that ~s England from France⟩ **c** : to hold (as brawlers) apart **d** : to separate by a process of extraction, elimination, or secretion **4 a** *archaic* : LEAVE, QUIT **b** *dial Brit* : RELINQUISH, GIVE UP ***syn*** see SEPARATE

[3]**part** *adv* (1513) : PARTLY

[4]**part** *adj* (1818) : PARTIAL 3

par·take \pär-ˈtāk, pər-\ *vb* **-took** \-ˈtu̇k\; **-tak·en** \-ˈtā-kən\; **-tak·ing** [back-formation fr. *partaker*, alter. of *part taker*] *vi* (1585) **1** : to take part in or experience something along with others ⟨~ in the revelry⟩ ⟨~ of the good life⟩ **2** : to have a portion (as of food or drink) **3** : to possess or share a certain nature or attribute ⟨the experience ~s of a mystical quality⟩ ~ *vt* : to take part in ***syn*** see SHARE — **par·tak·er** *n*

part·ed \ˈpärt-əd\ *adj* (1590) **1 a** : divided into parts **b** : cleft so that the divisions reach nearly but not quite to the base — usu. used in combination ⟨a 3-*parted* corolla⟩ **2** *archaic* : DEAD

par·terre \pär-ˈte(ə)r\ *n* [F, fr. MF, fr. *par terre* on the ground] (1639) **1** : an ornamental garden with paths between the beds **2** : the part of the main floor of a theater that is behind the orchestra; *esp* : PARQUET CIRCLE

par·the·no·car·py \ˈpär-thə-nō-ˌkär-pē\ *n* [ISV, fr. Gk *parthenos* virgin + *karpos* fruit — more at HARVEST] (ca. 1911) : the production of fruits without fertilization ⟨bananas set fruit by ~ and without pollination⟩ — **par·the·no·car·pic** \ˌpär-thə-nō-ˈkär-pik\ *adj*

par·the·no·gen·e·sis \ˌpär-thə-nō-ˈjen-ə-səs\ *n* [NL, fr. Gk *parthenos* + L *genesis* genesis] (1849) : reproduction by development of an unfertilized gamete that occurs esp. among lower plants and invertebrate animals

par·the·no·ge·net·ic \-jə-ˈnet-ik\ *adj* (1872) : of, characterized by, or produced by parthenogenesis — **par·the·no·ge·net·i·cal·ly** \-i-k(ə-)lē\ *adv*

Par·the·non \ˈpär-thə-ˌnän\ *n* [L, fr. Gk *Parthenōn*] (ca. 1847) : a celebrated Doric temple of Athena built on the acropolis at Athens in the 5th century B.C.

Par·thi·an \ˈpär-thē-ən\ *adj* (1590) **1** : of, relating to, or characteristic of ancient Parthia or its people **2** : relating to, being, or having the effect of a shot fired while in real or feigned retreat — **Parthian** *n*

[1]**par·tial** \ˈpär-shəl\ *adj* [ME *parcial*, fr. MF *partial*, fr. ML *partialis*, fr. LL, of a part, fr. L *part-, pars* part] (15c) **1** : inclined to favor one party more than the other : BIASED **2** : markedly fond of someone or something — used with *to* ⟨~ to beans⟩ **3** : of or relating to a part rather than the whole : not general or total ⟨a ~ solution to the problem⟩ — **par·tial·ly** \ˈpärsh-(ə-)lē\ *adv*

[2]**partial** *n* (1880) : OVERTONE 1a

partial denture *n* (1860) : a usu. removable artificial replacement of one or more teeth

partial derivative *n* (1889) : the derivative of a function of several variables with respect to one of them and with the remaining variables treated as constants

partial differential equation *n* (ca. 1889) : a differential equation containing at least one partial derivative

partial differentiation *n* (ca. 1890) : the process of finding a partial derivative

partial fraction *n* (1816) : one of the simpler fractions into the sum of which the quotient of two polynomials may be decomposed

par·tial·i·ty \ˌpär-shē-ˈal-ət-ē, pär-ˈshal-\ *n, pl* **-ties** (15c) **1** : the quality or state of being partial : BIAS **2** : a special taste or liking

partially ordered *adj* (1941) : having some or all elements connected by a relation that is transitive and antisymmetric

partial pressure *n* (1857) : the pressure exerted by a (specified) component in a mixture of gases

partial product *n* (1924) : a product obtained by multiplying a multiplicand by one digit of a multiplier having more than one digit

part·ible \ˈpärt-ə-bəl\ *adj* (1540) : capable of being parted : DIVISIBLE

par·tic·i·pant \pər-ˈtis-ə-pənt, pär-\ *n* (1562) : one that participates — **participant** *adj*

par·tic·i·pate \pər-ˈtis-ə-ˌpāt, pär-\ *vb* **-pat·ed; -pat·ing** [L *participatus*, pp. of *participare*, fr. *particip-, particeps* participant, fr. *part-, pars* part + *capere* to take — more at HEAVE] *vt, archaic* (1531) : PARTAKE ~ *vi* **1** : to possess something of the nature of a person, thing, or quality **2 a** : to take part ⟨always tried to ~ in class discussions⟩ **b** : to have a part or share in something ***syn*** see SHARE — **par·tic·i·pa·tive** \-ˌpāt-iv\ *adj* — **par·tic·i·pa·tor** \-ˌpāt-ər\ *n*

par·tic·i·pa·tion \pər-ˌtis-ə-ˈpā-shən, (ˌ)pär-\ *n* (14c) **1** : the act of participating **2** : the state of being related to a larger whole

par·tic·i·pa·tion·al \-ˈpāsh-nəl, -ˈpā-shən-ᵊl\ *adj* (1959) : PARTICIPATORY

par·tic·i·pa·to·ry \pər-ˈtis-ə-pə-ˌtōr-ē, pär-, -ˌtȯr-\ *adj* (1881) : characterized by or involving participation; *esp* : providing the opportunity for individual participation ⟨~ democracy⟩

par·ti·cip·i·al \ˌpärt-ə-ˈsip-ē-əl\ *adj* [L *participialis*, fr. *participium*] (1591) : of, relating to, or formed with or from a participle — **par·ti·cip·i·al·ly** \-ē-ə-lē\ *adv*

par·ti·ci·ple \ˈpärt-ə-ˌsip-əl\ *n* [ME, fr. MF, modif. of L *participium*, fr. *particip-, particeps*] (14c) : a word having the characteristics of both verb and adjective; *esp* : an English verbal form that has the function of an adjective and at the same time shows such verbal features as tense and voice and capacity to take an object

par·ti·cle \ˈpärt-i-kəl\ *n* [ME, fr. L *particula*, fr. dim. of *part-, pars*] (14c) **1** *archaic* : a clause or article of a composition or document **2** : one of the basic units of matter and energy (as a molecule, atom, proton, electron, or photon) **3 a** : a minute quantity or fragment **b** : a relatively small or the smallest possible discrete portion or amount of something **4 a** : a unit of speech expressing some general aspect of meaning or some connective or limiting relation and including the articles, most prepositions and conjunctions, and some interjections and adverbs **b** : an element that resembles a word but that is used only in composition (as *un-* in *unfair* and *-ward* in *backward*) **5** : a small eucharistic wafer distributed to a Roman Catholic layman at Communion

particle accelerator *n* (1946) : ACCELERATOR d

par·ti·cle·board \-ˌbō(ə)rd, -ˌbȯ(ə)rd\ *n* (ca. 1957) : a composition board made of very small pieces of wood bonded together (as with a synthetic resin)

particle physics *n* (1946) : HIGH-ENERGY PHYSICS — **particle physicist** *n*

par·ti–col·or \ˌpärt-ē-ˈkəl-ər\ *or* **par·ti–col·ored** \-ərd\ *adj* [obs. E *party* (parti-colored) + E *color* or *colored*] (1535) : showing different colors or tints; *esp* : having patches of two or more colors ⟨~ Persian cats⟩ — **parti–color** *n*

[1]**par·tic·u·lar** \pə(r)-ˈtik-(y)ə-lər, -ˈtik-lər\ *adj* [ME *particuler*, fr. MF, fr. LL *particularis*, fr. L *particula* small part] (14c) **1** : of, relating to, or being a single person or thing ⟨the ~ person I had in mind⟩ **2** *obs* : PARTIAL **3** : of, relating to, or concerned with details ⟨gave us a very ~ account of her day⟩ **4 a** : distinctive among other examples or cases of the same general category : notably unusual ⟨suffered from measles of ~ severity⟩ **b** : being one unit or element among others ⟨~ incidents in a story⟩ **5 a** : denoting an individual member or subclass in logic **b** : affirming or denying a predicate to a part of the subject — used of a proposition in logic ⟨"some men are wise" is a ~ affirmative⟩ **6 a** : concerned over or attentive to details : METICULOUS ⟨a very ~ housekeeper⟩ **b** : nice in taste : FASTIDIOUS **c** : hard to please : EXACTING ***syn*** see SPECIAL, CIRCUMSTANTIAL

[2]**particular** *n* (15c) **1** *archaic* : a separate part of a whole **2 a** : an individual fact, point, circumstance, or detail **b** : a specific item or detail of information or news ⟨bill of ~s⟩ **3 a** : an individual or a specific subclass in logic falling under some general concept or term **b** : a particular proposition in logic ***syn*** see ITEM — **in particular** : in distinction from others : SPECIFICALLY

par·tic·u·lar·ism \pə(r)-ˈtik-(yə-)lə-ˌriz-əm *also* pär-\ *n* (1824) **1** : exclusive or special devotion to a particular interest **2** : a political theory that each political group has a right to promote its own interests and esp. independence without regard to the interests of larger groups **3** : a tendency to explain complex social phenomena in terms of a single causative factor — **par·tic·u·lar·ist** \-rəst\ *n* — **par·tic·u·lar·is·tic** \-ˌtik-(yə-)lə-ˈris-tik\ *adj*

par·tic·u·lar·i·ty \pə(r)-ˌtik-yə-ˈlar-ət-ē *also* (ˌ)pär-\ *n, pl* **-ties** (1528) **1 a** : a minute detail : PARTICULAR **b** : an individual characteristic : PECULIARITY; *also* : SINGULARITY **2 a** : the quality or state of being particular as distinguished from universal **b** : attentiveness to detail : EXACTNESS **c** : the quality or state of being fastidious in behavior or expression

par·tic·u·lar·iza·tion \-ˌtik-(yə-)lə-rə-ˈzā-shən\ *n* (1657) : the act of particularizing : the condition of being particularized

par·tic·u·lar·ize \pə(r)-ˈtik-(yə-)lə-ˌrīz *also* pär-\ *vb* **-ized; -iz·ing** *vt* (1593) : to state in detail : SPECIFY ~ *vi* : to go into details

par·tic·u·lar·ly \pə(r)-ˈtik-yə-(lər-)lē, -yə-lə-lē; pə(r)-ˈtik-(ə-)lē; *also* pär-\ *adv* (14c) **1** : in a particular manner : in detail **2** : to an unusual degree

[1]**par·tic·u·late** \pär-ˈtik-yə-lət *also* -ˌlāt\ *adj* [L *particula*] (1871) : of or relating to minute separate particles

[2]**particulate** *n* (1942) : a particulate substance

particulate inheritance *n* (1889) : inheritance of characters specif. transmitted by genes in accord with Mendel's laws

[1]**part·ing** \ˈpärt-iŋ\ *n* (15c) : a place or point where a division or separation occurs — **parting of the ways** **1** : a point of separation or divergence **2** : a place or time at which a choice must be made

[2]**parting** *adj* (1577) : given, taken, or performed at parting ⟨a ~ kiss⟩

par·ti pris \ˌpär-ˌtē-ˈprē\ *n, pl* **par·tis pris** \-ˌtē-ˈprē(z)\ [F, lit., side taken] (1860) : a preconceived opinion : PREJUDICE — **parti pris** *adj*

[1]**par·ti·san** *also* **par·ti·zan** \ˈpärt-ə-zən, -sən, -ˌzan, *chiefly Brit* ˌpärt-ə-ˈzan\ *n* [MF *partisan*, fr. OIt *partigiano*, fr. *parte* part, party, fr. L *part-, pars* part] (1555) **1** : a firm adherent to a party, faction, cause, or person; *esp* : one exhibiting blind, prejudiced, and unreasoning allegiance **2 a** : a member of a body of detached light troops making forays and harassing an enemy **b** : a member of a guerrilla band operating within enemy lines ***syn*** see FOLLOWER — **partisan** *adj* — **par·ti·san·ship** \-ˌship\ *n*

[2]**par·ti·san** *or* **par·ti·zan** \ˈpärt-ə-zən, -sən\ *n* [MF *partisane*, fr. OIt *partigiana*, fem. of *partigiano*] (1556) : a weapon of the 16th and 17th centuries with long shaft and broad blade

par·ti·ta \pär-ˈtēt-ə\ *n* [It. fr. *partire*, to divide, fr. L — more at PART] (1880) **1** : VARIATION 5 **2** : SUITE 2b(1)

par·tite \ˈpär-ˌtīt\ *adj* [L *partitus*, fr. pp. of *partire*] (ca. 1570) **1** : divided into a usu. specified number of parts **2** : PARTED 1b ⟨a ~ leaf⟩

[1]**par·ti·tion** \pär-ˈtish-ən, pər-\ *n* (15c) **1 a** : the action of parting : the state of being parted : DIVISION **b** (1) : separation of a class or whole into constituent elements (2) : the separation of a set (as the points of a line) into subsets such that every element belongs to one set and no two subsets have an element in common **2** : something that divides; *esp* : an interior dividing wall **3** : one of the parts or sections of a whole

[2]**partition** *vt* (1741) **1 a** : to divide into parts or shares **b** : to divide (as a country) into two or more territorial units having separate political status **2** : to separate or divide by a partition (as a wall) — often

used with *off* ⟨~*ed* off a closet from the storage area⟩ — **par·ti·tion·er** \-'tish-(ə-)nər\ *n*

par·ti·tion·ist \-'tish-(ə-)nəst\ *n* (ca. 1900) : an advocate of political partition

par·ti·tive \'pärt-ət-iv\ *adj* (1520) **1** : serving to part or divide into parts **2** **a** : of, relating to, or denoting a part ⟨a ~ construction⟩ **b** : serving to indicate the whole of which a part is specified ⟨~ genitive⟩ — **par·ti·tive·ly** *adv*

part·let \'pärt-lət\ *n* [ME (Sc) *patelet,* fr. MF *patelette,* fr. dim. of *patte* paw] (1519) : a 16th century chemisette with a band or collar

part·ly \'pärt-lē\ *adv* (1523) : in some measure or degree : PARTIALLY

[1]part·ner \'pärt-nər *also* 'pärd-\ *n* [ME *partener,* alter. of *parcener,* fr. AF, coparcener — more at PARCENER] (13c) **1** *archaic* : one that shares : PARTAKER **2** **a** : ASSOCIATE, COLLEAGUE **b** : either of two persons who dance together **c** : one of two or more persons who play together in a game against an opposing side **d** : HUSBAND, WIFE **3** : a member of a partnership **4** : one of the heavy timbers that strengthen a ship's deck to support a mast — usu. used in pl.

[2]partner *vt* (1611) **1** : to join as partner **2** : to provide with a partner ~ *vi* : to act as a partner

part·ner·ship \-,ship\ *n* (1576) **1** : the state of being a partner : PARTICIPATION **2** **a** : a legal relation existing between two or more persons contractually associated as joint principals in a business **b** : the persons joined together in a partnership **3** : a relationship resembling a legal partnership and usu. involving close cooperation between parties having specified and joint rights and responsibilities

part of speech (15c) : a traditional class of words distinguished according to the kind of idea denoted and the function performed in a sentence

par·ton \'pär-,tän\ *n* [[1]*part* + [2]*-on*] (1969) : a hypothetical particle (as a quark or gluon) that is held to be a constituent of hadrons

par·tridge \'pär-trij, *dial* 'pa-trij\ *n, pl* **partridge** *or* **par·tridg·es** [ME *partrich,* modif. of OF *perdris,* modif. of L *perdic-, perdix,* fr. Gk *perdik-, perdix*] (13c) **1** : any of various typically medium-sized stout-bodied Old World gallinaceous game birds (*Perdix, Alectoris,* and related genera) with variegated plumage **2** : any of numerous gallinaceous birds (as the American ruffed grouse or bobwhite) somewhat like the Old World partridges in size, habits, or value as game

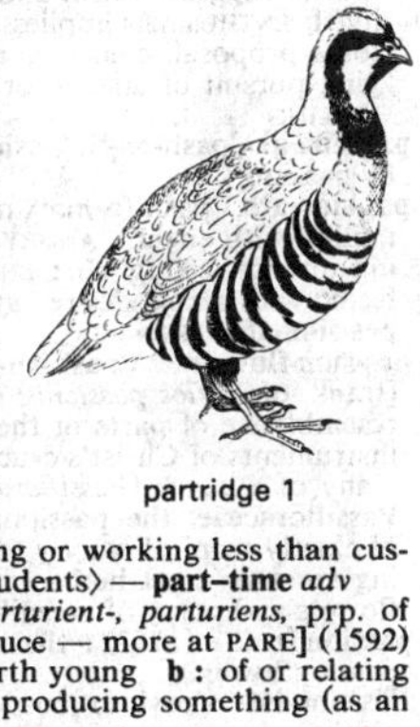
partridge 1

par·tridge·ber·ry \-,ber-ē\ *n* (1714) : an American trailing evergreen plant (*Mitchella repens*) of the madder family with insipid scarlet berries; *also* : its fruit

part–song \'pärt-,sȯŋ\ *n* (1850) : a usu. unaccompanied song consisting of two or more voice parts with one part carrying the melody

part–time \'pärt-'tīm\ *adj* (1891) : involving or working less than customary or standard hours ⟨a ~ job⟩ ⟨~ students⟩ — **part–time** *adv*

[1]par·tu·ri·ent \pär-'t(y)ür-ē-ənt\ *adj* [L *parturient-, parturiens,* prp. of *parturire* to be in labor, fr. *parere* to produce — more at PARE] (1592) **1** **a** : bringing forth or about to bring forth young **b** : of or relating to parturition **2** : being at the point of producing something (as an idea, discovery, or literary work)

[2]parturient *n* (1947) : a parturient individual

par·tu·ri·tion \,pärt-ə-'rish-ən, ,pär-chə-, ,pär-tyü-\ *n* [LL *parturition-, parturitio,* fr. L *parturitus,* pp. of *parturire*] (1646) : the action or process of giving birth to offspring

part·way \'pärt-'wā\ *adv* (1859) : to some extent : PARTIALLY, PARTLY

[1]par·ty \'pärt-ē\ *n, pl* **parties** [ME *partie* part, party, fr. OF, fr. *partir* to divide — more at PART] (13c) **1** : a person or group taking one side of a question, dispute, or contest **2** : a group of persons organized for the purpose of directing the policies of a government **3** : a person or group participating in an action or affair ⟨mountain-climbing ~⟩ ⟨a ~ to the transaction⟩ **4** : a particular individual : PERSON ⟨a coquettish little ~⟩ **5** : a detail of soldiers **6** : a social gathering; *also* : the entertainment provided for it — **party** *adj*

[2]party *vi* **par·tied; par·ty·ing** (1919) : to attend or give parties; *broadly* : REVEL 1

party line *n* (1834) **1** : the policy or practice of a political party **2** : a single telephone circuit connecting two or more subscribers with the exchange — called also *party wire* **3** : the principles or policies of an individual or organization; *esp* : the official policies of the Communist party — **par·ty–lin·er** \,pärt-ē-'lī-nər\ *n*

party poop·er \-'pü-pər\ *n* [[3]*poop* + *-er*] (1954) : one who refuses to join in the fun of a party; *broadly* : one who refuses to go along with everyone else

party wall *n* (ca. 1798) : a wall which divides two adjoining properties and in which each of the owners shares the rights

pa·rure \pə-'rù(ə)r\ *n* [F, lit., adornment, fr. OF *pareure,* fr. *parer* to prepare, adorn — more at PARE] (1818) : a matched set of ornaments (as jewelry)

par value *n* (1807) : PAR 1b(1)

par·ve \'pär-və\ *var of* PAREVE

par·ve·nu \'pär-və-,n(y)ü\ *n* [F, fr. pp. of *parvenir* to arrive, fr. L *pervenire,* fr. *per* through + *venire* to come — more at FOR, COME] (1802) : one that has recently or suddenly risen to an unaccustomed position of wealth or power and has not yet gained the prestige, dignity, or manner associated with it — **parvenu** *adj*

par·ve·nue \'pär-və-,n(y)ü\ *n* [F, fr. *parvenue,* fem. of *parvenum* pp.] (1826) : a female parvenu — **parvenue** *adj*

par·vis *also* **par·vise** \'pär-vəs\ *n* [ME *parvis,* fr. MF, modif. of LL *paradisus* enclosed park — more at PARADISE] (14c) **1** : a court or enclosed space before a building (as a church) **2** : a single portico or colonnade before a church

pas \'pä\ *n, pl* **pas** \'pä(z)\ [F, fr. L *passus* step — more at PACE] (1707) **1** : the right of precedence **2** : a dance step or combination of steps

pas·cal \pas-'kal, päs-'käl\ *n* [Blaise *Pascal*] (1956) **1** : a unit of pressure in the meter-kilogram-second system equivalent to one newton per square meter **2** *usu cap P or all cap* : a structured computer programming language developed from Algol and designed to process both numerical and textual data

Pas·cal's triangle \pas-'kalz-, päs-'kälz-\ *n* (1886) : a system of numbers triangularly arranged in rows that consist of the coefficients in the expansion of $(a + b)^n$ for $n = 0, 1, 2, 3, \ldots$

Pasch \'pask\ *n* [ME *pasche* Passover, Easter, fr. OF, fr. LL *pascha,* fr. LGk, fr. Gk, Passover, fr. Heb *pesaḥ*] (13c) **1** : PASSOVER **2** : EASTER — **pas·chal** \'pas-kəl\ *adj*

paschal full moon *n* (1892) : the 14th day of a lunar month occurring on or next after March 21 according to a fixed set of ecclesiastical calendar rules and without regard to the real moon

Paschal Lamb *n* (15c) : AGNUS DEI 2

pas de bour·rée \,päd-ə-bù-'rā\ *n, pl* **pas de bour·rée** *same*\ *or* **pas de bour·rées** \-'rā(z)\ [F, lit., bourrée step] (ca. 1914) : a walking or running ballet step usu. executed on the points of the toes

pas de deux \,päd-ə-'də(r), -'dü\ *n, pl* **pas de deux** \-'dər(z), -'də(z), -'dü(z)\ [F, lit., step for two] (ca. 1762) **1** : a dance or figure for two performers **2** : an intricate relationship or activity involving two parties or things

pas de qua·tre \,päd-ə-'kat(-rə), -'kätrᵊ\ *n, pl* **pas de qua·tre** *same*\ [F, lit., step for four] (1884) : a dance or figure for four performers

pas de trois \-'trwä, -trə-'wä\ *n, pl* **pas de trois** \-'trwä(z), -trə-'wä(z)\ [F, lit., step for three] (ca. 1762) : a dance or figure for three performers

pa·se \'päs-(,)ā\ *n* [Sp, lit., feint, fr. *pase* let him pass, fr. *pasar* to pass, fr. (assumed) VL *passare*] (1937) : a movement of a cape by a matador in drawing a bull and taking his charge

pa·seo \pə-'sā-(,)ō, pä-\ *n, pl* **paseos** [Sp, fr. *pasear* to take a stroll, fr. (assumed) VL *passare*] (1832) **1** **a** : a leisurely stroll : PROMENADE **b** : a public walk or boulevard **2** : a formal entrance march of bullfighters into an arena

[1]pash \'pash\ *vt* [ME *passhen*] *dial Eng* (14c) : SMASH

[2]pash *n* [origin unknown] *dial Eng* (1611) : HEAD

pa·sha \'päsh-ə, 'pash-; pə-'shä, -'shȯ\ *n* [Turk *paşa*] (1646) : a man of high rank or office (as in Turkey or northern Africa)

Pash·to \'pəsh-(,)tō\ *n* [Per *pashtu,* fr. Pashto] (1784) : the Iranian language of the Pathan people which is the chief vernacular of eastern Afghanistan and adjacent parts of Pakistan

Pa·siph·aë \pə-'sif-ə-,ē\ *n* [L, fr. Gk *Pasiphaē*] : the wife of Minos and mother of the Minotaur by a white bull

pasque·flow·er \'pask-,flaù(-ə)r\ *n* [alter. (influenced by MF *pasque* Easter, fr. OF) of earlier *passeflower,* fr. MF *passefleur,* fr. *passer* to pass (fr. OF) + *fleur* flower, fr. L *flor-, flos* — more at BLOW] (1578) : any of several low perennial herbs (genus *Anemone*) of the buttercup family with palmately compound leaves and large usu. white or purple early spring flowers

pas·qui·nade \,pas-kwə-'nād\ *n* [MF, fr. It *pasquinata,* fr. *Pasquino,* name given to a statue in Rome on which lampoons were posted] (1658) **1** : a lampoon posted in a public place **2** : satirical writing : SATIRE — **pasquinade** *vt*

[1]pass \'pas\ *vb* [ME *passen,* fr. OF *passer,* fr. (assumed) VL *passare,* fr. L *passus* step — more at PACE] *vi* (13c) **1** : MOVE, PROCEED, GO **2** **a** : to go away : DEPART **b** : DIE — often used with *on* **3** **a** : to go by : move past **b** : to run the normal course — used of time or a period of time ⟨the hours ~ quickly⟩ **c** : to move past another vehicle going in the same direction **4** **a** : to go or make one's way through ⟨allow no one to ~⟩ **b** : to go uncensured, unchallenged, or seemingly unnoticed ⟨let his remark ~⟩ **5** : to go from one quality, state, or form to another ⟨~*es* from a liquid to a gaseous state⟩ **6** **a** : to sit in inquest or judgment **b** (1) : to render a judgment, verdict, or opinion ⟨the court ~*ed* on the legality of wiretapping⟩ (2) : to become legally rendered ⟨judgment ~*ed* for the plaintiff⟩ **7** : to go from the control, ownership, or possession of one person or group to that of another ⟨the throne ~*ed* to the king's son⟩ ⟨title ~*es* from the seller to the buyer upon payment in full⟩ **8** **a** : HAPPEN, OCCUR **b** : to take place or be exchanged as or in a social, personal, or business interaction ⟨words ~*ed*⟩ **9** **a** : to become approved by a legislature or body empowered to sanction or reject ⟨the proposal ~*ed*⟩ **b** : to undergo an inspection, test, or course of study successfully **10** **a** : to serve as a medium of exchange **b** : to be accepted or regarded ⟨drivel that ~*es* for literature⟩ **c** : to identify oneself or accept identification as a white person though having some Negro ancestry **11** **a** *obs* : to make a pass in fencing **b** : to throw or hit a ball or puck to a teammate — often used with *off* **12** **a** : to decline to bid, double, or redouble in a card game **b** : to withdraw from the current poker pot ~ *vt* **1** : to go beyond: as **a** : SURPASS, EXCEED ⟨~*es* all expectations⟩ **b** : to advance or develop beyond **c** : to go past (one moving in the same direction) **2** : to omit a regularly scheduled declaration and payment of (a dividend) **3** **a** : to go across, over, or through : CROSS **b** : to live through (as an experience or peril) : UNDERGO **c** : to go through (as a test) successfully **4** **a** : to secure the approval of ⟨the bill ~*ed* the Senate⟩ **b** : to cause or permit to win approval or legal or official sanction ⟨~ a law⟩ **c** : to give approval or a passing grade to ⟨~ the students⟩ **5** **a** : to let (as time or a period of time) go by esp. while involved in a leisure activity ⟨I'll read to ~ the time⟩ **b** : to let go unnoticed : OVERLOOK, DISREGARD **6** **a** : PLEDGE **b** : to transfer the right to or property in ⟨~ title to a house⟩ **7** **a** : to put in circulation ⟨~ bad checks⟩ **b** (1) : to transfer or transmit from one to another (2) : to relay or communicate (as information) to another **c** : to cause or enable to go : TRANSPORT **d** : to throw or hit (a ball or puck) esp. to a teammate **8** **a** : to pronounce (as a sentence or opinion) esp. judicially **b** : UTTER **9** **a** : to cause or permit to go past or through a barrier **b** : to move or cause to move in a particular manner or direction ⟨~*ed* my hand over my face⟩ ⟨~ the rope through the loop⟩ **c** : to cause to march or go by in order ⟨~ the troops in review⟩ **10** : to emit or discharge from a bodily part and esp. the bowels **11** **a** : to give a base on balls to **b**

: to hit a ball past (an opponent) in a game (as tennis) — **pass·er** *n* — **pass muster :** to secure approval or acceptance — **pass the buck :** to shift a responsibility to someone else — **pass the hat :** to take up a collection for money — **pass the time of day :** to exchange greetings or engage in pleasant conversation

[2]pass *n* (14c) **1 :** a means (as an opening, road, or channel) by which a barrier may be passed or access to a place may be gained; *esp* : a low place in a mountain range **2 :** a position to be held usu. against odds

[3]pass *n* (15c) **1 :** the act or an instance of passing : PASSAGE **2 :** REALIZATION ⟨brought his dream to ~⟩ **3 :** a usu. distressing or bad state of affairs ⟨what has brought you to such a ~?⟩ **4 a :** a written permission to move about freely in a place or to leave or enter it **b :** a written leave of absence from a military post or station for a brief period **c :** a permit or ticket allowing free transportation or free admission **5** *archaic* : a thrust or lunge in fencing **6 a :** a transference of objects by sleight of hand or other deceptive means **b :** a moving of the hands over or along something **7** *archaic* : an ingenious sally (as of wit) **8 :** the passing of an examination or course of study; *also* : the mark or certification of such passing **9 :** a single complete mechanical operation; *also* : a single complete cycle of operations (as for processing, manufacturing, or printing) **10 a (1) :** a transfer of a ball or a puck from one player to another on the same team **(2) :** a ball or puck so transferred **b :** a ball hit to the side and out of reach of an opponent in a game (as tennis or paddleball) **11 :** BASE ON BALLS **12 :** an election not to bid, bet, or draw an additional card in a card game **13 :** a throw of dice in the game of craps that wins the shooter his bet — compare [3]CRAP 2, MISSOUT **14 :** a single passage or movement (as of an airplane) over a place or toward a target **15 a :** EFFORT, TRY **b :** a sexually inviting gesture or approach **16 :** PASE ***syn*** see JUNCTURE

pass·able \'pas-ə-bəl\ *adj* (15c) **1 a :** capable of being passed, crossed, or traveled on ⟨~ roads⟩ **b :** capable of being freely circulated **2 :** just good enough : TOLERABLE — **pass·ably** \-blē\ *adv*

pas·sa·ca·glia \ˌpäs-ə-'käl-yə, ˌpas-ə-'kal-yə\ *n* [modif. of Sp *pasacalle,* fr. *pasar* to pass + *calle* street, fr. L *callis* path — more at PASE] (1659) **1 a :** an old Italian or Spanish dance tune **b :** an instrumental musical composition consisting of variations usu. on a ground bass in moderately slow triple time **2 :** an old dance performed to a passacaglia

pas·sa·do \pə-'säd-(ˌ)ō\ *n, pl* **-dos** *or* **-does** [modif. of F *passade* (fr. It *passata*) or It *passata,* fr. *passare* to pass, fr. (assumed) VL] *archaic* (1588) : a thrust in fencing with one foot advanced

[1]pas·sage \'pas-ij\ *n* (13c) **1 a :** the action or process of passing from one place, condition, or stage to another **b** *obs* : DEATH **c :** a continuous movement or flow ⟨the ~ of time⟩ **2 a :** a way of exit or entrance : a road, path, channel, or course by which something passes **b :** a corridor or lobby giving access to the different rooms or parts of a building or apartment **3 a (1) :** a specific act of traveling or passing esp. by sea or air **(2) :** a privilege of conveyance as a passenger : ACCOMMODATIONS **b :** the passing of a legislative measure or law : ENACTMENT **4 :** a right, liberty, or permission to pass **5 a :** something that happens or is done : INCIDENT **b :** something that takes place between two persons mutually **6 a :** a usu. brief portion of a written work or speech that is relevant to a point under discussion or noteworthy for content or style **b :** a phrase or short section of a musical composition **c :** a detail of a work of art (as a painting) **7 :** the act or action of passing something or undergoing a passing **8 :** incubation of a pathogen (as a virus) in culture, a living organism, or a developing egg

[2]passage *vb* **pas·saged; pas·sag·ing** *vi* (1824) : to go past or across : CROSS ~ *vt* : to subject to passage ⟨*passaged* a virus⟩

pas·sage·way \-ij-ˌwā\ *n* (1649) : a way that allows passage

pas·sage·work \-ij-ˌwərk\ *n* (1865) : a section of a musical composition characteristically unimportant thematically and consisting esp. of ornamental figures

pas·sant \'pas-ᵊnt\ *adj* [MF, fr. prp. of *passer* to pass] (1500) : walking with the farther forepaw raised — used of a heraldic animal

pass away *vi* (14c) **1 :** to go out of existence **2 :** DIE

pass·band \'pas-ˌband\ *n* (1922) : a band of frequencies (as in a radio circuit or a light filter) that is transmitted with maximum efficiency

pass·book \-ˌbu̇k\ *n* (1828) : BANKBOOK

pass degree *n* (1868) : a bachelor's degree without honors that is taken at a British university

pas·sé \pa-'sā\ *adj* [F, fr. pp. of *passer*] (1775) **1 :** past one's prime **2 a :** OUTMODED **b :** behind the times

passed ball *n* (1861) : a pitched baseball not hit by the batter that passes the catcher when he should have stopped it and allows a base runner to advance a base — compare WILD PITCH

passed pawn *n* (1797) : a chess pawn that has no enemy pawn in front of it on its own or an adjacent file

pas·sel \'pas-əl\ *n* [alter. of *parcel*] (1835) : a large number : GROUP

passe·men·terie \pas-'men-trē, -'ment-ə-rē\ *n* [F, fr. *passement* ornamental braid, fr. *passer*] (1794) : a fancy edging or trimming made of braid, cord, gimp, beading, or metallic thread

pas·sen·ger \'pas-ᵊn-jər\ *n* [ME *passager,* fr. MF, fr. *passager,* adj., passing, fr. *passage* act of passing, fr. OF, fr. *passer*] (14c) **1 :** WAYFARER **2 :** a traveler in a public or private conveyance

passenger pigeon *n* (1802) : an extinct but formerly abundant No. American migratory pigeon (*Ectopistes migratorius*)

passe–par·tout \ˌpas-pər-'tü, -ˌpär-\ *n* [F, fr. *passe partout* pass everywhere] (1645) **1 :** MASTER KEY **2 a :** [5]MAT 1 **b :** a method of framing in which a picture, a mat, a glass, and a back (as of cardboard) are held together by strips of paper or cloth pasted over the edges **3 :** a strong paper gummed on one side and used esp. for mounting pictures

pass·er·by \ˌpas-ər-'bī, 'pas-ər-ˌ\ *n, pl* **pass·ers·by** \-ərz-\ (1568) : one who passes by

pas·ser·ine \'pas-ə-ˌrīn\ *adj* [L *passerinus* of sparrows, fr. *passer* sparrow] (1776) **1 :** of or relating to the largest order (Passeriformes) of birds which includes more than half of all living birds and consists chiefly of altricial songbirds of perching habits **2 :** of or relating to a suborder (Passeres) of passerine birds comprising the true songbirds with specialized vocal apparatus — **passerine** *n*

pas seul \ˌpä-'səl, -'sər(-ə)l\ *n* [F, lit., solo step] (1813) : a solo dance or dance figure

pass–fail \'pas-'fā(ə)l\ *n* (1959) : a system of grading whereby the grades "pass" and "fail" replace the traditional letter grades — **pass–fail** *adj*

pas·si·ble \'pas-ə-bəl\ *adj* [ME, fr. MF, fr. LL *passibilis,* fr. L *passus,* pp. of *pati* to suffer — more at PATIENT] (14c) : capable of feeling or suffering

pas·sim \'pas-əm; 'pas-ˌim, 'päs-\ *adv* [L, fr. *passus* scattered, fr. pp. of *pandere* to spread — more at FATHOM] (1803) : HERE AND THERE

[1]pass·ing \'pas-iŋ\ *n* (14c) : the act of one that passes or causes to pass; *esp* : DEATH — **in passing :** by the way : PARENTHETICALLY

[2]passing *adj* (14c) **1 :** going by or past ⟨a ~ pedestrian⟩ **2 :** having a brief duration ⟨a ~ whim⟩ **3** *obs* : SURPASSING **4 :** SUPERFICIAL **5 a :** of, relating to, or used in or for the act or process of passing ⟨~ lanes⟩ **b :** given on satisfactory completion of an examination or course of study ⟨a ~ grade⟩

[3]passing *adv* (14c) : to a surpassing degree : EXCEEDINGLY ⟨~ fair⟩

passing note *n* (1730) : a nonharmonic tone interposed between essential harmonic tones of adjacent chords — called also *passing tone*

passing shot *n* (ca 1949) : a stroke (as in tennis) that drives the ball to one side and beyond the reach of an opponent

pas·sion \'pash-ən\ *n* [ME, fr. OF, fr. LL *passion-, passio* suffering, being acted upon, fr. L *passus,* pp. of *pati* to suffer — more at PATIENT] (12c) **1** *often cap* **a :** the sufferings of Christ between the night of the Last Supper and his death **b :** an oratorio based on a gospel narrative of the Passion **2** *obs* : SUFFERING **3 :** the state or capacity of being acted on by external agents or forces **4 a (1) :** EMOTION ⟨his ruling ~ is greed⟩ **(2)** *pl* : the emotions as distinguished from reason **b :** intense, driving, or overmastering feeling or conviction ⟨driven to paint by a ~ beyond his control⟩ **c :** an outbreak of anger **5 a :** ardent affection : LOVE **b :** a strong liking or desire for or devotion to some activity, object, or concept **c :** sexual desire **d :** an object of desire or deep interest — **pas·sion·less** \-ləs\ *adj*

syn PASSION, FERVOR, ARDOR, ENTHUSIASM, ZEAL mean intense emotion compelling action. PASSION applies to an emotion that is deeply stirring or ungovernable; FERVOR implies a warm and steady emotion; ARDOR suggests warm and excited feeling likely to be fitful or short-lived; ENTHUSIASM applies to lively or eager interest in or admiration for a proposal, cause, or activity; ZEAL implies energetic and unflagging pursuit of an aim or devotion to a cause. ***syn*** see in addition FEELING

pas·sion·al \'pash-ən-ᵊl, 'pash-nəl\ *adj* (1700) : of, relating to, or marked by passion

pas·sion·ate \'pash-(ə-)nət\ *adj* (15c) **1 a :** easily aroused to anger **b :** filled with anger : ANGRY **2 a :** capable of, affected by, or expressing intense feeling **b :** ENTHUSIASTIC, ARDENT **3 :** swayed by or affected with sexual desire ***syn*** see IMPASSIONED — **pas·sion·ate·ly** *adv* — **pas·sion·ate·ness** *n*

pas·sion·flow·er \'pash-ən-ˌflau̇(-ə)r\ *n* [trans. of L *flos passionis;* fr. the fancied resemblance of parts of the flower to the instruments of Christ's crucifixion] (1633) : any of a genus (*Passiflora* of the family Passifloraceae, the passionflower family) of chiefly tropical woody tendriled climbing vines or erect herbs with usu. showy flowers and pulpy often edible berries

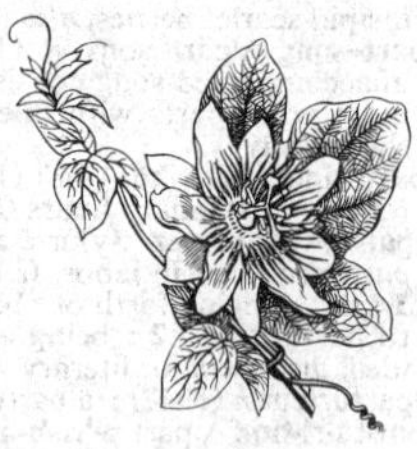

passionflower

passion fruit *n* (1752) : the edible fruit of a passionflower

Pas·sion·ist \'pash-(ə-)nəst\ *n* [It *passionista,* fr. *passione* passion, fr. LL *passion-, passio*] (1832) : a member of a Roman Catholic mendicant order founded by St. Paul of the Cross in Italy in 1720 and devoted chiefly to missionary work and retreats

passion play *n, often cap 1st P* (1870) : a dramatic representation of the scenes connected with the passion and crucifixion of Christ

Passion Sunday *n* (15c) : the fifth Sunday in Lent

Pas·sion·tide \'pash-ən-ˌtīd\ *n* (1847) : the last two weeks of Lent

Passion Week *n* (15c) **1 :** HOLY WEEK **2 :** the week between Passion Sunday and Palm Sunday

pas·siv·ate \'pas-iv-ˌāt\ *vt* **-at·ed; -at·ing** (1913) **1 :** to make inactive or less reactive ⟨~ the surface of steel by chemical treatment⟩ **2 :** to protect (as a solid-state device) against contamination by coating or surface treatment — **pas·siv·ation** \ˌpas-iv-'ā-shən\ *n*

[1]pas·sive \'pas-iv\ *adj* [ME, fr. L *passivus,* fr. *passus,* pp.] (14c) **1 a (1) :** acted upon by an external agency **(2) :** receptive to outside impressions or influences **b (1) :** asserting that the grammatical subject of a verb is subjected to or affected by the action represented by that verb **(2) :** containing or yielding a passive verb form **c (1) :** lacking in energy or will : LETHARGIC **(2) :** tending not to take an active or dominant part **d :** induced by an outside agency ⟨~ exercise of a paralyzed leg⟩ **2 a :** not active or operating : INERT **b :** of, relating to, or making direct use of the sun's heat usu. without the intervention of mechanical devices ⟨~ technique⟩ ⟨~ solar house⟩ **c :** LATENT **d (1) :** of, relating to, or characterized by a state of chemical inactivity; *esp* : resistant to corrosion **(2) :** not involving expenditure of chemical energy ⟨~ transport across a cell membrane⟩ **e :** exhibiting no gain or control — used of an electronic device (as a capacitor or resistor) **f :** operating solely by means of the power of an input signal ⟨a ~ communication satellite that reflects television signals⟩ **g :** relating to the detection of or to orientation by means of an object through its emission of energy **3 a :** receiving or enduring without resistance : SUBMISSIVE **b :** existing or occurring without being active, open, or direct ⟨~ support⟩ ***syn*** see INACTIVE — **pas·sive·ly** *adv* — **pas·sive·ness** *n* — **pas·siv·i·ty** \pa-'siv-ət-ē\ *n*

[2]passive *n* (1530) **1 :** a passive verb form **2 :** the passive voice of a language

passive immunity *n* (1895) : immunity acquired by transfer of antibodies (as by injection of serum from an individual with active immunity) — **passive immunization** *n*

passive resistance *n* (1819) : resistance esp. to a government or an occupying power characterized mainly by noncooperation

passive restraint *n* (1970) : a restraint (as a self-locking seat belt) that acts automatically to protect an automobile rider during a crash

passive transfer *n* (1941) **:** a local transfer of skin sensitivity from an allergic to a normal person by injection of serum from the former that is used esp. for identifying specific allergens when a high degree of allergic sensitivity is suspected

pas·siv·ism \'pas-iv-,iz-əm\ *n* (1872) **:** a passive attitude, behavior, or way of life — **pas·siv·ist** \-əst\ *n*

pass·key \'pas-,kē\ *n* (1817) **1 :** MASTER KEY **2 :** SKELETON KEY

pass off *vt* (1799) **1 :** to make public or offer for sale with intent to deceive **2 :** to give a false identity or character to

pass out *vi* (1899) **1 :** DIE **2 :** to lose consciousness ~ *vt* **:** to reject (a deal in bridge) as unplayable because everyone has passed on the first round of bidding

Pass·over \'pas-,ō-vər\ *n* [fr. the exemption of the Israelites from the slaughter of the first-born in Egypt in Exod 12:23-27] (1530) **:** a Jewish holiday beginning on the 14th of Nisan and commemorating the Hebrews' liberation from slavery in Egypt

pass over \(')pas-'ō-vər\ *vt* (14c) **1 :** to ignore in passing **2 :** to pay no attention to the claims of **:** DISREGARD

pass·port \'pas-,pō(ə)rt, -,pȯ(ə)rt\ *n* [MF *passeport,* fr. *passer* to pass + *port* port, fr. L *portus* — more at FORD] (1500) **1 a :** a formal document that is issued by an authorized official of a country to one of its citizens and usu. necessary for exit from and reentry into the country, that allows him to travel in a foreign country in accordance with visa requirements, and that requests protection for him while abroad **b :** a license issued by a country permitting a foreign citizen to pass or take goods through its territory **:** SAFE-CONDUCT **c :** a document of identification required by law to be carried by persons residing or traveling within a country **2 a :** a permission or authorization to go somewhere **b :** something that secures admission or acceptance ⟨education as a ~ to success⟩

pass–through *n* (1951) **1 :** the act, action, or process of offsetting increased costs by raising prices **2 :** an opening in a wall between two rooms through which something (as dishes) may be passed

pass up *vt* (1896) **:** to let go by without accepting or taking advantage of ⟨*pass up* a chance for promotion⟩; *also* **:** DECLINE, REJECT

pass·word \'pas-,wərd\ *n* (1817) **1 :** something that enables one to pass or gain admission: as **a :** a spoken word or phrase required to pass by a guard **b :** a sequence of characters required for access to a computer system **2 :** WATCHWORD

[1]**past** \'past\ *adj* [ME, fr. pp. of *passen* to pass] (14c) **1 a :** AGO ⟨12 years ~⟩ **b :** just gone or elapsed ⟨for the ~ few months⟩ **2 :** having existed or taken place in a period before the present **:** BYGONE **3 :** of, relating to, or constituting a verb tense that is expressive of elapsed time and that in English is usu. formed by internal vowel change (as in *sang*) or by the addition of a suffix (as in *laughed*) **4 :** having served as a specified officer in an organization ⟨~ president⟩

[2]**past** *prep* (14c) **1 a :** beyond the age for or of ⟨~ playing with dolls⟩ **b :** AFTER ⟨half ~ two⟩ **2 a :** at the farther side of **:** BEYOND **b :** in a course or direction going close to and then beyond ⟨drove ~ the house⟩ **3** *obs* **:** more than **4 :** beyond the capacity, range, or sphere of ⟨~ belief⟩

[3]**past** *n* (1590) **1 a :** time gone by **b :** something that happened or was done in the past ⟨regret the ~⟩ **2 a :** the past tense of a language **b :** a verb form in the past tense **3 :** a past life, history, or course of action; *esp* **:** one that is kept secret

[4]**past** *adv* (1805) **1 :** so as to reach and go beyond a point near at hand **2 :** at an end **:** OVER

pas·ta \'päs-tə\ *n* [It, fr. LL] (1874) **1 :** a paste in processed form (as spaghetti) or in the form of fresh dough (as ravioli) **2 :** a dish of cooked pasta

[1]**paste** \'pāst\ *n* [ME, fr. MF, fr. LL *pasta* dough, paste] (14c) **1 a :** a dough that contains a considerable proportion of fat and is used for pastry crust or fancy rolls **b :** a confection made by evaporating fruit with sugar or by flavoring a gelatin, starch, or gum arabic preparation **c :** a smooth food product made by evaporation or grinding ⟨tomato ~⟩ ⟨almond ~⟩ **d :** a shaped dough (as spaghetti or ravioli) prepared from semolina, farina, or wheat flour **2 :** a soft plastic mixture or composition: as **a :** a preparation usu. of flour or starch and water used as an adhesive or a vehicle for mordant or color **b :** clay or a clay mixture used in making pottery or porcelain **3 :** a brilliant glass of high lead content used for the manufacture of artificial gems

[2]**paste** *vt* **past·ed; past·ing** (1561) **1 :** to cause to adhere by or as if by paste **:** STICK **2 :** to cover with something pasted on

[3]**paste** *vt* **past·ed; past·ing** [alter. of *baste*] (1846) **:** to strike hard at

[1]**paste·board** \'pās(t)-,bō(ə)rd, -,bȯ(ə)rd\ *n* (1562) **1 :** a solid paperboard with a paper facing; *broadly* **:** PAPERBOARD **2 :** TICKET

[2]**pasteboard** *adj* (1599) **1 :** made of pasteboard **2 :** SHAM, UNSUBSTANTIAL

paste·down \-,dau̇n\ *n* (ca. 1888) **:** the outer leaf of an endpaper that is pasted down to the inside of the front or back cover of a book

[1]**pas·tel** \pas-'tel\ *n* [F, fr. It *pastello,* fr. LL *pastellus* woad, fr. dim. of *pasta*] (1662) **1 :** a paste made of powdered pigment and used for making crayons; *also* **:** a crayon made of such paste **2 a :** a drawing in pastel **b :** the process or art of drawing with pastels **3 :** a light literary sketch **4 :** any of various pale or light colors

[2]**pastel** *adj* (1884) **1 a :** of or relating to a pastel **b :** made with pastels **2 :** pale and light in color **3 :** lacking in body or vigor **:** DELICATE

pas·tel·ist *or* **pas·tel·list** \-'tel-əst\ *n* (1881) **:** an artist who works with pastels

pas·tern \'pas-tərn\ *n* [MF *pasturon,* fr. *pasture* pasture, tether attached to a horse's foot] (ca. 1530) **1 :** a part of the foot of an equine extending from the fetlock to the top of the hoof — see HORSE illustration **2 :** a part of the leg of an animal other than an equine that corresponds to the pastern

paste·up \'pā-,stəp\ *n* (ca. 1930) **:** MECHANICAL; *also* **:** the process of making mechanicals

pas·teur·iza·tion \,pas-chə-rə-'zā-shən, ,pas-tə-\ *n* (1886) **1 :** partial sterilization of a substance and esp. a liquid (as milk) at a temperature and for a period of exposure that destroys objectionable organisms without major chemical alteration of the substance **2 :** partial sterilization of perishable food products (as fruit or fish) with radiation (as gamma rays)

pas·teur·ize \'pas-chə-,rīz, 'pas-tə-\ *vt* **-ized; -iz·ing** [Louis *Pasteur*] (1881) **:** to subject to pasteurization — **pas·teur·iz·er** *n*

Pasteur treatment *n* (1926) **:** a method of aborting rabies by stimulating production of antibodies through successive inoculations with attenuated virus of gradually increasing strength

pas·tic·cio \pas-'tē-ch(ē-,)ō, päs-\ *n, pl* **-ci** \-(,)chē\ *or* **-cios** [It, lit., pasty, fr. ML *pasticius,* fr. LL *pasta*] (1752) **:** PASTICHE

pas·tiche \pas-'tēsh, päs-\ *n* [F, fr. It *pasticcio*] (1878) **1 :** a literary, artistic, or musical work that imitates the style of previous work; *also* **:** such stylistic imitation **2 a :** a musical, literary, or artistic composition made up of selections from different works **:** POTPOURRI **b :** HODGEPODGE — **pas·ti·cheur** \,pas-tē-'shər, ,päs-\ *n*

past·ies \'pā-stēz\ *n pl* [[2]*paste*] (ca. 1954) **:** small round coverings for a woman's nipples worn esp. by a stripteaser

pas·tille \pas-'tē(ə)l\ *also* **pas·til** \'pas-tᵊl\ *n* [F *pastille,* fr. L *pastillus* small loaf, lozenge; akin to L *panis* bread — more at FOOD] (1658) **1 :** a small mass of aromatic paste for fumigating or scenting the air of a room **2 :** an aromatic or medicated lozenge **:** TROCHE

pas·time \'pas-,tīm\ *n* (15c) **:** something that amuses and serves to make time pass agreeably **:** DIVERSION

pas·ti·na \'päs-tē-nə\ *n* [It, dim of *pasta* pasta] (ca. 1945) **:** very small bits of pasta used in soup or broth

past·i·ness \'pā-stē-nəs\ *n* (1608) **:** the quality or state of being pasty

past master *n* (1762) **1 :** one who has held the office of worshipful master in a lodge of Freemasons or of master in a guild, club, or society **2** [alter. of *passed master*] **:** one who is expert **:** ADEPT

past·ness \'pas(t)-nəs\ *n* (1829) **1 :** the quality or state of being past **2 :** the subjective quality of something being remembered rather than immediately experienced

[1]**pas·tor** \'pas-tər\ *n* [ME *pastour,* fr. MF, fr. L *pastor* herdsman, fr. *pastus,* pp. of *pascere* to feed — more at FOOD] (14c) **:** a spiritual overseer; *esp* **:** a clergyman serving a local church or parish — **pas·tor·ship** \-,ship\ *n*

[2]**pastor** *vt* **pas·tored; pas·tor·ing** \-t(ə-)riŋ\ (1623) **:** to serve as pastor of (as a church)

[3]**pas·tor** \päs-'tȯ(ə)r\ *n* [Sp, fr. L] *chiefly Southwest* (1849) **:** HERDSMAN

[1]**pas·to·ral** \'pas-t(ə-)rəl\ *adj* [ME, fr. L *pastoralis,* fr. *pastor* herdsman] (15c) **1 a** **:** (1) **:** of, relating to, or composed of shepherds or herdsmen (2) **:** devoted to or based on livestock raising **b :** of or relating to the countryside **:** not urban **c :** portraying or expressive of the life of shepherds or country people esp. in an idealized and conventionalized manner ⟨~ poetry⟩ **d :** pleasingly peaceful and innocent **:** IDYLLIC **2 a :** of or relating to spiritual care or guidance esp. of a congregation **b :** of or relating to the pastor of a church — **pas·to·ral·ly** \-t(ə-)rə-lē\ *adv* — **pas·to·ral·ness** *n*

[2]**pastoral** \'pas-t(ə-)rəl; *1d is often* ,pas-tə-'räl, -'ral\ *n* (1584) **1 a :** a literary work (as a poem or play) dealing with shepherds or rural life in a usu. artificial manner and typically drawing a contrast between the innocence and serenity of the simple life and the misery and corruption of city and esp. court life **b :** pastoral poetry or drama **c :** a rural picture or scene **d :** PASTORALE 1b **2 :** CROSIER 1 **3 :** a letter of a pastor to his charge: as **a :** a letter addressed by a bishop to his diocese **b :** a letter of the house of bishops of the Protestant Episcopal Church to be read in each parish

pas·to·rale \,pas-tə-'räl, -'ral *also* -'räl-ē\ *n* [It, fr. *pastorale* of herdsmen, fr. L *pastoralis,* fr. *pastor*] (1724) **1 a :** an opera of the 16th or 17th centuries having a pastoral plot **b :** an instrumental or vocal composition having a pastoral theme **2 :** PASTORAL 1a

Pastoral Epistle *n* (1836) **:** one of three New Testament letters including two addressed to Timothy and one to Titus that give advice on matters of church government and discipline

pas·to·ral·ism \'pas-t(ə-)rə-,liz-əm\ *n* (1854) **1 :** the quality or style characteristic of pastoral writing **2 a :** livestock raising **b :** social organization based on livestock raising as the primary economic activity — **pas·to·ral·ist** \-ləst\ *n*

pas·tor·ate \'pas-t(ə-)rət\ *n* (1795) **1 :** the office, state, jurisdiction, or tenure of office of a pastor **2 :** a body of pastors

pas·to·ri·um \pas-'tōr-ē-əm, -'tȯr-\ *n* [irreg. fr. *pastor* + *-orium*] *chiefly Southern* (1898) **:** a Protestant parsonage

past participle *n* (1798) **:** a participle that typically expresses completed action, that is traditionally one of the principal parts of the verb, and that is traditionally used in English in the formation of perfect tenses in the active voice and of all tenses in the passive voice

past perfect *adj* (1889) **:** of, relating to, or constituting a verb tense that is traditionally formed in English with *had* and denotes an action or state as completed at or before a past time spoken of — **past perfect** *n*

pas·tra·mi *also* **pas·tro·mi** \pə-'sträm-ē\ *n* [Yiddish, fr. Rom *pastramă*] (1936) **:** a highly seasoned smoked beef prepared esp. from shoulder cuts

past·ry \'pā-strē\ *n, pl* **pastries** [[1]*paste*] (1539) **1 a :** PASTE 1a **b :** sweet baked goods made of dough having a high fat content **2 :** a piece of pastry

past tense *n* (1813) **:** a verb tense expressing action or state in or as if in the past: **a :** a verb tense expressive of elapsed time (as *wrote* in "on arriving I wrote a letter") **b :** a verb tense expressing action or state in progress or continuance or habitually done or customarily occurring at a past time (as *was writing* in "I was writing while he dictated" or *loved* in "their sons loved fishing")

pas·tur·age \'pas-chə-rij\ *n* (1533) **:** PASTURE

[1]**pas·ture** \'pas-chər\ *n* [ME, fr. MF, fr. LL *pastura,* fr. L *pastus,* pp. of *pascere* to feed — more at FOOD] (14c) **1 :** plants (as grass) grown for the feeding esp. of grazing animals **2 :** land or a plot of land used for grazing **3 :** the feeding of livestock **:** GRAZING

[2]**pasture** *vb* **pas·tured; pas·tur·ing** *vi* (14c) **:** GRAZE, BROWSE ~ *vt* **1 :** to feed (as cattle) on pasture **2 :** to use as pasture

pas·ture·land \'pas-chər-,land\ *n* (1591) **:** PASTURE 2

[1]pas·ty \'pas-tē\ *n, pl* **pasties** [ME *pastee*, fr. MF *pasté*, fr. *paste* dough, paste] (14c) **1 :** [2]PIE 1, 2; *esp* **:** a meat pie **2 :** TURNOVER 5

[2]pasty \'pā-stē\ *adj* **past·i·er; -est** (1659) **:** resembling paste; *esp* **:** pallid and unhealthy in appearance

PA system \pē-'ā-\ *n* (ca. 1936) **:** PUBLIC-ADDRESS SYSTEM

[1]pat \'pat\ *n* [ME *patte*] (15c) **1 :** a light blow esp. with the hand or a flat instrument **2 :** a light tapping often rhythmical sound **3 :** something (as butter) shaped into a small flat usu. square individual portion — **pat on the back :** an expression of approval

[2]pat *adv* (1578) **:** in a pat manner **:** APTLY, PERFECTLY

[3]pat *vb* **pat·ted; pat·ting** *vt* (1591) **1 :** to strike lightly with a flat instrument **2 :** to flatten, smooth, or put into place or shape with light blows **3 :** to tap or stroke gently with the hand to soothe, caress, or show approval ~ *vi* **:** to strike or beat gently

[4]pat *adj* (1646) **1 a :** exactly suited to the purpose or occasion **:** APT **b :** suspiciously appropriate **:** CONTRIVED **2 :** learned, mastered, or memorized exactly **3 :** FIRM, UNYIELDING **4 :** reduced to a simple or mechanical form **:** STANDARD, TRITE

pa·ta·ca \pə-'täk-ə\ *n* [Pg] (1830) — see MONEY table

pa·ta·gi·um \pə-'tā-jē-əm\ *n, pl* **-gia** \-jē-ə\ [NL, fr. L, gold edging on a tunic] (1826) **:** a wing membrane: as **a :** the fold of skin connecting the forelimbs and hind limbs of a flying squirrel or dragon lizard **b :** the fold of skin in front of the main segments of a bird's wing

[1]patch \'pach\ *n* [ME *pacche*] (14c) **1 :** a piece of material used to mend or cover a hole or a weak spot **2 :** a tiny piece of black silk or court plaster worn on the face or neck esp. by women to hide a blemish or to heighten beauty **3 a :** a piece of adhesive plaster or other cover applied to a wound **b :** a shield worn over the socket of an injured or missing eye **4 a :** a small piece **:** SCRAP **b :** a part or area distinct from that about it ⟨cabbage ~⟩ **5 :** a piece of cloth sewed on a garment as an ornament or insignia; *esp* **:** SHOULDER PATCH **6 :** a temporary connection in a communication system (as a telephone hookup) **7 :** a temporary correction in a faulty computer program

[2]patch *vt* (1516) **1 :** to mend, cover, or fill up a hole or weak spot in **2 :** to provide with a patch **3 a :** to make of patches or fragments **b :** to mend or put together esp. in hasty or shabby fashion — usu. used with *up* **c :** to make a patch in (a computer program) **4 :** to connect (as circuits) by a patch cord ***syn*** see MEND

[3]patch *n* [perh. by folk etymology fr. It dial. *paccio*] (1549) **:** FOOL, DOLT

patch·board \'pach-,bō(ə)rd, -,bȯ(ə)rd\ *n* (1934) **:** a switchboard in which circuits are interconnected by patch cords

patch cord *n* (1926) **:** a wire with a plug at each end that is used to effect a communication patch

pa·tchou·li *also* **pa·tchou·ly** \'pach-ə-lē, pə-'chü-lē\ *n* [Tamil *paccuḷi*] (1845) **1 :** a heavy perfume made from patchouli oil **2 :** an East Indian shrubby mint (*Pogostemon cablin*) that yields a fragrant essential oil

patch pocket *n* (1895) **:** a flat pocket applied to the outside of a garment

patch test *n* (1933) **:** a test for determining allergic sensitivity that is made by applying to the unbroken skin small pads soaked with the allergen to be tested

patch·work \'pach-,wərk\ *n* (1692) **1 :** something composed of miscellaneous or incongruous parts **:** HODGEPODGE **2 :** pieces of cloth of various colors and shapes sewn together to form a covering

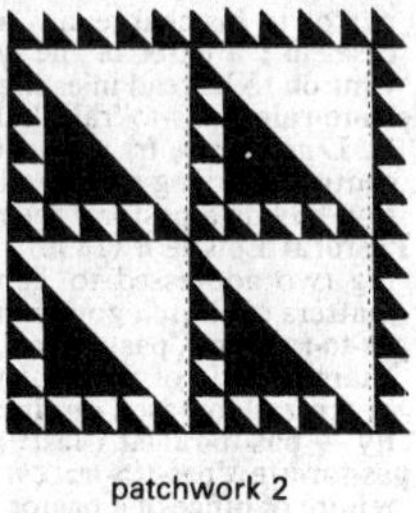
patchwork 2

patchy \'pach-ē\ *adj* **patch·i·er; -est** (1798) **:** marked by, consisting of, or diversified with patches **:** IRREGULAR — **patch·i·ly** \'pach-ə-lē\ *adv* — **patch·i·ness** \'pach-ē-nəs\ *n*

pate \'pāt\ *n* [ME] (14c) **1 :** HEAD **2 :** the crown of the head **3 :** BRAIN — used chiefly disparagingly — **pat·ed** \'pāt-əd\ *adj*

pâte \'pät\ *n* [F, lit., paste, fr. OF *paste*] (1863) **:** PASTE 2b

pâ·té \pä-'tā, pa-\ *n* [F, fr. OF *pasté*, fr. *paste*] (1706) **1 :** a meat or fish pie or patty **2 :** a spread of finely chopped or pureed seasoned meat ⟨chicken liver ~⟩

pâ·té de foie gras \(,)pä-,tād-ə-,fwä-'grä, (,)pa-,tād-\ *n, pl* **pâ·tés de foie gras** \-,tā(z)d-ə-\ [F] (1827) **:** a rich pâté of fat goose liver and truffles sometimes with added fat pork

pa·tel·la \pə-'tel-ə\ *n, pl* **-lae** \-'tel-(,)ē, -,ī\ *or* **-las** [L, fr. dim. of *patina* shallow dish] (1693) **:** a thick flat triangular movable bone that forms the anterior point of the knee and protects the front of the joint — called also *kneecap* — **pa·tel·lar** \-'tel-ər\ *adj*

pa·tel·li·form \pə-'tel-ə-,fȯrm\ *adj* [NL *Patella*, genus including the limpet, fr. L, small shallow dish] (1819) **1 :** resembling a limpet or limpet shell **2 :** disk-shaped with a narrow rim

pat·en \'pat-ᵊn\ *n* [ME, fr. MF *patene*, fr. ML & L; ML *patina*, fr. L, shallow dish, fr. Gk *patanē*; akin to L *patēre* to be open] (14c) **1 a :** plate usu. made of precious metal and used to carry the bread at the Eucharist **2 a :** PLATE **b :** something (as a metal disk) resembling a plate

pa·ten·cy \'pat-ᵊn-sē, 'pāt-\ *n* (1656) **:** the quality or state of being patent

[1]pa·tent *1-3 are* 'pat-ᵊnt, *chiefly Brit* 'pāt-; *4* 'pāt-; *5* 'pāt-, 'pat-; *6-7* 'pat-, 'pāt-, *Brit usu* 'pāt-\ *adj* [ME, fr. MF, fr. L *patent-, patens*, fr. prp. of *patēre* to be open — more at FATHOM] (14c) **1 a :** open to public inspection — used chiefly in the phrase *letters patent* **b** (1) **:** secured by letters patent or by a patent to the exclusive control and possession of a particular individual or party (2) **:** protected by a patent **:** made under a patent ⟨~ locks⟩ **c :** protected by a trademark or a trade name so as to establish proprietary rights analogous to those conveyed by letters patent or a patent **:** PROPRIETARY ⟨~ drugs⟩ **2 :** of, relating to, or concerned with the granting of patents esp. for inventions ⟨a ~ lawyer⟩ **3 :** making exclusive or proprietary claims or pretensions **4 :** affording free passage **:** UNOBSTRUCTED ⟨a ~ opening⟩ **5 :** PATULOUS, SPREADING ⟨a ~ calyx⟩ **6** *archaic* **:** ACCESSIBLE, EXPOSED **7 :** readily visible or intelligible **:** OBVIOUS ***syn*** see EVIDENT — **pa·tent·ly** *adv*

[2]pat·ent \'pat-ᵊnt, *Brit also* 'pāt-\ *n* (14c) **1 :** an official document conferring a right or privilege **:** LETTERS PATENT **2 a :** a writing securing to an inventor for a term of years the exclusive right to make, use, or sell his invention **b :** the monopoly or right so granted **c :** a patented invention **3 :** PRIVILEGE, LICENSE **4 :** an instrument making a conveyance of public lands; *also* **:** the land so conveyed **5 :** PATENT LEATHER

[3]pat·ent *vt* (1675) **1 :** to obtain or grant a patent right to **2 :** to grant a privilege, right, or license to by patent **3 :** to obtain or secure by patent; *esp* **:** to secure by letters patent exclusive right to make, use, or sell — **pat·ent·abil·i·ty** \,pat-ᵊn-tə-'bil-ət-ē, *Brit also* ,pāt-\ *n* — **pat·ent·able** \'pat-ᵊn-tə-bəl, *Brit also* 'pāt-\ *adj*

pat·ent·ed \'pat-ᵊnt-əd, *Brit also* 'pāt-\ *adj* (1951) **:** originated by or peculiar to one person or group **:** INDIVIDUALIZED

pat·en·tee \,pat-ᵊn-'tē, *Brit also* ,pāt-\ *n* (15c) **:** one to whom a grant is made or a privilege secured by patent

pat·ent flour \,pat-ᵊnt(t)-, *Brit also* ,pāt-\ *n* (1886) **:** a high-grade wheat flour that consists solely of endosperm

pat·ent leather \,pat-ᵊn(t)-, *Brit usu* ,pāt-\ *n* (1829) **:** a leather with a hard smooth glossy surface

patent medicine *n* (1770) **:** a packaged nonprescription drug which is protected by a trademark and whose contents are incompletely disclosed; *also* **:** any drug that is a proprietary

patent office *n* (1696) **:** a government office for examining claims to patents and granting patents

pat·en·tor \'pat-ᵊn-tər, ,pat-ᵊn-'tȯ(ə)r, *Brit also* 'pāt-, ,pāt-\ *n* (1641) **:** one that grants a patent

patent right *n* (1805) **:** a right granted by letters patent; *esp* **:** the exclusive right to an invention

pa·ter *n* (14c) **1** *often cap* \'pä-,te(ə)r\ **:** PATERNOSTER **2** \'pāt-ər\ [L] *chiefly Brit* **:** FATHER

pa·ter·fa·mil·i·as \,pat-ər-fə-'mil-ē-əs, ,pät-, ,pāt-\ *n, pl* **pa·tres·fa·mil·i·as** \,pā-,trēz-, ,pä-,träs-\ [L, fr. *pater* father + *familias*, archaic gen. of *familia* household — more at FATHER, FAMILY] (15c) **1 :** the male head of a household **2 :** the father of a family

pa·ter·nal \pə-'tərn-ᵊl\ *adj* [L *paternus*, fr. *pater*] (1605) **1 a :** of or relating to a father **b :** like that of a father ⟨~ benevolence⟩ **2 :** received or inherited from one's male parent **3 :** related through one's father ⟨~ grandfather⟩ — **pa·ter·nal·ly** \-ᵊl-ē\ *adv*

pa·ter·nal·ism \pə-'tərn-ᵊl-,iz-əm\ *n* (1881) **1 :** a system under which an authority undertakes to supply needs or regulate conduct of those under its control in matters affecting them as individuals as well as in their relations to authority and to each other **2 :** a policy or practice based on or characteristic of paternalism — **pa·ter·nal·ist** \-ᵊl-əst\ *n or adj* — **pa·ter·nal·is·tic** \-,tərn-ᵊl-'is-tik\ *adj* — **pa·ter·na·lis·ti·cal·ly** \-ti-k(ə-)lē\ *adv*

pa·ter·ni·ty \pə-'tər-nət-ē\ *n* (1582) **1 :** the quality or state of being a father **2 :** origin or descent from a father

paternity test *n* (1926) **:** a test to determine whether a given man could be the biological father of a given child that is made by comparison of genetic traits (as blood groups) of the mother, child, and suspected man

pa·ter·nos·ter \,pät-ər-'näs-tər, 'pat-ər-,, 'pä-,te(ə)r-', -'näs-,te(ə)r\ *n* [ME, fr. OE, fr. ML, fr. L *pater noster* our father, fr. the opening words] (bef. 12c) **1** *often cap* **:** LORD'S PRAYER **2 :** a word formula repeated as a prayer or magical charm

path \'path, 'pȧth\ *n, pl* **paths** \'pathz, 'paths, 'pȧthz, 'pȧths\ [ME, fr. OE *pæth*; akin to OHG *pfad* path] (bef. 12c) **1 :** a trodden way **2 :** a track specially constructed for a particular use **3 a :** COURSE, ROUTE **b :** a way of life, conduct, or thought **4 a :** the continuous series of positions or configurations that can be assumed in any motion or process of change by a moving or varying system **b :** a sequence of arcs in a network that can be traced continuously without retracing any arc **5 :** a line of communication over interconnecting neurons extending from one organ or center to another

path- *or* **patho-** *comb form* [NL, fr. Gk, fr. *pathos*, lit., suffering — more at PATHOS] **:** pathological state **:** disease ⟨*pathogen*⟩

-path \,path\ *n comb form* [G, back-formation fr. *-pathie* -pathy] **1 :** practitioner of a (specified) system of medicine that emphasizes one aspect of disease or its treatment ⟨naturo*path*⟩ **2** [ISV, fr. Gk *-pathēs*, adj., suffering, fr. *pathos*] **:** one suffering from a disorder (of such a part or system) ⟨psycho*path*⟩

Pa·than \pə-'tän *also* 'pä-thən\ *n* [Hindi *Paṭhān*] (1638) **:** a member of the principal ethnic group of Afghanistan

pa·thet·ic \pə-'thet-ik\ *adj* [MF or LL; MF *pathetique*, fr. LL *patheticus*, fr. Gk *pathētikos* capable of feeling, pathetic, fr. *paschein* to experience, suffer — more at PATHOS] (1598) **1 :** having a capacity to move one to either compassionate or contemptuous pity **2 :** marked by sorrow or melancholy **:** SAD ***syn*** see MOVING — **pa·thet·i·cal** \-i-kəl\ *adj* — **pa·thet·i·cal·ly** \-i-k(ə-)lē\ *adv*

pathetic fallacy *n* (1858) **:** the ascription of human traits or feelings to inanimate nature (as in *cruel sea*)

path·find·er \'path-,fīn-dər, 'pȧth-\ *n* (1840) **:** one that discovers a way; *esp* **:** one that explores untraversed regions to mark out a new route — **path·find·ing** \-diŋ\ *n or adj*

path·less \-ləs\ *adj* (1591) **:** UNTRODDEN, TRACKLESS — **path·less·ness** *n*

patho·bi·ol·o·gy \,path-ō-bī-'äl-ə-jē\ *n* (ca. 1909) **:** PATHOLOGY

patho·gen \'path-ə-jən\ *n* [ISV] (1880) **:** a specific causative agent (as a bacterium or virus) of disease

patho·gen·e·sis \,path-ə-'jen-ə-səs\ *n* [NL] (1876) **:** the origination and development of a disease

patho·ge·net·ic \-jə-'net-ik\ *adj* [ISV] (1838) **1 :** of or relating to pathogenesis **2 :** PATHOGENIC 2

patho·gen·ic \-'jen-ik\ *adj* [ISV] (1852) **1 :** PATHOGENETIC 1 **2 :** causing or capable of causing disease — **patho·ge·nic·i·ty** \-jə-'nis-ət-ē\ *n*

pa·tho·gno·mon·ic \,path-ə(g)-nō-'män-ik\ *adj* [Gk *pathognōmonikos*, fr. *path-* + *gnōmonikos* fit to judge, fr. *gnōmōn* interpreter; akin to Gk *gignōskein* to know — more at KNOW] (1625) **:** distinctively characteristic of a particular disease

patho·log·i·cal \,path-ə-'läj-i-kəl\ *also* **patho·log·ic** \-ik\ *adj* (1688) **1 :** of or relating to pathology **2 :** altered or caused by disease — **patho·log·i·cal·ly** \-i-k(ə-)lē\ *adv*

pa·thol·o·gist \pə-'thäl-ə-jəst, pa-\ *n* (1650) **:** a specialist in pathology; *specif* **:** one who interprets and diagnoses the changes caused by disease in tissues and body fluids

pa·thol·o·gy \-jē\ *n, pl* **-gies** [NL *pathologia* & MF *pathologie,* fr. Gk *pathologia* study of the emotions, fr. *path-* + *-logia* -logy] (1611) **1** : the study of the essential nature of diseases and esp. of the structural and functional changes produced by them **2** : something abnormal: **a** : the anatomic and physiologic deviations from the normal that constitute disease or characterize a particular disease **b** : deviation from propriety or from an assumed normal state of something nonliving or nonmaterial

patho·phys·i·ol·o·gy \ˌpath-ō-ˌfiz-ē-ˈäl-ə-jē\ *n* (1947) : the physiology of abnormal states; *specif* : the functional changes that accompany a particular syndrome or disease — **patho·phys·i·o·log·i·cal** \-ē-ə-ˈläj-i-kəl\ *also* **patho·phys·i·o·log·ic** \-ik\ *adj*

pa·thos \ˈpā-ˌthäs, -ˌthȯs, -ˌthōs *also* ˈpa-\ *n* [Gk, suffering, experience, emotion, fr. *paschein* to experience, suffer; akin to Lith *kesti* to suffer] (1591) **1** : an element in experience or in artistic representation evoking pity or compassion **2** : an emotion of sympathetic pity

path·way \ˈpath-ˌwā, ˈpȧth-\ *n* (1536) **1** : PATH, COURSE **2** : the sequence of enzyme catalyzed reactions by which an energy-yielding substance is utilized by protoplasm ⟨metabolic ~*s*⟩

-p·a·thy \p-ə-thē\ *n comb form* [L *-pathia,* fr. Gk *-patheia,* fr. *-pathēs* suffering — more at -PATH] **1** : feeling : suffering ⟨em*pathy*⟩ : being acted upon ⟨tele*pathy*⟩ **2** : disorder of (such) a part or kind ⟨neuro*pathy*⟩ **3** : system of medicine based on (such) a factor ⟨osteo*pathy*⟩

pa·tience \ˈpā-shən(t)s\ *n* (13c) **1** : the capacity, habit, or fact of being patient **2** *chiefly Brit* : SOLITAIRE 2

1**pa·tient** \ˈpā-shənt\ *adj* [ME *pacient,* fr. MF, fr. L *patient-, patiens,* fr. prp. of *pati* to suffer; akin to L *paene* almost, *penuria* need, Gk *pēma* suffering] (14c) **1** : bearing pains or trials calmly or without complaint **2** : manifesting forbearance under provocation or strain **3** : not hasty or impetuous **4** : steadfast despite opposition, difficulty, or adversity **5 a** : able or willing to bear — used with *of* **b** : SUSCEPTIBLE, ADMITTING ⟨~ of one interpretation⟩ — **pa·tient·ly** *adv*

2**patient** *n* (14c) **1 a** : an individual awaiting or under medical care and treatment **b** : the recipient of any of various personal services **2** : one that is acted upon

pa·ti·na \pə-ˈtē-nə, ˈpat-ə-nə\ *n, pl* **pa·ti·nas** \-nəz\ *or* **pa·ti·nae** \-ˌnē, -ˌnī\ [NL, fr. L, shallow dish — more at PATEN] (1748) **1 a** : a usu. green film formed naturally on copper and bronze by long exposure or artificially (as by acids) and often valued aesthetically for its color **b** : a surface appearance of something grown beautiful esp. with age or use **2** : an appearance or aura that is derived from association, habit, or established character **3** : a superficial covering or exterior

pat·i·nate \ˈpat-ə-ˌnāt\ *vb* **-nat·ed; -nat·ing** *vt* (1880) : to give a patina to ~ *vi* : to take on a patina — usu. used in the past participle ⟨*patinated* bronze⟩— **pat·i·na·tion** \ˌpat-ə-ˈnā-shən\ *n*

1**pa·tine** \pa-ˈtēn\ *n* [F, fr. NL *patina*] (1883) : PATINA

2**patine** *vt* **pa·tined; pa·tin·ing** (1896) : to cover with a patina

pa·tio \ˈpat-ē-ˌō *also* ˈpät-\ *n, pl* **pa·ti·os** [Sp] (1828) **1** : COURTYARD; *esp* : an inner court open to the sky **2** : a recreation area that adjoins a dwelling, is often paved, and is adapted esp. to outdoor dining

pa·tois \ˈpa-ˌtwä, ˈpä-\ *n, pl* **pa·tois** \-ˌtwäz\ [F] (1642) **1 a** : a dialect other than the standard or literary dialect **b** : illiterate or provincial speech **2** : the characteristic special language of an occupational or social group : JARGON

patr- *or* **patri-** *or* **patro-** *comb form* [*patr-, patri-* fr. L, fr. *patr-, pater; patr-, patro-* fr. Gk, fr. *patr-, patēr* — more at FATHER] : father ⟨*patri*stic⟩

pa·tri·arch \ˈpā-trē-ˌärk\ *n* [ME *patriarche,* fr. OF, fr. LL *patriarcha,* fr. Gk *patriarchēs,* fr. *patria* lineage (fr. *patr-, patēr* father) + *-archēs* -arch — more at FATHER] (12c) **1 a** : one of the scriptural fathers of the human race or of the Hebrew people **b** : a man who is father or founder **c** (1) : the oldest member or representative of a group (2) : a venerable old man **d** : a man who is head of a patriarchy **2 a** : any of the bishops of the ancient or Eastern Orthodox sees of Constantinople, Alexandria, Antioch, and Jerusalem or the ancient and Western see of Rome with authority over other bishops **b** : the head of any of various Eastern churches **c** : a Roman Catholic bishop next in rank to the pope with purely titular or with metropolitan jurisdiction **3** : a Mormon of the Melchizedek priesthood empowered to perform the ordinances of the church and pronounce blessings within a stake or prescribed jurisdiction — **pa·tri·ar·chal** \ˌpā-trē-ˈär-kəl\ *adj*

patriarchal cross *n* (1682) : a chiefly heraldic cross denoting a cardinal's or archbishop's rank and having two crossbars of which the lower is the longer and intersects the upright above or at its center — see CROSS illustration

pa·tri·arch·ate \ˈpā-trē-ˌär-kət, -ˌkāt\ *n* (1617) **1 a** : the office, jurisdiction, or time in office of a patriarch **b** : the residence or headquarters of a patriarch **2** : PATRIARCHY

pa·tri·ar·chy \-ˌär-kē\ *n, pl* **-chies** (1561) **1** : social organization marked by the supremacy of the father in the clan or family, the legal dependence of wives and children, and the reckoning of descent and inheritance in the male line **2** : a society organized according to the principles of patriarchy

pa·tri·cian \pə-ˈtrish-ən\ *n* [ME *patricion,* fr. MF *patricien,* fr. L *patricius,* fr. *patres* senators, fr. pl. of *pater* father — more at FATHER] (1533) **1** : a member of one of the original citizen families of ancient Rome **2 a** : a person of high birth : ARISTOCRAT **b** : a person of breeding and cultivation — **patrician** *adj*

pa·tri·ci·ate \-ˈtrish-ē-ət, -ē-ˌāt\ *n* (1656) **1** : the position or dignity of a patrician **2** : a patrician class

pat·ri·cide \ˈpa-trə-ˌsīd\ *n* (1593) **1** [L *patricida,* fr. *patr-* + *-cida* -cide] : one who murders his own father **2** [LL *patricidium,* fr. L *patr-* + *-cidium* -cide] : the murder of one's own father — **pat·ri·cid·al** \ˌpa-trə-ˈsīd-ᵊl\ *adj*

pat·ri·lin·eal \ˌpa-trə-ˈlin-ē-əl\ *adj* (1904) : relating to, based on, or tracing descent through the paternal line ⟨~ society⟩

pat·ri·mo·ny \ˈpa-trə-ˌmō-nē\ *n* [ME *patrimonie,* fr. MF, fr. L *patrimonium,* fr. *patr-, pater* father] (14c) **1 a** : an estate inherited from one's father or ancestor **b** : anything derived from one's father or ancestors : HERITAGE **2** : an estate or endowment belonging by ancient right to a church — **pat·ri·mo·ni·al** \ˌpa-trə-ˈmō-nē-əl\ *adj*

pa·tri·ot \ˈpā-trē-ət, -trē-ˌät, *chiefly Brit* ˈpa-trē-ət\ *n* [MF *patriote* compatriot, fr. LL *patriota,* fr. Gk *patriōtēs,* fr. *patrios* of one's father, fr. *patr-, patēr* father] (1605) : one who loves his country and supports its authority and interests

pa·tri·ot·ic \ˌpā-trē-ˈät-ik, *chiefly Brit* ˌpa-\ *adj* (1757) **1** : inspired by patriotism **2** : befitting or characteristic of a patriot — **pa·tri·ot·i·cal·ly** \-i-k(ə-)lē\ *adv*

pa·tri·o·tism \ˈpā-trē-ə-ˌtiz-əm, *chiefly Brit* ˈpa-\ *n* (ca. 1726) : love for or devotion to one's country

Patriots' Day *n* (1894) : the third Monday in April observed as a legal holiday in Maine and Massachusetts in commemoration of the battles of Lexington and Concord in 1775

pa·tris·tic \pə-ˈtris-tik\ *adj* (ca. 1828) : of or relating to the church fathers or their writings — **pa·tris·ti·cal** \-ti-kəl\ *adj*

pa·tris·tics \-tiks\ *n pl but sing in constr* (1897) : the study of the writings and background of the church fathers

Pa·tro·clus \pə-ˈtrō-kləs, -ˈträk-ləs\ *n* [L, fr. Gk *Patroklos*] : a Greek hero and friend of Achilles slain by Hector at Troy

1**pa·trol** \pə-ˈtrōl\ *n* (1664) **1 a** : the action of traversing a district or beat or of going the rounds along a chain of guards for observation or the maintenance of security **b** : the person performing such an action **c** : a unit of persons or vehicles employed for reconnaissance, security, or combat **2** : a subdivision of a Boy Scout troop or Girl Scout troop

2**patrol** *vb* **pa·trolled; pa·trol·ling** [F *patrouiller,* fr. MF, to tramp around in the mud, fr. *patte* paw — more at PATTEN] *vi* (1691) : to carry out a patrol ~ *vt* : to carry out a patrol of — **pa·trol·ler** *n*

pa·trol·man \pə-ˈtrōl-mən\ *n* (1867) : one who patrols; *esp* : a policeman assigned to a beat

patrol wagon *n* (1887) : an enclosed motortruck used by police to carry prisoners — called also *Black Maria, paddy wagon*

pa·tron \ˈpā-trən, *for 6 also* pa-ˈtrō^{n}\ *n* [ME, fr. MF, fr. ML & L; ML *patronus* patron saint, patron of a benefice, pattern, fr. L, defender, fr. *patr-, pater*] (14c) **1 a** : a person chosen, named, or honored as a special guardian, protector, or supporter **b** : a wealthy or influential supporter of an artist or writer **c** : a social or financial sponsor of a social function (as a ball or concert) **2** : one that uses wealth or influence to help an individual, an institution, or a cause **3** : one who buys the goods or uses the services offered esp. by an establishment **4** : the holder of the right of presentation to an English ecclesiastical benefice **5** : a master in ancient times who freed his slave but retained some rights over him **6** [F, fr. MF] : the proprietor of an establishment (as an inn) esp. in France **7** : the chief male officer in some fraternal lodges having both men and women members — **pa·tron·al** \ˈpā-trən-ᵊl; *Brit* pə-ˈtrō-n-ᵊl, pa-\ *adj*

pa·tron·age \ˈpa-trə-nij, ˈpā-\ *n* (15c) **1** : ADVOWSON **2** : the support or influence of a patron **3** : kindness done with an air of superiority **4** : business or activity provided by patrons ⟨the new branch library is expected to have a heavy ~⟩ **5 a** : the power to make appointments to government jobs esp. for political advantage **b** : the distribution of jobs on the basis of patronage **c** : jobs distributed by patronage

pa·tron·ess \ˈpā-trə-nəs\ *n* (15c) : a woman who is a patron

pa·tron·ize \ˈpā-trə-ˌnīz, ˈpa-\ *vt* **-ized; -iz·ing** (1589) **1** : to act as patron of : provide aid or support for **2** : to adopt an air of condescension toward **3** : to be a patron of — **pa·tron·iza·tion** \ˌpā-trə-nə-ˈzā-shən, pa-\ *n* — **pa·tron·iz·ing·ly** \ˈpā-trə-ˌnī-ziŋ-lē, ˈpa-\ *adv*

patron saint *n* (1717) **1** : a saint to whose protection and intercession a person, a society, a church, or a place is dedicated **2** : an original leader or prime exemplar

pat·ro·nym·ic \ˌpa-trə-ˈnim-ik\ *n* [LL *patronymicum,* fr. neut. of *patronymicus* of a patronymic, fr. Gk *patronymikos,* fr. *patronymia* patronymic, fr. *patr-* + *onyma* name — more at NAME] (1612) : a name derived from that of the father or a paternal ancestor usu. by the addition of an affix — **patronymic** *adj*

pa·troon \pə-ˈtrün\ *n* [F *patron* & Sp *patrón,* fr. ML *patronus,* fr. L, patron] (1743) **1** *archaic* : the captain or officer commanding a ship **2** [D, fr. F *patron*] : the proprietor of a manorial estate esp. in New York orig. granted under Dutch rule but in some cases existing until the mid-19th century

pat·sy \ˈpat-sē\ *n, pl* **pat·sies** [perh. fr. It *pazzo* fool] (1903) : one who is easily manipulated or victimized : SUCKER

pat·ten \ˈpat-ᵊn\ *n* [ME *patin,* fr. MF, fr. *patte* paw, hoof, fr. (assumed) VL *patta*] (14c) : a clog, sandal, or overshoe often with a wooden sole or metal device to elevate the foot and increase the wearer's height or aid in walking in mud

1**pat·ter** \ˈpat-ər\ *vb* [ME *patren,* fr. *paternoster*] *vt* (15c) : to say or speak in a rapid or mechanical manner ~ *vi* **1** : to recite prayers (as paternosters) rapidly or mechanically **2** : to talk glibly and volubly **3** : to speak or sing rapid-fire words in a theatrical performance — **pat·ter·er** \-ər-ər\ *n*

2**patter** *n* (1758) **1** : a specialized lingo : CANT; *esp* : the jargon of criminals (as thieves) **2** : the spiel of a street hawker or of a circus barker **3** : empty chattering talk **4 a** (1) : the rapid-fire talk of a comedian (2) : the talk with which an entertainer accompanies his routine **b** : the words of a comic song or of a rapidly spoken usu. humorous monologue introduced into such a song

3**patter** *vb* [freq. of 3*pat*] *vi* (1611) **1** : to strike or pat rapidly and repeatedly **2** : to run with quick light-sounding steps ~ *vt* : to cause to patter

4**patter** *n* (1844) : a quick succession of light sounds or pats

1**pat·tern** \ˈpat-ərn\ *n* [ME *patron,* fr. MF, fr. ML *patronus*] (14c) **1** : a form or model proposed for imitation : EXEMPLAR **2** : something designed or used as a model for making things ⟨a dressmaker's ~⟩ **3** : a model for making a mold into which molten metal is poured to form a casting **4** : an artistic, musical, literary, or mechanical design or form **5** : a natural or chance configuration ⟨frost ~⟩ ⟨the ~ of events⟩ **6** : a length of fabric sufficient for an article (as of clothing) **7 a** : the distribution of shrapnel, bombs on a target, or shot from a shotgun **b** : the grouping made on a target by bullets **8** : a reliable sample of traits, acts, tendencies, or other observable characteristics of a person, group, or institution ⟨behavior ~⟩ ⟨spending ~⟩ **9 a :** the flight path prescribed for an airplane that is coming in for a landing **b :** a prescribed route to be followed by a pass receiver in football **10 :** a standard diagram transmitted for testing television circuits **11 :** a discernible coherent system based on the intended interrelationship of component parts ⟨foreign policy ~*s*⟩ **12 :** frequent or widespread incidence ⟨a ~ of dissent⟩ ***syn*** see MODEL — **pat·terned** \-ərnd\ *adj* — **pat·tern·less** *adj*

2pattern *vt* (1599) **1 :** to make or fashion according to a pattern **2** *dial chiefly Eng* **a :** MATCH **b :** IMITATE **3 :** to furnish, adorn, or mark with a design ~ *vi* **:** to form a pattern

pat·tern·ing *n* (1862) **1 :** decoration, composition, or configuration according to a pattern **2 :** physiotherapy that is designed to improve malfunctioning nervous control by means of feedback from muscular activity imposed by an outside source or induced by other muscles

pat·ty *also* **pat·tie** \'pat-ē\ *n, pl* **patties** [F *pâté* pâté] (1710) **1 :** a little pie **2 a :** a small flat cake of chopped food ⟨a hamburger ~⟩ **b :** a small flat candy ⟨a peppermint ~⟩ **3 :** PATTY SHELL

patty shell *n* (1909) **:** a shell of puff paste made to hold a creamed meat, fish, or vegetable filling

pat·u·lous \'pach-ə-ləs\ *adj* [L *patulus,* fr. *patēre* to be open — more at FATHOM] (1616) **:** spreading widely from a center ⟨a tree with ~ branches⟩

pat·zer \'pät-sər, 'pat-\ *n* [prob. fr. G *patzer* bungler, fr. *patzen* to blunder] (1959) **:** an inept chess player

pau·ci·ty \'pȯ-sət-ē\ *n* [ME *paucite,* fr. MF or L; MF *paucité,* fr. L *paucitat-, paucitas,* fr. *paucus* little — more at FEW] (15c) **1 :** smallness of number **:** FEWNESS **2 :** smallness of quantity **:** DEARTH

Paul \'pȯl\ *n* [L *Paulus,* fr. Gk *Paulos*] **:** an early Christian apostle and missionary and author of several New Testament epistles

Paul Bun·yan \-'bən-yən\ *n* **:** a giant lumberjack of American folklore

Pau·li exclusion principle \'pau̇-lē-\ *n* [Wolfgang *Pauli*] (1926) **:** EXCLUSION PRINCIPLE — called also *Pauli principle*

Pau·line \'pȯ-,līn\ *adj* (1817) **:** of or relating to the apostle Paul, his epistles, or the doctrine or theology implicit in his epistles

Paul·ist \'pȯ-ləst\ *n* (1883) **:** a member of the Roman Catholic Congregation of the Missionary Priests of St. Paul the Apostle founded by I. T. Hecker in the U.S. in 1858

pau·low·nia \pȯ-'lō-nē-ə\ *n* [NL, fr. Anna *Paulovna* †1865 Russ. princess] (1847) **:** any of a genus (*Paulownia*) of Chinese trees of the figwort family; *esp* **:** one (*P. tomentosa*) widely cultivated for its panicles of fragrant violet flowers

paunch \'pȯnch, 'pänch\ *n* [ME, fr. MF *panche,* fr. L *pantic-, pantex*] (14c) **1 a :** the belly and its contents **b :** POTBELLY **2 :** RUMEN

paunchy \'pȯn-chē, 'pän-\ *adj* **paunch·i·er; -est** (1598) **:** having a potbelly — **paunch·i·ness** *n*

pau·per \'pȯ-pər\ *n* [L, poor] (1561) **1 :** a person destitute of means except such as are derived from charity; *specif* **:** one who receives aid from public poor funds **2 :** a very poor person — **pau·per·ism** \-pə-,riz-əm\ *n*

pau·per·ize \'pȯ-pə-,rīz\ *vt* **-ized; -iz·ing** (1834) **:** to reduce to poverty

pau·piette \pō-'pyet\ *n* [F *paupiette, poupiette,* deriv. of MF *poulpe* fleshy part, pulp — more at PULP] (1889) **:** a thin slice of meat or fish wrapped around a forcemeat filling

1pause \'pȯz\ *n* [ME, fr. L *pausa,* fr. Gk *pausis,* fr. *pauein* to stop; akin to Gk *paula* rest] (15c) **1 :** a temporary stop **2 a :** a break in a verse **b :** a brief suspension of the voice to indicate the limits and relations of sentences and their parts **3 :** temporary inaction esp. as caused by uncertainty **:** HESITATION **4 a :** the sign denoting a fermata **b :** a mark (as a period or comma) used in writing or printing to indicate or correspond to a pause of voice **5 :** a reason or cause for pausing ⟨a thought that should give one ~⟩

2pause *vb* **paused; paus·ing** *vi* (1526) **1 :** to stop temporarily **2 :** to linger for a time ~ *vt* **:** to cause to pause **:** STOP

pa·vane \pə-'vän, -'van\ *also* **pa·van** *same or* 'pav-ən\ *n* [MF *pavane,* fr. OSp *pavana,* fr. OIt] (1535) **1 :** a stately court dance by couples that was introduced from southern Europe into England in the 16th century **2 :** music for the pavane; *also* **:** music having the slow duple rhythm of a pavane

pave \'pāv\ *vt* **paved; pav·ing** [ME *paven,* fr. MF *paver,* fr. L *pavire* to strike, stamp; akin to OHG *arfūrian* to castrate, L *putare* to prune, reckon, think, Gk *paiein* to strike] (14c) **1 :** to lay or cover with material (as stone or concrete) that forms a firm level surface for travel **2 :** to cover firmly and solidly as if with paving material **3 :** to serve as a covering or pavement of — **pav·er** *n* — **pave the way :** to prepare a smooth easy way **:** facilitate development

pa·vé \pa-'vā\ *also* **pa·véed** *or* **pa·véd** \pa-'vād\ *adj* [*pavé* fr. F, fr. pp. of *paver* to pave] *of jewels* (1871) **:** set as close together as possible to conceal a metal base

pave·ment \'pāv-mənt\ *n* [ME, fr. OF, fr. L *pavimentum,* fr. *pavire*] (13c) **1 :** a paved surface: as **a :** the artificially covered surface of a public thoroughfare **b** *chiefly Brit* **:** SIDEWALK **2 :** the material with which something is paved **3 :** something that suggests a pavement (as in flatness, hardness, and extent of surface)

pav·id \'pav-əd\ *adj* [L *pavidus,* fr. *pavēre* to be frightened; akin to L *pavire*] (1656) **:** TIMID

1pa·vil·ion \pə-'vil-yən\ *n* [ME *pavilon,* fr. OF *paveillon,* fr. L *papilion-, papilio* butterfly; akin to OHG *fīfaltra* butterfly, Lith *petelīške* flighty] (13c) **1 a :** a large often sumptuous tent **b :** something resembling a canopy or tent ⟨tree ferns spread their delicate ~*s* —Blanche E. Baughan⟩ **2 a :** a part of a building projecting from the rest **b :** one of several detached or semidetached units into which a building is sometimes divided **3 a :** a light sometimes ornamental structure in a garden, park, or place of recreation that is used for entertainment or shelter **b :** a temporary structure erected at an exposition by an individual exhibitor **4 :** the lower faceted part of a brilliant between the girdle and the culet — see BRILLIANT illustration

2pavilion *vt* (14c) **:** to furnish or cover with or put in a pavilion

pav·ing \'pā-viŋ\ *n* (15c) **:** PAVEMENT

pav·ior *or* **pav·iour** \'pāv-yər\ *n* [ME *pavier,* fr. *paven* to pave] *Brit* (15c) **:** one that paves

Pav·lov·ian \pav-'lȯ-vē-ən, -'lō-; -'lȯ-fē-\ *adj* (1926) **1 :** of or relating to Ivan Pavlov or to his work and theories ⟨~ conditioning⟩ **2 :** being or expressing a conditioned or predictable reaction **:** AUTOMATIC ⟨the candidates gave ~ answers⟩

1paw \'pȯ\ *n* [ME, fr. MF *poue*] (14c) **1 :** the foot of a quadruped (as a lion or dog) that has claws; *broadly* **:** the foot of an animal **2 :** a human hand esp. when large or clumsy

2paw *vt* (1604) **1 :** to feel or touch clumsily, rudely, or sexually **2 :** to touch or strike at with a paw **3 :** to scrape or beat with or as if with a hoof **4 :** to flail at or grab for wildly ~ *vi* **1 :** to beat or scrape something with or as if with a hoof **2 :** to touch or strike with a paw **3 :** to feel or touch someone or something clumsily, rudely, or sexually **4 :** to flail or grab wildly

paw·ky \'pȯ-kē\ *adj* [obs. E dial. *pawk* (trick)] *chiefly Brit* (1676) **:** artfully shrewd **:** CANNY

pawl \'pȯl\ *n* [perh. modif. of D *pal* pawl] (1626) **:** a pivoted tongue or sliding bolt on one part of a machine that is adapted to fall into notches or interdental spaces on another part (as a ratchet wheel) so as to permit motion in only one direction

1pawn \'pȯn, 'pän\ *n* [ME *pown,* fr. MF *poon,* fr. ML *pedon-, pedo* foot soldier, fr. LL, one with broad feet, fr. L *ped-, pes* foot — more at FOOT] (14c) **1 :** one of the chessmen of least value having the power to move only forward ordinarily one square at a time, to capture only diagonally forward, and be promoted to any piece except a king upon reaching the eighth rank **2 :** one that can be used to further the purposes of another

2pawn *n* [ME *paun,* modif. of MF *pan*] (15c) **1 a :** something delivered to or deposited with another as security for a loan **b :** HOSTAGE **2 :** the state of being pledged **3 :** something used as a pledge **:** GUARANTY **4 :** the act of pawning

3pawn *vt* (1570) **:** to deposit in pledge or as security — **pawn·er** \'pȯ-nər, 'pän-ər\ *or* **paw·nor** *same or* pȯ-'nȯ(ə)r, pä-\ *n*

pawn·bro·ker \'pȯn-,brō-kər, 'pän-\ *n* (1687) **:** one who loans money on the security of personal property pledged in his keeping — **pawn·bro·king** \-kiŋ\ *n*

Paw·nee \pȯ-'nē, pä-\ *n, pl* **Pawnee** *or* **Pawnees** (1770) **:** a member of an American Indian people orig. of Kansas and Nebraska

pawn·shop \'pȯn-,shäp, 'pän-\ *n* (1849) **:** a pawnbroker's shop

paw·paw *var of* PAPAW

pax \'paks, 'päks\ *n* [ME, fr. ML, fr. L, peace — more at PEACE] (14c) **1 :** a tablet decorated with a sacred figure (as of Christ) and sometimes ceremonially kissed by participants at mass **2 :** the kiss of peace in the Mass **3 :** PEACE

1pay \'pā\ *vb* **paid** \'pād\ *also in sense 7* **payed; pay·ing** [ME *payen,* fr. OF *paier,* fr. L *pacare* to pacify, fr. *pac-, pax* peace] *vt* (13c) **1 a :** to make due return to for services rendered or property delivered **b :** to engage for money **:** HIRE ⟨you couldn't ~ me to do that⟩ **2 a :** to give in return for goods or service ⟨~ wages⟩ **b :** to discharge indebtedness for **:** SETTLE ⟨~ a bill⟩ **c :** to make a disposal or transfer of (money) **3 :** to give or forfeit in expiation or retribution ⟨~ the penalty⟩ **4 a :** to make compensation for **b :** to requite according to what is deserved ⟨~ them back⟩ **5 :** to give, offer, or make freely or as fitting ⟨~ attention⟩ **6 a :** to return value or profit to ⟨it ~*s* you to stay open⟩ **b :** to bring in as a return ⟨an investment ~*ing* five percent⟩ **7 :** to slacken (as a rope) and allow to run out — used with *out* ~ *vi* **1 :** to discharge a debt or obligation **2 :** to be worth the expense or effort ⟨it ~*s* to advertise⟩ — **pay one's dues 1 :** to earn a right or position through experience, suffering, or hard work **2** *also* **pay dues :** to suffer the consequences of or penalty for an act

syn PAY, COMPENSATE, REMUNERATE, SATISFY, REIMBURSE, INDEMNIFY, REPAY, RECOMPENSE mean to give money or its equivalent in return for something. PAY implies the discharge of an obligation incurred; COMPENSATE implies a making up for services rendered or help given; REMUNERATE more clearly suggests paying for services rendered and may extend to payment that is generous or not contracted for; SATISFY implies paying a person what is demanded or required by law; REIMBURSE implies a return of money that has been expended for another's benefit; INDEMNIFY implies making good a loss suffered through accident, disaster, warfare; REPAY stresses paying back an equivalent in kind or amount; RECOMPENSE suggests due return in amends, friendly repayment, or reward.

2pay *n* (14c) **1 a :** the act or fact of paying or being paid **b :** the status of being paid by an employer **:** EMPLOY **2 :** something paid for a purpose and esp. as a salary or wage **:** REMUNERATION **3 :** a person viewed with respect to reliability or promptness in paying debts or bills **4 a :** ore or a natural situation that yields metal and esp. gold in profitable amounts **b :** an oil-yielding stratum or zone ***syn*** see WAGE

3pay *adj* (ca. 1798) **1 :** containing or leading to something precious or valuable **2 :** equipped with a coin slot for receiving a fee for use ⟨~ telephone⟩ **3 :** requiring payment

4pay *vt* **payed** *also* **paid; pay·ing** [obs. F *peier,* fr. L *picare,* fr. *pic-, pix* pitch] (1627) **:** to coat with a waterproof composition

pay·able \'pā-ə-bəl\ *adj* (15c) **1 :** that may, can, or must be paid **2 :** PROFITABLE

pay–as–you–go *adj* (1840) **:** of or relating to a system or policy of paying bills when due or of paying for goods and services when purchased

pay·back \'pā-,bak\ *n* (1955) **:** a return on an investment equal to the original capital outlay; *also* **:** the period of time elapsed before an investment is recouped

pay–cable *n* (1975) **:** pay-TV sending programs through a cable television system to customers provided with a special signal decoder — compare SUBSCRIPTION TV

pay·check \'pā-,chek\ *n* (1899) **1 :** a check in payment of wages or salary **2 :** WAGES, SALARY

pay·day \-,dā\ *n* (1529) **:** a regular day on which wages are paid

pay dirt *n* (1856) **1 :** earth or ore that yields a profit to a miner **2 :** a useful or remunerative discovery or object

pay·ee \pā-'ē\ *n* (1758) **:** one to whom money is or is to be paid

pay envelope *n* (1901) **:** an envelope containing one's wages; *also* **:** WAGES

pay·er \'pā-ər\ *also* **pay·or** \'pā-ər, pā-'ȯ(ə)r\ *n* (14c) **:** one that pays; *esp* **:** the person by whom a bill or note has been or should be paid

pay·load \'pā-,lōd\ *n* (ca. 1922) **1 :** the revenue-producing or useful load that a vehicle of transport can carry **2 :** the explosive charge carried in the warhead of a missile **3 :** the load that is carried by a spacecraft and that consists of things (as passengers or instruments) that relate directly to the purpose of the flight as opposed to things (as fuel) that are necessary for operation; *also* **:** the weight of such a load

pay·mas·ter \ˈ-ˌmas-tər\ *n* (1550) **:** an officer or agent whose duty it is to pay salaries or wages

pay·ment \ˈpā-mənt\ *n* (14c) **1 :** the act of paying **2 :** something that is paid **:** PAY **3 :** REQUITAL

pay·nim \ˈpā-nəm\ *n* [ME *painim,* fr. OF *paienime* heathendom, fr. LL *paganismus,* fr. *paganus* pagan] *archaic* (13c) **:** PAGAN; *esp* **:** MUSLIM

1pay·off \ˈpā-ˌȯf\ *n* (1905) **1 a :** PROFIT, REWARD; *esp* **:** an amount received by a player in a game **b :** RETRIBUTION **2 :** the act or occasion of paying employees' wages or distributing gains (as profits or bribe money) **3 :** the climax of an incident or enterprise; *specif* **:** the denouement of a narrative **4 :** a decisive fact or factor resolving a situation or bringing about a definitive conclusion

2payoff *adj* (1934) **:** yielding results in the final test **:** DECISIVE

pay off \(ˌ)pā-ˈȯf\ *vt* (1710) **1 a :** to give all due wages to; *esp* **:** to pay in full and discharge (an employee) **b :** to pay (a debt or a creditor) in full **c :** BRIBE **2 :** to inflict retribution on **3 :** to allow (a thread or rope) to run off a spool or drum **~** *vi* **:** to yield returns

pay·ola \pā-ˈō-lə\ *n* [prob. alter. (influenced by *Victrola,* trademark for a phonograph) of *1payoff*] (1938) **:** undercover or indirect payment (as to a disc jockey) for a commercial favor (as for promoting a particular record)

pay·out \ˈpā-ˌau̇t\ *n* (1943) **:** the act of paying out **:** PAYOFF

pay·roll \ˈpā-ˌrōl\ *n* (1740) **1 :** a paymaster's or employer's list of those entitled to pay and of the amounts due to each **2 :** the sum necessary for distribution to those on a payroll; *also* **:** the money to be distributed

pay station *n* (1919) **:** a public telephone usu. equipped with a coin-operated mechanism for payment of tolls

pay–TV *n* (ca. 1956) **:** a service providing special noncommercial television programming (as recent movies and entertainment specials) by means of a scrambled signal over the air or through a cable television system to subscribers who are provided with a signal decoding device — called also *pay television;* compare PAY-CABLE, SUBSCRIPTION TV

pay up *vi* (15c) **:** to pay what is due **~** *vt* **:** to pay in full

PBB \ˌpē-ˌbē-ˈbē\ *n* (ca. 1975) **:** POLYBROMINATED BIPHENYL

PCB \ˌpē-ˌsē-ˈbē\ *n* (1966) **:** POLYCHLORINATED BIPHENYL

PCP \ˌpē-ˌsē-ˈpē\ *n* (ca. 1970) **:** PHENCYCLIDINE

PDQ \ˌpē-ˌdē-ˈkyü\ *adv, often not cap* [abbr. of *pretty damned quick*] (1875) **:** IMMEDIATELY

pe \ˈpā\ *n* [Heb *pē*] (ca. 1899) **:** the 17th letter of the Hebrew alphabet — see ALPHABET table

pea \ˈpē\ *n, pl* **peas** *also* **pease** \ˈpēz\ *often attrib* [back-formation fr. ME *pease* (taken as a pl.), fr. OE *pise,* fr. L *pisa,* pl. of *pisum,* fr. Gk *pison*] (bef. 12c) **1 a :** a variable annual leguminous vine (*Pisum sativum*) that is cultivated for its rounded smooth or wrinkled edible protein-rich seeds **b :** the seed of the pea **c** *pl* **:** the immature pods of the pea with their included seeds **2 :** any of various leguminous plants related to or resembling the pea — usu. used with a qualifying term ⟨chick-*pea*⟩ ⟨black-eyed **~**⟩; *also* **:** the seed of such a plant **3 :** something resembling a pea (as in size or shape)

pea aphid *n* (1925) **:** a widely distributed aphid (*Acyrthosiphon pisum*) that is a serious pest on legumes (as alfalfa, pea, and clover)

pea bean *n* (ca. 1887) **:** any of various kidney beans cultivated for their small white seeds which are used dried (as for baking)

1peace \ˈpēs\ *n* [ME *pees,* fr. OF *pais,* fr. L *pac-, pax;* akin to L *pacisci* to agree — more at PACT] (13c) **1 :** a state of tranquillity or quiet: as **a :** freedom from civil disturbance **b :** a state of security or order within a community provided for by law or custom ⟨a breach of the **~**⟩ **2 :** freedom from disquieting or oppressive thoughts or emotions **3 :** harmony in personal relations **4 a :** a state or period of mutual concord between governments **b :** a pact or agreement to end hostilities between those who have been at war or in a state of enmity **5 —** used interjectionally as a command or request for silence or calm or as a greeting or farewell — **at peace :** in a state of concord or tranquillity

2peace *vi, obs* (14c) **:** to be, become, or keep silent or quiet

peace·able \ˈpē-sə-bəl\ *adj* (14c) **1 a :** disposed to peace **:** not contentious or quarrelsome **b :** quietly behaved **2 :** marked by freedom from strife or disorder — **peace·able·ness** *n* — **peace·ably** \-blē\ *adv*

peace corps *n* (1960) **:** a body of trained personnel sent as volunteers esp. to assist underdeveloped nations

peace·ful \ˈpēs-fəl\ *adj* (14c) **1 :** PEACEABLE 1 **2 :** untroubled by conflict, agitation, or commotion **:** QUIET, TRANQUIL **3 :** of or relating to a state or time of peace **4 :** devoid of violence or force ***syn*** see CALM — **peace·ful·ly** \-fə-lē\ *adv* — **peace·ful·ness** *n*

peaceful coexistence *n* (1920) **:** a living together in peace rather than in constant hostility

peace·keep·ing \ˈpē-ˌskē-piŋ\ *n* (1945) **:** the preserving of peace; *esp* **:** international enforcement and supervision of a truce between hostile states or communities — **peace·keep·er** \-pər\ *n*

peace·mak·er \ˈpē-ˌsmā-kər\ *n* (15c) **:** one who makes peace esp. by reconciling parties at variance — **peace·mak·ing** \-kiŋ\ *n or adj*

peace offering *n* (1535) **:** a gift or service for the purpose of procuring peace or reconciliation

peace officer *n* (1714) **:** a civil officer (as a policeman) whose duty it is to preserve the public peace

peace pipe *n* (1760) **:** CALUMET

peace sign *n* (1969) **:** a sign made by holding the palm outward and forming a V with the index and middle fingers and used to indicate the desire for peace

peace·time \ˈpē-ˌstīm\ *n* (1551) **:** a time when a nation is not at war

1peach \ˈpēch\ *n* [ME *peche,* fr. MF (the fruit), fr. LL *persica,* fr. L *persicum,* fr. neut. of *persicus* Persian, fr. *Persia*] (14c) **1 a :** a low spreading freely branching Chinese tree (*Prunus persica*) of the rose family that is cosmopolitan in cultivation in temperate areas and has lanceolate leaves, sessile usu. pink flowers borne on the naked twigs in early spring, and a fruit which is a single-seeded drupe with a hard endocarp, a pulpy white or yellow mesocarp, and a thin downy epicarp **b :** the edible fruit of the peach **2 :** a variable color averaging a moderate yellowish pink

2peach *vb* [ME *pechen,* short for *apechen* to accuse, fr. (assumed) AF *apecher,* fr. LL *impedicare* to entangle — more at IMPEACH] *vt* (1570) **:** to inform against **:** BETRAY **~** *vi* **:** to turn informer **:** BLAB

peach leaf curl *n* (1888) **:** leaf curl of the peach that is caused by a fungus (*Taphrina deformans*)

peach tree borer *n* (1850) **:** a blue-black orange-marked clearwing moth (*Sanninoidea exitiosa*) whose white brown-headed larva bores in the wood of stone fruit trees (as the peach) in eastern No. America

peachy \ˈpē-chē\ *adj* **peach·i·er; -est** (1599) **1 :** resembling a peach **2 :** unusually fine **:** DANDY

1pea·cock \ˈpē-ˌkäk\ *n* [ME *pecok,* fr. *pe-* (fr. OE *pēa* peafowl, fr. L *pavon-, pavo* peacock) + *cok* cock] (14c) **1 :** a male peafowl distinguished by a crest of upright plumules and by greatly elongated loosely webbed upper tail coverts which are mostly tipped with ocellated spots and can be erected and spread at will in a fan shimmering with iridescent color; *broadly* **:** PEAFOWL **2 :** one making a proud display of himself **:** SHOW-OFF — **pea·cock·ish** \-ish\ *adj* — **pea·cocky** \-ē\ *adj*

2peacock *vi* (1586) **:** SHOW OFF

peacock blue *n* (1881) **:** a variable color averaging a moderate greenish blue

peacock flower *n* (1884) **:** ROYAL POINCIANA

pea·fowl \ˈpē-ˌfau̇l\ *n* [*pea-* (as in *peacock*) + *fowl*] (1804) **:** a very large terrestrial pheasant (genus *Pavo*) of southeastern Asia and the East Indies that is often reared as an ornamental fowl

pea green *n* (1752) **:** a variable color averaging a moderate yellow-green

pea·hen \ˈpē-ˌhen, -ˈhen\ *n* [ME *pehenne,* fr. *pe-* + *henne* hen] (14c) **:** a female peafowl

pea jacket \ˈpē-\ *n* [by folk etymology fr. D *pijjekker,* fr. *pij,* a kind of cloth + *jekker* jacket] (1721) **:** a heavy woolen double-breasted jacket orig. worn by sailors — called also *pea·coat* \ˈpē-ˌkōt\

1peak \ˈpēk\ *n* [perh. alter. of *pike*] (1530) **1 :** a pointed or projecting part of a garment; *esp* **:** the visor of a cap or hat **2 :** PROMONTORY **3 :** a sharp or pointed end **4 a** (1) **:** the top of a hill or mountain ending in a point (2) **:** a prominent mountain usu. having a well-defined summit **b :** something resembling a mountain peak **5 a :** the upper aftermost corner of a fore-and-aft sail **b :** the narrow part of a ship's bow or stern or the part of the hold in it **6 a :** the highest level or greatest degree **b :** a high point in a course of development esp. as represented on a graph **7 :** a point formed by the hair on the forehead ***syn*** see SUMMIT

2peak *vi* (1577) **:** to reach a maximum (as of capacity, value, or activity) — often used with *out* **~** *vt* **:** to cause to come to a peak, point, or maximum

3peak *adj* (1711) **:** being at or reaching the maximum

4peak *vi* [origin unknown] (1573) **1 :** to grow thin or sickly **2 :** to dwindle away

5peak *vt* [fr. *apeak* (held vertically)] (1626) **1 :** to set (as a gaff) nearer the perpendicular **2 :** to hold (oars) with blades well raised

1peaked \ˈpēkt *also* ˈpē-kəd\ *adj* (15c) **:** having a peak **:** POINTED — **peaked·ness** \ˈpēk(t)-nəs, ˈpē-kəd-nəs\ *n*

2peak·ed \ˈpē-kəd *also* ˈpik-əd\ *adj* (1835) **:** looking pale and wan

1peal \ˈpē(ə)l\ *n* [ME, appeal, summons to church, short for *appel* appeal, fr. *appelen* to appeal] (14c) **1 a :** the loud ringing of bells **b :** a complete set of changes on a given number of bells **c :** a set of bells tuned to the tones of the major scale for change ringing **2 :** a loud sound or succession of sounds ⟨**~***s* of laughter⟩

2peal *vi* (1632) **:** to give out peals **~** *vt* **:** to utter or give forth loudly

pea·like \ˈpē-ˌlīk\ *adj* (1774) **1 :** resembling a garden pea esp. in size, firmness, and shape ⟨a **~** lump under the skin⟩ **2** *of a flower* **:** being showy and papilionaceous

1pea·nut \ˈpē-(ˌ)nət\ *n* (1807) **1 a :** a low-branching widely cultivated leguminous annual herb (*Arachis hypogaea*) with showy yellow flowers having a peduncle which elongates and bends into the soil where the ovary ripens into a pod containing one to three oily edible seeds **b :** the seed or seed-containing pod of the peanut **2 :** an insignificant or tiny person **3** *pl* **:** a trifling amount

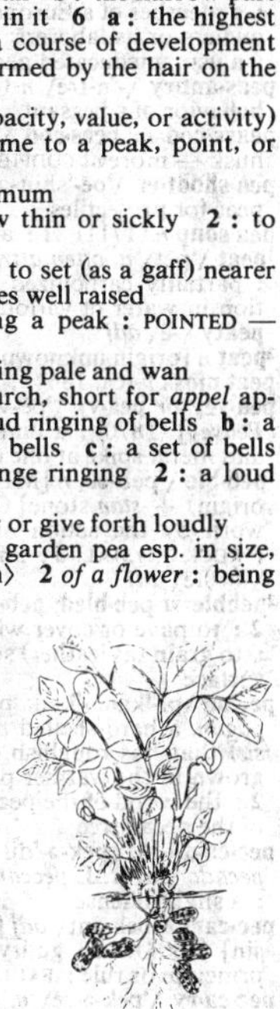

peanut 1a

2peanut *adj* (1836) **:** INSIGNIFICANT, PETTY ⟨**~** politics⟩

peanut oil *n* (1882) **:** a colorless to yellow fatty nondrying oil that is obtained from peanuts and is used chiefly as a salad oil, in margarine, in soap, and as a vehicle in pharmaceutical preparations and cosmetics

pear \ˈpa(ə)r, ˈpe(ə)r\ *n* [ME *pere,* fr. OE *peru,* fr. L *pirum*] (bef. 12c) **1 :** a fleshy pome fruit that is borne by a tree (genus *Pyrus,* esp. *P. communis*) of the rose family and is usu. larger at the apical end **2 :** a tree bearing pears

1pearl \ˈpər(-ə)l\ *n* [ME *perle,* fr. MF, fr. (assumed) VL *pernula,* dim. of L *perna* haunch, sea mussel; akin to OE *fiersn* heel, Gk *pternē*] (14c) **1 a :** a dense variously colored and usu. lustrous concretion formed of concentric layers of nacre as an abnormal growth within the shell of some mollusks and used as a gem **b :** MOTHER-OF-PEARL **2 :** one that is very choice or precious **3 :** something resembling a pearl intrinsically or physically **4 :** a nearly neutral slightly bluish medium gray

2pearl *vt* (14c) **1 :** to set or adorn with pearls **2 :** to sprinkle or bead with pearly drops **3 :** to form into small round grains **4 :** to give a pearly color or luster to **~** *vi* **1 :** to form drops or beads like pearls **2 :** to fish or search for pearls — **pearl·er** \ˈpər-lər\ *n*

3pearl *adj* (1610) **1 a :** of, relating to, or resembling pearl **b :** made of or adorned with pearls **2 :** having medium-sized grains

4pearl *n or vt* [alter. of *purl*] *Brit* (1824) **:** PICOT

pearl·es·cent \ˌpər-ˈles-ᵊnt\ *adj* (1936) **:** having a pearly luster ⟨a **~** lacquer⟩ — **pearl·es·cence** \-ᵊn(t)s\ *n*

pearl essence *n* (ca. 1909) **:** a translucent substance that occurs in the silvery scales of various fish (as herring) and is used in making artificial pearls, lacquers, and plastics

pearl gray *n* (1796) **1 :** a yellowish to light gray **2 :** a variable color averaging a pale blue

Pearl Harbor *n* [*Pearl Harbor,* Oahu, Hawaii, Am. naval station attacked without warning by the Japanese] (1942) **:** a sneak attack usu. with devastating effect

pearl·ite \ˈpər(-ə)l-ˌīt\ *n* [F *perlite,* fr. *perle* pearl] (1888) **1 :** the lamellar mixture of ferrite and cementite in slowly cooled iron-carbon alloys occurring normally as a principal constituent of both steel and cast iron **2 :** PERLITE — **pearl·it·ic** \ˌpər-ˈlit-ik\ *adj*

pearl·ized \ˈpər(-ə)l-ˌīzd\ *adj* (1937) **:** given a pearlescent surface or finish

pearl millet *n* (ca. 1890) **:** a tall cereal grass (*Pennisetum glaucum*) that has large leaves and dense round spikes and is widely grown for its seeds and for forage

pearl onion *n* (ca. 1890) **:** a very small usu. pickled onion used esp. in appetizers and as a garnish

pearly \ˈpər-lē\ *adj* **pearl·i·er; -est** (15c) **1 :** resembling, containing, or adorned with pearls or mother-of-pearl **2 :** highly precious

pearly everlasting *n* (1857) **:** an American everlasting (*Anaphalis margaritacea*) that has herbage covered with white woolly hairs and corymbose heads with white scarious involucres

pearly nautilus *n* (1822) **:** NAUTILUS 1

pear psylla *n* (1904) **:** a yellowish or greenish jumping plant louse (*Psylla pyricola*) that is often destructive to the pear

pear–shaped \ˈpa(ə)r-ˌshāpt, ˈpe(ə)r-\ *adj* (1758) **1 :** having an oval shape markedly tapering at one end **2** *of a vocal tone* **:** free from harshness, thinness, or nasality

peart \ˈpi(ə)rt\ *adj* [alter. of *pert*] *chiefly Southern & Midland* (15c) **:** being in good spirits **:** LIVELY — **peart·ly** *adv*

peas·ant \ˈpez-ᵊnt\ *n* [ME *paissaunt,* fr. MF *paisant,* fr. OF, fr. *païs* country, fr. LL *pagensis* inhabitant of a district, fr. L *pagus* district] (15c) **1 :** a member of a European class of persons tilling the soil as small landowners or as laborers; *also* **:** a member of a similar class elsewhere **2 :** a usu. uneducated person of low social status

peas·ant·ry \-ᵊn-trē\ *n* (1553) **1 :** PEASANTS **2 :** the position, rank, or behavior of a peasant

pease·cod *or* **peas·cod** \ˈpēz-ˌkäd\ *n* [ME *pesecod,* fr. *pese* + *cod* bag, husk — more at CODPIECE] (14c) **:** a pea pod

pea·shoot·er \ˈpē-ˈshüt-ər, -ˌshüt-\ *n* (1803) **:** a toy blowgun that uses peas for projectiles

pea soup *n* (1711) **1 :** a thick purée made of dried peas **2 :** a heavy fog

1peat \ˈpēt\ *n, often attrib* [ME *pete,* fr. ML *peta*] (14c) **1 :** TURF 2b **2 :** partially carbonized vegetable tissue formed by partial decomposition in water of various plants (as mosses of the genus *Sphagnum*) — **peaty** \-ē\ *adj*

2peat *n* [origin unknown] (1599) **:** a bold lively woman

peat moss *n* (ca. 1864) **:** SPHAGNUM

pea·vey *or* **pea·vy** \ˈpē-vē\ *n, pl* **peaveys** *or* **peavies** [prob. fr. the name *Peavey*] (1870) **:** a lumberman's lever that has a pivoting hooked arm and metal spike at one end — called also *cant dog;* compare CANT HOOK

1peb·ble \ˈpeb-əl\ *n* [ME *pobble,* fr. OE *papolstān,* fr. *papol-* (of unknown origin) + *stān* stone] (13c) **1 :** a small usu. rounded stone esp. when worn by the action of water **2 :** transparent and colorless quartz **:** ROCK CRYSTAL **3 :** an irregular, crinkled, or grainy surface — **peb·bly** \-(ə-)lē\ *adj*

2pebble *vt* **peb·bled; peb·bling** \-(ə-)liŋ\ (1605) **1 :** to pelt with pebbles **2 :** to pave or cover with pebbles or something resembling pebbles **3 :** to grain (as leather) so as to produce a rough and irregularly indented surface

pe·can \pi-ˈkän, -ˈkan; ˈpē-ˌkan\ *n* [of Algonquian origin; akin to Ojibwa *pagân,* a hard-shelled nut] (1773) **1 :** a large hickory (*Carya illinoensis*) that has roughish bark and hard but brittle wood and is widely grown in the warmer parts of the U.S. and in Mexico for its edible nut **2 :** the wood of the pecan tree **3 :** the smooth oblong thin-shelled nut of the pecan tree

pec·ca·dil·lo \ˌpek-ə-ˈdil-(ˌ)ō\ *n, pl* **-loes** *or* **-los** [Sp *pecadillo,* dim. of *pecado* sin, fr. L *peccatum,* fr. neut. of *peccatus,* pp. of *peccare*] (1591) **:** a slight offense

pec·cant \ˈpek-ənt\ *adj* [L *peccant-, peccans,* prp. of *peccare* to stumble, sin] (1604) **1 :** guilty of a moral offense **:** SINNING **2 :** violating a principle or rule **:** FAULTY — **pec·cant·ly** *adv*

pec·ca·ry \ˈpek-ə-rē\ *n, pl* **-ries** [of Cariban origin; akin to Chaima *paquera* peccary] (1613) **:** either of two largely nocturnal gregarious American mammals resembling the related pigs: **a :** a grizzled animal (*Tayassu angulatus*) with an indistinct white collar **b :** a blackish animal (*Tayassu pecari*) with whitish cheeks

pec·ca·vi \pe-ˈkä-(ˌ)wē, -(ˌ)vē; -ˈkā-ˌvī\ *n* [L, I have sinned, fr. *peccare*] (1553) **:** an acknowledgment of sin

1peck \ˈpek\ *n* [ME *pek,* fr. MF] (14c) **1** — see WEIGHT table **2 :** a large quantity or number

2peck *vb* [ME *pecken,* alter. of *piken* to pierce — more at PICK] *vt* (14c) **1 a :** to strike or pierce esp. repeatedly with the bill or a pointed tool **b :** to make by pecking ⟨~ a hole⟩ **2 :** to pick up with the bill ~ *vi* **1 a :** to strike, pierce, or pick up something with or as if with the bill **b :** CARP, NAG **2 :** to eat reluctantly and in small bites ⟨~ at food⟩

3peck *n* (1591) **1 :** an impression or hole made by pecking **2 :** a quick sharp stroke

peck·er \ˈpek-ər\ *n* (1587) **1 :** one that pecks **2** *chiefly Brit* **:** COURAGE **3 :** PENIS — often considered vulgar

peck·er·wood \ˈpek-ər-ˌwu̇d\ *n* [prob. inversion of *woodpecker*] (1927) **:** a rural white Southerner — often used disparagingly

pecking order *also* **peck order** *n* (1928) **1 :** the basic pattern of social organization within a flock of poultry in which each bird pecks another lower in the scale without fear of retaliation and submits to pecking by one of higher rank **2 :** a social hierarchy

Peck·sniff·ian \pek-ˈsnif-ē-ən\ *adj* [Seth *Pecksniff,* character in *Martin Chuzzlewit* (1843-44) by Charles Dickens] (1851) **:** unctuously hypocritical **:** PHARISAICAL

pecky \ˈpek-ē\ *adj* [3*peck*] (1848) **1 :** marked by lenticular or finger-shaped pockets of decay caused by fungi ⟨~ cypress⟩ **2 :** containing discolored or shriveled grains ⟨~ rice⟩

pec·ten \ˈpek-tən\ *n, pl* **pectens** [NL *pectin-, pecten,* fr. L, comb, scallop] (15c) **1** *pl usu* **pec·ti·nes** \-tə-ˌnēz\ **:** a body part that resembles a comb; *esp* **:** a folded vascular pigmented membrane projecting into the vitreous humor in the eye of a bird or reptile **2 :** 1SCALLOP 1a

pec·tic \ˈpek-tik\ *adj* [F *pectique,* fr. Gk *pēktikos* coagulating, fr. *pēgnynai* to fix, coagulate — more at PACT] (1831) **:** of, relating to, or derived from pectin

pectic acid *n* (1831) **:** any of various water-insoluble substances formed by hydrolyzing the methyl ester groups of pectins

pec·tin \ˈpek-tən\ *n* [F *pectine,* fr. *pectique*] (1838) **:** any of various water-soluble substances that bind adjacent cell walls in plant tissues and yield a gel which is the basis of fruit jellies; *also* **:** a commercial product rich in pectins

pec·tin·aceous \ˌpek-tə-ˈnā-shəs\ *adj* (1844) **:** of, relating to, or containing pectin

pec·ti·nate \ˈpek-tə-ˌnāt\ *adj* [L *pectinatus,* fr. *pectin-, pecten* comb; akin to Gk *kten-, kteis* comb, L *pectere* to comb — more at FEE] (1793) **:** having narrow parallel projections or divisions suggestive of the teeth of a comb ⟨~ antennae⟩ — **pec·ti·na·tion** \ˌpek-tə-ˈnā-shən\ *n*

pec·tin·es·ter·ase \ˌpek-tə-ˈnes-tə-ˌrās, -ˌrāz\ *n* (1945) **:** an enzyme that catalyzes the hydrolysis of pectins into pectic acids and methanol

1pec·to·ral \ˈpek-t(ə-)rəl\ *n* (15c) **:** something worn on the breast

2pectoral *adj* [MF or L; MF, fr. L *pectoralis,* fr. *pector-, pectus* breast] (1578) **1 :** of, situated in or on, or worn on the chest **2 :** coming from the breast or heart as the seat of emotion

pectoral cross *n* (1727) **:** a cross worn on the breast esp. by a prelate

pectoral fin *n* (1769) **:** either of the fins of a fish that correspond to the forelimbs of a quadruped

pectoral girdle *n* (ca. 1890) **:** the bony or cartilaginous arch that supports the forelimbs of a vertebrate

pectoral muscle *n* (1615) **:** any of the muscles which connect the ventral walls of the chest with the bones of the upper arm and shoulder and of which there are two on each side in man

pec·u·late \ˈpek-yə-ˌlāt\ *vt* **-lat·ed; -lat·ing** [L *peculatus,* pp. of *peculari,* fr. *peculium*] (1802) **:** EMBEZZLE — **pec·u·la·tion** \ˌpek-yə-ˈlā-shən\ *n* — **pec·u·la·tor** \ˈpek-yə-ˌlāt-ər\ *n*

1pe·cu·liar \pi-ˈkyül-yər\ *adj* [ME *peculier,* fr. L *peculiaris* of private property, special, fr. *peculium* private property, fr. *pecu* cattle; akin to L *pecus* cattle — more at FEE] (15c) **1 :** characteristic of only one person, group, or thing **:** DISTINCTIVE **2 :** different from the usual or normal: **a :** SPECIAL, PARTICULAR **b :** ODD, CURIOUS **c :** ECCENTRIC, QUEER ***syn*** see CHARACTERISTIC, STRANGE — **pe·cu·liar·ly** *adv*

2peculiar *n* (1562) **:** something exempt from ordinary jurisdiction; *esp* **:** a church or parish exempt from the jurisdiction of the ordinary in whose territory it lies

pe·cu·liar·i·ty \pi-ˌkyül-ˈyar-ət-ē, -ˌkyü-lē-ˈar-\ *n, pl* **-ties** (1646) **1 :** the quality or state of being peculiar **2 :** a distinguishing characteristic **3 :** ODDITY, QUIRK

pe·cu·ni·ary \pi-ˈkyü-nē-ˌer-ē\ *adj* [L *pecuniarius,* fr. *pecunia* money — more at FEE] (1502) **1 :** consisting of or measured in money **2 :** of or relating to money **:** MONETARY — **pe·cu·ni·ari·ly** \-ˌkyü-nē-ˈer-ə-lē\ *adv*

ped \ˈped\ *n* [Gk *pedon* ground; akin to L *ped-, pes* foot — more at FOOT] (ca. 1951) **:** a natural soil aggregate

ped- *or* **pedo-** *or* **paed-** *or* **paedo-** *comb form* [Gk *paid-, paido-,* fr. *paid-, pais* child, boy — more at FEW] **:** child ⟨*ped*iatric⟩ **:** childhood ⟨*paedo*genesis⟩

-ped \ˌped *also* pəd\ *or* **-pede** \ˌpēd\ *n comb form* [L *ped-, pes*] **:** foot ⟨pinni*ped*⟩ ⟨cirri*pede*⟩

ped·a·gog·i·cal \ˌped-ə-ˈgäj-i-kəl, -ˈgōj-\ *also* **ped·a·gog·ic** \-ik\ *adj* (1781) **:** of, relating to, or befitting a teacher or education — **ped·a·gog·i·cal·ly** \-i-k(ə-)lē\ *adv*

ped·a·gog·ics \-iks\ *n pl but sing in constr* (ca. 1864) **:** PEDAGOGY

ped·a·gogue *also* **ped·a·gog** \ˈped-ə-ˌgäg\ *n* [ME *pedagoge,* fr. MF, fr. L *paedagogus,* fr. Gk *paidagōgos,* slave who escorted children to school, fr. *paid-* ped- + *agōgos* leader, fr. *agein* to lead — more at AGENT] (14c) **:** TEACHER, SCHOOLMASTER

ped·a·go·gy \ˈped-ə-ˌgōj-ē *also* -ˌgäj-, *esp Brit* -ˌgäg-\ *n* (1583) **:** the art, science, or profession of teaching; *esp* **:** EDUCATION 2

1ped·al \ˈped-ᵊl\ *n* [MF *pedale,* fr. It, fr. L *pedalis,* adj.] (ca. 1611) **1 :** a lever pressed by the foot in the playing of a musical instrument (as an organ or piano) **2 :** a foot lever or treadle by which a part is activated in a mechanism

2ped·al *adj* [L *pedalis,* fr. *ped-, pes*] (1625) **1** \ˈped-ᵊl *also* ˈpēd-\ **:** of or relating to the foot **2** \ˈped-\ **:** of, relating to, or involving a pedal

3ped·al \ˈped-ᵊl\ *vb* **ped·aled** *also* **ped·alled; ped·al·ing** *also* **ped·al·ling** \ˈped-ᵊl-iŋ, ˈped-liŋ\ *vi* (1866) **1 :** to use or work a pedal **2 :** to ride a bicycle ~ *vt* **:** to work the pedals of

pedal bone *n* (1881) **:** COFFIN BONE

pe·dal·fer \pə-ˈdal-fər, -ˌfe(ə)r\ *n* [Gk *pedon* ground + E *al*umen + L *fer*rum iron] (1928) **:** a soil that lacks a hardened layer of accumulated carbonates

ped·al–note \ˈped-ᵊl-ˌnōt\ *n* [fr. the playing of the lowest notes on the organ by means of pedals] (ca. 1850) **1 :** PEDAL POINT **2 :** one of the lowest tones that can be sounded on a brass instrument being an octave below the normal usable range and representing the fundamental of the harmonic series

pedal point *n* (ca. 1852) **:** a single tone usu. the tonic or dominant that is normally sustained in the bass and sounds against changing harmonies in the other parts

pedal pushers *n pl* (1944) **:** women's and girls' calf-length trousers

pedal steel *n* (1971) **:** a box-shaped musical instrument with legs that has usu. 10 strings which can be altered in pitch by the use of foot pedals and that are plucked while being pressed with a movable steel bar — called also *pedal steel guitar*

ped·ant \ˈped-ᵊnt\ *n* [MF, fr. It *pedante*] (1588) **1** *obs* **:** a male schoolteacher **2 a :** one who parades his learning **b :** one who is unimaginative or who unduly emphasizes minutiae in the presentation or use of knowledge **c :** a formalist or precisionist in teaching

pe·dan·tic \pi-ˈdant-ik\ *adj* (1600) **1 :** of, relating to, or being a pedant **2 :** narrowly, stodgily, and often ostentatiously learned **3 :** UNIMAGINATIVE, PEDESTRIAN — **pe·dan·ti·cal·ly** \-ˈdant-i-k(ə-)lē\ *adv*

ped·ant·ry \ˈped-ᵊn-trē\ *n, pl* **-ries** (1612) **1 :** pedantic presentation or application of knowledge or learning **2 :** an instance of pedantry

ped·dle \'ped-ᵊl\ *vb* **ped·dled; ped·dling** \'ped-liŋ, -ᵊl-iŋ\ [back-formation fr. *peddler*, fr. ME *pedlere*] *vi* (1532) **1 :** to travel about with wares for sale; *broadly* **:** SELL **2 :** to be busy with trifles **:** PIDDLE ~ *vt* **1 :** to sell or offer for sale from place to place **:** HAWK; *broadly* **:** SELL **2 :** to deal out or seek to disseminate

ped·dler *also* **ped·lar** \'ped-lər\ *n* (14c) **:** one who peddles: as **a :** one who offers merchandise (as fresh produce) for sale along the street or from door to door **b :** one who deals in or promotes something intangible (as a personal asset or an idea) ⟨influence ~*s*⟩

ped·er·ast \'ped-ə-,rast\ *n* [Gk *paiderastēs*, lit., lover of boys, fr. *paid-* paed- + *erastēs* lover, fr. *erasthai* to love — more at EROS] (ca. 1730) **:** one that practices anal intercourse esp. with a boy — **ped·er·as·tic** \,ped-ə-'ras-tik\ *adj* — **ped·er·as·ty** \'ped-ə-,ras-tē\ *n*

[1]**ped·es·tal** \'ped-əs-tᵊl\ *n* [MF *piedestal*, fr. OIt *piedestallo*, fr. *pie di stallo* foot of a stall] (1563) **1 a :** the support or foot of a late classic or neoclassic column — see COLUMN illustration **b :** the base of an upright structure **2 :** BASE, FOUNDATION **3 :** a position of esteem

[2]**pedestal** *vt* **-taled** *or* **-talled; -tal·ing** *or* **-tal·ling** (1648) **:** to place on or furnish with a pedestal

[1]**pe·des·tri·an** \pə-'des-trē-ən\ *adj* [L *pedestr-, pedester*, lit., going on foot, fr. *pedes* one going on foot, fr. *ped-, pes* foot — more at FOOT] (1716) **1 :** COMMONPLACE, UNIMAGINATIVE **2 a :** going or performed on foot **b :** of, relating to, or designed for walking ⟨a ~ mall⟩

[2]**pedestrian** *n* (1793) **:** a person going on foot **:** WALKER

pe·des·tri·an·ism \-,iz-əm\ *n* (1809) **1 a :** the practice of walking **b :** fondness for walking for exercise or recreation **2 :** the quality or state of being unimaginative or commonplace

pe·di·at·ric \,pēd-ē-'a-trik\ *adj* (1880) **:** of or relating to pediatrics

pe·di·a·tri·cian \,pēd-ē-ə-'trish-ən\ *or* **pe·di·a·trist** \,pēd-ē-'a-trəst, pē-'dī-ə-\ *n* (ca. 1903) **:** a specialist in pediatrics

pe·di·at·rics \,pēd-ē-'a-triks\ *n pl but sing or pl in constr* (1884) **:** a branch of medicine dealing with the development, care, and diseases of children

pedi·cab \'ped-i-,kab\ *n* [L *ped-, pes* + E *cab*] (1945) **:** a tricycle with a 2-seat passenger compartment covered by a usu. folding top and a separate seat for a driver who pedals

ped·i·cel \'ped-ə-,sel\ *n* [NL *pedicellus*, dim. of L *pediculus*] (1676) **:** a slender basal part of an organism or one of its parts: as **a :** a plant stalk that supports a fruiting or spore-bearing organ — see CORYMB illustration **b :** a narrow basal attachment (as of the abdomen of an ant) of an animal organ or part — **ped·i·cel·late** \,ped-ə-'sel-ət\ *adj*

ped·i·cle \'ped-i-kəl\ *n* [L *pediculus*, fr. dim. of *ped-, pes*] (1626) **1 :** PEDICEL b **2 :** the part of a skin or tissue graft left attached to the original site during the preliminary stages of union — **ped·i·cled** \-kəld\ *adj*

pe·dic·u·late \pi-'dik-yə-lət\ *adj* [deriv. of L *pediculus* little foot, pedicel] (ca. 1890) **:** of or relating to an order (Pediculati) of marine teleost fishes with jugular ventral fins, pectoral fins at the end of an armlike process, and part of the dorsal fin modified into a lure — **pediculate** *n*

pe·dic·u·lo·sis \pi-,dik-yə-'lō-səs\ *n* [NL, fr. L *pediculus* louse, dim. of *pedis* louse] (ca. 1890) **:** infestation with lice

pe·dic·u·lous \pi-'dik-yə-ləs\ *adj* [L *pediculosus*, fr. *pediculus*] (1550) **:** infested with lice **:** LOUSY

pedi·cure \'ped-i-,kyu̇(ə)r\ *n* [F *pédicure*, fr. L *ped-, pes* foot + *curare* to take care, fr. *cura* care — more at CURE] (ca. 1842) **1 :** one who practices chiropody **2 a :** care of the feet, toes, and nails **b :** a single treatment of these parts — **pedi·cur·ist** \-,kyu̇r-əst\ *n*

ped·i·gree \'ped-ə-,grē\ *n* [ME *pedegru*, fr. MF *pie de grue* crane's foot; fr. the shape made by the lines of a genealogical chart] (15c) **1 :** a register recording a line of ancestors **2 a :** an ancestral line **:** LINEAGE **b :** the origin and the history of something **3 a :** a distinguished ancestry **b :** the recorded purity of breed of an individual or strain — **ped·i·greed** \-,grēd\ *or* **pedigree** *adj*

ped·i·ment \'ped-ə-mənt\ *n* [obs. E *periment*, prob. alter. of E *pyramid*] (1592) **1 :** a triangular space forming the gable of a low-pitched roof in classic architecture; *also* **:** a similar form used as a decoration **2 :** a broad gently sloping bedrock surface with low relief that is situated at the base of a steeper slope and is usu. thinly covered with alluvial gravel and sand — **ped·i·men·tal** \,ped-ə-'ment-ᵊl\ *adj*

pedi·palp \'ped-ə-,palp\ *n* [NL *pedipalpus*, fr. *ped-, pes* foot + *palpus* palpus] (1826) **:** either of the second pair of appendages of an arachnid (as a spider) that are borne near the mouth and are often modified for a special (as sensory) function

pedo- — see PED-

ped·o·cal \'ped-ə-,kal\ *n* [Gk *pedon* earth + L *calc-, calx* lime — more at PED, CHALK] (1928) **:** a soil that includes a definite hardened layer of accumulated carbonates — **ped·o·cal·ic** \,ped-ə-'kal-ik\ *adj*

[1]**pe·do·gen·e·sis** \,pēd-ə-'jen-ə-səs\ *var of* PAEDOGENESIS

[2]**pedo·gen·e·sis** \,ped-ə-'jen-ə-səs\ *n* [NL, fr. Gk *pedon* + L *genesis*] (1936) **:** the formation and development of soil — **pedo·gen·ic** \-'jen-ik\ *also* **pedo·ge·net·ic** \-jə-'net-ik\ *adj*

pe·dol·o·gy \pi-'däl-ə-jē, pe-\ *n* [Gk *pedon* + ISV *-logy*] (1912) **:** SOIL SCIENCE — **pe·do·log·ic** \,ped-ᵊl-'äj-ik\ *or* **pe·do·log·i·cal** \-i-kəl\ *adj* — **pe·dol·o·gist** \pi-'däl-ə-jəst, pe-\ *n*

pe·dom·e·ter \pi-'däm-ət-ər\ *n* [F *pédomètre*, fr. L *ped-, pes* foot + F *-mètre* -meter — more at FOOT] (1723) **:** an instrument usu. in watch form that records the distance a person covers on foot by responding to the body motion at each step

pe·do·phile \'pēd-ə-,fīl\ *n* (1951) **:** one affected with pedophilia

pe·do·phil·ia \,pēd-ə-'fil-ē-ə\ *n* [NL] (ca. 1906) **:** sexual perversion in which children are the preferred sexual object — **pe·do·phil·i·ac** \-'fil-ē-,ak\ *or* **pe·do·phil·ic** \-'fil-ik\ *adj*

pe·dun·cle \'pē-,dəŋ-kəl, pi-'\ *n* [NL *pedunculus*, dim. of L *ped-, pes*] (ca. 1753) **1 :** a stalk bearing a flower or flower cluster or a fructification — see CORYMB illustration **2 :** a narrow part by which some larger part or the whole body of an organism is attached **:** STALK, PEDICEL **3 :** a narrow stalk by which a tumor or polyp is attached — **pe·dun·cled** \-kəld\ *adj* — **pe·dun·cu·lar** \pi-'dəŋ-kyə-lər\ *adj*

pe·dun·cu·lat·ed \pi-'dəŋ-kyə-,lāt-əd\ *also* **pe·dun·cu·late** \-lət\ *adj* [NL *pedunculus*] (1760) **:** having, growing on, or being attached by a peduncle ⟨a ~ tumor⟩

[1]**pee** \'pē\ *n* (1612) **1 :** the letter *p* **2** *pl* **pee** *Brit* **:** PENNY

[2]**pee** *vi* **peed; pee·ing** [euphemism fr. the initial letter of *piss*] (1788) **:** URINATE — sometimes considered vulgar

[1]**peek** \'pēk\ *vi* [ME *piken*] (14c) **1 a :** to look furtively **b :** to peer through a crack or hole or from a place of concealment — often used with *in* or *out* **2 :** to take a brief look **:** GLANCE

[2]**peek** *n* (1843) **1 :** a surreptitious look **2 :** a brief look **:** GLANCE

[1]**peek·a·boo** \,pē-kə-'bü\ *n* [[1]*peek* + [1]*boo*] (1599) **:** a game for amusing a baby in which one repeatedly hides his face or body and pops back into view exclaiming "Peekaboo!"

[2]**peek·a·boo** \-,bü\ *adj* (1895) **1 :** trimmed with eyelet embroidery ⟨a ~ blouse⟩ **2 :** made of a sheer or transparent fabric

[1]**peel** \'pē(ə)l\ *n* (14c) **1 :** the skin or rind of a fruit **2 :** a thin layer of organic material that is embedded in a film of collodion and stripped from the surface of an object (as a plant fossil) for microscopic study

[2]**peel** *vb* [ME *pelen*, fr. MF *peler*, fr. L *pilare* to remove the hair from, fr. *pilus* hair — more at PILE] *vt* (14c) **1 :** to strip off an outer layer of ⟨~ an orange⟩ **2 :** to remove by stripping ⟨~ the label off the can⟩ ~ *vi* **1 a :** to come off in sheets or scales **b :** to lose an outer layer (as of skin) ⟨his face is ~*ing*⟩ **2 :** to take off one's clothes **3 :** to break away from a group or formation — often used with *off* — **peel·able** \'pē-lə-bəl\ *adj*

[3]**peel** *n* [ME *pel* stockade, stake, fr. AF, stockade & MF, stake, fr. L *palus* stake — more at POLE] (14c) **:** a medieval small massive fortified tower along the Scottish-English border

[4]**peel** *n* [ME *pele*, fr. MF, fr. L *pala*] (15c) **:** a usu. long-handled spade-shaped instrument that is used chiefly by bakers for getting something (as bread or pies) into or out of the oven

[1]**peel·er** \'pē-lər\ *n* (1597) **1 :** one that peels **2 :** a log of wood (as Douglas fir) suitable for cutting into rotary veneer — called also *peeler log*

[2]**peeler** *n* [Sir Robert *Peel*] *Brit* (1817) **:** POLICEMAN

peel·ing \'pē-liŋ\ *n* (1597) **:** a peeled-off piece or strip (as of skin or rind)

peel off *vi* (1941) **1 :** to veer away from an airplane formation esp. for diving or landing **2 :** DEPART, LEAVE

[1]**peen** \'pēn\ *vt* (1513) **:** to draw, bend, or flatten by or as if by hammering with a peen

[2]**peen** *n* [prob. of Scand origin; akin to Norw *penn* peen] (1683) **:** a usu. hemispherical or wedge-shaped end of the head of a hammer that is opposite the face and is used esp. for bending, shaping, or cutting the material struck

[1]**peep** \'pēp\ *vi* [ME *pepen*, of imit. origin] (15c) **1 :** to utter a feeble shrill sound as of a bird newly hatched **:** CHEEP **2 :** to utter the slightest sound

[2]**peep** *n* (15c) **1 :** a feeble shrill sound **:** CHEEP **2 :** a slight utterance esp. of complaint or protest ⟨don't let me hear another ~ out of you⟩ **3 :** any of several small sandpipers

[3]**peep** *vb* [ME *pepen*, perh. alter. of *piken* to peek] *vi* (15c) **1 a :** to peer through or as if through a crevice **b :** to look cautiously or slyly **2 :** to begin to emerge from or as if from concealment **:** show slightly ~ *vt* **:** to put forth or cause to protrude slightly

[4]**peep** *n* (1530) **1 :** a first glimpse or faint appearance ⟨at the ~ of dawn⟩ **2 a :** a brief look **:** GLANCE **b :** a furtive look

[1]**peep·er** \'pē-pər\ *n* (ca. 1611) **1 :** one that makes a peeping sound **2 :** any of various tailless amphibians (as a tree frog or a spring peeper) that peep shrilly

[2]**peeper** *n* (1652) **1 :** one that peeps; *specif* **:** VOYEUR **2 :** EYE

peep·hole \'pēp-,hōl\ *n* (1681) **:** a hole or crevice to peep through

Peep·ing Tom \,pē-piŋ-'täm\ *n* [*Peeping Tom*, legendary citizen of Coventry who watched Lady Godiva riding naked] (ca. 1796) **:** a prurient prying person **:** VOYEUR — **Peeping Tom·ism** \-'täm-,iz-əm\ *n*

peep show *n* (1851) **:** an entertainment (as a film) or object (as a small painting) viewed through a small opening or a magnifying glass

peep sight *n* (1881) **:** a rear sight for a gun having an adjustable metal piece pierced with a small hole to peep through in aiming

[1]**peer** \'pi(ə)r\ *n* [ME, fr. MF *per*, fr. *per*, adj., equal, fr. L *par*] (14c) **1 :** one that is of equal standing with another **:** EQUAL; *esp* **:** one belonging to the same societal group esp. based on age, grade, or status **2** *archaic* **:** COMPANION **3 a :** a member of one of the five ranks (as duke, marquess, earl, viscount, or baron) of the British peerage **b :** NOBLE 1 — **peer** *adj*

[2]**peer** *vt, archaic* (14c) **:** RIVAL, MATCH

[3]**peer** *vi* [perh. by shortening & alter. fr. *appear*] (1591) **1 :** to look narrowly or curiously; *esp* **:** to look searchingly at something difficult to discern **2 :** to come slightly into view **:** emerge partly ***syn*** see GAZE

peer·age \'pi(ə)r-ij\ *n* (15c) **1 :** the body of peers **2 :** the rank or dignity of a peer **3 :** a book containing a list of peers with their genealogy, history, and titles

peer·ess \'pir-əs\ *n* (1689) **1 :** the wife or widow of a peer **2 :** a woman who holds in her own right the rank of a peer

peer·less \'pi(ə)r-ləs\ *adj* (14c) **:** MATCHLESS, INCOMPARABLE

[1]**peeve** \'pēv\ *vt* **peeved; peev·ing** [back-formation fr. *peevish*] (1908) **:** to make peevish or resentful **:** ANNOY

[2]**peeve** *n* (1910) **1 :** a feeling or mood of resentment **2 :** a particular grievance **:** GRUDGE

pee·vish \'pē-vish\ *adj* [ME *pevish* spiteful] (1530) **1 :** querulous in temperament or mood **:** FRETFUL **2 :** perversely obstinate **3 :** marked by ill temper — **pee·vish·ly** *adv* — **pee·vish·ness** *n*

pee·wee \'pē-(,)wē\ *n* [imit.] (ca. 1796) **1 :** PEWEE **2 :** one that is diminutive or small; *esp* **:** a small child — **peewee** *adj*

pee·wit \'pē-,wit, 'pyü-ət\ *n* [imit.] (1529) **:** any of several birds; *esp* **:** LAPWING

[1]**peg** \'peg\ *n* [ME *pegge*, prob. fr. MD; akin to L *baculum* staff, Gk *baktērion*] (15c) **1 a :** a small usu. cylindrical pointed or tapered piece (as of wood) used to pin down or fasten things or to fit into or close holes **:** PIN, PLUG **b** *Brit* **:** CLOTHESPIN **c :** a predetermined level at which something (as a price) is fixed **2 a :** a projecting piece used as a support or boundary marker **b :** something (as a fact or opinion) used as a support, pretext, or reason **3 a :** one of the movable

\ə\ abut \ᵊ\ kitten, F table \ər\ further \a\ ash \ā\ ace \ä\ cot, cart \au̇\ out \ch\ chin \e\ bet \ē\ easy \g\ go \i\ hit \ī\ ice \j\ job \ŋ\ sing \ō\ go \ȯ\ law \ȯi\ boy \th\ thin \th\ the \ü\ loot \u̇\ foot \y\ yet \zh\ vision \à, k̲, ⁿ, œ, œ̄, ue, ue̅, ʸ\ see Guide to Pronunciation

wooden pegs set in the head of a stringed instrument (as a violin) that are turned to regulate the pitch of the strings — see VIOLIN illustration **b :** a step or degree esp. in estimation **4 :** a pointed prong or claw for catching or tearing **5** *Brit* **:** DRINK ⟨poured himself out a stiff ~ — Dorothy Sayers⟩ **6 :** something (as a leg) resembling a peg **7 :** THROW; *esp* **:** a hard throw in baseball made in an attempt to put out a base runner — **off the peg :** READY-MADE

2peg *vb* **pegged; peg·ging** *vt* (1543) **1 a :** to put a peg into **b** *Brit* **:** to pin (laundry) on a clothesline **2 :** to attach or fix as if with a peg: as **a :** to pin down **:** RESTRICT **b :** to fix or hold (as prices or wage increases) at a predetermined level or rate **c :** to place in a definite category **:** IDENTIFY **3 :** to mark by pegs **4 :** THROW ~ *vi* **1 :** to work steadily and diligently — often used with *away* **2 :** to move along vigorously or hastily **:** HUSTLE

3peg \ˈpeg\ *or* **pegged** \ˈpegd\ *adj* (1681) **:** wide at the top and narrow at the bottom ⟨~ pants⟩

Peg·a·sus \ˈpeg-ə-səs\ *n* [L (gen. *Pegasi*), fr. Gk *Pēgasos*] **1 :** a winged horse that causes the stream Hippocrene to spring from Mount Helicon with a blow of his hoof **2 :** poetic inspiration **3 :** a northern constellation near the vernal equinoctial point

peg·board \ˈpeg-ˌbō(ə)rd, -ˌbȯ(ə)rd\ *n* (1899) **:** a small board perforated with a pattern of holes into which pegs are stuck in playing certain games; *also* **:** a game played on a pegboard in which a player tries to remove one peg at a time in systematic fashion

Peg–Board *trademark* — used for material (as fiberboard) with regularly spaced perforations into which hooks may be inserted for the storage or display of articles

peg leg *n* [3*peg*] (1769) **:** an artificial leg; *esp* **:** one fitted at the knee

peg·ma·tite \ˈpeg-mə-ˌtīt\ *n* [F, fr. Gk *pēgmat-*, *pēgma* something fastened together, fr. *pēgnynai* to fasten together — more at PACT] (ca. 1828) **1 :** a coarse variety of granite occurring in dikes or veins **2 :** a formation similar to pegmatite in other rocks ⟨syenite ~⟩ — **peg·ma·tit·ic** \ˌpeg-mə-ˈtit-ik\ *adj*

peg–top \ˈpeg-ˈtäp\ *or* **peg–topped** \-ˈtäpt\ *adj* (1858) **:** PEG

peg top *n* (1788) **1** \ˈpeg-ˈtäp\ **:** a pear-shaped top that is made to spin on the sharp metal peg in its base by the unwinding of a string wound round its center **2** *pl* \-ˌtäps\ **:** peg trousers

Peh·le·vi \ˈpel-ə-(ˌ)vē\ *var of* PAHLAVI

pei·gnoir \pān-ˈwär, pen-\ *n* [F, lit., garment worn while combing the hair, fr. MF, fr. *peigner* to comb the hair, fr. L *pectinare*, fr. *pectin-*, *pecten* comb — more at PECTINATE] (1835) **:** a woman's loose negligee or dressing gown

pein *var of* PEEN

pe·jo·ra·tive \pi-ˈjȯr-ət-iv, -ˈjär-; ˈpej-(ə-)rət-, ˈpej-ə-ˌrāt-, ˈpēj-\ *adj* [LL *pejoratus*, pp. of *pejorare* to make or become worse, fr. L *pejor* worse; akin to L *pessimus* worst, Gk *pedon* ground — more at PARALLELEPIPED] (1888) **:** having negative connotations; *esp* **:** tending to disparage or belittle **:** DEPRECIATORY — **pe·jo·ra·tive·ly** *adv*

peke \ˈpēk\ *n, often cap* (1915) **:** PEKINGESE 2

Pe·kin \pi-ˈkin, ˈpē-\ *n* [*Peking, Pekin*, China] (ca. 1885) **:** any of a breed of large white ducks of Chinese origin used for meat production

Pe·king duck \ˌpē-ˌkiŋ-\ *n* (1955) **:** a Chinese dish consisting of roasted duck meat and strips of crispy duck skin topped with scallions and sauce and wrapped in thin pancakes

Pe·king·ese *or* **Pe·kin·ese** \ˌpē-kən-ˈēz, -kiŋ-, -ˈēs\ *n, pl* **Pekingese** *or* **Pekinese** (1849) **1 a :** the Chinese dialect of Peking **b :** a native or resident of Peking **2 :** any of a Chinese breed of small short-legged dogs with a broad flat face and a profuse long soft coat

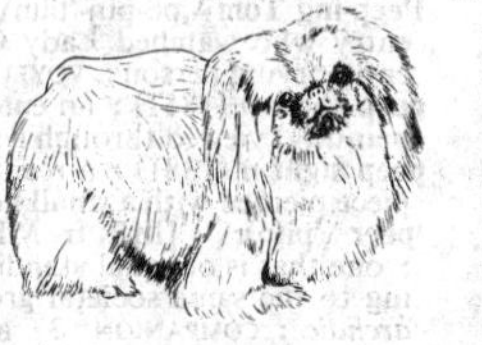

Pekingese 2

Peking man *n* (1926) **:** an extinct Pleistocene man that is known from skeletal and cultural remains in cave deposits at Cho-k'ou-tien, China and is now classified with the pithecanthropines

pe·koe \ˈpē-(ˌ)kō\ *n* [Chin (Amoy) *pek-ho*] (1712) **:** a tea made from the two youngest leaves and the end bud of the shoot

pel·age \ˈpel-ij\ *n* [F, fr. MF, fr. *poil* hair, fr. L *pilus* — more at PILE] (ca. 1828) **:** the hairy covering of a mammal

1Pe·la·gian \pə-ˈlā-j(ē-)ən\ *n* (1532) **:** one agreeing with Pelagius in denying original sin and consequently in holding that man has perfect freedom to do either right or wrong

2Pelagian *adj* (1579) **:** of or relating to Pelagians or Pelagianism

Pe·la·gian·ism \-ˌiz-əm\ *n* (1503) **:** the teaching of Pelagius or Pelagians

pe·lag·ic \pə-ˈlaj-ik\ *adj* [L *pelagicus*, fr. Gk *pelagikos*, fr. *pelagos* sea — more at FLAKE] (1656) **:** of, relating to, or living or occurring in the open sea **:** OCEANIC

pel·ar·go·ni·um \ˌpel-är-ˈgō-nē-əm, ˌpel-ər-\ *n* [NL, irreg. fr. Gk *pelargos* stork; akin to Gk *polios* gray — more at FALLOW] (1835) **:** any of a genus (*Pelargonium*) of southern African herbs (as a garden geranium) of the geranium family with showy flowers of various shades of red, pink, or white distinguished by a spurred calyx and irregular corolla

Pe·las·gian \pə-ˈlaz-j(ē-)ən, -ˈlaz-gē-ən\ *n* [Gk *pelasgios*, adj., Pelasgian, fr. *Pelasgoi* Pelasgians] (15c) **:** a member of an ancient people mentioned by classical writers as early inhabitants of Greece and the eastern islands of the Mediterranean — **Pelasgian** *adj* — **Pe·las·gic** \-jik, -gik\ *adj*

pe·le·cy·pod \pə-ˈles-ə-ˌpäd\ *n* [NL *Pelecypoda*, group name, fr. Gk *pelekys* axe + *pod-*, *pous* foot — more at FOOT] (ca. 1890) **:** LAMELLIBRANCH

pel·er·ine \ˌpel-ə-ˈrēn, ˈpel-ə-rən\ *n* [obs. F, neckerchief, fr. F *pèlerine*, fem. of *pèlerin* pilgrim, fr. LL *pelegrinus* — more at PILGRIM] (1744) **:** a woman's narrow cape made of fabric or fur and usu. with long ends hanging down in front

Pe·leus \ˈpēl-ˌyüs, ˈpē-lē-əs\ *n* [L, fr. Gk *Pēleus*] **:** a son of Aeacus who becomes by the goddess Thetis the father of Achilles

pelf \ˈpelf\ *n* [ME, fr. MF *pelfre* booty] (1500) **:** MONEY, RICHES

pel·i·can \ˈpel-i-kən\ *n* [ME, fr. OE *pellican*, fr. LL *pelecanus*, fr. Gk *pelekan*] (bef. 12c) **:** any of a genus (*Pelecanus*) of large web-footed birds with a very large bill and distensible gular pouch in which fish are caught

pe·lisse \pə-ˈlēs, pe-\ *n* [F, fr. LL *pellicia*, fr. fem. of *pellicius* made of skin, fr. L *pellis* skin — more at FELL] (1717) **1 :** a long cloak or coat made of fur or lined or trimmed with fur **2 :** a woman's loose lightweight cloak with wide collar and fur trimming

pel·la·gra \pə-ˈlag-rə, -ˈlāg-, -ˈläg-\ *n* [It, fr. *pelle* skin (fr. L *pellis*) + *-agra* (as in *podagra*, fr. L)] (1811) **:** a disease marked by dermatitis, gastrointestinal disorders, and central nervous symptoms and associated with a diet deficient in niacin and protein — **pel·la·grous** \-rəs\ *adj*

pel·la·grin \-rən\ *n* [irreg. fr. *pellagra*] (1865) **:** one that is affected with pellagra

1pel·let \ˈpel-ət\ *n* [ME *pelote*, fr. MF, fr. (assumed) VL *pilota*, dim. of L *pila* ball — more at PILE] (14c) **1 :** a usu. small rounded or spherical body (as of food, medicine, debris, or snow) **2 a :** a usu. stone ball used as a missile in medieval times **b :** CANNONBALL **c :** BULLET **d :** a piece of shot **e :** a substitute for a bullet; *specif* **:** an often bullet-shaped projectile fired from an air gun — **pel·let·al** \-ət-ᵊl\ *adj*

2pellet *vt* (1597) **1 :** PELLETIZE **2 :** to strike with pellets

pel·let·ize \ˈpel-ət-ˌīz\ *vt* **-ized; -iz·ing** (1942) **:** to form or compact into pellets ⟨~ ore⟩ — **pel·let·iza·tion** \ˌpel-ət-ə-ˈzā-shən\ *n* — **pel·let·iz·er** \ˈpel-ət-ˌī-zər\ *n*

pel·li·cle \ˈpel-i-kəl\ *n* [MF *pellicule*, fr. ML *pellicula*, fr. L, dim. of *pellis*] (1541) **:** a thin skin or film: as **a :** an outer membrane of some protozoans (as euglenoids or paramecia) **b :** a film that reflects a part of the light falling upon it and transmits the rest of the light through it and that is used for dividing a beam of light (as in a photographic device)

1pel·li·to·ry \ˈpel-ə-ˌtōr-ē, -ˌtȯr-\ *n, pl* **-ries** [ME *peletre*, fr. MF *piretre*, fr. L *pyrethrum*] (1533) **:** a southern European composite plant (*Anacyclus pyrethrum*) resembling yarrow — called also *pellitory-of-Spain*

2pellitory *n* [ME *paritorie*, fr. MF *paritaire*, fr. LL *parietaria*, fr. fem. of *parietarius* of a wall, fr. L *pariet-*, *paries* wall — more at PARIETAL] (1548) **:** any of a genus (*Parietaria*) of herbs of the nettle family with alternate leaves and inconspicuous flowers — called also *pellitory-of-the-wall*

pell–mell \ˈpel-ˈmel\ *adv* [MF *pelemele*] (1596) **1 :** in mingled confusion or disorder **2 :** in confused haste — **pell–mell** *adj or n*

pel·lu·cid \pə-ˈlü-səd\ *adj* [L *pellucidus*, fr. *per* through + *lucidus* lucid — more at FOR] (1619) **1 :** admitting maximum passage of light without diffusion or distortion **2 :** reflecting light evenly from all surfaces **3 :** easy to understand — **pel·lu·cid·ly** \pə-ˈlü-səd-lē\ *adv*

Pe·lops \ˈpē-ˌläps, ˈpel-ˌäps\ *n* [L, fr. Gk] **:** a son of Tantalus served by his father to the gods for food but later restored to life by them

pe·lo·rus \pə-ˈlōr-əs, -ˈlȯr-\ *n* [origin unknown] (1854) **:** a navigational instrument resembling a mariner's compass without magnetic needles and having two sight vanes by which bearings are taken

pe·lo·ta \pə-ˈlōt-ə\ *n* [Sp, fr. OF *pelote* little ball — more at PELLET] (1844) **1 :** a court game related to jai alai **2 :** the ball used in jai alai

1pelt \ˈpelt\ *n* [ME] (15c) **1 :** a usu. undressed skin with its hair, wool, or fur **2 :** a skin stripped of hair or wool for tanning

2pelt *vt* (1596) **:** to strip off the skin or pelt of (an animal)

3pelt *vb* [ME *pelten*] *vt* (1500) **1 :** to strike with a succession of blows or missiles ⟨~*ed* him with stones⟩ **2 :** HURL, THROW ⟨hand me anything hard . . . to ~ at her —Charles Dickens⟩ **3 :** to beat or dash repeatedly against ⟨hailstones ~*ing* the roof⟩ ~ *vi* **1 :** to deliver a succession of blows or missiles **2 :** to beat incessantly **3 :** to move rapidly and vigorously **:** HURRY — **pelt·er** *n*

4pelt *n* (1513) **:** BLOW, WHACK

pel·tate \ˈpel-ˌtāt\ *adj* [prob. fr. (assumed) NL *peltatus*, fr. L *pelta* small shield, fr. Gk *peltē*] (ca. 1760) **:** shaped like a shield; *specif* **:** having the stem or support attached to the lower surface instead of at the base or margin ⟨a ~ leaf⟩

pelt·ing \ˈpel-tiŋ\ *adj* [prob. fr. E dial. *pelt* piece of trash] *archaic* (1540) **:** PALTRY, INSIGNIFICANT

pelt·ry \ˈpel-trē\ *n, pl* **peltries** [ME, fr. AF *pelterie*] (15c) **:** PELTS, FURS; *esp* **:** raw undressed skins — often used in pl.

pel·vic \ˈpel-vik\ *adj* (1830) **:** of, relating to, or located in or near the pelvis — **pelvic** *n*

pelvic fin *n* (ca. 1909) **:** one of the paired fins of a fish that are homologous with the hind limbs of a quadruped

pelvic girdle *n* (1883) **:** a bony or cartilaginous arch that supports the hind limbs of a vertebrate

pel·vis \ˈpel-vəs\ *n, pl* **pel·vis·es** \-və-səz\ *or* **pel·ves** \-ˌvēz\ [NL, fr. L, basin; akin to OE & ON *full* cup, Gk *pella* wooden bowl] (1615) **1 :** a basin-shaped structure in the skeleton of many vertebrates that is formed by the pelvic girdle and adjoining bones of the spine **2 :** the cavity of the pelvis **3 :** the funnel-shaped cavity of the kidney into which urine is discharged

pel·y·co·saur \ˈpel-i-kə-ˌsȯ(ə)r\ *n* [deriv. of Gk *pelyc-*, *pelyx* wooden bowl + *sauros* lizard] (1904) **:** any of an order (Pelycosauria) of primitive Permian reptiles that resemble mammals and often have extreme development of the dorsal vertebral processes

Pem·broke table \ˈpem-ˌbrōk, -ˌbru̇k\ *n* (1778) **:** a small 4-legged table originating in the Georgian period and having two drop leaves and a drawer

Pembroke Welsh corgi *n* [*Pembroke*, Wales] (1938) **:** any of a breed of Welsh corgis with pointed ears, straight legs, and short tail — called also *Pembroke;* see WELSH CORGI illustration

pem·mi·can *also* **pem·i·can** \ˈpem-i-kən\ *n* [Cree *pimikân*] (1791) **:** a concentrated food used by No. American Indians and consisting of lean meat dried, pounded fine, and mixed with melted fat; *also* **:** a similar preparation (as of dried beef, flour, molasses, suet) used for emergency rations

pem·o·line \ˈpem-ə-ˌlēn\ *n* [origin unknown] (1961) **:** a synthetic organic drug $C_9H_8N_2O_2$ that is usu. mixed with magnesium hydroxide, is a mild stimulant of the central nervous system, and is used experimentally to improve memory

pem·phi·gus \ˈpem(p)-fi-gəs, pem-ˈfī-\ *n* [NL, fr. Gk *pemphig-*, *pemphix* breath, pustule] (ca. 1779) **:** a disease characterized by large blisters on skin and mucous membranes and often by itching or burning

1pen \ˈpen\ *n* [ME, fr. OE *penn*] (bef. 12c) **1 a :** a small enclosure for animals **b :** the animals in a pen ⟨a ~ of sheep⟩ **2 :** a small place of confinement or storage **3 :** a dock or slip for reconditioning submarines

2pen *vt* **penned; pen·ning** (13c) **:** to shut in or as if in a pen

[3]**pen** *n* [ME *penne,* fr. MF, feather, pen, fr. L *penna, pinna* feather; akin to Gk *pteron* wing — more at FEATHER] (14c) **1 :** an implement for writing or drawing with ink or a similar fluid: as **a :** QUILL **b :** PEN POINT **c :** a penholder containing a pen point **d :** FOUNTAIN PEN **e :** BALLPOINT **2 a :** a writing instrument regarded as a means of expression ⟨enlisted the ~s of the best writers —F. H. Chase⟩ **b :** WRITER **3 :** the internal horny feather-shaped shell of a squid

[4]**pen** *vt* **penned; pen·ning** (15c) **:** WRITE, INDITE ⟨~ a letter⟩

[5]**pen** *n* [origin unknown] (1550) **:** a female swan

[6]**pen** *n* (1848) **:** PENITENTIARY

pe·nal \ˈpēn-ᵊl\ *adj* [ME, fr. MF, fr. L *poenalis,* fr. *poena* punishment — more at PAIN] (15c) **1 :** of, relating to, or involving punishment, penalties, or punitive institutions **2 :** liable to punishment ⟨a ~ offense⟩ **3 :** used as a place of confinement and punishment ⟨a ~ colony⟩ — **pe·nal·ly** \-ᵊl-ē\ *adv*

penal code *n* (1845) **:** a code of laws concerning crimes and offenses and their punishment

pe·nal·ize \ˈpēn-ᵊl-ˌīz, ˈpen-\ *vt* **-ized; -iz·ing** (1868) **1 :** to inflict a penalty on **2 :** to put at a serious disadvantage — **pe·nal·iza·tion** \-ᵊl-ə-ˈzā-shən\ *n*

pen·al·ty \ˈpen-ᵊl-tē\ *n, pl* **-ties** [ML *poenalitas,* fr. L *poenalis*] (1512) **1 :** the suffering in person, rights, or property that is annexed by law or judicial decision to the commission of a crime or public offense **2 :** the suffering or the sum to be forfeited to which a person subjects himself by agreement in case of nonfulfillment of stipulations **3 a :** disadvantage, loss, or hardship due to some action **b :** a disadvantage (as loss of yardage, time, or possession of the ball or an addition to or subtraction from the score) imposed on a team or competitor for violation of the rules of a sport **4 :** points scored in bridge by the side that defeats the opposing contract — usu. used in pl. — **penalty** *adj*

penalty box *n* (1931) **:** an area alongside an ice hockey rink to which penalized players are confined for the duration of their penalty

penalty kick (1889) **1 :** a free kick in rugby **2 :** a free kick at the goal in soccer made from a point 12 yards in front of the goal and allowed for certain violations within a designated area around the goal

penalty shot *n* (ca. 1948) **:** an unhindered shot at the goal in ice hockey awarded to an individual for certain violations by an opponent

[1]**pen·ance** \ˈpen-ən(t)s\ *n* [ME, fr. OF, fr. ML *poenitentia* penitence] (13c) **1 :** an act of self-abasement, mortification, or devotion performed to show sorrow or repentance for sin **2 :** a sacramental rite that is practiced in Roman, Eastern, and some Anglican churches and that consists of private confession, absolution, and a penance directed by the confessor

[2]**penance** *vt* **pen·anced; pen·anc·ing** (1600) **:** to impose penance on

Pe·na·tes \pə-ˈnāt-ēz, -ˈnät-\ *n pl* [L — more at PENETRATE] (ca. 1513) **:** the Roman gods of the household worshiped in close connection with Vesta and with the Lares

pence \ˈpen(t)s\ *pl of* PENNY

pen·cel *or* **pen·cil** \ˈpen(t)-səl\ *n* [ME *pencel,* modif. of OF *penoncel*] (13c) **:** PENNONCEL

pen·chant \ˈpen-chənt, *esp Brit* ˈpäⁿ-ˌshäⁿ\ *n* [F, fr. prp. of *pencher* to incline, fr. (assumed) VL *pendicare,* fr. L *pendere* to weigh] (1672) **:** a strong and continued inclination; *broadly* **:** LIKING *syn* see LEANING

[1]**pen·cil** \ˈpen(t)-səl\ *n* [ME *pensel,* fr. MF *pincel,* fr. (assumed) VL *penicellus,* fr. L *penicillus,* lit., little tail, fr. dim. of *penis* tail, penis] (14c) **1 :** an artist's brush **2 :** an artist's individual skill or style **3 a :** an implement for writing, drawing, or marking consisting of or containing a slender cylinder or strip of a solid marking substance **b :** a small medicated or cosmetic roll or stick for local applications **4 a :** an aggregate of rays of radiation (as light) esp. when diverging from or converging to a point **b :** a set of geometric objects each pair of which has a common property ⟨the lines in a plane through a point comprise a ~ of lines⟩ **5 :** something long and thin like a pencil

[2]**pencil** *vt* **-ciled** *or* **-cilled; -cil·ing** *or* **-cil·ling** \-s(ə-)liŋ\ (1532) **:** to paint, draw, write, or mark with a pencil — **pen·cil·ler** \-s(ə-)lər\ *n*

pen·cil·ing *or* **pen·cil·ling** *n* (1706) **:** the work of the pencil or brush; *also* **:** a product of this

pencil pusher *n* (1881) **:** one (as a clerk) who does predominantly paperwork

pen·dant *also* **pen·dent** \ˈpen-dənt; *3 & 4 are also* ˈpen-ənt, *6 is also* päⁿ-däⁿ\ *n* [ME *pendaunt,* fr. MF *pendant,* fr. prp. of *pendre* to hang, fr. (assumed) VL *pendere,* fr. L *pendēre;* akin to L *pendere* to weigh, estimate, pay, *pondus* weight — more at SPIN] (14c) **1 :** something suspended: as **a :** an ornament allowed to hang free **b :** an electrical fixture suspended from the ceiling **2 :** a hanging ornament of roofs or ceilings much used in the later styles of Gothic architecture **3 :** a short rope hanging from a spar and having at its free end a block or spliced thimble **4** *chiefly Brit* **:** PENNANT 1a **5 :** the shank on a pocket watch stem to which the ring for suspension attaches **6 a :** COMPANION PIECE **b :** something secondary or supplementary

pen·den·cy \ˈpen-dən-sē\ *n* (1637) **:** the state of being pending

pen·dent *or* **pen·dant** \ˈpen-dənt\ *adj* [ME *pendaunt*] (15c) **1 :** jutting or leaning over **:** OVERHANGING ⟨a ~ cliff⟩ **2 :** supported from above **:** SUSPENDED ⟨icicles ~ from the eaves⟩ **3 :** remaining undetermined **:** PENDING — **pen·dent·ly** *adv*

pen·den·tive \pen-ˈdent-iv\ *n* [F *pendentif,* fr. L *pendent-, pendens,* prp. of *pendēre*] (1727) **:** one of the concave triangular members that supports a dome over a square space

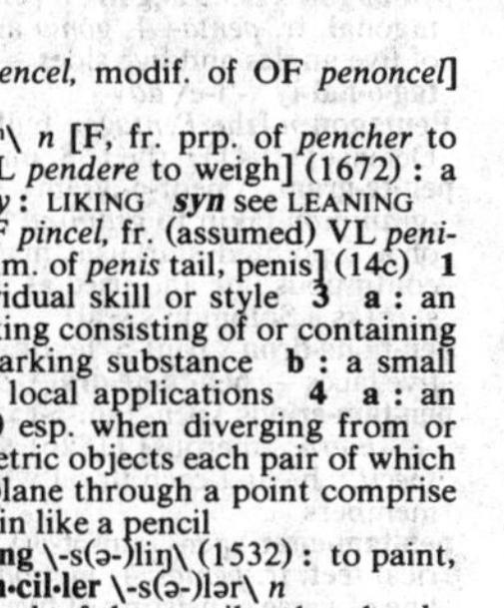

1 pendentive

[1]**pend·ing** \ˈpen-diŋ\ *prep* [F *pendant,* fr. prp. of *pendre*] (1726) **1 :** DURING **2 :** while awaiting

[2]**pending** *adj* (1797) **1 :** not yet decided **:** being in continuance **2 :** IMMINENT, IMPENDING

pen·du·lar \ˈpen-jə-lər, ˈpen-d(y)ə-\ *adj* (1878) **:** being or resembling the movement of a pendulum

pen·du·lous \-ləs\ *adj* [L *pendulus,* fr. *pendēre* to hang] (1605) **1** *archaic* **:** poised without visible support **2 a :** suspended so as to swing freely ⟨branches hung with ~ vines⟩ **b :** inclined or hanging downward ⟨~ jowls⟩ **3 :** marked by vacillation, indecision, or uncertainty — **pen·du·lous·ness** *n*

pen·du·lum \-ləm\ *n* [NL, fr. L, neut. of *pendulus*] (1660) **1 :** a body suspended from a fixed point so as to swing freely to and fro under the action of gravity and commonly used to regulate movements (as of clockwork) **2 :** something (as a state of affairs) that alternates between opposites

Pe·nel·o·pe \pə-ˈnel-ə-pē\ *n* [L, fr. Gk *Pēnelopē*] **:** the wife of Odysseus who waits faithfully for him during his 20 years' absence

pe·ne·plain *also* **pe·ne·plane** \ˈpē-ni-ˌplān, ˈpen-\ *n* [L *paene, pene* almost + E *plain* or *plane* — more at PATIENT] (1889) **:** a land surface of considerable area and slight relief shaped by erosion

pen·e·tra·ble \ˈpen-ə-trə-bəl\ *adj* (1538) **:** capable of being penetrated — **pen·e·tra·bil·i·ty** \ˌpen-ə-trə-ˈbil-ət-ē\ *n*

pen·e·tra·lia \ˌpen-ə-ˈtrā-lē-ə\ *n pl* [L, neut. pl. of *penetralis* inner, fr. *penetrare* to penetrate] (1668) **:** the innermost or most private parts

pen·e·trance \ˈpen-ə-trən(t)s\ *n* [*penetr*ant + *-ance*] (1934) **:** the proportion of individuals of a particular genotype that express its phenotypic effect in a given environment

[1]**pen·e·trant** \-trənt\ *adj* (1543) **:** PENETRATING

[2]**penetrant** *n* (1734) **:** one that penetrates or is capable of penetrating

pen·e·trate \ˈpen-ə-ˌtrāt\ *vb* **-trat·ed; -trat·ing** [L *penetratus,* pp. of *penetrare;* akin to L *penitus* inward, *Penates* household gods, Lith *peneti* to nourish] *vt* (ca. 1530) **1 a :** to pass into or through **b :** to enter by overcoming resistance **:** PIERCE **c :** to gain entrance to **2 a :** to see into or through **b :** to discover the inner contents or meaning of **3 :** to affect profoundly with feeling **4 :** to diffuse through or into ~ *vi* **1 a :** to pass, extend, pierce, or diffuse into or through something **b :** to pierce something with the eye or mind **2 :** to affect deeply the senses or feelings *syn* see ENTER

pen·e·trat·ing *adj* (1598) **1 :** having the power of entering, piercing, or pervading ⟨a ~ shriek⟩ **2 :** ACUTE, DISCERNING ⟨~ insights into life⟩ — **pen·e·trat·ing·ly** \-ˌtrāt-iŋ-lē\ *adv*

pen·e·tra·tion \ˌpen-ə-ˈtrā-shən\ *n* (1605) **1 a :** the depth to which something penetrates **b :** the power to penetrate; *esp* **:** the ability to discern deeply and acutely **c :** the extent to which a commercial product or agency is familiar or sells in a market **2 :** the act or process of penetrating: as **a :** the act of entering a country so that actual establishment of influence is accomplished **b :** an attack that penetrates the enemy's front or territory *syn* see DISCERNMENT

pen·e·tra·tive \ˈpen-ə-ˌtrāt-iv\ *adj* (15c) **1 :** tending to penetrate **:** PIERCING **2 :** ACUTE ⟨~ observations⟩ **3 :** IMPRESSIVE ⟨a ~ speaker⟩ — **pen·e·tra·tive·ly** *adv* — **pen·e·tra·tive·ness** *n*

pen·e·trom·e·ter \ˌpen-ə-ˈträm-ət-ər\ *n* [L *penetrare* + ISV *-meter*] (1905) **:** an instrument for measuring firmness or consistency (as of soil)

pen·gö \ˈpeŋ-ˌgə(r), -ˌgœ\ *n, pl* **pengö** *or* **pengös** [Hung *pengő,* lit., jingling] (ca. 1925) **:** the basic monetary unit of Hungary from 1925 to 1946

pen·guin \ˈpen-gwən, ˈpeŋ-\ *n* [origin unknown] (1588) **:** any of various erect short-legged flightless aquatic birds (family Spheniscidae) of the southern hemisphere

pen·hold·er \ˈpen-ˌhōl-dər\ *n* (1815) **:** a holder or handle for a pen point

pen·i·cil·la·mine \ˌpen-ə-ˈsil-ə-ˌmēn\ *n* (ca. 1943) **:** an amino acid $C_5H_{11}NO_2S$ that is obtained from penicillins and is used esp. in the treatment of poisoning by metals (as copper or lead) and of cystinuria

pen·i·cil·late \ˌpen-ə-ˈsil-ət, -ˌāt\ *adj* [prob. fr. (assumed) NL *penicillatus,* fr. L *penicillus* brush — more at PENCIL] (ca. 1819) **:** furnished with a tuft of fine filaments ⟨a ~ stigma⟩

pen·i·cil·lin \ˌpen-ə-ˈsil-ən\ *n* [NL *Penicillium*] (1929) **1 :** any of several relatively nontoxic antibiotic acids of the general constitution $C_9H_{11}N_2O_4SR$ that are produced by molds (genus *Penicillium* and esp. *P. notatum* or *P. chrysogenum*) or synthetically and are used esp. against cocci; *also* **:** a mixture of such acids **2 :** a salt or ester of a penicillin or a mixture of such salts or esters

pen·i·cil·lin·ase \-ˈsil-ə-ˌnās, -ˌnāz\ *n* (1940) **:** an enzyme that inactivates the penicillins by hydrolyzing them and that is found esp. in bacteria

pen·i·cil·li·um \-ˈsil-ē-əm\ *n, pl* **-lia** \-ē-ə\ [NL, fr. L *penicillus*] (1867) **:** any of a genus (*Penicillium* of the family Moniliaceae) of fungi (as a blue mold) that are found chiefly on moist nonliving organic matter

pe·nile \ˈpē-ˌnīl\ *adj* (1861) **:** of, relating to, or affecting the penis

pen·in·su·la \pə-ˈnin(t)-s(ə-)lə, -ˈnin-chə-lə\ *n* [L *paeninsula,* fr. *paene* almost + *insula* island — more at PATIENT] (1538) **:** a portion of land nearly surrounded by water and connected with a larger body by an isthmus; *also* **:** a piece of land jutting out into the water whether with or without a well-defined isthmus — **pen·in·su·lar** \-s(ə-)lər, -chə-lər\ *adj*

pe·nis \ˈpē-nəs\ *n, pl* **pe·nes** \ˈpē-(ˌ)nēz\ *or* **pe·nis·es** [L, penis, tail; akin to OHG *faselt* penis, Gk *peos*] (1676) **:** a male organ of copulation

penis envy *n* (ca. 1924) **:** the supposed coveting of the penis by a young human female which is held in psychoanalytic theory to lead to feelings of inferiority and defensive or compensatory behavior

pen·i·tence \ˈpen-ə-tən(t)s\ *n* [ME, fr. OF, fr. ML *poenitentia,* alter. of L *paenitentia* regret, fr. *paenitent-, paenitens,* prp.] (13c) **:** the quality or state of being penitent **:** sorrow for sins or faults

syn PENITENCE, REPENTANCE, CONTRITION, COMPUNCTION, REMORSE mean regret for sin or wrongdoing. PENITENCE implies sad and humble realization of and regret for one's misdeeds ⟨the attitude that no sin is beyond forgiveness if it is followed by true *penitence* —K. S. Latourette⟩ REPENTANCE adds the implication of a resolve to change ⟨I came not to call the righteous, but sinners to *repentance* —Lk 5:32 (AV)⟩ CONTRITION stresses the sorrowful regret that constitutes true penitence ⟨the tears of my *contrition* . . . repentance for things past —Edmund Spenser⟩ COMPUNCTION implies a painful sting of conscience esp. for contemplated wrongdoing ⟨they no longer felt *compunctions* about replacing men with machines —J. S. Vandiver⟩ REMORSE suggests prolonged and insistent self-reproach and mental anguish for past

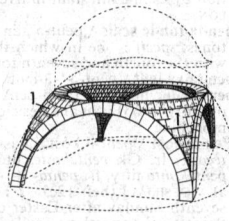

wrongs and esp. for those whose consequences cannot be remedied ⟨*remorse* that makes one walk on thorns —Oscar Wilde⟩

[1]**pen·i·tent** \-tənt\ *adj* [ME, fr. MF, fr. L *paenitent-, paenitens,* fr. prp. of *paenitēre* to be sorry; akin to L *paene* almost — more at PATIENT] (14c) : feeling or expressing humble or regretful pain or sorrow for sins or offenses : REPENTANT — **pen·i·tent·ly** *adv*

[2]**penitent** *n* (15c) **1** : a person who repents of sin **2** : a person under church censure but admitted to penance esp. under the direction of a confessor

pen·i·ten·tial \,pen-ə-'ten-chəl\ *adj* (1508) : of or relating to penitence or penance — **pen·i·ten·tial·ly** \-'tench-(ə-)lē\ *adv*

[1]**pen·i·ten·tia·ry** \,pen-ə-'tench-(ə-)rē\ *n, pl* **-ries** [ME *penitenciary,* fr. ML *poenitentiarius,* fr. *poenitentia*] (15c) **1 a** : an officer in some Roman Catholic dioceses vested with power from the bishop to deal with cases of a nature normally handled only by the bishop **b** *cap* : a cardinal presiding over a tribunal of the Roman curia concerned with dispensations and indulgences **2** : a public institution in which offenders against the law are confined for detention or punishment; *specif* : a state or federal prison in the U.S.

[2]**pen·i·ten·tia·ry** \,pen-ə-'tench-(ə-)rē, *1 also* -'tench-ē-,er-ē\ *adj* (1577) **1** : PENITENTIAL **2** : of, relating to, or incurring confinement in a penitentiary

pen·knife \'pen-,nīf\ *n* [fr. its original use for mending quill pens] (15c) : a small pocketknife usu. with only one blade

pen·light *or* **pen·lite** \'pen-,līt\ *n* (1945) : a small flashlight resembling a fountain pen in size or shape

pen·man \'pen-mən\ *n* (1591) **1 a** : CALLIGRAPHER **b** : COPYIST, SCRIBE **c** : a person with a specified quality or kind of handwriting ⟨a poor ~⟩ **2** : AUTHOR

pen·man·ship \-,ship\ *n* (1695) **1** : the art or practice of writing with the pen **2** : quality or style of handwriting

pen name *n* (ca. 1864) : an author's pseudonym

pen·nant \'pen-ənt\ *n* [alter. of *pendant*] (1698) **1 a** : any of various nautical flags tapering usu. to a point or swallowtail and used for identification or signaling **b** : a flag or banner longer in the fly than in the hoist; *esp* : one that tapers to a point **2** : a flag emblematic of championship (as in a professional baseball league)

pen·nate \'pen-,āt\ *adj* [irreg. fr. NL *Pennales*] (1938) : of, relating to, or being diatoms of an order (Pennales) characterized by a raphe or a structure resembling a raphe and by ornamentation of the valves that is always bilaterally arranged in relation to a line rather than to a point

pen·ni \'pen-ē\ *n, pl* **pen·nia** \-ē-ə\ *also* **penni** *or* **pen·nis** \-ēz\ [Finn] (1893) — see *markka* at MONEY table

pen·ni·less \'pen-i-ləs, 'pen-ᵊl-əs\ *adj* (14c) : destitute of money

pen·non \'pen-ən\ *n* [ME, fr. MF *penon,* aug. of *penne* feather — more at PEN] (14c) **1 a** : a long usu. triangular or swallow-tailed streamer typically attached to the head of a lance as an ensign **b** : PENNANT 1a **2** : WING, PINION

pen·non·cel *or* **pen·on·cel** \'pen-ən-,sel\ *n* [ME *penoncell,* fr. MF *penoncel,* dim. of *penon*] (14c) : a small pennon borne esp. at the head of a lance in late medieval or Renaissance times

Penn·syl·va·nia Dutch \,pen(t)-səl-,vā-nyə-, -nē-ə-\ *n* (1824) **1** : a people living mostly in eastern Pennsylvania whose characteristic cultural traditions go back to the German migrations of the 18th century **2** : a dialect of High German spoken in parts of Pennsylvania and Maryland — **Pennsylvania Dutchman** *n*

Pennsylvania German *n* (1869) : PENNSYLVANIA DUTCH 2

Penn·syl·va·nian \-'vā-nyən, -nē-ən\ *adj* (1698) **1** : of or relating to Pennsylvania or its people **2** : of, relating to, or being the period of the Paleozoic era in No. America between the Mississippian and Permian or the corresponding system of rocks — **Pennsylvanian** *n*

pen·ny \'pen-ē\ *n, pl* **pennies** \-ēz\ *or* **pence** \'pen(t)s\ *often attrib* [ME, fr. OE *penning, penig;* akin to OHG *pfenning,* a coin] (bef. 12c) **1 a** : a monetary unit of the United Kingdom formerly equal to $^1/_{240}$ pound but now equal to $^1/_{100}$ pound **b** : a similar monetary unit of any of various other countries in or formerly in the Commonwealth — see *lira, pound* at MONEY table **c** : a coin representing one penny **2** : DENARIUS **3** *pl pennies* : CENT **4** : a trivial amount **5** : a piece or sum of money ⟨that will cost a pretty ~⟩

-pen·ny \,pen-ē\ *adj comb form* [*penny;* perh. fr. the original price per hundred] : being a (designated) nail size — compare EIGHTPENNY NAIL, FOURPENNY NAIL, SIXPENNY NAIL, TENPENNY NAIL

pen·ny–an·te \,pen-ē-,ant-ē\ *adj* (1868) : SMALL-TIME, TWO-BIT

pen·ny an·te \'pen-ē-'ant-ē\ *n* (1855) : poker played for very low stakes

penny arcade *n* (1908) : an amusement center having coin-operated devices for entertainment

pen·ny·cress \'pen-ē-,kres\ *n* (ca. 1713) : a Eurasian herb (*Thlaspi arvense*) with round flat pods that is widely naturalized in the New World

penny dreadful *n* (1873) : a novel of violent adventure or crime

pen·ny–pinch·ing \'pen-ē-,pin-chiŋ\ *n* (ca. 1905) : FRUGALITY, PARSIMONY — **pen·ny–pinch·er** \-chər\ *n* — **penny–pinching** *adj*

pen·ny·roy·al \,pen-ē-'rȯi(-ə)l, 'pen-i-,rīl\ *n* [prob. by folk etymology fr. MF *poullieul,* modif. of L *pulegium*] (ca. 1530) **1** : a European perennial mint (*Mentha pulegium*) with small aromatic leaves **2** : an aromatic American mint (*Hedeoma pulegioides*) that has blue or violet flowers borne in axillary tufts and yields an oil used in folk medicine or to drive away mosquitoes

pen·ny·weight \'pen-ē-,wāt\ *n* (14c) — see WEIGHT table

pen·ny–wise \'pen-ē-,wīz\ *adj* [fr. the phrase *penny-wise and pound-foolish*] (1607) : wise or prudent only in dealing with small sums or matters

pen·ny·wort \-,wərt, -,wȯ(ə)rt\ *n* (15c) : any of several round-leaved plants: as **a** : any of several low creeping plants (genus *Hydrocotyle*) of the carrot family with crenate leaves and umbellate flowers **b** : a leafless perennial (*Obolaria virginica*) of the gentian family with white or purplish flowers

pen·ny·worth \'pen-ē-,wərth, *Brit often* 'pen-ərth\ *n, pl* **pennyworth** *or* **pennyworths** (bef. 12c) **1** : a penny's worth **2** : value for the money spent : BARGAIN **3** : a small quantity : MODICUM

Pe·nob·scot \pə-'näb-,skät, -skət\ *n, pl* **-scot** *or* **-scots** (1624) : a member of an American Indian people of the Penobscot river valley and Penobscot Bay region of Maine

pe·no·che \pə-'nō-chē\ *var of* PENUCHE

pe·nol·o·gy \pi-'näl-ə-jē\ *n* [Gk *poinē* penalty + E *-logy* — more at PAIN] (1838) : a branch of criminology dealing with prison management and the treatment of offenders — **pe·no·log·i·cal** \,pē-nə-'läj-i-kəl\ *adj* — **pe·nol·o·gist** \pi-'näl-ə-jəst\ *n*

pen pal *n* (1938) : a friend made and kept through correspondence

pen point *n* (ca. 1864) : a small thin convex metal device that tapers to a split point, fits into a holder, and is used for writing or drawing

pen pusher *n* (ca. 1905) : PENCIL PUSHER

pen·sile \'pen-,sīl\ *adj* [L *pensilis,* fr. *pensus,* pp. of *pendēre* to hang] (1603) : PENDENT, HANGING ⟨~ nests⟩

[1]**pen·sion** *n* [ME, fr. MF, fr. L *pension-, pensio,* fr. *pensus,* pp. of *pendere* to pay — more at PENDANT] (14c) **1** \'pen-chən\ : a fixed sum paid regularly to a person: **a** *archaic* : WAGE **b** : a gratuity granted (as by a government) as a favor or reward **c** : one paid under given conditions to a person following his retirement from service or to his surviving dependents **2** \päⁿs-yōⁿ\ [F, fr. MF] **a** : accommodations esp. at a continental European hotel or boardinghouse : ROOM AND BOARD **b** *also* **pen·sio·ne** \pen(t)-'syō-(,)nā\ [*pensione,* It] : a hotel or boardinghouse esp. in continental Europe — **pen·sion·less** \'pen-chən-ləs\ *adj*

[2]**pen·sion** \'pen-chən\ *vt* **pen·sioned; pen·sion·ing** \'pench-(ə-)niŋ\ (1702) **1** : to grant or pay a pension to **2** : to dismiss or retire from service with a pension ⟨~*ed* off his faithful old servant⟩ — **pen·sion·able** \'pench-(ə-)nə-bəl\ *adj*

pen·sion·ary \'pen-chə-,ner-ē\ *n, pl* **-ar·ies** (1536) : PENSIONER; *esp* : HIRELING — **pensionary** *adj*

pen·sion·er \'pench-(ə-)nər\ *n* (15c) **1** : a person who receives or lives on a pension **2** *obs* **a** : GENTLEMAN-AT-ARMS **b** : RETAINER **c** : MERCENARY, HIRELING

pen·sive \'pen(t)-siv\ *adj* [ME *pensif,* fr. MF, fr. *penser* to think, fr. L *pensare* to ponder, fr. *pensus,* pp. of *pendere* to weigh — more at PENDANT] (14c) **1** : musingly or dreamily thoughtful **2** : suggestive of sad thoughtfulness — **pen·sive·ly** *adv* — **pen·sive·ness** *n*

pen·stock \'pen-,stäk\ *n* (ca. 1607) **1** : a sluice or gate for regulating a flow (as of water) **2** : a conduit or pipe for conducting water

pent \'pent\ *adj* [prob. fr. pp. of obs. E *pend* (to confine)] (1550) : shut up : CONFINED ⟨a ~ crowd⟩ ⟨*pent-*up feelings⟩

penta- *or* **pent-** *comb form* [ME, fr. Gk, fr. *pente* — more at FIVE] **1** : five ⟨*penta*hedron⟩ **2** : containing five atoms, groups, or equivalents ⟨*pent*ane⟩

pen·ta·chlo·ro·phe·nol \,pent-ə-,klōr-ə-'fē-,nōl, -,klȯr-, -fi-'\ *n* [*penta-* + *chlor-* + *phenol*] (1879) : a crystalline compound C_6Cl_5OH used esp. as a wood preservative and fungicide and a disinfectant

pen·ta·cle \'pent-i-kəl\ *n* [(assumed) ML *pentaculum,* prob. fr. Gk *pente*] (1594) : PENTAGRAM

pen·tad \'pen-,tad\ *n* [Gk *pentad-, pentas,* fr. *pente*] (1653) : a group of five

pen·ta·gon \'pent-ə-,gän\ *n* [Gk *pentagōnon,* fr. neut. of *pentagōnos* pentagonal, fr. *penta-* + *gōnia* angle — more at -GON] (1571) : a polygon of five angles and five sides — **pen·tag·o·nal** \pen-'tag-ən-ᵊl\ *adj* — **pen·tag·o·nal·ly** \-ᵊl-ē\ *adv*

Pentagon *n* [the *Pentagon* building, headquarters of the Department of Defense] (1941) : the U.S. military leadership

pen·ta·gram \'pent-ə-,gram\ *n* [Gk *pentagrammon,* fr. *penta-* + *-grammon* (akin to *gramma* letter) — more at GRAM] (1833) : a figure of a 5-pointed star usu. made with alternate points connected by a continuous line and used as a magic symbol; *also* : a similar 6-pointed star (as a Solomon's seal)

pen·ta·he·dron \,pent-ə-'hē-drən\ *n* [NL] (ca. 1775) : a solid bounded by five faces — **pen·ta·he·dral** \-drəl\ *adj*

pen·tam·er·ous \pen-'tam-ə-rəs\ *adj* [NL *pentamerus,* fr. *penta-* (fr. Gk) + *-merus* -merous] (1826) : divided into or consisting of five parts; *specif* : having each floral whorl consisting of five or a multiple of five members

pen·tam·e·ter \pen-'tam-ət-ər\ *n* [L, fr. Gk *pentametros* having five metrical feet, fr. *penta-* + *metron* measure — more at MEASURE] (1589) : a line of verse consisting of five metrical feet

pen·tane \'pen-,tān\ *n* [ISV] (1877) : any of three isomeric hydrocarbons C_5H_{12} of the methane series occurring in petroleum

pen·tan·gle \'pent-,aŋ-gəl, 'pen-,taŋ-\ *n* (14c) : PENTAGRAM

pen·ta·pep·tide \,pent-ə-'pep-,tīd\ *n* (1907) : a polypeptide that contains five amino acid residues

pen·ta·ploid \'pent-ə-,plȯid\ *adj* (1921) : having or being a chromosome number that is five times the basic number — **pentaploid** *n* — **pen·ta·ploi·dy** \-,plȯid-ē\ *n*

pen·tar·chy \'pen-'tär-kē\ *n* [Gk *pentarchia,* fr. *penta-* + *-archia* -archy] (1611) : a group of five countries or districts each under its own ruler or government

Pen·ta·teuch \'pent-ə-,t(y)ük\ *n* [LL *Pentateuchus,* fr. Gk *Pentateuchos,* fr. *penta-* + *teuchos* tool, vessel, book; akin to Gk *teuchein* to make — more at DOUGHTY] (ca. 1530) : the first five books of Jewish and Christian Scriptures

pen·tath·lete \pen-'tath-,lēt\ *n* (1828) : an athlete participating in a pentathlon

pen·tath·lon \pen-'tath-lən, -,län\ *n* [Gk, fr. *penta-* + *athlon* contest — more at ATHLETE] (ca. 1706) : an athletic contest involving participation by each contestant in five different events; *esp* : MODERN PENTATHLON

pen·ta·ton·ic scale \,pent-ə-,tän-ik-\ *n* (ca. 1864) : a musical scale of five tones; *specif* : one in which the tones are arranged like a major scale with the fourth and seventh tones omitted

pen·ta·va·lent \,pent-ə-'vā-lənt\ *adj* (1871) : having a valence of five

pen·taz·o·cine \pen-'taz-ə-,sēn\ *n* [*penta-* + *azo* + *-cine* (of unknown origin)] (1963) : an analgesic drug $C_{19}H_{27}NO$ that is less addictive than morphine

Pen·te·cost \'pent-i-,kȯst, -,käst\ *n* [ME, fr. OE *pentecosten,* fr. LL *pentecoste,* fr. Gk *pentēkostē,* lit., fiftieth day, fr. *pentēkostos* fiftieth, fr. *pentēkonta* fifty, fr. *penta-* + *-konta* (akin to L *viginti* twenty) — more at VIGESIMAL] (bef. 12c) **1** : SHABUOTH **2** : a Christian feast on the seventh Sunday after Easter commemorating the descent of the Holy Spirit on the apostles — called also *Whitsunday*

[1]**Pen·te·cos·tal** \,pent-i-'käs-tᵊl, -'kȯs-\ *adj* (1663) **1** : of, relating to, or suggesting Pentecost **2** : of, relating to, or constituting any of various Christian religious bodies that emphasize revivalistic worship, baptism,

glossolalia, faith healing, and premillennial teaching — **Pen·te·cos·tal·ism** \-tə-ˌliz-əm\ *n* — **Pen·te·cos·tal·ist** \-tə-ləst\ *n*

²**Pentecostal** *n* (1904) **:** a member of a Pentecostal religious body

pent·house \ˈpent-ˌhau̇s\ *n* [ME *pentis,* fr. MF *appentis,* prob. fr. ML *appenticium* appendage, fr. L *appendic-, appendix* — more at APPENDIX] (14c) **1 a :** a shed or roof attached to and sloping from a wall or building **b :** a smaller structure joined to a building **:** ANNEX **2 :** a structure or dwelling built on the roof of a building

pent·land·ite \ˈpent-lən-ˌdīt\ *n* [F, fr. Joseph *Pentland* †1873 Irish scientist] (ca. 1858) **:** a bronzy yellow mineral $(Fe,Ni)_9S_8$ that is an isometric nickel iron sulfide and the principal ore of nickel

pen·to·bar·bi·tal \ˌpent-ə-ˈbär-bə-ˌtȯl\ *n* [*penta-* + *-o-* + *barbital*] (1931) **:** a granular barbiturate $C_{11}H_{18}N_2O_3$ used esp. in the form of its sodium or calcium salt as a sedative, hypnotic, and antispasmodic

pen·to·bar·bi·tone \-ˌtōn\ *n* [*penta-* + *-o-* + *barbitone* (barbital)] *Brit* (1938) **:** PENTOBARBITAL

pen·to·san \ˈpent-ə-ˌsan\ *n* (1892) **:** any of various polysaccharides that yield only pentoses on hydrolysis and are widely distributed in plants

pen·tose \ˈpen-ˌtōs, -ˌtōz\ *n* [ISV] (1890) **:** any monosaccharide $C_5H_{10}O_5$ (as ribose) that contains five carbon atoms in the molecule

Pen·to·thal \ˈpent-ə-ˌthȯl\ *trademark* — used for thiopental

pent·ox·ide \pent-ˈäk-ˌsīd\ *n* [ISV] (1863) **:** an oxide containing five atoms of oxygen in the molecule

pent·ste·mon *or* **pen·ste·mon** \pent-ˈstē-mən, ˈpen(t)-stə-\ *n* [NL *pentstemon,* alter. of *Penstemon,* fr. Gk *penta-* + *stēmōn* thread — more at STAMEN] (ca. 1741) **:** any of a genus (*Penstemon*) of chiefly American herbs of the figwort family with showy blue, purple, red, yellow, or white tubular flowers

pen·tyl \ˈpent-ᵊl\ *n* [*pentane* + *-yl*] (1877) **:** AMYL

pen·tyl·ene·tet·ra·zol \ˌpent-ᵊl-ˌēn-ˈte-trə-ˌzȯl, -ˌzōl\ *n* [*pent*-amethy*lene*= *tetrazole*] (1949) **:** an analeptic drug $C_6H_{10}N_4$

pe·nu·che \pə-ˈnü-chē\ *n* [MexSp *panocha* raw sugar, fr. dim. of Sp *pan* bread, fr. L *panis* — more at FOOD] (1871) **:** fudge made usu. of brown sugar, butter, cream or milk, and nuts

pe·nult \ˈpē-ˌnəlt, pi-ˈ\ *n* [L *paenultima* penult, fr. fem. of *paenultimus* almost last, fr. *paene* almost + *ultimus* last — more at ULTIMATE] (1572) **:** the next to the last member of a series; *esp* **:** the next to the last syllable of a word

pen·ul·ti·ma \pi-ˈnəl-tə-mə\ *n* [L] (ca. 1589) **:** PENULT

pen·ul·ti·mate \pi-ˈnəl-tə-mət\ *adj* (1677) **1 :** next to the last ⟨the ~ chapter of a book⟩ **2 :** of or relating to a penult ⟨a ~ accent⟩ — **pen·ul·ti·mate·ly** *adv*

pen·um·bra \pə-ˈnəm-brə\ *n, pl* **-brae** \-(ˌ)brē, -ˌbrī\ *or* **-bras** [NL, fr. L *paene* almost + *umbra* shadow — more at PATIENT, UMBRAGE] (1666) **1 :** a space of partial illumination (as in an eclipse) between the perfect shadow on all sides and the full light **2 :** a shaded region surrounding the dark central portion of a sunspot **3 :** a surrounding or adjoining region in which something exists in a lesser degree **:** FRINGE — **pen·um·bral** \-brəl\ *adj*

pe·nu·ri·ous \pə-ˈn(y)u̇r-ē-əs\ *adj* (1596) **1 :** marked by or suffering from penury **2 :** given to or marked by extreme stinting frugality ***syn*** see STINGY — **pe·nu·ri·ous·ly** *adv* — **pe·nu·ri·ous·ness** *n*

pen·u·ry \ˈpen-yə-rē\ *n* [ME, fr. L *penuria* want — more at PATIENT] (15c) **1 :** a cramping and oppressive lack of resources (as money); *esp* **:** severe poverty **2 :** extreme and often niggardly frugality ***syn*** see POVERTY

pe·on \ˈpē-ˌän, -ən *also* pā-ˈōn *for 2, Brit also* ˈpyün *for 1*\ *n, pl* **peons** *or* **pe·o·nes** \pā-ˈō-nēz\ [Pg *peão* & F *pion,* fr. ML *pedon-, pedo* foot soldier — more at PAWN] (1609) **1 :** any of various Indian or Ceylonese workers: as **a :** INFANTRYMAN **b :** ORDERLY **2** [Sp *peón,* fr. L *pedon-, pedo*] **:** a member of the landless laboring class in Spanish America **3** *pl* **peons a :** a person held in compulsory servitude to a master for the working out of an indebtedness **b :** DRUDGE, MENIAL

pe·on·age \ˈpē-ə-nij\ *n* (1844) **1 a :** the use of laborers bound in servitude because of debt **b :** a system of convict labor by which convicts are leased to contractors **2 :** the condition of a peon

pe·o·ny \ˈpē-ə-nē\ *n, pl* **-nies** [ME *piony,* fr. MF *pioine,* fr. L *paeonia,* fr. Gk *paiōnia,* fr. *Paiōn* Paeon, physician of the gods] (bef. 12c) **:** any of a genus (*Paeonia*) of plants of the buttercup family with large usu. double flowers of red, pink, or white

¹**peo·ple** \ˈpē-pəl\ *n, pl* **people** [ME *peple,* fr. OF *peuple,* fr. L *populus*] (13c) **1** *pl* **:** human beings making up a group or assembly or linked by a common interest **2** *pl* **:** HUMAN BEINGS, PERSONS — often used in compounds instead of *persons* ⟨salespeople⟩ **3** *pl* **:** the members of a family or kinship **4** *pl* **:** the mass of a community as distinguished from a special class ⟨disputes between the ~ and the nobles⟩ — often used by Communists to distinguish Communists or those under Communist control from other people ⟨the *People's* Court⟩ ⟨Bulgarian *People's* Republic⟩ **5** *pl* **peoples :** a body of persons that are united by a common culture, tradition, or sense of kinship, that typically have common language, institutions, and beliefs, and that often constitute a politically organized group **6 :** lower animals usu. of a specified kind or situation ⟨squirrels and chipmunks: the little furry ~⟩ **7 :** the body of enfranchised citizens of a state — **peo·ple·less** \-pəl-(l)əs\ *adj*

usage Use of *people* to designate a mass or indefinite number of persons has never been questioned, but some commentators have insisted upon *persons* when a definite number is specified. *Persons* is still used formally in such instances ⟨occupancy by more than 86 *persons* is prohibited⟩ but similar use of *people* meets less resistance nowadays and is even recommended by some stylebooks.

²**people** *vt* **peo·pled; peo·pling** \-p(ə-)liŋ\ [MF *peupler,* fr. OF, fr. *peuple*] (15c) **1 :** to supply or fill with people **2 :** to dwell in **:** INHABIT

peo·ple·hood \ˈpē-pəl-ˌhu̇d\ *n* (ca. 1899) **1 :** the quality or state of constituting a people **2 :** the awareness of the underlying unity that makes the individual a part of a people

people mover *n* (1968) **:** any of various rapid-transit systems (as of moving sidewalks or automated driverless cars) for shuttling people

¹**pep** \ˈpep\ *n* [short for *pepper*] (1912) **:** brisk energy or initiative and high spirits

²**pep** *vt* **pepped; pep·ping** (1925) **:** to inject pep into ⟨~ him up⟩

pep·los \ˈpep-ləs, -ˌläs\ *also* **pep·lus** \-ləs\ *n* [L *peplus,* fr. Gk *peplos*] (1776) **:** a garment worn like a shawl by women of ancient Greece

pep·lum \-ləm\ *n* [L, fr. Gk *peplon* peplos] (1866) **:** a short section attached to the waistline of a blouse, jacket, or dress — **pep·lumed** \-ləmd\ *adj*

pe·po \ˈpē-(ˌ)pō\ *n, pl* **pepos** [L, a melon — more at PUMPKIN] (ca. 1861) **:** an indehiscent fleshy 1-celled or falsely 3-celled many-seeded berry (as a pumpkin, squash, melon, or cucumber) that has a hard rind and is the characteristic fruit of the gourd family

¹**pep·per** \ˈpep-ər\ *n* [ME *peper,* fr. OE *pipor,* fr. L *piper* pepper, fr. Gk *peperi*] (bef. 12c) **1 a :** either of two pungent products from the fruit of an East Indian plant that are used as a condiment, carminative, or stimulant: (1) **:** BLACK PEPPER (2) **:** WHITE PEPPER **b :** any of a genus (*Piper* of the family Piperaceae, the pepper family) of tropical mostly jointed climbing shrubs with aromatic leaves; *esp* **:** a woody vine (*P. nigrum*) with ovate leaves and spicate flowers that is widely cultivated in the tropics for its red berries from which black pepper and white pepper are prepared **2 a :** any of several products similar to pepper that are obtained from close relatives of the pepper plant **b :** any of various pungent condiments obtained from plants of other genera than that of the pepper — used with a qualifying term ⟨cayenne ~⟩ **3 a :** CAPSICUM 1; *esp* **:** a New World capsicum (*Capsicum frutescens*) whose fruits are hot peppers or sweet peppers **b :** the fruit of a pepper that is usu. red or yellow when ripe — **pepper** *adj*

²**pepper** *vt* **pep·pered; pep·per·ing** \ˈpep-(ə-)riŋ\ (1581) **1 a :** to sprinkle, season, or cover with or as if with pepper **b :** to shower with or as if with shot or other missiles **2 :** to hit with rapid repeated blows **3 :** to sprinkle as pepper is sprinkled ⟨~*ed* his report with statistics⟩ — **pep·per·er** \-ər-ər\ *n*

pep·per–and–salt \ˌpep-ər(-ə)n-ˈsȯlt\ *adj* (1774) **:** having black and white or dark and light color intermingled in small flecks ⟨a ~ overcoat⟩

pep·per·box \ˈpep-ər-ˌbäks\ *n* (1546) **1 :** a small usu. cylindrical box or bottle with a perforated top used for sprinkling ground pepper on food **2 :** a late 18th century pistol with five or six revolving barrels

pep·per·corn \-ˌkȯ(ə)rn\ *n* (bef. 12c) **:** a dried berry of the black pepper

peppered moth *n* (ca. 1832) **:** a European geometrid moth (*Biston betularia*) that typically has white wings with small black specks but also occurs as a solid black form esp. in areas where the air is heavily polluted by industry

pep·per·grass \ˈpep-ər-ˌgras\ *n* (15c) **:** any of a genus (*Lepidium*) of cresses; *esp* **:** GARDEN CRESS

pepper mill *n* (1858) **:** a hand mill for grinding peppercorns

pep·per·mint \-ˌmint, -mənt, *in rapid speech* ˈpep-mənt *or* -ᵊm-ənt\ *n* (1696) **1 a :** a pungent and aromatic mint (*Mentha piperita*) with dark green lanceolate leaves and whorls of small pink flowers in spikes **b :** any of several mints (as *M. arvensis*) that are related to the peppermint **2 :** candy flavored with peppermint — **pep·per·minty** \ˈpep-ər-ˌmint-ē\ *adj*

pep·per·o·ni \ˌpep-ə-ˈrō-nē\ *n* [It *peperoni* chilies, pl. of *peperone* chili, aug. of *pepe* pepper, fr. L *piper* — more at PEPPER] (1921) **:** a highly seasoned beef and pork sausage

pepper pot *n* (1679) **1** *Brit* **:** PEPPERBOX 1 **2 a :** a highly seasoned West Indian stew of vegetables and meat or fish **b :** a thick soup of tripe, meat, dumplings, and vegetables highly seasoned esp. with crushed peppercorns — called also *Philadelphia pepper pot*

pepper shaker *n* (1895) **:** a container with a perforated top for sprinkling pepper

pep·per·tree \ˈpep-ər-ˌtrē\ *n* (1691) **:** a Peruvian evergreen tree (*Schinus molle*) of the sumac family grown as a shade tree in mild regions

pep·pery \ˈpep-(ə-)rē\ *adj* (1826) **1 :** of, relating to, or having the qualities of pepper **:** HOT, PUNGENT ⟨a ~ taste⟩ **2 :** having a hot temper **:** TOUCHY ⟨a ~ boss⟩ **3 :** FIERY, STINGING ⟨a ~ satire⟩

pep pill *n* (1937) **:** any of various stimulant drugs in pill or tablet form

pep·py \ˈpep-ē\ *adj* **pep·pi·er; -est** (ca. 1918) **:** full of pep — **pep·pi·ness** *n*

pep·sin \ˈpep-sən\ *n* [G, fr. Gk *pepsis* digestion, fr. *pessein*] (ca. 1844) **1 :** a proteinase of the stomach that breaks down most proteins to polypeptides **2 :** a preparation containing pepsin that is obtained from the stomach esp. of the hog and is used esp. as a digestive

pep·sin·o·gen \pep-ˈsin-ə-jən\ *n* [ISV *pepsin* + *-o-* + *-gen*] (ca. 1890) **:** a granular zymogen of the gastric glands that is readily converted into pepsin in a slightly acid medium

pep talk *n* (1925) **:** a usu. brief, high-pressure, and emotional talk designed to influence or encourage an audience

pep·tic \ˈpep-tik\ *adj* [L *pepticus,* fr. Gk *peptikos,* fr. *peptos* cooked, fr. *peptein, pessein* to cook, digest — more at COOK] (1651) **1 :** relating to or promoting digestion **:** DIGESTIVE **2 :** of, relating to, producing, or caused by pepsin ⟨~ digestion⟩ **3 :** connected with or resulting from the action of digestive juices ⟨a ~ ulcer⟩

pep·ti·dase \ˈpep-tə-ˌdās, -ˌdāz\ *n* (1918) **:** an enzyme that hydrolyzes simple peptides or their derivatives

pep·tide \ˈpep-ˌtīd\ *n* [ISV, fr. *peptone*] (1915) **:** any of various amides that are derived from two or more amino acids by combination of the amino group of one acid with the carboxyl group of another and are usu. obtained by partial hydrolysis of proteins — **pep·tid·ic** \pep-ˈtid-ik\ *adj*

peptide bond *n* (1935) **:** the chemical bond between carbon and nitrogen in a peptide linkage

peptide linkage *n* (ca. 1927) **:** the bivalent group CONH that unites the amino acid residues in a peptide

pep·ti·do·gly·can \ˌpep-təd-ō-ˈglī-ˌkan\ *n* [*peptide* + *-o-* + *glycan* (polysaccharide)] (1966) **:** a polymer that is composed of polysaccharide and peptide chains and is found esp. in bacterial cell walls — called also *mucopeptide, murein*

pep·tize \ˈpep-ˌtīz\ *vt* **pep·tized; pep·tiz·ing** [prob. fr. Gk *peptein*] (1864) **:** to cause to disperse in a medium; *specif* **:** to bring into colloidal solution — **pep·ti·za·tion** \ˌpep-tə-ˈzā-shən\ *n* — **pep·tiz·er** \ˈpep-ˌtī-zər\ *n*

\ə\ **abut** \ᵊ\ **kitten, F table** \ər\ **further** \a\ **ash** \ā\ **ace** \ä\ **cot, cart**
\au̇\ **out** \ch\ **chin** \e\ **bet** \ē\ **easy** \g\ **go** \i\ **hit** \ī\ **ice** \j\ **job**
\ŋ\ **sing** \ō\ **go** \ȯ\ **law** \ȯi\ **boy** \th\ **thin** \t͟h\ **the** \ü\ **loot** \u̇\ **foot**
\y\ **yet** \zh\ **vision** \à, k̟, ⁿ, œ, œ̄, ue, ue̅, ʸ\ *see* Guide to Pronunciation

pep·tone \'pep-,tōn\ *n* [G *pepton,* fr. Gk, neut. of *peptos* cooked] (1860) : any of various water-soluble products of partial hydrolysis of proteins

Pe·quot \'pē-,kwät\ *n* [prob. modif. of Narraganset *paquatanog* destroyers] (1631) : a member of an American Indian people of what is now eastern Connecticut

1per \(')pər\ *prep* [L, through, by means of, by — more at FOR] (14c) **1** : by the means or agency of : THROUGH ⟨~ bearer⟩ **2** : with respect to every member of a specified group : for each **3** : according to — often used with *as* ⟨as ~ instructions⟩

usage *Per* occurs most frequently in business contexts; its use outside such contexts is often criticized but is quite widespread, esp. in sense 2. Its most common and natural nonbusiness uses always involve figures, usu. in relation to price ⟨$150 *per* performance⟩, automobiles ⟨32 miles *per* gallon⟩ ⟨55 miles *per* hour⟩, or sports ⟨averages 15 points and 9 rebounds *per* game⟩

2per \'pər\ *adv* (1899) : for each : APIECE ⟨a bargain at $3.50 ~⟩

per- *prefix* [L, through, throughout, thoroughly, to destruction, fr. *per*] **1** : throughout : thoroughly ⟨*per*chlorinate⟩ **2 a** : containing the largest possible or a relatively large proportion of a (specified) chemical element ⟨*per*chloride⟩ **b** : containing an element in its highest or a high oxidation state ⟨*per*chloric acid⟩

1per·ad·ven·ture \'pər-əd-,ven-chər, 'per-; ,pər-əd-', ,per-\ *adv* [ME *per aventure,* fr. OF, by chance] *archaic* (13c) : PERHAPS, POSSIBLY

2peradventure *n* (15c) : DOUBT, CHANCE

per·am·bu·late \pə-'ram-byə-,lāt\ *vb* **-lat·ed; -lat·ing** [L *perambulatus,* pp. of *perambulare,* fr. *per-* through + *ambulare* to walk] *vt* (1568) **1** : to travel over or through esp. on foot : TRAVERSE **2** : to make an official inspection of (a boundary) on foot ~ *vi* : STROLL — **per·am·bu·la·tion** \-,ram-byə-'lā-shən\ *n* — **per·am·bu·la·to·ry** \-'ram-byə-lə-,tōr-ē, -,tȯr-\ *adj*

per·am·bu·la·tor \pə-'ram-byə-,lāt-ər, *for 2 also* 'pram-\ *n* (1611) **1** : one that perambulates **2** *chiefly Brit* : a baby carriage

per an·num \(,)pər-'an-əm\ *adv* [ML] (1601) : in or for each year

per·bo·rate \(')pər-'bō(ə)r-,āt, -'bȯ(ə)r-\ *n* [ISV] (1881) : a salt that is a compound of a borate with hydrogen peroxide

per·cale \(,)pər-'kā(ə)l, 'pər-,; (,)pər-'kal\ *n* [Per *pargālah*] (1621) : a fine closely woven cotton cloth variously finished for clothing, sheeting, and industrial uses

per·ca·line \,pər-kə-'lēn\ *n* [F, fr. *percale*] (ca. 1858) : a lightweight cotton fabric; *esp* : a glossy fabric used for bookbindings

per cap·i·ta \(,)pər-'kap-ət-ə\ *adv or adj* [ML, by heads] (1682) **1** : equally to each individual **2** : per unit of population : by or for each person ⟨the highest income *per capita* of any state in the union⟩

per·ceive \pər-'sēv\ *vt* **per·ceived; per·ceiv·ing** [ME *perceiven,* fr. MF *perceivre,* fr. L *percipere,* fr. *per-* thoroughly + *capere* to take — more at PER-, HEAVE] (14c) **1** : to attain awareness or understanding of **2** : to become aware of through the senses; *esp* : SEE, OBSERVE — **per·ceiv·able** \-'sē-və-bəl\ *adj* — **per·ceiv·ably** \-blē\ *adv* — **per·ceiv·er** *n*

1per·cent \pər-'sent\ *adv* [earlier *per cent,* fr. *per* + L *centum* hundred — more at HUNDRED] (1568) : in the hundred : of each hundred

2percent *adj* (1822) **1** : reckoned on the basis of a whole divided into one hundred parts **2** : paying interest at a specified percent

3percent *n, pl* **percent** *or* **percents** (1850) **1** *pl percent* **a** : one part in a hundred **b** : PERCENTAGE ⟨a large ~ of his income⟩ **2** *percents pl, Brit* : securities bearing a specified rate of interest

per·cent·age \pər-'sent-ij\ *n* (1786) **1 a** : a part of a whole expressed in hundredths **b** : the result obtained by multiplying a number by a percent **2 a** : a share of winnings or profits **b** : ADVANTAGE, PROFIT ⟨no ~ in going around looking like an old sack of laundry —Wallace Stegner⟩ **3** : an indeterminate part : PROPORTION **4 a** : PROBABILITY **b** : favorable odds

per·cen·tile \pər-'sen-,tīl\ *n* [prob. fr. *percent* + *-ile* (as in *quartile*)] (1885) : a value on a scale of one hundred that indicates the percent of a distribution that is equal to or below it ⟨a ~ score of 95 is a score equal to or better than 95 percent of the scores⟩

per cen·tum \pər-'sent-əm\ *n* [*per* + L *centum*] (1565) : PERCENT

per·cept \'pər-,sept\ *n* [back-formation fr. *perception*] (1837) : an impression of an object obtained by use of the senses : SENSE-DATUM

per·cep·ti·ble \pər-'sep-tə-bəl\ *adj* (1603) : capable of being perceived esp. by the senses ⟨a ~ change in her tone⟩ ⟨the light became increasingly ~⟩ — **per·cep·ti·bil·i·ty** \-,sep-tə-'bil-ət-ē\ *n* — **per·cep·ti·bly** \-blē\ *adv*

syn PERCEPTIBLE, SENSIBLE, PALPABLE, TANGIBLE, APPRECIABLE, PONDERABLE mean apprehensible as real or existent. PERCEPTIBLE applies to what can be discerned by the senses often to a minimal extent; SENSIBLE applies to whatever is clearly apprehended through the senses or impresses itself strongly on the mind; PALPABLE applies either to what has physical substance or to what is obvious and unmistakable; TANGIBLE suggests what is capable of being handled or grasped both physically and mentally; APPRECIABLE applies to what is distinctly discernible by the senses or definitely measurable; PONDERABLE suggests having definitely measurable weight or importance esp. as distinguished from eluding such determination.

per·cep·tion \pər-'sep-shən\ *n* [L *perception-, perceptio* act of perceiving, fr. *perceptus,* pp. of *percipere*] (ca. 1611) **1** *obs* : CONSCIOUSNESS **2 a** : a result of perceiving : OBSERVATION **b** : a mental image : CONCEPT **3 a** : awareness of the elements of environment through physical sensation ⟨color ~⟩ **b** : physical sensation interpreted in the light of experience **4 a** : quick, acute, and intuitive cognition : APPRECIATION **b** : a capacity for comprehension ***syn*** see DISCERNMENT — **per·cep·tion·al** \-shnəl, -shən-ᵊl\ *adj*

per·cep·tive \pər-'sep-tiv\ *adj* (1656) **1** : responsive to sensory stimulus : DISCERNING ⟨a ~ eye⟩ **2 a** : capable of or exhibiting keen perception : OBSERVANT ⟨a ~ scholar⟩ **b** : characterized by sympathetic understanding or insight — **per·cep·tive·ly** *adv* — **per·cep·tive·ness** *n* — **per·cep·tiv·i·ty** \(,)pər-,sep-'tiv-ət-ē\ *n*

per·cep·tu·al \(,)pər-'sep-chə(-wə)l, -'sepsh-wəl\ *adj* [L *perceptus*] (1878) : of, relating to, or involving perception esp. in relation to immediate sensory experience — **per·cep·tu·al·ly** \-ē\ *adv*

Per·ce·val \'pər-sə-vəl\ *n* [OF, modif. of MW *Peredur*] : a knight of King Arthur who wins a sight of the Holy Grail

1perch \'pərch\ *n* [ME *perche,* fr. MF, fr. L *pertica* pole] (14c) **1** : a bar or peg on which something is hung **2 a** : a roost for a bird **b** : a resting place or vantage point : SEAT **c** : a prominent position ⟨his new ~ as president⟩ **3 a** *chiefly Brit* : ROD 2 **b** : any of various units of measure for stonework

2perch *vi* (14c) : to alight, settle, or rest on a perch, a height, or a precarious spot ~ *vt* : to place on a perch, a height, or a precarious spot

3perch *n, pl* **perch** *or* **perch·es** [ME *perche,* fr. MF, fr. L *perca,* fr. Gk *perkē;* akin to OHG *faro* colored, L *porcus,* a spiny fish] (14c) **1 a** : a small European freshwater spiny-finned fish (*Perca fluviatilis*) **b** : an American fish (*P. flavescens*) that is closely related to the perch **2** : any of numerous teleost fishes (as of the families Percidae, Centrarchidae, Serranidae)

per·chance \pər-'chan(t)s\ *adv* [ME *per chance,* fr. MF, by chance] (14c) : PERHAPS, POSSIBLY

Per·che·ron \'pər-chə-,rän, -shə-\ *n* [F] (1875) : any of a breed of powerful rugged draft horses that originated in the Perche region of France

per·chlo·rate \(')pər-'klō(ə)r-,āt, -'klȯ(ə)r-, -ət\ *n* [ISV] (1826) : a salt or ester of perchloric acid

per·chlo·ric acid \(,)pər-,klōr-ik-, -,klȯr-\ *n* (1818) : a fuming corrosive strong acid $HClO_4$ that is the highest oxygen acid of chlorine and a powerful oxidizing agent when heated

per·chlo·ro·eth·y·lene \(,)pər-,klōr-ə-'weth-ə-,lēn, -,klȯr-\ *n* [*per-* + *chlor-* + *ethylene*] (1873) : a colorless nonflammable liquid used often as a solvent in dry cleaning and for removal of grease from metals

per·cip·i·ence \pər-'sip-ē-ən(t)s\ *n* (1768) : PERCEPTION

per·cip·i·ent \-ənt\ *adj* [L *percipient-, percipiens,* prp. of *percipere* to perceive] (1692) : capable of or characterized by perception : DISCERNING — **percipient** *n*

per·coid \'pər-,kȯid\ *adj* [deriv. of L *perca* perch] (1840) : of or relating to a very large suborder (Percoidea) of spiny-finned fishes including the true perches, sunfishes, sea basses, and sea breams — **percoid** *n*

per·co·late \'pər-kə-,lāt, ÷-kyə-\ *vb* **-lat·ed; -lat·ing** [L *percolatus,* pp. of *percolare,* fr. *per-* through + *colare* to sieve — more at PER-, COLANDER] *vt* (1626) **1 a** : to cause (a solvent) to pass through a permeable substance (as a powdered drug) esp. for extracting a soluble constituent **b** : to prepare (coffee) in a percolator **2** : to be diffused through : PENETRATE ~ *vi* **1** : to ooze or trickle through a permeable substance : SEEP **2 a** : to become percolated **b** : to become lively or effervescent **3** : to spread gradually ⟨allow the sunlight to ~ into our rooms —Norman Douglas⟩ — **per·co·la·tion** \,pər-kə-'lā-shən\ *n*

per·co·la·tor \'pər-kə-,lāt-ər, ÷-kyə-\ *n* (ca. 1842) : one that percolates; *specif* : a coffeepot in which boiling water rising through a tube is repeatedly deflected downward through a perforated basket containing ground coffee beans to extract their essence

per con·tra \(,)pər-'kän-trə\ *adv* [It, by the opposite side (of the ledger)] (1554) **1 a** : on the contrary **b** : by way of contrast **2** : as an offset

per cu·ri·am decision \(,)pər-,k(y)u̇r-ē-,äm-\ *n* [ML *per curiam,* lit., by the court] (1927) : a very brief usu. unanimous decision of a court rendered without elaborate discussion

per·cuss \pər-'kəs\ *vt* [L *percussus*] (1626) : to tap sharply; *esp* : to practice percussion on

per·cus·sion \pər-'kəsh-ən\ *n* [L *percussion-, percussio,* fr. *percussus,* pp. of *percutere* to beat, fr. *per-* thoroughly + *quatere* to shake — more at PER-, QUASH] (1544) **1** : the act of percussing: as **a** : the striking of a percussion cap so as to set off the charge in a firearm **b** : the beating or striking of a musical instrument **c** : the act or technique of tapping the surface of a body part to learn the condition of the parts beneath by the resultant sound **2** : the striking of sound on the ear **3** : percussion instruments that form a section of a band or orchestra — **percussion** *adj*

percussion cap *n* (1823) : CAP 5

percussion instrument *n* (1872) : a musical instrument (as a drum, xylophone, or maraca) sounded by striking, shaking, or scraping

per·cus·sion·ist \pər-'kəsh-(ə-)nəst\ *n* (1939) : one skilled in the playing of percussion instruments

per·cus·sive \pər-'kəs-iv\ *adj* (1793) **1** : of or relating to percussion; *esp* : operative or operated by striking **2** : having powerful impact — **per·cus·sive·ly** *adv* — **per·cus·sive·ness** *n*

per·cu·ta·ne·ous \,pər-kyu̇-'tā-nē-əs\ *adj* (1887) : effected or performed through the skin — **per·cu·ta·ne·ous·ly** *adv*

per·die \(,)pər-'dē, per-\ *var of* PARDIE

1per di·em \(,)pər-'dē-əm, -'dī-\ *adv* [ML] (1520) : by the day : for each day

2per diem *adj* (1809) **1** : based on use or service by the day : DAILY **2** : paid by the day

3per diem *n, pl* **per diems** (1812) **1** : a daily allowance **2** : a daily fee

per·di·tion \pər-'dish-ən\ *n* [ME *perdicion,* fr. LL *perdition-, perditio,* fr. L *perditus,* pp. of *perdere* to destroy, fr. *per-* to destruction + *dare* to give — more at PER-, DATE] (14c) **1 a** *archaic* : utter destruction **b** *obs* : LOSS **2 a** : eternal damnation **b** : HELL

1per·du *or* **per·due** \'pər-(,)d(y)ü, (,)pər-'\ *n* [F *sentinelle perdue,* lit., lost sentinel] *obs* (1591) : a soldier assigned to extremely hazardous duty

2per·du *or* **per·due** \per-dü̅\ *adj* [F *perdu,* masc., & *perdue,* fem., fr. pp. of *perdre* to lose, fr. L *perdere*] (1591) : remaining out of sight

per·du·ra·ble \(,)pər-'d(y)u̇r-ə-bəl, 'pər-jə-rə-\ *adj* [ME, fr. MF, fr. LL *perdurabilis,* fr. L *perdurare* to endure, fr. *per-* throughout + *durare* to last — more at DURING] (14c) : very durable — **per·du·ra·bil·i·ty** \(,)pər-,d(y)u̇r-ə-'bil-ət-ē, ,pər-jə-rə-\ *n* — **per·du·ra·bly** \(,)pər-'d(y)u̇r-ə-blē, 'pər-jə-rə-\ *adv*

per·dure \(,)pər-'d(y)u̇(ə)r\ *vi* **per·dured; per·dur·ing** [ME *perduren,* fr. L *perdurare*] (15c) : to continue to exist : LAST

per·e·gri·nate \'per-ə-grə-,nāt\ *vb* **-nat·ed; -nat·ing** *vi* (1593) : to travel esp. on foot : WALK ~ *vt* : to walk or travel over : TRAVERSE — **per·e·gri·na·tion** \,per-ə-grə-'nā-shən\ *n*

1per·e·grine \'per-ə-grən, -,grēn\ *adj* [ME, fr. ML *peregrinus,* fr. L, foreign — more at PILGRIM] (14c) : having a tendency to wander

2peregrine *n* (1555) : a swift nearly cosmopolitan falcon (*Falco pere-*

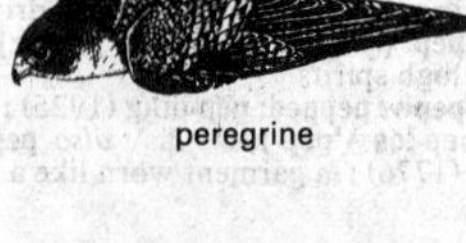

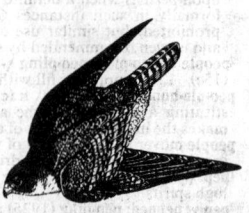

peregrine

grinus) that is much used in falconry — called also *peregrine falcon*

pe·rei·on \pə-ˈrī-ˌän\ *or* **pe·re·on** \-ˈrē-\ *n* [NL, fr. Gk *peraiōn*, prp. of *peraioun* to transport, fr. *peraios* situated beyond, fr. *pera* beyond; akin to Gk *poros* passage — more at FARE] (1855) **:** the thorax or the seven metameres comprising the thorax of some crustaceans (as a decapod)

pe·rei·o·pod \pə-ˈrī-ə-ˌpäd\ *or* **pe·reo·pod** \-ˈrē-\ *n* [NL *perion* + E *-pod*] (1893) **:** an appendage of the pereion

pe·remp·to·ry \pə-ˈrem(p)-t(ə-)rē\ *adj* [LL & L; LL *peremptorius*, fr. L, destructive, fr. *peremptus*, pp. of *perimere* to take entirely, destroy, fr. *per-* to destruction + *emere* to take — more at REDEEM] (1530) **1 a :** putting an end to or precluding a right of action, debate, or delay ⟨a ~ mandamus⟩ **b :** admitting of no contradiction ⟨a ~ conclusion based on absolute evidence⟩ **2 :** expressive of urgency or command ⟨a ~ call⟩ **3 a :** characterized by often imperious or arrogant self-assurance ⟨how insolent of late he is become, how proud, how ~ —Shak.⟩ **b :** indicative of a peremptory attitude or nature **:** HAUGHTY ⟨a ~ tone⟩ ⟨~ disregard of an objection⟩ ***syn*** see MASTERFUL — **pe·remp·to·ri·ly** \-ˈrem(p)-t(ə-)rə-lē; -ˌrem(p)-ˈtōr-ə-lē, -ˈtȯr-\ *adv* — **pe·remp·to·ri·ness** \-ˈrem(p)-t(ə-)rē-nəs\ *n*

pe·ren·nate \ˈper-ə-ˌnāt, pə-ˈren-ˌāt\ *vi* **-nat·ed; -nat·ing** [L *perennatus*, pp. of *perennare*, fr. *perennis*] (ca. 1623) **:** to live over from season to season ⟨a *perennating* rhizome⟩ — **per·en·na·tion** \ˌper-ə-ˈnā-shən\ *n*

pe·ren·ni·al \pə-ˈren-ē-əl\ *adj* [L *perennis*, fr. *per-* throughout + *annus* year — more at PER-, ANNUAL] (1644) **1 :** present at all seasons of the year **2 :** persisting for several years usu. with new herbaceous growth from a perennating part ⟨~ asters⟩ **3 a :** PERSISTENT, ENDURING **b :** continuing without interruption **:** CONSTANT **c :** regularly repeated or renewed **:** RECURRENT ***syn*** see CONTINUAL — **perennial** *n* — **pe·ren·ni·al·ly** \-ē-ə-lē\ *adv*

1per·fect \ˈpər-fikt\ *adj* [ME *parfit*, fr. OF, fr. L *perfectus*, fr. pp. of *perficere* to carry out, perfect, fr. *per-* thoroughly + *facere* to make, do — more at DO] (13c) **1 a :** being entirely without fault or defect **:** FLAWLESS ⟨a ~ crime⟩ **b :** satisfying all requirements **:** ACCURATE **c :** corresponding to an ideal standard or abstract concept ⟨a ~ gentleman⟩ **d :** faithfully reproducing the original; *specif* **:** LETTER-PERFECT **e :** legally valid **2 :** EXPERT, PROFICIENT ⟨practice makes ~⟩ **3 a :** PURE, TOTAL **b :** lacking in no essential detail **:** COMPLETE **c** *obs* **:** SANE **d :** ABSOLUTE, UNEQUIVOCAL **e :** of an extreme kind **:** UNMITIGATED **4** *obs* **:** MATURE **5 :** of, relating to, or constituting a verb form or verbal that expresses an action or state completed at the time of speaking or at a time spoken of **6** *obs* **a :** CERTAIN, SURE **b :** CONTENTED, SATISFIED **7** *of a musical interval* **:** belonging to the consonances unison, fourth, fifth, and octave which retain their character when inverted and when raised or lowered by a half step become augmented or diminished **8 a :** sexually mature and fully differentiated ⟨a ~ insect⟩ **b :** MONOCLINOUS ⟨a ~ flower⟩ — **per·fect·ness** \-fik(t)-nəs\ *n*

syn PERFECT, WHOLE, ENTIRE, INTACT mean not lacking or faulty in any particular. PERFECT implies the soundness and the excellence of every part, element, or quality of a thing frequently as an unattainable or theoretical state; WHOLE suggests a completeness or perfection that can be sought, gained, or regained; ENTIRE implies perfection deriving from integrity, soundness, or completeness of a thing; INTACT implies retention of perfection of a thing in its natural or original state.

2per·fect \pər-ˈfekt *also* ˈpər-fikt\ *vt* (14c) **1 :** to bring to final form **2 :** to make perfect **:** IMPROVE, REFINE — **per·fect·er** *n*

3per·fect \ˈpər-fikt\ *n* (1841) **:** the perfect tense of a language; *also* **:** a verb form in the perfect tense

per·fec·ta \pər-ˈfek-tə\ *n* [AmerSp *quiniela perfecta* perfect quiniela] (1967) **:** a system of betting (as on dog races) in which the bettor must pick the first and second place finishers in this sequence in order to win — compare QUINIELA, TRIFECTA

perfect binding *n* (1926) **:** a book binding in which a layer of adhesive holds the pages and cover together — **per·fect–bound** \ˈper-fik(t)-ˈbau̇nd\ *adj*

perfect game *n* (ca. 1949) **1 :** a baseball game in which a pitcher allows no hits, no runs, and no opposing batter to reach first base **2 :** a game in bowling in which a bowler gets 12 consecutive strikes

per·fect·ible \pər-ˈfek-tə-bəl *also* ˈpər-fik-\ *adj* (1635) **:** capable of improvement or perfection — **per·fect·ibil·i·ty** \pər-ˌfek-tə-ˈbil-ət-ē *also* ˌpər-fik-\ *n*

per·fec·tion \pər-ˈfek-shən\ *n* [ME *perfeccioun*, fr. OF *perfection*, fr. L *perfection-, perfectio*, fr. *perfectus*] (13c) **1 :** the quality or state of being perfect: as **a :** freedom from fault or defect **:** FLAWLESSNESS **b :** MATURITY **c :** the quality or state of being saintly **2 a :** an exemplification of supreme excellence **b :** an unsurpassable degree of accuracy or excellence **3 :** the act or process of perfecting

per·fec·tion·ism \-shə-ˌniz-əm\ *n* (ca. 1846) **1 a :** the doctrine that the perfection of moral character constitutes man's highest good **b :** the theological doctrine that a state of freedom from sin is attainable on earth **2 :** a disposition to regard anything short of perfection as unacceptable — **per·fec·tion·ist** \-sh(ə-)nəst\ *n or adj*

per·fec·tive \pər-ˈfek-tiv *also* ˈpər-fik-\ *adj* (1596) **1** *archaic* **a :** tending to make perfect **b :** becoming better **2 :** expressing action as complete or as implying the notion of completion, conclusion, or result ⟨~ verb⟩ — **perfective** *n* — **per·fec·tive·ly** *adv* — **per·fec·tive·ness** *n* — **per·fec·tiv·i·ty** \pər-ˌfek-ˈtiv-ət-ē *also* ˌpər-fik-\ *n*

per·fect·ly \ˈpər-fik-(t)lē\ *adv* (14c) **1 :** in a perfect manner **2 :** to a complete or adequate extent **:** QUITE

perfect number *n* (15c) **:** an integer (as 6 or 28) the sum of whose integral factors including 1 but excluding itself is equal to itself

per·fec·to \pər-ˈfek-(ˌ)tō\ *n, pl* **-tos** [Sp, perfect, fr. L *perfectus*] (1894) **:** a cigar that is thick in the middle and tapers almost to a point at each end

perfect participle *n* (1862) **:** PAST PARTICIPLE

perfect pitch *n* (1949) **:** ABSOLUTE PITCH 2

perfect square *n* (ca. 1936) **:** an integer whose square root is an integer ⟨9 is a *perfect square* because it is the square of 3⟩

perfect year *n* (ca. 1909) **:** a common year of 355 days or a leap year of 385 days in the Jewish calendar

per·fer·vid \(ˌ)pər-ˈfər-vəd, ˈpər-\ *adj* [NL *perfervidus*, fr. L *per-* thoroughly + *fervidus* fervid] (1856) **:** marked by overwrought or exaggerated emotion **:** excessively fervent ***syn*** see IMPASSIONED

per·fid·i·ous \(ˌ)pər-ˈfid-ē-əs\ *adj* (ca. 1598) **:** of, relating to, or characterized by perfidy ***syn*** see FAITHLESS — **per·fid·i·ous·ly** *adv* — **per·fid·i·ous·ness** *n*

per·fi·dy \ˈpər-fəd-ē\ *n, pl* **-dies** [L *perfidia*, fr. *perfidus* faithless, fr. *per fidem decipere* to betray, lit., to deceive by trust] (1592) **1 :** the quality or state of being faithless or disloyal **:** TREACHERY **2 :** an act or an instance of disloyalty

per·fo·li·ate \ˌpər-ˈfō-lē-ət, ˈpər-\ *adj* [NL *perfoliata*, an herb having leaves pierced by the stem, fr. L *per* through + *foliata*, fem. of *foliatus* foliate] (1687) **:** having the basal part naturally united around the stem ⟨a ~ leaf of a honeysuckle⟩

per·fo·rate \ˈpər-fə-ˌrāt\ *vb* **-rat·ed; -rat·ing** [L *perforatus*, pp. of *perforare* to bore through, fr. *per-* through + *forare* to bore — more at BORE] *vt* (ca. 1538) **1 :** to make a hole through ⟨an ulcer ~*s* the duodenal wall⟩; *specif* **:** to make a line of holes in to facilitate separation **2 :** to pass through or into by or as if by making a hole ~ *vi* **:** to penetrate a surface — **per·fo·rate** \ˈpər-f(ə-)rət, -fə-ˌrāt\ *adj* — **per·fo·ra·tor** \-fə-ˌrāt-ər\ *n*

per·fo·rat·ed \-fə-ˌrāt-əd\ *adj* (15c) **1 :** having a hole or series of holes; *esp* **:** having a specified number of perforations in 20 millimeters ⟨the stamps are ~ 10⟩ **2 :** characterized by perforation ⟨a ~ ulcer⟩

per·fo·ra·tion \ˌpər-fə-ˈrā-shən\ *n* (15c) **1 :** the act or process of perforating **2 a :** a hole or pattern made by or as if by piercing or boring **b :** one of the series of holes between rows of postage stamps in a sheet that serve as an aid in separation

per·force \pər-ˈfō(ə)rs, -ˈfȯ(ə)rs\ *adv* [ME *par force*, fr. MF, by force] (14c) **1** *obs* **:** by physical coercion **2 :** by force of circumstances

per·form \pə(r)-ˈfȯ(ə)rm\ *vb* [ME *performen*, fr. AF *performer*, alter. of OF *perfournir*, fr. *per-* thoroughly (fr. L) + *fournir* to complete — more at FURNISH] *vt* (14c) **1 :** to adhere to the terms of **:** FULFILL ⟨~ a contract⟩ **2 :** CARRY OUT, DO **3 a :** to do in a formal manner or according to prescribed ritual **b :** to give a rendition of **:** PRESENT ~ *vi* **1 :** to carry out an action or pattern of behavior **:** ACT, FUNCTION **2 :** to give a performance **:** PLAY — **per·form·abil·i·ty** \-ˌfȯr-mə-ˈbil-ət-ē\ *n* — **per·form·able** \-ˈfȯr-mə-bəl\ *adj* — **per·form·er** \-ˈfȯr-mər\ *n*

syn PERFORM, EXECUTE, DISCHARGE, ACCOMPLISH, ACHIEVE, EFFECT, FULFILL mean to carry out or into effect. PERFORM implies action that follows established patterns or procedures or fulfills agreed-upon requirements and often connotes special skill; EXECUTE stresses the carrying out of what exists in plan or in intent; DISCHARGE implies execution and completion of appointed duties or tasks; ACCOMPLISH stresses the successful completion of a process rather than the means of carrying it out; ACHIEVE adds to ACCOMPLISH the implication of conquered difficulties; EFFECT adds to ACHIEVE an emphasis on the inherent force in the agent capable of surmounting obstacles; FULFILL implies a complete realization of ends or possibilities.

per·for·mance \pə(r)-ˈfȯr-mən(t)s\ *n* (15c) **1 a :** the execution of an action **b :** something accomplished **:** DEED, FEAT **2 :** the fulfillment of a claim, promise, or request **:** IMPLEMENTATION **3 a :** the action of representing a character in a play **b :** a public presentation or exhibition ⟨a benefit ~⟩ **4 a :** the ability to perform **:** EFFICIENCY **b :** the manner in which a mechanism performs ⟨engine ~⟩ **5 :** the manner of reacting to stimuli **:** BEHAVIOR **6 :** linguistic behavior — compare COMPETENCE 3 — **per·for·ma·to·ry** \-mə-ˌtōr-ē, -ˌtȯr-\ *adj*

per·for·ma·tive \-ˈfȯr-mət-iv\ *n* (ca. 1955) **:** an expression that serves to effect a transaction or that constitutes the performance of the specified act by virtue of its utterance ⟨many ~*s* are *contractual* ("I bet") or *declaratory* ("I declare war") utterances —J. L. Austin⟩

per·form·ing *adj* (1886) **:** of, relating to, or constituting an art (as drama) that involves public performance ⟨the ~ arts⟩

1per·fume \ˈpər-ˌfyüm, (ˌ)pər-ˈ\ *n* [MF *perfum*, prob. fr. OProv, fr. *perfumar* to perfume, fr. *per-* thoroughly (fr. L) + *fumar* to smoke, fr. L *fumare*, fr. *fumus* smoke — more at FUME] (1533) **1 :** the scent of something sweet-smelling **2 :** a substance that emits a pleasant odor; *esp* **:** a fluid preparation of floral essences or synthetics and a fixative used for scenting ***syn*** see FRAGRANCE

2per·fume \(ˌ)pər-ˈfyüm, ˈpər-ˌ\ *vt* **per·fumed; per·fum·ing** (ca. 1538) **:** to fill or imbue with an odor

per·fum·er \pə(r)-ˈfyü-mər, ˈpər-ˌ\ *n* (ca. 1573) **:** one that makes or sells perfumes

per·fum·ery \pə(r)-ˈfyüm-(ə-)rē\ *n, pl* **-er·ies** (1800) **1 a :** the art or process of making perfume **b :** the products made by a perfumer **2 :** an establishment where perfumes are made

per·func·to·ry \pər-ˈfəŋ(k)-t(ə-)rē\ *adj* [LL *perfunctorius*, fr. L *perfunctus*, pp. of *perfungi* to accomplish, get through with, fr. *per-* through + *fungi* to perform — more at PER-, FUNCTION] (1593) **1 :** characterized by routine or superficiality **:** MECHANICAL ⟨a ~ smile⟩ **2 :** lacking in interest or enthusiasm **:** APATHETIC — **per·func·to·ri·ly** \-t(ə-)rə-lē\ *adv* — **per·func·to·ri·ness** \-t(ə-)rē-nəs\ *n*

per·fus·ate \(ˌ)pər-ˈfyü-ˌzāt, -zət\ *n* (1915) **:** a fluid (as a solution pumped through the heart) that is perfused

per·fuse \(ˌ)pər-ˈfyüz\ *vt* **per·fused; per·fus·ing** [L *perfusus*, pp. of *perfundere* to pour over, fr. *per-* through + *fundere* to pour — more at FOUND] (1526) **1 :** SUFFUSE **2 a :** to cause to flow or spread **:** DIFFUSE **b :** to force a fluid through (an organ or tissue) esp. by way of the blood vessels — **per·fu·sion** \-ˈfyü-zhən\ *n*

per·go·la \ˈpər-gə-lə, pər-ˈgō-\ *n* [It, fr. L *pergula* projecting roof] (1675) **1 :** ARBOR, TRELLIS **2 :** a structure usu. consisting of parallel colonnades supporting an open roof of girders and cross rafters

1per·haps \pər-ˈ(h)aps, ˈpraps\ *adv* [*per* + *hap*] (1528) **:** possibly but not certainly **:** MAYBE

2perhaps *n* (1534) **:** something open to doubt or conjecture

pe·ri \ˈpi(ə)r-ē\ *n* [Per *perī* fairy, genius, modif. of Av *pairikā* witch; akin to L *paelex* concubine] (1777) **1 :** a supernatural being in Persian folklore descended from fallen angels and excluded from paradise until penance is accomplished **2 :** a beautiful and graceful girl

\ə\ abut \ᵊ\ kitten, F table \ər\ further \a\ ash \ā\ ace \ä\ cot, cart \au̇\ out \ch\ chin \e\ bet \ē\ easy \g\ go \i\ hit \ī\ ice \j\ job \ŋ\ sing \ō\ go \ȯ\ law \ȯi\ boy \th\ thin \t͟h\ the \ü\ loot \u̇\ foot \y\ yet \zh\ vision \à, k̲, ⁿ, œ, œ̄, ue, ūe, ʸ\ *see* Guide to Pronunciation

peri- *prefix* [L, fr. Gk, around, in excess, fr. *peri;* akin to Gk *peran* to pass through — more at FARE] **1 :** all around : about ⟨*periscope*⟩ **2 :** near ⟨*perihelion*⟩ **3 :** enclosing : surrounding ⟨*perineurium*⟩

peri·anth \'per-ē-,an(t)th\ *n* [NL *perianthium,* fr. peri- + Gk *anthos* flower — more at ANTHOLOGY] (1785) **:** the external envelope of a flower esp. when not differentiated into a calyx and corolla — see FLOWER illustration

peri·apt \'per-ē-,apt\ *n* [MF or Gk; MF *periapte,* fr. Gk *periapton,* fr. *periaptein* to fasten around (oneself), fr. peri- + *haptein* to fasten] (1584) **:** AMULET

peri·car·di·al \,per-ē-'kärd-ē-əl\ *adj* (1654) **:** of, relating to, or affecting the pericardium; *also* **:** situated around the heart

peri·car·di·tis \-,kär-'dīt-əs\ *n* [NL] (ca. 1799) **:** inflammation of the pericardium

peri·car·di·um \,per-ə-'kärd-ē-əm\ *n, pl* **-dia** \-ē-ə\ [NL, fr. Gk *perikardion,* neut. of *perikardios* around the heart, fr. peri- + *kardia* heart — more at HEART] (ca. 1576) **1 :** the conical sac of serous membrane that encloses the heart and the roots of the great blood vessels of vertebrates **2 :** a cavity or space that contains the heart of an invertebrate and in arthropods is a part of the hemocoel

peri·carp \'per-ə-,kärp\ *n* [NL *pericarpium,* fr. Gk *perikarpion* pod, fr. peri- + -*karpion* -carp] (1759) **:** the ripened and variously modified walls of a plant ovary — see ENDOCARP illustration

peri·chon·dri·um \,per-ə-'kän-drē-əm\ *n, pl* **-dria** \-drē-ə\ [NL, fr. peri- + Gk *chondros* grain, cartilage — more at GRIND] (ca. 1741) **:** the membrane of fibrous connective tissue that invests cartilage except at joints — **peri·chon·dral** \-drəl\ *adj*

pe·ric·o·pe \pə-'rik-ə-pē\ *n* [LL, fr. Gk *perikopē* section, fr. peri- + *kopē* act of cutting; akin to Gk *koptein* to cut — more at CAPON] (1658) **:** a selection from a book; *specif* **:** LECTION 1

peri·cra·ni·um \,per-ə-'krā-nē-əm\ *n, pl* **-nia** \-nē-ə\ [NL, fr. Gk *perikranion* neut. of *perikranios* around the skull, fr. peri- + *kranion* skull — more at CRANIUM] (1541) **:** the external periosteum of the skull — **peri·cra·ni·al** \-nē-əl\ *adj*

peri·cy·cle \'per-ə-,sī-kəl\ *n* [F *péricycle,* fr. Gk *perikyklos* spherical, fr. peri- + *kyklos* circle — more at WHEEL] (ca. 1892) **:** a thin layer of parenchymatous or sclerenchymatous cells that surrounds the stele in most vascular plants — **peri·cy·clic** \,per-ə-'sī-klik, -'sik-lik\ *adj*

peri·cyn·thi·on \,per-ə-'sin(t)-thē-ən\ *n* [NL, fr. peri- + *Cynthia* + -*on* (as in perihelion)] (ca. 1959) **:** PERILUNE

peri·derm \'per-ə-,dərm\ *n* [NL *peridermis,* fr. peri- + -*dermis*] (1849) **:** an outer layer of tissue; *specif* **:** a cortical protective layer of many roots and stems that typically consists of phellem, phellogen, and phelloderm

pe·rid·i·um \pə-'rid-ē-əm\ *n, pl* **pe·rid·ia** \-ē-ə\ [NL, fr. Gk *pēridion,* dim. of *pēra* leather bag] (ca. 1823) **:** the outer envelope of the sporophore of many fungi

per·i·dot \'per-ə-,dō(t), -,dät\ *n* [F *péridot*] (ca. 1706) **:** a deep yellowish green transparent olivine used as a gem — **per·i·dot·ic** \,per-ə-'dōt-ik, -'dät-\ *adj*

pe·ri·do·tite \pə-'rid-ə-,tīt; 'per-ə-,dōt-,īt, -,dät-\ *n* [F *péridotite,* fr. *péridot*] (1878) **:** any of a group of granitoid igneous rocks composed of ferromagnesian minerals and esp. olivine — **pe·ri·do·tit·ic** \pə-,rid-ə-'tit-ik, ,per-əd-ə-\ *adj*

peri·gee \'per-ə-(,)jē\ *n* [Gk *gē* earth] (1594) **:** the point in the orbit of a satellite of the earth or of a vehicle orbiting the earth that is nearest to the center of the earth; *also* **:** the point nearest a planet or a satellite (as the moon) reached by any object orbiting it — compare APOGEE — **peri·ge·an** \-ə-'jē-ən\ *adj*

pe·rig·y·nous \pə-'rij-ə-nəs\ *adj* [NL *perigynus,* fr. peri- + -*gynus*

-gynous] (1807) **:** borne on a ring or cup of the receptacle surrounding a pistil ⟨~ petals⟩; *also* **:** having perigynous stamens and petals ⟨~ flowers⟩ — **pe·rig·y·ny** \-nē\ *n*

peri·he·lion \,per-ə-'hēl-yən\ *n, pl* **-he·lia** \-'hēl-yə\ [NL, fr. peri- + Gk *hēlios* sun — more at SOLAR] (1666) **:** the point in the path of a celestial body (as a planet) that is nearest to the sun — compare APHELION — **peri·he·lial** \-'hēl-yəl\ *adj*

peri·kary·on \-'kar-ē-,än, -ən\ *n, pl* **-karya** \-ē-ə\ [NL, fr. peri- + Gk *karyon* nut, kernel — more at CAREEN] (1897) **:** the cytoplasmic body of a nerve cell — **peri·kary·al** \-ē-əl\ *adj*

¹per·il \'per-əl\ *n* [ME, fr. OF, fr. L *periculum* — more at FEAR] (13c) **1 :** exposure to the risk of being injured, destroyed, or lost : DANGER ⟨fire put the city in ~⟩ **2 :** something that imperils : RISK ⟨lessen the ~s of the streets⟩

²peril *vt* **-iled** *also* **-illed; -il·ing** *also* **-il·ling** (1567) **:** to expose to danger

per·il·la \pə-'ril-ə\ *n* [NL] (1900) **:** any of a genus (*Perilla*) of Asian mints that have four didynamous stamens, a bilabiate fruiting calyx, and rugose nutlets

perilla oil *n* (1917) **:** a light yellow drying oil that is obtained from seeds of perillas and is used chiefly in varnish, printing ink, and linoleum and in the Orient as an edible oil

per·il·ous \'per-ə-ləs\ *adj* (13c) **:** full of or involving peril : HAZARDOUS *syn* see DANGEROUS — **per·il·ous·ly** *adv* — **per·il·ous·ness** *n*

peri·lune \'per-ə-,lün\ *n* [peri- + L *luna* moon] (1960) **:** the point in the path of a body orbiting the moon that is nearest to the center of the moon — compare APOLUNE

peri·lymph \-,lim(p)f\ *n* [ISV] (1836) **:** the fluid between the membranous and bony labyrinths of the ear

pe·rim·e·ter \pə-'rim-ət-ər\ *n* [F *périmètre,* fr. L *perimetros,* fr. Gk, fr. peri- + *metron* measure — more at MEASURE] (ca. 1592) **1 a :** the boundary of a closed plane figure **b :** the length of a perimeter **2 :** a line or strip bounding or protecting an area **3 :** outer limits

peri·morph \'per-ə-,mȯrf\ *n* [ISV] (ca. 1879) **:** a crystal of one species enclosing one of another species

peri·my·si·um \,per-ə-'miz(h)-ē-əm\ *n, pl* **-sia** \-ē-ə\ [NL, irreg. fr. peri- + Gk *mys* mouse, muscle — more at MOUSE] (ca. 1842) **:** the connective-tissue sheath that surrounds a muscle and forms sheaths for the bundles of muscle fibers

peri·na·tal \-'nāt-ᵊl\ *adj* (1952) **:** occurring in, concerned with, or being in the period around the time of birth ⟨~ mortality⟩ ⟨~ care⟩ — **peri·na·tal·ly** \-ᵊl-(l)ē\ *adv*

per·i·ne·um \,per-ə-'nē-əm\ *n, pl* **-nea** \-'nē-ə\ [NL, fr. LL *perinaion,* fr. Gk, fr. peri- + *inein* to empty out; akin to L *ira* ire] (ca. 1632) **:** an area of tissue that marks externally the approximate boundary of the outlet of the pelvis and gives passage to the urinogenital ducts and rectum; *also* **:** the area between the anus and the posterior part of the external genitalia esp. in the female — **per·i·ne·al** \-'nē-əl\ *adj*

peri·neu·ri·um \,per-ə-'n(y)ȯr-ē-əm\ *n, pl* **-ria** \-ē-ə\ [NL, fr. peri- + Gk *neuron* nerve — more at NERVE] (ca. 1842) **:** the connective-tissue sheath that surrounds a bundle of nerve fibers

¹pe·ri·od \'pir-ē-əd\ *n* [ME *pariode,* fr. MF *periode,* fr. ML, L, & Gk; ML *periodus* period of time, punctuation mark, fr. L & Gk; L, rhetorical period, fr. Gk *periodos* circuit, period of time, rhetorical period, fr. peri- + *hodos* way — more at CEDE] (1530) **1 :** the completion of a cycle, a series of events, or a single action : CONCLUSION **2 a** (1): an utterance from one full stop to another : SENTENCE (2) : a well-proportioned sentence of several clauses (3) : PERIODIC SENTENCE **b :** a musical structure or melodic section usu. composed of two or more contrasting or complementary phrases and ending with a cadence **3**

PERIODIC TABLE

This is a common form of the table. Roman numerals and letters heading the vertical columns indicate the groups (there are differences of opinion regarding the letter designations, those given here being probably the most generally used). The horizontal rows represent the periods, with two series removed from the two very long periods and represented below the main table. Atomic numbers are given above the symbols for the elements. Compare ELEMENT table.

IA																VIIA	Zero
1 H	IIA											IIIA	IVA	VA	VIA	1 H	2 He
3 Li	4 Be											5 B	6 C	7 N	8 O	9 F	10 Ne
11 Na	12 Mg	IIIB	IVB	VB	VIB	VIIB		VIII		IB	IIB	13 Al	14 Si	15 P	16 S	17 Cl	18 Ar
19 K	20 Ca	21 Sc	22 Ti	23 V	24 Cr	25 Mn	26 Fe	27 Co	28 Ni	29 Cu	30 Zn	31 Ga	32 Ge	33 As	34 Se	35 Br	36 Kr
37 Rb	38 Sr	39 Y	40 Zr	41 Nb	42 Mo	43 Tc	44 Ru	45 Rh	46 Pd	47 Ag	48 Cd	49 In	50 Sn	51 Sb	52 Te	53 I	54 Xe
55 Cs	56 Ba	57 *La	72 Hf	73 Ta	74 W	75 Re	76 Os	77 Ir	78 Pt	79 Au	80 Hg	81 Tl	82 Pb	83 Bi	84 Po	85 At	86 Rn
87 Fr	88 Ra	89 #Ac	104 Unq	105 Unp	106 Unh												

	58 Ce	59 Pr	60 Nd	61 Pm	62 Sm	63 Eu	64 Gd	65 Tb	66 Dy	67 Ho	68 Er	69 Tm	70 Yb	71 Lu
*LANTHANIDE SERIES														
#ACTINIDE SERIES	90 Th	91 Pa	92 U	93 Np	94 Pu	95 Am	96 Cm	97 Bk	98 Cf	99 Es	100 Fm	101 Md	102 No	103 Lr

a : the full pause with which the utterance of a sentence closes b : END, STOP 4 *obs* : GOAL, PURPOSE 5 a : a point . used to mark the end (as of a declarative sentence or an abbreviation) b : a rhythmical unit in Greek verse composed of a series of two or more cola 6 a : a portion of time determined by some recurring phenomenon b (1) : the interval of time required for a cyclic motion or phenomenon to complete a cycle and begin to repeat itself (2) : a number *k* that does not change the value of a periodic function *f* when added to the independent variable: $f(x + k) = f(x)$; *esp* : the smallest such number c : a single cyclic occurrence of menstruation 7 a : a chronological division : STAGE b : a division of geologic time longer than an epoch and included in an era c : a stage of culture having a definable place in time and space 8 a : one of the divisions of the academic day b : one of the divisions of the playing time of a game

syn PERIOD, EPOCH, ERA, AGE mean a division of time. PERIOD may designate an extent of time of any length ⟨*periods* of economic prosperity⟩ EPOCH applies to a period begun or set off by some significant or striking quality, change, or series of events ⟨the steam engine marked a new *epoch* in industry⟩ ERA suggests a period of history marked by a new or distinct order of things ⟨the *era* of global communications⟩ AGE is used frequently of a fairly definite period dominated by a prominent figure or feature ⟨the *age* of Samuel Johnson⟩

²**period** *adj* (1905) : of, relating to, or representing a particular historical period ⟨~ furniture⟩ ⟨~ costumes⟩

pe·ri·od·ic \ˌpir-ē-ˈäd-ik\ *adj* (1642) 1 : occurring or recurring at regular intervals 2 a : consisting of or containing a series of repeated stages, processes, or digits : CYCLIC ⟨~ decimals⟩ ⟨a ~ vibration⟩ b : being a function any value of which recurs at regular intervals 3 : expressed in or characterized by periodic sentences

per·iod·ic acid \ˌpər-(ˌ)ī-ˌäd-ik-\ *n* [ISV *per-* + *iodic*] (1903) : any of the strongly oxidizing acids (as H_5IO_6 or HIO_4) that are the highest oxygen acids of iodine

¹**pe·ri·od·i·cal** \ˌpir-ē-ˈäd-i-kəl\ *adj* (1601) 1 : PERIODIC 1 2 a : published with a fixed interval between the issues or numbers b : published in, characteristic of, or connected with a periodical — **pe·ri·od·i·cal·ly** \-k(ə-)lē\ *adv*

²**periodical** *n* (1798) : a periodical publication

periodical cicada *n* (ca. 1890) : SEVENTEEN-YEAR LOCUST

pe·ri·od·ic·i·ty \ˌpir-ē-ə-ˈdis-ət-ē\ *n* (1833) : the quality, state, or fact of being regularly recurrent or having periods

periodic law *n* (1872) : a law in chemistry: the elements when arranged in the order of their atomic numbers show a periodic variation in most of their properties

periodic sentence *n* (ca. 1900) : a usu. complex sentence that has no subordinate or trailing elements following its principal clause (as in "yesterday while I was walking down the street, I saw him")

periodic table *n* (1895) : an arrangement of chemical elements based on the periodic law

pe·ri·od·iza·tion \ˌpir-ē-əd-ə-ˈzā-shən\ *n* (1938) : division (as of history) into periods

peri·odon·tal \ˌper-ē-ō-ˈdänt-ᵊl\ *adj* (1854) 1 : investing or surrounding a tooth 2 : of or affecting periodontal tissues or regions ⟨~ diseases⟩ — **peri·odon·tal·ly** \-ᵊl-ē\ *adv*

periodontal membrane *n* (ca. 1903) : the fibrous connective-tissue layer covering the cementum of a tooth and holding it in place in the jawbone

peri·odon·tics \-ˈdänt-iks\ *n pl but sing or pl in constr* [NL *periodontium*, fr. *peri-* + Gk *odont-*, *odous*, *odōn* tooth — more at TOOTH] (ca. 1944) : a branch of dentistry that deals with diseases of the supporting and investing structures of the teeth including the gums, cementum, periodontal membranes, and alveolar bone — **peri·odon·tist** \-ˈdänt-əst\ *n*

peri·odon·tol·o·gy \-ˌdän-ˈtäl-ə-jē\ *n* (1914) : PERIODONTICS

period piece *n* (1940) : a piece (as of fiction, art, furniture, or music) whose special value lies in its evocation of an historical period

peri·onych·i·um \ˌper-ē-ō-ˈnik-ē-əm\ *n, pl* **-ia** \-ē-ə\ [NL, fr. *peri-* + Gk *onych-*, *onyx* nail — more at NAIL] (ca. 1903) : the tissue bordering the root and sides of a fingernail or toenail

periost- *or* **perioste-** *or* **periosteo-** *comb form* [NL *periosteum*] : periosteum ⟨*periosteo*myelitis⟩ ⟨*periosteo*ma⟩ ⟨*perios*titis⟩

peri·os·te·al \ˌper-ē-ˈäs-tē-əl\ *adj* (1830) 1 : situated around or produced external to bone 2 : of, relating to, or involving the periosteum

peri·os·te·um \-tē-əm\ *n, pl* **-tea** \-tē-ə\ [NL, fr. LL *periosteon*, fr. Gk, neut. of *periosteos* around the bone, fr. *peri-* + *osteon* bone — more at OSSEOUS] (1597) : the membrane of connective tissue that closely invests all bones except at the articular surfaces

peri·os·ti·tis \-ˌäs-ˈtīt-əs\ *n* [NL] (1843) : inflammation of the periosteum

¹**peri·pa·tet·ic** \ˌper-ə-pə-ˈtet-ik\ *n* (15c) 1 *cap* : a follower of Aristotle or adherent of Aristotelianism 2 : PEDESTRIAN, ITINERANT 3 *pl* : movement or journeys hither and thither

²**peripatetic** *adj* [MF & L; MF *peripatetique*, fr. L *peripateticus*, fr. Gk *peripatētikos*, fr. *peripatein* to walk up and down, discourse while pacing (as did Aristotle), fr. *peri-* + *patein* to tread; akin to Skt *patha* path — more at FIND] (1566) 1 *cap* : ARISTOTELIAN 2 a : of, relating to, or given to walking b : moving or traveling from place to place : ITINERANT — **peri·pa·tet·i·cal·ly** \-i-k(ə-)lē\ *adv* — **Peri·pa·tet·i·cism** \-ˈtet-ə-ˌsiz-əm\ *n*

pe·rip·a·tus \pə-ˈrip-ət-əs\ *n* [NL, genus name, fr. Gk *peripatos* act of walking about, fr. *peri-* + *patein* to tread] (ca. 1931) : any of a class (Onychophora) of primitive tropical arthropods that in some respects are intermediate between annelid worms and typical arthropods

peri·pe·teia \ˌper-ə-pə-ˈtē-(y)ə, -ˈtī-ə\ *n* [Gk, fr. *peripiptein* to fall around, change suddenly, fr. *peri-* + *piptein* to fall — more at FEATHER] (1591) : a sudden or unexpected reversal of circumstances or situation esp. in a literary work

pe·rip·e·ty \pə-ˈrip-ət-ē\ *n, pl* **-ties** (1753) : PERIPETEIA

¹**pe·riph·er·al** \pə-ˈrif-(ə-)rəl\ *adj* (1808) 1 : of, relating to, involving, or forming a periphery or surface part 2 : of, relating to, or being part of the peripheral nervous system ⟨~ nerves⟩ 3 : of, relating to, or being the outer part of the field of vision ⟨good ~ vision⟩ 4 : AUXILIARY, SUPPLEMENTARY ⟨~ equipment⟩ — **pe·riph·er·al·ly** \-ē\ *adv*

²**peripheral** *n* (1966) : a device connected to a computer to provide communication (as input and output) or auxiliary functions (as additional storage)

peripheral nervous system *n* (1935) : the part of the nervous system that is outside the central nervous system and comprises the cranial nerves excepting the optic nerve, the spinal nerves, and the autonomic nervous system

pe·riph·ery \pə-ˈrif-(ə-)rē\ *n, pl* **-er·ies** [MF *peripherie*, fr. LL *peripheria*, fr. Gk *periphereia*, fr. *peripherein* to carry around, fr. *peri-* + *pherein* to carry — more at BEAR] (1571) 1 : the perimeter of a circle or other closed curve; *also* : the perimeter of a polygon 2 : the external boundary or surface of a body 3 a : the outward bounds of something as distinguished from its internal regions or center : CONFINES b : an area lying beyond the strict limits of a thing

pe·riph·ra·sis \pə-ˈrif-rə-səs\ *n, pl* **-ra·ses** \-ˌsēz\ [L, fr. Gk, fr. *periphrazein* to express periphrastically, fr. *peri-* + *phrazein* to point out] (ca. 1533) 1 : use of a longer phrasing in place of a possible shorter form of expression 2 : an instance of periphrasis

peri·phras·tic \ˌper-ə-ˈfras-tik\ *adj* (1805) 1 : of, relating to, or characterized by periphrasis 2 : formed by the use of function words or auxiliaries instead of by inflection ⟨*more fair* is a ~ comparative⟩ — **peri·phras·ti·cal·ly** \-ti-k(ə-)lē\ *adv*

pe·riph·y·ton \pə-ˈrif-ə-ˌtän\ *n* [NL, fr. Gk *periphytos* (verbal of *periphyein* to grow around, fr. *peri-* + *phyein* to bring forth, grow) + *-on* (as in *plankton*) — more at BE] (1945) : organisms (as some algae) that live attached to underwater surfaces — **peri·phyt·ic** \ˌper-ə-ˈfit-ik\ *adj*

peri·plast \ˈper-ə-ˌplast\ *n* (1853) : PLASMA MEMBRANE; *also* : a proteinaceous subcellular layer below the plasma membrane esp. of a euglena

peri·proct \-ˌpräkt\ *n* [ISV *peri-* + Gk *prōktos* anus] (1877) : the well-defined area surrounding the anus of various invertebrates (as a sea urchin)

pe·rique \pə-ˈrēk\ *n* [LaF *périque*] (1882) : an aromatic fermented Louisiana tobacco used in smoking mixtures

peri·sarc \ˈper-ə-ˌsärk\ *n* [ISV *peri-* + Gk *sark-*, *sarx* flesh — more at SARCASM] (ca. 1871) : the outer usu. chitinous integument of a hydroid

peri·scope \-ˌskōp\ *n* [ISV] (1879) : a tubular optical instrument containing lenses and mirrors by which an observer obtains an otherwise obstructed field of view

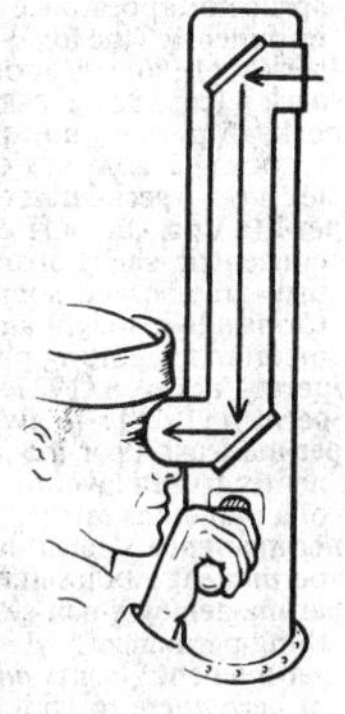
periscope

peri·scop·ic \ˌper-ə-ˈskäp-ik\ *adj* (1804) 1 : providing a view all around or on all sides ⟨~ lens⟩ 2 : of or relating to a periscope

per·ish \ˈper-ish\ *vb* [ME *perisshen*, fr. OF *periss-*, stem of *perir*, fr. L *perire*, fr. *per-* to destruction + *ire* to go — more at PER-, ISSUE] *vi* (13c) 1 : to become destroyed or ruined : DIE ⟨recollection of a past already long since ~*ed* —Philip Sherrard⟩ ⟨guard against your mistakes or your attempts (~ the thought) to cheat —C. B. Davis⟩ 2 *chiefly Brit* : DETERIORATE, SPOIL ~ *vt* 1 *chiefly Brit* : to cause to die : DESTROY 2 : WEAKEN, BENUMB

per·ish·able \ˈper-ish-ə-bəl\ *adj* (ca. 1611) : liable to perish : liable to spoil or decay ⟨such ~ products as fruit, vegetables, butter, and eggs⟩ — **per·ish·abil·i·ty** \ˌper-ish-ə-ˈbil-ət-ē\ *n* — **perishable** *n*

pe·ris·so·dac·tyl \pə-ˈris-ə-ˌdak-tᵊl\ *n* [NL *Perissodactyla*, fr. Gk *perissos* excessive, odd in number + *daktylos* finger, toe] (1849) : any of an order (Perissodactyla) of nonruminant ungulate mammals (as a horse, a tapir, or a rhinoceros) that usu. have an odd number of toes, molar teeth with transverse ridges on the grinding surface, and the posterior premolars resembling true molars — **perissodactyl** *adj*

peri·stal·sis \ˌper-ə-ˈstȯl-səs, -ˈstäl-, -ˈstal-\ *n, pl* **-stal·ses** \-ˌsēz\ [NL, fr. Gk *peristaltikos* peristaltic] (1859) : successive waves of involuntary contraction passing along the walls of the intestine or other hollow muscular structure and forcing the contents onward

peri·stal·tic \-tik\ *adj* [Gk *peristaltikos*, fr. *peristellein* to wrap around, fr. *peri-* + *stellein* to place — more at STALL] (1655) 1 : of, relating to, resulting from, or being peristalsis ⟨~ contractions force the food through the alimentary canal⟩ 2 : having an action suggestive of peristalsis — **peri·stal·ti·cal·ly** \-ti-k(ə-)lē\ *adv*

peristaltic pump *n* (1962) : a pump in which fluid is forced along by waves of contraction produced mechanically on flexible tubing

peri·stome \ˈper-ə-ˌstōm\ *n* [NL *peristoma*, fr. *peri-* + Gk *stoma* mouth — more at STOMACH] (ca. 1796) 1 : the fringe of teeth surrounding the orifice of a moss capsule 2 : the region around the mouth in various invertebrates — **peri·sto·mi·al** \ˌper-ə-ˈstō-mē-əl\ *adj*

peri·style \ˈper-ə-ˌstīl\ *n* [F *péristyle*, fr. L *peristylum*, fr. Gk *peristylon*, fr. neut. of *peristylos* surrounded by a colonnade, fr. *peri-* + *stylos* pillar — more at STEER] (1612) 1 : a colonnade surrounding a building or court 2 : an open space enclosed by a colonnade

peri·the·ci·um \ˌper-ə-ˈthē-s(h)ē-əm\ *n, pl* **-cia** \-s(h)ē-ə\ [NL, fr. *peri-* + Gk *thēkion*, dim. of *thēkē* case — more at TICK] (ca. 1832) : a spherical, cylindrical, or flask-shaped hollow fruiting body in various ascomycetous fungi that contains the asci and usu. opens by a terminal pore — **peri·the·cial** \-ˈthē-sh(ē-)əl, -sē-əl\ *adj*

periton- *or* **peritone-** *or* **peritoneo-** *comb form* [LL *peritoneum*] : peritoneum ⟨*periton*itis⟩

peri·to·ne·um \ˌper-ət-ᵊn-ˈē-əm\ *n, pl* **-ne·ums** \-ˈē-əmz\ *or* **-nea** \-ˈē-ə\ [LL, fr. Gk *peritonaion*, neut. of *peritonaios* stretched around, fr. *peri-* + *teinein* to stretch — more at THIN] (ca. 1540) : the smooth transparent serous membrane that lines the cavity of the abdomen of a mammal and is folded inward over the abdominal and pelvic viscera — **peri·to·ne·al** \-ˈē-əl\ *adj* — **peri·to·ne·al·ly** \-ə-lē\ *adv*

peri·to·ni·tis \ˌper-ət-ᵊn-ˈīt-əs\ *n* [NL] (1776) : inflammation of the peritoneum

pe·rit·ri·chous \pə-ˈri-tri-kəs\ *adj* [*peri-* + Gk *trich-*, *thrix* hair — more at TRICH-] (1877) 1 : having flagella uniformly distributed over the body ⟨~ bacteria⟩ **2 :** having a spiral line of modified cilia around the oral disk ⟨~ protozoa⟩ — **pe·rit·ri·chous·ly** *adv*

peri·wig \ˈper-i-ˌwig\ *n* [modif. of MF *perruque*] (1529) : PERUKE — **peri·wigged** \-ˌwigd\ *adj*

[1]**per·i·win·kle** \ˈper-i-ˌwiŋ-kəl\ *n* [ME *perwinke*, fr. OE *perwince*, fr. L *pervinca*, prob. fr. *per* through + *-vinca* (akin to L *vincire* to bind) — more at VETCH] (bef. 12c) : any of several trailing or woody evergreen herbs (genus *Vinca*) of the dogbane family: as **a :** a European creeper (*V. minor*) widely cultivated as a ground cover and for its blue or white flowers — called also *myrtle* **b :** a commonly cultivated subshrub (*V. rosea*) of the Old World tropics that is the source of several antineoplastic drugs — called also *Madagascar periwinkle*

[2]**periwinkle** *n* [(assumed) ME, alter. of OE *pinewincle*, fr. L *pina*, a kind of mussel (fr. Gk) + OE *-wincle* (akin to Dan *vincle* snail shell); akin to OE *wincian* to wink] (ca. 1530) : any of various gastropod mollusks: as **a :** any of a genus (*Littorina*) of edible littoral marine snails; *also* : any of various similar or related marine snails (as various American members of *Thais*) **b :** any of several No. American freshwater snails

per·jure \ˈpər-jər\ *vt* **per·jured; per·jur·ing** \ˈpərj-(ə-)riŋ\ [MF *perjurer*, fr. L *perjurare*, fr. *per-* to destruction, to the bad + *jurare* to swear — more at PER-, JURY] (1555) **1** *obs* : to cause to commit perjury **2 :** to make a perjurer of (oneself)

per·jur·er \ˈpər-jər-ər\ *n* (1553) : a person guilty of perjury

per·ju·ri·ous \(ˌ)pər-ˈju̇r-ē-əs\ *adj* (1602) : marked by perjury ⟨~ testimony⟩ — **per·ju·ri·ous·ly** *adv*

per·ju·ry \ˈpərj-(ə-)rē\ *n* (14c) : the voluntary violation of an oath or vow either by swearing to what is untrue or by omission to do what has been promised under oath : false swearing

[1]**perk** \ˈpərk\ *vb* [ME *perken*] *vi* (14c) **1 a :** to thrust up the head, stretch out the neck, or carry the body in a bold or insolent manner **b :** to stick up or out jauntily **2 :** to gain in vigor or cheerfulness esp. after a period of weakness or depression — usu. used with *up* ⟨he ~*ed* up noticeably when the letter arrived⟩ ~ *vt* **1 :** to make smart or spruce in appearance : FRESHEN, IMPROVE **2 :** to thrust up quickly or impudently ⟨the fox ~*ed* its ears⟩

[2]**perk** *vi* (1656) : PERCOLATE

[3]**perk** *n* (ca. 1824) : PERQUISITE — usu. used in pl.

perky \ˈpər-kē\ *adj* **perk·i·er; -est** (1855) **1 :** briskly self-assured : COCKY **2 :** JAUNTY ⟨a ~ . . . waltz —*New Yorker*⟩ — **perk·i·ly** \-kə-lē\ *adv* — **perk·i·ness** \-kē-nəs\ *n*

per·lite \ˈpər-ˌlīt\ *n* [F, fr. *perle* pearl] (1833) : volcanic glass that has a concentric shelly structure, appears as if composed of concretions, is usu. grayish and sometimes spherulitic, and when expanded by heat forms a lightweight aggregate used esp. in concrete and plaster and as a medium for potting plants — **per·lit·ic** \ˌpər-ˈlit-ik\ *adj*

[1]**perm** \ˈpərm\ *n* (1927) : PERMANENT

[2]**perm** *vt* (1928) : to give (hair) a permanent wave

per·ma·frost \ˈpər-mə-ˌfrȯst\ *n* [*permanent* + *frost*] (1943) : a permanently frozen layer at variable depth below the surface in frigid regions of a planet (as earth)

per·ma·nence \ˈpərm(-ə)-nən(t)s\ *n* (15c) : the quality or state of being permanent : DURABILITY

per·ma·nen·cy \-nən-sē\ *n, pl* **-cies** (1555) **1 :** PERMANENCE **2 :** something permanent

[1]**per·ma·nent** \-nənt\ *adj* [ME, fr. MF, fr. L *permanent-*, *permanens*, prp. of *permanēre* to endure, fr. *per-* throughout + *manēre* to remain — more at PER-, MANSION] (15c) : continuing or enduring without fundamental or marked change : STABLE ***syn*** see LASTING — **per·ma·nent·ly** *adv* — **per·ma·nent·ness** *n*

[2]**permanent** *n* (1925) : a long-lasting hair wave or straightening produced by mechanical and chemical means — called also *permanent wave*

permanent magnet *n* (1828) : a magnet that retains its magnetism after removal of the magnetizing force

permanent press *n* (1964) **1 :** the process of treating a fabric with a chemical (as a resin) and heat for setting the shape and for aiding wrinkle resistance **2 :** material treated by permanent press **3 :** the condition of material treated by permanent press — **permanent–press** *adj*

permanent tissue *n* (ca. 1928) : tissue that has completed its growth and differentiation and is generally incapable of meristematic activity

permanent tooth *n* (1836) : any of the second set of teeth of a mammal that follow the milk teeth, typically persist into old age, and in man are 32 in number

per·man·ga·nate \(ˌ)pər-ˈmaŋ-gə-ˌnāt\ *n* (1841) : a dark purple crystalline compound that is a salt of permanganic acid

per·man·gan·ic acid \ˌpər-(ˌ)man-ˌgan-ik-, -(ˌ)maŋ-\ *n* [ISV] (ca. 1836) : an unstable strong acid $HMnO_4$ known chiefly in purple-colored strongly oxidizing aqueous solutions

per·me·abil·i·ty \ˌpər-mē-ə-ˈbil-ət-ē\ *n* (1759) **1 :** the quality or state of being permeable **2 :** the property of a magnetizable substance that determines the degree in which it modifies the magnetic flux in the region occupied by it in a magnetic field

per·me·able \ˈpər-mē-ə-bəl\ *adj* (15c) : capable of being permeated : PENETRABLE; *esp* : having pores or openings that permit liquids or gases to pass through ⟨a ~ membrane⟩ ⟨~ limestone⟩

per·me·ance \-ən(t)s\ *n* (1845) **1 :** PERMEATION **2 :** the reciprocal of magnetic reluctance

per·me·ase \-ˌās, -ˌāz\ *n* [ISV *perme-* (fr. *permeate*) + *-ase*] (1957) : a substance that catalyzes the transport of another substance across a cell membrane

per·me·ate \ˈpər-mē-ˌāt\ *vb* **-at·ed; -at·ing** [L *permeatus*, pp. of *permeare*, fr. *per-* through + *meare* to go, pass; akin to MW *mynet* to go, OSlav *minǫti* to pass] *vi* (1656) : to diffuse through or penetrate something ~ *vt* **1 :** to spread or diffuse through ⟨a room *permeated* with tobacco smoke⟩ **2 :** to pass through the pores or interstices of — **per·me·ative** \-ˌāt-iv\ *adj*

per·me·ation \ˌpər-mē-ˈā-shən\ *n* (ca. 1623) **1 :** the quality or state of being permeated **2 :** the action or process of permeating

per men·sem \(ˌ)pər-ˈmen(t)-səm\ *adv* [ML] (1647) : by the month

Perm·ian \ˈpər-mē-ən, ˈper-\ *adj* [*Perm*, region in eastern Russia] (1841) : of, relating to, or being the last period of the Paleozoic era or the corresponding system of rocks — **Permian** *n*

per mill \(ˌ)pər-ˈmil\ *adv* [*per* + L *mille* thousand] (1902) : per thousand — **per·mil·lage** \(ˌ)pər-ˈmil-ij\ *n*

per·mis·si·ble \pər-ˈmis-ə-bəl\ *adj* [ME, fr. ML *permissibilis*, fr. L *permissus*, pp.] (15c) : that may be permitted : ALLOWABLE — **per·mis·si·bil·i·ty** \-ˌmis-ə-ˈbil-ət-ē\ *n* — **per·mis·si·ble·ness** \-ˈmis-ə-bəl-nəs\ *n* — **per·mis·si·bly** \-blē\ *adv*

per·mis·sion \pər-ˈmish-ən\ *n* [ME, fr. MF, fr. L *permission-*, *permissio*, fr. *permissus*, pp. of *permittere*] (15c) **1 :** the act of permitting **2 :** formal consent : AUTHORIZATION

per·mis·sive \pər-ˈmis-iv\ *adj* [ME *permyssyf*, fr. MF *permissif*, fr. L *permissus*, pp.] (15c) **1** *archaic* : granted on sufferance : TOLERATED **2 :** granting or tending to grant permission : TOLERANT **3 :** allowing discretion : OPTIONAL ⟨reduced the ~ retirement age from 65 to 62⟩ — **per·mis·sive·ly** *adv* — **per·mis·sive·ness** *n*

[1]**per·mit** \pər-ˈmit\ *vb* **per·mit·ted; per·mit·ting** [ME *permitten*, fr. L *permittere* to let through, permit, fr. *per-* through + *mittere* to let go, send] *vt* (15c) **1 :** to consent to expressly or formally ⟨~ access to records⟩ **2 :** to give leave : AUTHORIZE **3 :** to make possible ~ *vi* : to give an opportunity : ALLOW ⟨if time ~*s*⟩ ***syn*** see LET — **per·mit·tee** \ˌpər-ˌmit-ˈē, ˌpər-mit-ˈē\ *n* — **per·mit·ter** *n*

[2]**per·mit** \ˈpər-ˌmit, pər-ˈ\ *n* (1682) **1 :** a written warrant or license granted by one having authority ⟨a gun ~⟩ **2 :** PERMISSION

per·mit·tiv·i·ty \ˌpər-ˌmi-ˈtiv-ət-ē, -mə-\ *n* [[1]*permit* + *-ivity* (as in *selectivity*)] (1887) : the ability of a dielectric to store electrical potential energy under the influence of an electric field measured by the ratio of the capacitance of a condenser with the material as dielectric to its capacitance with vacuum as dielectric

per·mu·ta·tion \ˌpər-myu̇-ˈtā-shən\ *n* [ME *permutacioun* exchange, transformation, fr. MF *permutation*, fr. L *permutation-*, *permutatio*, fr. *permutatus*, pp. of *permutare*] (14c) **1 :** often major or fundamental change (as in character or condition) based primarily on rearrangement of existent elements ⟨land-owners and peasants . . . in the ~*s* of their tortured interdependence —P. E. Mosley⟩ **2 a :** the act or process of changing the lineal order of an ordered set of objects **b :** an ordered arrangement of a set of objects — **per·mu·ta·tion·al** \-shnəl, -shən-ᵊl\ *adj*

permutation group *n* (1904) : a group whose elements are permutations and in which the product of two permutations is a permutation whose effect is the same as the successive application of the first two

per·mute \pər-ˈmyüt\ *vt* **per·mut·ed; per·mut·ing** [ME *permuten* to exchange, fr. MF or L; MF *permuter*, fr. L *permutare*, fr. *per-* + *mutare* to change — more at MISS] (1878) : to change the order or arrangement of; *esp* : to arrange in all possible ways — **per·mut·able** \-ə-bəl\ *adj*

per·ni·cious \pər-ˈnish-əs\ *adj* [MF *pernicieus*, fr. L *perniciosus*, fr. *pernicies* destruction, fr. *per-* + *nec-*, *nex* violent death — more at NOXIOUS] (1521) **1 :** highly injurious or destructive : DEADLY **2** *archaic* : WICKED — **per·ni·cious·ly** *adv* — **per·ni·cious·ness** *n*

syn PERNICIOUS, BANEFUL, NOXIOUS, DELETERIOUS, DETRIMENTAL mean exceedingly harmful. PERNICIOUS and BANEFUL both imply causing irreparable or deadly injury, PERNICIOUS through evil or insidious corrupting or undermining, BANEFUL through poisoning or destroying; NOXIOUS applies to what is both offensive and injurious to the health of a body or mind; DELETERIOUS applies to what has an often unsuspected harmful effect; DETRIMENTAL implies obvious harmfulness to something specified.

pernicious anemia *n* (1874) : a severe anemia marked by a progressive decrease in number and increase in size and hemoglobin content of the red blood cells and by pallor, weakness, and gastrointestinal and nervous disturbances and associated with reduced ability to absorb vitamin B_{12} due to the absence of intrinsic factor

per·nick·e·ty \pər-ˈnik-ət-ē\ *adj* [perh. alter. of *particular*] (ca. 1808) : PERSNICKETY

Per·nod \per-ˈnō, ˌpər-\ *trademark* — used for an aromatic French liqueur

pe·ro·ne·al \ˌper-ō-ˈnē-əl, pə-ˈrō-nē-\ *adj* [NL *peroneus*, fr. *perone* fibula, fr. Gk *peronē*, lit., pin; akin to L *per* through — more at FOR] (1831) : of, relating to, or located near the fibula

per·oral \(ˌ)pər-ˈōr-əl, pe(ə)r-, -ˈȯr-, -ˈär-\ *adj* [ISV, fr. L *per* through + *or-*, *os* mouth — more at ORAL] (1908) : occurring through or by way of the mouth — **per·oral·ly** \-ə-lē\ *adv*

per·orate \ˈper-ər-ˌāt *also* ˈpər-\ *vi* **-orat·ed; -orat·ing** [L *peroratus*, pp. of *perorare* to declaim at length, wind up an oration, fr. *per-* through + *orare* to speak — more at PER-, ORATION] (1603) **1 :** to deliver a long or grandiloquent oration **2 :** to make a peroration

per·ora·tion \ˌper-ər-ˈā-shən, ˌpər-\ *n* [ME *peroracyon*, fr. L *peroration-*, *peroratio*, fr. *peroratus*, pp.] (15c) **1 :** the concluding part of a discourse and esp. an oration **2 :** a highly rhetorical speech — **per·ora·tion·al** \ˌper-ər-ˈā-shnəl, ˌpər-, -shən-ᵊl\ *adj*

per·ox·i·dase \pə-ˈräk-sə-ˌdās, -ˌdāz\ *n* (ca. 1900) : an enzyme that catalyzes the oxidation of various substances by peroxides

[1]**per·ox·ide** \pə-ˈräk-ˌsīd\ *n* [ISV] (ca. 1804) : an oxide containing a high proportion of oxygen; *esp* : a compound (as hydrogen peroxide) in which oxygen is visualized as joined to oxygen — **per·ox·id·ic** \-ˌräk-ˈsid-ik\ *adj*

[2]**peroxide** *vt* **-id·ed; -id·ing** (1906) : to treat with a peroxide; *esp* : to bleach (hair) with hydrogen peroxide

per·oxi·some \pə-ˈräk-sə-ˌsōm\ *n* [*peroxide* + [3]*-some*] (1965) : a cytoplasmic cell organelle containing enzymes for the production and decomposition of hydrogen peroxide — **per·oxi·som·al** \-ˌräk-sə-ˈsō-məl\ *adj*

per·oxy- \pə-ˈräk-si\ *comb form* [ISV *per-* + *oxy-*] : containing the bivalent group O–O

per·pend \(ˌ)pər-ˈpend\ *vb* [L *perpendere*, fr. *per-* thoroughly + *pendere* to weigh — more at PER-, PENDANT] *vt* (1527) : to reflect on carefully : PONDER ~ *vi* : to be attentive : REFLECT

[1]**per·pen·dic·u·lar** \ˌpər-pən-ˈdik-yə-lər\ *adj* [ME *perpendiculer*, fr. MF, fr. L *perpendicularis*, fr. *perpendiculum* plumb line, fr. *per-* + *pendēre* to hang — more at PENDANT] (14c) **1 a :** standing at right angles to the plane of the horizon : exactly upright **b :** being at right angles to a given line or plane **2 :** extremely steep : PRECIPITOUS **3 :** of or relating to a medieval English Gothic style of architecture in which vertical lines predominate **4 :** relating to, uniting, or consisting of individuals of dissimilar type or on different levels ***syn*** see VERTICAL — **per·pen·dic·u·lar·i·ty** \-ˌdik-yə-ˈlar-ət-ē\ *n* — **per·pen·dic·u·lar·ly** \-ˈdik-yə-lər-lē\ *adv*

²**perpendicular** *n* (1571) : a line at right angles to a line or plane (as of the horizon)

per·pe·trate \'pər-pə-ˌtrāt\ *vt* **-trat·ed; -trat·ing** [L *perpetratus,* pp. of *perpetrare,* fr. *per-* through + *patrare* to accomplish] (1542) : to bring about or carry out (as a crime) : COMMIT — **per·pe·tra·tion** \ˌpər-pə-'trā-shən\ *n* — **per·pe·tra·tor** \'pər-pə-ˌtrāt-ər\ *n*

per·pet·u·al \pər-'pech-(ə-)wəl, -'pech-əl\ *adj* [ME *perpetuel,* fr. MF, fr. L *perpetuus,* fr. *per-* through + *petere* to go to — more at FEATHER] (14c) **1 a** : continuing forever : EVERLASTING **b** (1) : valid for all time (2) : holding (as an office) for life or for an unlimited time **2** : occurring continually : indefinitely long-continued **3** : blooming continuously throughout the season ***syn*** see CONTINUAL — **per·pet·u·al·ly** \-ē\ *adv*

perpetual calendar *n* (1895) : a table for finding the day of the week for any one of a wide range of dates

perpetual check *n* (ca. 1909) : an endless succession of checks to which an opponent's king may be subjected to force a draw in chess

per·pet·u·ate \pər-'pech-ə-ˌwāt\ *vt* **-at·ed; -at·ing** [L *perpetuatus,* pp. of *perpetuare,* fr. *perpetuus*] (1530) : to make perpetual or cause to last indefinitely ⟨~ the species⟩ — **per·pet·u·a·tion** \-ˌpech-ə-'wā-shən\ *n* — **per·pet·u·a·tor** \-'pech-ə-ˌwāt-ər\ *n*

per·pe·tu·ity \ˌpər-pə-'t(y)ü-ət-ē\ *n, pl* **-ities** [ME *perpetuite,* fr. MF *perpetuité,* fr. L *perpetuitat-, perpetuitas,* fr. *perpetuus*] (15c) **1** : ETERNITY 2 **2** : the quality or state of being perpetual ⟨bequeathed to them in ~⟩ **3 a** : the condition of an estate limited so that it will not take effect or vest within the period fixed by law **b** : an estate so limited **4** : an annuity payable forever

per·phe·na·zine \(ˌ)pər-'fē-nə-ˌzēn, -'fen-ə-\ *n* [blend of *piperazine* and *phen-*] (1957) : a tranquilizing drug $C_{21}H_{26}ClN_3OS$ that is used to control tension, anxiety, and agitation esp. in psychotic conditions

per·plex \pər-'pleks\ *vt* [obs. *perplex,* adj., involved, perplexed, fr. L *perplexus,* fr. *per-* thoroughly + *plexus* involved, fr. pp. of *plectere* to braid, twine — more at PER-, PLY] (1595) **1** : to make unable to grasp something clearly or to think logically and decisively about something ⟨her attitude ~*es* me⟩ ⟨a ~*ing* problem⟩ **2** : to make intricate or involved : COMPLICATE ***syn*** see PUZZLE

per·plexed \-'plekst\ *adj* (15c) **1** : filled with uncertainty : PUZZLED **2** : full of difficulty — **per·plexed·ly** \-'plek-səd-lē, -'pleks-tlē\ *adv*

per·plex·i·ty \pər-'plek-sət-ē\ *n, pl* **-ties** [ME *perplexite,* fr. MF *perplexité,* fr. LL *perplexitat-, perplexitas,* fr. L *perplexus*] (14c) **1** : the state of being perplexed : BEWILDERMENT **2** : something that perplexes **3** : ENTANGLEMENT

per·qui·site \'pər-kwə-zət\ *n* [ME, property acquired by other means than inheritance, fr. ML *perquisitum,* fr. neut. of *perquisitus,* pp. of *perquirere* to purchase, acquire, fr. L, to search for thoroughly, fr. *per-* thoroughly + *quaerere* to seek] (1552) **1** : a privilege, gain, or profit incidental to regular salary or wages; *esp* : one expected or promised **2** : GRATUITY, TIP **3** : something held or claimed as an exclusive right or possession ⟨concepts . . . not the ~*s* of any particular groups — Gilbert Ryle⟩

per·ron \'per-ən, pe-rōⁿ\ *n* [F, fr. OF, aug. of *perre, pierre* rock, stone, fr. L *petra,* fr. Gk] (1723) : an outdoor stairway leading up to a building entrance; *also* : a platform at its top

per·ry \'per-ē\ *n* [ME *peirrie,* fr. MF *peré,* fr. (assumed) VL *piratum,* fr. L *pirum* pear] (14c) : fermented pear juice often made sparkling

perse \'pərs\ *adj* [ME *pers,* fr. MF, fr. ML *persus*] (14c) : of a dark grayish blue resembling indigo

per se \(ˌ)pər-'sā *also* pe(ə)r-'sā *or* (ˌ)pər-'sē\ *adv* [L] (14c) : by, of, or in itself or oneself or themselves : as such : INTRINSICALLY

per second per second *adv* (1922) : per second every second — used of acceleration

per·se·cute \'pər-si-ˌkyüt\ *vt* **-cut·ed; -cut·ing** [ME *persecuten,* fr. MF *persecuter,* back-formation fr. *persecuteur* persecutor, fr. LL *persecutor,* fr. *persecutus,* pp. of *persequi* to persecute, fr. L, to pursue, fr. *per-* through + *sequi* to follow — more at SUE] (15c) **1** : to harass in a manner designed to injure, grieve, or afflict; *specif* : to cause to suffer because of belief **2** : to annoy with persistent or urgent approaches (as attacks, pleas, or importunities) : PESTER ***syn*** see WRONG — **per·se·cu·tee** \ˌpər-si-ˌkyü-'tē\ *n* — **per·se·cu·tive** \'pər-si-ˌkyüt-iv\ *adj* — **per·se·cu·tor** \-ˌkyüt-ər\ *n* — **per·se·cu·to·ry** \-kyü-ˌtōr-ē, -ˌtȯr-; -ˌkyüt-ə-rē\ *adj*

per·se·cu·tion \ˌpər-si-'kyü-shən\ *n* (14c) **1** : the act or practice of persecuting esp. those who differ in origin, religion, or social outlook **2** : the condition of being persecuted, harassed, or annoyed

Per·se·id \'pər-sē-əd\ *n* [L *Perseus;* fr. their appearing to radiate from a point in Perseus] (1876) : any of a group of meteors that appear annually about August 11

Per·seph·o·ne \pər-'sef-ə-nē\ *n* [L, fr. Gk *Persephonē*] : a daughter of Zeus and Demeter abducted by Pluto to reign with him over the underworld

Per·seus \'pər-ˌsüs, -sē-əs\ *n* [L, fr. Gk] **1** : a son of Zeus and Danaë and slayer of Medusa **2** [L (gen. *Persei*), fr. Gk] : a northern constellation between Taurus and Cassiopeia

per·se·ver·ance \ˌpər-sə-'vir-ən(t)s\ *n* (14c) : the action or condition or an instance of persevering : STEADFASTNESS

per·sev·er·a·tion \pər-ˌsev-ə-'rā-shən\ *n* [L *perseveration-, perseveratio,* fr. *perseveratus,* pp. of *perseverare*] (1612) : continuation of something (as repetition of a word) usu. to an exceptional degree or beyond a desired point — **per·sev·er·ate** \-'sev-ə-ˌrāt\ *vi*

per·se·vere \ˌpər-sə-'vi(ə)r\ *vi* **-vered; -ver·ing** [ME *perseveren,* fr. MF *perseverer,* fr. L *perseverare,* fr. *per-* through + *severus* severe] (14c) : to persist in a state, enterprise, or undertaking in spite of counter influences, opposition, or discouragement — **per·se·ver·ing·ly** *adv*

Per·sian \'pər-zhən, *esp Brit* -shən\ *n* (14c) **1** : one of the people of Persia: as **a** : one of the ancient Iranian Caucasians who under Cyrus and his successors became the dominant Asian race **b** : a member of one of the peoples forming the modern Iranian nationality **2 a** : any of several Iranian languages dominant in Persia at different periods **b** : the modern language of Iran and western Afghanistan used also in Pakistan and by Indian Muslims as a literary language — see INDO-EUROPEAN LANGUAGES table **3** : a thin soft silk formerly used esp. for linings **4** : PERSIAN CAT — **Persian** *adj*

Persian cat *n* (1824) : a stocky round-headed domestic cat that has a long silky coat and thick ruff — see CAT illustration

Persian lamb *n* (1889) **1** : a pelt that is obtained from karakul lambs older than those yielding broadtail and that is characterized by very silky tightly curled fur **2** : the young of the karakul sheep that furnishes skins used in furriery

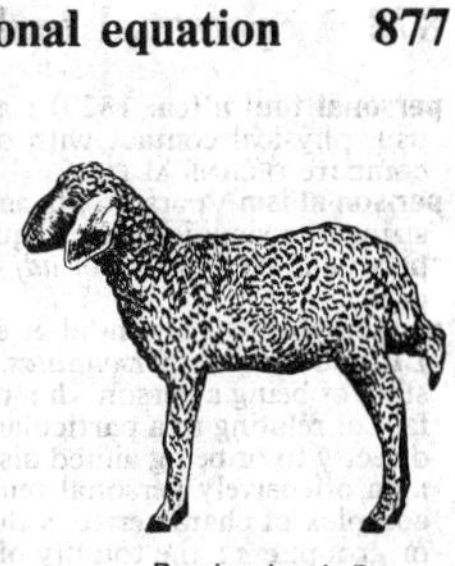

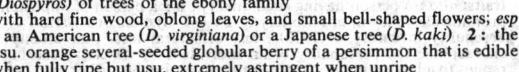

Persian lamb 2

per·si·flage \'pər-si-ˌfläzh, 'per-\ *n* [F, fr. *persifler* to banter, fr. *per-* thoroughly + *siffler* to whistle, hiss, boo, fr. L *sibilare,* of imit. origin] (1757) : frivolous bantering talk : light raillery

per·sim·mon \pər-'sim-ən\ *n* [of Algonquian origin; akin to Cree *pasiminan* dried fruit] (1612) **1** : any of a genus (*Diospyros*) of trees of the ebony family with hard fine wood, oblong leaves, and small bell-shaped flowers; *esp* : an American tree (*D. virginiana*) or a Japanese tree (*D. kaki*) **2** : the usu. orange several-seeded globular berry of a persimmon that is edible when fully ripe but usu. extremely astringent when unripe

per·sist \pər-'sist, -'zist\ *vi* [MF *persister,* fr. L *persistere,* fr. *per-* + *sistere* to take a stand, stand firm; akin to L *stare* to stand — more at STAND] (1538) **1** : to go on resolutely or stubbornly in spite of opposition, importunity, or warning **2** *obs* : to remain unchanged or fixed in a specified character, condition, or position **3** : to be insistent in the repetition or pressing of an utterance (as a question or an opinion) **4** : to continue to exist esp. past a usual, expected, or normal time ***syn*** see CONTINUE — **per·sist·er** *n*

per·sis·tence \pər-'sis-tən(t)s, -'zis-\ *n* (1546) **1** : the action or fact of persisting **2** : the quality or state of being persistent; *esp* : PERSEVERANCE

per·sis·ten·cy \-tən-sē\ *n* (1597) : PERSISTENCE 2

per·sis·tent \-tənt\ *adj* [L *persistent-, persistens,* prp. of *persistere*] (1826) **1** : existing for a long or longer than usual time or continuously: as **a** : retained beyond the usual period ⟨a ~ leaf⟩ **b** : continuing without change in function or structure ⟨~ gills⟩ **c** : effective in the open for an appreciable time usu. through slow volatilizing ⟨mustard gas is ~⟩ **d** : degraded only slowly by the environment ⟨~ pesticides⟩ **e** : remaining infective for a relatively long time in a vector after an initial period of incubation ⟨~ viruses⟩ **2 a** : continuing or inclined to persist in a course **b** : continuing to exist in spite of interference or treatment ⟨a ~ cough⟩ — **per·sis·tent·ly** *adv*

per·snick·e·ty \pər-'snik-ət-ē\ *adj* [alter. of *pernickety*] (ca. 1905) **1 a** : fussy about small details : FASTIDIOUS ⟨a ~ teacher⟩ **b** : having the characteristics of a snob **2** : requiring great precision ⟨a ~ job⟩

per·son \'pərs-ᵊn\ *n* [ME, fr. OF *persone,* fr. L *persona* actor's mask, character in a play, person, prob. fr. Etruscan *phersu* mask] (13c) **1** : HUMAN, INDIVIDUAL — sometimes used in combination esp. by those who prefer to avoid *man* in compounds applicable to both sexes ⟨chair*person*⟩ ⟨spokes*person*⟩ **2** : a character or part in or as if in a play : GUISE **3 a** : one of the three modes of being in the Trinitarian Godhead as understood by Christians **b** : the unitary personality of Christ that unites the divine and human natures **4 a** *archaic* : bodily appearance **b** : the body of a human being ⟨unlawful search of the ~⟩ **5** : the individual personality of a human being : SELF **6** : one (as a human being, a partnership, or a corporation) that is recognized by law as the subject of rights and duties **7** : reference of a segment of discourse to the speaker, to one spoken to, or to one spoken of as indicated by means of certain pronouns or in many languages by verb inflection ***usage*** see PEOPLE — **per·son·hood** \-ˌhu̇d\ *n* — **in person** : in one's bodily presence

per·so·na \pər-'sō-nə, -ˌnä\ *n* [L] (1704) **1** *pl* **per·so·nae** \-(ˌ)nē, -ˌnī\ : the characters of a fictional presentation (as a novel or play) ⟨comic *personae*⟩ **2** *pl* **personas** [NL, fr. L] : an individual's social facade or front that esp. in the analytic psychology of C. G. Jung reflects the role in life the individual is playing — compare ANIMA

per·son·able \'pərs-nə-bəl, -ᵊn-ə-bəl\ *adj* (15c) : pleasing in person : ATTRACTIVE — **per·son·able·ness** *n*

per·son·age \'pərs-nij, -ᵊn-ij\ *n* (15c) **1** : a human individual : PERSON **2** : a person of rank, note, or distinction; *esp* : one distinguished for presence and personal power **3** : a dramatic, fictional, or historical character; *also* : IMPERSONATION

per·so·na gra·ta \pər-ˌsō-nə-'grat-ə, -'grät-\ *adj* [NL, acceptable person] (1882) : personally acceptable or welcome

¹**per·son·al** \'pərs-nəl, -ᵊn-əl\ *adj* [ME, fr. MF, fr. LL *personalis,* fr. L *persona*] (14c) **1** : of, relating to, or affecting a person : PRIVATE ⟨done purely for ~ financial gain⟩ **2 a** : done in person without the intervention of another; *also* : proceeding from a single person **b** : carried on between individuals directly ⟨a ~ interview⟩ **3** : relating to the person or body **4** : relating to an individual or his character, conduct, motives, or private affairs often in an offensive manner ⟨a ~ insult⟩ **5 a** : being rational and self-conscious ⟨~, responsive government is still possible —John Fischer⟩ **b** : having the qualities of a person rather than a thing or abstraction ⟨a ~ devil⟩ **6** : of, relating to, or constituting personal property ⟨a ~ estate⟩ **7** : denoting grammatical person

²**personal** *n* (1861) **1** : a short newspaper paragraph relating to the activities of a person or a group or to personal matters **2** : a short personal or private communication in a special column of the classified ads section of a newspaper or periodical

personal computer *n* (1977) : MICROCOMPUTER 1

personal effects *n pl* (1843) : privately owned items (as clothing and toilet articles) normally worn or carried on the person

personal equation *n* (1845) : variation (as in observation) occasioned by the personal peculiarities of an individual; *also* : a correction or allowance made for such variation

personal foul *n* (ca. 1829) **:** a foul in a game (as basketball) involving usu. physical contact with or deliberate roughing of an opponent — compare TECHNICAL FOUL

per·son·al·ism \ˈpərs-nə-ˌliz-əm, -ᵊn-ə-\ *n* (ca. 1846) **:** a doctrine emphasizing the significance, uniqueness, and inviolability of personality — **per·son·al·ist** \-ləst\ *n or adj* — **per·son·al·is·tic** \ˌpərs-nə-ˈlis-tik, -ᵊn-ə-\ *adj*

per·son·al·i·ty \ˌpərs-ᵊn-ˈal-ət-ē, ˌpər-ˈsnal-\ *n, pl* **-ties** [ME *personalite,* fr. LL *personalitat-, personalitas,* fr. *personalis*] (14c) **1 a :** the quality or state of being a person **b :** personal existence **2 a :** the condition or fact of relating to a particular person; *specif* **:** the condition of referring directly to or being aimed disparagingly or hostilely at an individual **b :** an offensively personal remark ⟨indulgence in *personalities*⟩ **3 :** the complex of characteristics that distinguishes an individual or a nation or group; *esp* **:** the totality of an individual's behavioral and emotional characteristics **4 a :** distinction or excellence of personal and social traits; *also* **:** a person having such quality **b :** a person of importance, prominence, renown, or notoriety ⟨a TV ~⟩ ***syn*** see DISPOSITION

personality inventory *n* (1932) **:** any of several tests that attempt to characterize the personality of an individual by objective scoring of replies to a large number of questions concerning his or her own behavior — compare MINNESOTA MULTIPHASIC PERSONALITY INVENTORY

personality test *n* (1914) **:** any of several tests that consist of standardized tasks designed to determine various aspects of the personality or the emotional status of the individual examined

per·son·al·ize \ˈpərs-nə-ˌlīz, -ᵊn-ə-\ *vt* **-ized; -iz·ing** (ca. 1727) **1 :** PERSONIFY **2 :** to make personal or individual; *specif* **:** to mark as the property of a particular person ⟨*personalized* stationery⟩ — **per·son·al·iza·tion** \ˌpərs-nə-lə-ˈzā-shən, -ᵊn-ə-\ *n*

per·son·al·ly \ˈpərs-nə-lē, -ᵊn-ə-\ *adv* (14c) **1 :** in person ⟨attend to the matter ~⟩ **2 :** as a person **:** in personality ⟨~ attractive but not very trustworthy⟩ **3 :** for oneself **:** as far as oneself is concerned

personal pronoun *n* (1668) **:** a pronoun (as *I, you,* or *they*) that expresses a distinction of person

personal property *n* (1838) **:** property other than real property consisting of things temporary or movable **:** CHATTELS

personal tax *n* (ca. 1935) **:** DIRECT TAX

per·son·al·ty \ˈpərs-nəl-tē, -ᵊn-əl-\ *n, pl* **-ties** [ME, fr. AF *personalté,* fr. LL *personalitat-, personalitas* personality] (15c) **:** PERSONAL PROPERTY

per·so·na non gra·ta \pər-ˌsō-nə-ˌnän-ˈgrat-ə, -ˈgrät-\ *adj* [NL, person not acceptable] (1904) **:** personally unacceptable or unwelcome

per·son·ate \ˈpərs-ᵊn-ˌāt\ *vt* **-at·ed; -at·ing** (1591) **1 a :** IMPERSONATE, REPRESENT **b :** to assume without authority and with fraudulent intent (some character or capacity) **2 :** to invest with personality or personal characteristics ⟨*personating* their gods ridiculous, and themselves past shame —John Milton⟩ — **per·son·ation** \ˌpərs-ᵊn-ˈā-shən\ *n* — **per·son·ative** \ˈpərs-ᵊn-ˌāt-iv\ *adj* — **per·son·a·tor** \-ˌāt-ər\ *n*

per·son·i·fi·ca·tion \pər-ˌsän-ə-fə-ˈkā-shən\ *n* (ca. 1755) **1 :** attribution of personal qualities; *esp* **:** representation of a thing or abstraction as a person or by the human form **2 :** a divinity or imaginary being representing a thing or abstraction **3 :** EMBODIMENT, INCARNATION

per·son·i·fy \pər-ˈsän-ə-ˌfī\ *vt* **-fied; -fy·ing** (1727) **1 :** to conceive of or represent as a person or as having human qualities or powers **2 :** to be the embodiment or personification of **:** INCARNATE ⟨a man who *personified* kindness⟩ — **per·son·i·fi·er** \-ˌfī(-ə)r\ *n*

per·son·nel \ˌpərs-ᵊn-ˈel\ *n* [F, fr. G *personale, personal,* fr. ML *personale,* fr. LL, neut. of *personalis* personal] (1837) **1 a :** a body of persons usu. employed (as in a factory, office, or organization) **b personnel** *pl* **:** PERSONS **2 :** a division of an organization concerned with personnel

1per·spec·tive \pər-ˈspek-tiv\ *n* [ME *perspectyf,* fr. ML *perspectivum,* fr. neut. of *perspectivus* of sight, optical, fr. L *perspectus,* pp. of *perspicere* to look through, see clearly, fr. *per-* through + *specere* to look — more at PER-, SPY] (14c) **:** an optical glass (as a telescope)

2perspective *n* [MF, prob. modif. of OIt *prospettiva,* fr. *prospetto* view, prospect, fr. L *prospectus* — more at PROSPECT] (1563) **1 a :** the technique or process of representing on a plane or curved surface the spatial relation of objects as they might appear to the eye; *specif* **:** LINEAR PERSPECTIVE **b :** a picture in linear perspective **2 a :** the interrelation in which a subject or its parts are mentally viewed ⟨places the issues in proper ~⟩; *also* **:** POINT OF VIEW **b :** the capacity to view things in their true relations or relative importance ⟨urge you to maintain your ~ and to view your own task in a larger framework —W. J. Cohen⟩ **3 a :** a visible scene; *esp* **:** one giving a distinctive impression of distance **:** VISTA **b :** a mental view or prospect ⟨to gain a broader ~ on the international scene —*Current Biog.*⟩ **4 :** the appearance to the eye of objects in respect to their relative distance and positions — **per·spec·tiv·al** \pər-ˈspek-tiv-əl\ *adj*

3perspective *adj* [ME, fr. ML *perspectivus*] (1570) **1** *obs* **:** aiding the vision ⟨his eyes should be like unto the wrong end of a ~ glass —Alexander Pope⟩ **2 :** of, relating to, employing, or seen in perspective ⟨~ drawing⟩ — **per·spec·tive·ly** *adv*

per·spi·ca·cious \ˌpər-spə-ˈkā-shəs\ *adj* [L *perspicac-, perspicax,* fr. *perspicere*] (1640) **:** of acute mental vision or discernment **:** KEEN ***syn*** see SHREWD — **per·spi·ca·cious·ly** *adv* — **per·spi·ca·cious·ness** *n* — **per·spi·cac·i·ty** \-ˈkas-ət-ē\ *n*

per·spic·u·ous \pər-ˈspik-yə-wəs\ *adj* [L *perspicuus* transparent, perspicuous, fr. *perspicere*] (1586) **:** plain to the understanding esp. because of clarity and precision of presentation ⟨a ~ argument⟩ ***syn*** see CLEAR — **per·spi·cu·i·ty** \ˌpər-spə-ˈkyü-ət-ē\ *n* — **per·spic·u·ous·ly** \pər-ˈspik-yə-wə-slē\ *adv* — **per·spic·u·ous·ness** *n*

per·spi·ra·tion \ˌpər-spə-ˈrā-shən\ *n* (1626) **1 :** the action or process of perspiring **2 :** a saline fluid secreted by the sweat glands **:** SWEAT

per·spi·ra·to·ry \pər-ˈspī-rə-ˌtōr-ē, ˈpər-sp(ə-)rə-, -ˌtȯr-\ *adj* (1725) **:** of, relating to, secreting, or inducing perspiration

per·spire \pər-ˈspī(ə)r\ *vi* **per·spired; per·spir·ing** [F *perspirer,* fr. MF, fr. L *per-* through + *spirare* to blow, breathe — more at PER-, SPIRIT] (1725) **:** to emit matter through the skin; *specif* **:** to secrete and emit perspiration

per·suad·able \pər-ˈswād-ə-bəl\ *adj* (ca. 1598) **:** capable of being persuaded

per·suade \pər-ˈswād\ *vt* **per·suad·ed; per·suad·ing** [L *persuadēre,* fr. *per-* thoroughly + *suadēre* to advise, urge — more at SWEET] (15c) **1 :** to move by argument, entreaty, or expostulation to a belief, position, or course of action **2 :** to plead with **:** URGE — **per·suad·er** *n*

per·sua·si·ble \-ˈswā-zə-bəl, -ˈswā-sə-\ *adj* [MF, fr. L *persuasibilis* persuasive, fr. *persuasus*] (1502) **:** PERSUADABLE

per·sua·sion \pər-ˈswā-zhən\ *n* [ME *persuasioun,* fr. MF or L; MF *persuasion,* fr. L *persuasion-, persuasio,* fr. *persuasus,* pp. of *persuadēre*] (14c) **1 a :** the act or process or an instance of persuading **b :** a persuading argument **c :** the ability to persuade **:** PERSUASIVENESS **2 :** the condition of being persuaded **3 a :** an opinion held with complete assurance **b :** a system of religious beliefs; *also* **:** a group adhering to a particular system of beliefs **4 :** KIND, SORT ***syn*** see OPINION

per·sua·sive \-ˈswā-siv, -ziv\ *adj* (15c) **:** tending to persuade — **per·sua·sive·ly** *adv* — **per·sua·sive·ness** *n*

pert \ˈpərt\ *adj* [ME, open, bold, pert, modif. of OF *apert,* fr. L *apertus* open, fr. pp. of *aperire* to open] (14c) **1 a :** saucily free and forward **:** flippantly cocky and assured **b :** being trim and chic **:** JAUNTY ⟨a ~ little hat⟩ **c :** piquantly stimulating ⟨is a ~ notion and one to fascinate the attention —G. J. Nathan⟩ **2 :** LIVELY, VIVACIOUS ***syn*** see SAUCY — **pert·ly** *adv* — **pert·ness** *n*

per·tain \pər-ˈtān\ *vi* [ME *perteinen,* fr. MF *partenir,* fr. L *pertinēre* to reach to, belong, fr. *per-* through + *tenēre* to hold — more at THIN] (14c) **1 a** (1) **:** to belong as a part, member, accessory, or product (2) **:** to belong as an attribute, feature, or function ⟨the destruction and havoc ~*ing* to war⟩ (3) **:** to belong as a duty or right ⟨responsibilities that ~ to fatherhood⟩ **b :** to be appropriate to something ⟨the criteria . . . will be different from those that ~ elsewhere —J. B. Conant⟩ **2 :** to have reference ⟨books ~*ing* to birds⟩

per·ti·na·cious \ˌpərt-ᵊn-ˈā-shəs\ *adj* [L *pertinac-, pertinax,* fr. *per-* thoroughly + *tenac-, tenax* tenacious, fr. *tenēre*] (1626) **1 a :** adhering resolutely to an opinion, purpose, or design **b :** perversely persistent **2 :** stubbornly unyielding or tenacious ***syn*** see OBSTINATE — **per·ti·na·cious·ly** *adv* — **per·ti·na·cious·ness** *n* — **per·ti·nac·i·ty** \-ˈas-ət-ē\ *n*

per·ti·nence \ˈpərt-ᵊn-ən(t)s, ˈpərt-nən(t)s\ *n* (1659) **:** the quality or state of being pertinent **:** RELEVANCE

per·ti·nen·cy \-ᵊn-ən-sē, -nən-sē\ *n* (1598) **:** PERTINENCE

per·ti·nent \ˈpərt-ᵊn-ənt, ˈpərt-nənt\ *adj* [ME, fr. MF, fr. L *pertinent-, pertinens,* prp. of *pertinēre*] (14c) **:** having a clear decisive relevance to the matter in hand ***syn*** see RELEVANT — **per·ti·nent·ly** *adv*

per·turb \pər-ˈtərb\ *vt* [ME *perturben,* fr. MF *perturber,* fr. L *perturbare* to throw into confusion, fr. *per-* + *turbare* to disturb — more at TURBID] (14c) **1 :** to disturb greatly in mind **:** DISQUIET **2 :** to throw into confusion **:** DISORDER **3 :** to cause to experience a perturbation ***syn*** see DISCOMPOSE — **per·turb·able** \-ˈtər-bə-bəl\ *adj*

per·tur·ba·tion \ˌpərt-ər-ˈbā-shən, ˌpər-ˌtər-\ *n* (14c) **1 :** the action of perturbing **:** the state of being perturbed **2 :** a disturbance of motion, course, arrangement, or state of equilibrium; *esp* **:** a disturbance of the regular and usu. elliptic course of motion of a celestial body that is produced by some force additional to that which causes its regular motion — **per·tur·ba·tion·al** \-shnəl, -shən-ᵊl\ *adj*

per·tus·sis \pər-ˈtəs-əs\ *n* [NL, fr. L *per-* thoroughly + *tussis* cough] (ca. 1799) **:** WHOOPING COUGH

pe·ruke \pə-ˈrük\ *n* [MF *perruque,* fr. OIt *parrucca, perrucca* hair, wig] (ca. 1565) **:** WIG; *specif* **:** one of a type popular from the 17th to the early 19th century

pe·ruse \pə-ˈrüz\ *vt* **pe·rused; pe·rus·ing** [ME *perusen,* prob. fr. L *per-* thoroughly + ME *usen* to use] (15c) **1 :** to examine or consider with attention and in detail **:** STUDY **2 :** READ — **pe·rus·al** \-ˈrü-zəl\ *n* — **pe·rus·er** *n*

per·vade \pər-ˈvād\ *vt* **per·vad·ed; per·vad·ing** [L *pervadere* to go through, pervade, fr. *per-* through + *vadere* to go — more at PER-, WADE] (1659) **:** to become diffused throughout every part of

per·va·sion \pər-ˈvā-zhən\ *n* (1661) **:** the action of pervading or condition of being pervaded

per·va·sive \pər-ˈvā-siv, -ziv\ *adj* (ca. 1750) **:** that pervades or tends to pervade — **per·va·sive·ly** *adv* — **per·va·sive·ness** *n*

per·verse \(ˌ)pər-ˈvərs, ˈpər-ˌ\ *adj* [ME, fr. L *perversus,* fr. pp. of *pervertere*] (14c) **1 a :** turned away from what is right or good **:** CORRUPT **b :** IMPROPER, INCORRECT **c :** contrary to the evidence or the direction of the judge on a point of law ⟨~ verdict⟩ **2 a :** obstinate in opposing what is right, reasonable, or accepted **:** WRONGHEADED **b :** arising from or indicative of stubbornness or obstinacy **3 :** marked by peevishness or petulance **:** CRANKY ***syn*** see CONTRARY — **per·verse·ly** *adv* — **per·verse·ness** *n* — **per·ver·si·ty** \pər-ˈvər-sət-ē, -stē\ *n*

per·ver·sion \pər-ˈvər-zhən, -shən\ *n* (14c) **1 :** the action of perverting **:** the condition of being perverted **2 :** a perverted form; *esp* **:** an aberrant sexual practice esp. when habitual and preferred to normal coitus

per·ver·sive \-ˈvər-siv, -ziv\ *adj* (1817) **1 :** that perverts or tends to pervert **2 :** arising from or indicative of perversion

1per·vert \pər-ˈvərt\ *vt* [ME *perverten,* fr. MF *pervertir,* fr. L *pervertere* to overturn, corrupt, pervert, fr. *per-* thoroughly + *vertere* to turn — more at PER-, WORTH] (14c) **1 a :** to cause to turn aside or away from what is good or true or morally right **:** CORRUPT **b :** to cause to turn aside or away from what is generally done or accepted **:** MISDIRECT **2 a :** to divert to a wrong end or purpose **:** MISUSE **b :** to twist the meaning or sense of **:** MISINTERPRET ***syn*** see DEBASE — **per·vert·er** *n*

2per·vert \ˈpər-ˌvərt\ *n* (ca. 1661) **:** one that has been perverted; *specif* **:** one given to some form of sexual perversion

per·vert·ed \pər-ˈvərt-əd\ *adj* (1667) **1 :** CORRUPT **2 :** marked by perversion — **per·vert·ed·ly** *adv* — **per·vert·ed·ness** *n*

per·vi·ous \ˈpər-vē-əs\ *adj* [L *pervius,* fr. *per-* through + *via* way — more at PER, VIA] (1614) **1 :** ACCESSIBLE ⟨~ to reason⟩ **2 :** PERMEABLE ⟨~ soil⟩ — **per·vi·ous·ness** *n*

Pe·sach \ˈpā-ˌsäk\ *n* [Heb *pesaḥ*] (1613) **:** PASSOVER

pe·se·ta \pə-ˈsāt-ə\ *n* [Sp, fr. dim. of *peso*] (1811) — see MONEY table

pe·se·wa \pə-ˈsā-wə\ *n* [native name in Ghana] (1965) — see *cedi* at MONEY table

pesky \ˈpes-kē\ *adj* **pes·ki·er; -est** [prob. irreg. fr. *pest* + *-y*] (1775) **:** TROUBLESOME, VEXATIOUS

pe·so \ˈpā-(ˌ)sō, ˈpes-(ˌ)ō\ *n, pl* **pesos** [Sp, lit., weight, fr. L *pensum* — more at POISE] (1555) **1 :** an old silver coin of Spain and Spanish America equal to eight reals **2** — see MONEY table **3 :** the former basic monetary unit of Chile replaced in 1960 by the escudo **4 a :** the former basic monetary unit of Argentina replaced in 1985 by the austral **b** — see *austral* at MONEY table

pes·sa·ry \ˈpes-ə-rē\ *n, pl* **-ries** [ME *pessarie,* fr. LL *pessarium,* fr. *pessus, pessum* pessary, fr. Gk *pessos* oval stone for playing checkers, pessary]

(15c) **1 :** a vaginal suppository **2 :** a device worn in the vagina to support the uterus, remedy a malposition, or prevent conception

pes·si·mism \'pə-sə-,miz-əm *also* 'pez-\ *n* [F *pessimisme,* fr. L *pessimus* worst — more at PEJORATIVE] (1815) **1 :** an inclination to emphasize adverse aspects, conditions, and possibilities or to expect the worst possible outcome **2 a :** the doctrine that reality is essentially evil **b :** the doctrine that evil overbalances happiness in life — **pes·si·mist** \-məst\ *n*

pes·si·mis·tic \,pes-ə-'mis-tik *also* ,pez-\ *adj* (1868) **:** of, relating to, or characterized by pessimism **:** GLOOMY ***syn*** see CYNICAL — **pes·si·mis·ti·cal·ly** \-ti-k(ə-)lē\ *adv*

pest \'pest\ *n* [MF *peste,* fr. L *pestis*] (1553) **1 :** an epidemic disease associated with high mortality; *specif* **:** PLAGUE **2 :** something resembling a pest in destructiveness; *esp* **:** a plant or animal detrimental to man **3 :** one that pesters or annoys **:** NUISANCE — **pesty** \'pes-tē\ *adj*

pes·ter \'pes-tər\ *vt* **pes·tered; pes·ter·ing** \-t(ə-)riŋ\ [modif. of MF *empestrer* to hobble, embarrass, fr. (assumed) VL *impastoriare,* fr. L *in-* + (assumed) VL *pastoria* hobble, fr. L *pastor* herdsman — more at PASTOR] (1548) **1** *obs* **:** OVERCROWD **2 :** to harass with petty irritations **:** ANNOY ***syn*** see WORRY

pest·hole \'pest-,hōl\ *n* (1903) **:** a place liable to epidemic disease

pest·house \-,hau̇s\ *n* (1611) **:** a shelter or hospital for those infected with a pestilential or contagious disease

pes·ti·cide \'pes-tə-,sīd\ *n* (ca. 1925) **:** an agent used to destroy pests

pes·tif·er·ous \pes-'tif-(ə-)rəs\ *adj* [ME, fr. L *pestifer* pestilential, noxious, fr. *pestis* + *-fer* -ferous] (15c) **1 :** dangerous to society **:** PERNICIOUS **2 a :** carrying or propagating infection **:** PESTILENTIAL **b :** infected with a pestilential disease **3 :** TROUBLESOME, ANNOYING — **pes·tif·er·ous·ly** *adv* — **pes·tif·er·ous·ness** *n*

pes·ti·lence \'pes-tə-lən(t)s\ *n* (14c) **1 :** a contagious or infectious epidemic disease that is virulent and devastating; *specif* **:** BUBONIC PLAGUE **2 :** something that is destructive or pernicious ⟨I'll pour this ~ into his ear —Shak.⟩

pes·ti·lent \-lənt\ *adj* [ME, fr. L *pestilent-, pestilens* pestilential, fr. *pestis*] (15c) **1 :** destructive of life **:** DEADLY **2 :** injuring or endangering society **:** PERNICIOUS **3 :** causing displeasure or annoyance **4 :** INFECTIOUS, CONTAGIOUS ⟨~ disease⟩ — **pes·ti·lent·ly** *adv*

pes·ti·len·tial \,pes-tə-'len-chəl\ *adj* (14c) **1 a :** causing or tending to cause pestilence **:** DEADLY **b :** of or relating to pestilence **2 :** morally harmful **:** PERNICIOUS **3 :** giving rise to vexation or annoyance **:** IRRITATING — **pes·ti·len·tial·ly** \-'lench-(ə-)lē\ *adv*

[1]pes·tle \'pes-əl, 'pes-tᵊl\ *n* [ME *pestel,* fr. MF, fr. L *pistillum;* akin to MLG *vīsel* pestle, L *pilum* pestle, javelin, *pinsere* to pound, crush] (14c) **1 :** a usu. club-shaped implement for pounding or grinding substances in a mortar **2 :** any of various devices for pounding, stamping, or pressing

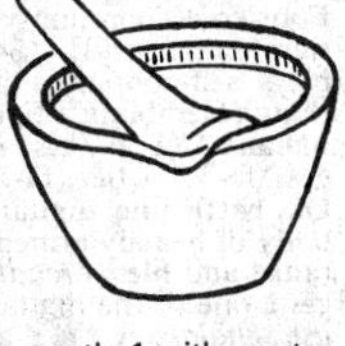
pestle 1 with mortar

[2]pestle *vb* **pes·tled; pes·tling** \'pes-(ə-)liŋ, 'pes-t(ə-)liŋ\ *vt* (15c) **:** to beat, pound, or pulverize with or as if with a pestle ~ *vi* **:** to work with a pestle **:** use a pestle

pes·to \'pes-(,)tō\ *n* [It, fr. *pesto,* adj., pounded, fr. *pestare* to pound, fr. LL *pistare,* freq. of L *pinsere*] (1937) **:** a sauce made esp. of fresh basil, garlic, oil, pine nuts, and grated cheese

[1]pet \'pet\ *n* [perh. back-formation fr. ME *pety* small — more at PETTY] (1508) **1 a :** a pampered and usu. spoiled child **b :** a person who is treated with unusual kindness or consideration **:** DARLING **2 :** a domesticated animal kept for pleasure rather than utility

[2]pet *adj* (1584) **1 :** kept or treated as a pet **2 :** expressing fondness or endearment ⟨a ~ name⟩ **3 :** FAVORITE ⟨his ~ project⟩

[3]pet *vb* **pet·ted; pet·ting** *vt* (1629) **1 a :** to treat as a pet **b :** to stroke in a gentle or loving manner **2 :** to treat with unusual kindness and consideration **:** PAMPER ~ *vi* **:** to engage in amorous embracing, caressing, and kissing **:** NECK — **pet·ter** *n*

[4]pet *n* [origin unknown] (1590) **:** a fit of peevishness, sulkiness, or anger

[5]pet *vi* **pet·ted; pet·ting** (1629) **:** to take offense **:** SULK

pet·al \'pet-ᵊl\ *n* [NL *petalum,* fr. Gk *petalon;* akin to Gk *petannynai* to spread out — more at FATHOM] (ca. 1726) **:** one of the modified leaves of a corolla of a flower — see FLOWER illustration — **pet·aled** *or* **pet·alled** \-ᵊld\ *adj* — **pet·al·like** \-ᵊl-,(l)īk\ *adj*

pet·al·oid \'pet-ᵊl-,ȯid\ *adj* (1730) **1 :** resembling a flower petal **2 :** consisting of petaloid elements

pet·al·ous \'pet-ᵊl-əs\ *adj* (ca. 1730) **1 :** having petals **2 :** having (such or so many) petals — used in combination ⟨poly*petalous*⟩

pe·tard \pə-'tär(d)\ *n* [MF, fr. *peter* to break wind, fr. *pet* expulsion of intestinal gas, fr. L *peditum,* fr. neut. of *peditus,* pp. of *pedere* to break wind; akin to Gk *bdein* to break wind] (1598) **1 :** a case containing an explosive to break down a door or gate or breach a wall **2 :** a firework that explodes with a loud report

pet·a·sos *or* **pet·a·sus** \'pet-ə-səs\ *n* [L & Gk; L *petasus,* fr. Gk *petasos;* akin to Gk *petannynai* to spread out] (ca. 1599) **:** a broad-brimmed low-crowned hat worn by ancient Greeks and Romans; *esp* **:** the winged hat of Hermes

pet·cock \'pet-,käk\ *n* [*pet-* (perh. fr. *petty*) + *cock*] (ca. 1864) **:** a small cock, faucet, or valve for letting out air, releasing compression, or draining

pe·te·chia \pə-'tē-kē-ə\ *n, pl* **-chi·ae** \-kē-,ī\ [NL, fr. It *petecchia,* deriv. of L *impetigo*] (1794) **:** a minute reddish or purplish spot containing blood that appears in skin or mucous membrane esp. in some infectious diseases (as typhoid fever) — **pe·te·chi·al** \-kē-əl\ *adj*

[1]pe·ter \'pēt-ər\ *vi* [origin unknown] (1846) **1 :** to diminish gradually and come to an end **:** GIVE OUT — usu. used with *out* ⟨novelists whose creative impetus seems largely to have ~*ed* out —*Times Lit. Supp.*⟩ **2 :** to become exhausted — usu. used with *out*

[2]peter *n* [fr. the name *Peter*] (ca. 1902) **:** PENIS — often considered vulgar

Pe·ter \'pēt-ər\ *n* [LL *Petrus,* fr. Gk *Petros,* fr. *petra* rock] **1 :** a fisherman of Galilee and one of the twelve apostles **2 :** either of two hortatory letters written to early Christians and included as books of the New Testament — see BIBLE table

Peter Pan \-'pan\ *n* **:** a boy in Sir James Barrie's play *Peter Pan* who lives without growing older in a never-never land

Peter Pan collar *n* (1923) **:** a usu. small flat close-fitting collar with rounded ends that meet in front

Peter Principle *n* [Laurence J. *Peter b*1919 Am. (Canad.-born) educator] (1968) **:** an observation: in a hierarchy every employee tends to rise to the level of his incompetence

Peter's pence *n pl but sing in constr* [fr. the tradition that St. Peter founded the papal see] (13c) **1 :** an annual tribute of a penny formerly paid by each householder in England to the papal see **2 :** a voluntary annual contribution made by Roman Catholics to the pope

pet·i·o·lar \,pet-ē-'ō-lər\ *adj* (ca. 1760) **:** of, relating to, or proceeding from a petiole

pet·i·o·late \'pet-ē-ə-,lāt, ,pet-ē-'ō-lət\ *adj* (ca. 1753) **:** having a stalk or petiole

pet·i·ole \'pet-ē-,ōl\ *n* [NL *petiolus,* fr. L, small foot, fruit stalk, alter. of *pediculus,* dim. of *ped-, pes* foot — more at FOOT] (1753) **1 :** a slender stem that supports the blade of a foliage leaf **2 :** PEDUNCLE; *specif* **:** a slender abdominal segment joining the rest of the abdomen to the thorax in some insects — **pet·i·oled** \-,ōld\ *adj*

pet·i·o·lule \'pet-ē-ō-,lül, ,pet-ē-'ōl-(,)yü(ə)l\ *n* [NL *petiolulus,* dim. of *petiolus*] (1832) **:** a stalk of a leaflet of a compound leaf

pet·it \'pet-ē\ *adj* [ME, small, minor, fr. MF, small] (14c) **:** PETTY 1 — used chiefly in legal compounds

pe·tit bourgeois \pə-'tē-, ,pet-ē-\ *n* [F, lit., small bourgeois] (1853) **1 :** a member of the petite bourgeoisie **2 :** PETITE BOURGEOISIE — **petit bourgeois** *adj*

[1]pe·tite \pə-'tēt\ *adj* [F, fem. of *petit*] (1784) **:** having a small trim figure — usu. used of a woman — **pe·tite·ness** *n*

[2]petite *n* (ca. 1929) **:** a clothing size for short women

pe·tite bourgeoisie \pə-,tēt-\ *n* [F, lit., small bourgeoisie] (1916) **:** the lower middle class including esp. small shopkeepers and artisans

pe·tit four \,pet-ē-'fō(ə)r, pə-,tē-, -'fȯ(ə)r; -'fu̇(ə)r\ *n, pl* **petits fours** *or* **petit fours** \-'fō(ə)rz, -'fȯ(ə)rz, -'fu̇(ə)r(z)\ [F, lit., small oven] (1884) **:** a small cake cut from pound or sponge cake and frosted

[1]pe·ti·tion \pə-'tish-ən\ *n* [ME, fr. MF, fr. L *petition-, petitio,* fr. *petitus,* pp. of *petere* to seek, request — more at FEATHER] (14c) **1 :** an earnest request **:** ENTREATY **2 a :** a formal written request made to a superior **b :** a document embodying such a formal written request **3 :** something asked or requested — **pe·ti·tion·ary** \-'tish-ə-,ner-ē\ *adj*

[2]petition *vb* **pe·ti·tioned; pe·ti·tion·ing** \-'tish-(ə-)niŋ\ *vt* (1607) **:** to make a request to **:** SOLICIT ~ *vi* **:** to make a request; *esp* **:** to make a formal written request — **pe·ti·tion·er** \-(ə-)nər\ *n*

pe·ti·tio prin·ci·pii \pə-'tēt-ē-,ō-(,)priŋ-'kip-ē-,ē\ *n* [ML, lit., postulation of the beginning, begging the question] (ca. 1531) **:** a logical fallacy in which a premise is assumed to be true without warrant or in which what is to be proved is implicitly taken for granted

pet·it jury \'pet-ē-\ *n* (15c) **:** a jury of 12 persons impaneled to try and to decide finally upon the facts at issue in causes for trial in a court

petit larceny *n* (1587) **:** larceny involving property of a value below a legally established minimum

pe·tit-maî·tre \pə-,tē-'mātrᵊ\ *n, pl* **petits-maîtres** *same*\ [F, lit., small master] (1711) **:** DANDY, FOP

pe·tit mal \'pet-ē-,mal, -,mäl\ *n* [F, lit., small illness] (ca. 1842) **:** epilepsy characterized by mild convulsive seizure with transient clouding of consciousness — compare GRAND MAL

pet·it point \'pet-ē-,pȯint\ *n* [F, lit., small point] (ca. 1882) **:** TENT STITCH; *also* **:** embroidery made with this stitch

pet·nap·ping \'pet-,nap-iŋ\ *n* [*pet* + *-napping* (as in *kidnapping*)] (1966) **:** the act of stealing a pet (as a cat or dog) usu. for profit — **pet·nap·per** \-,nap-ər\ *n*

pet peeve *n* (ca. 1919) **:** a frequent subject of complaint

petr- *or* **petri-** *or* **petro-** *comb form* [NL, fr. Gk *petr-, petro-,* fr. *petros* stone & *petra* rock] **1 :** stone **:** rock ⟨*petrology*⟩ **2 :** petroleum ⟨*petrodollars*⟩

Pe·trar·chan sonnet \pi-,trär-kən-, ,pē-, (,)pe-\ *n* [*Petrarch* (Francesco Petrarca)] (ca. 1909) **:** ITALIAN SONNET

pe·trel \'pe-trəl, 'pē-\ *n* [alter. of earlier *pitteral*] (1676) **:** any of numerous seabirds (families Procellariidae and Hydrobatidae); *esp* **:** one of the smaller long-winged birds that fly far from land — compare STORM PETREL

pe·tri dish \,pē-trē-\ *n* [Julius R. *Petri* †1921 Ger. bacteriologist] (ca. 1892) **:** a small shallow dish of thin glass with a loose cover used esp. for cultures in bacteriology

pet·ri·fac·tion \,pe-trə-'fak-shən\ *n* (1646) **1 :** the process of petrifying **2 :** something petrified **3 :** the quality or state of being petrified

pet·ri·fi·ca·tion \,pe-trə-fə-'kā-shən\ *n* (1611) **:** PETRIFACTION

pet·ri·fy \'pe-trə-,fī\ *vb* **-fied; -fy·ing** [MF *petrifier,* fr. *petr-* + *-ifier* -ify] *vt* (1544) **1 :** to convert into stone or a stony substance **2 :** to make rigid or inert like stone: **a :** to make lifeless or inactive **:** DEADEN ⟨slogans are apt to ~ a man's thinking —*Saturday Rev.*⟩ **b :** to confound with fear, amazement, or awe ⟨a novel about an airline pilot that will ~ you —Martin Levin⟩ ~ *vi* **:** to become stone or of stony hardness or rigidity

Pe·trine \'pē-,trīn\ *adj* [LL *Petrus* Peter] (1846) **1 :** of, relating to, or characteristic of the apostle Peter or the doctrines associated with his name **2 :** of, relating to, or characteristic of Peter the Great or his reign

pet·ro·chem·i·cal \,pe-trō-'kem-i-kəl\ *n* (1942) **:** a chemical isolated or derived from petroleum or natural gas — **pet·ro·chem·is·try** \-'kem-ə-strē\ *n*

pet·ro·dol·lars \'pe-trō-,däl-ərz\ *n pl* (1974) **:** foreign exchange obtained by petroleum-exporting countries through sales abroad — **pe·tro·dol·lar** \-ər\ *adj*

pet·ro·gen·e·sis \,pe-trō-'jen-ə-səs\ *n* [NL] (1901) **:** the origin or formation of rocks — **pet·ro·ge·net·ic** \-jə-'net-ik\ *adj*

pet·ro·glyph \'pe-trə-,glif\ *n* [F *pétroglyphe,* fr. *pétr-* petr- + *-glyphe* (as in *hiéroglyphe* hieroglyph)] (1870) **:** a carving or inscription on a rock

pe·trog·ra·phy \pə-ˈträg-rə-fē, pe-\ *n* [NL *petrographia,* fr. *petr-* + L *-graphia* -graphy] (1651) **:** the description and systematic classification of rocks — **pe·trog·ra·pher** \-fər\ *n* — **pet·ro·graph·ic** \ˌpe-trə-ˈgraf-ik\ *or* **pet·ro·graph·i·cal** \-i-kəl\ *adj* — **pet·ro·graph·i·cal·ly** \-i-k(ə-)lē\ *adv*

pet·rol \ˈpe-trəl, -ˌträl\ *n* [F *essence de pétrole,* lit., essence of petroleum] *chiefly Brit* (1895) **:** GASOLINE

pet·ro·la·tum \ˌpe-trə-ˈlāt-əm, -ˈlät-\ *n* [NL, fr. ML *petroleum*] (1887) **:** a neutral unctuous odorless tasteless substance obtained from petroleum and used esp. in ointments and dressings

pe·tro·leum \pə-ˈtrō-lē-əm, -ˈtrōl-yəm\ *n* [ML, fr. L *petr-* + *oleum* oil — more at OIL] (1526) **:** an oily flammable bituminous liquid that may vary from almost colorless to black, occurs in many places in the upper strata of the earth, is a complex mixture of hydrocarbons with small amounts of other substances, and is prepared for use as gasoline, naphtha, or other products by various refining processes

petroleum jelly *n* (ca. 1897) **:** PETROLATUM

pe·trol·o·gy \pə-ˈträl-ə-jē, pe-\ *n* [ISV] (ca. 1811) **:** a science that deals with the origin, history, occurrence, structure, chemical composition, and classification of rocks — **pet·ro·log·ic** \ˌpe-trə-ˈläj-ik\ *or* **pet·ro·log·i·cal** \-i-kəl\ *adj* — **pet·ro·log·i·cal·ly** \-i-k(ə-)lē\ *adv* — **pe·trol·o·gist** \pə-ˈträl-ə-jəst, pe-\ *n*

pet·ro·nel \ˌpe-trə-ˈnel\ *n* [perh. modif. of MF *poitrinal, petrinal,* fr. *poitrinal* of the chest, fr. *poitrine* chest, deriv. of L *pector-, pectus* — more at PECTORAL] (ca. 1577) **:** a portable firearm resembling a carbine of large caliber

pe·tro·sal \pə-ˈtrō-səl\ *adj* [NL *petrosa* petrous portion of the temporal bone, fr. L, fem. of *petrosus*] (1741) **:** of, relating to, or situated in the region of the petrous portion of the temporal bone or capsule of the internal ear

pe·trous \ˈpe-trəs, ˈpē-\ *adj* [MF *petreux,* fr. L *petrosus,* fr. *petra* rock, fr. Gk] (ca. 1541) **:** of, relating to, or constituting the exceptionally hard and dense portion of the temporal bone of man that contains the internal auditory organs

[1]**pet·ti·coat** \ˈpet-ē-ˌkōt\ *n* [ME *petycote* short tunic, petticoat, fr. *pety* small + *cote* coat] (15c) **1 :** a skirt worn by women, girls, or young children: as **a :** an outer skirt formerly worn by women and small children **b :** a fancy skirt made to show below a draped-up overskirt **c :** an underskirt usu. a little shorter than outer clothing and often made with a ruffled, pleated, or lace edge **d** *archaic* **:** the skirt of a woman's riding habit **2 a :** a garment characteristic or typical of women **b :** WOMAN **3 :** something (as a valance) resembling a petticoat — **pet·ti·coat·ed** \-əd\ *adj*

[2]**petticoat** *adj* (1660) **:** of, relating to, or exercised by women **:** FEMALE

pet·ti·fog·ger \ˈpet-ē-ˌfȯg-ər, -ˌfäg-\ *n* [prob. fr. *petty* + obs. E *fogger* (pettifogger)] (1564) **1 :** a lawyer whose methods are petty, underhanded, or disreputable **:** SHYSTER **2 :** one given to quibbling over trifles — **pet·ti·fog** \-ˌfȯg, -ˌfäg\ *vi* — **pet·ti·fog·gery** \-(ə-)rē\ *n*

pet·tish \ˈpet-ish\ *adj* [prob. fr. [4]*pet*] (ca. 1552) **:** FRETFUL, PEEVISH — **pet·tish·ly** *adv* — **pet·tish·ness** *n*

pet·ti·skirt \ˈpet-ē-ˌskərt\ *n* [*petticoat* + *skirt*] (1945) **:** PETTICOAT 1c

pet·ti·toes \ˈpet-ē-ˌtōz\ *n pl* [pl. of obs. *pettytoe* (offal)] (1555) **1 :** the feet of a pig used as food **2 :** TOES, FEET

pet·ty \ˈpet-ē\ *adj* **pet·ti·er; -est** [ME *pety* small, minor, alter. of *petit*] (1523) **1 :** having secondary rank or importance **:** MINOR, SUBORDINATE **2 :** having little or no importance or significance **3 :** marked by or reflective of narrow interests and sympathies **:** SMALL-MINDED — **pet·ti·ly** \ˈpet-ᵊl-ē\ *adv* — **pet·ti·ness** \ˈpet-ē-nəs\ *n*

petty cash *n* (ca. 1834) **:** cash kept on hand for payment of minor items

petty larceny *n* (1818) **:** PETIT LARCENY

petty officer *n* (1760) **:** a subordinate officer in the navy or coast guard appointed from among the enlisted men — compare NONCOMMISSIONED OFFICER

petty officer first class *n* (ca. 1942) **:** an enlisted man in the navy or coast guard ranking above a petty officer second class and below a chief petty officer

petty officer second class *n* (ca. 1942) **:** an enlisted man in the navy or coast guard ranking above a petty officer third class and below a petty officer first class

petty officer third class *n* (ca. 1942) **:** an enlisted man in the navy or coast guard ranking above a seaman and below a petty officer second class

pet·u·lance \ˈpech-ə-lən(t)s\ *n* (1610) **:** the quality or state of being petulant **:** PEEVISHNESS

pet·u·lan·cy \-lən-sē\ *n, archaic* (1559) **:** PETULANCE

pet·u·lant \-lənt\ *adj* [L or MF; MF, fr. L *petulant-, petulans;* akin to L *petere* to go to, attack, seek — more at FEATHER] (1605) **1 :** insolent or rude in speech or behavior **2 :** characterized by temporary or capricious ill humor **:** PEEVISH — **pet·u·lant·ly** *adv*

pe·tu·nia \pi-ˈt(y)ün-yə\ *n* [NL, fr. obs. F *petun* tobacco, fr. Tupi *petyn*] (ca. 1825) **:** any of a genus (*Petunia*) of tropical American herbs of the nightshade family with funnel-shaped corollas

pew \ˈpyü\ *n* [ME *pewe,* fr. MF *puie* balustrade, fr. L *podia,* pl. of *podium* parapet, podium, fr. Gk *podion* base, dim. of *pod-, pous* foot — more at FOOT] (14c) **1 :** a compartment in the auditorium of a church providing seats for several persons **2 :** one of the benches with backs and sometimes doors fixed in rows in a church

pe·wee \ˈpē-(ˌ)wē\ *n* [imit.] (ca. 1796) **:** any of various small olivaceous flycatchers

pew·hold·er \ˈpyü-ˌhōl-dər\ *n* (1845) **:** a renter or owner of a church pew

pe·wit *var of* PEEWIT

pew·ter \ˈpyüt-ər\ *n* [ME, fr. MF *peutre;* akin to It *peltro* pewter] (14c) **1 :** any of various alloys having tin as chief component; *esp* **:** a dull alloy with lead formerly used for domestic utensils **2 :** utensils of pewter — **pewter** *adj*

pew·ter·er \ˈpyüt-ər-ər\ *n* (14c) **:** one that makes pewter utensils

pey·o·te \pā-ˈōt-ē\ *also* **pey·otl** \-ˈōt-ᵊl\ *n* [MexSp *peyote,* fr. Nahuatl *peyotl*] (1885) **1 :** any of several American cacti (genus *Lophophora*); *esp* **:** MESCAL **2 :** a stimulant drug derived from mescal buttons

pfen·nig \ˈfen-ig, -ik, *G* ˈ(p)fen-ik\ *n, pl* **pfennig** *also* **pfen·nigs** \ˈfen-igz, -iks\ *or* **pfen·ni·ge** \ˈ(p)fen-i-gə, -i-yə\ [G, fr. OHG *pfenning* — more at PENNY] (1547) — see *deutsche mark* at MONEY table

PG \ˈpē-ˈjē\ *adj* [parental guidance] *of a motion picture* (ca. 1968) **:** of such a nature that all ages may be allowed admission but parental guidance is suggested — compare G, PG-13, R, X

PG–13 \-ˌthər(t)-ˈtēn\ *adj, of a motion picture* (1984) **:** of such a nature that persons of all ages may be admitted but parental guidance is suggested esp. for children under 13 — compare G, PG, R, X

pH \(ˈ)pē-ˈāch\ *n* [G, fr. *potenz* (power) + *H* (symbol for hydrogen)] (1909) **:** a measure of acidity and alkalinity of a solution that is a number on a scale on which a value of 7 represents neutrality and lower numbers indicate increasing acidity and higher numbers increasing alkalinity and on which each unit of change represents a tenfold change in acidity or alkalinity and that is the negative logarithm of the effective hydrogen-ion concentration or hydrogen-ion activity in gram equivalents per liter of the solution

Phae·dra \ˈfē-drə\ *n* [L, fr. Gk *Phaidra*] **:** a daughter of Minos who marries Theseus and falls in love with her stepson Hippolytus

Pha·ë·thon \ˈfā-ət-ᵊn; ˈfā-ə-tən, -ˌthän\ *n* [L, fr. Gk *Phaethōn*] **:** a son of Helios who drives his father's sun-chariot through the sky but loses control and is struck down by a thunderbolt of Zeus

pha·eton \ˈfā-ət-ᵊn\ *n* [*Phaëthon*] (1742) **1 :** any of various light four-wheeled horse-drawn vehicles **2 :** TOURING CAR

phage \ˈfāj *also* ˈfäzh\ *n* [by shortening] (ca. 1928) **:** BACTERIOPHAGE

-phage \ˌfāj *also* ˌfäzh\ *n comb form* [Gk *-phagos,* fr. *-phagos* -phagous] **:** one that eats ⟨bacterio*phage*⟩

-pha·gia \ˈfā-j(ē-)ə\ *n comb form* [NL, fr. Gk] **:** -PHAGY ⟨dys*phagia*⟩

phago·cyte \ˈfag-ə-ˌsīt\ *n* [ISV, fr. Gk *phagein* + NL *-cyta* -cyte] (ca. 1884) **:** a cell (as a leukocyte) that engulfs foreign material and consumes debris and foreign bodies — **phago·cyt·ic** \ˌfag-ə-ˈsit-ik\ *adj*

phago·cy·tize \ˈfag-ə-sə-ˌtīz, -ˌsīt-ˌīz\ *vt* **-tized; -tiz·ing** (1913) **:** PHAGOCYTOSE

phago·cy·tose \-sə-ˌtōs, -sī-, -ˌtōz\ *vt* **-tosed; -tos·ing** [back-formation fr. *phagocytosis*] (1912) **:** to consume by phagocytosis

phago·cy·to·sis \ˌfag-ə-sə-ˈtō-səs, -sī-\ *n, pl* **-to·ses** \-ˌsēz\ [NL] (1889) **:** the engulfing and usu. the destruction of particulate matter by phagocytes — **phago·cy·tot·ic** \-ˈtät-ik\ *adj*

-ph·a·gous \f-ə-gəs\ *adj comb form* [Gk *-phagos,* fr. *phagein* to eat — more at BAKSHEESH] **:** eating ⟨sapro*phagous*⟩

-ph·a·gy \f-ə-jē\ *n comb form, pl* **-ph·a·gies** [Gk *-phagia,* fr. *phagein*] **:** eating of a (specified) type or substance ⟨geo*phagy*⟩

pha·lange \ˈfā-ˌlanj, fə-ˈ, fā-ˈ\ *n* [F, fr. Gk *phalang-, phalanx*] (ca. 1860) **:** PHALANX 2

pha·lan·ge·al \ˌfā-lən-ˈjē-əl, ˌfal-ən-; fə-ˈlan-jē-, fā-\ *adj* (1831) **:** of or relating to a phalanx or the phalanges

pha·lan·ger \fə-ˈlan-jər, ˈfā-ˌ\ *n* [NL, fr. Gk *phalang-, phalanx*] (ca. 1774) **:** any of various marsupial mammals (family Phalangeridae) of the Australian region ranging in size from a mouse to a large cat

phal·an·stery \ˈfal-ən-ˌster-ē\ *n, pl* **-ster·ies** [F *phalanstère* dwelling of a Fourierist community, fr. L *phalang-, phalanx* + F *-stère* (as in *monastère* monastery)] (1846) **1 a :** a Fourierist cooperative community **b :** a self-contained structure housing such a community **2 :** something resembling a Fourierist phalanstery

pha·lanx \ˈfā-ˌlaŋ(k)s, *Brit usu* ˈfal-ˌaŋ(k)s\ *n, pl* **pha·lanx·es** *or* **pha·lan·ges** \fə-ˈlan-(ˌ)jēz, fā-, ˈfā-ˌ, *Brit usu* fal-ˈan-\ [L *phalang-, phalanx,* fr. Gk, battle line, digital bone, lit., log — more at BALK] (ca. 1553) **1 :** a body of heavily armed infantry in ancient Greece formed in close deep ranks and files; *broadly* **:** a body of troops in close array **2** *pl* **phalanges :** one of the digital bones of the hand or foot of a vertebrate **3** *pl usu* **phalanxes a :** a massed arrangement of persons, animals, or things **b :** an organized body of persons

phal·a·rope \ˈfal-ə-ˌrōp\ *n, pl* **-ropes** *also* **-rope** [F, fr. NL *phalaropod-, phalaropus,* fr. Gk *phalaris* coot + *pod-, pous* foot; akin to Gk *phalios* having a white spot — more at BALD, FOOT] (ca. 1776) **:** any of various small shorebirds (family Phalaropodidae) that resemble sandpipers but have lobate toes and are good swimmers

phal·lic \ˈfal-ik\ *adj* (1789) **1 :** of or relating to phallicism ⟨a ~ cult⟩ **2 :** of, relating to, or resembling a phallus **3 :** relating to or being the stage of psychosexual development in psychoanalytic theory during which a child becomes interested in his or her own sexual organs — **phal·li·cal·ly** \-i-k(ə-)lē\ *adv*

phal·li·cism \ˈfal-ə-ˌsiz-əm\ *n* (1884) **:** the worship of the generative principle as symbolized by the phallus

phal·lus \ˈfal-əs\ *n, pl* **phal·li** \ˈfal-ˌī, -ˌē\ *or* **phal·lus·es** [L, fr. Gk *phallos* penis, representation of the penis — more at BLOW] (ca. 1613) **1 :** a symbol or representation of the penis **2 :** PENIS

-phane \ˌfān\ *n comb form* [Gk *phanēs* appearing, fr. *phainein* to show — more at FANCY] **:** substance having a (specified) form, quality, or appearance ⟨hydro*phane*⟩

pha·nero·gam \ˈfan-ə-rə-ˌgam, fə-ˈner-ə-\ *n* [F *phanérogame,* deriv. of Gk *phaneros* visible (fr. *phainein*) + *gamos* marriage — more at BIGAMY] (1861) **:** a seed plant or flowering plant **:** SPERMATOPHYTE

pha·nero·phyte \ˈfan-ə-rə-ˌfīt, fə-ˈner-ə-\ *n* [Gk *phaneros* + ISV *-phyte*] (1913) **:** a perennial plant that bears its overwintering buds well above the surface of the ground

Pha·nero·zo·ic \ˌfan-ə-rə-ˈzō-ik\ *adj* [Gk *phaneros* + E [2]*-zoic*] (1930) **:** of, relating to, or being a period of geologic time that comprises the Paleozoic, Mesozoic, and Cenozoic

phan·tasm \ˈfan-ˌtaz-əm\ *n* [ME *fantasme,* fr. OF, fr. L *phantasma,* fr. Gk, fr. *phantazein* to present to the mind — more at FANCY] (13c) **1 :** a product of fantasy: as **a :** delusive appearance **:** ILLUSION **b :** GHOST, SPECTER **c :** a figment of the imagination **2 :** a mental representation of a real object — **phan·tas·mal** \fan-ˈtaz-məl\ *adj* — **phan·tas·mic** \-mik\ *adj*

phan·tas·ma \fan-ˈtaz-mə\ *n, pl* **-ma·ta** \-mət-ə\ [L] (1598) **:** PHANTASM 1

phan·tas·ma·go·ria \(ˌ)fan-ˌtaz-mə-ˈgōr-ē-ə, -ˈgȯr-\ *n* [F *phantasmagorie,* fr. *phantasme* phantasm (fr. OF *fantasme*) + *-agorie* (prob. fr. Gk *ageirein* to assemble, collect) — more at GREGARIOUS] (ca. 1802) **1 :** an optical effect by which figures on a screen appear to dwindle into the distance or to rush toward the observer with enormous increase of size **2 a :** a constantly shifting complex succession of things seen or imagined **b :** a scene that constantly changes — **phan·tas·ma·go·ric** \-ˈgōr-ik, -ˈgȯr-, -ˈgär-\ *adj*

phantasy *var of* FANTASY

[1]**phan·tom** \ˈfant-əm\ *n* [ME *fantosme, fantome,* fr. MF *fantosme,* modif. of L *phantasma*] (14c) **1 a :** something (as a specter) apparent to sense but with no substantial existence **:** APPARITION **b :** something elusive or visionary **:** WILL-O'-THE-WISP **c :** an object of continual dread or abhorrence **:** BUGBEAR ⟨the ~ of disease and want⟩ **2 :** something

existing in appearance only **3** : a representation of something abstract, ideal, or incorporeal ⟨she was a ~ of delight —William Wordsworth⟩ — **phan·tom·like** \-ˌlīk\ *adv or adj*

²**phantom** *adj* (15c) **1** : of the nature of, suggesting, or being a phantom : ILLUSORY **2** : FICTITIOUS, DUMMY ⟨~ voters⟩

pha·raoh \ˈfe(ə)r-(ˌ)ō, ˈfa(ə)r-(ˌ)ō, ˈfā-(ˌ)rō\ *n, often cap* [ME *pharao,* fr. OE, fr. LL *pharaon-, pharao,* fr. Gk *pharaō,* fr. Heb *parʽōh,* fr. Egypt *pr-ʿ3*] (bef. 12c) **1** : a ruler of ancient Egypt **2** : TYRANT — **phar·a·on·ic** \ˌfer-ā-ˈän-ik, ˌfar-\ *adj, often cap*

pharaoh ant *n* (ca. 1947) : a little red ant (*Monomorium pharaonis*) that is a common household pest

phar·i·sa·ic \ˌfar-ə-ˈsā-ik\ *adj* [LL *pharisaicus,* fr. LGk *pharisaikos,* fr. Gk *pharisaios* Pharisee] (1618) **1** : PHARISAICAL **2** *cap* : of or relating to the Pharisees

phar·i·sa·ical \-ˈsā-ə-kəl\ *adj* (1531) : marked by hypocritical censorious self-righteousness — **phar·i·sa·ical·ly** \-k(ə-)lē\ *adv* — **phar·i·sa·ical·ness** \-kəl-nəs\ *n*

phar·i·sa·ism \ˈfar-ə-(ˌ)sā-ˌiz-əm\ *n* [NL *pharisaismus,* fr. Gk *pharisaios*] (1610) **1** *cap* : the doctrines or practices of the Pharisees **2** *often cap* : pharisaical character, spirit, or attitude : HYPOCRISY

phar·i·see \ˈfar-ə-(ˌ)sē\ *n* [ME *pharise,* fr. OE *farise,* fr. LL *pharisaeus,* fr. Gk *pharisaios,* fr. Aram *pĕrīshayyā,* pl. of *pĕrīshā,* lit., separated] (bef. 12c) **1** *cap* : a member of a Jewish sect of the intertestamental period noted for strict observance of rites and ceremonies of the written law and for insistence on the validity of their own oral traditions concerning the law **2** : a pharisaical person

¹**phar·ma·ceu·ti·cal** \ˌfär-mə-ˈsüt-i-kəl\ *adj* [LL *pharmaceuticus,* fr. Gk *pharmakeutikos,* fr. *pharmakeuein* to administer drugs — more at PHARMACY] (1648) : of, relating to, or engaged in pharmacy or the manufacture and sale of pharmaceuticals ⟨a ~ company⟩ — **phar·ma·ceu·ti·cal·ly** \-i-k(ə-)lē\ *adv*

²**pharmaceutical** *n* (1881) : a medicinal drug

phar·ma·cist \ˈfär-mə-səst\ *n* (1834) : one engaged in pharmacy

pharmaco- *comb form* [Gk *pharmako-,* fr. *pharmakon*] : medicine : drug ⟨*pharmaco*logy⟩

phar·ma·co·dy·nam·ics \ˌfär-mə-kō-dī-ˈnam-iks, -də-\ *n pl but sing in constr* (ca. 1842) : a branch of pharmacology dealing with the reactions between drugs and living systems — **phar·ma·co·dy·nam·ic** \-ik\ *adj* — **phar·ma·co·dy·nam·i·cal·ly** \-i-k(ə-)lē\ *adv*

phar·ma·cog·no·sy \ˌfär-mə-ˈkäg-nə-sē\ *n* [ISV, fr. Gk *pharmakon* + *-gnōsia* knowledge, fr. *gnōsis* — more at GNOSIS] (ca. 1885) : descriptive pharmacology dealing with crude drugs and simples — **phar·ma·cog·nos·tic** \-ˌkäg-ˈnäs-tik\ *or* **phar·ma·cog·nos·ti·cal** \-ti-kəl\ *adj*

phar·ma·co·ki·net·ics \-kō-kə-ˈnet-iks, -kō-kī-\ *n pl but sing in constr* (1960) **1** : the study of the bodily absorption, distribution, metabolism, and excretion of drugs **2** : the characteristic interactions of a drug and the body in terms of its absorption, distribution, metabolism, and excretion — **phar·ma·co·ki·net·ic** \-ik\ *adj*

phar·ma·col·o·gy \ˌfär-mə-ˈkäl-ə-jē\ *n* (ca. 1771) **1** : the science of drugs including materia medica, toxicology, and therapeutics **2** : the properties and reactions of drugs esp. with relation to their therapeutic value — **phar·ma·co·log·i·cal** \-kə-ˈläj-i-kəl\ *also* **phar·ma·co·log·ic** \-ik\ *adj* — **phar·ma·co·log·i·cal·ly** \-i-k(ə-)lē\ *adv* — **phar·ma·col·o·gist** \-ˈkäl-ə-jəst\ *n*

phar·ma·co·poe·ia *also* **phar·ma·co·pe·ia** \-kə-ˈpē-(y)ə\ *n* [NL, fr. LGk *pharmakopoiia* preparation of drugs, fr. Gk *pharmako-* + *poiein* to make — more at POET] (1621) **1** : a book describing drugs, chemicals, and medicinal preparations; *esp* : one issued by an officially recognized authority and serving as a standard **2** : a collection or stock of drugs — **phar·ma·co·poe·ial** *also* **phar·ma·co·pe·ial** \-(y)əl\ *adj*

phar·ma·co·ther·a·py \ˌfär-mə-kō-ˈther-ə-pē\ *n* (ca. 1909) : the treatment of disease and esp. mental illness with drugs

phar·ma·cy \ˈfär-mə-sē\ *n, pl* **-cies** [LL *pharmacia* administration of drugs, fr. Gk *pharmakeia,* fr. *pharmakeuein* to administer drugs, fr. *pharmakon* magic charm, poison, drug] (1651) **1** : the art or practice of preparing, preserving, compounding, and dispensing drugs **2 a** : a place where medicines are compounded or dispensed **b** : DRUGSTORE **3** : PHARMACOPOEIA 2

phar·os \ˈfa(ə)r-ˌäs, ˈfe(ə)r-\ *n* [Gk, fr. *Pharos,* island in the bay of Alexandria, Egypt, famous for its lighthouse] (1552) : a lighthouse or beacon to guide seamen

pharyng- *or* **pharyngo-** *comb form* [Gk, fr. *pharyng-, pharynx*] : pharynx ⟨*pharyng*itis⟩ ⟨*pharyngo*logy⟩

pha·ryn·geal \ˌfar-ən-ˈjē-əl, fə-ˈrin-j(ē-)əl\ *adj* [NL *pharyngeus,* fr. *pharyng-, pharynx*] (1828) : relating to or located or produced in the region of the pharynx

phar·yn·gi·tis \ˌfar-ən-ˈjīt-əs\ *n, pl* **-git·i·des** \-ˈjit-ə-ˌdēz\ (ca. 1844) : inflammation of the pharynx

phar·ynx \ˈfar-iŋ(k)s\ *n, pl* **pha·ryn·ges** \fə-ˈrin-(ˌ)jēz\ *also* **phar·ynx·es** [NL *pharyng-, pharynx,* fr. Gk, throat, pharynx; akin to ON *barki* throat, L *forare* to bore — more at BORE] (ca. 1693) **1** : the part of the vertebrate alimentary canal between the cavity of the mouth and the esophagus **2** : a differentiated part of the alimentary canal in some invertebrates that may be thickened and muscular, eversible and toothed, or adapted as a suctorial organ

¹**phase** \ˈfāz\ *n* [NL *phasis,* fr. Gk, appearance of a star, phase of the moon, fr. *phainein* to show (middle voice, to appear) — more at FANCY] (1812) **1** : a particular appearance or state in a regularly recurring cycle of changes ⟨~*s* of the moon⟩ **2 a** : a distinguishable part in a course, development, or cycle ⟨the early ~*s* of his career⟩ **b** : an aspect or part (as of a problem) under consideration **3** : the point or stage in a period of uniform circular motion, harmonic motion, or the periodic changes of any magnitude varying according to a simple harmonic law to which the rotation, oscillation, or variation has advanced considered in its relation to a standard position or assumed instant of starting **4** : a homogeneous, physically distinct, and mechanically separable portion of matter present in a nonhomogeneous physical-chemical system **5** : an individual or subgroup distinguishably different in appearance or behavior from the norm of the group to which it belongs; *also* : the distinguishing peculiarity — **pha·sic** \ˈfā-zik\ *adj* — **in phase** : in a synchronized or correlated manner — **out of phase** : in an unsynchronized manner : not in correlation

²**phase** *vt* **phased; phas·ing** (1904) **1** : to adjust so as to be in a synchronized condition **2** : to conduct or carry out by planned phases **3** : to introduce in stages — often used with *in* ⟨~ in new models⟩

phase–contrast *adj* (1934) : of or employing the phase-contrast microscope

phase–contrast microscope *n* (1947) : a microscope that translates differences in phase of the light transmitted through or reflected by the object into differences of intensity in the image — called also *phase microscope*

phase·down \ˈfāz-ˌdau̇n\ *n* (1964) : a gradual reduction (as in operations)

phase modulation *n* (1930) : modulation of the phase of a radio carrier wave by voice or other signal

phase·out \ˈfā-ˌzau̇t\ *n* (1958) : a gradual stopping of operations or production : a closing down by phases

phase out \ˈfā-ˈzau̇t\ *vt* (ca. 1940) : to discontinue the practice, production, or use of by phases ⟨*phase out* the old machinery⟩ ~ *vi* : to stop production or operation by phases

-pha·sia \ˈfā-zh(ē-)ə\ *n comb form* [NL, fr. Gk, speech, fr. *phasis* utterance, fr. *phanai* to speak, say — more at BAN] : speech disorder of a (specified) type ⟨dys*phasia*⟩

phas·mid \ˈfaz-məd\ *n* [NL *Phasmida,* group name, fr. *Phasma,* type genus, fr. Gk, apparition, fr. *phainein* to show — more at FANCY] (1872) : any of an order or suborder (Phasmatodea) of large cylindrical or sometimes flattened chiefly tropical insects (as a walking stick) with long strong legs, strictly phytophagous habits, and slight metamorphosis

phat·ic \ˈfat-ik\ *adj* [Gk *phatos,* verbal of *phanai* to speak] (1923) : revealing or sharing feelings or establishing an atmosphere of sociability rather than communicating ideas — **phat·i·cal·ly** \-i-k(ə-)lē\ *adv*

pheas·ant \ˈfez-ᵊnt\ *n, pl* **pheasant** *or* **pheasants** [ME *fesaunt,* fr. AF, fr. OF *fesan,* fr. L *phasianus,* fr. Gk *phasianos,* fr. *phasianos* of the Phasis river, fr. *Phasis,* river in Colchis] (13c) **1** : any of numerous large often long-tailed and brightly colored Old World gallinaceous birds (*Phasianus* and related genera of the family Phasianidae) many of which are raised as ornamental or game birds **2** : any of various birds resembling a pheasant

phel·lem \ˈfel-ˌem\ *n* [Gk *phellos* cork + E *-em* (as in *phloem*)] (1887) : a layer of usu. suberized cells produced outwardly by a phellogen

phel·lo·derm \ˈfel-ə-ˌdərm\ *n* [Gk *phellos* + ISV *-derm*] (1875) : a layer of parenchyma produced inwardly by a phellogen

phel·lo·gen \ˈfel-ə-jən\ *n* [Gk *phellos* + ISV *-gen*] (1875) : a secondary meristem that initiates phellem and phelloderm in the periderm of a stem

phen- *or* **pheno-** *comb form* [obs. *phene* (benzene), fr. F *phène,* fr. Gk *phainein* to show; fr. its occurrence in illuminating gas — more at FANCY] : related to or derived from benzene ⟨*phen*ol⟩ : containing phenyl ⟨*pheno*barbital⟩

phe·na·caine \ˈfē-nə-ˌkān, ˈfen-ə-\ *n* [prob. fr. *phen*etidine + *acet-* + *-caine*] (1907) : a crystalline base $C_{18}H_{22}N_2O_2$ or its hydrochloride used as a local anesthetic

phen·ac·e·tin \fi-ˈnas-ət-ən\ *n* [ISV] (ca. 1887) : a white crystalline compound $C_{10}H_{13}NO_2$ that is used to ease pain or fever — called also *acetophenetidin*

phen·a·kite \ˈfen-ə-ˌkīt, ˈfēn-\ *or* **phen·a·cite** \-ˌsīt\ *n* [G *phenakit,* fr. Gk *phenak-, phenax* deceiver; fr. its being easily mistaken for quartz] (ca. 1834) : a glassy mineral Be_2SiO_4 that consists of a beryllium silicate and occurs in rhombohedral crystals

phen·an·threne \fə-ˈnan-ˌthrēn\ *n* [ISV *phen-* + *anthracene*] (1882) : a crystalline aromatic hydrocarbon $C_{14}H_{10}$ of coal tar isomeric with anthracene

phen·azine \ˈfen-ə-ˌzēn\ *n* [ISV] (ca. 1900) : a yellowish crystalline base $C_{12}H_8N_2$ that is the parent compound of many azine dyes and a few antibiotics

phen·cy·cli·dine \(ˈ)fen-ˈsik-lə-ˌdēn, -ˈsī-klə-, -dən\ *n* [*phen-* + *cycl-* + *-idin*] (1959) : a piperidine derivative $C_{17}H_{25}N$ used medicinally as an anesthetic and sometimes illicitly as a psychedelic drug to induce vivid mental imagery — called also *PCP*

phe·net·ic \fi-ˈnet-ik\ *adj* [*phen*otype + *-etic* (as in *genetic*)] (1960) : of, relating to, or being classificatory systems and procedures that are based on overall similarity usu. of many characters without regard to the evolutionary history of the organisms involved

phe·net·ics \-iks\ *n pl but sing in constr* (ca. 1960) : biological systematics based on phenetic relationships — **phe·net·i·cist** \-ˈnet-ə-səst\ *n*

phe·net·i·dine \fə-ˈnet-ə-ˌdēn\ *n* [*phenetole* + *-idine*] (ca. 1865) : any of three liquid basic amino derivatives $C_8H_{11}NO$ of phenetole used esp. in manufacturing dyestuffs

phe·ne·tole \ˈfen-ə-ˌtōl\ *n* [ISV *phen-* + *ethyl* + *-ole*] (ca. 1850) : the aromatic liquid ethyl ether $C_8H_{10}O$ of phenol

phen·met·ra·zine \(ˈ)fen-ˈme-trə-ˌzēn\ *n* [*phenyl* + *methyl* + *tetra-* + *oxazine*] (1956) : a sympathomimetic stimulant $C_{11}H_{15}NO$ used in the hydrochloride as an appetite suppressant

phe·no·bar·bi·tal \ˌfē-nō-ˈbär-bə-ˌtȯl\ *n* (1918) : a crystalline barbiturate $C_{12}H_{12}N_2O_3$ used as a hypnotic and sedative

phe·no·bar·bi·tone \-bə-ˌtōn\ *n, chiefly Brit* (ca. 1932) : PHENOBARBITAL

phe·no·copy \ˈfē-nə-ˌkäp-ē\ *n* [*phenotype* + *copy*] (1937) : a phenotypic variation that is caused by unusual environmental conditions and resembles the normal expression of a genotype other than its own

phe·no·cryst \-ˌkrist\ *n* [F *phénocryste,* fr. Gk *phainein* to show + *krystallos* crystal — more at FANCY] (ca. 1893) : one of the prominent embedded crystals of a porphyry — **phe·no·crys·tic** \ˌfē-nə-ˈkris-tik\ *adj*

phe·nol \ˈfē-ˌnōl, -ˌnȯl, fi-ˈ\ *n* [ISV *phen-* + *-ol*] (ca. 1852) **1** : a caustic poisonous crystalline acidic compound C_6H_5OH present in coal tar and wood tar that in dilute solution is used as a disinfectant **2** : any of various acidic compounds analogous to phenol and regarded as hydroxyl derivatives of aromatic hydrocarbons

phe·no·late \ˈfēn-ᵊl-ˌāt\ *n* (1885) : PHENOXIDE

\ə\ abut \ᵊ\ kitten, F table \ər\ further \a\ ash \ā\ ace \ä\ cot, cart
\au̇\ out \ch\ chin \e\ bet \ē\ easy \g\ go \i\ hit \ī\ ice \j\ job
\ŋ\ sing \ō\ go \ȯ\ law \ȯi\ boy \th\ thin \th\ the \ü\ loot \u̇\ foot
\y\ yet \zh\ vision \à, k̲, ⁿ, œ, œ̄, ue, ue̅, ʸ\ see Guide to Pronunciation

phe·no·lat·ed \'fēn-ᵊl-ˌāt-əd\ *adj* (1923) **:** treated, mixed, or impregnated with phenol

[1]**phe·no·lic** \fi-'nō-lik, -'näl-ik\ *adj* (1872) **1 a :** of, relating to, or having the characteristics of a phenol **b :** containing or derived from a phenol **2 :** of, relating to, or being a phenolic

[2]**phenolic** *n* (1924) **:** a usu. thermosetting resin or plastic made by condensation of a phenol with an aldehyde and used esp. for molding and insulating and in coatings and adhesives — called also *phenolic resin*

phe·nol·o·gy \fi-'näl-ə-jē\ *n* [*phenomena* + *-logy*] (ca. 1884) **1 :** a branch of science dealing with the relations between climate and periodic biological phenomena (as bird migration or plant flowering) **2 :** periodic biological phenomena (as of a kind of organism) that are correlated with climatic conditions — **phe·no·log·i·cal** \ˌfēn-ᵊl-'äj-i-kəl\ *adj* — **phe·no·log·i·cal·ly** \-k(ə-)lē\ *adv*

phe·nol·phtha·lein \ˌfēn-ᵊl-'thal-ē-ən, -'thal-ˌēn, -'thāl-\ *n* [ISV] (ca. 1875) **:** a white or yellowish white crystalline compound $C_{20}H_{14}O_4$ used in analysis as an indicator because its solution is brilliant red in alkalies and is decolorized by acids and in medicine as a laxative

phenol red *n* (1916) **:** a red crystalline compound $C_{19}H_{14}O_5S$ used esp. as an acid-base indicator

phe·nom \'fē-ˌnäm, fi-'näm\ *n* (ca. 1914) **:** PHENOMENON; *esp* **:** a person of phenomenal ability or promise

phe·nom·e·nal \fi-'näm-ən-ᵊl\ *adj* (1825) **:** relating to or being a phenomenon: as **a :** known through the senses rather than through thought or intuition **b :** concerned with phenomena rather than with hypotheses **c :** EXTRAORDINARY, REMARKABLE ***syn*** see MATERIAL — **phe·nom·e·nal·ly** \-ᵊl-ē\ *adv*

phe·nom·e·nal·ism \-ən-ᵊl-ˌiz-əm\ *n* (ca. 1868) **1 :** a theory that limits knowledge to phenomena only **2 :** a theory that all knowledge is of phenomena and all existence is phenomenal — **phe·nom·e·nal·ist** \-ᵊl-əst\ *n* — **phe·nom·e·nal·is·tic** \-ˌnäm-ən-ᵊl-'is-tik\ *adj* — **phe·nom·e·nal·is·ti·cal·ly** \-ti-k(ə-)lē\ *adv*

phe·nom·e·no·log·i·cal \fi-ˌnäm-ən-ᵊl-'äj-i-kəl\ *adj* (ca. 1858) **1 :** of or relating to phenomenology **2 :** PHENOMENAL **3 :** of or relating to phenomenalism — **phe·nom·e·no·log·i·cal·ly** \-k(ə-)lē\ *adv*

phe·nom·e·nol·o·gy \fi-ˌnäm-ə-'näl-ə-jē\ *n, pl* **-gies** [G *phänomenologie,* fr. *phänomenon* phenomenon + *-logie* -logy] (ca. 1797) **1 :** the study of the development of human consciousness and self-awareness as a preface to philosophy or a part of philosophy **2 a** (1) **:** the description of the formal structure of the objects of awareness and of awareness itself in abstraction from any claims concerning existence ⟨the ~ of internal time-consciousness⟩ (2) **:** the typological classification of a class of phenomena ⟨the ~ of religion⟩ **b :** an analysis produced by phenomenological investigation — **phe·nom·e·nol·o·gist** \-jəst\ *n*

phe·nom·e·non \fi-'näm-ə-ˌnän, -nən\ *n, pl* **-na** \-nə, -ˌnä\ *or* **-nons** [LL *phaenomenon,* fr. Gk *phainomenon,* fr. neut. of *phainomenos,* prp. of *phainesthai* to appear, middle voice of *phainein* to show — more at FANCY] (1605) **1** *pl* *phenomena* **:** an observable fact or event **2** *pl* *phenomena* **a :** an object or aspect known through the senses rather than by thought or nonsensuous intuition **b :** a temporal or spatiotemporal object of sensual experience as distinguished from a noumenon **c :** a fact or event of scientific interest susceptible of scientific description and explanation **3 a :** a rare or significant fact or event **b** *pl* *phenomenons* **:** an exceptional, unusual, or abnormal person, thing, or occurrence

usage The plural *phenomena* is occas. used as a singular ⟨a detailed analysis of this *phenomena*⟩ This singular use appears to be somewhat less frequent than the similar use of *criteria,* and while it may one day establish itself, it has not done so yet and will generally be considered an error.

phe·no·thi·azine \ˌfē-nō-'thī-ə-ˌzēn\ *n* [ISV] (1894) **1 :** a greenish yellow crystalline compound $C_{12}H_9NS$ used as an anthelmintic and insecticide esp. in veterinary practice **2 :** any of various phenothiazine derivatives (as chlorpromazine) that are used as tranquilizing agents esp. in the treatment of schizophrenia

phe·no·type \'fē-nə-ˌtīp\ *n* [G *phänotypus,* fr. Gk *phainein* to show + *typos* type] (ca. 1911) **:** the visible properties of an organism that are produced by the interaction of the genotype and the environment — **phe·no·typ·ic** \ˌfē-nə-'tip-ik\ *also* **phe·no·typ·i·cal** \-i-kəl\ *adj* — **phe·no·typ·i·cal·ly** \-i-k(ə-)lē\ *adv*

phen·ox·ide \fi-'näk-ˌsīd\ *n* (ca. 1920) **:** a salt of a phenol esp. in its capacity as a weak acid

phen·oxy- \fi-'näk-sē\ *comb form* [*phenyl* + *oxy-*] **:** containing the univalent radical C_6H_5O

phen·tol·amine \fen-'täl-ə-ˌmēn, -mən\ *n* [*phen-* + *toluidine* + *amine*] (ca. 1952) **:** an adrenergic blocking agent $C_{17}H_{19}N_3O$ that is used esp. in the diagnosis of pheochromocytoma

phe·nyl \'fen-ᵊl, 'fēn-\ *n* [ISV] (ca. 1850) **:** a univalent radical C_6H_5 that is an aryl group derived from benzene by removal of one hydrogen atom — often used in combination — **phe·nyl·ic** \fi-'nil-ik\ *adj*

phe·nyl·al·a·nine \ˌfen-ᵊl-'al-ə-ˌnēn, ˌfēn-\ *n* [ISV] (1883) **:** an essential amino acid $C_9H_{11}NO_2$ that is converted in the normal body to tyrosine

phen·yl·bu·ta·zone \ˌfen-ᵊl-'byüt-ə-ˌzōn\ *n* [*phenyl* + *butyric* acid + *pyrazalone* $(C_3H_4N_2O)$] (1952) **:** a drug $C_{19}H_{20}N_2O_2$ that is used for its analgesic and anti-inflammatory properties esp. in the treatment of arthritis, gout, and bursitis

phen·yl·ene \'fen-ᵊl-ˌēn\ *n* [ISV] (1862) **:** any of three bivalent radicals C_6H_4 derived from benzene by removal of two hydrogen atoms

phen·yl·eph·rine \-'ef-ˌrēn, -rən\ *n* [*phenyl* + epinephrine] (ca. 1943) **:** a sympathomimetic agent $C_9H_{13}NO_2$ that is used in the form of the hydrochloride as a vasoconstrictor, a mydriatic, and by injection to raise the blood pressure

phe·nyl·ke·ton·uria \ˌfen-ᵊl-ˌkēt-ᵊn-'(y)ür-ē-ə, ˌfēn-\ *n* [*phenyl* + *ketone* + *-uria*] (1935) **:** an inherited metabolic disease in man that is characterized by inability to oxidize a metabolic product of phenylalanine and by severe mental deficiency — abbr. *PKU* — **phe·nyl·ke·ton·uric** \-'(y)ür-ik\ *adj*

phen·yl·pro·pa·nol·amine \ˌfen-ᵊl-ˌprō-pə-'nōl-ə-ˌmēn, -'nōl-; -nō-'lam-ˌēn\ *n* [*phenyl* + *propane* + *-ol* + *amine*] (1947) **:** a sympathomimetic drug $C_9H_{13}NO$ used in the hydrochloride esp. as a nasal and bronchial decongestant and as an appetite suppressant

phen·yl·thio·car·ba·mide \ˌfen-ᵊl-ˌthī-ō-'kär-bə-ˌmīd\ *n* (1879) **:** a crystalline compound $C_7H_8N_2S$ that is extremely bitter or tasteless depending on the presence or absence of a single dominant gene in the taster — called also *phenylthiourea, PTC*

phen·yl·thio·urea \-ˌthī-ō-yü-'rē-ə\ *n* (1896) **:** PHENYLTHIOCARBAMIDE

phe·nyt·o·in \fə-'nit-ə-wən\ *n* [di*phenyl*hydan*toin*] (1941) **:** a crystalline compound $C_{15}H_{12}N_2O_2$ used in the form of its sodium salt in the treatment of epilepsy — called also *diphenylhydantoin;* compare DILANTIN

pheo·chro·mo·cy·to·ma \ˌfē-ə-ˌkrō-mə-sə-'tō-mə, -sī-\ *n, pl* **-mas** *or* **-ma·ta** \-mət-ə\ [NL, fr. ISV *pheochromocyte* (chromaffin cell) + NL *-oma*] (ca. 1929) **:** a tumor that is derived from chromaffin cells and is usu. associated with paroxysmal or sustained hypertension

pher·o·mone \'fer-ə-ˌmōn\ *n* [ISV *phero-* (fr. Gk *pherein* to carry) + *-mone* (as in *hormone*) — more at BEAR] (1959) **:** a chemical substance that is produced by an animal and serves esp. as a stimulus to other individuals of the same species for one or more behavioral responses — **pher·o·mon·al** \ˌfer-ə-'mōn-ᵊl\ *adj*

phew *a voiceless whistling breath usu followed by a voiceless* (y)ü *or* ue *sound; often read as* 'f(y)ü\ *interj* [imit.] (1604) — usu. used to express relief or fatigue

phi \'fī\ *n* [MGk, fr. Gk *phei*] (ca. 1899) **:** the 21st letter of the Greek alphabet — see ALPHABET table

phi·al \'fī(-ə)l\ *n* [ME, fr. L *phiala,* fr. Gk *phialē*] (14c) **:** VIAL

Phi Be·ta Kap·pa \ˌfī-ˌbāt-ə-'kap-ə\ *n* [*Phi Beta Kappa (Society),* fr. *phi* + *beta* + *kappa,* initials of the society's Gk motto *philosophia biou kybernētēs* philosophy the guide of life] (1912) **:** a person winning high scholastic distinction in an American college or university and being elected to membership in a national honor society founded in 1776

phil- *or* **philo-** *comb form* [ME, fr. OF, fr. L, fr. Gk, fr. *philos* dear, friendly] **:** loving **:** having an affinity for ⟨*philo*progenitive⟩

[1]**-phil** \ˌfil\ *or* **-phile** \ˌfīl\ *n comb form* [F *-phile,* fr. Gk *-philos* -philous] **:** lover **:** one having an affinity for or a strong attraction to ⟨acido*phil*⟩ ⟨Slavo*phile*⟩

[2]**-phil** *or* **-phile** *adj comb form* [NL *-philus,* fr. L, fr. Gk *-philos*] **:** loving **:** having a fondness or affinity for ⟨hemo*phile*⟩ ⟨Franco*phil*⟩

Phil·a·del·phia lawyer \ˌfil-ə-ˌdel-fyə-, -fē-ə-\ *n* [*Philadelphia,* Pa.] (1788) **:** a shrewd lawyer adept at exploiting legal technicalities

Philadelphia pepper pot *n* (ca. 1929) **:** PEPPER POT 2b

phil·a·del·phus \ˌfil-ə-'del-fəs\ *n* [NL, fr. Gk *philadelphos* brotherly, fr. *phil-* + *adelphos* brother — more at -ADELPHOUS] (1950) **:** any of a genus of ornamental shrubs of the saxifrage family of which several are widely grown in temperate regions for their showy white flowers — called also *mock orange, syringa*

phi·lan·der \fə-'lan-dər\ *vi* **-dered; -der·ing** \-d(ə-)riŋ\ [fr. obs. *philander* (lover, philanderer), prob. fr. the name *Philander*] (1788) **1 :** to make love to someone with whom marriage is impossible (as because of an existing marriage) or with no intention of proposing marriage **2 :** to have many love affairs — **phi·lan·der·er** \-dər-ər\ *n*

phil·an·throp·ic \ˌfil-ən-'thräp-ik\ *also* **phil·an·throp·i·cal** \-i-kəl\ *adj* (1789) **1 :** of, relating to, or characterized by philanthropy **:** HUMANITARIAN **2 :** dispensing or receiving aid from funds set aside for humanitarian purposes ⟨a ~ foundation⟩ — **phil·an·throp·i·cal·ly** \-i-k(ə-)lē\ *adv*

phi·lan·thro·pist \fə-'lan(t)-thrə-pəst\ *n* (ca. 1730) **:** one who practices philanthropy

phi·lan·thro·py \-pē\ *n, pl* **-pies** [LL *philanthropia,* fr. Gk *philanthrōpia,* fr. *philanthrōpos* loving mankind, fr. *phil-* + *anthrōpos* man] (ca. 1623) **1 :** goodwill to fellowmen; *esp* **:** active effort to promote human welfare **2 a :** a philanthropic act or gift **b :** an organization distributing or supported by philanthropic funds

phi·lat·e·list \fə-'lat-ᵊl-əst\ *n* (ca. 1865) **:** a specialist in philately **:** one who collects or studies stamps

phi·lat·e·ly \fə-'lat-ᵊl-ē\ *n* [F *philatélie,* fr. *phil-* + Gk *ateleia* tax exemption, fr. *atelēs* free from tax, fr. *a-* + *telos* tax; akin to Gk *telein* to pay, *tlēnai* to bear; fr. the fact that a stamped letter frees the recipient from paying the mailing charges — more at TOLERATE] (ca. 1865) **:** the collection and study of postage and imprinted stamps **:** stamp collecting — **phil·a·tel·ic** \ˌfil-ə-'tel-ik\ *adj* — **phil·a·tel·i·cal·ly** \-i-k(ə-)lē\ *adv*

Phi·le·mon \fə-'lē-mən, fī-\ *n* [Gk *Philēmōn*] **1 :** a friend and probable convert of the apostle Paul **2 :** a letter written by St. Paul to a Christian living in the area of Colossae and included as a book in the New Testament — see BIBLE table **3 :** a poor aged Phrygian in Greek mythology who with his wife Baucis treats a disguised Zeus hospitably and is rewarded by him with a splendid temple

Phil·har·mon·ic \ˌfil-ər-'män-ik, ˌfil-(ˌ)(h)är-\ *n* [F *philharmonique,* lit., loving harmony, fr. It *filarmonico,* fr. *fil-* phil- + *armonia* harmony, fr. L *harmonia*] (1843) **:** SYMPHONY ORCHESTRA

phil·hel·lene \(ˈ)fil-'hel-ˌēn\ *or* **phil·hel·len·ic** \ˌfil-hə-'len-ik\ *adj* [Gk *philellēn,* fr. *phil-* + *Hellēn* Hellene] (1823) **:** admiring Greece or the Greeks — **philhellene** *n* — **phil·hel·le·nism** \(ˈ)fil-'hel-ə-ˌniz-əm\ *n* — **phil·hel·le·nist** \-nəst\ *n*

-phil·ia \'fil-ē-ə\ *n comb form* [NL, fr. Gk *philia* friendship, fr. *philos* dear] **1 :** tendency toward ⟨hemo*philia*⟩ **2 :** abnormal appetite or liking for ⟨necro*philia*⟩

-phil·i·ac \'fil-ē-ˌak\ *n comb form* [NL *-philia* + Gk *-akos,* adj. suffix] **1 :** one having a tendency toward ⟨hemo*philiac*⟩ **2 :** one having an abnormal appetite or liking for ⟨copro*philiac*⟩

-phil·ic \'fil-ik\ *adj comb form* [Gk *-philos* -philous] **:** having an affinity for **:** loving ⟨photo*philic*⟩

Phi·lip·pi·ans \fə-'lip-ē-ənz\ *n pl but sing in constr* [short for *Epistle to the Philippians*] **:** a hortatory letter written by St. Paul to the Christians of Philippi and included as a book in the New Testament — see BIBLE table

phi·lip·pic \fə-'lip-ik\ *n* [MF *philippique,* fr. L & Gk; L *philippica, orationes philippicae,* speeches of Cicero against Mark Antony, trans. of Gk *philippikoi logoi,* speeches of Demosthenes against Philip II of Macedon, lit., speeches relating to Philip] (1542) **:** a discourse or declamation full of bitter condemnation **:** TIRADE

Phil·ip·pine mahogany \ˌfil-ə-ˌpēn-\ *n* [*Philippine* islands] (ca. 1924) **:** any of several Philippine timber trees (family Dipterocarpaceae) with wood resembling that of the true mahoganies; *also* **:** its wood

phi·lis·tia \fə-'lis-tē-ə\ *n pl, often cap* [*Philistia,* ancient country of southwest Palestine] (1857) **:** the class or world of cultural philistines

Phi·lis·tine \'fil-ə-ˌstēn; fə-'lis-tən, -ˌtēn; 'fil-ə-stən\ *n* (14c) **1 :** a native or inhabitant of ancient Philistia **2** *often not cap* **a :** a crass prosaic often priggish individual guided by material rather than intellectual or artistic values : BABBITT **b** : one uninformed in a special area of knowledge — **philistine** *adj, often cap* — **phi·lis·tin·ism** \-ˌstē-ˌniz-əm, -tə-, -stə-\ *n, often cap*

Phil·lips \ˈfil-əps\ *trademark* — used for screws having a special head with a cross slot for use with a special screwdriver

phil·lu·men·ist \fi-ˈlü-mə-nəst\ *n* [*phil-* + L *lumen* light — more at LUMINARY] (1943) : one who collects matchbooks or matchbox labels

Phi·loc·te·tes \fi-ˈläk-tə-ˌtēz\ *n* [Gk *Philoktētēs*] : a Greek archer who uses the bow of Hercules to slay Paris at Troy

philo·den·dron \ˌfil-ə-ˈden-drən\ *n, pl* **-drons** *or* **-dra** \-drə\ [NL, fr. Gk, neut. of *philodendros* loving trees, fr. *phil-* + *dendron* tree — more at DENDR-] (1899) : any of various aroid plants (as of the genus *Philodendron*) that are cultivated for their showy foliage

phi·lol·o·gy \fə-ˈläl-ə-jē *also* fi-\ *n* [F *philologie*, fr. L *philologia* love of learning and literature, fr. Gk, fr. *philologos* fond of learning and literature, fr. *phil-* + *logos* word, speech — more at LEGEND] (1612) **1** : the study of literature and of disciplines relevant to literature or to language as used in literature **2 a** : LINGUISTICS; *esp* : historical and comparative linguistics **b** : the study of human speech esp. as the vehicle of literature and as a field of study that sheds light on cultural history — **phil·o·log·i·cal** \ˌfil-ə-ˈläj-i-kəl\ *adj* — **phil·o·log·i·cal·ly** \-k(ə-)lē\ *adv* — **phi·lol·o·gist** \fə-ˈläl-ə-jəst *also* fi-\ *n*

Phil·o·mel \ˈfil-ə-ˌmel\ *n* [L *Philomela* Philomela, nightingale] (15c) : NIGHTINGALE

Phil·o·me·la \ˌfil-ə-ˈmē-lə\ *n* [L, fr. Gk *Philomēlē*] : an Athenian princess in Greek mythology raped and deprived of her tongue by her brother-in-law Tereus, avenged by the killing of his son, and changed into a nightingale while fleeing from him

philo·pro·gen·i·tive \ˌfil-ə-prō-ˈjen-ət-iv\ *adj* [*phil-* + L *progenitus*, pp. of *progignere* to beget — more at PROGENITOR] (1865) **1** : tending to produce offspring : PROLIFIC **2** : of, relating to, or characterized by love of offspring — **philo·pro·gen·i·tive·ness** *n*

phi·lo·sophe \ˌfē-lə-ˈzȯf\ *n* [F, lit., philosopher] (1774) : one of the deistic or materialistic writers and thinkers of the 18th century French Enlightenment

phi·los·o·pher \fə-ˈläs-(ə-)fər\ *n* [ME, modif. of MF *philosophe*, fr. L *philosophus*, fr. Gk *philosophos*, fr. *phil-* + *sophia* wisdom, fr. *sophos* wise] (14c) **1 a** : one who seeks wisdom or enlightenment : SCHOLAR, THINKER **b** : a student of philosophy **2 a** : a person whose philosophical perspective enables him to meet trouble with equanimity **b** : the expounder of a theory in a particular area of experience **c** : one who philosophizes

philosophers' stone *n* (14c) : an imaginary stone, substance, or chemical preparation believed to have the power of transmuting baser metals into gold and sought for by alchemists

philo·soph·i·cal \ˌfil-ə-ˈsäf-i-kəl *also* -ˈzäf-\ *or* **philo·soph·ic** \-ik\ *adj* (14c) **1 a** : of or relating to philosophers or philosophy **b** : based on philosophy **2** : characterized by the attitude of a philosopher; *specif* : calm in face of trouble — **philo·soph·i·cal·ly** \-i-k(ə-)lē\ *adv*

philosophical analysis *n* (1943) : an Anglo-American philosophical movement that seeks the solution of philosophical problems in the analysis of propositions or sentences — called also *analytic philosophy, linguistic analysis;* compare ORDINARY-LANGUAGE PHILOSOPHY

phi·los·o·phize \fə-ˈläs-ə-ˌfīz\ *vb* **-phized; -phiz·ing** *vi* (1594) **1** : to reason in the manner of a philosopher **2** : to expound a moralizing and often superficial philosophy ~ *vt* : to consider from or bring into conformity with a philosophical point of view — **phi·los·o·phiz·er** *n*

phi·los·o·phy \fə-ˈläs-(ə-)fē\ *n, pl* **-phies** [ME *philosophie*, fr. OF, fr. L *philosophia*, fr. Gk, fr. *philosophos* philosopher] (13c) **1 a** (1) *archaic* : PHYSICAL SCIENCE (2) : ETHICS **b** (1) : all learning exclusive of technical precepts and practical arts (2) : the sciences and liberal arts exclusive of medicine, law, and theology ⟨a doctor of ~⟩ (3) : the 4-year college course of a major seminary **c** : a discipline comprising as its core logic, aesthetics, ethics, metaphysics, and epistemology **2 a** : pursuit of wisdom **b** : a search for a general understanding of values and reality by chiefly speculative rather than observational means **c** : an analysis of the grounds of and concepts expressing fundamental beliefs **3 a** : a system of philosophical concepts ⟨Kantian ~⟩ **b** : a theory underlying or regarding a sphere of activity or thought ⟨the ~ of cooking⟩ ⟨~ of science⟩ **4 a** : the most general beliefs, concepts, and attitudes of an individual or group ⟨the hippie ~⟩ **b** : calmness of temper and judgment befitting a philosopher

philosophy of life (1853) **1** : an overall vision of or attitude toward life and the purpose of life **2** [trans. of G *Lebensphilosophie*] : any of various philosophies that emphasize human life or life in general

-phi·lous \f-(ə-)ləs\ *adj comb form* [Gk *-philos*, fr. *philos* dear, friendly] : loving : having an affinity for ⟨acidophilous⟩

phil·ter *or* **phil·tre** \ˈfil-tər\ *n* [MF *philtre*, fr. L *philtrum*, fr. Gk *philtron;* akin to Gk *philos* dear] (1587) **1** : a potion, drug, or charm held to have the power to arouse sexual passion **2** : a potion credited with magical power

phi phenomenon \ˌfī-\ *n* (ca. 1928) : apparent motion resulting from an orderly sequence of stimuli (as lights flashed in rapid succession a short distance apart on a sign) without any actual motion being presented to the eye

phleb- *or* **phlebo-** *comb form* [ME *fleb-*, fr. MF, fr. LL *phlebo-*, fr. Gk *phleb-, phlebo-*, fr. *phleb-, phleps;* akin to L *fluere* to flow — more at FLUID] : vein ⟨phlebitis⟩

phle·bi·tis \fli-ˈbīt-əs\ *n* [NL] (ca. 1822) : inflammation of a vein

phle·bo·gram \ˈflē-bə-ˌgram\ *n* [ISV] (1885) : a figure of a vein or a record of its movements (as by roentgenography following injection of a radiopaque substance)

phle·bog·ra·phy \fli-ˈbäg-rə-fē\ *n* [ISV] (ca. 1842) : the art of making phlebograms — **phle·bo·graph·ic** \ˌflē-bə-ˈgraf-ik\ *adj*

phle·bol·o·gy \fli-ˈbäl-ə-jē\ *n* [ISV] (1893) : a branch of medicine concerned with the veins

phle·bo·to·mus fever \fli-ˌbät-ə-məs-\ *n* [NL *Phlebotomus*, genus of sand flies] (ca. 1923) : SANDFLY FEVER

phle·bot·o·my \fli-ˈbät-ə-mē\ *n, pl* **-mies** [ME *fleobotomie*, fr. MF *flebotomie*, fr. LL *phlebotomia*, fr. Gk, fr. *phleb-* + *-tomia* -tomy] (15c) : the letting of blood in the treatment of disease : VENESECTION — **phle·bot·o·mist** \-məst\ *n*

Phleg·e·thon \ˈfleg-ə-ˌthän\ *n* [L, fr. Gk *Phlegethōn*] : a river of fire in Hades

phlegm \ˈflem\ *n* [ME *fleume*, fr. MF, fr. LL *phlegmat-, phlegma*, fr. Gk, flame, inflammation, phlegm, fr. *phlegein* to burn — more at BLACK] (14c) **1** : the one of the four humors in early physiology that was considered to be cold and moist and to cause sluggishness **2** : viscid mucus secreted in abnormal quantity in the respiratory passages **3 a** : dull or apathetic coldness or indifference **b** : intrepid coolness or calm fortitude — **phlegmy** \-ē\ *adj*

phleg·mat·ic \fleg-ˈmat-ik\ *adj* (14c) **1** : resembling, consisting of, or producing the humor phlegm **2** : having or showing a slow and stolid temperament *syn* see IMPASSIVE — **phleg·mat·i·cal·ly** \-i-k(ə-)lē\ *adv*

phlo·em \ˈflō-ˌem\ *n* [G, fr. Gk *phloios, phloos* bark; akin to Gk *phallos* penis — more at BLOW] (ca. 1875) : a complex tissue in the vascular system of higher plants that consists mainly of sieve tubes and elongated parenchyma cells usu. with fibers and that functions in translocation and in support and storage — compare XYLEM

phloem necrosis *n* (1923) : a pathological state in a plant characterized by brown discoloration and disintegration of the phloem; *esp* : a fatal virus disease of the American elm

phloem ray *n* (ca. 1875) : a vascular ray or part of a vascular ray that is located in phloem — compare XYLEM RAY

phlo·gis·tic \flō-ˈjis-tik\ *adj* (1733) **1** [NL *phlogiston*] : of or relating to phlogiston **2** [Gk *phlogistos*] : of or relating to inflammations and fevers

phlo·gis·ton \-tən\ *n* [NL, fr. Gk, neut. of *phlogistos* inflammable, fr. *phlogizein* to set on fire, fr. *phlog-, phlox* flame, fr. *phlegein*] (1733) : the hypothetical principle of fire regarded formerly as a material substance

phlog·o·pite \ˈfläg-ə-ˌpīt\ *n* [G *phlogopit*, fr. Gk *phlogōpos* fiery-looking, fr. *phlog-, phlox* + *ōps* face — more at EYE] (1850) : a usu. brown to red form of mica

phlox \ˈfläks\ *n, pl* **phlox** *or* **phlox·es** [NL, fr. L, a flower, fr. Gk, flame, wallflower] (1601) : any of a genus (*Phlox* of the family Polemoniaceae, the phlox family) of American annual or perennial herbs that have red, purple, white, or variegated flowers, a salverform corolla with the stamens on its tube, and a 3-valved capsular fruit

-phobe \ˌfōb\ *n comb form* [Gk *-phobos* fearing] : one fearing or averse to (something specified) ⟨Francophobe⟩

pho·bia \ˈfō-bē-ə\ *n* [NL, fr. LL *-phobia*, fr. Gk, fr. *-phobos* fearing, fr. *phobos* fear, flight; akin to Gk *phebesthai* to flee, be frightened, Lith *bėgti* to flee] (ca. 1786) : an exaggerated usu. inexplicable and illogical fear of a particular object or class of objects

pho·bic \ˈfō-bik\ *adj* (1897) : of, relating to, affected with, or constituting phobia — **phobic** *n*

-pho·bic \ˈfō-bik\ *or* **-ph·o·bous** \f-ə-bəs\ *adj comb form* [*-phobic* fr. F *-phobique*, fr. LL *-phobicus*, fr. Gk *-phobikos*, fr. *-phobia; -phobous* fr. LL *-phobus*, fr. Gk *-phobos*] **1** : having an aversion for ⟨calciphobous⟩ **2** : lacking affinity for ⟨lyophobic⟩

phoe·be \ˈfē-(ˌ)bē\ *n* [alter. of *pewee*] (1700) : any of several American flycatchers (genus *Sayornis*); *esp* : one (*S. phoebe*) of the eastern U.S. that has a slight crest and is plain grayish brown above and yellowish white below

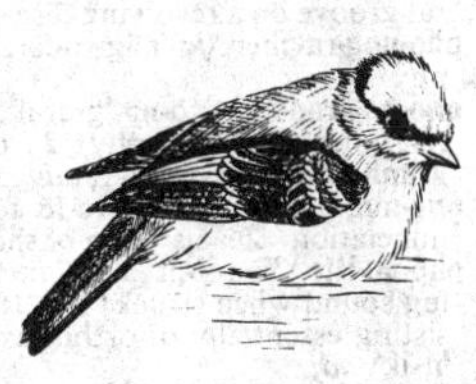
phoebe

Phoe·be \ˈfē-bē\ *n* [L, fr. Gk *Phoibē*, fr. *phoibē*, fem. of *phoibos*] : ARTEMIS

Phoe·bus \ˈfē-bəs\ *n* [L, fr. Gk *Phoibos*, fr. *phoibos* radiant] **1** : APOLLO **2** *not cap* : SUN

Phoe·ni·cian \fi-ˈnish-ən, -ˈnē-shən\ *n* (14c) **1** : a native or inhabitant of ancient Phoenicia **2** : the Semitic language of ancient Phoenicia — **Phoenician** *adj*

phoe·nix \ˈfē-niks\ *n* [ME *fenix*, fr. OE, fr. L *phoenix*, fr. Gk *phoinix* purple, crimson, Phoenician, phoenix, date palm, fr. *phoinos* bloodred; akin to Gk *phonos* murder, *theinein* to strike — more at DEFEND] (bef. 12c) : a legendary bird which according to one account lived 500 years, burned itself to ashes on a pyre, and rose alive from the ashes to live another period; *also* : a person or thing likened to the phoenix — **phoe·nix·like** \-ˌlīk\ *adj*

phon \ˈfän\ *n* [ISV, fr. Gk *phōnē* voice, sound] (1932) : the unit of loudness on a scale beginning at zero for the faintest audible sound and corresponding to the decibel scale of sound intensity with the number of phons of a given sound being equal to the decibels of a pure 1000-cycle tone judged by the average listener to be equal in loudness to the given sound

phon- *or* **phono-** *comb form* [L, fr. Gk *phōn-, phōno-*, fr. *phōnē* — more at BAN] : sound : voice : speech ⟨phonate⟩ ⟨phonograph⟩

pho·nate \ˈfō-ˌnāt\ *vi* **pho·nat·ed; pho·nat·ing** (1876) : to produce vocal sounds and esp. speech — **pho·na·tion** \fō-ˈnā-shən\ *n*

¹phone \ˈfōn\ *n* [by shortening] (1884) **1** : EARPHONE **2** : TELEPHONE

²phone *vb* **phoned; phon·ing** (1889) : TELEPHONE

³phone *n* [Gk *phōnē*] (1866) : a speech sound considered as a physical event without regard to its place in the sound system of a language

-phone \ˌfōn\ *n comb form* [Gk *-phōnos* sounding, fr. *phōnē*] : sound ⟨homophone⟩ — often in names of musical instruments and sound-transmitting devices ⟨radiophone⟩ ⟨xylophone⟩

pho·ne·mat·ic \ˌfō-ni-ˈmat-ik\ *adj* (1936) : PHONEMIC

pho·neme \ˈfō-ˌnēm\ *n* [F *phonème*, fr. Gk *phōnēmat-, phōnēma* speech sound, utterance, fr. *phōnein* to sound] (ca. 1916) : a member of the set of the smallest units of speech that serve to distinguish one utterance from another in a language or dialect ⟨the \p\ of *pat* and the \f\ of *fat* are two different ~s in English⟩

pho·ne·mic \fə-ˈnē-mik, fō-\ *adj* (ca. 1931) **1** : of, relating to, or having the characteristics of a phoneme **2 a** : constituting members of different phonemes ⟨in English \n\ and \ŋ\ are ~⟩ **b** : DISTINCTIVE 2 — **pho·ne·mi·cal·ly** \-mi-k(ə-)lē\ *adv*

pho·ne·mics \-miks\ *n pl but sing in constr* (1936) **1 :** a branch of linguistic analysis that consists of the study of phonemes **2 :** the structure of a language in terms of phonemes — **pho·ne·mi·cist** \-mə-səst\ *n*

pho·net·ic \fə-ˈnet-ik\ *adj* [NL *phoneticus,* fr. Gk *phōnētikos,* fr. *phōnein* to sound with the voice, fr. *phōnē* voice] (1826) **1 a :** of or relating to spoken language or speech sounds **b :** of or relating to the science of phonetics **2 :** representing the sounds and other phenomena of speech: **a :** constituting an alteration of ordinary spelling that better represents the spoken language, that employs only characters of the regular alphabet, and that is used in a context of conventional spelling **b :** representing speech sounds by means of symbols that have one value only **c :** employing for speech sounds more than the minimum number of symbols necessary to represent the significant differences in a speaker's speech — **pho·net·i·cal** \-i-kəl\ *adj* — **pho·net·i·cal·ly** \-i-k(ə-)lē\ *adv*

phonetic alphabet *n* (1848) **1 :** a set of symbols used for phonetic transcription **2 :** any of various systems of identifying letters of the alphabet by means of code words in voice communication

pho·ne·ti·cian \ˌfō-nə-ˈtish-ən *also* ˌfän-ə-\ *n* (1848) **:** a specialist in phonetics

pho·net·ics \fə-ˈnet-iks\ *n pl but sing in constr* (1836) **1 :** the system of speech sounds of a language or group of languages **2 a :** the study and systematic classification of the sounds made in spoken utterance **b :** the practical application of this science to language study

pho·nic \ˈfän-ik *also* ˈfō-nik\ *adj* (1823) **1 :** of, relating to, or producing sound **:** ACOUSTIC **2 a :** of or relating to the sounds of speech **b :** of or relating to phonics — **pho·ni·cal·ly** \-(ə-)lē\ *adv*

pho·nics \ˈfän-iks, *1 is also* ˈfō-niks\ *n pl but sing in constr* (ca. 1683) **1 :** the science of sound **:** ACOUSTICS **2 :** a method of teaching beginners to read and pronounce words by learning the phonetic value of letters, letter groups, and esp. syllables

pho·no \ˈfō-(ˌ)nō\ *n, pl* **phonos** (1909) **:** PHONOGRAPH

pho·no·car·dio·gram \ˌfō-nə-ˈkärd-ē-ə-ˌgram\ *n* [ISV] (1912) **:** a graphic record of heart sounds made by means of a microphone, amplifier, and galvanometer

pho·no·car·di·og·ra·phy \-ˌkärd-ē-ˈäg-rə-fē\ *n* (1916) **:** the process of producing a phonocardiogram — **pho·no·car·dio·graph** \-ˈkärd-ē-ə-ˌgraf\ *n* — **pho·no·car·dio·graph·ic** \-ˌkärd-ē-ə-ˈgraf-ik\ *adj*

pho·no·gram \ˈfō-nə-ˌgram\ *n* [ISV] (1860) **1 :** a character or symbol used to represent a word, syllable, or phoneme **2 :** a succession of orthographic letters that occurs with the same phonetic value in several words (as the *ight* of *bright, fight,* and *flight*) — **pho·no·gram·mic** *or* **pho·no·gram·ic** \ˌfō-nə-ˈgram-ik\ *adj* — **pho·no·gram·mi·cal·ly** *or* **pho·no·gram·i·cal·ly** \-i-k(ə-)lē\ *adv*

pho·no·graph \ˈfō-nə-ˌgraf\ *n* (1877) **:** an instrument for reproducing sounds by means of the vibration of a stylus or needle following a spiral groove on a revolving disc or cylinder

pho·nog·ra·pher \fə-ˈnäg-rə-fər, fō-\ *n* (1851) **:** a specialist in phonography

pho·no·graph·ic \ˌfō-nə-ˈgraf-ik, *1 is also* ˌfän-ə-\ *adj* (1828) **1 :** of or relating to phonography **2 :** of or relating to a phonograph — **pho·no·graph·i·cal·ly** \-i-k(ə-)lē\ *adv*

pho·nog·ra·phy \fə-ˈnäg-rə-fē, fō-\ *n* (1701) **1 :** spelling based on pronunciation **2 :** a system of shorthand writing based on sound

pho·no·lite \ˈfōn-ᵊl-ˌīt\ *n* [F, fr. G *phonolith,* fr. *phon-* + *-lith;* fr. its ringing sound when struck] (ca. 1828) **:** a gray or green volcanic rock consisting essentially of orthoclase and nepheline — **pho·no·lit·ic** \ˌfōn-ᵊl-ˈit-ik\ *adj*

pho·nol·o·gy \fə-ˈnäl-ə-jē, fō-\ *n* (1799) **1 :** the science of speech sounds including esp. the history and theory of sound changes in a language or in two or more related languages **2 :** the phonetics and phonemics of a language at a particular time — **pho·no·log·i·cal** \ˌfōn-ᵊl-ˈäj-i-kəl *also* ˌfän-ᵊl-\ *also* **pho·no·log·ic** \-ik\ *adj* — **pho·no·log·i·cal·ly** \-i-k(ə-)lē\ *adv* — **pho·nol·o·gist** \fə-ˈnäl-ə-jəst, fō-\ *n*

pho·non \ˈfō-ˌnän\ *n* [*phon-* + ²*-on*] (1932) **:** a quantum of vibrational energy (as in a crystal)

pho·no·rec·ord \ˈfō-nō-ˌrek-ərd\ *n* (1950) **:** a phonograph record

¹**pho·ny** *or* **pho·ney** \ˈfō-nē\ *adj* **pho·ni·er; -est** [origin unknown] (1900) **:** not genuine or real: as **a** (1) **:** intended to deceive or mislead (2) **:** intended to defraud **:** COUNTERFEIT ⟨a ~ $10 bill⟩ ⟨a ~ check⟩ **b :** arousing suspicion **:** probably dishonest ⟨something ~ about his alibi⟩ **c :** having no genuine existence **:** FICTITIOUS ⟨~ publicity stories⟩ **d :** FALSE, SHAM ⟨a ~ name⟩ ⟨~ pearls⟩ **e :** making a false show: as (1) **:** HYPOCRITICAL (2) **:** SPECIOUS ⟨has a ~ poetic elegance —*New Republic*⟩ — **pho·ni·ly** \ˈfōn-ᵊl-ē\ *adv* — **pho·ni·ness** \ˈfō-nē-nəs\ *n*

²**phony** *or* **phoney** *n, pl* **pho·nies** (1902) **:** one that is phony

³**phony** *or* **phoney** *vt* **pho·nied** *or* **pho·neyed; pho·ny·ing** *or* **pho·ney·ing** (1949) **:** COUNTERFEIT, FAKE — often used with *up* ⟨a paper *phonied* up on the spur of the moment —William Faulkner⟩

-pho·ny \f-ə-nē, ˌfō-nē\ *also* **-pho·nia** \ˈfō-nē-ə\ *n comb form* [ME *-phonie,* fr. OF, fr. L *-phonia,* fr. Gk *-phōnia,* fr. *-phōnos* sounding — more at -PHONE] **1 :** sound ⟨tele*phony*⟩ **2** *usu* **-phonia :** speech disorder of a (specified) type ⟨dys*phonia*⟩

phoo·ey \ˈfü-ē\ *interj* [imit.] (1929) — used to express repudiation or disgust

pho·rate \ˈfō(ə)r-ˌāt, ˈfȯ(ə)r-\ *n* [phos*phor*us + thion*ate*] (1959) **:** a very toxic organophosphate systemic insecticide $C_7H_{17}O_2PS_3$ that is used esp. in seed treatments

-phore \ˌfō(ə)r, ˌfȯ(ə)r\ *n comb form* [NL *-phorus,* fr. Gk *-phoros,* fr. *-phoros* (adj. comb. form) carrying, fr. *pherein* to carry — more at BEAR] **:** carrier ⟨gameto*phore*⟩

-pho·re·sis \fə-ˈrē-səs\ *n comb form, pl* **-pho·re·ses** \-ˌsēz\ [NL, fr. Gk *phorēsis* act of carrying, fr. *phorein* to carry, wear, freq. of *pherein*] **:** transmission ⟨electro*phoresis*⟩

phos- *comb form* [Gk *phōs-,* fr. *phōs*] **:** light ⟨*phos*gene⟩

phos·gene \ˈfäz-ˌjēn\ *n* [fr. its originally having been obtained by the action of sunlight] (ca. 1812) **:** a colorless gas $COCl_2$ of unpleasant odor that is a severe respiratory irritant

phosph- *or* **phospho-** *comb form* [*phosphorus*] **1 :** phosphorus ⟨*phosphide*⟩ **2 :** phosphate ⟨*phospho*fructokinase⟩

phos·pham·i·don \fäs-ˈfam-ə-ˌdän\ *n* [*phosphate* + *amide* + *-on,* of unknown origin] (ca. 1960) **:** a contact and systemic organophosphorus insecticide and miticide $C_{10}H_{19}ClNO_5P$

phos·pha·tase \ˈfäs-fə-ˌtās, -ˌtāz\ *n* (1911) **:** an enzyme that accelerates the hydrolysis and synthesis of organic esters of phosphoric acid and the transfer of phosphate groups to other compounds: **a :** ALKALINE PHOSPHATASE **b :** ACID PHOSPHATASE

phos·phate \ˈfäs-ˌfāt\ *n* [F, fr. *acide phosphorique* phosphoric acid] (1795) **1 a :** a salt or ester of a phosphoric acid **b :** an organic compound of phosphoric acid in which the acid group is bound to nitrogen or a carboxyl group in a way that permits useful energy to be released (as in metabolism) **2 :** a trivalent anion PO_4 derived from phosphoric acid H_3PO_4 **3 :** a phosphatic material used for fertilizers

phosphate group *n* (1953) **:** a group or radical derived from phosphoric acid H_3PO_4 by removal of one or more hydrogen atoms

phosphate rock *n* (1890) **:** a rock that consists largely of calcium phosphate usu. together with other minerals (as calcium carbonate), is used in making fertilizers, and is a source of phosphorus compounds

phos·phat·ic \fäs-ˈfat-ik, -ˈfāt-\ *adj* (1843) **:** of, relating to, or containing phosphoric acid or phosphates ⟨~ fertilizers⟩

phos·pha·tide \ˈfäs-fə-ˌtīd\ *n* [ISV] (1884) **:** PHOSPHOLIPID — **phos·pha·tid·ic** \ˌfäs-fə-ˈtid-ik\ *adj*

phos·pha·ti·dyl \ˌfäs-fə-ˈtīd-ᵊl, fäs-ˈfat-əd-ᵊl\ *n* (1941) **:** any of several univalent groups $(RCOO)_2C_3H_5OPO(OH)$ that are derived from phosphatidic acids

phos·pha·ti·dyl·cho·line \ˌfäs-fə-ˌtīd-ᵊl-ˈkō-ˌlēn, (ˌ)fäs-ˌfat-əd-ᵊl-\ *n* (ca. 1954) **:** LECITHIN

phos·pha·ti·dyl·eth·a·nol·amine \-ˌeth-ə-ˈnäl-ə-ˌmēn, -ˈnōl-\ *n* (1942) **:** any of a group of phospholipids that occur esp. in blood plasma and in the white matter of the central nervous system — called also *cephalin*

phos·pha·tize \ˈfäs-fə-ˌtīz\ *vt* **-tized; -tiz·ing** (1883) **1 :** to change to a phosphate or phosphates **2 :** to treat with phosphoric acid or a phosphate — **phos·pha·ti·za·tion** \ˌfäs-fət-ə-ˈzā-shən, -ˌfāt-\ *n*

phos·pha·tu·ria \ˌfäs-fə-ˈt(y)u̇r-ē-ə\ *n* [NL, fr. ISV *phosphate* + NL *-uria*] (1876) **:** the excessive discharge of phosphates in the urine

phos·phene \ˈfäs-ˌfēn\ *n* [ISV *phos-* + Gk *phainein* to show — more at FANCY] (ca. 1860) **:** a luminous impression due to excitation of the retina

phos·phide \-ˌfīd\ *n* [ISV] (1849) **:** a binary compound of phosphorus usu. with a more electropositive element or group

phos·phine \-ˌfēn\ *n* [ISV] (1873) **1 :** a colorless poisonous flammable gas PH_3 that is a weaker base than ammonia and that is used esp. to fumigate stored grain **2 :** any of various derivatives of phosphine analogous to amines but weaker as bases

phos·phite \-ˌfīt\ *n* (1799) **:** a salt or ester of phosphorous acid

phos·pho·cre·atine \ˌfäs-(ˌ)fō-ˈkrē-ə-ˌtēn\ *n* [ISV] (1927) **:** a compound $C_4H_{10}N_3O_5P$ of creatine and phosphoric acid that is found esp. in vertebrate muscle where it is an energy source for muscle contraction

phos·pho·di·es·ter·ase \-dī-ˈes-tə-ˌrās, -ˌrāz\ *n* [*phosph-* + *diester* + *-ase*] (1932) **:** a phosphatase (as from snake venom) that acts on diesters (as some nucleotides) to hydrolyze only one of the two ester groups

phos·pho·enol·pyr·uvate \ˈfäs-ˌfō-ə-ˌnȯl-pī-ˈrü-ˌvāt, -ˌnōl-, -ˌpī(ə)r-ˈyü-\ *n* (1956) **:** a salt or ester of phosphoenolpyruvic acid

phos·pho·enol·pyr·uvic acid \-pī-ˌrü-vik-, -ˌpī(ə)r-ˌyü-vik-\ *n* (1959) **:** the phosphate $H_2C{=}C(OPO_3H_2)COOH$ of the enol form of pyruvic acid that is formed as an intermediate in carbohydrate metabolism (as in the reversible dehydration of phosphoglyceric acid)

phos·pho·fruc·to·ki·nase \ˈfäs-(ˌ)fō-ˌfrək-tō-ˈkī-ˌnās, -ˌfrük-, -ˌfru̇k-, -ˌnāz\ *n* [*phosph-* + *fructose* + *kinase*] (1947) **:** an enzyme that functions in carbohydrate metabolism and esp. in glycolysis by catalyzing the transfer of a second phosphate (as from ATP) to fructose

phos·pho·glu·co·mu·tase \-ˌglü-kō-ˈmyü-ˌtās, -ˌtāz\ *n* [*phosph-* + *gluc-* + *mutase*] (1938) **:** an enzyme that is found in all plant and animal cells and that catalyzes the reversible isomerization of glucose-1-phosphate to glucose-6-phosphate

phos·pho·glyc·er·al·de·hyde \-ˌglis-ə-ˈral-də-ˌhīd\ *n* (1941) **:** a phosphate of glyceraldehyde $C_3H_5O_3(H_2PO_3)$ that is formed esp. in anaerobic metabolism of carbohydrates by the splitting of a diphosphate of fructose

phos·pho·glyc·er·ate \ˌfäs-fō-ˈglis-ə-ˌrāt\ *n* [*phosph-* + *glycer-* + *-ate*] (1901) **:** a salt or ester of phosphoglyceric acid

phos·pho·gly·cer·ic acid \-glis-ˌer-ik-\ *n* (1857) **:** either of two isomeric phosphates $HOOCC_2H_3(OH)OPO_3H_2$ of glyceric acid that are formed as intermediates in photosynthesis and in carbohydrate metabolism

phos·pho·ki·nase \ˌfäs-fō-ˈkī-ˌnās, -ˌnāz\ *n* (1946) **:** KINASE

phos·pho·li·pase \-ˈlī-ˌpās, -ˌpāz\ *n* (1945) **:** any of several enzymes that hydrolyze lecithins or phosphatidylethanolamines — called also *lecithinase*

phos·pho·lip·id \-ˈlip-əd\ *n* (1928) **:** any of numerous lipids (as lecithins and phosphatidylethanolamines) in which phosphoric acid as well as a fatty acid is esterified to glycerol and which are found in all living cells and in the bilayers of plasma membranes

phos·pho·mono·es·ter·ase \-ˌmän-ō-ˈes-tə-ˌrās, -ˌrāz\ *n* (1932) **:** a phosphatase that acts on monoesters

phos·pho·ni·um \fäs-ˈfō-nē-əm\ *n* [NL] (ca. 1866) **:** a univalent cation PH_4 analogous to ammonium and derived from phosphine; *also* **:** an organic derivative of phosphonium (as $(C_2H_5)_4P+$)

phos·pho·pro·tein \ˌfäs-fō-ˈprō-ˌtēn, -ˈprōt-ē-ən\ *n* (ca. 1908) **:** any of various proteins (as casein) that contain combined phosphoric acid

phos·phor \ˈfäs-fər, -ˌfō(ə)r\ *also* **phos·phore** \-ˌfō(ə)r, -ˌfȯ(ə)r, -fər\ *n* [L *phosphorus,* fr. Gk *phōsphoros,* lit., light bringer, fr. *phōsphoros* light-bearing, fr. *phōs-* + *pherein* to carry, bring — more at BEAR] (1705) **:** a phosphorescent substance; *specif* **:** a substance that emits light when excited by radiation

phosphor- *or* **phosphoro-** *comb form* **:** phosphorus ⟨*phosphor*ism⟩ **:** phosphoric acid ⟨*phosphoro*lysis⟩

phosphor bronze *n* (1875) **:** a bronze of great hardness, elasticity, and toughness that contains a small amount of phosphorus

phos·pho·resce \ˌfäs-fə-ˈres\ *vi* **-resced; -resc·ing** [prob. back-formation fr. *phosphorescent*] (1794) **:** to exhibit phosphorescence

phos·pho·res·cence \-ˈres-ᵊn(t)s\ *n* (1796) **1 :** luminescence that is caused by the absorption of radiations and continues for a noticeable time after these radiations have stopped **2 :** an enduring luminescence without sensible heat

phos·pho·res·cent \-ᵊnt\ *adj* (1766) **:** exhibiting phosphorescence — **phos·pho·res·cent·ly** *adv*

phos·pho·ric \fäs-'fȯr-ik, -'fär-; 'fäs-f(ə-)rik\ *adj* (1791) : of, relating to, or containing phosphorus esp. with a valence higher than in phosphorous compounds

phosphoric acid *n* (1791) **1** : a syrupy or deliquescent tribasic acid H₃PO₄ used esp. in preparing phosphates (as for fertilizers), in rust-proofing metals, and as a flavoring in soft drinks — called also *orthophosphoric acid* **2** : a compound (as pyrophosphoric acid or metaphosphoric acid) consisting of phosphate groups linked directly to each other by oxygen

phos·pho·rite \'fäs-fə-ˌrīt\ *n* (1796) **1** : a fibrous concretionary apatite **2** : PHOSPHATE ROCK — **phos·pho·rit·ic** \ˌfäs-fə-'rit-ik\ *adj*

phos·pho·rol·y·sis \ˌfäs-fə-'räl-ə-səs\ *n* [NL] (1937) : a reversible reaction analogous to hydrolysis in which phosphoric acid functions in a manner similar to that of water with the formation of a phosphate (as glucose-1-phosphate in the breakdown of liver glycogen) — **phos·pho·ro·lyt·ic** \-rō-'lit-ik\ *adj*

phos·pho·rous \'fäs-f(ə-)rəs; fäs-'fȯr-əs, -'fȯr-\ *adj* (1794) : of, relating to, or containing phosphorus esp. with a valence lower than in phosphoric compounds

phosphorous acid *n* (1794) : a deliquescent crystalline acid H₃PO₃ used esp. as a reducing agent and in making phosphites

phos·pho·rus \'fäs-f(ə-)rəs\ *n, often attrib* [NL, fr. Gk *phōsphoros* light-bearing — more at PHOSPHOR] (1645) **1** : a phosphorescent substance or body; *esp* : one that shines or glows in the dark **2** : a nonmetallic element of the nitrogen family that occurs widely esp. as phosphates — see ELEMENT table

phos·pho·ryl \'fäs-fə-ˌril\ *n* [ISV] (1871) : a usu. trivalent group PO consisting of phosphorus and oxygen

phos·phor·y·lase \fäs-'fȯr-ə-ˌlās, -ˌlāz\ *n* [*phosphoryl* + *-ase*] (1939) : any enzyme that catalyzes phosphorolysis with the formation of organic phosphates

phos·phor·y·late \-ˌlāt\ *vt* **-lat·ed; -lat·ing** (1931) : to cause (an organic compound) to take up or combine with phosphoric acid or a phosphorus-containing group — **phos·phor·y·la·tive** \-ˌlāt-iv\ *adj*

phos·phor·y·la·tion \ˌfäs-ˌfȯr-ə-'lā-shən\ *n* (1925) : the process of phosphorylating a chemical compound either by reaction with inorganic phosphate or by transfer of phosphate from another organic phosphate; *esp* : the enzymatic conversion of carbohydrates into their phosphoric esters in metabolic processes

phot \'fōt\ *n* [ISV, fr. Gk *phōt-, phōs* light] (ca. 1894) : the centimeter-gram-second unit of illumination equal to one lumen per square centimeter

phot- *or* **photo-** *comb form* [Gk *phōt-, phōto-*, fr. *phōt-, phōs* — more at FANCY] **1** : light : radiant energy ⟨*photon*⟩ ⟨*photography*⟩ **2** : photograph : photographic ⟨*photoengraving*⟩ **3** : photoelectric ⟨*photocell*⟩

pho·tic \'fōt-ik\ *adj* (1843) **1** : of, relating to, or involving light esp. in relation to organisms **2** : penetrated by light esp. of the sun ⟨~ zone of the ocean⟩ — **pho·ti·cal·ly** \'fōt-i-k(ə-)lē\ *adv*

¹pho·to \'fōt-ō\ *n, pl* **photos** (1860) : PHOTOGRAPH

²photo *vb* (1868) : PHOTOGRAPH

³photo *adj* (1889) : PHOTOGRAPH 1

pho·to·au·to·troph \ˌfōt-ō-'ȯt-ə-ˌtrōf\ *n* (1949) : a photoautotrophic organism

pho·to·au·to·tro·phic \-ˌȯt-ə-'trō-fik\ *adj* (1943) : autotrophic and utilizing energy from light ⟨green plants are ~⟩ — **pho·to·au·to·tro·phi·cal·ly** \-fi-k(ə-)lē\ *adv*

pho·to·bi·ol·o·gy \ˌfōt-ō-(ˌ)bī-'äl-ə-jē\ *n* [ISV] (1935) : a branch of biology that deals with the effects on living beings of radiant energy (as light) — **pho·to·bi·o·log·i·cal** \-ˌbī-ə-'läj-i-kəl\ *also* **pho·to·bi·o·log·ic** \-'läj-ik\ *adj* — **pho·to·bi·ol·o·gist** \-(ˌ)bī-'äl-ə-jəst\ *n*

pho·to·cath·ode \-'kath-ˌōd\ *n* [ISV] (1930) : a cathode that emits electrons when exposed to radiant energy and esp. light

pho·to·cell \'fōt-ə-ˌsel\ *n* [ISV] (1891) : PHOTOELECTRIC CELL

pho·to·chem·i·cal \ˌfōt-ō-'kem-i-kəl\ *adj* (1859) **1** : of, relating to, or resulting from the chemical action of radiant energy and esp. light ⟨~ smog⟩ **2** : of or relating to photochemistry ⟨~ studies⟩ — **pho·to·chem·i·cal·ly** \-k(ə-)lē\ *adv*

pho·to·chem·is·try \-'kem-ə-strē\ *n* (1867) **1** : a branch of chemistry that deals with the effect of radiant energy in producing chemical changes **2 a** : photochemical properties ⟨the ~ of gases⟩ **b** : photochemical processes ⟨the ~ of vision⟩ — **pho·to·chem·ist** \-'kem-əst\ *n*

pho·to·chro·mic \ˌfōt-ə-'krō-mik\ *adj* [*phot-* + *chrom-* + *-ic*] (1953) **1** : capable of changing color on exposure to radiant energy (as light) ⟨~ glass⟩ **2** : of, relating to, or utilizing the change of color shown by a photochromic substance ⟨a ~ process⟩ — **pho·to·chro·mism** \-ˌmiz-əm\ *n*

pho·to·co·ag·u·la·tion \-kō-ˌag-yə-'lā-shən\ *n* (1961) : a surgical process of coagulating tissue by means of a precisely oriented high-energy light source (as a light beam)

pho·to·com·pose \ˌfōt-ō-kəm-'pōz\ *vt* (1929) : to set (as reading matter) by photocomposition — **pho·to·com·pos·er** *n*

pho·to·com·po·si·tion \-ˌkäm-pə-'zish-ən\ *n* (1929) : composition of reading matter directly on film or photosensitive paper for reproduction

pho·to·con·duc·tive \-kən-'dək-tiv\ *adj* (1929) : having, involving, or operating by photoconductivity

pho·to·con·duc·tiv·i·ty \-ˌkän-ˌdək-'tiv-ət-ē, -kən-\ *n* (1929) : electrical conductivity that is affected by exposure to light or other electromagnetic radiation

¹pho·to·copy \'fōt-ə-ˌkäp-ē\ *n* [ISV] (ca. 1909) : a photographic reproduction of graphic matter

²photocopy *vt* (1939) : to make a photocopy of ~ *vi* : to make a photocopy — **pho·to·cop·i·er** *n*

pho·to·cur·rent \'fōt-ō-ˌkər-ənt, -ˌkə-rənt\ *n* [*photo*electric *current*] (1913) : a stream of electrons produced by photoelectric or photovoltaic effects

pho·to·de·com·po·si·tion \-ˌdē-ˌkäm-pə-'zish-ən\ *n* (1888) : chemical breaking down (as of a pesticide) by means of radiant energy

pho·to·de·grad·able \-di-'grād-ə-bəl\ *adj* (1971) : chemically degradable by the action of light ⟨~ plastics⟩

pho·to·de·tec·tor \ˌfōt-ō-di-'tek-tər\ *n* (1947) : any of various devices for detecting and measuring the intensity of radiant energy through photoelectric action

pho·to·di·ode \'fōt-ō-ˌdī-ˌōd\ *n* (1945) : a semiconductor device for detecting and measuring radiant energy (as light) by means of its conversion into an electric current

pho·to·dis·in·te·gra·tion \'fōt-ō-dis-ˌint-ə-'grā-shən\ *n* (1935) : disintegration of the nucleus of an atom produced by absorption of radiant energy (as light) — **pho·to·dis·in·te·grate** \-'int-ə-ˌgrāt\ *vt*

pho·to·dis·so·ci·a·tion \-dis-ˌō-sē-'ā-shən, -shē-\ *n* (1925) : dissociation (as of water) under the influence of radiant energy — **pho·to·dis·so·ci·ate** \-'ō-s(h)ē-ˌāt\ *vt* — **pho·to·dis·so·ci·a·tive** \-s(h)ē-ˌāt-iv, -shət-iv\ *adj*

pho·to·dra·ma \'fōt-ə-ˌdräm-ə, -ˌdram-\ *n* (ca. 1916) : MOTION PICTURE 2

pho·to·du·pli·cate \ˌfōt-ō-'d(y)ü-plə-ˌkāt\ *vb* (1953) : PHOTOCOPY — **pho·to·du·pli·cate** \-pli-kət\ *n* — **pho·to·du·pli·ca·tion** \-ˌd(y)ü-plə-'kā-shən\ *n*

pho·to·dy·nam·ic \-(ˌ)dī-'nam-ik\ *adj* [ISV] (ca. 1890) : of, relating to, or having the property of intensifying or inducing a toxic reaction to light and esp. sunlight in living systems — **pho·to·dy·nam·i·cal·ly** \-i-k(ə-)lē\ *adv*

pho·to·elec·tric \ˌfōt-ō-i-'lek-trik\ *adj* [ISV] (ca. 1879) : involving, relating to, or utilizing any of various electrical effects due to the interaction of radiation (as light) with matter — **pho·to·elec·tri·cal·ly** \-tri-k(ə-)lē\ *adv*

photoelectric cell *n* (1891) : a cell whose electrical properties are modified by the action of light

pho·to·elec·tron \ˌfōt-ō-i-'lek-ˌträn\ *n* [ISV] (1912) : an electron released in photoemission — **pho·to·elec·tron·ic** \-ˌlek-'trän-ik\ *adj*

pho·to·emis·sion \-i-'mish-ən\ *n* (1916) : the release of electrons from a usu. solid material (as a metal) by means of energy supplied by incidence of radiation and esp. light — **pho·to·emis·sive** \-'mis-iv\ *adj*

pho·to·en·grave \-in-'grāv\ *vt* [back-formation fr. *photoengraving*] (1881) : to make a photoengraving of — **pho·to·en·grav·er** *n*

pho·to·en·grav·ing *n* (1872) **1** : a photomechanical process for making linecuts and halftone cuts by photographing an image on a metal plate and then etching **2 a** : a plate made by photoengraving **b** : a print made from such a plate

photo finish *n* (1936) **1** : a race finish in which contestants are so close that a photograph of them as they cross the finish line has to be examined to determine the winner **2** : a close contest

pho·to·flash \'fōt-ə-ˌflash\ *n* (1930) : an electrically or mechanically operated flash lamp; *esp* : FLASHBULB

pho·to·flood \-ˌfləd\ *n* (1933) : an electric lamp using excess voltage to give intense sustained illumination for taking photographs

pho·to·flu·o·ro·gram \ˌfōt-ə-'flür-ə-ˌgram\ *n* (1942) : a photograph made by photofluorography

pho·to·flu·o·rog·ra·phy \-(ˌ)flü(-ə)r-'äg-rə-fē\ *n* (1942) : the photography of the image produced on a fluorescent screen by X rays — **pho·to·flu·o·ro·graph·ic** \-ˌflür-ə-'graf-ik\ *adj*

pho·tog \fə-'täg\ *n* [short for *photographer*] (ca. 1906) : one who takes photographs : PHOTOGRAPHER

pho·to·gen·ic \ˌfōt-ə-'jen-ik, -'jēn-\ *adj* (ca. 1847) **1** : produced or precipitated by light ⟨~ dermatitis⟩ **2** : producing or generating light : PHOSPHORESCENT ⟨~ bacteria⟩ **3** : suitable for being photographed ⟨a ~ smile⟩ — **pho·to·gen·i·cal·ly** \-i-k(ə-)lē\ *adv*

pho·to·ge·ol·o·gy \ˌfōt-ō-jē-'äl-ə-jē\ *n* (1941) : a branch of geology concerned with the identification of geological features through the study of aerial photographs — **pho·to·geo·log·ic** \-ˌjē-ə-'läj-ik\ *also* **pho·to·geo·log·i·cal** \-i-kəl\ *adj*

pho·to·gram \'fōt-ə-ˌgram\ *n* [ISV] (1859) : a shadowlike photograph made by placing objects between light-sensitive paper and a light source

pho·to·gram·met·ric \ˌfōt-ə-grə-'me-trik, -gra-\ *adj* (1897) : of, made by, or relating to photogrammetry

pho·to·gram·me·try \-'gram-ə-trē\ *n* [ISV *photogram* photograph (fr. *phot-* + *-gram*) + *-metry*] (1875) : the science of making reliable measurements by the use of photographs and esp. aerial photographs (as in surveying) — **pho·to·gram·me·trist** \-trəst\ *n*

¹pho·to·graph \'fōt-ə-ˌgraf\ *n* (1839) : a picture or likeness obtained by photography

²photograph *vt* (1839) : to take a photograph of ~ *vi* **1** : to take a photograph **2** : to undergo being photographed ⟨an actress who ~s well⟩ — **pho·tog·ra·pher** \fə-'täg-rə-fər\ *n*

pho·to·graph·ic \ˌfōt-ə-'graf-ik\ *adj* (1839) **1** : relating to, obtained by, or used in photography **2** : representing nature and human beings with the exactness of a photograph **3** : capable of retaining vivid impressions ⟨a ~ mind⟩ — **pho·to·graph·i·cal·ly** \-i-k(ə-)lē\ *adv*

pho·tog·ra·phy \fə-'täg-rə-fē\ *n* (1839) : the art or process of producing images on a sensitized surface (as a film) by the action of radiant energy and esp. light

pho·to·gra·vure \ˌfōt-ə-grə-'vyü(ə)r\ *n* [F, fr. *phot-* + *gravure*] (1879) : a process for printing from an intaglio plate prepared by photographic methods

pho·to·in·duced \ˌfōt-ō-in-'d(y)üst\ *adj* (1947) : induced by the action of light — **pho·to·in·duc·tion** \-'dək-shən\ *n* — **pho·to·in·duc·tive** \-'dək-tiv\ *adj*

pho·to·ion·iza·tion \-ˌī-ə-nə-'zā-shən\ *n* (1914) : ionization (as in the ionosphere) resulting from collision of a molecule or atom with a photon

pho·to·jour·nal·ism \ˌfōt-ō-'jərn-ᵊl-ˌiz-əm\ *n* (ca. 1938) : journalism in which written copy is subordinate to pictorial usu. photographic presentation of news stories or in which a high proportion of pictorial presentation is used — **pho·to·jour·nal·ist** \-ᵊl-əst\ *n* — **pho·to·jour·nal·is·tic** \-ˌjərn-ᵊl-'is-tik\ *adj*

pho·to·ki·ne·sis \-kə-'nē-səs, -kī-\ *n* [NL, fr. *phot-* + Gk *kinēsis* motion — more at -KINESIS] (1905) : motion or activity induced by light — **pho·to·ki·net·ic** \-'net-ik\ *adj*

pho·to·li·thog·ra·phy \-lith-'äg-rə-fē\ *n* [ISV] (1856) **1** : lithography in which photographically prepared plates are used **2** : a process involving the photographic transfer of a pattern to a surface for etching (as in

---

\ə\ abut \ᵊ\ kitten, F table \ər\ further \a\ ash \ā\ ace \ä\ cot, cart
\aú\ out \ch\ chin \e\ bet \ē\ easy \g\ go \i\ hit \ī\ ice \j\ job
\ŋ\ sing \ō\ go \ȯ\ law \ȯi\ boy \th\ thin \t̲h̲\ the \ü\ loot \ú\ foot
\y\ yet \zh\ vision \â, k̲, ⁿ, œ, œ̄, ᵫ, ǖ, �\ see Guide to Pronunciation

producing an integrated circuit) — **pho·to·litho·graph** \-'lith-ə-ˌgraf\ *n or vt* — **pho·to·li·thog·ra·pher** \-lith-'äg-rə-fər, -'lith-ə-ˌgraf-ər\ *n* — **pho·to·litho·graph·ic** \-ˌlith-ə-'graf-ik\ *adj* — **pho·to·litho·graph·i·cal·ly** \-i-k(ə-)lē\ *adv*

pho·tol·y·sis \fō-'täl-ə-səs\ *n* [NL] (ca. 1920) : chemical decomposition by the action of radiant energy — **pho·to·lyt·ic** \ˌfōt-ᵊl-'it-ik\ *adj* — **pho·to·lyt·i·cal·ly** \-i-k(ə-)lē\ *adv*

pho·to·lyze \'fōt-ᵊl-ˌīz\ *vb* **-lyzed; -lyz·ing** *vt* (1936) : to cause to undergo photolysis ~ *vi* : to undergo photolysis — **pho·to·lyz·able** \-ˌī-zə-bəl\ *adj*

[1]**pho·to·map** \'fōt-ō-ˌmap\ *n* (1942) : a photograph which is taken vertically from above (as from an airplane) and upon which a grid and data pertinent to maps have been added

[2]**photomap** *vt* (1942) : to make a photomap of ~ *vi* : to make a photomap

pho·to·me·chan·i·cal \ˌfōt-ō-mi-'kan-i-kəl\ *adj* [ISV] (ca. 1889) : relating to or involving any of various processes for producing printed matter from a photographically prepared surface — **pho·to·me·chan·i·cal·ly** \-i-k(ə-)lē\ *adv*

pho·tom·e·ter \fō-'täm-ət-ər\ *n* [NL *photometrum,* fr. *phot-* + *-metrum* -meter] (1884) : an instrument for measuring luminous intensity, luminous flux, illumination, or brightness

pho·to·met·ric \ˌfōt-ə-'me-trik\ *adj* (ca. 1828) : of or relating to photometry or the photometer — **pho·to·met·ri·cal·ly** \-tri-k(ə-)lē\ *adv*

pho·tom·e·try \fō-'täm-ə-trē\ *n* [NL *photometria,* fr. *phot-* + *-metria* -metry] (1824) : a branch of science that deals with measurement of the intensity of light; *also* : the practice of using a photometer

pho·to·mi·cro·graph \ˌfōt-ə-'mī-krə-ˌgraf\ *n* [*phot-* + *micr-* + *-graph*] (ca. 1858) : a photograph of a magnified image of a small object — **pho·to·mi·cro·graph·ic** \-ˌmī-krə-'graf-ik\ *adj* — **pho·to·mi·crog·ra·phy** \-mī-'kräg-rə-fē\ *n*

pho·to·mi·cro·scope \-'mī-krə-ˌskōp\ *n* (ca. 1909) : an instrument or system that combines a microscope, camera, and light source and is used for making photomicrographs — **pho·to·mi·cro·scop·ic** \-ˌmī-krə-'skäp-ik\ *adj*

pho·to·mon·tage \-män-'täzh, -mōⁿ(n)-, -'täzh\ *n* [ISV] (ca. 1935) : montage using photographic images; *also* : a picture made by photomontage

pho·to·mor·pho·gen·e·sis \ˌfōt-ə-ˌmȯr-fə-'jen-ə-səs\ *n* [NL] (1962) : plant morphogenesis controlled by radiant energy (as light) — **pho·to·mor·pho·gen·ic** \-'jen-ik\ *adj*

pho·to·mul·ti·pli·er \ˌfōt-ō-'məl-tə-ˌplī(-ə)r\ *n* (1941) : an electron multiplier in which electrons released by photoelectric emission are multiplied in successive stages by dynodes that produce secondary emission

pho·to·mu·ral \-'myu̇r-əl\ *n* (1927) : an enlarged photograph usu. several yards long used on walls esp. as decoration

pho·ton \'fō-ˌtän\ *n* [*phot-* + [2]*-on*] (ca. 1922) **1** : a quantum of radiant energy **2** : a unit of intensity of light at the retina equal to the illumination received per square millimeter of a pupillary area from a surface having a brightness of one candle per square meter — **pho·ton·ic** \fō-'tän-ik\ *adj*

pho·to·neg·a·tive \ˌfōt-ō-'neg-ət-iv\ *adj* (1922) : exhibiting negative phototropism or phototaxis

pho·to·nu·cle·ar \-'n(y)ü-klē-ər, ÷-'n(y)ü-kyə-lər\ *adj* (1941) : relating to or caused by the incidence of radiant energy (as gamma rays) on atomic nuclei

pho·to–off·set \-'ȯf-ˌset\ *n* (1926) : offset printing from photolithographic plates

pho·to·ox·i·da·tion \-ˌäk-sə-'dā-shən\ *n* (1888) : oxidation under the influence of radiant energy (as light) — **pho·to·ox·i·da·tive** \-'äk-sə-ˌdāt-iv\ *adj* — **pho·to·ox·i·dize** \-'äk-sə-ˌdīz\ *vb*

pho·to·pe·ri·od \-'pir-ē-əd\ *n* (ca. 1920) : a recurring cycle of light and dark periods of constant length; *also* : PHOTOPHASE 2 — **pho·to·pe·ri·od·ic** \-ˌpir-ē-'äd-ik\ *adj* — **pho·to·pe·ri·od·i·cal·ly** \-i-k(ə-)lē\ *adv* — **pho·to·pe·ri·od·ism** \-'pir-ē-əd-ˌiz-əm\ *n*

pho·to·phase \'fōt-ə-ˌfāz\ *n* (1944) **1** : LIGHT REACTION **2** : the light period of a photoperiodic cycle of light and dark

pho·to·pho·bia \ˌfōt-ə-'fō-bē-ə\ *n* [NL] (ca. 1799) : intolerance to light; *esp* : painful sensitiveness to strong light

pho·to·pho·bic \-'fō-bik\ *adj* (1858) **1 a** : shunning or avoiding light **b** : growing best under reduced illumination **2** : of or relating to photophobia

pho·to·phore \'fōt-ə-ˌfō(ə)r, -ˌfȯ(ə)r\ *n* [ISV] (1898) : a light-emitting organ; *esp* : one of the luminous spots on various marine mostly deep-sea fishes

pho·to·phos·phor·y·la·tion \'fōt-ō-ˌfäs-ˌfȯr-ə-'lā-shən\ *n* (1954) : the synthesis of ATP from ADP and phosphate that occurs in a plant using radiant energy absorbed during photosynthesis

phot·opic \fōt-'ō-pik, -'äp-ik\ *adj* (1915) : relating to or being vision in bright light with light-adapted eyes that is mediated by the cones of the retina

pho·to·play \'fōt-ō-ˌplā\ *n* (1910) : MOTION PICTURE 2

pho·to·po·la·rim·e·ter \ˌfōt-ō-ˌpō-lə-'rim-ət-ər\ *n* (ca. 1890) : a polariscope combined with a telescope for producing an image (as of a planet) by means of polarized light

pho·to·poly·mer \ˌfōt-ō-'päl-ə-mər\ *n* (1932) : a photosensitive plastic used in the manufacture of printing plates

pho·to·pos·i·tive \-'päz-ət-iv, -'päz-tiv\ *adj* (1914) : exhibiting positive phototropism or phototaxis

pho·to·print \'fōt-ō-ˌprint\ *n* (1888) : a reproduction of graphic matter on photographic paper

pho·to·prod·uct \ˌfōt-ō-'präd-(ˌ)əkt\ *n* (1926) : a product of a photochemical reaction

pho·to·pro·duc·tion \-prə-'dək-shən\ *n* (1949) : the production of elementary particles (as mesons) as a result of the action of photons on atomic nuclei; *also* : the production of a substance (as hydrogen) by a photochemical reaction (as in photosynthetic bacteria)

pho·to·re·ac·tion \-rē-'ak-shən\ *n* (1920) : a photochemical reaction

pho·to·re·ac·ti·va·tion \-rē-ˌak-tə-'vā-shən\ *n* (1949) : repair of DNA (as of a bacterium) esp. by a light-dependent enzymatic reaction after damage by ultraviolet irradiation — **pho·to·re·ac·ti·vat·ing** \-'ak-tə-ˌvāt-iŋ\ *adj*

photo–realism *n* (1961) : realism in painting characterized by extremely meticulous depiction of detail — **photo–realist** *n or adj*

pho·to·re·cep·tion \-ri-'sep-shən\ *n* (1902) : perception of waves in the range of visible light; *specif* : VISION — **pho·to·re·cep·tive** \-'sep-tiv\ *adj*

pho·to·re·cep·tor \-'sep-tər\ *n* (1906) : a receptor for light stimuli

pho·to·re·con·nais·sance \ˌfōt-ō-ri-'kän-ə-zən(t)s *also* -sən(t)s\ *n* (1940) : reconnaissance in which aerial photographs are taken

pho·to·re·duc·tion \-ri-'dək-shən\ *n* (1888) : chemical reduction under the influence of radiant energy (as light) : photochemical reduction — **pho·to·re·duce** \-ri-'d(y)üs\ *vt*

pho·to·re·sist \'fōt-ō-ri-ˌzist, ˌfōt-ō-ri-'\ *n* (1953) : a photosensitive resist that is used esp. in producing an integrated circuit on a silicon chip by photographically transferring the circuit pattern to the resist and by selective chemical etching

pho·to·res·pi·ra·tion \ˌfōt-ō-ˌres-pə-'rā-shən\ *n* (1945) : oxidation involving production of carbon dioxide during photosynthesis

pho·to·sen·si·tive \-'sen(t)-sət-iv, -'sen(t)-stiv\ *adj* (1886) : sensitive or sensitized to the action of radiant energy — **pho·to·sen·si·tiv·i·ty** \-ˌsen(t)-sə-'tiv-ət-ē\ *n*

pho·to·sen·si·ti·za·tion \-ˌsen(t)-sət-ə-'zā-shən, -ˌsen(t)-stə-'zā-\ *n* (ca. 1923) **1** : the process of photosensitizing **2** : the condition of being photosensitized; *esp* : the development of an abnormal capacity to react to sunlight typically by edematous swelling and dermatitis

pho·to·sen·si·tize \-'sen(t)-sə-ˌtīz\ *vt* (ca. 1923) : to make sensitive to the influence of radiant energy and esp. light — **pho·to·sen·si·tiz·er** *n*

pho·to·set \'fōt-ō-ˌset\ *vt* **-set; -set·ting** (1957) : PHOTOCOMPOSE — **pho·to·set·ter** *n*

pho·to·sphere \'fōt-ə-ˌsfi(ə)r\ *n* (1664) **1** : a sphere of light or radiance **2** : the luminous surface layer of the sun or a star — **pho·to·spher·ic** \ˌfōt-ə-'sfi(ə)r-ik, -'sfer-\ *adj*

pho·to·stat \'fōt-ə-ˌstat\ *vt* (1914) : to copy by a Photostat device

Photostat *trademark* — used for a device for making a photographic copy of graphic matter

pho·to·stat·ic \ˌfōt-ə-'stat-ik\ *adj* (1919) : of, made by, or using a Photostat device ⟨a ~ copy⟩ ⟨a ~ process⟩

pho·to·syn·thate \ˌfōt-ō-'sin-ˌthāt\ *n* [*photosynthesis* + *-ate*] (1913) : a product of photosynthesis

pho·to·syn·the·sis \-'sin(t)-thə-səs\ *n* [NL] (1898) : synthesis of chemical compounds with the aid of radiant energy and esp. light; *esp* : formation of carbohydrates in the chlorophyll-containing tissues of plants exposed to light — **pho·to·syn·the·size** \-ˌsīz\ *vi* — **pho·to·syn·thet·ic** \-sin-'thet-ik\ *adj* — **pho·to·syn·thet·i·cal·ly** \-i-k(ə-)lē\ *adv*

pho·to·sys·tem \'fōt-ō-ˌsis-təm\ *n* (1964) : either of two photochemical reactions occurring in chloroplasts: **a** : one that proceeds best in long wavelength light — called also *photosystem I* **b** : one that proceeds best in short wavelength light — called also *photosystem II*

pho·to·tac·tic \ˌfōt-ō-'tak-tik\ *adj* [ISV] (1882) : of, relating to, or exhibiting phototaxis — **pho·to·tac·ti·cal·ly** \-ti-kə-lē\ *adv*

pho·to·tax·is \-'tak-səs\ *n* [NL] (ca. 1890) : a taxis in which light is the directive factor

pho·to·te·leg·ra·phy \-tə-'leg-rə-fē\ *n* [ISV] (ca. 1886) : FACSIMILE 2

pho·to·tox·ic \-'täk-sik\ *adj* (1942) **1** : rendering the skin susceptible to damage (as sunburn or blisters) upon exposure to light and esp. ultraviolet light **2** : induced by a phototoxic substance — **pho·to·tox·ic·i·ty** \-täk-'sis-ət-ē\ *n*

pho·to·tro·pic \ˌfōt-ə-'trōp-ik, -'träp-\ *adj* (ca. 1890) : of, relating to, or capable of phototropism — **pho·to·tro·pi·cal·ly** \-i-k(ə-)lē\ *adv*

pho·tot·ro·pism \fō-'tä-trə-ˌpiz-əm\ *n* [ISV] (1899) : a tropism in which light is the orienting stimulus

pho·to·tube \'fōt-ō-ˌt(y)üb\ *n* (ca. 1930) : an electron tube having a photoemissive cathode whose released electrons are drawn to the anode by reason of its positive potential

pho·to·type·set·ting \ˌfōt-ō-'tīp-ˌset-iŋ\ *n* (1931) : PHOTOCOMPOSITION; *esp* : photocomposition done on a keyboard or tape-operated composing machine — **pho·to·type·set·ter** *n*

pho·to·ty·pog·ra·phy \-tī-'päg-rə-fē\ *n* [ISV] (ca. 1890) : PHOTOCOMPOSITION — **pho·to·ty·po·graph·ic** \-ˌtī-pə-'graf-ik\ *adj*

pho·to·vol·ta·ic \-väl-'tā-ik, -vōl-\ *adj* [ISV] (ca. 1890) : of, relating to, or utilizing the generation of a voltage when radiant energy falls on the boundary between dissimilar substances (as two different semiconductors) — **photovoltaic** *n*

phrag·mo·plast \'frag-mō-ˌplast\ *n* [ISV *phragmo-* (fr. Gk *phragmos* fence, fr. *phrassein* to enclose) + *-plast* — more at FARCE] (1912) : the enlarged barrel-shaped spindle that is characteristic of the later stages of plant mitosis and within which the cell plate forms

phras·al \'frā-zəl\ *adj* (1871) : of, relating to, or consisting of a phrase ⟨~ prepositions⟩ — **phras·al·ly** \-zə-lē\ *adv*

[1]**phrase** \'frāz\ *n* [L *phrasis,* fr. Gk, fr. *phrazein* to point out, explain, tell] (1530) **1** : a characteristic manner or style of expression : DICTION **2 a** : a brief expression; *esp* : CATCHWORD **b** : WORD **3** : a short musical thought typically two to four measures long closing with a cadence **4** : a group of two or more grammatically related words that bear to one another the modifying relation, the coordinate relation, or the composite relation ⟨an adverbial ~⟩ **5** : a series of dance movements comprising a section of a pattern

[2]**phrase** *vt* **phrased; phras·ing** (1570) **1 a** : to express in words or in appropriate or telling terms **b** : to designate by a descriptive word or phrase **2** : to divide into melodic phrases

phrase book *n* (1594) : a book containing idiomatic expressions of a foreign language and their translation

phrase·mak·er \'frāz-ˌmā-kər\ *n* (1822) **1** : one who coins impressive phrases **2** : one given to making fine-sounding but often hollow and meaningless phrases — **phrase·mak·ing** \-kiŋ\ *n*

phrase·mon·ger \-ˌməŋ-gər, -ˌmäŋ-\ *n* (1815) : PHRASEMAKER 2 — **phrase·mon·ger·ing** \-g(ə-)riŋ\ *n*

phra·seo·gram \'frā-zē-ə-ˌgram\ *n* [*phraseo-* (as in *phraseology*) + *-gram*] (1847) : a symbol for a phrase in some shorthand systems

phra·seo·graph \-ˌgraf\ *n* (1847) : PHRASEOGRAM

phra·seo·log·i·cal \ˌfrā-zē-ə-'läj-i-kəl\ *adj* (1664) **1 a** : expressed in formal often sententious phrases **b** : marked by frequently insincere use of such phrases **2** : of or relating to phraseology

phrase·ol·o·gist \ˌfrā-zē-'äl-ə-jəst, frā-'zäl-\ *n* (1713) : one who uses sententious or insincere phrases

phrase·ol·o·gy \-jē\ *n, pl* **-gies** [NL *phraseologia,* fr. Gk *phrase-, phrasis* + *-logia* -logy] (1664) **1** : a manner of organization of words and phrases into longer elements : STYLE **2** : choice of words

phras·ing \'frā-ziŋ\ *n* (1611) **1 :** style of expression : PHRASEOLOGY **2 :** the act, method, or result of grouping notes into musical phrases

phra·try \'frā-trē\ *n, pl* **phratries** [Gk *phratria,* fr. *phratēr* member of the same clan, member of a phratry — more at BROTHER] (1833) **1 :** a kinship group forming a subdivision of a Greek phyle **2 :** a tribal subdivision; *specif* : an exogamous group typically comprising several totemic clans

phre·at·ic \frē-'at-ik\ *adj* [Gk *phreat-, phrear* well; akin to L *fervēre* to boil — more at BURN] (ca. 1890) **1 :** of, relating to, or being groundwater **2 :** of, relating to, or being an explosion caused by steam derived from groundwater

phre·ato·phyte \frē-'at-ə-,fīt\ *n* [Gk *phreat-, phrear* well + E *-o-* + *-phyte*] (1920) : a deep-rooted plant that obtains its water from the water table or the layer of soil just above it — **phre·ato·phyt·ic** \-,at-ə-'fit-ik\ *adj*

phren- *or* **phreno-** *comb form* [Gk, fr. *phren-, phrēn* diaphragm, mind] **1 :** mind ⟨*phren*ology⟩ **2 :** diaphragm ⟨*phren*ic⟩

phre·net·ic \fri-'net-ik\ *adj* [L *phreneticus* — more at FRENETIC] (14c) : FRENETIC

-phre·nia \'frē-nē-ə\ *n comb form* [NL, fr. Gk *phren-, phrēn*] : disordered condition of mental functions ⟨hebe*phrenia*⟩

phren·ic \'fren-ik\ *adj* [NL *phrenicus,* fr. *phren-*] (1704) **1 :** of or relating to the diaphragm **2 :** of or relating to the mind

phre·nol·o·gy \fri-'näl-ə-jē\ *n* (1805) : the study of the conformation of the skull based on the belief that it is indicative of mental faculties and character — **phre·no·log·i·cal** \,fren-ᵊl-'äj-i-kəl, ,frēn-\ *adj* — **phre·nol·o·gist** \fri-'näl-ə-jəst\ *n*

phren·sy *var of* FRENZY

Phry·gian \'frij-(ē-)ən\ *n* (15c) **1 :** a native or inhabitant of ancient Phrygia **2 :** the language of the Phrygians usu. assumed to be Indo-European — see INDO-EUROPEAN LANGUAGES table — **Phrygian** *adj*

phtha·lein \'thal-ē-ən, 'thal-,ēn, 'thāl-\ *n* [ISV, fr. *phthalic acid*] (1875) : any of various xanthene dyes that are intensely colored in alkaline solution

phthal·ic acid \,thal-ik-\ *n* [ISV, short for obs. *naphthalic acid,* fr. *naphthalene*] (1857) : any of three isomeric acids $C_8H_6O_4$ obtained by oxidation of various benzene derivatives

phthalic anhydride *n* (1855) : a crystalline cyclic acid anhydride $C_8H_4O_3$ used esp. in making alkyd resins

phtha·lo·cy·a·nine \,thal-ō-'sī-ə-,nēn, ,thā-lō-\ *n* [ISV *phthal*ic acid + *-o-* + *cyanine*] (1933) : a bright greenish blue crystalline compound $C_{32}H_{18}N_8$; *also* : any of several metal derivatives that are brilliant fast blue to green dyes or pigments

phthis·ic \'tiz-ik\ *n* [ME *tisike,* fr. MF *tisique,* fr. *tisique* tubercular, fr. L *phthisicus,* fr. Gk *phthisikos,* fr. *phthisis*] (14c) : PHTHISIS — **phthisic** *or* **phthis·i·cal** \-i-kəl\ *adj*

phthi·sis \'t(h)ī-səs, 't(h)is-əs\ *n, pl* **phthi·ses** \'t(h)ī-,sēz, 't(h)is-,ēz\ [L, fr. Gk, fr. *phthinein* to waste away; akin to Skt *kṣiṇoti* he destroys] (1543) : a progressively wasting or consumptive condition; *esp* : pulmonary tuberculosis

phy·co·cy·a·nin \,fī-kō-'sī-ə-nən\ *n* [ISV *phyco-* (fr. Gk *phykos*) + *cyan-* + *-in*] (1875) : any of various bluish green protein pigments in the cells of blue-green algae

phy·co·er·y·thrin \-'er-i-thrən\ *n* [ISV *phyco-* + *erythr-* + *-in*] (ca. 1866) : any of the red protein pigments in the cells of red algae

phy·col·o·gy \fī-'käl-ə-jē\ *n* [Gk *phykos* seaweed + ISV *-logy* — more at FUCUS] (ca. 1847) : ALGOLOGY — **phy·co·log·i·cal** \,fī-kə-'läj-i-kəl\ *adj* — **phy·col·o·gist** \fī-'käl-ə-jəst\ *n*

phy·co·my·cete \,fī-kō-'mī-,sēt, -,mī-'sēt\ *n* [deriv. of Gk *phykos* + *mykēt-, mykēs* fungus — more at MYC-] (ca. 1900) : any of a large class (Phycomycetes) of highly variable lower fungi in many respects similar to algae — **phy·co·my·ce·tous** \-,mī-'sēt-əs\ *adj*

phyl- *or* **phylo-** *comb form* [L, fr. Gk, fr. *phylē, phylon;* akin to Gk *phyein* to bring forth — more at BE] : tribe : race : phylum ⟨*phylo*geny⟩

phy·lac·tery \fə-'lak-t(ə-)rē\ *n, pl* **-ter·ies** [ME *philaterie,* fr. ML *philaterium,* alter. of LL *phylacterium,* fr. Gk *phylaktērion* amulet, phylactery, fr. *phylassein* to guard, fr. *phylak-, phylax* guard] (14c) **1 :** one of two small square leather boxes containing slips inscribed with scriptural passages and traditionally worn on the left arm and on the head by Jewish men during morning weekday prayers **2 :** AMULET

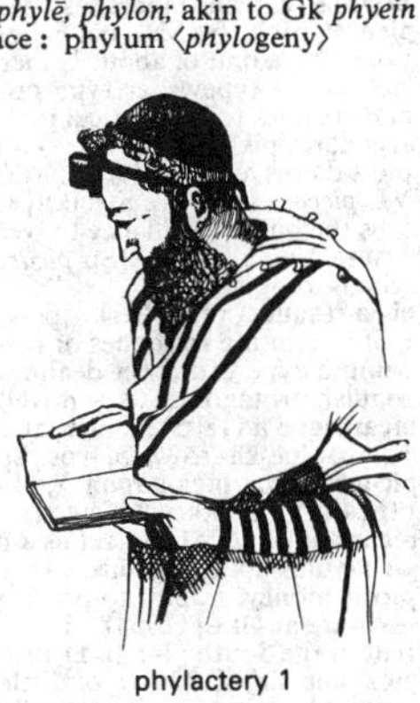

phylactery 1

phy·le \'fī-(,)lē\ *n, pl* **phy·lae** \-,lē\ [Gk *phylē* tribe, phyle] (1863) : the largest political subdivision among the ancient Athenians

phy·le·sis \fī-'lē-səs, 'fī-lə-\ *n* [NL, fr. *phyl-* + *-esis* (as in *genesis*)] (1923) : phyletic development

phy·let·ic \fī-'let-ik\ *adj* (1881) : of or relating to the course of evolutionary or phylogenetic development — **phy·let·i·cal·ly** \-i-k(ə-)lē\ *adv*

phyll- *or* **phyllo-** *comb form* [NL, fr. Gk, fr. *phyllon* — more at BLADE] : leaf ⟨*phyllo*me⟩

-phyll \,fil\ *n comb form* [NL *-phyllum,* fr. Gk *phyllon* leaf] : leaf ⟨sporo*phyll*⟩

phyl·la·ry \'fil-ə-rē\ *n, pl* **-ries** [NL *phyllarium,* fr. Gk *phyllarion,* dim. of *phyllon* leaf] (1857) : one of the involucral bracts subtending the flower head of a composite plant

phyl·lo \'fē-(,)lō, 'fī-\ *n* [modif. of NGk *phyllon* leaf, sheet (of pastry), fr. Gk — more at BLADE] (ca. 1950) : extremely thin pastry dough that produces a flaky pastry

phyl·lo·clade \'fil-ə-,klād\ *n* [NL *phyllocladium,* fr. *phyll-* + Gk *klados* branch — more at GLADIATOR] (1858) : a flattened stem or branch (as a joint of a cactus) that functions as a leaf

phyl·lode \'fil-,ōd\ *n* [NL *phyllodium,* fr. Gk *phyllōdēs* like a leaf, fr. *phyllon* leaf] (1848) : a flat expanded petiole that replaces the blade of a foliage leaf, fulfills the same functions, and is analogous to a cladophyll

phyl·lo·di·um \fil-'ōd-ē-əm\ *n, pl* **-dia** \-ē-ə\ [NL] (ca. 1847) : PHYLLODE

phyl·lome \'fil-,ōm\ *n* [ISV] (1875) : a plant part that is a leaf or is phylogenetically derived from a leaf

phyl·lo·tac·tic \,fil-ə-'tak-tik\ *adj* (1857) : of or relating to phyllotaxy

phyl·lo·taxy \'fil-ə-,tak-sē\ *also* **phyl·lo·tax·is** \,fil-ə-'tak-səs\ *n* [NL *phyllotaxis,* fr. *phyll-* + *-taxis*] (1857) **1 :** the arrangement of leaves on a stem and in relation to one another **2 :** the study of phyllotaxy and of the laws that govern it

-phyl·lous \'fil-əs\ *adj comb form* [NL *-phyllus,* fr. Gk *-phyllos,* fr. *phyllon* leaf — more at BLADE] : having (such or so many) leaves, leaflets, or leaflike parts ⟨di*phyllous*⟩

phyl·lox·e·ra \,fil-,äk-'sir-ə, fə-'läk-sə-rə\ *n* [NL, fr. *phyll-* + Gk *xēros* dry — more at SERENE] (1868) : any of various plant lice (esp. genus *Phylloxera*) that differ from aphids esp. in wing structure and in being continuously oviparous

phy·lo·ge·net·ic \,fī-lō-jə-'net-ik\ *adj* [ISV, fr. NL *phylogenesis* phylogeny, fr. *phyl-* + *genesis*] (1877) **1 :** of or relating to phylogeny **2 :** based on natural evolutionary relationships **3 :** acquired in the course of phylogenetic development : RACIAL — **phy·lo·ge·net·i·cal·ly** \-i-k(ə-)lē\ *adv*

phy·log·e·ny \fī-'läj-ə-nē\ *n, pl* **-nies** [ISV] (1872) **1 :** the racial history of a kind of organism **2 :** the evolution of a genetically related group of organisms as distinguished from the development of the individual organism **3 :** the history or course of the development of something (as a word or custom)

phy·lum \'fī-ləm\ *n, pl* **phy·la** \-lə\ [NL, fr. Gk *phylon* tribe, race — more at PHYL-] (ca. 1876) **1 a :** a direct line of descent within a group **b :** a group that constitutes or has the unity of a phylum; *esp* : one of the usu. primary divisions of the animal kingdom ⟨the ~ Arthropoda⟩ **2 :** a group of languages related more remotely than those of a family or stock

phys ed \(')fiz-'ed\ *n* (1955) : PHYSICAL EDUCATION

physi- *or* **physio-** *comb form* [L, fr. Gk, fr. *physis* — more at PHYSICS] **1 :** nature ⟨*physio*graphy⟩ **2 :** physical ⟨*physio*therapy⟩

phys·iat·rist \,fiz-ē-'a-trəst\ *n* [Gk *physis* + ISV *-iatrics* + *-ist*] (ca. 1947) : a physician who specializes in physical medicine

[1]**phys·ic** \'fiz-ik\ *n* [ME *physik* natural science, art of medicine, fr. OF *fisique,* fr. L *physica,* sing., natural science, fr. Gk *physikē,* fr. fem. of *physikos* — more at PHYSICS] (13c) **1 a :** the art or practice of healing disease **b :** the practice or profession of medicine **2 :** a medicinal agent or preparation; *esp* : PURGATIVE **3** *archaic* : NATURAL SCIENCE

[2]**physic** *vt* **phys·icked; phys·ick·ing** (14c) **1 :** to treat with or administer medicine to; *esp* : PURGE **2 :** HEAL, CURE

[1]**phys·i·cal** \'fiz-i-kəl\ *adj* [ME, fr. ML *physicalis,* fr. L *physica* physics] (1597) **1 a :** having material existence : perceptible esp. through the senses and subject to the laws of nature ⟨everything ~ is measurable by weight, motion, and resistance — Thomas De Quincey⟩ **b :** of or relating to material things **2 a :** of or relating to natural science **b** (1) **:** of or relating to physics (2) **:** characterized or produced by the forces and operations of physics **3 a :** of or relating to the body **b :** concerned or preoccupied with the body and its needs : CARNAL **c :** characterized by esp. rugged and forceful physical activity : ROUGH ⟨a ~ hockey game⟩ ***syn*** see MATERIAL — **phys·i·cal·ly** \-k(ə-)lē\ *adv* — **phys·i·cal·ness** \-kəl-nəs\ *n*

[2]**physical** *n* (1934) : PHYSICAL EXAMINATION

physical anthropology *n* (1873) : anthropology concerned with the comparative study of human evolution, variation, and classification esp. through measurement and observation — compare CULTURAL ANTHROPOLOGY — **physical anthropologist** *n*

physical education *n* (1838) : instruction in the development and care of the body ranging from simple calisthenic exercises to a course of study providing training in hygiene, gymnastics, and the performance and management of athletic games

physical examination *n* (1884) : an examination of the bodily functions and condition of an individual

physical geography *n* (1808) : geography that deals with the exterior physical features and changes of the earth

phys·i·cal·ism \'fiz-i-kə-,liz-əm\ *n* (ca. 1931) : a thesis that the descriptive terms of scientific language are reducible to terms which refer to spatiotemporal things or events or to their properties — **phys·i·cal·ist** \-ləst\ *n* — **phys·i·cal·is·tic** \,fiz-i-kə-'lis-tik\ *adj*

phys·i·cal·i·ty \,fiz-ə-'kal-ət-ē\ *n, pl* **-ties** (1660) **1 :** intensely physical orientation : predominance of the physical usu. at the expense of the mental, spiritual, or social **2 :** a physical aspect or quality

physical medicine *n* (1939) : a branch of medicine concerned with the diagnosis and treatment of disease and disability by physical means (as radiation, heat, and electricity) — compare PHYSICAL THERAPY

physical science *n* (1845) : the natural sciences (as physics, chemistry, and astronomy) that deal primarily with nonliving materials — **physical scientist** *n*

physical therapy *n* (1922) : the treatment of disease by physical and mechanical means (as massage, regulated exercise, water, light, heat, and electricity) — **physical therapist** *n*

phy·si·cian \fə-'zish-ən\ *n* [ME *fisicien,* fr. OF, fr. *fisique* medicine, [1]physic] (13c) **1 :** a person skilled in the art of healing; *specif* : a doctor of medicine **2 :** one exerting a remedial or salutary influence

phys·i·cist \'fiz-(ə-)səst\ *n* (1840) **1 :** a specialist in physics **2** *archaic* : a person skilled in natural science

phys·i·co·chem·i·cal \,fiz-i-kō-'kem-i-kəl\ *adj* (1664) **1 :** being physical and chemical **2 :** of or relating to chemistry that deals with the physicochemical properties of substances — **phys·i·co·chem·i·cal·ly** \-k(ə-)lē\ *adv*

phys·ics \'fiz-iks\ *n pl but sing or pl in constr* [L *physica,* pl., natural science, fr. Gk *physika,* fr. neut. pl. of *physikos* of nature, fr. *physis* growth, nature, fr. *phyein* to bring forth — more at BE] (1715) **1 :** a science that deals with matter and energy and their interactions in the fields of mechanics, acoustics, optics, heat, electricity, magnetism, radiation,

\ə\ abut \ᵊ\ kitten, F table \ər\ further \a\ ash \ā\ ace \ä\ cot, cart \au̇\ out \ch\ chin \e\ bet \ē\ easy \g\ go \i\ hit \ī\ ice \j\ job \ŋ\ sing \ō\ go \ȯ\ law \ȯi\ boy \th\ thin \th\ the \ü\ loot \u̇\ foot \y\ yet \zh\ vision \à, k̲, ⁿ, œ, œ̄, ue, ue̅, ʸ\ *see* Guide to Pronunciation

atomic structure, and nuclear phenomena **2 a :** the physical processes and phenomena of a particular system **b :** the physical properties and composition of something

Phys·io·crat \'fiz-ē-ə-,krat\ *n* [F *physiocrate,* fr. *physi-* physi- + *-crate* -crat] (1798) **:** a member of a school of political economists founded in 18th century France and characterized chiefly by a belief that government policy should not interfere with the operation of natural economic laws and that land is the source of all wealth — **phys·io·crat·ic** \,fiz-ē-ə-'krat-ik\ *adj, often cap*

phys·i·og·nom·ic \,fiz-ē-ə(g)-'näm-ik\ *also* **phys·i·og·nom·i·cal** \-i-kəl\ *adj* (ca. 1755) **:** of, relating to, or characteristic of physiognomy or the physiognomy — **phys·i·og·nom·i·cal·ly** \-i-k(ə-)lē\ *adv*

phys·i·og·no·my \,fiz-ē-'ä(g)-nə-mē\ *n, pl* **-mies** [ME *phisonomie,* fr. MF, fr. LL *physiognomonia, physiognomia,* fr. Gk *physiognōmonia,* fr. *physiognōmōn* judging character by the features, fr. *physis* nature, physique, appearance + *gnōmōn* interpreter — more at GNOMON] (14c) **1 :** the art of discovering temperament and character from outward appearance **2 :** the facial features held to show qualities of mind or character by their configuration or expression **3 :** external aspect; *also* **:** inner character or quality revealed outwardly ⟨the ~ of a political party⟩

phys·i·og·ra·phy \,fiz-ē-'äg-rə-fē\ *n* [prob. fr. (assumed) NL *physiographia,* fr. NL *physi-* + L *-graphia* -graphy] (ca. 1828) **:** PHYSICAL GEOGRAPHY — **phys·i·og·ra·pher** \-fər\ *n* — **phys·io·graph·ic** \,fiz-ē-ō-'graf-ik\ *also* **phys·io·graph·i·cal** \-i-kəl\ *adj*

phys·i·o·log·i·cal \,fiz-ē-ə-'läj-i-kəl\ *or* **phys·i·o·log·ic** \-ik\ *adj* (1814) **1 :** of or relating to physiology **2 :** characteristic of or appropriate to an organism's healthy or normal functioning **3 :** differing in, involving, or affecting physiological factors ⟨a ~ strain of bacteria⟩ — **phys·i·o·log·i·cal·ly** \-i-k(ə-)lē\ *adv*

physiological psychology *n* (1888) **:** a branch of psychology that deals with the effects of normal and pathological physiological processes on mental life — called also *psychophysiology*

physiological saline *n* (1896) **:** a solution of a salt or salts that is essentially isotonic with tissue fluids or blood

phys·i·ol·o·gy \,fiz-ē-'äl-ə-jē\ *n* [L *physiologia* natural science, fr. Gk, fr. *physi-* + *-logia* -logy] (1597) **1 :** a branch of biology that deals with the functions and activities of life or of living matter (as organs, tissues, or cells) and of the physical and chemical phenomena involved — compare ANATOMY **2 :** the organic processes and phenomena of an organism or any of its parts or of a particular bodily process — **phys·i·ol·o·gist** \-jəst\ *n*

phys·io·pa·thol·o·gy \'fiz-ē-ō-pə-'thäl-ə-jē, -pa-\ *n* (ca. 1885) **:** a branch of biology or medicine that combines physiology and pathology esp. in the study of altered bodily function in disease — **phys·io·path·o·log·ic** \-,path-ə-'läj-ik\ *or* **phys·io·path·o·log·i·cal** \-i-kəl\ *adj*

phys·io·ther·a·py \,fiz-ē-ō-'ther-ə-pē\ *n* [NL *physiotherapia,* fr. *physi-* + *therapia* therapy] (ca. 1903) **:** PHYSICAL THERAPY — **phys·io·ther·a·pist** \-pəst\ *n*

phy·sique \fə-'zēk\ *n* [F, fr. *physique* physical, bodily, fr. L *physicus* of nature, fr. Gk *physikos*] (1813) **:** the form or structure of a person's body **:** bodily makeup

phy·so·stig·mine \,fī-sə-'stig-,mēn\ *n* [ISV, fr. NL *Physostigma,* genus of vines whose fruit is the Calabar bean] (1864) **:** a crystalline tasteless alkaloid $C_{15}H_{21}N_3O_2$ from the Calabar bean that is used in medicine esp. in the form of its salicylate

phyt- *or* **phyto-** *comb form* [NL, fr. Gk, fr. *phyton,* fr. *phyein* to bring forth — more at BE] **:** plant ⟨*phyto*phagous⟩

phy·tane \'fī-,tān\ *n* (1907) **:** an isoprenoid hydrocarbon $C_{20}H_{42}$ that is found esp. associated with fossilized plant remains from the Precambrian and later eras

-phyte \,fīt\ *n comb form* [ISV, fr. Gk *phyton* plant] **1 :** plant having a (specified) characteristic or habitat ⟨xero*phyte*⟩ **2 :** pathological growth ⟨osteo*phyte*⟩

-phyt·ic \'fit-ik\ *adj comb form* [ISV, fr. Gk *phyton* plant] **:** like a plant ⟨holo*phytic*⟩

phy·to·alex·in \,fīt-ō-ə-'lek-sən\ *n* [*phyt-* + *alexin* (substance combating infection), fr. G, fr. Gk *alexein* to ward off, protect] (1949) **:** a chemical substance produced by a plant to combat infection by a pathogen (as a fungus)

phy·to·chem·i·cal \-'kem-i-kəl\ *adj* (ca. 1858) **:** of, relating to, or being phytochemistry — **phy·to·chem·i·cal·ly** \-i-k(ə-)lē\ *adv*

phy·to·chem·is·try \-'kem-ə-strē\ *n* (1837) **:** the chemistry of plants, plant processes, and plant products — **phy·to·chem·ist** \-'kem-əst\ *n*

phy·to·chrome \'fīt-ə-,krōm\ *n* (ca. 1893) **:** a chromoprotein that is present in traces in many plants and that plays a significant role in initiating floral and developmental processes when activated by red or far-red radiation

phy·to·fla·gel·late \,fīt-ō-'flaj-ə-lət, -,lāt; -flə-'jel-ət\ *n* (1935) **:** any of various organisms (as dinoflagellates) that are considered a subclass (as Phytomastigina) usu. of algae by botanists and of protozoans by zoologists and that have many characteristics in common with typical algae

phy·to·ge·og·ra·phy \,fīt-ō-jē-'äg-rə-fē\ *n* [ISV] (1847) **:** the biogeography of plants — **phy·to·geo·graph·i·cal** \-,jē-ə-'graf-i-kəl\ *or* **phy·to·geo·graph·ic** \-ik\ *adj* — **phy·to·geo·graph·i·cal·ly** \-i-k(ə-)lē\ *adv*

phy·to·he·mag·glu·ti·nin *also* **phy·to·hae·mag·glu·ti·nin** \'fīt-ō-,hē-mə-'glüt-ᵊn-ən\ *n* (1949) **:** a proteinaceous hemagglutinin of plant origin used esp. to induce mitosis (as in lymphocytes)

phy·to·hor·mone \,fīt-ə-'hȯr-,mōn\ *n* [ISV] (1933) **:** PLANT HORMONE

phy·ton \'fī-,tän\ *n* [NL, fr. Gk, plant] (1848) **1 :** a structural unit of a plant consisting of a leaf and its associated portion of stem **2 :** the smallest part of a stem, root, or leaf that when severed may grow into a new plant — **phy·ton·ic** \fī-'tän-ik\ *adj*

phy·to·patho·gen \,fīt-ō-'path-ə-jən\ *n* (ca. 1930) **:** an organism parasitic on a plant host — **phy·to·patho·gen·ic** \-,path-ə-'jen-ik\ *adj*

phy·to·pa·thol·o·gy \-pə-'thäl-ə-jē, -pa-\ *n* [ISV] (ca. 1864) **:** plant pathology — **phy·to·path·o·log·i·cal** \-,path-ə-'läj-i-kəl\ *adj*

phy·toph·a·gous \fī-'täf-ə-gəs\ *adj* (1826) **:** feeding on plants ⟨~ insect⟩

phy·to·plank·ter \,fīt-ō-'plaŋ(k)-tər\ *n* (1944) **:** a planktonic plant

phy·to·plank·ton \-'plaŋ(k)-tən, -,tän\ *n* [ISV] (1897) **:** planktonic plant life — **phy·to·plank·ton·ic** \-plaŋ(k)-'tän-ik\ *adj*

phy·to·so·ci·ol·o·gy \-,sō-sē-'äl-ə-jē, -shē-\ *n* (ca. 1928) **:** a branch of ecology that deals with the interrelations among the flora of particular areas and esp. with plant communities — **phy·to·so·cio·log·i·cal** \-sē-ə-'läj-i-kəl\ *adj*

phy·tos·ter·ol \fī-'täs-tə-,rȯl, -,rōl\ *n* [ISV] (1898) **:** any of various sterols derived from plants — compare ZOOSTEROL

phy·to·tox·ic \,fīt-ə-'täk-sik\ *adj* (1926) **:** poisonous to plants — **phy·to·tox·ic·i·ty** \-,täk-'sis-ət-ē\ *n*

1**pi** *also* **pie** \'pī\ *n, pl* **pies** [origin unknown] (ca. 1659) **1 :** type that is spilled or mixed **2 :** a pi character or matrix

2**pi** *also* **pie** *vb* **pied; pi·ing** *or* **pie·ing** *vt* (1870) **:** to spill or throw (type or type matter) into disorder ~ *vi* **:** to become pied

3**pi** *adj* (ca. 1940) **1 :** not intended to appear in final printing ⟨~ lines⟩ **2 :** capable of being inserted only by hand ⟨~ characters⟩

4**pi** *n, pl* **pis** \'pīz\ [MGk, fr. Gk *pei,* of Sem origin; akin to Heb *pē* pe] (1823) **1 :** the 16th letter of the Greek alphabet — see ALPHABET table **2 a :** the symbol π denoting the ratio of the circumference of a circle to its diameter **b :** the ratio itself **:** a transcendental number having a value to eight decimal places of 3.14159265

pi·al \'pī-əl, 'pē-\ *adj* (1889) **:** of or relating to the pia mater

pia ma·ter \'pī-ə-,māt-ər, 'pē-ə-,mät-\ *n* [ME, fr. ML, fr. L, tender mother] (15c) **:** the thin vascular membrane that invests the brain and spinal cord internal to the arachnoid and dura mater

pi·a·nism \'pē-ə-,niz-əm\ *n* (1844) **:** the art or technique of piano playing

1**pi·a·nis·si·mo** \,pē-ə-'nis-ə-,mō\ *adv or adj* [It, fr. *piano* softly] (1724) **:** very softly — used as a direction in music

2**pianissimo** *n, pl* **-mi** \-(,)mē\ *or* **-mos** (1883) **:** a passage played, sung, or spoken very softly

pi·a·nist \pē-'an-əst, 'pē-ə-nəst\ *n* (ca. 1828) **:** one who plays the piano; *esp* **:** a skilled or professional performer on the piano

pi·a·nis·tic \,pē-ə-'nis-tik\ *adj* (1881) **1 :** of, relating to, or characteristic of the piano **2 :** skilled in or well adapted to piano playing — **pi·a·nis·ti·cal·ly** \-ti-k(ə-)lē\ *adv*

1**pi·a·no** \pē-'än-(,)ō\ *adv or adj* [It, fr. LL *planus* smooth, fr. L, level — more at FLOOR] (1683) **:** in a soft or quiet manner — used as a direction in music

2**pi·ano** \pē-'an-(,)ō *also* -'än-\ *n, pl* **pianos** [It, short for *pianoforte,* fr. *piano e forte* soft and loud; fr. the fact that its tones could be varied in loudness] (1803) **:** a stringed instrument having steel wire strings that sound when struck by felt-covered hammers operated from a keyboard

piano accordion *n* (1860) **:** an accordion with a keyboard for the right hand resembling and corresponding to the middle register of a piano keyboard

pi·ano·forte \pē-'an-ə-,fō(ə)rt, -'än-, -,fȯ(ə)rt, -,fȯrt-ē; -,an-ə-'fȯrt-ē, -,än-\ *n* [It] (1767) **:** PIANO

piano hinge *n* (1926) **:** a hinge that has a thin pin joint and extends along the full length of the part to be moved

pi·as·sa·va \,pē-ə-'säv-ə\ *n* [Pg *piassaba,* fr. Tupi *piaçaba*] (1835) **1 :** any of several stiff coarse fibers obtained from palms and used esp. in cordage or brushes **2 :** a palm yielding piassava; *esp* **:** either of two Brazilian palms (*Attalia funifera* and *Leopoldinia piassaba*)

pi·as·tre *also* **pi·as·ter** \pē-'as-tər, -'äs-\ *n* [F *piastre,* fr. It *piastra* thin metal plate, coin, fr. L *emplastra, emplastrum* plaster] (1592) **1 :** PIECE OF EIGHT **2 a —** see *pound* at MONEY table **b —** see *lira* at MONEY table

pi·az·za \pē-'az-ə, -'äz-ə, *1 is usu* -'at-sə, -'ät-\ *n, pl* **piazzas** *or* **pi·az·ze** \-'at-(,)sā, -'ät-\ [It, fr. L *platea* broad street — more at PLACE] (1563) **1** *pl piazze* **:** an open square esp. in an Italian town **2 a :** an arcaded and roofed gallery **b** *dial* **:** VERANDA, PORCH

pi·broch \'pē-,bräk, -,bräk\ *n* [ScGael *piobaireachd* pipe-music] (1719) **:** a set of martial or mournful variations for the Scottish Highland bagpipe

1**pic** \'pik\ *n, pl* **pics** *or* **pix** \'piks\ [short for *picture*] (1884) **1 :** PHOTOGRAPH **2 :** MOTION PICTURE

2**pic** \'pik, 'pēk\ *n* [Sp *pica,* fr. *picar* to prick] (1926) **:** the picador's lance

1**pi·ca** \'pī-kə\ *n* [NL, fr. L, magpie — more at PIE] (1563) **:** an abnormal desire to eat substances (as chalk or ashes) not normally eaten

2**pica** *n* [prob. fr. ML, collection of church rules] (1588) **1 :** 12-point type **2 :** a unit of about $^1/_6$ inch used in measuring typographical material **3 :** a typewriter type providing 10 characters to the linear inch and six lines to the vertical inch

pic·a·dor \'pik-ə-,dȯ(ə)r, ,pik-ə-'\ *n, pl* **picadors** \-,dȯ(ə)rz, -'dȯ(ə)rz\ *or* **pic·a·do·res** \,pik-ə-'dōr-ēz, -'dȯr-\ [Sp, fr. *picar* to prick, fr. (assumed) VL *piccare* — more at PIKE] (1797) **:** a horseman in a bullfight who jabs the bull with a lance to weaken its neck and shoulder muscles

pi·ca·ra \'pē-kä-,rä\ *n* [Sp *pícara,* fem. of *pícaro*] (ca. 1930) **:** a woman who is a rogue

1**pi·ca·resque** \,pik-ə-'resk, ,pē-kə-\ *adj* [Sp *picaresco,* fr. *pícaro*] (1810) **:** of or relating to rogues or rascals; *also* **:** of, relating to, suggesting, or being a type of fiction dealing with the episodic adventures of a usu. roguish protagonist ⟨a ~ novel⟩

2**picaresque** *n* (1895) **:** one that is picaresque

pi·ca·ro \'pē-kä-,rō\ *n, pl* **-ros** [Sp *pícaro*] (1623) **:** ROGUE, BOHEMIAN

1**pic·a·roon** *or* **pick·a·roon** \,pik-ə-'rün\ *n* [Sp *picarón,* aug. of *pícaro*] (1624) **1 :** PICARO **2 :** PIRATE

2**picaroon** *vi* (1675) **:** to act as a pirate

1**pic·a·yune** \,pik-ē-'(y)ün\ *n* [F *picaillon* halfpenny, fr. Prov *picaioun,* fr. *picaio* money, fr. *pica* to prick, jingle, fr. (assumed) VL *piccare* to prick — more at PIKE] (1804) **1 a :** a Spanish half real piece formerly current in the South **b :** HALF DIME **2 :** something trivial

2**picayune** *adj* (1836) **:** of little value **:** PALTRY; *also* **:** PETTY, SMALL-MINDED — **pic·a·yun·ish** \-'(y)ü-nish\ *adj*

pic·ca·lil·li \,pik-ə-'lil-ē\ *n* [prob. alter. of *pickle*] (1769) **:** a pungent relish of chopped vegetables and spices

1**pic·co·lo** \'pik-ə-,lō\ *adj* [It, small] (ca. 1854) **:** smaller than ordinary size ⟨~ banjo⟩

2**piccolo** *n, pl* **-los** [It, short for *piccolo flauto* small flute] (1856) **:** a small shrill flute whose range is an octave higher than that of an ordinary flute — **pic·co·lo·ist** \-,lō-əst\ *n*

pice \'pīs\ *n, pl* **pice** [Hindi *paisā*] (1615) **:** PAISA

pi·ce·ous \'pi-sē-əs\ *adj* [L *piceus,* fr. *pic-, pix* pitch — more at PITCH] (1646) **:** of, relating to, or resembling pitch; *esp* **:** glossy brownish black in color ⟨an insect with a ~ brown abdomen⟩

1**pick** \'pik\ *vb* [ME *piken,* partly fr. (assumed) OE *pīcian* (akin to MD *picken* to prick); partly fr. MF *piquer* to prick — more at PIKE] *vt* (14c) **1 :** to pierce, penetrate, or break up with a pointed instrument ⟨~*ed* the hard clay⟩ **2 a :** to remove bit by bit ⟨~ meat from bones⟩ **b :** to remove covering or adhering matter from ⟨~ the bones⟩ **3 a :** to gather by plucking ⟨~ apples⟩ **b :** CHOOSE, SELECT ⟨tried to ~ the shortest route⟩ ⟨she ~*ed* out the most expensive dress⟩ **c :** to make (one's way) slowly and carefully ⟨~*ed* his way through the rubble⟩ **4 :** PILFER, ROB ⟨~ pockets⟩ **5 :** PROVOKE ⟨~ a quarrel⟩ **6 a :** to dig into : PROBE ⟨~ his teeth⟩ **b :** to pluck (as a guitar) with a pick or with the fingers **c :** to loosen or pull apart with a sharp point ⟨~ wool⟩ **7 :** to unlock with a device (as a wire) other than the key ⟨~ a lock⟩ **~** *vi* **1 :** to use or work with a pick **2 :** to gather or harvest something by plucking **3 :** PILFER — used in the phrase *picking and stealing* **4 :** to eat sparingly or mincingly ⟨~*ing* listlessly at his dinner⟩ — **pick and choose :** to select with care and deliberation — **pick at :** to criticize repeatedly esp. for minor faults : NAG — **pick on 1 :** to pick at : HARASS ⟨*picked on* smaller boys⟩ **2 :** to single out for a particular purpose or for special attention

[2]**pick** *n* (1513) **1 :** a blow or stroke with a pointed instrument **2 a :** the act or privilege of choosing or selecting : CHOICE ⟨take your ~⟩ **b :** the best or choicest one ⟨the ~ of the herd⟩ **3 :** the portion of a crop gathered at one time ⟨the first ~ of peaches⟩ **4 :** a screen in basketball

[3]**pick** *n* [ME *pik*] (14c) **1 :** a heavy wooden-handled iron or steel tool pointed at one or both ends — compare MATTOCK **2 a :** TOOTHPICK **b :** PICKLOCK **c :** a small thin piece (as of plastic or metal) used to pluck the strings of a stringed instrument **3 :** one of the points of the forepart of a figure skate blade

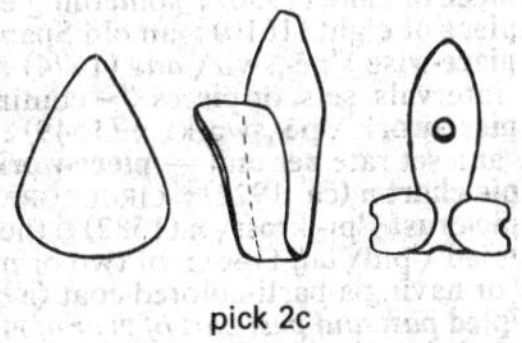

pick 2c

[4]**pick** *vt* [ME *pykken* to pitch (a tent), alter. of *picchen* to pitch] (1523) **1** *chiefly dial* **:** to throw or thrust with effort : HURL **2 :** to throw (a shuttle) across the loom

[5]**pick** *n* (1627) **1** *dial Eng* **a :** the act of pitching or throwing **b :** something thrown **2 a :** a throw of the shuttle **b :** one filling thread taken as a unit of fineness of fabric

pick·a·back \'pig-ē-ˌbak, 'pik-ə-\ *var of* PIGGYBACK

pick–and–shovel *adj* (1895) **:** done with or as if with a pick and shovel : LABORIOUS

pick·a·nin·ny *or* **pic·a·nin·ny** \'pik-ə-ˌnin-ē, ˌpik-ə-'\ *n, pl* **-nies** [prob. modif. of Pg *pequenino* very little] (1653) **:** a Negro child — often taken to be offensive

pick·ax \'pik-ˌaks\ *n* [alter. of ME *pikois,* fr. OF *picois,* fr. *pic* pick, fr. L *picus* woodpecker — more at PIE] (14c) **:** [3]PICK 1

[1]**pick·ed** \'pik-əd\ *adj* [ME, fr. [3]*pick*] *chiefly dial* (15c) **:** POINTED, PEAKED

[2]**picked** \'pikt\ *adj* [[1]*pick*] (ca. 1548) **:** CHOICE, PRIME

pick·eer \pik-'i(ə)r\ *vi* [prob. modif. of F *picorer* to steal sheep, maraud, fr. MF *pecore* sheep, fr. OIt *pecora,* fr. L, neut. pl. of *pecor-, pecus* cattle — more at FEE] *archaic* (ca. 1645) **:** to skirmish in advance of an army; *also* **:** SCOUT, RECONNOITER

pick·er \'pik-ər\ *n* (1624) **:** one that picks: as **a :** a worker who picks something (as crops) **b :** a tool, implement, or machine used in picking something

pick·er·el \'pik(-ə)-rəl\ *n, pl* **-el** *or* **-els** [ME *pikerel,* dim. of *pike*] (14c) **1 a** *dial chiefly Brit* **:** a young or small pike **b :** any of several comparatively small fishes (genus *Esox*) — usu. used with a qualifying term ⟨grass ~⟩ **2 :** WALLEYE 3

pick·er·el·weed \-rəl-ˌwēd\ *n* (1653) **:** any of various monocotyledonous aquatic plants: as **a :** any of a genus (*Pontederia*); *esp* **:** a blue-flowered American shallow-water herb (*P. cordata*) **b :** any of several still-water herbs (genus *Potamogeton*)

[1]**pick·et** \'pik-ət\ *n* [F *piquet,* fr. MF, fr. *piquer* to prick — more at PIKE] (1702) **1 :** a pointed or sharpened stake, post, or pale **2 a :** a detached body of soldiers serving to guard an army from surprise **b :** a detachment kept ready in camp for such duty **c :** SENTINEL **3 :** a person posted by a labor organization at a place of work affected by a strike; *also* **:** a person posted for a demonstration or protest

[2]**picket** *vt* (1745) **1 :** to enclose, fence, or fortify with pickets **2 a :** to guard with a picket **b :** to post as a picket **3 :** TETHER **4 a :** to post pickets at **b :** to walk or stand in front of as a picket **~** *vi* **:** to serve as a picket — **pick·et·er** *n*

pick·et·boat \'pik-ət-ˌbōt\ *n* (1866) **:** a craft used (as by the coast guard) for harbor patrol

picket line *n* (1856) **1 :** a position held by a line of military pickets **2 :** a line of individuals (as workers) picketing a business, organization, or institution

pick·ings \'pik-iŋz, -ənz\ *n pl* (1642) **:** something that is picked or picked up: as **a :** gleanable or eatable fragments : SCRAPS **b :** yield or return for effort expended

[1]**pick·le** \'pik-əl\ *n* [ME *pekille*] (15c) **1 :** a solution or bath for preserving or cleaning: as **a :** a brine or vinegar solution in which foods are preserved **b :** any of various baths used in industrial cleaning or processing **2 :** a difficult situation : PLIGHT ⟨could see no way out of the ~ I was in —R. L. Stevenson⟩ **3 :** an article of food that has been preserved in brine or in vinegar; *specif* **:** a cucumber that has been so preserved **4** *Brit* **:** a mischievous or troublesome person

[2]**pickle** *vt* **pick·led; pick·ling** \-(ə-)liŋ\ (1552) **1 :** to treat, preserve, or clean in or with a pickle **2 :** to give a light finish to (as furniture) by bleaching or painting and wiping

[3]**pickle** *n* [perh. fr. Sc *pickle* (to trifle, pilfer)] (1552) **1** *Scot* **:** GRAIN, KERNEL **2** *Scot* **:** a small quantity

pick·led *adj* (ca. 1552) **1 :** preserved in or cured with pickle ⟨~ herring⟩ **2 :** DRUNK ⟨gets thoroughly ~ before dinner —*New Yorker*⟩

pick·lock \'pik-ˌläk\ *n* (1553) **1 :** BURGLAR **2 :** a tool for picking locks

pick–me–up \'pik-mē-ˌəp\ *n* (1867) **:** something that stimulates or restores : TONIC, BRACER

pick·off \'pik-ˌȯf\ *n* (1939) **:** a baseball play in which a base runner is picked off

pick–off \'pik-ˌȯf\ *n* (1938) **:** a sensing device that responds to angular movement and produces a signal or effects control

pick off \(ˈ)pik-'ȯf\ *vt* (1810) **1 :** to shoot or bring down esp. one by one **2 :** to put out (a base runner who is off base) with a quick throw (as from the pitcher or catcher) **3 :** INTERCEPT ⟨*picked off* a pass⟩

pick out *vt* (1893) **1 :** DISCERN, MAKE OUT **2 :** to play the notes of by ear or one by one ⟨learned to *pick out* tunes on the piano⟩

pick over *vt* (1839) **:** to examine in order to select the best or remove the unwanted

pick·pock·et \'pik-ˌpäk-ət\ *n* (1591) **:** one who steals from pockets

pick·proof \-ˌprüf\ *adj* (1933) **:** designed to prevent picking ⟨a ~ lock⟩

pick·thank \-ˌthaŋk\ *n* [fr. *pick a thank* to seek someone's favor] *archaic* (ca. 1500) **:** SYCOPHANT

[1]**pick·up** \'pik-ˌəp\ *n* (1848) **1 :** the act or process of picking up: as **a :** a revival of business activity **b :** ACCELERATION **2 :** one that is picked up: as **a :** a hitchhiker who is given a ride **b :** a temporary chance acquaintance **3 :** the conversion of mechanical movements into electrical impulses in the reproduction of sound; *also* **:** a device (as on a phonograph) for making such conversion **4 a (1) :** the reception of sound or an image into a radio or television transmitting apparatus for conversion into electrical signals **(2) :** interference (as with such reception) from an adjacent electrical circuit or system **b :** a device (as a microphone or a television camera) for converting sound or the image of a scene into electrical signals **c :** the place where a broadcast originates **d :** the electrical system for connecting to a broadcasting station a program produced outside the studio **5 :** a light truck having an enclosed cab and an open body with low sides and tailgate — called also *pickup truck*

[2]**pickup** *adj* (ca. 1890) **:** utilizing or comprising local or available personnel esp. without formal organization ⟨a ~ basketball game⟩

pick up \(ˈ)pik-'əp\ *vt* (14c) **1 a :** to take hold of and lift up **b :** to gather together : COLLECT ⟨*picked up* all the pieces⟩ **c :** to clean up : TIDY **2 :** to take (passengers or freight) into a vehicle **3 a :** to acquire casually or by chance ⟨*picked up* a valuable antique at an auction⟩ **b :** to acquire by study or experience : LEARN ⟨*picking up* a great deal of knowledge in the process —Robert Schleicher⟩ **c :** to obtain esp. by payment : BUY ⟨*picked up* some groceries⟩ **d :** to acquire (a player) esp. from another team through a trade or by financial recompense **e :** to accept for the purpose of paying ⟨offered to *pick up* the tab⟩ **f :** to come down with : CATCH ⟨*picked up* a cold⟩ **g :** GAIN ⟨*picked up* a few yards on the last play⟩ **4 a :** to enter informally into conversation or companionship with (a previously unknown person) ⟨had a brief affair with a girl he *picked up* in a bar⟩ **b :** to take into custody ⟨the police *picked up* the fugitive⟩ **5 a :** to catch sight of : PERCEIVE ⟨*pick up* the harbor lights⟩ **b :** to come to and follow ⟨*picked up* the outlaw's trail⟩ **c :** to bring within range of sight or hearing ⟨*pick up* distant radio signals⟩ **d :** UNDERSTAND, CATCH ⟨didn't *pick up* the hint⟩ **6 a :** REVIVE **b :** INCREASE **7 :** to resume after a break : CONTINUE ⟨*pick up* the discussion tomorrow⟩ **8 :** to assume responsibility for guarding (an opponent) in an athletic contest **~** *vi* **1 :** to recover speed, vigor, or activity : IMPROVE ⟨after the strike, business *picked up*⟩ **2 :** to put things in order ⟨was always *picking up* after her⟩ **3 :** to pack up one's belongings ⟨couldn't just *pick up* and leave⟩ — **pick up on 1 a :** UNDERSTAND, APPRECIATE **b :** to become aware of : NOTICE **2 :** to adopt as one's own : TAKE UP

Pick·wick·ian \(ˈ)pik-'wik-ē-ən\ *adj* [Samuel *Pickwick,* character in the novel *Pickwick Papers* (1836–37) by Charles Dickens] (1836) **1 :** marked by simplicity and generosity **2 :** intended or taken in a sense other than the obvious or literal one

picky \'pik-ē\ *adj* **pick·i·er; -est** (ca 1867) **:** FUSSY, CHOOSY ⟨a ~ eater⟩

pi·clo·ram \'pik-lə-ˌram, 'pīk-\ *n* [*pi*coline + ch*lor*- + *am*ine] (1965) **:** a systemic herbicide $C_6H_3Cl_3N_2O_2$ that breaks down only very slowly in the soil

[1]**pic·nic** \'pik-(ˌ)nik\ *n, often attrib* [G or F; G *picknick,* fr. F *pique-nique*] (1748) **1 :** an excursion or outing with food usu. provided by members of the group and eaten in the open; *also* **:** the food provided for a picnic **2 a :** a pleasant or amusingly carefree experience ⟨I don't expect being married to be a ~ —Josephine Pinckney⟩ **b :** an easy task or feat **3 :** a shoulder of pork with much of the butt removed — see PORK illustration — **pic·nic·ky** \-(ˌ)nik-ē\ *adj*

[2]**picnic** *vi* **pic·nicked; pic·nick·ing** (1842) **:** to go on a picnic : eat in picnic fashion — **pic·nick·er** *n*

picnometer *var of* PYCNOMETER

pi·co- \'pē-(ˌ)kō, -kə\ *comb form* [ISV, perh. fr. It *piccolo* small] **1 :** one trillionth (10^{-12}) part of ⟨*pico*gram⟩ **2 :** very small ⟨*pico*rnavirus⟩

pi·co·far·ad \ˌpē-kō-'far-ˌad, -əd\ *n* [ISV] (ca. 1926) **:** one trillionth of a farad

pi·co·gram \'pē-kō-ˌgram, -kə-\ *n* [ISV] (1951) **:** one trillionth of a gram

pic·o·line \'pik-ə-ˌlēn, 'pī-k-\ *n* [L *pic-, pix* pitch + ISV *-ol* + *-ine* — more at PITCH] (1853) **:** any of the three liquid pyridine bases C_6H_7N found esp. in coal tar, ammonia liquor, and bone oil and used chiefly as solvents and in organic synthesis

pi·co·mole \'pē-kō-ˌmōl, -kə-\ *n* (1968) **:** one trillionth of a mole

pi·cor·na·vi·rus \(ˌ)pē-ˌkȯr-nə-'vī-rəs\ *n* [*pico-* + *RNA* + *virus*] (1962) **:** any of a group of RNA-containing viruses that includes the enteroviruses and rhinoviruses

pi·co·sec·ond \ˌpē-kō-'sek-ənd, -ənt\ *n* [ISV] (ca. 1962) **:** one trillionth of a second

[1]**pi·cot** \'pē-(ˌ)kō, pē-'\ *n* [F, lit., small point, fr. MF, fr. *pic* prick, fr. *piquer* to prick — more at PIKE] (ca. 1882) **:** one of a series of small ornamental loops forming an edging on ribbon or lace

[2]**picot** *vt* (1926) **:** to finish with picots

pic·o·tee \ˌpik-ə-'tē\ *n* [F *picoté* pointed, fr. *picoter* to mark with points, fr. *picot*] (1727) **:** a flower (as some carnations or tulips) having one basic color with a margin of another color

picr- *or* **picro-** *comb form* [F, fr. Gk *pikr-, pikro-,* fr. *pikros* — more at PAINT] **1 :** bitter ⟨*picr*ic acid⟩ **2 :** picric acid ⟨*picr*ate⟩

pic·rate \'pik-ˌrāt\ *n* (ca. 1866) **:** a salt or ester of picric acid

pic·ric acid \ˌpik-rik-\ *n* [ISV] (1852) **:** a bitter toxic explosive yellow crystalline strong acid $C_6H_3N_3O_7$ used esp. in high explosives, as a dye, or in medicine

\ə\ abut \ᵊ\ kitten, F table \ər\ further \a\ ash \ā\ ace \ä\ cot, cart \au̇\ out \ch\ chin \e\ bet \ē\ easy \g\ go \i\ hit \ī\ ice \j\ job \ŋ\ sing \ō\ go \ȯ\ law \ȯi\ boy \th\ thin \t͟h\ the \ü\ loot \u̇\ foot \y\ yet \zh\ vision \à, k̟, ⁿ, œ, œ̄, ue, ue̅, ʸ\ *see* Guide to Pronunciation

pic·ro·tox·in \ˌpik-rō-ˈtäk-sən\ *n* [ISV] (1815) **:** a poisonous bitter crystalline stimulant and convulsive drug $C_{30}H_{34}O_{13}$ used intravenously as an antidote for barbiturate poisoning

Pict \ˈpikt\ *n* [ME *Pictes,* pl., Picts, fr. OE *Pihtas,* fr. LL *Picti*] (bef. 12c) **:** a member of a possibly non-Celtic people who once occupied Great Britain, carried on continual border wars with the Romans, and about the ninth century became amalgamated with the Scots — **Pict·ish** \ˈpik-tish\ *adj or n*

pic·to·gram \ˈpik-tə-ˌgram\ *n* [ISV *picto-* (fr. L *pictus*) + *-gram*] (1910) **:** PICTOGRAPH

pic·to·graph \-ˌgraf\ *n* [L *pictus* + E *-o-* + *-graph*] (1851) **1 :** an ancient or prehistoric drawing or painting on a rock wall **2 :** one of the symbols belonging to a pictorial graphic system **3 :** a diagram representing statistical data by pictorial forms — **pic·to·graph·ic** \ˌpik-tə-ˈgraf-ik\ *adj*

pic·tog·ra·phy \pik-ˈtäg-rə-fē\ *n* (1851) **:** use of pictographs **:** PICTURE WRITING 1

[1]pic·to·ri·al \pik-ˈtōr-ē-əl, -ˈtȯr-\ *adj* [LL *pictorius,* fr. L *pictor* painter] (1646) **1 :** of or relating to a painter, a painting, or the painting or drawing of pictures ⟨~ perspective⟩ **2 a :** consisting of pictures ⟨~ records⟩ **b :** illustrated by pictures ⟨~ weekly⟩ **c :** consisting of or displaying the characteristics of pictographs **d :** suggesting or conveying visual images ⟨~ poetry⟩ ***syn*** see GRAPHIC — **pic·to·ri·al·ly** \-ē-ə-lē\ *adv* — **pic·to·ri·al·ness** *n*

[2]pictorial *n* (1844) **:** a periodical having much pictorial matter

pic·to·ri·al·ism \-ē-ə-ˌliz-əm\ *n* (1869) **:** the use or creation of pictures or visual images — **pic·to·ri·al·ist** \-ē-ə-ləst\ *n*

pic·to·ri·al·ize \pik-ˈtōr-ē-ə-ˌlīz, -ˈtȯr-\ *vt* **-ized; -iz·ing** (1870) **:** to represent by a picture or illustrate with pictures — **pic·to·ri·al·iza·tion** \-ˌtōr-ē-ə-lə-ˈzā-shən, -ˌtȯr-\ *n*

[1]pic·ture \ˈpik-chər\ *n* [ME, fr. L *pictura,* fr. *pictus,* pp. of *pingere* to paint — more at PAINT] (15c) **1 :** a design or representation made by various means (as painting, drawing, or photography) **2 a :** a description so vivid or graphic as to suggest a mental image or give an accurate idea of something ⟨the book gives a detailed ~ of what is happening⟩ **b :** a mental image **3 :** IMAGE, COPY ⟨he was the ~ of his father⟩ **4 a :** a transitory visible image or reproduction **b :** MOTION PICTURE **c** *pl, chiefly Brit* **:** MOVIES **5 :** TABLEAU 1, 2 ⟨stage ~s⟩ **6 :** SITUATION ⟨took a hard look at his financial ~⟩

[2]picture *vt* **pic·tured; pic·tur·ing** \ˈpik-chə-riŋ, ˈpik-shriŋ\ (15c) **1 :** to paint or draw a representation, image, or visual conception of **:** DEPICT; *also* **:** ILLUSTRATE **2 :** to describe graphically in words **3 :** to form a mental image of **:** IMAGINE

picture–book *adj* (1922) **:** suitable for or suggestive of a picture book **:** PICTURESQUE

picture book *n* (1847) **:** a book that consists wholly or chiefly of pictures

picture hat *n* (1887) **:** a woman's dressy hat with a broad brim

Pic·ture·phone \ˈpik-chər-ˌfōn\ *service mark* — used for a combined telephone and television apparatus

picture puzzle *n* (1898) **:** JIGSAW PUZZLE

pic·tur·esque \ˌpik-chə-ˈresk\ *adj* [F & It; F *pittoresque,* fr. It *pittoresco,* fr. *pittore* painter, fr. L *pictor,* fr. *pictus,* pp.] (1703) **1 a :** resembling a picture **:** suggesting a painted scene **b :** charming or quaint in appearance **2 :** evoking mental images **:** VIVID ***syn*** see GRAPHIC — **pic·tur·esque·ly** *adv* — **pic·tur·esque·ness** *n*

picture tube *n* (1937) **:** a cathode-ray tube having at one end a screen of luminescent material on which are produced visible images

picture window *n* (1938) **:** an outsize usu. single-paned window designed to frame an exterior view

picture writing *n* (1741) **1 :** the recording of events or expression of messages by pictures representing actions or facts **2 :** the record or message represented by picture writing

pic·tur·ize \ˈpik-chə-ˌrīz\ *vt* **-ized; -iz·ing** (ca. 1846) **:** to make a picture of **:** present in pictures; *esp* **:** to make into a motion picture — **pic·tur·iza·tion** \ˌpik-chə-rə-ˈzā-shən\ *n*

pic·ul \ˈpik-əl\ *n* [Malay *pikul* to carry a heavy load] (1588) **:** any of various units of weight used in China and southeast Asia; *esp* **:** a Chinese unit equal to 133.33 pounds (60.477 kilograms)

pid·dle \ˈpid-ᵊl\ *vi* **pid·dled; pid·dling** \ˈpid-liŋ, -ᵊl-iŋ\ [origin unknown] (1545) **1 :** DAWDLE, PUTTER **2 :** URINATE

pid·dling \ˈpid-lən, -liŋ, -ᵊl-ən, -ᵊl-iŋ\ *adj* (1559) **:** TRIVIAL, PALTRY

pid·dock \ˈpid-ək, -ik\ *n* [origin unknown] (1851) **:** a bivalve mollusk (genus *Pholas* or family Pholadidae) that bores holes in wood, clay, and rocks

pid·gin \ˈpij-ən\ *n* [*Pidgin English*] (1876) **:** a simplified speech used for communication between people with different languages — **pid·gin·iza·tion** \ˌpij-ə-nə-ˈzā-shən\ *n* — **pid·gin·ize** \-ə-ˌnīz\ *vt*

Pidgin English *n* [Pidgin E, modif. of E *business English*] (1859) **:** an English-based pidgin; *esp* **:** one orig. used in parts of the Orient

[1]pie \ˈpī\ *n* [ME, fr. OF, fr. L *pica;* akin to L *picus* woodpecker, OHG *speh*] (13c) **:** MAGPIE

[2]pie *n* [ME] (14c) **1 :** a meat dish baked with biscuit or pastry crust — compare POTPIE **2 :** a dessert consisting of a filling (as of fruit or custard) in a pastry shell or topped with pastry or both **3 a :** AFFAIR, BUSINESS ⟨she wanted her finger . . . in every possible social ~ —Mary Deasy⟩ **b :** a whole regarded as divisible into shares ⟨giving the less fortunate . . . a larger share of the economic ~ —R. M. Hutchins⟩

[3]pie *var of* PI

[1]pie·bald \ˈpī-ˌbȯld\ *adj* (1594) **1 :** of different colors; *esp* **:** spotted or blotched with black and white **2 :** composed of incongruous parts **:** HETEROGENEOUS

[2]piebald *n* (1765) **:** a piebald animal (as a horse)

[1]piece \ˈpēs\ *n* [ME, fr. OF, fr. (assumed) VL *pettia,* of Gaulish origin; akin to Bret *pez* piece] (13c) **1 :** a part of a whole: as **a :** FRAGMENT ⟨broke off a ~ of glass⟩ **b :** any of the individual members comprising a unit — often used in combination ⟨a five-*piece* band⟩ ⟨a three-*piece* suit⟩ **2 :** an object or individual regarded as a unit of a kind or class **:** EXAMPLE ⟨a ~ of fruit⟩ **3 :** a short distance ⟨down the road a ~⟩ **4 :** a standard quantity (as of length, weight, or size) in which something is made or sold **5 :** a literary, artistic, dramatic, or musical composition **6 :** FIREARM **7 :** COIN; *also* **:** TOKEN **8 :** a man used in playing a board game; *specif* **:** a chessman of superior rank **9 :** OPINION, VIEW ⟨spoke his ~⟩ **10 a :** an act of copulation — usu. considered vulgar **b :** the female partner in sexual intercourse — usu. considered vulgar ***syn*** see PART — **of a piece :** ALIKE, CONSISTENT — **piece of one's mind :** a severe scolding **:** TONGUE-LASHING — **piece of the action :** a share in activity or profit — **to pieces 1 :** without reserve or restraint **:** COMPLETELY **2 :** into fragments; *also* **:** into component parts **3 :** out of control ⟨went *to pieces* from shock⟩

[2]piece *vt* **pieced; piec·ing** (14c) **1 :** to repair, renew, or complete by adding pieces **:** PATCH **2 :** to join into a whole — often used with *together* ⟨his new book . . . has been *pieced* together from talks —Merle Miller⟩ — **piec·er** *n*

piece by piece *adv* (1560) **:** by degrees **:** PIECEMEAL

pièce de ré·sis·tance \pē-ˌes-də-rə-ˌzē-ˈstän(t)s, -rā-, -ˈstäⁿs\ *n, pl* **pièces de ré·sis·tance** *same*\ [F, lit., piece of resistance] (1839) **1 :** the chief dish of a meal **2 :** an outstanding item **:** SHOWPIECE

piece–dye \ˈpēs-ˌdī\ *vt* (1920) **:** to dye after weaving or knitting

piece goods *n pl* (1665) **:** cloth fabrics sold from the bolt at retail in lengths specified by the customer — called also *yard goods*

[1]piece·meal \ˈpē-ˌsmēl, -ˈsmē(ə)l\ *adv* (13c) **1 :** one piece at a time **:** GRADUALLY **2 :** in pieces or fragments **:** APART

[2]piecemeal *adj* (1600) **:** done, made, or accomplished piece by piece or in a fragmentary way ⟨~ reforms in the system⟩

piece of cake (1936) **:** something easily done **:** CINCH, BREEZE

piece of eight (1610) **:** an old Spanish peso of eight reals

piece·wise \ˈpē-ˌswīz\ *adv* (1674) **:** with respect to a number of discrete intervals, sets, or pieces ⟨~ continuous functions⟩

piece·work \ˈpē-ˌswərk\ *n* (1549) **:** work done by the piece and paid for at a set rate per unit — **piece·work·er** \-ˌswər-kər\ *n*

pie chart *n* (ca. 1922) **:** CIRCLE GRAPH

pie·crust \ˈpī-ˌkrəst\ *n* (1582) **:** the pastry shell of a pie

[1]pied \ˈpīd\ *adj* (14c) **:** of two or more colors in blotches; *also* **:** wearing or having a parti-colored coat ⟨a ~ horse⟩

[2]pied *past and past part of* PI *or of* PIE

pied–à–terre \pē-ˌād-ə-ˈte(ə)r, -ˌād-ä-, ˌpyā-\ *n, pl* **pieds–à–terre** *same*\ [F, lit., foot to the ground] (1829) **:** a temporary or second lodging

pied·mont \ˈpēd-ˌmänt\ *adj* [*Piedmont,* region of Italy] (1855) **:** lying or formed at the base of mountains — **piedmont** *n*

pied piper *n, often cap both Ps* [*The Pied Piper of Hamelin,* title & hero of a poem (1842) by Robert Browning] (1925) **1 :** one that offers strong but delusive enticement **2 :** a leader who makes irresponsible promises

pie–eyed \ˈpī-ˈīd\ *adj* (1904) **:** INTOXICATED

pie–faced \-ˈfāst\ *adj* (ca. 1912) **:** having a round, smooth, or blank face

pie·fort *or* **pied·fort** \pē-ˌā-ˈfō(ə)r\ *n, often attrib* [F *pied-fort,* lit., strong-footed one] (ca. 1917) **:** a coin struck on an unusually thick flan

pieing *pres part of* PI *or of* PIE

pie in the sky (1911) **:** a prospect or promise of deferred happiness or prosperity — **pie-in-the-sky** *adj*

pie·plant \ˈpī-ˌplant\ *n* (ca. 1847) **:** garden rhubarb

pier \ˈpi(ə)r\ *n* [ME *per,* fr. OE, fr. ML *pera*] (bef. 12c) **1 :** an intermediate support for the adjacent ends of two bridge spans **2 :** a structure (as a breakwater) extending into navigable water for use as a landing place or promenade or to protect or form a harbor **3 :** a vertical structural support: as **a :** the wall between two openings **b :** PILLAR, PILASTER **c :** a vertical member that supports the end of an arch or lintel **d :** an auxiliary mass of masonry used to stiffen a wall **4 :** a structural mount (as for a telescope) usu. of stonework, concrete, or steel

pierce \ˈpi(ə)rs\ *vb* **pierced; pierc·ing** [ME *percen,* fr. OF *percer*] *vt* (13c) **1 a :** to run into or through as a pointed weapon does **:** STAB **b :** to enter or thrust into sharply or painfully **2 :** to make a hole through **:** PERFORATE **3 :** to force or make a way into or through **4 :** to penetrate with the eye or mind **:** DISCERN **5 :** to penetrate so as to move or touch the emotions of ~ *vi* **:** to force a way into or through something ***syn*** see ENTER

pierced *adj* (15c) **1 :** having holes; *esp* **:** decorated with perforations **2 :** having the earlobe punctured for an earring ⟨~ ears⟩ **3 :** designed for pierced ears ⟨~ earrings⟩

pierc·ing *adj* (15c) **:** PENETRATING: as **a :** LOUD, SHRILL ⟨~ cries⟩ **b :** PERCEPTIVE ⟨~ eyes⟩ **c :** penetratingly cold **:** BITING ⟨a ~ wind⟩ **d :** CUTTING, INCISIVE ⟨~ sarcasm⟩ — **pierc·ing·ly** \ˈpir-siŋ-lē\ *adv*

pier glass *n* (1703) **:** a large high mirror; *esp* **:** one designed to occupy the wall space between windows — called also *pier mirror*

Pi·eri·an \pī-ˈir-ē-ən, -ˈer-\ *adj* (1591) **1 :** of or relating to the region of Pieria in ancient Macedonia or to the Muses who were early worshiped there **2 :** of or relating to learning or poetry

pie·ro·gi \pə-ˈrō-gē, pi(ə)r-ˈō-\ *n, pl* **-gi** *also* **-gies** [Pol, pl. of *pieróg* dumpling, pierogi] (1927) **:** PIROSHKI

Pier·rot \ˈpē-ə-ˌrō\ *n* [F, dim. of *Pierre* Peter] (ca. 1741) **:** a stock comic character of old French pantomime usu. having a whitened face and wearing loose white clothes

pier table *n* (1803) **:** a table to be placed under a pier glass

pies *pl of* PI *or of* PIE

pie safe *n* (1951) **:** a cupboard whose doors have decoratively pierced tin panels for ventilation

pie·tà \ˌpē-(ˌ)ā-ˈtä, pyā-\ *n, often cap* [It, lit., pity, fr. L *pietat-, pietas*] (1644) **:** a representation of the Virgin Mary mourning over the dead body of Christ

pi·etism \ˈpī-ə-ˌtiz-əm\ *n* (1697) **1** *cap* **:** a 17th century religious movement originating in Germany in reaction to formalism and intellectualism and stressing Bible study and personal religious experience **2 a :** emphasis on devotional experience and practices **b :** affectation of devotion — **pi·etist** \ˈpī-ət-əst\ *n, often cap*

pi·etis·tic \ˌpī-ə-ˈtis-tik\ *or* **pi·etis·ti·cal** \-ˈtis-ti-kəl\ *adj* (1830) **1 :** of or relating to Pietism **2 a :** of or relating to religious devotion or devout persons **b :** marked by overly sentimental or emotional devotion to religion **:** RELIGIOSE — **pi·etis·ti·cal·ly** \-ti-k(ə-)lē\ *adv*

pi·ety \ˈpī-ət-ē\ *n, pl* **pi·eties** [F *piété* piety, pity, fr. L *pietat-, pietas,* fr. *pius* dutiful — more at PIOUS] (1579) **1 :** the quality or state of being pious: as **a :** fidelity to natural obligations (as to parents) **b :** dutifulness in religion **:** DEVOUTNESS **2 :** an act inspired by piety **3 :** a conventional belief or standard **:** ORTHODOXY ***syn*** see FIDELITY

piezo- *comb form* [Gk *piezein* to press; akin to Skt *pīdayati* he squeezes] **:** pressure ⟨*piezo*meter⟩

pi·ezo·elec·tric \pē-ˌā-(ˌ)zō-ə-ˈlek-trik, pē-ˌāt-(ˌ)sō-\ *adj* [ISV] (1883) **:** of, relating to, marked by, or functioning by means of piezoelectricity — **pi·ezo·elec·tri·cal·ly** \-tri-k(ə-)lē\ *adv*

pi·ezo·elec·tric·i·ty \-ˌlek-ˈtris-ət-ē, -ˈtris-tē\ *n* [ISV] (1883) **:** electricity or electric polarity due to pressure esp. in a crystalline substance (as quartz)

pi·ezom·e·ter \ˌpē-ə-ˈzäm-ət-ər, pē-ˌāt-ˈsäm-\ *n* (1820) **:** an instrument for measuring pressure or compressibility; *esp* **:** one for measuring the change of pressure of a material subjected to hydrostatic pressure — **pi·ezo·met·ric** \pē-ˌā-zə-ˈme-trik, pē-ˌāt-sə-\ *adj* — **pi·ezom·e·try** \ˌpē-ə-ˈzäm-ə-trē, pē-ˌāt-ˈsäm-\ *n*

¹pif·fle \ˈpif-əl\ *vi* **pif·fled; pif·fling** \-(ə-)liŋ\ [perh. blend of *piddle* and *trifle*] (ca. 1847) **:** to talk or act in a trivial, inept, or ineffective way

²piffle *n* (1890) **:** trivial nonsense **:** INEPTITUDE

pif·fling \ˈpif-lən, ˈpif(-ə)-liŋ\ *adj* (1894) **:** of little worth or importance **:** TRIVIAL

¹pig \ˈpig\ *n, often attrib* [ME *pigge*] (13c) **1 :** a young swine not yet sexually mature; *broadly* **:** a wild or domestic swine **2 a :** PORK **b :** the dressed carcass of a young swine weighing less than 130 pounds (59.0 kilograms) **c :** PIGSKIN **3 a :** one thought to resemble a pig — usu. used disparagingly **b :** an animal related to or resembling the pig **4 :** a crude casting of metal (as iron) **5 :** an immoral woman **6** *slang* **:** POLICEMAN — usu. used disparagingly

²pig *vb* **pigged; pig·ging** *vi* (ca. 1532) **1 :** FARROW **2 :** to live like a pig ⟨~ it⟩ ~ *vt* **:** FARROW

³pig *n* [ME *pygg*] *chiefly Scot* (15c) **:** an earthenware vessel **:** CROCK

pig bed *n* (ca. 1864) **:** a bed of sand in which iron is cast into pigs

pig·boat \ˈpig-ˌbōt\ *n* (1921) **:** SUBMARINE

pi·geon \ˈpij-ən\ *n* [ME, fr. MF *pijon,* fr. LL *pipion-, pipio* young bird, fr. L *pipire* to chirp] (14c) **1 :** any of a widely distributed family (Columbidae, order Columbiformes) of birds with a stout body, rather short legs, and smooth and compact plumage; *esp* **:** a member of any of many varieties of the rock pigeon that exist in domestication and in the feral state in cities and towns throughout most of the world **2 :** a young woman **3 :** an easy mark **:** DUPE **4 :** CLAY PIGEON **5** [alter. of *pidgin*] **:** an object of special concern **:** BUSINESS

pigeon breast *n* (1842) **:** a rachitic deformity of the chest marked by sharp projection of the sternum

pigeon hawk *n* (ca. 1728) **1 :** a falcon of the No. American population of the merlin **2 :** SHARP-SHINNED HAWK

¹pi·geon·hole \ˈpij-ən-ˌhōl\ *n* (1577) **1 :** a hole or small recess for pigeons to nest **2 :** a small open compartment (as in a desk or cabinet) for keeping letters or documents **3 :** a neat category which usu. fails to reflect actual complexities

²pigeonhole *vt* (1840) **1 a :** to place in or as if in the pigeonhole of a desk **b :** to lay aside **:** SHELVE ⟨his reports continued to be *pigeonholed* and his advice not taken —Walter Mills⟩ **2 :** to assign to a category **:** CLASSIFY — **pi·geon·hol·er** \-ˌhō-lər\ *n*

pi·geon·ite \ˈpij-ə-ˌnīt\ *n* [*Pigeon* Point, northeast Minn. + *-ite*] (1900) **:** a monoclinic mineral $(Mg,Fe,Ca)_2Si_2O_6$ of the pyroxene group

pi·geon–liv·ered \ˌpij-ən-ˈliv-ərd\ *adj* (1602) **:** GENTLE, MILD

pigeon pea *n* (1725) **:** a leguminous woody herb (*Cajanus cajan*) that has trifoliate leaves, yellow flowers, and somewhat flat pods and is much cultivated esp. in the tropics; *also* **:** its small highly nutritious seed

pi·geon–toed \ˌpij-ən-ˈtōd\ *adj* (1801) **:** having the toes turned in

pi·geon·wing \ˈpij-ən-ˌwiŋ\ *n* (ca. 1807) **:** a fancy dance step executed by jumping and striking the legs together

pig·fish \ˈpig-ˌfish\ *n* (1807) **:** a saltwater grunt (*Orthopristis chrysopterus*) that is a food fish found from Long Island southward

pig·gery \ˈpig-ə-rē\ *n, pl* **-ger·ies** (1781) **1 :** a place where swine are kept **2 :** swinish behavior

pig·gin \ˈpig-ən\ *n* [origin unknown] (1554) **:** a small wooden pail with one stave extended upward as a handle

pig·gish \ˈpig-ish\ *adj* [¹*pig*] (1792) **1 :** GREEDY **2 :** STUBBORN — **pig·gish·ly** *adv* — **pig·gish·ness** *n*

¹pig·gy·back \ˈpig-ē-ˌbak\ *adv* [alter. of earlier *a pick pack,* of unknown origin] (1565) **1 :** up on the back and shoulders **2 :** on a railroad flatcar ⟨the trailer rode ~ from coast to coast⟩

²piggyback *n* (ca. 1590) **1 :** the act of carrying piggyback **2 :** the movement of loaded truck trailers on railroad flatcars or cars of special design — compare BIRDYBACK, FISHYBACK

³piggyback *adj* (1823) **1 :** marked by being up on the shoulders and back ⟨a child needs hugging, tussling, and ~ rides —Benjamin Spock⟩ **2 :** of or relating to the hauling of truck trailers on railroad flatcars **3 :** of, relating to, or being a radio or television commercial that is presented in addition to other commercials during one commercial break **4 :** being or relating to something carried into space as an extra load by a vehicle (as a spacecraft)

⁴piggyback *vt* (1952) **1 :** to carry up on the shoulders and back **2 :** to haul (as a truck trailer) by railroad car **3 :** to set up or cause to function in conjunction with something larger or more important ~ *vi* **1 :** to haul truck trailers on railroad cars **2 :** to function or be carried as if on the back of another

piggy bank *n* (1941) **:** a coin bank often in the shape of a pig

pig·head·ed \ˈpig-ˈhed-əd\ *adj* (1620) **:** OBSTINATE, STUBBORN — **pig·head·ed·ly** *adv* — **pig·head·ed·ness** *n*

pig in a poke (1562) **:** something offered in such a way as to obscure its real nature or worth ⟨unwilling to buy a *pig in a poke*⟩

pig iron *n* (1665) **:** crude iron that is the direct product of the blast furnace and is refined to produce steel, wrought iron, or ingot iron

pig latin *n, often cap L* (1931) **:** a jargon that is made by systematic alteration of English (as *ipskay the ointjay* for *skip the joint*)

pig lead *n* (1791) **:** lead cast in pigs

pig·let \ˈpig-lət\ *n* (1883) **:** a small usu. young hog

¹pig·ment \ˈpig-mənt\ *n* [L *pigmentum,* fr. *pingere* to paint — more at PAINT] (14c) **1 :** a substance that imparts black or white or a color to other materials; *esp* **:** a powdered substance that is mixed with a liquid in which it is relatively insoluble and used esp. to impart color to coating materials (as paints) or to inks, plastics, and rubber **2 :** a coloring matter in animals and plants esp. in a cell or tissue; *also* **:** any of various related colorless substances — **pig·men·tary** \-mən-ˌter-ē\ *adj*

²pig·ment \-mənt, -ˌment\ *vt* (1900) **:** to color with or as if with pigment

pig·men·ta·tion \ˌpig-mən-ˈtā-shən, -ˌmen-\ *n* (1866) **:** coloration with or deposition of pigment; *esp* **:** an excessive deposition of bodily pigment

pigmy *var of* PYGMY

pi·gno·lia \pēn-ˈyō-lē-ə\ *or* **pi·gno·li** \-lē\ *n* [It *pignolo,* fr. (assumed) VL *pineolus,* dim. of L *pineus* of the pine, fr. *pinus* pine] (1898) **:** PINE NUT

pig·nut \ˈpig-ˌnət\ *n* (1666) **1 :** any of several bitter-flavored hickory nuts **2 :** a hickory (as *Carya glabra, C. ovalis,* or *C. cordiformis*) bearing pignuts

pig out *vi, slang* (1978) **:** to eat greedily **:** GORGE

pig·pen \-ˌpen\ *n* (1803) **1 :** a pen for pigs **2 :** a dirty slovenly place

pig·skin \-ˌskin\ *n* (1855) **1 :** the skin of a swine or leather made of it **2 a :** a jockey's saddle **b :** FOOTBALL 2a

pig·stick \-ˌstik\ *vi* (1890) **:** to hunt the wild boar on horseback with a spear — **pig·stick·er** *n*

pig·sty \ˈpig-ˌstī\ *n* (ca. 1591) **:** PIGPEN 1

pig·tail \-ˌtāl\ *n* (1688) **1 :** tobacco in small twisted strands or rolls **2 :** a tight braid of hair

pig·tailed \-ˌtāld\ *adj* (1754) **:** wearing a pigtail ⟨~ little girls⟩

pig·weed \-ˌwēd\ *n* (1801) **:** any of various strongly growing weedy plants esp. of the goosefoot or amaranth families

piing *pres part of* PI *or of* PIE

pi·ka \ˈpē-kə, ˈpī-\ *n* [Tungusic *piika*] (1827) **:** any of various short-eared small lagomorph mammals (family Ochotonidae) of rocky uplands of Asia and western No. America that are related to the rabbits

pi·ka·ke \ˈpē-kə-ˌkā\ *n* [Hawaiian *pīkake*] (1938) **:** an East Indian vine (*Jasminum sambuc*) that is cultivated for its profuse fragrant white flowers

¹pike \ˈpīk\ *n* [ME, fr. OE *pīc* pickax] (13c) **1 :** PIKESTAFF 1 **2 :** a sharp point or spike; *also* **:** the tip of a spear — **piked** \ˈpīkt\ *adj*

²pike *n* [ME, perh. of Scand origin; akin to Norw dial. *pīk* pointed mountain] (13c) **1** *dial Eng* **:** a mountain or hill having a peaked summit — used esp. in place names **2** [Sp *pico,* fr. *picar* to prick — more at PICADOR] *archaic* **:** PEAK

³pike *n, pl* **pike** *or* **pikes** [ME, fr. ¹*pike*] (14c) **1 a :** a large elongate long-snouted teleost fish (*Esox lucius*) valued for food and sport and widely distributed in cooler parts of the northern hemisphere — called also *northern, northern pike* **b :** any of various fishes (family Esocidae) related to the pike: as **(1) :** MUSKELLUNGE **(2) :** PICKEREL **2 :** any of various fishes resembling the pike in appearance or habits

⁴pike *n* [MF *pique,* fr. *piquer* to prick, fr. (assumed) VL *piccare,* fr. *piccus* woodpecker, fr. L *picus* — more at PIE] (ca. 1511) **:** a weapon formed of a long wooden shaft with a pointed steel head and used by the foot soldier until superseded by the bayonet

⁵pike *vt* **piked; pik·ing** (1798) **:** to pierce, kill, or wound with a pike

⁶pike *vi* **piked; pik·ing** [ME *pyken* (refl.)] (1526) **1 :** to leave abruptly ⟨get lonely and sore, and ~ out —Sinclair Lewis⟩ **2 :** to make one's way ⟨~ along⟩

⁷pike *n* (1812) **1 :** TURNPIKE **2 :** a railroad or railroad line or system

⁸pike *n* [prob. fr. ³*pike*] (1928) **:** a body position (as in diving) in which the hips are bent, the knees are straight, the head is pressed forward, and the hands touch the toes or clasp the legs behind or just above the knees

pike·man \ˈpīk-mən\ *n* (1566) **:** a soldier armed with a pike

pike perch *n* (1842) **:** a fish (as the walleye) of the perch group that resembles the pike

pik·er \ˈpī-kər\ *n* [*Pike* county, Missouri, thought to be the original home of many shiftless farmers] (1872) **1 :** one who gambles or speculates with small amounts of money **2 :** one who does things in a small way; *also* **:** TIGHTWAD, CHEAPSKATE

pike·staff \ˈpīk-ˌstaf\ *n* (14c) **1 :** a spiked staff for use on slippery ground **2 :** the staff of a foot soldier's pike

pil- *or* **pili-** *or* **pilo-** *comb form* [L *pilus* — more at PILE] **:** hair ⟨*pil*eous⟩ ⟨*pili*ferous⟩

pi·laf *or* **pi·laff** \pi-ˈläf, ˈpē-ˌ\ *or* **pi·lau** *also* **pi·law** \pi-ˈlō, -ˈlȯ, ˈpē-(ˌ); *Southern often* ˈpər-(ˌ)lü, -(ˌ)lō\ *n* [Per & Turk *pilāv*] (1612) **:** a dish made of seasoned rice and often meat

pi·las·ter \ˈpī-ˌlas-tər *also* pə-ˈlas- *or* pī-ˈ\ *n* [MF *pilastre,* fr. It *pilastro*] (1575) **:** an upright architectural member that is rectangular in plan and is structurally a pier but architecturally treated as a column and that usu. projects a third of its width or less from the wall

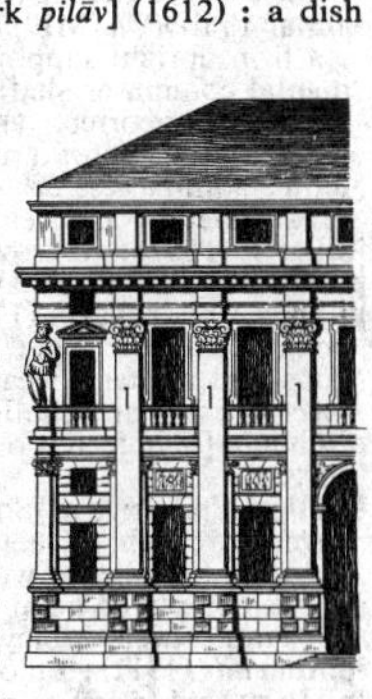

1 pilaster

pil·chard \ˈpil-chərd\ *n* [origin unknown] (ca. 1530) **1 :** a fish (*Sardinia pilchardus*) of the herring family resembling the herring and occurring in great schools along the coasts of Europe **2 :** any of several sardines related to the European pilchard

¹pile \ˈpī(ə)l\ *n* [ME, dart, stake, fr. OE *pīl,* fr. L *pilum* javelin — more at PESTLE] (bef. 12c) **1 :** a long slender column usu. of timber, steel, or reinforced concrete driven into the ground to carry a vertical load **2 :** a wedge-shaped heraldic charge usu. placed vertically with the broad end up **3 a :** a target-shooting arrowhead without cutting edges **b** [L *pilum*] **:** an ancient Roman foot soldier's heavy javelin

²pile *vt* **piled; pil·ing** (15c) **:** to drive piles into

³pile *n* [ME, fr. MF, fr. L *pila* pillar] (15c) **1 a (1) :** a quantity of things heaped together **(2) :** a heap of wood for burning a corpse or a sacrifice **b :** any great number or quantity **:** LOT **2 :** a large building or group of buildings **3 :** a great amount of money **:** FORTUNE **4 a :** a vertical series of alternate disks of two dissimilar metals (as copper and zinc) with disks of cloth or paper moistened with an electrolyte between them for producing a current of electricity **b :** a battery made up of cells similarly constructed **5 :** REACTOR 3b

⁴pile *vb* **piled; pil·ing** *vt* (15c) **1 :** to lay or place in a pile **:** STACK **2 :** to heap in abundance **:** LOAD ⟨*piled* potatoes on his plate⟩ ~ *vi* **1 :** to form a pile : ACCUMULATE **2 :** to move or press forward in or as if in a mass : CROWD ⟨*piled* into a car⟩

⁵pile *n* [ME, fr. L *pilus* hair; akin to L *pila* ball, *pilleus, pileus* felt cap, Gk *pilos*] (15c) **1 :** a coat or surface of usu. short close fine furry hairs **2 :** a velvety surface produced by an extra set of filling yarns that form raised loops which are cut and sheared — **pile·less** \'pī(ə)l-ləs\ *adj*

⁶pile *n* [ME, fr. L *pila* ball] (15c) **1 :** a single hemorrhoid **2** *pl* **:** HEMORRHOIDS; *also* **:** the condition of one affected with hemorrhoids

pi·le·at·ed \'pī-lē-,āt-əd, 'pil-ē-\ *adj* (ca. 1728) **:** having a crest covering the pileum ⟨a ~ woodpecker⟩

piled \'pī(ə)ld\ *adj* (15c) **:** having a pile ⟨a deep-*piled* rug⟩

pile driver *n* (1772) **1 :** a machine for driving down piles with a drop hammer or a steam or air hammer **2 :** an operator of a pile driver

pi·le·um \'pī-lē-əm\ *n, pl* **pi·lea** \-lē-ə\ [NL, fr. L *pileus, pileum* felt cap] (1874) **:** the top of the head of a bird from the bill to the nape

pile·up \'pī-,ləp\ *n* (ca. 1929) **1 :** a collision involving usu. several motor vehicles and causing damage or injury **2 :** a jammed tangled mass or pile (as of motor vehicles or people) resulting from collision or accumulation

pi·le·us \'pī-lē-əs\ *n, pl* **pi·lei** \-lē-,ī\ [NL, fr. L] (1760) **1 :** the umbrella-shaped fruiting body of many fungi (as the mushrooms) **2** [L] **:** a pointed or close-fitting cap worn by ancient Romans

pile·wort \'pī(ə)l-,wərt, -,wȯ(ə)rt\ *n* [⁶*pile;* fr. its use in treating piles] (1578) **1 :** CELANDINE 2 **2 :** a coarse hairy perennial figwort (*Scrophularia marilandica*) of the eastern and central U.S.

pil·fer \'pil-fər\ *vb* **pil·fered; pil·fer·ing** \-f(ə-)riŋ\ [MF *pelfrer,* fr. *pelfre* booty] *vi* (ca. 1548) **:** to steal stealthily in small amounts and often again and again ~ *vt* **:** to steal in small quantities ***syn*** see STEAL — **pil·fer·able** \-f(ə-)rə-bəl\ *adj* — **pil·fer·age** \-f(ə-)rij\ *n* — **pil·fer·er** \-fər-ər\ *n*

pil·gar·lic \pil-'gär-lik\ *n* [*pilled garlic*] (ca. 1529) **1 a :** a bald head **b :** a bald-headed man **2 :** a man looked upon with humorous contempt or mock pity

pil·grim \'pil-grəm\ *n* [ME, fr. OF *peligrin,* fr. LL *pelegrinus,* alter. of L *peregrinus* foreigner, fr. *peregrinus,* adj., foreign, fr. *pereger* being abroad, fr. *per* through + *agr-, ager* land — more at FOR, ACRE] (13c) **1 :** one who journeys in foreign lands **:** WAYFARER **2 :** one who travels to a shrine or holy place as a devotee **3** *cap* **:** one of the English colonists settling at Plymouth in 1620

¹pil·grim·age \'pil-grə-mij\ *n* (13c) **1 :** a journey of a pilgrim; *esp* **:** one to a shrine or a sacred place **2 :** the course of life on earth

²pilgrimage *vi* **-aged; -ag·ing** (14c) **:** to go on a pilgrimage

pilgrim bottle *n* (1874) **:** COSTREL

pil·ing \'pī-liŋ\ *n* (15c) **:** a structure of piles; *also* **:** PILES

Pi·li·pi·no \,pil-ə-'pē-(,)nō, ,pēl-\ *n* [Pilipino, fr. Sp *Filipino* Philippine] (1963) **:** the Tagalog-based official language of the Republic of the Philippines

¹pill \'pil\ *vb* [ME *pilen, pillen,* partly fr. OE *pilian* to peel, partly fr. MF *piller* to plunder] *vi, dial chiefly Eng* (12c) **:** to come off in flakes or scales **:** PEEL ~ *vt* **1** *archaic* **:** to subject to depredation or extortion **2** *dial* **:** to peel or strip off

²pill *n* [L *pilula,* fr. dim. of *pila* ball — more at PILE] (15c) **1 a :** medicine in a small rounded mass to be swallowed whole **b** *often cap* **:** an oral contraceptive — usu. used with *the* **2 :** something repugnant or unpleasant that must be accepted or endured **3 :** something resembling a pill in size or shape **4 :** a disagreeable or tiresome person

³pill *vt* (1736) **1 :** to dose with pills **2 :** BLACKBALL ~ *vi* **:** to become rough with or mat into little balls ⟨brushed woolens often ~⟩

¹pil·lage \'pil-ij\ *n* [ME, fr. MF, fr. *piller* to plunder, fr. *peille* rag, fr. L *pilleum, pilleus* felt cap] (14c) **1 :** the act of looting or plundering esp. in war **2 :** something taken as booty ***syn*** see SPOIL

²pillage *vb* **pil·laged; pil·lag·ing** *vt* (ca. 1592) **:** to plunder ruthlessly **:** LOOT ~ *vi* **:** to take booty ***syn*** see RAVAGE — **pil·lag·er** *n*

¹pil·lar \'pil-ər\ *n* [ME *piler,* fr. OF, fr. ML *pilare,* fr. L *pila*] (13c) **1 a :** a firm upright support for a superstructure **:** POST **b :** a usu. ornamental column or shaft; *esp* **:** one standing alone for a monument **2 :** a chief supporter **:** PROP **3 :** a solid mass of coal, rock, or ore left standing to support a mine roof **4 :** a body part that resembles a column — **pil·lar·less** *adj* — **from pillar to post :** from one place or one predicament to another

²pillar *vt* (1607) **:** to provide or strengthen with or as if with pillars

pil·lar–box \'pil-ər-,bäks\ *n, Brit* (1858) **:** a pillar-shaped mailbox

pill·box \'pil-,bäks\ *n* (1730) **1 :** a box for pills; *esp* **:** a shallow round box of pasteboard **2 :** a small low concrete emplacement for machine guns and antitank weapons **3 :** a small round hat without a brim; *specif* **:** a woman's shallow hat with a flat crown and straight sides

pill bug *n* [²*pill;* fr. its rolling into a ball when disturbed] (1843) **:** WOOD LOUSE

¹pil·lion \'pil-yən\ *n* [ScGael or IrGael; ScGael *pillean,* dim. of *peall* covering, couch; IrGael *pillīn,* dim. of *peall* covering, couch] (1503) **1 a :** a light saddle for women consisting chiefly of a cushion **b :** a pad or cushion put on behind a man's saddle chiefly for a woman to ride on **2 :** a motorcycle or bicycle saddle for a passenger

²pillion *adv* (1911) **:** on or as if on a pillion ⟨ride ~⟩

¹pil·lo·ry \'pil-(ə-)rē\ *n, pl* **-ries** [ME, fr. OF *pilori*] (13c) **1 :** a device for publicly punishing offenders consisting of a wooden frame with holes in which the head and hands can be locked **2 :** a means for exposing one to public scorn or ridicule

²pillory *vt* **-ried; -ry·ing** (ca. 1600) **1 :** to set in a pillory as punishment **2 :** to expose to public contempt, ridicule, or scorn

¹pil·low \'pil-(,)ō, -ə(-w)\ *n* [ME *pilwe,* fr. OE *pyle,* fr. L *pulvinus* pillow] (bef. 12c) **1 a :** a support for the head of a reclining person; *esp* **:** a cloth bag filled with feathers, down, sponge rubber, or plastic fiber **b :** something resembling a pillow esp. in form **2 :** a block or support used esp. to equalize or distribute pressure **3 :** a cushion or pad tightly stuffed and used as a support for the design and tools in making lace with a bobbin — **pil·lowy** \'pil-ə-wē\ *adj*

²pillow *vt* (1629) **1 :** to rest or lay on or as if on a pillow **2 :** to serve as a pillow for ~ *vi* **:** to lay or rest one's head on or as if on a pillow

pillow block *n* (1844) **:** a block or standard to support a journal (as of a shaft) **:** BEARING

pil·low·case \'pil-ə-,kās, -ō-\ *n* (1724) **:** a removable covering for a pillow

pillow lace *n* [fr. its being worked over a pillow on which the pattern is marked] (1858) **:** lace made with a bobbin

pillow sham *n* (1871) **:** an ornamental covering for a bed pillow

pillow slip *n* (ca. 1828) **:** PILLOWCASE

pilo- — see PIL-

pi·lo·car·pine \,pī-lə-'kär-,pēn\ *n* [ISV, fr. NL *Pilocarpus jaborandi,* species of tropical shrubs] (1875) **:** a muscarinic alkaloid $C_{11}H_{16}N_2O_2$ that is obtained from jaborandi and is a strong sialagogue and diaphoretic

pi·lose \'pī-,lōs\ *adj* [L *pilosus,* fr. *pilus* hair — more at PILE] (1753) **:** covered with usu. soft hair — **pi·los·i·ty** \pī-'läs-ət-ē\ *n*

¹pi·lot \'pī-lət\ *n* [MF *pilote,* fr. It *pilota,* alter. of *pedota,* fr. (assumed) MGk *pēdōtēs,* fr. Gk *pēda* steering oars, pl. of *pēdon* oar; akin to Gk *pod-, pous* foot — more at FOOT] (1530) **1 a :** one employed to steer a ship **:** HELMSMAN **b :** a person who is qualified and usu. licensed to conduct a ship into and out of a port or in specified waters, often for fixed fees **2 :** GUIDE, LEADER **3 :** COWCATCHER **4 :** one who handles or is qualified to handle the controls of an aircraft or spacecraft **5 :** a piece that guides a tool or machine part **6 :** a television show produced and filmed or taped as a sample of a proposed series **7 :** PILOT BURNER — **pi·lot·less** \-ləs\ *adj*

²pilot *vt* (1693) **1 :** to act as a guide to **:** lead or conduct over a usu. difficult course **2 a :** to set and conn the course of ⟨~ a ship⟩ **b :** to act as pilot of ⟨~ a plane⟩ ***syn*** see GUIDE

³pilot *adj* (1791) **:** serving as a guiding or tracing device, an activating or auxiliary unit, or a trial apparatus or operation ⟨a ~ study⟩

pi·lot·age \'pī-lət-ij\ *n* (1618) **1 :** the action or business of piloting **2 :** the compensation paid to a pilot

pilot balloon *n* (1802) **:** a small unmanned balloon sent up to show the direction and speed of the wind

pilot biscuit *n* (1836) **:** HARDTACK — called also *pilot bread*

pilot burner *n* (1902) **:** a small burner kept lighted to rekindle a principal burner

pilot engine *n* (1838) **:** a locomotive going in advance of a train to make sure that the way is clear

pilot fish *n* (1634) **:** a pelagic carangid fish (*Naucrates ductor*) that often swims in company with a shark

pi·lot·house \'pī-lət-,hau̇s\ *n* (1846) **:** a deckhouse for a ship's helmsman containing the steering wheel, compass, and navigating equipment

pilot light *n* (1890) **1 :** an indicator light showing where a switch or circuit breaker is located or whether a motor is in operation or power is on — called also *pilot lamp* **2 :** a small permanent flame used to ignite gas at a burner

pilot officer *n* (1919) **:** a commissioned officer in the British air force who ranks with a second lieutenant in the army

pil·sner *also* **pil·sen·er** \'pilz-(ə-)nər, 'pil-snər\ *n* [G, lit., of Pilsen, city in Czechoslovakia (now Plzen)] (1877) **1 :** a light beer with a strong flavor of hops **2 :** a tall slender footed glass for beer

Pilt·down man \,pilt-,dau̇n-\ *n* [*Piltdown,* East Sussex, England] (ca. 1918) **:** a supposedly very early primitive man erroneously reconstructed from a combination of human and animal skeletal remains the latter of which were later found to have been planted by a hoaxer

pil·u·lar \'pil-yə-lər\ *adj* (1802) **:** of, relating to, or resembling a pill

pil·ule \'pil-(,)yü(ə)l\ *n* [MF, fr. L *pilula* pill — more at PILE] (1543) **:** a little pill

pi·lus \'pī-ləs\ *n, pl* **pi·li** \-,lī\ [L — more at PILE] (ca. 1890) **:** a hair or a structure (as of a bacterium) resembling a hair

pi·ma cotton \,pē-mə-, ,pim-ə-\ *n* [*Pima* county, Arizona] (1925) **:** a cotton that produces fiber of exceptional strength and firmness and that was developed in the southwestern U.S. by selection and breeding of Egyptian cottons

Pi·man \'pē-mən\ *adj* (1891) **:** of, relating to, or constituting a language family of the Uto-Aztecan phylum

pi·men·to \pə-'ment-(,)ō\ *n, pl* **-tos** *or* **-to** [Sp *pimienta* allspice, pepper, fr. LL *pigmenta,* pl. of *pigmentum* plant juice, fr. L, pigment] (1660) **1 :** PIMIENTO 1 **2 :** ALLSPICE

pimento cheese *n* (1916) **:** a Neufchâtel, process, cream, or occas. cheddar cheese to which ground pimientos have been added

pi–me·son \'pī-'mez-,än, -'mes-; -'mā-,zän, -'mē-, -,sän\ *n* [⁴*pi*] (1948) **:** PION

pi·mien·to \pə-'ment-(,)ō, pəm-'yent-\ *n, pl* **-tos** [Sp. fr. *pimienta*] (1845) **1 :** any of various bluntly conical thick-fleshed sweet peppers of European origin that have a distinctive mild sweet flavor and are used esp. as a garnish, as a stuffing for olives, and as a source of paprika **2 :** a plant that bears pimientos

¹pimp \'pimp\ *n* [origin unknown] (1607) **:** a man who solicits clients for a prostitute

²pimp *vi* (1636) **:** to work as a pimp

pim·per·nel \'pim-pər-,nel, -pər-nəl\ *n* [ME *pimpernele,* fr. MF *pimprenelle,* fr. LL *pimpinella,* a medicinal herb] (15c) **:** any of a genus (*Anagallis*) of herbs of the primrose family; *esp* **:** SCARLET PIMPERNEL

pimp·ing \'pim-pən, -piŋ\ *adj* [origin unknown] (1687) **1 :** PETTY, INSIGNIFICANT **2** *chiefly dial* **:** PUNY, SICKLY

pim·ple \'pim-pəl\ *n* [ME *pinple*] (15c) **1 :** a small inflamed elevation of the skin **:** PAPULE; *esp* **:** PUSTULE **2 :** a swelling or protuberance like a pimple — **pim·pled** \-pəld\ *adj* — **pim·ply** \-p(ə-)lē\ *adj*

pimp·mo·bile \'pimp-mō-,bēl, -mə-\ *n* [*pimp* + *automobile*] (1971) **:** an ostentatious customized luxury car characteristic of a kind used by a pimp

¹pin \'pin\ *n* [ME, fr. OE *pinn;* akin to OHG *pfinn* peg] (bef. 12c) **1 a :** a piece of solid material (as wood or metal) used esp. for fastening separate articles together or as a support by which one article may be suspended from another **b** *obs* **:** the center peg of a target; *also* **:** the center itself **c :** something that resembles a pin esp. in slender elongated form ⟨an electrical connector ~⟩ **d (1) :** one of the wooden pieces constituting the target in various games (as bowling) **(2) :** the peg at which a quoit is pitched **(3) :** the staff of the flag marking a hole on a golf course **e :** a peg for regulating the tension of the strings of a musical instrument **f :** the part of a key stem that enters a lock **g (1) :** THOLE 2 **(2) :** a belaying pin **2 a (1) :** a small pointed piece of wire with a head used esp. for fastening cloth **(2) :** something of small value **:** TRIFLE **b :** an ornament or emblem fastened to clothing with a pin **c (1) :** BOBBY PIN **(2) :** HAIRPIN **(3) :** SAFETY PIN **3 :** LEG — usu. used in pl. ⟨wobbly on his ~*s*⟩ **4 :** a fall in wrestling

2pin *vt* **pinned; pin·ning** (14c) **1 a :** to fasten, join, or secure with a pin **b :** to hold fast or immobile **c :** to present (a girl) with a fraternity pin as a pledge of affection **2 a :** ATTACH, HANG ⟨*pinned* his hopes on a miracle⟩ **b :** to assign the blame or responsibility for ⟨~ the robbery on a night watchman⟩ **3 a :** to make (a chess opponent's man) unable to move without exposing the king to check or a valuable piece to capture **b** *of a wrestler* **:** to secure a fall over (an opponent)

3pin *adj* (15c) **1 :** of or relating to a pin **2** *of leather* **:** having a grain suggesting the heads of pins

pi·ña cloth \ˌpēn-yə-\ *n* [Sp *piña* pineapple, fr. L *pinea* pinecone — more at PINEAL] (1858) **:** a lustrous transparent cloth of Philippine origin that is woven of silky pineapple fibers

pi·ña co·la·da \ˌpēn-yə-kō-ˈläd-ə\ *n* [Sp, lit., strained pineapple] (1923) **:** a tall drink made of rum, cream of coconut, and pineapple juice mixed with ice

pin·afore \ˈpin-ə-ˌfō(ə)r, -ˌfȯ(ə)r\ *n* [²*pin* + *afore*] (1782) **:** a sleeveless usu. low-necked garment fastened in the back and worn as an apron or dress — **pin·afored** \-ˌfō(ə)rd, -ˌfȯ(ə)rd\ *adj*

pi·ña·ta *or* **pi·na·ta** \pēn-ˈyät-ə\ *n* [Sp *piñata*, lit., pot] (ca. 1887) **:** a decorated pottery jar filled with candies, fruits, and gifts and hung from the ceiling to be broken with sticks by blindfolded persons as part of Latin-American festivities (as at Christmas or for a birthday party)

pin·ball machine \ˈpin-ˌbȯl-\ *n* (1936) **:** an amusement device in which a ball propelled by a plunger scores points as it rolls down a slanting surface among pins and targets — called also *pinball game*

pin·bone \ˈpin-ˈbōn, -ˌbōn\ *n* (1640) **:** the hipbone esp. of a quadruped — see COW illustration

pince–nez \paⁿ-ˈsnā, pan(t)-\ *n, pl* **pince–nez** \-ˈsnā(z)\ [F, fr. *pincer* to pinch + *nez* nose, fr. L *nasus* — more at NOSE] (1876) **:** eyeglasses clipped to the nose by a spring

pin·cer \ˈpin(t)-sər, *esp for 1 US often* ˈpin-chər\ *n* [ME *pinceour*] (14c) **1** *pl but sing or pl in constr* **a :** an instrument having two short handles and two grasping jaws working on a pivot and used for gripping things **b :** a claw (as of a lobster) resembling a pair of pincers **:** CHELA **2 :** one part of a double envelopment in which two military forces converge on opposite sides of an enemy position — **pin·cer·like** \-ˌlīk\ *adj*

1pinch \ˈpinch\ *vb* [ME *pinchen*, fr. (assumed) ONF *pinchier*] *vt* (14c) **1 a :** to squeeze between the finger and thumb or between the jaws of an instrument **b :** to prune the tip of (a plant or shoot) usu. to induce branching **c :** to squeeze or compress painfully **d :** to cause physical or mental pain to **e** (1) **:** to cause to appear thin or shrunken (2) **:** to cause to shrivel or wither **2 :** to subject to strict economy or want **:** STRAITEN **3 a :** STEAL **b :** ARREST **4 :** to sail too close to the wind ~ *vi* **1 :** COMPRESS, SQUEEZE **2 :** to be miserly or closefisted **3 :** to press painfully **4 :** NARROW, TAPER ⟨the road ~*ed* down to a trail — Cecelia Holland⟩ — **pinch pennies :** to practice strict economy

2pinch *n* (15c) **1 a :** a critical juncture **:** EMERGENCY **b** (1) **:** PRESSURE, STRESS (2) **:** HARDSHIP, PRIVATION **c :** DEFICIT **2 a :** an act of pinching **:** SQUEEZE **b :** as much as may be taken between the finger and thumb ⟨a ~ of snuff⟩ **c :** a very small amount **3 :** a marked thinning of a vein or bed **4 a :** THEFT **b :** a police raid; *also* **:** ARREST ***syn*** see JUNCTURE — **with a pinch of salt :** with doubts about the truth of something proposed or related

3pinch *adj* [²*pinch*] (1912) **1 :** SUBSTITUTE ⟨~ runner⟩ **2 :** made by a pinch hitter ⟨~ homer⟩

pinch bar *n* (1837) **:** a bar similar in form and use to a crowbar and sometimes having an end adapted for pulling spikes or inserting under a heavy wheel that is to be rolled

pinch·beck \ˈpinch-ˌbek\ *n* [Christopher *Pinchbeck* †1732 Eng. watchmaker] (1734) **1 :** an alloy of copper and zinc used esp. to imitate gold in jewelry **2 :** something counterfeit or spurious — **pinchbeck** *adj*

pinch·cock \-ˌkäk\ *n* (1873) **:** a clamp used on a flexible tube to regulate the flow of a fluid through the tube

pinch·er \ˈpin-chər\ *n* (15c) **1 :** one that pinches **2** *pl* **:** PINCERS

pinch–hit \(ˈ)pinch-ˈhit\ *vi* [back-formation fr. *pinch hitter*] (1915) **1 :** to bat in the place of another player esp. in an emergency when a hit is particularly needed **2 :** to act or serve in place of another

pinch hit *n* (1927) **:** a hit made by a pinch hitter

pinch hitter *n* (1912) **:** one that pinch-hits

pin curl *n* (1896) **:** a curl made usu. by dampening a strand of hair with water or lotion, coiling it, and securing it by a hairpin or clip

pin·cush·ion \ˈpin-ˌku̇sh-ən\ *n* (1632) **:** a small cushion in which pins may be stuck ready for use

1Pin·dar·ic \pin-ˈdar-ik\ *adj* (1640) **1 :** of or relating to the poet Pindar **2 :** written in the manner or style characteristic of Pindar

2Pindaric *n* (1685) **1 :** a Pindaric ode **2** *pl* **:** loose irregular verses similar to those used in Pindaric odes

pin·dling \ˈpin-(d)lən, -(d)liŋ, -dᵊl-ən, -dᵊl-iŋ\ *adj* [perh. alter. of *spindling*] *dial* (1861) **:** PUNY, FRAIL

1pine \ˈpīn\ *n, often attrib* [ME, fr. OE *pin*, fr. L *pinus*; akin to Gk *pitys* pine, L *opimus* fat — more at FAT] (bef. 12c) **1 :** any of a genus (*Pinus* of the family Pinaceae, the pine family) of coniferous evergreen trees which have slender elongated needles and some of which are valuable timber trees or ornamentals **2 :** the straight-grained white or yellow usu. durable and resinous wood of a pine varying from extreme softness in the white pine to hardness in the longleaf pine **3 :** any of various Australian coniferous trees (as of the genera *Callitris*, *Araucaria*, or *Cupressus*) **4 :** PINEAPPLE — **piny** *or* **pin·ey** \ˈpī-nē\ *adj*

2pine *vi* **pined; pin·ing** [ME *pinen*, fr. OE *pīnian* to suffer, fr. (assumed) OE *pīn* punishment, fr. L *poena* — more at PAIN] (15c) **1 :** to lose vigor, health, or flesh (as through grief) **:** LANGUISH **2 :** to yearn intensely and persistently esp. for something unattainable ⟨they still *pined* for their lost wealth⟩ ***syn*** see LONG

pi·ne·al \ˈpī-nē-əl, pī-ˈ\ *adj* [F *pinéal*, fr. MF, fr. L *pinea* pinecone, fr. fem. of *pineus* of pine, fr. *pinus*] (1681) **:** of, relating to, or being the pineal gland

pi·ne·al·ec·to·my \ˌpī-nē-ə-ˈlek-tə-mē, pī-ˌnē-\ *n* (1915) **:** surgical removal of the pineal gland — **pi·ne·al·ec·to·mize** \-tə-ˌmīz\ *vt*

pineal gland *n* (1712) **:** a small usu. conical appendage of the brain of all craniate vertebrates that in a few reptiles has the essential structure of an eye, that functions in some birds as part of a time-measuring system, and that is variously postulated to be a vestigial third eye, an endocrine organ, or the seat of the soul — called also *pineal*, *pineal body*, *pineal organ*

pine·ap·ple \ˈpī-ˌnap-əl\ *n* (1664) **1 a :** a tropical monocotyledonous plant (*Ananas comosus* of the family Bromeliaceae, the pineapple family) that has rigid spiny-margined recurved leaves and a short stalk with a dense oblong head of small abortive flowers **b :** the multiple fruit of the pineapple that consists of the succulent fleshy inflorescence **2 a :** a dynamite bomb **b :** a hand grenade

pine·cone \ˈpīn-ˌkōn\ *n* (1695) **:** a cone of a pine tree

pine·drops \ˈpīn-ˌdräps\ *n pl but sing or pl in constr* (1857) **1 :** a purplish brown leafless saprophytic plant (*Pterospora andromedea*) of the wintergreen family with racemose drooping white flowers **2 :** BEECHDROPS

pine·land \ˈpīn-ˌland, -lənd\ *n* (1658) **:** land naturally predominantly forested with pine

pi·nene \ˈpī-ˌnēn\ *n* [ISV, fr. L *pinus*] (1885) **:** either of two liquid isomeric unsaturated bicyclic terpene hydrocarbons $C_{10}H_{16}$ of which one is a major constituent of wood turpentine

pine nut *n* (bef. 12c) **:** the edible seed of any of several pines — compare PIÑON

pin·ery \ˈpīn-(ə-)rē\ *n, pl* **-er·ies** (1758) **1 :** a hothouse or area where pineapples are grown **2 :** a grove or forest of pine

pine·sap \ˈpīn-ˌsap\ *n* (1840) **:** any of several yellowish or reddish parasitic or saprophytic herbs (genus *Monotropa*) of the wintergreen family resembling the Indian pipe

pine siskin *n* (1887) **:** a No. American finch (*Carduelis pinus*) with streaked plumage

pine snake *n* (1791) **1 :** a large constricting snake (*Pituophis melanoleucus*) of the eastern U.S. that is typically white and black and is found esp. in coastal regions from New Jersey southward **2 :** any of various snakes related to the pine snake

pine tar *n* (1880) **:** tar obtained by destructive distillation of the wood of the pine tree and used esp. in roofing and soaps and in the treatment of skin diseases

pi·ne·tum \pī-ˈnēt-əm\ *n, pl* **pi·ne·ta** \-ˈnēt-ə\ [L, fr. *pinus*] (1842) **:** a plantation of pine trees; *esp* **:** a scientific collection of living coniferous trees

pine·wood \ˈpīn-ˌwu̇d\ *n* (1673) **1 :** a wood of pines — often used in pl. but sing. or pl. in constr. **2 :** the wood of the pine tree

pin·ey woods \ˈpī-nē-ˌwu̇dz\ *n pl* (1800) **:** woodland of the southern U.S. in which pines are the dominant tree

pin·feath·er \ˈpin-ˌfet͟h-ər\ *n* (ca. 1775) **:** a feather not fully developed; *esp* **:** a feather just emerging through the skin

pin·fish \-ˌfish\ *n* (1878) **:** a small compressed dark green grunt (*Lagodon rhomboides*) that has sharp dorsal spines and is found along the Atlantic coast

pin·fold \-ˌfōld\ *n* [ME, fr. OE *pundfald*, fr. *pund-* enclosure + *fald* fold] (13c) **1 :** ⁴POUND 1a **2 :** a place of restraint

ping \ˈpiŋ\ *n* [imit.] (1835) **1 :** a sharp sound like that of a striking bullet **2 :** ignition knock — **ping** *vi*

ping·er \ˈpiŋ-ər\ *n* (1964) **:** a device for producing pulses of sound (as for marking an underwater site or detecting an underwater object)

pin·go \ˈpiŋ-(ˌ)gō\ *n* [Esk] (ca. 1938) **:** a low hill or mound forced up by hydrostatic pressure in an area underlain by permafrost

Ping–Pong \ˈpiŋ-ˌpäŋ, -ˌpȯŋ\ *trademark* — used for table tennis

pin·head \ˈpin-ˌhed\ *n* (1662) **1 :** something very small or insignificant **2 :** a very dull or stupid person **:** FOOL

pin·head·ed \-ˈhed-əd\ *adj* (1901) **:** lacking intelligence or understanding **:** DULL, STUPID — **pin·head·ed·ness** *n*

pin·hole \-ˌhōl\ *n* (1676) **:** a small hole made by, for, or as if by a pin

1pin·ion \ˈpin-yən\ *n* [ME, fr. MF *pignon*] (15c) **1 :** the terminal section of a bird's wing including the carpus, metacarpus, and phalanges; *broadly* **:** WING **2 :** FEATHER, QUILL; *also* **:** FLIGHT FEATHERS — **pin·ioned** \-yənd\ *adj*

2pinion *vt* (1577) **1 :** to restrain (a bird) from flight esp. by cutting off the pinion of one wing **2 a :** to disable or restrain by binding the arms **b :** to bind fast **:** SHACKLE

3pinion *n* [F *pignon*, fr. MF *peignon*, fr. *peigne* comb, fr. L *pecten* — more at PECTINATE] (1659) **1 :** a gear with a small number of teeth designed to mesh with a larger wheel or rack **2 :** the smaller of a pair or the smallest of a train of gear wheels

1pink \ˈpiŋk\ *n* [ME, fr. MD *pinke*] (15c) **:** a ship with a narrow overhanging stern — called also *pinkie*

2pink *n* [origin unknown] (1573) **1 :** any of a genus (*Dianthus* of the family Caryophyllaceae, the pink family) of plants having a cylindrical many-veined calyx with bracts at its base **2 a :** the very embodiment **:** PARAGON **b** (1) **:** one dressed in the height of fashion (2) **:** ELITE **c :** highest degree possible **:** HEIGHT ⟨keep their house in the ~ of repair —Rebecca West⟩ — **in the pink :** in the best of health

3pink *n* (1678) **1 :** any of a group of colors bluish red to red in hue, of medium to high lightness, and of low to moderate saturation **2 a** (1) **:** the scarlet color of a fox hunter's coat (2) **:** a fox hunter's coat of this color **b :** pink-colored clothing **c** *pl* **:** light-colored trousers formerly worn by army officers **3 :** a person who holds advanced liberal or moderately radical political or economic views

4pink *adj* (1720) **1 :** of the color pink **2 :** holding moderately radical and usu. socialistic political or economic views **3 :** emotionally moved **:** EXCITED — often used as an intensive ⟨was tickled ~ by her flattery⟩ — **pink·ness** *n*

5pink *vt* [ME *pinken* to thrust] (1598) **1 a :** PIERCE, STAB **b :** to wound by irony, criticism, or ridicule **2 a :** to perforate in an ornamental pattern **b :** to cut a saw-toothed edge on

pink bollworm *n* (1906) **:** a small dark brown moth (*Pectinophora gossypiella*) whose pinkish larva bores into the flowers and bolls of cotton and is a destructive pest in most cotton-growing regions

pink–collar *adj* (1977) **:** of, relating to, or constituting a class of employees in occupations (as nursing and clerical jobs) traditionally held by women
pink elephants *n pl* (1940) **:** any of various hallucinations arising esp. from heavy drinking or use of narcotics ⟨began to see *pink elephants*⟩
pink•eye \ˈpiŋ-ˌkī\ *n* (1855) **:** an acute highly contagious conjunctivitis of man and various domestic animals
¹pin•kie \ˈpiŋ-kē\ *n* [prob. fr. D *pinkje* small pink, dim. of *pink*, fr. MD *pinke*] (1685) **:** ¹PINK
²pinkie *or* **pin•ky** \ˈpiŋ-kē\ *n, pl* **pinkies** [prob. fr. D *pinkje*, dim. of *pink* little finger] (1808) **:** LITTLE FINGER
pinking shears *n pl* (ca. 1939) **:** shears with a saw-toothed inner edge on the blades for making a zigzag cut
pink•ish \ˈpiŋ-kish\ *adj* (1784) **:** somewhat pink; *esp* **:** tending to be pink in politics — **pink•ish•ness** *n*
pink lady *n* (1936) **:** a cocktail consisting of gin, brandy, lemon juice, grenadine, and white of egg shaken with ice and strained
pink•ly \ˈpiŋ-klē\ *adv* (1836) **:** in a pink manner **:** with a pink hue
pin knot *n* (ca. 1906) **:** a sound knot in lumber that is not over $^1/_2$ inch in diameter
pinko \ˈpiŋ-(ˌ)kō\ *n, pl* **pink•os** *also* **pink•oes** (1936) **:** ³PINK 3
pink•root \ˈpiŋ-ˌkrüt, -ˌkru̇t\ *n* (1763) **:** any of several plants (genus *Spigelia*) related to the nux vomica and used as anthelmintics; *esp* **:** an American woodland herb (*S. marilandica*) sometimes cultivated for its showy red and yellow flowers
pink slip *n* (1915) **:** a notice from an employer that a recipient's employment is being terminated
pin money *n* (1697) **1 a :** money given by a man to his wife for her own use **b :** money set aside for the purchase of incidentals **2 :** a trivial amount of money ⟨worked for *pin money*⟩
pin•na \ˈpin-ə\ *n, pl* **pin•nae** \ˈpin-ˌē, -ˌī\ *or* **pinnas** [NL, fr. L, feather, wing — more at PEN] (1785) **1 :** a leaflet or primary division of a pinnate leaf or frond **2 a :** a projecting body part (as a feather, wing, or fin) **b :** the largely cartilaginous projecting portion of the external ear — see EAR illustration
pin•nace \ˈpin-əs\ *n* [MF *pinace*, prob. fr. OSp *pinaza*, fr. *pino* pine, fr. L *pinus*] (ca. 1550) **1 :** a light sailing ship; *esp* **:** one used as a tender **2 :** any of various ship's boats
¹pin•na•cle \ˈpin-i-kəl\ *n* [ME *pinacle*, fr. MF, fr. LL *pinnaculum* gable, fr. dim. of L *pinna* wing, battlement] (14c) **1 :** an upright architectural member generally ending in a small spire and used esp. in Gothic construction to give weight to a buttress or angle pier **2 :** a structure or formation suggesting a pinnacle; *specif* **:** a lofty peak **3 :** the highest point of development or achievement **:** ACME ***syn*** see SUMMIT

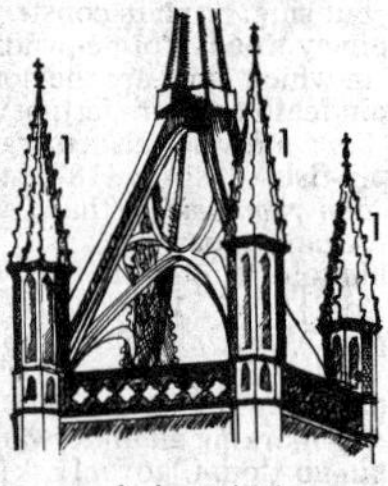

1 pinnacle 1

²pinnacle *vt* **-cled; -cling** \-k(ə-)liŋ\ (14c) **1 :** to surmount with a pinnacle **2 :** to raise or rear on a pinnacle
pin•nate \ˈpin-ˌāt\ *adj* [NL *pinnatus*, fr. L, feathered, fr. *pinna*] (1727) **:** resembling a feather esp. in having similar parts arranged on opposite sides of an axis like the barbs on the rachis of a feather ⟨~ leaf⟩ — **pin•nate•ly** *adv*
pinnati- *comb form* [NL, fr. *pinnatus*] **:** pinnately ⟨*pinnatisect*⟩
pin•nati•fid \pə-ˈnat-ə-fəd, -ˌfid\ *adj* [NL *pinnatifidus*, fr. *pinnati-* + L *-fidus* -fid] (1753) **:** cleft in a pinnate manner ⟨a ~ leaf⟩
pin•ner \ˈpin-ər\ *n* (1652) **1 :** a woman's cap with long lappets worn in the 17th and 18th centuries **2 :** one that pins
pin•ni•ped \ˈpin-ə-ˌped\ *n* [deriv. of L *pinna* + *ped-*, *pes* foot — more at FOOT] (ca. 1855) **:** any of a suborder (Pinnipedia) of aquatic carnivorous mammals (as a seal or walrus) with all four limbs modified into flippers — **pinniped** *adj*
pin•nule \ˈpin-(ˌ)yü(ə)l\ *n* [NL *pinnula*, fr. L, dim. of *pinna*] (1748) **1 :** any of the secondary branches of a plumose organ esp. of a crinoid **2 :** one of the ultimate divisions of a twice pinnate leaf
pi•noch•le \ˈpē-ˌnək-əl\ *n* [prob. modif. of G dial. *binokel*, a game resembling bezique, fr. F dial. *binocle*] (1864) **:** a card game played with a 48-card pack containing two each of A, K, Q, J, 10, 9 in each suit with the object to score points by melding certain combinations of cards or by winning tricks that contain scoring cards; *also* **:** the meld of queen of spades and jack of diamonds scoring 40 points in this game
pi•no•cy•to•sis \ˌpin-ə-sə-ˈtō-səs, ˌpīn-, -ˌsī-\ *n, pl* **-to•ses** \-ˌsēz\ [NL, fr. Gk *pinein* to drink + NL *cyt-* + *-osis* — more at POTABLE] (1895) **:** the uptake of fluid by a cell by invagination and pinching off of the plasma membrane
pi•no•cy•tot•ic \-ˈtät-ik\ *or* **pi•no•cyt•ic** \ˌpin-ə-ˈsit-ik, ˌpīn-\ *adj* (1959) **:** of, relating to, or being pinocytosis — **pi•no•cy•tot•i•cal•ly** \-i-k(ə-)lē\ *adv*
pi•no•le \pi-ˈnō-lē\ *n* [AmerSp, fr. Nahuatl *pinolli*] (1842) **1 :** a finely ground flour made from parched corn **2 :** any of various flours resembling pinole and ground from the seeds of other plants
pi•ñon *or* **pin•yon** \ˈpin-ˌyōn, -ˌyän, -yən; pin-ˈyōn\ *n, pl* **pi•ñons** *or* **pin•yons** *or* **pi•ño•nes** \pin-ˈyō-nēz\ [AmerSp *piñón*, fr. Sp, pine nut, fr. *piña* pinecone, fr. L *pinea* — more at PINEAL] (1831) **:** any of various low-growing pines (as *Pinus parryana*, *P. cembroides*, *P. edulis*, and *P. monophylla*) of western No. America with edible seeds; *also* **:** the edible seed of a piñon
Pi•not \pē-ˈnō, ˈpē-(ˌ)nō\ *n* [F] (1912) **1 :** any of several purple or white grapes grown chiefly in California and used esp. for wine-making **2 :** a wine made from Pinot grapes
¹pin•point \ˈpin-ˌpȯint\ *n* (1849) **1 :** something that is extremely small or insignificant **2 :** the point of a pin **3 :** an extremely small or sharp point
²pinpoint *vt* (1917) **1 :** to locate or aim with great precision or accuracy **2 a :** to fix, determine, or identify with precision **b :** to cause to stand out conspicuously **:** HIGHLIGHT
³pinpoint *adj* (1942) **1 :** extremely fine or precise **2 :** located, fixed, or directed with extreme precision ⟨~ targets⟩
¹pin•prick \ˈpin-ˌprik\ *n* (1862) **1 :** a small puncture made by or as if by a pin **2 :** a petty irritation or annoyance
²pinprick *vt* (1899) **:** to administer pinpricks to ~ *vi* **:** to administer pinpricks
pins and needles *n pl* (1813) **:** a pricking tingling sensation in a limb growing numb or recovering from numbness — **on pins and needles :** in a nervous or jumpy state of anticipation
pin•set•ter \ˈpin-ˌset-ər\ *n* (1916) **:** an employee or a mechanical device that spots pins in a bowling alley
pin•spot•ter \-ˌspät-ər\ *n* (1946) **:** PINSETTER
pin•stripe \-ˌstrīp\ *n* (1897) **:** a very thin stripe esp. on a fabric; *also* **:** a suit with such stripes — **pin–striped** \-ˌstrīpt\ *adj*
pint \ˈpīnt\ *n* [ME *pinte*, fr. MF, fr. ML *pincta*, prob. fr. (assumed) VL, fem. of *pinctus*, pp. of L *pingere* to paint — more at PAINT] (15c) **1 —** see WEIGHT table **2 :** a pint pot or vessel
pin•ta \ˈpint-ə, ˈpin-ˌtä\ *n* [AmerSp, fr. Sp, spot, mark, fr. (assumed) VL *pincta*] (1825) **:** a chronic skin disease that is endemic in tropical America, that occurs successively as an initial papule, a generalized eruption, and a patchy loss of pigment, and that is caused by a spirochete (*Treponema careteum*) morphologically indistinguishable from the causative agent of syphilis
pin•tail \ˈpin-ˌtāl\ *n, pl* **pintail** *or* **pintails** (1768) **:** a bird having elongated central tail feathers: as **a :** a slender gray and white river duck (*Anas acuta*) of which the male has a white line on the side of the neck and head **b :** any of several grouse
pin•tle \ˈpint-ᵊl\ *n* [ME *pintel*, lit., penis, fr. OE; akin to MLG *pint* penis, OE *pinn* pin] (15c) **:** a usu. upright pivot pin on which another part turns
¹pin•to \ˈpin-(ˌ)tō\ *n, pl* **pintos** *also* **pintoes** [AmerSp, fr. *pinto* spotted, fr. obs. Sp, fr. (assumed) VL *pinctus*] (1860) **:** a horse or pony marked with patches of white and another color — compare PIEBALD, SKEWBALD

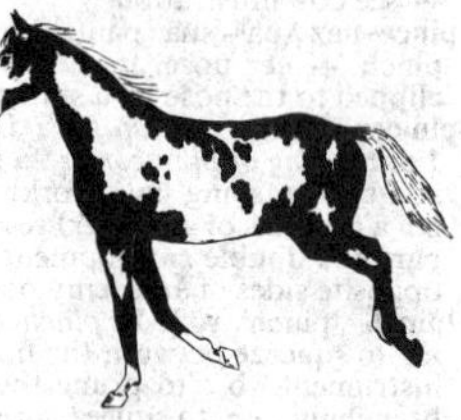

pinto

²pinto *adj* (1865) **:** PIED, MOTTLED
pinto bean *n* (1916) **:** a mottled kidney bean that is grown in the southwestern U.S. for food and for stock feed
pint–size \ˈpīnt-ˌsīz\ *or* **pint–sized** \-ˌsīzd\ *adj* (1936) **:** SMALL
¹pin•up \ˈpin-ˌəp\ *n* (1943) **:** something fastened to a wall: as **a :** a photograph of a pinup girl **b :** something (as a lamp) designed for wall attachment
²pinup *adj* (1941) **1 :** of or relating to pinup girls **2 :** designed for hanging on a wall
pinup girl *n* (1941) **1 :** a girl or woman whose glamorous qualities make her a suitable subject of a photograph for pinning up on an admirer's wall **2 :** a photograph of a pinup girl
pin•wale \ˈpin-ˌwāl\ *adj, of a fabric* (1949) **:** made with narrow wales
pin•weed \-ˌwēd\ *n* (1814) **:** any of a genus (*Lechea*) of herbs of the rock-rose family with slender stems and leaves
pin•wheel \-ˌhwēl, -ˌwēl\ *n* (1869) **1 :** a fireworks device in the form of a revolving wheel of colored fire **2 :** a toy consisting of lightweight vanes that revolve at the end of a stick
pin•work \-ˌwərk\ *n* (ca. 1890) **:** fine stitches raised from the surface of a design in needlepoint lace to add lightness to the effect
pin•worm \-ˌwərm\ *n* (ca. 1864) **1 :** any of numerous small nematode worms (family Oxyuridae) that infest the intestines and esp. the cecum of various vertebrates; *esp* **:** a worm (*Enterobius vermicularis*) parasitic in man **2 :** any of several rather slender insect larvae that burrow in plant tissue
pinx•ter flower \ˈpiŋ(k)-stər-\ *n* [D *pinkster* Whitsuntide] (1857) **:** a deciduous pink-flowered azalea (*Rhododendron nudiflorum*) that is native to rich moist woodlands of eastern No. America
pin•yin \ˈpin-ˈyin\ *n, often cap* [Chin (Pek) *p'in¹ yin¹* to spell phonetically, fr. *p'in¹* to arrange + *yin¹* sound, pronunciation] (1963) **:** a system for romanizing Chinese ideograms
pi•o•let \ˌpē-ə-ˈlā\ *n* [F] (1868) **:** an ice ax used in mountaineering
pi•on \ˈpī-ˌän\ *n* [contr. of *pi-meson*] (1950) **:** a short-lived meson that is primarily responsible for the nuclear force and that exists as a positive or negative particle with mass 273.2 times the electron mass or as a neutral particle with mass 264.2 times the electron mass — **pi•on•ic** \pī-ˈän-ik\ *adj*
¹pi•o•neer \ˌpī-ə-ˈni(ə)r\ *n* [MF *pionier*, fr. OF *peonier* foot soldier, fr. *peon* foot soldier, fr. ML *pedon-*, *pedo* — more at PAWN] (1523) **1 :** a member of a military unit usu. of construction engineers **2 a :** a person or group that originates or helps open up a new line of thought or activity or a new method or technical development **b :** one of the first to settle in a territory **3 :** a plant or animal capable of establishing itself in a bare or barren area and initiating an ecological cycle
²pioneer *vi* (1780) **:** to act as a pioneer ⟨~*ed* in the development of nuclear reactors⟩ ~ *vt* **1 :** to open or prepare for others to follow; *also* **:** SETTLE **2 :** to originate or take part in the development of
³pioneer *adj* (1840) **1 :** ORIGINAL, EARLIEST **2 :** relating to or being a pioneer; *esp* **:** of, relating to, or characteristic of early settlers or their time
pi•ous \ˈpī-əs\ *adj* [L *pius*; akin to L *piare* to appease] (1603) **1 a :** marked by or showing reverence for deity and devotion to divine worship **b :** marked by conspicuous religiosity ⟨a hypocrite — a thing all ~ words and uncharitable deeds —Charles Reade⟩ **2 :** sacred or devotional as distinct from the profane or secular **:** RELIGIOUS ⟨a ~ opinion⟩ **3 :** showing loyal reverence for a person or thing **:** DUTIFUL **4 a :** marked by sham or hypocrisy **b :** marked by self-conscious virtue **:** VIRTUOUS **5 :** deserving commendation **:** WORTHY ⟨a ~ effort⟩ — **pi•ous•ly** *adv* — **pi•ous•ness** *n*
¹pip \ˈpip\ *n* [ME *pippe*, fr. MD, fr. (assumed) VL *pipita*, alter. of L *pituita* phlegm, pip; akin to L *opimus* fat — more at FAT] (15c) **1 a :** a disorder of a bird marked by formation of a scale or crust on the tongue **b :** the scale or crust of this disorder **2 :** any of various human ailments; *esp* **:** a slight nonspecific disorder
²pip *vb* **pipped; pip•ping** [imit.] *vi* (1598) **1 :** ¹PEEP 1 **2 :** to break through the shell of the egg ⟨the chick *pipped*⟩ ~ *vt* **:** to break open (the shell of an egg) in hatching

3pip *n* [origin unknown] (1604) **1 a :** one of the dots used on dice and dominoes to indicate numerical value **b :** SPOT 2c **2 a :** SPOT, SPECK **b :** an inverted V or a spot of light on a radarscope indicating the return of radar waves reflected from an object; *broadly* **:** BLIP **3 :** an individual rootstock of the lily of the valley **4 :** a diamond-shaped insignia worn to indicate rank by a second lieutenant, lieutenant, or captain in the British army

4pip *n* [short for *pippin*] (1797) **1 :** a small fruit seed; *esp* **:** one of a several-seeded fleshy fruit **2 :** one extraordinary of its kind

5pip *vt* **pipped; pip·ping** *Brit* (1880) **:** BEAT, DEFEAT

6pip *n* [imit.] (1907) **:** a short high-pitched tone

pip·age *or* **pipe·age** \'pī-pij\ *n* (1612) **1 a :** transportation by means of pipes **b :** the charge for such transportation **2 :** material for pipelines **:** PIPING

pi·pal \'pē-(,)pəl\ *n* [Hindi *pipal,* fr. Skt *pippala*] (1788) **:** a large long-lived fig (*Ficus religiosa*) of India that yields a product like lac and lacks prop roots

1pipe \'pīp\ *n* [ME, fr. OE *pīpa* (akin to OHG *pfīfa* pipe), fr. (assumed) VL *pipa* pipe, fr. L *pipare* to peep, of imit. origin] (bef. 12c) **1 a :** a tubular wind instrument; *specif* **:** a small fipple flute held in and played by the left hand **b :** one of the tubes of a pipe organ: (1) **:** FLUE PIPE (2) **:** REED PIPE **c :** BAGPIPE — usu. used in pl. **d** (1) **:** VOICE, VOCAL CORD — usu. used in pl. (2) **:** PIPING 1 **2 :** a long tube or hollow body for conducting a liquid, gas, or finely divided solid or for structural purposes **3 a :** a tubular or cylindrical object, part, or passage **b :** a roughly cylindrical and vertical geological formation **c :** the eruptive channel opening into the crater of a volcano **4 a :** a large cask of varying capacity used esp. for wine and oil **b :** any of various units of liquid capacity based on the size of a pipe; *esp* **:** a unit equal to 2 hogsheads **5 :** a device for smoking usu. consisting of a tube having a bowl at one end and a mouthpiece at the other **6 :** something easy **:** SNAP ⟨considered the course a ~⟩ — **pipe·ful** \-,fu̇l\ *n* — **pipe·less** \'pī-pləs\ *adj* — **pipe·like** \-,plīk\ *adj*

2pipe *vb* **piped; pip·ing** *vi* (bef. 12c) **1 a :** to play on a pipe **b :** to convey orders by signals on a boatswain's pipe **2 a :** to speak in a high or shrill voice **b :** to emit a shrill sound ~ *vt* **1 a :** to play (a tune) on a pipe **b :** to utter in the shrill tone of a pipe **2 a :** to lead or cause to go with pipe music **b** (1) **:** to call or direct by the boatswain's pipe (2) **:** to receive aboard or attend the departure of by sounding a boatswain's pipe **3 :** to trim with piping **4 :** to furnish or equip with pipes **5 :** to convey by or as if by pipes; *specif* **:** to transmit by wire or coaxial cable **6 :** NOTICE

pipe–clay *vt* (1864) **:** to whiten or clean with pipe clay

pipe clay *n* (1758) **:** highly plastic grayish white clay used esp. in making tobacco pipes and for whitening leather

pipe cleaner *n* (1870) **:** something used to clean the inside of a pipe; *specif* **:** a piece of flexible wire in which tufted fabric is twisted and which is used to clean the stem of a tobacco pipe

pipe cutter *n* (ca. 1890) **:** a tool or machine for cutting pipe; *esp* **:** a hand tool comprising a grasping device and three sharp-edged wheels forced inward by screw pressure that cut into the pipe as the tool is rotated

pipe down *vi* [2*pipe*] (1850) **:** to stop talking or making noise

pipe dream *n* [fr. the fantasies brought about by the smoking of opium] (1896) **:** an illusory or fantastic plan, hope, or story

pipe·fish \'pīp-,fish\ *n* (1769) **:** any of various long slender fishes (of *Syngnathus* and related genera) that are related to the sea horses and have a tube-shaped snout and an angular body covered with bony plates

pipe fitter *n* (ca. 1890) **:** one who installs and repairs piping

pipe fitting *n* (ca. 1890) **1 :** a piece (as a coupling or elbow) used to connect pipes or as accessory to a pipe **2 :** the work of a pipe fitter

pipe·line \'pī-,plīn\ *n* (1860) **1 :** a line of pipe with pumps, valves, and control devices for conveying liquids, gases, or finely divided solids **2 :** a direct channel for information **3 :** the processes through which supplies pass from or as if from source to user

pipe of peace (ca. 1691) **:** CALUMET

pipe organ *n* (1885) **:** ORGAN 1b(1)

pip·er \'pī-pər\ *n* (bef. 12c) **:** one that plays on a pipe

pi·per·a·zine \pī-'per-ə-,zēn\ *n* [ISV, blend of *piperidine* and *az-*] (1889) **:** a crystalline heterocyclic base $C_4H_{10}N_2$ or $C_4H_{10}N_2 \cdot 6H_2O$ used esp. as an anthelmintic

pi·per·i·dine \pī-'per-ə-,dēn\ *n* [ISV, blend of *piperine* and *-ide*] (1854) **:** a liquid heterocyclic base $C_5H_{11}N$ that has a peppery ammoniacal odor and is obtained usu. by hydrolysis of piperine

pip·er·ine \'pip-ə-,rēn\ *n* [ISV, fr. L *piper* pepper] (1820) **:** a white crystalline alkaloid $C_{17}H_{19}NO_3$ that is the chief active constituent of pepper

pi·per·o·nal \pī-'per-ə-,nal\ *n* [ISV *piperine* + *-one* + *-al*] (1869) **:** a crystalline aldehyde $C_8H_6O_3$ with an odor of heliotrope that is used esp. in perfumery

pi·per·o·nyl bu·tox·ide \pī-'per-ə-,nil-byü-'täk-,sīd, -ən-ᵊl-\ *n* [*piperonal* + *-yl* + *but-* + *oxide*] (1945) **:** an insecticide $C_{19}H_{30}O_5$; *esp* **:** an oily liquid containing this compound that is used chiefly as a synergist (as for pyrethrum insecticides)

pipe·stone \'pīp-,stōn\ *n* (1804) **:** a pink or mottled pink-and-white argillaceous stone carved by the Indians into tobacco pipes

pipe stop *n* (ca. 1909) **:** an organ stop composed of flue pipes

pi·pette *or* **pi·pet** \pī-'pet\ *n* [F *pipette,* dim. of *pipe* pipe, cask, fr. (assumed) VL *pipa, pippa* pipe] (1839) **:** a small piece of apparatus which typically consists of a narrow tube into which fluid is drawn by suction (as for dispensing or measurement) and retained by closing the upper end

pipe up *vi* (1889) **:** SPEAK UP

pipe wrench *n* (ca. 1890) **:** a wrench for gripping and turning a cylindrical object (as a pipe) usu. by use of two serrated jaws so designed as to grip the pipe when turning in one direction only

1pip·ing \'pī-piŋ\ *n* (13c) **1 a :** the music of a pipe **b :** a sound, note, or call like that of a pipe **2 :** a quantity or system of pipes **3 :** trimming stitched in seams or along edges of clothing, slipcovers, or curtains

2piping *adj* (1594) **1 :** SHRILL ⟨a ~ voice⟩ **2 :** TRANQUIL ⟨~ times of peace —Shak.⟩

piping hot *adj* (14c) **:** very hot

pip·it \'pip-ət\ *n* [imit.] (1768) **:** any of various small singing birds (family Motacillidae and esp. genus *Anthus*) resembling the lark

pip·kin \'pip-kən\ *n* [perh. fr. *pipe*] (1565) **:** a small earthenware or metal pot usu. with a horizontal handle

pip·pin \'pip-ən\ *n* [ME *pepin,* fr. MF] (15c) **1 :** any of numerous apples that have usu. yellow or greenish yellow skins strongly flushed with red and are used esp. for cooking **2 :** a highly admired or very admirable person or thing

pip–pip \pip-'ip, 'pip-'pip\ *interj* [origin unknown] *Brit* (ca. 1904) **:** GOOD-BYE

pip·sis·se·wa \pip-'sis-ə-,wȯ\ *n* [Cree *pipisisikweu*] (1789) **:** any of a genus (*Chimaphila,* esp. *C. umbellata*) of evergreen herbs of the wintergreen family with astringent leaves used as a tonic and diuretic

pip–squeak \'pip-,skwēk\ *n* (1910) **:** one that is small or insignificant

pi·quance \'pē-kən(t)s, -kwən(t)s\ *n* (1883) **:** PIQUANCY

pi·quan·cy \'pē-kən-sē, 'pik-wən-\ *n* (1664) **:** the quality or state of being piquant

pi·quant \'pē-kənt, -,känt; 'pik-wənt\ *adj* [MF, fr. prp. of *piquer*] (1630) **1 :** agreeably stimulating to the palate; *esp* **:** SPICY **2 :** engagingly provocative; *also* **:** having a lively arch charm ***syn*** see PUNGENT — **pi·quant·ly** *adv* — **pi·quant·ness** *n*

1pique \'pēk\ *n* (1592) **:** a transient feeling of wounded vanity **:** a fit of resentment ***syn*** see OFFENSE

2pique *vt* **piqued; piqu·ing** [F *piquer,* lit., to prick — more at PIKE] (1669) **1 :** to arouse anger or resentment in **:** IRRITATE ⟨what ~s linguistic conservatives —T.H. Middleton⟩ **2 a :** to excite or arouse by a provocation, challenge, or rebuff ⟨sly remarks to ~ their interest⟩ **b :** PRIDE ⟨he ~s himself on his skill as a cook⟩ ***syn*** see PROVOKE

pi·qué *or* **pi·que** \pi-'kā, 'pē-,\ *n* [F *piqué,* fr. pp. of *piquer* to prick, quilt] (1852) **:** a durable ribbed clothing fabric of cotton, rayon, or silk

pi·quet \pi-'kā, pik-'et\ *n* [F] (1646) **:** a two-handed card game played with 32 cards

pi·ra·cy \'pī-rə-sē\ *n, pl* **-cies** [ML *piratia,* fr. LGk *peirateia,* fr. Gk *peiratēs* pirate] (ca. 1552) **1 :** robbery on the high seas **2 :** the unauthorized use of another's production, invention, or conception esp. in infringement of a copyright **3 a :** an act of piracy **b :** an act resembling piracy

pi·ra·gua \pə-'räg-wə, -'rag-\ *n* [Sp] (1609) **1 :** DUGOUT 1 **2 :** a 2-masted flat-bottomed boat

pi·ra·nha \pə-'ran-yə, -'rän-(y)ə\ *n* [Pg, fr. Tupi] (1869) **:** a small So. American characin fish (genus *Serrasalmo*) that often attacks and inflicts dangerous wounds upon men and large animals — called also *caribe*

pi·ra·ru·cu \pi-,rär-ə-'kü\ *n* [Pg, fr. Tupi *pirá-rucú*] (1840) **:** a very large food fish (*Arapaima gigas,* order Isospondyli) of the rivers of northern So. America

1pi·rate \'pī-rət\ *n* [ME, fr. MF or L; MF, fr. L *pirata,* fr. Gk *peiratēs,* fr. *peiran* to attempt — more at FEAR] (15c) **:** one who commits or practices piracy — **pi·rat·i·cal** \pə-'rat-i-kəl, pī-\ *adj* — **pi·rat·i·cal·ly** \-k(ə-)lē\ *adv*

2pirate *vb* **pi·rated; pi·rat·ing** *vt* (1574) **1 :** to commit piracy on **2 :** to take or appropriate by piracy: as **a :** to reproduce without authorization esp. in infringement of copyright **b :** to lure away from another employer by offers of betterment ~ *vi* **:** to commit or practice piracy

pirn \'pərn, *2 is also* 'pi(ə)rn\ *n* [ME] (15c) **1 :** QUILL 1a(1) **2** *chiefly Scot* **:** a device resembling a reel

pi·ro·gi \pə-'rō-gē, pi(ə)r-'ō-\ *n, pl* **-gi** *or* **-gies** [Pol] (1927) **:** PIROSHKI

pi·rogue \'pē-,rōg\ *n* [F, fr. Sp *piragua,* of Cariban origin; akin to Galibi *piraua* pirogue] (1666) **1 :** DUGOUT 1 **2 :** a boat like a canoe

piro·plasm \'pir-ə-,plaz-əm\ *or* **piro·plas·ma** \,pir-ə-'plaz-mə\ *n, pl* **piro·plasms** *or* **piro·plas·ma·ta** \,pir-ə-'plaz-mət-ə\ [NL *Piroplasma,* genus of piroplasms] (1901) **:** BABESIA

pi·rosh·ki *or* **pi·rozh·ki** \,pir-əsh-'kē\ *n pl* [Russ *pirozhki,* pl. of *pirozhok* small tart] (1912) **:** small cases of dough with meat, cheese, or vegetable filling

pir·ou·ette \,pir-ə-'wet\ *n* [F, lit., teetotum] (1706) **:** a rapid whirling about of the body; *specif* **:** a full turn on the toe or ball of one foot in ballet — **pirouette** *vi*

pis *pl of* PI

pis al·ler \,pē-za-'lā\ *n, pl* **pis al·lers** \-'lā(z)\ [F, lit., to go worst] (1676) **:** a last resource or device **:** EXPEDIENT

pis·ca·to·ri·al \,pis-kə-'tōr-ē-əl, -'tȯr-\ *adj* (1828) **:** PISCATORY

pis·ca·to·ry \'pis-kə-,tōr-ē, -,tȯr-\ *adj* [L *piscatorius,* fr. *piscatus,* pp. of *piscari* to fish, fr. *piscis*] (1633) **:** of, relating to, or dependent on fish or fishing

Pi·sce·an \'pī-sē-ən, 'pis-ē-, 'pis-kē-\ *n* (1925) **:** PISCES 2b

Pi·sces \'pī-(,)sēz, 'pis-,ēz, 'pis-,kās\ *n pl but sing in constr* [ME, fr. L (gen. *Piscium*), fr. pl. of *piscis* fish — more at FISH] **1 :** a zodiacal constellation directly south of Andromeda **2 a :** the 12th sign of the zodiac in astrology — see ZODIAC table **b :** one born under this sign

pi·sci·cul·ture \'pī-sə-,kəl-chər, 'pis-(k)ə-\ *n* [prob. F, fr. L *piscis* + F *culture* culture] (1859) **:** fish culture

pi·sci·na \pə-'sē-nə, -'sī-\ *n* [ML, fr. L, fishpond, fr. *piscis*] (1793) **:** a basin with a drain near the altar of a church for disposing of water from liturgical ablutions

pi·scine \'pī-,sēn, 'pis-,(k)īn\ *adj* [L *piscinus,* fr. *piscis*] (1799) **:** of, relating to, or characteristic of fish

pi·sciv·o·rous \pə-'siv-ə-rəs, pī-\ *adj* [L *piscis* + E *-vorous*] (1668) **:** feeding on fishes

pish \'pish\ *interj* (1592) — used to express disdain or contempt

1pi·si·form \'pī-sə-,fȯrm\ *adj* [L *pisum* pea + E *-iform* — more at PEA] (1767) **:** resembling a pea in size or shape

2pisiform *n* (1808) **:** a bone on the ulnar side of the carpus in most mammals

pis·mire \'pis-,mī(ə)r, 'piz-\ *n* [ME *pissemire,* fr. *pisse* urine + *mire* ant, of Scand. origin; akin to ON *maurr* ant; akin to L *formica* ant, Gk *myrmēx*] (14c) **:** ANT

pis·mo clam \ˌpiz-(ˌ)mō-\ *n, often cap P* [*Pismo* Beach, Calif.] (1913) : a thick-shelled clam (*Tivela stultorum*) of the southwest coast of No. America used extensively for food

pi·so·lite \ˈpī-sə-ˌlīt\ *n* [NL *pisolithus,* fr. Gk *pisos* pea + *-lithos* -lith] (1708) : a limestone composed of pisiform concretions — **pi·so·lit·ic** \ˌpī-sə-ˈlit-ik\ *adj*

¹piss \ˈpis\ *vb* [ME *pissen,* fr. OF *pissier,* fr. (assumed) VL *pissiare*] *vi* (13c) : URINATE — sometimes considered vulgar ~ *vt* : to urinate in or on — sometimes considered vulgar

²piss *n* (14c) **1** : URINE — sometimes considered vulgar **2** : an act of urinating — often used with *take;* sometimes considered vulgar

pissed \ˈpist\ *adj* (1846) **1** : ANGRY, DISGUSTED — sometimes considered vulgar **2** *Brit* : DRUNK — sometimes considered vulgar

piss off *vi, Brit* (1953) : to leave forthwith : get out — usu. used as a command; sometimes considered vulgar ~ *vt* : ANGER, IRRITATE — sometimes considered vulgar

pis·soir \pi-ˈswär\ *n* [F, fr. MF, fr. *pisser* to urinate, fr. OF *pissier*] (1919) : a public urinal usu. located on the street in some European countries

pis·ta·chio \pə-ˈstash-(ē-ˌ)ō, -ˈstäsh-\ *n, pl* **-chios** [It *pistacchio,* fr. L *pistacium* pistachio nut, fr. Gk *pistakion,* fr. *pistakē* pistachio tree, fr. Per *pistah*] (15c) : a small tree (*Pistacia vera*) of the sumac family whose drupaceous fruit contains a greenish edible seed; *also* : its seed

pis·ta·reen \ˌpis-tə-ˈrēn\ *n* [prob. modif. of Sp *peseta* peseta] (1744) : an old Spanish silver piece circulating at a debased rate

piste \ˈpēst\ *n* [F, fr. MF, fr. OIt *pista,* fr. *pistare* to trample down, pound—more at PISTON] (ca. 1727) : TRAIL; *esp* : a downhill ski trail

pis·til \ˈpis-tᵊl\ *n* [NL *pistillum,* fr. L, pestle — more at PESTLE] (1726) : the ovule-bearing organ of a seed plant that consists of the ovary with its appendages — see FLOWER illustration

pis·til·late \ˈpis-tə-ˌlāt\ *adj* (ca. 1828) : having pistils; *specif* : having pistils but no stamens

pis·tol \ˈpis-tᵊl\ *n* [MF *pistole,* fr. G, fr. MHG dial. *pischulle,* fr. Czech *pišťal,* lit., pipe; akin to Russ *pischal* harquebus] (1570) : a handgun whose chamber is integral with the barrel — **pistol** *vt*

pis·tole \pis-ˈtōl\ *n* [ME] (1592) : an old gold 2-escudo piece of Spain; *also* : any of several old gold coins of Europe of approximately the same value

pis·tol·eer \ˌpis-tə-ˈli(ə)r\ *n* (1577) : one who is armed with a pistol

pistol grip *n* (1874) **1** : a grip of a shotgun or rifle shaped like a pistol stock **2** : a handle shaped like a pistol stock

pistol–whip *vt* (1930) : to beat with a pistol

pis·ton \ˈpis-tən\ *n* [F, fr. It *pistone,* fr. *pistare* to pound, fr. OIt, fr. ML, fr. L *pistus,* pp. of *pinsere* to crush — more at PESTLE] (1704) **1** : a sliding piece moved by or moving against fluid pressure which usu. consists of a short cylinder fitting within a cylindrical vessel along which it moves back and forth **2** **a** : a valve sliding in a cylinder in a brass instrument and serving when depressed by a finger knob to lower its pitch **b** : a button on an organ console to bring in a previously selected registration

piston pin *n* (1897) : WRIST PIN

piston ring *n* (1867) : a springy split metal ring for sealing the gap between a piston and the cylinder wall

piston rod *n* (1786) : a rod by which a piston is moved or by which it communicates motion

¹pit \ˈpit\ *n* [ME, fr. OE *pytt;* akin to OHG *pfuzzi* well] (bef. 12c) **1** **a** (1) : a hole, shaft, or cavity in the ground (2) : MINE (3) : a scooped-out place used for burning something (as charcoal) **b** : an area often sunken or depressed below the adjacent floor area: as (1) : an enclosure in which animals are made to fight each other (2) : a space at the front of a theater for the orchestra (3) : an area in a securities or commodities exchange in which members do trading **2** **a** : HELL — used with *the* **b** : a place or situation of futility, misery, or degradation **c** *pl* : WORST ⟨it's the ~*s*⟩ **3** : a hollow or indentation esp. in the surface of an organism: as **a** : a natural hollow in the surface of the body **b** : one of the indented scars left in the skin by a pustular disease : POCKMARK **c** : a minute depression in the secondary wall of a plant cell functioning in the intercellular movement of water and dissolved material **4** : any of the areas alongside an auto racecourse used for refueling and repairing the cars during a race — often used in pl. with *the*

²pit *vb* **pit·ted; pit·ting** *vt* (15c) **1** **a** : to place, cast, bury, or store in a pit **b** : to make pits in; *esp* : to scar or mark with pits **2** **a** : to set (as gamecocks) into or as if into a pit to fight **b** : to set into opposition or rivalry — usu. used with *against* ~ *vi* **1** : to become marked with pits; *esp* : to preserve for a time an indentation made by pressure **2** : to make a pit stop

³pit *n* [D, fr. MD — more at PITH] (1841) : the stone of a drupaceous fruit

⁴pit *vt* **pit·ted; pit·ting** (ca. 1923) : to remove the pit from (a fruit)

¹pi·ta \ˈpēt-ə\ *n* [Sp & Pg] (1698) **1** : any of several fiber-yielding plants (as an agave) **2** : the fiber of a pita; *also* : any of several fibers from other sources

²pita *n* [NGk, lit., pie, cake] (ca. 1951) : a thin flat bread

pit–a–pat \ˌpit-i-ˈpat\ *n* [imit.] (1582) : PITTER-PATTER — **pit–a–pat** *adv or adj* — **pit–a–pat** *vi*

pit bull *n* (1930) **1** : any of various smooth-coated stocky muscular terriers orig. developed for dogfighting and noted for their strength and stamina **2** : STAFFORDSHIRE BULL TERRIER **3** : AMERICAN STAFFORDSHIRE TERRIER — called also *pit bull terrier*

¹pitch \ˈpich\ *n* [ME *pich,* fr. OE *pic,* fr. L *pic-, pix;* akin to L *opimus* fat — more at FAT] (bef. 12c) **1** : a black or dark viscous substance obtained as a residue in the distillation of organic materials and esp. tars **2** : any of various bituminous substances **3** : resin obtained from various conifers and often used medicinally **4** : any of various artificial mixtures resembling resinous or bituminous pitches

²pitch *vt* (bef. 12c) : to cover, smear, or treat with or as if with pitch

³pitch *vb* [ME *pichen*] *vt* (13c) **1** : to erect and fix firmly in place ⟨~ a tent⟩ **2** : to throw usu. with a particular objective or toward a particular point ⟨~ hay onto a wagon⟩: as **a** : to throw (a baseball) to a batter **b** : to toss (as coins) so as to fall at or near a mark ⟨~ pennies⟩ **c** : to put aside or discard by throwing ⟨~*ed* his cigarette into the fire⟩ **3** : to sell or advertise esp. in a high-pressure way **4** **a** (1) : to cause to be at a particular level or of a particular quality (2) : to set in a particular musical key **b** : to cause to be set at a particular angle : SLOPE **5** : to utter glibly and insincerely **6** **a** : to use as a starting pitcher **b** : to play as pitcher **7** : to hit (a golf ball) in a high arc with backspin so that it rolls very little after striking the green ~ *vi* **1** **a** : to fall precipitately or headlong **b** (1) *of a ship* : to have the bow alternately plunge precipitately and rise abruptly (2) *of an aircraft* : to turn about a lateral axis so that the nose rises or falls in relation to the tail (3) *of a missile or spacecraft* : to turn about a lateral axis that is both perpendicular to the longitudinal axis and horizontal with respect to the earth **c** : BUCK 1 **2** : ENCAMP **3** : to hit upon or happen upon something ⟨~ upon the perfect gift⟩ **4** : to incline downward : SLOPE **5** **a** : to throw a ball to a batter **b** : to play ball as a pitcher **c** : to pitch a golf ball ***syn*** see THROW — **pitch into** **1** : ATTACK, ASSAIL **2** : to set to work on energetically

⁴pitch *n* (1500) **1** : the action or a manner of pitching; *esp* : an up-and-down movement — compare YAW **2** **a** : SLOPE; *also* : degree of slope : RAKE **b** : the distance between any of various things: as (1) : distance between one point on a gear tooth and the corresponding point on the next tooth (2) : distance from any point on the thread of a screw to the corresponding point on an adjacent thread measured parallel to the axis **c** : the theoretical distance a propeller would advance longitudinally in one revolution **d** : the number of teeth or of threads per inch **3** *archaic* : TOP, ZENITH **4** **a** : the relative level, intensity, or extent of some quality or state **b** (1) : the property of a sound and esp. a musical tone that is determined by the frequency of the waves producing it : highness or lowness of sound (2) : a standard frequency for tuning instruments **c** (1) : the difference in the relative vibration frequency of the human voice that contributes to the total meaning of speech (2) : a definite relative pitch that is a significant phenomenon in speech **5** : a steep place : DECLIVITY **6** *chiefly Brit* **a** : an outdoor site (as for camping or doing business) **b** : a playing field **7** : an all-fours game in which the first card led is a trump **8** **a** : an often high-pressure sales talk **b** : ADVERTISEMENT **9** **a** : the delivery of a baseball by a pitcher to a batter **b** : a baseball so thrown **c** : PITCHOUT 2 — **pitched** \ˈpicht\ *adj*

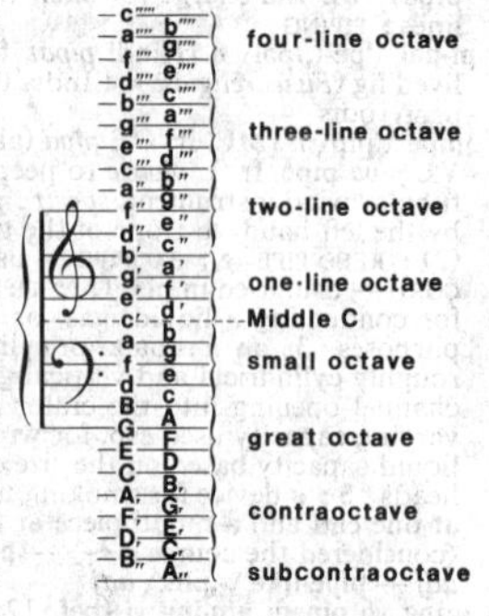

staff notation of pitch 4b(1)

pitch–black \ˈpich-ˈblak\ *adj* (1599) : extremely dark or black

pitch·blende \ˈpich-ˌblend\ *n* [part trans. of G *pechblende,* fr. *pech* pitch + *blende* blende] (1770) : a brown to black mineral that consists of massive uraninite, has a distinctive luster, contains radium, and is the chief ore-mineral source of uranium

pitch–dark \ˈpich-ˈdärk\ *adj* (1827) : extremely dark : PITCH-BLACK

pitched battle \ˈpich(t)-\ *n* (ca. 1549) : an intensely fought battle in which the opposing forces are locked in close combat

¹pitch·er \ˈpich-ər\ *n* [ME *picher,* fr. OF *pichier,* fr. ML *bicarius* goblet — more at BEAKER] (13c) **1** : a container for holding and pouring liquids that usu. has a lip or spout and a handle **2** : ASCIDIUM; *esp* : a modified leaf of a pitcher plant in which the hollowed petiole and base of the blade form an elongated receptacle

²pitcher *n* (1845) : one that pitches; *specif* : the player that pitches in a game of baseball

pitcher plant *n* (1819) : a plant (esp. family Sarraceniaceae, the pitcher-plant family) with leaves modified into pitchers in which insects are trapped and digested by means of liquids secreted by the leaves

pitch·fork \ˈpich-ˌfȯ(ə)rk\ *n* [ME *pikfork,* fr. *pik* pick + *fork*] (15c) : a long-handled fork that has two or three long somewhat curved prongs and is used esp. in pitching hay — **pitchfork** *vt*

pitch in *vi* (1843) **1** : to begin to work **2** : to contribute to a common endeavor

pitch·man \ˈpich-mən\ *n* (ca. 1926) : one who makes a sales pitch: as **a** : one who sells merchandise on the streets or from a concession **b** : one who does radio or TV commercials

pitch·out \ˈpich-ˌau̇t\ *n* (1912) **1** : a pitch in baseball deliberately out of reach of the batter to enable the catcher to check or put out a base runner **2** : a lateral pass in football between two backs behind the scrimmage line — **pitch out** *vi*

pitch pine *n* (1754) **1** : any of several pines that yield pitch; *esp* : a 3-leaved pine (*Pinus rigida*) of eastern No. America **2** : the wood of a pitch pine

pitch pipe *n* (1711) : a small reed pipe or flue pipe producing one or more tones to establish the pitch in singing or in tuning an instrument

pitch·stone \ˈpich-ˌstōn\ *n* (ca. 1784) : a glassy rock with a resinous luster that contains more water than obsidian does

pitch·wom·an \-ˌwu̇m-ən\ *n* (1957) : a woman who makes a sales pitch

pitchy \ˈpich-ē\ *adj* (1513) **1** **a** : full of pitch : TARRY **b** : of, relating to, or having the qualities of pitch **2** : PITCH-BLACK

pit·e·ous \ˈpit-ē-əs\ *adj* (13c) : of a kind to move to pity or compassion — **pit·e·ous·ly** *adv* — **pit·e·ous·ness** *n*

pit·fall \ˈpit-ˌfȯl\ *n* (14c) **1** : TRAP, SNARE; *specif* : a pit flimsily covered or camouflaged and used to capture and hold animals or men **2** : a hidden or not easily recognized danger or difficulty

¹pith \ˈpith\ *n* [ME, fr. OE *pitha;* akin to MD & MLG *pit* pith, pit] (bef. 12c) **1** **a** : a usu. continuous central strand of spongy tissue in the stems of most vascular plants that prob. functions chiefly in storage **b** : any of various loose spongy plant tissues that resemble true pith **c** : the soft or spongy interior of a part of the body **2** **a** : the essential part : CORE **b** : substantial quality (as of meaning) **3** : IMPORTANCE

²pith *vt* (1805) **1** **a** : to kill (as cattle) by piercing or severing the spinal cord **b** : to destroy the spinal cord or central nervous system of (as a frog) usu. by passing a wire or needle up and down the vertebral canal **2** : to remove the pith from (a plant stem)

pit·head \ˈpit-ˌhed\ *n* (1839) : the top of a mining pit or coal shaft; *also* : the immediately adjacent ground and buildings

pith·ec·an·thro·pine \ˌpith-i-ˈkan(t)-thrə-ˌpīn\ *n* (1925) : any of a group of Pleistocene hominids (as Java man, Peking man, and Heidelberg man) that have a smaller cranial capacity than modern man (*Homo sapiens*) but a greater cranial capacity than the australopithecines, prominent eyebrow ridges, a receding forehead, constriction of the skull behind the eye sockets, and relatively large canine and incisor teeth and that were formerly considered to comprise a genus (*Pithecanthropus*) but are now grouped in a single species (*Homo erectus*) — **pithecanthropine** *adj*

pith·ec·an·thro·pus \-'kan(t)-thrə-pəs, -ˌkan-'thrō-\ *n, pl* **-pi** \-ˌpī, -ˌpē\ [NL, fr. Gk *pithēkos* ape + *anthrōpos* human being; akin to OHG *bibēn* to tremble, L *foedus* ugly] (1905) : PITHECANTHROPINE

pith helmet *n* (1889) : TOPEE

pith ray *n* (1902) : MEDULLARY RAY

pithy \'pith-ē\ *adj* **pith·i·er; -est** (1562) **1 :** consisting of or abounding in pith **2 :** having substance and point : tersely cogent ***syn*** see CONCISE — **pith·i·ly** \'pith-ə-lē\ *adv* — **pith·i·ness** \'pith-ē-nəs\ *n*

piti·able \'pit-ē-ə-bəl\ *adj* (15c) **1 :** deserving or exciting pity : LAMENTABLE **2 :** of a kind to evoke mingled pity and contempt esp. because of inadequacy ⟨a ~ excuse⟩ ***syn*** see CONTEMPTIBLE — **piti·able·ness** *n* — **piti·ably** \-blē\ *adv*

piti·er \'pit-ē-ər\ *n* (1601) : one that pities

piti·ful \'pit-i-fəl\ *adj* (15c) **1 a :** deserving or arousing pity or commiseration **b :** exciting pitying contempt (as by meanness or inadequacy) **2** *archaic* : full of pity : COMPASSIONATE — **piti·ful·ly** \-f(ə-)lē\ *adv* — **piti·ful·ness** \-fəl-nəs\ *n*

piti·less \'pit-i-ləs, 'pit-ᵊl-əs\ *adj* (15c) : devoid of pity : MERCILESS — **piti·less·ly** *adv* — **piti·less·ness** *n*

pit·man \'pit-mən\ *n* (1761) **1** *pl* **pit·men** \-mən\ : one who works in or near a pit (as in a coal mine) **2** *pl* **pitmans :** CONNECTING ROD

pi·ton \'pē-ˌtän\ *n* [F] (1893) : a spike, wedge, or peg that is driven into a rock or ice surface as a support (as for a mountain climber)

pi·tot–stat·ic tube \ˌpē-ˌtō-'stat-ik-\ *n, often cap P* (1926) : a device that consists of a pitot tube and a static tube and that measures pressures in such a way that the relative speed of a fluid can be determined

pi·tot tube \ˌpē-ˌtō-\ *n, often cap P* [F (*tube de*) *Pitot*, fr. Henri *Pitot* †1771 Fr. physicist] (ca. 1859) **1 :** a device that consists of a tube having a short right-angled bend which is placed vertically in a moving body of fluid with the mouth of the bent part directed upstream and that is used with a manometer to measure the velocity of fluid flow **2 :** PITOT-STATIC TUBE

pit saw *n* (1679) : a handsaw worked by two persons one of whom stands on or above the log being sawed into planks and the other below it usu. in a pit

pit stop *n* (1932) **1 :** a stop at the pits during an automobile race **2 :** a stop for food, fuel, rest, or relief (as during a trip); *also* : a place where such a stop can be made

pit·tance \'pit-ᵊn(t)s\ *n* [ME *pitance*, fr. OF, piety, pity, fr. ML *pietantia*, fr. *pietant-*, *pietans*, prp. of *pietari* to be charitable, fr. L *pietas* piety — more at PITY] (14c) : a small portion, amount, or allowance; *also* : a meager wage or remuneration

pit·ted \'pit-əd\ *adj* (bef. 12c) : marked with pits

pit·ter–pat·ter \'pit-ər-ˌpat-ər, 'pit-ē-ˌ\ *n* [redupl. of [4]*patter*] (15c) : a rapid succession of light sounds or beats : PATTER — **pitter–patter** \ˌpit-ər-', ˌpit-ē-'\ *adv or adj* — **pitter–patter** *like adv*\ *vi*

pit·ting *n* (1665) **1 :** an arrangement of pits **2 :** the action or process of forming pits **3 :** the bringing of gamecocks together to fight

[1]**pi·tu·itary** \pə-'t(y)ü-ə-ˌter-ē\ *adj* [L *pituita* phlegm; fr. the former belief that the pituitary gland secreted phlegm — more at PIP] (1615) **1 :** of or relating to the pituitary gland **2 :** caused or characterized by secretory disturbances of the pituitary gland ⟨a ~ dwarf⟩

[2]**pituitary** *n, pl* **-itar·ies** (1845) : PITUITARY GLAND

pituitary gland *n* (1615) : a small oval endocrine organ that is attached to the infundibulum of the brain, consists of an epithelial anterior lobe joined by an intermediate part to a posterior lobe of nervous origin, and produces various internal secretions directly or indirectly impinging on most basic body functions — called also *pituitary body;* see BRAIN illustration

pit viper *n* (ca. 1885) : any of various mostly New World specialized venomous snakes (family Crotalidae) with a sensory pit on each side of the head and hollow perforated fangs

[1]**pity** \'pit-ē\ *n, pl* **pit·ies** [ME *pite*, fr. OF *pité*, fr. L *pietat-*, *pietas* piety, pity, fr. *pius* pious] (13c) **1 a :** sympathetic sorrow for one suffering, distressed, or unhappy **b :** capacity to feel pity **2 :** something to be regretted ⟨it's a ~ you can't go⟩

[2]**pity** *vb* **pit·ied; pity·ing** *vt* (1529) : to feel pity for ~ *vi* : to feel pity

pity·ing *adj* (1650) : expressing or feeling pity — **pity·ing·ly** \-iŋ-lē\ *adv*

pit·y·ri·a·sis \ˌpit-i-'rī-ə-səs\ *n* [NL, fr. Gk, fr. *pityron* scurf] (ca. 1693) : a condition of man or domestic animals marked by dry scaling or scurfy patches of skin

più \(ˌ)pyü, pē-ˌü\ *adv* [It, fr. L *plus*] (1724) : MORE — used to qualify an adverb or adjective used as a direction in music

Pi·ute *var of* PAIUTE

[1]**piv·ot** \'piv-ət\ *n* [F] (ca. 1611) **1 :** a shaft or pin on which something turns **2 a :** a person, thing, or factor having a major or central role, function, or effect **b :** a key player or position; *specif* : an offensive position of a basketball player who stands usu. with his back to his own basket to relay passes, shoot, or provide a screen for teammates **3 :** the action of pivoting

[2]**pivot** *adj* (1796) **1 :** turning on or as if on a pivot **2 :** PIVOTAL

[3]**pivot** *vi* (1841) : to turn on or as if on a pivot ~ *vt* **1 :** to provide with, mount on, or attach by a pivot **2 :** to cause to pivot — **pivot·able** \-ə-bəl\ *adj*

piv·ot·al \'piv-ət-ᵊl\ *adj* (1844) **1 :** of, relating to, or constituting a pivot **2 :** vitally important : CRUCIAL — **piv·ot·al·ly** \-ᵊl-ē\ *adv*

piv·ot·man \'piv-ət-ˌman\ *n* (ca. 1814) : one who plays the pivot; *specif* : a center on a basketball team

pivot tooth *n* (1842) : an artificial crown attached to the root of a tooth by a usu. metallic pin — called also *pivot crown*

pix *pl of* PIC

pix·el \'pik-səl, -ˌsel\ *n* [*pix* + *element*] (1969) : any of the small discrete elements that together constitute an image (as on a television screen)

[1]**pix·ie** *or* **pixy** \'pik-sē\ *n, pl* **pix·ies** [origin unknown] (1746) : FAIRY; *specif* : a cheerful mischievous sprite — **pix·ie·ish** \-sē-ish\ *adj*

[2]**pixie** *or* **pixy** *adj* (1943) : playfully mischievous — **pixi·ness** *n*

pix·i·lat·ed *or* **pix·il·lat·ed** \'pik-sə-ˌlāt-əd\ *adj* [irreg. fr. *pixie*] (1848) **1 :** somewhat unbalanced mentally; *also* : BEMUSED **2 :** WHIMSICAL — **pix·i·la·tion** \ˌpik-sə-'lā-shən\ *n*

piz·za \'pēt-sə\ *n* [It, prob. deriv. of ML *pinsa* kneading board, fr. L *pinsere* to beat, pound; akin to L *pistor* miller, baker—more at PESTLE] (1935) : an open pie made typically of thinly rolled bread dough spread with a spiced mixture (as of tomatoes, cheese, and ground meat) and baked — called also *pizza pie*

piz·zazz *or* **pi·zazz** \pə-'zaz\ *n* [origin unknown] (1937) : the quality of being exciting or attractive: as **a :** GLAMOUR **b :** VITALITY

piz·ze·ria \ˌpēt-sə-'rē-ə\ *n* [It, fr. *pizza*] (1943) : an establishment where pizzas are made or sold

[1]**piz·zi·ca·to** \ˌpit-si-'kät-(ˌ)ō\ *n, pl* **-ca·ti** \-'kät-(ˌ)ē\ (1845) : a note or passage played by plucking strings

[2]**pizzicato** *adv or adj* [It, pp. of *pizzicare* to pluck] (ca. 1854) : by means of plucking instead of bowing — used as a direction in music; compare ARCO

piz·zle \'piz-əl\ *n* [prob. fr. Flem *pezel;* akin to LG *pesel* pizzle] (1523) **1 :** the penis of an animal **2 :** a whip made of a bull's pizzle

pj's \(')pē-'jāz\ *n pl* [*pa*jama*s*] (1951) : PAJAMAS

PK \'pē-'kā\ *n* (1943) : PSYCHOKINESIS

pla·ca·ble \'plak-ə-bəl, 'plā-kə-\ *adj* (1586) : easily placated : TOLERANT, TRACTABLE — **pla·ca·bil·i·ty** \ˌplak-ə-'bil-ət-ē, ˌplā-kə-\ *n* — **pla·ca·bly** \'plak-ə-blē, 'plā-kə-\ *adv*

[1]**plac·ard** \'plak-ərd, -ˌärd\ *n* [ME *placquart*, a formal document, fr. MF, fr. *plaquier* to plate — more at PLAQUE] (1560) **1 :** a notice posted in a public place : POSTER **2 :** a small card or metal plaque

[2]**plac·ard** \-ˌärd, -ərd\ *vt* (1813) **1 a :** to cover with or as if with posters **b :** to post in a public place **2 :** to announce by or as if by posting

pla·cate \'plā-ˌkāt, 'plak-ˌāt\ *vt* **pla·cat·ed; pla·cat·ing** [L *placatus*, pp. of *placare* — more at PLEASE] (1678) : to soothe or mollify esp. by concessions : APPEASE ***syn*** see PACIFY — **pla·cat·er** *n* — **pla·ca·tion** \plā-'kā-shən, pla-\ *n* — **pla·ca·tive** \'plā-ˌkāt-iv, 'plak-ˌāt-\ *adj* — **pla·ca·to·ry** \'plā-kə-ˌtōr-ē, 'plak-ə-, -ˌtȯr-\ *adj*

[1]**place** \'plās\ *n* [ME, fr. OF, open space, fr. L *platea* broad street, fr. Gk *plateia* (*hodos*), fr. fem. of *platys* broad, flat; akin to Skt *pṛthu* broad, L *planta* sole of the foot] (13c) **1 a :** a way for admission or transit **b :** physical environment : SPACE **c :** physical surroundings : ATMOSPHERE **2 a :** an indefinite region or expanse ⟨all over the ~⟩ **b :** a building or locality used for a special purpose ⟨a ~ of learning⟩ ⟨a fine eating ~⟩ **c** *archaic* : the three-dimensional compass of a material object **3 a :** a particular region, center of population, or location ⟨a nice ~ to visit⟩ **b :** HOUSE, DWELLING ⟨lovely ~ you have here⟩ ⟨our summer ~⟩ **4 :** a particular part of a surface or body : SPOT **5 :** relative position in a scale or series: as **a :** position in a social scale ⟨kept them in their ~⟩ **b :** a step in a sequence ⟨in the first ~, you're wrong⟩ **c :** a position at the conclusion of a competition ⟨finished in last ~⟩ **6 a :** a proper or designated niche ⟨the ~ of education in society⟩ **b :** an appropriate moment or point ⟨this is not the ~ to discuss compensation —Robert Moses⟩ **7 a :** an available seat or accommodation ⟨needs a ~ to stay⟩ **b :** an empty or vacated position ⟨new ones will take their ~⟩ **8 :** the position of a figure in relation to others of a row or series; *esp* : the position of a digit within a numeral ⟨12 is a two ~ number⟩ ⟨in 316 the figure 1 is in the tens ~⟩ **9 a :** remunerative employment : JOB **b :** prestige accorded to one of high rank : STATUS ⟨an endless quest for preferment and ~ —*Time*⟩ **10 :** a public square : PLAZA **11 :** second place at the finish (as of a horse race)

[2]**place** *vb* **placed; plac·ing** *vt* (1548) **1 :** to distribute in an orderly manner : ARRANGE **2 a :** to put in or as if in a particular place : SET **b :** to present for consideration ⟨a question *placed* before the group⟩ **c :** to put in a particular state ⟨~ a performer under contract⟩ **d :** to direct to a desired spot **e :** to cause (the voice) to produce free and well resonated singing or speaking tones **3 :** to appoint to a position **4 :** to find a place (as a home or employment) for **5 a :** to assign to a position in a series or category : RANK **b :** ESTIMATE ⟨*placed* the value of the estate too high⟩ **c :** to identify by connecting with an associated context ⟨couldn't quite ~ her face⟩ **6 a :** to give (an order) to a supplier **b :** to give an order for ⟨~ a bet⟩ ~ *vi* : to earn a given spot in a competition; *specif* : to come in second (as in a horse race) — **placeable** \'plā-sə-bəl\ *adj*

pla·ce·bo *n, pl* **-bos** (13c) **1** \plä-'chā-(ˌ)bō\ [ME, fr. L, I shall please, fr. *placēre* to please — more at PLEASE] : the Roman Catholic vespers for the dead **2** \plə-'sē-\ [L, I shall please] **a (1) :** a medication prescribed more for the mental relief of the patient than for its actual effect on his disorder **(2) :** an inert or innocuous substance used esp. in controlled experiments testing the efficacy of another substance (as a drug) **b :** something tending to soothe

placebo effect *n* (1950) : improvement in the condition of a sick person that occurs in response to treatment but cannot be considered due to the specific treatment used

place·hold·er \'plās-ˌhōl-dər\ *n* (1958) : a symbol in a mathematical or logical expression that may be replaced by the name of any element of a set

[1]**place·kick** \'plā-ˌskik\ *n* (ca. 1856) : the kicking of a ball (as a football) placed or held in a stationary position on the ground

[2]**placekick** *vt* (1856) **1 :** to kick (a ball) from a stationary position **2 :** to score by means of a placekick — **place·kick·er** *n*

place·less \'plā-sləs\ *adj* (14c) : lacking a fixed location — **place·less·ly** *adv*

place·man \'plā-smən\ *n* (1741) : a political appointee to a public office esp. in 18th century Britain

place mat *n* (1928) : a small often rectangular table mat on which a place setting is laid

place·ment \'plā-smənt\ *n* (1844) **1 :** an act or instance of placing: as **a :** an accurately hit ball (as in tennis) that an opponent cannot return

---

b : the assignment of a person to a suitable place (as a job or a class in school) 2 : PLACEKICK

placement test *n* (1928) : a test usu. given to a student entering an educational institution to determine his knowledge or proficiency in various subjects so that he may be assigned to appropriate courses or classes

place–name \'plā-,snām\ *n* (1868) : the name of a geographical locality

pla·cen·ta \plə-'sent-ə\ *n, pl* **-centas** *or* **-cen·tae** \-'sent-(,)ē\ [NL, fr. L, flat cake, fr. Gk *plakount-, plakous,* fr. *plak-, plax* flat surface — more at PLEASE] (1691) **1** : the vascular organ in mammals except monotremes and marsupials that unites the fetus to the maternal uterus and mediates its metabolic exchanges through a more or less intimate association of uterine mucosal with chorionic and usu. allantoic tissues; *also* : an analogous organ in another animal **2** : a sporangium-bearing surface; *esp* : the part of the carpel bearing ovules — **pla·cen·tal** \-'sent-^{ə}l\ *adj or n*

pla·cen·ta·tion \,plas-^{ə}n-'tā-shən, plə-,sen-\ *n* (1760) **1** : the arrangement of placentas and ovules in a plant ovary **2 a** : the development of the placenta and attachment of the fetus to the uterus during pregnancy **b** : the morphological type of a placenta

[1]**plac·er** \'plā-sər\ *n* (1579) : one that places: as **a** : one that deposits or arranges **b** : one of the winners in a competition

[2]**plac·er** \'plas-ər\ *n* [Sp, fr. Catal, submarine plain, fr. *plaza* place, fr. L *platea* broad street — more at PLACE] (1842) : an alluvial, marine, or glacial deposit containing particles of valuable mineral and esp. of gold

place setting *n* (1944) : a table service for one person

place value *n* (1911) : the value of the location of a digit in a numeral ⟨in 425 the location of the digit 2 has a *place value* of ten while the digit itself indicates that there are two tens⟩

plac·id \'plas-əd\ *adj* [L *placidus,* fr. *placēre* to please — more at PLEASE] (1626) **1** : serenely free of interruption or disturbance : QUIET ⟨~ summer skies⟩ ⟨a ~ disposition⟩ **2** : COMPLACENT ***syn*** see CALM — **pla·cid·i·ty** \pla-'sid-ət-ē, plə-\ *n* — **plac·id·ly** \'plas-əd-lē\ *adv* — **plac·id·ness** *n*

plack·et \'plak-ət\ *n* [origin unknown] (1605) **1 a** : a slit in a garment (as a skirt) often forming the closure **b** *archaic* : a pocket esp. in a woman's skirt **2** *archaic* **a** : PETTICOAT **b** : WOMAN

plac·oid \'plak-,ȯid\ *adj* [Gk *plak-, plax* flat surface] (1842) : of, relating to, or being a scale of dermal origin with an enamel-tipped spine characteristic of the elasmobranchs

pla·fond \plȧ-fō^{n}\ *n* [F, fr. MF, fr. *plat* flat + *fond* bottom, fr. L *fundus* — more at PLATE, BOTTOM] (1664) : a usu. elaborate ceiling

pla·gal \'plā-gəl\ *adj* [ML *plagalis,* deriv. of Gk *plagios* oblique, sideways, fr. *plagos* side; akin to L *plaga* net, region, Gk *pelagos* sea — more at FLAKE] (1597) **1** *of a church mode* : having the keynote on the 4th scale step — compare AUTHENTIC 4a **2** *of a cadence* : progressing from the subdominant chord to the tonic — compare AUTHENTIC 4b

plage \'pläzh\ *n* [F, beach, luminous surface, fr. It *piaggia* beach, fr. LL *plagia,* fr. Gk *plagios* oblique] (1888) **1** : the beach of a seaside resort **2** : a bright region on the sun that is caused by the light emitted by clouds of calcium or hydrogen and that is often associated with a sunspot

plagiarise *Brit var of* PLAGIARIZE

pla·gia·rism \'plā-jə-,riz-əm *also* -jē-ə-\ *n* (1621) **1** : an act or instance of plagiarizing **2** : something plagiarized — **pla·gia·rist** \-rəst\ *n* — **pla·gia·ris·tic** \,plā-jə-'ris-tik *also* -jē-ə-\ *adj*

pla·gia·rize \'plā-jə-,rīz *also* -jē-ə-\ *vb* **-rized; -riz·ing** *vt* [*plagiary*] (1716) : to steal and pass off (the ideas or words of another) as one's own : use (a created production) without crediting the source ~ *vi* : to commit literary theft : present as new and original an idea or product derived from an existing source — **pla·gia·riz·er** *n*

pla·gia·ry \'plā-jē-,er-ē, -jə-rē\ *n, pl* **-ries** [L *plagiarius,* lit., plunderer, fr. *plagium* hunting net, fr. *plaga* net] (1601) **1** *archaic* : one that plagiarizes **2** : PLAGIARISM

pla·gio·clase \'plā-j(ē-)ə-,klās, 'plaj-(ē-)ə-, -,klāz\ *n* [Gk *plagios* oblique + *klasis* breaking, fr. *klan* to break — more at HALT] (ca. 1868) : a triclinic feldspar; *esp* : one having calcium or sodium in its composition

pla·gio·tro·pic \,plā-j(ē-)ə-'trōp-ik, ,plaj-(ē-)ə-, -'träp-\ *adj* [Gk *plagios* + ISV *-tropic*] (1882) : having the longer axis inclined away from the vertical ⟨~ lateral branches⟩

[1]**plague** \'plāg\ *n* [ME *plage,* fr. MF, fr. LL *plaga,* fr. L, blow; akin to L *plangere* to strike — more at PLAINT] (14c) **1 a** : a disastrous evil or affliction : CALAMITY **b** : a destructively numerous influx ⟨a ~ of locusts⟩ **2 a** : an epidemic disease causing a high rate of mortality : PESTILENCE **b** : a virulent contagious febrile disease that is caused by a bacterium (*Yersinia pestis*) and that occurs in several forms — called also *black death* **3 a** : a cause of irritation : NUISANCE **b** : a sudden unwelcome outbreak ⟨a ~ of burglaries⟩

[2]**plague** *vt* **plagued; plagu·ing** (15c) **1** : to smite, infest, or afflict with or as if with disease, calamity, or natural evil **2 a** : to cause worry or distress to : HAMPER, BURDEN **b** : to disturb or annoy persistently ***syn*** see WORRY — **plagu·er** *n*

plagu·ey *or* **plaguy** \'plā-gē, 'pleg-ē\ *adj, chiefly dial* (1615) : causing irritation or annoyance : TROUBLESOME — **plaguey** *adv* — **plagu·i·ly** \'plā-gə-lē, 'pleg-ə-\ *adv*

plaice \'plās\ *n, pl* **plaice** [ME *plaice,* fr. MF *plaïs,* fr. LL *platensis*] (14c) : any of various flatfishes; *esp* : a large European flounder (*Pleuronectes platessa*)

plaid \'plad\ *n* [ScGael *plaide*] (1512) **1** : a rectangular length of tartan worn over the left shoulder as part of the Scottish national costume **2 a** : a twilled woolen fabric with a tartan pattern **b** : a fabric with a pattern of tartan or an imitation of tartan **3 a** : TARTAN 1 **b** : a pattern of unevenly spaced repeated stripes crossing at right angles — **plaid** *adj* — **plaid·ed** \-əd\ *adj*

[1]**plain** \'plān\ *vi* [ME *plainen,* fr. OF *plaindre,* fr. L *plangere* lament — more at PLAINT] *archaic* (13c) : COMPLAIN

[2]**plain** *n* [ME, fr. OF, fr. L *planum,* fr. neut. of *planus* flat, plain — more at FLOOR] (13c) **1 a** : an extensive area of level or rolling treeless country **b** : a broad unbroken expanse **2** : something free from artifice, ornament, or extraneous matter

[3]**plain** *adj* (14c) **1** *archaic* : EVEN, LEVEL **2** : lacking ornament : UNDECORATED **3** : free of extraneous matter : PURE **4** : free of impediments to view : UNOBSTRUCTED **5 a** (1) : evident to the mind or senses : OBVIOUS ⟨it's perfectly ~ that they will resist⟩ (2) : CLEAR ⟨let me make my meaning ~⟩ **b** : marked by outspoken candor : free from duplicity or subtlety : BLUNT ⟨~ talk⟩ **6 a** : belonging to mankind in general **b** : lacking special distinction or affectation : ORDINARY **7** : characterized by simplicity : not complicated ⟨~ home-cooked meals⟩ **8** : lacking beauty or ugliness ***syn*** see COMMON, EVIDENT, FRANK — **plain·ly** *adv* — **plain·ness** \'plān-nəs\ *n*

[4]**plain** *adv* (14c) **1** : in a plain manner ⟨saw them clearly and told you ~ —*Amer. Documentation*⟩ **2** : SIMPLY, CLEARLY ⟨some people just ~ love to sew —Gloria Phillips⟩

[5]**plain** *adv* [partly fr. ME *plein* entire, complete, fr. MF, full, fr. L *plenus;* partly fr. [4]*plain* — more at FULL] (1535) : ABSOLUTELY ⟨it ~ galled me to pay fancy prices —F. R. Buckley⟩

plain·chant \'plān-,chant\ *n* [F *plain-chant,* lit., plain song] (ca. 1727) : PLAINSONG

plain·clothes \'plān-'klō(th)z\ *adj* (1866) : not wearing a uniform while on duty

plain·clothes·man \'plān-'klō(th)z-mən, -,man\ *n* (1903) : a plainclothes police officer : DETECTIVE

plain–Jane \'plān-'jān\ *adj* [fr. the name *Jane*] (1936) : not fancy or glamorous : ORDINARY

plain–laid \'plān-'lād\ *adj, of a rope* (ca. 1890) : consisting of three strands laid right-handed

Plain People *n* (1904) : members of any of various Protestant groups (as Mennonites) esp. in the U.S. who wear distinctively plain clothes and adhere to a simple and traditional style of life excluding many conveniences of modern technology (as motorcars)

Plains \'plānz\ *adj* (1697) : of or relating to No. American Indians of the Great Plains or to their culture

plain sailing *n* (1756) : easy progress over an unobstructed course

plains·man \'plānz-mən\ *n* [Great *Plains* + *man*] (1870) : an inhabitant of the plains

plain·song \'plān-,sȯŋ\ *n* (1513) **1** : GREGORIAN CHANT **2** : a liturgical chant of any of various Christian rites

plain·spo·ken \-'spō-kən\ *adj* (1678) : CANDID, FRANK — **plain·spo·ken·ness** \-kən-nəs\ *n*

plaint \'plānt\ *n* [ME, fr. MF, fr. L *planctus,* fr. *planctus,* pp. of *plangere* to strike, beat one's breast, lament; akin to OHG *fluokhōn* to curse, Gk *plēssein* to strike] (15c) **1** : LAMENTATION, WAIL **2** : PROTEST, COMPLAINT

plain·text \'plān-,tekst\ *n* (1918) : the intelligible form of an encrypted text or of its elements — compare CIPHERTEXT

plaint·ful \'plānt-fəl\ *adj* (14c) : MOURNFUL

plain·tiff \'plānt-əf\ *n* [ME *plaintif,* fr. MF, fr. *plaintif,* adj.] (15c) **1** : one who commences a personal action or lawsuit to obtain a remedy for an injury to his rights **2** : the complaining party in a litigation — compare DEFENDANT

plain·tive \'plānt-iv\ *adj* [ME *plaintif* grieving, fr. MF, fr. *plaint*] (1579) : expressive of suffering or woe : MELANCHOLY — **plain·tive·ly** *adv* — **plain·tive·ness** *n*

plain weave *n* (1888) : a weave in which the threads interlace alternately

plain–woven *adj* (ca. 1907) : made in plain weave

plais·ter \'plas-tər, 'plās-\ *var of* PLASTER

[1]**plait** \'plāt, 'plat\ *vt* (14c) **1** : PLEAT 1 **2 a** : to interweave the strands or locks of : BRAID **b** : to make by plaiting — **plait·er** *n*

[2]**plait** *n* [ME *pleit,* fr. MF, fr. (assumed) VL *plictus,* fr. *plictus,* pp. of L *plicare* to fold — more at PLY] (15c) **1** : PLEAT **2** : a braid of material (as hair or straw); *specif* : PIGTAIL

plait·ing *n* (15c) : the interlacing of strands : BRAIDING

[1]**plan** \'plan\ *n* [F, plane, foundation, ground plan; partly fr. L *planum* level ground, fr. neut. of *planus* level; partly fr. F *planter* to plant, fix in place, fr. LL *plantare* — more at FLOOR, PLANT] (1678) **1** : a drawing or diagram drawn on a plane: as **a** : a top or horizontal view of an object **b** : a large-scale map of a small area **2 a** : a method for achieving an end **b** : an often customary method of doing something : PROCEDURE **c** : a detailed formulation of a program of action **d** : GOAL, AIM **3** : an orderly arrangement of parts of an overall design or objective **4** : a detailed program (as for payment or the provision of some service) ⟨pension~⟩ — **plan·less** \-ləs\ *adj* — **plan·less·ly** *adv* — **plan·less·ness** *n*

syn PLAN, DESIGN, PLOT, SCHEME, PROJECT mean a method devised for making or doing something or achieving an end. PLAN always implies mental formulation and sometimes graphic representation; DESIGN often suggests a particular pattern and some degree of achieved order or harmony; PLOT implies a laying out in clearly distinguished sections with attention to their relations and proportions; SCHEME stresses calculation of the end in view and may apply to a plan motivated by craftiness and self-interest; PROJECT often stresses imaginative scope and vision.

[2]**plan** *vb* **planned; plan·ning** *vt* (1728) **1** : to arrange the parts of : DESIGN **2** : to devise or project the realization or achievement of ⟨~ a program⟩ **3** : to have in mind : INTEND ~ *vi* : to make plans — **plan·ner** *n*

[1]**plan-** *or* **plano-** *comb form* [prob. fr. NL, fr. Gk, wandering, fr. *planos;* akin to Gk *planasthai* to wander — more at PLANET] : moving about : motile ⟨*plano*blast⟩

[2]**plan-** *or* **plano-** *comb form* [L *planus*] **1** : flat ⟨*plano*sol⟩ **2** : flatly ⟨*plano*spiral⟩ **3** : flat and ⟨*plano*-concave⟩

pla·nar \'plā-nər, -,när\ *adj* (1850) **1** : of, relating to, or lying in a plane **2** : two-dimensional in quality — **pla·nar·i·ty** \plā-'nar-ət-ē\ *n*

pla·nar·ia \plə-'nar-ē-ə, -'ner-\ *n* [NL *Planaria,* fr. fem. of LL *planarius* lying on a plane, fr. L *planum* plane] (ca. 1909) : PLANARIAN; *esp* : any of a genus (*Planaria*) of 2-eyed planarian worms

pla·nar·i·an \-ē-ən\ *n* [NL *Planaria*] (ca. 1858) : any of a family (Planariidae) or order (Tricladida) of small soft-bodied ciliated mostly aquatic turbellarian worms

pla·na·tion \plā-'nā-shən\ *n* (1877) : the condition or process of becoming flattened; *esp* : mechanical erosion producing smoothed or flattened surfaces

plan·chet \'plan-chət\ *n* [dim. of *planch* (flat plate)] (1611) **1** : a metal disk to be stamped as a coin **2** : a small metal or plastic disk

plan·chette \plan-'shet\ *n* [F, fr. dim. of *planche* plank, fr. L *planca*] (1860) : a small triangular or heart-shaped board supported on casters at two points and a vertical pencil at a third and believed to produce automatic writing when lightly touched by the fingers; *also* : a similar board without a pencil

Planck's constant \'plaŋ(k)s-, 'pläŋ(k)s-\ *n* [Max K.E.L. *Planck*] (1910) : a constant *h* that gives the unvarying ratio of the frequency of radiation to its quanta of energy and that has an approximate value of 6.625 × 10^{-27} erg second (gcm^2 per second)

¹plane \'plān\ *vb* **planed; plan·ing** [ME *planen,* fr. MF *planer,* fr. LL *planare,* fr. L *planus* level — more at FLOOR] *vt* (14c) **1 a :** to make smooth or even : LEVEL **b :** to make plane by use of a plane ⟨*planed* the sides of the door⟩ **2 :** to remove by planing — often used with *away* or *off* ~ *vi* **1 :** to work with a plane **2 :** to do the work of a plane — **plan·er** *n*

²plane *n* [ME, fr. MF, fr. L *platanus,* fr. Gk *platanos;* akin to Gk *platys* broad — more at PLACE] (14c) : any of a genus (*Platanus* of the family Platanaceae, the plane-tree family) of trees with large palmately lobed leaves and flowers in globose heads — called also *buttonwood, plane tree, sycamore*

³plane *n* [ME, fr. MF, fr. LL *plana,* fr. *planare*] (15c) : a tool for smoothing or shaping a wood surface

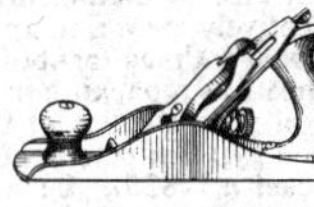

plane

⁴plane *n* [L *planum,* fr. neut. of *planus* level] (1570) **1 a :** a surface of such nature that a straight line joining two of its points lies wholly in the surface **b :** a flat or level surface **2 :** a level of existence, consciousness, or development ⟨on the intellectual ~⟩ **3 a :** one of the main supporting surfaces of an airplane **b** [by shortening] **:** AIRPLANE

⁵plane *adj* [L *planus*] (1570) **1 :** having no elevations or depressions : FLAT **2 a :** of, relating to, or dealing with geometric planes **b :** lying in a plane ⟨a ~ curve⟩ ***syn*** see LEVEL

⁶plane *vi* **planed; plan·ing** [F *planer,* fr. *plan* plane; fr. the plane formed by the wings of a soaring bird] (1611) **1 a :** to fly while keeping the wings motionless **b :** to skim across the surface of the water **2 :** to travel by airplane

plane angle *n* (1570) : an angle formed by two intersecting lines each of which lies on a face of a dihedral angle and is perpendicular to the edge of the face

plane geometry *n* (1747) : a branch of elementary geometry that deals with plane figures

plane·load \'plān-'lōd\ *n* (1941) : a load that fills an airplane

pla·ner tree \'plā-nər-\ *n* [J. J. *Planer* †1789 Ger. botanist] (ca. 1810) : a small-leaved No. American tree (*Planera aquatica*) of the elm family with an oval ribbed fruit

plan·et \'plan-ət\ *n* [ME *planete,* fr. OF, fr. LL *planeta,* modif. of Gk *planēt-, planēs,* lit., wanderer, fr. *planasthai* to wander; akin to ON *flana* to rush around] (13c) **1 a :** any of the seven celestial bodies sun, moon, Venus, Jupiter, Mars, Mercury, and Saturn that in ancient belief have motions of their own among the fixed stars **b (1) :** one of the bodies except a comet, asteroid, or satellite that revolves around the sun in the solar system **(2) :** a similar body associated with another star **c :** EARTH — usu. used with *the* **2 :** a celestial body held to influence the fate of human beings **3 :** a person or thing of great importance : LUMINARY

PLANETS

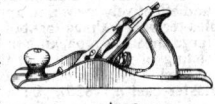

SYMBOL	NAME	MEAN DISTANCE FROM THE SUN astronomical units	million miles	PERIOD OF REVOLUTION IN DAYS OR YEARS	EQUATORIAL DIAMETER IN MILES
☿	Mercury	0.387	36.0	87.97 d.	3,031
♀	Venus	0.723	67.2	224.70 d.	7,521
⊕	Earth	1.000	92.9	365.26 d.	7,926
♂	Mars	1.524	141.5	686.98 d.	4,216
♃	Jupiter	5.203	483.4	11.86 y.	88,700
♄	Saturn	9.569	889.0	29.46 y.	74,500
⛢	Uranus	19.309	1793.8	84.01 y.	31,600
♆	Neptune	30.284	2813.4	164.79 y.	30,200
♇	Pluto	39.781	3695.7	247.69 y.	1,900

plane table *n* (1607) : an instrument that consists essentially of a drawing board on a tripod with a ruler pointed at the object observed and is used for plotting the lines of a survey directly from the observation

plan·e·tar·i·um \,plan-ə-'ter-ē-əm\ *n, pl* **-i·ums** *or* **-ia** \-ē-ə\ (1860) **1 :** a model or representation of the solar system **2 a :** an optical device for projecting various celestial images and effects **b :** a building or room housing such a projector

plan·e·tary \'plan-ə-,ter-ē\ *adj* (1607) **1 a :** of, relating to, or being a planet **b :** ERRATIC, WANDERING **c :** having a motion like that of a planet ⟨~ electrons⟩ **d :** IMMENSE ⟨the scope of this project has reached ~ proportions⟩ **2 a :** of, relating to, or belonging to the earth : TERRESTRIAL **b :** GLOBAL, WORLDWIDE **3 :** having or consisting of an epicyclic train of gear wheels

plan·e·tes·i·mal \,plan-ə-'tes-ə-məl, -'tez-\ *n* [*planet* + *-esimal* (as in *infinitesimal*)] (1903) : one of numerous small solid celestial bodies that may have existed at an early stage of the development of the solar system

planetesimal hypothesis *n* (1904) : a hypothesis in astronomy: the planets have evolved by aggregation from planetesimals

plan·e·toid \'plan-ə-,tȯid\ *n* (1803) **1 :** a body resembling a planet **2 :** ASTEROID — **plan·e·toi·dal** \,plan-ə-'tȯid-ᵊl\ *adj*

plan·e·tol·o·gy \,plan-ə-'täl-ə-jē\ *n, pl* **-gies** (1907) : a study that deals with the condensed matter (as the planets, natural satellites, comets, and meteorites) of the solar system — **plan·e·to·log·i·cal** \,plan-ət-ᵊl-'äj-i-kəl\ *adj* — **plan·e·tol·o·gist** \,plan-ə-'täl-ə-jəst\ *n*

plan·et–strick·en \'plan-ət-,strik-ən\ *or* **plan·et–struck** \-,strək\ *adj* (1600) **1** *archaic* : affected by the influence of a planet **2** *archaic* : PANIC-STRICKEN

planet wheel *n* (ca. 1827) : a gear wheel that revolves around the wheel with which it meshes in an epicyclic train

plan·form \'plan-,fȯrm\ *n* (1908) : the contour of an object (as an airplane) as viewed from above

plan·gen·cy \'plan-jən-sē\ *n* (1858) : the quality or state of being plangent

plan·gent \-jənt\ *adj* [L *plangent-, plangens,* prp. of *plangere* to strike, lament — more at PLAINT] (1858) **1 :** having a loud reverberating sound **2 :** having an expressive and esp. plaintive quality — **plan·gent·ly** *adv*

pla·nim·e·ter \plā-'nim-ət-ər, plə-\ *n* [F *planimètre,* fr. L *planum* plane + F *-mètre* -meter] (ca. 1858) : an instrument for measuring the area of a plane figure by tracing its boundary line

pla·ni·met·ric \,plā-nə-'me-trik\ *adj* (ca. 1828) **1 :** of, relating to, or made by means of a planimeter ⟨~ measurements⟩ **2** *of a map* : having no indications of relief

plan·ish \'plan-ish\ *vt* [MF *planiss-,* stem of *planir* to make smooth, fr. *plan* level, fr. L *planus*] (1688) : to toughen and finish (metal) by hammering lightly — **plan·ish·er** *n*

pla·ni·sphere \'plā-nə-,sfi(ə)r\ *n* [ME *planisperie,* fr. ML *planisphaerium,* fr. L *planum* plane + *sphaera* sphere] (14c) : a representation of the circles of the sphere on a plane; *esp* : a polar projection of the celestial sphere and the stars on a plane with adjustable circles or other appendages for showing celestial phenomena for any given time — **pla·ni·spher·ic** \,plā-nə-'sfi(ə)r-ik, -'sfer-\ *adj*

¹plank \'plaŋk\ *n* [ME, fr. ONF *planke,* fr. L *planca*] (14c) **1 a :** a heavy thick board; *specif* : one 2 to 4 inches (5.1 to 10 centimeters) thick and at least 8 inches (20 centimeters) wide **b :** an object made of a plank or planking **c :** PLANKING **2 a :** an article in the platform of a political party ⟨insisted on a strong civil rights ~⟩ **b :** a principal item of a policy or program

²plank *vt* (15c) **1 :** to cover or floor with planks **2 :** SET DOWN 1,2 **3 :** to cook and serve on a board usu. with an elaborate garnish

plank·ing *n* (15c) **1 :** the act or process of covering or fitting with planks **2 :** a quantity of planks

plank·ter \'plaŋ(k)-tər\ *n* [Gk *planktēr* wanderer, fr. *plazesthai*] (ca. 1935) : a planktonic organism

plank·ton \'plaŋ(k)-tən, -,tän\ *n* [G, fr. Gk, neut. of *planktos* drifting, fr. *plazesthai* to wander, drift, pass. of *plazein* to drive astray; akin to L *plangere* to strike — more at PLAINT] (1889) : the passively floating or weakly swimming usu. minute animal and plant life of a body of water — **plank·ton·ic** \plaŋ(k)-'tän-ik\ *adj*

Planned Parenthood *service mark* — used for research and dissemination of information on family planning

plan·ning *n* (1748) : the act or process of making or carrying out plans; *specif* : the establishment of goals, policies, and procedures for a social or economic unit ⟨city ~⟩ ⟨business ~⟩

plano- — see PLAN-

pla·no–con·cave \,plā-nō-(,)kän-'kāv, -'kän-,\ *adj* (1693) : flat on one side and concave on the other

pla·no–con·vex \-(,)kän-'veks, -'kän-,, -kən-'\ *adj* (1665) : flat on one side and convex on the other

pla·nog·ra·phy \plā-'näg-rə-fē, plə-\ *n* (ca. 1909) : a process (as lithography) for printing from a plane surface — **pla·no·graph·ic** \,plā-nə-'graf-ik\ *adj*

pla·no·sol \'plā-nə-,säl, -,sȯl\ *n* [²*plan-* + L *solum* ground, soil] (ca. 1938) : any of an intrazonal group of soils that have a strongly leached upper layer over a compacted clay or silt and occur on smooth flat uplands

plan position indicator *n* (1932) : PPI

¹plant \'plant\ *vb* [ME *planten,* fr. OE *plantian,* fr. LL *plantare* to plant, fix in place, fr. L, to plant, fr. *planta* plant] *vt* (bef. 12c) **1 a :** to put or set in the ground for growth ⟨~ seeds⟩ **b :** to set or sow with seeds or plants **c :** IMPLANT **2 a :** ESTABLISH, INSTITUTE **b :** COLONIZE, SETTLE **c :** to place (animals) in a new locality **d :** to stock with animals **3 a :** to place in or on the ground **b :** to place firmly or forcibly ⟨~*ed* a hard blow on his chin⟩ **4 a :** CONCEAL **b :** to covertly place for discovery, publication, or dissemination ~ *vi* : to plant something — **plant·able** \-ə-bəl\ *adj*

²plant *n* [ME *plante,* fr. OE, fr. L *planta*] (bef. 12c) **1 a :** a young tree, vine, shrub, or herb planted or suitable for planting **b :** any of a kingdom (Plantae) of living beings typically lacking locomotive movement or obvious nervous or sensory organs and possessing cellulose cell walls **2 a :** the land, buildings, machinery, apparatus, and fixtures employed in carrying on a trade or an industrial business **b :** a factory or workshop for the manufacture of a particular product **c :** the total facilities available for production or service **d :** the buildings and other physical equipment of an institution ⟨the school ~⟩ **3 :** an act of planting **4 :** something or someone planted ⟨left muddy footprints as a ~ to confuse the police⟩ — **plant·like** \-,līk\ *adj*

Plan·tag·e·net \plan-'taj-(ə-)nət\ *adj* [*Plantagenet,* nickname of the family adopted as surname] (1868) : of or relating to the English royal house that ruled from 1154 to 1399 — **Plantagenet** *n*

¹plan·tain \'plant-ᵊn\ *n* [ME, fr. OF, fr. L *plantagin-, plantago,* fr. *planta* sole of the foot; fr. its broad leaves — more at PLACE] (13c) : any of a genus (*Plantago* of the family Plantaginaceae, the plantain family) of short-stemmed elliptic-leaved herbs with spikes of minute greenish flowers

²plantain *n* [Sp *plántano, plátano* plane tree, banana tree, fr. ML *plantanus* plane tree, alter. of L *platanus* — more at PLANE] (1555) **1 :** a banana plant (*Musa paradisiaca*) **2 :** the angular greenish starchy fruit of the plantain that is a staple food in the tropics when cooked

plantain lily *n* (1882) : a plant (genus *Hosta*) of the lily family with plaited basal leaves and racemose white or violet flowers

plan·tar \'plant-ər, 'plan-,tär\ *adj* [L *plantaris,* fr. *planta* sole — more at PLACE] (ca. 1706) : of or relating to the sole of the foot

plan·ta·tion \plan-'tā-shən\ *n* (1569) **1 :** a usu. large group of plants and esp. trees under cultivation **2 :** a settlement in a new country or region : COLONY ⟨Plymouth *Plantation*⟩ **3 a :** a place that is planted or under cultivation **b :** an agricultural estate usu. worked by resident labor

plant·er \'plant-ər\ *n* (14c) **1 :** one that cultivates plants: as **a :** FARMER **b :** one who owns or operates a plantation **2 :** one who settles or founds a place and esp. a new colony **3 :** a container in which ornamental plants are grown
planter's punch *n* (1924) **:** a punch of rum, lime or lemon juice, sugar, water, and sometimes bitters
plant food *n* (1869) **1 :** FOOD 1b **2 :** FERTILIZER
plant hormone *n* (1935) **:** an organic substance other than a nutrient that in minute amounts modifies a plant physiological process; *esp* **:** one produced by a plant and active elsewhere than at the site of production
plan·ti·grade \'plant-ə-,grād\ *adj* [F, fr. L *planta* sole + F *-grade*] (1831) **:** walking on the sole with the heel touching the ground ⟨man is a ~ animal⟩ — **plantigrade** *n*
plant·ing *n* (1632) **1 :** PLANTATION 1 **2 :** an area where plants are grown for commercial or decorative purposes
plant kingdom *n* (1884) **:** the one of the three basic groups of natural objects that includes all living and extinct plants — compare ANIMAL KINGDOM, MINERAL KINGDOM
plant·let \'plant-lət\ *n* (1816) **:** a small or young plant
plant louse *n* (1805) **:** APHID; *also* **:** any of various small insects (as a jumping plant louse) of similar habits
plan·toc·ra·cy \plan-'täk-rə-sē\ *n* [*planter* + *-o-* + *-cracy*] (ca. 1846) **1 :** a ruling class made up of planters **2 :** government by planters
plan·u·la \'plan-yə-lə\ *n, pl* **-lae** \-,lē, -,lī\ [NL, fr. L *planus* level, flat — more at FLOOR] (1870) **:** the very young usu. flattened oval or oblong free-swimming ciliated larva of a coelenterate
plaque \'plak\ *n* [F, fr. MF, metal sheet, fr. *plaquier* to plate, fr. MD *placken* to piece, patch; akin to MD *placke* piece, MHG *placke* patch] (1848) **1 a :** an ornamental brooch; *esp* **:** the badge of an honorary order **b :** a flat thin piece (as of metal) used for decoration **c :** a commemorative or identifying inscribed tablet **2 a :** a localized abnormal patch on a body part or surface **b :** a film of mucus that harbors bacteria on a tooth **c :** an atherosclerotic lesion **3 :** a clear area in a bacterial culture produced by destruction of cells by a virus
¹plash \'plash\ *n* [prob. imit.] (1513) **:** SPLASH
²plash *vt* (1582) **:** to break the surface of (water) **:** SPLASH ~ *vi* **:** to cause a splashing or spattering effect
-pla·sia \'plā-zh(ē-)ə\ *or* **-pla·sy** \,plā-sē, ,plas-ē, p-lə-sē\ *n comb form* [NL *-plasia*, fr. Gk *plasis* molding, fr. *plassein*] **:** development **:** formation ⟨hyper*plasia*⟩ ⟨homo*plasy*⟩
plasm \'plaz-əm\ *n* [LL *plasma* something molded] (1747) **:** PLASMA
plasm- *or* **plasmo-** *comb form* [F, fr. NL *plasma*] **:** plasma ⟨*plasmo*dium⟩ ⟨*plasmo*lysis⟩
-plasm \,plaz-əm\ *n comb form* [G *-plasma*, fr. NL *plasma*] **:** formative or formed material (as of a cell or tissue) ⟨endo*plasm*⟩
plas·ma \'plaz-mə\ *n* [G, fr. LL, something molded, fr. Gk, fr. *plassein* to mold; akin to L *planus* level, flat — more at FLOOR] (1772) **1 :** a green faintly translucent quartz **2** [NL, fr. LL] **a :** the fluid part of blood, lymph, or milk as distinguished from suspended material **b :** the juice that can be expressed from muscle **3 :** PROTOPLASM **4 :** a collection of charged particles (as in the atmospheres of stars or in a metal) containing about equal numbers of positive ions and electrons and exhibiting some properties of a gas but differing from a gas in being a good conductor of electricity and in being affected by a magnetic field — **plas·mat·ic** \plaz-'mat-ik\ *adj*
plasma cell *n* (1888) **:** a lymphocyte that is a mature antibody-secreting B cell
plas·ma·gel \'plaz-mə-,jel\ *n* (1923) **:** gelated protoplasm; *esp* **:** the outer firm zone of a pseudopodium
plas·ma·gene \-,jēn\ *n* [ISV] (1939) **:** an extranuclear determiner of hereditary characteristics with a capacity for replication similar to that of a nuclear gene
plasma jet *n* (1957) **:** a stream of very hot ionized plasma; *also* **:** a device for producing such a stream
plas·ma·lem·ma \,plaz-mə-'lem-ə\ *n* [NL, fr. *plasma* + Gk *lemma* husk — more at LEMMA] (1923) **:** the differentiated protoplasmic surface bounding a cell
plasma membrane *n* (1900) **:** a semipermeable limiting layer of cell protoplasm — see CELL illustration
plas·ma·pher·e·sis \,plaz-mə-'fer-ə-səs\ *n* [NL, fr. *plasma* + Gk *aphairesis* taking off — more at APHAERESIS] (1914) **:** a process in which blood constituents and esp. red blood cells are separated from the plasma of a blood donor or patient and returned to his circulatory system
plas·ma·sol \'plaz-mə-,säl, -,sȯl, -,sōl\ *n* (1923) **:** solated protoplasm; *esp* **:** the inner fluid zone of a pseudopodium or amoeboid cell
plasma torch *n* (1959) **:** a device that heats a gas by electrical means to form a plasma for high-temperature operations (as melting metal)
plas·mid \'plaz-məd\ *n* [*plasma* + ²*-id*] (1952) **:** an extrachromosomal ring of DNA that replicates autonomously in bacteria
plas·min \-mən\ *n* (ca. 1866) **:** a proteolytic enzyme that dissolves the fibrin of blood clots
plas·min·o·gen \plaz-'min-ə-jən\ *n* (1945) **:** the precursor of plasmin that is found in blood plasma and serum
plas·mo·des·ma \,plaz-mə-'dez-mə\ *also* **plas·mo·desm** \'plaz-mə-,dez-əm\ *n, pl* **-des·ma·ta** \-'dez-mət-ə\ *or* **-des·mas** \-'dez-məz\ [NL *plasmodesma*, fr. *plasma* + Gk *desmat-*, *desma* bond, fr. *dein* to bind — more at DIADEM] (ca. 1923) **:** one of the cytoplasmic strands that pass through openings in some plant cell walls and provide living bridges between cells
plas·mo·di·um \plaz-'mōd-ē-əm\ *n, pl* **-dia** \-ē-ə\ [NL, fr. *plasm-* + *-odium* thing resembling, fr. Gk *-ōdēs* like] (1875) **1 a :** a motile multinucleate mass of protoplasm resulting from fusion of uninucleate amoeboid cells; *also* **:** an organism (as a stage of a slime mold) that consists of such a structure **b :** SYNCYTIUM 1 **2 :** an individual malaria parasite
plas·mog·a·my \plaz-'mäg-ə-mē\ *n* [ISV] (1912) **:** fusion of the cytoplasm of two or more cells as distinguished from fusion of nuclei
plas·mol·y·sis \plaz-'mäl-ə-səs\ *n* [NL] (1883) **:** shrinking of the cytoplasm away from the wall of a living cell due to outward osmotic flow of water to a medium more concentrated than the protoplasm — **plas·mo·lyt·ic** \,plaz-mə-'lit-ik\ *adj*
plas·mo·lyze \'plaz-mə-,līz\ *vb* **-lyzed; -lyz·ing** *vt* (1883) **:** to subject to plasmolysis ~ *vi* **:** to undergo plasmolysis
-plast \,plast\ *n comb form* [MF *-plaste* thing molded, fr. LL *-plastus*, fr. Gk *-plastos*, fr. *plastos* molded, fr. *plassein*] **:** organized particle or granule **:** cell ⟨chromo*plast*⟩
¹plas·ter \'plas-tər\ *n* [ME, fr. OE, fr. L *emplastrum*, fr. Gk *emplastron*, fr. *emplassein* to plaster on, fr. *en-* + *plassein* to mold, plaster; akin to L *planus* level, flat — more at FLOOR] (bef. 12c) **1 :** a medicated or protective dressing that consists of a film (as of cloth or plastic) spread with a usu. medicated substance ⟨adhesive ~⟩; *broadly* **:** something applied to heal and soothe **2 :** a pasty composition (as of lime, water, and sand) that hardens on drying and is used for coating walls, ceilings, and partitions — **plas·tery** \-t(ə-)rē\ *adj*
²plaster *vb* **plas·tered; plas·ter·ing** \-t(ə-)riŋ\ *vt* (14c) **1 :** to overlay or cover with plaster **:** COAT **2 :** to apply a plaster to **3 a :** to cover over or conceal as if with a coat of plaster **b :** to apply as a coating or incrustation **c :** to smooth down with a sticky or shiny substance ⟨~*ed* his hair down⟩ **4 :** to fasten or apply tightly to another surface **5 :** to treat with plaster of paris **6 :** to affix to or place on esp. conspicuously or in quantity **7 :** to inflict heavy damage, injury, or casualties on esp. by a concentrated or unremitting attack **:** strike heavily and effectively ~ *vi* **:** to apply plaster — **plas·ter·er** \-tər-ər\ *n*
plas·ter·board \'plas-tər-,bō(ə)rd, -,bȯ(ə)rd\ *n* (1906) **:** a board used in large sheets as a backing or as a substitute for plaster in walls and consisting of several plies of fiberboard, paper, or felt usu. bonded to a hardened gypsum plaster core
plaster cast *n* (1825) **1 :** a sculptor's model in plaster of paris **2 :** a rigid dressing of gauze impregnated with plaster of paris
plas·tered \'plas-tərd\ *adj* (1902) **:** DRUNK, INTOXICATED
plas·ter·ing *n* (15c) **1 :** a coating of or as if of plaster **2 :** a decisive defeat
plaster of par·is \-'par-əs\ *often cap 2d P* [*Paris*, France] (15c) **:** a white powdery slightly hydrated calcium sulfate $CaSO_4 \cdot {}^1\!/_2H_2O$ or $2CaSO_4 \cdot H_2O$ made by calcining gypsum and used chiefly for casts and molds in the form of a quick-setting paste with water
plas·ter·work \'plas-tər-,wərk\ *n* (1600) **:** plastering used to finish architectural constructions
¹plas·tic \'plas-tik\ *adj* [L *plasticus* of molding, fr. Gk *plastikos*, fr. *plassein* to mold, form] (1632) **1 :** FORMATIVE, CREATIVE ⟨~ forces in nature⟩ **2 a :** capable of being molded or modeled ⟨~ clay⟩ **b :** capable of adapting to varying conditions **:** PLIABLE ⟨ecologically ~ animals⟩ **3 :** SCULPTURAL **4 :** made or consisting of a plastic **5 :** capable of being deformed continuously and permanently in any direction without rupture **6 :** of, relating to, or involving plastic surgery **7 :** formed by or adapted to an artificial or conventional standard; *esp* **:** not genuine or sincere **:** SYNTHETIC ⟨this is the ~ age, the era of the sham and the bogus — Logan Gourlay⟩
syn PLASTIC, PLIABLE, PLIANT, DUCTILE, MALLEABLE, ADAPTABLE mean susceptible of being modified in form or nature. PLASTIC applies to substances soft enough to be molded yet capable of hardening into the desired fixed form; PLIABLE suggests something easily bent, folded, twisted, or manipulated; PLIANT may stress flexibility and sometimes connote springiness and so lack some of the suggestion of submissiveness found in PLIABLE; DUCTILE applies to what can be drawn out or extended with ease; MALLEABLE applies to what may be pressed or beaten into shape; ADAPTABLE implies the capability of being easily modified to suit other conditions, needs, or uses.
²plastic *n* (ca. 1909) **:** a plastic substance; *specif* **:** any of numerous organic synthetic or processed materials that are mostly thermoplastic or thermosetting polymers of high molecular weight and that can be molded, cast, extruded, drawn, or laminated into objects, films, or filaments — often used in pl. with sing. constr.
-plas·tic \'plas-tik\ *adj comb form* [Gk *-plastikos*, fr. *plassein*] **1 :** developing **:** forming ⟨thrombo*plastic*⟩ **2 :** of or relating to (something designated by a term ending in *-plasm*, *-plast*, *-plasty*, or *-plasy*) ⟨homo*plastic*⟩ ⟨neo*plastic*⟩
plas·ti·cal·ly \'plas-ti-k(ə-)lē\ *adv* (1835) **1 :** in a plastic manner **2 :** with respect to plastic qualities
plastic art *n* (ca. 1904) **1 :** art (as sculpture or bas-relief) characterized by modeling **:** three-dimensional art **2 :** one of the visual arts (as painting, sculpture, or film) esp. as distinguished from those that are written (as poetry or music)
plastic foam *n* (1943) **:** EXPANDED PLASTIC
plas·tic·i·ty \pla-'stis-ət-ē\ *n* (ca. 1782) **1 :** the quality or state of being plastic; *esp* **:** capacity for being molded or altered **2 :** the ability to retain a shape attained by pressure deformation **3 :** the capacity of organisms with the same genotype to vary in developmental pattern, in phenotype, or in behavior according to varying environmental conditions
plas·ti·cize \'plas-tə-,sīz\ *vt* **-cized; -ciz·ing** (1919) **1 :** to make plastic **2 :** to treat with a plastic ⟨a *plasticized* mattress cover⟩ — **plas·ti·ci·za·tion** \,plas-tə-sə-'zā-shən\ *n*
plas·ti·ciz·er \'plas-tə-,sī-zər\ *n* (1925) **:** one that plasticizes; *specif* **:** a chemical added esp. to rubbers and resins to impart flexibility, workability, or stretchability
plastic surgeon *n* (1946) **:** a specialist in plastic surgery
plastic surgery *n* (1842) **:** a branch of surgery concerned with the repair, restoration, or improvement of lost, injured, defective, or misshapen body parts
plas·tid \'plas-təd\ *n* [G, fr. Gk *plastos* molded] (1885) **:** any of various cytoplasmic organelles of photosynthetic cells that serve in many cases as centers of special metabolic activities — **plas·tid·i·al** \pla-'stid-ē-əl\ *adj*
plas·ti·sol \'plas-tə-,säl, -,sȯl\ *n* [*plastic* + ⁴*sol*] (1946) **:** a substance consisting of a mixture of a resin and a plasticizer that can be molded, cast, or made into a continuous film by application of heat
plas·to·cy·a·nin \,plas-tō-'sī-ə-nən\ *n* [Gk *plastos* + E *cyan-* + *-in*] (1961) **:** a copper-containing protein that acts as an intermediary in photosynthetic electron transport
plas·to·gene \'plas-tə-,jēn\ *n* [*plastid* + *-o-* + *-gene*] (1937) **:** a hereditary determinant in a plant cell plastid
plas·to·qui·none \,plas-(,)tō-kwin-'ōn, -'kwin-,ōn\ *n* [*plasto-* (fr. Gk *plastos* molded) + *quinone* — more at -PLAST] (1958) **:** a plant substance that is related to vitamin K and plays a role in photosynthetic phosphorylation
plas·tral \'plas-trəl\ *adj* (1889) **:** of or relating to a plastron

plas·tron \'plas-trən\ *n* [MF, fr. OIt *piastrone,* aug. of *piastra* thin metal plate — more at PIASTER] (ca. 1506) **1 a :** a metal breastplate formerly worn under the hauberk **b :** a quilted pad worn in fencing practice to protect the chest, waist, and the side on which the weapon is held **2 :** the ventral part of the shell of a tortoise or turtle consisting typically of nine symmetrically placed bones overlaid by horny plates **3 a :** a trimming like a bib for a woman's dress **b :** DICKEY 1a **4 :** a thin film of air held by water-repellent hairs of some aquatic insects

-plas·ty \,plas-tē\ *n comb form* [F *-plastie,* fr. LGk *-plastia* molding, fr. Gk *-plastēs* molder, fr. *plassein*] **:** plastic surgery ⟨osteo*plasty*⟩

-plasy — see -PLASIA

[1]plat \'plat\ *vt* **plat·ted; plat·ting** [ME *platen,* alter. of *plaiten*] (14c) **:** PLAIT

[2]plat *n* (1535) **:** PLAIT

[3]plat *n* [prob. alter. of *plot*] (1517) **1 :** a small piece of ground (as a lot or quadrat) **:** PLOT **2 :** a plan, map, or chart of a piece of land with actual or proposed features (as lots); *also* **:** the land represented

[4]plat *vt* **plat·ted; plat·ting** (1751) **:** to make a plat of

plat·an \'plat-ᵊn\ *n* [ME, fr. L *platanus*] (14c) **:** [2]PLANE

plat du jour \,pläd-ə-'zhü(ə)r, ,plad-\ *n, pl* **plats du jour** *same*\ [F, lit., plate of the day] (1906) **:** a dish that is featured by a restaurant on a particular day

[1]plate \'plāt\ *n* [ME, fr. OF, fr. *plate,* fem. of *plat* flat, fr. (assumed) VL *plattus,* prob. fr. Gk *platys* broad, flat — more at PLACE] (13c) **1 a :** a smooth flat thin piece of material **b** (1) **:** forged, rolled, or cast metal in sheets usu. thicker than ¼ inch (2) **:** a very thin layer of metal deposited on a surface of base metal by plating **c :** one of the broad metal pieces used in armor; *also* **:** armor of such plates **d** (1) **:** a lamina or plaque (as of bone or horn) that forms part of an animal body; *esp* **:** SCUTE (2) **:** the thin under portion of the forequarter of beef; *esp* **:** the fatty back part — see BEEF illustration **e :** HOME PLATE **f :** any of the huge movable segments into which the earth's crust is divided and which are held to float on and travel over the mantle **2** [ME; partly fr. OF *plate* plate, piece of silver; partly fr. OSp *plata* silver, fr. (assumed) VL *plattus* flat] **a** *obs* **:** a silver coin **b :** precious metal; *esp* **:** silver bullion **3** [ME, fr. MF *plat* dish, plate, fr. *plat* flat] **a :** domestic hollowware made of or plated with gold, silver, or base metals **b :** a shallow usu. circular vessel from which food is eaten or served **c** (1) **:** PLATEFUL (2) **:** a main course served on a plate (3) **:** food and service supplied to one person ⟨a dinner at $10 a ~⟩ **d** (1) **:** a prize given to the winner in a contest (2) **:** a horse race in which the contestants compete for a prize rather than stakes **e :** a dish or pouch passed in taking collections **f :** a flat glass dish used chiefly for culturing microorganisms **4 a :** a prepared surface from which printing is done **b :** a sheet of material (as glass) coated with a light-sensitive photographic emulsion **c** (1) **:** the usu. flat or grid-formed anode of an electron tube at which electrons collect (2) **:** a metallic grid with its interstices filled with active material that forms one of the structural units of a battery **d :** LICENSE PLATE **5 :** a horizontal structural member that provides bearing and anchorage esp. for the trusses of a roof or the rafters **6 :** the part of a denture that fits to the mouth; *broadly* **:** DENTURE **7 :** a full-page illustration often on different paper from the text pages — **plate·ful** \-,fu̇l\ *n* — **plate·like** \-,līk\ *adj*

[2]plate *vt* **plat·ed; plat·ing** (14c) **1 :** to cover or equip with plate: as **a :** to arm with armor plate **b :** to cover with an adherent layer mechanically, chemically, or electrically; *also* **:** to deposit (as a layer) on a surface **2 :** to make a printing surface from or for **3 :** to fix or secure with a plate

[1]pla·teau \pla-'tō, 'pla-,\ *n, pl* **plateaus** *or* **pla·teaux** \-'tōz, -,tōz\ [F, fr. MF, platter, fr. *plat* flat] (1796) **1 a :** a usu. extensive land area having a relatively level surface raised sharply above adjacent land on at least one side **:** TABLELAND **b :** a similar undersea feature **2 a :** a region of little or no change in a graphic representation **b :** a relatively stable level, period, or condition

[2]plateau *vi* (1939) **:** to reach a level, period, or condition of stability

plate glass *n* (ca. 1727) **:** rolled, ground, and polished sheet glass

plate·let \'plāt-lət\ *n* (1895) **:** a minute flattened body (as of ice or a mineral); *esp* **:** BLOOD PLATELET

plate·mak·er \'plāt-,mā-kər\ *n* (1904) **:** a machine for making printing plates and esp. offset printing plates — **plate·mak·ing** \-kiŋ\ *n*

plat·en \'plat-ᵊn\ *n* [MF *plateine,* fr. *plate*] (1541) **1 :** a flat plate; *esp* **:** one that exerts or receives pressure **2 :** the roller of a typewriter

plat·er \'plāt-ər\ *n* (1777) **1 :** one that plates **2 a :** a horse that runs chiefly in plate races **b :** an inferior racehorse

plate rail *n* (1902) **:** a rail or narrow shelf along the upper part of a wall for holding plates or ornaments

plat·er·esque \,plat-ə-'resk\ *adj, often cap* [Sp *plateresco,* fr. *platero* silversmith, fr. *plata* silver] (ca. 1842) **:** of, relating to, or being a 16th century Spanish architectural style characterized by elaborate ornamentation suggestive of silver plate

plate tectonics *n pl but sing in constr* (1969) **:** a theory that the lithosphere of the earth is divided into a small number of plates which float on and travel independently over the mantle and that much of the earth's seismic activity occurs at the boundaries of these plates

plat·form \'plat-,fȯrm\ *n, often attrib* [MF *plate-forme* diagram, map, lit., flat form] (1574) **1 :** PLAN, DESIGN **2 :** a declaration of the principles on which a group of persons stands; *esp* **:** a declaration of principles and policies adopted by a political party or a candidate **3 a** (1) **:** a horizontal flat surface usu. higher than the adjoining area; *also* **:** a device incorporating or providing a platform (2) **:** a raised flooring (as for speakers or performers) **b :** a place or opportunity for public discussion **4 a :** a usu. thick layer (as of cork) between the inner sole and outer sole of a shoe **b :** a shoe having such a sole

platform rocker *n* (1944) **:** a chair that rocks on a stable platform

platform scale *n* (1834) **:** a weighing machine with a flat platform on which objects are weighed — called also *platform balance*

platform tennis *n* (1955) **:** a variation of paddle tennis that is played on a platform enclosed by a wire fence

platin- *or* **platino-** *comb form* [NL *platinum*] **:** platinum ⟨*platino*type⟩

[1]pla·ti·na \plə-'tē-nə\ *n* [Sp] (1750) **:** PLATINUM; *esp* **:** crude native platinum

[2]platina *adj* (1940) **:** of the color platinum

plat·ing \'plāt-iŋ\ *n* (1831) **1 :** the act or process of plating **2 a :** a coating of metal plates **b :** a thin coating of metal

pla·tin·ic \plə-'tin-ik\ *adj* (1842) **:** of, relating to, or containing platinum esp. with a valence of four — compare PLATINOUS

plat·i·nize \'plat-ᵊn-,īz\ *vt* **-nized; -niz·ing** (1825) **:** to cover, treat, or combine with platinum or a compound of platinum

plat·i·no·cy·a·nide \,plat-ᵊn-ō-'sī-ə-,nīd\ *n* (1845) **:** a fluorescent complex salt formed by the union of platinous cyanide with another cyanide

plat·i·nous \'plat-nəs, -ᵊn-əs\ *adj* (1842) **:** of, relating to, or containing platinum esp. with a valence of two — compare PLATINIC

plat·i·num \'plat-nəm, -ᵊn-əm\ *n, often attrib* [NL, fr. Sp *platina,* fr. dim. of *plata* silver, fr. (assumed) VL *plattus* plate — more at PLATE] (1812) **1 :** a heavy precious grayish white noncorroding ductile malleable metallic element that fuses with difficulty and is used esp. in chemical ware and apparatus, as a catalyst, and in dental and jewelry alloys — see ELEMENT table **2 :** a moderate gray

platinum black *n* (ca. 1847) **:** a soft dull black powder of metallic platinum obtained by reduction and precipitation from solutions of its salts and used as a catalyst

platinum blonde *n* (1931) **1 :** a person whose hair is of a pale silvery blonde color that is usu. produced by bleach and a bluish rinse **2 :** the color of the hair of a platinum blonde

plat·i·tude \'plat-ə-,t(y)üd\ *n* [F, fr. *plat* flat, dull] (1812) **1 :** the quality or state of being dull or insipid **2 :** a banal, trite, or stale remark

plat·i·tu·di·nal \,plat-ə-'t(y)üd-nəl, -ᵊn-əl\ *adj* (1870) **:** PLATITUDINOUS

plat·i·tu·di·nar·i·an \-,t(y)üd-ᵊn-'er-ē-ən\ *n* (1855) **:** one given to the use of platitudes

plat·i·tu·di·nize \-'t(y)üd-ᵊn-,īz\ *vi* **-nized; -niz·ing** [*platitudinous*] (1885) **:** to utter platitudes

plat·i·tu·di·nous \-'t(y)üd-nəs, -ᵊn-əs\ *adj* [*platitude* + *-inous* (as in *multitudinous*)] (1862) **:** having the characteristics of a platitude **:** full of platitudes ⟨~ remarks⟩ — **plat·i·tu·di·nous·ly** *adv*

pla·ton·ic \plə-'tän-ik, plā-\ *adj* [L *platonicus,* fr. Gk *platōnikos,* fr. *Platōn* Plato] (1533) **1** *cap* **:** of, relating to, or characteristic of Plato or Platonism **2 a :** relating to or based on platonic love; *also* **:** experiencing or professing platonic love **b :** NOMINAL, THEORETICAL — **pla·ton·i·cal·ly** \-i-k(ə-)lē\ *adv*

platonic love *n, often cap P* (1631) **1 :** love conceived by Plato as ascending from passion for the individual to contemplation of the universal and ideal **2 :** a close relationship between two persons in which sexual desire has been suppressed or sublimated

Pla·to·nism \'plāt-ᵊn-,iz-əm\ *n* (ca. 1570) **1 a :** the philosophy of Plato stressing esp. that actual things are copies of transcendent ideas and that these ideas are the objects of true knowledge apprehended by reminiscence **b :** NEOPLATONISM **2 :** PLATONIC LOVE — **Pla·to·nist** \-ᵊn-əst\ *n* — **Pla·to·nis·tic** \,plāt-ᵊn-'is-tik\ *adj*

Pla·to·nize \'plāt-ᵊn-,īz\ *vb* **-nized; -niz·ing** *vi* (1608) **:** to adopt, imitate, or conform to Platonic opinions ~ *vt* **:** to explain in accordance with or adapt to Platonic doctrines; *esp* **:** IDEALIZE

[1]pla·toon \plə-'tün, pla-\ *n* [F *peloton* small detachment, lit., ball, fr. MF *pelote* little ball — more at PELLET] (1637) **1 :** a subdivision of a company-size military unit normally consisting of two or more squads or sections **2 :** a group of persons sharing a common characteristic or activity ⟨a ~ of waiters⟩; *esp* **:** a group of football players who are trained for either offense or defense and are sent into or withdrawn from the game as a body

[2]platoon *vt* (1963) **:** to play (one player) alternately with another player in the same position (as on a baseball team) ~ *vi* **1 :** to alternate with another player at the same position **2 :** to use alternate players at the same position

platoon sergeant *n* (1915) **:** a noncommissioned officer in the army ranking above a staff sergeant and below a first sergeant

Platt·deutsch \'plat-,dȯich, 'plät-\ *n* [G, fr. D *Platduitsch,* lit., Low German, fr. *plat* flat, low + *duitsch* German] (1834) **:** a colloquial language of northern Germany comprising several Low German dialects

plat·ter \'plat-ər\ *n* [ME *plater,* fr. AF, fr. MF *plat* plate] (14c) **1 a :** a large plate used esp. for serving meat **b :** PLATE 3c(2) **2 :** a phonograph record — **plat·ter·ful** \-,fu̇l\ *n* — **on a platter :** without effort **:** very easily ⟨can have the presidency *on a platter* —Jonathan Daniels⟩

[1]platy \'plāt-ē\ *adj* (1533) **:** resembling a plate; *also* **:** consisting of plates or flaky layers — used chiefly of soil or mineral formations

[2]platy \'plat-ē\ *n, pl* **platy** *or* **plat·ys** *or* **plat·ies** [NL *Platypoecilus,* former genus name of the fish] (1931) **:** either of two live-bearers (*Xiphophorus maculatus* and *X. variatus* of the family Poeciliidae) that are popular for tropical aquariums and are noted for variability and brilliant color — called also *platy·fish* \-,fish\

platy·hel·minth \,plat-i-'hel-,min(t)th\ *n* [deriv. of Gk *platys* broad, flat + *helminth-, helmis* helminth] (ca. 1890) **:** any of a phylum (Platyhelminthes) of soft-bodied usu. much flattened worms (as the planarians, flukes, and tapeworms) — **platy·hel·min·thic** \-hel-'min(t)-thik, -'mint-ik\ *adj*

platy·pus \'plat-i-pəs, -,pu̇s\ *n, pl* **platy·pus·es** *also* **platy·pi** \-,pī, -,pē\ [NL, fr. Gk *platypous* flat-footed, fr. *platys* broad, flat + *pous* foot — more at PLACE, FOOT] (1832) **:** a small aquatic oviparous mammal (*Ornithorhynchus anatinus*) of southern and eastern Australia and Tasmania that has a fleshy bill resembling that of a duck, dense fur, webbed feet, and a broad flattened tail

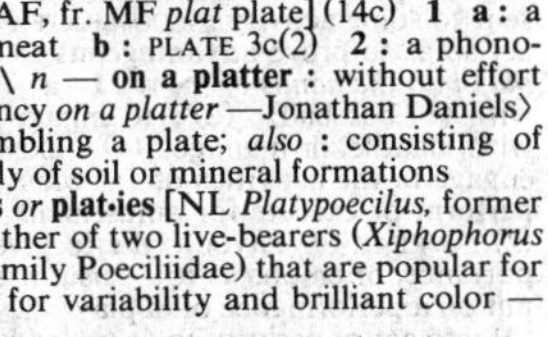

platypus

plat·yr·rhine \'plat-i-,rīn\ *adj* (1857) **1** [NL *Platyrrhina,* fr. Gk *platyrrhin-, platyrrhis* broad-nosed, fr. *platys* + *-rrhin* -rrhine] **:** of, relating to, or being any of a division (Platyrrhina) of monkeys all of which are New World monkeys and are characterized by a broad nasal septum, usu. 36 teeth, and often a prehensile tail **2** [Gk *platyrrhin-, platyrrhis*] **:** having a short broad nose — **platyrrhine** *n*

plau·dit \'plȯd-ət\ *n* [L *plaudite* applaud, pl. imper. of *plaudere* to applaud] (1624) **1 :** an act or round of applause **2 :** enthusiastic approval — usu. used in pl. ⟨received the ~*s* of the critics⟩

plau·si·bil·i·ty \ˌplȯ-zə-'bil-ət-ē\ *n, pl* **-ties** (1649) **1 :** the quality or state of being plausible **2 :** something plausible

plau·si·ble \'plȯ-zə-bəl\ *adj* [L *plausibilis* worthy of applause, fr. *plausus,* pp. of *plaudere*] (1565) **1 :** superficially fair, reasonable, or valuable but often specious ⟨a ~ pretext⟩ **2 :** superficially pleasing or persuasive ⟨a swindler . . . , then a quack, then a smooth, ~ gentleman —R. W. Emerson⟩ **3 :** appearing worthy of belief ⟨his argument was both powerful and ~⟩ — **plau·si·ble·ness** *n* — **plau·si·bly** \-blē\ *adv*

plau·sive \'plȯ-ziv, -siv\ *adj* [L *plausus,* pp.] (1600) **1 :** manifesting praise or approval **:** APPLAUDING **2** *obs* **:** PLEASING **3** *archaic* **:** SPECIOUS

[1]**play** \'plā\ *n* [ME, fr. OE *plega;* akin to OE *plegan* to play, MD *pleyen*] (bef. 12c) **1 a :** SWORDPLAY **b** *archaic* **:** GAME, SPORT **c :** the conduct, course, or action of a game **d :** a particular act or maneuver in a game: as **(1) :** the action during an attempt to advance the ball in football **(2) :** the action in which a player is put out in baseball **e :** the action in which cards are played after bidding in a card game **f :** the moving of a piece in a board game (as chess) **2 a** *obs* **:** SEXUAL INTERCOURSE **b :** DALLIANCE **3 a :** recreational activity; *esp* **:** the spontaneous activity of children **b :** absence of serious or harmful intent **:** JEST ⟨said it in ~⟩ **c :** the act or an instance of playing on words or speech sounds **d :** GAMING, GAMBLING **4 a (1) :** an act, way, or manner of proceeding **:** MANEUVER ⟨that was a ~ to get your fingerprints —Erle Stanley Gardner⟩ **(2) :** DEAL, VENTURE **b (1) :** OPERATION, ACTIVITY ⟨other motives surely come into ~ —M. R. Cohen⟩ **(2) :** brisk, fitful, or light movement ⟨the gem presented a dazzling ~ of colors⟩ **(3) :** free or unimpeded motion (as of a part of a machine); *also* **:** the length or measure of such motion **(4) :** scope or opportunity for action **5 :** emphasis or publicity esp. in the news media ⟨wished the country received a better ~ in the American press —Hugh MacLennan⟩ **6 :** a move or series of moves calculated to arouse friendly feelings — usu. used with *make* ⟨made a big ~ for the girl —Will Herman⟩ **7 a :** the stage representation of an action or story **b :** a dramatic composition **:** DRAMA ***syn*** see FUN — **in play :** in condition or position to be legitimately played — **out of play :** not in play

[2]**play** *vi* (bef. 12c) **1 a :** to engage in sport or recreation **:** FROLIC **b :** to have sexual relations; *esp* **:** to have promiscuous or illicit sexual relations — usu. used in the phrase *play around* **c (1) :** to move aimlessly about **:** TRIFLE **(2) :** to deal or behave frivolously or mockingly **:** JEST **(3) :** to deal in a light, speculative, or sportive manner **(4) :** to make use of double meaning or of the similarity of sound of two words for stylistic or humorous effect **2 a :** to take advantage ⟨~*ing* on fears⟩ **b (1) :** FLUTTER, FRISK **(2) :** to move or operate in a lively, irregular, or intermittent manner **c :** to move or function freely within prescribed limits **d :** to discharge, eject, or fire repeatedly or so as to make a stream ⟨hoses ~*ing* on a fire⟩ **3 a (1) :** to perform music ⟨~ on a violin⟩ **(2) :** to sound in performance ⟨the organ is ~*ing*⟩ **(3) :** to emit sounds ⟨his radio is ~*ing*⟩ **(4) :** to reproduce recorded sounds ⟨a record is ~*ing*⟩ **b (1) :** to act in a dramatic production **(2) :** SHOW, RUN ⟨what's ~*ing* at the theater⟩ **c :** to be suitable for dramatic performance **d :** to act with special consideration so as to gain favor, approval, or sympathy ⟨might ~ to popular prejudices to serve his political ends —V. L. Parrington⟩ — often used in the phrase *play up to* **4 a :** to engage or take part in a game **b :** to perform in a position in a specified manner ⟨the outfielders were ~*ing* deep⟩ **c :** to play a card or move a piece during one's turn in a game **d :** GAMBLE **e (1) :** to behave or conduct oneself in a specified way ⟨~ safe⟩ **(2) :** to feign a specified state or quality ⟨~ dead⟩ **(3) :** to take part in or assent to some activity **:** COOPERATE ⟨~ along with his scheme⟩ **(4) :** to act so as to prove advantageous to another — usu. used in the phrase *play into the hands of* ~ *vt* **1 a (1) :** to engage in or occupy oneself with ⟨~ baseball⟩ **(2) :** to engage in or as if in a game **(3) :** to deal with, handle, or manage **(4) :** EXPLOIT, MANIPULATE **b :** to pretend to engage in the activities of ⟨~ war⟩ ⟨children ~*ing* house⟩ **c (1) :** to perform or execute for amusement or to deceive or mock ⟨~ a trick⟩ **(2) :** WREAK ⟨~ havoc⟩ **d :** to give an indicated degree of value, importance, or emphasis to — usu. used with *up* or *down* **2 a (1) :** to put on a performance of (a play) **(2) :** to act in the character or part of **(3) :** to act or perform in ⟨~*ed* leading theaters⟩ **b :** to perform or act the part of ⟨~ the fool⟩ **3 a (1) :** to contend against in a game **(2) :** to use as a contestant in a game ⟨the coach did not ~ him⟩ **(3) :** to perform the duties associated with (a certain position) ⟨~*ed* quarterback⟩ **(4) :** to guard or move into position to defend against (an opponent) in a specified manner **b (1) :** to wager in a game **:** STAKE **(2) :** to make wagers on ⟨~ the races⟩ **(3) :** to operate on the basis of ⟨~ a hunch⟩ **c :** to put into action in a game; *esp* **:** to remove (a playing card) from one's hand and place usu. faceup on a table in one's turn either as part of a scoring combination or as one's contribution to a trick **d :** to catch or pick up (a batted ball) **:** FIELD ⟨~*ed* the ball barehanded⟩ **e :** to direct the course of (as a ball) **:** HIT ⟨~*ed* a wedge shot to the green⟩; *also* **:** to cause (a ball or puck) to rebound ⟨~*ed* the ball off the backboard⟩ **4 a :** to perform (music) on an instrument ⟨~ a waltz⟩ **b :** to perform music on ⟨~ the violin⟩ **c :** to perform music of (a certain composer) **d (1) :** to cause (as a radio or phonograph) to emit sounds **(2) :** to cause the recorded sound or image of (as a record or a magnetic tape) to be reproduced **5 a :** WIELD, PLY **b :** to discharge, fire, or set off with continuous effect ⟨~*ed* the hose on the burning building⟩ **c :** to cause to move or operate lightly and irregularly or intermittently **d :** to keep (a hooked fish) in action — **play·abil·i·ty** \ˌplā-ə-'bil-ət-ē\ *n* — **play·able** \'plā-ə-bəl\ *adj* — **play ball :** COOPERATE — **play both ends against the middle :** to set opposing interests against each other to one's own ultimate profit — **play by ear :** to deal with something without previous planning or instructions — **play possum :** to pretend to be asleep or dead — **play second fiddle :** to take a subordinate position — **play the field :** to have dates with more than one member of the opposite sex — **play the game :** to act according to a code or set of standards — **play with oneself :** MASTURBATE

pla·ya \'plī-ə\ *n* [Sp, lit., beach, fr. LL *plagia* — more at PLAGE] (1854) **:** the flat-floored bottom of an undrained desert basin that becomes at times a shallow lake

play·act \'plā-ˌakt\ *vb* [back-formation fr. *playacting*] *vi* (1925) **1 a :** to take part in theatrical performances esp. as a professional **b :** to make believe **2 :** to engage in theatrical or insincere behavior ~ *vt* **:** ACT OUT 1a — **play·act·ing** *n*

play–action pass *n* (1964) **:** a pass play in football in which the quarterback fakes a handoff before passing the ball

play·back \'plā-ˌbak\ *n* (1929) **1 :** the action of reproducing recorded sound or pictures often immediately after recording **2 :** a tape or disc sound or picture reproducing device

play back \(ˈ)plā-'bak\ *vt* (1949) **:** to perform a playback of (a usu. recently recorded disc or tape)

play·bill \'plā-ˌbil\ *n* (1673) **:** a bill advertising a play and usu. announcing the cast

Playbill *trademark* — used for a theater program

play·book \-ˌbu̇k\ *n* (1535) **1 :** one or more plays in book form **2 :** a notebook containing diagramed football plays

play·boy \-ˌbȯi\ *n* (1907) **:** a man who lives a life devoted chiefly to the pursuit of pleasure

play–by–play \ˌplā-bə-ˌplā, -ˌbī-\ *adj* (1931) **1 :** being a running commentary on a sports event **2 :** relating each event as it occurs

played out *adj* (1859) **1 :** worn out or used up **2 :** tired out **:** SPENT

play·er \'plā-ər\ *n* (14c) **:** one that plays: as **a :** a person who plays a game **b :** MUSICIAN **c :** ACTOR **d :** a mechanical device for automatically playing a musical instrument (as a piano)

player piano *n* (1908) **:** a piano containing a mechanical piano player

play·fel·low \'plā-ˌfel-(ˌ)ō, -ə(-w)\ *n* (1513) **:** PLAYMATE

play·field \-ˌfēld\ *n* (1883) **:** a playground designed for outdoor athletics

play·ful \'plā-fəl\ *adj* (13c) **1 :** full of play **:** FROLICSOME, SPORTIVE ⟨a ~ kitten⟩ **2 :** HUMOROUS, JOCULAR ⟨the ~ tone of her voice —Ellen Glasgow⟩ — **play·ful·ly** \-fə-lē\ *adv* — **play·ful·ness** *n*

play·girl \-ˌgər(-ə)l\ *n* (1938) **:** a woman who lives a life devoted chiefly to the pursuit of pleasure

play·go·er \-ˌgō(-ə)r\ *n* (1822) **:** one who frequently attends plays

play·ground \-ˌgrau̇nd\ *n* (1794) **1 :** a piece of land used for and usu. equipped with facilities for recreation esp. by children **2 :** the area of a specific activity ⟨that town was a gambling ~⟩

play·house \-ˌhau̇s\ *n* (bef. 12c) **1 :** THEATER **2 :** a small house for children to play in

playing card *n* (1543) **:** one of a set of 24 to 78 thin rectangular pieces of paperboard or plastic marked on one side to show its rank and suit and used in playing any of numerous games

playing field *n* (ca. 1583) **:** a field for various games; *esp* **:** the part of a field officially marked off for play

play·land \'plā-ˌland\ *n* (1918) **:** PLAYGROUND

play·let \-lət\ *n* (1884) **:** a short play

play·list \-ˌlist\ *n* (1972) **:** a list of recordings to be played on the air by a radio station

play·mak·er \-ˌmā-kər\ *n* (1945) **:** a player who leads the offense for a team (as in basketball or hockey)

play·mate \-ˌmāt\ *n* (1642) **:** a companion in play

play–off \'plā-ˌȯf\ *n* (1895) **1 :** a final contest or series of contests to determine the winner between contestants or teams that have tied **2 :** a series of contests played after the end of the regular season to determine a championship

play off \(ˈ)plā-'ȯf\ *vt* (1807) **1 :** to complete the playing of (an interrupted contest) **2 :** to break (a tie) by a play-off **3 :** to set in opposition for one's own gain

play out *vt* (1596) **1 a :** to perform to the end ⟨*play out* a role⟩ **b :** USE UP, FINISH **2 :** UNREEL, UNFOLD ⟨*played out* a length of line —Gordon Webber⟩ ~ *vi* **:** to become spent or exhausted

play·pen \'plā-ˌpen\ *n* (1931) **:** a portable usu. collapsible enclosure in which a baby or young child may play

play·room \-ˌrüm, -ˌru̇m\ *n* (1819) **:** RUMPUS ROOM

play·suit \-ˌsüt\ *n* (1908) **:** a sports and play outfit for women and children that consists usu. of a blouse and shorts

play therapy *n* (1939) **:** psychotherapy in which a child is encouraged to reveal his feelings and conflicts in play rather than by verbalization

play·thing \'plā-ˌthiŋ\ *n* (1675) **:** TOY

play·time \-ˌtīm\ *n* (1661) **:** a time for play or diversion

play·wear \'plā-ˌwa(ə)r, -ˌwe(ə)r\ *n* (1964) **:** informal clothing worn for leisure activities

play·wright \'plā-ˌrīt\ *n* [[1]*play* + obs. *wright* (maker) — more at WRIGHT] (1687) **:** a person who writes plays

pla·za \'plaz-ə, 'pläz-\ *n* [Sp, fr. L *platea* broad street — more at PLACE] (1683) **1 :** a public square in a city or town **2 :** an open-air area used for the parking or servicing of motor vehicles **3 :** the section of a toll road at which the tollbooths are located ⟨a toll ~⟩ **4 :** an area adjacent to an expressway which has service facilities (as a restaurant, service station, and rest rooms) **5 :** SHOPPING CENTER **6 :** an open area often featuring walkways and shops and usu. located near urban buildings

plea \'plē\ *n* [ME *plaid, plai,* fr. OF *plait, plaid,* fr. ML *placitum,* fr. L decision, decree, fr. neut. of *placitus,* pp. of *placēre* to please, be decided — more at PLEASE] (13c) **1 :** a legal suit or action **2 :** an allegation made by a party in support of his cause: as **a :** an allegation of fact — compare DEMURRER **b (1) :** a defendant's answer to a plaintiff's declaration in common-law practice **(2) :** an accused person's answer to a charge or indictment in criminal practice **c :** a plea of guilty to an indictment **3 :** something offered by way of excuse or justification ⟨left early with the ~ of a headache⟩ **4 :** an earnest entreaty **:** APPEAL ⟨their ~ for understanding must be answered⟩ ***syn*** see APOLOGY

plea bargaining *n* (ca. 1963) **:** the negotiation of an agreement between a prosecutor and a defendant whereby the defendant is permitted to plead guilty to a reduced charge — **plea–bargain** *vi*

pleach \'plēch, 'plāch\ *vt* [ME *plechen,* fr. ONF *plechier,* fr. L *plexus,* pp. of *plectere* to braid — more at PLY] (14c) **:** INTERLACE, PLAIT

plead \'plēd\ *vb* **plead·ed** \'plēd-əd\ *or* **pled** \'pled\; **plead·ing** [ME *plaiden* to institute a lawsuit, fr. MF *plaidier,* fr. *plaid* plea] *vi* (14c) **1 :** to argue a case or cause in a court of law **2 a :** to make an allegation in an action or other legal proceeding; *esp* **:** to answer the previous pleading of the other party by denying facts therein stated or by alleging new facts **b** : to conduct pleadings **3** : to make a plea of a specified nature ⟨~ not guilty⟩ **4** **a** : to argue for or against a claim **b** : to entreat or appeal earnestly : IMPLORE **~** *vt* **1** : to maintain (as a case or cause) in a court of law or other tribunal **2** : to allege in or by way of a legal plea **3** : to offer as a plea usu. in defense, apology, or excuse — **plead·able** \ˈplēd-ə-bəl\ *adj* — **plead·er** *n* — **plead·ing·ly** \ˈplēd-iŋ-lē\ *adv*

plead·ing *n* (13c) **1** : advocacy of a cause in a court of law **2** **a** : one of the formal usu. written allegations and counter allegations made alternately by the parties in a legal action or proceeding **b** : the action or process performed by the parties in presenting such formal allegations until a single point at issue is produced **c** : the introduction of one of these allegations and esp. the first one **d** : the body of rules according to which these allegations are framed **3** : the act or an instance of making a plea **4** : a sincere entreaty

pleas·ance \ˈplez-ᵊn(t)s\ *n* (14c) **1** *archaic* : a feeling of pleasure : DELIGHT **2** : a pleasant rest or recreation place usu. attached to a mansion

pleas·ant \ˈplez-ᵊnt\ *adj* [ME *plesaunt,* fr. MF *plaisant,* fr. prp. of *plaisir*] (14c) **1** : having qualities that tend to give pleasure : AGREEABLE ⟨a ~ day⟩ **2** : having or characterized by pleasing manners, behavior, or appearance — **pleas·ant·ly** *adv* — **pleas·ant·ness** *n*

pleas·ant·ry \-ᵊn-trē\ *n, pl* **-ries** (1655) **1** : an agreeable playfulness in conversation : BANTER **2** : a humorous act or remark : JEST

¹please \ˈplēz\ *vb* **pleased; pleas·ing** [ME *plesen,* fr. MF *plaisir,* fr. L *placēre;* akin to L *placare* to placate, OE *flōh* flat stone, Gk *plak-, plax* flat surface] *vi* (14c) **1** : to afford or give pleasure or satisfaction **2** : LIKE, WISH ⟨do as you ~⟩ **3** *archaic* : to have the kindness ⟨will you ~ to enter the carriage —Charles Dickens⟩ **~** *vt* **1** : to give pleasure to : GRATIFY **2** : to be the will or pleasure of ⟨may it ~ your Majesty⟩

²please *adv* (1622) **1** — used as a function word to express politeness or emphasis in a request ⟨~ come in⟩ **2** — used as a function word to express polite affirmation ⟨have some tea? *Please*⟩

pleas·ing \ˈplē-ziŋ\ *adj* (14c) : giving pleasure : AGREEABLE ⟨he found the sun's warmth ~⟩ — **pleas·ing·ly** \-ziŋ-lē\ *adv* — **pleas·ing·ness** *n*

plea·sur·able \ˈplezh-(ə-)rə-bəl, ˈplāzh-\ *adj* (1579) : PLEASANT, GRATIFYING — **plea·sur·abil·i·ty** \ˌplezh-(ə-)rə-ˈbil-ət-ē, ˌplāzh-\ *n* — **plea·sur·able·ness** \ˈplezh-(ə-)rə-bəl-nəs, ˈplāzh-\ *n* — **plea·sur·ably** \-blē\ *adv*

¹plea·sure \ˈplezh-ər, ˈplāzh-\ *n* [ME *plesure,* alter. of *plesir,* fr. MF *plaisir,* fr. *plaisir* to please] (14c) **1** : DESIRE, INCLINATION ⟨wait upon his ~ —Shak.⟩ **2** : a state of gratification **3** **a** : sensual gratification **b** : frivolous amusement **4** : a source of delight or joy

²pleasure *vb* **plea·sured; plea·sur·ing** \-(ə-)riŋ\ *vi* (1538) **1** : to take pleasure : DELIGHT **2** : to seek pleasure **~** *vt* **1** : to give pleasure to : GRATIFY **2** : to give sexual pleasure to

pleasure dome *n* (1797) : a place of pleasurable entertainment or recreation : RESORT

plea·sure·less \ˈplezh-ər-ləs, ˈplāzh-\ *adj* (1814) : giving no pleasure

pleasure principle *n* (1912) : a tendency for individual behavior to be directed toward immediate satisfaction of instinctual drives and immediate relief from pain or discomfort

¹pleat \ˈplēt\ *vt* [ME *pleten,* fr. *pleit, plete* plait] (14c) **1** : FOLD; *esp* : to arrange in pleats ⟨~ a skirt⟩ **2** : PLAIT 2 — **pleat·er** *n*

²pleat *n* [ME *plete*] (1581) : a fold in cloth made by doubling material over on itself; *also* : something resembling such a fold — **pleat·ed** *adj* — **pleat·less** \-ləs\ *adj*

pleb \ˈpleb\ *n* (1865) : PLEBEIAN

plebe \ˈplēb\ *n* [obs. *plebe* (common people), fr. F *plèbe,* fr. L *plebs*] (1833) : a freshman at a military or naval academy

¹ple·be·ian \pli-ˈbē-(y)ən\ *n* [L *plebeius* of the common people, fr. *plebs* common people; akin to Gk *plēthos* throng, *plēthein* to be full — more at FULL] (1533) **1** : a member of the Roman plebs **2** : one of the common people — **ple·be·ian·ism** \-ˌiz-əm\ *n*

²plebeian *adj* (1566) **1** : of or relating to plebeians **2** : crude or coarse in manner or style : COMMON — **ple·be·ian·ly** *adv*

pleb·i·scite \ˈpleb-ə-ˌsīt, -sət *also* -ˌsēt\ *n* [L *plebis scitum* law voted by the comitia, lit., decree of the common people] (1860) : a vote by which the people of an entire country or district express an opinion for or against a proposal esp. on a choice of government or ruler — **ple·bi·sci·ta·ry** \ple-ˈbis-ə-ˌter-ē, pli-; ˌpleb-ə-ˈsīt-ə-rē\ *adj*

plebs \ˈplebz, ˈpleps\ *n, pl* **ple·bes** \ˈplē-(ˌ)bēz, ˈplā-ˌbās\ [L] (1647) **1** : the general populace **2** : the common people of ancient Rome

ple·cop·ter·an \pli-ˈkäp-tə-rən\ *n* [NL *Plecoptera,* group name, fr. Gk *plekein* to braid + *pteron* wing — more at PLY, FEATHER] (ca. 1890) : STONE FLY — **plecopteran** *adj*

plec·trum \ˈplek-trəm\ *n, pl* **plec·tra** \-trə\ *or* **plectrums** [L, fr. Gk *plēktron,* fr. *plēssein* to strike — more at PLAINT] (1626) : ³PICK 2c

¹pledge \ˈplej\ *n* [ME, security, fr. MF *plege,* fr. LL *plebium,* fr. (assumed) LL *plebere* to pledge] (14c) **1** **a** : a bailment of a chattel as security for a debt or other obligation without involving transfer of title **b** : the chattel so delivered **c** : the contract incidental to such a bailment **2** **a** : the state of being held as a security or guaranty **b** : something given as security for the performance of an act **3** : a token, sign, or earnest of something else **4** : a gage of battle **5** : TOAST 3 **6** **a** : a binding promise or agreement to do or forbear **b** (1) : a promise to join a fraternity or secret society (2) : a person who has so promised

²pledge *vt* **pledged; pledg·ing** (15c) **1** : to make a pledge of; *specif* : PAWN **2** : to drink the health of **3** : to bind by a pledge **4** : to promise the performance of by a pledge — **pledg·er** \ˈplej-ər\ *n* — **pledg·or** \ˈplej-ər, ple-ˈjȯ(ə)r\ *n*

pledg·ee \ple-ˈjē\ *n* (1766) : one to whom a pledge is given

pled·get \ˈplej-ət\ *n* [origin unknown] (ca. 1540) : a compress or pad used to apply medication to or absorb discharges (as from a wound)

-ple·gia \ˈplē-j(ē-)ə\ *n comb form* [NL, fr. Gk *-plēgia,* fr. *plēssein* to strike — more at PLAINT] : paralysis ⟨di*plegia*⟩

ple·iad \ˈplē-əd, ˈplā-, -ˌad, *chiefly Brit* ˈplī-\ *n* [F *Pléiade,* group of seven 16th cent. Fr. poets, fr. MF, group of seven tragic poets of ancient Alexandria, fr. Gk *Pleiad-, Pleias,* fr. sing. of *Pleiades*] (ca. 1822) : a group of usu. seven illustrious or brilliant persons or things

Pleiad *n* : any of the Pleiades

Ple·ia·des \ˈplē-ə-ˌdēz, ˈplā-, *chiefly Brit* ˈplī-\ *n pl* [L, fr. Gk] **1** : the seven daughters of Atlas turned into a group of stars in Greek mythology **2** : a conspicuous loose cluster of stars in the constellation Taurus that includes six stars visible to the average eye

plein air \plā-ˈna(ə)r, ple-, -ˈne(ə)r\ *adj* [F, open air] (1894) **1** : of or relating to painting in outdoor daylight **2** : of or relating to a branch of impressionism that attempts to represent outdoor light and air — **plein-air·ism** \-ˌiz-əm\ *n* — **plein-air·ist** \-əst\ *n*

pleio- *or* **pleo-** *or* **plio-** *comb form* [Gk *pleiōn, pleōn* — more at PLUS] : more ⟨*pleio*tropic⟩ ⟨*pleo*morphism⟩ ⟨*Plio*cene⟩

pleio·tro·pic \ˌplī-ə-ˈtrōp-ik, -ˈträp-\ *adj* (ca. 1910) : producing more than one genic effect; *specif* : having multiple phenotypic expressions ⟨a ~ gene⟩ — **plei·ot·ro·py** \plī-ˈä-trə-pē\ *n*

Pleis·to·cene \ˈplī-stə-ˌsēn\ *adj* [Gk *pleistos* most + ISV *-cene;* akin to Gk *pleiōn* more] (ca. 1839) : of, relating to, or being the earlier epoch of the Quaternary or the corresponding system of rocks — **Pleistocene** *n*

ple·na·ry \ˈplē-nə-rē, ˈplen-ə-\ *adj* [LL *plenarius,* fr. L *plenus* full — more at FULL] (1517) **1** : complete in every respect : ABSOLUTE, UNQUALIFIED ⟨~ power⟩ **2** : fully attended or constituted by all entitled to be present ⟨a ~ session⟩ ***syn*** see FULL

plenary indulgence *n* (1675) : a remission of the entire temporal punishment for sin

ple·nip·o·tent \pli-ˈnip-ət-ənt\ *adj* [LL *plenipotent-, plenipotens,* fr. L *plenus* + *potent-, potens* powerful — more at POTENT] (1658) : PLENIPOTENTIARY

¹pleni·po·ten·tia·ry \ˌplen-ə-pə-ˈtench-(ə-)rē, -ˈten-chē-ˌer-ē\ *adj* [ML *plenipotentiarius,* adj. & n., fr. (assumed) *plenipotentia,* investment with full power, fr. LL *plenipotent-, plenipotens*] (ca. 1645) **1** : invested with full power **2** : of or relating to a plenipotentiary

²plenipotentiary *n, pl* **-ries** (1656) : a person and esp. a diplomatic agent invested with full power to transact business

plen·ish \ˈplen-ish\ *vt* [ME (Sc) *plenyssen* to fill up, fr. MF *pleniss-,* stem of *plenir,* fr. *plen* full, fr. L *plenus*] *chiefly Brit* (15c) : EQUIP

plen·i·tude \ˈplen-ə-ˌt(y)üd\ *n* [ME *plenitude,* fr. MF or L; MF, fr. L *plenitudo,* fr. *plenus* full] (15c) **1** : the quality or state of being full : COMPLETENESS **2** : a great sufficiency : ABUNDANCE

plen·i·tu·di·nous \ˌplen-ə-ˈt(y)üd-nəs, -ᵊn-əs\ *adj* [L *plenitudin-, plenitudo*] (1812) **1** : PORTLY **2** : characterized by plenitude

plen·te·ous \ˈplent-ē-əs\ *adj* [ME *plentevous, plenteous,* fr. MF *plentiveus,* fr. *plentif* abundant, fr. *plenté* plenty] (14c) **1** : FRUITFUL, PRODUCTIVE ⟨a ~ harvest —J. G. Frazer⟩ — usu. used with *in* or *of* ⟨the seasons had been ~ in corn —George Eliot⟩ **2** : constituting or existing in plenty ⟨~ grace with thee is found —Charles Wesley⟩ — **plen·te·ous·ly** *adv* — **plen·te·ous·ness** *n*

plen·ti·ful \ˈplent-i-fəl\ *adj* (15c) **1** : containing or yielding plenty ⟨a ~ land⟩ **2** : characterized by, constituting, or existing in plenty — **plen·ti·ful·ly** \-fə-lē\ *adv* — **plen·ti·ful·ness** *n*

syn PLENTIFUL, AMPLE, ABUNDANT, COPIOUS mean more than sufficient without being excessive. PLENTIFUL implies a great or rich supply; AMPLE implies a generous sufficiency to satisfy a particular requirement; ABUNDANT suggests an even greater or richer supply than does PLENTIFUL; COPIOUS stresses largeness of supply rather than fullness or richness.

plen·ti·tude \ˈplen(t)-ə-ˌt(y)üd\ *n* [by alter. (influenced by *plenty*)] (1615) : PLENITUDE

¹plen·ty \ˈplent-ē\ *n* [ME *plente,* fr. OF *plenté,* fr. LL *plenitat-, plenitas,* fr. L, fullness, fr. *plenus* full — more at FULL] (13c) **1** **a** : a full or more than adequate amount or supply ⟨had ~ of time to finish the job⟩ **b** : a large number or amount ⟨he's in ~ of trouble⟩ **2** : the quality or state of being copious : PLENTIFULNESS

²plenty *adj* (14c) **1** : plentiful in amount, number, or supply ⟨if reasons were as ~ as blackberries —Shak.⟩ **2** : AMPLE ⟨~ work to be done —*Time*⟩

usage Many commentators object to use of sense 2 in writing; it appears to be limited chiefly to spoken English. Sense 1 is literary but is no longer in common use.

³plenty *adv* (1842) : to a considerable or extreme degree : ABUNDANTLY ⟨the nights were ~ cold —F. B. Gipson⟩

usage Many handbooks advise avoiding the adverb *plenty* in writing; "use *very, quite,* or a more precise word," they advise. Actually *plenty* is often a more precise word than its recommended replacements; *very, fully,* or *quite* will not work as well in these typical quotations ⟨it's already *plenty* hot for us in the kitchen without some dolt opening the oven —C.H. Bridges⟩ ⟨may not be rising quite as rapidly as other health costs, but it is going up *plenty* fast —*Changing Times*⟩ It is not used in more formal writing.

ple·num \ˈplen-əm, ˈplēn-əm\ *n, pl* **-nums** *or* **-na** \-ə\ [NL, fr. L, neut. of *plenus*] (1678) **1** **a** : a space or all space every part of which is full of matter **b** (1) : a condition in which the pressure of the air in an enclosed space is greater than that of the outside atmosphere (2) : an enclosed space in which such a condition exists **2** : a general assembly of all members esp. of a legislative body **3** : the quality or state of being full

ple·och·ro·ism \plē-ˈäk-rə-ˌwiz-əm\ *n* [ISV *pleochroic* (fr. *pleio-* + Gk *chrōs* skin, color) + *-ism* — more at GRIT] (1857) : the property of a crystal of showing different colors when viewed by light that vibrates parallel to different axes — **pleo·chro·ic** \ˌplē-ə-ˈkrō-ik\ *adj*

pleo·mor·phic \ˌplē-ə-ˈmȯr-fik\ *adj* (1886) : POLYMORPHIC ⟨~ bacteria⟩ ⟨a ~ sarcoma⟩ — **pleo·mor·phism** \-ˌfiz-əm\ *n*

ple·o·nasm \ˈplē-ə-ˌnaz-əm\ *n* [LL *pleonasmus,* fr. Gk *pleonasmos,* fr. *pleonazein* to be excessive, fr. *pleiōn, pleōn* more — more at PLUS] (1586) **1** : the use of more words than those necessary to denote mere sense (as in *the man he said*) : REDUNDANCY **2** : an instance or example of pleonasm — **ple·o·nas·tic** \ˌplē-ə-ˈnas-tik\ *adj* — **ple·o·nas·ti·cal·ly** \-ti-k(ə-)lē\ *adv*

ple·oph·a·gous \plē-ˈäf-ə-gəs\ *adj, of a parasite* (1951) : not restricted to a single kind of host

pleo·pod \'plē-ə-,päd\ *n* [Gk *plein* to sail + E *-o-* + *-pod;* fr. its use in swimming — more at FLOW] (1855) : an abdominal limb of a crustacean

ple·ro·cer·coid \,plir-ō-'sər-,kȯid\ *n* [Gk *plērēs* full + *kerkos* tail — more at FULL] (ca. 1885) : the solid elongate infective larva of some tapeworms usu. occurring in the muscles of fishes

ple·sio·saur \'plē-sē-ə-,sȯ(ə)r, -zē-\ *n* [deriv. of Gk *plēsios* close (fr. *pelas* near) + *sauros* lizard — more at FELT] (1839) : any of a suborder (Plesiosauria) of Mesozoic marine reptiles with dorsoventrally flattened bodies and limbs modified into paddles

pleth·o·ra \'pleth-ə-rə\ *n* [ML, fr. Gk *plēthōra,* lit., fullness, fr. *plēthein* to be full — more at FULL] (1541) **1 :** a bodily condition characterized by an excess of blood and marked by turgescence and a florid complexion **2 :** EXCESS, SUPERFLUITY ⟨a ~ of regulations⟩ — **ple·tho·ric** \plə-'thȯr-ik, ple-, -'thär-; 'pleth-ə-rik\ *adj*

ple·thys·mo·gram \ple-'thiz-mə-,gram, plə-\ *n* (1894) : a tracing made by a plethysmograph

ple·thys·mo·graph \-,graf\ *n* [ISV, fr. Gk *plēthysmos* increase, fr. *plēthynein* to increase, fr. *plēthys* mass, quantity, fr. *plēthein* to be full] (1872) : an instrument for determining and registering variations in the size of an organ or limb and in the amount of blood present or passing through it — **ple·thys·mo·graph·ic** \-,thiz-mə-'graf-ik\ *adj* — **ple·thys·mo·graph·i·cal·ly** \-i-k(ə-)lē\ *adv* — **pleth·ys·mog·ra·phy** \,pleth-iz-'mäg-rə-fē\ *n*

pleur- *or* **pleuro-** *comb form* [NL, fr. *pleura*] **1 a :** pleura ⟨*pleuro*pneumonia⟩ **b :** pleura and ⟨*pleuro*peritoneum⟩ **2** [Gk, fr. *pleura*] : side : lateral ⟨*pleuro*dont⟩

pleu·ra \'plu̇r-ə\ *n, pl* **pleu·rae** \'plu̇(ə)r-,ē, -,ī\ *or* **pleuras** [Gk, rib, side] (1664) : the delicate serous membrane that lines each half of the thorax of mammals and is folded back over the surface of the lung of the same side — **pleu·ral** \'plu̇r-əl\ *adj*

pleu·ri·sy \'plu̇r-ə-sē\ *n* [ME *pluresie,* fr. MF *pleuresie,* fr. LL *pleurisis,* alter. of L *pleuritis,* fr. Gk, fr. *pleura* side] (14c) : inflammation of the pleura usu. with fever, painful and difficult respiration, cough, and exudation of fluid or fibrinous material into the pleural cavity — **pleu·rit·ic** \plü-'rit-ik\ *adj*

pleur·odont \'plu̇r-ə-,dänt\ *adj* [Gk *pleura* side + ISV *-odont*] (1872) **1 :** consolidated with the inner surface of the alveolar ridge without sockets ⟨~ teeth⟩ **2 :** having pleurodont teeth

pleu·ro·pneu·mo·nia \'plu̇r-ō-n(y)u̇-'mō-nyə\ *n* [NL] (1725) **1 :** combined inflammation of the pleura and lungs **2 :** an acute febrile and often fatal respiratory disorder of cattle and related animals caused by microorganisms (family Mycoplasmataceae) of uncertain affinities

pleuropneumonia–like organism \-,līk-\ *n* (1935) : MYCOPLASMA

pleus·ton \'plü-stən, -,stän\ *n* [(assumed) Gk *pleustos* (verbal of *plein* to sail, float) + ISV *-on* (as in *plankton*)] (1943) : macroscopic floating organisms forming mats on or near the surface of a body of fresh water — **pleus·ton·ic** \plü-'stän-ik\ *adj*

plexi·form \'plek-sə-,fȯrm\ *adj* [NL *plexus* + E *-iform*] (ca. 1828) : of, relating to, or having the form or characteristics of a plexus

Plexi·glas \-si-,glas\ *trademark* — used for acrylic plastic sheets and molding powders

plex·us \'plek-səs\ *n* [NL, fr. L, braid, network, fr. *plexus,* pp. of *plectere* to braid — more at PLY] (1682) **1 :** a network of anastomosing or interlacing blood vessels or nerves **2 :** an interwoven combination of parts or elements in a structure or system

pli·able \'plī-ə-bəl\ *adj* [ME, fr. MF, fr. *plier* to bend, fold — more at PLY] (15c) **1 a :** supple enough to bend freely or repeatedly without breaking **b :** yielding readily to others : COMPLAISANT **2 :** adjustable to varying conditions ***syn*** see PLASTIC — **pli·abil·i·ty** \,plī-ə-'bil-ət-ē\ *n* — **pli·able·ness** \'plī-ə-bəl-nəs\ *n* — **pli·ably** \-blē\ *adv*

pli·an·cy \'plī-ən-sē\ *n* (1699) : the quality or state of being pliant

pli·ant \'plī-ənt\ *adj* (14c) **1 :** PLIABLE 1a **2 :** easily influenced : YIELDING **3 :** suitable for varied uses ***syn*** see PLASTIC — **pli·ant·ly** *adv* — **pli·ant·ness** *n*

pli·ca \'plī-kə\ *n, pl* **pli·cae** \-,kē, -,sē\ [ML, fr. L *plicare* to fold — more at PLY] (ca. 1706) : a fold or folded part; *esp* : a groove or fold of skin

pli·cate \'plī-,kāt\ *adj* [L *plicatus,* pp. of *plicare*] (1760) **1 :** folded lengthwise like a fan ⟨a ~ leaf⟩ **2 :** having the surface thrown up into or marked with parallel ridges ⟨~ wing cases⟩

pli·ca·tion \plī-'kā-shən\ *n* (15c) **1 :** the act or process of folding : the state of being folded **2 :** FOLD

plié \plē-'ā\ *n* [F, fr. pp. of *plier* to bend] (1892) : a bending of the knees by a ballet dancer with the back held straight

pli·ers \'plī(-ə)rz\ *n pl but sing or pl in constr* (ca. 1568) : a small pincers for holding small objects or for bending and cutting wire

¹plight \'plīt\ *vt* [ME *plighten,* fr. OE *plihtan* to endanger, fr. *pliht* danger; akin to OHG *pflegan* to take care of] (13c) : to put or give in pledge : ENGAGE ⟨~ one's troth⟩ — **plight·er** *n*

²plight *n* (13c) : a solemnly given pledge : ENGAGEMENT

³plight *n* [ME *plit,* fr. AF, fr. (assumed) VL *plictus* fold — more at PLAIT] (14c) : CONDITION, STATE; *esp* : bad state or condition

plim·soll \'plim(p)-səl, 'plim-,sōl\ *n* [prob. fr. the supposed resemblance of the upper edge of the mudguard to the Plimsoll mark on a ship] *Brit* (1907) : a shoe with rubber sole, mudguard, and canvas top

Plimsoll mark *n* [Samuel *Plimsoll* †1898 Eng. shipping reformer] (1881) : a load line or a set of load-line markings on an ocean-going cargo ship — called also *Plimsoll line*

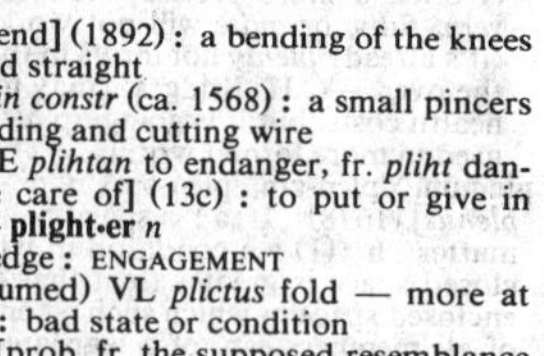

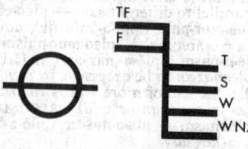

Plimsoll mark: *TF* tropical freshwater mark; *F* freshwater mark; *T* tropical load line; *S* summer load line; *W* winter load line; *WNA* winter load line, North Atlantic

¹plink \'pliŋk\ *vi* [imit.] (1941) **1 :** to make a tinkling sound **2 :** to shoot at random targets in an informal and noncompetitive manner ~ *vt* **1 :** to cause to make a tinkling sound **2 :** to shoot at esp. in a casual manner — **plink·er** *n*

²plink *n* (1949) : a tinkling metallic sound

plinth \'plin(t)th\ *n* [L *plinthus,* fr. Gk *plinthos*] (1563) **1 a :** the lowest member of a base : SUBBASE **b :** a block upon which the moldings of an architrave or trim are stopped at the bottom **2 :** a usu. square block serving as a base; *broadly* : any of various bases or lower parts — see BASE illustration **3 :** a course of stones forming a continuous foundation or base course

plio- — see PLEIO-

Plio·cene \'plī-ə-,sēn\ *adj* (1831) : of, relating to, or being the latest epoch of the Tertiary or the corresponding system of rocks — **Pliocene** *n*

Plio·film \'plī-ə-,film\ *trademark* — used for a glossy membrane made of rubber hydrochloride and used chiefly for water-resistant and packaging materials

plique–à–jour \,plē-(,)kä-'zhu̇(ə)r\ *n* [F, lit., braid letting in daylight] (ca. 1878) : a style of enameling in which usu. transparent enamels are fused into the openings of a metal filigree to produce an effect suggestive of stained glass

plis·kie *or* **plis·ky** \'plis-kē\ *n, pl* **pliskies** [origin unknown] *chiefly Scot* (1706) : PRACTICAL JOKE, TRICK

plis·sé *or* **plis·se** \pli-'sā\ *n* [F *plissé,* fr. pp. of *plisser* to pleat, fr. MF, fr. *pli* fold, fr. *plier* to fold — more at PLY] (1873) **1 :** a textile finish of permanently puckered designs formed by treating with a sodium hydroxide solution **2 :** a fabric usu. of cotton, rayon, or nylon with a plissé finish

plod \'pläd\ *vb* **plod·ded; plod·ding** [origin unknown] *vi* (ca. 1566) **1 a :** to walk heavily or slowly : TRUDGE **b :** to proceed slowly or tediously ⟨the movie just ~s along⟩ **2 :** to work laboriously and monotonously : DRUDGE ⟨*plodding* through stacks of unanswered mail⟩ ~ *vt* : to tread slowly or heavily along or over — **plod** *n* — **plod·der** *n* — **plod·ding·ly** \'pläd-iŋ-lē\ *adv*

-ploid \,plȯid\ *adj comb form* [ISV, fr. *diploid & haploid*] : having or being a chromosome number that bears (such) a relationship to or is (so many) times the basic chromosome number of a given group ⟨*polyploid*⟩

ploi·dy \'plȯid-ē\ *n* [fr. such words as *diploidy, hexaploidy*] (1939) : degree of repetition of the basic number of chromosomes

PL/1 \(,)pē-,el-'wən\ *n* [*p*rogramming *l*anguage (version) *1*] (1965) : a general-purpose language for programming a computer

¹plonk \'pläŋk, 'plȯŋk\ *var of* PLUNK

²plonk *n* [short for earlier *plink-plonk,* perh. modif. of F *vin blanc* white wine] *chiefly Brit* (ca. 1930) : cheap or inferior wine

plop \'pläp\ *vb* **plopped; plop·ping** [imit.] *vi* (1821) **1 :** to fall, drop, or move suddenly with a sound like that of something dropping into water **2 :** to allow the body to drop heavily ⟨*plopped* into a chair⟩ ~ *vt* : to set, drop, or throw heavily — **plop** *n*

plo·sion \'plō-zhən\ *n* (1899) : EXPLOSION 2 — **plo·sive** \'plō-siv, -ziv\ *adj or n*

¹plot \'plät\ *n* [ME, fr. OE] (bef. 12c) **1 a :** a small area of planted ground ⟨a vegetable ~⟩ **b :** a small piece of land in a cemetery **c :** a measured piece of land : LOT **2 :** GROUND PLAN, PLAT **3 :** the plan or main story of a literary work **4 :** a secret plan for accomplishing a usu. evil or unlawful end : INTRIGUE **5 :** a graphic representation (as a chart) — **plot·less** \-ləs\ *adj* — **plot·less·ness** *n*

syn PLOT, INTRIGUE, MACHINATION, CONSPIRACY, CABAL mean a plan secretly devised to accomplish an evil or treacherous end. PLOT implies careful foresight in planning a complex scheme; INTRIGUE suggests secret underhanded maneuvering in an atmosphere of duplicity; MACHINATION implies a contriving of annoyances, injuries, or evils by indirect means; CONSPIRACY implies a secret agreement among several people usu. involving treason or great treachery; CABAL typically applies to political intrigue involving persons of some eminence. ***syn*** see in addition PLAN

²plot *vb* **plot·ted; plot·ting** *vt* (1588) **1 a :** to make a plot, map, or plan of **b :** to mark or note on or as if on a map or chart **2 :** to lay out in plots **3 a :** to locate (a point) by means of coordinates **b :** to locate (a curve) by plotted points **c :** to represent (an equation) by means of a curve so constructed **4 :** to plan or contrive esp. secretly **5 :** to invent or devise the plot of (a literary work) ~ *vi* **1 :** to form a plot : SCHEME **2 :** to be located by means of coordinates ⟨the data ~ at a single point⟩ — **plot·ter** *n*

Plo·ti·nism \plō-'tī-,niz-əm, 'plōt-ᵊn-,iz-əm\ *n* (ca. 1890) : the Neoplatonic ideas of the philosopher Plotinus — **Plo·ti·nist** \-'tī-nəst, -ᵊn-əst\ *n*

plot·tage \'plät-ij\ *n* (1936) : the area included in a plot of land

plot·ty \'plät-ē\ *adj* **plot·ti·er; -est** (1897) : marked by intricacy of plot or intrigue

plo·ver \'pləv-ər, 'plō-vər\ *n, pl* **plover** *or* **plovers** [ME, fr. MF, fr. (assumed) VL *pluviarius,* fr. L *pluvia* rain — more at PLUVIAL] (14c) **1 :** any of numerous shore-inhabiting birds (family Charadriidae) that differ from the sandpipers in having a short hard-tipped bill and usu. a stouter more compact build **2 :** any of various birds (as a turnstone or sandpiper) related to the plovers

¹plow *or* **plough** \'plau̇\ *n* [ME, fr. OE *plōh* hide of land; akin to OHG *pfluog* plow] (13c) **1 :** an implement used to cut, lift, and turn over soil esp. in preparing a seedbed **2 :** any of various devices operating like a plow

²plow *or* **plough** *vt* (15c) **1 a :** to turn, break up, or work with a plow **b :** to make (as a furrow) with a plow **2 :** to cut into, open, or make furrows or ridges in with or as if with a plow — often used with *up* **3 :** to cleave the surface of or move through (water) ⟨whales ~*ing* the ocean⟩ ~ *vi* **1 a :** to use a plow **b :** to bear or admit of plowing **2 a :** to move in a way resembling that of a plow cutting into or going through the soil ⟨the car ~*ed* into a fence⟩ **b :** to proceed steadily and laboriously : PLOD ⟨had to ~ through a summer reading list⟩ — **plow·able** \-ə-bəl\ *adj* — **plow·er** \'plau̇(-ə)r\ *n*

plow back \(')plau̇-'bak\ *vt* (1930) : to reinvest (profits) in a business — **plow·back** \'plau̇-,bak\ *n*

plow·boy \'plau̇-,bȯi\ *n* (1596) **1 :** a boy who leads the team drawing a plow **2 :** a country youth

plow·man \-mən, -,man\ *n* (13c) **1 :** a man who guides a plow **2 :** a farm laborer

plow·share \'plau̇-,she(ə)r, -,sha(ə)r\ *n* [ME *ploughshare,* fr. *plough* plow + *schare* plowshare — more at SHARE] (14c) : the part of a moldboard plow that cuts the furrow

plow sole *n* (1907) : a layer of earth at the bottom of the furrow compacted by repeated plowing at the same depth

plow under *vt* (1900) : to cause to disappear : BURY, OVERWHELM

ploy \'plȯi\ *n* [prob. fr. *employ*] (1722) **1** : ESCAPADE, FROLIC **2** : a tactic intended to embarrass or frustrate an opponent; *also* : something devised or contrived : DEVICE ⟨may have issued his threat merely as a bargaining ~ —*N.Y. Times*⟩

[1]pluck \'plək\ *vb* [ME *plucken,* fr. OE *pluccian;* akin to MHG *pflücken* to pluck] *vt* (bef. 12c) **1** : to pull or pick off or out **2** **a** : to remove something (as hairs) from by or as if by plucking ⟨~ one's eyebrows⟩ **b** : ROB, FLEECE **3** : to move or separate forcibly ⟨~*ed* the child from the middle of the street⟩ **4** **a** : to pick, pull, or grasp at **b** : to play by sounding the strings with the fingers or a pick **5** : to remove (a person) from one situation in life and transfer him to another ~ *vi* : to make a sharp pull or twitch — **pluck·er** *n*

[2]pluck *n* (15c) **1** : an act or instance of plucking or pulling **2** : the heart, liver, lungs, and windpipe of a slaughtered animal esp. as an item of food **3** : courageous readiness to fight or continue against odds : dogged resolution

plucky \'plək-ē\ *adj* **pluck·i·er; -est** (1842) : marked by courage : SPIRITED — **pluck·i·ly** \'plək-ə-lē\ *adv* — **pluck·i·ness** \'plək-ē-nəs\ *n*

[1]plug \'pləg\ *n* [D, fr. MD *plugge;* akin to MHG *pfloc* plug] (1627) **1** **a** : a piece used to fill a hole : STOPPER **b** : an obtruding or obstructing mass of material resembling a stopper **2** : a flat compressed cake of tobacco **3** : SHOT **4** : a small core or segment removed from a larger object **5** : something inferior; *esp* : an inferior often aged or unsound horse; *also* : a quiet steady cold-blooded horse usu. of light or moderate weight **6** **a** : HYDRANT, FIREPLUG **b** : SPARK PLUG **7** : an artificial angling lure used primarily for casting and made with one or more sets of gang hooks **8** : any of various devices resembling or functioning like a plug: as **a** : a male fitting for making an electrical connection to a circuit by insertion in a receptacle or body of electrical equipment **b** : a device for connecting electric wires to a jack **9** : a piece of favorable publicity usu. incorporated in general matter

[2]plug *vb* **plugged; plug·ging** *vt* (1630) **1** : to stop, make tight, or secure by inserting a plug **2** : to hit with a bullet : SHOOT **3** : to advertise or publicize insistently ~ *vi* **1** : to become plugged — usu. used with *up* **2** : to work doggedly and persistently ⟨*plugged* away at his homework⟩ **3** : to fire shots — **plug·ger** *n* — **plug into** : to connect or become connected to by or as if by means of a plug ⟨the city was *plugged into* the new highway system⟩ ⟨the generator *plugs into* the power grid⟩

plugged \'pləgd\ *adj* (1694) **1** *of a coin* : altered by the insertion of a plug of base metal **2** : closed by or as if by a plug : OBSTRUCTED

plug hat *n* (1863) : a man's stiff hat (as a bowler or top hat)

plug–in \'pləg-,in\ *adj* (1922) : designed to be connected to an electric circuit by plugging in ⟨a ~ toy⟩ — **plug–in** *n*

plug in \'pləg-'in, ,pləg-\ *vi* (1903) : to establish an electric circuit by inserting a plug ~ *vt* : to attach or connect to a service outlet

plug–ug·ly \'pləg-,əg-lē\ *n* (1856) : THUG, TOUGH; *esp* : one hired to intimidate

plum \'pləm\ *n* [ME, fr. OE *plūme,* modif. of L *prunum* plum, fr. Gk *proumnon*] (bef. 12c) **1** **a** : any of numerous trees and shrubs (genus *Prunus*) with globular to oval smooth-skinned fruits that are drupes with oblong seeds **b** : the edible fruit of a plum **2** : any of various trees with edible fruits resembling plums; *also* : its fruit **3** **a** : a raisin when used in desserts (as puddings or cake) **b** : SUGARPLUM **4** : something superior or very desirable; *esp* : something desirable given in return for a favor ⟨political ~*s*⟩ **5** : a variable color averaging a dark reddish purple — **plum·like** \-,līk\ *adj*

plum·age \'plü-mij\ *n* [ME, fr. MF, fr. OF, fr. *plume* feather — more at PLUME] (15c) : the entire clothing of feathers of a bird — **plum·aged** \-mijd\ *adj*

[1]plumb \'pləm\ *n* [ME, fr. (assumed) OF *plomb,* fr. OF *plon* lead, fr. L *plumbum*] (14c) **1** : a lead weight attached to a line and used to indicate a vertical direction **2** : any of various weights (as a sinker for a fishing line or a lead for sounding) — **out of plumb** *or* **off plumb** : out of vertical or true

[2]plumb *adv* (15c) **1** : straight down or up : VERTICALLY **2** *chiefly dial* : to a complete degree : ABSOLUTELY ⟨'you're ~ crazy', she remarked, with easy candor —*Harper's Weekly*⟩ **3** : in a direct manner : EXACTLY; *also* : without interval of time : IMMEDIATELY

[3]plumb *vt* (15c) **1** : to weight with lead **2** **a** : to measure the depth of with a plumb **b** : to examine minutely and critically ⟨~*ing* the book's complexities⟩ **3** : to adjust or test by a plumb line **4** : to seal with lead **5** [back-formation fr. *plumber*] : to supply with or install as plumbing ~ *vi* : to work as a plumber

[4]plumb *adj* (15c) **1** : exactly vertical or true **2** : THOROUGH, COMPLETE *syn* see VERTICAL

plumb- *or* **plumbo-** *comb form* [L *plumb-,* fr. *plumbum*] : lead ⟨*plumb*ism⟩

plum·bag·i·nous \,pləm-'baj-ə-nəs\ *adj* (1796) : resembling, consisting of, or containing graphite

plum·ba·go \,pləm-'bā-(,)gō\ *n, pl* **-gos** [L *plumbagin-, plumbago* galena, fr. *plumbum*] (1747) **1** [NL, fr. L] : any of a genus (*Plumbago* of the family Plumbaginaceae, the plumbago family) of woody chiefly tropical plants with alternate leaves and spikes of showy flowers **2** : GRAPHITE

plumb bob *n* (ca. 1835) : the metal bob of a plumb line

plumb·er \'pləm-ər\ *n* [ME, fr. MF *plommier, plombier,* fr. L *plumbarius,* deriv. of *plumbum* lead] (14c) **1** *obs* : a dealer or worker in lead **2** : one who installs, repairs, and maintains piping, fittings, and fixtures involved in the distribution and use of water in a building

plumber's helper *n* (1952) : PLUNGER e — called also *plumber's friend*

plumber's snake *n* (1938) : a long flexible rod or cable usu. of steel that is used to free clogged pipes

plum·bic \'pləm-bik\ *adj* (1799) : of, relating to, or containing lead esp. with a valence of four

plum·bif·er·ous \,pləm-'bif-(ə-)rəs\ *adj* (1796) : containing lead

plumb·ing \'pləm-iŋ\ *n* (1666) **1** : the act of using a plumb **2** : a plumber's occupation or trade **3** : the apparatus (as pipes and fixtures) concerned in the distribution and use of water in a building

plum·bism \'pləm-,biz-əm\ *n* (1876) : lead poisoning esp. when chronic

plumb line *n* (1538) **1** : a line (as of cord) that has at one end a weight (as a plumb bob) and is used esp. to determine verticality **2** : a line directed to the center of gravity of the earth : a vertical line

plum·bous \'pləm-bəs\ *adj* (1854) : of, relating to, or containing lead esp. with a valence of two

[1]plume \'plüm\ *n* [ME, fr. MF, fr. L *pluma* small soft feather — more at FLEECE] (14c) **1** : a feather of a bird: as **a** : a large conspicuous or showy feather **b** : CONTOUR FEATHER **c** : PLUMAGE **d** : a cluster of distinctive feathers **2** **a** : material (as a feather, cluster of feathers, or a tuft of hair) worn as an ornament **b** : a token of honor or prowess : PRIZE **3** : something resembling a feather (as in shape, appearance, or lightness): as **a** : a plumose appendage of a plant **b** : an elongated and usu. open and mobile column or band (as of smoke, exhaust gases, or blowing snow) **c** : a plumate animal structure; *esp* : a full bushy tail

[2]plume *vt* **plumed; plum·ing** (15c) **1** **a** : to provide or deck with feathers **b** : to array showily **2** : to indulge (oneself) in pride with an obvious or vain display of self-satisfaction **3** **a** : to preen and arrange the feathers of (itself) — used of a bird **b** : to preen and arrange (feathers)

plumed \'plümd\ *adj* (1526) : provided with or adorned with or as if with a plume — often used in combination ⟨a white-*plumed* egret⟩

plume·let \'plüm-lət\ *n* (ca. 1847) : a small tuft or plume

[1]plum·met \'pləm-ət\ *n* [ME *plomet,* fr. MF *plombet* ball of lead, fr. *plomb* lead, fr. (assumed) OF — more at PLUMB] (14c) : PLUMB; *also* : PLUMB LINE

[2]plummet *vi* (1937) **1** : to fall perpendicularly ⟨the plane ~*ed* to earth⟩ **2** : to drop sharply and abruptly ⟨prices ~*ed*⟩

plum·my \'pləm-ē\ *adj* **plum·mi·er; -est** (1759) **1** **a** : full of plums ⟨a rich ~ cake⟩ **b** : CHOICE, DESIRABLE ⟨got a ~ role in the movie⟩ **2** **a** : having a plum color **b** : rich and mellow often to the point of affectation ⟨a ~ singing voice⟩

plu·mose \'plü-,mōs\ *adj* (ca. 1727) **1** : having feathers or plumes : FEATHERED **2** : FEATHERY

[1]plump \'pləmp\ *vb* [ME *plumpen*] *vi* (14c) **1** : to drop, sink, or come in contact suddenly or heavily ⟨~*ed* down in the chair⟩ **2** : to favor someone or something strongly — used with *for* ~ *vt* **1** : to drop, cast, or place suddenly or heavily **2** : to give support and favorable publicity to

[2]plump *n* (15c) : a sudden plunge, fall, or blow; *also* : the sound made by a plump

[3]plump *adv* (1594) **1** : with a sudden or heavy drop **2** **a** : straight down **b** : straight ahead **3** : without qualification : DIRECTLY

[4]plump *n* [ME *plumpe*] *chiefly dial* (15c) : GROUP, FLOCK ⟨a ~ of ducks rose at the same time —H. D. Thoreau⟩

[5]plump *vb* [ME, adj., dull, blunt] *vt* (1533) : to make plump ~ *vi* : to become plump

[6]plump *adj* (1569) **1** : having a full rounded usu. pleasing form ⟨a ~ woman⟩ **2** : AMPLE, ABUNDANT — **plump·ish** \'pləm-pish\ *adj*

plump·en \'pləm-pən\ *vb* (1687) : [5]PLUMP

[1]plump·er \'pləm-pər\ *n* [[5]*plump*] (1690) : an object carried in the mouth to fill out the cheeks

[2]plumper *n* [[1]*plump*] *chiefly Brit* (1785) : a vote for only one candidate when two or more are to be elected to the same office

[1]plump·ly \'pləm-plē\ *adv* (ca. 1611) : in a plump way ⟨a ~ pretty girl⟩

[2]plumply *adv* [[3]*plump*] (1786) : in a wholehearted manner and without hesitation or circumlocution : FORTHRIGHTLY

[1]plump·ness \'pləmp-nəs\ *n* (1545) : the quality or state of being plump

[2]plumpness *n* (1780) : freedom from hesitation or circumlocution : FORTHRIGHTNESS

plum pudding *n* (1711) : a rich boiled or steamed pudding containing fruits and spices

plu·mule \'plü-(,)myü(ə)l\ *n* [NL *plumula,* fr. L, dim. of *pluma* small soft feather — more at FLEECE] (ca. 1727) **1** : the primary bud of a plant embryo usu. situated at the apex of the hypocotyl and consisting of leaves and an epicotyl **2** : a down feather

plumy \'plü-mē\ *adj* **plum·i·er; -est** (1582) **1** : DOWNY **2** : having or resembling plumes

[1]plun·der \'plən-dər\ *vb* **plun·dered; plun·der·ing** \-d(ə-)riŋ\ [G *plündern*] *vt* (1632) **1** : PILLAGE, SACK **2** : to take esp. by force (as in war) : STEAL ~ *vi* : to commit robbery or looting — **plun·der·er** \-dər-ər\ *n*

[2]plunder *n* (1643) **1** : an act of plundering : PILLAGING **2** : something taken by force, theft, or fraud : LOOT **3** *chiefly dial* : personal or household effects *syn* see SPOIL

plun·der·able \'plən-d(ə-)rə-bəl\ *adj* (ca. 1802) **1** : capable of being plundered : subject to plunder **2** : worth plundering

plun·der·age \-d(ə-)rij\ *n* (1796) **1** : an act or instance of plundering; *esp* : embezzlement of goods on shipboard **2** : property obtained by plunderage

plun·der·ous \-d(ə-)rəs\ *adj* (1845) : given to plundering

[1]plunge \'plənj\ *vb* **plunged; plung·ing** [ME *plungen,* fr. MF *plonger,* fr. (assumed) VL *plumbicare,* fr. L *plumbum* lead] *vt* (14c) **1** **a** : to cause to penetrate or enter quickly and forcibly into something **b** : to sink (a potted plant) in the ground or a prepared bed **2** : to cause to enter a state or course of action usu. suddenly, unexpectedly, or violently ~ *vi* **1** : to thrust or cast oneself into or as if into water **2** **a** : to become pitched or thrown headlong or violently forward and downward; *also* : to move oneself in such a manner **b** : to act with reckless haste : enter suddenly or unexpectedly **c** : to bet or gamble heavily and recklessly **3** : to descend or dip suddenly ⟨the road ~*s* along the slope⟩

[2]plunge *n* (15c) : an act or instance of plunging : DIVE; *also* : SWIM

plung·er \'plən-jər\ *n* (1611) : one that plunges: as **a** : DIVER **b** : a reckless gambler or speculator **c** : the rod carrying the valves in the inner assembly of an automobile tire valve unit **d** (1) : a sliding reciprocating piece driven by or against fluid pressure; *esp* : PISTON (2) : a piece with a motion more or less like that of a ram or piston **e** : a rubber suction cup on a handle used to free plumbing traps and waste outlets of obstructions

plunk \'pləŋk\ *vb* [imit.] *vt* (1805) **1 :** to pluck or hit so as to produce a quick, hollow, metallic, or harsh sound **2 :** to set down suddenly **:** PLUMP ~ *vi* **1 :** to make a plunking sound **2 :** to drop abruptly **:** DIVE **3 :** to come out in favor of someone or something — used with *for* — **plunk** *n* — **plunk·er** *n*

plunk down *vi* (1891) **:** to drop abruptly **:** settle into position ~ *vt* **1 a :** to put down usu. firmly or abruptly ⟨*plunked* his money *down* on the counter⟩ **b :** to settle (oneself) into position ⟨*plunked* himself *down* on the bench⟩ **2 :** to pay out

plu·per·fect \(')plü-'pər-fikt\ *adj* [modif. of LL *plusquamperfectus,* lit., more than perfect] (1530) **:** PAST PERFECT — **pluperfect** *n*

plu·ral \'plu̇r-əl\ *adj* [ME, fr. MF & L; MF *plurel,* fr. L *pluralis,* fr. *plur-, plus* more — more at PLUS] (14c) **1 :** of, relating to, or constituting a class of grammatical forms usu. used to denote more than one or in some languages more than two ⟨*genetics* is ~ in form but takes a singular verb⟩ **2 :** relating to or consisting of or containing more than one or more than one kind or class ⟨a ~ society⟩ — **plural** *n* — **plu·ral·ly** \-ə-lē\ *adv*

plu·ral·ism \'plu̇r-ə-,liz-əm\ *n* (1818) **1 :** the holding of two or more offices or positions (as benefices) at the same time **2 :** the quality or state of being plural **3 a :** a theory that there are more than one or more than two kinds of ultimate reality **b :** a theory that reality is composed of a plurality of entities **4 a :** a state of society in which members of diverse ethnic, racial, religious, or social groups maintain an autonomous participation in and development of their traditional culture or special interest within the confines of a common civilization **b :** a concept, doctrine, or policy advocating this state — **plu·ral·ist** \-ləst\ *adj or n* — **plu·ral·is·tic** \,plu̇r-ə-'lis-tik\ *adj* — **plu·ral·is·ti·cal·ly** \-ti-k(ə-)lē\ *adv*

plu·ral·i·ty \plu̇-'ral-ət-ē\ *n, pl* **-ties** (14c) **1 a :** the state of being plural **b :** the state of being numerous **c :** a large number or quantity **2 :** PLURALISM 1; *also* **:** a benefice held by pluralism **3 a :** a number greater than another **b :** an excess of votes over those cast for an opposing candidate **c :** a number of votes cast for a candidate in a contest of more than two candidates that is greater than the number cast for any other candidate but not more than half the total votes cast

plu·ral·ize \'plu̇r-ə-,līz\ *vt* **-ized; -iz·ing** (1803) **:** to make plural or express in the plural form — **plu·ral·iza·tion** \,plu̇r-ə-lə-'zā-shən\ *n*

pluri- *comb form* [L, fr. *plur-, plus*] **:** having or being more than one **:** MULTI- ⟨*pluri*axial⟩

plu·rip·o·tent \plu̇-'rip-ət-ənt\ *adj* (1916) **:** not fixed as to developmental potentialities **:** having developmental plasticity

[1]plus \'pləs\ *adj* [L, adv., more, fr. neut. of *plur-, plus,* adj.; akin to Gk *pleion* more, L *plenus* full — more at FULL] (1579) **1 :** algebraically positive **2 :** having, receiving, or being in addition to what is anticipated **3 a :** falling high in a specified range ⟨a grade of C ~⟩ **b :** greater than that specified **c :** possessing a specified quality to a high degree **4 :** electrically positive **5 :** relating to or being a particular one of the two mating types that are required for successful fertilization in sexual reproduction in some lower plants (as a fungus)

[2]plus *n, pl* **plus·es** \'pləs-əz\ *also* **plus·ses** (1654) **1 :** PLUS SIGN **2 :** an added quantity **3 :** a positive factor or quality **4 :** SURPLUS

[3]plus *prep* (1668) **1 :** increased by **:** with the addition of ⟨four ~ five⟩ ⟨the principal ~ interest⟩ **2 :** BESIDES — chiefly in oral use ⟨~ which, we were traveling in an area exposed to few blacks —Linda Harris⟩

[4]plus *adv* (1950) **:** in addition **:** BESIDES — chiefly in oral use ⟨I think he would like me to be there. *Plus,* to totally heal, I have to do these things —Diana Munson⟩

[5]plus *conj* (1968) **:** AND — chiefly in oral use ⟨if you want to make a super investment, ~ you don't happen to be rich —*radio advt*⟩

usage The preposition *plus* has long been used with a meaning equivalent to *and* (as in "two *plus* two"); it is not, therefore, very surprising that in time people have begun to use it as a conjunction like *and.* It occurs mainly in spoken English and is likely to attract unfavorable notice in serious writing.

plus fours *n pl* (1920) **:** loose sports knickers made four inches longer than ordinary knickers

[1]plush \'pləsh\ *n* [MF *peluche*] (1594) **:** a fabric with an even pile longer and less dense than velvet pile

[2]plush *adj* (ca. 1645) **1 :** relating to, resembling, or made of plush **2 :** notably luxurious — **plush·ly** *adv* — **plush·ness** *n*

plushy \'pləsh-ē\ *adj* **plush·i·er; -est** (1611) **1 :** having the texture of or covered with plush **2 :** LUXURIOUS, SHOWY — **plush·i·ness** *n*

plus·sage \'pləs-ij\ *n* (1924) **:** an amount over and above another amount

plus sign *n* (ca. 1907) **:** a sign + denoting addition or a positive quantity

Plu·to \'plüt-(,)ō\ *n* [L *Pluton-, Pluto,* fr. Gk *Ploutōn*] **1 :** the Greek god of the underworld — compare DIS **2** [NL] **:** the planet farthest from the sun — see PLANET table

plu·toc·ra·cy \plü-'täk-rə-sē\ *n, pl* **-cies** [Gk *ploutokratia,* fr. *ploutos* wealth; akin to L *pluere* to rain] (1652) **1 :** government by the wealthy **2 :** a controlling class of the wealthy — **plu·to·crat** \'plüt-ə-,krat\ *n* — **plu·to·crat·ic** \,plüt-ə-'krat-ik\ *adj* — **plu·to·crat·i·cal·ly** \-i-k(ə-)lē\ *adv*

plu·ton \'plü-,tän\ *n* [prob. back-formation fr. *plutonic*] (1936) **:** a typically large body of intrusive igneous rock

plu·to·ni·an \plü-'tō-nē-ən\ *adj, often cap* (1667) **:** of, relating to, or characteristic of Pluto or the lower world **:** INFERNAL

plu·ton·ic \plü-'tän-ik\ *adj* [L *Pluton-, Pluto*] (1833) **1 :** formed by solidification of magma deep within the earth and crystalline throughout ⟨~ rock⟩ **2** *often cap* **:** PLUTONIAN

plu·to·ni·um \plü-'tō-nē-əm\ *n* [NL, fr. *Pluton-, Pluto,* the planet Pluto] (1942) **:** a radioactive metallic element similar chemically to uranium that is formed as the isotope 239 by decay of neptunium and found in minute quantities in pitchblende, that undergoes slow disintegration with the emission of a helium nucleus to form uranium 235, and that is fissionable with slow neutrons to yield atomic energy — see ELEMENT table

[1]plu·vi·al \'plü-vē-əl\ *adj* [L *pluvialis,* fr. *pluvia* rain, fr. fem. of *pluvius* rainy, fr. *pluere* to rain — more at FLOW] (ca. 1656) **1 a :** of or relating to rain **b :** characterized by abundant rain **2** *of a geologic change* **:** resulting from the action of rain

[2]pluvial *n* (1929) **:** a prolonged period of wet climate ⟨the ~*s* of the early Pleistocene⟩

[1]ply \'plī\ *vt* **plied; ply·ing** [ME *plien* to fold, fr. MF *plier,* fr. L *plicare;* akin to OHG *flehtan* to braid, L *plectere,* Gk *plekein*] (14c) **:** to twist together ⟨~ two single yarns⟩

[2]ply *n, pl* **plies** (1532) **1 a :** one of the strands in a yarn **b :** one of several layers (as of cloth) usu. sewn or laminated together **c :** one of the veneer sheets forming plywood **d :** a layer of a paper or paperboard **2 :** INCLINATION, BIAS

[3]ply *vb* **plied; ply·ing** [ME *plien,* short for *applien* to apply] *vt* (14c) **1 a :** to use or wield diligently ⟨busily ~*ing* his pen⟩ **b :** to practice or perform diligently ⟨~*ing* his trade⟩ **2 :** to keep furnishing or supplying something to ⟨*plied* us with liquor⟩ **3 :** to make a practice of rowing or sailing over or on ⟨the boat *plies* the river⟩ ~ *vi* **1 :** to apply oneself steadily **2 :** to go or travel regularly ⟨a steamer ~*ing* between opposite shores of the lake⟩

Plym·outh Rock \,plim-əth-\ *n* [fr. *Plymouth Rock,* on which the Pilgrims are supposed to have landed in 1620] (1849) **:** any of an American breed of medium-sized single-combed dual-purpose domestic fowls

ply·wood \'plī-,wu̇d\ *n* (1907) **:** a structural material consisting of sheets of wood glued or cemented together with the grains of adjacent layers arranged at right angles or at a wide angle

-pnea *or* **-pnoea** \(p)-nē-ə\ *n comb form* [NL, fr. Gk *-pnoia,* fr. *pnoia,* fr. *pnein* to breathe] **:** breath **:** breathing ⟨hyper*pnea*⟩ ⟨a*pnoea*⟩

pneum- *or* **pneumo-** *comb form* [NL, partly fr. Gk *pneum-* (fr. *pneuma*); partly fr. Gk *pneumōn* lung] **1 :** air **:** gas ⟨*pneumo*thorax⟩ **2 :** lung ⟨*pneum*ectomy⟩ **:** pulmonary and ⟨*pneumo*gastric⟩ **3 :** respiration ⟨*pneumo*graph⟩ **4 :** pneumonia ⟨*pneumo*coccus⟩

pneu·ma \'n(y)ü-mə\ *n* [Gk] (1884) **:** SOUL, SPIRIT

pneumat- *or* **pneumato-** *comb form* [Gk, fr. *pneumat-, pneuma*] **1 :** air **:** vapor **:** gas ⟨*pneumat*ics⟩ **2 :** respiration ⟨*pneumato*meter⟩

pneu·mat·ic \n(y)u̇-'mat-ik\ *adj* [L *pneumaticus,* fr. Gk *pneumatikos,* fr. *pneumat-, pneuma* air, breath, spirit, fr. *pnein* to breathe — more at SNEEZE] (1659) **1 :** of, relating to, or using gas (as air or wind): **a :** moved or worked by air pressure **b (1) :** adapted for holding or inflated with compressed air **(2) :** having air-filled cavities **2 :** of or relating to the pneuma **:** SPIRITUAL **3 :** having a well-proportioned feminine figure; *esp* **:** having a full bust — **pneu·mat·i·cal·ly** \-i-k(ə-)lē\ *adv* — **pneu·ma·tic·i·ty** \,n(y)ü-mə-'tis-ət-ē\ *n*

pneu·mat·ics \n(y)u̇-'mat-iks\ *n pl but sing in constr* (1660) **:** a branch of mechanics that deals with the mechanical properties of gases

pneu·ma·tol·o·gy \,n(y)ü-mə-'täl-ə-jē\ *n* [NL *pneumatologia,* fr. Gk *pneumat-, pneuma* + NL *-logia* -logy] (1678) **:** the study of spiritual beings or phenomena

pneu·ma·to·lyt·ic \,n(y)ü-mət-ᵊl-'it-ik, (,)n(y)ü-,mat-ᵊl-\ *adj* [ISV] (1896) **:** formed or forming by hot vapors or superheated liquids under pressure — used esp. of minerals and ores

pneu·mato·phore \n(y)u̇'mat-ə-,fō(ə)r, -,fȯ(ə)r\ *n* [ISV] (1859) **1 :** a muscular gas-containing sac that serves as a float on a siphonophore colony **2 :** a root often functioning as a respiratory organ in a marsh plant

pneu·mo·coc·cus \,n(y)ü-mə-'käk-əs\ *n, pl* **-coc·ci** \-'käk-(s)ī, -'käk-(,)(s)ē\ [NL] (ca. 1890) **:** a bacterium (*Diplococcus pneumoniae*) that causes an acute pneumonia involving one or more lobes of the lung — **pneu·mo·coc·cal** \-'käk-əl\ *adj*

pneu·mo·co·ni·o·sis \'n(y)ü-mō-,kō-nē-'ō-səs\ *n, pl* **-o·ses** \-,sēz\ [NL, fr. *pneum-* + Gk *konis* dust — more at INCINERATE] (1881) **:** a disease of the lungs caused by the habitual inhalation of irritant mineral or metallic particles — compare BLACK LUNG, SILICOSIS

pneu·mo·graph \'n(y)ü-mə-,graf\ *n* [ISV] (1878) **:** an instrument for recording the thoracic movements or volume change during respiration

pneu·mo·nec·to·my \,n(y)ü-mə-'nek-tə-mē\ *n, pl* **-mies** [Gk *pneumōn* + ISV *-ectomy*] (ca. 1895) **:** excision of an entire lung or of one or more lobes of a lung

pneu·mo·nia \n(y)u̇-'mō-nyə\ *n* [NL, fr. Gk, fr. *pneumōn* lung, alter. of *pleumōn* — more at PULMONARY] (1603) **:** a disease of the lungs characterized by inflammation and consolidation followed by resolution and caused by infection or irritants

pneu·mon·ic \n(y)u̇-'män-ik\ *adj* [NL *pneumonicus,* fr. Gk *pneumonikos,* fr. *pneumōn*] (1675) **1 :** of or relating to the lungs **:** PULMONIC, PULMONARY **2 :** of, relating to, or affected with pneumonia

pneu·mo·tho·rax \,n(y)ü-mə-'thō(ə)r-,aks, -'thȯ(ə)r-\ *n* [NL] (1821) **:** a state in which air or other gas is present in the pleural cavity and which occurs spontaneously as a result of disease or injury of lung tissue or puncture of the chest wall or is induced as a therapeutic measure to collapse the lung

pneu·mo·tro·pic \,n(y)ü-mə-'trōp-ik, -'träp-\ *adj* (ca. 1929) **:** turning, directed toward, or having an affinity for lung tissues — used esp. of infective agents

[1]poach \'pōch\ *vt* [ME *pochen,* fr. MF *pocher,* fr. OF *pochier,* lit., to put into a bag, fr. *poche* bag, pocket, of Gmc origin; akin to OE *pocca* bag] (14c) **:** to cook in simmering liquid

[2]poach *vb* [MF *pocher,* of Gmc origin; akin to ME *poken* to poke] *vt* (1677) **1 :** to trespass on ⟨a field ~*ed* too frequently by the amateur —*Times Lit. Supp.*⟩ **2 a :** to take (game or fish) by illegal methods **b :** to appropriate (something) as one's own ~ *vi* **1 :** to trespass for the purpose of stealing game; *also* **:** to take game or fish illegally **2 :** to encroach esp. for the purpose of taking something

[1]poach·er \'pō-chər\ *n* [[2]*poach*] (1667) **1 :** one that trespasses or steals **2 :** one who kills or takes game or fish illegally

[2]poacher *n* [[1]*poach*] (1861) **1 :** a covered pan containing a plate with depressions or shallow cups in each of which an egg can be cooked over steam rising from boiling water in the bottom of the pan **2 :** a shallow baking dish in which food (as fish) can be poached

po'boy \'pō-,bȯi\ *var of* POOR BOY

po·chard \'pō-chərd\ *n* [origin unknown] (1552) **:** any of numerous rather heavy-bodied diving ducks (esp. genus *Aythya*) with a large head and with feet and legs placed far back under the body

[1]pock \'päk\ *n* [ME *pokke,* fr. OE *pocc;* akin to MLG & MD *pocke* pock, L *bucca* cheek, mouth] (bef. 12c) **:** a pustule in an eruptive disease (as smallpox); *also* **:** a spot suggesting such a pustule

[2]pock *vt* (1841) **:** to mark with or as if with pocks **:** PIT

[1]pock·et \'päk-ət\ *n* [ME *poket,* fr. ONF *pokete,* dim. of *poke* bag, of Gmc origin; akin to OE *pocca* bag] (15c) **1 a :** a small bag carried by a person : PURSE **b** : a small bag that is sewed or inserted in a garment so that it is open at the top or side ⟨coat ~⟩ **2** : supply of money : MEANS **3** : RECEPTACLE, CONTAINER: as **a** : an opening at the corner or side of a billiard table **b** : a superficial pouch in some animals **4** : a small often isolated area or group ⟨~*s* of unemployment⟩: **a** (1) : a cavity containing a deposit (as of gold, water, or gas) (2) : a small body of ore **b** : AIR HOLE **5** : a place for a spar made by sewing a strip of canvas on a sail **6 a** : BLIND ALLEY **b** : the position of a contestant in a race hemmed in by others **c** : an area formed by blockers from which a football quarterback attempts to pass **7** : the concave area at the base of the finger sections of a baseball glove or mitt in which the ball is normally caught — **pock·et·ful** \-ˌfu̇l\ *n* — **in one's pocket** : in one's control or possession — **in pocket 1** : provided with funds **2** : in the position of having made a profit — **out of pocket 1** : low on money or funds **2** : having suffered a loss

[2]**pocket** *vt* (1589) **1 a** : to put or enclose in or as if in one's pocket ⟨~*ed* his change⟩ **b** : to appropriate to one's own use : STEAL **c** : to refuse assent to (a bill) by a pocket veto **2** : to put up with : ACCEPT **3** : to set aside : SUPPRESS ⟨~*ed* his pride⟩ **4 a** : to hem in **b** : to drive (a ball) into a pocket of a pool table **5** : to cover or supply with pockets — **pock·et·able** \-ə-bəl\ *adj*

[3]**pocket** *adj* (1612) **1 a** : small enough to be carried in the pocket **b** : SMALL, MINIATURE ⟨a ~ park⟩ **2 a** : of or relating to money **b** : carried in or paid from one's own pocket

pocket battleship *n* (1930) : a small battleship built so as to come within treaty limitations of tonnage and armament

pocket billiards *n pl but usu sing in constr* (1913) : POOL 2b

[1]**pock·et·book** \ˈpäk-ət-ˌbu̇k\ *n* (1617) **1** *often* **pocket book** : a small esp. paperback book that can be carried in the pocket **2** : a flat typically leather folding case for money or personal papers that can be carried in a pocket or handbag **3 a** : PURSE **b** : HANDBAG 2 **4** : financial resources : INCOME

[2]**pocketbook** *adj* (1894) : relating to or involving economic interests ⟨~ issues⟩

pocket borough *n* (1856) : an English constituency controlled before parliamentary reform by a single person or family

pocket edition *n* (1715) **1** : POCKETBOOK 1 **2** : a miniature form of something

pocket gopher *n* (1873) : GOPHER 2a

pocket-handkerchief *n* (1645) : a handkerchief carried in the pocket

pock·et·knife \ˈpäk-ət-ˌnīf\ *n* (1727) : a knife that has one or more blades that fold into the handle and that can be carried in the pocket

pocket money *n* (1632) : money for small personal expenses

pocket mouse *n* (1884) : any of various nocturnal burrowing rodents (family Heteromyidae) that resemble mice, live in arid parts of western No. America, and have long hind legs and tail and fur-lined cheek pouches

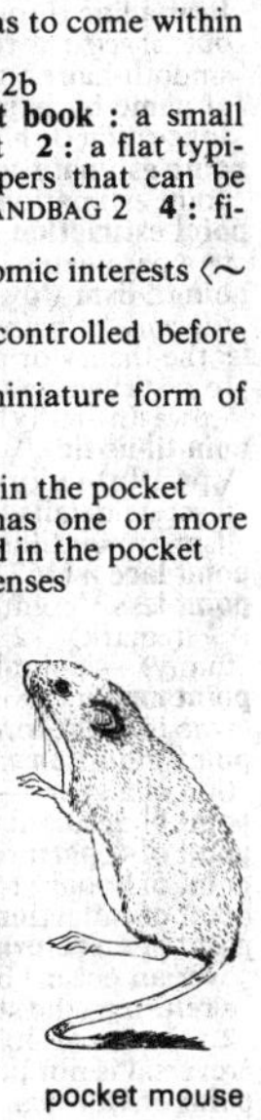
pocket mouse

pock·et–size \ˈpäk-ət-ˌsīz\ *also* **pock·et–sized** \-ˌsīzd\ *adj* (1907) **1** : of a size convenient for carrying in the pocket **2** : SMALL ⟨a ~ country⟩

pocket veto *n* (1842) : an indirect veto of a legislative bill by an executive through retention of the bill unsigned until after adjournment of the legislature — **pocket veto** *vt*

[1]**pock·mark** \ˈpäk-ˌmärk\ *n* (ca. 1673) : a mark, pit, or depressed scar caused by smallpox or acne; *also* : an imperfection suggesting a pockmark

[2]**pockmark** *vt* (1756) : to cover with or as if with pockmarks : PIT

pocky \ˈpäk-ē\ *adj* (14c) : covered with pocks

po·co \ˌpō-(ˌ)kō, ˌpȯ-\ *adv* [It, little, fr. L *paucus* — more at FEW] (1724) : to a slight degree : SOMEWHAT — used to qualify a direction in music ⟨~ allegro⟩

po·co a po·co \ˌpō-kō-(ˌ)ä-ˈpō-(ˌ)kō, ˌpȯ-kō-(ˌ)ä-ˈpȯ-\ *adv* [It] (ca. 1854) : little by little : GRADUALLY — used as a direction in music

po·co·cu·ran·te \ˌpō-kō-k(y)u̇-ˈrant-ē\ *adj* [It *poco curante* caring little] (1815) : INDIFFERENT, NONCHALANT — **po·co·cu·ran·tism** \-ˈran-ˌtiz-əm\ *n*

po·co·sin \pə-ˈkōs-ᵊn\ *n* [Delaware *pâkwesen*] (1634) : an upland swamp of the coastal plain of the southeastern U.S.

[1]**pod** \ˈpäd\ *n* [origin unknown] (1573) **1** : a bit socket in a brace **2** : a straight groove or channel in the barrel of an auger

[2]**pod** *n* [prob. alter. of *cod* bag — more at CODPIECE] (1688) **1** : a dry dehiscent pericarp or fruit that is composed of one or more carpels; *esp* : LEGUME **2 a** : an anatomical pouch **b** : a grasshopper egg case **3** : a tapered and roughly cylindrical body of ore or mineral **4** : a streamlined compartment under the wings or fuselage of an aircraft used as a container (as for fuel); *broadly* : a protective container or housing ⟨a submarine with its reactor in an external ~⟩ **5** : a detachable compartment (as for personnel, a power unit, or an instrument) on a spacecraft

[3]**pod** *vi* **pod·ded; pod·ding** (1734) : to produce pods

[4]**pod** *n* [origin unknown] (1832) : a number of animals (as seals) clustered together

-pod \ˌpäd\ *n comb form* [Gk *-podos*, fr. *pod-*, *pous* foot — more at FOOT] : foot : part resembling a foot ⟨pleo*pod*⟩

po·dag·ra \pə-ˈdag-rə\ *n* [ME, fr. L, fr. Gk, fr. *pod-*, *pous* + *agra* hunt, catch; akin to L *agere* to drive — more at AGENT] (14c) : GOUT

pod corn *n* (ca. 1893) : an Indian corn that has each kernel enclosed in a chaffy shell similar to that of other cereals

po·de·sta \ˌpōd-ə-ˈstä\ *n* [It *podestà*, lit., power, fr. L *potestat-*, *potestas*, irreg. fr. *potis* able — more at POTENT] (1548) : a chief magistrate in a medieval Italian municipality

podgy \ˈpäj-ē\ *adj* **podg·i·er; -est** [*podge* (something pudgy)] *chiefly Brit* (1846) : PUDGY

po·di·a·try \pə-ˈdī-ə-trē, pō-\ *n* [Gk *pod-*, *pous* + E *-iatry*] (1911) : the care and treatment of the human foot in health and disease — called also *chiropody* — **po·di·at·ric** \ˌpōd-ē-ˈa-trik\ *adj* — **po·di·a·trist** \pə-ˈdī-ə-trəst, pō-\ *n*

pod·ite \ˈpäd-ˌīt\ *n* [ISV *pod-* (fr. Gk *pod-*, *pous*) + *-ite*] (1875) : a limb segment of an arthropod

po·di·um \ˈpōd-ē-əm\ *n, pl* **podiums** *or* **po·dia** \-ē-ə\ [L — more at PEW] (1743) **1** : a low wall serving as a foundation or terrace wall: as **a** : one around the arena of an ancient amphitheater serving as a base for the tiers of seats **b** : the masonry under the stylobate of a temple **2 a** : a dais esp. for an orchestral conductor **b** : LECTERN

-po·di·um \ˈpōd-ē-əm\ *n comb form, pl* **-po·dia** \-ē-ə\ [NL, fr. Gk *podion*, dim. of *pod-*, *pous* foot — more at FOOT] : foot : part resembling a foot ⟨pseudo*podium*⟩

podo·phyl·lin \ˌpäd-ə-ˈfil-ən\ *n* [ISV, fr. NL *Podophyllum*] (1851) : a resin obtained from podophyllum and used in medicine as a caustic

podo·phyl·lum \-ˈfil-əm\ *n, pl* **-phyl·li** \-ˈfil-ˌī\ *or* **-phyllums** [NL, fr. *Podophyllum*, genus of herbs including the mayapple] (ca. 1760) : the rhizome and rootlet of the mayapple that is used as a caustic or as a source of the more effective podophyllin

Po·dunk \ˈpō-ˌdəŋk\ *n* [*Podunk*, village in Mass. or locality in Conn.] (1846) : a small, unimportant, and isolated town

pod·zol \ˈpäd-ˌzȯl\ *n* [Russ] (1908) : any of a group of zonal soils that develop in a moist climate esp. under coniferous or mixed forest and have an organic mat and a thin organic-mineral layer above a light gray leached layer resting on a dark illuvial horizon enriched with amorphous clay — **pod·zol·ic** \päd-ˈzäl-ik, -ˈzȯl-\ *adj*

pod·zol·iza·tion \ˌpäd-ˌzȯ-lə-ˈzā-shən\ *n* (1912) : a process of soil formation esp. in humid regions involving principally leaching of the upper layers with accumulation of material in lower layers and development of characteristic horizons; *specif* : the development of a podzol — **pod·zol·ize** \ˈpäd-ˌzȯ-ˌlīz\ *vb*

po·em \ˈpō-əm, -im, ˈpōm *also* ˈpȯ(-)m, ˈpō-ˌem\ *n* [MF *poeme*, fr. L *poema*, fr. Gk *poiēma*, fr. *poiein*] (1548) **1** : a composition in verse **2** : a creation, experience, or object suggesting a poem ⟨the house we stayed in . . . was itself a ~ —H. J. Laski⟩

po·esy \ˈpō-ə-zē, -sē\ *n, pl* **po·esies** [ME *poesie*, fr. MF, fr. L *poesis*, fr. Gk *poiēsis*, lit., creation, fr. *poiein*] (14c) **1 a** : a poem or body of poems **b** : POETRY **c** : artificial or sentimentalized poetic writing **2** : poetic inspiration

po·et \ˈpō-ət, -it *also* ˈpȯ(-)it\ *n* [ME, fr. MF *poete*, fr. L *poeta*, fr. Gk *poiētēs* maker, poet, fr. *poiein* to make, create; akin to Skt *cinoti* he heaps up] (14c) **1** : one who writes poetry : a maker of verses **2** : one (as a creative artist) of great imaginative and expressive gifts and special sensitivity to his medium

po·et·as·ter \ˈpō-ət-ˌas-tər\ *n* [NL, fr. L *poeta* + *-aster* -aster] (1599) : an inferior poet

po·et·ess \ˈpō-ət-əs, -it- *also* ˈpȯ(-)-it-\ *n* (1530) : a girl or woman who writes poetry

po·et·ic \pō-ˈet-ik\ *adj* (1530) **1 a** : of, relating to, or characteristic of poets or poetry **b** : given to writing poetry **2** : written in verse

po·et·i·cal \-i-kəl\ *adj* (14c) **1** : POETIC **2** : being beyond or above the truth of history or nature : IDEALIZED ⟨had ~ ideas about marriage⟩ — **po·et·i·cal·ly** \-k(ə-)lē\ *adv* — **po·et·i·cal·ness** \-i-kəl-nəs\ *n*

po·et·i·cism \pō-ˈet-ə-ˌsiz-əm\ *n* (1847) : an archaic, trite, or strained expression in poetry

po·et·i·cize \-ˌsīz\ *vt* **-cized; -ciz·ing** (1804) : to give a poetic quality to

poetic justice *n* (1679) : an outcome in which vice is punished and virtue rewarded usu. in a manner peculiarly or ironically appropriate

poetic license *n* (1530) : LICENSE 4

po·et·ics \pō-ˈet-iks\ *n pl but sing or pl in constr* (ca. 1727) **1 a** : a treatise on poetry or aesthetics **b** *also* **po·et·ic** \-ik\ : poetic theory or practice **2** : poetic feelings or utterances

po·et·ize \ˈpō-ət-ˌīz\ *vb* **-ized; -iz·ing** *vi* (1581) : to compose poetry ~ *vt* : POETICIZE — **po·et·iz·er** *n*

poet laureate *n, pl* **poets laureate** *or* **poet laureates** (14c) **1** : a poet honored for achievement in his art **2** : a poet appointed for life by an English sovereign as a member of the royal household and formerly expected to compose poems for court and national occasions **3** : one regarded by a country or region as its most eminent or representative poet

po·et·ry \ˈpō-ə-trē, -i-trē *also* ˈpȯ(-)i-trē\ *n* (14c) **1 a** : metrical writing : VERSE **b** : the productions of a poet : POEMS **2** : writing that formulates a concentrated imaginative awareness of experience in language chosen and arranged to create a specific emotional response through meaning, sound, and rhythm **3 a** : something likened to poetry esp. in beauty of expression **b** : poetic quality or aspect ⟨the ~ of dance⟩

po–faced \ˈpō-ˌfāst\ *adj* [origin unknown] *Brit* (1934) : woodenly expressionless : DEADPAN

pog·o·nip \ˈpäg-ə-ˌnip\ *n* [Paiute] (1865) : a dense winter fog containing frozen particles that is formed in deep mountain valleys of the western U.S.

po·go·noph·o·ran \ˌpō-gə-ˈnäf-ə-rən\ *n* [NL *Pogonophora*, fr. Gk *pōgōnophora*, neut. pl. of *pōgōnophoros* wearing a beard, fr. *pōgōn* beard + *-phoros* -phore] (1962) : any of a phylum or class (Pogonophora) of marine worms of uncertain systematic relationships that superficially resemble polychaetes but have a dorsal nervous system and obscure segmentation — **pogonophoran** *adj*

po·go stick \ˈpō-(ˌ)gō-\ *n* [fr. *Pogo*, a trademark] (1921) : a pole with a strong spring at the bottom and two footrests on which a person stands and propels himself along with a series of jumps

[1]**po·grom** \ˈpō-grəm; pō-ˈgräm, pə-; ˈpäg-rəm\ *n* [Yiddish, fr. Russ, lit., devastation] (1882) : an organized massacre of helpless people; *specif* : such a massacre of Jews

[2]**pogrom** *vt* (1915) : to massacre or destroy in a pogrom

po·grom·ist \-əst\ *n* (1907) : one who organizes or takes part in a pogrom

po·gy \ˈpō-gē\ *n, pl* **pogies** [of Algonquian origin; akin to Abnaki *p8kangan* menhaden] (ca. 1847) : MENHADEN

poi \ˈpȯi\ *n, pl* **poi** *or* **pois** [Hawaiian & Samoan] (1823) : a Hawaiian food of taro root cooked, pounded, and kneaded to a paste and often allowed to ferment

-poi·e·sis \(ˌ)pȯi-ˈē-səs\ *n comb form, pl* **-poi·e·ses** \-ˈē-ˌsēz\ [NL, fr. Gk *poiēsis* creation — more at POESY] : production : formation ⟨lympho*poiesis*⟩

\ə\ abut \ᵊ\ kitten, F table \ər\ further \a\ ash \ā\ ace \ä\ cot, cart \au̇\ out \ch\ chin \e\ bet \ē\ easy \g\ go \i\ hit \ī\ ice \j\ job \ŋ\ sing \ō\ go \ȯ\ law \ȯi\ boy \th\ thin \th\ the \ü\ loot \u̇\ foot \y\ yet \zh\ vision \à, k̟, ⁿ, œ, œ̄, ue, ue̅, ʸ\ *see* Guide to Pronunciation

-poi·et·ic \(,)pȯi-ˈet-ik\ *adj comb form* [Gk *poiētikos* creative, fr. *poiētēs* maker — more at POET] **:** productive **:** formative ⟨lympho*poietic*⟩

poi·gnan·cy \ˈpȯi-nyən-sē *sometimes* ˈpȯi(g)-nən-sē\ *n, pl* **-cies** (1730) **1 :** the quality or state of being poignant **2 :** an instance of poignancy

poi·gnant \ˈpȯi-nyənt *sometimes* ˈpȯi(g)-nənt\ *adj* [ME *poinaunt,* fr. MF *poignant,* prp. of *poindre* to prick, sting, fr. L *pungere* — more at PUNGENT] (14c) **1 :** pungently pervasive ⟨a ~ perfume⟩ **2 a** (1) **:** painfully affecting the feelings **:** PIERCING (2) **:** deeply affecting **:** TOUCHING **b :** designed to make an impression **:** CUTTING ⟨~ satire⟩ **3 a :** pleasurably stimulating **b :** being to the point **:** APT ***syn*** see PUNGENT, MOVING — **poi·gnant·ly** *adv*

poi·ki·lo·therm \pȯi-ˈkē-lə-,thərm, -ˈkil-ə-\ *n* [Gk *poikilos* variegated + ISV *-therm;* akin to L *pingere* to paint — more at PAINT] (1920) **:** an organism (as a frog) with a variable body temperature that is usu. slightly higher than the temperature of its environment **:** a cold-blooded organism — **poi·ki·lo·ther·mic** \,pȯi-kə-lō-ˈthər-mik\ *adj*

poi·lu \pwäl-ˈ(y)ü, ˈpwäl-,; pwȧ-lᵫ\ *n* [F, fr. *poilu* hairy, fr. MF, fr. *poil* hair, fr. L *pilus* — more at PILE] (1914) **:** a French soldier; *esp* **:** a front-line soldier in World War I

poin·ci·ana \,pȯin(t)-sē-ˈan-ə, ,p(w)än(t)-\ *n* [NL, fr. De *Poinci,* 17th cent. governor of part of the French West Indies] (1824) **:** any of a small genus (*Poinciana*) of ornamental tropical leguminous trees or shrubs with bright orange or red flowers; *also* **:** a showy closely related tree (*Delonix regia*) with immense racemes of scarlet and orange flowers, flat woody pods, and twice-pinnate leaves

poin·set·tia \÷pȯin-ˈset-ə, -ˈset-ē-ə\ *n* [NL, fr. Joel R. *Poinsett* †1851 Am. diplomat] (1836) **:** any of various spurges (genus *Euphorbia*) with flower clusters subtended by showy involucral bracts; *esp* **:** a showy Mexican and So. American plant (*E. pulcherrima*) with tapering scarlet bracts that suggest petals and surround small yellow flowers

[1]point \ˈpȯint\ *n* [ME, partly fr. OF, puncture, small spot, point in time or space, fr. L *punctum,* fr. neut. of *punctus,* pp. of *pungere* to prick; partly fr. OF *pointe* sharp end, fr. (assumed) VL *puncta,* fr. L, fem. of *punctus,* pp. — more at PUNGENT] (13c) **1 a** (1) **:** an individual detail **:** ITEM (2) **:** a distinguishing detail ⟨tact is one of her strong ~*s*⟩ **b :** the most important essential in a discussion or matter ⟨missed the whole ~ of the joke⟩ **c :** COGENCY **2** *obs* **:** physical condition **3 :** an end or object to be achieved **:** PURPOSE ⟨did not see what ~ there was in continuing the discussion⟩ **4 a** (1) **:** a geometric element of which it is postulated that at least two exist and that two suffice to determine a line (2) **:** a geometric element determined by an ordered set of coordinates **b** (1) **:** a narrowly localized place having a precisely indicated position ⟨walked to a ~ 50 yards north of the building⟩ (2) **:** a particular place **:** LOCALITY ⟨have come from distant ~*s*⟩ **c** (1) **:** an exact moment ⟨at this ~ he was interrupted⟩ (2) **:** a time interval immediately before something indicated **:** VERGE ⟨at the ~ of death⟩ **d** (1) **:** a particular step, stage, or degree in development ⟨had reached the ~ where nothing seemed to matter anymore⟩ (2) **:** a definite position in a scale **5 a :** the terminal usu. sharp or narrowly rounded part of something **:** TIP **b :** a weapon or tool having such a part and used for stabbing or piercing **c** (1) **:** the contact or discharge extremity of an electric device (as a spark plug) (2) *chiefly Brit* **:** an electric outlet **6 a :** a projecting usu. tapering piece of land or a sharp prominence **b** (1) **:** the tip of a projecting body part (2) **:** TINE 2 (3) *pl* **:** the extremities or markings of the extremities of an animal esp. when of a color differing from the rest of the body **c** (1) **:** a railroad switch (2) **:** the tip of the angle between two rails in a railroad frog **d :** the head of the bow of a stringed instrument **7 :** a short musical phrase; *esp* **:** a phrase in contrapuntal music **8 a :** a very small mark **b** (1) **:** PUNCTUATION MARK; *esp* **:** PERIOD (2) **:** DECIMAL POINT **9 :** a lace for tying parts of a garment together used esp. in the 16th and 17th centuries **10 :** one of usu. 11 divisions of a heraldic shield that determines the position of a charge **11 a :** one of the 32 equidistant spots of a compass card **b :** the difference of 11¼ degrees between two such successive points **12 :** a small detachment ahead of an advance guard or behind a rear guard **13 a :** NEEDLEPOINT 1 **b :** lace made with a bobbin **14 :** one of 12 spaces marked off on each side of a backgammon board **15 :** a unit of measurement: as **a** (1) **:** a unit of counting in the scoring of a game or contest (2) **:** a unit used in evaluating the strength of a bridge hand **b :** a unit of academic credit **c** (1) **:** a unit used in quoting prices (as of stocks, bonds, and commodities) (2) *pl* **:** a percentage of the face value of a loan often added as a placement fee or service charge (3) **:** a percentage of the profits of a business venture (as a motion-picture production) **d :** a unit of about $1/72$ inch used esp. to measure the size of type **16 :** the action of pointing: as **a :** the rigidly intent attitude of a hunting dog marking game for a gunner **b :** the action in dancing of extending one leg so that only the tips of the toes touch the floor **17 :** a position of a player in various games (as lacrosse); *also* **:** the player of such a position **18 :** a number thrown on the first roll of the dice in craps which the player attempts to repeat before throwing a seven — compare MISSOUT, PASS 13 **19 :** credit accruing from creating an advantageous impression ⟨working overtime so as to score ~*s* with the boss⟩ — **beside the point :** IRRELEVANT — **in point of :** with regard to **:** in the matter of ⟨*in point of* law⟩ ⟨*in point of* fact⟩ — **to the point :** RELEVANT, PERTINENT ⟨a suggestion that was *to the point*⟩

[2]point *vt* (14c) **1 a :** to furnish with a point **:** SHARPEN ⟨~*ing* a pencil with a knife⟩ **b :** to give added force, emphasis, or piquancy to ⟨~ up a remark⟩ **2 :** to scratch out the old mortar from the joints of (as a brick wall) and fill in with new material **3 a** (1) **:** to mark the pauses or grammatical divisions in **:** PUNCTUATE (2) **:** to separate (a decimal fraction) from an integer by a decimal point — usu. used with *off* **b :** to mark (as Hebrew words) with diacritics (as vowel points) **4 a** (1) **:** to indicate the position or direction of esp. by extending a finger ⟨~ the way home⟩ (2) **:** to direct somone's attention to ⟨~ the way to new knowledge —Elizabeth Hall⟩ — usu. used with *out* ⟨~ out a mistake⟩ **b** *of a hunting dog* **:** to indicate the presence and place of (game) by a point **5 a :** to cause to be turned in a particular direction ⟨~ a gun⟩ ⟨~*ed* the boat upstream⟩ **b :** to extend (a leg) in executing a point in dancing ~ *vi* **1 a :** to indicate the fact or probability of something specified ⟨everything ~*s* to a bright future⟩ **b :** to indicate the position or direction of something esp. by extending a finger ⟨~ at the map⟩ **c :** to point game ⟨a dog that ~*s* well⟩ **2 a :** to lie extended, aimed, or turned in a particular direction ⟨a directional arrow that ~*ed* to the north⟩ **b :** to execute a point in dancing **3** *of a ship* **:** to sail close to the wind **4 :** to train for a particular contest

point–blank \ˈpȯint-ˈblaŋk\ *adj* (1591) **1 a :** marked by no appreciable drop below initial horizontal line of flight **b :** so close to a target that a missile fired will travel in a straight line to the mark **2 :** DIRECT, BLUNT ⟨a ~ refusal⟩ — **point–blank** *adv*

point count *n* (1950) **:** a method of evaluating the strength of a hand in bridge by counting points for each high card and often for long or short suits; *also* **:** the value of a hand so evaluated

point d'ap·pui \,pwaⁿ(n)-dap-ˈwē\ *n, pl* **points d'appui** *same*\ [F, lit., point of support] (1819) **:** FOUNDATION, BASE; *esp* **:** a base for a military operation

point–de·vice \,pȯint-di-ˈvīs\ *adj* [ME *at point devis* at a fixed point] *archaic* (1526) **:** marked by punctilious attention to detail **:** METICULOUS — **point–device** *adv, archaic*

pointe \ˈpwaⁿ(n)t\ *n* [F, lit., point] (1846) **:** a ballet position in which the body is balanced on the extreme tip of the toe

[1]point·ed \ˈpȯint-əd\ *adj* (13c) **1 a :** having a point **b :** being an arch with a pointed crown; *also* **:** marked by the use of a pointed arch ⟨~ architecture⟩ **2 a :** being to the point **:** PERTINENT **b :** aimed at a particular person or group **3 :** CONSPICUOUS, MARKED ⟨~ indifference⟩ — **point·ed·ly** *adv* — **point·ed·ness** *n*

[2]pointed *adj* [short for *appointed*] *obs* (1523) **:** SET, FIXED

point·er \ˈpȯint-ər\ *n* (1574) **1 a** *pl, cap* **:** the two stars in the Great Bear a line through which points to the North Star **b :** one that points out; *specif* **:** a rod used to direct attention **2 :** a large strong slender smooth-haired gundog that hunts by scent and indicates the presence of game by pointing **3 :** one that furnishes with points **4 :** a useful suggestion or hint **:** TIP

point estimate *n* (1966) **:** the single value assigned to a parameter in point estimation

point estimation *n* (1962) **:** estimation in which a single value is assigned to a parameter

poin·til·lism \ˈpwaⁿ(n)-tē-,(y)iz-əm, ˈpȯint-ᵊl-,iz-əm\ *n, often cap* [F *pointillisme,* fr. *pointiller* to stipple, fr. *point* spot — more at POINT] (1901) **:** the theory or practice in art of applying small strokes or dots of color to a surface so that from a distance they blend together — **poin·til·list** \,pwaⁿ(n)-tē-ˈ(y)ēst, ˈpȯint-ᵊl-əst\ *n*

poin·til·lis·tic \,pwaⁿ(n)-tē-ˈ(y)is-tik, ,pȯint-ᵊl-ˈis-\ *also* **point·til·list** \,pwaⁿ(n)-tē-ˈ(y)ēst, ˈpȯint-ᵊl-əst\ *adj* (1922) **1 :** composed of many discrete details or parts **2 :** of, relating to, or characteristic of pointillism or pointillists

point lace *n* (1672) **:** NEEDLEPOINT 1

point·less \ˈpȯint-ləs\ *adj* (1726) **1 :** devoid of meaning **:** SENSELESS ⟨a ~ remark⟩ **2 :** devoid of effectiveness **:** FLAT ⟨~ attempts to be funny⟩ — **point·less·ly** *adv* — **point·less·ness** *n*

point man *n* (1903) **:** a soldier who goes ahead of a patrol; *broadly* **:** one who is in the forefront (as on a political issue)

point mutation *n* (1928) **:** mutation due to intramolecular reorganization of a gene — called also *gene mutation*

point of accumulation (1929) **:** LIMIT POINT

point of departure (1857) **:** a starting point esp. in a discussion

point of honor (1612) **:** a matter seriously affecting one's honor

point of inflection (1743) **:** INFLECTION POINT

point of no return (ca. 1941) **1 :** the point in the flight of an aircraft (as over an ocean) beyond which the remaining fuel will be insufficient for a return to the starting point with the result that the craft must proceed **2 :** a critical point (as in a course of action) at which turning back or reversal is not possible

point of view (ca. 1727) **:** a position from which something is considered or evaluated **:** STANDPOINT

point set topology *n* (1957) **:** a branch of topology concerned with the properties and theory of topological spaces and metric spaces developed with emphasis on set theory

point source *n* (1903) **:** a source of radiation (as light) that is concentrated at a point and considered as having no spatial extension

pointy \ˈpȯint-ē\ *adj* **point·i·er; -est** (1644) **1 :** coming to a rather sharp point **2 :** having parts that stick out sharply here and there

pointy–head \ˈpȯint-ē-,hed\ *n* (1968) **:** INTELLECTUAL — usu. used disparagingly — **pointy–head·ed** \-,hed-əd\ *adj*

[1]poise \ˈpȯiz\ *vb* **poised; pois·ing** [ME *poisen* to weigh, ponder, fr. MF *pois-,* stem of *peser,* fr. L *pensare* — more at PENSIVE] *vt* (1598) **1 a :** BALANCE; *esp* **:** to hold or carry in equilibrium ⟨walked along gracefully with a water jar *poised* on her head⟩ **b :** to hold supported or suspended without motion in a steady position ⟨*poised* her fork and gave her guest a knowing look —Louis Bromfield⟩ **2 :** to hold or carry (the head) in a particular way **3 :** to put into readiness **:** BRACE ~ *vi* **1 :** to become drawn up into readiness **2 :** HOVER

[2]poise *n* [ME *poyse* weight, heaviness, fr. MF *pois,* fr. L *pensum,* fr. neut. of *pensus,* pp. of *pendere* to weigh — more at PENDANT] (1555) **1 :** a stably balanced state **:** EQUILIBRIUM ⟨a ~ between widely divergent impulses —F. R. Leavis⟩ **2 a :** easy self-possessed assurance of manner **:** gracious tact in coping or handling; *also* **:** the pleasantly tranquil interaction between persons of poise ⟨no angry outbursts marred the ~ of the meeting⟩ **b :** a particular way of carrying oneself **:** BEARING, CARRIAGE ***syn*** see TACT

[3]poise \ˈpwäz\ *n* [F, fr. Jean Louis Marie *Poiseuille* †1869 Fr. physician and anatomist] (ca. 1924) **:** a centimeter-gram-second unit of viscosity equal to the viscosity of a fluid that would require a shearing force of one dyne to move a square-centimeter area of either of two parallel layers of fluid one centimeter apart with a velocity of one centimeter per second relative to the other layer with the space between the layers being filled with the fluid

poised \ˈpȯizd\ *adj* (ca. 1643) **:** having poise: **a :** marked by balance or equilibrium **b :** marked by easy composure of manner or bearing

[1]poi·son \ˈpȯiz-ᵊn\ *n* [ME, fr. MF, drink, poisonous drink, poison, fr. L *potion-, potio* drink — more at POTION] (14c) **1 a :** a substance that through its chemical action usu. kills, injures, or impairs an organism **b** (1) **:** something destructive or harmful (2) **:** an object of aversion or abhorrence **2 :** a substance that inhibits the activity of another substance or the course of a reaction or process ⟨a catalyst ~⟩

[2]poison *vb* **poi·soned; poi·son·ing** \ˈpȯiz-niŋ, -ᵊn-iŋ\ *vt* (14c) **1 a :** to injure or kill with poison **b :** to treat, taint, or impregnate with poison **2 :** to exert a baneful influence on **:** CORRUPT ⟨~*ed* their minds⟩ **3 :** to inhibit the activity, course, or occurrence of ~ *vi* : to put poison into or on something — **poi·son·er** \'pȯiz-nər, -ᵊn-ər\ *n*

³**poison** *adj* (1530) **1** : POISONOUS, VENOMOUS ⟨a ~ plant⟩ ⟨a ~ tongue⟩ **2** : impregnated with poison : POISONED ⟨a ~ arrow⟩

poison gas *n* (1915) : a poisonous gas or a liquid or a solid giving off poisonous vapors designed (as in chemical warfare) to kill, injure, or disable by inhalation or contact

poison hemlock *n* (ca. 1817) **1** : a large branching biennial poisonous herb (*Conium maculatum*) of the carrot family with finely divided leaves and white flowers **2** : WATER HEMLOCK

poison ivy *n* (1784) **1** : a climbing plant (*Rhus toxicodendron*) of the sumac family that is esp. common in the eastern and central U.S., that has ternate leaves, greenish flowers, and white berries, and that produces an acutely irritating oil causing a usu. intensely itching skin rash; *also* : any of several congeneric plants **2** : a skin rash caused by poison ivy

poison oak *n* (1743) : any of several poison ivies or congeneric plants producing an oil with similar irritating properties: **a** : POISON SUMAC **b** : a bushy plant (*Rhus diversiloba*) of the Pacific coast **c** : a bushy plant (*Rhus quercifolia*) of the southeastern U.S.

poi·son·ous \'pȯiz-nəs, -ᵊn-əs\ *adj* (ca. 1573) : having the properties or effects of poison : VENOMOUS — **poi·son·ous·ly** *adv*

poison–pen *adj* (1925) : written with malice and spite and usu. anonymously ⟨~ letter⟩

poison pill *n* (1983) : a financial tactic (as increasing indebtedness) used by a company to deter an unwanted takeover by another company

poison sumac *n* (1922) : a smooth American swamp shrub (*Rhus vernix*) that has pinnate leaves, greenish flowers, and greenish white berries and produces an irritating oil — called also *poison dogwood*

poi·son·wood \'pȯiz-ᵊn-,wu̇d\ *n* (1721) : a caustic or poisonous tree (*Metopium toxiferum*) of Florida and the West Indies that has compound leaves, greenish paniculate flowers, and orange-yellow fruits

Pois·son distribution \pwä-'sōⁿ-\ *n* [Siméon D. Poisson †1840 Fr. mathematician] (1922) : a probability density function that is often used as a mathematical model of the number of outcomes (as traffic accidents, atomic disintegrations, or organisms) obtained in a suitable interval of time and space, that has its mean equal to its variance, that is used as an approximation to the binomial distribution, and that has the form

$$f(x) = \frac{e^{-\mu}\mu^x}{x!} \quad \text{where } \mu$$

is the mean and *x* takes on nonnegative integral values

¹**poke** \'pōk\ *n* [ME, fr. ONF — more at POCKET] (13c) **1** *chiefly Southern & Midland* : BAG, SACK **2 a** : WALLET **b** : PURSE

²**poke** *vb* **poked; pok·ing** [ME *poken*, akin to MD *poken* to poke] *vt* (14c) **1 a** (1) : PROD, JAB ⟨*poked* him in the ribs⟩ (2) : to urge or stir by prodding or jabbing (3) : to cause to prod ⟨*poked* a stick at the snake⟩ **b** (1) : PIERCE, STAB (2) : to produce by piercing, stabbing, or jabbing ⟨~ a hole⟩ **c** (1) : HIT, PUNCH ⟨*poked* him in the nose⟩ (2) : to deliver (a blow) with the fist **2 a** : to cause to project ⟨*poked* her head out of the window⟩ **b** : to make (one's way) by poking ⟨*poked* his way through the ruins⟩ **c** : to interpose or interject in a meddlesome manner ⟨asked him not to ~ his nose into other people's business⟩ ~ *vi* **1 a** : to make a prodding, jabbing, or thrusting movement esp. repeatedly **b** : to strike out at something **2 a** : to look about or through something without system : RUMMAGE ⟨*poking* around in the attic⟩ **b** : MEDDLE **3** : to move or act slowly or aimlessly ⟨just *poked* around and didn't accomplish much⟩ **4** : to become stuck out or forward : PROTRUDE — **poke fun at** : RIDICULE, MOCK

³**poke** *n* (1796) **1 a** : a quick thrust : JAB **b** : a blow with the fist : PUNCH **2** : a projecting brim on the front of a woman's bonnet

⁴**poke** *n* [modif. of *puccoon* (in some Algonquian language of Virginia), a plant used in dyeing] (1708) : POKEWEED

poke·ber·ry \'pōk-,ber-ē\ *n* (1774) : the berry of the pokeweed; *also* : POKEWEED

poke bonnet *n* (1820) : a woman's bonnet with a projecting brim at the front

¹**pok·er** \'pō-kər\ *n* (1534) : one that pokes; *esp* : a metal rod for stirring a fire

²**po·ker** \'pō-kər\ *n* [prob. modif. of F *poque*, a card game similar to poker] (1834) : one of several card games in which a player bets that the value of his hand is greater than that of the hands held by others, in which each subsequent player must either equal or raise the bet or drop out, and in which the player holding the highest hand at the end of the betting wins the pot

poker hands in descending value: *1* five of a kind, *2* royal flush, *3* straight flush, *4* four of a kind, *5* full house, *6* flush, *7* straight, *8* three of a kind, *9* two pairs, *10* one pair

poker face *n* [²*poker*; fr. the need of the poker player to conceal the true quality of his hand] (ca. 1885) : an inscrutable face that reveals no hint of a person's thoughts or feelings — **po·ker–faced** \pō-kər-'fāst\ *adj*

poke·weed \'pō-,kwēd\ *n* (1751) : a coarse American perennial herb (*Phytolacca americana* of the family Phytolaccaceae, the pokeweed family) with racemose white flowers, dark purple juicy berries, a poisonous root, and young shoots sometimes used as potherbs

po·key \'pō-kē\ *n, pl* **pokeys** [origin unknown] *slang* (ca. 1919) : JAIL

poky *or* **pok·ey** \'pō-kē\ *adj* **pok·i·er; -est** [²*poke*] (1849) **1** : small and cramped **2** : SHABBY, DULL **3** : annoyingly slow — **pok·i·ly** \-kə-lē\ *adv* — **pok·i·ness** \-kē-nəs\ *n*

pol \'päl\ *n* (ca. 1942) : POLITICIAN

Po·la·bi·an \pō-'läb-ē-ən, -'läb-\ *n* [*Polab*, of Slavic origin; akin to Pol *po* on, and to Pol *Laba*, Elbe river] (1866) **1** *or* **Polab** : a Slavic people formerly dwelling in the basin of the Elbe and on the Baltic coast of Germany **2** : the extinct West Slavic language of the Polabians

Po·lack \'pō-,läk, -,lak\ *n* [Pol *Polak*] (1574) **1** *obs* : POLE 1 **2** : a person of Polish birth or descent — usu. used disparagingly

Po·land Chi·na \pō-lən(d)-'chī-nə\ *n* [*Poland*, Europe + *China*, Asia] (1879) : any of an American breed of large white-marked black swine

¹**po·lar** \'pō-lər\ *adj* [NL *polaris*, fr. L *polus* pole] (1551) **1 a** : of or relating to a geographical pole or the region around it **b** : coming from or having the characteristics of such a region **c** (1) : passing over a planet's north and south poles ⟨a satellite in a ~ orbit⟩ (2) : traveling in a polar orbit ⟨a ~ satellite⟩ **2** : of or relating to one or more poles (as of a magnet) **3** : serving as a guide **4** : diametrically opposite **5** : exhibiting polarity; *esp* : having a dipole or characterized by molecules having dipoles ⟨a ~ solvent⟩ **6** : resembling a pole or axis around which all else revolves : PIVOTAL **7** : of, relating to, or expressed in polar coordinates ⟨~ equations⟩; *also* : of or relating to a polar coordinate system

²**polar** *n* (1848) : a straight line related to a point; *specif* : the straight line joining the points of contact of the tangents from a point exterior to a conic section

polar bear *n* (1781) : a large creamy-white bear (*Thalarctos maritimus*) that inhabits arctic regions

polar body *n* (1888) : a cell that separates from an oocyte during meiosis and that contains a nucleus produced in the first or second meiotic division but very little cytoplasm

polar bear

polar circle *n* (ca. 1551) : one of the two parallels of latitude each at a distance from a pole of the earth equal to about 23 degrees 27 minutes

polar coordinate *n* (1816) : either of two numbers that locate a point in a plane by its distance from a fixed point on a line and the angle this line makes with a fixed line

polar front *n* (1920) : the boundary between the cold air of a polar region and the warmer air of lower latitudes

po·lar·im·e·ter \,pō-lə-'rim-ət-ər\ *n* [ISV, fr. *polarization*] (ca. 1859) **1** : an instrument for determining the amount of polarization of light or the proportion of polarized light in a partially polarized ray **2** : a polariscope for measuring the amount of rotation of the plane of polarization esp. by liquids — **po·lari·met·ric** \pō-,lar-ə-'me-trik\ *adj* — **po·lar·im·e·try** \,pō-lə-'rim-ə-trē\ *n*

Po·lar·is \pə-'lar-əs, -'lär-\ *n* [NL, fr. *polaris* polar] : NORTH STAR

po·lari·scope \pō-'lar-ə-,skōp\ *n* [ISV, fr. *polarization*] (ca. 1829) **1** : an instrument for studying the properties of or examining substances in polarized light **2** : POLARIMETER 2 — **po·lari·scop·ic** \-,lar-ə-'skäp-ik\ *adj*

po·lar·i·ty \pō-'lar-ət-ē, pə-\ *n, pl* **-ties** (1646) **1** : the quality or condition inherent in a body that exhibits opposite properties or powers in opposite parts or directions or that exhibits contrasted properties or powers in contrasted parts or directions **2** : attraction toward a particular object or in a specific direction **3** : the particular state either positive or negative with reference to the two poles or to electrification **4 a** : diametrical opposition **b** : an instance of such opposition

po·lar·iza·tion \,pō-lə-rə-'zā-shən\ *n* (1812) **1** : the action of polarizing or state of being or becoming polarized: as **a** (1) : the action or process of affecting radiation and esp. light so that the vibrations of the wave assume a definite form (2) : the state of radiation affected by this process **b** : the deposition of gas on one or both electrodes of an electrolytic cell increasing the resistance and setting up a counter electromotive force **c** : MAGNETIZATION **2 a** : division into two opposites **b** : concentration about opposing extremes of groups or interests formerly ranged on a continuum

po·lar·ize \'pō-lə-,rīz\ *vb* **-ized; -iz·ing** [F *polariser*, fr. NL *polaris* polar] *vt* (1811) **1** : to cause (as light waves) to vibrate in a definite pattern **2** : to give physical polarity to **3** : to break up into opposing factions or groupings **4** : CONCENTRATE 1 ⟨recreate a cohesive rock community by *polarizing* . . . an amorphous, fragmented audience —Ellen Willis⟩ ~ *vi* : to become polarized — **po·lar·iz·abil·i·ty** \,pō-lə-,rī-zə-'bil-ət-ē\ *n* — **po·lar·iz·able** \'pō-lə-,rī-zə-bəl\ *adj*

polar nucleus *n* (1882) : either of the two nuclei of a seed plant embryo sac that are destined to form endosperm

po·lar·og·ra·phy \,pō-lə-'räg-rə-fē\ *n* [ISV, fr. *polarization*] (1936) : a method of qualitative or quantitative analysis based on current-voltage curves obtained during electrolysis of a solution with a steadily increasing electromotive force — **po·laro·graph·ic** \pō-,lar-ə-'graf-ik\ *adj* — **po·laro·graph·i·cal·ly** \-i-k(ə-)lē\ *adv*

Po·lar·oid \'pō-lə-,rȯid\ *trademark* — used esp. for a light-polarizing material used esp. in eyeglasses and lamps to prevent glare and in various optical devices

po·lar·on \'pō-lə-ˌrän\ *n* [ISV *polar* + [2]*-on*] (1946) **:** a conducting electron in an ionic crystal together with the induced polarization of the surrounding lattice

pol·der \'pōl-dər, 'päl-\ *n* [D] (1604) **:** a tract of low land reclaimed from a body of water (as the sea)

[1]**pole** \'pōl\ *n* [ME, fr. OE *pāl* stake, pole, fr. L *palus* stake; akin to L *pangere* to fix — more at PACT] (bef. 12c) **1 a :** a long slender usu. cylindrical object (as a length of wood) **b :** a shaft which extends from the front axle of a wagon between wheelhorses and by which the wagon is drawn **:** TONGUE **c :** a long staff of wood, metal, or fiberglass used in the pole vault **2 a :** a varying unit of length; *esp* **:** one measuring 16½ feet (5.03 meters) **b :** a unit of area equal to a square rod (25.293 square meters) **3 :** a tree with a breast-high diameter of from 4 to 12 inches (10 to 30 centimeters) **4 :** the inside front row position on the starting line for a race

[2]**pole** *vb* **poled; pol·ing** *vt* (ca. 1753) **1 :** to act upon with a pole **2 :** to impel or push with a pole ~ *vi* **1 :** to propel a boat with a pole **2 :** to use ski poles to gain speed

[3]**pole** *n* [ME *pool,* fr. L *polus,* fr. Gk *polos* pivot, pole; akin to Gk *kyklos* wheel — more at WHEEL] (14c) **1 :** either extremity of an axis of a sphere and esp. of the earth's axis **2 a :** either of two related opposites **b :** a point of guidance or attraction **3 a :** one of the two terminals of an electric cell, battery, or dynamo **b :** one of two or more regions in a magnetized body at which the magnetic flux density is concentrated **4 :** either of two morphologically or physiologically differentiated areas at opposite ends of an axis in an organism or cell — see BLASTULA illustration **5 a :** the fixed point in a system of polar coordinates that serves as the origin **b :** the point of origin of two tangents to a conic section that determine a polar — **poles apart :** as diametrically opposed as possible ⟨the two voters were *poles apart* on that issue⟩

Pole \'pōl\ *n* [G, of Slavic origin; akin to Pol *Polak* Pole] (1589) **1 :** a native or inhabitant of Poland **2 :** a person of Polish descent

[1]**pole·ax** \'pō-ˌlaks\ *n* [ME *polax, pollax,* fr. *pol, polle* poll + *ax*] (14c) **1 :** a battle-ax with short handle and often a hook or spike opposite the blade; *also* **:** one with a long handle used as an ornamental weapon **2 :** an ax used in slaughtering cattle

[2]**poleax** *vt* (1882) **:** to attack, strike, or fell with or as if with a poleax

pole bean *n* (1770) **:** a cultivated bean that is usu. trained to grow upright on supports

pole·cat \'pōl-ˌkat\ *n, pl* **polecats** *or* **polecat** [ME *polcat,* prob. fr. MF *poul, pol* cock + ME *cat;* prob. fr. its preying on poultry — more at PULLET] (14c) **1 :** a European carnivorous mammal (*Mustela putorius*) of which the ferret is considered a domesticated variety **2 :** SKUNK

pole horse *n* (1823) **1 :** a horse harnessed beside the pole of a wagon **2 :** the horse having a starting position next to the inside rail in a harness race

poleis *pl of* POLIS

pole·less \'pōl-ləs\ *adj* (1647) **:** having no pole

po·lem·ic \pə-'lem-ik\ *n* [F *polémique,* fr. MF, fr. *polemique* controversial, fr. Gk *polemikos* warlike, hostile, fr. *polemos* war; akin to OE *ealfelo* baleful, Gk *pallein* to brandish] (1638) **1 a :** an aggressive attack on or refutation of the opinions or principles of another **b :** the art or practice of disputation or controversy — usu. used in pl. but sing. or pl. in constr. **2 :** an aggressive controversialist **:** DISPUTANT — **po·lem·i·cist** \-'lem-ə-səst\ *n*

po·lem·i·cal \-i-kəl\ *also* **po·lem·ic** \-ik\ *adj* (1640) **1 :** of, relating to, or being a polemic **:** CONTROVERSIAL **2 :** engaged in or addicted to polemics **:** DISPUTATIOUS — **po·lem·i·cal·ly** \-i-k(ə-)lē\ *adv*

po·lem·i·cize \-'lem-ə-ˌsīz\ *vi* **-cized; -ciz·ing** (1950) **:** to engage in controversy **:** deliver a polemic

po·le·mist \pə-'lem-əst, 'päl-ə-məst\ *n* [irreg. fr. *polemic*] (1825) **:** one skilled in or given to polemics

pol·e·mize \'päl-ə-ˌmīz\ *vi* **-mized; -miz·ing** (1828) **:** POLEMICIZE

pol·e·mo·ni·um \ˌpäl-ə-'mō-nē-əm\ *n* [NL, fr. Gk *polemōnion,* a plant] (1900) **:** JACOB'S LADDER

po·len·ta \pō-'lent-ə, pə-, -'len-ˌtä\ *n* [It, fr. L, pearl barley — more at POLLEN] (1598) **:** mush made of chestnut meal, cornmeal, semolina, or farina

pol·er \'pō-lər\ *n* (ca. 1864) **:** one that poles; *esp* **:** one that poles a boat

pole·star \'pōl-ˌstär\ *n* (1555) **1 :** NORTH STAR **2 a :** a directing principle **:** GUIDE **b :** a center of attraction

pole vault *n* (ca. 1890) **:** a vault with the aid of a pole; *specif* **:** a field event consisting of a vault for height over a crossbar — **pole–vault** *vi* — **pole–vault·er** *n*

pole·ward \'pōl-wərd\ *adv or adj* (1875) **:** toward or in the direction of a pole of the earth ⟨as the sun moves ~⟩ ⟨~ variation in temperature⟩

[1]**po·lice** \pə-'lēs\ *vt* **po·liced; po·lic·ing** (1589) **1** *archaic* **:** GOVERN **2 :** to control, regulate, or keep in order by use of police **3 :** to make clean and put in order **4 a :** to supervise the operation, execution, or administration of to prevent or detect and prosecute violations of rules and regulations **b :** to exercise such supervision over the policies and activities of **5 :** to perform the functions of a police force in or over

[2]**police** *n, pl* **police** *often attrib* [F, fr. LL *politia,* government, administration, fr. Gk *politeia,* fr. *politeuein* to be a citizen, engage in political activity, fr. *politēs* citizen, fr. *polis* city, state; akin to Skt *pur* city] (1716) **1 a :** the internal organization or regulation of a political unit through exercise of governmental powers esp. with respect to general comfort, health, morals, safety, or prosperity **b :** control and regulation of affairs affecting the general order and welfare of any unit or area **c :** the system of laws for effecting such control **2 a :** the department of government concerned primarily with maintenance of public order, safety, and health and enforcement of laws and possessing executive, judicial, and legislative powers **b :** the department of government charged with prevention, detection, and prosecution of public nuisances and crimes **3 a :** POLICE FORCE **b** *pl* **:** POLICEMEN **4 a :** a private organization resembling a police force ⟨campus ~⟩ **b** *pl* **:** the members of a private police organization **5 a :** the action or process of cleaning and putting in order **b :** military personnel detailed to perform this function

police action *n* (1933) **:** a localized military action undertaken without formal declaration of war by regular forces against persons held to be violators of international peace and order

police court *n* (1823) **:** a court of record that has jurisdiction over various minor offenses (as breach of the peace) and the power to bind over for trial in a superior court or for a grand jury persons accused of more serious offenses

police dog *n* (1908) **1 :** a dog trained to assist police (as in drug detection) **2 :** GERMAN SHEPHERD

police force *n* (1838) **:** a body of trained officers entrusted by a government with maintenance of public peace and order, enforcement of laws, and prevention and detection of crime

po·lice·man \pə-'lē-smən\ *n* (1801) **1 :** a member of a police force **2 :** one held to resemble a policeman ⟨making the United States the ~ for the whole wide world — R.B. Long⟩

police officer *n* (1800) **:** a member of a police force

police power *n* (1827) **:** the inherent power of a government to exercise reasonable control over persons and property within its jurisdiction in the interest of the general security, health, safety, morals, and welfare except where legally prohibited

police reporter *n* (1834) **:** a reporter regularly assigned to cover police news (as crimes and arrests)

police state *n* (1865) **:** a political unit characterized by repressive governmental control of political, economic, and social life usu. by an arbitrary exercise of power by police and esp. secret police in place of regular operation of administrative and judicial organs of the government according to publicly known legal procedures

police station *n* (1846) **:** the headquarters of the police for a particular locality

po·lice·wom·an \pə-'lē-ˌswu̇m-ən\ *n* (1853) **:** a woman who is a member of a police force

[1]**pol·i·cy** \'päl-ə-sē\ *n, pl* **-cies** *often attrib* [ME *policie,* government, policy, fr. MF, government, regulation, fr. LL *politia* — more at POLICE] (15c) **1 a :** prudence or wisdom in the management of affairs **:** SAGACITY **b :** management or procedure based primarily on material interest **2 a :** a definite course or method of action selected from among alternatives and in light of given conditions to guide and determine present and future decisions **b :** a high-level overall plan embracing the general goals and acceptable procedures esp. of a governmental body

[2]**policy** *n, pl* **-cies** [alter. of earlier *police,* fr. MF, certificate, fr. OIt *polizza,* modif. of ML *apodixa* receipt, fr. MGk *apodeixis,* fr. Gk, proof, fr. *apodeiknynai* to demonstrate — more at APODICTIC] (1565) **1 :** a writing whereby a contract of insurance is made **2 a :** a daily lottery in which participants bet that certain numbers will be drawn from a lottery wheel **b :** NUMBER 7a

pol·i·cy·hold·er \'päl-ə-sē-ˌhōl-dər\ *n* (1851) **:** the owner of an insurance policy

pol·i·cy–mak·ing \-ˌmā-kiŋ\ *n* (1942) **:** the high-level elaboration of policy and esp. of governmental policy — **pol·i·cy·mak·er** \-kər\ *n*

policy science *n* (1950) **:** a social science dealing with the making of high-level policy (as in a government or business)

po·lio \'pō-lē-ˌō\ *n* (1931) **:** POLIOMYELITIS

po·lio·my·eli·tis \ˌpō-lē-(ˌ)ō-ˌmī-ə-'lit-əs\ *n* [NL, fr. Gk *polios* gray + *myelos* marrow — more at FALLOW, MYEL-] (1878) **:** an acute infectious virus disease characterized by fever, motor paralysis, and atrophy of skeletal muscles often with permanent disability and deformity and marked by inflammation of nerve cells in the anterior horns of the spinal cord — called also *infantile paralysis*

po·lio·vi·rus \'pō-lē-(ˌ)ō-ˌvī-rəs\ *n* [NL, fr. *polio*myelitis + *virus*] (1953) **:** an enterovirus that occurs in several antigenically distinct forms and is the causative agent of human poliomyelitis

po·lis \'päl-əs\ *n, pl* **po·leis** \'päl-ˌās\ [Gk — more at POLICE] (1894) **:** a Greek city-state; *broadly* **:** a state or society esp. when characterized by a sense of community

-p·o·lis \p-(ə-)ləs\ *n comb form* [LL, fr. Gk, fr. *polis*] **:** city ⟨megalo*polis*⟩

[1]**pol·ish** \'päl-ish\ *vb* [ME *polisshen,* fr. MF *poliss-,* stem of *polir,* fr. L *polire*] *vt* (14c) **1 :** to make smooth and glossy usu. by friction **:** BURNISH **2 :** to smooth, soften, or refine in manners or condition **3 :** to bring to a highly developed, finished, or refined state **:** PERFECT ~ *vi* **:** to become smooth or glossy by or as if by friction — **pol·ish·er** *n*

[2]**polish** *n* (1704) **1 a :** a smooth glossy surface **:** LUSTER **b :** freedom from rudeness or coarseness **:** CULTURE **c :** a state of high development or refinement **2 :** the action or process of polishing **3 :** a preparation that is used to produce a gloss and often a color for the protection and decoration of a surface ⟨furniture ~⟩ ⟨nail ~⟩

[1]**Pol·ish** \'pō-lish\ *adj* [*Pole*] (1674) **:** of, relating to, or characteristic of Poland, the Poles, or Polish

[2]**Polish** *n* (1784) **:** the Slavic language of the Poles

polish off *vt* (1829) **:** to finish off or dispose of rapidly or completely

po·lit·bu·ro \'päl-ət-ˌbyu̇(ə)r-(ˌ)ō, 'pō-lət-, pə-'lit-\ *n* [Russ *politbyuro,* fr. *politicheskoe byuro* political bureau] (1925) **:** the principal policy-making and executive committee of a Communist party

po·lite \pə-'līt\ *adj* **po·lit·er; -est** [L *politus,* fr. pp. of *polire*] (1501) **1 a :** of, relating to, or having the characteristics of advanced culture **b :** marked by refined cultural interests and pursuits esp. in arts and belles lettres **2 a :** showing or characterized by correct social usage **b :** marked by an appearance of consideration, tact, deference, or courtesy **c :** marked by a lack of roughness or crudities ⟨uses terms seldom met with in ~ literature⟩ ***syn*** see CIVIL — **po·lite·ly** *adv* — **po·lite·ness** *n*

po·li·tesse \ˌpäl-i-'tes, ˌpȯ-li-\ *n* [F, fr. MF, cleanness, fr. OIt *pulitezza,* fr. *pulito,* pp. of *pulire* to polish, clean, fr. L *polire*] (1717) **:** formal politeness **:** DECOROUSNESS

pol·i·tic \'päl-ə-ˌtik\ *adj* [ME *politik,* fr. MF *politique,* fr. L *politicus,* fr. Gk *politikos,* fr. *politēs* citizen — more at POLICE] (15c) **1 :** POLITICAL **2 :** characterized by shrewdness in managing, contriving, or dealing **3 :** sagacious in promoting a policy **4 :** shrewdly tactful ***syn*** see EXPEDIENT, SUAVE

po·lit·i·cal \pə-'lit-i-kəl\ *adj* [L *politicus*] (1551) **1 a :** of or relating to government, a government, or the conduct of government **b :** of, relating to, or concerned with the making as distinguished from the administration of governmental policy **2 a :** of, relating to, or involving politics and esp. party politics **b :** adept at, sensitive to, or engrossed in politics ⟨highly ~ students⟩ **3 :** organized in governmental terms ⟨~ units⟩ **4 :** involving or charged or concerned with acts against a government or a political system ⟨~ criminals⟩ — **po·lit·i·cal·ly** \-k(ə-)lē\ *adv*

political economy *n* (1740) **1 :** a 19th century social science comprising the modern science of economics **2 :** a modern social science dealing with the interrelationship of political and economic processes — **political economist** *n*

po·lit·i·cal·ize \pə-ˈlit-i-kə-ˌlīz\ *vt* **-ized; -iz·ing** (1869) **:** to make political — **po·lit·i·cal·iza·tion** \-ˌlit-i-kə-lə-ˈzā-shən\ *n*

political science *n* (1779) **:** a social science concerned chiefly with the description and analysis of political and esp. governmental institutions and processes — **political scientist** *n*

pol·i·ti·cian \ˌpäl-ə-ˈtish-ən\ *n* (1589) **1 :** a person experienced in the art or science of government; *esp* **:** one actively engaged in conducting the business of a government **2 a :** a person engaged in party politics as a profession **b :** a person primarily interested in political offices from selfish or other narrow usu. short-run interests

po·lit·i·cize \pə-ˈlit-ə-ˌsīz\ *vt* **-cized; -ciz·ing** (1846) **:** to give a political tone or character to — **po·lit·i·ci·za·tion** \-ˌlit-ə-sə-ˈzā-shən\ *n*

pol·i·tick \ˈpäl-ə-ˌtik\ *vi* [back-formation fr. *politicking,* n., fr. *politics* + *-ing*] (ca. 1934) **:** to engage in political discussion or activity — **pol·i·tick·er** *n*

po·lit·i·co \pə-ˈlit-i-ˌkō\ *n, pl* **-cos** *also* **-coes** [It *politico* or Sp *político,* derivs. of L *politicus* political] (1630) **:** POLITICIAN 2

politico- *comb form* [L *politicus*] **:** political and ⟨*politico*-diplomatic⟩

pol·i·tics \ˈpäl-ə-ˌtiks\ *n pl but sing or pl in constr* [Gk *politika,* fr. neut. pl. of *politikos* political] (ca. 1529) **1 a :** the art or science of government **b :** the art or science concerned with guiding or influencing governmental policy **c :** the art or science concerned with winning and holding control over a government **2 :** political actions, practices, or policies **3 a :** political affairs or business; *specif* **:** competition between competing interest groups or individuals for power and leadership (as in a government) **b :** political life esp. as a principal activity or profession **c :** political activities characterized by artful and often dishonest practices **4 :** the political opinions or sympathies of a person **5 :** the total complex of relations between people in society

pol·i·ty \ˈpäl-ət-ē\ *n, pl* **-ties** [LL *politia* — more at POLICE] (1538) **1 :** political organization **2 :** a specific form of political organization **3 :** a politically organized unit **4 a :** the form or constitution of a politically organized unit **b :** the form of government of a religious denomination

pol·ka \ˈpōl-kə, ˈpō-kə\ *n* [Czech, fr. Pol *Polka* Polish woman, fem. of *Polak* Pole] (ca. 1844) **1 :** a vivacious couple dance of Bohemian origin in duple time with a basic pattern of hop-step-close-step **2 :** a lively Bohemian dance tune in 2/4 time — **polka** *vi*

pol·ka dot \ˈpō-kə-ˌdät\ *n* (1884) **:** a dot in a pattern of regularly distributed dots in textile design — **polka–dot** *or* **pol·ka–dot·ted** \-ˌdät-əd\ *adj*

1poll \ˈpōl\ *n* [ME *pol, polle,* fr. MLG] (13c) **1 :** HEAD **2 a :** the top or back of the head **b :** NAPE **3 :** the broad or flat end of a striking tool (as a hammer) **4 a (1) :** the casting or recording of the votes of a body of persons **(2) :** a counting of votes cast **b :** the place where votes are cast or recorded — usu. used in pl. ⟨at the ~s⟩ **c :** the period of time during which votes may be cast at an election **d :** the total number of votes recorded ⟨a heavy ~⟩ **5 a :** a questioning or canvassing of persons selected at random or by quota to obtain information or opinions to be analyzed **b :** a record of the information so obtained

2poll *vt* (14c) **1 a :** to cut off or cut short the hair or wool of **:** CROP, SHEAR **b :** to cut off or cut short (as wool) **2 a :** to cut off or back the top of (as a tree); *specif* **:** POLLARD **b :** to cut off or cut short the horns of (cattle) **3 a :** to receive and record the votes of **b :** to request each member of to declare his vote individually ⟨~ the assembly⟩ **4 :** to receive (as votes) in an election **5 :** to question or canvass in a poll **6 :** to test (as several computer terminals sharing a single line) in sequence for messages to be transmitted ~ *vi* **:** to cast one's vote at a poll — **poll·ee** \pō-ˈlē\ *n* — **poll·er** \ˈpō-lər\ *n*

pol·lack *or* **pol·lock** \ˈpäl-ək\ *n, pl* **pollack** *or* **pollock** [Sc *podlok,* of unknown origin] (15c) **:** a commercially important north Atlantic food fish (*Pollachius virens*) related to and resembling the cods but darker

1pol·lard \ˈpäl-ərd\ *n* [2*poll*] (1546) **:** a tree cut back to the trunk to promote the growth of a dense head of foliage

2pollard *vt* (1670) **:** to make a pollard of (a tree)

polled \ˈpōld\ *adj* (1607) **:** having no horns

pol·len \ˈpäl-ən\ *n* [NL *pollin-, pollen,* fr. L, fine flour; akin to L *pulvis* dust, *polenta* pearl barley, Gk *palē* fine meal] (1760) **1 :** a mass of microspores in a seed plant appearing usu. as a fine dust **2 :** a dusty bloom on the body of an insect

pollen basket *n* (1860) **:** a smooth area on each hind tibia of a bee that is edged by a fringe of stiff hairs and serves to collect and transport pollen — called also *corbicula*

pollen grain *n* (1835) **:** one of the granular microspores that occur in pollen and give rise to the male gametophyte of a seed plant

pol·len·iz·er *also* **pol·lin·iz·er** \ˈpäl-ə-ˌnī-zər\ *n* [*pollenize* (to pollinate)] (1897) **1 :** a plant that is a source of pollen **2 :** POLLINATOR a

pollen mother cell *n* (1884) **:** a cell that is derived from the hypodermis of the pollen sac and that gives rise by meiosis to four cells, each of which develops into a pollen grain

pollen sac *n* (1875) **:** one of the pouches of a seed plant anther in which pollen is formed

pollen tube *n* (1835) **:** a tube that is formed by a pollen grain, passes down the style, and conveys the sperm nuclei to the embryo sac of a flower

pol·lex \ˈpäl-ˌeks\ *n, pl* **pol·li·ces** \ˈpäl-ə-ˌsēz\ [NL *pollic-, pollex,* fr. L, thumb, big toe] (ca. 1835) **:** the first digit of the forelimb **:** THUMB

pollin- *or* **pollini-** *comb form* [NL *pollin-, pollen*] **:** pollen ⟨*pollin*ate⟩

pol·li·nate \ˈpäl-ə-ˌnāt\ *vt* **-nat·ed; -nat·ing** (1875) **1 :** to place pollen on the stigma of **2 :** to mark or smudge with pollen

pol·li·na·tion \ˌpäl-ə-ˈnā-shən\ *n* (1875) **:** the transfer of pollen from a stamen to an ovule

pol·li·na·tor \ˈpäl-ə-ˌnāt-ər\ *n* (1903) **:** one that pollinates: as **a :** an agent that pollinates flowers **b :** POLLENIZER 1

pol·lin·i·um \pä-ˈlin-ē-əm\ *n, pl* **-ia** \-ē-ə\ [NL, fr. *pollin-*] (ca. 1862) **:** a coherent mass of pollen grains often with a stalk bearing an adhesive disk that clings to insects

pol·li·nose \ˈpäl-ə-ˌnōs\ *adj, of an insect* (ca. 1826) **:** covered with pollen

pol·li·no·sis *or* **pol·len·osis** \ˌpäl-ə-ˈnō-səs\ *n* [NL *pollinosis,* fr. *pollin-*] (1925) **:** an acute recurrent catarrhal disorder caused by allergic sensitivity to specific pollens

poll·ster \ˈpōl-stər\ *n* (1939) **:** one that conducts a poll or compiles data obtained by a poll

poll tax *n* (1692) **:** a tax of a fixed amount per person levied on adults

pol·lut·ant \pə-ˈlüt-ᵊnt\ *n* (1892) **:** something that pollutes

pol·lute \pə-ˈlüt\ *vt* **pol·lut·ed; pol·lut·ing** [ME *polluten,* fr. L *pollutus,* pp. of *polluere,* fr. *por-* (akin to L *per* through) + *-luere* (akin to L *lutum* mud, Gk *lyma* dirt, defilement) — more at FOR] (14c) **1 a :** to make ceremonially or morally impure **:** DEFILE **b :** DEBASE 1 ⟨using language to deceive or mislead ~*s* language —Linda C. Lederman⟩ **2 a :** to make physically impure or unclean **:** BEFOUL, DIRTY **b :** to contaminate (an environment) esp. with man-made waste ***syn*** see CONTAMINATE — **pol·lut·er** *n* — **pol·lut·ive** \-ˈlüt-iv\ *adj*

pol·lu·tion \pə-ˈlü-shən\ *n* (14c) **1 :** emission of semen at other times than in coitus **2 a :** the action of polluting **:** the condition of being polluted **b :** POLLUTANT

Pol·lux \ˈpäl-əks\ *n* [L, modif. of Gk *Polydeukēs*] **1 :** one of the Dioscuri **2 :** a first-magnitude star in the constellation Gemini

Pol·ly·an·na \ˌpäl-ē-ˈan-ə\ *n* [*Pollyanna,* heroine of the novel *Pollyanna* (1913) by Eleanor Porter †1920 Am. fiction writer] (1918) **:** one characterized by irrepressible optimism and a tendency to find good in everything — **Pollyanna** *adj* — **Pol·ly·an·na·ish** \-ˈan-ə-ish\ *or* **Pol·ly·an·nish** \-ˈan-ish\ *adj*

pol·ly·wog *or* **pol·li·wog** \ˈpäl-ē-ˌwäg, -ˌwȯg\ *n* [alter. of ME *polwygle,* prob. fr. *pol* poll + *wiglen* to wiggle] (15c) **:** TADPOLE

po·lo \ˈpō-(ˌ)lō\ *n* [Balti, ball] (1872) **1 :** a game of oriental origin played by teams of players on horseback using mallets with long flexible handles to drive a wooden ball **2 :** WATER POLO — **po·lo·ist** \ˈpō-(ˌ)lō-əst\ *n*

polo coat *n* (1910) **:** a tailored overcoat that is made of soft fabric and esp. tan camel's hair and often has stitched edges and a half-belt on the back

po·lo·naise \ˌpäl-ə-ˈnāz, ˌpō-lə-\ *n* [F, fr. fem. of *polonais* Polish, fr. *Pologne* Poland, fr. ML *Polonia*] (1773) **1 :** an elaborate overdress with a short-sleeved fitted waist and a draped cutaway overskirt **2 a :** a stately Polish processional dance popular in 19th century Europe **b :** music for this dance in moderate 3/4 time

polonaise 1

Po·lo·nia \pə-ˈlō-nē-ə, -nyə\ *n* [ML] (1944) **:** people of Polish descent living outside Poland

po·lo·ni·um \pə-ˈlō-nē-əm\ *n* [NL, fr. ML *Polonia* Poland] (1898) **:** a radioactive metallic element that is similar chemically to tellurium and bismuth, occurs esp. in pitchblende and radium-lead residues, and emits a helium nucleus to form an isotope of lead — see ELEMENT table

Po·lo·ni·us \pə-ˈlō-nē-əs\ *n* **:** a garrulous courtier and father of Ophelia and Laertes in Shakespeare's *Hamlet*

polo shirt *n* (1920) **:** a close-fitting pullover often knit shirt with short or long sleeves and turnover collar or banded neck

pol·ter·geist \ˈpōl-tər-ˌgīst\ *n* [G, fr. *poltern* to knock + *geist* spirit, fr. OHG — more at GHOST] (1848) **:** a noisy usu. mischievous ghost held to be responsible for unexplained noises (as rappings)

1pol·troon \päl-ˈtrün\ *n* [MF *poultron,* fr. OIt *poltrone,* prob. akin to *poltro* colt, deriv. of L *pullus* young of an animal — more at FOAL] (ca. 1529) **:** a spiritless coward **:** CRAVEN

2poltroon *adj* (1645) **:** characterized by complete cowardice

pol·troon·ery \-ˈtrün-(ə-)rē\ *n* (1590) **:** mean pusillanimity **:** COWARDICE

1poly \ˈpäl-ē\ *n, pl* **pol·ys** \-ēz\ [by shortening] (ca. 1923) **:** a polymorphonuclear leukocyte

2poly *n, pl* **polys** [*poly*mer] (1942) **:** a polymerized plastic or something made of this; *esp* **:** a polyester fiber, fabric, or garment

poly- *comb form* [ME, fr. L, fr. Gk, fr. *polys;* akin to OE *full* full] **1 a :** many **:** several **:** much **:** MULTI- ⟨*poly*chotomous⟩ ⟨*poly*gyny⟩ **b :** excessive **:** abnormal **:** HYPER- ⟨*poly*phagia⟩ **2 a :** containing an indefinite number more than one of a (specified) substance ⟨*poly*sulfide⟩ **b :** polymeric **:** polymer of a (specified) monomer ⟨*poly*ethylene⟩ ⟨*poly*adenylic acid⟩

poly·acryl·amide \ˌpäl-ē-ə-ˈkril-ə-ˌmīd\ *n* (1944) **:** a polyamide of acrylic acid

poly·ac·ry·lo·ni·trile \ˈpäl-ē-ˌak-rə-lō-ˈnī-trəl, -ˌtrēl\ *n* (1935) **:** a polymer of acrylonitrile used often as fibers

poly·ad·e·nyl·ic acid \ˈpäl-ē-ˌad-ᵊn-ˌil-ik-\ *n* (1956) **:** RNA or a segment of RNA that is composed of a polynucleotide chain consisting entirely of adenylic acid residues and that codes for polylysine when functioning as messenger RNA in protein synthesis

poly·al·co·hol \ˌpäl-ē-ˈal-kə-ˌhȯl\ *n* (1900) **:** an alcohol (as ethylene glycol) that contains more than one hydroxyl group

polyalphabetic substitution \ˌpäl-ē-ˌal-fə-ˈbet-ik-\ *n* (1939) **:** substitution in cryptography that uses several cipher alphabets so that each plaintext letter will have a continually changing cipher equivalent — compare MONOALPHABETIC SUBSTITUTION

poly·am·ide \ˌpäl-ē-ˈam-ˌīd, -əd\ *n* [ISV] (1929) **:** a compound characterized by more than one amide group; *esp* **:** a polymeric amide (as nylon)

poly·amine \ˈpäl-ē-ə-ˌmēn, ˌpäl-ē-ˈam-ˌēn\ *n* (1861) **:** a compound characterized by more than one amino group

poly·an·dry \ˈpäl-ē-ˌan-drē\ *n* [Gk *polyandros,* adj., having many husbands, fr. *poly-* + *andr-, anēr* man, husband — more at ANDR-] (1780) **:** the state or practice of having more than one husband or male mate at one time — compare POLYGAMY, POLYGYNY — **poly·an·drous** \ˌpäl-ē-ˈan-drəs\ *adj*

\ə\ abut \ᵊ\ kitten, F table \ər\ further \a\ ash \ā\ ace \ä\ cot, cart \au̇\ out \ch\ chin \e\ bet \ē\ easy \g\ go \i\ hit \ī\ ice \j\ job \ŋ\ sing \ō\ go \ȯ\ law \ȯi\ boy \th\ thin \t͟h\ the \ü\ loot \u̇\ foot \y\ yet \zh\ vision \à, k̲, ⁿ, œ, œ̄, ue, ue̅, ʸ\ *see* Guide to Pronunciation

poly·an·tha \ˌpäl-ē-ˈan(t)-thə\ *n* [NL, fr. Gk *polyanthos* blooming] (1889) : any of numerous dwarf hybrid bush roses characterized by many large clusters of small flowers

poly·an·thus \-ˈan(t)-thəs\ *n, pl* **-an·thus·es** *or* **-an·thi** \-ˈan-ˌthī, -ˌthē\ [NL, fr. Gk *polyanthos* blooming, fr. *poly-* + *anthos* flower — more at ANTHOLOGY] (1727) **1 :** any of various hybrid primroses **2 :** a narcissus (*Narcissus tazetta*) having small white or yellow flowers arranged in umbels and having a spreading perianth

poly·ba·site \ˌpäl-i-ˈbā-ˌsīt\ *n* [G *polybasit*, fr. *poly-* + *basi-* (fr. L *basis* base) + *-it* -ite] (1830) **:** an iron-black metallic-looking ore $(Ag,Cu)_{16}Sb_2S_{11}$ of silver consisting of silver, copper, sulfur, and antimony

poly·bro·mi·nat·ed biphenyl \ˌpäl-i-ˌbrō-mə-ˌnāt-əd-\ *n* (1975) **:** any of several compounds that are similar to polychlorinated biphenyls in environmental toxicity and in structure but that have various hydrogen atoms replaced by bromine rather than chlorine — called also *PBB*

poly·car·bon·ate \ˌpäl-i-ˈkär-bə-ˌnāt, -nət\ *n* (1930) **:** any of various tough transparent thermoplastics characterized by high impact strength and high softening temperature

poly·cen·tric \ˌpäl-i-ˈsen-trik\ *adj* (1887) **:** having more than one center (as of development or control): as **a :** having several centromeres ⟨~ chromosomes⟩ ⟨~ cells⟩ **b :** characterized by polycentrism

poly·cen·trism \-ˌtriz-əm\ *n* (1956) **:** the existence of many centers of communist ideological thought; *esp* **:** the existence of a number of autonomous national communist movements

poly·chaete \ˈpäl-i-ˌkēt\ *adj* [deriv. of Gk *polychaitēs* having much hair, fr. *poly-* + *chaitē* long hair] (1886) **:** of or relating to a class (Polychaeta) of chiefly marine annelid worms usu. with paired segmental appendages, separate sexes, and a free-swimming trochophore larva — **polychaete** *n*

poly·chlo·ri·nat·ed biphenyl \ˌpäl-i-ˈklōr-ə-ˌnāt-əd-, -ˈklȯr-\ *n* (1962) **:** any of several compounds that are produced by replacing hydrogen atoms in biphenyl with chlorine, have various industrial applications, and are poisonous environmental pollutants which tend to accumulate in animal tissues — called also *PCB*

poly·chot·o·mous \-ˈkät-ə-məs\ *adj* [*poly-* + *-chotomous* (as in *dichotomous*)] (1858) **:** dividing or marked by division into many parts, branches, or classes — **poly·chot·o·my** \-mē\ *n*

poly·chro·mat·ic \-krō-ˈmat-ik\ *adj* [Gk *polychrōmatos*, fr. *poly-* + *chrōmat-, chrōma* color — more at CHROMATIC] (ca. 1847) **1 :** showing a variety or a change of colors **:** MULTICOLORED **2 :** being or relating to radiation that is composed of more than one wavelength

poly·chro·mato·phil·ic \-krō-ˌmat-ə-ˈfil-ik\ *adj* (1897) **:** stainable with more than one type of stain and esp. with both acid and basic dyes ⟨~ erythroblasts⟩ — **poly·chro·mato·phil·ia** \-ˈfil-ē-ə\ *n*

poly·chrome \ˈpäl-i-ˌkrōm\ *adj* [Gk *polychrōmos*, fr. *poly-* + *chrōma*] (1837) **:** relating to, made with, or decorated in several colors ⟨~ pottery⟩ — **poly·chro·my** \-ˌkrō-mē\ *n*

poly·cis·tron·ic \ˌpäl-i-sis-ˈträn-ik\ *adj* (1963) **:** containing the genetic information of a number of cistrons ⟨~ messenger RNA⟩

poly·clin·ic \ˌpäl-i-ˈklin-ik\ *n* [ISV] (ca. 1890) **:** a clinic or hospital treating diseases of many sorts

poly·con·den·sa·tion \-ˌkän-ˌden-ˈsā-shən, -dən-\ *n* [ISV] (1936) **:** a chemical condensation leading to the formation of a compound of high molecular weight

poly·con·ic projection \ˌpäl-i-ˌkän-ik-\ *n* (ca. 1864) **:** a map projection consisting of a composite series of concentric cones each of which before being unrolled has been placed over a sphere so as to be tangent to a different parallel of latitude

poly·crys·tal·line \-ˈkris-tə-lən\ *adj* (1918) **1 :** consisting of crystals variously oriented **2 :** composed of more than one crystal — **poly·crys·tal** \ˈpäl-i-ˌkris-tᵊl\ *n*

poly·cy·clic \ˌpäl-i-ˈsī-klik, -ˈsik-lik\ *adj* [ISV] (1869) **:** having more than one cyclic component; *esp* **:** having two or more usu. fused rings in the molecule

poly·cys·tic \-ˈsis-tik\ *adj* (1872) **:** having or involving more than one cyst ⟨~ kidneys⟩ ⟨~ disease⟩

poly·cy·the·mia \-(ˌ)sī-ˈthē-mē-ə\ *n* [NL, fr. *poly-* + *cyt-* + *-hemia*] (ca. 1857) **:** a condition marked by an abnormal increase in the number of circulating red blood cells; *specif* **:** POLYCYTHEMIA VERA — **poly·cy·the·mic** \-mik\ *adj*

polycythemia ve·ra \-ˈvir-ə\ *n* [NL, true polycythemia] (ca. 1925) **:** polycythemia of unknown cause that is characterized by increase in total blood volume and accompanied by nosebleed, distension of the circulatory vessels, and enlargement of the spleen — called also *erythremia*

poly·cyt·i·dyl·ic acid \ˌpäl-i-ˌsit-ə-ˈdil-ik-\ *n* (1965) **:** RNA or a segment of RNA that is composed of a polynucleotide chain consisting entirely of cytosine-containing nucleotides and that codes for a polypeptide chain consisting of proline residues when functioning as messenger RNA in protein synthesis

poly·dac·tyl \ˌpäl-i-ˈdak-tᵊl\ *adj* [Gk *polydaktylos*, fr. *poly-* + *daktylos* digit] (ca. 1890) **:** having several to many and esp. abnormally many digits — **poly·dac·ty·ly** \-tə-lē\ *n*

poly·dip·sia \ˌpäl-i-ˈdip-sē-ə\ *n* [NL, fr. *poly-* + Gk *dipsa* thirst] (1660) **:** excessive or abnormal thirst — **poly·dip·sic** \-sik\ *adj*

poly·dis·perse \-dis-ˈpərs\ *adj* [*poly-* + L *dispersus* dispersed, fr. pp. of *dispergere* to disperse] (1915) **:** of, relating to, or characterized by or as particles of varied sizes in the dispersed phase of a disperse system — **poly·dis·per·si·ty** \-ˈpər-sət-ē\ *n*

poly·elec·tro·lyte \ˌpäl-ē-ə-ˈlek-trə-ˌlīt\ *n* (ca. 1947) **:** a substance of high molecular weight (as a protein or a nucleotide) that is an electrolyte

poly·em·bry·o·ny \-ˈem-brē-ə-nē, -(ˌ)em-ˈbrī-\ *n* [ISV *poly-* + *embryon-* + *-y*] (1849) **1 :** the condition of having several embryos **2 :** the production of two or more embryos from one ovule or egg — **poly·em·bry·on·ic** \-ˌem-brē-ˈän-ik\ *adj*

poly·ene \ˈpäl-ē-ˌēn\ *n* [ISV] (1928) **:** an organic compound containing many double bonds; *esp* **:** one having the double bonds in a long aliphatic hydrocarbon chain — **poly·enic** \-ˈē-nik\ *adj*

poly·es·ter \ˈpäl-ē-ˌes-tər\ *n* [ISV] (1929) **:** any of a group of polymers that consist basically of repeated units of an ester and are used esp. in making fibers or plastics — **poly·es·ter·i·fi·ca·tion** \-e-ˌster-ə-fə-ˈkā-shən\ *n*

poly·es·trous \ˌpäl-ē-ˈes-trəs\ *adj* (1900) **:** having more than one period of estrus in a year

poly·eth·yl·ene \-ˈeth-ə-ˌlēn\ *n* (ca. 1862) **:** a polymer of ethylene; *esp* **:** any of various partially crystalline lightweight thermoplastics $(CH_2CH_2)_x$ that are resistant to chemicals and moisture, have good insulating properties, and are used esp. in packaging and insulation

po·lyg·a·la \pə-ˈlig-ə-lə\ *n* [NL, genus name, fr. L, milkwort, fr. Gk *polygalon*, fr. *poly-* + *gala* milk — more at GALAXY] (1578) **:** MILKWORT

poly·gam·ic \ˌpäl-i-ˈgam-ik\ *adj* (1819) **:** POLYGAMOUS

po·lyg·a·mous \pə-ˈlig-ə-məs\ *adj* [Gk *polygamos*, fr. *poly-* + *-gamos* -gamous] (1613) **1 a :** relating to or practicing polygamy **b :** having more than one mate at one time ⟨baboons are ~⟩ **2 :** bearing both hermaphrodite and unisexual flowers on the same plant

po·lyg·a·my \-mē\ *n* (ca. 1591) **1 :** marriage in which a spouse of either sex may have more than one mate at the same time — compare POLYANDRY, POLYGYNY **2 :** the state of being polygamous — **po·lyg·a·mist** \-məst\ *n* — **po·lyg·a·mize** \-ˌmīz\ *vi*

poly·gene \ˈpäl-i-ˌjēn\ *n* [ISV] (1941) **:** any of a group of nonallelic genes that collectively control the inheritance of a quantitative character or modify the expression of a qualitative character — **poly·gen·ic** \ˌpäl-i-ˈjē-nik\ *adj*

poly·gen·e·sis \ˌpäl-i-ˈjen-ə-səs\ *n* [NL] (ca. 1882) **:** development from more than one source

poly·ge·net·ic \-jə-ˈnet-ik\ *adj* (1861) **1 :** POLYPHYLETIC **2 :** having many distinct sources

¹poly·glot \ˈpäl-i-ˌglät\ *n* (1645) **1 :** one who is polyglot **2** *cap* **:** a book containing versions of the same text in several languages; *esp* **:** the Scriptures in several languages **3 :** a mixture or confusion of languages or nomenclatures

²polyglot *adj* [Gk *polyglōttos*, fr. *poly-* + *glōtta* language — more at GLOSS] (1656) **1 a :** speaking or writing several languages **:** MULTILINGUAL **b :** composed of numerous linguistic groups ⟨a ~ population⟩ **2 :** containing matter in several languages ⟨a ~ sign⟩ **3 :** composed of elements from different languages

poly·glot·ism *or* **poly·glot·tism** \-ˌglät-ˌiz-əm\ *n* (1882) **:** the use of many languages **:** the ability to speak many languages

poly·gon \ˈpäl-i-ˌgän\ *n* [LL *polygonum*, fr. Gk *polygōnon*, fr. neut. of *polygōnos* polygonal, fr. *poly-* + *gōnia* angle — more at -GON] (1571) **1 :** a closed plane figure bounded by straight lines **2 :** a closed figure on a sphere bounded by arcs of great circles — **po·lyg·o·nal** \pə-ˈlig-ən-ᵊl\ *adj* — **po·lyg·o·nal·ly** \-ᵊl-ē\ *adv*

po·lyg·o·num \pə-ˈlig-ə-nəm\ *n* [NL, fr. Gk *polygonon* knotgrass, fr. *poly-* + *gony* knee — more at KNEE] (ca. 1706) **:** any of a genus (*Polygonum*) of herbs of the buckwheat family with a prominent tubular sheath around the base of each petiole, thickened nodes, and flowers that are solitary and axillary or in spiked racemes — called also *knotweed*

poly·graph \ˈpäl-i-ˌgraf\ *n* (1871) **:** an instrument for recording variations of several different pulsations (as of physiological variables) simultaneously; *broadly* **:** LIE DETECTOR — **poly·graph·ic** \ˌpäl-i-ˈgraf-ik\ *adj*

po·lyg·ra·pher \ˈpäl-i-ˌgraf-ər, pə-ˈlig-rə-fər\ *n* (ca. 1934) **:** one who operates a polygraph

po·lyg·ra·phist \ˈpäl-i-ˌgraf-əst, pə-ˈlig-rə-fəst\ *n* (1954) **:** POLYGRAPHER

po·lyg·y·nous \pə-ˈlij-ə-nəs\ *adj* (1874) **:** relating to or practicing polygyny

po·lyg·y·ny \-nē\ *n* (1780) **:** the state or practice of having more than one wife or female mate at one time — compare POLYANDRY, POLYGAMY

polyhedral angle *n* (ca. 1864) **:** a portion of space partly enclosed by three or more planes whose intersections meet in a vertex

poly·he·dron \ˌpäl-i-ˈhē-drən\ *n, pl* **-drons** *or* **-dra** \-drə\ [NL] (1570) **:** a solid formed by plane faces — **poly·he·dral** \-drəl\ *adj*

poly·he·dro·sis \ˌpäl-i-hē-ˈdrō-səs\ *n, pl* **-droses** [NL, fr. *polyhedron*] (1947) **:** any of several virus diseases of insect larvae characterized by dissolution of tissues and accumulation of polyhedral granules in the resultant fluid

poly·his·tor \ˌpäl-i-ˈhis-tər\ *n* [Gk *polyistōr* very learned, fr. *poly-* + *istōr, histōr* learned — more at HISTORY] (1588) **:** POLYMATH — **poly·his·tor·ic** \-his-ˈtȯr-ik, -ˈtär-\ *adj*

poly·hy·droxy \-hī-ˈdräk-sē\ *adj* [*poly-* + *hydroxyl*] (ca. 1929) **:** containing more than one hydroxyl group in the molecule

Poly·hym·nia \ˌpäl-i-ˈhim-nē-ə\ *n* [L, fr. Gk *Polyymnia*] **:** the Greek Muse of sacred song

poly I:C \ˌpäl-ē-ˈī-ˈsē\ *or* **poly I·poly C** \ˌpäl-ē-ˈī-ˌpäl-ē-ˈsē\ *n* [*poly-* + *inosinic acid* + *cytidylic acid*] (1969) **:** a synthetic 2-stranded RNA composed of one strand of polyinosinic acid and one strand of polycytidylic acid that induces interferon formation and has been used experimentally as an anticancer and antiviral agent

poly·ino·sin·ic acid \ˌpäl-ē-ˌin-ə-ˌsin-ik-, -ˌī-nə-\ *n* [*poly-* + *inosinic acid* ($C_{10}H_{13}N_4O_8P$), part trans. of G *inosinsäure*, fr. *inosin* (fr. Gk *inos*, gen. of *is* sinew) + *säure* acid — more at WITHY] (1965) **:** RNA or a segment of RNA that is composed of a polynucleotide chain consisting entirely of inosinic acid residues

poly·ly·sine \ˌpäl-i-ˈlī-ˌsēn\ *n* (1947) **:** a protein whose polypeptide chain consists entirely of lysine residues

poly·math \ˈpäl-i-ˌmath\ *n* [Gk *polymathēs* very learned, fr. *poly-* + *manthanein* to learn — more at MATHEMATICAL] (1621) **:** one of encyclopedic learning — **polymath** *or* **poly·math·ic** \ˌpäl-i-ˈmath-ik\ *adj* — **po·ly·ma·thy** \pə-ˈlim-ə-thē, ˈpäl-ə-ˌmath-ē\ *n*

poly·mer \ˈpäl-ə-mər\ *n* [ISV, back-formation fr. *polymeric*] (1866) **:** a chemical compound or mixture of compounds formed by polymerization and consisting essentially of repeating structural units

poly·mer·ase \-mə-ˌrās, -ˌrāz\ *n* [*polymer* + *-ase*] (1958) **:** any of several enzymes that catalyze the formation of DNA or RNA from precursor substances in the presence of preexisting DNA or RNA acting as a template

poly·mer·ic \ˌpäl-ə-ˈmer-ik\ *adj* [ISV, fr. Gk *polymerēs* having many parts, fr. *poly-* + *meros* part — more at MERIT] (1833) **:** of, relating to, or constituting a polymer — **poly·mer·i·cal·ly** \-i-k(ə-)lē\ *adv* — **po·ly·mer·ism** \pə-ˈlim-ə-ˌriz-əm, ˈpäl-ə-mə-\ *n*

po·ly·mer·iza·tion \pə-ˌlim-ə-rə-ˈzā-shən, ˌpäl-ə-mə-rə-\ *n* [ISV] (1872) **1 :** a chemical reaction in which two or more small molecules combine to form larger molecules that contain repeating structural units of the

original molecules — compare ASSOCIATION 5 **2 :** reduplication of parts in an organism
po·ly·mer·ize \pə-ˈlim-ə-ˌrīz, ˈpäl-ə-mə-\ *vb* **-ized; -iz·ing** *vt* (1865) **:** to subject to polymerization ~ *vi* **:** to undergo polymerization
poly·meth·yl methacrylate \ˈpäl-i-ˌmeth-əl-\ *n* (1936) **:** a thermoplastic resin of polymerized methyl methacrylate which is characterized by its optical clarity (as in a contact lens)
poly·morph \ˈpäl-i-ˌmȯrf\ *n* [ISV] (ca. 1828) **1 :** a polymorphic organism; *also* **:** one of the several forms of such an organism **2 :** any of the crystalline forms of a polymorphic substance
poly·mor·phism \ˌpäl-i-ˈmȯr-ˌfiz-əm\ *n* (1839) **:** the quality or state of being able to assume different forms: as **a :** existence of a species in several forms independent of the variations of sex **b :** the property of crystallizing in two or more forms with distinct structure — **poly·mor·phic** \-fik\ *adj* — **poly·mor·phi·cal·ly** \-fi-k(ə-)lē\ *adv*
poly·mor·pho·nu·cle·ar \-ˌmȯr-fə-ˈn(y)ü-klē-ər\ *adj, of a leukocyte* (1897) **:** having the nucleus complexly lobed — **polymorphonuclear** *n*
poly·mor·phous \-ˈmȯr-fəs\ *adj* [Gk *polymorphous,* fr. *poly-* + *-morphos* -morphous] (1785) **:** having, assuming, or occurring in various forms, characters, or styles **:** POLYMORPHIC ⟨a ~ rash⟩ ⟨~ sexuality⟩ — **poly·mor·phous·ly** *adv*
polymorphous perverse *adj* (1909) **:** relating to or exhibiting infantile sexual tendencies in which the genitals are not yet identified as the sole or principal sexual organs nor coitus as the goal of erotic activity
poly·myx·in \ˌpäl-i-ˈmik-sən\ *n* [ISV, fr. NL *polymyxa,* fr. *poly-* + Gk *myxa* mucus — more at MUCUS] (1947) **:** any of several toxic antibiotics obtained from a soil bacterium (*Bacillus polymyxa*) and active against gram-negative bacteria
Poly·ne·sian \ˌpäl-ə-ˈnē-zhən, -shən\ *n* (1807) **1 :** a member of any of the native peoples of Polynesia **2 :** a group of Austronesian languages spoken in Polynesia — **Polynesian** *adj*
poly·neu·ri·tis \ˌpäl-i-n(y)u̇-ˈrīt-əs\ *n* [NL] (1886) **:** neuritis of several peripheral nerves at the same time caused by alcoholism, poisons, infectious disease, or vitamin deficiency (as of thiamine)
Poly·ni·ces \ˌpäl-ə-ˈnī-sēz\ *n* [L, fr. Gk *Polyneikēs*] **:** a son of Oedipus for whom the Seven against Thebes mount their expedition
¹**poly·no·mi·al** \ˌpäl-ə-ˈnō-mē-əl\ *n* [*poly-* + *-nomial* (as in *binomial*)] (1674) **:** a mathematical expression of one or more algebraic terms each of which consists of a constant multiplied by one or more variables raised to a nonnegative integral power ⟨$a + bx + cx^2$ is a ~⟩
²**polynomial** *adj* (ca. 1704) **:** relating to, composed of, or expressed as one or more polynomials ⟨~ functions⟩ ⟨~ equations⟩
poly·nu·cle·ar \ˌpäl-i-ˈn(y)ü-klē-ər, ÷-kyə-lər\ *adj* [ISV] (1876) **:** chemically polycyclic esp. with respect to the benzene ring — used chiefly of aromatic hydrocarbons that are important as pollutants and possibly as carcinogens
poly·nu·cle·o·tide \-ˈn(y)ü-klē-ə-ˌtīd\ *n* [ISV] (1911) **:** a polymeric chain of mononucleotides
po·lyn·ya \ˌpäl-ən-ˈyä\ *n* [Russ *polyn'ya*] (1853) **:** an area of open water in sea ice
poly·oma virus \ˌpäl-ē-ˈō-mə-\ *n* [NL *polyoma,* fr. *poly-* + *-oma*] (1958) **:** a papovavirus of rodents that is associated with various kinds of tumors — called also *polyoma*
poly·on·y·mous \ˌpäl-ē-ˈän-ə-məs\ *adj* [Gk *polyōnymos,* fr. *poly-* + *onoma, onyma* name] (1678) **:** having or known by various names
pol·yp \ˈpäl-əp\ *n* [MF *polype* octopus, nasal tumor, fr. L *polypus,* fr. Gk *polypous,* fr. *poly-* + *pous* foot — more at FOOT] (1742) **1 :** a coelenterate that has typically a hollow cylindrical body closed and attached at one end and opening at the other by a central mouth surrounded by tentacles armed with nematocysts **2 :** a projecting mass of swollen and hypertrophied or tumorous membrane — **pol·yp·oid** \-ə-ˌpȯid\ *adj*
poly·pep·tide \ˌpäl-i-ˈpep-ˌtīd\ *n* [ISV] (1903) **:** a molecular chain of amino acids — **poly·pep·tid·ic** \-(ˌ)pep-ˈtid-ik\ *adj*
poly·pet·al·ous \-ˈpet-ᵊl-əs\ *adj* [NL *polypetalus,* fr. *poly-* + *petalum* petal] (ca. 1704) **:** having or consisting of separate petals
poly·pha·gia \-ˈfā-j(ē-)ə\ *n* [Gk *polyphagia,* fr. *polyphagos*] (ca. 1693) **:** excessive appetite or eating
po·lyph·a·gous \pə-ˈlif-ə-gəs\ *adj* [Gk *polyphagos* eating too much, fr. *poly-* + *-phagos* -phagous] (1815) **:** feeding on or utilizing many kinds of food — **po·lyph·a·gy** \-ə-jē\ *n*
poly·phase \ˈpäl-i-ˌfāz\ *adj* [ISV] (1922) **:** having or producing two or more phases ⟨a ~ machine⟩ ⟨a ~ current⟩
poly·pha·sic \ˌpäl-i-ˈfā-zik\ *adj* (ca. 1939) **:** consisting of two or more phases
Poly·phe·mus \ˌpäl-ə-ˈfē-məs\ *n* [L, fr. Gk *Polyphēmos*] **:** a Cyclops whom Odysseus blinds in order to escape from his cave
poly·phe·nol \ˌpäl-i-ˈfē-ˌnōl, -fi-ˈ\ *n* [ISV] (1897) **:** a polyhydroxy phenol — **poly·phe·no·lic** \-fi-ˈnō-lik, -ˈnäl-ik\ *adj*
poly·phone \ˈpäl-i-ˌfōn\ *n* (1872) **:** a symbol or sequence of symbols having more than one phonemic value (as *a* in English)
poly·phon·ic \ˌpäl-i-ˈfän-ik\ *or* **po·lyph·o·nous** \pə-ˈlif-ə-nəs\ *adj* (1782) **1 :** of, relating to, or marked by polyphony **2 :** being a polyphone — **poly·phon·i·cal·ly** \ˌpäl-i-ˈfän-i-k(ə-)lē\ *or* **po·lyph·o·nous·ly** *adv*
polyphonic prose *n* (1916) **:** a freely rhythmical prose employing characteristic devices of verse (as alliteration and assonance)
po·lyph·o·ny \pə-ˈlif-ə-nē\ *n* [Gk *polyphōnia* variety of tones, fr. *polyphōnos* having many tones or voices, fr. *poly-* + *phōnē* voice — more at BAN] (ca. 1864) **:** a style of musical composition in which two or more independent melodies are juxtaposed in harmony
poly·phy·let·ic \ˌpäl-i-(ˌ)fī-ˈlet-ik\ *adj* [ISV, fr. Gk *polyphylos* of many tribes, fr. *poly-* + *phylē* tribe — more at PHYL-] (1875) **:** of or relating to more than one stock; *specif* **:** derived from more than one ancestral line — **poly·phy·let·i·cal·ly** \-i-k(ə-)lē\ *adv*
pol·yp·ide \ˈpäl-ə-ˌpīd\ *n* [*polyp* + Gk *-idēs,* patronymic suffix] (1877) **:** one of the individual zooids of a bryozoan colony
poly·ploid \ˈpäl-i-ˌplȯid\ *adj* [ISV] (1920) **:** having or being a chromosome number that is a multiple greater than two of the monoploid number — **polyploid** *n* — **poly·ploi·dy** \-ˌplȯid-ē\ *n*
po·lyp·nea \pä-ˈlip-nē-ə, pə-\ *n* [NL] (ca. 1890) **:** rapid or panting respiration
poly·po·dy \ˈpäl-ə-ˌpōd-ē\ *n, pl* **-dies** [ME *polypodie,* fr. L *polypodium,* fr. Gk *polypodion,* fr. *poly-* + *pod-, pous* foot — more at FOOT] (15c) **:** a widely distributed fern (*Polypodium vulgare*) that has creeping rootstocks and pinnatifid fronds with entire segments
poly·pro·pyl·ene \ˌpäl-i-ˈprō-pə-ˌlēn\ *n* (1935) **:** any of various thermoplastic plastics or fibers that are polymers of propylene
po·lyp·tych \ˈpäl-əp-ˌtik, pə-ˈlip-tik\ *n* [Gk *polyptychos* having many folds, fr. *poly-* + *ptychē* fold, fr. *ptyssein* to fold] (1859) **:** an arrangement of four or more panels (as of a painting) usu. hinged and folding together
poly·rhythm \ˈpäl-i-ˌrith-əm\ *n* (1929) **:** the simultaneous combination of contrasting rhythms in music — **poly·rhyth·mic** \ˌpäl-i-ˈrith-mik\ *adj* — **poly·rhyth·mi·cal·ly** \-mi-k(ə-)lē\ *adv*
poly·ri·bo·nu·cle·o·tide \ˌpäl-i-ˌrī-bō-ˈn(y)ü-klē-ə-ˌtīd\ *n* (1956) **:** a polynucleotide in which the mononucleotides are ribonucleotides
poly·ri·bo·some \-ˈrī-bə-ˌsōm\ *n* (1962) **:** a cluster of ribosomes linked together by a molecule of messenger RNA and forming the site of protein synthesis — **poly·ri·bo·som·al** \-ˌrī-bə-ˈsō-məl\ *adj*
poly·sac·cha·ride \-ˈsak-ə-ˌrīd\ *n* [ISV] (1892) **:** a carbohydrate that can be decomposed by hydrolysis into two or more molecules of monosaccharides; *esp* **:** one of the more complex carbohydrates (as cellulose, starch, or glycogen)
poly·sa·pro·bic \-sə-ˈprō-bik\ *adj* [ISV] (1925) **:** living in a medium that is rich in decomposable organic matter and is nearly free from dissolved oxygen
po·ly·se·mous \ˌpäl-i-ˈsē-məs, pə-ˈlis-ə-məs\ *adj* [LL *polysemus,* fr. Gk *polysēmos,* fr. *poly-* + *sēma* sign — more at SEMANTIC] (1884) **:** marked by multiplicity of meaning — **po·ly·se·my** \-mē\ *n*
poly·some \ˈpäl-i-ˌsōm\ *n* (1962) **:** POLYRIBOSOME
poly·sor·bate \-ˈsȯr-ˌbāt\ *n* (1950) **:** any of several emulsifiers used in the preparation of some pharmaceuticals or foods
po·lys·ti·chous \pə-ˈlis-ti-kəs\ *adj* [Gk *polystichos,* fr. *poly-* + *stichos* row — more at DISTICH] (ca. 1890) **:** arranged in several rows
poly·sty·rene \ˌpäl-i-ˈstī(ə)r-ˌēn\ *n* (1927) **:** a polymer of styrene; *esp* **:** a rigid transparent thermoplastic of good physical and electrical insulating properties used esp. in molded products, foams, and sheet materials
poly·sul·fide \-ˈsəl-ˌfīd\ *n* [ISV] (1849) **:** a sulfide containing two or more atoms of sulfur in the molecule
poly·syl·lab·ic \ˌpäl-i-sə-ˈlab-ik\ *adj* [ML *polysyllabus,* fr. Gk *polysyllabos,* fr. *poly-* + *syllabē* syllable] (1782) **1 :** having more than one and usu. more than three syllables **2 :** characterized by words of many syllables — **poly·syl·lab·i·cal·ly** \-i-k(ə-)lē\ *adv*
poly·syl·la·ble \ˈpäl-i-ˌsil-ə-bəl, ˌpäl-i-ˈ\ *n* [modif. of ML *polysyllaba,* fr. fem. of *polysyllabus*] (1585) **:** a polysyllabic word
poly·syn·ap·tic \ˌpäl-i-sə-ˈnap-tik\ *adj* (1964) **:** involving two or more synapses in the central nervous system ⟨~ reflexes⟩ — **poly·syn·ap·ti·cal·ly** \-ti-k(ə-)lē\ *adv*
poly·syn·de·ton \-ˈsin-də-ˌtän\ *n* [NL, fr. LGk, neut. of *polysyndetos* using many conjunctions, fr. Gk *poly-* + *syndetos* bound together, conjunctive — more at ASYNDETON] (1589) **:** repetition of conjunctions in close succession (as in *we have ships and men and money and stores*)
¹**poly·tech·nic** \-ˈtek-nik\ *adj* [F *polytechnique,* fr. Gk *polytechnos* skilled in many arts, fr. *poly-* + *technē* art — more at TECHNICAL] (1805) **:** relating to or devoted to instruction in many technical arts or applied sciences
²**polytechnic** *n* (1836) **:** a polytechnic school
poly·tene \ˈpäl-i-ˌtēn\ *adj* [ISV] (1935) **:** relating to, being, or having chromosomes each of which consists of many strands with the corresponding chromomeres in contact — **poly·te·ny** \-ˌtē-nē\ *n*
poly·the·ism \ˈpäl-i-(ˌ)thē-ˌiz-əm\ *n* [F *polythéisme,* fr. LGk *polytheos* polytheistic, fr. Gk, of many gods, fr. *poly-* + *theos* god] (1613) **:** belief in or worship of more than one god — **poly·the·ist** \-ˌthē-əst\ *adj or n* — **poly·the·is·tic** \ˌpäl-i-thē-ˈis-tik\ *also* **poly·the·is·ti·cal** \-ˈis-ti-kəl\ *adj*
poly·thene \ˈpäl-ə-ˌthēn\ *n* [by contr.] *chiefly Brit* (1939) **:** POLYETHYLENE
poly·to·nal·i·ty \ˌpäl-i-tō-ˈnal-ət-ē\ *n* (1923) **:** the simultaneous use of two or more musical keys — **poly·ton·al** \-ˈtōn-ᵊl\ *adj* — **poly·ton·al·ly** \-ᵊl-ē\ *adv*
poly·typ·ic \ˌpäl-i-ˈtip-ik\ *adj* (1888) **:** represented by several or many types or subdivisions ⟨a ~ species of organism⟩
poly·un·sat·u·rat·ed \ˈpäl-ē-ˌən-ˈsach-ə-ˌrāt-əd\ *adj, of an oil or fatty acid* (1932) **:** rich in unsaturated chemical bonds
poly·ure·thane \ˌpäl-ē-ˈyu̇r-ə-ˌthān\ *n* [ISV] (1944) **:** any of various polymers that contain NHCOO linkages and are used esp. in flexible and rigid foams, elastomers, and resins
poly·uria \ˌpäl-ē-ˈyu̇r-ē-ə\ *n* [NL] (ca. 1842) **:** excessive secretion of urine
poly·va·lent \ˌpäl-i-ˈvā-lənt\ *adj* [ISV] (1881) **1 a :** having a valence greater usu. than two **b :** having variable valence **2 :** effective against, sensitive toward, or counteracting more than one exciting agent (as a toxin or antigen) — **poly·va·lence** \-lən(t)s\ *n*
poly·vi·nyl \-ˈvīn-ᵊl\ *adj* [ISV] (1927) **:** of, relating to, or being a polymerized vinyl compound, resin, or plastic — often used in combination
poly·wa·ter \ˈpäl-i-ˌwȯt-ər, -ˌwät-\ *n* [*poly*meric *water*] (1969) **:** water condensed into a glass capillary tube and formerly held to be a stable form with special properties
pom·ace \ˈpəm-əs, ˈpäm-\ *n* [prob. fr. ML *pomacium* cider, fr. LL *pomum* apple, fr. L, fruit] (1572) **1 :** the dry or pulpy residue of material (as fruit, seeds, or fish) from which a liquid (as juice or oil) has been pressed or extracted **2 :** something crushed to a pulpy mass
po·ma·ceous \pō-ˈmā-shəs\ *adj* [NL *pomaceus,* fr. LL *pomum*] (1708) **1 :** of or relating to apples **2** [*pome*] **:** resembling a pome
po·made \pō-ˈmād, -ˈmäd\ *n* [MF *pommade* ointment formerly made from apples, fr. It *pomata,* fr. *pomo* apple, fr. LL *pomum*] (1562) **:** a perfumed ointment; *esp* **:** a fragrant hair dressing — **pomade** *vt*
po·man·der \ˈpō-ˌman-dər, pō-ˈ\ *n* [ME, modif. of MF *pome d'ambre,* lit., apple or ball of amber] (15c) **:** a mixture of aromatic substances enclosed in a perforated bag or box and used to scent clothes and lin-

\ə\ abut \ᵊ\ kitten, F table \ər\ further \a\ ash \ā\ ace \ä\ cot, cart \au̇\ out \ch\ chin \e\ bet \ē\ easy \g\ go \i\ hit \ī\ ice \j\ job \ŋ\ sing \ō\ go \ȯ\ law \ȯi\ boy \th\ thin \th\ the \ü\ loot \u̇\ foot \y\ yet \zh\ vision \à, k, ⁿ, œ, œ̄, ue, ue̅, ʸ\ see Guide to Pronunciation

ens or formerly carried as a guard against infection; *also* **:** a clove-studded orange or apple used for the same purposes

po·ma·tum \pō-ˈmāt-əm, -ˈmät-\ *n* [NL, fr. LL *pomum* apple] (1562) **:** POMADE

pome \ˈpōm\ *n* [ME, fr. MF *pome, pomme* apple, pome, ball, fr. LL *pomum* apple, fr. L, fruit] (15c) **:** a fleshy fruit consisting of an outer thickened fleshy layer and a central core with usu. five seeds enclosed in a capsule

pome·gran·ate \ˈpäm-(ə-)ˌgran-ət, ˈpəm-ˌgran-\ *n* [ME *poumgarnet,* fr. MF *pomme grenate,* lit., seedy apple] (14c) **1 :** a thick-skinned several-celled reddish berry that is about the size of an orange and has many seeds with pulpy crimson arils of tart flavor **2 :** a widely cultivated tropical Old World tree (*Punica granatum* of the family Punicaceae) bearing pomegranates

pomegranate 1

pom·e·lo \ˈpäm-ə-ˌlō\ *n, pl* **-los** [alter. of earlier *pompelmous,* fr. D *pompelmoes*] (1858) **1 :** SHADDOCK **2 :** GRAPEFRUIT

Pom·er·a·nian \ˌpäm-ə-ˈrā-nē-ən, -nyən\ *n* (1760) **1 :** any of a breed of very small compact long-haired dogs **2 :** a native or inhabitant of Pomerania — **Pomeranian** *adj*

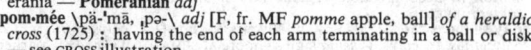

pom·mée \pä-ˈmā, ˌpə-\ *adj* [F, fr. MF *pomme* apple, ball] *of a heraldic cross* (1725) **:** having the end of each arm terminating in a ball or disk — see CROSS illustration

[1]pom·mel \ˈpəm-əl, ˈpäm-\ *n* [ME *pomel,* fr. MF, fr. (assumed) VL *pomellum* ball, knob, fr. dim. of LL *pomum* apple] (14c) **1 :** the knob on the hilt of a sword or saber **2 :** the protuberance at the front and top of a saddle **3 :** either of a pair of removable rounded or U-shaped handles used on the top of a pommel horse

[2]pom·mel \ˈpəm-əl\ *vt* **-meled** *or* **-melled; -mel·ing** *or* **-mel·ling** \-(ə-)liŋ\ [[1]*pommel*] (1530) **:** PUMMEL

pommel horse *n* (1908) **1 :** a gymnastics apparatus for swinging and balancing feats that consists of a padded rectangular or cylindrical form with two pommels on the top and that is supported in a horizontal position above the floor **2 :** an event in which the pommel horse is used

pom·my *or* **pom·mie** \ˈpäm-ē\ *n, pl* **pommies** [origin unknown] *Austral* (1915) **:** BRITON; *esp* **:** an English immigrant — called also *pom* \ˈpäm\; often used disparagingly

po·mol·o·gy \pō-ˈmäl-ə-jē\ *n* [NL *pomologia,* fr. L *pomum* fruit + *-logia* -logy] (1818) **:** the science and practice of fruit growing — **po·mo·log·i·cal** \ˌpō-mə-ˈläj-i-kəl\ *adj* — **po·mol·o·gist** \pō-ˈmäl-ə-jəst\ *n*

pomp \ˈpämp\ *n* [ME, fr. MF *pompe,* fr. L *pompa* procession, pomp, fr. Gk *pompē* act of sending, escort, procession, pomp] (14c) **1 :** a show of magnificence **:** SPLENDOR ⟨every day begins . . . in a ~ of flaming colours —F. D. Ommanney⟩ **2 :** a ceremonial or festival display (as a train of followers or a pageant) **3 a :** ostentatious display **:** VAINGLORY **b :** an ostentatious gesture or act

pom·pa·dour \ˈpäm-pə-ˌdō(ə)r, -ˌdȯ(ə)r\ *n* [Marquise de *Pompadour*] (ca. 1887) **1 a :** a man's style of hairdressing in which the hair is combed into a high mound in front **b :** a woman's style of hairdressing in which the hair is brushed into a loose full roll around the face **2 :** hair dressed in a pompadour — **pom·pa·doured** \-ˌdō(ə)rd, -ˌdȯ(ə)rd\ *adj*

pom·pa·no \ˈpäm-pə-ˌnō, ˈpəm-\ *n, pl* **-no** *or* **-nos** [Sp *pámpano* gilthead, lit., vine leaf, fr. L *pampinus*] (1778) **1 :** a marine percoid food fish (*Trachinotus carolinus*) of the southern Atlantic and Gulf coasts of No. America; *broadly* **:** any of several related fishes **2 :** a small bluish or greenish butterfish (*Peprilus simillimus*) of the Pacific coast

[1]pom–pom \ˈpäm-ˌpäm\ *n* [imit.; fr. the sound of its discharge] (1899) **:** an automatic gun of 20 to 40 millimeters mounted on ships in pairs, fours, or eights

[2]pom–pom *n* [alter. of *pompon*] (1904) **:** an ornamental ball or tuft used esp. on clothing, caps, or costumes

pom·pon \ˈpäm-ˌpän\ *n* [F, fr. MF *pompe* tuft of ribbons] (1861) **1 :** [2]POM-POM **2 :** a chrysanthemum or dahlia with small rounded flower heads

pom·pos·i·ty \päm-ˈpäs-ət-ē\ *n, pl* **-ties** (15c) **1 :** pompous demeanor, speech, or behavior **2 :** a pompous gesture, habit, or act

pomp·ous \ˈpäm-pəs\ *adj* (15c) **1 :** relating to or suggestive of pomp **:** MAGNIFICENT **2 :** having or exhibiting self-importance **:** ARROGANT ⟨a ~ politician⟩ **3 :** excessively elevated or ornate ⟨~ rhetoric⟩ ***syn*** see SHOWY — **pomp·ous·ly** *adv* — **pomp·ous·ness** *n*

ponce \ˈpän(t)s\ *n* [origin unknown] *Brit* (1872) **:** PIMP

pon·cho \ˈpän-(ˌ)chō\ *n, pl* **ponchos** [AmerSp, fr. Araucanian *pontho* woolen fabric] (1717) **1 :** a cloak resembling a blanket with a slit in the middle for the head **2 :** a waterproof garment resembling a poncho worn chiefly as a raincoat

[1]pond \ˈpänd\ *n* [ME *ponde* artificially confined body of water, alter. of *pounde* enclosure — more at POUND] (14c) **:** a body of water usu. smaller than a lake

[2]pond *vt* (1603) **:** to block (as a stream) to create a pond ~ *vi* **:** to collect in or form a pond

pon·der \ˈpän-dər\ *vb* **pon·dered; pon·der·ing** \-d(ə-)riŋ\ [ME *ponderen,* fr. MF *ponderer,* fr. L *ponderare* to weigh, ponder, fr. *ponder-, pondus* weight — more at PENDANT] *vt* (14c) **1 :** to weigh in the mind **:** APPRAISE ⟨~*ed* their chances of success⟩ **2 :** to think about **:** reflect on ⟨~*ed* the events of the day⟩ ~ *vi* **:** to think or consider esp. quietly, soberly, and deeply — **pon·der·er** \-dər-ər\ *n*

syn PONDER, MEDITATE, MUSE, RUMINATE mean to consider or examine attentively or deliberately. PONDER implies a careful weighing of a problem or, often, prolonged inconclusive thinking about a matter; MEDITATE implies a definite focusing of one's thoughts on something so as to understand it deeply; MUSE suggests a more or less focused daydreaming as in remembrance; RUMINATE implies going over the same matter in one's thoughts again and again but suggests little of either purposive thinking or rapt absorption.

pon·der·a·ble \ˈpän-d(ə-)rə-bəl\ *adj* [LL *ponderabilis,* fr. *ponderare*] (1813) **:** significant enough to be worth considering **:** APPRECIABLE ***syn*** see PERCEPTIBLE

pon·der·o·sa pine \ˌpän-də-ˌrō-sə-, -zə-\ *n* [NL *ponderosa,* specific epithet of *Pinus ponderosa,* fr. L, fem. of *ponderosus* ponderous] (1878) **:** a tall timber tree (*Pinus ponderosa*) of western No. America with long needles in groups of 2 to 5; *also* **:** its strong reddish straight-grained wood — called also *ponderosa*

pon·der·ous \ˈpän-d(ə-)rəs\ *adj* [ME, fr. MF *pondereux,* fr. L *ponderosus,* fr. *ponder-, pondus* weight] (15c) **1 :** of very great weight **2 :** unwieldy or clumsy because of weight and size **3 :** oppressively or unpleasantly dull **:** LIFELESS ⟨~ prose⟩ ***syn*** see HEAVY — **pon·der·ous·ly** *adv* — **pon·der·ous·ness** *n*

pond lily *n* (1748) **:** WATER LILY

pond scum *n* (ca. 1890) **1 :** SPIROGYRA; *also* **:** any of various related algae **2 :** a mass of tangled algal filaments in stagnant waters

pond skater *n* (1895) **:** WATER STRIDER

pond·weed \ˈpän-ˌdwēd\ *n* (1578) **:** any of a genus (*Potamogeton* of the family Zannichelliaceae, the pondweed family) of aquatic plants with jointed usu. rooting stems, 2-ranked floating or submerged leaves, and spikes of greenish flowers

pone \ˈpōn\ *n* [of Algonquian origin; akin to Delaware *äpân* baked] *Southern & Midland* (1612) **:** CORN PONE

pon·gee \(ˈ)pän-ˈjē, ˈpän-ˌ\ *n* [Chin (Pek) *pen³ chi¹,* fr. *pen³* own + *chi¹* loom] (1711) **:** a thin soft fabric of Chinese origin woven from raw silk; *also* **:** an imitation of this fabric in cotton or a synthetic fiber (as of polyester or rayon)

pon·gid \ˈpän-jəd, ˈpäŋ-gəd\ *n* [deriv. of Kongo *mpungu* ape] (1950) **:** APE 1b — **pongid** *adj*

[1]pon·iard \ˈpän-yərd\ *n* [MF *poignard,* fr. *poing* fist, fr. L *pugnus* fist — more at PUNGENT] (1586) **:** a dagger with a usu. slender blade of triangular or square cross section

[2]poniard *vt* (1593) **:** to pierce or kill with a poniard

pons \ˈpänz\ *n, pl* **pon·tes** \ˈpän-ˌtēz\ [NL, short for *pons Varolii*] (1831) **:** a broad mass of chiefly transverse nerve fibers conspicuous on the ventral surface of the brain of man and lower mammals at the anterior end of the medulla oblongata — see BRAIN illustration

pons asi·no·rum \ˈpän-ˌzas-ə-ˈnōr-əm, -ˈnȯr-\ *n* [NL, lit., asses' bridge, name applied to the proposition that the base angles of an isosceles triangle are equal] (1751) **:** a critical test of ability or understanding; *also* **:** STUMBLING BLOCK

pons Va·ro·lii \-və-ˈrō-lē-ˌī, -lē-ˌē\ *n* [NL, lit., bridge of Varoli, fr. Costanzo *Varoli* †1575 Ital. surgeon and anatomist] (ca. 1693) **:** PONS

pon·ti·fex \ˈpänt-ə-ˌfeks\ *n, pl* **pon·tif·i·ces** \pän-ˈtif-ə-ˌsēz\ [L *pontific-, pontifex,* lit., bridge maker, fr. *pont-, pons* bridge + *facere* to make — more at FIND, DO] (ca. 1579) **:** a member of the council of priests in ancient Rome

pon·tiff \ˈpänt-əf\ *n* [F *pontif,* fr. L *pontific-, pontifex*] (1626) **1 :** PONTIFEX **2 :** BISHOP; *specif* **:** POPE

[1]pon·tif·i·cal \pän-ˈtif-i-kəl\ *n* (14c) **1 :** episcopal attire; *specif* **:** the insignia of the episcopal order worn by a prelate when celebrating a pontifical mass — usu. used in pl. **2 :** a book containing the forms for sacraments and rites performed by a bishop

[2]pontifical *adj* [ME, fr. L *pontificalis,* fr. *pontific-, pontifex*] (15c) **1 a :** of or relating to a pontiff or pontifex **b :** celebrated by a prelate of episcopal rank with distinctive ceremonies ⟨~ mass⟩ **2 :** POMPOUS **3 :** pretentiously dogmatic — **pon·tif·i·cal·ly** \-k(ə-)lē\ *adv*

[1]pon·tif·i·cate \pän-ˈtif-i-kət, -ə-ˌkāt\ *n* [L *pontificatus,* fr. *pontific-, pontifex*] (1581) **:** the state, office, or term of office of a pontiff

[2]pon·tif·i·cate \pän-ˈtif-ə-ˌkāt\ *vi* **-cat·ed; -cat·ing** [ML *pontificatus,* pp. of *pontificare,* fr. L *pontific-, pontifex*] (1818) **1 a :** to officiate as a pontiff **b :** to celebrate pontifical mass **2 :** to speak or express opinions in a pompous or dogmatic way — **pon·tif·i·ca·tion** \(ˌ)pän-ˌtif-ə-ˈkā-shən\ *n* — **pon·tif·i·ca·tor** \-ˌkāt-ər\ *n*

pon·til \ˈpänt-ᵊl\ *n* [F, perh. fr. It *puntello,* dim. of *punto* point, fr. L *punctus* — more at POINT] (1832) **:** PUNTY — called also *pontil rod*

pon·tine \ˈpän-ˌtīn\ *adj* [ISV *pont-* (fr. NL *pont-, pons*) + *-ine*] (1889) **:** of or relating to the pons

Pont l'É·vêque \ˌpōⁿ-lā-ˈvek\ *n* [*Pont l'Évêque,* town in France] (ca. 1890) **:** a soft surface-ripened cheese firmer, yellower, and having less surface mold than Camembert

pon·ton \ˈpänt-ᵊn, pän-ˈtün\ *n* [F] (1676) **:** PONTOON

pon·ton·ier \ˌpänt-ᵊn-ˈi(ə)r\ *n* [F *pontonnier,* fr. *ponton*] (ca. 1830) **:** an individual engaged in constructing a pontoon bridge

[1]pon·toon \pän-ˈtün\ *n* [F *ponton,* floating bridge, punt, fr. L *ponton-, ponto,* fr. *pont-, pons* bridge] (1676) **1 :** a flat-bottomed boat (as a lighter); *esp* **:** a flat-bottomed boat or portable float used in building a floating temporary bridge **2 :** a float esp. of an airplane

[2]pontoon *n* [perh. alter. of *vingt-et-un*] *Brit* (ca. 1917) **:** BLACKJACK 5

po·ny \ˈpō-nē\ *n, pl* **ponies** [prob. fr. obs. F *poulenet,* dim. of F *poulain* colt, fr. ML *pullanus,* fr. L *pullus* young of an animal, foal — more at FOAL] (1659) **1 a :** a small horse; *esp* **:** one of any of several breeds of very small stocky animals noted for their gentleness and endurance **b :** a bronco, mustang, or similar horse of the western U.S. **c :** RACEHORSE — usu. used in pl. **2 :** something smaller than standard: as **a :** a small beer glass **b :** a small liqueur glass typically holding one ounce **3 :** a literal translation of a foreign language text; *esp* **:** one used surreptitiously by students in preparing or reciting lessons

pony express *n* (1860) **:** a rapid postal and express system that operated across the western U.S. in 1860–1861 by relays of horses and riders

po·ny·tail \ˈpō-nē-ˌtāl\ *n* (1951) **:** a style of arranging hair to resemble a pony's tail; *also* **:** hair arranged in this style — **po·ny·tailed** \-ˌtāld\ *adj*

po·ny up \ˌpō-nē-ˈəp\ *vb* **po·nied up; po·ny·ing up** [origin unknown] *vt* (1824) **:** to pay (money) in settlement of an account ⟨*ponied up* $12.50 for the fine —*Newsweek*⟩ ~ *vi* **:** PAY

Pon·zi scheme \ˈpän-zē-\ *n* [Charles A. *Ponzi* †1949 Am. (Ital.-born) swindler] (1926) **:** an investment swindle in which some early investors are paid off with money put up by later ones in order to encourage more and bigger risks

-poo \ˌpü, ˈpü\ *suffix* [origin unknown] — used as a disparaging diminutive ⟨cutesy-*poo*⟩

[1]pooch \ˈpüch\ *vb* [alter. of [1]*pouch*] *chiefly dial* (ca. 1923) **:** BULGE

[2]pooch *n* [origin unknown] (1924) **:** DOG

pood \ˈpüd, ˈpüt\ *n* [Russ *pud,* fr. ON *pund* pound — more at POUND] (1554) **:** a Russian unit of weight equal to about 36.11 pounds (16.38 kilograms)

poo·dle \ˈpüd-ᵊl\ *n* [G *pudel,* short for *pudelhund,* fr. *pudeln* to splash (fr. *pudel* puddle, fr. LG) + *hund* dog (fr. OHG *hunt*) — more at PUDDLE, HOUND] (1820) **1 :** any of a breed of active intelligent heavy-coated solid-colored dogs that occur in three sizes **2 :** a fabric with a

nubby or coarsely looped surface that resembles a poodle's coat — called also *poodle cloth*
¹poof \'püf, 'pu̇f\ *interj* [imit.] (1824) — used to express disdain or dismissal or to suggest instantaneous occurrence
²poof *also* **poove** \'püv, 'pu̇v\ *n, pl* **poofs** *also* **pooves** [prob. alter. of ²*puff*] *Brit* (1850) : a male homosexual — often used disparagingly
poof·ter \'püf-tər, 'pu̇f-\ *also* **poof·tah** \-tə\ *n, Brit* (ca. 1910) : POOF — often used disparagingly
pooh \'pü, 'pu̇\ *interj* (1602) — used to express contempt or disapproval
pooh–bah *also* **poo–bah** \'pü-,bä, -,bȯ\ *n, often cap P&B* [*Pooh-Bah,* character in Gilbert and Sullivan's opera *The Mikado* (1885) bearing the title Lord-High-Everything-Else] (1888) **1 :** a person holding many public or private offices **2 :** a person in high position or of great influence
pooh–pooh \'pü-(,)pü, pü-'\ *also* **pooh** \'pü\ *vb* [*pooh*] *vi* (1827) : to express contempt or impatience ~ *vt* : to express contempt for
¹pool \'pül\ *n* [ME, fr. OE *pōl;* akin to OHG *pfuol* pool] (bef. 12c) **1 a** (1) : a small and rather deep body of usu. fresh water (2) : a quiet place in a stream (3) : a body of water forming above a dam **b** : something resembling a pool ⟨a ~ of light⟩ **2 :** a small body of standing liquid **3 :** a continuous area of porous sedimentary rock that yields petroleum or gas **4 :** SWIMMING POOL
²pool *vi* (1626) **1 :** to form a pool **2** *of blood* **:** to accumulate or become static (as in the veins of a bodily part) ⟨blood~*ed* in his legs⟩
³pool *n* [F *poule,* lit., hen, fr. OF, fem. of *poul* cock — more at PULLET] (ca. 1711) **1 a :** an aggregate stake to which each player of a game has contributed **b :** all the money bet by a number of persons on a particular event **2 a :** a game played on an English billiard table in which each of the players stakes a sum and the winner takes all **b** : any of various games of billiards played on an oblong table having 6 pockets with usu. 15 object balls **3 :** an aggregation of the interests or property of different persons made to further a joint undertaking by subjecting them to the same control and a common liability **4 :** a readily available supply: as **a :** the whole quantity of a particular material present in the body and available for function or the satisfying of metabolic demands **b :** a body product (as blood) collected from many donors and stored for later use **c :** a group of people available for some purpose ⟨a shrinking ~ of applicants⟩ ⟨stenographic ~⟩
⁴pool *vt* (1879) : to contribute to a common fund or effort : make a common interest of
pool·room \'pül-,rüm, -,ru̇m\ *n* (1861) **1 :** a room in which bookmaking is carried on **2 :** a room for the playing of pool
pool·side \-,sīd\ *n* (1921) : the area surrounding a swimming pool
¹poop \'püp\ *n* [ME, fr. MF *poupe,* fr. L *puppis*] (15c) **1** *obs* : STERN **2** : an enclosed superstructure at the stern of a ship above the main deck
²poop *vt* (1748) **1 :** to break over the stern of **2 :** to ship (a sea or wave) over the stern
³poop *vb* [origin unknown] *vt, slang* (1932) : to put out of breath; *also* : to tire out ~ *vi, slang* : to become exhausted ⟨~ out⟩
⁴poop *n* [origin unknown] *slang* (1943) : INFORMATION
poop deck *n* (1840) : a partial deck above a ship's main afterdeck
poor \'pu̇(ə)r, 'pō(ə)r\ *adj* [ME *poure,* fr. OF *povre,* fr. L *pauper;* akin to L *paucus* little and to L *parere* to produce, *parare* to acquire — more at FEW, PARE] (13c) **1 a :** lacking material possessions **b :** of, relating to, or characterized by poverty **2 a :** less than adequate : MEAGER **b** : small in worth **3 :** exciting pity **4 a :** inferior in quality or value **b :** HUMBLE, UNPRETENTIOUS **c :** MEAN, PETTY **5 :** LEAN, EMACIATED **6** : BARREN, UNPRODUCTIVE — used of land **7 :** INDIFFERENT, UNFAVORABLE — **poor·ly** *adv* — **poor·ness** *n*
poor box *n* (1621) : a box (as in a church) for alms for the poor
poor boy \'pō(r)-,bȯi\ *n* (ca. 1920) : SUBMARINE 2
Poor Clare \-'kla(ə)r, -'kle(ə)r\ *n* (1818) : a member of an austere order of nuns founded by St. Clare under the direction of St. Francis in Assisi, Italy, in 1212
poor farm \'pu̇(ə)r-,färm, 'pō(ə)r-\ *n* (1852) : a farm maintained at public expense for the support and employment of needy persons
poor·house \-,hau̇s\ *n* (1745) : a place maintained at public expense to house needy or dependent persons
poor·ish \'pu̇(ə)r-ish, 'pō(ə)r-\ *adj* (1657) : rather poor
poor law *n* (1752) : a law providing for or regulating the public relief or support of the poor
poor·ly \'pu̇(ə)r-lē, 'pō(ə)r-\ *adj* (1573) : somewhat ill : INDISPOSED
poor–mouth \-,mau̇t͟h, -,mau̇th\ *vi* (1967) : to plead poverty as a defense or excuse ~ *vt* : to speak disparagingly of
poor mouth \-,mau̇th\ *n* (1822) : an exaggerated claim of poverty
poor–spir·it·ed \-'spir-ət-əd\ *adj* (1670) : lacking zest, confidence, or courage — **poor–spir·it·ed·ly** *adv* — **poor–spir·it·ed·ness** *n*
poor white *n* (1819) : a member of an inferior or underprivileged white social group — often taken to be offensive
¹pop \'päp\ *vb* **popped; pop·ping** [ME *poppen,* of imit. origin] *vt* (14c) **1** : to strike or knock sharply : HIT **2 :** to push, put, or thrust suddenly **3 :** to cause to explode or burst open **4 :** to fire at : SHOOT **5 :** to take (drugs) orally or by injection ⟨they *popped* pills⟩ ~ *vi* **1 a :** to go, come, enter, or appear suddenly — often used with *up* **b :** to escape or break away from something (as a point of attachment) usu. suddenly or unexpectedly **2 :** to make or burst with a sharp sound : EXPLODE **3** : to protrude from the sockets **4 :** to shoot with a firearm **5 :** to hit a pop fly — often used with *up* or *out* — **pop the question :** to propose marriage
²pop *n* (1591) **1 :** a sharp explosive sound **2 :** a shot from a gun **3 :** a flavored carbonated beverage **4 :** POP FLY
³pop *adv* (1621) : like or with a pop : SUDDENLY
⁴pop *n* [short for *poppa*] (1838) : FATHER
⁵pop *adj* [by shortening] (1880) **1 :** POPULAR ⟨~ music⟩: as **a :** of or relating to pop music ⟨~ singer⟩ **b :** of or relating to the popular culture disseminated through the mass media ⟨~ psychology⟩ ⟨~ grammarians⟩ ⟨~ society⟩ **2 a :** of or relating to pop art ⟨~ painter⟩ **b :** having, using, or imitating themes or techniques characteristic of pop art ⟨~ movie⟩
⁶pop *n* (1963) **1 :** pop music **2 :** POP ART **3 :** pop culture
pop art *n* (1962) : art in which commonplace objects (as road signs, hamburgers, comic strips, or soup cans) are used as subject matter and are often physically incorporated in the work — **pop artist** *n*
pop·corn \'päp-,kȯ(ə)rn\ *n* (1819) : an Indian corn (*Zea mays everta*) whose kernels on exposure to heat burst open to form a white starchy mass; *also* : the popped kernels
pope \'pōp\ *n* [ME, fr. OE *pāpa,* fr. LL *papa,* fr. Gk *pappas, papas,* title of bishops, lit., papa] (bef. 12c) **1** *often cap* : a prelate who as bishop of Rome is the head of the Roman Catholic Church **2 :** one that resembles a pope (as in authority) **3 a :** the Eastern Orthodox or Coptic patriarch of Alexandria **b :** a priest of an Eastern church
pop·ery \'pō-p(ə-)rē\ *n* (ca. 1534) : ROMAN CATHOLICISM — usu. used disparagingly
pop eye \'päp-,ī\ *n* [back-formation fr. *pop-eyed*] (1828) : an eye staring and bulging (as from excitement) — **pop–eyed** \-'īd\ *adj*
pop fly *n* (1887) : a high fly ball in baseball
pop·gun \'päp-,gən\ *n* (1662) : a toy gun that usu. shoots a cork and produces a popping sound
pop·in·jay \'päp-ən-,jā\ *n* [ME *papejay* parrot, fr. MF *papegai, papejai,* fr. Ar *babghā'*] (1528) : a strutting supercilious person
pop·ish \'pō-pish\ *adj* [*pope*] (1528) : ROMAN CATHOLIC — often used disparagingly
pop·ish·ly *adv* (1538) : in accordance with Roman Catholicism — often used disparagingly
pop·lar \'päp-lər\ *n* [ME *poplere,* fr. MF *pouplier,* fr. *pouple* poplar, fr. L *populus*] (14c) **1 a :** any of a genus (*Populus*) of slender quick-growing trees (as an aspen or cottonwood) of the willow family **b** : the wood of a poplar **2 :** TULIP TREE 1
pop·lin \'päp-lən\ *n* [F *papeline*] (1710) : a strong fabric in plain weave with crosswise ribs
pop·li·te·al \,päp-lə-'tē-əl *also* päp-'lit-ē-\ *adj* [NL *popliteus,* fr. L *poplit-, poples* ham of the knee] (1786) : of or relating to the back part of the leg behind the knee joint
pop off \(')päp-'ȯf\ *vi* (1761) **1 a :** to leave suddenly **b :** to die unexpectedly **2 :** to talk thoughtlessly and often loudly or angrily
pop·over \'päp-,ō-vər\ *n* (1876) : a hollow quick bread shaped like a muffin and made from a thin batter of eggs, milk, and flour
pop·pa \'päp-ə\ *var of* PAPA
pop·per \'päp-ər\ *n* (1750) **1 :** one that pops; *esp* : a utensil for popping corn **2** *slang* : a vial of amyl nitrite or butyl nitrite esp. when used as an aphrodisiac
pop·pet \'päp-ət\ *n* [ME *popet* doll, puppet — more at PUPPET] (1718) **1** *chiefly Brit* : DEAR **2 a** *Midland* : DOLL **b** *obs* : MARIONETTE **3 a** : an upright support or guide of a machine that is fastened at the bottom only **b :** a valve that rises perpendicularly to or from its seat **4** : any of the small pieces of wood on a boat's gunwale supporting or forming the rowlocks
pop·pied \'päp-ēd\ *adj* (1818) **1** *archaic* : growing or overgrown with poppies **2 :** DROWSY
¹pop·ple \'päp-əl\ *n* [ME *popul,* fr. OE, fr. L *populus*] *chiefly dial* (bef. 12c) : POPLAR 1
²popple *n* [*popple,* vb., fr. ME *poplen* to bubble, ripple, prob. of imit. origin] (1875) : a choppy sea
pop·py \'päp-ē\ *n, pl* **poppies** [ME *popi,* fr. OE *popæg, popig,* modif. of L *papaver*] (bef. 12c) **1 a :** any of a genus (*Papaver* of the family Papaveraceae, the poppy family) of chiefly annual or perennial herbs with milky juice, showy regular flowers, and capsular fruits including one (*P. somniferum*) that is the source of opium and several that are cultivated as ornamentals **b :** an extract or decoction of poppy used medicinally **2 :** a strong reddish orange
pop·py·cock \'päp-ē-,käk\ *n* [D dial. *pappekak,* lit., soft dung, fr. D *pap* pap + *kak* dung] (1863) : empty talk : NONSENSE
pop·py·head \-,hed\ *n* (1839) : a raised ornament often in the form of a finial generally used on the tops of the upright ends of seats in Gothic churches
Pop·si·cle \'päp-,sik-əl\ *trademark* — used for flavored and colored water frozen in a rectangular shape on two flat handles
pop·u·lace \'päp-yə-ləs\ *n* [MF, fr. It *popolaccio* rabble, pejorative of *popolo* the people, fr. L *populus*] (1572) **1 :** the common people : MASSES **2 :** POPULATION
pop·u·lar \'päp-yə-lər\ *adj* [L *popularis,* fr. *populus* the people, a people] (1548) **1 :** of or relating to the general public **2 :** suitable to the majority: as **a :** easy to understand : PLAIN ⟨a ~ history of the war⟩ **b :** suited to the means of the majority : INEXPENSIVE ⟨sold at ~ prices⟩ **3 :** frequently encountered or widely accepted **4 :** commonly liked or approved ⟨a very ~ girl⟩ ***syn*** see COMMON — **pop·u·lar·ly** *adv*
popular front *n, often cap P&F* (1936) : a coalition esp. of leftist political parties against a common opponent; *specif* : one sponsored and dominated by Communists as a device for gaining power
pop·u·lar·i·ty \,päp-yə-'lar-ət-ē\ *n* (1601) : the quality or state of being popular
pop·u·lar·ize \'päp-yə-lə-,rīz\ *vb* **-ized; -iz·ing** *vi* (1593) : to cater to popular taste ~ *vt* : to make popular: as **a :** to cause to be liked or esteemed **b :** to present in generally understandable or interesting form — **pop·u·lar·iza·tion** \,päp-yə-lə-rə-'zā-shən\ *n* — **pop·u·lar·iz·er** \'päp-yə-lə-,rī-zər\ *n*
popular sovereignty *n* (1848) **1 :** a doctrine in political theory that government is created by and subject to the will of the people **2 :** a pre-Civil War doctrine asserting the right of the people living in a newly organized territory to decide by vote of their territorial legislature whether or not slavery would be permitted there
pop·u·late \'päp-yə-,lāt\ *vt* **-lat·ed; -lat·ing** [ML *populatus,* pp. of *populare* to people, fr. L *populus* people] (1578) **1 :** to have a place in : OCCUPY, INHABIT **2 a :** to furnish or provide with inhabitants : PEOPLE **b** : to provide with members
pop·u·la·tion \,päp-yə-'lā-shən\ *n* [LL *population-, populatio,* fr. L *populus*] (1612) **1 a :** the whole number of people or inhabitants in a country or region **b :** the total of individuals occupying an area or making up a whole **c :** the total of particles in a particular energy level — used esp. of atoms in a laser **2 :** the act or process of populat-

\ə\ abut \ᵊ\ kitten, F table \ər\ further \a\ ash \ā\ ace \ä\ cot, cart \au̇\ out \ch\ chin \e\ bet \ē\ easy \g\ go \i\ hit \ī\ ice \j\ job \ŋ\ sing \ō\ go \ȯ\ law \ȯi\ boy \th\ thin \t͟h\ the \ü\ loot \u̇\ foot \y\ yet \zh\ vision \à, ḵ, ⁿ, œ, œ̄, ue, ue̅, ʸ\ see Guide to Pronunciation

ing 3 **a** : a body of persons or individuals having a quality or characteristic in common **b** (1) : the organisms inhabiting a particular locality (2) : a group of interbreeding organisms that represents the level of organization at which speciation begins **4** : a group of individual persons, objects, or items from which samples are taken for statistical measurement — **pop·u·la·tion·al** \-shnəl, -shən-ᵊl\ *adj*

population explosion *n* (1953) : a pyramiding of numbers of a biological population; *esp* : the recent great increase in human numbers resulting from both increased survival and exponential population growth

pop·u·list \'päp-yə-ləst\ *n* [L *populus* the people] (1892) **1** : a member of a political party claiming to represent the common people; *esp, often cap* : a member of a U.S. political party formed in 1891 primarily to represent agrarian interests and to advocate the free coinage of silver and government control of monopolies **2** : a believer in the rights, wisdom, or virtues of the common people — **pop·u·lism** \-,liz-əm\ *n* — **populist** *also* **pop·u·lis·tic** \,päp-yə-'lis-tik\ *adj, often cap*

pop·u·lous \'päp-yə-ləs\ *adj* [L *populosus,* fr. *populus* people] (15c) **1 a** : densely populated **b** : having a large population **2 a** : NUMEROUS **b** : filled to capacity — **pop·u·lous·ly** *adv* — **pop·u·lous·ness** *n*

pop–up \'päp-,əp\ *n* (1906) : POP FLY

por·bea·gle \'pȯ(ə)r-,bē-gəl\ *n* [Corn *porgh-bugel*] (1758) : a small viviparous shark (*Lamna nasus*) of the north Atlantic and Pacific oceans with a pointed nose and crescent-shaped tail

por·ce·lain \'pōr-s(ə-)lən, 'pȯr-\ *n* [MF *porcelaine* cowrie shell, porcelain, fr. It *porcellana,* fr. *porcello* vulva, lit., little pig, fr. L *porcellus,* dim. of *porcus* pig, vulva; fr. the shape of the shell — more at FARROW] (ca. 1540) : a hard, fine-grained, sonorous, nonporous, and usu. translucent and white ceramic ware that consists essentially of kaolin, quartz, and feldspar and is fired at high temperatures — **por·ce·lain·like** \-,līk\ *adj* — **por·ce·la·ne·ous** *or* **por·cel·la·ne·ous** \,pōr-sə-'lā-nē-əs, ,pȯr-\ *adj*

porcelain enamel *n* (1883) : VITREOUS ENAMEL

por·ce·lain·ize \'pōr-s(ə-)lə-,nīz, 'pȯr-\ *vt* **-ized; -iz·ing** (1951) : to fire a glassy coating on (as steel)

porch \'pō(ə)rch, 'pȯ(ə)rch\ *n* [ME *porche,* fr. OF, fr. L *porticus* portico, fr. *porta* gate; akin to L *portus* port — more at FORD] (13c) **1** : a covered entrance to a building usu. with a separate roof **2** *obs* : PORTICO

por·cine \'pȯr-,sīn\ *adj* [L *porcinus,* fr. *porcus* pig — more at FARROW] (1660) : of, relating to, or suggesting swine

por·ci·no \pȯr-'chē-(,)nō\ *n, pl* **-ni** \-(,)nē\ [It] (1976) : a wild edible mushroom of the genus *Boletus* (esp. *B. edulis*)

por·cu·pine \'pȯr-kyə-,pīn\ *n, often attrib* [ME *porkepin,* fr. MF *porc espin,* fr. OIt *porcospino,* fr. L *porcus* pig + *spina* spine, prickle] (15c) : any of various relatively large rodents having stiff sharp erectile bristles mingled with the hair and constituting an Old World terrestrial family (Hystricidae) and a New World arboreal family (Erethizontidae)

¹pore \'pō(ə)r, 'pȯ(ə)r\ *vi* **pored; por·ing** [ME *pouren*] (14c) **1** : to gaze intently **2** : to read studiously or attentively — usu. used with *over* **3** : to reflect or meditate steadily

²pore *n* [ME, fr. MF, fr. L *porus,* fr. Gk *poros* passage, pore — more at FARE] (14c) **1** : a minute opening esp. in an animal or plant; *esp* : one by which matter passes through a membrane **2** : a small interstice (as in soil) admitting absorption or passage of liquid — **pored** \'pō(ə)rd, 'pȯ(ə)rd\ *adj*

pore fungus *n* (ca. 1922) : a fungus (family Boletaceae or Polyporaceae) having the spore-bearing surface within tubes or pores

por·gy \'pȯr-gē\ *n, pl* **porgies** *also* **porgy** [partly fr. earlier *pargo* (porgy); partly fr. earlier *scuppaug* (porgy)] (1671) **1** : a blue-spotted crimson percoid food fish (*Pagrus pagrus*) of the coasts of Europe and America; *also* : any of various related fishes (family Sparidae) **2** [alter. of *pogy*] : any of various teleost fishes (as a menhaden) of families other than that of the porgy

pork \'pō(ə)rk, 'pȯ(ə)rk\ *n* [ME, fr. OF *porc,* pig, fr. L *porcus* — more at FARROW] (13c) **1** : the fresh or salted flesh of swine when dressed for food **2** : government money, jobs, or favors used by politicians as patronage

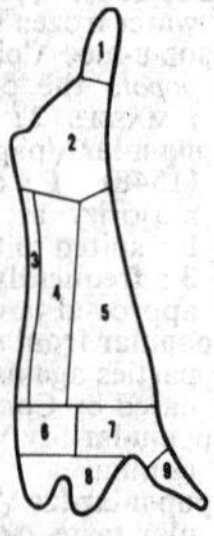

pork 1: *1* hind foot, *2* ham, *3* fatback, *4* loin, *5* side, *6* Boston butt, *7* picnic, *8* jowl, *9* forefoot

pork barrel *n* (1904) : a government project or appropriation yielding benefits (as patronage positions, increased employment, or public spending) to a political district and its political representative

pork belly *n* (ca. 1950) : an uncured side of pork

pork·er \'pōr-kər, 'pȯr-\ *n* (1657) : HOG; *esp* : a young pig fattened for table use as fresh pork

pork·pie hat \,pōrk-,pī-, ,pȯrk-\ *n* [fr. its shape] (1860) : a felt, straw, or cloth hat with a low telescoped crown, flat top, and brim turned up all around or up in back and down in front

por·ky \'pȯr-kē\ *n, pl* **porkies** (1900) : PORCUPINE

porn \'pȯ(ə)rn\ *or* **por·no** \'pȯr-(,)nō\ *n* [by shortening] (1962) : PORNOGRAPHY — **porn** *or* **porno** *adj*

por·nog·ra·pher \pȯr-'näg-rə-fər\ *n* (1850) : one who produces pornography

por·nog·ra·phy \-fē\ *n* [Gk *pornographos,* adj., writing of harlots, fr. *pornē* harlot + *graphein* to write; akin to Gk *pernanai* to sell, *poros* journey — more at FARE, CARVE] (ca. 1864) **1** : the depiction of erotic behavior (as in pictures or writing) intended to cause sexual excitement **2** : material (as books or a photograph) that depicts erotic behavior and is intended to cause sexual excitement — **por·no·graph·ic** \,pȯr-nə-'graf-ik\ *adj* — **por·no·graph·i·cal·ly** \-i-k(ə-)lē\ *adv*

po·ros·i·ty \pə-'räs-ət-ē, pōr-'äs-, pȯ-'räs-\ *n, pl* **-ties** (14c) **1 a** : the quality or state of being porous **b** : the ratio of the volume of interstices of a material to the volume of its mass **2** : PORE

po·rous \'pōr-əs, 'pȯr-\ *adj* (15c) **1 a** : possessing or full of pores **b** : containing vessels ⟨hardwood is ~⟩ **2** : permeable to fluids — **po·rous·ly** *adv* — **po·rous·ness** *n*

por·phyr·ia \pȯr-'fir-ē-ə\ *n* [NL, fr. ISV *porphyrin*] (1923) : any of several usu. hereditary abnormalities of porphyrin metabolism characterized by excretion of excess porphyrins in the urine and by extreme sensitivity to light

por·phy·rin \'pȯr-fə-rən\ *n* [ISV, fr. Gk *porphyra* purple] (1910) : any of various compounds with a structure that consists essentially of four pyrrole rings joined by four =C— groups; *esp* : one (as chlorophyll or hemoglobin) containing a central metal atom and usu. exhibiting biological activity

por·phy·rit·ic \,pȯr-fə-'rit-ik\ *adj* [ML *porphyriticus,* fr. Gk *porphyritikos,* fr. *porphyritēs* (*lithos*) porphyry] (15c) **1** : of or relating to porphyry **2** : having distinct crystals (as of feldspar) in a relatively fine-grained base

por·phy·roid \'pȯr-fə-,rȯid\ *n* [*porphyry*] (1796) : a more or less schistose metamorphic rock with porphyritic texture

por·phy·rop·sin \,pȯr-fə-'räp-sən\ *n* [Gk *porphyra* purple + E *-opsin* (as in *rhodopsin*)] (1930) : a purple pigment in the retinal rods of freshwater fishes that resembles rhodopsin

por·phy·ry \'pȯr-f(ə-)rē\ *n, pl* **-ries** [ME *porfurie,* fr. ML *porphyrium,* alter. of L *porphyrites,* fr. Gk *porphyritēs* (*lithos*), lit., stone like Tyrian purple, fr. *porphyra* purple] (15c) **1** : a rock consisting of feldspar crystals embedded in a compact dark red or purple groundmass **2** : an igneous rock of porphyritic texture

por·poise \'pȯr-pəs\ *n* [ME *porpoys,* fr. MF *porpois,* fr. ML *porcopiscis,* fr. L *porcus* pig + *piscis* fish — more at FARROW, FISH] (14c) **1** : any of several small gregarious toothed whales (genus *Phocaena*); *esp* : a blunt-snouted usu. largely black whale (*P. phocaena*) of the north Atlantic and Pacific 5 to 8 feet (1.5 to 2.4 meters) long **2** : any of several dolphins (as the bottle-nosed dolphin)

por·rect \pə-'rekt, pä-\ *adj* [L *porrectus,* pp. of *porrigere* to stretch out, fr. *por-* forward + *regere* to direct — more at PORTEND, RIGHT] (15c) : extended forward ⟨~ antennae⟩

por·ridge \'pȯr-ij, 'pär-\ *n* [alter. of *pottage*] (ca. 1643) : a soft food made by boiling meal of grains or legumes in milk or water until thick

por·rin·ger \-ən-jər\ *n* [alter. of ME *poteger, potinger,* fr. AF *potageer,* fr. MF *potager* of pottage, fr. *potage* pottage] (1522) : a low metal bowl with a single and usu. flat and pierced handle

¹port \'pō(ə)rt, 'pȯ(ə)rt\ *n* [ME, fr. OE & OF, fr. L *portus* — more at FORD] (bef. 12c) **1** : a place where ships may ride secure from storms : HAVEN **2 a** : a harbor town or city where ships may take on or discharge cargo **b** : AIRPORT **3** : PORT OF ENTRY

²port *n* [ME *porte,* fr. MF, gate, door, fr. L *porta* passage, gate; akin to L *portus* port] (bef. 12c) **1** *chiefly Scot* : GATE **2 a** : an opening for intake or exhaust of a fluid esp. in a valve seat or valve face **b** : the area of opening in a cylinder face of a passageway for the working fluid in an engine; *also* : such a passageway **c** : a place of access to a system **3 a** : an opening in a ship's side to admit light or air or to load cargo **b** *archaic* : the cover for a porthole **4** : a hole in an armored vehicle or fortification through which guns may be fired

³port *n* [ME, fr. MF, fr. *porter* to carry fr. L *portare*] (14c) **1** : the manner in which one bears himself **2** *archaic* : STATE 3 **3** : the position in which a military weapon is carried at the command *port arms*

⁴port *vt* (1580) : to turn or put (a helm) to the left — used chiefly as a command

⁵port *n* [prob. fr. ¹*port* or ²*port*] (ca. 1625) : the left side of a ship or aircraft looking forward — called also *larboard;* compare STARBOARD — **port** *adj*

⁶port *n* [*Oporto,* Portugal] (1691) : a sweet fortified wine of rich taste and aroma made in Portugal; *also* : a similar wine made elsewhere

¹por·ta·ble \'pōrt-ə-bəl, 'pȯrt-\ *adj* [ME, fr. MF, fr. LL *portabilis,* fr. L *portare* to carry — more at FARE] (15c) **1** : capable of being carried or moved about ⟨a ~ TV⟩ ⟨a ~ sawmill⟩ **2** *obs* : BEARABLE — **por·ta·bil·i·ty** \,pōrt-ə-'bil-ət-ē, ,pȯrt-\ *n* — **por·ta·bly** \'pōrt-ə-blē, 'pȯrt-\ *adv*

²portable *n* (1883) : something that is portable

¹por·tage \'pōrt-ij, 'pȯrt-, *3 is also* pȯr-'täzh\ *n* [ME, fr. MF, fr. *porter* to carry] (15c) **1** : the labor of carrying or transporting **2** *archaic* : the cost of carrying : PORTERAGE **3 a** : the carrying of boats or goods overland from one body of water to another or around an obstacle (as a rapids) **b** : the route followed in making such a transfer

²por·tage \'pōrt-ij, 'pȯrt-; pȯr-'täzh\ *vb* **por·taged; por·tag·ing** *vt* (1864) : to carry over a portage ~ *vi* : to move gear over a portage

¹por·tal \'pōrt-ᵊl, 'pȯrt-\ *n* [ME, fr. MF, fr. ML *portale* city gate, porch, fr. neut. of *portalis* of a gate, fr. L *porta* gate — more at PORT] (14c) **1** : DOOR, ENTRANCE; *esp* : a grand or imposing one **2** : the whole architectural composition surrounding and including the doorways and porches of a church **3** : the approach or entrance to a bridge or tunnel **4** : a communicating part or area of an organism; *specif* : the point at which something (as a pathogen) enters the body

²portal *adj* [NL *porta* transverse fissure of the liver, fr. L, gate] (1845) **1** : of or relating to the transverse fissure on the underside of the liver where most of the vessels enter **2** : of, relating to, or being a portal vein

portal system *n* [*portal vein*] (1851) : a system of veins that begins and ends in capillaries

portal–to–portal *adj* (1943) : of or relating to the time spent by a worker in traveling between the entrance to his employer's property and his actual working place (as in a mine) ⟨~ pay⟩

portal vein *n* [²*portal*] (1845) : a vein that collects blood from one part of the body and distributes it in another through capillaries; *esp* : a vein carrying blood from the digestive organs and spleen to the liver

por·ta·men·to \,pōrt-ə-'men-(,)tō, ,pȯrt-\ *n, pl* **-men·ti** \-(,)tē\ [It, lit., act of carrying, fr. *portare* to carry, fr. L] (1771) : a continuous gliding movement from one tone to another by the voice, a trombone, or a bowed stringed instrument

por·ta·pak *or* **por·ta·pack** \'pōrt-ə-,pak, 'pȯrt-\ *n* [*portable* + *pack*] (1970) : a small portable combined videotape recorder and camera

port arms *n* [fr. the command *port arms!*] (ca. 1890) : a position in the manual of arms in which the rifle is held diagonally in front of the body with the muzzle pointing upward to the left; *also* : a command to assume this position

por·ta·tive \'pōrt-ət-iv, 'pȯrt-\ *adj* [ME *portatif,* fr. MF, fr. L *portatus,* pp. of *portare*] (14c) : PORTABLE

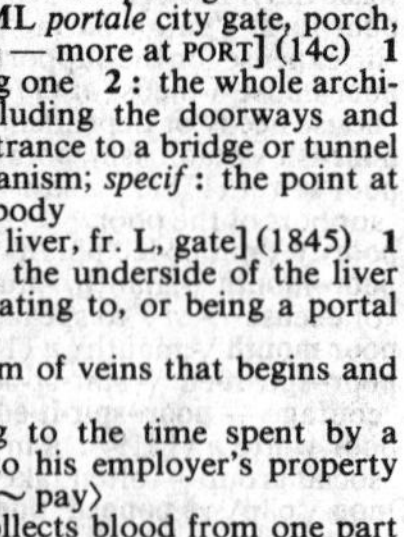

portcullis

port·cul·lis \pōrt-'kəl-əs, pȯrt-\ *n* [ME *port colice,* fr. MF *porte coleïce,* lit., sliding door]

(14c) : a grating of iron hung over the gateway of a fortified place and lowered between grooves to prevent passage

port de bras \ˌpȯrd-ə-ˈbrä\ *n* [F, lit., carriage of the arm] (1912) : the technique and practice of arm movement in ballet

Port du Sa·lut \ˌpōrd-ə-səl-ˈ(y)ü, ˌpȯrd-, -sal-\ *n* [F *port-du-salut, port=salut,* fr. *Port du Salut,* Trappist abbey in northwest France] (1881) : a semisoft pressed ripened cheese of usu. mild flavor originated by Trappist monks in France — called also *Port Salut*

Porte \ˈpō(ə)rt, ˈpȯ(ə)rt\ *n* [F, short for *Sublime Porte,* lit., sublime gate; fr. the gate of the sultan's palace where justice was administered] (15c) : the government of the Ottoman empire

porte co·chere \ˌpōrt-kō-ˈshe(ə)r, ˌpȯrt-\ *n* [F *porte cochère,* lit., coach door] (1698) **1** : a passageway through a building or screen wall designed to let vehicles pass from the street to an interior courtyard **2** : a roofed structure extending from the entrance of a building over an adjacent driveway and sheltering those getting in or out of vehicles

por·tend \pȯr-ˈtend, pōr-\ *vt* [ME *portenden,* fr. L *portendere,* fr. *por-* forward (akin to *per* through) + *tendere* to stretch — more at FOR, THIN] (15c) **1** : to give an omen or anticipatory sign of : BODE **2** : INDICATE, SIGNIFY

por·tent \ˈpō(ə)r-ˌtent, ˈpō(ə)r-\ *n* [L *portentum,* fr. neut. of *portentus,* pp. of *portendere*] (ca. 1563) **1** : something that foreshadows a coming event : OMEN **2** : prophetic indication or significance **3** : MARVEL, PRODIGY

por·ten·tous \pȯr-ˈtent-əs, pōr-\ *adj* (ca. 1540) **1** : of, relating to, or constituting a portent **2** : eliciting amazement or wonder : PRODIGIOUS **3** : self-consciously weighty : POMPOUS ***syn*** see OMINOUS — **por·ten·tous·ly** *adv* — **por·ten·tous·ness** *n*

[1]**por·ter** \ˈpōrt-ər, ˈpȯrt-\ *n* [ME, fr. OF *portier,* fr. LL *portarius,* fr. L *porta* gate — more at PORT] *chiefly Brit* (13c) : a person stationed at a door or gate to admit or assist those entering

[2]**porter** *n* [ME *portour,* fr. MF *porteour,* fr. LL *portator,* fr. L *portatus,* pp. of *portare* to carry — more at FARE] (14c) **1** : a person who carries burdens; *specif* : one employed to carry baggage for patrons at a hotel or transportation terminal **2** : a parlor-car or sleeping-car attendant who waits on passengers and makes up berths **3** [short for *porter's beer*] : a heavy dark brown beer brewed from browned or charred malt **4** : a person who does routine cleaning of the premises, furniture, and equipment (as in a hospital or office)

por·ter·age \-ə-rij\ *n* (15c) : a porter's work; *also* : the charge for it

por·ter·house \ˈpōrt-ər-ˌhau̇s, ˈpȯrt-\ *n* (1758) **1** *archaic* : a house where malt liquor (as porter) is sold **2** : a large steak cut from the thick end of the short loin to contain a T-shaped bone and a large piece of tenderloin — see BEEF illustration

port·fo·lio \pōrt-ˈfō-lē-ˌō, pȯrt-\ *n, pl* **-li·os** [It *portafoglio,* fr. *portare* to carry (fr. L) + *foglio* leaf, sheet, fr. L *folium* — more at BLADE] (1722) **1** : a hinged cover or flexible case for carrying loose papers, pictures, or pamphlets **2** [fr. the use of such a case to carry documents of state] : the office and functions of a minister of state or member of a cabinet **3** : the securities held by an investor : the commercial paper held by a financial house (as a bank) **4** : a set of pictures (as drawings or photographs) either bound in book form or loose in a folder

port·hole \ˈpōrt-ˌhōl, ˈpȯrt-\ *n* [[2]*port*] (ca. 1591) **1** : an opening (as a window) with a cover or closure esp. in the side of a ship or aircraft **2** : a port through which to shoot **3** : [2]PORT 2

Por·tia \ˈpōr-shə, ˈpȯr-\ *n* : the heroine in Shakespeare's *The Merchant of Venice*

por·ti·co \ˈpōrt-i-ˌkō, ˈpȯrt-\ *n, pl* **-coes** *or* **-cos** [It, fr. L *porticus* — more at PORCH] (1605) : a colonnade or covered ambulatory esp. in classical architecture and often at the entrance of a building

por·tiere \pōr-ˈtye(ə)r, pȯr-, -ˈti(ə)r; ˈpōrt-ē-ər, ˈpȯrt-\ *n* [F *portière,* fr. OF, fem. of *portier* porter, doorkeeper] (1843) : a curtain hanging across a doorway

[1]**por·tion** \ˈpōr-shən, ˈpȯr-\ *n* [ME, fr. OF, fr. L *portion-, portio;* akin to L *part-, pars* part] (14c) **1** : an individual's part or share of something: as **a** : a share received by gift or inheritance **b** : DOWRY **c** : a helping of food **2** : an individual's lot, fate, or fortune : one's share of good and evil **3** : an often limited part set off or abstracted from a whole ⟨give but that ~ which yourself proposed —Shak.⟩ ***syn*** see PART, FATE

[2]**portion** *vt* **por·tioned; por·tion·ing** \-sh(ə-)niŋ\ (14c) **1** : to divide into portions : DISTRIBUTE **2** : to allot a dowry to : DOWER

por·tion·less \-shən-ləs\ *adj* (1782) : having no portion; *esp* : having no dowry or inheritance

port·land cement \ˌpōrt-lən(d)-, ˌpȯrt-\ *n* [Isle of *Portland,* England; fr. its resemblance to a limestone found there] (1824) : a hydraulic cement made by finely pulverizing the clinker produced by calcining to incipient fusion a mixture of clay and limestone or similar materials

port·ly \ˈpōrt-lē, ˈpȯrt-\ *adj* **port·li·er; -est** [[3]*port*] (ca. 1529) **1** : DIGNIFIED, STATELY **2** : heavy or rotund of body : STOUT — **port·li·ness** *n*

[1]**port·man·teau** \pōrt-ˈman-(ˌ)tō, pȯrt-\ *n, pl* **-teaus** *or* **-teaux** \-(ˌ)tōz\ [MF *portemanteau,* fr. *porter* to carry + *manteau* mantle, fr. L *mantellum* — more at PORT] (1579) : a large traveling bag

[2]**portmanteau** *adj* (1872) : combining more than one use or quality

portmanteau word *n* (1882) : BLEND 1b

port of call (1884) **1** : an intermediate port where ships customarily stop for supplies, repairs, or transshipment of cargo **2** : a stop included on an itinerary

port of entry (1840) **1** : a place where foreign goods may be cleared through a customhouse **2** : a place where an alien may be permitted to enter a country

por·trait \ˈpōr-trət, ˈpȯr-, -ˌtrāt\ *n* [MF, fr. pp. of *portraire*] (1570) **1** : PICTURE; *esp* : a pictorial representation (as a painting) of a person usu. showing his face **2** : a sculptured figure : BUST, STATUE **3** : a graphic portrayal in words

por·trait·ist \-əst\ *n* (1866) : a maker of portraits

por·trai·ture \ˈpōr-trə-ˌchu̇(ə)r, ˈpȯr-, -chər, -ˌt(y)u̇(ə)r\ *n* (14c) **1** : the making of portraits : PORTRAYAL **2** : PORTRAIT

por·tray \pōr-ˈtrā, pȯr-, pər-\ *vt* [ME *portraien,* fr. MF *portraire,* fr. L *protrahere* to draw forth, reveal, expose — more at PROTRACT] (14c) **1** : to make a picture of : DEPICT **2** **a** : to describe in words **b** : to play the role of : ENACT — **por·tray·er** *n*

por·tray·al \-ˈtrā(-ə)l\ *n* (ca. 1847) **1** : the act or process or an instance of portraying : REPRESENTATION **2** : PORTRAIT

por·tress \ˈpōr-trəs, ˈpȯr-\ *n* (15c) : a female porter: as **a** : a doorkeeper in a convent or apartment house **b** : CHARWOMAN

Port Roy·al·ist \pōrt-ˈrȯi-ə-ləst, pȯrt-\ *n* [F *port-royaliste,* fr. *Port-Royal,* a convent near Versailles, France] (ca. 1727) : a member or adherent of a 17th century French Jansenist lay community noted for its logicians and educators

Port Sa·lut \ˌpōr-səl-ˈ(y)ü, ˌpȯr-, -sal-\ *n* (1902) : PORT DU SALUT

Por·tu·guese \ˌpōr-chə-ˈgēz, ˌpȯr-, -ˈgēs\ *n, pl* **Portuguese** [Pg *português,* adj. & n., fr. *Portugal*] (1615) **1** : the Romance language of Portugal and Brazil **2** **a** : a native or inhabitant of Portugal **b** : one who is of Portuguese descent — **Portuguese** *adj*

Portuguese man-of-war *n* (1707) : any of several large siphonophores (genus *Physalia*) having a large bladderlike sac or cyst with a broad crest on the upper side by means of which the colony floats at the surface of the sea

Portuguese man-of-war

por·tu·laca \ˌpōr-chə-ˈlak-ə, ˌpȯr-\ *n* [NL, fr. L, purslane, fr. *portula,* dim. of *porta* gate; fr. the lid of its capsule — more at PORT] (1548) : any of a genus (*Portulaca*) of mainly tropical succulent herbs of the purslane family; *esp* : a plant (*P. grandiflora*) cultivated for its showy flowers

po·sa·da \pə-ˈsäd-ə\ *n* [Sp, fr. *posar* to lodge, fr. LL *pausare*] (1763) : an inn in Spanish-speaking countries

[1]**pose** \ˈpōz\ *vb* **posed; pos·ing** [ME *posen,* fr. MF *poser,* fr. (assumed) VL *pausare,* fr. LL, to stop, rest, pause, fr. L *pausa* pause] *vt* (14c) **1** **a** : to put or set in place **b** : to place (as a model) in a studied attitude **2** **a** : to put or set forth : OFFER ⟨this attitude ~s a threat to our hopes for peace⟩ **b** : to present for attention or consideration ⟨let me ~ a question⟩ ~ *vi* **1** : to assume a posture or attitude usu. for artistic purposes **2** : to affect an attitude or character usu. to deceive or impress

[2]**pose** *n* (1818) **1** : a sustained posture; *esp* : one assumed for artistic effect **2** : an attitude, role, or characteristic assumed for effect

syn POSE, AIR, AIRS, AFFECTATION, MANNERISM mean an adopted way of speaking or behaving. POSE implies an attitude deliberately assumed in order to impress others ⟨her shyness was just a *pose*⟩ AIR may suggest natural acquirement through environment or way of life, but AIRS always implies artificiality and pretentiousness ⟨a snobby couple much given to putting on *airs*⟩ AFFECTATION applies to a trick of speech or behavior that strikes the observer as insincere ⟨his foreign accent is an *affectation*⟩ MANNERISM applies to an acquired eccentricity that has become a habit ⟨gesturing with a cigarette was her most noticeable *mannerism*⟩

[3]**pose** *vt* **posed; pos·ing** [short for earlier *appose,* fr. ME *apposen,* alter. of *opposen* to oppose] (1593) : PUZZLE, BAFFLE

Po·sei·don \pə-ˈsīd-ᵊn\ *n* [L, fr. Gk *Poseidōn*] : the Greek god of the sea — compare NEPTUNE

[1]**pos·er** \ˈpō-zər\ *n* [[3]*pose*] (1793) : a puzzling or baffling question

[2]**poser** *n* [[1]*pose*] (1888) : a person who poses

po·seur \pō-ˈzər\ *n* [F, lit., poser, fr. *poser*] (1872) : a person who pretends to be what he is not : an affected or insincere person

posh \ˈpäsh\ *adj* [origin unknown] (1918) : ELEGANT, FASHIONABLE — **posh·ly** *adv* — **posh·ness** *n*

pos·it \ˈpäz-ət\ *vt* **pos·it·ed** \ˈpäz-ət-əd, ˈpäz-təd\; **pos·it·ing** \ˈpäz-ət-iŋ, ˈpäz-tiŋ\ [L *positus,* pp.] (1647) **1** : to dispose or set firmly : FIX **2** : to assume or affirm the existence of : POSTULATE **3** : to propose as an explanation : SUGGEST

[1]**po·si·tion** \pə-ˈzish-ən\ *n* [ME *posycion,* fr. MF *position,* fr. L *position-, positio,* fr. *positus,* pp. of *ponere* to lay down, put, place, fr. (assumed) OL *posinere,* fr. *po-* away (akin to Gk *apo-*) + L *sinere* to lay, leave — more at OF, SITE] (14c) **1** : an act of placing or arranging: as **a** : the laying down of a proposition or thesis **b** : an arranging in order **2** : a point of view adopted and held to ⟨made his ~ on the issue clear⟩ **3** : a market commitment in securities or commodities; *also* : the inventory of a market trader **4** **a** : the point or area occupied by a physical object ⟨took her ~ at the head of the line⟩ **b** : a certain arrangement of bodily parts ⟨rose to a standing ~⟩ **5** **a** : relative place, situation, or standing ⟨is now in a ~ to make important decisions on his own⟩ **b** : social or official rank or status **c** : an employment for which one has been hired : JOB ⟨a ~ with a brokerage firm⟩ **d** : a situation that confers advantage or preference

[2]**position** *vt* **po·si·tioned; po·si·tion·ing** \-ˈzish-(ə-)niŋ\ (1817) : to put in proper position; *also* : LOCATE

po·si·tion·al \pə-ˈzish-nəl, -ən-ᵊl\ *adj* (1571) **1** : of, relating to, or fixed by position ⟨~ astronomy⟩ **2** : involving little movement ⟨~ warfare⟩ **3** : dependent on position or environment or context ⟨the front=articulated \k\ in \kē\ *key* and the back-articulated \k\ in \kül\ *cool* are ~ variants⟩ — **po·si·tion·al·ly** \-ē\ *adv*

positional notation *n* (1941) : a system of expressing numbers in which the digits are arranged in succession, the position of each digit has a place value, and the number is equal to the sum of the products of each digit by its place value

position effect *n* (1930) : genic effect that is due to interaction of adjacent genes and that is modified when the spatial relationships of the genes change (as by chromosomal inversion)

position paper *n* (1949) : a detailed report that recommends a course of action on a particular issue

[1]**pos·i·tive** \ˈpäz-ət-iv, ˈpäz-tiv\ *adj* [ME, fr. MF *positif,* fr. L *positivus,* fr. *positus*] (14c) **1** **a** : formally laid down or imposed : PRESCRIBED ⟨~ laws⟩ **b** : expressed clearly or peremptorily ⟨her answer was a ~ *no*⟩ **c** : fully assured : CONFIDENT **2** **a** : of, relating to, or constituting the degree of comparison that is expressed in English by the unmodified and uninflected form of an adjective or adverb and denotes no increase

or diminution **b** (1) **:** independent of changing circumstances **:** UNCONDITIONED (2) **:** relating to or constituting a motion or device that is definite, unyielding, constant, or certain in its action ⟨a ~ system of levers⟩ **c** (1) **:** INCONTESTABLE ⟨~ proof⟩ (2) **:** UNQUALIFIED ⟨a ~ disgrace⟩ **3 a :** not fictitious **:** REAL ⟨a ~ influence for good in the community⟩ **b :** active and effective in social or economic function rather than merely maintaining peace and order ⟨a ~ government⟩ **4 a :** having or expressing actual existence or quality as distinguished from deprivation or deficiency ⟨~ change in temperature⟩: as (1) **:** capable of being constructively applied (2) **:** not speculative **:** EMPIRICAL **b :** having rendition of light and shade similar in tone to the tones of the original subject ⟨a ~ photographic image⟩ **c :** that is or is generated in a direction arbitrarily or customarily taken as that of increase or progression ⟨~ rotation of the earth⟩ ⟨we are making some ~ progress⟩ **d :** directed or moving toward a source of stimulation ⟨a ~ taxis⟩ **e :** real and numerically greater than zero ⟨+2 is a ~ integer⟩ **5 a** (1) **:** being, relating to, or charged with electricity of which the proton is the elementary unit and which predominates in a glass body after being rubbed with silk (2) **:** losing electrons **b** (1) **:** having higher electric potential and constituting the part from which the current flows to the external circuit ⟨the ~ terminal of a discharging storage battery⟩ (2) **:** being an electron-collecting electrode of an electron tube **6 a :** marked by or indicating acceptance, approval, or affirmation **b :** affirming the presence of that sought or suspected to be present ⟨a ~ test for blood⟩ **7** *of a lens* **:** converging light rays and forming a real inverted image ***syn*** see SURE — **pos·i·tive·ly** \-lē, *for emphasis often* ˌpäz-ə-ˈtiv-\ *adv* — **pos·i·tive·ness** \ˈpäz-ət-iv-nəs, ˈpäz-tiv-\ *n*

²**positive** *n* (15c) **:** something positive: as **a** (1) **:** the positive degree of comparison in a language (2) **:** a positive form of an adjective or adverb **b :** something of which an affirmation can be made **:** REALITY **c :** a positive photograph or a print from a negative

positive definite *adj* (1907) **1 :** having a positive value for all values of the constituent variables ⟨*positive definite* quadratic forms⟩ **2** *of a matrix* **:** having the characteristic roots real and positive

positive law *n* (14c) **:** law established or recognized by governmental authority — compare NATURAL LAW

pos·i·tiv·ism \ˈpäz-ət-iv-ˌiz-əm, ˈpäz-tiv-\ *n* [F *positivisme*, fr. *positif* positive + *-isme* -ism] (1847) **1 a :** a theory that theology and metaphysics are earlier imperfect modes of knowledge and that positive knowledge is based on natural phenomena and their properties and relations as verified by the empirical sciences **b :** LOGICAL POSITIVISM **2 :** the quality or state of being positive — **pos·i·tiv·ist** \-əst\ *adj or n* — **pos·i·tiv·is·tic** \ˌpäz-ət-iv-ˈis-tik, ˌpäz-tiv-\ *adj*

pos·i·tiv·i·ty \ˌpäz-ə-ˈtiv-ət-ē\ *n, pl* **-ties** (1659) **1 :** the quality or state of being positive **2 :** something that is positive

pos·i·tron \ˈpäz-ə-ˌträn\ *n* [*positive* + *-tron* (as in *electron*)] (1933) **:** a positively charged particle having the same mass and magnitude of charge as the electron and constituting the antiparticle of the electron — called also *positive electron*

pos·i·tro·ni·um \ˌpäz-ə-ˈtrō-nē-əm\ *n* [*positron* + *-ium*] (1945) **:** a short-lived system suggestive of an atom and analogous to the hydrogen atom consisting of a positron and an electron bound together

pos·se \ˈpäs-ē\ *n* [ML *posse comitatus*, lit., power or authority of the county] (1645) **1 :** a large group often with a common interest **2 :** a body of persons summoned by a sheriff to assist in preserving the public peace usu. in an emergency **3 :** a group of people temporarily organized to make a search (as for a lost child)

pos·sess \pə-ˈzes *also* -ˈses\ *vt* [ME *possessen*, fr. MF *possesser* to have possession of, take possession of, fr. L *possessus*, pp. of *possidēre*, fr. *potis* able, in power + *sedēre* to sit — more at POTENT, SIT] (15c) **1 a** *obs* **:** to instate as owner **b :** to make the owner or holder — used in passive construction to indicate simple possession ⟨~*ed* of riches⟩ ⟨~*ed* of knowledge and experience⟩ **2 a :** to have and hold as property **:** OWN **b :** to have as an attribute, knowledge, or skill **3 a :** to take into one's possession **b :** to enter into and control firmly **:** DOMINATE ⟨was ~*ed* by demons⟩ **c :** to bring or cause to fall under the influence, possession, or control of some emotional or intellectual reaction ⟨melancholy ~*es* her⟩ ***syn*** see HAVE — **pos·ses·sor** *n*

pos·sessed *adj* (1595) **1** *obs* **:** held as a possession **2 a** (1) **:** influenced or controlled by something (as an evil spirit or a passion) (2) **:** MAD, CRAZED **b :** urgently desirous to do or have something **3 :** SELF-POSSESSED, CALM — **pos·sessed·ly** \-ˈzes-əd-lē, -ˈzes-tlē *also* -ˈses-\ *adv* — **pos·sessed·ness** \-ˈzes-əd-nəs, -ˈzest-nəs *also* -ˈses- & -ˈsest-\ *n*

pos·ses·sion \-ˈzesh-ən, *also* -ˈsesh-\ *n* (14c) **1 a :** the act of having or taking into control **b :** control or occupancy of property without regard to ownership **c :** OWNERSHIP **2 :** something owned, occupied, or controlled **:** PROPERTY **3 a :** domination by something (as an evil spirit, a passion, or an idea) **b :** a psychological state in which an individual's normal personality is replaced by another **c :** the fact or condition of being self-controlled — **pos·ses·sion·al** \-ˈzesh-nəl, -ən-ᵊl *also* -ˈsesh-\ *adj*

¹**pos·ses·sive** \pə-ˈzes-iv *also* -ˈses-\ *adj* (1530) **1 :** of, relating to, or constituting a word, a word group, or a grammatical case that denotes ownership or a relation analogous to ownership **2 :** manifesting possession or the desire to own or dominate — **pos·ses·sive·ly** *adv* — **pos·ses·sive·ness** *n*

²**possessive** *n* (1591) **1 a :** the possessive case **b :** a word in the possessive case **2 :** a possessive word or word group

possessive adjective *n* (1870) **:** a pronominal adjective expressing possession

possessive pronoun *n* (1530) **:** a pronoun that derives from a personal pronoun and denotes possession and analogous relationships

pos·ses·so·ry \pə-ˈzes-(ə-)rē *also* -ˈses-\ *adj* (1586) **1 :** of, arising from, or having the nature of possession **2 :** having possession **3 :** characteristic of a possessor **:** POSSESSIVE

pos·set \ˈpäs-ət\ *n* [ME *poshet, possot*] (15c) **:** a hot drink of sweetened and spiced milk curdled with ale or wine

pos·si·bil·i·ty \ˌpäs-ə-ˈbil-ət-ē\ *n, pl* **-ties** (14c) **1 :** the condition or fact of being possible **2 :** something that is possible **3** *archaic* **:** one's utmost power, capacity, or ability **4 :** potential or prospective value — usu. used in pl. ⟨the house had great *possibilities*⟩

pos·si·ble \ˈpäs-ə-bəl\ *adj* [ME, fr. MF, fr. L *possibilis*, fr. *posse* to be able, fr. *potis, pote* able + *esse* to be — more at POTENT, IS] (14c) **1 a :** being within the limits of ability, capacity, or realization **b :** being what may be done or may occur according to nature, custom, or manners **2 a :** being something that may or may not occur **b :** being something that may or may not be true or actual ⟨~ explanation⟩ **3 :** having an indicated potential ⟨a ~ housing site⟩ — **pos·si·bly** \-blē\ *adv*

syn POSSIBLE, PRACTICABLE, FEASIBLE mean capable of being realized. POSSIBLE implies that a thing may certainly exist or occur given the proper conditions; PRACTICABLE implies that something may be easily or readily effected by available means or under current conditions; FEASIBLE applies to what is likely to work or be useful in attaining the end desired.

pos·sum \ˈpäs-əm\ *n* (1613) **:** OPOSSUM

¹**post** \ˈpōst\ *n* [ME, fr. OE, fr. L *postis*; akin to Gk *pro* before and to Gk *histasthai* to stand — more at FOR, STAND] (bef. 12c) **1 :** a piece (as of timber or metal) fixed firmly in an upright position esp. as a stay or support **:** PILLAR, COLUMN **2 :** a pole or stake set up to mark or indicate something; *esp* **:** a pole that marks the starting or finishing point of a horse race **3 :** a metallic fitting attached to an electrical device (as a storage battery) for convenience in making connections **4 :** GOALPOST

²**post** *vt* (1650) **1 :** to affix to a usual place (as a wall) for public notices **:** PLACARD **2 a :** to publish, announce, or advertise by or as if by use of a placard **b :** to denounce by public notice **c :** to enter on a public listing **d :** to forbid (property) to trespassers under penalty of legal prosecution by notices placed along the boundaries **e :** SCORE

³**post** *n* [MF *poste* relay station, courier, fr. OIt *posta* relay station, fr. fem. of *posto*, pp. of *porre* to place, fr. L *ponere* — more at POSITION] (1507) **1** *obs* **:** COURIER **2** *archaic* **a :** one of a series of stations for keeping horses for relays **b :** the distance between any two such consecutive stations **:** STAGE **3** *chiefly Brit* **a :** a nation's organization for handling mail; *also* **:** the mail handled **b :** a single dispatch of mail **c :** POST OFFICE **d :** POSTBOX

⁴**post** *vi* (1533) **1 :** to travel with post-horses **2 :** to ride or travel with haste **:** HURRY **3 :** to rise from the saddle and return to it in rhythm with a horse's trot ~ *vt* **1** *archaic* **:** to dispatch in haste **2 :** MAIL ⟨~ a letter⟩ **3 a :** to transfer or carry from a book of original entry to a ledger **b :** to make transfer entries in **4 :** to make familiar with a subject **:** INFORM ⟨kept her ~*ed* on the latest gossip⟩

⁵**post** *adv* (1549) **:** with post-horses **:** EXPRESS

⁶**post** *n* [MF *poste*, fr. OIt *posto*, fr. pp. of *porre* to place] (1598) **1 a :** the place at which a soldier is stationed; *esp* **:** a sentry's beat or station **b :** a station or task to which one is assigned **c :** the place at which a body of troops is stationed **:** CAMP **d :** a local subdivision of a veterans' organization **e :** one of two bugle calls sounded (as in the British Army) at tattoo **2 a :** an office or position to which a person is appointed **b :** a player position in basketball that is the focal point of the offense; *specif* **:** PIVOT 2b **3 a :** TRADING POST, SETTLEMENT **b :** a trading station on the floor of a stock exchange

⁷**post** *vt* (1683) **1 a :** to station in a given place ⟨guards were ~*ed* at the doors⟩ **b :** to carry ceremoniously to a position ⟨~*ing* the colors⟩ **2** *chiefly Brit* **:** to assign to a unit, position, or location (as in the military or civil service) **3 :** to put up (as bond)

post- *prefix* [ME, fr. L, fr. *post*; akin to Skt *paśca* behind, after, Gk *apo* away from — more at OF] **1 a :** after **:** subsequent **:** later ⟨*post*date⟩ **b :** behind **:** posterior **:** following after ⟨*post*lude⟩ ⟨*post*consonantal⟩ **2 a :** subsequent to **:** later than ⟨*post*operative⟩ ⟨*post*-Pleistocene⟩ **b :** posterior to ⟨*post*orbital⟩

post·abor·tion	**post·elec·tion**	**post·mat·ing**
post·ac·ci·dent	**post·em·bry·o·nal**	**post·me·di·eval**
post·ad·o·les·cent	**post·em·bry·on·ic**	**post·mid·night**
post·am·pu·ta·tion	**post·emer·gen·cy**	**post·mortal**
post·ar·rest	**post·en·ceph·a·lit·ic**	**post·neo·na·tal**
post·atom·ic	**post·ep·i·lep·tic**	**post·or·gas·mic**
post·at·tack	**post·erup·tive**	**post·phle·bit·ic**
post·au·dit	**post·ex·er·cise**	**post·pol·li·na·tion**
post·bac·ca·lau·re·ate	**post·ex·pe·ri·ence**	**post·pres·i·den·tial**
post·bach·e·lor	**post·ex·per·i·men·tal**	**post·pri·ma·ry**
post·base	**post·ex·plo·sion**	**post·pris·on**
post·bib·li·cal	**post·ex·po·sure**	**post·psy·cho·an·a·lyt·ic**
post·bour·geois	**post·fault**	**post·pu·ber·ty**
post·burn	**post·flight**	**post·pu·bes·cent**
post·cap·i·tal·ist	**post·frac·ture**	**post·race**
post·chlo·ri·na·tion	**post·freeze**	**post·re·ces·sion**
post–Chris·tian	**post–Freud·ian**	**post–Ref·or·ma·tion**
post·civ·i·li·za·tion	**post·game**	**post·res·ur·rec·tion**
post·civ·i·lized	**post·gla·cial**	**post·re·tire·ment**
post·co·ital	**post·grad·u·a·tion**	**post·rev·o·lu·tion·ary**
post·col·lege	**post·har·vest**	**post·ri·ot**
post·col·le·giate	**post·heat**	**post·ro·man·tic**
post·co·lo·nial	**post·hem·or·rhag·ic**	**post·ro·man·ti·cism**
post·con·cep·tion	**post·hi·ber·na·tion**	**post·sea·son**
post·con·cert	**post·hos·pi·tal**	**post·sec·ond·ary**
post·con·quest	**post·hu·man**	**post·stim·u·la·tion**
post·con·so·nan·tal	**post·im·pact**	**post·stim·u·la·to·ry**
post·con·ven·tion	**post·im·pe·ri·al**	**post·stim·u·lus**
post·cop·u·la·to·ry	**post·in·au·gu·ral**	**post·strike**
post·cor·o·nary	**post·in·cu·nab·u·la**	**post·sur·gi·cal**
post·coup	**post·in·de·pen·dence**	**post·sync**
post·cri·sis	**post·in·dus·tri·al**	**post·syn·chro·ni·za·tion**
post·crys·tal·li·za·tion	**post·in·fec·tion**	**post·teen**
post–Dar·win·ian	**post·in·jec·tion**	**post·trau·mat·ic**
post·dead·line	**post·in·oc·u·la·tion**	**post·treat·ment**
post·de·bate	**post·ir·ra·di·a·tion**	**post·trial**
post·deb·u·tante	**post·isch·emic**	**post·vac·ci·nal**
post·de·liv·ery	**post·iso·la·tion**	**post·vac·ci·na·tion**
post·de·po·si·tion·al	**post·land·ing**	**post·va·got·o·my**
post·de·pres·sion	**post·lar·val**	**post·va·sec·to·my**
post·de·val·u·a·tion	**post·launch**	**post–Vic·to·ri·an**
post·dive	**post·lib·er·a·tion**	**post·war**
post·drug	**post·lit·er·ate**	**post·wean·ing**
post·ed·it·ing	**post·mar·i·tal**	**post·work·shop**
post·ed·u·ca·tion·al	**post·mas·tec·to·my**	

post·age \'pō-stij\ *n* (1654) **1 :** the fee for postal service **2 :** adhesive stamps or printed indicia representing postal fees
postage–due stamp *n* (1893) **:** a special adhesive stamp that is applied by a post office to mail bearing insufficient postage to make up an amount equal to the deficient postage with often an additional fee and that is paid for by the addressee immediately prior to delivery
postage meter *n* (1927) **:** a machine that prints postal indicia on pieces of mail, records the amount of postage given in the indicia, and subtracts it from a total amount which has been paid at a post office and for which the machine has been set
postage–stamp *adj* (1938) **:** resembling a postage stamp in size **:** very small
postage stamp *n* (1840) **:** a government adhesive stamp or imprinted stamp for use on mail as evidence of prepayment of postage
post·al \'pōs-tᵊl\ *adj* (1843) **1 :** of or relating to the mails or the post office **2 :** conducted by mail ⟨~ chess⟩
postal card *n* (1872) **1 :** a card officially stamped and issued by the government for use in the mail **2 :** POSTCARD
postal order *n, Brit* (1883) **:** MONEY ORDER
postal service *n* (ca. 1920) **:** POST OFFICE 1
postal union *n* (1875) **:** an association of governments setting up uniform regulations and practices for international mail
post·ax·i·al \(ˈ)pō-'stak-sē-əl\ *adj* (1872) **:** located behind an axis of the body; *esp* **:** of or relating to the posterior side of the axis of a vertebrate limb
post·bag \'pōs(t)-ˌbag\ *n* (1813) **1** *Brit* **:** MAILBAG **2** *Brit* **:** a single batch of mail **:** LETTERS
post·bel·lum \(ˈ)pōs(t)-'bel-əm\ *adj* [L *post bellum* after the war] (1874) **:** of, relating to, or characteristic of the period following a war and esp. following the American Civil War
post·box \'pōs(t)-ˌbäks\ *n* (1754) **:** MAILBOX; *esp* **:** a public mailbox
post·boy \-ˌbȯi\ *n* (1707) **:** POSTILION
post·card \'pōs(t)-ˌkärd\ *n* (1870) **1 :** POSTAL CARD 1 **2 :** a card on which a message may be written for mailing without an envelope and to which the sender must affix a stamp
post·ca·va \'pōs(t)-'kā-və\ *n* [NL] (1866) **:** the inferior vena cava of vertebrates higher than fishes — **post·ca·val** \-vəl\ *adj*
post chaise *n* (1712) **:** a carriage usu. having a closed body on four wheels and seating two to four persons
post·clas·si·cal \(ˈ)pōs(t)-'klas-i-kəl\ *or* **post·clas·sic** \-ik\ *adj* (1867) **:** of or relating to a period (as in art, literature, or civilization) following a classical one
post–com·mu·nion \ˌpōs(t)-kə-'myü-nyən\ *n, often cap P&C* [ME, fr. ML *postcommunion-, postcommunio,* fr. L *post-* + LL *communio* communion] (15c) **:** a liturgically variable prayer following the communion at Mass
post·cra·ni·al \(ˈ)pōs(t)-'krā-nē-əl\ *adj* (1913) **:** of or relating to the part of the body caudal to the head ⟨~ skeleton⟩ ⟨~ fossil remains⟩ — **post·cra·ni·al·ly** \-ē\ *adv*
post·date \(ˈ)pōs(t)-'dāt\ *vt* (1624) **1 a :** to date with a date later than that of execution ⟨~ a check⟩ **b :** to assign (an event) to a date subsequent to that of actual occurrence **2 :** to follow in time
1**post·di·lu·vi·an** \ˌpōs(t)-də-'lü-vē-ən, -dī-\ *adj* [*post-* + L *diluvium* flood — more at DELUGE] (1680) **:** of or relating to the period after the flood described in the Bible
2**postdiluvian** *n* (1684) **:** one living after the flood described in the Bible
post·doc·tor·al \(ˈ)pōs(t)-'däk-t(ə-)rəl\ *also* **post·doc·tor·ate** \-t(ə-)rət\ *adj* (1936) **:** being beyond the doctoral level: **a :** of or relating to advanced academic or professional work beyond a doctor's degree ⟨a ~ fellowship⟩ **b :** engaged in such work ⟨~ scholars⟩
post·emer·gence \ˌpō-sti-'mər-jən(t)s\ *adj* (1940) **:** used or occurring in the stage between the emergence of a seedling and the maturity of a crop plant ⟨~ herbicides⟩ ⟨~ development⟩
1**post·er** \'pō-stər\ *n* [4*post*] *archaic* (1605) **:** a swift traveler
2**poster** *n* [2*post*] (1838) **:** a bill or placard for posting often in a public place; *specif* **:** one that is decorative or pictorial
poster color *n* (1925) **:** an opaque watercolor paint with a gum or glue-size binder sold usu. in jars — called also *poster paint*
poste res·tante \ˌpō-ˌstres-'tä(ⁿ)nt, -'täⁿt\ *n* [F, lit., waiting mail] *chiefly Brit* (1768) **:** GENERAL DELIVERY
1**pos·te·ri·or** \pō-'stir-ē-ər, pä-\ *adj* [L, compar. of *posterus* coming after, fr. *post* after — more at POST-] (1534) **1 :** later in time **:** SUBSEQUENT **2 :** situated behind: as **a :** CAUDAL **b** *of the human body or its parts* **:** DORSAL **3** *of a plant part* **:** ADAXIAL, SUPERIOR — **pos·te·ri·or·ly** *adv*
2**pos·te·ri·or** \pä-'stir-ē-ər, pō-\ *n* (1619) **:** the hinder parts of the body; *specif* **:** BUTTOCKS
pos·te·ri·or·i·ty \(ˌ)pō-ˌstir-ē-'ȯr-ət-ē, (ˌ)pä-, -'är-\ *n* [ME *posteriorite,* fr. ML *posterioritas,* fr. L *posterior*] (14c) **:** the quality or state of being later or subsequent
pos·ter·i·ty \pä-'ster-ət-ē\ *n* [ME *posterite,* fr. MF *posterité,* fr. L *posteritat-, posteritas,* fr. *posterus* coming after] (14c) **1 :** the offspring of one progenitor to the furthest generation **:** DESCENDANTS **2 :** all future generations
pos·tern \'pōs-tərn, 'päs-\ *n* [ME *posterne,* fr. OF, alter. of *posterle,* fr. LL *posterula,* dim. of *postera* back door, fr. L, fem. of *posterus*] (13c) **1 :** a back door or gate **2 :** a private or side entrance or way — **postern** *adj*
pos·tero·lat·er·al \ˌpäs-tə-rō-'lat-ə-rəl, -'la-trəl\ *adj* [*posterior* + *-o-* + *lateral*] (1852) **:** posterior and lateral in position or direction ⟨~ aspect of the leg⟩
post exchange *n* (1892) **:** a store at a military installation that sells merchandise and services to military personnel and authorized civilians
post·ex·il·ic \ˌpō-(ˌ)steg-'zil-ik\ *adj* (1871) **:** of or relating to the period of Jewish history between the end of the exile in Babylon in 538 B.C. and A.D. 1
post·face \'pōs(t)-fəs, -ˌfās; pȯs-fás\ *n* [F, fr. *post-* + *-face* (as in *préface* preface)] (1782) **:** a brief article or note (as of explanation) placed at the end of a publication
post·form \(ˈ)pōs(t)-'fȯ(ə)rm\ *vt* (1945) **:** to shape (a fully or partially cured laminate) by reheating over a mold
post–free \'pōs(t)-'frē\ *adj, chiefly Brit* (1723) **:** POSTPAID
post·gan·gli·on·ic \ˌpōs(t)-ˌgaŋ-glē-'än-ik\ *adj* (1897) **:** distal to a ganglion; *specif* **:** of, relating to, or being an axon arising from a cell body within an autonomic ganglion — compare PREGANGLIONIC
1**post·grad·u·ate** \-'graj-(ə-)wət, -ə-ˌwāt\ *adj* (1858) **:** GRADUATE 2
2**postgraduate** *n* (ca. 1890) **:** a student continuing his education after graduation from high school or college
1**post·haste** \'pōst-'hāst\ *n* [3*post*] *archaic* (1545) **:** great haste
2**posthaste** *adv* (1593) **:** with all possible speed
3**posthaste** *adj, obs* (1604) **:** SPEEDY, IMMEDIATE ⟨requires your . . . ~ appearance —Shak.⟩
post hoc \'pōst-'häk\ *n* [NL *post hoc, ergo propter hoc* after this, therefore because of this] (1704) **:** the fallacy of arguing from temporal sequence to a causal relation
post·hole \'pōst-ˌhōl\ *n* (1703) **:** a hole sunk in the ground to hold a fence post
post horn *n* (ca. 1675) **:** a simple straight or coiled brass or copper wind instrument with cupped mouthpiece used esp. by guards of mail coaches of the 18th and 19th centuries
post–horse \'pōst-ˌhȯ(ə)rs\ *n* [3*post*] (1527) **:** a horse for use esp. by couriers or mail carriers
post·hu·mous \'päs-chə-məs *also* -t(y)ə-, -thə-; päst-'(h)yü-məs, 'pōst-\ *adj* [L *posthumus,* alter. of *postumus* late-born, posthumous, fr. superl. of *posterus* coming after — more at POSTERIOR] (1619) **1 :** born after the death of the father **2 :** published after the death of the author **3 :** following or occurring after death ⟨~ fame⟩ — **post·hu·mous·ly** *adv* — **post·hu·mous·ness** *n*
post·hyp·not·ic \ˌpōst-(h)ip-'nät-ik\ *adj* [ISV] (1890) **:** of, relating to, or characteristic of the period following a hypnotic trance
pos·tiche \pȯ-stēsh\ *n* [F, fr. Sp. *postizo*] (1886) **:** WIG; *esp* **:** TOUPEE 2
pos·til·ion *or* **pos·til·lion** \pō-'stil-yən, pə-\ *n* [MF *postillon* mail carrier using post-horses, fr. It *postiglione,* fr. *posta* post] (ca. 1611) **:** one who rides as a guide on the near horse of one of the pairs attached to a coach or post chaise esp. without a coachman
Post·im·pres·sion·ism \ˌpō-stim-'presh-ə-ˌniz-əm\ *n* [F *postimpressionisme,* fr. *post-* + *impressionisme* impressionism] (1910) **:** a theory or practice of art originating in France in the last quarter of the 19th century that in revolt against impressionism stresses variously volume, picture structure, or expressionism — **Post·im·pres·sion·ist** \-'presh-(ə-)nəst\ *adj or n* — **Post·im·pres·sion·is·tic** \-ˌpresh-ə-'nis-tik\ *adj*
1**post·ing** *n* [4*post*] (1682) **1 :** the act of transferring an entry or item from a book of original entry to the proper account in a ledger **2 :** the record in a ledger account resulting from the transfer of an entry or item from a book of original entry
2**posting** *n* [7*post*] (1945) **:** appointment to a post or a command
post–Kant·ian \(ˈ)pōs(t)-'kant-ē-ən, -'känt-\ *adj* (1843) **:** of or relating to the idealist philosophers (as Fichte, Schelling, and Hegel) following Kant and developing some of his ideas
post·lude \'pōst-ˌlüd\ *n* [*post-* + *-lude* (as in *prelude*)] (1851) **1 :** a closing piece of music; *esp* **:** an organ voluntary at the end of a church service **2 :** a closing phase (as of an epoch or a literary work)
post·man \'pōs(t)-mən, -ˌman\ *n* (1529) **:** MAILMAN
1**post·mark** \-ˌmärk\ *n* (1678) **:** an official postal marking on a piece of mail; *specif* **:** a cancellation mark showing the post office and date of mailing
2**postmark** *vt* (1716) **:** to put a postmark on
post·mas·ter \-ˌmas-tər\ *n* (1513) **1 :** one who has charge of a post office **2 :** one who has charge of a station for the accommodation of travelers or who supplies post-horses — **post·mas·ter·ship** \-ˌship\ *n*
postmaster general *n, pl* **postmasters general** (1626) **:** an official in charge of a national post office department or agency
post·meno·paus·al \ˌpōs(t)-ˌmen-ə-'pȯ-zəl\ *adj* (1928) **1 :** having undergone menopause **2 :** occurring after menopause
post me·ri·di·em \'pōs(t)-mə-'rid-ē-əm, -ē-ˌem\ *adj* [L] (1647) **:** being after noon — abbr. *p.m.*
post·mil·le·nar·i·an·ism \'pōs(t)-ˌmil-ə-'ner-ē-ə-ˌniz-əm\ *n* (ca. 1890) **:** POSTMILLENNIALISM — **postmillenarian** *adj or n*
post·mil·len·ni·al \ˌpōs(t)-mə-'len-ē-əl\ *adj* (1851) **1 :** coming after or relating to the period after the millennium **2 :** holding or relating to postmillennialism
post·mil·len·ni·al·ism \-ē-ə-ˌliz-əm\ *n* (1879) **:** the view that Christ will return only at the end of the millennium — **post·mil·len·ni·al·ist** \-ē-ə-ləst\ *n*
post·mis·tress \'pōs(t)-ˌmis-trəs\ *n* (1697) **:** a female postmaster
post·mod·ern \(ˈ)pōs(t)-'mäd-ərn, ÷-'mäd-(ə-)rən\ *adj* (1949) **:** of or relating to a movement that is in reaction against the theory and practice of modern art or literature — **post·mod·ern·ism** \-ər-ˌniz-əm\ *n* — **post·mod·ern·ist** \-nəst\ *adj or n*
1**post·mor·tem** \(ˈ)pōs(t)-'mȯrt-əm\ *adj* [L *post mortem* after death] (1742) **1 :** done, occurring, or collected after death ⟨~ tissue specimens⟩ **2 :** following the event
2**postmortem** *n* (1844) **1 :** an analysis or discussion of an event after it is over **2 :** POSTMORTEM EXAMINATION
postmortem examination *n* (1837) **:** an examination of a body after death for determining the cause of death or the character and extent of changes produced by disease
postnasal drip *n* (1949) **:** flow of mucous secretion from the posterior part of the nasal cavity onto the wall of the pharynx occurring usu. as a chronic accompaniment of an allergic state
post·na·tal \(ˈ)pōs(t)-'nāt-ᵊl\ *adj* [ISV] (ca. 1859) **:** subsequent to birth; *specif* **:** of or relating to an infant immediately after birth ⟨~ care⟩ — **post·na·tal·ly** \-ᵊl-ē\ *adv*
post·nup·tial \-'nəp-shəl, -chəl, ÷-chə-wəl\ *adj* (1807) **:** made or occurring after marriage or mating
1**post–obit** \pō-'stō-bət, *esp Brit* -'stäb-it\ *n* (1751) **:** POST-OBIT BOND
2**post–obit** *adj* [L *post obitum* after death] (1788) **:** occurring or taking effect after death
post–obit bond *n* (ca. 1890) **:** a bond made by a reversioner to secure a loan and payable out of his reversion
post office *n* (1652) **1 :** a government department or agency handling the transmission of mail **2 :** a local branch of a national post office

handling the mail for a particular place or area **3 :** a game in which a player acting as postmaster or postmistress may exact a kiss from one of the opposite sex as payment for the pretended delivery of a letter

post·op·er·a·tive \(ˈ)pō-ˈstäp-(ə-)rət-iv, -ˈstäp-ə-ˌrāt-\ *adj* [ISV] (ca. 1889) **:** following a surgical operation — **post·op·er·a·tive·ly** *adv*

post·or·bit·al \-ˈstȯr-bət-ᵊl\ *adj* (ca. 1835) **:** situated behind the eye socket

post·paid \ˈpōs(t)-ˈpād\ *adj* (1653) **:** having the postage paid by the sender and not chargeable to the receiver

post·par·tum \(ˈ)pōs(t)-ˈpärt-əm\ *adj* [NL *post partum* after birth] (1846) **1 :** following parturition ⟨~ period⟩ **2 :** being in the postpartum period ⟨~ mothers⟩ — **postpartum** *adv*

post·pone \pōs(t)-ˈpōn\ *vt* **post·poned; post·pon·ing** [L *postponere* to place after, postpone, fr. *post-* + *ponere* to place — more at POSITION] (ca. 1500) **1 :** to put off to a later time **:** DEFER **2 a :** to place later (as in a sentence) than the normal position in English ⟨~ an adjective⟩ **b :** to place later in order of precedence, preference, or importance ***syn*** see DEFER — **post·pon·able** \-ˈpō-nə-bəl\ *adj* — **post·pone·ment** \-ˈpōn-mənt\ *n* — **post·pon·er** *n*

post·po·si·tion \ˌpōs(t)-pə-ˈzish-ən, ˈpōs(t)-pə-ˌ\ *n* [F, fr. *postposer* to place after, fr. L *postponere* (perf. indic. *postposui*)] (ca. 1638) **:** the placing of a grammatical element after a word to which it is primarily related in a sentence; *also* **:** such a word or particle esp. when functioning as a preposition — **post·po·si·tion·al** \ˌpōs(t)-pə-ˈzish-nəl, -ən-ᵊl\ *adj* — **post·po·si·tion·al·ly** \-ē\ *adv*

post·pos·i·tive \(ˈ)pōs(t)-ˈpäz-ət-iv, -ˈpäz-tiv\ *adj* (1786) **:** placed after or at the end of another word — **post·pos·i·tive·ly** *adv*

post·pran·di·al \pōs(t)-ˈpran-dē-əl\ *adj* (1820) **:** following a meal

post·pro·duc·tion \ˌpōs(t)-prə-ˈdək-shən, ˈpōs(t)-prə-ˌ, -prō-\ *n* (1953) **:** the period following filming or taping in which a motion picture or television show is readied (as by editing and scoring) for public presentation

post road *n* (1657) **:** a route over which mail is carried

post·script \ˈpō(s)-ˌskript\ *n* [NL *postscriptum*, fr. L, neut. of *postscriptus*, pp. of *postscribere* to write after, fr. *post-* + *scribere* to write — more at SCRIBE] (1523) **:** a note or series of notes appended to a completed letter, article, or book

post·syn·ap·tic \ˌpōs(t)-sə-ˈnap-tik\ *adj* (1909) **1 :** occurring after synapsis ⟨a ~ chromosome⟩ **2 :** relating to, occurring in, or being part of a nerve cell by which a wave of excitation is conveyed away from a synapse — **post·syn·ap·ti·cal·ly** \-ti-k(ə-)lē\ *adv*

post·ten·sion \(ˈ)pōs(t)-ˈten-chən\ *vt* (1950) **:** to apply tension to (reinforcing steel) after concrete has set

post·test \ˈpōs(t)-ˌtest\ *n* (1946) **:** a test given to students after completion of an instructional program or segment and often used in conjunction with a pretest to measure their achievement and the effectiveness of the program

post time *n* [1*post*] (1845) **:** the designated time for the start of a horse race

post·tran·scrip·tion·al \ˌpōs(t)-tran(t)s-ˈkrip-shnəl, -shən-ᵊl\ *adj* (1969) **:** occurring, acting, or existing after genetic transcription ⟨~ control of messenger-RNA production⟩

post·trans·fu·sion \-tran(t)s-ˈfyü-zhən\ *adj* (1944) **1 :** caused by transfused blood ⟨malpractice suits for ~ hepatitis⟩ **2 :** occurring after blood transfusion ⟨induction of ~ shock⟩

post·trans·la·tion·al \-tran(t)s-ˈlā-shnəl, -shən-ᵊl\ *adj* (1975) **:** occurring or existing after genetic translation

pos·tu·lan·cy \ˈpäs-chə-lən-sē\ *n, pl* **-cies** (ca. 1882) **1 :** the quality or state of being a postulant **2 :** the period during which a person remains a postulant

pos·tu·lant \ˈpäs-chə-lənt\ *n* [F, petitioner, candidate, postulant, fr. MF, fr. prp. of *postuler* to demand, solicit, fr. L *postulare*] (1759) **1 :** a person admitted to a religious order as a probationary candidate for membership **2 :** a person on probation before being admitted as a candidate for holy orders in the Episcopal Church

1pos·tu·late \ˈpäs-chə-ˌlāt\ *vt* **-lat·ed; -lat·ing** [L *postulatus*, pp. of *postulare*, fr. (assumed) *postus*, pp. of *poscere* to ask; akin to OHG *forsca* question, Skt *pṛcchati* he asks] (1593) **1 :** DEMAND, CLAIM **2 a :** to assume or claim as true, existent, or necessary **:** depend upon or start from the postulate of **b :** to assume as a postulate or axiom (as in logic or mathematics) — **pos·tu·la·tion** \ˌpäs-chə-ˈlā-shən\ *n* — **pos·tu·la·tion·al** \-shnəl, -shən-ᵊl\ *adj*

2pos·tu·late \ˈpäs-chə-lət, -ˌlāt\ *n* [ML *postulatum*, fr. neut. of *postulatus*, pp. of *postulare* to assume, fr. L, to demand] (1646) **1 :** a hypothesis advanced as an essential presupposition, condition, or premise of a train of reasoning **2 :** AXIOM 3

pos·tu·la·tor \-ˌlāt-ər\ *n* (1863) **:** an official who presents a plea for beatification or canonization in the Roman Catholic Church — compare DEVIL'S ADVOCATE

pos·tur·al \ˈpäs-chə-rəl\ *adj* (1857) **:** of, relating to, or involving posture

1pos·ture \ˈpäs-chər\ *n* [F, fr. It *postura*, fr. L *positura*, fr. *positus*, pp. of *ponere* to place — more at POSITION] (ca. 1586) **1 a :** the position or bearing of the body whether characteristic or assumed for a special purpose ⟨erect ~⟩ **b :** the pose of a model or artistic figure **2 :** state or condition at a given time esp. with respect to capability in particular circumstances ⟨maintain a competitive ~ in the market⟩ ⟨put the country in a ~ of defense⟩ **3 :** a conscious mental or outward behavioral attitude ⟨his ~ of moral superiority ⟩ ⟨takes a neutral ~ toward the discussions⟩

2posture *vb* **pos·tured; pos·tur·ing** *vt* (ca. 1645) **:** to cause to assume a given posture **:** POSE ~ *vi* **1 :** to assume a posture; *esp* **:** to strike a pose for effect **2 :** to assume an artificial or pretended attitude **:** ATTITUDINIZE — **pos·tur·er** \-chər-ər\ *n*

post·vo·cal·ic \ˌpōst-vō-ˈkal-ik, -və-\ *adj* [ISV] (1892) **:** immediately following a vowel

po·sy \ˈpō-zē\ *n, pl* **posies** [alter. of *poesy*] (15c) **1 :** a brief sentiment, motto, or legend **2 a :** BOUQUET, NOSEGAY **b :** FLOWER

1pot \ˈpät\ *n* [ME, fr. OE *pott;* akin to MLG *pot* pot] (bef. 12c) **1 a :** a usu. rounded metal or earthen container used chiefly for domestic purposes (as in cooking or for holding liquids or growing plants); *also* **:** any of various technical or industrial vessels or enclosures resembling or likened to a household pot ⟨the ~ of a still⟩ **b :** POTFUL ⟨a ~ of coffee⟩ **2 :** an enclosed framework of wire, wood, or wicker for catching fish or lobsters **3 a :** a large amount (as of money) **b (1) :** the total of the bets at stake at one time **(2) :** one round in a poker game **c :** the common fund of a group **4 :** POTSHOT **5 :** POTBELLY **6 :** RUIN, DETERIORATION ⟨business went to ~⟩ **7** *Brit* **:** a shot in snooker in which a ball is pocketed **8 :** MARIJUANA

2pot *vb* **pot·ted; pot·ting** *vt* (1616) **1 a :** to place in a pot **b :** to pack or preserve (as cooked and chopped meat) in a sealed pot, jar, or can often with aspic **2 :** to shoot with a potshot **3 :** to make or shape (earthenware) as a potter **4 :** to embed (as electronic components) in a container with an insulating or protective material (as plastic) ~ *vi* **:** to take a potshot

1po·ta·ble \ˈpōt-ə-bəl\ *adj* [LL *potabilis*, fr. L *potare* to drink; akin to L *bibere* to drink, Gk *pinein*] (1572) **:** suitable for drinking — **po·ta·bil·i·ty** \ˌpōt-ə-ˈbil-ət-ē\ *n* — **po·ta·ble·ness** \ˈpōt-ə-bəl-nəs\ *n*

2potable *n* (1623) **:** a liquid that is suitable for drinking; *esp* **:** an alcoholic beverage

po·tage \pō-ˈtäzh\ *n* [MF, fr. OF, pottage] (1567) **:** a thick soup

pot ale *n* (1812) **:** the residue of fermented wort left in a still after the distillation of whiskey or alcohol and used for feeding swine

pot·ash \ˈpät-ˌash\ *n* [sing. of *pot ashes*] (1648) **1 a :** potassium carbonate esp. from wood ashes **b :** POTASSIUM HYDROXIDE **2 :** potassium or a potassium compound esp. as used in agriculture or industry

po·tas·sic \pə-ˈtas-ik\ *adj* (1858) **:** of, relating to, or containing potassium

po·tas·si·um \pə-ˈtas-ē-əm\ *n, often attrib* [NL, fr. *potassa* potash, fr. E *potash*] (ca. 1807) **:** a silver-white soft light low-melting univalent metallic element of the alkali metal group that occurs abundantly in nature esp. combined in minerals — see ELEMENT table

potassium–argon *adj* (1953) **:** being or relating to a method of dating archaeological or geological materials based on the radioactive decay of potassium to argon that has taken place in a specimen

potassium bromide *n* (1873) **:** a crystalline salt KBr with a saline taste that is used as a sedative and in photography

potassium carbonate *n* (1885) **:** a white salt K_2CO_3 that forms a strongly alkaline solution and is used in making glass and soap

potassium chlorate *n* (1885) **:** a crystalline salt $KClO_3$ that is used as an oxidizing agent in matches, fireworks, and explosives

potassium chloride *n* (1885) **:** a crystalline salt KCl occurring as a mineral and in natural waters and used as a fertilizer

potassium cyanide *n* (1885) **:** a very poisonous crystalline salt KCN used esp. in gold and silver extraction from ore

potassium dichromate *n* (1885) **:** a soluble salt $K_2Cr_2O_7$ forming large orange-red crystals used esp. in dyeing, in photography, and as an oxidizing agent

potassium hydroxide *n* (1885) **:** a white deliquescent solid KOH that dissolves in water with much heat to form a strongly alkaline and caustic liquid and is used chiefly in making soap and as a reagent

potassium nitrate *n* (1885) **:** a crystalline salt KNO_3 that occurs as a product of nitrification in arable soils, is a strong oxidizer, and is used esp. in making gunpowder, as a fertilizer, and in medicine

potassium permanganate *n* (1869) **:** a dark purple salt $KMnO_4$ used as an oxidizer and disinfectant

potassium phosphate *n* (1885) **:** any of various phosphates of potassium; *esp* **:** any of the three orthophosphates

potassium sulfate *n* (1885) **:** a white crystalline compound K_2SO_4 used esp. as a fertilizer

po·ta·tion \pō-ˈtā-shən\ *n* [ME *potacioun*, fr. MF *potation*, fr. L *potation-, potatio* act of drinking, fr. *potatus*, pp. of *potare* to drink — more at POTABLE] (15c) **1 :** a usu. alcoholic drink or brew **2 :** the act or an instance of drinking or inhaling; *also* **:** the portion taken in one such act

po·ta·to \pə-ˈtāt-(ˌ)ō, pət-ˈāt-, -ə(-w)\ *n, pl* **-toes** *often attrib* [Sp *batata*, fr. Taino] (1555) **1 :** SWEET POTATO **2 a :** an erect American herb (*Solanum tuberosum*) of the nightshade family widely cultivated as a vegetable crop **b :** the edible starchy tuber of a potato — called also *Irish potato, white potato*

potato beetle *n* (1821) **:** COLORADO POTATO BEETLE

potato blight *n* (1879) **:** any of several destructive fungus diseases of the potato

potato bug *n* (1799) **:** COLORADO POTATO BEETLE

potato chip *n* (1878) **:** a thin slice of white potato that has been fried until crisp and then usu. salted

potato leafhopper *n* (1921) **:** a small green white-spotted leafhopper (*Empoasca fabae*) of the eastern and southern U.S. that is a serious pest on many cultivated plants and esp. on the potato

potato psyllid *n* (1944) **:** a hemipterous insect (*Paratrioza cockerelli*) that feeds on tomato and potato plants and transmits a virus disease

potato tu·ber·worm \-ˈt(y)ü-bər-ˌwərm\ *n* (1920) **:** a grayish brown moth (*Phthorimaea operculella* of the family Gelechiidae) whose larva mines the leaves and bores in the stems esp. of potato and tobacco plants and commonly overwinters in potato tubers

pot–au–feu \ˌpät-ō-ˈfə(r), pȯ-tō-fœ\ *n, pl* **pot–au–feu** [F, lit., pot on the fire] (1791) **:** a French boiled dinner of meat and vegetables

pot·bel·lied \ˈpät-ˈbel-ēd\ *adj* (1657) **:** having a potbelly

potbellied stove *n* (1933) **:** a stove with a rounded or bulging body — called also *potbelly stove*

pot·bel·ly \ˈpät-ˌbel-ē\ *n* (ca. 1714) **1 :** an enlarged, swollen, or protruding abdomen **2 :** POTBELLIED STOVE

pot·boil \-ˌbȯil\ *vi* (1867) **:** to produce potboilers

pot·boil·er \-ˌbȯi-lər\ *n* (1864) **:** a usu. inferior work (as of art or literature) produced chiefly for profit

pot·boy \-ˌbȯi\ *n* (1795) **:** a boy who serves drinks in a tavern

pot cheese *n* (1812) **:** COTTAGE CHEESE

po·teen *also* **po·theen** \pə-ˈtēn, -ˈchēn, -ˈtyēn, -ˈthēn\ *n* [IrGael *poitīn*] (1812) **:** whiskey illicitly distilled in Ireland

Po·tem·kin village \pə-ˌtem(p)-kən-\ *n* [Grigori *Potëmkin*, who supposedly built impressive fake villages along a route Catherine the Great was to travel] (ca. 1938) **:** an impressive facade or show designed to hide an undesirable fact or condition

po·tence \ˈpōt-ᵊn(t)s\ *n* (15c) **:** POTENCY

po·ten·cy \ˈpōt-ᵊn-sē\ *n, pl* **-cies** (1539) **1 a :** the quality or state of being potent **b :** FORCE, POWER **c :** the ability or capacity to achieve or bring about a particular result **2 :** POTENTIALITY 1

1po·tent \ˈpōt-ᵊnt\ *adj* [L *potent-, potens*, fr. prp. of (assumed) L *potēre* to be powerful, fr. L *potis, pote* able; akin to Goth bruth*faths* bridegroom,

Gk *posis* husband, Skt *pati* master] (ca. 1500) **1 :** having or wielding force, authority, or influence : POWERFUL **2 :** achieving or bringing about a particular result : EFFECTIVE **3 a :** chemically or medicinally effective ⟨a ~ vaccine⟩ **b :** rich in a characteristic constituent ⟨~ tea⟩ **4 :** able to copulate — usu. used of the male — **po·tent·ly** *adv*

2potent *adj* [obs. E *potent* crutch] *of a heraldic cross* (1610) **:** having flat bars across the ends of the arms — see CROSS illustration

po·ten·tate \ˈpōt-ᵊn-ˌtāt\ *n* (15c) **:** RULER, SOVEREIGN; *broadly* **:** one who wields great power or sway

1po·ten·tial \pə-ˈten-chəl\ *adj* [ME, fr. LL *potentialis,* fr. *potentia* potentiality, fr. L, power, fr. *potent-, potens*] (14c) **1 :** existing in possibility **:** capable of development into actuality ⟨~ benefits⟩ **2 :** expressing possibility; *specif* **:** of, relating to, or constituting a verb phrase expressing possibility, liberty, or power by the use of an auxiliary with the infinitive of the verb (as in "it may rain") ***syn*** see LATENT — **po·ten·tial·ly** \-ˈtench-(ə-)lē\ *adv*

2potential *n* (1817) **1 a :** something that can develop or become actual ⟨a ~ for violence⟩ **b :** PROMISE 2 **2 a :** any of various functions from which the intensity or the velocity at any point in a field may be readily calculated **b :** the work required to move a unit positive charge from a reference point (as at infinity) to a point in question **c :** POTENTIAL DIFFERENCE

potential difference *n* (1896) **:** the voltage difference between two points that represents the work involved or the energy released in the transfer of a unit quantity of electricity from one point to the other

potential energy *n* (1853) **:** the energy that a piece of matter has because of its position or because of the arrangement of parts

po·ten·ti·al·i·ty \pə-ˌten-chē-ˈal-ət-ē\ *n, pl* **-ties** (1625) **1 :** the ability to develop or come into existence **2 :** POTENTIAL 1

po·ten·ti·ate \pə-ˈten-chē-ˌāt\ *vt* **-at·ed; -at·ing** (1817) **:** to make effective or active or more effective or more active; *also* **:** to augment the activity of (as a drug) synergistically — **po·ten·ti·a·tion** \-ˌten-chē-ˈā-shən\ *n* — **po·ten·ti·a·tor** \-ˈten-chē-ˌāt-ər\ *n*

po·ten·til·la \ˌpōt-ᵊn-ˈtil-ə\ *n* [NL, fr. ML, garden heliotrope, fr. L *potent-, potens*] (1548) **:** any of a large genus (*Potentilla*) of herbs and shrubs (as a cinquefoil) of the rose family that have opposite pinnate or palmate leaves

po·ten·ti·om·e·ter \pə-ˌten-chē-ˈäm-ət-ər\ *n* [ISV *potential* + *-o-* + *-meter*] (1881) **1 :** an instrument for measuring electromotive forces **2 :** VOLTAGE DIVIDER — **po·ten·tio·met·ric** \-ch(ē-)ə-ˈme-trik\ *adj*

pot·ful \ˈpät-ˌfu̇l\ *n* (14c) **1 :** as much or as many as a pot will hold **2 :** a large amount ⟨make a ~ of money —John Corry⟩

pot hat *n* (1798) **:** a hat with a stiff crown; *esp* **:** DERBY

1poth·er \ˈpät͟h-ər\ *n* [origin unknown] (1591) **1 a :** confused or fidgety flurry or activity : COMMOTION **b :** agitated talk or controversy usu. over a trivial matter **2 :** a choking cloud of dust or smoke **3 :** mental turmoil

2pother *vb* **poth·ered; poth·er·ing** \-(ə-)riŋ\ *vt* (1692) **:** to put into a pother ~ *vi* **:** to be in a pother

pot·herb \ˈpät-ˌ(h)ərb\ *n* (1538) **:** an herb whose leaves or stems are cooked for use as greens; *also* **:** one (as mint) used to season food

pot holder *n* (1944) **:** a small cloth pad used for handling hot cooking utensils

pot·hole \ˈpät-ˌhōl\ *n* (1826) **1 a :** a circular hole formed in the rocky bed of a river by the grinding action of stones or gravel whirled round by the water **b :** a sizable rounded often water-filled depression in land **2 :** a pot-shaped hole in a road surface — **pot·holed** \-ˌhōld\ *adj*

pot·hook \-ˌhu̇k\ *n* (15c) **1 :** an S-shaped hook for hanging pots and kettles over an open fire **2 :** a written character resembling a pothook

pot·house \-ˌhau̇s\ *n* (1724) **:** TAVERN 1

pot·hunt·er \-ˌhənt-ər\ *n* (1781) **1 :** one who hunts game for food **2 :** an amateur archaeologist — **pot·hunt·ing** \-iŋ\ *n*

po·tion \ˈpō-shən\ *n* [ME *pocioun,* fr. MF *potion,* fr. L *potion-, potio* drink, potion, fr. *potus,* pp. of *potare* to drink — more at POTABLE] (14c) **:** a mixture of liquids (as liquor or medicine)

1pot·latch \ˈpät-ˌlach\ *vt* (1847) **1 :** to hold or give a potlatch for (as a tribe or group) **2 :** to give (as a gift) esp. with the expectation of a gift in return ~ *vi* **:** to hold or give a potlatch

2potlatch *n* [Chinook Jargon, fr. Nootka *patshatl* giving] (ca. 1861) **1 :** a ceremonial feast of the Indians of the northwest coast marked by the host's lavish distribution of gifts requiring reciprocation **2** *Northwest* **:** a social event or celebration

pot·line \ˈpät-ˌlīn\ *n* (1944) **:** a row of electrolytic cells used in the production of aluminum

pot liquor *n* (1744) **:** the liquid left in a pot after cooking

pot·luck \ˈpät-ˈlək\ *n* (1592) **1 :** the regular meal available to a guest for whom no special preparations have been made **2 :** whatever is offered or available in given circumstances or at a given time ⟨without reservations you have to take ~ on hotel accommodations⟩

pot marigold *n* (1814) **:** a calendula (*Calendula officinalis*) grown esp. for ornament

po·tom·e·ter \pō-ˈtäm-ət-ər\ *n* [Gk *poton* drink (akin to Gk *pinein* to drink) + E *-meter* — more at POTABLE] (1884) **:** an apparatus for measuring the rate of transpiration in a plant by determining the amount of water absorbed

pot·pie \ˈpät-ˈpī\ *n* (ca. 1792) **:** pastry-covered meat and vegetables cooked in a deep dish

pot·pour·ri \ˌpō-pu̇-ˈrē\ *n* [F *pot pourri,* lit., rotten pot] (1749) **1 :** a mixture of flowers, herbs, and spices that is usu. kept in a jar and used for scent **2 :** a miscellaneous collection : MEDLEY ⟨a ~ of the best songs and sketches —*Current Biog.*⟩

pot roast *n* (1881) **:** a piece of beef cooked by braising usu. on top of the stove — see BEEF illustration

pot·sherd \ˈpät-ˌshərd\ *n* [ME *pot-sherd,* fr. *pot* + *sherd* shard] (14c) **:** a pottery fragment

1pot·shot \-ˌshät\ *n* [fr. the notion that such a shot is unsportsmanlike and worthy only of one whose object is to fill his cooking pot] (1858) **1 :** a shot taken from ambush or at a random or easy target **2 :** a critical remark made in a random or sporadic manner

2potshot *vb* **potshot; pot·shot·ting** *vi* (1918) **:** to take a potshot ~ *vt* **:** to attack or shoot with a potshot

pot still *n* (1799) **:** a still used esp. in the distillation of Irish grain whiskey and Scotch malt whiskey in which the heat of the fire is applied directly to the pot containing the mash

pot·stone \ˈpät-ˌstōn\ *n* (1771) **:** a more or less impure steatite used esp. in prehistoric times to make cooking vessels

pot·tage \ˈpät-ij\ *n* [ME *potage,* fr. OF, fr. *pot* pot, of Gmc origin; akin to OE *pott* pot] (13c) **:** a thick soup of vegetables or vegetables and meat

pot·ted \ˈpät-əd\ *adj* (1849) **1 :** planted or grown in a pot **2** *chiefly Brit* **:** briefly and superficially summarized ⟨a dull, pedestrian ~ history —*Times Lit. Supp.*⟩ **3** *slang* **:** DRUNK

1pot·ter \ˈpät-ər\ *n* (12c) **:** one that makes pottery

2potter *vi* [prob. freq. of E dial. *pote* to poke] (1829) **:** PUTTER — **pot·ter·er** \ˈpät-ər-ər\ *n* — **pot·ter·ing·ly** \ˈpät-ə-riŋ-lē\ *adv*

potter's clay *n* (1616) **:** a plastic clay suitable for making pottery — called also *potter's earth*

potter's field *n* [fr. the mention in Mt 27:7 of the purchase of a potter's field for use as a graveyard] (1526) **:** a public burial place for paupers, unknown persons, and criminals

potter's wheel *n* (ca. 1727) **:** a usu. horizontal disk revolving on a vertical spindle and carrying the clay being shaped by a potter

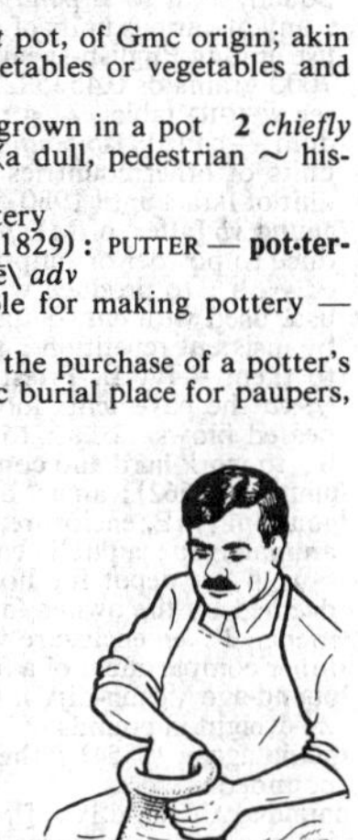
potter's wheel

pot·tery \ˈpät-ə-rē\ *n, pl* **-ter·ies** (15c) **1 :** a place where clayware is made and fired **2 a :** the art or craft of the potter **b :** the manufacture of clayware **3 :** CLAYWARE; *esp* **:** earthenware as distinguished on the one hand from porcelain and stoneware and on the other from brick and tile

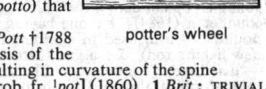

pot·tle \ˈpät-ᵊl\ *n* [ME *potel,* fr. MF, fr. *pot*] (14c) **1** *archaic* **:** a measure equal to a half gallon **2 :** a container holding a half gallon (1.9 liters)

pot·to \ˈpät-(ˌ)ō\ *n, pl* **pottos** [of Niger-Congo origin; akin to Wolof *pata,* a tailless monkey] (1705) **:** any of several African primates (genera *Arctocebus* and *Perodicticus*); *esp* **:** a West African primate (*P. potto*) that has a vestigial index finger and tail

Pott's disease \ˈpäts-\ *n* [Percivall *Pott* †1788 Eng. surgeon] (1835) **:** tuberculosis of the spine with destruction of bone resulting in curvature of the spine

1pot·ty \ˈpät-ē\ *adj* **pot·ti·er; -est** [prob. fr. 1pot] (1860) **1** *Brit* **:** TRIVIAL, INSIGNIFICANT **2** *chiefly Brit* **:** slightly crazy **3 :** SNOBBISH

2potty *n, pl* **potties** (ca. 1942) **:** a small child's pot for urination or defecation

pot·ty–chair \-ˌche(ə)r, -ˌcha(ə)r\ *n* (1943) **:** a child's chair having an open seat under which a receptacle is placed for toilet training

1pouch \ˈpau̇ch\ *n* [ME *pouche,* fr. MF, of Gmc origin; akin to OE *pocca* bag] (14c) **1 :** a small drawstring bag carried on the person **2 a :** a bag of small or moderate size for storing or transporting goods; *specif* **:** a lockable bag for first-class mail or diplomatic dispatches **b** *chiefly Scot* **:** POCKET **c :** PACKET **3 :** an anatomical structure resembling a pouch — **pouched** \ˈpau̇cht\ *adj*

2pouch *vt* (1566) **1 :** to put or form into or as if into a pouch **2 :** to transmit by pouch ~ *vi* **1 :** to bulge or stick out or down in a manner suggesting a pouch ⟨~*ing* cheeks⟩ **2 :** to transmit mail or dispatches by pouch

pouchy \ˈpau̇-chē\ *adj* **pouch·i·er; -est** (1828) **:** having, tending to have, or resembling a pouch ⟨~ insomniac eyes —Graham Greene⟩

pouf *also* **pouff** *or* **pouffe** \ˈpüf\ *n* [F *pouf,* something inflated, of imit. origin] (1893) **1 :** PUFF 3b(3) **2 :** a bouffant or fluffy part of a garment or accessory **3 :** OTTOMAN — **poufed** *or* **pouffed** \ˈpüft\ *adj*

pouil·ly–fuis·sé \pü-ˈyē-fwē-ˈsā\ *n* [Solutré-*Pouilly* and *Fuissé,* Fr. villages] (ca. 1929) **:** a dry white Burgundy

pou·larde *also* **pou·lard** \pü-ˈlärd\ *n* [F *poularde*] (1732) **:** a pullet sterilized to produce fattening

poult \ˈpōlt\ *n* [ME *polet, pulte* young fowl — more at PULLET] (15c) **:** a young fowl; *esp* **:** a young turkey

poul·ter·er \ˈpōl-tər-ər\ *n* [alter. of ME *pulter,* fr. MF *pouletier*] (1534) **:** one that deals in poultry

poul·ter's measure \ˈpōl-tərz-\ *n* [obs. *poulter* poulterer, fr. ME *pulter;* fr. the former practice of occas. giving one or two extra when counting eggs by dozens] (1576) **:** a meter in which lines of 12 and 14 syllables alternate

1poul·tice \ˈpōl-təs\ *n* [ML *pultes* pap, fr. L, pl. of *pult-, puls* porridge] (ca. 1542) **:** a soft usu. heated and sometimes medicated mass spread on cloth and applied to sores or other lesions

2poultice *vt* **-ticed; -tic·ing** (1730) **:** to apply a poultice to

poul·try \ˈpōl-trē\ *n* [ME *pultrie,* fr. MF *pouleterie,* fr. OF, fr. *pouletier* poulterer, fr. *poulet* — more at PULLET] (14c) **:** domesticated birds kept for eggs or meat

poul·try·man \-mən\ *n* (ca. 1573) **1 :** one who raises domestic fowls esp. on a commercial scale for the production of eggs and meat **2 :** one who deals in poultry or poultry products

1pounce \ˈpau̇n(t)s\ *n* [ME, talon] (15c) **:** the claw of a bird of prey

2pounce *vi* **pounced; pounc·ing** (1744) **1 a :** to swoop upon and seize something with or as if with talons **b :** to seize upon and make capital of something (as another's blunder or an opportunity) **2 :** to make a sudden assault or approach

3pounce *n* (1841) **:** the act of pouncing

4pounce *vt* **pounced; pounc·ing** [MF *poncer,* fr. *ponce*] (1580) **:** to dust, rub, finish, or stencil with pounce

5pounce *n* [F *ponce* pumice, fr. MF, fr. LL *pomic-, pomex,* alter. of L *pumic-, pumex* — more at FOAM] (1706) **1 :** a fine powder formerly used to prevent ink from spreading **2 :** a fine powder for making stenciled patterns

poun·cet–box \ˈpau̇n(t)-sət-\ *n* [prob. fr. (assumed) MF *poncette* small pounce bag] *archaic* (1596) **:** a box for carrying pomander

[1]**pound** \ˈpau̇nd\ *n, pl* **pounds** *also* **pound** [ME, fr. OE *pund,* fr. L *pondo* pound; akin to L *pondus* weight — more at PENDANT] (bef. 12c) **1** : any of various units of mass and weight; *specif* : a unit now in general use among English-speaking peoples equal to 16 avoirdupois ounces or 7000 grains or 0.45359237 kilogram — called also *avoirdupois pound;* see WEIGHT table **2 a** : the basic monetary unit of the United Kingdom — called also *pound sterling* **b** : any of numerous basic monetary units of other countries — see MONEY table **c** : the basic monetary unit of Israel until 1980

[2]**pound** *vb* [alter. of ME *pounen,* fr. OE *pūnian*] *vt* (bef. 12c) **1** : to reduce to powder or pulp by beating **2 a** : to strike heavily or repeatedly **b** : to produce with or as if with repeated vigorous strokes — usu. used with *out* ⟨~ out a story on the typewriter⟩ **c** : to inculcate by insistent repetition : DRIVE ⟨day after day the facts were ~*ed* home to them —Ivy B. Priest⟩ **3** : to move along heavily or persistently ⟨~*ed* the pavements looking for work⟩ ~ *vi* **1** : to strike heavy repeated blows **2 a** : to move with or make a heavy repetitive sound **b** : to work hard and continuously — used with *away*

[3]**pound** *n* (1562) : an act or sound of pounding

[4]**pound** *n* [ME, enclosure, fr. OE *pund-*] (15c) **1 a** : an enclosure for animals; *esp* : a public enclosure for stray or unlicensed animals ⟨a dog ~⟩ **b** : a depot for holding impounded personal property until redeemed by the owner ⟨a car ~⟩ **2** : a place or condition of confinement **3** : an enclosure within which fish are kept or caught; *esp* : the inner compartment of a fish trap or pound net

[1]**pound·age** \ˈpau̇n-dij\ *n* (ca. 1500) **1** : a charge per pound of weight **2** : weight in pounds

[2]**poundage** *n* (1554) : the act of impounding : the state of being impounded

pound·al \ˈpau̇n-dᵊl\ *n* [[1]*pound* + *-al* (as in *quintal*)] (1879) : a unit of force equal to the force that would give a free mass of one pound an acceleration of one foot per second per second

pound cake *n* [fr. the original recipe prescribing a pound of each of the principal ingredients] (1747) : a rich butter cake made with a large proportion of eggs and shortening

[1]**pound·er** \ˈpau̇n-dər\ *n* (bef. 12c) : one that pounds

[2]**pounder** *n* (1684) **1** : one having a usu. specified weight or value in pounds — usu. used in combination ⟨caught a ten-*pounder* with his new fishing rod⟩ **2** : a gun throwing a projectile of a specified weight — usu. used in combination ⟨the ship was armed with six-*pounders*⟩

pound–fool·ish \ˈpau̇n(d)-ˈfü-lish\ *adj* [fr. the phrase *penny-wise and pound-foolish*] (1607) : imprudent in dealing with large sums or large matters

pound mile *n* (1939) : the transport of one pound of mail or express for one mile

pound net *n* (1856) : a fish trap consisting of a netting arranged into a directing wing and an enclosure with a narrow entrance

[1]**pour** \ˈpō(ə)r, ˈpȯ(ə)r\ *vb* [ME *pouren*] *vt* (14c) **1 a** : to cause to flow in a stream **b** : to dispense from a container ⟨~*ed* drinks for everyone⟩ **2** : to supply or produce freely or copiously **3** : to give full expression to : VENT ⟨~*ed* out his feelings⟩ ~ *vi* **1** : to move with a continuous flow **2** : to rain hard **3** : to move or come continuously : STREAM ⟨complaints ~*ed* in⟩ — **pour·able** \ˈpōr-ə-bəl, ˈpȯr-\ *adj* — **pour·er** \-ər\ *n* — **pour·ing·ly** \-iŋ-lē\ *adv*

[2]**pour** *n* (1790) **1** : the action of pouring : STREAM **2 a** : an instance of pouring or an amount poured ⟨a ~ of concrete⟩ **b** : a heavy fall of rain : DOWNPOUR

pour·boire \pu̇(ə)rb-ˈwär\ *n* [F, fr. *pour boire* for drinking] (1815) : TIP, GRATUITY

pour·par·ler \ˌpu̇(ə)r-pär-ˈlā\ *n* [F] (1795) : a discussion preliminary to negotiations

pour·point \ˈpu̇(ə)r-ˌpȯint, -ˌpwant\ *n* [ME *purpoint,* fr. MF *pourpoint*] (15c) : a padded and quilted doublet

pour point \ˈpō(ə)r-ˌpȯint, ˈpȯ(ə)r-\ *n* (ca. 1922) : the lowest temperature at which a substance flows under specified conditions

pousse–ca·fé \ˌpü-(ˌ)skä-ˈfā\ *n* [F, lit., coffee chaser] (1880) : an after-dinner drink consisting of several liqueurs of different colors and specific gravities poured so as to remain in separate layers

pous·sette \pü-ˈset\ *vi* **pous·sett·ed; pous·sett·ing** [F, game in which contestants cross pins with each attempting to get his pin on top, fr. *pousser* to push] (1812) : to swing in a semicircle with hands joined with one's partner in a country-dance

[1]**pout** \ˈpau̇t\ *vb* [ME *pouten*] *vi* (14c) **1 a** : to show displeasure by thrusting out the lips or wearing a sullen expression **b** : SULK **2** : PROTRUDE ~ *vt* : to cause to protrude ⟨~*ed* her lips⟩

[2]**pout** *n* (1591) **1** : a protrusion of the lips expressive of displeasure **2** *pl* : a fit of pique

[3]**pout** *n, pl* **pout** *or* **pouts** [prob. fr. (assumed) ME *poute,* a fish with a large head, fr. OE *-pūte;* akin to ME *pouten* to pout, Skt *budbuda* bubble] (1591) : any of several large-headed fishes (as a bullhead or eelpout)

pout·er \ˈpau̇t-ər\ *n* (1809) **1** : one that pouts **2** : a domestic pigeon of a breed characterized by erect carriage and a dilatable crop

pouty \ˈpau̇t-ē\ *adj* (1863) : SULKY

pov·er·ty \ˈpäv-ərt-ē\ *n, often attrib* [ME *poverte,* fr. OF *poverté,* fr. L *paupertat-, paupertas,* fr. *pauper* poor — more at POOR] (12c) **1 a** : the state of one who lacks a usual or socially acceptable amount of money or material possessions **b** : renunciation as a member of a religious order of the right as an individual to own property **2** : SCARCITY, DEARTH **3 a** : debility due to malnutrition **b** : lack of fertility ⟨~ of the soil⟩

syn POVERTY, INDIGENCE, PENURY, WANT, DESTITUTION mean the state of one with insufficient resources. POVERTY may cover a range from extreme want of necessities to an absence of material comforts; INDIGENCE implies seriously straitened circumstances; PENURY suggests a cramping or oppressive lack of money; WANT and DESTITUTION imply extreme poverty that threatens life itself through starvation or exposure.

poverty line *n* (1901) : a level of personal or family income below which one is classified as poor according to governmental standards — called also *poverty level*

pov·er·ty–strick·en \-ˌstrik-ən\ *adj* (1803) : very poor : DESTITUTE

[1]**pow** \ˈpō, ˈpau̇\ *n* [alter. of POLL] (1724) : HEAD, POLL

[2]**pow** \ˈpau̇\ *n* [imit.] (1881) : a sound of a blow or explosion

POW \ˌpē(ˌ)ō-ˈdəb-əl-(ˌ)yü, -yə(-w), -ˈdəb(-ə)-yə(-w), -ˈdəb-yē\ *n* (ca. 1919) : PRISONER OF WAR

[1]**pow·der** \ˈpau̇d-ər\ *n, often attrib* [ME *poudre,* fr. OF, fr. L *pulver-, pulvis* dust — more at POLLEN] (13c) **1** : matter in a finely divided state : particulate matter **2 a** : a preparation in the form of fine particles esp. for medicinal or cosmetic use **b** : fine dry light snow **3** : any of various solid explosives used chiefly in gunnery and blasting

[2]**powder** *vb* **pow·dered; pow·der·ing** \ˈpau̇d-(ə-)riŋ\ *vt* (14c) **1** : to sprinkle or cover with or as if with powder **2** : to reduce or convert to powder **3** : to hit (as a ball) very hard ~ *vi* **1** : to become powder **2** : to apply cosmetic powder — **pow·der·er** \-ər-ər\ *n*

powder blue *n* (1896) : a variable color averaging a pale blue

powder horn *n* (1533) : a flask for carrying gunpowder; *esp* : one made of the horn of an ox or cow

powder keg *n* (1855) **1** : a small usu. metal cask for holding gunpowder or blasting powder **2** : something liable to explode

powder metallurgy *n* (1933) : a branch of science or an art concerned with the production of powdered metals or of metallic objects by compressing a powdered metal or alloy with or without other materials and heating without thoroughly melting to solidify and strengthen

powder monkey *n* (1682) : one who carries or has charge of explosives (as in blasting operations)

powder–puff *adj* (1939) : of, relating to, or being a competitive activity or event for women ⟨a ~ football game⟩

powder puff *n* (ca. 1704) : a small fluffy device (as a pad) for applying cosmetic powder

powder room *n* (ca. 1937) **1** : a rest room for women **2** : a lavatory in the main living area of a house

pow·dery \ˈpau̇d-ə-rē\ *adj* (15c) **1 a** : resembling or consisting of powder ⟨~ snow⟩ **b** : easily reduced to powder : CRUMBLING **2** : covered with or as if with powder

powdery mildew *n* (1889) **1** : a perfect fungus (family Erysiphaceae) or an imperfect fungus (genus *Oidium*) producing abundant powdery conidia on the host **2** : a plant disease caused by a powdery mildew

[1]**pow·er** \ˈpau̇(-ə)r\ *n, often attrib* [ME, fr. OF *poeir,* fr. *poeir* to be able, fr. (assumed) L *potēre* to be powerful — more at POTENT] (13c) **1 a** : possession of control, authority, or influence over others **b** : one having such power; *specif* : a sovereign state **c** : a controlling group : ESTABLISHMENT — often used in the phrase *the powers that be* **d** *archaic* : a force of armed men **e** *chiefly dial* : a large number or quantity **2 a** (1) : ability to act or produce an effect (2) : ability to get extra-base hits (3) : capacity for being acted upon or undergoing an effect **b** : legal or official authority, capacity, or right **3 a** : physical might **b** : mental or moral efficacy **c** : political control or influence **4** *pl* : an order of angels — see CELESTIAL HIERARCHY **5 a** : the number of times as indicated by an exponent that a number occurs as a factor in a product; *also* : the product itself **b** : CARDINAL NUMBER 2 **6 a** : a source or means of supplying energy; *esp* : ELECTRICITY **b** : MOTIVE POWER **c** : the time rate at which work is done or energy emitted or transferred **7** : MAGNIFICATION 2b **8** : SCOPE, COMPREHENSIVENESS **9** : the probability of rejecting the null hypothesis in a statistical test when a particular alternative hypothesis happens to be true

syn POWER, AUTHORITY, JURISDICTION, CONTROL, COMMAND, SWAY, DOMINION mean the right to govern or rule or determine. POWER implies possession of ability to wield force, permissive authority, or substantial influence; AUTHORITY implies the granting of power for a specific purpose within specified limits; JURISDICTION applies to official power exercised within prescribed limits; CONTROL stresses the power to direct and restrain; COMMAND implies the power to make arbitrary decisions and compel obedience; SWAY suggests the extent or scope of exercised power or influence; DOMINION stresses sovereign power or supreme authority.

syn POWER, FORCE, ENERGY, STRENGTH, MIGHT mean the ability to exert effort. POWER may imply latent or exerted physical, mental, or spiritual ability to act or be acted upon; FORCE implies the actual effective exercise of power; ENERGY applies to power expended or capable of being transformed into work; STRENGTH applies to the quality or property of a person or thing that makes possible the exertion of force or the withstanding of strain, pressure, or attack; MIGHT implies great or overwhelming power or strength.

[2]**power** *vt* (1540) **1** : to supply with power and esp. motive power **2** : to give impetus to

power base *n* (1959) : a base of political support

pow·er·boat \ˈpau̇(-ə)r-ˈbōt\ *n* (1908) : MOTORBOAT

power broker *n* (1961) : a person (as in politics) able to exert strong influence because of votes or individuals that he controls

pow·er–dive \-ˈdīv\ *vi* (1937) : to make a power dive ~ *vt* : to cause to power-dive

power dive *n* (1930) : a dive of an airplane accelerated by the power of the engine

pow·er·ful \ˈpau̇(-ə)r-fəl\ *adj* (15c) **1** : having great power, prestige, or influence **2** : leading to many or important deductions ⟨a ~ set of postulates⟩ — **pow·er·ful·ly** \-f(ə-)lē\ *adv*

power function *n* (1957) **1** : a function of a parameter under statistical test whose value for a particular value of the parameter is the probability of rejecting the null hypothesis if that value of the parameter happens to be true **2** : a function (as $f(x) = ax^k$) that equals the product of a constant and a power of the independent variable

pow·er·house \ˈpau̇(-ə)r-ˌhau̇s\ *n* (ca. 1890) **1 a** : POWER PLANT 1 **b** : a source of influence or inspiration **2** : one having great drive, energy, or ability

pow·er·less \-ləs\ *adj* (ca. 1552) **1** : devoid of strength or resources **2** : lacking the authority or capacity to act — **pow·er·less·ly** *adv* — **pow·er·less·ness** *n*

power mower *n* (1940) : a motor-driven lawn mower

power of attorney (1747) : a legal instrument authorizing one to act as the attorney or agent of the grantor

power pack *n* (1936) : a unit for converting a power supply (as from a battery or household electrical circuit) to a voltage suitable for an electronic device

power plant *n* (1890) **1** : an electric utility generating station **2** : an engine and related parts supplying the motive power of a self-propelled object (as a rocket or automobile)

power play *n* (1947) **1 :** a military, diplomatic, political, or administrative maneuver in which power is brought to bear **2 a :** a concentrated attack in football in which the ballcarrier is preceded by a mass of blockers **b :** a situation in ice hockey in which one team temporarily has more players on the ice than the other team because of a penalty

power politics *n pl but sing or pl in constr* (1926) **:** politics based primarily on the use of power as a coercive force rather than on ethical precepts; *esp* **:** international politics characterized by attempts to advance national interests through coercion on the basis of military and economic strength

power series *n* (1893) **:** an infinite series whose terms are successive integral powers of a variable multiplied by constants

power shovel *n* (1909) **:** a power-operated excavating machine consisting of a boom or crane that supports a lever arm with a large bucket at the end of it

power station *n* (1901) **:** POWER PLANT 1

power steering *n* (1932) **:** automotive steering with engine power used to amplify the torque applied at the steering wheel by the driver

power structure *n* (1950) **1 :** a group of persons having control of an organization **:** ESTABLISHMENT **2 :** the hierarchical interrelationships existing within a controlling group

power sweep *n* (1964) **:** SWEEP 3e

power take–off *n* (1929) **:** a supplementary mechanism (as on a tractor) enabling the engine power to be used to operate nonautomotive apparatus (as a pump or saw)

power train *n* (1943) **:** the intervening mechanism by which power is transmitted from an engine to a propeller or axle that it drives

[1]**pow·wow** \ˈpau̇-ˌwau̇\ *n* [of Algonquian origin; akin to Natick *pauwau* conjurer] (1625) **1 :** an American Indian medicine man **2 :** an American Indian ceremony (as for victory in war) **3 a :** a social get-together **b :** a meeting for discussion

[2]**powwow** *vi* (1642) **:** to hold a powwow

[1]**pox** \ˈpäks\ *n, pl* **pox** *or* **pox·es** [alter. of *pocks,* pl. of *pock*] (14c) **1 a :** a virus disease (as chicken pox) characterized by pustules or eruptions **b** *archaic* **:** SMALLPOX **c :** SYPHILIS **2 :** a disastrous evil **:** PLAGUE, CURSE ⟨a ~ on him⟩

[2]**pox** *vt, archaic* (1601) **:** to infect with a pox and esp. with syphilis

pox·vi·rus \ˈpäks-ˌvī-rəs\ *n* (1941) **:** any of a group of relatively large round, brick-shaped, or ovoid animal viruses (as the causative agent of smallpox) that have a fluffy appearance caused by a covering of tubules and threads

poz·zo·la·na \ˌpät-sə-ˈlän-ə\ *or* **poz·zo·lan** \ˈpät-sə-lən\ *n* [It *pozzolana*] (1706) **:** finely divided siliceous or siliceous and aluminous material that reacts chemically with slaked lime at ordinary temperature and in the presence of moisture to form a strong slow-hardening cement — **poz·zo·la·nic** \-ˈlan-ik, -ˈlän-\ *adj*

PPI \ˌpē-(ˌ)pē-ˈī\ *n* [*p*lan *p*osition *i*ndicator] (1945) **:** a radarscope on which spots of light representing reflections of radar waves indicate the range and bearing of objects

prac·ti·ca·ble \ˈprak-ti-kə-bəl\ *adj* (1670) **1 :** possible to practice or perform **:** FEASIBLE **2 :** capable of being used **:** USABLE — **prac·ti·ca·bil·i·ty** \ˌprak-ti-kə-ˈbil-ət-ē\ *n* — **prac·ti·ca·ble·ness** \ˈprak-ti-kə-bəl-nəs\ *n* — **prac·ti·ca·bly** \-blē\ *adv*

syn PRACTICABLE, PRACTICAL mean capable of being put to use or put into practice. PRACTICABLE applies to what has been proposed and seems feasible but has not been actually tested in use; PRACTICAL applies to things and to persons and implies proven success in meeting the demands made by actual living or use. ***syn*** see in addition POSSIBLE

[1]**prac·ti·cal** \ˈprak-ti-kəl\ *adj* [LL *practicus,* fr. Gk *praktikos,* fr. *prassein* to pass over, fare, do; akin to Gk *peran* to pass through — more at FARE] (1604) **1 :** actively engaged in some course of action or occupation ⟨a ~ farmer⟩ **2 a :** of, relating to, or manifested in practice or action **:** not theoretical or ideal ⟨a ~ question⟩ ⟨for all ~ purposes⟩ **b :** being such in practice or effect **:** VIRTUAL ⟨a ~ failure⟩ **3 :** capable of being put to use or account **:** USEFUL ⟨he had a ~ knowledge of French⟩ **4 a :** disposed to action as opposed to speculation or abstraction **b (1) :** qualified by practice or practical training ⟨a good ~ mechanic⟩ **(2) :** designed to supplement theoretical training by experience **5 :** concerned with voluntary action and ethical decisions ⟨~ reason⟩ ***syn*** see PRACTICABLE — **prac·ti·cal·i·ty** \ˌprak-ti-ˈkal-ət-ē\ *n* — **prac·ti·cal·ness** \ˈprak-ti-kəl-nəs\ *n*

[2]**practical** *n* (1925) **:** an examination requiring demonstration of some practical skill ⟨a zoology ~⟩

practical art *n* (ca. 1924) **:** an art (as woodworking) that serves ordinary or material needs — usu. used in pl.

practical joke *n* (ca. 1847) **:** a prank intended to trick or embarrass someone or cause him physical discomfort — **practical joker** *n*

prac·ti·cal·ly \ˈprak-ti-k(ə-)lē\ *adv* (1623) **1 :** in a practical manner ⟨talked ~ about the problem⟩ **2 :** ALMOST, NEARLY ⟨~ everyone went to the party⟩

practical nurse *n* (1921) **:** a nurse who cares for the sick professionally without having the training or experience required of a registered nurse; *esp* **:** LICENSED PRACTICAL NURSE

practical theology *n* (ca. 1909) **:** the study of the institutional activities of religion (as preaching, church administration, pastoral care, and liturgics)

[1]**prac·tice** *or* **prac·tise** \ˈprak-təs\ *vb* **prac·ticed** *or* **prac·tised; prac·tic·ing** *or* **prac·tis·ing** [ME *practisen,* fr. MF *practiser,* fr. *practique* practice, n., fr. LL *practice,* fr. Gk *praktikē,* fr. fem. of *praktikos*] *vt* (15c) **1 a :** to perform or work at repeatedly so as to become proficient ⟨~ his act⟩ **b :** to train by repeated exercises ⟨~ pupils in penmanship⟩ **2 a :** CARRY OUT, APPLY ⟨~ what you preach⟩ **b :** to do or perform often, customarily, or habitually ⟨~ politeness⟩ **c :** to be professionally engaged in ⟨~ medicine⟩ **3** *obs* **:** PLOT ~ *vi* **1 :** to do repeated exercises for proficiency **2 :** to pursue a profession actively **3** *archaic* **:** INTRIGUE **4 :** to do something customarily **5 :** to take advantage of someone ⟨he *practised* on their credulity with huge success —*Times Lit. Supp.*⟩ — **prac·tic·er** *n*

[2]**practice** *also* **practise** *n* (15c) **1 a :** actual performance or application ⟨ready to carry out in ~ what they advocated in principle⟩ **b :** a repeated or customary action ⟨he had an irritating ~ of watching his fellows⟩ **c :** the usual way of doing something ⟨it is wise to conform to local ~*s*⟩ **d :** the form, manner, and order of conducting legal suits and prosecutions **2 a :** systematic exercise for proficiency ⟨~ makes perfect⟩ **b :** the condition of being proficient through systematic exercise ⟨get in ~⟩ **3 a :** the continuous exercise of a profession **b :** a professional business; *esp* **:** one constituting an incorporeal property ***syn*** see HABIT

prac·ticed *or* **prac·tised** \ˈprak-təst\ *adj* (1568) **1 :** EXPERIENCED, SKILLED **2 :** learned by practice

prac·tice–teach \-təs-ˌtēch\ *vi* **-taught** \-ˌtȯt\; **-teach·ing** [back-formation fr. *practice teaching*] (1952) **:** to engage in practice teaching — **practice teacher** *n*

practice teaching *n* (ca. 1913) **:** teaching in which a student practices educational skills and methods under the supervision of an experienced teacher in preparation for professional teaching

prac·tic·ing *or* **prac·tis·ing** *adj* (1625) **:** actively engaged in a specified career or way of life ⟨a ~ physician⟩

prac·ti·cum \ˈprak-ti-kəm\ *n* [G *praktikum,* fr. LL *practicum,* neut. of *practicus* practical] (ca. 1909) **:** a course of study designed esp. for the preparation of teachers and clinicians that involves the supervised practical application (as in a classroom or clinic) of previously studied theory

prac·ti·tio·ner \prak-ˈtish-(ə-)nər\ *n* [alter. of earlier *practician,* fr. ME (Sc) *pratician,* fr. MF *practicien,* fr. *pratique*] (1535) **1 :** one who practices; *esp* **:** one who practices a profession **2** *Christian Science* **:** an authorized healer

prae·ci·pe \ˈpres-ə-ˌpē, ˈprēs-\ *n* [ML, fr. L *praecipe,* imper. of *praecipere* to instruct — more at PRECEPT] (ca. 1500) **1 :** any of various legal writs commanding a person to do something or to appear and show cause why he should not **2 :** a written order requesting a clerk or prothonotary of a court to issue a writ and specifying the contents of the writ

prae·di·al *var of* PREDIAL

prae·mu·ni·re \ˌprē-myu̇-ˈnī(ə)r-ē\ *n* [ME *praemunire facias,* fr. ML, that you cause to warn; fr. prominent words in the writ] (15c) **:** an offense against the English Crown punishable chiefly by forfeiture and orig. committed by asserting papal legal supremacy in England

prae·no·men \prē-ˈnō-mən\ *n, pl* **-nomens** *or* **-no·mi·na** \-ˈnäm-ə-nə, -ˈnō-mə-\ [L, fr. *prae-* pre- + *nomen* name — more at NAME] (1706) **:** the first of the usual three names of an ancient Roman

prae·sid·i·um *var of* PRESIDIUM

prae·tor \ˈprēt-ər\ *n* [ME *pretor,* fr. L *praetor*] (15c) **:** an ancient Roman magistrate ranking below a consul and having chiefly judicial functions — **prae·to·ri·al** \prē-ˈtōr-ē-əl, -ˈtȯr-\ *adj* — **prae·tor·ship** \ˈprēt-ər-ˌship\ *n*

prae·to·ri·an \prē-ˈtōr-ē-ən, -ˈtȯr-\ *adj* (1598) **1 :** of or relating to a praetor **2** *often cap* **:** of, forming, or resembling the Roman imperial bodyguard — **praetorian** *n, often cap*

prag·mat·ic \prag-ˈmat-ik\ *also* **prag·mat·i·cal** \-i-kəl\ *adj* [L *pragmaticus* skilled in law or business, fr. Gk *pragmatikos,* fr. *pragmat-, pragma* deed, fr. *prassein* to do — more at PRACTICAL] (1616) **1** *archaic* **a (1) :** BUSY **(2) :** OFFICIOUS **b :** OPINIONATED **2 :** relating to matters of fact or practical affairs often to the exclusion of intellectual or artistic matters **:** practical as opposed to idealistic ⟨the problem-solving mentality, the product of science and ~ effort —T. F. O'Dea⟩ ⟨~ men of power have had no time or inclination to deal with . . . social morality —K. B. Clark⟩ **3 :** relating to or being in accordance with philosophical pragmatism — **pragmatic** *n* — **prag·mat·i·cal·ly** \-i-k(ə-)lē\ *adv*

prag·mat·i·cism \prag-ˈmat-ə-ˌsiz-əm\ *n* (1905) **:** the philosophic doctrine of C. S. Peirce — **prag·mat·i·cist** \-səst\ *n*

prag·mat·ics \prag-ˈmat-iks\ *n pl but sing or pl in constr* (1937) **:** a branch of semiotic that deals with the relation between signs or linguistic expressions and their users

pragmatic sanction *n* (1643) **:** a solemn decree of a sovereign on a matter of primary importance and with the force of fundamental law

prag·ma·tism \ˈprag-mə-ˌtiz-əm\ *n* (ca. 1864) **1 :** a practical approach to problems and affairs ⟨tried to strike a balance between principles and ~⟩ **2 :** an American movement in philosophy founded by C. S. Peirce and William James and marked by the doctrines that the meaning of conceptions is to be sought in their practical bearings, that the function of thought is to guide action, and that truth is preeminently to be tested by the practical consequences of belief — **prag·ma·tist** \-mət-əst\ *adj or n* — **prag·ma·tis·tic** \ˌprag-mə-ˈtis-tik\ *adj*

prai·rie \ˈpre(ə)r-ē\ *n, often attrib* [F, fr. (assumed) VL *prataria,* fr. L *pratum* meadow; akin to L *pravus* crooked, MIr *rāth* earthworks] (ca. 1682) **1 :** land in or predominantly in grass **2 :** a tract of grassland: as **a :** a large area of level or rolling land in the Mississippi valley that in its natural uncultivated state usu. has deep fertile soil, a cover of tall coarse grasses, and few trees **b :** one of the dry treeless plateaus into which the prairies proper merge on the west

prairie chicken *n* (1691) **:** a grouse (*Tympanuchus cupido pinnatus*) of the Mississippi valley; *also* **:** a closely related American grouse (*T. pallidicinctus*)

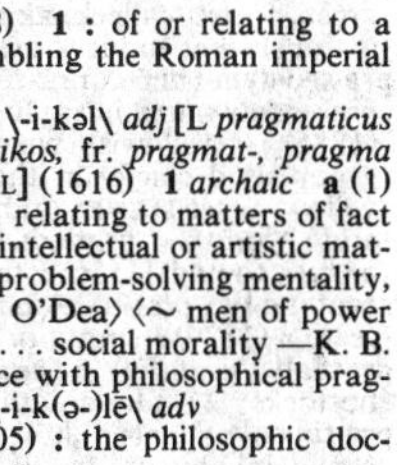
prairie chicken

prairie dog *n* (1774) **:** a colonial American burrowing rodent (genus *Cynomys,* esp. *C. ludovicianus* of the prairies) related to the marmots

prairie schooner *n* (1841) **:** a covered wagon used by pioneers in cross-country travel — called also *prairie wagon*

prairie soil *n* (1817) **:** any of a zonal group of soils developed in a temperate relatively humid climate under tall grass

prairie wolf *n* (1804) **:** COYOTE

[1]**praise** \ˈprāz\ *vb* **praised; prais·ing** [ME *praisen,* fr. OF *preisier* to prize, praise, fr. LL *pretiare* to prize, fr. L *pretium* price — more at PRICE] *vt* (13c) **1 :** to express a favorable judgment of **:** COMMEND **2 :** to glorify (a god

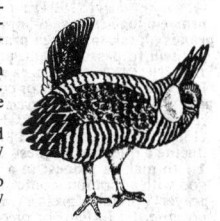

or saint) esp. by the attribution of perfections ~ *vi* : to express praise — **prais·er** *n*

²**praise** *n* (15c) **1** **a** : an expression of approval : COMMENDATION **b** : WORSHIP **2** **a** : VALUE, MERIT **b** *archaic* : one that is praised

praise·wor·thy \'prāz-ˌwər-t͟hē\ *adj* (1538) : LAUDABLE — **praise·wor·thi·ly** \-t͟hə-lē\ *adv* — **praise·wor·thi·ness** \-t͟hē-nəs\ *n*

Pra·krit \'präk-ˌrit, -rət\ *n* [Skt *prākṛta*, fr. *prākṛta* natural, vulgar] (1766) **1** : any or all of the ancient Indic languages or dialects other than Sanskrit — see INDO-EUROPEAN LANGUAGES table **2** : any of the modern Indic languages

pra·line \'prä-ˌlēn, 'prā-, 'prō-\ *n* [F, fr. Count Plessis-*Praslin* †1675 Fr. soldier] (ca. 1727) : a confection of nut kernels: **a** : almonds cooked in boiling sugar until brown and crisp **b** : a patty of creamy brown sugar and pecan meats

prall·tril·ler \'präl-ˌtril-ər\ *n* [G] (ca. 1841) : a musical ornament made by a quick alternation of a principal tone with the tone above

¹**pram** \'präm, 'pram\ *n* [D *praam*; akin to MLG *prām* pram] (1548) : a small lightweight nearly flat-bottomed boat with a broad transom and usu. squared-off bow

²**pram** \'pram\ *n* [by shortening & alter. fr. *perambulator*] *chiefly Brit* (1884) : BABY CARRIAGE

¹**prance** \'pran(t)s\ *vb* **pranced; pranc·ing** [ME *prauncen*] *vi* (14c) **1** : to spring from the hind legs or move by so doing **2** : to ride on a prancing horse **3** : to walk or move in a spirited manner : STRUT; *also* : to dance about ~ *vt* : to cause (a horse) to prance — **pranc·er** \'pran(t)-sər\ *n*

²**prance** *n* (1751) : an act or instance of prancing; *specif* : a prancing movement

pran·di·al \'pran-dē-əl\ *adj* [L *prandium* late breakfast, luncheon] (1820) : of or relating to a meal

¹**prang** \'praŋ\ *vt* [origin unknown] (1941) : to have an accident with : cause to crash

²**prang** *n* (1942) : ACCIDENT, CRASH

¹**prank** \'praŋk\ *n* [obs. *prank* to play tricks] (ca. 1529) : TRICK: **a** *obs* : a malicious act **b** : a mildly mischievous act **c** : a ludicrous act

²**prank** *vb* [prob. fr. D *pronken* to strut; akin to MHG *gebrunkel* glitter of metal] *vt* (1546) : to dress or adorn gaily or showily ~ *vi* : to show oneself off

prank·ish \'praŋ-kish\ *adj* (1827) **1** : full of pranks ⟨a ~ writer⟩ **2** : having the nature of a prank ⟨~ acts⟩ — **prank·ish·ly** *adv* — **prank·ish·ness** *n*

prank·ster \'praŋ(k)-stər\ *n* (1927) : one who plays pranks

prase \'prāz, 'prās\ *n* [F, fr. L *prasius*, fr. Gk *prasios*, fr. *prasios*, adj., leek green, fr. *prason* leek; akin to L *porrum* leek] (14c) : a chalcedony that is translucent and leek green

pra·seo·dym·i·um \ˌprā-zē-ō-'dim-ē-əm, ˌprā-sē-\ *n* [NL, alter. of *praseodidymium*, irreg. fr. Gk *prasios*, adj. + NL *didymium* didymium] (1885) : a yellowish white trivalent metallic element of the rare-earth group used chiefly in the form of its salts in coloring glass greenish yellow — see ELEMENT table

¹**prate** \'prāt\ *vi* **prat·ed; prat·ing** [ME *praten*, fr. MD; akin to MLG *pratten* to pout] (15c) : to talk long and idly : CHATTER — **prat·er** *n* — **prat·ing·ly** \'prāt-iŋ-lē\ *adv*

²**prate** *n* (1579) : empty or meaningless talk

prat·fall \'prat-ˌfȯl\ *n* [*prat* (buttocks) + *fall*] (1938) **1** : a fall on the buttocks **2** : a humiliating mishap or blunder

pra·tin·cole \'prat-ᵊn-ˌkōl, 'prāt-, -iŋ-\ *n* [deriv. of L *pratum* meadow + *incola* inhabitant, fr. *in-* + *colere* to cultivate — more at PRAIRIE, WHEEL] (1773) : any of a genus (*Glareola*) of Old World limicoline birds

pra·tique \pra-'tēk\ *n* [F, lit., practice — more at PRACTICE] (1609) : clearance given an incoming ship by the health authority of a port

¹**prat·tle** \'prat-ᵊl\ *vb* **prat·tled; prat·tling** \'prat-liŋ, -ᵊl-iŋ\ [LG *pratelen*; akin to MD *praten* to prate] *vi* (1532) **1** : PRATE **2** : to utter or make meaningless sounds suggestive of the chatter of children : BABBLE ~ *vt* : to say in an unaffected or childish manner — **prat·tler** \'prat-lər, -ᵊl-ər\ *n* — **prat·tling·ly** \-liŋ-lē, -ᵊl-iŋ-\ *adv*

²**prattle** *n* (1555) **1** : trifling or empty talk **2** : a sound that is meaningless, repetitive, and suggestive of the chatter of children

prau \'prau̇, 'prä-ˌü\ *n* [Malay *pĕrahu*] (1582) : any of several Indonesian boats usu. without a deck that are propelled by sails, oars, or paddles

¹**prawn** \'prȯn, 'prän\ *n* [ME *prane*] (15c) : any of numerous widely distributed edible decapod crustaceans (as of the genera *Pandalus* and *Peneus*) that resemble shrimps with large compressed abdomens; *also* : SHRIMP

²**prawn** *vi* (1886) : to fish for or with prawns — **prawn·er** *n*

prax·e·ol·o·gy \ˌprak-sē-'äl-ə-jē\ *n* [alter. of earlier *praxiology*, fr. *praxis* + *-o-* + *-logy*] (1904) : the study of human action and conduct — **prax·e·o·log·i·cal** \-sē-ə-'läj-i-kəl\ *adj*

prax·is \'prak-səs\ *n, pl* **prax·es** \-ˌsēz\ [ML, fr. Gk, doing, action, fr. *prassein* to pass through, practice — more at PRACTICAL] (1581) : ACTION, PRACTICE: as **a** : exercise or practice of an art, science, or skill **b** : customary practice or conduct

pray \'prā\ *vb* [ME *prayen*, fr. OF *preier*, fr. L *precari*, fr. *prec-*, *prex* request, prayer; akin to OHG *frāgēn* to ask, Skt *pṛcchati* he asks] *vt* (13c) **1** : ENTREAT, IMPLORE — often used as a function word in introducing a question, request, or plea **2** : to get or bring by praying ~ *vi* **1** : to make a request in a humble manner **2** : to address God or a god with adoration, confession, supplication, or thanksgiving

¹**prayer** \'pra(ə)r, 'pre(ə)r\ *n, often attrib* [ME, fr. MF *preiere*, fr. ML *precaria*, fr. L, fem. of *precarius* obtained by entreaty, fr. *prec-*, *prex*] (14c) **1** **a** (1) : an address (as a petition) to God or a god in word or thought ⟨said a ~ for the success of the voyage⟩ (2) : a set order of words used in praying ⟨repeat a ~⟩ **b** : an earnest request or wish **2** : the act or practice of praying to God or a god ⟨kneeling in ~⟩ **3** : a religious service consisting chiefly of prayers — often used in pl. **4** : something prayed for **5** : a slight chance ⟨tried hard but didn't have a ~⟩

²**pray·er** \'prā-ər, 'pre(-ə)r\ *n* [ME *prayere*, fr. *prayen* to pray + *-er*] (15c) : one that prays : SUPPLIANT

prayer beads \'pra(ə)r-, 'pre(ə)r-\ *n pl* (1630) : a string of beads by which prayers are counted; *specif* : ROSARY

prayer book *n* (ca. 1596) : a book containing prayers and often other forms and directions for worship

prayer·ful \'pra(ə)r-fəl, 'pre(ə)r-\ *adj* (1626) **1** : DEVOUT **2** : EARNEST, SINCERE — **prayer·ful·ly** \-fə-lē\ *adv* — **prayer·ful·ness** *n*

prayer meeting *n* (1780) : a Protestant worship service usu. held on a week night — called also *prayer service*

prayer rug *n* (ca. 1890) : a small Oriental rug used by Muslims to kneel on when praying

prayer shawl *n* (1905) : TALLITH

prayer wheel *n* (1814) : a cylinder of wood or metal that revolves on an axis and contains written prayers and that is used in praying by Tibetan Buddhists

praying mantid *n* (1901) : MANTIS

praying mantis *n* (ca. 1890) : MANTIS

pre- *prefix* [ME, fr. OF & L; OF, fr. L *prae-*, fr. *prae* in front of, before — more at FOR] **1** **a** (1) : earlier than : prior to : before ⟨*Pre*cambrian⟩ ⟨*pre*historic⟩ ⟨*pre*-English⟩ (2) : preparatory or prerequisite to ⟨*pre*medical⟩ ⟨*pre*journalism⟩ **b** : in advance : beforehand ⟨*pre*cancel⟩ ⟨*pre*pay⟩ **2** **a** : in front of : anterior to ⟨*pre*axial⟩ ⟨*pre*molar⟩ **b** : front : anterior ⟨*pre*abdomen⟩

pre·ad·mis·sion	**pre·for·mu·late**	**pre·punch**
pre·adult	**pre·fresh·man**	**pre·pu·pal**
pre·ag·ri·cul·tur·al	**pre·game**	**pre·pur·chase**
pre·an·es·thet·ic	**pre·gen·i·tal**	**pre·qual·i·fi·ca·tion**
pre·an·nounce	**pre·har·vest**	**pre·qual·i·fy**
pre·ar·range	**pre·head·ache**	**pre·race**
pre·ar·range·ment	**pre·hir·ing**	**pre·re·ces·sion**
pre·as·sign	**pre–His·pan·ic**	**pre·re·hears·al**
pre·au·dit	**pre·hol·i·day**	**pre·re·lease**
pre·bat·tle	**pre·hu·man**	**pre·re·quire**
pre·boom	**pre·in·au·gu·ral**	**pre·re·tire·ment**
pre·civ·i·li·za·tion	**pre·in·cor·po·ra·tion**	**pre·re·turn**
pre·clear	**pre·in·duc·tion**	**pre·re·view**
pre·clear·ance	**pre·in·dus·tri·al**	**pre·re·vi·sion·ist**
pre·code	**pre·in·ter·view**	**pre·rev·o·lu·tion**
pre·co·ital	**pre·in·va·sion**	**pre·rev·o·lu·tion·ary**
pre·col·lege	**pre·launch**	**pre·rinse**
pre·co·lo·nial	**pre·life**	**pre·ri·ot**
pre·com·bus·tion	**pre·lit·er·ary**	**pre·rock**
pre·com·mit·ment	**pre·log·i·cal**	**pre·ro·man·tic**
pre·com·pute	**pre·lunch**	**pre·sale**
pre·con·so·nan·tal	**pre·lun·cheon**	**pre·sched·ule**
pre·con·so·nan·tal·ly	**pre·man·u·fac·ture**	**pre·screen**
pre·con·struct	**pre·mar·ket**	**pre·sea·son**
pre·con·ven·tion	**pre·mar·ket·ing**	**pre·sen·tence**
pre·con·vic·tion	**pre·mar·riage**	**pre·sen·tenc·ing**
pre·cool	**pre·meal**	**pre·ser·vice**
pre·cop·u·la·to·ry	**pre·mea·sure**	**pre·show**
pre·coup	**pre·med·i·cate**	**pre·slaugh·ter**
pre·crash	**pre·me·di·eval**	**pre·sleep**
pre·crease	**pre·meet**	**pre·slice**
pre·cut	**pre·meno·paus·al**	**pre·song**
pre·dawn	**pre·merg·er**	**pre·sort**
pre·de·fine	**pre·meta·mor·phic**	**pre·spec·i·fy**
pre·de·liv·ery	**pre·mi·gra·tion**	**pre·split**
pre·dem·o·crat·ic	**pre·mi·gra·to·ry**	**pre·stamp**
pre·de·par·ture	**pre·mix**	**pre·ster·il·ize**
pre·des·ig·nate	**pre·mod·ern**	**pre·stor·age**
pre·des·ig·na·tion	**pre·mod·i·fi·ca·tion**	**pre·strike**
pre·de·val·u·a·tion	**pre·mod·i·fy**	**pre·struc·ture**
pre·de·vel·op·ment	**pre·moist·en**	**pre·sum·mit**
pre·din·ner	**pre·mold**	**pre·sweet·en**
pre·dis·charge	**pre·molt**	**pre·tape**
pre·dis·cov·ery	**pre·mor·al**	**pre·tech·no·log·i·cal**
pre·dive	**pre·my·cot·ic**	**pre·tele·vi·sion**
pre·drill	**pre·noon**	**pre·ter·mi·na·tion**
pre·dy·nas·tic	**pre·no·ti·fi·ca·tion**	**pre·the·ater**
pre·ed·it	**pre·no·ti·fy**	**pre·tour·na·ment**
pre·elec·tion	**pre·num·ber**	**pre·train**
pre·elec·tric	**pre·open·ing**	**pre·trav·el**
pre·em·bar·go	**pre·op·er·a·tion·al**	**pre·treat**
pre·em·ploy·ment	**pre·or·der**	**pre·treat·ment**
pre·en·roll·ment	**pre·paste**	**pre·trial**
pre·erect	**pre·pill**	**pre·trim**
pre·es·tab·lish	**pre·plan**	**pre·type**
pre·eth·i·cal	**pre·por·tion**	**pre·uni·fi·ca·tion**
pre·ex·per·i·ment	**pre·pres·i·den·tial**	**pre·uni·ver·si·ty**
pre·fade	**pre·price**	**pre·vi·a·ble**
pre·fas·cist	**pre·pri·ma·ry**	**pre·war**
pre·fight	**pre·prim·er**	**pre·wash**
pre·file	**pre·pro·duc·tion**	**pre·wean·ing**
pre·fi·nance	**pre·pro·gram**	**pre·whal·ing**
pre·fire	**pre·psy·che·del·ic**	**pre·work**
pre·flame	**pre·pub·li·ca·tion**	**pre·wrap**
pre·for·mat		

preach \'prēch\ *vb* [ME *prechen*, fr. OF *prechier*, fr. LL *praedicare*, fr. L, to proclaim publicly, fr. *prae-* pre- + *dicare* to proclaim — more at DICTION] *vi* (13c) **1** : to deliver a sermon **2** : to urge acceptance or abandonment of an idea or course of action; *specif* : to exhort in an officious or tiresome manner ~ *vt* **1** : to set forth in a sermon ⟨~ the gospel⟩ **2** : to advocate earnestly ⟨~*ed* revolution⟩ **3** : to deliver (as a sermon) publicly **4** : to bring, put, or affect by preaching ⟨~*ed* the . . . church out of debt —*Amer. Guide Series: Va.*⟩ — **preach·er** *n* — **preach·ing·ly** \'prē-chiŋ-lē\ *adv*

preach·ify \'prē-chə-ˌfī\ *vi* **-ified; -ify·ing** (1775) : to preach ineptly or tediously

preach·ment \'prēch-mənt\ *n* (14c) **1** : the act or practice of preaching **2** : SERMON, EXHORTATION; *specif* : a tedious or unwelcome one

preachy \'prē-chē\ *adj* **preach·i·er; -est** (1819) : marked by obvious moral exhortation : DIDACTIC — **preach·i·ly** \-chə-lē\ *adv* — **preach·i·ness** \-chē-nəs\ *n*

pre·ad·ap·ta·tion \ˌprē-ˌad-ˌap-ˈtā-shən\ *n* (ca. 1886) **1 :** the possession by an organism or group of characters that are not adapted to the ancestral environment but favor its survival in some other environment **2 :** a preadaptive character

pre·adapt·ed \ˌprē-ə-ˈdap-təd\ *adj* (1915) **:** characterized by preadaptation

pre·adap·tive \-ˈdap-tiv\ *adj* (1915) **:** of, relating to, or characterized by preadaptation

pre·ad·o·les·cence \ˈprē-ˌad-ᵊl-ˈes-ᵊn(t)s\ *n* (1930) **:** the period of human development just preceding adolescence; *specif* **:** the period between the approximate ages of 9 and 12 — **pre·ad·o·les·cent** \-ᵊnt\ *adj or n*

pre·am·ble \ˈprē-ˌam-bəl, prē-ˈ\ *n* [ME, fr. MF *preambule,* fr. ML *preambulum,* fr. LL, neut. of *praeambulus* walking in front of, fr. L *prae-* + *ambulare* to walk] (14c) **1 :** an introductory statement; *specif* **:** the introductory part of a constitution or statute that usu. states the reasons for and intent of the law **2 :** an introductory fact or circumstance; *esp* **:** one indicating what is to follow

pre·amp \ˈprē-ˌamp\ *n* [by shortening] (1949) **:** PREAMPLIFIER

pre·am·pli·fi·er \(ˈ)prē-ˈam-plə-ˌfī(-ə)r\ *n* (1935) **:** an amplifier designed to amplify extremely weak signals from a device (as a microphone, phonograph pickup, tuner, or television camera) before the signals are fed to additional amplifier circuits

pre·atom·ic \ˌprē-ə-ˈtäm-ik\ *adj* (1914) **:** of or relating to a time before the use of the atom bomb and atomic energy

pre·ax·i·al \(ˈ)prē-ˈak-sē-əl\ *adj* (1872) **:** situated in front of an axis of the body

preb·end \ˈpreb-ənd\ *n* [ME *prebende,* fr. MF, fr. ML *praebenda,* fr. LL, subsistence allowance granted by the state, fr. L, fem. of *praebendus,* gerundive of *praebēre* to offer, fr. *prae-* + *habēre* to hold — more at GIVE] (15c) **1 :** a stipend furnished by a cathedral or collegiate church to a clergyman (as a canon) in its chapter **2 :** PREBENDARY — **pre·ben·dal** \pri-ˈben-dᵊl, ˈpreb-ən-\ *adj*

preb·en·dary \ˈpreb-ən-ˌder-ē\ *n, pl* **-dar·ies** (15c) **1 :** a clergyman receiving a prebend for officiating and serving in the church **2 :** an honorary canon in a cathedral chapter

pre·bi·o·log·i·cal \ˌprē-ˌbī-ə-ˈläj-i-kəl\ *also* **pre·bi·o·log·ic** \-ik\ *adj* (1953) **:** of, relating to, or being chemical or environmental precursors of the origin of life ⟨~ molecules⟩

pre·bi·ot·ic \ˌprē-bī-ˈät-ik\ *adj* (1958) **:** PREBIOLOGICAL

pre·cal·cu·lus \(ˈ)prē-ˈkal-kyə-ləs\ *adj* (1964) **:** relating to or being mathematical prerequisites for the study of calculus — **precalculus** *n*

Pre·cam·bri·an \(ˈ)prē-ˈkam-brē-ən, -ˈkām-\ *adj* (1864) **:** of, relating to, or being the earliest era of geological history equivalent to the Archeozoic and Proterozoic eras or the corresponding system of rocks — **Precambrian** *n*

[1]**pre·can·cel** \(ˈ)prē-ˈkan(t)-səl\ *vt* (1921) **:** to cancel (a postage stamp) in advance of use — **pre·can·cel·la·tion** \ˌprē-ˌkan(t)-sə-ˈlā-shən\ *n*

[2]**precancel** *n* (1929) **:** a precanceled postage stamp

pre·can·cer·ous \(ˈ)prē-ˈkan(t)s-(ə-)rəs\ *adj* [ISV] (1882) **:** tending to become cancerous ⟨a ~ lesion⟩

pre·car·i·ous \pri-ˈkar-ē-əs, -ˈker-\ *adj* [L *precarius* obtained by entreaty, uncertain — more at PRAYER] (1646) **1** *archaic* **:** depending on the will or pleasure of another **2 :** dependent on uncertain premises **:** DUBIOUS ⟨~ generalizations⟩ **3 a :** dependent on chance circumstances, unknown conditions, or uncertain developments **b :** characterized by a lack of security or stability that threatens with danger ***syn*** see DANGEROUS — **pre·car·i·ous·ly** *adv* — **pre·car·i·ous·ness** *n*

pre·cast \ˈprē-ˈkast\ *adj* (1914) **:** being concrete that is cast in the form of a structural element (as a panel or beam) before being placed in final position

prec·a·to·ry \ˈprek-ə-ˌtōr-ē, -ˌtȯr-\ *adj* [LL *precatorius,* fr. L *precatus,* pp. of *precari* to pray — more at PRAY] (1636) **:** expressing a wish

pre·cau·tion \pri-ˈkȯ-shən\ *n* [F *précaution,* fr. LL *praecaution-, praecautio,* fr. L *praecautus,* pp. of *praecavēre* to guard against, fr. *prae-* + *cavēre* to be on one's guard — more at HEAR] (1603) **1 :** care taken in advance **:** FORESIGHT ⟨warned of the need for ~⟩ **2 :** a measure taken beforehand to prevent harm or secure good **:** SAFEGUARD — **pre·cau·tion·ary** \-shə-ˌner-ē\ *adj*

pre·cede \pri-ˈsēd\ *vb* **pre·ced·ed; pre·ced·ing** [ME *preceden,* fr. MF *preceder,* fr. L *praecedere,* fr. *prae-* pre- + *cedere* to go — more at CEDE] *vt* (15c) **1 :** to surpass in rank, dignity, or importance **2 :** to be, go, or come ahead or in front of **3 :** to be earlier than **4 :** to cause to be preceded **:** PREFACE ~ *vi* **:** to go or come before

pre·ce·dence \ˈpres-əd-ən(t)s, pri-ˈsēd-ᵊn(t)s\ *n* (1588) **1 a** *obs* **:** ANTECEDENT **b :** the fact of preceding in time **2 a :** the right to superior honor on a ceremonial or formal occasion **b :** the order of ceremonial or formal preference **c :** priority of importance **:** PREFERENCE

pre·ce·den·cy \-ən-sē, -ᵊn-sē\ *n* (1612) **:** PRECEDENCE

[1]**pre·ce·dent** \pri-ˈsēd-ᵊnt, ˈpres-əd-ənt\ *adj* [ME, fr. MF, fr. L *praecedent-, praecedens,* prp. of *praecedere*] (14c) **:** prior in time, order, arrangement, or significance

[2]**prec·e·dent** \ˈpres-əd-ənt\ *n* (15c) **1 :** an earlier occurrence of something similar **2 a :** something done or said that may serve as an example or rule to authorize or justify a subsequent act of the same or an analogous kind ⟨a verdict that had no ~⟩ **b :** the convention established by such a precedent or by long practice

pre·ced·ing \pri-ˈsēd-iŋ\ *adj* (15c) **:** that immediately precedes in time or place ⟨the ~ day⟩ ⟨~ paragraphs⟩

syn PRECEDING, ANTECEDENT, FOREGOING, PREVIOUS, PRIOR, FORMER, ANTERIOR mean being before. PRECEDING usu. implies being immediately before in time or in place; ANTECEDENT applies to order in time and may suggest a causal relation; FOREGOING applies chiefly to statements; PREVIOUS and PRIOR imply existing or occurring earlier, but PRIOR often adds an implication of greater importance; FORMER implies always a definite comparison or contrast with something that is latter; ANTERIOR applies to position before or ahead of usu. in space, sometimes in time or order.

pre·cen·sor \(ˈ)prē-ˈsen(t)-sər\ *vt* (1942) **:** to censor (a publication or film) before its release to the public

pre·cen·tor \pri-ˈsent-ər\ *n* [LL *praecentor,* fr. L *praecentus,* pp. of *praecinere* to sing before, fr. *prae-* + *canere* to sing — more at CHANT] (1613) **:** a leader of the singing of a choir or congregation — **pre·cen·to·ri·al** \ˌprē-ˌsen-ˈtōr-ē-əl, -ˈtȯr-\ *adj* — **pre·cen·tor·ship** \pri-ˈsent-ər-ˌship\ *n*

pre·cept \ˈprē-ˌsept\ *n* [ME, fr. L *praeceptum,* fr. neut. of *praeceptus,* pp. of *praecipere* to take beforehand, instruct, fr. *prae-* + *capere* to take — more at HEAVE] (14c) **1 :** a command or principle intended as a general rule of action **2 :** an order issued by legally constituted authority to a subordinate official ***syn*** see LAW

pre·cep·tive \pri-ˈsep-tiv\ *adj* (15c) **:** giving precepts **:** DIDACTIC

pre·cep·tor \pri-ˈsep-tər, ˈprē-ˌ\ *n* (15c) **1 a :** TEACHER, TUTOR **b :** the headmaster or principal of a school **2 :** the head of a preceptory of Knights Templars — **pre·cep·tor·ship** \-tər-ˌship\ *n*

[1]**pre·cep·to·ri·al** \pri-ˌsep-ˈtōr-ē-əl, ˌprē-, -ˈtȯr-\ *adj* (1727) **:** of, relating to, or making use of preceptors

[2]**preceptorial** *n* (ca. 1951) **:** a college course that emphasizes independent reading, discussion in small groups, and individual conferences with the teacher

pre·cep·to·ry \pri-ˈsep-t(ə-)rē, ˈprē-ˌ\ *n, pl* **-ries** (1540) **1 :** a subordinate house or community of the Knights Templars; *broadly* **:** COMMANDERY 1 **2 :** COMMANDERY 2

pre·cess \prē-ˈses, ˈprē-ˌ\ *vb* [back-formation fr. *precession*] *vi* (1529) **:** to progress with a movement of precession ~ *vt* **:** to cause to precess

pre·ces·sion \prē-ˈsesh-ən\ *n* [NL *praecession-, praecessio,* fr. ML, act of preceding, fr. L *praecessus,* pp. of *praecedere* to precede] (1594) **:** a comparatively slow gyration of the rotation axis of a spinning body about another line intersecting it so as to describe a cone caused by the application of a torque tending to change the direction of the rotation axis — **pre·ces·sion·al** \-ˈsesh-nəl, -ən-ᵊl\ *adj*

precession of the equinoxes (1621) **:** a slow westward motion of the equinoxes along the ecliptic caused by the gravitational action of sun and moon upon the protuberant matter about the earth's equator

pre–Chel·le·an \(ˈ)prē-ˈshel-ē-ən\ *adj* (1916) **:** of or relating to a lower Paleolithic culture preceding the Abbevillian and characterized by crudely flaked stone hand axes

pre–Chris·tian \-ˈkris(h)-chən\ *adj* (1828) **:** of, relating to, or being a time before the beginning of the Christian era

pré·cieux \prā-syœ̄\ *or* **pré·cieuse** \-syœ̄z\ *adj* [F *précieux,* masc., & *précieuse,* fem., lit., precious, fr. MF *precios*] (1727) **:** PRECIOUS 3

pre·cinct \ˈprē-ˌsiŋ(k)t\ *n* [ME, fr. ML *praecinctum,* fr. L, neut. of *praecinctus,* pp. of *praecingere* to gird about, fr. *prae-* pre- + *cingere* to gird — more at CINCTURE] (15c) **1 :** a part of a territory with definite bounds or functions often established for administrative purposes **:** DISTRICT: as **a :** a subdivision of a county, town, city, or ward for election purposes **b :** a division of a city for police control **2 a :** an enclosure bounded by the walls of a building — often used in pl. **b :** a sphere of thought, action, or influence — often used in pl. **3** *pl* **:** the region immediately surrounding a place **:** ENVIRONS **4 :** BOUNDARY — often used in pl. ⟨a ruined tower within the ~s of the squire's grounds —T. L. Peacock⟩

pre·ci·os·i·ty \ˌpres(h)-ē-ˈäs-ət-ē\ *n, pl* **-ties** (14c) **1 :** fastidious refinement **2 :** an instance of preciosity

[1]**pre·cious** \ˈpresh-əs\ *adj* [ME, fr. MF *precios,* fr. L *pretiosus,* fr. *pretium* price — more at PRICE] (14c) **1 :** of great value or high price **2 :** highly esteemed or cherished **3 :** excessively refined **:** AFFECTED **4 :** GREAT, THOROUGHGOING ⟨~ scoundrel⟩ — **pre·cious·ness** *n*

[2]**precious** *adv* (1595) **:** VERY, EXTREMELY ⟨has ~ little to say⟩

pre·cious·ly *adv* (14c) **1 :** in a precious manner **2 :** PRECIOUS

pre·ci·pe *var of* PRAECIPE

prec·i·pice \ˈpres(-ə-)pəs\ *n* [MF, fr. L *praecipitium,* fr. *praecipit-, praeceps* headlong, fr. *prae-* + *caput* head — more at HEAD] (1613) **1 :** a very steep or overhanging place **2 :** a hazardous situation; *broadly* **:** BRINK

pre·cip·i·ta·ble \pri-ˈsip-ət-ə-bəl\ *adj* (1670) **:** capable of being precipitated

pre·cip·i·tance \pri-ˈsip-ət-ən(t)s\ *n* (1667) **:** PRECIPITANCY

pre·cip·i·tan·cy \-ən-sē\ *n* (1646) **:** undue hastiness or suddenness

[1]**pre·cip·i·tant** \-ənt\ *adj* (1671) **:** PRECIPITATE — **pre·cip·i·tant·ly** *adv* — **pre·cip·i·tant·ness** *n*

[2]**precipitant** *n* (ca. 1684) **:** a precipitating agent; *esp* **:** one that causes the formation of a precipitate

[1]**pre·cip·i·tate** \pri-ˈsip-ə-ˌtāt\ *vb* **-tat·ed; -tat·ing** [L *praecipitatus,* pp. of *praecipitare,* fr. *praecipit-, praeceps*] *vt* (1575) **1 a :** to throw violently **:** HURL ⟨the quandaries into which the release of nuclear energy has *precipitated* mankind —A. B. Arons⟩ **b :** to throw down **2 :** to bring about esp. abruptly ⟨~ a scandal that would end with his expulsion —John Cheever⟩ **3 a :** to cause to separate from solution or suspension **b :** to cause (vapor) to condense and fall or deposit ~ *vi* **1 a :** to fall headlong **b :** to fall or come suddenly into some condition **2 :** to move or act precipitately **3 a :** to separate from solution or suspension **b :** to condense from a vapor and fall as rain or snow — **pre·cip·i·ta·tive** \-ˌtāt-iv\ *adj* — **pre·cip·i·ta·tor** \-ˌtāt-ər\ *n*

[2]**pre·cip·i·tate** \pri-ˈsip-ət-ət, -ə-ˌtāt\ *n* [NL *praecipitatum,* fr. L, neut. of *praecipitatus*] (1594) **1 :** a substance separated from a solution or suspension by chemical or physical change usu. as an insoluble amorphous or crystalline solid **2 :** a product, result, or outcome of some process or action

[3]**pre·cip·i·tate** \pri-ˈsip-ət-ət\ *adj* (1658) **1 :** exhibiting violent or unwise speed **2 a :** falling, flowing, or rushing with steep descent **b :** PRECIPITOUS — **pre·cip·i·tate·ly** *adv* — **pre·cip·i·tate·ness** *n*

syn PRECIPITATE, HEADLONG, ABRUPT, IMPETUOUS, SUDDEN mean showing undue haste or unexpectedness. PRECIPITATE stresses lack of due deliberation and implies prematureness of action ⟨the army's *precipitate* withdrawal⟩ HEADLONG stresses rashness and lack of forethought ⟨a *headlong* flight from arrest⟩ ABRUPT stresses curtness and a lack of warning or ceremony ⟨an *abrupt* refusal⟩ IMPETUOUS stresses extreme impatience or impulsiveness ⟨an *impetuous* lover⟩ SUDDEN stresses unexpectedness and sharpness or violence of action ⟨flew into a *sudden* rage⟩

pre·cip·i·ta·tion \pri-ˌsip-ə-ˈtā-shən\ *n* (1502) **1 :** the quality or state of being precipitate **:** HASTE **2 :** an act, process, or instance of precipitating; *esp* : the process of forming a precipitate **3** : something precipitated: as **a** : a deposit on the earth of hail, mist, rain, sleet, or snow; *also* : the quantity of water deposited **b** : PRECIPITATE 1

pre·cip·i·tin \pri-ˈsip-ət-ən\ *n* [ISV, fr. *precipitate*] (1900) : an antibody that forms an insoluble precipitate when it unites with its antigen

pre·cip·i·tin·o·gen \pri-ˌsip-ə-ˈtin-ə-jən\ *n* (1904) : an antigen that stimulates the production of a specific precipitin

pre·cip·i·tous \pri-ˈsip-ət-əs\ *adj* [F *précipiteux,* fr. MF, fr. L *precipitium* precipice] (1613) **1** : PRECIPITATE 1 **2 a** : very steep, perpendicular, or overhanging in rise or fall ⟨a ~ slope⟩ **b** : having precipitous sides ⟨a ~ gorge⟩ **c** : having a very steep ascent ⟨a ~ street⟩ ***syn*** see STEEP — **pre·cip·i·tous·ly** *adv* — **pre·cip·i·tous·ness** *n*

pré·cis \prā-ˈsē, ˈprā-(ˌ)sē\ *n, pl* **pré·cis** \-ˈsēz, -(ˌ)sēz\ [F, fr. *précis* precise] (1760) : a concise summary of essential points, statements, or facts

pre·cise \pri-ˈsīs\ *adj* [MF *precis,* fr. L *praecisus,* pp. of *praecidere* to cut off, fr. *prae-* + *caedere* to cut — more at CONCISE] (1526) **1** : exactly or sharply defined or stated **2** : minutely exact **3** : strictly conforming to a pattern, standard, or convention **4** : distinguished from every other ⟨at just that ~ moment⟩ ***syn*** see CORRECT — **pre·cise·ness** *n*

pre·cise·ly \-ˈsī-slē\ *adv* (15c) **1** : EXACTLY **2** — used as an intensive ⟨was popular ~ because he was so kind⟩

pre·ci·sian \pri-ˈsizh-ən\ *n* (1571) **1** : a person who stresses or practices scrupulous adherence to a strict standard esp. of religious observance or morality **2** : PURITAN 1

1pre·ci·sion \pri-ˈsizh-ən\ *n* (1740) **1** : the quality or state of being precise : EXACTNESS **2 a** : the degree of refinement with which an operation is performed or a measurement stated **b** : the accuracy (as in binary or decimal places) with which a number can be represented usu. expressed in terms of the number of computer words available for representation ⟨double ~ arithmetic permits the representation of an expression by two computer words⟩ **3** : RELEVANCE 2 — **pre·ci·sion·ist** \-ˈsizh-(ə-)nəst\ *n*

2precision *adj* (1875) **1** : adapted for extremely accurate measurement or operation **2** : held to low tolerance in manufacture **3** : marked by precision of execution

pre·clin·i·cal \(ˈ)prē-ˈklin-i-kəl\ *adj* (1926) : of, relating to, or concerned with the period preceding clinical manifestations

pre·clude \pri-ˈklüd\ *vt* **pre·clud·ed; pre·clud·ing** [L *praecludere,* fr. *prae-* + *claudere* to close — more at CLOSE] (1629) **1** *archaic* : CLOSE **2** : to make impossible by necessary consequence : rule out in advance — **pre·clu·sion** \-ˈklü-zhən\ *n* — **pre·clu·sive** \-ˈklü-siv, -ziv\ *adj* — **pre·clu·sive·ly** *adv*

pre·co·cial \pri-ˈkō-shəl\ *adj* [NL *praecoces* precocial birds, fr. L, pl. of *praecoc-, precox*] (ca. 1872) : capable of a high degree of independent activity from birth ⟨ducklings are ~⟩ — compare ALTRICIAL

pre·co·cious \pri-ˈkō-shəs\ *adj* [L *praecoc-, praecox* early ripening, precocious, fr. *prae-* + *coquere* to cook — more at COOK] (1650) **1** : exceptionally early in development or occurrence **2** : exhibiting mature qualities at an unusually early age — **pre·co·cious·ly** *adv* — **pre·co·cious·ness** *n* — **pre·coc·i·ty** \pri-ˈkäs-ət-ē\ *n*

pre·cog·ni·tion \ˌprē-(ˌ)käg-ˈnish-ən\ *n* [LL *praecognition-, praecognitio,* fr. L *praecognitus,* pp. of *praecognoscere* to know beforehand, fr. *prae-* + *cognoscere* to know — more at COGNITION] (ca. 1611) : clairvoyance relating to an event or state not yet experienced — **pre·cog·ni·tive** \(ˈ)prē-ˈkäg-nət-iv\ *adj*

pre–Co·lum·bi·an \ˌprē-kə-ˈləm-bē-ən\ *adj* (1888) : preceding or belonging to the time before the arrival of Columbus in America

pre·con·ceive \ˌprē-kən-ˈsēv\ *vt* (1597) : to form (as an opinion) prior to actual knowledge or experience ⟨*preconceived* notions⟩

pre·con·cep·tion \-ˈsep-shən\ *n* (1625) **1** : a preconceived idea **2** : PREJUDICE

pre·con·cert \ˌprē-kən-ˈsərt\ *vt* (1748) : to settle by prior agreement

1pre·con·di·tion \-ˈdish-ən\ *n* (1825) : PREREQUISITE

2precondition *vt* (1922) : to put in a proper or desired condition or frame of mind esp. in preparation

1pre·con·scious \(ˈ)prē-ˈkän-chəs\ *adj* (1860) : not present in consciousness but capable of being recalled without encountering any inner resistance or repression — **pre·con·scious·ly** *adv*

2preconscious *n* (ca. 1922) : the preconscious part of the psyche esp. in psychoanalysis

pre·cook \(ˈ)prē-ˈku̇k\ *vt* (1926) : to cook partially or entirely before final cooking or reheating

pre·crit·i·cal \-ˈkrit-i-kəl\ *adj* (1899) : prior to the development of critical capacity

pre·cur·sor \pri-ˈkər-sər, ˈprē-ˌ\ *n* [L *praecursor,* fr. *praecursus,* pp. of *praecurrere* to run before, fr. *prae-* pre- + *currere* to run — more at CURRENT] (1504) **1 a** : one that precedes and indicates the approach of another **b** : PREDECESSOR **2** : a substance from which another substance is formed ***syn*** see FORERUNNER — **pre·cur·so·ry** \-ˈkərs-(ə-)rē\ *adj*

pre·da·ceous *or* **pre·da·cious** \pri-ˈdā-shəs\ *adj* [L *praedari* to prey upon (fr. *praeda* prey) + E *-aceous* or *-acious* (as in *rapacious*) — more at PREY] (1713) **1** : living by preying on other animals : PREDATORY **2** *usu predacious* : tending to devour or despoil : RAPACIOUS— **pre·da·ceous·ness** *n* — **pre·dac·i·ty** \-ˈdas-ət-ē\ *n*

pre·date \(ˈ)prē-ˈdāt\ *vt* (ca. 1864) : ANTEDATE

pre·da·tion \pri-ˈdā-shən\ *n* [L *praedation-, praedatio,* fr. *praedatus,* pp. of *praedari*] (15c) **1** : the act of preying or plundering : DEPREDATION **2** : a mode of life in which food is primarily obtained by the killing and consuming of animals

predation pressure *n* (1942) : the effects of predation on a natural community esp. with respect to the survival of species preyed upon

pred·a·tor \ˈpred-ət-ər, -ə-ˌtȯ(ə)r\ *n* (1912) **1** : one that preys, destroys, or devours **2** : an animal that lives by predation

pred·a·to·ry \ˈpred-ə-ˌtōr-ē, -ˌtȯr-\ *adj* (1589) **1 a** : of, relating to, or practicing plunder, pillage, or rapine **b** : showing a disposition to injure or exploit others for one's own gain **2** : living by predation : PREDACEOUS; *also* : adapted to predation

pre·de·cease \ˌprēd-i-ˈsēs\ *vb* **-ceased; -ceas·ing** *vt* (1593) : to die before (another person) ~ *vi* : to die first — **predecease** *n*

pre·de·ces·sor \ˈpred-ə-ˌses-ər, ˈprēd-; ˌpred-ə-ˈ, ˌprēd-\ *n* [ME *predecessour,* fr. MF *predecesseur,* fr. LL *praedecessor,* fr. L *prae-* pre- + *decessor* retiring governor, fr. *decessus,* pp. of *decedere* to depart, retire from office — more at DECEASE] (14c) **1** : one that precedes; *esp* : a person who has previously occupied a position or office to which another has succeeded **2** *archaic* : ANCESTOR

pre·des·ti·nar·i·an \(ˌ)prē-ˌdes-tə-ˈner-ē-ən\ *n* [*predestination* + *-arian*] (1667) : one who believes in predestination — **predestinarian** *adj* — **pre·des·ti·nar·i·an·ism** \-ē-ə-ˌniz-əm\ *n*

1pre·des·ti·nate \prē-ˈdes-tə-nət, -ˌnāt\ *adj* [ME, fr. L *praedestinatus,* pp. of *praedestinare*] (14c) : destined, fated, or determined beforehand

2pre·des·ti·nate \-ˌnāt\ *vt* **-nat·ed; -nat·ing** [ME *predestinaten,* fr. L *praedestinatus,* pp.] (15c) **1** : to foreordain to an earthly or eternal lot or destiny by divine decree **2** *archaic* : PREDETERMINE

pre·des·ti·na·tion \(ˌ)prē-ˌdes-tə-ˈnā-shən\ *n* (14c) **1** : the act of predestinating : the state of being predestinated **2** : the doctrine that God in consequence of his foreknowledge of all events infallibly guides those who are destined for salvation

pre·des·ti·na·tor \prē-ˈdes-tə-ˌnāt-ər\ *n* (1700) **1** : one that predestinates **2** *archaic* : PREDESTINARIAN

pre·des·tine \(ˈ)prē-ˈdes-tən\ *vt* [ME *predestinen,* fr. MF or L; MF *predestiner,* fr. L *praedestinare,* fr. *prae-* + *destinare* to determine — more at DESTINE] (14c) : to destine, decree, determine, appoint, or settle beforehand; *esp* : PREDESTINATE 1

pre·de·ter·mi·na·tion \ˌprēd-i-ˌtər-mə-ˈnā-shən\ *n* (1647) **1** : the act of predetermining : the state of being predetermined: as **a** : the ordaining of events beforehand **b** : a fixing or settling in advance **2** : a purpose formed beforehand

pre·de·ter·mine \-ˈtər-mən\ *vt* [LL *praedeterminare,* fr. L *prae-* + *determinare* to determine] (1625) **1 a** : FOREORDAIN, PREDESTINE **b** : to determine beforehand **2** : to impose a direction or tendency on beforehand

pre·de·ter·min·er \-ˈtərm-(ə-)nər\ *n* (1959) : a limiting noun modifier (as *both* or *all*) characterized by occurrence before the determiner in a noun phrase

pre·di·a·be·tes \ˌprē-ˌdī-ə-ˈbēt-ēz, -ˈbēt-əs\ *n* (1935) : an inapparent abnormal state that precedes the development of clinically evident diabetes — **pre·di·a·bet·ic** \-ˈbet-ik\ *adj or n*

pre·di·al \ˈprēd-ē-əl\ *adj* [ML *praedialis,* fr. L *praedium* landed property, fr. *praed-, praes* bondsman] (ca. 1529) : of or relating to land or its products

1pred·i·ca·ble \ˈpred-i-kə-bəl\ *n* [ML *praedicabile,* fr. neut. of *praedicabilis*] (1551) : something that may be predicated; *esp* : one of the five most general kinds of attribution in traditional logic that include genus, species, difference, property, and accident

2predicable *adj* [ML *praedicabilis,* fr. LL *praedicare* to predicate] (ca. 1598) : capable of being asserted

pre·dic·a·ment \pri-ˈdik-ə-mənt, *1 is usu* ˈpred-i-kə-\ *n* [ME, fr. LL *praedicamentum,* fr. *praedicare*] (14c) **1** : the character, status, or classification assigned by a predication; *specif* : CATEGORY 1 **2** : CONDITION, STATE; *esp* : a difficult, perplexing, or trying situation

1pred·i·cate \ˈpred-i-kət\ *n* [LL *praedicatum,* fr. neut. of *praedicatus*] (1532) **1 a** : something that is affirmed or denied of the subject in a proposition in logic ⟨in "paper is white," whiteness is the ~⟩ **b** : a term designating a property or relation **2** : the part of a sentence or clause that expresses what is said of the subject and that usu. consists of a verb with or without objects, complements, or adverbial modifiers — **pred·i·ca·tive** \-kət-iv, ˈpred-ə-ˌkāt-\ *adj*

2pred·i·cate \ˈpred-ə-ˌkāt\ *vt* **-cat·ed; -cat·ing** [LL *praedicatus,* pp. of *praedicare* to assert, predicate logically, preach, fr. L, to proclaim publicly, assert — more at PREACH] (1552) **1 a** : AFFIRM, DECLARE **b** *archaic* : PREACH **2 a** : to assert to be a quality, attribute, or property — used with following *of* ⟨~s intelligence of man⟩ **b** : to make (a term) the predicate in a proposition **3** : FOUND, BASE ⟨his theory is *predicated* on recent findings⟩ **4** : IMPLY

3pred·i·cate \ˈpred-i-kət\ *adj* (1887) : completing the meaning of a copula ⟨~ adjective⟩ ⟨~ noun⟩

predicate calculus *n* (1950) : the branch of symbolic logic that uses symbols for quantifiers and for arguments and predicates of propositions as well as for unanalyzed propositions and logical connectives — called also *functional calculus;* compare PROPOSITIONAL CALCULUS

predicate nominative *n* (1887) : a noun or pronoun in the nominative or common case completing the meaning of a copula

pred·i·ca·tion \ˌpred-ə-ˈkā-shən\ *n* [ME *predicacion,* fr. MF *predication,* fr. L *praedication-, praedicatio,* fr. *praedicatus,* pp.] (14c). **1** *archaic* **a** : an act of proclaiming or preaching **b** : SERMON **2** : an act or instance of predicating: as **a** : the expression of action, state, or quality by a grammatical predicate **b** : the logical affirmation of something about another; *esp* : assignment of something to a class

pred·i·ca·to·ry \ˈpred-i-kə-ˌtōr-ē, -ˌtȯr-\ *adj* [LL *praedicatorius,* fr. *praedicatus,* pp. of *praedicare* to preach] (1652) : of or relating to preaching

pre·dict \pri-ˈdikt\ *vb* [L *praedictus,* pp. of *praedicere,* fr. *prae-* pre- + *dicere* to say — more at DICTION] *vt* (1632) : to declare in advance; *esp* : foretell on the basis of observation, experience, or scientific reason ~ *vi* : to make a prediction ***syn*** see FORETELL — **pre·dict·abil·i·ty** \-ˌdik-tə-ˈbil-ət-ē\ *n* — **pre·dict·able** \-ˈdik-tə-bəl\ *adj* — **pre·dict·ably** \-blē\ *adv* — **pre·dic·tive** \-ˈdik-tiv\ *adj* — **pre·dic·tive·ly** \-lē\ *adv* — **pre·dic·tor** \-ˈdik-tər\ *n*

pre·dic·tion \pri-ˈdik-shən\ *n* (1561) **1** : an act of predicting **2** : something that is predicted : FORECAST

pre·di·gest \ˌprēd-ī-ˈjest, ˌprēd-ə-\ *vt* (1663) **1** : to subject to predigestion **2** : to simplify for easy use ⟨~*ed* classics for children⟩

pre·di·ges·tion \-ˈjes(h)-chən\ *n* (ca. 1607) : artificial partial digestion of food esp. for use in cases of illness or impaired digestion

pre·di·lec·tion \ˌpred-ᵊl-ˈek-shən, ˌprēd-\ *n* [F *prédilection,* fr. ML *praedilectus,* pp. of *praediligere* to love more, prefer, fr. L *prae-* + *diligere* to love — more at DILIGENT] (1742) : a prepossession in favor of something : TASTE 6

syn PREDILECTION, PREPOSSESSION, PREJUDICE, BIAS mean an attitude of mind that predisposes one to favor something. PREDILECTION implies a strong liking deriving from one's temperament or experience; PREPOSSESSION suggests a fixed conception likely to preclude objective judgment of anything counter to it; PREJUDICE usu. implies an unfavorable prepossession and connotes a feeling rooted in suspicion, fear, or intolerence; BIAS implies an unreasoned and unfair distortion of judgment in favor of or against a person or thing.

pre·dis·pose \ˌprēd-is-ˈpōz\ *vt* (1646) **1 :** to dispose in advance ⟨a good teacher ~*s* children to learn⟩ **2 :** to make susceptible ⟨~ the miner to rheumatism —Lewis Mumford⟩ ~ *vi* **:** to bring about susceptibility *syn* see INCLINE — **pre·dis·po·si·tion** \ˌprē-ˌdis-pə-ˈzish-ən\ *n*

pred·nis·o·lone \pred-ˈnis-ə-ˌlōn\ *n* [blend of *prednisone* and *-ol*] (1955) **:** a glucocorticoid $C_{21}H_{28}O_5$ that is a dehydrogenated analogue of cortisol and is used often in the form of an ester or methyl derivative esp. as an anti-inflammatory drug in the treatment of arthritis

pred·ni·sone \ˈpred-nə-ˌsōn *also* -ˌzōn\ *n* [prob. fr. *pregnane* ($C_{21}H_{36}$) + *diene* (compound containing two double bonds) + *cortisone*] (1955) **:** a glucocorticoid $C_{21}H_{26}O_5$ that is a dehydrogenated analogue of cortisone and is used as an anti-inflammatory agent esp. in the treatment of arthritis, as an antineoplastic agent, and as an immunosuppressant

pre·doc·tor·al \(ˈ)prē-ˈdäk-t(ə-)rəl\ *adj* (1937) **1 a :** of or relating to the level before the doctoral in a program of academic study **b :** of or relating to academic study leading to the doctoral degree **2 :** being engaged in predoctoral academic work

pre·dom·i·nance \pri-ˈdäm(-ə)-nən(t)s\ *n* (1602) **:** the quality or state of being predominant

pre·dom·i·nan·cy \-nən-sē\ *n* (1598) **:** PREDOMINANCE

pre·dom·i·nant \-nənt\ *adj* [MF, fr. ML *praedominant-, praedominans,* prp. of *praedominari* to predominate, fr. L *prae-* + *dominari* to rule, govern — more at DOMINATE] (1576) **1 :** having superior strength, influence, or authority **:** PREVAILING **2 :** being most frequent or common *syn* see DOMINANT

pre·dom·i·nant·ly \-nənt-lē\ *adv* (1681) **:** for the most part **:** MAINLY

1**pre·dom·i·nate** \-nət\ *adj* [alter. of *predominant*] (1591) **:** PREDOMINANT — **pre·dom·i·nate·ly** *adv*

2**pre·dom·i·nate** \pri-ˈdäm-ə-ˌnāt\ *vb* [ML *praedominatus,* pp. of *praedominari*] *vi* (1594) **1 :** to hold advantage in numbers or quantity **:** PREPONDERATE **2 :** to exert controlling power or influence **:** PREVAIL ~ *vt* **:** to exert control over **:** DOMINATE — **pre·dom·i·na·tion** \-ˌdäm-ə-ˈnā-shən\ *n*

pree \ˈprē\ *vt* **preed; pree·ing** [alter. of *preve* to prove, test, fr. ME *preven,* fr. OF *preuv-,* stem of *prover* to prove] *Scot* (ca. 1700) **:** to taste tentatively **:** SAMPLE

pre·emer·gence \ˌprē-ə-ˈmər-jən(t)s\ *adj* (1935) **:** used or occurring before emergence of seedlings above the ground ⟨~ weed control⟩

pre·emer·gent \-jənt\ *adj* (1959) **:** PREEMERGENCE

pree·mie \ˈprē-mē\ *n* [*premature* + *-ie*] (1927) **:** a baby born prematurely

pre·em·i·nence \prē-ˈem-ə-nən(t)s\ *n* (15c) **:** the quality or state of being preeminent **:** SUPERIORITY

pre·em·i·nent \-nənt\ *adj* [LL *praeeminent-, praeeminens,* fr. L, prp. of *praeeminēre* to be outstanding, fr. *prae-* + *eminēre* to stand out — more at EMINENT] (15c) **:** having paramount rank, dignity, or importance **:** OUTSTANDING — **pre·em·i·nent·ly** *adv*

pre·empt \prē-ˈem(p)t\ *vb* [back-formation fr. *preemption*] *vt* (1850) **1 :** to acquire (as land) by preemption **2 :** to seize upon to the exclusion of others **:** take for oneself ⟨the movement was then ~*ed* by a lunatic fringe⟩ **3 :** to take the place of **:** take precedence over ⟨the program did not appear, having been ~*ed* by a baseball game —Robert MacNeil⟩ **4 :** to gain a commanding or preeminent place in ~ *vi* **:** to make a preemptive bid in bridge — **pre·emp·tor** \-ˈem(p)-tər\ *n*

pre·emp·tion \-ˈem(p)-shən\ *n* [ML *praeemptus,* pp. of *praeemere* to buy before, fr. L *prae-* pre- + *emere* to buy — more at REDEEM] (1602) **1 a :** the right of purchasing before others; *esp* **:** one given by the government to the actual settler upon a tract of public land **b :** the purchase of something under this right **2 :** a prior seizure or appropriation **:** a taking possession before others

pre·emp·tive \-ˈem(p)-tiv\ *adj* (1855) **1 a :** of or relating to preemption **b :** having power to preempt **2** *of a bid in bridge* **:** higher than necessary and designed to shut out bids by the opponents **3 :** giving a stockholder first option to purchase new stock in an amount proportionate to his existing holdings ⟨a ~ right⟩ **4 :** marked by the seizing of the initiative **:** initiated by oneself ⟨a ~ attack⟩ — **pre·emp·tive·ly** *adv*

1**preen** \ˈprēn\ *n* [ME *prene,* fr. OE *prēon;* akin to MHG *pfrieme* awl] (bef. 12c) **1** *dial chiefly Brit* **:** PIN **2** *dial chiefly Brit* **:** BROOCH

2**preen** *vt, chiefly Scot* (1572) **:** 2PIN

3**preen** *vb* [ME *preinen*] *vt* (14c) **1 :** to dress or smooth (oneself) up **:** PRIMP **2 :** to trim or dress with or as if with a bill **3 :** to pride or congratulate (oneself) for achievement ~ *vi* **1 :** to make oneself sleek **2 :** GLOAT, SWELL — **preen·er** *n*

pre–en·gi·neered \ˌprē-ˌen-jə-ˈni(ə)rd\ *adj* (1951) **:** constructed of or employing prefabricated modules ⟨a ~ building⟩

pre·ex·il·ian \ˌprē-eg-ˈzil-ē-ən, -ˈzil-yən\ *or* **pre·ex·il·ic** \-ˈzil-ik\ *adj* (1863) **:** previous to the exile of the Jews to Babylon in about 600 B.C.

pre·ex·ist \ˌprē-ig-ˈzist\ *vi* (1599) **:** to exist earlier or before ~ *vt* **:** ANTEDATE

pre·ex·is·tence \-ˈzis-tən(t)s\ *n* (ca. 1652) **:** existence in a former state or previous to something else; *specif* **:** existence of the soul before its union with the body — **pre·ex·is·tent** \-tənt\ *adj*

pre·fab \(ˈ)prē-ˈfab, ˈprē-ˌ\ *n* (1937) **:** a prefabricated structure — **prefab** *adj*

pre·fab·ri·cate \(ˈ)prē-ˈfab-ri-ˌkāt\ *vt* (1932) **1 :** to fabricate the parts of at a factory so that construction consists mainly of assembling and uniting standardized parts **2 :** to produce artificially — **pre·fab·ri·ca·tion** \ˌprē-ˌfab-ri-ˈkā-shən\ *n*

1**pref·ace** \ˈpref-əs\ *n* [ME, fr. MF, fr. ML *prephatia,* alter. of L *praefation-, praefatio* foreword, fr. *praefatus,* pp. of *praefari* to say beforehand, fr. *prae-* pre- + *fari* to say — more at BAN] (14c) **1** *often cap* **:** a variable doxology beginning with the Sursum Corda and ending with the Sanctus in traditional eucharistic liturgies **2 :** the introductory remarks of a speaker or author **3 :** APPROACH, PRELIMINARY

2**preface** *vb* **pref·aced; pref·ac·ing** *vi* (1619) **:** to make introductory remarks ~ *vt* **1 :** to say or write as preface ⟨a note *prefaced* to the manuscript⟩ **2 :** PRECEDE, HERALD **3 :** to introduce by or begin with a preface **4 :** to stand in front of ⟨a porch ~*s* the entrance⟩ **5 :** to be a preliminary to — **pref·ac·er** *n*

pref·a·to·ry \ˈpref-ə-ˌtōr-ē, -ˌtȯr-\ *adj* [L *praefatus,* pp.] (1675) **1 :** of, relating to, or constituting a preface **2 :** located in front

pre·fect \ˈprē-ˌfekt\ *n* [ME, fr. MF, fr. L *praefectus,* fr. pp. of *praeficere* to place at the head of, fr. *prae-* + *facere* to make — more at DO] (14c) **1 :** any of various high officials or magistrates of differing functions and ranks in ancient Rome **2 :** a chief officer or chief magistrate **3 :** a student monitor in a private school

prefect apostolic *n* (ca. 1909) **:** a Roman Catholic clergyman and usu. a priest with quasi-episcopal jurisdiction over a district of a missionary territory

pre·fec·ture \ˈprē-ˌfek-chər\ *n* (1608) **1 :** the office or term of office of a prefect **2 :** the official residence of a prefect **3 :** the district governed by a prefect — **pre·fec·tur·al** \-chə-rəl, pri-ˈ\ *adj*

prefecture apostolic *n* (ca. 1911) **:** the district under a prefect apostolic

pre·fer \pri-ˈfər\ *vt* **pre·ferred; pre·fer·ring** [ME *preferren,* fr. MF *preferer,* fr. L *praeferre* to put before, prefer, fr. *prae-* + *ferre* to carry — more at BEAR] (14c) **1** *archaic* **:** to promote or advance to a rank or position **2 :** to like better or best ⟨~*s* sports to reading⟩ ⟨~*s* to watch TV⟩ **3 :** to give (a creditor) priority **4** *archaic* **:** to put or set forward or before someone **:** RECOMMEND **5 :** to bring or lay against someone ⟨won't ~ charges⟩ **6 :** to bring forward or lay before one for consideration — **pre·fer·rer** *n*

pref·er·a·ble \ˈpref-(ə-)rə-bəl, ˈpref-ər-bəl *also* pri-ˈfər-ə-bəl\ *adj* (1648) **:** having greater value or desirability **:** being preferred — **pref·er·a·bil·i·ty** \ˌpref-(ə-)rə-ˈbil-ət-ē\ *n* — **pref·er·a·bly** \-blē\ *adv*

pref·er·ence \ˈpref-ərn(t)s, ˈpref-(ə-)rən(t)s\ *n* [F *préférence,* fr. ML *praeferentia,* fr. L *praeferent-, praeferens,* prp. of *praeferre*] (1656) **1 a :** the act of preferring **:** the state of being preferred **b :** the power or opportunity of choosing **2 :** one that is preferred **3 :** the act, fact, or principle of giving advantages to some over others **4 :** priority in the right to demand and receive satisfaction of an obligation *syn* see CHOICE

pref·er·en·tial \ˌpref-ə-ˈren-chəl\ *adj* (1849) **1 :** showing preference **2 :** employing or creating a preference in trade relations **3 :** designed to permit expression of preference among candidates ⟨a ~ primary⟩ **4 :** giving preference esp. in hiring to union members ⟨a ~ shop⟩ — **pref·er·en·tial·ly** \-ˈrench-(ə-)lē\ *adv*

pre·fer·ment \pri-ˈfər-mənt\ *n* (15c) **1 a :** advancement or promotion in dignity, office, or station **b :** a position or office of honor or profit **2 :** priority or seniority in right esp. to receive payment or to purchase property on equal terms with others **3 :** the act of bringing forward (as charges)

preferred stock *n* (ca. 1859) **:** stock guaranteed priority by a corporation's charter over common stock in the payment of dividends and usu. in the distribution of assets

pre·fig·u·ra·tion \(ˌ)prē-ˌfig-(y)ə-ˈrā-shən\ *n* (14c) **1 :** the act of prefiguring **:** the state of being prefigured **2 :** something that prefigures

pre·fig·u·ra·tive \(ˈ)prē-ˈfig-(y)ə-rət-iv\ *adj* (1504) **:** of, relating to, or showing by prefiguration — **pre·fig·u·ra·tive·ly** *adv* — **pre·fig·u·ra·tive·ness** *n*

pre·fig·ure \(ˈ)prē-ˈfig-yər, *esp Brit* -ˈfig-ər\ *vt* [ME *prefiguren,* fr. LL *praefigurare,* fr. L *prae-* pre- + *figurare* to shape, picture, fr. *figura* figure] (15c) **1 :** to show, suggest, or announce by an antecedent type, image, or likeness **2 :** to picture or imagine beforehand **:** FORESEE — **pre·fig·ure·ment** \-mənt\ *n*

1**pre·fix** *vt* [ME *prefixen,* fr. MF *prefixer,* fr. *pre-* + *fixer* to fix, fr. *fix* fixed, fr. L *fixus* — more at FIX] (15c) **1** \(ˈ)prē-ˈfiks\ **:** to fix or appoint beforehand **2** \ˈprē-ˌ, prē-ˈ\ [partly fr. 2*prefix*] **:** to place in front; *esp* **:** to add as a prefix ⟨~ a syllable to a word⟩

2**pre·fix** \ˈprē-ˌfiks\ *n* [NL *praefixum,* fr. L, neut. of *praefixus,* pp. of *praefigere* to fasten before, fr. *prae-* + *figere* to fasten — more at DIKE] (1646) **1 :** an affix attached to the beginning of a word, base, or phrase and serving to produce a derivative word or an inflectional form — compare SUFFIX **2 :** a title used before a person's name — **pre·fix·al** \ˈprē-ˌfik-səl, prē-ˈ\ *adj*

pre·flight \ˈprē-ˈflīt\ *adj* (1922) **:** preparing for or preliminary to flight

pre·fo·cus \(ˈ)prē-ˈfō-kəs\ *vt* (1948) **:** to focus beforehand (as automotive headlights before installation)

pre·form \ˈprē-ˈfȯ(ə)rm\ *vt* [L *praeformare,* fr. *prae-* + *formare* to form, fr. *forma* form] (1601) **1 :** to form or shape beforehand **2 :** to bring to approximate shape and size — **pre·form** \-ˌfȯrm\ *n*

pre·for·ma·tion \ˌprē-fȯr-ˈmā-shən\ *n* (1732) **1 :** previous formation **2 :** the now discredited theory that every germ cell contains the organism of its kind fully formed and that development consists merely in increase in size

1**pre·fron·tal** \(ˈ)prē-ˈfrənt-ᵊl\ *adj* (1854) **:** anterior to or involving the anterior part of a frontal structure ⟨a ~ bone⟩

2**prefrontal** *n* (1854) **:** a prefrontal part (as a bone)

pre·gan·gli·on·ic \ˌprē-ˌgaŋ-glē-ˈän-ik\ *adj* (1895) **:** proximal to a ganglion; *specif* **:** of, relating to, or being a usu. medullated axon arising from a cell body in the central nervous system and terminating in an autonomic ganglion — compare POSTGANGLIONIC

preg·na·ble \ˈpreg-nə-bəl\ *adj* [alter. of ME *prenable,* fr. MF — more at IMPREGNABLE] (15c) **:** vulnerable to capture ⟨a ~ fort⟩ — **preg·na·bil·i·ty** \ˌpreg-nə-ˈbil-ət-ē\ *n*

preg·nan·cy \ˈpreg-nən-sē\ *n, pl* **-cies** (15c) **1 :** the quality of being pregnant (as in meaning) **2 :** the condition of being pregnant **:** GESTATION **3 :** an instance of being pregnant

1**preg·nant** \ˈpreg-nənt\ *adj* [ME *preignant,* fr. MF, fr. prp. of *preindre* to press, fr. L *premere* — more at PRESS] *archaic* (14c) **:** COGENT

2**pregnant** *adj* [ME, fr. L *praegnant-, praegnans,* alter. of *praegnas,* fr. *prae-* pre- + *-gnas* (akin to *gignere* to produce) — more at KIN] (15c) **1 :** abounding in fancy, wit, or resourcefulness **:** INVENTIVE ⟨all this has been said . . . by great and ~ artists —*Times Lit. Supp.*⟩ **2 :** rich in significance or implication **:** MEANINGFUL, PROFOUND ⟨the ~ phrases of the Bible —Edmund Wilson⟩ ⟨a ~ pause⟩ **3 :** containing unborn young within the body **:** GRAVID **4 :** having possibilities of development or consequence **:** involving important issues **:** MOMENTOUS ⟨draw inspiration from the heroic achievements of that ~ age —Kemp Malone⟩ **5** *obs* **:** INCLINED, DISPOSED ⟨your own most ~ and vouchsafed ear —Shak.⟩ **6 :** FULL, TEEMING — **preg·nant·ly** *adv*

preg·nen·o·lone \preg-ˈnen-ᵊl-ˌōn\ *n* [ISV *pregnene* ($C_{21}H_{34}$) + *-ol* + *-one*] (1936) : an unsaturated hydroxy steroid ketone $C_{21}H_{32}O_2$ that is formed by the oxidation of steroids (as cholesterol) and yields progesterone on dehydrogenation

pre·heat \(ˈ)prē-ˈhēt\ *vt* (1898) : to heat beforehand; *esp* : to heat (an oven) to a designated temperature before using for cooking — **pre·heat·er** *n*

pre·hen·sile \prē-ˈhen(t)-səl, -ˈhen-ˌsīl\ *adj* [F *préhensile*, fr. L *prehensus*, pp. of *prehendere* to seize — more at GET] (ca. 1781) **1** : adapted for seizing or grasping esp. by wrapping around ⟨~ tail⟩ **2** : gifted with mental grasp or moral or aesthetic perception — **pre·hen·sil·i·ty** \(ˌ)prē-ˌhen-ˈsil-ət-ē\ *n*

pre·hen·sion \prē-ˈhen-chən\ *n* (ca. 1828) **1** : the act of taking hold, seizing, or grasping **2 a** : mental understanding : COMPREHENSION **b** : apprehension by the senses

pre·his·to·ri·an \ˌprē-(h)is-ˈtōr-ē-ən, -ˈtȯr-\ *n* (1893) : an archaeologist who specializes in prehistoric man and his culture

pre·his·tor·ic \ˌprē-(h)is-ˈtȯr-ik, -ˈtär-\ *also* **pre·his·tor·i·cal** \-i-kəl\ *adj* (1851) **1** : of, relating to, or existing in times antedating written history **2** : of or relating to a language in a period of its development from which contemporary records of its sounds and forms have not been preserved — **pre·his·tor·i·cal·ly** \-i-k(ə-)lē\ *adv*

pre·his·to·ry \(ˈ)prē-ˈhis-t(ə-)rē\ *n* (1871) **1** : the study of prehistoric man **2** : a history of the antecedents of an event, situation, or thing **3** : the prehistoric period of man's evolution

pre·hom·i·nid \-ˈhäm-ə-nəd\ *n* [deriv. of L *pre-* + *homin-*, *homo* man] (1939) : any of the extinct manlike primates that are often classified as a family (Prehominidae) — **prehominid** *adj*

pre·ig·ni·tion \ˌprē-ig-ˈnish-ən\ *n* (1898) : ignition in an internal-combustion engine while the inlet valve is open or before compression is completed

pre·im·plan·ta·tion \ˌprē-ˌim-ˌplan-ˈtā-shən\ *adj* (1945) : of, involving, or being an embryo before uterine implantation

pre·judge \(ˈ)prē-ˈjəj\ *vt* [MF *prejuger*, fr. L *praejudicare*, fr. *prae-* + *judicare* to judge — more at JUDGE] (1579) : to judge before hearing or before full and sufficient examination — **pre·judg·er** *n* — **pre·judg·ment** \-ˈjəj-mənt\ *n*

¹prej·u·dice \ˈprej-əd-əs\ *n* [ME, fr. OF, fr. L *praejudicium* previous judgment, damage, fr. *prae-* + *judicium* judgment — more at JUDICIAL] (13c) **1** : injury or damage resulting from some judgment or action of another in disregard of one's rights; *esp* : detriment to one's legal rights or claims **2 a** (1) : preconceived judgment or opinion (2) : an adverse opinion or leaning formed without just grounds or before sufficient knowledge **b** : an instance of such judgment or opinion **c** : an irrational attitude of hostility directed against an individual, a group, a race, or their supposed characteristics ***syn*** see PREDILECTION

²prejudice *vt* **-diced; -dic·ing** (15c) **1** : to injure or damage by some judgment or action (as in a case of law) **2** : to cause to have prejudice

prej·u·diced \-dəst\ *adj* (1579) : having or resulting from a prejudice or bias for or esp. against

prej·u·di·cial \ˌprej-ə-ˈdish-əl\ *adj* (15c) **1** : tending to injure or impair : DETRIMENTAL **2** : leading to premature judgment or unwarranted opinion — **prej·u·di·cial·ly** \-ˈdish-(ə-)lē\ *adv* — **prej·u·di·cial·ness** \-əl-nəs\ *n*

prej·u·di·cious \-ˈdish-əs\ *adj* (1579) : PREJUDICIAL

prel·a·cy \ˈprel-ə-sē\ *n, pl* **-cies** (14c) **1** : the office or dignity of a prelate **2** : episcopal church government

pre·lap·sar·i·an \ˌprē-ˌlap-ˈser-ē-ən\ *adj* [*pre-* + L *lapsus* slip, fall — more at LAPSE] (1879) : characteristic of or belonging to the time or state before the fall of man

prel·ate \ˈprel-ət *also* ˈprē-ˌlāt\ *n* [ME *prelat*, fr. OF, fr. ML *praelatus*, lit., one receiving preferment, fr. L (pp. of *praeferre* to prefer), fr. *prae-* + *latus*, pp. of *ferre* to carry — more at TOLERATE, BEAR] (13c) : an ecclesiastic (as a bishop or abbot) of superior rank

prelate nul·li·us \-nü-ˈlē-əs\ *n* [*nullius* fr. NL *nullius dioecesis* of no diocese] (ca. 1911) : a Roman Catholic prelate who is usu. a titular bishop and who has ordinary jurisdiction over a district independent of any diocese

prel·a·ture \ˈprel-ə-ˌchu̇(ə)r, -chər, -ˌt(y)u̇(ə)r\ *n* (1607) **1** : PRELACY 1 **2** : a body of prelates

pre·lect \pri-ˈlekt\ *vi* [L *praelectus*, pp. of *praelegere*, fr. *prae-* + *legere* to read — more at LEGEND] (1785) : to discourse publicly : LECTURE — **pre·lec·tion** \-ˈlek-shən\ *n*

pre·li·ba·tion \ˌprē-lī-ˈbā-shən\ *n* [L *praelibation-*, *praelibatio*, fr. *praelibatus*, pp. of *praelibare* to taste beforehand, fr. *prae-* + *libare* to pour as an offering, taste — more at LIBATION] (1526) : FORETASTE

pre·lim \ˈprē-ˌlim, pri-ˈ\ *n or adj* (1891) : PRELIMINARY

¹pre·lim·i·nary \pri-ˈlim-ə-ˌner-ē\ *n, pl* **-nar·ies** [F *préliminaires*, pl., fr. ML *praeliminaris*, adj., preliminary, fr. L *prae-* pre- + *limin-*, *limen* threshold — more at LIMB] (1656) : something that precedes or is introductory or preparatory: as **a** : a preliminary scholastic examination **b** *pl, Brit* : FRONT MATTER **c** : a minor match preceding the main event (as of a boxing card)

²preliminary *adj* (ca. 1667) : coming before and usu. forming a necessary prelude to something else — **pre·lim·i·nar·i·ly** \-ˌlim-ə-ˈner-ə-lē\ *adv*

pre·lit·er·ate \(ˈ)prē-ˈlit-ə-rət, -ˈli-trət\ *adj* (1925) **1 a** : not yet employing writing as a cultural medium **b** : lacking the use of writing **2** : antedating the use of writing — **preliterate** *n*

¹pre·lude \ˈprel-ˌ(y)üd, ˈprā-ˌl(y)üd, *sense 1 also* ˈprē-ˌlüd\ *n* [MF, fr. ML *praeludium*, fr. L *praeludere* to play beforehand, fr. *prae-* + *ludere* to play — more at LUDICROUS] (1561) **1** : an introductory performance, action, or event preceding and preparing for the principal or a more important matter **2 a** : a musical section or movement introducing the theme or chief subject (as of a fugue or suite) or serving as an introduction to an opera or oratorio **b** : an opening voluntary **c** : a separate concert piece usu. for piano or orchestra and based entirely on a short motive

²prelude *vb* **pre·lud·ed; pre·lud·ing** *vi* (1655) : to give or serve as a prelude; *esp* : to play a musical introduction ~ *vt* **1** : to serve as a prelude to **2** : to play as a prelude — **pre·lud·er** *n*

pre·lu·sion \pri-ˈlü-zhən\ *n* [L *praelusion-*, *praelusio*, fr. *praelusus*, pp. of *praeludere*] (1597) : PRELUDE, INTRODUCTION

pre·lu·sive \-ˈlü-siv, -ziv\ *adj* (1605) : constituting or having the form of a prelude : INTRODUCTORY — **pre·lu·sive·ly** *adv*

pre·ma·lig·nant \ˌprē-mə-ˈlig-nənt\ *adj* (ca. 1897) : PRECANCEROUS

pre·man \ˈprē-ˈman, -ˌman\ *n* (1921) : a hypothetical ancient primate constituting the immediate ancestor of man : PREHOMINID

pre·mar·i·tal \(ˈ)prē-ˈmar-ət-ᵊl\ *adj* (1886) : existing or occurring before marriage — **pre·mar·i·tal·ly** *adv*

pre·ma·ture \ˌprē-mə-ˈt(y)u̇(ə)r, -ˈchu̇(ə)r *also* ˌprem-ə-\ *adj* [L *praematurus* too early, fr. *prae-* + *maturus* ripe, mature] (ca. 1529) : happening, arriving, existing, or performed before the proper or usual time; *esp* : born after a gestation period of less than 37 weeks ⟨~ babies⟩ — **premature** *n* — **pre·ma·ture·ly** *adv* — **pre·ma·ture·ness** *n* — **pre·ma·tu·ri·ty** \-ˈt(y)u̇r-ət-ē, -ˈchu̇r-\ *n*

pre·max·il·la \ˌprē-mak-ˈsil-ə\ *n* [NL] (1866) : either of a pair of bones of the upper jaw of vertebrates between and in front of the maxillae — **pre·max·il·lary** \(ˈ)prē-ˈmak-sə-ˌler-ē, *chiefly Brit* ˌprē-mak-ˈsil-ə-rē\ *adj or n*

¹pre·med \ˈprē-ˈmed\ *n* (1928) : a premedical student or course of study

²premed *adj* (1950) : PREMEDICAL

pre·med·i·cal \(ˈ)prē-ˈmed-i-kəl\ *adj* (1904) : preceding and preparing for the professional study of medicine

pre·med·i·tate \pri-ˈmed-ə-ˌtāt, ˈprē-\ *vb* [L *praemeditatus*, pp. of *praemeditari*, fr. *prae-* + *meditari* to meditate] *vt* (ca. 1548) : to think about and revolve in the mind beforehand ~ *vi* : to think, consider, or deliberate beforehand — **pre·med·i·ta·tor** \-ˌtāt-ər\ *n*

pre·med·i·tat·ed *adj* (1590) : characterized by fully conscious willful intent and a measure of forethought and planning ⟨~ murder⟩ — **pre·med·i·tat·ed·ly** *adv*

pre·med·i·ta·tion \pri-ˌmed-ə-ˈtā-shən, ˌprē-\ *n* (15c) : an act or instance of premeditating; *specif* : consideration or planning of an act beforehand that shows intent to commit that act

pre·med·i·ta·tive \pri-ˈmed-ə-ˌtāt-iv, ˈprē-\ *adj* (1858) : given to or characterized by premeditation

pre·mei·ot·ic \ˌprē-mī-ˈät-ik\ *adj* (1905) : of, occurring in, or typical of a stage prior to meiosis ⟨~ DNA synthesis⟩ ⟨~ tissue⟩

pre·men·stru·al \(ˈ)prē-ˈmen(t)-strə(-wə)l\ *adj* (1885) : of, relating to, occurring, or being in the period just preceding menstruation ⟨~ tension⟩ ⟨~ women⟩ — **pre·men·stru·al·ly** \-ē\ *adv*

pre·mie *var of* PREEMIE

¹pre·mier \pri-ˈm(y)i(ə)r; ˈprē-mē-ər, ˈprem-ē-\ *adj* [ME *primier*, fr. MF *premier* first, chief, fr. L *primarius* of the first rank — more at PRIMARY] (15c) **1** : first in position, rank, or importance **2** : first in time : EARLIEST

²premier *n* [F, fr. *premier*, adj.] (1711) : PRIME MINISTER — **pre·mier·ship** \-ˌship\ *n*

pre·mier dan·seur \prə-myā-däⁿ-sœr\ *n* [F] (1828) : the principal male dancer in a ballet company

¹pre·miere \pri-ˈmye(ə)r, -ˈmi(ə)r; ˌprim-ē-ˈe(ə)r\ *adj* [alter. of ¹*premier*] (1768) : PREMIER

²premiere *n* [F *première*, fr. fem. of *premier* first] (1889) **1** : a first performance or exhibition ⟨the ~ of a play⟩ **2** : the chief actress of a theatrical cast

³premiere *or* **pre·mier** *like* ¹PREMIERE\ *vb* **pre·miered; pre·mier·ing** *vt* (1933) : to give a first public performance of ~ *vi* **1** : to have a first public performance **2** : to appear for the first time as a star performer

pre·miere dan·seuse \prə-myer-däⁿ-sœ̄z\ *n* [F *première danseuse*] (1828) : the principal female dancer in a ballet company

pre·mil·le·nar·i·an·ism \ˈprē-ˌmil-ə-ˈner-ē-ə-ˌniz-əm\ *n* (1844) : PREMILLENNIALISM — **pre·mil·le·nar·i·an** \-ē-ən\ *adj or n*

pre·mil·len·ni·al \ˌprē-mə-ˈlen-ē-əl\ *adj* (1846) **1** : coming before a millennium **2** : holding or relating to premillennialism — **pre·mil·len·ni·al·ly** \-ē-ə-lē\ *adv*

pre·mil·len·ni·al·ism \-ē-ə-ˌliz-əm\ *n* (ca. 1882) : the view that Christ's return will precede and usher in a future millennium of Messianic rule mentioned in Revelation — **pre·mil·len·ni·al·ist** \-ē-ə-ləst\ *n*

¹prem·ise *also* **pre·miss** \ˈprem-əs\ *n* [in sense 1, fr. ME *premisse*, fr. MF, fr. ML *praemissa*, fr. L, fem. of *praemissus*, pp. of *praemittere* to place ahead, fr. *prae-* pre- + *mittere* to send; in other senses, fr. ME *premisses*, fr. ML *praemissa*, fr. L, neut. pl. of *praemissus*] (14c) **1 a** : a proposition antecedently supposed or proved as a basis of argument or inference; *specif* : either of the first two propositions of a syllogism from which the conclusion is drawn **b** : something assumed or taken for granted : PRESUPPOSITION **2** *pl* : matters previously stated; *specif* : the preliminary and explanatory part of a deed or of a bill in equity **3** *pl* [fr. its being identified in the premises of the deed] **a** : a tract of land with the buildings thereon **b** : a building or part of a building usu. with its appurtenances (as grounds)

²pre·mise \ˈprem-əs *also* pri-ˈmīz\ *vt* **pre·mised; pre·mis·ing** (1526) **1 a** : to set forth beforehand as an introduction or a postulate **b** : to offer as a premise in an argument **2** : POSTULATE **3** : to base on certain assumptions

¹pre·mi·um \ˈprē-mē-əm\ *n* [L *praemium* booty, profit, reward, fr. *prae-* + *emere* to take, buy — more at REDEEM] (1601) **1 a** : a reward or recompense for a particular act **b** : a sum over and above a regular price paid chiefly as an inducement or incentive ⟨willing to pay a ~ for immediate delivery⟩ **c** : a sum in advance of or in addition to the nominal value of something ⟨bonds callable at a ~ of six percent⟩ **d** : something given free or at a reduced price with the purchase of a product or service **2** : the consideration paid for a contract of insurance **3** : a high value or a value in excess of that normally or usu. expected ⟨put a ~ on accuracy⟩

²premium *adj* (1844) : of exceptional quality or amount; *also* : higher-priced

pre·mo·lar \(ˈ)prē-ˈmō-lər\ *adj* (1880) : situated in front of or preceding the molar teeth; *esp* : being or relating to those teeth of a mammal in front of the true molars and behind the canines when the latter are present — **premolar** *n*

pre·mon·ish \-ˈmän-ish\ *vt, archaic* (1526) : FOREWARN ~ *vi, archaic* : to give warning in advance

pre·mo·ni·tion \ˌprē-mə-ˈnish-ən, ˌprem-ə-\ *n* [ME, fr. MF, fr. LL *praemonition-*, *praemonitio*, fr. L *praemonitus*, pp. of *praemonēre* to warn in advance, fr. *prae-* + *monēre* to warn — more at MENTAL] (15c) **1** : previous notice or warning : FOREWARNING **2** : anticipation of an event without conscious reason : PRESENTIMENT

pre·mon·i·to·ry \pri-ˈmän-ə-ˌtōr-ē, -ˌtȯr-\ *adj* (1647) : giving warning ⟨a ~ symptom⟩ — **pre·mon·i·to·ri·ly** \-ˌmän-ə-ˈtōr-ə-lē, -ˈtȯr-\ *adv*

Pre·mon·stra·ten·sian \ˌprē-ˌmän(t)-strə-ˈten-chən\ *n* [ML *praemonstratensis,* fr. *praemonstratensis* of Prémontré, fr. *Praemonstratus* Prémontré] (1695) : a member of an order of canons regular founded by St. Norbert at Prémontré near Laon, France, in 1120

pre·mune \(ˈ)prē-ˈmyün\ *adj* [back-formation fr. *premunition*] (1948) : exhibiting premunition

pre·mu·ni·tion \ˌprē-myu̇-ˈnish-ən\ *n* [L *praemunition-, praemunitio* advance fortification, fr. *praemunitus,* pp. of *praemunire* to fortify in advance, fr. *prae-* + *munire* to fortify — more at MUNITION] (1607) **1** *archaic* : an advance provision of protection **2 a** : resistance to a disease due to the existence of its causative agent in a state of physiological equilibrium in the host **b** : immunity to a particular infection due to previous presence of the causative agent

pre·name \ˈprē-ˌnām\ *n* (1894) : FORENAME

pre·na·tal \(ˈ)prē-ˈnāt-ᵊl\ *adj* (1826) : occurring, existing, or taking place before birth ⟨~ care⟩ ⟨the ~ period⟩ — **pre·na·tal·ly** \-ᵊl-ē\ *adv*

[1]**pre·nom·i·nate** \(ˈ)prē-ˈnäm-ə-nət\ *adj* [LL *praenominatus,* pp. of *praenominare* to name before, fr. L *prae-* + *nominare* to name — more at NOMINATE] *obs* (1513) : previously mentioned

[2]**pre·nom·i·nate** \-ˌnāt\ *vt, obs* (1547) : to mention previously — **pre·nom·i·na·tion** \(ˌ)prē-ˌnäm-ə-ˈnā-shən\ *n, obs*

pre·no·tion \(ˈ)prē-ˈnō-shən, ˈprē-ˌ\ *n* [L *praenotion-, praenotio* preconception, fr. *prae-* + *notio* idea, conception — more at NOTION] (1588) **1** : PRESENTIMENT, PREMONITION **2** : PRECONCEPTION

[1]**pren·tice** \ˈprent-əs\ *n* [ME *prentis,* short for *apprentis*] (14c) : APPRENTICE 1, LEARNER — **prentice** *adj*

[2]**prentice** *vt* **pren·ticed; pren·tic·ing** (1598) : APPRENTICE

pre·nup·tial \(ˈ)prē-ˈnəp-shəl, -chəl, ÷-chə-wəl\ *adj* (1869) : made or occurring before marriage

pre·oc·cu·pan·cy \(ˈ)prē-ˈäk-yə-pən-sē\ *n* (ca. 1755) **1** : an act or the right of taking possession before another **2** : the condition of being completely busied or preoccupied

pre·oc·cu·pa·tion \(ˌ)prē-ˌäk-yə-ˈpā-shən\ *n* [L *praeoccupation-, praeoccupatio* act of seizing beforehand, fr. *praeoccupatus,* pp. of *praeoccupare* to seize beforehand, fr. *prae-* + *occupare* to seize, occupy] (1603) **1** : an act of preoccupying : the state of being preoccupied **2 a** : extreme or excessive concern with something **b** : something that preoccupies one

pre·oc·cu·pied \(ˈ)prē-ˈäk-yə-ˌpīd\ *adj* (1849) **1 a** : lost in thought; *also* : absorbed in some preoccupation **b** : already occupied **2** : previously applied to another group and unavailable for use in a new sense — used of a biological generic or specific name

pre·oc·cu·py \-ˌpī\ *vt* [*pre-* + *occupy*] (1567) **1** : to engage or engross the interest or attention of beforehand or preferentially **2** : to take possession of or fill beforehand or before another

pre·op·er·a·tive \(ˈ)prē-ˈäp-(ə-)rət-iv, -ˈäp-ə-ˌrāt-\ *adj* (1904) : occurring before and usu. close to a surgical operation — **pre·op·er·a·tive·ly** *adv*

pre·or·bit·al \-ˈȯr-bət-ᵊl\ *adj* (ca. 1961) : occurring before going into orbit

pre·or·dain \ˌprē-ȯr-ˈdān\ *vt* (1533) : to decree or ordain in advance : FOREORDAIN — **pre·or·dain·ment** \-mənt\ *n* — **pre·or·di·na·tion** \(ˌ)prē-ˌȯrd-ᵊn-ˈā-shən\ *n*

pre·ovi·po·si·tion \ˌprē-ˌō-və-pə-ˈzish-ən\ *adj* (1935) : of, relating to, or being the period before oviposition of the first eggs by an adult female (as of an insect)

pre·ovu·la·to·ry \(ˈ)prē-ˈäv-yə-lə-ˌtōr-ē, -ˌtȯr-, -ˈōv-\ *adj* (1935) : occurring or being in or typical of the period immediately preceding ovulation

pre–owned \(ˈ)prē-ˈōnd\ *adj* (1964) : SECONDHAND

[1]**prep** \ˈprep\ *n* [by shortening] (1862) **1** : PREPARATION **2** : PREPARATORY SCHOOL **3** : a preliminary trial for a racehorse

[2]**prep** *vb* **prepped; prep·ping** *vi* (1914) **1** : to attend preparatory school **2** [short for *prepare*]: to get ready for ~ *vt* : PREPARE; *esp* : to prepare for operation or examination

pre·pack·age \(ˈ)prē-ˈpak-ij\ *vt* (1944) : to package (as food or a manufactured article) before offering for sale to the consumer

prep·a·ra·tion \ˌprep-ə-ˈrā-shən\ *n* [ME *preparacion,* fr. MF *preparation,* fr. L *praeparation-, praeparatio,* fr. *praeparatus,* pp. of *praeparare* to prepare] (14c) **1** : the action or process of making something ready for use or service or of getting ready for some occasion, test, or duty **2** : a state of being prepared : READINESS **3** : a preparatory act or measure **4** : something that is prepared; *specif* : a medicinal substance made ready for use ⟨a ~ for colds⟩

[1]**pre·par·a·tive** \pri-ˈpar-ət-iv\ *n* (15c) : something that prepares the way for or serves as a preliminary to something else : PREPARATION

[2]**preparative** *adj* (1530) : PREPARATORY — **pre·par·a·tive·ly** *adv*

pre·par·a·tor \pri-ˈpar-ət-ər\ *n* (1762) : one that prepares; *specif* : a person who prepares scientific specimens or museum displays

[1]**pre·pa·ra·to·ry** \pri-ˈpar-ə-ˌtōr-ē, -ˌtȯr- *also* ˈprep-(ə-)rə-\ *adj* (15c) : preparing or serving to prepare for something : INTRODUCTORY — **pre·pa·ra·to·ri·ly** \pri-ˌpar-ə-ˈtōr-ə-lē, -ˈtȯr- *also* ˌprep-(ə-)rə-\ *adv*

[2]**preparatory** *adv* (1649) : by way of preparation : in a preparatory manner — usu. used with *to* ⟨took a deep breath ~ to drinking⟩

preparatory school *n* (1822) **1** : a usu. private school preparing students primarily for college **2** *Brit* : a private elementary school preparing students primarily for British public schools

pre·pare \pri-ˈpa(ə)r, -ˈpe(ə)r\ *vb* **pre·pared; pre·par·ing** [ME *preparen,* fr. MF *preparer,* fr. L *praeparare,* fr. *prae-* pre- + *parare* to procure, prepare — more at PARE] *vt* (15c) **1 a** : to make ready beforehand for some purpose, use, or activity ⟨~ food for dinner⟩ **b** : to put in a proper state of mind ⟨is *prepared* to listen⟩ **2** : to work out the details of : plan in advance ⟨*preparing* strategy for the coming campaign⟩ **3 a** : to put together : COMPOUND ⟨~ a prescription⟩ **b** : to put into written form ⟨~ a report⟩ ~ *vi* : to get ready ⟨*preparing* for a career⟩ — **pre·par·er** *n*

pre·pared \-ˈpa(ə)rd, -ˈpe(ə)rd\ *adj* (1526) : subjected to a special process or treatment — **pre·pared·ly** \-lē; -ˈpar-əd-lē, -ˈper-\ *adv*

pre·pared·ness \pri-ˈpar-əd-nəs, -ˈper- *also* -ˈpa(ə)rd-nəs *or* -ˈpe(ə)rd-nəs\ *n* (1590) : the quality or state of being prepared; *esp* : a state of adequate preparation in case of war

pre·pay \(ˈ)prē-ˈpā\ *vt* **-paid** \-ˈpād\; **-pay·ing** (1839) : to pay or pay the charge on in advance — **pre·pay·ment** \-ˈpā-mənt\ *n*

pre·pense \pri-ˈpen(t)s\ *adj* [by shortening & alter. fr. earlier *purpensed,* fr. ME, pp. of *purpensen* to deliberate, premeditate, fr. MF *purpenser,* fr. OF, fr. *pur-* for (modif. of L *pro-*) + *penser* to think — more at PRO-, PENSIVE] (1702) : planned beforehand : PREMEDITATED — usu. used postpositively ⟨malice ~⟩ — **pre·pense·ly** *adv*

pre·plant \ˈprē-ˈplant\ *also* **pre·plant·ing** \-iŋ\ *adj* (1961) : occurring or used before planting a crop ⟨~ soil fertilization⟩

pre·pon·der·ance \pri-ˈpän-d(ə-)rən(t)s\ *n* (1681) **1** : a superiority in weight, power, importance, or strength **2 a** : a superiority or excess in number or quantity **b** : MAJORITY

pre·pon·der·an·cy \-d(ə-)rən-sē\ *n* (1646) : PREPONDERANCE

pre·pon·der·ant \pri-ˈpän-d(ə-)rənt\ *adj* (1664) **1** : having superior weight, force, or influence **2** : having greater prevalence ***syn*** see DOMINANT — **pre·pon·der·ant·ly** *adv*

[1]**pre·pon·der·ate** \pri-ˈpän-də-ˌrāt\ *vb* **-at·ed; -at·ing** [L *praeponderatus,* pp. of *praeponderare,* fr. *prae-* + *ponder-, pondus* weight — more at PENDANT] *vt* (1651) **1** *archaic* : OUTWEIGH **2** *archaic* : to weigh down ~ *vi* **1** : to exceed in weight **2** : to exceed in influence, power, or importance **3** : to exceed in numbers — **pre·pon·der·a·tion** \-ˌpän-də-ˈrā-shən, ˌprē-\ *n*

[2]**pre·pon·der·ate** \-ˈpän-də-rət\ *adj* (1802) : PREPONDERANT — **pre·pon·der·ate·ly** *adv*

prep·o·si·tion \ˌprep-ə-ˈzish-ən\ *n* [ME *preposicioun,* fr. L *praeposition-, praepositio,* fr. *praepositus,* pp. of *praeponere* to put in front, fr. *prae-* pre- + *ponere* to put — more at POSITION] (14c) : a linguistic form that combines with a noun, pronoun, or noun equivalent to form a phrase that typically has an adverbial, adjectival, or substantival relation to some other word — **prep·o·si·tion·al** \-ˈzish-nəl, -ən-ᵊl\ *adj* — **prep·o·si·tion·al·ly** \-ē\ *adv*

pre·pos·i·tive \pri-ˈpäz-ət-iv, -ˈpäz-tiv\ *adj* [LL *praepositivus,* fr. L *praepositus*] (1583) : put before : PREFIXED — **pre·pos·i·tive·ly** *adv*

pre·pos·sess \ˌprē-pə-ˈzes *also* -ˈses\ *vt* (1614) **1** *obs* : to take previous possession of **2** : to cause to be preoccupied **3** : to influence beforehand esp. favorably

pre·pos·sess·ing *adj* (1642) **1** *archaic* : creating prejudice **2** : tending to create a favorable impression : ATTRACTIVE

pre·pos·ses·sion \ˌprē-pə-ˈzesh-ən *also* -ˈsesh-\ *n* (1648) **1** *archaic* : prior possession **2** : an attitude, belief, or impression formed beforehand : PREJUDICE **3** : an exclusive concern with one idea or object : PREOCCUPATION ***syn*** see PREDILECTION

pre·pos·ter·ous \pri-ˈpäs-t(ə-)rəs\ *adj* [L *praeposterus,* lit., with the hind-side in front, fr. *prae-* + *posterus* hinder, following — more at POSTERIOR] (1542) : contrary to nature, reason, or common sense : ABSURD — **pre·pos·ter·ous·ly** *adv* — **pre·pos·ter·ous·ness** *n*

pre·po·ten·cy \(ˈ)prē-ˈpōt-ᵊn-sē\ *n* (1646) **1** : the quality or state of being prepotent : PREDOMINANCE **2** : unusual ability of an individual or strain to transmit its characters to offspring because of homozygosity for numerous dominant genes

pre·po·tent \-ᵊnt\ *adj* [ME, fr. L *praepotent-, praepotens,* fr. *prae-* + *potens* powerful — more at POTENT] (15c) **1 a** : having exceptional power, authority, or influence **b** : exceeding others in power **2** : exhibiting genetic prepotency — **pre·po·tent·ly** *adv*

[1]**prep·py** *or* **prep·pie** \ˈprep-ē\ *n, pl* **prep·pies** [[1]*prep* + *-ie*] (1967) **1** : a student at or a graduate of a preparatory school **2** : a person deemed to dress or behave like a preppy

[2]**preppy** *or* **preppie** *adj* (1967) **1** : relating to, characteristic of, or being a preppy **2** : relating to or being a style of dress characterized esp. by classic clothing and neat appearance — **prep·pi·ly** \ˈprep-ə-lē\ *adv* — **prep·pi·ness** \ˈprep-ē-nəs\ *n*

pre·pran·di·al \(ˈ)prē-ˈpran-dē-əl\ *adj* (1822) : of, relating to, or suitable for the time just before dinner ⟨a ~ drink⟩

pre·preg \ˈprē-ˈpreg\ *n* [*pre-* + im*preg*nated] (1954) : a reinforcing or molding material (as paper or glass cloth) already impregnated with a synthetic resin

[1]**pre·print** \ˈprē-ˌprint, -ˈprint\ *n* (1889) **1** : an issue of a technical paper often in preliminary form before its publication in a journal **2** : something (as an advertisement) printed before the rest of the publication in which it is to appear

[2]**pre·print** \(ˈ)prē-ˈprint\ *vt* (1926) : to print in advance for later use

pre·pro·cess \(ˈ)prē-ˈpräs-ˌes, -ˈprōs-, -əs\ *vt* (1942) : to do preliminary processing of (as data) — **pre·pro·ces·sor** \-ˌes-ər, -ə-sər, -ə-ˌsō(ə)r\ *n*

pre·pro·fes·sion·al \ˌprē-prə-ˈfesh-nəl, -ən-ᵊl\ *adj* (1926) : of or relating to the period preceding specific study for or practice of a profession

prep school *n* (1895) : PREPARATORY SCHOOL

pre·pu·ber·al \(ˈ)prē-ˈpyü-b(ə-)rəl\ *adj* (ca. 1935) : PREPUBERTAL

pre·pu·ber·tal \-bərt-ᵊl\ *adj* (1859) : of or relating to prepuberty

pre·pu·ber·ty \-bərt-ē\ *n* (1922) : the period immediately preceding puberty

pre·pu·bes·cence \ˌprē-pyü-ˈbes-ᵊn(t)s\ *n* (1916) : PREPUBERTY

pre·pu·bes·cent \-ᵊnt\ *adj* (1904) : PREPUBERTAL — **prepubescent** *n*

pre·puce \ˈprē-ˌpyüs\ *n* [ME, fr. MF, fr. L *praeputium,* fr. *prae-* + *-putium* (akin to Belorussian *potka* penis)] (15c) : FORESKIN; *also* : a similar fold investing the clitoris — **pre·pu·tial** \prē-ˈpyü-shəl\ *adj*

Pre–Raph·a·el·ite \(ˈ)prē-ˈraf-ē-ə-ˌlīt, -ˈrā-fē-, -ˈrāf-ē-\ *n* (1849) **1 a** : a member of a brotherhood of artists formed in England in 1848 to restore the artistic principles and practices regarded as characteristic of Italian art before Raphael **b** : an artist or writer influenced by this brotherhood **2** : a modern artist dedicated to restoring early Renaissance ideals or methods — **Pre–Raphaelite** *adj* — **Pre–Ra·pha·el·it·ism** \-ˌlīt-ˌiz-əm\ *n*

pre·re·cord \ˌprē-ri-ˈkȯ(ə)rd\ *vt* (ca. 1941) : to record (as a radio or television program) in advance of presentation or use

pre·reg·is·tra·tion \ˌprē-ˌrej-ə-ˈstrā-shən\ *n* (1967) : a special registration (as for returning students) prior to an official registration period — **pre·reg·is·ter** \(ˈ)prē-ˈrej-ə-stər\ *vi*

pre·req·ui·site \(ˈ)prē-ˈrek-wə-zət\ *n* (1633) : something that is necessary to an end or to the carrying out of a function — **prerequisite** *adj*

\ə\ abut \ᵊ\ kitten, F table \ər\ further \a\ ash \ā\ ace \ä\ cot, cart \au̇\ out \ch\ chin \e\ bet \ē\ easy \g\ go \i\ hit \ī\ ice \j\ job \ŋ\ sing \ō\ go \ȯ\ law \ȯi\ boy \th\ thin \t͟h\ the \ü\ loot \u̇\ foot \y\ yet \zh\ vision \à, k̲, ⁿ, œ, œ̄, ue, ue̅, ʸ\ see Guide to Pronunciation

pre·rog·a·tive \pri-ˈräg-ət-iv\ *n* [ME, fr. MF & L; MF, fr. L *praerogativa,* Roman century voting first in the comitia, privilege, fr. fem. of *praerogativus* voting first, fr. *praerogatus,* pp. of *praerogare* to ask for an opinion before another, fr. *prae-* + *rogare* to ask — more at RIGHT] (15c) **1 a :** an exclusive or special right, power, or privilege: as (1) **:** one belonging to an office or an official body (2) **:** one belonging to a person, group, or class of individuals (3) **:** one possessed by a nation as an attribute of sovereignty **b :** the discretionary power inhering in the British Crown **2 :** a distinctive excellence — **pre·rog·a·tived** \-ivd\ *adj*

pre·sa \ˈprā-sə, -(ˌ)sä, -zə\ *n, pl* **pre·se** \-(ˌ)sā, -(ˌ)zā\ [It, lit., act of taking, fr. *prendere* to take, fr. L *prehendere* to grasp — more at GET] (1724) **:** a mark or cue (as :S:) indicating the point of entry of the successive voice parts of a canon

¹pres·age \ˈpres-ij, *also* pri-ˈsāj\ *n* [ME, fr. L *praesagium,* fr. *praesagire* to forebode, fr. *prae-* + *sagire* to perceive keenly — more at SEEK] (14c) **1 :** something that foreshadows or portends a future event **:** OMEN **2 :** an intuition or feeling of what is going to happen in the future **3** *archaic* **:** PROGNOSTICATION **4 :** warning or indication of the future — **pre·sage·ful** \pri-ˈsāj-fəl\ *adj*

²pre·sage \ˈpres-ij, pri-ˈsāj\ *vb* **pre·saged; pre·sag·ing** *vt* (1562) **1 :** to give an omen or warning of **:** FORESHADOW, PORTEND **2 :** FORETELL, PREDICT ~ *vi* **:** to make or utter a prediction — **pre·sag·er** *n, obs*

pre·sanc·ti·fied \(ˈ)prē-ˈsaŋ(k)-ti-ˌfīd\ *adj* (1758) **:** consecrated at a previous service — used of eucharistic elements

presby- *or* **presbyo-** *comb form* [NL, fr. Gk *presby-* elder, fr. *presbys* old man] **:** old age ⟨*presby*opia⟩ ⟨*presbyo*phrenia⟩

pres·by·ope \ˈprez-bē-ˌōp; ˈpres-bē-, -pē-\ *n* [prob. fr. F, fr. Gk *presby-* + *ōps* eye — more at EYE] (ca. 1857) **:** one affected with presbyopia

pres·by·opia \ˌprez-bē-ˈō-pē-ə, ˌpres-\ *n* [NL] (1793) **:** a visual condition which becomes apparent esp. in middle age and in which loss of elasticity of the lens of the eye causes defective accommodation and inability to focus sharply for near vision — **pres·by·opic** \-ˈō-pik, -ˈäp-ik\ *adj or n*

pres·by·ter \ˈprez-bət-ər, ˈpres-\ *n* [LL, elder, priest, fr. Gk *presbyteros,* compar. of *presbys*] (1597) **1 :** a member of the governing body of an early Christian church **2 :** a member of the order of priests in churches having episcopal hierarchies that include bishops, priests, and deacons **3 :** ELDER 4b — **pres·byt·er·ate** \prez-ˈbit-ə-rət, pres-, -ˌrāt\ *n*

¹pres·by·te·ri·al \ˌprez-bə-ˈtir-ē-əl, ˌpres-\ *adj* (ca. 1600) **:** of or relating to presbyters or a presbytery — **pres·by·te·ri·al·ly** \-ē-ə-lē\ *adv*

²presbyterial *n, often cap* (1928) **:** an organization of Presbyterian women associated with a presbytery

¹Pres·by·te·ri·an \-ē-ən\ *adj* (1641) **1** *often not cap* **:** characterized by a graded system of representative ecclesiastical bodies (as presbyteries) exercising legislative and judicial powers **2 :** of, relating to, or constituting a Protestant Christian church that is presbyterian in government and traditionally Calvinistic in doctrine — **Pres·by·te·ri·an·ism** \-ē-ə-ˌniz-əm\ *n*

²Presbyterian *n* (1641) **:** a member of a Presbyterian church

pres·by·tery \ˈprez-bə-ˌter-ē, ˈpres-, -bə-trē\ *n, pl* **-ter·ies** [ME & LL; ME *presbytory* part of church reserved for clergy, fr. LL *presbyterium* group of presbyters, part of church reserved for clergy, fr. Gk *presbyterion* group of presbyters, fr. *presbyteros* elder, priest] (15c) **1 :** the part of a church reserved for the officiating clergy **2 :** a ruling body in presbyterian churches consisting of the ministers and representative elders from congregations within a district **3 :** the jurisdiction of a presbytery **4 :** the house of a Roman Catholic parish priest

¹pre·school \ˈprē-ˈskül\ *adj* (1914) **:** of, relating to, or constituting the period in a child's life from infancy to the age of five or six that ordinarily precedes attendance at elementary school

²pre·school \-ˌskül\ *n* (ca. 1925) **:** NURSERY SCHOOL, KINDERGARTEN

pre·school·er \-ˈskü-lər\ *n* (1946) **1 :** a child not yet old enough for school **2 :** a child attending a preschool

pre·science \ˈpresh(-ē)-ən(t)s, ˈpresh-; ˈprēs-ē-ən(t)s, ˈpres-\ *n* [ME, fr. LL *praescientia,* fr. L *praescient-, praesciens,* prp. of *praescire* to know beforehand, fr. *prae-* + *scire* to know — more at SCIENCE] (14c) **:** foreknowledge of events: **a :** divine omniscience **b :** human anticipation of the course of events **:** FORESIGHT — **pre·scient** \-ənt\ *adj* — **pre·scient·ly** *adv*

pre·sci·en·tif·ic \ˌprē-ˌsī-ən-ˈtif-ik\ *adj* (1896) **:** of, relating to, or having the characteristics of a period before the rise of modern science or a state prior to the application of the scientific method

pre·scind \pri-ˈsind\ *vb* [L *praescindere* to cut off in front, fr. *prae-* + *scindere* to cut — more at SHED] *vt* (1650) **:** to detach for purposes of thought ~ *vi* **:** to withdraw one's attention

pre·score \(ˈ)prē-ˈskō(ə)r, -ˈskȯ(ə)r\ *vt* (1930) **:** to record (as sound) in advance for use when the corresponding scenes are photographed in making movies

pre·scribe \pri-ˈskrīb\ *vb* **pre·scribed; pre·scrib·ing** [L *praescribere* to write at the beginning, dictate, order, fr. *prae-* + *scribere* to write — more at SCRIBE] *vi* (1531) **1** [ME *prescriben,* fr. ML *praescribere,* fr. L, to write at the beginning] **:** to claim a title to something by right of prescription **2 :** to lay down a rule **:** DICTATE **3 :** to write or give medical prescriptions **4 :** to become by prescription invalid or unenforceable ~ *vt* **1 a :** to lay down as a guide, direction, or rule of action **:** ORDAIN **b :** to specify with authority **2 :** to designate or order the use of as a remedy — **pre·scrib·er** *n*

pre·script \ˈprē-ˌskript, pri-ˈ\ *adj* [ME, fr. L *praescriptus,* pp.] (ca. 1540) **:** prescribed as a rule — **pre·script** \ˈprē-ˌskript\ *n*

pre·scrip·tion \pri-ˈskrip-shən\ *n* [partly fr. ME *prescripcion* establishment of a claim, fr. MF *prescription,* fr. LL *praescription-, praescriptio,* fr. L, act of writing at the beginning, order, limitation of subject matter, fr. *praescriptus,* pp. of *praescribere;* partly fr. L *praescription-, praescriptio* order] (14c) **1 a :** the establishment of a claim of title to something under common law usu. by use and enjoyment for a period fixed by statute **b :** the right or title acquired under common law by such possession **2 :** the process of making claim to something by long use and enjoyment **3 :** the action of laying down authoritative rules or directions **4 a :** a written direction for a therapeutic or corrective agent; *specif* **:** one for the preparation and use of a medicine **b :** a prescribed medicine **5 a :** ancient or long continued custom **b :** a claim founded upon ancient custom or long continued use **6 :** something prescribed as a rule

prescription drug *n* (1951) **:** a drug that can be obtained only by means of a physician's prescription

pre·scrip·tive \pri-ˈskrip-tiv\ *adj* (1765) **1 :** acquired by, founded on, or determined by prescription or by long-standing custom **2 :** serving to prescribe — **pre·scrip·tive·ly** *adv*

pre·se·lect \ˌprē-sə-ˈlekt\ *vt* (ca. 1864) **:** to choose in advance usu. on the basis of a particular criterion — **pre·se·lec·tion** \-ˈlek-shən\ *n*

pre·sell \(ˈ)prē-ˈsel\ *vt* **-sold** \-ˈsōld\; **-sell·ing** (1947) **:** to precondition by advertising and devices of salesmanship for a subsequent purchase

pres·ence \ˈprez-ᵊn(t)s\ *n* (14c) **1 :** the fact or condition of being present **2 a :** the part of space within one's immediate vicinity **b :** the neighborhood of one of superior esp. royal rank **3** *archaic* **:** COMPANY 2a **4 :** one that is present: as **a :** the actual person or thing that is present **b :** something present of a visible or concrete nature **5 a :** the bearing, carriage, or air of a person; *esp* **:** stately or distinguished bearing **b :** a quality of poise and effectiveness that enables a performer to achieve a close relationship with his audience **6 :** something (as a spirit) felt or believed to be present

presence of mind (1665) **:** self-control so maintained in an emergency or in an embarrassing situation that one can say and do the right thing

¹pres·ent \ˈprez-ᵊnt\ *n* [ME, fr. OF, fr. *presenter*] (13c) **:** something presented **:** GIFT

²pre·sent \pri-ˈzent\ *vb* [ME *presenten,* fr. OF *presenter,* fr. L *praesentare,* fr. *praesent-, praesens,* adj.] *vt* (13c) **1 a :** to bring or introduce into the presence of someone; *esp* **:** to introduce socially **b :** to bring (as a play) before the public **2 :** to make a gift to **3 :** to give or bestow formally **4 a :** to lay (as a charge) before a court as an object of inquiry **b :** to bring a formal public charge, indictment, or presentment against **5 :** to nominate to a benefice **6 :** to offer to view **:** SHOW **7 :** to act the part of **:** PERFORM **8 :** to aim, point, or direct (as a weapon) so as to face something or in a particular direction ~ *vi* **1 :** to present a weapon **2 :** to become manifest **3 :** to come forward as a patient ***syn*** see GIVE — **pre·sent·er** *n*

³pres·ent \ˈprez-ᵊnt\ *adj* [ME, fr. OF, fr. L *praesent-, praesens,* fr. prp. of *praeesse* to be before one, fr. *prae-* pre- + *esse* to be — more at IS] (14c) **1 :** now existing or in progress **2 a :** being in view or at hand **b :** existing in something mentioned or under consideration **3 :** constituting the one actually involved, at hand, or being considered **4 :** of, relating to, or constituting a verb tense that is expressive of present time or the time of speaking **5** *obs* **:** ATTENTIVE **6** *archaic* **:** INSTANT, IMMEDIATE — **pres·ent·ness** *n*

⁴pres·ent \ˈprez-ᵊnt\ *n* (14c) **1 a** *obs* **:** present occasion or affair **b** *pl* **:** the present words or statements; *specif* **:** the legal instrument or other writing in which these words are used **2 a :** the present tense of a language **b :** a verb form in the present tense **3 :** the present time

pre·sent·able \pri-ˈzent-ə-bəl\ *adj* (ca. 1626) **1 :** capable of being presented **2 :** being in condition to be seen or inspected esp. by the critical — **pre·sent·abil·i·ty** \-ˌzent-ə-ˈbil-ət-ē\ *n* — **pre·sent·able·ness** \-ˈzent-ə-bəl-nəs\ *n* — **pre·sent·ably** \-blē\ *adv*

pre·sent arms \pri-ˌzent-\ *n* [fr. the command *present arms!*] (1759) **1 :** a position in the manual of arms in which the rifle is held vertically in front of the body **2 :** a command to assume the position of present arms or to give a hand salute

pre·sen·ta·tion \ˌprē-ˌzen-ˈtā-shən, ˌprez-ᵊn-, ˌprēz-ᵊn-\ *n* (15c) **1 a :** the act of presenting **b :** the act, power, or privilege esp. of a patron of applying to the bishop or ordinary for the institution of one nominated to a benefice **2 :** something presented: as **a :** a symbol or image that represents something **b :** something offered or given **:** GIFT **c :** something set forth for the attention of the mind **d :** a descriptive or persuasive account (as by a salesman of his product) **3 :** the position in which the fetus lies in the uterus in labor with respect to the mouth of the uterus **4 :** an immediate object of perception, cognition, or memory **5** *often cap* **:** a church feast on November 21 celebrating the presentation of the Virgin Mary in the temple **6 :** the method by which radio, navigation, or radar information is given to the operator (as the pilot of an airplane) — **pre·sen·ta·tion·al** \-shnəl, -shən-ᵊl\ *adj*

pre·sen·ta·tive \pri-ˈzent-ət-iv, ˈprez-ᵊn-ˌtāt-\ *adj* (ca. 1842) **:** known, knowing, or capable of being known directly rather than through cogitation

pres·ent–day \ˈprez-ᵊnt-ˈdā\ *adj* (1887) **:** now existing or occurring

pre·sen·tee \ˌprez-ᵊn-ˈtē, pri-ˌzen-\ *n* (15c) **:** one who is presented or to whom something is presented

pre·sen·tient \pri-ˈsen-ch(ē-)ənt, ˈprē-; pri-ˈzen-\ *adj* [L *praesentient-, praesentiens,* prp. of *praesentire*] (1814) **:** having a presentiment

pre·sen·ti·ment \pri-ˈzent-ə-mənt\ *n* [F *pressentiment,* fr. MF, fr. *pressentir* to have a presentiment, fr. L *praesentire* to feel beforehand, fr. *prae-* + *sentire* to feel — more at SENSE] (1714) **:** a feeling that something will or is about to happen **:** PREMONITION — **pre·sen·ti·men·tal** \-ˌzent-ə-ˈment-ᵊl\ *adj*

pres·ent·ism \ˈprez-ᵊn-ˌtiz-əm\ *n* [³*present*] (ca. 1923) **:** an outlook dominated by present-day attitudes and experiences — **pres·ent·ist** \-ᵊnt-əst\ *adj*

pres·ent·ly \ˈprez-ᵊnt-lē\ *adv* (15c) **1 a** *archaic* **:** at once **b :** before long **:** without undue delay **2 :** at the present time **:** NOW

usage Both senses 1b and 2 are flourishing in current English, but many commentators have objected to sense 2. Since this sense has been in continuous use since the 15th century, it is not clear why it is objectionable. Perhaps a note in the *Oxford English Dictionary* (1909) that the sense has been obsolete since the 17th century in literary English is to blame, but the note goes on to observe that the sense is in regular use in most English dialects. The last citation in that dictionary is from a 1901 Leeds newspaper, written in Standard English. Sense 2 is most common in contexts relating to business and politics ⟨the fastest-rising welfare cost is Medicaid, *presently* paid by the states and cities —William Safire (1982)⟩

pre·sent·ment \pri-ˈzent-mənt\ *n* (14c) **1 :** the act of presenting to an authority a formal statement of a matter to be dealt with; *specif* **:** the notice taken or statement made by a grand jury of an offense from their own knowledge without a bill of indictment laid before them **2 :** the act of offering at the proper time and place a document (as a bill of exchange) that calls for acceptance or payment by another **3 a :** the act of presenting to view or consciousness **b :** something set forth, presented, or exhibited **c :** the aspect in which something is presented

present participle *n* (14c) : a participle that typically expresses present action in relation to the time expressed by the finite verb in its clause and that in English is formed with the suffix *-ing* and is used in the formation of the progressive tenses
present perfect *adj* (1580) : of, relating to, or constituting a verb tense that is formed in English with *have* and that expresses action or state completed at the time of speaking — **present perfect** *n*
present tense *n* (1669) : the tense of a verb that expresses action or state in the present time and is used of what occurs or is true at the time of speaking and of what is habitual or characteristic or is always or necessarily true, that is sometimes used to refer to action in the past (as in the historical present), and that is sometimes used for future events
present value *n* (1831) : the sum of money which if invested now at a given rate of compound interest will accumulate exactly to a specified amount at a specified future date ⟨at 12% interest the *present value* of $112 due one year from now is $100⟩
pres·er·va·tion·ist \ˌprez-ər-ˈvā-sh(ə-)nəst\ *n* (1927) : one that advocates preservation (as of a biological species or a historical landmark)
1**pre·ser·va·tive** \pri-ˈzər-vət-iv\ *adj* (14c) : having the power of preserving
2**preservative** *n* (1526) : something that preserves or has the power of preserving; *specif* : an additive used to protect against decay, discoloration, or spoilage
1**pre·serve** \pri-ˈzərv\ *vb* **pre·served; pre·serv·ing** [ME *preserven*, fr. MF *preserver*, fr. ML *praeservare*, fr. LL, to observe beforehand, fr. L *prae-* + *servare* to keep, guard, observe — more at CONSERVE] *vt* (14c) **1** : to keep safe from injury, harm, or destruction : PROTECT **2 a** : to keep alive, intact, or free from decay **b** : MAINTAIN **3 a** : to keep or save from decomposition **b** : to can, pickle, or similarly prepare for future use **4** : to keep up and reserve for personal or special use ~ *vi* **1** : to make preserves **2** : to raise and protect game for purposes of sport **3** : to stand preserving (as by canning) — **pre·serv·abil·i·ty** \-ˌzər-və-ˈbil-ət-ē\ *n* — **pre·serv·able** \-ˈzər-və-bəl\ *adj* — **pres·er·va·tion** \ˌprez-ər-ˈvā-shən\ *n* — **pre·serv·er** \pri-ˈzər-vər\ *n*
2**preserve** *n* (1600) **1** : fruit canned or made into jams or jellies or cooked whole or in large pieces in a syrup so as to keep its shape — often used in pl. **2** : an area restricted for the protection and preservation of natural resources (as animals or trees); *esp* : one used primarily for regulated hunting or fishing **3** : something regarded as reserved for certain persons
pre·set \(ˌ)prē-ˈset\ *vt* (1929) : to set beforehand — **pre·set·ta·ble** \-ˈset-ə-bəl\ *adj*
pre·shrunk \ˈprē-ˈshrəŋk, *esp Southern* -ˈsrəŋk\ *adj* (1929) : of, relating to, or being material (as a textile fabric) subjected to a shrinking process during manufacture usu. to reduce later shrinking
pre·side \pri-ˈzīd\ *vi* **pre·sid·ed; pre·sid·ing** [L *praesidēre* to guard, preside over, lit., to sit in front of, sit at the head of, fr. *prae-* + *sedēre* to sit — more at SIT] (1611) **1 a** : to occupy the place of authority : act as president, chairman, or moderator **b** : to occupy a position similar to that of a president or chairman **2** : to exercise guidance, direction, or control **3** : to occupy a position of featured instrumental performer — usu. used with *at* ⟨*presided* at the organ⟩ — **pre·sid·er** *n*
pres·i·den·cy \ˈprez-əd-ən-sē, ˈprez-dən- *also* ˈprez-ə-ˌden(t)-sē\ *n*, *pl* **-cies** (1591) **1 a** : the office of president **b** (1) : the office of president of the U.S. (2) : the American governmental institution comprising the office of president and various associated administrative and policy-making agencies **2** : the term during which a president holds office **3** : the action or function of one that presides : SUPERINTENDENCE **4** : a Mormon executive council of the church or a stake consisting of a president and two counselors
pres·i·dent \ˈprez-əd-ənt, ˈprez-dənt, ˈprez-ə-ˌdent *also* ˈprez-əd-ᵊnt, *in rapid speech* ˈprez-ᵊnt\ *n* [ME, fr. MF, fr. L *praesident-, praesidens*, fr. prp. of *praesidēre*] (14c) **1** : an official chosen to preside over a meeting or assembly **2** : an appointed governor of a subordinate political unit **3** : the chief officer of an organization (as a corporation or institution) usu. entrusted with the direction and administration of its policies **4** : the presiding officer of a governmental body **5 a** : an elected official serving as both chief of state and chief political executive in a republic having a presidential government **b** : an elected official having the position of chief of state but usu. only minimal political powers in a republic having a parliamentary government — **pres·i·den·tial** \ˌprez(-ə)-ˈden-chəl\ *adj* — **pres·i·den·tial·ly** \-ˈdench-(ə-)lē\ *adv* — **pres·i·dent·ship** \ˈprez-əd-ənt-ˌship, ˈprez-dənt-, ˈprez-ə-ˌdent- *also* ˈprez-əd-ᵊnt-\ *n*
presidential government *n* (1902) : a system of government in which the president is constitutionally independent of the legislature
Presidents' Day *n* (1952) : WASHINGTON'S BIRTHDAY 2
pre·sid·i·al \pri-ˈsid-ē-əl, prī-, -ˈzid-\ *adj* [LL *praesidialis*, fr. L *praesidium* garrison, fr. *praesid-, praeses* guard, governor, fr. *praesidēre*] (1598) **1** : of, having, or constituting a garrison **2** : of or relating to a president : PRESIDENTIAL **3** [F *présidial*, fr. MF, alter. of *presidal*, fr. LL *praesidalis* of a provincial governor, fr. L *praesid-, praeses*] : PROVINCIAL 1
pre·sid·i·ary \-ē-ˌer-ē\ *adj* (1599) : PRESIDIAL 1
pre·si·dio \pri-ˈsēd-ē-ˌō, -ˈsid-, -ˈzēd-, -ˈzid-\ *n*, *pl* **-di·os** [Sp, fr. L *praesidium*] (1763) : a garrisoned place; *esp* : a military post or fortified settlement in areas currently or orig. under Spanish control
pre·sid·i·um \pri-ˈsid-ē-əm, prī-, -ˈzid-\ *n*, *pl* **-ia** \-ē-ə\ *or* **-iums** [Russ *prezidium*, fr. L *praesidium* garrison] (1920) **1** : a permanent executive committee selected esp. in Communist countries to act for a larger body **2** : a nongovernmental executive committee
pre·sig·ni·fy \(ˌ)prē-ˈsig-nə-ˌfī\ *vt* [L *praesignificare*, fr. *prae-* + *significare* to signify] (1586) : to intimate or signify beforehand : PRESAGE
1**pre·soak** \(ˌ)prē-ˈsōk\ *vt* (1919) : to soak beforehand
2**pre·soak** \ˈprē-ˈsōk\ *n* (1919) **1** : an instance of presoaking **2** : a preparation used in presoaking clothes
pre–So·crat·ic \ˌprē-sə-ˈkrat-ik, -sō-\ *adj* (1871) : of or relating to Greek philosophers before Socrates — **pre–Socratic** *n*
1**press** \ˈpres\ *n* [ME *presse*, fr. OF, fr. *presser* to press] (13c) **1 a** : a crowd or crowded condition : THRONG **b** : a thronging or crowding forward or together **2 a** : an apparatus or machine by which a substance is cut or shaped, an impression of a body is taken, a material is compressed, pressure is applied to a body, liquid is expressed, or a cutting tool is fed into the work by pressure **b** : a building containing presses or a business using presses **3** : CLOSET, CUPBOARD **4 a** : an action of pressing or pushing : PRESSURE **b** : an aggressive pressuring defense employed in basketball often over the entire court area **5** : the properly smoothed and creased condition of a freshly pressed garment ⟨out of ~⟩ **6 a** : PRINTING PRESS **b** : the act or the process of printing **c** : a printing or publishing establishment **7 a** : the gathering and publishing or broadcasting of news : JOURNALISM **b** : newspapers, periodicals, and often radio and television news broadcasting **c** : news reporters, publishers, and broadcasters **d** : comment or notice in newspapers and periodicals ⟨is getting a good ~⟩ **8** : any of various pressure devices (as one for keeping sporting gear from warping when not in use) **9** : a lift in weight lifting in which the weight is raised to shoulder height and then smoothly extended overhead without assist from the legs — compare CLEAN AND JERK, SNATCH
2**press** *vb* [ME *pressen*, fr. MF *presser*, fr. L *pressare*, fr. *pressus*, pp. of *premere* to press; akin to L *prelum* press and perh. to Russ *peret'* to press] *vt* (14c) **1** : to act upon through steady pushing or thrusting force exerted in contact : SQUEEZE **2 a** : ASSAIL, HARASS **b** : AFFLICT, OPPRESS **3 a** : to squeeze out the juice or contents of **b** : to squeeze with apparatus or instruments to a desired density, smoothness, or shape **4 a** : to exert influence on : CONSTRAIN **b** : to try hard to persuade : BESEECH, ENTREAT **5** : to move by means of pressure **6 a** : to lay stress or emphasis on **b** : to insist on or request urgently **7** : to follow through (a course of action) **8** : to clasp in affection or courtesy **9** : to make (a phonograph record) from a matrix ~ *vi* **1** : to crowd closely : MASS **2** : to force or push one's way **3** : to seek urgently : CONTEND **4** : to require haste or speed in action **5** : to exert pressure **6** : to take or hold a press **7** : to employ a press in basketball — **press·er** *n* — **press the flesh** : to greet and shake hands with people esp. while campaigning for political office
3**press** *vb* [alter. of obs. *prest* (to enlist by giving pay in advance)] *vt* (1543) **1** : to force into service esp. in an army or navy : IMPRESS **2 a** : to take by authority esp. for public use : COMMANDEER **b** : to take and force into any usu. emergency service ~ *vi* : to impress men as soldiers or sailors
4**press** *n* (1592) **1** : impressment into service esp. in a navy **2** *obs* : a warrant for impressing recruits
press agent *n* [1*press*] (1883) : an agent employed to establish and maintain good public relations through publicity — **press–agent** *vb* — **press–agent·ry** \-ˈā-jən-trē\ *n*
press·board \ˈpres-ˌbō(ə)rd, -ˌbȯ(ə)rd\ *n* (1849) **1** : IRONING BOARD; *esp* : a small one for sleeves **2** : a strong highly glazed composition board resembling vulcanized fiber
press box *n* (1889) : a space reserved for reporters (as at a stadium)
press conference *n* (1937) : an interview given by a public figure to the press by appointment
press–gang \ˈpres-ˌgaŋ\ *n* [4*press*] (1693) : a detachment of men under command of an officer empowered to force men into military or naval service — **press–gang** *vt*
press·ing *adj* (1616) **1** : urgently important : CRITICAL **2** : EARNEST, WARM — **press·ing·ly** \-iŋ-lē\ *adv*
press kit *n* (1968) : a collection of promotional materials for distribution to the press
press·man \ˈpres-mən, -ˌman\ *n* (ca. 1598) **1** : an operator of a press; *esp* : the operator of a printing press **2** *Brit* : NEWSPAPERMAN
press·mark \-ˌmärk\ *n* [1*press* (closet)] *chiefly Brit* (1802) : a mark assigned to a book to indicate its location in a library
press of sail (1592) : the fullest amount of sail that a ship can crowd on — called also *press of canvas*
pres·sor \ˈpres-ˌȯ(ə)r, -ər\ *adj* [LL, one that presses, fr. L *pressus*, pp. of *premere* to press — more at PRESS] (ca. 1890) : raising or tending to raise blood pressure; *also* : involving vasoconstriction
press·room \ˈpres-ˌrüm, -ˌru̇m\ *n* (1683) **1** : a room in a printing plant containing the printing presses **2** : a room (as at the White House) for the use of members of the press
press·run \-ˌrən, -ˈrən\ *n* (1945) : a continuous operation of a printing press producing a specified number of copies; *also* : the number of copies printed
press secretary *n* (1951) : a person officially in charge of press relations for a usu. prominent public figure ⟨the President's *press secretary*⟩
1**pres·sure** \ˈpresh-ər\ *n* [ME, fr. LL *pressura*, fr. L, action of pressing, pressure, fr. *pressus*, pp. — more at PRESS] (14c) **1 a** : the burden of physical or mental distress **b** : the constraint of circumstance : the weight of social or economic imposition **2** : the application of force to something by something else in direct contact with it : COMPRESSION **3** *archaic* : IMPRESSION, STAMP **4 a** : the action of a force against an opposing force **b** : the force or thrust exerted over a surface divided by its area **c** : ELECTROMOTIVE FORCE **5** : the stress or urgency of matters demanding attention : EXIGENCY ⟨people who work well under ~⟩ **6** : the force of selection that results from one or more agents and tends to reduce a population of organisms ⟨population ~⟩ ⟨predation ~⟩ **7** : atmospheric pressure **8** : a sensation aroused by moderate compression of a body part or surface — **pres·sure·less** *adj*
2**pressure** *vt* **pres·sured; pres·sur·ing** \-(ə-)riŋ\ (1938) **1** : to apply pressure to **2** : PRESSURIZE **3** : to cook in a pressure cooker
pressure cabin *n* (1935) : a pressurized cabin
pressure cooker *n* (1915) **1** : an airtight utensil for quick cooking or preserving of foods by means of superheated steam under pressure **2** : a situation or environment that is fraught with emotional or social pressures — **pressure–cook** *vb*
pressure gauge *n* (1862) : a gauge for indicating fluid pressure
pressure group *n* (1928) : an interest group that is organized to influence public and esp. governmental policy but not to elect candidates to office
pressure point *n* (1909) : a point where a blood vessel runs near a bone and can be compressed (as to check bleeding) by the application of pressure against the bone

pressure suit *n* (1936) : an inflatable suit for high-altitude or space flight to protect the body from low pressure

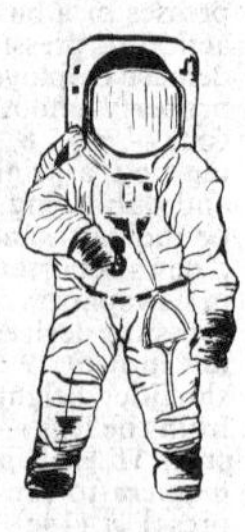

pressure suit

pres·sur·ize \'presh-ə-ˌrīz\ *vt* **-ized; -iz·ing** (1940) **1** : to maintain near-normal atmospheric pressure in during high-altitude or spaceflight (as by means of a supercharger) **2** : to apply pressure to **3** : to design to withstand pressure — **pres·sur·iza·tion** \ˌpresh-(ə-)rə-'zā-shən\ *n* — **pres·sur·iz·er** *n*

press·work \'pres-ˌwərk\ *n* (1771) : the operation, management, or product of a printing press; *esp* : the branch of printing concerned with the actual transfer of ink from form or plates to paper

prest \'prest\ *adj* [ME, fr. OF, fr. L *praestus* — more at PRESTO] *obs* (13c) : READY

pre·ster·num \'prē-'stər-nəm\ *n* [NL] (1872) : the anterior segment of the sternum of a mammal : MANUBRIUM

pres·ti·dig·i·ta·tion \ˌpres-tə-ˌdij-ə-'tā-shən\ *n* [F, fr. *prestidigitateur* prestidigitator, fr. *preste* nimble, quick (fr. It *presto*) + L *digitus* finger — more at DIGIT] (1859) : SLEIGHT OF HAND, LEGERDEMAIN — **pres·ti·dig·i·ta·tor** \-'dij-ə-ˌtāt-ər\ *n*

pres·tige \pre-'stēzh, -'stēj\ *n, often attrib* [F, fr. MF, conjuror's trick, illusion, fr. LL *praestigium,* fr. L *praestigiae,* pl., conjuror's tricks, irreg. fr. *praestringere* to tie up, blindfold, fr. *prae-* + *stringere* to bind tight — more at STRAIN] (1815) **1** : standing or estimation in the eyes of people : weight or credit in general opinion **2** : commanding position in people's minds ***syn*** see INFLUENCE — **pres·tige·ful** \-fəl\ *adj*

pres·ti·gious \pre-'stij-əs, -'stē-j- *also* prə-\ *adj* [L *praestigiosus,* fr. *praestigiae*] (1546) **1** *archaic* : of, relating to, or marked by illusion, conjuring, or trickery **2** : having prestige : HONORED — **pres·ti·gious·ly** *adv* — **pres·ti·gious·ness** *n*

pres·tis·si·mo \pres-'tis-ə-ˌmō\ *adv or adj* [It, fr. *presto* + *-issimo,* suffix denoting a high degree] (ca. 1724) : faster than presto — used as a direction in music

[1]**pres·to** \'pres-(ˌ)tō\ *adv or adj* [It, quick, quickly, fr. L *praestus* ready, fr. *praesto,* adv., on hand; akin to L *prae* before — more at FOR] (1683) **1** : suddenly as if by magic : IMMEDIATELY **2** : at a rapid tempo — used as a direction in music

[2]**presto** *n, pl* **prestos** (1807) : a presto musical passage or movement

[1]**pre·stress** \(ˈ)prē-'stres\ *vt* (1934) : to introduce internal stresses into (as a structural beam) to counteract the stresses that will result from applied load (as in incorporating cables under tension in concrete)

[2]**pre·stress** \'prē-'stres\ *n* (1934) **1** : the stresses introduced in prestressing **2** : the process of prestressing **3** : the condition of being prestressed

pre·sum·able \pri-'zü-mə-bəl\ *adj* (1692) : capable of being presumed : acceptable as an assumption — **pre·sum·ably** \-blē\ *adv*

pre·sume \pri-'züm\ *vb* **pre·sumed; pre·sum·ing** [ME *presumen,* fr. LL & MF; LL *praesumere* to dare, fr. L, to anticipate, assume, fr. *prae-* + *sumere* to take; MF *presumer* to assume, fr. L *praesumere* — more at CONSUME] *vt* (14c) **1** : to undertake without leave or clear justification : DARE **2** : to expect or assume esp. with confidence **3** : to suppose to be true without proof ⟨*presumed* innocent until proved guilty⟩ **4** : to take for granted : IMPLY ~ *vi* **1** : to act or proceed presumptuously or on a presumption **2** : to go beyond what is right or proper — **pre·sumed·ly** \-'zü-məd-lē, -'züm-dlē\ *adv* — **pre·sum·er** *n*

pre·sum·ing *adj* (1582) : PRESUMPTUOUS — **pre·sum·ing·ly** \-'zü-miŋ-lē\ *adv*

pre·sump·tion \pri-'zəm(p)-shən\ *n* [ME *presumpcioun,* fr. OF *presumption,* fr. LL & L; LL *praesumption-, praesumptio* presumptuous attitude, fr. L, assumption, fr. *praesumptus,* pp. of *praesumere*] (13c) **1** : presumptuous attitude or conduct : AUDACITY **2 a** : an attitude or belief dictated by probability : ASSUMPTION **b** : the ground, reason, or evidence lending probability to a belief **3** : a legal inference as to the existence or truth of a fact not certainly known that is drawn from the known or proved existence of some other fact

pre·sump·tive \-'zəm(p)-tiv\ *adj* (1561) **1** : giving grounds for reasonable opinion or belief **2** : based on probability or presumption **3** : being an embryonic precursor with the potential for forming a particular structure or tissue in the normal course of development ⟨~ retina⟩ — **pre·sump·tive·ly** *adv*

pre·sump·tu·ous \pri-'zəm(p)-ch(ə-w)əs, -shəs\ *adj* [ME, fr. MF *presumptueux,* fr. LL *praesumptuosus,* irreg. fr. *praesumptio*] (14c) : overstepping due bounds (as of propriety or courtesy) : taking liberties — **pre·sump·tu·ous·ly** *adv* — **pre·sump·tu·ous·ness** *n*

pre·sup·pose \ˌprē-sə-'pōz\ *vt* [ME *presupposen,* fr. MF *presupposer,* fr. ML *praesupponere* (perf. indic. *praesupposui*), fr. L *prae-* + ML *supponere* to suppose — more at SUPPOSE] (15c) **1** : to suppose beforehand **2** : to require as an antecedent in logic or fact — **pre·sup·po·si·tion** \(ˌ)prē-ˌsəp-ə-'zish-ən\ *n* — **pre·sup·po·si·tion·al** \-'zish-nəl, -'zish-ən-ᵊl\ *adj*

pre·syn·ap·tic \ˌprē-sə-'nap-tik\ *adj* (1909) : situated or occurring just before a nerve synapse — **pre·syn·ap·ti·cal·ly** \-ti-k(ə-)lē\ *adv*

prêt–à–por·ter \ˌpret-ä-pȯr-'tā\ *n* [F, ready to wear] (1959) : ready-to-wear clothes

pre·tax \'prē-'taks\ *adj* (1942) : existing before provision for taxes

[1]**pre·teen** \'prē-'tēn\ *n* (1952) : a boy or girl not yet 13 years old

[2]**preteen** *adj* (1954) **1** : relating to or produced for children esp. in the 9 to 12 year-old age group ⟨~ fashions⟩ **2** : being younger than 13

pre·teen–ag·er \-'tē-nā-jər\ *n* (1965) : PRETEEN

[1]**pre·tend** \pri-'tend\ *vb* [ME *pretenden,* fr. L *praetendere* to allege as an excuse, lit., to stretch in front of like a curtain, fr. *prae-* pre- + *tendere* to stretch — more at THIN] *vt* (15c) **1** : to give a false appearance of being, possessing, or performing : PROFESS ⟨does not ~ to be a psychiatrist⟩ **2 a** : to make believe : FEIGN ⟨he ~*ed* deafness⟩ **b** : to claim, represent, or assert falsely ⟨~*ing* an emotion he could not really feel⟩ **3** : VENTURE, UNDERTAKE ~ *vi* **1** : to feign an action, part, or role in play **2** : to put in a claim ***syn*** see ASSUME

[2]**pretend** *adj* (1911) : IMAGINARY, MAKE-BELIEVE

pre·tend·ed *adj* (15c) : professed or avowed but not genuine ⟨~ affection⟩ — **pre·tend·ed·ly** *adv*

pre·tend·er \pri-'ten-dər\ *n* (1591) : one that pretends: as **a** : one who lays claim to something; *specif* : a claimant to a throne who is held to have no just title **b** : one who makes a false or hypocritical show

pre·tense *or* **pre·tence** \'prē-ˌten(t)s, pri-'\ *n* [ME, fr. MF *pretensse,* fr. (assumed) ML *praetensa,* fr. LL, fem. of *praetensus,* pp. of L *praetendere*] (1526) **1** : a claim made or implied; *esp* : one not supported by fact **2 a** : mere ostentation : PRETENTIOUSNESS ⟨confuse dignity with pomposity and ~ —Bennett Cerf⟩ **b** : a pretentious act or assertion **3** : an inadequate or insincere attempt to attain a certain condition or quality **4** : professed rather than real intention or purpose : PRETEXT ⟨was there under false ~*s*⟩ **5** : MAKE-BELIEVE, FICTION **6** : false show : SIMULATION ⟨saw through his ~ of indifference⟩

[1]**pre·ten·sion** \pri-'ten-chən\ *n* (1609) **1** : an allegation of doubtful value : PRETEXT **2** : a claim or an effort to establish a claim **3** : a claim or right to attention or honor because of merit **4** : ASPIRATION, INTENTION **5** : VANITY, PRETENTIOUSNESS ***syn*** see AMBITION — **pre·ten·sion·less** \-ləs\ *adj*

[2]**pre·ten·sion** \(ˈ)prē-'ten-chən\ *vt* [*pre-* + [2]*tension*] (1937) : PRESTRESS

pre·ten·tious \pri-'ten-chəs\ *adj* [F *prétentieux,* fr. *prétention* pretension, fr. ML *praetention-, praetentio,* fr. L *praetentus,* pp. of *praetendere*] (1837) **1** : making usu. unjustified or excessive claims (as of value or standing) ⟨the ~ fraud who assumes a love of culture that is alien to him —Richard Watts⟩ **2** : making demands on one's skill, ability, or means : AMBITIOUS ⟨the ~ daring of the Green Mountain Boys in crossing the lake —*Amer. Guide Series: Vt.*⟩ ***syn*** see SHOWY — **pre·ten·tious·ly** *adv* — **pre·ten·tious·ness** *n*

pret·er·it *or* **pret·er·ite** \'pret-ə-rət\ *adj* [ME *preterit,* fr. MF, fr. L *praeteritus,* fr. pp. of *praeterire* to go by, pass, fr. *praeter* beyond, past, by (fr. compar. of *prae* before) + *ire* to go — more at FOR, ISSUE] (14c) **1** *archaic* : BYGONE, FORMER **2** : of, relating to, or constituting a verb tense that indicates action in the past without reference to duration, continuance, or repetition — **preterit** *n*

pre·ter·mi·nal \(ˈ)prē-'tərm-nəl, -ən-ᵊl\ *adj* (1947) : occurring before death

pre·ter·mis·sion \ˌprēt-ər-'mish-ən\ *n* [L *praetermission-, praetermissio,* fr. *praetermissus,* pp. of *praetermittere*] (1583) : the act or an instance of pretermitting : OMISSION

pre·ter·mit \-'mit\ *vt* **-mit·ted; -mit·ting** [L *praetermittere,* fr. *praeter* by, past + *mittere* to let go, send] (1538) **1** : to let pass without mention or notice : OMIT **2** : to leave undone : NEGLECT **3** : SUSPEND, BREAK OFF

pre·ter·nat·u·ral \ˌprēt-ər-'nach(-ə)-rəl\ *adj* [ML *praeternaturalis,* fr. L *praeter naturam* beyond nature] (1580) **1** : existing outside of nature **2** : exceeding what is natural or regular : EXTRAORDINARY ⟨wits trained to ~ acuteness by the debates —G. L. Dickinson⟩ **3** : inexplicable by ordinary means; *esp* : PSYCHIC ⟨~ phenomena⟩ — **pre·ter·nat·u·ral·ly** \-rə-lē, -'nach-ər-lē\ *adv* — **pre·ter·nat·u·ral·ness** \-'nach(-ə)-rəl-nəs\ *n*

pre·test \(ˈ)prē-'test\ *n* (1926) : a preliminary test: as **a** : a test of the effectiveness or safety of a product prior to its sale **b** : a test to evaluate the preparedness of students for further studies — **pretest** *vt*

pre·text \'prē-ˌtekst\ *n* [L *praetextus,* fr. *praetextus,* pp. of *praetexere* to assign as a pretext, lit., to weave in front, fr. *prae-* + *texere* to weave — more at TECHNICAL] (1513) : a purpose or motive alleged or an appearance assumed in order to cloak the real intention or state of affairs ***syn*** see APOLOGY

pre·tor, pre·to·ri·an *var of* PRAETOR, PRAETORIAN

pret·ti·fy \'prit-i-ˌfī, 'pu̇rt-, 'pru̇t-\ *vt* **-fied; -fy·ing** (1850) : to make pretty — **pret·ti·fi·ca·tion** \ˌprit-i-fə-'kā-shən, ˌpu̇rt-, ˌpru̇t-\ *n*

pret·ti·ness \'prit-ē-nəs, 'pu̇rt-, 'pru̇t-\ *n* (1649) **1** : the quality or state of being pretty **2** : something pretty

[1]**pret·ty** \'prit-ē, 'pu̇rt- *also* 'pru̇t-\ *adj* **pret·ti·er; -est** [ME *praty, prety,* fr. OE *prættig* tricky, fr. *prætt* trick; akin to ON *prettr* trick] (bef. 12c) **1 a** : ARTFUL, CLEVER **b** : PAT, APT **2 a** : pleasing by delicacy or grace **b** : having conventionally accepted elements of beauty **c** : appearing or sounding pleasant or nice but lacking strength, force, manliness, purpose, or intensity ⟨~ words that make no sense —Elizabeth B. Browning⟩ **3 a** : MISERABLE, TERRIBLE ⟨a ~ mess you've gotten us into⟩ **b** *chiefly Scot* : STOUT **4** : moderately large : CONSIDERABLE ⟨a very ~ profit⟩ ***syn*** see BEAUTIFUL — **pret·ti·ly** \-ᵊl-ē\ *adv* — **pret·ty·ish** \-ē-ish\ *adj*

[2]**pret·ty** \ˌpu̇rt-ē, pərt-ē, ˌprit-ē *also* ˌpru̇t-ē; *before "near(ly)" often without* -ē\ *adv* (1565) **1** : in some degree : MODERATELY ⟨~ cold weather⟩ **2** *archaic* : in a pretty manner : PRETTILY

usage Some handbooks complain that *pretty* is overworked and recommend the selection of a more specific word or restrict *pretty* to informal or colloquial contexts. *Pretty* is used to tone down a statement and is in wide use across the whole spectrum of English. It is common in informal speech and writing but is neither rare nor wrong in serious discourse ⟨he may, if he be *pretty* well off or clever, qualify himself as a doctor —G.B. Shaw⟩ ⟨dramaturgy and government may seem to be *pretty* distant analogues of one another —Scott Buchanan⟩ ⟨a return to those traditions of American foreign policy which worked *pretty* well for over a century —H.S. Commager⟩ ⟨the arguments for buying expensive books have to be *pretty* cogent —*Times Lit. Supp.*⟩

[3]**pret·ty** \'prit-ē, 'pu̇rt-ē *also* 'pru̇t-ē\ *n, pl* **pretties** (1736) **1** *pl* : dainty clothes; *esp* : LINGERIE **2** : a pretty person or thing

[4]**pret·ty** *like*[3]\ *vt* **pret·tied; pret·ty·ing** (1909) : to make pretty — usu. used with *up* ⟨curtains to ~ up the room⟩

pret·zel \'pret-səl\ *n* [G *brezel,* deriv. of L *brachiatus* having branches like arms, fr. *brachium* arm — more at BRACE] (ca. 1824) : a usu. brittle glazed and salted cracker typically shaped like a loose knot

pre·vail \pri-'vā(ə)l\ *vi* [ME *prevailen,* fr. L *praevalēre,* fr. *prae-* pre- + *valēre* to be strong — more at WIELD] (15c) **1** : to gain ascendancy through strength or superiority : TRIUMPH **2** : to be or become effective or effectual **3** : to use persuasion successfully ⟨~*ed* on him to sing⟩ **4** : to be frequent : PREDOMINATE ⟨the west winds that ~ in the mountains⟩ **5** : to be or continue in use or fashion : PERSIST ⟨a custom that still ~*s*⟩

pre·vail·ing \-'vā-liŋ\ *adj* (ca. 1586) **1** : having superior force or influence **2 a** : most frequent ⟨~ winds⟩ **b** : generally current : COMMON — **pre·vail·ing·ly** \-liŋ-lē\ *adv*

prev·a·lence \'prev(-ə)-lən(t)s\ *n* (1713) **1** : the quality or state of being prevalent **2** : the degree to which something is prevalent; *esp* : the percentage of a population that is affected with a particular disease at a given time

prev·a·lent \-lənt\ *adj* [L *praevalent-, praevalens* very powerful, fr. prp. of *praevalēre*] (1576) **1** *archaic* **:** POWERFUL **2** *archaic* **:** being in ascendancy **:** DOMINANT **3 :** generally or widely accepted, practiced, or favored **:** WIDESPREAD — **prevalent** *n* — **prev·a·lent·ly** *adv*

pre·var·i·cate \pri-ˈvar-ə-ˌkāt\ *vi* **-cat·ed; -cat·ing** [L *praevaricatus,* pp. of *praevaricari* to walk crookedly, fr. *prae-* + *varicari* to straddle, fr. *varus* bent, knock-kneed] (ca. 1631) **:** to deviate from the truth **:** EQUIVOCATE *syn* see LIE — **pre·var·i·ca·tion** \-ˌvar-ə-ˈkā-shən\ *n* — **pre·var·i·ca·tor** \-ˈvar-ə-ˌkāt-ər\ *n*

pre·ve·nient \pri-ˈvēn-yənt\ *adj* [L *praevenient-, praeveniens,* prp. of *praevenire*] (1656) **:** ANTECEDENT, ANTICIPATORY — **pre·ve·nient·ly** *adv*

pre·vent \pri-ˈvent\ *vb* [ME *preventen* to anticipate, fr. L *praeventus,* pp. of *praevenire* to come before, anticipate, forestall, fr. *prae-* + *venire* to come — more at COME] *vt* (15c) **1** *archaic* **a :** to be in readiness for (as an occasion) **b :** to meet or satisfy in advance **c :** to act ahead of **d :** to go or arrive before **2 :** to deprive of power or hope of acting or succeeding **3 :** to keep from happening or existing ⟨steps to ~ war⟩ **4 :** to hold or keep back **:** HINDER, STOP — often used with *from* ~ *vi* **:** to interpose an obstacle — **pre·vent·abil·i·ty** \-ˌvent-ə-ˈbil-ət-ē\ *n* — **pre·vent·able** *also* **pre·vent·ible** \-ˈvent-ə-bəl\ *adj* — **pre·vent·er** *n*

syn PREVENT, ANTICIPATE, FORESTALL mean to deal with beforehand. PREVENT implies taking advance measures against something possible or probable; ANTICIPATE may imply merely getting ahead of another by being a precursor or forerunner or it may imply checking another's intention by acting first; FORESTALL implies a getting ahead so as to stop or interrupt something in its course.

pre·ven·ta·tive \-ˈvent-ət-iv\ *adj or n* (ca. 1654) **:** PREVENTIVE

pre·ven·tion \pri-ˈven-chən\ *n* (1582) **:** the act of preventing or hindering

¹pre·ven·tive \-ˈvent-iv\ *n* (ca. 1639) **:** something that prevents; *esp* **:** something used to prevent disease

²preventive *adj* (1639) **1 :** devoted to or concerned with prevention **:** PRECAUTIONARY ⟨~ steps against soil erosion⟩ **2 :** undertaken to forestall anticipated hostile action ⟨a ~ coup⟩ — **pre·ven·tive·ly** *adv* — **pre·ven·tive·ness** *n*

pre·ver·bal \(ˈ)prē-ˈvər-bəl\ *adj* (1921) **1 :** occurring before the verb **2 :** having not yet acquired the faculty of speech ⟨a ~ child⟩

¹pre·view \ˈprē-ˌvyü\ *vt* (1607) **1 :** to see beforehand; *specif* **:** to view or to show in advance of public presentation **2 :** to give a preliminary survey of — **pre·view·er** \-ˌvyü-ər\ *n*

²preview *n* (1922) **1 :** an advance showing or performance (as of a motion picture or play) **2** *also* **pre·vue** \-ˌvyü\ **:** a showing of snatches from a motion picture advertised for appearance in the near future — called also *trailer* **3 :** an advance statement, sample, or survey

pre·vi·ous \ˈprē-vē-əs\ *adj* [L *praevius* leading the way, fr. *prae-* pre- + *via* way — more at VIA] (1625) **1 :** going before in time or order **:** PRIOR **2 :** acting too soon **:** PREMATURE *syn* see PRECEDING — **pre·vi·ous·ly** *adv* — **pre·vi·ous·ness** *n*

previous question *n* (ca. 1700) **:** a parliamentary motion to put the pending question to an immediate vote without further debate or amendment that if defeated has the effect of permitting resumption of debate

previous to *prep* (1702) **:** PRIOR TO, BEFORE

¹pre·vi·sion \prē-ˈvizh-ən\ *n* [LL *praevision-, praevisio,* fr. L *praevisus,* pp. of *praevidēre* to foresee, fr. *prae-* + *vidēre* to see — more at WIT] (1612) **1 :** FORESIGHT, PRESCIENCE **2 :** FORECAST, PROGNOSTICATION — **pre·vi·sion·al** \-ˈvizh-nəl, -ən-ᵊl\ *adj* — **pre·vi·sion·ary** \-ˈvizh-ə-ˌner-ē\ *adj*

²prevision *vt* **pre·vi·sioned; pre·vi·sion·ing** \-ˈvizh-(ə-)niŋ\ (1891) **:** FORESEE

pre·vo·cal·ic \ˌprē-vō-ˈkal-ik, -və-\ *adj* [ISV] (1899) **:** immediately preceding a vowel

pre·vo·ca·tion·al \ˌprē-vō-ˈkā-shnəl, -shən-ᵊl\ *adj* (1914) **:** given or required before admission to a vocational school

pre·writ·ing \ˈprē-ˌrīt-iŋ\ *n* (1968) **:** the formulation and organization of ideas preparatory to writing

prexy \ˈprek-sē\ *also* **prex** \ˈpreks\ *n, pl* **prex·ies** *also* **prex·es** [*prexy* fr. *prex,* by shortening & alter. fr. *president*] *slang* (1871) **:** PRESIDENT — used chiefly of a college president

¹prey \ˈprā\ *n, pl* **preys** [ME *preie,* fr. OF, fr. L *praeda;* akin to L *prehendere* to grasp, seize — more at GET] (13c) **1** *archaic* **:** SPOIL, BOOTY **2 a :** an animal taken by a predator as food **b :** one that is helpless or unable to resist attack **:** VICTIM ⟨was ~ to his own appetites⟩ **3 :** the act or habit of preying

²prey *vi* [ME *preyen,* fr. OF *preier,* fr. L *praedari,* fr. *praeda*] (13c) **1 :** to make raids for the sake of booty **2 a :** to seize and devour prey **b :** to commit violence or robbery or fraud **3 :** to have an injurious, destructive, or wasting effect — **prey·er** *n*

Pri·am \ˈprī-əm, -ˌam\ *n* [L *Priamus,* fr. Gk *Priamos*] **:** the father of Hector and Paris and king of Troy during the Trojan War

pri·a·pic \prī-ˈā-pik, -ˈap-ik\ *adj* [L *priapus* lecher, fr. *Priapus*] (1786) **1 :** PHALLIC **2 :** relating to or preoccupied with virility

Pri·a·pus \prī-ˈā-pəs\ *n* [L, fr. Gk *Priapos*] **:** a Greek and Roman god of gardens and male generative power

¹price \ˈprīs\ *n* [ME *pris,* fr. OF, fr. L *pretium* price, money; akin to Skt *prati-* against, in return — more at PROS-] (13c) **1** *archaic* **:** VALUE, WORTH **2 a :** the quantity of one thing that is exchanged or demanded in barter or sale for another **b :** the amount of money given or set as consideration for the sale of a specified thing **3 :** the terms for the sake of which something is done or undertaken: as **a :** an amount sufficient to bribe one ⟨believed every man had his ~⟩ **b :** a reward for the apprehension or death of a person ⟨a man with a ~ on his head⟩ **4 :** the cost at which something is obtained ⟨the ~ of freedom is restraint —J. Irwin Miller⟩

²price *vt* **priced; pric·ing** (14c) **1 :** to set a price on **2 :** to find out the price of **3 :** to drive by raising prices excessively ⟨*priced* themselves out of the market⟩ — **pric·er** *n*

price–cut·ter \ˈprī-ˌskət-ər\ *n* (1901) **:** one that reduces prices esp. to a level designed to cripple competition — **price–cut·ting** \-iŋ\ *n*

-priced \ˈprīst\ *adj comb form* **:** having (such) a price set ⟨low-*priced* merchandise⟩

price–earn·ings ratio \ˈprī-ˈsər-niŋz-\ *n* (1961) **:** a measure of the value of a common stock determined as the ratio of its market price to its earnings per share and usu. expressed as a simple numeral

price–fix·ing \ˈprīs-ˌfik-siŋ\ *n* (1920) **:** the setting of prices artificially (as by producers or government) contrary to free market operations

price index *n* (1886) **:** an index number expressing the level of a group of commodity prices relative to the level of the prices of the same commodities during an arbitrarily chosen base period and used to indicate changes in the level of prices from one period to another

price·less \ˈprī-sləs\ *adj* (1593) **1 a :** having a value beyond any price **:** INVALUABLE **b :** costly because of rarity or quality **:** PRECIOUS **2 :** having worth in terms of other than market value **3 :** surprisingly amusing, odd, or absurd — **price·less·ly** *adv*

price support *n* (1945) **:** artificial maintenance of prices (as of a raw material) at some predetermined level usu. through government action

price tag *n* (1881) **1 :** a tag on merchandise showing the price at which it is offered for sale **2 :** PRICE, COST

price war *n* (1925) **:** a period of commercial competition characterized by the repeated cutting of prices below those of competitors

pric·ey *also* **pricy** \ˈprī-sē\ *adj* **pric·i·er; -est** (1932) **:** EXPENSIVE ⟨a ~, handcrafted . . . antique —*Apartment Life*⟩

¹prick \ˈprik\ *n* [ME *prikke,* fr. OE *prica;* akin to MD *pric* prick] (bef. 12c) **1 :** a mark or shallow hole made by a pointed instrument **2 a :** a pointed instrument or weapon **b :** a sharp projecting organ or part **3 :** an instance of pricking or the sensation of being pricked: as **a :** a nagging or sharp feeling of remorse, regret, or sorrow **b :** a slight sharply localized discomfort ⟨the ~ of a needle⟩ **4 :** PENIS — usu. considered vulgar **5 :** a spiteful or contemptible person often having some authority — usu. considered vulgar

²prick *vt* (bef. 12c) **1 :** to pierce slightly with a sharp point **2 :** to affect with anguish, grief, or remorse ⟨doubt began to ~ him —Philip Hale⟩ **3 :** to ride, guide, or urge on with or as if with spurs **:** GOAD **4 :** to mark, distinguish, or note by means of a small mark **5 :** to trace or outline with punctures **6 :** to remove (a young seedling) from the seedbed to another suitable for further growth **7 :** to cause to be or stand erect ⟨a dog ~*ing* his ears⟩ ~ *vi* **1 a :** to prick something or cause a pricking sensation **b :** to feel discomfort as if from being pricked **2 a :** to urge a horse with the spur **b :** to ride fast **3 :** THRUST **4 :** to become directed upward **:** POINT — **prick up one's ears :** to listen intently

prick·er \ˈprik-ər\ *n* (14c) **1 :** one that pricks: as **a :** a rider of horses **b :** a military light horseman **2 :** BRIAR, PRICKLE, THORN

prick·et \ˈprik-ət\ *n* [ME *priket,* fr. *prikke*] (15c) **1 a :** a spike on which a candle is stuck **b :** a candlestick with such a point **2 :** a buck in his second year

¹prick·le \ˈprik-əl\ *n* [ME *prikle,* fr. OE *pricle;* akin to OE *prica* prick] (15c) **1 :** a fine sharp process or projection; *esp* **:** a sharp pointed emergence arising from the epidermis or bark of a plant **2 :** a prickling sensation

²prickle *vb* **prick·led; prick·ling** \-(ə-)liŋ\ *vt* (1513) **1 :** to prick slightly **2 :** to produce prickles in ~ *vi* **:** to cause or feel a prickling or stinging sensation **:** TINGLE

prick·ly \ˈprik-lē, -ə-lē\ *adj* **prick·li·er; -est** (1578) **1 :** full of or covered with prickles; *esp* **:** distinguished from related kinds by the presence of prickles **2 :** marked by prickling **:** STINGING ⟨a ~ sensation⟩ **3 a :** TROUBLESOME, VEXATIOUS ⟨~ issues⟩ **b :** easily irritated ⟨had a ~ disposition⟩ — **prick·li·ness** *n*

prickly ash *n* (1709) **:** a prickly aromatic shrub or small tree (*Zanthoxylum americanum*) of the rue family with yellowish flowers

prickly heat *n* (1736) **:** a noncontagious cutaneous eruption of red pimples with intense itching and tingling caused by inflammation around the sweat ducts

prickly pear *n* (1612) **:** any of a large genus (*Opuntia*) of cacti with usu. yellow flowers and flat or terete joints usu. studded with tubercles bearing spines or prickly hairs; *also* **:** its pulpy pear-shaped edible fruit

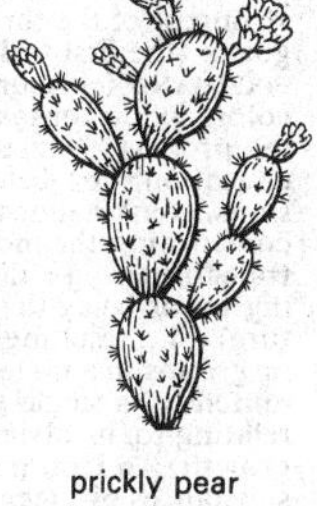

prickly pear

prickly poppy *n* (1724) **:** any of a genus (*Argemone*) of plants of the poppy family with prickly leaves and white or yellow flowers; *esp* **:** a yellow-flowered Mexican annual (*A. mexicana*)

¹pride \ˈprīd\ *n* [ME, fr. OE *prȳde,* fr. *prūd* proud — more at PROUD] (bef. 12c) **1 :** the quality or state of being proud: as **a :** inordinate self-esteem **:** CONCEIT **b :** a reasonable or justifiable self-respect **c :** delight or elation arising from some act, possession, or relationship ⟨parental ~⟩ **2 :** proud or disdainful behavior or treatment **:** DISDAIN **3 a :** ostentatious display **b :** highest pitch **:** PRIME **4 :** a source of pride **:** the best in a group or class **5 :** a company of lions **6 :** a showy or impressive group ⟨a ~ of dancers⟩

²pride *vt* **prid·ed; prid·ing** (13c) **:** to indulge in pride

pride·ful \ˈprīd-fəl\ *adj* (15c) **:** full of pride: as **a :** DISDAINFUL, HAUGHTY **b :** EXULTANT, ELATED — **pride·ful·ly** \-fə-lē\ *adv* — **pride·ful·ness** *n*

pride of place (1623) **:** the highest or first position

prie–dieu \(ˈ)prē-ˈdyə(r), prē-dyœ\ *n, pl* **prie–dieux** \-ˈdyə(r)(z), -dyœ(z)\ [F, lit., pray God] (1760) **1 :** a kneeling bench designed for use by a person at prayer and fitted with a raised shelf on which the elbows or a book may be rested **2 :** a low armless upholstered chair with a high straight back

pri·er \ˈprī(-ə)r\ *n* (1552) **:** one that pries; *esp* **:** an inquisitive person

priest \ˈprēst\ *n* [ME *preist,* fr. OE *prēost,* modif. of LL *presbyter* — more at PRESBYTER] (bef. 12c) **:** one authorized to perform the sacred rites of a religion esp. as a mediatory agent between man and God;

specif : an Anglican, Eastern Orthodox, or Roman Catholic clergyman ranking below a bishop and above a deacon
priest·ess \ˈprē-stəs\ *n* (1693) **1** : a woman authorized to perform the sacred rites of a religion **2** : a woman regarded as a leader (as of a movement)
priest·hood \ˈprēst-ˌhu̇d, ˈprē-ˌstu̇d\ *n* (bef. 12c) **1** : the office, dignity, or character of a priest **2** : the whole body of priests
priest·ly \ˈprēst-lē\ *adj* (bef. 12c) **1** : of or relating to a priest or the priesthood : SACERDOTAL **2** : characteristic of or befitting a priest — **priest·li·ness** *n*
priest–rid·den \ˈprē-ˌstrid-ᵊn\ *adj* (1653) : controlled or oppressed by a priest
[1]prig \ˈprig\ *n* [*prig* (to steal)] (1610) : THIEF
[2]prig *n* [prob. fr. [1]*prig*] (1676) **1** *archaic* : FELLOW, PERSON **2** *archaic* : FOP **3** : one who offends or irritates by observance of proprieties (as of speech or manners) in a pointed manner or to an obnoxious degree — **prig·gery** \-ə-rē\ *n* — **prig·gish** \ˈprig-ish\ *adj* — **prig·gish·ly** *adv* — **prig·gish·ness** *n*
prig·gism \ˈprig-ˌiz-əm\ *n* (ca. 1805) : stilted adherence to convention
[1]prill \ˈpril\ *vt* [perh. fr. E dial. *prill* (a running stream)] (1944) **1** : to convert (as a molten solid) into spherical pellets **2** : to make (as granular material) free flowing
[2]prill *n* (1952) : prilled material : a prilled substance
[1]prim \ˈprim\ *vt* **primmed; prim·ming** [origin unknown] (1706) **1** : to give a prim or demure expression to ⟨*primming* her thin lips after every mouthful —John Buchan⟩ **2** : to dress primly
[2]prim *adj* **prim·mer; prim·mest** (1771) **1 a** : stiffly formal and proper : DECOROUS **b** : PRUDISH **2** : NEAT, TRIM ⟨~ hedges⟩ — **prim·ly** *adv* — **prim·ness** *n*
pri·ma ballerina \ˌprē-mə-\ *n* [It, leading ballerina] (1782) : the principal female dancer in a ballet company
pri·ma·cy \ˈprī-mə-sē\ *n* (14c) **1** : the state of being first (as in importance, order, or rank) : PREEMINENCE ⟨the ~ of intellectual and esthetic over materialistic values —T. R. McConnell⟩ **2** : the office, rank, or preeminence of an ecclesiastical primate
pri·ma don·na \ˌprim-ə-ˈdän-ə, ˌprē-mə-\ *n, pl* **prima donnas** [It, lit., first lady] (1812) **1** : a principal female singer in an opera or concert organization **2** : an extremely sensitive, vain, or undisciplined person
[1]pri·ma fa·cie \ˌprī-mə-ˈfā-shə, -s(h)ē *also* -s(h)ē-ˌē\ *adv* [L] (15c) : at first view : on the first appearance ⟨the arguments . . . seem *prima facie* true —*Trans-Action*⟩
[2]prima facie *adj* (1800) **1** : true, valid, or sufficient at first impression : APPARENT ⟨the theory . . . gives a *prima facie* solution —R. J. Butler⟩ **2** : SELF-EVIDENT **3** : legally sufficient to establish a fact or a case unless disproved ⟨*prima facie* evidence⟩
pri·mal \ˈprī-məl\ *adj* [ML *primalis*, fr. L *primus* first — more at PRIME] (1602) **1** : ORIGINAL, PRIMITIVE ⟨village life continued in its ~ innocence —Van Wyck Brooks⟩ **2** : first in importance : FUNDAMENTAL ⟨our ~ concern⟩ — **pri·mal·i·ty** \prī-ˈmal-ət-ē\ *n*
primal scream therapy *n* (1971) : psychotherapy in which the patient recalls and reenacts a particularly disturbing past experience and expresses normally repressed anger or frustration esp. through spontaneous and unrestrained screams, hysteria, or violence — called also *primal therapy*
pri·mar·i·ly \prī-ˈmer-ə-lē *also* prə-\ *adv* (1601) **1** : for the most part : CHIEFLY ⟨has now become ~ a residential town —S. P. B. Mais⟩ **2** : in the first place : ORIGINALLY
[1]pri·ma·ry \ˈprī-ˌmer-ē, ˈprīm-(ə-)rē\ *adj* [LL *primarius* basic, primary, fr. L, principal, fr. *primus*] (15c) **1 a** : first in order of time or development : PRIMITIVE ⟨the ~ stage of civilization⟩ **b** : of or relating to formations of the Paleozoic and earlier periods **2 a** : of first rank, importance, or value : PRINCIPAL ⟨the ~ purpose⟩ **b** : BASIC, FUNDAMENTAL ⟨security is a ~ need⟩ **c** : of, relating to, or constituting the principal quills of a bird's wing **d** : of or relating to agriculture, forestry, and the extractive industries or their products **e** : expressive of present or future time ⟨~ tense⟩ **f** : of, relating to, or constituting the strongest of the three or four degrees of stress recognized by most linguists ⟨the first syllable of *basketball* carries ~ stress⟩ **3 a** : DIRECT, FIRSTHAND ⟨~ sources of information⟩ **b** : not derivable from other colors, odors, or tastes **c** : preparatory to something else in a continuing process ⟨~ instruction⟩ **d** : of or relating to a primary school ⟨~ education⟩ **e** : belonging to the first group or order in successive divisions, combinations, or ramifications ⟨~ nerves⟩ **f** : of, relating to, or constituting the inducing current or its circuit in an induction coil or transformer **g** : directly derived from ores ⟨~ metals⟩ **h** : of, relating to, or being the amino acid sequence in proteins ⟨~ protein structure⟩ **4** : resulting from the substitution of one of two or more atoms or groups in a molecule; *esp* : being or characterized by a carbon atom united by a single valence to only one chain or ring member **5** : of, relating to, involving, or derived from primary meristem ⟨~ tissue⟩ ⟨~ growth⟩ **6** : of, relating to, or involved in the production of organic substances by green plants ⟨~ productivity⟩
[2]primary *n, pl* **-ries** (ca. 1760) **1** : something that stands first in rank, importance, or value : FUNDAMENTAL — usu. used in pl. **2 a** [short for *primary planet*] : a planet as distinguished from its satellites **b** : the brighter component of a double star **3** : one of the usu. 9 or 10 strong quills on the distal joint of a bird's wing — see BIRD illustration **4 a** : PRIMARY COLOR **b** : a primary-color sensation **5 a** : CAUCUS **b** : an election in which qualified voters nominate or express a preference for a particular candidate or group of candidates for political office, choose party officials, or select delegates for a party convention **6** : the coil that is connected to the source of electricity in an induction coil or transformer — called also *primary coil*
primary atypical pneumonia *n* (ca. 1944) : a usu. mild pneumonia believed to be caused by a virus
primary cell *n* (1902) : a cell that converts chemical energy into electrical energy by irreversible chemical reactions
primary color *n* (1612) : any of a set of colors from which all other colors may be derived
primary consumer *n* (1965) : HERBIVORE
primary meristem *n* (1875) : meristem consisting of direct derivatives of embryonic cells that are always active in growth
primary root *n* (ca. 1890) : the root of a plant that develops first and originates from the radicle
primary school *n* (1802) **1** : a school usu. including the first three grades of elementary school but sometimes also including kindergarten **2** : ELEMENTARY SCHOOL
primary syphilis *n* (ca. 1903) : the first stage of syphilis that is marked by the development of a chancre and the spread of the causative spirochete in the tissues of the body
primary tooth *n* (ca. 1898) : MILK TOOTH
primary wall *n* (1933) : the first-formed wall of a plant cell that is produced around the protoplast and usu. has plasmodesmata
pri·mate \ˈprī-ˌmāt *or esp for 1* -mət\ *n* [ME *primat*, fr. OF, fr. ML *primat-, primas* archbishop, fr. L, leader, fr. *primus*] (13c) **1** *often cap* : a bishop who has precedence in a province, group of provinces, or a nation **2** *archaic* : one first in authority or rank : LEADER **3** : any of an order (Primates) of mammals comprising man together with the apes, monkeys, and related forms (as lemurs and tarsiers) — **pri·mate·ship** \-ˌship\ *n* — **pri·ma·tial** \prī-ˈmā-shəl\ *adj*
pri·ma·tol·o·gy \ˌprī-mə-ˈtäl-ə-jē\ *n* (1926) : the study of primates esp. other than recent man — **pri·ma·to·log·i·cal** \-mət-ᵊl-ˈäj-i-kəl\ *adj* — **pri·ma·tol·o·gist** \-mə-ˈtäl-ə-jəst\ *n*
[1]prime \ˈprīm\ *n* [ME, fr. OE *prim*, fr. L *prima hora* first hour] (bef. 12c) **1 a** *often cap* : the second of the canonical hours **b** : the first hour of the day usu. considered either as 6 a.m. or the hour of sunrise **2 a** : the earliest stage **b** : SPRING **c** : YOUTH **3** : the most active, thriving, or successful stage or period ⟨in the ~ of his life⟩ **4** : the chief or best individual or part : PICK ⟨~ of the flock, and choicest of the stall —Alexander Pope⟩ **5** : PRIME NUMBER **6 a** : the first note or tone of a musical scale : TONIC **b** : the interval between two notes on the same staff degree **7** : the symbol ′ **8** : PRIME RATE
[2]prime *adj* [ME, fr. MF, fem. of *prin* first, fr. L *primus*; akin to L *prior*] (14c) **1** : first in time : ORIGINAL **2 a** : of, relating to, or being a prime number — compare RELATIVELY PRIME **b** : having no polynomial factors other than itself and no monomial factors other than 1 ⟨a ~ polynomial⟩ **c** : expressed as a product of prime factors (as prime numbers and prime polynomials) ⟨a ~ factorization⟩ **3 a** : first in rank, authority, or significance : PRINCIPAL **b** : having the highest quality or value ⟨~ farmland⟩ **c** : of the highest grade regularly marketed — used of meat and esp. beef **4** : not deriving from something else : PRIMARY — **prime·ly** *adv* — **prime·ness** *n*
[3]prime *vb* **primed; prim·ing** [prob. fr. [1]*prime*] *vt* (1513) **1** : FILL, LOAD **2 a** : to prepare for firing by supplying with priming **b** : to insert a primer into (a cartridge case) **3** : to apply the first color, coating, or preparation to ⟨~ a wall⟩ **4** : to put into working order by filling or charging with something ⟨~ a pump with water⟩ **5** : to instruct beforehand : COACH ⟨*primed* the witness⟩ **6** : STIMULATE ~ *vi* : to become prime — **prime the pump** : to take steps to encourage the growth or functioning of something
prime cost *n* (1718) : the combined total of raw material and direct labor costs incurred in production; *broadly* : cost less vendor's or agent's commission for charges
prime meridian *n* (ca. 1859) : the meridian of 0 degrees longitude which runs through the original site of the Royal Observatory at Greenwich, England, and from which other longitudes are reckoned east and west
prime minister *n* (1655) **1** : the chief minister of a ruler or state **2** : the official head of a cabinet or ministry; *esp* : the chief executive of a parliamentary government — **prime ministerial** *adj* — **prime ministership** *n* — **prime ministry** *n*
prime mover *n* [trans. of ML *primus motor*] (ca. 1864) **1** : the self-moved being that is the source of all motion **2 a** : an initial source of motive power (as a windmill, waterwheel, turbine, or internal-combustion engine) designed to receive and modify force and motion as supplied by some natural source and apply them to drive machinery **b** : a powerful tractor or truck usu. with all-wheel drive **3** : the original or most effective force in an undertaking or work ⟨education is . . . a *prime mover* of cultural and societal change —R. C. Buck⟩
prime number *n* (ca. 1570) : any integer other than 0 or ± 1 that is not divisible without remainder by any other integers except ± 1 and ± the integer itself
[1]prim·er \ˈprim-ər, *chiefly Brit* ˈprī-mər\ *n* [ME, fr. ML *primarium*, fr. LL, neut. of *primarius* primary] (14c) **1** : a small book for teaching children to read **2** : a small introductory book on a subject
[2]prim·er \ˈprī-mər\ *n* (1819) **1 a** : a device for priming; *esp* : a cap, tube, or wafer containing percussion powder or compound used to ignite an explosive charge **b** : a molecule (as of DNA) whose presence is required for formation of more molecules of the same kind **2** : material used in priming a surface — called also *prime coat*
prime rate *n* (1958) : an interest rate formally announced by a bank to be the lowest available at a particular time to its most credit-worthy customers — called also *prime interest rate*
pri·me·ro \pri-ˈme(ə)r-(ˌ)ō, -ˈmi(ə)r-\ *n* [modif. of Sp *primera*] (1533) : a card game popular in the 16th and 17th centuries
prime time *n* (1958) : the evening period generally from 7 to 11 p.m. during which television has its largest number of viewers — **prime-time** *adj*
pri·me·val \prī-ˈmē-vəl\ *adj* [L *primaevus*, fr. *primus* first + *aevum* age — more at AYE] (1653) **1** : of or relating to the earliest ages (as of the world or human history) : ANCIENT, PRIMITIVE ⟨100 acres of ~ forest which has never felt an ax —Mary R. Zimmer⟩ **2** : existing in or persisting from the beginning (as of a solar system or universe) ⟨a ~ gas cloud⟩ — **pri·me·val·ly** \-və-lē\ *adv*
prim·ing *n* (15c) **1** : the act of one that primes **2** : the explosive used in priming a charge **3** : [2]PRIMER 2
pri·mip·a·ra \prī-ˈmip-ə-rə\ *n, pl* **-ras** *or* **-rae** \-ˌrē, -ˌrī\ [L, fr. *primus* first + *-para* -para] (ca. 1842) **1** : an individual bearing a first offspring **2** : an individual that has borne only one offspring — **pri·mip·a·rous** \prī-ˈmip-ə-rəs\ *adj*
[1]prim·i·tive \ˈprim-ət-iv\ *adj* [ME *primitif*, fr. L *primitivus*, fr. *primitus* originally, fr. *primus* first — more at PRIME] (15c) **1 a** : not derived : ORIGINAL, PRIMARY **b** : assumed as a basis; *esp* : AXIOMATIC ⟨~ concepts⟩ **2 a** : of or relating to the earliest age or period : PRIMEVAL ⟨the ~ church⟩ **b** : closely approximating an early ancestral type : little evolved **c** : belonging to or characteristic of an early stage of development : CRUDE, RUDIMENTARY ⟨~ technology⟩ **d** : of, relating to, or constituting the assumed parent speech of related languages ⟨~ Germanic⟩ **3 a** : ELEMENTAL, NATURAL ⟨our ~ feelings of vengeance

—John Mackwood⟩ **b :** of, relating to, or produced by a relatively simple people or culture ⟨~ art⟩ **c :** NAIVE **d** (1) **:** SELF-TAUGHT, UNTUTORED ⟨~ craftsmen⟩ (2) **:** produced by a self-taught artist ⟨a ~ painting⟩ — **prim·i·tive·ly** *adv* — **prim·i·tive·ness** *n* — **prim·i·tiv·i·ty** \ˌprim-ə-ˈtiv-ət-ē\ *n*

2**primitive** *n* (1600) **1 a :** something primitive; *specif* **:** a primitive idea, term, or proposition **b :** a root word **2 a** (1) **:** an artist of an early period of a culture or artistic movement (2) **:** a later imitator or follower of such an artist **b** (1) **:** a self-taught artist (2) **:** an artist whose work is marked by directness and naïveté **c :** a work of art produced by a primitive artist **3 a :** a member of a primitive people **b :** an unsophisticated person

primitive area *n* (1932) **:** a tract within a U.S. national forest set aside for preservation in natural condition with no alteration or development beyond measures for fire prevention being permitted

prim·i·tiv·ism \ˈprim-ət-iv-ˌiz-əm\ *n* (1861) **1 a :** belief in the superiority of a simple way of life close to nature **b :** belief in the superiority of nonindustrial society to that of the present **2 :** the style of art of primitive peoples or primitive artists — **prim·i·tiv·ist** \-iv-əst\ *n or adj* — **prim·i·tiv·is·tic** \ˌprim-ət-iv-ˈis-tik\ *adj*

1**pri·mo** \ˈprē-(ˌ)mō\ *n, pl* **primos** [It, fr. *primo* first, fr. L *primus*] (1792) **:** the first or leading part (as in a duet or trio)

2**pri·mo** \ˈprē-(ˌ)mō, ˈprī-\ *adv* [L, fr. *primus*] (ca. 1901) **:** in the first place

pri·mo·gen·i·tor \ˌprī-mō-ˈjen-ət-ər\ *n* [LL, fr. L *primus* + *genitor* begetter, fr. *genitus*, pp. of *gignere* to beget — more at KIN] (1654) **:** ANCESTOR, FOREFATHER

pri·mo·gen·i·ture \-ˈjen-ə-ˌchu̇(ə)r, -i-chər, -ə-ˌt(y)u̇(ə)r\ *n* [LL *primogenitura*, fr. L *primus* + *genitura* birth, fr. *genitus*, pp.] (1594) **1 :** the state of being the firstborn of the children of the same parents **2 :** an exclusive right of inheritance belonging to the eldest son

pri·mor·di·al \prī-ˈmȯrd-ē-əl\ *adj* [ME, fr. LL *primordialis*, fr. L *primordium* origin, fr. neut. of *primordius* original, fr. *primus* first + *ordiri* to begin — more at PRIME, ORDER] (14c) **1 a :** first created or developed **:** PRIMEVAL **b :** earliest formed in the growth of an individual or organ **:** PRIMITIVE **2 :** FUNDAMENTAL, PRIMARY ⟨~ human joys —Sir Winston Churchill⟩ — **pri·mor·di·al·ly** \-ē-ə-lē\ *adv*

pri·mor·di·um \-ē-əm\ *n, pl* **-dia** \-ē-ə\ [NL, fr. L] (1671) **:** the rudiment or commencement of a part or organ

primp \ˈprimp\ *vb* [perh. alter. of 1*prim*] *vt* (1801) **:** to dress, adorn, or arrange in a careful or finicky manner ~ *vi* **:** to dress or groom oneself carefully ⟨~*s* for hours before a date⟩

prim·rose \ˈprim-ˌrōz\ *n* [ME *primerose*, fr. MF] (15c) **:** any of a genus (*Primula* of the family Primulaceae, the primrose family) of perennial herbs with large tufted basal leaves and showy variously colored flowers — compare EVENING PRIMROSE

primrose path *n* (1602) **1 :** a path of ease or pleasure and esp. sensual pleasure ⟨himself the *primrose path* of dalliance treads —Shak.⟩ **2 :** a path of least resistance

primrose yellow *n* (ca. 1904) **1 :** a light to moderate greenish yellow **2 :** a light to moderate yellow

prim·u·la \ˈprim-yə-lə\ *n* [ML, fr. *primula veris*, lit., firstling of spring] (1753) **:** PRIMROSE

pri·mum mo·bi·le \ˌprī-məm-ˈmō-bə-lē, ˌprē-\ *n, pl* **primum mobiles** [ME, fr. ML, lit., first moving thing] (14c) **:** the outermost concentric sphere conceived in medieval astronomy as carrying the spheres of the fixed stars and the planets in its daily revolution

pri·mus \ˈprī-məs\ *n, often cap* [ML, one who is first, magnate, fr. L, first — more at PRIME] (1724) **:** the presiding bishop of the Scottish Episcopal Church

pri·mus in·ter pa·res \ˈprī-mə-ˌsint-ər-ˈpar-ēz, ˈprē-\ *n* [L] (1813) **:** first among equals

prince \ˈprin(t)s\ *n* [ME, fr. OF, fr. L *princip-*, *princeps*, lit., one who takes the first part, fr. *primus* first + *capere* to take — more at HEAVE] (13c) **1 a :** MONARCH, KING **b :** the ruler of a principality or state **2 :** a male member of a royal family; *esp* **:** a son of the sovereign **3 :** a nobleman of varying rank and status **4 :** a person of high rank or of high standing in his class or profession — **prince·ship** \ˈprin(t)s-ˌship\ *n*

Prince Al·bert \prin-ˈsal-bərt\ *n* [*Prince Albert* Edward (later Edward VII king of England)] (1884) **:** a long double-breasted frock coat

Prince Charming *n* [*Prince Charming*, hero of the fairy tale *Cinderella* by Charles Perrault] (1862) **:** a suitor who fulfills the dreams of his beloved; *also* **:** a man of often specious charm toward women

prince consort *n, pl* **princes consort** (1861) **:** the husband of a reigning female sovereign

prince·dom \ˈprin(t)s-dəm, -təm\ *n* (1560) **1 :** the jurisdiction, sovereignty, rank, or estate of a prince **2 :** PRINCIPALITY 3 — usu. used in pl.

prince·let \ˈprin(t)-slət\ *n* (1682) **:** PRINCELING

prince·li·ness \-slē-nəs\ *n* (1571) **1 :** princely conduct or character **2 :** LUXURY, MAGNIFICENCE

prince·ling \ˈprin(t)-sliŋ\ *n* (ca. 1618) **:** a petty or insignificant prince

prince·ly \ˈprin(t)-slē\ *adj* **prince·li·er; -est** (15c) **1 :** of or relating to a prince **:** ROYAL **2 :** befitting a prince **:** NOBLE, MAGNIFICENT ⟨~ manners⟩ ⟨a ~ sum⟩ — **princely** *adv*

Prince of Wales \-ˈwā(ə)lz\ (14c) **:** the male heir apparent to the British throne — used as a title only after it has been specif. conferred by the sovereign

prince's–feath·er \ˈprin(t)-səz-ˌfeth-ər\ *n* (1629) **:** a showy annual plant (*Amaranthus hybridus hypochondriacus*) of the amaranth family often cultivated for its dense usu. red spikes of bloom

1**prin·cess** \ˈprin(t)-səs, ˈprin-ˌses, (*usual Brit*) prin-ˈses\ *n* (15c) **1** *archaic* **:** a woman having sovereign power **2 :** a female member of a royal family; *esp* **:** a daughter or granddaughter of a sovereign **3 :** the consort of a prince **4 :** one very outstanding in a specified respect ⟨a ~ of a seamstress⟩ ⟨a winding ~ of a river⟩

2**princess** *like* 1\ *or* **prin·cesse** \prin-ˈses\ *adj* [F *princesse* princess, fr. *prince*] (1867) **:** close-fitting and usu. with gores from neck to flaring hemline ⟨a ~ gown⟩

princess royal *n, pl* **princesses royal** (ca. 1646) **:** the eldest daughter of a sovereign

1**prin·ci·pal** \ˈprin(t)-s(ə-)pəl, -sə-bəl\ *adj* [ME, fr. OF, fr. L *principalis*, fr. *princip-*, *princeps* — more at PRINCE] (13c) **1 :** most important, consequential, or influential **:** CHIEF **2 :** of, relating to, or constituting principal or a principal *usage* see PRINCIPLE — **prin·ci·pal·ly** \-ē, ˈprin(t)-splē\ *adv*

2**principal** *n* (14c) **1 :** a person who has controlling authority or is in a leading position: as **a :** a chief or head man or woman **b :** the chief executive officer of an educational institution **c :** one who employs another to act for him subject to his general control and instruction; *specif* **:** the person from whom an agent's authority derives **d :** the chief or an actual participant in a crime **e :** the person primarily or ultimately liable on a legal obligation **f :** a leading performer **:** STAR **2 :** a matter or thing of primary importance: as **a** (1) **:** a capital sum placed at interest, due as a debt, or used as a fund (2) **:** the corpus of an estate, portion, devise, or bequest **b :** the construction that gives shape and strength to a roof and is usu. one of several trusses; *broadly* **:** the most important member of a piece of framing *usage* see PRINCIPLE — **prin·ci·pal·ship** \ˈprin(t)-s(ə-)pəl-ˌship, -sə-bəl-\ *n*

principal diagonal *n* (1964) **:** the diagonal in a square matrix that runs from upper left to lower right

prin·ci·pal·i·ty \ˌprin(t)-sə-ˈpal-ət-ē\ *n, pl* **-ties** (14c) **1 a :** the state, office, or authority of a prince **b :** the position or responsibilities of a principal (as of a school) **2 :** the territory or jurisdiction of a prince **:** the country that gives title to a prince **3** *pl* **:** an order of angels — see CELESTIAL HIERARCHY

principal parts *n pl* (1870) **:** a series of verb forms from which all the other forms of a verb can be derived including in English the infinitive, the past tense, and the present and past participles

prin·cip·i·um \prin-ˈsip-ē-əm, priŋ-ˈkip-\ *n, pl* **-ia** \-ē-ə\ [L, beginning, basis] (1600) **:** a fundamental principle

prin·ci·ple \ˈprin(t)-s(ə-)pəl, -sə-bəl\ *n* [ME, modif. of MF *principe*, fr. L *principium* beginning, fr. *princip-*, *princeps* one taking the first part — more at PRINCE] (15c) **1 a :** a comprehensive and fundamental law, doctrine, or assumption **b** (1) **:** a rule or code of conduct (2) **:** habitual devotion to right principles ⟨a man of ~⟩ **c :** the laws or facts of nature underlying the working of an artificial device **2 :** a primary source **:** ORIGIN **3 a :** an underlying faculty or endowment ⟨such ~*s* of human nature as greed and curiosity⟩ **b :** an ingredient (as a chemical) that exhibits or imparts a characteristic quality **4** *cap, Christian Science* **:** a divine principle **:** GOD

usage Although nearly every handbook and many dictionaries warn against confusing *principle* and *principal*, many people still do. *Principle* is only a noun; *principal* is both adjective and noun. If you are unsure which noun you want, read the definitions in this dictionary.

— **in principle :** with respect to fundamentals ⟨prepared to accept the proposition *in principle*⟩

prin·ci·pled \-s(ə-)pəld, -sə-bəld\ *adj* (1642) **:** exhibiting, based on, or characterized by principle — often used in combination

prin·cox \ˈprin-ˌkäks, ˈpriŋ-\ *n* [origin unknown] *archaic* (1540) **:** a pert youth **:** COXCOMB

prink \ˈpriŋk\ *vb* [prob. alter. of 2*prank*] (1576) **:** PRIMP — **prink·er** *n*

1**print** \ˈprint\ *n* [ME *preinte*, fr. MF, fr. *preint*, pp. of *preindre* to press, fr. L *premere* — more at PRESS] (14c) **1 a :** a mark made by pressure **:** IMPRESSION **b :** something impressed with a print or formed in a mold **2 :** a device or instrument for impressing or forming a print **3 a :** printed state or form **b :** the printing industry **4 a :** PRINTED MATTER **b** *pl* **:** printed publications **5 :** printed letters **:** TYPE **6 a** (1) **:** a copy made by printing (2) **:** a reproduction of an original work of art (as a painting) made by a photomechanical process (3) **:** an original work of art (as a woodcut, etching, or lithograph) intended for graphic reproduction and produced by or under the supervision of the artist who designed it **b :** cloth with a pattern or figured design applied by printing; *also* **:** an article of such cloth **c :** a photographic or motion-picture copy; *esp* **:** one made from a negative — **in print :** procurable from the publisher — **out of print :** not procurable from the publisher

2**print** *vt* (14c) **1 a :** to impress something in or on **b :** to stamp (as a mark) in or on something **2 a :** to make a copy of by impressing paper against an inked printing surface **b** (1) **:** to impress (as wallpaper) with a design or pattern (2) **:** to impress (a pattern or design) on something **c :** to publish in print **d :** to display on a surface (as a computer screen) for viewing **3 :** to write in letters shaped like those of ordinary roman text type **4 :** to make (a positive picture) on a sensitized photographic surface from a negative or a positive ~ *vi* **1 a :** to work as a printer **b :** to produce printed matter **2 :** to produce something in printed form **3 :** to write or hand-letter in imitation of unjoined printed characters

3**print** *adj* (1629) **:** of, relating to, or writing for printed publications ⟨~ journalists⟩

print·able \ˈprint-ə-bəl\ *adj* (1837) **1 :** capable of being printed or of being printed from **2 :** considered fit to publish — **print·abil·i·ty** \ˌprin(t)-ə-ˈbil-ət-ē\ *n*

printed circuit *n* (1946) **:** a circuit for electronic apparatus made by depositing conductive material in continuous paths from terminal to terminal on an insulating surface

printed matter *n* (1876) **:** matter printed by any of various mechanical processes that is eligible for mailing at a special rate

print·er \ˈprint-ər\ *n* (1567) **:** one that prints: as **a :** a person engaged in printing **b :** a device used for printing; *esp* **:** a machine for printing from photographic negatives **c :** a device (as a chain printer) that produces printout

printer's devil *n* (1763) **:** an apprentice in a printing office

print·ery \ˈprint-ə-rē\ *n, pl* **-er·ies** (1638) **:** PRINTING OFFICE

print·ing *n* (14c) **1 :** the act or product of one that prints **2 :** reproduction in printed form **3 :** the art, practice, or business of a printer **4 :** IMPRESSION 4c **5** *pl* **:** paper to be printed on

printing office *n* (1733) **:** an establishment where printing is done

printing press *n* (1588) **:** a machine that produces printed copies

print·less \ˈprint-ləs\ *adj* (1610) **:** making, bearing, or taking no imprint

\ə\ abut \ᵊ\ kitten, F table \ər\ further \a\ ash \ā\ ace \ä\ cot, cart \au̇\ out \ch\ chin \e\ bet \ē\ easy \g\ go \i\ hit \ī\ ice \j\ job \ŋ\ sing \ō\ go \ȯ\ law \ȯi\ boy \th\ thin \th\ the \ü\ loot \u̇\ foot \y\ yet \zh\ vision \à, k̲, ⁿ, œ, œ̄, ue, ue̅, ʸ\ *see* Guide to Pronunciation

print·mak·ing \-ˌmā-kiŋ\ *n* (1928) **:** the design and production of prints by an artist — **print·mak·er** \-kər\ *n*

print·out \ˈprint-ˌau̇t\ *n* (1953) **:** a printed record produced automatically (as by a computer)

print out \(ˈ)print-ˈau̇t\ *vt* (1953) **:** to make a printout of

[1]**pri·or** \ˈprī(-ə)r\ *n* [ME, fr. OE & OF; both fr. ML, fr. LL, administrator, fr. L, former, superior] (bef. 12c) **1 :** the superior ranking next to the abbot of a monastery **2 :** the superior of a house or group of houses of any of various religious communities — **pri·or·ate** \ˈprī-ə-rət\ *n* — **pri·or·ship** \ˈprī(-ə)r-ˌship\ *n*

[2]**pri·or** \ˈprī(-ə)r\ *adj* [L, former, superior, compar. of OL *pri* before; akin to L *priscus* ancient, *prae* before — more at FOR] (1714) **1 :** earlier in time or order **2 :** taking precedence (as in importance) ***syn*** see PRECEDING — **pri·or·ly** *adv*

pri·or·ess \ˈprī-ə-rəs\ *n* (13c) **:** a nun corresponding in rank to a prior

pri·or·i·tize \prī -ˈȯr-ə-ˌtīz, -ˈär-; ˈprī-ə-rə-\ *vt* **-tized; -tiz·ing** [*priority* + *-ize*] (1966) **:** to list or rate (as projects or goals) in order of priority ***usage*** see -IZE — **pri·or·i·ti·za·tion** \prī-ˌȯr-ət-ə-ˈzā-shən, -är-; ˌprī-ə-rət-\ *n*

pri·or·i·ty \prī-ˈȯr-ət-ē, -ˈär-\ *n, pl* **-ties** (14c) **1 a** (1) **:** the quality or state of being prior (2) **:** precedence in date or position of publication — used of taxa **b** (1) **:** superiority in rank, position, or privilege (2) **:** legal precedence in exercise of rights over the same subject matter **2 :** a preferential rating; *esp* **:** one that allocates rights to goods and services usu. in limited supply ⟨that project has top ~⟩ **3 :** something meriting prior attention

prior to *prep* (1714) **:** in advance of **:** BEFORE
usage Sometimes termed pompous or affected, *prior to* is a synonym of *before* that most often appears in rather formal contexts, such as the annual reports of corporations. It may occas. emphasize the notion of anticipation ⟨if page makeup decisions are verified and approved *prior to* typesetting, proofreading of pages afterward becomes unnecessary —*Publishers Weekly*⟩

pri·o·ry \ˈprī-(ə-)rē\ *n, pl* **-ries** [ME *priorie*, fr. AF, fr. ML *prioria*, fr. *prior* [1]prior] (13c) **:** a religious house under a prior or prioress

prise \ˈprīz\ *chiefly Brit var of* PRIZE

prism \ˈpriz-əm\ *n* [LL *prismat-, prisma*, fr. Gk, lit., anything sawn, fr. *priein* to saw] (1570) **1 :** a polyhedron with two polygonal faces lying in parallel planes and with the other faces parallelograms — see VOLUME table **2 a :** a transparent body that is bounded in part by two nonparallel plane faces and is used to deviate or disperse a beam of light **b :** a prism-shaped decorative glass luster **3 :** a crystal form whose faces are parallel to one axis; *esp* **:** one whose faces are parallel to the vertical axis **4 :** a medium that distorts, slants, or colors whatever is viewed through it

pris·mat·ic \priz-ˈmat-ik\ *adj* (1709) **1 :** relating to, resembling, or constituting a prism **2 a :** formed by a prism **b :** resembling the colors formed by refraction of light through a prism ⟨~ effects⟩ **3 :** highly colored **:** BRILLIANT **4 :** having such symmetry that a general form with faces cutting all axes at unspecified intercepts is a prism ⟨~ crystals⟩ — **pris·mat·i·cal·ly** \-i-k(ə-)lē\ *adv*

pris·ma·toid \ˈpriz-mə-ˌtȯid\ *n* [LL *prismat-, prisma* prism] (ca. 1890) **:** a polyhedron that has all of its vertices in two parallel planes

pris·moid \ˈpriz-ˌmȯid\ *n* (1704) **:** a prismatoid whose parallel bases have the same number of sides — **pris·moi·dal** \priz-ˈmȯid-ᵊl\ *adj*

[1]**pris·on** \ˈpriz-ᵊn\ *n* [ME, fr. OF, fr. L *prehension-, prehensio* act of seizing, fr. *prehensus*, pp. of *prehendere* to seize — more at GET] (12c) **1 :** a state of confinement or captivity **2 :** a place of confinement: as **a :** a building in which persons are confined for safe custody while on trial for an offense or for punishment after trial and conviction **b :** an institution for the imprisonment of persons convicted of serious crimes **:** PENITENTIARY

[2]**prison** *vt* (14c) **:** IMPRISON, CONFINE

prison camp *n* (ca. 1908) **1 :** a camp for the confinement of reasonably trustworthy prisoners usu. employed on government projects **2 :** a camp for prisoners of war

pris·on·er \ˈpriz-nər, -ᵊn-ər\ *n* (14c) **:** a person deprived of his liberty and kept under involuntary restraint, confinement, or custody; *esp* **:** one on trial or in prison

prisoner of war (1678) **:** a person captured in war; *esp* **:** a member of the armed forces of a nation who is taken by the enemy during combat

prisoner's base *n* (ca. 1755) **:** a game in which players on each of two teams seek to tag and imprison players of the other team who have ventured out of their home territory

pris·sy \ˈpris-ē\ *adj* **pris·si·er; -est** [prob. blend of *prim* and *sissy*] (1895) **:** being prim and precise **:** FINICKY — **pris·si·ly** \ˈpris-ə-lē\ *adv* — **pris·si·ness** \ˈpris-ē-nəs\ *n*

pris·tane \ˈpris-ˌtān\ *n* [L *pristis* shark, sawfish; fr. its occurrence in the liver oils of sharks] (1923) **:** an isoprenoid hydrocarbon $C_{19}H_{40}$ that usu. accompanies phytane

pris·tine \ˈpris-ˌtēn, pris-ˈtēn, *esp Brit* ˈpris-ˌtīn\ *adj* [L *pristinus*; akin to L *prior* [2]prior] (1534) **1 :** belonging to the earliest period or state ⟨the hypothetical ~ lunar atmosphere⟩ **2 a :** uncorrupted by civilization ⟨~ innocence⟩ **b :** free from soil or decay **:** being fresh and clean — **pris·tine·ly** *adv*

prith·ee \ˈprith-ē, ˈprith-\ *interj* [alter. of (*I*) *pray thee*] *archaic* (ca. 1522) — used to express a wish or request

pri·va·cy \ˈprī-və-sē, *esp Brit* ˈpriv-ə-\ *n, pl* **-cies** (15c) **1 a :** the quality or state of being apart from company or observation **:** SECLUSION **b :** freedom from unauthorized intrusion ⟨one's right to ~⟩ **2** *archaic* **:** a place of seclusion **3 :** SECRECY

pri·vat·do·cent *or* **pri·vat·do·zent** \pri-ˈvät-dō(t)-ˌsent\ *n* [G *privatdozent*, fr. *privat* private + *dozent* teacher, fr. L *docent-, docens*, prp. of *docēre* to teach — more at DOCILE] (1854) **:** an unsalaried university lecturer or teacher in German-speaking countries remunerated directly by students' fees

[1]**pri·vate** \ˈprī-vət\ *adj* [ME *privat*, fr. L *privatus*, fr. pp. of *privare* to deprive, release, fr. *privus* private, set apart; akin to L *pro* for — more at FOR] (14c) **1 a :** intended for or restricted to the use of a particular person, group, or class ⟨a ~ park⟩ **b :** belonging to or concerning an individual person, company, or interest ⟨a ~ house⟩ **c** (1) **:** restricted to the individual or arising independently of others ⟨~ opinion⟩ (2) **:** carried on by the individual independently of the usual institutions ⟨~ study⟩; *also* **:** being educated by independent study or a tutor or in a private school ⟨~ students⟩ **d :** not general in effect ⟨a ~ statute⟩ **e :** of, relating to, or receiving hospital service in which the patient has more privileges than a semiprivate or ward patient **2 a** (1) **:** not holding public office or employment ⟨a ~ citizen⟩ (2) **:** not related to one's official position **:** PERSONAL ⟨~ correspondence⟩ **b :** being a private ⟨a ~ soldier⟩ **3 a :** withdrawn from company or observation **:** SEQUESTERED ⟨a ~ retreat⟩ **b :** not known or intended to be known publicly **:** SECRET **c :** preferring to keep personal affairs private **:** valuing privacy highly ⟨a quiet ~ man⟩ **d :** unsuitable for public use or display — **pri·vate·ly** *adv* — **pri·vate·ness** *n*

[2]**private** *n* (15c) **1** *archaic* **:** one not in public office **2** *obs* **:** PRIVACY **3** *pl* **:** PRIVATE PARTS **4 a :** a person of low rank in various organizations (as a police or fire department) **b :** an enlisted man of the lowest rank in the marine corps or of one of the two lowest ranks in the army — **in private :** not openly or in public

private detective *n* (1868) **:** a person concerned with the maintenance of lawful conduct or the investigation of crime either as a regular employee of a private interest (as a hotel) or as a contractor for fees

private enterprise *n* (1844) **:** FREE ENTERPRISE

pri·va·teer \ˌprī-və-ˈti(ə)r\ *n* (1664) **1 :** an armed private ship commissioned to cruise against the commerce or warships of an enemy **2 :** the commander or one of the crew of a privateer — **privateer** *vi*

private eye *n* (1938) **:** PRIVATE DETECTIVE

private first class *n* (1918) **:** an enlisted man ranking in the army above a private and below a corporal and in the marine corps above a private and below a lance corporal

private investigator *n* (ca. 1961) **:** PRIVATE DETECTIVE

private law *n* (1940) **:** a branch of law concerned with private persons, property, and relationships — compare PUBLIC LAW

private parts *n pl* (1773) **:** the external genital and excretory organs

private school *n* (1857) **:** a school that is established, conducted, and primarily supported by a nongovernmental agency

private treaty *n* (1858) **:** a sale of property on terms determined by conference of the seller and buyer — compare AUCTION

pri·va·tion \prī-ˈvā-shən\ *n* [ME *privacion*, fr. MF *privation*, fr. L *privation-, privatio*, fr. *privatus*, pp. of *privare* to deprive] (14c) **1 :** an act or instance of depriving **:** DEPRIVATION **2 :** the state of being deprived; *esp* **:** lack of what is needed for existence

pri·vat·ism \ˈprī-və-ˌtiz-əm\ *n* [*private*] (1950) **:** the attitude of being uncommitted to or avoiding involvement in anything beyond one's immediate interests

[1]**priv·a·tive** \ˈpriv-ət-iv\ *n* (1588) **:** a privative term, expression, or proposition; *also* **:** a privative prefix or suffix

[2]**privative** *adj* (1598) **:** constituting or predicating privation or absence of a quality ⟨*a-, un-, non-* are ~ prefixes⟩ ⟨*blind* is a ~ term⟩ — **priv·a·tive·ly** *adv*

pri·vat·ize \ˈprī-vət-ˌīz\ *vt* [[1]*private* + *-ize*] (1948) **:** to make private; *esp* **:** to change (as a business or industry) from public to private control or ownership — **pri·vat·iza·tion** \ˌprī-vət-ə-ˈzā-shən\ *n*

priv·et \ˈpriv-ət\ *n* [origin unknown] (1542) **:** an ornamental shrub (*Ligustrum vulgare*) of the olive family with half-evergreen leaves and small white flowers widely used for hedges; *broadly* **:** any of various similar shrubs of the same genus

[1]**priv·i·lege** \ˈpriv(-ə)-lij\ *n* [ME, fr. OF, fr. L *privilegium* law for or against a private person, fr. *privus* private + *leg-, lex* law — more at LEGAL] (12c) **:** a right or immunity granted as a peculiar benefit, advantage, or favor **:** PREROGATIVE; *esp* **:** such a right or immunity attached specif. to a position or an office

[2]**privilege** *vt* **-leged; -leg·ing** (14c) **:** to grant a privilege to

priv·i·leged \-lijd\ *adj* (14c) **1 :** having or enjoying one or more privileges ⟨~ classes⟩ **2 :** not subject to the usual rules or penalties because of some special circumstance; *esp* **:** not subject to disclosure in a court of law ⟨a ~ communication⟩ **3 :** having a plenary indulgence attached to a mass celebrated thereon ⟨a ~ altar⟩

priv·i·ly \ˈpriv-ə-lē\ *adv* (13c) **:** in a privy manner **:** PRIVATELY, SECRETLY

priv·i·ty \ˈpriv-ət-ē\ *n, pl* **-ties** [ME *privite* privacy, secret, fr. OF *privité*, fr. ML *privitat-, privitas*, fr. L *privus* private — more at PRIVATE] (1523) **1 a :** a relationship between persons who successively have a legal interest in the same right or property **b :** an interest in a transaction, contract, or legal action to which one is not a party arising out of a relationship to one of the parties **2 :** private or joint knowledge of a private matter; *esp* **:** cognizance implying concurrence

[1]**privy** \ˈpriv-ē\ *adj* [ME *prive*, fr. OF *privé*, fr. L *privatus* private] (14c) **1 :** belonging or relating to a person in his individual rather than his official capacity **2 a :** PRIVATE, WITHDRAWN **b :** SECRET **3 :** admitted as one sharing in a secret ⟨~ to the conspiracy⟩

[2]**privy** *n, pl* **priv·ies** (ca. 1548) **1 :** a person having a legal interest of privity **2 a :** a small building having a bench with holes through which the user may defecate or urinate **b :** TOILET 3b

privy council *n* (14c) **1** *archaic* **:** a secret or private council **2** *cap P&C* **:** a body of officials and dignitaries chosen by the British monarch as an advisory council to the Crown usu. functioning through its committees **3 :** a usu. appointive advisory council to an executive — **privy councillor** *n*

privy purse *n* (1664) **:** an allowance for the private expenses of the British sovereign

prix fixe \ˈprē-ˈfēks, -ˈfiks\ *n* [F, fixed price] (1883) **1 :** TABLE D'HÔTE **2 :** the price charged for a table d'hôte meal

[1]**prize** \ˈprīz\ *n* [ME *pris* prize, price — more at PRICE] (14c) **1 :** something offered or striven for in competition or in contests of chance; *also* **:** PREMIUM 1d **2 :** something exceptionally desirable **3** *archaic* **:** a contest for a reward **:** COMPETITION

[2]**prize** *adj* (1803) **1 a :** awarded or worthy of a prize **b :** awarded as a prize **c :** entered for the sake of a prize ⟨a ~ drawing⟩ **2 :** outstanding of a kind ⟨raised ~ hogs⟩

[3]**prize** *vt* **prized; priz·ing** [ME *prisen*, fr. MF *prisier*, fr. LL *pretiare*, fr. L *pretium* price, value — more at PRICE] (14c) **1 :** to estimate the value of **:** RATE **2 :** to value highly **:** ESTEEM ***syn*** see APPRECIATE

[4]**prize** *n* [ME *prise*, fr. MF, act of taking, fr. *prendre* to take, fr. L *prehendere* — more at GET] (14c) **1 :** something taken by force, stratagem, or threat; *esp* **:** property lawfully captured at sea in time of war **2 :** an act of capturing or taking; *esp* **:** the wartime capture of a ship and its cargo at sea ***syn*** see SPOIL

5**prize** \ˈprīz\ *vt* **prized; priz·ing** [*prize* (lever)] (1686) **:** to press, force, or move with a lever **:** PRY

prize·fight \ˈprīz-ˌfīt\ *n* (1824) **:** a professional boxing match — **prize·fight·er** \-ər\ *n*

prize·fight·ing \-iŋ\ *n* (1720) **:** 2BOXING

prize money *n* (1749) **1 :** a part of the proceeds of a captured ship formerly divided among the officers and men making the capture **2 :** money offered in prizes

priz·er \ˈprī-zər\ *n, archaic* (1599) **:** one that contends for a prize

prize·win·ner \ˈprīz-ˌwin-ər\ *n* (1893) **:** a winner of a prize

prize·win·ning \-ˌwin-iŋ\ *adj* (1919) **:** having won or of a quality to win a prize ⟨a ~ design⟩

1**pro** \ˈprō\ *n, pl* **pros** [ME, fr. L, prep., for — more at FOR] (15c) **1 :** an argument or evidence in affirmation ⟨an appraisal of the ~*s* and cons⟩ **2 :** the affirmative side or one holding it

2**pro** *adv* [*pro-*] (15c) **:** on the affirmative side **:** in affirmation ⟨much has been written ~ and con⟩

3**pro** \(ˌ)prō\ *prep* [L] (15c) **:** in favor of **:** FOR

4**pro** \ˈprō\ *n or adj* (1848) **:** PROFESSIONAL

1**pro-** *prefix* [ME, fr. OF, fr. L, fr. Gk, before, forward, forth, for, fr. *pro* — more at FOR] **1 a :** earlier than **:** prior to **:** before ⟨*pro*thalamion⟩ **b :** rudimentary **:** PROT- ⟨*pro*nucleus⟩ **2 a :** located in front of or at the front of **:** anterior to ⟨*pro*cephalic⟩ ⟨*pro*ventriculus⟩ **b :** front **:** anterior ⟨*pro*thorax⟩ **3 :** projecting ⟨*pro*gnathous⟩

2**pro-** *prefix* [L *pro* in front of, before, for — more at FOR] **1 :** taking the place of **:** substituting for ⟨*pro*cathedral⟩ ⟨*pro*caine⟩ **2 :** favoring **:** supporting **:** championing ⟨*pro*-American⟩

proa \ˈprō-ə\ *var of* PRAU

pro·ac·tive \(ˈ)prō-ˈak-tiv\ *adj* [L *pro-* forward] (1933) **1 :** relating to, caused by, or being interference between previous learning and the recall or performance of later learning ⟨~ inhibition of memory⟩ **2 :** acting in anticipation of future problems, needs, or changes

prob·a·bi·lism \ˈpräb-ə-bə-ˌliz-əm\ *n* [F *probabilisme,* fr. L *probabilis* probable] (ca. 1847) **1 :** a theory that certainty is impossible esp. in the sciences and that probability suffices to govern belief and action **2 :** a theory that in disputed moral questions any solidly probable course may be followed even though an opposed course is or appears more probable — **prob·a·bi·list** \-ləst\ *adj or n*

prob·a·bi·lis·tic \ˌpräb-ə-bə-ˈlis-tik\ *adj* (ca. 1864) **1 :** of or relating to probabilism **2 :** of, relating to, or based on probability

prob·a·bil·i·ty \ˌpräb-ə-ˈbil-ət-ē\ *n, pl* **-ties** (15c) **1 :** the quality or state of being probable **2 :** something (as an event or circumstance) that is probable **3 a (1) :** the ratio of the number of outcomes in an exhaustive set of equally likely outcomes that produce a given event to the total number of possible outcomes **(2) :** the chance that a given event will occur **b :** a branch of mathematics concerned with the study of probabilities **4 :** a logical relation between statements such that evidence confirming one confirms the other to some degree

probability density *n* (1939) **:** PROBABILITY DENSITY FUNCTION; *also* **:** a particular value of a probability density function

probability density function *n* (1957) **1 :** PROBABILITY FUNCTION **2 :** a function of a continuous random variable whose integral over an interval gives the probability that its value will fall within the interval

probability distribution *n* (1937) **:** PROBABILITY FUNCTION; *also* **:** PROBABILITY DENSITY FUNCTION 2

probability function *n* (1906) **:** a function of a discrete random variable that gives the probability that a specified value will occur

prob·a·ble \ˈpräb-(ə-)bəl\ *adj* [ME, fr. MF, fr. L *probabilis,* fr. *probare* to test, approve, prove — more at PROVE] (1606) **1 :** supported by evidence strong enough to establish presumption but not proof ⟨a ~ hypothesis⟩ **2 :** establishing a probability ⟨~ evidence⟩ **3 :** likely to be or become true or real ⟨~ events⟩

probable cause *n* (1676) **:** a reasonable ground for supposing that a criminal charge is well-founded

prob·a·bly \ˈpräb-(ə-)blē, ˈpräb-lē\ *adv* (1613) **:** insofar as seems reasonably true, factual, or to be expected **:** without much doubt ⟨is ~ happy⟩ ⟨it will ~ rain⟩

pro·band \ˈprō-ˌband, prō-ˈ\ *n* [L *probandus,* gerundive of *probare*] (ca. 1929) **:** SUBJECT 3c(2)

pro·bang \ˈprō-ˌbaŋ\ *n* [origin unknown] (1657) **:** a slender flexible rod with a sponge on one end used esp. for removing obstructions from the esophagus

1**pro·bate** \ˈprō-ˌbāt, *Brit also* -bit\ *n* [ME *probat,* fr. L *probatum,* neut. of *probatus,* pp. of *probare*] (1534) **1 a :** the action or process of proving before a competent judicial authority that a document offered for official recognition and registration as the last will and testament of a deceased person is genuine **b :** the judicial determination of the validity of a will **2 :** the officially authenticated copy of a probated will

2**pro·bate** \-ˌbāt\ *vt* **pro·bat·ed; pro·bat·ing** (1570) **1 :** to establish (a will) by probate as genuine and valid **2 :** to put (a convicted offender) on probation

probate court *n* (ca. 1847) **:** a court that has jurisdiction chiefly over the probate of wills and administration of deceased persons' estates

pro·ba·tion \prō-ˈbā-shən\ *n* [ME *probacioun,* fr. MF *probation,* fr. L *probation-, probatio,* fr. *probatus*] (15c) **1 :** critical examination and evaluation or subjection to such examination and evaluation **2 a :** subjection of an individual to a period of testing and trial to ascertain fitness (as for a job or school) **b :** the action of suspending the sentence of a convicted offender and giving him freedom during good behavior under the supervision of a probation officer **c :** the state or a period of being subject to probation — **pro·ba·tion·al** \-shnəl, -shən-ᵊl\ *adj* — **pro·ba·tion·al·ly** \-ē\ *adv* — **pro·ba·tion·ary** \-shə-ˌner-ē\ *adj*

pro·ba·tion·er \-sh(ə-)nər\ *n* (1603) **1 :** one whose fitness is being tested during a trial period **2 :** a convicted offender on probation

probation officer *n* (1880) **:** an officer appointed to investigate, report on, and supervise the conduct of convicted offenders on probation

pro·ba·tive \ˈprō-bət-iv\ *adj* (15c) **1 :** serving to test or try **:** EXPLORATORY **2 :** serving to prove **:** SUBSTANTIATING

pro·ba·to·ry \ˈprō-bə-ˌtōr-ē, -ˌtȯr-\ *adj* (ca. 1670) **:** PROBATIVE

1**probe** \ˈprōb\ *n* [ML *proba* examination, fr. L *probare*] (1580) **1 :** a slender instrument for surgical exploration (as of a wound or bodily cavity) **2 a :** a pointed metal tip for making electrical contact with a circuit element being checked **b :** a device used to penetrate or send back information esp. from outer space or a celestial body **c :** a pipe on the receiving airplane thrust into the drogue of the delivering airplane in air refueling **3 a :** the action of probing **b :** a penetrating or critical investigation **c :** a tentative exploratory advance or survey

2**probe** *vb* **probed; prob·ing** *vt* (1649) **1 :** to subject to a penetrating investigation **2 :** to examine with or as if with a probe ~ *vi* **:** to make an exploratory investigation ***syn*** see ENTER — **prob·er** *n*

pro·ben·e·cid \prō-ˈben-ə-səd\ *n* [irreg. fr. *propyl* + *benzoic acid*] (1950) **:** a drug $C_{13}H_{19}NO_4S$ that acts on renal tubular function and is used to increase the concentration of some drugs (as penicillin) in the blood by inhibiting their excretion and to increase the excretion of urates in gout

prob·it \ˈpräb-ət\ *n* [*prob*ability *unit*] (1934) **:** a unit of measurement of statistical probability based on deviations from the mean of a normal distribution

pro·bi·ty \ˈprō-bət-ē\ *n* [MF *probité,* fr. L *probitat-, probitas,* fr. *probus* honest — more at PROVE] (1514) **:** adherence to the highest principles and ideals **:** UPRIGHTNESS ***syn*** see HONESTY

1**prob·lem** \ˈpräb-ləm, ˈpräb-ᵊm, -ˌlem\ *n* [ME *probleme,* fr. MF, fr. L *problema,* fr. Gk *problēma,* lit., something thrown forward, fr. *proballein* to throw forward, fr. *pro-* forward + *ballein* to throw — more at PRO-, DEVIL] (14c) **1 a :** a question raised for inquiry, consideration, or solution **b :** a proposition in mathematics or physics stating something to be done **2 a :** an intricate unsettled question **b :** a source of perplexity, distress, or vexation ***syn*** see MYSTERY

2**problem** *adj* (1894) **1 :** dealing with a problem of conduct or social relationship ⟨a ~ play⟩ **2 :** difficult to deal with ⟨a ~ child⟩

prob·lem·at·ic \ˌpräb-lə-ˈmat-ik\ *or* **prob·lem·at·i·cal** \-i-kəl\ *adj* (1609) **1 a :** difficult to solve or decide **:** PUZZLING **b :** not definite or settled ⟨their future remains ~⟩ **c :** open to question or debate **:** QUESTIONABLE **2 :** expressing or supporting a possibility ***syn*** see DOUBTFUL — **prob·lem·at·i·cal·ly** \-i-k(ə-)lē\ *adv*

pro·bos·ci·de·an \prə-ˌbäs-ə-ˈdē-ən\ *or* **pro·bos·cid·i·an** \prə-ˌbäs-ˈid-ē-ən, (ˌ)prō-\ *n* [deriv. of L *proboscid-, proboscis*] (ca. 1859) **:** any of an order (Proboscidea) of large mammals comprising the elephants and extinct related forms — **proboscidean** *adj*

pro·bos·cis \prə-ˈbäs-əs, -kəs\ *n, pl* **-bos·cis·es** *also* **-bos·ci·des** \-ˈbäs-ə-ˌdēz\ [L, fr. Gk *proboskis,* fr. *pro-* + *boskein* to feed] (1576) **1 a :** the trunk of an elephant; *also* **:** any long flexible snout **b :** the human nose esp. when prominent **2 :** any of various elongated or extensible tubular processes (as the sucking organ of a butterfly) of the oral region of an invertebrate

pro·caine \ˈprō-ˌkān\ *n* [ISV 2*pro-* + *cocaine*] (1918) **:** a basic ester $C_{13}H_{20}N_2O_2$ of para-aminobenzoic acid; *also* **:** its crystalline hydrochloride used as a local anesthetic

pro·cam·bi·um \(ˈ)prō-ˈkam-bē-əm\ *n* [NL] (1875) **:** the part of a plant meristem that forms cambium and primary vascular tissues — **pro·cam·bi·al** \-bē-əl\ *adj*

pro·car·ba·zine \prō-ˈkär-bə-ˌzēn, -zən\ *n* [2*pro-* + *carb-* + *azine*] (1965) **:** an antineoplastic drug $C_{12}H_{19}N_3O$ that is a monoamine oxidase inhibitor used as the hydrochloride esp. in the palliative treatment of Hodgkin's disease

procaryote, procaryotic *var of* PROKARYOTE, PROKARYOTIC

pro·ca·the·dral \ˌprō-kə-ˈthē-drəl\ *n* (1868) **:** a parish church used as a cathedral

pro·ce·dur·al \prə-ˈsēj-(ə-)rəl\ *adj* (1889) **:** of or relating to procedure; *esp* **:** of or relating to the procedure used by courts or other bodies administering substantive law — **pro·ce·dur·al·ly** \-ē\ *adv*

pro·ce·dure \prə-ˈsē-jər\ *n* [F *procédure,* fr. MF, fr. *proceder*] (ca. 1611) **1 a :** a particular way of accomplishing something or of acting **b :** a step in a procedure **2 a :** a series of steps followed in a regular definite order ⟨legal ~⟩ **b :** a series of instructions for a computer that has a name by which it can be called into action **3 a :** a traditional or established way of doing things **b :** PROTOCOL 3a

pro·ceed \prō-ˈsēd, prə-\ *vi* [ME *proceden,* fr. MF *proceder,* fr. L *procedere,* fr. *pro-* forward + *cedere* to go — more at PRO-, CEDE] (14c) **1 :** to come forth from a source **:** ISSUE **2 a :** to continue after a pause or interruption **b :** to go on in an orderly regulated way **3 a :** to begin and carry on an action, process, or movement **b :** to be in the process of being accomplished **4 :** to move along a course **:** ADVANCE ***syn*** see SPRING

pro·ceed·ing *n* (1546) **1** *pl* **:** legal action ⟨divorce ~*s*⟩ **2 :** PROCEDURE **3** *pl* **:** EVENTS, HAPPENINGS **4 :** TRANSACTION **5** *pl* **:** an official record of things said or done

pro·ceeds \ˈprō-ˌsēdz\ *n pl* (1665) **1 :** the total amount brought in ⟨the ~ of a sale⟩ **2 :** the net amount received (as for a check or from an insurance settlement) after deduction of any discount or charges

pro·ce·phal·ic \ˌprō-sə-ˈfal-ik\ *adj* (1874) **:** relating to, forming, or situated on or near the front of the head

pro·cer·coid \(ˈ)prō-ˈsər-ˌkȯid\ *n* [*pro-* + Gk *kerkos* tail] (1926) **:** the solid first parasitic larva of some tapeworms that develops usu. in the body cavity of a copepod

1**pro·cess** \ˈpräs-ˌes, ˈprōs-, -əs\ *n, pl* **pro·cess·es** \-ˌes-əz, -ə-səz, -ə-ˌsēz\ [ME *proces,* fr. MF, fr. L *processus,* fr. *processus,* pp. of *procedere*] (14c) **1 a :** PROGRESS, ADVANCE **b :** something going on **:** PROCEEDING **2 a :** a natural phenomenon marked by gradual changes that lead toward a particular result ⟨the ~ of growth⟩ **b :** a series of actions or operations conducing to an end; *esp* **:** a continuous operation or treatment esp. in manufacture **3 a :** the whole course of proceedings in a legal action **b :** the summons, mandate, or writ used by a court to compel the appearance of the defendant in a legal action or compliance with its orders **4 :** a prominent or projecting part of an organism or organic structure ⟨a bone ~⟩ **5 :** 5CONK

2**process** *vt* (1532) **1 a :** to proceed against by law **:** PROSECUTE **b (1) :** to take out a summons against **(2) :** to serve a summons on **2 a :** to subject to a special process or treatment (as in the course of manufacture) **b :** to work (hair) into a conk

3**process** *adj* (1888) **1 :** treated or made by a special process esp. when involving synthesis or artificial modification **2 :** made by or used in a

mechanical or photomechanical duplicating process **3 :** of or involving illusory effects usu. introduced during processing of the film
⁴process \prə-ˈses\ *vi* [back-formation fr. ¹*procession*] *chiefly Brit* (1814) **:** to move in a procession
pro·cess cheese \ˌpräs-ˌes-, ˌprōs-, -əs-\ *n* (1926) **:** a cheese made by blending several lots of cheese
pro·cess·ible *or* **pro·cess·able** \ˈpräs-ˌes-ə-bəl, ˈprōs-\ *adj* (1954) **:** suitable for processing **:** capable of being processed — **pro·cess·ibil·i·ty** *or* **pro·cess·abil·i·ty** \ˌpräs-ˌes-ə-ˈbil-ət-ē, ˌprōs-\ *n*
¹pro·ces·sion \prə-ˈsesh-ən\ *n* [ME *processioun*, fr OF *procession*, fr. LL & L; LL *procession-, processio* religious procession, fr. L, act of proceeding, fr. *processus*, pp.] (12c) **1 a :** a group of individuals moving along in an orderly often ceremonial way **b :** SUCCESSION, SEQUENCE **2 a :** continuous forward movement **:** PROGRESSION **b :** EMANATION ⟨the Holy Ghost's ~ from the Father⟩
²procession *vi, archaic* (1691) **:** to go in procession
¹pro·ces·sion·al \prə-ˈsesh-nəl, -ən-ᵊl\ *n* (15c) **1 :** a book containing material for a procession **2 :** a musical composition (as a hymn) designed for a procession **3 :** a ceremonial procession
²processional *adj* (ca. 1611) **:** of, relating to, or moving in a procession — **pro·ces·sion·al·ly** \-ē\ *adv*
pro·ces·sor \ˈpräs-ˌes-ər, ˈprōs-\ *n* (1909) **1 :** one that processes ⟨scrap ~⟩ **2 a (1) :** COMPUTER **(2) :** the part of a computer system that operates on data — called also *central processing unit* **b :** a computer program (as a compiler) that puts another program into a form acceptable to the computer
process printing *n* (1931) **:** a method of printing from halftone plates in usu. three or more colors so that nearly any hue may be reproduced
pro·cès–ver·bal \prō-ˌsā-vər-ˈbäl, -(ˌ)ver-\ *n, pl* **pro·cès–ver·baux** \-ˈbō\ [F, lit., verbal trial] (1635) **:** an official written record
pro–choice \(ˈ)prō-ˈchȯis\ *adj* (1975) **:** favoring legalized abortion — **pro–choic·er** \-ˈchȯi-sər\ *n*
pro·claim \prō-ˈklām, prə-\ *vt* [ME *proclamen*, fr. MF or L; MF *proclamer*, fr. L *proclamare*, fr. *pro-* before + *clamare* to cry out — more at PRO-, CLAIM] (15c) **1 a :** to declare publicly, typically insistently, proudly, or defiantly and in either speech or writing **:** ANNOUNCE **b :** to give outward indication of **:** SHOW **2 :** to declare or declare to be solemnly, officially, or formally ⟨~ an amnesty⟩ ⟨~ the country a republic⟩ **3 :** to praise or glorify openly or publicly **:** EXTOL ***syn*** see DECLARE — **pro·claim·er** *n*
proc·la·ma·tion \ˌpräk-lə-ˈmā-shən\ *n* [ME *proclamacion*, fr. MF *proclamation*, fr. L *proclamation-, proclamatio*, fr. *proclamatus*, pp. of *proclamare*] (15c) **1 :** the action of proclaiming **:** the state of being proclaimed **2 :** something proclaimed; *specif* **:** an official formal public announcement
pro·clit·ic \prō-ˈklit-ik\ *adj* [NL *procliticus*, fr. Gk *pro-* + LL *-cliticus* (as in *encliticus* enclitic)] (1846) **:** of, relating to, or constituting a word or particle without sentence stress that is accentually dependent upon a following stressed word and is pronounced with it as a phonetic unit — **proclitic** *n*
pro·cliv·i·ty \prō-ˈkliv-ət-ē\ *n, pl* **-ties** [L *proclivitas*, fr. *proclivis* sloping, prone, fr. *pro-* forward + *clivus* hill — more at PRO-, DECLIVITY] (ca. 1591) **:** an inclination or predisposition toward something; *esp* **:** a strong inherent inclination toward something objectionable ***syn*** see LEANING
Proc·ne \ˈpräk-nē\ *n* [L, fr. Gk *Proknē*] **:** the wife of Tereus who is changed into a swallow while fleeing from him
pro·con·sul \(ˈ)prō-ˈkän(t)-səl\ *n* [ME, fr. L, fr. *pro consule* for a consul] (14c) **1 :** a governor or military commander of an ancient Roman province **2 :** an administrator in a modern colony, dependency, or occupied area usu. with wide powers — **pro·con·su·lar** \-s(ə-)lər\ *adj* — **pro·con·su·late** \-s(ə-)lət\ *n* — **pro·con·sul·ship** \-səl-ˌship\ *n*
pro·cras·ti·nate \p(r)ə-ˈkras-tə-ˌnāt, prō-\ *vb* **-nat·ed; -nat·ing** [L *procrastinatus*, pp. of *procrastinare*, fr. *pro-* forward + *crastinus* of tomorrow, fr. *cras* tomorrow] *vt* (1588) **:** to put off intentionally and habitually ~ *vi* **:** to put off intentionally the doing of something that should be done ***syn*** see DELAY — **pro·cras·ti·na·tion** \-ˌkras-tə-ˈnā-shən\ *n* — **pro·cras·ti·na·tor** \-ˈkras-tə-ˌnāt-ər\ *n*
pro·cre·ant \ˈprō-krē-ənt\ *adj* (1588) **1 :** producing offspring **2** *archaic* **:** of or relating to procreation
pro·cre·ate \-ˌāt\ *vb* **-at·ed; -at·ing** [L *procreatus*, pp. of *procreare*, fr. *pro-* forth + *creare* to create — more at PRO-, CREATE] *vt* (1536) **:** to beget or bring forth (offspring) **:** PROPAGATE ~ *vi* **:** to beget or bring forth offspring **:** REPRODUCE — **pro·cre·ation** \ˌprō-krē-ˈā-shən\ *n* — **pro·cre·ative** \ˈprō-krē-ˌāt-iv\ *adj* — **pro·cre·ator** \-ˌāt-ər\ *n*
pro·crus·te·an \p(r)ə-ˈkrəs-tē-ən, prō-\ *adj, often cap* (ca. 1846) **1 :** of, relating to, or typical of Procrustes **2 :** marked by arbitrary often ruthless disregard of individual differences or special circumstances
procrustean bed *n, often cap P* (1848) **:** a scheme or pattern into which someone or something is arbitrarily forced
Pro·crus·tes \p(r)ə-ˈkrəs-(ˌ)tēz, prō-\ *n* [L, fr. Gk *Prokroustēs*] **:** a villainous son of Poseidon in Greek myth who forces travelers to fit into his bed by stretching their bodies or cutting off their legs
pro·cryp·tic \(ˈ)prō-ˈkrip-tik\ *adj* [*pro-* (as in *protect*) + *cryptic*] (1891) **:** of, relating to, or being a concealing pattern or shade of coloring esp. in insects
proc·to·dae·um \ˌpräk-tə-ˈdē-əm\ *n, pl* **-daea** \-ˈdē-ə\ *or* **-dae·ums** [NL, fr. Gk *prōktos* anus + *hodos* way — more at CEDE] (1878) **:** the posterior ectodermal part of the alimentary canal formed in the embryo by invagination of the outer body wall
proc·tol·o·gy \präk-ˈtäl-ə-jē\ *n* [Gk *prōktos* + E *-logy*] (1899) **:** a branch of medicine dealing with the structure and diseases of the anus, rectum, and sigmoid colon — **proc·to·log·ic** \ˌpräk-tə-ˈläj-ik\ *or* **proc·to·log·i·cal** \-i-kəl\ *adj* — **proc·tol·o·gist** \präk-ˈtäl-ə-jəst\ *n*
proc·tor \ˈpräk-tər\ *n* [ME *procutour* procurator, proctor, alter. of *procuratour*] (14c) **:** SUPERVISOR, MONITOR; *specif* **:** one appointed to supervise students (as at an examination) — **proctor** *vb* — **proc·to·ri·al** \präk-ˈtōr-ē-əl, -ˈtȯr-\ *adj* — **proc·tor·ship** \ˈpräk-tər-ˌship\ *n*
pro·cum·bent \prō-ˈkəm-bənt\ *adj* [L *procumbent-, procumbens*, prp. of *procumbere* to fall or lean forward, fr. *pro-* forward + *-cumbere* to lie down — more at HIP] (1668) **1 :** being or having stems that trail along the ground without rooting **2 :** lying face down
proc·u·ra·tion \ˌpräk-yə-ˈrā-shən\ *n* [ME *procuracioun*, fr. MF *procuration*, fr. L *procuration-, procuratio*, fr. *procuratus*, pp. of *procurare*] (15c) **1 a :** the act of appointing another as one's agent or attorney **b :** the authority vested in one so appointed **2 :** the action of obtaining something (as supplies) **:** PROCUREMENT
proc·u·ra·tor \ˈpräk-yə-ˌrāt-ər\ *n* (13c) **1 :** one that manages another's affairs **:** AGENT **2 :** an officer of the Roman empire entrusted with management of the financial affairs of a province and often having administrative powers as agent of the emperor — **proc·u·ra·to·ri·al** \ˌpräk-yə-rə-ˈtōr-ē-əl, -ˈtȯr-\ *adj*
pro·cure \prə-ˈkyu̇(ə)r, prō-\ *vb* **pro·cured; pro·cur·ing** [ME *procuren*, fr. LL *procurare*, fr. L, to take care of, fr. *pro-* for + *cura* care] *vt* (13c) **1 a :** to get possession of **:** obtain by particular care and effort **b :** to get and make available for promiscuous sexual intercourse **2 :** to bring about **:** ACHIEVE ~ *vi* **:** to procure women — **pro·cur·able** \-ˈkyu̇r-ə-bəl\ *adj* — **pro·cur·ance** \-ən(t)s\ *n* — **pro·cure·ment** \-ˈkyu̇(ə)r-mənt\ *n*
pro·cur·er \-ˈkyu̇r-ər\ *n* (1538) **:** one that procures; *esp* **:** PANDER
Pro·cy·on \ˈprō-sē-ˌän, ˈpräs-ē-, -ən\ *n* [L, fr. Gk *Prokyōn*, lit., fore-dog; fr. its rising before Sirius] **:** a star of magnitude 0.38 in Canis Minor
¹prod \ˈpräd\ *vb* **prod·ded; prod·ding** [origin unknown] *vt* (1535) **1 a :** to thrust a pointed instrument into **:** PRICK **b :** to incite to action **:** STIR **2 :** to poke or stir as if with a prod ~ *vi* **:** to urge someone on — **prod·der** *n*
²prod *n* (ca. 1787) **1 :** a pointed instrument used to prod **2 :** an incitement to act
¹prod·i·gal \ˈpräd-i-gəl\ *adj* [L *prodigus*, fr. *prodigere* to drive away, squander, fr. *pro-, prod-* forth + *agere* to drive — more at PRO-, AGENT] (1500) **1 :** recklessly extravagant **2 :** characterized by wasteful expenditure **:** LAVISH **3 :** yielding abundantly **:** LUXURIANT ***syn*** see PROFUSE — **prod·i·gal·i·ty** \ˌpräd-ə-ˈgal-ət-ē\ *n* — **prod·i·gal·ly** \ˈpräd-i-g(ə-)lē\ *adv*
²prodigal *n* (1596) **:** one who spends or gives lavishly and foolishly
pro·di·gious \prə-ˈdij-əs\ *adj* (15c) **1 a** *obs* **:** being an omen **:** PORTENTOUS **b** *archaic* **:** resembling or befitting a prodigy **:** STRANGE, UNUSUAL **2 :** exciting amazement or wonder **3 :** extraordinary in bulk, quantity, or degree **:** ENORMOUS ***syn*** see MONSTROUS — **pro·di·gious·ly** *adv* — **pro·di·gious·ness** *n*
prod·i·gy \ˈpräd-ə-jē\ *n, pl* **-gies** [L *prodigium* omen, monster, fr. *pro-, prod-* + *-igium* (akin to *aio* I say) — more at ADAGE] (15c) **1 a :** a portentous event **:** OMEN **b :** something extraordinary or inexplicable **2 a :** an extraordinary, marvelous, or unusual accomplishment, deed, or event **b :** a highly talented child
pro·dro·mal \(ˈ)prō-ˈdrō-məl\ *adj* (1716) **:** PRECURSORY; *esp* **:** marked by prodromes
pro·drome \ˈprō-ˌdrōm\ *n* [F, lit., precursor, fr. Gk *prodromos*, fr. *pro-* before + *dromos* running — more at PRO-, DROMEDARY] (1822) **:** a premonitory symptom of disease
¹pro·duce \prə-ˈd(y)üs, prō-\ *vb* **pro·duced; pro·duc·ing** [ME (Sc) *producen*, fr. L *producere*, fr. *pro-* forward + *ducere* to lead — more at TOW] *vt* (15c) **1 :** to offer to view or notice **:** EXHIBIT **2 :** to give birth or rise to **:** YIELD **3 :** to extend in length, area, or volume ⟨~ a side of a triangle⟩ **4 :** to present to the public on the stage or screen or over radio or television **5 :** to give being, form, or shape to **:** MAKE; *esp* **:** MANUFACTURE **6 :** to accrue or cause to accrue ~ *vi* **:** to bear, make, or yield something ⟨labored literally day and night to ~ —Vera M. Dean⟩ — **pro·duc·ible** \-ˈd(y)ü-sə-bəl\ *adj*
²pro·duce \ˈpräd-(ˌ)üs, ˈprōd- *also* -(ˌ)yüs\ *n* (1695) **1 a :** something produced **b :** the amount produced **:** YIELD **2 :** agricultural products and esp. fresh fruits and vegetables as distinguished from grain and other staple crops **3 :** the progeny usu. of a female animal
pro·duced \prə-ˈd(y)üst, prō-\ *adj* (1669) **:** disproportionately elongated ⟨a ~ leaf⟩
pro·duc·er \prə-ˈd(y)ü-sər, prō-\ *n* (1513) **1 :** one that produces; *esp* **:** one that grows agricultural products or manufactures crude materials into articles of use **2 :** a furnace or apparatus that produces combustible gas to be used for fuel by circulating air or a mixture of air and steam through a layer of incandescent fuel **3 :** a person who supervises or finances the production of a stage or screen production or radio or television program **4 :** any of various organisms (as a green plant) which produce their own organic compounds from simple precursors (as carbon dioxide and inorganic nitrogen) and many of which are food sources for other organisms — compare CONSUMER b
producer gas *n* (1895) **:** gas made in a producer and consisting chiefly of carbon monoxide, hydrogen, and nitrogen
producer goods *n pl* (1948) **:** goods (as tools and raw materials) that are used to produce other goods and satisfy human wants only indirectly
prod·uct \ˈpräd-(ˌ)əkt\ *n* [in sense 1, fr. ME, fr. ML *productum*, fr. L, something produced, fr. neut. of *productus*, pp. of *producere*; in other senses, fr. L *productum*] (15c) **1 :** the number or expression resulting from the multiplication together of two or more numbers or expressions **2 :** something produced **3 :** the amount, quantity, or total produced **4 :** CONJUNCTION 5
pro·duc·tion \prə-ˈdək-shən, prō-\ *n* (15c) **1 a :** something produced **:** PRODUCT **b (1) :** a literary or artistic work **(2) :** a work presented on the stage or screen or over the air **c :** an exaggerated action **2 a :** the act or process of producing **b :** the creation of utility; *esp* **:** the making of goods available for use **3 :** total output esp. of a commodity or an industry — **pro·duc·tion·al** \-shnəl, -shən-ᵊl\ *adj*
production control *n* (ca. 1944) **:** systematic planning, coordinating, and directing of all manufacturing activities and influences to insure having goods made on time, of adequate quality, and at reasonable cost
production line *n* (1935) **:** LINE 6j
pro·duc·tive \prə-ˈdək-tiv, prō-\ *adj* (1612) **1 :** having the quality or power of producing esp. in abundance ⟨~ fishing waters⟩ **2 :** effective in bringing about **:** ORIGINATIVE ⟨investigating committees have been ~ of much good —R. K. Carr⟩ **3 a :** yielding or furnishing results, benefits, or profits **b :** yielding or devoted to the satisfaction of wants or the creation of utilities **4 :** continuing to be used in the formation of new words or constructions ⟨*un-* is a ~ prefix⟩ **5 :** raising mucus or sputum (as from the bronchi) ⟨a ~ cough⟩ — **pro·duc·tive·ly** *adv* — **pro·duc·tive·ness** *n*
pro·duc·tiv·i·ty \(ˌ)prō-ˌdək-ˈtiv-ət-ē, ˌpräd-(ˌ)ək-, prə-ˌdək-\ *n* (1809) **1 :** the quality or state of being productive **2 :** rate of production esp. of food by the utilization of solar energy by producer organisms

pro·em \ˈprō-ˌem, -əm\ *n* [ME *proheme,* fr. MF, fr. L *prooemium,* fr. Gk *prooimion,* fr. *pro-* + *oimē* song] (14c) **1 :** preliminary comment **:** PREFACE **2 :** PRELUDE — **pro·emi·al** \prō-ˈē-mē-əl, -ˈem-ē-\ *adj*

pro·en·zyme \(ˈ)prō-ˈen-ˌzīm\ *n* [ISV] (ca. 1900) **:** ZYMOGEN

pro·es·trus \(ˈ)prō-ˈes-trəs\ *n* [NL] (1923) **:** a period immediately preceding estrus characterized by preparatory physiological changes

prof \ˈpräf\ *n* (1838) **:** PROFESSOR

pro·fa·na·tion \ˌpräf-ə-ˈnā-shən, ˌprō-fə-\ *n* (1552) **:** the act or an instance of profaning

pro·fa·na·to·ry \prō-ˈfan-ə-ˌtōr-ē, prə-, -ˈfā-nə-, -ˌtȯr-\ *adj* (1853) **:** tending to profane **:** DESECRATING

[1]**pro·fane** \prō-ˈfān, prə-\ *vt* **pro·faned; pro·fan·ing** (14c) **1 :** to treat (something sacred) with abuse, irreverence, or contempt **:** DESECRATE **2 :** to debase by a wrong, unworthy, or vulgar use — **pro·fan·er** *n*

[2]**profane** *adj* [ME *prophane,* fr. MF, fr. L *profanus,* fr. *pro-* before + *fanum* temple — more at PRO-, FEAST] (15c) **1 :** not concerned with religion or religious purposes **:** SECULAR **2 :** not holy because unconsecrated, impure, or defiled **:** UNSANCTIFIED **3 :** serving to debase or defile what is holy **:** IRREVERENT **4 a :** not being among the initiated **b :** not possessing esoteric or expert knowledge — **pro·fane·ly** *adv* — **pro·fane·ness** \-ˈfān-nəs\ *n*

pro·fan·i·ty \prō-ˈfan-ət-ē, prə-\ *n, pl* **-ties** (1607) **1 a :** the quality or state of being profane **b :** the use of profane language **2 a :** profane language **b :** an utterance of profane language

pro·fess \prə-ˈfes, prō-\ *vb* [in sense 1, fr. ME *professen,* fr. *profes,* adj., having professed one's vows, fr. MF, fr. LL *professus,* fr. L, pp. of *profiteri* to profess, confess, fr. *pro-* before + *fateri* to acknowledge; in other senses, fr. L *professus,* pp. — more at CONFESS] *vt* (14c) **1 :** to receive formally into a religious community following a novitiate by acceptance of the required vows **2 a :** to declare or admit openly or freely **:** AFFIRM **b :** to declare in words or appearances only **:** PRETEND **3 :** to confess one's faith in or allegiance to **4 :** to practice or claim to be versed in (a calling or profession) ~ *vi* **1 :** to make a profession or avowal **2** *obs* **:** to profess friendship

pro·fessed \-ˈfest\ *adj* (1569) **1 :** openly and freely declared or acknowledged **:** AFFIRMED **2 :** professing to be qualified; *also* **:** EXPERT

pro·fessed·ly \prə-ˈfes-əd-lē, -ˈfest-lē\ *adv* (1570) **1 :** by profession or declaration **:** AVOWEDLY **2 :** with pretense **:** ALLEGEDLY

pro·fes·sion \prə-ˈfesh-ən\ *n* [ME *professioun,* fr. OF *profession,* fr. LL & L; LL *profession-, professio,* fr. L, public declaration, fr. *professus,* pp.] (13c) **1 :** the act of taking the vows of a religious community **2 :** an act of openly declaring or publicly claiming a belief, faith, or opinion **:** PROTESTATION **3 :** an avowed religious faith **4 a :** a calling requiring specialized knowledge and often long and intensive academic preparation **b :** a principal calling, vocation, or employment **c :** the whole body of persons engaged in a calling

[1]**pro·fes·sion·al** \prə-ˈfesh-nəl, -ən-ᵊl\ *adj* (15c) **1 a :** of, relating to, or characteristic of a profession **b :** engaged in one of the learned professions **c :** characterized by or conforming to the technical or ethical standards of a profession **2 a :** participating for gain or livelihood in an activity or field of endeavor often engaged in by amateurs ⟨a ~ golfer⟩ **b :** having a particular profession as a permanent career ⟨a ~ soldier⟩ **c :** engaged in by persons receiving financial return ⟨~ football⟩ **3 :** following a line of conduct as though it were a profession ⟨a ~ patriot⟩ — **pro·fes·sion·al·ly** \-ē\ *adv*

[2]**professional** *n* (1811) **:** one that is professional; *esp* **:** one that engages in a pursuit or activity professionally

professional corporation *n* (1970) **:** a corporation organized by one or more licensed individuals (as a doctor or lawyer) esp. for the purpose of providing professional services and obtaining tax advantages

pro·fes·sion·al·ism \-ˌiz-əm\ *n* (1856) **1 :** the conduct, aims, or qualities that characterize or mark a profession or a professional person **2 :** the following of a profession (as athletics) for gain or livelihood

pro·fes·sion·al·ize \-ˌīz\ *vt* **-ized; -iz·ing** (1856) **:** to give a professional character to — **pro·fes·sion·al·iza·tion** \-ˌfesh-nə-lə-ˈzā-shən, -ən-ᵊl-ə-\ *n*

pro·fes·sor \prə-ˈfes-ər\ *n* (14c) **1 :** one that professes, avows, or declares **2 a :** a faculty member of the highest academic rank at an institution of higher education **b :** a teacher at a university, college, or sometimes secondary school **c :** one that teaches or professes special knowledge of an art, sport, or occupation requiring skill — **pro·fes·so·ri·al** \ˌprō-fə-ˈsōr-ē-əl, ˌpräf-ə-, -ˈsȯr-\ *adj* — **pro·fes·so·ri·al·ly** \-ē-ə-lē\ *adv*

pro·fes·sor·ate \prə-ˈfes-ə-rət\ *n* (1860) **:** the office, term of office, or position of a professor

pro·fes·so·ri·at \ˌprō-fə-ˈsōr-ē-ət, ˌpräf-ə-, -ˈsȯr-, -ē-ˌat\ *or* **pro·fes·so·ri·ate** \-ət, -ˌāt\ *n* [modif. of F *professorat,* fr. *professeur* professor, fr. L *professor,* fr. *professus*] (1858) **1 :** the body of college and university teachers at an institution or in society **2 :** PROFESSORSHIP

pro·fes·sor·ship \prə-ˈfes-ər-ˌship\ *n* (1641) **:** the office, duties, or position of an academic professor

[1]**prof·fer** \ˈpräf-ər\ *vt* **prof·fered; prof·fer·ing** \-(ə-)riŋ\ [ME *profren,* fr. AF *profrer,* fr. OF *poroffrir,* fr. *por-* forth (fr. L *pro-*) + *offrir* to offer — more at PRO-] (14c) **:** to present for acceptance **:** TENDER, OFFER

[2]**proffer** *n* (13c) **:** OFFER, SUGGESTION

pro·fi·cien·cy \prə-ˈfish-ən-sē\ *n* (1544) **1 :** advancement in knowledge or skill **:** PROGRESS **2 :** the quality or state of being proficient

pro·fi·cient \prə-ˈfish-ənt\ *adj* [L *proficient-, proficiens,* prp. of *proficere* to go forward, accomplish, fr. *pro-* forward + *facere* to make — more at PRO-, DO] (1590) **:** well advanced in an art, occupation, or branch of knowledge — **proficient** *n* — **pro·fi·cient·ly** *adv*

syn PROFICIENT, ADEPT, SKILLED, SKILLFUL, EXPERT mean having great knowledge and experience in a trade or profession. PROFICIENT implies a thorough competence derived from training and practice; ADEPT implies special aptitude as well as proficiency; SKILLED stresses mastery of technique; SKILLFUL implies individual dexterity in execution or performance; EXPERT implies extraordinary proficiency and often connotes knowledge as well as technical skill.

[1]**pro·file** \ˈprō-ˌfīl\ *n* [It *profilo,* fr. *profilare* to draw in outline, fr. *pro-* forward (fr. L) + *filare* to spin, fr. LL — more at FILE] (ca. 1656) **1 :** a representation of something in outline; *esp* **:** a human head or face represented or seen in a side view **2 :** an outline seen or represented in sharp relief **:** CONTOUR **3 :** a side or sectional elevation: as **a :** a drawing showing a vertical section of the ground **b :** a vertical section of a soil from the ground surface to the underlying unweathered material **4 :** a set of data often in graphic form portraying the significant features of something ⟨a corporation's earnings ~⟩; *esp* **:** a graph representing the extent to which an individual exhibits traits or abilities as determined by tests or ratings **5 :** a concise biographical sketch **6 :** degree or level of public exposure ⟨trying to keep a low ~⟩ ⟨a job with a high ~⟩ ***syn*** see OUTLINE

[2]**profile** *vt* **pro·filed; pro·fil·ing** (1715) **1 :** to represent in profile or by a profile **:** produce (as by drawing, writing, or graphing) a profile of **2 :** to shape the outline of by passing a cutter around — **pro·fil·er** *n*

[1]**prof·it** \ˈpräf-ət\ *n, often attrib* [ME, fr. MF, fr. L *profectus* advance, profit, fr. *profectus,* pp. of *proficere*] (14c) **1 :** a valuable return **:** GAIN **2 :** the excess of returns over expenditure in a transaction or series of transactions; *esp* **:** the excess of the selling price of goods over their cost **3 :** net income usu. for a given period of time **4 :** the ratio of profit for a given year to the amount of capital invested or to the value of sales **5 :** the compensation accruing to entrepreneurs for the assumption of risk in business enterprise as distinguished from wages or rent — **prof·it·less** \-ləs\ *adj*

[2]**profit** *vi* (14c) **1 :** to be of service or advantage **:** AVAIL **2 :** to derive benefit **:** GAIN ~ *vt* **:** to be of service to **:** BENEFIT

prof·it·able \ˈpräf-ət-ə-bəl, ˈpräf-tə-bəl\ *adj* (14c) **:** affording profits **:** yielding advantageous returns or results — **prof·it·abil·i·ty** \ˌpräf-ət-ə-ˈbil-ət-ē\ *n* — **prof·it·able·ness** \ˈpräf-ət-ə-bəl-nəs\ *n* — **prof·it·ably** \-blē\ *adv*

profit and loss *n* (1588) **:** a summary account used at the end of an accounting period to collect the balances of the nominal accounts so that the net profit or loss may be shown

prof·i·teer \ˌpräf-ə-ˈti(ə)r\ *n* (1912) **:** one who makes what is considered an unreasonable profit esp. on the sale of essential goods during times of emergency — **profiteer** *vi*

pro·fit·er·ole \prə-ˈfit-ə-ˌrōl\ *n* [F, fr. *profiter* to profit] (1515) **:** a miniature cream puff with a sweet or savory filling

profit sharing *n* (1881) **:** a system or process under which employees receive a part of the profits of an industrial or commercial enterprise

profit system *n* (1945) **:** FREE ENTERPRISE

prof·li·ga·cy \ˈpräf-li-gə-sē\ *n* (1738) **:** the quality or state of being profligate

[1]**prof·li·gate** \ˈpräf-li-gət, -lə-ˌgāt\ *adj* [L *profligatus,* fr. pp. of *profligare* to strike down, fr. *pro-* forward, down + *-fligare* (akin to *fligere* to strike); akin to Gk *phlibein* to squeeze] (1647) **1 :** completely given up to dissipation and licentiousness **2 :** wildly extravagant **:** PRODIGAL — **prof·li·gate·ly** *adv*

[2]**profligate** *n* (1709) **:** a person given to wildly extravagant and usu. grossly self-indulgent expenditure

pro·flu·ent \ˈpräf-ˌlü-ənt, ˈprōf-; prō-ˈflü-\ *adj* [ME, fr. L *profluent-, profluens,* prp. of *profluere* to flow forth, fr. *pro-* forth + *fluere* to flow — more at PRO-, FLUENT] (15c) **:** flowing copiously or smoothly

pro for·ma \(ˈ)prō-ˈfȯr-mə\ *adj* [L, for form] (1573) **1 :** made or carried out in a perfunctory manner or as a formality **2 :** provided in advance to prescribe form or describe items ⟨*pro forma* invoice⟩

[1]**pro·found** \prə-ˈfau̇nd, prō-\ *adj* [ME, fr. MF *profond* deep, fr. L *profundus,* fr. *pro-* before + *fundus* bottom — more at PRO-, BOTTOM] (14c) **1 a :** having intellectual depth and insight **b :** difficult to fathom or understand **2 a :** extending far below the surface **b :** coming from, reaching to, or situated at a depth **:** DEEP-SEATED ⟨a ~ sigh⟩ **3 a :** characterized by intensity of feeling or quality **b :** all encompassing **:** COMPLETE ⟨~ sleep⟩ — **pro·found·ly** \-ˈfau̇n-(d)lē\ *adv* — **pro·found·ness** \-ˈfau̇n(d)-nəs\ *n*

[2]**profound** *n, archaic* (1621) **:** something that is very deep; *specif* **:** the depths of the sea

pro·fun·di·ty \prə-ˈfən-dət-ē\ *n, pl* **-ties** [ME *profundite,* fr. MF *profundité,* fr. L *profunditat-, profunditas* depth, fr. *profundus*] (15c) **1 a :** intellectual depth **b :** something profound or abstruse **2 :** the quality or state of being profound or deep

pro·fuse \prə-ˈfyüs, prō-\ *adj* [ME, fr. L *profusus,* pp. of *profundere* to pour forth, fr. *pro-* forth + *fundere* to pour — more at FOUND] (15c) **1 :** pouring forth liberally **:** EXTRAVAGANT ⟨~ in their thanks⟩ **2 :** exhibiting great abundance **:** BOUNTIFUL ⟨a ~ harvest⟩ — **pro·fuse·ly** *adv* — **pro·fuse·ness** *n*

syn PROFUSE, LAVISH, PRODIGAL, LUXURIANT, LUSH, EXUBERANT mean giving or given out in great abundance. PROFUSE implies pouring forth without restraint; LAVISH suggests an unstinted or unmeasured profusion; PRODIGAL implies reckless or wasteful lavishness threatening to lead to early exhaustion of resources; LUXURIANT suggests a rich and splendid abundance; LUSH suggests rich, soft luxuriance; EXUBERANT implies marked vitality or vigor in what produces abundantly.

pro·fu·sion \-ˈfyü-zhən\ *n* (1545) **1 :** lavish expenditure **:** EXTRAVAGANCE **2 :** the quality or state of being profuse **3 :** great quantity **:** lavish display or supply ⟨snow falling in ~⟩

[1]**prog** \ˈpräg\ *vi* **progged; prog·ging** [origin unknown] *chiefly dial* (1624) **:** to search about; *esp* **:** FORAGE

[2]**prog** *n, chiefly dial* (1655) **:** FOOD, VICTUALS

pro·ga·mete \ˌprō-gə-ˈmēt, (ˈ)prō-ˈgam-ˌēt\ *n* [ISV] (1892) **:** a cell giving rise to gametes: **a :** OOCYTE **b :** SPERMATOCYTE

pro·gen·i·tor \prō-ˈjen-ət-ər, prə-\ *n* [ME, fr. MF *progeniteur,* fr. L *progenitor,* fr. *progenitus,* pp. of *progignere* to beget, fr. *pro-* forth + *gignere* to beget — more at KIN] (14c) **1 a :** an ancestor in the direct line **:** FOREFATHER **b :** a biologically ancestral form **2 :** PRECURSOR, ORIGINATOR ⟨~*s* of socialist ideas —*Times Lit. Supp.*⟩

prog·e·ny \ˈpräj-(ə-)nē\ *n, pl* **-nies** [ME *progenie,* fr. MF, fr. L *progenies,* fr. *progignere*] (14c) **1 a :** DESCENDANTS, CHILDREN **b :** offspring of animals or plants **2 :** OUTCOME, PRODUCT **3 :** a body of followers, disciples, or successors

pro·ges·ta·tion·al \ˌprō-ˌjes-ˈtā-shnəl, -shən-ᵊl\ *adj* (1923) **:** preceding pregnancy or gestation; *esp* **:** of, relating to, inducing, or constituting the modifications of the female mammalian system associated with ovulation and corpus luteum formation ⟨~ hormones⟩

pro·ges·ter·one \prō-'jes-tə-ˌrōn\ *n* [*progestin* + *sterol* + *-one*] (1935) : a steroid progestational hormone $C_{21}H_{30}O_2$

pro·ges·tin \-'jes-tən\ *n* [*pro-* + *gestation* + *-in*] (1930) : a progestational hormone; *esp* : PROGESTERONE

pro·ges·to·gen \-'jes-tə-jən\ *n* [*progestational* + *-ogen* (as in *estrogen*)] (1942) : any of several progestational steroids (as progesterone) — **pro·ges·to·gen·ic** \-ˌjes-tə-'jen-ik\ *adj*

pro·glot·tid \(ˈ)prō-'glät-əd\ *n* [NL *proglottis*] (1878) : a segment of a tapeworm containing both male and female reproductive organs

pro·glot·tis \(ˈ)prō-'glät-əs\ *n, pl* **-glot·ti·des** \-'glät-ə-ˌdēz\ [NL *proglottid-, proglottis,* fr. Gk *proglōttis* tip of the tongue, fr. *pro-* + *glōtta* tongue — more at GLOSS] (1855) : PROGLOTTID

prog·na·thism \'präg-nə-ˌthiz-əm, präg-'nā-\ *n* (ca. 1864) : prognathous condition

prog·na·thous \-thəs\ *adj* (1836) : having the jaws projecting beyond the upper part of the face

prog·no·sis \präg-'nō-səs\ *n, pl* **-no·ses** \-ˌsēz\ [LL, fr. Gk *prognōsis,* lit., foreknowledge, fr. *progignōskein* to know before, fr. *pro-* + *gignōskein* to know — more at KNOW] (1655) **1** : the prospect of recovery as anticipated from the usual course of disease or peculiarities of the case **2** : FORECAST, PROGNOSTICATION

prog·nos·tic \präg-'näs-tik\ *n* [ME *pronostique,* fr. MF, fr. L *prognosticum,* fr. Gk *prognōstikon,* fr. neut. of *prognōstikos* foretelling, fr. *progignōskein*] (14c) **1** : something that foretells : PORTENT **2** : PROGNOSTICATION, PROPHECY — **prognostic** *adj*

prog·nos·ti·cate \präg-'näs-tə-ˌkāt\ *vt* **-cat·ed; -cat·ing** (1529) **1** : to foretell from signs or symptoms : PREDICT **2** : PRESAGE ***syn*** see FORETELL — **prog·nos·ti·ca·tive** \-ˌkāt-iv\ *adj* — **prog·nos·ti·ca·tor** \-ˌkāt-ər\ *n*

prog·nos·ti·ca·tion \(ˌ)präg-ˌnäs-tə-'kā-shən\ *n* (15c) **1** : an indication in advance : FORETOKEN **2** **a** : an act, the fact, or the power of prognosticating : FORECAST **b** : FOREBODING

pro·grade \'prō-'grād\ *adj* [L *pro-* forward + *gradi* to go — more at PRO-, GRADE] (1967) : being or relating to orbital or rotational motion of a body that is in the same direction as that of another celestial body ⟨~ orbit of a satellite⟩

¹pro·gram \'prō-ˌgram, -grəm\ *n* [F *programme* agenda, public notice, fr. Gk *programma,* fr. *prographein* to write before, fr. *pro-* before + *graphein* to write] (1633) **1** [LL *programma,* fr. Gk] : a public notice **2** **a** : a brief usu. printed outline of the order to be followed, of the features to be presented, and the persons participating (as in a public exercise or performance) **b** : the performance of a program; *esp* : a performance broadcast on radio or television **3** : a plan or system under which action may be taken toward a goal **4** : CURRICULUM **5** : PROSPECTUS, SYLLABUS **6** **a** : a plan for the programming of a mechanism (as a computer) **b** : a sequence of coded instructions that can be inserted into a mechanism (as a computer) or that is part of an organism

²program *also* **programme** *vt* **-grammed** *or* **-gramed; -gram·ming** *or* **-gram·ing** (1896) **1** **a** : to arrange or furnish a program of or for : BILL **b** : to enter in a program **2** : to work out a sequence of operations to be performed by (a mechanism) : provide with a program **3** **a** : to insert a program for (a particular action) into or as if into a mechanism **b** : to control by or as if by a program **c** (1) : to code in an organism's program (2) : to provide with a biological program ⟨cells that have been *programmed* to synthesize hemoglobin⟩ **4** : to direct or predetermine (as thinking of behavior) completely as if by computer programming ⟨children *programmed* into violence⟩ — **pro·gram·ma·bil·i·ty** \(ˌ)prō-ˌgram-ə-'bil-ət-ē\ *n* — **pro·gram·ma·ble** \'prō-ˌgram-ə-bəl\ *adj or n*

program director *n* (1953) : one in charge of planning and scheduling program material for a radio or television station or network

pro·gram·mat·ic \ˌprō-grə-'mat-ik\ *adj* (1896) **1** : relating to program music **2** : of, relating to, resembling, or having a program — **pro·gram·mat·i·cal·ly** \-i-k(ə-)lē\ *adv*

programme *chiefly Brit var of* PROGRAM

programmed instruction *n* (1962) : instruction through information given in small steps with each requiring a correct response by the learner before going on to the next step

pro·gram·mer *or* **pro·gram·er** \'prō-ˌgram-ər, -grə-mər\ *n* (ca. 1890) : one that programs: as **a** : one that prepares and tests programs for mechanisms **b** : a person or device that programs a mechanism **c** : one that prepares educational programs

pro·gram·ming *or* **pro·gram·ing** \-ˌgram-iŋ, -grə-miŋ\ *n* (1940) **1** : the planning, scheduling, or performing of a program **2** **a** : the process of instructing or learning by means of an instructional program **b** : the process of preparing an instructional program

program music *n* (1879) : music intended to suggest a sequence of images or incidents

¹prog·ress \'präg-rəs, -ˌres, *US also & Brit usu* 'prō-ˌgres\ *n* [ME, fr. L *progressus* advance, fr. *progressus,* pp. of *progredi* to go forth, fr. *pro-* forward + *gradi* to go — more at PRO-, GRADE] (15c) **1** **a** (1) : a royal journey marked by pomp and pageant (2) : a state procession **b** : a tour or circuit made by an official (as a judge) **c** : an expedition, journey, or march through a region **2** : a forward or onward movement (as to an objective or to a goal) : ADVANCE **3** : gradual betterment; *esp* : the progressive development of mankind — **in progress** : going on : OCCURRING

²pro·gress \prə-'gres\ *vi* (1590) **1** : to move forward : PROCEED **2** : to develop to a higher, better, or more advanced stage

pro·gres·sion \prə-'gresh-ən\ *n* (15c) **1** : a sequence of numbers in which each term is related to its predecessor by a uniform law **2** **a** : the action or process of progressing : ADVANCE **b** : a continuous and connected series : SEQUENCE **3** **a** : succession of musical tones or chords **b** : the movement of musical parts in harmony **c** : SEQUENCE 2c — **pro·gres·sion·al** \-'gresh-nəl, -ən-ᵊl\ *adj*

¹pro·gres·sive \prə-'gres-iv\ *adj* (1607) **1** **a** : of, relating to, or characterized by progress **b** : making use of or interested in new ideas, findings, or opportunities **c** : of, relating to, or constituting an educational theory marked by emphasis on the individual child, informality of classroom procedure, and encouragement of self-expression **2** : of, relating to, or characterized by progression **3** : moving forward or onward : ADVANCING **4** **a** : increasing in extent or severity ⟨a ~ disease⟩ **b** : increasing in rate as the base increases ⟨a ~ tax⟩ **5** *often cap* : of or relating to political Progressives **6** : of, relating to, or constituting a verb form that expresses action or state in progress at the time of speaking or a time spoken of — **pro·gres·sive·ly** *adv* — **pro·gres·sive·ness** *n*

²progressive *n* (1846) **1** **a** : one that is progressive **b** : one believing in moderate political change and esp. social improvement by governmental action **2** *cap* : a member of any of various U.S. political parties: as **a** : a member of a predominantly agrarian minor party that around 1912 split off from the Republicans; *specif* : BULL MOOSE **b** : a follower of Robert M. La Follette in the presidential campaign of 1924 **c** : a follower of Henry A. Wallace in the presidential campaign of 1948

Progressive Conservative *adj* (1942) : of or relating to a major political party in Canada traditionally advocating economic nationalism and close ties with the United Kingdom and the Commonwealth — **Progressive Conservative** *n*

pro·gres·siv·ism \prə-'gres-iv-ˌiz-əm\ *n* (1892) **1** : the principles, beliefs, or practices of progressives **2** *cap* : the political and economic doctrines advocated by the Progressives **3** : the theories of progressive education — **pro·gres·siv·ist** \-iv-əst\ *n or adj* — **pro·gres·siv·is·tic** \-ˌgres-iv-'is-tik\ *adj*

pro·hib·it \prō-'hib-ət, prə-\ *vt* [ME *prohibiten,* fr. L *prohibitus,* pp. of *prohibēre* to hold away, fr. *pro-* forward + *habēre* to hold] (15c) **1** : to forbid by authority : ENJOIN **2** **a** : to prevent from doing something **b** : PRECLUDE ***syn*** see FORBID

pro·hi·bi·tion \ˌprō-ə-'bish-ən *also* ˌprō-hə-\ *n* (14c) **1** : the act of prohibiting by authority **2** : an order to restrain or stop **3** *often cap* : the forbidding by law of the manufacture, transportation, and sale of alcoholic liquors except for medicinal and sacramental purposes

pro·hi·bi·tion·ist \-'bish-(ə-)nəst\ *n* (ca. 1846) : one who favors prohibition; *esp, cap* : a member of a minor U.S. political party advocating prohibition

pro·hib·i·tive \prō-'hib-ət-iv, prə-\ *adj* (1602) **1** : tending to prohibit or restrain **2** : tending to preclude use or purchase ⟨~ costs⟩ **3** : almost certain to win ⟨a ~ favorite⟩ — **pro·hib·i·tive·ly** *adv* — **pro·hib·i·tive·ness** *n*

pro·hib·i·to·ry \-'hib-ə-ˌtōr-ē, -ˌtȯr-\ *adj* (1591) : PROHIBITIVE

pro·insulin \(ˈ)prō-'in(t)-s(ə-)lən\ *n* (1916) : a single-chain pancreatic polypeptide precursor of insulin that gives rise to the double chain of insulin by loss of the middle part of the molecule

¹proj·ect \'präj-ˌekt, -ikt *also* 'prōj-\ *n* [ME *proiecte,* modif. of MF *pourjet,* fr. *pourjeter* to throw out, spy, plan, fr. *pour-* (fr. L *porro* forward) + *jeter* to throw; akin to Gk *pro* forward — more at FOR, JET] (15c) **1** : a specific plan or design : SCHEME **2** *obs* : IDEA **3** : a planned undertaking: as **a** : a definitely formulated piece of research **b** : a large usu. government-supported undertaking **c** : a task or problem engaged in usu. by a group of students to supplement and apply classroom studies **4** : a group of houses or apartments built and arranged according to a single plan ***syn*** see PLAN

²pro·ject \prə-'jekt\ *vb* [partly modif. of MF *pourjeter;* partly fr. L *projectus,* pp. of *proicere* to throw forward, fr. *pro-* + *jacere* to throw — more at JET] *vt* (15c) **1** **a** : to devise in the mind : DESIGN **b** : to plan, figure, or estimate for the future ⟨~ expenditures for the coming year⟩ **2** : to throw or cast forward : THRUST **3** : to put or set forth : present for consideration **4** : to cause to protrude **5** : to cause (light or shadow) to fall into space or (an image) to fall on a surface ⟨~ a beam of light⟩ **6** : to reproduce (as a point, line, or area) on a surface by motion in a prescribed direction **7** : to communicate vividly esp. to an audience ⟨~ an image⟩ ⟨an actress who could ~ amorality —*Current Biog.*⟩ **8** : to attribute or assign (something in one's own mind or a personal characteristic) to a person, group, or object ⟨a nation is an entity on which one can ~ many of the worst of one's instincts —*Times Lit. Supp.*⟩ **~** *vi* **1** : to jut out : PROTRUDE **2** **a** : to come across vividly : give an impression **b** : to make oneself heard clearly — **pro·ject·able** \-'jek-tə-bəl\ *adj*

¹pro·jec·tile \prə-'jek-tᵊl *also* -ˌtīl, *chiefly Brit* 'präj-ik-ˌtīl\ *n* (1665) **1** : a body projected by external force and continuing in motion by its own inertia; *esp* : a missile for a weapon (as a firearm) **2** : a self-propelling weapon (as a rocket)

²projectile *adj* (1715) **1** : projecting or impelling forward ⟨a ~ force⟩ **2** : capable of being thrust forward

pro·jec·tion \prə-'jek-shən\ *n* (1557) **1** **a** : a systematic presentation of intersecting coordinate lines on a flat surface upon which features from the curved surface of the earth or the celestial sphere may be mapped **b** : the process or technique of reproducing a spatial object upon a plane or curved surface or a line by projecting its points; *also* : a graph or figure so formed **2** : a transforming change **3** : the act of throwing or thrusting forward **4** : the forming of a plan : SCHEMING **5** **a** (1) : a jutting out (2) : a part that juts out **b** : a view of a building or architectural element **6** **a** : the act of perceiving a mental object as spatially and sensibly objective; *also* : something so perceived **b** : the attribution of one's own ideas, feelings, or attitudes to other people or to objects; *esp* : the externalization of blame, guilt, or responsibility as a defense against anxiety **7** : the display of motion pictures by projecting an image from them upon a screen **8** **a** : the act of projecting esp. to an audience **b** : control of the volume, clarity, and distinctness of a voice to gain greater audibility **9** : an estimate of future possibilities based on a current trend — **pro·jec·tion·al** \-shnəl, -shən-ᵊl\ *adj*

syn PROJECTION, PROTRUSION, PROTUBERANCE, BULGE mean an extension beyond the normal line or surface. PROJECTION implies a jutting out esp. at a sharp angle; PROTRUSION suggests a thrusting out so that the extension seems a deformity; PROTUBERANCE implies a growing or swelling out in rounded form; BULGE suggests an expansion caused by internal pressure.

projection booth *n* (ca. 1928) : a booth in a theater or hall for housing and operating a projector and esp. a motion-picture projector

pro·jec·tion·ist \prə-'jek-sh(ə-)nəst\ *n* (1922) : one that makes projections: as **a** : CARTOGRAPHER **b** : one that operates a motion-picture projector or television equipment

projection room *n* (1914) **1** : PROJECTION BOOTH **2** : a room equipped with a projector and screen for the private viewing of motion pictures

pro·jec·tive \prə-'jek-tiv\ *adj* (1682) **1** : relating to, produced by, or involving geometric projection **2** : of or relating to a test or device

designed to analyze the psychodynamic constitution of an individual — **pro·jec·tive·ly** *adv*
projective geometry *n* (1885) **:** a branch of geometry that deals with the properties of configurations that are unaltered by projection
pro·jec·tor \prə-'jek-tər\ *n* (1596) **1 :** one that plans a project; *specif* **:** PROMOTER **2 :** one that projects: as **a :** a device for projecting a beam of light **b :** an optical instrument for projecting an image upon a surface **c :** a machine for projecting motion pictures on a screen **3 :** an imagined line from an object to a surface along which projection takes place
pro·jet \prō-'zhā, 'prō-,\ *n, pl* **projets** \-'zhā(z), -,zhā(z)\ [F, fr. MF *pourjet*] (1808) **1 :** PLAN; *esp* **:** a draft of a proposed measure or treaty **2 :** a projected or proposed design
pro·kary·ote \(')prō-'kar-ē-,ōt\ *n* [*pro-* + *kary-* + *-ote* (as in *zygote*)] (1963) **:** a cellular organism (as a bacterium or a blue-green alga) that does not have a distinct nucleus — compare EUKARYOTE — **pro·kary·ot·ic** \-,kar-ē-'ät-ik\ *adj*
pro·lac·tin \prō-'lak-tən\ *n* [²*pro-* + *lact-* + *-in*] (ca. 1932) **:** a protein hormone of the anterior lobe of the pituitary that induces lactation
pro·la·min *or* **pro·la·mine** \'prō-lə-mən, -,mēn\ *n* [ISV *proline* + *ammonia* + *-in, -ine*] (1908) **:** any of various simple proteins found esp. in seeds and insoluble in absolute alcohol or water
pro·lan \'prō-,lan\ *n* [G, fr. L *proles* progeny] (1931) **:** either of two gonadotrophic hormones: **a :** FOLLICLE-STIMULATING HORMONE **b :** LUTEINIZING HORMONE
¹**pro·lapse** \prō-'laps, 'prō-,\ *n* [NL *prolapsus*, fr. LL, fall, fr. L *prolapsus*, pp. of *prolabi* to fall or slide forward, fr. *pro-* forward + *labi* to slide — more at PRO-, SLEEP] (1822) **:** the falling down or slipping of a body part from its usual position or relations
²**pro·lapse** \prō-'laps\ *vi* **pro·lapsed; pro·laps·ing** (1876) **:** to undergo prolapse
pro·late \'prō-,lāt\ *adj* [L *prolatus* (pp. of *proferre* to bring forward, extend) fr. *pro-* forward + *latus*, pp. of *ferre* to carry — more at BEAR, TOLERATE] (1694) **:** EXTENDED; *esp* **:** elongated in the direction of a line joining the poles ⟨a ~ spheroid⟩
prole \'prōl\ *n or adj* (1887) **:** PROLETARIAN
pro·leg \'prō-,leg, -,lāg\ *n* (1816) **:** a fleshy leg that occurs on an abdominal segment of some insect larvae but not in the adult
pro·le·gom·e·non \,prō-li-'gäm-ə-,nän, -nən\ *n, pl* **-e·na** \-nə\ [Gk, neut. pres. pass. part. of *prolegein* to say beforehand, fr. *pro-* before + *legein* to say — more at LEGEND] (1652) **:** prefatory remarks; *specif* **:** a formal essay or critical discussion serving to introduce and interpret an extended work — **pro·le·gom·e·nous** \-nəs\ *adj*
pro·lep·sis \prō-'lep-səs\ *n, pl* **-lep·ses** \-,sēz\ [Gk *prolēpsis*, fr. *prolambanein* to take beforehand, fr. *pro-* before + *lambanein* to take — more at LATCH] (1578) **:** ANTICIPATION: as **a :** the representation or assumption of a future act or development as if presently existing or accomplished **b :** the application of an adjective to a noun in anticipation of the result of the action of the verb (as in "while yon slow oxen turn the *furrowed* plain") — **pro·lep·tic** \-'lep-tik\ *adj*
pro·le·tar·i·an \,prō-lə-'ter-ē-ən\ *n* [L *proletarius*, fr. *proles* progeny (fr. *pro-* forth) + *-olescere* (fr. *alescere* to grow) — more at OLD] (1658) **:** a member of the proletariat — **proletarian** *adj*
pro·le·tar·i·an·ize \-'ter-ē-ə-,nīz\ *vt* **-ized; -iz·ing** (1887) **:** to reduce to a proletarian status or level — **pro·le·tar·i·an·iza·tion** \-,ter-ē-ə-nə-'zā-shən\ *n*
pro·le·tar·i·at \,prō-lə-'ter-ē-ət, -'tar-, -ē-,at\ *n* [F *prolétariat*, fr. L *proletarius*] (1853) **1 :** the lowest social or economic class of a community **2 :** the laboring class; *esp* **:** the class of industrial workers who lack their own means of production and hence sell their labor to live
pro–life \(')prō-'līf\ *adj* (1972) **:** ANTIABORTION ⟨~ lobbyists⟩ — **pro–lif·er** \-'lī-fər\ *n*
pro·lif·er·ate \prə-'lif-ə-,rāt\ *vb* **-at·ed; -at·ing** [back-formation fr. *proliferation*, fr. F *prolifération*, fr. *proliférer* to proliferate, fr. L *proles* + *-fer* -ferous] *vi* (1873) **1 :** to grow by rapid production of new parts, cells, buds, or offspring **2 :** to increase in number as if by proliferating **:** MULTIPLY ~ *vt* **:** to cause to grow by proliferating — **pro·lif·er·a·tion** \-,lif-ə-'rā-shən\ *n* — **pro·lif·er·a·tive** \-'lif-ə-,rāt-iv, -'lif-(ə-)rət-\ *adj*
pro·lif·ic \prə-'lif-ik\ *adj* [F *prolifique*, fr. L *proles* progeny] (1650) **1 :** producing young or fruit esp. freely **:** FRUITFUL **2** *archaic* **:** causing abundant growth, generation, or reproduction **3 :** marked by abundant inventiveness or productivity ⟨a ~ writer⟩ *syn* see FERTILE — **pro·lif·i·ca·cy** \-'lif-i-kə-sē\ *n* — **pro·lif·i·cal·ly** \-i-k(ə-)lē\ *adv* — **pro·lif·ic·ness** \-ik-nəs\ *n*
pro·li·fic·i·ty \,prō-lə-'fis-ət-ē\ *n* (1725) **:** prolific power or character
pro·line \'prō-,lēn\ *n* [G *prolin*] (1904) **:** an amino acid $C_5H_9NO_2$ that can be synthesized by animals from glutamate
pro·lix \prō-'liks, 'prō-(,)\ *adj* [ME, fr. MF & L; MF *prolixe*, fr. L *prolixus* extended, fr. *pro-* forward + *liquēre* to be fluid — more at LIQUID] (15c) **1 :** unduly prolonged or drawn out **:** too long **2 :** marked by or using an excess of words *syn* see WORDY — **pro·lix·i·ty** \prō-'lik-sət-ē\ *n* — **pro·lix·ly** *adv*
pro·loc·u·tor \prō-'läk-yət-ər\ *n* [L, fr. *pro-* for + *locutor* speaker, fr. *locutus*, pp. of *loqui* to speak] (15c) **1 :** one who speaks for another **:** SPOKESMAN **2 :** presiding officer **:** CHAIRMAN
pro·lo·gize \'prō-,lȯg-,īz, -,läg-; -lə-,jīz\ *or* **pro·logu·ize** \-,lȯg-,īz, -,läg-\ *vi* **-lo·gized** *or* **-logu·ized; -lo·giz·ing** *or* **-logu·iz·ing** (1608) **:** to write or speak a prologue
pro·logue *also* **pro·log** \'prō-,lȯg, -,läg\ *n* [ME *prolog*, fr. MF *prologue*, fr. L *prologus* preface to a play, fr. Gk *prologos* part of a Greek play preceding the entry of the chorus, fr. *pro-* before + *legein* to speak — more at PRO-, LEGEND] (14c) **1 :** the preface or introduction to a literary work **2 a :** a speech often in verse addressed to the audience by an actor at the beginning of a play **b :** the actor speaking such a prologue **3 :** an introductory or preceding event or development
pro·long \prə-'lȯŋ\ *vt* [ME *prolongen*, fr. MF *prolonguer*, fr. LL *prolongare*, fr. L *pro-* forward + *longus* long] (15c) **1 :** to lengthen in time **:** CONTINUE **2 :** to lengthen in extent, scope, or range *syn* see EXTEND — **pro·long·er** \-'lȯŋ-ər\ *n*
pro·lon·ga·tion \(,)prō-,lȯŋ-'gā-shən, prə-\ *n* (15c) **1 :** an extension or lengthening in time or duration **2 :** an expansion or continuation in extent, scope, or range
pro·lu·sion \prō-'lü-zhən\ *n* [L *prolusion-*, *prolusio*, fr. *prolusus*, pp. of *proludere* to play beforehand, fr. *pro-* before + *ludere* to play — more at LUDICROUS] (1601) **1 :** a preliminary trial or exercise **:** PRELUDE **2 :** an introductory and often tentative discourse — **pro·lu·so·ry** \-'lüs-(ə-)rē, -'lüz-\ *adj*
prom \'präm\ *n* [short for *promenade*] (1894) **1 :** a formal dance given by a high school or college class **2** *Brit* **:** PROMENADE 2
¹**prom·e·nade** \,präm-ə-'nād, -'näd\ *n* [F, fr. *promener* to take for a walk, fr. L *prominare* to drive forward, fr. *pro-* forward + *minare* to drive — more at AMENABLE] (1567) **1 :** a leisurely walk or ride esp. in a public place for pleasure or display **2 :** a place for strolling **3 a :** a ceremonious opening of a formal ball consisting of a grand march of all the guests **b :** a figure in a square dance in which couples move counterclockwise in a circle
²**promenade** *vb* **-nad·ed; -nad·ing** *vi* (1801) **1 :** to take or go on a promenade **2 :** to perform a promenade in a dance ~ *vt* **:** to walk about in or on — **prom·e·nad·er** *n*
promenade deck *n* (1829) **:** an upper deck or an area on a deck of a passenger ship where passengers stroll
Pro·me·the·an \prə-'mē-thē-ən\ *adj* (1588) **:** of, relating to, or resembling Prometheus, his experiences, or his art; *esp* **:** daringly original or creative
Pro·me·theus \-thē-əs, -,th(y)üs\ *n* [L, fr. Gk *Promētheus*] **:** a Titan who is chained and tortured by Zeus for stealing fire from heaven and giving it to man
pro·me·thi·um \-thē-əm\ *n* [NL, fr. L *Prometheus*] (1948) **:** a radioactive metallic element of the rare-earth group obtained as a fission product of uranium or from neutron-irradiated neodymium — see ELEMENT table
prom·i·nence \'präm(-ə)-nən(t)s\ *n* (1598) **1 :** something prominent **:** PROJECTION ⟨a rocky ~⟩ **2 :** the quality, state, or fact of being prominent or conspicuous **3 :** a mass of gas resembling a cloud that arises from the chromosphere of the sun
prom·i·nent \-nənt\ *adj* [L *prominent-*, *prominens*, fr. prp. of *prominēre* to jut forward, fr. *pro-* forward + *-minēre* (akin to *mont-*, *mons* mountain) — more at MOUNT] (1545) **1 :** standing out or projecting beyond a surface or line **:** PROTUBERANT **2 a :** readily noticeable **:** CONSPICUOUS **b :** widely and popularly known **:** LEADING *syn* see NOTICEABLE — **prom·i·nent·ly** *adv*
pro·mis·cu·ity \,präm-əs-'kyü-ət-ē, ,prō-məs-\ *n, pl* **-ities** (1849) **1 :** a miscellaneous mixture or mingling of persons or things **2 :** promiscuous sexual behavior
pro·mis·cu·ous \prə-'mis-kyə-wəs\ *adj* [L *promiscuus*, fr. *pro-* forth + *miscēre* to mix — more at PRO-, MIX] (1603) **1 :** composed of all sorts of persons or things **2 :** not restricted to one class, sort, or person **:** INDISCRIMINATE ⟨education . . . cheapened through the ~ distribution of diplomas —Norman Cousins⟩; *esp* **:** not restricted to one sexual partner **3 :** CASUAL, IRREGULAR ⟨~ eating habits⟩ — **pro·mis·cu·ous·ly** *adv* — **pro·mis·cu·ous·ness** *n*
¹**prom·ise** \'präm-əs\ *n* [ME *promis*, fr. L *promissum*, fr. neut. of *promissus*, pp. of *promittere* to send forth, promise, fr. *pro-* forth + *mittere* to send] (15c) **1 a :** a declaration that one will do or refrain from doing something specified **b :** a legally binding declaration that gives the person to whom it is made a right to expect or to claim the performance or forbearance of a specified act **2 :** reason to expect something ⟨little ~ of relief⟩; *esp* **:** ground for expectation of success, improvement, or excellence ⟨shows considerable ~⟩ **3 :** something that is promised
²**promise** *vb* **prom·ised; prom·is·ing** *vt* (15c) **1 :** to pledge to do, bring about, or provide ⟨~ aid⟩ **2** *archaic* **:** WARRANT, ASSURE **3** *chiefly dial* **:** BETROTH **4 :** to suggest beforehand **:** give promise of ⟨dark clouds ~ rain⟩ ~ *vi* **1 :** to make a promise **2 :** to give ground for expectation **:** be imminent — **prom·is·ee** \,präm-ə-'sē\ *n* — **prom·i·sor** \-'sȯ(ə)r\ *also* **prom·is·er** \'präm-ə-sər\ *n*
promised land *n* (1667) **:** a place or condition believed to promise final satisfaction or realization of hopes
prom·is·ing \'präm-ə-siŋ\ *adj* (1601) **:** full of promise **:** likely to succeed or to yield good results — **prom·is·ing·ly** \-siŋ-lē\ *adv*
prom·is·so·ry \'präm-ə-,sōr-ē, -,sȯr-\ *adj* [ML *promissorius*, fr. L *promissus*, pp.] (1649) **:** containing or conveying a promise or assurance
promissory note *n* (1710) **:** a written promise to pay at a fixed or determinable future time a sum of money to a specified individual or to bearer
prom·on·to·ry \'präm-ən-,tōr-ē, -,tȯr-\ *n, pl* **-ries** [L *promunturium*, *promonturium*; prob. akin to *prominēre* to jut forth — more at PROMINENT] (1548) **1 a :** a high point of land or rock projecting into a body of water **b :** a prominent mass of land overlooking or projecting into a lowland **2 :** a bodily prominence
pro·mote \prə-'mōt\ *vt* **pro·mot·ed; pro·mot·ing** [L *promotus*, pp. of *promovēre*, lit., to move forward, fr. *pro-* forward + *movēre* to move] (14c) **1 a :** to advance in station, rank, or honor **:** RAISE **b :** to change (a pawn) into a piece in chess by moving to the eighth rank **c :** to advance (a student) from one grade to the next higher grade **2 a :** to contribute to the growth or prosperity of **:** FURTHER ⟨~ international understanding⟩ **b :** to help bring (as an enterprise) into being **:** LAUNCH **c :** to present (merchandise) for buyer acceptance through advertising, publicity, or discounting **3** *slang* **:** to get possession of by doubtful means or by ingenuity *syn* see ADVANCE — **pro·mot·abil·i·ty** \-,mōt-ə-'bil-ət-ē\ *n* — **pro·mot·able** \-'mōt-ə-bəl\ *adj*
pro·mot·er \-'mōt-ər\ *n* (15c) **1 :** one that promotes; *esp* **:** one who assumes the financial responsibilities of a sporting event (as a boxing match) including contracting with the principals, renting the site, and collecting gate receipts **2** *obs* **:** PROSECUTOR **3 :** a substance that in very small amounts is able to increase the activity of a catalyst **4 :** the region of a genetic operon where transcription is initiated by binding with an appropriate polymerase

\ə\ abut \ᵊ\ kitten, F table \ər\ further \a\ ash \ā\ ace \ä\ cot, cart \au̇\ out \ch\ chin \e\ bet \ē\ easy \g\ go \i\ hit \ī\ ice \j\ job \ŋ\ sing \ō\ go \ȯ\ law \ȯi\ boy \th\ thin \t͟h\ the \ü\ loot \u̇\ foot \y\ yet \zh\ vision \á, k̲, ⁿ, œ, œ̄, ue, ue̅, ʸ\ *see* Guide to Pronunciation

pro•mo•tion \prə-'mō-shən\ *n* (15c) **1 :** the act or fact of being raised in position or rank : PREFERMENT **2 :** the act of furthering the growth or development of something; *esp* **:** the furtherance of the acceptance and sale of merchandise through advertising, publicity, or discounting — **pro•mo•tion•al** \-shnəl, -shən-ᵊl\ *adj*

pro•mo•tive \-'mōt-iv\ *adj* (1644) **:** tending or serving to promote — **pro•mo•tive•ness** *n*

[1]**prompt** \'präm(p)t\ *vt* [ME *prompten,* fr. ML *promptare,* fr. L *promptus* prompt] (14c) **1 :** to move to action : INCITE **2 :** to assist (one acting or reciting) by suggesting or saying the next words of something forgotten or imperfectly learned : CUE **3 :** to serve as the inciting cause of — **prompt•er** *n*

[2]**prompt** *adj* (1784) **:** of or relating to prompting actors

[3]**prompt** *adj* [ME, fr. MF or L; MF, fr. L *promptus* ready, prompt, fr. pp. of *promere* to bring forth, fr. *pro-* forth + *emere* to take — more at REDEEM] (15c) **1 :** being ready and quick to act as occasion demands **2 :** performed readily or immediately ⟨~ assistance⟩ ***syn*** see QUICK — **prompt•ly** \'präm(p)-tlē, 'präm-plē\ *adv* — **prompt•ness** \'prämt-nəs, 'prämp-nəs\ *n*

[4]**prompt** *n, pl* **prompts** \'präm(t)s, 'prämps\ (1597) **1** [[1]*prompt*] **:** something that prompts : REMINDER **2** [[3]*prompt*] **:** a limit of time given for payment of an account for goods purchased; *also* **:** the contract by which this time is fixed

prompt•book \'prämt-,bu̇k, 'prämp-,bu̇k\ *n* (1809) **:** a copy of a play with directions for performance used by a theater prompter

promp•ti•tude \'präm(p)-tə-,t(y)üd\ *n* [ME, fr. MF or LL; MF, fr. LL *promptitudo,* fr. L *promptus*] (15c) **:** the quality or habit of being prompt : PROMPTNESS

prompt side *n* (1824) **1 :** the side of the stage adjacent to the prompter's corner **2 :** the side of the stage to the right of an actor facing the audience

pro•mul•gate \'präm-əl-,gāt; prō-'məl-, prə-', 'prō-(,)\ *vt* **-gat•ed; -gat•ing** [L *promulgatus,* pp. of *promulgare*] (ca. 1530) **1 :** to make known by open declaration : PROCLAIM **2 a :** to make known or public the terms of (a proposed law) **b :** to put (a law) into action or force ***syn*** see DECLARE — **pro•mul•ga•tion** \,präm-əl-'gā-shən; ,prō-(,)məl-, (,)prō-, , prə-,\ *n* — **pro•mul•ga•tor** \'präm-əl-,gāt-ər; prō-'məl-, prə-', 'prō-(,)\ *n*

pro•na•tion \prō-'nā-shən\ *n* [*pronate* (fr. LL *pronatus,* pp. of *pronare* to bend forward, fr. L *pronus*) + *-ion*] (1666) **1 :** rotation of the hand and forearm so that the palm faces backwards or downwards **2 :** rotation of the medial bones in the midtarsal region of the foot inward and downward so that in walking the foot tends to come down on its inner margin — **pro•nate** \'prō-,nāt\ *vb*

pro•na•tor \'prō-,nāt-ər\ *n* (1727) **:** a muscle that produces pronation

prone \'prōn\ *adj* [ME, fr. L *pronus* bent forward, tending; akin to L *pro* forward — more at FOR] (14c) **1 :** having a tendency or inclination **:** being likely ⟨devices ~ to fail⟩ ⟨~ to forget names⟩ ⟨accident-*prone*⟩ **2 :** having the front or ventral surface downward — **prone** *adv* — **prone•ly** *adv* — **prone•ness** \'prōn-nəs\ *n*

syn PRONE, SUPINE, PROSTRATE, RECUMBENT mean lying down. PRONE implies a position with the front of the body turned toward the supporting surface; SUPINE implies lying on one's back and suggests inertness or abjectness; PROSTRATE implies lying full-length as in submission, defeat, or physical collapse; RECUMBENT implies the posture of one sleeping or resting. ***syn*** see in addition LIABLE

pro•neph•ros \(')prō-'nef-rəs, -,räs\ *n* [NL, fr. Gk *pro-* + *nephros* kidney — more at NEPHRITIS] (1881) **:** either member of the first and most anterior pair of the three successive paired vertebrate renal organs that functions in the adults of amphioxus and some lampreys, functions temporarily in larval fishes and amphibians, and is present but nonfunctional in embryos of reptiles, birds, and mammals — compare MESONEPHROS, METANEPHROS — **pro•neph•ric** \-rik\ *adj*

[1]**prong** \'prȯŋ, 'präŋ\ *n* [ME *pronge*] (15c) **1 :** FORK **2 :** a tine of a fork **3 :** a slender pointed or projecting part: as **a :** a fang of a tooth **b :** a point of an antler **4 :** something resembling a prong — **pronged** \'prȯŋd, 'präŋd\ *adj*

[2]**prong** *vt* (1848) **:** to stab, pierce, or break up with a pronged device

prong•horn \'prȯŋ-,hȯ(ə)rn, 'präŋ-\ *n, pl* **pronghorn** *also* **pronghorns** (1823) **:** a ruminant mammal (*Antilocapra americana*) of treeless parts of western No. America that resembles an antelope — called also *pronghorn antelope*

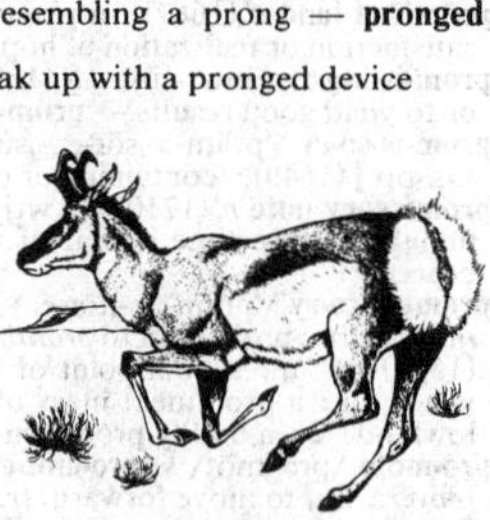

pronghorn

pro•nom•i•nal \prō-'näm-ən-ᵊl, -'näm-nəl\ *adj* [LL *pronominalis,* fr. L *pronomin-, pronomen*] (1680) **1 :** of, relating to, or constituting a pronoun **2 :** resembling a pronoun in identifying or specifying without describing ⟨the ~ adjective *this* in *this* dog⟩ — **pro•nom•i•nal•ly** \-ē\ *adv*

pro•noun \'prō-,nau̇n\ *n* [ME *pronom,* fr. L *pronomin-, pronomen,* fr. *pro-* for + *nomin-, nomen* name — more at PRO-, NAME] (1530) **:** a word belonging to one of the major form classes in any of a great many languages that is used as a substitute for a noun or noun equivalent, takes noun constructions, and refers to persons or things named or understood in the context

pro•nounce \prə-'nau̇n(t)s\ *vb* **pro•nounced; pro•nounc•ing** [ME *pronouncen,* fr. MF *prononcier,* fr. L *pronuntiare,* fr. *pro-* forth + *nuntiare* to report, fr. *nuntius* messenger — more at PRO-] *vt* (14c) **1 :** to declare officially or ceremoniously ⟨the minister *pronounced* them man and wife⟩ **2 :** to declare authoritatively or as an opinion ⟨doctors *pronounced* him fit to resume duties⟩ **3 a :** to employ the organs of speech to produce ⟨~ these words⟩; *esp* **:** to say correctly ⟨I can't ~ his name⟩ **b :** to represent in printed characters the spoken counterpart of (an orthographic representation) ⟨both dictionaries ~ *clique* the same⟩ **4 :** RECITE ⟨speak the speech, I pray you, as I *pronounced* it to you —Shak.⟩ ~ *vi* **1 :** to pass judgment **2 :** to produce the components of spoken language — **pro•nounce•abil•i•ty** \-,nau̇n(t)-sə-'bil-ət-ē\ *n* — **pro•nounce•able** \-'nau̇n(t)-sə-bəl\ *adj* — **pro•nounc•er** *n*

pro•nounced \-'nau̇n(t)st\ *adj* (1727) **:** strongly marked : DECIDED — **pro•nounced•ly** \-'nau̇n(t)-səd-lē, -'nau̇n(t)s-tlē\ *adv*

pro•nounce•ment \prə-'nau̇n(t)-smənt\ *n* (1593) **1 :** a usu. formal declaration of opinion **2 :** an authoritative announcement

pro•nounc•ing *adj* (1764) **:** relating to or indicating pronunciation ⟨a ~ dictionary⟩

pron•to \'prän-,tō\ *adv* [Sp, fr. L *promptus* prompt] (ca. 1740) **:** without delay

[1]**pro•nu•clear** \(')prō-'n(y)ü-klē-ər, ÷-kyə-lər\ *adj* [[1]*pro-* + *nuclear*] (ca. 1890) **:** of, relating to, or resembling a pronucleus

[2]**pronuclear** *adj* [[2]*pro-* + *nuclear*] (1971) **:** advocating the use of nuclear-powered generating stations

pro•nu•cle•us \(')prō-'n(y)ü-klē-əs\ *n* [NL] (1880) **:** the haploid nucleus of a male or female gamete (as an egg or sperm) up to the time of fusion with that of another gamete in fertilization

pro•nun•ci•a•men•to \prō-,nən(t)-sē-ə-'ment-(,)ō\ *n, pl* **-tos** *or* **-toes** [Sp *pronunciamiento,* fr. *pronunciar* to pronounce, fr. L *pronuntiare*] (1835) **:** PROCLAMATION, PRONOUNCEMENT

pro•nun•ci•a•tion \prə-,nən(t)-sē-'ā-shən *also* ÷-,nau̇n(t)-\ *n* [ME *pronunciacion,* fr. MF *prononciation,* fr. L *pronuntiation-, pronuntiatio,* fr. *pronuntiatus,* pp. of *pronuntiare*] (15c) **:** the act or manner of pronouncing something — **pro•nun•ci•a•tion•al** \-shnəl, -shən-ᵊl\ *adj*

[1]**proof** \'prüf\ *n* [ME, alter. of *preove,* fr. OF *preuve,* fr. LL *proba,* fr. L *probare* to prove — more at PROVE] (13c) **1 a :** the cogency of evidence that compels acceptance by the mind of a truth or a fact **b :** the process or an instance of establishing the validity of a statement esp. by derivation from other statements in accordance with principles of reasoning **2** *obs* **:** EXPERIENCE **3 :** something that induces certainty or establishes validity **4** *archaic* **:** the quality or state of having been tested or tried; *esp* **:** unyielding hardness **5 :** evidence operating to determine the finding or judgment of a tribunal **6 a** *pl* **proofs** *or* **proof :** a copy (as of typeset text) made for examination or correction **b :** a test impression of an engraving, etching, or lithograph **c :** a coin that is struck from a highly-polished die on a polished planchet, is not intended for circulation, and sometimes differs in metallic content from coins of identical design struck for circulation **d :** a test photographic print made from a negative **7 :** a test applied to articles or substances to determine whether they are of standard or satisfactory quality **8 a :** the minimum alcoholic strength of proof spirit **b :** strength with reference to the standard for proof spirit; *specif* **:** alcoholic strength indicated by a number that is twice the percent by volume of alcohol present ⟨whiskey of 90 ~ is 45% alcohol⟩

[2]**proof** *adj* (1592) **1 :** able to resist or repel ⟨makes literature somehow ~ against the facts of science —Jonathan Miller⟩ — often used in combination ⟨water*proof*⟩ **2 :** used in proving or testing or as a standard of comparison **3 :** of standard strength or quality or alcoholic content

[3]**proof** *vt* (1745) **1 a :** to make or take a proof or test of **b :** PROOFREAD **2 :** to give a resistant quality to **3 :** to activate (yeast) by mixing with water and sometimes sugar or milk — **proof•er** *n*

proof•like \'prü-,flīk\ *adj* (1966) **:** resembling a proof coin esp. because of a mirrorlike surface

proof•read \'prü-,frēd\ *vt* **-read** \-,fred\; **-read•ing** [back-formation fr. *proofreader*] (1920) **:** to read and mark corrections in (as a proof)

proof•read•er \-,frēd-ər\ *n* (1832) **:** one that proofreads

proof•room \'prü-,früm, -,fru̇m\ *n* (1903) **:** a room in which proofreading is done

proof spirit *n* (1790) **:** an alcoholic liquor or mixture of ethanol and water that contains 50% ethanol by volume at 60°F

[1]**prop** \'präp\ *n* [ME *proppe,* fr. MD, stopper; akin to MLG *proppe* stopper] (15c) **:** something that props or sustains : SUPPORT

[2]**prop** *vt* **propped; prop•ping** (1538) **1 a :** to support by placing something under or against — often used with *up* **b :** to support by placing against something **2 :** SUSTAIN, STRENGTHEN

[3]**prop** *n* (1841) **:** PROPERTY 3

[4]**prop** *n* (1914) **:** PROPELLER

prop- *comb form* [ISV, fr. *propionic (acid)*] **:** related to propionic acid ⟨*propane*⟩ ⟨*propyl*⟩

pro•pae•deu•tic \,prō-pi-'d(y)üt-ik\ *n* [Gk *propaideuein* to teach beforehand, fr. *pro-* before + *paideuein* to teach, fr. *paid-, pais* child — more at PRO-, FEW] (1798) **:** preparatory study or instruction — **propaedeutic** *adj*

pro•pa•gan•da \,präp-ə-'gan-də, ,prō-pə-\ *n* [NL, fr. *Congregatio de propaganda fide* Congregation for propagating the faith, organization established by Pope Gregory XV †1623] (1718) **1** *cap* **:** a congregation of the Roman curia having jurisdiction over missionary territories and related institutions **2 :** the spreading of ideas, information, or rumor for the purpose of helping or injuring an institution, a cause, or a person **3 :** ideas, facts, or allegations spread deliberately to further one's cause or to damage an opposing cause; *also* **:** a public action having such an effect — **pro•pa•gan•dist** \-dəst\ *n or adj* — **pro•pa•gan•dis•tic** \-,gan-'dis-tik\ *adj*

pro•pa•gan•dize \-'gan-,dīz\ *vb* **-dized; -diz•ing** *vt* (1844) **:** to subject to propaganda; *also* **:** to carry on propaganda for ~ *vi* **:** to carry on propaganda — **pro•pa•gan•diz•er** \-,dī-zər\ *n*

prop•a•gate \'präp-ə-,gāt\ *vb* **-gat•ed; -gat•ing** [L *propagatus,* pp. of *propagare* to set slips, propagate, fr. *propages* slip, offspring, fr. *pro-* before + *pangere* to fasten — more at PRO-, PACT] *vt* (ca. 1570) **1 :** to cause to continue or increase by sexual or asexual reproduction **2 :** to pass along to offspring **3 a :** to cause to spread out and affect a greater number or greater area : EXTEND **b :** to foster growing knowledge of, familiarity with, or acceptance of (as an idea or belief) : PUBLICIZE **c :** to transmit (as sound or light) through a medium ~ *vi* **1 :** to multiply sexually or asexually **2 :** INCREASE, EXTEND **3 :** to travel through space or a material — used of wave energy (as light, sound, or radio waves) — **prop•a•ga•ble** \'präp-ə-gə-bəl\ *adj* — **prop•a•ga•tive** \-,gāt-iv\ *adj* — **prop•a•ga•tor** \-,gāt-ər\ *n*

prop•a•ga•tion \,präp-ə-'gā-shən\ *n* (15c) **:** the act or action of propagating: as **a :** increase (as of a kind of organism) in numbers **b :** the spreading of something (as a belief) abroad or into new regions : DISSEMINATION **c :** enlargement or extension (as of a crack) in a solid body

PROOFREADERS' MARKS

⸎ or ɣ or ⸋	delete; take *it* out
⟆	close up; print as *o*ne word
⸕	delete and clo*s*e up
⋀ or > or ⋏	caret; insert here ⎨*something*
#	insert a space
eq#	space evenly ⋀ where indicated
stet	let marked ~~text~~ stand as set
tr	transpo*se*; change ⟨order ⟨the⟩
/	used to separate two or more marks and often as a concluding stroke at the end of an insertion
⌈ ⌊	set farther to the left
⌉ set⌊	farther to the right
⌢	set æ or fl as ligatures æ or fl
═	straighten alignment
‖ ‖	straighten or align
✗	imperfect or broken character
⎕	indent or insert em quad space
¶	begin a new paragraph
ⓢⓟ	spell out ⟨set ⟨5 lbs.⟩ as five pounds⟩
cap	set in <u>capitals</u> ⟨CAPITALS⟩
sm cap or *s.c.*	set in <u>small capitals</u> ⟨SMALL CAPITALS⟩
lc	set in ⟨lowercase ⟨lowercase⟩
ital	set in <u>italic</u> ⟨*italic*⟩
rom	set in <u>roman</u> ⟨roman⟩
bf	set in boldface ⟨**boldface**⟩
= or -/ or ⌵ or /H/	hyphen
⸍N⸍ or *en* or /N/	en dash ⟨1965–72⟩
⸍M⸍ or *em* or /M/	em — or long — dash
⌄	superscript or superior ⟨*3*as in π*r*²⟩
⌃	subscript or inferior ⟨⌃as in H₂O⟩
⌄ or ✗	centered ⟨⌖for a centered dot in *p · q*⟩
⌻	comma
⸌	apostrophe
⊙	period
; or ;/	semicolon
: or ⊙	colon
❝❞ or ⸜⸝	quotation marks
(/)	parentheses
⌊/⌋	brackets
OK/?	query to author: has this been set as intended?
⌐ or ⌐¹	push down a ▮ work-up
⊚ ¹	turn over an inve*r*ted letter
wf ¹	wrong font; a character of the w*r*ong size or esp. st*y*le

¹ The last three symbols are unlikely to be needed in marking proofs of photocomposed matter.

prop·a·gule \'präp-ə-ˌgyü(ə)l\ *n* [NL *propagulum,* fr. L *propages* slip] (1858) : a structure (as a cutting, a seed, or a spore) that propagates a plant

pro·pane \'prō-ˌpān\ *n* [ISV *prop-* + *-ane*] (1866) : a heavy flammable gaseous paraffin hydrocarbon C₃H₈ found in crude petroleum and natural gas and used esp. as fuel and in chemical synthesis

pro·pel \prə-'pel\ *vt* **pro·pelled; pro·pel·ling** [ME *propellen,* fr. L *propellere,* fr. *pro-* before + *pellere* to drive — more at FELT] (15c) : to drive forward or onward by or as if by means of a force that imparts motion *syn* see PUSH

¹**pro·pel·lant** *or* **pro·pel·lent** \-'pel-ənt\ *adj* (1644) : capable of propelling
²**propellant** *also* **propellent** *n* (1814) : something that propels: as **a** : an explosive for propelling projectiles **b** : fuel plus oxidizer used by a rocket engine **c** : a gas in a pressure bottle for expelling the contents when the pressure is released

pro·pel·ler *also* **pro·pel·lor** \prə-'pel-ər\ *n* (1780) **1** : one that propels **2** : a device that consists of a central hub with radiating blades placed and twisted so that each forms part of a helical surface and that is used to propel a vehicle (as a ship or airplane)

pro·pend \prō-'pend\ *vi* [L *propendere,* fr. *pro-* before + *pendere* to hang — more at PENDANT] *obs* (1545) : INCLINE

pro·pense \prō-'pen(t)s\ *adj* [L *propensus,* pp. of *propendere*] *archaic* (1528) : leaning or inclining toward : DISPOSED

pro·pen·si·ty \prə-'pen(t)-sət-ē\ *n, pl* **-ties** (1570) : an often intense natural inclination or preference *syn* see LEANING

¹**prop·er** \'präp-ər\ *adj* [ME *propre* proper, own, fr. MF, fr. L *proprius* own] (13c) **1 a** : referring to one individual only **b** : belonging to one : OWN **c** : appointed for the liturgy of a particular day **d** : represented heraldically in natural color **2** : belonging characteristically to a species or individual : PECULIAR **3** *chiefly dial* : BECOMING, HANDSOME **4** : very good : EXCELLENT **5** *chiefly Brit* : UTTER, ABSOLUTE **6** : strictly limited to a specified thing, place, or idea ⟨the city ∼⟩ **7 a** : strictly accurate : CORRECT **b** *archaic* : VIRTUOUS, RESPECTABLE **c** : strictly decorous : GENTEEL **8** : marked by suitability, rightness, or appropriateness : FIT **9** : being a mathematical subset (as a subgroup) that does not contain all the elements of the inclusive set from which it is derived *syn* see FIT — **prop·er·ly** *adv* — **prop·er·ness** *n*
²**proper** *n* (15c) **1** : the parts of the Mass that vary according to the liturgical calendar **2** : the part of a missal or breviary containing the proper of the Mass and the offices proper to the holy days of the liturgical year
³**proper** *adv, chiefly dial* (15c) : in a thorough manner : COMPLETELY

proper adjective *n* (1905) : an adjective that is formed from a proper noun and that is usu. capitalized in English

pro·per·din \prō-'pərd-ⁿn\ *n* [prob. fr. ¹*pro-* + L *perdere* to destroy + E *-in* — more at PERDITION] (1954) : a serum protein that participates in destruction of bacteria, neutralization of viruses, and lysis of red blood cells

proper fraction *n* (1674) : a fraction in which the numerator is less or of lower degree than the denominator

proper noun *n* (ca. 1890) : a noun that designates a particular being or thing, does not take a limiting modifier, and is usu. capitalized in English — called also *proper name*

prop·er·tied \'präp-ərt-ēd\ *adj* (1760) : possessing property

prop·er·ty \'präp-ərt-ē\ *n, pl* **-ties** [ME *proprete,* fr. MF *propreté,* fr. L *proprietat-, proprietas,* fr. *proprius* own] (14c) **1 a** : a quality or trait belonging and esp. peculiar to an individual or thing **b** : an effect that an object has on another object or on the senses **c** : VIRTUE 3 **d** : an attribute common to all members of a class **2 a** : something owned or possessed; *specif* : a piece of real estate **b** : the exclusive right to possess, enjoy, and dispose of a thing : OWNERSHIP **c** : something to which a person has a legal title **d** : one (as a performer) under contract whose work is esp. valuable **3** : an article or object used in a play or motion picture except painted scenery and costumes *syn* see QUALITY — **prop·er·ty·less** \-ē-ləs\ *adj*

property damage insurance *n* (ca. 1946) : insurance protecting against all or part of an individual's legal liability for damage done (as by his or her automobile) to the property of another

property right *n* (1903) : a legal right or interest in or against specific property

property tax *n* (1808) : a tax levied on real or personal property

pro·phage \'prō-ˌfāj, -ˌfäzh\ *n* (1951) : an intracellular form of a bacteriophage in which it is harmless to the host, is usu. integrated into the hereditary material of the host, and reproduces when the host does

pro·phase \-ˌfāz\ *n* [ISV] (1884) **1** : the initial phase of mitosis in which chromosomes are condensed from the resting form and split into paired chromatids **2** : the initial stage of meiosis in which the chromosomes become visible, homologous pairs of chromosomes undergo synapsis and become shortened and thickened, individual chromosomes become visibly double as paired chromatids, chiasmata occur, and the nuclear membrane disappears — compare DIAKINESIS, DIPLOTENE, LEPTOTENE, PACHYTENE, ZYGOTENE — **pro·pha·sic** \(')prō-'fā-zik\ *adj*

proph·e·cy *also* **proph·e·sy** \'präf-ə-sē\ *n, pl* **-cies** *also* **-sies** [ME *prophecie,* fr. OF, fr. LL *prophetia,* fr. Gk *prophēteia,* fr. *prophētēs* prophet] (13c) **1** : the function or vocation of a prophet; *specif* : the inspired declaration of divine will and purpose **2** : an inspired utterance of a prophet **3** : a prediction of something to come

proph·e·sy \'präf-ə-ˌsī\ *vb* **-sied; -sy·ing** [ME *prophesien,* fr. MF *prophesier,* fr. OF, fr. *prophecie*] *vt* (14c) **1** : to utter by or as if by divine inspiration **2** : to predict with assurance or on the basis of mystic knowledge **3** : PREFIGURE ∼ *vi* **1** : to speak as if divinely inspired **2** : to give instruction in religious matters : PREACH **3** : to make a prediction *syn* see FORETELL — **proph·e·si·er** \-ˌsī(-ə)r\ *n*

proph·et \'präf-ət\ *n* [ME *prophete,* OF, fr. L *propheta,* fr. Gk *prophētēs,* fr. *pro* for + *phanai* to speak — more at FOR, BAN] (12c) **1** : one who utters divinely inspired revelations; *specif, often cap* : the writer of one of the prophetic books of the Old Testament **2 :** one gifted with more than ordinary spiritual and moral insight; *esp* **:** an inspired poet **3 :** one who foretells future events **:** PREDICTOR **4 :** an effective or leading spokesman for a cause, doctrine, or group **5** *Christian Science* **a :** a spiritual seer **b :** disappearance of material sense before the conscious facts of spiritual Truth

proph·et·ess \ˈpräf-ət-əs\ *n* (14c) **:** a woman who is a prophet

pro·phet·ic \prə-ˈfet-ik\ *or* **pro·phet·i·cal** \-ˈfet-i-kəl\ *adj* (15c) **1 :** of, relating to, or characteristic of a prophet or prophecy **2 :** foretelling events **:** PREDICTIVE — **pro·phet·i·cal·ly** \-i-k(ə-)lē\ *adv*

Proph·ets \ˈpräf-əts\ *n pl* **:** the second part of the Jewish scriptures — see BIBLE table

¹pro·phy·lac·tic \ˌprō-fə-ˈlak-tik *also* ˌpräf-ə-\ *adj* [Gk *prophylaktikos,* fr. *prophylassein* to keep guard before, fr. *pro-* before + *phylassein* to guard, fr. *phylak-, phylax* guard] (ca. 1574) **1 :** guarding from or preventing disease **2 :** tending to prevent or ward off **:** PREVENTIVE — **pro·phy·lac·ti·cal·ly** \-ti-k(ə-)lē\ *adv*

²prophylactic *n* (1642) **:** something that is prophylactic: as **a :** something (as a condom) for preventing venereal infection **b :** a contraceptive device

pro·phy·lax·is \-ˈlak-səs\ *n, pl* **-lax·es** \-ˈlak-ˌsēz\ [NL, fr. Gk *prophylaktikos*] (ca. 1842) **:** measures designed to preserve health (as of the body or of society) and prevent the spread of disease

¹pro·pine \prə-ˈpēn, -ˈpīn\ *vt* **pro·pined; pro·pin·ing** [ME *propinen,* fr. MF *propiner,* fr. L *propinare* to present, drink to someone's health, fr. Gk *propinein* lit., to drink first, fr. *pro-* ¹pro- + *pinein* to drink — more at POTABLE] *chiefly Scot* (15c) **:** to present or give esp. as a token of friendship

²propine *n, Scot* (15c) **:** a gift in return for a favor

pro·pin·qui·ty \prə-ˈpiŋ-kwət-ē\ *n* [ME *propinquite,* fr. L *propinquitat-, propinquitas* kinship, proximity, fr. *propinquus* near, akin, fr. *prope* near — more at APPROACH] (14c) **1 :** nearness of blood **:** KINSHIP **2 :** nearness in place or time **:** PROXIMITY

pro·pi·o·nate \ˈprō-pē-ə-ˌnāt\ *n* [ISV] (1862) **:** a salt or ester of propionic acid

pro·pi·on·ic acid \ˌprō-pē-ˌän-ik-\ *n* [ISV ¹*pro-* + Gk *piōn* fat; akin to L *opimus* fat — more at FAT] (1850) **:** a liquid sharp-odored fatty acid $C_3H_6O_2$ found in milk and distillates of wood, coal, and petroleum

pro·pi·ti·ate \prō-ˈpish-ē-ˌāt\ *vt* **-at·ed; -at·ing** [L *propitiatus,* pp. of *propitiare,* fr. *propitius* propitious] (1645) **:** to gain or regain the favor or goodwill of **:** APPEASE, CONCILIATE ***syn*** see PACIFY — **pro·pi·ti·able** \-ē-ə-bəl\ *adj* — **pro·pi·ti·ator** \-ē-ˌāt-ər\ *n*

pro·pi·ti·a·tion \prō-ˌpis(h)-ē-ˈā-shən\ *n* (14c) **1 :** the act of propitiating **2 :** something that propitiates; *specif* **:** an atoning sacrifice

pro·pi·tia·to·ry \prō-ˈpish-(ē-)ə-ˌtōr-ē, -ˌtȯr-\ *adj* (1551) **1 :** intended to propitiate **:** EXPIATORY **2 :** of or relating to propitiation

pro·pi·tious \prə-ˈpish-əs\ *adj* [ME *propicious,* fr. L *propitius,* fr. *pro-* for + *petere* to seek — more at PRO-, FEATHER] (15c) **1 :** favorably disposed **:** BENEVOLENT **2 :** being of good omen **:** AUSPICIOUS ⟨~ sign⟩ **3 :** tending to favor **:** ADVANTAGEOUS ***syn*** see FAVORABLE — **pro·pi·tious·ly** *adv* — **pro·pi·tious·ness** *n*

prop·jet engine \ˈpräp-ˌjet-\ *n* (1947) **:** TURBO-PROPELLER ENGINE

pro·plas·tid \(ˈ)prō-ˈplas-təd\ *n* [ISV] (1922) **:** a minute cytoplasmic body from which a plastid is formed

prop·man \ˈpräp-ˌman\ *n* (ca. 1937) **:** a man in charge of stage properties

prop·o·lis \ˈpräp-ə-ləs\ *n* [L, fr. Gk, fr. *pro-* for + *polis* city — more at PRO-, POLICE] (1601) **:** a brownish resinous material of waxy consistency collected by bees from the buds of trees and used as a cement

pro·pone \prə-ˈpōn\ *vt* **pro·poned; pro·pon·ing** [ME (Sc) *proponen,* fr. L *proponere* — more at PROPOUND] (14c) **1** *Scot* **:** PROPOSE, PROPOUND **2** *Scot* **:** to put forward (a defense)

pro·po·nent \prə-ˈpō-nənt, ˈprō-ˌ\ *n* [L *proponent-, proponens,* prp. of *proponere*] (1588) **:** one who argues in favor of something **:** ADVOCATE

¹pro·por·tion \p(r)ə-ˈpōr-shən, -ˈpȯr-\ *n* [ME *proporcion,* fr. MF *proportion,* fr. L *proportion-, proportio,* fr. *pro* for + *portion-, portio* portion — more at FOR] (14c) **1 :** the relation of one part to another or to the whole with respect to magnitude, quantity, or degree **:** RATIO **2 :** harmonious relation of parts to each other or to the whole **:** BALANCE, SYMMETRY **3 :** a statement of equality between two ratios in which the first of the four terms divided by the second equals the third divided by the fourth (as in $4/2 = 10/5$) **4 a :** proper or equal share ⟨each did his ~ of the work⟩ **b :** QUOTA, PERCENTAGE **5 :** SIZE, DIMENSION — **in proportion :** PROPORTIONAL 1

²proportion *vt* **pro·por·tioned; pro·por·tion·ing** \-sh(ə-)niŋ\ (14c) **1 :** to adjust (a part or thing) in size relative to other parts or things **2 :** to make the parts of harmonious or symmetrical **3 :** APPORTION, ALLOT

pro·por·tion·able \-sh(ə-)nə-bəl\ *adj, archaic* (14c) **:** PROPORTIONAL, PROPORTIONATE — **pro·por·tion·ably** \-blē\ *adv, archaic*

¹pro·por·tion·al \p(r)ə-ˈpōr-shnəl, -ˈpȯr-, -shən-ᵊl\ *n* (14c) **:** a number or quantity in a proportion

²proportional *adj* (1570) **1 a :** corresponding in size, degree, or intensity **b :** having the same or a constant ratio ⟨corresponding sides of similar triangles are ~⟩ **2 :** regulated or determined in size or degree with reference to proportions ⟨a ~ system of immigration quotas⟩ — **pro·por·tion·al·i·ty** \-ˌpōr-shə-ˈnal-ət-ē, -ˌpȯr-\ *n* — **pro·por·tion·al·ly** \-ˈpōr-shnə-lē, -ˈpȯr-, -shən-ᵊl-ē\ *adv*

proportional parts *n pl* (ca. 1890) **:** fractional parts of the difference between successive entries in a table for use in linear interpolation

proportional representation *n* (1870) **:** an electoral system designed to represent in a legislative body each political group or party in proportion to its actual voting strength in the electorate

proportional tax *n* (ca. 1942) **:** a tax in which the tax rate remains constant regardless of the amount of the tax base

¹pro·por·tion·ate \p(r)ə-ˈpōr-sh(ə-)nət, -ˈpȯr-\ *adj* (14c) **:** PROPORTIONAL 1 — **pro·por·tion·ate·ly** *adv*

²pro·por·tion·ate \-shə-ˌnāt\ *vt* **-at·ed; -at·ing** (1570) **:** to make proportionate **:** PROPORTION

pro·pos·al \prə-ˈpō-zəl\ *n* (1653) **1 :** an act of putting forward or stating something for consideration **2 a :** something proposed **:** SUGGESTION **b :** OFFER; *specif* **:** an offer of marriage

pro·pose \prə-ˈpōz\ *vb* **pro·posed; pro·pos·ing** [ME *proposen,* fr. MF *proposer,* fr. L *proponere* (perf. indic. *proposui*) — more at PROPOUND] *vi* (14c) **1 :** to form or put forward a plan or intention ⟨man ~*s,* but God disposes⟩ **2** *obs* **:** to engage in talk or discussion **3 :** to make an offer of marriage ~ *vt* **1 a :** to set before the mind (as for discussion, imitation, or action) ⟨*proposed* a plan for settling the dispute⟩ **b :** to set before someone and esp. oneself as an aim or intent ⟨*proposed* to spend the summer in study⟩ **2 a :** to set forth for acceptance or rejection ⟨~ terms for peace⟩ ⟨~ a topic for debate⟩ **b :** to recommend to fill a place or vacancy **:** NOMINATE ⟨agreed to ~ him for membership⟩ **c :** to offer as a toast ⟨~ the health of the ladies⟩ — **pro·pos·er** *n*

¹prop·o·si·tion \ˌpräp-ə-ˈzish-ən\ *n* (14c) **1 a** (1) **:** something offered for consideration or acceptance **:** PROPOSAL (2) **:** a request for sexual intercourse **b :** the point to be discussed or maintained in argument usu. stated in sentence form near the outset **c :** a theorem or problem to be demonstrated or performed **2 a :** an expression in language or signs of something that can be believed, doubted, or denied or is either true or false **b :** the objective meaning of a proposition **3 :** something with which one is involved or with which one must deal ⟨the mine was never a paying ~⟩ — **prop·o·si·tion·al** \-ˈzish-nəl, -ən-ᵊl\ *adj*

²proposition *vt* **-si·tioned; -si·tion·ing** \-ˈzish-(ə-)niŋ\ (1924) **:** to make a proposal to; *esp* **:** to suggest sexual intercourse to

propositional calculus *n* (1903) **:** the branch of symbolic logic that uses symbols for unanalyzed propositions and logical connectives only — called also *sentential calculus;* compare PREDICATE CALCULUS

propositional function *n* (1903) **1 :** SENTENTIAL FUNCTION **2 :** something that is designated or expressed by a sentential function

pro·pos·i·tus \prō-ˈpäz-ət-əs\ *n, pl* **-i·ti** \-ə-ˌtī\ [NL, fr. L, pp. of *proponere*] (ca. 1899) **:** the person immediately concerned **:** SUBJECT

pro·pound \prə-ˈpau̇nd\ *vt* [alter. of earlier *propone,* fr. ME (Sc) *proponen,* fr. L *proponere* to display, propound, fr. *pro-* before + *ponere* to put, place — more at PRO-, POSITION] (1537) **:** to offer for discussion or consideration — **pro·pound·er** *n*

pro·poxy·phene \prō-ˈpäk-sə-ˌfēn\ *n* [*prop-* + *oxy-* + *-phene* (alter. of *phenyl*)] (1955) **:** an analgesic $C_{22}H_{29}NO_2$ structurally related to methadone but less addicting that is administered in the form of its hydrochloride

pro·prae·tor *or* **pro·pre·tor** \(ˈ)prō-ˈprēt-ər\ *n* [L *propraetor,* fr. *pro-* (as in *proconsul*) + *praetor*] (1579) **:** a praetor of ancient Rome sent out to govern a province

pro·pran·o·lol \prō-ˈpran-ə-ˌlȯl, -ˌlōl\ *n* [prob. alter. of earlier *propanolol,* fr. *propanol* (propyl alcohol) + *-ol*] (1964) **:** a beta-adrenergic blocking agent $C_{16}H_{21}NO_2$ used in the form of its hydrochloride in the treatment of abnormal heart rhythms and angina pectoris

¹pro·pri·etary \p(r)ə-ˈprī-ə-ˌter-ē\ *n, pl* **-etar·ies** (15c) **1 :** one that possesses, owns, or holds exclusive right to something; *specif* **:** one granted ownership of a colony (as one of the original American colonies) and full prerogatives of establishing a government and distributing land **2 :** something that is used, produced, or marketed under exclusive legal right of the inventor or maker; *specif* **:** a drug (as a patent medicine) that is protected by secrecy, patent, or copyright against free competition as to name, product, composition, or process of manufacture **3 :** a business secretly owned by and run as a cover for an intelligence organization

²proprietary *adj* [LL *proprietarius,* fr. L *proprietas* property — more at PROPERTY] (1589) **1 :** of, relating to, or characteristic of a proprietor ⟨~ rights⟩ **2 :** used, made, or marketed by one having the exclusive legal right ⟨a ~ process⟩ **3 :** privately owned and managed and run as a profit-making organization ⟨a ~ clinic⟩

pro·pri·etor \p(r)ə-ˈprī-ət-ər\ *n* [alter. of ¹*proprietary*] (1637) **1 :** a proprietary of a colony **2 a :** one who has the legal right or exclusive title to something **:** OWNER **b :** one having an interest (as control or present use) less than absolute and exclusive right — **pro·pri·etor·ship** \-ˌship\ *n*

pro·pri·etress \-ˈprī-ə-trəs\ *n* (1692) **:** a woman who is a proprietor

pro·pri·ety \p(r)ə-ˈprī-ət-ē\ *n, pl* **-eties** [ME *propriete,* fr. MF *proprieté* property, quality of a person or thing — more at PROPERTY] (15c) **1** *obs* **:** true nature **2** *obs* **:** a special characteristic **:** PECULIARITY **3 :** the quality or state of being proper **:** APPROPRIATENESS **4 a :** conformity to what is socially acceptable in conduct or speech **b :** fear of offending against conventional rules of behavior esp. between the sexes **c** *pl* **:** the customs and manners of polite society

pro·prio·cep·tion \ˌprō-prē-ō-ˈsep-shən\ *n* [*proprioceptive* + *-ion*] (1906) **:** the reception of stimuli produced within the organism

pro·prio·cep·tive \-ˈsep-tiv\ *adj* [L *proprius* own + E *-ceptive* (as in *receptive*)] (1906) **:** of, relating to, or being stimuli arising within the organism

pro·prio·cep·tor \-tər\ *n* (1906) **:** a sensory receptor excited by proprioceptive stimuli

prop root *n* (1905) **:** a root that serves as a prop or support to the plant

pro·pto·sis \(ˈ)prō-ˈtō-səs, präp-ˈtō-\ *n* [NL, fr. LL, falling forward, fr. Gk *proptōsis,* fr. *propiptein* to fall forward, fr. *pro-* + *piptein* to fall — more at PRO-, FEATHER] (ca. 1676) **:** forward projection or displacement esp. of the eyeball

pro·pul·sion \prə-ˈpəl-shən\ *n* [L *propulsus,* pp. of *propellere* to propel] (1626) **1 :** the action or process of propelling **2 :** something that propels

pro·pul·sive \-ˈpəl-siv\ *adj* [L *propulsus*] (1758) **:** tending or having power to propel

pro·pyl \ˈprō-pəl\ *n* (1850) **:** either of two isomeric alkyl radicals C_3H_7 derived from propane or an isomer — **pro·pyl·ic** \prō-ˈpil-ik\ *adj*

pro·py·lae·um \ˌpräp-ə-ˈlē-əm, ˌprōp-\ *n, pl* **-laea** \-ˈlē-ə\ [L, fr. Gk *propylaion,* fr. *pro-* before + *pylē* gate — more at PRO-] (ca. 1706) **:** a vestibule or entrance of architectural importance before a building or enclosure — often used in pl.

pro·pyl·ene \ˈprō-pə-ˌlēn\ *n* (1850) **:** a flammable gaseous hydrocarbon C_3H_6 obtained by cracking petroleum hydrocarbons and used chiefly in organic synthesis

propylene glycol *n* (1885) **:** a sweet hygroscopic viscous liquid $C_3H_8O_2$ made esp. from propylene and used esp. as an antifreeze and solvent and in brake fluids

pro ra·ta \(ˈ)prō-ˈrāt-ə, -ˈrät-, -ˈrat-\ *adv* [L] (1575) **:** proportionately according to an exactly calculable factor (as share or liability) — **pro rata** *adj*

pro·rate \(ˈ)prō-ˈrāt\ *vb* **pro·rat·ed; pro·rat·ing** [*pro rata*] *vt* (1860) **:** to divide, distribute, or assess proportionately ~ *vi* **:** to make a pro rata distribution

pro·ra·tion \prō-'rā-shən\ *n* (ca. 1919) **:** an act or an instance of prorating; *specif* **:** a cutback on production (as of crude oil) through allocations or quotas

pro·ro·gate \'prōr-ō-,gāt, 'prȯr-\ *vt* **-gat·ed; -gat·ing** (15c) **:** PROROGUE — **pro·ro·ga·tion** \,prōr-ō-'gā-shən, ,prȯr-\ *n*

pro·rogue \p(r)ə-'rōg\ *vb* **pro·rogued; pro·rogu·ing** [ME *prorogen,* fr. MF *proroguer,* fr. L *prorogare,* fr. *pro-* before + *rogare* to ask — more at PRO-, RIGHT] *vt* (15c) **1 :** DEFER, POSTPONE **2 :** to terminate a session of (as a British parliament) by royal prerogative ~ *vi* **:** to suspend or end a legislative session

pros *pl of* PRO

pros- *prefix* [LL, fr. Gk, fr. *proti, pros* face to face with, toward, in addition to, near; akin to Skt *prati-* near, toward, against, in return, Gk *pro* before — more at FOR] **1 :** near **:** toward ⟨*pros*enchyma⟩ **2 :** in front ⟨*pros*encephalon⟩

pro·sa·ic \prō-'zā-ik\ *adj* [LL *prosaicus,* fr. L *prosa* prose] (ca. 1656) **1 a :** characteristic of prose as distinguished from poetry **:** FACTUAL **b :** DULL, UNIMAGINATIVE **2 :** EVERYDAY, ORDINARY — **pro·sa·i·cal·ly** \-'zā-ə-k(ə-)lē\ *adv*

pro·sa·ism \'prō-(,)zā-,iz-əm\ *n* (1787) **1 :** a prosaic manner, style, or quality **2 :** a prosaic expression

pro·sa·ist *n* [L *prosa* prose] (1803) **1** \'prō-(,)zā-əst, -zā-,ist\ **:** a prose writer **2** \prō-'zā-əst\ **:** a prosaic person

pro·sa·teur \,prō-zə-'tər\ *n* [F, fr. It *prosatore,* fr. ML *prosator,* fr. L *prosa*] (1880) **:** a writer of prose

pro·sce·ni·um \prō-'sē-nē-əm\ *n* [L, fr. Gk *proskēnion* front of the building forming the background for a dramatic performance, stage, fr. *pro-* + *skēnē* building forming the background for a dramatic performance — more at SCENE] (1606) **1 a :** the stage of an ancient Greek or Roman theater **b :** the part of a modern stage in front of the curtain **c :** the wall that separates the stage from the auditorium and provides the arch that frames it **2 :** FOREGROUND

pro·sciut·to \prō-'shü-(,)tō\ *n, pl* **-ti** \-(,)tē\ *or* **-tos** [It, alter. of obs. *presciutto*] (ca. 1929) **:** dry-cured spiced Italian ham usu. sliced thin

pro·scribe \prō-'skrīb\ *vt* **pro·scribed; pro·scrib·ing** [L *proscribere* to publish, proscribe, fr. *pro-* before + *scribere* to write — more at SCRIBE] (15c) **1 :** to condemn or forbid as harmful or unlawful **:** PROHIBIT **2 :** to publish the name of (a person) as condemned to death with his property forfeited to the state — **pro·scrib·er** *n*

pro·scrip·tion \prō-'skrip-shən\ *n* [ME *proscripcion,* fr. L *proscription-, proscriptio,* fr. *proscriptus,* pp. of *proscribere*] (14c) **1 :** the act of proscribing **:** the state of being proscribed **2 :** an imposed restraint or restriction **:** PROHIBITION — **pro·scrip·tive** \-'skrip-tiv\ *adj* — **pro·scrip·tive·ly** *adv*

¹prose \'prōz\ *n* [ME, fr. MF, fr. L *prosa,* fr. fem. of *prorsus, prosus,* straightforward, being in prose, contr. of *proversus,* pp. of *provertere* to turn forward, fr. *pro-* forward + *vertere* to turn — more at PRO-, WORTH] (14c) **1 a :** the ordinary language people use in speaking or writing **b :** a literary medium distinguished from poetry esp. by its greater irregularity and variety of rhythm and its closer correspondence to the patterns of everyday speech **2 :** a prosaic style, quality, or condition

²prose *adj* (14c) **1 :** of, relating to, or written in prose **2 :** PROSAIC

³prose *vi* **prosed; pros·ing** (1641) **1 :** to write prose **2 :** to write or speak in a prosaic manner

pro·sec·tor \prō-'sek-tər\ *n* [prob. fr. F *prosecteur,* fr. LL *prosector* anatomist, fr. L *prosectus,* pp. of *prosecare* to cut away, fr. *pro-* forth + *secare* to cut — more at PRO-, SAW] (ca. 1857) **:** one that makes dissections for anatomic demonstrations

pros·e·cute \'präs-i-,kyüt\ *vb* **-cut·ed; -cut·ing** [ME *prosecuten,* fr. L *prosecutus,* pp. of *prosequi* to pursue — more at PURSUE] *vt* (15c) **1 :** to follow to the end **:** pursue until finished ⟨was . . . ordered to ~ the war with . . . vigor —Marjory S. Douglas⟩ **2 :** to engage in **:** PERFORM **3 a :** to bring legal action against for redress or punishment of a crime or violation of law ⟨*prosecuted* them for fraud⟩ **b :** to institute legal proceedings with reference to ⟨~ a claim⟩ ~ *vi* **:** to institute and carry on a legal suit or prosecution — **pros·e·cut·able** \-,kyüt-ə-bəl\ *adj*

prosecuting attorney *n* (1832) **:** an attorney who conducts proceedings in a court on behalf of the government **:** DISTRICT ATTORNEY

pros·e·cu·tion \,präs-i-'kyü-shən\ *n* (1567) **1 :** the act or process of prosecuting; *specif* **:** the institution and continuance of a criminal suit involving the process of pursuing formal charges against an offender to final judgment **2 :** the party by whom criminal proceedings are instituted or conducted **3** *obs* **:** PURSUIT

pros·e·cu·tor \'präs-i-,kyüt-ər\ *n* (1621) **1 :** a person who institutes an official prosecution before a court **2 :** PROSECUTING ATTORNEY

pros·e·cu·to·ri·al \,präs-i-kyü-'tōr-ē-əl, -'tȯr-\ *adj* (1968) **:** of, relating to, or being a prosecutor or prosecution

¹pros·e·lyte \'präs-ə-,līt\ *n* [ME *proselite,* fr. LL *proselytus* proselyte, alien resident, fr. Gk *prosēlytos,* fr. *pros* near + *-ēlytos* (akin to *elthein* to go); akin to Gk *elaunein* to drive — more at PROS-, ELASTIC] (14c) **:** a new convert; *specif* **:** a convert to Judaism

²proselyte *vb* **-lyt·ed; -lyt·ing** (1624) **:** PROSELYTIZE

pros·e·ly·tism \'präs-ə-,līt-,iz-əm, 'präs-(ə-)lə-,tiz-\ *n* (1660) **1 :** the act of becoming or condition of being a proselyte **:** CONVERSION **2 :** the act or process of proselytizing

pros·e·ly·tize \'präs-(ə-)lə-,tīz\ *vb* **-tized; -tiz·ing** *vi* (1679) **1 :** to induce someone to convert to one's faith **2 :** to recruit someone to join one's party, institution, or cause ~ *vt* **:** to recruit or convert esp. to a new faith, institution, or cause — **pros·e·ly·ti·za·tion** \,präs-(ə-)lət-ə-'zā-shən, ,präs-ə-,līt-\ *n* — **pros·e·ly·tiz·er** \'präs-(ə-)lə-,tī-zər\ *n*

pro·sem·i·nar \(')prō-'sem-ə-,när\ *n* (1921) **:** a directed course of study conducted in the manner of a graduate seminar but often open to advanced undergraduate students

pros·en·ceph·a·lon \,präs-,en-'sef-ə-,län, -lən\ *n* [NL] (1846) **:** FOREBRAIN — **pros·en·ce·phal·ic** \-sə-'fal-ik\ *adj*

prose poem *n* (1842) **:** a composition in prose that has some of the qualities of a poem (as rhythm, imagery, and compactness of expression) — **prose poet** *n*

pros·er \'prō-zər\ *n* (1627) **1 :** a writer of prose **2 :** one who talks or writes tediously

Pro·ser·pi·na \prə-'sər-pə-nə\ *or* **Pros·er·pine** \'präs-ər-,pīn\ *n* [L] **:** PERSEPHONE

pro·sit \'prō-zət, -sət\ *or* **prost** \'prōst\ *interj* [G, fr. L *prosit* may it be beneficial, fr. *prodesse* to be useful — more at PROUD] (1846) — used to wish good health esp. before drinking

pro·so \'prō-(,)sō\ *n* [Russ] (1917) **:** MILLET 1a

proso·branch \'präs-ə-,braŋk\ *n, pl* **-branchs** [NL *Prosobranchia,* fr. *proso-* in front (fr. Gk *prosō* forward) + L *branchia* branchia] (1851) **:** any of a subclass (Streptoneura, Prosobranchia, or Prosobranchiata) of gastropods that have the loop of visceral nerves twisted into a figure 8, the sexes usu. separate, and usu. an operculum — **prosobranch** *adj*

pro·sod·ic \prə-'säd-ik *also* -'zäd-\ *or* **pro·sod·i·cal** \-i-kəl\ *adj* (1774) **:** of or relating to prosody — **pro·sod·i·cal·ly** \-i-k(ə-)lē\ *adv*

pros·o·dy \'präs-əd-ē *also* 'präz-\ *n, pl* **-dies** [ME, fr. L *prosodia* accent of a syllable, fr. Gk *prosōidia* song sung to instrumental music, accent, fr. *pros* in addition to + *ōidē* song — more at PROS-, ODE] (15c) **1 :** the study of versification; *esp* **:** the systematic study of metrical structure **2 :** a particular system, theory, or style of versification — **pros·o·dist** \-əd-əst\ *n*

pro·so·ma \(')prō-'sō-mə\ *n* [NL, fr. Gk *pro-* + *sōma* body; akin to L *tumēre* to swell — more at THUMB] (1872) **:** the anterior region of the body of an invertebrate when not readily analyzable into its primitive segmentation; *esp* **:** CEPHALOTHORAX

pros·o·pog·ra·phy \,präs-ə-'päg-rə-fē\ *n* [NL *prosopographia,* fr. Gk *prosōpon* person + *-graphia* -graphy] (1929) **:** a study that identifies and relates a group of persons or characters within a particular historical or literary context — **pros·o·po·graph·i·cal** \-pə-'graf-i-kəl\ *adj*

pro·so·po·poe·ia \prə-,sō-pə-'pē-(y)ə, ,präs-ə-pə-\ *n* [L, fr. Gk *prosōpopoiia,* fr. *prosōpon* mask, person (fr. *pros-* + *ōps* face) + *poiein* to make — more at EYE, POET] (1561) **1 :** a figure of speech in which an imaginary or absent person is represented as speaking or acting **2 :** PERSONIFICATION

¹pros·pect \'präs-,pekt\ *n* [ME, fr. L *prospectus* view, prospect, fr. *prospectus,* pp. of *prospicere* to look forward, exercise foresight, fr. *pro-* forward + *specere* to look — more at PRO-, SPY] (15c) **1 :** EXPOSURE 3b **2 a** (1) **:** an extensive view (2) **:** a mental consideration **:** SURVEY **b :** a place that commands an extensive view **:** LOOKOUT **c :** something extended to the view **:** SCENE **d** *archaic* **:** a sketch or picture of a scene **3** *obs* **:** ASPECT **4 a :** the act of looking forward **:** ANTICIPATION **b :** a mental picture of something to come **:** VISION **c :** something that is awaited or expected **:** POSSIBILITY **d** *pl* (1) **:** financial expectations (2) **:** CHANCES **5 a :** a place showing signs of containing a mineral deposit **b :** a partly developed mine **c :** the mineral yield of a tested sample of ore or gravel **6 a :** a potential buyer or customer **b :** a likely candidate

syn PROSPECT, OUTLOOK, ANTICIPATION, FORETASTE mean an advance realization of something to come. PROSPECT implies expectation of a particular event, condition, or development of definite interest or concern; OUTLOOK suggests a forecasting of the future; ANTICIPATION implies a prospect or outlook that involves advance suffering or enjoyment of what is foreseen; FORETASTE implies an actual though brief or partial experience of something forthcoming.

— **in prospect :** possible or likely for the future

²pros·pect \'präs-,pekt, *chiefly Brit* prəs-'\ *vi* (1841) **:** to explore an area esp. for mineral deposits ~ *vt* **:** to inspect (a region) for mineral deposits; *broadly* **:** EXPLORE — **pros·pec·tor** \-,pek-tər, -'pek-\ *n*

pro·spec·tive \prə-'spek-tiv *also* 'prä-,, prō-', prä-'\ *adj* (1795) **1 :** relating to or effective in the future **2 a :** likely to come about **:** EXPECTED ⟨the ~ benefits of this law⟩ **b :** likely to be or become ⟨a ~ mother⟩ — **pro·spec·tive·ly** *adv*

pro·spec·tus \prə-'spek-təs, prä-\ *n, pl* **-tus·es** [L, prospect] (1765) **1 :** a preliminary printed statement that describes an enterprise (as a business or publication) and that is distributed to prospective buyers, investors, or participants **2 :** something (as a statement or situation) that forecasts the course or nature of something

pros·per \'präs-pər\ *vb* **pros·pered; pros·per·ing** \-p(ə-)riŋ\ [ME *prosperen,* fr. MF *prosperer,* fr. L *prosperare* to cause to succeed, fr. *prosperus* favorable] *vi* (15c) **1 :** to succeed in an enterprise or activity; *esp* **:** to achieve economic success **2 :** to become strong and flourishing ~ *vt* **:** to cause to succeed or thrive

pros·per·i·ty \prä-'sper-ət-ē\ *n* (13c) **:** the condition of being successful or thriving; *esp* **:** economic well-being

Pros·pero \'präs-pə-,rō\ *n* **:** the rightful duke of Milan in Shakespeare's *The Tempest*

pros·per·ous \'präs-p(ə-)rəs\ *adj* [ME, fr. MF *prospereux,* fr. *prosperer* to prosper + *-eux* -ous] (15c) **1 :** AUSPICIOUS, FAVORABLE **2 a :** marked by success or economic well-being **b :** enjoying vigorous and healthy growth **:** FLOURISHING — **pros·per·ous·ly** *adv* — **pros·per·ous·ness** *n*

pross \'präs\ *or* **pros·sie** \'präs-ē\ *or* **pros·tie** \'präs-tē\ *n, slang* (ca. 1902) **:** PROSTITUTE

pros·ta·glan·din \,präs-tə-'glan-dən\ *n* [*prostate gland* + *-in;* fr. its occurrence in the seminal fluid of animals] (1936) **:** any of various oxygenated unsaturated cyclic fatty acids of animals that may perform a variety of hormonelike actions (as in controlling blood pressure or smooth muscle contraction)

¹pros·tate \'präs-,tāt\ *n* [NL *prostata* prostate gland, fr. Gk *prostatēs,* fr. *proïstanai* to put in front, fr. *pro-* before + *histanai* to cause to stand — more at PRO-, STAND] (1646) **:** PROSTATE GLAND

²prostate \'präs-,tāt\ *also* **pros·tat·ic** \prä-'stat-ik\ *adj* (ca. 1828) **:** of, relating to, or being the prostate gland

pros·ta·tec·to·my \,präs-tə-'tek-tə-mē\ *n, pl* **-mies** (ca. 1890) **:** surgical removal of the prostate gland

prostate gland *n* (1840) **:** a firm partly muscular partly glandular body that is situated about the base of the mammalian male urethra and secretes an alkaline viscid fluid which is a major constituent of the ejaculatory fluid

prostatic utricle *n* (1925) **:** a small blind pouch that projects from the posterior wall of the urethra into the prostate

pros·ta·tism \'präs-tə-ˌtiz-əm\ *n* (ca. 1900) **:** disease of the prostate; *esp* **:** a disorder resulting from obstruction of the bladder neck by an enlarged prostate

pros·ta·ti·tis \ˌpräs-tə-'tīt-əs\ *n* [NL] (ca. 1890) **:** inflammation of the prostate gland

pros·the·sis \präs-'thē-səs, 'präs-thə-\ *n, pl* **-the·ses** \-ˌsēz\ [NL, fr. Gk, addition, fr. *prostithenai* to add to, fr. *pros-* in addition to + *tithenai* to put — more at PROS-, DO] (1900) **:** an artificial device to replace a missing part of the body

pros·thet·ic \präs-'thet-ik\ *adj* (ca. 1890) **1 :** of or relating to a prosthesis or prosthetics **2 :** of, relating to, or constituting a nonprotein group of a conjugated protein — **pros·thet·i·cal·ly** \-i-k(ə-)lē\ *adv*

pros·thet·ics \-iks\ *n pl but sing or pl in constr* (ca. 1894) **:** the surgical and dental specialties concerned with the artificial replacement of missing parts

prosth·odon·tics \ˌpräs-thə-'dänt-iks\ *n pl but sing or pl in constr* [NL *prosthodontia,* fr. *prosthesis* + *-odontia*] (1947) **:** prosthetic dentistry

prosth·odon·tist \-'dänt-əst\ *n* (1917) **:** a specialist in prosthodontics

[1]pros·ti·tute \'präs-tə-ˌt(y)üt\ *vt* **-tut·ed; -tut·ing** [L *prostitutus,* pp. of *prostituere,* fr. *pro-* before + *statuere* to station — more at PRO-, STATUTE] (ca. 1530) **1 :** to offer indiscriminately for sexual intercourse esp. for money **2 :** to devote to corrupt or unworthy purposes **:** DEBASE ⟨~ one's talents⟩ — **pros·ti·tu·tor** \-ˌt(y)üt-ər\ *n*

[2]prostitute *adj* (1563) **:** devoted to corrupt purposes **:** PROSTITUTED

[3]prostitute *n* (1613) **1 a :** a woman who engages in promiscuous sexual intercourse esp. for money **:** WHORE **b :** a male who engages in sexual practices for money **2 :** a person (as a writer or painter) who deliberately debases himself or his talents (as for money)

pros·ti·tu·tion \ˌpräs-tə-'t(y)ü-shən\ *n* (1553) **1 :** the act or practice of indulging in promiscuous sexual relations esp. for money **2 :** the state of being prostituted **:** DEBASEMENT

pro·sto·mi·um \prō-'stō-mē-əm\ *n, pl* **-mia** \-mē-ə\ [NL, fr. Gk *pro-* + *stoma* mouth — more at STOMACH] (1870) **:** the portion of the head of various worms and mollusks that is situated in front of the mouth and is usu. considered to be nonmetameric — **pro·sto·mi·al** \-mē-əl\ *adj*

[1]pros·trate \'präs-ˌtrāt\ *adj* [ME *prostrat,* fr. L *prostratus,* pp. of *prosternere,* fr. *pro-* before + *sternere* to spread out, throw down — more at STREW] (14c) **1 :** stretched out with face on the ground in adoration or submission; *also* **:** lying flat **2 :** completely overcome and lacking vitality, will, or power to rise ⟨was ~ from the heat⟩ **3 :** trailing on the ground **:** PROCUMBENT ⟨~ shrub⟩ ***syn*** see PRONE

[2]pros·trate \'präs-ˌtrāt, *esp Brit* präs-'\ *vt* **pros·trat·ed; pros·trat·ing** (15c) **1 :** to throw or put into a prostrate position **2 :** to put (oneself) in a humble and submissive posture or state ⟨the whole town had to ~ itself in official apology —Claudia Cassidy⟩ **3 :** to reduce to submission, helplessness, or exhaustion **:** OVERCOME ⟨was *prostrated* with grief⟩

pros·tra·tion \prä-'strā-shən\ *n* (1526) **1 a :** the act of assuming a prostrate position **b :** the state of being in a prostrate position **:** ABASEMENT **2 a :** complete physical or mental exhaustion **:** COLLAPSE **b :** the process of being made powerless or the condition of powerlessness ⟨the country suffered economic ~ after the war⟩

prosy \'prō-zē\ *adj* **pros·i·er; -est** [[1]*prose*] (1837) **:** lacking in qualities that seize the attention or strike the imagination **:** COMMONPLACE; *esp* **:** tediously dull in speech or manner — **pros·i·ly** \-zə-lē\ *adv* — **pros·i·ness** \-zē-nəs\ *n*

prot- *or* **proto-** *comb form* [ME *protho-,* fr. MF, fr. LL *proto-,* fr. Gk *prōt-, prōto-,* fr. *prōtos;* akin to Gk *pro* before — more at FOR] **1 a :** first in time ⟨*proto*lithic⟩ ⟨*proto*nymph⟩ **b :** beginning **:** giving rise to ⟨*proto*planet⟩ **2 a :** first or lowest of a series and as such usu. having the smallest relative amount of a (specified) element or radical ⟨*prot*oxide⟩ **b :** parent substance of a (specified) substance ⟨*prot*actinium⟩ **3 :** first formed **:** primary ⟨*proto*xylem⟩ **4** *cap* **:** relating to or constituting the recorded or assumed language that is ancestral to a language or to a group of related languages or dialects ⟨*Proto*-Indo-European⟩

prot·ac·tin·i·um \ˌprōt-ˌak-'tin-ē-əm\ *n* [NL] (1918) **:** a shiny metallic radioelement of relatively short life — see ELEMENT table

pro·tag·o·nist \prō-'tag-ə-nəst\ *n* [Gk *prōtagōnistēs,* fr. *prōt-* prot- + *agōnistēs* competitor at games, actor, fr. *agōnizesthai* to compete, fr. *agōn* contest, competition at games — more at AGONY] (1671) **1 :** the principal character in a story **2 :** the leader of a cause **:** CHAMPION **3 :** a muscle that by its contraction actually causes a particular movement

prot·amine \'prōt-ə-ˌmēn\ *n* [ISV *prot-* + *amine*] (1874) **:** any of various strongly basic proteins of relatively low molecular weight that are associated with nucleic acids, can be obtained in quantity from sperm cells, and typically contain much arginine

prot·a·sis \'prät-ə-səs\ *n, pl* **-a·ses** \-ˌsēz\ [LL, fr. Gk, premise of a syllogism, conditional clause, fr. *proteinein* to stretch out before, put forward, fr. *pro-* + *teinein* to stretch — more at THIN] (ca. 1568) **1 :** the introductory part of a play or narrative poem **2 :** the subordinate clause of a conditional sentence — compare APODOSIS — **pro·tat·ic** \prä-'tat-ik, prō-\ *adj*

prote- *or* **proteo-** *comb form* [ISV, fr. F *protéine*] **:** protein ⟨*proteo*lysis⟩ ⟨*prote*ose⟩

pro·tea \'prōt-ē-ə\ *n* [NL, fr. L *Proteus* Proteus] (1825) **:** any of a genus (*Protea* of the family Proteaceae, the protea family) of evergreen shrubs often grown for their showy bracts and dense flower heads

pro·te·an \'prōt-ē-ən, prō-'tē-\ *adj* (1598) **1 :** of or resembling Proteus in having a varied nature or ability to assume different forms **2 :** displaying great diversity or variety **:** VERSATILE

pro·te·ase \'prōt-ē-ˌās, -ˌāz\ *n* [ISV] (1903) **:** PROTEINASE, PEPTIDASE

pro·tect \prə-'tekt\ *vt* [L *protectus,* pp. of *protegere,* fr. *pro-* in front + *tegere* to cover — more at PRO-, THATCH] (1526) **1 :** to cover or shield from exposure, injury, or destruction **:** GUARD **2 :** to maintain the status or integrity of esp. through financial or legal guarantees: as **a :** to save from contingent financial loss **b :** to foster or shield from infringement or restriction ⟨salesmen with *~ed* territories⟩; *specif* **:** to restrict competition for (as domestic industries) by means of tariffs or trade controls ***syn*** see DEFEND — **pro·tec·tive** \-'tek-tiv\ *adj* — **pro·tec·tive·ly** *adv* — **pro·tec·tive·ness** *n*

pro·tec·tant \prə-'tek-tənt\ *n* (1935) **:** a protecting agent

pro·tec·tion \prə-'tek-shən\ *n* (14c) **1 :** the act of protecting **:** the state of being protected **2 a :** one that protects **b :** supervision or support of one that is smaller and weaker **3 :** the freeing of the producers of a country from foreign competition in their home market by restrictions (as high duties) on foreign competitive goods **4 a :** immunity from prosecution purchased by criminals through bribery **b :** money extorted by racketeers posing as a protective association **5 :** COVERAGE 2a

pro·tec·tion·ist \-sh(ə-)nəst\ *n* (1844) **:** an advocate of government economic protection for domestic producers through restrictions on foreign competitors — **pro·tec·tion·ism** \-shə-ˌniz-əm\ *n* — **protectionist** *adj*

protective tariff *n* (1838) **:** a tariff intended primarily to protect domestic producers rather than to yield revenue — compare REVENUE TARIFF

pro·tec·tor \prə-'tek-tər\ *n* (14c) **1 a :** one that protects **:** GUARDIAN **b :** a device used to prevent injury **:** GUARD **2 a :** one having the care of a kingdom during the king's minority **:** REGENT **b :** the executive head of the Commonwealth of England, Scotland, and Ireland from 1653 to 1659 — called also *Lord Protector of the Commonwealth* — **pro·tec·tor·ship** \-ˌship\ *n*

pro·tec·tor·al \-'tek-t(ə-)rəl\ *adj* (1657) **:** of or relating to a protector or protectorate

pro·tec·tor·ate \-'tek-t(ə-)rət\ *n* (1692) **1 a :** government by a protector **b** *cap* **:** the government of England (1653–59) under the Cromwells **c :** the rank, office, or period of rule of a protector **2 a :** the relationship of superior authority assumed by one power or state over a dependent one **b :** the dependent political unit in such a relationship

pro·tec·to·ry \-'tek-t(ə-)rē\ *n, pl* **-ries** (1868) **:** an institution for the protection and care usu. of homeless or delinquent children

pro·tec·tress \-'tek-trəs\ *n* (1570) **:** a woman who is a protector

pro·té·gé \'prōt-ə-ˌzhā, ˌprōt-ə-'\ *n* [F, fr. pp. of *protéger* to protect, fr. L *protegere*] (1778) **:** one who is protected or trained or whose career is furthered by a person of experience, prominence, or influence

pro·té·gée \'prōt-ə-ˌzhā, ˌprōt-ə-'\ *n* [F, fem. of *protégé*] (1778) **:** a female protégé

pro·tein \'prō-ˌtēn, 'prōt-ē-ən\ *n, often attrib* [F *protéine,* fr. LGk *prōteios* primary, fr. Gk *prōtos* first — more at PROT-] (ca. 1844) **1 :** any of numerous naturally occurring extremely complex combinations of amino acids that contain the elements carbon, hydrogen, nitrogen, oxygen, usu. sulfur, and occas. other elements (as phosphorus or iron), are essential constituents of all living cells, and are synthesized from raw materials by plants but assimilated as separate amino acids by animals **2 :** the total nitrogenous material in plant or animal substances

pro·tein·aceous \ˌprōt-ᵊn-'ā-shəs, ˌprō-ˌtēn-, ˌprōt-ē-ən-\ *adj* (ca. 1844) **:** of, relating to, resembling, or being protein

pro·tein·ase \'prōt-ᵊn-ˌās, 'prō-ˌtēn-, 'prōt-ē-ən-, -ˌāz\ *n* [ISV] (ca. 1929) **:** an enzyme that hydrolyzes proteins esp. to peptides

pro·tein·uria \ˌprōt-ᵊn-'(y)ür-ē-ə, ˌprō-ˌtēn-, ˌprōt-ē-ən-\ *n* [NL, fr. ISV *protein* + NL *-uria*] (1911) **:** the presence of excess protein in the urine

pro tem \(ˈ)prō-'tem\ *adv* (1828) **:** PRO TEMPORE

pro tem·po·re \prō-'tem-pə-rē\ *adv* [L] (15c) **:** for the time being

pro·tend \prō-'tend\ *vb* [ME *protenden,* fr. L *protendere,* fr. *pro-* + *tendere* to stretch — more at THIN] *vt* (15c) **1** *archaic* **:** to stretch forth **2** *archaic* **:** EXTEND ~ *vi, archaic* **:** STICK OUT, PROTRUDE

pro·ten·sive \-'ten(t)-siv\ *adj* [L *protensus,* pp. of *protendere*] (1671) **1** *archaic* **:** having continuance in time **2** *archaic* **:** having lengthwise extent or extensiveness — **pro·ten·sive·ly** *adv*

pro·te·ol·y·sis \ˌprōt-ē-'äl-ə-səs\ *n* [NL] (1880) **:** the hydrolysis of proteins or peptides with formation of simpler and soluble products

pro·teo·lyt·ic \ˌprōt-ē-ə-'lit-ik\ *adj* (1877) **:** of, relating to, or producing proteolysis — **pro·teo·lyt·i·cal·ly** \-i-k(ə-)lē\ *adv*

pro·te·ose \'prōt-ē-ˌōs, -ˌōz\ *n* [ISV] (ca. 1890) **:** any of various water-soluble protein derivatives formed by partial hydrolysis of proteins

Pro·tero·zo·ic \ˌprät-ə-rə-'zō-ik, ˌprōt-\ *adj* [Gk *proteros* former, earlier (fr. *pro* before) + ISV *-zoic* — more at FOR] (1899) **:** of, relating to, or being an era of geological history that includes the interval between the Archeozoic and the Paleozoic, perhaps exceeds in length all of subsequent geological time, and is marked by rocks that contain a few fossils indicating the existence of annelid worms and algae; *also* **:** relating to the system of rocks formed in this era — see GEOLOGIC TIME table — **Proterozoic** *n*

[1]pro·test \'prō-ˌtest\ *n* (15c) **1 :** a solemn declaration of opinion and usu. of dissent: as **a :** a sworn declaration that payment of a note or bill has been refused and that all responsible signers or debtors are liable for resulting loss or damage **b :** a declaration made esp. before or while paying that a tax is illegal and that payment is not voluntary **2 :** the act of objecting or a gesture of disapproval ⟨resigned in ~⟩; *esp* **:** a usu. organized public demonstration of disapproval ⟨staged a ~ against the war⟩ **3 :** a complaint, objection, or display of unwillingness usu. to an idea or a course of action ⟨went to the dentist under ~⟩ **4 :** an objection made to an official or a governing body of a sport

[2]pro·test \prə-'test, 'prō-ˌ, ˌprō-'\ *vb* [ME *protesten,* fr. MF *protester,* fr. L *protestari,* fr. *pro-* forth + *testari* to call to witness — more at PRO-, TESTAMENT] *vt* (15c) **1 :** to make solemn declaration or affirmation of ⟨~ my innocence⟩ **2 :** to execute or have executed a formal protest against (as a bill or note) **3 :** to make a statement or gesture in objection to ⟨*~ed* the abuses of human rights⟩ ~ *vi* **1 :** to make a protestation **2 :** to make or enter a protest ***syn*** see ASSERT — **pro·test·er** *or* **pro·tes·tor** \-'tes-tər, -ˌtes-\ *n*

[1]prot·es·tant \'prät-əs-tənt, *2 is also* prə-'tes-\ *n* [MF, fr. L *protestant-, protestans,* prp. of *protestari*] (1539) **1** *cap* **a :** one of a group of German princes and cities presenting a defense of freedom of conscience against an edict of the Diet of Spires in 1529 intended to suppress the Lutheran movement **b :** a member of any of several church denominations denying the universal authority of the Pope and affirming the Reformation principles of justification by faith alone, the priesthood of all believers, and the primacy of the Bible as the only source of revealed truth; *broadly* **:** a Christian not of a Catholic or Eastern church **2 :** one who makes or enters a protest — **Prot·es·tant·ism** \'prät-əs-tənt-ˌiz-əm\ *n*

[2]protestant *adj* (1539) **1** *cap* **:** of or relating to Protestants, their churches, or their religion **2 :** making or sounding a protest ⟨the two ~ ladies up and marched out —*Time*⟩

Protestant ethic *n* (1926) **:** an ethic that stresses the virtue of hard work, thrift, and self-discipline

pro·tes·ta·tion \ˌprät-əs-ˈtā-shən, ˌprō-ˌtes-, ˌprōt-əs-, ˌprät-ˌes-\ *n* (14c) : the act of protesting : a solemn declaration or avowal

pro·te·us \ˈprōt-ē-əs\ *n, pl* **-tei** \-ē-ˌī\ [NL, fr. L, Proteus] (1896) : any of a genus (*Proteus*) of aerobic gram-negative usu. motile bacteria that include saprophytes in decaying organic matter and forms associated with gastrointestinal disorders

Pro·teus \ˈprō-ˌt(y)üs, ˈprōt-ē-əs\ *n* [L, fr. Gk *Prōteus*] : a Greek sea god capable of assuming different forms

pro·tha·la·mi·on \ˌprō-thə-ˈlā-mē-ən, -ˌän\ *or* **pro·tha·la·mi·um** \-mē-əm\ *n, pl* **-mia** \-mē-ə\ [NL, fr. Gk *pro-* + *-thalamion* (as in *epithalamion*)] (ca. 1597) : a song in celebration of a marriage

pro·thal·li·um \prō-ˈthal-ē-əm\ *n, pl* **-thal·lia** \-ē-ə\ [NL, fr. *pro-* + *thallus*] (1858) **1** : the gametophyte of a pteridophyte (as a fern) that is typically a small flat green thallus attached to the soil by rhizoids **2** : a greatly reduced structure of a seed plant corresponding to the pteridophyte prothallium

pro·thal·lus \(ˈ)prō-ˈthal-əs\ *n* [NL] (1854) : PROTHALLIUM

proth·e·sis \ˈpräth-ə-səs\ *n, pl* **-e·ses** \-ˌsēz\ [LL, alter. of *prosthesis*, fr. Gk, lit., addition — more at PROSTHESIS] (ca. 1550) : the addition of a sound to the beginning of a word (as in Old French *estat* — whence English *estate* — from Latin *status*) — **pro·thet·ic** \prä-ˈthet-ik\ *adj*

pro·tho·no·ta·ry \prō-ˈthän-ə-ˌter-ē, ˌprō-thə-ˈnōt-ə-rē\ *or* **pro·to·no·ta·ry** \prō-ˈtän-ə-ˌter-ē, ˌprōt-ə-ˈnōt-ə-rē\ *n, pl* **-ries** [ME *prothonotarie*, fr. LL *protonotarius*, fr. *prot-* + L *notarius* notary] (15c) : a chief clerk of any of various courts of law — **pro·tho·no·tar·i·al** \prō-ˌthän-ə-ˈter-ē-əl, ˌprō-thə-nō-ˈter-ē-əl\ *adj*

pro·tho·rac·ic \ˌprō-thə-ˈras-ik\ *adj* (1826) : of or relating to the prothorax

prothoracic gland *n* (1887) : one of a pair of thoracic endocrine organs in some insects that control molting

pro·tho·rax \(ˈ)prō-ˈthō(ə)r-ˌaks, -ˈthȯ(ə)r-\ *n* [NL *prothorac-*, *prothorax*, fr. [1]*pro-* + *thorax*] (1826) : the anterior segment of the thorax of an insect — see INSECT illustration

pro·throm·bin \(ˈ)prō-ˈthräm-bən\ *n* [ISV] (1898) : a plasma protein produced in the liver in the presence of vitamin K and converted into thrombin in the clotting of blood

pro·tist \ˈprōt-əst, ˈprō-ˌtist\ *n* [deriv. of Gk *prōtistos* very first, primal, fr. superl. of *prōtos* first — more at PROT-] (1889) : any of a kingdom or other group (Protista) of unicellular or acellular organisms comprising bacteria, protozoans, various algae and fungi, and sometimes viruses — **pro·tis·tan** \prō-ˈtis-tən\ *adj or n*

pro·ti·um \ˈprōt-ē-əm, ˈprō-shē-\ *n* [NL, fr. Gk *prōtos* first] (1933) : the ordinary light hydrogen isotope of atomic mass 1

proto- — see PROT-

pro·to·col \ˈprōt-ə-ˌkȯl, -ˌkōl, -ˌkäl, -kəl\ *n* [MF *prothocole*, fr. ML *protocollum*, fr. LGk *prōtokollon* first sheet of a papyrus roll bearing data of manufacture, fr. Gk *prōt-* prot- + *kollan* to glue together, fr. *kolla* glue; akin to MD *helen* to glue] (1541) **1** : an original draft, minute, or record of a document or transaction **2 a** : a preliminary memorandum often formulated and signed by diplomatic negotiators as a basis for a final convention or treaty **b** : the records or minutes of a diplomatic conference or congress that show officially the agreements arrived at by the negotiators **3 a** : a code prescribing strict adherence to correct etiquette and precedence (as in diplomatic exchange and in the military services) **b** : a set of conventions governing the treatment and esp. the formatting of data in an electronic communications system **4** : the plan of a scientific experiment or treatment

pro·to·derm \ˈprōt-ə-ˌdərm\ *n* [ISV] (ca. 1932) : DERMATOGEN

pro·to·gal·axy \ˌprōt-ō-ˈgal-ək-sē\ *n* (1950) : a hypothetical cloud of gas believed to have condensed into stars and formed a galaxy

pro·to·his·to·ry \-ˈhis-t(ə-)rē\ *n* [ISV] (1903) : the study of human beings in the times that immediately antedate recorded history — **pro·to·his·to·ri·an** \-(h)is-ˈtȯr-ē-ən, -ˈtȯr-\ *n* — **pro·to·his·tor·ic** \-ˈtȯr-ik, -ˈtär-\ *adj*

pro·to·hu·man \-ˈhyü-mən, -ˈyü-\ *adj* (ca. 1909) : of, relating to, or resembling an early primitive man or a manlike primate — **protohuman** *n*

pro·to·lan·guage \ˈprōt-ō-ˌlaŋ-gwij\ *n* (1948) : an assumed or recorded ancestral language

pro·to·lith·ic \ˌprōt-ə-ˈlith-ik\ *adj* (1897) : of or relating to the earliest period of the Stone Age : EOLITHIC

pro·to·mar·tyr \ˈprōt-ō-ˌmärt-ər\ *n* [ME *prothomartir*, fr. MF, fr. LL *protomartyr*, fr. LGk *prōtomartyr-*, *prōtomartys*, fr. Gk *prōt-* + *martyr-*, *martys* martyr] (15c) : the first martyr in a cause or region

pro·ton \ˈprō-ˌtän\ *n* [Gk *prōton*, neut. of *prōtos* first — more at PROT-] (1920) : an elementary particle that is identical with the nucleus of the hydrogen atom, that along with neutrons is a constituent of all other atomic nuclei, that carries a positive charge numerically equal to the charge of an electron, and that has a mass of 1.673×10^{-24} gram — **pro·ton·ic** \prō-ˈtän-ik\ *adj*

pro·ton·ate \ˈprōt-ə-ˌnāt\ *vb* **-at·ed; -at·ing** *vt* (1945) : to add a proton to ~ *vi* : to acquire an additional proton — **pro·ton·ation** \ˌprōt-ə-ˈnā-shən\ *n*

pro·to·ne·ma \ˌprōt-ə-ˈnē-mə\ *n, pl* **-ne·ma·ta** \-ˈnē-mət-ə, -ˈnem-ət-\ [NL *protonemat-*, *protonema*, fr. *prot-* + Gk *nēma* thread — more at NEMAT-] (ca. 1857) : the primary usu. filamentous thalloid stage of the gametophyte in mosses and in some liverworts comparable to the prothallium in ferns — **pro·to·ne·mal** \-ˈnē-məl\ *adj* — **pro·to·ne·ma·tal** \-ˈnē-mət-ᵊl, -ˈnem-ət-\ *adj*

protonotary apostolic *or* **prothonotary apostolic** *n, pl* **protonotaries apostolic** *or* **prothonotaries apostolic** (1682) : a priest of the chief college of the papal curia who keeps records of consistories and canonizations and signs papal bulls; *also* : an honorary member of this college

pro·ton–syn·chro·tron \ˈprō-ˌtän-ˈsiŋ-k(r)ə-ˌträn, -ˈsin-\ *n* (1947) : a synchrotron in which protons are accelerated by means of frequency modulation of the radio-frequency accelerating voltage so that they have energies of billions of electron volts

pro·to·path·ic \ˌprōt-ə-ˈpath-ik\ *adj* [ISV, fr. MGk *prōtopathēs* affected first, fr. Gk *prōt-* prot- + *pathos* experience, suffering — more at PATHOS] (ca. 1905) : of, relating to, or being cutaneous sensory reception responsive only to rather gross stimuli

pro·to·phlo·em \-ˈflō-ˌem\ *n* (1884) : the first-formed phloem that develops from procambium, consists of narrow thin-walled cells capable of a limited amount of stretching, and is usu. associated with a region of rapid growth

pro·to·plan·et \ˈprōt-ō-ˌplan-ət\ *n* (1949) : a hypothetical whirling gaseous mass within a giant cloud of gas and dust that rotates around a sun and is believed to give rise to a planet

pro·to·plasm \ˈprōt-ə-ˌplaz-əm\ *n* [G *protoplasma*, fr. *prot-* + NL *plasma*] (1848) **1** : the organized colloidal complex of organic and inorganic substances (as proteins and water) that constitutes the living nucleus, cytoplasm, plastids, and mitochondria of the cell and is regarded as the only form of matter in which the vital phenomena are manifested **2** : CYTOPLASM — **pro·to·plas·mic** \ˌprōt-ə-ˈplaz-mik\ *adj*

pro·to·plast \ˈprōt-ə-ˌplast\ *n* [MF *protoplaste*, fr. LL *protoplastus* first man, fr. Gk *prōtoplastos* first formed, fr. *prōt-* prot- + *plastos* formed, fr. *plassein* to mold — more at PLASTER] (1532) **1** : one that is formed first : PROTOTYPE **2** : the nucleus, cytoplasm, and plasma membrane of a cell as distinguished from inert walls and inclusions

pro·to·por·phy·rin \ˌprōt-ō-ˈpȯr-f(ə-)rən\ *n* [ISV] (1925) : a purple porphyrin acid $C_{34}H_{34}N_4O_4$ obtained from hemin or heme by removal of bound iron

pro·to·star \ˈprōt-ō-ˌstär\ *n* (1947) : a hypothetical cloud of gas and dust in space believed to develop into a star

pro·to·stele \ˈprōt-ə-ˌstēl, ˌprōt-ə-ˈstē-lē\ *n* (ca. 1909) : a stele forming a solid rod with the phloem surrounding the xylem — **pro·to·ste·lic** \ˌprōt-ə-ˈstē-lik\ *adj*

pro·to·troph \ˈprōt-ə-ˌtrōf, -ˌträf\ *n* [back-formation fr. *prototrophic*] (1947) : a prototrophic individual

pro·to·tro·phic \ˌprōt-ə-ˈtrō-fik\ *adj* [ISV] (1900) : having the nutritional requirements of the normal or wild type — **pro·to·tro·phy** \prō-ˈtä-trə-fē\ *n*

pro·to·typ·al \ˌprōt-ə-ˈtī-pəl\ *adj* (1693) : PROTOTYPICAL

pro·to·type \ˈprōt-ə-ˌtīp\ *n* [F, fr. Gk *prōtotypon*, fr. neut. of *prōtotypos* archetypal, fr. *prōt-* + *typos* type] (1552) **1** : an original model on which something is patterned : ARCHETYPE **2** : an individual that exhibits the essential features of a later type **3** : a standard or typical example **4** : a first full-scale and usu. functional form of a new type or design of a construction (as an airplane)

pro·to·typ·i·cal \ˌprōt-ə-ˈtip-i-kəl\ *also* **pro·to·typ·ic** \-ik\ *adj* (1650) : of, relating to, or being a prototype — **pro·to·typ·i·cal·ly** \-i-k(ə-)lē\ *adv*

pro·to·xy·lem \ˌprōt-ə-ˈzī-ləm, -ˌlem\ *n* (1887) : the first-formed xylem developing from procambium and consisting of narrow cells with annular, spiral, or scalariform wall thickenings

pro·to·zo·al \ˌprōt-ə-ˈzō-əl\ *adj* (1890) : of or relating to protozoans

pro·to·zo·an \-ˈzō-ən\ *n* [NL *Protozoa*, fr. *prot-* + *-zoa*] (ca. 1864) : any of a phylum or subkingdom (Protozoa) of minute protoplasmic acellular or unicellular animals which have varied morphology and physiology and often complex life cycles which are represented in almost every kind of habitat, and some of which are serious parasites of man and domestic animals — **protozoan** *adj*

pro·to·zo·ol·o·gy \-zō-ˈäl-ə-jē, -zə-ˈwäl-\ *n* [NL *Protozoa* + ISV *-logy*] (1904) : a branch of zoology dealing with protozoans — **pro·to·zo·ol·o·gist** \-zō-ˈäl-ə-jəst, -zə-ˈwäl-\ *n*

pro·to·zo·on \-ˈzō-ˌän\ *n, pl* **-zoa** \-ˈzō-ə\ [NL, fr. sing. of *Protozoa*] (1834) : PROTOZOAN

pro·tract \prō-ˈtrakt, p(r)ə-\ *vt* [L *protractus*, pp. of *protrahere*, lit., to draw forward, fr. *pro-* forward + *trahere* to draw — more at PRO-, DRAW] (15c) **1** *archaic* : DELAY, DEFER **2** : to prolong in time or space : CONTINUE **3** : to lay down the lines and angles of with scale and protractor : PLOT **4** : to extend forward or outward — compare RETRACT 1 ***syn*** see EXTEND — **pro·trac·tive** \-ˈtrak-tiv\ *adj*

protracted meeting *n* (1832) : a revival meeting extending over a period of time

pro·trac·tile \-ˈtrak-tᵊl, -ˌtīl\ *adj* [L *protractus*] (1828) : capable of being thrust out ⟨~ jaws⟩

pro·trac·tion \-ˈtrak-shən\ *n* [LL *protraction-*, *protractio* act of drawing out, fr. *protractus*] (1535) **1** : the act of protracting : the state of being protracted **2** : the drawing to scale of an area of land

pro·trac·tor \-ˈtrak-tər\ *n* (ca. 1611) **1 a** : one that protracts **b** : a muscle that extends a part **2** : an instrument for laying down and measuring angles in drawing and plotting

pro·trep·tic \prō-ˈtrep-tik\ *n* [LL *protrepticus* hortatory, encouraging, fr. Gk *protreptikos*, fr. *protrepein* to turn forward, urge on, fr. *pro-* + *trepein* to turn — more at TROPE] (ca. 1656) : an utterance (as a speech) designed to instruct and persuade — **protreptic** *adj*

pro·trude \prō-ˈtrüd\ *vb* **pro·trud·ed; pro·trud·ing** [L *protrudere*, fr. *pro-* + *trudere* to thrust — more at THREAT] *vt* (1620) **1** *archaic* : to thrust forward **2** : to cause to project ~ *vi* : to jut out from the surrounding surface or context ⟨a handkerchief *protruding* from his breast pocket⟩ — **pro·tru·si·ble** \-ˈtrü-sə-bəl, -zə-\ *adj*

pro·tru·sion \prō-ˈtrü-zhən\ *n* [L *protrusus*, pp. of *protrudere*] (1646) **1** : the act of protruding : the state of being protruded **2** : something (as a part or excrescence) that protrudes ***syn*** see PROJECTION

pro·tru·sive \-ˈtrü-siv, -ziv\ *adj* (1676) **1** *archaic* : thrusting forward **2** : PROMINENT, PROTUBERANT ⟨a ~ jaw⟩ **3** : OBTRUSIVE, PUSHING ⟨a coarse ~ manner⟩ — **pro·tru·sive·ly** *adv* — **pro·tru·sive·ness** *n*

pro·tu·ber·ance \prō-ˈt(y)ü-b(ə-)rən(t)s\ *n* (1646) **1** : something that is protuberant **2** : the quality or state of being protuberant ***syn*** see PROJECTION

pro·tu·ber·ant \-b(ə-)rənt\ *adj* [LL *protuberant-*, *protuberans*, prp. of *protuberare* to bulge out, fr. L *pro-* forward + *tuber* hump, swelling — more at THUMB] (1646) **1** : thrusting out from a surrounding or adjacent surface often as a rounded mass : PROMINENT **2** : forcing itself into consciousness : OBTRUSIVE — **pro·tu·ber·ant·ly** *adv*

proud \ˈpraud\ *adj* [ME, fr. OE *prūd*, prob. fr. OF *prod, prud, prou* capable, good, valiant, fr. LL *prode* advantage, advantageous, back= formation fr. L *prodesse* to be advantageous, fr. *pro-*, *prod-* for, in favor + *esse* to be — more at PRO-, IS] (bef. 12c) **1** : feeling or showing pride: as **a** : having or displaying excessive self-esteem **b** : much pleased : EXULTANT **c** : having proper self-respect **2 a** : marked by stateliness : MAGNIFICENT **b** : giving reason for pride : GLORIOUS ⟨the

\ə\ abut \ᵊ\ kitten, F table \ər\ further \a\ ash \ā\ ace \ä\ cot, cart \au̇\ out \ch\ chin \e\ bet \ē\ easy \g\ go \i\ hit \ī\ ice \j\ job \ŋ\ sing \ō\ go \ȯ\ law \ȯi\ boy \th\ thin \t͟h\ the \ü\ loot \u̇\ foot \y\ yet \zh\ vision \à, k̟, ⁿ, œ, œ̄, ue, ue̅, ʸ\ see Guide to Pronunciation

~*est* moment in her life⟩ **3 :** VIGOROUS, SPIRITED ⟨a ~ steed⟩ **4** *chiefly Brit* **:** raised above a surrounding area ⟨a ~ design on a stamp⟩ — **proud·ly** *adv*

syn PROUD, ARROGANT, HAUGHTY, LORDLY, INSOLENT, OVERBEARING, SUPERCILIOUS, DISDAINFUL mean showing scorn for inferiors. PROUD may suggest an assumed superiority or loftiness; ARROGANT implies a claiming for oneself of more consideration or importance than is warranted; HAUGHTY suggests a consciousness of superior birth or position; LORDLY implies pomposity or an arrogant display of power; INSOLENT implies contemptuous haughtiness; OVERBEARING suggests a tyrannical manner or an intolerable insolence; SUPERCILIOUS implies a cool, patronizing haughtiness; DISDAINFUL suggests a more active and openly scornful superciliousness.

proud flesh *n* (15c) **:** an excessive growth of granulation tissue (as in an ulcer)

proud·ful \'prau̇d-fəl\ *adj, chiefly dial* (14c) **:** marked by or full of pride

proud·heart·ed \-'härt-əd\ *adj* (14c) **:** proud in spirit **:** HAUGHTY

proust·ite \'prü-,stīt\ *n* [F, fr. Joseph L. *Proust* †1826 Fr. chemist] (1835) **:** a mineral Ag_3AsS_3 that consists of a red silver arsenic sulfide and occurs in crystals or massively

pro·vas·cu·lar \(')prō-'vas-kyə-lər\ *adj* (1938) **:** of, relating to, or being procambium

prove \'prüv\ *vb* **proved; proved** *or* **prov·en** \'prü-vən, *Brit also* 'prō-\; **prov·ing** \'prü-viŋ\ [ME *proven,* fr. OF *prover,* fr. L *probare* to test, approve, prove, fr. *probus* good, honest, fr. *pro-* for, in favor + *-bus* (akin to OE *bēon* to be)] *vt* (12c) **1** *archaic* **:** to learn or find out by experience **2 a :** to test the truth, validity, or genuineness of ⟨the exception ~*s* the rule⟩ ⟨~ a will at probate⟩ **b :** to test the worth or quality of; *specif* **:** to compare against a standard — sometimes used with *up* or *out* **c :** to check the correctness of (as an arithmetic result) **3 a :** to establish the existence, truth, or validity of (as by evidence or logic) ⟨~ a theorem⟩ ⟨the charges were never *proved* in court⟩ ⟨they *proved* their appeal at the box office⟩ **b :** to demonstrate as having a particular quality or worth ⟨the vaccine has been *proven* effective after years of tests⟩ ⟨*proved* herself a great actress⟩ **4 :** to show (oneself) to be worthy or capable ⟨eager to ~ myself in the new job⟩ ~ *vi* **:** to turn out esp. after trial or test ⟨the new drug *proved* effective⟩ — **prov·able** \'prü-və-bəl\ *adj* — **prov·able·ness** *n* — **prov·ably** \-blē\ *adv* — **prov·er** \'prü-vər\ *n*

usage The past participle *proven,* orig. the past participle of *preve,* a Middle English variant of *prove* that survived in Scotland, has gradually worked its way into standard English over the past three and a half centuries. It seems to have first become established in legal use and to have come only slowly into literary use. Tennyson was one of its earliest frequent users, prob. for metrical reasons. It was disapproved by 19th century grammarians, one of whom included it in a list of "words that are not words." Surveys made some 30 or 40 years ago indicated that *proved* was about four times as frequent as *proven.* But our evidence from the last 10 or 15 years shows this no longer to be the case. As a past participle *proven* is now about as frequent as *proved* in all contexts. As an attributive adjective ⟨*proved* or *proven* gas reserves⟩ *proven* is much more common than *proved.*

prov·e·nance \'präv(-ə)-nən(t)s, -,näⁿ(t)s\ *n* [F, fr. *provenir* to come forth, originate, fr. L *provenire,* fr. *pro-* forth + *venire* to come — more at PRO-, COME] (1785) **:** ORIGIN, SOURCE

¹Pro·ven·çal \,prä-vən-'säl, ,prōv-, -,äⁿ-; prə'ven(t)-səl\ *adj* [MF, fr. *Provence* Provence] (1589) **1 :** of, relating to, or characteristic of Provence or the people of Provence **2** *or* **Pro·ven·çale :** cooked with garlic, onion, mushrooms, olive oil and herbs ⟨frogs' legs ~⟩

²Provençal *n* (1600) **1 :** a native or inhabitant of Provence **2 :** a Romance language spoken in southeastern France

prov·en·der \'präv-ən-dər\ *n* [ME, fr. MF *provende, provendre,* fr. ML *provenda,* alter. of *praebenda* prebend] (14c) **1 :** dry food for domestic animals **:** FEED **2 :** FOOD, VICTUALS

pro·ve·nience \prə-'vē-nyən(t)s, -nē-ən(t)s\ *n* [alter. of *provenance*] (1882) **:** ORIGIN, SOURCE

prov·en·ly \'prü-vən-lē, *Brit also* 'prō-\ *adv* (1887) **:** demonstrably as stated **:** without doubt or uncertainty

pro·ven·tric·u·lus \,prō-ven-'trik-yə-ləs\ *n, pl* **-li** \-,lī, -,lē\ [NL] (1835) **1 :** the glandular or true stomach of a bird that is situated between the crop and gizzard **2 :** a muscular dilatation of the foregut in most mandibulate insects that is armed internally with chitinous teeth or plates for triturating food **3 :** the thin-walled sac in front of the gizzard of an earthworm

prove out *vi* (1941) **:** to turn out to be satisfactory or as expected

¹prov·erb \'präv-,ərb\ *n* [ME *proverbe,* fr. MF, fr. L *proverbium,* fr. *pro-* + *verbum* word — more at WORD] (14c) **1 :** a brief popular epigram or maxim **:** ADAGE **2 :** BYWORD 4

²proverb *vt* (14c) **1 :** to speak of proverbially **2** *obs* **:** to provide with a proverb

pro–verb \'prō-,vərb, -'vərb\ *n* (1901) **:** a form of the verb *do* used to avoid repetition of a verb ⟨the word *do* in "act as I do" is a ~⟩

pro·ver·bi·al \prə-'vər-bē-əl\ *adj* (1548) **1 :** of, relating to, or resembling a proverb **2 :** that has become a proverb or byword **:** commonly spoken of — **pro·ver·bi·al·ly** \-ə-lē\ *adv*

Prov·erbs \'präv-,ərbz\ *n pl but sing in constr* **:** a collection of moral sayings and counsels forming a book of canonical Jewish and Christian Scripture — see BIBLE table

pro·vide \prə-'vīd\ *vb* **pro·vid·ed; pro·vid·ing** [ME *providen,* fr. L *providēre,* lit., to see ahead, fr. *pro-* forward + *vidēre* to see — more at PRO-, WIT] *vi* (15c) **1 :** to take precautionary measures ⟨~ for the common defense —*U.S. Constitution*⟩ **2 :** to make a proviso or stipulation ⟨the constitution . . . ~*s* for an elected two-chamber legislature —*Current Biog.*⟩ **3 :** to make preparation to meet a need ⟨~ for entertainment⟩; *esp* **:** to supply something for sustenance or support ⟨~*s* for the poor⟩ ~ *vt* **1** *archaic* **:** to prepare or get ready in advance **2 a :** to supply or make available (something wanted or needed) ⟨*provided* new uniforms for the band⟩; *also* **:** AFFORD ⟨curtains ~ privacy⟩ **b :** to make something available to ⟨~ the children with free balloons⟩ **3 :** to have as a condition **:** STIPULATE ⟨the contract ~*s* that certain deadlines will be met⟩

pro·vid·ed *conj* [pp. of *provide*] (15c) **:** on condition that **:** with the understanding **:** IF ***usage*** see PROVIDING

prov·i·dence \'präv-əd-ən(t)s, -ə-,den(t)s\ *n* [ME, fr. MF, fr. L *providentia,* fr. *provident-, providens*] (14c) **1 a** *often cap* **:** divine guidance or care **b** *cap* **:** God conceived as the power sustaining and guiding human destiny **2 :** the quality or state of being provident

prov·i·dent \-əd-ənt, -ə-,dent\ *adj* [L *provident-, providens,* fr. prp. of *providēre*] (15c) **1 :** making provision for the future **:** PRUDENT **2 :** FRUGAL, SAVING — **prov·i·dent·ly** *adv*

prov·i·den·tial \,präv-ə-'den-chəl\ *adj* (1648) **1 :** of, relating to, or determined by Providence **2** *archaic* **:** marked by foresight **:** PRUDENT **3 :** occurring by or as if by an intervention of Providence **:** FORTUNATE ⟨a ~ escape⟩ ***syn*** see LUCKY — **prov·i·den·tial·ly** \-'dench-(ə-)lē\ *adv*

pro·vid·er \prə-'vīd-ər\ *n* (1523) **:** one that provides; *esp* **:** BREADWINNER

pro·vid·ing *conj* [prp. of *provide*] (15c) **:** on condition that **:** in case

usage Although occas. still disapproved, *providing* is as well established as a conjunction as *provided* is. *Provided* is somewhat more common.

prov·ince \'präv-ən(t)s\ *n* [ME, fr. MF, fr. L *provincia*] (14c) **1 a :** a country or region brought under the control of the ancient Roman government **b :** an administrative district or division of a country **c** *pl* **:** all of a country except the metropolises **2 a :** a division of a country forming the jurisdiction of an archbishop or metropolitan **b :** a territorial unit of a religious order **3 a :** a biogeographic division of less rank than a region **b :** an area that exhibits essential continuity of geological history; *also* **:** one characterized by particular structural or petrological features **4 a :** proper or appropriate function or scope **:** SPHERE **b :** a department of knowledge or activity ***syn*** see FUNCTION

¹pro·vin·cial \prə-'vin-chəl\ *n* [in sense 1, fr. ME, fr. MF or ML; MF, fr. ML *provincialis,* fr. *provincia* ecclesiastical province; in other senses, fr. L *provincialis,* fr. *provincia* province] (14c) **1 :** the superior of a province of a Roman Catholic religious order **2 :** one living in or coming from a province **3 a :** a person of local or restricted interests or outlook **b :** a person lacking urban polish or refinement

²provincial *adj* (14c) **1 :** of, relating to, or coming from a province **2 a :** limited in outlook **:** NARROW **b :** lacking the polish of urban society **:** UNSOPHISTICATED **3 :** of or relating to a decorative style (as in furniture) marked by simplicity, informality, and relative plainness; *esp* **:** FRENCH PROVINCIAL — **pro·vin·cial·ly** \-'vinch-(ə-)lē\ *adv*

pro·vin·cial·ism \-chə-,liz-əm\ *n* (1770) **1 :** a dialectal or local word, phrase, or idiom **2 :** the quality or state of being provincial

pro·vin·cial·ist \-'vinch-(ə-)ləst\ *n* (1656) **:** a native or inhabitant of a province

pro·vin·ci·al·i·ty \prə-,vin-chē-'al-ət-ē\ *n, pl* **-ties** (1782) **1 :** PROVINCIALISM 2 **2 :** an act or instance of provincialism

pro·vin·cial·ize \-'vin-chə-,līz\ *vt* **-ized; -iz·ing** (1829) **:** to make provincial — **pro·vin·cial·iza·tion** \-,vinch-(ə-)lə-'zā-shən\ *n*

proving ground *n* (ca. 1890) **1 :** a place for scientific experimentation or testing (as of vehicles or weapons) **2 :** a place where something is developed or tried out

pro·vi·rus \(')prō-'vī-rəs\ *n* [NL] (ca. 1949) **:** a form of a virus that is integrated into the genetic material of a host cell and by replicating with it can be transmitted from one cell generation to the next without causing lysis — **pro·vi·ral** \-rəl\ *adj*

¹pro·vi·sion \prə-'vizh-ən\ *n* [ME, fr. MF, fr. LL & L; LL *provision-, provisio* act of providing, fr. L, foresight, fr. *provisus,* pp. of *providēre* to see ahead — more at PROVIDE] (15c) **1 a :** the act or process of providing **b :** the fact or state of being prepared beforehand **c :** a measure taken beforehand to deal with a need or contingency **:** PREPARATION ⟨made no ~ for replacements⟩ **2 :** a stock of needed materials or supplies; *esp* **:** a stock of food — usu. used in pl. **3 :** PROVISO, STIPULATION

²provision *vt* **pro·vi·sioned; pro·vi·sion·ing** \-'vizh-(ə-)niŋ\ (1809) **:** to supply with provisions

¹pro·vi·sion·al \prə-'vizh-nəl, -ən-ᵊl\ *adj* (1601) **:** serving for the time being **:** TEMPORARY — **pro·vi·sion·al·ly** \-ē\ *adv*

²provisional *n* (1886) **:** a postage stamp for use until a regular issue appears — compare DEFINITIVE

pro·vi·sion·ary \prə-'vizh-ə-,ner-ē\ *adj* (1617) **:** PROVISIONAL

pro·vi·sion·er \-'vizh-(ə-)nər\ *n* (1866) **:** a furnisher of provisions

pro·vi·so \prə-'vī-(,)zō\ *n, pl* **-sos** *or* **-soes** [ME, fr. ML *proviso quod* provided that] (15c) **1 :** an article or clause (as in a contract) that introduces a condition **2 :** a conditional stipulation

pro·vi·so·ry \-'vīz-(ə-)rē\ *adj* (ca. 1611) **1 :** containing or subject to a proviso **:** CONDITIONAL **2 :** PROVISIONAL

pro·vi·ta·min \(')prō-'vīt-ə-mən\ *n* (1927) **:** a precursor of a vitamin convertible into the vitamin in an organism

Pro·vo \'prō-(,)vō\ *n, pl* **Provos** [by shortening & alter. fr. *provisional* (wing), name of the faction] (ca. 1971) **:** a member of the extremist faction of the Irish Republican Army

pro·vo·ca·teur \prō-,väk-ə-'tər\ *n* (1919) **:** AGENT PROVOCATEUR

prov·o·ca·tion \,präv-ə-'kā-shən\ *n* [ME *provocacioun,* fr. MF *provocation,* fr. L *provocation-, provocatio,* fr. *provocatus,* pp. of *provocare*] (15c) **1 :** the act of provoking **:** INCITEMENT **2 :** something that provokes, arouses, or stimulates

pro·voc·a·tive \prə-'väk-ət-iv\ *adj* (1621) **:** serving or tending to provoke, excite, or stimulate — **provocative** *n* — **pro·voc·a·tive·ly** *adv* — **pro·voc·a·tive·ness** *n*

pro·voke \prə-'vōk\ *vt* **pro·voked; pro·vok·ing** [ME *provoken,* fr. MF *provoquer,* fr. L *provocare,* fr. *pro-* forth + *vocare* to call — more at PRO-, VOICE] (15c) **1 a** *archaic* **:** to arouse to a feeling or action **b :** to incite to anger **2 a :** to call forth (as a feeling or action) **:** EVOKE ⟨~ laughter⟩ **b :** to stir up purposely ⟨~ a fight⟩ **c :** to provide the needed stimulus for ⟨will ~ a lot of discussion⟩ — **pro·vok·er** *n*

syn PROVOKE, EXCITE, STIMULATE, PIQUE, QUICKEN mean to arouse as if by pricking. PROVOKE directs attention to the response called forth ⟨my stories usually *provoke* laughter⟩ EXCITE implies a stirring up or moving profoundly ⟨news that *excited* anger and frustration⟩ STIMULATE suggests a rousing out of lethargy, quiescence, or indifference ⟨*stimulating* conversation⟩ PIQUE suggests stimulating by mild irritation or challenge ⟨that remark *piqued* my interest⟩ QUICKEN implies beneficially stimulating and making active or lively ⟨the high salary *quickened* her desire to have the job⟩

pro·vok·ing \-'vō-kiŋ\ *adj* (1642) **:** causing mild anger **:** ANNOYING — **pro·vok·ing·ly** \-kiŋ-lē\ *adv*

pro·vo·lo·ne \ˌprō-və-'lō-nē\ n [It, aug. of *provola*, a kind of cheese] (1912) : a hard friable often smoked cheese of Italian origin

pro·vost \'prō-ˌvōst, 'präv-əst, 'prō-vəst, *esp attrib* ˌprō-(ˌ)vō\ n [ME, fr. OE *profost* & OF *provost*, fr. ML *propositus*, alter. of *praepositus*, fr. L, one in charge, director, fr. pp. of *praeponere* to place at the head — more at PREPOSITION] (bef. 12c) 1 : the chief dignitary of a collegiate or cathedral chapter 2 : the chief magistrate of a Scottish burgh 3 : the keeper of a prison 4 : a high-ranking university administrative officer

provost court n (1864) : a military court usu. for the trial of minor offenses within an occupied hostile territory

provost guard n (1862) : a police detail of soldiers under the authority of the provost marshal

provost marshal n (1535) : an officer who supervises the military police of a command

¹**prow** \'prau̇\ *adj* [ME, fr. MF *prou* — more at PROUD] *archaic* (15c) : VALIANT, GALLANT

²**prow** \'prau̇, *archaic* 'prō\ n [MF *proue*, prob. fr. OIt dial. *prua*, fr. L *prora*, fr. Gk *prōira*] (1555) 1 : the bow of a ship : STEM 2 : a pointed projecting front part (as of an airplane)

prow·ess \'prau̇-əs *also* 'prō-\ n [ME *prouesse*, fr. OF *proesse*, fr. *prou* valiant — more at PROUD] (13c) 1 : distinguished bravery; *esp* : military valor and skill 2 : extraordinary ability ⟨his ~ on the football field⟩

¹**prowl** \'prau̇(ə)l\ *vb* [ME *prollen*] *vi* (14c) : to move about or wander stealthily in or as if in search of prey ~ *vt* : to roam over in a predatory manner — **prowl·er** \'prau̇-lər\ n

²**prowl** n (1803) : an act or instance of prowling — **on the prowl** : in the act of prowling; *also* : in search of something (as a sexual partner) ⟨his fourth wife had just left him, and he was *on the prowl* again —Mary McCarthy⟩

prowl car n (1937) : SQUAD CAR

prox·e·mics \präk-'sē-miks\ n pl but sing or pl in constr [proximity + -emics (as in phonemics)] (1963) : the study of the nature, degree, and effect of the spatial separation individuals naturally maintain (as in various social and interpersonal situations) and of how this separation relates to environmental and cultural factors — **prox·e·mic** \-mik\ adj

prox·i·mal \'präk-sə-məl\ adj [L *proximus*] (1727) 1 : situated close to : PROXIMATE 2 : next to or nearest the point of attachment or origin, a central point, or the point of view; *esp* : located toward the center of the body — compare DISTAL 3 : of, relating to, or being the mesial and distal surfaces of a tooth — **prox·i·mal·ly** \-mə-lē\ adv

proximal convoluted tubule n (ca. 1899) : the convoluted portion of the vertebrate nephron that lies between Bowman's capsule and the loop of Henle, is made up of a single layer of cuboidal cells with striated borders, and is held to be concerned esp. with resorption of sugar, sodium and chloride ions, and water from the glomerular filtrate — called also *proximal tubule*

prox·i·mate \'präk-sə-mət\ adj [L *proximatus*, pp. of *proximare* to approach, fr. *proximus* nearest, next, superl. of *prope* near — more at APPROACH] (1661) 1 : immediately preceding or following (as in a chain of events, causes, or effects) ⟨an interest in ~, rather than ultimate, goals —Reinhold Niebuhr⟩ 2 : very near : CLOSE **b** : soon forthcoming : IMMINENT — **prox·i·mate·ly** adv — **prox·i·mate·ness** n

prox·im·i·ty \präk-'sim-ət-ē\ n [MF *proximité*, fr. L *proximitat-, proximitas*, fr. *proximus*] (15c) : the quality or state of being proximate : CLOSENESS

proximity fuze n (1945) : an electronic device that detonates a projectile within effective range of the target by means of the radio waves sent out from a tiny radio set in the nose of the projectile and reflected back to the set from the target

prox·i·mo \'präk-sə-ˌmō\ adj [L *proximo mense* in the next month] (1855) : of or occurring in the next month after the present

proxy \'präk-sē\ n, pl **prox·ies** [ME *procucie*, contr. of *procuracie*, fr. AF, fr. ML *procuracia*, alter. of L *procuratio* procuration] (15c) 1 : the agency, function, or office of a deputy who acts as a substitute for another 2 **a** : authority or power to act for another **b** : a document giving such authority; *specif* : a power of attorney authorizing a specified person to vote corporate stock 3 : a person authorized to act for another : PROCURATOR — **proxy** adj

proxy marriage n (1900) : a marriage celebrated in the absence of one of the contracting parties who authorizes a proxy to represent him at the ceremony

prude \'prüd\ n [F, good woman, prudish woman, short for *prude-femme* good woman, fr. OF *prode femme*] (1704) : a person who is excessively or priggishly attentive to propriety or decorum; *esp* : a woman who shows or affects extreme modesty

pru·dence \'prüd-ᵊn(t)s\ n [ME, fr. MF, fr. L *prudentia*, alter. of *providentia* — more at PROVIDENCE] (14c) 1 : the ability to govern and discipline oneself by the use of reason 2 : sagacity or shrewdness in the management of affairs 3 : skill and good judgment in the use of resources 4 : caution or circumspection as to danger or risk

pru·dent \-ᵊnt\ adj [ME, fr. MF, fr. L *prudent-, prudens*, contr. of *provident-, providens* — more at PROVIDENT] (14c) : characterized by, arising from, or showing prudence: as **a** : marked by wisdom or judiciousness **b** : shrewd in the management of practical affairs **c** : marked by circumspection : DISCREET **d** : PROVIDENT, FRUGAL *syn* see WISE — **pru·dent·ly** adv

pru·den·tial \prü-'den-chəl\ adj (1641) 1 : of, relating to, or proceeding from prudence 2 : exercising prudence esp. in business matters — **pru·den·tial·ly** \-'dench-(ə-)lē\ adv

prud·ery \'prüd-(ə-)rē\ n, pl **-er·ies** (1709) 1 : the characteristic quality or state of a prude : a prudish act or remark

prud·ish \'prüd-ish\ adj (1717) : marked by prudery : PRIGGISH — **prud·ish·ly** adv — **prud·ish·ness** n

pru·inose \'prü-ə-ˌnōs\ adj [L *pruinosus* covered with hoarfrost, fr. *pruina* hoarfrost — more at FREEZE] (ca. 1826) : covered with whitish dust or bloom ⟨~ stems⟩

¹**prune** \'prün\ n [ME, fr. MF, plum, fr. L *prunum* — more at PLUM] (14c) : a plum dried or capable of drying without fermentation

²**prune** vb **pruned; prun·ing** [ME *pruynen*, fr. MF *proignier*, prob. alter. of *provigner* to layer, fr. *provain* layer, fr. L *propagin-, propago*, fr. *pro-* forward + *pangere* to fix — more at PRO-, PACT] vt (15c) 1 **a** : to reduce esp. by eliminating superfluous matter ⟨*pruned* the text⟩ ⟨~ the budget⟩ **b** : to remove as superfluous ⟨~ away all ornamentation⟩ 2 : to cut off or cut back parts of for better shape or more fruitful growth ~ vi : to cut away what is unwanted or superfluous — **prun·er** n

pru·nel·la \pru̇-'nel-ə\ *also* **pru·nelle** \-'nel\ n [F *prunelle*, lit., sloe, fr. dim. of *prune* plum] (1670) 1 : a twilled woolen dress fabric 2 : a heavy woolen fabric used for the uppers of shoes

pruning hook n (1611) : a pole bearing a curved blade for pruning plants

pru·ri·ence \'pru̇r-ē-ən(t)s\ n (ca. 1755) : the quality or state of being prurient

pru·ri·en·cy \-ən-sē\ n (1711) : PRURIENCE

pru·ri·ent \-ənt\ adj [L *prurient-, pruriens*, prp. of *prurire* to itch, crave, be wanton; akin to L *pruna* glowing coal, Skt *plosati* he singes] (1652) : marked by or arousing an immoderate or unwholesome interest or desire; *esp* : marked by, arousing, or appealing to unusual sexual desire — **pru·ri·ent·ly** adv

pru·ri·go \pru̇-'rī-(ˌ)gō, -'rē-\ n [NL, fr. L, itch, fr. *prurire*] (1646) : a chronic inflammatory skin disease marked by itching papules

pru·rit·ic \-'rit-ik\ adj (1899) : of, relating to, or marked by itching

pru·ri·tus \-'rīt-əs, -'rēt-\ n [NL, fr. L *pruritus*, pp. of *prurire*] (1653) : ITCH 1

Prus·sian blue \ˌprəsh-ən-\ n [*Prussia*, Germany] (1724) 1 : any of numerous blue iron pigments formerly regarded as ferric ferrocyanide 2 : a dark blue crystalline hydrated ferric ferrocyanide $Fe_4[Fe(CN)_6]_3 \cdot xH_2O$ used as a test for ferric iron 3 : a variable color averaging a moderate to strong greenish blue

Prus·sian·ism \'prəsh-ə-ˌniz-əm\ n (1856) : the practices or policies (as the advocacy of militarism) held to be typically Prussian

prus·sian·ize \-ˌnīz\ vt **-ized; -iz·ing** *often cap* (1861) : to make Prussian in character or principle (as in authoritarian control or rigid discipline) — **prus·sian·iza·tion** \ˌprəsh-ə-nə-'zā-shən\ n

prus·si·ate \'prəs-ē-ˌāt\ n [F, fr. (*acide*) *prussique*] (1790) 1 : a salt of hydrocyanic acid : CYANIDE 2 **a** : FERROCYANIDE **b** : FERRICYANIDE

pru·tah or **pru·ta** \'prü-'tä\ n, pl **pru·toth** or **pru·tot** \-'tōt(h), -'tōs\ [NHeb *perūṭāh*, fr. LHeb, a small coin] (1949) 1 : a former monetary unit of Israel equivalent to ¹/₁₀₀₀ pound 2 : a coin representing one prutah

¹**pry** \'prī\ vi **pried; pry·ing** [ME *prien*] (14c) : to look closely or inquisitively; *also* : to make a nosy or presumptuous inquiry

²**pry** vt **pried; pry·ing** [alter. of ⁵*prize*] (ca. 1806) 1 : to raise, move, or pull apart with a lever : PRIZE 2 : to extract, detach, or open with difficulty ⟨*pried* the secret out of my sister⟩

³**pry** n (1823) 1 : a tool for prying 2 : LEVERAGE

pry·er *var of* PRIER

pry·ing adj (1552) : impertinently or officiously inquisitive or interrogatory *syn* see CURIOUS — **pry·ing·ly** \-iŋ-lē\ adv

psalm \'sä(l)m, *NewEng also* 'säm\ n, *often cap* [ME, fr. OE *psealm*, fr. LL *psalmus*, fr. Gk *psalmos*, lit., twanging of a harp, fr. *psallein* to pluck, play a stringed instrument] (bef. 12c) 1 : a sacred song or poem used in worship; *esp* : one of the biblical hymns collected in the Book of Psalms

psalm·book \-ˌbu̇k\ n, archaic (bef. 12c) : PSALTER

psalm·ist \'säm-əst, 'säl-məst, *NewEng also* 'säm-əst\ n (15c) : a writer or composer of psalms esp. biblical psalms

psalm·o·dy \'säm-əd-ē, 'säl-məd-, *NewEng also* 'säm-əd-ē\ n [ME *psalmodie*, fr. LL *psalmodia*, fr. LGk *psalmōidia*, lit., singing to the harp, fr. Gk *psalmos* + *aidein* to sing — more at ODE] (14c) 1 : the act, practice, or art of singing psalms in worship 2 : a collection of psalms

Psalms \'sä(l)mz, *NewEng also* 'sämz\ n pl but sing in constr : a collection of sacred poems forming a book of canonical Jewish and Christian Scripture — see BIBLE table

Psal·ter \'sȯl-tər\ n [ME, fr. OE *psalter* & OF *psaltier*, fr. LL *psalterium*, fr. LGk *psaltērion*, fr. Gk, psaltery] (bef. 12c) : the Book of Psalms; *also* : a collection of Psalms for liturgical or devotional use

psal·te·ri·um \sȯl-'tir-ē-əm\ n, pl **-ria** \-ē-ə\ [NL, fr. LL, psalter; fr. the resemblance of the folds to the pages of a book] (ca. 1846) : OMASUM

psal·tery *also* **psal·try** \'sȯl-t(ə-)rē\ n, pl **-ter·ies** *also* **-tries** [ME *psalterie*, fr. MF, fr. L *psalterium*, fr. Gk *psaltērion*, fr. *psallein* to play on a stringed instrument] (14c) : an ancient musical instrument resembling the zither

p's and q's \ˌpēz-ᵊn-'kyüz\ n pl [fr. the phrase *mind one's p's and q's*, alluding to the difficulty a child learning to write has in distinguishing between *p* and *q*] (1779) 1 : something (as one's manners) that one should be mindful of ⟨better watch his *p's and q's* when I get a six-gun of my own —Jean Stafford⟩ 2 : best behavior ⟨being on her *p's and q's* for two solid days was too much —Guy McCrone⟩

pse·phol·o·gy \sē-'fäl-ə-jē\ n [Gk *psēphos* pebble, ballot, vote; fr. the use of pebbles by the ancient Greeks in voting] (1952) : the scientific study of elections — **pse·pho·log·i·cal** \ˌsē-fə-'läj-i-kəl\ adj — **pse·phol·o·gist** \sē-'fäl-ə-jəst\ n

pseud \'süd\ n [short for *pseudo-intellectual*] *Brit* (ca. 1962) : a person who pretends to be an intellectual

pseud- or **pseudo-** comb form [ME, fr. LL, fr. Gk, fr. *pseudēs*] : false : spurious ⟨*pseudaxis*⟩ ⟨*pseudoclassic*⟩ ⟨*pseudopodium*⟩

pseud·epig·ra·graph \süd-'ep-ə-ˌgraf\ n (1884?) : PSEUDEPIGRAPHON 2

pseud·epig·ra·phon \ˌsüd-i-'pig-rə-ˌfän\ n, pl **-pha** \-fə\ [NL, sing. of *pseudepigrapha*, fr. Gk, neut. pl. of *pseudepigraphos* falsely inscribed, fr. *pseud-* + *epigraphein* to inscribe — more at EPIGRAM] (1692) 1 pl : APOCRYPHA 2 : any of various pseudonymous or anonymous Jewish religious writings of the period 200 B.C. to 200 A.D.; *esp* : such writings (as the Psalms of Solomon) not included in any canon of biblical Scripture — usu. used in pl.

pseud·epig·ra·phy \-fē\ n [Gk *pseudepigraphos*] (ca. 1842) : the ascription of false names of authors to works

pseu·do \'süd-(ˌ)ō\ adj [ME, fr. *pseudo-*] (15c) : being apparently rather than actually as stated : SHAM, SPURIOUS ⟨distinction between true and ~ humanism —K. F. Reinhardt⟩

\ə\ abut \ᵊ\ kitten, F table \ər\ further \a\ ash \ā\ ace \ä\ cot, cart
\au̇\ out \ch\ chin \e\ bet \ē\ easy \g\ go \i\ hit \ī\ ice \j\ job
\ŋ\ sing \ō\ go \ȯ\ law \ȯi\ boy \th\ thin \t̷h\ the \ü\ loot \u̇\ foot
\y\ yet \zh\ vision \ä, k̲, ⁿ, œ, œ̄, ᵫ, ᵫ̄, �\ see Guide to Pronunciation

pseu·do·al·lele \ˌsüd-ō-ə-ˈlē(ə)l\ *n* (ca. 1948) **:** any of two or more closely linked genes that act usu. as if a single member of an allelic pair but occas. undergo crossing-over and recombination — **pseu·do·al·le·lic** \-ˈlē-lik, -ˈlel-ik\ *adj* — **pseu·do·al·lel·ism** \-ˈlē(ə)l-ˌiz-əm, -ˈlel-ˌiz-\ *n*

pseu·do·cho·lin·es·ter·ase \ˈsüd-ō-ˌkō-lə-ˈnes-tə-ˌrās, -ˌrāz\ *n* (1943) **:** CHOLINESTERASE 2

pseu·do·clas·sic \ˌsüd-ō-ˈklas-ik\ *adj* (1899) **:** pretending to be or erroneously regarded as classic — **pseudoclassic** *n*

pseu·do·clas·si·cism \-ˈklas-ə-ˌsiz-əm\ *n* (1871) **:** imitative representation of classicism in literature and art

pseu·do·coel \ˈsüd-ə-ˌsēl\ *n* (1887) **:** a body cavity that is not a product of gastrulation and is not lined with a well-defined mesodermal membrane

pseu·do·coe·lom·ate \ˌsüd-ō-ˈsē-lə-ˌmāt\ *adj* (1940) **:** having a body cavity that is a pseudocoel — **pseudocoelomate** *n*

pseu·do·cy·e·sis \-sī-ˈē-səs\ *n* [NL, fr. *pseud-* + *cyesis* pregnancy, fr. Gk *kyēsis,* fr. *kyein* to be pregnant — more at CAVE] (1817) **:** a psychosomatic state that occurs without conception and is marked by some of the physical symptoms and changes in hormonal balance of pregnancy

pseu·do·mo·nad \ˌsüd-ə-ˈmō-ˌnad, -nəd\ *n* [NL *Pseudomonad-, Pseudomonas*] (1921) **:** any of a genus (*Pseudomonas*) of short rod-shaped bacteria many of which produce a greenish fluorescent water-soluble pigment and some of which are saprophytes or plant or animal pathogens

pseu·do·mo·nas \-nəs\ *n, pl* **-mo·na·des** \-ˈmō-nə-ˌdēz, -ˈmän-ə-\ [NL, fr. *pseud-* + *monad-, monas* monad] (1903) **:** PSEUDOMONAD

pseu·do·morph \ˈsüd-ə-ˌmȯrf\ *n* [prob. fr. F *pseudomorphe,* fr. *pseud-* + *-morphe* -morph] (1849) **1 :** a mineral having the characteristic outward form of another species **2 :** a deceptive or irregular form — **pseu·do·mor·phic** \ˌsüd-ə-ˈmȯr-fik\ *adj* — **pseu·do·mor·phism** \-ˌfiz-əm\ *n* — **pseu·do·mor·phous** \-fəs\ *adj*

pseud·onym \ˈsüd-ᵊn-ˌim\ *n* [F *pseudonyme,* fr. Gk *pseudōnymos* bearing a false name, fr. *pseud-* + *onyma* name — more at NAME] (1833) **:** a fictitious name; *esp* **:** PEN NAME

pseud·onym·i·ty \ˌsüd-ᵊn-ˈim-ət-ē\ *n* (1877) **:** the use of a pseudonym; *also* **:** the fact or state of being signed with a pseudonym

pseud·on·y·mous \sü-ˈdän-ə-məs\ *adj* [Gk *pseudōnymos*] (ca. 1706) **:** bearing or using a fictitious name ⟨a ~ report⟩; *also* **:** being a pseudonym — **pseud·on·y·mous·ly** *adv* — **pseud·on·y·mous·ness** *n*

pseu·do·pa·ren·chy·ma \ˌsüd-ō-pə-ˈreŋ-kə-mə\ *n* [NL] (1875) **:** compactly interwoven short-celled filaments in a thallophyte that resemble parenchyma of higher plants — **pseu·do·par·en·chy·ma·tous** \-ˌpar-ən-ˈkim-ət-əs, -ˈkī-mət-\ *adj*

pseu·do·pod \ˈsüd-ə-ˌpäd\ *n* [NL *pseudopodium*] (1874) **:** PSEUDOPODIUM — **pseu·dop·o·dal** \sü-ˈdäp-əd-ᵊl\ *or* **pseu·do·po·di·al** \ˌsüd-ə-ˈpōd-ē-əl\ *adj*

pseu·do·po·di·um \ˌsüd-ə-ˈpōd-ē-əm\ *n, pl* **-po·dia** \-ē-ə\ [NL] (1854) **1 :** a temporary protrusion or retractile process of the protoplasm of a cell that serves a locomotor or food-gathering function **2 :** a slender leafless branch of the gametophyte in various mosses that often bears gemmae

pseu·do·preg·nan·cy \ˌsüd-ō-ˈpreg-nən-sē\ *n* (ca. 1860) **1 :** PSEUDOCYESIS **2 :** an anestrous state resembling pregnancy that occurs in various mammals usu. after an infertile copulation — **pseu·do·preg·nant** \-nənt\ *adj*

pseu·do·ran·dom \-ˈran-dəm\ *adj* (1949) **:** being or involving entities (as numbers) that are selected by a definite computational process (as one involving a computer) but that satisfy one or more standard tests for statistical randomness

pseu·do·salt \ˈsüd-ō-ˌsȯlt\ *n* (1910) **:** a compound analogous in formula to a salt but not ionized as such

pseu·do·sci·ence \ˌsüd-ō-ˈsī-ən(t)s\ *n* (1844) **:** a system of theories, assumptions, and methods erroneously regarded as scientific — **pseu·do·sci·en·tif·ic** \-ˌsī-ən-ˈtif-ik\ *adj* — **pseu·do·sci·en·tist** \-ˈsī-ənt-əst\ *n*

pseu·do·scor·pi·on \-ˈskȯr-pē-ən\ *n* [NL *Pseudoscorpiones,* fr. *pseud-* + L *scorpion-, scorpio* scorpion] (1835) **:** any of an order (Pseudoscorpiones, Pseudoscorpionida, or Pseudoscorpionidea) of minute arachnids that have no caudal sting and feed on minute animals (as insects and mites)

pseu·do·so·phis·ti·ca·tion \ˈsüd-ō-sə-ˌfis-tə-ˈkā-shən\ *n* (1965) **:** false or feigned sophistication — **pseu·do·so·phis·ti·cat·ed** \-sə-ˈfis-ti-ˌkāt-əd\ *adj*

pseu·do·tu·ber·cu·lo·sis \-t(y)u̇-ˌbər-kyə-ˈlō-səs\ *n* [NL] (ca. 1900) **:** any of several diseases that are characterized by the formation of granulomas resembling tubercular nodules but are not caused by the tubercle bacillus

pshaw \ˈshȯ\ *interj* (1673) — used to express irritation, disapproval, contempt, or disbelief

¹psi \ˈsī, ˈpsī\ *n* [LGk, fr. Gk *psei*] (15c) **:** the 23d letter of the Greek alphabet — see ALPHABET table

²psi \ˈsī\ *adj* (1942) **:** relating to, concerned with, or being parapsychological psychic events or powers

psi·lo·cy·bin \ˌsī-lə-ˈsī-bən\ *n* [NL *Psilocybe* + *-in*] (1958) **:** a hallucinogenic indole $C_{12}H_{17}N_2O_4P$ obtained from a fungus (*Psilocybe mexicana*)

psi·lo·phyte \ˈsī-lə-ˌfīt\ *n* [NL *Psilophyton,* genus of plants, fr. Gk *psilos* bare, mere (akin to Gk *psēn to rub*) + *phyton* plant — more at PHYT-, SAND] (ca. 1911) **:** any of an order (Psilophytales) of Paleozoic simple dichotomously branched plants of Europe and eastern Canada that include the oldest known land plants with vascular structure — **psi·lo·phyt·ic** \ˌsī-lə-ˈfit-ik\ *adj*

psi particle \ˈsī-, ˈpsī-\ *n* (1974) **:** J PARTICLE

psit·ta·cine \ˈsit-ə-ˌsīn\ *adj* [L *psittacinus,* fr. *psittacus* parrot, fr. Gk *psittakos*] (1874) **:** of or relating to the parrots — **psittacine** *n*

psit·ta·co·sis \ˌsit-ə-ˈkō-səs\ *n* [NL, fr. L *psittacus*] (1897) **:** an infectious disease of birds caused by a rickettsia (*Chlamydia psittaci*), marked by diarrhea and wasting, and transmissible to man in whom it usu. occurs as an atypical pneumonia accompanied by high fever — **psit·ta·co·tic** \-ˈkät-ik, -ˈkōt-\ *adj*

pso·cid \ˈsō-səd\ *n* [deriv. of NL *Psocus,* genus of lice] (1891) **:** any of an order (Corrodentia) of minute usu. winged primitive insects (as a book louse)

pso·ri·a·sis \sə-ˈrī-ə-səs\ *n* [NL, fr. Gk *psōriasis,* fr. *psōrian* to have the itch, fr. *psōra* itch; akin to Gk *psēn* to rub — more at SAND] (ca. 1684) **:** a chronic skin disease characterized by circumscribed red patches covered with white scales — **pso·ri·at·ic** \ˌsōr-ē-ˈat-ik, ˌsȯr-\ *adj or n*

psych *also* **psyche** \ˈsīk\ *vt* **psyched; psych·ing** [by shortening] (1917) **1 :** PSYCHOANALYZE **2 a :** to anticipate correctly the intentions or actions of **:** OUTGUESS **b :** to analyze or figure out (as a problem or course of action) ⟨I *~ed* it all out by myself and decided —David Hulburd⟩ **3 a :** to make psychologically uneasy **:** INTIMIDATE, SCARE ⟨pressure doesn't ~ me —Jerry Quarry⟩ — often used with *out* **b :** to make (oneself) psychologically ready for performance — usu. used with *up* ⟨*~ed* himself up for the race⟩

psych- *or* **psycho-** *comb form* [Gk, fr. *psychē* breath, principle of life, life, soul; akin to Gk *psychein* to breathe, blow, cool, Skt *babhasti* he blows] **1 :** mind **:** mental processes and activities ⟨*psycho*dynamic⟩ ⟨*psycho*logy⟩ **2 :** psychological methods ⟨*psycho*analysis⟩ ⟨*psycho*therapy⟩ **3 :** brain ⟨*psycho*surgery⟩ **4 :** mental and ⟨*psycho*somatic⟩

psych·as·the·nia \ˌsī-kəs-ˈthē-nē-ə\ *n* [NL] (1900) **:** a neurotic state characterized esp. by phobias, obsessions, or compulsions that one knows are irrational — **psych·as·then·ic** \-ˈthen-ik\ *adj or n*

Psy·che \ˈsī-kē\ *n* [L, fr. Gk *psychē* soul] **1 :** a princess loved by Cupid **2** *not cap* [Gk *psychē*] **a :** SOUL, SELF **b :** MIND

psy·che·de·lia \ˌsī-kə-ˈdēl-yə\ *n* [NL, fr. E *psychedelic* + NL *-ia*] (1967) **:** the world of people, phenomena, or items associated with psychedelic drugs

¹psy·che·del·ic \ˌsī-kə-ˈdel-ik\ *n* [Gk *psychē* soul + *dēloun* to show] (1956) **:** a psychedelic drug (as LSD)

²psychedelic *adj* (1957) **1 a :** of, relating to, or being drugs (as LSD) capable of producing abnormal psychic effects (as hallucinations) and sometimes psychic states resembling mental illness **b :** produced by or associated with the use of psychedelic drugs ⟨a ~ experience⟩ **2 :** imitating, suggestive of, or reproducing effects (as distorted or bizarre images or sounds) resembling those produced by psychedelic drugs ⟨~ color schemes⟩ — **psy·che·del·i·cal·ly** \-ˈdel-i-k(ə-)lē\ *adv*

Psy·che knot \ˌsī-kē-\ *n* [fr. the frequent representation of Psyche in works of art with this style] (ca. 1888) **:** a woman's hair style in which the hair is brushed back and twisted into a conical coil usu. just above the nape

psy·chi·a·try \sə-ˈkī-ə-trē, sī-\ *n* [prob. fr. (assumed) NL *psychiatria,* fr. *psych-* + *-iatria* -iatry] (ca. 1846) **:** a branch of medicine that deals with mental, emotional, or behavioral disorders — **psy·chi·at·ric** \ˌsī-kē-ˈa-trik\ *adj* — **psy·chi·at·ri·cal·ly** \-tri-k(ə-)lē\ *adv* — **psy·chi·a·trist** \sə-ˈkī-ə-trəst, sī-\ *n*

¹psy·chic \ˈsī-kik\ *also* **psy·chi·cal** \-ki-kəl\ *adj* [Gk *psychikos* of the soul, fr. *psychē* soul] (1642) **1 :** of or relating to the psyche **:** PSYCHOGENIC **2 :** lying outside the sphere of physical science or knowledge **:** immaterial, moral, or spiritual in origin or force **3 :** sensitive to nonphysical or supernatural forces and influences **:** marked by extraordinary or mysterious sensitivity, perception, or understanding — **psy·chi·cal·ly** \-ki-k(ə-)lē\ *adv*

²psychic *n* (1871) **1 a :** a person apparently sensitive to nonphysical forces **b :** MEDIUM 2d **2 :** psychic phenomena

psychic energizer *n* (ca. 1958) **:** ANTIDEPRESSANT

psy·cho \ˈsī-(ˌ)kō\ *n, pl* **psychos** [short for *psychoneurotic*] (1942) **:** a victim of severe mental or emotional disorder; *esp* **:** a psychoneurotic person — **psycho** *adj*

psy·cho·acous·tics \ˌsī-kō-ə-ˈkü-stiks\ *n pl but sing in constr* (1948) **:** a branch of science dealing with hearing, the sensations produced by sounds, and the problems of communication — **psy·cho·acous·tic** \-stik\ *adj*

psy·cho·ac·tive \ˌsī-kō-ˈak-tiv\ *adj* (ca. 1961) **:** affecting the mind or behavior ⟨~ drugs⟩

psy·cho·anal·y·sis \ˌsī-kō-ə-ˈnal-ə-səs\ *n* [ISV] (1906) **:** a method of analyzing psychic phenomena and treating emotional disorders that emphasizes the importance of the patient's talking freely about himself while under treatment and esp. about early childhood experiences and about his dreams — **psy·cho·an·a·lyst** \-ˈan-ᵊl-əst\ *n*

psy·cho·an·a·lyt·ic \-ˌan-ᵊl-ˈit-ik\ *also* **psy·cho·an·a·lyt·i·cal** \-i-kəl\ *adj* (1906) **:** of, relating to, or employing psychoanalysis or its principles and techniques — **psy·cho·an·a·lyt·i·cal·ly** \-i-k(ə-)lē\ *adv*

psy·cho·an·a·lyze \-ˈan-ᵊl-ˌīz\ *vt* (1911) **:** to treat by means of psychoanalysis

psy·cho·bi·og·ra·phy \-bī-ˈäg-rə-fē, -bē-\ *n* (1931) **:** a biography written from a psychodynamic or psychoanalytic point of view — **psy·cho·bi·og·ra·pher** \-fər\ *n* — **psy·cho·bio·graph·i·cal** \-ˌbī-ə-ˈgraf-i-kəl\ *adj*

psy·cho·bi·ol·o·gy \-bī-ˈäl-ə-jē\ *n* [ISV] (1902) **:** the study of mental life and behavior in relation to other biological processes — **psy·cho·bi·o·log·i·cal** \-ˌbī-ə-ˈläj-i-kəl\ *also* **psy·cho·bi·o·log·ic** \-ik\ *adj* — **psy·cho·bi·ol·o·gist** \-bī-ˈäl-ə-jəst\ *n*

psy·cho·chem·i·cal \-ˈkem-i-kəl\ *n* (1956) **:** a psychoactive chemical — **psychochemical** *adj*

psy·cho·dra·ma \ˌsī-kə-ˈdräm-ə, -ˈdram-\ *n* (1937) **:** an extemporized dramatization designed to afford catharsis and social relearning for one or more of the participants from whose life history the plot is abstracted — **psy·cho·dra·mat·ic** \-kō-drə-ˈmat-ik\ *adj*

psy·cho·dy·nam·ics \ˌsī-kō-dī-ˈnam-iks, -də-\ *n pl but sing or pl in constr* (ca. 1874) **1 :** the psychology of mental or emotional forces or processes developing esp. in early childhood and their effects on behavior and mental states **2 :** explanation or interpretation (as of behavior or mental states) in terms of mental or emotional forces or processes **3 :** motivational forces acting esp. at the unconscious level — **psy·cho·dy·nam·ic** \-ik\ *adj* — **psy·cho·dy·nam·i·cal·ly** \-i-k(ə-)lē\ *adv*

psy·cho·gen·e·sis \ˌsī-kə-ˈjen-ə-səs\ *n* [NL] (1838) **1 :** the origin and development of mental functions, traits, or states **2 :** development from mental as distinguished from physical origins — **psy·cho·ge·net·ic** \-jə-ˈnet-ik\ *adj*

psy·cho·gen·ic \-ˈjen-ik\ *adj* (1902) **:** originating in the mind or in mental or emotional conflict — **psy·cho·gen·i·cal·ly** \-i-k(ə-)lē\ *adv*

psy·cho·graph \ˈsī-kə-ˌgraf\ *n* (1916) **:** PSYCHOBIOGRAPHY

psy·cho·his·to·ry \ˈsī-kō-ˌhis-t(ə-)rē\ *n* (1934) **1 :** an analysis of an historical person or issue by psychological and psychoanalytic methods **2 :** a branch of history that applies psychological and psychoanalytic methods to the interpretation of history — **psy·cho·his·to·ri·an** \ˌsī-kō-(h)is-ˈtōr-ē-ən, -ˈtȯr-, -ˈtär-\ *n* — **psy·cho·his·to·ri·cal** \-ˈtȯr-i-kəl, -ˈtär-\ *adj*

psy·cho·ki·ne·sis \ˌsī-kō-kə-ˈnē-səs, -kī-\ *n* [NL, fr. *psych-* + Gk *kinēsis* motion — more at KINESIOLOGY] (1914) **:** movement of physical objects by the mind without use of physical means — compare PRECOGNITION, TELEKINESIS — **psy·cho·ki·net·ic** \-'net-ik\ *adj*

psy·cho·lin·guis·tics \,sī-kō-liŋ-'gwis-tiks\ *n pl but sing in constr* (1936) : the study of linguistic behavior as conditioning and conditioned by psychological factors — **psy·cho·lin·guist** \-'liŋ-gwəst\ *n* — **psy·cho·lin·guis·tic** \-tik\ *adj*

psy·cho·log·i·cal \,sī-kə-'läj-i-kəl\ *also* **psy·cho·log·ic** \-ik\ *adj* (1688) **1 a** : of or relating to psychology **b** : MENTAL **2** : directed toward the will or toward the mind specif. in its conative function ⟨~ warfare⟩ — **psy·cho·log·i·cal·ly** \-i-k(ə-)lē\ *adv*

psychological moment *n* (1871) : the occasion when the mental atmosphere is most certain to be favorable to the full effect of an action or event

psy·chol·o·gism \sī-'käl-ə-,jiz-əm\ *n* (1858) : a theory that applies psychological conceptions to the interpretation of historical events or logical thought

psy·chol·o·gize \-,jīz\ *vb* **-gized; -giz·ing** *vi* (1830) : to speculate in psychological terms or on psychological motivations ~ *vt* : to explain or interpret in psychological terms

psy·chol·o·gy \-jē\ *n, pl* **-gies** [NL *psychologia,* fr. *psych-* + *-logia* -logy] (1653) **1** : the science of mind and behavior **2 a** : the mental or behavioral characteristics of an individual or group **b** : the study of mind and behavior in relation to a particular field of knowledge or activity **3** : a treatise on psychology — **psy·chol·o·gist** \-jəst\ *n*

psy·cho·met·ric \,sī-kə-'me-trik\ *adj* (1854) : of or relating to psychometrics or psychometry — **psy·cho·met·ri·cal·ly** \-tri-k(ə-)lē\ *adv*

psy·cho·me·tri·cian \-mə-'trish-ən\ *n* (ca. 1939) **1** : a person (as a clinical psychologist) who is skilled in the administration and interpretation of objective psychological tests **2** : a psychologist who devises, constructs, and standardizes psychometric tests

psy·cho·met·rics \-'me-triks\ *n pl but sing in constr* (1923) : the psychological theory or technique of mental measurement

psy·chom·e·try \sī-'käm-ə-trē\ *n* (ca. 1842) **1** : divination of facts concerning an object or its owner through contact with or proximity to the object **2** : PSYCHOMETRICS

psy·cho·mo·tor \,sī-kə-'mōt-ər\ *adj* [ISV] (1878) : of or relating to motor action directly proceeding from mental activity

psy·cho·neu·ro·sis \,sī-kō-n(y)ü-'rō-səs\ *n* [NL] (1883) : NEUROSIS; *esp* : a neurosis based on emotional conflict in which an impulse that has been blocked seeks expression in a disguised response or symptom — **psy·cho·neu·rot·ic** \-'rät-ik\ *adj or n*

psy·cho·path \'sī-kə-,path\ *n* [ISV] (1885) : a mentally ill or unstable person; *esp* : a person having a psychopathic personality

¹psy·cho·path·ic \,sī-kə-'path-ik\ *adj* (1847) : of, relating to, or characterized by psychopathy — **psy·cho·path·i·cal·ly** \-i-k(ə-)lē\ *adv*

²psychopathic *n* (ca. 1890) : PSYCHOPATH

psychopathic personality *n* (ca. 1923) **1** : an emotionally and behaviorally disordered state characterized by clear perception of reality except for the individual's social and moral obligations and often by the pursuit of immediate personal gratification in criminal acts, drug addiction, or sexual perversion **2** : an individual having a psychopathic personality

psy·cho·pa·thol·o·gy \,sī-kō-pə-'thäl-ə-jē, -pa-\ *n* [ISV] (1847) : the study of psychological and behavioral dysfunction occurring in mental disorder or in social disorganization; *also* : such dysfunction — **psy·cho·patho·log·ic** \,sī-kō-,path-ə-'läj-ik\ *or* **psy·cho·patho·log·i·cal** \-i-kəl\ *adj* — **psy·cho·patho·log·i·cal·ly** \-i-k(ə-)lē\ *adv* — **psy·cho·pa·thol·o·gist** \-pə-'thäl-ə-jəst, -pa-\ *n*

psy·chop·a·thy \sī-'käp-ə-thē\ *n* [ISV] (1847) : mental disorder; *esp* : extreme mental disorder marked usu. by egocentric and antisocial activity

psy·cho·phar·ma·col·o·gy \'sī-kō-,fär-mə-'käl-ə-jē\ *n* (1920) : the study of the effect of drugs on the mind and behavior — **psy·cho·phar·ma·co·log·i·cal** \-mə-kə-'läj-i-kəl\ *or* **psy·cho·phar·ma·co·log·ic** \-ik\ *adj* — **psy·cho·phar·ma·col·o·gist** \-'käl-ə-jəst\ *n*

psy·cho·phys·i·cal \,sī-kō-'fiz-i-kəl\ *adj* (1847) : of or relating to psychophysics; *also* : sharing mental and physical qualities — **psy·cho·phys·i·cal·ly** \-k(ə-)lē\ *adv*

psychophysical parallelism *n* (1894) : PARALLELISM 4

psy·cho·phys·ics \,sī-kō-'fiz-iks\ *n pl but sing in constr* [ISV] (ca. 1877) : a branch of psychology that studies the effect of physical processes (as intensity of stimulation) on the mental processes of an organism — **psy·cho·phys·i·cist** \-'fiz-(ə-)səst\ *n*

psy·cho·phys·i·o·log·i·cal \'sī-kō-,fiz-ē-ə-'läj-i-kəl\ *also* **psy·cho·phys·i·o·log·ic** \-ik\ *adj* (1839) **1** : of or relating to physiological psychology **2** : combining or involving mental and bodily processes — **psy·cho·phys·i·o·log·i·cal·ly** \-i-k(ə-)lē\ *adv*

psy·cho·phys·i·ol·o·gy \-ē-'äl-ə-jē\ *n* [ISV] (1839) : PHYSIOLOGICAL PSYCHOLOGY — **psy·cho·phys·i·ol·o·gist** \-jəst\ *n*

psy·cho·sex·u·al \,sī-kō-'seksh-(ə-)wəl, -'sek-shəl\ *adj* (1897) **1** : of or relating to the mental, emotional, and behavioral aspects of sexual development **2** : of or relating to mental or emotional attitudes concerning sexual activity **3** : of or relating to the physiological psychology of sex — **psy·cho·sex·u·al·ly** \-ē\ *adv*

psy·cho·sex·u·al·i·ty \-,sek-shə-'wal-ət-ē\ *n* (1910) : the psychic factors of sex

psy·cho·sis \sī-'kō-səs\ *n, pl* **-cho·ses** \-,sēz\ [NL] (1847) : fundamental mental derangement (as paranoia) characterized by defective or lost contact with reality — **psy·chot·ic** \-'kät-ik\ *adj or n* — **psy·chot·i·cal·ly** \-i-k(ə-)lē\ *adv*

psy·cho·so·cial \,sī-kō-'sō-shəl\ *adj* (1899) **1** : involving both psychological and social aspects ⟨~ adjustment in marriage⟩ **2** : relating social conditions to mental health ⟨~ medicine⟩ — **psy·cho·so·cial·ly** \-'sōsh-(ə-)lē\ *adv*

psy·cho·so·mat·ic \,sī-kə-sə-'mat-ik\ *adj* [ISV] (1863) **1** : of, relating to, concerned with, or involving both mind and body ⟨the ~ nature of man —Herbert Ratner⟩ **2** : of, relating to, involving, or concerned with bodily symptoms caused by mental or emotional disturbance ⟨~ illness⟩ ⟨~ medicine⟩ — **psy·cho·so·mat·i·cal·ly** \-i-k(ə-)lē\ *adv*

psy·cho·so·mat·ics \,sī-kə-sə-'mat-iks\ *n pl but sing in constr* (1938) : a branch of medical science dealing with interrelationships between the mind or emotions and the body and esp. with the relation of psychic conflict to somatic symptomatology

psy·cho·sur·gery \-'sərj-(ə-)rē\ *n* (1936) : cerebral surgery employed in treating psychic symptoms — **psy·cho·sur·geon** \-'sər-jən\ *n* — **psy·cho·sur·gi·cal** \-'sər-ji-kəl\ *adj*

psy·cho·syn·the·sis \,sī-kō-'sin(t)-thə-səs\ *n* (1919) : a form of psychotherapy combining psychoanalytic techniques with meditation and exercise

psy·cho·ther·a·peu·tic \-,ther-ə-'pyüt-ik\ *adj* [ISV] (ca. 1888) : of, relating to, or used in psychotherapy — **psy·cho·ther·a·peu·ti·cal·ly** \-i-k(ə-)lē\ *adv*

psy·cho·ther·a·py \-'ther-ə-pē\ *n* [ISV] (1853) : treatment of mental or emotional disorder or of related bodily ills by psychological means — **psy·cho·ther·a·pist** \-pəst\ *n*

psy·choto·mi·met·ic \sī-,kät-ō-mə-'met-ik, -mī-\ *adj* [*psychotic* + *-o-* + *mimetic*] (1956) : of, relating to, involving, or inducing psychotic alteration of behavior and personality ⟨~ drugs⟩ — **psychotomimetic** *n* — **psy·choto·mi·met·i·cal·ly** \-i-k(ə-)lē\ *adv*

psy·cho·tro·pic \,sī-kə-'trō-pik\ *adj* (1948) : acting on the mind ⟨~ drugs⟩ — **psychotropic** *n*

psychro- *comb form* [Gk, fr. *psychros,* fr. *psychein* to cool — more at PSYCH-] : cold ⟨*psychro*meter⟩

psy·chrom·e·ter \sī-'kräm-ət-ər\ *n* [ISV] (1838) : a hygrometer consisting essentially of two similar thermometers with the bulb of one being kept wet so that the cooling that results from evaporation makes it register a lower temperature than the dry one and with the difference between the readings constituting a measure of the dryness of the atmosphere — **psy·chro·met·ric** \,sī-krə-'me-trik\ *adj* — **psy·chrom·e·try** \sī-'kräm-ə-trē\ *n*

psy·chro·phil·ic \,sī-krō-'fil-ik\ *adj* (ca. 1903) : thriving at a relatively low temperature ⟨~ bacteria⟩

psyl·la \'sil-ə\ *n* [NL, genus name, fr. Gk, flea; akin to L *pulex* flea, Skt *pluṣi*] (1852) : any of various plant lice (family Psyllidae) including economically important plant pests — compare PEAR PSYLLA

psyl·lid \'sil-əd\ *n* [deriv. of NL *Psylla*] (1899) : PSYLLA — **psyllid** *adj*

psyl·li·um seed \'sil-ē-əm-\ *n* [NL *psyllium,* fr. Gk *psyllion* fleawort, fr. *psylla*] (1930) : the seed of a fleawort (esp. *Plantago psyllium*) that has the property of swelling and becoming gelatinous when moist and is used as a mild laxative — called also *psyllium*

ptar·mi·gan \'tär-mi-gən\ *n, pl* **-gan** *or* **-gans** [modif. of ScGael *tàrmachan*] (1599) : any of various grouses (genus *Lagopus*) of northern regions with completely feathered feet

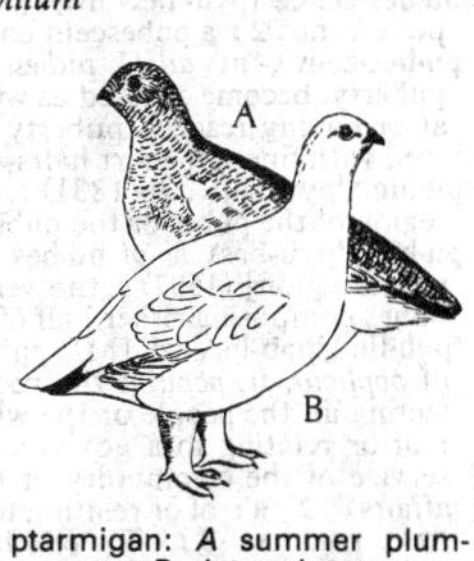

ptarmigan: *A* summer plumage; *B* winter plumage

PT boat \(')pē-'tē-\ *n* [*p*atrol *t*orpedo] (1941) : a high-speed 60 to 100 foot motorboat usu. equipped with torpedoes, machine guns, and depth charges — called also *PT*

PTC \,pē-,tē-'sē\ *n* (1932) : PHENYLTHIOCARBAMIDE

pterid- *or* **pterido-** *comb form* [Gk *pterid-, pteris;* akin to Gk *pteron* wing, feather — more at FEATHER] : fern ⟨*pterid*oid⟩ ⟨*pterido*logy⟩

pter·i·dine \'ter-ə-,dēn\ *n* [ISV *pter-* (fr. Gk *pteron*) + *-id* + *-ine;* fr. its being a factor in the pigments of butterfly wings] (ca. 1943) : a yellow crystalline bicyclic base $C_6H_4N_4$ that is a structural constituent esp. of various animal pigments

pter·i·dol·o·gy \,ter-ə-'däl-ə-jē\ *n* (1855) : the study of ferns — **pter·i·do·log·i·cal** \,ter-ə-də-'läj-i-kəl\ *adj* — **pter·i·dol·o·gist** \-'däl-ə-jəst\ *n*

pte·ri·do·phyte \tə-'rid-ə-,fīt, 'ter-əd-ō-\ *n* [deriv. of Gk *pterid-, pteris* fern + *phyton* plant — more at PHYT-] (1880) : any of a division (Pteridophyta) of vascular plants (as a fern) that have roots, stems, and leaves but lack flowers or seeds

pte·ri·do·sperm \tə-'rid-ə-,spərm, 'ter-əd-ō-\ *n* [ISV] (1904) : SEED FERN

pter·in \'ter-ən\ *n* [ISV *pter-* (fr. Gk *pteron* wing) + *-in*] (1934) : a compound that contains the bicyclic ring system characteristic of pteridine

ptero·dac·tyl \,ter-ə-'dak-tᵊl\ *n* [NL *Pterodactylus,* genus of reptiles, fr. Gk *pteron* wing + *daktylos* finger — more at FEATHER] (1830) : any of an order (Pterosauria) of extinct flying reptiles existing from the Lower Jurassic nearly to the close of the Mesozoic and having a featherless wing membrane that extends from the side of the body along the arm to the end of the greatly enlarged fourth digit

ptero·pod \'ter-ə-,päd\ *n* [NL *Pteropoda,* fr. Gk *pteron* wing + NL *-poda*] (1835) : any of a group (Pteropoda) of small gastropod mollusks having the anterior lobes of the foot expanded into broad thin winglike organs with which they swim

ptero·saur \'ter-ə-,só(ə)r\ *n* [deriv. of Gk *pteron* wing + *sauros* lizard] (1862) : PTERODACTYL

pter·o·yl·glu·tam·ic acid \'ter-ə-,wil-glü-,tam-ik-\ *n* [ISV *pteroyl* (the radical $(C_{13}H_{11}N_6O)CO$) + *glutamic acid*] (1943) : FOLIC ACID

pter·y·goid \'ter-ə-,gȯid\ *adj* [NL *pterygoides,* fr. Gk *pterygoeidēs,* lit., shaped like a wing, fr. *pteryg-, pteryx* wing; akin to Gk *pteron* wing — more at FEATHER] (1722) : of, relating to, or lying in the region of the inferior part of the sphenoid bone of the vertebrate skull — **pterygoid** *n*

pterygoid bone *n* (1722) : a horizontally placed bone or group of bones of the upper jaw or roof of the mouth in most lower vertebrates

pterygoid process *n* (1741) : a process extending downward from each side of the sphenoid bone in man and other mammals

pter·y·la \'ter-ə-lə\ *n, pl* **-lae** \-,lē, -,lī\ [NL, fr. Gk *pteron* + *hylē* wood, forest] (1867) : one of the definite areas of the skin of a bird on which feathers grow

Ptol·e·ma·ic \,täl-ə-'mā-ik\ *adj* [Gk *Ptolemaikos,* fr. *Ptolemaios* Ptolemy] (1674) **1** : of or relating to Ptolemy the geographer and astronomer who flourished at Alexandria about A.D. 130 **2** : of or relating to the Greco-Egyptian Ptolemies ruling Egypt from 323 to 30 B.C.

Ptolemaic system *n* (ca. 1771) : the system of planetary motions according to which the earth is at the center with the sun, moon, and planets revolving around it

pto·maine \'tō-ˌmān, tō-'\ *n* [It *ptomaina,* fr. Gk *ptōma* fall, fallen body, corpse, fr. *piptein* to fall — more at FEATHER] (1880) : any of various organic bases which are formed by the action of putrefactive bacteria on nitrogenous matter and some of which are poisonous

ptomaine poisoning *n* (1893) : food poisoning caused by bacteria or bacterial products

pto·sis \'tō-səs\ *n, pl* **pto·ses** \-ˌsēz\ [NL, fr. Gk *ptōsis* act of falling, fr. *piptein*] (1743) : a sagging or prolapse of an organ or part; *esp* : a drooping of the upper eyelid

pty·a·lin \'tī-ə-lən\ *n* [Gk *ptyalon* saliva, fr. *ptyein* to spit — more at SPEW] (1845) : an amylase found in the saliva of many animals that converts starch into sugar

pty·a·lism \-ˌliz-əm\ *n* [NL *ptyalismus,* fr. Gk *ptyalismos,* fr. *ptyalizein* to salivate, fr. *ptyalon*] (1676) : an excessive flow of saliva

pub \'pəb\ *n* (ca. 1859) **1** *chiefly Brit* : PUBLIC HOUSE 2 **2** : an establishment where alcoholic beverages are sold and consumed

pub crawler *n* (1910) : one who goes from bar to bar — **pub–crawl** *vi* — **pub crawl** *n*

pu·ber·tal \'pyü-bərt-ᵊl\ *or* **pu·ber·al** \'pyü-bə-rəl\ *adj* [*pubertal* fr. *puberty; puberal* fr. ML *puberalis,* fr. L *puber*] (1836) : of or relating to puberty

pu·ber·ty \'pyü-bərt-ē\ *n* [ME *puberte,* fr. L *pubertas,* fr. *puber* pubescent] (14c) **1** : the condition of being or the period of becoming first capable of reproducing sexually marked by maturing of the genital organs, development of secondary sex characteristics, and in the human and in higher primates by the first occurrence of menstruation in the female **2** : the age at which puberty occurs often construed legally as 14 in boys and 12 in girls

pu·ber·u·lent \pyü-'ber-(y)ə-lənt\ *adj* [L *puber* pubescent + E *-ulent* (as in *pulverulent*)] (ca. 1864) : covered with fine pubescence

pu·bes \'pyü-(ˌ)bēz\ *n, pl* **pubes** [NL, fr. L, manhood, body hair, pubic region; akin to L *puber* pubescent] (1570) **1** : the hair that appears on the lower part of the hypogastric region at puberty **2** : the pubic region

pu·bes·cence \pyü-'bes-ᵊn(t)s\ *n* (1646) **1** : the quality or state of being pubescent **2** : a pubescent covering or surface

pu·bes·cent \-ᵊnt\ *adj* [L *pubescent-, pubescens,* prp. of *pubescere* to reach puberty, become covered as with hair, fr. *pubes*] (1646) **1 a** : arriving at or having reached puberty **b** : of or relating to puberty **2** : covered with fine soft short hairs — compare VILLOUS

pu·bic \'pyü-bik\ *adj* (1831) : of, relating to, or situated in or near the region of the pubes or the pubis

pu·bis \'pyü-bəs\ *n, pl* **pu·bes** \-(ˌ)bēz\ [NL *os pubis,* lit., bone of the pubic region] (1597) : the ventral and anterior of the three principal bones composing either half of the pelvis

[1]**pub·lic** \'pəb-lik\ *adj* [ME *publique,* fr. MF, fr. L *publicus,* prob. alter. of *poplicus,* fr. *populus* the people] (15c) **1 a** : of, relating to, or affecting all the people or the whole area of a nation or state ⟨~ law⟩ **b** : of or relating to a government **c** : of, relating to, or being in the service of the community or nation ⟨an eminent figure in ~ life⟩ ⟨~ affairs⟩ **2 a** : of or relating to people in general : UNIVERSAL **b** : GENERAL, POPULAR **3** : of or relating to business or community interests as opposed to private affairs : SOCIAL **4** : devoted to the general or national welfare : HUMANITARIAN **5 a** : accessible to or shared by all members of the community **b** : capitalized in shares that can be freely traded on the open market ⟨a ~ company⟩ — compare CLOSE CORPORATION **6 a** : exposed to general view : OPEN **b** : WELL-KNOWN, PROMINENT **c** : PERCEPTIBLE, MATERIAL — **pub·lic·ness** *n*

[2]**public** *n* (15c) **1** : a place accessible or visible to the public — usu. used in the phrase *in public* **2** : the people as a whole : POPULACE **3** : a group of people having common interests or characteristics; *specif* : the group at which a particular activity or enterprise aims

public–address system *n* (1923) : an apparatus including a microphone and loudspeakers used for broadcasting to a large audience in an auditorium or out of doors

pub·li·can \'pəb-li-kən\ *n* [ME, fr. OF, fr. L *publicanus* tax farmer, fr. *publicum* public revenue, fr. neut. of *publicus*] (13c) **1 a** : a Jewish tax collector for the ancient Romans **b** : a collector of taxes or tribute **2** *chiefly Brit* : the licensee of a public house

public assistance *n* (1901) : government aid to needy, blind, aged, or disabled persons and to dependent children

pub·li·ca·tion \ˌpəb-lə-'kā-shən\ *n* [ME *publicacioun,* fr. MF *publication,* fr. LL *publication-, publicatio,* fr. L *publicatus,* pp. of *publicare,* fr. *publicus* public] (14c) **1** : the act or process of publishing **2** : a published work

public defender *n* (1918) : a lawyer usu. holding public office whose duty is to defend accused persons unable to pay for legal assistance

public domain *n* (1832) **1** : land owned directly by the government **2** : the realm embracing property rights that belong to the community at large, are unprotected by copyright or patent, and are subject to appropriation by anyone

public health *n* (1617) : the art and science dealing with the protection and improvement of community health by organized community effort and including preventive medicine and sanitary and social science

public house *n* (1658) **1** : INN, HOSTELRY **2** *chiefly Brit* : a licensed saloon or bar

pub·li·cist \'pəb-lə-səst\ *n* (1792) **1 a** : an expert in international law **b** : an expert or commentator on public affairs **2** : one that publicizes; *specif* : PRESS AGENT

pub·lic·i·ty \(ˌ)pə-'blis-ət-ē, -'blis-tē\ *n* (1791) **1** : the quality or state of being public **2 a** : an act or device designed to attract public interest; *specif* : information with news value issued as a means of gaining public attention or support **b** : the dissemination of information or promotional material **c** : paid advertising **d** : public attention or acclaim

pub·li·cize \'pəb-lə-ˌsīz\ *vt* **-cized; -ciz·ing** (1925) : to give publicity to

public land *n* (1789) : land owned by a government; *specif* : that part of the U.S. public domain subject to sale or disposal under the homestead laws

public law *n* (1773) **1** : a legislative enactment affecting the public at large **2** : a branch of law concerned with regulating the relations of individuals with the government and the organization and conduct of the government itself — compare PRIVATE LAW

pub·lic·ly \'pəb-li-klē\ *adv* (1567) **1** : in a manner observable by or in a place accessible to the public : OPENLY **2 a** : by the people generally **b** : by a government

public officer *n* (1925) : a person who holds a post to which he has been legally elected or appointed and who exercises governmental functions

public relations *n pl but usu sing in constr* (1807) : the business of inducing the public to have understanding for and goodwill toward a person, firm, or institution; *also* : the degree of understanding and goodwill achieved

public sale *n* (1678) : AUCTION 1

public school *n* (1580) **1** : an endowed secondary boarding school in Great Britain offering a classical curriculum and preparation for the universities or public service **2** : a free tax-supported school controlled by a local governmental authority

public servant *n* (1676) : a government official or employee

public service *n* (1570) **1** : the business of supplying a commodity (as electricity or gas) or service (as transportation) to any or all members of a community **2** : a service rendered in the public interest **3** : governmental employment; *esp* : CIVIL SERVICE

public–service corporation *n* (ca. 1904) : a quasi-public corporation

public speaking *n* (1762) **1** : the act or process of making speeches in public **2** : the art or science of effective oral communication with an audience ⟨took a course in *public speaking*⟩

pub·lic–spir·it·ed \ˌpəb-lik-'spir-ət-əd\ *adj* (1677) : motivated by devotion to the general welfare — **pub·lic–spir·it·ed·ness** *n*

public television *n* (1965) : television that provides cultural, informational, and instructional programs without commercials

public utility *n* (1903) : a business organization (as an electric company) performing a public service and subject to special governmental regulation

public works *n pl* (1676) : works (as schools, highways, docks) constructed for public use or enjoyment esp. when financed and owned by the government

pub·lish \'pəb-lish\ *vb* [ME *publishen,* modif. of MF *publier,* fr. L *publicare,* fr. *publicus* public] *vt* (14c) **1 a** : to make generally known **b** : to make public announcement of **2 a** : to place before the public : DISSEMINATE **b** : to produce or release for publication; *specif* : PRINT **c** : to issue the work of (an author) ~ *vi* **1** : to put out an edition **2** : to have one's work accepted for publication ⟨a ~*ing* scholar⟩ ***syn*** see DECLARE — **pub·lish·able** \-ə-bəl\ *adj*

pub·lish·er \-ər\ *n* (15c) : one that publishes; *esp* : a person or corporation whose business is publishing

pub·lish·ing \-iŋ\ *n* (ca. 1580) : the business or profession of the commercial production and issuance of literature, information, musical scores or sometimes recordings, or art ⟨newspaper ~⟩ ⟨microfilm ~⟩

puc·coon \(ˈ)pə-'kün\ *n* [fr. *puccoon* (in some Algonquian language of Virginia)] (ca. 1612) **1** : any of several American plants (as bloodroot) yielding a red or yellow pigment **2** : a pigment from a puccoon

puce \'pyüs\ *n* [F, lit., flea, fr. L *pulic-, pulex* — more at PSYLLA] (1787) : a dark red

[1]**puck** \'pək\ *n* [ME *puke,* fr. OE *pūca;* akin to ON *pūki* devil] (bef. 12c) **1** *archaic* : an evil spirit : DEMON **2** : a mischievous sprite : HOBGOBLIN; *specif, cap* : ROBIN GOODFELLOW

[2]**puck** *n* [E dial. *puck* to poke, hit, alter. of E [2]*poke*] (ca. 1890) : a vulcanized rubber disk used in ice hockey

pucka *var of* PUKKA

[1]**puck·er** \'pək-ər\ *vb* **puck·ered; puck·er·ing** \-(ə-)riŋ\ [prob. irreg. fr. [1]*poke*] *vi* (ca. 1598) : to become wrinkled or constricted ~ *vt* : to contract into folds or wrinkles

[2]**pucker** *n* (1744) : a fold or wrinkle in a normally even surface

puck·ery \'pək-(ə-)rē\ *adj* (1830) : that puckers or causes puckering

puck·ish \'pək-ish\ *adj* [[1]*puck*] (1874) : IMPISH, WHIMSICAL — **puck·ish·ly** *adv* — **puck·ish·ness** *n*

pud \'pu̇d\ *n, Brit* (1706) : PUDDING

pud·ding \'pu̇d-iŋ\ *n* [ME] (14c) **1** : BLOOD SAUSAGE **2 a** (1) : a boiled or baked soft food usu. with a cereal base ⟨corn ~⟩ (2) : a dessert of a soft, spongy, or thick creamy consistency ⟨chocolate ~⟩ (3) *Brit* : DESSERT 1 **b** : a dish often containing suet or having a suet crust and orig. boiled in a bag ⟨steak and kidney ~⟩

pudding stone *n* (1753) : CONGLOMERATE

[1]**pud·dle** \'pəd-ᵊl\ *n* [ME *podel;* akin to LG *pudel* puddle, OE *pudd* ditch] (14c) **1** : a very small pool of usu. dirty or muddy water **2 a** : an earthy mixture (as of clay, sand, and gravel) worked while wet into a compact mass that becomes impervious to water when dry **b** : a thin mixture of soil and water for puddling plants

[2]**puddle** *vb* **pud·dled; pud·dling** \'pəd-liŋ, -ᵊl-iŋ\ *vi* (15c) : to dabble or wade around in a puddle ~ *vt* **1** : to make muddy or turbid : MUDDLE **2 a** : to work (a wet mixture of earth or concrete) into a dense impervious mass **b** : to subject (iron) to the process of puddling **3 a** : to strew with puddles **b** : to compact (soil) esp. by working when too wet **c** : to dip the roots of (a plant) in a thin mud before transplanting — **pud·dler** \-lər, -ᵊl-ər\ *n*

puddle duck *n* (1877) : DABBLER b

puddle jumper *n, slang* (ca. 1942) : LIGHTPLANE

pud·dling \'pəd-liŋ, -ᵊl-iŋ\ *n* (1839) : the process of converting pig iron into wrought iron or rarely steel by subjecting it to heat and frequent stirring in a furnace in the presence of oxidizing substances

pu·den·cy \'pyüd-ᵊn-sē\ *n* [L *pudentia,* fr. *pudent-, pudens,* prp. of *pudēre* to be ashamed, make ashamed] (1611) : MODESTY

pu·den·dum \pyü-'den-dəm\ *n, pl* **-da** \-də\ [NL, sing. of L *pudenda,* fr. neut. pl. of *pudendus,* gerundive of *pudēre* to be ashamed] (1634) : the external genital organs of a human being and esp. of a woman — usu. used in pl. — **pu·den·dal** \-dᵊl\ *adj*

pudgy \'pəj-ē\ *adj* **pudg·i·er; -est** [origin unknown] (1836) : being short and plump : CHUBBY — **pudg·i·ness** *n*

pu·di·bund \'pyüd-ə-ˌbənd\ *adj* [L *pudibundus,* fr. *pudēre* to be ashamed + *-bundus* (as in *moribundus* moribund)] (ca. 1656) : PRUDISH

pueb·lo \pü-'eb-(ˌ)lō, 'pweb-, pyü-'eb-\ *n, pl* **-los** [Sp, village, lit., people, fr. L *populus*] (1808) **1 a** : the communal dwelling of an Indian village of Arizona, New Mexico, and adjacent areas consisting of contiguous flat-roofed stone or adobe houses in groups sometimes several stories high **b** : an Indian village of the southwestern U.S. **2** *cap* **a**

: a group of Indian peoples of the southwestern U.S. **b** : a member of any of these peoples

pu·er·ile \'pyů(-ə)r-əl, -,īl\ *adj* [F or L; F *puéril,* fr. L *puerilis,* fr. *puer* boy, child; akin to Gk *pais* boy, child — more at FEW] (1661) **1** : JUVENILE **2** : CHILDISH, SILLY ⟨~ remarks⟩ — **pu·er·ile·ly** \-ə(l)-lē, -,īl-lē\ *adv* — **pu·er·il·i·ty** \,pyů(-ə)r-'il-ət-ē\ *n*

pu·er·il·ism \'pyů(-ə)r-ə-,liz-əm, 'pyů(-ə)r-,ī-\ *n* (ca. 1924) : childish behavior esp. as a symptom of mental disorder

pu·er·per·al \pyü-'ər-p(ə-)rəl\ *adj* [L *puerpera* woman in childbirth, fr. *puer* child + *parere* to give birth to — more at PARE] (1768) : of, relating to, or occurring during childbirth or the period immediately following ⟨~ infection⟩ ⟨~ depression⟩

puerperal fever *n* (1768) : an abnormal condition that results from infection of the placental site following delivery or abortion and is characterized in mild form by fever but in serious cases may spread through the uterine wall or pass into the bloodstream — called also *childbed fever, puerperal sepsis*

pu·er·pe·ri·um \,pyü-ər-'pir-ē-əm\ *n, pl* **-ria** \-ē-ə\ [L, fr. *puerpera*] (ca. 1890) : the period between childbirth and the return of the uterus to its normal size

1puff \'pəf\ *vb* [ME *puffen,* fr. OE *pyffan*] *vi* (bef. 12c) **1 a** (1) : to blow in short gusts (2) : to exhale forcibly **b** : to breathe hard : PANT **c** : to emit small whiffs or clouds (as of smoke) often as an accompaniment to vigorous action ⟨~ at a pipe⟩ **2** : to speak or act in a scornful, conceited, or exaggerated manner **3 a** : to become distended : SWELL — usu. used with *up* **b** : to open or appear in or as if in a puff **4** : to form a chromosomal puff ~ *vt* **1 a** : to emit, propel, blow, or expel by or as if by puffs : WAFT **b** : to draw on (as a cigar, cigarette, or pipe) with intermittent exhalations of smoke **2 a** : to distend with or as if with air or gas : INFLATE **b** : to make proud or conceited : ELATE **c** (1) : to praise extravagantly and usu. with exaggeration (2) : ADVERTISE

2puff *n* (13c) **1 a** : an act or instance of puffing : WHIFF **b** : a slight explosive sound accompanying a puff **c** : a perceptible cloud or aura emitted in a puff **d** : DRAW 1a **2** : a light round hollow pastry made of puff paste **3 a** : a slight swelling : PROTUBERANCE **b** : a fluffy mass: as (1) : POUF 2 (2) : a small fluffy pad for applying cosmetic powder (3) : a soft loose roll of hair (4) : a quilted bed covering **4** : a commendatory notice or review **5** : an enlarged region of a chromosome that is associated with intensely active genes involved in RNA synthesis — **puff·i·ness** \'pəf-ē-nəs\ *n* — **puffy** \'pəf-ē\ *adj*

puff adder *n* (1789) : HOGNOSE SNAKE

puff·ball \'pəf-,bȯl\ *n* (1649) : any of various globose and often edible fungi (esp. family Lycoperdaceae) that discharge ripe spores in a smokelike cloud when pressed or struck

puff·er \'pəf-ər\ *n* (1629) **1** : one that puffs **2 a** : any of a family (Tetraodontidae) of chiefly tropical marine spiny-finned fishes which can distend themselves to a globular form and most of which are highly poisonous — called also *blowfish, globefish* **b** : any of various fish of the same order (Plectognathi) as the puffers

puff·ery \'pəf-(ə-)rē\ *n* (1782) : exaggerated commendation esp. for promotional purposes : HYPE

puf·fin \'pəf-ən\ *n* [ME *pophyn*] (1502) : any of several seabirds (genera *Fratercula* and *Lunda*) having a short neck and a deep grooved parti-colored laterally compressed bill

puff paste *n* (1611) : a pastry dough containing many alternating layers of butter and dough and used for making light flaky pastries

1pug \'pəg\ *n* [obs. *pug* (hobgoblin, monkey)] (1749) **1** : a small sturdy compact dog of a breed of Asian origin with a close coat, tightly curled tail, and broad wrinkled face **2 a** : PUG NOSE **b** : a close knot or coil of hair : BUN

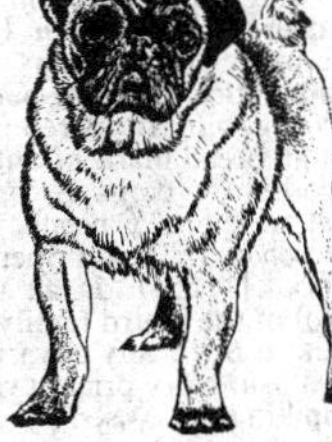

pug 1

2pug *vt* **pugged; pug·ging** [perh. alter. of *2poke*] (1843) **1** : to work and mix (as clay) when wet esp. to make more homogeneous and easier to handle (as in throwing or molding wares) **2** : to plug or pack with a substance (as clay or mortar) esp. for deadening sound

3pug *n* [by shortening & alter. fr. *pugilist*] (1858) : 1BOXER

4pug *n* [Hindi *pag* foot] (1865) : FOOTPRINT; *esp* : a print of a wild mammal

pug·ga·ree *or* **pug·a·ree** *or* **pug·gree** \'pəg-(ə-)rē\ *n* [Hindi *pagrī* turban] (1665) : a light scarf wrapped around a sun helmet or used as a hatband

pu·gi·lism \'pyü-jə-,liz-əm\ *n* [L *pugil* boxer; akin to L *pugnus* fist — more at PUNGENT] (1791) : 2BOXING — **pu·gi·lis·tic** \,pyü-jə-'lis-tik\ *adj*

pu·gi·list \'pyü-jə-ləst\ *n* (1790) : FIGHTER; *esp* : a professional boxer

pug·mark \'pəg-,märk\ *n* (1922) : 4PUG

pug mill *n* [2*pug*] (1824) : a machine in which materials (as clay and water) are mixed, blended, or kneaded into a desired consistency

pug·na·cious \,pəg-'nā-shəs\ *adj* [L *pugnac-, pugnax,* fr. *pugnare* to fight — more at PUNGENT] (1642) : having a belligerent nature : TRUCULENT, COMBATIVE **syn** see BELLIGERENT — **pug·na·cious·ly** *adv* — **pug·na·cious·ness** *n* — **pug·nac·i·ty** \-'nas-ət-ē\ *n*

pug nose *n* [1*pug*] (1778) : a nose having a slightly concave bridge and flattened nostrils — **pug–nosed** \'pəg-'nōzd\ *adj*

puis·ne \'pyü-nē\ *adj* [MF *puisné* younger — more at PUNY] *chiefly Brit* (1688) : inferior in rank ⟨~ judge⟩ — **puisne** *n*

puis·sance \'pwis-ᵊn(t)s, 'pyü-ə-sən(t)s, pyü-'is-ᵊn(t)s\ *n* [ME, fr. MF, fr. OF, fr. *puissant* powerful, fr. *poeir* to be able, be powerful — more at POWER] (15c) : STRENGTH, POWER — **puis·sant** \-ᵊnt, -sənt\ *adj* — **puis·sant·ly** *adv*

puke \'pyük\ *vb* **puked; puk·ing** [origin unknown] (1600) : VOMIT — **puke** *n*

puk·ka \'pək-ə\ *adj* [Hindi *pakkā* cooked, ripe, solid, fr. Skt *pakva;* akin to Gk *pessein* to cook — more at COOK] (1698) : GENUINE, AUTHENTIC; *also* : FIRST-CLASS

pul \'pül\ *n, pl* **puls** \'pülz\ *or* **pul** [Per *pūl*] (1927) — see *afghani* at MONEY table

pu·la \'p(y)ü-lə\ *n, pl* **pula** [native name in Botswana] (1976) — see MONEY table

Pu·las·ki \pə-'las-kē, pyü-\ *n* [Edward C. *Pulaski,* 20th cent. Am. forest ranger] (1924) : a single-bit ax with an adz-shaped hoe extending from the back

pul·chri·tude \'pəl-krə-,t(y)üd\ *n* [ME, fr. L *pulchritudin-, pulchritudo,* fr. *pulchr-, pulcher* beautiful] (15c) : physical comeliness — **pul·chri·tu·di·nous** \,pəl-krə-'t(y)üd-nəs, -ᵊn-əs\ *adj*

pule \'pyü(ə)l\ *vi* **puled; pul·ing** [prob. imit.] (1534) : WHINE, WHIMPER — **pul·er** *n*

pu·li \'pu̇l-ē, 'pyül-\ *n, pl* **pu·lik** \-ik\ *or* **pulis** \-ēz\ [Hung] (1936) : any of a breed of medium-sized Hungarian sheepdogs that have a long usu. corded coat

Pu·lit·zer prize \,pu̇l-ət-sər-, ,pyü-lət-\ *n* (1918) : any of various annual prizes (as for outstanding literary or journalistic achievement) established by the will of Joseph Pulitzer

1pull \'pu̇l\ *vb* [ME *pullen,* fr. OE *pullian*] *vt* (bef. 12c) **1 a** : to draw out from the skin ⟨~ feathers from a rooster's tail⟩ **b** : to pluck from a plant or by the roots ⟨~ flowers⟩ ⟨~ turnips⟩ **c** : EXTRACT ⟨~ a tooth⟩ **2 a** : to exert force upon so as to cause or tend to cause motion toward the force **b** : to stretch (cooling candy) repeatedly ⟨~ taffy⟩ **c** : to strain abnormally ⟨~ a tendon⟩ **d** : to hold back (a racehorse) from winning **e** : to work (an oar) by drawing back strongly **3** : to hit (a ball) toward the left from a right-handed swing or toward the right from a left-handed swing — compare PUSH **4** : to draw apart : REND, TEAR **5** : to print (as a proof) by impression **6** : REMOVE ⟨~ a crankshaft⟩ ⟨~*ed* the pitcher in the third inning⟩ **7** : to bring (a weapon) into the open ⟨~*ed* a knife⟩ **8** : COMMIT, PERPETRATE ⟨~ a robbery⟩ **9** : to draw the support or attention of : ATTRACT ⟨~ votes⟩ **10** : to demand or obtain an advantage over someone by the assertion of (as rank or superiority) ~ *vi* **1 a** : to use force in drawing, dragging, or tugging **b** : to move esp. through the exercise of mechanical energy ⟨the car ~*ed* out of the driveway⟩ **c** (1) : to take a drink (2) : to draw hard in smoking ⟨~*ed* at a pipe⟩ **d** : to strain against the bit **2** : to draw a gun **3** : to admit of being pulled **4** : to feel or express strong sympathy : ROOT ⟨~*ing* for my team to win⟩ **5** *of an offensive lineman in football* : to move back from the line of scrimmage and toward one flank to provide blocking for a ballcarrier — **pull·er** *n*

syn PULL, DRAW, DRAG, HAUL, TUG mean to cause to move in the direction determined by an applied force. PULL is the general term but may emphasize the force exerted rather than resulting motion; DRAW implies a smoother, steadier motion and generally a lighter force than PULL; DRAG suggests great effort overcoming resistance or friction; HAUL implies sustained pulling or dragging of heavy or bulky objects; TUG applies to strenuous often spasmodic efforts to move.

— **pull a fast one** : to perpetrate a trick or fraud — **pull a punch** *or* **pull punches** : to refrain from using all the force at one's disposal — **pull oneself together** : to regain one's self-possession — **pull one's leg** : to deceive someone playfully : HOAX — **pull one's weight** : to do one's full share of the work — **pull out all the stops** : to use all one's resources without restraint — **pull stakes** *or* **pull up stakes** : to move out : LEAVE — **pull strings** *or* **pull wires** : to exert secret influence or control — **pull the rug from under** : to remove support or assistance from — **pull the string** : to throw a change-up — **pull the wool over one's eyes** : to blind to the true situation : HOODWINK — **pull together** : to work in harmony : COOPERATE

2pull *n, often attrib* (14c) **1 a** : the act or an instance of pulling **b** (1) : a draft of liquid (2) : an inhalation of smoke **c** : the effort expended in moving ⟨a long ~ uphill⟩ **d** : force required to overcome resistance to pulling ⟨trigger ~⟩ **2 a** : ADVANTAGE **b** : special influence **3** : PROOF 6a **4** : a device for pulling something or for operating by pulling ⟨drawer ~⟩ **5** : a force that attracts, compels, or influences : ATTRACTION

pull away *vi* (ca. 1934) **1** : to draw oneself back or away : WITHDRAW **2** : to move off or ahead

pull·back \'pu̇l-,bak\ *n* (1668) : a pulling back; *esp* : an orderly withdrawal of troops from a position or area

pull down *vt* (1513) **1 a** : DEMOLISH, DESTROY **b** : to hunt down : OVERCOME **2 a** : to bring to a lower level : REDUCE **b** : to depress in health, strength, or spirits **3** : to draw as wages or salary

pul·let \'pu̇l-ət\ *n* [ME *polet* young fowl, fr. MF *poulet,* fr. OF, dim. of *poul* cock, fr. LL *pullus,* fr. L, young of an animal, chicken, sprout — more at FOAL] (14c) : a young hen; *specif* : a hen of the domestic fowl less than a year old

pul·ley \'pu̇l-ē\ *n, pl* **pulleys** [ME *pouley,* fr. MF *poulie,* prob. deriv. of Gk *polos* axis, pole] (14c) **1** : a sheave or small wheel with a grooved rim and with or without the block in which it runs used singly with a rope or chain to change the direction and point of application of a pulling force and in various combinations to increase the applied force esp. for lifting weights **2** : a pulley or pulleys with ropes to form a tackle that constitutes one of the simple machines **3** : a wheel used to transmit power by means of a band, belt, cord, rope, or chain passing over its rim

pull in *vt* (1605) **1** : CHECK, RESTRAIN **2** : ARREST ~ *vi* : to arrive at a destination or come to a stop

Pull·man \'pu̇l-mən\ *n* [George M. *Pullman*] (1867) **1** : a railroad passenger car with specially comfortable furnishings for day or esp. for night travel **2** : a large suitcase — called also *Pullman case*

pull off *vt* (1883) : to carry out despite difficulties : accomplish successfully against odds

pul·lo·rum disease \pə-'lōr-əm-, -'lȯr-\ *n* [NL *pullorum,* fr. L, of chickens (gen. pl. of *pullus*)] (1929) : a destructive typically diarrheal salmonellosis of the chicken and less often other birds caused by a bacterium (*Salmonella pullorum*) which is transmitted either through the egg or from chick to chick

\ə\ abut \ᵊ\ kitten, F table \ər\ further \a\ ash \ā\ ace \ä\ cot, cart \au̇\ out \ch\ chin \e\ bet \ē\ easy \g\ go \i\ hit \ī\ ice \j\ job \ŋ\ sing \ō\ go \ȯ\ law \ȯi\ boy \th\ thin \t͟h\ the \ü\ loot \u̇\ foot \y\ yet \zh\ vision \à, k̟, ⁿ, œ, œ̄, ue, ue̅, ʸ\ see Guide to Pronunciation

pull·out \'pu̇l-ˌau̇t\ *n* (1825) **1 :** the act or an instance of pulling out: as **a :** the action in which an airplane goes from a dive to horizontal flight **b :** PULLBACK **2 :** something that can be pulled out

pull out \pu̇l-'au̇t\ *vi* (1855) **1 :** LEAVE, DEPART **2 :** WITHDRAW

[1]**pull·over** \'pu̇l-ˌō-vər\ *n* (1899) **:** a pullover garment

[2]**pullover** \ˌpu̇l-ˌō-vər\ *adj* (1907) **:** put on by being pulled over the head

pull over \pu̇-'lō-vər\ *vi* (1930) **:** to steer one's vehicle to the side of the road

pull round *vi* (1891) **:** to regain one's health **~** *vt* **:** to restore to good health

pull through *vi* (1852) **:** to survive a dangerous or difficult situation **~** *vt* **:** to help survive a dangerous or difficult situation

pul·lu·late \'pəl-yə-ˌlāt\ *vi* **-lat·ed; -lat·ing** [L *pullulatus,* pp. of *pullulare,* fr. *pullulus,* dim. of *pullus* chicken, sprout — more at FOAL] (1619) **1 a :** GERMINATE, SPROUT **b :** to breed or produce freely **2 :** SWARM, TEEM — **pul·lu·la·tion** \ˌpəl-yə-'lā-shən\ *n*

pull–up \'pu̇l-ˌəp\ *n* (1938) **:** CHIN-UP

pull up \pu̇l-'əp\ *vt* (1623) **1 :** to bring to a stop **:** HALT **2 :** CHECK, REBUKE **~** *vi* **1 a :** to check oneself **b :** to come to a halt **:** STOP **2 :** to draw even with others in a race

pul·mo·nary \'pu̇l-mə-ˌner-ē, 'pəl-\ *adj* [L *pulmonarius,* fr. *pulmon-, pulmo* lung; akin to Gk *pleumōn* lung] (1704) **1 :** relating to, functioning like, or associated with the lungs **2 :** PULMONATE **3 :** carried on by the lungs

pulmonary artery *n* (1704) **:** an artery that conveys venous blood from the heart to the lungs — see HEART illustration

pulmonary vein *n* (1704) **:** a valveless vein that returns oxygenated blood from the lungs to the heart

[1]**pul·mo·nate** \'pu̇l-mə-ˌnāt, 'pəl-\ *n* (ca. 1842) **:** a pulmonate gastropod

[2]**pulmonate** *adj* [L *pulmon-, pulmo* lung] (1862) **1 :** having lungs or organs resembling lungs **2 :** of or relating to a large order (Pulmonata) of gastropod mollusks having a lung or respiratory sac and comprising most land snails and slugs and many freshwater snails

pul·mon·ic \pu̇l-'män-ik, ˌpəl-\ *adj* [L *pulmon-, pulmo*] (1661) **:** PULMONARY

pul·mo·tor \'pu̇l-ˌmōt-ər, 'pəl-\ *n* [fr. *Pulmotor,* a trademark] (1909) **:** a respiratory apparatus for pumping oxygen or air into and out of the lungs (as of an asphyxiated person)

[1]**pulp** \'pəlp\ *n* [MF *poulpe,* fr. L *pulpa* flesh, pulp] (1563) **1 a** (1) **:** the soft, succulent part of a fruit usu. composed of mesocarp (2) **:** stem pith when soft and spongy **b :** a soft mass of vegetable matter (as of apples) from which most of the water has been extracted by pressure **c :** the soft sensitive tissue that fills the central cavity of a tooth **d :** a material prepared by chemical or mechanical means from various materials (as rags but chiefly from wood) and used in making paper and cellulose products **2 :** pulverized ore mixed with water **3 a :** pulpy condition or character **b :** something in such a condition or having such a character **4 :** a magazine or book printed on cheap paper (as newsprint) and often dealing with sensational material — **pulp·i·ness** \'pəl-pē-nəs\ *n* — **pulpy** \'pəl-pē\ *adj*

[2]**pulp** *vt* (1683) **1 :** to reduce to pulp **:** cause to appear pulpy **2 :** to deprive of the pulp **3 :** to produce or reproduce (written matter) in pulp form **~** *vi* **:** to become pulp or pulpy — **pulp·er** *n*

pulp·al \'pəl-pəl\ *adj* (1903) **:** of or relating to pulp esp. of a tooth ⟨a ~ abscess⟩ — **pulp·al·ly** \'pəl-pə-lē\ *adv*

pul·pit \'pu̇l-ˌpit *also* 'pəl-, -pət\ *n* [ME, fr. LL *pulpitum,* fr. L, staging, platform] (14c) **1 :** an elevated platform or high reading desk used in preaching or conducting a worship service **2 a :** the preaching profession **b :** a preaching position

pulp·wood \'pəlp-ˌwu̇d\ *n* (1885) **:** a wood (as of aspen, hemlock, pine, or spruce) used in making pulp for paper

pul·que \'pül-ˌkā; 'pül-kē, 'pu̇l-\ *n* [MexSp] (1693) **:** a Mexican beverage made from the fermented juice of various magueys

pul·sant \'pəl-sənt\ *adj* (1709) **:** pulsating with activity

pul·sar \'pəl-ˌsär\ *n* [*pulse* + *-ar* (as in *quasar*)] (1968) **:** a celestial source of pulsating radio waves, X rays, or visible light characterized by a short relatively invariable interval (as .033 second) between pulses that is held to be a rotating neutron star

pul·sate \'pəl-ˌsāt *also* ˌpəl-'\ *vi* **pul·sat·ed; pul·sat·ing** [L *pulsatus,* pp. of *pulsare,* fr. *pulsus,* pp. of *pellere*] (1794) **1 :** to exhibit a pulse or pulsation **:** BEAT **2 :** to throb or move rhythmically **:** VIBRATE

pul·sa·tile \'pəl-sət-ᵊl, -sə-ˌtīl\ *adj* (1541) **:** of or marked by pulsation

pul·sa·tion \ˌpəl-'sā-shən\ *n* (1541) **1 :** rhythmical throbbing or vibrating (as of an artery); *also* **:** a single beat or throb **2 :** a periodically recurring alternate increase and decrease of a quantity (as pressure, volume, or voltage)

pul·sa·tor \'pəl-ˌsāt-ər, ˌpəl-'\ *n* (1890) **:** something (as a pulsometer pump) that beats or throbs in working

[1]**pulse** \'pəls\ *n* [ME *puls,* fr. OF *pouls* porridge, fr. L *pult-, puls;* akin to L *pollen* fine flour — more at POLLEN] (13c) **:** the edible seeds of various leguminous crops (as peas, beans, or lentils); *also* **:** a plant yielding pulse

[2]**pulse** *n* [ME *puls,* fr. MF *pouls,* fr. L *pulsus,* lit., beating, fr. *pulsus,* pp. of *pellere* to drive, push, beat — more at FELT] (14c) **1 :** a regular throbbing caused in the arteries by the contractions of the heart; *also* **:** a single excursion of such throbbing **2 a :** underlying sentiment or opinion or an indication of it **b :** VITALITY **3 a :** rhythmical beating, vibrating, or sounding **b :** BEAT, THROB **4 a :** a transient variation of a quantity (as electrical current or voltage) whose value is normally constant **b** (1) **:** an electromagnetic wave or modulation thereof of brief duration (2) **:** a brief disturbance of pressure in a medium; *esp* **:** a sound wave or short train of sound waves **5 :** a dose of a substance esp. when applied over a short period of time ⟨*pulse*-labeled DNA⟩

[3]**pulse** *vb* **pulsed; puls·ing** *vt* (1549) **1 :** to drive by or as if by a pulsation **2 :** to cause to pulsate **3 a :** to produce or modulate (as electromagnetic waves) in the form of pulses ⟨*pulsed* waves⟩ **b :** to cause (an apparatus) to produce pulses **~** *vi* **:** to exhibit a pulse or pulsation **:** THROB — **puls·er** *n*

pulse–jet engine \ˌpəls-ˌjet-\ *n* (1949) **:** a jet engine designed to produce a pulsating thrust by the intermittent flow of hot gases

pul·sion \'pəl-shən\ *n* [LL *pulsion-, pulsio,* fr. L *pulsus,* pp.] (1656) **:** PROPULSION

pul·som·e·ter \ˌpəl-'säm-ət-ər\ *n* [ISV] (ca. 1875) **:** a pump with valves for raising water by steam and atmospheric pressure without intervention of a piston

pul·ver·a·ble \'pəlv-(ə-)rə-bəl\ *adj* (ca. 1657) **:** capable of being pulverized

pul·ver·ize \'pəl-və-ˌrīz\ *vb* **-ized; -iz·ing** [MF *pulveriser,* fr. LL *pulverizare,* fr. L *pulver-, pulvis* dust, powder — more at POLLEN] *vt* (1585) **1 :** to reduce (as by crushing, beating, or grinding) to very small particles **:** ATOMIZE **2 :** ANNIHILATE, DEMOLISH **~** *vi* **:** to become pulverized — **pul·ver·iz·able** \-ˌrī-zə-bəl\ *adj* — **pul·ver·i·za·tion** \ˌpəlv-(ə-)rə-'zā-shən\ *n* — **pul·ver·iz·er** \'pəl-və-ˌrī-zər\ *n*

pul·ver·u·lent \ˌpəl-'ver-(y)ə-lənt\ *adj* [L *pulverulentus* dusty, fr. *pulver-, pulvis*] (ca. 1656) **1 :** consisting of or reducible to fine powder **2 :** being or looking dusty **:** CRUMBLY

pul·vil·lus \ˌpəl-'vil-əs\ *n, pl* **-vil·li** \-'vil-ˌī, -(ˌ)ē\ [NL, fr. L, dim. of *pulvinus*] (ca. 1826) **:** one of the lobed hairy adhesive organs that terminate the feet of true flies

pul·vi·nus \ˌpəl-'vī-nəs, -'vē-\ *n, pl* **-vi·ni** \-'vī-ˌnī, -'vē-(ˌ)nē\ [NL, fr. L, cushion] (1857) **:** a mass of large thin-walled cells surrounding a vascular strand at the base of a petiole or petiolule and functioning in turgor movements of leaves or leaflets

pu·ma \'p(y)ü-mə\ *n, pl* **pumas** *also* **puma** [Sp, fr. Quechua] (1777) **:** COUGAR; *also* **:** the fur or pelt of a cougar

[1]**pum·ice** \'pəm-əs\ *n* [ME *pomis,* fr. MF, fr. L *pumic-, pumex* — more at FOAM] (15c) **:** a volcanic glass full of cavities and very light in weight used esp. in powder form for smoothing and polishing — **pu·mi·ceous** \pyü-'mish-əs, ˌpə-\ *adj*

[2]**pumice** *vt* **pum·iced; pum·ic·ing** (15c) **:** to dress or finish with pumice

pum·ic·ite \'pəm-ə-ˌsīt\ *n* (1916) **:** PUMICE

pum·mel \'pəm-əl\ *vb* **-meled** *also* **-melled; -mel·ing** *also* **-mel·ling** \-(ə-)liŋ\ [alter. of *pommel*] (1548) **:** POUND, BEAT

[1]**pump** \'pəmp\ *n* [ME *pumpe, pompe,* fr. MLG *pumpe* or MD *pompe,* prob. fr. Sp *bomba,* of imit. origin] (15c) **1 :** a device that raises, transfers, or compresses fluids or that attenuates gases esp. by suction or pressure or both **2 :** HEART **3 :** an act or the process of pumping **4 :** electromagnetic radiation for pumping atoms or molecules **5 :** a mechanism (as the sodium pump) for pumping atoms, ions, or molecules

[2]**pump** *vi* (1508) **1 :** to work a pump **:** raise or move a fluid with a pump **2 :** to exert oneself to pump or as if to pump something **3 :** to move in a manner that resembles the action of a pump handle **~** *vt* **1 a :** to raise (as water) with a pump **b :** to draw fluid from with a pump **2 :** to pour forth, deliver, or draw with or as if with a pump ⟨~*ed* money into the economy⟩ ⟨~ new life into the classroom⟩ **3 a :** to question persistently **b :** to elicit by persistent questioning **4 a :** to operate by manipulating a lever **b :** to manipulate as if operating a pump handle ⟨~*ed* his hand warmly⟩ **c :** to cause to move with an action resembling that of a pump handle ⟨a runner ~*ing* her arms⟩ **5 :** to transport (as ions) against a concentration gradient by the expenditure of energy **6 a :** to raise (atoms or molecules) to a higher energy level by exposure to usu. electromagnetic radiation at one of the resonant frequencies so that reemission may occur at another frequency resulting in amplification or sustained oscillation **b :** to expose (as a laser, semiconductor, or crystal) to radiation in the process of pumping — **pump iron :** to lift weights

[3]**pump** *n* [origin unknown] (1555) **:** a low shoe that grips the foot chiefly at the toe and heel

pumped storage *n* (1927) **:** a hydroelectric system in which electricity is generated during periods of greatest consumption by the use of water that has been pumped into a reservoir at a higher altitude during periods of low consumption

pump·er \'pəm-pər\ *n* (1660) **:** one that pumps; *esp* **:** a fire truck equipped with a pump

pum·per·nick·el \'pəm-pər-ˌnik-əl\ *n* [G, perh. fr. *pumpern* flatulence + *nickel* goblin; fr. its reputed indigestibility] (1839) **:** a dark coarse sourdough bread made of unbolted rye flour

pump·kin \÷'pəŋ-kən, 'pəm(p)-kən\ *n, often attrib* [alter. of earlier *pumpion,* modif. of F *popon, pompon* melon, pumpkin, fr. L *pepon-, pepo,* fr. Gk *pepōn,* fr. *pepōn* ripened; akin to Gk *pessein* to cook, ripen — more at COOK] (1654) **1 a :** the usu. round orange fruit of a vine (*Cucurbita pepo*) of the gourd family widely cultivated as food **b :** WINTER CROOKNECK **c** *Brit* **:** any of various large-fruited winter squashes (*C. maxima*) **2 :** a usu. hairy prickly vine that produces pumpkins

pump·kin·seed \-ˌsēd\ *n* (1814) **1 :** a small brilliantly colored No. American freshwater sunfish (*Lepomis gibbosus*) **2 :** BLUEGILL

pump priming *n* (1936) **:** government investment expenditures designed to induce a self-sustaining expansion of economic activity

pump up *vt* (1791) **1 a :** to fill with enthusiasm or excitement **b :** to fill with or as if with air **:** INFLATE **2 :** to work up by effort

[1]**pun** \'pən\ *n* [perh. fr. It *puntiglio* fine point, quibble — more at PUNCTILIO] (1662) **:** the usu. humorous use of a word in such a way as to suggest two or more of its meanings or the meaning of another word similar in sound

[2]**pun** *vi* **punned; pun·ning** (1670) **:** to make puns

pu·na \'pü-nə\ *n* [AmerSp, fr. Quechua] (1613) **1 :** a treeless windswept tableland or basin in the higher Andes **2 :** a cold mountain wind in Peru

[1]**punch** \'pənch\ *vb* [ME *punchen,* fr. MF *poinçonner* to prick, stamp, fr. *poinçon* puncheon] *vt* (14c) **1 a :** PROD, POKE **b :** DRIVE, HERD ⟨~*ing* cattle⟩ **2 a :** to strike with a forward thrust esp. of the fist **b :** to drive or push forcibly by or as if by a punch **c :** to hit (a ball) with less than a full swing **3 :** to emboss, cut, perforate, or make with or as if with a punch **4 a :** to push down so as to produce a desired result ⟨~ buttons on a jukebox⟩ **b :** to hit or press down the operating mechanism of ⟨~ a time clock⟩ ⟨~ a typewriter⟩ **c :** to produce by or as if by punching keys ⟨~ out a tune on the piano⟩ ⟨a teletypewriter ~*ing* out the news⟩ **d :** to enter (as data) by punching keys **5 :** to give emphasis to **~** *vi* **:** to perform the action of punching something — **punch·er** *n*

[2]**punch** *n* (1580) **1 :** the action of punching **2 :** a quick blow with or as if with the fist **3 :** effective energy or forcefulness ⟨a story that packs a ~⟩ ⟨political ~⟩ — **punch·less** \'pənch-ləs\ *adj* — **to the punch :** to the first blow or to decisive action — usu. used with *beat*

³**punch** *n* [prob. short for *puncheon*] (1505) **1 a** : a tool usu. in the form of a short rod of steel that is variously shaped at one end for different operations (as forming, perforating, embossing, or cutting) **b** : a short tapering steel rod for driving the heads of nails below a surface **c** : a steel die faced with a letter in relief that is forced into a softer metal to form an intaglio matrix from which foundry type is cast **d** : a device or machine for cutting holes or notches (as in paper or cardboard) **2** : a hole or notch from a perforating operation

⁴**punch** *n* [perh. fr. Hindi *pāc* five, fr. Skt *pañca*; akin to Gk *pente* five; fr. its orig. having five ingredients — more at FIVE] (1632) : a hot or cold drink that is usu. a combination of hard liquor, wine, or beer and nonalcoholic beverages; *also* : a drink that is a mixture of nonalcoholic beverages

Punch–and–Judy show \ˌpən-chən-ˈjüd-ē-\ *n* (1876) : a traditional puppet show in which the little hook-nosed humpback Punch fights comically with his wife Judy

punch-ball \ˈpənch-ˌbȯl\ *n* (1932) : baseball adapted to playing in small areas and marked by the use of a rubber ball hit with a closed fist instead of a bat

punch-board \-ˌbȯ(ə)rd, -ˌbȯ(ə)rd\ *n* (ca. 1912) : a small board that has many holes each filled with a rolled-up printed slip to be punched out on payment of a nominal sum in an effort to obtain a slip that entitles the player to a designated prize

punch bowl *n* (1692) : a large bowl from which a beverage (as punch) is served

punch card *n* (1921) : a card in which holes are punched in designated positions to represent data — called also *Hollerith card, punched card*

punch–drunk \ˈpənch-ˌdrəŋk\ *adj* [²punch] (1918) **1** : suffering cerebral injury from many minute brain hemorrhages as a result of repeated head blows received in boxing **2** : behaving as if punch-drunk : DAZED, CONFUSED

¹**pun-cheon** \ˈpən-chən\ *n* [ME *ponson*, fr. MF *poinçon* pointed tool, king post, fr. (assumed) VL *punction-, punctio* pointed tool, fr. *punctiare* to prick, fr. L *punctus*, pp. of *pungere* to prick — more at PUNGENT] (14c) **1** : a pointed tool for piercing or for working on stone **2 a** : a short upright framing timber **b** : a split log or heavy slab with the face smoothed **3** : a figured stamp die or punch used esp. by goldsmiths, cutlers, and engravers

²**puncheon** *n* [ME *poncion*, fr. MF *ponchon, poinçon*, of unknown origin] (15c) **1** : a large cask of varying capacity **2** : any of various units of liquid capacity (as a unit equal to 70 gallons)

punch in *vi* (1926) : to record the time of one's arrival or beginning work by punching a time clock

pun-chi-nel-lo \ˌpən-chə-ˈnel-(ˌ)ō\ *n* [modif. of It dial. *polecenella*] (1666) **1** *cap* : a fat short humpbacked clown or buffoon in Italian puppet shows **2** *pl* **-los** : a squat grotesque person

punching bag *n* (ca. 1889) : a stuffed or inflated bag that is usu. suspended for free movement and that is punched for exercise or for training in boxing

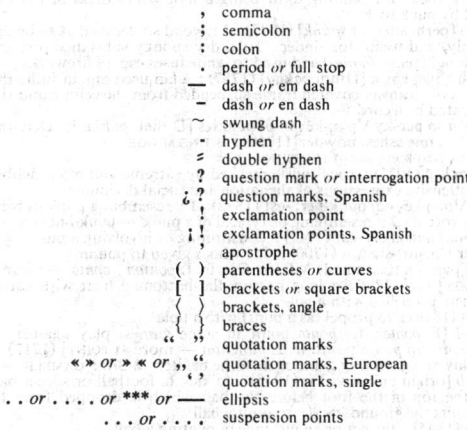

Punchinello

punch line *n* (1921) : the sentence, statement, or phrase (as in a joke) that makes the point

punch–out \ˈpən-ˌchaůt\ *n* (1928) : FIST-FIGHT

punch out \ˌpən-ˈchaůt\ *vi* (1973) : to record the time of one's stopping work or departure by punching a time clock ~ *vt* : to beat up

punch press *n* (1911) : a press equipped with cutting, shaping, or combination dies for working on material (as metal)

punch–up \ˈpən-ˌchəp\ *n, chiefly Brit* (1958) : FISTFIGHT

punchy \ˈpən-chē\ *adj* **punch·i·er; -est** (1917) **1** : having punch : FORCEFUL **2** : PUNCH-DRUNK

punc-tate \ˈpəŋ(k)-ˌtāt\ *adj* [NL *punctatus*, fr. L *punctum* point — more at POINT] (ca. 1760) **1** : marked with minute spots or depressions ⟨a ~ leaf⟩ **2** : characterized by dots or points ⟨~ skin lesions⟩ — **punc-ta-tion** \ˌpəŋ(k)-ˈtā-shən\ *n*

punc-til-io \ˌpəŋ(k)-ˈtil-ē-ˌō\ *n, pl* **-i-os** [It & Sp; It *puntiglio* point of honor, scruple, fr. Sp *puntillo*, fr. dim. of *punto* point, fr. L *punctum*] (1596) **1** : a minute detail of conduct in a ceremony or in observance of a code **2** : careful observance of forms (as in social conduct)

punc-til-i-ous \-ē-əs\ *adj* (1634) : marked by or concerned about precise exact accordance with the details of codes or conventions *syn* see CAREFUL — **punc-til-i-ous-ly** *adv* — **punc-til-i-ous-ness** *n*

punc-tu-al \ˈpəŋ(k)-chə(-wə)l\ *adj* [ME, fr. ML *punctualis*, fr. L *punctus* pricking, point, fr. *punctus*, pp. of *pungere* to prick — more at PUNGENT] (1675) : being on time : PROMPT — **punc-tu-al-i-ty** \ˌpəŋ(k)-chə-ˈwal-ət-ē\ *n* — **punc-tu-al-ly** \ˈpəŋ(k)-chə-(wə)-lē\ *adv*

punc-tu-ate \ˈpəŋ(k)-chə-ˌwāt\ *vb* **-at·ed; -at·ing** [ML *punctuatus*, pp. of *punctuare* to point, provide with punctuation marks, fr. L *punctus* point] *vt* (ca. 1818) **1** : to mark or divide (written matter) with punctuation marks **2** : to break into or interrupt at intervals ⟨the steady click of her needles *punctuated* the silence —Edith Wharton⟩ ~ *vi* : to use punctuation marks — **punc-tu-a-tor** \-ˌwāt-ər\ *n*

punc-tu-a-tion \ˌpəŋ(k)-chə-ˈwā-shən\ *n* (1539) **1** : the act of punctuating : the state of being punctuated **2** : the act or practice of inserting standardized marks or signs in written matter to clarify the meaning and separate structural units; *also* : a system of punctuation

punctuation mark *n* (1860) : any of various standardized marks or signs used in punctuation

¹**punc-ture** \ˈpəŋ(k)-chər\ *n* [L *punctura*, fr. *punctus*, pp. of *pungere*] (15c) **1** : an act of puncturing **2** : a hole, wound, or perforation made by puncturing **3** : a minute depression

²**puncture** *vb* **punc-tured; punc-tur-ing** \ˈpəŋ(k)-chə-riŋ, ˈpəŋ(k)-chə-shriŋ\ *vt* (1699) **1** : to pierce with or as if with a pointed instrument or object **2** : to make useless or ineffective as if by a puncture : DEFLATE ~ *vi* : to become punctured

puncture vine *n* (1911) : a European annual prostrate weed (*Tribulus terrestris* of the family Zygophyllaceae) that has been introduced into

the western U.S. and has compound leaves and hard spiny pods noted for puncturing automobile tires and for lowering the quality of hay and forage crops — called also *caltrop, puncture-weed*

pun-dit \ˈpən-dət\ *n* [Hindi *paṇḍit*, fr. Skt *paṇḍita*, fr. *paṇḍita* learned] (1672) **1** : PANDIT **2** : a learned man : TEACHER **3** : one who gives opinions in an authoritative manner : CRITIC — **pun-dit-ry** \-də-trē\ *n*

pung \ˈpəŋ\ *n* [short for earlier *tow-pong*, of Algonquian origin; akin to Micmac *tobágun* drag made with skin] *NewEng* (1825) : a sleigh with a box-shaped body

pun-gen-cy \ˈpən-jən-sē\ *n* (1649) : the quality or state of being pungent

pun-gent \-jənt\ *adj* [L *pungent-, pungens*, prp. of *pungere* to prick, sting; akin to L *pugnus* fist, *pugnare* to fight, Gk *pygmē* fist] (1597) **1** : sharply painful **2** : having a stiff and sharp point ⟨~ leaves⟩ **3 a** : marked by a sharp incisive quality : CAUSTIC ⟨a ~ critic⟩ ⟨~ language⟩ **b** : being sharp and to the point ⟨ask a few ~ questions⟩ **4** : causing a sharp or irritating sensation; *esp* : ACRID — **pun-gent-ly** *adv*
syn PUNGENT, PIQUANT, POIGNANT, RACY mean sharp and stimulating to the mind or the senses. PUNGENT implies a sharp, stinging, or biting quality esp. of odors; PIQUANT suggests a power to whet the appetite or interest through tartness or mild pungency; POIGNANT suggests something is sharply or piercingly effective in stirring one's consciousness or emotions; RACY implies having a strongly characteristic natural quality fresh and unimpaired.

pun-gle \ˈpəŋ-gəl\ *vb* **pun-gled; pun-gling** \ˈpəŋ-g(ə-)liŋ\ [Sp *póngale* put it down] *vt* (1851) : to make a payment or contribution of (money) — usu. used with *up* ~ *vi* : PAY, CONTRIBUTE — usu. used with *up*

¹**Pu-nic** \ˈpyü-nik\ *adj* [L *punicus*, fr. *Poenus* inhabitant of Carthage, modif. of Gk *Phoinix* Phoenician] (1533) **1** : of or relating to Carthage or the Carthaginians **2** : FAITHLESS, TREACHEROUS

²**Punic** *n* (1673) : the Phoenician dialect of ancient Carthage

pun-ish \ˈpən-ish\ *vb* [ME *punisshen*, fr. MF *puniss-*, stem of *punir*, fr. L *punire*, fr. *poena* penalty — more at PAIN] *vt* (14c) **1 a** : to impose a penalty on for a fault, offense, or violation **b** : to inflict a penalty for the commission of (an offense) in retribution or retaliation **2 a** : to deal with roughly or harshly **b** : to inflict injury on : HURT ~ *vi* : to inflict punishment — **pun-ish-abil-i-ty** \ˌpən-ish-ə-ˈbil-ət-ē\ *n* — **pun-ish-able** \ˈpən-ish-ə-bəl\ *adj* — **pun-ish-er** *n*
syn PUNISH, CHASTISE, CASTIGATE, CHASTEN, DISCIPLINE, CORRECT mean to inflict a penalty on in requital for wrongdoing. PUNISH implies subjecting to a penalty for wrongdoing; CHASTISE may apply to either the infliction of corporal punishment or to verbal censure or denunciation; CASTIGATE implies a severe, typically public censure; CHASTEN suggests any affliction or trial that leaves one humbled or subdued; DISCIPLINE implies a punishing or chastening in order to bring under control; CORRECT implies punishing aimed at reforming an offender.

pun-ish-ment \ˈpən-ish-mənt\ *n* (15c) **1** : the act of punishing **2 a** : suffering, pain, or loss that serves as retribution **b** : a penalty inflicted on an offender through judicial procedure **3** : severe, rough, or disastrous treatment

pu-ni-tion \pyü-ˈnish-ən\ *n* [ME *punicion*, fr. MF *punition*, fr. L *punition-, punitio*, fr. *punitus*] (15c) : PUNISHMENT

pu-ni-tive \ˈpyü-nət-iv\ *adj* [F *punitif*, fr. ML *punitivus*, fr. L *punitus*, pp. of *punire*] (1624) : inflicting, involving, or aiming at punishment — **pu-ni-tive-ly** *adv* — **pu-ni-tive-ness** *n*

punitive damages *n pl* (ca. 1890) : damages awarded in excess of normal compensation to the plaintiff to punish a defendant for a serious wrong

Pun-ja-bi \ˌpən-ˈjäb-ē, -ˈjab-\ *n* [Hindi *pañjābī*, fr. *pañjābī* of Punjab, fr. Per, fr. *Pañjāb* Punjab] (1846) **1** : PANJABI **2** : a native or inhabitant of the Punjab region of the northwestern Indian subcontinent — **Punjabi** *adj*

¹**punk** \ˈpəŋk\ *n* [origin unknown] (1596) **1** *archaic* : PROSTITUTE **2** [prob. partly fr. ³punk] : NONSENSE, FOOLISHNESS **3 a** : a young inex-

\ə\ abut \ᵊ\ kitten, F table \ər\ further \a\ ash \ā\ ace \ä\ cot, cart \aů\ out \ch\ chin \e\ bet \ē\ easy \g\ go \i\ hit \ī\ ice \j\ job \ŋ\ sing \ō\ go \ȯ\ law \ȯi\ boy \th\ thin \t͟h\ the \ü\ loot \ů\ foot \y\ yet \zh\ vision \à, ᵏ, ⁿ, œ, œ̄, ᵫ, ᵮ, ᵞ\ *see* Guide to Pronunciation

perienced person : BEGINNER, NOVICE; *esp* : a young man **b** : a usu. petty gangster, hoodlum, or ruffian **c** : a youth used as a homosexual partner **4 a** : PUNK ROCK **b** : a punk rock musician

2**punk** *adj* (1896) **1** : very poor : INFERIOR ⟨played a ~ game⟩ **2** : being in poor health ⟨said that she was feeling ~⟩ **3 a** : of or relating to punk rock **b** : relating to or being a style (as of dress or hair) inspired by punk rock

3**punk** *n* [perh. alter. of *spunk*] (1687) **1** : wood so decayed as to be dry, crumbly, and useful for tinder **2** : a dry spongy substance prepared from fungi (genus *Fomes*) and used to ignite fuses esp. of fireworks

pun·kah \ˈpəŋ-kə\ *n* [Hindi *pākhā*] (1787) : a fan used esp. in India that consists of a canvas-covered frame suspended from the ceiling and that is operated by a cord

pun·kie *also* **pun·ky** \ˈpəŋ-kē\ *n, pl* **punkies** [D dial. *punki*, fr. Delaware *punk*, lit., fine ashes, powder] (1769) : BITING MIDGE

pun·kin \ˈpəŋ-kən\ *var of* PUMPKIN

punk rock *n* (1971) : rock music marked by extreme and often deliberately offensive expressions of alienation and social discontent

punky \ˈpəŋ-kē\ *adj* **punk·i·er; -est** (1872) **1** : resembling punk in being soft or rotted **2** : resembling or typical of a punk — **punk·i·ness** *n*

pun·ny *adj* **pun·ni·er; -est** (1947) : constituting or involving a pun

pun·ster \ˈpən(t)-stər\ *n* (1700) : one who is given to punning

1**punt** \ˈpənt\ *n* [(assumed) ME, fr. OE, fr. L *ponton-, ponto* — more at PONTOON] (bef. 12c) : a long narrow flat-bottomed boat with square ends usu. propelled with a pole

2**punt** *vt* (1816) : to propel (as a punt) with a pole

3**punt** *vi* [F *ponter*, fr. *ponte* point in some games, play against the banker, fr. Sp *punto* point, fr. L *punctum* — more at POINT] (1712) **1** : to play at a gambling game against the banker **2** *Brit* : GAMBLE

4**punt** *vb* [origin unknown] *vt* (1845) : to kick (a football or soccer ball) with the top of the foot before the ball which is dropped from the hands hits the ground ~ *vi* : to punt a ball

5**punt** *n* (1845) : the act or an instance of punting a ball

punt·er \ˈpənt-ər\ *n* (ca. 1706) : one that punts: as **a** *chiefly Brit* : one that gambles; *esp* : one that bets against a bookmaker **b** : one that uses a punt in boating **c** : one that punts a ball

punt formation *n* (1949) : an offensive football formation in which a back making a punt stands approximately 10 yards behind the line and the other backs are in blocking position close to the line

pun·ty \ˈpənt-ē\ *n, pl* **punties** [F *pontil*] (1662) : a metal rod used for fashioning hot glass

pu·ny \ˈpyü-nē\ *adj* **pu·ni·er; -est** [MF *puisné* younger, lit., born afterward, fr. *puis* afterward + *né* born] (1577) : slight or inferior in power, size, or importance : WEAK — **pu·ni·ly** \ˈpyün-ᵊl-ē\ *adv* — **pu·ni·ness** \ˈpyü-nē-nəs\ *n*

1**pup** \ˈpəp\ *n* [short for *puppy*] (1773) : a young dog; *also* : one of the young of various animals (as a seal or rat)

2**pup** *vi* **pupped; pup·ping** (1773) : to give birth to pups

pu·pa \ˈpyü-pə\ *n, pl* **pu·pae** \-(ˌ)pē *also* -ˌpī\ *or* **pupas** [NL, fr. L *pupa* girl, doll] (1815) : an intermediate usu. quiescent stage of a metamorphic insect (as a bee, moth, or beetle) that occurs between the larva and the imago, is usu. enclosed in a cocoon or case, and undergoes internal changes by which larval structures are replaced by those typical of the imago — **pu·pal** \ˈpyü-pəl\ *adj*

pu·par·i·um \pyü-ˈpar-ē-əm, -ˈper-\ *n, pl* **pu·par·ia** \-ē-ə\ [NL, fr. *pupa*] (ca. 1815) : the outer shell formed from the larval skin that covers a coarctate pupa

pu·pate \ˈpyü-ˌpāt\ *vi* **pu·pat·ed; pu·pat·ing** (ca. 1879) : to become a pupa : pass through a pupal stage — **pu·pa·tion** \pyü-ˈpā-shən\ *n*

pup·fish \ˈpəp-ˌfish\ *n* (1949) : any of several killifishes (genus *Cyprinodon* of the family Cyprinodontidae) esp. of warm streams and springs of the western U.S.

1**pu·pil** \ˈpyü-pəl\ *n* [ME *pupille* minor ward, fr. MF, fr. L *pupillus* male ward (fr. dim. of *pupus* boy) & *pupilla* female ward, fr. dim. of *pupa* girl, doll, puppet] (1542) **1** : a child or young person in school or in the charge of a tutor or instructor : STUDENT **2** : one who has been taught or influenced by a famous or distinguished person

2**pupil** *n* [MF *pupille*, fr. L *pupilla*, fr. dim. of *pupa* doll; fr. the tiny image of oneself seen reflected in another's eye] (1567) : the contractile usu. round aperture in the iris of the eye — **pu·pil·lary** \ˈpyü-pə-ˌler-ē\ *adj*

pu·pil·age *or* **pu·pil·lage** \ˈpyü-pə-lij\ *n* (ca. 1599) : the state or period of being a pupil

pup·pet \ˈpəp-ət\ *n* [ME *popet*, fr. MF *poupette*, dim. of (assumed) *poupe* doll, fr. L *pupa*] (1538) **1 a** : a small-scale figure (as of a person or animal) usu. with a cloth body and hollow head that fits over and is moved by the hand **b** : MARIONETTE **2** : DOLL 1 **3** : one whose acts are controlled by an outside force or influence

pup·pe·teer \ˌpəp-ə-ˈti(ə)r\ *n* (ca. 1923) : one who manipulates puppets

pup·pet·ry \ˈpəp-ə-trē\ *n, pl* **-ries** (1528) **1** : the production or creation of puppets or puppet shows **2** : the art of manipulating puppets

pup·py \ˈpəp-ē\ *n, pl* **puppies** [ME *popi*, fr. MF *poupée* doll, toy, fr. (assumed) *poupe* doll] (1591) : a young domestic dog; *specif* : one less than a year old — **pup·py·ish** \-ish \ *adj* — **pup·py·like** \-ˌlīk\ *adj*

puppy dog *n* (1595) : a domestic dog; *esp* : one having the lovable attributes of a puppy

puppy love *n* (1834) : transitory affection felt by a boy or girl for one of the opposite sex

pup tent *n* (1863) : a low small tent for two persons usu. consisting of two halves fastened together

Pu·ra·na \pu̇-ˈrän-ə\ *n, often cap* [Skt *purāṇa*, fr. *purāṇa* ancient, fr. *purā* formerly; akin to OE *fore* earlier] (1696) : one of a class of Hindu sacred writings chiefly from A.D. 300 to A.D. 750 comprising popular myths and legends and other traditional lore — **Pu·ra·nic** \-ik\ *adj*

pur·blind \ˈpər-ˌblīnd\ *adj* [ME *pur blind*, fr. *pur* purely, wholly, fr. *pur* pure] (13c) **1 a** *obs* : wholly blind **b** : partly blind **2** : lacking in vision, insight, or understanding : OBTUSE — **pur·blind·ly** \-ˌblīn-(d)lē\ *adv* — **pur·blind·ness** \-ˌblīn(d)-nəs\ *n*

1**pur·chase** \ˈpər-chəs\ *vb* **pur·chased; pur·chas·ing** [ME *purchacen*, fr. OF *purchacier* to seek to obtain, fr. *por-, pur-* for, forward (modif. of L *pro-*) + *chacier* to pursue, chase — more at PRO-] *vt* (13c) **1 a** *archaic* : GAIN, ACQUIRE **b** : to acquire (real estate) by means other than descent or inheritance **c** : to obtain by paying money or its equivalent : BUY **d** : to obtain by labor, danger, or sacrifice **2** : to apply a device for obtaining a mechanical advantage to (as something to be moved); *also* : to move by a purchase **3** : to constitute the means for buying ⟨our dollars ~ less each year⟩ ~ *vi* : to purchase something — **pur·chas·able** \-chə-sə-bəl\ *adj* — **pur·chas·er** *n*

2**purchase** *n* (13c) **1** : an act or instance of purchasing **2** : something obtained esp. for a price in money or its equivalent **3 a** (1) : a mechanical hold or advantage applied to the raising or moving of heavy bodies (2) : an apparatus or device by which advantage is gained **b** (1) : an advantage used in applying one's power (2) : a means of exerting power

pur·dah \ˈpərd-ə\ *n* [Hindi *parda*, lit., screen, veil] (1865) : seclusion of women from public observation among Muslims and some Hindus esp. in India

pure \ˈpyu̇(ə)r\ *adj* **pur·er; pur·est** [ME *pur*, fr. OF, fr. L *purus*; akin to Skt *punāti* he cleanses, MIr *ūr* fresh, green] (13c) **1 a** (1) : unmixed with any other matter ⟨~ gold⟩ (2) : free from dust, dirt, or taint ⟨~ food⟩ (3) : SPOTLESS, STAINLESS **b** : free from harshness or roughness and being in tune — used of a musical tone **c** *of a vowel* : characterized by no appreciable alteration of articulation during utterance **2 a** : SHEER, UNMITIGATED ⟨~ folly⟩ **b** (1) : ABSTRACT, THEORETICAL (2) : A PRIORI ⟨~ mechanics⟩ **c** : not directed toward exposition of reality or solution of practical problems ⟨~ literature⟩ **d** : being nonobjective and to be appraised on formal and technical qualities only ⟨~ form⟩ **3 a** (1) : free from what vitiates, weakens, or pollutes (2) : containing nothing that does not properly belong **b** : free from moral fault or guilt **c** : marked by chastity : CONTINENT **d** (1) : of pure blood and unmixed ancestry (2) : homozygous in and breeding true for one or more characters **e** : ritually clean ***syn*** see CHASTE — **pure·ness** *n*

pure–blood·ed \ˈpyu̇(ə)r-ˈbləd-əd\ *or* **pure–blood** \-ˌbləd\ *adj* (1821) : of unmixed ancestry : PUREBRED — **pure·blood** \-ˌbləd\ *n*

pure·bred \-ˈbred\ *adj* (1868) : bred from members of a recognized breed, strain, or kind without admixture of other blood over many generations — **pure·bred** \-ˌbred\ *n*

pure democracy *n* (ca. 1910) : democracy in which the power is exercised directly by the people rather than through representatives

1**pu·ree** \pyu̇-ˈrā, -ˈrē\ *n* [F *purée*, fr. MF, fr. fem. of *puré*, pp. of *purer* to purify, strain, fr. L *purare* to purify, fr. *purus*] (1707) **1** : a paste or thick liquid suspension usu. made from cooked food ground finely **2** : a thick soup made of pureed vegetables

2**puree** *vt* **pu·reed; pu·ree·ing** (1928) : to make a puree of

pure imaginary *n* (1947) : the product of a real number other than zero and the imaginary unit

pure·ly \ˈpyu̇(ə)r-lē\ *adv* (13c) **1** : WHOLLY, COMPLETELY ⟨a selection based ~ on merit⟩ **2** : without admixture of anything injurious or foreign **3** : SIMPLY, MERELY ⟨read ~ for relaxation⟩ **4** : in a chaste or innocent manner

pur·fle \ˈpər-fəl\ *vt* **pur·fled; pur·fling** \-f(ə-)liŋ\ [ME *purfilen*, fr. MF *porfiler*, fr. (assumed) VL *profilare*, fr. L *pro-* forward + LL *filare* to spin — more at PRO-, FILE] (14c) : to ornament the border or edges of — **purfle** *n*

pur·ga·tion \ˌpər-ˈgā-shən\ *n* (14c) : the act or result of purging

1**pur·ga·tive** \ˈpər-gət-iv\ *adj* [ME *purgatif*, fr. MF, fr. LL *purgativus*, fr. L *purgatus*, pp.] (15c) : purging or tending to purge

2**purgative** *n* (1626) : a purging medicine : CATHARTIC

pur·ga·to·ri·al \ˌpər-gə-ˈtōr-ē-əl, -ˈtȯr-\ *adj* (15c) **1** : cleansing of sin : EXPIATORY **2** : of or relating to purgatory

pur·ga·to·ry \ˈpər-gə-ˌtōr-ē, -ˌtȯr-\ *n, pl* **-ries** [ME, fr. AF or ML; AF *purgatorie*, fr. ML *purgatorium*, fr. LL, neut. of *purgatorius* purging, fr. L *purgatus*, pp. of *purgare*] (13c) **1** : an intermediate state after death for expiatory purification; *specif* : a place or state of punishment wherein according to Roman Catholic doctrine the souls of those who die in God's grace may make satisfaction for past sins and so become fit for heaven **2** : a place or state of temporary suffering or misery

1**purge** \ˈpərj\ *vb* **purged; purg·ing** [ME *purgen*, fr. MF *purgier*, fr. L *purigare, purgare* to purify, purge, fr. *purus* pure + *-igare* (akin to *agere* to drive, do) — more at ACT] *vt* (13c) **1 a** : to clear of guilt **b** : to free from moral or ceremonial defilement **2 a** : to cause evacuation from (as the bowels) **b** (1) : to make free of something unwanted ⟨~ a manhole of gas⟩ ⟨find yourself *purged* of fear⟩ (2) : to free (as a boiler) of sediment or relieve (as a steam pipe) of trapped air by bleeding **c** (1) : to rid (as a nation or party) by a purge (2) : to get rid of (as someone or something undesirable) ⟨the leaders had been *purged*⟩ ⟨~ money-losing operations⟩ ~ *vi* **1** : to become purged **2** : to have or produce frequent evacuations **3** : to cause purgation — **purg·er** *n*

2**purge** *n* (1563) **1** : something that purges; *esp* : PURGATIVE **2 a** : an act or instance of purging **b** : the removal of elements or members regarded as undesirable and esp. as treacherous or disloyal

pu·ri·fi·ca·tion \ˌpyu̇r-ə-fə-ˈkā-shən\ *n* (14c) : the act or an instance of purifying or of being purified

pu·ri·fi·ca·tor \ˈpyu̇r-ə-fə-ˌkāt-ər\ *n* (1853) **1** : a linen cloth used to wipe the chalice after celebration of the Eucharist **2** : one that purifies

pu·ri·fi·ca·to·ry \pyu̇r-ˈif-i-kə-ˌtōr-ē, ˈpyu̇r-(ə-)fə-kə-, -ˌtȯr-\ *adj* (1610) : serving, tending, or intended to purify

pu·ri·fy \ˈpyu̇r-ə-ˌfī\ *vb* **-fied; -fy·ing** [ME *purifien*, fr. MF *purifier*, fr. L *purificare*, fr. L *purus* + *-ificare* -ify] *vt* (14c) : to make pure: as **a** : to clear from material defilement or imperfection **b** : to free from guilt or moral or ceremonial blemish **c** : to free from undesirable elements ~ *vi* : to grow or become pure or clean — **pu·ri·fi·er** \-ˌfī(-ə)r\ *n*

Pu·rim \ˈpu̇r-(ˌ)im, pu̇r-ˈ\ *n* [Heb *pūrīm*, lit., lots; fr. the casting of lots by Haman in Esth 9:24–26] (14c) : a Jewish holiday celebrated on the 14th of Adar in commemoration of the deliverance of the Jews from the massacre plotted by Haman

pu·rine \ˈpyu̇(ə)r-ˌēn\ *n* [G *purin*, fr. L *purus* pure + NL *uricus* uric (fr. E *uric*) + G *-in* -ine] (1898) **1** : a crystalline base $C_5H_4N_4$ that is the parent of compounds of the uric-acid group **2** : a derivative of purine; *esp* : a base (as adenine or guanine) that is a constituent of DNA or RNA

pur·ism \ˈpyu̇(ə)r-ˌiz-əm\ *n* (1803) **1** : an example of rigid adherence to or insistence on purity or nicety esp. in use of words; *esp* : a word, phrase, or sense used chiefly by purists **2** : the quality or practice of adherence to purity esp. in language

pur·ist \ˈpyu̇r-əst\ *n* (ca. 1706) : one who adheres strictly and often excessively to a tradition; *esp* : one preoccupied with the purity of a language and its protection from the use of foreign or altered forms — **pu·ris·tic** *adj*

¹pu·ri·tan \'pyůr-ət-ᵊn\ *n* [prob. fr. LL *puritas* purity] (1572) **1** *cap* : a member of a 16th and 17th century Protestant group in England and New England opposing as unscriptural the ceremonial worship and the prelacy of the Church of England **2** : one who practices or preaches a more rigorous or professedly purer moral code than that which prevails

²puritan *adj, often cap* (1589) : of or relating to puritans, the Puritans, or puritanism

pu·ri·tan·i·cal \,pyůr-ə-'tan-i-kəl\ *adj* (1607) **1** : PURITAN **2** : of, relating to, or characterized by a rigid morality : SEVERE, AUSTERE ⟨~ censors of literature⟩ — **pu·ri·tan·i·cal·ly** \-k(ə-)lē\ *adv*

pu·ri·tan·ism \'pyůr-ət-ᵊn-,iz-əm\ *n* (1573) **1** *cap* : the beliefs and practices characteristic of the Puritans **2** : strictness and austerity esp. in matters of religion or conduct

pu·ri·ty \'pyůr-ət-ē\ *n* [ME *purete*, fr. OF *pureté*, fr. LL *puritat-, puritas*, fr. L *purus* pure] (13c) **1** : the quality or state of being pure **2** : SATURATION 4a

Pur·kin·je cell \(,)pər-,kin-jē-\ *n* [Johannes E. *Purkinje*] (ca. 1890) : any of numerous nerve cells that occupy the middle layer of the cerebellar cortex and are characterized by a large globose body with massive dendrites directed outward and a single slender axon directed inward

Purkinje fiber *n* (ca. 1890) : any of the modified cardiac muscle fibers that have few nuclei, granulated central cytoplasm, and sparse peripheral striations and make up a network of conducting tissue in the myocardium

¹purl \'pər(-ə)l\ *vb* [obs. *pirl* (to twist)] *vt* (1526) **1 a** : to embroider with gold or silver thread **b** : to edge or border with gold or silver embroidery **2** : to knit in purl stitch ~ *vi* : to do knitting in purl stitch

²purl *n* (1535) **1** : gold or silver thread or wire for embroidering or edging **2** : the intertwisting of thread that knots a stitch usu. along an edge **3** : PURL STITCH

³purl *n* [perh. of Scand origin; akin to Norw *purla* to ripple] (1552) **1** : a purling or swirling stream or rill **2** : a gentle murmur or movement (as of purling water)

⁴purl *vi* (1591) **1** : EDDY, SWIRL **2** : to make a soft murmuring sound like that of a purling stream

pur·lieu \'pərl-(,)(y)ü\ *n* [ME *purlewe* land severed from an English royal forest by perambulation, fr. AF *puralé* perambulation, fr. OF *puraler* to go through, fr. *pur-* for, through + *aler* to go — more at PURCHASE, ALLEY] (15c) **1 a** : an outlying or adjacent district **b** *pl* : ENVIRONS, NEIGHBORHOOD **2 a** : a frequently visited place : HAUNT **b** *pl* : CONFINES, BOUNDS

pur·lin \'pər-lən\ *n* [origin unknown] (15c) : a horizontal member in a roof supporting the rafters

pur·loin \(,)pər-'lȯin, 'pər-,\ *vt* [ME *purloinen* to put away, render ineffectual, fr. AF *purloigner*, fr. OF *porloigner* to put off, delay, fr. *por-* forward + *loing* at a distance, fr. L *longe*, fr. *longus* long] (1548) : to appropriate wrongfully and often by a breach of trust ***syn*** see STEAL — **pur·loin·er** *n*

purl stitch *n* [²*purl*] (1885) : a knitting stitch usu. made with the yarn at the front of the work by inserting the right needle into the front of a loop on the left needle from the right, catching the yarn with the right needle, and bringing it through to form a new loop — compare KNIT STITCH

pu·ro·my·cin \,pyůr-ə-'mīs-ᵊn\ *n* [*purine* + *-o-* + *-mycin*] (1953) : an antibiotic $C_{22}H_{29}N_7O_5$ that is obtained from an actinomycete (*Streptomyces alboniger*) and is used esp. as a potent inhibitor of protein synthesis in microorganisms and mammalian cells

¹pur·ple \'pər-pəl\ *adj* **pur·pler** \-p(ə-)lər\; **pur·plest** \-p(ə-)ləst\ [ME *purpel*, alter. of *purper*, fr. OE *purpuran* of purple, gen. of *purpure* purple color, fr. L *purpura*, fr. Gk *porphyra*] (bef. 12c) **1** : REGAL, IMPERIAL **2** : of the color purple **3 a** : highly rhetorical : ORNATE **b** : marked by profanity

²purple *n* (15c) **1 a** (1) : TYRIAN PURPLE (2) : any of various colors that fall about midway between red and blue in hue **b** (1) : cloth dyed purple (2) : a garment of such color; *esp* : a purple robe worn as an emblem of rank or authority **c** (1) : a mollusk (as of the genus *Purpura*) yielding a purple dye and esp. the Tyrian purple of ancient times (2) : a pigment or dye that colors purple **2 a** : imperial or regal rank or power **b** : high rank or station

³purple *vb* **pur·pled; pur·pling** \-p(ə-)liŋ\ *vt* (15c) : to make purple ~ *vi* : to become purple

Purple Heart *n* (1932) : a U.S. military decoration awarded to any member of the armed forces wounded or killed in action

purple loosestrife *n* (1548) : a marsh herb (*Lythrum salicaria*) of Europe and the eastern U.S. that has a long spike of purple flowers

purple passage *n* [trans. of L *pannus purpureus* purple patch; fr. the traditional splendor of purple cloth as contrasted with more shabby materials] (1895) **1** : a passage conspicuous for brilliance or effectiveness in a work that is dull, commonplace, or uninspired **2** : a piece of obtrusively ornate writing — called also *purple patch*

purple scale *n* (ca. 1909) : a brownish or purplish armored scale (*Lepidosaphes beckii*) that is destructive to citrus fruit

pur·plish \'pər-p(ə-)lish\ *adj* (1562) : somewhat purple

pur·ply \'pər-p(ə-)lē\ *adj* (1725) : PURPLISH

¹pur·port \'pər-,pō(ə)rt, -,pȯ(ə)rt\ *n* [ME, fr. AF, content, tenor, fr. *purporter* to contain, fr. OF *porporter* to convey, fr. *por-* forward + *porter* to carry — more at PURCHASE, PORT] (15c) : meaning conveyed, professed, or implied : IMPORT; *also* : SUBSTANCE, GIST

²pur·port \(,)pər-'pō(ə)rt, -'pȯ(ə)rt\ *vt* (1528) **1** : to have the often specious appearance of being, intending, or claiming (something implied or inferred) : PROFESS ⟨a book that ~s to be an objective analysis⟩ **2** : INTEND, PURPOSE

pur·port·ed *adj* (1894) : REPUTED, RUMORED — **pur·port·ed·ly** *adv*

¹pur·pose \'pər-pəs\ *n* [ME *purpos*, fr. OF, fr. *purposer* to purpose, fr. L *proponere* (perf. indic. *proposui*) to propose — more at PROPOSE] (13c) **1 a** : something set up as an object or end to be attained : INTENTION **b** : RESOLUTION, DETERMINATION **2** : a subject under discussion or an action in course of execution ***syn*** see INTENTION — **on purpose** : by intent : INTENTIONALLY

²purpose *vt* **pur·posed; pur·pos·ing** (14c) : to propose as an aim to oneself

pur·pose·ful \'pər-pəs-fəl\ *adj* (1853) **1** : having a purpose or aim : MEANINGFUL ⟨~ activities⟩ **2** : full of determination ⟨a ~ man⟩ — **pur·pose·ful·ly** \-fə-lē\ *adv* — **pur·pose·ful·ness** *n*

pur·pose·less \-ləs\ *adj* (ca. 1552) : having no purpose : AIMLESS, MEANINGLESS — **pur·pose·less·ly** *adv* — **pur·pose·less·ness** *n*

pur·pose·ly \-lē\ *adv* (15c) : with a deliberate or express purpose

pur·po·sive \'pər-pə-siv, (,)pər-'pō-\ *adj* (1855) **1** : serving or effecting a useful function though not as a result of planning or design **2** : having or tending to fulfill a conscious purpose or design : PURPOSEFUL — **pur·po·sive·ly** *adv* — **pur·po·sive·ness** *n*

pur·pu·ra \'pər-p(y)ə-rə\ *n* [NL, fr. L, purple color] (1753) : any of several hemorrhagic states characterized by patches of purplish discoloration resulting from extravasation of blood into the skin and mucous membranes — **pur·pu·ric** \,pər-'pyů(ə)r-ik\ *adj*

pur·pure \'pər-pyər\ *n* [ME, fr. OE, purple] (1535) : the heraldic color purple

¹purr \'pər\ *n* [imit.] (1601) : a low vibratory murmur typical of an apparently contented or pleased cat

²purr *vi* (1620) **1** : to make a purr **2 a** : to speak in a manner that resembles a purr **b** : to speak in a malicious catty manner — **purr·ing·ly** \-iŋ-lē\ *adv*

¹purse \'pərs\ *n* [ME *purs*, fr. OE, modif. of ML *bursa*, fr. LL, ox-hide, fr. Gk *byrsa*] (bef. 12c) **1 a** (1) : a small bag for money (2) : a receptacle (as a pocketbook) for carrying money and often other small objects **b** : a receptacle (as a pouch) shaped like a purse **2 a** : RESOURCES, FUNDS **b** : a sum of money offered as a prize or present; *also* : the total amount of money offered in prizes for a given event — **purse·like** \-,līk\ *adj*

²purse *vt* **pursed; purs·ing** (14c) **1** : to put into a purse **2** : PUCKER, KNIT

purse–proud \'pər-,spraůd\ *adj* (1681) : proud because of one's wealth esp. in the absence of other distinctions

purs·er \'pər-sər\ *n* (15c) **1** : an official on a ship responsible for papers and accounts and on a passenger ship also for the comfort and welfare of passengers **2** : an official on an airliner responsible esp. for the comfort and welfare of passengers

purse seine *n* (1870) : a large seine designed to be set by two boats around a school of fish and so arranged that after the ends have been brought together the bottom can be closed — **purse seiner** *n*

purse strings *n pl* (15c) : financial resources

purs·lane \'pər-slən, -,slān\ *n* [ME, fr. MF *porcelaine*, fr. LL *porcillagin-, porcillago*, alter. of L *porcillaca*, alter. of *portulaca*] (14c) : any of a family (Portulacaceae, the purslane family) of usu. succulent herbs having perfect regular flowers with 2 sepals and 4 to 5 hypogynous petals; *esp* : a fleshy-leaved trailing plant (*Portulaca oleracea*) with tiny yellow flowers that is a common troublesome weed but is sometimes eaten as a potherb or in salads

pur·su·ance \pər-'sü-ən(t)s\ *n* (1596) : the act of pursuing; *esp* : a carrying out or into effect : PROSECUTION ⟨in ~ of his duties⟩

pur·su·ant to \-ənt-\ *prep* (1648) : in carrying out : in conformity with : ACCORDING TO

pur·sue \pər-'sü\ *vb* **pur·sued; pur·su·ing** [ME *pursuen*, fr. AF *pursuer*, fr. OF *poursuir*, fr. L *prosequi*, fr. *pro-* forward + *sequi* to follow — more at PRO-, SUE] *vt* (13c) **1** : to follow in order to overtake, capture, kill, or defeat **2** : to find or employ measures to obtain or accomplish : SEEK ⟨~ a goal⟩ **3** : to proceed along ⟨~s a northern course⟩ **4 a** : to engage in ⟨~ a hobby⟩ **b** : to follow up ⟨~ an argument⟩ **5** : to continue to afflict : HAUNT ⟨was *pursued* by horrible memories⟩ **6** : COURT, ²CHASE 1c ⟨*pursued* by dozens of women⟩ ~ *vi* : to go in pursuit ***syn*** see CHASE — **pur·su·er** *n*

pur·suit \pər-'süt\ *n* [ME, fr. MF *poursuite*, fr. *poursuir*] (15c) **1** : the act of pursuing **2** : an activity that one engages in as a vocation, profession, or avocation : OCCUPATION ***syn*** see WORK

pursuit plane *n* (1921) : a fighter plane designed for pursuit of enemy airplanes

pur·sui·vant \'pər-s(w)i-vənt\ *n* [ME *pursevant* attendant of a herald, fr. MF *poursuivant*, lit., follower, fr. prp. of *poursuir, poursuivre* to pursue] (14c) **1** : an officer of arms ranking below a herald but having similar duties **2** : FOLLOWER, ATTENDANT

¹pur·sy \'pəs-ē, 'pər-sē\ *adj* **pur·si·er; -est** [ME, fr. AF *pursif*, alter. of MF *polsif*, fr. *poulser, polser* to beat, push, pant — more at PUSH] (15c) **1** : short-winded esp. because of corpulence **2** : FAT — **pur·si·ness** *n*

²pursy \'pər-sē\ *adj* **purs·i·er; -est** [¹*purse*] (1552) **1** : having a puckered appearance **2** : PURSE-PROUD

pur·te·nance \'pərt-nən(t)s, -ᵊn-ən(t)s\ *n* [ME, lit., appendage, modif. of MF *partenance*, fr. *partenir* to pertain — more at PERTAIN] (15c) : ENTRAILS, PLUCK

pu·ru·lence \'pyůr-(y)ə-lən(t)s\ *n* (1597) : the quality or state of being purulent; *also* : PUS

pu·ru·lent \-lənt\ *adj* [L *purulentus*, fr. *pur-, pus* pus] (1597) **1** : containing, consisting of, or being pus ⟨a ~ discharge⟩ **2** : accompanied by suppuration

pur·vey \(,)pər-'vā, 'pər-,\ *vt* **pur·veyed; pur·vey·ing** [ME *purveien*, fr. MF *porveeir*, fr. L *providēre* to provide] (13c) **1** : to supply (as provisions) usu. as a matter of business **2** : CIRCULATE, DISSEMINATE

pur·vey·ance \-ən(t)s\ *n* (14c) : the act or process of purveying or procuring

pur·vey·or \-ər\ *n* (14c) **1** : one that purveys **2** : VICTUALLER, CATERER

pur·view \'pər-,vyü\ *n* [ME *purveu*, fr. AF *purveu est* it is provided (opening phrase of a statute)] (15c) **1 a** : the body or enacting part of a statute **b** : the limit, purpose, or scope of a statute **2** : the range or limit of authority, competence, responsibility, concern, or intention **3** : range of vision, understanding, or cognizance

pus \'pəs\ *n* [L *pur-, pus* — more at FOUL] (1541) : thick opaque usu. yellowish white fluid matter formed by suppuration and composed of exudate containing leukocytes, tissue debris, and microorganisms

\ə\ abut \ᵊ\ kitten, F table \ər\ further \a\ ash \ā\ ace \ä\ cot, cart
\aů\ out \ch\ chin \e\ bet \ē\ easy \g\ go \i\ hit \ī\ ice \j\ job
\ŋ\ sing \ō\ go \ȯ\ law \ȯi\ boy \th\ thin \t͟h\ the \ü\ loot \ů\ foot
\y\ yet \zh\ vision \á, k̟, ⁿ, œ, œ̄, ue, ue̅, ʸ\ *see* Guide to Pronunciation

Pu·sey·ism \'pyü-zē-,iz-əm, -sē-\ *n* [Edward Bouverie *Pusey*] (1838) : TRACTARIANISM — **Pu·sey·ite** \-,īt\ *n*

[1]**push** \'püsh\ *vb* [ME *pusshen*, fr. MF *poulser* to beat, push, fr. OF, fr. L *pulsare*, fr. *pulsus*, pp. of *pellere* to drive, strike — more at FELT] *vt* (14c) **1 a :** to press against with force in order to drive or impel **b :** to move or endeavor to move away or ahead by steady pressure without striking **2 a :** to thrust forward, downward, or outward **b :** to hit (a ball) toward the right from a right-handed swing or toward the left from a left-handed swing — compare PULL **3 a :** to press or urge forward to completion **b :** to urge or press the advancement, adoption, or practice of ⟨~*ed* a bill in the legislature⟩; *esp* : to make aggressive efforts to sell ⟨a drive to ~ canned goods⟩ **c :** to engage in the illicit sale of (narcotics) **4 :** to bear hard upon so as to involve in difficulty ⟨grinding poverty ~*ed* them to the breaking point⟩ **5 :** to approach in age or number ⟨grandmother must have been ~*ing* 75⟩ ~ *vi* **1 :** to press against something with steady force in or as if in order to impel **2 :** to press forward energetically against opposition **3 :** to exert oneself continuously, vigorously, or obtrusively to gain an end ⟨unions ~*ing* for higher wages⟩

syn PUSH, SHOVE, THRUST, PROPEL mean to cause to move ahead or aside by force. PUSH implies application of force by a body already in contact with the body to be moved; SHOVE implies a fast or rough pushing of something usu. along a surface; THRUST suggests less steadiness and greater violence than PUSH; PROPEL suggests rapidly driving forward or onward by force applied in any manner.

— **push one's luck :** to take an increasing risk

[2]**push** *n* (1563) **1 :** a vigorous effort to attain an end : DRIVE: **a :** a military assault or offensive **b :** an advance that overcomes obstacles **c :** a campaign to promote a product **2 :** a time for action : EMERGENCY **3 a :** an act of pushing : SHOVE **b** (1) : a physical force steadily applied in a direction away from the body exerting it ⟨the ~ of the water against the wharf⟩ (2) : a nonphysical pressure : INFLUENCE, URGE **c :** vigorous enterprise or energy **4 a :** an exertion of influence to promote another's interests **b :** stimulation to activity : IMPETUS

push around *vt* (1930) : to impose on contemptuously

push·ball \'püsh-,bȯl\ *n* (1896) : a game in which each of two sides endeavors to push an inflated leather-covered ball six feet in diameter across its opponents' goal; *also* : the ball used

push–bike \-,bīk\ *n, Brit* (1913) : a pedal bicycle — called also *push bicycle*

push broom *n* (1926) : a long-handled wide brush that is designed to be pushed and is used for sweeping

push–button *adj* (1916) : using or dependent on complex and more or less self-operating mechanisms that are put in operation by a simple act comparable to pushing a button ⟨~ warfare⟩

push button *n* (1878) : a small button or knob that when pushed operates something esp. by closing an electric circuit

push·cart \'püsh-,kärt\ *n* (1893) : a cart or barrow pushed by hand

push·chair \-,che(ə)r, -,cha(ə)r\ *n, chiefly Brit* (ca. 1909) : STROLLER

push·down \-,daůn\ *n* (1961) : a store of data (as in a computer) from which the most recently stored item must be the first retrieved — called also *pushdown list, pushdown stack*

push·er \'püsh-ər\ *n* (1591) : one that pushes; *esp* : one that pushes illegal drugs

push·ful \-fəl\ *adj* (1896) : PUSHING — **push·ful·ness** *n*

push·ing *adj* (1692) **1 :** marked by ambition, energy, enterprise, and initiative **2 :** marked by tactless forwardness or officious intrusiveness ***syn*** see AGGRESSIVE

push off *vi* (1925) : SET OUT ⟨we *pushed off* for home⟩

push on *vi* (1718) : to continue on one's way : PROCEED

push·over \'püsh-,ō-vər\ *n* (1906) **1 :** something accomplished without difficulty : SNAP **2 :** an opponent who is easy to defeat or a victim who is capable of no effective resistance **3 :** someone unable to resist an attraction or appeal : SUCKER

push·pin \-,pin\ *n* (1907) : a pin that has a roughly cylindrical head and that is easily inserted into or withdrawn from a surface (as a map) with the fingers

push–pull \-'pül\ *adj* (1922) : relating to or being an arrangement of two electronic circuit elements (as transistors) such that an alternating input causes them to send current through a load alternately ⟨a ~ circuit⟩ — **push–pull** *n*

Push·tu \'pəsh-(,)tü\ *var of* PASHTO

push–up \'püsh-,əp\ *n* (1942) : a conditioning exercise performed in a prone position by raising and lowering the body with the straightening and bending of the arms while keeping the back straight and supporting the body on the hands and toes

pushy \'püsh-ē\ *adj* **push·i·er; -est** (1936) : aggressive often to an objectionable degree : FORWARD — **push·i·ly** \'püsh-ə-lē\ *adv* — **push·i·ness** \'püsh-ē-nəs\ *n*

pu·sil·la·nim·i·ty \,pyü-sə-lə-'nim-ət-ē *also* ,pyü-zə-\ *n* (14c) : the quality or state of being pusillanimous : COWARDLINESS

pu·sil·lan·i·mous \-'lan-ə-məs\ *adj* [LL *pusillanimis*, fr. L *pusillus* very small (dim. of *pusus* small child) + *animus* spirit; akin to L *puer* child — more at PUERILE, ANIMATE] (1586) : lacking courage and resolution : marked by contemptible timidity ***syn*** see COWARDLY — **pu·sil·lan·i·mous·ly** *adv*

[1]**puss** \'püs\ *n* [origin unknown] (1530) **1 :** CAT **2 :** GIRL

[2]**puss** *n* [IrGael *pus* mouth, fr. MIr *bus*] *slang* (1890) : FACE

puss·ley \'pəs-lē\ *n* [by alter.] (1833) : PURSLANE

[1]**pussy** \'püs-ē\ *n, pl* **puss·ies** (1583) **1 :** CAT **2 :** a catkin of the pussy willow

[2]**pus·sy** \'püs-ē\ *n, pl* **pussies** [earlier *puss* (perh. of LG or Scand origin) + *-y*; akin to ON *pūss* pocket, pouch, LG *pūse* vulva, OE *pusa* bag, Gk *byein* to stuff, plug] (1878) **1 :** VULVA — usu. considered vulgar **2 a :** SEXUAL INTERCOURSE — usu. considered vulgar **b :** the female partner in sexual intercourse — usu. considered vulgar

[3]**pus·sy** \'pəs-ē\ *var of* [1]PURSY

[4]**pus·sy** \'pəs-ē\ *adj* **pus·si·er; -est** (ca. 1890) : full of or resembling pus

pussy·cat \'püs-ē-,kat\ *n* (1805) **1 :** CAT **2 :** one that is weak, compliant, or amiable : SOFTY

pussy·foot \'püs-ē-,füt\ *vi* (1903) **1 :** to tread or move warily or stealthily **2 :** to refrain from committing oneself — **pussy·foot·er** *n*

pussy·toes \'püs-ē-,tōz\ *or* **puss·y's–toes** \-ēz-\ *n pl but sing or pl in constr* (1892) : any of a genus (*Antennaria*) of woolly or hoary composite herbs that are natives mostly of temperate regions and have small whitish discoid flower heads and a pappus formed of club-shaped bristles

pussy willow \,püs-ē-\ *n* (1869) : a willow (as the American *Salix discolor*) having large cylindrical silky aments

[1]**pus·tu·lant** \'pəs-chə-lənt, 'pəs-t(y)ə-\ *n* (1871) : an agent (as a chemical) that induces pustule formation

[2]**pustulant** *adj* (ca. 1890) : producing pustules

pus·tu·lar \-lər\ *adj* (1739) **1 :** of, relating to, or resembling pustules **2 :** covered with pustular prominences : PUSTULATED

pus·tu·lat·ed \-,lāt-əd\ *adj* (1732) : covered with pustules

pus·tu·la·tion \,pəs-chə-'lā-shən, ,pəs-t(y)ə-\ *n* (1875) **1 :** the act of producing pustules : the state of having pustules **2 :** PUSTULE

pus·tule \'pəs-(,)chü(ə)l, -(,)t(y)ü(ə)l\ *n* [ME, fr. L *pustula* — more at FOG] (14c) **1 :** a small circumscribed elevation of the skin containing pus and having an inflamed base **2 :** a small often distinctively colored elevation or spot resembling a blister or pimple

[1]**put** \'püt\ *vb* **put; put·ting** [ME *putten*; akin to OE *putung* instigation, MD *poten* to plant] *vt* (bef. 12c) **1 a :** to place in a specified position or relationship : LAY ⟨~ the book on the table⟩ **b :** to move in a specified direction **c** (1) : to send (as a weapon or missile) into or through something : THRUST (2) : to throw with an overhand pushing motion ⟨~ the shot⟩ **d :** to bring into a specified state or condition ⟨a reapportionment . . . that was ~ into effect at the September primaries — *Current Biog.*⟩ **2 a :** to cause to endure or suffer something : SUBJECT ⟨~ traitors to death⟩ **b :** IMPOSE, INFLICT ⟨~ a special tax on luxuries⟩ **3 a :** to set before one for judgment or decision ⟨~ the question⟩ **b :** to call for a formal vote on ⟨~ the motion⟩ **4 a** (1) : to turn into language or literary form ⟨want to ~ my feelings into words⟩ (2) : to translate into another language ⟨~ the poem into English⟩ (3) : ADAPT ⟨lyrics ~ to music⟩ **b :** EXPRESS, STATE ⟨*putting* it mildly⟩ **5 a :** to devote (oneself) to an activity or end ⟨~ himself to winning back their confidence⟩ **b :** APPLY ⟨~ her mind to the problem⟩ **c :** ASSIGN ⟨~ them to work⟩ **d :** to cause to perform an action : URGE ⟨~ the horse over the fence⟩ **e :** IMPEL, INCITE ⟨~ them into a frenzy⟩ **6 a :** REPOSE, REST ⟨~*s* his faith in reason⟩ **b :** INVEST ⟨~ her money in the company⟩ **7 a :** to give as an estimate ⟨~ the time as about eleven⟩ **b :** ATTACH, ATTRIBUTE ⟨~*s* a high value on their friendship⟩ **c :** IMPUTE ⟨~ the blame on the partners⟩ **8 :** BET, WAGER ⟨~ $2 on the favorite⟩ ~ *vi* **1 :** to start in motion : GO; *esp* : to leave in a hurry **2** *of a ship* : to take a specified course ⟨~ down the river⟩ — **put forth 1 a :** ASSERT, PROPOSE **b :** to make public : ISSUE **2 :** to bring into action : EXERT **3 :** to produce or send out by growth ⟨*put forth* leaves⟩ **4 :** to start out — **put forward :** PROPOSE ⟨*put forward* a theory⟩ — **put in mind :** REMIND — **put one's finger on :** IDENTIFY ⟨*put his finger on* the cause of the trouble⟩ — **put one's foot down :** to take a firm stand — **put one's foot in one's mouth :** to make a tactless or embarrassing blunder — **put paid to** *Brit* : to finish off : WIPE OUT — **put the arm on** *or* **put the bite on :** to ask for money — **put the finger on :** to inform on ⟨*put the finger on* . . . heroin pushers —Barrie Zwicker⟩ — **put the make on :** to make sexual advances toward — **put to bed :** to make the final preparations for printing (as a newspaper) — **put together 1 :** to create as a unified whole : CONSTRUCT **2 :** ADD, COMBINE — **put to it :** to give difficulty to : press hard ⟨had been *put to it* to keep up⟩

[2]**put** *n* (14c) **1 :** a throw made with an overhand pushing motion; *specif* : the act or an instance of putting the shot **2 :** an option to sell a specified amount of a security (as a stock) or commodity (as wheat) at a fixed price at or within a specified time — compare [2]CALL 3d

[3]**put** *adj* (1848) : being in place : FIXED, SET ⟨stay ~ until I call⟩

put about *vi, of a ship* (1748) : to change direction : go on another tack ~ *vt* : to cause to change course or direction

put across *vt* (1919) **1 :** to achieve or carry through by deceit or trickery **2 :** to convey effectively or forcefully

put–and–take \,püt-ᵊn-'tāk\ *n* (1922) : any of various games of chance played with a teetotum or with dice in which players contribute to a pool and take from it according to the instructions on the top or dice

pu·ta·tive \'pyüt-ət-iv\ *adj* [ME, fr. LL *putativus*, fr. L *putatus*, pp. of *putare* to think] (15c) **1 :** commonly accepted or supposed **2 :** assumed to exist or to have existed — **pu·ta·tive·ly** *adv*

put away *vt* (14c) **1 a :** DISCARD, RENOUNCE ⟨to *put* grief *away* is disloyal to the memory of the departed —H. A. Overstreet⟩ **b :** DIVORCE **2 :** to eat or drink up : CONSUME **3 a :** to confine esp. in a mental institution **b :** BURY **c :** KILL

put by *vt* (15c) **1** *archaic* : REJECT **2 :** to lay aside : SAVE

put–down \'püt-,daůn\ *n* (1962) : an act or instance of putting down; *esp* : a humiliating remark : SQUELCH

put down \,püt-'daůn, 'püt-\ *vt* (14c) **1 :** to bring to an end : STOP ⟨*put down* a riot⟩ **2 a :** DEPOSE, DEGRADE **b :** DISPARAGE, BELITTLE ⟨mentioned his poetry only to *put* it *down*⟩ **c :** DISAPPROVE, CRITICIZE ⟨was *put down* for the way she dressed⟩ **d :** HUMILIATE, SQUELCH ⟨*put* him *down* with a sharp retort⟩ **3 :** to make ineffective : CHECK ⟨*put down* the gossip⟩ **4 a :** to put in writing ⟨*put* it *down* truthfully⟩ **b :** to enter in a list ⟨*put* me *down* for a donation⟩ **5 a :** to place in a category ⟨I *put* him *down* as a hypochondriac —O. S. J. Gogarty⟩ **b :** ATTRIBUTE ⟨*put* it *down* to inexperience⟩ **6 :** CONSUME ⟨*putting down* helping after helping —Carson McCullers⟩ **7 :** to pack or preserve for future use — **put down roots :** to establish a permanent residence

put in *vt* (15c) **1 :** to make a formal offer or declaration of ⟨*put in* a plea of guilty⟩ **2 :** to come in with : INTERPOSE ⟨*put in* a word for his brother⟩ **3 :** to spend (time) at some occupation or job ⟨*put in* six hours at the office⟩ **4 :** PLANT ⟨*put in* a crop⟩ ~ *vi* **1 :** to call at or enter a place; *esp* : to enter a harbor or port **2 :** to make an application, request, or offer — often used with *for* ⟨had to retire and *put in* for a pension —Seymour Nagan⟩

put·log \'püt-,lȯg, 'pət-, -,läg\ *n* [prob. alter. of earlier *putlock*, perh. fr. [3]*put* + *lock*] (1645) : one of the short timbers that support the flooring of a scaffold

put off *vt* (14c) **1 :** DISCONCERT, REPEL **2 a :** to hold back to a later time **b :** to induce to wait ⟨*put* the bill collector *off*⟩ **3 :** to take off : rid oneself of **4 :** to sell or pass fraudulently

[1]**put–on** \,püt-,ȯn, -,än\ *adj* (1621) : PRETENDED, ASSUMED

[2]**put–on** \'püt-,ȯn, -,än\ *n* (ca. 1927) : an instance of putting someone on ⟨conversational ~*s* are related to old-fashioned joshing —Jacob Brack-

man〉; *also* : PARODY, SPOOF 〈a kind of ~ of every pretentious film ever made —C. A. Ridley〉

put on \(ˈ)pu̇t-ˈȯn, -ˈän\ *vt* (15c) **1 a** : to dress oneself in : DON **b** : to make part of one's appearance or behavior **c** : FEIGN 〈*put* a saintly manner *on*〉 **2** : to cause to act or operate : APPLY 〈*put on* more speed〉 **3 a** : ADD 〈*put on* weight〉 **b** : EXAGGERATE, OVERSTATE 〈he's *putting* it *on* when he makes such claims〉 **4** : PERFORM, PRODUCE 〈*put on* a play〉 **5 a** : to mislead deliberately esp. for amusement 〈the interviewer . . . must be put down — or possibly, *put on* —Melvin Maddocks〉 **b** : KID 〈you're *putting* me *on*〉

put·out \ˈpu̇t-ˌau̇t\ *n* (1885) : the retiring of a base runner or batter by a defensive player in baseball

put out \ˌpu̇t-ˈau̇t, ˈpu̇t-\ *vt* (14c) **1** : EXTINGUISH 〈*put* the fire *out*〉 **2** : EXERT, USE 〈*put out* considerable effort〉 **3** : PUBLISH, ISSUE **4** : to produce for sale **5 a** : DISCONCERT, EMBARRASS **b** : ANNOY, IRRITATE **c** : INCONVENIENCE 〈don't *put* yourself *out* for us〉 **6** : to cause to be out (as in baseball or cricket) ~ *vi* **1** : to set out from shore **2** : to make an effort **3** : to engage in sexual intercourse

put over *vt* (1528) **1** : POSTPONE, DELAY **2** : PUT ACROSS

pu·tre·fac·tion \ˌpyü-trə-ˈfak-shən\ *n* [ME *putrefaccion*, fr. LL *putrefaction-, putrefactio*, fr. L *putrefactus*, pp. of *putrefacere*] (15c) **1** : the decomposition of organic matter; *esp* : the typically anaerobic splitting of proteins by bacteria and fungi with the formation of foul-smelling incompletely oxidized products **2** : the state of being putrefied : CORRUPTION — **pu·tre·fac·tive** \-ˈfak-tiv\ *adj*

pu·tre·fy \ˈpyü-trə-ˌfī\ *vb* **-fied; -fy·ing** [ME *putrefien*, fr. MF & L; MF *putrefier*, fr. L *putrefacere*, fr. *putrēre* to be rotten + *facere* to make — more at DO] *vt* (15c) : to make putrid ~ *vi* : to undergo putrefaction *syn* see DECAY

pu·tres·cence \pyü-ˈtres-ᵊn(t)s\ *n* (1646) : the state of being putrescent

pu·tres·cent \-ᵊnt\ *adj* [L *putrescent-, putrescens*, prp. of *putrescere* to grow rotten, incho. of *putrēre*] (1732) **1** : undergoing putrefaction : becoming putrid **2** : of or relating to putrefaction

pu·tres·ci·ble \-ˈtres-ə-bəl\ *adj* (1797) : liable to become putrid

pu·tres·cine \-ˈtres-ˌēn\ *n* [ISV, fr. L *putrescere*] (1887) : a crystalline slightly poisonous ptomaine $C_4H_{12}N_2$ that is formed by decarboxylation of ornithine, occurs widely but scantily in living things, and is found esp. in putrid flesh

pu·trid \ˈpyü-trəd\ *adj* [L *putridus*, fr. *putrēre* to be rotten, fr. *puter, putris* rotten; akin to L *putēre* to stink — more at FOUL] (1598) **1 a** : being in a state of putrefaction : ROTTEN **b** : of, relating to, or characteristic of putrefaction : FOUL 〈a ~ odor〉 **2 a** : morally corrupt **b** : totally objectionable *syn* see MALODOROUS — **pu·trid·i·ty** \pyü-ˈtrid-ət-ē\ *n* — **pu·trid·ly** \ˈpyü-trəd-lē\ *adv*

putsch \ˈpu̇ch\ *n* [G] (1920) : a secretly plotted and suddenly executed attempt to overthrow a government

putsch·ist \ˈpu̇ch-əst\ *n* (1898) : one who takes part in a putsch

putt \ˈpət\ *n* [alter. of ²*put*] (1743) : a golf stroke made on a putting green to cause the ball to roll into or near the hole — **putt** *vb*

put·tee \ˌpə-ˈtē, pu̇-; ˈpət-ē\ *n* [Hindi *paṭṭī* strip of cloth, fr. Skt *paṭṭikā*] (1886) **1** : a cloth strip wrapped around the leg from ankle to knee **2** : a usu. leather legging secured by a strap or catch or by laces

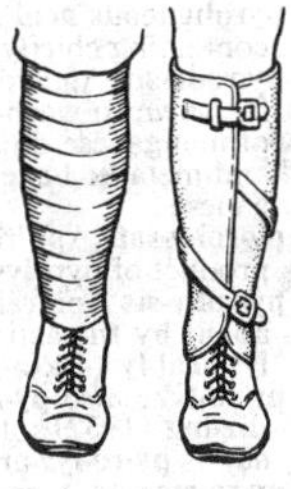

puttee

¹put·ter \ˈpu̇t-ər\ *n* (15c) : one that puts 〈a ~ of questions〉

²putt·er \ˈpət-ər\ *n* (1743) **1** : a golf club used in putting **2** : one that putts

³put·ter \ˈpət-ər\ *vi* [alter. of *potter*] (ca. 1877) **1** : to move or act aimlessly or idly **2** : to work at random : TINKER — **put·ter·er** \-ər-ər\ *n*

put through *vt* (1852) **1** : to carry to a successful conclusion 〈*put through* a number of reforms〉 **2 a** : to make a telephone connection for **b** : to obtain a connection for (a telephone call)

putt·ing green \ˈpət-iŋ-\ *n* (1841) : a smooth grassy area at the end of a golf fairway containing the hole; *also* : a similar area usu. with many holes that is used for practice

put·to \ˈpüt-(ˌ)ō\ *n, pl* **put·ti** \-(ˌ)ē\ [It, lit., boy, fr. L *putus*; akin to Skt *putra* son — more at FEW] (1644) : a figure of an infant boy esp. in European art of the Renaissance — usu. used in pl.

put to *vi, of a ship* (1797) : to put in to shore (as for shelter)

¹put·ty \ˈpət-ē\ *n, pl* **putties** [F *potée*, lit., potful, fr. OF, fr. *pot* pot] (1633) **1** : a pasty substance consisting of hydrated lime and water **2** : a polishing material containing chiefly an oxide of tin **3 a** : a cement usu. made of whiting and boiled linseed oil beaten or kneaded to the consistency of dough and used esp. in fastening glass in sashes and stopping crevices in woodwork **b** : any of various substances resembling such cement in appearance, consistency, or use: as **(1)** : an acid-resistant mixture of ferric oxide and boiled linseed oil **(2)** : a mixture of red and white lead and boiled linseed oil used as a lute in pipe fitting **4** : a light brownish gray to light grayish brown textile color **5** : one who is easily manipulated 〈is ~ in her hands〉

²putty *vt* **put·tied; put·ty·ing** (1734) : to use putty on or apply putty to

put·ty·root \ˈpət-ē-ˌrüt, -ˌru̇t\ *n* (1817) : a No. American orchid (*Aplectrum hyemale*) having a slender naked rootstock and producing brown flowers

put–up \ˌpu̇t-ˌəp\ *adj* (ca. 1810) : arranged secretly beforehand

put up \ˌpu̇t-ˈəp, ˈpu̇t-\ *vt* (14c) **1 a** : to place in a container or receptacle 〈*put* his lunch *up* in a bag〉 **b** : to put away (as a sword) in a scabbard : SHEATHE **c** : to prepare so as to preserve for later use : CAN **d** : to put in storage **2** : to start (game) from cover **3** : to nominate for election **4** : to offer up (as a prayer) **5** : SET 16 **6** : to offer for public sale 〈*puts* his possessions *up* for auction〉 **7** : to give food and shelter to : ACCOMMODATE **8** : to arrange (as a plot or scheme) with others 〈*put up* a job to steal the jewels〉 **9** : BUILD, ERECT **10 a** : to make a display of 〈*put up* a bluff〉 **b** : to engage in 〈*put up* a struggle against odds〉 **11 a** : CONTRIBUTE, PAY **b** : to offer as a prize or stake **12** : to increase the amount of : RAISE ~ *vi* : LODGE — **put up to** : INCITE, INSTIGATE 〈they *put* him *up to* playing the prank〉 — **put up with** : to endure or tolerate without complaint or attempt at reprisal

put–up·on \ˈpu̇t-ə-ˌpȯn, -ˌpän\ *adj* (1920) : imposed upon : taken advantage of

¹puz·zle \ˈpəz-əl\ *vb* **puz·zled; puz·zling** \-(ə-)liŋ\ [origin unknown] *vt* (1602) **1** : to offer or represent to (a person or his mind) a problem difficult to solve or a situation difficult to resolve : challenge mentally; *also* : to exert (as oneself) over such a problem or situation 〈they *puzzled* their wits to find a solution〉 **2** *archaic* : COMPLICATE, ENTANGLE **3** : to solve with difficulty or ingenuity 〈~ out an answer to a riddle〉 ~ *vi* **1** : to be uncertain as to action or choice **2** : to attempt a solution of a puzzle by guesswork or experiment — **puz·zler** \-(ə-)lər\ *n*

syn PUZZLE, PERPLEX, BEWILDER, DISTRACT, NONPLUS, CONFOUND, DUMBFOUND mean to baffle and disturb mentally. PUZZLE implies existence of a problem difficult to solve 〈a persistent fever which *puzzled* the doctor〉 PERPLEX adds a suggestion of worry and uncertainty esp. about making a necessary decision 〈new and *perplexing* challenges face higher education today —M. S. Eisenhower〉 BEWILDER stresses a confusion of mind that hampers clear and decisive thinking 〈the *bewildering* confusion of our times —Matthew Arnold〉 DISTRACT implies agitation or uncertainty induced by conflicting preoccupations or interests 〈that conflict of races and religions which had so long *distracted* the island —T. B. Macaulay〉 NONPLUS implies a bafflement that makes orderly planning or deciding impossible 〈doing the unexpected in a way likely to *nonplus* a conventionally-minded enemy —*Times Lit. Supp.*〉 CONFOUND implies temporary mental paralysis caused by astonishment or profound abasement 〈so spoke the son of God; and Satan stood a while as mute, *confounded* —John Milton〉 DUMBFOUND suggests intense but momentary confounding; often the idea of astonishment is so stressed that it becomes a near synonym of *astound* 〈I was *dumbfounded* to hear him say that I was on a quixotic enterprise —William Lawrence〉

²puzzle *n* (1607) **1** : the state of being puzzled : PERPLEXITY **2 a** : something that puzzles **b** : a question, problem, or contrivance designed for testing ingenuity *syn* see MYSTERY

puz·zle·head·ed \ˌpəz-əl-ˈhed-əd\ *adj* (1780) : having or based on confused attitudes or ideas — **puz·zle·head·ed·ness** *n*

puz·zle·ment \ˈpəz-əl-mənt\ *n* (1822) **1** : the state of being puzzled : PERPLEXITY **2** : PUZZLE

puz·zling *adj* (1666) : difficult to understand or solve — **puz·zling·ly** *adv*

py- *or* **pyo-** *comb form* [Gk, fr. *pyon* pus — more at FOUL] : pus 〈*pyemia*〉 〈*pyorrhea*〉

pya \pē-ˈ(y)ä\ *n* [Burmese] (1952) — see *kyat* at MONEY table

pyc·nid·i·um \pik-ˈnid-ē-əm\ *n, pl* **-ia** \-ē-ə\ [NL, fr. Gk *pyknos* dense; akin to Gk *pyka* thickly, Alb *puth* kiss] (1857) : a flask-shaped fruiting body bearing conidiophores and conidia on the interior and occurring in various imperfect fungi and ascomycetes — **pyc·nid·i·al** \-ē-əl\ *adj*

pyc·no·go·nid \pik-ˈnäg-ə-nəd, ˌpik-nə-ˈgän-əd\ *n* [deriv. of Gk *pyknos* + *gony* knee — more at KNEE] (1881) : SEA SPIDER

pyc·nom·e·ter \pik-ˈnäm-ət-ər\ *n* [Gk *pyknos* + ISV *-meter*] (1858) : a standard vessel often provided with a thermometer for measuring and comparing the densities of liquids or solids

pye–dog \ˈpī-ˌdȯg, -ˈdȯg\ *n* [prob. by shortening and alter. fr. *pariah dog*] (1864) : a half-wild dog common about Asian villages

pyel- *or* **pyelo-** *comb form* [NL, pelvis, fr. Gk *pyelos* trough; akin to Gk *plein* to sail — more at FLOW] : renal pelvis 〈*pyelography*〉

py·eli·tis \ˌpī-ə-ˈlīt-əs\ *n* [NL] (ca. 1842) : inflammation of the lining of the renal pelvis

py·elo·ne·phri·tis \ˌpī-(ə-)lō-ni-ˈfrīt-əs\ *n* [NL] (1866) : inflammation of both the lining of the pelvis and the parenchyma of the kidney — **py·elo·ne·phrit·ic** \-ˈfrit-ik\ *adj*

py·emia \pī-ˈē-mē-ə\ *n* [NL] (ca. 1857) : septicemia caused by pus-forming bacteria and accompanied by multiple abscesses

py·gid·i·um \pī-ˈjid-ē-əm\ *n, pl* **-ia** \-ē-ə\ [NL, fr. Gk *pygidion*, dim. of *pygē* rump; akin to L *pustula* pustule] (ca. 1849) : a caudal structure or the terminal body region of various invertebrates — **py·gid·i·al** \-ē-əl\ *adj*

pyg·mae·an *or* **pyg·me·an** \pig-ˈmē-ən, ˈpig-mē-\ *adj* [L *pygmaeus*] (1667) : PYGMY

Pyg·ma·lion \pig-ˈmāl-yən, -ˈmā-lē-ən\ *n* [L, fr. Gk *Pygmaliōn*] : a king of Cyprus who makes a female figure of ivory that is brought to life for him by Aphrodite

pyg·moid \ˈpig-ˌmȯid\ *adj* (ca. 1930) : resembling or having the characteristics of the Pygmies

pyg·my \ˈpig-mē\ *n, pl* **pygmies** [ME *pigmei*, fr. L *pygmaeus* of a pygmy, dwarfish, fr. Gk *pygmaios*, fr. *pygmē* fist, measure of length — more at PUNGENT] (14c) **1** *often cap* : any of a race of dwarfs described by ancient Greek authors **2** *cap* : any of a small people of equatorial Africa ranging under five feet in height **3** : a short insignificant person : DWARF — **pygmy** *adj*

py·ja·mas \pə-ˈjä-məz\ *chiefly Brit var of* PAJAMAS

pyk·nic \ˈpik-nik\ *adj* [ISV, fr. Gk *pyknos* dense, stocky — more at PYCNIDIUM] (1925) : characterized by shortness of stature, broadness of girth, and powerful muscularity : ENDOMORPHIC 2 — **pyknic** *n*

py·lon \ˈpī-ˌlän, -lən\ *n* [Gk *pylōn*, fr. *pylē* gate] (1850) **1 a** : a usu. massive gateway **b** : an ancient Egyptian gateway building in a truncated pyramidal form **c** : a monumental mass flanking an entranceway or an approach to a bridge **2** : a tower for supporting either end of a wire over a long span; *broadly* : any of various towerlike structures **3** : a projection (as a post or tower) marking a prescribed course of flight for an airplane **4** : a rigid structure on the outside of an aircraft for supporting something (as an engine, tank, or bomb) — see AIRPLANE illustration **5** : a conical marker used on a road (as for directing traffic)

py·lo·ric \pī-ˈlȯr-ik, pə-, -ˈlōr-\ *adj* (1807) : of or relating to the pylorus; *also* : of, relating to, or situated in or near the posterior part of the stomach

py·lo·rus \-əs\ *n, pl* **py·lo·ri** \-ˈlō(ə)r-ˌī, -(ˌ)ē\ [LL, fr. Gk *pylōros*, lit., gatekeeper, fr. *pylē*] (1615) : the opening from the vertebrate stomach into the intestine

\ə\ abut \ᵊ\ kitten, F table \ər\ further \a\ ash \ā\ ace \ä\ cot, cart \au̇\ out \ch\ chin \e\ bet \ē\ easy \g\ go \i\ hit \ī\ ice \j\ job \ŋ\ sing \ō\ go \ȯ\ law \ȯi\ boy \th\ thin \t͟h\ the \ü\ loot \u̇\ foot \y\ yet \zh\ vision \á, k̲, ⁿ, œ, œ̄, ue, ue̅, ʸ\ *see* Guide to Pronunciation

pyo·der·ma \ˌpī-ə-ˈdər-mə\ *n* [NL] (1930) **:** a bacterial skin inflammation marked by pus-filled lesions

pyo·gen·ic \-ˈjen-ik\ *adj* [ISV] (1839) **:** producing pus ⟨~ bacteria⟩ **:** marked by pus production

py·or·rhea \ˌpī-ə-ˈrē-ə\ *n* [NL] (1875) **:** purulent inflammation of the sockets of the teeth leading usu. to loosening of the teeth

pyr- *or* **pyro-** *comb form* [ME, fr. MF, fr. LL, fr. Gk, fr. *pyr* — more at FIRE] **1 :** fire **:** heat ⟨*pyro*meter⟩ ⟨*pyr*heliometer⟩ **2 a :** produced by or as if by the action of heat ⟨*pyro*electricity⟩ **b :** derived from a corresponding ortho acid by loss usu. of one molecule of water from two molecules of acid ⟨*pyro*phosphoric acid⟩ **3 :** fever ⟨*pyro*toxin⟩

pyr·acan·tha \ˌpī-rə-ˈkan(t)-thə\ *n* [NL, fr. Gk *pyrakantha,* a tree, fr. *pyr-* + *akantha* thorn — more at ACANTH-] (1705) **:** any of a small genus (*Pyracantha*) of Eurasian thorny evergreen or semievergreen shrubs of the rose family with alternate leaves, corymbs of white flowers, and small reddish pomes

py·ral·id \pī-ˈral-əd\ *n* [deriv. of L *pyralis,* fly fabled as living in fire, fr. Gk, fr. *pyr* fire] (ca. 1890) **:** any of a very large heterogeneous family (Pyralidae) of mostly small slender long-legged moths — **pyralid** *adj*

py·ral·i·did \pī-ˈral-əd-əd, -əˌdid\ *n* [deriv. of L *pyralis*] (ca. 1934) **:** PYRALID — **pyralidid** *adj*

[1]**pyr·a·mid** \ˈpir-əˌmid\ *n* [L *pyramid-, pyramis,* fr. Gk, of unknown origin] (1549) **1 a :** an ancient massive structure found esp. in Egypt having typically a square ground plan, outside walls in the form of four triangles that meet in a point at the top, and inner sepulchral chambers **b :** a structure or object of similar form **2 :** a polyhedron having for its base a polygon and for faces triangles with a common vertex — see VOLUME table **3 :** a crystalline form each face of which intersects the vertical axis and either two lateral axes or in the tetragonal system one lateral axis **4 :** an anatomical structure resembling a pyramid: as **a :** any of the conical masses that project from the renal medulla into the kidney pelvis **b :** either of two large bundles of motor fibers from the cerebral cortex that reach the medulla oblongata and are continuous with the pyramidal tracts of the spinal cord **5 :** an immaterial structure built on a broad supporting base and narrowing gradually to an apex ⟨the socioeconomic ~⟩ — **py·ra·mi·dal** \pə-ˈram-əd-ᵊl, ˌpir-ə-ˈmid-\ *adj* — **py·ra·mi·dal·ly** \-ē\ *adv* — **pyr·a·mid·i·cal** \ˌpir-ə-ˈmid-i-kəl\ *adj*

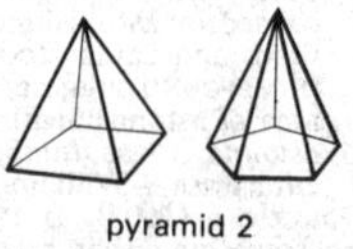

pyramid 2

[2]**pyramid** *vi* (ca. 1900) **1 :** to speculate (as on a security or commodity exchange) by using paper profits as margin for additional transactions **2 :** to increase rapidly and progressively step by step on a broad base ~ *vt* **1 :** to arrange or build up as if on the base of a pyramid **2 :** to use (as profits) in speculative pyramiding **3 :** to increase the impact of (as a tax assessed at the production level) on the ultimate consumer by treating as a cost subject to markup

pyramidal tract *n* (ca. 1890) **:** any of four columns of motor fibers that run in pairs on each side of the spinal cord and are continuations of the pyramids of the medulla oblongata

Pyr·a·mus \ˈpir-ə-məs\ *n* [L, fr. Gk *Pyramos*] **:** a legendary youth of Babylon who dies for love of Thisbe

py·ran \ˈpī(ə)r-ˌan\ *n* [ISV] (1904) **:** either of two cyclic compounds C_5H_6O that contain five carbon atoms and one oxygen atom in the ring

py·ra·nose \ˈpī-rə-ˌnōs, -ˌnōz\ *n* [ISV *pyran* + *-ose*] (1927) **:** a monosaccharide in the form of a cyclic hemiacetal containing a pyran ring

py·ran·o·side \pī-ˈran-əˌsīd\ *n* (1932) **:** a glycoside containing the pyran ring

pyr·ar·gy·rite \pī-ˈrär-jəˌrīt\ *n* [G *pyrargyrit,* fr. Gk *pyr-* + *argyros* silver — more at ARGENT] (1849) **:** a mineral Ag_3SbS_3 consisting of silver antimony sulfide that occurs in rhombohedral crystals or in massive form and has a dark red or black color with a metallic adamantine luster

pyre \ˈpī(ə)r\ *n* [L *pyra,* fr. Gk, fr. *pyr* fire — more at FIRE] (1658) **:** a combustible heap for burning a dead body as a funeral rite; *broadly* **:** a pile of material to be burned ⟨a ~ of dead leaves⟩

py·re·noid \pī-ˈrē-ˌnȯid, ˈpī-rə-\ *n* [ISV, fr. NL *pyrena*] (ca. 1875) **:** one of the protein bodies in the chromatophores of various lower organisms (as some algae) that act as centers for starch deposition

py·re·thrin \pī-ˈrē-thrən, -ˈreth-rən\ *n* [ISV, fr. L *pyrethrum*] (1924) **:** either of two oily liquid esters $C_{21}H_{28}O_3$ and $C_{22}H_{28}O_5$ that have insecticidal properties and that occur esp. in pyrethrum flowers

py·re·throid \-ˈrēˌthrȯid, -ˈreth-ˌrȯid\ *n* [*pyrethrin* + *-oid*] (1949) **:** any of various synthetic compounds that are related to the pyrethrins and resemble them in insecticidal properties — **pyrethroid** *adj*

py·re·thrum \pī-ˈrē-thrəm, -ˈreth-rəm\ *n* [L, pellitory, fr. Gk *pyrethron,* fr. *pyr* fire] (1562) **1 :** any of several chrysanthemums with finely divided often aromatic leaves including ornamentals as well as important sources of insecticides **2 :** an insecticide consisting of the dried heads of any of several Old World chrysanthemums

py·ret·ic \pī-ˈret-ik\ *adj* [NL *pyreticus,* fr. Gk *pyretikos,* fr. *pyretos* fever, fr. *pyr*] (ca. 1858) **:** of or relating to fever **:** FEBRILE

Py·rex \ˈpī(ə)r-ˌeks\ *trademark* — used for glass and glassware that contains appreciable oxide of boron and is resistant to heat, chemicals, and electricity

py·rex·ia \pī-ˈrek-sē-ə\ *n* [NL, fr. Gk *pyressein* to be feverish, fr. *pyretos*] (1769) **:** abnormal elevation of body temperature **:** FEVER — **py·rex·i·al** \-sē-əl\ *adj* — **py·rex·ic** \-sik\ *adj*

pyr·he·li·om·e·ter \ˈpī(ə)r-ˌhē-lē-ˈäm-ət-ər, ˈpi(ə)r-\ *n* [ISV] (1863) **:** an instrument for measuring the sun's radiant energy as received at the earth — **pyr·he·lio·met·ric** \-lē-ə-ˈme-trik\ *adj*

py·ric \ˈpī-rik, ˈpir-ik\ *adj* [F *pyrique,* fr. Gk *pyr*] (1946) **:** resulting from, induced by, or associated with burning

pyr·i·dine \ˈpir-əˌdēn\ *n* [*pyr-* + *-id* + *-ine*] (1851) **:** a toxic water-soluble flammable liquid base C_5H_5N of pungent odor that is obtained by distillation of bone oil or as a by-product of coking, is the parent of many naturally occurring organic compounds, and is used as a solvent and a denaturant for alcohol and in the manufacture of pharmaceuticals and waterproofing agents

pyr·i·dox·al \ˌpir-ə-ˈdäk-ˌsal\ *n* [ISV, fr. *pyridoxine*] (1944) **:** a crystalline aldehyde $C_8H_9NO_3$ of the vitamin B_6 group that occurs as a phosphate active as a coenzyme

pyr·i·dox·amine \ˌpir-ə-ˈdäk-sə-ˌmēn\ *n* [ISV *pyridoxine* + *amine*] (1939) **:** a crystalline amine $C_8H_{12}N_2O_2$ of the vitamin B_6 group that occurs as a phosphate active as a coenzyme

pyr·i·dox·ine \ˌpir-ə-ˈdäk-ˌsēn, -sən\ *n* [*pyridine* + *ox-* + *-ine*] (1940) **:** a crystalline phenolic alcohol $C_8H_{11}NO_3$ of the vitamin B_6 group found esp. in cereals and convertible in the organism into pyridoxal and pyridoxamine

pyr·i·form \ˈpir-əˌfȯrm\ *adj* [NL *pyriformis,* fr. ML *pyrum* pear (alter. of L *pirum*) + L *-iformis* -iform — more at PEAR] (1741) **:** having the form of a pear

py·ri·meth·amine \ˌpī-rə-ˈmeth-əˌmēn\ *n* [*pyrimidine* + *ethyl* + *amine*] (1952) **:** a folic acid antagonist $C_{12}H_{13}ClN_4$ used in the treatment of malaria and of toxoplasmosis

py·rim·i·dine \pī-ˈrim-əˌdēn, pə-\ *n* [ISV, alter. of *pyridine*] (1885) **1 :** a feeble organic base $C_4H_4N_2$ of penetrating odor **2 :** a derivative of pyrimidine; *esp* **:** a base (as cytosine, thymine, or uracil) that is a constituent of DNA or RNA

py·rite \ˈpīˌrīt\ *n* [L *pyrites*] (1588) **:** a common mineral that consists of iron disulfide FeS_2, has a pale brass-yellow color and metallic luster, and is burned in making sulfur dioxide and sulfuric acid

py·rites \pə-ˈrīt-ēz, pī-; ˈpīˌrīts\ *n, pl* **pyrites** [L, flint, fr. Gk *pyritēs* of or in fire, fr. *pyr* fire] (1567) **:** any of various metallic-looking sulfides of which pyrite is the commonest — **py·rit·ic** \-ˈrit-ik\ *adj*

py·ro·cat·e·chol \ˌpī-rō-ˈkat-əˌkȯl, -ˌkōl\ *n* [ISV *pyr-* + *catechol* ($C_{15}H_{14}O_6$)] (1890) **:** a crystalline phenol $C_6H_6O_2$ obtained by pyrolysis of various natural substances (as resins and lignins) but usu. made synthetically and used esp. as a photographic developer and in organic synthesis

Py·ro·ce·ram \ˌpī-rō-sə-ˈram\ *trademark* — used for glass-ceramic materials and articles made from them

py·ro·clas·tic \-ˈklas-tik\ *adj* (1887) **:** formed by or involving fragmentation as a result of volcanic or igneous action

py·ro·elec·tric·i·ty \ˈpī-rō-əˌlek-ˈtris-ət-ē, -ˈtris-tē\ *n* [ISV] (ca. 1834) **:** a state of electrical polarization produced (as in a crystal) by a change of temperature — **py·ro·elec·tric** \-ˈlek-trik\ *adj*

py·ro·gal·lic acid \ˌpī-rōˌgal-ik-, -ˌgȯ-lik-\ *n* [ISV] (1836) **:** PYROGALLOL

py·ro·gal·lol \-ˈgal-ˌȯl, -ˌōl; -ˈgȯ-ˌlȯl, -ˌlōl\ *n* [ISV *pyrogallic* (acid) + *-ol*] (1876) **:** a poisonous bitter crystalline phenol $C_6H_6O_3$ with weak acid properties that is obtained usu. by pyrolysis of gallic acid and used esp. as a mild reducing agent (as in photographic developing)

py·ro·gen \ˈpī-rə-jən\ *n* [ISV] (ca. 1890) **:** a fever-producing substance

py·ro·gen·ic \ˌpī-rō-ˈjen-ik\ *adj* [ISV] (1853) **1 :** producing or produced by heat or fever **2 :** of or relating to igneous origin — **py·ro·ge·nic·i·ty** \ˌpī-rō-jə-ˈnis-ət-ē\ *n*

py·ro·la \pī-ˈrō-lə\ *n* [NL, prob. fr. L *pirum* pear] (1578) **:** any of a genus (*Pyrola*) of short-stemmed perennial herbs that have basal persistent leaves and racemes of white, pink, or purple pentamerous flowers containing 10 straight or declined stamens

py·ro·lig·ne·ous \ˌpī-rō-ˈlig-nē-əs\ *adj* [F *pyroligneux,* fr. *pyr-* + *ligneux* woody, fr. L *lignosus,* fr. *lignum* wood — more at LIGNEOUS] (ca. 1790) **:** obtained by destructive distillation of wood

pyroligneous acid *n* (ca. 1790) **:** an acid reddish brown aqueous liquid containing chiefly acetic acid, methanol, wood oils, and tars

py·ro·lu·site \ˌpī-rō-ˈlü-ˌsīt\ *n* [G *pyrolusit,* fr. Gk *pyr-* + *lousis* washing, fr. *louein* to wash — more at LYE] (1828) **:** a mineral MnO_2 consisting of manganese dioxide that is of an iron-black or dark steel-gray color and metallic luster, is usu. soft, and is the most important ore of manganese

py·rol·y·sate \pī-ˈräl-əˌzāt, -ˌsāt\ *or* **py·rol·y·zate** \-ˌzāt\ *n* (1944) **:** a product of pyrolysis

py·rol·y·sis \pī-ˈräl-ə-səs\ *n* [NL] (1890) **:** chemical change brought about by the action of heat — **py·ro·lyt·ic** \ˌpī-rə-ˈlit-ik\ *adj* — **py·ro·lyt·i·cal·ly** \-i-k(ə-)lē\ *adv*

py·ro·lyze *also* **py·ro·lize** \ˈpī-rəˌlīz\ *vt* **-lyzed** *also* **-lized; -lyz·ing** *also* **-liz·ing** (1932) **:** to subject to pyrolysis — **py·ro·lyz·able** \-ˌlī-zə-bəl\ *adj* — **py·ro·lyz·er** *n*

py·ro·man·cy \-ˌman(t)-sē\ *n* [ME *pyromancie,* fr. MF, fr. LL *pyromantia,* fr. Gk *pyromanteia,* fr. *pyr* fire + *manteia* divination — more at -MANCY] (14c) **:** divination by means of fire or flames

py·ro·ma·nia \ˌpī-rō-ˈmā-nē-ə, -nyə\ *n* [NL] (ca. 1842) **:** an irresistible impulse to start fires — **py·ro·ma·ni·ac** \-nē-ˌak\ *n* — **py·ro·ma·ni·a·cal** \-mə-ˈnī-ə-kəl\ *adj*

py·ro·met·al·lur·gy \-ˈmet-ᵊl-ˌər-jē, *esp Brit* -mə-ˈtal-ər-\ *n* [ISV] (ca. 1908) **:** chemical metallurgy depending on heat action (as roasting and smelting) — **py·ro·met·al·lur·gi·cal** \-ˌmet-ᵊl-ˈər-ji-kəl\ *adj*

py·rom·e·ter \pī-ˈräm-ət-ər\ *n* [ISV] (1796) **:** an instrument for measuring temperatures esp. when beyond the range of mercurial thermometers usu. by the increase of electric resistance in a metal, by the generation of electric current by a thermocouple, or by the increase in intensity of light radiated by an incandescent body — **py·ro·met·ric** \ˌpī-rə-ˈme-trik\ *adj* — **py·ro·met·ri·cal·ly** \-tri-k(ə-)lē\ *adv* — **py·rom·e·try** \pī-ˈräm-ə-trē\ *n*

py·ro·mor·phite \ˌpī-rə-ˈmȯr-ˌfīt\ *n* [G *pyromorphit,* fr. Gk *pyr-* + *morphē* form] (ca. 1814) **:** a mineral $Pb_5(PO_4)_3Cl$ consisting essentially of a lead chloride and phosphate and occurring in green, yellow, brown, gray, or white crystals or masses

py·ro·nine \ˈpī-rəˌnēn\ *n* [ISV *pyr-* + *-on* + *-ine*] (1895) **:** any of several basic xanthene dyes used chiefly as biological stains

py·ro·nin·o·phil·ic \ˌpī-rəˌnē-nə-ˈfil-ik\ *adj* (1946) **:** staining selectively with pyronines ⟨~ cells⟩

py·rope \ˈpī(ə)r-ˌōp\ *n* [ME *pirope,* a red gem, fr. MF, fr. L *pyropus,* a red bronze, fr. Gk *pyrōpos,* lit., fiery-eyed, fr. *pyr-* + *ōp-, ōps* eye — more at EYE] (1804) **:** a magnesium-aluminum garnet that is deep red in color and is frequently used as a gem

py·ro·phor·ic \ˌpī-rə-ˈfȯr-ik, -ˈfär-\ *adj* [NL *pyrophorus,* fr. Gk *pyrophoros* fire-bearing, fr. *pyr-* + *-phoros* carrying, from *pherein* to carry — more at BEAR] (1836) **1 :** igniting spontaneously **2 :** emitting sparks when scratched or struck esp. with steel

py·ro·phos·phate \-ˈfäs-ˌfāt\ *n* (1836) **:** a salt or ester of pyrophosphoric acid — **py·ro·phos·phat·ic** \-fäs-ˈfat-ik\ *adj*

py·ro·phos·pho·ric acid \-fäsˌfȯr-ik-, -ˌfär-; -ˌfäs-f(ə-)rik-\ *n* [ISV] (1832) **:** a crystalline acid $H_4P_2O_7$ formed when orthophosphoric acid is heated or prepared in the form of salts by heating acid salts of orthophosphoric acid

py·ro·phyl·lite \ˌpī-rō-'fil-ˌīt, pī-'räf-ə-ˌlīt\ *n* [G *pyrophyllit*, fr. Gk *pyr-* + *phyllon* leaf — more at BLADE] (1830) : a white or greenish mineral AlSi₂O₅(OH) that is a hydrous aluminum silicate, resembles talc, occurs in a foliated form or in compact masses, and is used esp. in ceramic wares

py·ro·sis \pī-'rō-səs\ *n* [NL, fr. Gk *pyrōsis* burning, fr. *pyroun* to burn, fr. *pyr* fire — more at FIRE] (1789) : HEARTBURN

py·ro·sul·fu·ric acid \ˌ-ˌsəl-ˌfyur-ik-\ *n* [ISV] (1872) : an unstable crystalline acid H₂S₂O₇ usu. handled commercially as a thick oily fuming liquid and converted to sulfuric acid when mixed with water

¹**py·ro·tech·nic** \ˌpī-rə-'tek-nik\ *also* **py·ro·tech·ni·cal** \-ni-kəl\ *adj* [F *pyrotechnique*, fr. Gk *pyr* fire + *technē* art] (1825) : of or relating to pyrotechnics — **py·ro·tech·ni·cal·ly** \-ni-k(ə-)lē\ *adv*

²**pyrotechnic** *n* (1840) **1 a** : FIREWORK **b** : any of various similar devices (as for igniting a rocket or producing an explosion) **2** : a combustible substance used in a firework

py·ro·tech·nics \ˌpī-rə-'tek-niks\ *n pl* (1729) **1** *sing or pl in constr* : the art of making or the manufacture and use of fireworks **2 a** : a display of fireworks **b** : a spectacular display (as of oratory or extreme virtuosity) ⟨his verbal ~ are entertaining —*Times Lit. Supp.*⟩ — **py·ro·tech·nist** \-'tek-nəst\ *n*

py·rox·ene \pī-'räk-ˌsēn, pə-\ *n* [F *pyroxène*, fr. Gk *pyr-* + *xenos* stranger] (1800) : any of a group of igneous-rock-forming silicate minerals that contain calcium, sodium, magnesium, iron, or aluminum, usu. occur in short prismatic crystals or massive form, are often laminated, and vary in color from white to dark green or black — **py·rox·e·nic** \ˌpī-räk-'sēn-ik, pə-, -'sen-\ *adj* — **py·rox·e·noid** \pī-'räk-sə-ˌnóid, pə-\ *adj or n*

py·rox·e·nite \pī-'räk-sə-ˌnīt, pə-\ *n* (ca. 1862) : an igneous rock that is free from olivine and is composed essentially of pyroxene — **py·rox·e·nit·ic** \ˌ-räk-sə-'nit-ik\ *adj*

py·rox·y·lin \pī-'räk-sə-lən, pə-\ *n* [ISV *pyr-* + Gk *xylon* wood] (ca. 1847) **1** : a flammable mixture of cellulose nitrates usu. with less than 12.5 percent nitrogen that is less explosive than guncotton, soluble in a mixture of ether and alcohol or other organic solvents, and used esp. in making plastics and coatings (as lacquers) **2** : a pyroxylin product

Pyr·rha \'pir-ə\ *n* [L, fr. Gk] : the wife of Deucalion

pyr·rhic \'pir-ik\ *n* [L *pyrrhichius*, fr. Gk (*pous*) *pyrrhichios*, fr. *pyrrhichē*, a kind of dance] (1626) : a metrical foot consisting of two short or unaccented syllables — **pyrrhic** *adj*

Pyr·rhic victory \ˌpir-ik-\ *n* [*Pyrrhus*, king of Epirus who sustained heavy losses in defeating the Romans] (1885) : a victory won at excessive cost

Pyr·rho·nism \'pir-ə-ˌniz-əm\ *n* [F *pyrrhonisme*, fr. *Pyrrhon* Pyrrho, 4th cent. B.C. Gk philosopher, fr. Gk *Pyrrhōn*] (ca. 1670) **1** : the doctrines of a school of ancient extreme skeptics who suspended judgment on every proposition — compare ACADEMICISM **2** : total or radical skepticism — **Pyr·rho·nist** \-nəst\ *n*

pyr·rho·tite \'pir-ə-ˌtīt\ *n* [modif. of G *pyrrhotin*, fr. Gk *pyrrhotēs* redness; fr. *pyrrhos* red, fr. *pyr* fire — more at FIRE] (1868) : a bronze-colored mineral FeS of metallic luster that consists of ferrous sulfide and is attracted by the magnet

Pyr·rhus \'pir-əs\ *n* [L, fr. Gk *Pyrrhos*] : a son of Achilles and slayer of Priam at the taking of Troy

pyr·role \'pi(ə)r-ˌōl\ *n* [Gk *pyrrhos*] (1835) : a toxic liquid heterocyclic compound C₄H₅N that has a ring consisting of four carbon atoms and one nitrogen atom, polymerizes readily in air, and is the parent compound of many biologically important substances (as bile pigments,

porphyrins, and chlorophyll); *broadly* : a derivative of pyrrole — **pyr·ro·lic** \pir-'ō-lik\ *adj*

py·ru·vate \pī-'rü-ˌvāt\ *n* (1855) : a salt or ester of pyruvic acid

py·ru·vic acid \pī-ˌrü-vik-\ *n* [ISV *pyr-* + L *uva* grape; fr. its importance in fermentation — more at UVULA] (1838) : a 3-carbon keto acid C₃H₄O₃ that is an intermediate in carbohydrate metabolism and can be formed either from glucose after phosphorylation or from glycogen by glycolysis

¹**Py·thag·o·re·an** \pə-ˌthag-ə-'rē-ən, (ˌ)pī-\ *n* (1550) : any of a group professing to be followers of the Greek philosopher Pythagoras

²**Pythagorean** *adj* (1579) : of, relating to, or associated with the Greek philosopher Pythagoras, his philosophy, or the Pythagoreans

Py·thag·o·re·an·ism \-ˌiz-əm\ *n* (ca. 1727) : the doctrines and theories of Pythagoras and the Pythagoreans who developed some basic principles of mathematics and astronomy, originated the doctrine of the harmony of the spheres, and believed in metempsychosis, the eternal recurrence of things, and the mystical significance of numbers

Pythagorean theorem *n* (ca. 1909) : a theorem in geometry: the square of the length of the hypotenuse of a right triangle equals the sum of the squares of the lengths of the other two sides

Pyth·i·ad \'pith-ē-ˌad, -ē-əd\ *n* [Gk *Pythia*, the Pythian games, fr. neut. pl. of *pythios*] (1842) : the 4-year period between celebrations of the Pythian games in ancient Greece

¹**Pyth·i·an** \'pith-ē-ən\ *adj* [L *pythius* of Delphi, fr. Gk *pythios*, fr. *Pythō* Pytho, former name of Delphi, Greece] (1603) **1** : of or relating to games celebrated at Delphi every four years **2** : of or relating to Delphi or its oracle of Apollo

²**Pythian** *n* (1903) : KNIGHT OF PYTHIAS

Pyth·i·as \'pith-ē-əs\ *n* [Gk] : a friend of Damon condemned to death by Dionysius of Syracuse

py·thon \'pī-ˌthän, -thən\ *n* [L, monstrous serpent killed by Apollo, fr. Gk *Pythōn*] (1836) : a large constricting snake (as a boa); *esp* : any of a genus (*Python*) that includes the largest of recent snakes

py·tho·ness \'pī-thə-nəs, 'pith-ə-\ *n* [ME *Phitonesse*, fr. MF *pithonisse*, fr. LL *pythonissa*, fr. Gk *Pythōn*, spirit of divination, fr. *Pythō*, seat of the Delphic oracle] (14c) **1** : a woman who practices divination **2** : a prophetic priestess of Apollo — **py·thon·ic** \pī-'thän-ik\ *adj*

py·uria \pī-'yùr-ē-ə\ *n* [NL] (ca. 1811) : pus in the urine; *also* : a condition characterized by pus in the urine

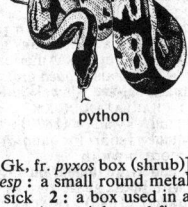

python

pyx \'piks\ *n* [ME, fr. ML *pyxis*, fr. L, box, fr. Gk, fr. *pyxos* box (shrub)] (15c) **1** : a container for the reserved host; *esp* : a small round metal receptacle used to carry the Eucharist to the sick **2** : a box used in a mint for deposit of sample coins reserved for testing weight and fineness

pyx·ie \'pik-sē\ *n* [by shortening & alter. fr. NL *Pyxidanthera*] (1882) : a creeping evergreen shrub (*Pyxidanthera barbulata*) of the sandy pine barrens of the Atlantic coast of the U.S. that is related to the true heaths and has usu. white star-shaped flowers

pyxie moss *n* (1892) : PYXIE

pyx·is \'pik-səs\ *n, pl* **pyx·i·des** \-sə-ˌdēz\ [NL, fr. L, box] (1845) : a capsular fruit that dehisces so that the upper part falls off like a cap

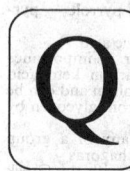

Q

q \ˈkyü\ *n, pl* **q's** *or* **qs** \ˈkyüz\ *often cap, often attrib* **1 a :** the 17th letter of the English alphabet **b :** a graphic representation of this letter **c :** a speech counterpart of orthographic *q* **2 :** a graphic device for reproducing the letter *q* **3 :** one designated *q* esp. as the 17th in order or class **4 :** something shaped like the letter Q

Q–boat \ˈkyü-ˌbōt\ *n* (ca. 1918) **:** Q-SHIP

Q fever \ˈkyü-\ *n* [*q*uery] (ca. 1937) **:** a mild disease characterized by high fever, chills, and muscular pains, caused by a rickettsia (*Coxiella burnetii*), and transmitted by raw milk, by contact, or by ticks

qin·tar \k(y)in-ˈtär\ *n, pl* **qin·dar·ka** \k(y)in-ˈdär-kə\ *or* **qintar** [Alb] (ca. 1929) — see *lek* at MONEY table

qi·vi·ut \ˈkē-vē-ət, -vē-ˌüt\ *n* [Esk] (ca. 1958) **:** the wool of the undercoat of the musk-ox

qoph \ˈkōf\ *n* [Heb *qōph*] (1873) **:** the 19th letter of the Hebrew alphabet — see ALPHABET table

Q–ship \ˈkyü-ˌship\ *n* (ca. 1919) **:** an armed ship disguised as a merchant or fishing ship and used to decoy enemy submarines into gun range

qt \ˈkyü-ˈtē\ *n, often cap Q&T* [abbr.] (ca. 1885) **:** QUIET — usu. used in the phrase *on the qt*

qua \ˈkwä *also* ˈkwā\ *prep* [L, which way, as, fr. abl. sing. fem. of *qui* who — more at WHO] (1647) **:** in the capacity or character of **:** AS ⟨the belief that all men ~ men have certain essential rights —W. K. Frankena⟩

Quaa·lude \ˈkwā-ˌlüd\ *trademark* — used for methaqualone

1quack \ˈkwak\ *n* [imit] (14c) **:** a noise made by quacking

2quack *vi* (1617) **:** to make the characteristic cry of a duck

3quack *vi* [*4quack*] (1628) **:** to play the quack

4quack *n* [short for *quacksalver*] (1638) **1 :** CHARLATAN 2 **2 :** a pretender to medical skill — **quack·ish** \-ish\ *adj*

5quack *adj* (1653) **:** of, relating to, or characteristic of a quack; *esp* **:** pretending to cure diseases

quack·ery \ˈkwak-(ə-)rē\ *n* (1709) **:** the practices or pretensions of a quack

quack grass \ˈkwak-\ *n* [alter. of *quick* (grass), alter. of *quitch* (grass)] (1712) **:** a European grass (*Agropyron repens*) that is naturalized throughout No. America as a weed and spreads by creeping rhizomes — called also *couch grass, quitch, twitch, witchgrass*

quack·sal·ver \ˈkwak-ˌsal-vər\ *n* [obs. D (now *kwakzalver*)] (1579) **:** CHARLATAN, QUACK

1quad \ˈkwäd\ *n* (1820) **:** QUADRANGLE

2quad *n* [short for *quadrat*] (ca. 1879) **:** a type-metal space that is 1 en or more in width

3quad *vt* **quad·ded; quad·ding** (ca. 1888) **:** to fill out (as a typeset line) with blank space

4quad *n* (1896) **:** QUADRUPLET

5quad *adj* [by shortening] (ca. 1970) **:** QUADRIPHONIC

6quad *n* [by shortening] (ca. 1971) **:** QUADRIPHONY

7quad *n* [short for *quadrillion*] (1974) **:** a unit of energy equal to one quadrillion British thermal units

quad·ran·gle \ˈkwäd-ˌraŋ-gəl\ *n* [ME, fr. MF, fr. LL *quadriangulum*, fr. L, neut. of *quadriangulus* quadrangular, fr. *quadri-* + *angulus* angle] (15c) **1 :** QUADRILATERAL **2 a :** a 4-sided enclosure esp. when surrounded by buildings **b :** the buildings enclosing a quadrangle **3 :** a tract of country represented by one of a series of map sheets (as published by the U.S. Geological Survey) — **qua·dran·gu·lar** \kwä-ˈdraŋ-gyə-lər\ *adj*

quad·rant \ˈkwäd-rənt\ *n* [ME, fr. L *quadrant-, quadrans* fourth part; akin to L *quattuor* four — more at FOUR] (15c) **1 a :** an instrument for measuring altitudes consisting commonly of a graduated arc of 90° with an index or vernier and usu. having a plumb line or spirit level for fixing the vertical or horizontal direction **b :** a device or mechanical part shaped like or suggestive of the quadrant of a circle **2 a :** an arc of 90° that is one quarter of a circle **b :** the area bounded by a quadrant and two radii **3 a :** any of the four parts into which a plane is divided by rectangular coordinate axes lying in that plane **b :** any of the four quarters into which something is divided by two real or imaginary lines that intersect each other at right angles — **qua·dran·tal** \kwä-ˈdrant-ᵊl\ *adj*

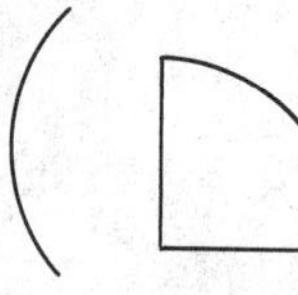

quadrant 2

Qua·dran·tid \kwä-ˈdrant-əd\ *n* [NL *Quadrant-, Quadrans* (*Muralis*) mural quadrant, a group of stars in the constellation Draco from which the shower appears to radiate] (ca. 1876) **:** one of the shooting stars constituting the meteoric shower that recurs near the 3d of January

quad·ra·phon·ic \ˌkwäd-rə-ˈfän-ik\ *adj* [*quadra-* (modif. of *quadri-*) + *phonic*] (ca. 1970) **:** of or relating to quadriphony **:** QUADRIPHONIC — **quad·ra·phon·ics** \-iks\ *n pl but sing in constr*

quad·rat \ˈkwäd-rət, -ˌrat\ *n* [alter. of *2quadrate*] (1683) **1 :** 2QUAD **2 :** a usu. rectangular plot used for ecological or population studies

1quad·rate \ˈkwäd-ˌrāt, -rət\ *adj* [ME, fr. L *quadratus*, pp. of *quadrare* to make square, fit; akin to L *quattuor* four] (14c) **1 :** being square or approximately square **2** *of a heraldic cross* **:** expanded into a square at the junction of the arms — see CROSS illustration **3 :** of, relating to, or constituting a bony or cartilaginous element of each side of the skull to which the lower jaw is articulated in most vertebrates below mammals

2quadrate *n* (15c) **1 :** an approximately square or cubical area, space, or body **2 :** a quadrate bone

qua·drat·ic \kwä-ˈdrat-ik\ *adj* (1668) **:** involving terms of the second degree at most ⟨~ function⟩ ⟨~ equations⟩ — **quadratic** *n* — **qua·drat·i·cal·ly** \-i-k(ə-)lē\ *adv*

quadratic form *n* (1859) **:** a homogeneous polynomial of the second degree ⟨$x^2 + 5xy + y^2$ is a *quadratic form*⟩

quad·ra·ture \ˈkwäd-rə-ˌchu̇(ə)r, -chər, -ˌt(y)u̇(ə)r\ *n* (1591) **1 a :** a configuration in which two celestial bodies have a separation of 90 degrees **b :** either of two points on an orbit in a middle position between the syzygies **2 :** the process of finding a square equal in area to a given area

qua·dren·ni·al \kwä-ˈdren-ē-əl\ *adj* (ca. 1656) **1 :** consisting of or lasting for four years **2 :** occurring or being done every four years — **quadrennial** *n* — **qua·dren·ni·al·ly** \-ē-ə-lē\ *adv*

qua·dren·ni·um \-ē-əm\ *n, pl* **-ni·ums** *or* **-nia** \-ē-ə\ [L *quadriennium*, fr. *quadri-* + *annus* year — more at ANNUAL] (ca. 1754) **:** a period of four years

quadri- *or* **quadr-** *or* **quadru-** *comb form* [ME, fr. L; akin to L *quattuor* four] **1 a :** four ⟨*quadri*lingual⟩ ⟨*quadru*manous⟩ **b :** square ⟨*quadr*ic⟩ **2 :** fourth ⟨*quadri*centennial⟩

quad·ric \ˈkwäd-rik\ *adj* [ISV] (1858) **:** QUADRATIC ⟨~ surface⟩ — used where there are more than two variables — **quadric** *n*

quad·ri·cen·ten·ni·al \ˌkwäd-rə-sen-ˈten-ē-əl\ *n* (1882) **:** a 400th anniversary or its celebration

quad·ri·ceps \ˈkwäd-rə-ˌseps\ *n* [NL *quadricipit-, quadriceps*, fr. *quadri-* + *-cipit-, -ceps* (as in *bicipit-, biceps* biceps] (1840) **:** the great extensor muscle of the front of the thigh divided above into four parts

qua·dri·ga \kwä-ˈdrē-gə\ *n, pl* **-gae** \-ˌgī\ [L, sing. of *quadrigae* team of four, contr. of *quadrijugae*, fem. pl. of *quadrijugus* yoked four abreast, fr. *quadri-* + *jungere* to yoke, join — more at YOKE] (1727) **:** a chariot drawn by four horses abreast

1quad·ri·lat·er·al \ˌkwäd-rə-ˈlat-ə-rəl, -ˈla-trəl\ *n* (1650) **1 :** a polygon of four sides **2 :** a combination or group that involves four parts or individuals

2quadrilateral *adj* [prob. fr. (assumed) NL *quadrilateralis*, fr. L *quadrilaterus*, fr. *quadri-* + *later-, latus* side] (1656) **:** having four sides

1qua·drille \kwä-ˈdril, k(w)ə-\ *n* [F, group of knights engaged in a carousel, fr. Sp. *cuadrilla* troop, fr. *cuarto* fourth] (1726) **1 :** a four-handed variant of ombre popular esp. in the 18th century **2 :** a square dance for four couples made up of five or six figures chiefly in 6/8 and 2/4 time; *also* **:** music for this dance

2quadrille *adj* [F *quadrillé*] (ca. 1885) **:** marked with squares or rectangles

qua·dril·lion \kwä-ˈdril-yən\ *n* [F, fr. MF, fr. *quadri-* + *-illion* (as in *million*)] (ca. 1674) — see NUMBER table — **quadrillion** *adj* — **qua·dril·lionth** \-yən(t)th\ *adj or n*

quad·ri·par·tite \ˌkwäd-rə-ˈpär-ˌtīt\ *adj* [ME, fr. L *quadripartitus*, fr. *quadri-* + *partitus*, pp. of *partire* to divide, fr. *part-, pars* part] (15c) **1 :** consisting of or divided into four parts **2 :** shared or participated in by four parties or persons ⟨a ~ agreement⟩

quad·ri·phon·ics \ˌkwäd-rə-ˈfän-iks\ *n pl but sing in constr* (ca. 1970) **:** QUADRIPHONY

quad·ri·phony \ˈkwäd-rə-ˌfän-ē\ *n* (1969) **:** the transmission, recording, or reproduction of sound by techniques that utilize four transmission channels — **quad·ri·phon·ic** *also* **quad·ro·phon·ic** \ˌkwäd-rə-ˈfän-ik\ *adj*

quad·ri·ple·gic \ˌkwäd-rə-ˈplē-jik\ *n* [*quadriplegia*, fr. NL, fr. *quadri-* + *-plegia*] (1921) **:** one affected with paralysis of both arms and both legs — **quad·ri·ple·gia** \-j(ē)ə\ *n*

1quad·ri·va·lent \-ˈvā-lənt\ *adj* [ISV] (1865) **1 :** TETRAVALENT **2 :** composed of four homologous chromosomes synapsed in meiotic prophase

2quadrivalent *n* (1923) **:** a quadrivalent chromosomal group

qua·driv·i·al \kwä-ˈdriv-ē-əl\ *adj* (15c) **1 :** of or relating to the quadrivium **2 :** having four ways or roads meeting in a point

qua·driv·i·um \-ē-əm\ *n* [LL, fr. L, crossroads, fr. *quadri-* + *via* way — more at VIA] (1804) **:** a group of studies consisting of arithmetic, music, geometry, and astronomy and forming the upper division of the seven liberal arts in medieval universities — compare TRIVIUM

qua·droon \kwä-ˈdrün\ *n* [modif. of Sp *cuarterón*, fr. *cuarto* fourth, fr. L *quartus*] (1707) **:** a person of one-quarter Negro ancestry

qua·dru·ma·nous \kwä-ˈdrü-mə-nəs\ *adj* [deriv. of L *quadri-* + *manus* hand + E *-ous* — more at MANUAL] (1699) **:** of, relating to, or being the primates excluding man which are distinguished by hand-shaped feet

qua·drum·vir \kwä-ˈdrəm-vər\ *n* [back-formation fr. *quadrumvirate*] (1790) **:** a member of a quadrumvirate

qua·drum·vi·rate \-və-rət\ *n* [*quadri-* + *-umvirate* (as in *triumvirate*)] (1752) **:** a group or association of four

quad·ru·ped \ˈkwäd-rə-ˌped\ *n* [L *quadruped-, quadrupes*, fr. *quadruped-, quadrupes*, adj., having four feet, fr. *quadri-* + *ped-, pes* foot — more at FOOT] (1646) **:** an animal having four feet — **quadruped** *adj* — **qua·dru·pe·dal** \kwä-ˈdrü-pəd-ᵊl, ˌkwäd-rə-ˈped-\ *adj*

1qua·dru·ple \kwä-ˈdrüp-əl, -ˈdrəp-; ˈkwäd-rəp-\ *vb* **qua·dru·pled; qua·dru·pling** \-(ə-)liŋ\ *vt* (14c) **:** to make four times as great or as many ~ *vi* **:** to become four times as great or as numerous

2quadruple *n* (1609) **:** a sum four times as great as another

3quadruple *adj* [MF or L; MF, fr. L *quadruplus*, fr. *quadri-* + *-plus* multiplied by — more at -FOLD] (ca. 1557) **1 :** having four units or members **2 :** being four times as great or as many **3 :** marked by four beats per measure ⟨~ meter⟩ — **qua·dru·ply** \-ˈdrüp-lē, -ˈdrəp-, -rəp-\ *adv* — **qua·dru·plic·i·ty** \ˌkwäd-rü-ˈplis-ət-ē\ *n*

qua·dru·plet \kwä-ˈdrü-plət, -ˈdrəp-lət; ˈkwäd-rə-plət\ *n* (1787) **1 :** one of four offspring born at one birth **2 :** a combination of four of a kind **3 :** a group of four musical notes to be performed in the time ordinarily given to three of the same kind

1qua·dru·pli·cate \kwä-ˈdrü-pli-kət\ *adj* [L *quadruplicatus*, pp. of *quadruplicare* to quadruple, fr. *quadruplic-, quadruplex* fourfold, fr. *quadri-* + *-plic-, -plex* fold — more at -FOLD] (1657) **1 :** consisting of or existing in four corresponding or identical parts or examples ⟨~ invoices⟩ **2 :** being the fourth of four things exactly alike

2qua·dru·pli·cate \-plə-ˌkāt\ *vt* **-cat·ed; -cat·ing** (ca. 1661) **1 :** to make quadruple or fourfold **2 :** to prepare in quadruplicate — **qua·dru·pli·ca·tion** \-ˌdrü-plə-ˈkā-shən\ *n*

3qua·dru·pli·cate \kwä-ˈdrü-pli-kət\ *n* (1790) **1 :** four copies all alike — used with *in* ⟨typed in ~⟩ **2 :** one of four things exactly alike; *specif* **:** one of four identical copies

quad·ru·pole \ˈkwäd-rə-ˌpōl\ *n* [ISV *quadri-* + *pole*] (1922) **:** a system composed of two dipoles of equal but oppositely directed moment

quae·re \ˈkwi(ə)r-ē, ˈkwe(ə)r-\ *n* [L, imper. of *quaerere* to seek, question] *archaic* (1589) **:** QUERY

quaes·tor \ˈkwes-tər, ˈkwē-stər\ *n* [ME *questor*, fr. L *quaestor*, fr. *quaestus*, pp. of *quaerere*] (14c) **:** one of numerous ancient Roman officials concerned chiefly with financial administration

quaff \ˈkwäf, ˈkwaf\ *vb* [origin unknown] *vi* (1523) **:** to drink deeply ~ *vt* **:** to drink (a beverage) deeply — **quaff** *n* — **quaff·er** *n*

quag \ˈkwag, ˈkwäg\ *n* [origin unknown] (1589) **:** MARSH, BOG

quag·ga \'kwag-ə, 'kwäg-\ *n* [obs. Afrik (now *kwagga*)] (ca. 1785) **:** an extinct wild ass (*Equus quagga*) of southern Africa related to the zebras
quag·gy \'kwag-ē, 'kwäg-\ *adj* (1610) **1 :** MARSHY **2 :** FLABBY, YIELDING
quag·mire \'kwag-,mī(ə)r, 'kwäg-\ *n* (1530) **1 :** soft miry land that shakes or yields under the foot **2 :** a difficult, precarious, or entrapping position **:** PREDICAMENT
qua·hog *also* **qua·haug** \'kō-,hȯg, 'kwȯ-, 'kwō-, -,häg\ *n* [Narraganset *poquaûhock*] (1753) **:** a thick-shelled American clam (*Mercenaria mercenaria*)
quai \'kā\ *n* [F, fr. MF *cai*] (14c) **:** QUAY
quaich *or* **quaigh** \'kwāk\ *n* [ScGael *cuach*] *chiefly Scot* (1673) **:** a small shallow drinking vessel with ears for use as handles
1**quail** \'kwā(ə)l\ *n, pl* **quail** *or* **quails** [ME *quaille*, fr. MF, fr. ML *quaccula*] (14c) **1 :** any of various Old World gallinaceous birds (genus *Coturnix*); *esp* **:** a migratory game bird (*C. coturnix* syn. *C. communis*) **2 :** any of various small American game birds (order Galliformes); *esp* **:** BOBWHITE
2**quail** *vb* [ME *quailen* to curdle, fr. MF *quailler*, fr. L *coagulare* — more at COAGULATE] *vi* (15c) **1 a** *chiefly dial* **:** WITHER, DECLINE **b :** to give way **:** FALTER ⟨his courage never ~*ed*⟩ **2 :** to recoil in dread or terror **:** COWER ⟨the strongest ~ before financial ruin —Samuel Butler †1902⟩ ~ *vt, archaic* **:** to make fearful ***syn*** see RECOIL
quaint \'kwānt\ *adj* [ME *cointe*, fr. OF, fr. L *cognitus*, pp. of *cognoscere* to know — more at COGNITION] (13c) **1** *obs* **:** EXPERT, SKILLED **2 a :** marked by skillful design ⟨~ with many a device in India ink —Herman Melville⟩ **b :** marked by beauty or elegance **3 a :** unusual or different in character or appearance **:** ODD ⟨figures of fun, ~ people —Herman Wouk⟩ **b :** pleasingly or strikingly old-fashioned or unfamiliar ***syn*** see STRANGE — **quaint·ly** *adv* — **quaint·ness** *n*
1**quake** \'kwāk\ *vi* **quaked; quak·ing** [ME *quaken*, fr. OE *cwacian*] (bef. 12c) **1 :** to shake or vibrate usu. from shock or instability **2 :** to tremble or shudder usu. from cold or fear
2**quake** *n* (14c) **:** an instance of shaking or trembling (as of the earth or moon); *esp* **:** EARTHQUAKE
quak·er \'kwā-kər\ *n* (1597) **1 :** one that quakes **2** *cap* **:** FRIEND 5 — **Quak·er·ish** \'kwā-k(ə-)rish\ *adj* — **Quak·er·ism** \-kə-,riz-əm\ *n* — **Quak·er·ly** \-kər-lē\ *adj*
Quaker gun *n* [fr. opposition to war as a basic Quaker tenet] (1809) **:** a dummy piece of artillery usu. made of wood
quak·er–la·dies \,kwā-kər-'lād-ēz\ *n pl* (1871) **:** BLUETS
quaking aspen *n* (1843) **:** an aspen (*Populus tremuloides*) of the U.S. and Canada that has small suborbicular leaves with flattened petioles and finely serrate margins
qua·le \'kwäl-ē, -,ā\ *n, pl* **qua·lia** \'kwäl-ē-ə\ [L, neut. of *qualis* of what kind] (1675) **1 :** a property (as redness) considered apart from things having the property **:** UNIVERSAL **2 :** a property as it is experienced as distinct from any source it might have in a physical object
qual·i·fi·able \'kwäl-ə-,fī-ə-bəl\ *adj* (1611) **:** capable of qualifying or being qualified
qual·i·fi·ca·tion \,kwäl-ə-fə-'kā-shən\ *n* (1543) **1 :** a restriction in meaning or application **:** a limiting modification ⟨this statement stands without ~⟩ **2 a** *obs* **:** NATURE **b** *archaic* **:** CHARACTERISTIC **3 a :** a quality or skill that fits a person (as for an office) ⟨the applicant with the best ~*s*⟩ **b :** a condition or standard that must be complied with (as for the attainment of a privilege) ⟨a ~ for membership⟩
qual·i·fied \'kwäl-ə-,fīd\ *adj* (1558) **1 a :** fitted (as by training or experience) for a given purpose **:** COMPETENT **b :** having complied with the specific requirements or precedent conditions (as for an office or employment) **:** ELIGIBLE **2 :** limited or modified in some way ⟨~ approval⟩ — **qual·i·fied·ly** \-,fī(-ə)d-lē\ *adv*
qual·i·fi·er \-,fī(-ə)r\ *n* (1561) **:** one that qualifies: as **a :** one that satisfies requirements or meets a specified standard **b :** a word (as an adjective) or word group that limits or modifies the meaning of another word (as a noun) or word group
qual·i·fy \'kwäl-ə-,fī\ *vb* **-fied; -fy·ing** [MF *qualifier*, fr. ML *qualificare*, fr. L *qualis*] *vt* (1533) **1 a :** to reduce from a general to a particular or restricted form **:** MODIFY **b :** to make less harsh or strict **:** MODERATE **c :** to alter the strength or flavor of **d :** to limit or modify the meaning of (as a noun) **2 :** to characterize by naming an attribute **:** DESCRIBE ⟨cannot ~ it as . . . either glad or sorry —T. S. Eliot⟩ **3 a :** to fit by training, skill, or ability for a special purpose **b (1) :** to declare competent or adequate **:** CERTIFY **(2) :** to invest with legal capacity **:** LICENSE ~ *vi* **1 :** to be or become fit (as for an office) **:** meet the required standard **2 :** to acquire legal or competent power or capacity ⟨has just *qualified* as a lawyer⟩ **3 a :** to exhibit a required degree of ability in a preliminary contest ⟨*qualified* for the finals⟩ **b :** to fire a score that makes one eligible for the award of a marksmanship badge
qual·i·ta·tive \'kwäl-ə-,tāt-iv\ *adj* (1607) **:** of, relating to, or involving quality or kind — **qual·i·ta·tive·ly** *adv*
qualitative analysis *n* (1842) **:** chemical analysis designed to identify the components of a substance or mixture
1**qual·i·ty** \'kwäl-ət-ē\ *n, pl* **-ties** [ME *qualite*, fr. OF *qualité*, fr. L *qualitat-, qualitas*, fr. *qualis* of what kind; akin to L *qui* who — more at WHO] (13c) **1 a :** peculiar and essential character **:** NATURE ⟨her ethereal ~ —Gay Talese⟩ **b :** an inherent feature **:** PROPERTY ⟨had a ~ of stridence, dissonance —Roald Dahl⟩ **c :** CAPACITY, ROLE ⟨in the ~ of reader and companion —Joseph Conrad⟩ **2 a :** degree of excellence **:** GRADE ⟨the ~ of competing air service —*Current Biog.*⟩ **b :** superiority in kind ⟨merchandise of ~⟩ **3 a :** social status **:** RANK **b :** ARISTOCRACY **4 a :** a distinguishing attribute **:** CHARACTERISTIC ⟨possesses many fine *qualities*⟩ **b** *archaic* **:** an acquired skill **:** ACCOMPLISHMENT **5 :** the character in a logical proposition of being affirmative or negative **6 :** vividness of hue **7 a :** TIMBRE **b :** the identifying character of a vowel sound determined chiefly by the resonance of the vocal chambers in uttering it **8 :** the attribute of an elementary sensation that makes it fundamentally unlike any other sensation
syn QUALITY, PROPERTY, CHARACTER, ATTRIBUTE mean an intelligible feature by which a thing may be identified. QUALITY is a general term applicable to any trait or characteristic whether individual or generic; PROPERTY implies a characteristic that belongs to a thing's essential nature and may be used to describe a type or species; CHARACTER applies to a peculiar and distinctive quality of a thing or a class; ATTRIBUTE implies a quality ascribed to a thing or a being.
2**quality** *adj* (1701) **:** being of high quality
quality control *n* (1935) **:** an aggregate of activities (as design analysis and statistical sampling with inspection for defects) designed to ensure adequate quality esp. in manufactured products —**quality controller** *n*
quality point *n* (ca. 1948) **:** GRADE POINT
quality point average *n* (ca. 1971) **:** GRADE POINT AVERAGE
qualm \'kwäm *also* 'kwȯm *or* 'kwälm\ *n* [origin unknown] (1530) **1 :** a sudden attack of illness, faintness, or nausea **2 :** a sudden access of usu. disturbing emotion (as doubt, fear, or tenderness) **3 :** a feeling of uneasiness about a point of conscience, honor, or propriety — **qualmy** \-ē\ *adj*
syn QUALM, SCRUPLE, COMPUNCTION, DEMUR mean a misgiving about what one is doing or going to do. QUALM implies an uneasy fear that one is not following one's conscience or better judgment; SCRUPLE implies doubt of the rightness of an act on grounds of principle; COMPUNCTION implies a spontaneous feeling of responsibility or compassion for a potential victim; DEMUR implies hesitation caused by objection to an outside suggestion or influence.
qualm·ish \-ish\ *adj* (1548) **1 a :** feeling qualms **:** NAUSEATED **b :** overly scrupulous **:** SQUEAMISH **2 :** of, relating to, or producing qualms — **qualm·ish·ly** *adv* — **qualm·ish·ness** *n*
qua·mash \'kwäm-ish\ *var of* CAMAS
quan·da·ry \'kwän-d(ə-)rē\ *n, pl* **-ries** [origin unknown] (1563) **:** a state of perplexity or doubt
quan·tal \'kwänt-ᵊl\ *adj* (1696) **1** [L *quanti* how many, pl. of *quantus*] **:** of, relating to, or having only two experimental alternatives (as dead or alive, all or none) **2** [*quantum*] **:** of or relating to a quantum
quan·ti·fi·ca·tion \,kwänt-ə-fə-'kā-shən\ *n* (1840) **:** the operation of quantifying — **quan·ti·fi·ca·tion·al** \-shnəl, -shən-ᵊl\ *adj* — **quan·ti·fi·ca·tion·al·ly** \-ē\ *adv*
quan·ti·fi·er \'kwänt-ə-,fī(-ə)r\ *n* (1876) **:** one that quantifies: as **a :** a prefixed operator that binds the variables in a logical formula by specifying their quantity **b :** a limiting noun modifier (as *five* in "the five young men") expressive of quantity and characterized by occurrence before the descriptive adjectives in a noun phrase
quan·ti·fy \-,fī\ *vt* **-fied; -fy·ing** [ML *quantificare*, fr. L *quantus* how much] (1840) **1 a (1) :** to limit by a quantifier **(2) :** to bind by prefixing a quantifier **b :** to make explicit the logical quantity of **2 :** to determine, express, or measure the quantity of — **quan·ti·fi·able** \-,fī-ə-bəl\ *adj*
quan·ti·tate \'kwän(t)-ə-,tāt\ *vt* **-tat·ed; -tat·ing** [back-formation fr. *quantitative*] (1927) **1 :** to measure or estimate the quantity of; *esp* **:** to measure or determine precisely **2 :** to express in quantitative terms — **quan·ti·ta·tion** \,kwän(t)-ə-'tā-shən\ *n*
quan·ti·ta·tive \'kwän(t)-ə-,tāt-iv\ *adj* [ML *quantitativus*, fr. L *quantitat-, quantitas* quantity + *-ivus* -ive] (1581) **1 :** of, relating to, or expressible in terms of quantity **2 :** of, relating to, or involving the measurement of quantity or amount **3 :** based on quantity; *specif, of classical verse* **:** based on temporal quantity or duration of sounds — **quan·ti·ta·tive·ly** *adv* — **quan·ti·ta·tive·ness** *n*
quantitative analysis *n* (ca. 1847) **:** chemical analysis designed to determine the amounts or proportions of the components of a substance
quantitative inheritance *n* (ca. 1929) **:** genic inheritance of a character (as skin color in man) controlled by a group of genes at different loci with each allelic pair having a specific quantitative effect
quan·ti·ty \'kwän(t)-ət-ē\ *n, pl* **-ties** [ME *quantite*, fr. MF *quantité*, fr. L *quantitat-, quantitas*, fr. *quantus* how much, how large; akin to L *quam* how, as, *quando* when, *qui* who — more at WHO] (14c) **1 a :** an indefinite amount or number **b :** a determinate or estimated amount ⟨precise *quantities* of four nucleic acids —*Current Biog.*⟩ **c :** total amount or number **d :** a considerable amount or number — often used in pl. ⟨generous *quantities* of luck —H. E. Putsch⟩ **2 a :** the aspect in which a thing is measurable in terms of greater, less, or equal or of increasing or decreasing magnitude **b :** the subject of a mathematical operation **c :** a factor to take into account ⟨an unknown ~ . . . as attorney general —Tom Wicker⟩ **3 a :** duration and intensity of speech sounds as distinct from their individual quality or phonemic character; *specif* **:** the relative length or brevity of a prosodic syllable in some languages (as Greek and Latin) **b :** the relative duration or time length of a speech sound or sound sequence **4 :** the character of a logical proposition as being universal, particular, or singular
quantity theory *n* (ca. 1896) **:** a theory in economics: changes in the price level tend to vary directly and in the value of money inversely with the amount of money in circulation and the velocity of its circulation
quan·tize \'kwän-,tīz\ *vt* **quan·tized; quan·tiz·ing** [*quantum*] (1921) **1 :** to subdivide (as energy) into small but measurable increments **2 :** to calculate or express in terms of quantum mechanics — **quan·ti·za·tion** \,kwänt-ə-'zā-shən\ *n* — **quan·tiz·er** \'kwän-,tī-zər\ *n*
1**quan·tum** \'kwänt-əm\ *n, pl* **quan·ta** \'kwänt-ə\ [L, neut. of *quantus* how much] (1567) **1 a :** QUANTITY, AMOUNT **b :** PORTION, PART **c :** gross quantity **:** BULK **2 a :** one of the very small increments or parcels into which many forms of energy are subdivided **b :** one of the small subdivisions of a quantized physical magnitude (as magnetic moment)
2**quantum** *adj* (1942) **:** LARGE, SIGNIFICANT ⟨a ~ improvement⟩
quantum jump *n* (ca. 1926) **1 :** an abrupt transition (as of an electron, an atom, or a molecule) from one discrete energy state to another **2 :** an abrupt change, sudden increase, or dramatic advance — called also *quantum leap*
quantum mechanics *n pl but sing or pl in constr* (1922) **:** a general mathematical theory dealing with the interactions of matter and radiation in terms of observable quantities only — **quantum mechanical** *adj* — **quantum mechanically** *adv*
quantum number *n* (1902) **:** any of a set of integers or odd half integers that indicate the magnitude of various discrete quantities (as electric charge) of a particle or system and that serve to define its state

quantum theory *n* (1911) **:** a theory in physics based on the concept of the subdivision of radiant energy into finite quanta and applied to numerous processes involving transference or transformation of energy in an atomic or molecular scale

[1]**quar·an·tine** \'kwȯr-ən-,tēn, 'kwär-\ *n* [It *quarantina,* fr. MF *quarantaine,* fr. OF, fr. *quarante* forty, fr. L *quadraginta,* fr. *quadra-* (akin to *quattuor* four) + *-ginta* (akin to *viginti* twenty) — more at FOUR, VIGESIMAL] (1609) **1 :** a period of 40 days **2 a :** a term during which a ship arriving in port and suspected of carrying contagious disease is held in isolation from the shore **b :** a regulation placing a ship in quarantine **c :** a place where a ship is detained during quarantine **3 a :** a restraint upon the activities or communication of persons or the transport of goods designed to prevent the spread of disease or pests **b :** a place in which those under quarantine are kept **4 :** a state of enforced isolation

[2]**quarantine** *vb* **-tined; -tin·ing** *vt* (1804) **1 :** to detain in or exclude by quarantine **2 :** to isolate from normal relations or communication ⟨~ an aggressor⟩ ~ *vi* **:** to establish or declare a quarantine

quare \'kwa(ə)r, 'kwe(ə)r, 'kwär\ *dial var of* [1]QUEER

quark \'kwȯ(ə)rk, 'kwärk\ *n* [coined by Murray Gell-Mann *b*1929 Am. physicist] (1964) **:** a hypothetical particle that carries a fractional electric charge, is thought to come in several types (as up, down, strange, charmed, and bottom), and is held to be a constituent of hadrons

[1]**quar·rel** \'kwȯr(-ə)l, 'kwär(-ə)l\ *n* [ME, fr. OF, square-headed arrow, building stone, fr. (assumed) VL *quadrellum,* dim. of L *quadrum* square; akin to L *quattuor* four — more at FOUR] (13c) **1 :** a square-headed bolt or arrow esp. for a crossbow **2 :** a small quadrangular building member (as a diamond-shaped pane of glass)

[2]**quarrel** *n* [ME *querele,* fr. MF, complaint, fr. L *querela,* fr. *queri* to complain — more at WHEEZE] (14c) **1 :** a ground of dispute or complaint ⟨have no ~ with a different approach⟩ **2 :** a usu. verbal conflict between antagonists **:** ALTERCATION

[3]**quarrel** *vi* **-reled** *or* **-relled; -rel·ing** *or* **-rel·ling** (14c) **1 :** to find fault ⟨many people ~ with the idea —*Johns Hopkins Mag.*⟩ **2 :** to contend or dispute actively ⟨~*ed* frequently with his superiors —*London Calling*⟩ — **quar·rel·er** *or* **quar·rel·ler** *n*

quar·rel·some \'kwȯr(-ə)l-səm, 'kwär(-ə)l-\ *adj* (1596) **:** apt or disposed to quarrel in an often petty manner **:** CONTENTIOUS ***syn*** see BELLIGERENT — **quar·rel·some·ly** *adv* — **quar·rel·some·ness** *n*

quar·ri·er \'kwȯr-ē-ər, 'kwär-\ *n* (14c) **:** a worker in a stone quarry

[1]**quar·ry** \'kwȯr-ē, 'kwär-\ *n, pl* **quarries** [ME *querre* entrails of game given to the hounds, fr. MF *cuiree*] (14c) **1** *obs* **:** a heap of the game killed in a hunt **2 :** GAME; *specif* **:** game hunted with hawks **3 :** one that is sought or pursued **:** PREY

[2]**quarry** *n, pl* **quarries** [ME *quarey,* alter. of *quarrere,* fr. MF *quarriere,* fr. (assumed) OF *quarre* squared stone, fr. L *quadrum* square] (15c) **1 :** an open excavation usu. for obtaining building stone, slate, or limestone **2 :** a rich source

[3]**quarry** *vb* **quar·ried; quar·ry·ing** *vt* (1774) **1 :** to dig or take from or as if from a quarry ⟨~ marble⟩ **2 :** to make a quarry in ⟨~ a hill⟩ ~ *vi* **:** to delve in or as if in a quarry

[4]**quarry** *n, pl* **quarries** [alter. of [1]*quarrel*] (1555) **:** a diamond-shaped pane of glass, stone, or tile

quar·ry·ing *n* (ca. 1828) **:** the business, occupation, or act of extracting useful material (as building stone) from quarries

quar·ry·man \'kwȯr-ē-mən, 'kwär-\ *n* (1611) **:** QUARRIER

quart \'kwȯ(ə)rt\ *n* [ME, one fourth of a gallon, fr. MF *quarte,* fr. OF, fr. fem. of *quart,* adj., fourth, fr. L *quartus;* akin to L *quattuor* four — more at FOUR] (14c) **1** — see WEIGHT table **2 a :** a vessel or measure having a capacity of one quart **b :** any of various units for bottled wine; *esp* **:** a unit for champagne containing 26 fluidounces

[1]**quar·tan** \'kwȯrt-ᵊn\ *adj* [ME *quarteyne,* fr. MF *(fievre) quartaine* quartan fever, fr. L *(febris) quartana,* fr. *quartanus* of the fourth, fr. *quartus*] (14c) **:** occurring every fourth day reckoning inclusively; *specif* **:** recurring at approximately 72-hour intervals

[2]**quartan** *n* (14c) **:** an intermittent fever that recurs at approximately 72-hour intervals; *esp* **:** a quartan malaria

[1]**quar·ter** \'kwȯ(r)t-ər\ *n* [ME, fr. OF *quartier,* fr. L *quartarius,* fr. *quartus* fourth] (13c) **1 :** one of four equal parts into which something is divisible **:** a fourth part ⟨in the top ~ of his class⟩ **2 :** any of various units of capacity or weight equal to or derived from one fourth of some larger unit **3 :** any of various units of length or area equal to one fourth of some larger unit **4 :** the fourth part of a measure of time: as **a :** one of a set of four 3-month divisions of a year ⟨business was up during the third ~⟩ **b :** a school term of about 12 weeks **c :** QUARTER HOUR ⟨a ~ after three⟩ **5 a :** a coin worth a quarter of a dollar **b :** the sum of 25 cents **6 a :** one limb of a quadruped with the adjacent parts; *esp* **:** one fourth part of the carcass of a slaughtered animal including a leg **b** *pl, Brit* **:** HINDQUARTER 2 **7 a :** the region or direction lying under any of the four divisions of the horizon **b :** one of the four parts into which the horizon is divided or the cardinal point corresponding to it **c :** a compass point or direction other than the cardinal points **d** (1) **:** an unspecified person or group ⟨financial help from many ~s —*Current Biog.*⟩ (2) **:** a point, direction, or place not definitely identified ⟨the view to the rear ~ —*Consumer Reports*⟩ **8 a :** a division or district of a town or city ⟨he describes the immigrant ~ —Alfred Kazin⟩ **b :** the inhabitants of such a quarter **9 a :** an assigned station or post **b** *pl* **:** an assembly of a ship's company for ceremony, drill, or emergency **c** *pl* **:** living accommodations **:** LODGINGS ⟨show you to your ~s⟩ **10 :** merciful consideration of an opponent; *specif* **:** the clemency of not killing a defeated enemy **11 :** a fourth part of the moon's period **12 :** the side of a horse's hoof between the toe and the heel — see HOOF illustration **13 a :** any of the four parts into which a heraldic field is divided **b :** a bearing or charge occupying the first fourth part of a heraldic field **14 :** the state of two machine parts that are exactly at right angles to one another or are spaced about a circle so as to subtend a right angle at the center of the circle **15 a :** the stern area of a ship's side **b :** the part of the yardarm outside the slings **16 :** one side of the upper of a shoe or boot from heel to vamp **17 :** one of the four equal periods into which the playing time of some games is divided

[2]**quarter** *vt* (14c) **1 a :** to divide into four equal or nearly equal parts **b :** to separate into either more or fewer than four parts ⟨~ an orange⟩ **c :** to divide (a human body) into four parts **2 :** to provide with lodging or shelter **3 :** to crisscross (an area) in many directions **4 a :** to arrange or bear (as different coats of arms) quarterly on one escutcheon **b :** to add (a coat of arms) to others on one escutcheon **c :** to divide (a shield) into distinct sections (as by stripes) **5 :** to adjust or locate (as cranks) at right angles in a machine ~ *vi* **1 :** LODGE, DWELL **2 :** to crisscross a district **3 :** to change from one quarter to another ⟨the moon ~s⟩ **4 :** to strike on a ship's quarter ⟨the wind was ~*ing*⟩

[3]**quarter** *adj* (14c) **:** consisting of or equal to a quarter

quar·ter·age \'kwȯ(r)t-ə-rij\ *n* (14c) **:** a quarterly payment, tax, wage, or allowance

[1]**quar·ter·back** \'kwȯ(r)t-ər-,bak\ *n* (1879) **:** an offensive back in football who usu. lines up behind the center, calls the signals, and directs the offensive play of his team

[2]**quarterback** *vt* (1944) **1 :** to direct the offensive play of (as a football team) **2 :** to give executive direction to **:** BOSS ⟨~*ed* the original buying syndicate —*Time*⟩ ~ *vi* **:** to play quarterback

quarterback sneak *n* (ca. 1923) **:** a usu. quick run with the ball by a quarterback into the middle of the offensive line

quar·ter–bound \,kwȯ(r)t-ər-'baund\ *adj, of a book* (ca. 1888) **:** bound in material of two qualities with the material of better quality on the spine only — **quarter binding** *n*

quarter day *n, chiefly Brit* (15c) **:** the day which begins a quarter of the year and on which a quarterly payment often falls due

quar·ter·deck \'kwȯ(r)t-ər-,dek\ *n* (1627) **1 :** the stern area of a ship's upper deck **2 :** a part of a deck on a naval vessel set aside by the captain for ceremonial and official use

[1]**quar·ter·fi·nal** \,kwȯ(r)t-ər-'fīn-ᵊl\ *n* (1927) **1** *pl* **:** a quarterfinal round **2 :** a quarterfinal match — **quar·ter·fi·nal·ist** \-ᵊl-əst\ *n*

[2]**quarterfinal** *adj* (ca. 1934) **1 :** immediately preceding the semifinal in an elimination tournament **2 :** of or participating in a quarterfinal

quarter horse *n* [fr. its high speed for distances up to a quarter of a mile] (1834) **:** a compact muscular saddle horse characterized by great endurance and by high speed for short distances

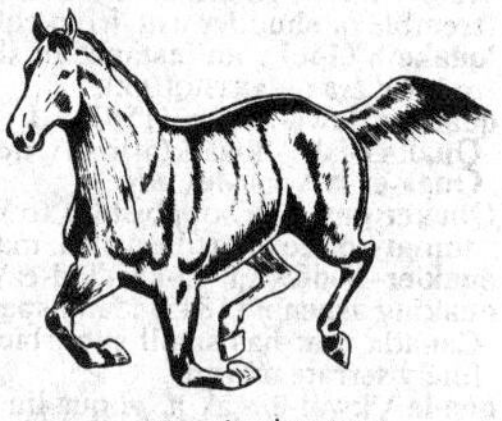
quarter horse

quarter hour *n* (1883) **1 :** any of the quarter points of an hour **2 :** fifteen minutes **3 :** a unit of academic credit representing an hour of class (as lecture class) or three hours of laboratory work each week for an academic quarter

[1]**quar·ter·ing** \'kwȯ(r)t-ə-riŋ\ *n* (1592) **1 a :** the division of an escutcheon containing different coats of arms into four or more compartments **b :** a quarter of an escutcheon or the coat of arms on it **2 :** a line of usu. noble or distinguished ancestry

[2]**quartering** *adj* (1692) **1 :** coming from a point well abaft the beam of a ship but not directly astern ⟨~ waves⟩ **2 :** lying at right angles

[1]**quar·ter·ly** \'kwȯ(r)t-ər-lē\ *adv* (15c) **1 :** in heraldic quarters or quarterings **2 :** at 3-month intervals

[2]**quarterly** *adj* (1563) **1 :** computed for or payable at 3-month intervals ⟨~ premium⟩ **2 :** recurring, issued, or spaced at 3-month intervals **3 :** divided into heraldic quarters or compartments

[3]**quarterly** *n, pl* **-lies** (1830) **:** a periodical published four times a year

Quarterly Meeting *n* (1675) **:** an organizational unit of the Society of Friends usu. composed of several Monthly Meetings

quar·ter·mas·ter \'kwȯ(r)t-ər-,mas-tər\ *n* (15c) **1 :** a petty officer who attends to a ship's helm, binnacle, and signals **2 :** an army officer who provides clothing and subsistence for a body of troops

quar·tern \'kwȯ(r)t-ərn\ *n* [ME *quarteron,* fr. OF, quarter of a pound, quarter of a hundred, fr. *quartier* quarter] (13c) **:** a fourth part

quarter note *n* (1763) **:** a musical note with the time value of $1/4$ of a whole note

quarter rest *n* (ca. 1890) **:** a musical rest corresponding in time value to a quarter note

quar·ter·sawed \,kwȯ(r)t-ər-'sȯd\ *also* **quar·ter·sawn** \-'sȯn\ *adj* (ca. 1890) **:** sawed from quartered logs so that the annual rings are nearly at right angles to the wide face — used of boards and planks

quarter section *n* (1804) **:** a tract of land that is half a mile square and contains 160 acres in the U.S. government system of land surveying

quarter sessions *n pl* (1577) **:** a former English local court with limited original and appellate criminal and sometimes civil jurisdiction and often administrative functions held quarterly usu. by two justices of the peace in a county or by a recorder in a borough

quar·ter·staff \'kwȯ(r)t-ər-,staf\ *n, pl* **-staves** \-,stavz, -,stāvz\ (1550) **:** a long stout staff formerly used as a weapon and wielded with one hand in the middle and the other between the middle and the end

quarter tone *n* (ca. 1776) **1 :** a musical interval of one half a semitone **2 :** a tone at an interval of one quarter

quar·tet *also* **quar·tette** \kwȯr-'tet\ *n* [It *quartetto,* fr. *quarto* fourth, fr. L *quartus* — more at QUART] (1773) **1 :** a musical composition for four instruments or voices **2 :** a group or set of four; *esp* **:** the performers of a quartet

quar·tic \'kwȯrt-ik\ *adj* [L *quartus* fourth] (ca. 1890) **:** of the fourth degree ⟨~ equation⟩ — **quartic** *n*

quar·tile \'kwȯr-,tīl, 'kwȯrt-ᵊl\ *n* [ISV, fr. L *quartus*] (1879) **:** the value that marks the boundary between two consecutive intervals in a frequency distribution of four intervals with each containing one quarter of the total population

quar·to \'kwȯrt-(,)ō\ *n, pl* **quartos** [L, abl. of *quartus* fourth] (1589) **1 :** the size of a piece of paper cut four from a sheet; *also* **:** paper or a page of this size **2 :** a book printed on quarto pages

quartz \'kwȯ(ə)rts\ *n* [G *quarz*] (ca. 1631) **:** a mineral SiO_2 consisting of a silicon dioxide that occurs in colorless and transparent or colored hexagonal crystals and also in crystalline masses — **quartz·ose** \'kwȯrt-,sōs\ *adj*

quartz glass *n* (1903) **:** vitreous silica prepared from pure quartz and noted for its transparency to ultraviolet radiation

quartz heater *n* (1980) **:** a portable electric radiant heater that has heating elements sealed in quartz-glass tubes producing infrared radiation in front of a reflective backing

quartz·if·er·ous \kwȯrt-ˈsif-(ə-)rəs\ *adj* (1832) **:** bearing quartz

quartz–iodine lamp *n* (ca. 1964) **:** an incandescent lamp that has a quartz bulb and a tungsten filament with the bulb containing iodine which reacts with the vaporized tungsten to prevent excessive blackening of the bulb

quartz·ite \ˈkwȯrt-ˌsīt\ *n* [ISV] (ca. 1847) **:** a compact granular rock composed of quartz and derived from sandstone by metamorphism — **quartz·it·ic** \kwȯrt-ˈsit-ik\ *adj*

qua·sar \ˈkwā-ˌzär *also* -ˌsär\ *n* [*quasi*-stell*ar*] (1964) **:** any of various celestial objects that resemble stars but are apparently far more distant and emit copious quantities of radiation usu. as bright blue and ultraviolet light and powerful radio waves

[1]**quash** \ˈkwäsh, ˈkwȯsh\ *vt* [ME *quassen,* fr. MF *casser, quasser* to annul, fr. LL *cassare,* fr. L *cassus* void; akin to L *carēre* to be without — more at CASTE] (14c) **:** to nullify esp. by judicial action ⟨~ an indictment⟩

[2]**quash** *vt* [ME *quashen* to smash, fr. MF *quasser, casser,* fr. L *quassare* to shake violently, shatter, fr. *quassus,* pp. of *quatere* to shake] (1609) **:** to suppress or extinguish summarily and completely ⟨~ a rebellion⟩

qua·si \ˈkwā-ˌzī, -ˌsī; ˈkwäz-ē, ˈkwäs-\ *adj* (1642) **1 :** having some resemblance usu. by possession of certain attributes ⟨a ~ corporation⟩ **2 :** having a legal status only by operation or construction of law and without reference to intent ⟨a ~ contract⟩

quasi- *comb form* [L *quasi* as if, as it were, approximately, fr. *quam* as + *si* if — more at QUANTITY, SO] **:** in some sense or degree ⟨*quasi*-historical⟩ ⟨*quasi*-officially⟩

qua·si–ju·di·cial \ˌkwā-ˌzī-jü-ˈdish-əl, -ˌsī-, ˌkwäz-ē-, ˌkwäs-ē-\ *adj* (1836) **1 :** having a partly judicial character by possession of the right to hold hearings on and conduct investigations into disputed claims and alleged infractions of rules and regulations and to make decisions in the general manner of courts ⟨~ bodies⟩ **2 :** essentially judicial in character but not within the judicial power or function esp. as constitutionally defined ⟨~ review⟩ — **qua·si–ju·di·cial·ly** \-ˈdish-(ə-)lē\ *adv*

qua·si–leg·is·la·tive \-ˈlej-ə-ˌslāt-iv\ *adj* (ca. 1934) **1 :** having a partly legislative character by possession of the right to make rules and regulations having the force of law ⟨a ~ agency⟩ **2 :** essentially legislative in character but not within the legislative power or function esp. as constitutionally defined ⟨~ powers⟩

Qua·si·mo·do \ˌkwäs-i-ˈmōd-(ˌ)ō, ˌkwäz-\ *n* [ML *quasi modo geniti infantes* as newborn babes (words of the introit for Low Sunday)] (ca. 1847) **:** LOW SUNDAY

qua·si·par·ti·cle \ˌkwā-ˌzī-ˈpärt-i-kəl, -ˌsī-, ˌkwäz-i-, ˌkwäs-i-\ *n* (1957) **:** a composite entity (as a vibration in a solid) that is analogous in its behavior to a single particle

qua·si–pub·lic \-ˈpəb-lik\ *adj* (1888) **:** essentially public (as in services rendered) although under private ownership or control

qua·si–stel·lar object \-ˈstel-ər-\ *n* (1964) **:** QUASAR

quas·sia \ˈkwäsh-ə\ *n* [NL, genus name of a So. American tree, fr. *Quassi* 18th cent. Surinam Negro slave who discovered the medicinal value of quassia] (1770) **:** a drug from the heartwood of various tropical trees of the ailanthus family used esp. as a bitter tonic and remedy for roundworms in children and as an insecticide

qua·ter·cen·te·na·ry \ˌkwät-ər-sen-ˈten-ə-rē, -ˈsent-ᵊn-ˌer-ē, -sen-ˈtē-nə-rē\ *n* [L *quater* four times + E *centenary* — more at QUATERNION] (1883) **:** a year marking a 400th anniversary

[1]**qua·ter·na·ry** \ˈkwät-ə(r)-ˌner-ē, kwə-ˈtər-nə-rē\ *adj* [L *quaternarius,* fr. *quaterni* four each] (1605) **1 a :** of, relating to, or consisting of four units or members **b :** of, relating to, or being a number system with a base of four **2** *cap* **:** of, relating to, or being the geological period from the end of the Tertiary to the present time or the corresponding system of rocks **3 :** consisting of, containing, or being an atom united by four bonds to carbon atoms

[2]**quaternary** *n, pl* **-ries** (1880) **1** *cap* **:** the Quaternary period or system of rocks **2 :** a member of a group fourth in order or rank

quaternary ammonium compound *n* (ca. 1934) **:** any of numerous strong bases and their salts derived from ammonium by replacement of the hydrogen atoms with organic radicals and important esp. as surface-active agents, disinfectants, and drugs

qua·ter·ni·on \kwə-ˈtər-nē-ən, kwä-\ *n* [ME *quaternyoun,* fr. LL *quaternion-, quaternio,* fr. L *quaterni* four each, fr. *quater* four times; akin to L *quattuor* four — more at FOUR] (14c) **1 :** a set of four parts, things, or persons **2 a :** a generalized complex number that is composed of a real number and a vector and that depends on one real and three imaginary units **b** *pl* **:** the calculus of quaternions

qua·ter·ni·ty \kwə-ˈtər-nət-ē, kwä-\ *n, pl* **-ties** [LL *quaternitas,* fr. L *quaterni* four each] (1529) **:** a union of a group or set of four

qua·train \ˈkwä-ˌtrān, kwä-ˈ\ *n* [MF, fr. *quatre* four, fr. L *quattuor*] (1582) **:** a unit or group of four lines of verse

qua·tre·foil \ˈkat-ər-ˌfȯil, ˈka-trə-\ *n* [ME *quaterfoil* set of four leaves, fr. MF *quatre* + ME *-foil* (as in *trefoil*)] (15c) **1 :** a conventionalized representation of a flower with four petals or of a leaf with four leaflets **2 :** a 4-lobed foliation in architecture

quat·tro·cen·to \ˌkwä-trō-ˈchen-(ˌ)tō\ *n, often cap* [It, lit., four hundred, fr. *quattro* four (fr. L *quattuor*) + *cento* hundred — more at CINQUECENTO] (ca. 1854) **:** the 15th century esp. with reference to Italian literature and art

quat·tu·or·de·cil·lion \ˌkwät-ə-ˌwȯr-di-ˈsil-yən\ *n, often attrib* [L *quattuordecim* fourteen (fr. *quattuor* four + *decem* ten) + E *-illion* (as in *million*) — more at TEN] (ca. 1903) — see NUMBER table

[1]**qua·ver** \ˈkwā-vər\ *vb* **qua·vered; qua·ver·ing** \ˈkwāv-(ə-)riŋ\ [ME *quaveren,* freq. of *quaven* to tremble] *vi* (15c) **1 :** TREMBLE **2 :** TRILL **3 :** to utter sound in tremulous tones ~ *vt* **:** to utter quaveringly — **qua·ver·ing·ly** \ˈkwāv-(ə-)riŋ-lē\ *adv* — **qua·very** \-(ə-)rē\ *adj*

[2]**quaver** *n* (1570) **1 :** EIGHTH NOTE **2 :** TRILL 1 **3 :** a tremulous sound

quay \ˈkē, ˈk(w)ā\ *n* [alter. of earlier *key,* fr. ME, fr. MF *cai,* fr. OF, of Celt origin; akin to Bret *kae* hedge, quay; akin to OE *hecg* hedge] (14c) **:** a structure built along the bank of a waterway for use as a landing place

quay·age \-ij\ *n* (14c) **1 :** a charge for use of a quay **2 :** room on or for quays **3 :** a system of quays

quay·side \-ˌsīd\ *n* (15c) **:** land bordering a quay

quean \ˈkwēn, ˈkwān\ *n* [ME *quene,* fr. OE *cwene;* akin to OE *cwēn* woman, queen] (bef. 12c) **1 :** a disreputable woman; *specif* **:** PROSTITUTE **2** *chiefly Scot* **:** WOMAN; *esp* **:** one that is young or unmarried

quea·sy *also* **quea·zy** \ˈkwē-zē\ *adj* **quea·si·er; -est** [ME *coysy, qwesye*] (15c) **1 :** full of doubt **:** HAZARDOUS **2 a :** causing nausea ⟨~ motion⟩ **b :** suffering from nausea **:** NAUSEATED **3 a :** causing uneasiness **b (1) :** DELICATE, SQUEAMISH **(2) :** ill at ease — **quea·si·ly** \-zə-lē\ *adv* — **quea·si·ness** \-zē-nəs\ *n*

Que·bec \kwi-ˈbek *also* ki-\ (ca. 1952) — a communications code word for the letter *q*

Que·be·cois *or* **Qué·be·cois** \ˌkā-bə-ˈkwä, -ˌbe-\ *n, pl* **Quebecois** *or* **Québecois** \-ˈkwä(z)\ [F *Québecois,* fr. *Québec* Quebec] (1873) **:** a native or inhabitant of Quebec; *specif* **:** a French-speaking native or inhabitant of Quebec

que·bra·cho \kā-ˈbräch-(ˌ)ō, ki-\ *n* [AmerSp, alter. of *quiebracha,* fr. Sp *quiebra* it breaks (fr. L *crepare* to crack, rattle) + *hacha* ax, fr MF *hache* — more at RAVEN, HASH] (ca. 1881) **1 :** any of several trees of southern So. America with hard wood: as **a :** a tree (*Aspidosperma quebracho*) of the dogbane family which occurs in Argentina and Chile and whose dried bark is used as a respiratory sedative in dyspnea and in asthma **b :** a chiefly Argentine tree (*Schinopsis lorentzii*) of the sumac family with dense wood rich in tannins **2 a :** the wood of a quebracho **b :** a tannin-rich extract of the Argentine quebracho used in tanning leather

Que·chua \ˈkech-(ə-)wə, kə-ˈchü-ə\ *n, pl* **Quechua** *or* **Quechuas** [Sp, fr. Quechua *kkechúwa* plunderer, robber] (1840) **1 a :** the language of the Quechua people widely spoken by other Indian peoples of Peru, Bolivia, Ecuador, Chile, and Argentina **b :** a language family comprising the Quechua language **2 a :** a member of an Indian people of central Peru **b :** a group of peoples constituting the dominant element of the Inca Empire — **Que·chu·an** \-(ə-)wən, -ˈchü-ən\ *adj or n*

[1]**queen** \ˈkwēn\ *n* [ME *quene,* fr. OE *cwēn* woman, wife, queen; akin to Goth *qens* wife, Gk *gynē* woman, wife] (bef. 12c) **1 a :** the wife or widow of a king **b :** the wife or widow of a tribal chief **2 a :** a female monarch **b :** a female chieftain **3 a :** a woman eminent in rank, power, or attractions ⟨a movie ~⟩ **b :** a goddess or a thing personified as female and having supremacy in a specified realm **c :** an attractive girl or woman; *esp* **:** a beauty contest winner **4 :** the most privileged piece of each color in a set of chessmen having the power to move in any direction across any number of unoccupied squares **5 :** a playing card marked with a stylized figure of a queen **6 :** the fertile fully developed female of social bees, ants, and termites whose function is to lay eggs — see HONEYBEE illustration **7 :** a mature female cat kept esp. for breeding **8 :** HOMOSEXUAL; *esp* **:** an effeminate one — often used disparagingly

[2]**queen** *vi* (1611) **1 :** to act like a queen; *esp* **:** to put on airs — usu. used with *it* ⟨~s it over her friends⟩ **2 :** to become a queen in chess ~ *vt* **:** to promote (a pawn) to a queen in chess

Queen Anne \kwē-ˈnan\ *adj* [*Queen Anne* of England] (1863) **1 :** of, relating to, or having the characteristics of a style of furniture originating in England under Dutch influence esp. during the first half of the 18th century that is marked by extensive use of upholstery, marquetry, and oriental fabrics **2 :** of, relating to, or having the characteristics of a style of English building of the early 18th century characterized by modified classic ornament and the use of red brickwork in which even relief ornament is carved

Queen Anne's lace *n* (1895) **:** WILD CARROT

queen consort *n, pl* **queens consort** (1765) **:** the wife of a reigning king

queen·ly \ˈkwēn-lē\ *adj* **queen·li·er; -est** (15c) **1 :** of, relating to, or befitting a queen **2 :** having royal rank **3 :** MONARCHICAL — **queen·li·ness** *n* — **queenly** *adv*

queen mother *n* (1577) **:** a queen dowager who is mother of the reigning sovereign

queen post *n* (1823) **:** one of two vertical tie posts in a truss (as of a roof)

queen regnant *n, pl* **queens regnant** (ca. 1847) **:** a queen reigning in her own right

Queen's Bench *n* (ca. 1860) — used instead of *King's Bench* when the British monarch is a queen

Queen's Counsel *n* (ca. 1860) — used instead of *King's Counsel* when the British monarch is a queen

queen·ship \ˈkwēn-ˌship\ *n* (1536) **1 :** the rank, dignity, or state of being a queen **2 :** a regal quality like that of a queen

queen·side \-ˌsīd\ *n* (ca. 1897) **:** the side of a chessboard containing the file on which the queen sits at the beginning of the game

queen–size *adj* (1959) **1 :** having dimensions of approximately 60 inches by 80 inches — used of a bed; compare FULL-SIZE, KING-SIZE, TWIN-SIZE **2 :** of a size that fits a queen-size bed ⟨a ~ sheet⟩

queen substance *n* (1954) **:** a pheromone that is secreted by queen bees, is consumed by worker bees, and inhibits the development of their ovaries

queen truss *n* (ca. 1864) **:** a truss framed with queen posts

[1]**queer** \ˈkwi(ə)r\ *adj* [origin unknown] (1508) **1 a :** differing in some odd way from what is usual or normal **b (1) :** ECCENTRIC, UNCONVENTIONAL **(2) :** mildly insane **:** TOUCHED **c :** absorbed or interested to an extreme or unreasonable degree **:** OBSESSED **d :** sexually deviate **:** HOMOSEXUAL — usu. used disparagingly **2 a :** WORTHLESS, COUNTERFEIT ⟨~ money⟩ **b :** QUESTIONABLE, SUSPICIOUS **3 :** not quite well *syn* see STRANGE — **queer·ish** \-ish\ *adj* — **queer·ly** *adv* — **queer·ness** *n*

[2]**queer** *vt* (ca. 1812) **1 :** to spoil the effect or success of ⟨~ one's plans⟩ **2 :** to put or get into an embarrassing or disadvantageous situation

[3]**queer** *n* (ca. 1812) **:** one that is queer; *esp* **:** HOMOSEXUAL — usu. used disparagingly

[1]**quell** \ˈkwel\ *vt* [ME *quellen* to kill, quell, fr. OE *cwellan* to kill; akin to OHG *quellen* to torture, kill, *quāla* torment, Gk *belonē* needle] (14c) **1 :** to thoroughly overwhelm and reduce to submission or passivity ⟨~ a riot⟩ **2 :** QUIET, PACIFY ⟨~ fears⟩ — **quell·er** *n*

[2]**quell** *n* [ME, fr. *quellen*] (15c) **1** *obs* **:** SLAUGHTER **2** *archaic* **:** the power of quelling

quench \ˈkwench\ *vb* [ME *quenchen,* fr. OE *-cwencan;* akin to OE *-cwincan* to vanish, OFris *quinka*] *vt* (bef. 12c) **1 a :** PUT OUT, EXTIN-

\ə\ abut \ᵊ\ kitten, F table \ər\ further \a\ ash \ā\ ace \ä\ cot, cart \au̇\ out \ch\ chin \e\ bet \ē\ easy \g\ go \i\ hit \ī\ ice \j\ job \ŋ\ sing \ō\ go \ȯ\ law \ȯi\ boy \th\ thin \t͟h\ the \ü\ loot \u̇\ foot \y\ yet \zh\ vision \à, k̲, ⁿ, œ, œ̄, ue, ue̅, ʸ\ see Guide to Pronunciation

GUISH **b** : to put out the light or fire of ⟨~ glowing coals with water⟩ **c** : to cool (as heated metal) suddenly by immersion (as in oil or water) **d** : to cause to lose heat or warmth ⟨you have ~*ed* the warmth of France toward you —Alfred Tennyson⟩ **2 a** : to bring (something immaterial) to an end typically by satisfying, damping, cooling, or decreasing ⟨a rational understanding of the laws of nature can ~ impossible desires —Lucius Garvin⟩ ⟨the praise that ~*es* all desire to read the book —T. S. Eliot⟩ **b** : to terminate by or as if by destroying : ELIMINATE ⟨the Commonwealth party ~*ed* a whole generation of play-acting —Margery Bailey⟩ ⟨~ a rebellion⟩ **c** : to relieve or satisfy with liquid ⟨~*ed* his thirst at a wayside spring⟩ ~ *vi* **1** : to become extinguished : COOL **2** : to become calm : SUBSIDE — **quench·able** \ˈkwen-chə-bəl\ *adj* — **quench·er** *n* — **quench·less** \ˈkwench-ləs\ *adj*

que·nelle \kə-ˈnel\ *n* [Fr, fr. G dial. *knödel* dumpling, fr. MHG; akin to OHG *knoto* knot — more at KNOT] (ca. 1845) : a poached oval dumpling made from pureed forcemeat (as of pike) and often served in a cream sauce

quer·ce·tin \ˈkwər-sət-ən\ *n* [ISV, fr. L *quercetum* oak forest, fr. *quercus* oak — more at FIR] (ca. 1833) : a yellow crystalline pigment $C_{15}H_{10}O_7$ occurring usu. in the form of glycosides in various plants

quer·cit·ron \ˈkwər-ˌsi-trən, ˌkwər-ˈ\ *n* [blend of NL *Quercus* and ISV *citron*] (1794) **1** : a large timber black oak (*Quercus velutina*) of the eastern and central U.S. **2** : the bark of a quercitron that is rich in tannin and yellow coloring matter and is used in tanning and dyeing

que·rist \ˈkwi(ə)r-əst, ˈkwe(ə)r-\ *n* [L *quaerere* to ask] (1633) : one who inquires

quern \ˈkwərn\ *n* [ME, fr. OE *cweorn*; akin to OHG *quirn* mill, OSlav *žrŭny*] (bef. 12c) : a primitive hand mill for grinding grain

quer·u·lous \ˈkwer-(y)ə-ləs *also* ˈkwir-\ *adj* [L *querulus*, fr. *queri* to complain] (1500) **1** : habitually complaining **2** : FRETFUL, WHINING ⟨a ~ voice⟩ — **quer·u·lous·ly** *adv* — **quer·u·lous·ness** *n*

[1]**que·ry** \ˈkwi(ə)r-ē, ˈkwe(ə)r-\ *n, pl* **queries** [alter. of earlier *quere*, fr. L *quaere*, imper. of *quaerere* to ask] (14c) **1** : QUESTION, INQUIRY **2** : a question in the mind : DOUBT **3** : QUESTION MARK

[2]**query** *vt* **que·ried; que·ry·ing** (1535) **1** : to ask questions about esp. in order to resolve a doubt **2** : to put as a question **3** : to ask questions of esp. with a desire for authoritative information **4** : to mark with a query *syn* see ASK — **que·ri·er** *n*

que·sa·dil·la \ˌkā-sə-ˈthē(l)-yə\ *n* [Sp, dim. of *quesada* cheese turnover, fr. *queso* cheese, fr. L *caseus* — more at CHEESE] (1944) : a wheat tortilla filled with a savory mixture, folded, fried in deep fat, and topped with cheese

[1]**quest** \ˈkwest\ *n* [ME, search, pursuit, investigation, inquest, fr. MF *queste* search, pursuit, fr. (assumed) VL *quaesta*, fr. L, fem. of *quaestus*] (14c) **1 a** : a jury of inquest **b** : INVESTIGATION **2** : an act or instance of seeking: **a** : PURSUIT, SEARCH **b** : a chivalrous enterprise in medieval romance usu. involving an adventurous journey **3** *obs* : ones who search or make inquiry

[2]**quest** *vi* (14c) **1** *of a dog* **a** : to search a trail **b** : BAY **2** : to go on a quest ~ *vt* **1** : to search for **2** : to ask for — **quest·er** *n*

[1]**ques·tion** \ˈkwes(h)-chən\ *n* [ME, fr. MF, fr. L *quaestion-, quaestio*, fr. *quaesitus, quaestus*, pp. of *quaerere* to seek, ask] (14c) **1 a** (1) : an interrogative expression often used to test knowledge (2) : an interrogative sentence or clause **b** : a subject or aspect in dispute or open for discussion : ISSUE; *broadly* : PROBLEM, MATTER **c** (1) : a subject or point of debate or a proposition to be voted on in a meeting (2) : the bringing of such to a vote **d** : the specific point at issue **2 a** : an act or instance of asking : INQUIRY **b** : INTERROGATION; *also* : a judicial or official investigation **c** : torture as part of an examination **d** (1) : OBJECTION, DISPUTE ⟨true beyond ~⟩ (2) : room for doubt or objection ⟨little ~ of his skill⟩ (3) : CHANCE, POSSIBILITY ⟨no ~ of escape⟩

[2]**question** *vt* (15c) **1** : to ask a question of or about **2** : to interrogate intensively : CROSS-EXAMINE **3 a** : DOUBT, DISPUTE **b** : to subject to analysis : EXAMINE ~ *vi* : to ask questions : INQUIRE *syn* see ASK — **ques·tion·er** *n*

ques·tion·able \ˈkwes(h)-chə-nə-bəl, *in rapid speech* ˈkwesh-nə-\ *adj* (1602) **1** *obs* : inviting inquiry **2** *obs* : liable to judicial inquiry or action **3** : affording reason for being doubted, questioned, or challenged : not certain or exact : PROBLEMATIC ⟨milk of ~ purity⟩ ⟨a ~ decision⟩ **4** : attended by well-grounded suspicions of being immoral, crude, false, or unsound : DUBIOUS ⟨~ motives⟩ *syn* see DOUBTFUL — **ques·tion·able·ness** *n* — **ques·tion·ably** \-blē\ *adv*

ques·tion·ary \ˈkwes(h)-chə-ˌner-ē\ *n, pl* **-ar·ies** (ca. 1901) : QUESTIONNAIRE

ques·tion·less \ˈkwes(h)-chən-ləs\ *adj* (1532) **1** : INDUBITABLE, UNQUESTIONABLE **2** : UNQUESTIONING

question mark *n* (1869) **1** : something unknown, unknowable, or uncertain **2** : a mark ? used in writing and printing at the conclusion of a sentence to indicate a direct question

ques·tion·naire \ˌkwes(h)-chə-ˈna(ə)r, -ˈne(ə)r\ *n* [F, fr. *questionner* to question, fr. MF, fr. *question*, n.] (1899) **1** : a set of questions for obtaining statistically useful or personal information from individuals **2** : a written or printed questionnaire often with spaces for answers **3** : a survey made by the use of a questionnaire

question time *n* (1885) : a period in a session of a British parliamentary body during which members may put to a minister questions on matters concerning his department

ques·tor \ˈkwes-tər\ *var of* QUAESTOR

quet·zal \ket-ˈsäl, -ˈsal\ *n, pl* **quetzals** *or* **quet·za·les** \-ˈsä-(ˌ)ās, -ˈsal-\ [AmerSp, fr. Nahuatl *quetzaltototl*, fr. *quetzalli* brilliant tail feather + *tototl* bird] (1827) **1** : a Central American trogon (*Pharomachrus mocinno*) that has brilliant plumage and in the male long upper tail coverts **2** *pl* *quetzales* — see MONEY table

Quet·zal·coatl \ket-ˈsäl-ˌkwät-ᵊl, -ˈsal-, -kə-ˌwät-\ *n* [Nahuatl] : a chief Toltec and Aztec god identified with the wind and air and represented by means of a feathered serpent

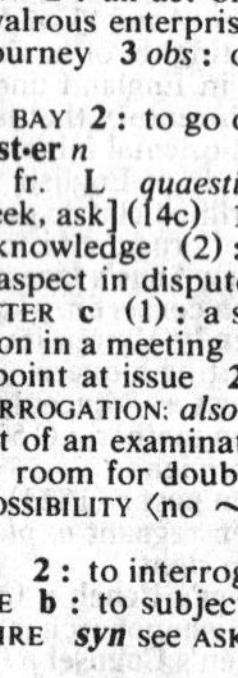

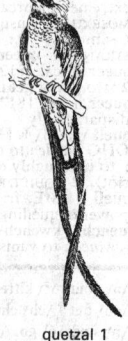

quetzal 1

[1]**queue** \ˈkyü\ *n* [F, lit., tail, fr. L *cauda, coda*] (1748) **1** : a braid of hair usu. worn hanging at the back of the head **2** : a waiting line esp. of persons or vehicles

[2]**queue** *vb* **queued; queu·ing** *or* **queue·ing** *vt* (1777) : to arrange or form in a queue ~ *vi* : to line up or wait in a queue — often used with *up* — **queu·er** *n*

[1]**quib·ble** \ˈkwib-əl\ *vb* **quib·bled; quib·bling** \-(ə-)liŋ\ *vi* (1656) **1 a** : CAVIL, CARP **b** : BICKER **2** : to evade the point of an argument by caviling about words ~ *vt* : to subject to quibbles — **quib·bler** \-(ə-)lər\ *n*

[2]**quibble** *n* [prob. dim. of obs. *quib* (quibble)] (1670) **1** : an evasion of or shift from the point **2** : a minor objection or criticism

quiche \ˈkēsh\ *n* [F, fr. G dial. (Lorraine) *küche*, dim. of *kuchen* cake, fr. OHG *kuocho* — more at CAKE] (ca. 1941) : an unsweetened custard pie usu. having a savory filling (as spinach, mushrooms, or ham)

quiche lor·raine \-lə-ˈrān, -lō-\ *n, often cap L* [F, fr. *lorraine*, fem. of *lorrain* of Lorraine] (ca. 1941) : a quiche containing cheese and crisp bacon bits

[1]**quick** \ˈkwik\ *adj* [ME *quik*, fr. OE *cwic*; akin to ON *kvikr* living, L *vivus* living, *vivere* to live, Gk *bios, zōē* life] (bef. 12c) **1** *archaic* : not dead : LIVING, ALIVE **2** : acting or capable of acting with speed: as **a** (1) : fast in understanding, thinking, or learning : mentally agile ⟨a ~ mind⟩ ⟨~ thinking⟩ (2) : reacting to stimuli with speed and keen sensitivity (3) : aroused immediately and intensely ⟨~ tempers⟩ **b** (1) : fast in development or occurrence ⟨a ~ succession of events⟩ (2) : done or taking place with rapidity ⟨gave them a ~ look⟩ **c** : marked by speed, readiness, or promptness of physical movement ⟨walked with ~ steps⟩ **d** : inclined to hastiness (as in action or response) ⟨too ~ to criticize⟩ **e** : capable of being easily and speedily prepared ⟨a ~ and tasty dinner⟩ **3** *archaic* **a** : not stagnant : RUNNING, FLOWING **b** : MOVING, SHIFTING ⟨~ mud⟩ **4** *archaic* : FIERY, GLOWING **5** *obs* **a** : PUNGENT **b** : CAUSTIC **6** *archaic* : PREGNANT **7** : having a sharp angle ⟨a ~ turn in the road⟩ — **quick·ly** *adv* — **quick·ness** *n*

syn QUICK, PROMPT, READY, APT mean able to respond without delay or hesitation or indicative of such ability. QUICK stresses instancy of response and is likely to connote native rather than acquired power ⟨very *quick* in perception⟩ ⟨a keen *quick* mind⟩ PROMPT is more likely to connote training and discipline that fits one for instant response ⟨*prompt* insight into the workings of complex apparatus —F. H. Garrison⟩ READY suggests facility or fluency in response ⟨reading maketh a full man, conference a *ready* man —Francis Bacon⟩ APT stresses the possession of qualities (as intelligence, a particular talent, or a strong bent) that makes quick effective response possible ⟨an *apt* student⟩ ⟨her answer was *apt* and to the point⟩ *syn* see in addition FAST

[2]**quick** *n* (bef. 12c) **1 quick** *pl* : living beings **2** [prob. of Scand origin; akin to ON *kvika* sensitive flesh, fr. *kvikr* living] **a** : a painfully sensitive spot or area of flesh (as that underlying a fingernail or toenail) **b** : the inmost sensibilities ⟨hurt to the ~ by the remark⟩ **c** : the very center of something : HEART **3** *archaic* : LIFE 1 1

[3]**quick** *adv* (13c) : in a quick manner

quick assets *n pl* (1891) : cash, accounts receivable, and other current assets excluding inventories

quick bread *n* (1918) : bread made with a leavening agent (as baking powder or baking soda) that permits immediate baking of the dough or batter mixture ⟨biscuits and muffins are *quick bread*⟩

quick·en \ˈkwik-ən\ *vb* **quick·ened; quick·en·ing** \-(ə-)niŋ\ *vt* (14c) **1 a** : to make alive : REVIVE **b** : to cause to be enlivened : STIMULATE **2** *archaic* **a** : KINDLE **b** : to cause to burn more intensely **3** : to make more rapid : HASTEN, ACCELERATE ⟨~*ed* her steps⟩ **4 a** : to make (a curve) sharper **b** : to make (a slope) steeper ~ *vi* **1** : to quicken something **2** : to come to life; *esp* : to enter into a phase of active growth and development ⟨seeds ~*ing* in the soil⟩ **3** : to reach the stage of gestation at which fetal motion is felt **4** : to shine more brightly ⟨watched the dawn ~*ing* in the east⟩ **5** : to become more rapid ⟨her pulse ~*ed* at the sight⟩ — **quick·en·er** \-(ə-)nər\ *n*

syn QUICKEN, ANIMATE, ENLIVEN, VIVIFY mean to make alive or lively. QUICKEN stresses a sudden renewal of life or activity esp. in something inert; ANIMATE emphasizes the imparting of motion or vitality to what is mechanical or artificial; ENLIVEN suggests a stimulus that arouses from dullness or torpidity; VIVIFY implies a freshening or energizing through renewal of vitality. *syn* see in addition PROVOKE

quick fix *n* (1970) : an expedient often inadequate solution to a problem

quick–freeze \ˈkwik-ˈfrēz\ *vt* **-froze** \-ˈfrōz\; **-fro·zen** \-ˈfrōz-ᵊn\; **-freez·ing** (1930) : to freeze (food) for preservation so rapidly that ice crystals formed are too small to rupture the cells and the natural juices and flavor are preserved

quick·ie \ˈkwik-ē\ *n* (ca. 1926) : something done or made in a hurry

quick kick *n* (ca. 1940) : a punt in football on first, second, or third down made from a running or passing formation and designed to take the opposing team by surprise

quick·lime \ˈkwik-ˌlīm\ *n* (15c) : the first solid product CaO that is obtained by calcining limestone and that develops great heat and becomes crumbly when treated with water

quick–lunch \-ˈlənch\ *n* (1903) : a luncheonette specializing in short-order food

quick·sand \ˈkwik-ˌsand\ *n* (15c) **1** : sand readily yielding to pressure; *esp* : a deep mass of loose sand mixed with water into which heavy objects readily sink **2** : something that entraps or frustrates

quick·set \-ˌset\ *n, chiefly Brit* (15c) : plant cuttings set in the ground to grow esp. in a hedgerow; *also* : a hedge or thicket esp. of hawthorn grown from quickset

[1]**quick·sil·ver** \-ˌsil-vər\ *n* (bef. 12c) : MERCURY 2a

[2]**quicksilver** *adj* (1655) : MERCURIAL 3

quick·step \-ˌstep\ *n* (ca. 1811) : a spirited march tune usu. accompanying a march in quick time

quick–tem·pered \-ˈtem-pərd\ *adj* (1830) : easily angered : IRASCIBLE

quick time *n* (ca. 1802) : a rate of marching in which 120 steps each 30 inches in length are taken in one minute

quick–wit·ted \ˈkwik-ˈwit-əd\ *adj* (1530) : quick in perception and understanding : mentally alert *syn* see INTELLIGENT — **quick–wit·ted·ly** *adv* — **quick–wit·ted·ness** *n*

[1]**quid** \ˈkwid\ *n, pl* **quid** *also* **quids** [origin unknown] *Brit* (1688) : a pound sterling

[2]quid *n* [E dial., cud, fr. ME *quide,* fr. OE *cwidu* — more at CUD] (1727) : a cut or wad of something chewable

quid·di·ty \'kwid-ət-ē\ *n, pl* **-ties** [ML *quidditas* essence, fr. L *quid* what, neut. of *quis* who — more at WHO] (1539) **1 a :** a trifling point : QUIBBLE **b :** CROTCHET, ECCENTRICITY **2 :** whatever makes something to be of the type that it is : ESSENCE

quid·nunc \'kwid-ˌnəŋk\ *n* [L *quid nunc* what now?] (1709) : one who seeks to know all the latest news or gossip : BUSYBODY

quid pro quo \ˌkwid-ˌprō-'kwō\ *n* [NL, something for something] (1539) : something given or received for something else

qui·es·cence \kwī-'es-ᵊn(t)s, kwē-\ *n* (1631) : the quality or state of being quiescent

qui·es·cent \-ᵊnt\ *adj* [L *quiescent-, quiescens,* prp. of *quiescere* to become quiet, rest, fr. *quies*] (1605) **1 :** marked by inactivity or repose : tranquilly at rest **2 :** causing no trouble or symptoms ⟨~ gallstones⟩ *syn* see LATENT — **qui·es·cent·ly** *adv*

[1]qui·et \'kwī-ət\ *n* [ME, fr. L *quiet-, quies* rest, quiet — more at WHILE] (14c) : the quality or state of being quiet : TRANQUILLITY — **on the quiet :** in a secretive manner

[2]quiet *adj* [ME, fr. MF, fr. L *quietus,* fr. pp. of *quiescere*] (14c) **1 a :** marked by little or no motion or activity : CALM ⟨a ~ sea⟩ **b :** GENTLE, EASYGOING ⟨a ~ temperament⟩ **c :** not interfered with ⟨~ reading⟩ **d :** enjoyed in peace and relaxation ⟨a ~ cup of tea⟩ **2 a :** free from noise or uproar : STILL **b :** UNOBTRUSIVE, CONSERVATIVE ⟨~ clothes⟩ **3 :** SECLUDED ⟨a ~ nook⟩ — **qui·et·ly** *adv* — **qui·et·ness** *n*

[3]quiet *adv* (1573) : in a quiet manner ⟨a *quiet*-running engine⟩

[4]quiet *vb* [LL *quietare* to set free, to calm, fr. L *quietus*] *vt* (1526) **1 :** to cause to be quiet : CALM **2 :** to make secure by freeing from dispute or question ⟨~ title to a property⟩ ~ *vi* : to become quiet — usu. used with *down* — **qui·et·er** *n*

qui·et·en \'kwī-ət-ᵊn\ *vb* **qui·et·ened; qui·et·en·ing** \-ət-niŋ, -ᵊn-iŋ\ *chiefly Brit* (ca. 1828) : QUIET

qui·et·ism \'kwī-ət-ˌiz-əm\ *n* (1687) **1 a :** a system of religious mysticism teaching that perfection and spiritual peace are attained by annihilation of the will and passive absorption in contemplation of God and divine things **b :** a passive withdrawn attitude or policy toward the world or worldly affairs **2 :** a state of calmness or passivity — **qui·et·ist** \-ət-əst\ *adj or n* — **qui·et·ist·ic** \ˌkwī-ət-'is-tik\ *adj*

qui·etude \'kwī-ə-ˌt(y)üd\ *n* [MF, fr. LL *quietudo,* fr. L *quietus*] (1597) : a quiet state : REPOSE

qui·etus \kwī-'ēt-əs\ *n* [ME *quietus est,* fr. ML, he is quit, formula of discharge from obligation] (1540) **1 :** final settlement (as of a debt) **2 :** removal from activity; *esp* : DEATH **3 :** something that quiets or represses

quiff \'kwif\ *n* [origin unknown] *Brit* (ca. 1890) : a prominent forelock

[1]quill \'kwil\ *n* [ME *quil* hollow reed, bobbin; akin to MHG *kil* large feather] (15c) **1 a (1) :** a bobbin, spool, or spindle on which filling yarn is wound **(2) :** a hollow shaft often surrounding another shaft and used in various mechanical devices **b :** a roll of dried bark ⟨cinnamon ~s⟩ **2 a (1) :** the hollow horny barrel of a feather **(2) :** FEATHER; *esp* : one of the large stiff feathers of the wing or tail **b :** one of the hollow sharp spines of a porcupine or hedgehog **3 :** something made from or resembling the quill of a feather; *esp* : a pen for writing **4 :** a float for a fishing line

[2]quill *vt* (1783) **1 :** to pierce with quills **2 a :** to wind (thread or yarn) on a quill **b :** to make a series of small rounded ridges in (cloth)

quill·back \'kwil-ˌbak\ *n, pl* **quillback** *or* **quillbacks** (ca. 1882) : any of several suckers; *esp* : a small fish (*Carpiodes cyprinus*) of central and eastern No. America that has the first ray of the dorsal fin much elongated

[1]quilt \'kwilt\ *n* [ME *quilte* mattress, quilt, fr. OF *cuilte,* fr. L *culcita* mattress] (13c) **1 :** a bed coverlet of two layers of cloth filled with wool, cotton, or down and held in place by stitched designs **2 :** something that is quilted or resembles a quilt

[2]quilt *vt* (1555) **1 a :** to fill, pad, or line like a quilt **b (1) :** to stitch, sew, or cover with lines or patterns like those used in quilts **(2) :** to stitch (designs) through layers of cloth **c :** to fasten between two pieces of material **2 :** to stitch or sew in layers with padding in between ~ *vi* **1 :** to make quilts **2 :** to do quilted work — **quilt·er** *n*

quilt·ing *n* (1609) **1 :** material that is quilted or used for making quilts **2 :** the process of quilting

quin- *or* **quino-** *comb form* [Sp *quina* — more at QUININE] **1 :** cinchona : cinchona bark ⟨*quinoline*⟩ **2 :** quinone ⟨*quinoid*⟩

quin·a·crine \'kwin-ə-ˌkrēn\ *n* [*quin-* + *acridine*] (ca. 1934) : an antimalarial drug derived from acridine and used esp. as the dihydrochloride $C_{23}H_{30}ClN_3O{\cdot}2HCl{\cdot}2H_2O$

quince \'kwin(t)s\ *n* [ME *quynce* quinces, pl. of *coyn, quyn* quince, fr. MF *coin,* fr. L *cydonium,* fr. Gk *kydōnion*] (14c) **1 :** the fruit of a central Asian tree (*Cydonia oblonga*) of the rose family that resembles a hard-fleshed yellow apple and is used for marmalade, jelly, and preserves **2 :** the tree that bears quinces

quin·cunx \'kwin-ˌkəŋ(k)s\ *n* [L *quincunc-, quincunx,* lit., five twelfths, fr. *quinque* five + *uncia* twelfth part — more at FIVE, OUNCE] (1658) : an arrangement of five things with one at each corner and one in the middle of a square or rectangle — **quin·cun·cial** \kwin-'kən-chəl\ *or* **quin·cunx·ial** \-'kəŋ(k)-sē-əl\ *adj*

quin·de·cil·lion \ˌkwin-di-'sil-yən\ *n, often attrib* [L *quindecim* fifteen (fr. *quinque* five + *decem* ten) + E *-illion* (as in *million*) — more at TEN] (ca. 1903) — see NUMBER table

quin·i·dine \'kwin-ə-ˌdēn\ *n* [ISV, fr. *quinine*] (1836) : an alkaloid $C_{20}H_{24}N_2O_2$ stereoisomeric with and resembling quinine that is used in treating cardiac rhythm irregularities

qui·nie·la \kēn-'yel-ə\ *or* **qui·nel·la** \kē-'nel-ə\ *n* [AmerSp *quiniela,* a game of chance resembling a lottery] (ca. 1942) : a system of betting (as on dog races) in which the bettor must pick the first and second place finishers but need not designate their order of finish in order to win — compare PERFECTA

qui·nine \'kwī-ˌnīn *also* 'kwin-ˌīn *or* kwin-'īn *or* k(w)in-'ēn\ *n* [Sp *quina* cinchona, short for *quinaquina,* fr. Quechua] (1826) **1 :** a bitter crystalline alkaloid $C_{20}H_{24}N_2O_2$ from cinchona bark used in medicine **2 :** a salt of quinine used esp. as an antipyretic, antimalarial, and bitter tonic

quinine water *n* (1953) : a carbonated beverage flavored with a small amount of quinine, lemon, and lime

qui·noa \ki-'nō-ə\ *n* [Sp, fr. Quechua *quinua*] (1625) : a pigweed (*Chenopodium quinoa*) of the high Andes whose seeds are ground and widely used as food in Peru

quin·o·line \'kwin-ᵊl-ˌēn\ *n* [ISV *quin-* + *-ol* + *-ine*] (1845) **1 :** a pungent oily nitrogenous base C_9H_7N that is obtained usu. by distillation of coal tar or by synthesis from aniline and is the parent compound of many alkaloids, drugs, and dyes **2 :** a derivative of quinoline

qui·none \kwin-'ōn, 'kwin-ˌ\ *n* [ISV *quinine* + *-one*] (1853) **1 :** either of two isomeric cyclic crystalline compounds $C_6H_4O_2$ that are di-keto derivatives of dihydro-benzene **2 :** any of various usu. yellow, orange, or red quinonoid compounds including several that are biologically important as coenzymes, hydrogen acceptors, or vitamins

qui·no·noid \kwin-'ō-ˌnȯid, 'kwin-ə-\ *or* **quin·oid** \'kwin-ˌȯid\ *adj* (1878) : resembling quinone esp. in having a benzene nucleus containing two double bonds within the nucleus

Quin·qua·ge·si·ma \ˌkwiŋ-kə-'jes-ə-mə, -'jā-zə-\ *n* [ML, fr. L, fem. of *quinquagesimus* fiftieth, fr. *quinquaginta* fifty, fr. *quinque* + *-ginta* (akin to *viginti* twenty — more at VIGESIMAL); fr. its being approximately 50 days before Easter] (14c) : the Sunday before Lent

quinque- *or* **quinqu-** *comb form* [L, fr. *quinque* — more at FIVE] : five ⟨*quinque*foliolate⟩

quin·quen·ni·al \kwin-'kwen-ē-əl, kwiŋ-\ *adj* (15c) **1 :** consisting of or lasting for five years **2 :** occurring or being done every five years — **quinquennial** *n* — **quin·quen·ni·al·ly** \-ē-ə-lē\ *adv*

quin·quen·ni·um \-ē-əm\ *n, pl* **-ni·ums** *or* **-nia** \-ē-ə\ [L, fr. *quinque-* + *annus* year — more at ANNUAL] (1621) : a period of five years

quin·que·va·lent \ˌkwiŋ-kwi-'vā-lənt\ *adj* (1877) : PENTAVALENT

quin·sy \'kwin-zē\ *n* [ME *quinesie,* fr. MF *quinancie,* fr. LL *cynanche,* fr. Gk *kynanchē,* fr. *kyn-, kyōn* dog + *anchein* to strangle — more at HOUND, ANGER] (14c) : a severe inflammation of the throat or adjacent parts with swelling and fever

quint \'kwint\ *n* (1935) : QUINTUPLET

quin·tain \'kwint-ᵊn\ *n* [ME *quintaine,* fr. MF, fr. L *quintana* street in a Roman camp separating the fifth maniple from the sixth where military exercises were performed, fr. fem. of *quintanus* fifth in rank, fr. *quintus* fifth] (15c) : an object to be tilted at; *esp* : a post with a revolving crosspiece that has a target at one end and a sandbag at the other end

quin·tal \'kwint-ᵊl, 'kant-\ *n* [ME, fr. MF, fr. ML *quintale,* fr. Ar *qinṭār,* fr. LGk *kentēnarion,* fr. LL *centenarium,* fr. L, neut. of *centenarius* consisting of a hundred — more at CENTENARY] (15c) **1 :** HUNDREDWEIGHT **2 :** a unit of weight equal to 100 kilograms (about 220.46 pounds)

quin·tes·sence \kwin-'tes-ᵊn(t)s\ *n* [ME, fr. MF *quinte essence,* fr. ML *quinta essentia,* lit., fifth essence] (15c) **1 :** the fifth and highest element in ancient and medieval philosophy that permeates all nature and is the substance composing the celestial bodies **2 :** the essence of a thing in its purest and most concentrated form **3 :** the most typical example or representative — **quint·es·sen·tial** \ˌkwint-ə-'sen-chəl\ *adj*

quin·tet *also* **quin·tette** \kwin-'tet\ *n* [*quintet* fr. It *quintetto,* fr. *quinto* fifth, fr. L *quintus; quintette* fr. F, fr. It *quintetto*] (1792) **1 :** a musical composition or movement for five instruments or voices **2 :** a group or set of five: as **a :** the performers of a quintet **b :** a basketball team

[1]quin·tic \'kwint-ik\ *adj* [L *quintus* fifth] (1853) : of the fifth degree

[2]quintic *n* (1856) : a polynomial or a polynomial equation of the fifth degree

quin·tile \'kwin-ˌtīl\ *n* [L *quintus* + E *-ile*] (ca. 1928) : any of the four values that divide the items of a frequency distribution into five classes

quin·til·lion \kwin-'til-yən\ *n* [L *quintus* + E *-illion* (as in *million*)] (ca. 1674) — see NUMBER table — **quintillion** *adj* — **quin·til·lionth** \-yən(t)th\ *adj or n*

[1]quin·tu·ple \kwin-'t(y)üp-əl, -'təp-; 'kwint-əp-\ *adj* [MF, fr. LL *quintuplex,* fr. L *quintus* fifth + *-plex* -fold; akin to L *quinque* five — more at FIVE, -FOLD] (1570) **1 :** being five times as great or as many **2 :** having five units or members **3 :** marked by five beats per measure ⟨~ meter⟩ — **quintuple** *n*

[2]quintuple *vb* **quin·tu·pled; quin·tu·pling** \-(ə-)liŋ\ *vt* (1639) : to make five times as great or as many ~ *vi* : to become five times as much or as numerous

quin·tu·plet \kwin-'təp-lət, -'t(y)üp-; 'kwint-əp-\ *n* (1873) **1 :** a combination of five of a kind **2 :** one of five offspring born at one birth

[1]quin·tu·pli·cate \kwin-'t(y)ü-pli-kət\ *adj* [L *quintuplicatus,* pp. of *quintuplicare* to quintuple, fr. *quintuplic-, quintuplex* quintuple] (1656) **1 :** consisting of or existing in five corresponding or identical parts or examples ⟨~ invoices⟩ **2 :** being the fifth of five things exactly alike ⟨file the ~ copy⟩

[2]quintuplicate *n* (1851) **1 :** one of five things exactly alike; *specif* : one of five identical copies **2 :** five copies all alike — used with *in* ⟨typed in ~⟩

[3]quin·tu·pli·cate \-plə-ˌkāt\ *vt* **-cat·ed; -cat·ing** (ca. 1890) **1 :** to make quintuple or fivefold **2 :** to prepare in quintuplicate

[1]quip \'kwip\ *n* [earlier *quippy,* perh. fr. L *quippe* indeed, to be sure (often ironical), fr. *quid* what — more at QUIDDITY] (1532) **1 a :** a clever usu. taunting remark : GIBE **b :** a witty or funny observation or response usu. made on the spur of the moment **2 :** QUIBBLE, EQUIVOCATION **3 :** something strange, droll, curious, or eccentric : ODDITY *syn* see JEST — **quip·ster** \-stər\ *n*

[2]quip *vb* **quipped; quip·ping** *vi* (1579) : to make quips : GIBE ~ *vt* : to jest or gibe at

qui·pu \'kē-(ˌ)pü\ *n* [Sp *quipo,* fr. Quechua *quipu*] (1704) : a device made of a main cord with smaller varicolored cords attached and knotted and used by the ancient Peruvians (as for calculating)

[1]quire \'kwī(ə)r\ *n* [ME *quair* four sheets of paper folded once, collection of sheets, fr. MF *quaer,* fr. (assumed) VL *quadernum,* alter. of L *quaterni* four each, set of four — more at QUATERNION] (15c) : a collection of 24 or sometimes 25 sheets of paper of the same size and quality : one twentieth of a ream

[2]quire *var of* CHOIR

Qui·ri·nus \kwə-'rī-nəs, -'rē-\ *n* [L] : an early state god of the Romans later identified with Romulus

¹quirk \'kwərk\ *n* [origin unknown] (1565) **1 a :** an abrupt twist or curve **b :** a peculiar trait : IDIOSYNCRASY **c :** ACCIDENT, VAGARY **2 :** a groove separating a bead or other molding from adjoining members — **quirk·i·ly** \'kwər-kə-lē\ *adv* — **quirk·i·ness** \-kē-nəs\ *n* — **quirky** \-kē\ *adj*

²quirk *vb* (1596) : CURL, TWIST

¹quirt \'kwərt\ *n* [MexSp *cuarta*] (1845) : a riding whip with a short handle and a rawhide lash

²quirt *vt* (1887) : to strike or drive with a quirt

quis·ling \'kwiz-liŋ\ *n* [Vidkun *Quisling* †1945 Norw. politician who collaborated with the Nazis] (1940) : a traitor who collaborates with the invaders of his country esp. by serving in a puppet government — **quis·ling·ism** \-liŋ-,iz-əm\ *n*

¹quit \'kwit\ *adj* [ME *quite, quit,* fr. OF *quite*] (13c) : released from obligation, charge, or penalty; *esp* : FREE

²quit *vb* **quit** *also* **quit·ted; quit·ting** [ME *quiten, quitten,* fr. MF *quiter, quitter,* fr. OF *quite* free of, released, lit., at rest, fr. L *quietus* quiet, at rest] *vt* (14c) **1 :** to set free : RELIEVE, RELEASE ⟨~ oneself of fear⟩ **2 :** to make full payment of : PAY UP ⟨~ a debt⟩ **3 :** CONDUCT, ACQUIT ⟨the youths ~ themselves like men⟩ **4 a :** to depart from or out of **b :** to leave the company of **c :** to relinquish, abandon, or give over (as a way of thinking, acting, or living) : FORSAKE **d :** to give up (an action, activity, or employment) : LEAVE ⟨~ a job⟩ ~ *vi* **1 :** to cease normal, expected, or necessary action **2 :** to give up employment **3 :** to admit defeat : GIVE UP *syn* see STOP

³quit *n* (ca. 1923) : the act of quitting a job

quitch \'kwich\ *n* [(assumed) ME *quicche,* fr. OE *cwice;* akin to OHG *quecca* couch grass, OE *cwic* living — more at QUICK] (bef. 12c) : QUACK GRASS

quit·claim \'kwit-,klām\ *vt* (14c) : to release or relinquish a legal claim to; *esp* : to release a claim to or convey by a quitclaim deed — **quitclaim** *n*

quitclaim deed *n* (1756) : a legal instrument used to release one person's right, title, or interest to another without providing a guarantee or warranty of title

quite \'kwīt\ *adv* [ME, fr. *quite,* adj., quit] (14c) **1 :** WHOLLY, COMPLETELY ⟨not ~ all⟩ **2 :** to an extreme : POSITIVELY ⟨~ sure⟩ **3 :** to a considerable extent : RATHER ⟨~ near⟩

quit·rent \'kwit-,rent\ *n* (15c) : a fixed rent payable to a feudal superior in commutation of services; *specif* : a fixed rent due from a socage tenant

quits \'kwits\ *adj* [ME, quit, prob. fr. ML *quittus,* alter. of L *quietus* at rest] (15c) : being on even terms by repayment or requital

quit·tance \'kwit-ⁿ(t)s\ *n* (14c) **1 a :** discharge from a debt or an obligation **b :** a document evidencing quittance **2 :** RECOMPENSE, REQUITAL

quit·ter \'kwit-ər\ *n* (1611) : one that quits; *esp* : one that gives up too easily : DEFEATIST

quit·tor \'kwit-ər\ *n* [ME *quiture* pus, prob. fr. OF, act of boiling, fr. L *coctura,* fr. *coctus,* pp. of *coquere* to cook — more at COOK] (1703) : a purulent inflammation of the feet esp. of horses and donkeys

¹quiv·er \'kwiv-ər\ *n* [ME, fr. MF *quivre,* of Gmc origin; akin to OE *cocer* quiver, OHG *kohhari*] (14c) **1 :** a case for carrying or holding arrows **2 :** the arrows in a quiver

²quiver *vi* **quiv·ered; quiv·er·ing** \-(ə-)riŋ\ [ME *quiveren,* prob. fr. *quiver* agile, quick, fr. (assumed) OE *cwifer*] (15c) : to shake or move with a slight trembling motion

³quiver *n* (1786) : the act or action of quivering : TREMOR

qui vive \kē-'vēv\ *n* [F *qui-vive,* fr. *qui vive?* long live who?, challenge of a French sentry] (1726) : ALERT, LOOKOUT — used in the phrase *on the qui vive*

qui·xote \'kwik-sət, kē-'(h)ōt-ē\ *n, often cap* [Don *Quixote,* hero of the novel *Don Quixote de la Mancha* (1605, 1615) by Cervantes] (1648) : a quixotic person — **quix·o·tism** \'kwik-sə-,tiz-əm\ *n* — **quix·o·try** \-sə-trē\ *n*

quix·ot·ic \kwik-'sät-ik\ *adj* [Don *Quixote*] (1815) **1 :** foolishly impractical esp. in the pursuit of ideals; *esp* : marked by rash lofty romantic ideas or extravagant chivalrous action **2 :** CAPRICIOUS, UNPREDICTABLE *syn* see IMAGINARY — **quix·ot·i·cal** \-i-kəl\ *adj* — **quix·ot·i·cal·ly** \-i-k(ə-)lē\ *adv*

¹quiz \'kwiz\ *n, pl* **quiz·zes** [origin unknown] (1749) **1 :** an eccentric person **2 :** PRACTICAL JOKE — *the act or action of quizzing; specif* : a short oral or written test

²quiz *vt* **quizzed; quiz·zing** (1796) **1 :** to make fun of : MOCK **2 :** to look at inquisitively **3 :** to question closely — **quiz·zer** *n*

quiz·mas·ter \'kwiz-,mas-tər\ *n* (1943) : one who puts the questions to contestants in a quiz show

quiz show *n* (1944) : an entertainment program (as on radio or television) in which contestants answer questions — called also *quiz program*

quiz·zi·cal \'kwiz-i-kəl\ *adj* (1800) **1 :** slightly eccentric : ODD **2 :** marked or characterized by bantering or teasing **3 :** INQUISITIVE, QUESTIONING — **quiz·zi·cal·i·ty** \,kwiz-ə-'kal-ət-ē\ *n* — **quiz·zi·cal·ly** \'kwiz-i-k(ə-)lē\ *adv*

quod \'kwäd\ *n* [origin unknown] *slang Brit* (ca. 1700) : PRISON

quod·li·bet \'kwäd-lə-,bet\ *n* [ME, fr. ML *quodlibetum,* fr. L *quodlibet,* neut. of *quilibet* any whatever, fr. *qui* who, what + *libet* it pleases, fr. *libēre* to please — more at WHO, LOVE] (14c) **1 :** a philosophical or theological point proposed for disputation; *also* : a disputation on such a point **2 :** a whimsical combination of familiar melodies or texts

¹quoin \'k(w)òin\ *n* [alter. of ¹*coin*] (14c) **1 a :** a solid exterior angle (as of a building) **b :** one of the members (as a block) forming a quoin and usu. differentiated from the adjoining walls by material, texture, color, size, or projection **2 :** the keystone or a voussoir of an arch **3 :** a wooden or expandable metal block used by printers to lock up a form within a chase

quoin 1b

²quoin *vt* (1683) **1 :** to equip (a type form) with quoins **2 :** to provide with quoins ⟨~ed walls⟩

¹quoit \'kwät, 'k(w)òit\ *n* [ME *coite*] (15c) **1 :** a flattened ring of iron or circle of rope used in a throwing game **2** *pl but sing in constr* : a game in which the quoits are thrown at an upright pin in an attempt to ring the pin or come as near to it as possible

²quoit *vi* (1597) : to throw like a quoit

quon·dam \'kwän-dəm, -,dam\ *adj* [L, at one time, formerly, fr. *quom, cum* when; akin to L *qui* who — more at WHO] (1586) : FORMER, SOMETIME ⟨a ~ friend⟩

Quon·set \,kwän(t)-sət, ,kwän-zət\ *trademark* — used for a prefabricated shelter set on a foundation of bolted steel trusses and built of a semicircular arching roof of corrugated metal insulated with wood fiber

quo·rum \'kwōr-əm, 'kwòr-\ *n* [ME, quorum of justices of the peace, fr. L, of whom, gen. pl. of *qui* who; fr. the wording of the commission formerly issued to justices of the peace] (15c) **1 :** the number usu. a majority of officers or members of a body that when duly assembled is legally competent to transact business **2 :** a select group **3 :** a Mormon body comprising those in the same grade of priesthood

quo·ta \'kwōt-ə\ *n* [ML, fr. L *quota pars* how great a part] (1618) **1 :** a proportional part or share; *esp* : the share or proportion assigned to each in a division or to each member of a body **2 :** the number or amount constituting a proportional share

quot·able \'kwōt-ə-bəl\ *adj* (1811) : fit for or worth quoting

quo·ta·tion \kwō-'tā-shən *also* kō-\ *n* (1646) **1 a :** the act or process of quoting **b** (1) : the naming or publishing of current bids and offers or prices of securities or commodities (2) : the bids, offers, or prices so named or published; *esp* : the highest bid and lowest offer for a particular security in a given market at a given time **2 :** something that is quoted; *esp* : a passage referred to, repeated, or adduced

quotation mark *n* (ca. 1883) : one of a pair of punctuation marks " " or ' ' used chiefly to indicate the beginning and the end of a quotation in which the exact phraseology of another or of a text is directly cited

¹quote \'kwōt *also* 'kōt\ *vb* **quot·ed; quot·ing** [ML *quotare* to mark the number of, number references, fr. L *quotus* of what number or quantity, fr. *quot* how many, (as) many as; akin to L *qui* who — more at WHO] *vt* (1582) **1 a :** to speak or write (a passage) from another usu. with credit acknowledgment **b :** to repeat a passage from esp. in substantiation or illustration **2 :** to cite in illustration ⟨~ cases⟩ **3 a :** to state (the current price or bid-offer spread) for a commodity, stock, or bond **b :** to give exact information on **4 :** to set off by quotation marks ~ *vi* : to inform a hearer or reader that matter following is quoted

²quote *n* (1888) **1 :** QUOTATION **2 :** QUOTATION MARK — often used orally to indicate the beginning of a direct quotation

quoth \(')kwōth\ *vb past* [ME, past of *quethen* to say, fr. OE *cwethan;* akin to OHG *quedan* to say] *archaic* (bef. 12c) : SAID — used chiefly in the first and third persons with a postpositive subject

quotha \'kwō-thə\ *interj* [alter. of *quoth he*] *archaic* (1519) — used esp. to express surprise or contempt

quo·tid·i·an \kwō-'tid-ē-ən\ *adj* [ME *cotidian,* fr. MF, fr. L *quotidianus, cotidianus,* fr. *quotidie* every day, fr. *quot* (as) many as + *dies* day — more at DEITY] (14c) **1 :** occurring every day ⟨~ fever⟩ **2 a :** belonging to each day : EVERYDAY ⟨~ routine⟩ **b :** COMMONPLACE, ORDINARY ⟨~ drabness⟩ — **quotidian** *n*

quo·tient \'kwō-shənt\ *n* [ME *quocient,* modif. of L *quotiens* how many times, fr. *quot* how many] (15c) **1 :** the number resulting from the division of one number by another **2 :** the numerical ratio usu. multiplied by 100 between a test score and a measurement on which that score might be expected largely to depend **3 :** QUOTA, SHARE

quotient group *n* (1893) : a group whose elements are the cosets of a normal subgroup of a given group —called also *factor group*

quotient ring *n* (ca. 1958) : a ring whose elements are the cosets of an ideal in a given ring

quo war·ran·to \,kwō-wə-'ränt-(,)ō, -'rant-; (')kwō-'wòr-ənt-,ō, -'wär-\ *n* [ML, by what warrant; fr. the wording of the writ] (1535) **1 a :** an English writ formerly requiring a person to show by what authority he exercises a public office, franchise, or liberty **b :** a legal proceeding for a like purpose begun by an information **2 :** the legal action begun by a quo warranto

Qur'an *or* **Qur·an** \kə-'ran, -'rän; kü(ə)r-'an, -'än\ *var of* KORAN

R

r \'är\ *n, pl* **r's** *or* **rs** \'ärz\ *often cap, often attrib* **1 a :** the 18th letter of the English alphabet **b :** a graphic representation of this letter **c :** a speech counterpart of orthographic *r* **2 :** a graphic device for reproducing the letter *r* **3 :** one designated *r* esp. as the 18th in order or class **4 :** something shaped like the letter R

R \'är\ *adj* [restricted] *of a motion picture* (1968) **:** of such a nature that admission is restricted to persons over a specified age (as 17) unless accompanied by a parent or guardian — compare G, PG, PG-13, X

Ra \'rä, 'rō\ *n* [Egypt *r*ʿ] **:** the Egyptian sun-god and chief deity

ra·ba·to \rə-'bät-(,)ō\ *n, pl* **-tos** [modif. of MF *rabat,* lit., act of turning down] (1591) **:** a wide lace-edged collar of the early 17th century often stiffened to stand high at the back

¹rab·bet \'rab-ət\ *n* [ME *rabet,* fr. MF *rabat* act of beating down, fr. OF *rabattre* to beat down, reduce — more at REBATE] (15c) **:** a channel, groove, or recess cut out of the edge or face of any body; *esp* **:** one intended to receive another member (as a panel)

²rabbet *vt* (1572) **1 :** to cut a rabbet in **2 :** to unite the edges of in a rabbet joint ~ *vi* **:** to become joined by a rabbet

rabbet joint *n* (ca. 1828) **:** a joint formed by fitting together rabbeted boards or timbers

rab·bi \'rab-,ī\ *n* [ME, fr. OE, fr. LL, fr. Gk *rhabbi,* fr. Heb *rabbī* my master, fr. *rabh* master + *-ī* my] (bef. 12c) **1 :** MASTER, TEACHER — used by Jews as a term of address **2 :** a Jew qualified to expound and apply the halakah and other Jewish law **3 :** a Jew trained and ordained for professional religious leadership; *specif* **:** the official leader of a Jewish congregation

rab·bin \'rab-ən\ *n* [F] (1579) **:** RABBI

rab·bin·ate \'rab-ə-nət, -,nāt\ *n* (1702) **1 :** the office or tenure of a rabbi **2 :** the whole body of rabbis

rab·bin·ic \rə-'bin-ik, ra-\ *or* **rab·bin·i·cal** \-i-kəl\ *adj* (1612) **1 :** of or relating to rabbis or their writings **2 :** of or preparing for the rabbinate **3 :** comprising or belonging to any of several sets of Hebrew characters simpler than the square Hebrew letters — **rab·bin·i·cal·ly** \-i-k(ə-)lē\ *adv*

Rabbinic Hebrew *n* (ca. 1959) **:** the Hebrew used esp. by medieval rabbis

rab·bin·ism \'rab-ə-,niz-əm\ *n* (1652) **:** rabbinic teachings and traditions

¹rab·bit \'rab-ət\ *n, pl* **rabbit** *or* **rabbits** *often attrib* [ME *rabet*] (14c) **1 :** any of a family (Leporidae) of long-eared short-tailed lagomorph mammals with long hind legs: **a :** any of various lagomorphs that are born naked, blind, and helpless, that are sometimes gregarious, and that include esp. the cottontails of the New World and a small Old World mammal (*Oryctolagus cuniculus*) that is the source of various domestic breeds **b :** HARE **2 :** the pelt of a rabbit **3 :** WELSH RABBIT **4 a :** a figure of a rabbit sped mechanically along the edge of a dog track as an object of pursuit **b :** a runner on a track team who sets a fast pace for a teammate in the first part of a long-distance race — **rab·bity** \-ē\ *adj*

²rabbit *vi* (1852) **:** to hunt rabbits — **rab·bit·er** *n*

rab·bit·brush \'rab-ət-,brəsh\ *n* (ca. 1890) **:** any of several low branching shrubs (genus *Chrysothamnus* and esp. *C. nauseosus*) of the alkali plains of western No. America that are characterized by linear entire leaves and clusters of golden yellow flowers

rabbit ears *n pl* (1952) **:** an indoor dipole television antenna consisting of two usu. extensible rods connected to a base to form a V shape

rabbit fever *n* (1925) **:** TULAREMIA

rabbit punch *n* (1915) **:** a short chopping blow delivered to the back of the neck or the base of the skull — **rabbit–punch** *vt*

rab·bit·ry \'rab-ə-trē\ *n, pl* **-ries** (1838) **:** a place where domestic rabbits are kept; *also* **:** a rabbit-raising enterprise

¹rabble \'rab-əl\ *n* [ME *rabel* pack of animals] (14c) **1 :** a disorganized or confused collection of things **2 a :** a disorganized or disorderly crowd of people **:** MOB **b :** the lowest class of people

²rabble *vt* **rab·bled; rab·bling** \-(ə-)liŋ\ (1644) **:** to insult or assault by or as a mob

³rabble *n* [F *râble* fire shovel, fr. ML *rotabulum,* alter. of L *rutabulum,* fr. *rutus,* pp. of *ruere* to dig up — more at RUG] (1864) **:** an iron bar with the end bent for use like a rake in puddling iron; *also* **:** a similar device used in a melting, refining, or roasting furnace

⁴rabble *vt* **rab·bled; rab·bling** \-(ə-)liŋ\ (1877) **:** to stir or skim with a rabble — **rab·bler** \'rab-(ə-)lər\ *n*

rab·ble·ment \'rab-əl-mənt\ *n* (1548) **1 :** RABBLE **2 :** DISTURBANCE

rab·ble–rous·er \'rab-əl-,rau̇-zər\ *n* (1843) **:** one that stirs up (as to hatred or violence) the masses of the people **:** DEMAGOGUE — **rab·ble–rous·ing** \-ziŋ\ *n or adj*

Ra·be·lai·sian \,rab-ə-'lā-zhən, -zē-ən\ *adj* (1817) **1 :** of, relating to, or characteristic of Rabelais or his works **2 :** marked by gross robust humor, extravagance of caricature, or bold naturalism

Ra·bi \'rə-bē\ *n* [Ar *rabīʿ*] (ca. 1769) **:** either of two months of the Islamic year: **a :** the 3d month **b :** the 4th month — see MONTH table

ra·bic \'rā-bik\ *adj* (1885) **:** of or relating to rabies

ra·bid \'rab-əd *also* 'rā-bəd\ *adj* [L *rabidus* mad, fr. *rabere*] (1611) **1 a :** extremely violent **:** FURIOUS **b :** going to extreme lengths in expressing or pursuing a feeling, interest, or opinion **2 :** affected with rabies — **ra·bid·i·ty** \rə-'bid-ət-ē, ra-, rā-\ *n* — **ra·bid·ly** \'rab-əd-lē *also* 'rā-bəd-\ *adv* — **ra·bid·ness** *n*

ra·bies \'rā-bēz\ *n, pl* **rabies** [NL, fr. L, madness, fr. *rabere* to rave — more at RAGE] (ca. 1598) **:** an acute virus disease of the nervous system of warm-blooded animals usu. transmitted through the bite of a rabid animal

rac·coon \ra-'kün *also* rə-\ *n, pl* **raccoon** *or* **raccoons** [*ärähkun* (in some Algonquian language of Virginia)] (1608) **1 a :** a small nocturnal carnivore (*Procyon lotor*) of No. America that is chiefly gray, has a bushy ringed tail, lives chiefly in trees, and has a varied diet including small animals, fruits, and nuts **b :** the pelt of this animal **2 :** any of several animals resembling or related to the raccoon

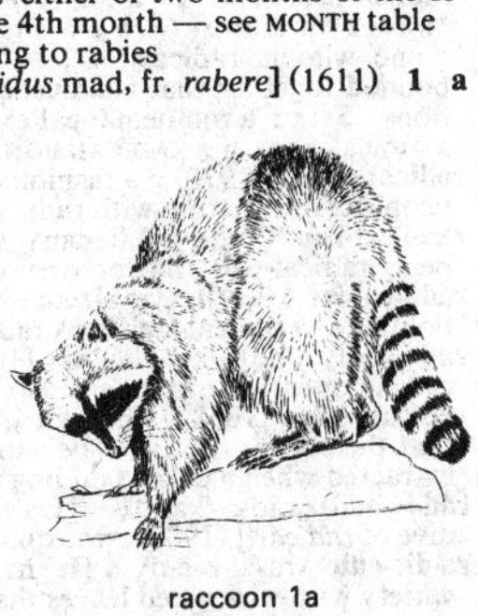

raccoon 1a

¹race \'rās\ *n* [ME *ras,* fr. ON *rās;* akin to OE *rǣs* rush, L *rorarii* skirmishers, Gk *erōē* rush] (14c) **1** *chiefly Scot* **:** the act of running **2 a :** a strong or rapid current of water flowing through a narrow channel **b :** a heavy or choppy sea **c :** a watercourse used industrially **d :** the current flowing in such a course **3 a :** a set course or duration of time **b :** the course of life **4 a :** a contest of speed **b** *pl* **:** a meeting in which several races (as for horses) are run **c :** a contest or rivalry involving progress toward a goal ⟨pennant ~⟩ **5 :** a track or channel in which something rolls or slides; *specif* **:** a groove (as for the balls) in a bearing **6 :** SLIPSTREAM

²race *vb* **raced; rac·ing** *vi* (1680) **1 :** to compete in a race **2 :** to go or move at top speed or out of control **3 :** to revolve too fast under a diminished load ~ *vt* **1 :** to engage in a race with **2 a :** to enter in a race **b :** to drive at high speed **c :** to transport or propel at maximum speed **3 :** to speed (as an engine) without a working load or with the transmission disengaged

³race *n* [MF, generation, fr. OIt *razza*] (1580) **1 :** a breeding stock of animals **2 a :** a family, tribe, people, or nation belonging to the same stock **b :** a class or kind of people unified by community of interests, habits, or characteristics ⟨the English ~⟩ **3 a :** an actually or potentially interbreeding group within a species; *also* **:** a taxonomic category (as a subspecies) representing such a group **b :** BREED **c :** a division of mankind possessing traits that are transmissible by descent and sufficient to characterize it as a distinct human type **4** *obs* **:** inherited temperament or disposition **5 :** distinctive flavor, taste, or strength

race·course \'rā-,skō(ə)rs, -,skȯ(ə)rs\ *n* (1764) **1 :** a course for racing **2 :** RACEWAY 1

race·horse \'rās-,hȯ(ə)rs\ *n* (1626) **:** a horse bred or kept for racing

ra·ce·mate \rā-'sē-,māt, rə-; 'ras-ə-\ *n* (1835) **1 :** a salt or ester of racemic acid **2 :** a racemic compound or mixture

ra·ceme \rā-'sēm, rə-\ *n* [L *racemus* bunch of grapes] (1785) **:** a simple inflorescence (as in the lily-of-the-valley) in which the flowers are borne on short stalks of about equal length at equal distances along an elongated axis and open in succession toward the apex — see INFLORESCENCE illustration

ra·ce·mic \-'sē-mik\ *adj* (1892) **:** of, relating to, or constituting a compound or mixture that is composed of equal amounts of dextrorotatory and levorotatory forms of the same compound and is optically inactive

ra·ce·mi·za·tion \rā-,sē-mə-'zā-shən, rə-; ,ras-ə-mə-\ *n* (1895) **:** the action or process of changing from an optically active compound into a racemic compound or mixture — **ra·ce·mize** \rā-'sē-,mīz, rə-; 'ras-ə-\ *vb*

ra·ce·mose \'ras-ə-,mōs; rā-'sē-, rə-\ *adj* [L *racemosus* full of clusters, fr. *racemus*] (1698) **:** having or growing in the form of a raceme

racemose gland *n* (1860) **:** a compound gland of freely branching ducts that end in acini

rac·er \'rā-sər\ *n* (1649) **1 :** one that races or is used for racing **2 :** any of various active American snakes (genus *Coluber* and *Mastigophis*); *esp* **:** BLACK RACER

race riot *n* (1890) **:** a riot caused by racial dissensions or hatreds

race runner *n* (1915) **:** a No. American lizard (*Cnemidophorus sexlineatus*) that moves swiftly

race·track \'rā-,strak\ *n* (1859) **:** a usu. oval course on which races are run

race·track·er \'rā-,strak-ər\ *n* (1953) **:** one who frequents a racetrack

race·way \'rā-,swā\ *n* (1828) **1 :** a canal for a current of water **2 :** a channel for loosely holding electrical wires in buildings **3 :** ¹RACE 5 **4 :** a course for racing; *esp* **:** a track for harness racing

rach·et \'rach-ət\ *var of* RATCHET

rachi- *or* **rachio-** *comb form* [Gk *rhachi-,* fr. *rhachis;* akin to Gk *rhachos* thorn, Lith *ražas* stubble] **:** spine ⟨*rachiodont*⟩

ra·chis \'rā-kəs, 'rak-əs\ *n, pl* **ra·chis·es** *also* **ra·chi·des** \'rak-ə-,dēz, 'rā-kə-\ [NL *rachid-, rachis,* modif. of Gk *rhachis*] (1842) **1 :** SPINAL COLUMN **2 :** an axial structure: as **a** (1) **:** the elongated axis of an inflorescence (2) **:** an extension of the petiole of a compound leaf that bears the leaflets **b :** the distal part of the shaft of a feather that bears the web

ra·chit·ic \rə-'kit-ik\ *adj* (1797) **:** RICKETY

ra·chi·tis \rə-'kīt-əs\ *n* [NL, fr. Gk *rhachitis* disease of the spine, fr. *rhachis*] (ca. 1727) **:** RICKETS

ra·cial \'rā-shəl\ *adj* (1862) **1 :** of, relating to, or based on a race **2 :** existing or occurring between races — **ra·cial·ly** \-shə-lē\ *adv*

ra·cial·ism \'rā-shə-,liz-əm\ *n* (1907) **:** RACISM — **ra·cial·ist** \-ləst\ *n or adj* — **ra·cial·is·tic** \,rā-shə-'lis-tik\ *adj*

rac·ing \'rā-siŋ\ *n* (1680) **:** the sport or profession of engaging in or holding races

racing form *n* (1946) **:** an information sheet giving details of past performance (as for racehorses) for use by bettors

rac·ism \'rā-,siz-əm, -,shiz-\ *n* (1936) **1 :** a belief that race is the primary determinant of human traits and capacities and that racial differences produce an inherent superiority of a particular race **2 :** racial prejudice or discrimination — **rac·ist** \-səst, -shəst\ *n or adj*

¹rack \'rak\ *n* [ME *rak,* prob. of Scand origin; akin to Sw dial. *rak* wreck; akin to OE *wrecan* to drive — more at WREAK] (14c) **:** a wind-driven mass of high often broken clouds

²rack *vi* (1590) **:** to fly or scud in high wind

³rack *n* [ME, prob. fr. MD *rec* framework; akin to OE *reccan* to stretch, Gk *oregein* — more at RIGHT] (15c) **1 :** a framework for holding fodder for livestock **2 :** an instrument of torture on which a body is stretched **3 a** (1) **:** a cause of anguish or pain (2) **:** acute suffering **b :** the action of straining or wrenching **4 :** a framework, stand, or grating on or in which articles are placed **5 :** a frame placed in a stream to stop fish and floating or suspended matter **6 a :** a bar with teeth on one face for gearing with a pinion or worm gear to transform rotary motion to linear motion or vice versa (as in an automobile steering mechanism or microscope drawtube) **b :** a notched bar used as a ratchet to engage with a pawl, click, or detent **7 :** a pair of antlers **8 :** a triangular frame used to set up the balls in a pool game; *also* **:** the balls as set up — **rack·ful** \-ˌfu̇l\ *n* — **on the rack :** under great mental or emotional stress

[4]rack *vt* (15c) **1 :** to torture on the rack **2 :** to cause to suffer torture, pain, or anguish **3 a :** to stretch or strain violently ⟨~*ed* his brains⟩ **b :** to raise (rents) oppressively **c :** to harass or oppress with high rents or extortions **4 :** to work or treat (material) on a rack **5 :** to work by a rack and pinion or worm so as to extend or contract ⟨~ a camera⟩ **6 :** to seize (as parallel ropes of a tackle) together **7 :** to place (as pool balls) in a rack ~ *vi* **:** to become forced out of shape or out of plumb ***syn*** see AFFLICT — **rack·er** *n* — **rack·ing·ly** \ˈrak-iŋ-lē\ *adv*

[5]rack *vt* [ME *rakken,* fr. OProv *arraca*] (15c) **:** to draw off (as wine) from the lees

[6]rack *vi* [prob. alter. of [1]*rock*] *of a horse* (1530) **:** to go at a rack

[7]rack *n* (1580) **:** either of two gaits of a horse: **a :** PACE 4b **b :** a fast showy 4-beat gait

[8]rack *n* [perh. fr. [3]*rack*] (1570) **1 :** the neck and spine of a forequarter of veal, pork, or esp. mutton **2 :** the rib section of a foresaddle of lamb used for chops or as a roast — see LAMB illustration

[9]rack *n* [alter. of *wrack*] (1599) **:** DESTRUCTION ⟨~ and ruin⟩

[1]rack·et *also* **rac·quet** \ˈrak-ət\ *n* [MF *raquette,* fr. Ar *rāḥah* palm of the hand] (1500) **1 :** a lightweight implement that consists of a netting (as of nylon) stretched in a usu. oval open frame with a handle attached and that is used for striking the ball or shuttlecock in various games (as tennis, racquets, or badminton) **2** *usu* **racquets** *pl but sing in constr* **:** a game for two or four players with ball and racket on a 4-walled court

[2]racket *n* [origin unknown] (1565) **1 :** confused clattering noise **:** CLAMOR **2 a :** social whirl or excitement **b :** the strain of exciting or trying experiences **3 a :** a fraudulent scheme, enterprise, or activity **b :** a usu. illegitimate enterprise made workable by bribery or intimidation **c :** an easy and lucrative means of livelihood **d** *slang* **:** OCCUPATION, BUSINESS

[3]racket *vi* (1760) **1 :** to engage in active social life **2 :** to move with or make a racket

[1]rack·e·teer \ˌrak-ə-ˈti(ə)r\ *n* (1928) **:** one who obtains money by an illegal enterprise usu. involving intimidation

[2]racketeer *vi* (1928) **:** to carry on a racket ~ *vt* **:** to practice extortion on

rack·ety \ˈrak-ət-ē\ *adj* (1773) **1 :** NOISY **2 :** FLASHY, ROWDY **3 :** RICKETY

rack·le \ˈrak-əl\ *adj* [ME *rakel*] *chiefly Scot* (14c) **:** IMPETUOUS

rack railway *n* (1884) **:** a railway having between its rails a rack that meshes with a gear wheel or pinion of the locomotive for traction on steep grades

rack–rent *vt* (1748) **:** to subject to rack rent

rack rent *n* [[4]*rack*] (1607) **1 :** an excessive or unreasonably high rent **2** *Brit* **:** the highest rent that can be earned on a property

rack–rent·er \ˈrak-ˈrent-ər\ *n* (1680) **:** one that pays or exacts rack rent

rack up *vt* (1949) **:** ACCUMULATE, GAIN ⟨*racked up* their tenth victory⟩

ra·clette \ra-ˈklet, rä-\ *n* [F, fr. *racler* to scrape] (ca. 1949) **:** a Swiss dish consisting of cheese melted over a fire and then scraped onto bread or boiled potatoes; *also* **:** the cheese used in this dish

ra·con \ˈrā-ˌkän\ *n* [*radar beacon*] (1945) **:** RADAR BEACON

ra·con·teur \ˌrak-ˌän-ˈtər, -ən-\ *n* [F, fr. MF, fr. *raconter* to tell, fr. OF, fr. *re-* + *aconter, acompter* to tell, count — more at ACCOUNT] (1828) **:** one who excels in telling anecdotes

ra·coon *var of* RACCOON

rac·quet·ball \ˈrak-ət-ˌbȯl\ *n* (1968) **:** a game similar to handball that is played on a 4-walled court with a short-handled racket and a larger ball

[1]racy \ˈrā-sē\ *adj* **rac·i·er; -est** [[3]*race*] (1650) **1 :** having the distinctive quality of something in its original or most characteristic form **2 a :** full of zest or vigor **b :** having a strongly marked quality **:** PIQUANT ⟨a ~ flavor⟩ **c :** RISQUÉ, SUGGESTIVE ***syn*** see PUNGENT — **rac·i·ly** \ˈrā-sə-lē\ *adv* — **rac·i·ness** \-sē-nəs\ *n*

[2]racy *adj* **rac·i·er; -est** [[1]*race*] (1841) **:** having a body fitted for racing **:** long-bodied and lean

rad \ˈrad\ *n* [*radiation absorbed dose*] (1918) **:** a unit of absorbed dose of ionizing radiation equal to an energy of 100 ergs per gram of irradiated material

ra·dar \ˈrā-ˌdär\ *n, often attrib* [*radio detecting and ranging*] (ca. 1941) **:** a radio device or system for locating an object by means of ultrahigh-frequency radio waves reflected from the object and received, observed, and analyzed by the receiving part of the device in such a way that characteristics (as distance and direction) of the object may be determined

radar astronomy *n* (1959) **:** astronomy dealing with investigations of celestial bodies in the solar system by analyzing radar waves directed toward and reflected from the object being studied

radar beacon *n* (1945) **:** a radar transmitter that upon receiving a radar signal emits a signal which reinforces the normal reflected signal or which introduces a code into the reflected signal esp. for identification purposes

ra·dar·scope \ˈrā-ˌdär-ˌskōp\ *n* [*radar* + *oscilloscope*] (1945) **:** the oscilloscope or screen serving as the visual indicator in a radar receiver

radar telescope *n* (1953) **:** a radar transmitter-receiver with an antenna for use in radar astronomy

[1]rad·dle \ˈrad-ᵊl\ *n* [prob. alter. of *ruddle*] (1523) **:** RED OCHER

[2]raddle *vt* **rad·dled; rad·dling** \ˈrad-liŋ, -ᵊl-iŋ\ (1631) **:** to mark or paint with raddle

[3]raddle *vt* **rad·dled; rad·dling** \ˈrad-liŋ, -ᵊl-iŋ\ [E dial. *raddle* (supple stick interwoven with others as in making a fence)] (1671) **:** to twist together **:** INTERWEAVE

rad·dled \ˈrad-ᵊld\ *adj* [origin unknown] (1694) **1 :** being in a state of confusion **:** lacking composure **2 :** BROKEN-DOWN, WORN

radi- *or* **radio-** *comb form* [F, fr. L *radius* ray] **1 a :** radial **:** radially ⟨*radio*symmetrical⟩ **b :** radial and ⟨*radio*bicipital⟩ **2 a :** radiant energy **:** radiation ⟨*radio*active⟩ ⟨*radio*paque⟩ **b :** radioactive ⟨*radio*-element⟩ **c :** radium **:** X rays ⟨*radio*therapy⟩ **d :** radioactive isotopes esp. as produced artificially ⟨*radio*carbon⟩ **e :** radio ⟨*radio*telegraphy⟩

[1]ra·di·al \ˈrād-ē-əl\ *adj* [ML *radialis,* fr. L *radius* ray] (1570) **1 :** arranged or having parts arranged like rays ⟨the ~ form of a starfish⟩ **2 a :** relating to, placed like, or moving along a radius **b :** characterized by divergence from a center **3 :** of, relating to, or adjacent to a bodily radius ⟨the thumb is on the ~ aspect of the hand⟩ **4 :** developing uniformly around a central axis ⟨~ cleavage of an egg⟩ — **ra·di·al·ly** \-ē-ə-lē\ *adv*

[2]radial *n* (1872) **1 a :** a radial part **b :** RAY **2 :** a body part (as an artery) lying near or following the course of the radius **3 :** a pneumatic tire in which the ply cords that extend to the beads are laid at approximately 90 degrees to the centerline of the tread — called also *radial-ply tire, radial tire*

ra·di·a·le \ˌrād-ē-ˈal-(ˌ)ē, -ˈāl-, -ˈäl-\ *n, pl* **-lia** \-ē-ə\ [NL, fr. ML, neut. of *radialis*] (1888) **:** a bone or cartilage of the carpus that articulates with the radius; *specif* **:** the navicular in man

radial engine *n* (ca. 1910) **:** a usu. internal-combustion engine with cylinders arranged radially like the spokes of a wheel

radial symmetry *n* (1890) **:** the condition of having similar parts regularly arranged around a central axis — **radially symmetrical** *adj*

ra·di·an \ˈrād-ē-ən\ *n* (1879) **:** a unit of plane angular measurement that is equal to the angle at the center of a circle subtended by an arc equal in length to the radius

ra·di·ance \ˈrād-ē-ən(t)s\ *n* (1601) **1 :** the quality or state of being radiant **2 :** a deep pink **3 :** the flux density of radiant energy per unit solid angle and per unit projected area of radiating surface

ra·di·an·cy \-ən-sē\ *n* (1646) **:** RADIANCE

[1]ra·di·ant \ˈrād-ē-ənt\ *adj* (15c) **1 a :** radiating rays or reflecting beams of light **b :** vividly bright and shining **:** GLOWING **2 :** marked by or expressive of love, confidence, or happiness ⟨a ~ smile⟩ **3 a :** emitted or transmitted by radiation **b :** emitting or relating to radiant heat **4 :** of, relating to, or exhibiting biological radiation ***syn*** see BRIGHT — **ra·di·ant·ly** *adv*

[2]radiant *n* (1727) **:** something that radiates: as **a :** a point in the heavens at which the visible parallel paths of meteors appear to meet when traced backward **b :** a point or object from which light emanates **c :** the part of a gas or electric heater that becomes incandescent

radiant energy *n* (ca. 1890) **:** energy traveling as a wave motion; *specif* **:** the energy of electromagnetic waves

radiant flux *n* (ca. 1925) **:** the rate of emission or transmission of radiant energy

radiant heat *n* (1794) **:** heat transmitted by radiation as contrasted with that transmitted by conduction or convection

radiant heating *n* (1937) **:** PANEL HEATING

[1]ra·di·ate \ˈrād-ē-ˌāt\ *vb* **-at·ed; -at·ing** [L *radiatus,* pp. of *radiare,* fr. *radius* ray] *vi* (1619) **1 :** to proceed in a direct line from or toward a center **2 :** to send out rays **:** shine brightly **3 a :** to issue in or as if in rays **b :** to evolve by radiation ~ *vt* **1 :** to send out in or as if in rays **2 :** IRRADIATE, ILLUMINATE **3 :** to spread abroad or around as if from a center

[2]ra·di·ate \ˈrād-ē-ət, -ē-ˌāt\ *adj* (1668) **:** having rays or radial parts: as **a :** having ray flowers **b :** characterized by radial symmetry **:** radially symmetrical — **ra·di·ate·ly** *adv*

ra·di·a·tion \ˌrād-ē-ˈā-shən\ *n* (1570) **1 a :** something that is radiated **b :** energy radiated in the form of waves or particles **2 a :** the action or process of radiating **b (1) :** the process of emitting radiant energy in the form of waves or particles **(2) :** the combined processes of emission, transmission, and absorption of radiant energy **3 :** radial arrangement **4 :** biological evolution in a group of organisms that is characterized by spreading into different environments and by divergence of structure **5 :** RADIATOR — **ra·di·a·tion·al** \-shnəl, -shən-ᵊl\ *adj* — **ra·di·a·tion·less** \-shən-ləs\ *adj* — **ra·di·a·tive** \ˈrād-ē-ˌāt-iv\ *adj*

radiation sickness *n* (1924) **:** sickness that results from exposure to radiation and is commonly marked by fatigue, nausea, vomiting, loss of teeth and hair, and in more severe cases by damage to blood-forming tissue with decrease in red and white blood cells and with bleeding

ra·di·a·tor \ˈrād-ē-ˌāt-ər\ *n* (1836) **:** one that radiates: as **a :** any of various devices (as a nest of pipes or tubes) for transferring heat from a fluid within to an area or object outside **b :** a transmitting antenna

[1]rad·i·cal \ˈrad-i-kəl\ *adj* [ME, fr. LL *radicalis,* fr. L *radic-, radix* root — more at ROOT] (14c) **1 :** of, relating to, or proceeding from a root: as **a (1) :** of or growing from the root of a plant ⟨~ tubers⟩ **(2) :** growing from the base of a stem, from a rootlike stem, or from a stem that does not rise above the ground ⟨~ leaves⟩ **b :** of, relating to, or constituting a linguistic root **c :** of or relating to a mathematical root **d :** designed to remove the root of a disease or all diseased tissue ⟨~ surgery⟩ **2 :** of or relating to the origin **:** FUNDAMENTAL **3 a :** marked by a considerable departure from the usual or traditional **:** EXTREME **b :** tending or disposed to make extreme changes in existing views, habits, conditions, or institutions **c :** of, relating to, or constituting a political group associated with views, practices, and policies of extreme change **d :** advocating extreme measures to retain or restore a political state of affairs ⟨the ~ right⟩ — **rad·i·cal·ness** *n*

[2]radical *n* (1641) **1 a :** a root part **b :** a basic principle **:** FOUNDATION **2 a :** ROOT 6 **b :** a sound or letter belonging to a radical **3 :** one who is radical **4 :** FREE RADICAL; *also* **:** a group of atoms bonded together that is considered an entity in various kinds of reactions **5 a :** a mathematical expression indicating a root by means of a radical sign **b :** RADICAL SIGN

radical chic *n* (1970) **:** a fashionable practice among socially prominent people of associating with radicals or members of minority groups

rad·i·cal·ism \ˈrad-i-kə-ˌliz-əm\ *n* (1820) **1 :** the quality or state of being radical **2 :** the doctrines or principles of radicals

rad·i·cal·ize \-kə-ˌlīz\ *vt* **-ized; -iz·ing** (1823) **:** to make radical esp. in politics — **rad·i·cal·iza·tion** \ˌrad-i-kə-lə-ˈzā-shən\ *n*

rad·i·cal·ly \ˈrad-i-k(ə-)lē\ *adv* (1609) **1 :** in origin or essence **2 :** in a radical or extreme manner

radical sign *n* (1668) **:** the sign $\surd$ placed before an expression to denote that the square root is to be extracted or that some other root is to be extracted when a corresponding index is placed over the sign

rad·i·cand \ˌrad-ə-ˈkand\ *n* [L *radicandum,* neut. of *radicandus,* gerundive of *radicari*] (1900) **:** the quantity under a radical sign

ra·dic·chio \ra-ˈdik-ē-ō\ *n* [It, lit., chicory] (1968) **:** a chicory of a red variety with variegated leaves that is used as a salad green

radices *pl of* RADIX
rad·i·cle \'rad-i-kəl\ *n* [L *radicula*, dim. of *radic-*, *radix*] (1671) **1 :** the lower part of the axis of a plant embryo or seedling: **a :** the embryonic root of a seedling **b :** HYPOCOTYL **c :** the hypocotyl and the root together **2 :** RADICAL
ra·dic·u·lar \rə-'dik-yə-lər, ra-\ *adj* [L *radicula* + E *-ar*] (1830) **1 :** of or relating to a plant radicle **2 :** of, relating to, or involving a nerve root ⟨~ pain⟩
radii *pl of* RADIUS
¹**ra·dio** \'rād-ē-,ō\ *n, pl* **ra·di·os** [short for *radiotelegraphy*] (1903) **1 a :** the wireless transmission and reception of electric impulses or signals by means of electromagnetic waves **b :** the use of these waves for the wireless transmission of electric impulses into which sound is converted **2 :** a radio message **3 :** a radio receiving set **4 a :** a radio transmitting station **b :** a radio broadcasting organization **c :** the radio broadcasting industry **d :** communication by radio
²**radio** *adj* (ca. 1887) **1 :** of, relating to, or operated by radiant energy **2 :** of or relating to electric currents or phenomena of frequencies between about 15,000 and 10^{11} hertz **3 a :** of, relating to, or used in radio or a radio set **b :** specializing in radio or associated with the radio industry **c (1) :** transmitted by radio **(2) :** making or participating in radio broadcasts **d :** controlled or directed by radio
³**radio** *vt* (1913) **1 :** to send or communicate by radio **2 :** to send a radio message to ~ *vi* **:** to send or communicate something by radio
radio- — see RADI-
ra·dio·ac·tive \,rād-ē-ō-'ak-tiv\ *adj* [ISV] (1898) **:** of, caused by, or exhibiting radioactivity — **ra·dio·ac·tive·ly** *adv*
ra·dio·ac·tiv·i·ty \-ak-'tiv-ət-ē\ *n* [ISV] (1899) **:** the property possessed by some elements (as uranium) of spontaneously emitting alpha or beta rays and sometimes also gamma rays by the disintegration of the nuclei of atoms; *also* **:** the rays emitted
radio astronomy *n* (1948) **:** astronomy dealing with electromagnetic radiations of radio frequency received from outside the earth's atmosphere — **radio astronomer** *n*
ra·dio·au·to·graph \,rād-ē-ō-'ȯt-ə-,graf\ *n* (1941) **:** AUTORADIOGRAPH — **ra·dio·au·to·graph·ic** \-,ȯt-ə-'graf-ik\ *adj* — **ra·dio·au·tog·ra·phy** \-ō-ȯ-'täg-rə-fē\ *n*
radio beacon *n* (1919) **:** a radio transmitting station that transmits special radio signals for use (as on a landing field) in determining the direction or position of those receiving them
ra·dio·bi·ol·o·gy \,rād-ē-ō-bī-'äl-ə-jē\ *n* (1919) **:** a branch of biology dealing with the interaction of biological systems and radiant energy or radioactive materials — **ra·dio·bi·o·log·i·cal** \-,bī-ə-'läj-i-kəl\ *also* **ra·dio·bi·o·log·ic** \-ik\ *adj* — **ra·dio·bi·o·log·i·cal·ly** \-i-k(ə-)lē\ *adv* — **ra·dio·bi·ol·o·gist** \-bī-'äl-ə-jəst\ *n*
ra·dio·broad·cast \-'brȯd-,kast\ *vt* (1925) **:** to broadcast (as music) by radio — **ra·dio·broad·cast·er** *n*
radio car *n* (1925) **:** an automobile equipped with radio communication
ra·dio·car·bon \,rād-ē-ō-'kär-bən\ *n* [ISV] (1939) **:** radioactive carbon; *esp* **:** CARBON 14
radiocarbon dating *n* (ca. 1951) **:** CARBON DATING
ra·dio·cast \'rād-ē-ō-,kast\ *vt* [*radio-* + broad*cast*] (1924) **:** RADIOBROADCAST — **ra·dio·cast·er** *n*
ra·dio·chem·is·try \,rād-ē-ō-'kem-ə-strē\ *n* (1904) **:** a branch of chemistry dealing with radioactive substances and phenomena including tracer studies — **ra·dio·chem·i·cal** \-'kem-i-kəl\ *adj* — **ra·dio·chem·i·cal·ly** \-k(ə-)lē\ *adv* — **ra·dio·chem·ist** \-'kem-əst\ *n*
ra·dio·chro·mato·gram \-krō-'mat-ə-,gram, -krə-\ *n* (ca. 1951) **:** a chromatogram revealing one or more radioactive substances
radio compass *n* (1918) **:** a direction finder used in navigation
ra·dio·ecol·o·gy \,rād-ē-ō-i-'käl-ə-jē\ *n* (1956) **:** the study of the effects of radiation and radioactive substances on ecological communities — **ra·dio·eco·log·i·cal** \-,ē-kə-'läj-i-kəl, -,ek-ə-\ *adj* — **ra·dio·ecol·o·gist** \-i-'käl-ə-jəst\ *n*
ra·dio·el·e·ment \-'el-ə-mənt\ *n* [ISV] (1903) **:** a radioactive element
radio frequency *n* (1915) **:** an electromagnetic wave frequency intermediate between audio frequencies and infrared frequencies used esp. in radio and television transmission

RADIO FREQUENCIES

CLASS	ABBREVIATION	RANGE
extremely low frequency	ELF	below 3 kilohertz
very low frequency	VLF	3 to 30 kilohertz
low frequency	LF	30 to 300 kilohertz
medium frequency	MF	300 to 3000 kilohertz
high frequency	HF	3 to 30 megahertz
very high frequency	VHF	30 to 300 megahertz
ultrahigh frequency	UHF	300 to 3000 megahertz
superhigh frequency	SHF	3 to 30 gigahertz
extremely high frequency	EHF	30 to 300 gigahertz

radio galaxy *n* (1960) **:** a galaxy that is a powerful source of radio waves
ra·dio·gen·ic \,rād-ē-ō-'jen-ik\ *adj* (1935) **:** produced by or determined from radioactivity
ra·dio·gram \'rād-ē-ō-,gram\ *n* (1896) **1 :** RADIOGRAPH **2 :** a message transmitted by radiotelegraphy **3** *Brit* **:** a combined radio receiver and record player
¹**ra·dio·graph** \-,graf\ *n* (1880) **:** a picture produced on a sensitive surface by a form of radiation other than light; *specif* **:** an X-ray or gamma ray photograph — **ra·dio·graph·ic** \,rād-ē-ō-'graf-ik\ *adj* — **ra·dio·graph·i·cal·ly** \-i-k(ə-)lē\ *adv*
²**radiograph** *vt* (1896) **:** to make a radiograph of
³**radiograph** *vt* [*radio-* + tele*graph*] (ca. 1933) **:** to send a radiogram to
ra·di·og·ra·phy \,rād-ē-'äg-rə-fē\ *n* [ISV] (1896) **:** the art, act, or process of making radiographs
ra·dio·im·mu·no·as·say \'rād-ē-,ō-im-yə-nō-'as-,ā, -im-,yü-, -a-'sā\ *n* (1961) **:** immunoassay of a substance (as insulin) that has been radioactively labeled — **ra·dio·im·mu·no·as·say·able** \-ə-bəl\ *adj*
ra·dio·iso·tope \,rād-ē-ō-'ī-sə-,tōp\ *n* [ISV] (1946) **:** a radioactive isotope — **ra·dio·iso·to·pic** \-,ī-sə-'täp-ik, -'tōp-ik\ *adj* — **ra·dio·iso·to·pi·cal·ly** \-i-k(ə-)lē\ *adv*
ra·dio·la·bel \-'lā-bəl\ *vt* (1953) **:** to label with a radioactive atom or substance
ra·di·o·lar·i·an \,rād-ē-ō-'lar-ē-ən, -'ler-\ *n* [deriv. of LL *radiolus* small sunbeam, fr. dim. of L *radius* ray — more at RAY] (1877) **:** any of a large order (Radiolaria) of marine protozoans having a siliceous skeleton of spicules and radiating threadlike pseudopodia — **radiolarian** *adj*
ra·dio·lo·ca·tion \-lō-'kā-shən\ *n* (1941) **:** the detection or the determination of the position and course of distant objects by radar
ra·dio·log·i·cal \,rād-ē-ə-'läj-i-kəl\ *or* **ra·dio·log·ic** \-ik\ *adj* (1909) **1 :** of or relating to radiology **2 :** of or relating to nuclear radiation — **ra·dio·log·i·cal·ly** \-k(ə-)lē\ *adv*
ra·di·ol·o·gist \,rād-ē-'äl-ə-jəst\ *n* (1906) **:** a physician specializing in the use of radiant energy for diagnostic and therapeutic purposes
ra·di·ol·o·gy \-jē\ *n* (1900) **1 :** a branch of medicine concerned with the use of radiant energy (as X rays and radium) in the diagnosis and treatment of disease **2 :** the science of radioactive substances and high-energy radiations
ra·dio·lu·cent \,rād-ē-ō-'lüs-ᵊnt\ *adj* (1917) **:** partly or wholly permeable to radiation ⟨~ tissues⟩ — **ra·dio·lu·cen·cy** \-ᵊn-sē\ *n*
ra·di·ol·y·sis \,rād-ē-'äl-ə-səs\ *n* [NL] (ca. 1948) **:** chemical decomposition by the action of radiation — **ra·dio·lyt·ic** \-ē-ə-'lit-ik\ *adj*
ra·dio·man \'rād-ē-ō-,man\ *n* (1921) **:** a radio operator or technician
ra·dio·me·te·or·o·graph \'rād-ē-ō-,mēt-ē-'ȯr-ə-,graf, -är-\ *n* (1936) **:** RADIOSONDE
ra·di·om·e·ter \,rād-ē-'äm-ət-ər\ *n* (1875) **:** an instrument for measuring the intensity of radiant energy by the torsional twist of suspended vanes that are blackened on one side and exposed to a source of radiant energy; *also* **:** an instrument for measuring electromagnetic or acoustic radiation — **ra·di·om·e·try** \-ə-trē\ *n*

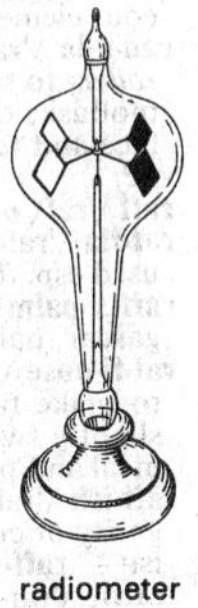
radiometer

ra·dio·met·ric \,rād-ē-ō-'me-trik\ *adj* [ISV] (1877) **1 :** relating to, using, or measured by a radiometer **2 :** of or relating to the measurement of geologic time by means of the rate of disintegration of radioactive elements — **ra·dio·met·ri·cal·ly** \-tri-k(ə-)lē\ *adv*
ra·dio·mi·met·ic \-mə-'met-ik, -mī-\ *adj* [ISV] (ca. 1947) **:** producing effects similar to those of radiation
ra·di·on·ics \,rād-ē-'än-iks\ *n pl but sing in constr* [*radio-* + electr*onics*] (1943) **:** ELECTRONICS
ra·dio·nu·clide \,rād-ē-ō-'n(y)ü-,klīd\ *n* (1947) **:** a radioactive nuclide
ra·di·opaque \,rād-ē-ō-'pāk\ *adj* (1917) **:** being opaque to various forms of radiation (as X rays)
ra·dio·phar·ma·ceu·ti·cal \'rād-ē-ō-,fär-mə-'süt-i-kəl\ *n* (1952) **:** a radioactive drug used for diagnostic or therapeutic purposes — **radiopharmaceutical** *adj*
ra·dio·phone \'rād-ē-ə-,fōn\ *n* (1881) **1 :** an apparatus for the production of sound by radiant energy **2 :** RADIOTELEPHONE
ra·dio·pho·to \,rād-ē-ō-'fōt-(,)ō\ *n* (1929) **1** *also* **ra·dio·pho·to·graph** \-'fōt-ə-,graf**:** a picture transmitted by radio **2 :** the process of transmitting a picture by radio
ra·dio·pro·tec·tive \-prə-'tek-tiv\ *adj* (1956) **:** serving to protect or aiding in protecting against the injurious effect of radiations ⟨~ drugs⟩ — **ra·dio·pro·tec·tion** \-'tek-shən\ *n*
radio range *n* (1929) **:** a radio facility aiding in the navigation of airplanes
ra·dio·sen·si·tive \,rād-ē-ō-'sen(t)-sət-iv, -'sen(t)-stiv\ *adj* (1920) **:** sensitive to the effects of radiant energy ⟨~ cancer cells⟩ — **ra·dio·sen·si·tiv·i·ty** \-,sen(t)-sə-'tiv-ət-ē\ *n*
ra·dio·sonde \'rād-ē-ō-,sänd\ *n* [ISV] (1937) **:** a miniature radio transmitter that is carried aloft (as by an unmanned balloon) with instruments for broadcasting (as by means of precise tone signals) the humidity, temperature, and pressure
radio spectrum *n* (1936) **:** the region of the electromagnetic spectrum usu. including frequencies below 30,000 megahertz in which radio or radar transmission and detection techniques may be used
radio star *n* (1948) **:** a cosmic radio source of very small dimensions and relatively strong radiation
ra·dio·stron·tium \,rād-ē-ō-'strän-ch(ē-)əm, -'stränt-ē-əm\ *n* [NL] (1941) **:** radioactive strontium; *esp* **:** STRONTIUM 90
ra·dio·tele·graph \-'tel-ə-,graf\ *n* [ISV] (1898) **:** WIRELESS TELEGRAPHY — **ra·dio·tele·graph·ic** \-,tel-ə-'graf-ik\ *adj* — **ra·dio·te·leg·ra·phy** \-tə-'leg-rə-fē\ *n*
ra·dio·te·lem·e·try \-tə-'lem-ə-trē\ *n* (1951) **1 :** TELEMETRY **2 :** BIOTELEMETRY — **ra·dio·tele·met·ric** \-,tel-ə-'me-trik\ *adj*
ra·dio·tele·phone \-'tel-ə-,fōn\ *n* [ISV] (1904) **:** an apparatus for carrying on wireless telephony by radio waves — **ra·dio·te·le·pho·ny** \-tə-'lef-ə-nē, -'tel-ə-,fō-nē\ *n*
radio telescope *n* (1929) **:** a radio receiver-antenna combination used for observation in radio astronomy
ra·dio·ther·a·py \,rād-ē-ō-'ther-ə-pē\ *n* [ISV] (ca. 1903) **:** the treatment of disease by means of X rays or radioactive substances — **ra·dio·ther·a·pist** \-pəst\ *n*
ra·dio·tho·ri·um \-'thōr-ē-əm, -'thȯr-\ *n* [NL] (1905) **:** a radioactive isotope of thorium with the mass number 228
ra·dio·trac·er \'rād-ē-ō-,trā-sər\ *n* (1946) **:** a radioactive tracer
ra·dio–ul·na \,rād-ē-ō-'əl-nə\ *n* [NL] (1960) **:** a single bone in the forelimb of an amphibian (as a frog) that represents fusion of the separate radius and ulna of higher forms
radio wave *n* (1916) **:** an electromagnetic wave with radio frequency
rad·ish \'rad-ish *also* 'red-\ *n* [ME, alter. of OE *rædic*, fr. L *radic-*, *radix* root, radish — more at ROOT] (bef. 12c) **:** the pungent fleshy root of a plant (*Raphanus sativus*) of the mustard family usu. eaten raw; *also* **:** the plant that produces radishes

ra·di·um \'rād-ē-əm\ *n, often attrib* [NL, fr. L *radius* ray] (1899) **:** an intensely radioactive shining white metallic element that resembles barium chemically, occurs in combination in minute quantities in minerals (as pitchblende or carnotite), emits alpha particles and gamma rays to form radon, and is used chiefly in luminous materials and in the treatment of cancer — see ELEMENT table

radium therapy *n* (1904) **:** RADIOTHERAPY

ra·di·us \'rād-ē-əs\ *n, pl* **ra·dii** \-ē-,ī\ *also* **ra·di·us·es** [L, ray, radius; perh. akin to L *radix* root — more at ROOT] (1615) **1 a :** the bone on the thumb side of the human forearm; *also* **:** a corresponding part of vertebrates above fishes **b :** the third and usu. largest vein of an insect's wing **2 :** a line segment extending from the center of a circle or sphere to the circumference or bounding surface **3 a :** the length of a radius ⟨a truck with a short turning ~⟩ **b :** the circular area defined by a stated radius **c :** a bounded or circumscribed area **4 :** a radial part **5 :** the distance from a center line or point to an axis of rotation

radius of curvature (1753) **:** the reciprocal of the curvature of a curve

radius vector *n* (1753) **1 a :** a line segment or its length from a fixed point to a variable point **b :** the linear polar coordinate of a variable point **2 :** a straight line joining the center of an attracting body (as the sun) with that of a body (as a planet) in orbit around it

ra·dix \'rād-iks\ *n, pl* **ra·di·ces** \'rād-ə-,sēz, 'rad-\ *or* **ra·dix·es** \'rād-ik-səz\ [L, root] (1798) **1 :** the base of a number system or of logarithms **2 :** the primary source

ra·dome \'rā-,dōm\ *n* [*radar dome*] (1944) **:** a plastic housing sheltering the antenna assembly of a radar set esp. on an airplane

ra·don \'rā-,dän\ *n* [ISV, fr. *radium*] (1918) **:** a heavy radioactive gaseous element formed by disintegration of radium — see ELEMENT table

rad·u·la \'raj-ə-lə\ *n, pl* **-lae** \-,lē, -,lī\ *also* **-las** [NL, fr. L, scraper, fr. *radere* to scrape — more at RAT] (ca. 1864) **:** a horny band or ribbon in mollusks other than bivalves that bears minute teeth on its dorsal surface and tears up food and draws it into the mouth — **rad·u·lar** \-lər\ *adj*

raff \'raf\ *n* [ME *raf* rubbish] (15c) **:** RIFFRAFF

raf·fia \'raf-ē-ə\ *n* [Malagasy *rafia*] (1882) **:** the fiber of the raffia palm used esp. for tying plants and making baskets and hats

raffia palm *n* (1897) **:** a pinnate-leaved palm (*Raphia ruffia*) of Madagascar that is valued for the fiber from its leafstalks

raf·fi·nose \'raf-ə-,nōs, -,nōz\ *n* [F, fr. *raffiner* to refine, fr. *re-* + *affiner* to make fine, fr. *a-* ad- (fr. L *ad-*) + *fin* fine] (1876) **:** a crystalline slightly sweet sugar $C_{18}H_{32}O_{16}$ obtained commercially from cottonseed meal and present in many plant products

raff·ish \'raf-ish\ *adj* (1801) **1 :** marked by or suggestive of flashy vulgarity or crudeness **2 :** marked by a careless unconventionality **:** RAKISH — **raff·ish·ly** *adv* — **raff·ish·ness** *n*

[1]**raffle** \'raf-əl\ *vb* **raf·fled; raf·fling** \'raf-(ə-)liŋ\ *vi* (1680) **:** to engage in a raffle ~ *vt* **:** to dispose of by means of a raffle ⟨~ off a turkey⟩

[2]**raffle** *n* [ME *rafle*, a dice game, fr. MF] (1766) **:** a lottery in which the prize is won by one of numerous persons buying chances

[3]**raffle** *n* [prob. fr. F *rafle* act of snatching, sweeping, fr. MF *rafle, raffe*, fr. MHG *raffen* to snatch; akin to OE *hreppan* to touch, *hearpe* harp — more at HARP] (1881) **:** RUBBISH; *specif* **:** a jumble or tangle of nautical equipment

raf·fle·sia \rə-'flē-zh(ē-)ə, ra-\ *n* [NL, fr. Sir Stamford *Raffles* †1826 Eng. colonial administrator] (1820) **:** any of a genus (*Rafflesia* of the family Rafflesiaceae) of Malaysian dicotyledonous plants that are parasitic in other plants and have fleshy usu. foul-smelling apetalous flowers emerging from the host, imbricated scales in place of leaves, and no stems

[1]**raft** \'raft\ *n* [ME *rafte* rafter, raft, fr. ON *raptr* rafter] (15c) **1 a :** a collection of logs or timber fastened together for conveyance by water **b :** a flat structure for support or transportation on water **2 :** a floating cohesive mass **3 :** an aggregation of animals (as waterfowl) resting on the water

[2]**raft** *vt* (1706) **1 :** to transport in the form of or by means of a raft; *also* **:** to convey (as pebbles) in floating ice or masses of organic material **2 :** to make into a raft ~ *vi* **:** to travel by raft

[3]**raft** *n* [alter. (influenced by [1]*raft*) of *raff* (jumble)] (1830) **:** a large collection

[1]**raf·ter** \'raf-tər\ *n* [ME, fr. OE *ræfter;* akin to ON *raptr* rafter] (bef. 12c) **:** any of the parallel beams that support a roof — see RIDGEPOLE illustration — **raf·tered** \-tərd\ *adj*

[2]**raft·er** \'raf-tər\ *n* [[2]*raft*] (1809) **1 :** one who maneuvers logs into position and binds them into rafts **2 :** one who travels by raft

rafts·man \'raf(t)-smən\ *n* (1776) **:** a man engaged in rafting

[1]**rag** \'rag\ *n* [ME *ragge*, fr. (assumed) OE *ragg*, fr. ON *rǫgg* tuft, shagginess — more at RUG] (14c) **1 a :** a waste piece of cloth **b** *pl* **:** clothes usu. in poor or ragged condition **c :** CLOTHING ⟨the ~ trade⟩ **2 :** something resembling a rag **3 :** NEWSPAPER **4 :** the stringy axis and white fibrous membrane of a citrus fruit

[2]**rag** *n* [origin unknown] (15c) **1 :** any of various hard rocks **2 :** a large roofing slate that is rough on one side

[3]**rag** *vt* **ragged** \'ragd\; **rag·ging** [origin unknown] (1739) **1 :** to rail at **:** SCOLD **2 :** TORMENT, TEASE

[4]**rag** *n, chiefly Brit* (1864) **:** an outburst of boisterous fun; *also* **:** PRANK

[5]**rag** *n* [short for *ragtime*] (ca. 1890) **:** a composition in ragtime

ra·ga \'räg-ə\ *n* [Skt *rāga*, lit., color, tone] (ca. 1909) **1 :** one of the ancient traditional melodic patterns or modes in Indian music **2 :** an improvisation based on a traditional raga — compare TALA

rag·a·muf·fin \'rag-ə-,məf-ən\ *n* [*Ragamoffyn*, a demon in *Piers Plowman* (1393), attributed to William Langland] (1581) **:** a ragged often disreputable person; *esp* **:** a poorly clothed often dirty child

rag·bag \'rag-,bag\ *n* (1820) **1 :** a bag for scraps **2 :** a miscellaneous collection

rag doll *n* (1853) **:** a stuffed usu. painted cloth doll

[1]**rage** \'rāj\ *n* [ME, fr. OF, fr. LL *rabia*, fr. L *rabies* rage, madness, fr. *rabere* to be mad; akin to Skt *rabhas* violence] (13c) **1 a :** violent and uncontrolled anger **b :** a fit of violent wrath **c** *archaic* **:** INSANITY **2 :** violent action (as of wind or sea) **3 :** an intense feeling **:** PASSION **4 :** a fad pursued with intense enthusiasm ⟨was all the ~⟩ ***syn*** see ANGER, FASHION

[2]**rage** *vi* **raged; rag·ing** (14c) **1 :** to be in a rage **2 :** to be in tumult **3 :** to prevail uncontrollably

rag·ged \'rag-əd\ *adj* (14c) **1 :** roughly unkempt **2 :** having an irregular edge or outline **3 a :** torn or worn to tatters **b :** worn-out from stress and strain ⟨ran herself ~⟩ **4 :** wearing tattered clothes **5 a :** STRAGGLY **b :** executed in an irregular or uneven manner **c** *of a sound* **:** HARSH, DISSONANT — **rag·ged·ly** *adv* — **rag·ged·ness** *n*

ragged robin *n* (1741) **:** a perennial herb (*Lychnis flos-cuculi*) cultivated for its pink flowers with narrow-lobed petals

rag·gedy \'rag-əd-ē\ *adj* (1890) **:** RAGGED

rag·gle \'rag-əl\ *n* [*raggle* (to cut a raggle in)] (1881) **:** a groove cut in masonry

rag·gle–tag·gle \'rag-əl-,tag-əl\ *adj* [irreg. fr. *ragtag*] (1904) **:** MOTLEY

ra·gi \'rag-ē, 'räg-\ *n* [Hindi *rāgī*] (1792) **:** an East Indian cereal grass (*Eleusine coracana*) yielding a staple food crop in the Orient; *also* **:** the seeds of ragi used for food

rag·ing \'rā-jiŋ\ *adj* (15c) **1 :** causing great pain or distress **2 :** VIOLENT, WILD **3 :** EXTRAORDINARY, TREMENDOUS ⟨a ~ success⟩

rag·lan \'rag-lən\ *n* [F.J.H. Somerset, Baron *Raglan* †1855 Brit. field marshal] (1863) **:** a loose overcoat with raglan sleeves

raglan sleeve *n* (ca. 1924) **:** a sleeve that extends to the neckline with slanted seams from the underarm to the neck

rag·man \'rag-,man\ *n* (1586) **:** a man who collects or deals in rags

Rag·na·rok \'rag-nə-,räk, -rək\ *n* [ON *ragna røkkr*, lit., twilight of the gods, prob. alter. of *ragna rǫk*, lit., history of the gods, fr. *ragna*, gen. pl. of *regin* the gods + *rǫk* history, origin] (1770) **:** the final destruction of the world in the conflict between the Aesir and the powers of Hel led by Loki — called also *Twilight of the Gods*

ra·gout \ra-'gü\ *n* [F *ragoût*, fr. *ragoûter* to revive the taste, fr. *re-* + *a-* ad- (fr. L *ad-*) + *goût* taste, fr. L *gustus;* akin to L *gustare* to taste — more at CHOOSE] (1664) **1 :** well-seasoned meat and vegetables cooked in a thick sauce **2 :** MIXTURE, MÉLANGE

rag·pick·er \'rag-,pik-ər\ *n* (1860) **:** one who collects rags and refuse for a livelihood

rag·tag \'rag-,tag\ *adj* [*ragtag and bobtail*] (1882) **1 :** RAGGED, UNKEMPT **2 :** MOTLEY 2 ⟨a ~ bunch of misfits⟩

ragtag and bobtail *n* [[1]*rag* + [1]*tag*] (1820) **:** RABBLE

rag·time \'rag-,tīm\ *n* [prob. fr. *ragged* + *time*] (1896) **1 :** rhythm characterized by strong syncopation in the melody with a regularly accented accompaniment **2 :** music having ragtime rhythm

rag·top \-,täp\ *n* (1953) **:** a convertible automobile

rag·weed \-,wēd\ *n* (1790) **1 :** any of various chiefly No. American weedy composite herbs (genus *Ambrosia*) that produce highly allergenic pollen **2 :** FRANSERIA

rag·wort \-,wərt, -,wȯ(ə)rt\ *n* (15c) **:** any of several composite herbs (genus *Senecio*); *esp* **:** TANSY RAGWORT

rah \'rä, 'rȯ\ *interj* (1870) **:** HURRAH — used esp. to cheer on a team

rah–rah \'rä-(,)rä, 'rȯ-(,)rȯ\ *adj* [redupl. of *rah*] (1914) **:** marked by the enthusiastic expression of college spirit

[1]**raid** \'rād\ *n* [Sc dial., fr. OE *rād* ride, raid — more at ROAD] (15c) **1 a :** a hostile or predatory incursion **b :** a surprise attack by a small force **2 a :** a brief foray outside one's usual sphere **b :** a sudden invasion by officers of the law **c :** a daring operation against a competitor **d :** the recruiting of personnel (as faculty, executives, or athletes) from competing organizations **3 :** the act of mulcting public money **4 :** an attempt by professional operators to depress stock prices by concerted selling

[2]**raid** *vt* (1865) **:** to make a raid on ~ *vi* **:** to conduct or take part in a raid

raid·er \'rād-ər\ *n* (1863) **:** one that raids: as **a :** a fast lightly armed ship operating against merchant shipping **b :** a soldier specially trained for close-range fighting

[1]**rail** \'rā(ə)l\ *n* [ME *raile*, fr. MF *reille* ruler, bar, fr. L *regula* ruler, fr. *regere* to keep straight, direct, rule — more at RIGHT] (14c) **1 a :** a bar extending from one post or support to another and serving as a guard or barrier **b :** a structural member or support **2 a :** RAILING 1 **b :** a light structure serving as a guard at the outer edge of a ship's deck **c :** a fence bounding a racetrack **3 a :** a bar of rolled steel forming a track for wheeled vehicles **b :** TRACK **c :** RAILROAD

[2]**rail** *vt* (14c) **:** to provide with a railing **:** FENCE

[3]**rail** *n, pl* **rail** *or* **rails** [ME *raile*, fr. MF *raale*] (15c) **:** any of numerous precocial wading birds (family Rallidae) that are structurally related to the cranes but are of small or medium size and have short rounded wings, a short tail, and usu. very long toes which enable them to run on the soft mud of swamps

[4]**rail** *vi* [ME *railen*, fr. MF *railler* to mock, fr. OProv *ralhar* to babble, joke, fr. (assumed) VL *ragulare* to bray, fr. LL *ragere* to neigh] (15c) **:** to revile or scold in harsh, insolent, or abusive language ***syn*** see SCOLD — **rail·er** *n*

rail·bird \'rā(ə)l-,bərd\ *n* (1892) **:** a racing enthusiast who sits on or near the track rail to watch a race or workout

rail·bus \-,bəs\ *n* (1933) **:** a passenger car with an automotive engine for operation on rails

rail·car \-,kär\ *n* (1834) **1 :** a railroad car **2 :** a self-propelled railroad car

rail·head \'rā(ə)l-,hed\ *n* (1896) **:** a point on a railroad at which traffic may originate or terminate

rail·ing \'rā-liŋ\ *n* (15c) **1 :** a barrier consisting of a rail and supports **2 :** RAILS; *also* **:** material for making rails

rail·lery \'rā-lə-rē\ *n, pl* **-ler·ies** [F *raillerie*, fr. MF, fr. *railler* to mock] (1653) **1 :** good-natured ridicule **:** BANTER **2 :** JEST

[1]**rail·road** \'rā(ə)l-,rōd, 're(ə)l-; 're(ə)r-,ōd\ *n* (1825) **:** a permanent road having a line of rails fixed to ties and laid on a roadbed and providing a track for cars or equipment drawn by locomotives or propelled by self-contained motors; *also* **:** such a road and its assets constituting a single property

[2]**railroad** *vt* (1891) **1 :** to transport by railroad **2 a :** to push through hastily or without due consideration **b :** to convict with undue haste and by means of false charges or insufficient evidence ~ *vi* **:** to work for a railroad company — **rail·road·er** *n*

railroad flat *n* (1947) **:** an apartment having a series of narrow rooms arranged in line

rail·road·ing *n* (1870) **:** construction or operation of a railroad

railroad worm *n* (1909) **1** [prob. fr. its dissemination by railroad] **:** APPLE MAGGOT **2** [fr. the rows of luminescent spots along its sides making it resemble a lighted train] **:** the larva or wingless female of any of

several So. American beetles (genus *Phrixothrix* of the family Cantharidae)
rail–split·ter \ˈrā(ə)l-ˌsplit-ər\ *n* (1860) : one that makes logs into fence rails
rail·way \-ˌwā\ *n* (1776) **1** : a line of track providing a runway for wheels **2** : RAILROAD; *esp* : a railroad operating with light equipment or within a small area
rai·ment \ˈrā-mənt\ *n* [ME *rayment,* short for *arrayment,* fr. *arrayen* to array] (15c) : CLOTHING, GARMENTS
[1]**rain** \ˈrān\ *n, often attrib* [ME *reyn,* fr. OE *regn, rēn;* akin to OHG *regan* rain] (bef. 12c) **1 a** : water falling in drops condensed from vapor in the atmosphere **b** : the descent of this water **c** : water that has fallen as rain : RAINWATER **2 a** : a fall of rain : RAINSTORM **b** *pl* : the rainy season **3** : rainy weather **4** : a heavy fall of particles or bodies
[2]**rain** *vi* (bef. 12c) **1** : to fall as water in drops from the clouds **2** : to send down rain **3** : to fall like rain ~ *vt* **1** : to pour down **2** : to bestow abundantly
rain·bird \ˈrān-ˌbərd\ *n* (1555) : any of numerous birds (esp. of the family Cuculidae) whose cries are popularly believed to augur rain
rain·bow \-ˌbō\ *n* (bef. 12c) **1** : an arc or circle that exhibits in concentric bands the colors of the spectrum and that is formed opposite the sun by the refraction and reflection of the sun's rays in raindrops, spray, or mist **2 a** : a multicolored array **b** : a wide assortment or range **3** [fr. the impossibility of reaching the rainbow, at whose foot a pot of gold is said to be buried] : an illusory goal or hope **4** : RAINBOW TROUT
rainbow fish *n* (1888) : any of numerous brilliantly colored fishes (as a wrasse, parrot fish, or guppy)
rainbow runner *n* (1940) : a large brilliantly marked blue and yellow food and sport fish (*Elagatis bipinnulatus*) common in warm seas
rainbow trout *n* (1882) : a large stout-bodied and sometimes anadromous trout (*Salmo gairdneri*) of western No. America that typically is greenish above and white on the belly with a pink, red, or lavender stripe along each side of the body and with profuse black dots
rain check *n* (1884) **1** : a ticket stub good for a later performance when the scheduled one is rained out **2** : an assurance of a deferred extension of an offer; *esp* : an assurance that a customer can take advantage of a sale later if the item or service offered is not available (as by being sold out)
rain·coat \ˈrān-ˌkōt\ *n* (1830) : a coat of waterproof or water-resistant material
rain·drop \-ˌdräp\ *n* (bef. 12c) : a drop of rain
rain·fall \-ˌfȯl\ *n* (1848) **1** : RAIN 2a **2** : the amount of precipitation usu. measured by the depth in inches
rain forest *n* (ca. 1903) **1** : a tropical woodland with an annual rainfall of at least 100 inches and marked by lofty broad-leaved evergreen trees forming a continuous canopy — called also *tropical rain forest* **2** : TEMPERATE RAIN FOREST
rain gauge *n* (1769) : an instrument for measuring the quantity of precipitation
rain·mak·ing \ˈrān-ˌmā-kiŋ\ *n* (1775) : the action or process of producing or attempting to produce rain by artificial means — **rain·mak·er** \-kər\ *n*
rain out *vt* (1928) : to interrupt or prevent by rain
rain·proof \ˈrān-ˈprüf\ *adj* (1831) : impervious to rain
rain·spout \-ˌspau̇t\ *n* (1922) : a pipe, duct, or orifice draining a roof gutter
rain·squall \-ˌskwȯl\ *n* (1849) : a squall accompanied by rain
rain·storm \-ˌstȯ(ə)rm\ *n* (1816) : a storm of or with rain
rain tree *n* (ca. 1900) : MONKEYPOD
rain·wash \ˈrān-ˌwȯsh, -ˌwäsh\ *n* (1876) : the washing away of material by rain; *also* : the material so washed away
rain·wa·ter \-ˌwȯt-ər, -ˌwät-\ *n* (bef. 12c) : water fallen as rain that has not collected soluble matter from the soil and is therefore soft
rain·wear \-ˌwa(ə)r, -ˌwe(ə)r\ *n* (1939) : waterproof or water-resistant clothing
rainy \ˈrā-nē\ *adj* **rain·i·er; -est** (bef. 12c) : marked by, abounding with, or bringing rain
rainy day *n* (1580) : a period of want or need
[1]**raise** \ˈrāz\ *vb* **raised; rais·ing** [ME *raisen,* fr. ON *reisa* — more at REAR] *vt* (13c) **1** : to cause or help to rise to a standing position **2 a** : AWAKEN, AROUSE **b** : to stir up : INCITE ⟨~ a rebellion⟩ **c** : to flush (game) from cover **d** : to recall from or as if from death **e** : to establish radio communication with **3 a** : to set upright by lifting or building **b** : to lift higher **c** : to place higher in rank or dignity : ELEVATE **d** : HEIGHTEN, INVIGORATE ⟨~ the spirits⟩ **e** : to end or suspend the operation or validity of ⟨~ a siege⟩ **4** : to get together for a purpose : COLLECT ⟨~ funds⟩ **5 a** : to breed and bring (an animal) to maturity **b** : GROW, CULTIVATE ⟨~ cotton⟩ **c** : to bring up (a child) : REAR **6 a** : to give rise to : PROVOKE ⟨~ a commotion⟩ **b** : to give voice to ⟨~ a cheer⟩ **7** : to bring up for consideration or debate ⟨~ an issue⟩ **8 a** : to increase the strength, intensity, or pitch of **b** : to increase the degree of **c** : to cause to rise in level or amount ⟨~ the rent⟩ **d** (1) : to increase the amount of (a poker bet) (2) : to bet more than (a previous bettor) **e** (1) : to make a higher bridge bid in (a partner's suit) (2) : to increase the bid of (one's partner) **9** : to make light and porous ⟨~ dough⟩ **10** : to cause to ascend **11** : to multiply (a quantity) by itself a specified number of times **12** : to bring in sight on the horizon by approaching ⟨~ land⟩ **13 a** : to bring up the nap of (cloth) **b** : to cause (as a blister) to form on the skin **14** : to increase the nominal value of fraudulently ⟨~ a check⟩ **15** : to articulate (a sound) with the tongue in a higher position ~ *vi* **1** *dial* : RISE **2** : to increase a bet or bid ***syn*** see LIFT — **rais·er** *n* — **raise cain** *or* **raise hell 1** : to act wildly : create a disturbance **2** : to scold or upbraid someone esp. loudly — **raise eyebrows** : to cause surprise or astonishment
[2]**raise** *n* (1538) **1** : an act of raising or lifting **2** : a rising stretch of road : an upward grade : RISE **3** : an increase in amount: as **a** : an increase of a bet or bid **b** : an increase in wages or salary **4** : a vertical or inclined opening or passageway connecting one mine working area with another at a higher level
raised *adj* (1582) **1 a** : done in relief **b** : having a nap **2** : leavened with yeast rather than with baking powder or baking soda
rai·sin \ˈrāz-ᵊn\ *n* [ME, fr. MF, grape, fr. L *racemus* cluster of grapes or berries] (13c) : a grape usu. of a special type dried in the sun or by artificial heat
rai·son d'être \ˌrā-ˌzōⁿ-ˈdetrᵊ\ *n* [F] (1864) : reason or justification for existence
raj \ˈräj\ *n* [Hindi *rāj,* fr. Skt *rājya;* akin to Skt *rājan* king] (1850) : RULE
ra·ja *or* **ra·jah** \ˈräj-ə, ˈräj-(ˌ)ä, ˈräzh-\ *n* [Hindi *rājā,* fr. Skt *rājan* king — more at ROYAL] (1555) **1** : an Indian or Malay prince or chief **2** : the bearer of a title of nobility among the Hindus
Ra·jab \rə-ˈjab\ *n* [Ar] (ca. 1769) : the 7th month of the Islamic year — see MONTH table
Ra·jas·tha·ni \ˌräj-ə-ˈstän-ē, ˌräzh-\ *n* [Hindi *Rājasthānī,* fr. *Rājasthān* Rajputana] (1901) : the Indic language of Rajasthan
Raj·put *or* **Raj·poot** \ˈräj-ˌpu̇t, ˈräzh-\ *n* [Hindi *rājpūt,* fr. Skt *rājaputra* king's son, fr. *rājan* king + *putra* son — more at FEW] (1598) : a member of an Indo-Aryan caste of northern India
[1]**rake** \ˈrāk\ *n* [ME, fr. OE *racu;* akin to OHG *rehho* rake] (bef. 12c) **1 a** : an implement equipped with projecting prongs to gather material (as grass) or for loosening or smoothing the surface of the ground **b** : a machine for gathering hay **2** : an implement like a rake
[2]**rake** *vt* **raked; rak·ing** (13c) **1** : to gather, loosen, or smooth with or as if with a rake **2** : to gain rapidly or in abundance ⟨~ in a fortune⟩ **3 a** : to touch in passing over lightly **b** : SCRATCH **4** : to censure severely **5** : to search through : RANSACK **6** : to sweep the length of esp. with gunfire : ENFILADE **7** : to glance over rapidly — **rak·er** *n*
[3]**rake** *n* [origin unknown] (1626) **1** : inclination from the perpendicular; *esp* : the overhang of a ship's bow or stern **2** : inclination from the horizontal : SLOPE **3** : the angle between the top cutting surface of a tool and a plane perpendicular to the surface of the work **4** : the angle between a wing-tip edge that is sensibly straight in planform and the plane of symmetry of an airplane
[4]**rake** *vi* **raked; rak·ing** (1691) : to incline from the perpendicular
[5]**rake** *n* [short for *rakehell*] (1653) : a dissolute person : LIBERTINE
rake·hell \ˈrāk-ˌhel\ *n* (1554) : LIBERTINE 2 — **rakehell** *or* **rake·helly** \-ˌhel-ē\ *adj*
rake–off \ˈrā-ˌkȯf\ *n* [[2]*rake* + *off;* fr. the use of a rake by a croupier to collect the operator's profits in a gambling casino] (1888) : a percentage or cut taken (as by an operator)
rake up *vt* (1581) : to make known or public : UNCOVER ⟨*rake up* a scandal⟩
[1]**rak·ish** \ˈrā-kish\ *adj* [[5]*rake*] (1706) : of, relating to, or characteristic of a rake : DISSOLUTE
[2]**rakish** *adj* [prob. fr. [4]*rake;* fr. the raking masts of pirate ships] (1824) **1** : having a trim or streamlined appearance suggestive of speed ⟨a ~ ship⟩ **2** : dashingly or carelessly unconventional : JAUNTY ⟨~ clothes⟩
rak·ish·ly *adv* (1838) : in a rakish manner
rak·ish·ness *n* (ca. 1828) : the quality or state of being rakish
rale \ˈral, ˈräl\ *n* [F *râle*] (1828) : an abnormal sound that accompanies the normal respiratory sounds
ral·len·tan·do \ˌräl-ən-ˈtän-(ˌ)dō\ *adv or adj* [It, lit., slowing down, verbal of *rallentare* to slow down again, fr. *re-* + *allentare* to slow down, fr. LL, fr. L *al-* ad- + *lentus* slow, pliant — more at LITHE] (1811) : with a gradual decrease in tempo — used as a direction in music
[1]**ral·ly** \ˈral-ē\ *vb* **ral·lied; ral·ly·ing** [F *rallier,* fr. OF *ralier,* fr. *re-* + *alier* to unite — more at ALLY] *vt* (1603) **1 a** : to muster for a common purpose **b** : to recall to order **2 a** : to arouse for action **b** : to rouse from depression or weakness ~ *vi* **1** : to come together again to renew an effort **2** : to join in a common cause **3** : RECOVER, REBOUND **4** : to engage in a rally
[2]**rally** *n, pl* **rallies** (1651) **1 a** : a mustering of scattered forces to renew an effort **b** : a summoning up of strength or courage after weakness or dejection **c** : a recovery of price after a decline **d** : a renewed offensive **2** : a mass meeting intended to arouse group enthusiasm **3** : a series of shots interchanged between players (as in tennis) before a point is won **4** *also* **ral·lye** [F *rallye,* fr. E [1]*rally*] : a competitive automobile run over public roads and under ordinary traffic rules with the object of maintaining a specified average speed between checkpoints over a route unknown to the participants until the start of the run
[3]**rally** *vt* **ral·lied; ral·ly·ing** [F *railler* to mock, rally — more at RAIL] (1668) : to attack with raillery : BANTER
ral·ly·ing \ˈral-ē-iŋ\ *n* (1957) : the sport of driving in automobile rallies
ral·ly·ist \ˈral-ē-əst\ *n* (1961) : one who participates in an automobile rally
ral·ly·mas·ter \-ˌmas-tər\ *n* (1967) : one who organizes and conducts an automobile rally
[1]**ram** \ˈram\ *n* [ME, fr. OE *ramm;* akin to OHG *ram*] (bef. 12c) **1 a** : a male sheep **b** *cap* : ARIES **2 a** : BATTERING RAM **b** : a warship with a heavy beak at the prow for piercing an enemy ship **3** : any of various guided pieces for exerting pressure or for driving or forcing something by impact: as **a** : the plunger of a hydrostatic press or force pump **b** : the weight that strikes the blow in a pile driver
[2]**ram** *vb* **rammed; ram·ming** [ME *rammen,* prob. fr. *ram,* n.] *vi* (14c) **1** : to strike with violence : CRASH **2** : to move with extreme rapidity ~ *vt* **1** : to force in by driving **2 a** : to make compact (as by pounding) **b** : CRAM, CROWD **3** : to force passage or acceptance of ⟨~ home an idea⟩ **4** : to strike against violently — **ram·mer** *n*
Ra·ma \ˈräm-ə\ *n* [Skt *Rāma*] : a deity or deified hero of later Hinduism worshiped as an avatar of Vishnu
Ram·a·dan \ˈram-ə-ˌdän, -ˌdan\ *n* [Ar *Ramaḍān*] (1601) : the 9th month of the Islamic year observed as sacred with fasting practiced daily from dawn to sunset — see MONTH table
ra·mate \ˈrā-ˌmāt\ *adj* [L *ramus* branch — more at RAMIFY] (ca. 1897) : having branches
[1]**ram·ble** \ˈram-bəl\ *vb* **ram·bled; ram·bling** \-b(ə-)liŋ\ [perh. fr. ME *romblen,* freq. of *romen* to roam] *vi* (1620) **1 a** : to move aimlessly from place to place **b** : to explore idly **2** : to talk or write in a desultory or long-winded wandering fashion **3** : to grow or extend irregu-

larly ~ *vt* : to wander over : ROAM ***syn*** see WANDER — **ram·bling·ly** \-b(ə-)liŋ-lē\ *adv*

2ramble *n* (1654) : a leisurely excursion for pleasure; *esp* : an aimless walk

ram·bler \'ram-blər\ *n* (1624) **1** : one that rambles **2** : any of various climbing roses with rather small often double flowers in large clusters

ram·bouil·let \,ram-bə-'lā, -bü-'yā\ *n, often cap* [*Rambouillet*, France] (1906) : a large sturdy sheep developed in France

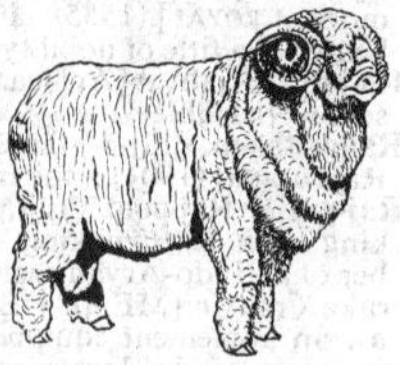

rambouillet

ram·bunc·tious \ram-'bəŋ(k)-shəs\ *adj* [prob. irreg. fr. *robust*] (1830) : marked by uncontrollable exuberance : UNRULY — **ram·bunc·tious·ly** *adv* — **ram·bunc·tious·ness** *n*

ram·bu·tan \ram-'büt-ᵊn\ *n* [Malay] (1613) : a bright red spiny Malayan fruit closely related to the litchi; *also* : a tree (*Nephelium lappaceum*) of the soapberry family that bears this fruit

ram·e·kin *or* **ram·e·quin** \'ram-(i-)kən\ *n* [F *ramequin*, fr. LG *ramken*, dim. of *ram* cream] (1706) **1** : a preparation of cheese with bread crumbs, puff paste, or eggs baked in a mold or shell **2** : an individual baking dish

ra·met \'rā-,met\ *n* [L *ramus* branch] (1929) : an independent member of a clone

ra·mie \'rā-mē, 'ram-ē\ *n* [Malay *rami*] (1817) : an Asian perennial plant (*Boehmeria nivea*) of the nettle family; *also* : the strong lustrous bast fiber of this plant

ram·i·fi·ca·tion \,ram-ə-fə-'kā-shən\ *n* (1665) **1 a** : the act or process of branching **b** : arrangement of branches (as on a plant) **2 a** : BRANCH, OFFSHOOT **b** : a branched structure **3** : CONSEQUENCE, OUTGROWTH ⟨the ~s of a problem⟩

ram·i·fy \'ram-ə-,fī\ *vb* **-fied; -fy·ing** [MF *ramifier*, fr. ML *ramificare*, fr. L *ramus* branch; akin to L *radix* root — more at ROOT] *vi* (1541) **1** : to split up into branches or constituent parts **2** : to send forth branches or extensions ~ *vt* **1** : to cause to branch **2** : to separate into divisions

Ra·mism \'rā-,miz-əm\ *n* [Petrus *Ramus* †1572 Fr. philosopher] (1710) : the doctrines of Ramus based on opposition to Aristotelianism and advocacy of a new logic blended with rhetoric — **Ra·mist** \-məst\ *n or adj*

ram·jet engine \,ram-,jet-\ *n* (1946) : a jet engine having in its forward end a continuous inlet of air that depends on the speed of flight for the compressing effect produced on the air rather than using a mechanical compressor

ra·mose \'rā-,mōs\ *adj* [L *ramosus*, fr. *ramus* branch] (1689) : consisting of or having branches ⟨a ~ sponge⟩

1ramp \'ramp\ *vi* [ME *rampen*, fr. MF *ramper* to crawl, rear, of Gmc origin; akin to OHG *rimpfan* to wrinkle — more at RUMPLE] (14c) **1 a** : to stand or advance menacingly with forelegs or with arms raised **b** : to move or act furiously **2** : to creep up — used esp. of plants

2ramp *n* (1671) : the act or an instance of ramping

3ramp *n* [back-formation fr. *ramps*, alter. of *rams*, fr. ME, fr. OE *hramsa*; akin to OHG *ramusia* ramp, Gk *kremyon*, a kind of onion] (1598) : any of various alliums used for food

4ramp *n* [F *rampe*, fr. *ramper*, fr. MF] (1778) **1** : a short bend, slope, or curve usu. in the vertical plane where a handrail or coping changes its direction **2** : a sloping way: as **a** : a sloping floor, walk, or roadway leading from one level to another **b** : a stairway for entering or leaving an airplane **c** : a slope for launching boats **3** : APRON 2j

1ram·page \'ram-,pāj, (')ram-'\ *vi* **ram·paged; ram·pag·ing** [Sc] (1808) : to rush wildly about

2ram·page \'ram-,pāj\ *n* (1861) : a course of violent, riotous, or reckless action or behavior — **ram·pa·geous** \ram-'pā-jəs\ *adj* — **ram·pa·geous·ly** *adv* — **ram·pa·geous·ness** *n*

ram·pan·cy \'ram-pən-sē\ *n* (1664) : the quality or state of being rampant

ram·pant \'ram-pənt *also* -,pant\ *adj* [ME, fr. MF, prp. of *ramper*] (14c) **1 a** : rearing upon the hind legs with forelegs extended **b** : standing on one hind foot with one foreleg raised above the other and the head in profile — used of a heraldic animal **2 a** : marked by a menacing wildness, extravagance, or absence of restraint **b** : WIDESPREAD **3** : having one impost or abutment higher than the other ⟨a ~ arch⟩ — **ram·pant·ly** *adv*

ram·part \'ram-,pärt, -pərt\ *n* [MF] (1583) **1** : a broad embankment raised as a fortification and usu. surmounted by a parapet **2** : a protective barrier : BULWARK **3** : a wall-like ridge (as of rock fragments, earth, or debris)

ram·pike \-,pīk\ *n* [origin unknown] (1594) : an erect broken or dead tree

ram·pi·on \'ram-pē-ən\ *n* [prob. modif. of MF *raiponce*, fr. OIt *raponzo*] (1573) : a European bellflower (*Campanula rapunculus*) with a tuberous root used with the leaves in salad

1ram·rod \'ram-,räd\ *n* (1757) **1** : a rod for ramming home the charge in a muzzle-loading firearm **2** : a cleaning rod for small arms **3** : BOSS, OVERSEER

2ramrod *adj* (1905) : marked by rigidity, severity, or stiffness

3ramrod *vt* (ca. 1940) : to direct, supervise, and control

ram·shack·le \'ram-,shak-əl\ *adj* [alter. of earlier *ransackled*, fr. pp. of obs. *ransackle*, freq. of *ransack*] (1830) **1** : appearing ready to collapse : RICKETY **2** : carelessly or loosely constructed

rams·horn \'ramz-,hȯ(ə)rn\ *n* (1901) : a snail (genus *Planorbis*) often used as an aquarium scavenger

ra·mus \'rā-məs\ *n, pl* **ra·mi** \-,mī\ [NL, fr. L, branch — more at RAMIFY] (1803) : a projecting part, elongated process, or branch: as **a** : the posterior more or less vertical part on each side of the lower jaw that articulates with the skull **b** : a branch of a nerve

ran *past of* RUN

1ranch \'ranch\ *n* [MexSp *rancho* small ranch, fr. Sp, camp, hut & Sp dial., small farm, fr. OSp *ranchear(se)* to take up quarters, fr. MF *(se) ranger* to take up a position, fr. *ranger* to set in a row — more at RANGE] (1831) **1** : a large farm for raising horses, beef cattle, or sheep **2** : a farm or area devoted to a particular specialty **3** : RANCH HOUSE

2ranch *vi* (1866) : to live or work on a ranch ~ *vt* **1** : to work as a rancher on **2** : to raise on a ranch

ranch·er \'ran-chər\ *n* (1836) : one who owns or works on a ranch

ran·che·ro \ran-'che(ə)r-(,)ō, rän-\ *n, pl* **-ros** [MexSp, fr. *rancho*] (1826) : RANCHER; *also* : RANCH 1

ranch house *n* (1862) **1** : the main dwelling house on a ranch **2** : a one-story house typically with a low-pitched roof and an open plan

ranch·man \'ranch-mən\ *n* (1856) : RANCHER

ran·cho \'ran-(,)chō, 'rän-\ *n, pl* **ranchos** [MexSp, small ranch] (1808) : RANCH 1

ran·cid \'ran(t)-səd\ *adj* [L *rancidus*, fr. *rancēre* to be rancid] (1646) **1** : having a rank smell or taste **2** : OFFENSIVE — **ran·cid·i·ty** \ran-'sid-ət-ē\ *n* — **ran·cid·ness** \'ran(t)-səd-nəs\ *n*

ran·cor \'raŋ-kər, -,kȯ(ə)r\ *n* [ME *rancour*, fr. MF *ranceur*, fr. LL *rancor* rancidity, rancor, fr. L *rancēre*] (13c) : bitter deep-seated ill will ***syn*** see ENMITY

ran·cor·ous \'raŋ-k(ə-)rəs\ *adj* (1590) : marked by rancor — **ran·cor·ous·ly** *adv*

ran·cour *Brit var of* RANCOR

rand \'rand, 'ränd, 'ränt\ *n, pl* **rand** [the *Rand*, So. Africa] (ca. 1932) **1** — see MONEY table **2** : a former monetary unit of Botswana, Lesotho, and Swaziland

R and D *n* (1966) : research and development

1ran·dom \'ran-dəm\ *n* [ME, impetuosity, fr. MF *randon*, fr. OF, fr. *randir* to run, of Gmc origin; akin to OHG *rinnan* to run — more at RUN] (1561) : a haphazard course — **at random** : without definite aim, direction, rule, or method

2random *adj* (1565) **1 a** : lacking a definite plan, purpose, or pattern **b** : made, done, or chosen at random ⟨read ~ passages from the book⟩ **2 a** : relating to, having, or being elements or events with definite probability of occurrence ⟨~ processes⟩ **b** : being or relating to a set or to an element of a set each of whose elements has equal probability of occurrence ⟨a ~ sample⟩; *also* : characterized by procedures designed to obtain such sets or elements ⟨~ sampling⟩ — **ran·dom·ly** *adv* — **ran·dom·ness** *n*

syn RANDOM, HAPHAZARD, CASUAL, DESULTORY mean determined by accident rather than design. RANDOM stresses lack of definite aim, fixed goal, or regular procedure; HAPHAZARD applies to what is done without regard for regularity or fitness or ultimate consequence; CASUAL suggests working or acting without deliberation, intention, or purpose; DESULTORY implies a jumping or skipping from one thing to another without method or system.

3random *adv* (1618) : in a random manner

random–access *adj* (1953) : permitting access to stored data in any order the user desires

random–access memory *n* (1955) : a computer memory that provides the main internal storage available to the user for programs and data — abbr. *RAM;* compare READ-ONLY MEMORY

ran·dom·iza·tion \,ran-də-mə-'zā-shən\ *n* (1926) : arrangement (as of samples) so as to simulate a chance distribution, reduce interference by irrelevant variables, and yield unbiased statistical data

ran·dom·ize \'ran-də-,mīz\ *vt* **-ized; -iz·ing** (1926) : to use randomization on — **ran·dom·iz·er** *n*

randomized block *n* (1942) : an experimental design (as in horticulture) in which different treatments are distributed in random order in a block or plot — called also *randomized block design*

random variable *n* (1949) : a variable that is itself a function of the result of a statistical experiment in which each outcome has a definite probability of occurrence ⟨the number of spots showing if two dice are thrown is a ~⟩ — called also *variate*

random walk *n* (1941) : a process (as Brownian movement or genetic drift) consisting of a sequence of steps (as movements or changes in gene frequency) each of whose characteristics (as magnitude and direction) is determined by chance

1randy \'ran-dē\ *adj* [prob. fr. obs. *rand* (to rant)] (1698) **1** *chiefly Scot* : having a coarse manner **2** : LUSTFUL, LECHEROUS

2randy *n, pl* **rand·ies** *chiefly Scot* (1762) : a scolding or dissolute woman

rang *past of* RING

1range \'rānj\ *n, often attrib* [ME, row of persons, fr. MF *renge*, fr. OF *rengier* to range] (14c) **1 a** (1) : a series of things in a line : ROW (2) : a series of mountains (3) : one of the north-south rows of townships in a U.S. public-land survey that are numbered east and west from the principal meridian of the survey **b** : an aggregate of individuals in one order **c** : a direction line **2** : a cooking stove that has an oven and a flat top with burners or heating elements **3 a** : a place that may be ranged over **b** : an open region over which animals (as livestock) may roam and feed **c** : the region throughout which a kind of organism or ecological community naturally lives or occurs **4** : the act of ranging about **5 a** (1) : the horizontal distance to which a projectile can be propelled (2) : the horizontal distance between a weapon and target **b** : the maximum distance a vehicle or craft can travel without refueling **c** (1) : a place where shooting is practiced (2) : DRIVING RANGE **6 a** : the space or extent included, covered, or used : SCOPE **b** : the extent of pitch covered by a melody or lying within the capacity of a voice or instrument **7 a** : a sequence, series, or scale between limits ⟨a wide ~ of patterns⟩ **b** : the limits of a series : the distance or extent between possible extremes **c** : the difference between the least and greatest values of an attribute or of the variable of a frequency distribution **8 a** : the set of values a function may take on **b** : the class of admissible values of a variable **9** : LINE 11

syn RANGE, GAMUT, COMPASS, SWEEP, SCOPE, ORBIT mean the extent that lies within the powers of something (as to cover or control). RANGE is a general term indicating the extent of one's perception or the extent of powers, capacities, or possibilities ⟨the entire *range* of human experience⟩ GAMUT suggests a graduated series running from one possible extreme to another ⟨a performance that included a *gamut* of emotions⟩ COMPASS implies a sometimes limited extent of perception, knowledge, or activity ⟨your concerns lie beyond the narrow *compass* of this study⟩ SWEEP suggests extent, often circular or arc-shaped, of motion or activity ⟨the book covers the entire *sweep* of criminal activity⟩ SCOPE is applicable to an area of activity, predetermined and limited, but somewhat flexible ⟨as time went on, the *scope* of the investigation widened⟩ ORBIT suggests an often circumscribed range of activity or influence within which forces work toward accommodation ⟨within that restricted *orbit* they tried to effect social change⟩

[2]**range** *vb* **ranged; rang·ing** [ME *rangen,* fr. MF *ranger,* fr. OF *rengier,* fr. *renc, reng* line, place, row — more at RANK] *vt* (14c) **1 a :** to set in a row or in the proper order **b :** to place among others in a position or situation **c :** to assign to a category : CLASSIFY **2 a :** to rove over or through **b :** to sail or pass along **3 :** to arrange (an anchor cable) on deck **4 :** to graze (livestock) on a range **5 :** to determine or give the elevation necessary for (a gun) to propel a projectile to a given distance ~ *vi* **1 a :** to roam at large or freely **b :** to move over an area so as to explore it **2 :** to take a position **3 a :** to correspond in direction or line : ALIGN **b :** to extend in a particular direction **4 :** to have range **5 :** to change or differ within limits **6** *of an organism* **:** to live or occur in or be native to a region **7 :** to obtain the range of an object by instrument (as radar or laser)

range finder *n* (1872) **1 :** an instrument used in gunnery to determine the distance of a target **2 :** TACHYMETER 1 **3 :** a usu. built-in adjustable optical device for focusing a camera that automatically indicates the correct focus (as when two parts of a split image are brought together)

range·land \ˈrānj-ˌland\ *n* (1935) **:** land used or suitable for range

range paralysis *n* (1935) **:** an avian leukosis involving flaccid paralysis esp. of the legs and wings of maturing chickens

rang·er \ˈrān-jər\ *n* (15c) **1 a :** the keeper of a British royal park or forest **b :** FOREST RANGER **2 :** one that ranges **3 a :** one of a body of organized armed men who range over a region esp. to enforce the law **b :** a soldier specially trained in close-range fighting and in raiding tactics

rangy \ˈrān-jē\ *adj* **rang·i·er; -est** (1868) **1 :** able to range for considerable distances **2 a :** long-limbed and long-bodied ⟨~ cattle⟩ **b :** being tall and slender **3 :** having room for ranging **4 :** having great scope — **rang·i·ness** *n*

ra·ni *or* **ra·nee** \rä-ˈnē, ˈrän-ˌē\ *n* [Hindi *rānī,* fr. Skt *rājñī,* fem. of *rājan* king — more at ROYAL] (1673) **:** a Hindu queen : a rajah's wife

ra·nid \ˈran-əd, ˈrā-nəd\ *n* [deriv. of L *rana* frog] (1934) **:** any of a large family (Ranidae) of frogs distinguished by slightly dilated transverse sacral processes

[1]**rank** \ˈraŋk\ *adj* [ME, fr. OE *ranc* overbearing, strong; akin to OE *riht* right — more at RIGHT] (13c) **1 :** luxuriantly or excessively vigorous in growth **2 :** offensively gross or coarse : FOUL **3** *obs* **:** grown too large **4 a :** shockingly conspicuous ⟨must lecture him on his ~ disloyalty —David Walden⟩ **b :** OUTRIGHT — used as an intensive ⟨~ beginners⟩ **5** *archaic* **:** LUSTFUL, RUTTISH **6 :** offensive in odor or flavor; *esp* **:** RANCID **7 :** PUTRID, FESTERING **8 :** high in amount : EXCESSIVE ***syn*** see MALODOROUS, FLAGRANT — **rank·ly** *adv* — **rank·ness** *n*

[2]**rank** *n* [MF *renc, reng,* of Gmc origin; akin to OHG *hring* ring — more at RING] (1570) **1 a :** ROW, SERIES **b :** a row of people **c** (1) **:** a line of soldiers ranged side by side in close order (2) *pl* **:** ARMED FORCES (3) *pl* **:** the body of enlisted personnel **d :** any of the rows of squares that extend across a chessboard perpendicular to the files **e** *Brit* **:** STAND 6 **2 :** an orderly arrangement : FORMATION **3 :** an aggregate of individuals classed together — usu. used in pl. **4 a :** relative standing or position **b :** a degree or position of dignity, eminence, or excellence : DISTINCTION ⟨soon took ~ as a leading attorney —J. D. Hicks⟩ **c :** high social position ⟨the privileges of ~⟩ **d :** a grade of official standing **5 :** the order according to some statistical characteristic (as the score on a test) **6 :** any of a series of classes of coal based on increasing alteration of the parent vegetable matter, increasing carbon content, and increasing fuel value **7 :** the number of linearly independent rows in a matrix

[3]**rank** *vt* (1573) **1 :** to arrange in lines or in a regular formation **2 :** to determine the relative position of : RATE **3 :** to take precedence of ~ *vi* **1 :** to form or move in ranks **2 :** to take or have a position in relation to others

rank and file *n* (1598) **1 :** the enlisted personnel of an armed force **2 :** the individuals who constitute the body of an organization, society, or nation as distinguished from the leaders — **rank and fil·er** \-ˈfī-lər\ *n*

rank correlation *n* (1907) **:** a measure of correlation depending on rank

rank·er \ˈraŋ-kər\ *n* (1878) **:** one who serves or has served in the ranks; *esp* **:** a commissioned officer promoted from the ranks

Ran·kine \ˈraŋ-kən\ *adj* [William J. M. *Rankine* †1872 Scot. engineer & physicist] (ca. 1926) **:** being, according to, or relating to an absolute-temperature scale on which the unit of measurement equals a Fahrenheit degree and on which the freezing point of water is 491.67° and the boiling point 671.67°

rank·ing *adj* (1862) **:** having a high position: as **a :** FOREMOST ⟨~ poet⟩ **b :** being next to the chairman in seniority ⟨~ committee member⟩

ran·kle \ˈraŋ-kəl\ *vb* **ran·kled; ran·kling** \-k(ə-)liŋ\ [ME *ranclen* to fester, fr. MF *rancler,* fr. OF *draoncler, raoncler,* fr. *draoncle, raoncle* festering sore, fr. ML *dracunculus,* fr. L, dim. of *draco* serpent — more at DRAGON] *vi* (1530) **1 :** to cause anger, irritation, or deep bitterness **2 :** to feel anger and irritation ~ *vt* **:** to cause irritation or bitterness in

ran·sack \ˈran-ˌsak, (ˈ)ran-ˈ\ *vt* [ME *ransaken,* fr. ON *rannsaka,* fr. *rann* house + *-saka* (akin to OE *sēcan* to seek) — more at SEEK] (13c) **1 a :** to search thoroughly **b :** to examine closely and carefully **2 :** to search through to commit robbery : PLUNDER — **ran·sack·er** *n*

[1]**ran·som** \ˈran(t)-səm\ *n* [ME *ransoun,* fr. OF *rançon,* fr. L *redemption-, redemptio* — more at REDEMPTION] (13c) **1 :** a consideration paid or demanded for the redemption of a captured person **2 :** the act of ransoming

[2]**ransom** *vt* (14c) **1 :** to deliver esp. from sin or its penalty **2 :** to free from captivity or punishment by paying a price ***syn*** see RESCUE — **ran·som·er** *n*

[1]**rant** \ˈrant\ *vb* [obs. D *ranten, randen*] *vi* (1602) **1 :** to talk in a noisy, excited, or declamatory manner **2 :** to scold vehemently ~ *vt* **:** to utter in a bombastic declamatory fashion — **rant·er** *n* — **rant·ing·ly** \-iŋ-lē\ *adv*

[2]**rant** *n* (1649) **1 a :** a bombastic extravagant speech **b :** bombastic extravagant language **2** *dial Brit* **:** a rousing good time

ran·u·la \ˈran-yə-lə\ *n* [NL, fr. L, swelling on the tongue of cattle, fr. dim. of *rana* frog] (15c) **:** a cyst formed under the tongue by obstruction of a gland duct

ra·nun·cu·lus \rə-ˈnəŋ-kyə-ləs\ *n, pl* **-lus·es** *or* **-li** \-ˌlī, -ˌlē\ [NL, fr. L, tadpole, crowfoot, dim. of *rana* frog] (1663) **:** any of a large widely distributed genus (*Ranunculus*) of dicotyledonous herbs (as a buttercup) that have simple or variously lobed leaves and usu. yellow flowers with five deciduous sepals and five nectar-producing petals

[1]**rap** \ˈrap\ *n* [ME *rappe*] (14c) **1 :** a sharp blow or knock **2 :** a sharp rebuke or criticism **3** *slang* **a :** the responsibility for or adverse consequences of an action **b :** a criminal charge **c :** a prison sentence

[2]**rap** *vb* **rapped; rap·ping** *vt* (14c) **1 :** to strike with a sharp blow **2 :** to utter suddenly and forcibly **3 :** to cause to be or come by raps ⟨~ the meeting to order⟩ **4 :** to criticize sharply **5** *slang* **:** to arrest, hold, or sentence on a criminal charge ~ *vi* **1 :** to strike a quick sharp blow **2 :** to make a short sharp sound

[3]**rap** *vt* **rapped** *also* **rapt; rap·ping** [back-formation fr. *rapt*] (1528) **1 :** to snatch away or upward **2 :** ENRAPTURE

[4]**rap** *n* [perh. fr. [1]*rap*] (1834) **:** a minimum amount or degree (as of care or consideration) : the least bit ⟨doesn't care a ~⟩

[5]**rap** *n* [perh. by shortening & alter. fr. *repartee*] (1932) **:** TALK, CONVERSATION; *also* **:** a line of talk : PATTER

[6]**rap** *vi* **rapped; rap·ping** (1929) **:** to talk freely and frankly ⟨a center where they could meet and ~ congenially . . . with people . . . with similar interests and problems —Robert Liebert⟩

ra·pa·cious \rə-ˈpā-shəs\ *adj* [L *rapac-, rapax,* fr. *rapere* to seize — more at RAPID] (1651) **1 :** excessively grasping or covetous ⟨~ invaders⟩ **2 :** living on prey **3 :** RAVENOUS ***syn*** see VORACIOUS — **ra·pa·cious·ly** *adv* — **ra·pa·cious·ness** *n*

ra·pac·i·ty \rə-ˈpas-ət-ē\ *n* (1543) **:** the quality of being rapacious

[1]**rape** \ˈrāp\ *n* [ME, fr. L *rapa, rapum* turnip, rape; akin to OHG *rāba* turnip, rape] (14c) **:** a European herb (*Brassica napus*) of the mustard family grown as a forage crop for sheep and hogs and for its seeds which yield rape oil and are a bird food

[2]**rape** *vt* **raped; rap·ing** [ME *rapen,* fr. L *rapere*] (14c) **1 a** *archaic* **:** to seize and take away by force **b :** DESPOIL **2 :** to commit rape on — **rap·er** *n* — **rap·ist** \ˈrā-pəst\ *n*

[3]**rape** *n* (15c) **1 :** an act or instance of robbing or despoiling or carrying away a person by force **2 a :** sexual intercourse with a woman by a man without her consent and chiefly by force or deception — compare STATUTORY RAPE **b :** unlawful sexual intercourse by force or threat other than by a man with a woman **3 :** an outrageous violation

[4]**rape** *n* [F *râpe* grape stalk] (1657) **:** grape pomace

rape oil *n* (1545) **:** a nondrying or semidrying oil obtained from rapeseed and turnip seed and used chiefly as a lubricant, illuminant, and food — called also *rapeseed oil*

rape·seed \ˈrāp-ˌsēd\ *n* (1577) **:** the seed of the rape plant

Ra·pha·el \ˈraf-ē-əl, ˈrā-fē-\ *n* [LL, fr. Gk *Rhaphaēl,* fr. Heb *Rĕphāʼēl*] **:** one of the four archangels named in Hebrew tradition

ra·phe \ˈrā-(ˌ)fē\ *n* [NL, fr. Gk *rhaphē* seam, fr. *rhaptein* to sew — more at RHAPSODY] (1753) **1 :** the seamlike union of the two lateral halves of a part or organ (as the tongue) having externally a ridge or furrow **2 a :** the part of the stalk of an anatropous ovary that is united in growth to the outside covering and forms a ridge along the body of the ovule **b :** the median line of a diatom's valve

ra·phia \ˈrā-fē-ə, ˈraf-ē-\ *n* [NL, genus of palms, fr. Malagasy *rafia* raffia] (1842) **:** RAFFIA

raph·ide \ˈraf-ˌīd\ *n, pl* **raph·ides** \ˈraf-ˌīdz, ˈraf-ə-ˌdēz\ [F & NL; F *raphide,* fr. NL *raphides,* pl., modif. of Gk *rhaphides,* pl. of *rhaphid-, rhaphis* needle, fr. *rhaptein*] (1842) **:** one of the needle-shaped crystals, usu. of calcium oxalate that develop as metabolic by-products in plant cells

[1]**rap·id** \ˈrap-əd\ *adj* [L *rapidus* seizing, sweeping, rapid, fr. *rapere* to seize, sweep away; akin to OE *refsan* to blame] (1634) **:** marked by a fast rate of motion, activity, succession, or occurrence ***syn*** see FAST — **rap·id·ly** *adv* — **rap·id·ness** *n*

[2]**rapid** *n* (1765) **:** a part of a river where the current is fast and the surface is usu. broken by obstructions — usu. used in pl. but sing. or pl. in constr.

rapid eye movement *n* (1916) **:** a rapid conjugate movement of the eyes associated esp. with REM sleep

rapid eye movement sleep *n* (1965) **:** REM SLEEP

rap·id–fire \ˌrap-əd-ˈfī(ə)r\ *adj* (1890) **1 :** firing or adapted for firing shots in rapid succession **2 :** marked by rapidity, liveliness, or sharpness

ra·pid·i·ty \rə-ˈpid-ət-ē, ra-\ *n* (ca. 1616) **:** the quality or state of being rapid

rapid transit *n* (1873) **:** fast passenger transportation (as by subway) in urban areas

ra·pi·er \ˈrā-pē-ər\ *n* [MF (*espee*) *rapiere*] (1553) **:** a straight 2-edged sword with a narrow pointed blade

rapier

rap·ine \ˈrap-ən, -ˌīn\ *n* [ME *rapyne,* fr. L *rapina,* fr. *rapere* to seize, rob] (15c) **:** PILLAGE, PLUNDER

rap·pa·ree \ˌrap-ə-ˈrē\ *n* [IrGael *rāpaire*] (1690) **1 :** an Irish irregular soldier or bandit **2 :** VAGABOND, PLUNDERER

rap·pee \ra-ˈpā\ *n* [F (*tabac*) *râpé,* lit., grated tobacco] (1740) **:** a pungent snuff made from dark rank tobacco leaves

rap·pel \rə-ˈpel, ra-\ *vi* [F, n., backward motion, recall, fr. OF *rapel,* fr. *rapeler* to recall, fr. *re-* + *apeler* to appeal, call — more at APPEAL] (1931) **:** to descend (as from a cliff) by sliding down a rope passed under one thigh, across the body, and over the opposite shoulder or through a special friction device — **rappel** *n*

rap·pen \ˈräp-ən\ *n, pl* **rappen** [G, lit., raven; akin to OHG *hraban* raven — more at RAVEN] (1838) **:** the centime of Switzerland

rap·per \ˈrap-ər\ *n* (1640) **:** one that raps or is used for rapping; *specif* **:** a door knocker

rap·pi·ni \ra-ˈpē-nē\ *n pl* [It *rapini,* pl. of *rapino,* dim. of *rapo*

\ə\ abut \ᵊ\ kitten, F table \ər\ further \a\ ash \ā\ ace \ä\ cot, cart \au̇\ out \ch\ chin \e\ bet \ē\ easy \g\ go \i\ hit \ī\ ice \j\ job \ŋ\ sing \ō\ go \ȯ\ law \ȯi\ boy \th\ thin \t͟h\ the \ü\ loot \u̇\ foot \y\ yet \zh\ vision \à, k̲, ⁿ, œ, œ̄, ue, ue̅, ʸ\ *see* Guide to Pronunciation

turnip, fr. L *rapum* — more at RAPE] (1942) : immature turnip plants for use as greens

rap·port \ra-'pō(ə)r, rə-, -'pò(ə)r\ *n* [F, fr. *rapporter* to bring back, refer, fr. OF *raporter* to bring back, fr. *re-* + *aporter* to bring, fr. L *apportare,* fr. *ad-* ad- + *portare* to carry — more at FARE] (1661) : RELATION; *esp* : relation marked by harmony, conformity, accord, or affinity

rap·por·teur \,ra-,pōr-'tər, -,pòr-\ *n* [MF, fr. *rapporter* to bring back, report] (1500) : one that gives reports (as at a meeting of a learned society)

rap·proche·ment \,rap-,rōsh-'mä^{n}, -,rósh-; ra-'prōsh-,\ *n* [F, fr. *rapprocher* to bring together, fr. MF, fr. *re-* + *approcher* to approach, fr. OF *aprochier*] (1809) : establishment of or state of having cordial relations

rap·scal·lion \rap-'skal-yən\ *n* [alter. of earlier *rascallion,* fr. 1*rascal*] (1649) : RASCAL, NE'ER-DO-WELL

rap sheet *n* (1960) : a police arrest record esp. for an individual

rapt \'rapt\ *adj* [ME, fr. L *raptus,* pp. of *rapere* to seize — more at RAPID] (15c) **1** : lifted up and carried away **2** : transported with emotion : ENRAPTURED **3** : wholly absorbed : ENGROSSED — **rapt·ly** \'rap-(t)lē\ *adv* — **rapt·ness** \'rap(t)-nəs\ *n*

rap·tor \'rap-tər, -,tò(ə)r\ *n* [deriv. of L *raptor* plunderer, fr. *raptus*] (1854) : BIRD OF PREY

rap·to·ri·al \rap-'tōr-ē-əl, -'tór-\ *adj* (1839) **1** : PREDACEOUS 1 **2** : adapted to seize prey **3** : of, relating to, or being a bird of prey

1rap·ture \'rap-chər\ *n* [L *raptus*] (1605) **1 a** : a state or experience of being carried away by overwhelming emotion **b** : a mystical experience in which the spirit is exalted to a knowledge of divine things **2** : an expression or manifestation of ecstasy or passion ***syn*** see ECSTASY — **rap·tur·ous** \'rap-chə-rəs, 'rap-shrəs\ *adj* — **rap·tur·ous·ly** *adv* — **rap·tur·ous·ness** *n*

2rapture *vt* **rap·tured; rap·tur·ing** (1637) : ENRAPTURE

rapture of the deep (1953) : NITROGEN NARCOSIS

ra·ra avis \,rar-ə-'ā-vəs, ,rer-; ,rär-ə-'ä-wəs\ *n, pl* **ra·ra avis·es** \-'ā-və-səz\ *or* **ra·rae aves** \,rär-,ī-'ä-,wās\ [L, rare bird] (1607) : RARITY 2

1rare \'ra(ə)r, 're(ə)r\ *adj* **rar·er; rar·est** [ME, fr. L *rarus*] (15c) **1** : marked by wide separation of component particles : THIN ⟨~ air⟩ **2 a** : marked by unusual quality, merit, or appeal : DISTINCTIVE **b** : superlative or extreme of its kind **3** : seldom occurring or found : UNCOMMON ***syn*** see CHOICE, INFREQUENT — **rare·ness** *n*

2rare *adj* **rar·er; rar·est** [alter. of earlier *rere,* fr. ME, fr. OE *hrēre* boiled lightly; akin to OE *hrēran* to stir, OHG *hruoren*] (1784) : cooked so that the inside is still red ⟨~ roast beef⟩

rare·bit \'ra(ə)r-bət, 're(ə)r-\ *n* [(*Welsh*) *rarebit*] (1725) : WELSH RABBIT

rare earth *n* (1875) **1** : any of a group of similar oxides of metals or a mixture of such oxides occurring together in widely distributed but relatively scarce minerals **2** : RARE EARTH ELEMENT

rare earth element *n* (1942) : any of a series of metallic elements of which the oxides are classed as rare earths and which include the elements with atomic numbers 58 through 71, usu. lanthanum, and sometimes yttrium and scandium — called also *rare earth metal;* compare ELEMENT table

rar·ee–show \'rar-ē-,shō, 'rer-\ *n* [alter. of *rare show*] (1681) : a small display or scene viewed in a box : PEEP SHOW; *broadly* : an unusual or amazing show or spectacle

rar·efac·tion \,rar-ə-'fak-shən, ,rer-\ *n* [F or ML; F *raréfaction,* fr. ML *rarefaction-, rarefactio,* fr. L *rarefactus,* pp. of *rarefacere* to rarefy] (1603) **1** : the action or process of rarefying **2** : the quality or state of being rarefied **3** : a state or region of minimum pressure in a medium traversed by compressional waves (as sound waves) — **rar·efac·tion·al** \-shnəl, -shən-^{ə}l\ *adj*

rar·efied *also* **rar·i·fied** \'rar-ə-,fīd, 'rer-\ *adj* (1941) **1** : of, relating to, or interesting to a select group : ESOTERIC **2** : very high

rar·efy *also* **rar·i·fy** \-ə-,fī\ *vb* **-efied; -efy·ing** [ME *rarefien, rarifien,* fr. MF *rarefier,* modif. of L *rarefacere,* fr. *rarus* rare + *facere* to make — more at DO] *vt* (14c) **1** : to make rare, thin, porous, or less dense : to expand without the addition of matter **2** : to make more spiritual, refined, or abstruse ~ *vi* : to become less dense

rare·ly \'ra(ə)r-lē, 're(ə)r-\ *adv* (1552) **1** : not often : SELDOM **2** : with rare skill : EXCELLENTLY **3** : in an extreme or exceptional manner

rare·ripe \'ra(ə)r-,rīp, 're(ə)r-\ *n* [E dial. *rare* (early) + E *ripe*] (1722) **1** : an early ripening fruit or vegetable **2** *dial* : GREEN ONION

rar·ing \'ra(ə)r-ən, 're(ə)r-, -iŋ\ *adj* [fr. prp. of E dial. *rare* to rear, alter. of E *rear*] (1909) : full of enthusiasm or eagerness

rar·i·ty \'rar-ət-ē, 'rer-\ *n, pl* **-ties** (1542) **1** : the quality, state, or fact of being rare **2** : one that is rare

ras·bo·ra \raz-'bōr-ə, -'bór-\ *n* [NL, fr. native name in the East Indies] (1931) : any of a genus (*Rasbora*) of tiny brilliantly colored cyprinid freshwater fishes often kept in tropical aquariums

ras·cal \'ras-kəl\ *n* [ME *rascaile* rabble, one of the rabble] (15c) **1** : a mean, unprincipled, or dishonest person **2** : a mischievous person or animal — **rascal** *adj*

ras·cal·i·ty \ra-'skal-ət-ē\ *n, pl* **-ties** (1577) **1** : RABBLE **2 a** : the character or actions of a rascal : KNAVERY **b** : a rascally act

ras·cal·ly \'ras-kə-lē\ *adj* (1596) : of or characteristic of a rascal — **rascally** *adv*

rase \'rāz\ *vt* **rased; ras·ing** [ME *rasen,* fr. MF *raser,* fr. (assumed) VL *rasare,* fr. L *rasus,* pp. of *radere* to scrape, shave — more at RAT] (14c) **1** : ERASE **2** : RAZE 1

1rash \'rash\ *adv, archaic* [ME (northern dial.) *rasch* quickly; akin to OHG *rasc* fast] (15c) : in a rash manner

2rash *adj* (1509) **1** : marked by or proceeding from undue haste or lack of deliberation or caution **2** *obs* : quickly effective ***syn*** see ADVENTUROUS — **rash·ly** *adv* — **rash·ness** *n*

3rash *n* [obs. F *rache* scurf, fr. (assumed) VL *rasica,* fr. *rasicare* to scratch, fr. L *rasus,* pp. of *radere*] (1709) **1** : an eruption on the body **2** : a large number of instances in a short period ⟨a ~ of complaints⟩

rash·er \'rash-ər\ *n* [perh. fr. obs. *rash* to cut, fr. ME *rashen*] (1592) : a thin slice of bacon or ham broiled or fried; *also* : a portion consisting of several such slices

1rasp \'rasp\ *vb* [ME *raspen,* fr. (assumed) MF *rasper,* of Gmc origin; akin to OHG *raspōn* to scrape together] *vt* (14c) **1** : to rub with something rough; *specif* : to abrade with a rasp **2** : to grate upon : IRRITATE **3** : to utter in an irritated tone ~ *vi* **1** : SCRAPE **2** : to produce a grating sound — **rasp·er** *n* — **rasp·ing·ly** \'ras-piŋ-lē\ *adv*

2rasp *n* (1541) **1** : a coarse file with cutting points instead of lines **2** : something used for rasping **3 a** : an act of rasping **b** : a rasping sound, sensation, or effect

rasp·ber·ry \'raz-,ber-ē, -b(ə-)rē\ *n* [E dial. *rasp* (raspberry) + E *berry*] (1623) **1 a** : any of various usu. black or red edible berries that are aggregate fruits consisting of numerous small drupes on a fleshy receptacle and that are usu. rounder and smaller than the closely related blackberries **b** : a plant (genus *Rubus*) that bears raspberries **2** : a sound of contempt made by protruding the tongue between the lips and expelling air forcibly to produce a vibration; *broadly* : an expression of disapproval

raspy \'ras-pē\ *adj* (1838) **1** : HARSH, GRATING **2** : IRRITABLE

Ras·ta \'ras-tə\ *n* (1955) : RASTAFARIAN — **Rasta** *adj*

Ras·ta·far·i·an \,ras-tə-'far-ē-ən\ *n* [*Ras Tafari,* precoronation name of Haile Selassie] (1955) : an adherent of Rastafarianism — **Rastafarian** *adj*

Ras·ta·far·i·an·ism \-ē-ə-,niz-əm\ *n* (1968) : a religious cult among black Jamaicans that teaches the eventual redemption of blacks and their return to Africa, employs the ritualistic use of marijuana, forbids the cutting of hair, and venerates Haile Selassie as a god

ras·ter \'ras-tər\ *n* [G, fr. L *raster, rastrum* rake, fr. *radere* to scrape] (ca. 1934) : a scan pattern (as of the electron beam in a cathode-ray tube) in which an area is scanned from side to side in lines from top to bottom; *also* : a pattern of closely spaced rows of dots that form the image on a cathode-ray tube (as of a television or computer display)

ra·sure \'rā-shər, -zhər\ *n* [MF, fr. L *rasura,* fr. *rasus,* pp. of *radere*] (1508) : ERASURE, OBLITERATION

1rat \'rat\ *n* [ME, fr. OE *ræt;* akin to OHG *ratta* rat, L *rodere* to gnaw, *radere* to scrape, shave] (bef. 12c) **1 a** : any of numerous rodents (*Rattus* and related genera) differing from the related mice by considerably larger size and by structural details (as of the teeth) **b** : any of various similar rodents **2** : a contemptible person: as **a** : one who betrays or deserts his party, friends, or associates **b** : SCAB 3b **c** : INFORMER 2 **3** : a pad over which a woman's hair is arranged — **rat·like** \-,līk\ *adj*

2rat *vb* **rat·ted; rat·ting** *vi* (1812) **1** : to betray, desert, or inform on one's associates — usu. used with *on* **2** : to catch or hunt rats **3** : to work as a scab ~ *vt* : to give (hair) the effect of greater quantity by use of a rat

rat·able *or* **rate·able** \'rāt-ə-bəl\ *adj* (1503) : capable of being rated, estimated, or apportioned — **rat·ably** \-blē\ *adv*

rat·a·fia \,rat-ə-'fē-ə\ *n* [F] (1699) **1** : a liqueur made from an infusion of macerated fruit or fruit juice in a liquor (as brandy) and often flavored with almonds **2** : a sweet biscuit made of almond paste

rat·a·plan \'rat-ə-,plan\ *n* [F, of imit. origin] (1847) : the iterative sound of beating ⟨a rolling ~ of drums —*Time*⟩

rat–a–tat \'rat-ə-,tat\ *or* **rat–a–tat–tat** \,rat-ə-,ta(t)-'tat\ *n* [imit.] (1681) : a sharp repeated knocking, tapping, or cracking sound

ra·ta·tou·ille \,ra-,ta-'tü-ē, ,rä-,tä-\ *n* [F, fr. *touiller* to stir, fr. L *tudiculare,* fr. *tudes* hammer; akin to L *tundere* to beat — more at STINT] (ca. 1877) : a seasoned stew made of eggplant, tomatoes, green peppers, squash, and sometimes meat

rat–bite fever *n* (1910) : either of two febrile bacterial diseases of man usu. transmitted by the bite of a rat

ratch \'rach\ *n* [G *ratsche,* fr. *ratschen* to rattle, fr. MHG *ratzen;* akin to MHG *razzeln* to rattle] (1721) **1** : RATCHET 2 **2** : a notched bar with which a pawl or detent works to prevent reversal of motion

rat cheese *n* (1939) : CHEDDAR

1ratch·et \'rach-ət\ *n* [alter. of earlier *rochet,* fr. F, alter. of MF *rocquet* lance head, of Gmc origin; akin to OHG *rocko* distaff — more at ROCK] (1654) **1** : a mechanism that consists of a bar or wheel having inclined teeth into which a pawl drops so that motion can be imparted to the wheel or bar, governed, or prevented and that is used in a hand tool (as a wrench or screwdriver) to allow effective motion in one direction only **2** : a pawl or detent for holding or propelling a ratchet wheel

2ratchet *vt* (1973) : to raise to progressively higher levels — used with *up* or *upward* ⟨inflation *ratcheting* up the cost of living⟩

ratchet wheel *n* (1777) : a toothed wheel held in position or turned by an engaging pawl

1rate \'rāt\ *vb* **rat·ed; rat·ing** [ME *raten*] *vt* (14c) **1** : to rebuke angrily or violently **2** *obs* : to drive away by scolding ~ *vi* : to voice angry reprimands

2rate *n* [ME, fr. MF, fr. ML *rata,* fr. L (*pro*) *rata* (*parte*) according to a fixed proportion] (15c) **1 a** : reckoned value : VALUATION **b** *obs* : ESTIMATION **2** *obs* : a fixed quantity **3 a** : a fixed ratio between two things **b** : a charge, payment, or price fixed according to a ratio, scale, or standard: as (1) : a charge per unit of a public-service commodity (2) : a charge per unit of freight or passenger service (3) : a unit charge or ratio used by a government for assessing property taxes (4) *Brit* : a local tax **4 a** : a quantity, amount, or degree of something measured per unit of something else **b** : an amount of payment or charge based on another amount; *specif* : the amount of premium per unit of insurance **5** : relative condition or quality : CLASS — **at any rate** : in any case : ANYWAY

3rate *vb* **rat·ed; rat·ing** *vt* (15c) **1** *obs* : ALLOT **2** : CONSIDER, REGARD ⟨was *rated* an excellent pianist⟩ **3 a** : to set an estimate on : VALUE, ESTEEM ⟨black is *rated* very high this season⟩ **b** : to determine or assign the relative rank or class of : GRADE ⟨~ a seaman⟩ **c** : to estimate the normal capacity or power of **4** : to fix the amount of premium to be charged per unit of insurance on **5** : to have a right to : DESERVE ⟨she *rated* special privileges⟩ ~ *vi* : to enjoy a status of special privilege ⟨really ~s with the boss⟩ ***syn*** see ESTIMATE

rated load *n* (ca. 1925) : the load a machine is designed to carry

ra·tel \'rāt-^{ə}l, 'rät-\ *n* [Afrik, lit., rattle, fr. MD — more at RATTLE] (1777) : an African or Asian nocturnal carnivorous mammal (genus *Mellivora*) resembling the badger

rate·me·ter \'rāt-,mēt-ər\ *n* (1949) : an instrument that indicates the counting rate of an electronic counter

rate of change (ca. 1937) : a value that results from dividing the change of a function of a variable by the change in the variable ⟨velocity is the *rate of change* of distance with respect to time⟩

rate of exchange (1727) : the amount of one currency that will buy a given amount of another

rate of interest (ca. 1924) **:** the percentage usu. on an annual basis that is paid for the use of money borrowed from another
rate·pay·er \'rāt-ˌpā-ər\ *n, Brit* (1845) **:** TAXPAYER
rat·er \'rāt-ər\ *n* (1611) **1 :** one that rates; *specif* **:** a person who estimates or determines a rating **2 :** one having a specified rating or class — usu. used in combination ⟨first-*rater*⟩
rat fink *n* (1964) **:** INFORMER 2, FINK
rat·fish \'rat-ˌfish\ *n* (1882) **:** CHIMAERA; *esp* **:** a silvery iridescent white-spotted chimaera (*Hydrolagus colliei*) of cold deep waters of the Pacific coast of No. America
rathe \'rāth, 'rath\ *adj* [ME, quick, fr. OE *hrœth,* alter. of *hrœd;* akin to OHG *hrad* quick] *archaic* (15c) **:** EARLY ⟨bring the ~ primrose that forsaken dies —John Milton⟩
rath·er \'rath-ər, 'räth-, 'rəth- *also* 'reth-; *interjectionally* 'ra-'thər, 'rä-, 'rə-\ *adv* [ME, fr. OE *hrathor,* compar. of *hrathe* quickly; akin to OHG *rado* quickly, OE *hrœd* quick] (bef. 12c) **1 :** with better reason or more propriety **:** more properly ⟨this you should pity ~ than despise —Shak.⟩ **2 :** more readily or willingly **:** PREFERABLY ⟨I'd ~ not go⟩ ⟨would ~ read than watch television⟩ — often used interjectionally to express affirmation **3 :** more correctly speaking ⟨my father, or ~ my stepfather⟩ **4 :** to the contrary **:** INSTEAD ⟨was no better but ~ grew worse —Mk 5:26 (RSV)⟩ **5 :** in some degree **:** SOMEWHAT ⟨it's ~ warm⟩ — often used as a mild intensive ⟨spent ~ a lot of money⟩ — **the rather** *archaic* **:** the more quickly or readily
raths·kel·ler \'rät-ˌskel-ər, 'rat(h)-\ *n* [obs. G (now *ratskeller*), city-hall basement restaurant, fr. *rat* council + *keller* cellar] (1900) **:** a usu. basement tavern or restaurant
rat·icide \'rat-ə-ˌsīd\ *n* (1908) **:** a substance for killing rats
rat·i·fy \'rat-ə-ˌfī\ *vt* **-fied; -fy·ing** [ME *ratifien,* fr. MF *ratifier,* fr. ML *ratificare,* fr. L *ratus* determined, fr. pp. of *reri* to calculate — more at REASON] (14c) **:** to approve and sanction formally **:** CONFIRM ⟨~ a treaty⟩ — **rat·i·fi·ca·tion** \ˌrat-ə-fə-'kā-shən\ *n*
ra·ti·né \ˌrat-ə-'nā\ *or* **ra·tine** \ˌrat-ə-'nā, ra-'tēn\ *n* [F *ratiné*] (1685) **1 :** a nubby ply yarn of various fibers made by twisting under tension a thick and a thin yarn **2 :** a rough bulky fabric usu. woven loosely in plain weave from ratiné yarns
rat·ing \'rāt-iŋ\ *n* (1702) **1 :** a classification according to grade; *specif* **:** a military or naval specialist classification **2** *chiefly Brit* **:** a naval enlisted man **3 a :** relative estimate or evaluation **:** STANDING ⟨the school has a good academic ~⟩ **b :** an estimate of an individual's or business's credit and responsibility **c :** an estimate of the percentage of the public listening to or viewing a particular radio or television program **4 :** a stated operating limit of a machine expressible in power units (as kilowatts of a direct-current generator) or in characteristics (as voltage)
ra·tio \'rā-(ˌ)shō, -shē-ˌō\ *n, pl* **ra·tios** [L, computation, reason — more at REASON] (1660) **1 a :** the indicated quotient of two mathematical expressions **b :** the relationship in quantity, amount, or size between two or more things **:** PROPORTION **2 :** the expression of the relative values of gold and silver as determined by a country's currency laws
ra·ti·o·ci·nate \ˌrat-ē-'ōs-ᵊn-ˌāt, ˌrash-ē-, -'äs-\ *vi* **-nat·ed; -nat·ing** [L *ratiocinatus,* pp. of *ratiocinari* to reckon, fr. *ratio*] (1643) **:** REASON — **ra·ti·o·ci·na·tor** \-ˌāt-ər\ *n*
ra·ti·o·ci·na·tion \-ˌōs-ᵊn-'ā-shən, -ˌäs-\ *n* (1530) **1 :** the process of exact thinking **:** REASONING **2 :** a reasoned train of thought — **ra·ti·o·ci·na·tive** \-'ōs-ᵊn-ˌāt-iv, -'äs-\ *adj*
[1]ra·tion \'rash-ən, 'rā-shən\ *n* [F, fr. L *ration-, ratio* computation, reason] (1702) **1 a :** a food allowance for one day **b** *pl* **:** FOOD, PROVISIONS **2 :** a share esp. as determined by supply
[2]ration *vt* **ra·tioned; ra·tion·ing** \'rash-(ə-)niŋ, 'rāsh-\ (1859) **1 :** to supply with or put on rations **2 a :** to distribute as rations — often used with *out* ⟨~*ed* out sugar and flour⟩ **b :** to distribute equitably **c :** to use sparingly
[1]ra·tio·nal \'rash-nəl, -ən-ᵊl\ *adj* [ME *racional,* fr. L *rationalis,* fr. *ration-, ratio*] (14c) **1 a :** having reason or understanding **b :** relating to, based on, or agreeable to reason **:** REASONABLE ⟨a ~ explanation⟩ ⟨~ behavior⟩ **2 :** involving only multiplication, division, addition, and subtraction and only a finite number of times **3 :** relating to, consisting of, or being one or more rational numbers — **ra·tio·nal·ly** \-ē\ *adv* — **ra·tio·nal·ness** *n*
[2]rational *n* (1606) **:** something rational; *specif* **:** RATIONAL NUMBER
ra·tio·nale \ˌrash-ə-'nal\ *n* [L, neut. of *rationalis*] (1657) **1 :** an explanation of controlling principles of opinion, belief, practice, or phenomena **2 :** an underlying reason **:** BASIS
rational function *n* (1904) **:** a function that is the quotient of two polynomials; *also* **:** POLYNOMIAL
ra·tio·nal·ism \'rash-nə-ˌliz-əm, -ən-ᵊl-ˌiz-\ *n* (1827) **1 :** reliance on reason as the basis for establishment of religious truth **2 a :** a theory that reason is in itself a source of knowledge superior to and independent of sense perceptions **b :** a view that reason and experience rather than the nonrational are the fundamental criteria in the solution of problems **3 :** FUNCTIONALISM — **ra·tio·nal·ist** \-nə-ləst, -ən-ᵊl-əst\ *n* — **rationalist** *or* **ra·tio·nal·is·tic** \ˌrash-nə-'lis-tik, -ən-ᵊl-'is-\ *adj* — **ra·tio·nal·is·ti·cal·ly** \-ti-k(ə-)lē\ *adv*
ra·tio·nal·i·ty \ˌrash-ə-'nal-ət-ē\ *n, pl* **-ties** (1628) **1 :** the quality or state of being rational **2 :** the quality or state of being agreeable to reason **:** REASONABLENESS **3 :** a rational opinion, belief, or practice — usu. used in pl.
ra·tio·nal·ize \'rash-nə-ˌlīz, -ən-ᵊl-ˌīz\ *vb* **-ized; -iz·ing** *vt* (1803) **1 :** to free (a mathematical expression) from irrational parts ⟨~ a denominator⟩ **2 :** to bring into accord with reason or cause something to seem reasonable: as **a :** to substitute a natural for a supernatural explanation of ⟨~ a myth⟩ **b :** to attribute (one's actions) to rational and creditable motives without analysis of true and esp. unconscious motives ⟨*rationalized* his dislike of his brother⟩ ~ *vi* **:** to provide plausible but untrue reasons for conduct — **ra·tio·nal·iza·tion** \ˌrash-nə-lə-'zā-shən, -ən-ᵊl-ə-\ *n* — **ra·tio·nal·iz·er** \'rash-nə-ˌlī-zər, -ən-ᵊl-ˌī-\ *n*
rational number *n* (1904) **:** an integer or the quotient of two integers
[1]rat·ite \'ra-ˌtīt\ *adj* [deriv. of L *ratitus* marked with the figure of a raft, fr. *ratis* raft] (1877) **:** having a flat breastbone
[2]ratite *n* (ca. 1890) **:** a bird with a flat breastbone; *esp* **:** any of a superorder (Ratitae) of birds (as an ostrich, an emu, a moa, and a kiwi) that have small or rudimentary wings and no keel to the breastbone
rat·line \'rat-lən\ *n* [ME *radelyng*] (15c) **:** one of the small transverse ropes attached to the shrouds of a ship so as to form the steps of a rope ladder
rat mite *n* (1942) **:** a widely distributed mite (*Bdellonyssus bacoti*) that usu. feeds on rodents but may cause dermatitis in and transmit typhus to man
[1]ra·toon \ra-'tün\ *n* [Sp *retoño,* fr. *retoñar* to sprout, fr. *re-* (fr. L) + *otoñar* to grow in autumn, fr. *otoño* autumn, fr. L *autumnus*] (1631) **1 :** a shoot of a perennial plant (as sugarcane) **2 :** a crop (as of bananas) produced on ratoons
[2]ratoon *vi* (1789) **:** to sprout or spring up from the root ~ *vt* **:** to grow or produce (a crop) from or on ratoons
rat race *n* (1939) **:** strenuous, wearisome, and usu. competitive activity or rush
rat snake *n* (1860) **:** any of numerous large harmless rat-eating colubrid snakes — called also *chicken snake*
rat·tail \'rat-ˌtāl\ *n* (1705) **1 :** a horse's tail with little or no hair **2 :** GRENADIER 2
rattail cactus *n* (1900) **:** a commonly cultivated tropical American cactus (*Aporocactus flagelliformis*) with creeping stems and showy crimson flowers
rat–tail file *n* (1744) **:** a round slender tapered file
rat·tan \ra-'tan, rə-\ *n* [Malay *rotan*] (1660) **1 :** a rattan cane or switch **2 a :** a climbing palm (esp. of the genera *Calamus* and *Daemonorops*) with very long tough stems **b :** a part of the stem of a rattan used esp. for walking sticks and wickerwork
rat·teen \ra-'tēn\ *n* [F *ratine*] *archaic* (1685) **:** a coarse woolen fabric
rat·ter \'rat-ər\ *n* (1857) **:** one that catches rats; *specif* **:** a rat-catching dog or cat
[1]rat·tle \'rat-ᵊl\ *vb* **rat·tled; rat·tling** \'rat-liŋ, -ᵊl-iŋ\ [ME *ratelen;* akin to MD *ratel* rattle, OE *hratian* to rush — more at CARDINAL] *vi* (14c) **1 :** to make a rapid succession of short sharp noises ⟨the windows *rattled* in the wind⟩ **2 :** to chatter incessantly and aimlessly **3 :** to move with a clatter or rattle; *also* **:** to be or move about in a place or station too large or grand ⟨*rattled* around the big old home⟩ ~ *vt* **1 :** to say, perform, or affect in a brisk lively fashion ⟨*rattled* off four magnificent backhands —Kim Chapin⟩ **2 :** to cause to make a rattling sound **3 :** ROUSE; *specif* **:** to beat (a cover) for game **4 :** to upset to the point of loss of poise and composure
[2]rattle *n* (1500) **1 a :** a rapid succession of sharp clattering sounds **b :** NOISE, RACKET **2 a :** a device that produces a rattle; *specif* **:** a case containing pellets used as a baby's toy **b :** the sound-producing organ on a rattlesnake's tail **3 :** a throat noise caused by air passing through mucus and heard esp. at the approach of death
[3]rattle *vt* **rat·tled; rat·tling** \'rat-liŋ, -ᵊl-iŋ\ [irreg. fr. *ratline*] (1729) **:** to furnish with ratlines
rat·tle·brain \'rat-ᵊl-ˌbrān\ *n* (1709) **:** a flighty or thoughtless person — **rat·tle·brained** \ˌrat-ᵊl-'brānd\ *adj*
rat·tler \'rat-lər, -ᵊl-ər\ *n* (15c) **1 :** one that rattles **2 :** RATTLESNAKE
rat·tle·snake \'rat-ᵊl-ˌsnāk\ *n* (1630) **:** any of various thick-bodied American venomous snakes (family Crotalidae, genera *Sistrurus* and *Crotalus*) with horny interlocking joints at the end of the tail that make a sharp rattling sound when shaken
rattlesnake plantain *n* (1778) **:** an orchid (genus *Goodyera*) with checked or mottled leaves
rattlesnake root *n* (1682) **:** any of various plants formerly believed to be distasteful to rattlesnakes or effective against their venom: as **a :** any of a genus (*Prenanthes* and esp. *P. altissima*) of composite plants that have lobed or pinnatifid leaves and small heads of drooping ligulate flowers **b :** SENECA SNAKEROOT
rattlesnake weed *n* (1760) **:** a hawkweed (*Hieracium venosum*) with purple-veined leaves
rat·tle·trap \'rat-ᵊl-ˌtrap\ *n* (1822) **:** something rattly or rickety; *esp* **:** an old car — **rattletrap** *adj*
[1]rat·tling \'rat-liŋ\ *adj* (1560) **1 :** LIVELY, BRISK ⟨moved at a ~ pace⟩ **2 :** extraordinarily good **:** SPLENDID — **rat·tling·ly** \-liŋ-lē\ *adv*
[2]rattling *adv* (1829) **:** to an extreme degree **:** VERY ⟨a ~ good argument —E. A. Betts⟩
rat·tly \'rat-lē, -ᵊl-ē\ *adj* (1881) **:** likely to rattle **:** making a rattle
rat·ton \'rat-ᵊn, 'rät-\ *n* [ME *ratoun,* fr. MF *raton,* dim. of *rat,* prob. of Gmc origin; akin to OE *rœt* rat] *chiefly dial* (14c) **:** RAT
rat·trap \'ra(t)-ˌtrap\ *n* (15c) **1 :** a trap for rats **2 :** a dirty dilapidated structure **3 :** a hopeless situation
rat trap cheese *n* (1927) **:** CHEDDAR
rat·ty \'rat-ē\ *adj* **rat·ti·er; -est** (1865) **1 a :** infested with rats **b :** of, relating to, or suggestive of a rat **2 :** SHABBY, UNKEMPT ⟨a ~ brown overcoat —John Lardner⟩ **3 a :** DESPICABLE, TREACHEROUS **b :** IRRITABLE ⟨feeling ~ as hell —Richard Bissell⟩
rau·cous \'rȯ-kəs\ *adj* [L *raucus* hoarse; akin to OE *rēon* to lament — more at RUMOR] (1769) **1 :** disagreeably harsh or strident **:** HOARSE ⟨~ voices⟩ **2 :** boisterously disorderly ⟨a . . . ~ frontier town —Truman Capote⟩ ***syn*** see LOUD — **rau·cous·ly** *adv* — **rau·cous·ness** *n*
raunch \'rȯnch, 'ränch\ *n* [back-formation fr. *raunchy*] (1964) **:** VULGARITY, LEWDNESS
raun·chy \'rȯn-chē, 'rän-\ *adj* **raun·chi·er; -est** [origin unknown] (1939) **1 :** SLOVENLY, DIRTY ⟨a ~ panhandler⟩ **2 :** OBSCENE, SMUTTY ⟨~ jokes⟩ — **raun·chi·ly** \'rȯn-chə-lē\ *adv* — **raun·chi·ness** \-chē-nəs\ *n*
rau·wol·fia \rau̇-'wu̇l-fē-ə, rȯ-\ *n* [NL, fr. Leonhard *Rauwolf* †1596 Ger. botanist] (1752) **1 :** any of a large pantropic genus (*Rauwolfia*) of the dogbane family of somewhat poisonous trees and shrubs yielding emetic and purgative substances **2 :** a medicinal extract from the root of an Indian rauwolfia (*Rauwolfia serpentina*) used in the treatment of hypertension and mental disorders
[1]rav·age \'rav-ij\ *n* [F, fr. MF, fr. *ravir* to ravish — more at RAVISH] (1611) **1 :** an act or practice of ravaging **2 :** damage resulting from ravaging **:** violently destructive effect ⟨the ~*s* of time⟩

\ə\ abut \ᵊ\ kitten, F table \ər\ further \a\ ash \ā\ ace \ä\ cot, cart \au̇\ out \ch\ chin \e\ bet \ē\ easy \g\ go \i\ hit \ī\ ice \j\ job \ŋ\ sing \ō\ go \ȯ\ law \ȯi\ boy \th\ thin \th\ the \ü\ loot \u̇\ foot \y\ yet \zh\ vision \à, k̲, ⁿ, œ, œ̄, ue, ue̅, ʸ\ see Guide to Pronunciation

[2]ravage *vb* **rav·aged; rav·ag·ing** *vt* (1611) **:** to wreak havoc on **:** visit destructively and often violently **~** *vi* **:** to commit destructive actions — **rav·age·ment** \-ij-mənt\ *n* — **rav·ag·er** *n*
syn RAVAGE, DEVASTATE, WASTE, SACK, PILLAGE, DESPOIL mean to lay waste by plundering or destroying. RAVAGE implies violent often cumulative depredation and destruction; DEVASTATE implies the complete ruin and desolation of a wide area; WASTE may imply producing the same result by a slow process rather than sudden and violent action; SACK implies carrying off all valuable possessions from a place; PILLAGE implies ruthless plundering at will but without the completeness suggested by SACK; DESPOIL applies to looting or robbing of a place or person without suggesting accompanying destruction.

[1]rave \'rāv\ *vb* **raved; rav·ing** [ME *raven*] *vi* (14c) **1 a :** to talk irrationally in or as if in delirium **b :** to declaim wildly **c :** to talk with extreme enthusiasm ⟨*raved* about her beauty⟩ **2 :** to move or advance violently **:** STORM ⟨the iced gusts still ~ and beat —John Keats⟩ **~** *vt* **:** to utter in madness or frenzy — **rav·er** *n*

[2]rave *n* (1598) **1 :** an act or instance of raving **2 :** an extravagantly favorable criticism ⟨the play received the critics' ~*s*⟩

[1]rav·el \'rav-əl\ *vb* **-eled** *or* **-elled; -el·ing** *or* **-el·ling** \-(ə-)liŋ\ [D *rafelen*, fr. *rafel* loose thread; akin to OE *ræfter* rafter] *vt* (1582) **1 a :** to separate or undo the texture of **:** UNRAVEL **b :** to undo the intricacies of **:** DISENTANGLE **2 :** ENTANGLE, CONFUSE **~** *vi* **1** *obs* **:** to become entangled or confused **2 :** to become unwoven, untwisted, or unwound **:** FRAY **3 :** BREAK UP, CRUMBLE — **rav·el·er** \-(ə-)lər\ *n* — **rav·el·ment** \-əl-mənt\ *n*

[2]ravel *n* (1634) **:** an act or result of raveling: as **a :** something tangled **b :** something raveled out; *specif* **:** a loose thread

rav·el·ing *or* **rav·el·ling** \'rav(-ə)-liŋ, -lən\ *n* (1658) **:** RAVEL b

[1]ra·ven \'rā-vən\ *n* [ME, fr. OE *hræfn;* akin to OHG *hraban* raven, L *corvus,* Gk *korax,* L *crepare* to rattle, crack] (bef. 12c) **:** a glossy black corvine bird (*Corvus corax*) of northern Europe, Asia, and America

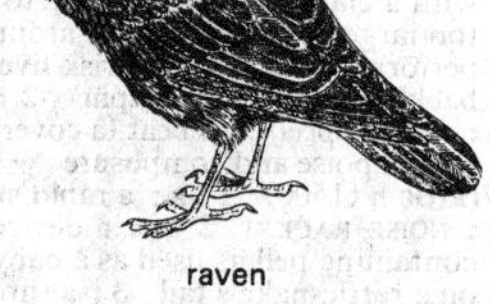
raven

[2]raven *adj* (1634) **:** shiny and black like a raven's feathers ⟨~ hair⟩

[3]rav·en \'rav-ən\ *vb* **rav·ened; rav·en·ing** \-(ə-)niŋ\ [MF *raviner* to rush, take by force, fr. *ravine* rapine] *vt* (1530) **1 :** to devour greedily **2 :** DESPOIL ⟨men . . . ~ the earth, destroying its resources —*New Yorker*⟩ **~** *vi* **1 :** to feed greedily **2 :** to prowl for food **:** PREY **3 :** PLUNDER — **rav·en·er** \-(ə-)nər\ *n*

rav·en·ous \'rav-(ə-)nəs\ *adj* (15c) **1 :** RAPACIOUS ⟨a ~ wolves⟩ **2 :** very eager for food, satisfaction, or gratification ⟨a ~ appetite⟩ ***syn*** see VORACIOUS — **rav·en·ous·ly** *adv* — **rav·en·ous·ness** *n*

rav·in \'rav-ən\ *n* [ME, fr. MF *ravine*] (14c) **1 :** PLUNDER, PILLAGE **2 a :** an act or habit of preying **b :** something seized as prey

ra·vine \rə-'vēn\ *n* [F, fr. MF, rapine, rush, fr. L *rapina* rapine] (1760) **:** a small narrow steep-sided valley that is larger than a gully and smaller than a canyon and that is usu. worn by running water

rav·ined \'rav-ənd\ *adj, obs* (15c) **:** RAVENOUS

[1]rav·ing \'rā-viŋ\ *n* (15c) **:** irrational, incoherent, wild, or extravagant utterance or declamation — usu. used in pl.

[2]raving *adj* (15c) **1 :** talking wildly or irrationally ⟨a ~ lunatic⟩ **2 :** RAVISHING ⟨a ~ beauty⟩

ra·vi·o·li \ˌrav-ē-'ō-lē, ˌräv-\ *n, pl* **ravioli** *or* **ra·vi·o·lis** \-lēz\ [It, fr. It dial., pl. of *raviolo,* lit., little turnip, dim. of *rava* turnip, fr. L *rapa* — more at RAPE] (1611) **:** pasta in the form of little cases of dough containing a savory filling (as of meat or cheese); *also* **:** a dish consisting of ravioli in a tomato sauce

rav·ish \'rav-ish\ *vt* [ME *ravisshen,* fr. MF *raviss-,* stem of *ravir,* fr. (assumed) VL *rapire,* alter. of L *rapere* to seize, rob — more at RAPID] (14c) **1 a :** to seize and take away by violence **b :** to overcome with emotion (as joy or delight) ⟨~*ed* by the beauty of the scene⟩ **c :** RAPE, VIOLATE **2 :** PLUNDER, ROB — **rav·ish·er** *n* — **rav·ish·ment** \-ish-mənt\ *n*

rav·ish·ing \'rav-ish-iŋ\ *adj* (15c) **:** unusually attractive, pleasing, or striking — **rav·ish·ing·ly** \-iŋ-lē\ *adv*

[1]raw \'rò\ *adj* **raw·er** \'rò(-ə)r\; **raw·est** \'rò-əst\ [ME, fr. OE *hrēaw;* akin to OHG *hrō* raw, L *crudus* raw, *cruor* blood, Gk *kreas* flesh] (bef. 12c) **1 :** not cooked **2 a (1) :** being in or nearly in the natural state **:** not processed or purified ⟨~ fibers⟩ ⟨~ sewage⟩ **(2) :** not diluted or blended ⟨~ spirits⟩ **b :** unprepared or imperfectly prepared for use **c :** not being in polished, finished, or processed form ⟨~ data⟩ ⟨a ~ draft of a thesis⟩ **3 a (1) :** having the surface abraded or chafed **(2) :** very irritated ⟨a ~ sore throat⟩ **b :** lacking covering **:** NAKED **4 a :** lacking experience or understanding **:** GREEN ⟨a ~ recruit⟩ **b (1) :** marked by absence of refinements **(2) :** VULGAR, COARSE **5 :** disagreeably damp or cold ***syn*** see RUDE — **raw·ly** *adv* — **raw·ness** *n*

[2]raw *n* (1823) **:** a raw place or state — **in the raw 1 :** in the natural or crude state ⟨life *in the raw*⟩ **2 :** NAKED ⟨slept *in the raw*⟩

raw·boned \'rò-'bōnd\ *adj* (1591) **1 :** having little flesh **:** GAUNT **2 :** having a coarse heavy frame that seems inadequately covered with flesh ***syn*** see LEAN

raw deal *n* (1920) **:** an instance of unfair treatment

[1]raw·hide \'rò-ˌhīd\ *n* (1829) **1 :** a whip of untanned hide **2 :** untanned cattle skin

[2]rawhide *vt* **raw·hid·ed; raw·hid·ing** (1858) **:** to whip or drive with or as if with a rawhide

ra·win·sonde \'rā-wən-ˌsänd\ *n* [*ra*dar + *win*d + radio*sonde*] (ca. 1946) **:** a radiosonde tracked by a radio direction-finding device to determine the velocity of winds aloft

raw material *n* (1796) **:** crude or processed material that can be converted by manufacture, processing, or combination into a new and useful product ⟨wheat . . . is *raw material* for the flour mill —C. A. Koepke⟩; *broadly* **:** something with a potential for improvement, development, or elaboration ⟨perplexities are often the *raw material* of discoveries —Agnes M. Clerke⟩

raw score *n* (ca. 1926) **:** an individual's actual achievement score (as on a test) unadjusted for relative position in the group tested

rax \'raks\ *vb* [ME (northern dial.) *raxen,* fr. OE *raxan;* akin to OE *reccan* to stretch — more at RACK] *chiefly Scot* (bef. 12c) **:** STRETCH

[1]ray \'rā\ *n* [ME *raye,* fr. MF *raie,* fr. L *raia*] (14c) **:** any of numerous elasmobranch fishes (order Hypotremata) having the body flattened dorsoventrally, the eyes on the upper surface, and a much-reduced caudal region

[2]ray *n* [ME, fr. MF *rai,* fr. L *radius* rod, ray; perh. akin to L *radix* root — more at ROOT] (14c) **1 a :** one of the lines of light that appear to radiate from a bright object **b :** a beam of radiant energy (as light) of small cross section **c (1) :** a stream of material particles traveling in the same line (as in radioactive phenomena) **(2) :** a single particle of such a stream **2 a :** light cast by rays **:** RADIANCE **b :** a moral or intellectual light **3 :** a thin line suggesting a ray: as **a :** any of a group of lines diverging from a common center **b :** HALF LINE **4 a :** one of the bony rods that extend and support the membrane in the fin of a fish **b :** one of the radiating divisions of the body of a radiate animal (as a starfish) **5 a :** a branch or flower stalk of an umbel **b (1) :** MEDULLARY RAY **(2) :** VASCULAR RAY **c :** RAY FLOWER 1 **6 :** PARTICLE, TRACE ⟨~ of hope⟩ — **rayed** \'rād\ *adj*

[3]ray *vi* (1598) **1 a :** to shine in or as if in rays **b :** to issue as rays **2 :** to extend like the radii of a circle **:** RADIATE **~** *vt* **1 :** to emit in rays **2 :** to furnish or mark with rays

ray flower *n* (1842) **1 :** one of the marginal flowers of the head in a composite plant (as the aster) that also has disk flowers **2 :** the entire head in a plant (as chicory) that lacks disk flowers

ray·less \'rā-ləs\ *adj* (1747) **:** having, admitting, or emitting no rays; *esp* **:** DARK — **ray·less·ness** *n*

rayless goldenrod *n* (1923) **:** any of several composite plants (*Haplopappus* or related genera) which lack ray flowers and some of which produce trembles in cattle

ray·on \'rā-ˌän\ *n* [irreg. fr. [2]*ray*] (1924) **1 :** any of a group of smooth textile fibers made in filament and staple form from cellulosic material by extrusion through minute holes **2 :** a rayon yarn, thread, or fabric

raze \'rāz\ *vt* **razed; raz·ing** [alter. of *rase*] (1547) **1 :** to destroy to the ground **:** DEMOLISH **2 a :** to scrape, cut, or shave off **b** *archaic* **:** ERASE — **raz·er** *n*

ra·zee \rā-'zē\ *n* [F (*vaisseau*) *rasé,* lit., cut-off ship] (1794) **:** a wooden ship with the upper deck cut away

ra·zor \'rā-zər\ *n* [ME *rasour,* fr. OF *raseor,* fr. *raser* to raze, shave — more at RASE] (13c) **:** a keen-edged cutting instrument for shaving or cutting hair

ra·zor·back \'rā-zər-ˌbak\ *n* (1849) **:** a thin-bodied long-legged half-wild mongrel hog chiefly of the southeastern U.S.

ra·zor–backed \ˌrā-zər-'bakt\ *or* **ra·zor·back** \'rā-zər-ˌbak\ *adj* (1829) **:** having a sharp narrow back ⟨a ~ horse⟩

ra·zor·bill \'rā-zər-ˌbil\ *n* (1674) **:** a No. Atlantic auk (*Alca torda*) with the plumage black above and white below and a compressed sharp-edged bill — called also *razor-billed auk*

razor clam *n* (1882) **:** any of numerous marine bivalve mollusks (family Solenidae) having a long narrow curved thin shell

[1]razz \'raz\ *n* [short for *razzberry* (sound of contempt), alter. of *raspberry*] (ca. 1919) **:** RASPBERRY 2

[2]razz *vt* (1921) **:** HECKLE, DERIDE ⟨the fans ~*ed* the visiting players⟩

raz·zle–daz·zle \ˌraz-əl-'daz-əl\ *n* [irreg. redupl. of *dazzle*] (1889) **1 :** a state of confusion or hilarity **2 :** a complex maneuver (as in sports) designed to confuse an opponent **3 :** a confusing or colorful often gaudy action or display — **razzle–dazzle** *adj*

razz·ma·tazz \ˌraz-mə-'taz\ *n* [prob. alter. of *razzle-dazzle*] (1942) **1 :** RAZZLE-DAZZLE 3 **2 :** DOUBLE-TALK 2 **3 :** VIM, ZING

RBI \ˌär-(ˌ)bē-'ī, 'rib-ē\ *n, pl* **RBIs** *or* **RBI** [*r*un *b*atted *i*n] (1948) **:** a run in baseball that is driven in by a batter; *also* **:** official credit to a batter for driving in a run ⟨led the league in ~*s*⟩

r color *n* (1937) **:** an acoustic effect of a simultaneously articulated \r\ imparted to a vowel by retroflexion or constriction of the tongue — **r–col·ored** \'är-ˌkəl-ərd\ *adj*

-rd *symbol* — used after the figure 3 to indicate the ordinal number *third* ⟨*3rd*⟩ ⟨*83rd*⟩

[1]re \'rā\ *n* [ML, fr. the syllable sung to this note in a medieval hymn to St. John the Baptist] (14c) **:** the 2d tone of the diatonic scale in solmization

[2]re \(')rā, (')rē\ *prep* [L, abl. of *res* thing — more at REAL] (1707) **:** with regard to **:** IN RE

re- *prefix* [ME, fr. OF, fr. L *re-, red-* back, again, against] **1 :** again **:** anew ⟨*re*tell⟩ **2 :** back **:** backward ⟨*re*call⟩

re·ac·cel·er·ate
re·ac·cept
re·ac·ces·sion
re·ac·cli·ma·tize
re·ac·cred·it
re·ac·cred·i·ta·tion
re·ac·quaint
re·ac·quire
re·ac·qui·si·tion
re·ac·ti·vate
re·ac·ti·va·tion
re·ad·dress
re·ad·just
re·ad·just·ment
re·ad·mis·sion
re·ad·mit
re·adopt
re·af·firm
re·af·fir·ma·tion
re·af·fix
re·al·lo·cate
re·al·lo·ca·tion
re·anal·y·sis
re·an·a·lyze
re·an·i·mate
re·an·i·ma·tion
re·an·nex
re·an·nex·ation
re·ap·pear
re·ap·pear·ance
re·ap·pli·ca·tion
re·ap·ply
re·ap·point
re·ap·point·ment
re·ap·prais·al
re·ap·praise
re·ap·pro·pri·ate
re·ap·prove
re·ar·gue
re·ar·gu·ment
re·arous·al
re·arouse
re·ar·range
re·ar·range·ment
re·ar·rest
re·as·cend
re·as·cent
re·as·sem·blage
re·as·sem·ble
re·as·sem·bly
re·as·sert
re·as·ser·tion
re·as·sess
re·as·sess·ment
re·as·sign
re·as·sign·ment
re·as·sume
re·at·tach
re·at·tach·ment
re·at·tain
re·at·tempt
re·at·tri·bute
re·at·tri·bu·tion
re·awak·en
re·bait
re·bal·ance
re·bap·tism
re·bap·tize
re·bid
re·bind
re·blend
re·bloom
re·board
re·body
re·boil
re·book
re·bore
re·bot·tle
re·buri·al
re·bury
re·buy
re·cal·cu·late
re·cal·cu·la·tion
re·cen·tral·iza·tion
re·cen·tri·fuge
re·cer·ti·fi·ca·tion
re·cer·ti·fy

re·chal·lenge
re·chan·nel
re·char·ter
re·check
re·cho·reo·graph
re·chris·ten
re·chro·mato·graph
re·chro·ma·tog·ra·phy
re·cir·cu·late
re·cir·cu·la·tion
re·clad
re·clas·si·fi·ca·tion
re·clas·si·fy
re·cock
re·cod·i·fi·ca·tion
re·cod·i·fy
re·col·o·ni·za·tion
re·col·o·nize
re·col·or
re·com·bine
re·com·mence
re·com·mence·ment
re·com·mis·sion
re·com·pi·la·tion
re·com·pile
re·com·pu·ta·tion
re·com·pute
re·con·ceive
re·con·cen·trate
re·con·cen·tra·tion
re·con·cep·tion
re·con·cep·tu·al·iza·tion
re·con·dense
re·con·fig·u·ra·tion
re·con·fig·ure
re·con·nect
re·con·nec·tion
re·con·quer
re·con·quest
re·con·se·crate
re·con·se·cra·tion
re·con·tact
re·con·tam·i·nate
re·con·tam·i·na·tion
re·con·tour
re·con·vene
re·con·vey
re·con·vict
re·con·vic·tion
re·con·vince
re·copy
re·cork
re·cross
re·cul·ti·vate
re·cut
re·date
re·ded·i·cate
re·ded·i·ca·tion
re·de·fect
re·de·liv·er
re·de·liv·ery
re·de·pos·it
re·de·ter·mi·na·tion
re·de·ter·mine
re·di·ges·tion
re·dis·cov·er
re·dis·cov·ery
re·dis·cuss
re·dis·pose
re·dis·po·si·tion
re·dis·solve
re·dis·till
re·dis·til·la·tion
re·di·vide
re·di·vi·sion
re·don
re·draft
re·draw
re·dream
re·drill
re·dub
re·el·i·gi·bil·i·ty
re·el·i·gi·ble
re·emerge
re·emer·gence
re·emission
re·emit
re·em·pha·sis
re·em·pha·size
re·en·dow
re·en·er·gize
re·en·gage
re·en·gi·neer
re·en·grave
re·en·list
re·en·list·ment
re·en·roll
re·en·throne
re·equip
re·equip·ment
re·erect
re·es·ca·late
re·es·ca·la·tion
re·es·tab·lish

re·es·tab·lish·ment
re·es·ti·mate
re·eval·u·ate
re·eval·u·a·tion
re·ex·am·i·na·tion
re·ex·am·ine
re·ex·pe·ri·ence
re·ex·plore
re·ex·port
re·ex·por·ta·tion
re·face
re·feed
re·feel
re·fence
re·fight
re·fig·ure
re·file
re·find
re·fix
re·float
re·fold
re·for·mat
re·for·mu·late
re·for·mu·la·tion
re·for·ti·fi·ca·tion
re·for·ti·fy
re·found
re·foun·da·tion
re·frame
re·freeze
re·fry
re·fur·nish
re·gain
re·gath·er
re·gear
re·gild
re·give
re·glaze
re·grade
re·graft
re·grant
re·green
re·grind
re·groom
re·groove
re·growth
re·han·dle
re·hang
re·heat
re·hinge
re·hire
re·hos·pi·tal·iza·tion
re·hos·pi·tal·ize
re·hu·man·ize
re·hyp·no·tize
re·iden·ti·fy
re·ig·nite
re·im·age
re·imag·ine
re·im·merse
re·im·plan·ta·tion
re·im·port
re·im·por·ta·tion
re·im·pose
re·im·po·si·tion
re·in·cor·po·rate
re·in·cor·po·ra·tion
re·in·dict
re·in·dict·ment
re·in·dus·tri·al·iza·tion
re·in·dus·tri·al·ize
re·in·fes·ta·tion
re·in·hab·it
re·ini·tiate
re·in·ject
re·in·jec·tion
re·in·jure
re·in·ju·ry
re·ink
re·in·ner·vate
re·in·ner·va·tion
re·in·oc·u·late
re·in·oc·u·la·tion
re·in·sert
re·in·ser·tion
re·in·spect
re·in·spec·tion
re·in·stall
re·in·stal·la·tion
re·in·sti·tute
re·in·sti·tu·tion·al·iza·tion
re·in·ter
re·in·ter·view
re·in·tro·duce
re·in·tro·duc·tion
re·in·vade
re·in·va·sion
re·in·ves·ti·gate
re·in·ves·ti·ga·tion
re·in·vig·o·rate
re·in·vig·o·ra·tion
re·in·vig·o·ra·tor
re·jack·et
re·judge

re·jug·gle
re·key
re·key·board
re·kin·dle
re·knit
re·la·bel
re·lac·quer
re·land·scape
re·launch
re·learn
re·lend
re·li·cense
re·li·cen·sure
re·light
re·link
re·liq·ue·fy
re·load
re·lock
re·lu·bri·cate
re·lu·bri·ca·tion
re·mar·ket
re·mar·riage
re·mar·ry
re·mate
re·ma·te·ri·al·ize
re·mea·sure
re·mea·sure·ment
re·meet
re·melt
re·merge
re·mi·gra·tion
re·mil·i·ta·ri·za·tion
re·mil·i·ta·rize
re·mix
re·mo·bi·li·za·tion
re·mo·bi·lize
re·moist·en
re·mold
re·mon·e·ti·za·tion
re·mon·e·tize
re·mo·ti·vate
re·mo·ti·va·tion
re·my·thol·o·gize
re·nail
re·name
re·na·tion·al·iza·tion
re·na·tion·al·ize
re·nest
re·ob·serve
re·oc·cu·pa·tion
re·oc·cu·py
re·oc·cur
re·oc·cur·rence
re·oil
re·op·er·ate
re·op·er·a·tion
re·or·ches·trate
re·or·ches·tra·tion
re·ori·ent
re·ori·en·tate
re·ori·en·ta·tion
re·out·fit
re·ox·i·da·tion
re·ox·i·dize
re·pack
re·paint
re·pat·tern
re·pave
re·peg
re·peo·ple
re·perk
re·pho·to·graph
re·phrase
re·plan
re·plate
re·pledge
re·plot
re·plumb
re·pol·ish
re·poll
re·pop·u·lar·ize
re·pop·u·late
re·pop·u·la·tion
re·pot
re·pres·sur·ize
re·price
re·pro·vi·sion
re·pump
re·punc·tu·a·tion
re·pur·chase
re·pu·ri·fy
re·rack
re·raise
re·read
re·re·cord
re·reg·is·ter
re·reg·is·tra·tion
re·re·mind
re·re·peat
re·re·view
re·roof
re·route
re·sail
re·sam·ple

re·saw
re·sched·ule
re·school
re·score
re·screen
re·sculpt
re·seal
re·season
re·seat
re·se·cure
re·see
re·seg·re·gate
re·seg·re·ga·tion
re·sell
re·sell·er
re·sen·si·tize
re·sen·tence
re·ser·vice
re·set·tle
re·set·tle·ment
re·sew
re·shave
re·shin·gle
re·shoe
re·shoot
re·show
re·sight
re·site
re·size
re·slate
re·soak
re·so·cial·iza·tion
re·so·cial·ize
re·sod
re·sol·der

re·so·lid·i·fi·ca·tion
re·so·lid·i·fy
re·sow
re·spec·i·fi·ca·tion
re·spec·i·fy
re·spir·i·tu·al·ize
re·spot
re·spray
re·sprout
re·sta·bi·lize
re·stack
re·stage
re·stamp
re·stan·dard·iza·tion
re·stan·dard·ize
re·start
re·stim·u·late
re·stim·u·la·tion
re·stock
re·strength·en
re·stress
re·stuff
re·style
re·sub·mis·sion
re·sub·mit
re·sum·mon
re·sup·ply
re·sur·vey
re·sus·pend
re·syn·the·sis
re·syn·the·size
re·sys·tem·atize
re·tack·le
re·tag
re·tar·get

re·taste
re·teach
re·team
re·tell
re·tex·ture
re·thread
re·tie
re·tight·en
re·time
re·trans·fer
re·trans·form
re·trans·for·ma·tion
re·trans·mis·sion
re·trans·mit
re·tune
re·type
re·up·hol·ster
re·uti·li·za·tion
re·uti·lize
re·vac·ci·nate
re·vac·ci·na·tion
re·val·i·date
re·val·i·da·tion
re·val·o·ri·za·tion
re·val·o·rize
re·vict·ual
re·vi·su·al·iza·tion
re·vote
re·warm
re·wash
re·weave
re·weigh
re·wet
re·wire
re·wrap

'**re** \ (ə)r\ *vb* : ARE ⟨you're right⟩
re·ab·sorb \ˌrē-əb-'sȯ(ə)rb, -'zȯ(ə)rb\ *vt* (1768) : to take up (something previously secreted or emitted) ⟨sugars ∼ed in the kidney⟩; *also* : RESORB 2

¹**reach** \'rēch\ *vb* [ME *rechen*, fr. OE *rǣcan*; akin to OHG *reichen* to reach, Lith *raižytis* to stretch oneself repeatedly] *vt* (bef. 12c) **1 a** : to stretch out : EXTEND **b** : THRUST **2 a** : to touch or grasp by extending a part of the body (as a hand) or an object ⟨couldn't ∼ the apple⟩ **b** : to pick up and draw toward one : TAKE **c** (1) : to extend to ⟨the shadow ∼ed the wall⟩ (2) : to get up to or as far as : come to ⟨your letter ∼ed me yesterday⟩ ⟨his voice ∼ed the last rows⟩ ⟨they hoped to ∼ an agreement⟩ **d** (1) : ENCOMPASS (2) : to make an impression on (3) : to communicate with **3** : to hand over : PASS ∼ *vi* **1 a** : to make a stretch with or as if with one's hand **b** : to strain after something **2 a** : PROJECT, EXTEND ⟨his land ∼es to the river⟩ **b** : to arrive at or come to something ⟨as far as the eye could ∼⟩ **3** : to sail on a reach — **reach·able** \'rē-chə-bəl\ *adj* — **reach·er** *n*

²**reach** *n* (1536) **1** : a continuous stretch or expanse; *esp* : a straight portion of a stream or river **2 a** (1) : the action or an act of reaching (2) : an individual part of a progression or journey **b** : the distance or extent of reaching or of ability to reach **c** : COMPREHENSION, RANGE **3** : a bearing shaft or coupling pole; *esp* : the rod joining the hind axle to the forward bolster of a wagon **4** : the tack sailed by a ship with the wind coming just forward of the beam or with the wind directly abeam or abaft the beam **5** : ECHELON, LEVEL — usu. used in pl. ⟨the higher ∼es of academic life⟩

reach–me–down \'rēch-mē-ˌdaun\ *adj or n, chiefly Brit* (1862) : HAND-ME-DOWN

re·act \rē-'akt\ *vb* [NL *reactus*, pp. of *reagere*, fr. L *re-* + *agere* to act — more at AGENT] *vi* (1644) **1** : to exert a reciprocal or counteracting force or influence — often used with *on* or *upon* **2** : to respond to a stimulus **3** : to act in opposition to a force or influence — usu. used with *against* **4** : to move or tend in a reverse direction **5** : to undergo chemical reaction ∼ *vt* : to cause to react

re·ac·tance \rē-'ak-tən(t)s\ *n* (1893) : the part of the impedance of an alternating-current circuit that is due to capacitance or inductance or both and that is expressed in ohms

re·ac·tant \-tənt\ *n* (ca. 1920) : a substance that enters into and is altered in the course of a chemical reaction

re·ac·tion \rē-'ak-shən\ *n* (1611) **1 a** : the act or process or an instance of reacting **b** : resistance or opposition to a force, influence, or movement, *esp* : tendency toward a former and usu. outmoded political or social order or policy **2** : bodily response to or activity aroused by a stimulus: **a** : an action induced by vital resistance to another action; *esp* : the response of tissues to a foreign substance (as an antigen or infective agent) **b** : depression or exhaustion due to excessive exertion or stimulation : **c** : heightened activity and overaction succeeding depression or shock **d** : a mental or emotional disorder forming an individual's response to his life situation **3** : the force that a body subjected to the action of a force from another body exerts in the opposite direction **4 a** (1) : chemical transformation or change : the interaction of chemical entities (2) : the state resulting from such a reaction : a process involving change in atomic nuclei

¹**re·ac·tion·ary** \rē-'ak-shə-ˌner-ē\ *adj* (1840) : relating to, marked by, or favoring reaction; *esp* : ultraconservative in politics — **re·ac·tion·ary·ism** \-ˌiz-əm\ *n*

²**reactionary** *n, pl* **-ar·ies** (1858) : a reactionary person

reaction engine *n* (1868) : an engine (as a jet engine) that develops thrust by expelling a jet of fluid or a stream of particles

re·ac·tive \rē-'ak-tiv\ *adj* (1794) **1** : of, relating to, or marked by reaction or reactance **2 a** : readily responsive to a stimulus **b** : occur-

---

\ə\ abut \ᵊ\ kitten, F table \ər\ further \a\ ash \ā\ ace \ä\ cot, cart
\aú\ out \ch\ chin \e\ bet \ē\ easy \g\ go \i\ hit \ī\ ice \j\ job
\ŋ\ sing \ō\ go \ȯ\ law \ȯi\ boy \th\ thin \th̸\ the \ü\ loot \ú\ foot
\y\ yet \zh\ vision \à, k̲, ⁿ, œ, œ̄, ᵫ, ᵫ̄, ᵊ\ *see* Guide to Pronunciation

ring as a result of stress or emotional upset ⟨~ depression⟩ — **re·ac·tive·ly** *adv* — **re·ac·tive·ness** *n* — **re·ac·tiv·i·ty** \(,)rē-,ak-'tiv-ət-ē\ *n*

re·ac·tor \rē-'ak-tər\ *n* (ca. 1904) **1 :** one that reacts **2 :** a device (as a coil, winding, or conductor of small resistance) used to introduce reactance into an alternating-current circuit **3 a :** a vat for an industrial chemical reaction **b :** a device for the controlled release of nuclear energy (as for producing heat)

¹read \'rēd\ *vb* **read** \'red\; **read·ing** \'rēd-iŋ\ [ME *reden* to advise, interpret, read, fr. OE *rǣdan;* akin to OHG *rātan* to advise, L *reri* to calculate — more at REASON] *vt* (bef. 12c) **1 a** (1) **:** to receive or take in the sense of (as letters or symbols) esp. by sight or touch (2) **:** to study the movements of (as lips) with mental formulation of the communication expressed (3) **:** to utter aloud the printed or written words of ⟨~ them a story⟩ **b :** to learn from what one has seen or found in writing or printing **c :** to deliver aloud by or as if by reading; *specif* **:** to utter interpretively **d** (1) **:** to become acquainted with or look over the contents of (as a book) **:** PERUSE (2) **:** to make a study of ⟨~ law⟩ (3) **:** to read the works of **e :** to check (as copy or proof) for errors **f** (1) **:** to receive and understand (a voice message) by radio (2) **:** UNDERSTAND, COMPREHEND **2 a :** to interpret the meaning or significance of ⟨~ palms⟩ **b :** FORETELL, PREDICT ⟨able to ~ his fortune⟩ **3 a :** to learn the nature of by observing outward expression or signs ⟨~*s* him like a book⟩ **b :** to note the action of in order to anticipate what will happen ⟨a good canoeist ~*s* the rapids⟩; *also* **:** to anticipate by observation ⟨the quarterback was able to ~ the blitz⟩ **4 a :** to attribute a meaning to (as something read) **:** INTERPRET ⟨how do you ~ this passage⟩ **b :** to attribute (a meaning) to something read or considered ⟨~ a nonexistent meaning into her words⟩ **5 :** to use as a substitute for or in preference to another word or phrase in a particular passage, text, or version ⟨~ *hurry* for *harry*⟩ **6 :** INDICATE ⟨the thermometer ~*s* zero⟩ **7 :** to interpret (a musical work) in performance **8 a :** to sense the meaning of (information) in recorded and coded form (as in storage) **:** acquire (information) from storage — used of a computer or data processor **b :** to read the coded information on (as tape or a punch card) **c :** to cause to be read and transferred to storage ⟨~ the contents of a punch card into a core⟩ ~ *vi* **1 a :** to perform the act of reading words **:** read something **b** (1) **:** to learn something by reading (2) **:** to pursue a course of study **2 a :** to yield a particular meaning or impression when read **b :** to be readable in a particular manner or to a particular degree ⟨this book ~*s* smoothly⟩ **3 :** to consist of specific words, phrases, or other similar elements ⟨a passage that ~*s* differently in older versions⟩ — **read between the lines :** to understand more than is directly stated — **read the riot act 1 :** to order a mob to disperse **2 a :** to order or warn to cease something **b :** to protest vehemently **c :** to reprimand severely

²read \'red\ *adj* (1586) **:** instructed by or informed through reading

³read \'rēd\ *n* (1825) **1** *chiefly Brit* **:** a period of reading ⟨it was a night . . . for a ~ and a long sleep —William Sansom⟩ **2 :** something (as a book) that is read ⟨a novel that's a good ~⟩ **3 :** the action or an instance of reading

read·able \'rēd-ə-bəl\ *adj* (1570) **:** able to be read easily: as **a :** LEGIBLE **b :** interesting to read — **read·abil·i·ty** \,rēd-ə-'bil-ət-ē\ *n* — **read·able·ness** \'rēd-ə-bəl-nəs\ *n* — **read·ably** \-blē\ *adv*

read·er \'rēd-ər\ *n* (bef. 12c) **1 a :** one that reads **b :** one appointed to read to others: as (1) **:** LECTOR (2) **:** one chosen to read aloud selected material in a Christian Science church or society **c** (1) **:** PROOFREADER (2) **:** one who evaluates manuscripts (3) **:** one who reads periodical literature to discover items of special interest or value **d :** an employee who reads and records the indications of meters **e :** a teacher's assistant who reads and marks student papers **2** *Brit* **:** one who reads lectures or expounds subjects to students **3 a :** a device for projecting a readable image of a transparency **b :** a unit that scans material recorded (as on punch cards) for storage or computation **4 a :** a book for instruction and practice esp. in reading **b :** ANTHOLOGY

read·er·ship \-,ship\ *n* (1719) **1 a :** the quality or state of being a reader **b :** the office or position of a reader **2 :** the mass or a particular group of readers ⟨a magazine's ~⟩

readi·ly \'red-ᵊl-ē\ *adv* (14c) **:** in a ready manner: as **a :** without hesitating **:** WILLINGLY ⟨~ accepted advice⟩ **b :** without much difficulty **:** EASILY ⟨for reasons that anyone could ~ understand⟩

read·ing \'rēd-iŋ\ *n* (bef. 12c) **1 :** the act of reading **2 a :** material read or for reading **b :** extent of material read **3 a :** a particular version **b :** data indicated by an instrument **4 a :** a particular interpretation of something (as a law) **b :** a particular performance of something (as a musical work) **5 :** an indication of a certain state of affairs ⟨a study to get some ~ of shoppers' preferences⟩

reading desk *n* (1703) **:** a desk to support a book in a convenient position for a standing reader

read–on·ly memory \'rēd-'ōn-lē-\ *n* (1961) **:** a usu. small computer memory that contains special-purpose information (as a program) which cannot be altered — abbr. *ROM;* compare RANDOM-ACCESS MEMORY

read·out \'rēd-,au̇t\ *n* (1652) **1 :** the process of reading **2 a :** the process of removing information from an automatic device (as an electronic computer) and displaying it in an understandable form **b :** the information removed from such a device and displayed or recorded (as by magnetic tape or printing device) **c :** an electronic device that presents information in visual form **3 :** the radio transmission of data or pictures from a space vehicle either immediately upon acquisition or later by means of playback of a tape recording

read out \(')rēd-'au̇t\ *vt* (1600) **1 a :** to read aloud **b :** to produce a readout of **2 :** to expel from an organization or group

¹ready \'red-ē\ *adj* **readi·er; -est** [ME *redy;* akin to OHG *reiti* ready, Goth *garaiths* arrayed, Gk *arariskein* to fit — more at ARM] (13c) **1 a :** prepared mentally or physically for some experience or action **b :** prepared for immediate use ⟨dinner is ~⟩ **2 a** (1) **:** willingly disposed **:** INCLINED ⟨~ to agree to his proposal⟩ (2) **:** likely to do something indicated ⟨a house that looks ~ to collapse⟩ **b :** spontaneously prompt **3 :** notably dexterous, adroit, or skilled ⟨a ~ wit⟩ **4 :** immediately available ⟨had little ~ cash⟩ ***syn*** see QUICK — **readi·ness** *n*

²ready *vt* **read·ied; ready·ing** (14c) **:** to make ready

³ready *n* (1837) **:** the state of being ready; *esp* **:** the state of preparation of a small arm for immediate aiming and firing ⟨kept their guns at the ~⟩

ready box *n* (1942) **:** a box placed near a gun (as on a ship) to hold ammunition kept ready for immediate use

¹ready–made \,red-ē-'mād\ *adj* (14c) **1 :** made beforehand esp. for general sale ⟨~ suits⟩ **2 :** lacking originality or individuality **3 :** readily available ⟨her illness provided a ~ excuse⟩

²ready–made *n* (1882) **1 :** something (as a garment) that is ready-made **2** *usu* **readymade :** an artifact (as a comb or a pair of ice tongs) selected and displayed as a work of art

ready room *n* (1941) **:** a room in which pilots or astronauts are briefed and await orders

ready–to–wear \,red-ēt-ə-'wa(ə)r, -'we(ə)r\ *adj, of clothing* (1895) **:** READY-MADE; *also* **:** dealing in ready-made clothes ⟨~ stores⟩

ready–wit·ted \,red-ē-'wit-əd\ *adj* (1581) **:** QUICK-WITTED

re·af·for·es·ta·tion \,rē-ə-,fȯr-ə-'stā-shən, -,fär-\ *n, chiefly Brit* (1884) **:** REFORESTATION — **re·af·for·est** \-'fȯr-əst, -'fär-\ *vt, chiefly Brit*

re·agent \rē-'ā-jənt\ *n* [NL *reagent-, reagens,* prp. of *reagere* to react — more at REACT] (1797) **:** a substance used (as in detecting or measuring a component, in preparing a product, or in developing photographs) because of its chemical or biological activity

re·ag·gre·gate \(')rē-'ag-ri-,gāt\ *vt* (1849) **:** to cause to re-form into an aggregate or a whole — **re·ag·gre·gate** \-gət\ *n* — **re·ag·gre·ga·tion** \(,)rē-,ag-ri-'gā-shən\ *n*

re·agin \rē-'ā-jən, -gən\ *n* [ISV, fr. *reagent*] (ca. 1911) **1 :** a substance in the blood of persons with syphilis responsible for positive serological reactions for syphilis **2 :** an antibody in the blood of individuals with some forms of allergy possessing the power of passively sensitizing the skin of normal individuals — **re·agin·ic** \,rē-ə-'jin-ik, -'gin-\ *adj*

¹re·al \'rē(-ə)l, 'ri(-ə)l\ *adj* [ME, real, relating to things (in law), fr. MF, fr. ML & LL; ML *realis* relating to things (in law), fr. LL, real, fr. L *res* thing, fact; akin to Skt *rai* property] (15c) **1 :** of or relating to fixed, permanent, or immovable things (as lands or tenements) **2 a :** not artificial, fraudulent, illusory, or apparent **:** GENUINE ⟨~ gold⟩; *also* **:** being precisely what the name implies ⟨a ~ professional⟩ **b** (1) **:** occurring in fact ⟨a story of ~ life⟩ (2) **:** of or relating to practical or everyday concerns or activities ⟨left school to live in the ~ world⟩ **c :** having objective independent existence ⟨unable to believe that what he saw was ~⟩ **d :** FUNDAMENTAL, ESSENTIAL **e** (1) **:** belonging to or having elements or components that belong to the set of real numbers ⟨the ~ roots of an equation⟩ ⟨a ~ matrix⟩ (2) **:** concerned with or containing real numbers ⟨~ analysis⟩ (3) **:** REAL-VALUED ⟨~ variable⟩ **f :** measured by purchasing power ⟨~ income⟩ ⟨~ dollars⟩ **g :** COMPLETE, UTTER ⟨considered him a ~ idiot⟩ — **re·al·ness** *n* — **for real 1 :** in earnest **:** SERIOUSLY ⟨they were fighting *for real*⟩ **2 :** GENUINE ⟨couldn't believe the threats were *for real*⟩

²real *n* (1626) **:** a real thing; *esp* **:** a mathematical real quantity

³real *adv* (1718) **:** VERY ⟨he was ~ cool —H. M. McLuhan⟩

usage Most handbooks consider the adverb *real* to be informal and more suitable to speech than writing. Our evidence bears out these observations.

⁴re·al \rā-'äl\ *n, pl* **reals** *or* **re·ales** \-'äl-(,)ās\ [Sp, fr. *real* royal, fr. L *regalis* — more at ROYAL] (1555) **:** a former monetary unit and coin of Spain and its possessions

⁵re·al \rā-'äl\ *n, pl* **reals** *or* **reis** \'rās(h), 'rāz(h)\ [Pg, fr. *real* royal, fr. L *regalis*] (1951) **:** a former monetary unit and coin of Portugal or Brazil

real estate *n* (1666) **:** property in buildings and land

real focus *n* (1909) **:** a point at which rays (as of light) converge or from which they diverge

re·al·gar \rē-'al-,gär, -gər\ *n* [ME, fr. ML, fr. Catal, fr. Ar *rahj al-ghār* powder of the mine] (15c) **:** an orange-red mineral consisting of arsenic sulfide and having a resinous luster

re·alia \rē-'al-ē-ə, -'ā-lē-\ *n pl* [LL, neut. pl. of *realis* real] (1937) **:** objects or activities used to relate classroom teaching to the real life esp. of peoples studied

re·align \,rē-ə-'līn\ *vt* (1899) **:** to align again; *esp* **:** to reorganize or make new groupings of — **re·align·ment** \-mənt\ *n*

real image *n* (1899) **:** an optical image formed of real foci

re·al·ism \'rē-ə-,liz-əm, 'ri-ə-\ *n* (1817) **1 :** concern for fact or reality and rejection of the impractical and visionary **2 a :** a doctrine that universals exist outside the mind; *specif* **:** the conception that an abstract term names an independent and unitary reality **b :** the conception that objects of sense perception or cognition exist independently of the mind — compare NOMINALISM **3 :** fidelity in art and literature to nature or to real life and to accurate representation without idealization — **re·al·ist** \-ləst\ *adj or n* — **re·al·is·tic** \,rē-ə-'lis-tik, ,ri-ə-\ *adj* — **re·al·is·ti·cal·ly** \-ti-k(ə-)lē\ *adv*

re·al·i·ty \rē-'al-ət-ē\ *n, pl* **-ties** (1550) **1 :** the quality or state of being real **2 a** (1) **:** a real event, entity, or state of affairs ⟨his dream became a ~⟩ (2) **:** the totality of real things and events ⟨trying to escape from ~⟩ **b :** something that is neither derivative nor dependent but exists necessarily — **in reality :** in actual fact

re·al·iza·tion \,rē-ə-lə-'zā-shən, ,ri-ə-\ *n* (1611) **1 :** the action of realizing **:** the state of being realized **2 :** something realized

re·al·ize \'rē-ə-,līz, 'ri-ə-\ *vt* **-ized; -iz·ing** [F *réaliser,* fr. MF *realiser,* fr. *real* real] (1611) **1 a :** to bring into concrete existence **:** ACCOMPLISH ⟨finally *realized* her goal⟩ **b :** to cause to seem real **:** make appear real ⟨a book in which the characters are carefully *realized*⟩ **2 a :** to convert into actual money ⟨*realized* assets⟩ **b :** to bring or get by sale, investment, or effort **:** GAIN **3 :** to conceive vividly as real **:** be fully aware of ⟨he did not ~ the risk he was taking⟩ ***syn*** see THINK — **re·al·iz·able** \-,lī-zə-bəl\ *adj* — **re·al·iz·er** *n*

real–life *adj* (1938) **:** existing or occurring in reality **:** drawn from or drawing on actual events or situations ⟨~ problems⟩ ⟨~ drama⟩

re·al·ly \'rē-(ə-)lē, 'ri(-ə)l-ē\ *adv* (15c) **1 a :** in reality **:** ACTUALLY ⟨~ didn't know the answer⟩ **b :** TRULY, UNQUESTIONABLY ⟨~ beautiful diamonds⟩ **2 :** INDEED 1 ⟨~, you're being ridiculous⟩

realm \'relm\ *n* [ME *realme,* fr. OF, modif. of L *regimen* rule — more at REGIMEN] (13c) **1 :** KINGDOM 2 **2 :** SPHERE, DOMAIN ⟨within the ~ of possibility⟩ **3 :** a primary marine or terrestrial biogeographic division of the earth's surface

real number *n* (1909) **:** one of the numbers that have no imaginary parts and comprise the rationals and the irrationals

re·al·po·li·tik \rā-'äl-,pō-li-,tēk\ *n* [G, fr. *real* practical + *politik* politics] (1917) **:** politics based on practical and material factors rather than on theoretical or ethical objectives

real presence *n, often cap R&P* (1559) **:** the doctrine that Christ is actually present in the Eucharist

real time *n* (1953) **:** the actual time during which something takes place ⟨the computer may partly analyze the data in *real time* (as it comes in) —R. H. March⟩ — **real–time** *adj*

Re·al·tor \ˈrē(-ə)l-tər, -ˌtȯ(ə)r, ÷ˈrē-lət-ər *also* rē-ˈal-tər\ *collective mark* — used for a real estate agent who is a member of the National Association of Realtors

re·al·ty \ˈrē(-ə)l-tē\ *n* [*real* + *-ty* (as in *property*)] (1670) **:** REAL ESTATE

re·al–val·ued \ˌrē-əl-ˈval-(ˌ)yüd, -yəd\ *adj* (1965) **:** taking on only real numbers for values ⟨a ~ function⟩

1**ream** \ˈrēm\ *n* [ME *reme,* fr. MF *raime,* fr. Ar *rizmah,* lit., bundle] (14c) **1 :** a quantity of paper being 20 quires or variously 480, 500, or 516 sheets **2 :** a great amount — usu. used in pl.

2**ream** *vt* [perh. fr. (assumed) ME dial. *remen* to open up, fr. OE dial. *rēman;* akin to OE *rȳman* to open up, *rūm* roomy — more at ROOM] (1815) **1 a :** to widen the opening of (a hole) **:** COUNTERSINK **b** (1) **:** to enlarge or dress out (a hole) with a reamer (2) **:** to enlarge the bore of (as a gun) in this way **c :** to remove by reaming **2 a :** to press out with a reamer **b :** to press out the juice of (as an orange) with a reamer **3 :** CHEAT, VICTIMIZE

ream·er \ˈrē-mər\ *n* (1825) **:** one that reams: as **a :** a rotating finishing tool with cutting edges used to enlarge or shape a hole **b :** a fruit juice extractor with a ridged and pointed center rising from a shallow dish

reap \ˈrēp\ *vb* [ME *repen,* fr. OE *repan*] *vt* (bef. 12c) **1 a** (1) **:** to cut with a sickle, scythe, or reaping machine (2) **:** to clear of a crop by reaping **b :** to gather by reaping **:** HARVEST **2 :** OBTAIN, WIN ~ *vi* **:** to reap something

reap·er \ˈrē-pər\ *n* (bef. 12c) **:** one that reaps; *esp* **:** any of various machines for reaping grain

reap·hook \ˈrēp-ˌhu̇k\ *n* (1591) **:** a hand implement with a hook-shaped blade used in reaping

re·ap·por·tion \ˌrē-ə-ˈpōr-shən, -ˈpȯr-\ *vt* (ca. 1828) **:** to apportion (as a house of representatives) anew ~ *vi* **:** to make a new apportionment — **re·ap·por·tion·ment** \-shən-mənt\ *n*

1**rear** \ˈri(ə)r, *vt4 & vi2 are also* ˈra(ə)r *or* ˈre(ə)r\ *vb* [ME *reren,* fr. OE *rǣran;* akin to ON *reisa* to raise, OE *rīsan* to rise] *vt* (bef. 12c) **1 :** to erect by building **:** CONSTRUCT **2 :** to raise upright **3 a** (1) **:** to breed and raise (an animal) for use or market (2) **:** BRING UP 1 **b :** to cause (as plants) to grow **4 :** to cause (a horse) to rise up on the hind legs ~ *vi* **1 :** to rise high **2** *of a horse* **:** to rise up on the hind legs *syn* see LIFT — **rear·er** *n*

2**rear** \ˈri(ə)r\ *n* [prob. fr. *rear* (in such terms as *rear guard*)] (1600) **1 :** the back part of something: as **a :** the unit (as of an army) or area farthest from the enemy **b :** the part of something located opposite its front ⟨the ~ of a house⟩ **c :** BUTTOCKS **2 :** the space or position at the back ⟨moved to the ~⟩

3**rear** \ˈri(ə)r\ *adj* (1600) **:** being at the back

4**rear** \ˈri(ə)r\ *adv* (1934) **:** toward or from the rear — usu. used in combination ⟨a *rear*-driven car⟩

rear admiral *n* (1589) **:** a commissioned officer in the navy who ranks above a commodore and in the coast guard who ranks above a captain and whose insignia is two stars

rear echelon *n* (ca. 1934) **:** an element of a military headquarters or unit located at a considerable distance from the front and concerned esp. with administrative and supply duties

rear end *n* (ca. 1930) **:** BUTTOCKS

rear·guard \ˈri(ə)r-ˌgärd\ *adj* (1898) **:** of or relating to resistance esp. to sweeping social forces ⟨fought a ~ action against automation⟩

rear guard \-ˈgärd, -ˌgärd\ *n* [ME *reregarde,* fr. MF, fr. OF, fr. *rere* backward, behind (fr. L *retro*) + *garde* guard — more at RETRO-] (1659) **:** a military detachment detailed to bring up and protect the rear of a main body or force

re·arm \(ˈ)rē-ˈärm\ *vt* (1871) **:** to arm (as a nation or a military force) again with new or better weapons ~ *vi* **:** to become armed again — **re·ar·ma·ment** \-ˈär-mə-mənt\ *n*

rear·most \ˈri(ə)r-ˌmōst\ *adj* (1718) **:** farthest in the rear **:** LAST

rear·view mirror \ˌri(ə)r-ˌvyü-\ *n* (1926) **:** a mirror (as in an automobile) that gives a view of the area behind a vehicle

1**rear·ward** \ˈri(ə)r-ˌwȯrd\ *n* [ME *rerewarde,* fr. AF; akin to OF *reregarde* rear guard] (14c) **:** REAR; *esp* **:** the rear division (as of an army)

2**rear·ward** \-wərd\ *adj* [2*rear* + *-ward*] (1598) **1 :** located at, near, or toward the rear **2 :** directed toward the rear

3**rear·ward** \-wərd\ *also* **rear·wards** \-wərdz\ *adv* (1625) **:** at, near, or toward the rear **:** BACKWARD

1**rea·son** \ˈrēz-ᵊn\ *n* [ME *resoun,* fr. OF *raison,* fr. L *ration-, ratio* reason, computation; akin to Goth *rathjo* account, advice, L *reri* to calculate, think, Gk *arariskein* to fit — more at ARM] (13c) **1 a :** a statement offered in explanation or justification ⟨gave ~*s* that were quite satisfactory⟩ **b :** a rational ground or motive ⟨a good ~ to act soon⟩ **c :** a sufficient ground of explanation or of logical defense; *esp* **:** something (as a principle or law) that supports a conclusion or explains a fact ⟨outlined the ~*s* behind his client's action⟩ **d :** the thing that makes some fact intelligible **:** CAUSE ⟨wanted to know the ~ for earthquakes⟩ **2 a** (1) **:** the power of comprehending, inferring, or thinking esp. in orderly rational ways **:** INTELLIGENCE (2) **:** proper exercise of the mind (3) **:** SANITY **b :** the sum of the intellectual powers **3** *archaic* **:** treatment that affords satisfaction *syn* see CAUSE — **in reason :** RIGHTLY, JUSTIFIABLY — **within reason :** within reasonable limits — **with reason :** with good cause

2**reason** *vb* **rea·soned; rea·son·ing** \ˈrēz-niŋ, -ᵊn-iŋ\ *vi* (14c) **1 a** *obs* **:** to take part in conversation, discussion, or argument **b :** to talk with another so as to influence his actions or opinions ⟨can't ~ with her⟩ **2 :** to use the faculty of reason so as to arrive at conclusions ~ *vt* **1** *archaic* **:** to justify or support with reasons **2 :** to persuade or influence by the use of reason **3 :** to discover, formulate, or conclude by the use of reason ⟨a carefully ~*ed* analysis⟩ *syn* see THINK — **rea·son·er** \-nər, -ᵊn-ər\ *n*

rea·son·able \ˈrēz-nə-bəl, -ᵊn-ə-bəl\ *adj* (14c) **1 a :** not conflicting with reason ⟨a ~ theory⟩ **b :** not extreme or excessive ⟨~ requests⟩ **c :** MODERATE, FAIR ⟨a ~ chance⟩ ⟨a ~ price⟩ **d :** INEXPENSIVE **2 a :** having the faculty of reason **b :** possessing sound judgment — **rea·son·abil·i·ty** \ˌrēz-nə-ˈbil-ət-ē, -ᵊn-ə-\ *n* — **rea·son·able·ness** \ˈrēz-nə-bəl-nəs, -ᵊn-ə-\ *n* — **rea·son·ably** \-blē\ *adv*

rea·son·ing *n* (14c) **1 :** the use of reason; *esp* **:** the drawing of inferences or conclusions through the use of reason **2 :** an instance of the use of reason **:** ARGUMENT

rea·son·less \ˈrēz-ᵊn-ləs\ *adj* (14c) **1 :** not having the faculty of reason ⟨a ~ brute⟩ **2 :** not reasoned **:** SENSELESS ⟨~ hostility⟩ **3 :** not based on or supported by reasons ⟨a ~ accusation⟩ — **rea·son·less·ly** *adv*

re·as·sur·ance \ˌrē-ə-ˈshu̇r-ən(t)s\ *n* (1611) **1 :** the action of reassuring **:** the state of being reassured **2 :** REINSURANCE

re·as·sure \ˌrē-ə-ˈshu̇(ə)r\ *vt* (1598) **1 :** to assure anew ⟨*reassured* him that the work was on schedule⟩ **2 :** to restore to confidence ⟨felt *reassured* by their earnest promise to do better⟩ **3 :** REINSURE — **re·as·sur·ing·ly** \-ˈshu̇r-iŋ-lē\ *adv*

re·ata \rē-ˈat-ə, -ˈät-\ *n* [AmerSp] (1846) **:** LARIAT

Re·au·mur \ˌrā-ō-ˈmyu̇(ə)r; rā-ˈō-mər, -ˌmyu̇(ə)r\ *adj* [René Antoine Ferchault de *Réaumur*] (1782) **:** relating or conforming to a thermometric scale on which the boiling point of water is at 80° above the zero of the scale and the freezing point is at zero

1**reave** \ˈrēv\ *vb* **reaved** *or* **reft** \ˈreft\; **reav·ing** [ME *reven,* fr. OE *rēafian;* akin to OHG *roubōn* to rob, L *rumpere* to break] *vi* (bef. 12c) **:** PLUNDER, ROB ~ *vt* **1** *archaic* **a** (1) **:** ROB, DESPOIL (2) **:** to deprive one of **b :** SEIZE **2** *archaic* **:** to carry or tear away — **reav·er** *n*

2**reave** *vt* **reaved** *or* **reft** \ˈreft\; **reav·ing** [ME *reven,* prob. modif. of ON *rīfa* to rive] *archaic* (13c) **:** BURST

reb \ˈreb\ *n* [short for *rebel*] (1862) **:** JOHNNY REB

Reb \(ˈ)reb\ *n* [Yiddish, fr. Heb *rabbī* my master, rabbi] (1882) **:** RABBI, MISTER — used as a title

re·bar·ba·tive \ri-ˈbär-bət-iv\ *adj* [F *rébarbatif,* fr. MF, fr. *rebarber* to be repellent, fr. *re-* + *barbe* beard, fr. L *barba* — more at BEARD] (1892) **:** REPELLENT, IRRITATING — **re·bar·ba·tive·ly** *adv*

1**re·bate** \ˈrē-ˌbāt, ri-ˈ\ *vb* **re·bat·ed; re·bat·ing** [ME *rebaten,* fr. MF *rabattre* to beat down again, fr. OF, fr. *re-* + *abattre* to beat down, fr. *a-* (fr. L *ad-*) + *battre* to beat, fr. L *battuere* — more at BATTLE] *vt* (15c) **1 :** to reduce the force or activity of **:** DIMINISH **2 :** to reduce the sharpness of **:** BLUNT **3 a :** to make a rebate of **b :** to give a rebate to ~ *vi* **:** to give rebates — **re·bat·er** *n*

2**re·bate** \ˈrē-ˌbāt\ *n* (1656) **:** a return of a part of a payment **:** ABATEMENT

3**re·bate** \ˈrab-ət, ˈrē-ˌbāt\ *var of* RABBET

re·ba·to \ri-ˈbät-(ˌ)ō\ *var of* RABATO

reb·be \ˈreb-ə\ *n* [Yiddish, fr. Heb *rabbī* rabbi] (1881) **:** a Jewish spiritual leader or teacher **:** RABBI

re·bec *or* **re·beck** \ˈrē-ˌbek, ˈreb-(ˌ)ek\ *n* [MF *rebec,* alter. of OF *rebebe,* fr. OProv *rebeb,* fr. Ar *rabāb*] (1509) **:** an ancient bowed usu. 3-stringed musical instrument with a pear-shaped body and slender neck

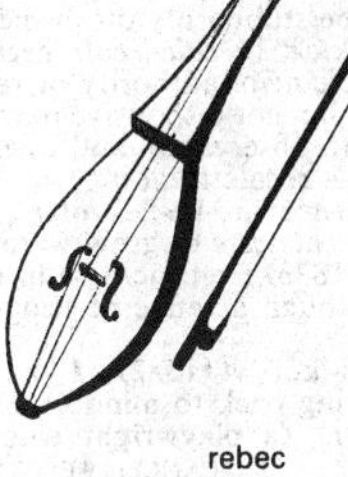

rebec

Re·bek·ah \ri-ˈbek-ə\ *n* [Heb *Ribhqāh*] **:** the wife of Isaac

1**reb·el** \ˈreb-əl\ *adj* [ME, fr. OF *rebelle,* fr. L *rebellis,* fr. *re-* + *bellum* war, fr. OL *duellum*] (13c) **1 a :** opposing or taking arms against a government or ruler **b :** of or relating to rebels ⟨the ~ camp⟩ **2 :** DISOBEDIENT, REBELLIOUS

2**rebel** *n* (14c) **:** one who rebels or participates in a rebellion

3**re·bel** \ri-ˈbel\ *vi* **re·belled; re·bel·ling** (14c) **1 a :** to oppose or disobey one in authority or control **b :** to renounce and resist by force the authority of one's government **2 a :** to act in or show opposition or disobedience ⟨*rebelled* against the conventions of polite society⟩ **b :** to feel or exhibit anger or revulsion ⟨*rebelled* at the injustice of life⟩

re·bel·lion \ri-ˈbel-yən\ *n* (14c) **1 :** opposition to one in authority or dominance **2 a :** open, armed, and usu. unsuccessful defiance of or resistance to an established government **b :** an instance of such defiance or resistance

syn REBELLION, REVOLUTION, UPRISING, REVOLT, INSURRECTION, MUTINY mean an armed outbreak against authority. REBELLION implies an open formidable resistance that is often unsuccessful; REVOLUTION applies to a successful rebellion resulting in a major change (as in government); UPRISING implies a brief, limited and often immediately ineffective rebellion; REVOLT and INSURRECTION imply an armed uprising that quickly fails or succeeds; MUTINY applies to group insubordination or insurrection esp. against naval authority.

re·bel·lious \-yəs\ *adj* (15c) **1 a :** given to or engaged in rebellion ⟨~ troops⟩ **b :** of, relating to, or characteristic of a rebel or rebellion ⟨a ~ speech⟩ **2 :** resisting treatment or management **:** REFRACTORY — **re·bel·lious·ly** *adv* — **re·bel·lious·ness** *n*

rebel yell *n* (1868) **:** a prolonged high-pitched yell often uttered by Confederate soldiers in the U.S. Civil War

re·birth \(ˈ)rē-ˈbərth, ˈrē-ˌ\ *n* (1837) **1 a :** a new or second birth **:** METEMPSYCHOSIS **b :** spiritual regeneration **2 :** RENAISSANCE, REVIVAL ⟨a ~ of nationalism⟩

Re·blo·chon \rə-blȯ-ˈshōⁿ\ *n* [F] (1908) **:** a semisoft creamy mild-flavored French cheese

reb·o·ant \ˈreb-ə-wənt\ *adj* [L *reboant-, reboans,* prp. of *reboare* to resound, fr. *re-* + *boare* to cry aloud, roar, fr. Gk *boan,* of imit. origin] (1830) **:** marked by reverberation

re·born \(ˈ)rē-ˈbȯ(ə)rn\ *adj* (1598) **:** born again **:** REGENERATED, REVIVED

1**re·bound** \ˈrē-ˈbau̇nd, ri-\ *vb* [ME *rebounden,* fr. MF *rebondir,* fr. OF, fr. *re-* + *bondir* to bound — more at BOUND] *vi* (14c) **1 a :** to spring back on or as if on collision or impact with another body **b :** to recover from setback or frustration **2 :** REECHO **3 :** to gain possession of a rebound in basketball ~ *vt* : to cause to rebound — **re·bound·er** \'rē-'bau̇n-dər, 'rē-,, ri-'\ *n*

[2]**re·bound** \'rē-,bau̇nd, ri-'\ *n* (1530) **1 a** : the action of rebounding : RECOIL **b** : an upward leap or movement : RECOVERY ⟨a sharp ~ in prices⟩ **2 a** : a basketball or hockey puck that rebounds **b** : the act or an instance of gaining possession of a basketball rebound ⟨leads the league in ~*s*⟩ **3** : a reaction to setback, frustration, or crisis ⟨on the ~ from an unhappy love affair⟩

re·bo·zo \ri-'bō-(,)zō, -(,)sō\ *n, pl* **-zos** [Sp, shawl, fr. *rebozar* to muffle prob. akin to L *bucca* cheek, mouth] (1807) : a long scarf worn chiefly by Mexican women

re·branch \(')rē-'branch\ *vi* (1888) : to form secondary branches

re·broad·cast \(')rē-'bro̊d-,kast\ *vt* **-cast; -cast·ing** (1923) **1** : to broadcast again (a radio or television program being simultaneously received from another source) **2** : to repeat (a broadcast) at a later time — **rebroadcast** *n*

re·buff \ri-'bəf\ *vt* [MF *rebuffer*, fr. OIt *ribuffare* to reprimand] (1586) : to reject or criticize sharply : SNUB — **rebuff** *n*

re·build \(')rē-'bild\ *vb* **-built** \-'bilt\; **-build·ing** *vt* (1611) **1 a** : to make extensive repairs to : RECONSTRUCT ⟨~ a war-torn city⟩ **b** : to restore to a previous state ⟨~ inventories⟩ **2** : to make extensive changes in : REMODEL ⟨~ society⟩ ~ *vi* : to build again ⟨planned to ~ after the fire⟩ ***syn*** see MEND

[1]**re·buke** \ri-'byük\ *vt* **re·buked; re·buk·ing** [ME *rebuken*, fr. ONF *rebuker*] (14c) **1 a** : to criticize sharply : REPRIMAND **b** : to serve as a rebuke to **2** : to turn back or keep down : CHECK ***syn*** see REPROVE — **re·buk·er** *n*

[2]**rebuke** *n* (15c) : an expression of strong disapproval : REPRIMAND

re·bus \'rē-bəs\ *n* [L, by things, abl. pl. of *res* thing — more at REAL] (1605) : a representation of words or syllables by pictures of objects or by symbols whose names resemble the intended words or syllables in sound; *also* : a riddle made up of such pictures or symbols

re·but \ri-'bət\ *vb* **re·but·ted; re·but·ting** [ME *rebuten*, fr. MF *reboter*, fr. *re-* + *boter* to butt — more at BUTT] *vt* (14c) **1** : to drive or beat back : REPEL **2 a** : to contradict or oppose by formal legal argument, plea, or countervailing proof **b** : to expose the falsity of : REFUTE ~ *vi* : to make or furnish an answer or counter proof — **re·but·ta·ble** \-'bət-ə-bəl\ *adj*

re·but·tal \ri-'bət-ᵊl\ *n* (1830) : the act of rebutting esp. in a legal suit; *also* : argument or proof that rebuts

[1]**re·but·ter** \-'bət-ər\ *n* [AF *rebuter*, fr. OF *reboter* to rebut] (1540) : the answer of a defendant in matter of fact to a plaintiff's surrejoinder

[2]**rebutter** *n* (1794) : one that rebuts

re·cal·ci·trance \ri-'kal-sə-trən(t)s\ *n* (1856) : the state of being recalcitrant

re·cal·ci·tran·cy \-trən-sē\ *n* (1869) : RECALCITRANCE

re·cal·ci·trant \-trənt\ *adj* [LL *recalcitrant-*, *recalcitrans*, prp. of *recalcitrare* to be stubbornly disobedient, fr. L, to kick back, fr. *re-* + *calcitrare* to kick, fr. *calc-*, *calx* heel — more at CALK] (1843) **1** : obstinately defiant of authority or restraint **2 a** : difficult to manage or operate **b** : not responsive to treatment **c** : RESISTANT ⟨this subject is ~ both to observation and to experiment —G. G. Simpson⟩ ***syn*** see UNRULY — **recalcitrant** *n*

re·ca·les·cence \,rē-kə-'les-ᵊn(t)s\ *n* [L *recalescere* to grow warm again, fr. *re-* + *calescere* to grow warm, incho. of *calēre* to be warm — more at LEE] (1873) : an increase in temperature that occurs while cooling metal through a range of temperatures in which change in structure occurs

[1]**re·call** \ri-'ko̊l\ *vt* (1582) **1 a** : to call back ⟨was ~*ed* to active duty⟩ **b** : to bring back to mind ⟨~*s* his early years⟩ **c** : to remind one of : RESEMBLE ⟨a playwright who ~*s* the Elizabethan dramatists⟩ **d** : RECOLLECT **2** : CANCEL, REVOKE **3** : RESTORE, REVIVE ***syn*** see REMEMBER — **re·call·abil·i·ty** \-,ko̊-lə-'bil-ət-ē\ *n* — **re·call·able** \-'ko̊-lə-bəl\ *adj* — **re·call·er** *n*

[2]**re·call** \ri-'ko̊l, 'rē-,\ *n* (1611) **1** : a call to return ⟨a ~ of workers after a layoff⟩ **2** : the right or procedure by which an official may be removed by vote of the people **3** : remembrance of what has been learned or experienced **4** : the act of revoking **5** : a public call by a manufacturer for the return of a product that may be defective or contaminated **6** : the ability (as of an information retrieval system) to retrieve stored material

re·ca·mier \,rā-käm-'yā\ *n* [fr. its appearance in a portrait of Mme. Récamier by Jacques-Louis David] (1938) : a usu. backless couch with a high curved headrest and low footrest

re·can·a·li·za·tion \(,)rē-,kan-ᵊl-ə-'zā-shən\ *n* (1953) : the process of reuniting an interrupted channel of a bodily tube (as a vas deferens) — **re·can·a·lize** \-kə-'nal-,īz, -'kan-ᵊl-,īz\ *vt*

re·cant \ri-'kant\ *vb* [L *recantare*, fr. *re-* + *cantare* to sing — more at CHANT] *vt* (1535) **1** : to withdraw or repudiate (a statement or belief) formally and publicly : RENOUNCE **2** : REVOKE ~ *vi* : to make an open confession of error ***syn*** see ABJURE — **re·can·ta·tion** \,rē-,kan-'tā-shən\ *n*

[1]**re·cap** \'rē-,kap, ri-'\ *vb* **re·capped; re·cap·ping** [by shortening] (1926) : RECAPITULATE

[2]**re·cap** \'rē-,kap\ *n* (ca. 1933) : RECAPITULATION

[3]**re·cap** \(')rē-'kap\ *vt* **re·capped; re·cap·ping** (ca. 1939) : [1]RETREAD — **re·cap·pa·ble** \-'kap-ə-bəl\ *adj*

[4]**re·cap** \'rē-,kap\ *n* (ca. 1939) : [2]RETREAD 2

re·cap·i·tal·iza·tion \(,)rē-,kap-ət-ᵊl-ə-'zā-shən, -,kap-tᵊl-\ *n* (1920) : a revision of the capital structure of a corporation

re·cap·i·tal·ize \(')rē-'kap-ət-ᵊl-,īz, -'kap-tᵊl-\ *vt* (1904) : to change the capital structure of

re·ca·pit·u·late \,rē-kə-'pich-ə-,lāt\ *vb* **-lat·ed; -lat·ing** [LL *recapitulatus*, pp. of *recapitulare* to restate by heads, sum up, fr. L *re-* + *capitulum* division of a book] *vt* (1570) : to repeat the principal points or stages of : SUMMARIZE ~ *vi* : SUM UP

re·ca·pit·u·la·tion \-,pich-ə-'lā-shən\ *n* (14c) **1** : a concise summary **2** : the hypothetical occurrence in an individual organism's development of successive stages resembling the series of ancestral types from which it has descended so that the ontogeny of the individual is a recapitulation of the phylogeny of its group **3** : the third section of a sonata form

[1]**re·cap·ture** \(')rē-'kap-chər\ *n* (1752) **1 a** : the act of retaking **b** : an instance of being retaken **2** : the retaking of a prize or goods under international law **3** : a government seizure under law of earnings or profits beyond a fixed amount

[2]**recapture** *vt* (1799) **1 a** : to capture again **b** : to experience again ⟨by no effort of the imagination could she ~ the ecstasy —Ellen Glasgow⟩ **2** : to take (as a portion of earnings or profits above a fixed amount) by law or through negotiations under law

re·cast \(')rē-'kast\ *vt* **-cast; -cast·ing** (1603) : to cast again ⟨~ a gun⟩ ⟨~ a play⟩; *also* : REMODEL, REFASHION ⟨~*s* his political image to fit the times⟩ — **re·cast** \'rē-,kast, (')rē-'\ *n*

[1]**re·cede** \ri-'sēd\ *vi* **re·ced·ed; re·ced·ing** [L *recedere* to go back, fr. *re-* + *cedere* to go — more at CEDE] (1605) **1 a** : to move back or away : WITHDRAW **b** : to slant backward **2** : to grow less or smaller : DIMINISH, DECREASE

syn RECEDE, RETREAT, RETROGRADE, RETRACT, BACK mean to move backward. RECEDE implies a gradual withdrawing from a forward or high fixed point in time or space; RETREAT implies withdrawal from a point or position reached; RETROGRADE implies movement contrary to a normally progressive direction; RETRACT implies drawing back from an extended position; BACK is used with *up, down, out,* or *off,* to refer to any retrograde motion.

[2]**re·cede** \(')rē-'sēd\ *vt* [*re-* + *cede*] (1771) : to cede back to a former possessor

[1]**re·ceipt** \ri-'sēt\ *n* [ME *receite*, fr. ONF, fr. ML *recepta*, prob. fr. L, neut. pl. of *receptus*, pp. of *recipere* to receive] (14c) **1** : RECIPE **2 a** *obs* : RECEPTACLE **b** *archaic* : a revenue office **3** : the act or process of receiving **4** : something received — usu. used in pl. **5** : a writing acknowledging the receiving of goods or money

[2]**receipt** *vt* (1787) **1** : to give a receipt for or acknowledge the receipt of **2** : to mark as paid

re·ceiv·able \ri-'sē-və-bəl\ *adj* (14c) **1** : capable of being received **2** : subject to call for payment ⟨notes ~⟩

re·ceiv·ables \-bəlz\ *n pl* (1917) : amounts of money receivable

re·ceive \ri-'sēv\ *vb* **re·ceived; re·ceiv·ing** [ME *receiven*, fr. ONF *receivre*, fr. L *recipere*, fr. *re-* + *capere* to take — more at HEAVE] *vt* (14c) **1** : to come into possession of : ACQUIRE ⟨~ a gift⟩ **2 a** : to act as a receptacle or container for ⟨the cistern ~*s* water from the roof⟩ **b** : to assimilate through the mind or senses ⟨~ new ideas⟩ **3 a** : to permit to enter : ADMIT **b** : WELCOME, GREET **c** : to react to in a specified manner **4** : to accept as authoritative, true, or accurate : BELIEVE **5 a** : to support the weight or pressure of : BEAR **b** : to take (a mark or impression) from the weight of something ⟨some clay ~*s* clear impressions⟩ **c** : ACQUIRE, EXPERIENCE ⟨*received* his early schooling at home⟩ **d** : to suffer the hurt or injury of ⟨*received* a broken nose⟩ ~ *vi* **1** : to be a recipient **2** : to be at home to visitors ⟨~*s* on Tuesdays⟩ **3** : to convert incoming radio waves into perceptible signals **4** : to catch or gain possession of a kicked ball in football

received *adj* (15c) : generally accepted : COMMON ⟨a healthy skepticism about ~ explanations —B. K. Lewalski⟩

Received Pronunciation *n* (1932) : the pronunciation of Received Standard

Received Standard *n* (ca. 1911) : the form of English spoken at the English public schools, at the universities of Oxford and Cambridge, and by many educated Englishmen elsewhere

re·ceiv·er \ri-'sē-vər\ *n* (14c) : one that receives: as **a** : TREASURER **b** (1) : a person appointed to hold in trust and administer property under litigation (2) : a person appointed to settle the affairs of a business involving a public interest or to manage a corporation during reorganization **c** : one that receives stolen goods : FENCE **d** : a vessel to receive and contain gases **e** : a device for converting electromagnetic waves or signals into audio or visual form: as (1) : TELEPHONE RECEIVER (2) : a radio receiver with a tuner and amplifier on one chassis **f** (1) : CATCHER (2) : a member of the offensive team in football eligible to catch a forward pass

receiver general *n, pl* **receivers general** (15c) : a public officer in charge of the treasury (as of Massachusetts)

re·ceiv·er·ship \ri-'sē-vər-,ship\ *n* (15c) **1** : the office or function of a receiver **2** : the state of being in the hands of a receiver

receiving blanket *n* (1926) : a small lightweight blanket used to wrap an infant (as after bathing)

receiving end *n* (1937) : the position of being a recipient or esp. a victim — usu. used in the phrase *on the receiving end* ⟨to help defend anyone on the *receiving end* of a libel action —*Reporter*⟩

receiving line *n* (1933) : a group of people who stand in a line and individually welcome guests (as at a wedding reception)

re·cen·cy \'rēs-ᵊn-sē\ *n* (1612) : the quality or state of being recent ⟨the eagerness of the people for ~ in their news —F. L. Mott⟩

re·cen·sion \ri-'sen-chən\ *n* [L *recension-*, *recensio* enumeration, fr. *recensēre* to review, fr. *re-* + *censēre* to assess, tax — more at CENSOR] (1818) **1** : a critical revision of a text **2** : a text established by critical revision

re·cent \'rēs-ᵊnt\ *adj* [MF or L; MF, fr. L *recent-*, *recens*; akin to Gk *kainos* new] (1533) **1 a** : of or relating to a time not long past **b** : having lately come into existence : NEW, FRESH **2** *cap* : of, relating to, or being the present or post-Pleistocene geologic epoch — **re·cent·ness** *n*

re·cent·ly *adv* (1533) : during a recent period of time : LATELY

re·cep·ta·cle \ri-'sep-ti-kəl\ *n* [L *receptaculum*, fr. *receptare* to receive, fr. *receptus*, pp. of *recipere* to receive] (15c) **1** : one that receives and contains something : CONTAINER **2** [NL *receptaculum*, fr. L] **a** : the end of the flower stalk upon which the floral organs are borne **b** : a modified branch bearing sporangia in a cryptogamous plant **3** : a mounted female electrical fitting that contains the live parts of the circuit

re·cep·tion \ri-'sep-shən\ *n* [ME *recepcion*, fr. MF or L; MF *reception*, fr. L *reception-*, *receptio*, fr. *receptus*, pp.] (15c) **1** : the act or action or an instance of receiving: as **a** : RECEIPT ⟨the ~ of American capital⟩ **b** : ADMISSION ⟨his ~ into the church⟩ **c** : RESPONSE, REACTION ⟨the play met with a mixed ~⟩ **d** : the receiving of a radio or television broadcast **2** : a social gathering often for the purpose of extending a formal welcome

re·cep·tion·ist \-sh(ə-)nəst\ *n* (1901) : one employed to greet telephone callers, visitors, patients, or clients

re·cep·tive \ri-'sep-tiv\ *adj* (1594) **1** : able or inclined to receive; *esp* : open and responsive to ideas, impressions, or suggestions **2 a** *of a* *sensory end organ* : fit to receive and transmit stimuli **b** : SENSORY — **re·cep·tive·ness** *n* — **re·cep·tiv·i·ty** \ˌrē-ˌsep-ˈtiv-ət-ē, ri-\ *n*

re·cep·tor \ri-ˈsep-tər\ *n* (1900) : RECEIVER: as **a** : a cell or group of cells that receives stimuli : SENSE ORGAN **b** : a chemical group or molecule in a plasma membrane or cell interior that has an affinity for a specific chemical group, molecule, or virus

1re·cess \ˈrē-ˌses, ri-ˈ\ *n* [L *recessus*, fr. *recessus*, pp. of *recedere* to recede] (1531) **1** : the action of receding : RECESSION **2** : a hidden, secret, or secluded place or part **3 a** : INDENTATION, CLEFT ⟨a deep ~ in the hill⟩ **b** : ALCOVE ⟨a pleasant ~ lined with books⟩ **4** : a suspension of business or procedure often for rest or relaxation ⟨children playing at ~⟩

2recess *vt* (1809) **1** : to put into a recess ⟨~*ed* lighting⟩ **2** : to make a recess in **3** : to interrupt for a recess ~ *vi* : to take a recess

1re·ces·sion \ri-ˈsesh-ən\ *n* (1652) **1** : the act or action of receding : WITHDRAWAL **2** : a departing procession (as of clergy and choir at the end of a church service) **3** : a period of reduced economic activity — **re·ces·sion·ary** \-ə-ˌner-ē\ *adj*

2re·ces·sion \(ˈ)rē-ˈsesh-ən\ *n* [*re-* + *cession*] (1828) : the act of ceding back to a former possessor

1re·ces·sion·al \ri-ˈsesh-nəl, -ən-ᵊl\ *adj* (1867) : of or relating to a withdrawal

2recessional *n* (1867) **1** : a hymn or musical piece at the conclusion of a service or program **2** : 1RECESSION 2

1re·ces·sive \ri-ˈses-iv\ *adj* (1672) **1 a** : tending to go back : RECEDING **b** : RETIRING, WITHDRAWN **2 a** : producing little or no phenotypic effect when occurring in heterozygous condition with a contrasting allele ⟨~ genes⟩ **b** : expressed only when the determining gene is in the homozygous condition ⟨~ traits⟩ — **re·ces·sive·ly** *adv* — **re·ces·sive·ness** *n*

2recessive *n* (1900) **1** : a recessive character or gene **2** : an organism possessing one or more recessive characters

re·charge \(ˈ)rē-ˈchärj\ *vi* (1598) **1** : to make a new attack **2** : to regain energy or spirit ~ *vt* **1** : to charge again; *esp* : to restore anew the active materials in (a storage battery) **2** : to inspire or invigorate afresh : RENEW — **re·charge** \(ˈ)rē-ˈchärj, ˈrē-ˌ\ *n* — **re·charge·able** \(ˈ)rē-ˈchär-jə-bəl\ *adj* — **re·charg·er** \-jər\ *n*

ré·chauf·fé \ˌrā-shō-ˈfā, -ˈshō-ˌ\ *n* [F, fr. *réchauffé* warmed-over, fr. pp. of *réchauffer* to warm over, fr. *ré-* re- + *chauffer* to warm, fr. MF *chaufer* — more at CHAFE] (1805) **1** : a warmed-over dish of food **2** : REHASH

re·cheat \ri-ˈchēt\ *n* [ME *rechate*, fr. *rechaten* to blow the recheat, fr. MF *rachater* to assemble, rally, fr. *re-* + *achater* to acquire, fr. (assumed) VL *accaptare*, fr. L *ac-* + *captare* to seek to obtain, intens. of *capere* to take, receive — more at HEAVE] (15c) : a hunting call sounded on a horn to assemble the hounds

re·cher·ché \rə-ˌsher-ˈshā, -ˈshe(ə)r-ˌ\ *adj* [F, fr. pp. of *rechercher* to seek out, fr. MF *recherchier* — more at RESEARCH] (1722) **1 a** : EXQUISITE, CHOICE **b** : EXOTIC, RARE **2** : excessively refined : AFFECTED **3** : PRETENTIOUS, OVERBLOWN

re·cid·i·vism \ri-ˈsid-ə-ˌviz-əm\ *n* (1886) : a tendency to relapse into a previous condition or mode of behavior; *esp* : relapse into criminal behavior

re·cid·i·vist \-vəst\ *n* [F *récidiviste*, fr. *récidiver* to relapse, fr. ML *recidivare*, fr. L *recidivus* recurring, fr. *recidere* to fall back, fr. *re-* + *cadere* to fall — more at CHANCE] (1880) : one who relapses; *specif* : an habitual criminal — **recidivist** *adj* — **re·cid·i·vis·tic** \-ˌsid-ə-ˈvis-tik\ *adj*

rec·i·pe \ˈres-ə-(ˌ)pē\ *n* [L, take, imper. of *recipere* to take, receive — more at RECEIVE] (1584) **1** : PRESCRIPTION 4a **2** : a set of instructions for making something (as a food dish) from various ingredients **3** : a formula or procedure for doing or attaining something ⟨a ~ for success⟩

re·cip·i·ent \ri-ˈsip-ē-ənt\ *n* [L *recipient-*, *recipiens*, prp. of *recipere*] (1558) : one that receives : RECEIVER — **recipient** *adj*

1re·cip·ro·cal \ri-ˈsip-rə-kəl\ *adj* [L *reciprocus* returning the same way, alternating, irreg. fr. *re-* + *pro-*] (1570) **1 a** : inversely related : OPPOSITE **b** : of, constituting, or resulting from paired crosses in which the kind that supplies the male parent of the first cross supplies the female parent of the second cross and vice versa **2** : shared, felt, or shown by both sides **3** : serving to reciprocate : consisting of or functioning as a return in kind ⟨the ~ devastation of nuclear war⟩ **4 a** : mutually corresponding ⟨agreed to extend ~ privileges to each other's citizens⟩ **b** : marked by or based on reciprocity ⟨~ trade agreements⟩ — **re·cip·ro·cal·ly** \-k(ə-)lē\ *adv*

2reciprocal *n* (1570) **1** : something in a reciprocal relationship to another **2** : one of a pair of numbers (as $^2/_3$, $^3/_2$) whose product is one; *broadly* : MULTIPLICATIVE INVERSE

reciprocal pronoun *n* (1844) : a pronoun (as *each other*) used to denote mutual action or cross relationship between the members comprised in a plural subject

re·cip·ro·cate \ri-ˈsip-rə-ˌkāt\ *vb* **-cat·ed; -cat·ing** *vt* (1611) **1** : to give and take mutually **2** : to return in kind or degree ⟨~ a compliment gracefully⟩ ~ *vi* **1** : to make a return for something ⟨we hope to ~ for your kindness⟩ **2** : to move forward and backward alternately ⟨a *reciprocating* valve⟩ — **re·cip·ro·ca·tor** \-ˌkāt-ər\ *n*

syn RECIPROCATE, RETALIATE, REQUITE, RETURN mean to give back usu. in kind or in quantity. RECIPROCATE implies a mutual or equivalent exchange or a paying back of what one has received ⟨*reciprocated* their hospitality by inviting them for a visit⟩ RETALIATE usu. implies a paying back of injury in exact kind, often vengefully ⟨the enemy *retaliated* by executing their prisoners⟩ REQUITE implies a paying back according to one's preference and often not equivalently ⟨*requited* her love with cold indifference⟩ RETURN implies a paying back of something usu. in kind but sometimes by way of contrast ⟨*returned* their kindness with ingratitude⟩

reciprocating engine *n* (1822) : an engine in which the to-and-fro motion of a piston is transformed into circular motion of the crankshaft

re·cip·ro·ca·tion \ri-ˌsip-rə-ˈkā-shən\ *n* (1561) **1 a** : a mutual exchange **b** : a return in kind or of like value **2** : an alternating motion — **re·cip·ro·ca·tive** \-ˈsip-rə-ˌkāt-iv, -kət-\ *adj*

rec·i·proc·i·ty \ˌres-ə-ˈpräs-ət-ē, -ˈpräs-tē\ *n, pl* **-ties** (1766) **1** : the quality or state of being reciprocal : mutual dependence, action, or influence **2** : a mutual exchange of privileges; *specif* : a recognition by one of two countries or institutions of the validity of licenses or privileges granted by the other

re·ci·sion \ri-ˈsizh-ən\ *n* [MF, alter. of *rescision*, fr. LL *rescission-*, *rescissio* rescission] (1611) : CANCELLATION

re·cit·al \ri-ˈsīt-ᵊl\ *n* (1550) **1 a** : the act or process or an instance of reciting **b** : a detailed account : ENUMERATION ⟨the ~ of his troubles⟩ **c** : DISCOURSE, NARRATION ⟨a colorful ~ of a night on the town⟩ **2 a** : a concert given by an individual musician or dancer or by a dance troupe **b** : a public exhibition of skill given by music or dance pupils — **re·cit·al·ist** \-ᵊl-əst\ *n*

rec·i·ta·tion \ˌres-ə-ˈtā-shən\ *n* (15c) **1** : the act of enumerating ⟨a ~ of relevant details⟩ **2** : the act or an instance of reading or repeating aloud esp. publicly **3 a** : a student's oral reply to questions **b** : a class period

rec·i·ta·tive \ˌres-(ə-)tə-ˈtēv\ *n* [It *recitativo*, fr. *recitare* to recite, fr. L] (1656) **1** : a rhythmically free vocal style that imitates the natural inflections of speech and that is used for dialogue and narrative in operas and oratorios; *also* : a passage to be delivered in this style **2** : RECITATION — **recitative** *adj*

rec·i·ta·ti·vo \ˌres-(ə-)tə-ˈtē-(ˌ)vō\ *n, pl* **-vi** \-(ˌ)vē\ *or* **-vos** [It] (1645) : RECITATIVE 1

re·cite \ri-ˈsīt\ *vb* **re·cit·ed; re·cit·ing** [ME *reciten* to state formally, fr. MF or L; MF *reciter* to recite, fr. L *recitare*, fr. *re-* + *citare* to summon — more at CITE] *vt* (15c) **1** : to repeat from memory or read aloud publicly **2 a** : to relate in full ⟨~*s* dull anecdotes⟩ **b** : ENUMERATE, DETAIL ⟨*recited* a catalog of offenses⟩ **3** : to repeat or answer questions about (a lesson) ~ *vi* **1** : to repeat or read aloud something memorized or prepared **2** : to reply to a teacher's question on a lesson — **re·cit·er** *n*

reck \ˈrek\ *vb* [ME *recken* to take heed, fr. OE *reccan*; akin to OHG *ruohhen* to take heed] *vi* (bef. 12c) **1** : WORRY, CARE **2** *archaic* : to be of account or interest : MATTER ~ *vt* **1** *archaic* : to care for : REGARD **2** *archaic* : to matter to : CONCERN

reck·less \ˈrek-ləs\ *adj* (bef. 12c) **1** : marked by lack of proper caution : careless of consequences **2** : NEGLIGENT ⟨~ mining practices devastated the countryside⟩ ***syn*** see ADVENTUROUS — **reck·less·ly** *adv* — **reck·less·ness** *n*

reck·on \ˈrek-ən\ *vb* **reck·oned; reck·on·ing** \-(ə-)niŋ\ [ME *rekenen*, fr. OE *-recenian* (as in *gerecenian* to narrate); akin to OE *reccan*] *vt* (13c) **1 a** : COUNT ⟨~ the days till Christmas⟩ **b** : ESTIMATE, COMPUTE ⟨~ the height of a building⟩ **c** : to determine by reference to a fixed basis ⟨the existence of the U.S. is ~*ed* from the Declaration of Independence⟩ **2** : to regard or think of as : CONSIDER **3** *chiefly dial* : THINK, SUPPOSE ⟨I ~ I've outlived my time —Ellen Glasgow⟩ ~ *vi* **1** : to settle accounts **2** : to make a calculation **3 a** : JUDGE **b** *chiefly dial* : SUPPOSE, THINK **4** : to accept something as certain : place reliance ⟨I ~ on your promise to help⟩ — **reckon with** : to take into consideration — **reckon without** : to fail to consider : IGNORE

reck·on·ing *n* (14c) **1** : the act or an instance of reckoning: as **a** : ACCOUNT, BILL **b** : COMPUTATION **c** : calculation of a ship's position **2** : a settling of accounts ⟨day of ~⟩ **3** : a summing up

re·claim \ri-ˈklām\ *vt* [ME *reclamen*, fr. MF *reclamer* to call back, fr. L *reclamare* to cry out against, fr. *re-* + *clamare* to cry out — more at CLAIM] (14c) **1 a** : to recall from wrong or improper conduct : REFORM **b** : TAME, SUBDUE **2 a** : to rescue from an undesirable state **b** : to make available for human use by changing natural conditions ⟨~ swampland⟩ **3** : to obtain from a waste product or by-product : RECOVER **4** : to demand or obtain the return of ***syn*** see RESCUE — **re·claim·able** \-ˈklā-mə-bəl\ *adj*

rec·la·ma·tion \ˌrek-lə-ˈmā-shən\ *n* [F *réclamation*, fr. L *reclamation-*, *reclamatio*, fr. *reclamatus*, pp. of *reclamare*] (1633) : the act or process of reclaiming: as **a** : REFORMATION, REHABILITATION **b** : restoration to use : RECOVERY

ré·clame \rā-ˈkläm\ *n* [F, advertising, fr. *réclamer* to appeal, fr. MF *reclamer*] (1870) **1** : public acclaim : VOGUE **2** : a gift for dramatization or publicity : SHOWMANSHIP

rec·li·nate \ˈrek-lə-ˌnāt\ *adj* (1753) : bent downward so that the apex is below the base ⟨~ leaves⟩

re·cline \ri-ˈklīn\ *vb* **re·clined; re·clin·ing** [ME *reclinen*, fr. MF or L; MF *recliner*, fr. L *reclinare*, fr. *re-* + *clinare* to bend — more at LEAN] *vt* (15c) : to cause or permit to incline backwards ~ *vi* **1** : to lean or incline backwards **2** : REPOSE, LIE

re·clin·er \-ˈklī-nər\ *n* (1955) : a chair with an adjustable back and footrest

re·clos·able \(ˈ)rē-ˈklō-zə-bəl\ *adj* (1965) : capable of being closed again tightly after opening ⟨~ packages of bacon⟩

1re·cluse \ˈrek-ˌlüs, ri-ˈklüs, ˈrek-ˌlüz\ *adj* [ME, fr. OF *reclus*, lit., shut up, fr. LL *reclusus*, pp. of *recludere* to shut up, fr. L *re-* + *claudere* to close — more at CLOSE] (13c) : marked by withdrawal from society : SOLITARY — **re·clu·sive** \ri-ˈklü-siv, -ziv\ *adj*

2recluse *n* (13c) : a person who leads a secluded or solitary life

re·clu·sion \ri-ˈklü-zhən\ *n* (15c) : the state of being recluse

rec·og·ni·tion \ˌrek-ig-ˈnish-ən, -əg-\ *n* [L *recognition-*, *recognitio*, fr. *recognitus*, pp. of *recognoscere*] (1558) **1** : the action of recognizing : the state of being recognized: as **a** : ACKNOWLEDGMENT; *esp* : formal acknowledgment of the political existence of a government or nation **b** : knowledge or feeling that someone or something present has been met before **2** : special notice or attention **3** : the sensing and encoding of printed or written data by a machine ⟨optical character ~⟩ ⟨magnetic ink character ~⟩

re·cog·ni·zance \ri-ˈkäg-nə-zən(t)s, -ˈkän-ə-\ *n* [alter. of ME *reconissaunce*, fr. MF *reconoissance* recognition, fr. *reconoistre* to recognize] (14c) **1 a** : an obligation of record entered into before a court or magistrate requiring the performance of an act (as appearance in court) usu. under penalty of a money forfeiture **b** : the sum liable to forfeiture upon such an obligation **2** *archaic* : TOKEN, PLEDGE

rec·og·nize \ˈrek-ig-ˌnīz, -əg-\ *vt* **-nized; -niz·ing** [modif. of MF *reconoiss-*, stem of *reconoistre*, fr. L *recognoscere*, fr. *re-* + *cognoscere* to know — more at COGNITION] (1531) **1 :** to acknowledge formally: as **a :** to admit as being lord or sovereign **b :** to admit as being of a particular status **c :** to admit as being one entitled to be heard **d :** to acknowledge the de facto existence or the independence of **2 :** to acknowledge or take notice of in some definite way: as **a :** to acknowledge with a show of appreciation ⟨~ an act of bravery with the award of a medal⟩ **b :** to acknowledge acquaintance with ⟨~ an old crony with a nod⟩ **3 a :** to perceive to be something or someone previously known ⟨*recognized* the word⟩ **b :** to perceive clearly **:** REALIZE — **rec·og·niz·abil·i·ty** \ˌrek-ig-ˌnī-zə-ˈbil-ət-ē, -əg-\ *n* — **rec·og·niz·able** \ˈrek-əg-ˌnī-zə-bəl, -ig-\ *adj* — **rec·og·niz·ably** \-blē\ *adv* — **rec·og·niz·er** *n*

[1]**re·coil** \ri-ˈkȯi(ə)l\ *vi* [ME *reculen*, fr. MF *reculer*, fr. *re-* + *cul* backside — more at CULET] (14c) **1 a :** to fall back under pressure **b :** to shrink back physically or emotionally **2 :** to spring back to or as if to a starting point **:** REBOUND **3** *obs* **:** DEGENERATE

syn RECOIL, SHRINK, FLINCH, WINCE, BLENCH, QUAIL mean to draw back in fear or distaste. RECOIL implies a start or movement away through shock, fear, or disgust; SHRINK suggests an instinctive recoil through sensitiveness, scrupulousness, or cowardice; FLINCH implies a failure to endure pain or face something dangerous or frightening with resolution; WINCE suggests a slight involuntary physical reaction (as a start or recoiling); BLENCH implies fainthearted flinching; QUAIL suggests shrinking and cowering in fear.

[2]**re·coil** \ˈrē-ˌkȯil, ri-ˈkȯi(ə)l\ *n* (14c) **1 :** the act or action of recoiling; *esp* **:** the kickback of a gun upon firing **2 :** REACTION ⟨the ~ from the rigors of Calvinism —Edmund Wilson⟩

re·coil·less \-ˌkȯil-ləs, -ˈkȯi(ə)l-\ *adj* (1943) **:** venting expanding propellant gas before recoil is produced ⟨~ rifle⟩ ⟨~ airgun⟩

re·coil–op·er·at·ed \ˌrē-ˌkȯil-ˈäp-(ə-)ˌrāt-əd\ *adj, of a firearm* (1942) **:** utilizing the movement of parts in recoil to operate the action

re·coin \(ˌ)rē-ˈkȯin\ *vt* (1685) **:** to coin again or anew; *esp* **:** REMINT — **re·coin·age** \-ˈkȯi-nij\ *n*

rec·ol·lect \ˌrek-ə-ˈlekt\ *vb* [ML *recollectus*, pp. of *recolligere*, fr. L, to gather again] *vt* (1559) **1 :** to bring back to the level of conscious awareness **:** REMEMBER ⟨trying to ~ a forgotten address⟩ **2 :** to remind (oneself) of something temporarily forgotten ~ *vi* **:** to call something to mind ***syn*** see REMEMBER

re–col·lect \ˌrē-kə-ˈlekt\ *vt* [partly fr. L *recollectus*, pp. of *recolligere*, fr. *re-* + *colligere* to collect; partly fr. *re-* + *collect*] (1607) **:** to collect again; *esp* **:** RALLY, RECOVER

rec·ol·lect·ed \ˌre-kə-ˈlek-təd\ *adj* (1627) **:** COMPOSED, CALM

rec·ol·lec·tion \ˌrek-ə-ˈlek-shən\ *n* (1624) **1 a :** tranquillity of mind **b :** religious contemplation **2 a :** the action or power of recalling to mind **b :** something recalled to the mind

re·com·bi·nant \(ˌ)rē-ˈkäm-bə-nənt\ *adj* (1942) **:** exhibiting genetic recombination ⟨~ progeny⟩ — **recombinant** *n*

recombinant DNA *n* (1975) **:** DNA prepared in the laboratory by breaking up and splicing together DNA from several different sources (as different species of organisms)

re·com·bi·na·tion \ˌrē-ˌkäm-bə-ˈnā-shən\ *n* (1924) **:** the formation by the processes of crossing-over and independent assortment of new combinations of genes in progeny that did not occur in the parents — **re·com·bi·na·tion·al** \-shnəl, -shən-ᵊl\ *adj*

rec·om·mend \ˌrek-ə-ˈmend\ *vt* [ME *recommenden* to praise, fr. ML *recommendare*, fr. L *re-* + *commendare* to commend] (14c) **1 a :** to present as worthy of acceptance or trial ⟨~*ed* the medicine⟩ **b :** to endorse as fit, worthy, or competent ⟨~*s* her for the position⟩ **2 :** ENTRUST, COMMIT ⟨~*ed* his soul to God⟩ **3 :** to make acceptable ⟨has other points to ~ it⟩ **4 :** ADVISE ⟨~ that the matter be dropped⟩ — **rec·om·mend·able** \-ˈmen-də-bəl\ *adj* — **rec·om·men·da·to·ry** \-də-ˌtōr-ē, -ˌtȯr-\ *adj*

rec·om·men·da·tion \ˌrek-ə-mən-ˈdā-shən, -ˌmen-\ *n* (15c) **1 a :** the act of recommending **b :** something (as a procedure) recommended **2 :** something that recommends or expresses commendation

re·com·mit \ˌrē-kə-ˈmit\ *vt* (1621) **1 :** to refer (as a bill) back to a committee **2 :** to entrust or consign again — **re·com·mit·ment** \-mənt\ *n* — **re·com·mit·tal** \-ˈmit-ᵊl\ *n*

[1]**rec·om·pense** \ˈrek-əm-ˌpen(t)s\ *vt* **-pensed; -pens·ing** [ME *recompensen*, fr. MF *recompenser*, fr. LL *recompensare*, fr. L *re-* + *compensare* to compensate] (15c) **1 a :** to give something to by way of compensation (as for a service rendered or damage incurred) **b :** to pay for **2 :** to return in kind **:** REQUITE ***syn*** see PAY

[2]**recompense** *n* (15c) **:** an equivalent or a return for something done, suffered, or given **:** COMPENSATION ⟨offered in ~ for injuries⟩

re·com·pose \ˌrē-kəm-ˈpōz\ *vt* (15c) **1 :** to compose again **:** REARRANGE **2 :** to restore to composure — **re·com·po·si·tion** \(ˌ)rē-ˌkäm-pə-ˈzish-ən\ *n*

re·con \ri-ˈkän\ *n* [by shortening] (1918) **:** RECONNAISSANCE

rec·on·cile \ˈrek-ən-ˌsīl\ *vb* **-ciled; -cil·ing** [ME *reconcilen*, fr. MF or L; MF *reconcilier*, fr. L *reconciliare*, fr. *re-* + *conciliare* to conciliate] *vt* (14c) **1 a :** to restore to friendship or harmony ⟨*reconciled* the factions⟩ **b :** SETTLE, RESOLVE ⟨~ differences⟩ **2 :** to make consistent or congruous ⟨~ an ideal with reality⟩ **3 :** to cause to submit to or accept something unpleasant ⟨was *reconciled* to hardship⟩ **4 a :** to check (a financial account) against another for accuracy **b :** to account for ~ *vi* **:** to become reconciled ***syn*** see ADAPT — **rec·on·cil·abil·i·ty** \ˌrek-ən-ˌsī-lə-ˈbil-ət-ē\ *n* — **rec·on·cil·able** \ˌrek-ən-ˈsī-lə-bəl, ˈrek-ən-ˌ\ *adj* — **rec·on·cile·ment** \ˈrek-ən-ˌsīl-mənt\ *n* — **rec·on·cil·er** *n*

rec·on·cil·i·a·tion \ˌrek-ən-ˌsil-ē-ˈā-shən\ *n* [ME, fr. L *reconciliation-, reconciliatio*, fr. *reconciliatus*, pp. of *reconciliare*] (14c) **1 :** the action of reconciling **:** the state of being reconciled **2 :** the Roman Catholic sacrament of penance — **rec·on·cil·ia·to·ry** \-ˈsil-yə-ˌtōr-ē, -ˈsil-ē-ə-, -ˌtȯr-\ *adj*

re·con·dite \ˈrek-ən-ˌdīt, ri-ˈkän-\ *adj* [L *reconditus*, pp. of *recondere* to conceal, fr. *re-* + *condere* to store up, fr. *com-* + *-dere* to put — more at DO] (1649) **1 :** hidden from sight **:** CONCEALED **2 :** difficult or impossible for one of ordinary understanding or knowledge to comprehend **:** DEEP ⟨a ~ subject⟩ **3 :** of, relating to, or dealing with something little known or obscure ⟨~ fact about the origin of the holiday —Floyd Dell⟩ — **re·con·dite·ly** *adv* — **re·con·dite·ness** *n*

re·con·di·tion \ˌrē-kən-ˈdish-ən\ *vt* (1920) **1 :** to restore to good condition (as by replacing parts) **2 :** to condition (as a person or his attitudes) anew; *also* **:** to reinstate (a response) in an organism

re·con·firm \ˌrē-kən-ˈfərm\ *vt* (1611) **:** to confirm again; *also* **:** to establish more strongly — **re·con·fir·ma·tion** \(ˌ)rē-ˌkän-fər-ˈmā-shən\ *n*

re·con·nais·sance \ri-ˈkän-ə-zən(t)s *also* -sən(t)s\ *n* [F, lit., recognition, fr. MF *reconoissance* — more at RECOGNIZANCE] (1810) **:** a preliminary survey to gain information; *esp* **:** an exploratory military survey of enemy territory

re·con·noi·ter *or* **re·con·noi·tre** \ˌrē-kə-ˈnȯit-ər *also* ˌrek-ə-\ *vb* **-noi·tered** *or* **-noi·tred; -noi·ter·ing** *or* **-noi·tring** \-ˈnȯit-ə-riŋ, -ˈnȯi-triŋ\ [obs. F *reconnoître*, lit., to recognize, fr. MF *reconoistre* — more at RECOGNIZE] *vt* (1707) **:** to make a reconnaissance of ~ *vi* **:** to engage in reconnaissance

re·con·sid·er \ˌrē-kən-ˈsid-ər\ *vt* (1571) **:** to consider again with a view to changing or reversing ~ *vi* **:** to consider something again — **re·con·sid·er·a·tion** \-ˌsid-ə-ˈrā-shən\ *n*

re·con·sti·tute \(ˌ)rē-ˈkän(t)-stə-ˌt(y)üt\ *vt* (1812) **:** to constitute again or anew; *esp* **:** to restore to a former condition by adding water — **re·con·sti·tu·tion** \(ˌ)rē-ˌkän(t)-stə-ˈt(y)ü-shən\ *n*

re·con·struct \ˌrē-kən-ˈstrəkt\ *vt* (1768) **:** to construct again **:** REESTABLISH, REASSEMBLE — **re·con·struct·ible** \-ˈstrək-tə-bəl\ *adj* — **re·con·struc·tive** \-tiv\ *adj* — **re·con·struc·tor** \-tər\ *n*

re·con·struc·tion \ˌrē-kən-ˈstrək-shən\ *n* (1791) **1 a :** the action of reconstructing **:** the state of being reconstructed **b** *often cap* **:** the reorganization and reestablishment of the seceded states in the Union after the American Civil War **2 :** something reconstructed

re·con·struc·tion·ism \-shə-ˌniz-əm\ *n, often cap* (1942) **1 :** a movement in 20th century American Judaism that advocates a creative adjustment to contemporary conditions through the cultivation of traditions and folkways shared by all Jews **2 :** advocacy of post-Civil War reconstruction — **re·con·struc·tion·ist** \-sh(ə-)nəst\ *adj or n, often cap*

re·con·ver·sion \ˌrē-kən-ˈvər-zhən, -shən\ *n* (1599) **:** conversion back to a previous state

re·con·vert \ˌrē-kən-ˈvərt\ *vt* (1611) **:** to cause to undergo reconversion ~ *vi* **:** to undergo reconversion

re·con·vey \ˌrē-kən-ˈvā\ *vt* (1506) **:** to convey back to a previous position or owner — **re·con·vey·ance** \-ˈvā-ən(t)s\ *n*

[1]**re·cord** \ri-ˈkȯ(ə)rd\ *vb* [ME *recorden*, lit., to recall, fr. OF *recorder*, fr. L *recordari*, fr. *re-* + *cord-, cor* heart — more at HEART] *vt* (14c) **1 a** (1) **:** to set down in writing **:** furnish written evidence of (2) **:** to deposit an authentic official copy of ⟨~ a deed⟩ **b :** to state as if for a record ⟨spoke in favor of the bill but also said he wanted to ~ certain reservations⟩ **c** (1) **:** to register permanently by mechanical means ⟨earthquake shocks ~*ed* by a seismograph⟩ (2) **:** INDICATE, READ ⟨the thermometer ~*ed* 90°⟩ **2 :** to give evidence of ⟨the intensity of the explosion is ~*ed* on the charred tree trunks⟩ **3 :** to cause (as sound, visual images, or data) to be registered on something (as a disc or magnetic tape) in reproducible form ~ *vi* **:** to record something — **re·cord·able** \-ˈkȯrd-ə-bəl\ *adj*

[2]**rec·ord** \ˈrek-ərd *also* -ˌȯ(ə)rd\ *n* (14c) **1 :** the state or fact of being recorded **2 :** something that records: as **a :** something that recalls or relates past events **b :** an official document that records the acts of a public body or officer **c :** an authentic official copy of a document deposited with a legally designated officer **d :** the official copy of the papers used in a law case **3 a** (1) **:** a body of known or recorded facts about something or someone esp. with reference to a particular sphere of activity that often forms a discernible pattern ⟨a good academic ~⟩ ⟨a liberal voting ~⟩ (2) **:** a collection of related items of information (as in a data base) treated as a unit **b** (1) **:** an attested top performance (2) **:** an unsurpassed statistic **4 :** something on which sound or visual images have been recorded; *specif* **:** a disc with a spiral groove carrying recorded sound for phonograph reproduction — **for the record :** for public knowledge **:** on the record — **off the record :** not for publication ⟨spoke *off the record*⟩ ⟨remarks that were *off the record*⟩ — **of record :** being documented or attested ⟨a partner *of record* in several firms⟩ — **on record 1 :** in the position of having publicly declared oneself ⟨went *on record* as opposed to higher taxes⟩ **2 :** being known, published, or documented ⟨the judge's opinion is *on record*⟩ — **on the record :** for publication

[3]**record** *like*[2]\ *adj* (1893) **:** of, relating to, or being one that is extraordinary among or surpasses others of its kind

re·cor·da·tion \ˌrek-ˌȯr-ˈdā-shən; ˌrē-ˌkȯr-, ri-\ *n* (1802) **:** the action or process of recording

record changer *n* (1931) **:** a phonograph with a device that automatically positions and plays successively each of a stack of records; *also* **:** the automatic device on a record changer

re·cord·er \ri-ˈkȯrd-ər\ *n* (15c) **1 a :** the chief judicial magistrate of some British cities and boroughs **b :** a municipal judge with criminal jurisdiction of first instance and sometimes limited civil jurisdiction **2 :** one that records **3 :** any of a group of wind instruments ranging from soprano to bass that are characterized by a conical tube, a whistle mouthpiece, and eight finger holes

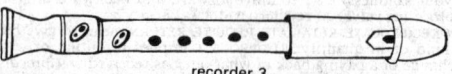

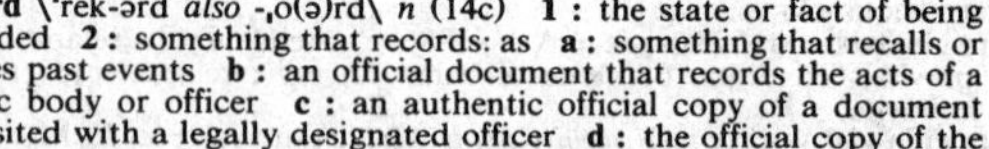
recorder 3

re·cord·ing \ri-ˈkȯrd-iŋ\ *n* (1932) **:** RECORD 4

re·cord·ist \ri-ˈkȯrd-əst\ *n* (1930) **:** one who records sound (as on magnetic tape)

record player *n* (1934) **:** an electronic instrument for playing phonograph records through a loudspeaker

[1]**re·count** \ri-ˈkau̇nt\ *vt* [ME *recounten*, fr. MF *reconter*, fr. *re-* + *conter* to count, relate — more at COUNT] (15c) **:** to relate in detail **:** NARRATE — **re·count·er** *n*

[2]**re·count** \(ˌ)rē-ˈkau̇nt\ *vt* [*re-* + *count*] (1764) **:** to count again

[3]**re·count** \ˈrē-ˌkau̇nt, (ˌ)rē-ˈ\ *n* (1884) **:** a second or fresh count

re·coup \ri-ˈküp\ *vb* [F *recouper* to cut back, fr. OF, fr. *re-* + *couper* to cut — more at COPE] *vt* (1628) **1 a :** to get an equivalent for (as losses) : make up for **b** : REIMBURSE, COMPENSATE ⟨~ a person for losses⟩ **2** : REGAIN ⟨an attempt to ~ his fortune⟩ ~ *vi* : to make good or make up for something lost — **re·coup·able** \-ˈkü-pə-bəl\ *adj* — **re·coup·ment** \-ˈküp-mənt\ *n*

re·course \ˈrē-ˌkō(ə)rs, -ˌkȯ(ə)rs, ri-ˈ\ *n* [ME *recours*, fr. MF, fr. LL *recursus*, fr. L, act of running back, fr. *recursus*, pp. of *recurrere* to run back — more at RECUR] (14c) **1 a** : a turning to someone or something for help or protection **b** : a source of help or strength : RESORT **2** : the right to demand payment from the maker or endorser of a negotiable instrument (as a check)

re·cov·er \ri-ˈkəv-ər\ *vb* **re·cov·ered; re·cov·er·ing** \-(ə-)riŋ\ [ME *recoveren*, fr. MF *recoverer*, fr. L *recuperare*; akin to L *recipere* to receive — more at RECEIVE] *vt* (14c) **1** : to get back : REGAIN **2 a** : to bring back to normal position or condition ⟨stumbled, then ~*ed* himself⟩ **b** *archaic* : RESCUE **3 a** : to make up for ⟨~ increased costs through higher prices⟩ **b** : to gain by legal process **4** *archaic* : REACH **5** : to find or identify again ⟨~ a comet⟩ **6 a** : to obtain from an ore, a waste product, or a by-product **b** : to save from loss and restore to usefulness : RECLAIM ~ *vi* **1** : to regain a normal position or condition (as of health) ⟨~*ing* from a cold⟩ **2** : to obtain a final legal judgment in one's favor — **re·cov·er·abil·i·ty** \-ˌkəv-(ə-)rə-ˈbil-ət-ē\ *adj* — **re·cov·er·able** \-ˈkəv-(ə-)rə-bəl\ *adj* — **re·cov·er·er** \-ˈkəv-ər-ər\ *n*

re–cov·er \(ˈ)rē-ˈkəv-ər\ *vt* (15c) : to cover again or anew

re·cov·ery \ri-ˈkəv-(ə-)rē\ *n, pl* **-er·ies** (15c) : the act, process, or an instance of recovering; *esp* : an economic upturn (as after a depression)

recovery room *n* (1916) : a hospital room equipped for meeting postoperative emergencies

1**rec·re·ant** \ˈrek-rē-ənt\ *adj* [ME, fr. MF, fr. prp. of *recroire* to renounce one's cause in a trial by battle, fr. *re-* + *croire* to believe, fr. L *credere* — more at CREED] (14c) **1** : crying for mercy : COWARDLY **2** : unfaithful to duty or allegiance

2**recreant** *n* (15c) **1** : COWARD **2** : APOSTATE, DESERTER

rec·re·ate \ˈrek-rē-ˌāt\ *vb* **-at·ed; -at·ing** [L *recreatus*, pp.] *vt* (1530) : to give new life or freshness to : REFRESH ~ *vi* : to take recreation — **rec·re·ative** \-ˌāt-iv\ *adj*

re–cre·ate \ˌrē-krē-ˈāt\ *vt* (1587) : to create again; *esp* : to form anew in the imagination — **re–cre·at·able** \-ˈāt-ə-bəl\ *adj* — **re–cre·ation** \-ˈā-shən\ *n* — **re–cre·ative** \-ˈāt-iv\ *adj* — **re–cre·ator** \-ˈāt-ər\ *n*

rec·re·ation \ˌrek-rē-ˈā-shən\ *n* [ME *recreacion*, fr. MF *recreation*, fr. L *recreation-*, *recreatio* restoration to health, fr. *recreatus*, pp. of *recreare* to create anew, restore, refresh, fr. *re-* + *creare* to create] (15c) : refreshment of strength and spirits after work; *also* : a means of refreshment or diversion : HOBBY — **rec·re·ation·al** \-shnəl, -shən-ᵊl\ *adj*

recreational vehicle *n* (1966) : a vehicle designed for recreational use (as in camping)

rec·re·ation·ist \-sh(ə-)nəst\ *n* (1904) : one who seeks recreation esp. in the outdoors

recreation room *n* (1854) **1** : a room (as a rumpus room) used for recreation and relaxation **2** : a public room (as in a hospital) for recreation and social activities — called also *rec room*

re·crim·i·nate \ri-ˈkrim-ə-ˌnāt\ *vi* **-nat·ed; -nat·ing** [ML *recriminatus*, pp. of *recriminare*, fr. L *re-* + *criminari* to accuse — more at CRIMINATE] (1611) **1** : to make a retaliatory charge against an accuser **2** : to retort bitterly — **re·crim·i·na·tion** \-ˌkrim-ə-ˈnā-shən\ *n* — **re·crim·i·na·tive** \-ˈkrim-ə-ˌnāt-iv\ *adj* — **re·crim·i·na·to·ry** \-ˈkrim-(ə-)nə-ˌtōr-ē, -ˌtȯr-\ *adj*

re·cru·desce \ˌrē-krü-ˈdes\ *vi* **-desced; -desc·ing** [L *recrudescere* to become raw again, fr. *re-* + *crudescere* to become raw, fr. *crudus* raw — more at RAW] (1884) : to break out or become active again

re·cru·des·cence \-ˈdes-ᵊn(t)s\ *n* (ca. 1721) : a new outbreak after a period of abatement or inactivity : RENEWAL

re·cru·des·cent \-ᵊnt\ *adj* (ca. 1727) : breaking out again : RENEWING

1**re·cruit** \ri-ˈkrüt\ *vt* (1643) **1 a** (1) : to fill up the number of (as an army) with new members : REINFORCE (2) : to enlist as a member of an armed service **b** : to increase or maintain the number of ⟨America ~*ed* her population from Europe⟩ **c** : to secure the services of : ENGAGE, HIRE **d** : to seek to enroll ⟨a college that ~*s* students from the ghettos⟩ **2** : REPLENISH **3** : to restore or increase the health, vigor, or intensity of ~ *vi* : to enlist new members — **re·cruit·er** *n* — **re·cruit·ment** \-ˈkrüt-mənt\ *n*

2**recruit** *n* [F *recrute*, *recrue* fresh growth, new levy of soldiers, fr. MF, fr. *recroistre* to grow up again, fr. L *recrescere*, fr. *re-* + *crescere* to grow — more at CRESCENT] (1648) **1** : a fresh or additional supply **2** : a newcomer to a field or activity; *specif* : a newly enlisted or drafted member of the armed forces **3** : a former enlisted man of the lowest rank in the army

re·crys·tal·lize \(ˈ)rē-ˈkris-tə-ˌlīz\ *vb* (1797) : to crystallize again or repeatedly — **re·crys·tal·li·za·tion** \(ˌ)rē-ˌkris-tə-lə-ˈzā-shən\ *n*

rect- *or* **recto-** *comb form* [NL *rectum*] : rectum ⟨rect*al*⟩

rec·tal \ˈrek-tᵊl\ *adj* (ca. 1864) : relating to, affecting, or being near the rectum — **rec·tal·ly** \-ē\ *adv*

rect·an·gle \ˈrek-ˌtaŋ-gəl\ *n* [ML *rectangulus* having a right angle, fr. L *rectus* right + *angulus* angle — more at RIGHT, ANGLE] (1571) : a parallelogram all of whose angles are right angles; *esp* : one with adjacent sides of unequal length

rect·an·gu·lar \rek-ˈtaŋ-gyə-lər\ *adj* (1624) **1** : shaped like a rectangle ⟨a ~ area⟩ **2 a** : crossing, lying, or meeting at a right angle ⟨~ axes⟩ **b** : having edges, surfaces, or faces that meet at right angles : having faces or surfaces shaped like rectangles ⟨~ parallelepipeds⟩ ⟨~ blocks⟩ — **rect·an·gu·lar·i·ty** \(ˌ)rek-ˌtaŋ-gyə-ˈlar-ət-ē\ *n* — **rect·an·gu·lar·ly** \rek-ˈtaŋ-gyə-lər-lē\ *adv*

rectangular coordinate *n* (ca. 1864) : a Cartesian coordinate of a Cartesian coordinate system whose straight-line axes or coordinate planes are perpendicular

rec·ti·fi·able \ˈrek-tə-ˌfī-ə-bəl\ *adj* [*rectify* (to determine the length of an arc)] (1816) : having finite length ⟨a ~ curve⟩ — **rec·ti·fi·abil·i·ty** \ˌrek-tə-ˌfī-ə-ˈbil-ət-ē\ *n*

rec·ti·fi·er \ˈrek-tə-ˌfī(-ə)r\ *n* (1611) : one that rectifies; *specif* : a device for converting alternating current into direct current

rec·ti·fy \ˈrek-tə-ˌfī\ *vt* **-fied; -fy·ing** [ME *rectifien*, fr. MF *rectifier*, fr. ML *rectificare*, fr. L *rectus* right] (15c) **1** : to set right : REMEDY **2** : to purify (as alcohol) esp. by repeated or fractional distillation **3** : to correct by removing errors : ADJUST ⟨~ the calendar⟩ **4** : to make (an alternating current) unidirectional *syn* see CORRECT — **rec·ti·fi·ca·tion** \ˌrek-tə-fə-ˈkā-shən\ *n*

rec·ti·lin·ear \ˌrek-tə-ˈlin-ē-ər\ *adj* [LL *rectilineus*, fr. L *rectus* + *linea* line] (1659) **1** : moving in or forming a straight line ⟨~ motion⟩ **2** : characterized by straight lines **3** : PERPENDICULAR 3 **4** : corrected for distortion so that straight lines are imaged accurately ⟨~ lens⟩ — **rec·ti·lin·ear·ly** *adv*

rec·ti·tude \ˈrek-tə-ˌt(y)üd\ *n* [ME, fr. MF, fr. LL *rectitudo*, fr. L *rectus* straight, right] (15c) **1** : the quality or state of being straight **2** : moral integrity : RIGHTEOUSNESS **3** : the quality or state of being correct in judgment or procedure

rec·ti·tu·di·nous \ˌrek-tə-ˈt(y)üd-nəs, -ᵊn-əs\ *adj* [LL *rectitudin-*, *rectitudo* rectitude] (1897) **1** : characterized by rectitude **2** : piously self-righteous

rec·to \ˈrek-(ˌ)tō\ *n, pl* **rectos** [NL *recto* (*folio*) the page being straight] (1824) **1** : the side of a leaf (as of a manuscript) that is to be read first **2** : a right-hand page — compare VERSO

rec·tor \ˈrek-tər\ *n* [L, fr. *rectus*, pp. of *regere* to direct — more at RIGHT] (14c) **1** : one that directs : LEADER **2 a** : a clergyman (as of the Protestant Episcopal Church) in charge of a parish **b** : an incumbent of a Church of England benefice in full possession of its rights **c** : a Roman Catholic priest directing a church with no pastor or one whose pastor has other duties **3** : the head of a university or school — **rec·tor·ate** \-t(ə-)rət\ *n* — **rec·to·ri·al** \rek-ˈtōr-ē-əl, -ˈtȯr-\ *adj* — **rec·tor·ship** \ˈrek-tər-ˌship\ *n*

rec·to·ry \ˈrek-t(ə-)rē\ *n, pl* **-ries** (1594) **1** : a benefice held by a rector **2** : a residence of a rector or a parish priest

rec·trix \ˈrek-triks\ *n, pl* **rec·tri·ces** \ˈrek-trə-ˌsēz, rek-ˈtrī-(ˌ)sēz\ [NL, fr. L, fem. of *rector* one that directs] (1768) : any of the quill feathers of a bird's tail that are important in controlling flight direction — see BIRD illustration

rec·tum \ˈrek-təm\ *n, pl* **rectums** *or* **rec·ta** \-tə\ [NL, fr. *rectum intestinum*, lit., straight intestine] (1541) : the terminal part of the intestine from the sigmoid flexure to the anus

rec·tus \ˈrek-təs\ *n, pl* **rec·ti** \-ˌtī, -ˌtē\ [NL, fr. *rectus musculus* straight muscle] (1733) : any of several straight muscles (as of the abdomen)

re·cum·ben·cy \ri-ˈkəm-bən-sē\ *n, pl* **-cies** (1646) : the state of leaning, resting, or reclining : REPOSE; *also* : a recumbent position

re·cum·bent \-bənt\ *adj* [L *recumbent-*, *recumbens*, prp. of *recumbere* to lie down, fr. *re-* + *-cumbere* to lie down — more at HIP] (1705) **1 a** : suggestive of repose : LEANING, RESTING **b** : lying down **c** : representing a person lying down ⟨a ~ statue⟩ **2** *of an anatomical structure* : tending to rest on the surface from which it extends *syn* see PRONE

re·cu·per·ate \ri-ˈk(y)ü-pə-ˌrāt\ *vb* **-at·ed; -at·ing** [L *recuperatus*, pp. of *recuperare* — more at RECOVER] *vt* (1547) : to get back : REGAIN ~ *vi* : to regain a former state or condition; *esp* : to recover health or strength — **re·cu·per·a·tion** \-ˌk(y)ü-pə-ˈrā-shən\ *n*

re·cu·per·a·tive \-ˈk(y)ü-pə-ˌrāt-iv\ *adj* (ca. 1828) **1** : of or relating to recuperation ⟨~ powers⟩ **2** : aiding in recuperation : RESTORATIVE

re·cur \ri-ˈkər\ *vi* **re·curred; re·cur·ring** [ME *recurren* to return, fr. L *recurrere*, lit., to run back, fr. *re-* + *currere* to run — more at CURRENT] (15c) **1** : to have recourse : RESORT **2** : to go back in thought or discourse **3 a** : to come up again for consideration **b** : to come again to mind **4** : to occur again after an interval — **re·cur·rence** \-ˈkər-ən(t)s, -ˈkə-rən(t)s\ *n*

re·cur·rent \-ˈkər-ənt, -ˈkə-rənt\ *adj* [L *recurrent-*, *recurrens*, prp. of *recurrere*] (1611) **1** : running or turning back in a direction opposite to a former course — used of various nerves and branches of vessels in the arms and legs **2** : returning or happening time after time ⟨~ complaints⟩ — **re·cur·rent·ly** *adv*

recurring decimal *n* (1801) : REPEATING DECIMAL

re·cur·sion \ri-ˈkər-zhən\ *n* [LL *recursion-*, *recursio*, fr. *recursus*, pp. of *recurrere*] (1616) **1** : RETURN **2** : the determination of a succession of elements (as numbers or functions) by operation on one or more preceding elements according to a rule or formula involving a finite number of steps

re·cur·sive \ri-ˈkər-siv\ *adj* (1934) **1** : of, relating to, or involving mathematical recursion **2** : of, relating to, or constituting a procedure that can repeat itself indefinitely or until a specified condition is met ⟨a ~ rule in a grammar⟩ — **re·cur·sive·ly** *adv* — **re·cur·sive·ness** *n*

re·curved \(ˈ)rē-ˈkərvd\ *adj* (1597) : curved backward or inward

re·cu·san·cy \ˈrek-yə-zən-sē, ri-ˈkyüz-ᵊn-\ *n* [*recusant*, n., fr. L *recusant-*, *recusans*, prp. of *recusare* to refuse, fr. *re-* + *causari* to give a reason, fr. *causa* cause, reason] (1563) : refusal to accept or obey established authority; *specif* : the refusal of Roman Catholics to attend services of the Church of England constituting a statutory offense from about 1570 till 1791 — **re·cu·sant** \-zənt, -ᵊnt\ *n or adj*

1**re·cy·cle** \(ˈ)rē-ˈsī-kəl\ *vt* (1926) **1** : to pass again through a series of changes or treatments: as **a** : to process (as liquid body waste, glass, or cans) in order to regain material for human use **b** : RECOVER 6 **2** : to adapt to a new use : ALTER **3** : to bring back : REUSE ⟨a light, chatty tribute that ~*s* a number of good anecdotes —Larry McMurtry⟩ **4** : to make ready for reuse ⟨the plan to ~ long-vacant tenements⟩ ~ *vi* **1** : to return to an earlier point in a countdown **2** : to return to an original condition so that operation can begin again — used of an electronic device — **re·cy·cla·ble** \-k(ə-)lə-bəl\ *adj* — **re·cy·cler** \-k(ə-)lər\ *n*

2**recycle** *n* (1942) : the process of recycling

1**red** \ˈred\ *adj* **red·der; red·dest** [ME, fr. OE *rēad*; akin to OHG *rōt* red, L *ruber* & *rufus*, Gk *erythros*] (bef. 12c) **1 a** : of the color red **b** : having red as a distinguishing color **2 a** (1) : flushed esp. with anger or embarrassment (2) : RUDDY, FLORID (3) : of a coppery hue **b** : BLOODSHOT ⟨eyes ~ from crying⟩ **c** : in the color range between a moderate orange and russet or bay **d** : tinged with red : REDDISH **3** : heated to redness : GLOWING **4 a** : inciting or endorsing radical social or political change esp. by force **b** *often cap* : COMMUNIST **c**

\ə\ abut \ᵊ\ kitten, F table \ər\ further \a\ ash \ā\ ace \ä\ cot, cart \au̇\ out \ch\ chin \e\ bet \ē\ easy \g\ go \i\ hit \ī\ ice \j\ job \ŋ\ sing \ō\ go \ȯ\ law \ȯi\ boy \th\ thin \t͟h\ the \ü\ loot \u̇\ foot \y\ yet \zh\ vision \à, k̲, ⁿ, œ, œ̄, ue, ūe, ʸ\ *see* Guide to Pronunciation

often cap : of or relating to a communist country and esp. to the U.S.S.R.
[2]red *n* (bef. 12c) **1** : a color whose hue resembles that of blood or of the ruby or is that of the long-wave extreme of the visible spectrum **2** : one that is of a red or reddish color: as **a** : RED WINE **b** : an animal with a reddish coat **3 a** : a pigment or dye that colors red **b** : a shade or tint of red **4 a** : one who advocates the violent overthrow of an existing social or political order **b** *cap* : COMMUNIST **5** [fr. the bookkeeping practice of entering debit items in red ink] : the condition of showing a loss — usu. used with *the* ⟨in the ~⟩ — compare BLACK **6** *pl, slang* : red drug capsules containing the sodium salt of secobarbital — called also *red devils*
re·dact \ri-ˈdakt\ *vt* [ME *redacten,* fr. L *redactus,* pp.] (15c) **1** : to put in writing : FRAME **2** : to select or adapt for publication : EDIT
re·dac·tion \-ˈdak-shən\ *n* [F *rédaction,* fr. LL *redaction-, redactio* act of reducing, compressing, fr. L *redactus,* pp. of *redigere* to bring back, reduce, fr. *re-, red-* re- + *agere* to lead — more at AGENT] (1788) **1** : an act or instance of redacting **2** : a work that has been redacted : EDITION, VERSION — **re·dac·tion·al** \-shnəl, -shən-ᵊl\ *adj*
re·dac·tor \-ˈdak-tər\ *n* (1816) : one who redacts; *esp* : EDITOR
red admiral *n* (1840) : a nymphalid butterfly (*Vanessa atalanta*) that is common in both Europe and America, has broad orange-red bands on the forewings, and feeds on nettles in the larval stage
red alert *n* (ca. 1951) : the final stage of alert in which enemy attack appears imminent; *broadly* : a state of alert brought on by impending danger
red alga *n* (1852) : an alga (division Rhodophyta) that has predominantly red pigmentation
red ant *n* (1667) : any of various reddish ants (as the pharaoh ant)
red·ar·gue \ri-ˈdär-(ˌ)gyü\ *vt* **-gued; -gu·ing** [ME *redarguen,* fr. L *redarguere,* fr. *red-* + *arguere* assert, make clear — more at ARGENT] *archaic* (1627) : CONFUTE, DISPROVE
red–bait \ˈred-ˌbāt\ *vb, often cap R, vt* (1940) : to subject (as a person or group) to red-baiting ~ *vi* : to engage in red-baiting — **red–bait·er** *n, often cap R*
red–bait·ing *n, often cap R* (1928) : the act of attacking or persecuting as a Communist or as communistic
red bay *n* (1730) : a small tree (*Persea borbonia*) of the southern U.S. that has dark red heartwood
red·bel·ly dace \ˌred-ˌbel-ē-\ *n* (ca. 1948) : either of two small brightly marked No. American cyprinid fishes (*Phoxinus eos* and *P. erythrogaster*) — called also *red-bel·lied dace* \-ˌbel-ēd-\
red birch *n* (1785) : the heartwood lumber of the yellow birch (*Betula lutea*) and of the sweet birch (*Betula lenta*)
red·bird \ˈred-ˌbərd\ *n* (1669) : any of several birds (as a cardinal, several tanagers, or the bullfinch) with predominantly red plumage
red blood cell *n* (1910) : any of the hemoglobin-containing cells that carry oxygen to the tissues and are responsible for the red color of vertebrate blood — called also *erythrocyte, red blood corpuscle, red cell, red corpuscle*
red–blood·ed \ˈred-ˈbləd-əd\ *adj* (1881) : VIGOROUS, LUSTY
red·bone \ˈred-ˌbōn\ *n* (1916) : a moderate-sized speedy dark red or red and tan American hound that is used esp. for hunting raccoons
red·breast \ˈred-ˌbrest\ *n* (15c) **1** : a bird (as a robin) with a reddish breast **2** : a reddish-bellied sunfish (*Lepomis auritus*) of the eastern U.S. — called also *red-breasted bream*
red·brick \-ˌbrik\ *adj* (ca. 1943) **1** : built of red brick **2** *often cap* [fr. the common use of red brick in constructing the buildings of recently founded universities] : of, relating to, or being the British Universities founded in modern times
red·bud \-ˌbəd\ *n* (1705) : an American leguminous tree (genus *Cercis*) with usu. pale rosy pink flowers
red bug *n, Southern & Midland* (1804) : CHIGGER 2
red·cap \ˈred-ˌkap\ *n* (1918) : a baggage porter (as at a railroad station)
red–carpet *adj* [fr. the traditional laying down of a red carpet for important guests to walk on] (1951) : marked by ceremonial courtesy ⟨~ treatment⟩
red carpet *n* (1952) : a greeting or reception marked by ceremonial courtesy — usu. used in the phrase *roll out the red carpet*
red cedar *n* (1682) **1** : an American juniper (*Juniperus virginiana*) that is common east of the Rocky mountains and has dark green closely imbricated needle-shaped leaves **2** : the fragrant close-grained red wood of the red cedar
red cent *n* (1839) : a trivial amount : PENNY 4, WHIT
red clover *n* (bef. 12c) : a Eurasian clover (*Trifolium pratense*) that has globose heads of reddish purple flowers and is widely cultivated as a hay, forage, and cover crop
red·coat \ˈred-ˌkōt\ *n* (1520) : a British soldier esp. in America during the Revolutionary War
red coral *n* (ca. 1864) : a gorgonian (*Corallium nobile*) of the Mediterranean and adjacent parts of the Atlantic having a hard stony skeleton of a delicate red or pink color used for ornaments and jewelry
Red Cross *n* (1863) : a red Greek cross on a white background used as the emblem of the International Red Cross
red currant *n* (1622) : any of numerous cultivated currants derived from either of two natural species (*Ribes sativum* and *R. rubrum*)
[1]redd \ˈred\ *vb* **redd·ed** *or* **redd; redd·ing** [ME *redden* to clear, prob. alter. of *ridden* — more at RID] *vt, chiefly dial* (1568) : to set in order — usu. used with *up* or *out* ~ *vi, chiefly dial* : to make things tidy — usu. used with *up*
[2]redd *n* [origin unknown] (1804) : the spawning ground or nest of various fishes
red deer *n* (15c) **1** : the common deer of temperate Europe and Asia (*Cervus elaphus*) that is related to but smaller than the elk of No. America **2** : the whitetail in its summer coat
red·den \ˈred-ᵊn\ *vb* **red·dened; red·den·ing** \ˈred-niŋ, -ᵊn-iŋ\ *vt* (1611) : to make red or reddish ~ *vi* : to become red; *esp* : BLUSH
red devils *n pl, slang* (ca. 1966) : RED 6
red·dish \ˈred-ish\ *adj* (14c) : tinged with red — **red·dish·ness** *n*
red dog *n* (1953) : BLITZ 2b — **red dog** *vb*
red drum *n* (1709) : CHANNEL BASS
[1]rede \ˈrēd\ *vt* [ME *reden* — more at READ] (bef. 12c) **1** *dial* : to give counsel to : ADVISE **2** *dial* : INTERPRET, EXPLAIN
[2]rede *n* (bef. 12c) **1** *chiefly dial* : COUNSEL, ADVICE **2** *archaic* : ACCOUNT, STORY
red·ear \ˈred-ˌi(ə)r\ *n* (ca. 1948) : a common sunfish (*Lepomis microlophus*) of the southern and eastern U.S. resembling the bluegill but having the back part of the operculum bright orange-red — called also *redear sunfish, shellcracker*
re·dec·o·rate \(ˈ)rē-ˈdek-ə-ˌrāt\ *vt* (1611) : to freshen or change in appearance : REFURBISH ~ *vi* : to freshen or change a decorative scheme — **re·dec·o·ra·tion** \(ˌ)rē-ˌdek-ə-ˈrā-shən\ *n* — **re·dec·o·ra·tor** \(ˈ)rē-ˈdek-ə-ˌrāt-ər\ *n*
re·deem \ri-ˈdēm\ *vt* [ME *redemen,* modif. of MF *redimer,* fr. L *redimere,* fr. *re-, red-* re- + *emere* to take, buy; akin to Lith *imti* to take] (15c) **1 a** : to buy back : REPURCHASE **b** : to get or win back **2** : to free from what distresses or harms: as **a** : to free from captivity by payment of ransom **b** : to extricate from or help to overcome something detrimental ⟨new interests that ~*ed* his life from futility⟩ **c** : to release from blame or debt : CLEAR **d** : to free from the consequences of sin **3** : to change for the better : REFORM **4** : REPAIR, RESTORE **5 a** : to free from a lien by payment of an amount secured thereby **b** (1) : to remove the obligation of by payment ⟨the U.S. Treasury ~*s* savings bonds on demand⟩ (2) : to convert into something of value ⟨~ trading stamps⟩ **c** : to make good : FULFILL **6 a** : to atone for : EXPIATE **b** (1) : to offset the bad effect of (2) : to make worthwhile : RETRIEVE ***syn*** see RESCUE — **re·deem·able** \-ˈdē-mə-bəl\ *adj*
re·deem·er \-ˈdē-mər\ *n* (15c) : a person who redeems; *esp, cap* : JESUS
re·de·fine \ˌrēd-i-ˈfīn\ *vt* (1872) **1** : to define (as a concept) again : REFORMULATE ⟨had to ~ their terms in order to deal with the problem⟩ **2** : to reexamine or reevaluate esp. with a view to change — **re·def·i·ni·tion** \(ˌ)rē-ˌdef-ə-ˈnish-ən\ *n*
re·demp·tion \ri-ˈdem(p)-shən\ *n* [ME *redempcioun,* fr. MF *redemption,* fr. L *redemption-, redemptio,* fr. *redemptus,* pp. of *redimere* to redeem] (14c) : the act, process, or an instance of redeeming — **re·demp·tion·al** \-shnəl, -shən-ᵊl\ *adj*
re·demp·tion·er \-sh(ə-)nər\ *n* (1771) : an immigrant to America in the 18th and 19th centuries who obtained passage by becoming an indentured servant
re·demp·tive \-ˈdem(p)-tiv\ *adj* (1647) : of, relating to, or bringing about redemption
Re·demp·tor·ist \ri-ˈdem(p)-t(ə-)rəst\ *n* [F *rédemptoriste,* fr. LL *redemptor* redeemer, fr. L, contractor, fr. *redemptus*] (ca. 1842) : a member of the Congregation of the Most Holy Redeemer founded by St. Alphonsus Liguori in Scala, Italy, in 1732 and devoted to preaching
re·demp·to·ry \ri-ˈdem(p)-t(ə-)rē\ *adj* (1602) : serving to redeem
re·de·ploy \ˌrēd-i-ˈplȯi\ *vt* (1945) : to transfer from one area or activity to another ~ *vi* : to relocate men or equipment — **re·de·ploy·ment** \-mənt\ *n*
re·de·scribe \ˌrēd-i-ˈskrīb\ *vt* (1871) : to describe anew or again; *esp* : to give a new and more complete description to (a biological taxon)
re·de·scrip·tion \-ˈskrip-shən\ *n* (1884) : a new and more complete description esp. of a biological taxon
re·de·sign \ˌrēd-i-ˈzīn\ *vt* (1891) : to revise in appearance, function, or content — **redesign** *n*
re·de·vel·op \ˌrēd-i-ˈvel-əp\ *vt* (1882) : to develop again; *esp* : REDESIGN, REBUILD — **re·de·vel·op·er** *n*
re·de·vel·op·ment \-əp-mənt\ *n* (1873) : the act or process of redeveloping; *esp* : renovation of a blighted area
red–eye \ˈred-ˌī\ *n* (1819) **1** : cheap whiskey **2** : a late night or overnight flight
red·eye gravy \ˌred-ˌī-\ *n* (1947) : gravy made from the juices of ham
red fescue *n* (ca. 1900) : a perennial pasture and turf grass (*Festuca rubra*) of Europe and America with creeping rootstocks, erect culms, and reddish spikelets
red·fish \ˈred-ˌfish\ *n* (15c) : any of various reddish fishes: as **a** (1) : a marine scorpaenid food fish (*Sebastes marinus*) of the northern coasts of Europe and America that is usu. bright rose-red when mature — called also *rosefish* (2) : a fish (*Sebastes mentella*) related to the redfish **b** : CHANNEL BASS
red flag *n* (1602) : something that incites to anger or vexation
red fox *n* (1632) : a fox (*Vulpes vulpes*) with bright orange-red to dusky reddish brown fur
red giant *n* (1916) : a star that has low surface temperature and a diameter that is large relative to the sun
red–green blindness *n* (1888) : dichromatism in which the spectrum is seen in tones of yellow and blue — called also *red-green color blindness*

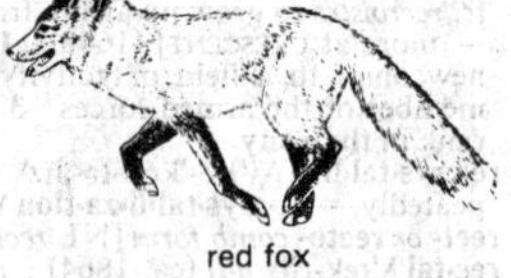
red fox

Red Guard *n* (1966) : a member of a teenage activist organization in China serving the Maoist party
red gum *n* (1788) **1 a** : any of several Australian trees of the genus *Eucalyptus* (esp. *E. camaldulensis, E. amygdalina,* and *E. calophylla*) **b** : eucalyptus gum **2** : SWEET GUM
red–hand·ed \ˈred-ˈhan-dəd\ *adv or adj* (1819) : in the act of committing a crime or misdeed ⟨caught ~⟩
red·head \ˈred-ˌhed\ *n* (1664) **1** : a person having red hair **2** : an American duck (*Aythya americana*) related to the canvasback but having in the male a brighter reddish head and shorter bill
red·head·ed *adj* (1565) : having red hair or a red head
red heat *n* (1686) : the state of being red-hot; *also* : the temperature at which a substance is red-hot
red herring *n* (15c) **1** : a herring cured by salting and slow smoking to a dark brown color **2** [fr. the practice of drawing a red herring across a trail to confuse hunting dogs] : something that distracts attention from the real issue
red·horse \ˈred-ˌhȯrs\ *n* (1796) : any of numerous large suckers (genera *Moxostoma* and *Placopharynx*) of No. American rivers and lakes that have in the male red fins esp. in the breeding season
[1]red–hot \ˈred-ˈhät\ *adj* (14c) **1** : glowing with heat : extremely hot **2** : exhibiting or marked by intense emotion, enthusiasm, or violence ⟨a ~ political campaign⟩ **3** : FRESH, NEW ⟨~ news⟩

[2]red-hot \-ˌhät\ *n* (1835) **1 :** one who shows intense emotion or partisanship **2 :** HOT DOG **3 :** a small red candy strongly flavored with cinnamon

re·dia \ˈrēd-ē-ə\ *n, pl* **re·di·ae** \-ē-ˌē\ *also* **re·di·as** [NL, fr. Francesco *Redi* †1698? Ital. naturalist] (1877) **:** a larva produced within the sporocyst of many trematodes that produces another generation of rediae or develops into a cercaria — **re·di·al** \-ē-əl\ *adj*

Red Indian *n* (1835) **:** AMERICAN INDIAN

red·in·gote \ˈred-iŋ-ˌgōt\ *n* [F, modif. of E *riding coat*] (1793) **:** a fitted outer garment: as **a :** a double-breasted coat with wide flat cuffs and collar worn by men in the 18th century **b :** a woman's lightweight coat open at the front **c :** a dress with a front gore of contrasting material

red ink *n* [fr. the use of red ink in financial statements to indicate a loss] (1926) **1 :** a business loss **:** DEFICIT **2 :** the condition of showing a business loss

red·in·te·grate \ri-ˈdint-ə-ˌgrāt, re-\ *vt* [ME *redintegraten,* fr. L *redintegratus,* pp. of *redintegrare,* fr. *re-, red-* re- + *integrare* to make complete — more at INTEGRATE] *archaic* (15c) **:** to restore to a former and esp. sound state

red·in·te·gra·tion \ri-ˌdint-ə-ˈgrā-shən, re-\ *n* (1501) **1** *archaic* **:** restoration to a former state **2 a :** revival of the whole of a previous mental state when a phase of it recurs **b :** arousal of any response by a part of the complex of stimuli that originally aroused that response — **red·in·te·gra·tive** \-ˈdint-ə-ˌgrāt-iv\ *adj*

re·di·rect \ˌrēd-ə-ˈrekt, ˌrē-(ˌ)dī-\ *vt* (1844) **:** to change the course or direction of — **re·di·rec·tion** \-ˈrek-shən\ *n*

[1]re·dis·count \(ˈ)rē-ˈdis-ˌkau̇nt, ˌrē-dis-ˈ\ *vt* (1866) **:** to discount again (as commercial paper) — **re·dis·count·able** \-ə-bəl\ *adj*

[2]re·dis·count \(ˈ)rē-ˈdis-ˌkau̇nt\ *n* (1896) **1 :** the act or process of rediscounting **2 :** negotiable paper that is rediscounted

re·dis·trib·ute \ˌrēd-ə-ˈstrib-yət\ *vt* (1611) **1 :** to alter the distribution of **:** REALLOCATE **2 :** to spread to other areas — **re·dis·tri·bu·tion** \(ˌ)rē-ˌdis-trə-ˈbyü-shən\ *n* — **re·dis·tri·bu·tion·al** \-shnəl, -shən-ᵊl\ *adj* — **re·dis·trib·u·tive** \ˌrēd-ə-ˈstrib-yət-iv\ *adj* — **re·dis·trib·u·to·ry** \-yə-ˌtōr-ē, -ˌtȯr-\ *adj*

re·dis·tri·bu·tion·ist \(ˈ)rē-ˌdis-trə-ˈbyü-sh(ə-)nəst\ *n* (1979) **:** one that believes in or advocates a welfare state

re·dis·trict \(ˈ)rē-ˈdis-(ˌ)trikt\ *vt* (1850) **:** to divide anew into districts; *specif* **:** to revise the legislative districts of ~ *vi* **:** to revise legislative districts

red·i·vi·vus \ˌred-ə-ˈvī-vəs, -ˈvē-\ *adj* [LL, fr. L, renovated] (1651) **:** brought back to life **:** REBORN

red jasmine *n* (1729) **1 :** a widely cultivated frangipani (*Plumeria rubra*) with large terminal cymes of pink, red, or purple fragrant flowers **2 :** CYPRESS VINE

red lead *n* (1732) **:** an orange-red to brick-red lead oxide Pb_3O_4 used in storage-battery plates, in glass and ceramics, and as a paint pigment — called also *minium*

red leaf *n* (1909) **:** any of several plant diseases characterized by reddening of the foliage

red·leg \ˈred-ˌleg, -ˌlāg\ *n* (1802) **1 :** any of several birds (as a redshank) with red legs **2 :** ARTILLERYMAN

red–legged grasshopper \ˌred-ˌleg(-ə)d-, -ˌlāg(-ə)d-\ *n* (1867) **:** a widely distributed and sometimes highly destructive small No. American grasshopper (*Melanoplus femur-rubrum*) with red hind legs — called also *red-legged locust*

red–let·ter \ˌred-ˌlet-ər\ *adj* [fr. the practice of marking holy days in red letters in church calendars] (1704) **:** of special significance

red light *n* (1849) **1 :** a warning signal; *esp* **:** a red traffic signal **2 :** a cautionary sign **:** DETERRENT

red–light district *n* (1900) **:** a district in which houses of prostitution are numerous

[1]red·line \ˈred-ˈlīn\ *n* (1953) **:** a recommended safety limit **:** the fastest, farthest, or highest point or degree considered safe; *also* **:** the red line which marks this point on a gauge

[2]red·line \ˈred-ˌlīn, -ˈlīn\ *vi* (1968) **:** to withhold home-loan funds or insurance from neighborhoods considered poor economic risks ~ *vt* **:** to discriminate against in housing or insurance

red·ly \ˈred-lē\ *adv* (ca. 1611) **:** in a red manner **:** with red color

red man *n* (1725) **1 :** AMERICAN INDIAN **2** *cap R&M* [Improved Order of *Red Men*] **:** a member of a major benevolent and fraternal order

red maple *n* (1770) **:** a common tree (*Acer rubrum*) of the eastern and central U.S. that grows chiefly on moist soils, has reddish twigs and somewhat pubescent leaves, and yields a lighter and softer wood than the sugar maple

red marrow *n* (1900) **:** reddish bone marrow that is the seat of blood-cell production

red mass *n, often cap R&M* (1889) **:** a votive mass of the Holy Ghost celebrated in red vestments esp. at the opening of courts and congresses

red mite *n* (1894) **:** any of several mites having a red color: as **a :** EUROPEAN RED MITE **b :** CITRUS RED MITE

red mulberry *n* (1717) **:** a No. American forest tree (*Morus rubra*) with soft weak but durable wood; *also* **:** its edible purple fruit

red mullet *n* (1762) **:** MULLET 2

red·neck \ˈred-ˌnek\ *n* (1830) **:** a white member of the Southern rural laboring class — sometimes used disparagingly — **redneck** *also* **red-necked** \-ˌnekt\ *adj*

red·ness \-nəs\ *n* (bef. 12c) **:** the quality or state of being red or red-hot

re·do \(ˈ)rē-ˈdü\ *vt* (1597) **1 :** to do over or again **2 :** REDECORATE — **re·do** \ˈrē-ˌdü, -ˈdü\ *n*

red oak *n* (1634) **1 :** any of numerous American oaks (as *Quercus rubra* and *Quercus falcata*) that have four stamens in each floret, acorns with the inner surface of the shell lined with woolly hairs, the acorn cap covered with thin scales, and leaf veins that usu. run beyond the margin of the leaf to form bristles **2 :** the wood of red oak

red ocher *n* (1572) **:** a red earthy hematite used as a pigment

red·o·lence \ˈred-ᵊl-ən(t)s\ *n* (15c) **1 :** SCENT, AROMA **2 :** the quality or state of being redolent *syn* see FRAGRANCE

red·o·lent \-ᵊl-ənt\ *adj* [ME, fr. MF, fr. L *redolent-, redolens,* prp. of *redolēre* to emit a scent, fr. *re-, red-* + *olēre* to smell — more at ODOR] (15c) **1 :** exuding fragrance **:** AROMATIC **2 a :** full of a specified fragrance **:** SCENTED ⟨air ~ of seaweed⟩ **b :** EVOCATIVE, SUGGESTIVE ⟨a city ~ of antiquity⟩ *syn* see ODOROUS — **red·o·lent·ly** *adv*

red osier *n* (1807) **:** a common No. American shrub (*Cornus stolonifera*) with reddish purple twigs, white flowers, and globose blue or whitish fruit

re·dou·ble \(ˈ)rē-ˈdəb-əl\ *vt* (15c) **1 :** to make twice as great in size or amount **:** INTENSIFY **2 a** *obs* **:** to echo back **b** *archaic* **:** REPEAT ~ *vi* **1 :** to become redoubled **2** *archaic* **:** RESOUND **3 :** to double an opponent's double in bridge — **redouble** *n*

re·doubt \ri-ˈdau̇t\ *n* [F *redoute,* fr. It *ridotto,* fr. ML *reductus* secret place, fr. L, withdrawn, fr. pp. of *reducere* to lead back — more at REDUCE] (1608) **1 a :** a small usu. temporary enclosed defensive work **b :** a defended position **:** protective barrier **2 :** a secure place

re·doubt·able \ri-ˈdau̇t-ə-bəl\ *adj* [ME *redoutable,* fr. MF, fr. *redouter* to dread, fr. *re-* + *douter* to doubt] (14c) **1 :** causing fear or alarm **:** FORMIDABLE **2 :** inspiring or worthy of awe or reverence **:** ILLUSTRIOUS — **re·doubt·ably** \-blē\ *adv*

re·dound \ri-ˈdau̇nd\ *vi* [ME *redounden,* fr. MF *redonder,* fr. L *redundare,* fr. *re-, red-* re- + *unda* wave — more at WATER] (14c) **1** *archaic* **:** to become swollen **:** OVERFLOW **2 :** to have an effect for good or ill ⟨new power alignments which may or may not ~ to the faculty's benefit —G. W. Bonham⟩ **3 :** to become transferred or added **:** ACCRUE **4 :** REBOUND, REFLECT

red·out \ˈred-ˌau̇t\ *n* (1942) **:** a condition in which centripetal acceleration drives blood to the head and causes reddening of the visual field and headache

re·dox \ˈrē-ˌdäks\ *adj* [*red*uction + *ox*idation] (1828) **:** of or relating to oxidation-reduction

red–pen·cil \ˈred-ˈpen(t)-səl\ *vt* (1946) **1 :** CENSOR **2 :** CORRECT, REVISE

red pepper *n* (ca. 1597) **:** CAYENNE PEPPER

red pine *n* (1809) **1 :** a No. American pine (*Pinosa resinosa*) that has reddish bark **2 :** the hard but not durable wood of the red pine that consists chiefly of sapwood

red·poll \ˈred-ˌpōl\ *n* (1738) **:** any of several small finches (genus *Carduelis* or *Acanthis*) which resemble siskins and in which the males usu. have a red or rosy crown; *esp* **:** one (*C. flammea*) found in northern regions of both the New and Old World

red poll *n, often cap R&P* [alter. of *red polled*] (1893) **:** any of a British breed of large hornless dual-purpose red cattle

[1]re·dress \ri-ˈdres\ *vt* [ME *redressen,* fr. MF *redresser,* fr. OF *redrecier,* fr. *re-* + *drecier* to make straight — more at DRESS] (14c) **1 a** (1) **:** to set right **:** REMEDY (2) **:** to make up for **:** COMPENSATE **b :** to remove the cause of (a grievance or complaint) **c :** to exact reparation for **:** AVENGE **2** *archaic* **a :** to requite (a person) for a wrong or loss **b :** HEAL *syn* see CORRECT — **re·dress·er** *n*

[2]re·dress \ri-ˈdres, ˈrē-ˌ\ *n* (14c) **1 a :** relief from distress **b :** means or possibility of seeking a remedy ⟨without ~⟩ **2 :** compensation for wrong or loss **:** REPARATION **3 a :** an act or instance of redressing **b :** RETRIBUTION, CORRECTION

red ribbon *n* (1927) **:** a red ribbon usu. with appropriate words or markings awarded the second-place winner in a competition

red·root \ˈred-ˌrüt, -ˌru̇t\ *n* (1709) **1 :** a perennial herb (*Lachnanthes tinctoria*) of the bloodwort family of the eastern U.S. whose red root is the source of a dye **2 :** a pigweed (*Amaranthus retroflexus*) that bears greenish flowers in dense spikes with bracts almost twice as long as the sepals

red rust *n* (1899) **1 :** the uredinial stage of a rust **2 :** the diseased condition produced by red rust

red salmon *n* (1881) **:** SOCKEYE

red seaweed *n* (1760) **:** RED ALGA; *specif* **:** any of a genus (*Polysiphonia*) having a filamentous much-branched thallus

red·shank \ˈred-ˌshaŋk\ *n* (1525) **:** a common Old World sandpiper (*Tringa totanus*) with pale red legs and feet

red·shift \ˈred-ˈshift\ *n* (1923) **:** a displacement of the spectrum of a celestial body toward longer wavelengths that is a consequence of the Doppler effect or the gravitational field of the source — **red·shift·ed** *adj*

red·shirt \ˈred-ˌshərt\ *n* [fr. the red jersey commonly worn by such a player in practice scrimmages against the regulars] (1952) **:** a college athlete who is kept out of varsity competition for a year in order to extend the period of his eligibility — **redshirt** *vb*

red–shoul·dered hawk \ˌred-ˌshōl-dərd-\ *n* (1812) **:** a common hawk (*Buteo lineatus*) of eastern No. America that has a banded tail and a light spot on the underside of the wings toward the tips

red sin·dhi \-ˈsin-dē\ *n* [[1]*red* + *sindhi* (one belonging to Sind, Pakistan)] (1946) **:** any of an Indian breed of rather small red humped dairy cattle extensively used for crossbreeding with European stock in tropical areas

red siskin *n* (1948) **:** a finch (*Carduelis cucullata*) of northern So. America that is scarlet with black head, wings, and tail

red·skin \ˈred-ˌskin\ *n* (1699) **:** AMERICAN INDIAN — usu. taken to be offensive

red snapper *n* (1755) **:** any of various reddish fishes (as of the genera *Lutjanus* and *Sebastodes*) including several food fishes

red snow *n* (1678) **:** snow colored by various airborne dusts or by a growth of algae (as of the genus *Chlamydomonas*) that contain red pigment and live in the upper layer of snow; *also* **:** an alga causing red snow

red soil *n* (1892) **:** any of a group of zonal soils that develop in a warm temperate moist climate under deciduous or mixed forests and that have thin organic and organic-mineral layers overlying a yellowish brown leached layer resting on an illuvial red horizon — called also *red podzolic soil*

red spider *n* (1646) **:** any of several small web-spinning mites (family Tetranychidae) that attack forage and crop plants

red spruce *n* (1777) **:** a coniferous tree (*Picea rubens*) of eastern No. America that has deeply furrowed brown or purplish bark and is an important source of lumber and pulpwood

\ə\ abut \ᵊ\ kitten, F table \ər\ further \a\ ash \ā\ ace \ä\ cot, cart
\au̇\ out \ch\ chin \e\ bet \ē\ easy \g\ go \i\ hit \ī\ ice \j\ job
\ŋ\ sing \ō\ go \ȯ\ law \ȯi\ boy \th\ thin \t͟h\ the \ü\ loot \u̇\ foot
\y\ yet \zh\ vision \à, k̲, ⁿ, œ, œ̄, ue, ue̅, ʸ\ *see* Guide to Pronunciation

red squill *n* (1738) **1 :** a red-bulbed form of squill (*Urginea maritima*) **2 :** a rat poison derived from the bulb of red squill

red squirrel *n* (1637) **:** a common and widely distributed No. American squirrel (*Tamiasciurus hudsonicus* or *Sciurus hudsonicus*) that has the upper parts chiefly red and is smaller than the gray squirrel

red star *n* (1903) **:** a star having a very low surface temperature and a red color

red·start \'red-ˌstärt\ *n* [*red* + obs. *start* (handle, tail)] (ca. 1570) **1 :** a small European singing bird (*Phoenicurus phoenicurus*) related to the redbreast **2 :** a fly-catching warbler (*Setophaga ruticilla*) chiefly of eastern No. America

red–tailed hawk \ˌred-ˌtāld-\ *n* (1805) **:** a widely distributed New World buteonine hawk (*Buteo jamaicensis*); *esp* **:** a common rodent-eating hawk (*Buteo jamaicensis borealis*) of eastern No. America that is mottled dusky above and white streaked dusky and tinged with buff below and has a rather short typically reddish tail

red tape *n* [fr. the red tape formerly used to bind legal documents in England] (1736) **:** official routine or procedure marked by excessive complexity which results in delay or inaction

red tide *n* (1904) **:** seawater discolored by the presence of large numbers of dinoflagellates (esp. of the genera *Gonyaulax* and *Gymnodinium*) which produce a toxin poisonous to many forms of marine life and to humans who consume infected shellfish — compare SAXITOXIN

red·top \'red-ˌtäp\ *n* (1790) **:** any of various grasses (genus *Agrostis*) with usu. reddish panicles; *esp* **:** an important forage and lawn grass (*A. alba*) of eastern No. America

re·duce \ri-'d(y)üs\ *vb* **re·duced; re·duc·ing** [ME *reducen* to lead back, fr. L *reducere*, fr. *re-* + *ducere* to lead — more at TOW] *vt* (14c) **1 a :** to draw together or cause to converge **:** CONSOLIDATE ⟨~ all the questions to one⟩ **b :** to diminish in size, amount, extent, or number ⟨~ taxes⟩ ⟨~ the likelihood of war⟩ ⟨add the wine and ~ the sauce for two minutes⟩ **c :** to narrow down **:** RESTRICT ⟨the Indians were *reduced* to small reservations⟩ **d :** to make shorter **:** ABRIDGE **2** *archaic* **:** to restore to righteousness **:** SAVE **3 :** to bring to a specified state or condition ⟨the impact of the movie *reduced* them to tears⟩ **4 a :** to force to capitulate **b :** FORCE, COMPEL **5 a :** to bring to a systematic form or character ⟨~ natural events to laws⟩ **b :** to put down in written or printed form ⟨~ an agreement to writing⟩ **6 :** to correct (as a fracture) by bringing displaced or broken parts back into their normal positions **7 a :** to lower in grade or rank **:** DEMOTE **b :** to lower in condition or status **:** DOWNGRADE **8 a :** to diminish in strength or density **b :** to diminish in value **9 a (1) :** to change the denominations or form of without changing the value **(2) :** to construct a geometrical figure similar to but smaller than (a given figure) **b :** to transpose from one form into another **:** CONVERT **c :** to change (an expression) to an equivalent but more fundamental expression ⟨~ a fraction⟩ **10 :** to break down (as by crushing or grinding) **:** PULVERIZE **11 a :** to bring to the metallic state by removal of nonmetallic elements ⟨~ an ore by heat⟩ **b :** DEOXIDIZE **c :** to combine with or subject to the action of hydrogen **d (1) :** to change (an element or ion) from a higher to a lower oxidation state **(2) :** to add one or more electrons to (an atom or ion or molecule) **12 :** to change (a stressed vowel) to an unstressed vowel ~ *vi* **1 a (1) :** to become diminished or lessened; *esp* **:** to lose weight by dieting **(2) :** to become reduced ⟨ferrous iron ~*s* to ferric iron⟩ **b :** to become concentrated or consolidated **c :** to undergo meiosis **2 :** to become converted or equated *syn* see DECREASE, CONQUER — **re·duc·er** *n* — **re·duc·ibil·i·ty** \-ˌd(y)ü-sə-'bil-ət-ē\ *n* — **re·duc·ible** \-'d(y)ü-sə-bəl\ *adj* — **re·duc·ibly** \-blē\ *adv*

reducing agent *n* (1885) **:** a substance that reduces a chemical compound usu. by donating electrons

re·duc·tant \ri-'dək-tənt\ *n* (1925) **:** REDUCING AGENT

re·duc·tase \-ˌtās, -ˌtāz\ *n* (1902) **:** an enzyme that catalyzes reduction

re·duc·tio ad ab·sur·dum \ri-'dək-tē-ˌō-ˌad-əb-'sərd-əm, -s(h)ē-ˌō-, -'zərd-\ *n* [LL, lit., reduction to the absurd] (1741) **:** disproof of a proposition by showing an absurdity to which it leads when carried to its logical conclusion

re·duc·tion \ri-'dək-shən\ *n* [ME *reduccion* restoration, fr. MF *reduction*, fr. LL & L; LL *reduction-, reductio* reduction (in a syllogism), fr. L, restoration, fr. *reductus*, pp. of *reducere*] (1546) **1 :** the act or process of reducing **:** the state of being reduced **2 a :** something made by reducing **b :** the amount by which something is reduced **3 :** MEIOSIS; *specif* **:** production of the gametic chromosome number in the first meiotic division — **re·duc·tion·al** \-shnəl, -shən-ᵊl\ *adj*

reduction division *n* (1891) **:** the usu. first division of meiosis in which chromosome reduction occurs; *also* **:** MEIOSIS 2

reduction gear *n* (1896) **:** a combination of gears used to reduce the input speed (as of a marine turbine) to a lower output speed (as of a ship's propeller)

re·duc·tion·ism \ri-'dək-shə-ˌniz-əm\ *n* (ca. 1943) **1 :** the attempt to explain all biological processes by the same explanations (as by physical laws) that chemists and physicists use to interpret inanimate matter; *also* **:** the theory that complete reductionism is possible **2 :** a procedure or theory that reduces complex data or phenomena to simple terms; *esp* **:** OVERSIMPLIFICATION — **re·duc·tion·ist** \-sh(ə-)nəst\ *n or adj* — **re·duc·tion·is·tic** \-ˌdək-shə-'nis-tik\ *adj*

re·duc·tive \ri-'dək-tiv\ *adj* (1633) **1 :** of, relating to, causing, or involving reduction **2 :** of or relating to reductionism **:** REDUCTIONISTIC

re·dun·dan·cy \ri-'dən-dən-sē\ *n, pl* **-cies** (1601) **1 a :** the quality or state of being redundant **:** SUPERFLUITY **b :** the use of redundant components; *also* **:** such components **c** *chiefly Brit* **:** dismissal from a job esp. by layoff or early retirement **2 :** PROFUSION, ABUNDANCE **3 a :** superfluous repetition **:** PROLIXITY **b :** an act or instance of needless repetition **4 :** the part of a message that can be eliminated without loss of essential information

re·dun·dant \-dənt\ *adj* [L *redundant-, redundans*, prp. of *redundare* to overflow — more at REDOUND] (ca. 1604) **1 a :** exceeding what is necessary or normal **:** SUPERFLUOUS **b :** characterized by or containing an excess; *specif* **:** using more words than necessary **c :** characterized by similarity or repetition ⟨a group of particularly ~ brick buildings⟩ **d** *chiefly Brit* **:** being out of work **:** laid off **2 :** PROFUSE, LAVISH **3 :** serving as a duplicate for preventing failure of an entire system (as a spacecraft) upon failure of a single component — **re·dun·dant·ly** *adv*

re·du·pli·cate \ri-'d(y)ü-pli-ˌkāt, 'rē-\ *vt* [LL *reduplicatus*, pp. of *reduplicare*, fr. L *re-* + *duplicare* to double — more at DUPLICATE] (ca. 1570) **1 :** to make or perform again **:** COPY, REPEAT **2 :** to form (a word) by reduplication — **re·du·pli·cate** \-kət\ *adj*

re·du·pli·ca·tion \ri-ˌd(y)ü-pli-'kā-shən, ˌrē-\ *n* (1589) **1 :** an act or instance of doubling or reiterating **2 a :** an often grammatically functional repetition of a radical element or a part of it occurring usu. at the beginning of a word and often accompanied by change of the radical vowel **b (1) :** a word or form produced by reduplication **(2) :** the repeated element in such a word or form **3 :** ANADIPLOSIS — **re·du·pli·ca·tive** \ri-'d(y)ü-pli-ˌkāt-iv, 'rē-\ *adj* — **re·du·pli·ca·tive·ly** *adv*

re·du·vi·id \ri-'d(y)ü-vē-əd\ *n* [deriv. of L *reduvia* hangnail] (1888) **:** any of a large and widely distributed family (Reduviidae) of blood-sucking hemipterous insects comprising the assassin bugs — **reduviid** *adj*

re·dux \(ˈ)rē-'dəks\ *adj* [L, fr. *reducere* to lead back] (1660) **:** brought back — used postpositively

red·ware \'red-ˌwa(ə)r, -ˌwe(ə)r\ *n* (ca. 1797) **:** earthenware pottery made of clay containing considerable iron oxide

red water *n* (1594) **:** any of several cattle diseases characterized by hematuria

red wheat *n* (1523) **:** a wheat that has red grains

red wine *n* (ca. 1754) **:** a wine with a predominantly red color derived during fermentation from the natural pigment in the skins of dark-colored grapes

red·wing \'red-ˌwiŋ\ *n* (1654) **1 :** a European thrush (*Turdus musicus*) having the underwing coverts red **2 :** RED-WINGED BLACKBIRD

red–winged blackbird \ˌred-ˌwiŋd-\ *n* (1797) **:** a No. American blackbird (*Agelaius phoeniceus*) of which the adult male is black with a patch of bright scarlet at the bend of the wings bordered behind with yellow or buff — called also *redwing blackbird*

red·wood \'red-ˌwu̇d\ *n* (1634) **1 :** any of various woods yielding a red dye **2 :** a tree that yields a red dyewood or produces red or reddish wood **3 a :** a commercially important coniferous timber tree (*Sequoia sempervirens*) of California that sometimes reaches a height of 360 feet (110 meters) **b :** the brownish red light wood of the California redwood

red worm *n* (1935) **:** BLOODWORM; *esp* **:** a small reddish aquatic oligochaete worm (genus *Tubifex*)

re·echo \(ˈ)rē-'ek-(ˌ)ō\ *vi* (1590) **:** to repeat or return an echo **:** echo again or repeatedly **:** REVERBERATE ~ *vt* **:** to echo back **:** REPEAT

¹reed \'rēd\ *n* [ME *rede*, fr. OE *hrēod*; akin to OHG *hriot* reed, Lith *krutėti* to stir] (bef. 12c) **1 a :** any of various tall grasses with slender often prominently jointed stems that grow esp. in wet areas **b :** a stem of a reed **c :** a person or thing too weak to rely on **:** one easily swayed or overcome **2 :** a growth or mass of reeds; *specif* **:** reeds for thatching **3 :** ARROW **4 :** a wind instrument made from the hollow joint of a plant **5 :** an ancient Hebrew unit of length equal to 6 cubits **6 a :** a thin elastic tongue (as of cane, wood, metal, or plastic) fastened at one end over an air opening in a wind instrument (as a clarinet, organ pipe, or accordion) and set in vibration by an air current **b :** a woodwind instrument that produces sound by the vibrating of a reed against the mouthpiece ⟨the ~*s* of an orchestra⟩ **7 :** a device on a loom resembling a comb and used to space warp yarns evenly **8 :** REEDING 1a

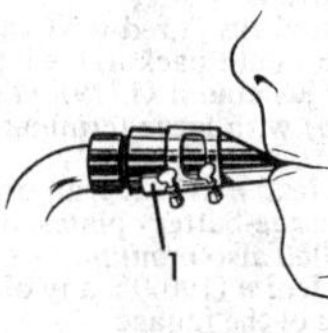

1 reed 6a

²reed *vt* (1951) **:** to make corrugations on (the edge of a coin)

reed·buck \'rēd-ˌbək\ *n, pl* **reedbuck** *also* **reedbucks** (1834) **:** any of a genus (*Redunca*) of fawn-colored African antelopes in which the females are hornless

re·ed·i·fy \(ˈ)rē-'ed-ə-ˌfī\ *vt* **-fied; -fy·ing** [ME *reedifien*, fr. MF *reedifier*, fr. LL *reaedificare*, fr. L *re-* + *aedificare* to build — more at EDIFY] *Brit* (15c) **:** REBUILD

reed·ing \'rēd-iŋ\ *n* (1815) **1 a :** a small convex molding — see MOLDING illustration **b :** decoration by series of reedings **2 :** corrugations on the edge of a coin

re·edit \(ˈ)rē-'ed-ət\ *vt* (1797) **:** to edit again **:** make a new edition of — **re·edi·tion** \ˌrē-ə-'dish-ən\ *n*

reed·man \'rēd-ˌman\ *n* (1938) **:** one who plays a reed instrument

reed organ *n* (1851) **:** a keyboard wind instrument in which the wind acts on a set of free reeds

reed pipe *n* (ca. 1727) **:** a pipe-organ pipe producing its tone by vibration of a beating reed in a current of air

re·ed·u·cate \(ˈ)rē-'ej-ə-ˌkāt\ *vt* (1808) **:** to train again; *esp* **:** to rehabilitate through education — **re·ed·u·ca·tion** \(ˌ)rē-ˌej-ə-'kā-shən\ *n* — **re·ed·u·ca·tive** \(ˈ)rē-'ej-ə-ˌkāt-iv\ *adj*

reedy \'rēd-ē\ *adj* **reed·i·er; -est** (14c) **1 :** abounding in or covered with reeds **2 :** made of or resembling reeds; *esp* **:** SLENDER, FRAIL **3 :** having the tone quality of a reed instrument

¹reef \'rēf\ *n* [ME *riff*, fr. ON *rif*; akin to OE *ribb* rib] (14c) **1 :** a part of a sail taken in or let out in regulating size **2 :** reduction in sail area by reefing

²reef *vt* (1667) **1 :** to reduce the area of (a sail) by rolling or folding a portion **2 :** to lower or bring inboard (a spar) wholly or partially ~ *vi* **:** to reduce a sail by taking in a reef

³reef *n* [D *rif*, prob. of Scand origin; akin to ON *rif* reef of a sail] (1584) **1 a :** a chain of rocks or ridge of sand at or near the surface of water **b :** a hazardous obstruction **2 :** LODE, VEIN — **reefy** \'rē-fē\ *adj*

¹reef·er \'rē-fər\ *n* (1818) **1 :** one that reefs **2 :** a close-fitting usu. double-breasted jacket or coat of thick cloth

²ree·fer \'rē-fər\ *n* [by shortening & alter.] (1914) **1 :** REFRIGERATOR **2 :** a refrigerator car, truck, trailer, or ship

³reef·er *n* [perh. fr. ²*reef*] (1931) **:** a marijuana cigarette; *also* **:** MARIJUANA 2

reef knot *n* (1841) **:** a square knot used in reefing a sail — see KNOT illustration

¹reek \'rēk\ *n* [ME *rek*, fr. OE *rēc*; akin to OHG *rouh* smoke] (bef. 12c) **1** *chiefly dial* **:** SMOKE **2 :** VAPOR, FOG **3 :** a strong or disagreeable fume or odor

²reek *vi* (bef. 12c) **1 :** to emit smoke or vapor **2 a :** to give off or become permeated with a strong or offensive odor **b :** to give a strong impression of some constituent quality or feature ⟨a neighborhood that ~*s* of poverty⟩ **3 :** EMANATE ~ *vt* **1 :** to subject to the action of smoke or vapor **2 :** to give off : EXUDE ⟨a politician who ~*s* charm⟩ — **reek·er** *n* — **reeky** \ˈrē-kē\ *adj*

[1]**reel** \ˈrē(ə)l\ *n* [ME, fr. OE *hrēol;* akin to ON *hrǣll* weaver's reed, Gk *krekein* to weave] (bef. 12c) **1 :** a revolvable device on which something flexible is wound: as **a :** a small windlass at the butt of a fishing rod for the line **b** *chiefly Brit* **:** a spool or bobbin for sewing thread **c :** a flanged spool for photographic film; *esp* **:** one for motion pictures **2 :** a quantity of something wound on a reel **3 :** a frame for drying clothes usu. having radial arms on a vertical pole

[2]**reel** *vt* (14c) **1 :** to wind on or as if on a reel **2 :** to draw by reeling a line ⟨~ a fish in⟩ ~ *vi* **:** to turn a reel — **reel·able** \ˈrē-lə-bəl\ *adj*

[3]**reel** *vb* [ME *relen,* prob. fr. *reel,* n.] *vi* (14c) **1 a :** to turn or move round and round **b :** to be in a whirl **2 :** to behave in a violent disorderly manner **3 :** to waver or fall back (as from a blow) **4 :** to walk or move unsteadily ~ *vt* **:** to cause to reel

[4]**reel** *n* (1572) **:** a reeling motion

[5]**reel** *n* [prob. fr. [4]*reel*] (1585) **1 :** a lively Scottish-Highland dance; *also* **:** the music for this dance **2 :** VIRGINIA REEL

re·elect \ˌrē-ə-ˈlekt\ *vt* (1601) **:** to elect for another term in office — **re·elec·tion** \-ˈlek-shən\ *n*

reel·er \ˈrē-lər\ *n* (ca. 1598) **1 :** one that reels **2 :** a motion picture having a specified number of reels ⟨a two-*reeler*⟩

reel off *vt* (1952) **1 :** to chalk up usu. as a series **2 :** to tell or recite readily and usu. at length ⟨*reel off* a few jokes to break the ice⟩

reel–to–reel *adj* (1961) **:** of, relating to, or utilizing magnetic tape that requires threading on a take-up reel ⟨a ~ tape recorder⟩

re·em·broi·der \ˌrē-əm-ˈbrȯid-ər\ *vt* (1927) **:** to outline a design (as on lace) with embroidery stitching

re·em·ploy \ˌrē-əm-ˈplȯi\ *vt* (ca. 1611) **:** to employ again; *esp* **:** to hire back — **re·em·ploy·ment** \-mənt\ *n*

re·en·act \ˌrē-ə-ˈnakt\ *vt* (1676) **1 :** to enact (as a law) again **2 :** to act or perform again **3 :** to repeat the actions of (an earlier event or incident) — **re·en·act·ment** \-ˈnak(t)-mənt\ *n*

re·en·force \ˌrē-ən-ˈfō(ə)rs, -ˈfȯ(ə)rs\ *var of* REINFORCE

re·en·ter \(ˈ)rē-ˈent-ər\ *vt* (15c) **1 :** to enter (something) again **2 :** to return to and enter ~ *vi* **:** to enter again

re·en·trance \(ˈ)rē-ˈen-trən(t)s\ *n* (1594) **:** REENTRY

[1]**re·en·trant** \-trənt\ *adj* (1781) **:** directed inward

[2]**reentrant** *n* (1899) **1 :** one that reenters **2 :** one that is reentrant **3 :** an indentation in a landform

re·en·try \(ˈ)rē-ˈen-trē\ *n* (15c) **1 :** a retaking possession; *esp* **:** entry by a lessor on leased premises on the tenant's failure to perform the conditions of the lease **2 :** a second or new entry **3 :** a playing card that will enable a player to regain the lead **4 :** the action of reentering the earth's atmosphere after travel in space

reest \ˈrēst\ *vi* [prob. short for Sc *arreest* to arrest, fr. ME (Sc) *arreisten,* fr. MF *arester* — more at ARREST] *chiefly Scot* (1786) **:** BALK

[1]**reeve** \ˈrēv\ *n* [ME *reve,* fr. OE *gerēfa,* fr. *ge-* (associative prefix) + *-rēfa* (akin to OE *-rōf* number, OHG *ruova*) — more at CO-] (bef. 12c) **1 :** a local administrative agent of an Anglo-Saxon king **2 :** a medieval English manor officer responsible chiefly for overseeing the discharge of feudal obligations **3 a :** the council president in some Canadian municipalities **b :** a local official charged with enforcement of specific regulations ⟨deer ~⟩

[2]**reeve** *vb* **rove** \ˈrōv\ *or* **reeved; reev·ing** [origin unknown] *vt* (1627) **1 :** to pass (as a rope) through a hole or opening **2 :** to fasten by passing through a hole or around something **3 :** to pass a rope through ~ *vi, of a rope* **:** to pass through a block or similar device

[3]**reeve** *n* [prob. alter. of *ruff*] (1634) **:** the female of the ruff (sandpiper)

ref \ˈref\ *n* (1899) **:** a referee in a game or sport

re·fash·ion \(ˈ)rē-ˈfash-ən\ *vt* (1803) **:** REMAKE, ALTER

re·fect \ri-ˈfekt\ *vt* [L *refectus,* pp.] *archaic* (15c) **:** to refresh with food or drink

re·fec·tion \ri-ˈfek-shən\ *n* [ME *refeccioun,* fr. MF *refection,* fr. L *refection-, refectio,* fr. *refectus,* pp. of *reficere* to restore, fr. *re-* + *facere* to make — more at DO] (14c) **1 :** refreshment of mind, spirit, or body; *esp* **:** NOURISHMENT **2 a :** the taking of refreshment **b :** food and drink together **:** REPAST

re·fec·to·ry \ri-ˈfek-t(ə-)rē\ *n, pl* **-ries** [LL *refectorium,* fr. L *refectus*] (15c) **:** a dining hall (as in a monastery or college)

refectory table *n* (1923) **:** a long table with heavy legs

re·fel \ri-ˈfel\ *vt* **re·felled; re·fel·ling** [L *refellere* to prove false, refute, fr. *re-* + *fallere* to deceive — more at FAIL] *obs* (1530) **:** REJECT, REPULSE

re·fer \ri-ˈfər\ *vb* **re·ferred; re·fer·ring** [ME *referren,* fr. L *referre* to bring back, report, refer, fr. *re-* + *ferre* to carry — more at BEAR] *vt* (14c) **1 a** (1) **:** to think of, regard, or classify within a general category or group (2) **:** to explain in terms of a general cause **b :** to allot to a particular place, stage, or period **c :** to regard as coming from or located in a specific area **2 a :** to send or direct for treatment, aid, information, or decision ⟨~ a patient to a specialist⟩ ⟨~ a bill back to a committee⟩ **b :** to direct for testimony or guaranty as to character or ability ~ *vi* **1 a :** to have relation or connection **:** RELATE **b :** to direct attention usu. by clear and specific mention ⟨no one *referred* to yesterday's quarrel⟩ **2 :** to have recourse **:** glance briefly ⟨*referred* frequently to his notes while speaking⟩ — **re·fer·able** \ˈref-(ə-)rə-bəl, ri-ˈfər-ə-\ *adj* — **re·fer·rer** \ri-ˈfər-ər\ *n*

[1]**ref·er·ee** \ˌref-ə-ˈrē\ *n* (1621) **1 :** one to whom a thing is referred: as **a :** a person to whom a legal matter is referred for investigation and report or for settlement **b :** a person who reviews an esp. technical paper before publication **c :** REFERENCE 4a **2 :** a sports official usu. having final authority in administering a game **3** *chiefly Brit* **:** REFERENCE 4a

[2]**referee** *vb* **-eed; -ee·ing** *vt* (1889) **1 :** to conduct (as a match or game) as referee **2 a :** to arbitrate (as a legal matter) as a judge or third party **b :** to review (as a technical paper) before publication ~ *vi* **:** to act as a referee

[1]**ref·er·ence** \ˈref-ərn(t)s, ˈref-(ə-)rən(t)s\ *n* (1589) **1 :** the act of referring or consulting **2 :** a bearing on a matter **:** RELATION ⟨in ~ to your recent letter⟩ **3 :** something that refers: as **a :** ALLUSION, MENTION **b :** something (as a sign or indication) that refers a reader or consulter to another source of information (as a book or passage) **c :** consultation of sources of information **4 :** one referred to or consulted: as **a :** a person to whom inquiries as to character or ability can be made **b :** a statement of the qualifications of a person seeking employment or appointment given by someone familiar with the person **c** (1) **:** a source of information (as a book or passage) to which a reader or consulter is referred (2) **:** a work (as a dictionary or encyclopedia) containing useful facts or information **d :** DENOTATION, MEANING

[2]**reference** *adj* (1856) **:** used or usable for reference; *esp* **:** constituting a standard for measuring or constructing

[3]**reference** *vt* **-enced; -enc·ing** (1891) **1 a :** to supply with references **b :** to cite in or as a reference **2 :** to put in a form (as a table) adapted to easy reference

reference mark *n* (1856) **:** a conventional mark (as *, †, or ‡) placed in written or printed text to direct the reader's attention esp. to a footnote

ref·er·en·dum \ˌref-ə-ˈren-dəm\ *n, pl* **-da** \-də\ *or* **-dums** [NL, fr. L, neut. of *referendus,* gerundive of *referre* to refer] (1847) **1 a :** the principle or practice of submitting to popular vote a measure passed on or proposed by a legislative body or by popular initiative **b :** a vote on a measure so submitted **2 :** a diplomatic agent's note asking his government for instructions

ref·er·ent \ˈref-(ə-)rənt\ *n* [L *referent-, referens,* prp. of *referre*] (1844) **:** one that refers or is referred to; *esp* **:** the thing that a symbol (as a word or sign) stands for — **referent** *adj*

ref·er·en·tial \ˌref-ə-ˈren-chəl\ *adj* (1660) **:** of, containing, or constituting a reference — **ref·er·en·tial·i·ty** \-ˌren-chē-ˈal-ət-ē\ *n* — **ref·er·en·tial·ly** \-ˈrench-(ə-)lē\ *adv*

re·fer·ral \ri-ˈfər-əl\ *n* (1927) **1 :** the act, action, or an instance of referring **2 :** one that is referred

[1]**re·fill** \(ˈ)rē-ˈfil\ *vt* (1681) **:** to fill again **:** REPLENISH ~ *vi* **:** to become filled again — **re·fill·able** \-ə-bəl\ *adj*

[2]**re·fill** \ˈrē-ˌfil\ *n* (1886) **1 :** a product or a container and a product used to refill the exhausted supply of a device **2 :** something provided again; *esp* **:** a second filling of a medical prescription

re·fi·nance \ˌrē-fə-ˈnan(t)s, (ˈ)rē-ˈfī-ˌ, ˌrē-(ˌ)fī-ˈ\ *vt* (1908) **:** to renew or reorganize the financing of ~ *vi* **:** to finance something anew

re·fine \ri-ˈfīn\ *vb* **re·fined; re·fin·ing** *vt* (1582) **1 :** to reduce (as metal, sugar, or oil) to a pure state **2 :** to free from moral imperfection **:** ELEVATE **3 :** to improve or perfect by pruning or polishing ⟨~ a poetic style⟩ **4 :** to reduce in vigor or intensity **5 :** to free from what is coarse, vulgar, or uncouth ~ *vi* **1 :** to become pure or perfected **2 :** to make improvement by introducing subtleties or distinctions — **re·fin·er** *n*

re·fined \ri-ˈfīnd\ *adj* (1588) **1 :** FASTIDIOUS, CULTIVATED **2 :** free from impurities **3 :** PRECISE, EXACT ⟨a ~ test for radioactivity⟩

re·fine·ment \ri-ˈfīn-mənt\ *n* (ca. 1611) **1 :** the action or process of refining **2 :** the quality or state of being refined **:** CULTIVATION **3 a :** a refined feature or method **b :** a highly refined distinction **:** SUBTLETY **c :** a contrivance or device intended to improve or perfect

re·fin·ery \ri-ˈfīn-(ə-)rē\ *n, pl* **-er·ies** (1727) **:** a building and equipment for refining or processing esp. metals, oil, or sugar

re·fin·ish \(ˈ)rē-ˈfin-ish\ *vt* (1931) **:** to give (as furniture) a new surface ~ *vi* **:** to refinish furniture — **re·fin·ish·er** *n*

[1]**re·fit** \(ˈ)rē-ˈfit\ *vt* (1666) **:** to fit out or supply again ~ *vi* **:** to obtain repairs or fresh supplies or equipment

[2]**re·fit** \ˈrē-ˌfit, (ˈ)rē-ˈ\ *n* (1799) **:** the action of refitting; *esp* **:** a refitting and renovating of a ship

re·fla·tion \(ˈ)rē-ˈflā-shən\ *n* [*re-* + *-flation* (as in *deflation*)] (1932) **:** restoration of deflated prices to a desirable level — **re·fla·tion·ary** \-shə-ˌner-ē\ *adj*

re·flect \ri-ˈflekt\ *vb* [ME *reflecten,* fr. L *reflectere* to bend back, fr. *re-* + *flectere* to bend] *vt* (15c) **1** *archaic* **:** to turn into or away from a course **:** DEFLECT **2 :** to turn, throw, or bend off or backward at an angle ⟨a mirror ~*s* light⟩ **3 :** to bend or fold back **4 :** to give back or exhibit as an image, likeness, or outline **:** MIRROR ⟨the clouds were ~*ed* in the water⟩ **5 :** to bring or cast as a result ⟨his attitude ~*s* little credit on his judgment⟩ **6 :** to make manifest or apparent **:** SHOW ⟨the pulse ~*s* the condition of the heart⟩ **7 :** REALIZE, CONSIDER ~ *vi* **1 :** to throw back light or sound **2 a :** to think quietly and calmly **b :** to express a thought or opinion resulting from reflection **3 a :** to tend to bring reproach or discredit ⟨an investigation that ~*s* on all the members of the department⟩ **b :** to bring about a specified appearance or characterization ⟨an act which ~*s* well on him⟩ **c :** to have a bearing or influence ***syn*** see THINK

re·flec·tance \ri-ˈflek-tən(t)s\ *n* (1926) **:** the fraction of the total radiant flux incident upon a surface that is reflected and that varies according to the wavelength distribution of the incident radiation — called also *re·flec·tiv·i·ty* \ˌrē-ˌflek-ˈtiv-ət-ē, ri-\

reflecting telescope *n* (1842) **:** REFLECTOR 2

re·flec·tion \ri-ˈflek-shən\ *n* [ME, alter. of *reflexion,* fr. LL *reflexion-, reflexio* act of bending back, fr. L *reflexus,* pp. of *reflectere*] (14c) **1 :** an instance of reflecting; *esp* **:** the return of light or sound waves from a surface **2 :** the production of an image by or as if by a mirror **3 a :** the action of bending or folding back **b :** a reflected part **:** FOLD **4 :** something produced by reflecting: as **a :** an image given back by a reflecting surface **b :** an effect produced by an influence ⟨a high crime rate is a ~ of an unstable society⟩ **5 :** an often obscure or indirect criticism **:** REPROACH ⟨the book was suppressed as a ~ on the regime⟩ **6 :** a thought, idea, or opinion formed or a remark made as a result of meditation **7 :** consideration of some subject matter, idea, or purpose **8** *obs* **:** turning back **:** RETURN **9 a :** a transformation of a figure in which each point is replaced by a point symmetric with respect to a line **b :** a transformation that involves reflection in more than one axis of a rectangular coordinate system — **re·flec·tion·al** \-shnəl, -shən-ᵊl\ *adj*

re·flec·tive \ri-ˈflek-tiv\ *adj* (1627) **1 :** capable of reflecting light, images, or sound waves **2 :** marked by reflection **:** THOUGHTFUL, DELIBERATIVE **3 :** of, relating to, or caused by reflection ⟨~ glare of the snow⟩ **4 :** REFLEXIVE ⟨~ verb⟩ — **re·flec·tive·ly** *adv* — **re·flec·tive·ness** *n*

\ə\ abut \ᵊ\ kitten, F table \ər\ further \a\ ash \ā\ ace \ä\ cot, cart
\au̇\ out \ch\ chin \e\ bet \ē\ easy \g\ go \i\ hit \ī\ ice \j\ job
\ŋ\ sing \ō\ go \ȯ\ law \ȯi\ boy \th\ thin \t͟h\ the \ü\ loot \u̇\ foot
\y\ yet \zh\ vision \à, k̲, ⁿ, œ, œ̄, ue, ue̅, ʸ\ *see* Guide to Pronunciation

re·flec·tom·e·ter \ˌrē-ˌflek-ˈtäm-ət-ər, ri-\ *n* (1665) **:** a device for measuring the reflectance of radiant energy (as light) — **re·flec·tom·e·try** \-ə-trē\ *n*

re·flec·tor \ri-ˈflek-tər\ *n* (1767) **1 :** one that reflects; *esp* **:** a polished surface for reflecting light or other radiation **2 :** a telescope in which the principal focusing element is a mirror

re·flec·tor·ize \-tə-ˌrīz\ *vt* **-ized; -iz·ing** (1940) **1 :** to make reflecting **2 :** to provide with reflectors

¹re·flex \ˈrē-ˌfleks\ *n* [L *reflexus,* pp. of *reflectere* to reflect] (1508) **1 a :** reflected heat, light, or color **b :** a mirrored image **c :** a copy exact in essential or peculiar features **2 a :** an automatic and often inborn response to a stimulus that involves a nerve impulse passing inward from a receptor to a nerve center and thence outward to an effector (as a muscle or gland) without reaching the level of consciousness — compare HABIT **b :** the process that culminates in a reflex and comprises reception, transmission, and reaction — called also *reflex action* **c** *pl* **:** the power of acting or responding with adequate speed **d :** a way of thinking or behaving **3 :** a linguistic element (as a word or sound) or system (as writing) that is derived from a prior and esp. an older element or system ⟨*boat* is the ~ of Old English *bāt*⟩

²reflex *adj* [L *reflexus*] (1649) **1 :** directed back on the mind or its operations **:** INTROSPECTIVE **2 :** bent, turned, or directed back **:** REFLECTED ⟨a stem with ~ leaves⟩ **3 :** produced or carried out in reaction, resistance, or return **4** *of an angle* **:** being between 180° and 360° **5 :** of, relating to, or produced by a reflex without intervention of consciousness — **re·flex·ly** *adv*

reflex arc *n* (1882) **:** the complete nervous path involved in a reflex

reflex camera *n* (1906) **:** a single- or double-lens camera in which the image formed by the focusing lens is reflected onto a usu. ground-glass screen for viewing

re·flexed \ˈrē-ˌflekst, ri-ˈ\ *adj* [L *reflexus* + E *-ed*] (1733) **:** bent or curved backward or downward ⟨~ petals⟩ ⟨~ leaves⟩

re·flex·ion *chiefly Brit var of* REFLECTION

¹re·flex·ive \ri-ˈflek-siv\ *adj* [ML *reflexivus,* fr. L *reflexus*] (1640) **1 a :** directed or turned back on itself **b :** marked by or capable of reflection **:** REFLECTIVE **2 :** of, relating to, characterized by, or being a relation that exists between an entity and itself ⟨the relation "is equal to" is ~ but the relation "is the father of" is not⟩ **3 :** of, relating to, or constituting an action (as in "he perjured himself") directed back on the agent or the grammatical subject **4 :** characterized by habitual and unthinking behavior — **re·flex·ive·ly** *adv* — **re·flex·ive·ness** *n* — **re·flex·iv·i·ty** \ˌrē-ˌflek-ˈsiv-ət-ē, ri-\ *n*

²reflexive *n* (1866) **:** REFLEXIVE PRONOUN

reflexive pronoun *n* (1867) **:** a pronoun referring to the subject of the sentence, clause, or verbal phrase in which it stands; *specif* **:** a personal pronoun compounded with *-self*

re·flex·ol·o·gy \ˌrē-ˌflek-ˈsäl-ə-jē\ *n* [ISV] (1923) **:** the study and interpretation of behavior in terms of simple and complex reflexes

re·flow \(ˈ)rē-ˈflō\ *vi* (14c) **1 :** to flow back **:** EBB **2 :** to flow in again — **re·flow** \ˈrē-ˌflō\ *n*

ref·lu·ence \ˈref-ˌlü-ən(t)s, re-ˈflü-\ *n* (1592) **:** REFLUX 1

re·flu·ent \-ənt\ *adj* [L *refluent-, refluens,* prp. of *refluere* to flow back, fr. *re-* + *fluere* to flow — more at FLUID] (1699) **:** flowing back

¹re·flux \ˈrē-ˌfləks\ *n* [ME, fr. ML *refluxus,* fr. L *re-* + *fluxus* flow — more at FLUX] (15c) **1 :** a flowing back **:** EBB **2 :** a process of refluxing or condition of being refluxed

²re·flux \ri-ˈfləks, ˈrē-ˌ\ *vt* (1927) **:** to cause to flow back or return; *esp* **:** to heat so that the vapors formed condense and return to be heated again

re·fo·cus \(ˈ)rē-ˈfō-kəs\ *vt* (1865) **1 :** to focus again **2 :** to change the emphasis or direction of ⟨had ~*ed* his life⟩ ~ *vi* **1 :** to focus something again **2 :** to change emphasis or direction

re·for·es·ta·tion \(ˌ)rē-ˌfȯr-ə-ˈstā-shən, -ˌfär-\ *n* (1887) **:** the action of renewing forest cover by planting seeds or young trees — **re·for·est** \(ˈ)rē-ˈfȯr-əst, -ˈfär-\ *vt*

re·forge \(ˈ)rē-ˈfō(ə)rj, -ˈfȯ(ə)rj\ *vt* [ME *reforgen,* fr. MF *reforgier,* fr. *re-* + *forgier* to forge] (15c) **:** to forge again **:** MAKE OVER

¹re·form \ri-ˈfȯ(ə)rm\ *vb* [ME *reformen,* fr. MF *reformer,* fr. L *reformare,* fr. *re-* + *formare* to form] *vt* (15c) **1 a :** to amend or improve by change of form or removal of faults or abuses **b :** to put or change into an improved form or condition **2 :** to put an end to (an evil) by enforcing or introducing a better method or course of action **3 :** to induce or cause to abandon evil ways ⟨~ a drunkard⟩ **4 a :** to subject (hydrocarbons) to cracking **b :** to produce (as gasoline or gas) by cracking ~ *vi* **:** to become changed for the better ***syn*** see CORRECT — **re·form·abil·i·ty** \-ˌfȯr-mə-ˈbil-ət-ē\ *n* — **re·form·able** \-ˈfȯr-mə-bəl\ *adj*

²reform *n* (1663) **1 :** amendment of what is defective, vicious, corrupt, or depraved **2 :** a removal or correction of an abuse, a wrong, or errors **3** *cap* **:** REFORM JUDAISM

³reform *adj* (1819) **:** relating to or favoring reform

re–form \(ˈ)rē-ˈfȯ(ə)rm\ *vt* (14c) **:** to form again ~ *vi* **:** to take form again ⟨the ice ~*ed* on the lake⟩

re·for·mate \ri-ˈfȯr-ˌmāt, -mət\ *n* (1949) **:** a product of hydrocarbon reforming

ref·or·ma·tion \ˌref-ər-ˈmā-shən\ *n* (15c) **1 :** the act of reforming **:** the state of being reformed **2** *cap* **:** a 16th century religious movement marked ultimately by rejection or modification of some Roman Catholic doctrine and practice and establishment of the Protestant churches — **ref·or·ma·tion·al** \-shnəl, -shən-ᵊl\ *adj*

re·for·ma·tive \ri-ˈfȯr-mət-iv\ *adj* (1593) **:** intended or tending to reform

¹re·for·ma·to·ry \ri-ˈfȯr-mə-ˌtōr-ē, -ˌtȯr-\ *adj* (1589) **:** REFORMATIVE

²reformatory *n, pl* **-ries** (1834) **:** a penal institution to which young or first offenders or women are committed for training and reformation

re·formed *adj* (1563) **1 :** changed for the better **2** *cap* **:** PROTESTANT; *specif* **:** of or relating to the chiefly Calvinist Protestant churches formed in various continental European countries

reformed spelling *n* (1896) **:** any of several methods of spelling English words that use letters with more phonetic consistency than conventional spelling and that usu. discard some silent letters (as in *pedagog* for *pedagogue*)

re·form·er \ri-ˈfȯr-mər\ *n* (1548) **1 :** one that works for or urges reform **2** *cap* **:** a leader of the Protestant Reformation **3 :** an apparatus for cracking oils or gases to form specialized products

re·form·ism \ri-ˈfȯr-ˌmiz-əm\ *n* (ca. 1904) **:** a doctrine, policy, or movement of reform — **re·form·ist** \-məst\ *n or adj*

Reform Judaism *n* (1905) **:** Judaism marked by a liberal approach in nonobservance of much legal tradition regarded as irrelevant to the present and in shortening and simplification of traditional ritual

reform school *n* (1847) **:** a reformatory for boys or girls

re·fract \ri-ˈfrakt\ *vt* [L *refractus,* pp. of *refringere* to break open, break up, refract, fr. *re-* + *frangere* to break — more at BREAK] (1612) **1 :** to subject (as a ray of light) to refraction ⟨to ~ that familiar world through the mind and heart of a romantic . . . woman—Anton Myrer⟩ **2 :** to determine the refracting power of

re·frac·tile \-ˈfrak-tᵊl, -ˌtīl\ *adj* (1847) **:** capable of refracting **:** REFRACTIVE

refracting telescope *n* (1764) **:** REFRACTOR

re·frac·tion \ri-ˈfrak-shən\ *n* (1603) **1 :** deflection from a straight path undergone by a light ray or energy wave in passing obliquely from one medium (as air) into another (as glass) in which its velocity is different **2 :** the change in the apparent position of a celestial body due to bending of the light rays emanating from it as they pass through the atmosphere; *also* **:** the correction to be applied to the apparent position of a body because of this bending **3 :** the action of distorting an image by viewing through a medium; *also* **:** an instance of this

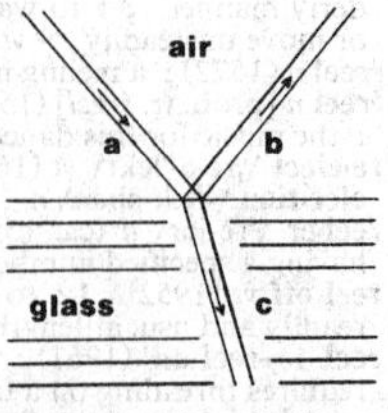

refraction 1: *a* light ray, *b* reflected ray, *c* refracted ray

re·frac·tive \ri-ˈfrak-tiv\ *adj* (1673) **1 :** having power to refract **2 :** relating or due to refraction — **re·frac·tive·ly** *adv* — **re·frac·tive·ness** *n* — **re·frac·tiv·i·ty** \ˌrē-ˌfrak-ˈtiv-ət-ē, ri-\ *n*

refractive index *n* (1839) **:** INDEX OF REFRACTION

re·frac·tom·e·ter \ˌrē-ˌfrak-ˈtäm-ət-ər, ri-\ *n* [ISV] (ca. 1876) **:** an instrument for measuring indices of refraction — **re·frac·to·met·ric** \ri-ˌfrak-tə-ˈme-trik\ *adj* — **re·frac·tom·e·try** \ˌrē-ˌfrak-ˈtäm-ə-trē, ri-\ *n*

re·frac·tor \ri-ˈfrak-tər\ *n* (1769) **:** a telescope whose principal focusing element is a lens

¹re·frac·to·ry \ri-ˈfrak-t(ə-)rē\ *adj* [alter. of *refractary,* fr. L *refractarius,* irreg. fr. *refragari* to oppose, fr. *re-* + *-fragari* (as in *suffragari* to support with one's vote)] (1606) **1 :** resisting control or authority **:** STUBBORN, UNMANAGEABLE **2 a :** resistant to treatment or cure ⟨a ~ lesion⟩ **b :** unresponsive to stimulus **c :** IMMUNE, INSUSCEPTIBLE ⟨after recovery they were ~ to infection⟩ **3 :** difficult to fuse, corrode, or draw out; *esp* **:** capable of enduring high temperature ***syn*** see UNRULY — **re·frac·to·ri·ly** \-t(ə-)rə-lē; ˌrē-ˌfrak-ˈtōr-ə-lē, ri-, -ˈtȯr-\ *adv* — **re·frac·to·ri·ness** \ri-ˈfrak-t(ə-)rē-nəs\ *n*

²refractory *n, pl* **-ries** (1627) **:** a refractory person or thing; *esp* **:** a heat-resisting ceramic material

refractory period *n* (1879) **:** the brief period immediately following the response esp. of a muscle or nerve before it recovers the capacity to make a second response — called also *refractory phase*

¹re·frain \ri-ˈfrān\ *vb* [ME *refreynen,* fr. MF *refraindre,* fr. L *refringere* to break up, destroy, check — more at REFRACT] *vt, archaic* (14c) **:** CURB, RESTRAIN ~ *vi* **:** to keep oneself from doing, feeling, or indulging in something and esp. from following a passing impulse — **re·frain·ment** \-mənt\ *n*

²refrain *n* [ME *refreyn,* fr. MF *refrain,* fr. *refraindre* to resound, fr. L *refringere* to break up, refract] (14c) **:** a regularly recurring phrase or verse esp. at the end of each stanza or division of a poem or song **:** CHORUS; *also* **:** the musical setting of a refrain

re·fran·gi·ble \ri-ˈfran-jə-bəl\ *adj* [irreg. fr. L *refringere* to refract] (1673) **:** capable of being refracted — **re·fran·gi·bil·i·ty** \-ˌfran-jə-ˈbil-ət-ē\ *n* — **re·fran·gi·ble·ness** \-ˈfran-jə-bəl-nəs\ *n*

re·fresh \ri-ˈfresh\ *vb* [ME *refresshen,* fr. MF *refreschir,* fr. OF, fr. *re-* + *freis* fresh — more at FRESH] *vt* (14c) **1 :** to restore strength and animation to **:** REVIVE **2 :** to freshen up **:** RENOVATE **3 a :** to restore or maintain by renewing supply **:** REPLENISH **b :** AROUSE, STIMULATE ⟨let me ~ your memory⟩ **4 :** to restore water to ~ *vi* **1 :** to become refreshed **2 :** to take refreshment **3 :** to lay in fresh provisions ***syn*** see RENEW

re·fresh·en \ri-ˈfresh-ən, (ˈ)rē-\ *vt* [*re-* + *freshen*] (1782) **:** REFRESH

re·fresh·er \ri-ˈfresh-ər\ *n* (1678) **1 :** something (as a drink) that refreshes **2 :** REMINDER **3 :** review or instruction designed esp. to keep one abreast of professional developments

re·fresh·ing \-iŋ\ *adj* (1580) **:** serving to refresh; *esp* **:** agreeably stimulating because of freshness or newness — **re·fresh·ing·ly** \-iŋ-lē\ *adv*

re·fresh·ment \ri-ˈfresh-mənt\ *n* (14c) **1 :** the act of refreshing **:** the state of being refreshed **2 a :** something (as food or drink) that refreshes **b** *pl* (1) **:** a light meal (2) **:** assorted light foods

re·fried beans \(ˌ)rē-ˌfrīd-\ *n pl* (1957) **:** beans cooked with seasonings, fried, then mashed and fried again

¹re·frig·er·ant \ri-ˈfrij-(ə-)rənt\ *adj* (1599) **:** allaying heat or fever

²refrigerant *n* (1676) **:** a refrigerant agent or agency: as **a :** a medication for reducing body heat **b :** a substance used in refrigeration

re·frig·er·ate \ri-ˈfrij-ə-ˌrāt\ *vt* **-at·ed; -at·ing** [L *refrigeratus,* pp. of *refrigerare,* fr. *re-* + *frigerare* to cool, fr. *frigor-, frigus* cold — more at FRIGID] (1534) **:** to make or keep cold or cool; *specif* **:** to freeze or chill (as food) for preservation — **re·frig·er·a·tion** \-ˌfrij-ə-ˈrā-shən\ *n*

re·frig·er·a·tor \ri-ˈfrij-ə-ˌrāt-ər\ *n* (1803) **:** something that refrigerates or keeps cool: **a :** a cabinet, room, or appliance for keeping food or other items cool **b :** an apparatus for rapidly cooling heated liquids or vapors in a distilling process

re·frin·gent \ri-ˈfrin-jənt\ *adj* [L *refringent-, refringens,* prp. of *refringere* to refract] (1778) **:** REFRACTIVE, REFRACTING

reft *past of* REAVE

re·fu·el \(ˈ)rē-ˈfyü-əl\ *vt* (1811) **:** to provide with additional fuel ~ *vi* **:** to take on additional fuel

¹ref·uge \ˈref-(ˌ)yüj, -(ˌ)yüzh\ *n* [ME, fr. MF, fr. L *refugium,* fr. *refugere* to escape, fr. *re-* + *fugere* to flee — more at FUGITIVE] (14c) **1 :** shelter or protection from danger or distress **2 :** a place that provides shelter or protection **3 :** something to which one has recourse in difficulty

²refuge *vb* **ref·uged; ref·ug·ing** *vt* (1594) **:** to give refuge to ~ *vi* **:** to seek or take refuge

ref·u·gee \ˌref-yu̇-ˈjē, ˈref-yu̇-ˌ\ *n* [F *réfugié,* pp. of *(se) réfugier* to take refuge, fr. L *refugium*] (1685) **:** one that flees; *esp* **:** one who flees to a foreign country or power to escape danger or persecution — **ref·u·gee·ism** \-ˌiz-əm\ *n*

re·fu·gi·um \ri-ˈfyü-jē-əm\ *n, pl* **-gia** \-jē-ə\ [NL, fr. L, refuge] (1943) **:** an area of relatively unaltered climate that is inhabited by plants and animals during a period of continental climatic change (as a glaciation) and remains as a center of relict forms from which a new dispersion and speciation may take place after climatic readjustment

re·ful·gence \ri-ˈfu̇l-jən(t)s, -ˈfəl-\ *n* [L *refulgentia,* fr. *refulgent-, refulgens,* prp. of *refulgēre* to shine brightly, fr. *re-* + *fulgēre* to shine — more at FULGENT] (1634) **:** a radiant or resplendent quality or state **:** BRILLIANCE — **re·ful·gent** \-jənt\ *adj*

¹**re·fund** \ri-ˈfənd, ˈrē-ˌ\ *vt* [ME *refunden,* fr. MF & L; MF *refonder,* fr. L *refundere,* lit., to pour back, fr. *re-* + *fundere* to pour — more at FOUND] (15c) **1 :** to give or put back **2 :** to return (money) in restitution, repayment, or balancing of accounts — **re·fund·abil·i·ty** \ri-ˌfən-də-ˈbil-ət-ē, (ˌ)rē-\ *n* — **re·fund·able** \-ə-bəl\ *adj*

²**re·fund** \ˈrē-ˌfənd\ *n* (1866) **1 :** the act of refunding **2 :** a sum refunded

³**re·fund** \(ˈ)rē-ˈfənd\ *vt* [*re-* + *fund*] (ca. 1860) **:** to fund again

re·fur·bish \ri-ˈfər-bish\ *vt* (ca. 1611) **:** to brighten or freshen up **:** RENOVATE — **re·fur·bish·er** *n* — **re·fur·bish·ment** \-bish-mənt\ *n*

re·fus·al \ri-ˈfyü-zəl\ *n* (15c) **1 :** the act of refusing or denying **2 :** the opportunity or right of refusing or taking before others

¹**re·fuse** \ri-ˈfyüz\ *vb* **re·fused; re·fus·ing** [ME *refusen,* fr. MF *refuser,* fr. (assumed) VL *refusare,* fr. L *refusus,* pp. of *refundere* to pour back] *vt* (14c) **1 :** to express oneself as unwilling to accept ⟨~ a gift⟩ ⟨~ a promotion⟩ **2 a :** to show or express unwillingness to do or comply with ⟨the motor *refused* to start⟩ **b :** DENY ⟨they were *refused* admittance to the game⟩ **3** *obs* **:** GIVE UP, RENOUNCE **4** *of a horse* **:** to decline to jump or leap over ~ *vi* **:** to withhold acceptance, compliance, or permission ***syn*** see DECLINE — **re·fus·er** *n*

²**ref·use** \ˈref-ˌyüs, -ˌyüz\ *n* [ME, fr. MF *refus* rejection, fr. OF, fr. *refuser*] (15c) **1 :** the worthless or useless part of something **:** LEAVINGS **2 :** TRASH, GARBAGE

³**ref·use** \ˈref-ˌyüs, -ˌyüz\ *adj* (15c) **:** thrown aside or left as worthless

re·fuse·nik *or* **re·fus·nik** \ri-ˈfyüz-(ˌ)nik\ *n* [¹*refuse* + *-nik*] (1974) **:** a Soviet citizen and esp. a Jew who is refused permission to emigrate

ref·u·ta·tion \ˌref-yu̇-ˈtā-shən\ *n* (1548) **:** the act or process of refuting

re·fute \ri-ˈfyüt\ *vt* **re·fut·ed; re·fut·ing** [L *refutare,* fr. *re-* + *-futare* to beat — more at BEAT] (1597) **1 :** to prove wrong by argument or evidence **:** show to be false or erroneous **2 :** to deny the truth or accuracy of ⟨*refuted* the election returns which showed him the loser⟩ — **re·fut·able** \-ˈfyüt-ə-bəl\ *adj* — **re·fut·ably** \-blē\ *adv* — **re·fut·er** *n*

reg \ˈreg\ *n* [by shortening] (ca. 1925) **:** REGULATION ⟨federal ~s⟩

re·gal \ˈrē-gəl\ *adj* [ME, fr. MF or L; MF, fr. L *regalis* — more at ROYAL] (14c) **1 :** of, relating to, or suitable for a king **2 :** of notable excellence or magnificence **:** SPLENDID — **re·gal·i·ty** \ri-ˈgal-ət-ē\ *n* — **re·gal·ly** \ˈrē-gə-lē\ *adv*

¹**re·gale** \ri-ˈgā(ə)l\ *vb* **re·galed; re·gal·ing** [F *régaler,* fr. MF, fr. *regale,* n.] *vt* (ca. 1656) **1 :** to entertain sumptuously **:** feast with delicacies **2 :** to give pleasure or amusement to ⟨*regaled* us with stories of his exploits⟩ ~ *vi* **:** to feast oneself **:** FEED

²**regale** *n* [F *régal,* fr. MF *regale,* fr. *re-* + *galer* to have a good time — more at GALLANT] (1670) **1 :** a sumptuous feast **2 :** a choice piece esp. of food

re·ga·lia \ri-ˈgāl-yə\ *n pl* [ML, fr. L, neut. pl. of *regalis*] (1540) **1 :** royal rights or prerogatives **2 a :** the emblems, symbols, or paraphernalia indicative of royalty **b :** decorations or insignia indicative of an office or membership **3 :** special dress; *esp* **:** FINERY

¹**re·gard** \ri-ˈgärd\ *n* [ME, fr. MF, fr. OF, fr. *regarder*] (14c) **1** *archaic* **:** APPEARANCE **2 a :** ATTENTION, CONSIDERATION ⟨due ~ should be given to all facets of the question⟩ **b :** a protective interest **:** CARE ⟨ought to have more ~ for his health⟩ **3 :** LOOK, GAZE **4 a :** the worth or estimation in which something or someone is held ⟨a man of small ~⟩ **b (1) :** a feeling of respect and affection **:** ESTEEM ⟨his hard work won him the ~ of his colleagues⟩ **(2)** *pl* **:** friendly greetings implying such feeling ⟨give him my ~s⟩ **5 :** a basis of action or opinion **:** MOTIVE **6 :** an aspect to be taken into consideration **:** RESPECT ⟨is a small school, and is fortunate in this ~⟩ **7** *obs* **:** INTENTION — **in regard to :** with respect to **:** CONCERNING — **with regard to :** in regard to

²**regard** *vb* [ME *regarden,* fr. MF *regarder* to look back at, regard, fr. OF, fr. *re-* + *garder* to guard, look at — more at GUARD] *vt* (15c) **1 :** to pay attention to **:** take into consideration or account **2 a :** to show respect or consideration for **b :** to hold in high esteem **3 :** to look at **4** *archaic* **:** to relate to **5 :** to consider and appraise usu. from a particular point of view ⟨is highly ~*ed* as a mechanic⟩ ~ *vi* **1 :** to look attentively **:** GAZE **2 :** to pay attention **:** HEED

syn REGARD, RESPECT, ESTEEM, ADMIRE mean to recognize the worth of a person or thing. REGARD is a general term that is usu. qualified ⟨he is not highly *regarded* in the profession⟩ RESPECT implies a considered evaluation or estimation ⟨after many years they came to *respect* her views⟩ ESTEEM implies greater warmth of feeling accompanying a high valuation ⟨no citizen of the town was more highly *esteemed*⟩ ADMIRE suggests usu. enthusiastic appreciation and often deep affection ⟨a friend that I truly *admire*⟩

— **as regards :** with respect to **:** CONCERNING

re·gar·dant \ri-ˈgärd-ᵊnt\ *adj* [MF, prp. of *regarder*] (15c) **:** looking backward over the shoulder — used of a heraldic animal

re·gard·ful \ri-ˈgärd-fəl\ *adj* (1586) **1 :** HEEDFUL, OBSERVANT **2 :** full or expressive of regard or respect **:** RESPECTFUL — **re·gard·ful·ly** \-fə-lē\ *adv* — **re·gard·ful·ness** *n*

re·gard·ing *prep* (1890) **:** with respect to **:** CONCERNING

¹**re·gard·less** \ri-ˈgärd-ləs\ *adj* (1591) **:** HEEDLESS, CARELESS — **re·gard·less·ly** *adv* — **re·gard·less·ness** *n*

²**regardless** *adv* (1872) **:** despite everything ⟨went ahead with their plans ~⟩

regardless of *prep* (1784) **:** without taking into account ⟨accepts all *regardless of* age⟩; *also* **:** in spite of ⟨*regardless of* our mistakes⟩

re·gat·ta \ri-ˈgät-ə, -ˈgat-\ *n* [It] (1652) **:** a rowing, speedboat, or sailing race or a series of such races

re·ge·la·tion \ˌrē-jə-ˈlā-shən\ *n* (1857) **:** the freezing again of water derived from ice melting under pressure when the pressure is relieved

re·gen·cy \ˈrē-jən-sē\ *n, pl* **-cies** (15c) **1 :** the office, jurisdiction, or government of a regent or body of regents **2 :** a body of regents **3 :** the period of rule of a regent or body of regents

Regency *adj* (1938) **:** of, relating to, or characteristic of the styles of George IV's regency as Prince of Wales during the period 1811–20

re·gen·er·a·cy \ri-ˈjen-(ə-)rə-sē\ *n* (1626) **:** the state of being regenerated

¹**re·gen·er·ate** \ri-ˈjen-(ə-)rət\ *adj* [ME *regenerat,* fr. L *regeneratus,* pp. of *regenerare* to regenerate, fr. *re-* + *generare* to beget — more at GENERATE] (15c) **1 :** formed or created again **2 :** spiritually reborn or converted **3 :** restored to a better, higher, or more worthy state — **re·gen·er·ate·ly** *adv* — **re·gen·er·ate·ness** *n*

²**re·gen·er·ate** \ri-ˈjen-ə-ˌrāt\ *vi* (1541) **1 :** to become formed again **2 :** to become regenerate **:** REFORM **3 :** to undergo regeneration ~ *vt* **1 a :** to subject to spiritual regeneration **b :** to change radically and for the better **2 a :** to generate or produce anew; *esp* **:** to replace (a body part) by a new growth of tissue **b :** to produce again chemically sometimes in a physically changed form **3 :** to restore to original strength or properties **4 :** to increase the amplification of (an electron current) by causing part of the power in the output circuit to act upon the input circuit — **re·gen·er·a·ble** \-ˈjen-(ə-)rə-bəl\ *adj*

³**re·gen·er·ate** \-ˈjen-(ə-)rət\ *n* (1569) **:** one that is regenerated: as **a :** an individual who is spiritually reborn **b (1) :** an organism that has undergone regeneration **(2) :** a regenerated body part

regenerated cellulose *n* (1904) **:** cellulose obtained in a changed form by chemical treatment (as of a cellulose solution or derivative)

re·gen·er·a·tion \ri-ˌjen-ə-ˈrā-shən, ˌrē-\ *n* (14c) **1 :** an act or the process of regenerating **:** the state of being regenerated **2 :** spiritual renewal or revival **3 :** renewal or restoration of a body or bodily part after injury or as a normal process **4 :** utilization by special devices of heat or other products that would ordinarily be lost

re·gen·er·a·tive \ri-ˈjen-ə-ˌrāt-iv, -ˈjen-(ə-)rət-\ *adj* (15c) **1 :** of, relating to, or marked by regeneration **2 :** tending to regenerate

re·gen·er·a·tor \ri-ˈjen-ə-ˌrāt-ər\ *n* (ca. 1550) **1 :** one that regenerates **2 :** a device used esp. with hot-air engines or gas furnaces in which incoming air or gas is heated by contact with masses (as of brick) previously heated by outgoing hot air or gas

re·gent \ˈrē-jənt\ *n* [ME, fr. MF or ML; MF, fr. ML *regent-, regens,* fr. L, prp. of *regere* to rule — more at RIGHT] (15c) **1 :** one who governs a kingdom in the minority, absence, or disability of the sovereign **2 :** one who rules or reigns **:** GOVERNOR **3 :** a member of a governing board (as of a state university) — **regent** *adj* — **re·gent·al** \-jənt-ᵊl\ *adj*

reg·gae \ˈreg-(ˌ)ā, ˈrāg-\ *n* [origin unknown] (1968) **:** popular music of Jamaican origin that combines indigenous styles with elements of rock 'n' roll and soul music and is performed at moderate tempos with the accent on the offbeat

reg·i·cide \ˈrej-ə-ˌsīd\ *n* (1548) **1** [prob. fr. (assumed) NL *regicida,* fr. L *reg-, rex* king + *-cida* -cide — more at ROYAL] **:** one who kills a king **2** [prob. fr. (assumed) NL *regicidium,* fr. L *reg-, rex* + *-cidium* -cide] **:** the killing of a king

re·gime *also* **ré·gime** \rā-ˈzhēm, ri- *also* ri-ˈjēm\ *n* [F *régime,* fr. L *regimin-, regimen*] (1776) **1 a :** REGIMEN 1 **b :** a regular pattern of occurrence or action (as of seasonal rainfall) **c :** the characteristic behavior or orderly procedure of a natural phenomenon or process **2 a :** mode of rule or management **b :** a form of government ⟨a socialist ~⟩ **c :** a government in power ⟨predicted that the new ~ would fall⟩ **d :** a period of rule

reg·i·men \ˈrej-ə-mən *also* ˈrezh-ə-\ *n* [ME, fr. L *regimin-, regimen* rule, fr. *regere* to rule] (15c) **1 a :** a systematic plan (as of diet, therapy, or medication) esp. when designed to improve and maintain the health of a patient **b :** a regular course of strenuous training ⟨the daily ~ of a top ballet dancer⟩ **2 :** GOVERNMENT, RULE **3 :** REGIME 1c

¹**reg·i·ment** \ˈrej-(ə-)mənt\ *n* [ME, fr. MF, fr. LL *regimentum,* fr. L *regere*] (14c) **1 :** governmental rule **2 :** a military unit consisting usu. of a number of battalions

²**reg·i·ment** \ˈrej-ə-ˌment\ *vt* (1617) **1 :** to form into or assign to a regiment **2 a :** to organize rigidly esp. for the sake of regulation or control ⟨~ an entire country⟩ **b :** to subject to order or uniformity — **reg·i·men·ta·tion** \ˌrej-ə-mən-ˈtā-shən, -ˌmen-\ *n*

reg·i·men·tal \ˌrej-ə-ˈment-ᵊl\ *adj* (1659) **1 :** of or relating to a regiment **2 :** AUTHORITATIVE, DICTATORIAL

reg·i·men·tals \-ᵊlz\ *n pl* (1742) **1 :** a regimental uniform **2 :** military dress

re·gion \ˈrē-jən\ *n* [ME, fr. MF, fr. L *region-, regio,* fr. *regere* to rule] (14c) **1 :** an administrative area, division, or district **2 a :** an indefinite area of the world or universe ⟨few unknown ~s left on earth⟩ **b :** a broad homogeneous geographical area ⟨the Appalachian ~⟩ **c (1) :** a major world area that supports a characteristic fauna **(2) :** an area characterized by the prevalence of one or more vegetational climax types **3 a :** any of the major subdivisions into which the body or one of its parts is divisible **b :** an indefinite area surrounding a specified body part ⟨a pain in the ~ of the heart⟩ **4 :** a sphere of activity of interest **:** FIELD **5 :** one of the zones into which the atmosphere is divided according to height or the sea according to depth **6 :** an open connected set together with none, some, or all of the points on its boundary ⟨a simple closed curve divides the plane into two ~s⟩

¹**re·gion·al** \ˈrēj-nəl, -ən-ᵊl\ *adj* (1654) **1 :** of, relating to, or characteristic of a region **2 :** affecting a particular region **:** LOCALIZED

²**regional** *n* (1946) **:** something (as a branch of an organization or an edition of a magazine) that serves a region

re·gion·al·ism \ˈrēj-nəl-ˌiz-əm, -ən-ᵊl-\ *n* (1881) **1 a :** consciousness of and loyalty to a distinct region with a homogeneous population **b :** development of a political or social system based on one or more such areas **2 :** emphasis on regional locale and characteristics in art or

\ə\ abut \ᵊ\ kitten, F table \ər\ further \a\ ash \ā\ ace \ä\ cot, cart \au̇\ out \ch\ chin \e\ bet \ē\ easy \g\ go \i\ hit \ī\ ice \j\ job \ŋ\ sing \ō\ go \ȯ\ law \ȯi\ boy \th\ thin \t͟h\ the \ü\ loot \u̇\ foot \y\ yet \zh\ vision \à, k̟, ⁿ, œ, œ̄, ue, ue̅, ʸ\ *see* Guide to Pronunciation

literature **3 :** a characteristic feature (as of speech) of a geographic area — **re·gion·al·ist** \-əst\ *n or adj* — **re·gion·al·is·tic** \ˌrēj-nəl-ˈis-tik, -ən-ᵊl-\ *adj*

re·gion·al·ize \ˈrēj-nəl-ˌīz, -ən-ᵊl-\ *vt* **-ized; -iz·ing** (1921) **:** to divide into regions or administrative districts **:** arrange regionally — **re·gion·al·iza·tion** \ˌrēj-nəl-ə-ˈzā-shən, -ən-ᵊl-ə-\ *n*

re·gion·al·ly \ˈrēj-nəl-ē, -ən-ᵊl-ē\ *adv* (1879) **:** on a regional basis

re·gis·seur \ˌrā-zhi-ˈsər\ *n* [F *régisseur, fr. régiss-* (stem of *régir* to direct, fr. L *regere* to rule) + *-eur* -or — more at RIGHT] (1828) **:** a director responsible for staging a theatrical work (as a ballet)

1reg·is·ter \ˈrej-ə-stər\ *n* [ME *registre,* fr. MF, fr. ML *registrum,* alter. of LL *regesta,* pl., register, fr. L, neut. pl. of *regestus,* pp. of *regerere* to bring back, fr. *re-* + *gerere* to bear — more at CAST] (14c) **1 :** a written record containing regular entries of items or details **2 a :** a book or system of public records **b :** a roster of qualified or available individuals ⟨a civil service ~⟩ **3 :** an entry in a register **4 a :** a set of organ pipes of like quality **:** STOP **b (1) :** the range of a human voice or a musical instrument **(2) :** a portion of such a range similarly produced or of the same quality **c :** a variety of a language that is appropriate to a particular subject or occasion **5 a :** a device regulating admission of air to fuel **b :** a grille often with shutters for admitting heated air or for ventilation **6 :** REGISTRATION, REGISTRY **7 a :** an automatic device registering a number or a quantity **b :** a number or quantity so registered **8 :** a condition of correct alignment or proper relative position **9 :** a device (as in a computer) for storing small amounts of data; *esp* **:** one in which data can be both stored and operated on

2register *vb* **reg·is·tered; reg·is·ter·ing** \-st(ə-)riŋ\ *vt* (14c) **1 a :** to make or secure official entry of in a register **b :** to enroll formally esp. as a voter or student **c :** to record automatically **:** INDICATE **d :** to make a record of **:** NOTE **e :** PERCEIVE; *also* **:** COMPREHEND **2 :** to make or adjust so as to correspond exactly **3 :** to secure special protection for (a piece of mail) by prepayment of a fee **4 :** to convey an impression of **:** EXPRESS **5 :** ACHIEVE ⟨~*ed* an impressive victory⟩ ~ *vi* **1 a :** to enroll one's name in a register ⟨~*ed* at the hotel⟩ **b :** to enroll one's name officially as a prerequisite for voting **c :** to enroll formally as a student **2 a :** to correspond exactly **b :** to be in correct alignment or register **3 :** to make or convey an impression

3register *n* [prob. alter. of ME *registrer*] (1531) **:** REGISTRAR

reg·is·tered *adj* (1861) **1 a :** having the owner's name entered in a register ⟨~ security⟩ **b :** recorded as the owner of a security **2 :** recorded on the basis of pedigree or breed characteristics in the studbook of a breed association **3 :** qualified formally or officially

registered mail *n* (1886) **:** mail recorded in the post office of mailing and at each successive point of transmission and guaranteed special care in delivery

registered nurse *n* (1896) **:** a graduate trained nurse who has been licensed by a state authority after qualifying for registration

register ton *n* (ca. 1909) **:** TON 1a

reg·is·tra·ble \ˈrej-ə-st(ə-)rə-bəl\ *adj* (ca. 1802) **:** capable of being registered

reg·is·trant \ˈrej-ə-strənt\ *n* (ca. 1890) **:** one that registers or is registered

reg·is·trar \ˈrej-ə-ˌsträr\ *n* [alter. of ME *registrer,* fr. MF *registreur,* fr. *registrer* to register, fr. ML *registrare,* fr. *registrum*] (1675) **:** an official recorder or keeper of records: as **a :** an officer of an educational institution responsible for registering students, keeping academic records, and corresponding with applicants and evaluating their credentials **b :** an admitting officer at a hospital

reg·is·tra·tion \ˌrej-ə-ˈstrā-shən\ *n* (1566) **1 :** the act of registering **2 :** an entry in a register **3 :** the number of individuals registered **:** ENROLLMENT **4 a :** the art or act of selecting and adjusting pipe organ stops **b :** the combination of stops selected for performing a particular organ work **5 :** a document certifying an act of registering

reg·is·try \ˈrej-ə-strē\ *n, pl* **-tries** (1589) **1 :** REGISTRATION, ENROLLMENT **2 :** the nationality of a ship according to its entry in a register **:** FLAG **3 :** a place of registration **4 a :** an official record book **b :** an entry in a registry

re·gius professor \ˌrē-j(ē-)əs-\ *n* [NL, royal professor] (1621) **:** a holder of a professorship founded by royal subsidy at a British university

reg·let \ˈreg-lət\ *n* [F *réglet,* fr. MF *reglet* straightedge, fr. *regle* rule, fr. L *regula* — more at RULE] (1664) **1 :** a flat narrow architectural molding **2 :** a strip of wood used like a lead between lines of type

reg·nal \ˈreg-nᵊl\ *adj* [ML *regnalis,* fr. L *regnum* reign — more at REIGN] (1612) **:** of or relating to a king or his reign; *specif* **:** calculated from a monarch's accession to the throne ⟨in his eighth ~ year⟩

reg·nant \ˈreg-nənt\ *adj* [L *regnant-, regnans,* prp. of *regnare* to reign, fr. *regnum*] (1600) **1 :** exercising rule **:** REIGNING **2 a :** having the chief power **b :** of common or widespread occurrence

reg·num \ˈreg-nəm\ *n, pl* **reg·na** \-nə\ [L] (1911) **:** KINGDOM

rego·lith \ˈreg-ə-ˌlith\ *n* [Gk *rhēgos* blanket + E *-lith;* akin to Skt *rāga* color] (1897) **:** unconsolidated residual or transported material that overlies the solid rock on the earth, moon, or a planet

rego·sol \ˈreg-ə-ˌsäl, -ˌsȯl\ *n* [*rego-* (as in *regolith*) + L *solum* soil — more at SOLE] (1949) **:** any of a group of azonal soils consisting chiefly of imperfectly consolidated material and having no clear-cut and specific morphology

re·greet \(ˈ)rē-ˈgrēt\ *vt, archaic* (1593) **:** to greet in return

regreets *n pl, obs* (1596) **:** GREETINGS

1re·gress \ˈrē-ˌgres\ *n* [ME, fr. L *regressus,* fr. *regressus,* pp. of *regredi* to go back, fr. *re-* + *gradi* to go — more at GRADE] (14c) **1 a :** an act or the privilege of going or coming back **b :** REENTRY 1 **2 :** movement backward to a previous and esp. worse or more primitive state or condition **3 :** the act of reasoning backward

2re·gress \ri-ˈgres\ *vi* (1552) **1 a :** to make or undergo regress **:** RETROGRADE **b :** to be subject to or exhibit regression **2 :** to tend to approach or revert to a mean ~ *vt* **:** to induce a state of psychological regression in — **re·gres·sor** \-ˈgres-ər\ *n*

re·gres·sion \ri-ˈgresh-ən\ *n* (1597) **1 :** the act or an instance of regressing **2 :** a trend or shift toward a lower or less perfect state: as **a :** progressive decline of a manifestation of disease **b (1) :** gradual loss of differentiation and function by a body part esp. as a physiological change accompanying aging **(2) :** gradual loss of memories and acquired skills **c :** reversion to an earlier mental or behavioral level **d :** a functional relationship between two or more correlated variables that is often empirically determined from data and is used esp. to predict values of one variable when given values of the others ⟨the ~ of *y* on *x* is linear⟩; *specif* **:** a function that yields the mean value of a random variable under the condition that one or more independent variables have specified values **3 :** retrograde motion

re·gres·sive \ri-ˈgres-iv\ *adj* (1634) **1 :** tending to regress or produce regression **2 :** being, characterized by, or developing in the course of an evolutionary process involving increasing simplification of bodily structure **3 :** decreasing in rate as the base increases ⟨a ~ tax⟩ — **re·gres·sive·ly** *adv* — **re·gres·sive·ness** *n*

1re·gret \ri-ˈgret\ *vb* **re·gret·ted; re·gret·ting** [ME *regretten,* fr. MF *regreter,* fr. OF, fr. *re-* + *-greter* (prob. of Gmc origin; akin to ON *grāta* to weep) — more at GREET] *vt* (14c) **1 a :** to mourn the loss or death of **b :** to miss very much **2 :** to be very sorry for ⟨~*s* his mistakes⟩ ~ *vi* **:** to experience regret — **re·gret·ter** *n*

2regret *n* (1590) **1 :** sorrow aroused by circumstances beyond one's control or power to repair **2 a :** an expression of distressing emotion (as sorrow or disappointment) **b** *pl* **:** a note politely declining an invitation ***syn*** see SORROW — **re·gret·ful** \-ˈgret-fəl\ *adj* — **re·gret·ful·ly** \-fə-lē\ *adv* — **re·gret·ful·ness** *n*

re·gret·ta·ble \ri-ˈgret-ə-bəl\ *adj* (1603) **:** deserving regret

re·gret·ta·bly \-blē\ *adv* (1866) **:** to a regrettable extent ⟨a ~ steep decline in wages⟩

re·group \(ˈ)rē-ˈgrüp\ *vt* (1885) **:** to form into a new grouping ⟨in order to subtract 129 from 531 ~ 531 into 5 hundreds, 2 tens, and 11 ones⟩ ⟨~ military forces⟩ ~ *vi* **1 :** to reorganize (as after a setback) for renewed activity **2 :** to alter the tactical formation of a military force

re·grow \(ˈ)rē-ˈgrō\ *vb* **-grew** \-ˈgrü\; **-grown** \-ˈgrōn\; **-grow·ing** *vt* (1872) **:** to grow (as a missing part) anew ~ *vi* **:** to continue growth after interruption or injury

1reg·u·lar \ˈreg-yə-lər, ˈreg(-ə)-lər\ *adj* [ME *reguler,* fr. MF, fr. LL *regularis* regular, fr. L, of a bar, fr. *regula* rule — more at RULE] (14c) **1 :** belonging to a religious order **2 a :** formed, built, arranged, or ordered according to some established rule, law, principle, or type **b (1) :** both equilateral and equiangular ⟨a ~ polygon⟩ **(2) :** having faces that are congruent regular polygons and all the polyhedral angles congruent ⟨a ~ polyhedron⟩ **c** *of a flower* **:** having the arrangement of floral parts exhibiting radial symmetry with members of the same whorl similar in form **d :** having or constituting an isometric system ⟨~ crystals⟩ **3 a :** ORDERLY, METHODICAL ⟨~ habits⟩ **b :** recurring, attending, or functioning at fixed or uniform intervals ⟨a ~ income⟩ ⟨a ~ churchgoer⟩ **4 a :** constituted, conducted, or done in conformity with established or prescribed usages, rules, or discipline **b :** NORMAL, STANDARD: as **(1) :** ABSOLUTE, COMPLETE ⟨a ~ fool⟩ ⟨the office seemed like a ~ madhouse⟩ **(2) :** thinking or behaving in an acceptable manner ⟨was a ~ guy⟩ **c (1) :** conforming to the normal or usual manner of inflection **(2) :** WEAK 7 **5 a :** of, relating to, or constituting the regular army of a state **b :** constituting or made up of individuals properly recognized as legitimate combatants in war

syn REGULAR, NORMAL, TYPICAL, NATURAL mean being of the sort or kind that is expected as usual, ordinary, or average. REGULAR stresses conformity to a rule, standard, or pattern; NORMAL implies lack of deviation from what has been discovered or established as the most usual or expected; TYPICAL implies showing all important traits of a type, class, or group and may suggest lack of strong individuality; NATURAL applies to what conforms to a thing's essential nature, function, or mode of being.

2regular *n* (1563) **1 :** one who is regular: as **a :** one of the regular clergy **b :** a soldier in a regular army **c :** one who can be trusted or depended on ⟨a party ~⟩ **d :** a player on an athletic team who usu. starts every game **e :** one who is usu. present or participating **2 :** a clothing size designed to fit a person of average height

regular army *n* (1854) **:** a permanently organized body constituting the standing army of a state

reg·u·lar·i·ty \ˌreg-yə-ˈlar-ət-ē\ *n, pl* **-ties** (1603) **1 :** the quality or state of being regular **2 :** something that is regular

reg·u·lar·ize \ˈreg-yə-lə-ˌrīz\ *vt* **-ized; -iz·ing** (1833) **:** to make regular by conformance to law, rules, or custom — **reg·u·lar·iza·tion** \ˌreg-yə-lə-rə-ˈzā-shən\ *n*

reg·u·lar·ly \ˈreg-yə-lər-lē, ˈreg-yə(r)-lē\ *adv* (1526) **1 :** on a regular basis **:** at regular intervals **2 :** in a regular manner

regular solid *n* (1841) **:** any of the five possible regular polyhedrons that include the regular tetrahedron, hexahedron, octahedron, dodecahedron, and icosahedron

regular year *n* (ca. 1900) **:** a common year of 354 days or a leap year of 384 days in the Jewish calendar

reg·u·late \ˈreg-yə-ˌlāt\ *vt* **-lat·ed; -lat·ing** [LL *regulatus,* pp. of *regulare,* fr. L *regula* rule] (1630) **1 a :** to govern or direct according to rule **b (1) :** to bring under the control of law or constituted authority **(2) :** to make regulations for or concerning ⟨~ the industries of a country⟩ **2 :** to bring order, method, or uniformity to ⟨~ one's habits⟩ **3 :** to fix or adjust the time, amount, degree, or rate of ⟨~ the pressure of a tire⟩ — **reg·u·la·tive** \-ˌlāt-iv\ *adj* — **reg·u·la·to·ry** \-lə-ˌtōr-ē, -ˌtȯr-\ *adj*

1reg·u·la·tion \ˌreg-yə-ˈlā-shən, ˌreg-ə-ˈlā-\ *n* (1665) **1 :** the act of regulating **:** the state of being regulated **2 a :** an authoritative rule dealing with details or procedure ⟨safety ~*s* in a factory⟩ **b :** a rule or order having the force of law issued by an executive authority of a government **3 a :** the process of redistributing material (as in an embryo) to restore a damaged or lost part independent of new tissue growth **b :** the mechanism by which an early embryo maintains normal development ***syn*** see LAW

2regulation *adj* (1836) **:** conforming to regulations **:** OFFICIAL

reg·u·la·tor \ˈreg-yə-ˌlāt-ər\ *n* (1655) **1 :** one that regulates **2 :** REGULATORY GENE

regulatory gene *or* **regulator gene** *n* (1961) **:** a gene controlling the production of a genetic repressor

reg·u·lus \ˈreg-yə-ləs\ *n* [NL, fr. L, petty king, fr. *reg-, rex* king — more at ROYAL] (1559) **1** *cap* **:** a first-magnitude star in the constellation Leo **2** [ML, metallic antimony, fr. L] **:** the more or less impure mass of metal formed beneath the slag in smelting and reducing ores

re·gur·gi·tate \(ˈ)rē-ˈgər-jə-ˌtāt\ *vb* **-tat·ed; -tat·ing** [ML *regurgitatus,* pp. of *regurgitare,* fr. L *re-* + LL *gurgitare* to engulf, fr. L *gurgit-, gurges* whirlpool — more at VORACIOUS] *vi* (1653) **:** to become thrown or poured back ~ *vt* : to throw or pour back or out from or as if from a cavity

re·gur·gi·ta·tion \(ˌ)rē-ˌgər-jə-ˈtā-shən\ *n* (1601) : an act of regurgitating: as **a** : the casting up of incompletely digested food (as by some birds in feeding their young) **b** : the backward flow of blood through a defective heart valve

re·hab \ˈrē-ˌhab\ *n, often attrib* [by shortening] (1941) **1** : REHABILITATION **2** : a rehabilitated house — **rehab** *vt* — **re·hab·ber** \-ər\ *n*

re·ha·bil·i·tant \ˌrē-(h)ə-ˈbil-ə-tənt\ *n* (1961) : a disabled person undergoing rehabilitation

re·ha·bil·i·tate \ˌrē-(h)ə-ˈbil-ə-ˌtāt\ *vt* **-tat·ed; -tat·ing** [ML *rehabilitatus,* pp. of *rehabilitare,* fr. L *re-* + LL *habilitare* to habilitate] (1580) **1 a** : to restore to a former capacity : REINSTATE **b** : to restore to good repute : reestablish the good name of **2 a** : to restore to a former state (as of efficiency, good management, or solvency) ⟨~ slum areas⟩ **b** : to restore or bring to a condition of health or useful and constructive activity — **re·ha·bil·i·ta·tion** \-ˌbil-ə-ˈtā-shən\ *n* — **re·ha·bil·i·ta·tive** \-ˈbil-ə-ˌtāt-iv\ *adj* — **re·ha·bil·i·ta·tor** \-ˌtāt-ər\ *n*

¹re·hash \(ˈ)rē-ˈhash\ *vt* (1822) **1** : to talk over or discuss again **2** : to present or use again in another form without substantial change or improvement

²re·hash \ˈrē-ˌhash\ *n* (1849) **1** : a product of rehashing : something presented in a new form without change of substance ⟨a book that was a ~ of stale ideas⟩ **2** : the action or process of rehashing

re·hear \(ˈ)rē-ˈhi(ə)r\ *vt* **-heard** \-ˈhərd\; **-hear·ing** \-ˈhi(ə)r-iŋ\ (1756) : to hear again or anew esp. judicially

re·hear·ing *n* (1686) : a second or new hearing by the same tribunal

re·hears·al \ri-ˈhər-səl\ *n* (14c) **1** : something recounted or told again : RECITAL **2 a** : a private performance or practice session preparatory to a public appearance **b** : a practice exercise : TRIAL

re·hearse \ri-ˈhərs\ *vb* **re·hearsed; re·hears·ing** [ME *rehersen,* fr. MF *rehercier,* lit., to harrow again, fr. *re-* + *hercier* to harrow, fr. *herce* harrow — more at HEARSE] *vt* (14c) **1 a** : to say again : REPEAT **b** : to recite aloud in a formal manner **2** : to present an account of : NARRATE, RELATE ⟨~ a familiar story⟩ **3** : to recount in order : ENUMERATE ⟨had *rehearsed* their grievances in a letter to the governor⟩ **4 a** : to give a rehearsal of **b** : to train or make proficient by rehearsal **5** : to perform or practice as if in a rehearsal ~ *vi* : to engage in a rehearsal — **re·hears·er** *n*

re·house \(ˈ)rē-ˈhau̇z\ *vt* (1820) : to house again or anew; *esp* : to establish in a new or different housing unit of a better quality

re·hy·drate \(ˈ)rē-ˈhī-ˌdrāt\ *vt* (1943) : to restore fluid to (something dehydrated) — **re·hy·drat·able** \-ˌdrāt-ə-bəl\ *adj* — **re·hy·dra·tion** \ˌrē-ˌhī-ˈdrā-shən\ *n*

reichs·mark \ˈrīk-ˌsmärk\ *n, pl* **reichsmarks** *also* **reichsmark** [G, fr. *reichs* (gen. of *reich* empire, kingdom, fr. OHG *rīhhi*) + *mark* mark — more at RICH] (1924) : the German mark from 1925 to 1948

re·ifi·ca·tion \ˌrā-ə-fə-ˈkā-shən, ˌrē-\ *n* (1846) : the process or result of reifying

re·ify \ˈrā-ə-ˌfī, rē-\ *vt* **re·ified; re·ify·ing** [L *res* thing — more at REAL] (1854) : to regard (something abstract) as a material or concrete thing

¹reign \ˈrān\ *n* [ME *regne,* fr. OF, fr. L *regnum,* fr. *reg-, rex* king — more at ROYAL] (13c) **1 a** : royal authority : SOVEREIGNTY ⟨under the ~ of the Stuart kings⟩ **b** : the dominion, sway, or influence of one resembling a monarch ⟨the ~ of the Puritan ministers⟩ **2** : the time during which one (as a sovereign) reigns

²reign *vi* (13c) **1 a** : to possess or exercise sovereign power : RULE **b** : to hold office as chief of state although possessing little governing power ⟨in England the sovereign ~*s* but does not rule⟩ **2** : to exercise authority in the manner of a monarch **3** : to be predominant or prevalent ⟨chaos ~*ed* in the classroom⟩

reign of terror [*Reign of Terror,* a period of the French Revolution that was conspicuous for mass executions of political suspects] (1801) : a state or a period of time marked by violence often committed by those in power that produces widespread terror

re·im·burse \ˌrē-əm-ˈbərs\ *vt* **-bursed; -burs·ing** [*re-* + obs. E *imburse* (to put in the pocket, pay), fr. ML *imbursare,* fr. L *in-* in- + ML *bursa* purse — more at PURSE] (ca. 1611) **1** : to pay back to someone : REPAY ⟨~ travel expenses⟩ **2** : to make restoration or payment of an equivalent to ⟨~ him for his traveling expenses⟩ ***syn*** see PAY — **re·im·burs·able** \-ˈbər-sə-bəl\ *adj* — **re·im·burse·ment** \-ˈbər-smənt\ *n*

re·im·pres·sion \ˌrē-əm-ˈpresh-ən\ *n* (1684) : REPRINT a

¹rein \ˈrān\ *n* [ME *reine,* fr. MF *rene,* fr. (assumed) VL *retina,* fr. L *retinēre* to restrain — more at RETAIN] (14c) **1** : a strap fastened to a bit by which a rider or driver controls an animal — usu. used in pl. **2 a** : a restraining influence : CHECK ⟨kept a tight ~ on the proceedings⟩ **b** : controlling or guiding power — usu. used in pl. ⟨the ~*s* of government⟩ **3** : opportunity for unhampered activity or use ⟨gave full ~ to her imagination⟩

²rein *vt* (1530) **1** : to check or stop by or as if by a pull at the reins ⟨~*ed* in his horse⟩ ⟨couldn't ~ his impatience⟩ **2** : to control or direct with or as if with reins ~ *vi* **1** *archaic* : to submit to the use of reins **2** : to stop or slow up one's horse or oneself by or as if by pulling the reins

re·in·car·nate \ˌrē-ən-ˈkär-ˌnāt, (ˈ)rē-ˈin-ˌ\ *vt* (1858) : to incarnate again

re·in·car·na·tion \(ˌ)rē-ˌin-ˌkär-ˈnā-shən\ *n* (1858) **1 a** : the action of reincarnating : the state of being reincarnated **b** : rebirth in new bodies or forms of life; *esp* : a rebirth of a soul in a new human body **2** : a fresh embodiment

rein·deer \ˈrān-ˌdi(ə)r\ *n* [ME *reindere,* fr. ON *hreinn* reindeer + ME *deer* animal, deer] (15c) : any of several large deer (subspecies of *Rangifer tarandus*) orig. of Old World arctic regions and Greenland but introduced elsewhere that have palmate antlers in both sexes and are grouped with the caribou in a single species

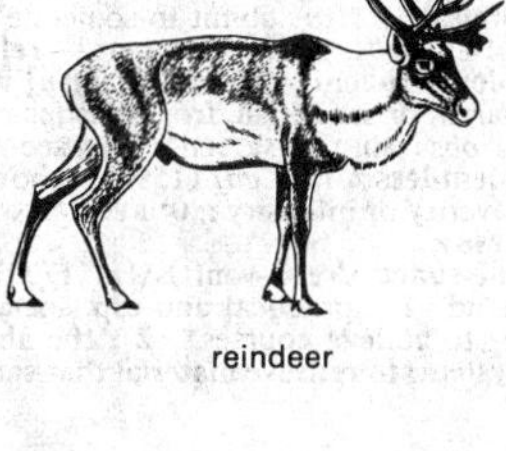
reindeer

reindeer moss *n* (ca. 1753) : a gray, erect, tufted, and much-branched lichen (*Cladonia rangiferina*) that forms extensive patches in arctic and north-temperate regions, constitutes a large part of the food of reindeer, and is sometimes eaten by man — called also *reindeer lichen*

re·in·fec·tion \ˌrē-ən-ˈfek-shən\ *n* (1882) : infection following recovery from or superimposed on infection of the same type

re·in·force \ˌrē-ən-ˈfō(ə)rs, -ˈfȯ(ə)rs\ *vb* [*re-* + *inforce,* alter. of *enforce*] *vt* (1600) **1** : to strengthen or increase by fresh additions ⟨~ the regular troops⟩ ⟨were *reinforcing* their pitching staff⟩ **2** : to strengthen by additional assistance, material, or support : make stronger or more pronounced ⟨~ the elbows of a jacket⟩ ⟨claimed that the media ~ destructive impulses⟩ **3** : to stimulate (as an experimental animal or a student) with a reinforcer following a correct or desired performance; *also* : to encourage (a response) with a reinforcer ~ *vi* : to seek or get reinforcements — **re·in·force·able** \-ə-bəl\ *adj*

reinforced concrete *n* (1902) : concrete in which metal (as steel) is embedded so that the two materials act together in resisting forces

re·in·force·ment \ˌrē-ən-ˈfōr-smənt, -ˈfȯr-\ *n* (1617) **1** : the action of reinforcing : the state of being reinforced **2** : something that reinforces

re·in·forc·er \-ˈfōr-sər, -ˈfȯr-\ *n* (1955) : a stimulus (as a reward or the removal of an electric shock) that increases the probability of a desired response in operant conditioning by being applied or effected following the desired response

reins \ˈrānz\ *n pl* [ME, fr. MF & L; MF, fr. L *renes*] (14c) **1 a** : KIDNEYS **b** : the region of the kidneys : LOINS **2** : the seat of the feelings or passions

reins·man \ˈrānz-mən\ *n* (1855) : a skilled driver or rider of horses

re·in·state \ˌrē-ən-ˈstāt\ *vt* **-stat·ed; -stat·ing** (1628) **1** : to place again (as in possession or in a former position) **2** : to restore to a previous effective state — **re·in·state·ment** \-ˈstāt-mənt\ *n*

re·in·sur·ance \ˌrē-ən-ˈshu̇r-ən(t)s, *esp Southern* (ˈ)rē-ˈin-ˌ\ *n* (1755) : insurance by another insurer of all or a part of a risk previously assumed by an insurance company

re·in·sure \ˌrē-ən-ˈshu̇(ə)r\ *vt* (1828) **1** : to insure again by transferring to another insurance company all or a part of a liability assumed **2** : to insure again by assuming all or a part of the liability of an insurance company already covering a risk ~ *vi* : to provide increased insurance — **re·in·sur·er** *n*

re·in·te·grate \(ˈ)rē-ˈint-ə-ˌgrāt\ *vt* [ML *reintegratus,* pp. of *reintegrare* to renew, reinstate, fr. L *re-* + *integrare* to integrate] (1626) : to integrate again into an entity : restore to unity — **re·in·te·gra·tion** \(ˌ)rē-ˌint-ə-ˈgrā-shən\ *n* — **re·in·te·gra·tive** \(ˈ)rē-ˈint-ə-ˌgrāt-iv\ *adj*

re·in·ter·pret \ˌrē-ən-ˈtər-prət, *rapid* -pət\ *vt* (ca. 1611) : to interpret again; *specif* : to give a new or different interpretation to — **re·in·ter·pre·ta·tion** \-ˌtər-prə-ˈtā-shən, *rapid* -pə-\ *n*

re·in·vent \ˌrē-ən-ˈvent\ *vt* (1686) **1** : to make as if for the first time something already invented ⟨realized they were ~*ing* a machine that had been designed a century before⟩ **2** : to remake or redo completely **3** : to bring into use again — **re·in·ven·tion** \-ˈven-chən\ *n*

re·in·vest \ˌrē-ən-ˈvest\ *vt* (ca. 1611) **1** : to invest again or anew **2 a** : to invest (as income from investments) in additional securities **b** : to invest (as earnings) in a business rather than distribute as dividends or profits

re·in·vest·ment \-ˈves(t)-mənt\ *n* (ca. 1611) **1** : the action of reinvesting : the state of being reinvested **2** : a second or repeated investment

reis *pl of* REAL

re·is·sue \(ˈ)rē-ˈish-(ˌ)ü, -ˈish-ə(-w), *chiefly Brit* -ˈis-(ˌ)yü\ *vi* (1618) : to come forth again ~ *vt* : to issue again; *esp* : to cause to become available again — **reissue** *n*

re·it·er·ate \rē-ˈit-ə-ˌrāt\ *vt* **-at·ed; -at·ing** [L *reiteratus,* pp. of *reiterare* to repeat, fr. *re-* + *iterare* to iterate] (1526) : to state or do over again or repeatedly sometimes with wearying effect — **re·it·er·a·tion** \(ˌ)rē-ˌit-ə-ˈrā-shən\ *n* — **re·it·er·a·tive** \rē-ˈit-ə-ˌrāt-iv, -rət-iv; -ˈi-trət-iv\ *adj* — **re·it·er·a·tive·ly** *adv*

Rei·ter's syndrome \ˈrīt-ərz-\ *n* [Hans *Reiter* †1969 Ger. physician] (ca. 1947) : a disease of uncertain cause that is characterized by arthritis, conjunctivitis, and urethritis — called also *Reiter's disease*

reive \ˈrēv\ *vb* **reived; reiv·ing** [ME (Sc) *reifen,* fr. OE *rēafian* to rob — more at REAVE] *Scot* (bef. 12c) : RAID — **reiv·er** *n, Scot*

¹re·ject \ri-ˈjekt\ *vt* [ME *rejecten,* fr. L *rejectus,* pp. of *reicere,* fr. *re-* + *jacere* to throw — more at JET] (15c) **1 a** : to refuse to accept, consider, submit to, take for some purpose, or use ⟨thought about her suggestion and then ~*ed* it⟩ ⟨~ a manuscript⟩ **b** : to refuse to hear, receive, or admit : REBUFF, REPEL ⟨parents who ~ their children⟩ **c** : to refuse as lover or spouse **2** *obs* : to cast off **3** : THROW BACK, REPULSE **4** : to spew out ***syn*** see DECLINE — **re·ject·er** *or* **re·jec·tor** \-ˈjek-tər\ *n* — **re·ject·ing·ly** \-tiŋ-lē\ *adv* — **re·jec·tive** \-ˈjek-tiv\ *adj*

²re·ject \ˈrē-ˌjekt\ *n* (1555) : a rejected person or thing; *esp* : one rejected as not wanted, unsatisfactory, or not fulfilling standard requirements

re·ject·ee \ri-ˌjek-ˈtē, ˌrē-\ *n* (1941) : one that is rejected; *specif* : a person rejected as unfit for military service

re·jec·tion \ri-ˈjek-shən\ *n* (ca. 1552) **1 a** : the action of rejecting : the state of being rejected **b** : the immunological process of sloughing off foreign tissue or an organ (as a transplant) by the recipient organism **2** : something rejected

rejection slip *n* (1906) : a printed slip enclosed with a rejected manuscript returned by an editor to an author

re·jig·ger \(ˈ)rē-ˈjig-ər\ *vt* [*re-* + ²*jigger*] (1942) : ALTER, REARRANGE

re·joice \ri-ˈjȯis\ *vb* **re·joiced; re·joic·ing** [ME *rejoicen,* fr. MF *rejoiss-,* stem of *rejoir,* fr. *re-* + *joir* to rejoice, fr. L *gaudēre* — more at JOY] *vt* (14c) : to give joy to : GLADDEN ~ *vi* : to feel joy or great delight — **re·joic·er** *n* — **re·joic·ing·ly** \-ˈjȯi-siŋ-lē\ *adv* — **rejoice in** : HAVE, POSSESS

re·joic·ing *n* (14c) **1** : the action of one that rejoices **2** : an instance, occasion, or expression of joy : FESTIVITY

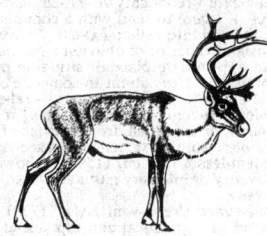

\ə\ abut \ᵊ\ kitten, F table \ər\ further \a\ ash \ā\ ace \ä\ cot, cart \au̇\ out \ch\ chin \e\ bet \ē\ easy \g\ go \i\ hit \ī\ ice \j\ job \ŋ\ sing \ō\ go \ȯ\ law \ȯi\ boy \th\ thin \th\ the \ü\ loot \u̇\ foot \y\ yet \zh\ vision \a, k, ⁿ, œ, œ̄, ue, ue̅, ʸ\ *see* Guide to Pronunciation

re·join \ri-ˈjȯin, *vt 1 is* (ˈ)rē-\ *vb* [ME *rejoinen* to answer to a legal charge, fr. MF *rejoin-*, stem of *rejoindre*, fr. *re-* + OF *joindre* to join — more at JOIN] *vi* (15c) : to answer the replication of the plaintiff ~ *vt* **1 :** to join again **2 :** to say often sharply or critically in response esp. as a reply to a reply ***syn*** see ANSWER

re·join·der \ri-ˈjȯin-dər\ *n* [ME *rejoiner*, fr. MF *rejoindre* to rejoin] (15c) **1 :** the defendant's answer to the plaintiff's replication **2 :** REPLY; *specif* **:** an answer to a reply

re·ju·ve·nate \ri-ˈjü-və-ˌnāt\ *vb* **-nat·ed; -nat·ing** [*re-* + L *juvenis* young — more at YOUNG] *vt* (1807) **1 a :** to make young or youthful again **:** REINVIGORATE **b :** to restore to an original or new state ⟨~ old cars⟩ **2 a :** to stimulate (a stream) to renewed erosive activity esp. by uplift **b :** to develop youthful features of topography in ~ *vi* **:** to cause or undergo rejuvenescence ***syn*** see RENEW — **re·ju·ve·na·tion** \ri-ˌjü-və-ˈnā-shən, ˌrē-\ *n* — **re·ju·ve·na·tor** \ri-ˈjü-və-ˌnāt-ər\ *n*

re·ju·ve·nes·cence \ri-ˌjü-və-ˈnes-ən(t)s, ˌrē-\ *n* [ML *rejuvenescere* to become young again, fr. L *re-* + *juvenescere* to become young, fr. *juvenis*] (1631) **:** a renewal of youthfulness **:** REJUVENATION — **re·ju·ve·nes·cent** \-ˀnt\ *adj*

[1]**re·lapse** \ri-ˈlaps, ˈrē-ˌ\ *n* [L *relapsus*, pp. of *relabi* to slide back, fr. *re-* + *labi* to slide — more at SLEEP] (1533) **1 :** the act or an instance of backsliding, worsening, or subsiding **2 :** a recurrence of symptoms of a disease after a period of improvement

[2]**re·lapse** \ri-ˈlaps\ *vi* **re·lapsed; re·laps·ing** (1568) **1 :** to slip or fall back into a former worse state **2 :** SINK, SUBSIDE ⟨~ into deep thought⟩ — **re·laps·er** *n*

relapsing fever *n* (1849) **:** a variable acute epidemic disease that is marked by recurring high fever lasting 5 to 7 days and that is caused by a spirochete (genus *Borrelia*) transmitted by the bites of lice and ticks

re·late \ri-ˈlāt\ *vb* **re·lat·ed; re·lat·ing** [L *relatus* (pp. of *referre* to carry back), fr. *re-* + *latus*, pp. of *ferre* to carry — more at TOLERATE, BEAR] *vt* (1530) **1 :** to give an account of **:** TELL **2 :** to show or establish logical or causal connection between ⟨seeks to ~ crime to poverty⟩ ~ *vi* **1 :** to apply or take effect retroactively **2 :** to have relationship or connection **:** REFER ⟨the readings ~ to his lectures⟩ **3 :** to have or establish a relationship **:** INTERACT ⟨the way a child ~*s* to a teacher⟩ **4 :** to respond esp. favorably ⟨can't ~ to that kind of music⟩ ***syn*** see JOIN — **re·lat·able** \-ˈlāt-ə-bəl\ *adj* — **re·lat·er** *or* **re·la·tor** \-ˈlāt-ər\ *n*

re·lat·ed *adj* (1662) **1 :** connected by reason of an established or discoverable relation **2 :** connected by common ancestry or sometimes by marriage **3 :** having close harmonic connection — used of tones, chords, or tonalities — **re·lat·ed·ly** *adv* — **re·lat·ed·ness** *n*

re·la·tion \ri-ˈlā-shən\ *n* [ME *relacioun*, fr. MF *relation*, fr. L *relation-*, *relatio*, fr. *relatus*, pp.] (14c) **1 :** the act of telling or recounting **:** ACCOUNT **2 :** an aspect or quality (as resemblance) that connects two or more things or parts as being or belonging or working together or as being of the same kind ⟨the ~ of time and space⟩; *specif* **:** a property (as one expressed by *is equal to, is less than,* or *is the brother of*) that holds between an ordered pair of objects **3 :** the referring by a legal fiction of an act to a prior date as the time of its taking effect **4 a** (1) **:** a person connected by consanguinity or affinity **:** RELATIVE (2) **:** a person legally entitled to a share of the property of an intestate **b :** relationship by consanguinity or affinity **:** KINSHIP **5 :** REFERENCE, RESPECT ⟨in ~ to⟩ **6 :** the attitude or stance which two or more persons or groups assume toward one another ⟨race ~*s*⟩ **7 a :** the state of being mutually or reciprocally interested (as in social or commercial matters) **b** *pl* (1) **:** DEALINGS, AFFAIRS ⟨foreign ~*s*⟩ (2) **:** INTERCOURSE (3) **:** SEXUAL INTERCOURSE

re·la·tion·al \-shnəl, -shən-ˀl\ *adj* (1662) **1 :** of or relating to kinship **2 :** characterized or constituted by relations **3 :** having the function chiefly of indicating a relation of syntax ⟨*has* is notional in *he has luck*, ~ in *he has gone*⟩ — **re·la·tion·al·ly** \-ē\ *adv*

re·la·tion·ship \-shən-ˌship\ *n* (1744) **1 :** the state of being related or interrelated ⟨entered into the marriage ~⟩ **2 :** the relation connecting or binding participants in a relationship: as **a :** KINSHIP **b :** a specific instance or type of kinship **3 a :** a state of affairs existing between those having relations or dealings ⟨had a good ~ with his family⟩ **b :** a romantic or passionate attachment

[1]**rel·a·tive** \ˈrel-ət-iv\ *n* (14c) **1 :** a word referring grammatically to an antecedent **2 :** a thing having a relation to or connection with or necessary dependence on another thing **3 a :** a person connected with another by blood or affinity **b :** an animal or plant related to another by common descent **4 :** a relative term

[2]**relative** *adj* (1530) **1 :** introducing a subordinate clause qualifying an expressed or implied antecedent ⟨~ pronoun⟩; *also* **:** introduced by such a connective ⟨~ clause⟩ **2 :** RELEVANT, PERTINENT ⟨matters ~ to world peace⟩ **3 :** not absolute or independent **:** COMPARATIVE ⟨the ~ isolation of life in the country⟩ **4 :** having the same key signature — used of major and minor keys and scales **5 :** expressed as the ratio of the specified quantity (as an error in measuring) to the total magnitude (as the value of a measured quantity) or to the mean of all the quantities involved

relative humidity *n* (1820) **:** the ratio of the amount of water vapor actually present in the air to the greatest amount possible at the same temperature

rel·a·tive·ly *adv* (1561) **:** to a relative degree or extent **:** SOMEWHAT

relatively prime *adj, of integers* (ca. 1890) **:** having no common factors except +1 and −1 ⟨12 and 25 are *relatively prime*⟩

relative to *prep* (1660) **:** with regard to **:** in connection with

relative wind *n* (1918) **:** the motion of the air relative to a body in it

rel·a·tiv·ism \ˈrel-ət-iv-ˌiz-əm\ *n* (1865) **1 a :** a theory that knowledge is relative to the limited nature of the mind and the conditions of knowing **b :** a view that ethical truths depend on the individuals and groups holding them **2 :** RELATIVITY — **rel·a·tiv·ist** \-əst\ *n*

rel·a·tiv·is·tic \ˌrel-ət-iv-ˈis-tik\ *adj* (1886) **1 :** of, relating to, or characterized by relativity or relativism **2 :** moving at a velocity such that there is a significant change in properties (as mass) in accordance with the theory of relativity ⟨a ~ electron⟩ — **rel·a·tiv·is·ti·cal·ly** \-ˈis-ti-k(ə-)lē\ *adv*

rel·a·tiv·i·ty \ˌrel-ə-ˈtiv-ət-ē\ *n, pl* **-ties** (1834) **1 a :** the quality or state of being relative **b :** something that is relative **2 :** the state of being dependent for existence on or determined in nature, value, or quality by relation to something else **3 a :** a theory which is based on the two postulates (1) that the speed of light in a vacuum is constant and independent of the source or observer and (2) that the mathematical forms of the laws of physics are invariant in all inertial systems and which leads to the assertion of the equivalence of mass and energy and of change in mass, dimension, and time with increased velocity — called also *special theory of relativity* **b :** an extension of the theory to include gravitation and related acceleration phenomena — called also *general theory of relativity* **4 :** RELATIVISM 1b

rel·a·tiv·ize \ˈrel-ət-iv-ˌīz\ *vt* **-ized; -iz·ing** (1937) **:** to treat or describe as relative

re·lax \ri-ˈlaks\ *vb* [ME *relaxen* to make less compact, fr. L *relaxare*, fr. *re-* + *laxare* to loosen, fr. *laxus* loose — more at SLACK] *vt* (1620) **1 :** to make less tense or rigid **:** SLACKEN ⟨~*ed* his muscles⟩ **2 :** to make less severe or stringent **:** MODIFY ⟨~ immigration laws⟩ **3 :** to make soft or enervated **4 :** to relieve from nervous tension ~ *vi* **1 :** to become lax, weak, or loose **:** REST **2 :** to become less intense or severe ⟨hoped the committee would ~ in its opposition⟩ **3** *of a muscle or muscle fiber* **:** to become inactive and lengthen **4 :** to cast off social restraint, nervous tension, or anxiety ⟨couldn't ~ in crowds⟩ **5 :** to seek rest or recreation ⟨~ at the seashore⟩ **6 :** to relieve constipation **7 :** to attain an equilibrium state following the abrupt removal of some influence (as light, high temperature, or stress) — **re·lax·er** *n*

[1]**re·lax·ant** \ri-ˈlak-sənt\ *adj* (1771) **:** of, relating to, or producing relaxation ⟨an anesthetic and ~ agent⟩

[2]**relaxant** *n* (1847) **:** a substance (as a drug) that relaxes; *specif* **:** one that relieves muscular tension

re·lax·ation \ˌrē-ˌlak-ˈsā-shən, ri-ˌlak- *esp Brit* ˌrel-ək-\ *n* (1526) **1 :** the act of relaxing or state of being relaxed **2 :** a relaxing or recreative state, activity, or pastime **:** DIVERSION **3 :** the lengthening that characterizes inactive muscle fibers or muscles

re·laxed \ri-ˈlakst\ *adj* (1638) **1 :** freed from or lacking in precision or stringency **2 :** set or being at rest or at ease **3 :** easy of manner **:** INFORMAL — **re·laxed·ly** \-ˈlak-səd-lē, -ˈlaks-tlē\ *adv* — **re·laxed·ness** \-ˈlak-səd-nəs, -ˈlaks(t)-nəs\ *n*

re·lax·in \ri-ˈlak-sən\ *n* (1930) **:** a sex hormone of the corpus luteum that facilitates birth by causing relaxation of the pelvic ligaments

[1]**re·lay** \ˈrē-ˌlā\ *n* (1659) **1 a :** a supply (as of horses) arranged beforehand for successive relief **b :** a number of persons who relieve others in some work ⟨worked in ~*s* around the clock⟩ **2 a :** a race between teams in which each team member successively covers a specified portion of the course **b :** one of the divisions of a relay **3 :** an electromagnetic device for remote or automatic control that is actuated by variation in conditions of an electric circuit and that operates in turn other devices (as switches) in the same or a different circuit **4 :** SERVOMOTOR **5 :** the act of passing along (as a message or ball) by stages; *also* **:** one of such stages

[2]**re·lay** \ˈrē-ˌlā, ri-ˈlā\ *vt* **re·layed; re·lay·ing** [ME *relayen* to hunt with relays, fr. MF *relaier*, fr. OF, fr. *re-* + *laier* to leave — more at DELAY] (1788) **1 a :** to place or dispose in relays **b :** to provide with relays **2 :** to pass along by relays ⟨news was ~*ed* to distant points⟩ **3 :** to control or operate by a relay

[3]**re·lay** \(ˈ)rē-ˈlā\ *vt* **-laid** \-ˈlād\; **-lay·ing** [*re-* + [1]*lay*] (1757) **:** to lay again ⟨~ track⟩

[1]**re·lease** \ri-ˈlēs\ *vt* **re·leased; re·leas·ing** [ME *relesen*, fr. MF *relessier*, fr. L *relaxare* to relax] (14c) **1 :** to set free from restraint, confinement, or servitude ⟨~ hostages⟩ ⟨~ pent-up emotions⟩ ⟨~ the brakes⟩; *also* **:** to let go **:** DISMISS ⟨*released* from her job⟩ **2 :** to relieve from something that confines, burdens, or oppresses ⟨was *released* from her promise⟩ **3 :** to give up in favor of another **:** RELINQUISH ⟨~ a claim to property⟩ **4 :** to give permission for publication, performance, exhibition, or sale of; *also* **:** PUBLISH, PRESENT ⟨the commission *released* its findings⟩ ⟨~ a new movie⟩ ***syn*** see FREE — **re·leas·able** \-ˈlē-sə-bəl\ *adj*

[2]**release** *n* (14c) **1 :** relief or deliverance from sorrow, suffering, or trouble **2 a :** discharge from obligation or responsibility **b** (1) **:** relinquishment of a right or claim (2) **:** an act by which a legal right is discharged; *specif* **:** a conveyance of a right in lands or tenements to another having an estate in possession **3 a :** the act or an instance of liberating or freeing (as from restraint) **b :** the act or manner of concluding a musical tone or phrase **c :** the act or manner of ending a sound **:** the movement of one or more vocal organs in quitting the position for a speech sound **4 :** an instrument effecting a legal release **5 a :** the permitting of a working fluid (as steam) to escape from the cylinder at the end of the working stroke **b :** the point in a cycle at which this act occurs **6 :** the state of being freed **7 :** a device adapted to hold or release a mechanism as required **8 a :** the act of permitting performance or publication; *also* **:** PERFORMANCE, PUBLICATION ⟨a record that immediately became a best-seller on its ~⟩ **b :** the matter released; *esp* **:** a statement prepared for the press

re–lease \(ˈ)rē-ˈlēs\ *vt* (1828) **:** to lease again

released time *n* (1941) **:** time off from regularly scheduled activities (as school) given to take part in some other specified activity (as religious instruction)

release print *n* (1937) **:** a motion-picture film released for public showing

re·leas·er \ri-ˈlē-sər\ *n* (1651) **:** one that releases; *specif* **:** a stimulus that serves as the initiator of complex reflex behavior

rel·e·gate \ˈrel-ə-ˌgāt\ *vt* **-gat·ed; -gat·ing** [L *relegatus*, pp. of *relegare*, fr. *re-* + *legare* to send with a commission — more at LEGATE] (1599) **1 :** to send into exile **:** BANISH **2 :** ASSIGN: as **a :** to assign to a place of insignificance or of oblivion **:** put out of sight or mind **b :** to assign to an appropriate place or situation on the basis of classification or appraisal **c :** to submit to someone or something for appropriate action **:** DELEGATE ***syn*** see COMMIT — **rel·e·ga·tion** \ˌrel-ə-ˈgā-shən\ *n*

re·lent \ri-ˈlent\ *vb* [ME *relenten*] *vi* (1526) **1 :** to become less severe, harsh, or strict usu. from reasons of humanity **2 :** LET UP, SLACKEN ~ *vt, obs* **:** SOFTEN, MOLLIFY ***syn*** see YIELD

re·lent·less \-ləs\ *adj* (1592) **:** showing or promising no abatement of severity or intensity **:** UNRELENTING — **re·lent·less·ly** *adv* — **re·lent·less·ness** *n*

rel·e·vance \ˈrel-ə-vən(t)s\ *n* (1733) **1 a :** relation to the matter at hand **b :** practical and esp. social applicability **:** PERTINENCE ⟨giving ~ to college courses⟩ **2 :** the ability (as of an information retrieval system) to retrieve material that satisfies the needs of the user

rel·e·van·cy \-vən-sē\ *n, pl* **-cies** (1561) : RELEVANCE; *also* : something relevant

rel·e·vant \'rel-ə-vənt\ *adj* [ML *relevant-, relevans,* fr. L, prp. of *relevare* to raise up — more at RELIEVE] (1560) **1 a :** having significant and demonstrable bearing on the matter at hand **b :** affording evidence tending to prove or disprove the matter at issue or under discussion ⟨~ testimony⟩ **c :** having social relevance **2 :** PROPORTIONAL, RELATIVE — **rel·e·vant·ly** *adv*

syn RELEVANT, GERMANE, MATERIAL, PERTINENT, APPOSITE, APPLICABLE, APROPOS mean relating to or bearing upon the matter in hand. RELEVANT implies a traceable, significant, logical connection; GERMANE may additionally imply a fitness for or appropriateness to the situation or occasion; MATERIAL implies so close a relationship that it cannot be dispensed with without serious alteration of the case; PERTINENT stresses a clear and decisive relevance; APPOSITE suggests a felicitous relevance; APPLICABLE suggests the fitness of bringing a general rule or principle to bear upon a particular case; APROPOS suggests being both relevant and opportune.

re·li·abil·i·ty \ri-ˌlī-ə-'bil-ət-ē\ *n* (1816) **1 :** the quality or state of being reliable **2 :** the extent to which an experiment, test, or measuring procedure yields the same results on repeated trials

¹re·li·able \ri-'lī-ə-bəl\ *adj* (1569) **1 :** suitable or fit to be relied on **:** DEPENDABLE **2 :** giving the same result on successive trials — **re·li·able·ness** *n* — **re·li·ably** \-blē\ *adv*

²reliable *n* (1890) : one that is reliable

re·li·ance \ri-'lī-ən(t)s\ *n* (1607) **1 :** the act of relying **:** the state of being reliant **2 :** something or someone relied on

re·li·ant \-ənt\ *adj* (1859) : having reliance on something or someone **:** DEPENDENT — **re·li·ant·ly** *adv*

rel·ic \'rel-ik\ *n* [ME *relik,* fr. OF *relique,* fr. ML *reliquia,* fr. LL *reliquiae,* pl., remains of a martyr, fr. L, remains, fr. *relinquere* to leave behind — more at RELINQUISH] (13c) **1 a :** an object esteemed and venerated because of association with a saint or martyr **b :** SOUVENIR, MEMENTO **2** *pl* **:** REMAINS, CORPSE **3 :** a survivor or remnant left after decay, disintegration, or disappearance **4 :** a trace of some past or outmoded practice, custom, or belief

¹rel·ict \'rel-ikt\ *n* [in sense 1, fr. LL *relicta,* fr. L, fem. of *relictus,* pp. of *relinquere;* in senses 2 & 3, fr. *relict* (residual), adj., fr. L *relictus*] (1545) **1 :** WIDOW **2 :** a persistent remnant of an otherwise extinct flora or fauna or kind of organism **3 a :** a relief feature or rock remaining after other parts have disappeared **b :** something left unchanged

²relict *adj* (1649) : of, relating to, or being a relict ⟨~ populations⟩

re·lic·tion \ri-'lik-shən\ *n* [L *reliction-, relictio* act of leaving behind, fr. *relictus*] (1676) **1 :** the gradual recession of water leaving land permanently uncovered **2 :** land uncovered by reliction

¹re·lief \ri-'lēf\ *n* [ME, fr. MF, fr. OF, fr. *relever* to relieve] (14c) **1 :** a payment made by a feudal tenant to his lord on succeeding to an inherited estate **2 a :** removal or lightening of something oppressive, painful, or distressing **b :** aid in the form of money or necessities for the poor, aged, or handicapped **c :** military assistance to an endangered post or force **d :** means of breaking or avoiding monotony or boredom **:** DIVERSION **3 :** release from a post or from the performance of duty **4 :** one that takes the place of another on duty **5 :** legal remedy or redress **6** [F] **a :** a mode of sculpture in which forms and figures are distinguished from a surrounding plane surface **b :** sculpture or a sculptural form executed in this mode **c :** projecting detail, ornament, or figures **7 :** sharpness of outline due to contrast ⟨a roof in bold ~ against the sky⟩ **8 :** the elevations or inequalities of a land surface

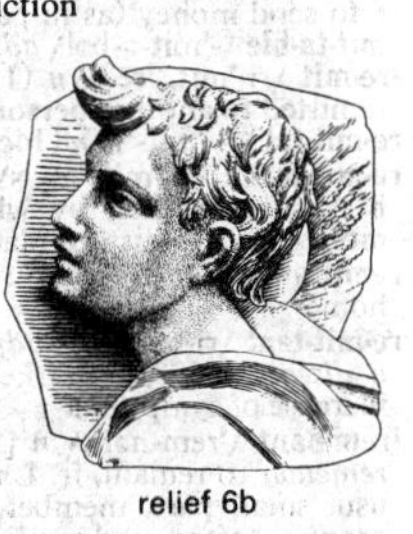
relief 6b

²relief *adj* (1838) **1 :** providing relief **2 :** characterized by surface inequalities **3 :** of or used in letterpress

relief map *n* (1876) : a map representing topographic relief

relief pitcher *n* (ca. 1949) : a baseball pitcher who takes over for another during a game

relief printing *n* (1875) : LETTERPRESS 1

re·lieve \ri-'lēv\ *vb* **re·lieved; re·liev·ing** [ME *releven,* fr. MF *relever* to raise, relieve, fr. L *relevare,* fr. *re-* + *levare* to raise — more at LEVER] *vt* (14c) **1 a :** to free from a burden **:** give aid or help to **b :** to set free from an obligation, condition, or restriction **c :** to ease of a burden, wrong, or oppression by judicial or legislative interposition **2 a :** to bring about the removal or alleviation of **:** MITIGATE **b :** ROB, DEPRIVE **3 a :** to release from a post, station, or duty **b :** to take the place of **4 :** to remove or lessen the monotony of **5 a :** to set off by contrast **b :** to raise in relief **6 :** to discharge the bladder or bowels of (oneself) ~ *vi* **1 :** to bring or give relief **2 :** to stand out in relief **3 :** to serve as a relief pitcher — **re·liev·able** \-'lē-və-bəl\ *adj* — **re·liev·er** *n*

syn RELIEVE, ALLEVIATE, LIGHTEN, ASSUAGE, MITIGATE, ALLAY mean to make something less grievous. RELIEVE implies a lifting of enough of a burden to make it tolerable; ALLEVIATE implies temporary or partial lessening of pain or distress; LIGHTEN implies reducing a burdensome or depressing weight; ASSUAGE implies softening or sweetening what is harsh or disagreeable; MITIGATE suggests a moderating or countering of the effect of something violent or painful; ALLAY implies an effective calming or soothing of fears or alarms.

re·lieved \ri-'lēvd\ *adj* (1869) : experiencing or showing relief esp. from anxiety or pent-up emotions — **re·liev·ed·ly** \-'lē-vəd-lē\ *adv*

re·lie·vo \ri-'lē-(ˌ)vō, rēl-'yā-\ *n, pl* **-vos** [It *rilievo,* fr. *rilevare* to raise, fr. L *relevare*] (1625) : RELIEF 6

re·li·gio- \ri-'lij-(ē-)ō\ *comb form* : religion ⟨*religio*centric⟩ : religion and ⟨*religio*philosophical⟩

re·li·gion \ri-'lij-ən\ *n* [ME *religioun,* fr. L *religion-, religio* reverence, religion] (13c) **1 a** (1) **:** the service and worship of God or the supernatural (2) **:** commitment or devotion to religious faith or observance **b :** the state of a religious ⟨a nun in her 20th year of ~⟩ **2 :** a personal set or institutionalized system of religious attitudes, beliefs, and practices **3** *archaic* **:** scrupulous conformity **:** CONSCIENTIOUSNESS **4 :** a cause, principle, or system of beliefs held to with ardor and faith — **re·li·gion·less** *adj*

re·li·gion·ist \-'lij-(ə-)nəst\ *n* (1653) : a person adhering to a religion

re·li·gi·ose \ri-'lij-ē-ˌōs\ *adj* [*religion* + *-ose*] (1853) : RELIGIOUS; *esp* : excessively, obtrusively, or sentimentally religious — **re·li·gi·os·i·ty** \-ˌlij-ē-'äs-ət-ē\ *n*

¹re·li·gious \ri-'lij-əs\ *adj* [ME, fr. OF *religieus,* fr. L *religiosus,* fr. *religio*] (13c) **1 :** relating to or manifesting faithful devotion to an acknowledged ultimate reality or deity ⟨a ~ person⟩ ⟨~ attitudes⟩ **2 :** of, relating to, or devoted to religious beliefs or observances **3 a :** scrupulously and conscientiously faithful **b :** FERVENT, ZEALOUS — **re·li·gious·ly** *adv* — **re·li·gious·ness** *n*

²religious *n, pl* **religious** [ME, fr. OF *religieus,* fr. *religieus,* adj.] (14c) : a member of a religious order under monastic vows

re·line \(ˈ)rē-'līn\ *vt* (1851) : to put new lines on or a new lining in

re·lin·quish \ri-'liŋ-kwish, -'lin-\ *vt* [ME *relinquisshen,* fr. MF *relinquiss-,* stem of *relinquir,* fr. L *relinquere* to leave behind, fr. *re-* + *linquere* to leave — more at LOAN] (15c) **1 :** to withdraw or retreat from **:** leave behind **2 :** GIVE UP ⟨~ a title⟩ **3 a :** to stop holding physically **:** RELEASE ⟨slowly ~*ed* his grip on the bar⟩ **b :** to give over possession or control of **:** YIELD ⟨few leaders willingly ~ power⟩ — **re·lin·quish·ment** \-mənt\ *n*

syn RELINQUISH, YIELD, RESIGN, SURRENDER, ABANDON, WAIVE mean to give up completely. RELINQUISH usu. does not imply strong feeling but may suggest some regret, reluctance, or weakness; YIELD implies concession or compliance or submission to force; RESIGN emphasizes voluntary relinquishment or sacrifice without struggle; SURRENDER implies a giving up after a struggle to retain or resist; ABANDON stresses finality and completeness in giving up; WAIVE implies conceding or forgoing with little or no compulsion.

rel·i·quary \'rel-ə-ˌkwer-ē\ *n, pl* **-quar·ies** [F *reliquaire,* fr. ML *reliquiarium,* fr. *reliquia* relic — more at RELIC] (ca. 1656) : a container or shrine in which sacred relics are kept

re·lique \ri-'lēk, 'rel-ik\ *archaic var of* RELIC

re·liq·ui·ae \ri-'lik-wē-ˌī, -wē-ˌē\ *n pl* [L — more at RELIC] (1654) : remains of the dead **:** RELICS

¹rel·ish \'rel-ish\ *n* [alter. of ME *reles* taste, fr. OF, something left behind, release, fr. *relessier* to release] (ca. 1530) **1 :** characteristic flavor; *esp* **:** pleasing or zestful flavor **2 :** a quantity just sufficient to flavor or characterize **:** TRACE **3 a :** enjoyment of or delight in something that satisfies one's tastes, inclinations, or desires ⟨eat with great ~⟩ **b :** a strong liking **:** INCLINATION ⟨has little ~ for sports⟩ **4 a :** something adding a zestful flavor; *esp* **:** a condiment (as of pickles or green tomatoes) eaten with other food to add flavor **b :** APPETIZER, HORS D'OEUVRE

²relish *vt* (1586) **1 :** to add relish to **2 :** to be pleased or gratified by **:** ENJOY **3 :** to eat or drink with pleasure **4 :** to appreciate with taste and discernment ~ *vi* **:** to have a characteristic or pleasing taste — **rel·ish·able** \-ə-bəl\ *adj*

re·live \(ˈ)rē-'liv\ *vi* (1548) : to live again ~ *vt* : to live over again; *esp* : to experience again in the imagination

re·lo·cate \(ˈ)rē-'lō-ˌkāt, ˌrē-lō-'\ *vt* (1834) : to locate again **:** establish or lay out in a new place ~ *vi* : to move to a new location — **re·lo·ca·tion** \ˌrē-lō-'kā-shən\ *n*

re·lo·cat·ee \ˌrē-lə-ˌkāt-'ē, ˌrē-ˌlō-kə-'tē\ *n* (1954) : one who moves to a new location **:** one that is relocated

re·lu·cent \ri-'lüs-ᵊnt\ *adj* [L *relucent-, relucens,* pp. of *relucēre* to shine back, fr. *re-* + *lucēre* to shine — more at LIGHT] (1507) : reflecting light **:** SHINING

re·luct \ri-'ləkt\ *vi* [L *reluctari*] (1547) : to show reluctance

re·luc·tance \ri-'lək-tən(t)s\ *n* (1710) **1 :** the quality or state of being reluctant **2 :** the opposition offered in a magnetic circuit to magnetic flux; *specif* **:** the ratio of the magnetic potential difference to the corresponding flux

re·luc·tan·cy \-tən-sē\ *n* (1634) : RELUCTANCE

re·luc·tant \ri-'lək-tənt\ *adj* [L *reluctant-, reluctans,* prp. of *reluctari* to struggle against, fr. *re-* + *luctari* to struggle — more at LOCK] (1706) : holding back **:** AVERSE, UNWILLING ⟨~ to get involved⟩ ***syn*** see DISINCLINED — **re·luc·tant·ly** *adv*

re·luc·tate \ri-'lək-ˌtāt\ *vi* **-tat·ed; -tat·ing** (1643) : RELUCT — **re·luc·ta·tion** \ri-ˌlək-'tā-shən, ˌrē-\ *n*

re·luc·tiv·i·ty \ri-ˌlək-'tiv-ət-ē, ˌrē-\ *n* [*reluctance* + *-ivity* (as in *conductivity*)] (ca. 1888) : the reciprocal of magnetic permeability

re·lume \(ˈ)rē-'lüm\ *vt* **re·lumed; re·lum·ing** [irreg. fr. LL *reluminare*] (1604) : to light or light up again **:** REKINDLE

re·ly \ri-'lī\ *vi* **re·lied; re·ly·ing** [ME *relien* to rally, fr. MF *relier* to connect, rally, fr. L *religare* to tie back, fr. *re-* + *ligare* to tie — more at LIGATURE] (1571) **1 :** to have confidence based on experience ⟨someone you can ~ on⟩ **2 :** to be dependent ⟨the system on which we ~ for water⟩ — **re·li·er** \-'lī(-ə)r\ *n*

rem *n* [*r*oentgen *e*quivalent *m*an] (1947) : the dosage of an ionizing radiation that will cause the same biological effect as one roentgen of X-ray or gamma-ray dosage

REM \'rem\ *n* (1962) : RAPID EYE MOVEMENT

¹re·main \ri-'mān\ *vi* [ME *remainen,* fr. MF *remaindre,* fr. L *remanēre,* fr. *re-* + *manēre* to remain — more at MANSION] (14c) **1 a :** to be a part not destroyed, taken, or used up ⟨only a few ruins ~⟩ **b :** to be something yet to be shown, done, or treated ⟨it ~*s* to be seen⟩ **2 :** to stay in the same place or with the same person or group; *esp* **:** to stay behind **3 :** to continue unchanged ⟨the fact ~*s* that nothing can be done⟩

²remain *n* (15c) **1** *obs* **:** STAY **2 :** a remaining part or trace — usu. used in pl. **3** *pl* **:** a dead body

¹re·main·der \ri-'mān-dər\ *n* [ME, fr. AF, fr. MF *remaindre*] (15c) **1 :** an interest or estate in property that follows and is dependent on the termination of a prior intervening possessory estate created at the same time by the same instrument **2 a :** a remaining group, part, or trace

b (1) : the number left after a subtraction **b** (2) : the final undivided part after division that is less or of lower degree than the divisor **3** : a book sold at a reduced price by the publisher after sales have slowed
[2]**remainder** *adj* (1567) : LEFTOVER, REMAINING
[3]**remainder** *vt* **-dered; -der·ing** \-d(ə-)riŋ\ (1904) : to dispose of as remainders
remainder theorem *n* (1886) : a theorem in algebra: if *f(x)* is a polynomial in *x* then the remainder on dividing *f(x)* by *x* — *a* is *f(a)*
[1]**re·make** \(ˈ)rē-ˈmāk\ *vt* **-made** \-ˈmād\; **-mak·ing** (1635) : to make anew or in a different form
[2]**re·make** \ˈrē-ˌmāk\ *n* (1936) : one that is remade; *esp* : a new version of a motion picture
re·man \(ˈ)rē-ˈman\ *vt* (1666) **1** : to man again or anew **2** : to imbue with courage again
re·mand \ri-ˈmand\ *vt* [ME *remaunden*, fr. MF *remander*, fr. LL *remandare* to send back word, fr. L *re-* + *mandare* to order — more at MANDATE] (15c) : to order back: as **a** : to send back (a case) to another court or agency for further action **b** : to return to custody pending trial or for further detention — **remand** *n*
re·ma·nence \ˈrem-ə-nən(t)s, ri-ˈmā-\ *n* (ca. 1880) : the magnetic induction remaining in a magnetized substance no longer under external magnetic influence
re·ma·nent \-nənt\ *adj* [ME, fr. L *remanent-, remanens*, prp. of *remanēre* to remain] (15c) **1** : RESIDUAL, REMAINING **2** : of, relating to, or characterized by remanence
re·man·u·fac·ture \(ˌ)rē-ˌman-(y)ə-ˈfak-chər\ *vt* (1851) : to manufacture into a new product — **remanufacture** *n* — **re·man·u·fac·tur·er** \-chər-ər\ *n*
re·map \(ˈ)rē-ˈmap\ *vt* (1931) : to map again; *also* : to lay out in a new pattern
[1]**re·mark** \ri-ˈmärk\ *n* [F *remarque*, fr. MF, fr. *remarquer* to remark, fr. *re-* re- + *marquer* to mark — more at MARQUE] (1660) **1** : the act of remarking : NOTICE **2** : mention of that which deserves attention or notice **3** : an expression of opinion or judgment
[2]**remark** *vt* (1675) **1** : to take notice of : OBSERVE **2** : to express as an observation or comment : SAY ~ *vi* : to notice something and comment thereon — used with *on* or *upon*
re·mark·able \ri-ˈmär-kə-bəl\ *adj* (ca. 1604) : worthy of being or likely to be noticed esp. as being uncommon or extraordinary ***syn*** see NOTICEABLE — **re·mark·able·ness** *n* — **re·mark·ably** \-blē\ *adv*
re·marque \ri-ˈmärk\ *n* [F *remarque* remark, note, fr. MF, fr. *remarquer*] (1882) **1** : a drawn, etched, or incised scribble or sketch done on the margin of a plate or stone and removed before the regular printing **2** : a proof taken before remarques have been removed
re·mas·ter \(ˈ)rē-ˈmas-tər\ *vt* (1964) : to create a new master of esp. by altering or enhancing the sound quality of an older recording
re·match \(ˈ)rē-ˈmach, ˈrē-ˌ\ *n* (1941) : a second match between the same contestants or teams
re·me·di·a·ble \ri-ˈmēd-ē-ə-bəl\ *adj* (ca. 1570) : capable of being remedied
re·me·di·al \ri-ˈmēd-ē-əl\ *adj* (1651) **1** : intended as a remedy **2** : concerned with the correction of faulty study habits and the raising of a pupil's general competence ⟨~ reading courses⟩ — **re·me·di·al·ly** \-ə-lē\ *adv*
remediate *adj, obs* (1605) : REMEDIAL
re·me·di·a·tion \ri-ˌmēd-ē-ˈā-shən\ *n* (1818) : the act or process of remedying ⟨~ of reading problems⟩
[1]**rem·e·dy** \ˈrem-əd-ē\ *n, pl* **-dies** [ME *remedie*, fr. AF, fr. L *remedium*, fr. *re-* + *mederi* to heal — more at MEDICAL] (13c) **1** : a medicine, application, or treatment that relieves or cures a disease **2** : something that corrects or counteracts **3** : the legal means to recover a right or to prevent or obtain redress for a wrong — **rem·e·di·less** *adj*
[2]**remedy** *vt* **-died; -dy·ing** (15c) : to provide or serve as a remedy for : RELIEVE ***syn*** see CURE, CORRECT
re·mem·ber \ri-ˈmem-bər\ *vb* **-bered; -ber·ing** \-b(ə-)riŋ\ [ME *remembren*, fr. MF *remembrer*, fr. LL *rememorari*, fr. L *re-* + LL *memorari* to be mindful of, fr. L *memor* mindful — more at MEMORY] *vt* (14c) **1** : to bring to mind or think of again ⟨~s the old days⟩ **2** *archaic* **a** : BETHINK 1b **b** : REMIND **3 a** : to keep in mind for attention or consideration ⟨~s friends at Christmas⟩ **b** : REWARD ⟨was ~*ed* in the will⟩ **4** : to retain in the memory ⟨~ the facts until the test is over⟩ **5** : to convey greetings from **6** : RECORD, COMMEMORATE ~ *vi* **1** : to exercise or have the power of memory **2** : to have a recollection or remembrance — **re·mem·ber·abil·i·ty** \-ˌmem-b(ə-)rə-ˈbil-ət-ē\ *n* — **re·mem·ber·able** \-ˈmem-b(ə-)rə-bəl\ *adj* — **re·mem·ber·er** \-bər-ər\ *n*
syn REMEMBER, RECOLLECT, RECALL, REMIND, REMINISCE mean to bring an image or idea from the past into the mind. REMEMBER implies a keeping in memory that may be effortless or unwilled; RECOLLECT implies a bringing back to mind what is lost or scattered; RECALL suggests an effort to bring back to mind and often to re-create in speech; REMIND suggests a jogging of one's memory by an association or similarity; REMINISCE implies a casual often nostalgic recalling of experiences long past and gone.
re·mem·brance \ri-ˈmem-brən(t)s *also* -bə-rən(t)s\ *n* (14c) **1** : the state of bearing in mind **2 a** : the ability to remember : MEMORY **b** : the period over which one's memory extends **3** : an act of recalling to mind **4** : a memory of a person, thing, or event **5 a** : something that serves to keep in or bring to mind : REMINDER **b** : COMMEMORATION, MEMORIAL **c** : a greeting or gift recalling or expressing friendship or affection
Remembrance Day *n* (1918) : November 11 set aside in commemoration of the end of hostilities in 1918 and 1945 and observed as a legal holiday in Canada
re·mem·branc·er \ri-ˈmem-brən-sər\ *n* (15c) **1** : any of several English officials **2** : one that reminds
Remembrance Sunday *n* (1942) : a Sunday that is usu. closest to November 11 and that in Great Britain is set aside in commemoration of the end of hostilities in 1918 and 1945
re·mex \ˈrē-ˌmeks\ *n, pl* **rem·i·ges** \ˈrem-ə-ˌjēz\ [NL *remig-, remex*, fr. L, oarsman, fr. *remus* oar + *agere* to drive — more at ROW, AGENT] (1767) : a primary or secondary quill feather of the wing of a bird
re·mil·i·ta·rize \(ˈ)rē-ˈmil-ə-tə-ˌrīz\ *vt* (1936) : to equip again with military forces and installations — **re·mil·i·ta·ri·za·tion** \(ˌ)rē-ˌmil-ət-ə-rə-ˈzā-shən\ *n*

re·mind \ri-ˈmīnd\ *vt* (1660) : to put in mind of something : cause to remember ***syn*** see REMEMBER — **re·mind·er** *n*
re·mind·ful \-ˈmīn(d)-fəl\ *adj* (1810) **1** : MINDFUL **2** : tending to remind : SUGGESTIVE, EVOCATIVE
rem·i·nisce \ˌrem-ə-ˈnis\ *vi* **-nisced; -nisc·ing** [back-formation fr. *reminiscence*] (1829) : to indulge in reminiscence ***syn*** see REMEMBER — **rem·i·nis·cer** \-ˈnis-ər\ *n*
rem·i·nis·cence \-ˈnis-ᵊn(t)s\ *n* (1589) **1** : apprehension of a Platonic idea as if it had been known in a previous existence **2 a** : recall to mind of a long-forgotten experience or fact **b** : the process or practice of thinking or telling about past experiences **3 a** : a remembered experience **b** : an account of a memorable experience — often used in pl. **4** : something so like another as to be regarded as an unconscious repetition, imitation, or survival
rem·i·nis·cent \-ᵊnt\ *adj* [L *reminiscent-, reminiscens*, prp. of *reminisci* to remember, fr. *re-* + *-minisci* (akin to L *ment-, mens* mind) — more at MENTAL] (1765) **1** : of the character of or relating to reminiscence **2** : marked by or given to reminiscence **3** : tending to remind : SUGGESTIVE — **rem·i·nis·cent·ly** *adv*
rem·i·nis·cen·tial \ˌrem-ə-(ˌ)nis-ˈen-chəl\ *adj* (1646) : REMINISCENT
re·mint \(ˈ)rē-ˈmint\ *vt* (1823) : to melt down (old or worn coin) and make into new coin
re·mise \ri-ˈmīz\ *vt* **re·mised; re·mis·ing** [ME *remisen*, fr. MF *remis*, pp. of *remettre* to put back, fr. L *remittere* to send back] (15c) : to give, grant, or release a claim to : DEED
re·miss \ri-ˈmis\ *adj* [ME, fr. L *remissus*, fr. pp. of *remittere* to send back, relax] (15c) **1** : negligent in the performance of work or duty : CARELESS **2** : showing neglect or inattention : LAX ***syn*** see NEGLIGENT — **re·miss·ly** *adv* — **re·miss·ness** *n*
re·mis·si·ble \ri-ˈmis-ə-bəl\ *adj* (1577) : capable of being forgiven ⟨~ sins⟩ — **re·mis·si·bly** \-blē\ *adv*
re·mis·sion \ri-ˈmish-ən\ *n* (13c) **1** : the act or process of remitting **2** : a state or period during which something is remitted
[1]**re·mit** \ri-ˈmit\ *vb* **re·mit·ted; re·mit·ting** [ME *remitten*, fr. L *remittere* to send back, fr. *re-* + *mittere* to send] *vt* (14c) **1 a** : to lay aside (a mood or disposition) partly or wholly **b** : to desist from (an activity) **c** : to let (as attention or diligence) slacken : RELAX **2 a** : to release from the guilt or penalty of ⟨~ sins⟩ **b** : to refrain from exacting ⟨~ a tax⟩ **c** : to cancel or refrain from inflicting ⟨~ the penalty of loss of pay⟩ **d** : to give relief from (suffering) **3** : to submit or refer for consideration, judgment, decision, or action; *specif* : REMAND **4** : to restore or consign to a former status or condition **5** : POSTPONE, DEFER **6** : to send (money) to a person or place esp. in payment of a demand, account, or draft ~ *vi* **1 a** : to abate in force or intensity : MODERATE **b** *of a disease or abnormality* : to abate symptoms for a period **2** : to send money (as in payment) — **re·mit·ment** \-ˈmit-mənt\ *n* — **re·mit·ta·ble** \-ˈmit-ə-bəl\ *adj* — **re·mit·ter** *n*
[2]**re·mit** \ri-ˈmit, ˈrē-ˌ\ *n* (15c) **1** : an act of remitting **2** : something remitted to another person or authority
re·mit·tal \ri-ˈmit-ᵊl\ *n* (14c) : REMISSION
re·mit·tance \ri-ˈmit-ᵊn(t)s\ *n* (1705) **1 a** : a sum of money remitted **b** : an instrument by which money is remitted **2** : transmittal of money (as to a distant place)
remittance man *n* (1886) : a person living abroad on remittances from home
re·mit·tent \ri-ˈmit-ᵊnt\ *adj* [L *remittent-, remittens*, prp. of *remittere*] *of a disease* (1693) : marked by alternating periods of abatement and increase of symptoms
[1]**rem·nant** \ˈrem-nənt\ *n* [ME, contr. of *remenant*, fr. MF, fr. prp. of *remenoir* to remain, fr. L *remanēre* — more at REMAIN] (14c) **1 a** : a usu. small part, member, or trace remaining **b** : a small surviving group — often used in pl. **2** : an unsold or unused end of piece goods
[2]**remnant** *adj* (1550) : still remaining
re·mod·el \(ˈ)rē-ˈmäd-ᵊl\ *vt* (1789) : to alter the structure of : REMAKE
re·mon·strance \ri-ˈmän(t)-strən(t)s\ *n* (1585) **1** : an earnest presentation of reasons for opposition or grievance; *esp* : a document formally stating such points **2** : an act or instance of remonstrating
re·mon·strant \-strənt\ *adj* (1641) : vigorously objecting or opposing — **remonstrant** *n* — **re·mon·strant·ly** *adv*
re·mon·strate \ri-ˈmän-ˌstrāt *also* ˈrem-ən-\ *vb* **-strat·ed; -strat·ing** [ML *remonstratus*, pp. of *remonstrare* to demonstrate, fr. L *re-* + *monstrare* to show — more at MUSTER] *vi* (1666) : to present and urge reasons in opposition : EXPOSTULATE ~ *vt* : to say or plead in protest, reproof, or opposition — **re·mon·stra·tion** \ri-ˌmän-ˈstrā-shən, ˌrem-ən-\ *n* — **re·mon·stra·tive** \ri-ˈmän(t)-strət-iv\ *adj* — **re·mon·stra·tive·ly** *adv* — **re·mon·stra·tor** \ri-ˈmän-ˌstrāt-ər *also* ˈrem-ən-\ *n*
rem·o·ra \ˈrem-ə-rə *also* ri-ˈmōr-ə *or* -ˈmȯr-\ *n* [L, lit., delay, fr. *remorari* to delay, fr. *re-* + *morari* to delay — more at MORATORIUM] (1567) **1** : any of several specialized fishes (of *Echeneis* and related genera) that have the anterior dorsal fin converted into a suctorial disk on the head by means of which they cling to other fishes and to ships **2** : HINDRANCE, DRAG

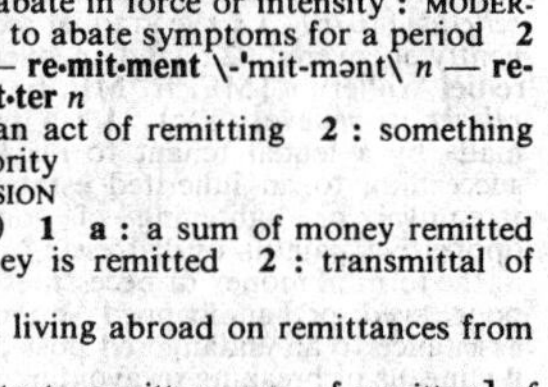
remoras on tiger shark

re·morse \ri-ˈmȯ(ə)rs\ *n* [ME, fr. MF *remors*, fr. ML *remorsus*, fr. LL, act of biting again, fr. L *remorsus*, pp. of *remordēre* to bite again, fr. *re-* + *mordēre* to bite — more at SMART] (15c) **1** : a gnawing distress arising from a sense of guilt for past wrongs : SELF-REPROACH **2** *obs* : COMPASSION ***syn*** see PENITENCE
re·morse·ful \-ˈmȯrs-fəl\ *adj* (1592) : motivated or marked by remorse — **re·morse·ful·ly** \-fə-lē\ *adv* — **re·morse·ful·ness** *n*
re·morse·less \-ˈmȯr-sləs\ *adj* (1593) **1** : having no remorse : MERCILESS **2** : RELENTLESS — **re·morse·less·ly** *adv* — **re·morse·less·ness** *n*
re·mote \ri-ˈmōt\ *adj* **re·mot·er; -est** [L *remotus*, fr. pp. of *removēre* to remove] (15c) **1** : separated by an interval or space greater than usual ⟨an involucre ~ from the flower⟩ **2** : far removed in space, time, or relation : DIVERGENT ⟨the ~ past⟩ ⟨comments ~ from the truth⟩ **3**

: OUT-OF-THE-WAY, SECLUDED ‹a ~ cabin in the hills› **4 :** acting, acted on, or controlled indirectly or from a distance ‹~ computer operation›; *also* : relating to the acquisition of information about a distant object (as by radar or photography) without coming into physical contact with it ‹~ sensing instruments› **5 :** not arising from a primary or proximate action **6 :** small in degree : SLIGHT ‹a ~ possibility› **7 :** distant in manner : ALOOF — **re·mote·ly** *adv* — **re·mote·ness** *n*

re·mo·tion \ri-ˈmō-shən\ *n* (15c) **1 :** the quality or state of being remote **2 :** the act of removing : REMOVAL **3** *obs* : DEPARTURE

[1]**re·mount** \(ˈ)rē-ˈmau̇nt\ *vb* [ME *remounten,* partly fr. *re-* + *mounten* to mount, partly fr. MF *remonter,* fr. *re-* + *monter* to mount] *vt* (15c) **1 :** to mount (something) again ‹~ a picture› **2 :** to furnish remounts to ~ *vi* **1 :** to mount again **2 :** REVERT

[2]**re·mount** \ˈrē-ˌmau̇nt, (ˈ)rē-ˈ\ *n* (1781) **:** a fresh horse to replace one no longer available

re·mov·al \ri-ˈmü-vəl\ *n* (1597) **:** the act or process of removing : the fact of being removed

[1]**re·move** \ri-ˈmüv\ *vb* **re·moved; re·mov·ing** [ME *removen,* fr. OF *removoir,* fr. L *removēre,* fr. *re-* + *movēre* to move] *vt* (14c) **1 a :** to change the location, position, station, or residence of ‹~ soldiers to the front› **b :** to transfer (a legal proceeding) from one court to another **2 :** to move by lifting, pushing aside, or taking away or off ‹~*s* his hat in church› **3 :** to dismiss from office **4 :** to get rid of : ELIMINATE ‹~ a tumor surgically› ~ *vi* **1 :** to change location, station, or residence ‹*removing* from the city to the suburbs› **2 :** to go away **3 :** to be capable of being removed — **re·mov·abil·i·ty** \-ˌmü-və-ˈbil-ət-ē\ *n* — **re·mov·able** *also* **re·move·able** \ri-ˈmü-və-bəl\ *adj* — **re·mov·able·ness** \-ˈmü-və-bəl-nəs\ *n* — **re·mov·ably** \-blē\ *adv* — **re·mov·er** *n*

[2]**remove** *n* (1553) **1 :** REMOVAL; *specif* : MOVE 2c **2 a :** a distance or interval separating one person or thing from another **b :** a degree or stage of separation

re·moved *adj* (1548) **1 a :** distant in degree of relationship **b :** of a younger or older generation ‹a second cousin's child is a second cousin once ~› **2 :** separate or remote in space, time, or character

REM sleep *n* (1970) **:** a state of sleep that recurs cyclically several times during a normal period of sleep and that is characterized by increased neuronal activity of the forebrain and midbrain, by depressed muscle tone, and esp. in man by dreaming, rapid eye movements, and vascular congestion of the sex organs — called also *paradoxical sleep, rapid eye movement sleep*

re·mu·da \ri-ˈm(y)üd-ə\ *n* [AmerSp, relay of horses, fr. Sp, exchange, fr. *remudar* to exchange, fr. *re-* + *mudar* to change, fr. L *mutare* — more at MISS] (ca. 1892) **:** the herd of horses from which those to be used for the day are chosen

re·mu·ner·ate \ri-ˈmyü-nə-ˌrāt\ *vt* **-at·ed; -at·ing** [L *remuneratus,* pp. of *remunerare* to recompense, fr. *re-* + *munerare* to give, fr. *muner-, munus* gift — more at MEAN] (1523) **1 :** to pay an equivalent for ‹their services were generously *remunerated*› **2 :** to pay an equivalent to for a service, loss, or expense : RECOMPENSE *syn* see PAY — **re·mu·ner·a·tor** \-ˌrāt-ər\ *n* — **re·mu·ner·a·to·ry** \-rə-ˌtōr-ē, -ˌtȯr-\ *adj*

re·mu·ner·a·tion \ri-ˌmyü-nə-ˈrā-shən\ *n* (15c) **1 :** something that remunerates : RECOMPENSE, PAY **2 :** an act or fact of remunerating

re·mu·ner·a·tive \ri-ˈmyü-nə-rət-iv, -ˌrāt-\ *adj* (1627) **1 :** serving to remunerate **2 :** providing remuneration : PROFITABLE — **re·mu·ner·a·tive·ly** *adv* — **re·mu·ner·a·tive·ness** *n*

Re·mus \ˈrē-məs\ *n* [L] **:** a son of Mars slain by his twin brother Romulus

re·nais·sance \ˌren-ə-ˈsän(t)s, -ˈzän(t)s, -ˈsä^{n}s, -ˈzä^{n}s, *chiefly Brit* ri-ˈnās-ᵊn(t)s\ *n, often attrib* [F, fr. MF, rebirth, fr. *renaistre* to be born again, fr. L *renasci,* fr. *re-* + *nasci* to be born — more at NATION] (1845) **1** *cap* **a :** the transitional movement in Europe between medieval and modern times beginning in the 14th century in Italy, lasting into the 17th century, and marked by a humanistic revival of classical influence expressed in a flowering of the arts and literature and by the beginnings of modern science **b :** the period of the Renaissance **c :** the neoclassic style of architecture prevailing during the Renaissance **2** *often cap* **:** a movement or period of vigorous artistic and intellectual activity **3 :** REBIRTH, REVIVAL

Renaissance man *n* (1906) **:** a person who has wide interests and is expert in several areas

re·nal \ˈrēn-ᵊl\ *adj* [F or LL; F *rénal,* fr. LL *renalis,* fr. L *renes* kidneys] (ca. 1656) **:** relating to, involving, or located in the region of the kidneys : NEPHRITIC

renal clearance *n* (1948) **:** CLEARANCE 3

re·na·scence \ri-ˈnas-ᵊn(t)s, -ˈnās-\ *n, often cap* (1864) **:** RENAISSANCE

re·na·scent \-ᵊnt\ *adj* [L *renascent-, renascens,* prp. of *renasci*] (ca. 1727) **:** rising again into being or vigor

re·na·ture \(ˈ)rē-ˈnā-chər\ *vt* **re·na·tured; re·na·tur·ing** \-ˈnāch-(ə-)riŋ\ [*re-* + *-nature* (as in *denature*)] (1926) **:** to restore (as a denatured protein) to an original or normal condition — **re·na·tur·ation** \(ˌ)rē-ˌnā-chə-ˈrā-shən\ *n*

ren·con·tre \rä^{n}-kō^{n}trᵊ, ren-ˈkänt-ər\ *or* **ren·coun·ter** \ren-ˈkau̇nt-ər\ *n* [*rencounter* fr. MF *rencontre,* fr. *rencontrer; rencontre* fr. F] (1523) **1 :** a hostile meeting or a contest between forces or individuals : COMBAT **2 :** a casual meeting

ren·coun·ter \ren-ˈkau̇nt-ər\ *vt* [MF *rencontrer* to meet by chance or in hostility, fr. *re-* + *encontrer* to encounter] *archaic* (1549) **:** to meet casually

rend \ˈrend\ *vb* **rent** \ˈrent\; **rend·ing** [ME *renden,* fr. OE *rendan;* akin to OFris *renda* to tear, Skt *randhra* hole] *vt* (bef. 12c) **1 :** to remove from place by violence : WREST **2 :** to split or tear apart or in pieces by violence **3 :** to tear (the hair or clothing) as a sign of anger, grief, or despair **4 a :** to lacerate mentally or emotionally **b :** to pierce with sound **c :** to divide (as a nation) into contesting factions ~ *vi* **1 :** to perform an act of tearing or splitting **2 :** to become torn or split *syn* see TEAR

[1]**ren·der** \ˈren-dər\ *vb* **ren·dered; ren·der·ing** \-d(ə-)riŋ\ [ME *rendren,* fr. MF *rendre* to give back, yield, fr. (assumed) VL *rendere,* alter. of L *reddere,* partly fr. *re-* + *dare* to give & partly fr. *re-* + *-dere* to put — more at DATE, DO] *vt* (14c) **1 a :** to melt down : extract by melting ‹~ lard› **b :** to treat so as to convert into industrial fats and oils or fertilizer **2 a :** to transmit to another : DELIVER **b :** GIVE UP, YIELD **c :** to furnish for consideration, approval, or information: as **(1) :** to hand down (a legal judgment) **(2) :** to agree on and report (a verdict) **3 a :** to give in return or retribution **b (1) :** GIVE BACK, RESTORE **(2) :** REFLECT, ECHO **c :** to give in acknowledgment of dependence or obligation : PAY **d :** to do (a service) for another **4 a (1) :** to cause to be or become : MAKE ‹enough rainfall . . . to ~ irrigation unnecessary —P. E. James› ‹~ a person helpless› **(2) :** IMPART **b (1) :** to reproduce or represent by artistic or verbal means : DEPICT **(2) :** to give a performance of **(3) :** to produce a copy or version of ‹the documents are ~*ed* in the original French› **(4) :** to execute the motions of ‹~ a salute› **c :** TRANSLATE **5 :** to direct the execution of : ADMINISTER ‹~ justice› **6 :** to apply a coat of plaster or cement directly to ~ *vi* **:** to give recompense — **ren·der·able** \-d(ə-)rə-bəl\ *adj* — **ren·der·er** \-dər-ər\ *n*

[2]**render** *n* (1647) **:** a return esp. in goods or services due from a feudal tenant to his lord

[1]**ren·dez·vous** \ˈrän-di-ˌvü, -dā-\ *n, pl* **ren·dez·vous** \-ˌvüz\ [MF, fr. *rendez vous* present yourselves] (1591) **1 a :** a place appointed for assembling or meeting **b :** a place of popular resort : HAUNT **2 :** a meeting at an appointed place and time **3 :** the process of bringing two spacecraft together

[2]**rendezvous** *vb* **-voused** \-ˌvüd\; **-vous·ing** \-ˌvü-iŋ\; **-vouses** \-ˌvüz\ *vi* (1645) **:** to come together at a rendezvous ~ *vt* **1 :** to bring together at a rendezvous **2 :** to meet at a rendezvous

ren·di·tion \ren-ˈdish-ən\ *n* [obs. F, fr. MF, alter. of *reddition,* fr. LL *reddition-, redditio,* fr. L *redditus,* pp. of *reddere* to return] (1601) **:** the act or result of rendering: as **a :** SURRENDER **b :** TRANSLATION **c :** PERFORMANCE, INTERPRETATION

ren·dzi·na \ren-ˈjē-nə\ *n* [Pol *rędzina* rich limy soil] (1922) **:** any of a group of dark grayish brown intrazonal soils developed in grassy regions of high to moderate humidity from soft calcareous marl or chalk

[1]**ren·e·gade** \ˈren-i-ˌgād\ *n* [Sp *renegado,* fr. ML *renegatus,* fr. pp. of *renegare* to deny, fr. L *re-* + *negare* to deny — more at NEGATE] (1583) **1 :** a deserter from one faith, cause, or allegiance to another **2 :** an individual who rejects lawful or conventional behavior

[2]**renegade** *vi* **-gad·ed; -gad·ing** (ca. 1611) **:** to become a renegade

[3]**renegade** *adj* (1705) **1 :** having deserted a faith, cause, or religion for a hostile one **2 :** having rejected tradition : UNCONVENTIONAL

re·nege \ri-ˈnig, -ˈneg, -ˈnēg, -ˈnāg\ *vb* **re·neged; re·neg·ing** [ML *renegare*] *vt* (1548) **:** DENY, RENOUNCE ~ *vi* **1** *obs* **:** to make a denial **2 :** REVOKE **3 :** to go back on a promise or commitment — **re·neg·er** *n*

re·ne·go·tia·ble \ˌrē-ni-ˈgō-sh(ē-)ə-bəl\ *adj* (1943) **:** subject to renegotiation ‹~ mortgages›

re·ne·go·ti·ate \ˌrē-ni-ˈgō-shē-ˌāt\ *vt* (ca. 1934) **:** to negotiate again; *esp* **:** to readjust by negotiation to eliminate or recover excessive profits — **re·ne·go·ti·a·tion** \ˌrē-ni-ˌgō-s(h)ē-ˈā-shən\ *n*

re·new \ri-ˈn(y)ü\ *vt* (14c) **1 :** to make like new : restore to freshness, vigor, or perfection ‹as we ~ our strength in sleep› **2 :** to make new spiritually : REGENERATE **3 a :** to restore to existence : REVIVE **b :** to make extensive changes in : REBUILD **4 :** to do again : REPEAT **5 :** to begin again : RESUME **6 :** REPLACE, REPLENISH ‹~ water in a tank› **7 a :** to grant or obtain an extension of or on **b :** to grant or obtain an extension on the loan of ‹~ a library book› ~ *vi* **1 :** to become new or as new **2 :** to begin again : RESUME **3 :** to make a renewal (as of a lease) — **re·new·er** *n*

syn RENEW, RESTORE, REFRESH, RENOVATE, REJUVENATE mean to make like new. RENEW implies so extensive a remaking that what had become faded or disintegrated now seems like new ‹efforts to *renew* a failing marriage› RESTORE implies a return to an original state after depletion or loss ‹*restored* a fine piece of furniture› REFRESH implies the supplying of something necessary to restore lost strength, animation, or power ‹lunch *refreshed* my energy› RENOVATE suggests a renewing by cleansing, repairing, or rebuilding ‹the apartment has been entirely *renovated*› REJUVENATE suggests the restoration of youthful vigor, powers, and appearance ‹the change in jobs *rejuvenated* her spirits›

re·new·able \-ˈn(y)ü-ə-bəl\ *adj* (1727) **1 :** capable of being renewed ‹~ contracts› **2 :** capable of being replaced by natural ecological cycles or sound management practices — **re·new·abil·i·ty** \-ˌn(y)ü-ə-ˈbil-ət-ē\ *n* — **re·new·ably** \-ˈn(y)ü-ə-blē\ *adv*

re·new·al \ri-ˈn(y)ü-əl\ *n* (1681) **1 :** the act or process of renewing : REPETITION **2 :** the quality or state of being renewed **3 :** something (as a subscription to a magazine) renewed **4 :** something used for renewing; *specif* : an expenditure that betters existing fixed assets **5 :** the rebuilding of a large area (as of a city) by a public authority

reni- *or* **reno-** *comb form* [L *renes* kidneys] **:** kidney ‹*reni*form›

re·ni·form \ˈrē-nə-ˌfȯrm, ˈren-ə-\ *adj* [NL *reniformis,* fr. *reni-* + *-formis* -form] (ca. 1753) **:** suggesting a kidney in outline

re·nin \ˈrē-nən, ˈren-ən\ *n* [ISV, fr. L *renes*] (1906) **:** a proteolytic enzyme of the kidney that plays a major role in the release of angiotensin

re·ni·ten·cy \ˈren-ə-tən-sē, ri-ˈnīt-ᵊn-\ *n* (1613) **:** RESISTANCE, OPPOSITION

re·ni·tent \ˈren-ə-tənt, ri-ˈnīt-ᵊnt\ *adj* [F or L; F *rénitent,* fr. L *renitent-, renitens,* prp. of *reniti* to struggle against, fr. *re-* + *niti* to strive — more at NISUS] (1701) **1 :** resisting physical pressure **2 :** resisting constraint or compulsion : RECALCITRANT

ren·min·bi \ˈren-ˈmin-ˈbē\ *n pl* [Chin (Pek) *ren²min²* (fr. *ren²* human + *min²* people) people's + *bi⁴* currency] (ca. 1957) **:** the currency of the People's Republic of China consisting of yuan

ren·net \ˈren-ət\ *n* [ME, fr. (assumed) ME *rennen* to cause to coagulate, fr. OE *gerennan,* fr. *ge-* together + (assumed) OE *rennan* to cause to run; akin to OHG *rennen* to cause to run, OE *rinnan* to run — more at CO-, RUN] (15c) **1 a :** the contents of the stomach of an unweaned animal and esp. a calf **b :** the lining membrane of a stomach or one of its compartments (as the fourth of a ruminant) used for curdling milk; *also* : a preparation of the stomach of animals used for this purpose **2 a :** RENNIN **b :** a substitute for rennin

ren·nin \ˈren-ən\ *n* (1897) **:** an enzyme that coagulates milk and is used in making cheese and junkets; *esp* : one from the mucous membrane of the stomach of a calf

\ə\ **abut** \ᵊ\ **kitten,** F **table** \ər\ **further** \a\ **ash** \ā\ **ace** \ä\ **cot, cart** \au̇\ **out** \ch\ **chin** \e\ **bet** \ē\ **easy** \g\ **go** \i\ **hit** \ī\ **ice** \j\ **job** \ŋ\ **sing** \ō\ **go** \ȯ\ **law** \ȯi\ **boy** \th\ **thin** \th̲\ **the** \ü\ **loot** \u̇\ **foot** \y\ **yet** \zh\ **vision** \à, k̲, ^{n}, œ, œ̄, ue, ue̅, ʸ\ *see* Guide to Pronunciation

re·no·gram \ˈrē-nə-ˌgram\ *n* (1952) **:** a photographic depiction of the course of renal excretion of a radioactively labeled substance — **re·no·graph·ic** \ˌrē-nə-ˈgraf-ik\ *adj* — **re·nog·ra·phy** \rē-ˈnäg-rə-fē\ *n*

re·nom·i·nate \(ˌ)rē-ˈnäm-ə-ˌnāt\ *vt* (1864) **:** to nominate again esp. for a succeeding term — **re·nom·i·na·tion** \(ˌ)rē-ˌnäm-ə-ˈnā-shən\ *n*

[1]**re·nounce** \ri-ˈnau̇n(t)s\ *vb* **re·nounced; re·nounc·ing** [ME *renouncen,* fr. MF *renoncer,* fr. L *renuntiare,* fr. *re-* + *nuntiare* to report, fr. *nuntius* messenger] *vt* (14c) **1 :** to give up, refuse, or resign usu. by formal declaration ⟨~ his errors⟩ **2 :** to refuse to follow, obey, or recognize any further **:** REPUDIATE ⟨~ the authority of the church⟩ **3 :** to fail to follow with a card from (the suit led) ~ *vi* **:** to make a renounce or renunciation ***syn*** see ABDICATE, ABJURE — **re·nounce·ment** \-ˈnau̇n(t)-smənt\ *n* — **re·nounc·er** *n*

[2]**re·nounce** \ri-ˈnau̇n(t)s, ˈrē-ˌ\ *n* (1747) **:** failure to follow suit in a card game

re·no·vas·cu·lar \ˌrē-nō-ˈvas-kyə-lər\ *adj* (1961) **:** of, relating to, or involving the blood vessels of the kidneys ⟨~ hypertension⟩

ren·o·vate \ˈren-ə-ˌvāt\ *vt* **-vat·ed; -vat·ing** [L *renovatus,* pp. of *renovare,* fr. *re-* + *novare* to make new, fr. *novus* new — more at NEW] (1552) **1 :** to restore to a former better state (as by cleaning, repairing, or rebuilding) **2 :** to restore to life, vigor, or activity **:** REVIVE ⟨the church was *renovated* by a new ecumenical spirit⟩ ***syn*** see RENEW — **ren·o·va·tion** \ˌren-ə-ˈvā-shən\ *n* — **ren·o·va·tive** \ˈren-ə-ˌvāt-iv\ *adj* — **ren·o·va·tor** \-ˌvāt-ər\ *n*

[1]**re·nown** \ri-ˈnau̇n\ *n* [ME, fr. MF *renon,* fr. OF, fr. *renomer* to celebrate, fr. *re-* + *nomer* to name, fr. L *nominare,* fr. *nomin-, nomen* name — more at NAME] (14c) **1 :** a state of being widely acclaimed and highly honored **:** FAME **2** *obs* **:** REPORT, RUMOR

[2]**renown** *vt* (1530) **:** to give renown to

re·nowned *adj* (14c) **:** having renown **:** CELEBRATED ***syn*** see FAMOUS

[1]**rent** \ˈrent\ *n* [ME *rente,* fr. OF, income from a property, fr. (assumed) VL *rendita,* fr. fem. of *renditus,* pp. of *rendere* to yield — more at RENDER] (13c) **1 a :** a usu. fixed periodical return made by a tenant or occupant of property to the owner for the possession and use thereof; *esp* **:** an agreed sum paid at fixed intervals by a tenant to his landlord for the use of land or its appendages **b :** the amount paid by a hirer of personal property to the owner for the use thereof **2 :** property (as a house) rented or for rent **3 a :** the portion of the income of an economy (as of a nation) attributable to land as a factor of production in addition to capital and labor **b :** ECONOMIC RENT — **for rent :** available for use or service in return for payment

[2]**rent** *vt* (1530) **1 :** to take and hold under an agreement to pay rent **2 :** to grant the possession and enjoyment of for rent ~ *vi* **1 :** to be for rent **2 a :** to obtain the possession and use of a place or article for rent **b :** to allow the possession and use of property for rent ***syn*** see HIRE — **rent·abil·i·ty** \ˌrent-ə-ˈbil-ət-ē\ *n* — **rent·able** \ˈrent-ə-bəl\ *adj*

[3]**rent** *past and past part of* REND

[4]**rent** *n* [E dial. *rent* (to rend)] (1535) **1 :** an opening made by or as if by rending **2 :** a split in a party or organized group **:** SCHISM **3 :** an act or instance of rending

rent–a–car \ˈrent-ə-ˌkär\ *n* [fr. the imper. phrase *rent a car*] (1935) **:** a rented car

[1]**rent·al** \ˈrent-ᵊl\ *n* (14c) **1 :** an amount paid or collected as rent **2 :** something that is rented **3 :** an act of renting **4 :** a business that rents something

[2]**rental** *adj* (15c) **1 a :** of or relating to rent **b :** available for rent **2 :** dealing in rental property ⟨a ~ agency⟩

rental library *n* (1928) **:** a commercially operated library (as in a store) that lends books at a fixed charge per book per day — called also *lending library*

rent control *n* (1931) **:** government regulation of the amount charged as rent for housing and often also of eviction — **rent–controlled** *adj*

rente \ˈräⁿ(n)t\ *n* [F] (1689) **1 a :** interest payable by the French and other European governments on the consolidated debt **b :** a government security yielding rente **2 :** annual income under French law resembling an annuity

rent·er \ˈrent-ər\ *n* (1655) **:** one that rents; *specif* **:** the lessee or tenant of property

ren·tier \räⁿ-tyā\ *n* [F, fr. OF, fr. *rente*] (ca. 1847) **1 :** one who owns rentes **2 :** a person who receives a fixed income (as from land or stocks)

rent strike *n* (1964) **:** a refusal by a group of tenants to pay rent (as in protest against high rates)

re·num·ber \(ˌ)rē-ˈnəm-bər\ *vt* (15c) **:** to number again or differently

re·nun·ci·a·tion \ri-ˌnən(t)-sē-ˈā-shən\ *n* [ME, fr. L *renuntiation-, renuntiatio,* fr. *renuntiatus,* pp. of *renuntiare* to renounce] (14c) **:** the act or practice of renouncing **:** REPUDIATION; *specif* **:** ascetic self-denial — **re·nun·ci·a·tive** \ri-ˈnən(t)-sē-ˌāt-iv\ *adj* — **re·nun·ci·a·to·ry** \-sē-ə-ˌtōr-ē, -ˌtȯr-\ *adj*

re·of·fer \(ˌ)rē-ˈȯf-ər, -ˈäf-\ *vt* (1920) **:** to offer (a security issue) for public sale

re·open \(ˌ)rē-ˈō-pən, -ˈōp-ᵊm\ *vt* (1733) **1 :** to open again **2 a :** to take up again **:** RESUME ⟨~ discussion⟩ **b :** to resume discussion or consideration of ⟨~ a contract⟩ **3 :** to begin again ~ *vi* **:** to open again ⟨school ~*s* in September⟩

[1]**re·or·der** \(ˌ)rē-ˈȯrd-ər\ *vt* (1656) **1 :** to arrange in a different way **2 :** to give a reorder for ~ *vi* **:** to place a reorder

[2]**reorder** *n* (1901) **:** an order like a previous order placed with the same supplier

re·or·ga·ni·za·tion \(ˌ)rē-ˌȯrg-(ə-)nə-ˈzā-shən\ *n* (1813) **:** the act or process of reorganizing **:** the state of being reorganized; *esp* **:** the financial reconstruction of a business concern — **re·or·ga·ni·za·tion·al** \-shnəl, -shən-ᵊl\ *adj*

re·or·ga·nize \(ˌ)rē-ˈȯr-gə-ˌnīz\ *vt* (1681) **:** to organize again or anew ~ *vi* **:** to reorganize something — **re·or·ga·niz·er** *n*

reo·vi·rus \ˌrē-ō-ˈvī-rəs\ *n* [*r*espiratory *e*nteric *o*rphan (i.e. unidentified) *virus*] (1959) **:** any of a group of rather large, widely distributed, and possibly tumorigenic viruses with double-stranded RNA

[1]**rep** \ˈrep\ *n, slang* (1705) **:** REPUTATION; *esp* **:** status in a group (as a gang)

[2]**rep** *n* (1848) **:** REPRESENTATIVE ⟨sales ~*s*⟩

[3]**rep** *or* **repp** \ˈrep\ *n* [F *reps,* modif. of E *ribs,* pl. of *rib*] (1860) **:** a plain-weave fabric with prominent rounded crosswise ribs

[4]**rep** *n* (1925) **:** REPERTORY 2b

[5]**rep** *n* [*r*oentgen *e*quivalent *p*hysical] (1947) **:** the dosage of an ionizing radiation that will develop the same amount of energy upon absorption in human tissue as one roentgen of X-ray or gamma-ray dosage

re·pack·age \(ˌ)rē-ˈpak-ij\ *vt* (1946) **:** to package again or anew; *specif* **:** to put into a more efficient or attractive form ⟨~ a candidate's public image⟩ — **re·pack·ag·er** *n*

[1]**re·pair** \ri-ˈpa(ə)r, -ˈpe(ə)r\ *vi* [ME *repairen,* fr. MF *repairier* to go back to one's country, fr. LL *repatriare,* fr. L *re-* + *patria* native country — more at EXPATRIATE] (14c) **1 a :** to betake oneself **:** GO ⟨~*ed* to his home⟩ **b :** RALLY **2** *obs* **:** RETURN

[2]**repair** *n* (14c) **1 :** the act of repairing **:** RESORT **2 :** a popular gathering place

[3]**repair** *vb* [ME *repairen,* fr. MF *reparer,* fr. L *reparare,* fr. *re-* + *parare* to prepare — more at PARE] *vt* (14c) **1 a :** to restore by replacing a part or putting together what is torn or broken **:** FIX ⟨~ a shoe⟩ **b :** to restore to a sound or healthy state **:** RENEW ⟨~ his strength⟩ **2 :** to make good **:** compensate for **:** REMEDY ⟨will ~ his earlier failure⟩ ~ *vi* **:** to make repairs ***syn*** see MEND — **re·pair·abil·i·ty** \-ˌpar-ə-ˈbil-ət-ē, -ˌper-\ *n* — **re·pair·able** \-ˈpar-ə-bəl, -ˈper-\ *adj* — **re·pair·er** \-ˈpar-ər, -ˈper-\ *n*

[4]**repair** *n* (1595) **1 a :** the act or process of repairing **b :** an instance or result of repairing **c :** the replacement of destroyed cells or tissues by new formations **2 a :** relative condition with respect to soundness or need of repairing **b :** the state of being in good or sound condition

re·pair·man \ri-ˈpa(ə)r-ˌman, -ˈpe(ə)r-, -mən\ *n* (1871) **:** one who repairs; *specif* **:** one whose occupation is to make repairs in a mechanism

re·pand \ri-ˈpand\ *adj* [L *repandus* bent backward, fr. *re-* + *pandus* bent; akin to ON *fattr* bent backward] (ca. 1760) **:** having a slightly undulating margin ⟨a ~ leaf⟩ ⟨a ~ colony of bacteria⟩

rep·a·ra·ble \ˈrep-(ə-)rə-bəl\ *adj* (1570) **:** capable of being repaired

rep·a·ra·tion \ˌrep-ə-ˈrā-shən\ *n* [ME, fr. MF, fr. LL *reparation-, reparatio,* fr. L *reparatus,* pp. of *reparare*] (15c) **1 a :** a repairing or keeping in repair **b** *pl* **:** REPAIRS **2 a :** the act of making amends, offering expiation, or giving satisfaction for a wrong or injury **b :** something done or given as amends or satisfaction **3 :** the payment of damages **:** INDEMNIFICATION; *specif* **:** compensation in money or materials payable by a defeated nation for damages to or expenditures sustained by another nation as a result of hostilities with the defeated nation — usu. used in pl.

re·par·a·tive \ri-ˈpar-ət-iv\ *adj* (1656) **1 :** of, relating to, or effecting repair **2 :** serving to make amends

rep·ar·tee \ˌrep-ər-ˈtē, -ˌär-, -ˈtā\ *n* [F *repartie,* fr. *repartir* to retort, fr. MF, fr. *re-* + *partir* to divide — more at PART] (1645) **1 a :** a quick and witty reply **b :** a succession or interchange of clever retorts **:** amusing and usu. light sparring with words **2 :** adroitness and cleverness in reply **:** skill in repartee ***syn*** see WIT

[1]**re·par·ti·tion** \ˌrep-ˌär-ˈtish-ən, ˌrē-ˌpär-\ *n* [prob. fr. Sp *repartición,* fr. *repartir* to distribute, fr. *re-* + *partir* to divide, fr. L *partire* — more at PART] (1555) **:** DISTRIBUTION

[2]**re·par·ti·tion** \ˌrē-ˌpär-ˈtish-ən\ *n* [*re-* + *partition*] (1835) **:** a second or additional dividing or distribution

re·pass \(ˌ)rē-ˈpas\ *vb* [ME *repassen,* fr. MF *repasser,* fr. OF, fr. *re-* + *passer* to pass] *vi* (15c) **:** to pass again esp. in the opposite direction **:** RETURN ~ *vt* **1 :** to pass through, over, or by again ⟨~ the house⟩ **2 :** to cause to pass again **3 :** to adopt again ⟨~*ed* the resolution⟩ — **re·pas·sage** \-ˈpas-ij\ *n*

[1]**re·past** \ri-ˈpast, ˈrē-ˌ\ *n* [ME, fr. MF, fr. OF, fr. *repaistre* to feed, fr. *re-* + *paistre* to feed, fr. L *pascere* — more at FOOD] (14c) **1 :** something taken as food **:** MEAL **2 :** the act or time of taking food

[2]**re·past** \ri-ˈpast\ *vt, obs* (15c) **:** FEED ~ *vi* **:** to take food **:** FEAST

re·pa·tri·ate \(ˌ)rē-ˈpā-trē-ˌāt, -ˈpa-\ *vt* **-at·ed; -at·ing** [LL *repatriatus,* pp. of *repatriare* to go back to one's country — more at REPAIR] (ca. 1611) **:** to restore or return to the country of origin, allegiance, or citizenship ⟨~ prisoners of war⟩ — **re·pa·tri·ate** \-trē-ət, -trē-ˌāt\ *n* — **re·pa·tri·a·tion** \(ˌ)rē-ˌpā-trē-ˈā-shən, -ˌpa-\ *n*

re·pay \(ˌ)rē-ˈpā\ *vb* **-paid** \-ˈpād\; **-pay·ing** *vt* (1530) **1 a :** to pay back **:** REFUND ⟨~ a loan⟩ **b :** to give or inflict in return or requital ⟨~ evil for evil⟩ **2 :** to make a return payment to **:** COMPENSATE, REQUITE **3 :** to make requital for **:** RECOMPENSE ⟨a company which ~*s* hard work⟩ ~ *vi* **:** to make return payment or requital ***syn*** see PAY — **re·pay·able** \-ˈpā-ə-bəl\ *adj* — **re·pay·ment** \-ˈpā-mənt\ *n*

re·peal \ri-ˈpē(ə)l\ *vt* [ME *repelen,* fr. MF *repeler,* fr. OF, fr. *re-* + *apeler* to appeal, call] (14c) **1 :** to rescind or annul by authoritative act; *esp* **:** to revoke or abrogate by legislative enactment **2 :** ABANDON, RENOUNCE **3** *obs* **:** to summon to return **:** RECALL — **repeal** *n* — **re·peal·able** \-ˈpē-lə-bəl\ *adj*

re·peal·er \ri-ˈpē-lər\ *n* (1765) **:** one that repeals; *specif* **:** a legislative act that abrogates an earlier act

[1]**re·peat** \ri-ˈpēt\ *vb* [ME *repeten,* fr. MF *repeter,* fr. L *repetere,* fr. *re-* + *petere* to go to, seek — more at FEATHER] *vt* (14c) **1 a :** to say or state again **b :** to say over from memory **:** RECITE **c :** to say after another **2 a :** to make, do, or perform again ⟨~ an experiment⟩ **b :** to make appear again **:** REPRODUCE ⟨a program ~*ed* on tape⟩ **c :** to go through or experience again ⟨had to ~ third grade⟩ **3 :** to express or present (oneself) again in the same words, terms, or form ~ *vi* **:** to say, do, or accomplish something again; *esp* **:** to vote illegally by casting more than one ballot in an election — **re·peat·abil·i·ty** \-ˌpēt-ə-ˈbil-ət-ē\ *n* — **re·peat·able** \-ˈpēt-ə-bəl\ *adj*

[2]**re·peat** \ri-ˈpēt, ˈrē-ˌ\ *n* (1556) **1 :** the act of repeating **2 a :** something repeated **:** REPETITION **b :** a musical passage to be repeated in performance; *also* **:** a sign placed before and after such a passage **c :** a usu. transcribed repetition of a radio or television program **d :** one of several adjacent genetic duplications

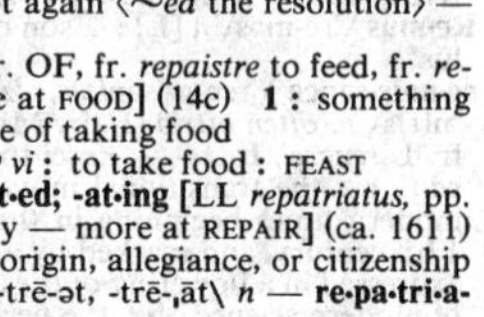

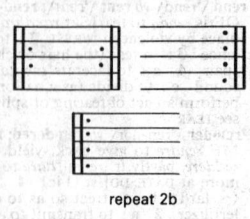

repeat 2b

re·peat·ed \ri-ˈpēt-əd\ *adj* (1611) **1 :** renewed or recurring again and again ⟨~ changes of plan⟩ **2 :** said, done, or presented again

re·peat·ed·ly *adv* (1718) **:** AGAIN AND AGAIN

re·peat·er \ri-ˈpēt-ər\ *n* (1598) **:** one that repeats: as **a :** one who relates or recites **b :** a watch or clock with a striking mechanism that upon pressure of a spring will indicate the time in hours or quarters and sometimes minutes **c :** a firearm having a magazine that holds a number of cartridges loaded into the chamber by the action of the piece **d :** an habitual violator of the laws **e :** one who votes illegally by casting more than one ballot in an election **f :** a student enrolled in a class or course for a second or subsequent time **g :** a device for receiving electronic communication signals and delivering corresponding amplified ones
re·peat·ing *adj, of a firearm* (1824) **:** designed to load cartridges from a magazine
repeating decimal *n* (1773) **:** a decimal in which after a certain point a particular digit or sequence of digits repeats itself indefinitely — compare TERMINATING DECIMAL
re·pe·chage \ˌrep-ə-ˈshäzh, rə-ˌpesh-ˈäzh\ *n* [F *repêchage* second chance, reexamination for a candidate who has failed, fr. *repêcher* to fish out, rescue, fr. *re-* + *pêcher* to fish, fr. L *piscari* — more at PISCATORY] (ca. 1928) **:** a trial heat (as in rowing) in which first-round losers are given another chance to qualify for the semifinals
re·pel \ri-ˈpel\ *vb* **re·pelled; re·pel·ling** [ME *repellen,* fr. L *repellere,* fr. *re-* + *pellere* to drive — more at FELT] *vt* (15c) **1 a :** to drive back **:** REPULSE **b :** to fight against **:** RESIST **2 :** TURN AWAY, REJECT ⟨*repelled* the insinuation⟩ **3 a :** to drive away **:** DISCOURAGE ⟨foul words and frowns must not ~ a lover —Shak.⟩ **b :** to be incapable of adhering to, mixing with, taking up, or holding **c :** to force away or apart or tend to do so by mutual action at a distance **4 :** to cause aversion in **:** DISGUST ~ *vi* **:** to cause aversion — **re·pel·ler** *n*
re·pel·len·cy \ri-ˈpel-ən-sē\ *n* (1747) **:** the quality or capacity of repelling
1re·pel·lent *also* **re·pel·lant** \ri-ˈpel-ənt\ *adj* [L *repellent-, repellens,* prp. of *repellere*] (1643) **1 :** serving or tending to drive away or ward off — often used in combination ⟨a mosquito-*repellent* spray⟩ **2 :** arousing aversion or disgust **:** REPULSIVE ***syn*** see REPUGNANT — **re·pel·lent·ly** *adv*
2repellent *also* **repellant** *n* (1661) **:** something that repels; *esp* **:** a substance used to prevent insect attacks
1re·pent \ri-ˈpent\ *vb* [ME *repenten,* fr. OF *repentir,* fr. *re-* + *pentir* to be sorry, fr. L *paenitēre* — more at PENITENT] *vi* (13c) **1 :** to turn from sin and dedicate oneself to the amendment of one's life **2 a :** to feel regret or contrition **b :** to change one's mind ~ *vt* **1 :** to cause to feel regret or contrition **2 :** to feel sorrow, regret, or contrition for — **re·pent·er** *n*
2re·pent \ˈrē-pənt\ *adj* [L *repent-, repens,* prp. of *repere* to creep — more at REPTILE] (1669) **:** CREEPING, PROSTRATE ⟨~ stems⟩
re·pen·tance \ri-ˈpent-ᵊn(t)s\ *n* (14c) **:** the action or process of repenting esp. for misdeeds or moral shortcomings ***syn*** see PENITENCE
re·pen·tant \-ᵊnt\ *adj* (13c) **1 :** experiencing repentance **:** PENITENT **2 :** expressive of repentance — **re·pen·tant·ly** *adv*
re·per·cus·sion \ˌrē-pər-ˈkəsh-ən, ˌrep-ər-\ *n* [L *repercussion-, repercussio,* fr. *repercussus,* pp. of *repercutere* to drive back, fr. *re-* + *percutere* to beat — more at PERCUSSION] (1536) **1 :** REFLECTION, REVERBERATION **2 a :** an action or effect given or exerted in return **:** a reciprocal action or effect **b :** a widespread, indirect, or unforeseen effect of an act, action, or event — usu. used in pl. — **re·per·cus·sive** \-ˈkəs-iv\ *adj*
rep·er·toire \ˈrep-ə(r)-ˌtwär\ *n* [F *répertoire,* fr. LL *repertorium*] (1847) **1 a :** a list or supply of dramas, operas, pieces, or parts that a company or person is prepared to perform **b :** a supply of skills, devices, or expedients ⟨part of the ~ of a quarterback⟩; *broadly* **:** AMOUNT, SUPPLY ⟨an endless ~ of summer clothes⟩ **c :** a list or supply of capabilities ⟨the instruction ~ of a computer⟩ **2 a :** the complete list or supply of dramas, operas, or musical works available for performance ⟨our modern orchestral ~⟩ **b :** the complete list or supply of skills, devices, or ingredients used in a particular field, occupation, or practice ⟨the ~ of literary criticism⟩
rep·er·to·ry \ˈrep-ə(r)-ˌtōr-ē, -ˌtȯr-\ *n, pl* **-ries** [LL *repertorium* list, fr. L *repertus,* pp. of *reperire* to find, fr. *re-* + *parere* to produce — more at PARE] (1593) **1 :** a place where something may be found **:** REPOSITORY **2 a :** REPERTOIRE **b :** a company that presents several different plays, operas, or pieces usu. alternately in the course of a season at one theater **c :** a theater housing such a company **3 :** the production and presentation of plays by a repertory company ⟨acting in ~⟩
rep·e·tend \ˈrep-ə-ˌtend\ *n* [L *repetendus* to be repeated, gerundive of *repetere* to repeat] (1874) **:** a repeated sound, word, or phrase; *specif* **:** REFRAIN
rep·e·ti·tion \ˌrep-ə-ˈtish-ən\ *n* [L *repetition-, repetitio,* fr. *repetitus,* pp. of *repetere* to repeat] (1526) **1 :** the act or an instance of repeating or being repeated **2 :** MENTION, RECITAL — **rep·e·ti·tion·al** \-ˈtish-nəl, -ən-ᵊl\ *adj*
rep·e·ti·tious \-ˈtish-əs\ *adj* (1675) **:** characterized or marked by repetition; *esp* **:** tediously repeating — **rep·e·ti·tious·ly** *adv* — **rep·e·ti·tious·ness** *n*
re·pet·i·tive \ri-ˈpet-ət-iv\ *adj* (1839) **1 :** containing repetition **:** REPEATING **2 :** REPETITIOUS — **re·pet·i·tive·ly** *adv* — **re·pet·i·tive·ness** *n*
re·pine \ri-ˈpīn\ *vi* (1530) **1 :** to feel or express dejection or discontent **2 :** to long for something — **re·pin·er** *n*
re·place \ri-ˈplās\ *vt* (1595) **1 :** to restore to a former place or position ⟨~ cards in a file⟩ **2 :** to take the place of esp. as a substitute or successor **3 :** to put something new in the place of ⟨~ a worn carpet⟩ — **re·place·able** \-ˈplā-sə-bəl\ *adj* — **re·plac·er** *n*
syn REPLACE, DISPLACE, SUPPLANT, SUPERSEDE mean to put out of a usual or proper place or into the place of another. REPLACE implies a filling of a place once occupied by something lost, destroyed, or no longer usable or adequate; DISPLACE implies either an ousting or dislodging preceding a replacing; SUPPLANT implies either a dispossessing or usurping of another's place, possessions, or privileges or an uprooting of something and its replacement with something else; SUPERSEDE implies replacing a person or thing that has become superannuated, obsolete, or otherwise inferior.
re·place·ment \ri-ˈplā-smənt\ *n* (1790) **1 :** the action or process of replacing **:** the state of being replaced **:** SUBSTITUTION **2 :** something that replaces; *esp* **:** an individual assigned to a military unit to replace a loss or complete a quota
re·plant \(ˈ)rē-ˈplant\ *vt* (1575) **1 :** to plant again or anew **2 :** to provide with new plants **3 :** to subject to replantation
re·plan·ta·tion \ˌrē-(ˌ)plan-ˈtā-shən\ *n* (1870) **:** reattachment or reinsertion of a bodily part (as a limb or tooth) after separation from the body
1re·play \(ˈ)rē-ˈplā\ *vt* (1884) **:** to play again or over
2re·play \ˈrē-ˌplā\ *n* (1895) **1 a :** an act or instance of replaying **b :** the playing of a tape (as a videotape) **2 :** REPETITION, REENACTMENT ⟨don't want a ~ of our old mistakes⟩
re·plead·er \(ˈ)rē-ˈplēd-ər\ *n* [*replead* (to plead again) + *-er* (as in *misnomer*)] (1607) **1 :** a second legal pleading **2 :** the right of pleading again granted usu. when the issue raised is immaterial or insufficient
re·plen·ish \ri-ˈplen-ish\ *vb* [ME *replenisshen,* fr. MF *repleniss-,* stem of *replenir* to fill, fr. OF, fr. *re-* + *plein* full, fr. L *plenus* — more at FULL] *vt* (14c) **1 a :** to fill with persons or animals **:** STOCK **b** *archaic* **:** to supply fully **:** PERFECT **c :** to fill with inspiration or power **:** NOURISH **2 a :** to fill or build up again ⟨~*ed* his glass⟩ **b :** to make good **:** REPLACE ~ *vi* **:** to become full **:** fill up again — **re·plen·ish·able** \-ə-bəl\ *adj* — **re·plen·ish·er** *n* — **re·plen·ish·ment** \-ish-mənt\ *n*
re·plete \ri-ˈplēt\ *adj* [ME, fr. MF & L; MF *replet,* fr. L *repletus,* pp. of *replēre* to fill up, fr. *re-* + *plēre* to fill — more at FULL] (14c) **1 :** fully or abundantly provided or filled ⟨a book ~ with . . . delicious details —William Safire⟩ **2 a :** abundantly fed **b :** FAT, STOUT **3 :** COMPLETE ***syn*** see FULL — **re·plete·ness** *n*
re·ple·tion \ri-ˈplē-shən\ *n* (14c) **1 :** the act of eating to excess **:** the state of being fed to excess **:** SURFEIT **2 :** the condition of being filled up or overcrowded **3 :** fulfillment of a need or desire **:** SATISFACTION
1re·plev·in \ri-ˈplev-ən\ *n* [ME, fr. AF *replevine,* fr. *replevir* to give security, fr. OF, fr. *re-* + *plevir* to pledge, fr. (assumed) LL *plebere*] (15c) **1 :** the recovery by a person of goods or chattels claimed to be wrongfully taken or detained upon the person's giving security to try the matter in court and return the goods if defeated in the action **2 :** the writ or the common-law action whereby goods and chattels are replevied
2replevin *vt* (1678) **:** REPLEVY
1re·plevy \ri-ˈplev-ē\ *n, pl* **re·plev·ies** [ME, fr. AF *replevir,* v.] (15c) **:** REPLEVIN
2replevy *vt* **re·plev·ied; re·plevy·ing** (1596) **:** to take or get back by a writ for replevin — **re·plevi·able** \-ē-ə-bəl\ *adj*
rep·li·ca \ˈrep-li-kə\ *n* [It, repetition, fr. *replicare* to repeat, fr. LL, fr. L, to fold back — more at REPLY] (1852) **1 :** a close reproduction or facsimile esp. by the maker of the original **2 :** COPY, DUPLICATE ***syn*** see REPRODUCTION
rep·li·case \ˈrep-li-ˌkās, -ˌkāz\ *n* [*replication* + *-ase*] (1963) **:** a polymerase that promotes synthesis of a particular RNA in the presence of a template of RNA
1rep·li·cate \ˈrep-lə-ˌkāt\ *vb* **-cat·ed; -cat·ing** [LL *replicatus,* pp. of *replicare*] *vt* (1607) **:** DUPLICATE, REPEAT ⟨~ a statistical experiment⟩ ~ *vi* **:** to undergo replication **:** produce a replica of itself ⟨virus particles *replicating* in cells⟩
2rep·li·cate \-li-kət\ *adj* (1922) **:** MANIFOLD, REPEATED
3rep·li·cate \-li-kət\ *n* (1929) **:** one of several identical experiments, procedures, or samples
rep·li·ca·tion \ˌrep-lə-ˈkā-shən\ *n* (14c) **1 a :** ANSWER, REPLY **b (1) :** an answer to a reply **:** REJOINDER **(2) :** a plaintiff's reply to a defendant's plea, answer, or counterclaim **2 :** ECHO, REVERBERATION **3 a :** COPY, REPRODUCTION **b :** the action or process of reproducing **4 :** performance of an experiment or procedure more than once; *esp* **:** systematic or random repetition of agricultural test rows or plats to reduce error
rep·li·ca·tive \ˈrep-li-ˌkāt-iv\ *adj* (ca. 1890) **:** of, relating to, involved in, or characterized by replication ⟨the ~ form of tobacco mosaic virus⟩
rep·li·con \ˈrep-li-ˌkän\ *n* [*replicate* + *2-on*] (1963) **:** a linear or circular section of DNA or RNA which replicates sequentially as a unit
1re·ply \ri-ˈplī\ *vb* **re·plied; re·ply·ing** [ME *replien,* fr. MF *replier* to fold again, fr. L *replicare* to fold back, fr. *re-* + *plicare* to fold — more at PLY] *vi* (14c) **1 a :** to respond in words or writing **b :** ECHO, RESOUND **c :** to make a legal replication **2 :** to do something in response; *specif* **:** to return gunfire or an attack ~ *vt* **:** to give as an answer ***syn*** see ANSWER — **re·pli·er** \-ˈplī(-ə)r\ *n*
2reply *n, pl* **replies** (1560) **1 :** something said, written, or done in answer or response **2 :** REPLICATION 1b(2)
re·po \ˈrē-ˌpō\ *n, pl* **repos** [by shortening & alter.] (1963) **:** REPURCHASE AGREEMENT
re·po·lar·iza·tion \ˌrē-ˌpō-lə-rə-ˈzā-shən\ *n* (1958) **:** polarization of a muscle fiber, cell, or membrane following depolarization — **re·po·lar·ize** \(ˈ)rē-ˈpō-lə-ˌrīz\ *vb*
1re·port \ri-ˈpō(ə)rt, -ˈpȯ(ə)rt\ *n* [ME, fr. MF, fr. OF, fr. *reporter* to report, fr. L *reportare,* fr. *re-* + *portare* to carry — more at FARE] (14c) **1 a :** common talk or an account spread by common talk **:** RUMOR **b :** quality of reputation ⟨a witness of good ~⟩ **2 a :** a usu. detailed account or statement ⟨a news ~⟩ **b :** an account or statement of a judicial opinion or decision **c :** a usu. formal record of the proceedings of a meeting or session **3 :** an explosive noise — **on report :** subject to disciplinary action
2report *vt* (14c) **1 a :** to give an account of **:** RELATE **b :** to describe as being in a specified state ⟨~*ed* him much improved⟩ **2 a :** to serve as carrier of (a message) **b :** to relate the words or sense of (something said) **c :** to make a written record or summary of **d (1) :** to watch for and write about the newsworthy aspects or developments of **:** COVER **(2) :** to prepare or present an account of for broadcast **3 a (1) :** to give a formal or official account or statement of ⟨the treasurer ~*ed* a balance of ten dollars⟩ **(2) :** to return or present (a matter referred for consideration) with conclusions or recommendations **b :** to announce or relate as the result of investigation ⟨~*ed* no sign of disease⟩ **c :** to announce the presence, arrival, or sighting of **d :** to make known to the proper authorities ⟨~ a fire⟩ **e :** to make a charge of misconduct against ~ *vi* **1 a :** to give an account **:** TELL **b :** to present oneself **c :** to account for oneself ⟨~*ed* sick on Friday⟩ **2 :** to

make, issue, or submit a report **3 :** to act in the capacity of a reporter — **re·port·able** \-ˈpōrt-ə-bəl, -ˈpȯrt-\ *adj*

re·port·age \ri-ˈpōrt-ij, -ˈpȯrt-, *esp for 2* ˌrep-ər-ˈtäzh, ˌrep-ˌȯr-ˈ\ *n* [F, fr. *reporter* to report] (ca. 1864) **1 a :** the act or process of reporting news **b :** something (as news) that is reported **2 :** writing intended to give an account of observed or documented events

report card *n* (1920) **1 :** a report on a student that is periodically submitted by a school to the student's parents or guardian **2 :** an evaluation of performance

re·port·ed·ly \ri-ˈpōrt-əd-lē, -ˈpȯrt-\ *adv* (1901) **:** according to report

re·port·er \ri-ˈpōrt-ər, -ˈpȯrt-\ *n* (14c) **:** one that reports: as **a :** one who makes authorized statements of law decisions or legislative proceedings **b :** one who makes a shorthand record of a speech or proceeding **c (1) :** one employed by a newspaper, magazine, or television company to gather and report news **(2) :** one who broadcasts news — **re·por·to·ri·al** \ˌrep-ə(r)-ˈtōr-ē-əl, ˌrēp-, -ˈtȯr-\ *adj* — **re·por·to·ri·al·ly** \-ē-ə-lē\ *adv*

report out *vt* (1907) **:** to return after consideration and often with revisions to a legislative body for action ⟨after much debate the committee *reported* the bill *out*⟩

report stage *n* (ca. 1906) **:** the stage in the British legislative process preceding the third reading and concerned esp. with amendments and details

re·pos·al \ri-ˈpō-zəl\ *n, obs* (1605) **:** the act of reposing

[1]**re·pose** \ri-ˈpōz\ *vb* **re·posed; re·pos·ing** [ME *reposen*, fr. MF *reposer*, fr. OF, fr. LL *repausare*, fr. L *re-* + LL *pausare* to stop, fr. L *pausa* pause] *vt* (15c) **:** to lay at rest ~ *vi* **1 a :** to lie at rest **b :** to lie dead ⟨*reposing* in state⟩ **c :** to remain still or concealed **2 :** to take a rest **3** *archaic* **:** RELY **4 :** to rest for support **:** LIE

[2]**repose** *n* (1509) **1 a :** a state of resting after exertion or strain; *esp* **:** rest in sleep **b :** eternal or heavenly rest ⟨pray for the ~ of a soul⟩ **2 a :** a place of rest **b :** PEACE, TRANQUILLITY ⟨the ~ of the bayous⟩ **c :** a harmony in the arrangement of parts and colors that is restful to the eye **3 a :** lack of activity **:** QUIESCENCE **b :** cessation or absence of activity, movement, or animation ⟨the appearance of his face in ~⟩ **4 :** composure of manner **:** POISE

[3]**re·pose** *vt* **re·posed; re·pos·ing** [ME *reposen* to replace, fr. L *reponere* (perf. indic. *reposui*)] (1548) **1** *archaic* **:** to put away or set down **:** DEPOSIT **2 a :** to place (as confidence or trust) in someone or something **b :** to place for control, management, or use

re·pose·ful \ri-ˈpōz-fəl\ *adj* (1852) **:** of a kind to induce ease and relaxation — **re·pose·ful·ly** \-fə-lē\ *adv* — **re·pose·ful·ness** *n*

re·pos·it *vt* **re·pos·it·ed** \-ˈpäz-ət-əd, -ˈpäz-təd\; **re·pos·it·ing** \-ˈpäz-ət-iŋ, -ˈpäz-tiŋ\ [L *repositus*, pp. of *reponere* to replace, fr. *re-* + *ponere* to place — more at POSITION] (1641) **1** \ri-ˈpäz-ət\ **:** DEPOSIT, STORE **2** \(ˈ)rē-\ **:** to put back in place **:** REPLACE

[1]**re·po·si·tion** \ˌrē-pə-ˈzish-ən, ˌrep-ə-\ *n* (1588) **:** the act of repositing **:** the state of being reposited

[2]**re·po·si·tion** \ˌrē-pə-ˈzish-ən\ *vt* (1859) **:** to change the position of

[1]**re·pos·i·to·ry** \ri-ˈpäz-ə-ˌtōr-ē, -ˌtȯr-\ *n, pl* **-ries** (15c) **1 :** a place, room, or container where something is deposited or stored **:** DEPOSITORY **2 :** a side altar in a Roman Catholic church where the consecrated Host is reserved from Maundy Thursday until Good Friday **3 :** one that contains or stores something nonmaterial ⟨considered the book a ~ of knowledge⟩ **4 :** a place or region richly supplied with a natural resource **5 :** a person to whom something is confided or entrusted

[2]**repository** *adj, of a drug* (1950) **:** designed to act over a prolonged period ⟨~ penicillin⟩

re·pos·sess \ˌrē-pə-ˈzes *also* -ˈses\ *vt* (15c) **1 a :** to regain possession of **b :** to resume possession of in default of the payment of installments due **2 :** to restore to possession — **re·pos·ses·sion** \-ˈzesh-ən *also* -ˈsesh-\ *n* — **re·pos·sess·or** \-ˈzes-ər *also* -ˈses-\ *n*

[1]**re·pous·sé** \rə-ˌpü-ˈsā, -ˈpü-ˌ\ *adj* [F, lit., pushed back] (1858) **1 :** shaped or ornamented with patterns in relief made by hammering or pressing on the reverse side — used esp. of metal **2 :** formed in relief

[2]**repoussé** *n* (ca. 1875) **1 :** repoussé work **2 :** repoussé decoration

re·pow·er \(ˈ)rē-ˈpau̇(-ə)r\ *vt* (1954) **:** to provide again or anew with power; *esp* **:** to provide (as a boat) with a new engine ~ *vi* **:** to repower something (as a boat)

repp *var of* REP

rep·re·hend \ˌrep-ri-ˈhend\ *vt* [ME *reprehenden*, fr. L *reprehendere*, lit., to hold back, fr. *re-* + *prehendere* to grasp — more at GET] (14c) **:** to voice disapproval of **:** CENSURE ***syn*** see CRITICIZE

rep·re·hen·si·ble \ˌrep-ri-ˈhen(t)-sə-bəl\ *adj* (14c) **:** worthy of or deserving reprehension **:** CULPABLE — **rep·re·hen·si·bil·i·ty** \-ˌhen(t)-sə-ˈbil-ət-ē\ *n* — **rep·re·hen·si·ble·ness** \-ˈhen(t)-sə-bəl-nəs\ *n* — **rep·re·hen·si·bly** \-blē\ *adv*

rep·re·hen·sion \-ˈhen-chən\ *n* [ME *reprehensioun*, fr. MF or L; MF *reprehension*, fr. L *reprehension-*, *reprehensio*, fr. *reprehensus*, pp. of *reprehendere*] (14c) **:** the act of reprehending **:** CENSURE

rep·re·hen·sive \-ˈhen(t)-siv\ *adj* (1589) **:** serving to reprehend **:** conveying reprehension or reproof

rep·re·sent \ˌrep-ri-ˈzent\ *vb* [ME *representen*, fr. MF *representer*, fr. L *repraesentare*, fr. *re-* + *praesentare* to present] *vt* (14c) **1 :** to bring clearly before the mind **:** PRESENT ⟨a book which ~*s* the character of early America⟩ **2 :** to serve as a sign or symbol of ⟨the flag ~*s* our country⟩ **3 :** to portray or exhibit in art **:** DEPICT **4 :** to serve as the counterpart or image of **:** TYPIFY ⟨a movie hero who ~*s* the ideals of the culture⟩ **5 a :** to produce on the stage **b :** to act the part or role of **6 a (1) :** to take the place of in some respect **(2) :** to act in the place of or for usu. by legal right **b :** to serve esp. in a legislative body by delegated authority usu. resulting from election **7 :** to describe as having a specified character or quality ⟨~*s* himself as a friend⟩ **8 a :** to give one's impression and judgment of **:** state in a manner intended to affect action or judgment **b :** to point out in protest or remonstrance **9 :** to serve as a specimen, example, or instance of **10 a :** to form an image or representation of in the mind **b (1) :** to apprehend (an object) by means of an idea **(2) :** to recall in memory **11 :** to correspond to in essence **:** CONSTITUTE ~ *vi* **:** to make representations against something **:** PROTEST — **rep·re·sent·able** \-ə-bəl\ *adj* — **rep·re·sent·er** *n*

re–pre·sent \ˌrē-pri-ˈzent\ *vt* (1564) **:** to present again or anew — **re–pre·sen·ta·tion** \ˈrē-ˌprē-ˌzen-ˈtā-shən, -ˌprez-ᵊn-, -ˌprēz-ᵊn-\ *n*

rep·re·sen·ta·tion \ˌrep-ri-ˌzen-ˈtā-shən, -zən-\ *n* (15c) **1 :** one that represents: as **a :** an artistic likeness or image **b (1) :** a statement or account made to influence opinion or action **(2) :** an incidental or collateral statement of fact on the faith of which a contract is entered into **c :** a dramatic production or performance **d (1) :** a usu. formal statement made against something or to effect a change **(2) :** a usu. formal protest **2 :** the act or action of representing **:** the state of being represented: as **a :** REPRESENTATIONALISM 2 **b (1) :** the action or fact of one person standing for another so as to have the rights and obligations of the person represented **(2) :** the substitution of an individual or class in place of a person (as a child for a deceased parent) **c :** the action of representing or the fact of being represented esp. in a legislative body **3 :** the body of persons representing a constituency — **rep·re·sen·ta·tion·al** \-shnəl, -shən-ᵊl\ *adj* — **rep·re·sen·ta·tion·al·ly** \-ē\ *adv*

rep·re·sen·ta·tion·al·ism \-shnəl-ˌiz-əm, -shən-ᵊl-\ *n* (1899) **1 :** the doctrine that the immediate object of knowledge is an idea in the mind distinct from the external object which is the occasion of perception **2 :** the theory or practice of realistic representation in art — **rep·re·sen·ta·tion·al·ist** \-əst\ *n*

[1]**rep·re·sen·ta·tive** \ˌrep-ri-ˈzent-ət-iv\ *adj* (14c) **1 :** serving to represent **2 a :** standing or acting for another esp. through delegated authority **b :** of, based on, or constituting a government in which the many are represented by persons chosen from among them usu. by election **3 :** serving as a typical or characteristic example ⟨a ~ moviegoer⟩ **4 :** of or relating to representation or representationalism — **rep·re·sen·ta·tive·ly** *adv* — **rep·re·sen·ta·tive·ness** *n* — **rep·re·sen·ta·tiv·i·ty** \-ˌzent-ə-ˈtiv-ət-ē\ *n*

[2]**representative** *n* (1647) **1 :** a typical example of a group, class, or quality **:** SPECIMEN **2 :** one that represents another or others: as **a (1) :** one that represents a constituency as a member of a legislative body **(2) :** a member of the house of representatives of the U.S. Congress or a state legislature **b :** one that represents another as agent, deputy, substitute, or delegate usu. being invested with the authority of the principal **c :** one that represents a business organization **d :** one that represents another as successor or heir

re·press \ri-ˈpres\ *vb* [ME *repressen*, fr. L *repressus*, pp. of *reprimere* to check, fr. *re-* + *premere* to press — more at PRESS] *vt* (14c) **1 a :** to check by or as if by pressure **:** CURB ⟨injustice was ~*ed*⟩ **b :** to put down by force **:** SUBDUE ⟨~ a disturbance⟩ **2 a :** to hold in by self-control ⟨~*ed* a laugh⟩ **b :** to prevent the natural or normal expression, activity, or development of ⟨~*ed* his anger⟩ **3 :** to exclude from consciousness **4 :** to inactivate (a gene or formation of a gene product) by allosteric combination at a DNA binding site ~ *vi* **:** to take repressive action — **re·press·ibil·i·ty** \-ˌpres-ə-ˈbil-ət-ē\ *n* — **re·press·ible** \-ˈpres-ə-bəl\ *adj* — **re·pres·sive** \-ˈpres-iv\ *adj* — **re·pres·sive·ly** *adv* — **re·pres·sive·ness** *n*

re–press \(ˈ)rē-ˈpres\ *vt* (14c) **:** to press again ⟨~ a record⟩

re·pressed \ri-ˈprest\ *adj* (1665) **1 :** subjected to or marked by repression **2 :** characterized by restraint

re·pres·sion \ri-ˈpresh-ən\ *n* (1533) **1 a :** the action or process of repressing **:** the state of being repressed ⟨~ of unpopular opinions⟩ **b :** an instance of repressing ⟨racial ~*s*⟩ **2 a :** a process by which unacceptable desires or impulses are excluded from consciousness and left to operate in the unconscious **b :** an item so excluded — **re·pres·sion·ist** \-(ə-)nəst\ *adj*

re·pres·sor \ri-ˈpres-ər\ *n* [NL] (15c) **:** one that represses; *esp* **:** a protein that is determined by a regulatory gene and that inhibits the function of a genetic operator

re·priev·al \ri-ˈprē-vəl\ *n, archaic* (1586) **:** REPRIEVE

[1]**re·prieve** \ri-ˈprēv\ *vt* **re·prieved; re·priev·ing** [perh. fr. MF *repris*, pp. of *reprendre* to take back] (1596) **1 :** to delay the punishment of (as a condemned prisoner) **2 :** to give relief or deliverance to for a time

[2]**reprieve** *n* (1598) **1 a :** the act of reprieving **:** the state of being reprieved **b :** a formal temporary suspension of the execution of a sentence esp. of death **2 :** an order or warrant for a reprieve **3 :** a temporary respite (as from pain or trouble)

[1]**rep·ri·mand** \ˈrep-rə-ˌmand\ *n* [F *réprimande*, fr. L *reprimenda*, fem. of *reprimendus*, gerundive of *reprimere* to check — more at REPRESS] (1634) **:** a severe or formal reproof

[2]**reprimand** *vt* (1681) **:** to reprove sharply or censure formally usu. from a position of authority ***syn*** see REPROVE

[1]**re·print** \(ˈ)rē-ˈprint\ *vt* (1551) **:** to print again **:** make a reprint of

[2]**re·print** \ˈrē-ˌprint, (ˈ)rē-ˈ\ *n* (ca. 1611) **:** a reproduction of printed matter: as **a :** a subsequent printing of a book already published that preserves the identical text of the previous printing **b :** OFFPRINT **c :** matter (as an article) that has appeared in print before

re·print·er \(ˈ)rē-ˈprint-ər\ *n* (1689) **:** one that publishes a reprint

re·pri·sal \ri-ˈprī-zəl\ *n* [ME *reprisail*, fr. MF *reprisaille*, fr. OIt *ripresaglia*, fr. *ripreso*, pp. of *riprendere* to take back, fr. *ri-* re- (fr. L *re-*) + *prendere* to take, fr. L *prehendere* — more at GET] (15c) **1 a :** the act or practice in international law of resorting to force short of war in retaliation for damage or loss suffered **b :** an instance of such action **2** *obs* **:** PRIZE **3 :** the regaining of something (as by recapture) **4 :** something (as a sum of money) given or paid in restitution — usu. used in pl. **5 :** a retaliatory act

[1]**re·prise** \ri-ˈprēz, *1 is also* -ˈprīz\ *n* [ME, fr. MF, lit., action of taking back, fr. OF, fr. *reprendre* to take back, fr. *re-* + *prendre* to take, fr. L *prehendere*] (15c) **1 :** a deduction or charge made yearly out of a manor or estate — usu. used in pl. **2 :** a recurrence, renewal, or resumption of an action **3 a :** a musical repetition: **(1) :** the repetition of the exposition preceding the development **(2) :** RECAPITULATION **b :** a repeated performance **:** REPETITION

[2]**re·prise** \ri-ˈprīz, *3 is* -ˈprēz\ *vt* **re·prised; re·pris·ing** [MF *reprise* action of taking back] (15c) **1** *archaic* **:** TAKE BACK; *esp* **:** to recover by force **2** *archaic* **:** COMPENSATE **3 a :** to repeat the performance of **b :** RECAPITULATE

re·pris·ti·nate \(ˈ)rē-ˈpris-tə-ˌnāt\ *vt* **-nat·ed; -nat·ing** [*re-* + *pristine* + *-ate*] (1659) **:** to restore to an original state or condition — **re·pris·ti·na·tion** \(ˌ)rē-ˌpris-tə-ˈnā-shən\ *n*

re·pro \ˈrē-(ˌ)prō\ *n, pl* **repros** [short for *reproduction*] (1946) **:** a clear sharp proof made esp. from a letterpress printing surface to serve as photographic copy for a printing plate

[1]**re·proach** \ri-ˈprōch\ *n* [ME *reproche*, fr. MF, fr. OF, fr. *reprochier* to reproach, fr. (assumed) VL *repropiare*, fr. L *re-* + *prope* near — more at

APPROACH] (15c) **1 a :** a cause or occasion of blame, discredit, or disgrace **b :** DISCREDIT, DISGRACE **2 :** the act or action of reproaching or disapproving ⟨was beyond ~⟩ **3 :** an expression of rebuke or disapproval **4** *obs* **:** one subjected to censure or scorn — **re·proach·ful** \-fəl\ *adj* — **re·proach·ful·ly** \-fə-lē\ *adv* — **re·proach·ful·ness** *n*

[2]**reproach** *vt* (15c) **1 :** to make (something) a matter of reproach **2 :** to express disappointment in or displeasure with (a person) for conduct that is blameworthy or in need of amendment **3 :** to bring into discredit ***syn*** see REPROVE — **re·proach·able** \-ˈprō-chə-bəl\ *adj* — **re·proach·er** *n* — **re·proach·ing·ly** \-ˈprō-chiŋ-lē\ *adv*

rep·ro·bance \ˈrep-rə-bən(t)s\ *n, archaic* (1604) **:** REPROBATION

[1]**rep·ro·bate** \ˈrep-rə-ˌbāt\ *vt* **-bat·ed; -bat·ing** [ME *reprobaten,* fr. LL *reprobatus,* pp. of *reprobare* — more at REPROVE] (15c) **1 :** to condemn strongly as unworthy, unacceptable, or evil ⟨*reprobating* the laxity of the age⟩ **2 :** to foreordain to damnation **3 :** to refuse to accept **:** REJECT ***syn*** see CRITICIZE — **rep·ro·ba·tive** \ˈrep-rə-ˌbāt-iv\ *adj* — **rep·ro·ba·to·ry** \-bə-ˌtōr-ē, -ˌtȯr-\ *adj*

[2]**reprobate** *adj* (1545) **1** *archaic* **:** rejected as worthless or not standing a test **:** CONDEMNED **2 a :** foreordained to damnation **b :** morally abandoned **:** DEPRAVED **3 :** expressing or involving reprobation **4 :** of, relating to, or characteristic of a reprobate

[3]**reprobate** *n* (1545) **:** a reprobate person

rep·ro·ba·tion \ˌrep-rə-ˈbā-shən\ *n* (1532) **:** the act of reprobating or the state of being reprobated

re·pro·cess \(ˈ)rē-ˈpräs-ˌes, -ˈprōs-, -əs\ *vt* (1921) **:** to subject to a special process or treatment in preparation for reuse; *esp* **:** to extract uranium and plutonium from (the spent fuel rods of a nuclear reactor) for use again as fuel

re·pro·duce \ˌrē-prə-ˈd(y)üs\ *vt* (ca. 1611) **:** to produce again: as **a :** to produce (new individuals of the same kind) by a sexual or asexual process **b :** to cause to exist again or anew ⟨~ water from steam⟩ **c :** to imitate closely ⟨sound-effects can ~ the sound of thunder⟩ **d :** to present again **e :** to make a representation (as an image or copy) of ⟨~ a face on canvas⟩ **f :** to revive mentally **:** RECALL **g :** to translate (a recording) into sound ~ *vi* **1 :** to undergo reproduction **2 :** to produce offspring — **re·pro·duc·er** *n* — **re·pro·duc·ibil·i·ty** \-ˌd(y)ü-sə-ˈbil-ət-ē\ *n* — **re·pro·duc·ible** \-ˈd(y)ü-sə-bəl\ *adj or n* — **re·pro·duc·ibly** \-blē\ *adv*

re·pro·duc·tion \ˌrē-prə-ˈdək-shən\ *n* (1659) **1 :** the act or process of reproducing; *specif* **:** the process by which plants and animals give rise to offspring and which fundamentally consists of the segregation of a portion of the parental body by a sexual or an asexual process and its subsequent growth and differentiation into a new individual **2 :** something reproduced **:** COPY **3 :** young seedling trees in a forest

syn REPRODUCTION, DUPLICATE, COPY, FACSIMILE, REPLICA mean a thing made to closely resemble another. REPRODUCTION implies an exact or close imitation of an existing thing; DUPLICATE implies a double or counterpart exactly corresponding to another thing; COPY applies esp. to one of a number of things reproduced mechanically; FACSIMILE suggests a close reproduction in the same materials that may differ in scale; REPLICA implies the exact reproduction of something in all respects.

[1]**re·pro·duc·tive** \ˌrē-prə-ˈdək-tiv\ *adj* (1753) **:** of, relating to, or capable of reproduction — **re·pro·duc·tive·ly** *adv*

[2]**reproductive** *n* (1934) **:** an actual or potential parent; *specif* **:** a sexually functional social insect

re·pro·gram \(ˈ)rē-ˈprō-ˌgram, -grəm\ *vt* (1959) **:** to program anew; *esp* **:** to write new programs for (as a computer) ~ *vi* **:** to rewrite or revise a program esp. of a computer

re·prog·ra·phy \ri-ˈpräg-rə-fē\ *n* [*repro*duction + *-graphy*] (1956) **:** facsimile reproduction (as by photocopying) of graphic matter — **re·prog·ra·pher** \-rə-fər\ *n* — **re·pro·graph·ic** \ˌrē-prə-ˈgraf-ik, ˌre-\ *adj* — **re·pro·graph·ics** \-iks\ *n pl*

re·proof \ri-ˈprüf\ *n* [ME *reprof,* fr. MF *reprove,* fr. OF, fr. *reprover*] (14c) **:** criticism for a fault **:** REBUKE

re·prove \ri-ˈprüv\ *vb* **re·proved; re·prov·ing** [ME *reproven,* fr. MF *reprover,* fr. LL *reprobare* to disapprove, condemn, fr. L *re-* + *probare* to test, approve — more at PROVE] *vt* (14c) **1 :** to scold or correct usu. gently or with kindly intent **2 :** to express disapproval of **:** CENSURE ⟨it is not for me to ~ popular taste —D.W. Brogan⟩ **3** *obs* **:** DISPROVE, REFUTE **4** *obs* **:** CONVINCE, CONVICT ~ *vi* **:** to express rebuke or reproof — **re·prov·er** *n* — **re·prov·ing·ly** \-ˈprü-viŋ-lē\ *adv*

syn REPROVE, REBUKE, REPRIMAND, ADMONISH, REPROACH, CHIDE mean to criticize adversely. REPROVE implies an often kindly intent to correct a fault; REBUKE suggests a sharp or stern reproof; REPRIMAND implies a severe, formal, often public or official rebuke; ADMONISH suggests earnest or friendly warning and counsel; REPROACH and CHIDE suggest displeasure or disappointment expressed in mild reproof or scolding.

[1]**rep·tile** \ˈrep-tᵊl, -ˌtīl\ *n* [ME *reptil,* fr. MF or LL; MF *reptile* (fem.), fr. LL *reptile* (neut.), fr. neut. of *reptilis* creeping, fr. L *reptus,* pp. of *repere* to creep; akin to OHG *reba* tendril] (14c) **1 :** an animal that crawls or moves on its belly (as a snake) or on small short legs (as a lizard) **2 a :** any of a class (Reptilia) of air-breathing vertebrates that include the alligators and crocodiles, lizards, snakes, turtles, and extinct related forms and are characterized by a completely ossified skeleton with a single occipital condyle, a distinct quadrate bone usu. immovably articulated with the skull, ribs attached to the sternum, and a body usu. covered with scales or bony plates **b :** AMPHIBIAN **3 :** a groveling or despised person

[2]**reptile** *adj* (1607) **:** characteristic of a reptile **:** REPTILIAN

[1]**rep·til·ian** \rep-ˈtil-ē-ən, -ˈtil-yən\ *adj* (ca. 1846) **1 :** resembling or having the characteristics of the reptiles **2 :** of or relating to the reptiles

[2]**reptilian** *n* (ca. 1847) **:** REPTILE 2a

re·pub·lic \ri-ˈpəb-lik\ *n* [F *république,* fr. MF *republique,* fr. L *respublica,* fr. *res* thing, wealth + *publica,* fem. of *publicus* public — more at REAL, PUBLIC] (1604) **1 a (1) :** a government having a chief of state who is not a monarch and who in modern times is usu. a president **(2) :** a political unit (as a nation) having such a form of government **b (1) :** a government in which supreme power resides in a body of citizens entitled to vote and is exercised by elected officers and representatives responsible to them and governing according to law **(2) :** a political unit (as a nation) having such a form of government **c :** a usu. specified republican government of a political unit ⟨the French Fourth Republic⟩ **2 :** a body of persons freely engaged in a specified activity ⟨the ~ of letters⟩ **3 :** a constituent political and territorial unit of Czechoslovakia, the U.S.S.R., or Yugoslavia

[1]**re·pub·li·can** \ri-ˈpəb-li-kən\ *n* (1697) **1 :** one that favors or supports a republican form of government **2** *cap* **a :** a member of a political party advocating republicanism **b :** a member of the Democratic-Republican party or of the Republican party of the U.S.

[2]**republican** *adj* (1712) **1 a :** of, relating to, or having the characteristics of a republic **b :** favoring, supporting, or advocating a republic **c :** belonging or appropriate to one living in or supporting a republic ⟨~ simplicity⟩ **2** *cap* **a :** DEMOCRATIC-REPUBLICAN **b :** of, relating to, or constituting the one of the two major political parties evolving in the U.S. in the mid-19th century that is usu. primarily associated with business, financial, and some agricultural interests and is held to favor a restricted governmental role in social and economic life

re·pub·li·can·ism \ri-ˈpəb-li-kə-ˌniz-əm\ *n* (1689) **1 :** adherence to or sympathy for a republican form of government **2 :** the principles or theory of republican government **3** *cap* **a :** the principles, policy, or practices of the Republican party of the U.S. **b :** the Republican party or its members

re·pub·li·can·ize \-kə-ˌnīz\ *vt* **-ized; -iz·ing** (1797) **:** to make republican in character, form, or principle

re·pub·li·ca·tion \(ˌ)rē-ˌpəb-lə-ˈkā-shən\ *n* (1730) **1 :** the act or action of republishing **:** the state of being republished **2 :** something that has been republished

re·pub·lish \(ˈ)rē-ˈpəb-lish\ *vt* (1625) **1 :** to publish again or anew **2 :** to execute (a will) anew — **re·pub·lish·er** *n*

re·pu·di·ate \ri-ˈpyüd-ē-ˌāt\ *vt* **-at·ed; -at·ing** [L *repudiatus,* pp. of *repudiare,* fr. *repudium* divorce] (1545) **1 :** to divorce or separate formally from (a woman) **2 :** to refuse to have anything to do with **:** DISOWN **3 a :** to refuse to accept; *esp* **:** to reject as unauthorized or as having no binding force **b :** to reject as untrue or unjust ⟨~ a charge⟩ **4 :** to refuse to acknowledge or pay ***syn*** see DECLINE — **re·pu·di·a·tor** \-ˌāt-ər\ *n*

re·pu·di·a·tion \ri-ˌpyüd-ē-ˈā-shən\ *n* (1545) **:** the act of repudiating **:** the state of being repudiated; *esp* **:** the refusal of public authorities to acknowledge or pay a debt — **re·pu·di·a·tion·ist** \-sh(ə-)nəst\ *n*

re·pugn \ri-ˈpyün\ *vb* [ME *repugnen,* fr. MF & L; MF *repugner,* fr. L *repugnare*] *vi, archaic* (14c) **:** to offer opposition, objection, or resistance ~ *vt* **:** to contend against **:** OPPOSE

re·pug·nance \ri-ˈpəg-nən(t)s\ *n* (14c) **1 a :** the quality or fact of being contradictory or inconsistent **b :** an instance of such contradiction or inconsistency **2 :** strong dislike, distaste, or antagonism

re·pug·nan·cy \-nən-sē\ *n, pl* **-cies** (14c) **:** REPUGNANCE

re·pug·nant \-nənt\ *adj* [ME, opposed, contradictory, incompatible, fr. MF, fr. L *repugnant-, repugnans,* prp. of *repugnare* to fight against, fr. *re-* + *pugnare* to fight — more at PUNGENT] (14c) **1 :** INCOMPATIBLE, INCONSISTENT **2** *archaic* **:** HOSTILE **3 :** exciting distaste or aversion — **re·pug·nant·ly** *adv*

syn REPUGNANT, REPELLENT, ABHORRENT, DISTASTEFUL, OBNOXIOUS, INVIDIOUS mean so unlikable as to arouse antagonism or aversion. REPUGNANT implies being alien to one's ideas, principles, or tastes and arousing resistance or loathing; REPELLENT suggests a generally forbidding or unpleasant quality that causes one to back away; ABHORRENT implies a repugnance causing active antagonism; DISTASTEFUL implies a contrariness to one's tastes or inclinations; OBNOXIOUS suggests an objectionableness too great to tolerate; INVIDIOUS applies to what cannot be used or performed without creating ill will, odium, or envy.

[1]**re·pulse** \ri-ˈpəls\ *vt* **re·pulsed; re·puls·ing** [L *repulsus,* pp. of *repellere* to repel] (1533) **1 :** to drive or beat back **:** REPEL **2 :** to repel by discourtesy, coldness, or denial **3 :** to cause repulsion in

[2]**repulse** *n* (1533) **1 :** REBUFF, REJECTION **2 :** the action of repelling an attacker **:** the fact of being repelled

re·pul·sion \ri-ˈpəl-shən\ *n* (1547) **1 :** the action of repulsing **:** the state of being repulsed **2 :** the action of repelling **:** the force with which bodies, particles, or like forces repel one another **3 :** a feeling of aversion **:** REPUGNANCE

re·pul·sive \-siv\ *adj* (1598) **1 :** tending to repel or reject **:** COLD, FORBIDDING **2 :** serving or able to repulse **3 :** arousing aversion or disgust — **re·pul·sive·ly** *adv* — **re·pul·sive·ness** *n*

re·pur·chase agreement \(ˌ)rē-ˌpər-chəs-\ *n* (ca. 1924) **:** a contract giving the seller of securities (as treasury bills) the right to repurchase after a specified period and the buyer the right to retain interest earnings

rep·u·ta·ble \ˈrep-yət-ə-bəl\ *adj* (1674) **1 :** enjoying good repute **:** held in esteem **2 :** employed widely or sanctioned by good writers — **rep·u·ta·bil·i·ty** \ˌrep-yət-ə-ˈbil-ət-ē\ *n* — **rep·u·ta·bly** \ˈrep-yət-ə-blē\ *adv*

rep·u·ta·tion \ˌrep-yə-ˈtā-shən\ *n* [ME *reputacioun,* fr. L *reputation-, reputatio* consideration, fr. *reputus,* pp. of *reputare*] (14c) **1 a :** overall quality or character as seen or judged by people in general **b :** recognition by other people of some characteristic or ability ⟨has the ~ of being clever⟩ **2 :** a place in public esteem or regard **:** good name — **rep·u·ta·tion·al** \-shnəl, -shən-ᵊl\ *adj*

[1]**re·pute** \ri-ˈpyüt\ *vt* **re·put·ed; re·put·ing** [ME *reputen,* fr. MF *reputer,* fr. L *reputare* to reckon up, think over, fr. *re-* + *putare* to reckon — more at PAVE] (15c) **:** BELIEVE, CONSIDER

[2]**repute** *n* (1551) **1 :** the character or status commonly ascribed to one **:** REPUTATION **2 :** the state of being favorably known, spoken of, or esteemed

re·put·ed *adj* (1549) **1 :** having a good repute **:** REPUTABLE **2 :** being such according to reputation or popular belief

re·put·ed·ly *adv* (1687) **:** according to reputation or general belief

[1]**re·quest** \ri-ˈkwest\ *n* [ME *requeste,* fr. MF, fr. (assumed) VL *requaesta,* fr. fem. of *requaestus,* pp. of *requaerere* to require] (14c) **1 :** the act or an instance of asking for something **2 :** something asked for **3 :** the condition or fact of being requested ⟨available on ~⟩ **4 :** the state of being sought after **:** DEMAND

\ə\ abut \ᵊ\ kitten, F table \ər\ further \a\ ash \ā\ ace \ä\ cot, cart \au̇\ out \ch\ chin \e\ bet \ē\ easy \g\ go \i\ hit \ī\ ice \j\ job \ŋ\ sing \ō\ go \ȯ\ law \ȯi\ boy \th\ thin \th\ the \ü\ loot \u̇\ foot \y\ yet \zh\ vision \á, k, ⁿ, œ, œ̄, ue, ue̅, ʸ\ *see* Guide to Pronunciation

[2]request *vt* (1533) **1 :** to make a request to or of ⟨~*ed* her to write a paper⟩ **2 :** to ask as a favor or privilege ⟨~*s* to be excused⟩ **3** *obs* **:** to ask (a person) to come or go to a thing or place **4 :** to ask for ⟨~*ed* a brief delay⟩ ***syn*** see ASK — **re·quest·er** *or* **re·quest·or** \-'kwes-tər\ *n*

re·qui·em \'rek-wē-əm *also* 'rāk- *or* 'rēk-\ *n* [ME, fr. L (first word of the introit of the requiem mass), acc. of *requies* rest, fr. *re-* + *quies* quiet, rest — more at WHILE] (14c) **1 :** a mass for the dead **2 a :** a solemn chant (as a dirge) for the repose of the dead **b :** something that resembles such a solemn chant **3 a :** a musical setting of the mass for the dead **b :** a musical composition in honor of the dead

requiem shark *n* (ca. 1900) **:** any of a family (Carcharhinidae) of sharks that includes some dangerous to man

re·qui·es·cat \,rek-wē-'es-,kät; -,at; ,rā-kwē-'es-,kät\ *n* [L, may he (or she) rest, fr. *requiescere* to rest, fr. *re-* + *quiescere* to be quiet, fr. *quies*] (1824) **:** a prayer for the repose of a dead person

re·quire \ri-'kwī(ə)r\ *vb* **re·quired; re·quir·ing** [ME *requeren,* fr. MF *requerre,* fr. (assumed) VL *requaerere* to seek for, need, require, alter. of L *requirere,* fr. *re-* + *quaerere* to seek, ask] *vt* (14c) **1 a :** to claim or ask for by right and authority ⟨this night your soul is *required* of you —Lk 12:20 (RSV)⟩ **b** *archaic* **:** REQUEST **2 a :** to call for as suitable or appropriate ⟨the occasion ~*s* formal dress⟩ **b :** to demand as necessary or essential **:** have a compelling need for ⟨all living beings ~ food⟩ **3 :** to impose a compulsion or command on **:** COMPEL **4** *chiefly Brit* **:** to feel or be obliged — used with a following infinitive ⟨one does not ~ to be a specialist —Elizabeth Bowen⟩ ~ *vi, archaic* **:** ASK ***syn*** see DEMAND

re·quire·ment \-'kwī(ə)r-mənt\ *n* (1662) **:** something required: **a :** something wanted or needed **:** NECESSITY ⟨production was not sufficient to satisfy military ~*s*⟩ **b :** something essential to the existence or occurrence of something else **:** CONDITION ⟨failed to meet the school's ~*s* for graduation⟩

req·ui·site \'rek-wə-zət\ *adj* [ME, fr. L *requisitus,* pp. of *requirere*] (15c) **:** ESSENTIAL, NECESSARY — **requisite** *n* — **req·ui·site·ness** *n*

req·ui·si·tion \,rek-wə-'zish-ən\ *n* [MF or ML; MF, fr. ML *requisition-, requisitio,* fr. L, act of searching, fr. *requisitus,* pp.] (1503) **1 a :** the act of formally requiring or calling upon someone to perform an action **b :** a formal demand made by one nation upon another for the surrender or extradition of a fugitive from justice **2 a :** the act of requiring something to be furnished **b :** a demand or application made usu. with authority: as (1) **:** a demand made by military authorities upon civilians for supplies or other needs (2) **:** a written request for something authorized but not made available automatically **3 :** the state of being in demand or use — **requisition** *vt*

re·quit·al \ri-'kwīt-ᵊl\ *n* (1582) **1 :** something given in return, compensation, or retaliation **2 :** the act or action of requiting **:** the state of being requited

re·quite \ri-'kwīt\ *vt* **re·quit·ed; re·quit·ing** [*re-* + obs. *quite* (to quit, pay), fr. ME *quiten* — more at QUIT] (1529) **1 a :** to make return for **:** REPAY **b :** to make retaliation for **:** AVENGE **2 :** to make suitable return to for a benefit or service or for an injury ***syn*** see RECIPROCATE, PAY — **re·quit·er** *n*

re·ra·di·ate \(')rē-'rād-ē-,āt\ *vt* (1913) **:** to radiate again or anew; *esp* **:** to emit (energy) in the form of radiation after absorbing incident radiation — **re·ra·di·a·tion** \(,)rē-,rād-ē-'ā-shən\ *n*

rere·dos \'rer-ə-,däs *also* 'rir-ə-,däs *or* 'ri(ə)r-,däs\ *n* [ME, fr. AF *areredos,* fr. MF *arrere* behind + *dos* back, fr. L *dorsum* — more at ARREAR] (15c) **1 :** a usu. ornamental wood or stone screen or partition wall behind an altar **2 :** the back of a fireplace or open hearth

[1]re·re·lease \,rē-ri-'lēs\ *n* (1945) **:** something that is rereleased

[2]rerelease *vt* (1967) **:** to release (as a movie or record) again

rereward *n* [ME *rerewarde,* fr. AF, fr. OF *rere* behind + ONF *warde* guard; akin to OF *garde* guard — more at REAR GUARD] *obs* (14c) **:** REAR GUARD

[1]re·run \(')rē-'rən\ *vt* **-ran** \-'ran\; **-run; -run·ning** (1903) **:** to run again or anew

[2]re·run \'rē-,rən, (')rē-'\ *n* (ca. 1934) **:** the act or action or an instance of rerunning **:** REPETITION; *esp* **:** a presentation of a motion-picture film or television program after its first run

res \'rās, 'rēz\ *n, pl* **res** [L — more at REAL] (1623) **:** a particular thing **:** MATTER — used esp. in legal phrases

res ad·ju·di·ca·ta \'rē-zə-,jüd-i-'kät-ə\ *n* [LL] (1902) **:** RES JUDICATA

re·sal·able \(')rē-'sā-lə-bəl\ *adj* (1866) **:** fit for resale

re·sale \'rē-,sāl, (')rē-'sā(ə)l\ *n* (1625) **1 :** the act of selling again usu. to a new party **2 a :** a secondhand sale **b :** an additional sale to the same buyer

re·scale \(')rē-'skā(ə)l\ *vt* (1944) **:** to plan, establish, or formulate on a new and usu. smaller scale

re·scind \ri-'sind\ *vt* [L *rescindere* to annul, fr. *re-* + *scindere* to cut — more at SHED] (1643) **1 :** to take away **:** REMOVE **2 a :** to take back **:** ANNUL, CANCEL ⟨refused to ~ the order⟩ **b :** to abrogate (a contract) by restoring to the opposite party what one has received from him **3 :** to make void (as an act) by action of the enacting authority or a superior authority **:** REPEAL — **re·scind·er** *n* — **re·scind·ment** \-'sin(d)-mənt\ *n*

re·scis·sion \ri-'sizh-ən\ *n* [LL *rescission-, rescissio,* fr. L *rescissus,* pp. of *rescindere*] (ca. 1611) **:** an act of rescinding

re·scis·so·ry \-'siz-ə-rē, -'sis-\ *adj* (1605) **:** relating to or tending to or having the effect of rescission

re·script \'rē-,skript\ *n* [L *rescriptum,* fr. neut. of *rescriptus,* pp. of *rescribere* to write in reply, fr. *re-* + *scribere* to write — more at SCRIBE] (1528) **1 :** a written answer of a Roman emperor or of a pope to a legal inquiry or petition **2 :** an official or authoritative order, decree, edict, or announcement **3 :** an act or instance of rewriting

res·cue \'res-(,)kyü\ *vt* **res·cued; res·cu·ing** [ME *rescuen,* fr. MF *rescourre,* fr. OF, fr. *re-* + *escourre* to shake out, fr. L *excutere,* fr. *ex-* + *quatere* to shake — more at QUASH] (14c) **:** to free from confinement, danger, or evil **:** SAVE, DELIVER: as **a :** to take (as a prisoner) forcibly from legal custody **b :** to recover (as a prize) by force **c :** to deliver (as a place under siege) by armed force — **res·cu·able** \-ə-bəl\ *adj* — **rescue** *n* — **res·cu·er** *n*

syn RESCUE, DELIVER, REDEEM, RANSOM, RECLAIM, SAVE mean to set free from confinement or danger. RESCUE implies freeing from imminent danger by prompt or vigorous action; DELIVER implies release usu. of a person from confinement, temptation, slavery, or suffering; REDEEM implies releasing from bondage or penalties by giving what is demanded or necessary; RANSOM specif. applies to buying out of captivity; RECLAIM suggests a bringing back to a former state or condition of someone or something abandoned or debased; SAVE may replace any of the foregoing terms; it may further imply a preserving or maintaining for usefulness or continued existence.

rescue mission *n* (1902) **:** a city religious mission seeking to convert and rehabilitate the down-and-out

[1]re·search \ri-'sərch, 'rē-,\ *n* [MF *recerche,* fr. *recerchier* to investigate thoroughly, fr. OF, fr. *re-* + *cerchier* to search — more at SEARCH] (1577) **1 :** careful or diligent search **2 :** studious inquiry or examination; *esp* **:** investigation or experimentation aimed at the discovery and interpretation of facts, revision of accepted theories or laws in the light of new facts, or practical application of such new or revised theories or laws **3 :** the collecting of information about a particular subject

[2]research *vt* (1593) **1 :** to search or investigate exhaustively ⟨~ a problem⟩ **2 :** to do research for ⟨~ a book⟩ ~ *vi* **:** to engage in research — **re·search·able** \-ə-bəl\ *adj* — **re·search·er** *n*

re·search·ist \-'sər-chəst, -,sər-\ *n* (1921) **:** one engaged in research

re·seau \rā-'zō, ri-\ *n, pl* **re·seaux** \-'zō(z)\ [F *réseau,* fr. OF *resel,* dim. of *rais* net, fr. L *retis, rete* — more at RETINA] (1578) **1 :** a net ground or foundation in lace **2 :** a system of lines forming small squares of standard size photographed by a separate exposure on the same plate with star images to facilitate measurements **3 :** a screen with minute elements of three colors in a regular geometric pattern used for taking color photographs

re·sect \ri-'sekt\ *vt* [L *resectus,* pp. of *resecare* to cut off, fr. *re-* + *secare* to cut — more at SAW] (1846) **:** to perform resection on — **re·sect·abil·i·ty** \-,sek-tə-'bil-ət-ē\ *n* — **re·sect·able** \-'sek-tə-bəl\ *adj*

re·sec·tion \ri-'sek-shən\ *n* (1775) **:** the surgical removal of part of an organ or structure

reseda \'rā-zə-,dä\ *n* [F *réséda,* fr. *réséda,* a mignonette] (1873) **:** a variable color averaging a grayish green

re·seed \(')rē-'sēd\ *vt* (1888) **1 :** to sow seed on again or anew **2 :** to maintain (itself) by self-sown seed ~ *vi* **:** to maintain itself by self-sown seed

re·sem·blance \ri-'zem-blən(t)s\ *n* (14c) **1 a :** the quality or state of resembling; *esp* **:** correspondence in appearance or superficial qualities **b :** a point of likeness **:** SIMILARITY **2 :** REPRESENTATION, IMAGE **3** *archaic* **:** characteristic appearance **4** *obs* **:** PROBABILITY ***syn*** see LIKENESS

re·sem·blant \-blənt\ *adj* (14c) **:** marked by or showing resemblance

re·sem·ble \ri-'zem-bəl\ *vt* **re·sem·bled; re·sem·bling** \-b(ə-)liŋ\ [ME *resemblen,* fr. MF *resembler, ressembler,* fr. OF, fr. *re-* + *sembler* to be like, seem, fr. L *similare* to copy, fr. *similis* like — more at SAME] (14c) **1 :** to be like or similar to **2** *archaic* **:** to represent as like

re·send \(')rē-'send\ *vt* **-sent** \-'sent\; **-send·ing** (1554) **:** to send again or back

re·sent \ri-'zent\ *vt* [F *ressentir* to be emotionally sensible of, fr. OF, fr. *re-* + *sentir* to feel, fr. L *sentire* — more at SENSE] (1628) **:** to feel or express annoyance or ill will at

re·sent·ful \-fəl\ *adj* (1656) **1 :** full of resentment **:** inclined to resent **2 :** caused or marked by resentment — **re·sent·ful·ly** \-fə-lē\ *adv* — **re·sent·ful·ness** *n*

re·sent·ment \ri-'zent-mənt\ *n* (1619) **:** a feeling of indignant displeasure or persistent ill will at something regarded as a wrong, insult, or injury ***syn*** see OFFENSE

re·ser·pine \ri-'sər-,pēn, -pən\ *n* [G *reserpin,* prob. irreg. fr. NL *Rauwolfia serpentina,* a species of rauwolfia] (1952) **:** a drug $C_{33}H_{40}N_2O_9$ extracted esp. from the root of rauwolfias and used in the treatment of hypertension, mental disorders, and tension states

res·er·va·tion \,rez-ər-'vā-shən\ *n* (14c) **1 :** an act of reserving something: as **a** (1) **:** the act or fact of a grantor's reserving some newly created thing out of the thing granted (2) **:** the right or interest so reserved **b :** the setting of limiting conditions or withholding from complete exposition ⟨answered without ~⟩ **c :** an arrangement to have something (as a hotel room) held for one's use; *also* **:** a promise, guarantee, or record of such engagement **2 :** something reserved: as **a :** a tract of public land set aside (as for the use of American Indians) **b :** an area in which hunting is not permitted; *esp* **:** one set aside as a secure breeding place **3 a :** a limiting condition ⟨agreed, but with ~*s*⟩ **b :** a specific objection ⟨had ~*s* about the finding⟩

[1]re·serve \ri-'zərv\ *vt* **re·served; re·serv·ing** [ME *reserven,* fr. MF *reserver,* fr. L *reservare,* lit., to keep back, fr. *re-* + *servare* to keep — more at CONSERVE] (14c) **1 a :** to hold in reserve **:** keep back ⟨~ grain for seed⟩ **b :** to set aside (part of the consecrated elements) at the Eucharist for future use **c :** to retain or hold over to a future time or place **:** DEFER ⟨~ one's judgment on a plan⟩ **d :** to make legal reservation of **2 :** to set or have set aside or apart ⟨~ a hotel room⟩ ***syn*** see KEEP

[2]reserve *n, often attrib* (1648) **1 :** something stored or kept available for future use or need **:** STOCK **2 :** something reserved or set aside for a particular purpose, use, or reason: as **a** (1) **:** a military force withheld from action for later decisive use — usu. used in pl. (2) **:** forces not in the field but available (3) **:** the military forces of a country not part of the regular services; *also* **:** RESERVIST **b :** a tract (as of public land) set apart **:** RESERVATION **3 :** an act of reserving **:** QUALIFICATION **4 a :** restraint, closeness, or caution in one's words and actions **b :** forbearance from making a full explanation, complete disclosure, or free expression of one's mind **5** *archaic* **:** SECRET **6 a :** money or its equivalent kept in hand or set apart usu. to meet liabilities **b :** the liquid resources of a nation for meeting international payments **7 :** SUBSTITUTE **8 :** RESERVE PRICE — **in reserve :** held back for future or special use

reserve bank *n* (1905) **:** a central bank holding reserves of other banks

reserve clause *n* (1944) **:** the clause in a professional athlete's contract that reserves for the club the exclusive right automatically to renew the contract and that binds the athlete to the club for his entire playing career or until he is traded or released

re·served \ri-'zərvd\ *adj* (1601) **1 :** restrained in words and actions **2 :** kept or set apart or aside for future or special use ***syn*** see SILENT — **re·serv·ed·ly** \-'zər-vəd-lē\ *adv* — **re·serv·ed·ness** \-'zər-vəd-nəs\ *n*

reserved power *n* (1835) **:** a political power reserved by a constitution to the exclusive jurisdiction of a specified political authority

reserve price *n* (1919) : a price announced at an auction as the lowest that will be considered

re·serv·ist \ri-'zər-vəst\ *n* (1876) : a member of a military reserve

res·er·voir \'rez-ə(r)v-،wär, -ə(r)v-،(w)ȯr *also* -ə(r)-،vȯi\ *n* [F *réservoir*, fr. MF, fr. *reserver*] (1690) **1 a** : a place where something is kept in store: as **a** : an artificial lake where water is collected and kept in quantity for use **b** : a part of an apparatus in which a liquid is held **c** : SUPPLY, STORE ⟨a large ~ of educated people⟩ **2** : an extra supply : RESERVE **3** : an organism in which a parasite that is pathogenic for some other species lives and multiplies without damaging its host; *also* : a noneconomic organism within which a pathogen of economic or medical importance flourishes

re·set \(')rē-'set\ *vt* -**set**; -**set·ting** (1655) **1** : to set again or anew ⟨~ type⟩ ⟨~ a diamond⟩ **2** : to change the reading of ⟨~ an odometer⟩ — **re·set·table** \-'set-ə-bəl\ *adj*

res ges·tae \'räs-'ges-،tī, 'rāz-'jes-(،)tē\ *n pl* [L] (1616) : things done; *esp* : the facts that form the environment of a litigated issue and are admissible in evidence

resh \'räsh\ *n* [Heb *rēsh*] (ca. 1899) : the 20th letter of the Hebrew alphabet — see ALPHABET table

re·shape \(')rē-'shāp\ *vt* (1827) : to give a new form or orientation to : REORGANIZE — **re·shap·er** *n*

re·ship \(')rē-'ship\ *vt* (1654) : to ship again; *specif* : to put on board a second time ~ *vi* : to embark on a ship again or anew; *specif* : to sign again for service on a ship — **re·ship·ment** \-mənt\ *n* — **re·ship·per** *n*

re·shuf·fle \(')rē-'shəf-əl\ *vt* (1830) **1** : to shuffle (as cards) again **2** : to reorganize usu. by the redistribution of existing elements ⟨the cabinet was *reshuffled* by the prime minister⟩ — **reshuffle** *n*

re·sid \ri-'zid\ *n* (1967) : RESIDUAL OIL

re·side \ri-'zīd\ *vi* **re·sid·ed; re·sid·ing** [ME *residen*, fr. MF or L; MF *resider*, fr. L *residēre* to sit back, remain, abide, fr. *re-* + *sedēre* to sit — more at SIT] (15c) **1 a** : to be in residence as the incumbent of a benefice or office **b** : to dwell permanently or continuously : occupy a place as one's legal domicile **2 a** : to be present as an element or quality **b** : to be vested as a right — **re·sid·er** *n*

res·i·dence \'rez-əd-ən(t)s, 'rez-dən(t)s, 'rez-ə-،den(t)s\ *n* (14c) **1 a** : the act or fact of dwelling in a place for some time **b** : the act or fact of living or regularly staying at or in some place for the discharge of a duty or the enjoyment of a benefit **2 a** (1) : the place where one actually lives as distinguished from his domicile or a place of temporary sojourn (2) : DOMICILE 2a **b** : the place where a corporation is actually or officially established **c** : the status of a legal resident **3 a** : a building used as a home : DWELLING **b** : housing or a unit of housing provided for students **4 a** : the period or duration of abode in a place ⟨after a ~ of 30 years⟩ **b** : a period of active and esp. full-time study, research, or teaching at a college or university **5** : the persistence of a substance that is suspended or dissolved in a medium ⟨the ~ time of a pollutant⟩ — **in residence** : engaged to live and work at a particular place often for a specified time ⟨poet *in residence* at a university⟩

res·i·den·cy \'rez-əd-ən-sē, 'rez-dən-, 'rez-ə-،den(t)-\ *n, pl* -**cies** (1579) **1** : a usu. official place of residence **2** : a territory in a protected state in which the powers of the protecting state are executed by a resident agent **3** : a period of advanced training in a medical specialty

¹res·i·dent \'rez-əd-ənt, 'rez-dənt, 'rez-ə-،dent\ *adj* [ME, fr. L *resident-, residens,* prp. of *residēre*] (14c) **1 a** : living in a place for some length of time : RESIDING **b** : serving in a regular or full-time capacity ⟨the ~ engineer for a highway department⟩; *also* : being in residence **2** : PRESENT, INHERENT **3** : not migratory

²resident *n* (15c) **1** : one who resides in a place **2** : a diplomatic agent residing at a foreign court or seat of government; *esp* : one exercising authority in a protected state as representative of the protecting power **3** : a physician serving a residency

resident commissioner *n* (1902) **1** : a nonvoting representative of a dependency in the U.S. House of Representatives **2** : a resident administrator in a British colony or possession

res·i·den·tial \،rez(-ə)-'den-chəl\ *adj* (1654) **1 a** : used as a residence or by residents **b** : providing living accommodations for students ⟨a ~ college⟩ **2** : restricted to or occupied by residences ⟨a ~ neighborhood⟩ **3** : of or relating to residence or residences — **res·i·den·tial·ly** \-'dench-(ə-)lē\ *adv*

¹res·id·u·al \ri-'zij-(ə-)wəl, -'zij-əl\ *adj* [L *residuum* residue] (1570) **1** : of, relating to, or constituting a residue **2** : leaving a residue that remains effective for some time — **re·sid·u·al·ly** \-ē\ *adv*

²residual *n* (1570) **1** : REMAINDER, RESIDUUM: as **a** : the difference between results obtained by observation and by computation from a formula or between the mean of several observations and any one of them **b** : a residual product or substance **c** : an internal aftereffect of experience or activity that influences later behavior; *esp* : a disability remaining from a disease or operation **2** : a payment (as to an actor or writer) for each rerun after an initial showing (as of a taped TV show)

residual oil *n* (ca. 1948) : fuel oil that remains after the removal of valuable distillates (as gasoline) from petroleum and that is used esp. by industry — called also *resid*

residual power *n* (1945) : power held to remain at the disposal of a governmental authority after an enumeration or delegation of specified powers to other authorities

re·sid·u·ary \ri-'zij-ə-،wer-ē\ *adj* (1726) : of, relating to, or constituting a residue ⟨~ estate⟩

res·i·due \'rez-ə-،d(y)ü\ *n* [ME, fr. MF *residu,* fr. L *residuum,* fr. neut. of *residuus* left over, fr. *residēre* to remain] (14c) : something that remains after a part is taken, separated, or designated : REMNANT, REMAINDER: as **a** : the part of a testator's estate remaining after the satisfaction of all debts, charges, allowances, and previous devises and bequests **b** : the remainder after subtracting a multiple of a modulus from an integer or a power of the integer that can appear as the second of the two terms in an appropriate congruence ⟨2 and 7 are ~s of 12 modulo 5⟩ ⟨9 is a quadratic ~ of 7 modulo 5 since $7^2 - 8 \times 5 = 9$⟩ **c** : a constituent structural unit (as a group or monomer) of a usu. complex molecule ⟨amino acid ~s left after hydrolysis of protein⟩

residue class *n* (1948) : the set of elements (as integers) that leave the same remainder when divided by a given modulus

re·sid·u·um \ri-'zij-ə-wəm\ *n, pl* **re·sid·ua** \-ə-wə\ [L] (1672) : something residual: as **a** : RESIDUE a **b** : a residual product (as from the distillation of petroleum)

re·sign \ri-'zīn\ *vb* [ME *resignen,* fr. MF *resigner,* fr. L *resignare,* lit., to unseal, cancel, fr. *re-* + *signare* to sign, seal — more at SIGN] *vt* (14c) **1** : RELEGATE, CONSIGN; *esp* : to give (oneself) over without resistance ⟨~ed herself to her fate⟩ **2** : to give up deliberately; *esp* : to renounce (as a right or position) by a formal act ~ *vi* **1** : to give up one's office or position : QUIT **2** : to accept something as inevitable : SUBMIT *syn* see RELINQUISH, ABDICATE — **re·sign·ed·ly** \-'zī-nəd-lē\ *adv* — **re·sign·ed·ness** \-'zī-nəd-nəs\ *n* — **re·sign·er** \-'zī-nər\ *n*

re–sign \(')rē-'sīn\ *vt* (1805) : to sign again

res·ig·na·tion \،rez-ig-'nā-shən\ *n* (14c) **1 a** : an act or instance of resigning something : SURRENDER **b** : a formal notification of resigning **2** : the quality or state of being resigned : SUBMISSIVENESS

re·sile \ri-'zī(ə)l\ *vi* **re·siled; re·sil·ing** [LL & L; LL *resilire* to withdraw, fr. L, to recoil] (1529) : RECOIL, RETRACT; *esp* : to return to a prior position

re·sil·ience \ri-'zil-yən(t)s\ *n* (1824) **1** : the capability of a strained body to recover its size and shape after deformation caused esp. by compressive stress **2** : an ability to recover from or adjust easily to misfortune or change

re·sil·ien·cy \-yən-sē\ *n* (1835) : RESILIENCE

re·sil·ient \-yənt\ *adj* [L *resilient-, resiliens,* prp. of *resilire* to jump back, recoil, fr. *re-* + *salire* to leap — more at SALLY] (1674) : characterized or marked by resilience: as **a** : capable of withstanding shock without permanent deformation or rupture **b** : tending to recover from or adjust easily to misfortune or change *syn* see ELASTIC — **re·sil·ient·ly** *adv*

¹res·in \'rez-ᵊn\ *n* [ME, fr. MF *resine,* fr. L *resina,* fr. Gk *rhētinē* pine resin] (14c) **1 a** : any of various solid or semisolid amorphous fusible flammable natural organic substances that are usu. transparent or translucent and yellowish to brown, are formed esp. in plant secretions, are soluble in organic solvents (as ether) but not in water, are electrical nonconductors, and are used chiefly in varnishes, printing inks, plastics, and sizes and in medicine **b** : ROSIN **2 a** : any of a large class of synthetic products that have some of the physical properties of natural resins but are different chemically and are used chiefly in plastics **b** : any of various products made from a natural resin or a natural polymer

²resin *vt* **res·ined; res·in·ing** \'rez-ᵊn-iŋ, 'rez-niŋ\ (1865) : to treat with resin

res·in·ate \'rez-ᵊn-،āt\ *vt* -**at·ed; -at·ing** (ca. 1890) : to impregnate or flavor with resin

resin canal *n* (1884) : a tubular intercellular space in gymnosperms and some angiosperms that is lined with epithelial cells which secrete resin — called also *resin duct*

re·sin·i·fy \'re-'zin-ə-،fī\ *vt* -**fied; -fy·ing** (1876) : to convert into or treat with resin

res·in·oid \'rez-ᵊn-،ȯid\ *n* (1880) **1** : a thermosetting synthetic resin **2** : GUM RESIN

res·in·ous \'rez-nəs, -ᵊn-əs\ *adj* (1646) : of, relating to, resembling, containing, or derived from resin

¹re·sist \ri-'zist\ *vb* [ME *resisten,* fr. MF or L; MF *resister,* fr. L *resistere,* fr. *re-* + *sistere* to take a stand; akin to L *stare* to stand — more at STAND] *vi* (14c) : to exert force in opposition ~ *vt* **1** : to exert oneself so as to counteract or defeat **2** : to withstand the force or effect of *syn* see OPPOSE

²resist *n* (1836) : something (as a coating) that protects against a chemical, electrical, or physical action

re·sis·tance \ri-'zis-tən(t)s\ *n* (15c) **1 a** : an act or instance of resisting : OPPOSITION **b** : a means of resisting **2** : the ability to resist; *esp* : the inherent capacity of a living being to resist untoward circumstances (as disease, malnutrition, or toxic agents) **3** : an opposing or retarding force **4 a** : the opposition offered by a body or substance to the passage through it of a steady electric current **b** : a source of resistance **5** *often cap* : an underground organization of a conquered country engaging in sabotage and secret operations against occupation forces and collaborators

¹re·sis·tant \-tənt\ *n* (1600) : one that resists : RESISTER

²resistant *adj* (1610) : giving or capable of resistance — often used in combination ⟨wrinkle-*resistant* clothes⟩

re·sist·er \ri-'zis-tər\ *n* (14c) : one that resists; *esp* : one who actively opposes the policies of a government

re·sist·ibil·i·ty \ri-،zis-tə-'bil-ət-ē\ *n* (1617) **1** : the quality or state of being resistible **2** : ability to resist

re·sist·ible \ri-'zis-tə-bəl\ *adj* (1608) : capable of being resisted

re·sis·tive \ri-'zis-tiv\ *adj* (1603) : marked by resistance — often used in combination ⟨fire-*resistive* material⟩ — **re·sis·tive·ly** *adv* — **re·sis·tive·ness** *n*

re·sis·tiv·i·ty \ri-،zis-'tiv-ət-ē, ،rē-\ *n, pl* -**ties** (1885) **1** : the longitudinal electrical resistance of a uniform rod of unit length and unit cross-sectional area : the reciprocal of conductivity **2** : capacity for resisting : RESISTANCE

re·sist·less \ri-'zist-ləs\ *adj* (1586) **1** : IRRESISTIBLE **2** : offering no resistance — **re·sist·less·ly** *adv* — **re·sist·less·ness** *n*

re·sis·tor \ri-'zis-tər\ *n* (1905) : a device that has electrical resistance and that is used in an electric circuit for protection, operation, or current control

re·sit·ting \(')rē-'sit-iŋ\ *n* (1661) : a sitting (as of a legislature) for a second time : another sitting

res ju·di·ca·ta \'rēz-،jüd-i-'kät-ə\ *n* [L, judged matter] (1693) : a matter finally decided on its merits by a court having competent jurisdiction and not subject to litigation again between the same parties

re·sole \(')rē-'sōl\ *vt* (1853) : to furnish (a shoe) with a new sole ~ *vi* : to resole a shoe

---

\ə\ abut \ᵊ\ kitten, F table \ər\ further \a\ ash \ā\ ace \ä\ cot, cart \au̇\ out \ch\ chin \e\ bet \ē\ easy \g\ go \i\ hit \ī\ ice \j\ job \ŋ\ sing \ō\ go \ȯ\ law \ȯi\ boy \th\ thin \th̲\ the \ü\ loot \u̇\ foot \y\ yet \zh\ vision \ā, k̲, ⁿ, œ, œ̄, ᵫ, ᵫ̄, �\ see Guide to Pronunciation

re·sol·u·ble \ri-ˈzäl-yə-bəl\ *adj* [LL *resolubilis,* fr. L *resolvere* to resolve] (1602) : capable of being resolved

[1]res·o·lute \ˈrez-ə-ˌlüt, -lət\ *adj* [L *resolutus,* pp. of *resolvere*] (1533) **1** : marked by firm determination : RESOLVED **2** : BOLD, STEADY ***syn*** see FAITHFUL — **res·o·lute·ly** \-ˌlüt-lē, -lət-; ˌrez-ə-ˈlüt-\ *adv* — **res·o·lute·ness** \-ˌlüt-nəs, -lət-, -ˈlüt-\ *n*

[2]resolute *n* (1602) : one who is resolute

res·o·lu·tion \ˌrez-ə-ˈlü-shən\ *n* [ME, fr. MF or L; MF *resolution,* fr. L *resolution-, resolutio,* fr. *resolutus,* pp.] (14c) **1** : the act or process of reducing to simpler form: as **a** : the act of analyzing a complex notion into simpler ones **b** : the act of answering : SOLVING **c** : the act of determining **d** : the passing of a voice part from a dissonant to a consonant tone or the progression of a chord from dissonance to consonance **e** : the separating of a chemical compound or mixture into its constituents **f** (1) : the division of a prosodic element into its component parts (2) : the substitution in Greek or Latin prosody of two short syllables for a long syllable **g** : the analysis of a vector into two or more vectors of which it is the sum **h** : the process or capability of making distinguishable the individual parts of an object, closely adjacent optical images, or sources of light **2** : the subsidence of inflammation esp. in a lung **3** **a** : something that is resolved **b** : firmness of resolve **4** : a formal expression of opinion, will, or intent voted by an official body or assembled group **5** : the point in a literary work at which the chief dramatic complication is worked out ***syn*** see COURAGE

[1]re·solve \ri-ˈzälv, -ˈzȯlv *also* -ˈzäv *or* -ˈzȯv\ *vb* **re·solved; re·solv·ing** [L *resolvere* to unloose, dissolve, fr. *re-* + *solvere* to loosen, release — more at SOLVE] *vt* (14c) **1** *obs* : DISSOLVE, MELT **2** **a** : to break up : SEPARATE ⟨the prism *resolved* the light into a play of color⟩; *also* : to change by disintegration **b** : to reduce by analysis ⟨~ the problem into simple elements⟩ **c** : to distinguish between or make independently visible adjacent parts of **d** : to separate (a racemic compound or mixture) into the two components **3** : to cause resolution of (as inflammation) **4** **a** : to deal with successfully : clear up ⟨~ doubts⟩ ⟨~ a dispute⟩ **b** : to find an answer to **c** : to make clear or understandable **d** : to find a mathematical solution of **e** : to split up (as a vector) into two or more components esp. in assigned directions **5** : to reach a firm decision about ⟨~ to get more sleep⟩ ⟨~ disputed points in a text⟩ **6** **a** : to declare or decide by a formal resolution and vote **b** : to change by resolution or formal vote ⟨the house *resolved* itself into a committee⟩ **7** : to make (as voice parts) progress from dissonance to consonance **8** : to work out the resolution of (as a play) ~ *vi* **1** : to become separated into component parts; *also* : to become reduced by dissolving or analysis **2** : to form a resolution : DETERMINE **3** : CONSULT, DELIBERATE **4** : to progress from dissonance to consonance ***syn*** see DECIDE — **re·solv·able** \-ˈzäl-və-bəl, -ˈzȯl- *also* -ˈzäv-ə- *or* -ˈzȯv-ə-\ *adj* — **re·solv·er** *n*

[2]resolve *n* (1591) **1** : something that is resolved **2** : fixity of purpose : RESOLUTENESS **3** : a legal or official determination; *esp* : a formal resolution

re·sol·vent \ri-ˈzäl-vənt, -ˈzȯl-\ *n* (1851) : a means of solving something (as an equation) — **resolvent** *adj*

resolving power *n* (1879) **1** : the ability of an optical system to form distinguishable images of objects separated by small angular distances **2** : the ability of a photographic film or plate to reproduce the fine detail of an optical image

res·o·nance \ˈrez-ᵊn-ən(t)s, ˈrez-nən(t)s\ *n* [ME, fr. MF, fr. L *resonatia* echo, fr. *resonant-, resonans,* prp. of *resonare* to resound] (15c) **1** **a** : the quality or state of being resonant **b** (1) : a vibration of large amplitude in a mechanical or electrical system caused by a relatively small periodic stimulus of the same or nearly the same period as the natural vibration period of the system (2) : the state of adjustment that produces resonance in a mechanical or electrical system **2** **a** : the intensification and enriching of a musical tone by supplementary vibration **b** : a quality imparted to voiced sounds by vibration in anatomical resonating chambers or cavities (as the mouth or the nasal cavity) **c** : a quality of richness or variety **3** : the sound elicited on percussion of the chest **4** : a phenomenon that relates to the general stability of a molecule, ion, or group to which two or more structures differing only in the distribution of electrons can be assigned and which is represented by the total combination of the assigned structures **5** **a** : the enhancement of an atomic, nuclear, or particle reaction or a scattering event by excitation of internal motion in the system **b** : MAGNETIC RESONANCE **6** : an extremely short-lived elementary particle **7** : the synchronous relationship involving gravitation that exists between orbital periods of two celestial bodies that orbit a third (as a planet)

res·o·nant \ˈrez-ᵊn-ənt, ˈrez-nənt\ *adj* (1592) **1** : continuing to sound : ECHOING **2** **a** : capable of inducing resonance **b** : relating to or exhibiting resonance **3** **a** : intensified and enriched by or as if by resonance **b** : marked by grandiloquence — **resonant** *n* — **res·o·nant·ly** *adv*

res·o·nate \ˈrez-ᵊn-ˌāt\ *vb* **-nat·ed; -nat·ing** [L *resonatus,* pp. of *resonare* to resound — more at RESOUND] *vi* (1873) **1** : to produce or exhibit resonance **2** : to respond as if by resonance ⟨~ to the music⟩; *also* : to have a repetitive pattern that resembles resonance **3** : to relate harmoniously ~ *vt* : to subject to resonating

res·o·na·tor \-ˌāt-ər\ *n* (1869) : something that resounds or resonates: as **a** : a hollow metallic container for producing microwaves or a piezoelectric crystal put into oscillation by the oscillations of an outside source **b** : a device for increasing the resonance of a musical instrument

re·sorb \(ˈ)rē-ˈsȯ(ə)rb, -ˈzȯ(ə)rb\ *vb* [L *resorbēre,* fr. *re-* + *sorbēre* to suck up] *vt* (1640) **1** : to swallow or suck in again **2** : to break down and assimilate (something previously differentiated) ~ *vi* : to undergo resorption

res·or·cin \rə-ˈzȯrs-ᵊn\ *n* [ISV *res-* (fr. L *resina* resin) + *orcin* (a phenol $C_7H_8O_2$)] (ca. 1868) : RESORCINOL

res·or·cin·ol \-ˌȯl, -ˌōl\ *n* (1881) : a crystalline phenol $C_6H_6O_2$ obtained from various resins or artificially and used esp. in making dyes, pharmaceuticals, and resins

re·sorp·tion \(ˈ)rē-ˈsȯrp-shən, -ˈzȯrp-\ *n* [L *resorptus,* pp. of *resorbēre*] (1818) : the action or process of resorbing something — **re·sorp·tive** \-tiv\ *adj*

[1]re·sort \ri-ˈzȯ(ə)rt\ *n* [ME, fr. MF, resource, recourse, fr. *resortir* to rebound, resort, fr. OF, fr. *re-* + *sortir* to escape, sally] (14c) **1** **a** : one who is looked to for help : REFUGE, RESOURCE **b** : RECOURSE **2** **a** : frequent, habitual, or general visiting ⟨a place of popular ~⟩ **b** : persons who frequent a place : THRONG **c** (1) : a frequently visited place : HAUNT (2) : a place providing recreation and entertainment esp. to vacationers ***syn*** see RESOURCE

[2]resort *vi* (15c) **1** : to go esp. frequently or habitually : REPAIR **2** : to have recourse ⟨~ to force⟩

re–sort \(ˈ)rē-ˈsȯ(ə)rt\ *vt* (1889) : to sort again

re·sort·er \ri-ˈzȯrt-ər\ *n* (1917) : a frequenter of resorts

re·sound \ri-ˈzau̇nd *also* -ˈsau̇nd\ *vb* [ME *resounen,* fr. MF *resoner,* fr. L *resonare,* fr. *re-* + *sonare* to sound; akin to L *sonus* sound — more at SOUND] *vi* (14c) **1** : to become filled with sound : REVERBERATE **2** **a** : to sound loudly **b** : to produce a sonorous or echoing sound **3** : to become renowned ~ *vt* **1** : to extol loudly or widely : CELEBRATE **2** : ECHO, REVERBERATE **3** : to sound or utter in full resonant tones

re·sound·ing *adj* (14c) **1** : producing or characterized by resonant sound : RESONATING **2** **a** : impressively sonorous **b** : EMPHATIC, UNEQUIVOCAL ⟨a ~ success⟩ — **re·sound·ing·ly** \-ˈzau̇n-diŋ-lē *also* -ˈsau̇n-\ *adv*

re·source \ˈrē-ˌsō(ə)rs, -ˌsȯ(ə)rs, -ˌzō(ə)rs, -ˌzȯ(ə)rs, ri-ˈ\ *n* [F *ressource,* fr. OF *ressourse* relief, resource, fr. *resourdre* to relieve, lit., to rise again, fr. L *resurgere* — more at RESURRECTION] (ca. 1611) **1** **a** : a source of supply or support : an available means — usu. used in pl. **b** : a natural source of wealth or revenue — usu. used in pl. **c** : computable wealth — usu. used in pl. **d** : a source of information or expertise **2** : something to which one has recourse in difficulty : EXPEDIENT **3** : a possibility of relief or recovery **4** : a means of spending one's leisure time **5** : an ability to meet and handle a situation : RESOURCEFULNESS

syn RESOURCE, RESORT, EXPEDIENT, SHIFT, MAKESHIFT, STOPGAP mean something one turns to in the absence of the usual means or source of supply. RESOURCE and RESORT apply to anything one falls back upon; EXPEDIENT may apply to any device or contrivance used when the usual one is not at hand or not possible; SHIFT implies a tentative or temporary imperfect expedient; MAKESHIFT implies an inferior expedient adopted because of urgent need or countenanced through indifference; STOPGAP applies to something used temporarily as an emergency measure.

re·source·ful \ri-ˈsōrs-fəl, -ˈsȯrs-, -ˈzōrs-, -ˈzȯrs-\ *adj* (1851) : able to meet situations : capable of devising ways and means — **re·source·ful·ly** \-fə-lē\ *adv* — **re·source·ful·ness** *n*

[1]re·spect \ri-ˈspekt\ *n* [ME, fr. L *respectus,* lit., act of looking back, fr. *respectus,* pp. of *respicere* to look back, regard, fr. *re-* + *specere* to look — more at SPY] (14c) **1** : a relation to or concern with something usu. specified : REFERENCE ⟨with ~ to your last letter⟩ **2** : an act of giving particular attention : CONSIDERATION **3** **a** : high or special regard : ESTEEM **b** : the quality or state of being esteemed **c** *pl* : expressions of respect or deference ⟨paid his ~*s*⟩ **4** : PARTICULAR, DETAIL ⟨a good plan in some ~*s*⟩ — **in respect of** : with regard to : CONCERNING

[2]respect *vt* (1560) **1** **a** : to consider worthy of high regard : ESTEEM **b** : to refrain from interfering with **2** : to have reference to : CONCERN ***syn*** see REGARD — **re·spect·er** *n*

[1]re·spect·able \ri-ˈspek-tə-bəl\ *adj* (1599) **1** : worthy of respect : ESTIMABLE **2** : decent or correct in character or behavior : PROPER **3** **a** : fair in size or quantity ⟨~ amount⟩ **b** : moderately good : TOLERABLE **4** : fit to be seen : PRESENTABLE ⟨~ clothes⟩ — **re·spect·abil·i·ty** \-ˌspek-tə-ˈbil-ət-ē\ *n* — **re·spect·able·ness** \-ˈspek-tə-bəl-nəs\ *n* — **re·spect·ably** \-blē\ *adv*

[2]respectable *n* (1814) : a respectable person

re·spect·ful \ri-ˈspekt-fəl\ *adj* (1687) : marked by or showing respect or deference — **re·spect·ful·ly** \-fə-lē\ *adv* — **re·spect·ful·ness** *n*

re·spect·ing *prep* (1611) **1** : in view of : CONSIDERING **2** : with regard to : CONCERNING

re·spec·tive \ri-ˈspek-tiv\ *adj* (1592) **1** *obs* : PARTIAL, DISCRIMINATIVE **2** : PARTICULAR, SEPARATE ⟨their ~ homes⟩ — **re·spec·tive·ness** *n*

re·spec·tive·ly *adv* (1626) **1** : in particular : SEPARATELY ⟨could not recognize the solutions as salty or sour, ~⟩ **2** : in the order given ⟨Mary and Anne were ~ 12 and 16 years old⟩

re·spell \(ˈ)rē-ˈspel\ *vt* (1806) : to spell again or in another way; *esp* : to spell out according to a phonetic system

re·spi·ra·ble \ˈres-p(ə-)rə-bəl, ri-ˈspī-rə-\ *adj* (1779) : fit for breathing; *also* : capable of being taken in by breathing ⟨~ particles of ash⟩

res·pi·ra·tion \ˌres-pə-ˈrā-shən\ *n* [ME *respiracioun,* fr. L *respiration-, respiratio,* fr. *respiratus,* pp. of *respirare*] (15c) **1** **a** : the placing of air or dissolved gases in intimate contact with the circulating medium of a multicellular organism (as by breathing) **b** : a single complete act of breathing **2** : the physical and chemical processes by which an organism supplies its cells and tissues with the oxygen needed for metabolism and relieves them of the carbon dioxide formed in energy-producing reactions **3** : any of various energy-yielding oxidative reactions in living matter — **re·spi·ra·to·ry** \ˈres-p(ə-)rə-ˌtōr-ē, ri-ˈspī-rə-, -ˌtȯr-\ *adj*

res·pi·ra·tor \ˈres-pə-ˌrāt-ər\ *n* (ca. 1836) **1** : a device worn over the mouth or nose for protecting the respiratory tract **2** : a device for maintaining artificial respiration

respiratory pigment *n* (1896) : any of various permanently or intermittently colored conjugated proteins that function in the transfer of oxygen in cellular respiration

respiratory quotient *n* (ca. 1890) : a ratio indicating the relation of the volume of carbon dioxide given off in respiration to that of the oxygen consumed

respiratory system *n* (ca. 1940) : a system of organs subserving the function of respiration and in air-breathing vertebrates consisting typically of the lungs and their nervous and circulatory supply and the channels by which these are continuous with the outer air

re·spire \ri-ˈspī(ə)r\ *vb* **re·spired; re·spir·ing** [ME *respiren,* fr. L *respirare,* fr. *re-* + *spirare* to blow, breathe — more at SPIRIT] *vi* (1592) **1** : BREATHE; *specif* : to inhale and exhale air successively **2** *of a cell or tissue* : to take up oxygen and produce carbon dioxide through oxidation ~ *vt* : BREATHE

res·pi·rom·e·ter \ˌres-pə-ˈräm-ət-ər\ *n* (ca. 1883) **:** an instrument for studying the character and extent of respiration — **res·pi·ro·met·ric** \-rō-ˈme-trik\ *adj* — **res·pi·rom·e·try** \-ˈräm-ə-trē\ *n*

¹**re·spite** \ˈres-pət *also* ri-ˈspīt, *Brit usu* ˈres-ˌpīt\ *n* [ME *respit*, fr. OF, fr. ML *respectus*, fr. L, act of looking back — more at RESPECT] (13c) **1 :** a period of temporary delay; *esp* **:** REPRIEVE 1b **2 :** an interval of rest or relief

²**respite** *vt* **re·spit·ed; re·spit·ing** (14c) **1 :** to grant a respite to **2 :** PUT OFF, DELAY

re·splen·dence \ri-ˈsplen-dən(t)s\ *n* (15c) **:** the quality or state of being resplendent **:** SPLENDOR

re·splen·den·cy \-dən-sē\ *n* (ca. 1611) **:** RESPLENDENCE

re·splen·dent \-dənt\ *adj* [L *resplendent-, resplendens*, prp. of *resplendēre* to shine back, fr. *re-* + *splendēre* to shine — more at SPLENDID] (15c) **:** shining brilliantly **:** characterized by a glowing splendor ⟨meadows ~ with wildflowers —*Outdoor World*⟩ ***syn*** see SPLENDID — **re·splen·dent·ly** *adv*

¹**re·spond** \ri-ˈspänd\ *n* (15c) **:** an engaged pillar supporting an arch or closing a colonnade or arcade

²**respond** *vb* [MF *respondre*, fr. L *respondēre* to promise in return, answer, fr. *re-* + *spondēre* to promise — more at SPOUSE] *vi* (1719) **1 :** to say something in return **:** make an answer **2 a :** to react in response **b :** to show favorable reaction ⟨~ to surgery⟩ **3 :** to be answerable ⟨~ in damages⟩ ~ *vt* **:** REPLY ***syn*** see ANSWER

¹**re·spon·dent** \ri-ˈspän-dənt\ *n* [L *respondent-, respondens*, prp. of *respondēre*] (1528) **1 :** one who responds: as **a :** one who maintains a thesis in reply **b** (1) **:** one who answers in various legal proceedings (as in equity cases) (2) **:** the prevailing party in the lower court **c :** a person who responds to a poll **2 :** a reflex that occurs in response to a specific external stimulus ⟨the knee jerk is a typical ~⟩ — compare OPERANT

²**respondent** *adj* (1726) **1 :** making response **:** RESPONSIVE; *esp* **:** being a respondent at law **2 :** relating to or being behavior or responses to a stimulus that are followed by a reward ⟨~ conditioning⟩ — compare OPERANT 3

re·spond·er \ri-ˈspän-dər\ *n* (1879) **:** one that responds; *esp* **:** the part of a transponder that transmits a radio signal

re·sponse \ri-ˈspän(t)s\ *n* [ME & L; ME *respounse*, fr. MF *respons*, fr. L *responsum* reply, fr. neut. of *responsus*, pp. of *respondēre*] (14c) **1 :** an act of responding **2 :** something constituting a reply or a reaction: as **a :** a verse, phrase, or word sung or said by the people or choir after or in reply to the officiant in a liturgical service **b :** the activity or inhibition of previous activity of an organism or any of its parts resulting from stimulation **c :** the output of a transducer or detecting device resulting from a given input

re·spon·si·bil·i·ty \ri-ˌspän(t)-sə-ˈbil-ət-ē\ *n, pl* **-ties** (1787) **1 :** the quality or state of being responsible: as **a :** moral, legal, or mental accountability **b :** RELIABILITY, TRUSTWORTHINESS **2 :** something for which one is responsible **:** BURDEN

re·spon·si·ble \ri-ˈspän(t)-sə-bəl\ *adj* (1643) **1 a :** liable to be called on to answer **b** (1) **:** liable to be called to account as the primary cause, motive, or agent ⟨a committee ~ for the job⟩ (2) **:** being the cause or explanation ⟨mechanical defects were ~ for the accident⟩ **c :** liable to legal review or in case of fault to penalties **2 a :** able to answer for one's conduct and obligations **:** TRUSTWORTHY **b :** able to choose for oneself between right and wrong **3 :** marked by or involving responsibility or accountability ⟨~ financial policies⟩ ⟨a ~ job⟩ **4 :** politically answerable; *esp* **:** required to submit to the electorate if defeated by the legislature — used esp. of the British cabinet — **re·spon·si·ble·ness** *n* — **re·spon·si·bly** \-blē\ *adv*

syn RESPONSIBLE, ANSWERABLE, ACCOUNTABLE, AMENABLE, LIABLE mean subject to being held to account. RESPONSIBLE implies holding a specific office, duty, or trust; ANSWERABLE suggests a relation between one having a moral or legal obligation and a court or other authority charged with oversight of its observance; ACCOUNTABLE suggests imminence of retribution for unfulfilled trust or violated obligation; AMENABLE and LIABLE stress the fact of subjection to review, censure, or control by a designated authority under certain conditions.

re·spon·sions \ri-ˈspän-chənz\ *n pl* [ME *responcioun* response, sum to be paid, fr. MF or ML; MF *responsion*, fr. ML *responsion-, responsio*, fr. L, answer, fr. *responsus*, pp.] (1813) **:** an examination required for matriculation as an undergraduate at Oxford

re·spon·sive \ri-ˈspän(t)-siv\ *adj* (1560) **1 :** giving response **:** constituting a response **:** ANSWERING ⟨a ~ glance⟩ ⟨~ aggression⟩ **2 :** quick to respond or react appropriately or sympathetically **:** SENSITIVE **3 :** using responses ⟨~ worship⟩ — **re·spon·sive·ly** *adv* — **re·spon·sive·ness** *n*

re·spon·so·ry \-ˈspän(t)s-(ə-)rē\ *n, pl* **-ries** [ME, fr. ML *responsorius*, fr. L *responsus*] (15c) **:** a set of versicles and responses sung or said after or during a lection

re·spon·sum \ri-ˈspän(t)-səm\ *n, pl* **-sa** \-sə\ [NL, fr. L, reply, formal opinion of a jurisconsult] (1896) **:** a written decision from a rabbinic authority in response to a submitted question or problem

res pu·bli·ca \(ˌ)rā-ˈspü-bli-ˌkä\ *n* [L — more at REPUBLIC] (ca. 1898) **1 :** COMMONWEALTH, STATE, REPUBLIC **2 :** COMMONWEAL

res·sen·ti·ment \rə-ˌsäⁿ-tē-ˈmäⁿ\ *n* [F, resentment, fr. *ressentir* to resent] (1941) **:** deep-seated resentment, frustration, and hostility accompanied by a sense of being powerless to express these feelings directly

¹**rest** \ˈrest\ *n* [ME, fr. OE; akin to OHG *rasta* rest, *ruowa* calm, Gk *erōē* respite, OE *aern* house] (bef. 12c) **1 :** REPOSE, SLEEP; *specif* **:** a bodily state characterized by minimal functional and metabolic activities — compare REM SLEEP **2 a :** freedom from activity or labor **b :** a state of motionlessness or inactivity **c :** the repose of death **3 :** a place for resting or lodging **4 :** peace of mind or spirit **5 a** (1) **:** a rhythmic silence in music (2) **:** a character representing such a silence **b :** a brief pause in reading **6 :** something used for support — **at rest 1 :** resting or reposing esp. in sleep or death **2 :** QUIESCENT, MOTIONLESS **3 :** free of anxieties

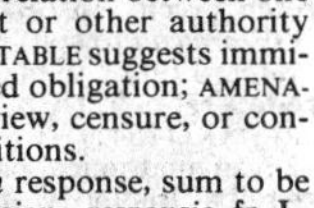

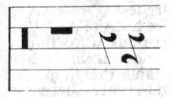

rest 5a(2)

²**rest** *vi* (bef. 12c) **1 a :** to get rest by lying down; *esp* **:** SLEEP **b :** to lie dead **2 :** to cease from action or motion **:** refrain from labor or exertion **3 :** to be free from anxiety or disturbance **4 :** to sit or lie fixed or supported ⟨a column ~s on its pedestal⟩ **5 a :** to remain confident **:** TRUST ⟨cannot ~ on that assumption⟩ **b :** to be based or founded ⟨the verdict ~*ed* on several sound precedents⟩ **6 :** to remain for action or accomplishment ⟨the answer ~s with him⟩ **7** *of farmland* **:** to remain idle or uncropped **8 :** to bring to an end voluntarily the introduction of evidence in a law case ~ *vt* **1 :** to give rest to **2 :** to set at rest **3 :** to place on or against a support **4 :** to cause to be firmly fixed ⟨~*ed* all hope in his son⟩ **5 :** to stop voluntarily from presenting evidence pertinent to (a case at law) — **rest·er** *n*

³**rest** *n* [ME *reste*, lit., stoppage, short for *areste*, fr. MF, fr. OF, fr. *arester* to arrest] (15c) **:** a projection or attachment on the side of the breastplate of medieval armor for supporting the butt of a lance

⁴**rest** *n* [ME, fr. MF *reste*, fr. *rester* to remain, fr. L *restare*, lit., to stand back, fr. *re-* + *stare* to stand — more at STAND] (1530) **:** something that remains over **:** REMAINDER ⟨ate the ~ of the candy⟩ — **for the rest :** with regard to remaining issues or needs

re·stage \(ˈ)rē-ˈstāj\ *vt* (1923) **:** to present again or anew on the stage

¹**re·start** \(ˈ)rē-ˈstärt\ *vt* (1845) **1 :** to start anew **2 :** to resume (as an activity) after interruption ~ *vi* **:** to resume operation — **re·start·able** \-ə-bəl\ *adj*

²**re·start** \ˈrē-ˌstärt, (ˈ)rē-ˈ\ *n* (1888) **:** the act or an instance of restarting

re·state \(ˈ)rē-ˈstāt\ *vt* (1713) **:** to state again or in another way

re·state·ment \-mənt\ *n* (1803) **1 :** something that is restated **2 :** the act of restating

res·tau·rant \ˈres-t(ə-)rənt, -tə-ˌränt, -ˌtränt, -tərnt\ *n* [F, fr. prp. of *restaurer* to restore, fr. L *restaurare*] (1827) **:** a public eating place

res·tau·ra·teur \ˌres-tə-rə-ˈtər\ *also* **res·tau·ran·teur** \-ˌrän-\ *n* [F *restaurateur*, fr. LL *restaurator* restorer, fr. L *restauratus*, pp. of *restaurare*] (1796) **:** the operator or proprietor of a restaurant

rest·ful \ˈrest-fəl\ *adj* (14c) **1 :** marked by, affording, or suggesting rest and repose ⟨a ~ color scheme⟩ **2 :** being at rest **:** QUIET — **rest·ful·ly** \-fə-lē\ *adv* — **rest·ful·ness** *n*

rest home *n* (1926) **:** an establishment that provides housing and general care for the aged or the convalescent

rest house *n* (1807) **:** a building used for shelter by travelers

rest·ing *adj* (14c) **1 :** being or characterized by dormancy **:** QUIESCENT ⟨a ~ spore⟩ ⟨bulbs in the ~ state⟩ **2 :** not undergoing or marked by division **:** VEGETATIVE ⟨a ~ nucleus⟩

res·ti·tute \ˈres-tə-ˌt(y)üt\ *vb* **-tut·ed; -tut·ing** [L *restitutus*, pp.] *vt* (1500) **1 :** to restore to a former state or position **2 :** GIVE BACK; *esp* **:** REFUND ~ *vi* **:** to undergo restitution

res·ti·tu·tion \ˌres-tə-ˈt(y)ü-shən\ *n* [ME, fr. MF, fr. L *restitution-, restitutio*, fr. *restitutus*, pp. of *restituere* to restore, fr. *re-* + *statuere* to set up — more at STATUTE] (14c) **1 :** an act of restoring or a condition of being restored: as **a :** a restoration of something to its rightful owner **b :** a making good of or giving an equivalent for some injury **2 :** a legal action serving to cause restoration of a previous state

res·tive \ˈres-tiv\ *adj* [ME *restyf*, fr. MF *restif*, fr. *rester* to stop behind, remain] (14c) **1 :** stubbornly resisting control **:** BALKY **2 :** marked by restlessness **:** FIDGETY ***syn*** see CONTRARY — **res·tive·ly** *adv* — **res·tive·ness** *n*

rest·less \ˈrest-ləs\ *adj* (bef. 12c) **1 :** lacking or denying rest **:** UNEASY ⟨a ~ night⟩ **2 :** continuously moving **:** UNQUIET ⟨the ~ sea⟩ **3 :** characterized by or manifesting unrest esp. of mind ⟨~ pacing⟩; *also* **:** CHANGEFUL, DISCONTENTED — **rest·less·ly** *adv* — **rest·less·ness** *n*

rest mass *n* (1914) **:** the mass of a body exclusive of additional mass acquired by the body when in motion according to the theory of relativity

re·stor·able \ri-ˈstōr-ə-bəl, -ˈstȯr-\ *adj* (ca. 1611) **:** fit for restoring or reclaiming

re·stor·al \-əl\ *n* (ca. 1611) **:** RESTORATION

res·to·ra·tion \ˌres-tə-ˈrā-shən\ *n* (1660) **1 :** an act of restoring or the condition of being restored: as **a :** a bringing back to a former position or condition **:** REINSTATEMENT ⟨the ~ of peace⟩ **b :** RESTITUTION **c :** a restoring to an unimpaired or improved condition ⟨the ~ of a painting⟩ **d :** the replacing of missing teeth or crowns **2 :** something that is restored; *esp* **:** a representation or reconstruction of the original form (as of a fossil or a building) **3** *cap* **a :** the reestablishing of the monarchy in England in 1660 under Charles II **b :** the period in English history usu. held to coincide with the reign of Charles II but sometimes to extend through the reign of James II

¹**re·stor·ative** \ri-ˈstōr-ət-iv, -ˈstȯr-\ *adj* (15c) **:** of or relating to restoration; *esp* **:** having power to restore

²**restorative** *n* (15c) **:** something that serves to restore to consciousness, vigor, or health

re·store \ri-ˈstō(ə)r, -ˈstȯ(ə)r\ *vt* **re·stored; re·stor·ing** [ME *restoren*, fr. OF *restorer*, fr. L *restaurare* to renew, rebuild, alter. of *instaurare* to renew — more at STORE] (13c) **1 :** GIVE BACK, RETURN **2 :** to put or bring back into existence or use **3 :** to bring back to or put back into a former or original state **:** RENEW **4 :** to put again in possession of something ***syn*** see RENEW — **re·stor·er** *n*

re·strain \ri-ˈstrān\ *vt* [ME *restraynen*, fr. MF *restraindre*, fr. L *restringere* to restrain, restrict, fr. *re-* + *stringere* to bind tight — more at STRAIN] (14c) **1 a :** to prevent from doing, exhibiting, or expressing something ⟨~*ed* the boy from jumping⟩ **b :** to limit, restrict, or keep under control ⟨try to ~ your anger⟩ **2 :** to moderate or limit the force, effect, development, or full exercise of ⟨~ trade⟩ **3 :** to deprive of liberty; *esp* **:** to place under arrest or restraint — **re·strain·able** \-ˈstrā-nə-bəl\ *adj* — **re·strain·er** *n*

syn RESTRAIN, CHECK, CURB, BRIDLE mean to hold back from or control in doing something. RESTRAIN suggests holding back by force or persuasion from acting or from going to extremes; CHECK implies restraining or impeding a progress, activity, or impetus; CURB suggests an abrupt or drastic checking; BRIDLE implies keeping under control by subduing or holding in.

re·strained \ri-ˈstrānd\ *adj* (1580) **:** marked by restraint **:** being without excess or extravagance — **re·strain·ed·ly** \-ˈstrā-nəd-lē\ *adv*

\ə\ abut \ᵊ\ kitten, F table \ər\ further \a\ ash \ā\ ace \ä\ cot, cart \au̇\ out \ch\ chin \e\ bet \ē\ easy \g\ go \i\ hit \ī\ ice \j\ job \ŋ\ sing \ō\ go \ȯ\ law \ȯi\ boy \th\ thin \t͟h\ the \ü\ loot \u̇\ foot \y\ yet \zh\ vision \à, ḵ, ⁿ, œ, œ̄, ue, ue̅, ʸ\ *see* Guide to Pronunciation

restraining order *n* (ca. 1876) : a preliminary legal order sometimes issued to keep a situation unchanged pending decision upon an application for an injunction
re·straint \ri-ˈstrānt\ *n* [ME, fr. MF *restrainte,* fr. *restraindre*] (15c) **1 a :** an act of restraining : the state of being restrained **b** (1) : a means of restraining : a restraining force or influence (2) : a device that restricts movement ⟨a ~ for children riding in cars⟩ **2 :** a control over the expression of one's emotions or thoughts
re·strict \ri-ˈstrikt\ *vt* [L *restrictus,* pp. of *restringere*] (1535) **1 :** to confine within bounds : RESTRAIN **2 :** to place under restrictions as to use or distribution ***syn*** see LIMIT
re·strict·ed *adj* (ca. 1828) : subject or subjected to restriction: as **a** : not general : LIMITED ⟨the decision had a ~ effect⟩ **b :** available to the use of particular groups or specif. excluding others ⟨a ~ neighborhood⟩ **c :** not intended for general circulation or release ⟨a ~ document⟩ — **re·strict·ed·ly** *adv*
re·stric·tion \ri-ˈstrik-shən\ *n* [ME *restriccioun,* fr. LL *restriction-, restrictio,* fr. *restrictus,* pp.] (15c) **1 :** something that restricts: as **a :** a regulation that restricts or restrains ⟨~s for hunters⟩ **b :** a limitation on the use or enjoyment of property or a facility **2 :** an act of restricting : the condition of being restricted
restriction enzyme *n* (1965) : any of various enzymes that break double-stranded DNA into fragments at specific sites in the interior of the molecule — called also *restriction endonuclease*
re·stric·tion·ism \-shə-ˌniz-əm\ *n* (1937) : a policy or philosophy favoring restriction (as of trade) — **re·stric·tion·ist** \-sh(ə-)nəst\ *adj or n*
re·stric·tive \ri-ˈstrik-tiv\ *adj* (1579) **1 a :** of or relating to restriction **b :** serving or tending to restrict ⟨~ regulations⟩ **2 :** limiting the reference of a modified word or phrase **3 :** prohibiting further negotiation — **restrictive** *n* — **re·stric·tive·ly** *adv* — **re·stric·tive·ness** *n*
restrictive clause *n* (ca. 1904) : a descriptive clause that is essential to the definiteness of the word it modifies (as "that you ordered" in "the book that you ordered is out of print")
re·strike \(ˈ)rē-ˈstrīk, ˈrē-ˌ\ *n* (ca. 1899) : a coin or medal struck from an original die at some time after the original issue
rest room *n* (1899) : a room or suite of rooms providing toilets and lavatories
re·struc·ture \(ˈ)rē-ˈstrək-chər\ *vt* (1942) : to change the makeup, organization, or pattern of ~ *vi* : to restructure something
re·study \(ˈ)rē-ˈstəd-ē\ *vt* (1811) : to study again or anew : make a new appraisal or evaluation of — **restudy** *n*
¹re·sult \ri-ˈzəlt\ *vi* [ME *resulten,* fr. ML *resultare,* fr. L, to rebound, fr. *re-* + *saltare* to leap — more at SALTATION] (15c) **1 a :** to proceed or arise as a consequence, effect, or conclusion ⟨death ~ed from the disease⟩ **b :** to have an issue or result ⟨the disease ~ed in death⟩ **2 :** REVERT 2
²result *n* (1647) **1 :** something that results as a consequence, issue, or conclusion; *also* : beneficial or tangible effect : FRUIT **2 :** something obtained by calculation or investigation ⟨showed us the ~ of the calculations⟩ ***syn*** see EFFECT — **re·sult·ful** \-fəl\ *adj* — **re·sult·less** \-ləs\ *adj*
¹re·sul·tant \ri-ˈzəlt-ᵊnt\ *adj* (1639) : derived from or resulting from something else — **re·sul·tant·ly** *adv*
²resultant *n* (1815) : something that results : OUTCOME; *specif* : the single vector that is the sum of a given set of vectors
re·sume \ri-ˈzüm\ *vb* **re·sumed; re·sum·ing** [ME *resumen,* fr. MF or L; MF *resumer,* fr. L *resumere,* fr. *re-* + *sumere* to take up, take — more at CONSUME] *vt* (15c) **1 :** to assume or take again : REOCCUPY ⟨*resumed* his seat by the fire —Thomas Hardy⟩ **2 :** to return to or begin again after interruption ⟨*resumed* her work⟩ **3 :** to take back to oneself **4 :** to pick up again **5 :** REITERATE, SUMMARIZE ~ *vi* : to begin again something interrupted
ré·su·mé *or* **re·su·me** *or* **re·su·mé** \ˈrez-ə-ˌmā, ˌrez-ə-ˈ *also* ˈrāz- *or* ˌrāz-\ *n* [F *résumé,* fr. pp. of *résumer* to resume, summarize, fr. MF *resumer*] (1804) : SUMMARY; *specif* : a short account of one's career and qualifications prepared typically by an applicant for a position
re·sump·tion \ri-ˈzəm(p)-shən\ *n* [ME, fr. MF or LL; MF *resomption,* fr. LL *resumption-, resumptio,* fr. L *resumptus,* pp. of *resumere*] (15c) **1 :** an act or instance of resuming : RECOMMENCEMENT **2 :** a return to payment in specie
re·su·pi·nate \ri-ˈsü-pə-ˌnāt\ *adj* [L *resupinatus,* pp. of *resupinare* to bend back to a supine position, fr. *re-* + *supinus* supine] (1776) **1 :** inverted in position **2 :** having or being a fruiting body lying flat on the substrate with the hymenium at the periphery or over the whole surface ⟨~ fungi⟩ ⟨~ sporophores⟩
re·sup·ply \ˌrē-sə-ˈplī\ *vt* (1636) : to supply again : provide anew with supplies — **resupply** *n*
re·sur·face \(ˈ)rē-ˈsər-fəs\ *vt* (1886) : to provide with a new or fresh surface ~ *vi* : to come again to the surface (as of the water); *broadly* : to appear or show up again
re·surge \ri-ˈsərj\ *vi* **re·surged; re·surg·ing** [L *resurgere*] (1606) : to undergo a resurgence
re·sur·gence \ri-ˈsər-jən(t)s\ *n* (1863) : a rising again into life, activity, or prominence : RENASCENCE
re·sur·gent \-jənt\ *adj* [L *resurgent-, resurgens,* prp. of *resurgere*] (1808) : undergoing or tending to produce resurgence
res·ur·rect \ˌrez-ə-ˈrekt\ *vt* [back-formation fr. *resurrection*] (1772) **1** : to raise from the dead **2 :** to bring to view, attention, or use again
res·ur·rec·tion \ˌrez-ə-ˈrek-shən\ *n* [ME, fr. LL *resurrection-, resurrectio* act of rising from the dead, fr. *resurrectus,* pp. of *resurgere* to rise from the dead, fr. L, to rise again, fr. *re-* + *surgere* to rise — more at SURGE] (13c) **1 a** *cap* : the rising of Christ from the dead **b** *often cap* : the rising again to life of all the human dead before the final judgment **c** : the state of one risen from the dead **2 :** RESURGENCE, REVIVAL **3** *Christian Science* : a spiritualization of thought : material belief that yields to spiritual understanding — **res·ur·rec·tion·al** \-shnəl, -shən-ᵊl\ *adj*
res·ur·rec·tion·ist \-sh(ə-)nəst\ *n* (1776) **1 :** BODY SNATCHER **2 :** one who resurrects
re·sus·ci·tate \ri-ˈsəs-ə-ˌtāt\ *vb* **-tat·ed; -tat·ing** [L *resuscitatus,* pp. of *resuscitare,* lit., to stir up again, fr. *re-* + *suscitare* to stir up, fr. *sub-, sus-* up + *citare* to put in motion, stir — more at SUB-, CITE] *vt* (1532) : to revive from apparent death or from unconsciousness; *also* : REVITALIZE ~ *vi* : COME TO, REVIVE — **re·sus·ci·ta·tion** \ri-ˌsəs-ə-ˈtā-shən, ˌrē-\ *n* — **re·sus·ci·ta·tive** \ri-ˈsəs-ə-ˌtāt-iv\ *adj*
re·sus·ci·ta·tor \ri-ˈsəs-ə-ˌtāt-ər\ *n* (ca. 1847) : one that resuscitates; *specif* : an apparatus used to restore the respiration of a partially asphyxiated person
ret \ˈret\ *vb* **ret·ted; ret·ting** [ME *reten,* fr. MD] *vt* (15c) : to soak (as flax) to loosen the fiber from the woody tissue ~ *vi* : to become retted
re·ta·ble \ˈrē-ˌtā-bəl, ˈret-ə-bəl\ *n* [F, fr. Sp *retablo,* deriv. of L *retro-* retro- + *tabula* board, tablet] (ca. 1823) : a raised shelf above an altar for the altar cross, the altar lights, and flowers
¹re·tail \ˈrē-ˌtāl, *esp for 2 also* ri-ˈtā(ə)l\ *vb* [ME *retailen,* fr. MF *retaillier* to cut back, divide into pieces, fr. OF, fr. *re-* + *taillier* to cut — more at TAILOR] *vt* (15c) **1 :** to sell in small quantities directly to the ultimate consumer **2 :** TELL, RETELL ~ *vi* : to sell at retail — **re·tail·er** *n*
²re·tail \ˈrē-ˌtāl\ *n* (15c) : the sale of commodities or goods in small quantities to ultimate consumers — **at retail 1 :** at a retailer's price **2 :** ⁴RETAIL
³re·tail \ˈrē-ˌtāl\ *adj* (1601) : of, relating to, or engaged in the sale of commodities at retail ⟨~ trade⟩
⁴re·tail \ˈrē-ˌtāl\ *adv* (1784) : in small quantities : from a retailer
re·tail·ing \ˈrē-ˌtā-liŋ\ *n* (14c) : the activities involved in the selling of goods to ultimate consumers for personal or household consumption
re·tain \ri-ˈtān\ *vt* [ME *reteinen, retainen,* fr. MF *retenir,* fr. L *retinēre* to hold back, keep, restrain, fr. *re-* + *tenēre* to hold — more at THIN] (15c) **1 a :** to keep in possession or use **b :** to keep in one's pay or service; *specif* : to employ by paying a retainer **c :** to keep in mind or memory : REMEMBER **2 :** to hold secure or intact ⟨lead ~s heat⟩ ***syn*** see KEEP
retained object *n* (ca. 1904) : an object in a passive construction ⟨*me* in *a book was given me* and *book* in *I was given a book* are *retained objects*⟩
¹re·tain·er \ri-ˈtā-nər\ *n* (1540) **1 :** one that retains **2 a :** a person attached or owing service to a household; *esp* : SERVANT **b :** EMPLOYEE **3 :** any of various devices used for holding something
²retainer *n* [ME *reteiner* act of withholding, fr. *reteinen* + AF *-er* (as in *weyver* waiver)] (1778) **1 :** the act of a client by which he engages the services of a lawyer, counselor, or adviser **2 :** a fee paid to a lawyer or professional adviser for advice or services or for a claim on his services in case of need
¹re·take \(ˈ)rē-ˈtāk\ *vt* **-took** \-ˈtu̇k\; **-tak·en** \-ˈtā-kən\; **-tak·ing** (15c) **1** : to take or receive again **2 :** RECAPTURE **3 :** to photograph again
²re·take \ˈrē-ˌtāk\ *n* (1916) : a second photographing or recording; *also* : an instance of this
re·tal·i·ate \ri-ˈtal-ē-ˌāt\ *vb* **-at·ed; -at·ing** [LL *retaliatus,* pp. of *retaliare,* fr. L *re-* + *talio* legal retaliation] *vt* (1611) : to repay (as an injury) in kind ~ *vi* : to return like for like; *esp* : to get revenge ***syn*** see RECIPROCATE — **re·tal·i·a·tion** \ri-ˌtal-ē-ˈā-shən, ˌrē-\ *n* — **re·tal·i·a·tive** \ri-ˈtal-ē-ˌāt-iv\ *adj* — **re·tal·ia·to·ry** \-ˈtal-yə-ˌtōr-ē, -ˈtal-ē-ə-, -ˌtȯr-\ *adj*
¹re·tard \ri-ˈtärd\ *vb* [ME *retarden,* fr. MF or L; MF *retarder,* fr. L *retardare,* fr. *re-* + *tardus* slow] *vt* (15c) **1 :** to slow up esp. by preventing or hindering advance or accomplishment : IMPEDE **2 :** to delay academic progress by failure to promote ~ *vi* : to undergo retardation ***syn*** see DELAY — **re·tard·er** *n*
²re·tard *n* (1788) **1** \ri-ˈtärd\ : a holding back or slowing down : RETARDATION **2** \ˈrē-ˌtärd\ : RETARDATE
re·tar·dant \ri-ˈtärd-ᵊnt\ *adj* (1642) : serving or tending to retard ⟨flame-*retardant* fabrics⟩ — **retardant** *n*
re·tar·date \-ˈtärd-ˌāt, -ət\ *n* (ca. 1915) : a mentally retarded person
re·tar·da·tion \ˌrē-ˌtär-ˈdā-shən, ri-\ *n* (15c) **1 :** an act or instance of retarding **2 :** the extent to which something is retarded **3 :** a musical suspension; *specif* : one that resolves upward **4 a :** an abnormal slowness of thought or action; *also* : less than normal intellectual competence usu. characterized by an IQ of less than 70 **b :** slowness in development or progress
re·tard·ed \ri-ˈtärd-əd\ *adj* (1895) : slow or limited in intellectual or emotional development or academic progress
retch \ˈrech, *esp Brit* ˈrēch\ *vb* [(assumed) ME *rechen* to spit, retch, fr. OE *hrǣcan* to spit, hawk; akin to L *crepare* to rattle — more at RAVEN] *vi* (ca. 1798) : to make an effort to vomit ~ *vt* : VOMIT — **retch** *n*
re·te \ˈrēt-ē, ˈrāt-\ *n, pl* **re·tia** \ˈrēt-ē-ə, ˈrāt-\ [NL, fr. L, net — more at RETINA] (1541) **1 :** a network esp. of blood vessels or nerves : PLEXUS **2 :** an anatomical part resembling or including a network
re·tell \(ˈ)rē-ˈtel\ *vt* **-told** \-ˈtōld\; **-tell·ing** (1593) **1 :** to tell again or in another form **2 :** to count again
re·tell·ing *n* (1883) : a new version of a story ⟨a ~ of a Greek legend⟩
re·tene \ˈrē-ˌtēn, ˈret-ˌēn\ *n* [Gk *rhētinē* resin] (1867) : a crystalline hydrocarbon $C_{18}H_{18}$ isolated esp. from pine tar and fossil resins or prepared artificially
re·ten·tion \ri-ˈten-chən\ *n* [ME *retencioun,* fr. L *retention-, retentio,* fr. *retentus,* pp. of *retinēre* to retain — more at RETAIN] (15c) **1 a :** the act of retaining : the state of being retained **b :** abnormal retaining of a fluid or secretion in a body cavity **2 a :** power of retaining : RETENTIVENESS **b :** an ability to retain things in mind; *specif* : a preservation of the aftereffects of experience and learning that makes recall or recognition possible **3 :** something retained
re·ten·tive \-ˈtent-iv\ *adj* [ME *retentif,* fr. MF & ML; MF, fr. ML *retentivus,* fr. L *retentus,* pp.] (14c) : having the power, property, or capacity of retaining ⟨soils ~ of moisture⟩; *esp* : retaining knowledge easily — **re·ten·tive·ly** *adv* — **re·ten·tive·ness** *n*
re·ten·tiv·i·ty \ˌrē-ˌten-ˈtiv-ət-ē, ri-\ *n* (1881) : the power of retaining; *specif* : the capacity for retaining magnetism after the action of the magnetizing force has ceased
¹re·test \(ˈ)rē-ˈtest\ *vt* (1863) : to test again
²re·test \ˈrē-ˌtest, (ˈ)rē-ˈ\ *n* (1887) : a repeated test
re·think \(ˈ)rē-ˈthiŋk\ *vb* **-thought** \-ˈthȯt\; **-think·ing** *vt* (1700) : to think about again : RECONSIDER ~ *vi* : to engage in reconsideration — **rethink** \ˈrē-ˌthiŋk, -ˈthiŋk\ *n* — **re·think·er** *n*
ret·i·cence \ˈret-ə-sən(t)s\ *n* (1603) **1 :** the quality or state of being reticent : RESERVE, RESTRAINT **2 :** an instance of being reticent **3** : RELUCTANCE
ret·i·cen·cy \-sən-sē\ *n, pl* **-cies** (1617) : RETICENCE
ret·i·cent \-sənt\ *adj* [L *reticent-, reticens,* prp. of *reticēre* to keep silent, fr. *re-* + *tacēre* to be silent — more at TACIT] (1834) **1 :** inclined to be silent or uncommunicative in speech : RESERVED **2 :** restrained in expression, presentation, or appearance ⟨the room has an aspect of ~ dignity —A. N. Whitehead⟩ **3 :** RELUCTANT ***syn*** see SILENT — **ret·i·cent·ly** *adv*

ret·i·cle \'ret-i-kəl\ *n* [L *reticulum* network] (ca. 1731) **:** a system of lines, dots, cross hairs, or wires in the focus of the eyepiece of an optical instrument

re·tic·u·lar \ri-'tik-yə-lər\ *adj* (1597) **1 :** RETICULATE; *esp* **:** of, relating to, or forming a reticulum **2 :** INTRICATE

reticular formation *n* (ca. 1890) **:** a mass of nerve cells and fibers situated primarily in the brain stem and functioning upon stimulation esp. in arousal of the organism

1re·tic·u·late \-lət, -,lāt\ *adj* [L *reticulatus,* fr. *reticulum*] (1658) **1 :** resembling a net; *esp* **:** having veins, fibers, or lines crossing ⟨a ~ leaf⟩ **2 :** of, relating to, or constituting evolutionary change dependent on genetic recombination involving diverse interbreeding populations — **re·tic·u·late·ly** *adv*

2re·tic·u·late \-,lāt\ *vb* **-lat·ed; -lat·ing** [back-formation fr. *reticulated,* adj. (reticulate)] *vt* (1787) **1 :** to divide, mark, or construct so as to form a network **2 :** to distribute (as electricity, water, or goods) by a network ~ *vi* **:** to become reticulated

re·tic·u·la·tion \ri-,tik-yə-'lā-shən\ *n* (1671) **:** a reticulated formation **:** NETWORK; *also* **:** something reticulated

ret·i·cule \'ret-i-,kyü(ə)l\ *n* [F *réticule,* fr. L *reticulum* network, network bag, fr. dim. of *rete* net — more at RETINA] (1727) **1 :** RETICLE **2 :** a woman's drawstring bag used esp. as a carryall

re·tic·u·lo·cyte \ri-'tik-yə-lō-,sīt\ *n* [NL *reticulum* + ISV *-cyte*] (1922) **:** a young red blood cell that appears esp. during active regeneration of lost blood and exhibits a fine reticulum when stained with basic stains

re·tic·u·lo·en·do·the·li·al \ri-'tik-yə-lō-,en-də-'thē-lē-əl\ *adj* [NL *reticulum* + *endothelium*] (ca. 1923) **:** of, relating to, or being the reticuloendothelial system

reticuloendothelial system *n* (ca. 1923) **:** a diffuse system of cells arising from mesenchyme and comprising all the phagocytic cells of the body except the circulating leukocytes

re·tic·u·lum \ri-'tik-yə-ləm\ *n* [NL, fr. L, network] (ca. 1658) **1 :** the second compartment of the stomach of a ruminant in which folds of the mucous membrane form hexagonal cells **2 :** a reticular formation **:** NETWORK; *esp* **:** interstitial tissue composed of reticulum cells

reticulum cell *n* (1912) **:** one of the branched anastomosing reticuloendothelial cells that form an intricate interstitial network ramifying through other tissues and organs

retin- *or* **retino-** *comb form* [*retina*] **:** retina ⟨*retin*itis⟩ ⟨*retino*scopy⟩

ret·i·na \'ret-ᵊn-ə, 'ret-nə\ *n, pl* **retinas** *or* **ret·i·nae** \-ᵊn-,ē, -,ī\ [ME *rethina,* fr. ML *retina,* prob. fr. L *rete* net; akin to Lith *rẽtis* sieve] (15c) **:** the sensory membrane that lines the eye, receives the image formed by the lens, is the immediate instrument of vision, and is connected with the brain by the optic nerve — see EYE illustration

ret·i·nac·u·lum \,ret-ᵊn-'ak-yə-ləm\ *n, pl* **-la** \-lə\ [NL, fr. L, halter, cable, fr. *retinēre* to hold back — more at RETAIN] (ca. 1825) **:** a small structure on the forewings of many lepidopterous insects (as a butterfly) that catches and holds the frenulum

1ret·i·nal \'ret-ᵊn-əl, 'ret-nəl\ *adj* (1838) **:** of, relating to, involving, or being a retina

2ret·i·nal \'ret-ᵊn-,al, -,ȯl\ *n* [*retin-* + *3-al*] (ca. 1960) **:** a yellowish to orange aldehyde $C_{20}H_{28}O$ derived from vitamin A that in combination with proteins forms the visual pigments of the retinal rods and cones

ret·i·nene \'ret-ᵊn-,ēn\ *n* (1934) **:** RETINAL

ret·i·ni·tis \,ret-ᵊn-'īt-əs\ *n* [NL] (1861) **:** inflammation of the retina

retinitis pig·men·to·sa \-,pig-mən-'tō-sə, -(,)men-, -zə\ *n* [NL, pigmented retinitis] (1861) **:** any of several hereditary progressive degenerative diseases of the eye marked by night blindness in the early stages, atrophy and pigment changes in the retina, constriction of the visual field, and eventual blindness

ret·i·no·blas·to·ma \,ret-ᵊn-ō-,blas-'tō-mə\ *n* [*retin-* + *blast-* + *-oma*] (1924) **:** a hereditary malignant tumor of the retina derived from retinal germ cells

ret·i·nol \'ret-ᵊn-,ȯl, -,ōl\ *n* [*retin-* + *1-ol;* fr. its being the source of retinal] (ca. 1838) **:** the chief and typical vitamin A

ret·i·nop·a·thy \,ret-ᵊn-'äp-ə-thē\ *n* (1932) **:** any of various noninflammatory disorders of the retina including some that are major causes of blindness

ret·i·nos·co·py \,ret-ᵊn-'äs-kə-pē\ *n* (1884) **:** observation of the retina of the eye esp. to determine the state of refraction

ret·i·no·tec·tal \,ret-ᵊn-ō-'tek-təl\ *adj* [*retin-* + *tect*um + *-al*] (1951) **:** of, relating to, or being the nerve fibers connecting the retina and the tectum of the midbrain ⟨~ pathways⟩

ret·i·nue \'ret-ᵊn-,(y)ü\ *n* [ME *retenue,* fr. MF, fr. fem. of *retenu,* pp. of *retenir* to retain] (14c) **:** a group of retainers or attendants

re·tin·u·la \re-'tin-yə-lə\ *n, pl* **-lae** \-,lē, -,lī\ *also* **-las** [NL, dim. of ML *retina*] (1878) **:** the neural receptor of a single facet of an arthropod compound eye — **re·tin·u·lar** \-lər\ *adj*

re·tir·ant \ri-'tī-rənt\ *n* (1948) **:** RETIREE

re·tire \ri-'tī(ə)r\ *vb* **re·tired; re·tir·ing** [MF *retirer,* fr. *re-* + *tirer* to draw] *vi* (1533) **1 :** to withdraw from action or danger **:** RETREAT **2 :** to withdraw esp. for privacy **3 :** to fall back **:** RECEDE **4 :** to withdraw from one's position or occupation **:** conclude one's working or professional career **5 :** to go to bed ~ *vt* **1 :** WITHDRAW: as **a :** to march (a military force) away from the enemy **b :** to withdraw from circulation or from the market **:** RECALL **c :** to withdraw from usual use or service **2 :** to cause to retire from one's position or occupation **3 a :** to put out (a batter or batsman) in baseball or cricket **b :** to cause (a side) to end a turn at bat in baseball **4 :** to win permanent possession of (as a trophy)

re·tired \ri-'tī(ə)rd\ *adj* (1590) **1 :** SECLUDED ⟨~ village⟩ **2 :** withdrawn from one's position or occupation **:** having concluded one's working or professional career **3 :** received by or due to one in retirement — **re·tired·ly** \-'tī-rəd-lē, -'tī(ə)rd-\ *adv* — **re·tired·ness** \-'tī(ə)rd-nəs\ *n*

re·tir·ee \ri-,tī-'rē\ *n* (1945) **:** a person who has retired from a working or professional career

1re·tire·ment \ri-'tī(ə)r-mənt\ *n* (1596) **1 a :** an act of retiring **:** the state of being retired **b :** withdrawal from one's position or occupation or from active working life **c :** the age at which one normally retires ⟨reached ~ but was asked to work another year⟩ **2 :** a place of seclusion or privacy

2retirement *adj* (1919) **:** of, relating to, or designed for retired persons

re·tir·ing \ri-'tī(ə)r-iŋ\ *adj* (1766) **:** RESERVED, SHY — **re·tir·ing·ly** \-iŋ-lē\ *adv* — **re·tir·ing·ness** *n*

re·tool \(')rē-'tül\ *vt* (1927) **1 :** to reequip with tools **2 :** REORGANIZE

1re·tort \ri-'tȯ(ə)rt\ *vb* [L *retortus,* pp. of *retorquēre,* lit., to twist back, hurl back, fr. *re-* + *torquēre* to twist — more at TORTURE] *vt* (1557) **1 :** to pay or hurl back **:** RETURN ⟨~ an insult⟩ **2 a :** to make a reply to **b :** to say in reply **3 :** to answer (as an argument) by a counter argument ~ *vi* **1 :** to answer back usu. sharply **2 :** to return an argument or charge **3 :** RETALIATE ***syn*** see ANSWER

2retort *n* (1600) **:** a quick, witty, or cutting reply; *esp* **:** one that turns the first speaker's words against him

3re·tort \ri-'tȯ(ə)rt, 'rē-,\ *n* [MF *retorte,* fr. ML *retorta,* fr. L, fem. of *retortus,* pp.; fr. its shape] (1605) **:** a vessel or chamber in which substances are distilled or decomposed by heat

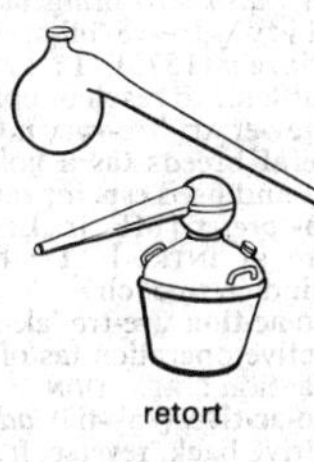

retort

4re·tort \ri-'tȯ(ə)rt, 'rē-,\ *vt* (1850) **:** to treat (as oil shale) by heating in a retort

re·tor·tion \ri-'tȯr-shən\ *n* (1609) **:** an act of retorting

1re·touch \(')rē-'təch\ *vb* [F *retoucher,* fr. MF, fr. *re-* + *toucher* to touch] *vt* (1685) **1 :** to rework in order to improve **:** TOUCH UP **2 :** to alter (as a photographic negative) to produce a more desirable appearance **3 :** to color (new growth of hair) to match previously dyed, tinted, or bleached hair ~ *vi* **:** to make or give retouches — **re·touch·er** *n*

2re·touch \'rē-,təch, (')rē-'\ *n* (1703) **:** the act, process, or an instance of retouching; *esp* **:** the retouching of a new growth of hair

re·trace \(')rē-'trās\ *vt* [F *retracer,* fr. MF *retracier,* fr. *re-* + *tracier* to trace] (1697) **:** to trace again or back

re·tract \ri-'trakt\ *vb* [ME *retracten,* fr. L *retractus,* pp. of *retrahere* — more at RETREAT] *vt* (15c) **1 :** to draw back or in ⟨cats ~ their claws⟩ **2 a :** TAKE BACK, WITHDRAW ⟨~ a confession⟩ **b :** DISAVOW ~ *vi* **1 :** to draw back **2 :** to recant or disavow something ***syn*** see ABJURE, RECEDE — **re·tract·able** \-'trak-tə-bəl\ *adj*

re·trac·tile \ri-'trak-tᵊl, -,tīl\ *adj* (1777) **:** capable of being drawn back or in ⟨~ claws⟩ — **re·trac·til·i·ty** \,rē-,trak-'til-ət-ē, ri-\ *n*

re·trac·tion \ri-'trak-shən\ *n* [ME *retraccioun,* fr. MF *retraction,* fr. L *retraction-, retractio* hesitation, refusal, fr. *retractus,* pp.] (14c) **1 :** an act of recanting; *specif* **:** a statement made by one retracting **2 :** an act of retracting **:** the state of being retracted **3 :** the ability to retract

re·trac·tor \ri-'trak-tər\ *n* (1837) **:** one that retracts: as **a :** a surgical instrument for holding open the edges of a wound **b :** a muscle that draws in an organ or part

re·train \(')rē-'trān\ *vt* (1918) **:** to train again or anew ~ *vi* **:** to become trained again — **re·train·able** \-'trā-nə-bəl\ *adj*

re·train·ee \(,)rē-,trā-'nē\ *n* (1942) **:** a person who is being retrained

re·tral \'rē-trəl, 're-\ *adj* [L *retro* back — more at RETRO-] (1875) **1 :** situated at or toward the back **:** POSTERIOR **2 :** BACKWARD, RETROGRADE — **re·tral·ly** \-trə-lē\ *adv*

re·trans·late \,rē-tran(t)s-'lāt, -tranz-\ *vt* (1860) **:** to translate (a translation) into another language; *also* **:** to give a new form to ~ *vi* **:** to retranslate something — **re·trans·la·tion** \-'lā-shən\ *n*

1re·tread \(')rē-'tred\ *vt* **re·tread·ed; re·tread·ing** (1907) **1 :** to bond or vulcanize a new tread to the prepared surface of (a worn tire) **2 :** to make over as if new ⟨~ an old plot⟩

2re·tread \'rē-,tred\ *n* (1914) **1 :** a new tread on a tire **2 :** a retreaded tire **3 :** something made or done again esp. in slightly revised form **:** REMAKE **4 a :** one (as a retired person) who is retrained for work **b :** one (as an athlete) who has previously held the same or a similar position

re–tread \(')rē-'tred\ *vt* **-trod** \-'träd\; **-trod·den** \-'träd-ᵊn\ *or* **-trod; -tread·ing** (1598) **:** to tread again

1re·treat \ri-'trēt\ *n* [ME *retret,* fr. MF *retrait,* fr. pp. of *retraire* to withdraw, fr. L *retrahere,* lit., to draw back, fr. *re-* + *trahere* to draw — more at DRAW] (14c) **1 a** (1) **:** an act or process of withdrawing esp. from what is difficult, dangerous, or disagreeable (2) **:** the process of receding from a position or state attained ⟨the ~ of a glacier⟩ ⟨the slow ~ of an epidemic⟩ **b** (1) **:** the usu. forced withdrawal of troops from an enemy or from an advanced position (2) **:** a signal for retreating **c** (1) **:** a signal given by bugle at the beginning of a military flag-lowering ceremony (2) **:** a military flag-lowering ceremony **2 :** a place of privacy or safety **:** REFUGE **3 :** a period of group withdrawal for prayer, meditation, study, and instruction under a director

2retreat *vi* (15c) **1 :** to make a retreat **:** WITHDRAW **2 :** to slope backward ~ *vt* **:** to draw or lead back **:** REMOVE; *specif* **:** to move (a piece) back in chess ***syn*** see RECEDE — **re·treat·er** *n*

re·treat·ant \-'trēt-ᵊnt\ *n* (1880) **:** one who is on a religious retreat

re·trench \ri-'trench\ *vb* [obs. F *retrencher* (now *retrancher*), fr. MF *retrenchier,* fr. *re-* + *trenchier* to cut] *vt* (1625) **1 a :** CUT DOWN, REDUCE **b :** to cut out **:** EXCISE **2 :** to pare away **:** REMOVE ~ *vi* **:** to make retrenchments; *specif* **:** ECONOMIZE ***syn*** see SHORTEN

re·trench·ment \-mənt\ *n* (1600) **:** REDUCTION, CURTAILMENT; *specif* **:** a cutting of expenses

re·tri·al \(')rē-'trī(-ə)l\ *n* (1875) **:** a second trial, experiment, or test

ret·ri·bu·tion \,re-trə-'byü-shən\ *n* [ME *retribucioun,* fr. MF *retribution,* fr. LL *retribution-, retributio,* fr. L *retributus,* pp. of *retribuere* to pay back, fr. *re-* + *tribuere* to pay — more at TRIBUTE] (14c) **1 :** RECOMPENSE, REWARD **2 :** the dispensing or receiving of reward or punishment esp. in the hereafter **3 :** something given or exacted in recompense; *esp* **:** PUNISHMENT

re·trib·u·tive \ri-'trib-yət-iv\ *adj* (1678) **:** of, relating to, or marked by retribution — **re·trib·u·tive·ly** *adv*

re·trib·u·to·ry \-yə-,tōr-ē, -,tȯr-\ *adj* (1612) **:** RETRIBUTIVE

\ə\ abut \ᵊ\ kitten, F table \ər\ further \a\ ash \ā\ ace \ä\ cot, cart \au̇\ out \ch\ chin \e\ bet \ē\ easy \g\ go \i\ hit \ī\ ice \j\ job \ŋ\ sing \ō\ go \ȯ\ law \ȯi\ boy \th\ thin \t͟h\ the \ü\ loot \u̇\ foot \y\ yet \zh\ vision \à, k̲, ⁿ, œ, œ̄, ue, u̅e, ʸ\ *see* Guide to Pronunciation

re·triev·al \ri-ˈtrē-vəl\ *n* (1643) **1 :** an act or process of retrieving **2 :** possibility of being retrieved or of recovering ⟨beyond ~⟩

[1]**re·trieve** \ri-ˈtrēv\ *vb* **re·trieved; re·triev·ing** [ME *retreven,* modif. of MF *retrouver* to find again, fr. *re-* + *trouver* to find, prob. fr. (assumed) VL *tropare* to compose — more at TROUBADOUR] *vt* (15c) **1 :** to discover and bring in (killed or wounded game) **2 :** to call to mind again **3 :** to get back again : REGAIN **4 a :** RESCUE, SALVAGE **b :** to return (as a ball or shuttlecock that is difficult to reach) successfully **5 :** RESTORE, REVIVE ⟨his writing ~*s* the past⟩ **6 :** to remedy the evil consequences of : CORRECT **7 :** to get and bring back; *esp* : to recover (as information) from storage ~ *vi* : to bring in game ⟨a dog that ~*s* well⟩; *also* : to bring back an object thrown by a person — **re·triev·abil·i·ty** \-ˌtrē-və-ˈbil-ət-ē\ *n* — **re·triev·able** \-ˈtrē-və-bəl\ *adj*

[2]**retrieve** *n* (1575) **1 :** RETRIEVAL **2 :** the successful return of a ball that is difficult to reach or control (as in tennis)

re·triev·er \ri-ˈtrē-vər\ *n* (15c) : one that retrieves; *esp* : a dog of any of several breeds (as a golden retriever) having a heavy water-resistant coat and used esp. for retrieving game

retro- *prefix* [ME, fr. L, fr. *retro,* fr. *re-* + *-tro* (as in *intro* within) — more at INTRO-] **1 :** backward : back ⟨*retro*-rocket⟩ **2 :** situated behind ⟨*retro*choir⟩

ret·ro·ac·tion \ˌre-trō-ˈak-shən\ *n* (ca. 1727) **1** [*retroactive* + *-ion*] : retroactive operation (as of a law or tax) **2** [*retro-* + *action*] : a reciprocal action : REACTION

ret·ro·ac·tive \-ˈak-tiv\ *adj* [F *retroactif,* fr. L *retroactus,* pp. of *retroagere* to drive back, reverse, fr. *retro-* + *agere* to drive — more at AGENT] (ca. 1611) : extending in scope or effect to a prior time or to conditions that existed or originated in the past; *esp* : made effective as of a date prior to enactment, promulgation, or imposition ⟨~ tax⟩ — **ret·ro·ac·tive·ly** *adv* — **ret·ro·ac·tiv·i·ty** \-ˌak-ˈtiv-ət-ē\ *n*

ret·ro·cede \ˌre-trō-ˈsēd\ *vb* **-ced·ed; -ced·ing** [L *retrocedere,* fr. *retro-* + *cedere* to go, cede — more at CEDE] *vi* (1805) : to go back : RECEDE ~ *vt* [F *rétrocéder,* fr. ML *retrocedere,* fr. L *retro-* + *cedere* to cede] : to cede back (as a territory) — **ret·ro·ces·sion** \-ˈsesh-ən\ *n*

ret·ro–engine \ˈre-trō-ˌen-jən\ *n* (1965) : a rocket engine that produces thrust in the direction opposite to that of the motion of the spacecraft

ret·ro·fire \-ˌfī(ə)r\ *vi, of a retro-engine or retro-rocket* (1961) : to become ignited ~ *vt* : to cause to retrofire — **retrofire** *n*

ret·ro·fit \ˌre-trō-ˈfit\ *vt* (1953) : to furnish (as a computer, airplane, or building) with new parts or equipment not available at the time of manufacture — **retrofit** *n*

ret·ro·flex \ˈre-trə-ˌfleks\ *also* **ret·ro·flexed** \-ˌflekst\ *adj* [ISV, fr. NL *retroflexus,* fr. L *retro-* + *flexus,* pp. of *flectere* to bend] (1776) **1 :** turned or bent abruptly backward **2 :** articulated with the tongue tip turned up or curled back just under the hard palate ⟨~ vowel⟩

ret·ro·flex·ion *or* **ret·ro·flec·tion** \ˌre-trə-ˈflek-shən\ *n* (1845) **1 :** the act or process of bending back **2 :** the state of being bent back; *esp* : the bending back of an organ (as a uterus) upon itself **3 :** retroflex articulation

ret·ro·gra·da·tion \ˌre-trō-grā-ˈdā-shən, -grə-\ *n* (1554) : the action or process of retrograding

[1]**ret·ro·grade** \ˈre-trə-ˌgrād\ *adj* [ME, fr. L *retrogradus,* fr. *retro-* + *gradus* step — more at GRADE] (14c) **1 a** (1) *of a celestial body* : having a direction contrary to that of the general motion of similar bodies (2) : being or relating to the rotation of a satellite in a direction opposite to that of the body orbited **b :** moving, directed, or treading backward ⟨a ~ step⟩ **c :** contrary to the normal order : INVERSE **2 :** tending toward or resulting in a worse state **3** *archaic* : CONTRADICTORY, OPPOSED **4 :** characterized by retrogression **5 :** affecting a period immediately prior to a precipitating cause ⟨~ amnesia⟩ — **ret·ro·grade·ly** *adv*

[2]**retrograde** *adv* (1619) : BACKWARD, REVERSELY

[3]**retrograde** *vb* [L *retrogradi,* fr. *retro-* + *gradi* to go — more at GRADE] *vt, archaic* (1582) : to turn back : REVERSE ~ *vi* **1 a :** to go back : RETREAT ⟨a glacier ~*s*⟩ **b :** to go back over or recapitulate something **2 :** to decline to a worse condition ***syn*** see RECEDE

ret·ro·gress \ˌre-trə-ˈgres\ *vi* [L *retrogressus,* pp. of *retrogradi*] (1819) : to move backward : REVERT

ret·ro·gres·sion \-ˈgresh-ən\ *n* (1646) **1 :** REGRESSION 3 **2 :** return to a former and less complex level of development or organization

ret·ro·gres·sive \-ˈgres-iv\ *adj* (1802) : characterized by retrogression: as **a :** going or directed backward **b :** declining from a better to a worse state **c :** passing from a higher to a lower level of organization ⟨~ evolution⟩ — **ret·ro·gres·sive·ly** *adv*

ret·ro·pack \ˈre-trō-ˌpak\ *n* (1962) : a system of auxiliary rockets on a spacecraft that produces thrust in the direction opposite to the motion of the spacecraft and that is used to reduce speed

ret·ro·per·i·to·ne·al \-ˌper-ət-ən-ˈē-əl\ *adj* (1874) : situated behind the peritoneum — **ret·ro·per·i·to·ne·al·ly** \-ə-lē\ *adv*

ret·ro·re·flec·tion \ˌre-trō-ri-ˈflek-shən\ *n* (ca. 1965) : the action or use of a retroreflector — **ret·ro·re·flec·tive** \-ˈflek-tiv\ *adj*

ret·ro·re·flec·tor \-ˈflek-tər\ *n* (1946) : a device that reflects radiation (as light) so that the paths of the rays are parallel to those of the incident rays

ret·ro–rock·et \ˈre-trō-ˌräk-ət\ *n* (1947) : an auxiliary rocket on an airplane, missile, or spacecraft that produces thrust in a direction opposite to or at an oblique angle to the motion of the object for deceleration

re·trorse \ˈrē-ˌtrȯ(ə)rs\ *adj* [L *retrorsus,* contr. of *retroversus* — more at RETROVERSION] (ca. 1825) : bent backward or downward

[1]**ret·ro·spect** \ˈre-trə-ˌspekt\ *n* [*retro-* + *-spect* (as in *prospect*)] (1602) **1** *archaic* : reference to or regard of a precedent or authority **2 :** a review of or meditation on past events — **in retrospect :** in considering the past or a past event

[2]**retrospect** *adj* (1709) : RETROSPECTIVE

[3]**retrospect** *vb* [L *retrospectus,* pp. of *retrospicere* to look back at, fr. *retro-* + *specere* to look — more at SPY] *vi* (1659) **1 :** to engage in retrospection **2 :** to refer back : REFLECT ~ *vt* : to go back over in thought

ret·ro·spec·tion \ˌre-trə-ˈspek-shən\ *n* (1674) : the act or process or an instance of surveying the past

[1]**ret·ro·spec·tive** \-ˈspek-tiv\ *adj* (1664) **1 a** (1) : of, relating to, or given to retrospection (2) : based on memory ⟨a ~ report⟩ **b :** being a retrospective ⟨a ~ exhibition⟩ **2 :** affecting things past : RETROACTIVE — **ret·ro·spec·tive·ly** *adv*

[2]**retrospective** *n* (1949) : a generally comprehensive exhibition or performance of the work of an artist over a span of years

re·trous·sé \rə-ˌtrü-ˈsā, rə-ˈtrü-ˌ, ˌre-trü-ˈ\ *adj* [F, fr. pp. of *retrousser* to tuck up, fr. MF, fr. *re-* + *trousser* to truss, tuck up] (1802) : turned up ⟨~ nose⟩

ret·ro·ver·sion \ˌre-trō-ˈvər-zhən *also* -shən\ *n* [L *retroversus* turned backward, fr. *retro-* + *versus,* pp. of *vertere* to turn — more at WORTH] (1587) **1 :** the act or process of turning back or regressing **2 :** the bending backward of the uterus and cervix

ret·ro·vi·rus \ˈre-trō-ˌvī-rəs\ *n* (1975) : any of a group of RNA-containing viruses (as the AIDS virus) that produce reverse transcriptase by means of which DNA is produced using their RNA as a template and incorporated into the genome of infected cells and that include numerous viruses causing tumors in animals including man

re·try \(ˈ)rē-ˈtrī\ *vt* (1673) : to try again

ret·si·na \ret-ˈsē-nə\ *n* [NGk, perh. fr. It *resina* resin, fr. L] (1940) : a resin-flavored Greek wine

[1]**re·turn** \ri-ˈtərn\ *vb* [ME *retournen,* fr. MF *retourner,* fr. *re-* + *tourner* to turn — more at TURN] *vi* (14c) **1 a :** to go back or come back again ⟨~ home⟩ **b :** to go back in thought or practice : REVERT ⟨soon ~*ed* to her old habit⟩ **2 :** to pass back to an earlier possessor **3 :** REPLY, RETORT ~ *vt* **1 a :** to give (as an official account) to a superior **b :** to elect (a candidate) as attested by official report or returns **c :** to bring back (as a writ or verdict) to an office or tribunal **2 a :** to bring, send, or put back to a former or proper place ⟨~ the gun to its holster⟩ **b :** to restore to a former or to a normal state **3 a :** to send back : VISIT — usu. used with *on* or *upon* **b** *obs* : RETORT **4 :** to bring in (as profit) : YIELD **5 a :** to give or perform in return : REPAY ⟨~ a compliment⟩ **b :** to give back to the owner **c :** REFLECT ⟨~ an echo⟩ **6 :** to cause (as a wall) to continue in a different direction (as at a right angle) **7 :** to lead (a specified suit or specified card of a suit) in response to a partner's earlier lead **8 a :** to hit back (a ball or shuttlecock) **b :** to run with (a football) after a kick by the opposing team ***syn*** see RECIPROCATE — **re·turn·er** *n*

[2]**return** *n* (14c) **1 a :** the act of coming back to or from a place or condition **b :** a regular or frequent returning : RECURRENCE **2 a** (1) : the delivery of a legal order (as a writ) to the proper officer or court (2) : the endorsed certificate of an official stating his action in the execution of such an order (3) : the sending back of a commission with the certificate of the commissioners **b :** an account or formal report **c** (1) : a report of the results of balloting — usu. used in pl. ⟨election ~*s*⟩ (2) : an official declaration of the election of a candidate (3) *chiefly Brit* : ELECTION **d** (1) : a formal statement on a required legal form showing taxable income, allowable deductions and exemptions, and the computation of the tax due (2) : a list of taxable property **3 a :** the continuation usu. at a right angle of the face or of a member of a building or of a molding or group of moldings **b :** a turn, bend, or winding back (as in a rod, stream, or trench) **c :** a means for conveying something (as water) back to its starting point **4 a :** a quantity of goods, consignment, or cargo coming back in exchange for goods sent out as a mercantile venture **b :** the value of or profit from such venture **c** (1) : the profit from labor, investment, or business : YIELD (2) *pl* : RESULTS **d :** the rate of profit in a process of production per unit of cost **5 a :** the act of returning something to a former place, condition, or ownership : RESTITUTION **b :** something returned; *esp, pl* : unsold publications returned to the publisher for cash or credit **6 a :** something given in repayment or reciprocation **b :** ANSWER, RETORT **7 :** an answering play: as **a :** a lead in a suit previously led by one's partner in a card game **b :** the action or an instance of returning a ball (as in football or tennis) — **in return :** in compensation or repayment

[3]**return** *adj* (1676) **1 a :** having or formed by a change of direction ⟨a ~ facade⟩ **b :** doubled on itself ⟨a ~ flue⟩ **2 :** played, delivered, or given in return : taking place for the second time ⟨a ~ meeting for the two champions⟩ **3 :** used or taken on returning ⟨the ~ road⟩ **4 :** returning or permitting return ⟨a ~ valve⟩ **5 :** of, relating to, or causing a return to a place or condition

[1]**re·turn·able** \ri-ˈtər-nə-bəl\ *adj* (15c) **1 :** legally required to be returned, delivered, or argued at a specified time or place ⟨a writ ~ on the date indicated⟩ **2 a :** capable of returning or of being returned (as for reuse) **b :** permitted to be returned

[2]**returnable** *n* (1963) : something designed to be returned (as for recycling); *esp* : a returnable beverage container

re·turn·ee \ri-ˌtər-ˈnē\ *n* (1944) : one who returns; *esp* : one returning to the U.S. after military service overseas

re·tuse \ri-ˈt(y)üs\ *adj* [L *retusus* blunted, fr. pp. of *retundere* to pound back, blunt, fr. *re-* + *tundere* to beat, pound — more at STINT] (ca. 1753) : having the apex rounded or obtuse with a slight notch

[1]**Reu·ben** \ˈrü-bən\ *n* [Heb *Rĕʼūbhēn*] : a son of Jacob and the traditional eponymous ancestor of one of the tribes of Israel

[2]**Reuben** *n* [*Reuben* L. Goldberg †1970 Am. cartoonist] (1958) : a statuette awarded annually by a professional organization for notable achievement in cartoon artistry

Reuben sandwich *n* [fr. the name *Reuben*] (ca. 1966) : a grilled sandwich of corned beef, Swiss cheese, and sauerkraut usu. on rye bread

re·uni·fy \(ˈ)rē-ˈyü-nə-ˌfī\ *vt* (ca. 1890) : to restore unity to — **re·uni·fi·ca·tion** \(ˌ)rē-ˌyü-nə-fə-ˈkā-shən\ *n*

re·union \(ˈ)rē-ˈyün-yən\ *n* (1610) **1 :** an act of reuniting : the state of being reunited **2 :** a reuniting of persons after separation

re·union·ist \-yə-nəst\ *n* (1806) : an advocate of reunion (as of sects or parties) — **re·union·is·tic** \(ˌ)rē-ˌyün-yə-ˈnis-tik\ *adj*

re·unite \ˌrē-yü-ˈnīt\ *vb* [ML *reunitus,* pp. of *reunire,* fr. L *re-* + LL *unire* to unite — more at UNITE] *vt* (1591) : to bring together again ~ *vi* : to come together again : REJOIN

re–up \(ˈ)rē-ˈəp\ *vi* [*re-* + sign *up*] (ca. 1906) : to enlist again

re·us·able \(ˈ)rē-ˈyü-zə-bəl\ *adj* (1943) : capable of being used again or repeatedly — **re·us·abil·i·ty** \(ˌ)rē-ˌyü-zə-ˈbil-ət-ē\ *n*

[1]**re·use** \(ˈ)rē-ˈyüz\ *vt* (1843) : to use again esp. after reclaiming or reprocessing ⟨the need to ~ scarce resources⟩

[2]**reuse** \-ˈyüs\ *n* (1866) : further or repeated use

[1]**rev** \ˈrev\ *n* [short for *revolution*] (ca. 1890) : a revolution of a motor

[2]**rev** *vb* **revved; rev·ving** *vt* (1920) **1 a :** to step up the number of revolutions per minute of — often used with *up* ⟨~ up the engine⟩ **b :** INCREASE — used with *up* ⟨~ up production⟩ **2 :** to drive or operate esp. at high speed — often used with *up* **3 :** to make more active or effec-

tive — used with *up* ~ *vi* **1** : to operate at an increased speed of revolution — usu. used with *up* **2** : to increase in amount or activity — used with *up*

re·val·u·ate \(ˈ)rē-ˈval-yə-ˌwāt\ *vt* [back-formation fr. *revaluation*] (1921) : REVALUE; *specif* : to increase the value of (currency) — **re·val·u·a·tion** \(ˌ)rē-ˌval-yə-ˈwā-shən\ *n*

re·val·ue \(ˈ)rē-ˈval-(ˌ)yü, -yə(-w)\ *vt* (ca. 1611) **1** : to value (as currency) anew **2** : to make a new valuation of : REAPPRAISE

re·vamp \(ˈ)rē-ˈvamp\ *vt* (1850) **1** : RENOVATE, RECONSTRUCT **2** : to make over : REVISE

re·vanche \rə-ˈvä^{n}sh\ *n* [F, fr. MF, alter. of *revenche* — more at REVENGE] (1858) : REVENGE; *esp* : a usu. political policy designed to recover lost territory or status

1re·vanch·ist \-ˈvä^{n}-shəst\ *n* (1926) : one who advocates a policy of revanche

2revanchist *adj* (1951) : of or relating to a policy of revanche

re·vas·cu·lar·iza·tion \ˈrē-ˌvas-kyə-lə-rə-ˈzā-shən\ *n* (1951) : a surgical procedure for the provision of a new, additional, or augmented blood supply to a body part or organ

1re·veal \ri-ˈvē(ə)l\ *vt* [ME *revelen*, fr. MF *reveler*, fr. L *revelare* to uncover, reveal, fr. *re-* + *velare* to cover, veil, fr. *velum* veil] (14c) **1** : to make known through divine inspiration **2** : to make (something secret or hidden) publicly or generally known ⟨~ a secret⟩ **3** : to open up to view : DISPLAY ⟨the uncurtained window ~*ed* a cluttered room⟩ — **re·veal·able** \-ˈvē-lə-bəl\ *adj* — **re·veal·er** *n*

syn REVEAL, DISCOVER, DISCLOSE, DIVULGE, TELL, BETRAY mean to make known what has been or should be concealed. REVEAL may apply to supernatural or inspired revelation of truths beyond the range of ordinary human vision or reason; DISCOVER implies an uncovering of matters kept secret and not previously known; DISCLOSE may also imply a discovering but more often an imparting of information previously kept secret; DIVULGE implies a disclosure involving some impropriety or breach of confidence; TELL implies an imparting of necessary or useful information; BETRAY implies a divulging that represents a breach of faith or an involuntary or unconscious disclosure.

2reveal *n* [alter. of earlier *revale*, fr. ME *revalen* to lower, fr. MF *revaler*, fr. *re-* + *val* valley — more at VALE] (1688) : the side of an opening (as for a window) between a frame and the outer surface of a wall; *also* : JAMB

re·veal·ing *adj* (ca. 1925) : allowing a look at or an understanding of something inner or hidden : INSIGHTFUL — **re·veal·ing·ly** *adv*

re·veal·ment \ri-ˈvē(ə)l-mənt\ *n* (1584) : an act of revealing

re·veg·e·tate \(ˈ)rē-ˈvej-ə-ˌtāt\ *vt* (1804) : to provide (barren or denuded land) with a new vegetative cover — **re·veg·e·ta·tion** \(ˌ)rē-ˌvej-ə-ˈtā-shən\ *n*

re·ve·hent \ˈrev-ə-hənt, ri-ˈvē-ənt\ *adj* [L *revehent-*, *revehens*, prp. of *revehere* to carry back, fr. *re-* + *vehere* to carry — more at WAY] (1876) : carrying back ⟨~ veins⟩

rev·eil·le \ˈrev-ə-lē, *Brit* ri-ˈval-i *or* -ˈvel-\ *n* [modif. of F *réveillez*, imper. pl. of *réveiller* to awaken, fr. MF *reveiller*, fr. *re-* + *eveiller* to awaken, fr. (assumed) VL *exvigilare*, fr. L *ex-* + *vigilare* to keep watch, stay awake — more at VIGILANT] (1644) **1** : a signal to get up mornings **2** : a bugle call at about sunrise signaling the first military formation of the day; *also* : the formation so signaled

1rev·el \ˈrev-əl\ *vi* **-eled** *or* **-elled; -el·ing** *or* **-el·ling** \-(ə-)liŋ\ [ME *revelen*, fr. MF *reveler*, lit., to rebel, fr. L *rebellare*] (14c) **1** : to take part in a revel : CAROUSE **2** : to take intense satisfaction

2revel *n* (14c) : a usu. wild party or celebration

rev·e·la·tion \ˌrev-ə-ˈlā-shən\ *n* [ME, fr. MF, fr. LL *revelation-*, *revelatio*, fr. L *revelatus*, pp. of *revelare* to reveal] (14c) **1 a** : an act of revealing or communicating divine truth **b** : something that is revealed by God to man **2** *cap* : an apocalyptic writing addressed to early Christians of Asia Minor and included as a book in the New Testament — see BIBLE table **3 a** : an act of revealing to view or making known **b** : something that is revealed; *esp* : an enlightening or astonishing disclosure

Rev·e·la·tions \-shənz\ *n pl but sing in constr* [alter. (influenced by such titles as *Galatians*) of *Revelation*] : REVELATION 2

rev·e·la·tor \ˈrev-ə-ˌlāt-ər\ *n* (1801) : one that reveals; *esp* : one that reveals the will of God

rev·e·la·to·ry \ˈrev-ə-lə-ˌtōr-ē, -ˌtȯr-, ri-ˈvel-ə-\ *adj* (1882) : of or relating to revelation : serving to reveal something

rev·el·er *or* **rev·el·ler** \ˈrev-(ə-)lər\ *n* (14c) : one who engages in revelry

rev·el·ry \ˈrev-əl-rē\ *n* (15c) : noisy partying or merrymaking

rev·e·nant \ˈrev-ə-ˌnän, -nənt\ *n* [F, fr. prp. of *revenir* to return] (1827) : one that returns after death or a long absence — **revenant** *adj*

1re·venge \ri-ˈvenj\ *vt* **re·venged; re·veng·ing** [ME *revengen*, fr. MF *revengier*, fr. OF, fr. *re-* + *vengier* to avenge — more at VENGENCE] (14c) **1** : to avenge (as oneself) usu. by retaliating in kind or degree **2** : to inflict injury in return for ⟨~ an insult⟩ — **re·veng·er** *n*

2revenge *n* [MF *revenge*, *revenche*, fr. *revengier*, *revenchier* to revenge] (1547) **1** : a desire for revenge **2** : an act or instance of retaliating in order to get even **3** : an opportunity for getting satisfaction

re·venge·ful \ri-ˈvenj-fəl\ *adj* (1586) : full of or prone to revenge : determined to get even — **re·venge·ful·ly** \-fə-lē\ *adv* — **re·venge·ful·ness** *n*

rev·e·nue \ˈrev-ə-ˌn(y)ü\ *n, often attrib* [ME, fr. MF, fr. *revenir* to return, fr. L *revenire*, fr. *re-* + *venire* to come — more at COME] (15c) **1** : the total income produced by a given source ⟨a property expected to yield a large annual ~⟩ **2** : the gross income returned by an investment **3** : the yield of sources of income (as taxes) that a political unit (as a nation or state) collects and receives into the treasury for public use **4** : a government department concerned with the collection of the national revenue

revenue bond *n* (1856) : a bond issued by a public agency authorized to build, acquire, or improve a revenue-producing property (as a toll road) and payable out of revenue derived from such property

rev·e·nu·er \ˈrev-ə-ˌn(y)ü-ər\ *n* (1880) : a revenue officer or boat

revenue stamp *n* (1870) : a stamp (as on a cigar box) for use as evidence of payment of a tax

revenue tariff *n* (1820) : a tariff intended wholly or primarily to produce public revenue — compare PROTECTIVE TARIFF

re·verb \ri-ˈvərb, ˈrē-ˌ\ *n* [short for *reverberation*] (1953) : an electronically produced echo effect in recorded music; *also* : a device for producing reverb

re·ver·ber·ant \ri-ˈvər-b(ə-)rənt\ *adj* (1807) **1** : tending to reverberate **2** : marked by reverberation : RESONANT — **re·ver·ber·ant·ly** *adv*

1re·ver·ber·ate \-bə-ˌrāt\ *vb* **-at·ed; -at·ing** [L *reverberatus*, pp. of *reverberare*, fr. *re-* + *verberare* to lash, fr. *verber* rod — more at VERVAIN] *vt* (1547) **1 a** : REPEL **b** : ECHO **c** : REFLECT **2** : to subject to the action of a reverberatory furnace ~ *vi* **1 a** : to become driven back **b** : to become reflected **2** : to continue in or as if in a series of echoes : RESOUND

2re·ver·ber·ate \-b(ə-)rət\ *adj* (1603) : REVERBERANT

re·ver·ber·a·tion \ri-ˌvər-bə-ˈrā-shən\ *n* [ME *reverberacioun*, fr. MF *reverberation*, fr. ML *reverberation-*, *reverberatio*, fr. L *reverberatus*, pp.] (14c) **1** : an act of reverberating : the state of being reverberated **2 a** : something that is reverberated **b** : an effect or impact that resembles an echo

re·ver·ber·a·tive \ri-ˈvər-bə-ˌrāt-iv, -b(ə-)rət-\ *adj* (1716) **1** : constituting reverberation **2** : tending to reverberate : REVERBERANT

1re·ver·ber·a·to·ry \ri-ˈvər-b(ə-)rə-ˌtōr-ē, -bə-ˌtōr-, -ˌtȯr-\ *adj* (1605) : acting by reverberation; *esp* : forced back or diverted onto material under treatment

2reverberatory *n, pl* **-ries** (1651) : a furnace or kiln in which heat is radiated from the roof onto the material treated

1re·vere \ri-ˈvi(ə)r\ *vt* **re·vered; re·ver·ing** [L *revereri*, fr. *re-* + *vereri* to fear, respect — more at WARY] (ca. 1661) : to show devoted deferential honor to : regard as worthy of great honor ⟨~ the aged⟩ ⟨~ tradition⟩

syn REVERE, REVERENCE, VENERATE, WORSHIP, ADORE mean to honor and admire profoundly and respectfully. REVERE stresses deference and tenderness of feeling ⟨that makes her loved at home, *revered* abroad —Robert Burns⟩ REVERENCE presupposes an intrinsic merit and inviolability in the one honored and a corresponding depth of feeling in the one honoring ⟨sincerity and simplicity! if I could only say how I *reverence* them —A. C. Benson⟩ VENERATE implies a holding as holy or sacrosanct because of character, association, or age ⟨those who *venerate* . . . Dante and Shakespeare and Milton —Havelock Ellis⟩ ⟨a *venerated* tradition⟩ WORSHIP implies homage usu. expressed in words or ceremony ⟨admire the poetry and *worship* the memory of the poet —William DuBois⟩ ADORE implies love and stresses the notion of an individual and personal attachment ⟨his staff *adored* him, his men worshiped him —W. A. White⟩

2revere *n* [by alter.] (ca. 1934) : REVERS

1rev·er·ence \ˈrev-(ə-)rən(t)s, ˈrev-ərn(t)s\ *n* [ME, fr. OF, fr. L *reverentia*, fr. *reverent-*, *reverens*, prp. of *revereri*] (13c) **1** : honor or respect felt or shown : DEFERENCE; *esp* : profound adoring awed respect **2** : a gesture of respect (as a bow) **3** : the state of being revered **4** : one held in reverence — used as a title for a clergyman ***syn*** see HONOR

2reverence *vt* **-enced; -enc·ing** (14c) : to regard or treat with reverence ***syn*** see REVERE — **rev·er·enc·er** *n*

1rev·er·end \ˈrev-(ə-)rənd, ˈrev-ərnd\ *adj* [ME, fr. MF, fr. L *reverendus*, gerundive of *revereri*] (15c) **1** : worthy of reverence : REVERED **2 a** : of or relating to the clergy **b** : being a member of the clergy — used as a title usu. preceded by *the* and followed by a title or a full name ⟨the *Reverend* Mr. Doe⟩ ⟨the *Reverend* John Doe⟩ ⟨the *Reverend* Mrs. Jane Doe⟩

2reverend *n* (1608) : a member of the clergy — used with *the*

rev·er·ent \ˈrev-(ə-)rənt, ˈrev-ərnt\ *adj* [ME, fr. L *reverent-*, *reverens*, prp. of *revereri*] (15c) : expressing or characterized by reverence : WORSHIPFUL — **rev·er·ent·ly** *adv*

rev·er·en·tial \ˌrev-ə-ˈren-chəl\ *adj* (1555) **1** : expressing or having a quality of reverence ⟨~ awe⟩ **2** : inspiring reverence — **rev·er·en·tial·ly** \-ˈrench-(ə-)lē\ *adv*

rev·er·ie *also* **rev·ery** \ˈrev-(ə-)rē\ *n, pl* **rev·er·ies** [F *rêverie*, fr. MF, delirium, fr. *resver*, *rever* to wander, be delirious] (1657) **1** : DAYDREAM **2** : the condition of being lost in thought

re·vers \ri-ˈvi(ə)r, -ˈve(ə)r\ *n, pl* **re·vers** \-ˈvi(ə)rz, -ˈve(ə)rz\ [F, lit., reverse, fr. MF, fr. *revers*, adj.] (ca. 1900) : a lapel esp. on a woman's garment

re·ver·sal \ri-ˈvər-səl\ *n* (15c) **1** : an act or the process of reversing **2** : a conversion of a photographic positive into a negative or vice versa **3** : a change of fortune usu. for the worse

1re·verse \ri-ˈvərs\ *adj* [ME *revers*, fr. MF, fr. L *reversus*, pp. of *revertere* to turn back — more at REVERT] (14c) **1 a** : opposite or contrary to a previous or normal condition ⟨~ order⟩ **b** : having the back presented to the observer or opponent **2** : coming from the rear of a military force **3** : acting, operating, or arranged in a manner contrary to the usual **4** : effecting reverse movement ⟨~ gear⟩ **5** : so made that the part which normally prints in color appears white against a colored background — **re·verse·ly** *adv*

2reverse *vb* **re·versed; re·vers·ing** *vt* (14c) **1 a** : to turn completely about in position or direction **b** : to turn upside down : INVERT **2** : ANNUL; as **a** : to overthrow, set aside, or make void (a legal decision) by a contrary decision **b** : to cause to take an opposite point of view **c** : to change to the contrary ⟨~ a policy⟩ **3** : to cause to go in the opposite direction; *esp* : to cause (as an engine) to perform its action in the opposite direction ~ *vi* **1** : to turn or move in the opposite direction **2** : to put a mechanism (as an engine) in reverse — **re·vers·er** *n*

syn REVERSE, TRANSPOSE, INVERT mean to change to the opposite position. REVERSE is the most general term and may imply change in order, side, direction, meaning; TRANSPOSE implies a change in order or relative position of units often through exchange of position; INVERT applies chiefly to turning upside down or inside out.

— **reverse field** : to turn and head in the opposite direction

3reverse *n* (14c) **1** : something directly contrary to something else : OPPOSITE **2** : an act or instance of reversing; *esp* : DEFEAT, SETBACK **3** : the back part of something **4 a (1)** : a gear that reverses something; *also* : the whole mechanism brought into play when such a gear is used **(2)** : movement in reverse **b** : an offensive play in football in which a back moving in one direction gives the ball to a player moving

\ə\ abut \ᵊ\ kitten, F table \ər\ further \a\ ash \ā\ ace \ä\ cot, cart \au̇\ out \ch\ chin \e\ bet \ē\ easy \g\ go \i\ hit \ī\ ice \j\ job \ŋ\ sing \ō\ go \ȯ\ law \ȯi\ boy \th\ thin \th\ the \ü\ loot \u̇\ foot \y\ yet \zh\ vision \à, k, ^{n}, œ, œ̄, ue, u̅e, ^{y}\ *see* Guide to Pronunciation

in the opposite direction — **in reverse :** in an opposite manner or direction
reverse discrimination *n* (1969) : discrimination against whites or males
reverse osmosis *n* (1955) : the flow of fresh water through a semipermeable membrane when pressure is applied to a solution (as seawater) on one side of it
reverse tran·scrip·tase \-ˌtran-ˈskrip-(ˌ)tās, -(ˌ)tāz\ *n* (1971) : a polymerase that catalyzes the formation of DNA using RNA as a template and that is found in many tumor-producing viruses containing RNA
1**re·vers·ible** \ri-ˈvər-sə-bəl\ *adj* (1648) : capable of being reversed or of reversing: as **a :** capable of going through a series of actions (as changes) either backward or forward ⟨a ~ chemical reaction⟩ **b :** having two finished usable sides ⟨~ fabric⟩ **c :** wearable with either side out ⟨a ~ coat⟩ — **re·vers·ibil·i·ty** \-ˌvər-sə-ˈbil-ət-ē\ *n* — **re·vers·ibly** \-ˈvər-sə-blē\ *adv*
2**reversible** *n* (1863) : a reversible cloth or article of clothing
re·ver·sion \ri-ˈvər-zhən, -shən\ *n* [ME, fr. MF, fr. L *reversion-, reversio* act of returning, fr. *reversus,* pp.] (15c) **1 a :** the part of a simple estate remaining in the control of its owner after he has granted therefrom a lesser particular estate **b :** a future interest in property left in the control of a grantor or his successor **2 :** the right of succession or future possession or enjoyment **3 a :** an act or the process of returning (as to a former condition) **b :** a return toward an ancestral type or condition : reappearance of an ancestral character **4 :** an act or instance of turning the opposite way : the state of being so turned **5 :** a product of reversion; *specif* : an organism with an atavistic character : THROWBACK
re·ver·sion·al \-ˈvərzh-nəl, -ˈvərsh-, -ən-ᵊl\ *adj* (1675) : REVERSIONARY
re·ver·sion·ary \-ˈvər-zhə-ˌner-ē, -shə-\ *adj* (1720) : of, relating to, constituting, or involving esp. a legal reversion
re·ver·sion·er \-ˈvərzh-nər, -ˈvərsh-, -ə-nər\ *n* (1614) : one that has or is entitled to a reversion
re·vert \ri-ˈvərt\ *vi* [ME *reverten,* fr. MF *revertir,* fr. L *revertere,* v.t., to turn back & *reverti,* v.i., to return, come back, fr. *re-* + *vertere, verti* to turn — more at WORTH] (15c) **1 :** to come or go back (as to a former condition, period, or subject) **2 :** to return to the proprietor or his heirs at the end of a reversion **3 :** to return to an ancestral type — **re·vert·er** *n* — **re·vert·ible** \-ˈvərt-ə-bəl\ *adj*
re·ver·tant \ri-ˈvərt-ᵊnt\ *n* (1955) : a mutant gene, individual, or strain that regains a former capability (as the production of a particular protein) by undergoing further mutation ⟨yeast ~s⟩ — **revertant** *adj*
re·vest \(ˈ)rē-ˈvest\ *vt* (1561) : REINSTATE, REINVEST
re·vet \ri-ˈvet\ *vt* **re·vet·ted; re·vet·ting** [F *revêtir,* lit., to clothe again, dress up, fr. L *revestire,* fr. *re-* + *vestire* to clothe — more at VEST] (1812) : to face (as an embankment) with a revetment
re·vet·ment \-ˈvet-mənt\ *n* (1771) **1 :** a facing (as of stone or concrete) to sustain an embankment **2 :** EMBANKMENT; *esp* : a barricade to provide shelter (as against bomb splinters or strafing)
1**re·view** \ri-ˈvyü\ *n* [MF *revue,* fr. *revoir* to look over, fr. *re-* + *voir* to see — more at VIEW] (1565) **1 :** REVISION 1a **2 a :** a formal military inspection **b :** a military ceremony honoring a person or an event **3 :** a general survey (as of the events of a period) **4 :** an act or the process of reviewing **5 :** judicial reexamination (as of the proceedings of a lower tribunal by a higher) **6 a :** a critical evaluation (as of a book or play) **b :** a magazine devoted chiefly to reviews and essays **7 a :** a retrospective view or survey (as of one's life) **b (1) :** renewed study of material previously studied **(2) :** an exercise facilitating such study **8 :** REVUE
2**re·view** \ri-ˈvyü, *1 is also* ˈrē-\ *vb* [in senses 1 & 2, fr. *re-* + *view;* in other senses, fr. 1*review*] *vt* (1576) **1 :** to view or see again **2 :** to examine or study again; *esp* : to reexamine judicially **3 :** to look back on : take a retrospective view of **4 a :** to go over or examine critically or deliberately ⟨~*ed* the results of the study⟩ **b :** to give a critical evaluation of ⟨~ a novel⟩ **5 :** to hold a review of ⟨~ troops⟩ ~ *vi* **1 :** to study material again : make a review ⟨~ for a test⟩ **2 :** to write reviews
re·view·er \ri-ˈvyü-ər\ *n* (1651) : one that reviews; *esp* : a writer of critical reviews
re·vile \ri-ˈvī(ə)l\ *vb* **re·viled; re·vil·ing** [ME *revilen,* fr. MF *reviler* to despise, fr. *re-* + *vil* vile] *vt* (14c) : to subject to verbal abuse : VITUPERATE ~ *vi* : to use abusive language : RAIL ***syn*** see SCOLD — **re·vile·ment** \-ˈvī(ə)l-mənt\ *n* — **re·vil·er** *n*
re·vis·al \ri-ˈvī-zəl\ *n* (1612) : an act of revising : REVISION
1**re·vise** \ˈrē-ˌvīz, ri-ˈ\ *n* (1591) **1 :** an act of revising : REVISION **2 :** a printing proof that incorporates changes marked in a previous proof
2**re·vise** \ri-ˈvīz\ *vt* **re·vised; re·vis·ing** [F *reviser,* fr. L *revisere* to look at again, fr. *revisus,* pp. of *revidēre* to see again, fr. *re-* + *vidēre* to see — more at WIT] (1596) **1 :** to look over again in order to correct or improve ⟨~ a manuscript⟩ **2 a :** to make a new, amended, improved, or up-to-date version of ⟨~ a dictionary⟩ **b :** to provide with a new taxonomic arrangement ⟨*revising* the alpine ferns⟩ ***syn*** see CORRECT — **re·vis·able** \-ˈvī-zə-bəl\ *adj* — **re·vis·er** *or* **re·vi·sor** \-ˈvī-zər\ *n*
Revised Standard Version *n* (1946) : a revision of the American Standard Version of the Bible published in 1946 and 1952
Revised Version *n* (1881) : a British revision of the Authorized Version of the Bible published in 1881 and 1885
re·vi·sion \ri-ˈvizh-ən\ *n* (ca. 1611) **1 a :** an act of revising **b :** a result of revising : ALTERATION **2 :** a revised version — **re·vi·sion·ary** \-ə-ˌner-ē\ *adj*
re·vi·sion·ism \ri-ˈvizh-ə-ˌniz-əm\ *n* (1921) **1 :** advocacy of revision (as of a doctrine or policy or in historical analysis) **2 :** a movement in revolutionary Marxian socialism favoring an evolutionary rather than a revolutionary spirit — **re·vi·sion·ist** \-nəst\ *n or adj*
1**re·vis·it** \(ˈ)rē-ˈviz-ət\ *vt* (1602) : to visit again : return to
2**revisit** *n* (1623) : a second or subsequent visit
re·vi·so·ry \ri-ˈvīz-(ə-)rē\ *adj* (ca. 1846) : having the power or purpose to revise ⟨a ~ committee⟩ ⟨a ~ function⟩
re·vi·tal·ise *Brit var of* REVITALIZE
re·vi·tal·ize \(ˈ)rē-ˈvīt-ᵊl-ˌīz\ *vt* **-ized; -iz·ing** (1869) : to give new life or vigor to — **re·vi·tal·iza·tion** \(ˌ)rē-ˌvīt-ᵊl-ə-ˈzā-shən\ *n*
re·viv·al \ri-ˈvī-vəl\ *n* (1651) **1 :** an act or instance of reviving : the state of being revived: as **a :** renewed attention to or interest in something **b :** a new presentation or publication of something old **c (1) :** a period of renewed religious interest **(2) :** an often highly emotional evangelistic meeting or series of meetings **2 :** restoration of force, validity, or effect (as to a contract)
re·viv·al·ism \-ˈvī-və-ˌliz-əm\ *n* (1815) **1 :** the spirit or methods characteristic of religious revivals **2 :** a tendency or desire to revive or restore
re·viv·al·ist \-ˈvīv-(ə-)ləst\ *n* (1820) **1 :** one who conducts religious revivals; *specif* : a clergyman who travels about to conduct revivals **2 :** one who revives or restores something disused — **revivalist** *adj* — **re·viv·al·is·tic** \-ˌvī-və-ˈlis-tik\ *adj*
re·vive \ri-ˈvīv\ *vb* **re·vived; re·viv·ing** [ME *reviven,* fr. MF *revivre,* fr. L *revivere* to live again, fr. *re-* + *vivere* to live — more at QUICK] *vi* (15c) **:** to return to consciousness or life : to become active or flourishing again ~ *vt* **1 :** to restore to consciousness or life **2 :** to restore from a depressed, inactive, or unused state : bring back **3 :** to renew in the mind or memory — **re·viv·able** \-ˈvī-və-bəl\ *adj* — **re·viv·er** *n*
re·viv·i·fy \rē-ˈviv-ə-ˌfī\ *vt* [F *révivifier,* fr. LL *revivificare,* fr. L *re-* + LL *vivificare* to vivify] (1675) : to give new life to : REVIVE — **re·viv·i·fi·ca·tion** \-ˌviv-ə-fə-ˈkā-shən\ *n*
re·vi·vis·cence \ˌrē-ˌvī-ˈvis-ᵊn(t)s, ri-\ *n* [L *reviviscere* to come to life again, fr. *re-* + *viviscere* to come to life, fr. *vivus* alive, living — more at QUICK] (1626) : an act of reviving : the state of being revived — **re·vi·vis·cent** \-ᵊnt\ *adj*
re·vo·ca·ble \ˈrev-ə-kə-bəl *also* ri-ˈvō-\ *also* **re·vok·able** \ri-ˈvō-kə-bəl\ *adj* [ME, fr. MF, fr. L *revocabilis,* fr. *revocare*] (15c) : capable of being revoked
re·vo·ca·tion \ˌrev-ə-ˈkā-shən; ri-ˌvō-, ˌrē-\ *n* [ME, fr. MF, fr. L *revocation-, revocatio,* fr. *revocatus,* pp. of *revocare*] (15c) : an act or instance of revoking
1**re·voke** \ri-ˈvōk\ *vb* **re·voked; re·vok·ing** [ME *revoken,* fr. MF *revoquer,* fr. L *revocare,* fr. *re-* + *vocare* to call — more at VOICE] *vt* (14c) **1 :** to annul by recalling or taking back : RESCIND ⟨~ a will⟩ **2 :** to bring or call back ~ *vi* : to fail to follow suit when able in a card game in violation of the rules — **re·vok·er** *n*
2**revoke** *n* (1709) : an act or instance of revoking in a card game
1**re·volt** \ri-ˈvōlt *also* -ˈvȯlt\ *vb* [MF *revolter,* fr. OIt *rivoltare* to overthrow, fr. (assumed) VL *revolvitare,* freq. of L *revolvere* to revolve, roll back] *vi* (1540) **1 :** to renounce allegiance or subjection (as to a government) : REBEL **2 a :** to experience disgust or shock **b :** to turn away with disgust ~ *vt* : to cause to turn away or shrink with disgust or abhorrence — **re·volt·er** *n*
2**revolt** *n* (1560) **1 :** a renouncing of allegiance (as to a government or party); *esp* : a determined armed uprising **2 :** a movement or expression of vigorous dissent ***syn*** see REBELLION
re·volt·ing *adj* (1806) : extremely offensive — **re·volt·ing·ly** *adv*
rev·o·lute \ˈrev-ə-ˌlüt\ *adj* [L *revolutus,* pp.] (ca. 1753) : rolled backward or downward ⟨a leaf with ~ margins⟩
rev·o·lu·tion \ˌrev-ə-ˈlü-shən\ *n* [ME *revolucioun,* fr. MF *revolution,* fr. LL *revolution-, revolutio,* fr. L *revolutus,* pp. of *revolvere* to revolve] (14c) **1 a (1) :** the action by a celestial body of going round in an orbit or elliptic course; *also* : apparent movement of such a body round the earth **(2) :** the time taken by a celestial body to make a complete round in its orbit **(3) :** the rotation of a celestial body on its axis **b :** completion of a course (as of years); *also* : the period made by the regular succession of a measure of time or by a succession of similar events **c (1) :** a progressive motion of a body round an axis so that any line of the body parallel to the axis returns to its initial position while remaining parallel to the axis in transit and usu. at a constant distance from it **(2) :** motion of any figure about a center or axis ⟨~ of a right triangle about one of its legs generates a cone⟩ **(3) :** ROTATION 1b **2 a :** a sudden, radical, or complete change **b :** a fundamental change in political organization; *esp* : the overthrow or renunciation of one government or ruler and the substitution of another by the governed **c :** activity or movement designed to effect fundamental changes in the socioeconomic situation ***syn*** see REBELLION
1**rev·o·lu·tion·ary** \-shə-ˌner-ē\ *adj* (1774) **1 a :** of, relating to, or constituting a revolution ⟨~ war⟩ **b :** tending to or promoting revolution ⟨a ~ party⟩ **c :** constituting or bringing about a major or fundamental change ⟨~ styling⟩ ⟨a ~ new product⟩ **2** *cap* : of or relating to the American Revolution or to the period in which it occurred — **rev·o·lu·tion·ari·ly** \-ˌlü-shə-ˈner-ə-lē\ *adv* — **rev·o·lu·tion·ari·ness** \-ˈlü-shə-ˌner-ē-nəs\ *n*
2**revolutionary** *n, pl* **-ar·ies** (1850) **1 :** one engaged in a revolution **2 :** an advocate or adherent of revolutionary doctrines
rev·o·lu·tion·ise *Brit var of* REVOLUTIONIZE
rev·o·lu·tion·ist \ˌrev-ə-ˈlü-sh(ə-)nəst\ *n* (1710) : REVOLUTIONARY — **revolutionist** *adj*
rev·o·lu·tion·ize \-shə-ˌnīz\ *vb* **-ized; -iz·ing** *vt* (1797) **1 :** to overthrow the established government of **2 :** to imbue with revolutionary doctrines **3 :** to change fundamentally or completely ~ *vi* : to engage in revolution — **rev·o·lu·tion·iz·er** *n*
re·volve \ri-ˈvälv, -ˈvȯlv *also* -ˈväv *or* -ˈvȯv\ *vb* **re·volved; re·volv·ing** [ME *revolven,* fr. L *revolvere* to roll back, cause to return, fr. *re-* + *volvere* to roll — more at VOLUBLE] *vt* (15c) **1 :** to turn over at length in the mind : PONDER ⟨~ a scheme⟩ **2 a :** to cause to go round in an orbit **b :** to cause to turn round on or as if on an axis : ROTATE ~ *vi* **1 :** RECUR **2 a :** to ponder something **b :** to remain under consideration ⟨ideas *revolved* in his mind⟩ **3 a :** to move in a curved path round a center or axis **b :** to turn or roll round on an axis **4 :** to center on : have as a main point ⟨the dispute *revolved* around wages⟩ — **re·volv·able** \-ˈväl-və-bəl, -ˈvȯl- *also* -ˈväv-ə- *or* -ˈvȯv-ə-\ *adj*
re·volv·er \ri-ˈväl-vər, -ˈvȯl- *also* -ˈväv-ər *or* -ˈvȯv-ər\ *n* (ca. 1835) **1 :** one that revolves **2 :** a handgun with a cylinder of several chambers brought successively into line with the barrel and discharged with the same hammer
re·volv·ing *adj* (1697) : tending to revolve or recur; *esp* : recurrently available
revolving charge account *n* (1967) : a charge account under which payment is made in monthly installments and includes a carrying charge
revolving credit *n* (1919) : a credit which may be used repeatedly up to the limit specified after partial or total repayments have been made
revolving fund *n* (1920) : a fund set up for specified purposes with the proviso that repayments to the fund may be used again for these purposes

re·vue \ri-ˈvyü\ *n* [F, fr. MF, review — more at REVIEW] (1872) **:** a theatrical production consisting typically of brief loosely connected often satirical skits, songs, and dances

re·vulsed \ri-ˈvəlst\ *adj* [L *revulsus,* pp. + E *-ed*] (ca. 1934) **:** affected with or having undergone revulsion

re·vul·sion \ri-ˈvəl-shən\ *n* [L *revulsion-, revulsio* act of tearing away, fr. *revulsus,* pp. of *revellere* to pluck away, fr. *re-* + *vellere* to pluck — more at VULNERABLE] (1607) **1 :** a strong pulling or drawing away **:** WITHDRAWAL **2 a :** a sudden or strong reaction or change **b :** a sense of utter distaste or repugnance — **re·vul·sive** \-ˈvəl-siv\ *adj*

revved *past and past part of* REV

revving *pres part of* REV

re·wake \(ˈ)rē-ˈwāk\ *vb* **-waked** *or* **-woke** \-ˈwōk\; **-waked** *or* **-wo·ken** \-ˈwō-kən\ *or* **-woke; -wak·ing** *vt* (1593) **:** to waken again or anew ~ *vi* **:** to become awake again

re·wak·en \(ˈ)rē-ˈwā-kən\ *vb* (1638) **:** REWAKE

[1]re·ward \ri-ˈwȯ(ə)rd\ *vt* [ME *rewarden,* fr. ONF *rewarder* to regard, reward, fr. *re-* + *warder* to watch, guard, of Gmc origin; akin to OHG *wartēn* to watch — more at WARD] (14c) **1 :** to give a reward to or for **2 :** RECOMPENSE — **re·ward·able** \-ˈwȯrd-ə-bəl\ *adj* — **re·ward·er** *n*

[2]reward *n* (14c) **1 :** something that is given in return for good or evil done or received and esp. that is offered or given for some service or attainment **2 :** a stimulus administered to an organism following a correct or desired response that increases the probability of occurrence of the response

re·ward·ing *adj* (1697) **1 :** yielding or likely to yield a reward **:** VALUABLE, SATISFYING ⟨a ~ experience⟩ **2 :** serving as a reward ⟨a ~ smile of thanks⟩ — **re·ward·ing·ly** *adv*

[1]re·wind \(ˈ)rē-ˈwīnd\ *vt* **-wound** \-ˈwau̇nd\; **-wind·ing** (1904) **:** to wind again; *esp* **:** to reverse the winding of (as film)

[2]re·wind \ˈrē-ˌwīnd, (ˈ)rē-ˈ \ *n* (1926) **1 :** something that rewinds or is rewound **2 :** an act of rewinding

re·word \(ˈ)rē-ˈwərd\ *vt* (1602) **1 :** to repeat in the same words **2 :** to alter the wording of; *also* **:** to restate in other words

re·work \(ˈ)rē-ˈwərk\ *vt* (1842) **:** to work again or anew: as **a :** REVISE **b :** to reprocess (as used material) for further use

[1]re·write \(ˈ)rē-ˈrīt\ *vb* **-wrote** \-ˈrōt\; **-writ·ten** \-ˈrit-ᵊn\; **-writ·ing** \-ˈrīt-iŋ\ *vt* (1567) **1 :** to write in reply **2 :** to make a revision of (as a story) **:** cause to be revised: as **a :** to put (contributed material) into form for publication **b :** to alter (previously published material) for use in another publication ~ *vi* **:** to revise something previously written — **re·writ·er** *n*

[2]re·write \ˈrē-ˌrīt\ *n* (1914) **1 :** a piece of writing (as a news story) constructed by rewriting **2 :** an act or instance of rewriting

re·write man \ˈrē-ˌrīt-ˌman\ *n* (1901) **:** a newspaperman who specializes in rewriting

re·write rule \ˈrē-ˌrīt-\ *n* (1961) **:** a rule in a grammar which specifies the constituents of a single symbol

rex \ˈreks\ *n, pl* **rex·es** *or* **rex** [F *castorrex, castorex,* a variety of rabbit, fr. L *castor* beaver + *rex* king — more at CASTOR, ROYAL] (1920) **:** an animal showing a genetic recessive variation in which the guard hairs are very short or entirely lacking; *esp* **:** any of a breed of slender domestic cats having a short curly undercoat and no guard hairs — see CAT illustration

Reye's syndrome \ˈrīz-, ˈrāz-\ *also* **Reye syndrome** \ˈrī-, ˈrā-\ *n* [R.D.K. *Reye* †1977 Austral. pathologist] (1965) **:** an often fatal encephalopathy esp. of childhood characterized by fever, vomiting, fatty infiltration of the liver, and swelling of the kidneys and brain

rey·nard \ˈrān-ərd, ˈren-, -ˌär(d)\ *n, often cap* [ME *Renard,* name of the fox who is hero of the Fr. beast epic *Roman de Renart,* fr. MF *Renart, Renard*] (14c) **:** FOX

re·zone \(ˈ)rē-ˈzōn\ *vt* (1944) **:** to alter the zoning of

R factor \ˈär-\ *n* [*r*esistance] (1962) **:** a group of genes present in some bacteria that provide a basis for resistance to antibiotics and can be transferred from cell to cell by conjugation

Rh \ˈär-ˈāch\ *adj* (1940) **:** of, relating to, or being an Rh factor ⟨~ antigens⟩ ⟨~ sensitization in pregnancy⟩

rhabd- *or* **rhabdo-** *comb form* [LGk, fr. Gk, fr. *rhabdos* rod — more at VERVAIN] **:** rodlike structure ⟨*rhabdo*virus⟩

rhab·do·coele \ˈrab-də-ˌsēl\ *n* [NL *Rhabdocoela,* fr. *rhabd-* + NL *-coela -coele*] (ca. 1909) **:** a turbellarian worm (order Rhabdocoela) with an unbranched intestine

rhab·dom \ˈrab-ˌdäm, -dəm\ *or* **rhab·dome** \-ˌdōm\ *n* [LGk *rhabdōma* bundle of rods, fr. Gk *rhabdos* rod] (1878) **:** one of the minute rodlike structures in the retinulae in the compound eyes of arthropods

rhab·do·man·cy \ˈrab-də-ˌman(t)-sē\ *n* [LGk *rhabdomanteia,* fr. Gk *rhabdos* rod + *-manteia* -mancy] (1646) **:** divination by rods or wands — **rhab·do·man·cer** \-ˌman(t)-sər\ *n*

rhab·do·mere \-ˌmi(ə)r\ *n* [blend of *rhabdom* and *-mere*] (ca. 1884) **:** a division of a rhabdom

rhab·do·myo·sar·co·ma \ˈrab-(ˌ)dō-ˌmī-ə-sär-ˈkō-mə\ *n, pl* **-mas** *or* **-ma·ta** \-mət-ə\ [NL, fr. *rhabd-* + *my-* + *sarcoma*] (1898) **:** a malignant tumor composed of striated muscle fibers

rhab·do·virus \-ˌvī-rəs\ *n* (1966) **:** any of a group of RNA-containing rod- or bullet-shaped viruses found in plants and animals and including the causative agents of rabies and vesicular stomatitis

rhad·a·man·thine \ˌrad-ə-ˈman(t)-thən, -ˈman-ˌthīn\ *adj, often cap* [*Rhadamanthus*] (1840) **:** rigorously strict or just

Rhad·a·man·thus \ˌrad-ə-ˈman(t)-thəs\ *n* **:** a judge of the underworld in Greek mythology

Rhae·to–Ro·man·ic \ˌrēt-ō-rō-ˈman-ik\ *n* [L *Rhaetus* of Rhaetia, ancient Roman province + E *Romanic*] (1867) **:** a Romance language of eastern Switzerland, northeastern Italy, and adjacent parts of Austria

rham·nose \ˈram-ˌnōs, -ˌnōz\ *n* [ISV, fr. NL *Rhamnus,* genus of the buckthorn; fr. its being produced from a plant of this genus] (1888) **:** a crystalline sugar $C_6H_{12}O_5$ that occurs combined in many plants and is obtained in the common dextrorotatory L form

rhap·sod·ic \rap-ˈsäd-ik\ *adj* (1782) **1 :** extravagantly emotional **:** RAPTUROUS **2 :** resembling or characteristic of a rhapsody — **rhap·sod·i·cal** \-i-kəl\ *adj* — **rhap·sod·i·cal·ly** \-i-k(ə-)lē\ *adv*

rhap·so·dist \ˈrap-səd-əst\ *n* (ca. 1656) **1 :** a professional reciter of epic poems **2 :** one who writes or speaks rhapsodically

rhap·so·dize \-sə-ˌdīz\ *vi* **-dized; -diz·ing** (1806) **:** to speak or write in a rhapsodic manner ⟨~ about a new book⟩

rhap·so·dy \ˈrap-səd-ē\ *n, pl* **-dies** [L *rhapsodia,* fr. Gk *rhapsōidia* recitation of selections from epic poetry, rhapsody, fr. *rhaptein* to sew, stitch together + *aidein* to sing; akin to OHG *worf* scythe handle, Gk *rhepein* to bend, incline — more at ODE] (1542) **1 :** a portion of an epic poem adapted for recitation **2** *archaic* **:** a miscellaneous collection **3 a** (1) **:** a highly emotional utterance (2) **:** a highly emotional literary work (3) **:** effusively rapturous or extravagant discourse **b :** RAPTURE, ECSTASY **4 :** a musical composition of irregular form having an improvisatory character

rhat·a·ny \ˈrat-ᵊn-ē\ *n* [Sp *ratania* & Pg *ratânhia,* fr. Quechua *ratánya*] (1808) **1 :** the dried root of either of two American shrubs (*Krameria triandra* and *K. argentea*) used as an astringent **2 :** a plant yielding rhatany

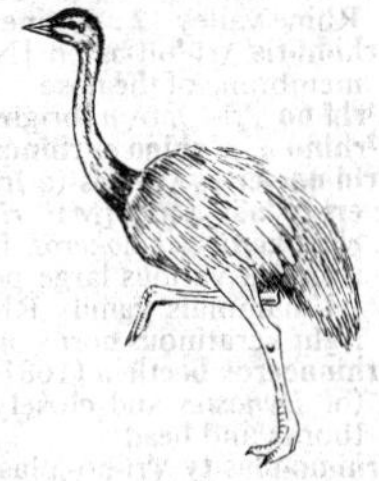
rhea

rhea \ˈrē-ə\ *n* [NL, genus of birds, prob. fr. L *Rhea,* mother of Zeus, fr. Gk] (1797) **:** any of several large tall flightless So. American birds (order Rheiformes) that resemble but are smaller than the African ostrich, have three toes, a fully feathered head and neck, an undeveloped tail, and pale gray to brownish feathers that droop over the rump and back

rhe·bok \ˈrē-ˌbäk\ *n* [Afrik *reebok,* fr. MD, male roe deer, fr. *ree* roe + *boc* buck] (1834) **:** a large gray southern African antelope (*Pelea capreolus*)

rhe·ni·um \ˈrē-nē-əm\ *n* [NL, fr. L *Rhenus* Rhine river] (1925) **:** a rare heavy metallic element that resembles manganese, is obtained either as a powder or as a silver-white hard metal, and is used in catalysts and thermocouples — see ELEMENT table

rheo- *comb form* [Gk *rhein* to flow — more at STREAM] **:** flow **:** current ⟨*rheo*stat⟩

rhe·ol·o·gy \rē-ˈäl-ə-jē\ *n* [ISV] (1929) **:** a science dealing with the deformation and flow of matter; *also* **:** the quality or state of being able to be deformed or to flow — **rhe·o·log·i·cal** \ˌrē-ə-ˈläj-i-kəl\ *adj* — **rhe·o·log·i·cal·ly** \-k(ə-)lē\ *adv* — **rhe·ol·o·gist** \rē-ˈäl-ə-jəst\ *n*

rhe·om·e·ter \rē-ˈäm-ət-ər\ *n* [ISV] (1877) **:** an instrument for measuring the flow of viscous substances

rheo·stat \ˈrē-ə-ˌstat\ *n* (1843) **:** a resistor for regulating a current by means of variable resistances — **rheo·stat·ic** \ˌrē-ə-ˈstat-ik\ *adj*

rhe·sus monkey \ˌrē-səs-\ *n* [NL *Rhesus,* genus of monkeys, fr. L, a mythical king of Thrace, fr. Gk *Rhēsos*] (1841) **:** a pale brown Indian monkey (*Macaca mulatta*) often used in medical research

rhe·tor \ˈrē-ˌtȯ(ə)r, ˈre-; ˈret-ər, ˈret-\ *n* [ME *rethor,* fr. L *rhetor,* fr. Gk *rhētōr*] (14c) **:** RHETORICIAN 1

rhet·o·ric \ˈret-ə-rik\ *n* [ME *rethorik,* fr. MF *rethorique,* fr. L *rhetorica,* fr. Gk *rhētorikē,* lit., art of oratory, fr. fem. of *rhētorikos* of an orator, fr. *rhētōr* orator, rhetorician, fr. *eirein* to say, speak — more at WORD] (14c) **1 :** the art of speaking or writing effectively; *specif* **:** the study of principles and rules of composition formulated by critics of ancient times **2 a :** skill in the effective use of speech **b :** a type or mode of language or speech; *also* **:** insincere or grandiloquent language **3 :** verbal communication **:** DISCOURSE

rhe·tor·i·cal \ri-ˈtȯr-i-kəl, -ˈtär-\ *also* **rhe·tor·ic** \ri-ˈtȯr-ik, -ˈtär-\ *adj* (15c) **1 a :** of, relating to, or concerned with rhetoric **b :** employed for rhetorical effect **2 a :** given to rhetoric **:** GRANDILOQUENT **b :** VERBAL — **rhe·tor·i·cal·ly** \-i-k(ə-)lē\ *adv*

rhetorical question *n* (1843) **:** a question asked merely for effect with no answer expected

rhet·o·ri·cian \ˌret-ə-ˈrish-ən\ *n* (15c) **1 a :** a master or teacher of rhetoric **b :** ORATOR **2 :** an eloquent or grandiloquent writer or speaker

rheum \ˈrüm\ *n* [ME *reume,* fr. MF, fr. L *rheuma,* fr. Gk, lit., flow, flux, fr. *rhein* to flow — more at STREAM] (14c) **1 :** a watery discharge from the mucous membranes esp. of the eyes or nose **2** *archaic* **:** TEARS — **rheumy** \ˈrü-mē\ *adj*

[1]rheu·mat·ic \ru̇-ˈmat-ik\ *adj* [ME *rewmatik* subject to rheum, fr. L *rheumaticus,* fr. Gk *rheumatikos,* fr. *rheumat-, rheuma*] (1711) **:** of, relating to, characteristic of, or affected with rheumatism — **rheu·mat·i·cal·ly** \-i-k(ə-)lē\ *adv*

[2]rheumatic *n* (1884) **:** one affected with rheumatism

rheumatic disease *n* (1927) **:** any of several diseases (as rheumatic fever or fibrositis) marked by inflammation and pain in muscles or joints

rheumatic fever *n* (1782) **:** an acute disease that occurs chiefly in children and young adults and is characterized by fever, by inflammation and pain in and around the joints, and by inflammatory involvement of the pericardium and heart valves

rheu·ma·tism \ˈrü-mə-ˌtiz-əm, ˈru̇m-ə-\ *n* [L *rheumatismus* flux, rheum, fr. Gk *rheumatismos,* fr. *rheumatizesthai* to suffer from a flux, fr. *rheumat-, rheuma* flux] (1688) **1 :** any of various conditions characterized by inflammation or pain in muscles, joints, or fibrous tissue ⟨muscular ~⟩ **2 :** RHEUMATOID ARTHRITIS

rheu·ma·tiz \-ˌtiz\ *n, chiefly dial* (1760) **:** RHEUMATISM

rheu·ma·toid \-ˌtȯid\ *adj* [ISV, fr. *rheumatism*] (1871) **:** characteristic of or affected with rheumatoid arthritis

rheumatoid arthritis *n* (1859) **:** a usu. chronic disease of unknown cause characterized esp. by pain, stiffness, inflammation, swelling, and sometimes destruction of joints

rheumatoid factor *n* (1960) **:** an autoantibody of high molecular weight that is usu. present in rheumatoid arthritis

rheu·ma·tol·o·gy \ˌrü-mə-ˈtäl-ə-jē, ˌru̇m-ə-\ *n* (ca. 1941) **:** a medical science dealing with rheumatic diseases — **rheu·ma·tol·o·gist** \-jəst\ *n*

Rh factor \ˈär-ˈāch-\ *n* [*rh*esus monkey (in which it was first detected)] (1942) **:** any of one or more genetically determined substances present

in the red blood cells of most persons and of higher animals and capable of inducing intense antigenic reactions
rhin- *or* **rhino-** *comb form* [NL, fr. Gk, fr. *rhin-, rhis*] : nose ⟨*rhin*itis⟩ : nose and ⟨*rhino*laryngology⟩
rhi·nal \ˈrīn-ᵊl\ *adj* (ca. 1864) : of or relating to the nose : NASAL
-rhine — see -RRHINE
rhin·en·ceph·a·lon \ˌrī-(ˌ)nen-ˈsef-ə-ˌlän, -lən\ *n* [NL] (1846) : the chiefly olfactory part of the forebrain — **rhin·en·ce·phal·ic** \ˌrī-ˌnen-sə-ˈfal-ik\ *adj*
rhine·stone \ˈrīn-ˌstōn\ *n* [*Rhine* river] (1888) : a colorless imitation stone of high luster made of glass, paste, or gem quartz — **rhine·stoned** \-ˌstōnd\ *adj*
Rhine wine \ˈrīn-\ *n* (1843) **1** : a usu. white wine produced in the Rhine valley **2** : a wine similar to Rhine wine produced elsewhere
rhi·ni·tis \rī-ˈnīt-əs\ *n* [NL] (ca. 1884) : inflammation of the mucous membrane of the nose
¹rhi·no \ˈrī-(ˌ)nō\ *n* [origin unknown] (1670) : MONEY, CASH
²rhino *n, pl* **rhino** *or* **rhinos** (1884) : RHINOCEROS
rhi·noc·er·os \rī-ˈnäs-(ə-)rəs, rə-\ *n, pl* **-noc·er·os·es** *or* **-noc·er·os** *or* **-noc·eri** \-ˈnäs-ə-ˌrī\ [ME *rinoceros*, fr. L *rhinocerot-, rhinoceros*, fr. Gk *rhinokerōt-, rhinokerōs*, fr. *rhin-* + *keras* horn — more at HORN] (14c) : any of various large powerful herbivorous thick-skinned perissodactyl mammals (family Rhinocerotidae) that have one or two heavy upright keratinous horns on the snout
rhinoceros beetle *n* (1681) : any of various large chiefly tropical beetles (of *Dynastes* and closely related genera) having projecting horns on thorax and head
rhi·no·plas·ty \ˈrī-nō-ˌplas-tē\ *n, pl* **-ties** (1842) : plastic surgery on the nose usu. for cosmetic purposes
rhi·nos·co·py \rī-ˈnäs-kə-pē\ *n* [ISV] (1861) : examination of the nasal passages
rhi·no·vi·rus \ˌrī-nō-ˈvī-rəs\ *n* [NL] (1961) : any of a group of picornaviruses that are related to the enteroviruses and are associated with disorders of the upper respiratory tract
rhiz- *or* **rhizo-** *comb form* [NL, fr. Gk, fr. *rhiza* — more at ROOT] : root ⟨*rhiz*anthous⟩ ⟨*rhizo*carpous⟩
-rhi·za *or* **-r·rhi·za** \ˈrī-zə\ *n comb form, pl* **-zae** \-(ˌ)zē\ *or* **-zas** [NL, fr. Gk *rhiza*] : root : part resembling or connected with a root ⟨coleo*rhiza*⟩ ⟨mycor*rhiza*⟩
rhi·zo·bi·um \rī-ˈzō-bē-əm\ *n, pl* **-bia** \-bē-ə\ [NL, fr. *rhiz-* + Gk *bios* life — more at QUICK] (1921) : any of a genus (*Rhizobium*) of small heterotrophic soil bacteria capable of forming symbiotic nodules on the roots of leguminous plants and of there becoming bacteroids that fix atmospheric nitrogen
rhi·zoc·to·nia \ˌrī-ˌzäk-ˈtō-nē-ə\ *n* [NL, fr. *rhiz-* + Gk *-ktonos* killing, fr. *kteinein* to kill; akin to Skt *kṣaṇoti* he wounds] (1897) : a fungus of a form genus (*Rhizoctonia*) that includes major plant pathogens
rhizoctonia disease *n* (ca. 1934) : a plant disease caused by a rhizoctonia; *esp* : one of potatoes characterized esp. by black scurfy spots on the tubers
rhi·zo·gen·e·sis \ˌrī-zə-ˈjen-ə-səs\ *n* [NL] (1949) : root development
rhi·zoid \ˈrī-ˌzȯid\ *n* (1875) : a rootlike structure — **rhi·zoi·dal** \rī-ˈzȯid-ᵊl\ *adj*
rhi·zo·ma·tous \rī-ˈzō-mət-əs\ *adj* [ISV, fr. NL *rhizomat-, rhizoma*] (1847) : having or resembling a rhizome ⟨~ plants⟩
rhi·zome \ˈrī-ˌzōm\ *n* [NL *rhizomat-, rhizoma*, fr. Gk *rhizōmat-, rhizōma* mass of roots, fr. *rhizoun* to cause to take root, fr. *rhiza* root — more at ROOT] (1845) : a somewhat elongate usu. horizontal subterranean plant stem that is often thickened by deposits of reserve food material, produces shoots above and roots below, and is distinguished from a true root in possessing buds, nodes, and usu. scalelike leaves — **rhi·zo·mic** \rī-ˈzō-mik, -ˈzäm-ik\ *adj*
rhi·zo·plane \ˈrī-zə-ˌplān\ *n* (ca. 1949) : the external surface of roots together with closely adhering soil particles and debris
rhi·zo·pod \ˈrī-zə-ˌpäd\ *n* [NL *Rhizopoda*, fr. *rhiz-* + *-poda* -pod] (1851) : any of a subclass (Rhizopoda) of usu. creeping protozoans (as an amoeba or a foraminifer) having lobate or rootlike pseudopodia
rhi·zo·pus \ˈrī-zə-pəs, -ˌpu̇s\ *n* [NL, fr. *rhiz-* + Gk *pous* foot — more at FOOT] (1887) : any of a genus (*Rhizopus*) of mold fungi including economic pests causing decay
rhi·zo·sphere \-ˌsfi(ə)r\ *n* [ISV] (1929) : soil that surrounds and is influenced by the roots of a plant
rhi·zot·o·my \rī-ˈzät-ə-mē\ *n, pl* **-mies** [ISV] (1911) : the operation of cutting the anterior or posterior spinal nerve roots
Rh–neg·a·tive \ˌär-ˌāch-ˈneg-ət-iv\ *adj* (1945) : lacking Rh factor in the blood
rho \ˈrō\ *n* [Gk *rhō*, of Sem origin; akin to Heb *rēsh* resh] (15c) : the 17th letter of the Greek alphabet — see ALPHABET table
rhod- *or* **rhodo-** *comb form* [NL, fr. L, fr. Gk, fr. *rhodon* rose] : rose : red ⟨*rhod*ium⟩ ⟨*rhodo*lite⟩
rho·da·mine \ˈrōd-ə-ˌmēn\ *n, often cap* [ISV] (1888) : any of a group of yellowish red to blue fluorescent dyes; *esp* : a brilliant bluish red dye made by fusing an amino derivative of phenol with phthalic anhydride and used esp. in coloring paper and as a biological stain
Rhode Is·land bent \rō-ˌdī-lən(d)-\ *n* [*Rhode Island*, state of U.S.] (1790) : a lawn grass (*Agrostis tenuis*) of eastern No. America
Rhode Island Red *n* (1896) : any of an American breed of general-purpose domestic fowls having a long heavy body, smooth yellow or reddish legs, and rich brownish red plumage
Rhode Island White *n* (1923) : any of an American breed of domestic fowls resembling Rhode Island Reds but having pure white plumage
Rhodes grass \ˈrōdz-\ *n* [Cecil J. *Rhodes*] (1915) : an African perennial grass (*Chloris gayana*) widely cultivated as a forage grass esp. in dry regions
Rho·de·sian man \rō-ˌdē-zh(ē-)ən-\ *n* [Northern *Rhodesia*, Africa] (1921) : an extinct African man (*Homo rhodesiensis* or *Africanthropus rhodesiensis*) having long bones of modern type, a skull with prominent brow ridges and large face but human palate and dentition, and a simple but relatively large brain
Rhodesian Ridge·back \-ˈrij-ˌbak\ *n* (1930) : any of an African breed of powerful long-bodied hunting dogs having a dense harsh short tan coat with a characteristic crest of reversed hair along the spine
Rhodes scholar \ˈrōd(z)-\ *n* (1902) : a holder of one of numerous scholarships founded under the will of Cecil J. Rhodes that can be used at Oxford University for two or three years and are open to candidates from the British Commonwealth and the U.S.
rho·di·um \ˈrōd-ē-əm\ *n* [NL, fr. Gk *rhodon* rose] (1804) : a white hard ductile metallic element that is resistant to attack by acids, occurs in platinum ores, and is used in alloys with platinum — see ELEMENT table
rho·do·chro·site \ˌrōd-ə-ˈkrō-ˌsīt, rə-ˈdäk-rə-\ *n* [G *rhodocrosit*, fr. Gk *rhodochrōs* rose-colored, fr. *rhod-* + *chrōs* color; akin to Gk *chrōma* color — more at CHROMATIC] (1836) : a rose red mineral $MnCO_3$ consisting essentially of manganese carbonate
rho·do·den·dron \ˌrōd-ə-ˈden-drən\ *n* [NL, fr. L, oleander, fr. Gk, fr. *rhod-* + *dendron* tree — more at DENDR-] (1664) : any of a genus (*Rhododendron*) of the heath family of widely cultivated shrubs and trees with alternate leaves and showy flowers; *esp* : one with leathery evergreen leaves as distinguished from a deciduous azalea
rho·do·lite \ˈrōd-ᵊl-ˌīt\ *n* (ca. 1897) : a pink or purple garnet used as a gem
rhodomontade *var of* RODOMONTADE
rho·do·nite \ˈrōd-ᵊn-ˌīt\ *n* [G *rhodonit*, fr. Gk *rhodon* rose] (1823) : a pale red triclinic mineral $MnSiO_3$ that consists essentially of manganese silicate and is used as an ornamental stone
rho·dop·sin \rō-ˈdäp-sən\ *n* [ISV *rhod-* + Gk *opsis* sight, vision + ISV *-in* — more at OPTIC] (1886) : a red photosensitive pigment in the retinal rods of marine fishes and most higher vertebrates that is important in vision in dim light — called also *visual purple*
rho·do·ra \rō-ˈdōr-ə, -ˈdȯr-\ *n* [NL, fr. L, a plant] (ca. 1731) : any of a genus (*Rhodora*) of the heath family of shrubs that are found in Canada and New England and have delicate pink flowers produced before or with the leaves in the spring
rhomb \ˈräm(b)\ *n, pl* **rhombs** \ˈrämz\ [MF *rhombe*, fr. L *rhombus*] (1578) **1** : RHOMBUS **2** : RHOMBOHEDRON
rhomb·en·ceph·a·lon \ˌräm-(ˌ)ben-ˈsef-ə-ˌlän, -lən\ *n* [NL] (ca. 1909) : the parts of the vertebrate brain that develop from the embryonic hindbrain; *also* : HINDBRAIN 1a
rhom·bic \ˈräm-bik\ *adj* (1701) **1** : having the form of a rhombus **2** : ORTHORHOMBIC
rhom·bo·he·dron \ˌräm-bō-ˈhē-drən\ *n, pl* **-drons** *or* **-dra** \-drə\ [NL, deriv. of Gk *rhombos* + NL *-hedron*] (1836) : a parallelepiped whose faces are rhombuses — **rhom·bo·he·dral** \-drəl\ *adj*
¹rhom·boid \ˈräm-ˌbȯid\ *n* [MF *rhomboïde*, fr. L *rhomboides*, fr. Gk *rhomboeidēs* resembling a rhombus, fr. *rhombos*] (1570) : a parallelogram with no right angles and with adjacent sides of unequal length
²rhomboid \ˈräm-ˌbȯid\ *or* **rhom·boi·dal** \räm-ˈbȯid-ᵊl\ *adj* (1693) : shaped somewhat like a rhombus or rhomboid
rhom·boi·de·us \räm-ˈbȯid-ē-əs\ *n, pl* **-dei** \-ē-ˌī\ [NL, fr. L *rhomboides* rhomboid] (1835) : either of two muscles that lie beneath the trapezius muscle and connect the spinous processes of various vertebrae with the medial border of the scapula
rhom·bus \ˈräm-bəs\ *n, pl* **rhom·bus·es** *or* **rhom·bi** \-ˌbī, -ˌbē\ [L, fr. Gk *rhombos*] (ca. 1567) : a parallelogram with four equal sides and esp. one with no right angles
rhon·chus \ˈräŋ-kəs\ *n, pl* **rhon·chi** \ˈräŋ-ˌkī\ [LGk, fr. *rhenchein* to snore, wheeze; akin to OIr *srennim* I snore] (1829) : a whistling or snoring sound heard on auscultation of the chest when the air channels are partly obstructed
Rh–pos·i·tive \ˌär-ˌāch-ˈpäz-ət-iv, -ˈpäz-tiv\ *adj* (1942) : containing Rh factor in the red blood cells
rhu·barb \ˈrü-ˌbärb\ *n* [ME *rubarbe*, fr. MF *reubarbe*, fr. ML *reubarbarum*, alter. of *rha barbarum*, lit., barbarian rhubarb] (15c) **1** : any of several plants (genus *Rheum*) of the buckwheat family having large leaves with thick succulent petioles often used as food **2** : the dried rhizome and roots of any of several rhubarbs grown in China and Tibet and used as a purgative and stomachic **3** : a heated dispute or controversy
rhumb \ˈrəm(b)\ *n, pl* **rhumbs** \ˈrəmz\ [Sp *rumbo* rhumb, rhumb line] (1578) **1** : a line or course on a single bearing **2** : any of the points of the mariner's compass
rhumba *var of* RUMBA
rhumb line *n* [Sp *rumbo*] (ca. 1795) : a line on the surface of the earth that follows a single compass bearing and makes equal oblique angles with all meridians
rhus \ˈrüs\ *n, pl* **rhus·es** *or* **rhus** [NL, fr. L, sumac, fr. Gk *rhous*] (ca. 1611) : any of a genus (*Rhus*) of shrubs and trees (as sumac or poison ivy) that are native to temperate and warm regions, have compound trifoliolate or pinnate leaves, and sometimes produce substances causing dermatitis
¹rhyme \ˈrīm\ *n* [alter. of ME *rime*, fr. OF] (13c) **1 a** (1) : rhyming verse (2) : POETRY **b** : a composition in verse that rhymes **2 a** : correspondence in terminal sounds of units of composition or utterance (as two or more words or lines of verse) **b** : one of two or more words thus corresponding in sound **c** : correspondence of other than terminal word sounds: as (1) : ALLITERATION (2) : INTERNAL RHYME **3** : RHYTHM, MEASURE — **rhymeless** *adj*
²rhyme *vb* **rhymed; rhym·ing** *vt* (13c) **1** : to relate or praise in rhyming verse **2 a** : to put into rhyme **b** : to compose (verse) in rhyme **c** : to cause to rhyme : use as rhyme ~ *vi* **1** : to make rhymes; *also* : to compose rhyming verse **2** *of a word or verse* : to end in syllables that are rhymes **3** : to be in accord : HARMONIZE — **rhym·er** *n*
rhyme or reason *n* (15c) : good sense or reason
rhyme royal \-ˈrȯi(-ə)l\ *n* (ca. 1841) : a stanza of seven lines in iambic pentameter with a rhyme scheme of *ababbcc*
rhyme scheme *n* (1917) : the arrangement of rhymes in a stanza or a poem
rhyme·ster \ˈrīm(p)-stər\ *n* (1589) : an inferior poet
rhyming slang *n* (1860) : slang in which the word intended is replaced by a word or phrase that rhymes with it (as *loaf of bread* for *head*) or the first part of the phrase (as *loaf* for *head*)
rhyn·cho·ce·pha·lian \ˌriŋ-kō-sə-ˈfāl-yən\ *n* [deriv. of Gk *rhynchos* beak, snout + *kephalē* head — more at CEPHALIC] (1886) : any of an order (Rhynchocephalia) of reptiles (as the tuatara) resembling lizards — **rhynchocephalian** *adj*
rhy·o·lite \ˈrī-ə-ˌlīt\ *n* [G *rhyolith*, fr. Gk *rhyax* stream, stream of lava (fr. *rhein*) + G *-lith* -lite] (1868) : a very acid volcanic rock that is the lava form of granite — **rhy·o·lit·ic** \ˌrī-ə-ˈlit-ik\ *adj*

rhythm \'rith-əm\ *n* [MF & L; MF *rhythme,* fr. L *rhythmus,* fr. Gk *rhythmos,* fr. *rhein* to flow — more at STREAM] (1560) **1 a :** an ordered recurrent alternation of strong and weak elements in the flow of sound and silence in speech **b :** a particular example or form of rhythm ⟨iambic ~⟩ **2 a :** the aspect of music comprising all the elements (as accent, meter, and tempo) that relate to forward movement **b :** a characteristic rhythmic pattern ⟨rumba ~⟩; *also* : [1]METER 2 **c :** the group of instruments in a band supplying the rhythm — called also *rhythm section* **3 a :** movement or fluctuation marked by the regular recurrence or natural flow of related elements **b :** the repetition in a literary work of phrase, incident, character type, or symbol **4 :** a regularly recurrent quantitative change in a variable biological process **5 :** the effect created by the elements in a play, movie, or novel that relate to the temporal development of the action **6 :** RHYTHM METHOD

rhythm and blues *n* (1949) **:** popular music with elements of blues and Negro folk music

rhythm band *n* (ca. 1943) **:** a band usu. composed of schoolchildren who play simple percussion instruments (as rhythm sticks, sleigh bells, or tambourines) to learn fundamentals of coordination and music

rhyth·mic \'rith-mik\ *or* **rhyth·mi·cal** \-mi-kəl\ *adj* (1603) **1 :** of, relating to, or involving rhythm **2 :** marked by or moving in pronounced rhythm — **rhyth·mi·cal·ly** \-mi-k(ə-)lē\ *adv*

rhyth·mic·i·ty \rith-'mis-ət-ē\ *n* (ca. 1885) **:** the state of being rhythmic or of responding rhythmically

rhyth·mics \'rith-miks\ *n pl but sing or pl in constr* (ca. 1864) **:** the science or theory of rhythms

rhyth·mist \'rith-(ə-)məst\ *n* (1864) **:** one who studies or has a feeling for rhythm

rhyth·mize \'rith-(ə-),mīz\ *vt* **-mized; -miz·ing** (1885) **:** to order or compose rhythmically — **rhyth·mi·za·tion** \,rith-(ə-)mə-'zā-shən\ *n*

rhythm method *n* (1940) **:** a method of birth control involving continence during the period in which ovulation is most likely to occur

rhythm stick *n* (1952) **:** one of a pair of plain or notched wood sticks that are struck or rubbed together to produce various percussive sounds and are used esp. by young children in rhythm bands

rhyt·i·dome \'rit-ə-,dōm, 'rīt-\ *n* [prob. fr. (assumed) NL *rhytidoma,* fr. Gk *rhytidōma* wrinkle, fr. *rhytidoun* to wrinkle, fr. *rhytid-, rhytis* wrinkle] (1881) **:** the bark external to the last formed periderm

rhy·ton \'rī-,tän\ *n* [Gk, neut. of *rhytos* flowing; akin to Gk *rhein* to flow — more at STREAM] (1850) **:** a drinking vessel of ancient times with a base in the shape of a woman's or animal's head

[1]**ri·al** \rē-'ȯl, -'äl\ *n* [Per, fr. Ar *riyāl* riyal] (1932) — see MONEY table

[2]**rial** *var of* RIYAL

ri·al·to \rē-'al-(,)tō\ *n, pl* **-tos** [*Rialto,* island and district in Venice] (ca. 1549) **1 :** EXCHANGE, MARKETPLACE **2 :** a theater district

ri·ant \'rī-ənt, 'rē-; rē-'äⁿ\ *adj* [MF, prp. of *rire* to laugh, fr. L *ridēre* — more at RIDICULOUS] (1567) **:** GAY, MIRTHFUL — **ri·ant·ly** \'rī-ənt-lē, 'rē-\ *adv*

ri·a·ta \rē-'at-ə, -'ät-\ *n* [modif. of AmerSp *reata*] (1846) **:** LARIAT

[1]**rib** \'rib\ *n* [ME, fr. OE *ribb;* akin to OHG *rippi* rib, Gk *erephein* to roof over] (bef. 12c) **1 a :** any of the paired curved bony or partly cartilaginous rods that stiffen the walls of the body of most vertebrates and protect the viscera **b :** a cut of meat including a rib — see BEEF illustration **c** [fr. the account of Eve's creation from Adam's rib in Gen 2:21–22] **:** WIFE **2 :** something resembling a rib in shape or function: as **a** (1) **:** a traverse member of the frame of a ship that runs from keel to deck (2) **:** a light fore-and-aft member in an airplane's wing **b :** one of the stiff strips supporting an umbrella's fabric **c :** one of the arches in Romanesque and Gothic vaulting meeting and crossing one another and dividing the whole vaulted space into triangles **3 :** an elongated ridge: as **a** (1) **:** a vein of an insect's wing (2) **:** one of the primary veins of a leaf **b :** one of the ridges in a knitted or woven fabric

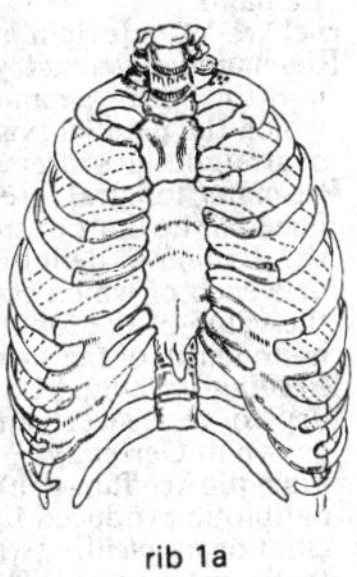

rib 1a

[2]**rib** *vt* **ribbed; rib·bing** (1547) **1 :** to furnish or enclose with ribs **2 :** to form vertical ridges in knitting — **rib·ber** *n*

[3]**rib** *n* [prob. fr. [1]*rib;* fr. the tickling of the ribs to cause laughter] (1929) **1 :** JOKE **2 :** PARODY

[4]**rib** *vt* **ribbed; rib·bing** (1930) **:** to poke fun at **:** KID — **rib·ber** *n*

[1]**rib·ald** \'rib-əld *also* 'rib-,ȯld, 'rī-,bȯld\ *n* [ME, fr. MF *ribaut, ribauld* wanton, rascal, fr. *riber* to be wanton, of Gmc origin; akin to OHG *rīban* to be wanton, lit., to twist; akin to Gk *rhiptein* to throw] (14c) **:** a ribald person

[2]**ribald** *adj* (1500) **1 :** CRUDE, OFFENSIVE ⟨~ language⟩ **2 :** characterized by or using coarse indecent humor ***syn*** see COARSE

rib·ald·ry \'rib-əl-drē *also* 'rīb-\ *n, pl* **-ries** (14c) **1 :** a ribald quality or element **2 :** ribald language or humor

rib·and \'rib-ənd\ *n* [ME, alter. of *riban*] (14c) **:** a ribbon used esp. as a decoration

rib·band \'rib-,(b)and, 'rib-ən(d)\ *n* [[1]*rib* + *band*] (1711) **:** a long narrow strip or bar used in shipbuilding; *esp* **:** one bent and bolted longitudinally to the frames to hold them in position during construction

rib·bing \'rib-iŋ\ *n* (1564) **:** an arrangement of ribs

[1]**rib·bon** \'rib-ən\ *n* [ME *riban,* fr. MF *riban, ruban*] (1545) **1 a :** a flat or tubular narrow closely woven fabric (as of silk or rayon) used for trimmings or knitting **b :** a narrow fabric used for tying packages **c :** a piece of usu. multicolored ribbon worn as a military decoration or in place of a medal **d :** a strip of colored satin given for winning a place in a competition **2 :** a long narrow strip resembling a ribbon: as **a :** a board framed into the studs to support the ceiling or floor joists **b :** a strip of inked fabric (as in a typewriter) **3** *pl* **:** reins for controlling an animal **4 :** TATTER, SHRED — usu. used in pl. **5 :** RIBBAND — **rib·bon·like** \-,līk\ *adj*

[2]**ribbon** *vt* (1716) **1 a :** to adorn with ribbons **b :** to divide into ribbons **c :** to cover with or as if with ribbons **2 :** to rip to shreds

ribbon development *n* (1927) **:** a system of buildings built side by side along a road

rib·bon·fish \'rib-ən-,fish\ *n* (1751) **:** any of a family (Trachipteridae) of elongate greatly compressed marine fishes (as a dealfish)

ribbon worm *n* (1855) **:** NEMERTEAN

rib·by \'rib-ē\ *adj* (1849) **:** showing or marked by ribs

rib cage *n* (1909) **:** the bony enclosing wall of the chest consisting chiefly of the ribs and their connectives

ri·bes \'rī-(,)bēz\ *n, pl* **ribes** [NL, fr. ML, currant, fr. Ar *rībās* rhubarb] (1562) **:** any of a genus (*Ribes*) of shrubs (as a currant or a gooseberry) of the saxifrage family that have small racemose variously colored flowers and pulpy two-seeded to many-seeded berries

rib eye *n* (1926) **:** the large piece of meat that lies along the outer side of the rib (as of a steer)

rib·grass \'rib-,gras\ *n* (1538) **:** [1]PLANTAIN; *specif* **:** an Old World plantain (*Plantago lanceolata*) with long narrow ribbed leaves

rib·let \'rib-lət\ *n* (1943) **:** one of the rib ends in the strip of breast of lamb or veal — see LAMB illustration

ri·bo·fla·vin \,rī-bə-'flā-vən, 'rī-bə-,\ *n* [ISV *ribose* + L *flavus* yellow — more at BLUE] (1935) **:** a yellow crystalline compound $C_{17}H_{20}N_4O_6$ that is a growth-promoting member of the vitamin B complex and occurs both free (as in milk) and combined (as in liver) — called also *vitamin* B_2, *vitamin G*

ri·bo·nu·cle·ase \,rī-bō-'n(y)ü-klē-,ās, -,āz\ *n* [*ribonucleic* (acid) + *-ase*] (1942) **:** an enzyme that catalyzes the hydrolysis of RNA

ri·bo·nu·cle·ic acid \,rī-bō-n(y)ü-,klē-ik-, -,klā-\ *n* [*ribose* + *nucleic acid*] (1931) **:** RNA

ri·bo·nu·cleo·pro·tein \-,n(y)ü-klē-ō-'prō-,tēn, -'prōt-ē-ən\ *n* [*ribonucleic* + *-o-* + *protein*] (1940) **:** a nucleoprotein that contains RNA

ri·bo·nu·cle·o·side \-'n(y)ü-klē-ə-,sīd\ *n* [*ribose* + *nucleoside*] (1940) **:** a nucleoside that contains ribose

ri·bo·nu·cle·o·tide \-,tīd\ *n* [*ribose* + *nucleotide*] (1929) **:** a nucleotide that contains ribose and occurs esp. as a constituent of RNA

ri·bose \'rī-,bōs, -,bōz\ *n* [ISV, fr. *ribonic acid* (an acid $C_5H_{10}O_6$ obtained by oxidation of ribose)] (1892) **:** a pentose $C_5H_{10}O_5$ found esp. in the D-form and obtained esp. from RNA

ribosomal RNA *n* (1961) **:** RNA that is a fundamental structural element of ribosomes

ri·bo·some \'rī-bə-,sōm\ *n* [*ribo*nucleic (acid) + *-some*] (ca. 1958) **:** any of the RNA-rich cytoplasmic granules that are sites of protein synthesis — **ri·bo·som·al** \,rī-bə-'sō-məl\ *adj*

rib roast *n* (ca. 1890) **:** a cut of meat containing the large piece that lies along the outer side of the rib — see BEEF illustration

rib·wort \'rib-,wərt, -,wȯ(ə)rt\ *n* (15c) **:** RIBGRASS

rice \'rīs\ *n* [ME *rys,* fr. OF *ris,* fr. OIt *riso,* fr. Gk *oryza, oryzon*] (13c) **1 :** the seed of rice **2 :** an annual cereal grass (*Oryza sativa*) widely cultivated in warm climates for its seed that is used for food and for its by-products

rice·bird \'rīs-,bərd\ *n* (1728) **:** any of several small birds common in rice fields; *esp* **:** BOBOLINK

rice paper *n* [fr. its resemblance to paper made from rice straw] (1822) **:** a thin papery material made from the pith of a small Asian tree or shrub (*Tetrapanax papyriferum*) of the ginseng family

rice polishings *n pl* (ca. 1934) **:** the inner bran layer of rice rubbed off in milling

ric·er \'rī-sər\ *n* (1896) **:** a kitchen utensil in which soft foods are pressed through a perforated container to produce strings about the diameter of a rice grain

rich \'rich\ *adj* [ME *riche,* fr. OE *rīce;* akin to OHG *rīhhi* rich, OE *rīce* kingdom, OHG *rīhhi,* n.; all fr. prehistoric Gmc words borrowed fr. Celt words akin to OIr *rī* (gen. *rīg*) king — more at ROYAL] (bef. 12c) **1 :** having abundant possessions and esp. material wealth **2 a :** having high value or quality **b :** well supplied ⟨a city ~ in traditions⟩ **3 :** magnificently impressive **:** SUMPTUOUS **4 a :** vivid and deep in color ⟨a ~ red⟩ **b :** full and mellow in tone and quality ⟨a ~ voice⟩ **c :** having a strong fragrance ⟨~ perfumes⟩ **5 :** highly productive or remunerative ⟨a ~ mine⟩ **6 a :** having abundant plant nutrients ⟨~ soil⟩ **b :** highly seasoned, fatty, oily, or sweet ⟨~ foods⟩ **c :** high in the combustible component ⟨a ~ fuel mixture⟩ **d :** high in some component ⟨cholesterol-*rich* foods⟩ **7 a :** ENTERTAINING; *also* **:** LAUGHABLE **b :** MEANINGFUL, SIGNIFICANT ⟨~ allusions⟩ **c :** LUSH ⟨~ meadows⟩ **8 :** pure or nearly pure ⟨~ lime⟩ — **rich·ness** *n*

syn RICH, WEALTHY, AFFLUENT, OPULENT mean having goods, property, and money in abundance. RICH implies having more than enough to gratify normal needs or desires; WEALTHY stresses the possession of property and intrinsically valuable things; AFFLUENT suggests prosperity and an increasing wealth; OPULENT suggests lavish expenditure and display of great wealth.

Rich·ard Roe \,rich-ər-'drō\ *n* (1768) **:** a party to legal proceedings whose true name is unknown — compare JOHN DOE

rich·en \'rich-ən\ *vt* **rich·ened; rich·en·ing** \-(ə-)niŋ\ (1878) **:** to make rich or richer

rich·es \'rich-əz\ *n pl* [ME, sing. or pl., fr. *richesse,* lit., richness, fr. OF, fr. *riche* rich, of Gmc origin; akin to OE *rīce* rich] (13c) **:** things that make one rich **:** WEALTH

rich·ly \'rich-lē\ *adv* [ME *richely,* fr. OE *rīclīce,* fr. *rīce* rich] (bef. 12c) **1 :** in a rich manner **2 :** in full measure **:** AMPLY ⟨praise ~ deserved⟩

Rich·ter scale \'rik-tər-\ *n* [Charles F. *Richter b*1900 Am. seismologist] (1938) **:** a logarithmic scale for expressing the magnitude of a seismic disturbance (as an earthquake) in terms of the energy dissipated in it with 2 indicating the smallest earthquake that can be felt, 4.5 an earthquake causing slight damage, and 8.5 a very devastating earthquake

ri·cin \'rīs-ᵊn, 'ris-\ *n* [L *ricinus* castor-oil plant] (1896) **:** a poisonous protein in the castor bean

ri·cin·ole·ic acid \,ris-ᵊn-ō-,lē-ik-, ,rīs-, -,lā-\ *n* [L *ricinus* + E *oleic*] (1848) **:** an oily unsaturated hydroxy fatty acid $C_{18}H_{34}O_3$ that occurs in castor oil as a glyceride and yields esters important as plasticizers

[1]rick \'rik\ *n* [ME *reek,* fr. OE *hrēac;* akin to ON *hraukr* rick] (bef. 12c) **1 :** a stack (as of hay) in the open air **2 :** a pile of material (as cordwood) split from short logs
[2]rick *vt* (1623) **:** to pile (as hay) in ricks
[3]rick *vt* [perh. fr. ME *wrikken* to move unsteadily] *chiefly Brit* (ca. 1798) **:** WRENCH, SPRAIN
rick·ets \'rik-əts\ *n pl but sing in constr* [origin unknown] (1634) **:** a deficiency disease that affects the young during the period of skeletal growth, is characterized esp. by soft and deformed bones, and is caused by failure to assimilate and use calcium and phosphorus normally due to inadequate sunlight or vitamin D
rick·ett·sia \rik-'et-sē-ə\ *n, pl* **-si·as** *or* **si·ae** \-sē-,ē, -,ī\ *also* **-sia** [NL, genus of microorganisms, fr. Howard T. *Ricketts* †1910 Am. pathologist] (1919) **:** any of a family (Rickettsiaceae) of pleomorphic rod-shaped nonfilterable microorganisms that cause various diseases (as typhus) — **rick·ett·si·al** \-sē-əl\ *adj*
rick·ety \'rik-ət-ē\ *adj* (1683) **1 :** affected with rickets **2 a :** feeble in the joints ⟨a ~ old man⟩ **b :** SHAKY, UNSOUND ⟨~ stairs⟩
rick·ey \'rik-ē\ *n, pl* **rickeys** [prob. fr. the name *Rickey*] (1895) **:** a drink containing liquor, lime juice, sugar, and soda water; *also* **:** a similar drink without liquor
rick·rack *or* **ric·rac** \'rik-,rak\ *n* [redupl. of [4]*rack*] (1884) **:** a flat braid woven to form zigzags and used esp. as trimming on clothing
rick·sha *or* **rick·shaw** \'rik-,shȯ\ *n* [alter. of *jinrikisha*] (1887) **:** a small covered 2-wheeled vehicle usu. for one passenger that is pulled by one man and that was used orig. in Japan
[1]ric·o·chet \'rik-ə-,shā, *Brit also* -,shet\ *n* [F] (1769) **:** a glancing rebound (as of a projectile off a flat surface); *also* **:** an object that ricochets
[2]ricochet *vi* **-cheted** \-,shād\ *or* **-chet·ted** \-,shet-əd\; **-chet·ing** \-,shā-iŋ\ *or* **-chet·ting** \-,shet-iŋ\ (1828) **:** to skip with or as if with glancing rebounds
ri·cot·ta \ri-'kȯt-ə\ *n* [It, fr. fem. of pp. of *ricuocere* to cook again, fr. L *recoquere,* fr. *re-* + *coquere* to cook — more at COOK] (1877) **:** a white unripened whey cheese of Italy that resembles cottage cheese; *also* **:** a similar cheese made in the U.S. from whole or skim milk
ric·tal \'rik-tᵊl\ *adj* (1825) **:** of or relating to the rictus
ric·tus \'rik-təs\ *n* [NL, fr. L, open mouth, fr. *rictus,* pp. of *ringi* to open the mouth; akin to OSlav *ręgnǫti* to gape] (1827) **1 :** the gape of a bird's mouth **2 a :** the mouth orifice **b :** a gaping grin or grimace
rid \'rid\ *vt* **rid** *also* **rid·ded; rid·ding** [ME *ridden* to clear, fr. ON *rythja;* akin to L *ruere* to dig up — more at RUG] (13c) **1** *archaic* **:** SAVE, RESCUE **2 :** to make free **:** RELIEVE, DISENCUMBER ⟨~ the language of impropriety⟩ ⟨be ~ of worries⟩ ⟨get ~ of that junk⟩
rid·dance \'rid-ᵊn(t)s\ *n* (1535) **1 :** an act of ridding **2 :** DELIVERANCE, RELIEF — often used in the phrase *good riddance*
rid·den \'rid-ᵊn\ *adj* (1653) **1 :** being harassed, oppressed, or obsessed by — usu. used in combination ⟨guilt-*ridden*⟩ ⟨debt-*ridden*⟩ **2 :** excessively full of or supplied with — usu. used in combination ⟨slum-*ridden*⟩
[1]rid·dle \'rid-ᵊl\ *n* [ME *redels, ridel,* fr. OE *rǣdelse* opinion, conjecture, riddle; akin to OE *rǣdan* to interpret — more at READ] (bef. 12c) **1 :** a mystifying, misleading, or puzzling question posed as a problem to be solved or guessed **:** CONUNDRUM, ENIGMA **2 :** something or someone difficult to understand ***syn*** see MYSTERY
[2]riddle *vb* **rid·dled; rid·dling** \'rid-liŋ, -ᵊl-iŋ\ *vi* (1571) **:** to speak in or propound riddles ~ *vt* **1 :** to find the solution of **:** EXPLAIN **2 :** to set a riddle for **:** PUZZLE — **rid·dler** \-lər, -ᵊl-ər\ *n*
[3]riddle *n* [ME *riddil,* fr. OE *hriddel;* akin to L *cribrum* sieve, *cernere* to sift — more at CERTAIN] (bef. 12c) **:** a coarse sieve
[4]riddle *vt* **rid·dled; rid·dling** \'rid-liŋ, -ᵊl-iŋ\ (13c) **1 :** to separate (as grain from chaff) with a riddle **:** SCREEN **2 :** to pierce with many holes ⟨*riddled* the car with bullets⟩ **3 :** to spread through **:** PERMEATE ⟨a book *riddled* with errors⟩
rid·dling \'rid-liŋ, -ᵊl-iŋ\ *adj* (1591) **:** containing or presenting riddles
[1]ride \'rīd\ *vb* **rode** \'rōd\ *or chiefly dial* **rid** \'rid\; **rid·den** \'rid-ᵊn\ *or chiefly dial* **rid** *or* **rode; rid·ing** \'rīd-iŋ\ [ME *riden,* fr. OE *rīdan;* akin to OHG *rītan* to ride, OIr *riadaim* I ride] *vi* (bef. 12c) **1 a :** to sit and travel on the back of an animal that one directs **b :** to travel in or on a conveyance **2 :** to travel as if on a conveyance **:** be borne ⟨*rode* on a wave of popularity⟩ **3 a :** to lie moored or anchored ⟨a ship ~*s* at anchor⟩ **b :** SAIL **c :** to move like a floating object ⟨the moon *rode* in the sky⟩ **4 :** to become supported on a point or surface **5 a :** to travel over a surface ⟨the car ~*s* well⟩ **b :** to move on the body ⟨shorts that ~ up⟩ **6 :** to continue without interference ⟨let it ~⟩ **7 a :** to be contingent **:** DEPEND ⟨plans on which the future ~*s*⟩ **b :** to become bet ⟨a lot of money *riding* on the favorite⟩ ~ *vt* **1 a :** to travel on ⟨~ a bike⟩ ⟨~ the bus⟩ **b :** to move with like a rider ⟨~ the waves⟩ **2 a :** to traverse by conveyance ⟨*rode* 500 miles⟩ **b :** to ride a horse in ⟨~ a race⟩ **3 :** SURVIVE, OUTLAST — usu. used with *out* ⟨*rode* out the gale⟩ **4 :** to traverse on horseback to inspect or maintain ⟨~ fence⟩ **5 :** to mount in copulation **6 a :** OBSESS, OPPRESS ⟨*ridden* by anxiety⟩ **b :** to harass persistently **:** NAG **c :** TEASE, RIB **7 :** CARRY, CONVEY **8 :** to project over **:** OVERLAP **9 :** to give with (a punch) to soften the impact **10 :** to keep in partial engagement by resting a foot continuously on the pedal ⟨~ the clutch⟩ — **rid·able** *or* **ride·able** \'rīd-ə-bəl\ *adj* — **ride circuit :** to hold court in the various towns of a judicial circuit — **ride for a fall :** to court disaster — **ride herd on :** to keep a check on — **ride high :** to experience success
[2]ride *n* (1759) **1 :** an act of riding; *esp* **:** a trip on horseback or by vehicle **2 :** a way (as a road or path) suitable for riding **3 :** any of various mechanical devices (as at an amusement park) for riding on **4 a :** a trip on which gangsters take a victim to murder him **b :** something resembling such a trip ⟨take the taxpayers for a ~⟩ **5 :** a means of transportation **6 :** the qualities of travel comfort in a vehicle
rid·er \'rīd-ər\ *n* (14c) **1 :** one that rides **2 a :** an addition to a document often attached on a separate piece of paper **b :** a clause appended to a legislative bill to secure a usu. distinct object **3 :** something used to overlie another or to move along on another piece — **rid·er·less** \-ləs\ *adj*
rid·er·ship \'rīd-ər-,ship\ *n* (1968) **:** the number of persons who ride a system of public transportation
[1]ridge \'rij\ *n* [ME *rigge,* fr. OE *hrycg;* akin to OHG *hrukki* ridge, back, L *cruc-, crux* cross, *curvus* curved — more at CROWN] (bef. 12c) **1 :** an elevated body part (as along the backbone) **2 a :** a range of hills or mountains **b :** an elongate elevation on an ocean bottom **3 :** an elongate crest or a linear series of crests **4 :** a raised strip (as of plowed ground) **5 :** the line of intersection at the top between the opposite slopes or sides of a roof — **ridged** \'rijd\ *adj*
[2]ridge *vb* **ridged; ridg·ing** *vt* (1523) **:** to form into a ridge ~ *vi* **:** to extend in ridges
ridge·ling *or* **ridg·ling** \'rij-liŋ\ *n* [perh. fr. [1]*ridge;* fr. the supposition that the undescended testis remains near the animal's back] (1555) **1 :** a partially castrated male animal **2 :** a male animal having one or both testes retained in the inguinal canal
ridge·pole \'rij-,pōl\ *n* (1788) **1 :** the horizontal pole at the top of a tent **2 :** the highest horizontal timber in a roof against which the upper ends of the rafters are fixed

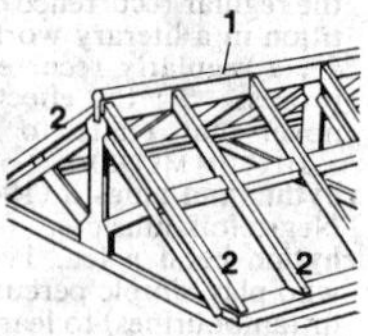

1 ridgepole, 2 rafters

ridgy \'rij-ē\ *adj* (1697) **:** having or rising in ridges
[1]rid·i·cule \'rid-ə-,kyü(ə)l\ *n* [F or L; F, fr. L *ridiculum* jest] (1690) **:** the act of exposing to laughter **:** DERISION, MOCKERY
[2]ridicule *vt* **-culed; -cul·ing** (ca. 1700) **:** to make fun of — **rid·i·cul·er** *n*
syn RIDICULE, DERIDE, MOCK, TAUNT, TWIT mean to make an object of laughter of. RIDICULE implies a deliberate often malicious belittling ⟨consistently *ridiculed* everything she said⟩ DERIDE suggests contemptuous and often bitter ridicule ⟨*derided* their efforts to start their own business⟩ MOCK implies scorn often ironically expressed as by mimicry or sham deference ⟨youngsters began to *mock* the helpless wino⟩ TAUNT suggests jeeringly provoking insult or challenge ⟨terrorists *taunted* the hostages⟩ TWIT usu. suggests mild or good-humored teasing ⟨students *twitted* their teacher about his tardiness⟩
ri·dic·u·lous \rə-'dik-yə-ləs\ *adj* [L *ridiculosus* (fr. *ridiculum* jest, fr. neut. of *ridiculus*) or *ridiculus,* lit., laughable, fr. *ridēre* to laugh; akin to Skt *vrīḍate* he is ashamed] (1550) **:** arousing or deserving ridicule **:** ABSURD, PREPOSTEROUS ***syn*** see LAUGHABLE — **ri·dic·u·lous·ly** *adv* — **ri·dic·u·lous·ness** *n*
[1]rid·ing \'rīd-iŋ\ *n* (14c) **:** the action or state of one that rides
[2]rid·ing *adj* (15c) **1 :** used for or when riding ⟨a ~ horse⟩ ⟨~ boots⟩ **2 :** operated by a rider ⟨a ~ mower⟩
[3]ri·ding \'rīd-iŋ\ *n* [ME *-redying* or *trithing,* alter. of (assumed) OE *thriding,* fr. ON *thrithjungr* third part, fr. *thrithi* third; akin to OE *thridda* third — more at THIRD] (1514) **1 :** one of the three administrative jurisdictions into which Yorkshire, England, was formerly divided **2 :** an administrative jurisdiction or electoral district in a British dominion (as Canada)
rid·ley \'rid-lē\ *n* [prob. fr. the name *Ridley*] (1942) **:** a sea turtle (*Caretta kempii* or *Lepidochelys kempii*) found off the Atlantic coast of the U.S.
ri·dot·to \ri-'dät-(,)ō\ *n, pl* **-tos** [It, retreat, place of entertainment, redoubt — more at REDOUBT] (1722) **:** a public entertainment consisting of music and dancing often in masquerade popular in 18th century England
ri·el \rē-'el\ *n* [origin unknown] (1956) — see MONEY table
Rie·mann·ian geometry \rē-,män-ē-ən-\ *n* [G. F. B. *Riemann*] (1904) **:** a non-Euclidean geometry in which straight lines are geodesics and in which the parallel postulate is replaced by the postulate that every pair of straight lines intersects
Rie·mann integral \,rē-,män-, -mən-\ *n* (1914) **:** a definite integral defined as the limit of sums found by partitioning the interval comprising the domain of definition into subintervals, by finding the sum of products each of which consists of the width of a subinterval multiplied by the value of the function at some point in it, and by letting the maximum width of the subintervals approach zero
Ries·ling \'rēz-liŋ, 'rē-sliŋ\ *n* [G] (1833) **:** a white wine that ranges from dry to very sweet and is made from a single variety of grape orig. grown in Germany
ri·fam·pin \rī-'fam-pən\ *or* **ri·fam·pi·cin** \rī-'fam-pə-sən\ *n* [*rif*amycin (an antibiotic produced from a bacterium, fr. which it is derived) + *ampi*cillin or *ampicillin* (which it resembles in efficacy)] (1966) **:** a semisynthetic antibiotic $C_{43}H_{58}N_4O_{12}$ that acts against some viruses and bacteria esp. by inhibiting RNA synthesis
rife \'rīf\ *adj* [ME *ryfe,* fr. OE *rȳfe;* akin to ON *rīfr* abundant] (12c) **1 :** prevalent esp. to an increasing degree ⟨fear was ~ in the people⟩ **2 :** ABUNDANT, COMMON **3 :** copiously supplied **:** ABOUNDING — usu. used with *with* ⟨~ with rumors⟩ — **rife** *adv* — **rife·ly** *adv*
[1]riff \'rif\ *n* [prob. by shortening & alter. fr. *refrain*] (1958) **:** an ostinato phrase in jazz typically supporting a solo improvisation; *also* **:** a piece based on such a phrase
[2]riff *vi* (1950) **:** to perform a jazz riff
[3]riff *vb* [short for *riffle*] (1952) **:** RIFFLE, SKIM ⟨~ pages⟩
Riff \'rif\ *n, pl* **Riffs** *or* **Riffi** \'rif-ē\ *or* **Riff** (1903) **:** a Berber of the Rif in northern Morocco
Riff·ian \'rif-ē-ən\ *n* (1867) **:** RIFF
[1]rif·fle \'rif-əl\ *vb* **rif·fled; rif·fling** \'rif-(ə-)liŋ\ *vi* (1752) **1 :** to form, flow over, or move in riffles **2 :** to flip cursorily **:** THUMB ⟨~ through files⟩ ~ *vt* **1 :** to ruffle slightly **:** RIPPLE **2 a :** to leaf through hastily; *specif* **:** to leaf (as a stack of paper) by sliding a thumb along the edge of the leaves **b :** to shuffle (playing cards) by separating the deck into two parts and riffling with the thumbs so the cards intermix **3 :** to manipulate (small objects) idly between the fingers
[2]riffle *n* [perh. alter. of *ruffle*] (1792) **1 a :** a shallow extending across a streambed and causing broken water **b :** a stretch of water flowing over a riffle **2 :** a small wave or succession of small waves **:** RIPPLE **3 a :** any of various contrivances (as blocks or rails) laid on the bottom of a sluice or launder to make a series of grooves or interstices to catch and retain a mineral (as gold) **b :** a groove or interstice so formed **4 :** a cleat or bar fastened to an inclined surface in a gold-washing apparatus to catch and hold mineral grains **5** [[1]*riffle*] **a :** the act or process of shuffling (as cards) **b :** the sound made while doing this
[3]riffle *vt* **rif·fled; rif·fling** \'rif-(ə-)liŋ\ (1949) **:** to run through a riffle or over a series of riffles ⟨~ ground ore⟩
rif·fler \'rif-lər\ *n* [F *rifloir,* fr. *rifler* to file, rifle] (ca. 1797) **:** a small filing or scraping tool

riff·raff \ˈrif-ˌraf\ *n* [ME *ryffe raffe,* fr. *rif and raf* every single one, fr. MF *rif et raf* completely, fr. *rifler* to scratch, plunder + *raffe* act of sweeping] (15c) **1 a :** disreputable persons **b :** RABBLE **c :** one of the riffraff **2 :** REFUSE, RUBBISH — **riffraff** *adj*

1**ri·fle** \ˈrī-fəl\ *vb* **ri·fled; ri·fling** \-f(ə-)liŋ\ [ME *riflen,* fr. MF *rifler* to scratch, file, plunder, of Gmc origin; akin to OHG *riffilōn* to saw, obs. D *rijffelen* to scrape] *vt* (14c) **1 :** to ransack esp. with the intent to steal **2 :** to steal and carry away ~ *vi* **:** to engage in ransacking and stealing — **ri·fler** \-f(ə-)lər\ *n*

2**rifle** *vt* **ri·fled; ri·fling** \-f(ə-)liŋ\ [F *rifler* to scratch, file] (1635) **:** to cut spiral grooves into the bore of ⟨*rifled* arms⟩ ⟨*rifled* pipe⟩

3**rifle** *n* (1772) **1 a :** a shoulder weapon with a rifled bore **b :** a rifled artillery piece **2** *pl* **:** a body of soldiers armed with rifles

4**rifle** *vt* **ri·fled; ri·fling** \-f(ə-)liŋ\ [3*rifle*] (1937) **:** to propel (as a ball) with great force or speed

ri·fle·bird \ˈrī-fəl-ˌbərd\ *n* (1831) **:** any of several birds of paradise (genus *Ptiloris*)

ri·fle·man \-mən\ *n* (1755) **1 :** a soldier armed with a rifle **2 :** one skilled in shooting with a rifle

ri·fle·ry \ˈrī-fəl-rē\ *n* (ca. 1935) **:** the practice of shooting at targets with a rifle

ri·fling \ˈrī-f(ə-)liŋ\ *n* (1797) **1 :** the act or process of making spiral grooves **2 :** a system of spiral grooves in the surface of the bore of a gun causing a projectile when fired to rotate about its longer axis

1**rift** \ˈrift\ *n* [ME, of Scand origin; akin to Dan & Norw *rift* fissure, ON *rifa* to rive — more at RIVE] (14c) **1 a :** FISSURE, CREVASSE **b :** a normal geological fault **2 :** a clear space or interval **3 :** BREACH, ESTRANGEMENT

2**rift** *vi* (14c) **:** to burst open ~ *vt* **1 :** CLEAVE, DIVIDE ⟨hills were ~*ed* by the earthquake⟩ **2 :** PENETRATE

3**rift** *n* [prob. alter. of E dial. *riff* (reef)] (1727) **:** a shallow or rocky place in a stream

rift valley *n* (1903) **:** an elongated valley formed by the depression of a block of the earth's crust between two faults or groups of faults of approximately parallel strike

1**rig** \ˈrig\ *vt* **rigged; rig·ging** [ME *riggen*] (15c) **1 :** to fit out (as a ship) with rigging **2 :** CLOTHE, DRESS — usu. used with *out* **3 :** to furnish with special gear **:** EQUIP **4 a :** to put in condition or position for use **:** ADJUST, ARRANGE ⟨a car *rigged* for manual control⟩ **b :** CONSTRUCT ⟨~ up a temporary shelter⟩

2**rig** *n* (1822) **1 :** the distinctive shape, number, and arrangement of sails and masts of a ship **2 :** EQUIPAGE; *esp* **:** a carriage with its horse **3 :** CLOTHING, DRESS **4 :** tackle, equipment, or machinery fitted for a specified purpose ⟨an oil-drilling ~⟩

3**rig** *vt* **rigged; rig·ging** [*rig* (swindle)] (1851) **1 :** to manipulate or control usu. by deceptive or dishonest means ⟨~ an election⟩ **2 :** to fix in advance for a desired result ⟨~ a quiz program⟩

rig·a·doon \ˌrig-ə-ˈdün\ *or* **ri·gau·don** \rē-gō-dōⁿ\ *n* [F *rigaudon*] (1691) **:** a lively dance of the 17th and 18th centuries; *also* **:** the music for a rigadoon

rig·a·ma·role *var of* RIGMAROLE

rig·a·to·ni \ˌrig-ə-ˈtō-nē\ *n* [It, pl., fr. *rigato* furrowed, fluted, fr. pp. of *rigare* to furrow, flute, fr. *riga* line, of Gmc origin; akin to OHG *riga* line — more at ROW] (ca. 1923) **:** macaroni made in short curved fluted pieces

Ri·gel \ˈrī-jəl, -gəl; ˈrij-əl\ *n* [Ar *Rijl,* lit., foot] **:** a first-magnitude star in the left foot of the constellation Orion

rig·ger \ˈrig-ər\ *n* (ca. 1611) **1 :** one that rigs **2 :** a long slender pointed sable paintbrush

rig·ging \ˈrig-iŋ, -ən\ *n* (1594) **1 a :** lines and chains used aboard a ship esp. in working sail and supporting masts and spars **b :** a similar network (as in theater scenery) used for support and manipulation **2 :** CLOTHING

1**right** \ˈrīt\ *adj* [ME, fr. OE *riht;* akin to OHG *reht* right, L *rectus* straight, right, *regere* to lead straight, direct, rule, *rogare* to ask, Gk *oregein* to stretch out] (bef. 12c) **1 :** RIGHTEOUS, UPRIGHT **2 :** being in accordance with what is just, good, or proper ⟨~ conduct⟩ **3 a :** agreeable to a standard **b :** conforming to facts or truth **:** CORRECT ⟨the ~ answer⟩ **4 :** SUITABLE, APPROPRIATE ⟨the ~ man for the job⟩ **5 :** STRAIGHT ⟨a ~ line⟩ **6 :** GENUINE, REAL **7 a :** of, relating to, situated on, or being the side of the body which is away from the heart and on which the hand is stronger in most people **b :** located nearer to the right hand than to the left **c :** located on the right of an observer facing the object specified or directed as his right arm would point when raised out to the side **d** (1) **:** located on the right of an observer facing in the same direction as the object specified ⟨stage ~⟩ (2) **:** located on the right when facing downstream ⟨the ~ bank of a river⟩ **8 :** having the axis perpendicular to the base ⟨~ cone⟩ **9 :** of, relating to, or constituting the principal or more prominent side of an object ⟨made sure his socks were ~ side out⟩ **10 :** acting or judging in accordance with truth or fact ⟨time proved him ~⟩ **11 a :** being in good physical or mental health or order ⟨not in his ~ mind⟩ **b :** being in a correct or proper state ⟨put things ~⟩ **12 :** most favorable or desired **:** PREFERABLE; *also* **:** socially acceptable ⟨knew all the ~ people⟩ **13** *often cap* **:** of, adhering to, or constituted by the Right esp. in politics *syn* see CORRECT — **right·ness** *n*

2**right** *n* [ME, fr. OE *riht,* fr. *riht,* adj.] (bef. 12c) **1 :** qualities (as adherence to duty or obedience to lawful authority) that together constitute the ideal of moral propriety or merit moral approval **2 :** something to which one has a just claim: as **a :** the power or privilege to which one is justly entitled **b** (1) **:** the interest that one has in a piece of property — often used in pl. ⟨mineral ~*s*⟩ (2) *pl* **:** the property interest possessed under law or custom and agreement in an intangible thing esp. of a literary and artistic nature ⟨film ~*s* of the novel⟩ **3 :** something that one may properly claim as due **4 :** the cause of truth or justice **5 a :** the right hand; *also* **:** a blow struck with this hand ⟨gave him a hard ~ on the jaw⟩ **b :** the location or direction of the right side ⟨woods on his ~⟩ **c :** the part on the right side **6 a :** the true account or correct interpretation **b :** the quality or state of being factually correct **7** *often cap* **a :** the part of a legislative chamber located to the right of the presiding officer **b :** the members of a continental European legislative body occupying the right as a result of holding more conservative political views than other members **8 a** (1) *cap* **:** individuals sometimes professing opposition to change in the established order and favoring traditional attitudes and practices and sometimes advocating the forced establishment of an authoritarian political order (2) **:** a group or party in another organization that favors conservative, traditional, or sometimes authoritarian attitudes and policies **b** *often cap* **:** a conservative position **9 a :** a privilege given stockholders to subscribe pro rata to a new issue of securities generally below market price **b :** the negotiable certificate evidencing such privilege — usu. used in pl. — **by rights :** with reason or justice **:** PROPERLY — **in one's own right :** by virtue of one's own qualifications or properties — **to rights :** into proper order

3**right** *adv* (bef. 12c) **1 :** according to right ⟨live ~⟩ **2 :** in the exact location or position **:** PRECISELY ⟨~ at his fingertips⟩ ⟨~ in the middle of the floor⟩ **3 :** in a suitable, proper, or desired manner ⟨knew he wasn't doing it ~⟩ **4 :** in a direct line or course **:** DIRECTLY, STRAIGHT ⟨go ~ home⟩ **5 :** according to fact or truth **:** TRULY ⟨guessed ~⟩ **6 a :** all the way ⟨windows ~ to the floor⟩ **b :** in a complete manner ⟨felt ~ at home⟩ **7 :** without delay **:** IMMEDIATELY ⟨~ after lunch⟩ **8 :** to a great degree **:** VERY ⟨a ~ pleasant day⟩ **9 :** on or to the right ⟨looked left and ~⟩

usage This ancient and homely adverb seems to make commentators nervous, esp. in senses 4, 6, and 8. Some commentators think senses 4 and 6 should not be used in formal prose; these senses do not seem to be much used in the most formal writing but are very common in ordinary edited prose. Sense 8 is variously described as archaic, not standard, or regional. None of these descriptors is accurate. It is in current good use. It does appear in most dialect areas but seems to be more common in the Southern and Midland areas than elsewhere. It seems to be more common in speech than writing, but it is not rare in edited prose ⟨it is the man and his London that count, and [the author] recognizes this *right* well —Newgate Callendar, *N.Y. Times Bk. Rev.*⟩ ⟨a defender of the language — you remember, he defended it *right* profitably in his earlier [book] —William Cole, *Saturday Rev.*⟩

4**right** *vt* (bef. 12c) **1 a :** to do justice to **:** redress the injuries of ⟨so just is God to ~ the innocent —Shak.⟩ **b :** JUSTIFY, VINDICATE ⟨felt the need to ~ himself in court⟩ **2 :** AVENGE ⟨vows to ~ the injustice done to his family⟩ **3 a :** to adjust or restore to the proper state or condition ⟨helps to ~ the imbalance of his previous work⟩ **b :** to bring or restore to an upright position ⟨~ a capsized boat⟩ ~ *vi* **:** to become upright — **right·er** *n*

right angle *n* (14c) **:** the angle bounded by two lines perpendicular to each other **:** an angle of 90° or $\frac{1}{2}\pi$ radians — **right–an·gled** \ˈrīt-ˈaŋ-gəld\ *or* **right–an·gle** \-gəl\ *adj*

right ascension *n* (1594) **:** the arc of the celestial equator between the vernal equinox and the point where the hour circle through the given body intersects the equator reckoned eastward commonly in terms of the corresponding interval of sidereal time in hours, minutes, and seconds

right away *adv* (1818) **:** without delay or hesitation **:** IMMEDIATELY

right circular cone *n* (ca. 1942) **:** CONE 2a

right circular cylinder *n* (ca. 1942) **:** a cylinder with circular bases such that any segment of a straight line lying wholly in the surface and joining the bases is perpendicular to them

righ·teous \ˈrī-chəs\ *adj* [alter. of earlier *rightuous,* alter. of ME *rightwise, rightwos,* fr. OE *rihtwīs,* fr. *riht,* n., right + *wīs* wise] (bef. 12c) **1 :** acting in accord with divine or moral law **:** free from guilt or sin **2 a :** morally right or justifiable ⟨a ~ decision⟩ **b :** arising from an outraged sense of justice or morality ⟨~ indignation⟩ **3** *slang* **:** GENUINE *syn* see MORAL — **righ·teous·ly** *adv* — **righ·teous·ness** *n*

right field *n* (1857) **1 :** the part of the baseball outfield to the right looking out from home plate **2 :** the position of the player defending right field — **right fielder** *n*

right·ful \ˈrīt-fəl\ *adj* (13c) **1 :** JUST, EQUITABLE **2 a :** having a just or legally established claim **:** LEGITIMATE ⟨the ~ owner⟩ **b :** held by right or just claim **:** LEGAL ⟨~ authority⟩ **3 :** PROPER, FITTING ⟨thought her ~ place was in the home⟩ — **right·ful·ly** \-fə-lē\ *adv* — **right·ful·ness** *n*

right–hand \ˈrīt-ˌhand\ *adj* (13c) **1 :** situated on the right **2 :** RIGHT-HANDED **3 :** chiefly relied on ⟨~ man⟩

right hand *n* (bef. 12c) **1 a :** the hand on a person's right side **b :** an indispensable person **2 a :** the right side **b :** a place of honor

right–hand·ed \-ˈhan-dəd\ *adj* (14c) **1 :** using the right hand habitually or more easily than the left; *also* **:** swinging from right to left ⟨a ~ batter⟩ **2 :** relating to, designed for, or done with the right hand **3 a :** having the same direction or course as the movement of the hands of a watch viewed from in front **:** CLOCKWISE **b :** having a spiral structure or form that ascends or advances to the right ⟨a ~ screw⟩ ⟨a ~ double helix of DNA⟩ **4** *of a door* **:** opening to the right away from one — **right–handed** *adv* — **right–hand·ed·ly** *adv* — **right–hand·ed·ness** *n*

right–hand·er \-ˈhan-dər\ *n* (1857) **1 :** a blow struck with the right hand **2 :** a right-handed person

right·ism \ˈrīt-ˌiz-əm\ *n, often cap* (1939) **1 :** the principles and views of the Right **2 :** advocacy of or adherence to the doctrines of the Right — **right·ist** \ˈrīt-əst\ *n or adj, often cap*

right·ly \ˈrīt-lē\ *adv* (bef. 12c) **1 :** in accordance with right conduct **:** FAIRLY, JUSTLY **2 :** in the right or proper manner **:** PROPERLY, FITLY **3 :** according to truth or fact **:** CORRECTLY, EXACTLY

right–mind·ed \-ˈmīn-dəd\ *adj* (1585) **:** having a right or honest mind **:** purposing well ⟨a ~ citizen⟩ — **right–mind·ed·ness** *n*

right now *adv* (14c) **1 :** RIGHT AWAY **2 :** at present

right off *adv* (1758) **:** RIGHT AWAY **:** at once — **right off the bat :** RIGHT OFF

right of search (1817) **:** the right to stop a merchant vessel on the high seas and make a reasonable search to determine its liability to capture by violation of international or revenue law

right–of–way \ˌrīt-ə(v)-ˈwā\ *n, pl* **rights–of–way** *also* **right–of–ways** (1768) **1 :** a legal right of passage over another person's ground **2 a**

\ə\ abut \ᵊ\ kitten, F table \ər\ further \a\ ash \ā\ ace \ä\ cot, cart \au̇\ out \ch\ chin \e\ bet \ē\ easy \g\ go \i\ hit \ī\ ice \j\ job \ŋ\ sing \ō\ go \ȯ\ law \ȯi\ boy \th\ thin \t͟h\ the \ü\ loot \u̇\ foot \y\ yet \zh\ vision \à, k̲, ⁿ, œ, œ̄, ue, ue̅, ʸ\ *see* Guide to Pronunciation

: the area over which a right-of-way exists **b** : the strip of land over which is built a public road **c** : the land occupied by a railroad esp. for its main line **d** : the land used by a public utility (as for a transmission line) **3 a** : a precedence in passing accorded to one vehicle over another by custom, decision, or statute **b** : the right of traffic to take precedence **c** : the right to take precedence over others ⟨gave the bill the ~ in the Senate⟩

right on *adj* (1970) **1** : exactly correct — often used interjectionally to express agreement **2** *usu* **right–on** : attuned to the spirit of the times

Right Reverend (15c) — used as a title for high ecclesiastical officials

right shoulder arms *n* (ca. 1902) : a position in the manual of arms in which the butt of the rifle is held in the right hand with the barrel resting on the right shoulder; *also* : a command to assume this position

right–to–life \ˈrīt-tə-ˈlīf\ *adj* (1972) : opposed to abortion — **right–to–lif•er** \-ˈlī-fər\ *n*

right–to–work *adj* (1949) : opposing or banning the closed shop and the union shop

right triangle *n* (ca. 1924) : a triangle having a right angle

right•ward \ˈrīt-wərd\ *adj* (1825) : being toward or on the right

right whale *n* (1725) : any of a family (Balaenidae) of whalebone whales having very long baleen, a large head on a stocky body, a smooth throat, and short, broad, rounded flippers

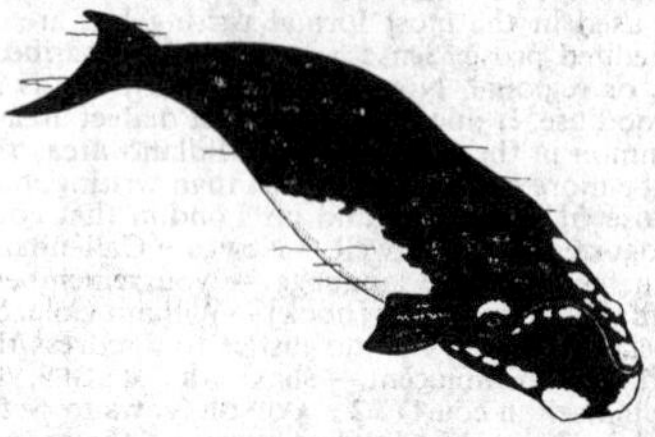

right whale

right wing *n* (1905) **1** : the rightist division of a group or party **2** : RIGHT 8 — **right–wing•er** \(ˈ)rīt-ˈwiŋ-ər\ *n*

rig•id \ˈrij-əd\ *adj* [MF or L; MF *rigide*, fr. L *rigidus*, fr. *rigēre* to be stiff] (1538) **1 a** : deficient in or devoid of flexibility ⟨~ price controls⟩ ⟨a ~ bar of metal⟩ **b** : appearing stiff and unyielding ⟨his face ~ with pain⟩ **2 a** : inflexibly set in opinion **b** : strictly observed ⟨adheres to a ~ schedule⟩ **3** : firmly inflexible rather than lax or indulgent ⟨a ~ disciplinarian⟩ **4** : precise and accurate in procedure ⟨~ control of the manufacturing process⟩ **5 a** : having the gas containers enclosed within compartments of a fixed fabric-covered framework ⟨a ~ airship⟩ **b** : having the outer shape maintained by a fixed framework — **rig•id•ly** *adv* — **rig•id•ness** *n*

syn RIGID, RIGOROUS, STRICT, STRINGENT mean extremely severe or stern. RIGID implies uncompromising inflexibility; RIGOROUS implies the imposition of hardship and difficulty; STRICT emphasizes undeviating conformity to rules, standards, or requirements; STRINGENT suggests restrictions or limitations that curb or coerce. *syn* see in addition STIFF

ri•gid•i•fy \rə-ˈjid-ə-ˌfī\ *vb* **-fied; -fy•ing** *vt* (1842) : to make rigid ~ *vi* : to become rigid — **ri•gid•i•fi•ca•tion** \-ˌjid-ə-fə-ˈkā-shən\ *n*

ri•gid•i•ty \rə-ˈjid-ət-ē\ *n, pl* **-ties** (1624) **1** : the quality or state of being rigid **2** : one that is rigid (as in form or conduct)

rig•ma•role \ˈrig-(ə-)mə-ˌrōl\ *n* [alter. of obs. *ragman roll* (long list, catalog)] (ca. 1736) **1** : confused or meaningless talk **2** : a complex and ritualistic procedure

rig•or \ˈrig-ər\ *n* [ME *rigour*, fr. MF *rigueur*, fr. L *rigor*, lit., stiffness, fr. *rigēre* to be stiff; akin to L *regere* to lead straight — more at RIGHT] (14c) **1 a** (1) : harsh inflexibility in opinion, temper, or judgment : SEVERITY (2) : the quality of being unyielding or inflexible : STRICTNESS (3) : severity of life : AUSTERITY **b** : an act or instance of strictness, severity, or cruelty **2** : a tremor caused by a chill **3** : a condition that makes life difficult, challenging, or uncomfortable; *esp* : extremity of cold **4** : strict precision : EXACTNESS ⟨logical ~⟩ **5 a** *obs* : RIGIDITY, STIFFNESS **b** : rigidness or torpor of organs or tissue that prevents response to stimuli

rig•or•ism \ˈrig-ə-ˌriz-əm\ *n* (1704) : rigidity in principle or practice — **rig•or•ist** \-ə-rəst\ *n or adj* — **rig•or•is•tic** \ˌrig-ə-ˈris-tik\ *adj*

rig•or mor•tis \ˌrig-ər-ˈmȯrt-əs *also chiefly Brit* ˌrī-ˌgȯ(ə)r-\ *n* [NL, stiffness of death] (1839) : temporary rigidity of muscles occurring after death

rig•or•ous \ˈrig-(ə-)rəs\ *adj* (14c) **1** : manifesting, exercising, or favoring rigor : very strict **2 a** : marked by extremes of temperature or climate **b** : HARSH, SEVERE **3** : scrupulously accurate : PRECISE *syn* see RIGID — **rig•or•ous•ly** *adv* — **rig•or•ous•ness** *n*

rig•our *chiefly Brit var of* RIGOR

Riks•mål *or* **Riks•maal** \ˈrik-ˌsmȯl, ˈrēk-\ *n* [Norw, fr. *rik* kingdom (akin to OE *rīce* kingdom) + *mål* speech, fr. ON *māl* — more at RICH, MAIL] (ca. 1913) : BOKMÅL

rile \ˈrī(ə)l\ *vt* **riled; ril•ing** [alter. of *roil*] (1825) **1** : to make agitated and angry : UPSET **2** : ROIL 1

ril•ey \ˈrī-lē\ *adj* (1805) **1** : TURBID **2** : ANGRY

1rill \ˈril\ *n* [D *ril* or LG *rille*; akin to OE *rīth* rivulet] (1538) : a very small brook

2rill *vi* (1610) : to flow like a rill

3rill \ˈril\ *or* **rille** \ˈril, ˈril-ə\ *n* [G *rille*, lit., channel made by a small stream, fr. LG, rill] (1868) : any of several long narrow valleys on the moon's surface

rill•et \ˈril-ət\ *n* (1538) : a little rill

1rim \ˈrim\ *n* [ME, fr. OE *rima*; akin to ON *rimi* strip of land] (15c) **1 a** : the outer part of a wheel joined to the hub usu. by spokes **b** : a removable outer metal band on an automobile wheel to which the tire is attached **2 a** : the outer often curved or circular edge or border of something **b** : BRINK **3** : FRAME 3d(1) — **rim•less** \-ləs\ *adj*

2rim *vb* **rimmed; rim•ming** *vt* (1794) **1** : to serve as a rim for : BORDER ⟨cliffs *rimming* the camp⟩ **2** : to run around the rim of ⟨putts that ~ the cup⟩ ~ *vi* : to form or show a rim

1rime \ˈrīm\ *n* [ME *rim*, fr. OE *hrīm*; akin to ON *hrīm* frost, Latvian *kreims* cream] (bef. 12c) **1** : FROST 1c **2** : an accumulation of granular ice tufts on the windward sides of exposed objects that is formed from supercooled fog or cloud and built out directly against the wind **3** : CRUST, INCRUSTATION ⟨a ~ of snow⟩

2rime *vt* **rimed; rim•ing** (ca. 1755) : to cover with or as if with rime

3rime, rimer, rimester *var of* RHYME, RHYMER, RHYMESTER

rim•fire \ˈrim-ˌfī(ə)r\ *adj, of a cartridge* (1868) : having the priming distributed in the rim of the shell — **rimfire** *n*

rim•land \ˈrim-ˌland\ *n* (1944) : a region on the periphery of the heartland

rimmed \ˈrimd\ *adj* (1729) : having a rim — usu. used in combination ⟨dark-*rimmed* glasses⟩ ⟨red-*rimmed* eyes⟩

rim•rock \ˈrim-ˌräk\ *n* (1860) **1** : a top stratum or overlying strata of resistant rock of a plateau that outcrops to form a vertical face **2** : the edge or face of a rimrock outcrop

rimy \ˈrī-mē\ *adj* **rim•i•er; -est** [OE *hrīmig*, fr. *hrīm*] (bef. 12c) : covered with rime : FROSTY

rind \ˈrīnd, ˈrīn\ *n* [ME, fr. OE; akin to OHG *rinda* bark, OE *rendan* to rend] (bef. 12c) **1** : the bark of a tree **2** : a usu. hard or tough outer layer : PEEL, CRUST ⟨grated lemon ~⟩ — **rind•ed** \-əd\ *adj*

rin•der•pest \ˈrin-dər-ˌpest\ *n* [G, fr. *rinder*, pl., cattle + *pest* pestilence, fr. L *pestis*] (1865) : an acute infectious febrile disease esp. of cattle caused by a virus and marked by diphtheritic inflammation of mucous membranes

1ring \ˈriŋ\ *n* [ME, fr. OE *hring*; akin to OHG *hring* ring, L *curvus* curved — more at CROWN] (bef. 12c) **1** : a circular band for holding, connecting, hanging, pulling, packing, or sealing ⟨a key ~⟩ ⟨a towel ~⟩ **2** : a circlet usu. of precious metal worn on the finger **3 a** : a circular line, figure, or object ⟨smoke ~⟩ **b** : an encircling arrangement ⟨a ~ of suburbs⟩ **c** : a circular or spiral course — often used in pl. in the phrase *run rings around* **4 a** (1) : an often circular space esp. for exhibitions or competitions; *esp* : such a space at a circus (2) : a structure containing such a ring **b** : a square enclosure in which boxers or wrestlers contest **5** : one of the concentric bands usu. believed to be composed of meteoric fragments revolving around a planet (as Saturn) **6** : ANNUAL RING **7 a** : an exclusive combination of persons for a selfish and often corrupt purpose (as to control a market) ⟨a wheat ~⟩ **b** : GANG **8** : the field of a political contest : RACE **9** : food in the shape of a circle **10** : an arrangement of atoms represented in formulas or models in a cyclic manner as a closed chain — called also *cycle* **11** : a set of mathematical elements that is closed under two binary operations of which the first forms a commutative group with the set and the second is associative over the set and is distributive with respect to the first operation **12** *pl* **a** : a pair of usu. rubber-covered metal rings suspended from a ceiling or crossbar to a height of approximately eight feet above the floor and used for hanging, swinging, and balancing feats in gymnastics **b** : an event in gymnastics competition in which the rings are used **13** : 2BOXING ⟨ended his ~ career⟩ — **ring•like** \ˈriŋ-ˌlīk\ *adj*

2ring *vb* **ringed; ring•ing** \ˈriŋ-iŋ\ *vt* (15c) **1** : to place or form a ring around : ENCIRCLE ⟨police ~*ed* the building⟩ **2** : to provide with a ring **3** : GIRDLE 3 **4** : to throw a ringer over (the peg) in a game (as horseshoes or quoits) ~ *vi* **1 a** : to move in a ring **b** : to rise in the air spirally **2** : to form or take the shape of a ring

3ring *vb* **rang** \ˈraŋ\; **rung** \ˈrəŋ\; **ring•ing** \ˈriŋ-iŋ\ [ME *ringen*, fr. OE *hringan*; akin to MD *ringen* to ring, Lith *krankti* to croak] *vi* (bef. 12c) **1** : to sound resonantly or sonorously ⟨the doorbell *rang*⟩ ⟨cheers *rang* out⟩ **2 a** : to be filled with a reverberating sound : RESOUND ⟨the halls *rang* with laughter⟩ **b** : to have the sensation of being filled with a humming sound ⟨his ears *rang*⟩ **3** : to cause something to ring ⟨~ for the waitress⟩ **4 a** : to be filled with talk or report ⟨the whole land *rang* with his fame⟩ **b** : to have great renown **c** : to sound repetitiously ⟨their praise *rang* in his ears⟩ **5** : to have a sound or character expressive of some quality ⟨a story that ~*s* true⟩ **6** *chiefly Brit* : to make a telephone call — usu. used with *up* ~ *vt* **1** : to cause to sound esp. by striking **2** : to make (a sound) by or as if by ringing a bell **3** : to announce by or as if by ringing **4** : to repeat often, loudly, or earnestly **5 a** : to summon esp. by bell **b** *chiefly Brit* : TELEPHONE — usu. used with *up* — **ring a bell** : to arouse a response ⟨that name *rings a bell*⟩ — **ring down the curtain** : to conclude a performance or an action — **ring the changes** *or* **ring changes** : to run through the range of possible variations — **ring up the curtain** : to begin a performance or an action

4ring *n* (1549) **1** : a set of bells **2** : a clear resonant sound made by or resembling that made by vibrating metal **3** : resonant tone : SONORITY **4** : a loud sound continued, repeated, or reverberated **5** : a sound or character expressive of some particular quality ⟨the sermon had a familiar ~⟩ **6 a** : the act or an instance of ringing **b** : a telephone call ⟨give me a ~ in the morning⟩

ring–a–lie•vo \ˌriŋ-ə-ˈlē-(ˌ)vō\ *or* **ring–a–le•vio** \-vē-ˌō\ *n* [alter. of earlier *ring relievo*, fr. 1*ring* + *relieve*] (ca. 1901) : a game in which players on one team are given time to hide and are then sought out by members of the other team who try to capture them, keep them in a place of confinement, and keep them from being released by their teammates

ring–around–a–rosy \ˌriŋ-ə-ˌraun-də-ˈrō-zē\ *or* **ring–around–the–rosy** \-ˌraun(d)-thə-\ *n* (1883) : a children's singing game in which players dance around in a circle and at a given signal squat — called also *ring-a-rosy*

ring•bark \ˈriŋ-ˌbärk\ *vt* (1892) : GIRDLE 3

ring binder *n* (ca. 1929) : a loose-leaf binder in which split metal rings attached to a metal back hold the perforated sheets of paper

ring•bolt \ˈriŋ-ˌbōlt\ *n* (1626) : an eyebolt with a ring through its eye

ring•bone \-ˌbōn\ *n* (1523) : an exostosis on the pastern bones of the horse usu. producing lameness

ring dance *n* (1600) : ROUND DANCE 1

ring•dove \ˈriŋ-ˌdəv\ *n* (1538) **1** : a common European pigeon (*Columba palumbus*) with a whitish patch on each side of the neck and wings edged with white **2** : a small dove (*Streptopelia risoria*) of southeastern Europe and Asia

ringed \ˈriŋd\ *adj* (14c) **1** : encircled or marked with or as if with rings **2** : composed or formed of rings

1ring•er \ˈriŋ-ər\ *n* (15c) **1** : one that sounds esp. by ringing **2 a** (1) : one that enters a competition under false representations (2) : IM-

POSTOR, FAKE **b :** one that strongly resembles another — often used with *dead* ⟨he's a dead ~ for the senator⟩
[2]ringer *n* (1863) **:** one that encircles or puts a ring around (as a quoit or horseshoe that lodges so as to surround the peg)
Ring·er's solution \'riŋ-ərz-\ *also* **Ring·er solution** \'riŋ-ər-\ *n* [Sidney *Ringer* †1910 Eng. physician] (1893) **:** a balanced aqueous solution that contains chloride, sodium, potassium, calcium, bicarbonate, and phosphate ions and that is used in physiological experiments to provide a medium essentially isotonic to many animal tissues
ring finger *n* (bef. 12c) **:** the third finger of the left hand counting the forefinger as the first
ring·git \'riŋ-git\ *n* [native name in Malaysia] (1967) —see MONEY table
ring·ing \'riŋ-iŋ\ *adj* (14c) **1 :** clear and full in tone **:** RESOUNDING ⟨a ~ baritone⟩ **2 :** vigorously unequivocal **:** DECISIVE ⟨a ~ condemnation of immorality⟩ — **ring·ing·ly** \-iŋ-lē\ *adv*
ring·lead·er \'riŋ-ˌlēd-ər\ *n* (1503) **:** a leader of a ring of individuals engaged esp. in improper or unlawful activities
ring·let \'riŋ-lət\ *n* (1555) **1 :** a small ring or circle **2 :** CURL; *esp* **:** a long curl of hair
ring·mas·ter \'riŋ-ˌmas-tər\ *n* (1873) **:** one in charge of performances in a ring (as of a circus)
ring·neck \-ˌnek\ *n* (1791) **:** a ring-necked bird or animal
ring–necked \'riŋ-'nekt\ *or* **ring–neck** \ˌriŋ-ˌnek\ *adj* (1831) **:** having a ring of color about the neck
ring–necked duck *n* (1831) **:** an American scaup duck (*Aythya collaris*) the male of which has a narrow chestnut ring encircling the neck, a black back, and light gray sides with a conspicuous white mark in front of the wings
ring–necked pheasant *n* (1834) **:** any of various pheasants with white neck rings that have been widely introduced in temperate regions as game birds and that are varieties of or hybrids between varieties of the common Old World pheasant (*Phasianus colchicus*)

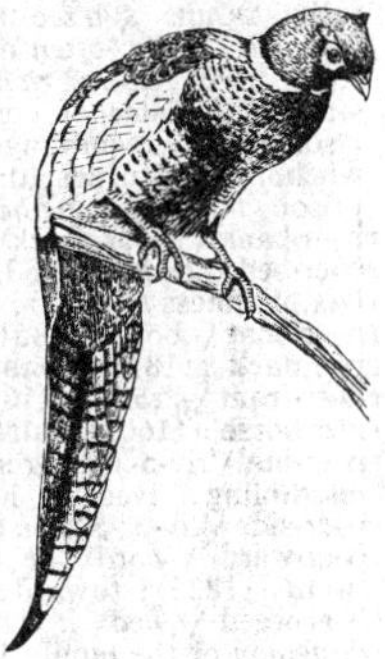

ring-necked pheasant

ring–po·rous \'riŋ-ˌpōr-əs, -ˌpȯr-\ *adj* (1902) **:** having vessels more numerous and usu. larger in cross section in the springwood with a resulting more or less distinct line between the springwood and the wood of the previous season — compare DIFFUSE-POROUS
[1]ring·side \'riŋ-ˌsīd\ *n* (1866) **1 :** the area just outside a ring esp. in which a contest occurs **2 :** a place from which one may have a close view
[2]ringside *adj* (1896) **:** being at the ringside ⟨a ~ seat⟩
ring spot *n* (1923) **1 :** a lesion of plant tissue consisting of yellowish, purplish, or necrotic, often concentric rings **2 :** a plant disease of which ring spots are the characteristic lesion
ring·straked \'riŋ-ˌstrākt\ *adj, archaic* (1611) **:** marked with circular stripes
ring·tail \-ˌtāl\ *n* (1844) **1 :** RACCOON **2 :** CACOMISTLE **3 :** CAPUCHIN 3
ring–tailed \-'tā(ə)ld\ *adj* (1729) **1 :** having a tail marked with rings of differing colors **2 :** having a tail carried in a form approximating a circle ⟨a ~ Afghan hound⟩
ring·taw \-ˌtȯ\ *n* (1828) **:** a game of marbles in which marbles are placed in a circle on the ground and shot at from the edge of the circle with the object being to knock them out of the circle
ring·toss \-ˌtȯs, -ˌtäs\ *n* (1871) **:** a game in which the object is to toss a ring so that it will fall over an upright stick
ring up *vt* [fr. the bell that rings when a sum is recorded by a cash register] (1957) **1 :** to total and record esp. by means of a cash register **2 :** ACHIEVE ⟨*rang up* many social triumphs⟩
ring·worm \'riŋ-ˌwərm\ *n* (15c) **:** any of several contagious diseases of the skin, hair, or nails of man and domestic animals caused by fungi and characterized by ring-shaped discolored patches on the skin that are covered with vesicles and scales
rink \'riŋk\ *n* [ME (Sc) *rinc* area in which a contest takes place, fr. MF *renc* place, row — more at RANK] (1787) **1 a :** a smooth extent of ice marked off for curling or ice hockey **b :** a surface of ice for ice-skating; *also* **:** a building containing such a rink **c :** an enclosure for roller-skating **2 :** an alley for lawn bowling **3 :** a team in bowls or curling
rinky–dink \'riŋ-kē-ˌdiŋk\ *adj* [origin unknown] (1913) **1 :** OLD-FASHIONED **2 :** SMALL-TIME
[1]rinse \'rin(t)s, *esp dial* 'rench\ *vt* **rinsed; rins·ing** [ME *rincen*, fr. MF *rincer*, fr. (assumed) VL *recentiare*, fr. L *recent-*, *recens* fresh, recent] (14c) **1 :** to cleanse by flushing with liquid (as water) — often used with *out* ⟨~ out the mouth⟩ **2 a :** to cleanse (as of soap used in washing) by clear water **b :** to treat (hair) with a rinse **3 :** to remove (dirt or impurities) by washing lightly or in water only — **rins·er** *n*
[2]rinse *n* (1837) **1 :** the act or process of rinsing **2 a :** liquid used for rinsing **b :** a solution that temporarily tints hair
rins·ing *n* (1818) **1 :** DREGS, RESIDUE — usu. used in pl. **2 :** water that has been used for rinsing — usu. used in pl.
rio·ja \rē-'ō-(ˌ)hä\ *n, often cap* (1907) **:** a wine from the Rioja region of Spain; *esp* **:** a dry red wine from this region
[1]ri·ot \'rī-ət\ *n* [ME, fr. OF, dispute] (13c) **1** *archaic* **a :** profligate behavior **:** DEBAUCHERY **b :** unrestrained revelry **c :** noise, uproar, or disturbance made by revelers **2 a :** public violence, tumult, or disorder **b :** a violent public disorder; *specif* **:** a tumultuous disturbance of the public peace by three or more persons assembled together and acting with a common intent **3 :** a random or disorderly profusion ⟨the woods were a ~ of color⟩ **4 :** one that is wildly amusing ⟨the new comedy is a ~⟩
[2]riot *vi* (14c) **1 :** to indulge in revelry or wantonness **2 :** to create or engage in a riot ~ *vt* **:** to waste or spend recklessly ⟨~*ed* away his whole inheritance⟩ — **ri·ot·er** *n*
riot act *n* [the *Riot Act*, English law of 1715 providing for the dispersal of riots upon command of legal authority] (1866) **:** a vigorous reprimand or warning — used in the phrase *read the riot act*
riot gun *n* (1916) **:** a small arm used to disperse rioters rather than to inflict serious injury or death; *esp* **:** a short-barreled shotgun
ri·ot·ous \'rī-ət-əs\ *adj* (15c) **1 a :** of the nature of a riot **:** TURBULENT **b :** participating in riot **2 :** ABUNDANT, EXUBERANT ⟨the garden was ~ with flowers⟩ — **ri·ot·ous·ly** *adv* — **ri·ot·ous·ness** *n*
[1]rip \'rip\ *vb* **ripped; rip·ping** [prob. fr. Flem *rippen* to strip off roughly] *vt* (1530) **1 a :** to tear or split apart or open **b :** to saw or split (wood) with the grain **2 :** to slash or slit with or as if with a sharp blade **3 :** to hit sharply ⟨*ripped* a double to left field⟩ **4 :** to utter violently **:** spit out ⟨*ripped* out an oath⟩ ~ *vi* **1 :** to become ripped **:** REND **2 :** to rush headlong ⟨*ripped* past second base⟩ *syn* see TEAR — **rip into :** to tear into **:** ATTACK
[2]rip *n* (1711) **:** a rent made by ripping **:** TEAR
[3]rip *n* [perh. fr. [2]*rip*] (1775) **1 :** a body of water made rough by the meeting of opposing tides, currents, or winds **2 :** a current of water roughened by passing over an irregular bottom
[4]rip *n* [perh. by shortening & alter. fr. *reprobate*] (1797) **:** a dissolute person **:** LIBERTINE
ri·par·i·an \rə-'per-ē-ən, rī-\ *adj* [L *riparius* — more at RIVER] (ca. 1841) **:** relating to or living or located on the bank of a natural watercourse (as a river) or sometimes of a lake or a tidewater
riparian right *n* (ca. 1860) **:** a right (as access to or use of the shore, bed, and water) of one owning riparian land
rip cord *n* (ca. 1907) **1 :** a cord by which the gasbag of a balloon may be ripped open for a limited distance to release the gas quickly and so cause immediate descent **2 :** a cord or wire pulled in making a descent to release the pilot parachute which lifts the main parachute out of its container
rip current *n* (1936) **:** a strong usu. narrow surface current flowing outward from a shore that results from the return flow of waves and wind-driven water
ripe \'rīp\ *adj* **rip·er; rip·est** [ME, fr. OE *ripe;* akin to OE *rīpan* to reap — more at REAP] (bef. 12c) **1 :** fully grown and developed **:** MATURE **2 :** having mature knowledge, understanding, or judgment **3 :** of advanced years **:** LATE ⟨lived to a ~ old age⟩ **4 a :** fully arrived **:** SUITABLE ⟨the time seemed ~ for the experiment⟩ **b :** fully prepared **:** READY ⟨the colonies were ~ for revolution⟩ **5 :** brought by aging to full flavor or the best state **:** MELLOW ⟨~ cheese⟩ **6 :** ruddy, plump, or full like ripened fruit — **ripe·ly** *adv* — **ripe·ness** *n*
rip·en \'rī-pən, 'rīp-ᵊm\ *vb* **rip·ened; rip·en·ing** \'rīp-(ə-)niŋ\ *vi* (1561) **:** to grow or become ripe ~ *vt* **1 :** to make ripe **2 a :** to bring to completeness or perfection **b :** to age or cure (cheese) to develop characteristic flavor, odor, body, texture, and color **c :** to improve flavor and tenderness of (beef or game) by aging under refrigeration — **rip·en·er** \'rīp-(ə-)nər\ *n*
ri·pie·no \ri-'pyā-(ˌ)nō, -'pyen-(ˌ)ō\ *n, pl* **-ni** \-(ˌ)nē, -(ˌ)ē\ *or* **-nos** [It, lit., filled up] (1933) **:** TUTTI
rip–off \'rip-ˌȯf\ *n* (1969) **1 :** an act or instance of stealing **:** THEFT; *also* **:** a financial exploitation **2 :** a usu. cheap exploitive imitation
rip off \(')rip-'ȯf\ *vb* (1967) **1 a :** ROB; *also* **:** CHEAT, DEFRAUD **b :** STEAL **2 :** PLAGIARIZE
ri·poste \ri-'pōst\ *n* [F, modif. of It *risposta*, lit., answer, fr. *rispondere* to respond, fr. L *respondēre*] (1707) **1 :** a fencer's quick return thrust following a parry **2 :** a retaliatory verbal sally **:** RETORT **3 :** a retaliatory maneuver or measure — **riposte** *vi*
ripped \'ript\ *adj, slang* (1970) **:** being under the influence of alcohol or drugs **:** HIGH, STONED
rip·per \'rip-ər\ *n* (ca. 1611) **1 :** one that rips: as **a :** RIPSAW **b :** a machine used to break up solid material (as rock or ore) **2 :** an excellent example or instance of its kind
rip·ping \'rip-iŋ\ *adj* [prob. fr. prp. of [1]*rip*] (1826) **:** EXCELLENT, DELIGHTFUL ⟨wrote me some ~ letters⟩ ⟨had a ~ time⟩
[1]rip·ple \'rip-əl\ *vb* **rip·pled; rip·pling** \-(ə-)liŋ\ [perh. freq. of [1]*rip*] *vi* (1670) **1 a :** to become lightly ruffled or covered with small waves **b :** to flow in small waves **c :** to fall in soft undulating folds ⟨her dress *rippled* to the floor⟩ **2 :** to flow with a light rise and fall of sound or inflection ⟨laughter *rippled* over the audience⟩ **3 :** to move with an undulating motion or so as to cause ripples ⟨the canoe *rippled* through the water⟩ **4 :** to run irregularly through a group or a population ⟨the news gradually *rippled* outwards⟩ ~ *vt* **1 :** to stir up small waves on **2 :** to impart a wavy motion or appearance to ⟨*rippling* his arm muscles⟩ **3 :** to utter or play with a slight rise and fall of sound — **rip·pler** \-(ə-)lər\ *n*
[2]ripple *n* (1755) **1 a :** a shallow stretch of rough water in a stream **b** (1) **:** the ruffling of the surface of water (2) **:** a small wave **2 a :** RIPPLE MARK **b :** a sound like that of rippling water ⟨a ~ of laughter⟩
ripple effect *n* (1966) **:** a spreading, pervasive, and usu. unintentional effect or influence ⟨the closing of one factory had *ripple effects* on the whole community⟩
ripple mark *n* (1833) **1 :** one of a series of small ridges produced esp. on sand by the action of wind, a current of water, or waves **2 :** a striation across the grain of wood esp. on the tangential surface — **rip·ple–marked** \'rip-əl-ˌmärkt\ *adj*
[1]rip·rap \'rip-ˌrap\ *n* [obs. *riprap* (sound of rapping)] (1833) **1 :** a foundation or sustaining wall of stones or chunks of concrete thrown together without order (as in deep water); *also* **:** a layer of this or similar material on an embankment slope to prevent erosion **2 :** material used for riprap
[2]riprap *vt* (1848) **1 :** to form a riprap in or upon **2 :** to strengthen or support with a riprap
rip–roar·ing \'rip-'rōr-iŋ, -'rȯr-\ *adj* (1834) **:** noisily excited or exciting
rip·saw \'rip-ˌsȯ\ *n* (1846) **:** a coarse-toothed saw used to cut wood in the direction of the grain — compare CROSSCUT SAW

rip·snort·er \'rip-'snȯrt-ər\ *n* (1840) : something extraordinary : HUMDINGER ⟨the finale was a ~⟩ — **rip·snort·ing** \-iŋ\ *adj*

rip·stop \'rip-ˌstäp\ *adj* (1949) : being a fabric woven with a double thread at regular intervals so that small tears do not spread ⟨~ nylon⟩ — **ripstop** *n*

rip·tide \'rip-ˌtīd\ *n* (1862) : RIP CURRENT

Rip·u·ar·i·an \ˌrip-yə-'wer-ē-ən\ *adj* [ML *Ripuarius*] (1781) : of, relating to, or constituting a group of Franks settling in the 4th century on the Rhine near Cologne

Rip van Win·kle \ˌrip-(ˌ)van-'wiŋ-kəl, -vən-\ *n* : a ne'er-do-well in a story in Washington Irving's *Sketch Book* who sleeps for 20 years

[1]**rise** \'rīz\ *vi* **rose** \'rōz\; **ris·en** \'riz-ᵊn\; **ris·ing** \'rī-ziŋ\ [ME *risen*, fr. OE *rīsan*; akin to OHG *rīsan* to rise, L *oriri* to rise, *rivus* stream, Gk *ornynai* to rouse, *oros* mountain] (bef. 12c) **1 a :** to assume an upright position esp. from lying, kneeling, or sitting **b :** to get up from sleep or from one's bed **2 :** to return from death **3 :** to take up arms ⟨~ in rebellion⟩ **4 :** to respond warmly : APPLAUD — usu. used with *to* ⟨the audience *rose* to her verve and wit⟩ **5 :** to end a session : ADJOURN **6 :** to appear above the horizon ⟨the sun ~*s* at six⟩ **7 a :** to move upward : ASCEND **b :** to increase in height, size, or volume ⟨the river *rose* after the heavy rains⟩ **8 :** to extend above other objects ⟨mountain peaks *rose* between the valleys⟩ **9 a :** to become heartened or elated ⟨his spirits *rose*⟩ **b :** to increase in fervor or intensity ⟨his anger *rose* as he thought about the insult⟩ **10 a :** to attain a higher level or rank ⟨officers who *rose* from the ranks⟩ **b :** to increase in quantity or number **11 a :** to take place : HAPPEN **b :** to come into being : ORIGINATE **12 :** to follow as a consequence : RESULT **13 :** to exert oneself to meet a challenge ⟨~ to the occasion⟩ ***syn*** see SPRING

[2]**rise** \'rīz *also* 'rīs\ *n* (1573) **1 :** an act of rising or a state of being risen: as **a :** a movement upward : ASCENT **b :** emergence (as of the sun) above the horizon **c :** the upward movement of a fish to seize food or bait **2 :** BEGINNING, ORIGIN ⟨the river had its ~ in the mountain⟩ **3 :** the distance or elevation of one point above another **4 a :** an increase esp. in amount, number, or volume **b :** an increase in price, value, rate, or sum ⟨a ~ in the cost of living⟩ **5 a :** an upward slope ⟨a ~ in the road⟩ **b :** a spot higher than surrounding ground : HILLTOP **6 :** an angry reaction ⟨got a ~ out of him⟩

ris·er \'rī-zər\ *n* (15c) **1 :** one that rises (as from sleep) **2 :** the upright member between two stair treads **3 :** a stage platform on which performers are placed for greater visibility **4 :** a vertical pipe (as for water or gas) or a vertical portion of an electric wiring system **5 :** one of the straps that connects a parachutist's harness with the shroud lines

ris·i·bil·i·ty \ˌriz-ə-'bil-ət-ē\ *n, pl* **-ties** (1620) **1 :** LAUGHTER **2 :** the ability or inclination to laugh — often used in pl. ⟨our *risibilities* support us as we skim over the surface of a deep issue —J. A. Pike⟩

ris·i·ble \'riz-ə-bəl\ *adj* [LL *risibilis*, fr. L *risus*, pp. of *ridēre* to laugh — more at RIDICULOUS] (1557) **1 a :** capable of laughing **b :** disposed to laugh **2 :** arousing or provoking laughter : FUNNY **3 :** associated with, relating to, or used in laughter ⟨~ muscles⟩

ris·i·bles \-bəlz\ *n pl* (1785) : sense of the ridiculous : sense of humor

[1]**ris·ing** \'rī-ziŋ\ *n* (14c) : INSURRECTION, UPRISING

[2]**rising** *adv* (1760) : approaching a stated age : NEARLY ⟨a red cow ~ four years old — *Lancaster (Pa.) Jour.*⟩

rising diphthong *n* (1888) : a diphthong in which the second element is more prominent than the first (as \wi\ in \'kwit\ *quit*)

rising rhythm *n* (1921) : rhythm with stress occurring regularly on the last syllable of each foot — compare FALLING RHYTHM

[1]**risk** \'risk\ *n* [F *risque*, fr. It *risco*] (ca. 1661) **1 :** possibility of loss or injury : PERIL **2 :** a dangerous element or factor **3 a :** the chance of loss or the perils to the subject matter of an insurance contract; *also* **:** the degree of probability of such loss **b :** a person or thing that is a specified hazard to an insurer ⟨a poor ~ for insurance⟩ **c :** an insurance hazard from a specified cause or source ⟨war ~⟩

[2]**risk** *vt* (1687) **1 :** to expose to hazard or danger ⟨~*ed* her life⟩ **2 :** to incur the risk or danger of ⟨~*ed* breaking his neck⟩ — **risk·er** *n*

risk capital *n* (1944) : VENTURE CAPITAL

risky \'ris-kē\ *adj* **risk·i·er; -est** (1827) : attended with risk or danger : HAZARDOUS ***syn*** see DANGEROUS — **risk·i·ness** *n*

ri·sor·gi·men·to \(ˌ)rē-ˌzȯr-ji-'men-(ˌ)tō, -ˌsȯr-\ *n, pl* **-tos** [It, lit., rising again, fr. *risorgere* to rise again (fr. L *resurgere*) + *-i-* + *-mento* -ment — more at RESURRECTION] (ca. 1902) : a time of renewal or renaissance : REVIVAL; *specif* : the 19th century movement for Italian political unity

ri·sot·to \ri-'sȯt-(ˌ)ō, -'zȯt-\ *n, pl* **-tos** [It] (1855) : rice cooked in meat stock and seasoned (as with Parmesan cheese or saffron)

ris·qué \ri-'skā\ *adj* [F, fr. pp. of *risquer* to risk, fr. *risque*] (1867) : verging on impropriety or indecency : OFF-COLOR

Rit·a·lin \'rit-ə-lən\ *trademark* — used for methylphenidate

ri·tard \ri-'tärd, 'rē-ˌ\ *n* (ca. 1890) : RITARDANDO

[1]**ri·tar·dan·do** \ri-ˌtär-'dän-(ˌ)dō, ˌrē-\ *adv or adj* [It, fr. L *retardandum*, gerund of *retardare* to retard] (1811) : with a gradual slackening in tempo — used as a direction in music

[2]**ritardando** *n, pl* **-dos** (ca. 1934) : a ritardando passage

rite \'rīt\ *n* [ME, fr. L *ritus*; akin to OE *rīm* number, Gk *arithmos* number — more at ARITHMETIC] (14c) **1 a :** a prescribed form or manner governing the words or actions for a ceremony **b :** the liturgy of a church or group of churches **2 :** a ceremonial act or action ⟨initiation ~*s*⟩ **3 :** a division of the Christian church using a distinctive liturgy

rite de pas·sage \ˌrēt-də-pa-'säzh, -pä-\ *n, pl* **rites de passage** \ˌrēt(s)-də-\ [F] (1911) : RITE OF PASSAGE

rite of passage [trans. of F *rite de passage*] (1938) : a ritual associated with a crisis or a change of status (as marriage, illness, or death) for an individual

ri·tor·nel·lo \ˌrit-ər-'nel-(ˌ)ō, ˌri-ˌtȯr-\ *n, pl* **-nel·li** \-'nel-(ˌ)ē\ *or* **-nellos** [It, dim. of *ritorno* return, fr. *ritornare* to return, fr. *ri-* re- + *tornare* to turn, fr. L, to turn on a lathe — more at TURN] (1675) **1 a :** a short recurrent instrumental passage in a vocal composition **b :** an instrumental interlude in early opera **2 :** a tutti passage in a concerto or rondo refrain

[1]**rit·u·al** \'rich-(ə-)wəl, 'rich-əl\ *adj* [L *ritualis*, fr. *ritus* rite] (1570) **1 :** of or relating to rites or a ritual : CEREMONIAL ⟨a ~ dance⟩ **2 :** according to religious law or social custom ⟨~ purity⟩ — **rit·u·al·ly** \-ē\ *adv*

[2]**ritual** *n* (1649) **1 :** the established form for a ceremony; *specif* : the order of words prescribed for a religious ceremony **2 a :** ritual observance; *specif* : a system of rites **b :** a ceremonial act or action **c :** any formal and customarily repeated act or series of acts

rit·u·al·ism \-ˌiz-əm\ *n* (1843) **1 :** the use of ritual **2 :** excessive devotion to ritual — **rit·u·al·ist** \-əst\ *n* — **rit·u·al·is·tic** \ˌrich-(ə-)wəl-'is-tik, ˌrich-əl-\ *adj* — **rit·u·al·is·ti·cal·ly** \-ti-k(ə-)lē\ *adv*

rit·u·al·ize \'rich-(ə-)wəl-ˌīz, 'rich-əl-\ *vb* **-ized; -iz·ing** *vi* (1842) : to practice ritualism ~ *vt* **1 :** to make a ritual of **2 :** to impose a ritual on — **rit·u·al·iza·tion** \ˌrich-(ə-)wəl-ə-'zā-shən, ˌrich-əl-\ *n*

ritzy \'rit-sē\ *adj* **ritz·i·er; -est** [*Ritz* hotels, noted for their opulence] (1920) **1 :** ostentatiously smart : FASHIONABLE, POSH **2 :** SNOBBISH — **ritz·i·ness** *n*

[1]**ri·val** \'rī-vəl\ *n* [MF or L; MF, fr. L *rivalis* one using the same stream as another, rival in love, fr. *rivalis* of a stream, fr. *rivus* stream — more at RISE] (1577) **1 a :** one of two or more striving to reach or obtain something that only one can possess **b :** one striving for competitive advantage **2** *obs* : COMPANION, ASSOCIATE **3 :** one that equals another in desired qualities : PEER

[2]**rival** *adj* (1590) : having the same pretensions or claims : COMPETING

[3]**rival** *vb* **ri·valed** *or* **ri·valled; ri·val·ing** *or* **ri·val·ling** \'rīv-(ə-)liŋ\ *vi* (1605) : to act as a rival : COMPETE ~ *vt* **1 :** to be in competition with **2 :** to strive to equal or excel : EMULATE **3 :** to possess qualities or aptitudes that approach or equal (those of another)

ri·val·rous \'rī-vəl-rəs\ *adj* (1812) : given to rivalry : COMPETITIVE

ri·val·ry \'rī-vəl-rē\ *n, pl* **-ries** (1598) : the act of rivaling : the state of being a rival : COMPETITION

rive \'rīv\ *vb* **rived** \'rīvd\; **riv·en** \'riv-ən\ *also* **rived; riv·ing** \'rī-viŋ\ [ME *riven*, fr. ON *rīfa*; akin to L *ripa* shore, Gk *ereipein* to tear down, OE *rāw* row] *vt* (14c) **1 a :** to wrench open or tear apart or to pieces : REND **b :** to split with force or violence ⟨lightning *rived* the tree⟩ **2 a :** to divide into pieces : SHATTER **b :** FRACTURE ~ *vi* : to become split : CRACK ***syn*** see TEAR

riv·er \'riv-ər\ *n, often attrib* [ME *rivere*, fr. OF, fr. (assumed) VL *riparia*, fr. L, fem. of *riparius* riparian, fr. *ripa*] (13c) **1 a :** a natural stream of water of considerable volume **b :** WATERCOURSE **2 a :** something resembling a river ⟨a ~ of lava⟩ **b** *pl* **:** large or overwhelming quantities ⟨drank ~*s* of coffee⟩ — **up the river :** to or in prison ⟨takes the rap and goes *up the river* —Nigel Balchin⟩

riv·er·bank \'riv-ər-ˌbaŋk\ *n* (1565) : the bank of a river

riv·er·bed \-ˌbed\ *n* (1833) : the channel occupied by a river

river blindness *n* (1953) : ONCHOCERCIASIS

riv·er·boat \-ˌbōt\ *n* (1851) : a boat for use on a river

river duck *n* (1837) : DABBLER b

riv·er·front \-ˌfrənt\ *n* (1855) : the land or area along a river

river horse *n* (1601) : HIPPOPOTAMUS

riv·er·ine \'riv-ə-ˌrīn, -ˌrēn\ *adj* (1860) **1 :** relating to, formed by, or resembling a river **2 :** living or situated on the banks of a river

riv·er·side \'riv-ər-ˌsīd\ *n* (14c) : the side or bank of a river

riv·er·ward \-wərd\ *or* **riv·er·wards** \-wərdz\ *adv* [[1]*river* + *-ward*, *-wards*] (1833) : toward a river

riv·er·weed \-ˌwēd\ *n* (1832) : any of a widely distributed genus (*Podostemon* of the family Podostemaceae) of rock-inhabiting submerged aquatic herbs that have sessile involucrate flowers and poorly developed leaves

[1]**riv·et** \'riv-ət\ *n* [ME *ryvette*, fr. MF *rivet*, fr. *river* to attach] (15c) : a headed pin or bolt of metal used for uniting two or more pieces by passing the shank through a hole in each piece and then beating or pressing down the plain end so as to make a second head

[2]**rivet** *vt* (15c) **1 :** to fasten with or as if with rivets **2 :** to upset the end or point of (as a metallic pin, rod, or bolt) by beating or pressing so as to form a head **3 :** to fasten firmly ⟨they ~ these feelings . . . tightly together —Michael Novak⟩ **4 :** to attract and hold (as the attention) completely — **riv·et·er** *n*

ri·vi·era \ˌriv-ē-'er-ə, ri-'vyer-\ *n, often cap* [fr. the *Riviera*, region in southeastern France and northwestern Italy] (ca. 1797) : a coastal region frequented as a resort area and usu. marked by a mild climate

ri·vi·ère \ˌriv-ē-'e(ə)r, ri-'vye(ə)r\ *n* [F, lit., river, fr. OF *rivere*] (1879) : a necklace of precious stones (as diamonds)

riv·u·let \'riv-(y)ə-lət\ *n* [It *rivoletto*, dim. of *rivolo*, fr. L *rivulus*, dim. of *rivus* stream — more at RISE] (1587) : a small stream : BROOK

[1]**ri·yal** \rē-'(y)ȯl, -'(y)äl\ *n* [Ar *riyāl*, fr. Sp *real* real] (1928) — see MONEY table

[2]**riyal** *var of* RIAL

RNA \ˌär-ˌen-'ā\ *n* [*ribonucleic acid*] (1948) : any of various nucleic acids that contain ribose and uracil as structural components and are associated with the control of cellular chemical activities — compare MESSENGER RNA, RIBOSOMAL RNA, TRANSFER RNA

RNA polymerase *n* (ca. 1962) : an enzyme that promotes the synthesis of RNA using DNA or RNA as a template

RN·ase \är-'en-ˌās, -ˌāz\ *or* **RNA·ase** \ˌär-ˌen-'ā-ˌās, -'ā-ˌāz\ *n* [*RNA* + *-ase*] (1957) : RIBONUCLEASE

[1]**roach** \'rōch\ *n, pl* **roach** *also* **roach·es** [ME *roche*, fr. MF] (14c) **1 :** a silver-white European freshwater cyprinid fish (*Rutilus rutilus*) with a greenish back; *also* : any of various related fishes (as some shiners) **2 :** any of several American freshwater sunfishes (family Centrarchidae)

[2]**roach** *n* [origin unknown] (1794) **1 :** a curved cut in the edge of a sail to prevent chafing or to secure a better fit **2 :** a roll of hair brushed straight back from the forehead or side of the head

[3]**roach** *vt* (1818) **1 :** to cut (as a horse's mane) so that the remainder stands upright **2 :** to cause to arch; *specif* : to brush (the hair) in a roach — often used with *up*

[4]**roach** *n* [by shortening] (1836) **1 :** COCKROACH **2 :** the butt of a marijuana cigarette

roach back *n* (1874) : an arched back (as of a dog)

roach clip *n* (1968) : a metal clip that resembles tweezers and is used by marijuana smokers to hold a roach — called also *roach holder*

road \'rōd\ *n* [ME *rode*, fr. OE *rād* ride, journey; akin to OE *rīdan* to ride] (14c) **1 :** ROADSTEAD — often used in pl. **2 a :** an open way for vehicles, persons,

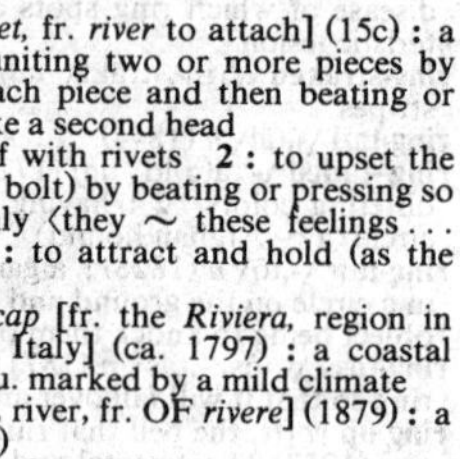

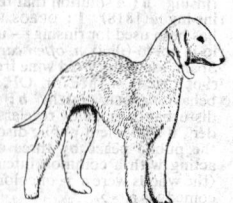

roach back

and animals; *esp* : one lying outside of an urban district : HIGHWAY **b** : ROADBED 2b **3** : ROUTE, PATH **4** : RAILWAY **5** : a series of scheduled visits or appearances (as games or performances) in several locations or the travel necessary to make these visits ⟨the team is on the ~⟩ ⟨on tour with the musical's ~ company⟩ — **road·less** \ˈrōd-ləs\ *adj* — **down the road** : in the future

road·abil·i·ty \ˌrōd-ə-ˈbil-ət-ē\ *n* (ca. 1914) : the qualities (as steadiness and balance) desirable in an automobile on the road

road agent *n* (1863) : a highwayman who formerly operated esp. on stage routes in unsettled districts

road·bed \ˈrōd-ˌbed\ *n* (ca. 1840) **1 a** : the bed on which the ties, rails, and ballast of a railroad rest **b** : the ballast or the upper surface of the ballast on which the ties rest **2 a** : the earth foundation of a road prepared for surfacing **b** : the part of the surface of a road traveled by vehicles

road·block \-ˌbläk\ *n* (1940) **1 a** : a barricade often with traps or mines for holding up an enemy at a point on a road covered by fire **b** : a road barricade set up esp. by law enforcement officers **2** : an obstruction in a road **3** : something (as a fact, condition, or countermeasure) that blocks progress or prevents accomplishment of an objective — **roadblock** *vt*

road hog *n* (1891) : a driver of an automotive vehicle who obstructs others esp. by occupying part of another's traffic lane

road·hold·ing \ˈrōd-ˌhōld-iŋ\ *n, chiefly Brit* (ca. 1932) : the qualities of an automobile that tend to make it hold the road

road·house \ˈrōd-ˌhau̇s\ *n* (1857) : an inn usu. outside city limits providing liquor and usu. meals, dancing, and often gambling

road·ie \ˈrōd-ē\ *n* [*road* + *-ie*] (1969) : one who works (as by moving heavy equipment) for traveling entertainers

road metal *n* (1818) : broken stone or cinders used in making and repairing roads or ballasting railroads

road racing *n* (1828) : racing over public roads; *specif* : automobile racing over roads or over a closed course designed to simulate public roads (as with left- and right-hand turns, sharp corners, and hills)

road roller *n* (1876) : one that rolls roadways; *specif* : a machine with heavy wide smooth rollers for compacting roadbeds

road·run·ner \ˈrō-ˌdrən-ər\ *n* (1856) : a largely terrestrial bird (*Geococcyx californianus*) of the cuckoo family that is a speedy runner and ranges from California to Mexico and eastward to Texas; *also* : a closely related Mexican bird (*G. velox*)

road show *n* (1908) **1** : a theatrical performance given by a troupe on tour **2** : a special engagement of a new motion picture usu. at increased prices

1road·side \ˈrōd-ˌsīd\ *n* (1744) : the strip of land along a road : the side of a road

2roadside *adj* (1810) : situated at the side of a road ⟨a ~ diner⟩

road·stead \ˈrōd-ˌsted\ *n* (1556) : a place less enclosed than a harbor where ships may ride at anchor

road·ster \ˈrōd-stər\ *n* (1818) **1 a** : a horse for riding or driving on roads **b** : a utility saddle horse of the hackney type **2 a** : a light carriage : BUGGY **b** : an automobile with an open body that seats two and has a folding fabric top and a luggage compartment in the rear

road test *n* (1906) **1** : a test of a vehicle under practical operating conditions on the road **2** : a test on the road of a person's driving ability as a requirement for a driver's license — **road test** *vt*

road·way \ˈrōd-ˌwā\ *n* (1600) **1 a** : the strip of land over which a road passes **b** : ROAD; *specif* : ROADBED 2b **2** : a railroad right-of-way with tracks, structures, and appurtenances **3** : the part of a bridge used by vehicles

road·work \-ˌwərk\ *n* (1903) : conditioning for an athletic contest (as a boxing match) consisting mainly of long runs

road·wor·thy \-ˌwər-t͟hē\ *adj* (1819) : fit for use on the road — **road·wor·thi·ness** *n*

roam \ˈrōm\ *vb* [ME *romen*] *vi* (14c) **1** : to go from place to place without purpose or direction : WANDER **2** : to travel purposefully unhindered through a wide area ⟨cattle ~*ing* in search of water⟩ ~ *vt* : to range or wander over ***syn*** see WANDER — **roam** *n* — **roam·er** *n*

1roan \ˈrōn *also* ˈrō-ən\ *adj* [MF, fr. OSp *roano*] (1530) : having the base color (as red, black, or brown) muted and lightened by admixture of white hairs ⟨a ~ horse⟩ ⟨a ~ calf⟩

2roan *n* (1580) **1** : an animal (as a horse) with a roan coat — usu. used of a red roan when unqualified **2** : the color of a roan horse — used esp. when the base color is red **3** : a sheepskin tanned with sumac and colored and finished to imitate morocco

1roar \ˈrō(ə)r, ˈrȯ(ə)r\ *vb* [ME *roren*, fr. OE *rārian*; akin to OHG *rērēn* to bleat, Skt *rāyati* he barks] *vi* (bef. 12c) **1 a** : to utter or emit a full loud prolonged sound **b** : to sing or shout with full force **2 a** : to make or emit a loud confused sound (as background reverberation or rumbling) **b** : to laugh loudly **3 a** : to be boisterous or disorderly **b** : to proceed or rush with great noise or commotion **4** : to make a loud noise during inhalation (as by a horse afflicted with roaring) ~ *vt* **1** : to utter or proclaim with a roar ⟨~*ed* his commands⟩ **2** : to cause to roar

2roar *n* (14c) **1** : the deep cry of a wild animal **2** : a loud deep cry (as of pain or anger) **3** : a loud continuous confused sound ⟨the ~ of conversation in the bar⟩ **4** : a boisterous outcry

roar·er \ˈrōr-ər, ˈrȯr-\ *n* (14c) **1** : one that roars **2** : a horse subject to roaring

1roar·ing \ˈrōr-iŋ, ˈrȯr-\ *adj* (14c) **1** : making or characterized by a sound resembling a roar : LOUD ⟨~ applause⟩ **2** : marked by prosperity esp. of a temporary nature : BOOMING **3** : INTENSE, UTTER ⟨in the ~ heat⟩ ⟨the ~ egotists . . . that we all find repugnant —Diane Wakoski⟩ — **roar·ing·ly** *adv*

2roaring *adv* (1697) : EXTREMELY ⟨was ~ hungry —Herman Wouk⟩

3roaring *n* (1823) : noisy inhalation in a horse caused by nerve paralysis and muscular atrophy and constituting an unsoundness

roaring boy *n* (1590) : a noisy street bully of Elizabethan and Jacobean England who intimidated passersby

1roast \ˈrōst\ *vb* [ME *rosten*, fr. OF *rostir*, of Gmc origin; akin to OHG *rōsten* to roast] *vt* (13c) **1 a** : to cook by exposing to dry heat (as in an oven or before a fire) or by surrounding with hot embers, sand, or stones ⟨~ a potato in ashes⟩ **b** : to dry and parch by exposure to heat ⟨~ coffee⟩ **2** : to heat (inorganic material) with access of air and without fusing to effect change (as expulsion of volatile matter, oxidation, or removal of sulfur from sulfide ores) **3** : to heat to excess ⟨~*ed* by the summer sun⟩ **4** : to criticize severely ⟨films have been ~*ed* by most critics —H. J. Seldes⟩ ~ *vi* **1** : to cook food by heat **2** : to undergo being roasted

2roast *n* (14c) **1** : a piece of meat suitable for roasting **2** : a gathering at which food is roasted before an open fire or in hot ashes or sand **3** : an act or process of roasting; *specif* : severe banter or criticism

3roast *adj* (14c) : that has been roasted ⟨~ beef⟩

roast·er \ˈrō-stər\ *n* (15c) **1** : one that roasts **2** : a device for roasting **3** : something adapted to roasting: as **a** : a suckling pig **b** : a young chicken (*Gallus gallus*)

roast·ing ear \ˈrō-stiŋ-ˌi(ə)r, *sense 2 usu* ˈrōs-ᵊn-ˌi(ə)r *or* ˈrōs-ˌni(ə)r\ *n* (1650) **1** : an ear of young corn roasted or suitable for roasting usu. in the husk **2** *chiefly Southern & Midland* : an ear of corn suitable for boiling or steaming

rob \ˈräb\ *vb* **robbed; rob·bing** [ME *robben*, fr. OF *rober*, of Gmc origin; akin to OHG *roubōn* to rob — more at REAVE] *vt* (13c) **1 a** (1) : to take something away from by force : steal from (2) : to take personal property from by violence or threat **b** (1) : to remove valuables without right from (a place) (2) : to take the contents of (a receptacle) **c** : to take away as loot : STEAL ⟨~ jewelry⟩ **2 a** : to deprive of something due, expected, or desired ⟨air power had . . . *robbed* sea power of its sovereign values —S. L. A. Marshall⟩ **b** : to withhold unjustly or injuriously ~ *vi* : to commit robbery — **rob·ber** *n*

usage Sense *vt* 1c, in which the direct object is the thing stolen, is sometimes considered to be wrong, or perhaps archaic. The sense has been in use since the 13th century and is found in earlier literature ⟨contrive to *rob* the honey and subvert the hive —John Dryden⟩ It is not as common now as other senses, however, although occas. encountered ⟨two men *robbed* $26,000 from the . . . bank —*radio newscast*⟩

ro·ba·lo \rō-ˈbäl-(ˌ)ō\ *n, pl* **-los** *or* **-lo** [Sp] (ca. 1890) : SNOOK 1

ro·band \ˈrō-ˌband, -bənd\ *n* [prob. fr. MD *rabant*] (1762) : a piece of spun yarn or marline used to fasten the head of a sail to a spar

robber baron *n* (1878) : an American capitalist of the latter part of the 19th century who became wealthy through exploitation (as of natural resources, governmental influence, or low wage scales)

robber fly *n* (1871) : any of numerous predaceous flies (family Asilidae) some of which closely resemble the bumblebees

rob·bery \ˈräb-(ə-)rē\ *n, pl* **-ber·ies** (13c) : the act or practice of robbing; *specif* : larceny from the person or presence of another by violence or threat

1robe \ˈrōb\ *n* [ME, fr. OF, robe, booty, of Gmc origin; akin to OHG *roubōn* to rob] (13c) **1 a** : a long flowing outer garment; *esp* : one used for ceremonial occasions or as a symbol of office or profession **b** : a loose garment (as a bathrobe) for informal wear esp. at home **2** : COVERING, MANTLE ⟨peaks on the axis of the range in their ~*s* of snow and light —John Muir †1914⟩ **3** : a covering of pelts or fabric for the lower body used while driving or at outdoor events

2robe *vb* **robed; rob·ing** *vt* (14c) : to clothe or cover with or as if with a robe ~ *vi* **1** : to put on a robe **2** : DRESS

robe de cham·bre \ˌrōb-də-ˈshäⁿbrᵊ, -ˈshäm-brə\ *n, pl* **robes de chambre** \ˌrōb(z)-\ [F] (1731) : DRESSING GOWN

rob·in \ˈräb-ən\ *n* [short for *robin redbreast*] (1549) **1 a** : a small European thrush (*Erithacus rubecula*) resembling a warbler and having a brownish olive back and yellowish red throat and breast **b** : any of various Old World songbirds that are related to or resemble the European robin **2** : a large No. American thrush (*Turdus migratorius*) with olivaceous gray upperparts, blackish head and tail, black and whitish streaked throat, and chiefly dull reddish breast and underparts

Rob·in Good·fel·low \ˌräb-ən-ˈgu̇d-ˌfel-(ˌ)ō, -ə(-w)\ *n* : a mischievous sprite in English folklore

Robin Hood \-ˈhu̇d\ *n* : a legendary English outlaw famed for his archery and for robbing the rich and giving to the poor

robin red·breast \-ˈred-ˌbrest\ *n* [ME, fr. *Robin*, nickname for *Robert*] (15c) : ROBIN

Rob·in·son Cru·soe \ˌräb-ə(n)-sən-ˈkrü-(ˌ)sō\ *n* : a shipwrecked sailor in Defoe's *Robinson Crusoe* who lives for many years on a desert island

ro·ble \ˈrō-(ˌ)blā\ *n* [AmerSp, fr. Sp, oak, fr. L *robur*] (1879) : any of several oaks of California and Mexico

ro·bot \ˈrō-ˌbät, -bət\ *n* [Czech, fr. *robota* work; akin to OHG *arabeit* trouble, L *orbus* orphaned] (1923) **1 a** : a machine that looks like a human being and performs various complex acts (as walking or talking) of a human being; *also* : a similar but fictional machine whose lack of capacity for human emotions is often emphasized **b** : an efficient, insensitive, often brutalized person **2** : an automatic apparatus or device that performs functions ordinarily ascribed to human beings or operates with what appears to be almost human intelligence **3** : a mechanism guided by automatic controls — **ro·bot·ic** \rō-ˈbät-ik, rə-\ *adj* — **ro·bot·ism** \ˈrō-ˌbät-ˌiz-əm, -bət-\ *n*

robot bomb *n* (1944) : a small pilotless jet-propelled airplane that is heavily loaded with explosives and that descends as an aerial bomb

ro·bot·ics \rō-ˈbät-iks\ *n pl but sing in constr* (1941) : technology dealing with the design, construction, and operation of robots in automation

ro·bot·iza·tion \ˌrō-ˌbät-ə-ˈzā-shən, -bət-\ *n* (ca. 1927) **1** : AUTOMATION **2** : the process of turning a human being into a robot

ro·bot·ize \ˈrō-ˌbät-ˌīz, -bət-\ *vt* **-ized; -iz·ing** (1927) **1** : to make automatic : equip with robots **2** : to turn (a human being) into a robot

Rob Roy \ˈräb-ˈrȯi\ *n* [prob. fr. *Rob Roy*, nickname of Robert McGregor †1734 Scot. freebooter] (1919) : a manhattan made with Scotch whisky

ro·bust \rō-ˈbəst, ˈrō-(ˌ)bəst\ *adj* [L *robustus* oaken, strong, fr. *robor-*, *robur* oak, strength] (1549) **1 a** : having or exhibiting strength or vigorous health : VIGOROUS **b** : firm in purpose or outlook ⟨a ~ faith⟩ **c** : strongly formed or constructed : STURDY ⟨a ~ plastic⟩ **2** : ROUGH, RUDE ⟨stories . . . laden with ~, down-home imagery —*Playboy*⟩ **3** : requiring strength or vigor ⟨~ work⟩ **4** : FULL-BODIED ⟨~ coffee⟩

\ə\ abut \ᵊ\ kitten, F table \ər\ further \a\ ash \ā\ ace \ä\ cot, cart \au̇\ out \ch\ chin \e\ bet \ē\ easy \g\ go \i\ hit \ī\ ice \j\ job \ŋ\ sing \ō\ go \ȯ\ law \ȯi\ boy \th\ thin \t͟h\ the \ü\ loot \u̇\ foot \y\ yet \zh\ vision \à, k̲, ⁿ, œ, œ̄, ue, uē, ʸ\ see Guide to Pronunciation

syn see HEALTHY — **ro·bust·ly** *adv* — **ro·bust·ness** \-ˈbəs(t)-nəs, -ˌ(t)bəs(t)-\ *n*
ro·bus·ta coffee \rō-ˌbəs-tə-\ *n* [NL *robusta,* specific epithet of *Coffea robusta,* syn. of *Coffea canephora*] (1909) **1 :** a coffee (*Coffea canephora*) that is indigenous to central Africa but has been introduced elsewhere (as in Java) **2 a :** the seed of robusta coffee **b :** coffee brewed from the seed of robusta coffee
ro·bus·tious \rō-ˈbəs-chəs\ *adj* (1548) **1 :** ROBUST **2 :** vigorous in a rough or unrefined way : BOISTEROUS — **ro·bus·tious·ly** *adv* — **ro·bus·tious·ness** *n*
roc \ˈräk\ *n* [Ar *rukhkh*] (1579) : a legendary bird of great size and strength believed to inhabit the Indian ocean area
Ro·chelle salt \rō-ˌshel-\ *n* [La *Rochelle,* France] (ca. 1753) : a crystalline salt $KNaC_4H_4O_6{\cdot}4H_2O$ that is a mild purgative
roche mou·ton·née \ˈrōsh-ˌmüt-ᵊn-ˈā, ˈrōsh-\ *n, pl* **roches mou·ton·nées** *same or* -ˈāz\ [F, lit., fleecy rock] (1843) : an elongate rounded ice-sculptured hillock of bedrock
roch·et \ˈräch-ət\ *n* [ME, fr. MF, fr. OF, fr. (assumed) OF *roc* coat, of Gmc origin; akin to OHG *roc* coat] (14c) : a white linen vestment resembling a surplice with close-fitting sleeves worn esp. by bishops and privileged prelates
[1]**rock** \ˈräk\ *vb* [ME *rokken,* fr. OE *roccian;* akin to OHG *rucken* to cause to move] *vt* (bef. 12c) **1 a :** to move back and forth in or as if in a cradle **b :** to wash (placer gravel) in a cradle **2 a :** to cause to sway back and forth ⟨a boat ~*ed* by the waves⟩ **b** (1) **:** to cause to shake violently (2) **:** DISTURB, UPSET ~ *vi* **1 :** to become moved backward and forward under impact **2 :** to move oneself or itself rhythmically back and forth ***syn*** see SHAKE — **rock the boat :** to do something that disturbs the equilibrium of a situation
[2]**rock** *n* (1823) **1 :** a rocking movement **2 :** popular music usu. played on electronically amplified instruments and characterized by a persistent heavily accented beat, much repetition of simple phrases, and often country, folk, and blues elements
[3]**rock** *n* [ME *roc,* fr. MD *rocke;* akin to OHG *rocko* distaff, *roc* coat] (14c) **1 :** DISTAFF **2 :** the wool or flax on a distaff
[4]**rock** *n* [ME *rokke,* fr. ONF *roque,* fr. (assumed) VL *rocca*] (14c) **1 :** a large mass of stone forming a cliff, promontory, or peak **2 :** a concreted mass of stony material; *also* **:** broken pieces of such masses **3 :** consolidated or unconsolidated solid mineral matter; *also* **:** a particular mass of it **4 a :** something like a rock in firmness: (1) **:** FOUNDATION, SUPPORT (2) **:** REFUGE ⟨a ~ of independent thought . . . in an ocean of parochialism —Thomas Molnar⟩ **b :** something that threatens or causes disaster — often used in pl. **5 a :** a flavored stick candy with color running through **b :** ROCK CANDY 1 **6** *slang* **a :** GEM **b :** DIAMOND — **rock** *adj* — **rock·like** \ˈräk-ˌlīk\ *adj* — **on the rocks 1 :** in or into a state of destruction or wreckage ⟨their marriage went *on the rocks*⟩ **2 :** on ice cubes ⟨bourbon *on the rocks*⟩
rock·a·bil·ly \ˈräk-ə-ˌbil-ē\ *n* [[2]*rock* + *-billy* (as in *hillbilly*)] (1956) : pop music marked by features of rock and country music
rock and roll *n* (ca. 1954) : [2]ROCK 2
rock and roller *n* (1956) : ROCKER 3
rock and rye *n* (1880) : a liqueur made with rock candy, rye whiskey, fruit juice, and sometimes fruit slices
rock·a·way \ˈräk-ə-ˌwā\ *n* [perh. fr. *Rockaway,* New Jersey] (1845) : a light low four-wheel carriage with a fixed top and open sides
rock bass *n* (1815) **1 :** a sunfish (*Ambloplites rupestris*) found esp. in the upper Mississippi valley and Great Lakes region **2 a :** STRIPED BASS **b :** any of several sea basses (genus *Paralabrax*) of the California and adjoining Mexican coast
rock–bottom *adj* (1866) : being the very lowest ⟨~ off-season rates⟩
rock bottom *n* (1884) : the lowest or most fundamental part or level
rock·bound \ˈräk-ˌbau̇nd\ *adj* (1840) : fringed, surrounded, or covered with rocks : ROCKY
rock brake *n* (1846) : any of several ferns that grow chiefly on or among rocks
rock candy *n* (1723) **1 :** boiled sugar crystallized in large masses on string and used esp. in rock and rye **2 :** [4]ROCK 5a
Rock Cornish *n* (ca. 1956) : a crossbred domestic fowl produced by interbreeding Cornish and white Plymouth Rock fowls and used esp. for small roasters
rock crystal *n* (1666) : transparent quartz
rock dove *n* (ca. 1611) : a bluish gray wild pigeon (*Columba livia*) of Europe and Asia that is the ancestor of many domesticated pigeons and of the feral pigeons found in cities and towns throughout most of the world — called also *rock pigeon*
rock·er \ˈräk-ər\ *n* (1760) **1 a :** either of two curving pieces of wood or metal on which an object (as a cradle) rocks **b :** any of various objects (as an infant's toy having a seat placed between side pieces) that rock on rockers **c :** any of various objects in the form of a rocker or with parts resembling a rocker (as a skate with a curved blade) **d :** one of the curved stripes at the lower part of a chevron worn by a noncommissioned officer above the rank of sergeant **2 :** any of various devices that work with a rocking motion **3 :** a rock performer, song, or enthusiast — **off one's rocker :** in a state of extreme confusion or insanity ⟨went *off her rocker,* and had to be put away —Mervyn Wall⟩
rocker arm *n* (1860) : a center-pivoted lever to push an automotive engine valve down
rock·ery \ˈräk-(ə-)rē\ *n, pl* **-er·ies** [[4]*rock* + *-ery*] *chiefly Brit* (1845) : ROCK GARDEN
[1]**rock·et** \ˈräk-ət, rä-ˈket\ *n* [MF *roquette,* fr. OIt *rochetta,* dim. of *ruca* garden rocket, fr. L *eruca*] (ca. 1530) : any of several plants of the mustard family: as **a :** GARDEN ROCKET **b :** DAME'S VIOLET
[2]**rock·et** \ˈräk-ət\ *n, often attrib* [It *rocchetta,* lit., small distaff, fr. dim. of *rocca* distaff, of Gmc origin; akin to OHG *rocko* distaff] (1611) **1 a :** a firework consisting of a case partly filled with a combustible composition fastened to a guiding stick and projected through the air by the reaction resulting from the rearward discharge of the gases liberated by combustion **b :** such a device used as an incendiary weapon or as a propelling unit (as for a lifesaving line or a whaling harpoon) **2 :** a jet engine that operates on the same principle as the firework rocket, consists essentially of a combustion chamber and an exhaust nozzle, carries either liquid or solid propellants which provide the fuel and oxygen needed for combustion and thus make the engine independent of the oxygen of the air, and is used esp. for the propulsion of a missile (as a bomb or shell) or a vehicle (as an airplane) **3 :** a rocket-propelled bomb, missile, or projectile
[3]**rock·et** \ˈräk-ət\ *vi* (1860) **1 :** to rise up swiftly, spectacularly, and with force **2 :** to travel rapidly in or as if in a rocket ~ *vt* **:** to convey by means of or as if by a rocket
rocket bomb *n* (ca. 1895) **1 :** an aerial bomb designed for release at low altitude and equipped with a rocket apparatus for giving it added momentum **2 :** a rocket-propelled bomb launched from the ground
rock·e·teer \ˌräk-ə-ˈti(ə)r\ *n* (1832) **1 :** one who fires, pilots, or rides in a rocket **2 :** a scientist who specializes in rocketry
rocket plane *n* (1932) : an airplane propelled by rockets or armed with rocket launchers
rock·et·ry \ˈräk-ə-trē\ *n* (1930) : the study of, experimentation with, or use of rockets
rocket ship *n* (1927) : a rocket-propelled craft capable of navigation beyond the earth's atmosphere
rocket sled *n* (1954) : a rocket-propelled vehicle that runs usu. on a single rail and that is used esp. in aeronautical experimentation
rock·fall \ˈräk-ˌfȯl\ *n* (1924) : a mass of falling or fallen rocks
rock·fish \-ˌfish\ *n* (1605) : any of various important market fishes that live among rocks or on rocky bottoms: as **a :** any of numerous scorpaenid fishes (esp. genus *Sebastes*) **b :** STRIPED BASS **c :** any of several groupers
rock garden *n* (1836) : a garden laid out among rocks or decorated with rocks and adapted for the growth of particular kinds of plants (as alpines)
rock hind *n* (ca. 1867) : any of various spotted groupers commonly found about rocky coasts or reefs
rock hound *n* (1915) **1 :** a specialist in geology; *esp* **:** one who searches for oil **2 :** an amateur rock and mineral collector — **rock·hound·ing** \ˈräk-ˌhau̇n-diŋ\ *n*
rock·i·ness \ˈräk-ē-nəs\ *n* (ca. 1611) : the quality or state of being rocky
rocking chair *n* (1766) : a chair mounted on rockers
rocking horse *n* (1724) : a toy horse mounted on rockers — called also *hobbyhorse*
rock·ling \ˈräk-liŋ\ *n* (1602) : any of several small rather elongate marine cods (family Gadidae)
rock lobster *n* (ca. 1884) **1 :** SPINY LOBSTER **2 :** the flesh of a spiny lobster esp. when canned or frozen for use as food
rock maple *n* (1775) : a sugar maple (*Acer saccharum*)
rock 'n' roll, rock 'n' roller *var of* ROCK AND ROLL, ROCK AND ROLLER
rock oil *n* (1668) : PETROLEUM
rock·oon \rä-ˈkün\ *n* [[2]*rocket* + *balloon*] (1953) : a small research rocket carried to a high altitude by a balloon and then fired
rock pigeon *n* (ca. 1611) : ROCK DOVE
rock rabbit *n* (1840) **1 :** HYRAX **2 :** PIKA
rock–ribbed \ˈräk-ˈribd\ *adj* (1776) **1 :** ROCKY **2 :** firm and inflexible in doctrine or integrity ⟨a ~ conservative community —John Hale⟩
rock·rose \ˈräk-ˈrōz\ *n* (ca. 1731) : any of various shrubs or woody herbs (family Cistaceae, the rockrose family) with simple entire leaves and a capsular fruit
rock salt *n* (1707) : common salt occurring in solid form as a mineral; *also* **:** salt artificially prepared in large crystals or masses
rock·shaft \ˈräk-ˌshaft\ *n* (ca. 1864) : a shaft that oscillates on its journals instead of revolving
rock tripe *n* (1854) : any of various dark leathery umbilicate foliose lichens (as of the genus *Umbilicaria*) that are widely distributed on rocks in boreal and alpine areas and that are sometimes used as emergency food
rock wallaby *n* (1841) : any of various medium-sized kangaroos (genus *Petrogale*)
rock·weed \ˈräk-ˌwēd\ *n* (1626) : any of various coarse brown seaweeds (family Fucaceae, esp. genera *Fucus* and *Ascophyllum*) growing attached to rocks
rock wool *n* (ca. 1909) : mineral wool made by blowing a jet of steam through molten rock (as limestone or siliceous rock) or through slag and used chiefly for heat and sound insulation
[1]**rocky** \ˈräk-ē\ *adj* **rock·i·er; -est** [[4]*rock*] (15c) **1 :** abounding in or consisting of rocks **2 :** difficult to impress or affect : INSENSITIVE **3 :** firmly held : STEADFAST
[2]**rocky** *adj* **rock·i·er; -est** [[1]*rock*] (1737) **1 :** UNSTABLE, WOBBLY **2 :** physically upset (as from drinking excessively) **3 :** marked by obstacles : DIFFICULT ⟨a financially ~ year —Michael Murray⟩
Rocky Mountain sheep *n* [*Rocky mountains,* No. America] (1804) : BIGHORN
Rocky Mountain spotted fever *n* (1903) : an acute rickettsial disease characterized by chills, fever, prostration, pains in muscles and joints, and a red to purple eruption and transmitted by the bite of a wood tick (*Dermacentor andersoni*)
[1]**ro·co·co** \rə-ˈkō-(ˌ)kō, rō-kə-ˈkō\ *n* (1840) : rococo work or style
[2]**rococo** *adj* [F, irreg. fr. *rocaille* rock work, fr. *roc* rock, alter. of MF *roche,* fr. (assumed) VL *rocca*] (1841) **1 a :** of or relating to an artistic style esp. of the 18th century characterized by fanciful curved spatial forms and elaborate ornamentation **b :** of or relating to an 18th century musical style marked by light gay ornamentation and departure from thorough-bass and polyphony **2 :** excessively ornate or intricate
rod \ˈräd\ *n* [ME, fr. OE *rodd;* akin to ON *rudda* club] (bef. 12c) **1 a** (1) **:** a straight slender stick growing on or cut from a tree or bush (2) **:** OSIER (3) **:** a stick or bundle of twigs used to punish; *also* **:** PUNISHMENT (4) **:** a shepherd's cudgel (5) **:** a pole with a line and usu. a reel attached for fishing **b** (1) **:** a slender bar (as of wood or metal) (2) **:** a bar or staff for measuring (3) **:** SCEPTER; *also* **:** a wand or staff carried as a badge of office (as of marshal) **2 a :** a unit of length — see WEIGHT table **b :** a square rod **3 :** any of the long rod-shaped photosensitive receptors in the retina responsive to faint light **4 :** a rod-shaped bacterium **5** *slang* **:** PISTOL — **rod·less** \-ləs\ *adj* — **rod·like** \-ˌlīk\ *adj*
rode *past and chiefly dial past part of* RIDE
ro·dent \ˈrōd-ᵊnt\ *n* [deriv. of L *rodent-, rodens,* prp. of *rodere* to gnaw — more at RAT] (1859) : any of an order (Rodentia) of relatively small gnawing mammals (as a mouse, a squirrel, or a beaver) that have in the

upper jaw a single pair of incisors with a chisel-shaped edge; *also* : a small mammal (as a rabbit or a shrew) — **rodent** *adj*

ro·den·ti·cide \rō-ˈdent-ə-ˌsīd\ *n* (ca. 1935) : an agent that kills, repels, or controls rodents

rodent ulcer *n* [L *rodent-, rodens* gnawing] (1835) : a chronic persisting ulcer of the exposed skin and esp. of the face that is destructive locally, spreads slowly, and is usu. a carcinoma derived from basal cells — called also *rodent cancer*

ro·deo \ˈrōd-ē-ˌō, rə-ˈdā-(ˌ)ō\ *n, pl* **ro·de·os** [Sp, fr. *rodear* to surround, fr. *rueda* wheel, fr. L *rota* — more at ROLL] (1834) **1** : ROUNDUP **2** **a** : a public performance featuring bronco riding, calf roping, steer wrestling, and Brahma bull riding **b** : a contest resembling a rodeo

rod·man \ˈräd-mən, -ˌman\ *n* (1853) : a surveyor's assistant who holds the leveling rod

ro·do·mon·tade \ˌräd-ə-mən-ˈtād, ˌrōd-, -ˈtäd\ *n* [MF, fr. It *Rodomonte,* character in *Orlando Innamorato* by Matteo M. Boiardo] (1612) **1** : a bragging speech **2** : vain boasting or bluster : RANT — **rodomontade** *adj*

[1]**roe** \ˈrō\ *n, pl* **roe** *or* **roes** [ME *ro,* fr. OE *rā;* akin to OHG *rēh* roe, OIr *riabach* dappled] (bef. 12c) : DOE

[2]**roe** *n* [ME *roof, roughe, row;* akin to OHG *rogo* roe, Lith *kurkulai* frog's eggs] (15c) **1** **a** : the eggs of a fish esp. when still enclosed in the ovarian membrane **b** : the eggs or ovaries of an invertebrate (as the coral of a lobster) **2** : a dark mottled or flecked figure appearing esp. in quartersawed lumber

roe·buck \ˈrō-ˌbək\ *n, pl* **roebuck** *or* **roebucks** (14c) : ROE DEER; *esp* : the male roe deer

roe deer *n* (bef. 12c) : a small European and Asian deer (*Capreolus capreolus*) that has erect cylindrical antlers forked at the summit, is reddish brown in summer and grayish in winter, has a white rump patch, and is noted for its nimbleness and grace

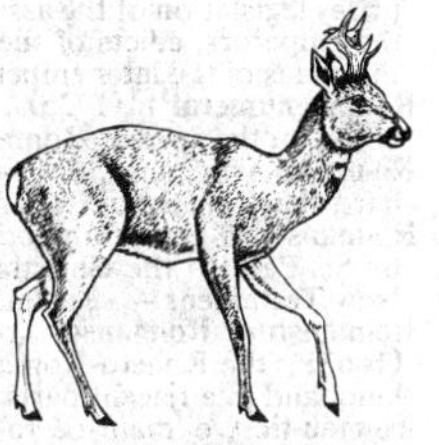
roe deer

[1]**roent·gen** \ˈrent-gən, ˈrənt-, -jən; ˈren-chən, ˈrən-\ *adj* [ISV, fr. Wilhelm *Röntgen*] (1896) : of or relating to X rays ⟨~ examinations⟩

[2]**roentgen** *n* (ca. 1929) : the international unit of x-radiation or gamma radiation equal to the amount of radiation that produces in one cubic centimeter of dry air at 0°C and standard atmospheric pressure ionization of either sign equal to one electrostatic unit of charge

roent·gen·o·gram \-ə-ˌgram\ *n* [ISV] (1904) : a photograph made with X rays

roent·gen·og·ra·phy \ˌrent-gən-ˈäg-rə-fē, ˌrənt-, -jən-; ˌren-chən-, ˌrən-\ *n* [ISV] (ca. 1905) : photography by means of X rays — **roent·gen·o·graph·ic** \-ə-ˈgraf-ik\ *adj* — **roent·gen·o·graph·i·cal·ly** \-i-k(ə-)lē\ *adv*

roent·gen·ol·o·gy \-ˈäl-ə-jē\ *n* [ISV] (ca. 1905) : a branch of radiology that deals with the use of X rays for diagnosis or treatment of disease — **roent·gen·o·log·ic** \-ə-ˈläj-ik\ *or* **roent·gen·o·log·i·cal** \-i-kəl\ *adj* — **roent·gen·o·log·i·cal·ly** \-i-k(ə-)lē\ *adv* — **roent·gen·ol·o·gist** \-ˈäl-ə-jəst\ *n*

roentgen ray *n, often cap 1st R* (ca. 1898) : X RAY

ro·ga·tion \rō-ˈgā-shən\ *n* [ME *rogacion,* fr. LL *rogation-, rogatio,* fr. L, questioning, fr. *rogatus,* pp. of *rogare* to ask — more at RIGHT] (14c) **1** *obs* : LITANY, SUPPLICATION **2** : the religious observance of the Rogation Days — often used in pl.

Rogation Day *n* (15c) : one of the days of prayer esp. for the harvest observed on the three days before Ascension Day and by Roman Catholics also on April 25

rog·er \ˈräj-ər\ *interj* [fr. *Roger,* former communications code word for the letter *r*] (1941) — used esp. in radio and signaling to indicate that a message has been received and understood

[1]**rogue** \ˈrōg\ *n* [origin unknown] (1561) **1** : VAGRANT, TRAMP **2** : a dishonest or worthless person : SCOUNDREL **3** : a mischievous person : SCAMP **4** : a horse inclined to shirk or misbehave **5** : an individual exhibiting a chance and usu. inferior biological variation — **rogu·ish** \ˈrō-gish\ *adj* — **rogu·ish·ly** *adv* — **rogu·ish·ness** *n*

[2]**rogue** *vi* **rogued; rogu·ing** *or* **rogue·ing** (1766) : to weed out inferior, diseased, or nontypical individuals from a crop plant or a field

[3]**rogue** *adj, of an animal* (1859) : being vicious and destructive

rogue elephant *n* (1859) : a vicious elephant that separates from the herd and roams alone

rogu·ery \ˈrō-g(ə-)rē\ *n, pl* **-er·ies** (1620) **1** : an act characteristic of a rogue **2** : mischievous play

rogues' gallery *n* (1859) : a collection of pictures of persons arrested as criminals

roil \ˈrȯi(ə)l, *vt 2 is also* ˈrī(ə)l\ *vb* [origin unknown] *vt* (1590) **1** **a** : to make turbid by stirring up the sediment or dregs of **b** : to stir up : DISTURB, DISORDER **2** : RILE 1 ~ *vi* : to move turbulently

roily \ˈrȯi-lē\ *adj* (1823) **1** : full of sediment or dregs : MUDDY **2** : TURBULENT ⟨the ~ waters rushed out in a wasting flood —V. L. Parrington⟩

rois·ter \ˈrȯi-stər\ *vi* **rois·tered; rois·ter·ing** \-st(ə-)riŋ\ [earlier *roister* (roisterer); fr. MF *rustre* lout] (1582) : to engage in noisy revelry : CAROUSE — **rois·ter·er** \-stər-ər\ *n* — **rois·ter·ous** \-st(ə-)rəs\ *adj* — **rois·ter·ous·ly** *adv*

rol·a·mite \ˈrō-lə-ˌmīt\ *n* [*roll* + *-amite,* of unknown origin] (1967) : a nearly frictionless elementary mechanism consisting of two or more rollers inserted in the loops of a flexible band with the band acting to turn the rollers whose movement can be directed to perform various functions

Ro·land \ˈrō-lənd\ *n* [F] : a stalwart defender of the Christians against the Saracens in the Charlemagne legends who is killed at Roncesvalles

role *also* **rôle** \ˈrōl\ *n* [F *rôle,* lit., roll, fr. OF *rolle*] (1606) **1** **a** (1) : a character assigned or assumed (2) : a socially expected behavior pattern usu. determined by an individual's position in a particular society **b** : a part played by an actor or singer **2** : FUNCTION **3** : an identifier attached to an index term to show functional relationships between terms

role model *n* (1957) : a person whose behavior in a particular role is imitated by others

role–play \ˈrōl-ˌplā, -ˈplā\ *vt* (1949) : ACT OUT ⟨students were asked to ~ the thoughts and feelings of each character —R.G. Lambert⟩ ~ *vi* : to play a role

Rolf·ing \ˈrȯlf-iŋ *also* ˈrȯf-\ *service mark* — used for a system of muscle massage intended to serve as both physical and emotional therapy

[1]**roll** \ˈrōl\ *n* [ME *rolle,* fr. OF, fr. L *rotulus,* dim. of *rota* wheel; akin to OHG *rad* wheel, L *rotundus* round, Skt *ratha* wagon] (13c) **1** **a** (1) : a written document that may be rolled up : SCROLL; *specif* : a document containing an official or formal record ⟨the ~*s* of parliament⟩ (2) : a manuscript book **b** : a list of names or related items : CATALOG **c** : an official list: as (1) : MUSTER ROLL (2) : a list of members of a school or class or of members of a legislative body **2** : something that is rolled up into a cylinder or ball or rounded as if rolled: as **a** : a quantity (as of fabric or paper) rolled up to form a single package **b** : a hairdo in which some or all of the hair is rolled or curled up or under ⟨a pageboy ~⟩ **c** : any of various food preparations rolled up for cooking or serving; *specif* : a small piece of baked yeast dough **d** : a cylindrical twist of tobacco **e** : a flexible case (as of leather) in which articles may be rolled and fastened by straps or clasps **f** (1) : paper money folded or rolled into a wad (2) *slang* : BANKROLL **3** : something that performs a rolling action or movement : ROLLER: as **a** : a wheel for making decorative lines on book covers; *also* : a design impressed by such a tool **b** : a typewriter platen

[2]**roll** *vt* (14c) **1** **a** : to impel forward by causing to turn over and over on a surface **b** : to cause to revolve by turning over and over on or as if on an axis **c** : to cause to move in a circular manner **d** : to form into a mass by turning over and over **e** : to impel forward with an easy continuous motion **2** **a** : to put a wrapping around : ENFOLD, ENVELOP **b** : to wrap round on itself : shape into a ball or roll **3** **a** : to press, spread, or level with a roller : make smooth, even, or compact **b** : to spread out : EXTEND ⟨~ out the red carpet⟩ **4** **a** : to move on rollers or wheels **b** : to cause to begin operating or moving ⟨~ the cameras⟩ **5** **a** : to sound with a full reverberating tone ⟨~*ed* out the words⟩ **b** : to make a continuous beating sound upon : sound a roll upon ⟨~*ed* their drums⟩ **c** : to utter with a trill ⟨~*ed* his *r*'s⟩ **d** : to play (a chord) in arpeggio style **6** : to rob (a drunk, sleeping, or unconscious person) usu. by going through the pockets ~ *vi* **1** **a** : to move along a surface by rotation without sliding **b** (1) : to turn over and over ⟨the children ~*ed* in the grass⟩ (2) : to luxuriate in an abundant supply : WALLOW ⟨fairly ~*ing* in money⟩ **2** **a** : to move onward or around as if by completing a revolution : ELAPSE, PASS ⟨the months ~ on⟩ **b** : to shift the gaze continually ⟨eyes ~*ing* in terror⟩ **c** : to revolve on an axis **3** : to move about : ROAM, WANDER **4** **a** : to go forward in an easy, gentle, or undulating manner ⟨the waves ~*ed* in⟩ **b** : to flow in a continuous stream : POUR ⟨money was ~*ing in*⟩ **c** : to flow as part of a stream of words **d** : to have an undulating contour ⟨~*ing* prairie⟩ **e** : to lie extended : STRETCH **5** **a** : to travel in a vehicle **b** : to become carried on a stream **c** : to move on wheels **6** **a** : to make a deep reverberating sound ⟨the thunder ~*s*⟩ **b** : TRILL **7** **a** : to swing from side to side ⟨the ship heaved and ~*ed*⟩ **b** : to walk with a swinging gait : SWAY **c** : to move so as to cushion the impact of a blow — used with *with* ⟨~*ed* with the punch⟩ **8** **a** : to take the form of a cylinder or ball **b** : to respond to rolling in a specified way **9** **a** : to get under way : begin to move or operate **b** : to move forward : develop and maintain impetus **10** **a** : BOWL **b** : to execute a somersault **11** *of a football quarterback* : to run toward one flank usu. parallel to the line of scrimmage esp. before throwing a pass — often used with *out* — **roll the bones** : to shoot craps

[3]**roll** *n* (1688) **1** **a** : a sound produced by rapid strokes on a drum **b** : a sonorous and often rhythmical flow of speech **c** : a heavy reverberatory sound ⟨the ~ of cannon⟩ **d** : a chord in arpeggio style **e** : a trill of some birds (as a canary) **2** : a rolling movement or an action or process involving such movement ⟨a ~ of the dice⟩: as **a** : a swaying movement of the body **b** : a side-to-side movement (as of a ship or train) **c** : a flight maneuver in which a complete revolution about the longitudinal axis of an airplane is made with the horizontal direction of flight being approximately maintained; *also* : the motion of a spacecraft about its longitudinal axis **d** : SOMERSAULT **e** : the movement of a curling stone after impact with another stone

roll·back \ˈrōl-ˌbak\ *n* (1942) : the act or an instance of rolling back ⟨a government-ordered ~ of gasoline prices⟩

roll back \ˈrōl-ˈbak\ *vt* (1942) **1** : to reduce (as a commodity price) to or toward a previous level on a national scale **2** : to cause to retreat or withdraw : push back **3** : RESCIND ⟨attempted to *roll back* antipollution standards⟩

roll bar *n* (ca. 1952) : an overhead metal bar on an automobile that is designed to protect the occupant in case of a turnover

roll cage *n* (1966) : a protective framework of metal bars encasing the driver of a racing car

roll call *n* (1775) **1** : the act or an instance of calling off a list of names (as for checking attendance); *also* : a time for a roll call **2** : [6]LIST 1

[1]**roll·er** \ˈrō-lər\ *n* (15c) **1** **a** : a revolving cylinder over or on which something is moved or which is used to press, shape, spread, or smooth something **b** : a cylinder or rod on which something (as a shade) is rolled up **2** **a** : a long heavy wave on a coast **b** : a tumbler pigeon **3** : one that rolls or performs a rolling operation

[2]**rol·ler** \ˈrō-lər\ *n* [G, fr. *rollen* to roll, reverberate, fr. MF *roller,* fr. (assumed) VL *rotulare,* fr. L *rotulus*] (1678) **1** : any of numerous mostly brightly colored nonpasserine Old World birds (family Coraciidae) related to the motmots **2** : a canary having a song in which the notes are soft and run together

roller bearing *n* (1857) : a bearing in which the journal rotates in peripheral contact with a number of rollers usu. contained in a cage

roll·er coast·er \ˈrō-lər-ˌkō-stər, ˈrō-lē-ˌkō-\ *n* (1888) **1** : an elevated railway (as in an amusement park) constructed with curves and inclines

on which cars roll **2 :** something resembling a roller coaster; *esp* **:** behavior, events, or experiences characterized by sudden and extreme changes
Roller Derby *service mark* — used for an entertainment involving two roller-skating teams on an oval track in which each team attempts to maneuver a skater into position to score points by circling the track and lapping opponents within a given time period
roller skate *n* (1863) **:** a shoe with a set of wheels attached for skating over a flat surface; *also* **:** a metal frame with wheels attached that can be fitted to the sole of a shoe — **roller–skate** *vi* — **roller skater** *n*
roller towel *n* (1845) **:** an endless towel hung from a roller
Rolle's theorem \ˈrōlz-, ˈrōlz-\ *n* [Michel *Rolle* †1719 Fr. mathematician] (ca. 1891) **:** a theorem in mathematics: if a curve is continuous, crosses the x-axis at two points, and has a tangent at every point between the two intercepts, its tangent is parallel to the x-axis at some point between the intercepts
roll film *n* (1895) **:** a strip of film for still camera use wound on a spool
rol·lick \ˈräl-ik\ *vi* [origin unknown] (1826) **:** to move or behave in a carefree joyous manner **:** FROLIC — **rollick** *n*
rolling hitch *n* (ca. 1769) **:** a hitch for fastening a line to a spar or to the standing part of another line that will not slip when the pull is parallel to the spar or line
rolling mill *n* (1787) **:** an establishment where metal is rolled into plates and bars
rolling pin *n* (ca. 1589) **:** a long cylinder for rolling out dough
rolling stock *n* (1853) **:** the wheeled vehicles owned and used by a railroad or motor carrier
roll–off \ˈrō-ˌlȯf\ *n* (1947) **:** a play-off match in bowling
roll·out \ˈrō-ˌlau̇t\ *n* (1952) **1 :** the public introduction of a new aircraft; *broadly* **:** the widespread public introduction of a new product **2 :** a football play in which the quarterback rolls to his left or right
roll out \(ˈ)rō-ˈlau̇t\ *vi* (1884) **:** to get out of bed
roll·over \ˈrō-ˌlō-vər\ *n* (ca. 1945) **1 :** the act or process of rolling over **2 :** a motor vehicle accident in which the vehicle overturns
roll over \(ˈ)rō-ˈlō-vər\ *vt* (1949) **1 a :** to defer payment of (an obligation) **b :** to renegotiate the terms of (a financial agreement) **2 :** REINVEST
roll–over arm *n* (ca. 1925) **:** a fully upholstered chair or sofa arm curving outward from the seat
roll·top desk \ˌrōl-ˌtäp-\ *n* (1887) **:** a writing desk with a sliding cover often of parallel slats fastened to a flexible backing
roll up *vt* (1859) **:** to increase by successive accumulations **:** ACCUMULATE ⟨*rolled up* a large majority⟩ ~ *vi* **1 :** to become larger by successive accumulations **2 :** to arrive in a vehicle
[1]**ro·ly–po·ly** \ˌrō-lē-ˈpō-lē\ *adj* [redupl. of *roly,* fr. [2]*roll*] (1820) **:** being short and pudgy **:** ROTUND
[2]**roly–poly** *n, pl* **-lies** (1836) **1 :** a roly-poly person or thing **2 :** a sweet dough spread with a filling, rolled, and baked or steamed
Rom \ˈrōm\ *n, pl* **Rom** *also* **Roma** \-ə\ [Romany, married man, husband, Gypsy male, fr. Skt *ḍomba, ḍoma* low caste male musician] (1841) **:** GYPSY 1
Ro·ma·ic \rō-ˈmā-ik\ *n* [NGk *Rhōmaikos,* fr. Gk *Rhōmaïkos* Roman, fr. *Rhōmē* Rome] (1810) **:** the modern Greek vernacular — **Romaic** *adj*
ro·maine \rō-ˈmān\ *n* [F, fr. fem. of *romain* Roman, fr. L *Romanus*] (1907) **:** a lettuce (*Lactuca sativa longifolia*) with long crisp leaves and columnar heads — called also *cos lettuce, romaine lettuce*
ro·man \rō-ˈmä^{n}\ *n* [F, fr. OF *romans* romance] (1765) **:** a metrical romance
[1]**Ro·man** \ˈrō-mən\ *n* [partly fr. ME, fr. OE, fr. L *Romanus,* adj. & n., fr. *Roma* Rome; partly fr. ME *Romain,* fr. OF, fr. L *Romanus*] (bef. 12c) **1 :** a native or resident of Rome **2 :** ROMAN CATHOLIC — often taken to be offensive **3** *not cap* **:** roman letters or type
[2]**Roman** *adj* (14c) **1 :** of or relating to Rome or the people of Rome; *specif* **:** characteristic of the ancient Romans ⟨~ fortitude⟩ **2 a :** LATIN 1a **b :** of or relating to the Latin alphabet **3** *not cap* **:** of or relating to a type style with upright characters — compare ITALIC **4 :** of or relating to the see of Rome or the Roman Catholic Church **5 :** having a semicircular intrados ⟨~ arch⟩ **6 :** having a prominent slightly aquiline bridge ⟨~ nose⟩
ro·man à clef \rō-ˌmä(n)n-(ˌ)ä-ˈklā\ *n, pl* **romans à clef** \-ˌmä^{n}-(ˌ)zä-\ [F, lit., novel with a key] (1893) **:** a novel in which real persons or actual events figure under disguise
Roman candle *n* (1834) **:** a cylindrical firework that discharges at intervals balls or stars of fire
[1]**Roman Catholic** *n* (1605) **:** a member of the Roman Catholic Church
[2]**Roman Catholic** *adj* (1614) **:** of, relating to, or being a Christian church having a hierarchy of priests and bishops under the pope, a liturgy centered in the Mass, veneration of the Virgin Mary and saints, clerical celibacy, and a body of dogma including transubstantiation and papal infallibility
Roman Catholicism *n* (1823) **:** the faith, doctrine, or polity of the Roman Catholic Church
[1]**ro·mance** \rō-ˈman(t)s, rə-; ˈrō-ˌ\ *n* [ME *romauns,* fr. OF *romans* French, something written in French, fr. L *romanice* in the Roman manner, fr. *romanicus* Roman, fr. *Romanus*] (13c) **1 a (1) :** a medieval tale based on legend, chivalric love and adventure, or the supernatural **(2) :** a prose narrative treating imaginary characters involved in events remote in time or place and usu. heroic, adventurous, or mysterious **(3) :** a love story **b :** a class of such literature **2 :** something (as an extravagant story or account) that lacks basis in fact **3 :** an emotional attraction or aura belonging to an esp. heroic era, adventure, or activity **4 :** LOVE AFFAIR **5** *cap* **:** the Romance languages
[2]**romance** *vb* **ro·manced; ro·manc·ing** *vi* (1671) **1 :** to exaggerate or invent detail or incident **2 :** to entertain romantic thoughts or ideas ~ *vt* **1 :** to try to influence or curry favor with esp. by lavishing personal attention, gifts, or flattery **2 :** to carry on a love affair with
[3]**romance** *n* (ca. 1797) **:** a short instrumental piece in ballad style
Ro·mance \rō-ˈman(t)s, rə-; ˈrō-ˌ\ *adj* (1690) **:** of, relating to, or being any of several languages developed from Latin (as Italian, French, and Spanish) — see INDO-EUROPEAN LANGUAGES table
ro·manc·er \-ər\ *n* (14c) **1 :** a writer of romance **2 :** one that romances
Roman collar *n* (ca. 1890) **:** CLERICAL COLLAR
Ro·man·esque \ˌrō-mə-ˈnesk\ *adj* (1819) **:** of or relating to a style of architecture developed in Italy and western Europe between the Roman and the Gothic styles and characterized in its development after 1000 by the use of the round arch and vault, substitution of piers for columns, decorative use of arcades, and profuse ornament — **Romanesque** *n*
ro·man–fleuve \rō-ˌmä^{n}-ˈflœv, -ˈflə(r)v\ *n, pl* **ro·mans–fleuves** \-ˌmä^{n}-ˈflœv, ˈflə(r)v(z)\ [F, lit., river novel] (1935) **:** a novel in the form of a long usu. easygoing chronicle of a social group (as a family or a community)
Roman holiday *n* (1818) **1 :** a time of debauchery or of sadistic enjoyment **2 :** a destructive or tumultuous disturbance **:** RIOT
Ro·ma·nian \ru̇-ˈmā-nē-ən, rō-, -nyən\ *n* (1868) **1 :** a native or inhabitant of Romania **2 :** RUMANIAN 2
Ro·man·ic \rō-ˈman-ik\ *adj* (1708) **:** ROMANCE — **Romanic** *n*
Ro·man·ism \ˈrō-mə-ˌniz-əm\ *n* (1674) **:** ROMAN CATHOLICISM — often taken to be offensive
Ro·man·ist \-nəst\ *n* (1523) **1 :** ROMAN CATHOLIC — often taken to be offensive **2 :** a specialist in the language, culture, or law of ancient Rome — **Romanist** *or* **Ro·man·is·tic** \ˌrō-mə-ˈnis-tik\ *adj*
ro·man·ize \ˈrō-mə-ˌnīz\ *vt* **-ized; -iz·ing** (1607) **1** *often cap* **:** to make Roman in character **2 :** to write or print (as a language) in the Latin alphabet ⟨~ Chinese⟩ **3** *cap* **a :** to convert to Roman Catholicism **b :** to give a Roman Catholic character to — **ro·man·iza·tion** \ˌrō-mə-nə-ˈzā-shən\ *n, often cap*
roman law *n, often cap R* (1660) **:** the legal system of the ancient Romans that includes written and unwritten law, is based on the traditional law and the legislation of the city of Rome, and in form comprises legislation of the assemblies, resolves of the senate, enactments of the emperors, edicts of the praetors, writings of the jurisconsults, and the codes of the later emperors
Roman numeral *n* (1735) **:** a numeral in a system of notation that is based on the ancient Roman system — see NUMBER table
Ro·ma·no \rə-ˈmän-(ˌ)ō, rō-\ *n* [It, Roman, fr. L *Romanus*] (1908) **:** a hard sharp cheese of Italian origin that is often served grated
Ro·mans \ˈrō-mənz\ *n pl but sing in constr* **:** a letter on doctrine written by St. Paul to the Christians of Rome and included as a book in the New Testament — see BIBLE table
Ro·mansh *or* **Ro·mansch** \rō-ˈmänch, -ˈmanch\ *n* [Romansh *romonsch*] (1663) **:** the Rhaeto-Romanic dialects spoken in the Grisons, Switzerland, and in adjacent parts of Italy
[1]**ro·man·tic** \rō-ˈmant-ik, rə-\ *n* (1628) **1 :** a romantic person, trait, or component **2** *cap* **:** a romantic writer, artist, or composer
[2]**romantic** *adj* [F *romantique,* fr. obs. *romant* romance, fr. OF *romans*] (1650) **1 :** consisting of or resembling a romance **2 :** having no basis in fact **:** IMAGINARY **3 :** impractical in conception or plan **:** VISIONARY **4 a :** marked by the imaginative or emotional appeal of what is heroic, adventurous, remote, mysterious, or idealized **b** *often cap* **:** of, relating to, or having the characteristics of romanticism **c :** of or relating to music of the 19th century characterized by an emphasis on subjective emotional qualities and freedom of form; *also* **:** of or relating to a composer of this music **5 a :** having an inclination for romance **:** responsive to the appeal of what is idealized, heroic, or adventurous **b :** marked by expressions of love or affection **c :** conducive to or suitable for lovemaking **6 :** of, relating to, or constituting the part of the hero esp. in a light comedy — **ro·man·ti·cal·ly** \-i-k(ə-)lē\ *adv*
ro·man·ti·cism \rō-ˈmant-ə-ˌsiz-əm, rə-\ *n* (1830) **1** *often cap* **a (1) :** a literary, artistic, and philosophical movement originating in the 18th century, characterized chiefly by a reaction against neoclassicism and an emphasis on the imagination and emotions, and marked esp. in English literature by sensibility and the use of autobiographical material, an exaltation of the primitive and the common man, an appreciation of external nature, an interest in the remote, a predilection for melancholy, and the use in poetry of older verse forms **(2)** an aspect of romanticism **b :** adherence to a romantic attitude or style **2 :** the quality or state of being romantic — **ro·man·ti·cist** \-səst\ *n, often cap*
ro·man·ti·cize \-ˈmant-ə-ˌsīz\ *vb* **-cized; -ciz·ing** *vt* (1818) **:** to make romantic **:** treat as idealized or heroic ~ *vi* **1 :** to hold romantic ideas **2 :** to present details, incidents, or people in a romantic way — **ro·man·ti·ci·za·tion** \-ˌmant-ə-sə-ˈzā-shən\ *n*
Ro·ma·ny \ˈräm-ə-nē, ˈrō-mə-\ *n, pl* **Romanies** [Romany *romani,* adj., Gypsy, fr. *rom* Gypsy man — more at ROM] (ca. 1812) **1 :** GYPSY 1 **2 :** the Indic language of the Gypsies — **Romany** *adj*
ro·maunt \rō-ˈmȯnt, -ˈmänt\ *n* [ME, fr. MF *romant*] *archaic* (1530) **:** ROMANCE 1a(1)
rom·el·dale \ˈräm-əl-ˌdāl\ *n, often cap* [blend of *Romney* (Marsh), *Rambouillet,* and *Corriedale*] (ca. 1948) **:** any of an American breed of utility sheep yielding a heavy fleece of fine wool and producing a quickly maturing high-grade market lamb
[1]**Ro·meo** \ˈrō-mē-ˌō, *in Shak also* ˈrōm-(ˌ)yō\ *n, pl* **Ro·me·os** **1 :** the hero of Shakespeare's *Romeo and Juliet* who dies for love of Juliet **2 :** a male lover
[2]**Romeo** (ca. 1952) — a communications code word for the letter *r*
Rom·ish \ˈrō-mish\ *adj* (1531) **:** ROMAN CATHOLIC — usu. used disparagingly — **Rom·ish·ly** *adv* — **Rom·ish·ness** *n*
Rom·ney Marsh \ˌräm-nē-, ˌrəm-\ *n* [*Romney Marsh,* pasture tract in England] (1832) **:** any of a British breed of hardy long-wooled mutton-type sheep esp. adapted to damp or marshy regions — called also *Romney*
[1]**romp** \ˈrämp, ˈrȯmp\ *n* [partly alter. of [2]*ramp;* partly alter. of *ramp* (bold woman)] (1706) **1 :** one that romps; *esp* **:** a romping girl or woman **2 a :** high-spirited, carefree, and boisterous play **b :** something suggestive of such play: as **(1) :** a light fast-paced narrative, dramatic, or musical work usu. in a comic mood **(2) :** an episode of lovemaking **3 :** an easy winning pace; *also* **:** RUNAWAY
[2]**romp** *vi* [alter. of [1]*ramp*] (1709) **1 :** to run or play in a lively, carefree, or boisterous manner **2 :** to move or proceed in a brisk, easy, or playful manner **3 :** to win a contest easily
romp·er \ˈräm-pər, ˈrȯm-\ *n* (1842) **1 :** one that romps **2 :** a one-piece garment esp. for children with the lower part shaped like bloomers — usu. used in pl.
Rom·u·lus \ˈräm-yə-ləs\ *n* [L] **:** a son of Mars and legendary founder of Rome

ron·deau \'rän-(,)dō, rän-'dō\ *n, pl* **ron·deaux** \-(,)dōz, -'dōz\ [MF *rondel, rondeau*] (1525) **1 a :** a fixed form of verse based on two rhyme sounds and consisting usu. of 13 lines in three stanzas with the opening words of the first line of the first stanza used as an independent refrain after the second and third stanzas — called also *rondel* **b :** a poem in this form **2 :** a monophonic trouvère song with a 2-part refrain

ron·del \'rän-d⁹l, rän-'del\ *or* **ron·delle** \rän-'del\ *n* [ME, fr. OF, lit., small circle — more at RONDEL] (13c) **1** usu *rondel* **:** a circular object; *esp* **:** a circular jewel or jeweled ring **2 a** usu *rondel* **:** a fixed form of verse based on two rhyme sounds and consisting usu. of 14 lines in three stanzas in which the first two lines of the first stanza are repeated as the refrain of the second and third stanzas **b :** a poem in this form **c :** RONDEAU 1

ron·de·let \rän-də-'let, -'lā\ *n* (1575) **:** a modified rondeau consisting usu. of seven lines in which the first line of four syllables is repeated as the third line and as the final line or refrain and the remaining lines are made up of eight syllables each

ron·do \'rän-(,)dō, rän-'dō\ *n, pl* **rondos** [It *rondò*, fr. MF *rondeau*] (1797) **1 :** an instrumental composition typically with a refrain recurring four times in the tonic and with three couplets in contrasting keys **2 :** the musical form of a rondo used esp. for a movement in a concerto or sonata

ron·dure \'rän-jər, -(,)d(y)ù(ə)r\ *n* [F *rondeur* roundness, fr. MF, fr. *rond* round, fr. OF *roont* — more at ROUND] (1600) **1 :** ROUND 1a **2 :** gracefully rounded curvature

ron·nel \'rän-⁹l\ *n* [fr. *Ronnel*, a trademark] (1960) **:** an organophosphate $C_8H_8Cl_3O_3PS$ that is used esp. as a systemic insecticide to protect cattle from pests

röntgen *var of* ROENTGEN

ron·yon \'rən-yən, 'rän-\ *n* [perh. modif. of F *rogne* scab] *obs* (1598) **:** a mangy or scabby creature

rood \'rüd\ *n* [ME, fr. OE *rōd* rod, rood; akin to OHG *ruota* rod, OSlav *ratište* shaft of a lance] (bef. 12c) **1 :** a cross or crucifix symbolizing the cross on which Jesus Christ died; *specif* **:** a large crucifix on a beam or screen at the entrance of the chancel of a medieval church **2 a :** any of various units of land area; *esp* **:** a British unit equal to ¼ acre **b :** any of various units of length; *esp* **:** a British unit equal to seven or eight yards or sometimes a rod

¹roof \'rüf, 'rùf\ *n, pl* **roofs** \'rüfs, 'rùfs *also* 'rüvz, 'rùvz\ [ME, fr. OE *hrōf*; akin to ON *hrōf* roof of a boathouse, OSlav *stropŭ* roof] (bef. 12c) **1 a** (1) **:** the cover of a building (2) **:** material used for a roof **:** ROOFING **b :** the roof of a dwelling conventionally designating the home itself ⟨didn't have a ~ over my head⟩ ⟨they share the same ~⟩ **2 a :** the highest point **:** SUMMIT **b :** an upper limit **:** CEILING **3 a :** the vaulted upper boundary of the mouth **b :** a covering structure of any of various parts of the body ⟨~ of the skull⟩ **4 :** something suggesting a roof: as **a :** a canopy of leaves and branches **b :** the top over the passenger section of a vehicle — **roofed** \'rüft, 'rùft\ *adj* — **roof·less** \'rüf-ləs, 'rùf-\ *adj* — **roof·like** \-,līk\ *adj*

roof 1a(1): *1* gambrel, *2* mansard, *3* hip, *4* lean-to

²roof *vt* (15c) **1 a :** to cover with or as if with a roof **b :** to provide with a particular kind of roof or roofing — often used in combination ⟨slate-*roofed* houses⟩ **2 :** to constitute a roof over — **roof·er** *n*

roof garden *n* (1893) **:** a restaurant or nightclub at the top of a building often in connection with or decorated to suggest an outdoor garden

roof·ing *n* (1611) **:** material for a roof

roof·line \'rüf-,līn, 'rùf-\ *n* (1857) **:** the profile of a roof (as of a house)

¹roof·top \-,täp\ *n* (1611) **:** ROOF; *esp* **:** the outer surface of a usu. flat roof ⟨sunning themselves on the ~⟩

²rooftop *adj* (1939) **:** situated or taking place on a rooftop

roof·tree \'rüf-,trē, 'rùf-\ *n* (15c) **:** RIDGEPOLE

¹rook \'rùk\ *n* [ME, fr. OE *hrōc*; akin to OE *hræfn* raven — more at RAVEN] (bef. 12c) **:** a common Old World gregarious bird (*Corvus frugilegus*) about the size and color of the related American crow

²rook *vt* (1590) **:** to defraud by cheating or swindling

³rook *n* [ME *rok*, fr. MF *roc*, fr. Ar *rukhkh*, fr. Per *rukh*] (14c) **:** either of two pieces of the same color in a set of chessmen having the power to move along the ranks or files across any number of unoccupied squares — called also *castle*

rook

rook·ery \'rùk-ə-rē\ *n, pl* **-er·ies** (1725) **1 a :** the nests or breeding place of a colony of rooks; *also* **:** a colony of rooks **b :** a breeding ground or haunt of gregarious birds or mammals; *also* **:** a colony of such birds or mammals **2 :** a crowded dilapi-

dated tenement or group of dwellings **3 :** a place teeming with like individuals

rook·ie \'rùk-ē\ *n* [perh. alter. of *recruit*] (1892) **1 :** RECRUIT; *also* **:** NOVICE **2 :** a first-year participant in a major professional sport

rooky \'rùk-ē\ *adj* (1605) **:** full of or containing rooks

¹room \'rüm, 'rùm\ *n* [ME, fr. OE *rūm*; akin to OHG *rūm* room, L *rur-, rus* open land] (bef. 12c) **1 :** an extent of space occupied by or sufficient or available for something ⟨in the country where there is ~ to run and play⟩ **2 a** *obs* **:** an appropriate or designated position, post, or station **b :** PLACE, STEAD ⟨in whose ~ I am now assuming the pen —Sir Walter Scott⟩ **3 a :** a partitioned part of the inside of a building; *esp* **:** such a part used as a lodging **b :** the people in a room **4 a :** suitable or fit occasion or opportunity **:** CHANCE ⟨left no ~ for doubt⟩

²room *vi* (1817) **:** to occupy a room esp. as a lodger ~ *vt* **:** to accommodate with lodgings

room and board *n* (1955) **:** lodging and food usu. furnished for a set price or as part of wages

room·er \'rü-mər, 'rùm-ər\ *n* (ca. 1871) **:** one who occupies a rented room in another's house

room·ette \rü-'met, rùm-'et\ *n* (1937) **:** a small private single room on a railroad sleeping car

room·ful \'rüm-,fùl, 'rùm-\ *n* (1710) **:** as much or as many as a room will hold; *also* **:** the persons or objects in a room

rooming house *n* (1893) **:** a house where lodgings are provided for rent

rooming–in \'rüm-iŋ-'in, 'rùm-\ *n* (1943) **:** an arrangement in a hospital whereby a newborn infant is kept in a crib at the mother's bedside instead of in a nursery

room·mate \'rüm-,māt, 'rùm-\ *n* (1789) **:** one of two or more persons sharing the same room or living quarters — called also *room·ie* \'rü-mē, 'rùm-ē\

room service *n* (1930) **:** the bringing of ordered food or drink to hotel guests in their rooms

roomy \'rü-mē, 'rùm-ē\ *adj* **room·i·er; -est** (1627) **1 :** having ample room **:** SPACIOUS **2** of a female mammal **:** having a large or well-proportioned body suited for breeding — **room·i·ness** *n*

roor·back \'rù(ə)r-,bak\ *n* [fr. an attack on James K. Polk in 1844 purporting to quote from an invented book by a Baron von *Roorback*] (1844) **:** a defamatory falsehood published for political effect

roose \'rüz\ *vt* [ME *rusen*, fr. ON *hrōsa*] *chiefly dial* (14c) **:** PRAISE

¹roost \'rüst\ *n* [ME, fr. OE *hrōst*; akin to MD *roest* roost, OSlav *krada* pile of wood] (bef. 12c) **1 a :** a support on which birds rest **b :** a place where birds customarily roost **2 :** a group of birds (as fowl) roosting together

²roost *vi* (1530) **1 :** to settle down for rest or sleep **:** PERCH **2 :** to settle oneself as if on a roost ~ *vt* **:** to supply a roost for or put to roost

roost·er \'rüs-tər *also* 'rùs-\ *n* (1822) **1 a :** an adult male domestic fowl **:** COCK **b :** an adult male of various birds other than the domestic fowl **2 :** a cocky or vain person

rooster tail *n* (1946) **:** a high arching spray of water thrown up behind a fast-moving motorboat

¹root \'rüt, 'rùt\ *n, often attrib* [ME, fr. OE *rōt*, fr. ON; akin to OE *wyrt* root, L *radix*, Gk *rhiza*] (bef. 12c) **1 a :** the usu. underground part of a seed plant body that originates usu. from the hypocotyl, functions as an organ of absorption, aeration, and food storage or as a means of anchorage and support, and differs from a stem esp. in lacking nodes, buds, and leaves **b :** any subterranean plant part (as a true root or a bulb, tuber, rootstock, or other modified stem) esp. when fleshy and edible **2 a :** the part of a tooth within the socket — see TOOTH illustration **b :** the enlarged basal part of a hair within the skin **c :** the proximal end of a nerve **d :** the part of an organ or physical structure by which it is attached to the body ⟨the ~ of the tongue⟩ **3 a :** something that is an active or source (as of a condition or quality) ⟨the love of money is the ~ of all evil —1 Tim 6:10 (AV)⟩ **b :** one or more progenitors of a group of descendants **c :** an underlying support **:** BASIS **d :** the essential core **:** HEART — often used in the phrase *at root* **:** close relationship with an environment **:** TIE — usu. used in pl. **4 a :** a quantity taken an indicated number of times as an equal factor ⟨2 is a fourth ~ of 16⟩ **b :** a number that reduces an equation to an identity when it is substituted for one variable **5 a :** the lower part **:** BASE **b :** the part by which an object is attached to something else **6 :** the simple element inferred as the basis from which a word is derived by phonetic change or by extension (as composition or the addition of an affix or inflectional ending) **7 :** the tone from whose overtones a chord is composed **:** the lowest tone of a chord in normal position **syn** see ORIGIN — **root·ed** \-əd\ *adj* — **root·less** \-ləs\ *adj* — **root·less·ness** *n* — **root·like** \-,līk\ *adj*

²root *vt* (14c) **1 a :** to furnish with or enable to develop roots **b :** to fix or implant by or as if by roots **2 :** to remove altogether by or as if by pulling out by the roots — usu. used with *out* ⟨~ out dissenters⟩ ~ *vi* **1 :** to grow roots or take root **2 :** to have an origin or base

³root *vb* [ME *wroten*, fr. OE *wrōtan*; akin to OHG *ruozzan* to root] *vi* (bef. 12c) **1 :** to turn up or dig in the earth with the snout **:** GRUB **2 :** to poke or dig about ~ *vt* **:** to turn over, dig up, or discover and bring to light — usu. used with *out* ⟨~ out the cause of the problem⟩

⁴root \'rüt *also* 'rùt\ *vi* [perh. alter. of ²*rout*] (1889) **1 :** to noisily applaud or encourage a contestant or team **:** CHEER **2 :** to wish the success of or lend support to someone or something — **root·er** *n*

root·age \'rüt-ij, 'rùt-\ *n* (ca. 1895) **1 :** a developed system of roots **2 :** ROOT 3a

root beer *n* (1843) **:** a sweetened carbonated beverage flavored with extracts of roots (as sarsaparilla) and herbs

root canal *n* (1893) **:** the part of the pulp cavity lying in the root of a tooth; *also* **:** a dental operation to save a tooth by removing the contents of its root canal and filling the cavity with a protective substance

root cap *n* (ca. 1879) **:** a protective cap of parenchyma cells that covers the terminal meristem in most root tips

---

root cellar *n* (1822) : a pit used for the storage esp. of root crops
root crop *n* (1834) : a crop (as turnips) grown for its enlarged roots
root·ed·ness \'rüt-əd-nəs, 'rùt-\ *n* (ca. 1642) : the quality or state of having roots
root hair *n* (1857) : a filamentous extension of an epidermal cell near the tip of a rootlet that functions in absorption of water and minerals
root·hold \'rüt-,hōld, 'rùt-\ *n* (1864) **1** : the anchorage of a plant to soil through the growing and spreading of roots **2** : a place where plants may obtain a roothold
root knot *n* (1889) : a plant disease caused by nematodes that produce characteristic enlargements on the roots and stunt the growth of the plant
root–knot nematode *n* (1922) : any of several small plant-parasitic nematodes (genus *Meloidogyne*) that cause root knot
root·let \-lət\ *n* (ca. 1793) : a small root
root–mean–square *n* (1895) : the square root of the arithmetic mean of the squares of a set of numbers
root pressure *n* (1875) : the chiefly osmotic pressure by which water rises into the stems of plants from the roots
root rot *n* (1883) : any of various plant diseases characterized by decay of the roots
root·stock \-,stäk\ *n* (1832) **1** : a rhizomatous underground part of a plant **2** : a stock for grafting consisting of a root or a piece of root; *broadly* : STOCK
rooty \'rüt-ē, 'rùt-\ *adj* (15c) : full or consisting of roots ⟨~ soil⟩
¹**rope** \'rōp\ *n* [ME, fr. OE *rāp*; akin to OHG *reif* hoop] (bef. 12c) **1 a** : a large stout cord of strands of fibers or wire twisted or braided together **b** : a long slender strip of material used as rope ⟨rawhide ~⟩ **c** : a hangman's noose **2** : a row or string consisting of things united by or as if by braiding, twining, or threading **3** *pl* : special techniques or procedures ⟨show him the ~s⟩ — **on the ropes** : in a defensive and often helpless position
²**rope** *vb* **roped; rop·ing** *vt* (14c) **1 a** : to bind, fasten, or tie with a rope or cord **b** : to partition, separate, or divide by a rope ⟨~ off the street⟩ **c** : LASSO **2** : to draw as if with a rope : LURE ~ *vi* : to take the form of or twist in the manner of rope — **rop·er** *n*
rope·danc·er \'rōp-,dan(t)-sər\ *n* (1648) : one that dances, walks, or performs acrobatic feats on a rope high in the air — **rope·danc·ing** \-siŋ\ *n*
rop·ery \'rō-p(ə-)rē\ *n* [prob. fr. the thought that the perpetrator deserved the gallows] *archaic* (1530) : roguish tricks or banter
rope·walk \'rōp-,wók\ *n* (1671) : a long covered walk, building, or room where ropes are manufactured
rope·walk·er \-,wó-kər\ *n* (1615) : an acrobat that walks on a rope high in the air
rope·way \-,wā\ *n* (1889) **1** : an endless aerial cable moved by a stationary engine and used to transport freight (as logs and ore) **2** : a fixed cable or a pair of fixed cables between supporting towers serving as a track for suspended passenger or freight carriers
ropy *also* **rop·ey** \'rō-pē\ *adj* **rop·i·er; -est** (15c) **1 a** : capable of being drawn into a thread : VISCOUS; *also* : tending to adhere in stringy masses **b** : having a gelatinous or slimy quality from bacterial or fungal contamination ⟨~ milk⟩ ⟨~ flour⟩ **2 a** : resembling rope **b** : MUSCULAR, SINEWY **3** *usu* *ropey, slang* : extremely unsatisfactory : LOUSY — **rop·i·ness** *n*
roque \'rōk\ *n* [alter. of *croquet*] (1899) : croquet played on a hard-surfaced court with a raised border
Roque·fort \'rōk-fərt\ *trademark* — used for a pungent French blue cheese made from sheep's milk
ro·que·laure \,rō-kə-'lō(ə)r, ,räk-ə-, -'lò(ə)r\ *n* [F, fr. the Duc de *Roquelaure* †1738 Fr. marshal] (1716) : a knee-length cloak worn esp. in the 18th and 19th centuries
ror·qual \'rò(ə)r-kwəl, -,kwòl\ *n* [F, fr. Norw *rørhval*, fr. ON *reytharhvalr*, fr. *reythr* rorqual + *hvalr* whale] (1827) : any of several large whalebone whales (genus *Balaenoptera* or *Sibbaldus*) having the skin of the throat marked with deep longitudinal furrows
Ror·schach \'rò(ə)r-,shäk\ *adj* (1927) : of, relating to, used in connection with, or resulting from the Rorschach test
Rorschach test *n* [Hermann *Rorschach* †1922 Swiss psychiatrist] (1927) : a personality and intelligence test in which a subject interprets inkblot designs in terms that reveal intellectual and emotional factors — called also *Rorschach inkblot test*
ro·sa·ceous \rō-'zā-shəs\ *adj* [deriv. of L *rosa*] (1731) **1** : of or relating to the rose family **2** : of, relating to, or resembling a rose esp. in having a 5-petaled regular corolla
ros·an·i·line \rō-'zan-ᵊl-ən\ *n* [L *rosa* rose + ISV *aniline*] (1862) **1** : a white crystalline compound $C_{20}H_{21}N_3O$ that is the parent of many dyes **2** : FUCHSINE
ro·sar·i·an \rō-'zar-ē-ən, -'zer-\ *n* (1864) : a cultivator of roses
ro·sa·ry \'rōz-(ə-)rē\ *n, pl* **-ries** [ML *rosarium*, fr. L, rose garden, fr. neut. of *rosarius* of roses, fr. *rosa* rose] (1547) **1** *often cap* : a Roman Catholic devotion consisting of meditation on usu. five sacred mysteries during recitation of five decades of Hail Marys of which each begins with an Our Father and ends with a Gloria Patri **2** : a string of beads used in counting prayers esp. of the Roman Catholic rosary
rosary pea *n* (ca. 1866) **1** : an East Indian leguminous twining herb (*Abrus precatorius*) that bears jequirity beans and has a root used as a substitute for licorice — called also *Indian licorice, jequirity bean* **2** : JEQUIRITY BEAN 1
ros·coe \'räs-(,)kō\ *n* [prob. fr. the name *Roscoe*] *slang* (1914) : HANDGUN
¹**rose** *past of* RISE
²**rose** \'rōz\ *n* [ME, fr. OE, fr. L *rosa*] (bef. 12c) **1 a** : any of a genus (*Rosa* of the family Rosaceae, the rose family) of usu. prickly shrubs with pinnate leaves and showy flowers having five petals in the wild state but being often double or partly double under cultivation **b** : the flower of a rose **2** : something resembling a rose in form: as **a** (1) : COMPASS CARD (2) : a circular card with radiating lines used in other instruments **b** : a rosette esp. on a shoe **c** (1) : a form in which gems (as diamonds) are cut that usu. has a flat circular base and facets in two ranges rising to a point (2) : a gem with a rose cut **3** *pl* : a comfortable situation or an easily accomplished task ⟨it was not all sunshine and ~s —Anthony Lewis⟩ **4** : a variable color averaging a moderate purplish red **5** : a plane curve which consists of three or more loops meeting at the origin and whose equation in polar coordinates is of the form $\rho = a \sin n\theta$ or $\rho = a \cos n\theta$ where *n* is an integer greater than 1 — **rose·like** \-,līk\ *adj* — **under the rose** : SUB ROSA
³**rose** *adj* (14c) **1 a** : of or relating to a rose **b** : containing or used for roses **c** : flavored, scented, or colored with or like roses **2** : of the color rose
ro·sé \rō-'zā\ *n* [F] (1897) : a light pink table wine made from red grapes by removing the skins after fermentation has begun
ro·se·ate \'rō-zē-ət, -zē-,āt\ *adj* [L *roseus* rosy, fr. *rosa*] (1589) **1** : resembling a rose esp. in color **2** : overly optimistic : viewed favorably — **ro·se·ate·ly** *adv*
roseate spoonbill *n* (ca. 1785) : a spoonbill (*Ajaia ajaja*) that is found from the southern U.S. to Patagonia and has chiefly pink plumage
rose·bay \'rōz-,bā\ *n* (1760) **1** : RHODODENDRON; *esp* : GREAT LAUREL **2** : FIREWEED b
rosebay rhododendron *n* (ca. 1949) : GREAT LAUREL
rose–breast·ed grosbeak \,rōz-,bres-təd-\ *n* (1810) : a grosbeak (*Pheucticus ludovicianus*) of eastern No. America that in the male is chiefly black and white with a rose-red breast and in the female is grayish brown with a streaked breast
rose·bud \'rōz-,bəd\ *n* (1611) : the bud of a rose
rose·bush \'rōz-,bùsh\ *n* (1587) : a shrubby rose
rose chafer *n* (ca. 1704) : a common No. American beetle (*Macrodactylus subspinosus*) that feeds on plant roots as a larva and on leaves and flowers (as of rose or grapevines) as an adult — called also *rose bug*
rose–col·ored \'rōz-,kəl-ərd\ *adj* (1526) **1** : having a rose color **2** : seeing or seen in a promising light : OPTIMISTIC
rose–colored glasses *n pl* (1950) : favorably disposed opinions : optimistic eyes ⟨views the world through *rose-colored glasses*⟩
rose fever *n* (1851) : hay fever occurring in the spring or early summer — called also *rose cold*
rose·fish \'rōz-,fish\ *n* (1721) : REDFISH a(1)
rose geranium *n* (ca. 1832) : any of several pelargoniums grown for their fragrant 3- to 5-lobed leaves and small pink flowers
ro·se·ma·ling \'rō-zə-,mäl-iŋ, -sə-\ *n* [Norw, fr. *rose* rose + *maling* painting] (1942) : painted or sometimes carved decoration (as on furniture, walls, or wooden dinnerware) in Scandinavian peasant style that consists esp. of floral designs and inscriptions
rose mallow *n* (ca. 1731) **1** : HOLLYHOCK **2** : any of several plants (genus *Hibiscus*) with large rose-colored flowers; *esp* : a showy plant (*H. moscheutos*) of the salt marshes of the eastern U.S.
rose·mary \'rōz-,mer-ē\ *n, pl* **-mar·ies** [ME *rosmarine*, fr. L *rosmarinus*, fr. *ror-, ros* dew + *marinus* of the sea; akin to ON *rās* race — more at RACE, MARINE] (15c) **1** : a fragrant shrubby mint (*Rosmarinus officinalis*) of southern Europe and Asia Minor used in cookery and in perfumery **2** : COSTMARY
rose of Jer·i·cho \-'jer-i-,kō\ [ME, fr. *Jericho*, ancient city in Palestine] (15c) : an Asian plant (*Anastatica hierochuntica*) of the mustard family that rolls up when dry and expands when moistened
rose of Shar·on \-'shar-ən, -'sher-\ [Plain of *Sharon*, Palestine] (ca. 1847) : a commonly cultivated Asian small shrubby tree (*Hibiscus syriacus*) having showy bell-shaped rose, purple, or white flowers
rose oil *n* (1552) : a fragrant essential oil obtained from roses and used chiefly in perfumery and in flavoring
ro·se·o·la \,rō-zē-'ō-lə, rō-'zē-ə-lə\ *n* [NL, fr. L *roseus* rosy, fr. *rosa* rose] (1818) : a rose-colored eruption in spots or a disease marked by such an eruption; *esp* : ROSEOLA INFANTUM — **ro·se·o·lar** \-lər\ *adj*
roseola in·fan·tum \-in-'fant-əm\ *n* [L, infant roseola] (ca. 1935) : a mild disease of infants and children characterized by fever lasting three days followed by an eruption of rose-colored spots
rose pink *n* (ca. 1864) : a variable color averaging a moderate pink
ros·ery \'rōz-(ə-)rē\ *n, pl* **-er·ies** (1864) : a place where roses are grown
rose slug *n* (1877) : the slimy green larva of either of two sawflies (*Claudius isomerus* and *Endelomyia aethiops*) that feed on the parenchyma of and skeletonize the leaves of roses
ro·set \'rō-zət\ *n* [alter. of ME *rosin*] *chiefly Scot* (1501) : RESIN
Ro·set·ta stone \rō-,zet-ə-\ *n* [*Rosetta*, Egypt] (ca. 1864) **1** : a black basalt stone found in 1799 that bears an inscription in hieroglyphics, demotic characters, and Greek and is celebrated for having given the first clue to the decipherment of Egyptian hieroglyphics **2** : one that gives a clue to understanding
ro·sette \rō-'zet\ *n* [F, lit., small rose, fr. OF, fr. *rose*, fr. L *rosa*] (1790) **1** : an ornament usu. made of material gathered or pleated so as to resemble a rose and worn as a badge of office, as evidence of having won a decoration (as the Medal of Honor), or as trimming **2** : a disk of foliage or a floral design usu. in relief used as a decorative motif **3** : a structure or color marking on an animal suggestive of a rosette; *esp* : one of the groups of spots on a leopard **4** : a cluster of leaves in crowded circles or spirals arising basally from a crown (as in the dandelion) or apically from an axis with greatly shortened internodes (as in many tropical palms)
rose·wa·ter \'rōz-,wòt-ər, -,wät-\ *adj* (1840) **1** : affectedly nice or delicate **2** : having the odor of rose water
rose water *n* (14c) : a watery solution of the odoriferous constituents of the rose used as a perfume
rose window *n* (ca. 1773) : a circular window filled with tracery
rose·wood \'rōz-,wùd\ *n* (1660) **1** : any of various tropical trees (as of the genus *Dalbergia*) yielding valuable cabinet woods of a dark red or purplish color streaked and variegated with black **2** : the wood of a rosewood
Rosh Ha·sha·nah \,rōsh-(h)ə-'shō-nə, ,räsh-, -'shän-ə\ *n* [LHeb *rōsh hashshānāh*, lit., beginning of the year] (1846) : the Jewish New Year observed on the first and by Orthodox and Conservative Jews also on the second of Tishri
Ro·si·cru·cian \,rō-zə-'krü-shən, ,räz-ə-\ *n* [Christian *Rosenkreutz* (NL *Rosae Crucis*) reputed 15th cent. founder of the movement] (1624) **1** : an adherent of a 17th and 18th century movement devoted to esoteric wisdom with emphasis on psychic and spiritual enlightenment **2** : a member of one of several organizations held to be descended from the Rosicrucians — **Rosicrucian** *adj* — **Ro·si·cru·cian·ism** \-shə-,niz-əm\ *n*
ros·i·ly \'rō-zə-lē\ *adv* (1809) **1** : in an optimistic manner **2** : with a rosy color or tinge
¹**ros·in** \'räz-ᵊn, 'ròz-, *dial* 'rò-zəm\ *n* [ME, modif. of MF *resine* resin] (14c) : a translucent amber-colored to almost black brittle friable resin

that is obtained by chemical means from the oleoresin or dead wood of pine trees or from tall oil and used esp. in making varnish, paper size, soap, and soldering flux and in rosining violin bows
[2]rosin *vt* **ros·ined; ros·in·ing** \'räz-niŋ, 'rȯz-, -ᵊn-iŋ\ (15c) **:** to rub or treat (as the bow of a violin) with rosin
ros·in·weed \'räz-ᵊn-,wēd, 'rȯz-\ *n* (1831) **:** any of several American plants having resinous foliage or a resinous odor; *esp* **:** COMPASS PLANT
ros·tel·lar \rä-'stel-ər\ *adj* (1877) **:** of, relating to, or having the form of a rostellum ⟨a ~ platform of an orchid⟩
ros·tel·lum \rä-'stel-əm\ *n* [NL, fr. L, dim. of *rostrum* beak] (ca. 1826) **:** a small process resembling a beak **:** a diminutive rostrum: as **a :** the apex of the gynoecium of an orchid flower **b :** the sucking beak of an insect (as a louse or aphid) **c :** an anterior prolongation of the head of a tapeworm bearing hooks
ros·ter \'räs-tər *also* 'rȯs- *or* 'rōs-\ *n* [D *rooster,* lit., gridiron; fr. the parallel lines] (1727) **1 a :** a roll or list of personnel; *esp* **:** one that gives the order in which a duty is to be performed **b :** the persons listed on a roster **2 :** an itemized list
ros·tral \'räs-trəl *also* 'rȯs-\ *adj* [NL *rostralis,* fr. L *rostrum*] (1709) **1 :** of or relating to a rostrum **2 :** situated toward the oral or nasal region: as **a** *of a part of the spinal cord* **:** SUPERIOR 6a **b** *of a part of the brain* **:** anterior or ventral — **ros·tral·ly** \-ē\ *adv*
ros·trate \'räs-,trāt, -trət *also* 'rȯs-\ *adj* (ca. 1819) **:** having a rostrum
ros·trum \'räs-trəm *also* 'rȯs-\ *n, pl* **rostrums** *or* **ros·tra** \-trə\ [L, beak, ship's beak, fr. *rodere* to gnaw — more at RAT] (1542) **1** [L *Rostra,* pl., a platform for speakers in the Roman Forum decorated with the beaks of captured ships, fr. pl. of *rostrum*] **a :** an ancient Roman platform for public orators **b :** a stage for public speaking **c :** a raised platform on a stage **2 :** the curved end of a ship's prow; *esp* **:** the beak of a war galley **3 :** a bodily part or process suggesting a bird's bill: as **a :** the beak, snout, or proboscis of any of various insects or arachnids **b :** the often spinelike anterior median prolongation of the carapace of a crustacean (as a crayfish or lobster)
rosy \'rō-zē\ *adj* **ros·i·er; -est** (14c) **1 a :** of the color rose **b :** having a pinkish usu. healthy-looking complexion **:** BLOOMING **c :** marked by blushes **2 :** characterized by or tending to promote optimism — **ros·i·ness** *n*
[1]rot \'rät\ *vb* **rot·ted; rot·ting** [ME *roten,* fr. OE *rotian;* akin to OHG *rōzzēn* to rot, L *rudus* rubble — more at RUDE] *vi* (bef. 12c) **1 a :** to undergo decomposition from the action of bacteria or fungi **b :** to become unsound or weak (as from use or chemical action) **2 a :** to go to ruin **:** DETERIORATE **b :** to become morally corrupt **:** DEGENERATE ~ *vt* **:** to cause to decompose or deteriorate with or as if with rot ***syn*** see DECAY
[2]rot *n* (14c) **1 a :** the process of rotting **:** the state of being rotten **:** DECAY **b :** something rotten or rotting **2 a** *archaic* **:** a wasting putrescent disease **b :** any of several parasitic diseases esp. of sheep marked by necrosis and wasting **c :** plant disease marked by breakdown of tissues and caused esp. by fungi or bacteria **3 :** NONSENSE — often used interjectionally
ro·ta \'rōt-ə\ *n* [L, wheel — more at ROLL] (1673) **1** *chiefly Brit* **a :** a fixed order of rotation (as of persons or duties) **b :** a roll or list of persons **:** ROSTER **2** *cap* [ML, fr. L] **:** a tribunal of the papal curia exercising jurisdiction esp. in matrimonial cases appealed from diocesan courts
ro·ta·me·ter \'rōt-ə-,mēt-ər, rō-'tam-ət-\ *n* [L *rota* + E *-meter*] (ca. 1907) **:** a gauge that consists of a graduated glass tube containing a free float for measuring the flow of a fluid
Ro·tar·i·an \rō-'ter-ē-ən\ *n* [*Rotary* (*club*)] (1912) **:** a member of a major national and international service club
[1]ro·ta·ry \'rōt-ə-rē\ *adj* [ML *rotarius,* fr. L *rota* wheel] (ca. 1731) **1 a :** turning on an axis like a wheel **b :** taking place about an axis ⟨~ motion⟩ **2 :** having an important part that turns on an axis ⟨~ cutter⟩ **3 :** characterized by rotation **4 :** of, relating to, or being a press in which paper is printed by rotation in contact with a curved printing surface attached to a cylinder
[2]rotary *n, pl* **-ries** (ca. 1888) **1 :** a rotary machine **2 :** a road junction formed around a central circle about which traffic moves in one direction only — called also *circle, traffic circle*
rotary cultivator *n* (1926) **:** an implement having blades or claws that revolve rapidly and till or stir the soil
rotary engine *n* (1837) **1 :** any of various engines (as a turbine) in which power is applied to vanes or similar parts constrained to move in a circular path **2 :** a radial engine in which the cylinders revolve about a stationary crankshaft
rotary plow *n* (1890) **1 :** a plow having a rotating propeller-shaped element for throwing snow aside **2 :** ROTARY CULTIVATOR
rotary–wing aircraft *n* (1935) **:** ROTORCRAFT
[1]ro·tate \'rō-,tāt\ *adj* [L *rota*] (1785) **:** having the parts flat and spreading or radiating like the spokes of a wheel ⟨~ blue flowers⟩
[2]ro·tate \'rō-,tāt, *esp Brit* rō-'\ *vb* **ro·tat·ed; ro·tat·ing** [L *rotatus,* pp. of *rotare,* fr. *rota* wheel — more at ROLL] *vi* (1808) **1 :** to turn about an axis or a center **:** REVOLVE; *esp* **:** to move in such a way that all particles follow circles with a common angular velocity about a common axis **2 a :** to perform an act, function, or operation in turn **b :** to pass or alternate in a series ~ *vt* **1 :** to cause to turn about an axis or a center **:** REVOLVE **2 :** to cause to grow in rotation ⟨~ crops⟩ **3 :** to cause to pass or act in a series **:** ALTERNATE **4 :** to exchange (individuals or units) with other personnel — **ro·tat·able** \'rō-,tāt-ə-bəl *also* rō-'\ *adj*
ro·ta·tion \rō-'tā-shən\ *n* (1555) **1 a** (1) **:** the action or process of rotating on or as if on an axis or center (2) **:** the act or an instance of rotating something **b :** one complete turn **:** the angular displacement required to return a rotating body or figure to its original orientation **2 a :** return or succession in a series ⟨~ of the seasons⟩ **b :** the growing of different crops in succession in one field usu. in a regular sequence **3 :** the turning of a body part about its long axis as if on a pivot **4 :** a game of pool in which all 15 object balls are shot in numerical order — **ro·ta·tion·al** \-shnəl, -shən-ᵊl\ *adj*
ro·ta·tive \'rō-,tāt-iv *also* rō-'\ *adj* (1778) **1 :** turning like a wheel **:** ROTARY **2 :** relating to, occurring in, or characterized by rotation — **ro·ta·tive·ly** *adv*
ro·ta·tor \'rō-,tāt-ər *also* rō-'\ *n* (1676) **:** one that rotates or causes rotation: as **a** *pl* **-tors** *or* **-tor·es** \,rōt-ə-'tōr-,ēz, -'tȯr-\ **:** a muscle that partially rotates a part on its axis **b :** a device for rotating a directional antenna **c :** a rotating planet or galaxy
ro·ta·to·ry \'rōt-ə-,tōr-ē, -,tȯr-, *Brit* -t(ə-)ri *also* rō-'tā-tə-ri\ *adj* (ca. 1755) **1 :** of, relating to, or producing rotation **2 :** occurring in rotation
[1]rote \'rōt\ *n* [ME, fr. MF, of Gmc origin; akin to OHG *hruozza* crowd] (14c) **:** [3]CROWD 1
[2]rote *n* [ME] (14c) **1 :** the use of memory usu. with little intelligence ⟨learn by ~⟩ **2 :** routine or repetition carried out mechanically or unthinkingly ⟨a joyless sense of order, ~, and commercial hustle —L. L. King⟩
[3]rote *adj* (1641) **1 :** learned or memorized by rote **2 :** MECHANICAL 3a
[4]rote *n* [perh. of Scand origin; akin to ON *rauta* to roar — more at ROUT] (1610) **:** the noise of surf on the shore
ro·te·none \'rōt-ᵊn-,ōn\ *n* [ISV, fr. Jp *roten* derris plant] (1924) **:** a crystalline insecticide $C_{23}H_{22}O_6$ that is of low toxicity for warm-blooded animals and is used esp. in home gardens
rot·gut \'rät-,gət\ *n* (1633) **:** cheap or inferior liquor
ro·ti·fer \'rōt-ə-fər\ *n* [deriv. of L *rota* + *-fer*] (1793) **:** any of a class (Rotifera of the phylum Aschelminthes) of minute usu. microscopic but many-celled aquatic invertebrate animals having the anterior end modified into a retractile disk bearing circles of strong cilia that often give the appearance of rapidly revolving wheels
ro·tis·ser·ie \rō-'tis-(ə-)rē\ *n* [F *rôtisserie,* fr. MF *rostisserie,* fr. *rostir* to roast — more at ROAST] (ca. 1920) **1 :** a restaurant specializing in broiled and barbecued meats **2 :** an appliance fitted with a spit on which food is rotated before or over a source of heat
rotl \'rät-ᵊl\ *n* [Ar *raṭl*] (1615) **:** any of various units of weight of Mediterranean and Near Eastern countries ranging from slightly less than one pound to more than six pounds
ro·to \'rōt-(,)ō\ *n, pl* **rotos** (1926) **:** ROTOGRAVURE
ro·to·gra·vure \,rōt-ə-grə-'vyu̇(ə)r\ *n* [L *rota* + E *-o-* + *gravure*] (1913) **1 :** PHOTOGRAVURE **2 :** a section of a newspaper devoted to rotogravure pictures
ro·tor \'rōt-ər\ *n* [contr. of *rotator*] (1903) **1 :** a part that revolves in a stationary part; *esp* **:** the rotating member of an electrical machine **2 :** a revolving vertical cylinder of a rotor ship **3 :** a complete system of more or less horizontal blades that supplies all or a major part of the force supporting an aircraft in flight
ro·tor·craft \-,kraft\ *n* (1948) **:** an aircraft (as a helicopter) supported in flight partially or wholly by rotating airfoils
rotor ship *n* (1924) **:** a ship propelled by the pressure and suction of the wind acting on one or more revolving vertical cylinders
ro·to·till \'rōt-ə-,til\ *vt* [back-formation fr. *Rototiller*] (1939) **:** to stir with a rotary cultivator
Ro·to·till·er \-,til-ər\ *trademark* — used for a rotary cultivator
[1]rot·ten \'rät-ᵊn\ *adj* [ME *roten,* fr. ON *rotinn;* akin to OE *rotian* to rot] (13c) **1 :** having rotted **:** PUTRID **2 :** morally corrupt **3 :** extremely unpleasant or inferior ⟨it was a ~ show —M. J. Arlen⟩ **4 :** marked by weakness or unsoundness ⟨feeling ~⟩ — **rot·ten·ly** *adv* — **rot·ten·ness** \-ᵊn-(n)əs\ *n*
[2]rotten *adv* (1596) **:** to an extreme degree ⟨spoiled ~⟩
rotten borough *n* (1812) **:** an election district that has many fewer inhabitants than other election districts with the same voting power
rot·ten·stone \'rät-ᵊn-,stōn\ *n* (1677) **:** a decomposed siliceous limestone used for polishing
rot·ter \'rät-ər\ *n* (1894) **:** a thoroughly objectionable person
rott·wei·ler \'rät-,wī-lər, 'rȯt-,vī-\ *n, often cap* [G, fr. *Rottweil,* Germany] (1907) **:** any of a German breed of tall powerful black-and-tan short-haired cattle dogs

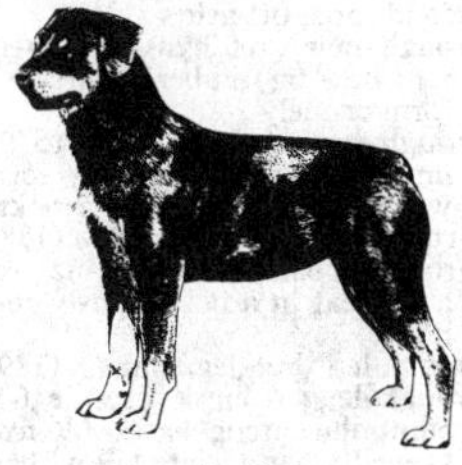

rottweiler

ro·tund \rō-'tənd, 'rō-,\ *adj* [L *rotundus* — more at ROLL] (1705) **1 :** marked by roundness **:** ROUNDED **2 :** marked by fullness of sound or cadence **:** OROTUND, SONOROUS ⟨a master of ~ phrase⟩ **3 :** notably plump **:** CHUBBY — **ro·tun·di·ty** \rō-'tən-dət-ē\ *n* — **ro·tund·ly** \-'tən-dlē, 'rō-,\ *adv* — **ro·tund·ness** \rō-'tən(d)-nəs, 'rō-,\ *n*
ro·tun·da \rō-'tən-də\ *n* [It *rotonda,* fr. L *rotunda,* fem. of *rotundus*] (1687) **1 :** a round building; *esp* **:** one covered by a dome **2 a :** a large round room **b :** a large central area (as in a hotel)
ro·tu·ri·er \rō-'t(y)u̇r-ē-,ā\ *n* [MF] (1586) **:** a person not of noble birth
rou·ble *var of* RUBLE
roué \rü-'ā\ *n* [F, lit., broken on the wheel, fr. pp. of *rouer* to break on the wheel, fr. ML *rotare,* fr. L, to rotate; fr. the feeling that such a person deserves this punishment] (1800) **:** a man devoted to a life of sensual pleasure **:** RAKE
[1]rouge \'rüzh, *esp Southern* 'rüj\ *n* [F, fr. MF, fr. *rouge* red, fr. L *rubeus* reddish — more at RUBY] (1753) **1 :** any of various cosmetics for coloring the cheeks or lips red **2 :** a red powder consisting essentially of ferric oxide used in polishing glass, metal, or gems and as a pigment
[2]rouge *vb* **rouged; roug·ing** *vi* (1782) **:** to use rouge ~ *vt* **1 :** to apply rouge to **2 :** to cause to redden
[1]rough \'rəf\ *adj* **rough·er; rough·est** [ME, fr. OE *rūh;* akin to L *ruga* wrinkle, Gk *oryssein* to dig, ON *rögg* tuft — more at RUG] (bef. 12c) **1 a :** marked by inequalities, ridges, or projections on the surface **:** COARSE **b :** covered with or made up of coarse and often shaggy hair ⟨*rough*-coated collie ~⟩ **c** (1) **:** having a broken, uneven, or bumpy surface ⟨~ terrain⟩ (2) **:** difficult to travel through or penetrate **:** WILD ⟨into the ~ woods —P. B. Shelley⟩ **2 a :** TURBULENT, TEMPESTUOUS ⟨~ seas⟩ **b** (1) **:** characterized by harshness, violence, or force (2) **:** presenting a challenge **:** DIFFICULT ⟨~ to deal with —R. M. McAlmon⟩ **3 :** coarse or rugged in character or appearance: as **a**

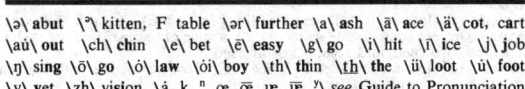

: harsh to the ear **b** : crude in style or expression **c** : INDELICATE **d** : marked by a lack of refinement or grace : UNCOUTH **4 a** : CRUDE, UNFINISHED ⟨~ carpentry⟩ **b** : executed or ventured hastily, tentatively, or imperfectly ⟨a ~ draft⟩ ⟨~ estimate⟩; *also* : APPROXIMATE ⟨this gives a ~ idea of what they meant⟩ — **rough·ish** \-ish\ *adj* — **rough·ness** *n*

syn ROUGH, HARSH, UNEVEN, RUGGED, SCABROUS mean not smooth or even. ROUGH implies points, bristles, ridges, or projections on the surface; HARSH implies a surface or texture distinctly unpleasant to the touch; UNEVEN implies a lack of uniformity in height, breadth, or quality; RUGGED implies irregularity or roughness of land surface and connotes difficulty of travel; SCABROUS implies scaliness or prickliness of surface. ***syn*** see in addition RUDE

[2]**rough** *n* (15c) **1** : uneven ground covered with high grass, brush, and stones; *specif* : such ground bordering a golf fairway **2** : the rugged or disagreeable side or aspect ⟨hiking-camping admirers of nature in the ~ —Eleanor Stirling⟩ **3 a** : something in a crude, unfinished, or preliminary state **b** : broad outline : general terms ⟨the question . . . has been discussed in ~ —*Manchester Guardian Weekly*⟩ **c** : a hasty preliminary drawing or layout **4** : ROWDY

[3]**rough** *adv* (1560) : ROUGHLY 1

[4]**rough** *vt* (1763) **1** : ROUGHEN **2 a** : to subject to abuse : MANHANDLE, BEAT — usu. used with *up* **b** : to subject to unnecessary and intentional violence in a sport **3** : to calk or otherwise roughen (a horse's shoes) to prevent slipping **4 a** : to shape, make, or dress in a rough or preliminary way **b** : to indicate the chief lines of ⟨~ out the structure of a building⟩ — **rough·er** *n* — **rough it** : to live under harsh or primitive conditions

rough·age \'rəf-ij\ *n* (ca. 1900) : coarse bulky food (as bran) that is relatively high in fiber and low in digestible nutrients and that by its bulk stimulates peristalsis

rough–and–ready \,rəf-ən-'red-ē\ *adj* (1810) : crude in nature, method, or manner but effective in action or use

[1]**rough–and–tum·ble** \-'təm-bəl\ *n* (1792) : rough disorderly unrestrained fighting or struggling; *also* : INFIGHTING

[2]**rough–and–tumble** *adj* (1832) **1** : marked by rough-and-tumble ⟨grew up in a ~ atmosphere —E. J. Kahn⟩; *also* : ROUGH-AND-READY **2** : put together haphazardly : MAKESHIFT ⟨a ~ fence⟩

rough bluegrass *n* (ca. 1923) : a European forage grass (*Poa trivialis*) naturalized in eastern No. America

rough breathing *n* (1899) **1** : a mark ʽ used in Greek over some initial vowels or over ρ to show that they are aspirated (as in ὡς pronounced \'hōs\ or ῥήτωρ pronounced \'hrā-,tōr\) **2** : the sound indicated by a mark ʽ over a Greek vowel or ρ

[1]**rough·cast** \'rəf-,kast, *for 2 also* -'kast\ *vt* **-cast; -cast·ing** (ca. 1565) **1** : to plaster (as a wall) with roughcast **2** : to shape or form roughly

[2]**rough·cast** \-,kast\ *n* (1579) **1** : a rough model **2** : a plaster of lime mixed with shells or pebbles used for covering buildings **3** : a rough surface finish (as of a plaster wall)

rough cut *n* (1937) : a print of an incompletely edited motion picture

[1]**rough–dry** \'rəf-'drī\ *vt* (1837) : to dry (laundry) without smoothing or ironing

[2]**rough–dry** \,rəf-,drī\ *adj* (1856) : being dry after laundering but not ironed or smoothed over ⟨~ clothes⟩

rough·en \'rəf-ən\ *vb* **rough·ened; rough·en·ing** \-(ə-)niŋ\ *vt* (1582) : to make rough or rougher ⟨her hands were ~*ed* by work —Ellen Glasgow⟩ ~ *vi* : to become rough

rough fish *n* (1843) : a fish that is neither a sport fish nor an important food for sport fishes

rough–hew \'rəf-'hyü\ *vt* **-hewed; -hewn** \-'hyün\; **-hew·ing** (ca. 1530) **1** : to hew (as timber) coarsely without smoothing or finishing **2** : to form crudely

rough–hewn \-'hyün\ *adj* (1530) **1** : being in a rough, unsmoothed, or unfinished state : crudely formed ⟨~ beams⟩ **2** : lacking polish ⟨he was rather attractive, in a ~ kind of way —Jan Speas⟩

[1]**rough·house** \'rəf-,hau̇s\ *n* (1887) : violence or rough boisterous play

[2]**rough·house** \-,hau̇s, -,hau̇z\ *vb* **rough·housed; rough·hous·ing** *vt* (1902) : to treat in a boisterously rough manner ~ *vi* : to engage in roughhouse

rough·leg \'rəf-,leg, -,lāg\ *n* (1895) : ROUGH-LEGGED HAWK

rough–legged hawk \,rəf-,leg(-ə)d-, -,lāg(-ə)d-\ *n* (1811) : a large circumpolar arctic hawk (*Buteo lagopus*) that winters southward and typically has a white tail with a wide black band or bands at the tip

rough lemon *n* (1900) **1** : a hybrid lemon that forms a large spreading thorny tree, bears rough-skinned nearly globular acid fruit, and is important chiefly as a rootstock for other citrus trees **2** : the fruit of a rough lemon

rough·ly \'rəf-lē\ *adv* (14c) **1** : in a rough manner: as **a** : with harshness or violence ⟨treated the prisoner ~⟩ **b** : in crude fashion : IMPERFECTLY ⟨~ dressed lumber⟩ **2** : without completeness or exactness : APPROXIMATELY ⟨~ 20 percent⟩

[1]**rough·neck** \'rəf-,nek\ *n* (1836) **1 a** : a rough or uncouth person **b** : ROWDY, TOUGH **2** : a worker of an oil-well-drilling crew other than the driller

[2]**roughneck** *adj* (1916) : having the characteristics of or suitable for a roughneck

rough·rid·er \'rəf-'rīd-ər\ *n* (1733) **1** : one who is accustomed to riding unbroken or little-trained horses **2** *usu* **Rough Rider** : a member of the 1st U.S. Volunteer Cavalry regiment in the Spanish-American War commanded by Theodore Roosevelt

[1]**rough·shod** \-'shäd\ *adj* (1688) **1** : shod with calked shoes **2** : marked by main force without justice or consideration ⟨a tyrant's ~ rule⟩

[2]**roughshod** *adv* (1813) : in a roughshod manner ⟨rode ~ over the opposition⟩

rough trade *n* (1935) : male homosexuals who are or affect to be rugged and potentially violent; *also* : such a homosexual

rouille \'rü-ē, rüy\ *n* [F, lit., rust; fr. its color] (1951) : a peppery garlic sauce

rou·lade \rü-'läd\ *n* [F, lit., act of rolling] (ca. 1706) **1** : a florid vocal embellishment sung to one syllable **2** : a slice of usu. stuffed meat that is rolled, browned, and steamed or braised

rou·leau \rü-'lō\ *n, pl* **rou·leaux** \-'lōz\ [F] (1693) : a little roll; *esp* : a roll of coins put up in paper

[1]**rou·lette** \rü-'let\ *n* [F, lit., small wheel, fr. OF *roelete,* dim. of *roele* small wheel, fr. LL *rotella,* dim. of L *rota* wheel — more at ROLL] (1745) **1** : a gambling game in which players bet on which compartment of a revolving wheel a small ball will come to rest in **2 a** : any of various toothed wheels or disks (as for producing rows of dots on engraved plates or for making short consecutive incisions in paper to facilitate subsequent division) **b** : tiny slits between rows of stamps in a sheet that are made by a roulette and serve as an aid in separation — compare PERFORATION

[2]**roulette** *vt* **rou·lett·ed; rou·lett·ing** (1867) : to make roulettes in

Rou·ma·nian \rü-'mā-nē-ən, -nyən\ *var of* RUMANIAN

[1]**round** \'rau̇nd\ *vt* [alter. of ME *rounen,* fr. OE *rūnian;* akin to OE *rūn* mystery — more at RUNE] (bef. 12c) **1** : WHISPER **2** : to speak to in a whisper

[2]**round** *adj* [ME, fr. OF *roont,* fr. L *rotundus* — more at ROLL] (13c) **1 a** (1) : having every part of the surface or circumference equidistant from the center (2) : CYLINDRICAL ⟨a ~ peg⟩ **b** : approximately round ⟨a ~ face⟩ **2** : well filled out : PLUMP, SHAPELY **3 a** : COMPLETE, FULL ⟨a ~ dozen⟩ ⟨a ~ ton⟩ **b** : approximately correct; *esp* : exact only to a specific decimal or place ⟨use the ~ number 1400 for the exact figure 1411⟩ **c** : substantial in amount : AMPLE ⟨a good ~ price —T. B. Costain⟩ **4** : direct in utterance : OUTSPOKEN ⟨a ~ oath⟩ **5** : moving in or forming a circle **6 a** : brought to completion or perfection : FINISHED **b** : presented with lifelike fullness or vividness **7** : delivered with a swing of the arm ⟨a ~ blow⟩ **8 a** : having full or unimpeded resonance or tone : SONOROUS **b** : pronounced with rounded lips : LABIALIZED **9** : of or relating to handwriting predominantly curved rather than angular — **round·ly** \'rau̇n-(d)lē\ *adv* — **round·ness** \'rau̇n(d)-nəs\ *n*

[3]**round** *adv* (13c) **1** : in a circular or curved path or progression **2** : AROUND **3** : with revolving or rotating motion ⟨the wheel turns ~⟩ **4** : to a particular person or place ⟨send ~ for the doctor⟩

[4]**round** *n* (14c) **1 a** : something (as a circle, globe, or ring) that is round **b** (1) : a knot of people (2) : a circle of things **2** : ROUND DANCE 1 **3** : a musical canon sung in unison in which each part is continuously repeated **4 a** : a rung of a ladder or a chair **b** : a rounded molding **5 a** : a circling or circuitous path or course **b** : motion in a circle or a curving path **6 a** : a route or circuit habitually covered (as by a watchman or policeman) **b** : a series of professional calls on hospital patients made by a doctor or nurse — usu. used in pl. **c** : a series of similar or customary calls or stops ⟨making the ~*s* of his friends —*Current Biog.*⟩ **7** : a drink of liquor apiece served at one time to each person in a group ⟨I'll buy the next ~⟩ **8** : a sequence of recurring routine or repetitive actions or events ⟨went about his ~ of chores⟩ ⟨the newest ~ of talks⟩ **9** : a period of time that recurs in a fixed pattern ⟨the daily ~⟩ **10 a** : one shot fired by a weapon or by each man in a military unit **b** : a unit of ammunition consisting of the parts necessary to fire one shot **11 a** : a unit of action in a contest or game which comprises a stated period, covers a prescribed distance, includes a specified number of plays, or gives each player one turn **b** : a division of a tournament in which each contestant plays an opponent **12** : a prolonged burst (as of applause) **13 a** : a cut of beef esp. between the rump and the lower leg — see BEEF illustration **b** : a slice of food ⟨a ~ of bread⟩ **14** : a rounded or curved part — **in the round 1** : in full sculptured form unattached to a background **2** : with an inclusive or comprehensive view or representation **3** : with a center stage surrounded by an audience ⟨theater *in the round*⟩

[5]**round** *vt* (14c) **1 a** : to make round **b** (1) : to make (the lips) round and protruded (as in the pronunciation of \ü\) (2) : to pronounce with lip rounding : LABIALIZE **2 a** : GO AROUND **b** : to pass part of the way around **3** : ENCIRCLE, ENCOMPASS **4** : to bring to completion or perfection — often used with *off* or *out* **5** : to express as a round number — often used with *off* ⟨11.3572 ~*ed* off to three decimals becomes 11.357⟩ ~ *vi* **1 a** : to become round, plump, or shapely **b** : to reach fullness or completion **2** : to follow a winding course : BEND — **round on** : to turn against : ASSAIL

[6]**round** \(')rau̇nd\ *prep* (1602) **1** : AROUND **2** : all during : THROUGHOUT ⟨~ the year⟩

[1]**round·about** \'rau̇n-də-,bau̇t\ *adj* (1608) : CIRCUITOUS, INDIRECT ⟨had to take a ~ course⟩ — **round·about·ness** *n*

[2]**roundabout** *n* (1755) **1** : a circuitous route : DETOUR **2** *Brit* : MERRY-GO-ROUND **3** : a short close-fitting jacket worn by men and boys esp. in the 19th century **4** *Brit* : ROTARY 2

round angle *n* (ca. 1934) : an angle of 360° or 2π radians

round clam *n* (ca. 1843) : QUAHOG

round dance *n* (1683) **1** : a folk dance in which participants form a ring and move in a prescribed direction **2** : a ballroom dance in which couples progress around the room **3** : a series of movements performed by a bee to indicate that a source of food is nearby

round·ed \'rau̇n-dəd\ *adj* (1712) **1** : made round : flowing rather than jagged or angular **2** : fully developed — **round·ed·ness** *n*

roun·del \'rau̇n-dᵊl\ *n* [ME, fr. OF *rondel,* fr. *roont* round — more at ROUND] (13c) **1** : a round figure or object (as a circular panel, window, or niche) **2 a** : RONDEL 2a **b** : an English modified rondeau

roun·de·lay \'rau̇n-də-,lā\ *n* [modif. of MF *rondelet,* dim. of *rondel*] (1573) **1** : a simple song with a refrain **2** : a poem with a refrain recurring frequently or at fixed intervals as in a rondel

round·er \'rau̇n-dər\ *n* (1828) **1** : a dissolute person : WASTREL **2** *pl but sing in constr* : a game of English origin that is played with ball and bat and that somewhat resembles baseball **3 a** : one that rounds by hand or by machine **b** : a tool for making an edge or a surface round **4** : a boxing match lasting a specified number of rounds — usu. used in combination ⟨a 10-*rounder*⟩

Round·head \'rau̇nd-,hed\ *n* [fr. the Puritans' cropping their hair short in contrast to the Cavaliers] (1642) **1** : PURITAN 1 **2** : a member of the parliamentary party in England at the time of Charles I and Oliver Cromwell

round·head·ed \-'hed-əd\ *adj* (1729) : having a round head; *specif* : BRACHYCEPHALIC — **round·head·ed·ness** *n*

round·house \'rau̇nd-,hau̇s\ *n* (1589) **1** *archaic* : LOCKUP **2** : a circular building for housing and repairing locomotives **3** : a cabin or apartment on the stern of a quarterdeck **4** : a blow delivered with a wide swing

round·ish \'raůn-dish\ *adj* (1545) : somewhat round
round·let \'raůn-(d)lət\ *n* [ME *roundelet,* fr. MF *rondelet* — more at ROUNDELAY] (14c) : a small circle or round object : DISK
round lot *n* (ca. 1902) : the standard unit of trading in a security market usu. amounting to 100 shares of stock
round–robin \'raůn-,dräb-ən\ *n* [fr. the name *Robin*] (ca. 1730) **1 a** : a written petition, memorial, or protest to which the signatures are affixed in a circle so as not to indicate who signed first **b** : a statement signed by several persons **c** : something (as a letter) sent in turn to the members of a group each of whom signs and forwards it sometimes after adding comment **2** : ROUND TABLE 2 **3** : a tournament in which every contestant meets every other contestant in turn **4** : SERIES, ROUND
round–shoul·dered \'raůn(d)-'shōl-dərd\ *adj* (1586) : having the shoulders stooping or rounded
rounds·man \'raůn(d)z-mən\ *n* (1795) **1** : one that makes rounds **2** : a supervisory police officer of the grade of sergeant or just below
round steak *n* (1876) : a steak cut from the round of beef — see BEEF illustration
round ta·ble \'raůn(d)-,tā-bəl\ *n* (14c) **1 a** *cap R&T* : the large circular table of King Arthur and his knights **b** : the knights of King Arthur **2** *usu* **round·ta·ble** : a conference for discussion or deliberation by several participants; *also* : the participants in such a conference
round–the–clock *adj* (ca. 1937) : AROUND-THE-CLOCK
round–trip \'raůn(d)-,trip\ *n* (1860) : a trip to a place and back usu. over the same route
round·up \'raůn-,dəp\ *n* (1873) **1 a** (1) : the act or process of collecting animals (as cattle) by riding around them and driving them in (2) : the men and horses so engaged **b** : a gathering in of scattered persons or things ⟨a ~ of all suspects⟩ **2** : a summary of information (as from news bulletins)
round up \'raůn-'dəp\ *vt* (1844) **1** : to collect (as cattle) by means of a roundup **2** : to gather in or bring together from various quarters
round window *n* (ca. 1903) : FENESTRA 1b
round·wood \'raůn-,důd\ *n* (1910) : timber used (as for poles) without being squared by sawing or hewing
round·worm \'raůn-,dwərm\ *n* (ca. 1565) : NEMATODE; *also* : a related round-bodied unsegmented worm (as a spiny-headed worm) as distinguished from a flatworm
roup \'rüp, 'raůp\ *n* [origin unknown] (ca. 1808) : a virus disease of poultry marked by cheesy lesions of the mouth, throat, and eyes
[1]**rouse** \'raůz\ *vb* **roused; rous·ing** [ME *rousen* to shake the feathers] *vt* (1531) **1** *archaic* : to cause to break from cover **2 a** : to stir up : EXCITE ⟨was *roused* to fury⟩ **b** : to arouse from or as if from sleep or repose : AWAKEN ~ *vi* **1** : to become aroused : AWAKEN **2** : to become stirred — **rouse·ment** \'raůz-mənt\ *n* — **rous·er** *n*
[2]**rouse** *n* (ca. 1802) : an act or instance of rousing; *esp* : an excited stir
[3]**rouse** *n* [alter. (resulting fr. incorrect division of *to drink carouse*) of *carouse*] (1602) **1** *obs* : DRINK, TOAST **2** *archaic* : CAROUSAL
rouse·about \'raů-zə-,baůt\ *n, Austral* (1881) : an unskilled worker
rous·ing \'raů-ziŋ\ *adj* (1641) **1 a** : giving rise to excitement : STIRRING **b** : BRISK, LIVELY **2** : EXCEPTIONAL, SUPERLATIVE — **rous·ing·ly** *adv*
Rous sarcoma \'raůs-\ *n* [F. Peyton *Rous* †1970 Am. physician] (ca. 1925) : a readily transplantable malignant fibrosarcoma of chickens that is caused by a specific carcinogenic virus
Rous·seau·ism \rü-'sō-,iz-əm\ *n* (1865) **1** : the philosophical, educational, and political doctrines of Jean Jacques Rousseau **2** : the return to or glorification of a simpler and more primitive way of life — **Rousseau·ist** \-əst\ *n* — **Rous·seau·is·tic** \,rü-,sō-'is-tik, rü-\ *adj*
roust \'raůst\ *vt* [alter. of [1]*rouse*] (1658) : to drive (as from bed) roughly or unceremoniously
roust·about \'raů-stə-,baůt\ *n* (1868) **1 a** : DECKHAND **b** : LONGSHOREMAN **2** : an unskilled or semiskilled laborer esp. in an oil field or refinery **3** : a circus worker who erects and dismantles tents, cares for the grounds, and handles animals and equipment
roust·er \'raů-stər\ *n* (1883) : ROUSTABOUT 1
[1]**rout** \'raůt\ *n* [ME *route,* fr. MF, troop, defeat, fr. (assumed) VL *rupta,* fr. L, fem. of *ruptus,* pp. of *rumpere* to break — more at REAVE] (13c) **1** : a crowd of people : THRONG; *specif* : RABBLE 2b **2 a** : DISTURBANCE **b** *archaic* : FUSS **3** : a fashionable gathering
[2]**rout** \'rōt, 'rüt\ *vi* [ME *rowten,* fr. ON *rauta;* akin to OE *rēotan* to weep, L *rudere* to roar] *dial chiefly Brit* (14c) : to low loudly : BELLOW — used of cattle
[3]**rout** \'raůt\ *vb* [alter. of [3]*root*] *vi* (1547) **1** : to poke around with the snout : ROOT ⟨pigs ~*ing* in the earth⟩ **2** : to search haphazardly ~ *vt* **1 a** *archaic* : to dig up with the snout **b** : to gouge out or make a furrow in (as wood or metal) **2 a** : to force out as if by digging — usu. used with *out* **b** : to cause to emerge esp. from bed **3** : to come up with : UNCOVER
[4]**rout** \'raůt\ *n* [MF *route* troop, defeat] (1598) **1** : a state of wild confusion or disorderly retreat **2 a** : a disastrous defeat : DEBACLE **b** : a precipitate flight
[5]**rout** \'raůt\ *vt* (1600) **1 a** : to disorganize completely : DEMORALIZE **b** : to put to precipitate flight **c** : to defeat decisively or disastrously ⟨the discomfiture of seeing their party ~*ed* at the polls —A. N. Holcombe⟩ **2** : to drive out : DISPEL
[1]**route** \'rüt, 'raůt\ *n* [ME, fr. OF, fr. (assumed) VL *rupta* (*via*), lit., broken way, fr. L *rupta,* fem. of *ruptus,* pp.] (13c) **1 a** : a traveled way : HIGHWAY ⟨the main ~ north⟩ **b** : a means of access : CHANNEL ⟨the ~ to social mobility —T. F. O'Dea⟩ **2** : a line of travel : COURSE **3 a** : an established or selected course of travel or action **b** : an assigned territory to be systematically covered ⟨a newspaper ~⟩
[2]**route** *vt* **rout·ed; rout·ing** (1832) **1 a** : to send by a selected route : DIRECT ⟨was *routed* along the scenic shore road⟩ **b** : to divert in a specified direction **2** : to prearrange and direct the order and execution of (a series of operations)
route·man \'rüt-mən, 'raůt-,man\ *n* (1918) : one who is responsible for making sales or deliveries on an assigned route
[1]**rout·er** \'raůt-ər\ *n* (1846) : one that routs: as **a** : a routing plane **b** : a machine with a revolving vertical spindle and cutter for milling out the surface of wood or metal
[2]**rout·er** \'rüt-ər, 'raůt-\ *n* (1903) : one that routes
[3]**rout·er** \'rüt-ər, 'raůt-\ *n* [*route* (race of a mile or more)] (ca. 1951) : a horse trained for distance races
route step *n* (1867) : a style of marching in which troops maintain prescribed intervals but are not required to keep in step or to maintain silence — called also *route march*
route·way \'rüt-,wā, 'raůt-\ *n* (1946) : ROUTE 3a
routh \'raůth, 'rüth\ *n* [origin unknown] *chiefly Scot* (1707) : PLENTY
[1]**rou·tine** \rü-'tēn\ *n* [F, fr. MF, fr. *route* traveled way] (1676) **1 a** : a regular course of procedure ⟨if resort to legal action becomes a campus ~ —J. A. Perkins⟩ **b** : habitual or mechanical performance of an established procedure ⟨the ~ of factory work⟩ **2** : a reiterated speech or formula ⟨the old "After you" ~ —Ray Russell⟩ **3** : a worked-out part (as of an entertainment or sports contest) that may be often repeated ⟨a dance ~⟩ ⟨a gymnastic ~⟩; *esp* : a theatrical number **4** : a sequence of computer instructions for performing a particular task
[2]**rou·tine** \rü-'tēn, ,rü-,\ *adj* (1817) **1** : of a commonplace or repetitious character : ORDINARY **2** : of, relating to, or being in accordance with established procedure ⟨~ business⟩ — **rou·tine·ly** *adv*
rou·tin·ize \rü-'tē-,nīz, 'rüt-ᵊn-,īz\ *vt* **-ized; -iz·ing** (1921) : to discipline in or reduce to a routine — **rou·tin·iza·tion** \(,)rü-,tē-nə-'zā-shən, ,rüt-ᵊn-ə-\ *n*
roux \'rü\ *n, pl* **roux** \'rüz\ [F, fr. *beurre roux* browned butter] (1813) : a cooked mixture of flour and fat used as a thickening agent in a soup or a sauce
[1]**rove** \'rōv\ *vb* **roved; rov·ing** [ME *roven* to shoot at random, wander] *vi* (1536) : to move aimlessly : ROAM ~ *vt* : to wander through or over **syn** see WANDER
[2]**rove** *n* (1742) : an act or instance of wandering
[3]**rove** *past and past part of* REEVE
[4]**rove** *vt* **roved; rov·ing** [origin unknown] (1789) : to join (textile fibers) with a slight twist and draw out into roving
[5]**rove** *n* (1789) : ROVING
rove beetle *n* [perh. fr. [1]*rove*] (ca. 1771) : any of a family (Staphylinidae) of numerous often predatory active beetles having a long body and very short wing covers beneath which the wings are folded transversely
[1]**ro·ver** \'rō-vər\ *n* [ME, fr. MD, fr. *roven* to rob; akin to OE *rēafian* to reave — more at REAVE] (14c) : PIRATE
[2]**rov·er** \'rō-vər\ *n* [ME, fr. *roven*] (15c) **1** : a random or long-distance mark in archery — usu. used in pl. **2** : WANDERER, ROAMER **3** : a player who is not assigned to a specific position on a team and who plays wherever needed
[1]**rov·ing** \'rō-viŋ\ *adj* [[1]*rove*] (1596) **1 a** : capable of being shifted from place to place : MOBILE **b** : not restricted as to location or area of concern **2** : inclined to ramble or stray ⟨a ~ fancy⟩
[2]**roving** *n* [[4]*rove*] (1802) : a slightly twisted roll or strand of usu. textile fibers
[1]**row** \'rō\ *vb* [ME *rowen,* fr. OE *rōwan;* akin to MHG *rüejen* to row, L *remus* oar] *vi* (bef. 12c) **1** : to propel a boat by means of oars **2** : to move by or as if by the propulsion of oars ~ *vt* **1 a** : to propel with or as if with oars **b** : to be equipped with (a specified number of oars) **c** (1) : to participate in (a rowing match) (2) : to compete against in rowing (3) : to pull (an oar) in a crew **2** : to transport in an oar-propelled boat — **row·er** \'rō(-ə)r\ *n*
[2]**row** *n* (1832) : an act or instance of rowing
[3]**row** *n* [ME *rawe;* akin to OE *rǣw, rāw* row, OHG *rīga* line, L *rima* slit] (13c) **1** : a number of objects arranged in a usu. straight line ⟨a ~ of bottles⟩; *also* : the line along which such objects are arranged ⟨planted the corn in parallel ~*s*⟩ **2 a** : WAY, STREET **b** : a street or area dominated by a specific kind of enterprise or occupancy ⟨doctors' ~⟩ **3** : TWELVE-TONE ROW **4 a** : a continuous strip usu. running horizontally or parallel to a base line **b** : a horizontal arrangement of items — **in a row** : one after another : SUCCESSIVELY
[4]**row** *vt* (1657) : to form into rows
[5]**row** \'raů\ *n* [origin unknown] (1746) : a noisy disturbance or quarrel
[6]**row** \'raů\ *vi* (1797) : to engage in a row : have a quarrel
row·an \'raů-ən, 'rō-ən\ *n* [of Scand origin; akin to ON *reynir* rowan; akin to OE *rēad* red — more at RED] (1548) **1 a** : a Eurasian tree (*Sorbus aucuparia*) of the rose family with flat corymbs of white flowers followed by small red pomes **b** : an American mountain ash (*Sorbus americana*) **2** : the fruit of a rowan
row·an·ber·ry \-,ber-ē\ *n* (1814) : ROWAN 2
row·boat \'rō-,bōt\ *n* (1538) : a small boat designed to be rowed
[1]**row·dy** \'raůd-ē\ *adj* **row·di·er; -est** [perh. irreg. fr. [5]*row*] (1819) : coarse or boisterous in behavior : ROUGH; *also* : characterized by such behavior ⟨~ local bars⟩ — **row·di·ly** \'raůd-ᵊl-ē\ *adv* — **row·di·ness** \'raůd-ē-nəs\ *n* — **row·dy·ish** \-ē-ish\ *adj*
[2]**rowdy** *n, pl* **rowdies** (1819) : a rowdy person : TOUGH
row·dy·ism \'raůd-ē-,iz-əm\ *n* (1842) : rowdy character or behavior
[1]**row·el** \'raů(-ə)l\ *n* [ME *rowelle,* fr. MF *rouelle* small wheel, fr. OF *roele* — more at ROULETTE] (15c) : a revolving disk with sharp marginal points at the end of a spur
[2]**rowel** *vt* **-eled** *or* **-elled; -el·ing** *or* **-el·ling** (1599) **1** : to goad with or as if with a rowel **2** : VEX, TROUBLE
row·en \'raů-ən\ *n* [ME *rowein,* fr. (assumed) ONF *rewain;* akin to OF *regaïn* aftermath, fr. *re-* + *gaaignier* to till — more at GAIN] (15c) : AFTERMATH 1
row house \'rō-\ *n* (1936) : one of a series of houses connected by common sidewalls and forming a continuous group
row·ing \'rō-iŋ\ *n* (bef. 12c) **1** : the propelling of a boat by means of oars : the action of one that rows **2** : the sport of racing in shells
rowing boat *n, chiefly Brit* (1820) : ROWBOAT
row·lock \'räl-ək, 'rəl-; 'rō-,läk\ *n* [prob. by alter.] *chiefly Brit* (ca. 1750) : OARLOCK
[1]**roy·al** \'rȯi(-ə)l\ *adj* [ME *roial,* fr. MF, fr. L *regalis,* fr. *reg-, rex* king; akin to OIr *rī* (gen. *rīg*) king, Skt *rājan,* L *regere* to rule — more at RIGHT] (14c) **1 a** : of kingly ancestry ⟨the ~ family⟩ **b** : of, relating to, or subject to the crown ⟨the ~ estates⟩ **c** : being in the crown's

service ⟨*Royal* Air Force⟩ **2 a :** suitable for royalty : MAGNIFICENT **b :** requiring no exertion : EASY ⟨there is no ~ road to logic —Justus Buchler⟩ **3 a :** of superior size, magnitude, or quality ⟨a patronage of ~ dimensions —J. H. Plumb⟩ — often used as an intensive ⟨a ~ pain⟩ **b :** established or chartered by the crown **4 :** of, relating to, or being a part (as a mast, sail, or yard) next above the topgallant — **roy·al·ly** \'rȯi-ə-lē\ *adv*

[2]**royal** *n* (15c) **1 :** a person of royal blood **2 :** a small sail on the royal mast immediately above the topgallant sail **3 :** a stag of 8 years or more having antlers with at least 12 points

royal blue *n* (1789) **:** a variable color averaging a vivid purplish blue

royal flush *n* (ca. 1868) **:** a straight flush having an ace as the highest card — see POKER illustration

roy·al·ism \'rȯi-ə-ˌliz-əm\ *n* (1793) **:** MONARCHISM

roy·al·ist \-ə-ləst\ *n* (1643) **1** *often cap* **:** an adherent of a king or of monarchical government: as **a :** CAVALIER 3 **b :** TORY 4 **2 :** a reactionary business tycoon — **royalist** *adj*

royal jelly *n* (ca. 1855) **:** a highly nutritious secretion of the pharyngeal glands of the honeybee that is fed to the very young larvae in a colony and to all queen larvae

royal palm *n* (ca. 1861) **:** any of several palms (genus *Roystonea*); *esp* **:** a tall graceful pinnate-leaved palm (*R. regia*) of southern Florida and Cuba that is widely planted for ornament

royal poinciana *n* (ca. 1900) **:** a showy tropical tree (*Delonix regia* syn. *Poinciana regia*) widely planted for its immense racemes of scarlet and orange flowers — called also *flamboyant, peacock flower*

royal purple *n* (1661) **:** a dark reddish purple

roy·al·ty \'rȯi(-ə)l-tē\ *n, pl* **-ties** [ME *roialte,* fr. MF *roialté,* fr. OF, fr. *roial*] (14c) **1 a :** royal status or power : SOVEREIGNTY **b :** a right or perquisite of a sovereign (as a percentage paid to the crown of gold or silver taken from mines) **2 :** regal character or bearing : NOBILITY **3 a :** persons of royal lineage **b :** a person of royal rank ⟨how to address *royalties* —George Santayana⟩ **c :** a privileged class **4 :** a right of jurisdiction granted to an individual or corporation by a sovereign **5 a :** a share of the product or profit reserved by the grantor esp. of an oil or mining lease **b :** a payment made to an author or composer for each copy of his work sold or to an inventor for each article sold under a patent

royster *var of* ROISTER

roz·zer \'räz-ər\ *n* [origin unknown] *slang Brit* (1893) **:** POLICEMAN

RPG \ˌär-(ˌ)pē-'jē\ *n* [report program generator] (1966) **:** a computer language that generates programs from the user's specifications esp. to produce business reports

-r·rha·gia \'rā-j(ē-)ə, 'rā-zhə; 'räj-ə, 'räzh-\ *n comb form* [NL, fr. Gk, fr. *rhēgnynai* to break, burst; akin to OSlav *rězati* to cut] **:** abnormal or excessive discharge or flow ⟨metro*rrhagia*⟩

-r·rhea *also* **-r·rhoea** \'rē-ə\ *n comb form* [ME *-ria,* fr. LL *-rrhoea,* fr. Gk *-rrhoia,* fr. *rhoia,* fr. *rhein* to flow — more at STREAM] **:** flow : discharge ⟨logo*rrhea*⟩ ⟨leuko*rrhea*⟩

-r·rhine *or* **-rhine** \ˌrīn\ *adj comb form* [ISV, fr. Gk *-rrhin-, -rrhis,* fr. *rhin-, rhis* nose] **:** having (such) a nose ⟨platy*rrhine*⟩

-r·rhi·za — see -RHIZA

rRNA \ˌär-ˌär-ˌen-'ā\ *n* (ca. 1965) **:** RIBOSOMAL RNA

ru·a·na \rü-'ä-nə\ *n* [AmerSp, fr. Sp, woolen fabric] (ca. 1903) **:** a woolen covering resembling a poncho

[1]**rub** \'rəb\ *vb* **rubbed; rub·bing** [ME *rubben;* akin to Icel *rubba* to scrape] *vi* (14c) **1 a :** to move along the surface of a body with pressure : GRATE **b (1) :** to fret or chafe with or as if with friction **(2) :** to cause discontent, irritation, or anger **2 :** to continue in a situation usu. with slight difficulty ⟨in spite of financial difficulties, he is *rubbing* along⟩ **3 :** to admit of being rubbed (as for erasure or obliteration) ~ *vt* **1 a :** to subject to or as if to the action of something moving esp. back and forth with pressure and friction **b (1) :** to cause (a body) to move with pressure and friction along a surface **(2) :** to treat in any of various ways by rubbing **c :** to bring into reciprocal back-and-forth or rotary contact **2 :** ANNOY, IRRITATE ⟨his attitude tended to ~ her⟩ — **rub elbows** *or* **rub shoulders :** to associate closely : MINGLE — **rub one's nose in :** to bring forcefully or repeatedly to one's attention — **rub the wrong way :** to arouse the antagonism or displeasure of : IRRITATE

[2]**rub** *n* (1586) **1 a :** an unevenness of surface (as of the ground in lawn bowling) **b :** OBSTRUCTION, DIFFICULTY ⟨the ~ is that so few of the scholars have any sense of this truth themselves —Benjamin Farrington⟩ **c :** something grating to the feelings (as a gibe or harsh criticism) **d :** something that mars serenity **2 :** the application of friction with pressure ⟨an alcohol ~⟩

Ru·bai·yat stanza \'rü-bē-ˌät-, -ˌat-; -ˌbī-ˌ(y)ät-, -ˌ(y)at-\ *n* [*The Rubáiyát of Omar Khayyám,* quatrains translated by Edward FitzGerald (1859)] (1940) **:** an iambic pentameter quatrain with a rhyme scheme *aaba*

ru·basse \rü-'bas, 'rü-ˌ\ *n* [F *rubace,* irreg. fr. *rubis* ruby — more at RUBY] (ca. 1890) **:** a quartz stained a ruby red

ru·ba·to \rü-'bät-(ˌ)ō\ *n, pl* **-tos** [It, lit., robbed] (ca. 1883) **:** a fluctuation of speed within a musical phrase typically against a rhythmically steady accompaniment

[1]**rub·ber** \'rəb-ər\ *n* (1536) **1 a :** one that rubs **b :** an instrument or object (as a rubber eraser) used in rubbing, polishing, scraping, or cleaning **c :** something that prevents rubbing or chafing **2** [fr. its use in erasers] **a :** an elastic substance that is obtained by coagulating the milky juice of any of various tropical plants (as of the genera *Hevea* and *Ficus*), is essentially a polymer of isoprene, and is prepared as sheets and then dried — called also *caoutchouc, india rubber* **b :** any of various synthetic rubberlike substances **c :** natural or synthetic rubber modified by chemical treatment to increase its useful properties (as toughness and resistance to wear) and used esp. in tires, electrical insulation, and waterproof materials **3 :** something made of or resembling rubber: as **a :** a rubber overshoe **b (1) :** a rubber tire **(2) :** the set of tires on a vehicle **c :** a rectangular slab of white rubber in the middle of a baseball infield on which a pitcher stands while pitching **d :** CONDOM — **rubber** *adj*

[2]**rubber** *n* [origin unknown] (1599) **1 :** a contest consisting of an odd number of games won by the side that takes a majority (as two out of three) **2 :** an odd game played to determine the winner of a tie

rubber band *n* (1895) **:** a continous band of rubber used in various ways (as for holding together a sheaf of papers)

rubber–base paint *n* (ca. 1937) **:** a paint having a rubber derivative or a synthetic resin as its binder or vehicle

rubber bridge *n* (1935) **:** a form of contract bridge in which settlement is made at the end of each rubber

rubber cement *n* (ca. 1890) **:** an adhesive consisting typically of a dispersion of vulcanized rubber in an organic solvent

rubber check *n* [fr. its coming back like a bouncing rubber ball] (1926) **:** a check returned by a bank because of insufficient funds in the payer's account

rub·ber·ize \'rəb-ə-ˌrīz\ *vt* **-ized; -iz·ing** (ca. 1908) **:** to coat or impregnate with rubber or a rubber solution

rub·ber·like \'rəb-ər-ˌlīk\ *adj* (1944) **:** resembling rubber esp. in physical properties (as elasticity and toughness)

rub·ber·neck \-ˌnek\ *vi* (1896) **1 :** to look about, stare, or listen with exaggerated curiosity **2 :** to go on a tour : SIGHTSEE

rub·ber·neck·er \-ˌnek-ər\ *also* **rub·ber·neck** \-ˌnek\ *n* (ca. 1896) **1 :** an inquisitive person **2 :** TOURIST; *esp* **:** one on a guided tour

rubber plant *n* (1888) **:** a plant that yields rubber; *esp* **:** a tall tropical Asian tree (*Ficus elastica*) frequently dwarfed as an ornamental

rubber–stamp *vt* (1918) **1 :** to approve, endorse, or dispose of as a matter of routine or at the command of another **2 :** to mark with a rubber stamp

rubber stamp *n* (1881) **1 :** a stamp of rubber for making imprints **2 a :** a person who echoes or imitates others **b :** a body or person that approves or endorses a program or policy with little or no dissent or discussion **3 a :** a stereotyped copy or expression ⟨the usual *rubber stamps* of criticism —H. L. Mencken⟩ **b :** a routine endorsement or approval — **rubber–stamp** *adj*

rubber tree *n* (1847) **:** a tree that yields rubber; *esp* **:** a So. American tree (*Hevea brasiliensis*) of the spurge family that is cultivated in plantations and is a chief source of rubber

rub·bery \'rəb-(ə-)rē\ *adj* (1907) **:** resembling rubber (as in elasticity, consistency, or texture) ⟨~ legs⟩

rub·bing \'rəb-iŋ\ *n* (1845) **:** an image of a raised, incised, or textured surface obtained by placing paper over it and rubbing the paper with a colored substance

rubbing alcohol *n* (ca. 1930) **:** a cooling and soothing liquid for external application that contains approximately 70 percent denatured ethyl alcohol or isopropanol

rub·bish \'rəb-ish, *dial* -ij\ *n* [ME *robys*] (15c) **1 :** useless waste or rejected matter : TRASH **2 :** something that is worthless or nonsensical ⟨few real masterpieces are forgotten and not much ~ survives —William Bridges-Adams⟩ — **rub·bishy** \-ē\ *adj*

[1]**rub·ble** \'rəb-əl\ *n* [ME *robyl*] (15c) **1 a :** broken fragments (as of rock) resulting from the decay or destruction of a building ⟨fortifications knocked into ~ —C. S. Forester⟩ **b :** a miscellaneous confused mass or group of usu. broken or worthless things ⟨lay in a pile of ~, only this time there was more of it, additional gear having hit the deck —K.M. Dodson⟩ **2 :** waterworn or rough broken stones or bricks used in coarse masonry or in filling courses of walls; *also* **:** RUBBLEWORK **3 :** rough stone as it comes from the quarry

[2]**rubble** *vt* **rub·bled; rub·bling** \-(ə-)liŋ\ (15c) **:** to reduce to rubble

rub·ble·work \'rəb-əl-ˌwərk\ *n* (1823) **:** masonry of stones that are rudely squared or not squared and are irregular in size and shape

rub·down \'rəb-ˌdau̇n\ *n* (1896) **:** a brisk rubbing of the body

rube \'rüb\ *n* [*Rube,* nickname for *Reuben*] (1896) **:** an awkward unsophisticated person : RUSTIC

[1]**ru·be·fa·cient** \ˌrü-bə-'fā-shənt\ *adj* [L *rubefacient-, rubefaciens,* prp. of *rubefacere* to make red, fr. *rubeus* reddish + *facere* to make — more at RUBY, DO] (1804) **:** causing redness (as of the skin)

[2]**rubefacient** *n* (1805) **:** a substance for external application that produces redness of the skin

Rube Gold·berg \'rüb-'gōl(d)-ˌbərg\ *also* **Rube Gold·berg·i·an** \-ˌbər-gē-ən, -ˌbərg-yən\ *adj* [Reuben (*Rube*) L. *Goldberg* †1970 Am. cartoonist] (1942) **:** accomplishing by complex means what seemingly could be done simply ⟨a kind of *Rube Goldberg* contraption . . . with five hundred moving parts —L. T. Grant⟩; *also* **:** characterized by such complex means

ru·bel·la \rü-'bel-ə\ *n* [NL, fr. L, fem. of *rubellus* reddish, fr. *ruber* red — more at RED] (1883) **:** GERMAN MEASLES

ru·bel·lite \rü-'bel-ˌīt, 'rü-bə-ˌlīt\ *n* [L *rubellus*] (ca. 1796) **:** a red tourmaline used as a gem

ru·be·o·la \ˌrü-bē-'ō-lə, rü-'bē-ə-lə\ *n* [NL, fr. neut. pl. of (assumed) NL *rubeolus* reddish, fr. L *rubeus* — more at RUBY] (1803) **:** MEASLES — **ru·be·o·lar** \-lər\ *adj*

Ru·bi·con \'rü-bi-ˌkän\ *n* [L *Rubicon-, Rubico,* river of northern Italy forming part of the boundary between Cisalpine Gaul and Italy whose crossing by Julius Caesar in 49 B.C. was regarded by the Senate as an act of war] (1626) **:** a bounding or limiting line; *esp* **:** one that when crossed commits a person irrevocably

ru·bi·cund \'rü-bi-(ˌ)kənd\ *adj* [L *rubicundus,* fr. *rubēre* to be red; akin to L *rubeus*] (1503) **:** RUDDY — **ru·bi·cun·di·ty** \ˌrü-bi-'kən-dət-ē\ *n*

ru·bid·i·um \rü-'bid-ē-əm\ *n* [NL, fr. L *rubidus* red, fr. *rubēre*] (1861) **:** a soft silvery metallic element that decomposes water with violence and bursts into flame spontaneously in air — see ELEMENT table

rub in *vt* (1851) **:** to harp on (as something unpleasant) : EMPHASIZE

ru·bi·ous \'rü-bē-əs\ *adj* (1601) **:** RED, RUBY

ru·ble \'rü-bəl\ *n* [Russ *rubl'*] (1554) — see MONEY table

rub off \'rəb-'ȯf\ *vi* (1818) **:** to become transferred ⟨bad habits were *rubbing off* on them⟩ ⟨carbon *rubs off* on your hands⟩ — **rub-off** \-ˌȯf\ *n*

rub out \-'au̇t\ *vt* (1567) **1 :** to obliterate or extinguish by rubbing **2 :** to destroy completely; *specif* **:** KILL, MURDER ⟨somebody *rubbed* him *out* . . . with a twenty-two —Raymond Chandler⟩ — **rub·out** \-ˌau̇t\ *n*

ru·bric \'rü-brik, -ˌbrik\ *n* [ME *rubrike* red ocher, heading in red letters of part of a book, fr. MF *rubrique,* fr. L *rubrica,* fr. *rubr-, ruber* red] (14c) **1 :** a heading of a part of a book or manuscript done or underlined in a color (as red) different from the rest **2 a (1) :** NAME, TITLE; *specif* **:** the title of a statute **(2) :** something under which a thing is classed : CATEGORY ⟨the sensations falling under the general ~, "pressure" —F. A. Geldard⟩ **b :** an authoritative rule; *esp* **:** a rule for conduct of a liturgical service **c :** an explanatory or introductory commentary : GLOSS; *specif* **:** an editorial interpolation **3 :** an established rule, tradition, or custom — **rubric** *or* **ru·bri·cal** \-bri-kəl\ *adj* — **ru·bri·cal·ly** \-bri-k(ə-)lē\ *adv*

ru·bri·cate \'rü-bri-,kāt\ *vt* **-cat·ed; -cat·ing** (1638) **1** : to write or print as a rubric **2** : to provide with a rubric — **ru·bri·ca·tion** \,rü-bri-'kā-shən\ *n* — **ru·bri·ca·tor** \'rü-bri-,kāt-ər\ *n*

rub up *vt* (1572) **1** : to revive or refresh knowledge of : RECALL **2** : to improve the keenness of (a mental faculty)

ru·bus \'rü-bəs\ *n, pl* **rubus** [NL, fr. L, blackberry] (ca. 1921) : any of a genus (*Rubus*) of plants (as a blackberry or a raspberry) of the rose family having 3- to 7-foliolate or simple lobed leaves, white or pink flowers, and a mass of carpels ripening into an aggregate fruit composed of many drupelets

1**ru·by** \'rü-bē\ *n, pl* **rubies** [ME, fr. MF *rubis, rubi,* irreg. fr. L *rubeus* reddish; akin to L *ruber* red — more at RED] (14c) **1 a** : a precious stone that is a red corundum **b** : something made of ruby; *esp* : a watch bearing or other part of ruby or a substitute material **2 a** : the dark red color of the ruby **b** : something resembling a ruby in color

2**ruby** *adj* (1508) : of the color ruby

ruby glass *n* (1797) : glass of a deep red color containing selenium, an oxide of copper, or a chloride of gold

ruby spinel *n* (1839) : a usu. red spinel used as a gem

ru·by·throat \'rü-bē-,thrōt\ *n* (ca. 1783) : RUBY-THROATED HUMMINGBIRD

ru·by–throat·ed hummingbird \,rü-bē-,thrōt-əd-\ *n* (ca. 1782) : a hummingbird (*Archilochus colubris*) of eastern No. America having a bright bronzy green back, whitish underparts, and in the adult male a red throat with metallic reflections

ruche \'rüsh\ *or* **ruch·ing** \'rü-shiŋ\ *n* [F *ruche*] (1827) : a pleated, fluted, or gathered strip of fabric used for trimming — **ruched** \'rüsht\ *adj*

1**ruck** \'rək\ *n* [ME *ruke* pile of combustible material, of Scand origin; akin to ON *hraukr* rick — more at RICK] (1601) **1 a** : an indistinguishable gathering : JUMBLE **b** : the usual run of persons or things : GENERALITY ⟨his verse compares well with the general ~ of poets of his day —Bonamy Dobrée⟩ **2** : the persons or things following the vanguard

2**ruck** *vb* [*ruck,* n. (wrinkle)] (1812) : PUCKER, WRINKLE

ruck·sack \'rək-,sak, 'rük-\ *n* [G, fr. *ruck-* (alter. of *rücken* back, fr. OHG *hrukki*) + *sack* sack — more at RIDGE] (1893) : KNAPSACK

ruck·us \'rək-əs, 'rük-, 'rük-\ *n* [prob. blend of *ruction* and *rumpus*] (ca. 1890) : ROW, DISTURBANCE ⟨raise a ~⟩

ruc·tion \'rək-shən\ *n* [perh. by shortening & alter. fr. *insurrection*] (ca. 1825) **1** : a noisy fight **2** : DISTURBANCE, UPROAR

rud·beck·ia \,rəd-'bek-ē-ə, rüd-\ *n* [NL, fr. Olof *Rudbeck* †1702 Swed. scientist] (1759) : any of a genus (*Rudbeckia*) of No. American perennial composite herbs having showy flower heads with mostly yellow ray flowers and a conical chaffy receptacle

rudd \'rəd, 'rüd\ *n* [prob. fr. *rud* redness, red ocher, fr. ME *rude,* fr. OE *rudu* — more at RUDDY] (1526) : a freshwater European cyprinid fish (*Scardinius erythrophthalmus*) resembling the roach

rud·der \'rəd-ər\ *n* [ME *rother,* fr. OE *rōther* paddle; akin to OE *rōwan* to row] (14c) **1** : a flat piece or structure of wood or metal attached upright to a ship's stern so that it can be turned causing the ship's head to turn in the same direction **2** : a movable auxiliary airfoil usu. attached at the rear end that serves to control direction of flight of an airplane in the horizontal plane — see AIRPLANE illustration — **rud·der·less** \-ləs\ *adj*

rud·der·post \-,pōst\ *n* (1691) **1** : RUDDERSTOCK **2** : an additional sternpost in a ship with a single screw propeller to which the rudder is attached

rud·der·stock \-,stäk\ *n* (ca. 1864) : the shaft of a rudder

1**rud·dle** \'rəd-ᵊl\ *n* [dim. of *rud* red ocher] (1523) : RED OCHER

2**ruddle** *vt* **rud·dled; rud·dling** \'rəd-liŋ, -ᵊl-iŋ\ (1631) : to color with or as if with red ocher : REDDEN

rud·dock \'rəd-ək, 'rüd-\ *n* [ME *ruddok,* fr. OE *rudduc;* akin to OE *rudu*] (bef. 12c) : ROBIN 1a

rud·dy \'rəd-ē\ *adj* **rud·di·er; -est** [ME *rudi,* fr. OE *rudig,* fr. *rudu* redness; akin to OE *rēad* red — more at RED] (bef. 12c) **1** : having a healthy reddish color **2** : RED, REDDISH **3** *Brit* — used as an intensive ⟨bellowed like a ~ bull when she wanted food —Doreen Tovey⟩ — **rud·di·ly** \'rəd-ᵊl-ē\ *adv* — **rud·di·ness** \'rəd-ē-nəs\ *n*

ruddy duck *n* (1813) : an American duck (*Oxyura jamaicensis*) which has a wedge-shaped tail of stiff sharp feathers, a broad bill, and white cheeks and the adult male of which has rich brownish red on the upper side

rude \'rüd\ *adj* **rud·er; rud·est** [ME, fr. MF, fr. L *rudis;* akin to L *rudus* rubble, *ruere* to fall — more at RUG] (14c) **1 a** : being in a rough or unfinished state : CRUDE **b** : NATURAL, RAW ⟨~ cotton⟩ **c** : PRIMITIVE, UNDEVELOPED ⟨peasants use ~ wooden plows —Jack Raymond⟩ **d** : SIMPLE, ELEMENTAL ⟨landscape done in ~ whites, blacks, deep browns —Richard Harris⟩ **2** : lacking refinement or delicacy: **a** : IGNORANT, UNLEARNED **b** : INELEGANT, UNCOUTH **c** : offensive in manner or action : DISCOURTEOUS **d** : UNCIVILIZED, SAVAGE **e** : COARSE, VULGAR **3** : marked by or suggestive of lack of training or skill : INEXPERIENCED ⟨~ workmanship⟩ **4** : ROBUST, STURDY **5** : FORCEFUL, ABRUPT ⟨a ~ awakening⟩ — **rude·ly** *adv*

syn RUDE, ROUGH, CRUDE, RAW mean lacking in social refinement. RUDE implies ignorance of or indifference to good form; it may suggest intentional discourtesy; ROUGH is likely to stress lack of polish and gentleness; CRUDE may apply to thought or behavior limited to the gross, the obvious, or the primitive and ignorant of civilized amenities; RAW suggests being untested, inexperienced, or unfinished.

rude·ness *n* (14c) **1** : the quality or state of being rude **2** : a rude action

1**ru·der·al** \'rüd-ə-rəl\ *adj* [NL *ruderalis,* fr. L *ruder-, rudus* rubble] (ca. 1858) : growing where the natural vegetational cover has been disturbed by man ⟨~ weeds of old fields and roadsides⟩

2**ruderal** *n* (ca. 1928) : a weedy and commonly introduced plant growing where the vegetational cover has been interrupted

ru·di·ment \'rüd-ə-mənt\ *n* [L *rudimentum* beginning, fr. *rudis* raw, rude] (1548) **1** : a basic principle or element or a fundamental skill — usu. used in pl. ⟨students . . . teaching themselves the ~*s* of rational government —G. B. Galanti⟩ **2 a** : something unformed or undeveloped : BEGINNING — usu. used in pl. ⟨the ~*s* of a plan⟩ **b** (1) : a body part so deficient in size or structure as to be entirely unable to perform its normal function (2) : an organ just beginning to develop : ANLAGE — **ru·di·men·tal** \,rüd-ə-'ment-ᵊl\ *adj*

ru·di·men·ta·ry \,rüd-ə-'ment-ə-rē, -'men-trē\ *adj* (1839) **1** : consisting in first principles : FUNDAMENTAL ⟨these ~ truths —M. R. Cohen⟩ **2** : of a primitive kind ⟨the equipment of these past empire-builders was ~ —A. J. Toynbee⟩ **3** : very imperfectly developed or represented only by a vestige ⟨the ~ tail of a hyrax⟩ — **ru·di·men·tari·ly** \-,men-'ter-ə-lē, -'men-trə-lē\ *adv* — **ru·di·men·tari·ness** \-'ment-ə-rē-nəs, -'men-trē-\ *n*

1**rue** \'rü\ *vb* **rued; ru·ing** [ME *ruen,* fr. OE *hrēowan;* akin to OHG *hriuwan* to regret] *vt* (bef. 12c) : to feel penitence, remorse, or regret for ~ *vi* : to feel sorrow, remorse, or regret

2**rue** *n* (bef. 12c) : REGRET, SORROW

3**rue** *n* [ME, fr. MF, fr. L *ruta,* fr. Gk *rhytē*] (14c) : a strong-scented perennial woody herb (*Ruta graveolens* of the family Rutaceae, the rue family) that has bitter leaves used in medicine

rue anemone *n* (ca. 1817) : a delicate vernal herb (*Anemonella thalictroides*) of the buttercup family with white flowers resembling those of the wood anemone

rue·ful \'rü-fəl\ *adj* (13c) **1** : exciting pity or sympathy : PITIABLE ⟨~ squalid poverty . . . by every wayside —John Morley⟩ **2** : MOURNFUL, REGRETFUL ⟨troubled her with a ~ disquiet —W. M. Thackeray⟩ — **rue·ful·ly** \-fə-lē\ *adv* — **rue·ful·ness** *n*

ru·fes·cent \rü-'fes-ᵊnt\ *adj* [L *rufescent-, rufescens,* prp. of *rufescere* to become reddish, fr. *rufus* red — more at RED] (1817) : REDDISH

1**ruff** \'rəf\ *n* [ME *ruf*] (15c) **1** *also* **ruffe** \'rəf\ : a small freshwater European perch (*Acerina cernua*) **2** : PUMPKINSEED 1

2**ruff** *n* [prob. back-formation fr. *ruffle*] (1555) **1** : a wheel-shaped stiff collar worn by men and women of the late 16th and early 17th centuries **2** : a fringe or frill of long hairs or feathers growing around or on the neck **3** : a common Eurasian sandpiper (*Philomachus pugnax*) whose male during the breeding season has a large ruff of erectile feathers on the neck — **ruffed** \'rəft\ *adj*

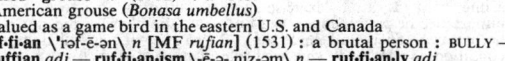

1 ruff 1

3**ruff** *vb* [MF *roffler*] *vi* (1598) : to take a trick with a trump ~ *vt* : to play a trump on (a card previously led or played)

4**ruff** *n* (ca. 1828) : the act of trumping

ruffed grouse *n* (1752) : a No. American grouse (*Bonasa umbellus*) valued as a game bird in the eastern U.S. and Canada

ruf·fi·an \'rəf-ē-ən\ *n* [MF *rufian*] (1531) : a brutal person : BULLY — **ruffian** *adj* — **ruf·fi·an·ism** \-ē-ə-,niz-əm\ *n* — **ruf·fi·an·ly** *adj*

1**ruf·fle** \'rəf-əl\ *vb* **ruf·fled; ruf·fling** \-(ə-)liŋ\ [ME *ruffelen;* akin to LG *ruffelen* to crumple] *vt* (14c) **1 a** : ROUGHEN, ABRADE **b** : TROUBLE, VEX ⟨*ruffled* his composure⟩ **2** : to erect (as feathers) in or like a ruff **3 a** : to flip through (as pages) **b** : SHUFFLE **4** : to make into a ruffle ~ *vi* : to become ruffled ⟨their dispositions ~ perceptibly —*Life*⟩

2**ruffle** *n* (1534) **1** : COMMOTION, BRAWL **2** : a state or cause of irritation **3 a** : a strip of fabric gathered or pleated on one edge **b** : 2RUFF 2 **4** : an unevenness or disturbance of surface : RIPPLE — **ruf·fly** \'rəf-(ə-)lē\ *adj*

3**ruffle** *n* [*ruff* (a drumbeat)] (1802) : a low vibrating drumbeat less loud than a roll

ru·fous \'rü-fəs\ *adj* [L *rufus* red — more at RED] (1782) : REDDISH

rug \'rəg\ *n* [(assumed) ME, rag, tuft, of Scand origin; akin to ON *rǫgg* tuft; akin to L *ruere* to rush, fall, dig up, Skt *ravate* he breaks up] (1810) **1** : a piece of thick heavy fabric that usu. has a nap or pile and is used as a floor covering **2** : a floor mat of an animal pelt ⟨a bearskin ~⟩ **3** : LAP ROBE **4** *slang* : TOUPEE 2

ru·ga \'rü-gə\ *n, pl* **ru·gae** \-,gī, -,gē, -,jē\ [NL, fr. L, wrinkle — more at ROUGH] (ca. 1775) : an anatomical fold or wrinkle esp. of the viscera — usu. used in pl.

rug·by \'rəg-bē\ *n, often cap* [*Rugby* School, Rugby, England] (1864) : a football game in which play is continuous without time-outs or substitutions, interference and forward passing are not permitted, and kicking, dribbling, lateral passing, and tackling are featured

rug·ged \'rəg-əd\ *adj* [ME, fr. (assumed) ME *rug*] (14c) **1** *obs* : SHAGGY, HAIRY **2** : having a rough uneven surface : JAGGED ⟨~ mountains⟩ **3** : TURBULENT, STORMY **4 a** : seamed with wrinkles and furrows : WEATHERED **b** : showing signs of strength : STURDY ⟨there was a certain ~ air of fidelity about him —Charles Dickens⟩ **5 a** : AUSTERE, STERN **b** : COARSE, RUDE **6 a** : presenting a severe test of ability, stamina, or resolution **b** : strongly built or constituted ⟨those that survive are stalwart, ~ men —L. D. Stamp⟩ ***syn*** see ROUGH — **rug·ged·ly** *adv* — **rug·ged·ness** *n*

rug·ged·ize \'rəg-əd-,īz\ *vt* **-ized; -iz·ing** (1950) : to strengthen (as a machine) for better resistance to wear, stress, and abuse ⟨a *ruggedized* camera⟩ — **rug·ged·iza·tion** \,rəg-əd-ə-'zā-shən\ *n*

rug·ger \'rəg-ər\ *n* [by alter.] *Brit* (1893) : RUGBY

ru·go·la \'rü-gə-lə\ *n* [alter. of *arugula*] (1973) : GARDEN ROCKET

ru·go·sa rose \rü-,gō-sə-, -zə-\ *n* [NL *rugosa,* specific epithet of *Rosa rugosa* rugose rose] (1892) : any of various garden roses descended from a rose introduced from China and Japan

ru·gose \'rü-,gōs\ *adj* [L *rugosus,* fr. *ruga*] (1706) **1** : full of wrinkles ⟨~ cheeks⟩ **2** : having the veinlets sunken and the spaces between elevated ⟨~ leaves of the sage⟩ — **ru·gos·i·ty** \rü-'gäs-ət-ē\ *n*

ru·gu·lose \'rü-gyə-,lōs\ *adj* [prob. fr. (assumed) NL *rugulosus,* fr. NL *rugula,* dim. of L *ruga*] (ca. 1819) : having small rugae : finely wrinkled

Ruhm·korff coil \ˈrüm-ˌkȯrf-, ˌrüm-\ *n* [Heinrich *Ruhmkorff* †1877 Ger. physicist] (1852) **:** INDUCTION COIL

[1]**ru·in** \ˈrü-ən, -ˌin\ *n* [ME *ruine,* fr. MF, fr. L *ruina;* akin to L *ruere* to fall — more at RUG] (14c) **1 a** *archaic* **:** a falling down **:** COLLAPSE ⟨from age to age . . . the crash of ~ fitfully resounds —William Wordsworth⟩ **b :** physical, moral, economic, or social collapse **2 a :** the state of being ruined ⟨the city lay in ~*s*⟩ **b :** the remains of something destroyed — usu. used in pl. ⟨the ~*s* of the ancient world —William Hazlitt †1830⟩ **3 :** a cause of destruction **4 a :** the action of destroying, laying waste, or wrecking **b :** DAMAGE, INJURY **5 :** a ruined building, person, or object — **ru·in·ate** \-ə-ˌnət, -ˌnāt\ *adj* — **ru·in·ate** \-ˌnāt\ *vt*

[2]**ruin** *vt* (1581) **1 :** to reduce to ruins **:** DEVASTATE **2 a :** to damage irreparably **b :** BANKRUPT, IMPOVERISH ⟨~*ed* by speculation⟩ **3 :** to subject to frustration, failure, or disaster ⟨will ~ your chances of promotion⟩ ~ *vi* **:** to become ruined — **ru·in·er** *n*

ru·in·ation \ˌrü-ə-ˈnā-shən\ *n* (1664) **:** RUIN, DESTRUCTION

ru·in·ous \ˈrü-ə-nəs\ *adj* (14c) **1 :** DILAPIDATED, RUINED **2 :** causing or tending to cause ruin — **ru·in·ous·ly** *adv* — **ru·in·ous·ness** *n*

[1]**rule** \ˈrül\ *n* [ME *reule,* fr. OF, fr. L *regula* straightedge, rule, fr. *regere* to lead straight — more at RIGHT] (13c) **1 a :** a prescribed guide for conduct or action **b :** the laws or regulations prescribed by the founder of a religious order for observance by its members **c :** an accepted procedure, custom, or habit **d** (1) **:** a usu. written order or direction made by a court regulating court practice or the action of parties (2) **:** a legal precept or doctrine **e :** a regulation or bylaw governing procedure or controlling conduct **2 a** (1) **:** a usu. valid generalization (2) **:** a generally prevailing quality, state, or mode ⟨fair weather was the ~ yesterday —*N.Y. Times*⟩ **b :** a standard of judgment **:** CRITERION **c :** a regulating principle **d :** a determinate method for performing a mathematical operation and obtaining a certain result **3 a :** the exercise of authority or control **:** DOMINION **b :** a period during which a specified ruler or government exercises control **4 a :** a strip of material marked off in units used for measuring or ruling off lengths **b :** a metal strip with a type-high face that prints a linear design; *also* **:** a linear design produced by or as if by such a strip ***syn*** see LAW — **as a rule :** for the most part **:** GENERALLY

[2]**rule** *vb* **ruled; rul·ing** *vt* (13c) **1 a :** to exert control, direction, or influence on ⟨the superstitions that ~ primitive minds⟩ **b :** to exercise control over esp. by curbing or restraining ⟨~ a fractious horse⟩ ⟨*ruled* his appetites firmly⟩ **2 a :** to exercise authority or power over often harshly or arbitrarily ⟨the speaker *ruled* the legislature with an iron hand⟩ **b :** to be preeminent in **:** DOMINATE **3 :** to determine and declare authoritatively; *esp* **:** to command or determine judicially **4 a** (1) **:** to mark with lines drawn along or as if along the straight edge of a ruler (2) **:** to mark (a line) on a paper with a ruler **b :** to arrange in a line ~ *vi* **1 a :** to exercise supreme authority **b :** to be first in importance or prominence **:** PREDOMINATE ⟨the physical did not ~ in her nature —Sherwood Anderson⟩ **2 :** to exist in a specified state or condition **3 :** to lay down a legal rule ***syn*** see GOVERN, DECIDE

ruled surface *n* (ca. 1862) **:** a surface generated by a moving straight line with the result that through every point on the surface a line can be drawn lying wholly in the surface

rule·less \ˈrül-ləs\ *adj* (15c) **:** not restrained or regulated by law

rule of the road (1871) **:** a customary practice (as driving always on a particular side of the road or yielding the right of way) developed in the interest of safety and often subsequently reinforced by law; *esp* **:** any of the rules making up a code governing ships in matters relating to mutual safety

rule of thumb (1692) **1 :** a method of procedure based on experience and common sense **2 :** a general principle regarded as roughly correct but not intended to be scientifically accurate

rule out *vt* (1869) **1 :** EXCLUDE, ELIMINATE **2 :** to make impossible **:** PREVENT ⟨heavy rain *ruled out* the picnic⟩

rul·er \ˈrü-lər\ *n* (14c) **1 :** one that rules; *specif* **:** SOVEREIGN **2 :** a worker or a machine that rules paper **3 :** a smooth-edged strip (as of wood or metal) that is usu. marked off in units (as inches) and is used as a straightedge or for measuring — **rul·er·ship** \-ˌship\ *n*

[1]**rul·ing** \ˈrü-liŋ\ *n* (1560) **:** an official or authoritative decision, decree, statement, or interpretation (as by a judge on a point of law)

[2]**ruling** *adj* (1593) **1 a :** exerting power or authority ⟨the ~ party⟩ **b :** CHIEF, PREDOMINATING ⟨a ~ passion⟩ **2 :** generally prevailing

[1]**rum** \ˈrəm\ *n* [prob. short for obs. *rumbullion* (rum)] (1654) **1 :** an alcoholic beverage distilled from a fermented cane product (as molasses) **2 :** alcoholic liquor ⟨the demon ~⟩

[2]**rum** *adj* **rum·mer; rum·mest** [earlier *rome,* perh. fr. Romany *rom* Gypsy man] (1752) **1** *chiefly Brit* **:** QUEER, ODD ⟨writing is a ~ trade . . . and what is all right one day is all wrong the next —Angela Thirkell⟩ **2** *chiefly Brit* **:** DIFFICULT, DANGEROUS

ru·ma·ki \rə-ˈmä-kē\ *n* [origin unknown] (1961) **:** a cooked appetizer made of pieces of usu. marinated chicken liver wrapped together with sliced water chestnuts in bacon slices

Ru·ma·nian \rü-ˈmā-nē-ən, -nyən\ *n* (1868) **1 :** ROMANIAN 1 **2 :** the Romance language of the Romanians — **Rumanian** *adj*

rum·ba \ˈrəm-bə, ˈrüm-, ˈrüm-\ *n* [AmerSp] (1922) **:** a ballroom dance of Cuban origin in $^2/_4$ or $^4/_4$ time with a basic pattern of step-close-step and marked by a delayed transfer of weight and pronounced hip movements; *also* **:** the music for this dance

[1]**rum·ble** \ˈrəm-bəl\ *vb* **rum·bled; rum·bling** \-b(ə-)liŋ\ [ME *rumblen;* akin to MHG *rummeln* to rumble] *vi* (14c) **1 :** to make a low heavy rolling sound ⟨thunder *rumbling* in the distance⟩ **2 :** to travel with a low reverberating sound ⟨wagons *rumbled* into town⟩ **3 :** to speak in a low rolling tone **4 :** to engage in a rumble ~ *vt* **1 :** to utter or emit in a low rolling voice **2 :** to polish or otherwise treat (metal parts) in a tumbling barrel — **rum·bler** \-b(ə-)lər\ *n*

[2]**rumble** *n* (14c) **1 a :** a low heavy continuous reverberating often muffled sound (as of thunder) **b :** low frequency noise in phonographic playback caused by the transmission of mechanical vibrations by the turntable to the pickup **2 :** a seat for servants behind the body of a carriage **3 :** TUMBLING BARREL **4 a :** widespread expression of dissatisfaction or unrest **b :** a street fight esp. among gangs

rumble seat *n* (1912) **:** a folding seat in the back of an automobile (as a coupe or roadster) not covered by the top

rum·bling \ˈrəm-bliŋ\ *n* (14c) **1 :** RUMBLE **2 :** general but unofficial talk or opinion often of dissatisfaction — usu. used in pl. ⟨occasional ~*s* about . . . government spending —Paul Potter⟩

rum·bly \ˈrəm-b(ə-)lē\ *adj* (1874) **:** tending to rumble or rattle

rum·bus·tious \ˌrəm-ˈbəs-chəs\ *adj* [alter. of *robustious*] *chiefly Brit* (1778) **:** RAMBUNCTIOUS — **rum·bus·tious·ly** *adv, chiefly Brit* — **rum·bus·tious·ness** *n, chiefly Brit*

ru·men \ˈrü-mən\ *n, pl* **ru·mi·na** \-mə-nə\ *or* **rumens** [NL *rumin-, rumen,* fr. L, gullet] (1728) **:** the large first compartment of the stomach of a ruminant in which cellulose is broken down by the action of symbionts — **ru·mi·nal** \-mən-ᵊl\ *adj*

[1]**ru·mi·nant** \ˈrü-mə-nənt\ *n* (1661) **:** a ruminant mammal

[2]**ruminant** *adj* (ca. 1679) **1 a** (1) **:** chewing the cud (2) **:** characterized by chewing again what has been swallowed **b :** of or relating to a suborder (Ruminantia) of even-toed hoofed mammals (as sheep, giraffes, deer, and camels) that chew the cud and have a complex 3- or 4-chambered stomach **2 :** given to or engaged in contemplation **:** MEDITATIVE ⟨stood there with her hands clasped in this attitude of ~ relish —Thomas Wolfe⟩ — **ru·mi·nant·ly** *adv*

ru·mi·nate \ˈrü-mə-ˌnāt\ *vb* **-nat·ed; -nat·ing** [L *ruminatus,* pp. of *ruminari* to chew the cud, muse upon, fr. *rumin-, rumen* gullet; akin to Skt *romantha* ruminant] *vt* (1533) **1 :** to go over in the mind repeatedly and often casually or slowly **2 :** to chew repeatedly for an extended period ~ *vi* **1 :** to chew again what has been chewed slightly and swallowed **:** chew the cud **2 :** to engage in contemplation **:** REFLECT ***syn*** see PONDER — **ru·mi·na·tion** \ˌrü-mə-ˈnā-shən\ *n* — **ru·mi·na·tive** \ˈrü-mə-ˌnāt-iv\ *adj* — **ru·mi·na·tive·ly** *adv* — **ru·mi·na·tor** \-ˌnāt-ər\ *n*

[1]**rum·mage** \ˈrəm-ij\ *vb* **rum·maged; rum·mag·ing** *vi* (1595) **1 :** to make a thorough search or investigation **2 :** to engage in an undirected or haphazard search ~ *vt* **1 :** to make a thorough search through **:** RANSACK ⟨*rummaged* the attic⟩ **2 :** to examine minutely and completely **3 :** to discover by searching — **rum·mag·er** *n*

[2]**rummage** *n* [obs. E *rummage* act of packing cargo, modif. of MF *arrimage*] (1598) **1 a :** a confused miscellaneous collection **b :** items for sale at a rummage sale **2 :** a thorough search esp. among a confusion of objects

rummage sale *n* (ca. 1858) **:** a usu. informal sale of miscellaneous goods; *esp* **:** a sale of donated articles conducted by a nonprofit organization (as a church or charity) to help support its programs

rum·mer \ˈrəm-ər\ *n* [G or D; G *römer,* fr. D *roemer*] (1654) **:** a large-bowled footed drinking glass often elaborately etched or engraved

[1]**rum·my** \ˈrəm-ē\ *adj* **rum·mi·er; -est** (1828) **:** QUEER, ODD ⟨were still feeling a little ~ from our trip up the escalator —*New Yorker*⟩

[2]**rummy** *n, pl* **rummies** (1851) **:** DRUNKARD

[3]**rummy** *n* [perh. fr. [1]*rummy*] (1915) **:** any of several card games for two or more players in which each player tries to assemble groups of three or more cards of the same rank or suit and to be the first to meld all his cards

[1]**ru·mor** \ˈrü-mər\ *n* [ME *rumour,* fr. MF, fr. L *rumor;* akin to OE *rēon* to lament, Gk *ōryesthai* to howl] (14c) **1 :** talk or opinion widely disseminated with no discernible source **2 :** a statement or report current without known authority for its truth **3** *archaic* **:** talk or report of a notable person or event **4 :** a soft low indistinct sound **:** MURMUR

[2]**rumor** *vt* **ru·mored; ru·mor·ing** \ˈrüm-(ə-)riŋ\ (1594) **:** to tell or spread by rumor

ru·mor·mon·ger \-ˌməŋ-gər, -ˌmäŋ-\ *n* (1917) **:** one who spreads rumors

ru·mour \ˈrü-mər\ *chiefly Brit var of* RUMOR

rump \ˈrəmp\ *n* [ME, of Scand origin; akin to Icel *rumpr* rump; akin to MHG *rumph* torso] (15c) **1 a :** the upper rounded part of the hindquarters of a quadruped mammal **b :** BUTTOCKS **c :** the sacral or dorsal part of the posterior end of a bird **2 :** a cut of beef between the loin and round — see BEEF illustration **3 :** a small fragment remaining after the separation of the larger part of a group or an area; *esp* **:** a group (as a parliament) carrying on in the name of the original body after the departure or expulsion of a large number of its members

[1]**rum·ple** \ˈrəm-pəl\ *n* (ca. 1500) **:** FOLD, WRINKLE

[2]**rumple** *vb* **rum·pled; rum·pling** \-p(ə-)liŋ\ [D *rompelen;* akin to OHG *rimpfan* to wrinkle, L *curvus* curved — more at CROWN] *vt* (1603) **1 :** WRINKLE, CRUMPLE **2 :** to make unkempt **:** TOUSLE ~ *vi* **:** to become rumpled

rum·ply \ˈrəm-p(ə-)lē\ *adj* **rum·pli·er; -est** (1833) **:** having rumples

rum·pus \ˈrəm-pəs\ *n* [origin unknown] (1764) **:** a usu. noisy commotion

rumpus room *n* (1939) **:** a room usu. in the basement of a home that is used for games, parties, and recreation

rum·run·ner \ˈrəm-ˌrən-ər\ *n* (1920) **:** a person or ship engaged in bringing prohibited liquor ashore or across a border — **rum–run·ning** \-ˌrən-iŋ\ *adj or n*

[1]**run** \ˈrən\ *vb* **ran** \ˈran\; **run; run·ning** [ME *ronnen,* alter. of *rinnen,* v.i. (fr. OE *iernan, rinnan* & ON *rinna*) & of *rennen,* v.t., fr. ON *renna;* akin to OHG *rinnan,* v.i., to run, OE *rīsan* to rise] *vi* (bef. 12c) **1 a :** to go faster than a walk; *specif* **:** to go steadily by springing steps so that both feet leave the ground for an instant in each step **b** *of a horse* **:** to move at a fast gallop **c :** FLEE, RETREAT, ESCAPE ⟨dropped the gun and *ran*⟩ **d :** to utilize a running play on offense — used of a football team **2 a :** to go without restraint **:** move freely about at will ⟨let chickens ~ loose⟩ **b :** to keep company **:** CONSORT ⟨a ram *running* with ewes⟩ ⟨*ran* with a wild crowd when he was young⟩ **c :** to sail before the wind in distinction from reaching or sailing close-hauled **d :** ROAM, ROVE ⟨*running* about with no overcoat⟩ **3 a :** to go rapidly or hurriedly **:** HASTEN ⟨~ and fetch the doctor⟩ **b :** to go in urgency or distress **:** RESORT ⟨~*s* to mother at every little difficulty⟩ **c :** to make a quick, easy, or casual trip or visit ⟨*ran* over to borrow some sugar⟩ **4 a :** to contend in a race **b :** to enter into an election contest **5 a :** to move on or as if on wheels **:** GLIDE ⟨file drawers *running* on ball bearings⟩ **b :** to roll forward rapidly or freely **c :** to pass or slide freely ⟨a rope ~*s* through the pulley⟩ **d :** to ravel lengthwise ⟨stockings guaranteed not to ~⟩ **6 :** to sing or play a musical passage quickly ⟨~ up the scale⟩ **7 a :** to go back and forth **:** PLY ⟨the train ~*s* between New York and Washington⟩ **b** *of fish* **:** to migrate or move in schools; *esp* **:** to ascend a river to spawn **8 a :** TURN, ROTATE ⟨a swiftly *running* grindstone⟩ **b :** FUNCTION, OPERATE ⟨the engine ~*s* on gasoline⟩ **9 a :** to continue in force or operation ⟨the contract has two more

years to ~⟩ **b :** to accompany as a valid obligation or right ⟨a right-of-way that ~*s* with the land⟩ **c :** to continue to accrue or become payable ⟨interest on the loan ~*s* from July 1st⟩ **10 :** to pass from one state to another ⟨~ into debt⟩ **11 a :** to flow rapidly or under pressure **b :** MELT, FUSE **c :** SPREAD, DISSOLVE ⟨colors guaranteed not to ~⟩ **d :** to discharge pus or serum ⟨a *running* sore⟩ **12 a :** to develop rapidly in some specific direction; *esp* **:** to throw out an elongated shoot of growth **b :** to tend to produce or develop a specified quality or feature ⟨they ~ to big noses in that family⟩ **13 a :** to lie in or take a certain direction ⟨the boundary line ~*s* east⟩ **b :** to lie or extend in relation to something **c :** to go back **:** REACH **d** (1) **:** to be in a certain form or expression ⟨the letter ~*s* as follows⟩ (2) **:** to be in a certain order of succession **14 a :** to occur persistently ⟨musical talent ~*s* in the family⟩ **b :** to remain of a specified size, amount, character, or quality ⟨profits were *running* high⟩ **c :** to exist or occur in a continuous range of variation ⟨shades ~ from white to dark gray⟩ **d :** to play on a stage a number of successive days or nights ⟨the musical *ran* for six months⟩ **15 a :** to spread or pass quickly from point to point ⟨chills *ran* up her spine⟩ **b :** to be current **:** CIRCULATE ⟨speculation *ran* rife⟩ ~ *vt* **1 a :** to cause (an animal) to go rapidly **:** ride or drive fast **b :** to bring to a specified condition by or as if by running ⟨*ran* himself to death⟩ **c :** to go in pursuit of **:** HUNT, CHASE ⟨dogs that ~ deer⟩ **d :** to follow the trail of backward **:** TRACE ⟨*ran* the rumor to its source⟩ **e :** to enter, register, or enroll as a contestant in a race **f :** to put forward as a candidate for office **2 a :** to drive (livestock) esp. to a grazing place **b :** to provide pasturage for (livestock) **c :** to keep or maintain (livestock) on or as if on pasturage **3 a :** to pass over or traverse with speed **b :** to accomplish or perform by or as if by running ⟨*ran* a great race⟩ ⟨*running* errands for a bank⟩ **c :** to slip through or past ⟨~ a blockade⟩ ⟨~ a red light⟩ **4 a :** to cause to penetrate or enter **:** THRUST ⟨*ran* a splinter into her toe⟩ **b :** STITCH **c :** to cause to pass **:** LEAD ⟨~ a wire in from the antenna⟩ **d :** to cause to collide ⟨*ran* his head into a post⟩ **e :** SMUGGLE ⟨~ guns⟩ **5 :** to cause to pass lightly or quickly over, along, or into something ⟨*ran* her eye down the list⟩ **6 a :** to cause or allow (as a vehicle or a vessel) to go in a specified manner or direction ⟨*ran* the car off the road⟩ **b :** OPERATE ⟨~ a lathe⟩ **c :** to direct the business or activities of **:** MANAGE, CONDUCT ⟨~ a factory⟩ **7 a :** to be full of or drenched with ⟨streets *ran* blood⟩ **b :** CONTAIN, ASSAY **8 :** to cause to move or flow in a specified way or into a specified position ⟨~ cards into a file⟩ **9 a :** to melt and cast in a mold ⟨~ bullets⟩ **b :** TREAT, PROCESS, REFINE ⟨~ oil in a still⟩ ⟨~ a problem through a computer⟩ **10 :** to make oneself liable to **:** INCUR ⟨*ran* the risk of discovery⟩ **11 :** to mark out **:** DRAW ⟨~ a contour line on a map⟩ **12 a :** to permit (as charges) to accumulate before settling ⟨~ an account at the grocery⟩ **b :** ²COST *vt* 1 ⟨rooms that ~ $50 a night⟩ **13 a :** to produce by or as if by printing — usu. used with *off* ⟨*ran* off 10,000 copies of the first edition⟩ **b :** to carry in a printed medium **:** PRINT ⟨every newspaper *ran* the story⟩ **14 a :** to make (a series of counts) without a miss ⟨~ 19 in an inning in billiards⟩ **b :** to lead winning cards of (a suit) successively **15 :** to make (a golf ball) roll forward after alighting — **run across :** to meet with or discover by chance — **run after 1 :** PURSUE, CHASE; *esp* **:** to seek the company of **2 :** to take up with **:** FOLLOW ⟨*run after* new theories⟩ — **run against 1 :** to meet suddenly or unexpectedly **2 :** to work or take effect unfavorably to **:** DISFAVOR, OPPOSE — **run a temperature :** to have a fever — **run false :** to save distance by running directly for the game instead of following the scent or track — **run foul of 1 :** to collide with ⟨*ran foul of* a hidden reef⟩ **2 :** to come into conflict with ⟨*run foul of* the law⟩ — **run into 1 a :** to change or transform into **:** BECOME **b :** to merge with **c :** to mount up to ⟨their yearly income often *runs into* six figures⟩ **2 a :** to collide with **b :** ENCOUNTER, MEET ⟨*ran into* an old classmate the other day⟩ — **run rings around :** to show marked superiority over **:** defeat decisively or overwhelmingly — **run riot 1 :** to act wildly or without restraint **2 :** to occur in profusion — **run short :** to become insufficient — **run short of :** to use up — **run to :** to mount up to ⟨the book *runs to* 500 pages⟩ — **run upon :** to run across **:** meet with

²run *n* (15c) **1 a :** an act or the action of running **:** continued rapid movement **b :** a quickened gallop **c** (1) **:** the act of migrating or ascending a river to spawn (2) **:** an assemblage of fish that migrate or ascend a river to spawn **d :** a running race ⟨a mile ~⟩ **e :** a score made in baseball by a runner reaching home plate safely **f :** strength or ability to run **g :** a gain of a usu. specified distance made on a running play in football ⟨scored on a 25-yard ~⟩ **2 a** *chiefly Midland* **:** CREEK 2 **b :** something that flows in the course of a certain operation or during a certain time ⟨the first ~ of sap in sugar maples⟩ **3 a :** the stern of the underwater body of a ship from where it begins to curve or slope upward and inward **b :** the direction in which a vein of ore lies **c :** a direction of secondary or minor cleavage **:** GRAIN ⟨the ~ of a mass of granite⟩ **d** (1) **:** the horizontal distance covered by a flight of steps (2) **:** the horizontal distance from the wall plate to the center line of a building **e :** general tendency or direction **4 :** a continuous series esp. of things of identical or similar sort: as **a :** a rapid passage up or down a scale in vocal or instrumental music **b :** a number of rapid small dance steps executed in even tempo **c :** the act of making successively a number of successful shots or strokes; *also* **:** the score thus made ⟨a ~ of 20 in billiards⟩ **d :** an unbroken course of performances or showings **e :** a set of consecutive measurements, readings, or observations **f :** persistent and heavy demands from depositors, creditors, or customers ⟨a ~ on a bank⟩ **g :** SEQUENCE 2b **5 :** the quantity of work turned out in a continuous operation ⟨a press ~ of 10,000 copies⟩ **6 :** the usual or normal kind, character, type, or group ⟨the average ~ of students⟩ **7 a :** the distance covered in a period of continuous traveling or sailing **b :** a course or route esp. if mapped out and traveled with regularity **:** TRIP **c :** a news reporter's regular territory **:** BEAT **d :** the distance a golf ball travels after touching the ground **e :** freedom of movement in or access to a place or area ⟨has the ~ of the house⟩ **8 a :** the period during which a machine or plant is in continuous operation **b :** the use of machinery for a single set of processing procedures ⟨a computer ~⟩ **9 a :** a way, track, or path frequented by animals **b :** an enclosure for domestic animals where they may feed or exercise **c** *Austral* (1) **:** a large area of land used for grazing ⟨a sheep ~⟩ (2) **:** RANCH, STATION ⟨*run-holder*⟩ **d :** an inclined passageway **10 a :** an inclined course (as for skiing or bobsledding) **b :** a support (as a track, pipe, or trough) on which something runs **11 a :** a ravel in a knitted fabric (as in hosiery) caused by the breaking of stitches **b :** a paint defect caused by excessive flow — **on the run 1 :** in haste **:** without pausing **2 :** in retreat **:** running away

³run *adj* (1774) **1 a :** being in a melted state ⟨~ butter⟩ **b :** made from molten material **:** cast in a mold ⟨~ metal⟩ **2** *of fish* **:** having made a migration or spawning run ⟨a fresh ~ salmon⟩ **3 :** exhausted or winded from running

run·about \ˈrən-ə-ˌbau̇t\ *n* (14c) **1 :** one who wanders about **:** STRAY **2 :** a light open wagon, roadster, or motorboat

run·a·gate \ˈrən-ə-ˌgāt\ *n* [alter. of *renegate*, fr. ML *renegatus* — more at RENEGADE] (1547) **1 :** VAGABOND **2 :** FUGITIVE, RUNAWAY

run along *vi* (1767) **:** to go away **:** be on one's way **:** DEPART

run·around \ˈrən-ə-ˌrau̇nd\ *n* (1915) **1 :** deceptive or delaying action esp. in response to a request **2 :** matter typeset in shortened measure to run around something (as a cut)

¹run·away \ˈrən-ə-ˌwā\ *n* (1547) **1 :** one that runs away from danger, duty, or restraint **:** FUGITIVE **2 :** the act of running away out of control; *also* **:** something (as a horse) that is running out of control **3 :** a one-sided or overwhelming victory

²runaway *adj* (1548) **1 a :** running away **:** FUGITIVE **b :** leaving to gain special advantages (as lower wages) or avoid disadvantages (as governmental or union restrictions) ⟨~ shipping firms⟩ ⟨a ~ shop⟩ **2 :** accomplished by elopement or during flight **3 :** won by or having a long lead ⟨a ~ success⟩ **4 :** subject to uncontrolled changes ⟨~ inflation⟩ **5 :** operating out of control ⟨a ~ oil well⟩ ⟨a ~ nuclear reactor⟩

run away \ˌrən-ə-ˈwā\ *vi* (14c) **1 a :** to leave quickly in order to avoid or escape something **b :** to leave home; *esp* **:** ELOPE **2 :** to run out of control **:** STAMPEDE, BOLT **3 :** to gain a substantial lead **:** win by a large margin — **run away with 1 :** to take away in haste or secretly; *esp* **:** STEAL **2 :** to outshine the others in (a theatrical performance) **3 :** to carry or drive beyond prudent or reasonable limits ⟨your imagination *ran away with* you⟩

run·back \ˈrən-ˌbak\ *n* (1929) **:** a run made in football after catching an opponent's kick or intercepting a pass

run·ci·ble spoon \ˌrən(t)-sə-bəl-\ *n* [coined with an obscure meaning by Edward Lear] (1889) **:** a sharp-edged fork with three broad curved prongs

run·ci·nate \ˈrən(t)-sə-ˌnāt\ *adj* [L *runcinatus*, pp. of *runcinare* to plane off, fr. *runcina* plane] (ca. 1776) **:** pinnately cut with the lobes pointing downward ⟨~ leaves of the dandelion⟩

run·dle \ˈrən-dᵊl\ *n* [ME *roundel* circle — more at ROUNDEL] (1565) **1 :** a step of a ladder **:** RUNG **2 :** the drum of a windlass or capstan

rund·let *or* **run·let** \ˈrən-(d)lət\ *n* [ME *roundelet* — more at ROUNDLET] (14c) **1 :** a small barrel **:** KEG **2 :** an old unit of liquid capacity equal to 18 U.S. gallons

run·down \ˈrən-ˌdau̇n\ *n* (1908) **1 :** a maneuver in baseball in which a base runner who is caught off base is chased by two or more opposing players who throw the ball from one to another in an attempt to tag him out **2 :** an item-by-item report **:** SUMMARY

run–down \ˈrən-ˈdau̇n\ *adj* (ca. 1892) **1 :** WORN-OUT, EXHAUSTED **2 :** completely unwound **3 :** being in poor repair **:** DILAPIDATED

run down \ˈrən-ˈdau̇n, ˌrən-\ *vt* (1578) **1 a :** to collide with and knock down **b :** to run against and cause to sink **2 a :** to chase to exhaustion or until captured **b :** to trace the source of **c :** to tag out (a base runner) between bases on a rundown **3 :** DISPARAGE ~ *vi* **1 :** to cease to operate because of the exhaustion of motive power ⟨the clock *ran down*⟩ **2 :** to decline in physical condition or vigor

rune \ˈrün\ *n* [ON & OE *rūn* mystery, runic character, writing; akin to OHG *rūna* secret discussion] (1685) **1 :** any of the characters of any of several alphabets used by the Germanic peoples from about the 3d to the 13th centuries **2 :** MYSTERY, MAGIC **3** [Finn *runo*, of Gmc origin; akin to ON *rūn*] **a :** a Finnish or Old Norse poem **b :** POEM, SONG — **ru·nic** \ˈrü-nik\ *adj*

rune 1: Anglo-Saxon runic alphabet

¹rung *past part of* RING

²rung \ˈrəŋ\ *n* [ME, fr. OE *hrung* crossbar; akin to OE *hring* ring — more at RING] (13c) **1 a :** a rounded part placed as a crosspiece between the legs of a chair **b :** one of the crosspieces of a ladder **2** *Scot* **:** a heavy staff or cudgel **3 :** a spoke of a wheel **4 :** a stage in an ascent ⟨rise a few ~*s* on the social scale —H. W. Van Loon⟩

run–in \ˈrən-ˌin\ *n* (1905) **1 :** something inserted as a substantial addition in copy or typeset matter **2 :** ALTERCATION, QUARREL

run in \ˈrən-ˈin, ˌrən-\ *vi* (ca. 1878) **:** to pay a casual visit ~ *vt* **1 a :** to make (typeset matter) continuous without a paragraph or other break **b :** to insert as additional matter **2 :** to arrest for a minor

\ə\ abut \ᵊ\ kitten, F table \ər\ further \a\ ash \ā\ ace \ä\ cot, cart \au̇\ out \ch\ chin \e\ bet \ē\ easy \g\ go \i\ hit \ī\ ice \j\ job \ŋ\ sing \ō\ go \ȯ\ law \ȯi\ boy \th\ thin \t͟h\ the \ü\ loot \u̇\ foot \y\ yet \zh\ vision \à, k̲, ⁿ, œ, œ̄, ue, ue̅, ʸ\ *see* Guide to Pronunciation

offense **3 :** to operate (a new machine) carefully until there is efficient running

run·less \'rən-ləs\ *adj* (1921) **:** scoring no runs

run·let \'rən-lət\ *n* (1755) **:** RUNNEL

run·nel \'rən-ᵊl\ *n* [alter. of ME *rinel*, fr. OE *rynel;* akin to OE *rinnan* to run — more at RUN] (bef. 12c) **:** RIVULET, STREAMLET

run·ner \'rən-ər\ *n* (14c) **1 a :** one that runs **:** RACER **b :** BASE RUNNER **c :** BALLCARRIER **2 a :** MESSENGER **b :** one that smuggles or distributes illicit or contraband goods (as drugs, liquor, or guns) **3 :** any of various large active carangid fishes **4 a :** either of the longitudinal pieces on which a sled or sleigh slides **b :** the part of a skate that slides on the ice **:** BLADE **c :** the support of a drawer or a sliding door **5 a :** a growth produced by a plant in running; *esp* **:** STOLON 1a **b :** a plant that forms or spreads by means of runners **c :** a twining vine (as a scarlet runner) **6 a :** a long narrow carpet for a hall or staircase **b :** a narrow decorative cloth cover for a table or dresser top

runner bean *n, chiefly Brit* (1882) **:** SCARLET RUNNER

run·ner–up \'rən-ə-,rəp, ,rən-ə-'\ *n, pl* **run·ners–up** \-ər-,zəp, -'zəp\ *also* **runner–ups** (1842) **:** the competitor that does not win first place in a contest; *esp* **:** one that finishes in second place

1run·ning \'rən-iŋ\ *n* (bef. 12c) **1 a :** the action of running **b :** RACE **2 :** physical condition for running **3 :** MANAGEMENT, CARE — **in the running 1 :** competing in a contest **2 :** having a chance to win a contest — **out of the running 1 :** not competing in a contest **2 :** having no chance of winning a contest

2running *adj* (13c) **1 :** CURSIVE, FLOWING **2 :** FLUID, RUNNY **3 a :** INCESSANT, CONTINUOUS ⟨a ~ battle⟩ **b :** made during the course of a process or activity ⟨a ~ commentary on the game⟩ **4 :** measured in a straight line ⟨cost of lumber per ~ foot⟩ **5 a :** initiated or performed while running or with a running start ⟨~ catch⟩ **b :** of, relating to, used in, or being a football play in which the ball is advanced by running rather than by passing ⟨their ~ game was off⟩ ⟨a ~ back⟩ **c :** designed for use for foot races ⟨a ~ track⟩ **6 :** fitted or trained for running rather than walking, trotting, or jumping ⟨a ~ horse⟩

3running *adv* (1911) **:** in succession **:** CONSECUTIVELY ⟨for three days ~⟩

running board *n* (1817) **:** a footboard esp. at the side of an automobile

running dog *n* (1927) **:** one who does someone else's bidding **:** LACKEY

running gear *n* (ca. 1864) **1 :** the working and carrying parts of a machine (as a locomotive) **2 :** the parts of an automobile chassis not used in developing, transmitting, and controlling power

running hand *n* (1648) **:** handwriting in which the letters are usu. slanted and the words formed without lifting the pen

running head *n* (1839) **:** a headline repeated on consecutive pages (as of a book) — called also *running headline*

running knot *n* (1648) **:** a knot that slips along the rope or line round which it is tied; *esp* **:** an overhand slipknot

running light *n* (1881) **:** one of the lights carried by a vehicle (as a ship) under way at night that indicate size, position, and direction

running mate *n* (1868) **1 :** a horse entered in a race to set the pace for a horse of the same owner or stable **2 :** a candidate running for a subordinate place on a ticket; *esp* **:** the candidate for vice-president **3 :** COMPANION

running start *n* (1926) **:** FLYING START

running stitch *n* (1850) **:** a small even stitch run in and out in cloth

running title *n* (1668) **:** the title or short title of a volume printed at the top of left-hand text pages or sometimes of all text pages

run·ny \'rən-ē\ *adj* (1817) **:** having a tendency to run ⟨a ~ nose⟩

run·off \'rən-,ȯf\ *n* (1893) **1 :** the portion of the precipitation on the land that ultimately reaches streams; *esp* **:** the water from rain or melted snow that flows over the surface **2 :** a final race, contest, or election to decide an earlier one that has not resulted in a decision in favor of any one competitor

run off \'rən-'ȯf, ,rən-\ *vt* (1683) **1 a :** to recite, compose, or produce rapidly **b :** to cause to be run or played to a finish **c :** to decide (as a race) by a runoff **d :** CARRY OUT **2 :** to drain off **:** DRAW OFF **3 a :** to drive off (as trespassers) **b :** to steal (as cattle) by driving away **~** *vi* **:** RUN AWAY 1 — **run off with :** to carry off **:** STEAL

run–of–paper \,rən-əv-'pā-pər\ *adj* (ca. 1923) **:** to be placed anywhere in a newspaper at the option of the editor ⟨~ advertisement⟩

run–of–the–mill \,rən-ə(v)-thə-'mil\ *adj* (1930) **:** not outstanding in quality or rarity **:** AVERAGE

run–of–the–mine \-'mīn\ *or* **run–of–mine** \-əv-'mīn\ *adj* (1903) **1 :** not graded ⟨~ coal⟩ **2 :** RUN-OF-THE-MILL

1run–on \'rən-'ȯn, -'än\ *adj* (1903) **:** continuing without rhetorical pause from one line of verse into another

2run–on \-,ȯn, -,än\ *n* (ca. 1909) **:** something (as a dictionary entry) that is run on

run on \'rən-'ȯn, ,rən-, -'än\ *vi* (1595) **1 :** to keep going **:** CONTINUE **2 :** to talk or narrate at length **~** *vt* **1 :** to continue (matter in type) without a break or a new paragraph **:** RUN IN **2 :** to place or add (as an entry in a dictionary) at the end of a paragraphed item

run–on sentence *n* (1914) **:** a sentence containing a comma fault

run out *vi* (14c) **1 a :** to come to an end **:** EXPIRE ⟨time *ran out*⟩ **b :** to become exhausted or used up ⟨the gasoline *ran out*⟩ **2 :** to jut out **~** *vt* **1 :** to finish out (as a course, series, or contest) **:** COMPLETE **2 a :** to fill out (a typeset line) with quads, leaders, or ornaments **b :** to set (as the first line of a paragraph) with a hanging indention **3 :** to exhaust (oneself) in running **4 :** to cause to leave by force or coercion **:** EXPEL — **run out of :** to use up the available supply of — **run out on :** DESERT

run·over \'rən-,ō-vər\ *n* (ca. 1934) **:** matter for publication that exceeds the space allotted

run–over \'rən-'ō-vər\ *adj* (ca. 1934) **:** extending beyond the allotted space

run over \,rən-'ō-vər\ *vi* (1526) **1 :** OVERFLOW **2 :** to exceed a limit **~** *vt* **1 :** to go over, examine, repeat, or rehearse quickly **2 :** to collide with, knock down, and often drive over ⟨*ran over* a dog⟩

runt \'rənt\ *n* [origin unknown] (1501) **1** *chiefly Scot* **:** a hardened stalk or stem of a plant **2 :** an animal unusually small of its kind; *esp* **:** the smallest of a litter of pigs **3 :** a person of small stature — **runt·i·ness** \'rənt-ē-nəs\ *n* — **runty** \'rənt-ē\ *adj*

run–through \'rən-,thrü\ *n* (1929) **:** a cursory reading, summary, or rehearsal

run through \,rən-'thrü\ *vt* (15c) **1 :** PIERCE **2 :** to spend or consume wastefully and rapidly **3 :** to read or rehearse without pausing **4 a :** CARRY OUT, DO **b :** to subject to a process

run–up \'rən-,əp\ *n* (1834) **1 :** the act of running up something **2 :** a usu. sudden increase in volume or price ⟨a ~ in stock prices⟩ ⟨~ in trading⟩

run up \'rən-'əp\ *vi* (14c) **:** to grow rapidly **:** shoot up **~** *vt* **1 :** to increase by bidding **:** bid up **2 :** to stitch together quickly **3 :** to erect hastily **4 :** ACCUMULATE ⟨*ran up* a large telephone bill⟩

run·way \'rən-,wā\ *n* (1833) **1 a :** a beaten path made by animals **b :** a passageway for animals **2 :** the channel of a stream **3 :** an artificially surfaced strip of ground on a landing field for the landing and takeoff of airplanes **4 :** a narrow platform from a stage into an auditorium **5 :** RUN 10b

ru·pee \rü-'pē, 'rü-,pē\ *n* [Hindi *rūpaiyā*, fr. Skt *rūpya* coined silver] (1610) — see MONEY table

ru·pi·ah \rü-'pē-ə\ *n, pl* **rupiah** *or* **rupiahs** [Hindi *rūpaiyā*] (1947) — see MONEY table

1rup·ture \'rəp-chər\ *n* [ME *ruptur*, fr. MF or L; MF *rupture*, fr. L *ruptura* fracture, fr. *ruptus*, pp. of *rumpere* to break — more at REAVE] (15c) **1 :** breach of peace or concord; *specif* **:** open hostility or war between nations **2 a :** the tearing apart of a tissue ⟨~ of the heart muscle⟩ ⟨~ of an intervertebral disk⟩ **b :** HERNIA **3 :** a breaking apart or the state of being broken apart

2rupture *vb* **rup·tured; rup·tur·ing** \-chə-riŋ, -shriŋ\ *vt* (1739) **1 a :** to part by violence **:** BREAK, BURST **b :** to create or induce a breach of **2 :** to produce a rupture in **~** *vi* **:** to have or undergo a rupture

ru·ral \'ru̇r-əl\ *adj* [ME, fr. MF, fr. L *ruralis*, fr. *rur-*, *rus* open land — more at ROOM] (15c) **:** of or relating to the country, country people or life, or agriculture — **ru·ral·i·ty** \ru̇-'ral-ət-ē\ *n* — **ru·ral·ly** \-ə-lē\ *adv*

rural dean *n* (15c) **:** DEAN 1b

rural free delivery *n* (1892) **:** free delivery of mail to a rural area — called also *rural delivery*

ru·ral·ist \'ru̇r-ə-ləst\ *n* (1739) **:** one who lives in a rural area

rural route *n* (1898) **:** a mail-delivery route in a rural free delivery area

rur·ban \'rər-bən, 'ru̇(ə)r-\ *adj* [blend of *rural* and *urban*] (1918) **:** of, relating to, or constituting an area which is chiefly residential but where some farming is carried on

Ru·ri·tan \'ru̇r-ə-tən\ *n* [*Ruritan National* (club)] (1968) **:** a member of a major national service club

Ru·ri·ta·ni·an \'ru̇r-ə-,tā-nē-ən, ,ru̇r-ə-'\ *adj* [*Ruritania*, fictional kingdom in the novel *Prisoner of Zenda* (1894) by Anthony Hope] (1896) **:** of, relating to, or having the characteristics of an imaginary place of high romance

ruse \'rüs, 'rüz\ *n* [F, fr. MF, fr. *ruser* to dodge, deceive] (1625) **:** a wily subterfuge ***syn*** see TRICK

1rush \'rəsh\ *n* [ME, fr. OE *risc;* akin to MHG *rusch* rush, L *restis* rope] (bef. 12c) **:** any of various monocotyledonous often tufted marsh plants (as of the genera *Juncus* and *Scirpus* of the family Juncaceae, the rush family) with cylindrical often hollow stems which are used in bottoming chairs and plaiting mats — **rushy** \-ē\ *adj*

2rush *vb* [ME *russhen*, fr. MF *ruser* to put to flight, repel, deceive, fr. L *recusare* to refuse — more at RECUSANCY] *vi* (14c) **1 :** to move forward, progress, or act with haste or eagerness or without preparation **2 :** to advance a football by running plays ⟨~*ed* for a total of 150 yards⟩ **~** *vt* **1 :** to push or impel on or forward with speed, impetuosity, or violence **2 :** to perform in a short time or at high speed **3 :** to urge to an unnatural or extreme speed ⟨don't ~ me⟩ **4 :** to run toward or against in attack **:** CHARGE **5 a :** to carry (a ball) forward in a running play **b :** to move in quickly on (a kicker or passer) to hinder, prevent, or block a kick or pass — used esp. of defensive linemen **6 a :** to lavish attention on **:** COURT **b :** to try to secure a pledge of membership (as in a fraternity) from

3rush *n* (14c) **1 a :** a violent forward motion **b :** ATTACK, ONSET **c :** a surging of emotion **2 a :** a burst of activity, productivity, or speed **b :** a sudden insistent demand **3 :** a thronging of people usu. to a new place in search of wealth ⟨gold ~⟩ **4 :** the act of carrying a football during a game **:** running play **5 a :** a round of attention usu. involving extensive social activity **b :** a drive by a fraternity or sorority to recruit new members **6 :** a print of a motion-picture scene processed directly after the shooting for review by the director or producer **7 a :** the immediate pleasurable feeling produced by a drug (as heroin or amphetamine) — called also *flash* **b :** a sudden feeling of intense pleasure or euphoria **:** THRILL

4rush *adj* (1887) **:** requiring or marked by special speed or urgency ⟨~ orders⟩ ⟨the ~ season⟩

rush candle *n* (1591) **:** RUSHLIGHT

rush·ee \,rəsh-'ē\ *n* (ca. 1916) **:** a college or university student who is being rushed by a fraternity or sorority

rush·er \'rəsh-ər\ *n* (1654) **:** one that rushes; *esp* **:** BALLCARRIER

rush hour *n* (1898) **:** a period of the day when the demands esp. of traffic or business are at a peak

rush·ing *n* (1883) **:** the act of advancing a football by running plays **:** the use of running plays; *also* **:** yardage gained by running plays

rush·light \'rəsh-,līt\ *n* (1710) **:** a candle that consists of the pith of a rush dipped in grease

rusk \'rəsk\ *n* [modif. of Sp & Pg *rosca* coil, twisted roll] (1595) **1 :** hard crisp bread orig. used as ship's stores **2 :** a sweet or plain bread baked, sliced, and baked again until dry and crisp

Russ \'rəs, 'rüs, 'ru̇s\ *n, pl* **Russ** *or* **Russ·es** [Russ *Rus'*] (1567) **:** RUSSIAN — **Russ** *adj*

1rus·set \'rəs-ət\ *n* [ME, fr. OF *rousset*, fr. *rousset*, adj., russet, fr. *rous* russet, fr. L *russus* red; akin to L *ruber* red — more at RED] (13c) **1 :** coarse homespun usu. reddish brown cloth **2 :** a variable color averaging a strong brown **3 :** any of various winter apples having russet rough skins

2russet *adj* (15c) **:** of the color russet

rus·set·ing *also* **rus·set·ting** \'rəs-ət-iŋ\ *n* (1912) **:** a brownish roughened area on the skin of fruit (as apples) caused by injury

Rus·sia leather \,rəsh-ə-\ *n* [*Russia*, Europe] (1658) **:** leather made by tanning various skins with willow, birch, or oak and then rubbing the flesh side with a phenolic oil distilled from a European birch — called also *Russia calf*

Rus·sian \'rəsh-ən\ n (1538) **1 a :** a native or inhabitant of Russia; *esp* : a member of the dominant Slavic-speaking Great Russian ethnic group of Russia **b :** one that is of Russian descent **2 a :** a Slavic language of the Russian people that is the official language of the U.S.S.R. **b :** the three Slavic languages of the Russian people including Belorussian and Ukrainian — **Russian** *adj* — **Rus·sian·ness** *n*

Russian blue *n, often cap B* (1889) : a slender long-bodied large-eared domestic cat with short silky bluish gray fur

Russian dressing *n* (1922) : a dressing (as of mayonnaise or oil and vinegar) with added chili sauce, chopped pickles, or pimientos

Rus·sian·ize \'rəsh-ə-ˌnīz\ *vt* **-ized; -iz·ing** (1831) : to make Russian — **Rus·sian·iza·tion** \ˌrəsh-ə-nə-'zā-shən\ *n*

Russian olive *n* (1913) : a chiefly silvery Eurasian large shrub or small tree (*Elaeagnus angustifolia*) cultivated in arid windy regions esp. as a shelterbelt plant

Russian roulette *n* (1937) : an act of bravado consisting of spinning the cylinder of a revolver loaded with one cartridge, pointing the muzzle at one's own head, and pulling the trigger

Russian thistle *n* (ca. 1894) : a prickly European saltwort (*Salsola kali*) that is a serious pest in No. America — called also *Russian tumbleweed*

Russian wolfhound *n* (1872) : BORZOI

Rus·si·fy \'rəs-ə-ˌfī\ *vt* **-fied; -fy·ing** (1865) : RUSSIANIZE — **Rus·si·fi·ca·tion** \ˌrəs-ə-fə-'kā-shən\ *n*

Rus·so- *comb form* [*Russia & Russian*] **1** \'rəs-ə, 'rəs-, -ō\ : Russia : Russians ⟨*Russophobia*⟩ **2** \'rəs(h)-(ˌ)ō, ˌrəs(h)-\ : Russian and ⟨*Russo*-Japanese⟩

¹rust \'rəst\ *n* [ME, fr. OE *rūst*; akin to OE *rēad* red — more at RED] (bef. 12c) **1 a :** the reddish brittle coating formed on iron esp. when chemically attacked by moist air and composed essentially of hydrated ferric oxide **b :** a comparable coating produced on a metal other than iron by corrosion **c :** something resembling rust : ACCRETION **2** : corrosive or injurious influence or effect **3 :** any of numerous destructive diseases of plants produced by fungi (order *Uredinales*) and characterized by reddish brown pustular lesions; *also* : a fungus causing this **4 :** a strong brown

²rust *vi* (13c) **1 :** to form rust : become oxidized ⟨iron ∼s⟩ **2 :** to degenerate esp. from inaction, lack of use, or passage of time ⟨most men would . . . have allowed their faculties to ∼ —T. B. Macaulay⟩ **3** : to become reddish brown as if with rust ⟨the leaves slowly ∼ed⟩ **4** : to be affected with a rust fungus ∼ *vt* **1 :** to cause (a metal) to form rust ⟨keep up your bright swords, for the dew will ∼ them —Shak.⟩ **2** : to impair or corrode by or as if by time, inactivity, or deleterious use **3 :** to cause to become reddish brown : turn the color of rust

rust belt *n, often cap R&B* (1983) : the northeastern and midwestern states of the U.S. in which heavy industry has declined

¹rus·tic \'rəs-tik\ *also* **rus·ti·cal** \-ti-kəl\ *adj* [ME *rustik*, fr. MF *rustique*, fr. L *rusticus*, fr. *rus* open land — more at ROOM] (15c) **1 :** of, relating to, or suitable for the country : RURAL **2 a :** made of the rough limbs of trees ⟨∼ furniture⟩ **b :** finished by rusticating ⟨a ∼ joint in masonry⟩ **3 a :** characteristic of or resembling country people **b** : lacking in social graces or polish **4 :** appropriate to the country (as in plainness or sturdiness) ⟨heavy ∼ boots⟩ — **rus·ti·cal·ly** \-ti-k(ə-)lē\ *adv* — **rus·tic·i·ty** \ˌrəs-'tis-ət-ē\ *n*

²rustic *n* (1550) **1 :** an inhabitant of a rural area **2 a :** an awkward coarse person **b :** an unsophisticated rural person

rus·ti·cate \'rəs-ti-ˌkāt\ *vb* **-cat·ed; -cat·ing** *vi* (1660) : to go into or reside in the country : follow a rustic life ∼ *vt* **1** ⟨*chiefly Brit*⟩ : to suspend from school or college **2 :** to bevel or rebate (as the edges of stone blocks) to make the joints conspicuous ⟨a *rusticated* stone wall⟩ **3 a** : to compel to reside in the country **b :** to cause to become rustic : implant rustic mannerisms in — **rus·ti·ca·tion** \ˌrəs-ti-'kā-shən\ *n* — **rus·ti·ca·tor** \'rəs-ti-ˌkāt-ər\ *n*

¹rus·tle \'rəs-əl\ *vb* **rus·tled; rus·tling** \'rəs-(ə-)liŋ\ [ME *rustelen*] *vi* (14c) **1 :** to make or cause a rustle **2 a :** to act or move with energy or speed **b :** to forage food **3 :** to steal cattle ∼ *vt* **1 :** to cause to rustle **2 :** to procure by rustling; *esp* : FORAGE **3 :** to take (as cattle) feloniously : STEAL — **rus·tler** \-(ə-)lər\ *n*

²rustle *n* (1759) : a quick succession or confusion of small sounds

rust mite *n* (1884) : any of various small gall mites that burrow in the surface of leaves or fruits usu. producing brown or reddish patches

rust·proof \'rəst-'prüf\ *adj* (1691) : incapable of rusting

¹rusty \'rəs-tē\ *adj* **rust·i·er; -est** (bef. 12c) **1 :** affected by or as if by rust; *esp* : stiff with or as if with rust **2 :** inept and slow through lack of practice or old age **3 a :** of the color rust **b :** dulled in color or appearance by age and use ⟨a ∼ old suit of clothes⟩ **4 :** OUTMODED **5** : HOARSE, GRATING — **rust·i·ly** \-tə-lē\ *adv* — **rust·i·ness** \-tē-nəs\ *n*

²rus·ty \'rəs-tē\ *adj* **rus·ti·er; -est** [alter. of *restive*] *chiefly dial* (1709) : ILL-NATURED, SURLY

¹rut \'rət\ *n* [ME *rutte*, fr. MF *rut* roar, fr. LL *rugitus*, fr. L *rugitus*, pp. of *rugire* to roar; akin to OE *rēoc* wild, MIr *rucht* roar] (15c) **1 :** an annually recurrent state of sexual excitement in the male deer; *broadly* : sexual excitement in a mammal (as estrus in the female) esp. when periodic **2 :** the period during which rut normally occurs — often used with *the*

²rut *vi* **rut·ted; rut·ting** (1625) : to be in or enter into a state of rut

³rut *n* [perh. modif. of MF *route* way, route] (1580) **1 a :** a track worn by a wheel or by habitual passage **b :** a groove in which something runs **c :** CHANNEL, FURROW **2 :** a usual or fixed practice; *esp* : a monotonous routine ⟨fall easily into a conversational ∼⟩

⁴rut *vt* **rut·ted; rut·ting** (1607) : to make a rut in : FURROW

ru·ta·ba·ga \ˌrüt-ə-'bā-gə, ˌrüt-, -'beg-ə; 'rüt-ə-ˌ, 'rüt-ə-ˌ\ *n* [Sw dial. *rotabagge*, fr. *rot* root + *bagge* bag] (1799) : a turnip (*Brassica napobrassica*) that usu. produces a very large yellowish root

ruth \'rüth\ *n* [ME *ruthe*, fr. *ruen* to rue] (12c) **1 :** compassion for the misery of another **2 :** sorrow for one's own faults : REMORSE

Ruth \'rüth\ *n* [Heb *Rūth*] **1 :** a Moabite woman who accompanied Naomi to Bethlehem and became the ancestress of David **2 :** a short narrative book of canonical Jewish and Christian Scriptures — see BIBLE table

ru·the·ni·um \rü-'thē-nē-əm\ *n* [NL, fr. ML *Ruthenia* Russia] (1848) : a hard brittle grayish polyvalent rare metallic element occurring in platinum ores and used in hardening platinum alloys — see ELEMENT table

ruth·er·ford·ium \ˌrəth-ə(r)-'fō(ə)rd-ē-əm\ *n* [Ernest *Rutherford* + *-ium*] (1969) : UNNILQUADIUM

ruth·ful \'rüth-fəl\ *adj* (13c) **1 :** full of ruth : TENDER **2 :** full of sorrow : WOEFUL **3 :** causing sorrow — **ruth·ful·ly** \-fə-lē\ *adv* — **ruth·ful·ness** *n*

ruth·less \'rüth-ləs\ *also* **'rüth-** *adj* (14c) : having no ruth : MERCILESS, CRUEL — **ruth·less·ly** *adv* — **ruth·less·ness** *n*

ru·ti·lant \'rüt-ᵊl-ənt\ *adj* [ME *rutilaunt*, fr. L *rutilant-, rutilans*, pp. of *rutilare* to be reddish, fr. *rutilus* reddish; akin to L *ruber* red — more at RED] (15c) : having a reddish glow

ru·tile \'rü-ˌtēl\ *n* [G *rutil*, fr. L *rutilus*] (1803) : a mineral TiO₂ that consists of titanium dioxide usu. with a little iron, is typically of a reddish brown color but sometimes deep red or black, and has a brilliant metallic or adamantine luster

rut·tish \'rət-ish\ *adj* (1601) : inclined to rut : LUSTFUL — **rut·tish·ly** *adv* — **rut·tish·ness** *n*

rut·ty \'rət-ē\ *adj* **rut·ti·er; -est** (1596) : full of ruts

R-value \'är-ˌval-(ˌ)yü, -ˌval-, -yə(-w)\ *n* [prob. fr. thermal *r*esistance] (1948) : a measure of the ability of a substance or combination of substances (as building material or insulation) to retard the flow of heat with higher numbers indicating better insulating properties

Rx \'är-'eks\ *n* [alter. of ℞ symbol used at the beginning of a prescription, abbr. for L *recipe*, lit., take — more at RECIPE] (1926) : a medical prescription

-ry \rē\ *n suffix* [ME *-rie*, fr. OF, short for *-erie -ery*] : -ERY ⟨*wizardry*⟩ ⟨*citizenry*⟩ ⟨*ancientry*⟩

rya \'rē-ə\ *n* [*Rya*, village in southwest Sweden] (1945) : a Scandinavian handwoven rug with a deep resilient comparatively flat pile; *also* : the weave typical of this rug

¹rye \'rī\ *n* [ME, fr. OE *ryge*; akin to OHG *rocko* rye, Lith *rugys*] (bef. 12c) **1 :** a hardy annual grass (*Secale cereale*) that is widely grown for grain and as a cover crop **2 :** the seeds of rye **3 :** RYE BREAD **4 :** RYE WHISKEY

²rye *n* [Romany *rai*, fr. Skt *rājan* king — more at ROYAL] (1851) : a male Gypsy

rye bread *n* (1579) : bread made wholly or in part of rye flour; *esp* : a light bread often with caraway seeds

rye·grass \'rī-ˌgras\ *n* (1747) : any of several grasses (genus *Lolium*); *esp* : either of two grasses (*L. perenne* and *L. multiflorum*) that are used esp. for pasture and as cover crops in the southern U.S. and in New Zealand

rye whiskey *n* (1785) : a whiskey distilled from rye or from rye and malt

S

s \ˈes\ *n, pl* **s's** *or* **ss** \ˈes-əz\, *often cap, often attrib* **1 a :** the 19th letter of the English alphabet **b :** a graphic representation of this letter **c :** a speech counterpart of orthographic *s* **2 :** a graphic device for reproducing the letter *s* **3 :** one designated *s* esp. as the 19th in order or class **4** [abbr. for *satisfactory*] **a :** a grade rating a student's work as satisfactory **b :** one graded or rated with an S **5 :** something shaped like the letter S

[1]**-s** \s *after a voiceless consonant sound,* z *after a voiced consonant sound or a vowel sound*\ *n pl suffix* [ME *-es, -s,* fr. OE *-as,* nom. & acc. pl. ending of some masc. nouns; akin to OS *-os*] — used to form the plural of most nouns that do not end in *s, z, sh, ch,* or postconsonantal *y* ⟨head*s*⟩ ⟨book*s*⟩ ⟨boy*s*⟩ ⟨belief*s*⟩, to form the plural of proper nouns that end in postconsonantal *y* ⟨Mary*s*⟩, and with or without a preceding apostrophe to form the plural of abbreviations, numbers, letters, and symbols used as nouns ⟨MC*s*⟩ ⟨Ph.D.'*s*⟩ ⟨4*s*⟩ ⟨the 1940'*s*⟩ ⟨$*s*⟩ ⟨B'*s*⟩; compare [1]-ES

[2]**-s** *adv suffix* [ME *-es, -s,* pl. ending of nouns, fr. *-es,* gen. sing. ending of nouns (functioning adverbially), fr. OE *-es*] — used to form adverbs denoting usual or repeated action or state ⟨always at home Sunday*s*⟩ ⟨morning*s* he stops by the newsstand⟩

[3]**-s** *vb suffix* [ME (Northern & North Midland dial.) *-es,* fr. OE (Northumbrian dial.) *-es, -as,* prob. fr. OE *-es, -as,* 2d sing. pres. indic. ending — more at -EST] — used to form the third person singular present of most verbs that do not end in *s, z, sh, ch,* or postconsonantal *y* ⟨fall*s*⟩ ⟨take*s*⟩ ⟨play*s*⟩; compare [2]-ES

[1]**'s** *like* -S\ *vb* [contr. of *is, has, does*] **1 a :** IS ⟨she'*s* here⟩ **b :** WAS ⟨when'*s* the last time you ate?⟩ **2 :** HAS ⟨he'*s* seen them⟩ **3 :** DOES ⟨what'*s* he want?⟩

[2]**'s** \s\ *pron* [by contr.] **:** US — used with *let* ⟨let'*s*⟩

-'s \s *after voiceless consonant sounds other than* s, sh, ch; z *after vowel sounds and voiced consonant sounds other than* z, zh, j; əz *after* s, sh, ch, z, zh, j\ *n suffix or pron suffix* [ME *-es, -s,* gen. sing. ending, fr. OE *-es;* akin to OHG *-es,* gen. sing. ending, Gk *-oio, -ou,* Skt *-asya*] — used to form the possessive of singular nouns ⟨boy'*s*⟩, of plural nouns not ending in *s* ⟨children'*s*⟩, of some pronouns ⟨anyone'*s*⟩, and of word groups functioning as nouns ⟨the man in the corner'*s* hat⟩ or pronouns ⟨someone else'*s*⟩

Saa·nen \ˈsän-ən, ˈzän-\ *n* [*Saanen,* locality in southwest Switzerland] (1906) **:** any of a Swiss breed of usu. white and hornless short-haired dairy goats

saba·dil·la \ˌsab-ə-ˈdil-ə, -ˈdē-(y)ə\ *n* [Sp *cebadilla*] (1812) **:** a Mexican plant (*Schoenocaulon officinalis*) of the lily family; *also* **:** its seeds that are used as a source of veratrine and in insecticides

sa·ba·yon \sä-bä-yō^{n}\ *n* [F, modif. of It *zabaione* — more at ZABAGLIONE] (1906) **:** ZABAGLIONE

sab·bat \ˈsab-ət, sa-ˈbä\ *n, often cap* [F, lit., sabbath, fr. L *sabbatum*] (1652) **:** a midnight assembly of diabolists (as witches and sorcerers) held esp. in medieval and Renaissance times to renew allegiance to the devil through mystic rites and orgies

[1]**Sab·ba·tar·i·an** \ˌsab-ə-ˈter-ē-ən\ *n* [L *sabbatarius,* fr. *sabbatum* sabbath] (1613) **1 :** one who observes the Sabbath on Saturday in conformity with the letter of the fourth commandment **2 :** an adherent of Sabbatarianism

[2]**Sabbatarian** *adj* (1631) **1 :** of or relating to the Sabbath **2 :** of or relating to Sabbatarians or Sabbatarianism

Sab·ba·tar·i·an·ism \-ˌiz-əm\ *n* (1673) **:** strict and often rigorous observance of the Sabbath

Sab·bath \ˈsab-əth\ *n* [ME *sabat,* fr. OF & OE, fr. L *sabbatum,* fr. Gk *sabbaton,* fr. Heb *shabbāth,* lit., rest] (bef. 12c) **1 a :** the seventh day of the week observed from Friday evening to Saturday evening as a day of rest and worship by Jews and some Christians **b :** Sunday observed among Christians as a day of rest and worship **2 :** a time of rest

[1]**sab·bat·i·cal** \sə-ˈbat-i-kəl\ *or* **sab·bat·ic** \-ik\ *adj* [LL *sabbaticus,* fr. Gk *sabbatikos,* fr. *sabbaton*] (1645) **1 :** of or relating to the sabbath ⟨~ laws⟩ **2 :** of or relating to a sabbatical year

[2]**sabbatical** *n* (ca. 1903) **1 :** SABBATICAL YEAR 2 **2 :** LEAVE 1b **3 :** a break or change from a normal routine (as of employment)

sabbatical year *n* (1635) **1** *often cap S* **:** a year of rest for the land observed every seventh year in ancient Judea **2 :** a leave often with pay granted usu. every seventh year (as to a college professor) for rest, travel, or research — called also *sabbatical leave*

Sa·bel·li·an \sə-ˈbel-ē-ən\ *n* [L *Sabellus* Sabine] (1601) **1 :** a member of one of a group of early Italian peoples including Sabines and Samnites **2 :** one or all of several little known languages or dialects of ancient Italy presumably closely related to Oscan and Umbrian — see INDO-EUROPEAN LANGUAGES table — **Sabellian** *adj*

[1]**sa·ber** *or* **sa·bre** \ˈsā-bər\ *n* [F *sabre,* modif. of G dial. *sabel,* fr. MHG, of Slav origin; akin to Russ *sablya* saber] (1680) **1 :** a cavalry sword with a curved blade, thick back, and guard **2 a :** a light fencing or dueling sword having an arched guard that covers the back of the hand and a tapering flexible blade with a full cutting edge along one side and a partial cutting edge on the back at the tip — compare ÉPÉE, FOIL **b :** the sport of fencing with the saber

[2]**saber** *or* **sabre** *vt* **sa·bered** *or* **sa·bred; sa·ber·ing** *or* **sa·bring** \-b(ə-)riŋ\ (1790) **:** to strike, cut, or kill with a saber

saber rattling *n* (1922) **:** ostentatious display of military power

saber saw *n* (1953) **:** a light portable electric saw with a pointed reciprocating blade

sa·ber–toothed \ˌsā-bər-ˈtütht\ *adj* (1849) **:** having long sharp canine teeth

saber–toothed tiger \-ˌtüth(t)-\ *n* (1849) **:** any of numerous extinct cats (as genus *Smilodon*) widely distributed from the Oligocene through the Pleistocene and characterized by extreme development of the upper canines into curved swordlike piercing or slashing weapons

sa·bin \ˈsā-bən\ *n* [Wallace C. W. *Sabine* †1919 Am. physicist] (1934) **:** a unit of acoustic absorption equivalent to the absorption by one square foot of a perfect absorber

Sa·bine \ˈsā-ˌbīn, *esp Brit* ˈsab-ˌīn\ *n* [ME *Sabin,* fr. L *Sabinus*] (14c) **1 :** a member of an ancient people of the Apennines northeast of Latium **2 :** the Italic language of the Sabine people — **Sabine** *adj*

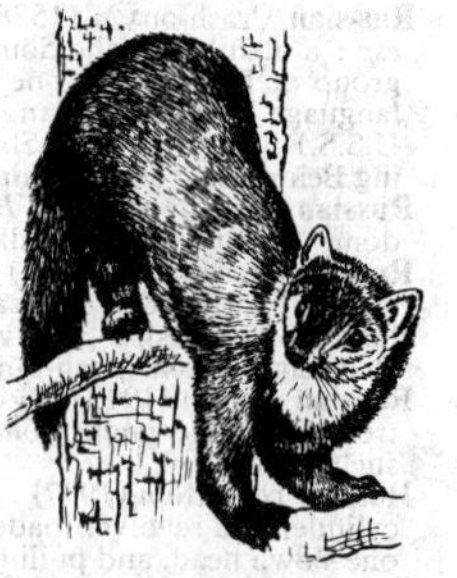

sable 2a

[1]**sa·ble** \ˈsā-bəl\ *n, pl* **sables** [ME, sable or its fur, the heraldic color black, black, fr. MF, sable or its fur, the heraldic color black, fr. MLG *sabel* sable or its fur, fr. MHG *zobel,* of Slav origin; akin to Russ *sobol'* sable or its fur] (14c) **1 a :** the color black **b :** black clothing worn in mourning — usu. used in pl. **2 a** *or pl* **sable (1) :** a carnivorous mammal (*Martes zibellina*) of northern Europe and parts of northern Asia related to the martens and supplying a valuable fur **(2) :** any of various animals related to the sable **b :** the fur or pelt of a sable **3 a :** the usu. dark brown color of the fur of the sable **b :** a grayish yellowish brown

[2]**sable** *adj* (15c) **1 :** of the color black **2 :** DARK

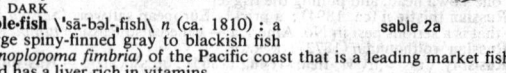

sa·ble·fish \ˈsā-bəl-ˌfish\ *n* (ca. 1810) **:** a large spiny-finned gray to blackish fish (*Anoplopoma fimbria*) of the Pacific coast that is a leading market fish and has a liver rich in vitamins

sa·bot \sa-ˈbō, ˈsab-(ˌ)ō, *for 1b also* ˈsab-ət\ *n* [F] (ca. 1607) **1 a :** a wooden shoe worn in various European countries **b (1) :** a strap across the instep in a shoe esp. of the sandal type **(2) :** a shoe having a sabot strap **2 :** a thrust-transmitting carrier that positions a missile in a gun barrel or launching tube and that prevents the escape of gas ahead of the missile

[1]**sab·o·tage** \ˈsab-ə-ˌtäzh\ *n* [F, fr. *saboter* to clatter with sabots, botch, sabotage, fr. *sabot*] (ca. 1891) **1 :** destruction of an employer's property (as tools or materials) or the hindering of manufacturing by discontented workers **2 :** destructive or obstructive action carried on by a civilian or enemy agent designed to hinder a nation's war effort **3 a :** an act or process tending to hamper or hurt **b :** deliberate subversion

[2]**sabotage** *vt* **-taged; -tag·ing** (ca. 1913) **:** to practice sabotage on

sab·o·teur \ˌsab-ə-ˈtər, -ˈt(y)ů(ə)r\ *n* [F, fr. *saboter*] (1921) **:** one that commits sabotage

sa·bra \ˈsäb-rə\ *n, often cap* [NHeb *ṣabhār,* lit., prickly pear] (1945) **:** a native-born Israeli

sac \ˈsak\ *n* [F, lit., bag, fr. L *saccus* — more at SACK] (1741) **:** a pouch within an animal or plant often containing a fluid ⟨a synovial ~⟩ — **sac·like** \-ˌlīk\ *adj*

sa·ca·huis·te \ˌsak-ə-ˈwis-tə, ˌsäk-, -tē\ *n* [AmerSp *zacahuiscle,* of Amer-Ind origin; akin to Nahuatl *zacatl* coarse grass] (1896) **:** a bear grass (*Nolina texana*) with long linear leaves that is used for forage

sac·a·ton \ˈsak-ə-ˌtōn\ *n* [AmerSp *zacatón,* fr. *zacate* coarse grass, fr. Nahuatl *zacatl*] (1846) **:** a coarse perennial grass (*Sporobolus wrightii*) of the southwestern U.S. that is used for hay in alkaline regions

sac·cade \sa-ˈkäd\ *n* [F, twitch, jerk, fr. MF, fr. *saquer* to pull, draw] (1938) **:** a small rapid jerky movement of the eye esp. as it jumps from fixation on one point to another (as in reading) — **sac·cad·ic** \-ˈkäd-ik\ *adj*

sac·cate \ˈsak-ˌāt\ *adj* [NL *saccatus,* fr. L *saccus*] (1830) **:** having the form of a sac or pouch ⟨~ pollen grains⟩

sacchar- *or* **sacchari-** *or* **saccharo-** *comb form* [L *saccharum,* fr. Gk *sakcharon,* fr. Pali *sakkharā,* fr. Skt *śarkarā* gravel, sugar] **:** sugar ⟨*sacchar*ic⟩ ⟨*sacchari*fy⟩ ⟨*saccharo*meter⟩

sac·cha·rase \ˈsak-ə-ˌrās, -ˌrāz\ *n* [ISV] (1920) **:** INVERTASE

sac·cha·ride \ˈsak-ə-ˌrīd\ *n* (1862) **:** a simple sugar, combination of sugars, or polymerized sugar **:** CARBOHYDRATE

sac·char·i·fi·ca·tion \sə-ˌkar-ə-fə-ˈkā-shən\ *n* (1839) **:** the process of breaking a complex carbohydrate (as starch or cellulose) into simple sugars — **sac·char·i·fy** \sə-ˈkar-ə-ˌfī, sa-\ *vt*

sac·cha·rim·e·ter \ˌsak-ə-ˈrim-ət-ər\ *n* [ISV] (1874) **:** a device for measuring the amount of sugar in a solution; *esp* **:** a polarimeter so used

sac·cha·rin \ˈsak-(ə-)rən\ *n* [ISV] (1885) **:** a crystalline compound $C_7H_5NO_3S$ that is unrelated to the carbohydrates, is several hundred times sweeter than cane sugar, and is used as a calorie-free sweetener

sac·cha·rine \ˈsak-(ə-)rən, -ə-ˌrēn, -ə-ˌrīn\ *adj* [L *saccharum*] (ca. 1674) **1 a :** of, relating to, or resembling that of sugar ⟨~ taste⟩ **b :** yielding or containing sugar ⟨~ vegetables⟩ **2 :** overly or sickishly sweet ⟨~ flavor⟩ **3 :** ingratiatingly or affectedly agreeable or friendly **4 :** overly sentimental **:** MAWKISH — **sac·cha·rin·i·ty** \ˌsak-ə-ˈrin-ət-ē\ *n*

sac·cha·roi·dal \ˌsak-ə-ˈrȯid-^{ə}l\ *adj* (1838) **:** having or being a fine granular texture like that of loaf sugar ⟨~ marble⟩

sac·cha·rom·e·ter \-ˈräm-ət-ər\ *n* (1784) **:** SACCHARIMETER; *esp* **:** a hydrometer with a special scale

sac·cha·ro·my·ces \-rō-ˈmī-(ˌ)sēz\ *n* [NL, fr. *sacchar-* + *-myces* fungus, fr. Gk *mykēs* — more at MYC-] (1873) **:** any of a genus (*Saccharomyces*) family Saccharomycetaceae) of usu. unicellular yeasts (as a brewer's yeast) that are distinguished by their sparse or absent mycelium and by their facility in reproducing asexually by budding

sac·cu·lar \ˈsak-yə-lər\ *adj* (1861) **:** resembling a sac ⟨a ~ aneurysm⟩

sac·cu·lat·ed \-ˌlāt-əd\ *also* **sac·cu·late** \-ˌlāt, -lət\ *adj* (1835) **:** having or formed of a series of saccular expansions — **sac·cu·la·tion** \ˌsak-yə-ˈlā-shən\ *n*

sac·cule \ˈsak-(ˌ)yü(ə)l\ *n* [NL *sacculus,* fr. L, dim. of *saccus* bag — more at SACK] (ca. 1836) **:** a little sac; *specif* **:** the smaller chamber of the membranous labyrinth of the ear

sac·cu·lus \ˈsak-yə-ləs\ *n, pl* **-li** \-ˌlī, -ˌlē\ [NL] (1748) **:** SACCULE

sac·er·do·tal \ˌsas-ər-ˈdōt-^{ə}l, ˌsak-\ *adj* [ME, fr. MF, fr. L *sacerdotalis,* fr. *sacerdot-, sacerdos* priest, fr. *sacer* sacred + *-dot-, -dos* (akin to *facere* to make) — more at SACRED, DO] (15c) **1 :** of or relating to priests or a priesthood **:** PRIESTLY **2 :** of, relating to, or suggesting sacerdotalism — **sac·er·do·tal·ly** \-^{ə}l-ē\ *adv*

sac·er·do·tal·ism \-^{ə}l-ˌiz-əm\ *n* (1856) **:** religious belief emphasizing the powers of priests as essential mediators between God and man — **sac·er·do·tal·ist** \-^{ə}l-əst\ *n*

sac fungus *n* (ca. 1929) **:** ASCOMYCETE

sa·chem \ˈsā-chəm, ˈsach-əm\ *n* [Narraganset *sachima*] (1622) **1 :** a No. American Indian chief; *esp* **:** the chief of a confederation of the

Algonquian tribes of the north Atlantic coast 2 : a Tammany leader — **sa·chem·ic** \sā-'chem-ik, sa-\ *adj*
Sa·cher torte \ˌsäk-ər-, ˌzäk-\ *n* [G *sachertorte,* fr. *Sacher* (name of a family of 19th and 20th cent. Austrian restaurant proprietors) + G *torte* torte] (1906) : a rich chocolate torte with an apricot jam filling
sa·chet \sa-'shā\ *n* [F, fr. OF, dim. of *sac* bag — more at SAC] (15c) **1** : a small bag or packet **2** : a small bag containing a perfumed powder or potpourri used to scent clothes and linens — **sa·cheted** \-'shād\ *adj*
1sack \'sak\ *n* [ME *sak* bag, sackcloth, fr. OE *sacc,* fr. L *saccus* bag & LL *saccus* sackcloth, both fr. Gk *sakkos* bag, sackcloth, of Sem origin; akin to Heb *śaq* bag, sackcloth] (bef. 12c) **1** : a usu. rectangular-shaped bag (as of paper, burlap, or canvas) **2** : the amount contained in a sack; *esp* : a fixed amount of a commodity used as a unit of measure **3 a** : a woman's loose-fitting dress **b** : a short usu. loose-fitting coat for women and children **c** : SACQUE 2 **4** : DISMISSAL ⟨the lazy worker got the ~⟩ **5 a** : HAMMOCK, BUNK **b** : BED **6** : a base in baseball **7** : an instance of sacking the quarterback in football — **sack·ful** \-ˌfu̇l\ *n*
2sack *vt* (14c) **1** : to put in or as if in a sack **2** : to dismiss esp. summarily **3** : to tackle (the quarterback) behind the line of scrimmage in football — **sack·er** *n*
3sack *n* [modif. of MF *sec* dry, fr. L *siccus;* akin to OHG *sihan* to filter, Gk *hikmas* moisture] (1531) : any of several white wines imported to England from Spain and the Canary islands during the 16th and 17th centuries
4sack *vt* [MF *sachier,* fr. *sac*] (1547) **1** : to plunder (as a town) esp. after capture **2** : to strip of valuables : LOOT ***syn*** see RAVAGE — **sack·er** *n*
5sack *n* [MF *sac,* fr. OIt *sacco,* lit., bag, fr. L *saccus*] (1549) : the plundering of a captured town
sack·but \'sak-(ˌ)bət\ *n* [MF *saqueboute,* lit., hooked lance, fr. OF, fr. *saquer* to pull + *bouter* to push — more at BUTT] (1533) : the medieval and Renaissance trombone
sack·cloth \'sak-ˌ(k)lȯth\ *n* [1*sack*] (14c) **1** : a coarse cloth of goat or camel's hair or of flax, hemp, or cotton **2** : a garment of sackcloth worn as a sign of mourning or penitence
sack coat *n* (1847) : a man's jacket with a straight back
sack·ing \'sak-iŋ\ *n* (1589) : material for sacks; *esp* : a coarse fabric (as burlap or gunny)
sack out \'sak-'au̇t\ *vi* [1*sack*] (1946) : to go to bed : go to sleep
sack race *n* (1859) : a jumping race in which each contestant has his legs enclosed in a sack
sacque \'sak\ *n* [alter. of 1*sack*] (1883) **1** : SACK 3a, 3b **2** : an infant's usu. short jacket that fastens at the neck
sacr- *or* **sacro-** *comb form* [NL, fr. *sacrum,* fr. L, neut. of *sacr-, sacer* sacred] **1** : sacrum ⟨*sacral*⟩ **2** : sacral and ⟨*sacroiliac*⟩
1sa·cral \'sak-rəl, 'sā-krəl\ *adj* (1767) : of, relating to, or lying near the sacrum
2sa·cral \'sā-krəl, 'sak-rəl\ *adj* [L *sacr-, sacer* — more at SACRED] (1882) : HOLY, SACRED
sac·ra·ment \'sak-rə-mənt\ *n* [ME *sacrement, sacrament,* fr. OF & LL; OF, fr. LL *sacramentum,* fr. L, oath of allegiance, obligation, fr. *sacrare* to consecrate] (12c) **1** : a formal religious act that is sacred as a sign or symbol of a spiritual reality; *esp* : one believed to have been instituted or recognized by Jesus Christ **2** *cap* : the eucharistic elements; *specif* : BLESSED SACRAMENT
1sac·ra·men·tal \ˌsak-rə-'ment-ᵊl\ *adj* (15c) **1** : of, relating to, or having the character of a sacrament **2** : suggesting a sacrament (as in sacredness) — **sac·ra·men·tal·ly** \-ᵊl-ē\ *adv*
2sacramental *n* (1529) : an action or object (as the rosary) of ecclesiastical origin that serves to express or increase devotion
sac·ra·men·tal·ism \-ᵊl-ˌiz-əm\ *n* (1861) : belief in or use of sacramental rites, acts, or objects; *specif* : belief that the sacraments are inherently efficacious and necessary for salvation
sac·ra·men·tal·ist \-ᵊl-əst\ *n* (1840) **1** : SACRAMENTARIAN **2** : an adherent of sacramentalism
Sac·ra·men·tar·i·an \ˌsak-rə-ˌmen-'ter-ē-ən, -mən-\ *n* (1535) **1** : one who interprets sacraments as merely visible symbols **2** : SACRAMENTALIST — **Sacramentarian** *adj* — **Sac·ra·men·tar·i·an·ism** \-ē-ə-ˌniz-əm\ *n*
sa·crar·i·um \sə-'krer-ē-əm, sa-, sā-\ *n, pl* **-ia** \-ē-ə\ [ML, fr. L, pagan Roman shrine, fr. *sacr-, sacer* sacred] (1708) **1 a** : SANCTUARY 1b **b** : SACRISTY **c** : PISCINA **2** : an ancient Roman shrine or sanctuary in a temple or a home holding sacred objects
sa·cred \'sā-krəd\ *adj* [ME, fr. pp. of *sacren* to consecrate, fr. OF *sacrer,* fr. L *sacrare,* fr. *sacr-, sacer* holy, cursed; akin to L *sancire* to make sacred, Hitt *saklais* rite] (14c) **1 a** : dedicated or set apart for the service or worship of deity ⟨a tree ~ to the gods⟩ **b** : devoted exclusively to one service or use (as of a person or purpose) ⟨a fund ~ to charity⟩ **2 a** : worthy of religious veneration : HOLY **b** : entitled to reverence and respect **3** : of or relating to religion : not secular or profane ⟨~ music⟩ **4** *archaic* : ACCURSED **5 a** : UNASSAILABLE, INVIOLABLE **b** : highly valued and important ⟨a ~ responsibility⟩ — **sa·cred·ly** *adv* — **sa·cred·ness** *n*
sacred baboon *n* [fr. its veneration by the ancient Egyptians] (ca. 1891) : HAMADRYAS BABOON
sacred cow *n* [fr. the veneration of the cow by Hindus] (1921) : one that is often unreasonably immune from criticism or opposition
sacred mushroom *n* (1930) **1** : any of various New World hallucinogenic fungi (as of the genus *Psilocybe*) used esp. in some Indian ceremonies **2** : MESCAL BUTTON
1sac·ri·fice \'sak-rə-ˌfīs, -fəs *also* -ˌfīz\ *n* [ME, fr. OF, fr. L *sacrificium,* fr. *sacr-, sacer* + *facere* to make — more at DO] (13c) **1** : an act of offering to deity something precious; *esp* : the killing of a victim on an altar **2** : something offered in sacrifice **3 a** : destruction or surrender of something for the sake of something else **b** : something given up or lost ⟨the ~*s* made by parents⟩ **4** : LOSS ⟨goods sold at a ~⟩ **5** : SACRIFICE HIT
2sac·ri·fice \-ˌfīs, -ˌfīz *also* -fəs\ *vb* **-ficed; -fic·ing** *vt* (13c) **1** : to offer as a sacrifice **2** : to suffer loss of, give up, renounce, injure, or destroy esp. for an ideal, belief, or end **3** : to sell at a loss ~ *vi* **1** : to make or perform the rites of a sacrifice **2** : to make a sacrifice hit in baseball — **sac·ri·fic·er** *n*
sacrifice fly *n* (1908) : an outfield fly in baseball caught by a fielder after which a runner scores
sacrifice hit *n* (1880) : a bunt in baseball that allows a runner to advance one base while the batter is put out
sac·ri·fi·cial \ˌsak-rə-'fish-əl\ *adj* (1607) **1** : of, relating to, of the nature of, or involving sacrifice **2** : of or relating to a metal that serves as the anode and is electrolytically consumed instead of another metal that is present — **sac·ri·fi·cial·ly** \-ə-lē\ *adv*
sac·ri·lege \'sak-rə-lij\ *n* [ME, fr. MF, fr. L *sacrilegium,* fr. *sacrilegus* one who steals sacred things, fr. *sacr-, sacer* + *legere* to gather, steal — more at LEGEND] (14c) **1** : a technical and not necessarily intrinsically outrageous violation (as improper reception of a sacrament) of what is sacred because consecrated to God **2** : gross irreverence toward a hallowed person, place, or thing — **sac·ri·le·gious** \÷ˌsak-rə-'lij-əs *also* -'lēj-\ *adj* — **sac·ri·le·gious·ly** *adv* — **sac·ri·le·gious·ness** *n*
sac·ris·tan \'sak-rə-stən\ *n* [ME, fr. ML *sacristanus,* fr. L *sacr-, sacer*] (14c) : a person in charge of the sacristy and ceremonial equipment; *also* : SEXTON
sac·ris·ty \'sak-rə-stē\ *n, pl* **-ties** [ML *sacristia,* fr. *sacrista* sacristan, fr. L *sacr-, sacer*] (ca. 1656) : a room in a church where sacred vessels and vestments are kept and where the clergy vests
1sa·cro·il·i·ac \ˌsak-rō-'il-ē-ˌak, ˌsā-krō-\ *adj* [ISV] (1831) : of, relating to, or being the region of juncture of the sacrum and ilium
2sacroiliac *n* (1936) : the sacroiliac region; *also* : its firm fibrous cartilage
sac·ro·sanct \'sak-rō-ˌsaŋ(k)t\ *adj* [L *sacrosanctus,* prob. fr. *sacro sanctus* hallowed by a sacred rite] (1601) : most sacred or holy; *also* : having an imputed rather than a genuine sacred character ⟨~ institutions that have outlived their usefulness to society⟩ — **sac·ro·sanc·ti·ty** \ˌsak-rō-'saŋ(k)-tət-ē\ *n*
sa·crum \'sak-rəm, 'sā-krəm\ *n, pl* **sa·cra** \'sak-rə, 'sā-krə\ [NL, fr. LL *os sacrum* last bone of the spine, lit., holy bone, trans. of Gk *hieron osteon*] (1753) : the part of the vertebral column that is directly connected with or forms a part of the pelvis and in man consists of five united vertebrae
sad \'sad\ *adj* **sad·der; sad·dest** [ME, fr. OE *sæd* sated; akin to OHG *sat* sated, L *satis* enough] (14c) **1 a** : affected with or expressive of grief or unhappiness : DOWNCAST **b (1)** : causing or associated with grief or unhappiness : DEPRESSING ⟨~ news⟩ **(2)** : REGRETTABLE, DEPLORABLE ⟨a ~ relaxation of morals —C. W. Cunnington⟩ **c** : of little worth **2** : of a dull somber color — **sad·ly** *adv* — **sad·ness** *n*
sad·den \'sad-ᵊn\ *vb* **sad·dened; sad·den·ing** \'sad-niŋ, -ᵊn-iŋ\ *vt* (1628) : to make sad ~ *vi* : to become sad
1sad·dle \'sad-ᵊl\ *n, often attrib* [ME *sadel,* fr. OE *sadol;* akin to OHG *satul* saddle] (bef. 12c) **1 a (1)** : a girthed usu. padded and leather-covered seat for the rider of an animal (as a horse) **(2)** : a part of a driving harness comparable to a saddle that is used to keep the breeching in place **b** : a seat to be straddled by the rider of a vehicle (as a bicycle) **2** : an often shaped mounted support for an object **3 a** : a ridge connecting two higher elevations **b** : COL 2 **4 a** : both sides of the unsplit back of a carcass including both loins **b** : a colored marking on the back of an animal **c** : the rear part of a male fowl's back extending to the tail — see COCK illustration **5** : the central part of the backbone of the binding of a book **6** : a piece of leather across the instep of a shoe — **sad·dle·less** \-ᵊl-(l)əs\ *adj* — **in the saddle** : in control

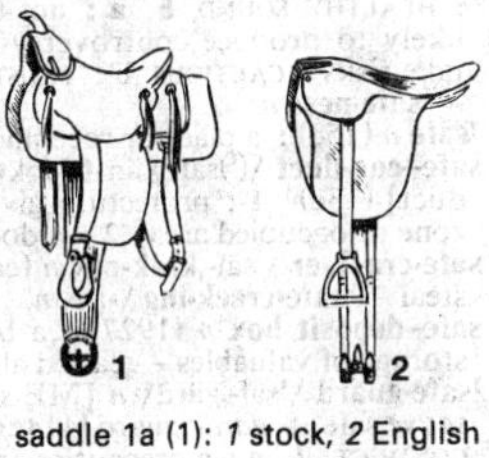
saddle 1a (1): *1* stock, *2* English

2saddle *vb* **sad·dled; sad·dling** \'sad-liŋ, -ᵊl-iŋ\ *vt* (bef. 12c) **1** : to put a saddle on **2 a** : to place under a burden or encumbrance **b** : to place (an onerous responsibility) on a person or group ~ *vi* : to mount a saddled horse
sad·dle·bag \'sad-ᵊl-ˌbag\ *n* (1773) : one of a pair of covered pouches laid across the back of a horse behind the saddle or hanging over the rear wheel of a bicycle or motorcycle
saddle blanket *n* (1737) : a folded blanket or pad under a saddle to prevent galling the horse
sad·dle·bow \'sad-ᵊl-ˌbō\ *n* (bef. 12c) : the arch in or the pieces forming the front of a saddle
sad·dle·cloth \-ˌklȯth\ *n* (15c) : a cloth placed under or over a saddle
sad·dled prominent \ˌsad-ᵊld-\ *n* [fr. the hump or prominence on the back of the larva] (1910) : a moth (*Heterocampa guttivitta*) whose larva is a serious defoliator of hardwood trees in the eastern and midwestern U.S.
saddle horn *n* (1856) : a hornlike prolongation of the pommel of a stock saddle
saddle horse *n* (1662) : a horse suited for or trained for riding
saddle leather *n* (1832) : leather made of the hide of cattle that is vegetable tanned and used for saddlery; *also* : smooth polished leather simulating this
sad·dler \'sad-lər\ *n* (14c) : one that makes, repairs, or sells saddles and other furnishings for horses
sad·dlery \'sad-lə-rē, 'sad-ᵊl-rē\ *n, pl* **-dler·ies** (15c) : the trade, articles of trade, or shop of a saddler
saddle seat *n* (1895) : a slightly concave chair seat (as of a Windsor chair) with sometimes a thickened ridge at the center front
saddle shoe *n* (1939) : an oxford-style shoe having a saddle of contrasting color or leather — called also *saddle oxford*
saddle soap *n* (1889) : a mild soap used for cleansing and conditioning leather
saddle sore *n* (1946) **1** : a gall or open sore developing on the back of a horse at points of pressure from an ill-fitting or ill-adjusted saddle **2** : an irritation or sore on parts of the rider chafed by the saddle

sad·dle·tree \ˈsad-ᵊl-ˌtrē\ *n* (15c) **:** the frame of a saddle

Sad·du·ce·an \ˌsaj-ə-ˈsē-ən, ˌsad-yə-\ *adj* (1593) **:** of or relating to the Sadducees

Sad·du·cee \ˈsaj-ə-ˌsē, ˈsad-yə-\ *n* [ME *saducee,* fr. OE *sadduce,* fr. LL *sadducaeus,* fr. Gk *saddoukaios,* fr. LHeb *ṣaddūqī*] (bef. 12c) **:** a member of a Jewish party of the intertestamental period consisting of a traditional ruling class of priests and rejecting doctrines not in the Law (as resurrection, retribution in a future life, and the existence of angels) — **Sad·du·cee·ism** \-ˌiz-əm\ *n*

sa·dhe \ˈ(t)säd-ə, -ē\ *n* [Heb *ṣādhē*] (ca. 1899) **:** the 18th letter of the Hebrew alphabet — see ALPHABET table

sa·dhu *or* **sad·dhu** \ˈsäd-(ˌ)ü\ *n* [Skt *sādhu*] (ca. 1845) **:** a usu. Hindu mendicant ascetic

sad·iron \ˈsad-ˌī(-ə)rn\ *n* [*sad* (compact, heavy) + *iron*] (ca. 1761) **:** a flatiron pointed at both ends and having a removable handle

sa·dism \sā-ˌdiz-əm, ˈsad-ˌiz-\ *n* [ISV, fr. Marquis de *Sade*] (1888) **1 :** a sexual perversion in which gratification is obtained by the infliction of physical or mental pain on others (as on a love object) — compare MASOCHISM **2 a :** delight in cruelty **b :** excessive cruelty — **sa·dist** \ˈsād-əst, ˈsad-\ *n* — **sa·dis·tic** \sə-ˈdis-tik *also* sā- *or* sa-\ *adj* — **sa·dis·ti·cal·ly** \-ti-k(ə-)lē\ *adv*

sa·do·mas·och·ism \ˌsād-(ˌ)ō-ˈmas-ə-ˌkiz-əm, ˌsad-, -ˈmaz-\ *n* [ISV *sadism* + *-o-* + *masochism*] (1922) **:** the derivation of pleasure from the infliction of physical or mental pain either on others or on oneself — **sa·do·mas·och·ist** \-kəst\ *n or adj* — **sa·do·mas·och·is·tic** \-ˌmas-ə-ˈkis-tik, -ˌmaz-\ *adj*

sad sack *n* (1943) **:** an inept person; *esp* **:** an inept soldier

Sa·far \sə-ˈfär\ *n* [Ar *ṣafar*] (ca. 1769) **:** the 2d month of the Islamic year — see MONTH table

sa·fa·ri \sə-ˈfär-ē, -ˈfar-\ *n* [Ar *safarīy* of a trip] (1896) **1 :** the caravan and equipment of a hunting expedition esp. in eastern Africa **2 :** a hunting expedition in eastern Africa **3 :** JOURNEY, EXPEDITION ⟨an arctic ~⟩ — **safari** *vi*

safari jacket *n* (1951) **:** a belted shirt jacket with pleated expansible pockets

safari suit *n* (1967) **:** a safari jacket with matching pants

[1]**safe** \ˈsāf\ *adj* **saf·er; saf·est** [ME *sauf,* fr. OF, fr. L *salvus* safe, healthy; akin to L *salus* health, safety, *salubris* healthful, *solidus* solid, Gk *holos* whole, safe] (13c) **1 :** freed from harm or risk **:** UNHURT **2 a :** secure from threat of danger, harm, or loss **b :** successful at getting to a base in baseball without being put out **3 :** affording safety or security from danger, risk, or difficulty **4** *obs, of mental or moral faculties* **:** HEALTHY, SOUND **5 a :** not threatening danger **:** HARMLESS **b :** unlikely to produce controversy or contradiction **6 a :** not likely to take risks **:** CAUTIOUS **b :** TRUSTWORTHY, RELIABLE — **safe** *or* **safe·ly** *adv* — **safe·ness** *n*

[2]**safe** *n* (15c) **:** a place or receptacle to keep articles (as valuables) safe

safe–con·duct \(ˈ)sāf-ˈkän-(ˌ)dəkt\ *n* [ME *sauf conduit,* fr. OF, safe conduct] (13c) **1 :** protection given a person passing through a military zone or occupied area **2 :** a document authorizing safe-conduct

safe·crack·er \ˈsāf-ˌkrak-ər\ *n* (ca. 1825) **:** one that breaks open safes to steal — **safe·crack·ing** \-iŋ\ *n*

safe–deposit box *n* (1927) **:** a box (as in the vault of a bank) for safe storage of valuables — called also *safety-deposit box*

[1]**safe·guard** \ˈsāf-ˌgärd\ *n* [ME *saufgarde,* fr. MF *saufegarde,* fr. OF, fr *sauve* safe + *garde* guard] (14c) **1 a :** CONVOY, ESCORT **b :** PASS, SAFE-CONDUCT **2 a :** a precautionary measure, stipulation, or device **b :** a technical contrivance to prevent accident

[2]**safeguard** *vt* (15c) **1 :** to provide a safeguard for **2 :** to make safe **:** PROTECT ***syn*** see DEFEND

safe house *n* (1946) **:** a place where one may engage in secret activities or take refuge

safe·keep·ing \ˈsāf-ˈkē-piŋ\ *n* (15c) **1 :** the act or process of preserving in safety **2 :** the state of being preserved in safety

safe·light \ˈsā-ˌflīt\ *n* (1903) **:** a darkroom lamp with a filter to screen out rays that are harmful to sensitive film or paper

[1]**safe·ty** \ˈsāf-tē\ *n, pl* **safeties** [ME *saufte,* fr. MF *sauveté,* fr. OF, fr. *sauve,* fem. of *sauf* safe] (14c) **1 :** the condition of being safe from undergoing or causing hurt, injury, or loss **2 :** a device (as on a gun, a mine, or a machine) designed to prevent inadvertent or hazardous operation **3 a (1) :** a situation in football in which a member of the offensive team is tackled behind its own goal line that counts two points for the defensive team — compare TOUCHBACK **(2) :** a member of a defensive backfield in football who occupies the deepest position in order to receive a kick, defend against a forward pass, or stop a ballcarrier — called also *safetyman* **b :** a billiard shot made with no attempt to score or so as to leave the balls in an unfavorable position for the opponent **c :** BASE HIT

[2]**safety** *vt* **safe·tied; safe·ty·ing** (1940) **:** to protect against failure, breakage, or accident ⟨~ a rifle⟩

safety belt *n* (ca. 1858) **:** a belt fastening a person to an object to prevent falling or injury

safety glass *n* (1919) **:** transparent material that is prepared by laminating a sheet of transparent plastic between sheets of clear glass and is used esp. for windows (as of automobiles) likely to be subjected to shock or impact

safety island *n* (1918) **:** an area within a roadway from which vehicular traffic is excluded (as by pavement markings or curbing)

safety lamp *n* (1816) **:** a miner's lamp constructed to avoid explosion in an atmosphere containing flammable gas usu. by enclosing the flame in fine wire gauze

safe·ty·man \ˈsāf-tē-ˌman\ *n* (1927) **:** SAFETY 3a(2)

safety match *n* (1863) **:** a match capable of being struck and ignited only on a specially prepared friction surface

safety pin *n* (1857) **:** a pin in the form of a clasp with a guard covering its point when fastened

safety razor *n* (ca. 1875) **:** a razor provided with a guard for the blade to prevent deep cuts in the skin

safety valve *n* (1813) **1 :** an automatic escape or relief valve (as for a steam boiler) **2 :** an outlet for pent-up energy or emotion **3 :** something that relieves the pressure of overcrowding

safety zone *n* (1915) **:** a safety island for pedestrians or for streetcar or bus passengers

saf·flow·er \ˈsaf-ˌlau̇(-ə)r\ *n* [MF *saffleur,* fr. OIt *saffiore,* fr. Ar *aṣfar,* a yellow plant] (1642) **:** a widely grown Old World composite herb (*Carthamus tinctorius*) with large orange or red flower heads and seeds rich in oil; *also* **:** a red dyestuff prepared from the flower heads

safflower oil *n* (ca. 1857) **:** an edible drying oil obtained from the seeds of the safflower

saf·fron \ˈsaf-rən\ *n* [ME, fr. OF *safran,* fr. ML *safranum,* fr. Ar *za'farān*] (13c) **1 :** the deep orange aromatic pungent dried stigmas of a purple-flowered crocus used to color and flavor foods and formerly as a dyestuff and in medicine **2 :** a moderate orange to orange yellow **3 :** a purple-flowered crocus (*Crocus sativus*)

saf·ra·nine \ˈsaf-rə-ˌnēn, -nən\ *or* **saf·ra·nin** \-nən\ *n* [ISV, fr. F or G *safran* saffron] (1868) **1 :** any of various usu. red synthetic dyes that are amino derivatives of bases **2 :** any of various mixtures of safranine salts used in dyeing and as microscopic stains

saf·role \ˈsaf-ˌrōl\ *n* [ISV, fr. G *sassafras* sassafras + *-ole*] (1869) **:** a poisonous oily cyclic ether $C_{10}H_{10}O_2$ that is the principal component of sassafras oil and is used chiefly for perfuming

[1]**sag** \ˈsag\ *vb* **sagged; sag·ging** [ME *saggen,* prob. of Scand origin; akin to Sw *sacka* to sag] *vi* (15c) **1 :** to droop, sink, or settle from or as if from pressure or loss of tautness **2 a :** to lose firmness, resiliency, or vigor ⟨spirits *sagging* from overwork⟩ **b :** to decline esp. from a thriving state **3 :** DRIFT **4 :** to fail to stimulate or retain interest **~** *vt* **:** to cause to sag **:** leave slack in

[2]**sag** *n* (1580) **1 :** a tendency to drift (as of a ship to leeward) **2 a :** a sagging part ⟨the ~ in a rope⟩ **b :** a drop or depression below the surrounding area **c :** an instance or amount of sagging ⟨~ is inevitable in a heavy unsupported span⟩ **3 :** a temporary economic decline (as in the price of a commodity)

sa·ga \ˈsäg-ə *also* ˈsag-\ *n* [ON — more at SAW] (1709) **1 :** a prose narrative recorded in Iceland in the 12th and 13th centuries of historic or legendary figures and events of the heroic age of Norway and Iceland **2 :** a modern heroic narrative resembling the Icelandic saga **3 :** a long detailed account ⟨the ~ of the winning of the West⟩

sa·ga·cious \sə-ˈgā-shəs, sig-ˈā-\ *adj* [L *sagac-, sagax* sagacious; akin to L *sagire* to perceive keenly — more at SEEK] (1607) **1** *obs* **:** keen in sense perception **2 a :** of keen and farsighted penetration and judgment **:** DISCERNING ⟨~ judge of character⟩ **b :** caused by or indicating acute discernment ⟨~ purchase of stock⟩ ***syn*** see SHREWD — **sa·ga·cious·ly** *adv* — **sa·ga·cious·ness** *n*

sa·gac·i·ty \sə-ˈgas-ət-ē, sig-ˈas-\ *n* (1548) **:** the quality of being sagacious

sag·a·more \ˈsag-ə-ˌmō(ə)r, -ˌmȯ(ə)r\ *n* [Abnaki *sāgimau,* lit., he prevails over] (1613) **1 :** a subordinate chief of the Algonquian Indians of the north Atlantic coast **2 :** SACHEM 1

saga novel *n* (1938) **:** ROMAN-FLEUVE

[1]**sage** \ˈsāj\ *adj* **sag·er; sag·est** [ME, fr. OF, fr. (assumed) VL *sapius,* fr. L *sapere* to taste, have good taste, be wise; akin to OE *sefa* mind, Oscan *sipus* knowing] (13c) **1 a :** wise through reflection and experience **b** *archaic* **:** GRAVE, SOLEMN **2 :** proceeding from or characterized by wisdom, prudence, and good judgment ⟨~ counsel⟩ ***syn*** see WISE — **sage·ly** *adv* — **sage·ness** *n*

[2]**sage** *n* (14c) **1 :** one (as a profound philosopher) distinguished for wisdom **2 :** a mature or venerable man of sound judgment

[3]**sage** *n* [ME, fr. MF *sauge,* fr. L *salvia,* fr. *salvus* healthy; fr. its use as a medicinal herb — more at SAFE] (14c) **1 :** a mint (*Salvia officinalis*) with grayish green aromatic leaves used esp. in flavoring meats; *broadly* **:** SALVIA **2 :** SAGEBRUSH

sage·brush \ˈsāj-ˌbrəsh\ *n* (1852) **:** any of several No. American hoary composite subshrubs (genus *Artemisia*); *esp* **:** a common plant (*A. tridentata*) having a bitter juice and an odor resembling sage and often covering vast tracts of alkaline plains in the western U.S.

sage cheese *n* (1699) **:** a cheese similar to mild cheddar flecked with green and flavored with sage

sage grouse *n* (1876) **:** a large grouse (*Centrocercus urophasianus*) of the dry sagebrush plains of western No. America that has mottled gray and buff plumage with a contrasting black belly

sag·ger *or* **sag·gar** \ˈsag-ər\ *n* [prob. alter. of *safeguard*] (1768) **:** a box made of fireclay in which delicate ceramic pieces are fired

sag·it·tal \ˈsaj-ət-ᵊl\ *adj* [L *sagitta* arrow] (1541) **1 :** of or relating to the suture between the parietal bones of the skull **2 :** of, relating to, situated in, or being the median plane of the body or any plane parallel thereto — **sag·it·tal·ly** \-ᵊl-ē\ *adv*

Sag·it·tar·i·an \ˌsaj-ə-ˈter-ē-ən\ *n* (1911) **:** SAGITTARIUS 2b

Sag·it·tar·i·us \-ē-əs\ *n* [L (gen. *Sagittarii*), lit., archer, fr. *sagitta*] **1 :** a southern constellation pictured as a centaur shooting an arrow **2 a :** the 9th sign of the zodiac in astrology — see ZODIAC table **b :** one born under this sign

sag·it·tate \ˈsaj-ə-ˌtāt\ *adj* [L *sagitta*] (1760) **:** shaped like an arrowhead; *specif* **:** elongated, triangular, and having the two basal lobes prolonged downward ⟨~ leaf⟩

sa·go \ˈsā-(ˌ)gō\ *n, pl* **sagos** [Malay *sagu* sago palm] (1580) **:** a dry granulated or powdered starch prepared from the pith of a sago palm and used in foods and as textile stiffening

sago palm *n* (1769) **:** a plant that yields sago; *esp* **:** any of various lofty pinnate-leaved Indian and Malaysian palms (genus *Metroxylon*)

sa·gua·ro \sə-ˈwär-ə, -ˈ(g)wär-(ˌ)ō\ *n, pl* **-ros** [MexSp] (1856) **:** an arborescent cactus (*Carnegiea gigantea*) of desert regions of the southwestern U.S. and Mexico that has a tall columnar simple or sparsely branched trunk of up to 60 feet and bears white flowers and edible fruit — called also *saguaro cactus*

sa·hib \ˈsä-ˌ(h)ib, -ˌ(h)ēb, ˌsä-ˈ\ *n* [Hindi *ṣāhib,* fr. Ar] (1673) **:** SIR, MASTER — used esp. among Hindus and Muslims in colonial India when addressing or speaking of a European of some social or official status

said \ˈsed\ *adj* [pp. of *say*] (14c) **:** AFOREMENTIONED

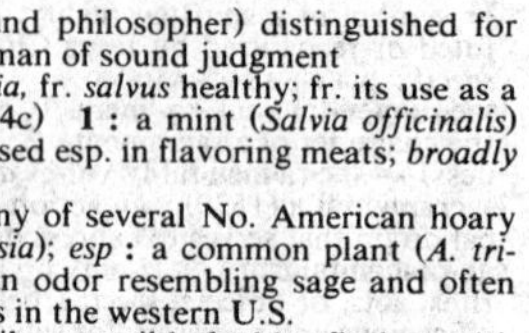

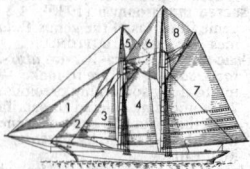

sail 1a (of a schooner): *1* flying jib, *2* jib, *3* forestaysail, *4* foresail, *5* fore gaff-topsail, *6* main-topmast staysail, *7* mainsail, *8* main gaff-topsail

[1]**sail** \'sā(ə)l, *as last element in compounds often* səl\ *n* [ME, fr. OE *segl;* akin to OHG *segal* sail, L *secare* to cut — more at SAW] (bef. 12c) **1 a** (1) : an extent of fabric (as canvas) by means of which wind is used to propel a ship through water (2) : the sails of a ship **b** *pl usu* **sail** : a ship equipped with sails **2 :** an extent of fabric used in propelling a wind-driven vehicle (as an iceboat) **3 :** something that resembles a sail **4 :** a passage by a sailing ship : CRUISE — **sailed** \'sā(ə)ld\ *adj* — **under sail :** in motion with sails set

[2]**sail** *vi* (bef. 12c) **1 a :** to travel on water in a ship **b :** YACHT **2 a :** to travel on water by the action of wind upon sails or by other means **b :** to move or proceed easily, gracefully, or without resistance ⟨she ~*ed* into the room⟩ ⟨the bill ~*ed* through the legislature⟩ **3 :** to begin a water voyage ⟨~ with the tide⟩ ~ *vt* **1 a :** to travel on (water) by means of motive power (as sail) **b :** to glide through **2 :** to direct or manage the motion of (as a ship) — **sail·able** \'sā-lə-bəl\ *adj* — **sail into :** to attack vigorously or sharply ⟨*sailed into* his dinner⟩ ⟨*sailed into* me for being late⟩

sail·board \'sā(ə)l-ˌbō(ə)rd, -ˌbȯ(ə)rd\ *n* (1962) : a small flat sailboat that is designed for one or two passengers

sail·boat \'sā(ə)l-ˌbōt\ *n* (1798) : a boat usu. propelled by sail — **sail·boat·er** \-ər\ *n* — **sail·boat·ing** \-iŋ\ *n*

sail·cloth \-ˌklȯth\ *n* (13c) : a heavy canvas used for sails, tents, or upholstery; *also* : a lightweight canvas used for clothing

sail·er \'sā-lər\ *n* (1582) : a ship or boat esp. having specified sailing qualities

sail·fish \'sā(ə)l-ˌfish\ *n* (1591) : any of a genus (*Istiophorus*) of large pelagic fishes related to the swordfish but having teeth, scales, and a very large dorsal fin

sail·ing \'sā-liŋ\ *n* (bef. 12c) **1 a :** the technical skill of managing a ship : NAVIGATION **b :** the method of determining the course to be followed to reach a given point **2 a :** the sport of handling or riding in a sailboat **b :** a departure from a port

sail·or \'sā-lər\ *n* [alter. of *sailer*] (1642) **1 a :** one that sails; *esp* : MARINER **b** (1) : a member of a ship's crew (2) : SEAMAN 2b **2 :** a traveler by water **3 :** a stiff straw hat with a low flat crown and straight circular brim

sailor collar *n* (1895) : a broad collar having a square flap across the back and tapering to a V in the front

sail·or's–choice \ˌsā-lərz-'chȯis\ *n* (1850) : any of several small grunts of the Western Atlantic: as **a :** PINFISH **b :** PIGFISH

sail·plane \'sā(ə)l-ˌplān\ *n* (1922) : a glider of such design that it is able to rise in an upward air current — **sailplane** *vi* — **sail·plan·er** *n*

sai·min \'sī-'min\ *n* [prob. fr. Chin (Cant) *sai mîn,* lit., fine noodles] (1949) : a Hawaiian noodle soup

sain \'sān\ *vt* [ME *sainen,* fr. OE *segnian,* fr. LL *signare,* fr. L, to mark — more at SIGN] (bef. 12c) **1** *dial Brit* : to make the sign of the cross on (oneself) **2** *dial Brit* : BLESS

sain·foin \'san-ˌfȯin, 'san-\ *n* [F, fr. MF, fr. *sain* healthy (fr. L *sanus*) + *foin* hay, fr. L *fenum*] (1626) : a pink-flowered perennial leguminous forage herb (*Onobrychis viciaefolia*) of Eurasia that has been introduced elsewhere

[1]**saint** \'sānt, *before a name* (ˌ)sānt *or* sənt\ *n* [ME, fr. OF, fr. LL *sanctus,* fr. L, sacred, fr. pp. of *sancire* to make sacred — more at SACRED] (12c) **1 :** one officially recognized esp. through canonization as preeminent for holiness **2 a :** one of the spirits of the departed in heaven **b** : ANGEL 1a **3 a :** one of God's chosen and usu. Christian people **b** *cap* : a member of any of various Christian bodies; *specif* : LATTER-DAY SAINT **4 :** one eminent for piety or virtue **5 :** an illustrious predecessor — **saint·dom** \'sānt-dəm\ *n* — **saint·like** \'sānt-ˌlīk\ *adj*

[2]**saint** \'sānt\ *vt* (13c) : to recognize or designate as a saint; *specif* : CANONIZE

Saint Ag·nes' Eve \-ˌag-nəs-(əz-)'ēv\ *n* [*St. Agnes*] (1820) : the night of January 20 when a woman is traditionally held to have a revelation of her future husband

Saint An·drew's cross \-ˌan-ˌdrüz-\ *n* [*St. Andrew* †*ab* A.D. 60, apostle who, according to tradition, was crucified on a cross of this type] (1615) : a figure of a cross that has the form of two intersecting oblique bars — see CROSS illustration

Saint An·tho·ny's cross \-ˌan(t)-thə-nēz-, *chiefly Brit* -ˌan-tə-\ *n* [*St. Anthony*] (1885) : TAU CROSS

Saint Anthony's fire *n* (1580) : any of several inflammations or gangrenous conditions (as erysipelas or ergotism) of the skin

saint au·gus·tine grass \-ˌȯ-gə-ˌstēn-\ *n, often cap S&A* [prob. fr. *St. Augustine,* Fla.] (ca. 1900) : a perennial much-branched creeping grass (*Stenotaphrum secundatum*) of the southern U.S. that is valuable as a sand binder and as sod grass

Saint Ber·nard \-bər-'närd\ *n* [the hospice of Grand *St. Bernard,* where such dogs were first bred] (1839) : any of a Swiss alpine breed of tall powerful working dogs used esp. formerly in aiding lost travelers

saint·ed \'sānt-əd\ *adj* (1598) **1 :** befitting or relating to a saint **2** : SAINTLY, PIOUS **3 :** entered into heaven : DEAD **4 :** much admired : IDOLIZED

Saint El·mo's fire \ˌsānt-ˌel-(ˌ)mōz-\ *n* [*St. Elmo* (*Erasmus*) †303 Ital. bishop & patron saint of sailors] (1814) : a flaming phenomenon sometimes seen in stormy weather at prominent points on an airplane or ship and on land that is of the nature of a brush discharge of electricity — called also *Saint Elmo's light*

Saint Emi·lion \ˌsaⁿ-tā-mēl-'yōⁿ\ *n* [*Saint-Émilion,* village in SW France] (1833) : a red Bordeaux wine

saint·hood \'sānt-ˌhu̇d\ *n* (1550) **1 :** the quality or state of being a saint **2 :** saints as a group

Saint John's bread \-'jänz-ˌbred\ *n* (ca. 1890) : CAROB 2

Saint–John's–wort \-'jänz-ˌwərt, -ˌwȯ(ə)rt\ *n* [*St. John* the Baptist] (1753) : any of a genus (*Hypericum* of the family Guttiferae, the Saint-John's-wort family) of herbs and shrubs with showy pentamerous yellow flowers

Saint Lou·is encephalitis \-ˌlü-əs-\ *n* [*St. Louis,* Mo.] (1938) : a No. American viral encephalitis that is transmitted by several culex mosquitoes

saint·ly \'sānt-lē\ *adj* (1660) : relating to, resembling, or befitting a saint : HOLY — **saint·li·ness** *n*

Saint Mar·tin's summer \-ˌmärt-ᵊn(z)-'səm-ər\ *n* [*Saint Martin's* Day, November 11] (1591) : Indian summer when occurring in November

Saint Pat·rick's Day \-'pa-triks-\ *n* (1844) : March 17 observed by the Roman Catholic Church in honor of St. Patrick and celebrated in Ireland in commemoration of his death

saint's day *n* (15c) : a day in a church calendar on which a saint is commemorated

saint·ship \'sānt-ˌship\ *n* (1631) : SAINTHOOD 1

Saint Val·en·tine's Day \-'val-ən-ˌtīnz-\ *n* [*St. Valentine* †*ab*270 Ital. priest] (14c) : February 14 observed in honor of St. Valentine and as a time for sending valentines

Saint Vi·tus' dance *also* **Saint Vitus's dance** \-ˌvīt-əs(-əz)-\ *n* [*St. Vitus,* 3d cent. Christian child martyr] (1621) : CHOREA

saith \(ˈ)seth, 'sā-əth\ *archaic pres 3d sing of* SAY

saithe \'sāth, 'sāth\ *n, pl* **saithe** [of Scand origin; akin to ON *seithr* coalfish] (1632) : POLLACK

Sai·va \'s(h)ī-və\ *n* [Skt *Śaiva,* fr. *Śiva* Siva] (1651) : a member of a major Hindu sect devoted to the cult of Siva — **Sai·vism** \-ˌviz-əm\ *n*

[1]**sake** \'sāk\ *n* [ME, dispute, guilt, purpose, fr. OE *sacu* guilt, action at law; akin to OHG *sahha* action at law, cause, OE *sēcan* to seek — more at SEEK] (13c) **1 :** END, PURPOSE ⟨for the ~ of argument⟩ **2 a :** the good, advantage, or enhancement of some entity (as an ideal) ⟨free to pursue learning for its own ~ —M. S. Eisenhower⟩ **b :** personal or social welfare, safety, or benefit

[2]**sa·ke** *or* **sa·ki** \'säk-ē\ *n* [Jp *sake*] (1687) : a Japanese alcoholic beverage of fermented rice usu. served hot

sa·ker \'sā-kər\ *n* [ME *sagre,* fr. MF *sacre,* fr. Ar *saqr*] (15c) : an Old World falcon (*Falco cherrug*) used in falconry

Sak·ti \'s(h)äk-tē\, **Saktism** *var of* SHAKTI, SHAKTISM

sal \'sal\ *n* [L — more at SALT] (14c) : SALT

[1]**sa·laam** \sə-'läm\ *n* [Ar *salām,* lit., peace] (1613) **1 :** a salutation or ceremonial greeting in the East **2 :** an obeisance performed by bowing very low and placing the right palm on the forehead

[2]**salaam** *vt* (1693) : to greet or pay homage to with a salaam ~ *vi* : to perform a salaam

sal·able *or* **sale·able** \'sā-lə-bəl\ *adj* (1530) : capable of being or fit to be sold : MARKETABLE — **sal·abil·i·ty** \ˌsā-lə-'bil-ət-ē\ *n*

sa·la·cious \sə-'lā-shəs\ *adj* [L *salac-, salax* fond of leaping, lustful, fr. *salire* to leap — more at SALLY] (1661) **1 :** arousing or appealing to sexual desire or imagination : LASCIVIOUS **2 :** LECHEROUS, LUSTFUL — **sa·la·cious·ly** *adv* — **sa·la·cious·ness** *n*

sal·ad \'sal-əd\ *n* [ME *salade,* fr. MF, fr. OProv *salada,* fr. *salar* to salt, fr. *sal* salt, fr. L — more at SALT] (15c) **1 :** a green vegetable or herb grown for salad; *esp* : LETTUCE **2 a :** green vegetables (as lettuce, endive, or romaine) and often tomatoes, cucumbers, or radishes served with dressing **b :** a dish of meat, fish, shellfish, eggs, fruits, or vegetables singly or in combination usu. served cold with a dressing **3 :** a usu. incongruous mixture : HODGEPODGE

salad bar *n* (1973) : a self-service counter in a restaurant featuring an array of salad makings and dressings

salad days *n pl* (1606) : time of youthful inexperience or indiscretion ⟨my *salad days* when I was green in judgment —Shak.⟩; *also* : an early flourishing period : HEYDAY

salad dressing *n* (1836) : a dressing either uncooked (as French dressing) or cooked (as a boiled dressing) that is used for salad

salad oil *n* (1558) : an edible vegetable oil (as olive oil) suitable for use in salad dressings

sa·lal \sə-'lal, sa-\ *n* [Chinook Jargon] (1825) : a small shrub (*Gaultheria shallon*) of the heath family found on the Pacific coast of No. America and bearing edible grape-sized dark purple berries

sal·a·man·der \'sal-ə-ˌman-dər *also* ˌsal-ə-'\ *n* [ME *salamandre,* fr. MF, fr. L *salamandra,* fr. Gk] (14c) **1 :** a mythical animal having the power to endure fire without harm **2 :** an elemental being in the theory of Paracelsus inhabiting fire **3 :** any of numerous amphibians (order Caudata) superficially resembling lizards but scaleless and covered with a soft moist skin and breathing by gills in the larval stage **4 :** an article used in connection with fire: as **a :** a cooking utensil for browning a food (as pastry or pudding) **b :** a portable stove **c :** an incinerator **d :** a stove with an overhead heat source that is used usu. to glaze a dish (as an au gratin dish) — **sal·a·man·drine** \ˌsal-ə-'man-drən\ *adj*

sa·la·mi \sə-'läm-ē\ *n* [It, pl. of *salame* salami, fr. *salare* to salt, fr. *sale* salt, fr. L *sal* — more at SALT] (1852) : highly seasoned sausage of pork and beef either dried or fresh

sal am·mo·ni·ac \ˌsal-ə-'mō-nē-ˌak\ *n* [ME *sal armoniak,* fr. L *sal ammoniacus,* lit., salt of Ammon] (14c) : AMMONIUM CHLORIDE

sa·lar·i·at \sə-'lar-ē-ət, -'ler-\ *n* [F, fr. *salaire* salary (fr. L *salarium*) + *-ariat* (as in *prolétariat* proletariat)] (1917) : the class or body of salaried persons usu. as distinguished from wage earners

sal·a·ry \'sal(-ə)-rē\ *n, pl* **-ries** [ME *salarie,* fr. L *salarium* salt money, pension, salary, fr. neut. of *salarius* of salt, fr. *sal* salt — more at SALT] (14c) : fixed compensation paid regularly for services — **sal·a·ried** \-rēd\ *adj*

sale \'sā(ə)l\ *n* [ME, fr. OE *sala,* fr. ON — more at SELL] (bef. 12c) **1 :** the act of selling; *specif* : the transfer of ownership of and title to property from one person to another for a price **2 a :** opportunity of selling or being sold : DEMAND **b :** distribution by selling **3 :** public disposal to the highest bidder : AUCTION **4 :** a selling of goods at bargain prices **5** *pl* **a :** operations and activities involved in promoting and selling goods or services ⟨vice-president in charge of ~*s*⟩ **b :** gross receipts — **for sale :** available for purchase — **on sale 1 :** for sale **2 :** available for purchase at a reduced price

sa·lep \'sal-əp, sə-'lep\ *n* [F or Sp, both fr. Ar dial. *saḥlab,* alter. of Ar (*khusy ath-*) *tha'lab,* lit., testicles of the fox] (1736) : the starchy or mucilaginous dried tubers of various Old World orchids (esp. genus *Orchis*) used for food or in medicine

sal·era·tus \ˌsal-ə-'rāt-əs\ *n* [NL *sal aeratus* aerated salt] (1837) : a leavening agent consisting of potassium or sodium bicarbonate

sale·room \'sā(ə)l-ˌrüm, -ˌru̇m\ *chiefly Brit var of* SALESROOM

\ə\ abut \ᵊ\ kitten, F table \ər\ further \a\ ash \ā\ ace \ä\ cot, cart \au̇\ out \ch\ chin \e\ bet \ē\ easy \g\ go \i\ hit \ī\ ice \j\ job \ŋ\ sing \ō\ go \ȯ\ law \ȯi\ boy \th\ thin \t͟h\ the \ü\ loot \u̇\ foot \y\ yet \zh\ vision \à, k̲, ⁿ, œ, œ̄, ue, ue̅, ʸ\ *see* Guide to Pronunciation

sales \'sā(ə)lz\ *adj* (1935) **:** of, relating to, or used in selling
sales check *n* (1926) **:** a strip or piece of paper used by retail stores as a memorandum, record, or receipt of a purchase or sale
sales·clerk \'sā(ə)lz-ˌklərk\ *n* (1926) **:** a salesman or saleswoman in a store
sales·girl \-ˌgər(-ə)l\ *n* (1887) **:** SALESWOMAN
Sa·le·sian \sə-'lē-zhən, sā-\ *n* (1884) **:** a member of the Society of St. Francis de Sales founded by St. John Bosco in Turin, Italy in the 19th century and devoted chiefly to education
sales·la·dy \'sā(ə)lz-ˌlād-ē\ *n* (1856) **:** SALESWOMAN
sales·man \'sā(ə)lz-mən\ *n* (1523) **:** one who sells either in a given territory or in a store — **sales·man·ship** \-ˌship\ *n*
sales·peo·ple \-ˌpē-pəl\ *n pl* (1876) **:** persons employed to sell goods or services
sales·per·son \-ˌpərs-ᵊn\ *n* (1901) **:** a salesman or saleswoman
sales·room \'sā(ə)lz-ˌrüm, -ˌrům\ *n* (1840) **:** a place where goods are displayed for sale; *esp* **:** an auction room
sales slip *n* (1926) **:** SALES CHECK
sales tax *n* (1921) **:** a tax levied on the sale of goods and services that is usu. calculated as a percentage of the purchase price and collected by the seller
sales·wom·an \'sā(ə)lz-ˌwům-ən\ *n* (1704) **:** a woman employed to sell merchandise esp. in a store
sali- *comb form* [L, fr. *sal* — more at SALT] **:** salt ⟨*sali*ferous⟩
sal·ic \'sal-ik\ *adj* [by alter.] (1902) **:** SIALIC
Sa·lic \'sā-lik, 'sal-ik\ *adj* [MF or ML; MF *salique,* fr. ML *Salicus,* fr. LL *Salii* Salic Franks] (1548) **:** of, relating to, or being a Frankish people that settled on the IJssel river early in the 4th century
sal·i·cin \'sal-ə-sən\ *n* [F *salicine,* fr. L *salic-, salix* willow — more at SALLOW] (1830) **:** a bitter white crystalline glucoside $C_{13}H_{18}O_7$ found in the bark and leaves of several willows and poplars and used in medicine like salicylic acid
Salic law *n* (1599) **1 :** the legal code of the Salic Franks **2 :** a rule held to derive from the Salic code excluding females from the line of succession to a throne
sa·lic·y·late \sə-'lis-ə-ˌlāt\ *n* (1842) **:** a salt or ester of salicylic acid
sal·i·cyl·ic acid \ˌsal-ə-ˌsil-ik-\ *n* [ISV, fr. *salicyl* (the group HOC_6H_4CO)] (1840) **:** a crystalline phenolic acid $C_7H_6O_3$ used esp. in the form of salts as an analgesic and antipyretic and in the treatment of rheumatism
sa·lience \'sā-lyən(t)s, -lē-ən(t)s\ *n* (1837) **1 :** a striking point or feature **:** HIGHLIGHT **2 :** the quality or state of being salient
sa·lien·cy \-lyən-sē, -lē-ən-\ *n, pl* **-cies** (1831) **:** SALIENCE
[1]**sa·lient** \'sā-lyənt, -lē-ənt\ *adj* [L *salient-, saliens,* prp. of *salire* to leap — more at SALLY] (1646) **1 :** moving by leaps or springs **:** JUMPING; *specif* **:** of, relating to, or being a salientian ⟨a ~ amphibian⟩ **2 :** jetting upward ⟨a ~ fountain⟩ **3 a :** projecting beyond a line, surface, or level **b :** standing out conspicuously **:** PROMINENT, STRIKING ⟨~ traits⟩ *syn* see NOTICEABLE — **sa·lient·ly** *adv*
[2]**salient** *n* (1828) **:** something (as a promontory) that projects outward or upward from its surroundings; *esp* **:** an outwardly projecting part of a fortification, trench system, or line of defense
sa·li·en·tian \ˌsā-lē-'en-chən\ *n* [deriv. of L *salient-, saliens*] (ca. 1944) **:** any of an order (Salientia) of amphibians comprising the frogs, toads, and tree toads all of which lack a tail in the adult stage and have long strong hind limbs suited to leaping and swimming — **salientian** *adj*
sa·li·na \sə-'lī-nə, -'lē-\ *n* [Sp, fr. L *salinae* saltworks, fr. fem. pl. of *salinus*] (1589) **1 :** a salt-encrusted playa or flat **2 :** a salt marsh, pond, or lake
[1]**sa·line** \'sā-ˌlēn, -ˌlīn\ *adj* [ME, fr. L *salinus,* fr. *sal* salt — more at SALT] (15c) **1 :** consisting of or containing salt ⟨a ~ solution⟩ **2 :** of, relating to, or resembling salt **:** SALTY ⟨a ~ taste⟩ **3 :** consisting of or relating to the salts of the alkali metals or of magnesium ⟨a ~ cathartic⟩ — **sa·lin·i·ty** \sā-'lin-ət-ē, sə-\ *n*
[2]**saline** *n* (15c) **1 :** a metallic salt; *esp* **:** a salt of potassium, sodium, or magnesium with a cathartic action **2 :** a saline solution; *esp* **:** one isotonic with body fluids
sa·li·nize \'sal-ə-ˌnīz *also* 'sā-lə-\ *vt* **-nized; -niz·ing** (1926) **:** to treat or impregnate with salt — **sa·li·ni·za·tion** \ˌsal-ə-nə-'zā-shən *also* ˌsā-lə-\ *n*
sa·li·nom·e·ter \ˌsal-ə-'näm-ət-ər, ˌsā-lə-\ *n* [ISV *saline* + *-o-* + *-meter*] (1844) **:** an instrument (as a hydrometer) for measuring the amount of salt in a solution
Sa·lique \'sā-lik, 'sal-ik; sa-'lēk, sā-\ *var of* SALIC
Salis·bury steak \ˌsȯlz-ˌber-ē-, ˌsalz-, -b(ə-)rē-\ *n* [J. H. *Salisbury,* 19th cent. Eng. physician] (ca. 1897) **:** ground beef mixed with egg, milk, bread crumbs, and seasonings and formed into a large patty and cooked
Sa·lish \'sā-lish\ *n* (1840) **1 :** the peoples speaking Salish dialects **2 :** a language stock of the Mosan phylum — **Sa·lish·an** \-ən\ *adj*
sa·li·va \sə-'lī-və\ *n* [L — more at SALLOW] (1676) **:** a slightly alkaline secretion of water, mucin, protein, salts, and often a starch-splitting enzyme that is secreted into the mouth by salivary glands, lubricates ingested food, and often begins the breakdown of starches
sal·i·vary \'sal-ə-ˌver-ē\ *adj* (1709) **:** of or relating to saliva or the glands that secrete it; *esp* **:** producing or carrying saliva
salivary chromosome *n* (1948) **:** one of the very large polytene chromosomal strands that are made up of many chromatids and are typical of the salivary gland cells of various insects
sal·i·vate \'sal-ə-ˌvāt\ *vb* **-vat·ed; -vat·ing** *vt* (1669) **:** to produce an abnormal flow of saliva in (as by the use of mercury) ~ *vi* **1 :** to have a flow of saliva esp. in excess **2 :** DROOL 2 — **sal·i·va·tion** \ˌsal-ə-'vā-shən\ *n* — **sal·i·va·tor** \'sal-ə-ˌvāt-ər\ *n*
Salk vaccine \'sȯ(l)k-\ *n* [Jonas *Salk*] (1954) **:** a vaccine consisting of poliomyelitis virus inactivated with formaldehyde
sal·let \'sal-ət\ *n* [ME, fr. MF *sallade*] (15c) **:** a light 15th century helmet with or without a visor and with a projection over the neck
[1]**sal·low** \'sal-(ˌ)ō, -ə(-w)\ *n* [ME, fr. OE *sealh;* akin to OHG *salha* sallow, L *salix* willow] (bef. 12c) **:** any of various Old World broad-leaved willows (as *Salix caprea*) including important sources of charcoal and tanbark
[2]**sallow** *adj* [ME *salowe,* fr. OE *salu;* akin to OHG *salo* murky, L *saliva* spittle] (bef. 12c) **:** of a grayish greenish yellow color — **sal·low·ish** \'sal-ə-wish\ *adj* — **sal·low·ness** \'sal-ō-nəs, 'sal-ə-\ *n*
[1]**sal·ly** \'sal-ē\ *n, pl* **sallies** [MF *saillie,* fr. OF, fr. *saillir* to rush forward, fr. L *salire* to leap; akin to Gk *hallesthai* to leap] (1560) **1 :** an action of rushing or bursting forth; *esp* **:** a sortie of troops from a defensive position to attack the enemy **2 a :** a brief outbreak **:** OUTBURST **b :** a witty or imaginative saying **:** QUIP **3 :** a venture or excursion usu. off the beaten track **:** JAUNT
[2]**sally** *vi* **sal·lied; sal·ly·ing** (1560) **1 :** to leap out or burst forth suddenly **2 :** SET OUT, DEPART — usu. used with *forth*
Sal·ly Lunn \ˌsal-ē-'lən\ *n* [*Sally Lunn,* 18th cent. Eng. baker] (1780) **:** a slightly sweetened yeast-leavened bread
sally port *n* (1649) **:** a gate or passage in a fortified place for use by troops making a sortie
sal·ma·gun·di \ˌsal-mə-'gən-dē\ *n* [F *salmigondis*] (1674) **1 :** a salad plate of chopped meats, anchovies, eggs, and vegetables arranged in rows for contrast and dressed with a salad dressing **2 :** a heterogeneous mixture **:** POTPOURRI
sal·mi \'sal-mē\ *n* [F *salmis,* short for *salmigondis*] (1759) **:** a ragout of partly roasted game stewed in a rich sauce
salm·on \'sam-ən\ *n, pl* **salmon** *also* **salmons** [ME *samon,* fr. MF, fr. L *salmon-, salmo*] (14c) **1 a :** a large soft-finned anadromous game fish (*Salmo salar*) of the northern Atlantic noted as a food fish — called also *Atlantic salmon* **b :** any of various anadromous fishes (family Salmonidae) other than the salmon; *esp* **:** any of several fishes (genus *Oncorhynchus*) that breed in rivers tributary to the northern Pacific **c :** a fish (as a barramunda) resembling a salmon **2 :** the variable color of salmon's flesh averaging a strong yellowish pink
salm·on·ber·ry \-ˌber-ē\ *n* (1844) **:** a showy red-flowered raspberry (*Rubus spectabilis*) of the Pacific coast; *also* **:** its edible salmon-colored fruit
sal·mo·nel·la \ˌsal-mə-'nel-ə\ *n, pl* **-nel·lae** \-'nel-(ˌ)ē, -ˌī\ *or* **-nellas** *or* **-nella** [NL, fr. Daniel E. *Salmon* †1914 Am. veterinarian] (1913) **:** any of a genus (*Salmonella*) of aerobic rod-shaped usu. motile bacteria that are pathogenic for man and other warm-blooded animals and cause food poisoning, gastrointestinal inflammation, or diseases of the genital tract
sal·mo·nel·lo·sis \ˌsal-mə-ˌnel-'ō-səs\ *n, pl* **-lo·ses** \-ˌsēz\ [NL] (ca. 1913) **:** infection with or disease caused by salmonellae
sal·mo·nid \'sa(l)m-ə-(ˌ)nid\ *n* [NL *Salmonidae,* fr. *Salmon-, Salmo,* genus name, fr. L *salmo* salmon] (1868) **:** any of a family (Salmonidae) of elongate soft-finned fishes (as a salmon or trout) that have the last vertebrae upturned — **salmonid** *adj*
salm·on·oid \'sam-ə-ˌnȯid\ *n* (1842) **:** SALMONID; *also* **:** a related fish — **salmonoid** *adj*
salmon pink *n* (1884) **:** a strong yellowish pink that is lighter and slightly redder than average salmon
Sa·lo·me \sə-'lō-mē\ *n* [LL, fr. Gk *Salōmē*] **:** a niece of Herod Antipas given the head of John the Baptist as a reward for her dancing
sa·lom·e·ter \sā-'läm-ət-ər, sə-\ *n* [L *sal* salt + E *-o-* + *-meter*] (1860) **:** a hydrometer for indicating the percentage of salt in a solution
sa·lon \sə-'län, 'sal-ˌän, sa-'lōⁿ\ *n* [F] (1699) **1 :** an elegant apartment or living room (as in a fashionable home) **2 :** a fashionable assemblage of notables (as literary figures, artists, or statesmen) held by custom at the home of a prominent person **3 a :** a hall for exhibition of art **b** *cap* **:** an annual exhibition of works of art **4 :** a stylish business establishment or shop ⟨a beauty ~⟩
sa·loon \sə-'lün\ *n* [F *salon,* fr. It *salone,* aug. of *sala* hall, of Gmc origin; akin to OHG *sal* hall; akin to Lith *sala* village] (1728) **1 :** SALON 1 **2 :** SALON 2 **3 a :** an often elaborately decorated public apartment or hall (as a large cabin for social use of a ship's passengers) **b :** SALON 4 **c :** a room or establishment in which alcoholic beverages are sold and consumed **4** *Brit* **a :** PARLOR CAR **b :** SEDAN 2a
sal·pa \'sal-pə\ *n* [NL, fr. L, a kind of stockfish, fr. Gk *salpē*] (1852) **:** a transparent barrel-shaped or fusiform free-swimming oceanic tunicate (family Salpidae and esp. genus *Salpa*) that is abundant in warm seas
sal·pi·glos·sis \ˌsal-pə-'gläs-əs\ *n* [NL, irreg. fr. Gk *salpinx* trumpet + *glōssa* tongue — more at GLOSS] (1827) **:** any of a small genus (*Salpiglossis*) of Chilean herbs of the nightshade family with large funnel-shaped varicolored flowers often strikingly marked
sal·pin·gi·tis \ˌsal-pən-'jīt-əs\ *n* [NL] (1861) **:** inflammation of a fallopian or eustachian tube
sal·pinx \'sal-(ˌ)piŋ(k)s\ *n, pl* **sal·pin·ges** \sal-'pin-(ˌ)jēz\ [NL *salping-, salpinx,* fr. Gk, trumpet] (1842) **1 :** EUSTACHIAN TUBE **2 :** FALLOPIAN TUBE
sal·sa \'sȯl-sə, 'säl-\ *n* [Sp] (ca. 1962) **1 :** a spicy sauce of tomatoes, onions, and hot peppers **2 :** popular music of Latin American origin that has absorbed characteristics of rhythm and blues, jazz, and rock
sal·si·fy \'sal-sə-fē, -ˌfī\ *n* [F *salsifis,* modif. of It *sassefrica,* fr. LL *saxifrica,* any of various herbs, fr. L *saxum* rock + *fricare* to rub — more at SAXIFRAGE, FRICTION] (ca. 1706) **:** a European biennial composite herb (*Tragopogon porrifolius*) with a long fusiform edible root — called also *oyster plant, vegetable oyster*
sal soda \'sal-'sōd-ə\ *n* (15c) **:** a transparent crystalline hydrated sodium carbonate $Na_2CO_3 \cdot 10H_2O$ — called also *washing soda*
[1]**salt** \'sȯlt\ *n* [ME, fr. OE *sealt;* akin to OHG *salz* salt, L *sal,* Gk *hals* salt, sea] (bef. 12c) **1 a :** a crystalline compound NaCl that is the chloride of sodium, is abundant in nature, and is used esp. to season or preserve food or in industry — called also *common salt* **b :** a substance (as sal soda) resembling common salt **c** *pl* (1) **:** a mineral or saline mixture (as Epsom salts) used as an aperient or cathartic (2) **:** SMELLING SALTS **d :** any of numerous compounds that result from replacement of part or all of the acid hydrogen of an acid by a metal or a group acting like a metal **:** an ionic crystalline compound **2 a :** an ingredient that gives savor, piquancy, or zest **:** FLAVOR ⟨a people . . . full of life, vigor, and the ~ of personality —Clifton Fadiman⟩ **b :** sharpness of wit **:** PUNGENCY **c :** COMMON SENSE **d :** RESERVE, SKEPTICISM — often used in the phrase *with a grain of salt* **e :** a scattered elite — usu. used in the phrase *salt of the earth* **3 :** SAILOR ⟨a tale worthy of an old ~⟩ **4 :** KEEP 3 — usu. used in the phrases *earn one's salt* and *worth one's salt* — **salt·like** \-ˌlīk\ *adj*
[2]**salt** *vt* (bef. 12c) **1 a :** to treat, provide, or season with common salt **b :** to preserve (food) with salt or in brine **c :** to supply (as an animal) with salt **2 :** to give flavor or piquancy to (as a story) **3 :** to enrich (as a mine) artificially by secretly placing valuable mineral in some of the working places **4 :** to sprinkle with or as if with a salt

[3]salt *adj* (bef. 12c) **1 a :** SALINE, SALTY **b :** being or inducing the one of the four basic taste sensations that is suggestive of seawater — compare BITTER, SOUR, SWEET **2 :** cured or seasoned with salt : SALTED **3 :** overflowed with salt water ⟨a ~ pond⟩ **4 :** SHARP, PUNGENT — **salt·ness** *n*

[4]salt *adj* [by shortening & alter. fr. *assaut,* fr. ME *a sawt,* fr. MF *a saut,* lit., on the jump] *obs* (1598) : LUSTFUL, LASCIVIOUS

salt–and–pepper *adj* (1915) : PEPPER-AND-SALT

sal·ta·rel·lo \ˌsal-tə-ˈrel-(ˌ)ō, ˌsäl-\ *n, pl* **-los** [It] (1597) : an Italian dance with a lively hop step beginning each measure

sal·ta·tion \sal-ˈtā-shən, sȯl-\ *n* [L *saltation-, saltatio,* fr. *saltatus,* pp. of *saltare* to leap, dance, fr. *saltus,* pp. of *salire* to leap — more at SALLY] (1646) **1 a :** the action or process of leaping or jumping **b :** DANCE **2 a :** the direct transformation of one organismic form into another when it occurs according to some evolutionary theories by major evolutionary steps; *broadly* : discontinuous variation **b :** MUTATION — used esp. of bacteria and fungi

sal·ta·to·ri·al \ˌsal-tə-ˈtōr-ē-əl, ˌsȯl-, -ˈtȯr-\ *adj* (1789) : relating to, marked by, or adapted for leaping ⟨~ legs of a grasshopper⟩

sal·ta·to·ry \ˈsal-tə-ˌtōr-ē, ˈsȯl-, -ˌtȯr-\ *adj* (1656) **1 :** of or relating to dancing ⟨the ~ art⟩ **2 :** proceeding by leaps rather than by gradual transitions : DISCONTINUOUS

salt away *vt* (ca. 1890) : to lay away (as money) safely : SAVE

salt·box \ˈsȯlt-ˌbäks\ *n* (1876) : a frame dwelling with two stories in front and one behind and a roof with a long rear slope

salt·bush \-ˌbu̇sh\ *n* (1863) : any of various shrubby plants of the goosefoot family that thrive in dry alkaline soil; *esp* : any of numerous oraches that are important browse plants in dry regions

salt·cel·lar \ˈsȯlt-ˌsel-ər\ *n* [ME *salt saler,* fr. *salt* + *saler* saltcellar fr. MF, fr. L *salarius* of salt — more at SALARY] (15c) : a small vessel for holding salt at the table

salt dome *n* (1908) : a domical anticline in sedimentary rock that has a mass of rock salt as its core

salt·er \ˈsȯl-tər\ *n* (bef. 12c) **1 :** one that manufactures or deals in salt **2 :** one that salts something (as meat, fish, or hides)

salt flat *n* (1816) : a salt-encrusted flat area resulting from evaporation of a former body of water

salt gland *n* (1950) : a gland (as of a marine bird) capable of excreting a concentrated salt solution

salt grass *n* (1704) : a grass (esp. *Distichlis spicata*) native to an alkaline habitat (as a salt meadow)

sal·tim·boc·ca \ˌsȯl-təm-ˈbäk-ə\ *n* [It, deriv. of *saltare* to leap (fr. L) + *bocca* mouth, fr. L *bucca* cheek — more at SALTATION, POCK] (1937) : scallops of veal prepared with sage, slices of ham, and sometimes cheese and served with a wine sauce

sal·tine \sȯl-ˈtēn\ *n* (1907) : a thin crisp cracker sprinkled with salt

salt·ing \ˈsȯl-tiŋ\ *n, chiefly Brit* (1712) : land flooded regularly by tides — usu. used in pl.

sal·tire \ˈsȯl-ˌti(ə)r, ˈsal-\ *n* [ME *sautire,* fr. MF *saultoir* X-shaped animal barricade that can be jumped over by people, saltire, fr. *saulter* to jump, fr. L *saltare* — more at SALTATION] (15c) : a heraldic charge consisting of a cross formed by a bend and a bend sinister crossing in the center

salt lake *n* (1763) : a landlocked body of water that has become salty through evaporation

salt·less \ˈsȯlt-ləs\ *adj* (14c) **1 :** having no salt **2 :** INSIPID

salt lick *n* (1751) : LICK 3

salt marsh *n* (bef. 12c) : flat land subject to overflow by salt water

salt–marsh caterpillar *n* (1854) : an American moth (*Estigmene acrea* of the family Arctiidae) whose larva is destructive to various crop plants

salt out *vt* (1939) : to precipitate, coagulate, or separate (as a dissolved substance or lyophilic sol) esp. from a solution by the addition of salt ~ *vi* : to become salted out

salt pan *n* (15c) : an undrained natural depression in which water gathers and leaves a deposit of salt on evaporation

salt·pe·ter \ˈsȯlt-ˈpēt-ər\ *n* [alter. of earlier *salpeter,* fr. ME, fr. MF *salpetre,* fr. ML *sal petrae,* lit., salt of the rock] (1501) **1 :** POTASSIUM NITRATE **2 :** SODIUM NITRATE

salt pork *n* (1723) : fat pork cured in salt or brine

salt·shak·er \ˈsȯlt-ˌshā-kər\ *n* (1895) : a container with a perforated top for sprinkling salt

salt·wa·ter \ˌsȯlt-ˌwȯt-ər, -ˌwät-\ *adj* (bef. 12c) : relating to, living in, or consisting of salt water

salt·works \ˈsȯlt-ˌwərks\ *n pl but sing or pl in constr* (1565) : a plant where salt is prepared commercially

salt·wort \-ˌwərt, -ˌwȯ(ə)rt\ *n* (1568) **1 :** any of a genus (*Salsola*) of plants (as the Russian thistle) of the goosefoot family of which some have been used in making soda ash **2 :** a low-growing strong-smelling coastal shrub (*Batis maritima*) of warm parts of the New World

salty \ˈsȯl-tē\ *adj* **salt·i·er; -est** (15c) **1 :** of, seasoned with, or containing salt **2 :** smacking of the sea or nautical life **3 a :** PIQUANT **b :** EARTHY 3b ⟨~ language⟩ — **salt·i·ly** \-tə-lē\ *adv* — **salt·i·ness** \-tē-nəs\ *n*

sa·lu·bri·ous \sə-ˈlü-brē-əs\ *adj* [L *salubris* — more at SAFE] (1547) : favorable to or promoting health or well-being ***syn*** see HEALTHFUL — **sa·lu·bri·ous·ly** *adv* — **sa·lu·bri·ous·ness** *n* — **sa·lu·bri·ty** \-brət-ē\ *n*

sa·lu·ki \sə-ˈlü-kē\ *n* [Ar *salūqīy* of Saluq, fr. *Salūq* Saluq, ancient city in Arabia] (1809) : any of an ancient northern African and Asian breed of tall swift slender hunting dogs having long narrow heads, long silky ears, and a smooth silky coat

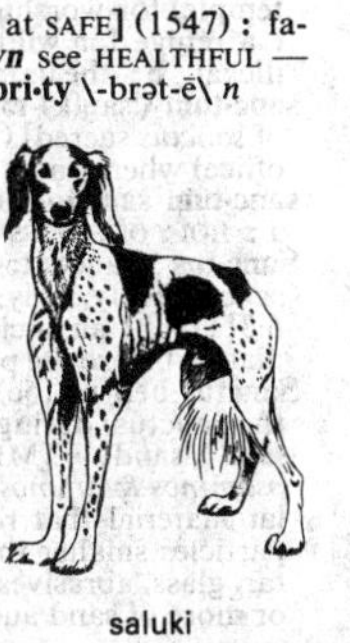

saluki

sal·u·tary \ˈsal-yə-ˌter-ē\ *adj* [MF *salutaire,* fr. L *salutaris,* fr. *salut-, salus* health] (15c) **1 :** producing a beneficial effect : REMEDIAL ⟨~ influences⟩ **2 :** promoting health : CURATIVE ***syn*** see HEALTHFUL — **sal·u·tari·ly** \ˌsal-yə-ˈter-ə-lē\ *adv* — **sal·u·tari·ness** \ˈsal-yə-ˌter-ē-nəs\ *n*

sal·u·ta·tion \ˌsal-yə-ˈtā-shən\ *n* (14c) **1 a :** an expression of greeting, goodwill, or courtesy by word, gesture, or ceremony **b** *pl* **:** REGARDS **2 :** the word or phrase of greeting (as *Gentlemen* or *Dear Sir*) that conventionally comes immediately before the body of a letter — **sal·u·ta·tion·al** \-shnəl, -shən-ᵊl\ *adj*

sa·lu·ta·to·ri·an \sə-ˌlüt-ə-ˈtōr-ē-ən, -ˈtȯr-\ *n* (ca. 1847) : the student usu. having the second highest rank in a graduating class who delivers the salutatory address at the commencement exercises

[1]sa·lu·ta·to·ry \sə-ˈlüt-ə-ˌtōr-ē, -ˌtȯr-\ *adj* (1702) : of or relating to a salutation : expressing or containing a welcome or greeting

[2]salutatory *n, pl* **-ries** (1779) : an address or statement of welcome or greeting

[1]sa·lute \sə-ˈlüt\ *vb* **sa·lut·ed; sa·lut·ing** [ME *saluten,* fr. L *salutare,* fr. *salut-, salus* health, safety, greeting — more at SAFE] *vt* (14c) **1 a :** to address with expressions of kind wishes, courtesy, or honor **b :** to give a sign of respect, courtesy, or goodwill to : GREET **2 :** to become apparent to (one of the senses) **3 a :** to honor (as a person, nation, or event) by a conventional military or naval ceremony **b :** to show respect and recognition to (a military superior) by assuming a prescribed position **c :** to express commendation of : PRAISE ~ *vi* : to make a salute — **sa·lut·er** *n*

[2]salute *n* (15c) **1 :** GREETING, SALUTATION **2 a :** a sign, token, or ceremony expressing goodwill, compliment, or respect ⟨the festival was a ~ to the arts⟩ **b :** the position (as of the hand) or the entire attitude of a person saluting a superior **3 :** FIRECRACKER

sal·u·tif·er·ous \ˌsal-yə-ˈtif-(ə-)rəs\ *adj* [L *salutifer,* fr. *salut-, salus* + *-i-* + *-fer* -ferous] (1540) : SALUTARY

salv·able \ˈsal-və-bəl\ *adj* [LL *salvare* to save — more at SAVE] (1667) : capable of being saved or salvaged

[1]sal·vage \ˈsal-vij\ *n* [F, fr. MF, fr. *salver* to save — more at SAVE] (1645) **1 a :** compensation paid for saving a ship or its cargo from the perils of the sea or for the lives and property rescued in a wreck **b :** the act of saving or rescuing a ship or its cargo **c :** the act of saving or rescuing property in danger (as from fire) **2 a :** property saved from destruction in a calamity (as a wreck or fire) **b :** something extracted (as from rubbish) as valuable or useful

[2]salvage *vt* **sal·vaged; sal·vag·ing** (1889) : to rescue or save (as from wreckage or ruin) — **sal·vage·abil·i·ty** \ˌsal-vij-ə-ˈbil-ət-ē\ *n* — **sal·vage·able** \-ə-bəl\ *adj* — **sal·vag·er** *n*

Sal·var·san \ˈsal-vər-ˌsan\ *trademark* — used for arsphenamine

sal·va·tion \sal-ˈvā-shən\ *n* [ME, fr. OF, fr. LL *salvation-, salvatio,* fr. *salvatus,* pp. of *salvare* to save — more at SAVE] (13c) **1 a :** deliverance from the power and effects of sin **b :** the agent or means that effects salvation **c** *Christian Science* **:** the realization of the supremacy of infinite Mind over all bringing with it the destruction of the illusion of sin, sickness, and death **2 :** liberation from ignorance or illusion **3 a :** preservation from destruction or failure **b :** deliverance from danger or difficulty — **sal·va·tion·al** \-shnəl, -shən-ᵊl\ *adj*

Salvation Army *n* (1878) : an international religious and charitable group organized on military lines and founded in 1865 by William Booth for evangelizing and social betterment (as of the poor)

sal·va·tion·ism \sal-ˈvā-shə-ˌniz-əm\ *n* (1883) : religious teaching emphasizing the saving of the soul

Sal·va·tion·ist \-sh(ə-)nəst\ *n* (1882) **1 :** a soldier or officer of the Salvation Army **2** *often not cap* **:** EVANGELIST — **salvationist** *adj, often cap*

[1]salve \ˈsav, ˈsäv, ˈsȧv, ˈsalv, ˈsälv\ *n* [ME, fr. OE *sealf;* akin to OHG *salba* salve, Gk *olpē* oil flask] (bef. 12c) **1 :** an unctuous adhesive substance for application to wounds or sores **2 :** a remedial or soothing influence or agency ⟨a ~ to their hurt feelings⟩

[2]salve *vt* **salved; salv·ing** (bef. 12c) **1 :** to remedy (as disease) with or as if with a salve **2 :** QUIET, ASSUAGE ⟨give him a raise in salary to ~ his feelings —Upton Sinclair⟩

[3]salve \ˈsalv\ *vt* **salved; salv·ing** [back-formation fr. *salvage*] (ca. 1706) : SALVAGE — **sal·vor** \ˈsal-vər, -ˌvȯ(ə)r\ *n*

sal·ver \ˈsal-vər\ *n* [modif. of F *salve,* fr. Sp *salva* sampling of food to detect poison, tray, fr. *salvar* to save, sample food to detect poison, fr. LL *salvare* to save — more at SAVE] (1661) : a tray esp. for serving food or beverages

sal·ver·form \ˈsal-vər-ˌfȯrm\ *adj* (1821) : tubular with a spreading limb — used of a gamopetalous corolla

sal·ver–shaped \ˈsal-vər-ˌshāpt\ *adj* (ca. 1760) : SALVERFORM

sal·via \ˈsal-vē-ə\ *n* [NL, fr. L, sage — more at SAGE] (1601) : any of a large and widely distributed genus (*Salvia*) of herbs or shrubs of the mint family having a 2-lipped open calyx and two anthers; *esp* : one (*S. splendens*) with scarlet flowers

sal·vif·ic \sal-ˈvif-ik\ *adj* [LL *salvificus,* fr. L *salvus* safe + *-ficus* -fic] (1591) : having the intent or power to save or redeem ⟨the ~ life and death of Christ —E. A. Walsh⟩

[1]sal·vo \ˈsal-(ˌ)vō\ *n, pl* **salvos** *or* **salvoes** [It *salva,* fr. F *salve,* fr. L, hail!, imper. of *salvēre* to be healthy, fr. *salvus* healthy — more at SAFE] (1591) **1 a :** a simultaneous discharge of two or more guns in military action or as a salute **b :** the release all at one time of a rack of bombs or rockets (as from an airplane) **c :** a series of shots by an artillery battery with each gun firing one round in turn after a prescribed interval **d :** the bombs or projectiles released in a salvo **2 :** something suggestive of a salvo: as **a :** a sudden burst ⟨a ~ of cheers⟩ **b :** a spirited verbal attack ⟨the first ~ of a political campaign⟩

[2]salvo *vt* (1839) : to release a salvo of ~ *vi* : to fire a salvo

[3]salvo *n, pl* **salvos** [ML *salvo jure* with the right reserved] (1621) **1 :** a mental reservation : PROVISO **2 :** a means of safeguarding one's name or honor or allaying one's conscience : SALVE

sal vo·la·ti·le \ˌsal-və-ˈlat-ᵊl-ē\ *n* [NL, lit., volatile salt] (1654) : SMELLING SALTS

SAM \ˈsam, ˌes-(ˌ)ā-ˈem\ *n* (1950) : SURFACE-TO-AIR MISSILE

sa·ma·ra \ˈsam-ə-rə; sə-ˈmar-ə, -ˈmär-\ *n* [NL, fr. L, seed of the elm] (1577) : a dry indehiscent usu. one-seeded winged fruit (as of an ash or elm tree) — called also *key*

Sa·mar·i·tan \sə-ˈmar-ət-ᵊn, -ˈmer-\ *n* [ME, fr. OE, fr. LL *samaritanus,* n. & adj., fr. Gk *samaritēs* inhabitant of Samaria, fr. *Samaria*] (bef. 12c)

\ə\ abut \ᵊ\ kitten, F table \ər\ further \a\ ash \ā\ ace \ä\ cot, cart \au̇\ out \ch\ chin \e\ bet \ē\ easy \g\ go \i\ hit \ī\ ice \j\ job \ŋ\ sing \ō\ go \ȯ\ law \ȯi\ boy \th\ thin \t͟h\ the \ü\ loot \u̇\ foot \y\ yet \zh\ vision \á, k̟, ⁿ, œ, œ̄, ue, ue̅, ʸ\ *see* Guide to Pronunciation

1 : a native or inhabitant of Samaria 2 *often not cap* [fr. the parable of the good Samaritan in Lk 10:30–37] : one ready and generous in helping those in distress — **samaritan** *adj, often cap*

sa·mar·i·um \sə-ˈmer-ē-əm, -ˈmar-\ *n* [NL, fr. F *samarskite*] (1879) : a pale gray lustrous metallic element used esp. in alloys that form permanent magnets — see ELEMENT table

sa·mar·skite \sə-ˈmär-ˌskīt, ˈsam-ər-\ *n* [F, fr. Col. von *Samarski,* 19th cent. Russ. mine official] (ca. 1849) : a black or brownish black orthorhombic mineral that is a complex oxide of rare earths, uranium, iron, lead, thorium, niobium, tantalum, titanium, and tin

sam·ba \ˈsam-bə, ˈsäm-\ *n* [Pg] (1885) : a Brazilian dance of African origin with a basic pattern of step-close-step-close and characterized by a dip and spring upward at each beat of the music; *also* : the music for this dance — **samba** *vi*

sam·bar *or* **sam·bur** \ˈsäm-bər, ˈsam-\ *n* [Hindi *sā̃bar,* fr. Skt *śambara*] (1698) : a large Asian deer (*Cervus unicolor*) having strong 3-pointed antlers and long coarse hair on the throat

sam·bo \ˈsam-(ˌ)bō, ˈsäm-\ *n* [Russ, fr. *samozashchita bez oruzhiya* self-defense without weapons] (1972) : an international style of wrestling employing judo techniques

Sam Browne belt \ˌsam-ˌbraün-\ *n* [Sir *Sam*uel James *Browne* †1901 Brit. army officer] (1915) : a leather belt for a dress uniform supported by a light strap passing over the right shoulder

[1]**same** \ˈsām\ *adj* [ME, fr. ON *samr;* akin to OHG *sama* same, L *simulis* like, *simul* together, at the same time, *similis* like, *sem-* one, Gk *homos* same, *hama* together, *hen-, heis* one] (13c) **1 a** : resembling in every relevant respect **b** : conforming in every respect — used with *as* **2 a** : being one without addition, change, or discontinuance : IDENTICAL **b** : being the one under discussion or already referred to **3** : corresponding so closely as to be indistinguishable ⟨the ~ day last year⟩ **4** : equal in size, shape, value, or importance — usu. used with a *th-* determiner (as *the, that, those*) in all senses

syn SAME, SELFSAME, VERY, IDENTICAL, EQUIVALENT, EQUAL mean not different or not differing from one another. SAME may imply and SELFSAME always implies that the things under consideration are one thing and not two or more things; VERY, like SELFSAME, may imply identity, or, like SAME, may imply likeness in kind; IDENTICAL may imply selfsameness or suggest absolute agreement in all details; EQUIVALENT implies amounting to the same thing in worth or significance; EQUAL implies being identical in value, magnitude, or some specified quality.

[2]**same** *pron* (14c) **1** : something identical with or similar to another **2** : something previously defined or described — often used with a *th-* determiner (as *the, that, those*) in both senses — **all the same** *or* **just the same** : despite everything : NEVERTHELESS

[3]**same** *adv* (1766) : in the same manner — used with a *th-* determiner (as *the, that, those*)

sa·mekh \ˈsäm-ˌek\ *n* [Heb *sāmekh*] (1823) : the 15th letter of the Hebrew alphabet — see ALPHABET table

same·ness \ˈsām-nəs\ *n* (1581) **1** : the quality or state of being the same : IDENTITY, SIMILARITY **2** : MONOTONY, UNIFORMITY

sam·i·sen \ˈsam-ə-ˌsen\ *n* [Jp] (1864) : a 3-stringed Japanese musical instrument resembling a banjo

sa·mite \ˈsam-ˌīt, ˈsā-ˌmīt\ *n* [ME *samit,* fr. MF, fr. ML *examitum, samitum,* fr. MGk *hexamiton,* fr. Gk, neut. of *hexamitos* of six threads, fr. *hexa-* + *mitos* thread of the warp] (14c) : a rich medieval silk fabric interwoven with gold or silver

sa·miz·dat \ˈsäm-ēz-ˌdät\ *n* [Russ, fr. *sam-* self- + *izdatel'stvo* publisher, fr. *izdat'* to publish, fr. *iz* out, from + *dat'* to give; akin to L *dare* to give — more at DATE] (1970) : the system in the U.S.S.R. by which government-suppressed literature is clandestinely printed and distributed; *also* : such literature

sam·let \ˈsam-lət\ *n* [irreg. fr. *salmon* + *-let*] (1655) : PARR

Sam·nite \ˈsam-ˌnīt\ *n* [*Samnium,* Italy] (ca. 1899) : a member of an ancient people of central Italy

Sa·mo·an \sə-ˈmō-ən\ *n* (1846) **1** : the Polynesian language of the Samoans **2** : a native or inhabitant of Samoa — **Samoan** *adj*

Samoa time *n* (1983) : the time of the 11th time zone west of Greenwich that includes American Samoa

sam·o·var \ˈsam-ə-ˌvär\ *n* [Russ, fr. *samo-* self + *varit'* to boil] (1830) **1** : an urn with a spigot at its base used esp. in Russia to boil water for tea **2** : an urn similar to a Russian samovar with a device for heating the contents

Sam·o·yed *also* **Sam·o·yede** \ˈsam-ə-ˌyed, ˈsam-ˌȯi-ˌed\ *n* [Russ *samoed*] (1589) **1** : a member of a people of the Nenets district of the Arkhangelsk region of the U.S.S.R. **2** : any of a group of Uralic languages spoken by the Samoyed people **3** : any of a Siberian breed of medium-sized white or cream-colored sled dogs — **Samoyed** *adj* — **Sam·o·yed·ic** \ˌsam-ə-ˈyed-ik, -ˌȯi-ˈed-\ *adj*

samp \ˈsamp\ *n* [Narraganset *nasaump* corn mush] (1643) : coarse hominy or a boiled cereal made from it

sam·pan \ˈsam-ˌpan\ *n* [Chin (Pek) *san[1] pan[3],* fr. *san[1]* three + *pan[3]* board, plank] (1620) : a flat-bottomed Chinese skiff usu. propelled by two short oars

sam·phire \ˈsam-ˌfī(ə)r\ *n* [alter. of earlier *sampiere,* fr. MF (*herbe de*) *Saint Pierre,* lit., St. Peter's herb] (1545) **1** : a fleshy European seacoast plant (*Crithmum maritimum*) of the carrot family that is sometimes pickled **2** : a common glasswort (*Salicornia europaea*) that is sometimes pickled

[1]**sam·ple** \ˈsam-pəl\ *n* [ME, fr. MF *essample,* fr. L *exemplum* — more at EXAMPLE] (15c) **1** : a representative part or a single item from a larger whole or group esp. when presented for inspection or shown as evidence of quality : SPECIMEN **2** : a finite part of a statistical population whose properties are studied to gain information about the whole *syn* see INSTANCE

[2]**sample** *vt* **sam·pled; sam·pling** \-p(ə-)liŋ\ (1767) : to take a sample of or from; *esp* : to judge the quality of by a sample : TEST ⟨*sampled* his output for defects⟩ ⟨~ a wine⟩

[3]**sample** *adj* (1820) : serving as an illustration or example ⟨~ questions⟩

[1]**sam·pler** \ˈsam-plər\ *n* (1523) : a decorative piece of needlework typically having letters or verses embroidered on it in various stitches as an example of skill

[2]**sam·pler** \-p(ə-)lər\ *n* (1778) **1** : one that collects, prepares, or examines samples **2** : something containing representative specimens or selections ⟨a ~ of nineteen poets —K. E. Judd⟩; *also* : ASSORTMENT

sample space *n* (1951) : a set in which all of the possible outcomes of a statistical experiment are represented as points

sam·pling \ˈsam-pliŋ, *for 1 & 3* -p(ə-)liŋ\ *n* (1778) **1** : the act, process, or technique of selecting a suitable sample; *specif* : the act, process, or technique of selecting a representative part of a population for the purpose of determining parameters or characteristics of the whole population **2** : a small part selected as a sample for inspection or analysis ⟨ask a ~ of people which candidate they favored⟩ **3** : the introduction or promotion of a product by distributing trial packages of it

sam·sa·ra \səm-ˈsär-ə\ *n* [Skt *saṁsāra,* lit., passing through] (1845) : the indefinitely repeated cycles of birth, misery, and death caused by karma

Sam·son \ˈsam(p)-sən\ *n* [LL, fr. Gk *Sampsōn,* fr. Heb *Shimshōn*] : a Hebrew hero who wreaked havoc among the Philistines by means of his great strength

Sam·so·ni·an \sam(p)-ˈsō-nē-ən\ *adj* [*Samson*] (1654) : of heroic strength or proportions : MIGHTY

Sam·u·el \ˈsam-yə(-wə)l\ *n* [LL, fr. Gk *Samouel,* fr. Heb *Shĕmū'ēl*] **1** : the early Hebrew judge who successively anointed Saul and David king **2** : either of two narrative and historical books of canonical Jewish and Christian Scriptures — see BIBLE table

sam·u·rai \ˈsam-(y)ə-ˌrī\ *n, pl* **samurai** [Jp] (1874) **1** : a military retainer of a Japanese daimyo practicing the chivalric code of Bushido **2** : the warrior aristocracy of Japan

san·a·tive \ˈsan-ət-iv\ *adj* [ME *sanatif,* fr. MF, fr. LL *sanativus,* fr. L *sanatus,* pp. of *sanare* to cure, fr. *sanus* healthy] (15c) : having the power to cure or heal : CURATIVE, RESTORATIVE

san·a·to·ri·um \ˌsan-ə-ˈtōr-ē-əm, -ˈtȯr-\ *n, pl* **-riums** *or* **-ria** \-ē-ə\ [NL, fr. LL, neut. of *sanatorius* curative, fr. *sanatus*] (1839) **1** : an establishment that provides therapy combined with a regimen (as of diet and exercise) for treatment or rehabilitation **2 a** : an institution for rest and recuperation (as of convalescents) **b** : an establishment for the treatment of the chronically ill

san·be·ni·to \ˌsan-bə-ˈnēt-(ˌ)ō, ˌsam-\ *n, pl* **-tos** [Sp *sambenito,* fr. *San Benito* St. Benedict of Nursia] (1560) **1** : a sackcloth coat worn by penitents on being reconciled to the church **2** : a Spanish Inquisition garment resembling a scapular and being either yellow with red crosses for the penitent or black with painted devils and flames for the impenitent condemned to an auto-da-fé

San·cho Pan·za \ˌsan-chō-ˈpan-zə, ˌsän-chō-ˈpän-\ *n* [Sp] : the squire of Don Quixote in Cervantes' *Don Quixote*

sanc·ti·fi·ca·tion \ˌsaŋ(k)-tə-fə-ˈkā-shən\ *n* (1526) **1** : an act of sanctifying **2 a** : the state of being sanctified **b** : the state of growing in divine grace as a result of Christian commitment after baptism or conversion

sanc·ti·fi·er \ˈsaŋ(k)-tə-ˌfī(-ə)r\ *n* (1548) : one that sanctifies; *specif, cap* : HOLY SPIRIT

sanc·ti·fy \-ˌfī\ *vt* **-fied; -fy·ing** [ME *sanctifien,* fr. MF *sanctifier,* fr. LL *sanctificare,* fr. L *sanctus* sacred — more at SAINT] (14c) **1** : to set apart to a sacred purpose or to religious use : CONSECRATE **2** : to free from sin : PURIFY **3** : to give moral or social sanction to **4** : to make productive of holiness or piety ⟨observe the day of the sabbath, to ~ it —Deut 5:12 (DV)⟩

sanc·ti·mo·nious \ˌsaŋ(k)-tə-ˈmō-nē-əs, -nyəs\ *adj* (1603) **1** : affecting piousness : hypocritically devout **2** *obs* : possessing sanctity : HOLY — **sanc·ti·mo·nious·ly** *adv* — **sanc·ti·mo·nious·ness** *n*

sanc·ti·mo·ny \ˈsaŋ(k)-tə-ˌmō-nē\ *n, pl* **-nies** [MF *sanctimonie,* fr. L *sanctimonia,* fr. *sanctus*] (1540) **1** *obs* : HOLINESS **2** : affected or hypocritical holiness

[1]**sanc·tion** \ˈsaŋ(k)-shən\ *n* [MF or L; MF, fr. L *sanction-, sanctio,* fr. *sanctus,* pp. of *sancire* to make holy — more at SACRED] (15c) **1** : a formal decree; *esp* : an ecclesiastical decree **2 a** *obs* : a solemn agreement : OATH **b** : something that makes an oath binding **3** : the detriment, loss of reward, or coercive intervention annexed to a violation of a law as a means of enforcing the law **4 a** : a consideration, principle, or influence (as of conscience) that impels to moral action or determines moral judgment **b** : a mechanism of social control for enforcing a society's standards **c** : explicit or official permission or ratification : APPROBATION **5** : an economic or military coercive measure adopted usu. by several nations in concert for forcing a nation violating international law to desist or yield to adjudication

[2]**sanction** *vt* **sanc·tioned; sanc·tion·ing** \-sh(ə-)niŋ\ (1778) **1** : to make valid or binding usu. by a formal procedure (as ratification) **2** : to give effective or authoritative approval or consent to *syn* see APPROVE

sanc·ti·ty \ˈsaŋ(k)-tət-ē\ *n, pl* **-ties** [ME *sauncite,* fr. MF *sainteté,* fr. L *sanctitat-, sanctitas,* fr. *sanctus* sacred] (14c) **1** : holiness of life and character : GODLINESS **2 a** : the quality or state of being holy or sacred : INVIOLABILITY **b** *pl* : sacred objects, obligations, or rights

sanc·tu·ary \ˈsaŋ(k)-chə-ˌwer-ē\ *n, pl* **-ar·ies** [ME *sanctuarie,* fr. MF *saintuarie,* fr. LL *sanctuarium,* fr. L *sanctus*] (14c) **1** : a consecrated place: as **a** : the ancient Hebrew temple at Jerusalem or its holy of holies **b** (1) : the most sacred part of a religious building (as the part of a Christian church in which the altar is placed) (2) : the room in which general worship services are held (3) : a place (as a church or a temple) for worship **2 a** (1) : a place of refuge and protection (2) : a refuge for wildlife where predators are controlled and hunting is illegal **b** : the immunity from law attached to a sanctuary

sanc·tum \ˈsaŋ(k)-təm\ *n, pl* **sanctums** *also* **sanc·ta** \-tə\ [LL, fr. L, neut. of *sanctus* sacred] (1577) **1** : a sacred place **2** : a place (as a study or office) where one is free from intrusion ⟨an editor's ~⟩

sanc·tum sanc·to·rum \ˌsaŋ(k)-təm-ˌsaŋ(k)-ˈtōr-əm, -ˈtȯr-\ *n* [LL] (15c) **1** : HOLY OF HOLIES **2** : SANCTUM 2

Sanc·tus \ˈsaŋ(k)-təs; ˈsäŋ(k)-təs, -ˌtüs\ *n* [ME, fr. LL *Sanctus, sanctus, sanctus* Holy, holy, holy, opening of a hymn sung by the angels in Isa 6:3] (14c) : an ancient Christian hymn of adoration sung or said immediately before the prayer of consecration in traditional liturgies

Sanctus bell *n* (15c) : a bell rung by the server at several points (as at the Sanctus) during the mass

[1]**sand** \ˈsand\ *n* [ME, fr. OE; akin to OHG *sant* sand, L *sabulum,* Gk *psammos & ammos* sand, *psēn* to rub] (bef. 12c) **1 a** : a loose granular material that results from the disintegration of rocks, consists of particles smaller than gravel but coarser than silt, and is used in mortar, glass, abrasives, and foundry molds **b** : soil containing 85 percent or more of sand and a maximum of 10 percent of clay; *broadly* : sandy

soil **2** **a :** a tract of sand : BEACH **b :** a sandbank or sandbar **3** : the sand in an hourglass; *also* : the moments of a lifetime — usu. used in pl. ⟨the ~*s* of this government run out very rapidly —H. J. Laski⟩ **4 :** an oil-producing formation of sandstone or unconsolidated sand **5 :** firm resolution **6 :** a variable color averaging a yellowish gray

2**sand** *vt* (14c) **1 :** to sprinkle or dust with or as if with sand **2 :** to cover or fill with sand **3 :** to smooth or dress by grinding or rubbing with an abrasive (as sandpaper)

san·dal \ˈsan-dᵊl\ *n* [ME *sandalie,* fr. L *sandalium,* fr. Gk *sandalion,* dim. of *sandalon* sandal] (14c) **1 :** a shoe consisting of a sole strapped to the foot **2 :** a low-cut shoe that fastens by an ankle strap **3 :** a strap to hold on a slipper or low shoe **4 :** a rubber overshoe cut very low — **san·daled** \ˈsan-dᵊld\ *adj*

san·dal·wood \-ˌwu̇d\ *n* [*sandal* sandalwood (fr. ME, fr. MF, fr. ML *sandalum,* fr. LGk *santalon,* deriv. of Skt *candana,* of Dravidian origin; akin to Tamil *cāntu* sandalwood tree) + *wood*] (1511) **1 :** the compact close-grained fragrant yellowish heartwood of a parasitic tree (*Santalum album* of the family Santalaceae, the sandalwood family) of southern Asia much used in ornamental carving and cabinetwork; *also* : the tree that yields this wood **2 :** any of various trees other than sandalwood some of which yield dyewoods; *also* : the fragrant wood of such a tree

sandalwood oil *n* (ca. 1909) : an essential oil obtained from sandalwood: as **a :** a pale yellow somewhat viscous aromatic liquid obtained from a sandalwood (*Santalum album*) and used chiefly in perfumes and soaps **b :** an oil obtained from a sandalwood (*Eucarya spicata*) of Western Australia

san·da·rac \ˈsan-də-ˌrak\ *n* [L *sandaraca* red coloring, fr. Gk *sandarakē* realgar, red pigment from realgar] (14c) : a brittle faintly aromatic translucent resin obtained from a large northern African tree (*Callitris articulata*) of the pine family and used chiefly in making varnish and as incense; *also* : a similar resin obtained from any of several related Australian trees

1**sand·bag** \ˈsan(d)-ˌbag\ *n* (1590) : a bag filled with sand and used in fortifications, as ballast, or as a weapon

2**sandbag** *vt* (1860) **1 :** to bank, stop up, or weight with sandbags **2** **a** : to hit or stun with a sandbag **b :** to treat unfairly or harshly **c :** to coerce by crude means ⟨are raiding the Treasury and *sandbagging* the government —C. W. Ferguson⟩ — **sand·bag·ger** *n*

sand·bank \ˈsan(d)-ˌbaŋk\ *n* (1584) : a large deposit of sand forming a mound, hillside, bar, or shoal

sand·bar \-ˌbär\ *n* (1766) : a ridge of sand built up by currents esp. in a river or in coastal waters

1**sand·blast** \-ˌblast\ *n* (1871) : a stream of sand projected by air or steam (as for engraving, cutting, or cleaning glass or stone)

2**sandblast** *vt* (1888) : to affect or treat with or as if with a sandblast — **sand·blast·er** *n*

sand–blind \ˈsan(d)-ˌblīnd\ *adj* [ME, prob. fr. (assumed) ME *samblind,* fr. OE *sam-* half (akin to OHG *sāmi-* half) + *blind* — more at SEMI-] (15c) : having poor eyesight : PURBLIND

sand bluestem *n* (ca. 1946) : a tall rhizomatous American grass (*Andropogon hallii*) used for forage and as a soil binder

sand·box \ˈsan(d)-ˌbäks\ *n* (1688) : a box or receptacle containing loose sand: as **a :** a shaker for sprinkling sand on wet ink **b :** a box that contains sand for children to play in

sand·bur \ˈsan(d)-ˌbər\ *n* (1830) : any of a genus (*Cenchrus,* esp. *C. tribuloides* and *C. pauciflorus*) of grasses producing spikelets enclosed in ovoid spiny involucres that form burs; *also* : one of these burs

sand–cast \-ˌkast\ *vt* **-cast; -cast·ing** (1928) : to make (a casting) by pouring metal in a sand mold

sand casting *n* (1926) : a casting made in a mold of sand

sand crack *n* (1754) : a fissure in the wall of a horse's hoof often causing lameness

sand dollar *n* (1883) : any of numerous flat circular sea urchins (order Exocycloida) that live chiefly in shallow water on sandy bottoms

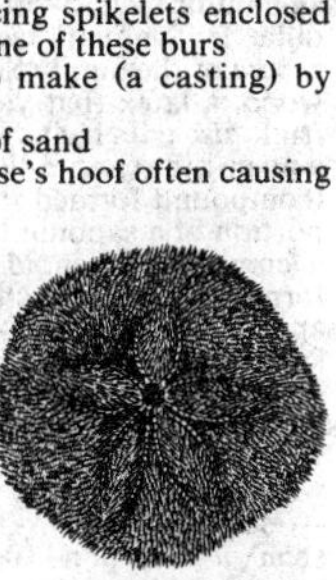
sand dollar

sand·er \ˈsan-dər\ *n* (1627) : one that sands: as **a :** a device for spreading sand on newly surfaced or icy roads; *also* : the device together with the truck that bears it **b :** a machine or device that smooths, polishes, or scours by means of abrasive material usu. in the form of a disk or belt — called also *sanding machine*

sand·er·ling \ˈsan-dər-liŋ\ *n* [perh. irreg. fr. *sand* + *-ling*] (1602) : a small sandpiper (*Calidris alba*) with largely gray-and-white plumage

sand flea *n* (1796) **1 :** a flea (as a chigoe) found in sandy places **2** : BEACH FLEA

sand fly *n* (1736) : any of various small biting two-winged flies (families Psychodidae, Simuliidae, and Ceratopogonidae)

sand·fly fever \ˌsan(d)-ˌflī-\ *n* (1910) : a virus disease of brief duration that is characterized by fever, headache, pain in the eyes, malaise, and leukopenia and is transmitted by the bite of a sand fly (*Phlebotomus papatasii*) — called also *phlebotomus fever*

sand·glass \ˈsan(d)-ˌglas\ *n* (1556) : an instrument (as an hourglass) for measuring time by the running of sand

sand grouse *n* (1783) : any of numerous birds (family Pteroclidae) of arid parts of southern Europe, Asia, and Africa that are closely related to the pigeons but have precocial downy young

san·dhi \ˈsän-dē, ˈsän-\ *n* [Skt *saṁdhi,* lit., placing together] (1874) : modification of the sound of a morpheme (as a word or affix) conditioned by context in which it is uttered ⟨pronunciation of *-ed* as \d\ in *glazed* and as \t\ in *paced,* and occurrence of *a* in *a cow* and of *an* in *an old cow,* are examples of ~⟩

sand·hill crane \ˌsand-ˌhil-\ *n* (1805) : a crane (*Grus canadensis*) of eastern and central No. America that is chiefly bluish gray tinged with a sandy yellow

sand·hog \ˈsand-ˌhȯg, -ˌhäg\ *n* (1903) : a laborer who works in a caisson in driving underwater tunnels

sand jack *n* (ca. 1901) : a device for lowering a heavy weight (as a bridge section) into place by allowing sand on which it is supported to run out

S and L *n* (1972) : SAVINGS AND LOAN ASSOCIATION

sand lance *n* (1776) : any of several small elongate marine teleost fishes (genus *Ammodytes*) that associate in large schools and remain buried in sandy beaches at ebb tide — called also *sand eel, sand launce*

sand lily *n* (ca. 1900) : a western No. American spring herb (*Leucocrinum montanum*) of the lily family with narrow linear leaves and fragrant salverform flowers

sand·lot \ˈsan-ˌ(d)lät\ *n* (1878) : a vacant lot esp. when used (as by children) for usu. unorganized sports — **sandlot** *adj* — **sand·lot·ter** \-ˌ(d)lät-ər\ *n*

sand·man \ˈsan(d)-ˌman\ *n* (1861) : a genie in folklore who makes children sleepy by sprinkling sand in their eyes

sand myrtle *n* (1814) : a variable low-branching evergreen upland shrub (*Leiophyllum buxifolium*) of the heath family found in the southeastern U.S.

sand painting *n* (1900) : a Navaho and Pueblo Indian ceremonial design made of various materials (as colored sands) on a flat surface of sand or buckskin

1**sand·pa·per** \ˈsan(d)-ˌpā-pər\ *n* (1825) : paper covered on one side with abrasive material (as sand) glued fast and used for smoothing and polishing — **sand·pa·pery** \-p(ə-)rē\ *adj*

2**sandpaper** *vt* (1846) : to rub with or as if with sandpaper

sand·pile \ˈsan(d)-ˌpīl\ *n* (1901) : a pile of sand; *esp* : sand for children to play in

sand·pip·er \-ˌpī-pər\ *n* (1674) : any of numerous small shorebirds (suborder Charadrii) distinguished from the related plovers chiefly by the longer and soft-tipped bill

sand·soap \ˈsan(d)-ˌsōp\ *n* (ca. 1855) : a gritty soap for all-purpose cleaning

sand·spur \-ˌspər\ *n* (ca. 1898) : SANDBUR

sand·stone \-ˌstōn\ *n* (ca. 1668) : a sedimentary rock consisting of usu. quartz sand united by some cement (as silica or calcium carbonate)

sand·storm \-ˌstȯ(ə)rm\ *n* (1774) : a windstorm (as in a desert) driving clouds of sand before it

sand table *n* (ca. 1910) **1 :** a table holding sand for children to mold **2** : a table bearing a relief model of a terrain built to scale for study or demonstration esp. of military tactics

sand trap *n* (1922) : an artificial hazard on a golf course consisting of a depression containing sand

sand verbena *n* (1898) : any of several western American herbs (genus *Abronia*) of the four-o'clock family having flowers like the verbena; *esp* : either of two plants (*A. latifolia* and *A. umbellata*) of the Pacific coast

1**sand·wich** \ˈsan-(ˌ)(d)wich\ *n* [John Montagu, 4th Earl of *Sandwich* †1792 Eng. diplomat] (1762) **1 :** a slice of bread covered with a filling (as of meat, cheese, fish, or various mixtures) which is usu. covered with another slice of bread; *also* : a partially split long or round roll stuffed with a filling **2 :** something resembling a sandwich; *esp* : composite structural material consisting of layers often of high-strength facings bonded to a low strength central core

2**sandwich** *vt* (1861) **1 :** to make into or as if into a sandwich; *esp* : to insert or enclose between usu. two things of another quality or character **2 :** to make a place for — often used with *in* or *between*

sandwich board *n* (1897) : two usu. hinged boards designed for hanging from the shoulders with one board before and one behind and used esp. for advertising or picketing

sandwich coin *n* (1965) : a clad coin

sandwich man *n* (1864) : one who advertises or pickets a place of business by wearing a sandwich board

sand·worm \ˈsan-ˌ(d)wərm\ *n* (1776) : any of various sand-dwelling polychaete worms: as **a :** any of several large burrowing worms (esp. genus *Nereis*) often used as bait **b :** LUGWORM

sand·wort \ˈsan-ˌ(d)wərt, -ˌ(d)wȯ(ə)rt\ *n* (1597) : any of a genus (*Arenaria*) of low tufted herbs of the pink family growing usu. in dry sandy regions

sandy \ˈsan-dē\ *adj* **sand·i·er; -est** (bef. 12c) **1 :** consisting of, containing, or sprinkled with sand **2 :** of the color sand — **sand·i·ness** *n*

sane \ˈsān\ *adj* **san·er; san·est** [L *sanus* healthy, sane] (1628) **1 :** free from hurt or disease : HEALTHY **2 :** mentally sound; *esp* : able to anticipate and appraise the effect of one's actions **3 :** proceeding from a sound mind : RATIONAL ***syn*** see WISE — **sane·ly** *adv* — **sane·ness** \ˈsān-nəs\ *n*

San·for·ized \ˈsan-fə-ˌrīzd\ *trademark* — used for fabrics that are shrunk by a mechanical process before being manufactured into articles (as clothing)

sang *past of* SING

san·ga·ree \ˌsaŋ-gə-ˈrē\ *n* [Sp *sangría,* lit., bleeding] (1736) **1 :** a sweetened iced drink of wine or sometimes of ale, beer, or liquor garnished with nutmeg **2 :** SANGRIA

sang·froid \ˈsä^{n}-ˈf(r)wä, ˌsä^{n}-frə-ˈwä\ *n* [F *sang-froid,* lit., cold blood] (1750) : self-possession or imperturbability esp. under strain

San·greal \ˈsan-ˈgrā(ə)l, ˈsaŋ-\ *n* [ME *Sangrayll,* fr. MF *Saint Graal* Holy Grail] (15c) : GRAIL

san·gria \saŋ-ˈgrē-ə, san-\ *n* [Sp] (1736) : a usu. iced punch made of red wine, fruit juice, and soda water

san·gui·nar·ia \ˌsaŋ-gwə-ˈner-ē-ə, -ˈnar-\ *n* [NL, fr. L, an herb that stanches blood, fr. fem. of *sanguinarius* sanguinary] (1808) **1 :** BLOODROOT **2 :** the rhizome and roots of a bloodroot used as an expectorant and emetic

san·gui·nary \ˈsaŋ-gwə-ˌner-ē\ *adj* [L *sanguinarius,* fr. *sanguin-, sanguis* blood] (1623) **1 :** BLOODTHIRSTY, MURDEROUS ⟨~ hatred⟩ **2 :** attended by bloodshed : BLOODY ⟨this bitter and ~ war —T. H. D. Mahoney⟩ **3 :** consisting of blood ⟨a ~ stream⟩ — **san·gui·nari·ly** \ˌsaŋ-gwə-ˈner-ə-lē\ *adv*

1**san·guine** \ˈsaŋ-gwən\ *adj* [ME *sanguin,* fr. MF, fr. L *sanguineus,* fr. *sanguin-, sanguis*] (14c) **1 :** BLOODRED **2** **a :** consisting of or relating to blood **b :** SANGUINARY 1 **c** *of the complexion* : RUDDY **3 :** having blood as the predominating bodily humor; *also* : having the bodily conformation and temperament held characteristic of such predominance and marked by sturdiness, high color, and cheerfulness **4** : CONFIDENT, OPTIMISTIC — **san·guine·ly** *adv* — **san·guine·ness** \-gwən-nəs\ *n* — **san·guin·i·ty** \saŋ-ˈgwin-ət-ē, san-\ *n*

²sanguine *n* (1500) : a moderate to strong red

san·guin·e·ous \san-ˈgwin-ē-əs, saŋ-\ *adj* [L *sanguineus*] (1520) **1** : BLOODRED **2** : of, relating to, or involving bloodshed : BLOODTHIRSTY **3** : of, relating to, or containing blood

San·he·drin \san-ˈhed-rən, sän-; san-ˈhēd-, ˈsan-əd-\ *n* [LHeb *sanhedhrin gĕdhōlāh* great council] (1588) : the supreme council and tribunal of the Jews during postexilic times headed by a High Priest and having religious, civil, and criminal jurisdiction

san·i·cle \ˈsan-i-kəl\ *n* [ME, fr. MF, fr. ML *sanicula*] (15c) : any of several plants sometimes held to have healing powers; *esp* : a plant (genus *Sanicula*) of the carrot family with a root used in folk medicine as an anodyne or astringent

sa·ni·ous \ˈsā-nē-əs\ *adj* [L *saniosus*, fr. *sanies* bloody discharge] (1562) : consisting of a thin mixture of serum and pus with a slightly bloody tinge

san·i·tar·i·an \ˌsan-ə-ˈter-ē-ən\ *n* (1859) : a specialist in sanitary science and public health ⟨milk ~⟩

san·i·tar·i·um \ˌsan-ə-ˈter-ē-əm\ *n, pl* **-i·ums** *or* **-ia** \-ē-ə\ [NL, fr. L *sanitat-, sanitas* health] (1851) : SANATORIUM

san·i·tary \ˈsan-ə-ˌter-ē\ *adj* [F *sanitaire*, fr. L *sanitas*] (1842) **1** : of or relating to health ⟨~ measures⟩ **2** : of, relating to, or used in the disposal esp. of domestic waterborne waste ⟨~ sewage⟩ **3** : characterized by or readily kept in cleanliness ⟨~ packages⟩ — **san·i·tari·ly** \ˌsan-ə-ˈter-ə-lē\ *adv*

sanitary landfill *n* (1968) : LANDFILL

sanitary napkin *n* (1917) : a disposable absorbent pad (as of cellulose) in a gauze covering used postpartum or during menstruation to absorb the uterine flow

sanitary ware *n* (1872) : ceramic plumbing fixtures (as sinks, lavatories, or toilet bowls)

san·i·tate \ˈsan-ə-ˌtāt\ *vt* **-tat·ed; -tat·ing** [back-formation fr. *sanitation*] (1882) : to make sanitary esp. by providing with sanitary appliances or facilities

san·i·ta·tion \ˌsan-ə-ˈtā-shən\ *n* (1848) **1** : the act or process of making sanitary **2** : the promotion of hygiene and prevention of disease by maintenance of sanitary conditions

san·i·tize \ˈsan-ə-ˌtīz\ *vt* **-tized; -tiz·ing** [L *sanitas*] (1836) **1** : to make sanitary (as by cleaning or sterilizing) **2** : to make more acceptable by removing unpleasant or undesired features ⟨~ a document⟩ — **san·i·ti·za·tion** \ˌsan-ət-ə-ˈzā-shən\ *n*

san·i·to·ri·um \ˌsan-ə-ˈtōr-ē-əm, -ˈtȯr-\ *n, pl* **-ri·ums** *or* **-ria** \-ē-ə\ [by alter. (influenced by *sanitarium*)] (1914) : SANATORIUM

san·i·ty \ˈsan-ət-ē\ *n* [ME *sanite*, fr. L *sanitat-, sanitas* health, sanity, fr. *sanus* healthy, sane] (1602) : the quality or state of being sane; *esp* : soundness or health of mind

San Ja·cin·to Day \ˌsan-jə-ˈsint-ə-, -hə-ˌsint-\ *n* (ca. 1907) : April 21 observed as a legal holiday in Texas in commemoration of the battle of San Jacinto in 1836 by which independence from Mexico was won

San Jo·se scale \ˌsan-ə-ˌzā-, -(h)ō-\ *n* [*San Jose*, Calif.] (1887) : a scale insect (*Quadraspidiotus perniciosus*) that is naturalized in the U.S. prob. from Asia and is a most damaging pest to fruit trees

sank *past of* SINK

San·khya \ˈsäŋ-kyə\ *n* [Skt *sāṁkhya*, lit., based on calculation] (1788) : an orthodox Hindu philosophy teaching salvation through knowledge of the distinction between matter and souls

sann hemp \ˈsən-, ˈsän-\ *n* [Hindi *san*] (1939) : SUNN

san·nup \ˈsan-əp\ *n* [Abnaki *senanbe*] (1628) : a married male American Indian

sann·ya·si \(ˌ)sən-ˈyäs-ē\ *or* **sann·ya·sin** \-ˈyäs-ᵊn\ *n* [Hindi *sannyāsī*, fr. Skt *sannyāsin*] (1613) : a Hindu mendicant ascetic

¹sans \(ˌ)sanz\ *prep* [ME *saun, sans*, fr. MF *san, sans*, modif. of L *sine* without — more at SUNDER] (14c) : WITHOUT ⟨my love to thee is sound, ~ crack or flaw —Shak.⟩

²sans \ˈsanz\ *n, pl* **sans** (ca. 1909) : SANS SERIF

sans·cu·lotte \ˌsan-sk(y)ü-ˈlät\ *n* [F *sans-culotte*, lit., without breeches] (1790) **1** : an extreme radical republican in France at the time of the Revolution **2** : a radical or violent extremist in politics — **sans-cu·lott·ic** \-ˈlät-ik\ *adj* — **sans·cu·lott·ish** \-ish\ *adj* — **sans·cu·lott·ism** \-ˌiz-əm, ˈsan-skyü-ˌlät-\ *n*

san·sei \(ˈ)sän-ˈsā, ˈsän-ˌ\ *n, pl* **sansei** *also* **sanseis** *often cap* [Jp *san* third + *sei* generation] (1940) : a son or daughter of nisei parents who is born and educated in America and esp. in the U.S.

san·se·vie·ria \ˌsan(t)-sə-ˈvir-ē-ə\ *n* [NL, fr. Raimondo di Sangro, prince of *San Severo* †1774 Ital. scholar] (1804) : any of a genus (*Sansevieria*) of tropical herbs of the lily family with showy mottled sword-shaped leaves usu. yielding a strong fiber

San·skrit \ˈsan-ˌskrit, ˈsan(t)-skrət\ *n* [Skt *saṁskṛta*, lit., perfected, fr. *sam* together (akin to OHG *sama* same) + *karoti* he makes — more at SAME] (1617) **1** : an ancient Indic language that is the classical language of India and of Hinduism as described by the Indian grammarians **2** : classical Sanskrit together with the older Vedic and various later modifications of classical Sanskrit — see INDO-EUROPEAN LANGUAGES table — **Sanskrit** *adj* — **San·skrit·ist** \-əst\ *n*

San·skrit·ic \san-ˈskrit-ik\ *n* (ca. 1909) : a group of Indic languages developed directly from Sanskrit — see INDO-EUROPEAN LANGUAGES table — **Sanskritic** *adj*

sans ser·if *or* **san·ser·if** \san-ˈser-əf, ˈsanz-\ *n* [prob. fr. *sans* + modif. of D *schreef* stroke — more at SERIF] (1830) : a letter or typeface with no serifs

San·ta Ana \ˌsant-ə-ˈan-ə\ *n* [*Santa Ana* mountains in southern Calif.] (1887) : a strong hot dry foehn wind from the north, northeast, or east in southern California

San·ta Claus \ˈsant-ē-ˌklȯz, ˈsant-ə-\ *n* [modif. of D Sinterklaas, alter. of *Sint Nikolaas* Saint Nicholas] : a plump white-bearded and red-suited old man in modern folklore who delivers presents to good children at Christmas time

San·ta Ger·tru·dis \ˌsant-ə-(ˌ)gər-ˈtrüd-əs\ *n* [*Santa Gertrudis*, section of the King Ranch, Kingsville, Texas] (1942) : any of a breed of red beef cattle developed from a Brahman-shorthorn cross and valued for their hardiness in hot climates

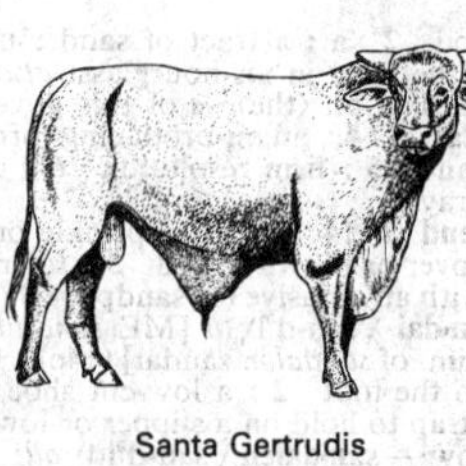
Santa Gertrudis

san·tir \san-ˈti(ə)r\ *or* **san·tour** \-ˈtü(ə)r\ *n* [Ar *santīr, santūr*, fr. Gk *psaltērion* psaltery] (1853) : a Persian dulcimer

san·to·li·na \ˌsant-ᵊl-ˈē-nə\ *n* [NL, alter. of L *santonica*, an herb, fem. of *santonicus* of the Santoni, fr. *Santoni*, a people of Aquitania] (1578) : any of a genus (*Santolina*) of Mediterranean composite subshrubs that have dissected leaves and clustered flower heads lacking ray flowers

san·to·nin \ˈsant-ᵊn-ən, san-ˈtän-ən\ *n* [ISV, fr. NL *santonica*, fr. L] (1838) : a poisonous slightly bitter crystalline compound $C_{15}H_{18}O_3$ found esp. in the unopened flower heads of several artemisias (esp. *Artemisia maritima* and *A. cina*) and used as an anthelmintic

¹sap \ˈsap\ *n* [ME, fr. OE *sæp*; akin to OHG *saf* sap] (bef. 12c) **1 a** : the fluid part of a plant; *specif* : a watery solution that circulates through a plant's vascular system **b** (1) : a body fluid (as blood) essential to life, health, or vigor (2) : bodily health and vigor **2** : a foolish gullible person **3** : BLACKJACK, BLUDGEON

²sap *vt* **sapped; sap·ping** (1725) **1** : to drain or deprive of sap **2** : to knock out with a sap

³sap *vb* **sapped; sap·ping** [MF *sapper*, fr. *sappe*] *vi* (1598) : to proceed by digging a sap ~ *vt* **1** : to subvert by digging or eroding the substratum or foundation : UNDERMINE **2** : to weaken or exhaust the energy or vitality of **3** : to operate against or pierce by a sap ***syn*** see WEAKEN

⁴sap *n* [MF & OIt; MF *sappe* hoe, fr. OIt *zappa*] (1642) : the extension of a trench from within the trench itself to a point beneath an enemy's fortifications

sap green *n* (1578) : a strong yellow green

sap·head \ˈsap-ˌhed\ *n* (1798) : a weak-minded stupid person : SAP — **sap·head·ed** \-ˈhed-əd\ *adj*

sa·phe·nous \sə-ˈfē-nəs, ˈsaf-ə-nəs\ *adj* [*saphena* (saphenous vein), fr. ME, fr. ML, fr. Ar *ṣāfin*] (1840) : of, relating to, associated with, or being either of the two chief superficial veins of the leg

sap·id \ˈsap-əd\ *adj* [L *sapidus* tasty, fr. *sapere* to taste — more at SAGE] (1634) **1 a** : affecting the organs of taste : possessing flavor **b** : having a strong agreeable flavor **2** : agreeable to the mind — **sa·pid·i·ty** \sa-ˈpid-ət-ē\ *n*

sa·pi·ence \ˈsā-pē-ən(t)s, ˈsap-ē-\ *n* [ME, fr. MF, fr. L *sapientia*, fr. *sapient-, sapiens*, prp.] (14c) : WISDOM, SAGENESS

sa·pi·ens \ˈsap-ē-ənz, ˈsā-pē-, -ˌenz\ *adj* [NL (specific epithet of *Homo sapiens*), fr. L, pp. of *sapere*] (1939) : of, relating to, or being recent man (*Homo sapiens*) as distinguished from various fossil men

sa·pi·ent \ˈsā-pē-ənt, ˈsap-ē-\ *adj* [ME, fr. MF, fr. L *sapient-, sapiens*, fr. prp. of *sapere* to taste, be wise — more at SAGE] (15c) : possessing or expressing great sagacity or discernment ***syn*** see WISE — **sa·pi·ent·ly** *adv*

sap·less \ˈsap-ləs\ *adj* (1591) **1** : destitute of sap : DRY **2** : lacking vitality or vigor : FEEBLE — **sap·less·ness** *n*

sap·ling \ˈsap-liŋ, -lən\ *n* (15c) **1** : a young tree; *specif* : one not over four inches in diameter at breast height **2** : YOUTH 2a

sap·o·dil·la \ˌsap-ə-ˈdil-ə, -ˈdē-(y)ə\ *n* [Sp *zapotillo*, dim. of *zapote* sapodilla, fr. Nahuatl *tzapotl*] (1697) : a tropical evergreen tree (*Achras zapota* of the family Sapotaceae, the sapodilla family) with hard reddish wood, a latex that yields chicle, and a rough-skinned brownish edible fruit; *also* : its fruit

sa·po·ge·nin \ˌsap-ə-ˈjen-ən, sə-ˈpäj-ə-nən\ *n* [ISV *saponin* + *-genin* (compound formed from another compound)] (ca. 1862) : a nonsugar portion of a saponin that is typically obtained by hydrolysis, has either a complex terpenoid or a steroidal structure, and in the latter case forms a practicable starting point in the synthesis of steroid hormones

sap·o·na·ceous \ˌsap-ə-ˈnā-shəs\ *adj* [NL *saponaceus*, fr. L *sapon-, sapo* soap, of Gmc origin; akin to OE *sāpe* soap] (1710) : resembling or having the qualities of soap — **sap·o·na·ceous·ness** *n*

sa·pon·i·fy \sə-ˈpän-ə-ˌfī\ *vb* **-fied; -fy·ing** [F *saponifier*, fr. L *sapon-, sapo*] *vt* (1821) : to convert (as fat) into soap; *specif* : to hydrolyze (a fat) with alkali to form a soap and glycerol ~ *vi* : to undergo saponifying — **sa·pon·i·fi·able** \-ˌfī-ə-bəl\ *adj* — **sa·pon·i·fi·ca·tion** \-ˌpän-ə-fə-ˈkā-shən\ *n* — **sa·pon·i·fi·er** \-ˌfī(-ə)r\ *n*

sa·po·nin \ˈsap-ə-nən, sə-ˈpō-\ *n* [F *saponine*, fr. L *sapon-, sapo*] (1831) : any of various mostly toxic glucosides that occur in plants (as soapwort or soapbark) and are characterized by the property of producing a soapy lather; *esp* : a hygroscopic amorphous saponin mixture used esp. as a foaming and emulsifying agent and detergent

sap·o·nite \ˈsap-ə-ˌnīt\ *n* [Sw *saponit*, fr. L *sapon-, sapo* soap] (ca. 1849) : a hydrous magnesium aluminum silicate occurring in soft soapy amorphous masses and filling veins and cavities (as in serpentine)

sap·per \ˈsap-ər\ *n* (1626) **1** : a military specialist in field fortification work (as sapping) **2** : a military specialist who lays, detects, and disarms mines

¹sap·phic \ˈsaf-ik\ *adj* (1501) **1** *cap* : of or relating to the Greek lyric poet Sappho **2** : of, relating to, or consisting of a 4-line strophe made up of chiefly trochaic and dactylic feet **3** : LESBIAN 2

²sapphic *n* (1586) **1** : a sapphic strophe **2** : a verse having the metrical pattern of one of the first three lines of a sapphic strophe

sap·phire \ˈsaf-ˌī(ə)r\ *n* [ME *safir*, fr. OF, fr. L *sapphirus*, fr. Gk *sappheiros*, fr. Heb *sappīr*, fr. Skt *śanipriya*, lit., dear to the planet Saturn, fr. *Śani* Saturn + *priya* dear] (13c) **1 a** : a gem variety of corundum in transparent or translucent crystals of a color other than red; *esp* : one of a transparent rich blue **b** : a gem of such corundum **2** : a variable color averaging a deep purplish blue — **sapphire** *adj*

sap·phi·rine \ˈsaf-ə-ˌrīn, ˈsaf-ˌī(ə)r-ˌēn, sa-ˈfī-rən\ *adj* (15c) **1** : made of sapphire **2** : resembling sapphire esp. in color

sap·phism \ˈsaf-ˌiz-əm\ *n* [*Sappho* + *-ism*; fr. the belief that Sappho was homosexual] (ca. 1890) : LESBIANISM

sap·pi·ness \ˈsap-ē-nəs\ *n* (1552) **1** : the state of being full of or smelling of sap **2** : the quality or state of being sappy : FOOLISHNESS

sap·py \'sap-ē\ *adj* **sap·pi·er; -est** (bef. 12c) **1 :** abounding with sap **2 :** resembling or consisting largely of sapwood **3 a :** foolishly or immaturely sentimental **b :** lacking in good sense : SILLY

sapr- *or* **sapro-** *comb form* [Gk, fr. *sapros*] **1 :** rotten : putrid ⟨*sapremia*⟩ **2 :** dead or decaying organic matter ⟨*sapro*phyte⟩

sap·ro·gen·ic \,sap-rə-'jen-ik\ *adj* (ca. 1876) : of, causing, or resulting from putrefaction — **sap·ro·ge·nic·i·ty** \-rō-jə-'nis-ət-ē\ *n*

sap·ro·lite \'sap-rə-,līt\ *n* (ca. 1894) : disintegrated rock that lies in its original place

sa·proph·a·gous \sa-'präf-ə-gəs\ *adj* [NL *saprophagus,* fr. *sapr-* + *-phagus* -phagous] (1819) : feeding on decaying matter

sap·ro·phyte \'sap-rə-,fīt\ *n* [ISV] (ca. 1875) : a saprophytic organism; *esp* : a plant living on dead or decaying organic matter

sap·ro·phyt·ic \,sap-rə-'fit-ik\ *adj* (1882) : obtaining food by absorbing dissolved organic material; *esp* : obtaining nourishment osmotically from the products of organic breakdown and decay — **sap·ro·phyt·i·cal·ly** \-i-k(ə-)lē\ *adv*

sap·ro·zo·ic \,sap-rə-'zō-ik\ *adj* (ca. 1920) : SAPROPHYTIC — used of animals (as protozoans)

sap·sa·go \sap-'sā-(,)gō, 'sap-sə-,gō\ *n* [modif. of G *schabziger*] (1846) : a very hard green skim-milk cheese flavored with the powdered leaves of an aromatic legume (*Trigonella coerulea*) and shaped in truncated cones

sap·suck·er \'sap-,sək-ər\ *n* (1805) : any of various small American woodpeckers (esp. genus *Sphyrapicus*) that drill holes in trees in order to obtain sap and insects for food

sap·wood \-,wu̇d\ *n* (ca. 1855) : the younger softer living or physiologically active outer portion of wood that lies between the cambium and the heartwood and is more permeable, less durable, and usu. lighter in color than the heartwood

sar·a·band *or* **sar·a·bande** \'sar-ə-,band\ *n* [F *sarabande,* fr. Sp *zarabanda*] (1616) **1 :** a stately court dance of the 17th and 18th centuries resembling the minuet **2 :** the music for the saraband in slow triple time with accent on the second beat

Sar·a·cen \'sar-ə-sən\ *n* [ME, fr. OE, fr. LL *Saracenus,* fr. LGk *Sarakēnos*] (bef. 12c) : a member of a nomadic people of the deserts between Syria and Arabia; *broadly* : ARAB — **Saracen** *adj* — **Sar·a·cen·ic** \,sar-ə-'sen-ik\ *adj*

Sa·rah \'ser-ə, 'sar-ə, 'sā-rə\ *n* [Heb *Śārāh*] **1 :** the wife of Abraham and mother of Isaac **2 :** a kinswoman of Tobias married to him

sa·ran \sə-'ran\ *n* [fr. *Saran,* a trademark] (ca. 1940) : a tough flexible thermoplastic resin

sarape \sə-'räp-ē\ *var of* SERAPE

Sar·a·to·ga trunk \,sar-ə-,tō-gə-\ *n* [*Saratoga* Springs, N.Y.] (1858) : a large traveling trunk usu. with a rounded top

sarc- *or* **sarco-** *comb form* [Gk *sark-, sarko-,* fr. *sark-, sarx*] **1 :** flesh ⟨*sarc*ous⟩ **2 :** striated muscle ⟨*sarco*lemma⟩

sar·casm \'sär-,kaz-əm\ *n* [F or LL; F *sarcasme,* fr. LL *sarcasmos,* fr. Gk *sarkasmos,* fr. *sarkazein* to tear flesh, bite the lips in rage, sneer, fr. *sark-, sarx* flesh; akin to Av *thwarəs-* to cut] (1579) **1 :** a sharp and often satirical or ironic utterance designed to cut or give pain ⟨tired of his contemptuous ∼*s*⟩ **2 a :** a mode of satirical wit depending for its effect on bitter, caustic, and often ironic language that is usu. directed against an individual **b :** the use or language of sarcasm ⟨this is no time to indulge in ∼⟩ ***syn*** see WIT

sar·cas·tic \sär-'kas-tik\ *adj* [fr. *sarcasm,* after such pairs as E *enthusiasm: enthusiastic*] (1695) **1 :** having the character of sarcasm ⟨∼ criticism⟩ **2 :** given to the use of sarcasm : CAUSTIC ⟨a ∼ critic⟩ — **sar·cas·ti·cal·ly** \-ti-k(ə-)lē\ *adv*

syn SARCASTIC, SATIRIC, IRONIC, SARDONIC mean marked by bitterness and a power or will to cut or sting. SARCASTIC implies an intentional inflicting of pain by deriding, taunting, or ridiculing ⟨a critic famous mainly for his *sarcastic* remarks⟩ SATIRIC implies that the intent of the ridiculing is censure and reprobation ⟨a *satiric* look at contemporary sexual mores⟩ IRONIC implies an attempt to be amusing or provocative by saying usu. the opposite of what is meant ⟨made the *ironic* observation that the government could always be trusted⟩ SARDONIC implies scorn, mockery, or derision that is manifested by either verbal or facial expression ⟨surveyed the scene with a *sardonic* smile⟩

sarce·net \'särs-nət\ *n* [ME, fr. AF *sarzinett*] (15c) : a soft thin silk in plain or twill weaves used for dresses, veils, or trimmings — **sarcenet** *adj*

sar·coid \'sär-,ku̇id\ *n* (1841) **1 :** any of various diseases characterized esp. by the formation of nodules in the skin **2 :** a nodule characteristic of sarcoid or of sarcoidosis

sar·coid·osis \,sär-,ku̇id-'ō-səs\ *n, pl* **-o·ses** \-,sēz\ [NL] (1936) : a chronic disease of unknown cause that is characterized by the formation of nodules resembling true tubercles esp. in the lymph nodes, lungs, bones, and skin

sar·co·lem·ma \,sär-kə-'lem-ə\ *n* [NL, fr. *sarc-* + Gk *lemma* husk — more at LEMMA] (1840) : the thin transparent homogeneous sheath enclosing a striated muscle fiber — **sar·co·lem·mal** \-əl\ *adj*

sar·co·ma \sär-'kō-mə\ *n, pl* **-mas** *or* **-ma·ta** \-mət-ə\ [NL, fr. Gk *sarkōmat-, sarkōma* fleshy growth, fr. *sarkoun* to grow flesh, fr. *sark-, sarx*] (1804) : a malignant neoplasm arising in tissue of mesodermal origin (as connective tissue, bone, cartilage, or striated muscle) — **sar·co·ma·tous** \sär-'kō-mət-əs\ *adj*

sar·co·ma·to·sis \(,)sär-,kō-mə-'tō-səs\ *n, pl* **-to·ses** \-,sēz\ [NL] (ca. 1890) : a disease characterized by the presence and spread of sarcomas

sar·co·mere \'sär-kə-,mi(ə)r\ *n* (1891) : any of the repeating structural units of striated muscle fibrils

sar·coph·a·gus \sär-'käf-ə-gəs\ *n, pl* **-gi** \-,gī, -,jī, -,gē\ *also* **-gus·es** [L *sarcophagus* (*lapis*) limestone used for coffins, fr. Gk (*lithos*) *sarkophagos,* lit., flesh-eating stone, fr. *sark-* sarc- + *phagein* to eat — more at BAKSHEESH] (1704) : a stone coffin; *broadly* : COFFIN

sar·co·plasm \'sär-kə-,plaz-əm\ *n* [NL *sarcoplasma*] (ca. 1909) : the cytoplasm of a striated muscle fiber — **sar·co·plas·mat·ic** \,sär-kə-,plaz-'mat-ik\ *adj* — **sar·co·plas·mic** \-'plaz-mik\ *adj*

sarcoplasmic reticulum *n* (1953) : the endoplasmic reticulum of a striated muscle fiber

sar·cop·tic mange \(,)sär-,käp-tik-\ *n* [NL *Sarcoptes,* fr. *sarc-* + Gk *koptein* to cut — more at CAPON] (ca. 1890) : mange caused by mites (genus *Sarcoptes*) burrowing in the skin esp. of the head and face

sar·co·some \'sär-kə-,sōm\ *n* [NL *sarcosoma,* fr. *sarc-* + *-soma* -some] (1899) : a mitochondrion of a striated muscle fiber — **sar·co·som·al** \,sär-kə-'sō-məl\ *adj*

sard \'särd\ *n* [F *sarde,* fr. L *sarda*] (14c) : a deep orange-red variety of chalcedony classed by some as a variety of carnelian

sardar *var of* SIRDAR

sar·dine \sär-'dēn\ *n, pl* **sardines** *also* **sardine** [ME *sardeine,* fr. MF *sardine,* fr. L *sardina*] (15c) **1 :** any of several small or immature clupeid fishes; *esp* : the young of the European pilchard (*Sardinia pilchardus*) when of a size suitable for preserving for food **2 :** any of various small fishes (as an anchovy) resembling the true sardines or similarly preserved for food

Sar·din·ian \sär-'din-ē-ən, -'din-yən\ *n* (1598) **1 :** a native or inhabitant of Sardinia **2 :** the Romance language of central and southern Sardinia — **Sardinian** *adj*

sar·don·ic \sär-'dän-ik\ *adj* [F *sardonique,* fr. Gk *sardonios*] (1638) : disdainfully or skeptically humorous : derisively mocking ⟨a ∼ comment⟩ ⟨his ∼ expression⟩ ***syn*** see SARCASTIC — **sar·don·i·cal·ly** \-i-k(ə-)lē\ *adv*

sar·don·i·cism \sär-'dän-ə-,siz-əm\ *n* (1926) : sardonic quality or humor

sard·onyx \sär-'dän-iks *also* 'särd-^{ə}n-\ *n* [ME *sardonix,* fr. L *sardonyx,* fr. Gk] (14c) : an onyx having parallel layers of sard

sar·gas·so \sär-'gas-(,)ō\ *n, pl* **-sos** [Pg *sargaço*] (1598) **1 :** GULFWEED, SARGASSUM **2 :** a mass of floating vegetation and esp. sargassums

sar·gas·sum \sär-'gas-əm\ *n* [NL, genus name, fr. ISV *sargasso*] (ca. 1890) : any of a genus (*Sargassum*) of brown algae that have a branching thallus with lateral outgrowths differentiated as leafy segments, air bladders, or spore-bearing structures : GULFWEED

sarge \'särj\ *n* [by shortening & alter.] (1867) : SERGEANT

sa·ri *also* **sa·ree** \'sär-ē\ *n* [Hindi *sāṛī,* fr. Skt *śāṭī*] (1578) : a garment of southern Asian women that consists of several yards of lightweight cloth draped so that one end forms a skirt or pajama and the other a head or shoulder covering

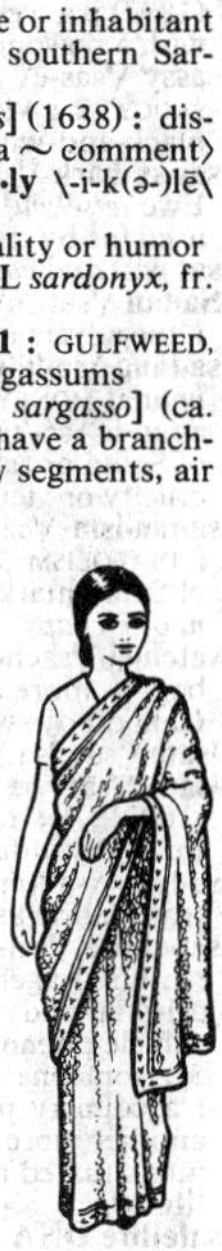
sari

sa·rin \'sär-ən, zä-'rēn\ *n* [G] (1951) : an extremely toxic chemical warfare agent $C_4H_{10}FO_2P$ that is a powerful cholinesterase inhibitor

sark \'särk\ *n* [ME (Sc) *serk,* fr. OE *serc;* akin to ON *serkr* shirt] *dial chiefly Brit* (bef. 12c) : SHIRT

sa·rod *also* **sa·rode** \sə-'rōd\ *n* [Hindi *sarod,* fr. Per] (1865) : a lute of northern India — **sa·rod·ist** \-'rōd-əst\ *n*

sa·rong \sə-'rȯŋ, -'räŋ\ *n* [Malay *kain sarong* cloth sheath] (1830) **1 :** a loose skirt made of a long strip of cloth wrapped around the body and worn by men and women of the Malay archipelago and the Pacific islands **2 :** cloth for sarongs

Sar·pe·don \sär-'pēd-^{ə}n\ *n* [L, fr. Gk *Sarpēdōn*] : a son of Zeus and Europa and king of Lycia killed in the Trojan War

sar·ra·ce·nia \,sar-ə-'sē-nē-ə, -'sen-ē-\ *n* [NL, fr. Michel *Sarrazin* †1734 Fr. physician & naturalist] (1884) : any of a genus (*Sarracenia* of the family Sarraceniaceae) that includes the insectivorous bog herbs of eastern No. America with pitcher-shaped or tubular leaves having an arched or hooded flap at the apex

sar·sa·pa·ril·la \,sas-(ə-)pə-'ril-ə, ,särs-, -'rel-\ *n* [Sp *zarzaparrilla*] (1577) **1 a :** any of various tropical American greenbriers **b :** the dried roots of a sarsaparilla used esp. as a flavoring **2 :** any of various plants (as wild sarsaparilla) that resemble or are used as a substitute for sarsaparilla **3 :** a sweetened carbonated beverage flavored with sassafras and oil distilled from a European birch

sarsenet *var of* SARCENET

sar·to·ri·al \sär-'tōr-ē-əl, sə(r)-, -'tȯr-\ *adj* [L *sartor*] (1823) : of or relating to a tailor or tailored clothes — **sar·to·ri·al·ly** \-ē-ə-lē\ *adv*

sar·to·ri·us \sär-'tōr-ē-əs, -'tȯr-\ *n, pl* **-rii** \-ē-,ī, -ē-,ē\ [NL, fr. L *sartor* tailor, fr. *sartus,* pp. of *sarcire* to mend — more at EXORCISE] (1704) : a muscle that crosses the front of the thigh obliquely, assists in rotating the leg to the cross-legged position in which the knees are spread wide apart, and in man is the longest muscle

Sar·um \'sar-əm, 'ser-\ *adj* [*Sarum,* old borough near Salisbury, England] (1570) : of or relating to the Roman rite as modified in Salisbury and used in England, Wales, and Ireland before the Reformation

^{1}**sash** \'sash\ *n* [Ar *shāsh* muslin] (1590) : a band worn about the waist or over one shoulder and used as a dress accessory or the emblem of an honorary or military order — **sashed** \'sasht\ *adj*

^{2}**sash** *n, pl* **sash** *also* **sash·es** [prob. modif. of F *châssis* chassis (taken as pl.)] (1681) : the framework in which panes of glass are set in a window or door; *also* : such a framework together with its panes forming a usu. movable part of a window

^{1}**sa·shay** \sa-'shā, sī-\ *vi* [alter. of *chassé*] (1836) **1 :** to make a chassé **2 a :** WALK, GLIDE, GO **b :** to strut or move about in an ostentatious or conspicuous manner **c :** to proceed or move in a diagonal or sideways manner

^{2}**sashay** *n* [by alter.] (1900) **1 :** CHASSÉ **2 :** TRIP, EXCURSION **3 :** a square-dance figure in which partners sidestep in a circle around each other with the man moving behind the woman

sa·shi·mi \'säsh-ə-mē\ *n* [Jp] (1880) : a Japanese dish consisting of thinly sliced raw fish

sas·ka·toon \,sas-kə-'tün\ *n* [*Saskatoon,* Saskatchewan, Canada] (1875) : SERVICEBERRY

Sas·quatch \'sas-,kwach, -,kwäch\ *n* [Salish *se'sxac* wild men] (ca. 1929) : a hairy manlike creature reported to exist in the northwestern U.S. and western Canada and said to be a primate between 6 and 15 feet tall — called also *bigfoot*

^{1}**sass** \'sas\ *n* [alter. of ^{1}*sauce*] (1835) : impudent speech

^{2}**sass** *vt* (1856) : to talk impudently or disrespectfully to

sas·sa·fras \'sas-(ə-),fras\ *n* [Sp *sasafrás*] (1577) **1 :** a tall eastern No. American tree (*Sassafras albidum*) of the laurel family with mucilaginous twigs and leaves **2 :** the dried root bark of the sassafras used esp. as a diaphoretic or flavoring agent

[1]**Sas·sa·ni·an** *or* **Sa·sa·ni·an** \sə-'sā-nē-ən, sa-'sā-\ *adj* (1788) **:** of, relating to, or having the characteristics of the Sassanid dynasty of ancient Persia or its art or architecture

[2]**Sassanian** *or* **Sasanian** *n* (1855) **:** SASSANID

Sas·sa·nid \sə-'sän-əd, -'san-; 'sas-ᵊn-\ *n* [NL *Sassanidae* Sassanids, fr. *Sassan,* founder of the dynasty] (1776) **:** a member of a dynasty of Persian kings of the 3d to 7th centuries — **Sassanid** *adj*

sass·wood \'sas-,wu̇d\ *n* [earlier *sassywood,* fr. *sassy* sasswood + *wood*] (1897) **:** a western African leguminous tree (*Erythrophloeum guineënse*) with a poisonous bark and a hard strong insect-resistant wood

sassy \'sas-ē\ *adj* **sass·i·er; -est** [alter. of *saucy*] (1815) **1 :** IMPUDENT, SAUCY **2 :** VIGOROUS, LIVELY **3 :** distinctively smart and stylish ⟨a ~ black-and-white bow tie —Jean Stafford⟩

sas·sy bark \'sas-ē-\ *n* [*sassy* sasswood, prob. of African origin; akin to Ewe *se³se³wu³*, an African timber tree] (1856) **:** sasswood bark formerly used (as by tribal Africans) as poison in ordeals

sat *past and past part of* SIT

Sa·tan \'sāt-ᵊn\ *n* [ME, fr. OE, fr. LL, fr. Gk, fr. Heb *śāṭān* adversary] **:** the adversary of God and lord of evil in Judaism and Christianity

sa·tang \sə-'täŋ\ *n, pl* **satang** *or* **satangs** [Thai *satān̄*] (ca. 1915) — see *baht* at MONEY table

sa·tan·ic \sə-'tan-ik, sā-\ *adj* (1667) **1 :** of, relating to, or characteristic of Satan or satanism ⟨~ pride⟩ ⟨~ rites⟩ **2 :** characterized by extreme cruelty or viciousness — **sa·tan·i·cal·ly** \-i-k(ə-)lē\ *adv*

sa·tan·ism \'sāt-ᵊn-,iz-əm\ *n, often cap* (1565) **1 :** innate wickedness **:** DIABOLISM **2 :** obsession with or affinity for evil; *specif* **:** the worship of Satan marked by the travesty of Christian rites — **sa·tan·ist** \-ᵊn-əst\ *n, often cap*

satch·el \'sach-əl\ *n* [ME *sachel,* fr. MF, fr. L *saccellus,* dim. of *saccus* bag — more at SACK] (14c) **:** a small bag often with a shoulder strap ⟨schoolboys with their ~*s*⟩ — **satch·el·ful** \-,fu̇l\ *n*

[1]**sate** \'sāt, 'sat\ *archaic past of* SIT

[2]**sate** \'sāt\ *vt* **sat·ed; sat·ing** [prob. by shortening & alter. fr. *satiate*] (1602) **1 :** to cloy with overabundance **:** GLUT **2 :** to appease (as a thirst) by indulging to the full ***syn*** see SATIATE

sa·teen \sa-'tēn, sə-\ *n* [alter. of *satin*] (1878) **:** a smooth durable lustrous fabric usu. made of cotton in satin weave

sat·el·lite \'sat-ᵊl-,īt\ *n* [MF, fr. L *satellit-, satelles* attendant] (1548) **1 :** a hired agent or obsequious follower **:** MINION, SYCOPHANT **2 a :** a celestial body orbiting another of larger size **b :** a man-made object or vehicle intended to orbit the earth, the moon, or another celestial body **3 :** someone or something attendant, subordinate, or dependent; *esp* **:** a country politically and economically dominated or controlled by another more powerful country **4 :** a usu. independent urban community situated near but not immediately adjacent to a large city — **satellite** *adj*

satellite DNA *n* (1969) **:** a DNA fraction differing in density from most of an organism's DNA as determined by centrifugation that apparently consists of repetitive nucleotide sequences, does not undergo transcription, and is found in some organisms (as the mouse) esp. in centromeric regions

sa·tem \'sät-əm\ *adj* [Av *satəm* hundred; fr. the fact that its initial sound (derived fr. an alveolar fricative) is the representative of an IE palatal stop — more at HUNDRED] (1901) **:** of, relating to, or constituting that part of the Indo-European language family in which the palatal stops became in prehistoric times palatal or alveolar fricatives — compare CENTUM

sa·ti \(,)sə-'tē, 'sə-,tē\ *var of* SUTTEE

sa·tia·ble \'sā-shə-bəl\ *adj* (1570) **:** capable of being appeased or satisfied

[1]**sa·tiate** \'sā-sh(ē-)ət\ *adj* (15c) **:** filled to satiety

[2]**sa·ti·ate** \'sā-shē-,āt\ *vt* **-at·ed; -at·ing** [L *satiatus,* pp. of *satiare,* fr. *satis* enough — more at SAD] (1532) **:** to satisfy (as a need or desire) fully or to excess — **sa·ti·a·tion** \,sā-s(h)ē-'ā-shən\ *n*

syn SATIATE, SATE, SURFEIT, CLOY, PALL, GLUT, GORGE mean to fill to repletion. SATIATE and SATE may sometimes imply only complete satisfaction but more often suggest repletion that has destroyed interest or desire; SURFEIT implies a nauseating repletion; CLOY stresses the disgust or boredom resulting from such surfeiting; PALL emphasizes the loss of ability to stimulate interest or appetite; GLUT implies excess in feeding or supplying; GORGE suggests glutting to the point of bursting or choking.

sa·ti·ety \sə-'tī-ət-ē *also* 'sā-sh(ē-)ət-\ *n* [MF *satieté,* fr. L *satietat-, satietas,* fr. *satis*] (1533) **1 :** the quality or state of being fed or gratified to or beyond capacity **:** SURFEIT, FULLNESS **2 :** the revulsion or disgust caused by overindulgence or excess

[1]**sat·in** \'sat-ᵊn\ *n* [ME, fr. MF] (14c) **:** a fabric (as of silk) in satin weave with lustrous face and dull back

[2]**satin** *adj* (1521) **1 :** made of or covered with satin **2 :** suggestive of satin esp. in smooth lustrous appearance or sleekness to touch

sat·in·et \,sat-ᵊn-'et\ *n* (1703) **1 :** a thin silk satin or imitation satin **2 :** a variation of satin weave used in making satinet

satin stitch *n* (1684) **:** an embroidery stitch nearly alike on both sides and worked so closely as to resemble satin

satin weave *n* (1897) **:** a weave in which warp threads interlace with filling threads to produce a smooth-faced fabric

sat·in·wood \'sat-ᵊn-,wu̇d\ *n* (1792) **1 a :** an East Indian tree (*Chloroxylon swietenia*) of the mahogany family that yields a lustrous yellowish brown wood **b :** a tree (as a yellowwood) with wood resembling true satinwood **2 :** the wood of a satinwood

sat·iny \'sat-nē, 'sat-ᵊn-ē\ *adj* (1786) **:** having or resembling the soft lustrous smoothness of satin

sat·ire \'sa-,tī(ə)r\ *n* [MF or L; MF, fr. L *satura, satira,* fr. (*lanx*) *satura* full plate, medley, fr. fem. of *satur* sated; akin to L *satis* enough — more at SAD] (1509) **1 :** a literary work holding up human vices and follies to ridicule or scorn **2 :** trenchant wit, irony, or sarcasm used to expose and discredit vice or folly ***syn*** see WIT

sa·tir·ic \sə-'tir-ik\ *or* **sa·tir·i·cal** \-i-kəl\ *adj* (1509) **1 :** of, relating to, or constituting satire ⟨~ writers⟩ ⟨the ~ undertone of his essay⟩ **2 :** manifesting or given to satire ⟨watched by his ~ companion⟩ ***syn*** see SARCASTIC — **sa·tir·i·cal·ly** \-i-k(ə-)lē\ *adv*

sat·i·rist \'sat-ə-rəst\ *n* (1589) **:** one that satirizes; *esp* **:** a writer of satire

sat·i·rize \-,rīz\ *vb* **-rized; -riz·ing** *vi* (1601) **:** to utter or write satire ~ *vt* **:** to censure or ridicule by means of satire

sat·is·fac·tion \,sat-əs-'fak-shən\ *n* [ME, fr. MF, fr. LL *satisfaction-, satisfactio,* fr. L, reparation, amends, fr. *satisfactus,* pp. of *satisfacere* to satisfy] (14c) **1 a :** the payment through penance of the temporal punishment incurred by a sin **b :** reparation for sin that meets the demands of divine justice **2 a :** fulfillment of a need or want **b :** the quality or state of being satisfied **:** CONTENTMENT **c :** a source or means of enjoyment **:** GRATIFICATION **3 a :** compensation for a loss or injury **:** ATONEMENT, RESTITUTION **b :** the discharge of a legal obligation or claim **c :** VINDICATION **4 :** convinced assurance or certainty ⟨proved to the ~ of the court⟩

sat·is·fac·to·ri·ly \-'fak-t(ə-)rə-lē\ *adv* (1587) **:** in a satisfactory manner

sat·is·fac·to·ry \,sat-əs-'fak-t(ə-)rē\ *adj* (1547) **:** giving satisfaction **:** ADEQUATE — **sat·is·fac·to·ri·ness** *n*

sat·is·fi·able \'sat-əs-,fī-ə-bəl\ *adj* (1609) **:** capable of being satisfied

sat·is·fy \'sat-əs-,fī\ *vb* **-fied; -fy·ing** [ME *satisfien,* fr. MF *satisfier,* modif. of L *satisfacere,* fr. *satis* enough + *facere* to do, make — more at SAD, DO] *vt* (15c) **1 a :** to carry out the terms of (as a contract) **:** DISCHARGE **b :** to meet a financial obligation to **2 :** to make reparation to (an injured party) **:** INDEMNIFY **3 a :** to make happy **:** PLEASE **b :** to gratify to the full **:** APPEASE **4 a :** CONVINCE **b :** to put an end to (doubt or uncertainty) **:** DISPEL **5 a :** to conform to (as specifications) **:** be adequate to (an end in view) **b :** to make true by fulfilling a condition ⟨values that ~ an equation⟩ ⟨~ a hypothesis⟩ **6 :** to respond to by chemical union ⟨~ valences⟩ ~ *vi* **:** to be adequate **:** SUFFICE; *also* **:** PLEASE ***syn*** see PAY — **sat·is·fy·ing·ly** \-iŋ-lē\ *adv*

sa·to·ri \sə-'tōr-ē, sä-, -'tȯr-\ *n* [Jp] (1727) **:** a state of intuitive illumination sought in Zen Buddhism

sa·trap \'sā-,trap *also* 'sa-,trap *or* 'sa-trəp\ *n* [ME, fr. L *satrapes,* fr. Gk *satrapēs,* fr. OPer *xshathrapāvan,* lit., protector of the dominion] (14c) **1 :** the governor of a province in ancient Persia **2 a :** RULER **b :** a subordinate official **:** HENCHMAN

sa·tra·py \'sā-trə-pē, 'sa-, -,trap-ē\ *n, pl* **-pies** (1603) **:** the territory or jurisdiction of a satrap

sat·su·ma \sat-'sü-mə, 'sat-sə-\ *n* [*Satsuma,* former province in Kyushu, Japan] (1882) **1 :** any of several cultivated mandarin trees that bear medium-sized largely seedless fruits with thin smooth skin **2 :** the fruit of a satsuma

sat·u·ra·ble \'sach-(ə-)rə-bəl\ *adj* (ca. 1570) **:** capable of being saturated

sat·u·rant \'sach-(ə-)rənt\ *n* (ca. 1775) **:** something that saturates

[1]**sat·u·rate** \'sach-ə-,rāt\ *vt* **-rat·ed; -rat·ing** [L *saturatus,* pp. of *saturare,* fr. *satur* sated — more at SATIRE] (1538) **1 :** to satisfy fully **:** SATIATE **2 :** to treat, furnish, or charge with something to the point where no more can be absorbed, dissolved, or retained ⟨water *saturated* with salt⟩ **3 a :** to fill completely with something that permeates or pervades ⟨book is *saturated* with Hollywood, old and new —Newgate Callendar⟩ **b :** to load to capacity **4 :** to cause to combine till there is no further tendency to combine ***syn*** see SOAK — **sat·u·ra·tor** \-,rāt-ər\ *n*

[2]**sat·u·rate** \'sach-(ə-)rət\ *adj* (1782) **:** SATURATED

sat·u·rat·ed \'sach-ə-,rāt-əd\ *adj* (1728) **1 :** full of moisture **:** made thoroughly wet **2 a :** being the most concentrated solution that can persist in the presence of an excess of the dissolved substance **b :** being a compound that does not tend to unite directly with another compound — used esp. of organic compounds containing no double or triple bonds **3** *of a color* **:** having high saturation **:** PURE

sat·u·ra·tion \,sach-ə-'rā-shən\ *n* (1554) **1 a :** the act of saturating **:** the state of being saturated **b :** SATIETY, SURFEIT **2 :** conversion of an unsaturated to a saturated chemical compound (as by hydrogenation) **3 :** a state of maximum impregnation: as **a :** complete infiltration **:** PERMEATION **b :** the presence in air of the most water possible under existent pressure and temperature **c :** magnetization to the point beyond which a further increase in the intensity of the magnetizing force will produce no further magnetization **4 a :** chromatic purity **:** freedom from dilution with white **b (1) :** degree of difference from the gray having the same lightness — used of an object color **(2) :** degree of difference from the achromatic light-source color of the same brightness — used of a light-source color **5 :** the supplying of a market with all the goods it will absorb **6 :** an overwhelming concentration of military forces or firepower

Sat·ur·day \'sat-ərd-ē, -(,)ā\ *n* [ME *saterday,* fr. OE *sæterndæg;* akin to OFris *sāterdei;* both fr. a prehistoric WGmc compound whose first component was borrowed fr. L *Saturnus* Saturn and whose second component is represented by OE *dæg* day] (bef. 12c) **:** the seventh day of the week — **Sat·ur·days** \-ēz\ *adv*

Saturday night special *n* (1968) **:** a cheap easily concealed handgun

Sat·urn \'sat-ərn\ *n* [L *Saturnus*] **1 :** a Roman god of agriculture and father by Ops of Jupiter **2 :** the planet 6th in order from the sun — see PLANET table

sat·ur·na·lia \,sat-ər-'nāl-yə, -'nā-lē-ə\ *n pl but sing or pl in constr* [L, fr. neut. pl. of *saturnalis* of Saturn, fr. *Saturnus*] (1591) **1** *cap* **:** the festival of Saturn in ancient Rome beginning on Dec. 17 **2** *sing, pl* **saturnalias** *also* **saturnalia a :** an unrestrained often licentious celebration **:** ORGY **b :** EXCESS, EXTRAVAGANCE — **sat·ur·na·lian** \-'nāl-yən, -'nā-lē-ən\ *adj* — **sat·ur·na·lian·ly** *adv*

Sa·tur·ni·an \sa-'tər-nē-ən, sə-\ *adj* (1557) **1 :** of, relating to, or influenced by the planet Saturn **2** *archaic* **:** of or relating to the god Saturn or the golden age of his reign

sa·tur·ni·id \-nē-əd\ *n* [deriv. of NL *Saturnia,* genus of moths, fr. L, daughter of the god Saturn] (1892) **:** any of a large family (Saturniidae) of stout strong-winged moths (as a luna moth or a cecropia moth) with hairy bodies — **saturniid** *adj*

sat·ur·nine \'sat-ər-,nīn\ *adj* (15c) **1 :** born under or influenced astrologically by the planet Saturn **2 a :** cold and steady in mood **:** slow to act or change **b :** of a gloomy or surly disposition **c :** having a sardonic aspect ⟨a ~ smile⟩ ***syn*** see SULLEN

sat·urn·ism \'sat-ər-,niz-əm\ *n* [*saturn* (lead)] (1855) **:** LEAD POISONING

sa·tya·gra·ha \(,)sə-'tyä-grə-hə\ *n* [Skt *satyāgraha,* lit., insistence on truth] (1919) **:** pressure for social and political reform through friendly passive resistance practiced by M. K. Gandhi and his followers in India

sa·tyr \ˈsāt-ər, ˈsat-\ *n* [ME, fr. L *satyrus*, fr. Gk *satyros*] (14c) **1** *often cap* : a sylvan deity in Greek mythology having certain characteristics of a horse or goat and fond of Dionysian revelry **2 a** : a lecherous man **b** : one having satyriasis **3** : any of various usu. brown and gray satyrid butterflies — **sa·tyr·ic** \sā-ˈtir-ik, sə-, sa-\ *adj*

sa·ty·ri·a·sis \ˌsāt-ə-ˈrī-ə-səs, ˌsat-\ *n* [LL, fr. Gk, fr. *satyros*] (1657) : excessive or abnormal sexual craving in the male

sa·ty·rid \sə-ˈtī-rəd\ *n* [NL *Satyridae*, deriv. of Gk *satyros*] (1901) : any of a family (Satyridae) of usu. brownish butterflies that feed on grasses as larvae and have one or more main wing veins swollen basally — **satyrid** *adj*

satyr play *n* (1929) : a comic play of ancient Greece burlesquing a mythological subject and having a chorus representing satyrs

1sauce \ˈsȯs, *usu* ˈsas *for 4*\ *n* [ME, fr. MF, fr. L *salsa*, fem. of *salsus* salted, fr. pp. of *sallere* to salt, fr. *sal* salt — more at SALT] (14c) **1 a** : a condiment or relish for food; *esp* : a fluid dressing or topping **2** : something that adds zest or piquancy **3** : stewed fruit eaten with other food or as a dessert ⟨apple ~⟩ **4** : pert or impudent language or actions **5** *slang* : LIQUOR

2sauce \ˈsȯs, *usu* ˈsas *for 3*\ *vt* **sauced; sauc·ing** (15c) **1** : to dress with relish or seasoning **2 a** *archaic* : to modify the harsh or unpleasant characteristics of **b** : to give zest or piquancy to **3** : to be rude or impudent to

sauce·boat \ˈsȯs-ˌbōt\ *n* (1747) : a low boat-shaped pitcher for serving sauces and gravies

sauce·box \ˈsas-ˌbäks *also* ˈsȯs-\ *n* (1588) : a saucy impudent person

sauce·pan \ˈsȯ-ˌspan, *esp Brit* -spən\ *n* (1686) : a small deep cooking pan with a handle

sau·cer \ˈsȯ-sər\ *n* [ME, plate containing sauce, fr. MF *saussier*, fr. *sausse, sauce*] (1607) **1** : a small shallow dish in which a cup is set at table **2** : something resembling a saucer esp. in shape; *esp* : FLYING SAUCER — **sau·cer·like** \-ˌlīk\ *adj*

saucy \ˈsas-ē *also* ˈsȯs-ē\ *adj* **sauc·i·er; -est** (1530) **1 a** : impertinently bold and impudent **b** : amusingly forward and flippant : IRREPRESSIBLE **2** : SMART, TRIM ⟨a ~ little hat⟩ — **sauc·i·ly** \-ə-lē\ *adv* — **sauc·i·ness** \-ē-nəs\ *n*

sau·er·bra·ten \ˈsau̇(-ə)r-ˌbrät-ᵊn\ *n* [G, fr. *sauer* sour (fr. OHG *sūr*) + *braten* roast meat — more at SOUR] (1889) : oven-roasted or pot-roasted beef marinated before cooking in vinegar with peppercorns, garlic, onions, and bay leaves

sau·er·kraut \ˈsau̇(-ə)r-ˌkrau̇t\ *n* [G, fr. *sauer* sour + *kraut* cabbage] (1617) : cabbage cut fine and fermented in a brine made of its own juice with salt

sau·ger \ˈsȯ-gər\ *n* [origin unknown] (ca. 1882) : a pike perch (*Stizostedion canadense*) similar to but smaller than the walleye

saugh *or* **sauch** \ˈsäk, ˈsȯk\ *n* [ME (Sc) *sauch*, fr. OE *salh*, alter. of *sealh* — more at SALLOW] *chiefly Scot* (14c) : SALLOW

Saul \ˈsȯl\ *n* [LL *Saulus*, fr. Gk *Saulos*, fr. Heb *Shāʼūl*] **1** : the first king of Israel **2** : the apostle Paul — called also *Saul of Tarsus*

sau·na \ˈsau̇-nə, ˈsȯ-nə\ *n* [Finn] (1891) **1** : a Finnish steam bath in which the steam is provided by water thrown on hot stones; *also* : a bathhouse or room used for such a bath **2** : a dry heat bath; *also* : a room or cabinet used for such a bath

saun·ter \ˈsȯnt-ər, ˈsänt-\ *vi* [prob. fr. ME *santren* to muse] (15c) : to walk about in an idle or leisurely manner : STROLL — **saunter** *n* — **saun·ter·er** \-ər-ər\ *n*

sau·rel \sȯ-ˈrel\ *n* [F, fr. LL *saurus* horse mackerel, fr. Gk *sauros*] (1882) : either of two carangid fishes (genus *Trachurus*): **a** : a horse mackerel (*T. trachurus*) **b** : a jack mackerel (*T. symmetricus*)

sau·ri·an \ˈsȯr-ē-ən\ *n* [deriv. of Gk *sauros* horse mackerel, lizard; akin to Gk *psauein* to touch, graze] (ca. 1801) : any of a group (Sauria) of reptiles including the lizards and in older classifications the crocodiles and various extinct forms (as the dinosaurs and ichthyosaurs) that resemble lizards — **saurian** *adj*

sau·ro·pod \ˈsȯr-ə-ˌpäd\ *n* [NL *Sauropoda*, fr. Gk *sauros* lizard + NL *-poda*] (ca. 1891) : any of a suborder (Sauropoda) of dinosaurs comprising herbivorous forms with long neck and tail, small head, and more or less plantigrade 5-toed limbs — **sauropod** *adj*

sau·ry \ˈsȯr-ē\ *n, pl* **sauries** [NL *saurus* lizard, fr. Gk *sauros*] (ca. 1771) **1** : a slender long-beaked fish (*Scombresox saurus*) related to the needlefishes and found in temperate parts of the Atlantic **2** : a widely distributed fish (*Cololabris saira*) of the Pacific similar to the related Atlantic saury

sau·sage \ˈsȯ-sij\ *n* [ME *sausige*, fr. ONF *saussiche*, fr. LL *salsicia*, fr. L *salsus* salted — more at SAUCE] (15c) : a highly seasoned minced meat (as pork) usu. stuffed in casings of prepared animal intestine

1sau·té \sō-ˈtā, sȯ-\ *n* [F, pp. of *sauter* to jump, fr. L *saltare* — more at SALTATION] (1813) : a sautéed dish — **sauté** *adj*

2sauté *vt* **sau·téed** *or* **sau·téd; sau·té·ing** (1813) : to fry in a small amount of fat

sau·ternes \sō-ˈtərn, sȯ-, -ˈte(ə)rn\ *n, often cap* [F *sauternes*, fr. *Sauternes*, commune in France] (1711) **1** : a full-bodied sweet white wine from the Bordeaux region of France **2** *usu* **sauterne** : a semidry to semisweet American white wine that is a blend of several grapes

sau·vi·gnon blanc \ˌsō-vēn-ˌyō^{n}-ˈblä^{n}\ *n* [F, white sauvignon (variety of grape)] (1941) : a dry white California wine made from a grape orig. grown in Bordeaux and the Loire valley

1sav·age \ˈsav-ij\ *adj* [ME *sauvage*, fr. MF, fr. ML *salvaticus*, alter. of L *silvaticus* of the woods, wild, fr. *silva* wood, forest] (14c) **1 a** : not domesticated or under human control : UNTAMED ⟨~ beasts⟩ **b** : lacking the restraints normal to civilized human beings : FIERCE, FEROCIOUS **2** : WILD, UNCULTIVATED ⟨seldom have I seen such ~ scenery —Douglas Carruthers⟩ **3** : BOORISH, RUDE ⟨the ~ bad manners of most motorists —M. P. O'Connor⟩ **4** : lacking complex or advanced culture : UNCIVILIZED ***syn*** see FIERCE — **sav·age·ly** *adv* — **sav·age·ness** *n*

2savage *vt* **sav·aged; sav·ag·ing** (1563) : to attack or treat brutally

3savage *n* (1575) **1** : a person belonging to a primitive society **2** : a brutal person **3** : a rude or unmannerly person

sav·age·ry \ˈsav-ij-(ə-)rē\ *n, pl* **-ries** (1595) **1 a** : the quality of being savage **b** : an act of cruelty or violence **2** : an uncivilized state

sav·ag·ism \ˈsav-ij-ˌiz-əm\ *n* (1796) : SAVAGERY

sa·van·na *also* **sa·van·nah** \sə-ˈvan-ə\ *n* [Sp *zavana*, fr. Taino *zabana*] (1555) **1** : a treeless plain esp. in Florida **2** : a tropical or subtropical grassland containing scattered trees and drought-resistant undergrowth

sa·vant \sa-ˈvänt, sə-, -ˈvä^{n}; sə-ˈvant, ˈsav-ənt\ *n* [F, fr. prp. of *savoir* to know, fr. L *sapere* to be wise — more at SAGE] (1719) : a man of learning; *esp* : a person with detailed knowledge in some specialized field (as of science or literature)

sav·a·rin \ˈsav-ə-rən\ *n* [F, fr. Anthelme Brillat-*Savarin* †1826 Fr. politician, writer, and gourmet] (1877) : a rich yeast cake baked in a ring mold and soaked in a rum or kirsch syrup

sa·vate \sə-ˈvät, sa-, -ˈvat\ *n* [F, lit., old shoe] (1862) : a form of boxing in which blows are delivered with either the hands or the feet

1save \ˈsāv\ *vb* **saved; sav·ing** [ME *saven*, fr. OF *salver*, fr. LL *salvare*, fr. L *salvus* safe — more at SAFE] *vt* (13c) **1 a** : to deliver from sin **b** : to rescue or deliver from danger or harm **c** : to preserve or guard from injury, destruction, or loss **2** : to put aside as a store or reserve : ACCUMULATE **3 a** : to make unnecessary : AVOID ⟨it ~*s* an hour's waiting⟩ **b** (1) : to keep from being lost to an opponent (2) : to prevent an opponent from scoring or winning **4** : MAINTAIN, PRESERVE ⟨~ appearances⟩ ~ *vi* **1** : to rescue or deliver someone **2 a** : to put aside money **b** : to avoid unnecessary waste or expense : ECONOMIZE **3** : to make a save ***syn*** see RESCUE — **sav·able** *or* **save·able** \ˈsā-və-bəl\ *adj* — **sav·er** *n*

2save *n* (1890) **1** : a play that prevents an opponent from scoring or winning **2** : the action of a relief pitcher in baseball in successfully protecting a team's lead

3save \(ˌ)sāv\ *prep* [ME *sauf*, fr. MF, fr. *sauf*, adj., safe — more at SAFE] (14c) : other than : BUT, EXCEPT ⟨no hope ~ one⟩

4save \(ˌ)sāv\ *conj* (14c) **1** : except for the fact that : ONLY — used with *that* ⟨of his earlier years little is known, ~ that he studied violin —J. N. Burk⟩ **2** : BUT, EXCEPT — used before a word often taken to be the subject of a clause ⟨no one knows about it ~ she⟩

save–all \ˈsā-ˌvȯl\ *n* (1645) : something that prevents waste, loss, or damage (as a receptacle for catching waste products for further utilization)

sav·e·loy \ˈsav-ə-ˌlȯi\ *n* [modif. of F *cervelas*, fr. MF, fr. OIt *cervellata* pig's brains, fr. *cervello* brain, fr. L *cerebellum* — more at CEREBELLUM] *Brit* (1837) : a ready-cooked highly seasoned dry sausage

sav·in \ˈsav-ən\ *n* [ME, fr. MF *savine*, fr. L *sabina*, fem. of *Sabinus*, lit., Sabine] (14c) **1** : a Eurasian juniper (*Juniperus sabina*) with dark foliage and small yellowish green berries **2** : RED CEDAR 1

1sav·ing \ˈsā-viŋ\ *n* [gerund of *save*] (14c) **1** : preservation from danger or destruction : DELIVERANCE **2** : the act or an instance of economizing **3 a** *pl* : money put by **b** : the excess of income over consumption expenditures — often used in pl.

2sav·ing \ˌsā-viŋ, ˈsā-\ *prep* [prp. of *save*] (14c) **1** : EXCEPT, SAVE **2** : without disrespect to

3sav·ing \ˌsā-viŋ, ˈsā-\ *conj* (14c) : EXCEPT, SAVE

saving grace *n* (1597) : a redeeming quality or factor

savings account *n* (1911) : an account (as in a bank) on which interest is usu. paid and from which withdrawals can be made usu. only by presentation of a passbook or by written authorization on a prescribed form

savings and loan association *n* (ca. 1924) : a cooperative association organized to hold savings of members in the form of dividend-bearing shares and to invest chiefly in home mortgage loans

savings bank *n* (1817) : a bank organized to hold funds of individual depositors in interest-bearing accounts and to make long-term investments (as in home mortgage loans)

savings bond *n* (1948) : a nontransferable registered U.S. bond issued in denominations of $50 to $10,000

sav·ior *or* **sav·iour** \ˈsāv-yər *also* -ˌyȯ(ə)r\ *n* [ME *saveour*, fr. MF, fr. LL *salvator*, fr. *salvatus*, pp. of *salvare* to save] (14c) **1** : one that saves from danger or destruction **2** : one who brings salvation; *specif, cap* : JESUS 1

sa·voir faire \ˌsav-ˌwär-ˈfa(ə)r, -ˈfe(ə)r\ *n* [F *savoir-faire*, lit., knowing how to do] (1815) : capacity for appropriate action; *esp* : a polished sureness in social behavior ***syn*** see TACT

1sa·vor *also* **sa·vour** \ˈsā-vər\ *n* [ME, fr. OF, fr. L *sapor*; akin to L *sapere* to taste — more at SAGE] (13c) **1** : the taste or smell of something **2** : a particular flavor or smell **3** : a distinctive quality — **sa·vor·less** \-ləs\ *adj* — **sa·vor·ous** \ˈsāv-(ə-)rəs\ *adj*

2savor *also* **savour** *vb* **sa·vored; sa·vor·ing** \ˈsāv-(ə-)riŋ\ *vi* (14c) : to have a specified smell or quality : SMACK ~ *vt* **1** : to give flavor to : SEASON **2 a** : to have experience of : TASTE **b** : to taste or smell with pleasure : RELISH **c** : to delight in : ENJOY — **sa·vor·er** \ˈsā-vər-ər\ *n*

1sa·vory *also* **sa·voury** \ˈsāv(-ə)-rē\ *adj* (13c) : having savor: as **a** : piquantly pleasant to the mind ⟨a ~ collection of essays⟩ **b** : morally exemplary : EDIFYING ⟨his reputation was anything but ~⟩ **c** : pleasing to the sense of taste esp. by reason of effective seasoning ***syn*** see PALATABLE — **sa·vor·i·ly** \-rə-lē\ *adv* — **sa·vor·i·ness** \-rē-nəs\ *n*

2savory *also* **savoury** *n, pl* **sa·vor·ies** *Brit* (1661) : a dish of stimulating flavor served usu. at the end of dinner but sometimes as an appetizer

3sa·vo·ry \ˈsāv(-ə)-rē\ *n, pl* **-ries** [ME *saverey*] (ca. 1890) : either of two aromatic mints: **a** : SUMMER SAVORY **b** : WINTER SAVORY

Sa·voy·ard \sə-ˈvȯi-ˌärd, ˌsav-ˌȯi-ˈärd, ˌsav-ˌwä-ˈyär(d)\ *n* [*Savoy* theater, London, built for the presentation of Gilbert and Sullivan operas] (1890) : a devotee, performer, or producer of the comic operas of W. S. Gilbert and A. S. Sullivan

sa·voy cabbage \sə-ˌvȯi-, ˌsav-ˌȯi-\ *n* [trans. of F *chou de Savoie* cabbage of Savoy] (1707) : a cabbage with compact heads of wrinkled and curled leaves

1sav·vy \ˈsav-ē\ *vb* **sav·vied; sav·vy·ing** [modif. of Sp *sabe* he knows, fr. *saber* to know, fr. L *sapere* to be wise — more at SAGE] (1785) : UNDERSTAND

2savvy *n* (ca. 1785) : practical know-how ⟨political ~⟩ — **savvy** *adj*

\ə\ abut \ᵊ\ kitten, F table \ər\ further \a\ ash \ā\ ace \ä\ cot, cart \au̇\ out \ch\ chin \e\ bet \ē\ easy \g\ go \i\ hit \ī\ ice \j\ job \ŋ\ sing \ō\ go \ȯ\ law \ȯi\ boy \th\ thin \th\ the \ü\ loot \u̇\ foot \y\ yet \zh\ vision \à, k, ^{n}, œ, œ̄, ue, ue̅, ʸ\ see Guide to Pronunciation

[1]saw *past of* SEE

[2]saw \'sȯ\ *n* [ME *sawe,* fr. OE *sagu;* akin to OHG *sega* saw, L *secare* to cut, *secula* sickle] (bef. 12c) : a hand or power tool or a machine used to cut hard material (as wood, metal, or bone) and equipped usu. with a toothed blade or disk — **saw·like** \-ˌlīk\ *adj*

[3]saw *vb* **sawed** \'sȯd\; **sawed** *or* **sawn** \'sȯn\; **saw·ing** \'sȯ(-)iŋ\ *vt* (13c) **1** : to cut with a saw **2** : to produce or form by cutting with a saw **3** : to slash as though with a saw ~ *vi* **1 a** : to use a saw **b** : to cut with or as if with a saw **2** : to undergo cutting with a saw **3** : to make motions as though using a saw ⟨~*ed* at the reins⟩ — **saw·er** \'sȯ(-ə)r\ *n*

[4]saw *n* [ME *sawe,* fr. OE *sagu* discourse; akin to OHG & ON *saga* tale, OE *secgan* to say — more at SAY] (bef. 12c) : MAXIM, PROVERB

saw·bones \'sȯ-ˌbōnz\ *n, pl* **sawbones** *or* **saw·bones·es** *slang* (1837) : PHYSICIAN, SURGEON

saw·buck \'sȯ-ˌbək\ *n* (1850) **1** *slang* : a 10-dollar bill **2** : SAWHORSE; *esp* : one with X-shaped ends

saw·dust \'sȯd-(ˌ)əst\ *n* (1530) : fine particles (as of wood) made by a saw in cutting

sawed–off \'sȯ-ˌdȯf\ *adj* (1869) **1** : having an end sawed off ⟨a ~ shotgun⟩ **2** : of less than average height

saw·fish \'sȯ-ˌfish\ *n* (1664) : any of a family (Pristidae) of several large elongate viviparous rays having a long flattened snout with a row of stout serrate structures along each edge and living in warm shallow seas and in or near the mouths of rivers principally in tropical America and Africa

saw·fly \-ˌflī\ *n* (1773) : any of numerous hymenopterous insects (superfamily Tenthredinoidea) whose female usu. has a pair of serrated blades in her ovipositor and whose larva resembles a plant-feeding caterpillar

saw grass *n* (1822) : any of various sedges (as of the genus *Cladium*) having the edges of the leaves set with minute sharp teeth

saw·horse \'sȯ-ˌhȯ(ə)rs\ *n* (1778) : a frame on which wood is laid for sawing by hand; *esp* : HORSE 2b

saw·log \-ˌlȯg, -ˌläg\ *n* (1756) : a log of suitable size for sawing into lumber

saw·mill \-ˌmil\ *n* (1553) : a mill or machine for sawing logs

saw·ney \'sȯ-nē\ *n* [prob. alter. of *zany*] *chiefly Brit* (ca. 1700) : FOOL, SIMPLETON — **sawney** *adj*

saw palmetto *n* (1797) : any of several shrubby palms with spiny-toothed petioles esp. of the southern U.S. and West Indies; *esp* : a common stemless palm (*Serenoa repens*) of the southern U.S.

saw set *n* (1846) : an instrument used to set the teeth of saws

saw·tim·ber \'sȯ-ˌtim-bər\ *n* (1901) : timber suitable for sawing into lumber

saw·tooth \-ˌtüth\ *adj* (1870) : having serrations : arranged or having parts arranged like the teeth of a saw ⟨a ~ roof⟩

saw–toothed \-'tütht\ *adj* (ca. 1857) **1** : having teeth like those of a saw ⟨a ~ shark⟩ **2** : SAWTOOTH

saw–whet \'sȯ-ˌ(h)wet\ *n* [fr. the resemblance of its cry to the sound made in filing a saw] (1834) : a very small harsh-voiced No. American owl (*Cryptoglaux acadica*) that is largely dark brown above and white beneath

saw·yer \'sȯ-yər, 'sȯi-ər\ *n* (14c) **1** : one that saws **2** : any of several large longicorn beetles whose larvae bore large holes in timber or dead wood **3** : a tree fast in the bed of a stream with its branches projecting to the surface

sax \'saks\ *n* (ca. 1923) : SAXOPHONE

sax·horn \'saks-ˌhȯ(ə)rn\ *n* [Antoine *Sax* †1894 Belgian instrument maker + E *horn*] (1844) : any of a group of valved brass instruments ranging from soprano to bass and characterized by a conical tube, oval shape, and cup-shaped mouthpiece

sax·ic·o·lous \sak-'sik-ə-ləs\ *adj* [L *saxum* rock (akin to L *secare* to cut) + *-cola* inhabitant; akin to L *colere* to inhabit — more at SAW, WHEEL] (1856) : inhabiting or growing among rocks ⟨~ lichens⟩

sax·i·frage \'sak-sə-frij, -ˌfrāj\ *n* [ME, fr. MF, fr. LL *saxifraga,* fr. L, fem. of *saxifragus* breaking rocks, fr. *saxum* rock + *frangere* to break — more at SAW, BREAK] (15c) : any of a genus (*Saxifraga* of the family Saxifragaceae, the saxifrage family) of mostly perennial herbs with showy pentamerous flowers and often with basal tufted leaves

saxi·tox·in \ˌsak-sə-'täk-sən\ *n* [*saxi-* (fr. NL *Saxidomus giganteus,* species of butter clam from which it is isolated) + E *toxin*] (1962) : a potent nonprotein poison $C_{10}H_{17}N_7O_4 \cdot 2HCl$ that originates in dinoflagellates (genus *Gonyaulax*) found in red tides and that sometimes occurs in and renders toxic normally edible mollusks which feed on them

Sax·on \'sak-sən\ *n* [ME, fr. LL *Saxones* Saxons, of Gmc origin; akin to OE *Seaxan* Saxons] (13c) **1 a (1)** : a member of a Germanic people that entered and conquered England with the Angles and Jutes in the 5th century A.D. and merged with them to form the Anglo-Saxon people **(2)** : an Englishman or lowlander as distinguished from a Welshman, Irishman, or Highlander **b** : a native or inhabitant of Saxony **2 a** : the Germanic language or dialect of any of the Saxon peoples **b** : the Germanic element in the English language esp. as distinguished from the French and Latin — **Saxon** *adj*

sax·o·ny \'sak-s(ə-)nē\ *n, pl* **-nies** *often cap* [*Saxony,* Germany] (1842) **1 a** : a fine soft woolen fabric **b** : a fine closely twisted knitting yarn **2** : a Wilton jacquard carpet

sax·o·phone \'sak-sə-ˌfōn\ *n* [F, fr. Antoine J. (known as Adolphe) *Sax* †1894 Belgian maker of musical instruments + F *-phone*] (1851) : one of a group of single-reed woodwind instruments ranging from soprano to bass and characterized by a conical metal tube and finger keys — **sax·o·phon·ic** \ˌsak-sə-'fōn-ik, -'fän-\ *adj* — **sax·o·phon·ist** \'sak-sə-ˌfō-nəst, *esp Brit* sak-'säf-ə-\ *n*

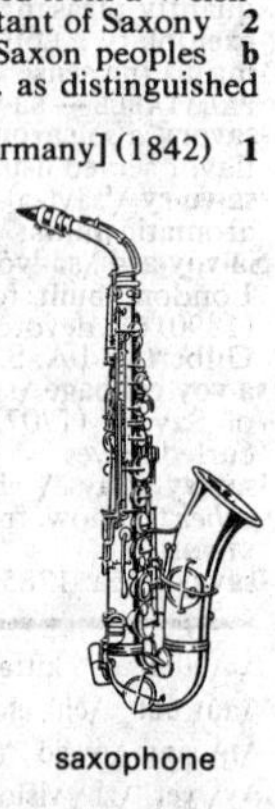

saxophone

sax·tu·ba \'sak-'st(y)ü-bə\ *n* [Antoine *Sax* + E *tuba*] (ca. 1864) : a bass saxhorn

[1]say \'sā, *Southern also* 'se\ *vb* **said** \'sed, *esp when subject follows* səd\; **say·ing** \'sā-iŋ\; **says** \'sez, *sometimes* 'sāz, *esp when subject follows* səz\ [ME *sayen,* fr. OE *secgan;* akin to OHG *sagēn* to say, L *inquam* I say, Gk *ennepein* to speak, tell] *vt* (bef. 12c) **1 a** : to express in words : STATE **b** : to state as opinion or belief : DECLARE **2 a** : UTTER, PRONOUNCE **b** : RECITE, REPEAT ⟨*said* his prayers⟩ **3 a** : INDICATE, SHOW ⟨the clock ~*s* five minutes after twelve⟩ **b** : to give expression to : COMMUNICATE ⟨a glance that *said* all that was necessary⟩ ~ *vi* : to express oneself : SPEAK — **say·er** \'sā-ər, 'se(-ə)r\ *n* — **say uncle** : to admit defeat — **that is to say** : in other words : in effect

[2]say *n, pl* **says** \'sāz, *Southern also* 'sez\ (1571) **1** *archaic* : something that is said : STATEMENT **2** : an expression of opinion ⟨had his ~⟩ **3** : a right or power to influence action or decision; *esp* : the authority to make final decisions

[3]say *adv* [fr. imper. of [1]*say*] (1596) **1** : ABOUT, APPROXIMATELY ⟨the property is worth, ~, four million dollars⟩ **2** : for example : AS ⟨if we compress any gas, ~ oxygen⟩

say·able \'sā-ə-bəl, 'se-\ *adj* (1856) **1** : capable of being said **2** : capable of being spoken effectively or easily ⟨readings in ~ Chinese —*Linguistic Reporter*⟩

say·est \'sā-əst\ *archaic 2d person sing of* SAY

say·ing \'sā-iŋ, 'se-\ *n* (15c) : something said; *esp* : ADAGE

say–so \'sā-(ˌ)sō, 'se-\ *n* (1637) **1 a** : one's unsupported assertion or assurance **b** : an authoritative pronouncement ⟨left the hospital on the ~ of his doctor⟩ **2** : a right of final decision ⟨has the ultimate ~ on what will be taught⟩

say·yid \'sī-(y)əd, 'sēd-ē\ *n* [Ar] (1788) **1** : an Islamic chief or leader **2** : LORD, SIR — used as a courtesy title for a Muslim of rank or lineage

Saz·e·rac \'saz-ə-ˌrak\ *trademark* — used for a cocktail with a whiskey base

[1]scab \'skab\ *n* [ME, of Scand origin; akin to OSw *skabbr* scab; akin to OE *sceabb* scab, L *scabies* mange, *scabere* to scratch — more at SHAVE] (13c) **1** : scabies of domestic animals **2** : a crust of hardened blood and serum over a wound **3 a** : a contemptible person **b (1)** : one who refuses to join a labor union **(2)** : a union member who refuses to strike or returns to work before a strike has ended **(3)** : a worker who accepts employment or replaces a union worker during a strike **(4)** : one who works for less than union wages or on nonunion terms **4** : any of various bacterial or fungus diseases of plants characterized by crustaceous spots; *also* : one of the spots

[2]scab *vi* **scabbed; scab·bing** (1683) **1** : to become covered with a scab **2** : to act as a scab

[1]scab·bard \'skab-ərd\ *n* [ME *scaubert,* fr. AF *escaubers*] (13c) : a sheath for a sword, dagger, or bayonet

[2]scabbard *vt* (1579) : to put in a scabbard

scab·by \'skab-ē\ *adj* **scab·bi·er; -est** (1526) **1 a** : covered with or full of scabs ⟨~ skin⟩ **b** : diseased with scab ⟨a ~ animal⟩ ⟨~ potatoes⟩ **2** : MEAN, CONTEMPTIBLE ⟨a ~ trick⟩

sca·bies \'skā-bēz\ *n, pl* **scabies** [L] (15c) : contagious itch or mange esp. with exudative crusts that is caused by parasitic mites (esp. *Sarcoptes scabiei*) — **sca·bi·et·ic** \ˌskā-bē-'et-ik\ *adj*

[1]sca·bi·ous \'skā-bē-əs, 'skab-ē-\ *n* [ME *scabiose,* fr. ML *scabiosa,* fr. L, fem. of *scabiosus,* adj.] (1526) : any of a genus (*Scabiosa*) of herbs of the teasel family with terminal flower heads subtended by a leafy involucre

[2]scabious *adj* [L *scabiosus,* fr. *scabies*] (1603) **1** : SCABBY **2** : of, relating to, or resembling scabies ⟨~ eruptions⟩

scab·land \'skab-ˌland\ *n* (1904) : a region characterized by elevated tracts of rocky land with little or no soil cover and traversed or isolated by postglacial dry stream channels — usu. used in pl.

sca·brous \'skab-rəs *also* 'skāb-\ *adj* [L *scabr-, scaber* rough, scurfy; akin to L *scabies* mange — more at SCAB] (1657) **1** : DIFFICULT, KNOTTY ⟨a ~ problem⟩ **2** : rough to the touch: as **a** : having small raised dots, scales, or points ⟨a ~ leaf⟩ **b** : covered with raised, roughened, or unwholesome patches ⟨~ paint⟩ ⟨yellowed ~ skin⟩ **3** : dealing with suggestive, indecent, or scandalous themes : SALACIOUS; *also* : SQUALID *syn* see ROUGH — **sca·brous·ly** *adv* — **sca·brous·ness** *n*

[1]scad \'skad\ *n, pl* **scad** *also* **scads** [origin unknown] (1602) : any of several carangid fishes (esp. of the genus *Decapterus*)

[2]scad *n* [prob. alter. of E dial. *scald* a multitude] (1869) **1** : a large number or quantity ⟨hooked a ~ of little fish —*Field & Stream*⟩ **2** *pl* : a great abundance ⟨~*s* of money⟩

scaf·fold \'skaf-əld *also* -ˌōld\ *n* [ME, fr. ONF *escafaut,* modif. of (assumed) VL *catafalicum,* fr. Gk *kata-* cata- + L *fala* tower] (14c) **1 a** : a temporary or movable platform for workers (as bricklayers, painters, or miners) to stand or sit on when working at a height above the floor or ground **b** : a platform on which a criminal is executed (as by hanging or beheading) **c** : a platform at a height above ground or floor level **2** : a supporting framework

scaf·fold·ing \-iŋ\ *n* (14c) : a system of scaffolds; *also* : material for scaffolds

scag \'skag\ *n* [origin unknown] *slang* (1967) : HEROIN

sca·glio·la \skal-'yō-lə, -'yȯ-\ *n* [It, lit., little chip] (1747) : an imitation of ornamental marble consisting of finely ground gypsum mixed with glue

scal·able \'skā-lə-bəl\ *adj* (1579) : capable of being scaled

sca·lade \skə-'lād, -'läd\ *or* **sca·la·do** \-'lād-(ˌ)ō, -'läd-\ *n, pl* **-lades** *or* **-lados** [obs. It *scalada,* fr. *scalare* to scale, fr. *scala* ladder, staircase, fr. LL — more at SCALE] *archaic* (1591) : ESCALADE

[1]sca·lar \'skā-lər, -ˌlär\ *adj* [L *scalaris,* fr. *scalae* stairs, ladder — more at SCALE] (1656) **1** : having an uninterrupted series of steps : GRADUATED ⟨~ chain of authority⟩ ⟨~ cells⟩ **2 a** : capable of being represented by a point on a scale ⟨~ quantity⟩ **b** : of or relating to a scalar or scalar product ⟨~ multiplication⟩

[2]scalar *n* (1853) **1** : a real number rather than a vector **2** : a quantity (as mass or time) that has a magnitude describable by a real number and no direction

sca·la·re \skə-'la(ə)r-ē, -'le(ə)r-, -'lär-\ *n* [NL, specific epithet, fr. L, neut. of *scalaris;* fr. the barred pattern on its body] (1928) : a black and silver laterally compressed So. American cichlid fish (*Pterophyllum scalare*) popular in aquariums

sca·lari·form \skə-'lar-ə-ˌfȯrm\ *adj* [NL *scalariformis,* fr. L *scalaris* + *-iformis* -iform] (1836) : resembling a ladder esp. in having transverse bars or markings like the rungs of a ladder ⟨~ cells in plants⟩ — **sca·lari·form·ly** *adv*

scalar product *n* (1878) : a real number that is the product of the lengths of two vectors and the cosine of the angle between them — called also *dot product, inner product*

scal·a·wag \'skal-i-ˌwag\ *n* [origin unknown] (ca. 1848) **1** : SCAMP, REPROBATE **2** : a white Southerner acting in support of the reconstruction governments after the American Civil War often for private gain

[1]scald \'skȯld\ *vb* [ME *scalden,* fr. ONF *escalder,* fr. LL *excaldare* to wash in warm water, fr. L *ex-* + *calida, calda* warm water, fr. fem. of *calidus* warm — more at CALDRON] *vt* (13c) **1 :** to burn with or as if with hot liquid or steam **2 a :** to subject to the action of boiling water or steam **b :** to bring to a temperature just below the boiling point ⟨~ milk⟩ **3 :** SCORCH ~ *vi* **1 :** to scald something **2 :** to become scalded

[2]scald *n* (1601) **1 :** an injury to the body caused by scalding **2 :** an act or process of scalding **3 a :** a plant disease marked esp. by discoloration suggesting injury by heat **b :** a burning and browning of plant tissues resulting from high temperatures or high temperature and intense light

[3]scald *adj* [*scall* + *-ed*] (1561) **1** *archaic* **:** SCABBY, SCURFY **2** *archaic* **:** SHABBY, CONTEMPTIBLE ⟨~ rogues⟩

[4]scald \'skȯld, 'skäld\ *var of* SKALD

[5]scald \'skȯld\ *adj* [alter. of *scalded*] (1830) **:** subjected to scalding ⟨like coffee . . . with ~ cream —Charles Kingsley⟩

scald•ing \'skȯl-diŋ\ *adj* (13c) **1 :** causing the sensation of scalding or burning **2 :** BOILING **3 :** ARDENT, SCORCHING ⟨the ~ sun⟩ **4 :** BITING, SCATHING ⟨a series of ~ editorials⟩

[1]scale \'skā(ə)l\ *n* [ME, bowl, scale of a balance, fr. ON *skāl;* akin to ON *skel* shell — more at SHELL] (14c) **1 a :** either pan or tray of a balance **b :** a beam that is supported freely in the center and has two pans of equal weight suspended from its ends — usu. used in pl. **2 :** an instrument or machine for weighing

[2]scale *vb* **scaled; scal•ing** *vt* (1603) **:** to weigh in scales ~ *vi* **:** to have a specified weight on scales

[3]scale *n* [ME, fr. MF *escale,* of Gmc origin; akin to OE *scealu* shell, husk — more at SHELL] (14c) **1 a :** a small, flattened, rigid, and definitely circumscribed plate forming part of the external body covering esp. of a fish **b :** a small thin plate suggesting a fish scale ⟨~*s* of mica⟩ ⟨the ~*s* on a moth's wing⟩ **c :** the scaly covering of a scaled animal **2 :** a small thin dry lamina shed (as in many skin diseases) from the skin **3 :** a thin coating, layer, or incrustation: **a** (1) **:** a black scaly coating of oxide (as magnetic oxide) forming on the surface of iron when heated for processing (2) **:** a similar coating forming on other metals **b :** a hard incrustation usu. rich in sulfate of calcium that is deposited on the inside of a vessel (as a boiler) in which water is heated **4 a :** a modified leaf protecting a seed plant bud before expansion **b :** a thin, membranous, chaffy, or woody bract **5 a :** one of the small overlapping usu. metal pieces forming the outer surface of scale armor **b :** SCALE ARMOR **6 a :** SCALE INSECT **b :** infestation with or disease caused by scale insects — **scaled** \'skā(ə)ld\ *adj* — **scale•less** \'skā(ə)l-ləs\ *adj*

[4]scale *vb* **scaled; scal•ing** *vt* (15c) **1 :** to remove the scale or scales from (as by scraping) ⟨~ a fish⟩ **2 :** to take off in thin layers or scales **3 :** to form scale on ⟨hard water ~*s* a boiler⟩ **4 :** to throw (as a thin flat stone) so that the edge cuts the air or so that it skips on water **:** SKIM ~ *vi* **1 :** to separate and come off in scales **:** FLAKE **2 :** to shed scales ⟨*scaling* skin⟩ **3 :** to become encrusted with scale

[5]scale *n* [ME, fr. LL *scala* ladder, staircase, fr. L *scalae,* pl., stairs, rungs, ladder; akin to L *scandere* to climb — more at SCAN] (15c) **1 a** *obs* **:** LADDER **b** *archaic* **:** a means of ascent **2 :** a graduated series of musical tones ascending or descending in order of pitch according to a specified scheme of their intervals **3 :** something graduated esp. when used as a measure or rule: as **a :** a series of marks or points at known intervals used to measure distances (as the height of the mercury in a thermometer) **b :** an indication of the relationship between the distances on a map and the corresponding actual distances **c :** an instrument consisting of a strip (as of wood, plastic, or metal) with one or more sets of spaces graduated and numbered on its surface for measuring or laying off distances or dimensions **4 a :** a graduated series or scheme of rank or order ⟨a ~ of taxation⟩ **b :** MINIMUM WAGE 2 **5 a :** a proportion between two sets of dimensions (as between those of a drawing and its original) **b :** a distinctive relative size, extent, or degree ⟨projects done on a large ~⟩ **6 :** a graded series of tests or of performances used in rating individual intelligence or achievement — **scale** *adj* — **to scale :** according to the proportions of an established scale of measurement ⟨floor plans drawn *to scale*⟩

[6]scale *vb* **scaled; scal•ing** *vt* (15c) **1 a :** to attack with or take by means of scaling ladders ⟨~ a castle wall⟩ **b :** to climb up or reach by means of a ladder **c :** to reach the highest point of **:** SURMOUNT **2 a :** to arrange in a graduated series ⟨~ a test⟩ **b** (1) **:** to measure by or as if by a scale (2) **:** to measure or estimate the sound content of (as logs) **c :** to pattern, make, regulate, set, or estimate according to some rate or standard **:** ADJUST ⟨a production schedule *scaled* to actual need⟩ — often used with *down* or *up* ⟨~ down imports⟩ ~ *vi* **1 :** to climb by or as if by a ladder **2 :** to rise in a graduated series **3 :** MEASURE

[7]scale *n* [[6]*scale*] (1577) **1** *obs* **:** ESCALADE **2 :** an estimate of the amount of sound lumber in logs or standing timber

scale armor *n* (1842) **:** armor of small metallic scales on leather or cloth

scale–down \'skā(ə)l-,dau̇n\ *n* (ca. 1931) **:** a reduction according to a fixed ratio ⟨a ~ of debts⟩

scale insect *n* (1840) **:** any of numerous small but very prolific homopterous insects (superfamily Coccoidea) which have winged males, degenerated scale-covered females attached to the host plant, and young that suck the juices of plants and some of which are economic pests — compare LAC

scale•like \'skā(ə)l-,līk\ *adj* (1883) **:** resembling a scale ⟨~ design⟩; *specif* **:** reduced to a minute appressed element resembling a scale

sca•lene \'skā-,lēn, skā-'\ *adj* [LL *scalenus,* fr. Gk *skalēnos,* lit., uneven; akin to Gk *skolios* crooked — more at CYLINDER] *of a triangle* (1734) **:** having the three sides of unequal length — see TRIANGLE illustration

scale•pan \'skā(ə)l-,pan\ *n* (1830) **:** a pan of a scale for weighing

scal•er \'skā-lər\ *n* (1568) **1 :** one that scales **2 :** a dental instrument for removing tartar from teeth **3 :** an electronic device that operates a recorder or produces an output pulse after a specified number of input impulses

scale•up \'skā-,ləp\ *n* (1945) **:** an increase according to a fixed ratio — **scale up** \'skā-'ləp\ *vb*

scall \'skȯl\ *n* [ME, fr. ON *skalli* bald head; akin to Sw *skulle* skull] (14c) **:** a scurf or scabby disorder (as of the scalp)

scal•lion \'skal-yən\ *n* [ME *scaloun,* fr. AF *scalun,* fr. (assumed) VL *escalonia,* fr. L *ascalonia (caepa)* onion of Ascalon, fr. fem. of *ascalonius* of Ascalon, fr. *Ascalon-, Ascalo* Ascalon, seaport in southern Palestine] (14c) **1 :** SHALLOT **2 :** LEEK **3 :** an onion forming a thick basal portion without a bulb; *also* **:** GREEN ONION

[1]scal•lop \'skäl-əp, 'skal-\ *n* [ME *scalop,* fr. MF *escalope* shell, of Gmc origin; akin to MD *schelpe* shell] (15c) **1 a :** any of many marine bivalve mollusks (family Pectinidae) that have a radially ribbed shell with the edge undulated and that swim by opening and closing the valves **b :** the adductor muscle of a scallop as an article of food **2 a :** a valve or shell of a scallop **b :** a baking dish shaped like a valve of a scallop **3 :** one of a continuous series of circle segments or angular projections forming a border **4 :** CYMLING **5** [F *escalope,* perh. fr. E [1]*scallop;* fr. its being served curled like a scallop valve] **:** a thin slice of boneless meat (as veal)

[2]scallop *vt* (1737) **1** [fr. earlier *escallop* scallop shell, alter. (influenced by MF *escalope* shell) of [1]*scallop*] **:** to bake in a sauce usu. covered with seasoned bread or cracker crumbs ⟨~*ed* potatoes⟩ **2** [[1]*scallop*] **a :** to shape, cut, or finish in scallops **b :** to form scallops in ~ *vi* **:** to gather or dredge scallops

scal•lop•er \-ər\ *n* (ca. 1881) **1 :** a person who dredges for or gathers scallops **2 :** a boat equipped and used to dredge for scallops

scal•ly•wag *var of* SCALAWAG

sca•lo•gram \'skā-lə-,gram\ *n* [[5]*scale* + *-o-* + *-gram*] (1944) **:** an arrangement of items (as problems on a test or features of speech) in ascending order so that the presence or accomplishment of an item at one level implies the presence of or the capability to accomplish items at all lower levels

sca•lop•pi•ne *or* **scal•lo•pi•ni** \,skäl-ə-'pē-nē, ,skal-\ *n* [It *scaloppine,* deriv. of F *escalope,* perh. fr. E [1]*scallop*] (1946) **:** thin slices of meat (as veal) sautéed or coated with flour and fried

[1]scalp \'skalp\ *n* [ME, of Scand origin; akin to ON *skālpr* sheath; akin to MD *schelpe* shell] (14c) **1 a :** the part of the integument of the human head usu. covered with hair in both sexes **b :** the part of a lower animal (as a wolf or fox) corresponding to the human scalp **2 a :** a part of the human scalp with attached hair cut or torn from an enemy as a token of victory (as by Indian warriors of No. America) **b :** a trophy of victory or accomplishment **3** *chiefly Scot* **:** a projecting mass of bare ground or rock

[2]scalp *vt* (1676) **1 a :** to deprive of the scalp **b :** to remove an upper part from **2 a :** to screen or sift (as ore or meal) in order to remove foreign materials or to separate out coarser grades **b :** to remove a desired constituent from and discard the rest **3 :** to buy and sell so as to make small quick profits ⟨~ stocks⟩ ⟨~ grain⟩; *esp* **:** to resell at greatly increased prices ⟨~ theater tickets⟩ ~ *vi* **1 :** to take scalps **2 :** to profit by slight market fluctuations — **scalp•er** *n*

scal•pel \'skal-pəl *also* skal-'pel\ *n* [L *scalpellus, scalpellum,* dim. of *scalper, scalprum* chisel, knife, fr. *scalpere* to carve — more at SHELF] (1742) **:** a small straight thin-bladed knife used esp. in surgery

scalp lock *n* (1826) **:** a long tuft of hair on the crown of the otherwise shaved head of a warrior of some American Indian tribes

scaly \'skā-lē\ *adj* **scal•i•er; -est** (1528) **1 a :** covered with, composed of, or rich in scale or scales **b :** FLAKY **2 :** of or relating to scaly animals **3 :** DESPICABLE, POOR **4 :** infested with scale insects ⟨~ fruit⟩ — **scal•i•ness** *n*

scaly anteater *n* (1840) **:** PANGOLIN

scam \'skam\ *n* [origin unknown] (1963) **:** a fraudulent or deceptive act or operation ⟨an insurance ~⟩

scam•mo•ny \'skam-ə-nē\ *n, pl* **-nies** [ME *scamonie,* fr. OE *scammoniam,* fr. L *scammonia,* fr. Gk *skammōnia*] (bef. 12c) **1 :** a twining convolvulus (*Convolvulus scammonia*) of Asia Minor with a large thick root **2 a :** the dried root of scammony **b :** a cathartic resin obtained from scammony

[1]scamp \'skamp\ *n* [obs. *scamp* (to roam about idly)] (1808) **1 :** RASCAL, ROGUE **2 :** an impish or playful young person — **scamp•ish** \'skam-pish\ *adj*

[2]scamp *vt* [perh. of Scand origin; akin to ON *skammr* short — more at SCANT] (1837) **:** to perform or deal with in a hasty, neglectful, or imperfect manner

[1]scam•per \'skam-pər\ *vi* **scam•pered; scam•per•ing** \-p(ə-)riŋ\ [prob. fr. obs. D *schampen* to flee, fr. MF *escamper,* fr. It *scampare,* fr. (assumed) VL *excampare* to decamp, fr. L *ex-* + *campus* field — more at CAMP] (1691) **:** to run nimbly and usu. playfully about

[2]scamper *n* (1697) **:** a playful or hurried run or movement

scam•pi \'skam-pē, 'skäm-\ *n, pl* **scampi** [It, pl. of *scampo,* a European lobster] (1925) **:** SHRIMP; *esp* **:** large shrimp prepared with a garlic-flavored sauce

[1]scan \'skan\ *vb* **scanned; scan•ning** [ME *scannen,* fr. LL *scandere,* fr. L, to climb; akin to Gk *skandalon* trap, stumbling block, offense, Skt *skandati* he leaps] *vt* (14c) **1 :** to read or mark so as to show metrical structure **2 :** to examine by point-by-point observation or checking: **a :** to investigate thoroughly by checking point by point and often repeatedly ⟨a fire lookout *scanning* the hills with binoculars⟩ **b :** to glance from point to point of often hastily, casually, or in search of a particular item ⟨~ the want ads looking for a job⟩ **3 a :** to examine successive small portions of (as an object) with a sensing device (as a photometer or a beam of radiation) **b :** to bring under a moving electron beam for conversion of light and dark picture or image values into corresponding electrical values to be transmitted by facsimile or television; *also* **:** to bring under a moving electron beam in the reconstruction of the image or picture **c :** to direct a succession of radar beams over in searching for a target **d :** to check (as a magnetic tape or a punch card) for recorded data by means of a mechanical or electronic device **e :** to make a scan of (as the human body) ~ *vi* **1 :** to scan verse **2 :** to conform to a metrical pattern ***syn*** see SCRUTINIZE — **scan•na•ble** \'skan-ə-bəl\ *adj*

[2]scan *n* (1706) **1 :** the act or process of scanning **2 :** a radar display **3 :** a radar or television trace **4 a :** a depiction (as a photograph) of the distribution of a radioactive material in something (as a bodily organ) **b :** an image of a bodily part produced by combining (as by computer) radiographic data obtained from several angles or sections **5 :** TRACE 5b

1scan·dal \'skan-dᵊl\ *n* [ME, fr. LL *scandalum* stumbling block, offense, fr. Gk *skandalon*] (13c) **1 a :** discredit brought upon religion by unseemly conduct in a religious person **b :** conduct that causes or encourages a lapse of faith or of religious obedience in another **2 :** loss of or damage to reputation caused by actual or apparent violation of morality or propriety : DISGRACE **3 a :** a circumstance or action that offends propriety or established moral conceptions or disgraces those associated with it **b :** a person whose conduct offends propriety or morality **4 :** malicious or defamatory gossip **5 :** indignation, chagrin, or bewilderment brought about by a flagrant violation of morality, propriety, or religious opinion ***syn*** see OFFENSE

2scandal *vt* (1592) **1** *obs* **:** DISGRACE **2** *chiefly dial* **:** DEFAME, SLANDER

scan·dal·ize \'skan-də-,līz\ *vt* **-ized; -iz·ing** (1566) **1 :** to speak falsely or maliciously of **2** *archaic* **:** to bring into reproach **3 :** to offend the moral sense of : SHOCK

scan·dal·mon·ger \'skan-dᵊl-,məŋ-gər, -,mäŋ-\ *n* (1721) **:** a person who circulates scandal — **scan·dal·mon·ger·ing** \-g(ə-)riŋ\ *n*

scan·dal·ous \'skan-d(ə-)ləs\ *adj* (1603) **1 :** LIBELOUS, DEFAMATORY **2 :** offensive to propriety or morality : SHOCKING — **scan·dal·ous·ly** *adv* — **scan·dal·ous·ness** *n*

scandal sheet *n* (1904) **:** a newspaper or periodical dealing to a large extent in scandal and gossip

scan·dent \'skan-dənt\ *adj* [L *scandent-, scandens,* prp. of *scandere* to climb — more at SCAN] (1682) **:** characterized by a climbing mode of growth ⟨~ stems⟩ ⟨~ vines⟩

Scan·di·an \'skan-dē-ən\ *adj* [L *Scandia*] (ca. 1909) **1 :** SCANDINAVIAN **2 :** of or relating to the languages of Scandinavia — **Scandian** *n*

Scan·di·na·vian \,skan-də-'nā-vē-ən, -vyən\ *n* (1830) **1 a :** a native or inhabitant of Scandinavia **b :** a person of Scandinavian descent **2 :** the North Germanic languages — **Scandinavian** *adj*

scan·di·um \'skan-dē-əm\ *n* [NL, fr. L *Scandia,* ancient name of southern Scandinavian peninsula] (1879) **:** a white metallic element found in association with rare-earth elements — see ELEMENT table

scan·ner \'skan-ər\ *n* (1557) **:** one that scans: as **a :** a device that automatically checks a process or condition and may initiate a desired corrective action **b :** a device for sensing recorded data **c :** a device used for scanning (as in television, facsimile, or radar) **d :** a device (as a CAT scanner) for making scans of the human body

scanning electron microscope *n* (1962) **:** an electron microscope in which a beam of focused electrons moves across the object with the secondary electrons produced by the object and the electrons scattered by the object being collected to form a three-dimensional image on a cathode-ray tube — called also *scanning microscope* — **scanning electron microscopy** *n*

scan·sion \'skan-chən\ *n* [LL *scansion-, scansio,* fr. L, act of climbing, fr. (assumed) L *scansus,* pp. of L *scandere*] (1671) **:** the analysis of verse to show its meter

1scant \'skant\ *adj* [ME, fr. ON *skamt,* neut. of *skammr* short; akin to Gk *koptein* to cut — more at CAPON] (15c) **1** *dial* **a :** excessively frugal **b :** not prodigal : CHARY **2 a :** barely or scarcely sufficient; *specif* **:** not quite coming up to a stated measure **b :** lacking in amplitude or quantity **3 :** having a small or insufficient supply ⟨he's fat, and ~ of breath —Shak.⟩ ***syn*** see MEAGER — **scant·ly** *adv* — **scant·ness** *n*

2scant *adv, dial* (15c) **:** SCARCELY, HARDLY

3scant *vt* (1590) **1 :** to make small, narrow, or meager : SKIMP **2 :** to provide with a meager or inadequate portion or allowance : STINT **3 :** to provide an incomplete supply of : WITHHOLD **4 :** to give scant attention to : SLIGHT

scant·ies \'skant-ēz\ *n pl* [blend of *1scant* and *panties*] (1934) **:** abbreviated panties for women

scant·ling \'skant-liŋ, -lən\ *n* [alter. of ME *scantilon,* lit., mason's or carpenter's gauge, fr. ONF *escantillon*] (1526) **1 a :** the dimensions of timber and stone used in building **b :** the dimensions of a frame or strake used in shipbuilding **2 :** a small quantity, amount, or proportion : MODICUM **3 :** a small piece of lumber (as an upright piece in house framing)

scanty \'skant-ē\ *adj* **scant·i·er; -est** [E dial. *scant* scanty supply, fr. ME, fr. ON *skamt,* fr. neut. of *skammr* short] (1660) **:** limited or less than sufficient in degree, quantity, or extent ***syn*** see MEAGER — **scant·i·ly** \'skant-ᵊl-ē\ *adv* — **scant·i·ness** \'skant-ē-nəs\ *n*

1scape \'skāp\ *vb* **scaped; scap·ing** [ME *scapen,* short for *escapen*] (13c) **:** ESCAPE

2scape *n* [L *scapus* shaft, stalk — more at SHAFT] (1601) **1 :** a peduncle arising at or beneath the surface of the ground in an acaulescent plant (as the tulip); *broadly* **:** a flower stalk **2 :** the shaft of an animal part (as an antenna or feather)

3scape *n* [*landscape*] (1773) **:** a view or picture of a scene — usu. used in combination ⟨city*scape*⟩

1scape·goat \'skāp-,gōt\ *n* [*1scape;* intended as trans. of Heb *'azāzēl* (prob. name of a demon), as if *'ēz 'ōzēl* goat that departs — Lev 16:8 (AV)] (1530) **1 :** a goat upon whose head are symbolically placed the sins of the people after which he is sent into the wilderness in the biblical ceremony for Yom Kippur **2 a :** one that bears the blame for others **b :** one that is the object of irrational hostility

2scapegoat *vt* (1943) **:** to make a scapegoat of — **scape·goat·ing** \-,gōt-iŋ\ *n* — **scape·goat·ism** \-,gōt-,iz-əm\ *n*

scape·grace \'skāp-,grās\ *n* [*1scape*] (1809) **:** an incorrigible rascal

scaph·oid \'skaf-,ȯid\ *n* [NL *scaphoides,* fr. Gk *skaphoeidēs,* fr. *skaphos* boat] (1741) **:** the bone of the thumb side of the carpus that is the largest in the proximal row; *also* **:** the navicular bone of the tarsus — **scaphoid** *adj*

scap·o·lite \'skap-ə-,līt\ *n* [F, fr. L *scapus* shaft + F *-o-* + *-lite;* fr. the prismatic shape of its crystals] (ca. 1802) **:** any of a group of minerals that are essentially complex silicates of aluminum, calcium, and sodium and that include some used as semiprecious stones

sca·pose \'skā-,pōs\ *adj* (ca. 1903) **:** bearing, resembling, or consisting of a scape ⟨~ flowering stems⟩

scap·u·la \'skap-yə-lə\ *n, pl* **-lae** \-,lē, -,lī\ *or* **-las** [NL, fr. L, shoulder blade, shoulder] (1578) **:** either of a pair of large triangular bones lying one in each dorsal lateral part of the thorax, being the principal bone of the corresponding half of the shoulder girdle, and articulating with the corresponding clavicle or coracoid — called also *shoulder blade*

1scap·u·lar \-lər\ *n* [ME *scapulare,* fr. LL, fr. L *scapula* shoulder] (bef. 12c) **1 a :** a long wide band of cloth with an opening for the head worn front and back over the shoulders as part of a monastic habit **b :** a pair of small cloth squares joined by shoulder tapes and worn under the clothing on the breast and back as a sacramental and often also as a badge of a third order or confraternity **2 a :** SCAPULA **b :** one of the feathers covering the base of a bird's wing — see BIRD illustration

2scapular *adj* [NL *scapularis,* fr. *scapula*] (1713) **:** of or relating to the shoulder, the scapula, or scapulars

scapular medal *n* (1910) **:** a medal worn in place of a sacramental scapular

1scar \'skär\ *n* [ME *skere,* fr. ON *sker* skerry; akin to ON *skera* to cut — more at SHEAR] (14c) **1 :** an isolated or protruding rock **2 :** a steep rocky eminence : a bare place on the side of a mountain

2scar *n* [ME *escare, scar,* fr. MF *escare* scab, fr. LL *eschara,* fr. Gk, hearth, scab] (14c) **1 :** a mark left (as in the skin) by the healing of injured tissue **2 a :** a mark left on a stem or branch by a fallen leaf or harvested fruit **b :** CICATRIX 2 **3 :** a mark or indentation resulting from damage or wear ⟨the *~s* of bullets on the . . . church door —Kay Boyle⟩ **4 :** a lasting moral or emotional injury ⟨one of his men had been killed . . . in a manner that left a ~ upon his mind —H. G. Wells⟩ — **scar·less** \-ləs\ *adj*

3scar *vb* **scarred; scar·ring** *vt* (1555) **1 :** to mark with a scar **2 :** to do lasting injury to ~ *vi* **1 :** to form a scar **2 :** to become scarred

scar·ab \'skar-əb\ *n* [MF *scarabee,* fr. L *scarabaeus*] (1579) **1 :** any of a family (Scarabaeidae) of stout-bodied beetles (as a dung beetle) with lamellate antennae **2 :** a stone or faience beetle used in ancient Egypt as a talisman, ornament, and a symbol of resurrection

scar·a·bae·us \,skar-ə-'bē-əs\ *n* [L] (1664) **:** SCARAB 2

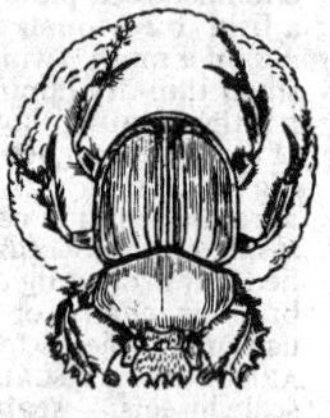
scarab 1

scar·a·mouch *or* **scar·a·mouche** \'skar-ə-,müsh, -,müch, -,mau̇ch\ *n* [F *Scaramouche,* fr. It *Scaramuccia*] (1662) **1** *cap* **:** a stock character in the Italian commedia dell'arte that burlesques the Spanish don and is characterized by boastfulness and cowardliness **2 a :** a cowardly buffoon **b :** RASCAL, SCAMP

1scarce \'ske(ə)rs, 'ska(ə)rs\ *adj* **scarc·er; scarc·est** [ME *scars,* fr. ONF *escars,* fr. (assumed) VL *excarpsus,* lit., plucked out, pp. of L *excerpere* to pluck out — more at EXCERPT] (13c) **1 :** deficient in quantity or number compared with the demand : not plentiful or abundant **2 :** intentionally absent ⟨made himself ~ at inspection time⟩ ***syn*** see INFREQUENT — **scarce·ness** *n*

2scarce *adv* (15c) **:** SCARCELY, HARDLY

scarce·ly *adv* (13c) **1 a :** by a narrow margin : only just ⟨had ~ rung the bell when the door flew open —Agnes S. Turnbull⟩ **b :** almost not ⟨~ ever wore this mantle —Arnold Bennett⟩ **2 a :** certainly not ⟨could ~ interfere between another man and his own beast —Owen Wister⟩ **b :** probably not ⟨there could ~ have been found a leader better equipped —V. L. Parrington⟩

scar·ci·ty \'sker-sət-ē, 'sker-stē, 'skar-\ *n, pl* **-ties** (14c) **:** the quality or state of being scarce; *esp* **:** want of provisions for the support of life

1scare \'ske(ə)r, 'ska(ə)r\ *vb* **scared; scar·ing** [ME *skerren,* fr. ON *skirra,* fr. *skjarr* shy, timid] (13c) *vt* **:** to frighten esp. suddenly : ALARM ~ *vi* **:** to become scared — **scar·er** *n*

2scare *n* (1548) **1 :** a sudden fright **2 :** a widespread state of alarm : PANIC — **scare** *adj*

scare·crow \'ske(ə)r-,krō, 'ska(ə)r-\ *n* (1589) **1 a :** something frightening but harmless **b :** an object usu. suggesting a human figure that is set up to frighten birds (as crows) away from crops **2 :** a skinny or ragged person

scared *adj* (1725) **:** thrown into or being in a state of fear, fright, or panic

scaredy–cat \'ske(ə)rd-ē-,kat, 'ska(ə)rd-\ *n* [*scared* (pp. of *scare*) + *-y* + *cat*] (1933) **:** an unduly fearful person

scare·head \'ske(ə)r-,hed, 'ska(ə)r-\ *n* (1887) **:** a big, sensational, or alarming newspaper headline

scare·mon·ger \-,məŋ-gər, -,mäŋ-\ *n* (1888) **:** one inclined to raise or excite alarms esp. needlessly

scare up *vt* (1841) **:** to find or get together with considerable labor or difficulty : to scrape ⟨managed to *scare up* the money⟩

1scarf \'skärf\ *n, pl* **scarves** \'skärvz\ *or* **scarfs** [ONF *escarpe* sash, sling] (1555) **1 :** a broad band of cloth worn about the shoulders, around the neck, or over the head **2 a :** a military or official sash usu. indicative of rank **b** *archaic* **:** TIPPET 3 **3 :** RUNNER 6b

2scarf *vt* (1598) **1 :** to wrap, cover, or adorn with or as if with a scarf **2 :** to wrap or throw on (a scarf or mantle) loosely

3scarf *n, pl* **scarfs** [ME *skarf,* prob. of Scand origin; akin to ON *skarfr* scarf; akin to Gk *skorpios* scorpion] (1580) **1 :** either of the chamfered or cutaway ends that fit together to form a scarf joint **2 :** a joint made by chamfering, halving, or notching two pieces to correspond and lapping and bolting them — called also *scarf joint*

4scarf *also* **scarph** \'skärf\ *vt* (1627) **1 :** to unite by a scarf joint **2 :** to form a scarf on

5scarf *vt* [by alter.] (ca. 1960) **:** 3SCOFF 1 ⟨~*ed* up bowls of chili⟩

scarf·pin \'skärf-,pin\ *n* (1859) **:** TIEPIN

scarf·skin \'skärf-,skin\ *n* [*1scarf*] (1615) **:** EPIDERMIS; *esp* **:** that forming the cuticle of a nail

scar·i·fi·ca·tion \,skar-ə-fə-'kā-shən, ,sker-\ *n* (15c) **1 :** the act or process of scarifying **2 :** a mark or marks made by scarifying

1scar·i·fy \'skar-ə-,fī, 'sker-\ *vt* **-fied; -fy·ing** [MF *scarifier,* fr. LL *scarificare,* alter. of L *scarifare,* fr. Gk *skariphasthai* to scratch an outline, sketch — more at SCRIBE] (1541) **1 :** to make scratches or small cuts in (as the skin) ⟨~ an area for vaccination⟩ **2 :** to lacerate the feelings of **3 :** to break up and loosen the surface of (as a field or road) **4 :** to cut or soften the wall of (a hard seed) to hasten germination — **scar·i·fi·er** \-,fī(-ə)r\ *n*

2scar·ify \'sker-ə-,fī, 'skar-\ *vt* **-fied; -fy·ing** (1794) **:** SCARE, FRIGHTEN

scar·i·ous \'sker-ē-əs, 'skar-\ *adj* [NL *scariosus*] (1806) **:** dry and membranous in texture ⟨a ~ bract⟩

scar·la·ti·na \ˌskär-lə-ˈtē-nə\ *n* [NL, fr. ML *scarlata* scarlet] (1803) : SCARLET FEVER — **scar·la·ti·nal** \-ˈtēn-ᵊl\ *adj*

[1]**scar·let** \ˈskär-lət\ *n* [ME *scarlat, scarlet,* fr. OF or ML; OF *escarlate,* fr. ML *scarlata,* fr. Per *saqalāt,* a kind of rich cloth] (13c) **1 :** scarlet cloth or clothes **2 :** any of various bright reds

[2]**scarlet** *adj* (14c) **1 :** of the color scarlet **2 a :** grossly and glaringly offensive ⟨sinning in flagrant and ~ fashion —G. W. Johnson⟩ **b** [fr. the use of the word in Isa 1:18 & Rev 17:1–6 (AV)] **:** of, characterized by, or associated with sexual immorality ⟨~ women⟩

scarlet fever *n* (1676) : an acute contagious febrile disease caused by hemolytic streptococci (esp. various strains of *Streptococcus pyogenes*) and characterized by inflammation of the nose, throat, and mouth, generalized toxemia, and a red rash

scarlet letter *n* [fr. the novel *The Scarlet Letter* (1850) by Nathaniel Hawthorne] (1850) : a scarlet A worn as a punitive mark of adultery

scarlet pimpernel *n* (1855) **1 :** a common pimpernel (*Anagallis arvensis*) having scarlet, white, or purplish flowers that close in cloudy weather **2** [*The Scarlet Pimpernel,* assumed name of the hero of *The Scarlet Pimpernel* (1905), novel by Baroness Orczy] **:** a person who rescues others from mortal danger by smuggling them across a border

scarlet runner *n* (1806) : a tropical American high-climbing bean (*Phaseolus coccineus*) that has large bright red flowers and red-and-black seeds and is grown widely as an ornamental and in Great Britain as a preferred food bean — called also *scarlet runner bean*

scarlet sage *n* (ca. 1910) : a garden salvia (*Salvia splendens*) of Brazil with long racemes of intense scarlet flowers

scarlet tanager *n* (1810) : a common American tanager (*Piranga olivacea*) of which the male is scarlet with black wings and the female and young are chiefly olive

[1]**scarp** \ˈskärp\ *n* [It *scarpa,* prob. of Gmc origin; akin to OE *scearp* sharp] (1589) **1 :** the inner side of a ditch below the parapet of a fortification **2 a :** a line of cliffs produced by faulting or erosion **b :** a low steep slope along a beach caused by wave erosion

[2]**scarp** *vt* (1803) : to cut down vertically or to a steep slope

scar·per \ˈskär-pər\ *vi* [perh. fr. It *scappare,* fr. (assumed) VL *excappare* — more at ESCAPE] *Brit* (ca. 1846) : FLEE, RUN AWAY; *broadly* : LEAVE, DEPART

scar·ry \ˈskär-ē\ *adj* [[2]*scar*] (1653) : bearing marks of wounds : SCARRED

[1]**scart** \ˈskärt\ *vb* [ME *skarten,* alter. of *scratten*] *chiefly Scot* (14c) : SCRATCH, SCRAPE

[2]**scart** *n, chiefly Scot* (1585) : SCRATCH, MARK; *esp* : one made in writing

scar tissue *n* (1885) : the connective tissue forming a scar and composed chiefly of fibroblasts in recent scars and largely of dense collagenous fibers in old scars

scary \ˈske(ə)r-ē, ˈska(ə)r-\ *adj* **scar·i·er; -est** (1582) **1 :** causing fright : ALARMING ⟨told us a ~ story⟩ **2 :** easily scared : TIMID **3 :** feeling alarm or fright : FRIGHTENED — **scar·i·ly** \ˈsker-ə-lē, ˈskar-\ *adv*

[1]**scat** \ˈskat\ *vi* **scat·ted; scat·ting** [*scat,* interj. used to drive away a cat] (1838) **1 :** to go away quickly **2 :** to move fast : SCOOT

[2]**scat** *n* [Gk *skat-, skōr* excrement — more at SCAT-] (1927) : an animal fecal dropping

[3]**scat** *n* [origin unknown] (1929) : jazz singing with nonsense syllables

[4]**scat** *vi* **scat·ted; scat·ting** (1935) : to improvise nonsense syllables to an instrumental accompaniment : sing scat

scat- *or* **scato-** *comb form* [Gk *skato-,* fr. *skat-, skōr* excrement; akin to OE *scearn* dung, L *muscerda* mouse dropping] : ordure ⟨scatology⟩

scat·back \ˈskat-ˌbak\ *n* [[1]*scat* + *back*] (1945) : an offensive back in football who is an esp. fast and elusive ballcarrier

[1]**scathe** \ˈskāth, ˈskāth\ *n* [ME *skathe,* fr. ON *skathi;* akin to OE *sceatha* injury, OHG *scado,* Gk *askēthēs* unharmed] (bef. 12c) : HARM, INJURY — **scathe·less** \-ləs\ *adj*

[2]**scathe** \ˈskāth\ *vt* **scathed; scath·ing** (13c) **1 :** to do harm to; *specif* : SCORCH, SEAR **2 :** to assail with withering denunciation

scath·ing \ˈskā-thiŋ\ *adj* (1794) : bitterly severe ⟨a ~ condemnation⟩ *syn* see CAUSTIC — **scath·ing·ly** \-thiŋ-lē\ *adv*

sca·tol·o·gy \ska-ˈtäl-ə-jē, skə-\ *n* (1876) **1 :** interest in or treatment of obscene matters esp. in literature **2 :** the biologically oriented study of excrement (as for taxonomic purposes or for the determination of diet) — **scat·o·log·i·cal** \ˌskat-ᵊl-ˈäj-i-kəl\ *adj*

scatt \ˈskat\ *n* [ON *skattr;* akin to OE *sceat* property, money, a small coin] *archaic* (1502) : TAX, TRIBUTE

[1]**scat·ter** \ˈskat-ər\ *vb* [ME *scateren*] *vt* (14c) **1 a :** to cause to separate widely **b :** to cause to vanish **2** *archaic* **:** to fling away heedlessly : SQUANDER **3 :** to distribute irregularly **4 :** to sow by casting in all directions : STREW **5 a :** to reflect irregularly and diffusely **b :** to diffuse or disperse (a beam of radiation) **6 :** to divide into ineffectual small portions ~ *vi* **1 :** to separate and go in various directions : DISPERSE **2 :** to occur or fall irregularly or at random — **scat·ter·er** \-ər-ər\ *n*

syn SCATTER, DISPERSE, DISSIPATE, DISPEL mean to cause to separate or break up. SCATTER implies a force that drives parts or units irregularly in many directions ⟨the bowling ball *scattered* the pins⟩ DISPERSE implies a wider separation and a complete breaking up of a mass or group ⟨police *dispersed* the crowd⟩ DISSIPATE stresses complete disintegration or dissolution and final disappearance ⟨the fog was *dissipated* by the morning sun⟩ DISPEL stresses a driving away or getting rid of as if by scattering ⟨an authoritative statement that *dispelled* all doubt⟩

[2]**scatter** *n* (1642) **1 :** the act of scattering **2 :** a small quantity or number irregularly distributed or strewn about **3 :** the state or extent of being scattered; *esp* : DISPERSION

scat·ter·ation \ˌskat-ə-ˈrā-shən\ *n* (1776) **1 :** the act or process of scattering : the state of being scattered **2 :** the movement of people and industry away from the city; *also* : the resulting regional urbanization **3 :** a policy of distributing funds and energies in too many ineffectively small units

scat·ter·brain \ˈskat-ər-ˌbrān\ *n* (1790) : a giddy heedless person

scat·ter·brained \-ˌbrānd\ *adj* (1747) : having the characteristics of a scatterbrain

scatter diagram *n* (1925) : a two-dimensional graph in rectangular coordinates consisting of points whose coordinates represent values of two variables under study

scat·ter·good \ˈskat-ər-ˌgu̇d\ *n* (1577) : a wasteful person : SPENDTHRIFT

scat·ter·gram \-ˌgram\ *n* (1938) : SCATTER DIAGRAM

scat·ter·gun \-ˌgən\ *n or adj* (1836) : SHOTGUN

[1]**scat·ter·ing** *n* (14c) **1 :** an act or process in which something scatters or is scattered **2 :** something scattered: as **a :** a small number or quantity interspersed here and there ⟨a ~ of visitors⟩ **b :** the random change in direction of a beam due to collision of the particles, photons, or waves constituting the radiation with the particles of the medium traversed

[2]**scattering** *adj* (15c) **1 :** going in various directions **2 :** found or placed far apart and in no order **3 :** divided among many or several ⟨~ votes⟩ — **scat·ter·ing·ly** \-ə-riŋ-lē\ *adv*

scatter rug *n* (1926) : a rug of such a size that several can be used (as to fill vacant places) in a room

scat·ter·shot \ˈskat-ər-ˌshät\ *adj* (1951) : broadly inclusive : SHOTGUN

scat·ty \ˈskat-ē\ *adj* **scat·ti·er; -est** [prob. fr. *scatter*brain + *-y*] *chiefly Brit* (ca. 1911) : CRAZY

scaup \ˈsko̊p\ *n, pl* **scaup** *or* **scaups** [perh. alter. of *scalp* (bed of shellfish); fr. its fondness for shellfish] (1797) : any of several diving ducks (genus *Aythya* and esp. *A. affinis* and *A. marila*)

scav·enge \ˈskav-ənj, -inj\ *vb* **scav·enged; scav·eng·ing** [back-formation fr. *scavenger*] *vt* (1644) **1 a (1) :** to remove (as dirt or refuse) from an area **(2) :** to clean away dirt or refuse from : CLEANSE ⟨~ a street⟩ **b :** to feed on (carrion or refuse) **2 a :** to remove (burned gases) from the cylinder of an internal-combustion engine after a working stroke **b :** to remove (as an undesirable constituent) from a substance or region by chemical or physical means **c :** to clean and purify (molten metal) by taking up foreign elements in chemical union **3 :** to salvage from discarded or refuse material; *also* : to salvage usable material from ~ *vi* : to work or act as a scavenger

scav·en·ger \ˈskav-ən-jər\ *n* [alter. of earlier *scavager,* fr. ME *skawager* collector of a toll on goods sold by nonresident merchants, fr. *skawage* toll on goods sold by nonresident merchants, fr. ONF *escauwage* inspection] (1530) **1** *chiefly Brit* **:** a person employed to remove dirt and refuse from streets **2 :** one that scavenges: as **a :** a garbage collector **b :** a junk collector **c :** a chemically active substance acting to make innocuous or remove an undesirable substance **3 :** an organism that feeds habitually on refuse or carrion

scavenger hunt *n* (1940) : a party contest in which usu. couples are sent out with a time limit in which to acquire without buying one or more articles that are esp. difficult to obtain

sce·na \ˈshā-(ˌ)nä\ *n* [It, lit., scene, fr. L] (1819) : an elaborate solo vocal composition that consists of a recitative usu. followed by one or more aria sections

sce·nar·io \sə-ˈnar-ē-ˌō, -ˈner-\ *n, pl* **-i·os** [It, fr. L *scaenarium,* fr. *scaena* stage] (1878) **1 a :** an outline or synopsis of a play; *esp* : a plot outline used by actors of the commedia dell'arte **b :** the libretto of an opera **2 a :** SCREENPLAY **b :** SHOOTING SCRIPT **3 :** a sequence of events esp. when imagined; *esp* : an account or synopsis of a projected course of action or events ⟨his ~ for a settlement envisages . . . reunification —Selig Harrison⟩

sce·nar·ist \-ˈnar-əst, -ˈner-\ *n* (1920) : a writer of scenarios

[1]**scend** \ˈsend\ *n* [alter. (influenced by *ascend*) of [2]*send*] (1625) **1 :** the upward movement of a pitching ship **2 :** the lift of a wave : SEND

[2]**scend** *vi* (1726) : to rise or heave upward under the influence of a natural force (as on a wave)

scene \ˈsēn\ *n* [MF, stage, fr. L *scena, scaena* stage, scene, fr. Gk *skēnē* temporary shelter, tent, building forming the background for a dramatic performance, stage; akin to Gk *skia* shadow — more at SHINE] (1540) **1 :** one of the subdivisions of a play: as **a :** a division of an act presenting continuous action in one place **b :** a single situation or unit of dialogue in a play ⟨the love ~⟩ **c :** a motion-picture or television episode or sequence **2 a :** a stage setting **b :** a real or imaginary prospect suggesting a stage setting ⟨a sylvan ~⟩ **3 :** the place of an occurrence or action : LOCALE ⟨~ of the crime⟩ **4 :** an exhibition of anger or indecorous behavior ⟨make a ~⟩ **5 a :** sphere of activity ⟨the drug ~⟩ **b :** SITUATION ⟨it was a bad ~ . . . all these teenyboppers coming from hundreds of miles around —Paul Newman⟩ — **behind the scenes 1 :** out of public view; *also* : in secret **2 :** in a position to see the hidden workings ⟨taken *behind the scenes* and told just how in fact the actual government . . . has operated —William Clark⟩

scen·ery \ˈsēn-(ə-)rē\ *n, pl* **-er·ies** (1729) **1 :** the painted scenes or hangings and accessories used on a theater stage **2 :** a picturesque view or landscape

scene·shift·er \-ˌshif-tər\ *n* (1752) : a worker who moves the scenes in a theater

scene–steal·er \ˈsēn-ˌstē-lər\ *n* (1949) : an actor who diverts attention to himself when he is not intended to be the center of attention

sce·nic \ˈsēn-ik *also* ˈsen-\ *also* **sce·ni·cal** \-i-kəl\ *adj* (1623) **1 :** of or relating to the stage, a stage setting, or stage representation **2 :** of or relating to natural scenery ⟨a ~ view⟩ **3 :** representing graphically an action, event, or episode ⟨a ~ bas-relief⟩ — **sce·ni·cal·ly** \-i-k(ə-)lē\ *adv*

scenic railway *n* (1894) : a miniature railway (as in an amusement park) with artificial scenery along the way

sce·nog·ra·phy \sē-ˈnäg-rə-fē\ *n* [Gk *skēnographia* painting of scenery, fr. *skēnē* + *-graphia* -graphy] (1645) : the art of perspective representation esp. as applied to the painting of stage scenery (as by the ancient Greeks) — **sce·no·graph·ic** \ˌsē-nə-ˈgraf-ik\ *adj*

[1]**scent** \ˈsent\ *n* (14c) **1 :** effluvia from a substance that affect the sense of smell: as **a :** an odor left by an animal on a surface passed over **b :** a characteristic or particular odor; *esp* : one that is agreeable **2 a :** power of smelling : sense of smell ⟨a keen ~⟩ **b :** power of detection : NOSE ⟨a ~ for heresy⟩ **3 :** a course of pursuit or discovery ⟨throw one off the ~⟩ **4 :** INKLING, INTIMATION ⟨a ~ of trouble⟩ **5 :** PERFUME 2 **6 :** bits of paper dropped in the game of hare and hounds **7 :** a mixture prepared for use as a lure in hunting or fishing ***syn*** see FRAGRANCE, SMELL — **scent·less** \ˈsent-ləs\ *adj*

\ə\ abut \ᵊ\ kitten, F table \ər\ further \a\ ash \ā\ ace \ä\ cot, cart \au̇\ out \ch\ chin \e\ bet \ē\ easy \g\ go \i\ hit \ī\ ice \j\ job \ŋ\ sing \ō\ go \o̊\ law \o̊i\ boy \th\ thin \th\ the \ü\ loot \u̇\ foot \y\ yet \zh\ vision \à, k̲, ⁿ, œ, ᵫ, ue, ue̅, ʸ\ *see* Guide to Pronunciation

[2]**scent** *vb* [ME *senten,* fr. MF *sentir* to feel, smell, fr. L *sentire* to perceive, feel — more at SENSE] *vt* (15c) **1 a :** to perceive by the olfactory organs : SMELL **b :** to get or have an inkling of ⟨~ trouble⟩ **2 :** to imbue or fill with odor ⟨~*ed* the air with perfume⟩ ~ *vi* **1 :** to yield an odor of some specified kind ⟨this ~*s* of sulfur⟩; *also* **:** to bear indication or suggestions **2 :** to use the nose in seeking or tracking prey

scent·ed *adj* (1579) **:** having scent: as **a :** having the sense of smell **b :** having a perfumed smell **c :** having or exhaling an odor

[1]**scep·ter** \'sep-tər\ *n* [ME *sceptre,* fr. MF *ceptre,* fr. L *sceptrum,* fr. Gk *skēptron* staff, scepter — more at SHAFT] (14c) **1 :** a staff or baton borne by a sovereign as an emblem of authority **2 :** royal or imperial authority **:** SOVEREIGNTY

[2]**scepter** *vt* **scep·tered; scep·ter·ing** \-t(ə-)riŋ\ (1526) **:** to invest with the scepter in token of royal authority

scep·tered \'sep-tərd\ *adj* (1513) **1 :** invested with a scepter or sovereign authority **2 :** of or relating to a sovereign or to royalty

sceptic, sceptical, scepticism *var of* SKEPTIC, SKEPTICAL, SKEPTICISM

sceptre *Brit var of* SCEPTER

scha·den·freu·de \'shäd-ᵊn-ˌfrȯid-ə\ *n* [G, fr. *schaden* damage (fr. OHG *scado*) + *freude* joy, fr. OHG *frewida;* akin to OHG *frō* happy — more at SCATHE, FROLIC] (1952) **:** enjoyment obtained from others' troubles

[1]**sched·ule** \'skej-(ˌ)ü(ə)l, 'skej-əl, *Canad also* 'shej-, *Brit usu* 'shed-(ˌ)yü(ə)l\ *n* [ME *cedule,* fr. MF, slip of paper, note, fr. LL *schedula* slip of paper, dim. of L *scheda, scida* sheet of papyrus, fr. (assumed) Gk *schidē;* akin to Gk *schizein* to split — more at SHED] (14c) **1 a** *obs* **:** a written document **b :** a statement of supplementary details appended to a legal or legislative document **2 :** a written or printed list, catalog, or inventory; *also* **:** TIMETABLE 1 **3 :** PROGRAM; *esp* **:** a procedural plan that indicates the time and sequence of each operation ⟨finished on ~⟩ **4 :** a body of items to be dealt with **:** AGENDA

[2]**schedule** *vt* **sched·uled; sched·ul·ing** (1862) **1 a :** to place in a schedule **b :** to make a schedule of **2 :** to appoint, assign, or designate for a fixed time — **sched·ul·er** *n*

schee·lite \'shā-ˌlīt\ *n* [G *scheelit,* fr. Karl W. *Scheele* †1786 Swed. chemist] (ca. 1837) **:** a mineral $CaWO_4$ consisting of the tungstate of calcium that is a source of tungsten and its compounds

Sche·her·a·zade \shə-ˌher-ə-'zäd(-ə), -'zäd(-ē)\ *n* [G *Scheherezade,* fr. Per *Shīrazād*] **:** the fictional wife of an oriental king and the narrator of the tales in the *Arabian Nights' Entertainments*

sche·ma \'skē-mə\ *n, pl* **sche·ma·ta** \-mət-ə\ *also* **schemas** [Gk *schēmat-, schēma*] (1796) **1 :** a diagrammatic presentation; *broadly* **:** a structured framework or plan **:** OUTLINE **2 :** a mental codification of experience that includes a particular organized way of perceiving cognitively and responding to a complex situation or set of stimuli

[1]**sche·mat·ic** \ski-'mat-ik\ *adj* [NL *schematicus,* fr. Gk *schēmat-, schēma*] (1701) **:** of or relating to a scheme or schema — **sche·mat·i·cal·ly** \-i-k(ə-)lē\ *adv*

[2]**schematic** *n* (1929) **:** a schematic drawing or diagram

sche·ma·tism \'skē-mə-ˌtiz-əm\ *n* (1660) **:** the disposition of constituents in a pattern or according to a scheme **:** DESIGN; *also* **:** a particular systematic disposition of parts

sche·ma·tize \'skē-mə-ˌtīz\ *vt* **-tized; -tiz·ing** [Gk *schēmatizein,* fr. *schēmat-, schēma*] (1828) **1 :** to form or to form into a scheme or systematic arrangement **2 :** to express or depict schematically — **sche·ma·ti·za·tion** \ˌskē-mət-ə-'zā-shən\ *n*

[1]**scheme** \'skēm\ *n* [L *schemat-, schema* arrangement, figure, fr. Gk *schēmat-, schēma,* fr. *echein* to have, hold, be in (such) a condition; akin to OE *sige* victory, Skt *sahate* he prevails] (1610) **1 a** *archaic* (1) **:** a mathematical or astronomical diagram (2) **:** a representation of the astrological aspects of the planets at a particular time **b :** a graphic sketch or outline **2 :** a concise statement or table **:** EPITOME **3 :** a plan or program of action; *esp* **:** a crafty or secret one **4 :** a systematic or organized framework **:** DESIGN ***syn*** see PLAN

[2]**scheme** *vb* **schemed; schem·ing** *vt* (1767) **:** to form a scheme for ~ *vi* **:** to form plans; *also* **:** PLOT, INTRIGUE — **schem·er** *n*

schem·ing *adj* (1813) **:** given to forming schemes; *esp* **:** shrewdly devious and intriguing

[1]**scher·zan·do** \skert-'sän-(ˌ)dō\ *adv or adj* [It, fr. verbal of *scherzare* to joke, of Gmc origin; akin to MHG *scherzen* to leap for joy, joke; akin to Gk *skairein* to gambol — more at CARDINAL] (ca. 1811) **:** in sportive manner **:** PLAYFULLY — used as a direction in music indicating style and tempo ⟨allegretto ~⟩

[2]**scherzando** *n, pl* **-dos** (1876) **:** a passage or movement in scherzando style

scher·zo \'ske(ə)rt-(ˌ)sō\ *n, pl* **scherzos** *or* **scher·zi** \-(ˌ)sē\ [It, lit., joke, fr. *scherzare*] (1852) **:** a sprightly humorous instrumental musical composition or movement commonly in quick triple time

Schick test \'shik-\ *n* [Béla *Schick*] (1916) **:** a serological test for susceptibility to diphtheria by cutaneous injection of a diluted diphtheria toxin that causes an area of reddening and induration in susceptible individuals

Schiff's reagent \ˌshifs-\ *or* **Schiff reagent** \ˌshif-\ *n* [Hugo *Schiff* †1915 Ger. chemist] (1897) **:** a solution of fuchsine decolorized by treatment with sulfur dioxide that gives a useful test for aldehydes because they restore the reddish violet color of the dye — compare FEULGEN REACTION

schil·ler \'shil-ər\ *n* [G] (1885) **:** a bronzy iridescent luster (as of a mineral)

schil·ling \'shil-iŋ\ *n* [G, fr. OHG *skilling,* a gold coin — more at SHILLING] (1753) — see MONEY table

schip·per·ke \'skip-ər-kē, 'ship-, -ərk(-ə)\ *n* [Flem, dim. of *schipper* skipper; fr. its use as a watchdog on boats — more at SKIPPER] (1887) **:** any of a Belgian breed of small stocky black dogs with foxy head and heavy coat

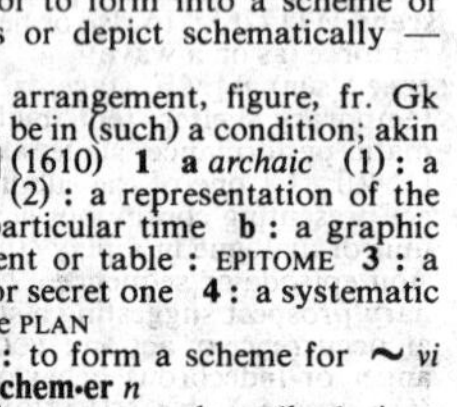

schipperke

schism \'siz-əm, 'skiz- *also* 'shiz-; *among clergy usu* 'siz-\ *n* [ME *scisme,* fr. MF *cisme,* fr. LL *schismat-, schisma,* fr. Gk, cleft, division, fr. *schizein* to split — more at SHED] (14c) **1 :** DIVISION, SEPARATION; *also* **:** DISCORD, DISHARMONY **2 a :** formal division in or separation from a church or religious body **b :** the offense of promoting schism

[1]**schis·mat·ic** \siz-'mat-ik, skiz-\ *n* (14c) **:** one who creates or takes part in schism

[2]**schismatic** *also* **schis·mat·i·cal** \-i-kəl\ *adj* (15c) **:** of, relating to, or guilty of schism — **schis·mat·i·cal·ly** \-i-k(ə-)lē\ *adv*

schis·ma·tize \-mə-ˌtīz\ *vb* **-tized; -tiz·ing** *vi* (1601) **:** to take part in schism; *esp* **:** to make a breach of union (as in the church) ~ *vt* **:** to induce into schism

schist \'shist\ *n* [F *schiste,* fr. L *schistos (lapis),* lit., fissile stone, fr. Gk *schistos* that may be split, fr. *schizein*] (1795) **:** a metamorphic crystalline rock having a closely foliated structure and admitting of division along approximately parallel planes

schis·tose \'shis-ˌtōs\ *also* **schis·tous** \-təs\ *adj* (1794) **:** of or relating to schist **:** having the character or structure of a schist — **schis·tos·i·ty** \shis-'täs-ət-ē\ *n*

schis·to·some \'shis-tə-ˌsōm\ *n* [NL *Schistosoma,* fr. Gk *schistos* + *sōma* body — more at SOMAT-] (1905) **:** any of a genus (*Schistosoma*) of elongated trematode worms with the sexes separate that parasitize the blood vessels of birds and mammals and in man cause destructive schistosomiases; *broadly* **:** a worm of the family (Schistosomatidae) that includes this genus — **schis·to·som·al** \ˌshis-tə-'sō-məl\ *adj* — **schistosome** *adj*

schis·to·so·mi·a·sis \ˌshis-tə-sə-'mī-ə-səs\ *n, pl* **-a·ses** \-ˌsēz\ [NL, fr. *Schistosoma*] (1906) **:** infestation with or disease caused by schistosomes; *specif* **:** a severe endemic disease of man in much of Asia, Africa, and So. America marked esp. by blood loss and tissue damage

schiz- *or* **schizo-** *comb form* [NL, fr. Gk *schizo-,* fr. *schizein* to split — more at SHED] **1 :** split **:** cleft ⟨*schizo*carp⟩ **2 :** characterized by or involving cleavage ⟨*schizo*genesis⟩ **3 :** schizophrenia ⟨*schizo*thymia⟩

schizo \'skit-(ˌ)sō\ *n, pl* **schiz·os** (1945) **:** a schizophrenic individual

schizo·carp \'skiz-ə-ˌkärp, 'skit-sə-\ *n* [ISV] (1870) **:** a dry compound fruit that splits at maturity into several indehiscent one-seeded carpels

schi·zog·o·ny \skiz-'äg-ə-nē, skit-'säg-\ *n* [NL *schizogonia,* fr. *schiz-* + L *-gonia* -gony] (1887) **:** asexual reproduction by multiple segmentation characteristic of sporozoans (as the malaria parasite) — **schi·zog·o·nous** \-nəs\ *or* **schizo·gon·ic** \ˌskiz-ə-'gän-ik, ˌskit-sə-\ *adj*

schiz·oid \'skit-ˌsȯid\ *adj* [ISV] (1924) **:** characterized by, resulting from, tending toward, or suggestive of schizophrenia — **schizoid** *n*

schiz·ont \'skiz-ˌänt, 'skit-ˌsänt\ *n* [ISV] (1900) **:** a multinucleate sporozoan that reproduces by schizogony

schizo·phrene \'skit-sə-ˌfrēn\ *n* [ISV, prob. back-formation fr. NL *schizophrenia*] (1925) **:** one affected with schizophrenia **:** SCHIZOPHRENIC

schizo·phre·nia \ˌskit-sə-'frē-nē-ə\ *n* [NL] (1912) **1 :** a psychotic disorder characterized by loss of contact with the environment, by noticeable deterioration in the level of functioning in everyday life, and by disintegration of personality expressed as disorder of feeling, thought, and conduct — called also *dementia praecox* **2 :** the presence of mutually contradictory or antagonistic parts or qualities — **schizo·phren·ic** \-'fren-ik\ *adj or n* — **schizo·phren·i·cal·ly** \-'fren-i-k(ə-)lē\ *adv*

schizy *or* **schiz·zy** \'skit-sē\ *adj* [by shortening & alter.] (ca. 1927) **:** SCHIZOID

schle·miel \shlə-'mē(ə)l\ *n* [Yiddish *shlumiel*] (1892) **:** an unlucky bungler **:** CHUMP

schlepp *or* **schlep** \'shlep\ *vb* [Yiddish *shleppen,* fr. MHG *sleppen,* fr. MLG *slēpen*] *vt* (1922) **:** DRAG, HAUL ~ *vi* **:** to proceed or move slowly, tediously, or awkwardly

schlie·ren \'shlir-ən\ *n pl* [G] (ca. 1885) **1 :** small masses or streaks in an igneous rock that differ in composition from the main body **2 :** regions of varying refraction in a transparent medium often caused by pressure or temperature differences and detectable esp. by photographing the passage of a beam of light — **schlie·ric** \'shli(ə)r-ik\ *adj*

schlock \'shläk\ *also* **schlocky** \-ē\ *adj* [Yiddish *shlak,* fr. *shlak* curse, cheap merchandise, lit., blow, fr. MHG *slag, slac,* fr. OHG *slag,* fr. *slahan* to strike — more at SLAY] (1915) **:** of low quality or value — **schlock** *n*

schm- *or* **shm-** \shm\ *comb form* [Yiddish *shm-,* fr. the initial consonant cluster of several derogatory terms] — used to form a rhyming term of derision by replacing the initial consonant or consonant cluster of a word or by preceding the initial vowel ⟨fancy, *schm*ancy, I prefer plain⟩ ⟨Godfather-*shm*odfather — enough already —Judith Crist⟩

schmaltz *also* **schmalz** \'shmȯlts, 'shmälts\ *n* [Yiddish *shmalts,* lit., rendered fat, fr. MHG *smalz;* akin to OHG *smelzan* to melt — more at SMELT] (1935) **1 :** sentimental or florid music or art **2 :** SENTIMENTALITY — **schmaltzy** \-ē\ *adj*

schmear *or* **schmeer** \'shmi(ə)r\ *n* [Yiddish *shmir* smear; akin to OHG *smero* grease — more at SMEAR] (1965) **:** an aggregate of related things ⟨the whole ~⟩

Schmidt system \'s(h)mit-\ *n* [B. *Schmidt* †1935 Ger. optical scientist] (1945) **:** an optical system (as for a telescope or camera) that utilizes an objective composed of a concave spherical mirror having in front of it a transparent plate to offset spherical aberration

schmo *or* **schmoe** \'shmō\ *n, pl* **schmoes** [prob. modif. of Yiddish *shmok* penis, fool, fr. G *schmuck* adornment] *slang* (1947) **:** JERK 4

schmooze *or* **shmooze** \'shmüz\ *vi* [Yiddish *shmuesn* to talk, chat, fr. *schmues* talk, fr. Heb *shĕmu'ōth* news, rumor] (1939) **:** to converse informally **:** CHAT

schmuck \'shmək\ *n* [Yiddish *shmok*] *slang* (1892) **:** JERK 4

schnapps \'shnaps\ *n, pl* **schnapps** [G *schnaps,* lit., dram of liquor, fr. LG *snaps* dram, mouthful, fr. *snappen* to snap] (1818) **:** any of various liquors of high alcoholic content; *esp* **:** strong Holland gin

schnau·zer \'shnaüt-sər, 's(h)naü-zər\ *n* [G, fr. *schnauze* snout — more at SNOUT] (1923) **:** a dog of any of three breeds that originated in Germany and are characterized by a long head, small ears, heavy eyebrows, mustache and beard, and a wiry coat: **a :** STANDARD SCHNAUZER **b :** GIANT SCHNAUZER **c :** MINIATURE SCHNAUZER

schnit·zel \'s(h)nit-səl\ *n* [G, lit., shaving, chip, fr. MHG *snitzel,* dim. of *sniz* slice; akin to OHG *snīdan* to cut, OE *snīthan,* Czech *snět* bough] (1854) **:** a seasoned and garnished veal cutlet

schnook \'shnu̇k\ *n* [origin unknown] *slang* (1947) **:** a stupid or unimportant person **:** DOLT

schnor·kel \'s(h)nȯr-kəl\ *var of* SNORKEL

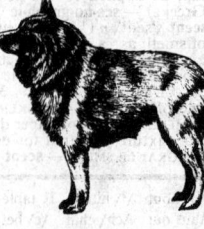

schnor·rer \ˈshnȯr-ər, ˈshnōr-\ *n* [Yiddish *shnorer*] (1892) **:** BEGGAR; *esp* **:** one who wheedles others into supplying his wants
schnoz·zle \ˈs(h)näz-əl\ *n* [prob. modif. of Yiddish *shnoitsl,* dim. of *shnoits* snout, fr. G *schnauze* snout, muzzle — more at SNOUT] *slang* (1937) **:** NOSE
scho·la can·to·rum \ˌskō-lə-kan-ˈtȯr-əm, -ˈtȯr-\ *n, pl* **scho·lae cantorum** \-ˌlē-, -ˌlā-, -ˌlī-\ [ML, school of singers] (1782) **1 :** a singing school esp. for church choristers; *specif* **:** the choir or choir school of a monastery or of a cathedral **2 :** an enclosure designed for a choir and located in the center of the nave in early church buildings
schol·ar \ˈskäl-ər\ *n* [ME *scoler,* fr. OE *scolere* & OF *escoler,* fr. ML *scholaris,* fr. LL, of a school, fr. L *schola* school] (bef. 12c) **1 :** one who attends a school or studies under a teacher **:** PUPIL **2 a :** one who has done advanced study in a special field **b :** a learned person **3 :** a holder of a scholarship
schol·ar·ly \-ər-lē\ *adj* (1638) **:** of, characteristic of, or suitable to learned persons **:** LEARNED, ACADEMIC
schol·ar·ship \-ər-ˌship\ *n* (1535) **1 :** a grant-in-aid to a student (as by a college or foundation) **2 :** the character, qualities, activity, or attainments of a scholar **:** LEARNING **3 :** a fund of knowledge and learning ⟨drawing on the ~ of the ancients⟩ ***syn*** see KNOWLEDGE
[1]**scho·las·tic** \skə-ˈlas-tik\ *adj* [ML & L; ML *scholasticus* of the schoolmen, fr. L, of a school, fr. Gk *scholastikos,* fr. *scholazein* to keep a school, fr. *scholē* school] (1596) **1 a** *often cap* **:** of or relating to Scholasticism ⟨~ theology⟩ ⟨~ philosophy⟩ **b :** suggestive or characteristic of a scholastic esp. in subtlety or aridity **:** PEDANTIC ⟨turned out dull ~ reports⟩ **2 :** of or relating to schools or scholars; *esp* **:** of or relating to high school or secondary school — **scho·las·ti·cal·ly** \-ti-k(ə-)lē\ *adv*
[2]**scholastic** *n* (1644) **1 a** *cap* **:** a Scholastic philosopher **b :** PEDANT, FORMALIST **2** [NL *scholasticus,* fr. L *scholasticus,* adj.] **:** a student in a scholasticate **3 :** one who adopts academic or traditional methods in art
scho·las·ti·cate \skə-ˈlas-tə-ˌkāt, -ti-kət\ *n* [NL *scholasticatus,* fr. *scholasticus* student in a scholasticate] (1875) **:** a college-level school of general study for those preparing for membership in a Roman Catholic religious order
scho·las·ti·cism \skə-ˈlas-tə-ˌsiz-əm\ *n* (1756) **1** *cap* **a :** a philosophical movement dominant in western Christian civilization from the 9th until the 17th century and combining religious dogma with the mystical and intuitional tradition of patristic philosophy esp. of St. Augustine and later with Aristotelianism **b :** NEO-SCHOLASTICISM **2 a :** close adherence to the traditional teachings or methods of a school or sect **b :** pedantic adherence to scholarly methods
scho·li·ast \ˈskō-lē-ˌast, -lē-əst\ *n* [MGk *scholiastēs,* fr. *scholiazein* to write scholia on, fr. Gk *scholion*] (1583) **:** a maker of scholia **:** COMMENTATOR, ANNOTATOR — **scho·li·as·tic** \ˌskō-lē-ˈas-tik\ *adj*
scho·li·um \ˈskō-lē-əm\ *n, pl* **-lia** \-lē-ə\ *or* **-li·ums** [NL, fr. Gk *scholion* comment, scholium, fr. dim. of *scholē* lecture] (1535) **1 :** a marginal annotation or comment (as on the text of a classic by an early grammarian) **2 :** a remark or observation subjoined but not essential to a demonstration or a train of reasoning
[1]**school** \ˈskül\ *n* [ME *scole,* fr. OE *scōl,* fr. L *schola,* fr. Gk *scholē* leisure, discussion, lecture, school; akin to Gk *echein* to hold — more at SCHEME] (bef. 12c) **1 :** an organization that provides instruction: as **a :** an institution for the teaching of children **b :** COLLEGE, UNIVERSITY **c** (1) **:** a group of scholars and teachers pursuing knowledge together that with similar groups constituted a medieval university (2) **:** one of the four faculties of a medieval university (3) **:** an institution for specialized higher education often associated with a university ⟨the ~ of engineering⟩ **d :** an establishment offering specialized instruction ⟨a secretarial ~⟩ ⟨driving ~s⟩ **2 a** (1) **:** the process of teaching or learning esp. at a school (2) **:** attendance at a school (3) **:** a session of a school **b :** a school building **c :** the students attending a school; *also* **:** its teachers and students **3 :** a source of knowledge ⟨experience was his ~⟩ **4 a :** persons who hold a common doctrine or follow the same teacher (as in philosophy, theology, or medicine) ⟨the Aristotelian ~⟩ **b :** a group of artists under a common influence **c :** persons of similar opinions or behavior ⟨other ~s of thought⟩ **5 :** the regulations governing military drill of individuals or units; *also* **:** the exercises carried out ⟨the ~ of the soldier⟩
[2]**school** *vt* (1577) **1 :** to educate in an institution of learning **2 a :** to teach or drill in a specific knowledge or skill ⟨well ~*ed* in languages⟩ **b :** to discipline or habituate to something ⟨~ oneself in patience⟩ ***syn*** see TEACH
[3]**school** *n* [ME *scole,* fr. MD *schole;* akin to OE *scolu* multitude, *scylian* to separate — more at SKILL] (15c) **:** a large number of fish or aquatic animals of one kind swimming together
[4]**school** *vi* (1597) **:** to swim or feed in a school ⟨bluefish are ~*ing*⟩
school–age *adj* (1879) **:** old enough to go to school ⟨~ children⟩
school·bag \ˈskül-ˌbag\ *n* (1895) **:** a bag for carrying schoolbooks and school supplies
school board *n* (1836) **:** a board in charge of local public schools
school·book \-ˌbu̇k\ *n* (1745) **:** a school textbook
school·boy \-ˌbȯi\ *n* (1588) **:** a boy attending school
school bus *n* (1908) **:** a vehicle used for transporting children to or from school or on activities connected with school
school·child \ˈskül-ˌchīld\ *n* (1840) **:** a child attending school
school committee *n* (1787) **:** SCHOOL BOARD
school district *n* (1809) **:** a unit for administration of a public-school system often comprising several towns within a state
-school·er \ˈskü-lər\ *comb form* **:** one who attends (such) a school ⟨grade-*schooler*⟩
school·fel·low \ˈskül-ˌfel-(ˌ)ō, -ə(-w)\ *n* (15c) **:** SCHOOLMATE
school·girl \-ˌgər(-ə)l\ *n* (1777) **:** a girl attending school
school·house \-ˌhau̇s\ *n* (15c) **:** a building used as a school and esp. as an elementary school
school·ing *n* (15c) **1 a :** instruction in school **:** EDUCATION **b :** training, guidance, or discipline derived from experience **2** *archaic* **:** REPROOF **3 :** the cost of instruction and maintenance at school **4 :** the training of a horse to service; *esp* **:** the teaching and exercising of horse and rider in the formal techniques of equitation
school–leav·er \ˈskül-ˌlē-vər\ *n, Brit* (1925) **:** one who has left school
school·man \ˈskül-mən, -ˌman\ *n* (1540) **1 a :** one skilled in academic disputation **b** *cap* **:** SCHOLASTIC 1a **2 :** EDUCATOR 1, 2b
school·marm \-ˌmä(r)m\ *or* **school·ma'am** \-ˌmäm, -ˌmam\ *n* [*school* + *marm,* alter. of ma'am] (1831) **1 :** a female schoolteacher esp. in a rural or small-town school **2 :** a person who exhibits characteristics attributed to schoolteachers (as strict adherence to arbitrary rules) — **school·marm·ish** \-ish\ *adj*
school·mas·ter \-ˌmas-tər\ *n* (13c) **1 :** a man who teaches school **2 :** one that disciplines or directs **3 :** a reddish brown edible snapper (*Lutjanus apodus*) of the tropical Atlantic and the Gulf of Mexico — **school·mas·ter·ish** \-ish\ *adj* — **school·mas·ter·ly** *adj*
school·mate \-ˌmāt\ *n* (1563) **:** a companion at school
school·mis·tress \-ˌmis-trəs\ *n* (1500) **:** a woman who teaches school
school·room \-ˌrüm, -ˌru̇m\ *n* (1773) **:** CLASSROOM
school·teach·er \-ˌtē-chər\ *n* (ca. 1847) **:** one who teaches school
school·time \-ˌtīm\ *n* (1740) **1 :** the time for beginning a session of school or during which school is held **2 :** the period of life spent in school or in study
school·work \-ˌwərk\ *n* (1857) **:** lessons done in class or assigned to be done at home
schoo·ner \ˈskü-nər\ *n* [origin unknown] (1716) **1 :** a typically 2-masted fore-and-aft rigged vessel with a foremast and a mainmast stepped nearly amidships **2 :** a larger-than-usual drinking glass (as for beer or sherry) **3 :** PRAIRIE SCHOONER
schooner rig *n* (1866) **:** FORE-AND-AFT RIG — **schoo·ner–rigged** \ˌskü-nə(r)-ˈrigd\ *adj*
schorl \ˈshȯr(ə)l\ *n* [G *schörl*] (1779) **:** TOURMALINE; *esp* **:** tourmaline of the black variety
schot·tische \ˈshät-ish, shä-ˈtēsh\ *n* [G, fr. *schottisch* Scottish, fr. *Schotte* Scotchman; akin to OE *Scottas* Scotchmen] (1849) **1 :** a round dance resembling a slow polka **2 :** music for the schottische
schrod *var of* SCROD
schtick *var of* SHTICK
schuss \ˈshu̇s, ˈshüs\ *vi* [G *schussen,* fr. *schuss,* lit., shot, fr. OHG *scuz* — more at SHOT] (1940) **:** to ski directly down a slope at high speed — **schuss** *n*
schuss·boom·er \-ˌbü-mər\ *n* (1953) **:** one who schusses
schwa \ˈshwä\ *n* [G, fr. Heb *shĕwā'*] (1895) **1 :** an unstressed mid-central vowel that is the usual sound of the first and last vowels of the English word *America* **2 :** the symbol ə used for the schwa sound and less widely for a similarly articulated stressed vowel (as in *cut*)
Schwann cell \ˈshwän-\ *n* [Theodor *Schwann* †1882 Ger. naturalist] (ca. 1909) **:** a cell of the neurilemma of a nerve fiber
schwar·me·rei \ˌshfer-mə-ˈrī\ *n* [G *schwärmerei,* fr. *schwärmen* to be enthusiastic, lit., to swarm] (1845) **:** excessive or unwholesome sentiment
sci·at·ic \sī-ˈat-ik\ *adj* [MF *sciatique,* fr. LL *sciaticus,* alter. of L *ischiadicus* of sciatica, fr. Gk *ischiadikos,* fr. *ischiad-, ischias* sciatica, fr. *ischion* ischium] (1547) **1 :** of, relating to, or situated near the hip **2 :** of, relating to, or caused by sciatica ⟨~ pains⟩
sci·at·i·ca \sī-ˈat-i-kə\ *n* [ME, fr. ML, fr. LL, fem. of *sciaticus*] (15c) **:** pain along the course of a sciatic nerve esp. in the back of the thigh; *broadly* **:** pain in the lower back, buttocks, hips, or adjacent parts
sciatic nerve *n* (1741) **:** either of the pair of largest nerves in the body that arise one on each side from the nerve plexus supplying the posterior limb and pelvic region and that pass out of the pelvis and down the back of the thigh
sci·ence \ˈsī-ən(t)s\ *n* [ME, fr. MF, fr. L *scientia,* fr. *scient-, sciens* having knowledge, fr. prp. of *scire* to know; akin to L *scindere* to cut — more at SHED] (14c) **1 :** the state of knowing **:** knowledge as distinguished from ignorance or misunderstanding **2 a :** a department of systematized knowledge as an object of study ⟨the ~ of theology⟩ **b :** something (as a sport or technique) that may be studied or learned like systematized knowledge ⟨have it down to a ~⟩ **c :** one of the natural sciences **3 a :** knowledge covering general truths or the operation of general laws esp. as obtained and tested through scientific method **b :** such knowledge concerned with the physical world and its phenomena **:** NATURAL SCIENCE **4 :** a system or method reconciling practical ends with scientific laws ⟨culinary ~⟩ **5** *cap* **:** CHRISTIAN SCIENCE
science fiction *n* (1851) **:** fiction dealing principally with the impact of actual or imagined science on society or individuals or having a scientific factor as an essential orienting component
sci·en·tial \sī-ˈen-chəl\ *adj* (15c) **1 :** relating to or producing knowledge or science **2 :** having efficient knowledge **:** CAPABLE
sci·en·tif·ic \ˌsī-ən-ˈtif-ik\ *adj* [ML *scientificus* producing knowledge, fr. L *scient-, sciens* + *-i-* + *-ficus* -fic] (1589) **:** of, relating to, or exhibiting the methods or principles of science — **sci·en·tif·i·cal·ly** \-i-k(ə-)lē\ *adv*
scientific method *n* (1854) **:** principles and procedures for the systematic pursuit of knowledge involving the recognition and formulation of a problem, the collection of data through observation and experiment, and the formulation and testing of hypotheses
scientific notation *n* (ca. 1934) **:** a widely used floating-point system in which numbers are expressed as products consisting of a number between 1 and 10 multiplied by an appropriate power of 10
sci·en·tism \ˈsī-ən-ˌtiz-əm\ *n* (1877) **1 :** methods and attitudes typical of or attributed to the natural scientist **2 :** an exaggerated trust in the efficacy of the methods of natural science applied to all areas of investigation (as in philosophy, the social sciences, and the humanities)
sci·en·tist \ˈsī-ənt-əst\ *n* [L *scientia*] (1834) **1 :** one learned in science and esp. natural science **:** a scientific investigator **2** *cap* **:** CHRISTIAN SCIENTIST
sci·en·tize \ˈsī-ən-ˌtīz\ *vt* **-tized; -tiz·ing** (1917) **:** to treat with a scientific approach ⟨the attempt to ~ reality, to name it and classify it —John Fowles⟩
sci–fi \ˈsī-ˈfī\ *adj* [*science fiction*] (1955) **:** of, relating to, or being science fiction ⟨a ~ story⟩
sci·li·cet \ˈskē-li-ˌket; ˈsī-lə-ˌset, ˈsil-ə-\ *adv* [ME, fr. L, surely, to wit, fr. *scire* to know + *licet* it is permitted, fr. *licēre* to be permitted — more at LICENSE] (14c) **:** TO WIT, NAMELY

scil·la \'s(k)il-ə\ *n* [NL, fr. L, squill — more at SQUILL] (1824) **:** any of a genus (*Scilla*) of Old World bulbous herbs of the lily family with narrow basal leaves and pink, blue, or white racemose flowers

scim·i·tar \'sim-ət-ər, -ə-,tär\ *n* [It *scimitarra*] (1548) **:** a saber made of a curved blade with the edge on the convex side and used chiefly by Arabs and Turks

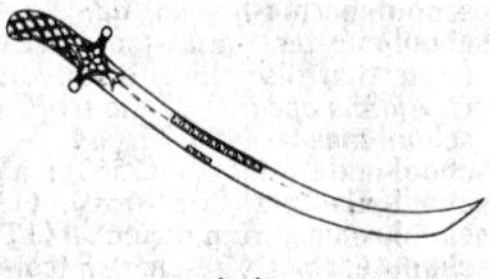
scimitar

scin·tig·ra·phy \sin-'tig-rə-fē\ *n* [*scintillation* + *-graphy;* fr. the scintillation counter used to record radiation on the picture] (1958) **:** a diagnostic technique in which a two-dimensional picture of a bodily radiation source is obtained by the use of radioisotopes — **scin·ti·graph·ic** \,sint-ə-'graf-ik\ *adj*

scin·til·la \sin-'til-ə\ *n* [L] (1692) **:** SPARK, TRACE

scin·til·lant \'sint-ᵊl-ənt\ *adj* (1737) **:** that scintillates **:** SPARKLING — **scin·til·lant·ly** *adv*

scin·til·late \'sint-ᵊl-,āt\ *vb* **-lat·ed; -lat·ing** [L *scintillatus,* pp. of *scintillare* to sparkle, fr. *scintilla* spark] *vi* (1623) **1 :** to emit sparks **:** SPARK **2 :** to emit quick flashes as if throwing off sparks **:** SPARKLE; ~ *vt* **:** to throw off as a spark or as sparkling flashes ⟨~ witticisms⟩ — **scin·til·la·tor** \-,āt-ər\ *n*

scin·til·lat·ing *adj* (1883) **:** brilliantly lively, stimulating, or witty ⟨~ conversation⟩

scin·til·la·tion \,sint-ᵊl-'ā-shən\ *n* (1623) **1 :** an act or instance of scintillating; *esp* **:** rapid changes in the brightness of a celestial body **2 a :** a spark or flash emitted in scintillating **b :** a flash of light produced in a phosphor by an ionizing event **3 :** a brilliant outburst (as of wit) **4 :** a flash of the eye

scintillation counter *n* (ca. 1948) **:** a device for detecting and registering individual scintillations (as in radioactive emission)

scin·til·lom·e·ter \,sint-ᵊl-'äm-ət-ər\ *n* [L *scintilla* + ISV *-o-* + *-meter*] (1877) **:** SCINTILLATION COUNTER

sci·o·lism \'sī-ə-,liz-əm\ *n* [LL *sciolus* smatterer, fr. dim. of L *scius* knowing, fr. *scire* to know — more at SCIENCE] (1816) **:** a superficial show of learning — **sci·o·list** \-ləst\ *n* — **sci·o·lis·tic** \,sī-ə-'lis-tik\ *adj*

sci·on \'sī-ən\ *n* [ME, fr. MF *cion,* of Gmc origin; akin to OHG *chinan* to sprout, split open, OE *cīnan* to gape] (14c) **1 :** a detached living portion of a plant joined to a stock in grafting and usu. supplying solely aerial parts to a graft **2 :** DESCENDANT, CHILD

sci·re fa·cias \,sī-rē-'fā-sh(ē-)əs\ *n* [ME, fr. ML, you should cause to know] (15c) **1 :** a judicial writ founded on some matter of record and requiring the party proceeded against to show cause why the record should not be enforced, annulled, or vacated **2 :** a legal proceeding instituted by a scire facias

sci·roc·co \shi-'räk-(,)ō, sə-\ *var of* SIROCCO

scir·rhous \'s(k)ir-əs\ *adj* (1563) **:** of, relating to, or being a hard slow-growing malignant tumor having a preponderance of fibrous tissue

scir·rhus \'s(k)ir-əs\ *n, pl* **scir·rhi** \'s(k)i(ə)r-,ī, 'ski(ə)r-,ē\ [NL, fr. Gk *skiros, skirrhos,* fr. *skiros* hard] (1615) **:** a scirrhous tumor

scis·sile \'sis-əl, -,īl\ *adj* [F, fr. L *scissilis,* fr. *scissus,* pp. of *scindere* to split — more at SHED] (1621) **:** capable of being cut smoothly or split easily ⟨a ~ peptide bond⟩

scis·sion \'sizh-ən\ *n* [F, fr. LL *scission-, scissio,* fr. L *scissus,* pp.] (15c) **1 :** a division or split in a group or union **:** SCHISM **2 :** an action or process of cutting, dividing, or splitting **:** the state of being cut, divided, or split

1**scis·sor** \'siz-ər\ *n* [ME *sisoure,* fr. MF *cisoire,* fr. LL *cisorium* cutting instrument, irreg. fr. L *caesus,* pp. of *caedere* to cut — more at CONCISE] (15c) **:** SCISSORS

2**scissor** *vt* **scis·sored; scis·sor·ing** \-(ə-)riŋ\ (1612) **:** to cut, cut up, or cut off with scissors or shears

scis·sors \'siz-ərz\ *n pl but sing or pl in constr* (14c) **1 :** a cutting instrument having two blades whose cutting edges slide past each other **2 a :** a gymnastic feat in which the leg movements suggest the opening and closing of scissors **b :** SCISSORS HOLD

scissors–and–paste *adj* (1902) **:** being a compilation rather than an effort of original and independent investigation

scissors hold *n* (1909) **:** a wrestling hold in which the legs are locked around the head or body of an opponent

scissors kick *n* (ca. 1934) **:** a swimming kick used esp. in sidestrokes in which the legs move like scissors

scis·sor·tail \'siz-ər-,tāl\ *n* (1839) **:** a flycatcher (*Muscivora forficata*) of the southern U.S. and Mexico with a deeply forked tail

sclaff \'sklaf\ *vi* [fr. earlier E (Sc) *sclaff,* n., a slight blow, slap] (1893) **:** to scrape the ground instead of hitting the ball cleanly on a golf stroke — **sclaff** *n* — **sclaff·er** *n*

scler- *or* **sclero-** *comb form* [NL, fr. Gk *sklēr-, sklēro-,* fr. *sklēros* — more at SKELETON] **1 a :** hard ⟨*scler*ite⟩ ⟨*sclero*derma⟩ **b :** hardness ⟨*sclero*meter⟩ **2 :** sclera ⟨*scler*itis⟩

scle·ra \'skler-ə\ *n* [NL, fr. Gk *sklēros*] (1888) **:** the dense fibrous opaque white outer coat enclosing the eyeball except the part covered by the cornea — see EYE illustration — **scler·al** \-əl\ *adj*

scler·e·id \'skler-ē-əd\ *n* [*scler*enchyma + *-id*] (ca. 1900) **:** a sclerenchymatous cell of a higher plant that is nearly isodiametric

scle·ren·chy·ma \sklə-'reŋ-kə-mə\ *n* [NL] (1875) **:** a protective or supporting tissue in higher plants composed of cells with walls thickened and lignified and often mineralized — **scler·en·chy·ma·tous** \,skler-ən-'kim-ət-əs, -'kī-mət-\ *adj*

scler·ite \'skle(ə)r-,īt\ *n* [ISV] (1861) **:** a hard chitinous or calcareous plate, piece, or spicule (as of the arthropod integument)

sclero·der·ma \,skler-ə-'dər-mə\ *n* [NL] (1866) **:** a usu. slowly progressive disease marked by the deposition of fibrous connective tissue in the skin and often in internal organs

scle·rom·e·ter \sklə-'räm-ət-ər\ *n* [ISV] (ca. 1879) **:** an instrument for determining the relative hardnesses of materials

sclero·pro·tein \,skler-ō-'prō-,tēn, -'prōt-ē-ən\ *n* [ISV] (1907) **:** any of various fibrous proteins esp. from connective and skeletal tissues

scle·ros·ing \sklə-'rō-siŋ, -ziŋ\ *adj* (ca. 1885) **:** causing or characterized by sclerosis ⟨~ agents⟩

scle·ro·sis \sklə-'rō-səs\ *n* [ME *sclirosis,* fr. ML, fr. Gk *sklērōsis* hardening, fr. *sklēroun* to harden, fr. *sklēros*] (14c) **1 :** pathological hardening of tissue esp. from overgrowth of fibrous tissue or increase in interstitial tissue; *also* **:** a disease characterized by sclerosis **2 :** hardening of plant cell walls usu. by lignification

1**scle·rot·ic** \sklə-'rät-ik\ *adj* (1543) **1 :** being or relating to the sclera **2 :** of, relating to, or affected with sclerosis

2**sclerotic** *n* [ML *sclerotica,* fr. (assumed) Gk *sklērōtos,* verbal of Gk *sklēroun* to harden — more at SKELETON] (1690) **:** SCLERA

sclerotic coat *n* (1741) **:** SCLERA

scler·o·tin \'skler-ət-ən, sklə-'rōt-ᵊn\ *n* [(assumed) Gk *sklērōtos* + ISV *-in*] (1940) **:** an insoluble tanned protein permeating and stiffening the chitin of the cuticle of arthropods

scle·ro·tium \sklə-'rō-sh(ē-)əm\ *n, pl* **-tia** \-sh(ē-)ə\ [NL, fr. (assumed) Gk *sklērōtos*] (1871) **:** a compact mass of hardened mycelium stored with reserve food material that in some higher fungi becomes detached and remains dormant until a favorable opportunity for growth occurs — **scle·ro·tial** \-'rō-shəl\ *adj*

scler·o·tized \'skler-ə-,tīzd\ *adj* [(assumed) Gk *sklērōtos* + E *-ize* + *-ed*] (ca. 1902) **:** hardened esp. by the formation of sclerotin ⟨~ insect cuticle⟩ — **scler·o·ti·za·tion** \,skler-ət-ə-'zā-shən\ *n*

1**scoff** \'skäf, 'skȯf\ *n* [ME *scof,* prob. of Scand origin; akin to obs. Dan *skof* jest; akin to OFris *skof* mockery] (14c) **1 :** an expression of scorn, derision, or contempt **:** GIBE **2 :** an object of scorn, mockery, or derision

2**scoff** *vi* (14c) **:** to show contempt by derisive acts or language ~ *vt* **:** to treat or address with derision **:** MOCK — **scoff·er** *n*

syn SCOFF, JEER, GIBE, FLEER, SNEER, FLOUT mean to show one's contempt in derision or mockery. SCOFF stresses insolence, disrespect, or incredulity as motivating the derision; JEER suggests a coarser more undiscriminating derision; GIBE implies taunting either good-naturedly or in sarcastic derision; FLEER suggests grinning or grimacing derisively; SNEER stresses insulting by contemptuous facial expression, phrasing, or tone of voice; FLOUT stresses contempt shown by refusal to heed.

3**scoff** *vb* [alter. of earlier *scaff,* of unknown origin] *vt* (ca. 1846) **1 :** to eat greedily **2 :** SEIZE — often used with *up* ~ *vi* **:** to eat something greedily

scoff·law \-,lȯ\ *n* (1924) **:** a contemptuous law violator

1**scold** \'skōld\ *n* [ME *scald, scold,* perh. of Scand origin; akin to ON *skāld* poet, skald, Icel *skālda* to make scurrilous verse] (13c) **1 a :** one who scolds habitually or persistently **b :** a woman who disturbs the public peace by noisy and quarrelsome or abusive behavior **2 :** SCOLDING

2**scold** *vi* (14c) **1** *obs* **:** to quarrel noisily **2 :** to find fault noisily or angrily ~ *vt* **:** to censure severely or angrily **:** REBUKE — **scold·er** *n*

syn SCOLD, UPBRAID, BERATE, RAIL, REVILE, VITUPERATE mean to reproach angrily and abusively. SCOLD implies rebuking in irritation or ill temper justly or unjustly; UPBRAID implies censuring on definite and usu. justifiable grounds; BERATE suggests prolonged and often abusive scolding; RAIL (*at* or *against*) stresses an unrestrained berating; REVILE implies a scurrilous, abusive attack prompted by anger or hatred; VITUPERATE suggests a violent reviling.

scold·ing *n* (15c) **1 :** the action of one who scolds **2 :** a harsh reproof

sco·le·cite \'skäl-ə-,sīt, 'skō-lə-\ *n* [G *skolezit,* fr. Gk *skōlēk-, skōlēx* worm; fr. the motion of some forms when heated] (ca. 1823) **:** a zeolite mineral $CaAl_2Si_3O_{10}·3H_2O$ that is a hydrous calcium aluminum silicate and occurs in radiating groups of crystals, in fibrous masses, and in nodules

sco·lex \'skō-,leks\ *n, pl* **sco·li·ces** \-lə-,sēz\ [NL *scolic-, scolex,* fr. Gk *skōlēk-, skōlēx* worm; akin to Gk *skolios* crooked — more at CYLINDER] (1855) **:** the head of a tapeworm either in the larva or adult stage

sco·li·o·sis \,skō-lē-'ō-səs\ *n, pl* **-o·ses** \-,sēz\ [NL, fr. Gk *skoliōsis* crookedness of a bodily part, fr. *skolios* crooked] (ca. 1706) **:** a lateral curvature of the spine — **sco·li·ot·ic** \-'ät-ik\ *adj*

scol·lop \'skäl-əp\ *var of* SCALLOP

scol·o·pen·dra \'skäl-ə-'pen-drə\ *n* [NL, genus of centipedes, fr. L, a kind of millipede, fr. Gk *skolopendra*] (1608) **:** CENTIPEDE

scom·broid \'skäm-,brȯid\ *n* [deriv. of Gk *skombros* mackerel] (1842) **:** any of a suborder (Scombroidea) of marine spiny-finned fishes (as mackerels, tunas, albacores, bonitos, and swordfishes) of great economic importance as food fishes — **scombroid** *adj*

1**sconce** \'skän(t)s\ *n* [ME, fr. MF *esconse* screened lantern, fr. OF, fr. fem. of *escons,* pp. of *escondre* to hide, fr. L *abscondere* — more at ABSCOND] (15c) **1 :** a bracket candlestick or group of candlesticks; *also* **:** an electric light fixture patterned on a candle sconce **2 :** HEAD, SKULL

2**sconce** *n* [D *schans,* fr. G *schanze*] (1571) **:** a detached defensive work

scone \'skōn, 'skän\ *n* [perh. fr. D *schoonbrood* fine white bread, fr. *schoon* pure, clean (fr. *schone* beautiful; akin to OE *scīene*) + *brood* bread — more at SHEEN] (1513) **:** a rich quick bread cut into usu. triangular shapes and cooked on a griddle or baked on a sheet

1**scoop** \'sküp\ *n* [ME *scope,* fr. MD *schope;* akin to OHG *skepfen* to shape — more at SHAPE] (14c) **1 a :** a large ladle **b :** a deep shovel or similar implement for digging, dipping, or shoveling **c :** a hemispherical utensil for dipping soft food **d :** a small spoon-shaped utensil or instrument for cutting or gouging **2 :** the action of scooping **3 a :** a hollow place **:** CAVITY **b :** a part forming or surrounding an opening for channeling a fluid (as air) into a desired path **4 a :** information esp. of immediate interest **b :** BEAT 7b **5 :** a rounded and usu. low-cut neckline on a woman's garment — called also *scoop neck* — **scoop·ful** \-,fu̇l\ *n*

2**scoop** *vt* (14c) **1 a :** to take out or up with or as if with a scoop **:** DIP **b :** to pick up quickly or surreptitiously with or as if with a sweep of the hand — often used with *up* **2 :** to empty by ladling out the contents **3 :** to make hollow **:** DIG OUT **4 :** BEAT 5a(2) — **scoop·er** *n*

scoot \'sküt\ *vi* [prob. of Scand origin; akin to ON *skjōta* to shoot — more at SHOOT] (1758) **1 :** to move swiftly **2 :** to slide esp. while seated ⟨~ over and let me sit down⟩ — **scoot** *n*

scoot·er \'sküt-ər\ *n* (1916) **1 :** a child's foot-operated vehicle consisting of a narrow footboard mounted between two wheels tandem with an upright steering handle attached to the front wheel **2 :** MOTOR SCOOTER

scop \'shōp, 'skōp, 'skäp\ *n* [OE; akin to OHG *schof* poet] (bef. 12c) **:** an Old English bard or poet

[1]**scope** \ˈskōp\ *n* [It *scopo* purpose, goal, fr. Gk *skopos;* akin to Gk *skeptesthai* to watch, look at — more at SPY] (1555) **1** : space or opportunity for unhampered motion, activity, or thought **2** : INTENTION, OBJECT **3** : extent of treatment, activity, or influence **4** : range of operation ***syn*** see RANGE

[2]**scope** *n* [*-scope*] (1603) **1** : any of various instruments for viewing: as **a** : MICROSCOPE **b** : TELESCOPE **c** : OSCILLOSCOPE **d** : RADARSCOPE **2** : HOROSCOPE

-scope \ˌskōp\ *n comb form* [NL *-scopium,* fr. Gk *-skopion;* akin to Gk *skeptesthai*] : means (as an instrument) for viewing or observing ⟨micro*scope*⟩

sco·pol·amine \skō-ˈpäl-ə-ˌmēn, -mən\ *n* [G *scopolamin,* fr. NL *Scopolia* + G *amin* amine] (1892) : a poisonous alkaloid $C_{17}H_{21}NO_4$ found in the roots of various plants (esp. genus *Scopolia*) of the nightshade family and used esp. as a truth serum or usu. with morphine as a sedative in surgery and obstetrics — called also *hyoscine*

scop·u·la \ˈskäp-yə-lə\ *n* [NL, fr. LL, dim. of L *scopa* broom — more at SCULLION] (1802) : a bushy tuft of hairs

-s·co·py \s-kə-pē\ *n comb form* [Gk *-skopia,* fr. *skeptesthai*] : viewing : observation ⟨radio*scopy*⟩

scor·bu·tic \skȯr-ˈbyüt-ik\ *adj* [NL *scorbuticus,* fr. *scorbutus* scurvy, prob. of Gmc origin; akin to OE *scurf*] (1655) : of, relating to, producing, or affected with scurvy — **scor·bu·ti·cal·ly** \-i-k(ə-)lē\ *adv*

[1]**scorch** \ˈskȯ(ə)rch\ *vb* [ME *scorcnen, scorchen,* prob. of Scand origin; akin to ON *skorpna* to shrivel up — more at SHRIMP] *vt* (15c) **1** : to burn a surface of so as to change its color and texture **2 a** : to parch with or as if with intense heat **b** : to afflict painfully with censure or sarcasm **3** : DEVASTATE; *esp* : to destroy (as property of possible use to an advancing enemy) before abandoning — used in the phrase *scorched earth* ~ *vi* **1** : to become scorched **2** : to travel at great and usu. excessive speed **3** : to cause intense heat or mental anguish ⟨~*ing* sun⟩ ⟨~*ing* fury⟩ — **scorch·ing·ly** \ˈskȯr-chiŋ-lē\ *adv*

[2]**scorch** *n* (1611) **1** : a result of scorching **2** : a browning of plant tissues usu. from disease or heat

[3]**scorch** *vt* [alter. of [2]*score*] *dial Brit* (1550) : CUT, SLASH

scorched *adj* (1593) : parched or discolored by scorching

scorch·er \ˈskȯr-chər\ *n* (1874) : one that scorches; *esp* : a very hot day

[1]**score** \ˈskō(ə)r, ˈskȯ(ə)r\ *n, pl* **scores** [ME *scor,* fr. ON *skor* notch, tally, twenty; akin to OE *scieran* to cut — more at SHEAR] (13c) **1** *or pl* **score a** : TWENTY **b** : a group of 20 things — often used in combination with a cardinal number ⟨four*score*⟩ **c** *pl* : a group of an indefinite large number **2 a** : a line (as a scratch or incision) made with or as if with a sharp instrument **b** (1) : a mark used as a starting point or goal (2) : a mark used for keeping account **3 a** : an account or reckoning orig. kept by making marks on a tally **b** : amount due : INDEBTEDNESS **4** : GRUDGE ⟨a ~ to settle⟩ **5 a** : REASON, GROUND **b** : SUBJECT, TOPIC **6 a** : the copy of a musical composition in written or printed notation **b** : a musical composition; *specif* : the music for a movie or theatrical production **c** : a complete description of a dance composition in choreographic notation **7 a** : a number that expresses accomplishment (as in a game or test) or excellence (as in quality) either absolutely in points gained or by comparison to a standard **b** : an act (as a goal, run, or touchdown) in any of various games or contests that gains points **8** : success in obtaining something (as money or drugs) esp. through illegal or irregular means **9** : the stark inescapable facts of a situation ⟨knows the ~⟩

[2]**score** *vb* **scored; scor·ing** *vt* (14c) **1 a** : to keep a record or account of by or as if by notches on a tally : RECORD **b** : to enter in a record **c** : to mark with significant lines or notches (as in keeping account) **2** : to mark with lines, grooves, scratches, or notches **3** : BERATE, SCOLD; *also* : DENOUNCE **4 a** (1) : to make (a score) in a game or contest ⟨*scored* a touchdown⟩ ⟨*scored* three points⟩ (2) : to enable (a base runner) to make a score (3) : to have as a value in a game or contest : COUNT ⟨a touchdown ~*s* six points⟩ **b** (1) : ACHIEVE, WIN ⟨*scored* a dazzling success⟩ (2) : ACQUIRE ⟨help a traveler ~ local drugs —Poitor Koper⟩ **5** : to determine the merit of : GRADE **6 a** : to write or arrange (music) for a specific performance medium **b** : to make an orchestration of **c** : to compose a score for (a movie) ~ *vi* **1** : to keep score in a game or contest **2** : to make a score in a game or contest **3 a** : to gain or have the advantage **b** : to be successful: as (1) : to succeed in having sexual intercourse (2) : to manage to obtain illicit drugs **c** : [3]RATE — **scor·er** *n* — **score points** : to gain favor, status, or advantage

score·board \ˈskō(ə)r-ˌbō(ə)rd, ˈskȯ(ə)r-ˌbȯ(ə)rd\ *n* (1826) : a large board for displaying the score of a game or match

score·card \-ˌkärd\ *n* (ca. 1877) : a card for recording the score of a game

score·keep·er \-ˌkē-pər\ *n* (1880) : one that keeps score; *specif* : an official who records the score during a game or contest

score·less \-ləs\ *adj* (1885) : having no score

sco·ria \ˈskōr-ē-ə, ˈskȯr-\ *n, pl* **-ri·ae** \-ē-ˌē, -ē-ˌī\ [ME, fr. L, fr. Gk *skōria,* fr. *skōr* excrement — more at SCAT-] (14c) **1** : the refuse from melting of metals or reduction of ores : SLAG **2** : rough vesicular cindery lava — **sco·ri·a·ceous** \ˌskōr-ē-ˈā-shəs, ˌskȯr-\ *adj*

[1]**scorn** \ˈskȯ(ə)rn\ *n* [ME, fr. OF *escarn,* of Gmc origin; akin to OHG *scern* jest; akin to Gk *skairein* to gambol — more at CARDINAL] (13c) **1** : open dislike and disrespect or derision often mixed with indignation **2** : an expression of contempt or derision **3** : an object of extreme disdain, contempt, or derision : something contemptible

[2]**scorn** *vt* (13c) : to treat with scorn : reject or dismiss as contemptible or unworthy ⟨~*ed* the traditions of their ancestors⟩ ⟨~*ed* to reply to the charge⟩ ~ *vi* : to show disdain or derision : SCOFF ***syn*** see DESPISE — **scorn·er** *n*

scorn·ful \ˈskȯrn-fəl\ *adj* (15c) : full of scorn : CONTEMPTUOUS — **scorn·ful·ly** \-fə-lē\ *adv* — **scorn·ful·ness** *n*

scor·pae·nid \skȯr-ˈpē-nəd\ *n* [deriv. of Gk *skorpaina,* a kind of fish] (1885) : any of a family (Scorpaenidae) of marine spiny-finned fishes comprising the scorpion fishes — **scorpaenid** *adj*

Scor·pio \ˈskȯr-pē-ˌō\ *n* [L (gen. *Scorpionis*), fr. Gk *Skorpios,* lit., scorpion] **1** : SCORPIUS **2 a** : the 8th sign of the zodiac in astrology — see ZODIAC table **b** : one born under this sign

scor·pi·on \ˈskȯr-pē-ən\ *n* [ME, fr. OF, fr. L *scorpion-, scorpio,* fr. Gk *skorpios;* akin to OE *scieran* to cut — more at SHEAR] (13c) **1 a** : any of an order (Scorpionida) of arachnids that have an elongated body and a narrow segmented tail bearing a venomous sting at the tip **b** *cap* : SCORPIO **2** : a scourge prob. studded with metal **3** : something that incites to action like the sting of an insect

scorpion fish *n* (1661) : a scorpaenid fish; *esp* : one with a venomous spine on the dorsal fin

scorpion fly *n* (1668) : any of a family (Panorpidae) of mecopterous insects that have cylindrical bodies and the male genitalia enlarged into a swollen bulb; *broadly* : a mecopterous insect

Scor·pi·us \ˈskȯr-pē-əs\ *n* [L (gen. *Scorpii*), fr. Gk *Skorpios,* lit., scorpion] : a southern constellation partly in the Milky Way and next to Libra

scot \ˈskät\ *n* [ME, fr. ON *skot* shot, contribution — more at SHOT] (13c) : money assessed or paid

Scot \ˈskät\ *n* [ME *Scottes* Scotchmen, fr. OE *Scottas* Irishmen, Scotchmen, fr. LL *Scotus* Irishman] (bef. 12c) **1** : one of a Gaelic people of northern Ireland settling in Scotland about A.D. 500 **2 a** : a native or inhabitant of Scotland **b** : a person of Scotch descent

scot and lot *n* (15c) **1** : a parish assessment formerly laid on subjects in Great Britain according to their ability to pay **2** : obligations of all kinds taken as a whole

[1]**scotch** \ˈskäch\ *vt* [ME *scocchen* to gash] (15c) **1** *archaic* : CUT, GASH, SCORE; *also* : WOUND ⟨we have ~*ed* the snake, not killed it —Shak.⟩ **2** : to put an end to ⟨~*ed* rumors of a military takeover⟩

[2]**scotch** *n* (15c) : a superficial cut : SCORE

[3]**scotch** *n* [origin unknown] (1639) : a chock to prevent rolling or slipping

[4]**scotch** *vt* (1642) **1** : to block with a chock **2** : HINDER, THWART

[1]**Scotch** \ˈskäch\ *adj* [contr. of *Scottish*] (1591) **1** : of, relating to, or characteristic of Scotland, the Scotch, or Scots **2** : inclined to frugality

[2]**Scotch** *n* (1700) **1** : SCOTS **2** *pl in constr* : the people of Scotland **3** *often not cap* : whiskey distilled in Scotland esp. from malted barley — called also *Scotch whisky*

[3]**Scotch** *trademark* —used for any of numerous adhesive tapes

Scotch broom *n* (1817) : a deciduous broom (*Cytisus scoparius*) of western Europe that is widely cultivated for its bright yellow or partly red flowers and that has become a pest in some areas (as California)

Scotch egg *n* (1809) : a hard-boiled egg wrapped in sausage meat, covered with bread crumbs, and fried

Scotch–Irish *adj* (1744) : of, relating to, or descended from Scotch settlers in northern Ireland

Scotch·man \ˈskäch-mən\ *n* (ca. 1570) : a man who is Scotch

Scotch pine *n* (1731) : a pine (*Pinus sylvestris*) of northern Europe and Asia with spreading or pendulous branches, short rigid twisted needles, and hard yellow wood that provides valuable timber

Scotch terrier *n* (1810) : SCOTTISH TERRIER

Scotch verdict *n* (1912) **1** : a verdict of not proven that is allowed by Scottish criminal law in some cases instead of a verdict of not guilty **2** : an inconclusive decision or pronouncement

Scotch·wom·an \ˈskäch-ˌwu̇m-ən\ *n* (1818) : a woman who is Scotch

Scotch woodcock *n* (1879) : buttered toast spread with anchovy paste and scrambled egg

sco·ter \ˈskōt-ər\ *n, pl* **scoters** *or* **scoter** [origin unknown] (ca. 1674) : any of several sea ducks (genera *Oidemia* and *Melanitta*) of northern coasts of Europe and No. America and some larger inland waters

scot–free \ˈskät-ˈfrē\ *adj* [*scot*] (13c) : completely free from obligation, harm, or penalty

sco·tia \ˈskō-sh(ē-)ə, ˈskōt-ē-ə\ *n* [L, fr. Gk *skotia,* fr. fem. of *skotios* dark, shadowy, fr. *skotos* darkness — more at SHADE] (1563) : a concave molding used esp. in classical architecture in the bases of columns — see BASE illustration, MOLDING illustration

Scot·ic \ˈskät-ik\ *adj* (1796) : of or relating to the ancient Scots

Sco·tism \ˈskōt-ˌiz-əm\ *n* (1871) : the doctrines of Duns Scotus (as voluntarism, realism, and the plurality of substantial forms) — **Sco·tist** \ˈskōt-əst\ *n*

Scot·land Yard \ˌskät-lən(d)-ˈyärd\ *n* [*Scotland Yard,* street in London formerly the headquarters of the metropolitan police] (1864) : the detective department of the London metropolitan police

sco·to·ma \skə-ˈtō-mə\ *n, pl* **-mas** *or* **-ma·ta** \-mət-ə\ [NL *scotomat-, scotoma,* fr. ML, dimness of vision, fr. Gk *skotōmat-, skotōma,* fr. *skotoun* to darken, fr. *skotos*] (1875) : a blind or dark spot in the visual field

sco·to·pic \skə-ˈtō-pik, -ˈtäp-ik\ *adj* [NL *scotopia* scotopic vision, fr. Gk *skotos* darkness + NL *-opia*] (1915) : relating to or being vision in dim light with dark-adapted eyes which involves only the retinal rods as light receptors

[1]**Scots** \ˈskäts\ *adj* [ME *Scottis,* alter. of *Scottish*] (14c) : SCOTCH 1 — used esp. of the people and language and in legal context

[2]**Scots** *n* (1542) : the English language of Scotland

Scots·man \ˈskät-smən\ *n* (14c) : SCOTCHMAN

Scots pine *n, chiefly Brit* (1797) : SCOTCH PINE

Scots·wom·an \ˈskät-ˌswu̇m-ən\ *n* (1820) : SCOTCHWOMAN

Scot·ti·cism \ˈskät-ə-ˌsiz-əm\ *n* [LL *scotticus* of the ancient Scots, fr. *Scotus* Scot] (1717) : a characteristic feature of Scottish English esp. as contrasted with standard English

Scot·tie \ˈskät-ē\ *n* (1918) **1** : SCOTCHMAN **2** : SCOTTISH TERRIER

[1]**Scot·tish** \ˈskät-ish\ *adj* [ME, fr. *Scottes* Scotchmen] (13c) : SCOTCH 1 — often preferred by natives of Scotland

[2]**Scottish** *n* (1759) : SCOTS

Scottish deerhound *n* (1935) : any of an old breed of large very tall dogs that have the general form of a greyhound but are larger and taller with a rough coat

Scottish Gaelic *n* (1956) : the Gaelic language of Scotland

Scottish rite *n* (1903) **1** : a ceremonial observed by one of the Masonic systems **2** : a system or organization that observes the Scottish rite and confers 33 degrees

Scottish terrier *n* (1837) : any of an old Scottish breed of terrier that has short legs, a large head with small erect ears and a powerful muzzle, a broad deep chest, and a very hard coat of wiry hair

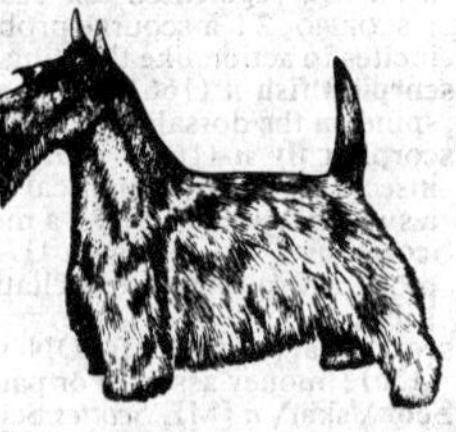

Scottish terrier

scoun·drel \ˈskau̇n-drəl\ *n* [origin unknown] (1589) : a disreputable person : RASCAL — **scoundrel** *adj* — **scoun·drel·ly** \-drə-lē\ *adj*

[1]**scour** \ˈskau̇(ə)r\ *vb* [ME *scuren,* prob. of Scand origin; akin to Sw *skura* to rush] *vi* (13c) : to move about quickly esp. in search ~ *vt* : to go through or range over in or as if in a search

[2]**scour** *vb* [ME *scouren*] *vt* (14c) **1 a** : to rub hard esp. with a rough material for cleansing **b** : to remove by rubbing hard and washing **2** *archaic* : to clear (a region) of enemies or outlaws **3** : to clean by purging : PURGE **4** : to remove dirt and debris from (as a pipe or ditch) **5** : to free from foreign matter or impurities by or as if by washing ⟨~ wool⟩ **6** : to clear, dig, or remove by or as if by a powerful current of water ~ *vi* **1** : to perform a process of scouring **2** : to suffer from diarrhea or dysentery **3** : to become clean and bright by rubbing

[3]**scour** *n* (1681) **1** : a place scoured by running water **2** : scouring action (as of a glacier) **3** : DIARRHEA, DYSENTERY — usu. used in pl. but sing. or pl. in constr. **4** : SCOURING 1; *also* : damage done by scouring action

scour·er \ˈskau̇r-ər\ *n* (15c) : one that scours

[1]**scourge** \ˈskərj *also* ˈskō(ə)rj, ˈskȯ(ə)rj, ˈsku̇(ə)rj\ *n* [ME, fr. AF *escorge,* fr. (assumed) OF *escorgier* to whip, fr. OF *es-* ex- + L *corrigia* whip] (13c) **1** : WHIP; *esp* : one used to inflict pain or punishment **2** : an instrument of punishment or criticism **3** : a cause of widespread or great affliction

[2]**scourge** *vt* **scourged; scourg·ing** (13c) **1** : FLOG, WHIP **2 a** : to punish severely **b** : AFFLICT **c** : to drive as if by blows of a whip **d** : CHASTISE — **scourg·er** *n*

scour·ing \ˈskau̇(ə)r-iŋ\ *n* (1588) **1** : material removed by scouring or cleaning **2** : the lowest rank of society — usu. used in pl.

scouring rush *n* (ca. 1817) : HORSETAIL; *esp* : one (*Equisetum hyemale*) with strongly siliceous stems formerly used for scouring

scouse \ˈskau̇s\ *n* (1840) **1** : LOBSCOUSE **2 a** : a native or inhabitant of Liverpool, England **b** : a dialect of English spoken in Liverpool

[1]**scout** \ˈskau̇t\ *vb* [ME *scouten,* fr. MF *escouter* to listen, fr. L *auscultare* — more at AUSCULTATION] *vi* (14c) **1** : to explore an area to obtain information (as about an enemy) **2 a** : to make a search **b** : to work as a talent scout ~ *vt* **1** : to observe in order to obtain information or evaluate **2** : to explore in order to obtain information **3** : to find by making a search — often used with *up*

[2]**scout** *n* (1553) **1 a** : the act of scouting **b** : a scouting expedition : RECONNAISSANCE **2 a** : one sent to obtain information; *esp* : a soldier, ship, or plane sent out in war to reconnoiter **b** : WATCHMAN, LOOKOUT **c** : TALENT SCOUT **3** *often cap* : a member of any of various scouting movements: as **a** : BOY SCOUT **b** : GIRL SCOUT **4** : INDIVIDUAL, PERSON — used chiefly in the phrase *good scout*

[3]**scout** *vb* [of Scand origin; akin to ON *skūti* taunt; akin to OE *scēotan* to shoot — more at SHOOT] *vt* (1605) **1** : MOCK **2** : SCORN ~ *vi* : SCOFF ***syn*** see DESPISE

scout car *n* (1933) **1** : a military reconnaissance vehicle **2** : SQUAD CAR

scout·craft \ˈskau̇t-ˌkraft\ *n* (1908) : the craft, skill, or practice of a scout

scout·er \ˈskau̇t-ər\ *n* (1642) **1** : one that scouts **2** *often cap* : an adult leader in the Boy Scouts of America

scouth \ˈsküth, ˈskau̇th\ *n* [origin unknown] *Scot* (1591) : PLENTY

scout·ing \ˈskau̇t-iŋ\ *n* (1644) **1** : the action of one that scouts **2** *often cap* : the activities of various national and worldwide organizations for youth directed to developing character, citizenship, and individual skills

scout·mas·ter \ˈskau̇t-ˌmas-tər\ *n* (1579) : the leader of a band of scouts; *specif* : the adult leader of a troop of Boy Scouts

scow \ˈskau̇\ *n* [D *schouw;* akin to OHG *scalta* punt pole] (1669) : a large flat-bottomed boat with broad square ends used chiefly for transporting bulk material (as ore, sand, or refuse)

[1]**scowl** \ˈskau̇(ə)l\ *vb* [ME *skoulen,* prob. of Scand origin; akin to Dan *skule* to scowl] *vi* (14c) **1** : to contract the brow in an expression of displeasure **2** : to exhibit a threatening aspect ~ *vt* : to express with a scowl — **scowl·er** *n*

[2]**scowl** *n* (1500) : a facial expression of displeasure : FROWN

[1]**scrab·ble** \ˈskrab-əl\ *vb* **scrab·bled; scrab·bling** \-(ə-)liŋ\ [D *schrabbelen* to scratch] *vi* (1537) **1** : SCRAWL, SCRIBBLE **2** : to scratch or claw about clumsily or frantically **3 a** : SCRAMBLE, CLAMBER **b** : to struggle by or as if by scraping or scratching ~ *vt* **1** : SCRAMBLE **2** : SCRIBBLE — **scrab·bler** \-(ə-)lər\ *n*

[2]**scrabble** *n* (1842) **1** : SCRIBBLE **2** : a repeated scratching or clawing **3** : SCRAMBLE

scrab·bly \ˈskrab-(ə-)lē\ *adj* (1945) **1** : SCRATCHY, RASPY **2** : SPARSE, SCRUBBY

[1]**scrag** \ˈskrag\ *n* [perh. alter. of [2]*crag*] (1542) **1** : a rawboned or scrawny person or animal **2** : the lean end of a neck of mutton or veal; *broadly* : NECK

[2]**scrag** *vt* **scragged; scrag·ging** (1756) **1 a** : to execute by hanging or garroting **b** : to wring the neck of **2 a** : CHOKE **b** : KILL, MURDER

scrag·gly \ˈskrag-(ə-)lē\ *adj* (1869) : ROUGH, IRREGULAR; *also* : UNKEMPT

scrag·gy \ˈskrag-ē\ *adj* **scrag·gi·er; -est** (1574) **1** : ROUGH, JAGGED **2** : being lean and long : SCRAWNY

[1]**scram** \ˈskram\ *vi* **scrammed; scram·ming** [short for *scramble*] (ca. 1928) : to go away at once ⟨~, you're not wanted⟩

[2]**scram** *n* (1953) : a rapid emergency shutdown of a nuclear reactor

[1]**scram·ble** \ˈskram-bəl\ *vb* **scram·bled; scram·bling** \-b(ə-)liŋ\ [perh. alter. of [1]*scrabble*] *vi* (1586) **1 a** : to move or climb hastily on all fours **b** : to move with urgency or panic **2 a** : to struggle eagerly or unceremoniously for possession of something ⟨~ for front seats⟩ **b** : to get or gather something with difficulty or in irregular ways ⟨~ for a living⟩ **3 a** : to spread or grow irregularly : SPRAWL, STRAGGLE **b** *of a plant* : to climb over a support **4** : to take off quickly in response to an alert **5** *of a football quarterback* : to run with the ball after the pass protection breaks down ~ *vt* **1** : to collect by scrambling **2 a** : to toss or mix together : JUMBLE **b** : to prepare (eggs) by stirring during frying **3** : to cause or order (a fighter-interceptor group) to scramble **4** : to disarrange the elements of telephone, teletype, facsimile, or television transmissions in order to make unintelligible to interception — **scram·bler** \-b(ə-)lər\ *n*

[2]**scramble** *n* (1674) **1** : a scrambling movement or struggle **2** : a disordered mess : JUMBLE **3** : a rapid emergency takeoff of fighter-interceptor planes

scran·nel \ˈskran-ᵊl\ *adj* [origin unknown] (1637) : HARSH, UNMELODIOUS

[1]**scrap** \ˈskrap\ *n* [ME, fr. ON *skrap* scraps; akin to ON *skrapa* to scrape] (14c) **1** *pl* : fragments of discarded or leftover food **2 a** : a small detached piece ⟨a ~ of paper⟩ **b** : a fragment of something written or printed **c** : the least bit ⟨not a ~ of evidence⟩ **3** *pl* : CRACKLINGS **4 a** : fragments of stock removed in manufacturing **b** : manufactured articles or parts rejected or discarded and useful only as material for reprocessing; *esp* : waste and discarded metal

[2]**scrap** *vt* **scrapped; scrap·ping** (ca. 1891) **1** : to convert into scrap **2** : to abandon or get rid of as no longer of enough worth or effectiveness to retain ⟨~ outworn methods⟩ ***syn*** see DISCARD

[3]**scrap** *n* [origin unknown] (ca. 1889) : FIGHT

[4]**scrap** *vi* **scrapped; scrap·ping** (ca. 1895) : QUARREL, FIGHT

scrap·book \ˈskrap-ˌbu̇k\ *n* (1825) : a blank book in which miscellaneous items (as newspaper clippings or pictures) are collected and preserved

[1]**scrape** \ˈskrāp\ *vb* **scraped; scrap·ing** [ME *scrapen,* fr. ON *skrapa;* akin to OE *scrapian* to scrape, L *scrobis* ditch, Gk *keirein* to cut — more at SHEAR] *vt* (14c) **1 a** : to remove from a surface by usu. repeated strokes of an edged instrument **b** : to make (a surface) smooth or clean with strokes of an edged instrument or an abrasive **2 a** : to grate harshly over or against **b** : to damage or injure the surface of by contact with a rough surface **c** : to draw roughly or noisily over a surface **3** : to collect by or as if by scraping — often used with *up* or *together* ⟨~ up the price of a ticket⟩ ~ *vi* **1** : to move in sliding contact with a rough surface **2** : to accumulate money by small economies **3** : to draw back the foot along the ground in making a bow **4** : to make one's way with difficulty or succeed by a narrow margin — **scrap·er** *n* — **scrape a leg** : to make a low bow

[2]**scrape** *n* (15c) **1 a** : the act or process of scraping **b** : a sound made by scraping **c** : damage or injury caused by scraping : ABRASION ⟨bumps and ~*s*⟩ **2** : a bow made with a drawing back of the foot along the ground **3 a** : a disagreeable predicament **b** : QUARREL, FIGHT

scrap heap *n* (ca. 1902) **1** : a pile of discarded metal **2** : the place where useless things are discarded

scra·pie \ˈskrā-pē\ *n* [[1]*scrape*] (1910) : a usu. fatal virus disease esp. of sheep that is characterized by twitching, excitability, intense itching, excessive thirst, emaciation, weakness, and finally paralysis

scrap·per \ˈskrap-ər\ *n* (1874) : FIGHTER, QUARRELER

scrap·pi·ness \ˈskrap-ē-nəs\ *n* (1867) : the quality or state of being scrappy

scrap·ple \ˈskrap-əl\ *n* [dim. of [1]*scrap*] (1855) : a seasoned mixture of ground meat (as pork) and cornmeal set in a mold and served sliced and fried

[1]**scrap·py** \ˈskrap-ē\ *adj* **scrap·pi·er; -est** (1837) : consisting of scraps — **scrap·pi·ly** \ˈskrap-ə-lē\ *adv*

[2]**scrappy** *adj* **scrap·pi·er; -est** (ca. 1896) **1** : QUARRELSOME **2** : having an aggressive and determined spirit

[1]**scratch** \ˈskrach\ *vb* [blend of E dial. *scrat* (to scratch) and obs. E *cratch* (to scratch)] *vt* (15c) **1** : to scrape or dig with the claws or nails **2** : to rub and tear or mark the surface of with something sharp or jagged **3** : to scrape or rub lightly (as to relieve itching) **4** : to scrape together : collect with difficulty or by effort **5** : to write or draw on a surface **6 a** : to cancel or erase by or as if by drawing a line through **b** : to withdraw (an entry) from competition **7** : SCRIBBLE, SCRAWL **8** : to scrape along a rough surface ⟨~ a match⟩ ~ *vi* **1** : to use the claws or nails in digging, tearing, or wounding **2** : to scrape or rub oneself lightly (as to relieve itching) **3** : to gather money or get a living by hard work and esp. through irregular means and sacrifice **4** : to make a thin grating sound **5** : to withdraw from a contest or engagement **6** : to make a scratch in billiards or pool — **scratch·er** *n* — **scratch one's back** : to accommodate with a favor esp. in expectation of like return — **scratch the surface** : to make a superficial effort or modest start

[2]**scratch** *n* (1586) **1** : a mark or injury produced by scratching; *also* : a slight wound **2** : SCRAWL, SCRIBBLE **3** : the sound made by scratching **4 a** : the starting line in a race **b** : a point at the beginning of a project at which nothing has been done ahead of time ⟨build a school system from ~⟩ **5 a** : a test of courage **b** : satisfactory condition or performance ⟨not up to ~⟩ **6** : a contestant whose name is withdrawn **7** : poultry feed (as mixed grains) scattered on the litter or ground esp. to induce birds to exercise — called also *scratch feed* **8 a** : a shot in billiards or pool that ends a player's turn; *specif* : a shot in pool in which the cue ball falls into the pocket **b** : a shot that scores by chance : FLUKE **9** *slang* : MONEY, FUNDS

[3]**scratch** *adj* (1897) **1** : made as or used for a tentative effort **2** : made or done by chance and not as intended ⟨a ~ shot⟩ **3** : arranged or put together with little selection : HAPHAZARD ⟨a ~ team⟩ **4** : having no handicap or allowance ⟨a ~ golfer⟩

scratch·board \ˈskrach-ˌbō(ə)rd, -ˌbȯ(ə)rd\ *n* (ca. 1908) : a black-surfaced cardboard having an undercoat of white clay on which an effect resembling engraving is achieved by scratching away portions of the surface to produce white lines

scratch hit *n* (1903) : a batted ball not solidly hit yet credited to the batter as a base hit

scratch pad *n* (1895) : a pad of scratch paper

scratch paper *n* (1899) : paper that may be used for casual writing

scratch sheet *n* (1939) : a racing publication listing competitors scratched from races and giving odds

scratch test *n* (1937) : a test for allergic susceptibility made by rubbing an extract of an allergy-producing substance into small breaks or scratches in the skin

scratchy \'skrach-ē\ *adj* **scratch·i·er; -est** (1866) **1** : likely to scratch : PRICKLY ⟨~ undergrowth⟩ **2** : making a scratching noise **3** : marked or made with scratches ⟨~ drawing⟩ ⟨~ handwriting⟩ **4** : uneven in quality : RAGGED **5** : causing tingling or itching : IRRITATING ⟨~ wool⟩ — **scratch·i·ness** *n*

scrawl \'skrȯl\ *vb* [origin unknown] *vt* (1612) : to write or draw awkwardly, hastily, or carelessly ~ *vi* : to write awkwardly or carelessly — **scrawl** *n* — **scrawl·er** *n* — **scrawly** \'skrȯ-lē\ *adj*

scraw·ny \'skrȯ-nē\ *adj* **scraw·ni·er; -est** [origin unknown] (1833) : exceptionally thin and slight or meager in body ⟨~ scrub cattle⟩ ***syn*** see LEAN — **scraw·ni·ness** *n*

screak \'skrēk\ *vi* [of Scand origin; akin to ON *skrækja* to screak; akin to ME *scremen* to scream] (1500) : to make a harsh shrill noise : SCREECH — **screak** *n* — **screaky** \-ē\ *adj*

[1]**scream** \'skrēm\ *vb* [ME *scremen;* akin to OHG *scrīan* to scream] *vi* (13c) **1 a** (1) : to voice a sudden sharp loud cry (2) : to produce harsh high tones **b** : to move with or make a noise resembling a scream ⟨the car ~*ed* to a stop⟩ ⟨a ~*ing* siren⟩ **2 a** : to speak or write with intense hysterical expressions **b** : to protest violently **3** : to produce a vivid startling effect ~ *vt* : to utter with or as if with a scream

[2]**scream** *n* (1605) **1** : a loud sharp penetrating cry or noise **2** : one that is very funny

scream·er \'skrē-mər\ *n* (1712) **1** : one that screams **2** : any of several So. American birds (family Anhimidae) with large stout bills, spurred wings, and more or less webbed feet **3** : a sensationally startling headline

scream·ing *adj* (1848) **1** : so striking or conspicuous as to attract notice as if by screaming ⟨~ headlines⟩ ⟨a ~ need for reform⟩ ⟨dressed in ~ red⟩ **2** : so funny as to provoke screams of laughter ⟨a ~ farce⟩ — **scream·ing·ly** *adv*

screaming mee·mies \-'mē-mēz\ *n pl but sing in constr* [origin unknown] (1942) : nervous hysteria : JITTERS

scree \'skrē\ *n* [of Scand origin; akin to ON *skritha* landslide, fr. *skrītha* to creep; akin to OHG *scrītan* to go, Lith *skrytis* felly, n.] (ca. 1781) : an accumulation of loose stones or rocky debris lying on a slope or at the base of a hill or cliff : TALUS

[1]**screech** \'skrēch\ *n* (1560) **1** : a high shrill piercing cry usu. expressing pain or terror **2** : a sound resembling a screech

[2]**screech** *vb* [alter. of earlier *scritch,* fr. ME *scrichen;* akin to ON *skrækja* to screak] *vi* (1577) **1** : to utter a high shrill piercing cry : make an outcry usu. in terror or pain **2** : to make a shrill high-pitched sound resembling a screech; *also* : to move with such a sound ⟨the train ~*ed* into the station⟩ ~ *vt* : to utter with or as if with a screech — **screech·er** *n*

screech owl *n* (1671) : any of numerous New World owls (genus *Otus*); *esp* : a small No. American owl (*O. asio*) with a pair of tufts of lengthened feathers on the head resembling ears

screechy \'skrē-chē\ *adj* (1830) : producing a screech

screed \'skrēd\ *n* [ME *screde* fragment, alter. of OE *scrēade* — more at SHRED] (1789) **1 a** : a lengthy discourse **b** : an informal piece of writing **2** : a strip (as of plaster of the thickness planned for the coat) laid on as a guide **3** : a leveling device drawn over freshly poured concrete

[1]**screen** \'skrēn\ *n* [ME *screne,* fr. MF *escren,* fr. MD *scherm;* akin to OHG *skirm* screen, L *corium* skin — more at CUIRASS] (15c) **1** : a protective or ornamental device (as a movable partition) shielding an area from heat or drafts or from view **2** : something that shelters, protects, or hides: as **a** : a growth or stand of trees, shrubs, or plants **b** : a protective formation of troops, ships, or planes **c** : something that covers or disguises the true nature (as of an activity or feeling) ⟨greets strangers with a ~ of excessive friendliness —Tony Schwartz⟩ **d** (1) : a maneuver in various sports (as basketball or ice hockey) whereby an opponent is legally impeded or his view of the play is momentarily blocked (2) : SCREEN PASS **3 a** : a perforated plate or cylinder or a meshed wire or cloth fabric usu. mounted and used to separate coarser from finer parts **b** : a system for examining and separating into different groups **c** : a piece of apparatus designed to prevent agencies in one part from affecting other parts ⟨an optical ~⟩ ⟨an electric ~⟩ ⟨a magnetic ~⟩ **d** : a frame holding a usu. metallic netting used esp. in a window or door to exclude pests (as insects) **4 a** : a flat surface on which a picture or series of pictures is projected or reflected **b** : the surface on which the image appears in an electronic display (as in a television set, radar receiver, or computer terminal) **5** : a glass plate ruled with crossing opaque lines through which an image is photographed in making a halftone **6** : the motion-picture medium or industry

[2]**screen** *vt* (15c) **1** : to guard from injury or danger **2 a** : to give shelter or protection to with or as if with a screen **b** : to separate with or as if with a screen; *also* : to shield (an opponent) from a play or from view of a play **3 a** : to pass (as coal, gravel, or ashes) through a screen to separate the fine part from the coarse; *also* : to remove by a screen **b** (1) : to examine usu. methodically in order to make a separation into different groups (2) : to select or eliminate by a screening process **4** : to provide with a screen to keep out pests (as insects) **5 a** (1) : to present (as a motion picture) for viewing on a screen (2) : to view the presentation of (as a motion picture) **b** : to present in a motion picture ~ *vi* **1** : to appear on a motion-picture screen **2** : to provide a screen in a game or sport ***syn*** see HIDE — **screen·able** \'skrē-nə-bəl\ *adj* — **screen·er** *n*

screen·ing \'skrē-niŋ\ *n* (1730) **1** : the act or process of one that screens **2** *pl but sing or pl in constr* : material (as waste or fine coal) separated out by passsage through or retention on a screen **3** : metal or plastic mesh (as for window screens) **4** : a showing of a motion picture

screen·land \'skrēn-,land\ *n* (1925) : FILMDOM

screen memory *n* (1923) : a recollection of early childhood that may be falsely recalled or magnified in importance and that masks another memory of deep emotional significance

screen pass *n* (ca. 1949) : a forward pass in football to a receiver at or behind the line of scrimmage who is protected by a screen of blockers

screen·play \'skrēn-,plā\ *n* (1916) : the script and often shooting directions of a story prepared for motion-picture production

screen test *n* (1927) : a short film sequence for assessing the ability or suitability of a person for a motion-picture role — **screen–test** *vt*

screen·writ·er \'skrēn-,rīt-ər\ *n* (1921) : a writer of screenplays

[1]**screw** \'skrü\ *n* [ME, fr. MF *escroe* female screw, nut, fr. ML *scrofa,* fr. L, sow] (15c) **1 a** : a simple machine of the inclined plane type consisting of a spirally grooved solid cylinder and a correspondingly grooved hollow cylinder into which it fits **b** : a nail-shaped or rod-shaped piece with a spiral groove and a slotted or recessed head designed to be inserted into material by rotating (as with a screwdriver) and used for fastening pieces of solid material together **2 a** : a screwlike form : SPIRAL **b** : a turn of a screw; *also* : a twist like the turn of a screw **c** : a screwlike device (as a corkscrew) **3** : a worn-out horse **4** *chiefly Brit* : a small packet (as of tobacco) **5** : a prison guard **6** : one who bargains shrewdly; *also* : SKINFLINT **7** : SCREW PROPELLER **8 a** : THUMBSCREW 2 **b** : pressure or punitive measures intended to coerce — used chiefly in the phrase *put the screws on* or *put the screws to* **9 a** : an act of sexual intercourse — usu. considered vulgar **b** : a partner in sexual intercourse — usu. considered vulgar — **screw·like** \-,līk\ *adj* — **have a screw loose** : to be mentally unbalanced

[2]**screw** *vt* (1605) **1 a** (1) : to attach, fasten, or close by means of a screw (2) : to unite or separate by means of a screw or a twisting motion ⟨~ the two pieces together⟩ (3) : to press tightly in a device (as a vise) operated by a screw (4) : to operate, tighten, or adjust by means of a screw (5) : to torture by means of a thumbscrew **b** : to cause to rotate spirally about an axis **2 a** (1) : to twist into strained configurations : CONTORT ⟨~*ed* up his face⟩ (2) : SQUINT (3) : CRUMPLE **b** : to furnish with a spiral groove or ridge : THREAD **3** : to increase the intensity, quantity, or capability of ⟨trying to ~ up courage to confess —Will Scott⟩ **4 a** (1) : to mistreat or exploit through extortion, trickery, or unfair actions; *esp* : to deprive of or cheat out of something due or expected ⟨~*ed* out of a job⟩ (2) : to treat so as to bring about injury or loss (as to a person's reputation) ⟨use the available Federal machinery to ~ our political enemies —J.W. Dean III⟩ — often used as a generalized curse ⟨~ you!⟩ **b** : to extract by pressure or threat **5** : to copulate with — usu. considered vulgar ~ *vi* **1** : to rotate like or as a screw **2** : to turn or move with a twisting or writhing motion **3** : COPULATE — usu. considered vulgar — **screw·er** *n*

screw around *vi* (1939) : to waste time with unproductive activity : DALLY

[1]**screw·ball** \'skrü-,bȯl\ *n* (1928) **1** : a baseball pitch that spins and breaks in the opposite direction to a curve **2** : a whimsical, eccentric, or crazy person : ZANY

[2]**screwball** *adj* (ca. 1936) : crazily eccentric or whimsical : ZANY

screw·bean \'skrü-,bēn\ *n* (1866) **1** : a leguminous shrub or small tree (*Prosopis pubescens*) of the southwestern U.S. — called also *screwbean mesquite* **2** : a spirally twisted sweet pod that is the fruit of the screwbean

screw·driv·er \'skrü-,drī-vər\ *n* (1779) **1** : a tool for turning screws **2** : vodka and orange juice served with ice

screw eye *n* (1873) : a wood screw with a head in the form of a loop

screw jack *n* (1719) : JACKSCREW

screw pine *n* (ca. 1901) : any of a genus (*Pandanus* of the family Pandanaceae, the screw-pine family) of tropical monocotyledonous plants with slender palmlike stems, often huge prop roots, and terminal crowns of swordlike leaves

screw propeller *n* (1839) : PROPELLER

screw thread *n* (ca. 1812) **1** : the projecting helical rib of a screw **2** : one complete turn of a screw thread

screw·up \'skrü-,əp\ *n* (1970) : [3]BOTCH, BLUNDER

screw up \(')skrü-'əp\ *vt* (1680) **1** : to tighten, fasten, or lock by or as if by a screw **2 a** : BUNGLE, BOTCH **b** : to cause to act or function in a crazy or confused way : CONFOUND, DISTURB ~ *vi* : to botch an activity or undertaking

screw·worm \'skrü-,wərm\ *n* (1879) : a two-winged fly (*Cochliomyia hominivorax*) of the warmer parts of America whose larva develops in sores or wounds or in the nostrils of mammals including man with serious or sometimes fatal results; *esp* : its larva **2** : any of several flies other than the screwworm and esp. their larvae which parasitize the flesh of mammals

screwy \'skrü-ē\ *adj* **screw·i·er; -est** (1887) **1** : crazily absurd, eccentric, or unusual **2** : CRAZY, INSANE — **screw·i·ness** *n*

scrib·al \'skrī-bəl\ *adj* (1857) : of, relating to, or due to a scribe

scrib·ble \'skrib-əl\ *vb* **scrib·bled; scrib·bling** \-(ə-)liŋ\ [ME *scriblen,* fr. ML *scribillare,* fr. L *scribere* to write] *vt* (15c) **1** : to write hastily or carelessly without regard to legibility or form **2** : to cover with careless or worthless writings or drawings ~ *vi* : to write or draw hastily and carelessly — **scribble** *n*

scrib·bler \'skrib-(ə-)lər\ *n* (1553) **1** : one that scribbles **2** : a minor or insignificant author

[1]**scribe** \'skrīb\ *n* [ME, fr. L *scriba* official writer, fr. *scribere* to write; akin to Gk *skariphasthai* to scratch an outline, *keirein* to cut — more at SHEAR] (14c) **1** : one of a learned class in ancient Israel through New Testament times studying the Scriptures and serving as copyists, editors, teachers, and jurists **2 a** : an official or public secretary or clerk **b** : a copier of manuscripts **3** : AUTHOR; *specif* : JOURNALIST

[2]**scribe** *vi* **scribed; scrib·ing** (1782) : to work as a scribe : WRITE

[3]**scribe** *vt* **scribed; scrib·ing** [prob. short for *describe*] (1678) **1** : to mark a line on by cutting or scratching with a pointed instrument **2** : to make by cutting or scratching

[4]**scribe** *n* (1812) : SCRIBER

scrib·er \'skrī-bər\ *n* (1834) : a sharp-pointed tool for making marks and esp. for marking off material (as wood or metal) to be cut

scrieve \'skrēv\ *vi* [of Scand origin; akin to ON *skrefa* to stride] *Scot* (1785) : to move along swiftly and smoothly

\ə\ abut \ᵊ\ kitten, F table \ər\ further \a\ ash \ā\ ace \ä\ cot, cart \au̇\ out \ch\ chin \e\ bet \ē\ easy \g\ go \i\ hit \ī\ ice \j\ job \ŋ\ sing \ō\ go \ȯ\ law \ȯi\ boy \th\ thin \th\ the \ü\ loot \u̇\ foot \y\ yet \zh\ vision \à, k, ⁿ, œ, œ̄, ue, ue̅, ʸ\ *see* Guide to Pronunciation

scrim \'skrim\ *n* [origin unknown] (1792) **1 :** a durable plain-woven usu. cotton fabric for use in clothing, curtains, building, and industry **2 :** a theater drop that appears opaque when a scene in front is lighted and transparent or translucent when a scene in back is lighted

[1]**scrim·mage** \'skrim-ij\ *n* [alter. of *skirmish*] (15c) **1 a :** a minor battle : SKIRMISH **b :** a confused fight : SCUFFLE **2 a :** the interplay between two football teams that begins with the snap of the ball and continues until the ball is dead **b :** practice play (as in football or basketball) between two squads

[2]**scrimmage** *vi* **scrim·maged; scrim·mag·ing** (1825) **:** to take part in a scrimmage — **scrim·mag·er** *n*

scrimmage line *n* (ca. 1909) **:** LINE OF SCRIMMAGE

scrimp \'skrimp\ *vb* [perh. of Scand origin; akin to Sw *skrympa* to shrink, ON *skorpna* to shrivel up — more at SHRIMP] *vt* (1774) **1 :** to be niggardly in providing for **2 :** to make too small, short, or scanty ~ *vi* **:** to be frugal or stingy — **scrimpy** \'skrim-pē\ *adj*

scrim·shan·der \'skrim-,shan-dər\ *n* [origin unknown] (1851) **:** a person who creates scrimshaw

[1]**scrim·shaw** \'skrim-,shȯ\ *vb* [origin unknown] *vt* (ca. 1825) **:** to carve or engrave into scrimshaw ~ *vi* **:** to produce scrimshaw

[2]**scrimshaw** *n* (1851) **1 :** any of various carved or engraved articles made esp. by American whalers usu. from whalebone or whale ivory **2 :** scrimshawed work **3 :** the art, practice, or technique of producing scrimshaw

[1]**scrip** \'skrip\ *n* [ME *scrippe*, fr. ML *scrippum* pilgrim's knapsack] *archaic* (14c) **:** a small bag or wallet

[2]**scrip** *n* [alter. of *script*] (1617) **1 :** a small piece **2 :** a short writing (as a certificate, schedule, or list) **3 a :** any of various documents used as evidence that the holder or bearer is entitled to receive something (as a fractional share of stock or an allotment of land) **b :** paper currency or a token issued for temporary use in an emergency

[1]**script** \'skript\ *n* [L *scriptum* thing written, fr. neut. of *scriptus*, pp. of *scribere* to write — more at SCRIBE] (14c) **1 a :** something written : TEXT **b :** an original or principal instrument or document **c** (1) **:** MANUSCRIPT 1 (2) **:** the written text of a stage play, screenplay, or broadcast; *specif* **:** the one used in production or performance **2 a :** a style of printed letters that resembles handwriting **b :** written characters : HANDWRITING **c :** ALPHABET **3 :** a plan of action

[2]**script** *vt* (1935) **:** to prepare a script for or from

scrip·to·ri·um \skrip-'tōr-ē-əm, -'tȯr-\ *n, pl* **-ria** \-ē-ə\ [ML, fr. L *scriptus*] (1774) **:** a copying room in a medieval monastery set apart for the scribes

scrip·tur·al \'skrip-chə-rəl, 'skrip-shrəl\ *adj* (1641) **:** of, relating to, contained in, or according to a sacred writing; *specif* **:** BIBLICAL — **scrip·tur·al·ly** \-ē\ *adv*

scrip·ture \'skrip-chər\ *n* [ME, fr. LL *scriptura*, fr. L, act or product of writing, fr. *scriptus*] (14c) **1 a** (1) *cap* **:** the books of the Bible — often used in pl. (2) *often cap* **:** a passage from the Bible **b :** a body of writings considered sacred or authoritative **2 :** something written ⟨the primitive man's awe for any ~ —George Santayana⟩

script·writ·er \'skrip-,trīt-ər\ *n* (1935) **:** one who writes scripts

scriv·en·er \'skriv-(ə-)nər\ *n* [ME *scriveiner*, alter. of *scrivein*, fr. MF *escrivein*, fr. (assumed) VL *scriban-*, *scriba*, alter. of L *scriba* scribe] (14c) **1 :** a professional or public copyist or writer : SCRIBE **2 :** NOTARY PUBLIC

scrod \'skräd\ *n* [perh. fr. obs. D *schrood* shred; akin to OE *scrēade* shred — more at SHRED] (1841) **:** a young fish (as a cod or haddock); *esp* **:** one split and boned for cooking

scrof·u·la \'skrȯf-yə-lə, 'skräf-\ *n* [ML, fr. LL *scrofulae*, pl., swellings of the lymph nodes of the neck, fr. pl. of *scrofula*, dim. of L *scrofa* breeding sow] (15c) **:** tuberculosis of lymph nodes esp. in the neck

scrof·u·lous \-ləs\ *adj* (1612) **1 :** of, relating to, or affected with scrofula **2 a :** having a diseased appearance **b :** morally contaminated

[1]**scroll** \'skrōl\ *n* [ME *scrowle*, alter. of *scrowe*, fr. MF *escroue* scrap, scroll, of Gmc origin; akin to OE *scrēade* shred] (15c) **1 a :** a roll (as of papyrus, leather, or parchment) for writing a document **b** *archaic* **:** a written message **c :** ROSTER, LIST **d :** a riband with rolled ends often inscribed with a motto **2 a :** something resembling a scroll in shape; *esp* **:** a spiral or convoluted form in ornamental design derived from the curves of a loosely or partly rolled parchment scroll **b :** the curved head of a bowed stringed musical instrument — see VIOLIN illustration

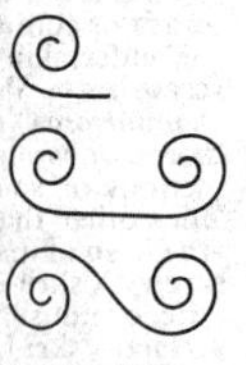

scroll 2a

[2]**scroll** *vi* (1973) **:** to move text across a display screen as if by unrolling a scroll

scroll saw *n* (1851) **1 :** a thin handsaw for cutting curves or irregular designs **2 :** FRETSAW **3 :** JIGSAW 1

scroll·work \'skrōl-,wərk\ *n* (1739) **:** ornamentation characterized by scrolls; *esp* **:** fancy designs in wood often made with a scroll saw

scrooge \'skrüj\ *n, often cap* [Ebenezer *Scrooge*, character in the story *A Christmas Carol* (1843) by Charles Dickens] (1899) **:** a miserly person

scro·tum \'skrōt-əm\ *n, pl* **scro·ta** \-ə\ *or* **scrotums** [L; akin to L *scrupus* sharp stone — more at SHRED] (1597) **:** the external pouch that in most mammals contains the testes — **scro·tal** \'skrōt-ᵊl\ *adj*

scrouge \'skrau̇j, 'skrüj\ *vb* **scrouged; scroug·ing** [alter. of E dial. *scruze* (to squeeze)] *chiefly dial* (1755) **:** CROWD, PRESS

scrounge \'skrau̇nj\ *vb* **scrounged; scroung·ing** [alter. of E dial. *scrunge* (to wander about idly)] *vt* (ca. 1909) **1 :** STEAL, SWIPE **2 a :** to get as needed by or as if by foraging, scavenging, or borrowing **b :** FINAGLE, WHEEDLE — often used with *up* ~ *vi* **:** to search about and turn up something needed from whatever source is available by any expedient means; *also* **:** to actively seek money, work, or sustenance from any available source — **scroung·er** *n*

[1]**scrub** \'skrəb\ *n, often attrib* [ME, alter. of *schrobbe* shrub — more at SHRUB] (14c) **1 a :** a stunted tree or shrub **b :** vegetation consisting chiefly of scrubs **c :** a tract covered with scrub **2 :** a domestic animal of mixed or unknown parentage and usu. inferior conformation : MONGREL **3 :** a person of insignificant size or standing **4 :** a player not belonging to the first string

[2]**scrub** *vb* **scrubbed; scrub·bing** [of LG or Scand origin; akin to MLG & MD *schrubben* to scrub, Sw *skrubba*] *vt* (1595) **1 a** (1) **:** to clean with hard rubbing : SCOUR (2) **:** to remove by scrubbing **b :** to subject to friction : RUB **2 :** WASH 6c(2) **3 :** CANCEL, ELIMINATE ~ *vi* **1 :** to use hard rubbing in cleaning **2 :** to prepare for surgery by scrubbing oneself

[3]**scrub** *n* (1621) **1 :** an act or instance of scrubbing; *esp* **:** CANCELLATION **2 :** one that scrubs

scrubbed *adj* [[1]*scrub*] (1596) **1** \'skrəb-əd\ *archaic* **:** SCRUBBY 1 **2** \'skrəbd\ **:** giving the impression of being clean or wholesome as if from scrubbing ⟨days when studios manufactured ~ public images for their stars —Sally Helgesen⟩

scrub·ber \'skrəb-ər\ *n* (1839) **:** one that scrubs; *esp* **:** an apparatus for removing impurities esp. from gases

scrub brush *n* (1950) **:** a brush with hard bristles for heavy cleaning — called also *scrubbing brush*

scrub·by \'skrəb-ē\ *adj* **scrub·bi·er; -est** [[1]*scrub*] (1591) **1 :** inferior in size or quality : STUNTED ⟨~ cattle⟩ **2 :** covered with or consisting of scrub **3 :** SHABBY, PALTRY

scrub·land \'skrəb-,land\ *n* (1852) **:** land covered with scrub

scrub pine *n* (1791) **:** a pine of dwarf, straggly, or scrubby growth usu. by reason of environmental conditions; *specif* **:** a pine tree unsuitable for lumber by reason of inferior or defective growth

scrub typhus *n* (1929) **:** TSUTSUGAMUSHI DISEASE

scrub·wom·an \'skrəb-,wu̇m-ən\ *n* (1873) **:** a woman whose occupation is cleaning : CHARWOMAN

scruff \'skrəf\ *n* [alter. of earlier *scuff*, of unknown origin] (1790) **:** the back of the neck : NAPE

scruffy \'skrəf-ē\ *adj* **scruff·i·er; -est** [E dial. *scruff* (something worthless)] (1871) **:** UNKEMPT, SLOVENLY — **scruff·i·ness** *n*

scrum \'skrəm\ *n* [short for *scrummage*, alter. of *scrimmage*] (1888) **1** *or* **scrum·mage** \'skrəm-ij\ **:** a rugby play in which the forwards of each side come together in a tight mass and struggle to gain possession of the ball when it is tossed in among them **2** *Brit* **:** MADHOUSE 2 — **scrummage** *vi*

scrump·tious \'skrəm(p)-shəs\ *adj* [prob. alter. of *sumptuous*] (1830) **:** DELIGHTFUL, EXCELLENT — **scrump·tious·ly** *adv*

[1]**scrunch** \'skrənch, 'skru̇nch\ *vb* [alter. of [1]*crunch*] *vt* (1790) **1 :** CRUNCH, CRUSH **2 a :** to draw or squeeze together tightly **b :** CRUMPLE, WRINKLE — often used with *up* ~ *vi* **1 :** to move with or make a crunching sound **2 :** CROUCH, HUNCH — often used with *up*

[2]**scrunch** *n* (1857) **:** a crunching sound

[1]**scru·ple** \'skrü-pəl\ *n* [ME *scriple*, fr. L *scrupulus* a unit of weight, small sharp stone] (14c) **1** — see WEIGHT table **2 :** a minute part or quantity : IOTA

[2]**scruple** *n* [MF *scrupule*, fr. L *scrupulus* small sharp stone, cause of mental discomfort, scruple, dim. of *scrupus* sharp stone — more at SHRED] (1526) **1 :** an ethical consideration or principle that inhibits action **2 :** the quality or state of being scrupulous ***syn*** see QUALM

[3]**scruple** *vi* **scru·pled; scru·pling** \-p(ə-)liŋ\ (1627) **1 :** to have scruples **2 :** to show reluctance on grounds of conscience : HESITATE

scru·pu·los·i·ty \,skrü-pyə-'läs-ət-ē\ *n* (1526) **1 :** the quality or state of being scrupulous **2 :** [2]SCRUPLE 1

scru·pu·lous \'skrü-pyə-ləs\ *adj* [ME, fr. L *scrupulosus*, fr. *scrupulus*] (15c) **1 :** having moral integrity **:** acting in strict regard for what is considered right or proper **2 :** punctiliously exact : PAINSTAKING ⟨working with ~ care⟩ ***syn*** see UPRIGHT, CAREFUL — **scru·pu·lous·ly** *adv* — **scru·pu·lous·ness** *n*

scru·ta·ble \'skrüt-ə-bəl\ *adj* [LL *scrutabilis* searchable, fr. L *scrutari* to search, investigate, examine — more at SCRUTINY] (1600) **:** capable of being deciphered : COMPREHENSIBLE

scru·ti·neer \,skrüt-ᵊn-'i(ə)r\ *n* (1557) **1 :** one that examines **2** *Brit* **:** one who takes or counts votes

scru·ti·nize \'skrüt-ᵊn-,īz\ *vb* **-nized; -niz·ing** *vt* (1671) **:** to examine closely and minutely ~ *vi* **:** to make a scrutiny — **scru·ti·niz·er** *n*

syn SCRUTINIZE, SCAN, INSPECT, EXAMINE mean to look at or over carefully and usu. critically. SCRUTINIZE stresses close attention to minute detail; SCAN implies a surveying from point to point often suggesting a cursory overall observation; INSPECT implies scrutinizing for errors or defects; EXAMINE suggests a scrutiny in order to determine the nature, condition, or quality of a thing.

scru·ti·ny \'skrüt-ᵊn-ē, 'skrüt-nē\ *n, pl* **-nies** [L *scrutinium*, fr. *scrutari* to search, examine, fr. *scruta* trash] (1604) **1 :** a searching study, inquiry, or inspection : EXAMINATION **2 :** a searching look **3 :** close watch : SURVEILLANCE

scu·ba \'sk(y)ü-bə\ *n* [self-contained underwater breathing apparatus] (1952) **:** an apparatus used for breathing while swimming under water

scuba diver *n* (ca. 1961) **:** one who swims under water with the aid of scuba gear — **scuba dive** *vi*

[1]**scud** \'skəd\ *vi* **scud·ded; scud·ding** [prob. of Scand origin; akin to Norw *skudda* to push; akin to L *quatere* to shake — more at QUASH] (1532) **1 :** to move or run swiftly esp. as if driven forward **2 :** to run before a gale

[2]**scud** *n* (1609) **1 :** the action of scudding : RUSH **2 a :** loose vapory clouds driven swiftly by the wind **b** (1) **:** a slight sudden shower (2) **:** mist, rain, snow, or spray driven by the wind **c :** a gust of wind

scu·do \'sküd-(,)ō\ *n, pl* **scu·di** \-(,)ē\ [It, lit., shield, fr. L *scutum* — more at ESQUIRE] (1644) **1 :** a gold or silver coin formerly used in Italy and approximately equivalent to a dollar **2 :** a unit of value equivalent to a scudo

[1]**scuff** \'skəf\ *vb* [prob. of Scand origin; akin to Sw *skuffa* to push] *vi* (1768) **1 a :** to walk without lifting the feet : SHUFFLE **b :** to poke or shuffle a foot in exploration or embarrassment **2 :** to become scratched, chipped, or roughened by wear ~ *vt* **1 :** [3]CUFF **2 a :** to scrape (the feet) along a surface while walking or back and forth while standing **b :** to poke at with the toe **3 :** to scratch, gouge, or wear away the surface of

[2]**scuff** *n* (1899) **1 a :** a noise of or as if of scuffing **b :** the act or an instance of scuffing **c :** a mark or injury caused by scuffing **2 :** a flat-soled slipper without quarter or heel strap

scuf·fle \'skəf-əl\ *vi* **scuf·fled; scuf·fling** \-(ə-)liŋ\ [prob. of Scand origin; akin to Sw *skuffa* to push] (1590) **1 a :** to struggle at close quarters with disorder and confusion **b :** to struggle (as by working odd jobs) to get by **2 a :** to move with a quick shuffling gait : SCURRY **b :** SHUFFLE — **scuffle** *n*

scuffle hoe *n* (1856) **:** a garden hoe that has both edges sharpened and can be pushed forward or drawn back

¹scull \ˈskəl\ *n* [ME *sculle*] (14c) **1 a :** an oar used at the stern of a boat to propel it forward with a thwartwise motion **b :** one of a pair of oars usu. less than 10 feet in length and operated by one person **2 :** a racing shell propelled by one or two persons using sculls

²scull *vt* (1624) **:** to propel (a boat) by sculls or by a large oar worked thwartwise ~ *vi* **:** to scull a boat — **scull·er** *n*

scul·lery \ˈskəl-(ə-)rē\ *n, pl* **-ler·ies** [ME, department of household in charge of dishes, fr. MF *escuelerie*, fr. *escuelle* bowl, fr. L *scutella* drinking bowl — more at SCUTTLE] (15c) **:** a room for cleaning and storing dishes and culinary utensils, washing vegetables, and similar coarse work

scul·lion \ˈskəl-yən\ *n* [ME *sculion*, fr. MF *escouillon* dishcloth, alter. of *escouvillon*, fr. *escouve* broom, fr. L *scopa*, lit., twig; akin to L *scapus* stalk — more at SHAFT] (15c) **:** a kitchen helper

scul·pin \ˈskəl-pən\ *n, pl* **sculpins** *also* **sculpin** [origin unknown] (1672) **1 :** any of a family (Cottidae) of numerous spiny large-headed broad-mouthed usu. scaleless fishes **2 :** a scorpion fish (*Scorpaena guttata*) of the southern California coast caught for food and sport

sculpt \ˈskəlpt\ *vb* [F *sculpter*, alter. of obs. *sculper*, fr. L *sculpere*] (1864) **:** CARVE, SCULPTURE

sculp·tor \ˈskəlp-tər\ *n* [L, fr. *sculptus*, pp. of *sculpere*] (1634) **:** one that sculptures **:** an artist who produces works of sculpture

sculp·tress \-trəs\ *n* (1662) **:** a woman who sculptures

sculp·tur·al \ˈskəlp-chə-rəl, ˈskəlp-shrəl\ *adj* (1819) **1 :** of or relating to sculpture **2 :** resembling sculpture **:** SCULPTURESQUE — **sculp·tur·al·ly** \-ē\ *adv*

¹sculp·ture \ˈskəlp-chər\ *n* [ME, fr. L *sculptura*, fr. *sculptus*, pp. of *sculpere* to carve, alter. of *scalpere* — more at SHELF] (14c) **1 a :** the action or art of processing (as by carving, modeling, or welding) plastic or hard materials into works of art **b (1) :** work produced by sculpture **(2) :** a three-dimensional work of art (as a statue) **2 :** impressed or raised markings or a pattern of such esp. on a plant or animal part

²sculpture *vb* **sculp·tured; sculp·tur·ing** \ˈskəlp-chə-riŋ, ˈskəlp-shriŋ\ *vt* (1645) **1 a :** to form an image or representation of from solid material (as wood or stone) **b :** to form into a three-dimensional work of art **2 :** to change (the form of the earth's surface) by natural processes (as erosion and deposition) **3 :** to shape by or as if by carving or molding ~ *vi* **:** to work as a sculptor

sculp·tur·esque \ˌskəlp-chə-ˈresk\ *adj* (1835) **:** done in the manner of or resembling sculpture — **sculp·tur·esque·ly** *adv*

¹scum \ˈskəm\ *n* [ME, fr. MD *schum*; akin to OHG *scūm* foam] (14c) **1 a :** extraneous matter or impurities risen to or formed on the surface of a liquid often as a foul filmy covering **b :** the scoria of metals in a molten state **:** DROSS **c :** a slimy film on a solid or gelatinous object **2 a :** REFUSE **b :** a low, vile, or worthless person or group of people — **scum·my** \ˈskə-mē\ *adj*

²scum *vi* **scummed; scum·ming** (1661) **:** to become covered with or as if with scum

¹scum·ble \ˈskəm-bəl\ *vt* **scum·bled; scum·bling** \-b(ə-)liŋ\ [freq. of ²*scum*] (1798) **1 a :** to make (as color or a painting) less brilliant by covering with a thin coat of opaque or semiopaque color **b :** to apply (a color) in this manner **2 :** to soften the lines or colors of (a drawing) by rubbing lightly

²scumble *n* (1834) **1 :** the act or effect of scumbling **2 :** a material used for scumbling

¹scun·ner \ˈskən-ər\ *vi* [ME (Sc dial.) *skunniren*] *chiefly Scot* (15c) **:** to be in a state of disgusted irritation

²scunner *n* (ca. 1500) **:** an unreasonable or extreme dislike or prejudice

scup \ˈskəp\ *n, pl* **scup** *also* **scups** [Narraganset *mishcùp*] (ca. 1848) **:** a porgy (*Stenotomus chrysops*) that is distributed along the Atlantic coast of the U.S. from So. Carolina to Maine and that is used as a panfish

scup·per \ˈskəp-ər\ *n* [ME *skopper*] (15c) **1 :** an opening cut through the waterway and bulwarks of a ship so that water falling on deck may flow overboard **2 :** an opening in the wall of a building through which water can drain from a floor or flat roof

scup·per·nong \-ˌnȯŋ, -ˌnäŋ\ *n* [*Scuppernong*, river and lake in No. Carolina] (1811) **1 :** MUSCADINE; *esp* **:** a cultivated muscadine with yellowish green plum-flavored fruits **2 :** a sweet aromatic amber-colored wine made from scuppernongs

scurf \ˈskərf\ *n* [ME, fr. OE, of Scand origin; akin to Icel *skurfa* scurf; akin to OHG *scorf* scurf, L *carpere* to pluck — more at HARVEST] (bef. 12c) **1 :** thin dry scales detached from the epidermis esp. in an abnormal skin condition; *specif* **:** DANDRUFF **2 a :** something like flakes or scales adhering to a surface **b :** the foul remains of something adherent **3 a :** a scaly deposit or covering on some plant parts; *also* **:** a localized or general darkening and roughening of a plant surface usu. more pronounced than russeting **b :** a plant disease characterized by scurf — **scurfy** \ˈskər-fē\ *adj*

scur·rile *or* **scur·ril** \ˈskər-əl, ˈskə-rəl\ *adj* [MF *scurrile*, fr. L *scurrilis*, fr. *scurra* buffoon] (1567) **:** SCURRILOUS

scur·ril·i·ty \skə-ˈril-ət-ē\ *n, pl* **-ties** (1589) **1 :** the quality or state of being scurrilous **2 a :** scurrilous or abusive language **b :** an offensively rude or abusive remark ***syn*** see ABUSE

scur·ri·lous \ˈskər-ə-ləs, ˈskə-rə-\ *adj* (1576) **1 a :** using or given to coarse language **b :** being vulgar and evil ⟨~ imposters who used a religious exterior to rob poor people —Edwin Benson⟩ **2 :** containing obscenities or coarse abuse ⟨a . . . campaign filled with ~ charges and countercharges —A. D. Graeff⟩ — **scur·ri·lous·ly** *adv* — **scur·ri·lous·ness** *n*

scur·ry \ˈskər-ē, ˈskə-rē\ *vi* **scur·ried; scur·ry·ing** [short for *hurry-scurry*, redupl. of *hurry*] (1810) **1 :** to move in or as if in a brisk rapidly alternating step **:** SCAMPER **2 :** to circulate in an agitated, confused, or fluttering manner — **scurry** *n*

¹scur·vy \ˈskər-vē\ *n* [*scurf*] (1565) **:** a disease marked by spongy gums, loosening of the teeth, and a bleeding into the skin and mucous membranes and caused by a lack of ascorbic acid

²scurvy *adj* (1579) **:** disgustingly mean or contemptible **:** DESPICABLE ⟨a ~ trick⟩ ***syn*** see CONTEMPTIBLE — **scur·vi·ly** \-və-lē\ *adv* — **scur·vi·ness** \-vē-nəs\ *n*

scurvy grass *n* (1597) **:** a cress (as *Cochlearia officinalis*) formerly believed useful in preventing or treating scurvy

scut \ˈskət\ *n* [origin unknown] (ca. 1530) **:** a short erect tail (as of a hare)

scu·tage \ˈsk(y)üt-ij\ *n* [ME, fr. ML *scutagium*, fr. L *scutum* shield — more at ESQUIRE] (15c) **:** a tax levied on a tenant of a knight's estate in place of military service

¹scutch \ˈskəch\ *vt* [obs. F *escoucher*, fr. (assumed) VL *excuticare* to beat out, fr. L *excutere*, fr. *ex-* + *quatere* to shake, strike — more at QUASH] (1733) **:** to separate the woody fiber from (flax or hemp) by beating

²scutch *n* (1791) **1 :** SCUTCHER **2 :** a bricklayer's hammer for cutting, trimming, and dressing bricks

scutch·eon \ˈskəch-ən\ *n* [ME *scochon*, fr. MF *escuchon*] (14c) **:** ESCUTCHEON

scutch·er \ˈskəch-ər\ *n* (1776) **:** an implement or machine for scutching flax or cotton

scute \ˈsk(y)üt\ *n* [NL *scutum*, fr. L, shield — more at ESQUIRE] (1898) **:** an external bony or horny plate or large scale

scu·tel·late \sk(y)ü-ˈtel-ət, ˈsk(y)üt-ᵊl-ˌāt\ *or* **scu·tel·lat·ed** \ˈsk(y)üt-ᵊl-ˌāt-əd\ *adj* (1785) **:** having or covered with scutella

scu·tel·lum \sk(y)ü-ˈtel-əm\ *n, pl* **-la** \-ə\ [NL, dim. of L *scutum* shield] (ca. 1760) **1 :** a hard plate or scale (as on the thorax of an insect or the tarsus of a bird) **2 :** the shield-shaped cotyledon of a monocotyledon (as a grass) — **scu·tel·lar** \-ər\ *adj*

scut·ter \ˈskət-ər\ *vi* [alter. of ⁴*scuttle*] (1781) **:** SCURRY, SCAMPER

¹scut·tle \ˈskət-ᵊl\ *n* [ME *scutel*, fr. L *scutella* drinking bowl, tray, dim. of *scutra* platter] (15c) **1 :** a shallow open basket for carrying something (as grain or garden produce) **2 :** a metal pail that usu. has a bail and a sloped lip and is used esp. for carrying coal

²scuttle *n* [ME *skottell*] (15c) **1 :** a small opening in a wall or roof furnished with a lid: as **a :** a small opening or hatchway in the deck of a ship large enough to admit a person and with a lid for covering it **b :** a small hole in the side or bottom of a ship furnished with a lid or glazed **2 :** a lid that closes a scuttle

³scuttle *vt* **scut·tled; scut·tling** \ˈskət-liŋ, -ᵊl-iŋ\ (1642) **1 :** to cut a hole through the bottom, deck, or side of (a ship); *specif* **:** to sink or attempt to sink by making holes through the bottom **2 :** DESTROY, WRECK; *also* **:** SCRAP 2

⁴scuttle *vi* **scut·tled; scut·tling** \ˈskət-liŋ, -ᵊl-iŋ\ [prob. blend of *scud* and *shuttle*] (15c) **:** SCURRY

⁵scuttle *n* (1623) **1 :** a quick shuffling pace **2 :** a short swift run

scut·tle·butt \ˈskət-ᵊl-ˌbət\ *n* [²*scuttle* + ³*butt*] (1805) **1 a :** a cask on shipboard to contain fresh water for a day's use **b :** a drinking fountain on a ship or at a naval or marine installation **2 :** RUMOR, GOSSIP

scu·tum \ˈsk(y)üt-əm\ *n, pl* **scu·ta** \-ə\ [NL, fr. L, shield — more at ESQUIRE] (1771) **:** a bony, horny, or chitinous plate **:** SCUTE

scut work \ˈskət-\ *n* [perh. fr. E slang *scut* junior intern] (ca. 1962) **:** routine and often menial labor

scuz·zy \ˈskəz-ē\ *adj* **scuz·zi·er; -est** [perh. alter. of *disgusting*] *slang* (1968) **:** dirty, shabby, or foul in condition or character

Scyl·la \ˈsil-ə\ *n* [L, fr. Gk *Skyllē*] **:** a nymph changed into a monster in Greek mythology who terrorizes mariners in the Strait of Messina — **between Scylla and Cha·ryb·dis** \-kə-ˈrib-dəs\ **:** between two equally hazardous alternatives

scy·phis·to·ma \sī-ˈfis-tə-mə\ *n, pl* **-mae** \-(ˌ)mē\ *also* **-mas** [NL, fr. L *scyphus* cup + Gk *stoma* mouth — more at STOMACH] (1878) **:** a sexually produced scyphozoan larva that ultimately repeatedly constricts transversely to form free-swimming medusae

scy·pho·zo·an \ˌsī-fə-ˈzō-ən\ *n* [NL *Scyphozoa*, fr. L *scyphus* + NL *-zoa*] (1892) **:** any of a class (Scyphozoa) of coelenterates that comprise jellyfishes lacking a true polyp and usu. a velum — **scyphozoan** *adj*

¹scythe \ˈsīth, ˈsī\ *n* [ME *sithe*, fr. OE *sīthe*; akin to OE *sagu* saw — more at SAW] (bef. 12c) **:** an implement used for mowing (as grass) and composed of a long curving blade fastened at an angle to a long handle

²scythe *vb* **scythed; scyth·ing** *vt* (1597) **:** to cut with or as if with a scythe ~ *vi* **:** to work with a scythe

Scyth·i·an \ˈsith-ē-ən, ˈsith-\ *n* [L *Scytha*, fr. Gk *Skythēs*] (15c) **1 :** a member of an ancient nomadic people inhabiting Scythia **2 :** the Iranian language of the Scythians — **Scythian** *adj*

sea \ˈsē\ *n* [ME *see*, fr. OE *sǣ*; akin to OS & OHG *sē* sea] (bef. 12c) **1 a :** a great body of salty water that covers much of the earth; *broadly* **:** the waters of the earth as distinguished from the land and air **b :** a body of salt water of second rank more or less landlocked ⟨the Mediterranean ~⟩ **c :** OCEAN **d :** an inland body of water esp. if large or if salt or brackish ⟨the Caspian ~⟩ **e :** a small freshwater lake ⟨the *Sea* of Galilee⟩ **2 a :** surface motion on a large body of water or its direction; *also* **:** rough water **:** a heavy swell or wave **b :** the disturbance of the ocean or other body of water due to the wind **3 :** something likened to the sea esp. in vastness ⟨the crowd was a ~ of faces⟩ **4 :** the seafaring life **5 :** ³MARE — **sea** *adj* — **at sea 1 :** on the sea; *specif* **:** on a sea voyage **2 :** LOST, BEWILDERED — **to sea :** to or on the open waters of the sea

sea anchor *n* (1769) **:** a drag typically of canvas thrown overboard to retard the drifting of a ship or seaplane and to keep its head to the wind

sea anemone *n* (1742) **:** any of numerous usu. solitary polyps (order Actiniaria) whose form, bright and varied colors, and cluster of tentacles superficially resemble a flower

sea·bag \ˈsē-ˌbag\ *n* (1919) **:** a cylindrical canvas bag used esp. by a sailor for clothes and other gear

sea bass *n* (1765) **1 :** any of numerous marine fishes (family Serranidae) that are usu. smaller and more active than the groupers; *esp* **:** a food and sport fish (*Centropristis striata*) of the Atlantic coast of the U.S. **2 :** any of numerous croakers or drums including noted sport and food fishes

sea·bed \-ˌbed\ *n* (1838) **:** the floor of a sea or ocean

Sea·bee \ˈsē-(ˌ)bē\ *n* [alter. of *cee* + *bee*; fr. the initials of *construction battalion*] (1942) **:** a member of one of the U.S. Navy construction battalions for building naval shore facilities in combat zones

sea·bird \ˈsē-ˌbərd\ *n* (1589) **:** a bird (as a gull or albatross) frequenting the open ocean

sea biscuit *n* (1680) **:** HARDTACK

\ə\ abut \ᵊ\ kitten, F table \ər\ further \a\ ash \ā\ ace \ä\ cot, cart \au̇\ out \ch\ chin \e\ bet \ē\ easy \g\ go \i\ hit \ī\ ice \j\ job \ŋ\ sing \ō\ go \ȯ\ law \ȯi\ boy \th\ thin \th\ the \ü\ loot \u̇\ foot \y\ yet \zh\ vision \à, k, ⁿ, œ, œ̄, ue, ue̅, ʸ\ see Guide to Pronunciation

sea·board \'sē-ˌbō(ə)rd, -ˌbȯ(ə)rd\ *n* (1788) : SEACOAST; *also* : the country bordering a seacoast — **seaboard** *adj*
sea·boot \-ˌbüt\ *n* (1851) : a very high waterproof boot used esp. by sailors and fishermen
sea·borne \-ˌbō(ə)rn, -ˌbȯ(ə)rn\ *adj* (1823) **1** : borne over or on the sea ⟨a ∼ invasion⟩ **2** : engaged in or carried on by oversea shipping ⟨∼ trade⟩
sea bread *n* (1837) : HARDTACK
sea bream *n* (1530) : any of numerous marine percoid fishes (as of the families Sparidae or Bramidae)
sea breeze *n* (1697) : a cooling breeze blowing generally in the daytime inland from the sea
sea captain *n* (1612) : the master esp. of a merchant vessel
sea change *n* (1610) **1** *archaic* : a change brought about by the sea **2** : TRANSFORMATION
sea chest *n* (1669) : a sailor's storage chest for personal property
sea·coast \'sē-ˌkōst\ *n* (14c) : the shore or border of the land adjacent to the sea
sea cow *n* (1613) : MANATEE, DUGONG
sea·craft \'sē-ˌkraft\ *n* (1919) **1** : seagoing ships **2** : skill in navigation
sea crayfish *n* (1748) : SPINY LOBSTER
sea cucumber *n* (1601) : HOLOTHURIAN; *esp* : one whose contracted body suggests a cucumber in form
sea devil *n* (1634) : DEVILFISH 1
sea·dog \'sē-ˌdȯg\ *n* (1825) : FOGBOW
sea dog *n* (1840) : a veteran sailor
sea·drome \-ˌdrōm\ *n* (1923) : a usu. floating airdrome on water serving esp. as an intermediate or emergency landing place
sea duck *n* (1753) : a diving duck (as a scoter, merganser, or eider) that frequents the sea
sea duty *n* (1946) : duty in the U.S. Navy performed outside the continental U.S. or specified dependencies thereof
sea eagle *n* (1668) : any of various fish-eating eagles (esp. genus *Haliaeetus*)
Sea Explorer *n* (1948) : an Explorer in a scouting program that teaches seamanship
sea fan *n* (ca. 1633) : a gorgonian with a fan-shaped skeleton; *esp* : one (*Gorgonia flabellum*) of Florida and the West Indies
sea·far·er \'sē-ˌfar-ər, -ˌfer-\ *n* [*sea* + 1*fare* + *-er*] (1513) : MARINER
sea·far·ing \-ˌfar-iŋ, -ˌfer-\ *n* (1592) : a mariner's calling — **seafaring** *adj*
sea fire *n* (1814) : marine bioluminescence
sea·floor \'sē-ˌflō(ə)r, -ˌflȯ(ə)r\ *n* (1855) : SEABED
sea·food \-ˌfüd\ *n* (1836) : edible marine fish and shellfish
sea·fowl \-ˌfau̇l\ *n* (14c) : SEABIRD
sea·front \-ˌfrənt\ *n* (1879) : the waterfront of a seaside place
sea gate *n* (1861) : a way (as a gate, beach, or channel) that gives access to the sea
sea·girt \'sē-ˌgərt\ *adj* (1621) : surrounded by the sea
sea·go·ing \-ˌgō-iŋ, -ˌgȯ(-)iŋ\ *adj* (1829) : OCEANGOING
sea grape *n* (1806) : a variable plant (*Coccoloba uvifera*) of sandy shores of Florida and tropical America that has rounded leaves with cordate bases and bears clusters of bluish edible berries
sea green *n* (1598) **1** : a moderate green or bluish green **2** : a moderate yellow green
sea gull *n* (1542) : a gull frequenting the sea; *broadly* : GULL
sea hare *n* (1593) : any of various large naked mollusks (genus *Aplysia*) with arched backs and anterior tentacles that project like ears
sea holly *n* (1548) : a European coastal herb (*Eryngium maritimum*) of the carrot family with spiny leaves and pale blue flowers
sea horse *n* (15c) **1** : WALRUS **2** : a mythical creature half horse and half fish **3** : any of numerous small fishes (family Syngnathidae) related to the pipefishes but stockier with the head and forepart of the body sharply flexed like the head and neck of a horse

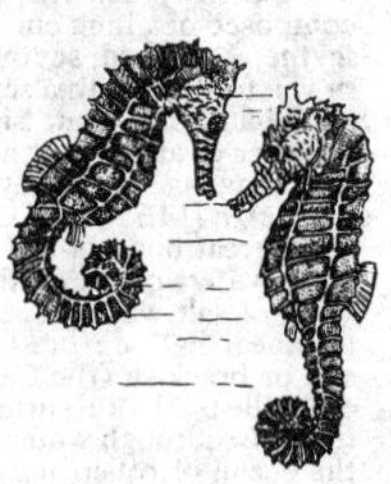
sea horse 3

sea is·land cotton \ˌsē-ˌī-lən(d)-\ *n, often cap S&I* [*Sea islands,* chain of islands in the Atlantic] (1805) : a cotton (*Gossypium barbadense*) with esp. long silky fiber — called also *sea island*
sea kale *n* (1699) : a European fleshy plant (*Crambe maritima*) of the mustard family used as a potherb
sea king *n* (1819) : a Norse pirate chief
1**seal** \'sē(ə)l\ *n, pl* **seals** *also* **seal** [ME *sele,* fr. OE *seolh;* akin to OHG *selah* seal] (bef. 12c) **1** : any of numerous marine aquatic carnivorous mammals (families Phocidae and Otariidae) that occur chiefly in cold regions and have limbs modified into webbed flippers adapted primarily to swimming; *esp* : FUR SEAL **2 a** : the pelt of a fur seal **b** : leather made from the skin of a seal **3** : a dark brown
2**seal** *vi* (1828) : to hunt seal
3**seal** *n* [ME *seel,* fr. OF, fr. L *sigillum* seal, fr. dim. of *signum* sign, seal — more at SIGN] (13c) **1 a** : something that confirms, ratifies, or makes secure : GUARANTEE, ASSURANCE **b** (1) : a device with a cut or raised emblem, symbol, or word used to certify a signature or authenticate a document (2) : a medallion or ring face bearing such a device incised so that it can be impressed on wax or moist clay; *also* : a piece of wax or a wafer bearing such an impression **c** : an impression, device, or mark given the effect of a common-law seal by statute law or by American local custom recognized by judicial decision **d** : a usu. ornamental adhesive stamp that may be used to close a letter or package; *esp* : one given in a fund-raising campaign **2 a** : something that secures (as a wax seal on a document) **b** : a closure that must be broken to be opened and that thus reveals tampering **c** (1) : a tight and perfect closure (as against the passage of gas or water) (2) : a device to prevent the passage or return of gas or air into a pipe or container **3** : a seal that is a symbol or mark of office — **under seal** : with an authenticating seal affixed
4**seal** *vt* (14c) **1 a** : to confirm or make secure by or as if by a seal **b** : to solemnize for eternity (as a marriage) by a Mormon rite **2 a** : to set or affix an authenticating seal to; *also* : AUTHENTICATE, RATIFY **b** : to mark with a stamp or seal usu. as an evidence of standard exactness, legal size, weight, or capacity, or merchantable quality **3 a** : to fasten with or as if with a seal to prevent tampering **b** : to close or make secure against access, leakage, or passage by a fastening or coating **c** : to fix in position or close breaks in with a filling (as of plaster) **4** : to determine irrevocably or indisputably ⟨that answer ∼*ed* our fate⟩
sea ladder *n* (1902) **1** : a rope ladder or set of steps to be lowered over a ship's side for use in coming aboard (as at sea) **2** : SEA STEPS
sea lamprey *n* (1879) : a large anadromous lamprey (*Petromyzon marinus*) that is sometimes used as food and is a pest destructive of native fish fauna in the Great Lakes
sea–lane \'sē-ˌlān\ *n* (1927) : an established sea route
seal·ant \'sē-lənt\ *n* (1944) : a sealing agent ⟨radiator ∼⟩
sea lavender *n* (1597) : any of a genus (*Limonium*) of mostly coastal plants of the plumbago family
sea lawyer *n* (1848) : an argumentative captious sailor
sealed–beam \'sē(ə)l(d)-'bēm\ *adj* (1941) : of, relating to, or being an electric light with prefocused reflector and lens sealed in the lamp vacuum
sea legs *n pl* (1712) : bodily adjustment to the motion of a ship indicated esp. by ability to walk steadily and by freedom from seasickness
1**seal·er** \'sē-lər\ *n* (15c) **1** : an official who attests or certifies conformity to a standard of correctness **2** : a coat (as of size) applied to prevent subsequent coats of paint or varnish from sinking in
2**sealer** *n* (1842) : a person or a ship engaged in hunting seals
sea lettuce *n* (1668) : any of several seaweeds (esp. genus *Ulva,* of the family Ulvaceae) with green fronds sometimes eaten as salad
sea level *n* (1806) : the level of the surface of the sea esp. at its mean position midway between mean high and low water
sea lily *n* (1903) : CRINOID; *esp* : a stalked crinoid
sealing wax *n* (14c) : a resinous composition that is plastic when warm and is used for sealing (as letters, dry cells, or cans)
sea lion *n* (1697) : any of several large Pacific eared seals (genus *Zalophus* and *Otaria*) that are related to the fur seals but lack their valuable coat
seal off *vt* (1948) : to close tightly
seal point *n* [1*seal* (the color)] (1939) : a Siamese cat with cream or fawn-colored body and dark brown points
seal ring *n* (1608) : a finger ring engraved with a seal : SIGNET RING
seal·skin \'sē(ə)l-ˌskin\ *n* (14c) **1** : the fur or pelt of a fur seal **2** : a garment (as a jacket, coat, or cape) of sealskin — **sealskin** *adj*
Sea·ly·ham terrier \ˌsē-lē-ˌham-, *esp Brit* -lē-əm-\ *n* [*Sealyham,* Pembrokeshire, Wales] (1907) : a short-legged long-headed strong-jawed heavy-boned chiefly white terrier of a breed developed in Wales
1**seam** \'sēm\ *n* [ME *seem,* fr. OE *sēam;* akin to OE *sīwian* to sew — more at SEW] (bef. 12c) **1 a** : the joining of two pieces (as of cloth or leather) by sewing usu. near the edge **b** : the stitching used in such a joining **2** : the space between adjacent planks or strakes of a ship **3 a** : a line, groove, or ridge formed by the abutment of edges **b** : a thin layer or stratum (as of rock) between distinctive layers; *also* : a bed of valuable mineral and esp. coal irrespective of thickness **c** : a line left by a cut or wound; *also* : WRINKLE — **seam·less** *adj* — **seam·less·ly** *adv* — **seam·less·ness** *n* — **seam·like** \-ˌlīk\ *adj* — **at the seams** : ENTIRELY, COMPLETELY ⟨falling apart *at the seams*⟩
2**seam** *vt* (1582) **1 a** : to join by sewing **b** : to join as if by sewing (as by welding, riveting, or heat-sealing) **2** : to mark with lines suggesting seams ∼ *vi* : to become fissured or ridgy — **seam·er** *n*
sea–maid \'sē-ˌmād\ *or* **sea–maid·en** \-ˌmād-ᵊn\ *n* (1590) : MERMAID; *also* : a goddess or nymph of the sea
sea·man \'sē-mən\ *n* (13c) **1** : SAILOR, MARINER **2 a** : one of the three ranks below petty officer in the navy or coast guard **b** : an enlisted man in the navy or coast guard ranking above a seaman apprentice and below a petty officer
seaman apprentice *n* (1947) : an enlisted man in the navy or coast guard ranking above a seaman recruit and below a seaman
sea·man·like \'sē-mən-ˌlīk\ *adj* (1796) : characteristic of or befitting a competent seaman
sea·man·ly \-lē\ *adj* (1798) : SEAMANLIKE
seaman recruit *n* (1947) : an enlisted man of the lowest rank in the navy or coast guard
sea·man·ship \'sē-mən-ˌship\ *n* (1766) : the art or skill of handling, working, and navigating a ship
sea·mark \-ˌmärk\ *n* (15c) **1** : a line on a coast marking the tidal limit **2** : an elevated object serving as a beacon to mariners
sea mew *n* (15c) : SEA GULL; *esp* : a European gull (*Larus canus*)
sea mile *n* (1796) : NAUTICAL MILE
sea·mount \'sē-ˌmau̇nt\ *n* (1948) : a submarine mountain rising above the deep-sea floor
sea mouse *n* (1520) : a large broad marine polychaete worm (esp. genus *Aphrodite*) covered with hairlike setae
seam·ster \'sēm(p)-stər *also* 'sem(p)-\ *n* [ME *semester, semster,* fr. OE *sēamestre* seamstress, tailor, fr. *sēam* seam] (bef. 12c) : a person employed at sewing; *esp* : TAILOR
seam·stress \-strəs\ *n* (1613) : a woman whose occupation is sewing
seamy \'sē-mē\ *adj* **seam·i·er; -est** (1604) **1** *archaic* : having the rough side of the seam showing **2 a** : UNPLEASANT **b** : DEGRADED, SORDID — **seam·i·ness** *n*
sé·ance \'sā-ˌän(t)s, -ˌäⁿs, sā-'\ *n* [F, fr. *seoir* to sit, fr. L *sedēre* — more at SIT] (1803) **1** : SESSION, SITTING **2** : a spiritualist meeting to receive spirit communications
sea nettle *n* (1601) : a stinging jellyfish
sea oats *n pl but sing or pl in constr* (1894) : a tall grass (*Uniola panicolata*) that has panicles resembling those of the oat, grows on the coast of the southern U.S., and is useful as a sand binder
sea onion *n* (1548) : SQUILL 1a
sea otter *n* (1664) : a rare large marine otter (*Enhydra lutris*) of the northern Pacific coasts that attains a maximum length of nearly six feet and feeds largely on shellfish
sea–otter's–cabbage *n* (1866) : a gigantic kelp (*Nereocystis lütkeana*) of the northern Pacific
sea pen *n* (1763) : any of numerous anthozoans (as of the genus *Pennatula*) whose colonies have a feathery form
sea·piece \'sē-ˌpēs\ *n* (1656) : SEASCAPE 2

sea·plane \-ˌplān\ *n* (1913) **:** an airplane designed to take off from and land on the water

sea·port \ˈsē-ˌpō(ə)rt, -ˌpȯ(ə)rt\ *n* (1596) **:** a port, harbor, or town accessible to seagoing ships

sea power *n* (1849) **1 :** a nation having formidable naval strength **2 :** naval strength

sea purse *n* (1856) **:** the horny egg case of skates and of some sharks

sea puss \-ˌpu̇s\ *n* [by folk etymology fr. a word of Algonquian origin; akin to Delaware *sepus* small brook] (1891) **:** a swirling or along shore undertow

sea·quake \ˈsē-ˌkwāk\ *n* [*sea* + *-quake* (as in *earthquake*)] (1680) **:** a submarine earthquake

[1]sear *var of* SERE

[2]sear \ˈsi(ə)r\ *vb* [ME *seren,* fr. OE *sēarian* to become sere, fr. *sēar* sere] *vi* (bef. 12c) **:** to cause withering or drying ~ *vt* **1 :** to make withered and dry **:** PARCH **2 :** to burn, scorch, or injure with or as if with sudden application of intense heat — **sear·ing·ly** \-iŋ-lē\ *adv*

[3]sear *n* (1874) **:** a mark or scar left by searing

[4]sear *n* [prob. fr. MF *serre* grasp, fr. *serrer* to press, grasp, fr. LL *serare* to bolt, latch, fr. L *sera* bar for fastening a door] (1596) **:** the catch that holds the hammer of a gunlock at cock or half cock

[1]search \ˈsərch\ *vb* [ME *cerchen,* fr. MF *cerchier* to go about, survey, search, fr. LL *circare* to go about, fr. L *circum* round about — more at CIRCUM-] *vt* (14c) **1 :** to look into or over carefully or thoroughly in an effort to find or discover something: as **a :** to examine in seeking something ⟨~*ed* the north field⟩ **b :** to look through or explore by inspecting possible places of concealment or investigating suspicious circumstances **c :** to read thoroughly **:** CHECK; *esp* **:** to examine a public record or register for information about ⟨~ land titles⟩ **d :** to examine for articles concealed on the person **e :** to look at as if to discover or penetrate intention or nature **2 :** to uncover, find, or come to know by inquiry or scrutiny — usu. used with *out* ~ *vi* **1 :** to look or inquire carefully ⟨~*ed* for the papers⟩ **2 :** to make painstaking investigation or examination — **search·able** \ˈsər-chə-bəl\ *adj* — **search·er** *n* — **search·ing·ly** \-chiŋ-lē\ *adv*

[2]search *n* (15c) **1 a :** an act of searching ⟨a ~ for food⟩ ⟨go in ~ of help⟩ **b :** an act of boarding and inspecting a ship on the high seas in exercise of right of search **2** *obs* **:** a party that searches **3 :** power or range of penetrating; *also* **:** a penetrating effect

search·less \ˈsərch-ləs\ *adj* (1605) **:** INSCRUTABLE, IMPENETRABLE

search·light \-ˌlīt\ *n* (1883) **1 :** an apparatus for projecting a beam of light; *also* **:** a beam of light projected by it **2 :** FLASHLIGHT 3

search warrant *n* (1818) **:** a warrant authorizing a search (as of a house) for stolen goods or unlawful possessions (as gambling implements)

sea robin *n* (1814) **:** any of various marine fishes (family Triglidae) with a spiny armored head and the bottom three rays of the pectoral fin on each side free of membrane and modified for use as feelers or in crawling — called also *gurnard*

sea room *n* (1554) **:** room for maneuver at sea

sea rover *n* (1579) **:** one that roves the sea; *specif* **:** PIRATE

sea–run \ˌsē-ˌrən\ *adj* (1885) **:** ANADROMOUS ⟨a ~ salmon⟩

sea·scape \ˈsē-ˌskāp\ *n* (1799) **1 :** a view of the sea **2 :** a picture representing a scene at sea

sea scorpion *n* (1896) **:** SCULPIN

Sea Scout *n* (1911) **:** SEA EXPLORER

sea serpent *n* (1774) **:** a large marine animal resembling a serpent often reported to have been seen but never proved to exist

sea·shell \ˈsē-ˌshel\ *n* (bef. 12c) **:** the shell of a marine animal and esp. a mollusk

sea·shore \-ˌshō(ə)r, -ˌshȯ(ə)r\ *n* (1526) **1 a :** land adjacent to the sea **:** SEACOAST **b :** NATIONAL SEASHORE **2 :** all the ground between the ordinary high-water and low-water marks **:** FORESHORE

sea·sick \-ˌsik\ *adj* (1566) **:** affected with or suggestive of seasickness

sea·sick·ness \-nəs\ *n* (1625) **:** motion sickness experienced on the water

sea·side \ˈsē-ˌsīd\ *n* (13c) **:** the district or land bordering the sea **:** country adjacent to the sea **:** SEASHORE — **seaside** *adj*

sea slug *n* (1779) **1 :** HOLOTHURIAN **2 :** a naked marine gastropod; *specif* **:** NUDIBRANCH

sea snake *n* (1755) **1 :** SEA SERPENT **2 :** any of numerous venomous aquatic viviparous snakes (family Hydrophidae) of warm seas

[1]sea·son \ˈsēz-ᵊn\ *n* [ME, fr. MF *saison,* fr. OF, fr. L *sation-, satio* action of sowing, fr. *satus,* pp. of *serere* to sow — more at SOW] (14c) **1 a :** a time characterized by a particular circumstance or feature ⟨in a ~ of religious awakening —F. A. Christie⟩ **b :** a suitable or natural time or occasion ⟨when my ~ comes to sit on David's throne —John Milton⟩ **c :** an indefinite period of time **:** WHILE ⟨sent home again to her father for a ~ —Francis Hackett⟩ **2 a :** a period of the year characterized by or associated with a particular activity or phenomenon ⟨hay fever ~⟩: as **(1) :** a period associated with some phase or activity of agriculture (as growth or harvesting) **(2) :** a period in which an animal engages in some activity (as migrating or mating); *also* **:** ESTRUS, HEAT **(3) :** the period normally characterized by a particular kind of weather ⟨a long rainy ~⟩ **(4) :** a period marked by special activity in some field ⟨the theatrical ~⟩ ⟨the hunting ~⟩ **(5) :** a period in which a place is most frequented **b :** one of the four quarters into which the year is commonly divided **c :** the time of a major holiday **3 :** YEAR ⟨a boy of seven ~*s*⟩ **4** [ME *sesoun,* fr. *sesounen* to season] **:** SEASONING **5 :** the schedule of official games played or to be played by a sports team during a playing season ⟨try to get through the ~ undefeated⟩ **6 :** OFF-SEASON ⟨closed for the ~⟩ — **sea·son·less** *adj* — **in season 1 :** at the right time **2 :** at the stage of greatest fitness (as for eating) ⟨peaches are *in season*⟩ **3 :** legally available to be hunted or caught — **out of season :** not in season

[2]season *vb* **sea·soned; sea·son·ing** \ˈsēz-niŋ, -ᵊn-iŋ\ [ME *sesounen,* fr. MF *assaisoner* to ripen, season, fr. OF, fr. *a-* (fr. L *ad-*) + *saison* season] *vt* (14c) **1 a :** to give (food) more flavor or zest by adding seasoning or savory ingredients **b :** to give a distinctive quality to as if by seasoning; *esp* **:** to make more agreeable ⟨advice ~*ed* with wit⟩ **c** *archaic* **:** to qualify by admixture **:** TEMPER **2 a :** to treat (as lumber) so as to prepare for use **b :** to make fit by experience ⟨a ~*ed* veteran⟩ ~ *vi* **:** to become seasoned

sea·son·able \ˈsēz-nə-bəl, -ᵊn-ə-bəl\ *adj* (14c) **1 :** suitable to the season or circumstances **:** TIMELY ⟨a ~ frost⟩ **2 :** occurring in good or proper time **:** OPPORTUNE ⟨a ~ time for discussion⟩ — **sea·son·able·ness** *n* — **sea·son·ably** \-blē\ *adv*

sea·son·al \ˈsēz-nəl, -ᵊn-əl\ *adj* (1838) **1 :** of, relating to, or varying in occurrence according to the season ⟨~ storms⟩ **2 :** affected or caused by seasonal need or availability ⟨~ unemployment⟩ ⟨~ industries⟩ — **sea·son·al·i·ty** \ˌsēz-ᵊn-ˈal-ət-ē\ *n* — **sea·son·al·ly** \ˈsēz-nə-lē, -ᵊn-ə-lē\ *adv*

sea·son·er \ˈsēz-nər, -ᵊn-ər\ *n* (1598) **:** one that seasons: as **a :** a user of seasonings ⟨a heavy ~⟩ **b :** SEASONING

sea·son·ing \ˈsēz-niŋ, -ᵊn-iŋ\ *n* (1580) **:** something that serves to season; *esp* **:** an ingredient (as a condiment, spice, or herb) added to food primarily for the savor that it imparts

season ticket *n* (1820) **:** a ticket (as to all of a club's home games or for specified daily transportation) valid during a specified time

sea spider *n* (1666) **:** any of various small long-legged marine arthropods (class Pycnogonida) that superficially resemble spiders

sea squirt *n* (1850) **:** a sessile tunicate **:** ASCIDIAN

sea star *n* (1569) **:** STARFISH

sea steps *n pl* (1899) **:** projecting metal plates or bars attached to the side of a ship by which it may be boarded

sea stores *n pl* (1659) **:** supplies (as of foodstuffs) laid in before starting on a sea voyage

sea·strand \ˈsē-ˌstrand\ *n* (bef. 12c) **:** SEASHORE

[1]seat \ˈsēt\ *n* [ME *sete,* fr. ON *sæti;* akin to OE *sittan* to sit] (13c) **1 a :** a special chair of one in eminence; *also* **:** the status represented by it **b :** a chair, stool, or bench intended to be sat in or on **c :** the particular part of something on which one rests in sitting ⟨the ~ of a chair⟩ ⟨trouser ~⟩ **d :** BUTTOCKS **2 a :** a seating accommodation ⟨a ~ for the game⟩ ⟨a 200-*seat* restaurant⟩ **b :** a right of sitting ⟨lost his ~ in Congress⟩ **c :** membership on an exchange **3 a :** a place occupied by something **b :** a place from which authority is exercised ⟨the county ~⟩ **c :** a bodily part in which some function or condition is centered ⟨the brain as the ~ of the mind⟩ **4 :** posture in or way of sitting on horseback **5 a :** a part at or forming the base of something **b :** a part (as a socket) or surface on or in which another part or surface rests

[2]seat *vt* (1593) **1 a :** to install in a seat of dignity or office **b (1) :** to cause to sit or assist in finding a seat **(2) :** to provide seats for ⟨a theater ~*ing* 1000 persons⟩ **c :** to put in a sitting position **2 :** to repair the seat of or provide a new seat for **3 :** to fit to or with a seat ⟨~ a valve⟩ ~ *vi* **1** *archaic* **:** to take one's seat or place **2 :** to fit correctly on a seat — **seat·er** *n*

seat belt *n* (1948) **:** an arrangement of straps designed to hold a person steady in a seat (as during the takeoff of an airplane or while driving an automobile)

-seat·er \ˈsēt-ər\ *n comb form* **:** one that has a specified number of seats ⟨the car was a 4-*seater*⟩

seat·ing \ˈsēt-iŋ\ *n* (1880) **1 :** the act of providing with seats **2 a :** material for covering or upholstering seats **b :** a seat on or in which something rests ⟨a valve ~⟩

seat·mate \ˈsēt-ˌmāt\ *n* (1859) **:** one with whom one shares a seat

seat–of–the–pants *adj* (1942) **:** employing or based on personal experience, judgment, and effort rather than technological aids ⟨~ navigation⟩ ⟨a ~ pilot⟩

sea·train \ˈsē-ˌtrān\ *n* (1932) **:** a seagoing ship equipped for carrying a train of railroad cars

sea trout *n* (1745) **1 :** any of various trouts or chars that as adults inhabit the sea but ascend rivers to spawn **2 :** any of various marine fishes felt to resemble trouts: as **a :** WEAKFISH 1 **b :** SPOTTED SEA TROUT

sea turtle *n* (1764) **:** any of two families (Cheloniidae and Dermochelyidae) of widely distributed marine turtles with the feet modified into paddles that include the green turtle, leatherback, hawksbill, loggerhead, and ridley

sea urchin *n* (1591) **:** any of a class (Echinoidea) of oblate echinoderms that are usu. enclosed in thin brittle shells covered with movable spines

sea·wall \ˈsē-ˌwȯl\ *n* (15c) **:** a wall or embankment to protect the shore from erosion or to act as a breakwater

[1]sea·ward \ˈsē-wərd\ *n* (14c) **:** the direction or side away from land and toward the open sea

[2]seaward *adj* (15c) **1 :** directed or situated toward the sea **2 :** coming from the sea ⟨a ~ wind⟩

[3]seaward *also* **sea·wards** \-wərdz\ *adv* (1540) **:** toward the sea

sea wasp *n* (1940) **:** any of various scyphozoan jellyfishes (order or suborder Cubomedusae) that sting virulently and sometimes fatally

sea·wa·ter \ˈsē-ˌwȯt-ər, -ˌwät-\ *n* (bef. 12c) **:** water in or from the sea

sea·way \-ˌwā\ *n* (bef. 12c) **1 :** the sea as a route for travel; *also* **:** an ocean traffic lane **2 :** a ship's headway **3 :** a moderate or rough sea **4 :** a deep inland waterway that admits ocean shipping

sea·weed \-ˌwēd\ *n* (1577) **1 :** a mass or growth of marine plants **2 :** a plant growing in the sea; *esp* **:** a marine alga (as a kelp)

sea whip *n* (1858) **:** a gorgonian with an elongated flexible unbranched or little-branched axis

sea·wor·thy \ˈsē-ˌwər-t͟hē\ *adj* (1807) **:** fit or safe for a sea voyage ⟨a ~ ship⟩ — **sea·wor·thi·ness** \-t͟hē-nəs\ *n*

sea wrack *n* (1551) **:** SEAWEED; *esp* **:** that cast ashore in masses

se·ba·ceous \si-ˈbā-shəs\ *adj* [L *sebaceus* made of tallow, fr. *sebum* tallow — more at SOAP] (1728) **1 :** secreting sebum ⟨~ glands⟩ **2 :** of, relating to, or being fatty material **:** FATTY ⟨a ~ exudate⟩

se·ba·cic acid \si-ˌbas-ik-, ˌsē-, -ˌbā-sik-\ *n* [ISV, fr. L *sebaceus*] (1790) **:** a crystalline dicarboxylic acid $C_{10}H_{18}O_4$ used esp. in the manufacture of synthetic resins

seb·or·rhea \ˌseb-ə-ˈrē-ə\ *n* [NL, fr. L *sebum* + NL *-rrhea*] (1876) **:** abnormally increased secretion and discharge of sebum — **seb·or·rhe·ic** \-ˈrē-ik\ *adj*

se·bum \ˈsēb-əm\ *n* [L, tallow, grease — more at SOAP] (1876) **:** fatty lubricant matter secreted by sebaceous glands of the skin

\ə\ abut \ᵊ\ kitten, F table \ər\ further \a\ ash \ā\ ace \ä\ cot, cart
\au̇\ out \ch\ chin \e\ bet \ē\ easy \g\ go \i\ hit \ī\ ice \j\ job
\ŋ\ sing \ō\ go \ȯ\ law \ȯi\ boy \th\ thin \t͟h\ the \ü\ loot \u̇\ foot
\y\ yet \zh\ vision \à, k̲, ⁿ, œ, œ̄, ue, ue̅, ʸ\ *see* Guide to Pronunciation

sec \'sek\ *adj* [F, lit., dry — more at SACK] *of champagne* (1889) **:** moderately dry

se·cant \'sē-ˌkant, -kənt\ *n* [NL *secant-, secans,* fr. L, prp. of *secare* to cut — more at SAW] (1593) **1 :** a straight line cutting a curve at two or more points **2 a :** a straight line drawn from the center of a circle through one end of a circular arc to a tangent drawn from the other end of the arc **b :** the trigonometric function that for an acute angle is the ratio of the hypotenuse of a right triangle of which the angle is considered part and the leg adjacent to the angle

se·ca·teur \ˌsek-ə-'tər, 'sek-ə-ˌ\ *n* [F *sécateur,* fr. L *secare* to cut] *chiefly Brit* (1881) **:** pruning shears — usu. used in pl.

[1]**sec·co** \'sek-(ˌ)ō\ *n* [It, fr. *secco* dry, fr. L *siccus* — more at SACK] (1852) **:** the art of painting on dry plaster

[2]**secco** *adj or adv* [It, lit., dry] (1876) **1 :** short and very staccato — used as a direction in music **2** *of a recitative* **:** accompanied only by the instruments playing the continuo

se·cede \si-'sēd\ *vi* **se·ced·ed; se·ced·ing** [L *secedere,* fr. *sed-, se-* apart (fr. *sed, se* without) + *cedere* to go — more at IDIOT, CEDE] (ca. 1755) **:** to withdraw from an organization (as a religious communion or political party or federation) — **se·ced·er** *n*

se·cern \si-'sərn\ *vt* [L *secernere* to separate — more at SECRET] (1656) **:** to discriminate in thought **:** DISTINGUISH

se·ces·sion \si-'sesh-ən\ *n* [L *secession-, secessio,* fr. *secessus,* pp. of *secedere*] (1604) **1 :** withdrawal into privacy or solitude **:** RETIREMENT **2 :** formal withdrawal from an organization

se·ces·sion·ism \-'sesh-ə-ˌniz-əm\ *n* (1851) **:** the doctrine or policy of secession — **se·ces·sion·ist** \-'sesh-(ə-)nəst\ *adj*

se·ces·sion·ist \-'sesh-(ə-)nəst\ *n* (1860) **:** one who joins in a secession or maintains that secession is a right

se·clude \si-'klüd\ *vt* **se·clud·ed; se·clud·ing** [ME *secluden* to keep away, fr. L *secludere* to separate, seclude, fr. *se-* apart + *claudere* to close — more at SECEDE, CLOSE] (15c) **1 :** to remove or separate from intercourse or outside influence **:** ISOLATE **2** *obs* **:** to exclude from a privilege, rank, or dignity **:** DEBAR **3 :** SHUT OFF, SCREEN

se·clud·ed *adj* (1604) **1 :** screened or hidden from view **:** SEQUESTERED ⟨a ~ valley⟩ **2 :** living in seclusion **:** SOLITARY ⟨~ monks⟩ — **se·clud·ed·ly** *adv* — **se·clud·ed·ness** *n*

se·clu·sion \si-'klü-zhən\ *n* [ML *seclusion-, seclusio,* fr. L *seclusus,* pp. of *secludere*] (1623) **1 :** the act of secluding **:** the condition of being secluded **2 :** a secluded or isolated place ***syn*** see SOLITUDE — **se·clu·sive** \-'klü-siv, -ziv\ *adj* — **se·clu·sive·ly** *adv* — **se·clu·sive·ness** *n*

seco·bar·bi·tal \ˌsek-ō-'bär-bə-ˌtȯl\ *n* [fr. *Seconal,* a trademark + *barbital*] (1951) **:** a barbiturate $C_{12}H_{18}N_2O_3$ that is used chiefly in the form of its bitter hygroscopic powdery sodium salt as a hypnotic and sedative

Sec·o·nal \'sek-ə-ˌnȯl, -ˌnal, -ən-ᵊl\ *trademark* — used for a preparation of secobarbital

[1]**sec·ond** \'sek-ənd *also* -ənt, *esp before a consonant* -ən, -ᵊŋ\ *adj* [ME, fr. OF, fr. L *secundus* second, following, favorable, fr. *sequi* to follow — more at SUE] (13c) **1 a :** next to the first in place or time ⟨was ~ in line⟩ **b** (1) **:** next to the first in value, excellence, or degree ⟨his ~ choice of schools⟩ (2) **:** INFERIOR, SUBORDINATE ⟨was ~ to none⟩ **c :** ranking next below the top of a grade or degree in authority or precedence ⟨~ mate⟩ **d :** ALTERNATE, OTHER ⟨elects a mayor every ~ year⟩ **e :** resembling or suggesting a prototype **:** ANOTHER ⟨a ~ Thoreau⟩ **f :** ingrained by discipline, training, or effort **:** ACQUIRED ⟨~ nature⟩ **g :** being the forward gear or speed next higher than first in a motor vehicle **2 :** relating to or having a part typically subordinate to and lower in pitch than the first part in concerted or ensemble music — **second** *or* **sec·ond·ly** *adv*

[2]**second** *n* [ME *secunde,* fr. ML *secunda,* fr. L, fem. of *secundus* second; fr. its being the second sexagesimal division of a unit, as a minute is the first] (14c) **1 a :** the 60th part of a minute of angular measure **b :** the 60th part of a minute of time **:** 1/86,400 part of the mean solar day; *specif* **:** an international unit of time equal to the duration of 9,192,631,770 periods of the radiation corresponding to the transition between the two hyperfine levels of the ground state of the cesium-133 atom **2 :** an instant of time **:** MOMENT

[3]**second** *n* (1567) **1 a** — see NUMBER table **b :** one that is next after the first in rank, position, authority, or precedence ⟨the ~ in line⟩ **2 :** one that assists or supports another; *esp* **:** the assistant of a duelist or boxer **3 a :** the musical interval embracing two diatonic degrees **b :** a tone at this interval; *specif* **:** SUPERTONIC **c :** the harmonic combination of two tones a second apart **4 a** *pl* **:** merchandise that is usu. slightly flawed and does not meet the manufacturer's standard for firsts or irregulars **b :** an article of such merchandise **5 :** the act or declaration by which a parliamentary motion is seconded **6 :** a place next below the first in a competition, examination, or contest **7 :** SECOND BASE **8 :** the second forward gear or speed of a motor vehicle **9** *pl* **:** a second helping of food

[4]**second** *vt* [L *secundare,* fr. *secundus* second, favorable] (1586) **1 a :** to give support or encouragement to **:** ASSIST **b :** to support (a fighting person or group) in combat **:** bring up reinforcements for **2 a :** to support or assist in contention or debate **b :** to endorse (a motion or a nomination) so that debate or voting may begin **3** *chiefly Brit* **:** to release (as a military officer) from a regularly assigned position for temporary duty with another unit or organization — **sec·ond·er** *n*

[1]**sec·ond·ary** \'sek-ən-ˌder-ē\ *adj* (14c) **1 a :** of second rank, importance, or value **b :** of, relating to, or constituting the second strongest of the three or four degrees of stress recognized by most linguists ⟨the fourth syllable of *basketball team* carries ~ stress⟩ **c** *of a tense* **:** expressive of past time **2 a :** immediately derived from something original, primary, or basic **b :** of or relating to the induced current or its circuit in an induction coil or transformer ⟨a ~ coil⟩ ⟨~ voltage⟩ **c :** characterized by or resulting from the substitution of two atoms or groups in a molecule ⟨a ~ salt⟩; *esp* **:** being or characterized by a carbon atom united by two valences to chain or ring members **d** (1) **:** not first in order of occurrence or development (2) **:** produced by activity of formative tissue and esp. cambium other than that at a growing point ⟨~ growth⟩ ⟨~ phloem⟩ **3 a :** of or relating to the second order or stage in a series **b :** of, relating to, or being the second segment of the wing of a bird or the quills of this segment **c :** of or relating to a secondary school ⟨~ education⟩ — **sec·ond·ari·ly** \ˌsek-ən-'der-ə-lē\ *adv* — **sec·ond·ari·ness** \'sek-ən-ˌder-ē-nəs\ *n*

[2]**secondary** *n, pl* **-ar·ies** (1595) **1 :** one occupying a subordinate or auxiliary position rather than that of a principal **2 :** a defensive football backfield **3 :** a secondary electrical circuit or coil **4 :** any of the quill feathers of the forearm of a bird — see BIRD illustration

secondary cell *n* (ca. 1909) **:** STORAGE CELL

secondary color *n* (1831) **:** a color formed by mixing primary colors in equal or equivalent quantities

secondary emission *n* (1931) **:** the emission of electrons from a surface that is bombarded by particles (as electrons or ions) from a primary source

secondary radiation *n* (1938) **:** rays (as X rays or beta rays) emitted by molecules or atoms as the result of the incidence of a primary radiation

secondary road *n* (1947) **1 :** a road not of primary importance **2 :** a feeder road

secondary root *n* (1861) **:** one of the branches of a primary root

secondary school *n* (1835) **:** a school intermediate between elementary school and college and usu. offering general, technical, vocational, or college-preparatory courses

secondary sex characteristic *n* (1927) **:** a physical characteristic (as the breasts of a female mammal or the nuptial plumage of a male bird) that appears in members of one sex at puberty or in seasonal breeders at the breeding season and is not directly concerned with reproduction — called also *secondary sexual characteristic*

secondary syphilis *n* (ca. 1909) **:** the second stage of syphilis that appears from 2 to 6 months after primary infection, that is marked by lesions esp. in the skin but also in organs and tissues, and that lasts from 3 to 12 weeks

second banana *n* (ca. 1954) **:** a comedian who plays a supporting role to a top banana; *broadly* **:** a person in a subservient position

second base *n* (1845) **1 :** the base that must be touched second by a base runner in baseball **2 :** the player position for defending the area of the baseball infield on the first-base side of second base — **second baseman** *n*

sec·ond–best \ˌsek-ən-'best, -ᵊŋ-\ *adj* (15c) **:** next to the best

[1]**second best** *n* (1708) **:** one that is below or after the best

[2]**second best** *adv* (1777) **:** in second place

second blessing *n* (1929) **:** sanctification as a second gift of the Holy Spirit that follows an initial experience of conversion

second childhood *n* (1901) **:** DOTAGE

second–class *adj* (1837) **1 :** of or relating to a second class **2 :** INFERIOR, MEDIOCRE; *also* **:** socially, politically, or economically deprived ⟨~ citizens⟩

second class *n* (1902) **1 :** the second and usu. next to highest group in a classification **2 :** CABIN CLASS **3 :** a class of U.S. or Canadian mail comprising periodicals sent to regular subscribers

Second Coming *n* (1644) **:** the coming of Christ as judge on the last day

second consonant shift *n* (1939) **:** CONSONANT SHIFT b

second–degree burn *n* (1937) **:** a burn marked by pain, blistering, and superficial destruction of dermis with edema and hyperemia of the tissues beneath the burn

Second Empire \ˌsek-ən-'dem-ˌpī(ə)r\ *adj* (ca. 1934) **:** of, relating to, or characteristic of a style (as of furniture) developed in France under Napoleon III and marked by heavy ornate modification of Empire styles

second estate *n, often cap S&E* (ca. 1935) **:** the second of the traditional political classes; *specif* **:** NOBILITY

second fiddle *n* (1884) **:** one that plays a supporting or subservient role

second growth *n* (1863) **:** forest trees that come up naturally after removal of the first growth by cutting or by fire

sec·ond–guess \ˌsek-ᵊŋ-'ges, -ən-\ *vt* (1949) **1 :** to think out alternative strategies or explanations for after the event **2 a :** OUTGUESS **b :** PREDICT — **sec·ond–guess·er** *n*

[1]**sec·ond·hand** \ˌsek-ən-'\ *adj* (1588) **1 a :** received from or through an intermediary **:** BORROWED **b :** DERIVATIVE ⟨~ ideas⟩ **2 a :** acquired after being used by another **:** not new ⟨~ books⟩ **b :** dealing in secondhand merchandise ⟨a ~ bookstore⟩

[2]**secondhand** *adv* (1682) **:** at second hand **:** INDIRECTLY

[1]**second hand** \ˌsek-ən-'hand\ *n* (1721) **:** an intermediate person or means **:** INTERMEDIARY — usu. used in the phrase *at second hand*

[2]**second hand** \'sek-ən-ˌ\ *n* (1759) **:** the hand marking seconds on a timepiece

second lieutenant *n* (1702) **:** a commissioned officer of the lowest rank in the army, air force, or marine corps

second mortgage *n* (1902) **:** a mortgage the lien of which is subordinate to that of a first mortgage

se·con·do \si-'kōn-(ˌ)dō, -'kän-\ *n, pl* **-di** \-(ˌ)dē\ [It, fr. *secondo,* adj., second, fr. L *secundus*] (ca. 1847) **:** the second part in a concerted piece; *esp* **:** the lower part (as in a piano duet)

second person *n* (1672) **1 a :** a set of linguistic forms (as verb forms, pronouns, and inflectional affixes) referring to the person or thing addressed in the utterance in which they occur **b :** a linguistic form belonging to such a set **2 :** reference of a linguistic form to the person or thing addressed in the utterance in which it occurs

sec·ond–rate \ˌsek-ən-'(d)rāt\ *adj* (1669) **:** of second or inferior quality or value **:** MEDIOCRE — **sec·ond–rate·ness** *n* — **sec·ond–rat·er** \-'(d)rāt-ər\ *n*

Second Reader *n* (1895) **:** a member of a Christian Science church or society chosen for a term of office to assist the First Reader in conducting services by reading aloud selections from the Bible

second reading *n* (1647) **1 :** the stage in the British legislative process following the first reading and usu. providing for debate on the principal features of a bill before its submission to a committee for consideration of details **2 :** the stage in the U.S. legislative process that occurs when a bill has been reported back from committee and that provides an opportunity for full debate and amendment before a vote is taken on the question of a third reading

second sight *n* (1616) **:** the capacity to see remote or future objects or events **:** CLAIRVOYANCE, PRECOGNITION

second–story man *n* (1903) **:** a burglar who enters a house by an upstairs window

sec·ond–string \ˌsek-ən-ˌstriŋ, ˌsek-ᵊŋ-\ *adj* [fr. the reserve bowstring carried by an archer in case the first breaks] (1643) **:** being a substitute as distinguished from a regular (as on a ball team)

second thought *n* (1633) **:** reconsideration or a revised opinion of a previous often hurried decision ⟨began to have *second thoughts*⟩
second wind *n* (1900) **:** renewed energy or endurance
second world *n, often cap S&W* [after *third world*] (1967) **:** the Communist nations as a political and economic bloc
se·cre·cy \'sē-krə-sē\ *n, pl* **-cies** [alter. of earlier *secretie,* fr. ME *secretee,* fr. *secre* secret, fr. MF *secré,* fr. L *secretus*] (15c) **1 :** the habit or practice of keeping secrets or maintaining privacy or concealment **2 :** the condition of being hidden or concealed
1**se·cret** \'sē-krət\ *adj* [ME, fr. MF, fr. L *secretus,* fr. pp. of *secernere* to separate, distinguish, fr. *se-* apart + *cernere* to sift — more at SECEDE, CERTAIN] (14c) **1 a :** kept from knowledge or view **:** HIDDEN **b :** marked by the habit of discretion **:** CLOSEMOUTHED **c :** working with hidden aims or methods **:** UNDERCOVER ⟨a ~ agent⟩ **d :** not acknowledged **:** UNAVOWED ⟨a ~ bride⟩ **e :** conducted in secret ⟨a ~ trial⟩ **2 :** remote from human frequentation or notice **:** SECLUDED **3 :** revealed only to the initiated **:** ESOTERIC **4 :** constructed so as to elude observation or detection ⟨a ~ panel⟩ **5 :** containing information whose unauthorized disclosure could endanger national security — compare CONFIDENTIAL, TOP SECRET — **se·cret·ly** *adv*
syn SECRET, COVERT, STEALTHY, FURTIVE, CLANDESTINE, SURREPTITIOUS, UNDERHANDED mean done without attracting observation. SECRET implies concealment on any grounds for any motive; COVERT stresses the fact of not being open or declared; STEALTHY suggests taking pains to avoid being seen or heard esp. in some misdoing; FURTIVE implies a sly or cautious stealthiness; CLANDESTINE implies secrecy usu. for an evil or illicit purpose; SURREPTITIOUS applies to action or behavior done secretly often with skillful avoidance of detection and in violation of custom, law, or authority; UNDERHANDED stresses fraud or deception.
2**secret** *n* (14c) **1 a :** something kept hidden or unexplained **:** MYSTERY **b :** something kept from the knowledge of others or shared only confidentially with a few **c :** a method, formula, or process used in an art or a manufacturing operation and divulged only to those of one's own company or craft **d** *pl* **:** the practices or knowledge making up the shared discipline or culture of an esoteric society **2 :** a prayer traditionally said inaudibly by the celebrant just before the preface of the mass **3 :** something taken to be a specific or key to a desired end ⟨the ~ of longevity⟩ — **in secret :** in a private place or manner **:** in secrecy
se·cre·ta·gogue \si-'krēt-ə-ˌgäg\ *n* [*secretion* + *-agogue*] (1919) **:** a substance stimulating secretion (as by the stomach or pancreas)
sec·re·tar·i·at \ˌsek-rə-'ter-ē-ət, -ē-ˌat\ *n* [F *secrétariat,* fr. ML *secretariatus,* fr. *secretarius*] (1811) **1 :** the office of secretary **2 :** a secretarial corps; *specif* **:** the clerical staff of an organization **3 :** the administrative department of a governmental organization
sec·re·tary \'sek-rə-ˌter-ē, 'sek-ə-ˌter-, *in rapid speech also* 'sek-ˌter-, *esp Brit* 'sek-(r)ə-trē\ *n, pl* **-tar·ies** [ME *secretarie,* fr. ML *secretarius,* confidential employee, secretary, fr. L *secretum* secret, fr. neut. of *secretus,* pp.] (15c) **1 :** one employed to handle correspondence and manage routine and detail work for a superior **2 a :** an officer of a business concern who may keep records of directors' and stockholders' meetings and of stock ownership and transfer and help supervise the company's legal interests **b :** an officer of an organization or society responsible for its records and correspondence **3 :** an officer of state who superintends a government administrative department **4 a :** WRITING DESK, ESCRITOIRE **b :** a writing desk with a top section for books — **sec·re·tari·al** \ˌsek-rə-'ter-ē-əl\ *adj* — **sec·re·tary·ship** \'sek-rə-ˌter-ē-ˌship\ *n*
secretary bird *n* [prob. fr. the resemblance of its crest to a bunch of quill pens stuck behind the ear] (1797) **:** a large long-legged African bird of prey (*Sagittarius serpentarius*) that feeds largely on reptiles

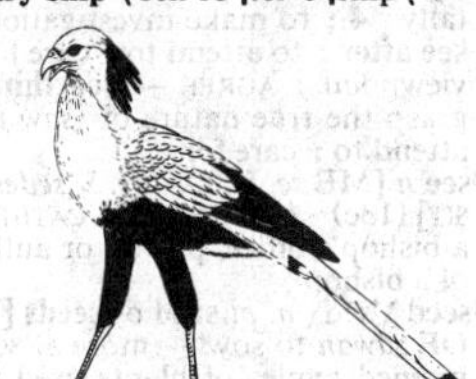
secretary bird

secretary–general *n, pl* **secretaries–general** (1701) **:** a principal administrative officer
secret ballot *n* (1914) **:** AUSTRALIAN BALLOT
1**se·crete** \si-'krēt\ *vt* **se·cret·ed; se·cret·ing** [back-formation fr. *secretion*] (1707) **:** to form and give off (a secretion)
2**se·crete** \si-'krēt, 'sē-krət\ *vt* **se·cret·ed; se·cret·ing** [alter. of obs. *secret,* fr. 1*secret*] (1741) **1 :** to deposit or conceal in a hiding place **2 :** to appropriate secretly **:** ABSTRACT ***syn*** see HIDE
se·cre·tin \si-'krēt-ᵊn\ *n* [*secretion* + *-in*] (1902) **:** an intestinal protein and hormone capable of stimulating secretion by the pancreas and liver
se·cre·tion \si-'krē-shən\ *n* [F *sécrétion,* fr. L *secretion-, secretio* separation, fr. *secretus,* pp. of *secernere* to separate — more at SECRET] (1646) **1 a :** the process of segregating, elaborating, and releasing some material either functionally specialized (as saliva) or isolated for excretion (as urine) **b :** a product of secretion formed by an animal or plant; *esp* **:** one performing a specific useful function in the organism **2** [2*secrete*] **:** the act of hiding something **:** CONCEALMENT — **se·cre·tion·ary** \-shə-ˌner-ē\ *adj*
se·cre·tive \'sē-krət-iv, si-'krēt-\ *adj* [back-formation fr. *secretiveness,* part trans. of F *secrétivité*] (1853) **:** disposed to secrecy **:** not open or outgoing in speech, activity, or purposes ***syn*** see SILENT — **se·cre·tive·ly** *adv* — **se·cre·tive·ness** *n*
se·cre·tor \si-'krēt-ər\ *n* (1947) **:** an individual of blood group A, B, or AB who secretes the antigens characteristic of these blood groups in bodily fluids (as saliva)
se·cre·to·ry \si-'krēt-ə-rē\ *adj* (1692) **:** of, relating to, or promoting secretion; *also* **:** produced by secretion
secret partner *n* (ca. 1909) **:** a partner whose membership in a partnership is kept secret from the public
secret police *n* (1921) **:** a police organization operating for the most part in secrecy and esp. for the political purposes of its government often with terroristic methods
secret service *n* (1737) **1 :** a governmental service of a secret nature **2** *cap both Ss* **:** a division of the U.S. Treasury Department charged chiefly with the suppression of counterfeiting and the protection of the president
secret society *n* (1829) **:** any of various oath-bound societies often devoted to brotherhood, moral discipline, and mutual assistance
sect \'sekt\ *n* [ME *secte,* fr. MF & LL & L; MF, group, sect, fr. LL *secta* organized ecclesiastical body, fr. L, way of life, class of persons, fr. *sequi* to follow — more at SUE] (14c) **1 a :** a dissenting or schismatic religious body; *esp* **:** one regarded as extreme or heretical **b :** a religious denomination **2** *archaic* **:** SEX ⟨so is all her ~ —Shak.⟩ **3 a :** a group adhering to a distinctive doctrine or to a leader **b :** PARTY **c :** FACTION
1**-sect** \ˌsekt\ *adj comb form* [L *sectus,* pp. of *secare* to cut — more at SAW] **:** cut **:** divided ⟨pinnati*sect*⟩
2**-sect** \ˌsekt, 'sekt\ *vb comb form* [L *sectus*] **:** cut **:** divide ⟨bi*sect*⟩
1**sec·tar·i·an** \sek-'ter-ē-ən\ *adj* (1819) **1 :** of, relating to, or characteristic of a sect or sectarian **2 :** limited in character or scope **:** PAROCHIAL — **sec·tar·i·an·ism** \-ē-ə-ˌniz-əm\ *n*
2**sectarian** *n* (1819) **1 :** an adherent of a sect **2 :** a narrow or bigoted person
sec·tar·i·an·ize \sek-'ter-ē-ə-ˌnīz\ *vb* **-ized; -iz·ing** *vi* (1842) **:** to act as sectarians ~ *vt* **:** to make sectarian
sec·ta·ry \'sek-tə-rē\ *n, pl* **-ries** (1558) **:** a member of a sect
sec·tile \'sek-tᵊl, -ˌtīl\ *adj* [L *sectilis,* fr. *sectus*] (1805) **:** capable of being severed by a knife with a smooth cut — **sec·til·i·ty** \sek-'til-ət-ē\ *n*
1**sec·tion** \'sek-shən\ *n* [L *section-, sectio,* fr. *sectus*] (1559) **1 a :** the action or an instance of cutting or separating by cutting **b :** a part set off by or as if by cutting **2 :** a distinct part or portion of something written (as a chapter, law, or newspaper) **3 a :** the profile of something as it would appear if cut through by an intersecting plane **b :** the plane figure resulting from the cutting of a solid by a plane **4 :** a natural subdivision of a taxonomic group **5 :** a character § used as a mark for the beginning of a section and as a reference mark **6 :** a piece of land one square mile in area forming one of the 36 subdivisions of a township **7 :** a distinct part of a territorial or political area, community, or group of people **8 a :** a part that is, may be, or is viewed as separated ⟨chop the stalks into ~*s*⟩ ⟨the northern ~ of the route⟩ **b :** one segment of a fruit **:** CARPEL **9 :** a basic military unit usu. having a special function **10 :** a very thin slice (as of tissue) suitable for microscopic examination **11 a :** one of the classes formed by dividing the students taking a course **b :** one of the discussion groups into which a conference or organization is divided **12 a :** a division of a railroad sleeping car with an upper and a lower berth **b :** a part of a permanent railroad way under the care of a particular crew **c :** one of two or more vehicles or trains which run on the same schedule **13 :** one of several component parts that may be assembled or reassembled ⟨a bookcase in ~*s*⟩ **14 :** a division of an orchestra composed of one class of instruments **15 :** SIGNATURE 3b ***syn*** see PART
2**section** *vb* **sec·tioned; sec·tion·ing** \-sh(ə-)niŋ\ *vt* (1819) **1 :** to cut or separate into sections **2 :** to represent in sections ~ *vi* **:** to become cut or separated into parts
1**sec·tion·al** \'sek-shnəl, -shən-ᵊl\ *adj* (1806) **1 a :** of or relating to a section **b :** local or regional rather than general in character ⟨~ interests⟩ **2 :** consisting of or divided into sections ⟨~ furniture⟩ — **sec·tion·al·ly** \-ē\ *adv*
2**sectional** *n* (1901) **:** a piece of furniture made up of modular units capable of use separately or in various combinations
sec·tion·al·ism \'sek-shnə-ˌliz-əm, -shən-ᵊl-ˌiz-\ *n* (1855) **:** an exaggerated devotion to the interests of a region
Section Eight *n* [*Section VIII,* Army Regulation 615-360, in effect from December 1922 to July 1944] (1945) **1 :** a discharge from the U.S. Army for military inaptitude or undesirable habits or traits of character **2 :** a soldier discharged for military inaptitude or undesirable habits or traits of character
section gang *n* (1890) **:** a crew of track workers employed to maintain a railroad section
section hand *n* (1873) **:** a laborer belonging to a section gang
1**sec·tor** \'sek-tər, -ˌtȯ(ə)r\ *n* [LL, fr. L, cutter, fr. *sectus,* pp. of *secare* to cut — more at SAW] (1570) **1 a :** a geometric figure bounded by two radii and the included arc of a circle **b (1) :** a subdivision of a defensive military position **(2) :** a portion of a military front or area of operation **2 :** a mathematical instrument consisting of two rulers connected at one end by a joint and marked with several scales **3 :** a distinctive part (as of an economy)
2**sec·tor** \-tər\ *vt* **sec·tored; sec·tor·ing** \-t(ə-)riŋ\ (1884) **:** to divide into or furnish with sectors
sec·to·ri·al \sek-'tōr-ē-əl, -'tȯr-\ *adj* (1803) **1 :** of, relating to, or having the shape of a sector of a circle **2** *of a chimera* **:** having a sector of variant growth interposed in an otherwise normal body of tissue
1**sec·u·lar** \'sek-yə-lər\ *adj* [ME, fr. OF *seculer,* fr. LL *saecularis,* fr. L, coming once in an age, fr. *saeculum* breed, generation; akin to L *serere* to sow — more at SOW] (13c) **1 a :** of or relating to the worldly or temporal ⟨~ concerns⟩ **b :** not overtly or specif. religious ⟨~ music⟩ **c :** not ecclesiastical or clerical ⟨~ courts⟩ ⟨~ landowners⟩ **2 :** not bound by monastic vows or rules; *specif* **:** of, relating to, or forming clergy not belonging to a religious order or congregation ⟨a ~ priest⟩ **3 a :** occurring once in an age or a century **b :** existing or continuing through ages or centuries **c :** of or relating to a long term of indefinite duration — **sec·u·lar·i·ty** \ˌsek-yə-'lar-ət-ē\ *n* — **sec·u·lar·ly** \'sek-yə-lər-lē\ *adv*
2**secular** *n, pl* **seculars** *or* **secular** (13c) **1 :** a secular ecclesiastic (as a diocesan priest) **2 :** LAYMAN
sec·u·lar·ism \'sek-yə-lə-ˌriz-əm\ *n* (1851) **:** indifference to or rejection or exclusion of religion and religious considerations — **sec·u·lar·ist** \-rəst\ *n* — **secularist** *or* **sec·u·lar·is·tic** \ˌsek-yə-lə-'ris-tik\ *adj*
sec·u·lar·ize \'sek-yə-lə-ˌrīz\ *vt* **-ized; -iz·ing** (1611) **1 :** to make secular **2 :** to transfer from ecclesiastical to civil or lay use, possession, or control **3 :** to convert to or imbue with secularism — **sec·u·lar·iza·tion** \ˌsek-yə-lə-rə-'zā-shən\ *n* — **sec·u·lar·iz·er** *n*

\ə\ abut \ᵊ\ kitten, F table \ər\ further \a\ ash \ā\ ace \ä\ cot, cart \au̇\ out \ch\ chin \e\ bet \ē\ easy \g\ go \i\ hit \ī\ ice \j\ job \ŋ\ sing \ō\ go \ȯ\ law \ȯi\ boy \th\ thin \th\ the \ü\ loot \u̇\ foot \y\ yet \zh\ vision \à, k, ⁿ, œ, œ̄, ue, ue̅, ʸ\ *see* Guide to Pronunciation

se·cund \si-ˈkənd, ˈsē-ˌ\ *adj* [L *secundus* following — more at SECOND] (1777) **:** having some part or element arranged on one side only **:** UNILATERAL ⟨~ racemes⟩

1se·cure \si-ˈkyu̇(ə)r\ *adj* **se·cur·er; -est** [L *securus* safe, secure, fr. *se* without + *cura* care — more at IDIOT, CURE] (1533) **1 a** *archaic* **:** unwisely free from fear or distrust **:** OVERCONFIDENT **b :** easy in mind **:** CONFIDENT **c :** assured in opinion or expectation **:** having no doubt **2 a :** free from danger **b :** free from risk of loss **c :** affording safety **:** INVIOLABLE ⟨a ~ hideaway⟩ **d :** TRUSTWORTHY, DEPENDABLE ⟨~ foundation⟩ **3 :** ASSURED, CERTAIN ⟨~ victory⟩ — **se·cure·ly** *adv* — **se·cure·ness** *n*

2secure *vb* **se·cured; se·cur·ing** *vt* (1593) **1 a :** to relieve from exposure to danger **:** act to make safe against adverse contingencies ⟨he locked the door to ~ them from interruption⟩ ⟨~ a supply line from enemy raids⟩ **b :** to put beyond hazard of losing or of not receiving **:** GUARANTEE ⟨~ the blessings of liberty —*U.S. Constitution*⟩ **c :** to give pledge of payment to (a creditor) or of (an obligation) ⟨~ a note by a pledge of collateral⟩ **2 a :** to take (a person) into custody **:** hold fast **:** PINION **b :** to make fast **:** SEAL ⟨~ a door⟩ **3 a :** to get secure usu. lasting possession or control of ⟨~ employment⟩ **b :** BRING ABOUT, EFFECT **4 :** to release (naval personnel) from work or duty ~ *vi* **1** *of naval personnel* **:** to stop work **:** go off duty **2** *of a ship* **:** to tie up **:** BERTH ***syn*** see ENSURE — **se·cur·er** *n*

se·cure·ment \si-ˈkyu̇(ə)r-mənt\ *n* (1622) **1** *obs* **:** PROTECTION **2 :** the act or process of securing

se·cu·ri·ty \si-ˈkyu̇r-ət-ē\ *n, pl* **-ties** (15c) **1 :** the quality or state of being secure: as **a :** freedom from danger **:** SAFETY **b :** freedom from fear or anxiety **c :** freedom from want or deprivation ⟨job ~⟩ **2 a :** something given, deposited, or pledged to make certain the fulfillment of an obligation **b :** SURETY **3 :** an evidence of debt or of ownership (as a stock certificate or bond) **4 a :** something that secures **:** PROTECTION **b (1) :** measures taken to guard against espionage or sabotage, crime, attack, or escape **(2) :** an organization or department whose task is security

security blanket *n* (1968) **1 :** a blanket carried by a child as a protection against anxiety **2 :** a usu. familiar object whose presence dispels anxiety

Security Council *n* (1945) **:** a permanent council of the United Nations having primary responsibility for the maintenance of peace and security

security interest *n* (1951) **:** the rights that a creditor has in the personal property of a debtor that secures an obligation **:** LIEN

security police *n* (1920) **1 :** police engaged in counterespionage **2 :** AIR POLICE

se·dan \si-ˈdan\ *n* [origin unknown] (1635) **1 :** a portable often covered chair that is designed to carry one person and that is borne on poles by two men **2 a :** an enclosed automobile seating 4 to 7 persons including the driver and having a single compartment, 2 or 4 doors, and a permanent top **b :** a motorboat having one passenger compartment

1se·date \si-ˈdāt\ *adj* [L *sedatus*, fr. pp. of *sedare* to calm; akin to *sedēre* to sit — more at SIT] (1663) **:** keeping a quiet steady attitude or pace **:** UNRUFFLED ***syn*** see SERIOUS — **se·date·ly** *adv* — **se·date·ness** *n*

2sedate *vt* **se·dat·ed; se·dat·ing** [back-formation fr. *sedative*] (1945) **:** to dose with sedatives

se·da·tion \si-ˈdā-shən\ *n* [MF or L; MF, fr. L *sedation-, sedatio*, fr. *sedatus*, pp.] (1543) **1 :** the inducing of a relaxed easy state esp. by the use of sedatives **2 :** a state resulting from or like that resulting from sedation

1sed·a·tive \ˈsed-ət-iv\ *adj* [ME *sedatyve*, fr. MF *sedatif*, fr. ML *sedativus*, fr. L *sedatus*] (15c) **:** tending to calm, moderate, or tranquilize nervousness or excitement

2sedative *n* (1797) **:** a sedative agent or drug

sed·en·tary \ˈsed-ᵊn-ˌter-ē\ *adj* [MF *sedentaire*, fr. L *sedentarius*, fr. *sedent-, sedens*, prp. of *sedēre* to sit] (1598) **1 :** not migratory **:** SETTLED ⟨~ birds⟩ **2 :** doing or requiring much sitting **3 :** permanently attached ⟨~ barnacles⟩

se·der \ˈsād-ər\ *n, often cap* [Heb *sēdher* order] (1865) **:** a Jewish home or community service including a ceremonial dinner held on the first evening of the Passover and repeated on the second by Orthodox Jews except in Israel in commemoration of the exodus from Egypt

se·de·runt \sə-ˈdir-ənt, -ˈder-\ *n* [L, there (they) sat (fr. *sedēre* to sit), word used to introduce list of those attending a session — more at SIT] (1825) **:** a prolonged sitting (as for discussion)

sedge \ˈsej\ *n* [ME *segge*, fr. OE *secg;* akin to MHG *segge* sedge, OE *sagu* saw — more at SAW] (bef. 12c) **:** any of a family (Cyperaceae, the sedge family) of usu. tufted marsh plants differing from the related grasses in having achenes and solid stems; *esp* **:** any of a cosmopolitan genus (*Carex*) — **sedgy** \ˈsej-ē\ *adj*

se·di·lia \sə-ˈdēl-yə, -ˈdil-, *esp Brit* -ˈdīl-\ *n pl* [L, pl. of *sedile* seat, fr. *sedēre*] (1793) **:** seats on the south side of the chancel for the celebrant, deacon, and subdeacon

1sed·i·ment \ˈsed-ə-mənt\ *n* [MF, fr. L *sedimentum* settling, fr. *sedēre* to sit, sink down] (1547) **1 :** the matter that settles to the bottom of a liquid **2 :** material deposited by water, wind, or glaciers

2sed·i·ment \-ˌment\ *vt* (1859) **:** to deposit as sediment ~ *vi* **1 :** to settle to the bottom in a liquid **2 :** to deposit sediment

sed·i·ment·able \ˌsed-ə-ˈment-ə-bəl\ *adj* (1944) **:** capable of being sedimented by centrifugation ⟨~ ribosomal particles⟩

sed·i·men·ta·ry \ˌsed-ə-ˈment-ə-rē, -ˈmen-trē\ *adj* (1830) **1 :** of, relating to, or containing sediment ⟨~ deposits⟩ **2 :** formed by or from deposits of sediment

sedimentary rock *n* (1839) **:** rock formed of mechanical, chemical, or organic sediment: as **a :** rock (as sandstone or shale) formed of fragments transported from their source and deposited elsewhere by water **b :** rock (as rock salt or gypsum) formed by precipitation or solution **c :** rock (as limestone) formed from inorganic remains (as shells and skeletons) of organisms

sed·i·men·ta·tion \ˌsed-ə-mən-ˈtā-shən, -ˌmen-\ *n* (1874) **:** the action or process of forming or depositing sediment **:** SETTLING

sed·i·men·tol·o·gy \ˌsed-ə-mən-ˈtäl-ə-jē, -ˌmen-\ *n* (1937) **:** a branch of science that deals with sedimentary rocks and their inclusions — **sed·i·men·to·log·ic** \-ˌment-ᵊl-ˈäj-ik\ *or* **sed·i·men·to·log·i·cal** \-i-kəl\ *adj* — **sed·i·men·to·log·i·cal·ly** \-i-k(ə-)lē\ *adv* — **sed·i·men·tol·o·gist** \-mən-ˈtäl-ə-jəst, -ˌmen-\ *n*

se·di·tion \si-ˈdish-ən\ *n* [ME, fr. MF, fr. L *sedition-, seditio*, lit., separation, fr. *se-* apart + *ition-, itio* act of going, fr. *itus*, pp. of *ire* to go — more at SECEDE, ISSUE] (14c) **:** incitement of resistance to or insurrection against lawful authority

se·di·tious \si-ˈdish-əs\ *adj* (15c) **1 :** disposed to arouse or take part in or guilty of sedition **2 :** of, relating to, or tending toward sedition — **se·di·tious·ly** *adv* — **se·di·tious·ness** *n*

se·duce \si-ˈd(y)üs\ *vt* **se·duced; se·duc·ing** [ME *seducen*, fr. LL *seducere*, fr. L, to lead away, fr. *se-* apart + *ducere* to lead — more at TOW] (15c) **1 :** to persuade to disobedience or disloyalty **2 :** to lead astray usu. by persuasion or false promises **3 :** to carry out the physical seduction of **4 :** ATTRACT ***syn*** see LURE — **se·duc·er** *n*

se·duce·ment \-ˈd(y)ü-smənt\ *n* (1586) **1 :** SEDUCTION **2 :** something that serves to seduce

se·duc·tion \si-ˈdək-shən\ *n* [MF, fr. LL *seduction-, seductio*, fr. L, act of leading aside, fr. *seductus*, pp. of *seducere*] (1526) **1 :** the act of seducing to wrong; *specif* **:** the enticement of a female to unlawful sexual intercourse without use of force **2 :** something that seduces **:** TEMPTATION **3 :** something that attracts or charms

se·duc·tive \-ˈdək-tiv\ *adj* (1766) **:** tending to seduce **:** having alluring or tempting qualities ⟨a ~ woman⟩ ⟨a ~ spring morning⟩ — **se·duc·tive·ly** *adv* — **se·duc·tive·ness** *n*

se·duc·tress \-ˈdək-trəs\ *n* [obs. *seductor* male seducer, fr. LL, fr. *seductus*, pp. of *seducere* to seduce] (1803) **:** a woman who seduces

se·du·li·ty \si-ˈd(y)ü-lət-ē\ *n* (1542) **:** sedulous activity **:** DILIGENCE

sed·u·lous \ˈsej-ə-ləs\ *adj* [L *sedulus*, fr. *sedulo* sincerely, diligently, fr. *se* without + *dolus* guile — more at IDIOT, TALE] (1540) **1 :** involving or accomplished with careful perseverance ⟨~ craftsmanship⟩ **2 :** diligent in application or pursuit ⟨a ~ student⟩ ***syn*** see BUSY — **sed·u·lous·ly** *adv* — **sed·u·lous·ness** *n*

se·dum \ˈsēd-əm\ *n* [NL, fr. L, houseleek] (15c) **:** any of a genus (*Sedum*) of fleshy widely distributed herbs of the orpine family **:** STONECROP

1see \ˈsē\ *vb* **saw** \ˈsȯ\; **seen** \ˈsēn\; **see·ing** \ˈsē-iŋ\ [ME *seen*, fr. OE *sēon;* akin to OHG *sehan* to see, OE *secgan* to say — more at SAY] *vt* (bef. 12c) **1 :** to perceive by the eye **2 a :** to have experience of **:** UNDERGO ⟨~ army service⟩ **b :** to come to know **:** DISCOVER **3 a :** to form a mental picture of **:** VISUALIZE ⟨can still ~ her as she was years ago⟩ **b :** to perceive the meaning or importance of **:** UNDERSTAND **c :** to be aware of **:** RECOGNIZE ⟨~*s* only our faults⟩ **d :** to imagine as a possibility **:** SUPPOSE ⟨couldn't ~ him as a crook⟩ **4 a :** EXAMINE, WATCH ⟨want to ~ how he handles the problem⟩ **b (1) :** READ **(2) :** to read of **c :** to attend as a spectator ⟨~ a play⟩ **5 a :** to take care of **:** provide for ⟨had enough money to ~ us through⟩ **b :** to make sure ⟨~ that order is kept⟩ **6 a :** to regard as **:** JUDGE **b :** to prefer to have ⟨I'll ~ him hanged first⟩ ⟨I'll ~ you dead before I accept your terms⟩ **c :** to find acceptable or attractive ⟨can't understand what he ~*s* in her⟩ **7 a :** to call on **:** VISIT **b (1) :** to keep company with esp. in courtship or dating ⟨had been ~*ing* each other for a year⟩ **(2) :** to grant an interview to **:** RECEIVE ⟨the president will ~ you⟩ **8 :** ACCOMPANY, ESCORT ⟨~ the girls home⟩ **9 :** to meet (a bet) in poker or to equal the bet of (a player) **:** CALL ~ *vi* **1 a :** to give or pay attention **b :** to look about **2 a :** to have the power of sight **b :** to apprehend objects by sight **3 :** to grasp something mentally **4 :** to make investigation or inquiry — **see·able** \-ə-bəl\ *adj* — **see after :** to attend to **:** care for — **see eye to eye :** to have a common viewpoint **:** AGREE — **see things :** HALLUCINATE — **see through :** to grasp the true nature of ⟨*saw through* their deceptions⟩ — **see to :** to attend to **:** care for

2see *n* [ME *se*, fr. OF, fr. L *sedes* seat; akin to L *sedēre* to sit — more at SIT] (13c) **1 a** *archaic* **:** CATHEDRA **b :** a cathedral town **c :** a seat of a bishop's office, power, or authority **2 :** the authority or jurisdiction of a bishop

1seed \ˈsēd\ *n, pl* **seed** *or* **seeds** [ME, fr. OE *sǣd;* akin to OHG *sāt* seed, OE *sāwan* to sow — more at SOW] (bef. 12c) **1 a (1) :** the grains or ripened ovules of plants used for sowing **(2) :** the fertilized ripened ovule of a flowering plant containing an embryo and capable normally of germination to produce a new plant; *broadly* **:** a propagative plant structure (as a spore or small dry fruit) **b :** a propagative animal structure: **(1) :** MILT, SEMEN **(2) :** a small egg (as of an insect) **(3) :** a developmental form of a lower animal suitable for transplanting; *specif* **:** SPAT **c :** the condition or stage of bearing seed ⟨in ~⟩ **2 :** PROGENY **3 :** a source of development or growth **:** GERM ⟨sowed the ~*s* of discord⟩ **4 :** something (as a tiny particle or a bubble in glass) that resembles a seed in shape or size **5 :** a competitor who has been seeded in a tournament — **seed** *adj* — **seed·ed** \-əd\ *adj* — **seed·less** \-ləs\ *adj* — **seed·like** \-ˌlīk\ *adj* — **go to seed** *or* **run to seed 1 :** to develop seed **2 :** DECAY

2seed *vi* (15c) **1 :** to sow seed **:** PLANT **2 :** to bear or shed seed ~ *vt* **1 a :** to plant seeds in **:** SOW ⟨~ land to grass⟩ **b :** to furnish with something that causes or stimulates growth or development **c :** INOCULATE **d :** to supply with nuclei (as of crystallization or condensation); *esp* **:** to treat (a cloud) with solid particles to convert water droplets into ice crystals in an attempt to produce precipitation **2 :** PLANT 1a **3 :** to extract the seeds from (as raisins) **4 a :** to schedule (tournament players or teams) so that superior ones will not meet in early rounds **b :** to rank (a contestant) relative to others in a tournament on the basis of previous record ⟨the top-*seeded* tennis star⟩

seed·bed \ˈsēd-ˌbed\ *n* (1660) **1 :** soil or a bed of soil prepared for planting seed **2 :** a place or source of growth or development

seed·cake \-ˌkāk\ *n* (1573) **1 :** a cake or cookie containing aromatic seeds (as sesame or caraway) **2 :** OIL CAKE

seed coat *n* (1796) **:** an outer protective covering of a seed

seed·eat·er \ˈsēd-ˌēt-ər\ *n* (ca. 1879) **:** a bird (as a finch) whose diet consists basically of seeds

seed·er \ˈsēd-ər\ *n* (1867) **1 :** an implement for planting or sowing seeds **2 :** a device for seeding fruit **3 :** one that seeds clouds

seed fern *n* (1927) **:** any of an order (Cycadofilicales) of extinct plants with foliage like that of ferns and with naked seeds

seed leaf *n* (1693) **:** COTYLEDON 2

seed·ling \'sēd-liŋ\ *n* (1660) **1 :** a young plant grown from seed **2 a :** a young tree before it becomes a sapling **b :** a nursery plant not yet transplanted — **seedling** *adj*

seed money *n* (1943) **:** money used for setting up a new enterprise

seed oyster *n* (1885) **:** a young oyster esp. of a size for transplantation

seed pearl *n* (1553) **1 :** a very small and often irregular pearl **2 :** minute pearls imbedded in some binding material

seed plant *n* (1707) **:** a plant that bears seeds; *specif* **:** SPERMATOPHYTE

seed·pod \'sēd-ˌpäd\ *n* (1718) **:** [2]POD 1

seeds·man \'sēdz-mən\ *n* (1601) **1 :** one who sows seeds **2 :** a dealer in seeds

seed stock *n* (1926) **:** a supply (as of seed) for planting; *broadly* **:** a source of new individuals ⟨a *seed stock* of trout in the streams⟩

seed tick *n* (1705) **:** the 6-legged larva of a tick

seed·time \'sēd-ˌtīm\ *n* (15c) **1 :** the season of sowing **2 :** a period of original development

seed vessel *n* (1668) **:** PERICARP

seedy \'sēd-ē\ *adj* **seed·i·er; -est** (1574) **1 a :** containing or full of seeds ⟨a ~ fruit⟩ **b :** containing many small similar inclusions ⟨glass ~ with air bubbles⟩ **2 :** inferior in condition or quality: as **a :** SHABBY, RUN-DOWN ⟨~ clothes⟩ **b :** somewhat disreputable **:** SQUALID ⟨a ~ district⟩ ⟨~ entertainment⟩ **c :** slightly unwell **:** DEBILITATED ⟨felt ~ and went home early⟩ — **seed·i·ly** \'sēd-ᵊl-ē\ *adv* — **seed·i·ness** \'sēd-ē-nəs\ *n*

see·ing \'sē-iŋ\ *conj* (1503) **:** INASMUCH AS

Seeing Eye *trademark* — used for a guide dog trained to lead the blind

seek \'sēk\ *vb* **sought** \'sȯt\; **seek·ing** [ME *seken,* fr. OE *sēcan;* akin to OHG *suohhen* to seek, L *sagire* to perceive keenly, Gk *hēgeisthai* to lead] *vt* (bef. 12c) **1 :** to resort to **:** go to **2 a :** to go in search of **:** look for **b :** to try to discover **3 :** to ask for **:** REQUEST ⟨~*s* advice⟩ **4 :** to try to acquire or gain **:** aim at ⟨~ fame⟩ **5 :** to make an attempt **:** TRY — used with an infinitive ⟨governments . . . ~ to keep the bulk of their people contented —D. M. Potter⟩ ~ *vi* **1 :** to make a search or inquiry **2 a :** to be sought **b :** to be lacking ⟨in critical judgment . . . they were sadly to ~ —*Times Lit. Supp.*⟩ — **seek·er** *n*

seel \'sē(ə)l\ *vt* [alter. of ME *silen,* fr. MF *siller,* fr. ML *ciliare,* fr. L *cilium* eyelid] (1500) **1 :** to close the eyes of (as a hawk) by drawing threads through the eyelids **2** *archaic* **:** to close up (one's eyes)

see·ly \'sē-lē\ *adj* [ME *sely* — more at SILLY] *archaic* (13c) **:** pitiable esp. because of weak physical or mental condition **:** FRAIL

seem \'sēm\ *vi* [ME *semen,* of Scand origin; akin to ON *sōma* to beseem, *samr* same — more at SAME] (13c) **1 :** to give the impression of being **2 :** to appear to the observation or understanding

[1]**seem·ing** *n* (14c) **:** external appearance as distinguished from true character **:** LOOK

[2]**seeming** *adj* (14c) **:** having an often deceptive or delusive appearance on superficial examination ⟨their wealth gave them a ~ security⟩ ***syn*** see APPARENT — **seem·ing·ly** \'sē-miŋ-lē\ *adv*

seem·ly \'sēm-lē\ *adj* **seem·li·er; -est** [ME *semely,* fr. ON *sœmiligr,* fr. *sœmr* becoming; akin to ON *sōma* to beseem] (13c) **1 a :** GOOD-LOOKING, HANDSOME **b :** agreeably fashioned **:** ATTRACTIVE **2 :** conventionally proper **:** DECOROUS **3 :** suited to the occasion, purpose, or person **:** FIT — **seem·li·ness** *n* — **seemly** *adv*

seen *past part of* SEE

[1]**seep** \'sēp\ *vi* [alter. of earlier *sipe,* fr. ME *sipen,* fr. OE *sipian;* akin to MLG *sipen* to seep] (1790) **:** to flow or pass slowly through fine pores or small openings **:** OOZE ⟨water ~*ed* in through a crack⟩

[2]**seep** *n* (ca. 1825) **1 a :** a spot where a fluid (as water, oil, or gas) contained in the ground oozes slowly to the surface and often forms a pool **b :** a small spring **2 :** SEEPAGE — **seepy** \'sē-pē\ *adj*

seep·age \'sē-pij\ *n* (ca. 1825) **1 :** the process of seeping **:** OOZING **2 :** a quantity of fluid that has seeped (as through porous material)

[1]**seer** \'si(ə)r, *esp for 1 also* 'sē-ər\ *n* (15c) **1 :** one that sees **2 a :** one that predicts events or developments **b :** a person credited with extraordinary moral and spiritual insight **3 :** one that practices divination esp. by concentrating on a glass or crystal globe

[2]**seer** \'si(ə)r\ *n, pl* **seers** *or* **seer** [Hindi *ser*] (1618) **1 :** any of various Indian units of weight; *esp* **:** a unit equal to 2.057 pounds (0.9330 kilograms) **2 :** an Afghan unit of weight equal to 15.6 pounds (7.08 kilograms)

seer·ess \'si(ə)r-əs\ *n* (1845) **:** a woman who predicts events or developments **:** PROPHETESS

seer·suck·er \'si(ə)r-ˌsək-ər\ *n* [Hindi *śīrśaker,* fr. Per *shīr-o-shakar,* lit., milk and sugar] (1722) **:** a light fabric of linen, cotton, or rayon usu. striped and slightly puckered

[1]**see·saw** \'sē-ˌsȯ\ *n* [prob. fr. redupl. of [3]*saw*] (1704) **1 :** an alternating up-and-down or backward-and-forward motion or movement; *also* **:** a contest or struggle in which now one side now the other has the lead **2 a :** a pastime in which two children or groups of children ride on opposite ends of a plank balanced in the middle so that one end goes up as the other goes down **b :** the plank or apparatus so used — **seesaw** *adj*

[2]**seesaw** *vi* (1712) **1 a :** to move backward and forward or up and down **b :** to play at seesaw **2 :** ALTERNATE ~ *vt* **:** to cause to move in seesaw fashion

[1]**seethe** \'sēth\ *vb* **seethed; seeth·ing** [ME *sethen,* fr. OE *sēothan;* akin to OHG *siodan* to seethe, Lith *siausti* to rage] *vt* (bef. 12c) **1** *archaic* **:** BOIL, STEW **2 :** to soak or saturate in a liquid ~ *vi* **1** *archaic* **:** BOIL **2 a :** to be in a state of rapid agitated movement **b :** to churn or foam as if boiling **3 :** to suffer violent internal excitement

[2]**seethe** *n* (1816) **:** a state of seething **:** EBULLITION

seeth·ing *adj* (14c) **1 :** intensely hot **:** BOILING ⟨a ~ inferno⟩ **2 :** constantly moving or active **:** AGITATED

see–through \'sē-ˌthrü\ *adj* (1945) **:** TRANSPARENT — **see–through** *n*

[1]**seg·ment** \'seg-mənt\ *n* [L *segmentum,* fr. *secare* to cut — more at SAW] (1570) **1 a :** a separate piece of something **:** BIT, FRAGMENT ⟨chop the stalks into short ~*s*⟩ **b :** one of the constituent parts into which a body, entity, or quantity is divided or marked off by or as if by natural boundaries ⟨all ~*s* of the population agree⟩ **2 :** a portion cut off from a geometric figure by one or more points, lines, or planes: as **a :** the part of a circular area bounded by a chord and an arc of that circle or so much of the area as is cut off by the chord **b :** the part of a sphere cut off by a plane or included between two parallel planes **c :** the finite part of a line between two points in the line ***syn*** see PART — **seg·men·tary** \-mən-ˌter-ē\ *adj*

[2]**seg·ment** \'seg-ˌment\ *vt* (1859) **:** to separate into segments **:** give off as segments

seg·men·tal \seg-'ment-ᵊl\ *adj* (1816) **1 :** of, relating to, or having the form of a segment and esp. the sector of a circle ⟨~ fanlight⟩ **2 :** of, relating to, or composed of somites or metameres **:** METAMERIC **3 a :** divided into segments ⟨~ knowledge⟩ **b :** PARTIAL, INCOMPLETE **c :** resulting from segmentation — **seg·men·tal·ly** \-ᵊl-ē\ *adv*

seg·men·ta·tion \ˌseg-mən-'tā-shən, -ˌmen-\ *n* (1851) **:** the process of dividing into segments; *esp* **:** the formation of many cells from a single cell (as in a developing egg)

segmentation cavity *n* (1888) **:** BLASTOCOEL

seg·ment·ed \'seg-ˌment-əd, seg-'\ *adj* (1854) **:** divided into or composed of segments or sections ⟨~ worms⟩

se·gno \'sān-(ˌ)yō\ *n, pl* **segnos** [It, sign, fr. L *signum* — more at SIGN] (1908) **:** a notational sign; *specif* **:** the sign that marks the beginning or end of a musical repeat

se·go lily \ˌsē-(ˌ)gō-\ *n* [*sego* (the bulb of the sego lily), fr. Paiute] (1913) **:** a mariposa lily (*Calochortus nuttallii*) of western No. America having mostly white or in some areas mostly yellow flowers mottled with variable amounts of a darker color

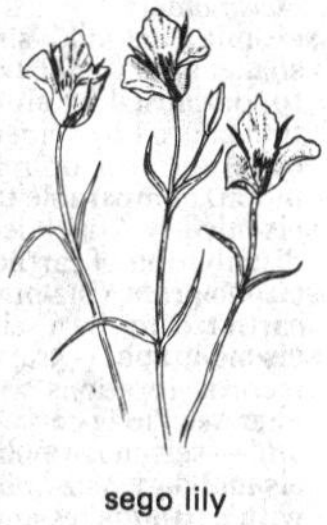

sego lily

seg·re·gant \'seg-ri-gənt\ *n* (1926) **:** a genetic segregate

[1]**seg·re·gate** \'seg-ri-ˌgāt\ *vb* **-gat·ed; -gat·ing** [L *segregatus,* pp. of *segregare,* fr. *se-* apart + *greg-, grex* herd — more at SECEDE, GREGARIOUS] *vt* (1542) **1 :** to separate or set apart from others or from the general mass **:** ISOLATE **2 :** to cause or force the separation of (as from the rest of society) ~ *vi* **1 :** SEPARATE, WITHDRAW **2 :** to practice or enforce a policy of segregation **3 :** to undergo genetic segregation — **seg·re·ga·tive** \-ˌgāt-iv\ *adj*

[2]**seg·re·gate** \'seg-ri-gət, -ˌgāt\ *n* (1871) **:** one that is in some respect segregated; *esp* **:** one that differs genetically from the parental line because of genetic segregation

seg·re·gat·ed *adj* (1652) **1 a :** set apart or separated from others of the same kind or group ⟨a ~ account in a bank⟩ **b :** divided in facilities or administered separately for members of different groups or races ⟨~ education⟩ **c :** restricted to members of one group or one race by a policy of segregation ⟨~ schools⟩ **2 :** practicing or maintaining segregation esp. of races ⟨~ states⟩

seg·re·ga·tion \ˌseg-ri-'gā-shən\ *n* (1555) **1 :** the act or process of segregating **:** the state of being segregated **2 a :** the separation or isolation of a race, class, or ethnic group by enforced or voluntary residence in a restricted area, by barriers to social intercourse, by separate educational facilities, or by other discriminatory means **b :** the separation for special treatment or observation of individuals or items from a larger group ⟨~ of gifted children into accelerated classes⟩ **3 :** the separation of allelic genes that occurs typically during meiosis

seg·re·ga·tion·ist \-sh(ə-)nəst\ *n* (1913) **:** a person who believes in or practices segregation esp. of races — **segregationist** *adj*

[1]**se·gue** \'sāg-(ˌ)wā, 'seg-\ *vb imper* [It, there follows, fr. *seguire* to follow, fr. L *sequi* — more at SUE] (ca. 1854) **1 :** proceed to what follows without pause — used as a direction in music **2 :** perform the music that follows like that which has preceded — used as a direction in music

[2]**segue** *vi* **se·gued; se·gue·ing** (ca. 1913) **1 :** to proceed without pause from one musical number or theme to another **2 :** to proceed without interruption from one activity, topic, scene, or part to another

[3]**segue** *n* (ca. 1961) **:** the act or an instance of segueing

se·gui·di·lla \ˌseg-ə-'dē-(y)ə, -'dēl-yə\ *n* [Sp, dim. of *seguida,* a dance, lit., sequence, fr. *seguido,* pp. of *seguir* to follow, fr. L *sequi*] (1763) **1 a :** a Spanish dance with many regional variations **b :** the music for such a dance **2 :** a Spanish stanza of four or seven short partly assonant verses

sei \'sā, 'sī\ *n* [short for *sei whale,* part trans. of Norw *seihval,* fr. *sei* coalfish + *hval* whale; fr. its habit of following the coalfish in search of food] (1912) **:** a common and widely distributed white-spotted rorqual (*Balaenoptera borealis*) that grows to a length of nearly 60 feet (18.3 meters) — called also *sei whale*

sei·cen·to \sā-'chen-(ˌ)tō\ *n* [It, lit., six-hundred, fr. *sei* six (fr. L *sex*) + *cento* hundred — more at SIX, CINQUECENTO] (1902) **:** the 17th century; *specif* **:** the 17th century period in Italian literature and art

seiche \'sāsh, 'sēch\ *n* [F] (1839) **:** an oscillation of the surface of a lake or landlocked sea that varies in period from a few minutes to several hours

sei·del \'sīd-ᵊl, 'zīd-\ *n* [G, fr. L *situla* bucket] (1908) **:** a large glass for beer

Seid·litz powders \'sed-ləts-\ *n pl* [*Sedlitz,* Bohemia, Czechoslovakia; fr. the similarity of their effect to that of the water of the village] (1815) **:** effervescing salts consisting of one powder of sodium bicarbonate and Rochelle salt and another of tartaric acid that are mixed in water and drunk as a mild cathartic

sei·gneur \sān-'yər\ *n, often cap* [MF, fr. ML *senior,* fr. L, adj., elder — more at SENIOR] (1592) **1 :** a man of rank or authority; *esp* **:** the feudal lord of a manor **2 :** a member of the landed gentry of Canada

sei·gneur·ial \-'yu̇r-ē-əl, -'yər-\ *adj* (1656) **:** of, relating to, or befitting a seigneur

sei·gneury \'sān-yə-rē\ *n, pl* **-gneur·ies** (1683) **1 a :** the territory under the government of a feudal lord **b :** a landed estate held in Canada by feudal tenure until 1854 **2 :** the manor house of a Canadian seigneur

sei·gnior \sān-'yō(ə)r, 'sān-ˌ\ *n* [ME *seignour,* fr. MF *seigneur*] (14c) **:** SEIGNEUR 1

sei·gnior·age *or* **sei·gnor·age** \'sān-yə-rij\ *n* [ME *seigneurage,* fr. MF, right of the lord (esp. to coin money), fr. *seigneur*] (15c) **:** a government

\ə\ abut \ᵊ\ kitten, F table \ər\ further \a\ ash \ā\ ace \ä\ cot, cart \au̇\ out \ch\ chin \e\ bet \ē\ easy \g\ go \i\ hit \ī\ ice \j\ job \ŋ\ sing \ō\ go \ȯ\ law \ȯi\ boy \th\ thin \th\ the \ü\ loot \u̇\ foot \y\ yet \zh\ vision \à, k̟, ⁿ, œ, œ̄, ue, ue̅, ʸ\ see Guide to Pronunciation

revenue from the manufacture of coins calculated as the difference between the face value and the metal value of the coins

sei·gniory *or* **sei·gnory** \'sān-yə-rē\ *n, pl* **-gnior·ies** *or* **-gnor·ies** (13c) **1** : LORDSHIP, DOMINION; *specif* : the power or authority of a feudal lord **2** : the territory over which a lord holds jurisdiction

sei·gno·ri·al \sān-'yōr-ē-əl, -'yȯr-\ *adj* (1818) : of, relating to, or befitting a seignior : MANORIAL

1**seine** \'sān\ *n* [ME, fr. OE *segne*, fr. L *sagena* seine, fr. Gk *sagēnē*] (bef. 12c) : a large net with sinkers on one edge and floats on the other that hangs vertically in the water and is used to enclose fish when its ends are pulled together or are drawn ashore

2**seine** *vb* **seined; sein·ing** *vi* (1836) : to fish with or catch fish with a seine ~ *vt* : to fish for or in with a seine — **sein·er** *n*

sei·sin *or* **sei·zin** \'sēz-ᵊn\ *n* [ME *seisine*, fr. OF *saisine*, fr. *saisir* to seize — more at SEIZE] (13c) **1** : the possession of land or chattels **2** : the possession of a freehold estate in land by one having title thereto

seism- *or* **seismo-** *comb form* [Gk, fr. *seismos*] : earthquake : vibration ⟨*seismo*meter⟩

seis·mic \'sīz-mik, 'sīs-\ *adj* [Gk *seismos* shock, earthquake, fr. *seiein* to shake; akin to Skt *tvesati* he is violently moved] (1858) **1** : of, subject to, or caused by an earthquake; *also* : of or relating to an earth vibration caused by something else (as an explosion or the impact of a meteorite) **2** : of or relating to a vibration on a celestial body (as the moon) comparable to a seismic event on earth

seis·mic·i·ty \sīz-'mis-ət-ē, sīs-\ *n* (1902) : the relative frequency and distribution of earthquakes

seis·mo·gram \'sīz-mə-,gram, 'sīs-\ *n* [ISV] (ca. 1891) : the record of an earth tremor by a seismograph

seis·mo·graph \-,graf\ *n* [ISV] (1858) : an apparatus to measure and record vibrations within the earth and of the ground — **seis·mog·ra·pher** \sīz-'mäg-rə-fər, sīs-\ *n* — **seis·mo·graph·ic** \,sīz-mə-'graf-ik, ,sīs-\ *adj* — **seis·mog·ra·phy** \sīz-'mäg-rə-fē, sīs-\ *n*

seis·mol·o·gy \sīz-'mäl-ə-jē, sīs-\ *n* [ISV] (1858) : a science that deals with earthquakes and with artificially produced vibrations of the earth — **seis·mo·log·i·cal** \,sīz-mə-'läj-i-kəl, ,sīs-\ *adj* — **seis·mol·o·gist** \sīz-'mäl-ə-jəst, sīs-\ *n*

seis·mom·e·ter \sīz-'mäm-ət-ər, sīs-\ *n* (1841) : a seismograph measuring the actual movements of the ground (as on the earth or the moon) — **seis·mo·met·ric** \,sīz-mə-'me-trik, ,sīs-\ *adj*

seis·mom·e·try \sīz-'mäm-ə-trē, sīs-\ *n* [ISV] (1858) : the scientific study of earthquakes

seize \'sēz\ *vb* **seized; seiz·ing** [ME *saisen*, fr. OF *saisir* to put in possession of, fr. ML *sacire*, of Gmc origin; akin to OHG *sezzen* to set — more at SET] *vt* (13c) **1 a** *usu* **seise** \'sēz\ : to vest ownership of a freehold estate in **b** *often* **seise** : to put in possession of something ⟨the biographer will be *seized* of all pertinent papers⟩ **2 a** : to take possession of : CONFISCATE **b** : to take possession of by legal process **3 a** : to possess or take by force : CAPTURE **b** : to take prisoner : ARREST **4 a** : to take hold of : CLUTCH **b** : to possess oneself of : GRASP **c** : to understand fully and distinctly : APPREHEND **5 a** : to attack or overwhelm physically : AFFLICT ⟨suddenly *seized* with an acute illness —H. G. Armstrong⟩ **b** : to possess (as one's mind) completely or overwhelmingly ⟨*seized* the popular imagination —Basil Davenport⟩ **6** : to bind or fasten together with a lashing of small stuff (as yarn, marline, or fine wire) ~ *vi* **1** : to take or lay hold suddenly or forcibly **2 a** : to cohere to a relatively moving part through excessive pressure, temperature, or friction — used esp. of machine parts (as bearings, brakes, or pistons) **b** : to fail to operate due to the seizing of a part — used of an engine ***syn*** see TAKE — **seiz·er** *n*

seiz·ing *n* (14c) **1 a** : the cord or lashing used in seizing **b** : the fastening so made — see KNOT illustration **2** : the operation of fastening together or lashing with tarred small stuff

sei·zure \'sē-zhər\ *n* (15c) **1 a** : the act, action, or process of seizing : the state of being seized **b** : the taking possession of person or property by legal process **2** : a sudden attack (as of disease) ⟨an epileptic ~⟩

se·jant \'sē-jənt\ *adj* [modif. of MF *seant*, prp. of *seoir* to sit, fr. L *sedēre* — more at SIT] (1500) : SITTING — used of a heraldic animal

sel \'sel\ *chiefly Scot var of* SELF

se·la·chi·an \sə-'lā-kē-ən\ *n* [deriv. of Gk *selachos* cartilaginous phosphorescent fish; akin to Gk *selas* brightness — more at SELENIUM] (1835) : any of a variously defined group (Selachii) of elasmobranch fishes that includes all the elasmobranchs or all elasmobranchs except the chimaeras, the existing sharks and rays or in its most restricted use the existing sharks as distinguished from the rays — **selachian** *adj*

se·lag·i·nel·la \sə-,laj-ə-'nel-ə\ *n* [NL, fr. L *selagin-*, *selago*, a plant resembling the savin] (1835) : any of a genus (*Selaginella*) of mossy lower tracheophytes that have branching stems and scalelike leaves and produce one-celled sporangia containing both megaspores and microspores

se·lah \'sē-lə, -,lä\ *interj* [Heb *selāh*] (1530) — a term of uncertain meaning found in the Hebrew text of the Psalms and Habakkuk carried over untranslated into some English versions

sel·couth \'sel-,küth\ *adj* [ME, fr. OE *seldcūth*, fr. *seldan* seldom + *cūth* known — more at UNCOUTH] *archaic* (bef. 12c) : UNUSUAL, STRANGE

1**sel·dom** \'sel-dəm\ *adv* [ME, fr. OE *seldan*; akin to OHG *seltan* seldom, L *sed*, *se* without — more at IDIOT] (bef. 12c) : in few instances : RARELY, INFREQUENTLY

2**seldom** *adj* (15c) : RARE, INFREQUENT

1**se·lect** \sə-'lekt\ *adj* [L *selectus*, pp. of *seligere* to select, fr. *se-* apart (fr. *sed*, *se* without) + *legere* to gather, select — more at LEGEND] (1565) **1** : chosen from a number or group by fitness or preference **2 a** : of special value or excellence : SUPERIOR, CHOICE **b** : exclusively or fastidiously chosen often with regard to social, economic, or cultural characteristics **3** : judicious or restrictive in choice : DISCRIMINATING ⟨pleased with the ~ appreciation of his books —Osbert Sitwell⟩ — **se·lect·ness** \sə-'lek(t)-nəs\ *n*

2**select** *vt* (1567) : to take by preference from a number or group : pick out : CHOOSE ~ *vi* : to make a choice

3**select** *n* (1610) : one that is select — often used in pl.

se·lect·ed *adj* (1590) : SELECT; *specif* : of a higher grade or quality than the ordinary

se·lect·ee \sə-,lek-'tē\ *n* (1940) : one inducted into military service under selective service

se·lec·tion \sə-'lek-shən\ *n* (1646) **1** : the act or process of selecting : the state of being selected **2** : one that is selected : CHOICE; *also* : a collection of selected things **3** : a natural or artificial process that results or tends to result in the survival and propagation of some individuals or organisms but not of others with the result that the inherited traits of the survivors are perpetuated — compare DARWINISM, NATURAL SELECTION ***syn*** see CHOICE

se·lec·tive \sə-'lek-tiv\ *adj* (1625) **1** : of, relating to, or characterized by selection : selecting or tending to select **2 a** : of, relating to, or constituting the ability of a radio circuit or apparatus to respond to a specific frequency without interference **b** : highly specific in activity or effect ⟨~ pesticides⟩ ⟨~ absorption⟩ — **se·lec·tive·ly** *adv* — **se·lec·tive·ness** *n* — **se·lec·tiv·i·ty** \sə-,lek-'tiv-ət-ē, ,sē-\ *n*

selective service *n* (1919) : a system under which men are called up for military service : DRAFT

se·lect·man \si-'lek(t)-,man, -,lek(t)-'man, -'lek(t)-mən; 'sē-,lek(t)-,man\ *n* (1635) : one of a board of officials elected in towns of all New England states except Rhode Island to serve as the chief administrative authority of the town

se·lec·tor \sə-'lek-tər\ *n* (1777) : one that selects

1**selen-** *or* **seleno-** *comb form* [L *selen-*, fr. Gk *selēn-*, fr. *selēnē* — more at SELENIUM] : moon ⟨*selen*ium⟩ ⟨*seleno*graphy⟩

2**selen-** *or* **seleni-** *or* **seleno-** *comb form* [Sw, fr. NL *selenium*] : selenium ⟨*seleni*ferous⟩ ⟨*selen*ious⟩

sel·e·nate \'sel-ə-,nāt\ *n* [Sw *selenat*, fr. *selen* selenic] (1818) : a salt or ester of selenic acid

Se·le·ne \sə-'lē-nē\ *n* : the Greek goddess of the moon

se·le·nic \sə-'lēn-ik, -'len-\ *adj* [Sw *selen*, fr. NL *selenium*] (1818) : of, relating to, or containing selenium esp. with a relatively high valence

selenic acid *n* (1818) : a strong acid H_2SeO_4 whose aqueous solution attacks gold and platinum

sel·e·nide \'sel-ə-,nīd\ *n* (1849) : a binary compound of selenium usu. with a more electropositive element or group

sel·e·nif·er·ous \,sel-ə-'nif-(ə-)rəs\ *adj* [ISV] (1823) : containing or yielding selenium ⟨~ vegetation⟩ ⟨~ soils⟩

se·le·ni·ous \sə-'lē-nē-əs\ *adj* [ISV] (1834) : of, relating to, or containing selenium esp. with a relatively low valence

sel·e·nite \'sel-ə-,nīt\ *n* [L *selenites*, fr. Gk *selēnitēs* (*lithos*), lit., stone of the moon, fr. *selēnē*; fr. the belief that it waxed and waned with the moon] (1668) : a variety of gypsum occurring in transparent crystals or crystalline masses

se·le·ni·um \sə-'lē-nē-əm\ *n* [NL, fr. Gk *selēnē* moon; akin to Gk *selas* brightness, L *sol* sun — more at SOLAR] (1818) : a nonmetallic element that resembles sulfur and tellurium chemically, is obtained chiefly as a by-product in copper refining, and occurs in allotropic forms of which a gray stable form varies in electrical conductivity with the intensity of its illumination and is used in electronic devices — see ELEMENT table

selenium cell *n* (1880) : an insulated strip of selenium mounted with electrodes and used as a photoconductive element

se·le·no·cen·tric \sə-,lē-nə-'sen-trik\ *adj* [ISV] (ca. 1852) : of or relating to the center of the moon; *also* : referred to or involving the moon as a center

sel·e·nog·ra·phy \,sel-ə-'näg-rə-fē\ *n* (1650) **1** : the science of the physical features of the moon **2** : the physical geography of the moon — **sel·e·nog·ra·pher** \-fər\ *n* — **se·le·no·graph·ic** \,sel-ə-nō-'graf-ik, sə-,lē-nə-\ *adj*

sel·e·nol·o·gy \,sel-ə-'näl-ə-jē\ *n* (1821) : a branch of astronomy that deals with the moon — **se·le·no·log·i·cal** \,sel-ə-nō-'läj-i-kəl, sə-,lēn-ᵊl-'äj-\ *adj* — **selenologist** *n*

1**self** \'self, *Southern also* 'sef\ *pron* [ME (intensive pron.), fr. OE; akin to OHG *selb*, intensive pron., L *sui* (reflexive pron.) of oneself — more at SUICIDE] (bef. 12c) : MYSELF, HIMSELF, HERSELF ⟨check payable to ~⟩

2**self** *adj* (bef. 12c) **1** *obs* : belonging to oneself : OWN **2** *obs* : IDENTICAL, SAME **3 a** : having a single character or quality throughout; *specif* : having one color only ⟨a ~ flower⟩ **b** : of the same kind (as in color, material, or pattern) as something with which it is used ⟨~ trimming⟩

3**self** *n, pl* **selves** \'selvz, *Southern also* 'sevz\ (13c) **1 a** : the entire person of an individual **b** : the realization or embodiment of an abstraction **2 a** (1) : an individual's typical character or behavior ⟨his true ~ was revealed⟩ (2) : an individual's temporary behavior or character ⟨his better ~⟩ **b** : a person in his best condition ⟨looked like his old ~⟩ **3** : the union of elements (as body, emotions, thoughts, and sensations) that constitute the individuality and identity of a person **4** : personal interest or advantage

4**self** *vt* (1914) **1** : INBREED **2** : to pollinate with pollen from the same flower or plant ~ *vi* : to undergo self-pollination

self- *comb form* [ME, fr. OE, fr. *self*] **1 a** : oneself or itself ⟨*self*-supporting⟩ **b** : of oneself or itself ⟨*self*-abasement⟩ **c** : by oneself or itself ⟨*self*-propelled⟩ ⟨*self*-acting⟩ **2 a** : to, with, for, or toward oneself or itself ⟨*self*-consistent⟩ ⟨*self*-addressed⟩ ⟨*self*-love⟩ **b** : of or in oneself or itself inherently ⟨*self*-evident⟩ **c** : from or by means of oneself or itself ⟨*self*-fertile⟩

self-abase·ment
self-ab·ne·gat·ing
self-ab·ne·ga·tion
self-ac·cel·er·at·ing
self-ac·cep·tance
self-ac·cu·sa·tion
self-ac·cu·sa·to·ry
self-ac·cus·ing
self-ac·knowl·edged
self-ac·quired
self-ad·just·ing
self-ad·min·is·ter
self-ad·mit·ted
self-ad·mit·ted·ly
self-ad·u·la·to·ry
self-ad·vance·ment
self-ad·ver·tise·ment
self-ad·ver·tis·er
self-af·fir·ma·tion
self-ag·gran·dize·ment
self-ag·gran·diz·ing
self-alien·ation
self-anoint·ed
self-ap·prais·al
self-ap·pro·ba·tion
self-as·sess·ment
self-as·sign·ment
self-au·then·ti·cat·ing
self-avowed
self-bet·ter·ment
self-can·cel
self-care
self-car·i·ca·ture
self-cas·ti·gate
self-cas·ti·ga·tion
self-cen·sor·ship
self-char·ac·ter·iza·tion
self-charg·ing
self-clas·si·fi·ca·tion
self-com·mand
self-com·mun·ing
self-com·mu·nion
self-com·pla·cen·cy
self-com·pla·cent
self-con·dem·na·tion
self-con·demned
self-con·firm·ing
self-con·se·cra·tion
self-con·sti·tut·ed
self-con·sum·ing
self-con·tempt
self-cre·at·ed
self-cre·ation
self-crit·i·cal
self-crit·i·cism
self-cul·ti·va·tion
self-damn·ing
self-de·base·ment
self-de·ceit
self-de·ceived

self-de·ceiv·er
self-de·ceiv·ing
self-de·cep·tion
self-de·cep·tive
self-de·feat·ing
self-de·lud·ed
self-de·lud·ing
self-de·lu·sion
self-den·i·grat·ing
self-den·i·gra·tion
self-de·pen·dence
self-de·pen·dent
self-dep·re·cat·ing
self-dep·re·cat·ing·ly
self-dep·re·ca·to·ry
self-de·pre·ci·a·tion
self-de·scribed
self-de·scrip·tion
self-de·scrip·tive
self-de·vel·op·ment
self-de·vour·ing
self-dif·fer·en·ti·a·tion
self-di·rect·ed
self-di·rect·ing
self-di·rec·tion
self-di·rec·tive
self-dis·sat·is·fac·tion
self-doubt
self-doubt·ing
self-ed·u·cat·ed
self-ed·u·cat·ing
self-ed·u·ca·tion
self-eman·ci·pa·tion
self-emas·cu·la·tion
self-en·grossed
self-en·hance·ment
self-eval·u·ate
self-eval·u·a·tion
self-ex·clu·sion
self-ex·cul·pa·tion
self-ex·hi·bi·tion
self-ex·is·tence
self-ex·is·tent
self-ex·plain·ing
self-ex·tinc·tion
self-fi·nance
self-formed
self-gen·er·at·ed
self-gen·er·at·ing
self-giv·ing
self-guid·ed
self-hate
self-hat·ing
self-ha·tred
self-heal·ing
self-help
self-humb·ling
self-hu·mil·i·a·tion
self-hyp·no·sis
self-idol·a·try
self-im·posed
self-im·prove·ment
self-in·fat·u·at·ed
self-in·flict·ed
self-ini·ti·at·ed
self-in·struct·ed
self-in·ter·pre·ta·tion
self-in·ter·view
self-iso·la·tion
self-la·beled
self-lac·er·at·ing
self-lac·er·a·tion
self-loath·ing
self-lock·ing
self-lu·bri·cat·ing
self-lu·mi·nous
self-main·te·nance
self-man·age·ment
self-mas·tery
self-mock·ery
self-mock·ing
self-mor·ti·fi·ca·tion
self-mo·ti·vat·ed
self-mu·ti·lat·ing
self-mu·ti·la·tion
self-ne·gat·ing
self-ob·sessed
self-op·er·at·ing
self-op·er·a·tive
self-or·dained
self-ori·ent·ed
self-par·o·dist
self-par·o·dy
self-per·pet·u·at·ing
self-per·pet·u·a·tion
self-pleas·ing
self-po·lic·ing
self-praise
self-pre·oc·cu·pa·tion
self-pre·oc·cu·pied
self-pre·serv·ing
self-pro·claimed
self-pro·duced
self-pro·fessed
self-pro·mot·er
self-pro·mo·tion
self-pro·tec·tion
self-pro·tec·tive
self-pro·tec·tive·ness
self-pun·ish·ing
self-pun·ish·ment
self-raised
self-re·crim·i·na·tion
self-ref·or·ma·tion
self-reg·u·la·tion
self-reg·u·la·tive
self-reg·u·la·tory
self-re·in·forc·ing
self-re·new·al
self-re·new·ing
self-re·nounc·ing
self-re·nun·ci·a·tion
self-re·proach
self-re·proach·ful
self-re·proach·ing
self-re·proach·ing·ly
self-re·proach·ing·ness
self-re·proof
self-re·prov·ing
self-re·prov·ing·ly
self-re·strain·ing
self-re·straint
self-rid·i·cule
self-se·lect·ed
self-se·lec·tion
self-set
self-ster·il·ized
self-sur·ren·der
self-sus·tained
self-ther·a·py
self-tor·ment
self-tor·ment·ing
self-tor·men·tor
self-tor·ture
self-tran·scen·dence
self-trans·for·ma·tion
self-un·der·stand·ing
self-val·i·dat·ing
self-wor·ship
self-wor·ship·er

self-aban·doned \\,sel-fə-'ban-dənd\\ *adj* (1791) **:** abandoned by oneself; *esp* **:** given up to one's impulses

self-aban·don·ment \\-dən-mənt\\ *n* (1818) **1 :** a surrender of one's selfish interests or desires **2 :** a lack of self-restraint

self-ab·sorbed \\,sel-fəb-'sȯ(ə)rbd, -'zȯ(ə)rbd\\ *adj* (1847) **:** absorbed in one's own thoughts, activities, or interests

self-ab·sorp·tion \\-'sȯrp-shən, -'zȯrp-\\ *n* (1862) **:** preoccupation with oneself

self-abuse \\,sel-fə-'byüs\\ *n* (1605) **1 :** reproach of oneself **2 :** MASTURBATION

self-act·ing \\'sel-'fak-tiŋ\\ *adj* (ca. 1680) **:** acting or capable of acting of or by itself **:** AUTOMATIC

self-ac·tiv·i·ty \\,sel-,fak-'tiv-ət-ē\\ *n* (1644) **:** independent and esp. self-determined activity

self-ac·tu·al·ize \\'sel-'fak-ch(ə-w)ə-,līz, -'faksh-wə-\\ *vi* (ca. 1969) **:** to realize fully one's potential — **self-ac·tu·al·iza·tion** \\,sel-,fak-ch(ə-w)ə-lə-'zā-shən, -,faksh-wə-\\ *n*

self-ad·dressed \\,sel-fə-'drest, 'sel-'fad-,rest\\ *adj* (1904) **:** addressed for return to the sender ⟨a ~ envelope⟩

self-ad·just·ment \\,sel-fə-'jəs(t)-mənt\\ *n* (ca. 1917) **:** adjustment to oneself or one's environment

self-ad·mi·ra·tion \\,sel-,fad-mə-'rā-shən\\ *n* (1661) **:** SELF-CONCEIT

self-af·fect·ed \\,sel-fə-'fek-təd\\ *adj* (1606) **:** CONCEITED, SELF-LOVING

self-anal·y·sis \\,sel-fə-'nal-ə-səs\\ *n* (1862) **:** a systematic attempt by an individual to understand his own personality without the aid of another person

self-an·a·lyt·i·cal \\,sel-,fan-ᵊl-'it-i-kəl\\ *also* **self-an·a·lyt·ic** *adj* (1953) **:** using self-analysis

self-an·ni·hi·la·tion \\,sel-fə-,nī-ə-'lā-shən\\ *n* (1647) **:** annihilation of the self (as in mystical contemplation of God)

self-ap·plaud·ing \\,sel-fə-'plȯd-iŋ\\ *adj* (1654) **:** marked by self-applause

self-ap·plause \\-'plȯz\\ *n* (1678) **:** an expression or feeling of approval of oneself

self-ap·point·ed \\,sel-fə-'pȯint-əd\\ *adj* (1799) **:** appointed by oneself **:** SELF-STYLED

self-as·sem·bly \\,sel-fə-'sem-blē\\ *n* (1964) **:** the process by which a complex macromolecule (as collagen) or a supramolecular system (as a virus) spontaneously assembles itself from its components

self-as·sert·ing \\,sel-fə-'sərt-iŋ\\ *adj* (1837) **1 :** asserting oneself or one's own rights, claims, or opinions **2 a :** SELF-ASSURED, CONFIDENT **b :** ARROGANT — **self-as·sert·ing·ly** \\-iŋ-lē\\ *adv*

self-as·ser·tion \\,sel-fə-'sər-shən\\ *n* (1805) **1 :** the act of asserting oneself or one's own rights, claims, or opinions **2 :** the act of asserting one's superiority over others

self-as·ser·tive \\-'sərt-iv\\ *adj* (1865) **:** given to or characterized by self-assertion *syn* see AGGRESSIVE — **self-as·ser·tive·ly** *adv* — **self-as·ser·tive·ness** *n*

self-as·sump·tion \\,sel-fə-'səm(p)-shən\\ *n* (1606) **:** SELF-CONCEIT

self-as·sur·ance \\,sel-fə-'shu̇r-ən(t)s\\ *n* (1594) **:** SELF-CONFIDENCE

self-as·sured \\-'shu̇(ə)rd\\ *adj* (1711) **:** sure of oneself **:** SELF-CONFIDENT — **self-as·sured·ly** \\-'shu̇r-əd-lē, -'shu̇(ə)rd-\\ *adv* — **self-as·sured·ness** \\-'shu̇r-əd-nəs, -'shu̇(ə)rd-\\ *n*

self-aware \\,sel-fə-'wa(ə)r, -'we(ə)r\\ *adj* (ca. 1934) **:** characterized by self-awareness

self-aware·ness *n* (1880) **:** an awareness of one's own personality or individuality

self-belt \\'self-'belt\\ *n* (1965) **:** a belt made of the same material as the garment with which it is worn — **self-belt·ed** \\-'bel-təd\\ *adj*

self-be·tray·al \\,self-bi-'trā(-ə)l\\ *n* (1857) **:** SELF-REVELATION

self-bind·er \\'self-'bīn-dər\\ *n* (1877) **:** a harvesting machine that cuts grain and binds it into bundles

self-born \\-'bȯ(ə)rn\\ *adj* (1587) **1 :** arising within the self ⟨~ sorrows⟩ **2 :** springing from a prior self ⟨phoenix rising ~ from the fire⟩

self-cen·tered \\'self-'sent-ərd\\ *adj* (1676) **1 :** independent of outside force or influence **:** SELF-SUFFICIENT **2 :** concerned solely with one's own desires, needs, or interests **:** SELFISH — **self-cen·tered·ly** *adv* — **self-cen·tered·ness** *n*

self-clos·ing \\-'klō-ziŋ\\ *adj* (1875) **:** closing or shutting automatically after being opened

self-cock·ing \\-'käk-iŋ\\ *adj, of a firearm* (1880) **:** cocked by the operation of some part of the action ⟨~ on pushing the bolt forward⟩

self-col·lect·ed \\,self-kə-'lek-təd\\ *adj* (1711) **:** SELF-POSSESSED

self-col·ored \\'self-'kəl-ərd\\ *adj* (1759) **:** of a single color ⟨a ~ flower⟩

self-com·pat·i·ble \\,self-kəm-'pat-ə-bəl\\ *adj* (ca. 1941) **:** capable of effective self-pollination that results in the production of seeds and fruits — **self-com·pat·i·bil·i·ty** \\-,pat-ə-'bil-ət-ē\\ *n*

self-com·posed \\,self-kəm-'pōzd\\ *adj* (ca. 1934) **:** having control over one's emotions **:** CALM — **self-com·pos·ed·ly** \\-'pō-zəd-lē\\ *adv* — **self-com·posed·ness** \\-'pō-zəd-nəs, -'pōz(d)-nəs\\ *n*

self-con·ceit \\,self-kən-'sēt\\ *n* (1588) **:** an exaggerated opinion of one's own qualities or abilities **:** VANITY — **self-con·ceit·ed** \\-əd\\ *adj*

self-con·cept \\'self-'kän-,sept\\ *n* (1925) **:** the mental image one has of oneself

self-con·cep·tion \\,self-kən-'sep-shən\\ *n* (ca. 1950) **:** SELF-CONCEPT

self-con·cern \\-'sərn\\ *n* (1681) **:** a selfish or morbid concern for oneself — **self-con·cerned** \\-'sərnd\\ *adj*

self-con·fessed \\-'fest\\ *adj* (1917) **:** openly acknowledged by oneself **:** AVOWED

self-con·fes·sion \\-'fesh-ən\\ *n* (ca. 1961) **:** open acknowledgment **:** AVOWAL

self-con·fi·dence \\'self-'kän-fəd-ən(t)s, -fə-,den(t)s\\ *n* (1637) **:** confidence in oneself and in one's powers and abilities — **self-con·fi·dent** \\-fəd-ənt, -fə-,dent\\ *adj* — **self-con·fi·dent·ly** *adv*

self-con·fron·ta·tion \\,self-,kän-(,)frən-'tā-shən\\ *n* (1970) **:** SELF-ANALYSIS

self-con·grat·u·la·tion \\-kən-,grach-ə-'lā-shən\\ *n* (1712) **:** congratulation of oneself; *esp* **:** a complacent acknowledgment of one's own superiority or good fortune

self-con·grat·u·la·to·ry \\-'grach-(ə-)lə-,tōr-ē, -,tȯr-\\ *adj* (1877) **:** indulging in self-congratulation

self-con·scious \\'self-'kän-chəs\\ *adj* (ca. 1680) **1 a :** conscious of one's own acts or states as belonging to or originating in oneself **:** aware of oneself as an individual **b :** intensely aware of oneself **:** CONSCIOUS ⟨a rising and ~ social class⟩; *also* **:** produced or done with such awareness ⟨~ art⟩ **2 :** uncomfortably conscious of oneself as an object of the observation of others **:** ILL AT EASE — **self-con·scious·ly** *adv* — **self-con·scious·ness** *n*

self-con·se·quence \\'self-'kän(t)-sə-,kwen(t)s, -si-kwən(t)s\\ *n* (1778) **:** SELF-IMPORTANCE

self-con·sis·ten·cy \\,self-kən-'sis-tən-sē\\ *n* (1692) **:** the quality or state of being self-consistent

self-con·sis·tent \\-tənt\\ *adj* (1683) **:** having each part logically consistent with the rest

self-con·tained \\,self-kən-'tānd\\ *adj* (1591) **1 a :** complete in itself **:** INDEPENDENT ⟨a ~ machine⟩ ⟨a ~ program of study⟩ **b :** BUILT-IN ⟨a lectern with a ~ light fixture⟩ **2 a :** showing self-command **b :** formal and reserved in manner — **self-con·tained·ly** \\-'tā-nəd-lē, -'tānd-lē\\ *adv* — **self-con·tained·ness** \\-'tā-nəd-nəs, -'tān(d)-nəs\\ *n* — **self-con·tain·ment** \\-'tān-mənt\\ *n*

self-con·tam·i·na·tion \\,self-kən-,tam-ə-'nā-shən\\ *n* (1955) **1 :** contamination by oneself **2 :** contamination from within

self-con·tent \\-kən-'tent\\ *n* (1654) **:** SELF-SATISFACTION

self-con·tent·ed \\-əd\\ *adj* (1818) **:** SELF-SATISFIED — **self-con·tent·ed·ly** *adv* — **self-con·tent·ed·ness** *n*

self-con·tent·ment \\-'tent-mənt\\ *n* (1875) **:** SELF-SATISFACTION

self-con·tra·dic·tion \\,self-,kän-trə-'dik-shən\\ *n* (1658) **1 :** contradiction of oneself **2 :** a self-contradictory statement or proposition

self-con·tra·dic·to·ry \\-'dik-t(ə-)rē\\ *adj* (1657) **:** consisting of two contradictory members or parts

self-con·trol \\,self-kən-'trōl\\ *n* (1711) **:** restraint exercised over one's own impulses, emotions, or desires — **self-con·trolled** \\-'trōld\\ *adj*

self-cor·rect·ing \\,self-kə-'rek-tiŋ\\ *adj* (ca. 1939) **:** correcting or compensating for one's own errors or weaknesses

self-cor·rec·tive \\-'rek-tiv\\ *adj* (ca. 1925) **:** SELF-CORRECTING

self-cul·ture \\'self-'kəl-chər\\ *n* (ca. 1832) **:** the development of one's mind or capacities through one's own efforts

self-deal·ing \\'self-'dē-liŋ\\ *n* (1940) **:** financial dealing that is not at arm's length; *esp* **:** borrowing from or lending to a company by a controlling individual primarily to his own advantage

self-ded·i·ca·tion \\,self-,ded-i-'kā-shən\\ *n* (1695) **:** dedication of oneself to a cause or ideal

self-de·fense \\,self-di-'fen(t)s\\ *n* (1651) **1 :** a plea of justification for the use of force or for homicide **2 :** the act of defending oneself, one's property, or a close relative

self-de·fen·sive \\-'fen(t)-siv\\ *adj* (1828) **:** of, relating to, or given to self-defense ⟨a ~ person⟩ ⟨a ~ attitude⟩

self-def·i·ni·tion \\,self-,def-ə-'nish-ən\\ *n* (1965) **:** the evaluation by oneself of one's worth as an individual in distinction from one's interpersonal or social roles

\\ə\\ abut \\ᵊ\\ kitten, F table \\ər\\ further \\a\\ ash \\ā\\ ace \\ä\\ cot, cart \\au̇\\ out \\ch\\ chin \\e\\ bet \\ē\\ easy \\g\\ go \\i\\ hit \\ī\\ ice \\j\\ job \\ŋ\\ sing \\ō\\ go \\ȯ\\ law \\ȯi\\ boy \\th\\ thin \\t͟h\\ the \\ü\\ loot \\u̇\\ foot \\y\\ yet \\zh\\ vision \\à, k̲, ⁿ, œ, œ̄, ue, ue̅, ʸ\\ *see* Guide to Pronunciation

self–de·ni·al \ˌself-di-ˈnī(-ə)l\ *n* (1642) **:** a restraint or limitation of one's own desires or interests
self–de·ny·ing \-ˈnī-iŋ\ *adj* (1632) **:** showing self-denial — **self–de·ny·ing·ly** \-iŋ-lē\ *adv*
self–de·spair \ˌself-di-ˈspa(ə)r, -ˈspe(ə)r\ *n* (1677) **:** despair of oneself **:** HOPELESSNESS
self–de·stroy·er \-di-ˈstrȯi(-ə)r\ *n* (1654) **:** one who destroys himself
self–de·stroy·ing \-ˈstrȯi-iŋ\ *adj* (1645) **:** SELF-DESTRUCTIVE
self–de·struct \ˌself-di-ˈstrəkt\ *vi* (1968) **:** to destroy itself — **self–destruct** *adj*
self–de·struc·tion \-ˈstrək-shən\ *n* (1586) **:** destruction of oneself; *esp* **:** SUICIDE
self–de·struc·tive \-ˈstrək-tiv\ *adj* (1654) **:** acting or tending to harm or destroy oneself; *also* **:** SUICIDAL — **self–de·struc·tive·ness** *n*
self–de·ter·mi·na·tion \ˌself-di-ˌtər-mə-ˈnā-shən\ *n* (ca. 1680) **1 :** free choice of one's own acts or states without external compulsion **2 :** determination by the people of a territorial unit of their own future political status
self–de·ter·mined \-ˈtər-mənd\ *adj* (ca. 1680) **:** determined by oneself
self–de·ter·min·ing \-ˈtərm-(ə-)niŋ\ *adj* (1662) **:** capable of determining one's or its own acts
self–de·ter·min·ism \-ˈtər-mə-ˌniz-əm\ *n* (1936) **:** a doctrine that the actions of a self are determined by itself
self–de·vot·ed \ˌself-di-ˈvōt-əd\ *adj* (1713) **:** characterized by self-devotion — **self–de·vot·ed·ly** *adv* — **self–de·vot·ed·ness** *n*
self–de·vot·ing \-ˈvōt-iŋ\ *adj* (1702) **:** SELF-DEVOTED
self–de·vo·tion \-ˈvō-shən\ *n* (1815) **:** devotion of oneself esp. in service or sacrifice ⟨his ~ to science cost him his life⟩
self–dis·ci·pline \ˈself-ˈdis-ə-plən\ *n* (1838) **:** correction or regulation of oneself for the sake of improvement ***syn*** see COOL
self–dis·ci·plined \-plənd\ *adj* (1932) **:** capable of or subject to self-discipline
self–dis·cov·ery \ˌself-dis-ˈkəv-(ə-)rē\ *n* (1924) **:** the act or process of achieving self-knowledge
self–dis·trib·ut·ing \-ˈtrib-yət-iŋ\ *adj* (ca. 1961) **:** distributing itself automatically
self–dis·trust \-ˈtrəst\ *n* (1789) **:** a lack of confidence in oneself **:** DIFFIDENCE — **self–dis·trust·ful** \-fəl\ *adj*
self·dom \ˈself-dəm, -təm\ *n* (1863) **:** the essence of one's self **:** INDIVIDUALITY
self–dra·ma·ti·za·tion \ˌself-ˌdram-ət-ə-ˈzā-shən, -ˌdräm-\ *n* (1937) **:** the act or an instance of dramatizing oneself
self–dra·ma·tiz·ing \ˈself-ˈdram-ə-ˌtī-ziŋ, -ˈdräm-\ *adj* (1938) **:** seeing and presenting oneself as an important or dramatic figure
self–drive \ˈself-ˈdrīv\ *adj, chiefly Brit* (1952) **:** being a rental car
self–ef·face·ment \ˌsel-fə-ˈfā-smənt\ *n* (1866) **:** the placing or keeping of oneself in the background
self–ef·fac·ing \-ˈfā-siŋ\ *adj* (1902) **:** RESERVED, SHY — **self–ef·fac·ing·ly** \-siŋ-lē\ *adv*
self–elect·ed \ˌsel-fə-ˈlek-təd\ *adj* (1818) **:** SELF-APPOINTED
self–em·ployed \ˌsel-fim-ˈplȯid\ *adj* (1946) **:** earning income directly from one's own business, trade, or profession rather than as a specified salary or wages from an employer — **self–employed** *n*
self–em·ploy·ment \-ˈplȯi-mənt\ *n* (1745) **:** the state of being self-employed
self–en·er·giz·ing \ˈsel-ˈfen-ər-ˌjī-ziŋ\ *adj* (ca. 1931) **:** containing means for augmentation of power within itself ⟨a ~ brake⟩
self–en·forc·ing \ˌsel-fin-ˈfōr-siŋ, -ˈfȯr-\ *adj* (1952) **:** containing in itself the authority or means that provide for its enforcement
self–en·rich·ment \ˌsel-fin-ˈrich-mənt\ *n* (ca. 1961) **:** the act or process of increasing one's intellectual or spiritual resources
self–es·teem \ˌsel-fə-ˈstēm\ *n* (1657) **1 :** a confidence and satisfaction in oneself **:** SELF-RESPECT **2 :** SELF-CONCEIT
self–ev·i·dence \ˈsel-ˈfev-əd-ənts, -ə-ˌden(t)s\ *n* (1671) **:** the quality or state of being self-evident
self–ev·i·dent \-əd-ənt, -ə-ˌdent\ *adj* (1671) **:** evident without proof or reasoning — **self–ev·i·dent·ly** *adv*
self–ex·am·i·na·tion \ˌsel-fig-ˌzam-ə-ˈnā-shən\ *n* (1647) **:** a reflective examination (as of one's beliefs or motives) **:** INTROSPECTION
self–ex·cit·ed \ˌsel-fik-ˈsīt-əd\ *adj* (ca. 1896) **:** excited by a current produced by the dynamo itself ⟨~ generator⟩
self–ex·e·cut·ing \ˈsel-ˈfek-sə-ˌkyüt-iŋ\ *adj* (1868) **:** taking effect immediately without implementing legislation ⟨a ~ treaty⟩
self–ex·iled \ˈsel-ˈfeg-ˌzīld, -ˈfek-ˌsīld\ *adj* (1737) **:** exiled by one's own wish or decision
self–ex·plan·a·to·ry \ˌsel-fik-ˈsplan-ə-ˌtōr-ē, -ˌtȯr-\ *adj* (1898) **:** explaining itself **:** capable of being understood without explanation
self–ex·plo·ra·tion \ˌsel-ˌfek-splə-ˈrā-shən, -ˌsplō-\ *n* (1959) **:** the examination and analysis of one's own unrealized spiritual or intellectual capacities
self–ex·pres·sion \ˌsel-fik-ˈspresh-ən\ *n* (1892) **:** the expression of one's own personality **:** assertion of one's individual traits — **self–ex·pres·sive** \-ˈspres-iv\ *adj*
self–feed \ˈself-ˈfēd\ *vt* **-fed** \-ˈfed\; **-feed·ing** (ca. 1924) **:** to provide rations to (animals) in bulk so as to permit selecting food in kind and quantity as wanted — compare HAND-FEED
self–feed·er \-ər\ *n* (1924) **:** a device for feeding livestock that is equipped with a feed hopper that automatically supplies a trough below
self–feel·ing \ˈself-ˈfē-liŋ\ *n* (1879) **:** self-centered emotion
self–fer·tile \ˈself-ˈfərt-ᵊl\ *adj* (1865) **:** fertile by means of its own pollen or sperm — **self–fer·til·i·ty** \ˌself-(ˌ)fər-ˈtil-ət-ē\ *n*
self–fer·til·iza·tion \ˌself-ˌfərt-ᵊl-ə-ˈzā-shən\ *n* (1859) **:** fertilization effected by union of ova with pollen or sperm from the same individual
self–fer·til·ized \ˈself-ˈfərt-ᵊl-ˌīzd\ *adj* (1871) **:** fertilized by one's own pollen or sperm
self–fer·til·iz·ing \-ˌī-ziŋ\ *adj* (1859) **:** SELF-FERTILIZED
self–flag·el·la·tion \ˌself-ˌflaj-ə-ˈlā-shən\ *n* (1845) **:** extreme criticism of oneself
self–flat·ter·ing \ˈself-ˈflat-ə-riŋ\ *adj* (1586) **:** given to self-flattery
self–flat·tery \-ə-rē\ *n* (1680) **:** the glossing over of one's own weaknesses or mistakes and the exaggeration of one's own good qualities and achievements
self–for·get·ful \ˌself-fər-ˈget-fəl\ *adj* (1864) **:** having or showing no thought of self or selfish interests — **self–for·get·ful·ly** \-fə-lē\ *adv* — **self–for·get·ful·ness** *n*
self–for·get·ting \-ˈget-iŋ\ *adj* (1847) **:** SELF-FORGETFUL — **self–for·get·ting·ly** \-iŋ-lē\ *adv*
self–fruit·ful \ˈself-ˈfrüt-fəl\ *adj* (1940) **:** capable of setting a crop of self-pollinated fruit — **self–fruit·ful·ness** *n*
self–ful·fill·ing \ˌself-fül-ˈfil-iŋ\ *adj* (1953) **1 :** marked by or achieving self-fulfillment **2 :** attaining fulfillment by virtue of having been predicted or assumed beforehand ⟨a ~ prophecy⟩
self–ful·fill·ment \-ˈfil-mənt\ *n* (ca. 1864) **:** fulfillment of oneself
self–giv·en \ˈself-ˈgiv-ən\ *adj* (1742) **1 :** derived from itself ⟨a ~ entity⟩ **2 :** given by oneself ⟨~ authority⟩
self–glo·ri·fi·ca·tion \ˌself-ˌglōr-ə-fə-ˈkā-shən, -ˌglȯr-\ *n* (1838) **:** a feeling or expression of one's own superiority
self–glo·ri·fy·ing \ˈself-ˈglōr-ə-ˌfī-iŋ, -ˈglȯr-\ *adj* (1860) **:** given to or marked by boasting **:** BOASTFUL
self–glo·ry \-ˈglōr-ē, -ˈglȯr-ē\ *n* (1647) **:** personal vanity **:** PRIDE
self–gov·er·nance \-ˈgəv-ər-nən(t)s\ *n* (1964) **:** SELF-GOVERNMENT 2
self–gov·erned \-ˈgəv-ərnd\ *adj* (1709) **1 :** not influenced or controlled by others **2 :** exercising self-control
self–gov·ern·ing \-ˈgəv-ər-niŋ\ *adj* (1845) **:** having control or rule over oneself; *specif* **:** having self-government **:** AUTONOMOUS
self–gov·ern·ment \-ˈgəv-ər(n)-mənt, -ˈgəv-ᵊm-ənt\ *n* (1734) **1 :** SELF-COMMAND, SELF-CONTROL **2 :** government under the control and direction of the inhabitants of a political unit rather than by an outside authority; *broadly* **:** control of one's own affairs
self–grat·i·fi·ca·tion \ˌself-ˌgrat-ə-fə-ˈkā-shən\ *n* (1677) **:** the act of pleasing oneself or of satisfying one's desires
self–grat·u·la·tion \-ˌgrach-ə-ˈlā-shən\ *n* (1802) **:** SELF-CONGRATULATION
self–grat·u·la·to·ry \ˈself-ˈgrach-(ə-)lə-ˌtōr-ē, -ˌtȯr-\ *adj* (1859) **:** SELF-CONGRATULATORY
self–hard·en·ing \-ˈhärd-niŋ, -ᵊn-iŋ\ *adj* (1902) **:** hardening by itself or without quenching after heating ⟨~ steel⟩
self–heal \ˈself-ˌhēl\ *n* (14c) **:** a blue-flowered Eurasian mint (*Prunella vulgaris*) naturalized throughout No. America and formerly considered to have medicinal properties
self·hood \-ˌhu̇d\ *n* (1649) **1 :** INDIVIDUALITY **2 :** the quality or state of being selfish
self–iden·ti·cal \ˌsel-fī-ˈdent-i-kəl, -fə-\ *adj* (1877) **:** having self-identity
self–iden·ti·fi·ca·tion \-ˌdent-ə-fə-ˈkā-shən\ *n* (1951) **:** identification with someone or something outside oneself
self–iden·ti·ty \-ˈden(t)-ət-ē\ *n* (1866) **1 :** sameness of a thing with itself **2 :** INDIVIDUALITY ⟨self-understanding is the necessary condition of a sense of ~ —J. C. Murray⟩
self–ig·nite \ˌsel-fig-ˈnīt\ *vi* (1943) **:** to become ignited without flame or spark (as under high compression)
self–ig·ni·tion \-ˈnish-ən\ *n* (1903) **:** ignition without flame or spark
self–im·age \ˈsel-ˈfim-ij\ *n* (1951) **:** one's conception of oneself or of one's role
self–im·mo·la·tion \ˌsel-ˌfim-ə-ˈlā-shən\ *n* (1817) **:** a deliberate and willing sacrifice of oneself
self–im·por·tance \ˌsel-fim-ˈpȯrt-ᵊn(t)s, -ən(t)s\ *n* (1775) **1 :** an exaggerated estimate of one's own importance **:** SELF-CONCEIT **2 :** arrogant or pompous behavior
self–important \-ᵊnt, -ənt\ *adj* (ca. 1775) **:** having an exaggerated notion of one's own importance — **self–im·por·tant·ly** *adv*
self–in·clu·sive \ˌsel-fin-ˈklü-siv, -ziv\ *adj* (ca. 1925) **1 :** enclosing itself **2 :** complete in itself
self–in·com·pat·i·ble \ˌsel-ˌfin-kəm-ˈpat-ə-bəl\ *adj* (1933) **:** incapable of effective self-pollination — **self–in·com·pat·i·bil·i·ty** \-ˌpat-ə-ˈbil-ət-ē\ *n*
self–in·crim·i·nat·ing \ˌsel-fin-ˈkrim-ə-ˌnāt-iŋ\ *adj* (1931) **:** serving or tending to incriminate oneself
self–in·crim·i·na·tion \-ˌkrim-ə-ˈnā-shən\ *n* (1923) **:** incrimination of oneself; *specif* **:** the giving of evidence or answering of questions the tendency of which would be to subject one to criminal prosecution
self–in·duced \ˌsel-fin-ˈd(y)üst\ *adj* (1886) **:** induced by oneself; *specif* **:** produced by self-induction ⟨a ~ voltage⟩
self–in·duc·tance \-ˈdək-tən(t)s\ *n* (1888) **:** inductance that induces an electromotive force in the same circuit as the one in which the current varies
self–in·duc·tion \-ˈdək-shən\ *n* (1873) **:** induction of an electromotive force in a circuit by a varying current in the same circuit
self–in·dul·gence \-ˈdəl-jən(t)s\ *n* (1753) **:** excessive or unrestrained gratification of one's own appetites, desires, or whims — **self–in·dul·gent** \-jənt\ *adj* — **self–in·dul·gent·ly** *adv*
self–in·struc·tion·al \ˌsel-fin-ˈstrək-shnəl, -shən-ᵊl\ *adj* (1963) **:** of, relating to, or designed for independent study
self–in·sur·ance \ˌsel-fin-ˈshu̇r-ən(t)s, ˈsel-ˈfin-ˌ\ *n* (ca. 1897) **:** insurance of oneself or of one's own interests by the setting aside of money at regular intervals to provide a fund to cover possible losses
self–in·sured \ˌsel-fin-ˈshu̇(ə)rd\ *adj* (ca. 1928) **:** insured by oneself
self–in·sur·er \-ˈshu̇r-ər\ *n* (ca. 1909) **:** one who practices self-insurance
self–in·ter·est \ˈsel-ˈfin-trəst, -ˈfint-ə-rəst, -ə-ˌrest, -ərst; -ˈfin-ˌtrest\ *n* (1649) **1 :** a concern for one's own advantage and well-being ⟨acted out of ~ and fear⟩ **2 :** one's own interest or advantage ⟨~ requires that we be generous in foreign aid⟩ — **self–in·ter·est·ed** \-əd\ *adj* — **self–in·ter·est·ed·ness** *n*
self–in·volved \ˌsel-fin-ˈvälvd, -ˈvȯlvd *also* -ˈvävd *or* ˈvȯvd\ *adj* (1842) **:** SELF-ABSORBED
self·ish \ˈsel-fish\ *adj* (1640) **1 :** concerned excessively or exclusively with oneself **:** seeking or concentrating on one's own advantage, pleasure, or well-being without regard for others **2 :** arising from concern with one's own welfare or advantage in disregard of others ⟨a ~ act⟩ — **self·ish·ly** *adv* — **self·ish·ness** *n*
self–jus·ti·fi·ca·tion \ˌself-ˌjəs-tə-fə-ˈkā-shən\ *n* (1775) **:** the act or an instance of making excuses for oneself
self–jus·ti·fy·ing \ˈself-ˈjəs-tə-ˌfī-iŋ\ *adj* (1740) **:** seeking to justify oneself
self–know·ing \ˈself-ˈnō-iŋ\ *adj* (1667) **:** having self-knowledge
self–knowl·edge \ˈself-ˈnäl-ij\ *n* (1613) **:** knowledge or understanding of one's own capabilities, character, feelings, or motivations
self·less \ˈsel-fləs\ *adj* (1825) **:** having no concern for self **:** UNSELFISH — **self·less·ly** *adv* — **self·less·ness** *n*

self–lim·it·ed \ˈsel-ˈflim-ət-əd\ *adj* (1845) **:** limited by one's or its own nature; *specif* **:** running a definite and limited course ⟨a ~ disease⟩

self–lim·it·ing \-ət-iŋ\ *adj* (1855) **:** limiting oneself or itself; *esp, of a disease* **:** SELF-LIMITED

self–liq·ui·dat·ing \ˈsel-ˈflik-wə-ˌdāt-iŋ\ *adj* (1919) **1 :** of or relating to a commercial transaction in which goods are converted into cash in a short time **2 :** generating funds from its own operations to repay the investment made to create it ⟨a ~ housing project⟩

self–load·er \ˈsel-ˈflōd-ər\ *n* (ca. 1936) **:** a semiautomatic firearm

self–load·ing \ˈsel-ˈflōd-iŋ\ *adj, of a firearm* (1899) **:** SEMIAUTOMATIC

self–love \ˈsel-ˈfləv\ *n* (1563) **:** love of self: **a :** CONCEIT **b :** regard for one's own happiness or advantage — **self–lov·ing** \-ˈfləv-iŋ\ *adj*

self–made \ˈself-ˈmād\ *adj* (1615) **1 :** made such by one's own actions **2 :** raised from poverty or obscurity by one's own efforts

self–mail·er \-ˈmā-lər\ *n* (ca. 1942) **:** a folder that can be sent by mail without enclosure in an envelope by use of a gummed sticker or a precanceled stamp to hold the leaves together

self–mail·ing \-liŋ\ *adj* (ca. 1948) **:** capable of being mailed without being enclosed in an envelope

self–moved \ˈself-ˈmüvd\ *adj* (ca. 1680) **:** moved by inherent power

self–mur·der \-ˈmərd-ər\ *n* (1563) **:** SELF-DESTRUCTION, SUICIDE

self·ness \ˈself-nəs\ *n* (1586) **1 :** EGOISM, SELFISHNESS **2 :** PERSONALITY, SELFHOOD

self–ob·ser·va·tion \ˌsel-ˌfäb-sər-ˈvā-shən, -zər-\ *n* (1832) **1 :** INTROSPECTION **2 :** observation of one's own appearance

self–opin·ion \ˌsel-fə-ˈpin-yən\ *n* (1579) **:** high or exaggerated opinion of oneself **:** SELF-CONCEIT

self–opin·ion·at·ed \-yə-ˌnāt-əd\ *adj* (1671) **1 :** CONCEITED **2 :** stubbornly holding to one's own opinion **:** OPINIONATED — **self–opin·ion·at·ed·ness** *n*

self–or·ga·ni·za·tion \ˌsel-ˌfȯrg-(ə-)nə-ˈzā-shən\ *n* (ca. 1938) **:** organization of oneself or itself; *specif* **:** the act or process of forming or joining a labor union

self–paced \ˈself-ˈpāst\ *adj* (1973) **:** designed to permit the student to learn at his own pace ⟨~ math course⟩

self–par·tial·i·ty \ˌself-ˌpär-shē-ˈal-ət-ē, -ˌpär-ˈshal-\ *n* (1628) **1 :** an excessive estimate of oneself as compared with others **2 :** a prejudice in favor of one's own claims or interests

self–per·cep·tion \ˌself-pər-ˈsep-shən\ *n* (1678) **:** perception of oneself; *esp* **:** SELF-CONCEPT

self–pity \ˈself-ˈpit-ē\ *n* (1621) **:** pity for oneself; *esp* **:** a self-indulgent dwelling on one's own sorrows or misfortunes — **self–pity·ing** \-ē-iŋ\ *adj* — **self–pity·ing·ly** \-iŋ-lē\ *adv*

self–pleased \-ˈplēzd\ *adj* (1809) **:** SELF-SATISFIED

self–poise \-ˈpȯiz\ *n* (1854) **:** the quality or state of being self-poised

self–poised \-ˈpȯizd\ *adj* (1621) **:** having poise through self-command

self–pol·li·nate \ˈself-ˈpäl-ə-ˌnāt\ *vi* (1900) **:** to undergo self-pollination ~ *vt* **:** SELF 2

self–pol·li·na·tion \ˌself-ˌpäl-ə-ˈnā-shən\ *n* (1876) **:** the transfer of pollen from the anther of a flower to the stigma of the same flower or sometimes to that of a genetically identical flower (as of the same plant or clone)

self–por·trait \ˈself-ˈpōr-trət, -ˈpȯr-, -ˌtrāt\ *n* (1840) **:** a portrait of oneself done by oneself

self–pos·sessed \ˌself-pə-ˈzest, *also* -ˈsest\ *adj* (1838) **:** having or showing self-possession **:** composed in mind or manner **:** CALM — **self–pos·sessed·ly** \-ˈzes-əd-lē, -ˈses-; -ˈzest-lē, -ˈsest-\ *adv*

self–pos·ses·sion \ˌself-pə-ˈzesh-ən, *also* -ˈsesh-\ *n* (1745) **:** control of one's emotions or reactions esp. when under stress **:** PRESENCE OF MIND, COMPOSURE ***syn*** see CONFIDENCE

self–pres·er·va·tion \ˌself-ˌprez-ər-ˈvā-shən\ *n* (1614) **1 :** preservation of oneself from destruction or harm **2 :** a natural or instinctive tendency to act so as to preserve one's own existence

self–pride \ˈself-ˈprīd\ *n* (1586) **:** pride in oneself or in that which relates to oneself

self–pro·pelled \ˌself-prə-ˈpeld\ *adj* (1899) **1 :** containing within itself the means for its own propulsion ⟨a ~ vehicle⟩ **2 :** mounted on or fired from a moving vehicle ⟨a ~ gun⟩

self–pro·pel·ling \-ˈpel-iŋ\ *adj* (1895) **:** SELF-PROPELLED 1

self–pro·pul·sion \-ˈpəl-shən\ *n* (ca. 1934) **:** propulsion by one's own power

self–pub·lished \ˌself-ˈpəb-lisht\ *adj* (1975) **:** published by the author ⟨~ book⟩

self–pu·ri·fi·ca·tion \ˌself-ˌpyu̇r-ə-fə-ˈkā-shən\ *n* (ca. 1919) **1 :** purification by natural process ⟨~ of water⟩ **2 :** purification of oneself

self–ques·tion \ˈself-ˈkwes(h)-chən\ *n* (1917) **:** a question put to a person by himself

self–ques·tion·ing \-chə-niŋ\ *n* (1862) **:** examination of one's own actions and motives

self–rat·ing \ˈsel-ˈfrāt-iŋ\ *n* (1925) **:** determination of one's own rating with reference to a standard scale

self–re·al·iza·tion \ˌsel-ˌfrē-ə-lə-ˈzā-shən, -ˌfri-ə-\ *n* (1874) **:** fulfillment by oneself of the possibilities of one's character or personality

self–re·al·iza·tion·ism \-shə-ˌniz-əm\ *n* (ca. 1874) **:** the ethical theory that the highest good for man consists in realizing or fulfilling himself usu. on the assumption that he has certain inborn abilities constituting his real or ideal self — **self–re·al·iza·tion·ist** \-sh(ə-)nəst\ *n*

self–rec·og·ni·tion \ˌsel-ˌfrek-ig-ˈnish-ən, -əg-\ *n* (1946) **1 :** recognition of one's own self **2 :** the process by which the immune system of an organism learns to distinguish between the body's own chemicals, cells, and tissues and intruders from the outside — compare SELF-TOLERANCE

self–re·cord·ing \ˌsel-fri-ˈkȯrd-iŋ\ *adj* (1875) **:** making an automatic record ⟨~ instruments⟩

self–re·flec·tion \-ˈflek-shən\ *n* (1652) **:** SELF-EXAMINATION

self–re·flec·tive \-ˈflek-tiv\ *adj* (1875) **:** marked by or engaging in self-reflection

self–re·gard \ˌsel-fri-ˈgärd\ *n* (1595) **1 :** regard for or consideration of oneself or one's own interests **2 :** SELF-RESPECT

self–re·gard·ing \-iŋ\ *adj* (1789) **:** concerned with oneself or one's own interests

self–reg·is·ter·ing \ˈsel-ˈfrej-ə-st(ə-)riŋ\ *adj* (1836) **:** registering automatically ⟨a ~ barometer⟩

self–reg·u·lat·ing \ˈsel-ˈfreg-yə-ˌlāt-iŋ\ *adj* (1837) **:** regulating oneself or itself; *esp* **:** AUTOMATIC ⟨a ~ mechanism⟩

self–re·li·ance \ˌsel-fri-ˈlī-ənts\ *n* (1833) **:** reliance on one's own efforts and abilities

self–re·li·ant \-ənt\ *adj* (1848) **:** having confidence in and exercising one's own powers or judgment

self–rep·li·cat·ing \ˈsel-ˈfrep-lə-ˌkāt-iŋ\ *adj* (ca. 1960) **:** reproducing itself autonomously ⟨DNA is a ~ molecule⟩ — **self–rep·li·ca·tion** \ˌsel-ˌfrep-lə-ˈkā-shən\ *n*

self–re·spect \ˌsel-fri-ˈspekt\ *n* (1795) **1 :** a proper respect for oneself as a human being **2 :** regard for one's own standing or position

self–re·spect·ing \-ˈspek-tiŋ\ *adj* (1786) **:** having or characterized by self-respect

self–re·veal·ing \ˌsel-fri-ˈvē-liŋ\ *adj* (1839) **:** marked by self-revelation

self–rev·e·la·tion \ˌsel-ˌfrev-ə-ˈlā-shən\ *n* (1852) **:** revelation of one's own thoughts, feelings, and attitudes esp. without deliberate intent

self–re·ward·ing \ˌsel-fri-ˈwȯrd-iŋ\ *adj* (1740) **:** containing or producing its own reward ⟨a ~ virtue⟩

self–righ·teous \ˈsel-ˈfrī-chəs\ *adj* (1680) **:** convinced of one's own righteousness esp. in contrast with the actions and beliefs of others **:** narrow-mindedly moralistic — **self–righ·teous·ly** *adv* — **self–righ·teous·ness** *n*

self–ris·ing flour \ˌsel-ˌfrī-ziŋ-\ *n* (1854) **:** a commercially prepared mixture of flour, salt, and a leavening agent

self–rule \ˈsel-ˈfrül\ *n* (ca. 1855) **:** SELF-GOVERNMENT

self–rul·ing \-ˈfrü-liŋ\ *adj* (ca. 1680) **:** SELF-GOVERNING

self–sac·ri·fice \ˈself-ˈsak-rə-ˌfīs, -fəs *also* -ˌfīz\ *n* (1805) **:** sacrifice of oneself or one's interest for others or for a cause or ideal

self–sac·ri·fic·er \-ˌfīs-ər, -ˌfīz- *also* -fəs-\ *n* (1668) **:** one that practices self-sacrifice

self–sa·cri·fic·ing \-ˌfīs-iŋ, -ˌfīz- *also* -fəs-\ *adj* (1817) **:** sacrificing oneself for others — **self–sac·ri·fic·ing·ly** \-iŋ-lē\ *adv*

self·same \ˈself-ˌsām\ *adj* (15c) **:** being the one mentioned or in question **:** IDENTICAL ⟨he left the ~ day⟩ ***syn*** see SAME — **self·same·ness** \-ˌsām-nəs, -ˈsām-\ *n*

self–sat·is·fac·tion \ˌself-ˌsat-əs-ˈfak-shən\ *n* (1793) **:** a usu. smug satisfaction with oneself or one's position or achievements

self–sat·is·fied \ˈself-ˈsat-əs-ˌfīd\ *adj* (1734) **:** feeling or showing self-satisfaction

self–scru·ti·ny \ˈself-ˈskrüt-ᵊn-ē, -ˈskrüt-nē\ *n* (1711) **:** SELF-EXAMINATION

self–seal·ing \ˈself-ˈsē-liŋ\ *adj* (1924) **1 :** capable of sealing itself (as after puncture) ⟨a ~ tire⟩ **2 :** capable of being sealed by pressure without the addition of moisture ⟨~ envelopes⟩

self–search·ing \-ˈsər-chiŋ\ *n* (1687) **:** SELF-QUESTIONING

self–seek·er \-ˈsē-kər\ *n* (1632) **:** one who is self-seeking

[1]**self–seek·ing** \-kiŋ\ *n* (1586) **:** the act or practice of selfishly advancing one's own ends

[2]**self–seeking** *adj* (1628) **:** seeking only to further one's own interests

self–se·lect·ed \ˌself-sə-ˈlek-təd\ *adj* (1964) **:** selected by oneself **:** SELF-APPOINTED ⟨~ community leaders⟩

self–se·lec·tion \-ˈlek-shən\ *n* (1952) **:** selection of or by oneself

self–serve \ˈself-ˈsərv\ *adj* (1926) **:** permitting self-service

self–ser·vice \ˈself-ˈsər-vəs\ *n* (1925) **:** the serving of oneself (as in a restaurant or service station) with goods or services to be paid for at a cashier's desk or by means of a coin-operated mechanism — **self–service** *adj*

self–serv·ing \-ˈsər-viŋ\ *adj* (ca. 1904) **:** serving one's own interests often in disregard of the truth or the interests of others

self–slaugh·ter \-ˈslȯt-ər\ *n* (1602) **:** SUICIDE

self–slaugh·tered \-ərd\ *adj* (1593) **:** killed by oneself

self–sow \ˈself-ˈsō\ *vi* **-sowed** \-ˈsōd\; **-sown** \-ˈsōn\ *or* **-sowed; -sow·ing** (1608) **:** to sow itself by dropping seeds or by natural action (as of wind or water)

self–start·er \-ˈstärt-ər\ *n* (1894) **1 :** a more or less automatic attachment for starting an engine; *esp* **:** an electric motor used to start an internal-combustion engine **2 :** a person who has initiative

self–start·ing \-ˈstärt-iŋ\ *adj* (1887) **:** capable of starting by oneself or itself

self–ster·ile \-ˈster-əl\ *adj* (1876) **:** sterile to its own pollen or sperm — **self–ste·ril·i·ty** \ˌself-stə-ˈril-ət-ē\ *n*

self–stick \ˈself-ˈstik\ *adj* (1947) **:** capable of adhering to a surface by application of pressure without the addition of moisture

self–stim·u·la·tion \ˌself-ˌstim-yə-ˈlā-shən\ *n* (1950) **:** stimulation of oneself as a result of one's own activity or behavior ⟨electrical ~ of the brain in rats⟩ — **self–stim·u·la·to·ry** \ˈself-ˈstim-yə-lə-ˌtōr-ē, -ˌtȯr-\ *adj*

self–study \ˈself-ˈstəd-ē\ *n* (1683) **:** study of oneself; *also* **:** a record of observations from such study

self–styled \-ˈstī(ə)ld\ *adj* (1823) **:** called by oneself ⟨~ experts⟩

self–sub·sis·tent \ˌself-səb-ˈsis-tənt\ *adj* (1647) **:** subsisting independently of anything external to itself — **self–sub·sis·tence** \-tən(t)s\ *n*

self–sub·sist·ing \-ˈsis-tiŋ\ *adj* (1667) **:** SELF-SUBSISTENT

self–suf·fi·cien·cy \ˌself-sə-ˈfish-ən-sē\ *n* (1623) **:** the quality or state of being self-sufficient

self–suf·fi·cient \-ˈfish-ənt\ *adj* (1589) **1 :** able to maintain oneself or itself without outside aid **:** capable of providing for one's own needs **2 :** having an extreme confidence in one's own ability or worth **:** HAUGHTY, OVERBEARING

self–suf·fic·ing \-ˈfī-siŋ *also* -ziŋ\ *adj* (1687) **:** SELF-SUFFICIENT — **self–suf·fic·ing·ly** \-siŋ-lē, -ziŋ-\ *adv* — **self–suf·fic·ing·ness** *n*

self–sug·ges·tion \ˌself-sə(g)-ˈjes(h)-chən\ *n* (1892) **:** AUTOSUGGESTION

self–sup·port \ˌself-sə-ˈpō(ə)rt, -ˈpȯ(ə)rt\ *n* (1774) **:** independent support of oneself or itself — **self–sup·port·ed** \-əd\ *adj*

self–sup·port·ing \-iŋ\ *adj* (1836) **:** characterized by self-support: as **a :** meeting one's needs by one's own efforts or output **b :** supporting itself or its own weight ⟨a ~ wall⟩

self–sur·ren·der \ˌself-sə-ˈren-dər\ *n* (1702) **:** surrender of the self **:** a yielding up (as to some influence) of oneself or one's will

\ə\ abut \ᵊ\ kitten, F table \ər\ further \a\ ash \ā\ ace \ä\ cot, cart
\au̇\ out \ch\ chin \e\ bet \ē\ easy \g\ go \i\ hit \ī\ ice \j\ job
\ŋ\ sing \ō\ go \ȯ\ law \ȯi\ boy \th\ thin \t͟h\ the \ü\ loot \u̇\ foot
\y\ yet \zh\ vision \à, k̲, ⁿ, œ, œ̄, ue, u̅e, ʸ\ *see* Guide to Pronunciation

self–sus·tain·ing \-sə-'stā-niŋ\ *adj* (1844) **1** : maintaining or able to maintain oneself or itself by independent effort **2** : maintaining or able to maintain itself once commenced ⟨a ~ nuclear reaction⟩

self–taught \'self-'tȯt\ *adj* (1725) **1** : having knowledge or skills acquired by one's own efforts without formal instruction ⟨a ~ musician⟩ **2** : learned by oneself ⟨~ knowledge⟩

self–tol·er·ance \'self-'tāl-(ə-)rən(t)s\ *n* (1971) : the physiological state that exists in an organism when its immune system has lost the capacity to attack and destroy its own bodily constituents — compare SELF-RECOGNITION

self–treat·ment \'self-'trēt-mənt\ *n* (ca. 1934) : medication of oneself or treatment of one's own disease without medical supervision or prescription

self–trust \-'trəst\ *n* (1583) : SELF-CONFIDENCE

self–will \'self-'wil\ *n* (15c) : stubborn or willful adherence to one's own desires or ideas : OBSTINACY

self–willed \-'wild\ *adj* (14c) : governed by one's own will : not yielding to the wishes of others : OBSTINATE — **self–willed·ly** \-'wil-(d)lē\ *adv* — **self–willed·ness** \-'wil(d)-nəs\ *n*

self–wind·ing \-'wīn-diŋ\ *adj* (1884) : not needing to be wound by hand ⟨a ~ watch⟩

self–worth \-'wərth\ *n* (1965) : SELF-ESTEEM

Sel·juk \'sel-,jük, sel-'\ *or* **Sel·ju·ki·an** \sel-'jü-kē-ən\ *adj* [Turk *Selçuk*, eponymous ancestor of the dynasties] (1834) **1** : of or relating to any of several Turkish dynasties ruling over a great part of western Asia in the 11th, 12th, and 13th centuries **2** : of, relating to, or characteristic of a Turkish people ruled over by a Seljuk dynasty — **Seljuk** *or* **Selju·kian** *n*

¹**sell** \'sel\ *vb* **sold** \'sōld\; **sell·ing** [ME *sellen*, fr. OE *sellan*; akin to OHG *sellen* to sell, ON *sala* sale, Gk *helein* to take] *vt* (bef. 12c) **1** : to deliver or give up in violation of duty, trust, or loyalty : BETRAY — often used with *out* **2 a** (1) : to give up (property) to another for money or other valuable consideration (2) : to offer for sale **b** : to give up in return for something else esp. foolishly or dishonorably ⟨*sold* his birthright for a mess of pottage⟩ **c** : to exact a price for ⟨*sold* their lives dearly⟩ **3 a** : to deliver into slavery for money **b** : to give into the power of another ⟨*sold* his soul to the devil⟩ **c** : to deliver the personal services of for money **4** : to dispose of or manage for profit instead of in accordance with conscience, justice, or duty ⟨*sold* their votes⟩ **5 a** : to develop a belief in the truth, value, or desirability of : gain acceptance for ⟨trying to ~ a program to the Congress⟩ **b** : to persuade or influence to a course of action or to the acceptance of something ⟨~ children on reading⟩ **6** : to impose on : CHEAT **7 a** : to cause or promote the sale of ⟨using television advertising to ~ books⟩ **b** : to make or attempt to make sales to **c** : to influence or induce to make a purchase **8** : to achieve a sale of ⟨*sold* a million copies⟩ ~ *vi* **1** : to dispose of something by sale **2** : to achieve a sale; *also* : to achieve satisfactory sales ⟨hoped that the new line would ~⟩ **3** : to have a specified price — **sell·able** \'sel-ə-bəl\ *adj* — **sell down the river** : to betray the faith of — **sell short 1** : to make a short sale **2** : to fail to value properly : UNDERESTIMATE

²**sell** *n* (1853) **1** : a deliberate deception : HOAX **2** : the act or an instance of selling

³**sell** *or* **selle** \'sel\ *n* [ME *selle*, fr. MF, fr. L *sella* — more at SETTLE] *archaic* (15c) : SADDLE

⁴**sell** *chiefly Scot var of* SELF

sell·er \'sel-ər\ *n* (13c) **1** : one that offers for sale **2** : a product offered for sale and selling well, to a specified extent, or in a specified manner ⟨a poor ~⟩

seller's market *n* (1932) : a market in which goods are scarce, buyers have a limited range of choice, and prices are high — compare BUYER'S MARKET

selling climax *n* (1949) : a sharp decline in stock prices for a short time on very heavy trading volume followed by a rally

sell·ing–plat·er \'sel-iŋ-,plāt-ər\ *n* (1886) : a horse that runs in selling races

selling point *n* (1923) : an aspect or detail of something that is emphasized (as in selling or promoting)

selling race *n* (ca. 1898) : a claiming race in which the winning horse is put up for auction

sell–off \'sel-,ȯf\ *n* (1946) : a usu. sudden sharp decline in security prices accompanied by increased volume of trading

sell off \(')sel-'ȯf\ *vi* (1700) : to suffer a drop in prices

sell–out \'sel-,aut\ *n* (1927) **1** : the act or an instance of selling out **2** : a show, exhibition, or contest for which all seats are sold **3** : one who sells out

sell out \(')sel-'aut\ *vt* (1796) **1** : to sell the goods of (a debtor) in order to satisfy creditors **2** : to sell security or commodity holdings of usu. to satisfy an uncovered margin ~ *vi* **1** : to dispose of one's goods by sale; *esp* : to sell one's business **2** : to betray one's cause or associates

sel·syn \'sel-,sin\ *n* [*self-synchronizing*] (1936) : a system comprising a generator and a motor so connected by wire that angular rotation or position in the generator is reproduced simultaneously in the motor — called also *synchro*

selt·zer \'selt-sər\ *n* [modif. of G *Selterser* (*wasser*) water of Selters, fr. Nieder *Selters*, Germany] (1741) : an artificially prepared carbonated mineral water

sel·vage *or* **sel·vedge** \'sel-vij\ *n* [ME *selvage*, prob. fr. MFlem *selvegge*, *selvage*, fr. *selv* self + *egge* edge; akin to OE *self* and to OE *ecg* edge — more at EDGE] (15c) **1 a** : the edge on either side of a woven or flat knitted fabric so finished as to prevent raveling; *specif* : a narrow border often of different or heavier threads than the fabric and sometimes in a different weave **b** : an edge (as of fabric or paper) meant to be cut off and discarded **2** : an outer or peripheral part: as **a** : BORDER, EDGE **b** : the edge plate of a lock through which the bolt is projected — **sel·vaged** *or* **sel·vedged** \-vijd\ *adj*

selves *pl of* SELF

se·man·tic \si-'mant-ik\ *also* **se·man·ti·cal** \-i-kəl\ *adj* [Gk *sēmantikos* significant, fr. *sēmainein* to signify, mean, fr. *sēma* sign, token; akin to Skt *dhyāti* he thinks] (1895) **1** : of or relating to meaning in language **2** : of or relating to semantics — **se·man·ti·cal·ly** \-i-k(ə-)lē\ *adv*

se·man·ti·cist \-'mant-ə-səst\ *n* (1902) : a specialist in semantics

se·man·tics \si-'mant-iks\ *n pl but sing or pl in constr* (ca. 1900) **1** : the study of meanings: **a** : the historical and psychological study and the classification of changes in the signification of words or forms viewed as factors in linguistic development **b** (1) : SEMIOTIC (2) : a branch of semiotic dealing with the relations between signs and what they refer to and including theories of denotation, extension, naming, and truth **2** : GENERAL SEMANTICS **3 a** : the meaning or relationship of meanings of a sign or set of signs; *esp* : connotative meaning **b** : the language used (as in advertising or political propaganda) to achieve a desired effect on an audience

¹**sema·phore** \'sem-ə-,fō(ə)r, -,fȯ(ə)r\ *n* [Gk *sēma* sign, signal + ISV *-phore*] (1816) **1** : an apparatus for visual signaling (as by the position of one or more movable arms) **2** : a system of visual signaling by two flags held one in each hand

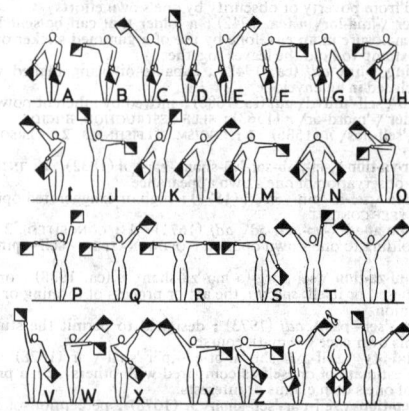

semaphore 2: alphabet; 3 positions following Z: error, end of word, numerals follow; numerals 1, 2, 3, 4, 5, 6, 7, 8, 9, 0 same as A through J

²**semaphore** *vb* **-phored; -phor·ing** *vt* (1893) : to convey (information) by or as if by semaphore ~ *vi* : to send signals by or as if by semaphore

se·ma·si·ol·o·gy \si-,mā-sē-'äl-ə-jē, -,mā-zē-\ *n* [ISV, fr. Gk *sēmasia* meaning, fr. *sēmainein* to mean] (1877) : SEMANTICS 1 — **se·ma·si·o·log·i·cal** \-sē-ə-'läj-i-kəl, -zē-\ *adj*

se·mat·ic \si-'mat-ik\ *adj* [Gk *sēmat-, sēma* sign] (1890) : warning of danger — used of conspicuous colors of a poisonous or noxious animal ⟨the ~ coloration of the skunk⟩

¹**sem·bla·ble** \'sem-blə-bəl\ *adj* [ME, fr. MF, fr. OF, fr. *sembler* to be like, seem] (14c) **1** : SIMILAR **2** : SUITABLE **3** : APPARENT, SEEMING — **sem·bla·bly** \-blə-blē\ *adv*

²**semblable** *n* (15c) **1** *archaic* : something similar : LIKE **2** : one that is like oneself : one's fellow

sem·blance \'sem-blən(t)s\ *n* [ME, fr. MF, fr. OF *sembler* to be like, seem — more at RESEMBLE] (14c) **1 a** : outward and often specious appearance or show : FORM ⟨wrapped in a ~ of composure —Harry Hervey⟩ **b** : MODICUM ⟨has been struggling to get some ~ of justice for his people —Bayard Rustin⟩ **2** : ASPECT, COUNTENANCE **3 a** : a phantasmal form : APPARITION **b** : IMAGE, LIKENESS **4** : actual or apparent resemblance

se·mé \sə-'mā, 'sem-(,)ā\ *adj* [MF, pp. of *semer* to sow, fr. L *seminare*, fr. *semen*] (1562) : having an ornamental pattern consisting of usu. regularly disposed separate objects or groups of small figures (as flowers or stars) : SOWN, DOTTED — **semé** *n*

se·mei·ol·o·gy *var of* SEMIOLOGY

Sem·e·le \'sem-ə-,lē\ *n* [L, fr. Gk *Semelē*] : a daughter of Cadmus consumed by flames when visited by Zeus in his divine splendor

se·men \'sē-mən\ *n* [NL, fr. L seed; akin to OHG *sāmo* seed, L *serere* to sow — more at SOW] (14c) : a viscid whitish fluid of the male reproductive tract consisting of spermatozoa suspended in secretions of accessory glands

se·mes·ter \sə-'mes-tər\ *n* [G, fr. L *semestris* half-yearly, fr. *sex* six + *mensis* month — more at SIX, MOON] (1827) **1** : a period of six months **2** : either of the two usu. 18-week periods of instruction into which an academic year is often divided — **se·mes·tral** \-trəl\ *or* **se·mes·tri·al** \-trē-əl\ *adj*

semester hour *n* (1922) : a unit of academic credit representing an hour of class (as lecture class) or three hours of laboratory work each week for an academic semester

semi \'sem-ē, -,ī\ *n* (1946) : SEMITRAILER

semi– \,sem-i, 'sem-, -,ī\ *prefix* [ME, fr. L; akin to OHG *sāmi-* half, Gk *hēmi-*] **1 a** : precisely half of: (1) : forming a bisection of ⟨*semiel*-lipse⟩ ⟨*semioval*⟩ (2) : being a usu. vertically bisected form of (a specified architectural feature) ⟨*semiarch*⟩ ⟨*semidome*⟩ **b** : half in quantity or value : half of or occurring halfway through a specified period of time ⟨*semiannual*⟩ ⟨*semicentenary*⟩ — compare BI- **2** : to some extent : partly : incompletely ⟨*semicivilized*⟩ ⟨*semi-independent*⟩ ⟨*semidry*⟩ — compare DEMI-, HEMI- **3 a** : partial : incomplete ⟨*semiconsciousness*⟩ ⟨*semidarkness*⟩ **b** : having some of the characteristics of ⟨*semiporcelain*⟩ **c** : QUASI- ⟨*semigovernmental*⟩ ⟨*semimonastic*⟩

semi·ab·stract \,sem-ē-ab-'strakt, ,sem-,ī-, -'ab-,\ *adj* (1945) : having subject matter that is easily recognizable although the form is stylized ⟨~ art⟩ — **semi·ab·strac·tion** \-ab-'strak-shən\ *n*

semi·an·nu·al \-'an-yə(-wə)l\ *adj* (1794) : occurring every six months or twice a year — **semi·an·nu·al·ly** \-ē\ *adv*

semi·an·tique \-an-'tēk\ *n* (ca. 1930) : a rug or carpet that is approximately 50 to 100 years old

semi–aquat·ic \-ə-'kwät-ik, -'kwat-\ *adj* (1833) : growing equally well in or adjacent to water; *also* : frequenting but not living wholly in water

semi·ar·bo·re·al \-är-ˈbōr-ē-əl, -ˈbȯr-\ *adj* (1938) : often inhabiting and frequenting trees but not completely arboreal
semi·ar·id \-ˈar-əd\ *adj* (1898) : characterized by light rainfall; *specif* : having from about 10 to about 20 inches of annual precipitation — **semi·arid·i·ty** \-ə-ˈrid-ət-ē, -a-ˈrid-\ *n*
semi·au·to·bio·graph·i·cal \-ˌȯt-ə-ˌbī-ə-ˈgraf-i-kəl\ *adj* (1939) : partly autobiographical ⟨a ~ comedy⟩
semi·au·to·mat·ic \-ˌȯt-ə-ˈmat-ik\ *adj* (ca. 1894) : not fully automatic: as **a** : operated partly automatically and partly by hand **b** *of a firearm* : employing gas pressure or force of recoil and mechanical spring action to eject the empty cartridge case after the first shot and load the next cartridge from the magazine but requiring release and another pressure of the trigger for each successive shot — **semiautomatic** *n* — **semi·au·to·mat·i·cal·ly** \-i-k(ə-)lē\ *adv*
semi·au·ton·o·mous \-ȯ-ˈtän-ə-məs\ *adj* (1915) : largely self-governing within a larger political or organizational entity
semi·breve \ˈsem-i-ˌbrēv, ˈsem-ˌī-, -ˌbrev\ *n* (1591) : WHOLE NOTE
semi·cen·te·na·ry \ˌsem-i-sen-ˈten-ə-rē, ˌsem-ˌī-, -ˈsent-ᵊn-ˌer-ē, -sen-ˈtē-nə-rē\ *n* (1870) : SEMICENTENNIAL — **semicentenary** *adj*
semi·cen·ten·ni·al \-sen-ˈten-ē-əl\ *n* (1859) : a 50th anniversary or its celebration — **semicentennial** *adj*
semi·cir·cle \ˈsem-i-ˌsər-kəl\ *n* [L *semicirculus*, fr. *semi-* + *circulus* circle] (1526) **1** : a half of a circle **2** : an object or arrangement of objects in the form of a half circle — **semi·cir·cu·lar** \ˌsem-i-ˈsər-kyə-lər\ *adj*
semicircular canal *n* (1748) : any of the loop-shaped tubular parts of the labyrinth of the ear that together constitute a sensory organ associated with the maintenance of bodily equilibrium — see EAR illustration
semi·civ·i·lized \ˌsem-i-ˈsiv-ə-ˌlīzd, ˌsem-ˌī-\ *adj* (1836) : partly civilized
semi·clas·sic \-ˈklas-ik\ *n* (1924) : a semiclassical work (as of music)
semi·clas·si·cal \-i-kəl\ *adj* (1904) : having some of the characteristics of the classical: as **a** : of, relating to, or being a musical composition that acts as a bridge between classical and popular music **b** : of, relating to, or being a classical composition that has developed popular appeal
semi·co·lon \ˈsem-i-ˌkō-lən\ *n* (1644) : a punctuation mark ; used chiefly in a coordinating function between major sentence elements (as independent clauses of a compound sentence)
semi·co·lo·nial \ˌsem-i-kə-ˈlō-nyəl, ˌsem-ˌī-, -nē-əl\ *adj* (1932) **1** : nominally independent but actually under foreign domination **2** : dependent on foreign nations as suppliers of manufactured goods and as purchasers of raw materials — **semi·co·lo·nial·ism** \-ˌiz-əm\ *n*
semi·col·o·ny \-ˈkäl-ə-nē\ *n* (1945) : a semicolonial state
semi·com·mer·cial \-kə-ˈmər-shəl\ *adj* (1926) : of, relating to, adapted to, or characterized by limited marketing of an experimental product
semi·con·duct·ing \ˌsem-i-kən-ˈdək-tiŋ, ˌsem-ˌī-\ *adj* (1787) : of, relating to, or having the characteristics of a semiconductor
semi·con·duc·tor \-ˈdək-tər\ *n* (1879) : any of a class of solids (as germanium or silicon) whose electrical conductivity is between that of a conductor and that of an insulator in being nearly as great as that of a metal at high temperatures and nearly absent at low temperatures
semi·con·scious \-ˈkän-chəs\ *adj* (1839) : incompletely conscious : imperfectly aware or responsive — **semi·con·scious·ness** *n*
semi·con·ser·va·tive \-kən-ˈsər-vət-iv\ *adj* (1961) : relating to or being replication (as of DNA) in which the original separates into parts each of which is incorporated into a new whole and serves as a template for the formation of the missing parts — **semi·con·ser·va·tive·ly** *adv*
semi·crys·tal·line \-ˈkris-tə-lən\ *adj* (1816) : incompletely or imperfectly crystalline
semi·cy·lin·dri·cal \-sə-ˈlin-dri-kəl\ *adj* (ca. 1731) : having the shape of a longitudinal half of a cylinder
semi·dark·ness \-ˈdärk-nəs\ *n* (1849) : partial darkness
semi·de·ify \-ˈdē-ə-ˌfī, -ˈdā-\ *vt* (1953) : to regard as somewhat godlike
semi·des·ert \-ˈdez-ərt\ *n* (1849) : an area that has some of the characteristics of a desert and is often located between a desert and grassland or woodland
semi·de·tached \-di-ˈtacht\ *adj* (1859) : forming one of a pair of residences joined into one building by a common sidewall
semi·di·am·e·ter \ˌsem-i-dī-ˈam-ət-ər\ *n* (ca. 1551) : RADIUS; *specif* : the apparent radius of a generally spherical celestial body
semi·di·ur·nal \-dī-ˈərn-ᵊl\ *adj* (1594) **1** : relating to or accomplished in half a day **2** : occurring twice a day **3** : occurring approximately every half day ⟨the ~ tides⟩
semi·di·vine \ˌsem-i-də-ˈvīn, ˌsem-ˌī-\ *adj* (1600) : more than mortal but not fully divine
semi·doc·u·men·ta·ry \-ˌdäk-yə-ˈment-ə-rē, -ˈmen-trē\ *n* (1945) : a motion picture that uses many details taken from actual events or situations in presenting a fictional story — **semidocumentary** *adj*
semi·dome \ˈsem-i-ˌdōm, ˈsem-ˌī-\ *n* (1788) : a roof or ceiling covering a semicircular or nearly semicircular room or recess — **semi·domed** \-ˌdōmd\ *adj*
semi·do·mes·ti·cat·ed \ˌsem-i-də-ˈmes-ti-ˌkāt-əd, ˌsem-ˌī-\ *or* **semi·do·mes·tic** \-ˈmes-tik\ *adj* (1847) : of, relating to, or living in semidomestication
semi·do·mes·ti·ca·tion \-ˌmes-ti-ˈkā-shən\ *n* (1835) : a captive state (as in a zoo) of a wild animal in which its living conditions and often its breeding are controlled by man
semi·dom·i·nant \-ˈdäm-(ə-)nənt\ *adj* (1942) : producing an intermediate phenotype in the heterozygous condition ⟨a ~ mutant gene⟩
semi·dry \ˌsem-i-ˈdrī\ *adj* (1878) : moderately dry
semi·dry·ing \-ˈdrī-iŋ\ *adj* (1905) : that dries imperfectly or slowly — used of some oils (as cottonseed oil)
semi·dwarf \ˌsem-i-ˈdwȯ(ə)rf, ˌsem-ˌī-\ *adj* (ca. 1959) : of or being a plant of a variety that is undersized but larger than a dwarf ⟨~ wheats⟩ — **semidwarf** *n*
semi·erect \ˌsem-ē-ə-ˈrekt, ˌsem-ˌī-\ *adj* (1822) **1** : incompletely upright in bodily posture ⟨~ primates⟩ **2** : erect for half the length ⟨~ stems⟩
semi·ev·er·green \-ˈev-ər-ˌgrēn\ *adj* (ca. 1901) **1** : having functional and persistent foliage during part of the winter or dry season **2** : tending to be evergreen in a mild climate but deciduous in a rigorous climate
semi·feu·dal \ˌsem-i-ˈfyüd-ᵊl, ˌsem-ˌī-\ *adj* (1898) : having some characteristics of feudalism
¹**semi·fi·nal** \ˌsem-i-ˈfīn-ᵊl\ *adj* (1884) **1** : being next to the last in an elimination tournament **2** : of or participating in a semifinal
²**semi·fi·nal** \ˈsem-i-ˌ\ *n* (1895) **1** : a semifinal match **2** : a semifinal round — **semi·fi·nal·ist** \ˌsem-i-ˈfīn-ᵊl-əst\ *n*
semi·fin·ished \ˌsem-i-ˈfin-isht, ˌsem-ˌī-\ *adj* (1902) : partially finished or processed; *esp, of steel* : rolled from raw ingots into shapes (as bars, billets, or plates) suitable for further processing
semi·fit·ted \-ˈfit-əd\ *adj* (ca. 1950) : conforming somewhat to the lines of the body
semi·flex·i·ble \-ˈflek-sə-bəl\ *adj* (1925) **1** : somewhat flexible **2** *of a book cover* : having a thin board stiffener under the covering material
semi·flu·id \-ˈflü-əd\ *adj* (ca. 1735) : having the qualities of both a fluid and a solid : VISCOUS ⟨fluid and ~ lubricants⟩ — **semifluid** *n*
semi·for·mal \-ˈfȯr-məl\ *adj* (1932) : being or suitable for an occasion of moderate formality ⟨a ~ dinner⟩ ⟨~ gowns⟩
semi·gloss \ˈsem-i-ˌgläs, ˈsem-ˌī-, -ˌglȯs\ *adj* (1937) : having a low luster; *specif* : producing a finish midway between gloss and flat
semi·gov·ern·men·tal \ˌsem-i-ˌgəv-ər(n)-ˈment-ᵊl, ˌsem-ˌī-, -ˌgəv-ᵊm-ˈent-\ *adj* (1919) : having some governmental functions and powers
semi·group \ˈsem-i-ˌgrüp, ˈsem-ˌī-\ *n* (ca. 1927) : a mathematical set that is closed under an associative binary operation
semi–in·de·pen·dent \ˈsem-ē-ˌin-də-ˈpen-dənt, ˈsem-ˌī-\ *adj* (1860) : partially independent; *specif* : SEMIAUTONOMOUS
semi–in·di·rect \-ˌin-də-ˈrekt, -dī-\ *adj, of lighting* (1920) : using a translucent reflector that transmits some primary light while reflecting most of it
semi·leg·end·ary \ˌsem-i-ˈlej-ən-ˌder-ē, ˌsem-ˌī-\ *adj* (1878) : having historical foundation but elaborated in legend
semi·le·thal \-ˈlē-thəl\ *n* (1927) : a mutation that in the homozygous condition produces more than 50 percent mortality but not complete mortality — **semilethal** *adj*
semi·liq·uid \-ˈlik-wəd\ *adj* (1684) : having the qualities of both a liquid and a solid : SEMIFLUID ⟨~ manure⟩ — **semiliquid** *n*
semi·lit·er·ate \-ˈlit-ə-rət, -ˈli-trət\ *adj* (1927) **1 a** : able to read and write on an elementary level **b** : able to read but unable to write **2** : having limited knowledge or understanding : not well-versed — **semiliterate** *n*
semi·log \-ˈlȯg, -ˈläg\ *adj* (1927) : SEMILOGARITHMIC
semi·log·a·rith·mic \-ˌlȯg-ə-ˈrith-mik, -ˌläg-\ *adj* (ca. 1923) : having one scale logarithmic and the other arithmetic — used of graph paper or of a graph on such paper
semi·lu·nar \-ˈlü-nər\ *adj* [NL *semilunaris*, fr. L *semi-* + *lunaris* lunar] (1597) : shaped like a crescent
semilunar valve *n* (ca. 1719) : any of the crescentic cusps that occur as a set of three between the heart and the aorta and another of three between the heart and the pulmonary artery, are forced apart by pressure in the ventricles during systole and pushed together by pressure in the arteries during diastole, and prevent regurgitation of blood into the ventricles; *also* : either set of three cusps
semi·lus·trous \ˌsem-i-ˈləs-trəs, ˌsem-ˌī-\ *adj* (1953) : slightly lustrous
semi·ma·jor axis \ˌsem-i-ˌmā-jər-, ˌsem-ˌī-\ *n* (1926) : one half of the longest diameter of an ellipse (as that formed by the orbit of a planet)
semi·man·u·fac·tures \-ˌman-(y)ə-ˈfak-chərz\ *n pl* (1929) : products (as steel or newsprint) that are made from raw materials and that require further processing to become finished goods
semi·matte *also* **semi·mat** *or* **semi·matt** \-ˈmat\ *adj* [*semi-* + ⁴*mat*] (1937) : having a slight luster
semi·met·al \-ˈmet-ᵊl\ *n* (ca. 1661) : an element (as arsenic) possessing metallic properties in an inferior degree and not malleable — **semi·me·tal·lic** \-mə-ˈtal-ik\ *adj*
semi·mi·cro \-ˈmī-(ˌ)krō\ *adj* (1936) : of, relating to, or dealing with quantities intermediate between those treated as micro and macro ⟨~ analysis for chlorine⟩ ⟨a ~ balance⟩
semi·mi·nor axis \-ˌmī-nər-\ *n* (1926) : one half of the shortest diameter of an ellipse (as that formed by the orbit of a planet)
semi·moist \-ˈmȯist\ *adj* (ca. 1903) : slightly moist
semi·mo·nas·tic \-mə-ˈnas-tik\ *adj* (1911) : having some features characteristic of a monastic order
¹**semi·month·ly** \-ˈmən(t)th-lē\ *n* (1851) : a semimonthly publication
²**semimonthly** *adj* (1860) : occurring twice a month
³**semimonthly** *adv* (ca. 1890) : twice a month
semi·mys·ti·cal \ˌsem-i-ˈmis-ti-kəl, ˌsem-ˌī-\ *adj* (1890) : having some of the qualities of mysticism
sem·i·nal \ˈsem-ən-ᵊl\ *adj* [ME, fr. MF, fr. L *seminalis*, fr. *semin-*, *semen* seed — more at SEMEN] (14c) **1** : of, relating to, or consisting of seed or semen **2** : containing or contributing the seeds of later development : CREATIVE, ORIGINAL ⟨a ~ book⟩ ⟨one of the most ~ of the great poets⟩ — **sem·i·nal·ly** \-ᵊl-ē\ *adv*
seminal duct *n* (ca. 1909) : a tube or passage serving esp. or exclusively as an efferent duct of the testis and in man being made up of the tubules of the epididymis, the vas deferens, and the ejaculatory duct
seminal fluid *n* (ca. 1929) **1** : SEMEN **2** : the part of the semen that is produced by various accessory glands : semen excepting the spermatozoa
seminal vesicle *n* (ca. 1889) : a pouch on either side of the male reproductive tract that is variously formed in different mammals, is connected with the seminal duct, and serves for temporary storage of semen
sem·i·nar \ˈsem-ə-ˌnär\ *n* [G, fr. L *seminarium* seminary] (1889) **1** : a group of advanced students studying under a professor with each doing original research and all exchanging results through reports and discussions **2 a** (1) : a course of study pursued by a seminar (2) : an advanced or graduate course often featuring informality and discussion **b** : a scheduled meeting of a seminar or a room for such meetings **3** : a meeting for giving and discussing information
sem·i·nar·i·an \ˌsem-ə-ˈner-ē-ən\ *n* (1794) : a student in a seminary esp. of the Roman Catholic Church
sem·i·na·rist \ˈsem-ə-nə-rəst\ *n* (1835) : SEMINARIAN

\ə\ abut \ᵊ\ kitten, F table \ər\ further \a\ ash \ā\ ace \ä\ cot, cart
\au̇\ out \ch\ chin \e\ bet \ē\ easy \g\ go \i\ hit \ī\ ice \j\ job
\ŋ\ sing \ō\ go \ȯ\ law \ȯi\ boy \th\ thin \th\ the \ü\ loot \u̇\ foot
\y\ yet \zh\ vision \à, k̲, ⁿ, œ, œ̄, ue, ue̅, ʸ\ *see* Guide to Pronunciation

sem·i·nary \ˈsem-ə-ˌner-ē\ *n, pl* **-nar·ies** [ME, seedbed, nursery, seminary, fr. L *seminarium,* fr. *semin-, semen* seed] (15c) **1 :** an environment in which something originates and from which it is propagated ⟨a ~ of vice and crime⟩ **2 a :** an institution of secondary or higher education; *esp* **:** an academy for girls **b :** an institution for the training of candidates for the priesthood, ministry, or rabbinate
semi·nat·u·ral \ˌsem-i-ˈnach-(ə-)rəl, ˌsem-ˌī-\ *adj* (ca. 1962) **:** modified by human influence but retaining many natural features ⟨~ temperate meadows⟩
sem·i·nif·er·ous \ˌsem-ə-ˈnif-(ə-)rəs\ *adj* [L *semin-, semen* seed + E *-iferous*] (1692) **:** producing or bearing seed or semen
seminiferous tubule *n* (1860) **:** any of the coiled threadlike tubules that make up the bulk of the testis and are lined with a germinal epithelium from which the spermatozoa are produced
Sem·i·nole \ˈsem-ə-ˌnōl\ *n, pl* **Seminoles** *or* **Seminole** [Creek *simaló-ni, simanó-li,* lit., wild, fr. AmerSp *cimarrón*] (1789) **:** a member of an American Indian people of Florida
semi·no·mad \ˌsem-i-ˈnō-ˌmad, ˌsem-ˌī-\ *n* (ca. 1934) **:** a member of a people living usu. in portable or temporary dwellings and practicing seasonal migration but having a base camp at which some crops are cultivated — **semi·no·mad·ic** \-nō-ˈmad-ik\ *adj*
semi·nude \-ˈn(y)üd\ *adj* (1849) **:** partially nude — **semi·nu·di·ty** \-ˈn(y)üd-ət-ē\ *n*
semi·of·fi·cial \ˌsem-ē-ə-ˈfish-əl, ˌsem-ˌī-\ *adj* (1806) **:** having some official authority or standing — **semi·of·fi·cial·ly** \-ˈfish-(ə-)lē\ *adv*
se·mi·ol·o·gy \ˌsē-mē-ˈäl-ə-jē, ˌsem-ē-, ˌsē-ˌmī-\ *n* [Gk *sēmeion* sign] (ca. 1890) **:** the study of signs; *esp* **:** SEMIOTIC — **se·mi·o·log·i·cal** \(ˌ)sē-ˌmī-ə-ˈläj-i-kəl\ *adj* — **se·mi·o·log·i·cal·ly** \-ə-ˈläj-i-k(ə-)lē\ *adv* — **se·mi·ol·o·gist** \-ˈäl-ə-jəst\ *n*
semi·opaque \ˌsem-ē-ō-ˈpāk, ˌsem-ˌī-\ *adj* (1691) **:** nearly opaque
se·mi·o·sis \ˌsē-mē-ˈō-səs, ˌsem-ē-, ˌsē-ˌmī-\ *n* [NL, fr. Gk *sēmeiōsis* observation of signs, fr. *sēmeioun* to observe signs, fr. *sēmeion*] (ca. 1907) **:** a process in which something functions as a sign to an organism
se·mi·ot·ic \-ˈät-ik\ *or* **se·mi·ot·ics** \-iks\ *n, pl* **semiotics** [Gk *sēmeiōtikos* observant of signs, fr. *sēmeiousthai* to interpret signs, fr. *sēmeion* sign; akin to Gk *sēma* sign — more at SEMANTIC] (1938) **:** a general philosophical theory of signs and symbols that deals esp. with their function in both artificially constructed and natural languages and comprises syntactics, semantics, and pragmatics — **semiotic** *adj* — **se·mi·o·ti·cian** \-ə-ˈtish-ən\ *n* — **se·mi·ot·i·cist** \-ˈät-ə-səst\ *n*
semi·pal·mat·ed \ˌsem-i-ˈpal-ˌmāt-əd, ˌsem-ˌī-, -ˈpä(l)m-ˌāt-\ *adj* (1785) **:** having the anterior toes joined only part way down with a web ⟨a plover with ~ feet⟩
semi·par·a·sit·ic \-ˌpar-ə-ˈsit-ik\ *adj* (1878) **:** of, relating to, or being a parasitic plant that contains some chlorophyll and is capable of photosynthesis
semi·per·ma·nent \-ˈpərm-(ə-)nənt\ *adj* (ca. 1890) **:** lasting or intended to last for a long time but not permanent
semi·per·me·able \-ˈpər-mē-ə-bəl\ *adj* (1888) **:** partially but not freely or wholly permeable; *specif* **:** permeable to some usu. small molecules but not to other usu. larger particles ⟨a ~ membrane⟩ — **semi·per·me·abil·i·ty** \-ˌpər-mē-ə-ˈbil-ət-ē\ *n*
semi·po·lit·i·cal \-pə-ˈlit-i-kəl\ *adj* (1857) **:** of, relating to, or involving some political features or activity
semi·pop·u·lar \-ˈpäp-yə-lər\ *adj* (1899) **:** somewhat popular
semi·por·ce·lain \-ˈpōr-s(ə-)lən, -ˈpȯr-\ *n* (1880) **:** any of several ceramic wares resembling or imitative of porcelain; *esp* **:** a relatively high-fired and hard-glazed white earthenware widely used for tableware
semi·por·no·graph·ic \-ˌpȯr-nə-ˈgraf-ik\ *adj* (1964) **:** somewhat pornographic — **semi·por·nog·ra·phy** \-pȯr-ˈnäg-rə-fē\ *n*
semi·post·al \ˌsem-i-ˈpōs-tᵊl, ˌsem-ˌī-\ *n* (1927) **:** a postage stamp sold at a premium over its postal value esp. for a humanitarian purpose
semi·pre·cious \-ˈpresh-əs\ *adj, of a gemstone* (ca. 1890) **:** of less commercial value than a precious stone
semi·pri·vate \-ˈprī-vət\ *adj* (ca. 1925) **:** of, receiving, or associated with hospital service giving a patient more privileges than a ward patient but fewer than a private patient
semi·pro \ˈsem-i-ˌprō, ˈsem-ˌī-\ *adj or n* (1908) **:** SEMIPROFESSIONAL
1**semi·pro·fes·sion·al** \ˌsem-i-prə-ˈfesh-nəl, -ən-ᵊl, ˌsem-ˌī-\ *adj* (1897) **1 :** engaging in an activity for pay or gain but not as a full-time occupation **2 :** engaged in by semiprofessional players ⟨~ baseball⟩ — **semi·pro·fes·sion·al·ly** \-ē\ *adv*
2**semiprofessional** *n* (ca. 1897) **:** one who engages in an activity (as a sport) semiprofessionally
semi·pub·lic \ˌsem-i-ˈpəb-lik, ˌsem-ˌī-\ *adj* (1804) **1 :** open to some persons outside the regular constituency **2 :** having some features of a public institution; *specif* **:** maintained as a public service by a private nonprofit organization
semi·quan·ti·ta·tive \-ˈkwän(t)-ə-ˌtāt-iv\ *adj* (ca. 1927) **:** constituting or involving less than quantitative precision — **semi·quan·ti·ta·tive·ly** *adv*
semi·qua·ver \ˈsem-i-ˌkwā-vər, ˈsem-ˌī-\ *n* (1576) **:** SIXTEENTH NOTE
semi·re·li·gious \-ri-ˈlij-əs\ *adj* (1864) **:** somewhat religious in character
semi·re·tired \-ri-ˈtī(ə)rd\ *adj* (1937) **:** working only part-time esp. because of age or ill health
semi·re·tire·ment \-ˈtī(ə)r-mənt\ *n* (1923) **:** the state or condition of being semiretired
semi·rig·id \ˌsem-i-ˈrij-əd, ˌsem-ˌī-\ *adj* (1908) **1 :** rigid to some degree or in some parts **2** *of an airship* **:** having a flexible cylindrical gas container with an attached stiffening keel that carries the load
semi·rur·al \-ˈrůr-əl\ *adj* (ca. 1864) **:** somewhat rural
semi·sa·cred \-ˈsā-krəd\ *adj* (ca. 1898) **:** SEMIRELIGIOUS
semi·se·cret \-ˈsē-krət\ *adj* (1917) **:** not publicly announced but widely known nevertheless
semi·sed·en·tary \-ˈsed-ᵊn-ˌter-ē\ *adj* (ca. 1930) **:** sedentary during part of the year and nomadic otherwise ⟨~ tribes⟩
semi·shrub·by \ˈsem-i-ˌshrəb-ē, ˈsem-ˌī-, *esp Southern* -ˌsrəb-\ *adj* (1930) **:** resembling or being a subshrub
semi·skilled \ˌsem-i-ˈskild, ˌsem-ˌī-\ *adj* (1916) **:** having or requiring less training than skilled labor and more than unskilled labor
semi·soft \-ˈsȯft\ *adj* (ca. 1903) **:** moderately soft; *specif* **:** firm but easily cut ⟨~ cheese⟩
semi·sol·id \-ˈsäl-əd\ *adj* (1834) **:** having the qualities of both a solid and a liquid **:** highly viscous — **semisolid** *n*
semi·sweet \-ˈswēt\ *adj* (1943) **:** slightly sweetened ⟨~ chocolate⟩
semi·syn·thet·ic \-sin-ˈthet-ik\ *adj* (1937) **1 :** produced by chemical alteration of a natural starting material ⟨~ penicillins⟩ **2 :** containing both chemically identified and complex natural ingredients ⟨a ~ diet⟩
Sem·ite \ˈsem-ˌīt, *esp Brit* ˈsē-ˌmīt\ *n* [F *sémite,* fr. *Sem* Shem, fr. LL, fr. Gk *Sēm,* fr. Heb *Shēm*] (1875) **:** a member of any of a group of peoples of southwestern Asia chiefly represented now by the Jews and Arabs but in ancient times also by the Babylonians, Assyrians, Aramaeans, Canaanites, and Phoenicians
semi·ter·res·tri·al \ˌsem-i-tə-ˈres-trē-əl, ˌsem-ˌī-, -ˈres(h)-chəl\ *adj* (1917) **1 :** growing on boggy ground **2 :** frequenting but not living wholly on land
1**Se·mit·ic** \sə-ˈmit-ik\ *adj* [G *semitisch,* fr. *Semit, Semite* Semite, prob. fr. NL *Semita,* fr. LL *Sem* Shem] (1826) **1 :** of, relating to, or characteristic of the Semites; *specif* **:** JEWISH **2 :** of, relating to, or constituting a subfamily of the Afro-Asiatic language family that includes Hebrew, Aramaic, Arabic, and Ethiopic
2**Semitic** *n* (1875) **:** any or all of the Semitic languages
Se·mit·i·cist \sə-ˈmit-ə-səst\ *n* (1956) **:** SEMITIST
Se·mit·ics \-ˈmit-iks\ *n pl but sing in constr* (1895) **:** the study of the language, literature, and history of Semitic peoples; *specif* **:** Semitic philology
Sem·i·tism \ˈsem-ə-ˌtiz-əm\ *n* (1851) **1 a :** Semitic character or qualities **b :** a characteristic feature of a Semitic language occurring in another language **2 :** policy favorable to Jews **:** predisposition in favor of Jews
Sem·i·tist \-ət-əst\ *n* (1885) **1 :** a scholar of the Semitic languages, cultures, or histories **2** *often not cap* **:** a person favoring or disposed to favor the Jews
semi·ton·al \ˌsem-i-ˈtōn-ᵊl, ˌsem-ˌī-\ *adj* (1863) **:** CHROMATIC 3a, SEMITONIC — **semi·ton·al·ly** \-ᵊl-ē\ *adv*
semi·tone \ˈsem-i-ˌtōn, ˈsem-ˌī-\ *n* (1609) **:** the tone at a half step; *also* **:** HALF STEP — **semi·ton·ic** \ˌsem-i-ˈtän-ik, ˌsem-ˌī-\ *adj* — **semi·ton·i·cal·ly** \-i-k(ə-)lē\ *adv*
semi·trail·er \ˈsem-i-ˌtrā-lər, ˈsem-ˌī-\ *n* (1919) **1 :** a freight trailer that when attached is supported at its forward end by the fifth wheel device of the truck tractor **2 :** a trucking rig made up of a tractor and a semitrailer
semi·trans·lu·cent \ˌsem-i-ˌtran(t)s-ˈlüs-ᵊnt, ˌsem-ˌī-, -ˌtranz-\ *adj* (1832) **:** somewhat translucent
semi·trans·par·ent \-ˌtran(t)s-ˈpar-ənt, -ˈper-\ *adj* (1793) **:** imperfectly transparent
semi·trop·i·cal \-ˈträp-i-kəl\ *also* **semi·trop·ic** \-ik\ *adj* (1860) **:** SUBTROPICAL
semi·trop·ics \-iks\ *n pl* (1908) **:** SUBTROPICS
semi·vow·el \ˈsem-i-ˌvau̇(-ə)l\ *n* (1530) **1 :** one of the glides (as English \y\, \w\, or \r\) **2 :** a letter representing a semivowel
1**semi·week·ly** \ˌsem-i-ˈwē-klē, ˌsem-ˌī-\ *adj* (1791) **:** occurring twice a week — **semiweekly** *adv*
2**semiweekly** *n* (1833) **:** a semiweekly publication
semi·works \ˈsem-i-ˌwərks, ˈsem-ˌī-\ *n pl, often attrib* (1926) **:** a manufacturing plant operating on a limited commercial scale to provide final tests of a new product or process
semi·year·ly \ˌsem-i-ˈyi(ə)r-lē, ˌsem-ˌī-\ *adj* (1928) **:** occurring twice a year
sem·o·li·na \ˌsem-ə-ˈlē-nə\ *n* [It *semolino,* dim. of *semola* bran, fr. L *simila* finest wheat flour] (1797) **:** the purified middlings of hard wheat (as durum) used esp. for pasta (as macaroni or spaghetti)
sem·per·vi·vum \ˌsem-pər-ˈvī-vəm\ *n* [NL, fr. L, neuter of *sempervivus* ever-living, fr. *semper* ever + *vivus* living — more at QUICK] (ca. 1591) **:** any of a large genus (*Sempervivum*) of Old World fleshy herbs of the orpine family often grown as ornamentals
sem·pi·ter·nal \ˌsem-pi-ˈtərn-ᵊl\ *adj* [ME, fr. LL *sempiternalis,* fr. L *sempiternus,* fr. *semper* ever, always, fr. *sem-* one, same (akin to ON *samr* same) + *per* through — more at SAME, FOR] (15c) **:** of never-ending duration **:** ETERNAL — **sem·pi·ter·nal·ly** \-ᵊl-ē\ *adv*
sem·pi·ter·ni·ty \-ˈtər-nət-ē\ *n* (1599) **:** ETERNITY
sem·ple \ˈsem-pəl\ *adj* [alter. of *simple*] *Scot* (1759) **:** of humble birth
sem·pli·ce \ˈsem-pli-ˌchā\ *adj or adv* [It, fr. L *simplic-, simplex* — more at SIMPLE] (ca. 1740) **:** SIMPLE — used as a direction in music
sem·pre \ˈsem-(ˌ)prā\ *adv* [It, fr. L *semper*] (ca. 1801) **:** ALWAYS — used in music directions ⟨~ legato⟩
semp·stress \ˈsem(p)-strəs\ *var of* SEAMSTRESS
1**sen** \ˈsen\ *n, pl* **sen** [Jp] (1727) — see *yen* at MONEY table
2**sen** *n, pl* **sen** [Indonesian *sén,* prob. fr. E *cent*] (1951) — see *rupiah* at MONEY table
3**sen** *n, pl* **sen** [prob. fr. Indonesian *sén*] (1954) — see *dollar, riel* at MONEY table
4**sen** *n, pl* **sen** [Malay, prob. fr. E *cent*] (1967) — see *ringgit* at MONEY table
se·nar·i·us \si-ˈnar-ē-əs, -ˈner-\ *n, pl* **se·nar·ii** \-ē-ˌī, -ē-ˌē\ [L, fr. *senarius* consisting of six each, fr. *seni* six each, fr. *sex* six — more at SIX] (1540) **:** a verse consisting of six feet esp. in Latin prosody
se·na·ry \ˈsen-ə-rē, ˈsēn-\ *adj* [L *senarius* consisting of six] (1661) **:** of, based on, or characterized by six **:** compounded of six things or six parts ⟨~ scale⟩ ⟨~ division⟩
sen·ate \ˈsen-ət\ *n* [ME *senat,* fr. OF, fr. L *senatus,* lit., council of elders, fr. *sen-, senex* old, old man — more at SENIOR] (13c) **1 :** an assembly or council usu. possessing high deliberative and legislative functions: as **a :** the supreme council of the ancient Roman republic and empire **b :** the second chamber in the bicameral legislature of a major political unit (as a nation, state, or province) **2 :** the hall or chamber in which a senate meets **3 :** a governing body of some universities charged with maintaining academic standards and regulations and usu. composed of the principal or representative members of the faculty
sen·a·tor \ˈsen-ət-ər, *as a title also* ˈsen-tər\ *n* [ME *senatour,* fr. OF *senateur,* fr. L *senator,* fr. *senatus*] (13c) **:** a member of a senate
sen·a·to·ri·al \ˌsen-ə-ˈtōr-ē-əl, -ˈtȯr-\ *adj* (1740) **:** of, relating to, or befitting a senator or a senate ⟨~ office⟩ ⟨~ rank⟩
senatorial courtesy *n* (1884) **:** a custom of the U.S. Senate of refusing to confirm a presidential appointment of an official in or from a state when the appointment is opposed by the senators or senior senator of the president's party from that state
senatorial district *n* (1829) **:** a territorial division from which a senator is elected — compare CONGRESSIONAL DISTRICT

sen·a·to·ri·an \ˌsen-ə-ˈtōr-ē-ən, -ˈtȯr-\ *adj* (1614) **:** SENATORIAL; *specif* **:** of or relating to the ancient Roman senate

sen·a·tor·ship \ˈsen-ət-ər-ˌship\ *n* (1602) **:** the office or position of senator

se·na·tus con·sul·tum \sə-ˌnät-ə-skən-ˈsəl-təm, -ˈsu̇l-\ *n, pl* **senatus con·sul·ta** \-tə\ [L, decree of the senate] (1696) **:** a decree of the ancient Roman senate

[1]**send** \ˈsend\ *vb* **sent** \ˈsent\; **send·ing** [ME *senden*, fr. OE *sendan*; akin to OHG *sendan* to send, OE *sith* road, journey, OIr *sēt*] *vt* (bef. 12c) **1 :** to cause to go: as **a :** to propel or throw in a particular direction **b :** DELIVER ⟨*sent* a blow to the chin⟩ **c :** DRIVE ⟨*sent* the ball between the goalposts⟩ **2 :** to cause to happen ⟨whatever fate may ~⟩ **3 :** to dispatch by a means of communication **4 a :** to direct, order, or request to go **b :** to permit or enable to attend a term or session ⟨~ a daughter to college⟩ **c :** to direct by advice or reference **d :** to cause or order to depart **:** DISMISS **5 a :** to force to go **:** drive away **b :** to cause to assume a specified state ⟨*sent* them into a rage⟩ **6 :** to cause to issue: as **a :** to pour out **:** DISCHARGE ⟨clouds ~*ing* forth rain⟩ **b :** UTTER ⟨~ forth a cry⟩ **c :** EMIT ⟨*sent* out waves of perfume⟩ **d :** to grow out (parts) in the course of development ⟨a plant ~*ing* forth shoots⟩ **7 :** to cause to be carried to a destination; *esp* **:** to consign to death or a place of punishment **8 :** to convey or cause to be conveyed or transmitted by an agent ⟨~ a package by mail⟩ ⟨*sent* out invitations⟩ **9 :** to strike or thrust so as to impel violently ⟨*sent* him sprawling⟩ **10 :** DELIGHT, THRILL ~ *vi* **1 a :** to dispatch someone to convey a message or do an errand — often used with *out* ⟨~ out for pizza⟩ **b :** to dispatch a request or order — often used with *away* **2 :** SCEND **3 :** TRANSMIT — **send·er** *n* — **send for :** to request by message to come **:** SUMMON — **send packing :** to send off or dismiss roughly or in disgrace

[2]**send** *n* (1726) **:** the lift of a wave

send down *vt, Brit* (1853) **:** to suspend or expel from a university

send in *vt* (1715) **1 :** to cause to be delivered ⟨*send in* a letter of complaint⟩ **2 :** to give (one's name or card) to a servant when making a call **3 :** to send (a player) into an athletic contest

send–off \ˈsen-ˌdȯf\ *n* (1872) **:** a demonstration of goodwill and enthusiasm for the beginning of a new venture (as a trip)

send–up \ˈsen-ˌdəp\ *n* (ca. 1964) **:** PARODY, TAKEOFF

send up \(ˈ)sen-ˈdəp\ *vt* (1852) **1 :** to sentence to imprisonment **:** send to jail **2 :** to make fun of **:** SATIRIZE, PARODY

se·ne \ˈsā-(ˌ)nā\ *n, pl* **sene** [Samoan, fr. E *cent*] (1967) — see *tala* at MONEY table

Sen·e·ca \ˈsen-i-kə\ *n, pl* **Seneca** *or* **Senecas** [D *Sennecaas*, pl., the Seneca, Oneida, Onondaga, and Cayuga peoples collectively, fr. Mahican *A'sinnika* Oneida, trans. of Iroquois *Onē̃yóde'*, lit., standing rock] (1614) **1 a :** an American Indian people of what is now western New York **b :** a member of this people **2 :** the language of the Seneca people

seneca snakeroot *n* (1789) **:** a No. American milkwort (*Polygala senega*) with tufted leafy stems terminated by small white flowers — called also *rattlesnake root, senega root;* compare SENEGA

se·ne·cio \si-ˈnē-sh(ē-ˌ)ō\ *n, pl* **-cios** [NL, fr. L, old man, groundsel (fr. its hoary pappus), fr. *sen-, senic-, senex* old man] (ca. 1890) **:** any of a genus (*Senecio*) of widely distributed composite plants that have alternate or basal leaves and flower heads with disk and ray flowers or only disk flowers and with the ray flowers mostly yellow and pistillate

se·nec·ti·tude \si-ˈnek-tə-ˌt(y)üd\ *n* [ML *senectitudo*, alter. of L *senectus* old age, fr. *sen-, senic-, senex* old, old man — more at SENIOR] (1796) **:** the final stage of the normal life span

sen·e·ga \ˈsen-i-gə\ *n* (1738) **:** the dried root of seneca snakeroot that contains an irritating saponin

senega root *n* [alter. of *Seneca root;* fr. its use by the Seneca as a remedy for snakebite] (ca. 1898) **1 :** SENECA SNAKEROOT **2 :** SENEGA

se·nes·cence \si-ˈnes-ᵊn(t)s\ *n* [*senescent*, fr. L *senescent-, senescens*, prp. of *senescere* to grow old, fr. *sen-, senex* old] (1695) **1 :** the state of being old **:** the process of becoming old **2 :** the plant growth phase from full maturity to death that is characterized by an accumulation of metabolic products, increase in respiratory rate, and a loss in dry weight esp. in leaves and fruit — **se·nes·cent** \-ᵊnt\ *adj*

sen·e·schal \ˈsen-ə-shəl\ *n* [ME, fr. MF, of Gmc origin; akin to Goth *sineigs* old, and to OHG *scalc* servant — more at SENIOR] (14c) **:** an agent or steward in charge of a lord's estate in feudal times

sen·gi \ˈseŋ-gē\ *n, pl* **sengi** [native name in Zaire] (1967) — see *zaire* at MONEY table

se·nhor \si-ˈnyō(ə)r, -ˈnyȯ(ə)r\ *n, pl* **senhors** *or* **se·nho·res** \-ˈnyōr-ēs(h), -ˈnyȯr-, -ēz(h)\ [Pg, fr. ML *senior* superior, lord, fr. L, adj., elder] (1795) **:** a Portuguese or Brazilian man — used as a title equivalent to *Mr.*

se·nho·ra \-ˈnyōr-ə, -ˈnyȯr-\ *n* [Pg, fem. of *senhor*] (1802) **:** a married Portuguese or Brazilian woman — used as a title equivalent to *Mrs.*

se·nho·ri·ta \ˌsē-nyə-ˈrēt-ə\ *n* [Pg, fr. dim. of *senhora*] (1874) **:** an unmarried Portuguese or Brazilian girl or woman — used as a title equivalent to *Miss*

se·nile \ˈsēn-ˌīl *also* ˈsen-\ *adj* [L *senilis*, fr. *sen-, senex* old, old man] (1661) **1 :** of, relating to, exhibiting, or characteristic of old age ⟨~ weakness⟩; *esp* **:** exhibiting a loss of mental faculties associated with old age **2 :** approaching the end of a geological cycle of erosion — **se·nile·ly** \-ˌīl-lē\ *adv*

se·nil·i·ty \si-ˈnil-ət-ē *also* se-\ *n* (1778) **:** the quality or state of being senile; *specif* **:** the physical and mental infirmity of old age

[1]**se·nior** \ˈsē-nyər\ *n* [ME, fr. L, fr. *senior*, adj.] (14c) **1 :** a person older than another ⟨five years his ~⟩ **2 a :** a person with higher standing or rank **b :** a senior fellow of a college at an English university **c :** a student in the year preceding graduation from a school of secondary or higher level **3 :** SENIOR CITIZEN

[2]**senior** *adj* [ME, fr. L, older, elder, compar. of *sen-, senex* old; akin to Goth *sineigs* old, Gk *henos*] (15c) **1 :** of prior birth, establishment, or enrollment — often used to distinguish a father with the same given name as his son **2 :** higher ranking **:** SUPERIOR ⟨~ officers⟩ **3 :** of or relating to seniors ⟨the ~ class⟩ **4 :** having a claim on corporate assets and income prior to other securities

senior airman *n* (ca. 1977) **:** an enlisted man in the air force who ranks above an airman first class but who has not been made sergeant

senior chief petty officer *n* (ca. 1960) **:** an enlisted man in the navy or coast guard ranking above a chief petty officer and below a master chief petty officer

senior citizen *n* (1954) **:** an elderly person; *esp* **:** one who has retired

senior high school *n* (1915) **:** a school usu. including grades 10 to 12

se·nior·i·ty \sēn-ˈyȯr-ət-ē, -ˈyär-\ *n* (15c) **1 :** the quality or state of being senior **:** PRIORITY **2 :** a privileged status attained by length of continuous service (as in a company)

senior master sergeant *n* (ca. 1961) **:** a noncommissioned officer in the air force ranking above a master sergeant and below a chief master sergeant

sen·i·ti \ˈsen-ə-tē\ *n, pl* **seniti** [Tongan, modif. of E *cent*] (1967) — see *pa'anga* at MONEY table

sen·na \ˈsen-ə\ *n* [NL, fr. Ar *sanā*] (1543) **1 :** any of a genus (*Cassia*) of leguminous herbs, shrubs, and trees native to warm regions; *esp* **:** one used medicinally **2 :** the dried leaflets or pods of various sennas (esp. *Cassia acutifolia* and *C. angustifolia*) used as a purgative

sen·net \ˈsen-ət\ *n* [prob. alter. of obs. *signet* (signal)] (1590) **:** a signal call on a trumpet or cornet for entrance or exit on the stage

sen·night *also* **se'n·night** \ˈsen-ˌīt\ *n* [ME, fr. OE *seofon nihta* seven nights] *archaic* (bef. 12c) **:** the space of seven nights and days **:** WEEK

sen·nit \ˈsen-ət\ *n* [perh. fr. F *coussinet*, dim. of *coussin* cushion; fr. its use to protect cables from fraying] (ca. 1769) **1 :** a braided cord or fabric (as of plaited rope yarns) **2 :** a straw or grass braid for hats

se·nor *or* **se·ñor** \sān-ˈyȯ(ə)r\ *n, pl* **senors** *or* **se·ño·res** \-ˈyō(ə)r-(ˌ)ās, -ˈyȯ(ə)r-\ [Sp *señor*, fr. ML *senior* superior, lord, fr. L, adj., elder] (1622) **:** a Spanish or Spanish-speaking man — used as a title equivalent to *Mr.*

se·no·ra *or* **se·ño·ra** \sān-ˈyōr-ə, -ˈyȯr-\ *n* [Sp *señora*, fem. of *señor*] (1579) **:** a married Spanish or Spanish-speaking woman — used as a title equivalent to *Mrs.*

se·no·ri·ta *or* **se·ño·ri·ta** \ˌsān-yə-ˈrēt-ə\ *n* [Sp *señorita*, fr. dim. of *señora*] (1823) **:** an unmarried Spanish or Spanish-speaking girl or woman — used as a title equivalent to *Miss*

sen·ryu \ˈsen-rē-(ˌ)ü\ *n, pl* **senryu** [Jp] (ca. 1965) **:** a 3-line unrhymed Japanese poem structurally similar to haiku but treating human nature usu. in an ironic or satiric vein

sensa *pl of* SENSUM

sen·sate \ˈsen-ˌsāt\ *adj* [ML, fr. LL, endowed with sense, fr. L *sensus* sense] (1500) **1 :** relating to, apprehending, or apprehended through the senses **2 :** preoccupied with things that can be experienced through a sense modality — **sen·sate·ly** *adv*

sen·sa·tion \sen-ˈsā-shən, sən-\ *n* [ML *sensation-, sensatio*, fr. LL *sensatus* endowed with sense] (1615) **1 a :** a mental process (as seeing, hearing, or smelling) due to immediate bodily stimulation often as distinguished from awareness of the process — compare PERCEPTION **b :** awareness (as of heat or pain) due to stimulation of a sense organ **c :** a state of consciousness of a kind usu. due to physical objects or internal bodily changes ⟨a burning ~ in his chest⟩ **d :** an indefinite bodily feeling ⟨a ~ of buoyancy⟩ **2 :** something (as a physical object, sense-datum, pain, or afterimage) that causes or is the object of sensation **3 a :** a state of excited interest or feeling ⟨their elopement caused a ~⟩ **b :** a cause of such excitement ⟨the show was the musical ~ of the season⟩; *esp* **:** one (as a person) in some respect exceptional or outstanding ⟨the rookie hitting ~ of the American League⟩

sen·sa·tion·al \-shnəl, -shən-ᵊl\ *adj* (1840) **1 :** of or relating to sensation or the senses **2 :** arousing or tending to arouse (as by lurid details) a quick, intense, and usu. superficial interest, curiosity, or emotional reaction **3 :** exceedingly or unexpectedly excellent or great — **sen·sa·tion·al·ly** \-ē\ *adv*

sen·sa·tion·al·ism \-ˌiz-əm\ *n* (1847) **1 :** empiricism that limits experience as a source of knowledge to sensation or sense perceptions **2 :** the use or effect of sensational subject matter or treatment — **sen·sa·tion·al·ist** \-əst\ *n* — **sen·sa·tion·al·is·tic** \-ˌsā-shnəl-ˈis-tik, -shən-ᵊl-\ *adj*

sen·sa·tion·al·ize \-ˌīz\ *vt* **-ized; -iz·ing** (1869) **:** to present in a sensational manner

[1]**sense** \ˈsen(t)s\ *n* [MF or L; MF *sens* sensation, feeling, mechanism of perception, meaning, fr. L *sensus*, fr. *sensus*, pp. of *sentire* to perceive, feel; akin to OHG *sin* mind, sense, OE *sith* journey — more at SEND] (1513) **1 :** a meaning conveyed or intended **:** IMPORT, SIGNIFICATION; *esp* **:** one of a set of meanings a word or phrase may bear esp. as segregated in a dictionary entry **2 a :** the faculty of perceiving by means of sense organs **b :** a specialized animal function or mechanism (as sight, hearing, smell, taste, or touch) basically involving a stimulus and a sense organ **c :** the sensory mechanisms constituting a unit distinct from other functions (as movement or thought) **3 :** conscious awareness or rationality — usu. used in pl. ⟨when he came to his ~*s* he was shocked to hear what he had done⟩ **4 a :** a particular sensation or kind or quality of sensation ⟨a good ~ of balance⟩ **b :** a definite but often vague awareness or impression ⟨felt a ~ of insecurity⟩ ⟨a ~ of danger⟩ **c :** a motivating awareness ⟨a ~ of shame⟩ **d :** a discerning awareness and appreciation ⟨her ~ of humor⟩ **5 :** CONSENSUS ⟨the ~ of the meeting⟩ **6 a :** capacity for effective application of the powers of the mind as a basis for action or response **:** INTELLIGENCE **b :** sound mental capacity and understanding typically marked by shrewdness and practicality; *also* **:** agreement with or satisfaction of such power ⟨this decision makes ~⟩ **7 :** one of two opposite directions esp. of motion (as of a point, line, or surface)

syn SENSE, COMMON SENSE, GUMPTION, JUDGMENT, WISDOM mean ability to reach intelligent conclusions. SENSE implies a reliable ability to judge and decide with soundness, prudence, and intelligence; COMMON SENSE suggests an average degree of such ability without sophistication or special knowledge; GUMPTION suggests a readiness to use or apply common sense; JUDGMENT implies sense tempered and refined by experience, training, and maturity; WISDOM implies sense and judgment far above average.

\ə\ **abut** \ᵊ\ **kitten, F table** \ər\ **further** \a\ **ash** \ā\ **ace** \ä\ **cot, cart**
\au̇\ **out** \ch\ **chin** \e\ **bet** \ē\ **easy** \g\ **go** \i\ **hit** \ī\ **ice** \j\ **job**
\ŋ\ **sing** \ō\ **go** \ȯ\ **law** \ȯi\ **boy** \th\ **thin** \t͟h\ **the** \ü\ **loot** \u̇\ **foot**
\y\ **yet** \zh\ **vision** \à, k̲, ⁿ, œ, œ̄, ue, ue̅, ʸ\ *see* **Guide to Pronunciation**

²sense *vt* **sensed; sens·ing** (1598) **1 a** : to perceive by the senses **b** : to be or become conscious of ⟨~ danger⟩ **2** : GRASP, COMPREHEND **3** : to detect (as a symbol or radiation) automatically

sense–datum *n, pl* **sense–data** (1921) : an immediate unanalyzable private object of sensation

sense·ful \'sen(t)s-fəl\ *adj* (1591) : REASONABLE, JUDICIOUS

sense·less \'sen(t)-sləs\ *adj* (1557) : destitute of, deficient in, or contrary to sense: as **a** : UNCONSCIOUS ⟨knocked ~⟩ **b** : FOOLISH, STUPID ⟨it was some ~ practical joke —A. Conan Doyle⟩ **c** : MEANINGLESS, PURPOSELESS ⟨a ~ murder⟩ — **sense·less·ly** *adv* — **sense·less·ness** *n*

sense organ *n* (1854) : a bodily structure that receives a stimulus (as heat or sound waves) and is affected in such a manner as to initiate a wave of excitation in associated sensory nerve fibers which convey specific impulses to the central nervous system where they are interpreted as corresponding sensations : RECEPTOR

sen·si·bil·ia \ˌsen(t)-sə-'bil-ē-ə, -'bil-yə\ *n pl* [LL, fr. neut. pl. of L *sensibilis* sensible] (1923) : what may be sensed

sen·si·bil·i·ty \ˌsen(t)-sə-'bil-ət-ē\ *n, pl* **-ties** (15c) **1** : ability to receive sensations : SENSITIVENESS ⟨tactile ~⟩ **2** : peculiar susceptibility to a pleasurable or painful impression (as from praise or a slight) — often used in pl. **3** : awareness of and responsiveness toward something (as emotion in another) **4** : refined or excessive sensitiveness in emotion and taste with especial responsiveness to the pathetic

¹sen·si·ble \'sen(t)-sə-bəl\ *adj* [ME, fr. MF, fr. L *sensibilis,* fr. *sensus,* pp.] (14c) **1** : of a kind to be felt or perceived: as **a** : perceptible to the senses or to reason or understanding ⟨felt a ~ chill⟩ ⟨her distress was ~ from her manner⟩ **b** *archaic* : perceptibly large : CONSIDERABLE **c** (1) : perceptible as real or material : SUBSTANTIAL ⟨the ~ world in which we live⟩ (2) : of a kind to arouse emotional response ⟨his whipping was a ~ expression of his father's anger⟩ **2 a** : capable of receiving sensory impressions ⟨~ to pain⟩ **b** : receptive to external influences : SENSITIVE ⟨the most ~ reaches of the spirit⟩ **3 a** : perceiving through the senses or mind : COGNIZANT ⟨~ of the increasing heat⟩; *also* : convinced by perceived evidence : SATISFIED ⟨~ of my error⟩ **b** : emotionally aware and responsive ⟨we are ~ of your problems⟩ **c** : CONSCIOUS **4** : having, containing, or indicative of good sense or reason : RATIONAL, REASONABLE ⟨~ people⟩ ⟨made a ~ answer⟩ ***syn*** see MATERIAL, PERCEPTIBLE, AWARE, WISE — **sen·si·ble·ness** *n* — **sen·si·bly** \-blē\ *adv*

²sensible *n* (1589) : something that can be sensed

sensible horizon *n* (ca. 1642) : HORIZON 1b(1)

sen·sil·lum \sen-'sil-əm\ *also* **sen·sil·la** \-'sil-ə\ *n, pl* **-sil·la** \-'sil-ə\ *also* **-sil·lae** \-'sil-(ˌ)ē\ [NL *sensillum,* dim. of ML *sensus* sense organ, fr. L, sense] (1925) : a simple epithelial sense organ usu. in the form of a spine, plate, rod, cone, or peg that is composed of one or a few cells with a nerve connection

¹sen·si·tive \'sen(t)-sət-iv, 'sen(t)-stiv\ *adj* [ME, fr. MF *sensitif,* fr. ML *sensitivus,* irreg. fr. L *sensus,* pp.] (15c) **1** : SENSORY 2 **2 a** : receptive to sense impressions **b** : capable of being stimulated or excited by external agents (as light, gravity, or contact) ⟨a photographic emulsion ~ to red light⟩ ⟨~ protoplasm⟩ **3** : highly responsive or susceptible: as **a** (1) : easily hurt or damaged; *esp* : easily hurt emotionally (2) : delicately aware of the attitudes and feelings of others or of the nuances of a work of art **b** : excessively or abnormally susceptible : HYPERSENSITIVE ⟨~ to egg protein⟩ **c** : readily fluctuating in price or demand ⟨~ commodities⟩ **d** : capable of indicating minute differences : DELICATE ⟨~ scales⟩ **e** : readily affected or changed by various agents (as light or mechanical shock) **f** : high in radio sensitivity **4 a** : concerned with highly classified government information or involving discretionary authority over important policy matters **b** : calling for tact, care, or caution in treatment : TOUCHY ⟨a ~ issue like race relations⟩ ***syn*** see LIABLE — **sen·si·tive·ly** *adv* — **sen·si·tive·ness** *n*

²sensitive *n* (1850) **1** : a person having occult or psychical abilities **2** : a sensitive person

sensitive plant *n* (1659) : any of several mimosas (esp. *Mimosa pudica*) with leaves that fold or droop when touched; *broadly* : a plant responding to touch with movement

sen·si·tiv·i·ty \ˌsen(t)-sə-'tiv-ət-ē\ *n, pl* **-ties** (1803) : the quality or state of being sensitive: as **a** : the capacity of an organism or sense organ to respond to stimulation : IRRITABILITY **b** : the quality or state of being hypersensitive **c** : the degree to which a radio receiving set responds to incoming waves **d** : the capacity of being easily hurt **e** : awareness of the needs and emotions of others

sen·si·ti·za·tion \ˌsen(t)-sət-ə-'zā-shən, ˌsen(t)-stə-'zā-\ *n* (1887) **1** : the action or process of sensitizing **2** : the quality or state of being sensitized (as to an antigen)

sen·si·tize \'sen(t)-sə-ˌtīz\ *vb* **-tized; -tiz·ing** [*sensitive* + *-ize*] *vt* (1880) : to make sensitive or hypersensitive ~ *vi* : to become sensitive — **sen·si·tiz·er** *n*

sen·si·tom·e·ter \ˌsen(t)-sə-'täm-ət-ər\ *n* [ISV *sensitive* + *-o-* + *-meter*] (1880) : an instrument for measuring sensitivity of photographic material — **sen·si·to·met·ric** \ˌsen(t)-sət-ə-'me-trik\ *adj* — **sen·si·tom·e·try** \-sə-'täm-ə-trē\ *n*

sen·sor \'sen-ˌsȯ(ə)r, 'sen(t)-sər\ *n* [L *sensus,* pp. of *sentire* to perceive — more at SENSE] (1928) : a device that responds to a physical stimulus (as heat, light, sound, pressure, magnetism, or a particular motion) and transmits a resulting impulse (as for measurement or operating a control); *also* : SENSE ORGAN

sen·so·ri·al \sen-'sōr-ē-əl, -'sȯr-\ *adj* (1768) : SENSORY — **sen·so·ri·al·ly** \-ə-lē\ *adv*

sen·so·ri·mo·tor \ˌsen(t)s-(ə-)rē-'mōt-ər\ *adj* (1855) : of, relating to, or functioning in both sensory and motor aspects of bodily activity

sen·so·ri·neu·ral \-'n(y)u̇r-əl\ *adj* [*sensory* + *neural*] (ca. 1977) : of, relating to, or involving the aspects of sense perception mediated by nerves ⟨~ hearing loss⟩

sen·so·ri·um \sen-'sōr-ē-əm, -'sȯr-\ *n, pl* **-ri·ums** *or* **-ria** \-ē-ə\ [LL, sense organ, fr. L *sensus* sense] (1647) : the parts of the brain or the mind concerned with the reception and interpretation of sensory stimuli; *broadly* : the entire sensory apparatus

sen·so·ry \'sen(t)s-(ə-)rē\ *adj* (1749) **1** : of or relating to sensation or to the senses **2** : conveying nerve impulses from the sense organs to the nerve centers : AFFERENT

sensory area *n* (1896) : an area of the cerebral cortex that receives afferent nerve fibers from lower sensory or motor areas

sen·su·al \'sench-(ə-)wəl, 'sen-shəl\ *adj* [ME, fr. LL *sensualis,* fr. L *sensus* sense + *-alis* -al] (15c) **1** : SENSORY **2** : relating to or consisting in the gratification of the senses or the indulgence of appetite : FLESHLY **3 a** : devoted to or preoccupied with the senses or appetites **b** : VOLUPTUOUS **c** : deficient in moral, spiritual, or intellectual interests : WORLDLY; *esp* : IRRELIGIOUS ***syn*** see CARNAL, SENSUOUS — **sen·su·al·i·ty** \ˌsen-chə-'wal-ət-ē\ *n* — **sen·su·al·ly** \'sench-(ə-)wə-lē, 'sen-shə-lē\ *adv*

sen·su·al·ism \'sench-(ə-)wə-ˌliz-əm, 'sen-shə-ˌliz-\ *n* (1813) : persistent or excessive pursuit of sensual pleasures and interests — **sen·su·al·ist** \-ləst\ *n* — **sen·su·al·is·tic** \ˌsench-(ə-)wə-'lis-tik, ˌsen-shə-'lis-\ *adj*

sen·su·al·ize \'sench-(ə-)wə-ˌlīz, 'sen-shə-ˌlīz\ *vt* **-ized; -iz·ing** (1687) : to make sensual — **sen·su·al·iza·tion** \ˌsench-(ə-)wə-lə-'zā-shən, ˌsen-shə-lə-\ *n*

sen·sum \'sen(t)-səm\ *n, pl* **sen·sa** \-sə\ [ML, fr. L, neut. of *sensus,* pp. of *sentire* to feel — more at SENSE] (1920) : SENSE-DATUM

sen·su·ous \'sench-(ə-)wəs\ *adj* [L *sensus* sense + E *-ous*] (1640) **1 a** : of or relating to the senses or sensible objects **b** : producing or characterized by gratification of the senses : having strong sensory appeal ⟨~ pleasure⟩ **2** : characterized by sense impressions or imagery aimed at the senses ⟨~ verse⟩ **3** : highly susceptible to influence through the senses — **sen·su·os·i·ty** \ˌsen-chə-'wäs-ət-ē\ *n* — **sen·su·ous·ly** \'sench-ə-wə-slē\ *adv* — **sen·su·ous·ness** *n*

syn SENSUOUS, SENSUAL, LUXURIOUS, VOLUPTUOUS mean relating to or providing pleasure through gratification of the senses. SENSUOUS implies gratification of the senses for the sake of aesthetic pleasure; SENSUAL tends to imply the gratification of the senses or the indulgence of the physical appetites as ends in themselves; LUXURIOUS suggests the providing of or indulgence of sensuous pleasure inducing bodily ease and languor; VOLUPTUOUS implies more strongly an abandonment esp. to sensual pleasure.

sent *past and past part of* SEND

¹sen·tence \'sent-ᵊn(t)s, -ᵊnz\ *n* [ME, fr. MF, fr. L *sententia,* lit., feeling, opinion, fr. (assumed) *sentent-, sentens,* irreg. prp. of *sentire* to feel — more at SENSE] (14c) **1** *obs* : OPINION; *esp* : a conclusion given on request or reached after deliberation **2 a** : JUDGMENT 2a; *specif* : one formally pronounced by a court or judge in a criminal proceeding and specifying the punishment to be inflicted upon the convict **b** : the punishment so imposed ⟨serve out a ~⟩ **3** *archaic* : MAXIM, SAW **4** : a grammatically self-contained speech unit consisting of a word or a syntactically related group of words that expresses an assertion, a question, a command, a wish, or an exclamation, that in writing usu. begins with a capital letter and concludes with appropriate end punctuation, and that in speaking is phonetically distinguished by various patterns of stress, pitch, and pauses **5** : PERIOD 2b **6** : a meaningful logical formula : PROPOSITION 2a

²sentence *vt* **sen·tenced; sen·tenc·ing** (1592) **1** : to impose a sentence on **2** : to cause to suffer something ⟨*sentenced* these most primitive cultures to extinction —E. W. Count⟩

sentence fragment *n* (1947) : a word, phrase, or clause that usu. has in speech the intonation of a sentence but lacks the grammatically self-contained structure usu. found in the sentences of formal and esp. written composition

sentence stress *n* (1884) : the manner in which stresses are distributed on the syllables of words assembled into sentences — called also *sentence accent*

sen·ten·tia \sen-'ten-ch(ē-)ə\ *n, pl* **-ti·ae** \-chē-ˌē\ [L, lit., feeling, opinion — more at SENTENCE] (1926) : APHORISM — usu. used in pl.

sen·ten·tial \sen-'ten-chəl\ *adj* (1646) **1** : of or relating to a sentence ⟨a relative clause with a ~ antecedent⟩ **2** : of, relating to, or involving a proposition in logic ⟨~ connective⟩

sentential calculus *n* (1937) : PROPOSITIONAL CALCULUS

sentential function *n* (1949) : an expression that contains one or more variables and becomes a declarative sentence when constants are substituted for the variables

sen·ten·tious \sen-'ten-chəs\ *adj* [ME, full of meaning, fr. L *sententiosus,* fr. *sententia* sentence, maxim] (1509) **1** : terse, aphoristic, or moralistic in expression : PITHY, EPIGRAMMATIC **2 a** : given to or abounding in aphoristic expression **b** : given to or abounding in excessive moralizing — **sen·ten·tious·ly** *adv* — **sen·ten·tious·ness** *n*

sen·ti \'sent-ē\ *n, pl* **senti** [Swahili, modif. of E *cent*] (1966) — see *shilling* at MONEY table

sen·tience \'sen-ch(ē-)ən(t)s, 'sent-ē-ən(t)s\ *n* (1839) **1** : a sentient quality or state **2** : feeling or sensation as distinguished from perception and thought

sen·tient \'sen-ch(ē-)ənt, 'sent-ē-ənt\ *adj* [L *sentient-, sentiens,* prp. of *sentire* to perceive, feel] (1632) **1** : responsive to or conscious of sense impressions **2** : AWARE **3** : finely sensitive in perception or feeling — **sen·tient·ly** *adv*

sen·ti·ment \'sent-ə-mənt\ *n* [F or ML; F, fr. ML *sentimentum,* fr. L *sentire*] (1639) **1 a** : an attitude, thought, or judgment prompted by feeling : PREDILECTION **b** : a specific view or notion : OPINION **2 a** : EMOTION **b** : refined feeling : delicate sensibility esp. as expressed in a work of art **c** : emotional idealism **d** : a romantic or nostalgic feeling verging on sentimentality **3 a** : an idea colored by emotion **b** : the emotional significance of a passage or expression as distinguished from its verbal context ***syn*** see FEELING, OPINION

sen·ti·men·tal \ˌsent-ə-'ment-ᵊl\ *adj* (1749) **1 a** : marked or governed by feeling, sensibility, or emotional idealism **b** : resulting from feeling rather than reason or thought **2** : having an excess of sentiment or sensibility — **sen·ti·men·tal·ly** \-ᵊl-ē\ *adv*

sen·ti·men·tal·ism \ˌsent-ə-'ment-ᵊl-ˌiz-əm\ *n* (1817) **1** : the disposition to favor or indulge in sentimentality **2** : an excessively sentimental conception or statement — **sen·ti·men·tal·ist** \-ᵊl-əst\ *n*

sen·ti·men·tal·i·ty \ˌsent-ə-ˌmen-'tal-ət-ē, -mən-\ *n, pl* **-ties** (1770) **1** : the quality or state of being sentimental esp. to excess or in affectation **2** : a sentimental idea or its expression

sen·ti·men·tal·ize \-'ment-ᵊl-ˌīz\ *vb* **-ized; -iz·ing** *vi* (1812) : to indulge in sentiment ~ *vt* : to look upon or imbue with sentiment — **sen·ti·men·tal·iza·tion** \-ˌment-ᵊl-ə-'zā-shən\ *n*

sen·ti·mo \sen-'tē-(ˌ)mō\ *n, pl* **-mos** [Pilipino, fr. Sp *céntimo*] (1968) — see *peso* at MONEY table

¹sen·ti·nel \'sent-nəl, -ᵊn-əl\ *n* [MF *sentinelle,* fr. OIt *sentinella,* fr. *sentina* vigilance, fr. *sentire* to perceive, fr. L] (1579) : SENTRY

²sentinel *vt* **-neled** *or* **-nelled; -nel·ing** *or* **-nel·ling** (1593) **1 :** to watch over as a sentinel **2 :** to furnish with a sentinel **3 :** to post as sentinel
sen·try \'sen-trē\ *n, pl* **sentries** [perh. fr. obs. *sentry* (sanctuary, watchtower)] (1632) **:** GUARD, WATCH; *esp* **:** a soldier standing guard at a point of passage (as a gate)
sentry box *n* (ca. 1728) **:** a shelter for a sentry on his post
se·pal \'sē-pəl, 'sep-\ *n* [NL *sepalum,* fr. *sepa-* (fr. Gk *skepē* covering) + *-lum* (as in *petalum* petal); akin to Lith *kepùrė* head covering] (1821) **:** one of the modified leaves comprising a calyx — see FLOWER illustration
se·pal·oid \-ə-,lȯid\ *adj* (1830) **:** resembling or functioning as a sepal
-sepal·ous \'sep-ə-ləs\ *adj comb form* [*sepal*] **:** having (such or so many) sepals ⟨gamo*sepalous*⟩
sep·a·ra·ble \'sep-(ə-)rə-bəl\ *adj* [ME, fr. L *separabilis,* fr. *separare*] (14c) **1 :** capable of being separated or dissociated **2** *obs* **:** causing separation — **sep·a·ra·bil·i·ty** \,sep-(ə-)rə-'bil-ət-ē\ *n* — **sep·a·ra·ble·ness** *n* — **sep·a·ra·bly** \-blē\ *adv*
¹sep·a·rate \'sep-(ə-),rāt\ *vb* **-rat·ed; -rat·ing** [ME *separaten,* fr. L *separatus,* pp. of *separare,* fr. *se-* apart + *parare* to prepare, procure — more at SECEDE, PARE] *vt* (15c) **1 a :** to set or keep apart **:** DISCONNECT, SEVER **b :** to make a distinction between **:** DISCRIMINATE, DISTINGUISH ⟨~ religion from magic⟩ **c :** SORT ⟨~ mail⟩ **d :** to disperse in space or time **:** SCATTER ⟨widely *separated* homesteads⟩ **2** *archaic* **:** to set aside for a special purpose **:** CHOOSE, DEDICATE **3 :** to part by a legal separation: **a :** to sever conjugal ties with **b :** to sever contractual relations with **:** DISCHARGE ⟨*separated* from the army⟩ **4 :** to block off **:** SEGREGATE **5 a :** to isolate from a mixture **:** EXTRACT ⟨~ cream from milk⟩ **b :** to divide into constituent parts ~ *vi* **1 :** to become divided or detached **2 a :** to sever an association **:** WITHDRAW **b :** to cease to live together as man and wife **3 :** to go in different directions **4 :** to become isolated from a mixture
syn SEPARATE, PART, DIVIDE, SEVER, SUNDER, DIVORCE mean to become or cause to become disunited or disjointed. SEPARATE may imply any of several causes such as dispersion, removal of one from others, or presence of an intervening thing; PART implies the separating of things or persons in close union or association; DIVIDE implies separating into pieces or sections by cutting or breaking; SEVER implies violence esp. in the removal of a part or member; SUNDER suggests violent rending or wrenching apart; DIVORCE implies separating two things that commonly interact and belong together.
²sep·a·rate \'sep-(ə-)rət\ *adj* (1600) **1 a** *archaic* **:** SOLITARY, SECLUDED **b :** IMMATERIAL, DISEMBODIED **c :** set or kept apart **:** DETACHED **2 a :** not shared with another **:** INDIVIDUAL ⟨~ rooms⟩ **b** *often cap* **:** estranged from a parent body ⟨~ churches⟩ **3 a :** existing by itself **:** AUTONOMOUS **b :** dissimilar in nature or identity ***syn*** see DISTINCT — **sep·a·rate·ly** \-(ə-)rət-lē, 'sep-ərt-lē\ *adv* — **sep·a·rate·ness** \-(ə-)rət-nəs\ *n*
³sep·a·rate \'sep-(ə-)rət\ *n* (1892) **1 :** OFFPRINT **2 :** an article of dress designed to be worn interchangeably with others to form various costume combinations — usu. used in pl.
sep·a·ra·tion \,sep-ə-'rā-shən\ *n* (15c) **1 :** the act or process of separating **:** the state of being separated **2 a :** a point, line, or means of division **b :** an intervening space **:** GAP **3 a :** cessation of cohabitation between husband and wife by mutual agreement or judicial decree **b :** termination of a contractual relationship (as employment or military service)
sep·a·ra·tion·ist \-sh(ə-)nəst\ *n* (1882) **:** SEPARATIST
sep·a·rat·ism \'sep-(ə-)rət-,iz-əm\ *n* (1628) **:** a belief in, movement for, or state of separation (as schism, secession, or segregation)
sep·a·rat·ist \'sep-(ə-)rət-əst, 'sep-ə-,rāt-\ *n* (1608) **:** one that favors separatism: as **a** *cap* **:** one of a group of 16th and 17th century English Protestants preferring to separate from rather than to reform the Church of England **b :** an advocate of independence or autonomy for a part of a political unit (as a nation) **c :** an advocate of racial or cultural separation — **separatist** *adj* — **sep·a·ra·tis·tic** \,sep-(ə-)rə-'tis-tik\ *adj*
sep·a·ra·tive \'sep-ə-,rāt-iv, 'sep-(ə-)rət-\ *adj* (1592) **:** tending toward, causing, or expressing separation
sep·a·ra·tor \'sep-(ə-),rāt-ər\ *n* (1607) **:** one that separates; *esp* **:** a device for separating liquids of different specific gravities (as cream from milk) or liquids from solids
Se·phar·di \sə-'färd-ē\ *n, pl* **Se·phar·dim** \-'färd-əm\ [LHeb *sĕphāradhī,* fr. *sĕphāradh* Spain, fr. Heb, region where Jews were once exiled (Obad 1: 20)] (1851) **:** a member of the occidental branch of European Jews settling in Spain and Portugal and later in Greece, the Levant, England, the Netherlands, and the Americas; *also* **:** one of their descendants — **Se·phar·dic** \-'färd-ik\ *adj*
¹se·pia \'sē-pē-ə\ *n* [L, cuttlefish, ink, fr. Gk *sēpia;* akin to Gk *sēpein* to make putrid, *sapros* rotten] (1821) **1 a :** the inky secretion of a cuttlefish **b :** a brown melanin-containing pigment from the ink of cuttlefishes **2 :** a print or photograph of a brown color resembling sepia **3 :** a brownish gray to dark olive brown
²sepia *adj* (1827) **1 :** made of or done in sepia **2 :** of the color sepia
se·pi·o·lite \'sē-pē-ə-,līt\ *n* [G *sepiolith,* fr. Gk *sēpion* cuttlebone (fr. *sēpia*) + G *-lith* -lite] (1854) **:** MEERSCHAUM 1
se·poy \'sē-,pȯi\ *n* [Pg *sipai,* fr. Hindi *sipāhī,* fr. Per, cavalryman] (1717) **:** a native of India employed as a soldier by a European power
sep·pu·ku \se-'pü-(,)kü, 'sep-ə-,kü\ *n* [Jp] (1904) **:** HARA-KIRI
sep·sis \'sep-səs\ *n, pl* **sep·ses** \'sep-,sēz\ [NL, fr. Gk *sēpsis* decay, fr. *sēpein* to make putrid] (1876) **:** a toxic condition resulting from the spread of bacteria or their products from a focus of infection; *esp* **:** SEPTICEMIA
sept \'sept\ *n* [prob. alter. of *sect*] (1517) **:** a branch of a family; *esp* **:** CLAN
sep·tal \'sep-tᵊl\ *adj* (1839) **:** of or relating to a septum
sep·tate \'sep-,tāt\ *adj* (1846) **:** divided by or having a septum
Sep·tem·ber \sep-'tem-bər, səp-\ *n* [ME *Septembre,* fr. OF & OE, both fr. L *September* (seventh month), fr. *septem* seven — more at SEVEN] (bef. 12c) **:** the 9th month of the Gregorian calendar
sep·te·nar·i·us \,sep-tə-'nar-ē-əs, -'ner-\ *n, pl* **-nar·ii** \-ē-,ī, -ē-,ē\ [L, fr. *septenarius* of seven, fr. *septeni* seven each, fr. *septem* seven] (1819) **:** a verse consisting of seven feet esp. in Latin prosody
sep·ten·de·cil·lion \(,)sep-,ten-di-'sil-yən\ *n, often attrib* [L *septendecim* seventeen (fr. *septem* seven + *decem* ten) + E *-illion* (as in *million*) — more at TEN] (ca. 1938) — see NUMBER table
sep·ten·ni·al \sep-'ten-ē-əl\ *adj* [LL *septennium* period of seven years, fr. L *septem* + *-ennium* (as in *biennium*)] (1640) **1 :** occurring or being done every seven years **2 :** consisting of or lasting for seven years — **sep·ten·ni·al·ly** \-ə-lē\ *adv*
sep·ten·tri·on \sep-'ten-trē-,än, -trē-ən\ *n* [ME, fr. MF, fr. L *septentrio,* sing. of *septentriones* the seven stars of Ursa Major or Ursa Minor, lit., the seven plow oxen, fr. *septem* seven + *trio* plow ox] *obs* (14c) **:** the northern regions **:** NORTH
sep·ten·tri·o·nal \-trē-ən-ᵊl\ *adj* (14c) **:** NORTHERN
sep·tet \sep-'tet\ *n* [G *septet,* fr. L *septem*] (1837) **1 :** a musical composition for seven instruments or voices **2 :** a group or set of seven; *esp* **:** the performers of a septet
sep·tic \'sep-tik\ *adj* [L *septicus,* fr. Gk *sēptikos,* fr. *sēpein* to make putrid — more at SEPIA] (1605) **1 :** PUTREFACTIVE **2 :** relating to, involving, or characteristic of sepsis
sep·ti·ce·mia \,sep-tə-'sē-mē-ə\ *n* [NL, fr. L *septicus* + NL *-emia*] (1866) **:** invasion of the bloodstream by virulent microorganisms from a local seat of infection accompanied esp. by chills, fever, and prostration — called also *blood poisoning;* compare SEPSIS — **sep·ti·ce·mic** \-'sē-mik\ *adj*
sep·ti·ci·dal \,sep-tə-'sīd-ᵊl\ *adj* [NL *septum* + L *-cidere* to cut, fr. *caedere* — more at CONCISE] (1819) **:** dehiscent longitudinally at or along a septum ⟨a ~ fruit⟩
septic sore throat *n* (1924) **:** an inflammatory sore throat caused by hemolytic streptococci and marked by fever, prostration, and toxemia
septic tank *n* (ca. 1902) **:** a tank in which the solid matter of continuously flowing sewage is disintegrated by bacteria
sep·tif·ra·gal \sep-'tif-ri-gəl\ *adj* [NL *septum* + L *frangere* to break — more at BREAK] (1819) **:** dehiscing by breaking away from the dissepiments ⟨a ~ pod⟩
sep·til·lion \sep-'til-yən\ *n, often attrib* [F, fr. L *septem* + F *-illion* (as in *million*) — more at SEVEN] (1690) — see NUMBER table
sep·tu·a·ge·nar·i·an \(,)sep-,t(y)ü-ə-jə-'ner-ē-ən, ,sep-tə-,waj-ə-\ *n* [LL *septuagenarius* seventy years old, fr. L, of or containing seventy, fr. *septuageni* seventy each, fr. *septuaginta*] (1805) **:** a person whose age is in the seventies — **septuagenarian** *adj*
Sep·tu·a·ge·si·ma \,sep-tə-wə-'jes-ə-mə, -'jā-zə-\ *n* [ME, fr. LL, fr. L, fem. of *septuagesimus* seventieth, fr. *septuaginta* seventy; fr. its being approximately seventy days before Easter] (14c) **:** the third Sunday before Lent
Sep·tu·a·gint \sep-'t(y)ü-ə-jənt, 'sep-tə-wə-,jint\ *n* [LL *Septuaginta,* fr. L, seventy, irreg. fr. *septem* seven + *-ginta* (akin to L *viginti* twenty); fr. the approximate number of its translators — more at SEVEN, VIGESIMAL] (1633) **:** a pre-Christian Greek version of the Jewish Scriptures redacted by Jewish scholars and adopted by Greek-speaking Christians — **Sep·tu·a·gin·tal** \(,)sep-,t(y)ü-ə-'jint-ᵊl, ,sep-tə-wə-\ *adj*
sep·tum \'sep-təm\ *n, pl* **sep·ta** \-tə\ [NL, fr. L *saeptum* enclosure, fence, wall, fr. *saepire* to fence in, fr. *saepes* fence, hedge; akin to Gk *haimasia* stone wall] (1726) **:** a dividing wall or membrane esp. between bodily spaces or masses of soft tissue — compare DISSEPIMENT
¹sep·ul·cher *or* **sep·ul·chre** \'sep-əl-kər\ *n* [ME *sepulcre,* fr. OF, fr. L *sepulcrum, sepulchrum,* fr. *sepelire* to bury; akin to Gk *hepein* to care for, Skt *sapati* he serves] (13c) **1 :** a place of burial **:** TOMB **2 :** a receptacle for religious relics esp. in an altar
²sepulcher *or* **sepulchre** *vt* **-chered** *or* **-chred; -chering** *or* **-chring** \-k(ə-)riŋ\ (1591) **1** *archaic* **:** to place in or as if in a sepulcher **:** BURY **2** *archaic* **:** to serve as a sepulcher for
se·pul·chral \sə-'pəl-krəl *also* -'pu̇l-\ *adj* (1615) **1 :** MORTUARY **2 :** suited to or suggestive of a sepulcher **:** FUNEREAL — **se·pul·chral·ly** \-krə-lē\ *adv*
sep·ul·ture \'sep-əl-,chu̇(ə)r\ *n* [ME, fr. OF, fr. L *sepultura,* fr. *sepultus,* pp. of *sepelire*] (13c) **1 :** BURIAL **2 :** SEPULCHER
se·qua·cious \si-'kwā-shəs\ *adj* [L *sequac-, sequax* inclined to follow, fr. *sequi*] (1643) **1** *archaic* **:** SUBSERVIENT, TRACTABLE **2 :** intellectually servile — **se·qua·cious·ly** *adv* — **se·quac·i·ty** \-'kwas-ət-ē\ *n*
se·quel \'sē-kwəl *also* -,kwel\ *n* [ME, fr. MF *sequelle,* fr. L *sequela,* fr. *sequi* to follow — more at SUE] (15c) **1 :** CONSEQUENCE, RESULT **2 a :** subsequent development **b :** the next installment (as of a speech or story); *esp* **:** a literary or cinematic work continuing the course of a story begun in a preceding one
se·quela \si-'kwel-ə\ *n, pl* **se·quel·ae** \-'kwel-(,)ē\ [NL, fr. L, sequel] (1793) **1 :** an aftereffect of disease or injury **2 :** a secondary result
¹se·quence \'sē-kwən(t)s, -,kwen(t)s\ *n* [ME, fr. ML *sequentia,* fr. LL, sequel, lit., act of following, fr. L *sequent-, sequens,* prp. of *sequi*] (14c) **1 :** a hymn in irregular meter between the gradual and Gospel in masses for special occasions (as Easter) **2 :** a continuous or connected series: as **a :** an extended series of poems united by a single theme ⟨a sonnet ~⟩ **b :** three or more playing cards usu. of the same suit in consecutive order of rank **c :** a succession of repetitions of a melodic phrase or harmonic pattern each in a new position **d :** a set of elements ordered as are the natural numbers **e** (1) **:** a succession of related shots or scenes developing a single subject or phase of a film story (2) **:** EPISODE **3 a :** order of succession **b :** an arrangement of the tenses of successive verbs in a sentence designed to express a coherent relationship esp. between main and subordinate parts **4 a :** CONSEQUENCE, RESULT **b :** a subsequent development **5 :** continuity of progression
²sequence *vt* **se·quenced; se·quenc·ing** (1941) **1 :** to arrange in a sequence **2 :** to determine the sequence of chemical constituents (as amino-acid residues) in ⟨*sequenced* biological marcromolecules⟩
se·quenc·er \'sē-kwən-sər, -,kwen(t)-sər\ *n* (1949) **:** any of various devices for arranging (as informational items or the events in the launching of a rocket) into or separating (as amino acids from protein) in a sequence

\ə\ abut \ᵊ\ kitten, F table \ər\ further \a\ ash \ā\ ace \ä\ cot, cart \au̇\ out \ch\ chin \e\ bet \ē\ easy \g\ go \i\ hit \ī\ ice \j\ job \ŋ\ sing \ō\ go \ȯ\ law \ȯi\ boy \th\ thin \t͟h\ the \ü\ loot \u̇\ foot \y\ yet \zh\ vision \à, k̟, ⁿ, œ, œ̄, ue, ue̅, ʸ\ *see* Guide to Pronunciation

se·quen·cy \'sē-kwən-sē\ *n* [LL *sequentia*] (1818) : SEQUENCE 3a, 5

se·quent \'sē-kwənt\ *adj* [L *sequent-, sequens*, prp.] (1601) **1 :** CONSECUTIVE, SUCCEEDING **2 :** CONSEQUENT, RESULTANT

se·quen·tial \si-'kwen-chəl\ *adj* (1854) **1 :** of, relating to, or arranged in a sequence : SERIAL ⟨~ file systems⟩ **2 :** following in sequence **3 :** relating to or based on a method of testing a statistical hypothesis that involves examination of a sequence of samples for each of which the decision is made to accept or reject the hypothesis or to continue sampling — **se·quen·tial·ly** \-'kwench-(ə-)lē\ *adv*

1**se·ques·ter** \si-'kwes-tər\ *vt* **-tered; -ter·ing** \-t(ə-)riŋ\ [ME *sequestren*, fr. MF *sequestrer*, fr. LL *sequestrare* to surrender for safekeeping, set apart, fr. L *sequester* agent, depositary, bailee; akin to L *sequi* to follow] (14c) **1 a :** to set apart : SEGREGATE **b :** SECLUDE, WITHDRAW **2 a :** to seize esp. by a writ of sequestration **b :** to place (property) in custody esp. in sequestration **3 :** to hold (as a metallic ion) in solution usu. by inclusion in an appropriate coordination complex

2**sequester** *n, obs* (1604) : SEPARATION, ISOLATION

se·ques·trate \'sēk-wəs-,trāt, 'sek-; si-'kwes-\ *vt* **-trat·ed; -trat·ing** [LL *sequestratus*, pp. of *sequestrare*] (1513) : SEQUESTER

se·ques·tra·tion \,sēk-wəs-'trā-shən, ,sek-; (,)sē-,kwes-\ *n* (15c) **1 :** the act of sequestering : the state of being sequestered **2 a :** a legal writ authorizing a sheriff or commissioner to take into custody the property of a defendant who is in contempt until he complies with the orders of a court **b :** a deposit whereby a neutral depositary agrees to hold property in litigation and to restore it to the party to whom it is adjudged to belong

se·ques·trum \si-'kwes-trəm\ *n, pl* **-trums** *also* **-tra** \-trə\ [NL, fr. L, legal sequestration; akin to L *sequester* bailee] (1831) : a fragment of dead bone detached from adjoining sound bone

se·quin \'sē-kwən\ *n* [F, fr. It *zecchino*, fr. *zecca* mint, fr. Ar *sikkah* die, coin] (1582) **1 :** an old gold coin of Italy and Turkey **2 :** a small plate of shining metal or plastic used for ornamentation esp. on clothing

se·quined *or* **se·quinned** \-kwənd\ *adj* (1582) : ornamented with or as if with sequins

se·qui·tur \'sek-wət-ər, -wə-,tu̇(ə)r\ *n* [L, it follows, 3d pers. sing. pres. indic. of *sequi* to follow — more at SUE] (1836) : the conclusion of an inference : CONSEQUENCE

se·quoia \si-'kwȯi-(y)ə\ *n* [NL, genus name, fr. *Sequoya* (George Guess)] (ca. 1866) : either of two huge coniferous California trees of the pine family that reach a height of over 300 feet: **a :** BIG TREE **b :** REDWOOD 3a

sera *pl of* SERUM

se·rac \sə-'rak, sā-\ *n* [F *sérac*, lit., a kind of white cheese, fr. ML *seracium* whey, fr. L *serum* whey — more at SERUM] (1860) : a pinnacle, sharp ridge, or block of ice among the crevasses of a glacier

se·ra·glio \sə-'ral-(,)yō, -'räl-\ *n, pl* **-glios** [It *serraglio* enclosure, seraglio, partly fr. ML *serraculum* enclosure, bar of a door, bolt, fr. LL *serare* to bolt; partly fr. Turk *saray* palace — more at SEAR] (1588) **1 :** HAREM 1a **2 :** a palace of a sultan

se·rai \sə-'rī\ *n* [Turk & Per; Turk *saray* mansion, palace, fr. Per *sarāī* mansion, inn] (1609) **1 :** CARAVANSARY **2 :** SERAGLIO 2

ser·al \'sir-əl\ *adj* (1916) : of, relating to, or constituting an ecological sere

se·ra·pe \sə-'räp-ē, -'rap-\ *n* [MexSp *sarape*] (1834) : a colorful woolen shawl worn over the shoulders esp. by Mexican men

ser·aph \'ser-əf\ *n, pl* **ser·a·phim** \-ə-,fim\ *or* **seraphs** [back-formation fr. *seraphim*] (1667) : SERAPHIM 2

ser·a·phim \'ser-ə-,fim\ *n pl* [LL *seraphim*, pl., seraphs, fr. Heb *śĕrāphīm*] (bef. 12c) **1 :** an order of angels — see CELESTIAL HIERARCHY **2** *sing, pl* **seraphim :** one of the 6-winged angels standing in the presence of God — **se·raph·ic** \sə-'raf-ik\ *adj* — **se·raph·i·cal·ly** \-i-k(ə-)lē\ *adv*

Se·ra·pis \sə-'rā-pəs\ *n* [L, fr. Gk *Sarapis*] : an Egyptian god combining attributes of Osiris and Apis and having a widespread cult throughout Greece and Rome

Serb \'sərb\ *n* [Serb *Srb*] (1860) **1 :** a native or inhabitant of Serbia **2 :** SERBIAN 2 — **Serb** *adj*

Ser·bi·an \'sər-bē-ən\ *n* (1848) **1 :** SERB 1 **2 a :** the Serbo-Croatian language as spoken in Serbia **b :** a literary form of Serbo-Croatian using the Cyrillic alphabet — **Serbian** *adj*

Ser·bo–Cro·atian \,sər-(,)bō-krō-'ā-shən\ *n* (1883) **1 :** the Slavic language of the Serbs and Croats consisting of Serbian written in the Cyrillic alphabet and Croatian written in the Roman alphabet **2 :** one whose native language is Serbo-Croatian — **Serbo–Croatian** *adj*

1**sere** \'si(ə)r\ *adj* [ME, fr. OE *sēar* dry; akin to OHG *sōrēn* to wither, Gk *hauos* dry] (bef. 12c) **1 :** being dried and withered **2** *archaic* **:** THREADBARE

2**sere** *n* [L *series* series] (1916) : a series of ecological communities formed in ecological succession

1**ser·e·nade** \,ser-ə-'nād\ *n* [F *sérénade*, fr. It *serenata*, fr. *sereno* clear, calm (of weather), fr. L *serenus* serene] (1649) **1 a :** a complimentary vocal or instrumental performance; *esp* : one given outdoors at night for a woman **b :** a work so performed **2 :** an instrumental composition in several movements, written for a small ensemble, and midway between the suite and the symphony in style

2**serenade** *vb* **-nad·ed; -nad·ing** *vt* (1672) : to perform a serenade in honor of **~** *vi* : to play a serenade — **ser·e·nad·er** *n*

ser·e·na·ta \,ser-ə-'nät-ə\ *n* [It, serenade] (ca. 1724) : an 18th century secular cantata of a dramatic character usu. composed in honor of an individual or event

ser·en·dip·i·tous \,ser-ən-'dip-ət-əs\ *adj* (1943) : obtained or characterized by serendipity ⟨~ discoveries⟩ — **ser·en·dip·i·tous·ly** *adv*

ser·en·dip·i·ty \-'dip-ət-ē\ *n* [fr. its possession by the heroes of the Persian fairy tale *The Three Princes of Serendip*] (1754) : the faculty of finding valuable or agreeable things not sought for

1**se·rene** \sə-'rēn\ *adj* [L *serenus;* akin to OHG *serawēn* to become dry, Gk *xēros* dry] (1503) **1 :** AUGUST — used as part of a title ⟨His *Serene* Highness⟩ **2 :** marked by or suggestive of utter calm and unruffled repose or quietude ⟨a ~ smile⟩ **3 a :** clear and free of storms or unpleasant change ⟨~ skies⟩ **b :** shining bright and steady ⟨the moon, ~ in glory —Alexander Pope⟩ *syn* see CALM — **se·rene·ly** *adv* — **se·rene·ness** \-'rēn-nəs\ *n*

2**serene** *n* (1644) **1 :** a serene condition or expanse (as of sky, sea, or light) **2 :** SERENITY, TRANQUILLITY

se·ren·i·ty \sə-'ren-ət-ē\ *n* [ME, fr. MF *serenité*, fr. L *serenitat-, serenitas*, fr. *serenus* serene] (15c) : the quality or state of being serene

serf \'sərf\ *n* [F, fr. L *servus* slave, servant, serf — more at SERVE] (1611) : a member of a servile feudal class bound to the soil and subject to the will of his lord — **serf·age** \'sər-fij\ *n* — **serf·dom** \'sərf-dəm, -təm\ *n*

serge \'sərj\ *n* [ME *sarge*, fr. MF, fr. (assumed) VL *sarica*, fr. L *serica*, fem. of *sericus* silken — more at SERICEOUS] (14c) : a durable twilled fabric having a smooth clear face and a pronounced diagonal rib on the front and the back

ser·gean·cy \'sär-jən-sē\ *n* (1670) : the function, office, or rank of a sergeant

ser·geant \'sär-jənt\ *n* [ME, servant, attendant, sergeant, fr. MF *sergent, serjant*, fr. L *servient-, serviens*, prp. of *servire* to serve] (14c) **1 :** SERGEANT AT ARMS **2** *obs* : an officer who enforces the judgments of a court or the commands of one in authority **3 :** a noncommissioned officer ranking in the army and marine corps above a corporal and below a staff sergeant and in the air force above an airman first class or senior airman and below a staff sergeant; *broadly* : NONCOMMISSIONED OFFICER **4 :** an officer in a police force ranking in the U.S. just below captain or sometimes lieutenant and in England just below inspector

sergeant at arms (14c) : an officer of an organization (as a legislative body or court of law) who preserves order and executes commands

sergeant first class *n* (1948) : a noncommissioned officer in the army ranking above a staff sergeant and below a master sergeant

sergeant fish *n* (ca. 1883) **1 :** COBIA **2 :** SNOOK 1

sergeant major *n, pl* **sergeants major** *or* **sergeant majors** (1802) **1 :** a noncommissioned officer in the army, air force, or marine corps serving as chief administrative assistant in a headquarters **2 :** a noncommissioned officer in the marine corps ranking above a first sergeant **3 :** a bluish green to yellow percoid fish (*Abudefduf saxatilis*) with black vertical stripes on the sides that is widely distributed in the western tropical Atlantic ocean

sergeant major of the army (1966) : the ranking noncommissioned officer of the army serving as adviser to the chief of staff

sergeant major of the marine corps (ca. 1971) : the ranking noncommissioned officer of the marine corps serving as adviser to the commandant

ser·geanty \'sär-jənt-ē\ *n, pl* **-geant·ies** [ME *sergeantie*, fr. MF *sergentie*, fr. *sergent* sergeant] (15c) : any of numerous feudal services of a personal nature by which an estate is held of the king or other lord distinct from military tenure and from socage tenure

serg·ing \'sər-jiŋ\ *n* [*serge*] (ca. 1909) : the process of overcasting the raw edges of a piece of fabric (as a carpet) to prevent raveling

1**se·ri·al** \'sir-ē-əl\ *adj* (1840) **1 :** of, relating to, consisting of, or arranged in a series, rank, or row ⟨~ order⟩ **2 :** appearing in successive parts or numbers ⟨a ~ story⟩ **3 :** belonging to a series maturing periodically rather than on a single date ⟨~ bonds⟩ **4 :** of, relating to, or being music based on a series of tones in an arbitrary but fixed pattern without regard for traditional tonality **5 :** relating to or being a connection in a computer system in which the bits of a byte are transmitted sequentially over a single wire — **se·ri·al·ly** \-ə-lē\ *adv*

2**serial** *n* (1846) **1 a :** a work appearing (as in a magazine or on television) in parts at intervals **b :** one part of a serial work : INSTALLMENT **2 :** a publication (as a newspaper or journal) issued as one of a consecutively numbered and indefinitely continued series

se·ri·al·ism \'sir-ē-ə-,liz-əm\ *n* (1958) : serial music; *also* : the theory or practice of composing serial music

se·ri·al·ist \-ləst\ *n* (1846) **1 :** a writer of serials **2 :** a composer of serial music

se·ri·al·ize \-,līz\ *vt* **-ized; -iz·ing** (1857) : to arrange or publish in serial form — **se·ri·al·iza·tion** \,sir-ē-ə-lə-'zā-shən\ *n*

serial number *n* (1896) : a number indicating place in a series and used as a means of identification

1**se·ri·ate** \'sir-ē-,āt, -ē-ət\ *adj* [(assumed) NL *seriatus*, fr. L *series*] (1846) : arranged in a series or succession — **se·ri·ate·ly** *adv*

2**se·ri·ate** \'sir-ē-,āt\ *vt* **-at·ed; -at·ing** (1872) : to arrange in a series

1**se·ri·a·tim** \,sir-ē-'āt-əm, -'at-\ *adv* [ML, fr. L *series*] (1680) : in a series

2**seriatim** *adj* (1871) : following seriatim

se·ri·ceous \sə-'rish-əs\ *adj* [LL *sericeus* silken, fr. L *sericum* silk garment, silk, fr. neut. of *sericus* silken, fr. Gk *sērikos*, fr. *Sēres*, an eastern Asian people producing silk in ancient times] (ca. 1777) : finely pubescent ⟨~ leaf⟩

ser·i·cin \'ser-ə-sən\ *n* [ISV, fr. L *sericum* silk] (ca. 1868) : a gelatinous protein that cements the two fibroin filaments in a silk fiber

seri·cul·ture \'ser-ə-,kəl-chər\ *n* [L *sericum* silk + E *culture*] (1851) : the production of raw silk by raising silkworms — **seri·cul·tur·al** \-'kəlch(-ə)-rəl\ *adj* — **seri·cul·tur·ist** \-rəst\ *n*

se·ries \'si(ə)r-(,)ēz\ *n, pl* **series** *often attrib* [L, fr. *serere* to join, link together; akin to L *sort-, sors* lot, Gk *eirein* to string together, *hormos* chain, necklace] (1611) **1 a :** a number of things or events of the same class coming one after another in spatial or temporal succession ⟨a concert ~⟩ ⟨the hall opened into a ~ of small rooms⟩ **b :** a set of regularly presented television programs each of which is complete in itself **2 :** the indicated sum of a usu. infinite sequence of numbers **3 a :** the coins or currency of a particular country and period **b :** a group of postage stamps in different denominations **4 :** a succession of volumes or issues published with related subjects or authors, similar format and price, or continuous numbering **5 :** a division of rock formations that is smaller than a system and comprises rocks deposited during an epoch **6 :** a group of chemical compounds related in composition and structure **7 :** an arrangement of the parts of or elements in an electric circuit whereby the whole current passes through each part or element without branching **8 :** a set of vowels connected by ablaut (as *i, a, u* in *ring, rang, rung*) **9 a :** a number of games (as of baseball) played usu. on consecutive days between two teams ⟨in town for a 3-game ~⟩ **b :** WORLD SERIES **10 :** a group of successive coordinate sentence elements joined together **11 :** SOIL SERIES **12 :** three consecutive games in bowling — **in series :** in a serial arrangement

series winding *n* (ca. 1909) : a winding in which the armature coil and the field-magnet coil are in series with the external circuit — **se·ries–wound** \,sir-ēz-'wau̇nd\ *adj*

ser·if \'ser-əf\ *n* [prob. fr. D *schreef* stroke, line, fr. MD, fr. *schriven* to write, fr. L *scribere* — more at SCRIBE] (1841) : any of the short lines stemming from and at an angle to the upper and lower ends of the strokes of a letter — **ser·ifed** *or* **ser·iffed** \-əft\ *adj*

1 serif

seri·graph \'ser-ə-ˌgraf\ *n* [L *seri*cum silk + Gk *graphein* to write, draw — more at CARVE] (ca. 1888) : an original silk-screen color print made by an artist — **se·rig·ra·pher** \sə-'rig-rə-fər\ *n* — **se·rig·ra·phy** \-fē\ *n*

se·rin \sə-'raⁿ\ *n* [F] (1530) : a small European finch (*Serinus serinus*) related to the canary

ser·ine \'se(ə)r-ˌēn\ *n* [ISV *seri*cin + *-ine*] (ca. 1909) : a crystalline amino acid $C_3H_7NO_3$ that occurs as a structural part of many proteins or cephalins

se·rio·com·ic \ˌsir-ē-ō-'käm-ik\ *adj* [*serious* + *-o-* + *comic*] (1783) : having a mixture of the serious and the comic ⟨a ~ novel⟩ — **se·rio·com·i·cal·ly** \-i-k(ə-)lē\ *adv*

se·ri·ous \'sir-ē-əs\ *adj* [ME *seryows,* fr. MF or LL; MF *serieux,* fr. LL *seriosus,* alter. of L *serius*] (15c) **1 :** thoughtful or subdued in appearance or manner : SOBER **2 a :** requiring much thought or work ⟨~ study⟩ **b :** of or relating to a matter of importance ⟨a ~ play⟩ **3 a :** not joking or trifling : being in earnest **b** *archaic* : PIOUS **c :** deeply interested : DEVOTED ⟨~ musician⟩ **4 a :** not easily answered or solved ⟨~ objections⟩ **b :** having important or dangerous possible consequences ⟨a ~ injury⟩ — **se·ri·ous·ness** *n*

syn SERIOUS, GRAVE, SOLEMN, SEDATE, STAID, SOBER, EARNEST mean not light or frivolous. SERIOUS implies a concern for what really matters; GRAVE implies both seriousness and dignity in expression or attitude; SOLEMN suggests an impressive gravity utterly free from levity; SEDATE implies a composed and decorous seriousness; STAID suggests a settled, accustomed sedateness and prim self-restraint; SOBER stresses seriousness of purpose and absence of levity or frivolity; EARNEST suggests sincerity or often zealousness of purpose.

se·ri·ous·ly *adv* (1509) **1 :** in a sincere manner : EARNESTLY **2 :** to a serious extent : SEVERELY

se·ri·ous–mind·ed \ˌsir-ē-ə-'smīn-dəd\ *adj* (1845) : having a serious disposition or trend of thought — **se·ri·ous–mind·ed·ly** *adv* — **se·ri·ous–mind·ed·ness** *n*

ser·jeant, ser·jeanty *var of* SERGEANT, SERGEANTY

ser·jeant–at–law \ˌsär-jənt-ət-'lȯ\ *n, pl* **ser·jeants–at–law** (1503) : a member of a former class of barristers of the highest rank

ser·mon \'sər-mən\ *n* [ME, fr. OF, fr. ML *sermon-, sermo,* fr. L, speech, conversation, fr. *serere* to link together — more at SERIES] (13c) **1 :** a religious discourse delivered in public usu. by a clergyman as a part of a worship service **2 :** a speech on conduct or duty — **ser·mon·ic** \ˌsər-'män-ik\ *adj*

ser·mon·ette \ˌsər-mə-'net\ *n* (1814) : a short sermon

ser·mon·ize \'sər-mə-ˌnīz\ *vb* **-ized; -iz·ing** *vi* (1635) **1 :** to compose or deliver a sermon **2 :** to speak didactically or dogmatically ~ *vt* : to preach to or on at length — **ser·mon·iz·er** *n*

Sermon on the Mount (1645) : an ethical discourse delivered by Jesus and recorded in Matthew 5–7 and paralleled briefly in Luke 6: 20–49

sero- *comb form* [L *serum*] : serum ⟨*serology*⟩

se·ro·di·ag·no·sis \ˌsir-ō-ˌdī-ig-'nō-səs\ *n* [NL] (1896) : diagnosis by the use of serum (as in the Wassermann test) — **se·ro·di·ag·nos·tic** \-'näs-tik\ *adj*

se·rol·o·gy \sə-'räl-ə-jē, sir-'äl-\ *n* [ISV] (ca. 1909) : a science dealing with serums and esp. their reactions and properties — **se·ro·log·i·cal** \ˌsir-ə-'läj-i-kəl\ *or* **se·ro·log·ic** \-ik\ *adj* — **se·ro·log·i·cal·ly** \-i-k(ə-)lē\ *adv* — **se·rol·o·gist** \sə-'räl-ə-jəst, sir-'äl-\ *n*

se·ro·pu·ru·lent \ˌsir-ō-'pyu̇r-(y)ə-lənt, ˌser-\ *adj* (1835) : consisting of a mixture of serum and pus ⟨a ~ exudate⟩

se·ro·sa \sə-'rō-zə\ *n* [NL, fr. fem. of *serosus* serous, fr. L *serum*] (ca. 1890) : a usu. enclosing serous membrane — **se·ro·sal** \-zəl\ *adj*

se·ro·ti·nal \sə-'rät-nəl, -ᵊn-əl; ˌser-ə-'tīn-ᵊl\ *adj* [L *serotinus* coming late] (ca. 1909) : of or relating to the latter and usu. drier part of summer

se·rot·i·nous \sə-'rät-nəs, -ᵊn-əs; ˌser-ə-'tī-nəs\ *adj* [L *serotinus* coming late, fr. *sero* late — more at SOIREE] (ca. 1656) : remaining closed on the tree with seed dissemination delayed or occurring gradually ⟨~ cones⟩

se·ro·to·ner·gic \ˌsir-ə-tə-'nər-jik\ *also* **se·ro·to·nin·er·gic** \ˌsir-ə-ˌtō-nə-'nər-jik\ *adj* [*serotonin* + *-ergic*] (1967) : liberating, activated by, or involving serotonin in the transmission of nerve impulses ⟨~ pathways⟩

se·ro·to·nin \ˌsir-ə-'tō-nən, ˌser-\ *n* [*sero-* + *tonic* + *-in*] (1948) : a phenolic amine $C_{10}H_{12}N_2O$ that is a powerful vasoconstrictor and is found esp. in the blood serum and gastric mucosa of mammals

se·ro·type \'sir-ə-ˌtīp, 'ser-\ *n* (1946) : a group of intimately related organisms distinguished by a common set of antigens; *also* : the set of antigens characteristic of such a group

se·rous \'sir-əs\ *adj* [MF *sereux,* fr. *serum,* fr. L] (1594) : of, relating to, or resembling serum; *esp* : of thin watery constitution ⟨a ~ exudate⟩

serous membrane *n* (1869) : a thin membrane (as the peritoneum) with cells that secrete a serous fluid; *esp* : SEROSA

se·row \sə-'rō\ *n* [Lepcha *sā-ro* long-haired Tibetan goat] (1847) : any of several goat antelopes (genus *Capricornis*) of eastern Asia which are usu. rather dark and heavily built and some of which have distinct manes

ser·pent \'sər-pənt\ *n* [ME, fr. MF, fr. L *serpent-, serpens,* fr. prp. of *serpere* to creep; akin to Gk *herpein* to creep, Skt *sarpati* he creeps] (14c) **1 a** *archaic* : a noxious creature that creeps, hisses, or stings **b** : SNAKE **2 :** DEVIL 1 **3 :** a treacherous person

[1]**ser·pen·tine** \'sər-pən-ˌtēn, -ˌtīn\ *adj* [ME, fr. MF *serpentin,* fr. LL *serpentinus,* fr. L *serpent-, serpens*] (15c) **1 :** of or resembling a serpent (as in form or movement) **2 :** subtly wily or tempting **3 a :** winding or turning one way and another **b :** having a compound curve whose central curve is convex — **ser·pen·tine·ly** *adv*

[2]**serpentine** *n* (1519) : something that winds sinuously

[3]**ser·pen·tine** \-ˌtēn\ *n* [ME, fr. ML *serpentina, serpentinum,* fr. LL fem. & neut. of *serpentinus* resembling a serpent] (15c) : a mineral or rock consisting essentially of a hydrous magnesium silicate $Mg_3Si_2O_7 \cdot 2H_2O$ usu. having a dull green color and often a mottled appearance

ser·pig·i·nous \(ˌ)sər-'pij-ə-nəs\ *adj* [ML *serpigin-, serpigo* creeping skin disease, fr. L *serpere* to creep] (1676) : CREEPING, SPREADING; *esp* : healing over in one portion while continuing to advance in another ⟨~ ulcer⟩ — **ser·pig·i·nous·ly** *adv*

ser·ra·nid \sə-'ran-əd, 'ser-ə-nəd\ *n* [deriv. of L *serra* saw] (ca. 1900) : any of a large family (Serranidae) of carnivorous marine percoid fishes which have an oblong compressed body covered with ctenoid scales and many of which are important food and sport fishes (as the sea basses) esp. of warm seas — **serranid** *adj*

[1]**ser·rate** \'se(ə)r-ˌāt, sə-'rāt\ *adj* [L *serratus,* fr. *serra* saw] (1668) : notched or toothed on the edge; *specif* : having marginal teeth pointing forward or toward the apex ⟨a ~ leaf⟩

[2]**ser·rate** \sə-'rāt, 'se(ə)r-ˌāt\ *vt* **ser·rat·ed; ser·rat·ing** [LL *serratus,* pp. of *serrare* to saw, fr. L *serra*] (1750) : to mark or make with serrations

ser·ra·tion \sə-'rā-shən, se-\ *n* (1842) **1 :** the condition of being serrate **2 :** a formation resembling the toothed edge of a saw **3 :** one of the teeth in a serrate margin

ser·ried \'ser-ēd\ *adj* (1667) **1 :** crowded or pressed together : COMPACT ⟨the crowd collected in a ~ mass —W. S. Maugham⟩ **2** [by alter.] : marked by ridges : SERRATE ⟨the ~ contours of the . . . mountains —*Amer. Guide Series: Oregon*⟩ — **ser·ried·ly** *adv* — **ser·ried·ness** *n*

ser·ry \'ser-ē\ *vb* **ser·ried; ser·ry·ing** [MF *serré,* pp. of *serrer* to press, crowd — more at SEAR] *vi, archaic* (1581) : to press together esp. in ranks ~ *vt* : to crowd together

Ser·to·li cell \sər-ˌtō-lē-\ *n* [Enrico *Sertoli* †1910 Ital. histologist] (ca. 1899) : one of the elongated striated cells lining the seminiferous tubules that support and apparently nourish the spermatids

Ser·to·man \(ˌ)sər-'tō-mən\ *n* [*Sertoma* (club)] (1956) : a member of a major international service club

se·rum \'sir-əm\ *n, pl* **serums** *or* **se·ra** \-ə\ [L, whey, serum; akin to Gk *oros* whey, serum, *hormē* onset, assault, Skt *sarati* it flows] (1665) **1 :** the watery portion of an animal fluid remaining after coagulation: **a :** BLOOD SERUM; *esp* : immune blood serum that contains specific immune bodies (as antitoxins or agglutinins) ⟨antitoxin ~⟩ **b :** WHEY **c :** a normal or pathological serous fluid (as in a blister) **2 :** the watery part of a plant fluid

serum albumin *n* (1879) : a crystallizable albumin or mixture of albumins that normally constitutes more than half of the protein in blood serum and serves to maintain the osmotic pressure of the blood

serum globulin *n* (ca. 1890) : a globulin or mixture of globulins occurring in blood serum and containing most of the antibodies of the blood

serum hepatitis *n* (1932) : a sometimes fatal hepatitis caused by a double-stranded DNA virus that tends to persist in the blood serum and is transmitted esp. by contact with infected blood (as by transfusion) or blood products — called also *serum jaundice;* compare INFECTIOUS HEPATITIS

serum sickness *n* (ca. 1913) : an allergic reaction to the injection of foreign serum manifested by urticaria, swelling, eruption, arthritis, and fever

ser·val \'sər-vəl, (ˌ)sər-'val\ *n* [F, fr. Pg *lobo cerval* lynx, fr. ML *lupus cervalis,* lit., cervine wolf] (1771) : a long-legged African wildcat (*Felis capensis*) having large untufted ears and a tawny black-spotted coat

serval

ser·vant \'sər-vənt\ *n* [ME, fr. OF, fr. prp. of *servir*] (13c) : one that serves others; *esp* : one that performs duties about the person or home of a master or personal employer — **ser·vant·hood** \-ˌhu̇d\ *n* — **ser·vant·less** *adj*

[1]**serve** \'sərv\ *vb* **served; serv·ing** [ME *serven,* fr. MF *servir,* fr. OF, fr. L *servire* to be a slave, serve, fr. *servus* slave, servant, perh. of Etruscan origin] *vi* (14c) **1 a :** to be a servant **b :** to do military or naval service **2 :** to assist a celebrant as server at mass **3 a :** to be of use ⟨in a day when few people could write, seals *served* as signatures —Elizabeth W. King⟩ **b :** to be favorable, opportune, or convenient **c :** STAND BY, ASSIST **d :** to hold an office : discharge a duty or function ⟨~ on a jury⟩ **4 :** to prove adequate or satisfactory : SUFFICE ⟨a safe-conduct that *served* not only for him but for the entire party⟩ **5 :** to help persons to food: as **a :** to wait at table **b :** to set out portions of food or drink **6 :** to wait on customers **7 :** to put the ball or shuttlecock in play in various games (as tennis, volleyball, or badminton) ~ *vt* **1 a :** to be a servant to : ATTEND **b :** to give the service and respect due to (a superior) **c :** to comply with the commands or demands of : GRATIFY **d :** to give military or naval service to **e :** to perform the duties of (an office or post) **2 :** to act as server at (mass) **3** *archaic* : to pay a lover's or suitor's court to (a lady) ⟨that gentle lady, whom I love and ~ —Edmund Spenser⟩ **4 a :** to work through or perform (a term of service) ⟨*served* his time as a mate⟩ **b :** to put in (a term of imprisonment) **5 a :** to wait on at table **b :** to bring (food) to a diner **6 a :** to furnish or supply with something needed or desired **b :** to wait on (a customer) in a store **c :** to furnish professional service to **7 a :** to answer the needs of : AVAIL **b :** to be enough for : SUFFICE **c :** to contribute or conduce to : PROMOTE **8 :** to treat or act toward in a specified way : REQUITE ⟨he *served* me ill⟩ **9 a :** to bring to notice, deliver, or execute as required by law **b :** to make legal service upon (a person named in a process) **10** *of a male animal* : to copulate with **11 :** to wind yarn or wire tightly around (a rope or stay) for protection **12 :** to provide services that benefit or help **13 :** to put (the ball or shuttlecock) in play (as in tennis or badminton) — **serve one right** : to be deserved

2serve *n* (1611) **:** the act or action of putting the ball or shuttlecock in play in various games (as volleyball, badminton, or tennis); *also* **:** a turn to serve

serv·er \'sər-vər\ *n* (15c) **1 :** one that serves food or drink **2 :** the player who serves (as in tennis) **3 :** something used in serving food or drink **4 :** one that serves legal processes upon another **5 :** the celebrant's assistant at low mass

1ser·vice \'sər-vəs\ *n* [ME *serves,* pl. of *serve* fruit of the service tree, service tree, fr. OE *syrfe,* fr. (assumed) VL *sorbea,* fr. L *sorbus* service tree] (bef. 12c) **:** an Old World tree (*Sorbus domestica*) resembling the related mountain ashes but having larger flowers and larger edible fruit; *also* **:** a related Old World tree (*S. torminalis*) with bitter fruits

2ser·vice \'sər-vəs\ *n* [ME, fr. MF, fr. L *servitium* condition of a slave, body of slaves, fr. *servus* slave] (14c) **1 a :** the occupation or function of serving ⟨in active ~⟩ **b :** employment as a servant ⟨entered his ~⟩ **2 a :** the work performed by one that serves ⟨gives good ~⟩ **b :** HELP, USE, BENEFIT ⟨be of ~ to them⟩ **c :** contribution to the welfare of others **d :** disposal for use ⟨put the capability of the entire system at his ~ —C. R. Bowen⟩ **3 a :** a form followed in worship or in a religious ceremony ⟨the burial ~⟩ **b :** a meeting for worship — often used in pl. ⟨held evening ~*s*⟩ **4 :** the act of serving: as **a :** a helpful act ⟨did him a ~⟩ **b :** useful labor that does not produce a tangible commodity — usu. used in pl. ⟨charge for professional ~*s*⟩ **c :** SERVE **5 :** a set of articles for a particular use ⟨a silver ~ for 12⟩ **6 a :** an administrative division (as of a government or business) ⟨the consular ~⟩ **b :** one of a nation's military forces (as the army or navy) **7 a :** a facility supplying some public demand ⟨telephone ~⟩ ⟨bus ~⟩ **b :** a facility providing maintenance and repair ⟨television ~⟩ **8 :** the materials (as spun yarn, small lines, or canvas) used for serving a rope **9 :** the act of bringing a legal writ, process, or summons to notice as prescribed by law **10 :** the act of copulating with a female animal **11 :** a branch of a hospital medical staff devoted to a particular specialty ⟨obstetrical ~⟩

3service *vt* **ser·viced; ser·vic·ing** (1893) **:** to perform services for: as **a :** to repair or provide maintenance for **b :** to meet interest and sinking fund payments on (as government debt) **c :** to perform any of the business functions auxiliary to production or distribution of **d** *of a male animal* **:** SERVE 10 — **ser·vic·er** *n*

4service *adj* (1929) **1 :** of or relating to the armed services **2 :** used in serving or supplying ⟨delivery men use the ~ entrance⟩ **3 :** intended for hard or everyday use **4 a :** providing services ⟨the ~ trades—from filling stations to universities —John Fischer⟩ **b :** offering repair, maintenance, or incidental services

ser·vice·able \'sər-və-sə-bəl\ *adj* (14c) **1 :** HELPFUL, USEFUL **2 :** fit for use ⟨her ~ but not exceptional voice —Irving Kolodin⟩ — **ser·vice·abil·i·ty** \ˌsər-və-sə-'bil-ət-ē\ *n* — **ser·vice·able·ness** \'sər-və-sə-bəl-nəs\ *n* — **ser·vice·ably** \-blē\ *adv*

ser·vice·ber·ry \'sər-vəs-ˌber-ē *also* 'sär-\ *n* (1805) **:** any of various No. American trees and shrubs (genus *Amelanchier*) of the rose family sometimes cultivated for their showy white flowers or edible purple or red fruits — called also *Juneberry, shadblow, shadbush*

service book *n* (1580) **:** a book setting forth forms of worship used in religious services

service box *n* (1898) **:** the area in which a player stands while serving in various court games (as squash racquets or handball)

service break *n* (ca. 1952) **:** a game won on an opponent's serve (as in tennis)

service cap *n* (ca. 1908) **:** a flat-topped visor cap worn as part of a military uniform — compare GARRISON CAP

service ceiling *n* (1920) **:** the altitude at which under standard air conditions a particular airplane can no longer rise at a rate greater than a small designated rate (as 100 feet per minute)

service charge *n* (1917) **:** a fee charged for a particular service often in addition to a standard or basic fee — called also *service fee*

service club *n* (1926) **1 :** a club of business or professional men or women organized for their common benefit and active in community service **2 :** a recreation center for enlisted men provided by one of the armed services

service court *n* (ca. 1878) **:** a part of the court into which the ball or shuttlecock must be served

service line *n* (1875) **:** a line marked on a court in various games (as handball or tennis) parallel to the front wall or to the net to mark a boundary of the service zone or service court

ser·vice·man \'sər-vəs-ˌman, -mən\ *n* (1899) **1 :** a male member of the armed forces **2 :** a man employed to repair or maintain equipment **3 :** a service station attendant

service mark *n* (1945) **:** a mark or device used to identify a service (as transportation or insurance) offered to customers

service medal *n* (ca. 1934) **:** a medal awarded to an individual for military service in a specified war or campaign

service module *n* (1961) **:** a space vehicle module that contains oxygen, water, fuel cells, propellant tanks, and the main rocket engine

service road *n* (1921) **:** FRONTAGE ROAD

service sideline *n* (1941) **:** either of the lines on a doubles tennis court inside and parallel to the sidelines and marking the edges of the service courts

service station *n* (1916) **1 :** a retail station for servicing motor vehicles esp. with gasoline and oil **2 :** a place at which some service is offered

service stripe *n* (1920) **:** a stripe worn on an enlisted man's left sleeve to indicate three years of service in the army or four years in the navy

service tree *n* (1600) **:** 1SERVICE

ser·vice·wom·an \'sər-vəs-ˌwu̇m-ən\ *n* (1943) **:** a female member of the armed forces

ser·vi·ette \ˌsər-vē-'et\ *n* [F, fr. MF, fr. *servir* to serve] *chiefly Brit* (15c) **:** a table napkin

ser·vile \'sər-vəl, -ˌvīl\ *adj* [ME, fr. L *servilis,* fr. *servus* slave — more at SERVE] (15c) **1 :** of or befitting a slave or a menial position **2 :** meanly or cravenly submissive **:** ABJECT ***syn*** see SUBSERVIENT — **ser·vile·ly** \-və(l)-lē, -ˌvīl-lē\ *adv* — **ser·vile·ness** \-vəl-nəs, -ˌvīl-\ *n* — **ser·vil·i·ty** \(ˌ)sər-'vil-ət-ē\ *n*

serv·ing \'sər-viŋ\ *n* (1864) **:** a helping of food or drink

Ser·vite \'sər-ˌvīt\ *n* [ML *Servitae,* pl., Servites, fr. L *servus*] (1550) **:** a member of the mendicant Order of Servants of Mary founded in Florence, Italy, in 1233 — **Servite** *adj*

ser·vi·tor \'sər-vət-ər, -və-ˌtȯ(ə)r\ *n* [ME *servitour,* fr. MF, fr. LL *servitor,* fr. L *servitus,* pp. of *servire* to serve] (14c) **:** a male servant

ser·vi·tude \'sər-və-ˌt(y)üd\ *n* [ME, fr. MF, fr. L *servitudo* slavery, fr. *servus* slave] (15c) **1 :** a condition in which one lacks liberty esp. to determine one's course of action or way of life **2 :** a right by which something (as a piece of land) owned by one person is subject to a specified use or enjoyment by another

ser·vo \'sər-(ˌ)vō\ *n, pl* **servos** (1947) **1 :** SERVOMOTOR **2 :** SERVOMECHANISM

ser·vo·mech·a·nism \'sər-vō-ˌmek-ə-ˌniz-əm\ *n* [*servo-* (as in *servomotor*) + *mechanism*] (1926) **:** an automatic device for controlling large amounts of power by means of very small amounts of power and automatically correcting performance of a mechanism

ser·vo·mo·tor \'sər-vō-ˌmōt-ər\ *n* [F *servo-moteur,* fr. L *servus* slave, servant + F *-o-* + *moteur* motor, fr. L *motor* one that moves — more at MOTOR] (1889) **:** a power-driven mechanism that supplements a primary control operated by a comparatively feeble force (as in a servomechanism)

-ses *pl of* -SIS

ses·a·me \'ses-ə-mē *also* 'sez-\ *n* [alter. of earlier *sesam, sesama,* fr. L *sesamum, sesama,* fr. Gk *sēsamon, sēsamē,* of Sem origin; akin to Assyr *šamaššamu* sesame, Ar *simsim*] (15c) **1 :** an East Indian annual erect herb (*Sesamum indicum* of the family Pedaliaceae); *also* **:** its small seeds used as a source of oil and a flavoring agent **2 :** OPEN SESAME

sesame oil *n* (1870) **:** a pale yellow bland semidrying fatty oil obtained from sesame seeds and used chiefly as an edible oil, as a vehicle for various pharmaceuticals, and in cosmetics and soaps

ses·a·moid \'ses-ə-ˌmȯid\ *n* [Gk *sēsamoeidēs,* lit., resembling sesame seed, fr. *sēsamon*] (1696) **:** a nodular mass of bone (as the patella) or cartilage in a tendon esp. at a joint or bony prominence — **sesamoid** *adj*

sesqui- *comb form* [L, one and a half, half again, lit., and a half, fr. *semis* half (fr. *semi-*) + *-que* (enclitic) and; akin to Gk *te* and, Skt *ca,* Goth *-h, -uh*] **1 :** one and a half times ⟨*sesqui*centennial⟩ **2 a :** containing three atoms or equivalents of a specified element or group esp. combined with two of another ⟨*sesqui*oxide⟩ **b :** intermediate **:** combination ⟨*sesqui*carbonate⟩

ses·qui·car·bon·ate \ˌses-kwi-'kär-bə-ˌnāt, -nət\ *n* (1825) **:** a salt that is neither a simple normal carbonate nor a simple bicarbonate but often (as $Na_2CO_3 \cdot NaHCO_3 \cdot 2H_2O$) a combination of the two

ses·qui·cen·te·na·ry \-kwi-sen-'ten-ə-rē, -'sent-ᵊn-ˌer-ē, -sen-'tē-nə-rē\ *n* (1954) **:** SESQUICENTENNIAL

ses·qui·cen·ten·ni·al \-sen-'ten-ē-əl\ *n* (1880) **:** a 150th anniversary or its celebration — **sesquicentennial** *adj*

ses·qui·pe·da·lian \ˌses-kwə-pə-'dāl-yən\ *adj* [L *sesquipedalis,* lit., a foot and a half long, fr. *sesqui-* + *ped-, pes* foot — more at FOOT] (1656) **1 :** having many syllables **:** LONG ⟨~ terms⟩ **2 :** given to or characterized by the use of long words ⟨a ~ orator⟩

ses·qui·ter·pene \ˌses-kwə-'tər-ˌpēn\ *n* (ca. 1888) **:** any of a class of terpenes $C_{15}H_{24}$; *also* **:** a derivative of such a terpene

ses·sile \'ses-ˌīl, -əl\ *adj* [L *sessilis* of or fit for sitting, low, dwarf (of plants), fr. *sessus,* pp.] (1753) **1 :** attached directly by the base **:** not raised upon a stalk or peduncle ⟨a ~ leaf⟩ ⟨~ bubbles⟩ **2 :** permanently attached or established **:** not free to move about ⟨~ polyps⟩

ses·sion \'sesh-ən\ *n* [ME, fr. MF, fr. L *session-, sessio,* lit., act of sitting, fr. *sessus,* pp. of *sedēre* to sit — more at SIT] (15c) **1 :** a meeting or series of meetings of a body (as a court or legislature) for the transaction of business ⟨morning ~⟩ **2** *pl* **a (1) :** a sitting of English justices of peace in execution of the powers conferred by their commissions **(2) :** an English court holding such sessions **b :** any of various courts similar to the English sessions **3 :** the period between the first meeting of a legislative or judicial body and the prorogation or final adjournment **4 :** the ruling body of a Presbyterian congregation consisting of the elders in active service **5 :** the period during the year or day in which a school conducts classes **6 :** a meeting or period devoted to a particular activity ⟨a recording ~⟩ — **ses·sion·al** \'sesh-nəl, -ən-ᵊl\ *adj*

session man *n* (1958) **:** a studio musician who backs up a performer at a recording session

ses·terce \'ses-ˌtərs\ *n* [L *sestertius,* fr. *sestertius* two and a half times as great (fr. its being equal orig. to two and a half asses), fr. *semis* half (fr. *semi-*) + *tertius* third — more at THIRD] (1598) **:** an ancient Roman coin equal to ¼ denarius

ses·ter·tium \se-'stər-sh(ē-)əm\ *n, pl* **-tia** \-sh(ē-)ə\ [L, fr. gen. pl. of *sestertius* (in the phrase *milia sestertium* thousands of sesterces)] (1540) **:** a unit of value in ancient Rome equal to 1000 sesterces

ses·tet \se-'stet\ *n* [It *sestetto,* fr. *sesto* sixth, fr. L *sextus* — more at SEXT] (1859) **:** a stanza or a poem of six lines; *specif* **:** the last six lines of an Italian sonnet

ses·ti·na \se-'stē-nə\ *n* [It, fr. *sesto* sixth] (1586) **:** a lyrical fixed form consisting of six 6-line usu. unrhymed stanzas in which the end words of the first stanza recur as end words of the following five stanzas in a successively rotating order and as the middle and end words of the three verses of the concluding tercet

1set \'set\ *vb* **set; set·ting** [ME *setten,* fr. OE *settan;* akin to OHG *sezzen* to set, OE *sittan* to sit] *vt* (bef. 12c) **1 :** to cause to sit **:** place in or on a seat **2 a :** to put (a fowl) on eggs to hatch them **b :** to put (eggs) for hatching under a fowl or into an incubator **3 :** to place (oneself) in position to start running in a race **4 a :** to place with care or deliberate purpose and with relative stability ⟨~ a ladder against the wall⟩ ⟨~ a stone on the grave⟩ **b :** TRANSPLANT 1 ⟨~ seedlings⟩ **c (1) :** to make (as a trap) ready to catch prey **(2) :** to fix (a hook) firmly into the jaw of a fish **d :** to put aside (as dough containing yeast) for fermenting **5 :** to direct with fixed attention ⟨~ your mind to it⟩ **6 :** to cause to assume a specified condition, relation, or occupation ⟨slaves were ~ free⟩ **7 a :** to appoint or assign to an office or duty **b :** POST, STATION **8 :** to cause to assume a specified posture or position ⟨~ the door ajar⟩ **9 a :** to fix as a distinguishing imprint, sign, or appearance ⟨the years have ~ their mark on him⟩ **b :** AFFIX **c :** APPLY ⟨~ a match to kindling⟩ **10 :** to fix or decide on as a time, limit, or regulation **:** PRESCRIBE ⟨~ a wedding day⟩ ⟨~ the rules for the game⟩ **11 a :** to establish as the highest level or best performance ⟨~ a record for the half mile⟩ **b :** to furnish as a pattern or model ⟨~ an example of generosity⟩ **c :** to allot as a task ⟨*setting* lessons for the children to work upon at home —*Manchester Examiner*⟩ **12 a :** to adjust (a device and esp. a measuring device) to a desired position ⟨~ the alarm for 7:00⟩ ⟨~ a thermostat at 68⟩; *also* : to adjust (as a clock) in conformity with a standard **b** : to restore to normal position or connection when dislocated or fractured ⟨~ a broken bone⟩ **c** : to spread to the wind ⟨~ the sails⟩ **13** **a** : to put in order for use ⟨~ a place for a guest⟩ **b** : to make scenically ready for a performance ⟨~ the stage⟩ **c** (1) : to arrange (type) for printing ⟨~ type by hand⟩ (2) : to put into type or its equivalent (as on film) ⟨~ the first word in italic⟩ **14** **a** : to put a fine edge on by grinding or honing ⟨~ a razor⟩ **b** : to bend slightly the tooth points of (a saw) alternately in opposite directions **c** : to sink (the head of a nail) below the surface **15** : to fix in a desired position (as by heating or stretching) **16** : to arrange (hair) in a desired style by using implements (as curlers, rollers, or clips) and gels or lotions **17** **a** : to adorn with something affixed or infixed : STUD, DOT ⟨clear sky ~ with stars⟩ **b** : to fix (as a precious stone) in a border of metal : place in a setting **18** **a** : to hold something in regard or esteem at the rate of ⟨~s a great deal by daily exercise⟩ **b** : to place in a relative rank or category ⟨~ duty before pleasure⟩ **c** : to fix at a certain amount ⟨~ bail at $500⟩ **d** : VALUE, RATE ⟨his promises were ~ at naught⟩ **e** : to place as an estimate of worth ⟨~ a high value on life⟩ **19** : to place in relation for comparison or balance ⟨theory ~ against practice⟩ **20** **a** : to direct to action **b** : to incite to attack or antagonism ⟨war ~s brother against brother⟩ **21** **a** : to place by transporting ⟨was ~ ashore on the island⟩ **b** : to put in motion **c** : to put and fix in a direction ⟨~ our faces toward home once more⟩ **d** *of a dog* : to point out the position of (game) by holding a fixed attitude **22** : to defeat (an opponent or his contract) in bridge **23** **a** : to fix firmly : make immobile : give rigid form or condition to ⟨~ his jaw in determination⟩ **b** : to make unyielding or obstinate **24** : to cause to become firm or solid ⟨~ milk for cheese⟩ **25** : to cause (as fruit) to develop ~ *vi* **1** *chiefly dial* : SIT **2** : to be becoming : be suitable : FIT ⟨his behavior does not ~ well with his years⟩ **3** : to cover and warm eggs to hatch them **4** **a** : to become lodged or fixed ⟨the pudding ~ heavily on his stomach⟩ **b** : to place oneself in position in preparation for an action (as running) **5** *of a plant part* : to undergo development usu. as a result of pollination **6** **a** : to pass below the horizon : go down ⟨the sun ~s⟩ **b** : to sink out of sight : pass away **7** : to apply oneself to some activity ⟨~ to work⟩ **8** : to have a specified direction in motion : FLOW, TEND ⟨the wind was *setting* from Pine Hill to the farm —Esther Forbes⟩ **9** *of a dog* : to indicate the position of game by crouching or pointing **10** : to dance face to face with another in a square dance ⟨~ to your partner and turn⟩ **11** **a** : to become solid or thickened by chemical or physical alteration ⟨the cement ~s rapidly⟩ **b** *of a dye or color* : to become permanent **c** *of a bone* : to become whole by knitting **d** *of metal* : to acquire a permanent twist or bend from strain — **set about** : to begin to do — **set apart** **1** : to reserve to a particular use **2** : to make noticeable or outstanding — **set aside** **1** : to put to one side : DISCARD **2** : to set apart for a purpose : RESERVE, SAVE **3** : DISMISS **4** : ANNUL, OVERRULE — **set at** : to mount an attack on : ASSAIL ⟨would go although . . . devils should *set at* me —Charlotte Yonge⟩ — **set eyes on** : to catch sight of — **set foot in** : ENTER — **set foot on** : to step onto — **set forth** **1** : PUBLISH **2** : to give an account or statement of **3** : to start out on a journey — **set forward** **1** : FURTHER **2** : to start out on a journey — **set in motion** : to give impulse to ⟨*sets* the story *in motion* vividly —Howard Thompson⟩ — **set one's hand to** : to become engaged in — **set one's heart on** : RESOLVE ⟨she *set her heart on* succeeding⟩ — **set one's house in order** : to organize one's affairs — **set one's sights on** : to determine to pursue — **set one straight** : to correct someone by providing accurate information — **set sail** : to start out on a course; *esp* : to begin a voyage ⟨*set sail* for Europe⟩ — **set store by** *or* **set store on** : to consider valuable, trustworthy, or worthwhile — **set the stage** : to provide the basis or background ⟨this trend will *set the stage* for higher earnings⟩ — **set to music** : to provide music or instrumental accompaniment for (a text) — **set upon** : to attack usu. with violence ⟨the dogs *set upon* the trespassers⟩

²set *n* (14c) **1** **a** : the act or action of setting **b** : the condition of being set **2** **a** : mental inclination, tendency, or habit : BENT ⟨a ~ toward mathematics⟩ **b** : a state of psychological preparedness usu. of limited duration for action in response to an anticipated stimulus or situation ⟨the influence of mental ~ on the effect experienced with marijuana⟩ **3** : a number of things of the same kind that belong or are used together **4** : direction of flow ⟨the ~ of the wind⟩ **5** : form or carriage of the body or of its parts **6** : the manner of fitting or of being placed or suspended ⟨in order to give the skirt a pretty ~ —Mary J. Howell⟩ **7** : amount of deflection from a straight line ⟨~ of a saw's teeth⟩ **8** : permanent change of form (as of metal) due to repeated or excessive stress **9** : the act or result of arranging hair by curling or waving **10** *also* **sett** \ˈset\ **a** : a young plant or rooted cutting ready for transplanting **b** : a small bulb, corm, or tuber or a piece of tuber used for propagation ⟨onion ~s⟩ **11** *or* **sett** : the burrow of a badger **12** : the width of the body of a piece of type **13** : an artificial setting for a scene of a theatrical or film production **14** *also* **sett** : a rectangular paving stone of sandstone or granite **15** : a division of a tennis match won by the side that wins at least six games beating the opponent by two games or by winning a tiebreaker **16** : a collection of books or periodicals forming a unit **17** : a clutch of eggs **18** : the basic formation in a country-dance or square dance **19** : a session of music (as jazz or dance music) usu. followed by an intermission; *also* : the music played at one session **20** : a group of persons associated by common interests **21** : a collection of elements and esp. mathematical ones (as numbers or points) — called also *class* **22** : an apparatus of electronic components assembled so as to function as a unit ⟨a television ~⟩ **23** : a usu. offensive formation in football

³set *adj* [ME *sett*, fr. pp. of *setten* to set] (15c) **1** : INTENT, DETERMINED ⟨~ upon going⟩ **2** : fixed by authority or appointment : PRESCRIBED, SPECIFIED ⟨~ hours of study⟩ **3** : INTENTIONAL, PREMEDITATED ⟨did it of ~ purpose⟩ **4** : reluctant to change ⟨~ in his ways⟩ **5** **a** : IMMOVABLE, RIGID ⟨~ frown⟩ **b** : BUILT-IN **6** : SETTLED, PERSISTENT ⟨~ defiance⟩ **7** : being in readiness : PREPARED ⟨~ for an early morning start⟩

se·ta \ˈsēt-ə\ *n, pl* **se·tae** \ˈsē-ˌtē\ [NL, fr. L *saeta, seta* bristle — more at SINEW] (1793) : a slender usu. rigid or bristly and springy organ or part of an animal or plant — **se·tal** \ˈsēt-ᵊl\ *adj*

se·ta·ceous \si-ˈtā-shəs\ *adj* [L *saeta, seta*] (1664) **1** : set with or consisting of bristles **2** : resembling a bristle in form or texture

set–aside \ˈset-ə-ˌsīd\ *n* (1943) : something (as a portion of receipts or production) that is set aside for a specified purpose

set·back \ˈset-ˌbak\ *n* (1674) **1** : a checking of progress **2** : DEFEAT, REVERSE **3** : ⁴PITCH 7 **4** : a placing of the face of a building on a line some distance to the rear of the building line or of the wall below; *also* : the rooftop area produced by a setback **5** : automatic scheduled adjustment to a lower temperature setting of a thermostat

set back \(ˈ)set-ˈbak\ *vt* [¹*set* + ²*back*] (1600) **1** : to slow the progress of : HINDER, DELAY **2** : COST ⟨a new suit *set* him *back* $200⟩

set by *vt* (1595) : to set apart for future use

set down *vt* (15c) **1** : to cause to sit down : SEAT **2** : to place at rest on a surface or on the ground **3** : to suspend (a jockey) from racing **4** : to cause or allow to get off a vehicle : DELIVER **5** : to land (an airplane) on the ground or water **6** **a** : ORDAIN, ESTABLISH **b** : to put in writing **7** **a** : REGARD, CONSIDER ⟨*set* him *down* as a liar⟩ **b** : ATTRIBUTE

se te·nant \sə-ˈten-ənt, ˌset-ə-ˈnäⁿ\ *adj* [F, lit., holding one another] *of postage stamps* (ca. 1911) : joined together as in the original sheet but differing in design, overprint, color, or perforation

Seth \ˈseth\ *n* [Heb *Shēth*] : a son of Adam

¹set–in \ˌset-ˌin\ *adj* (1534) **1** : placed, located, or built as a part of some other construction ⟨a ~ bookcase⟩ ⟨a ~ washbasin⟩ **2** : cut separately and stitched in ⟨~ sleeves⟩

²set–in \ˈset-ˌin\ *n* (1953) : INSERT

set in *vt* (15c) : INSERT; *esp* : to stitch (a small part) within a large article ⟨*set in* a sleeve of a dress⟩ ~ *vi* **1** : to become established **2** : to blow or flow toward shore ⟨the wind was beginning to *set in*⟩

set·line \ˈset-ˌlīn\ *n* (1865) : a long heavy fishing line to which several hooks are attached in series

set·off \ˈset-ˌȯf\ *n* (1621) **1** : something that is set off against another thing: **a** : DECORATION, ORNAMENT **b** : COMPENSATION, COUNTERBALANCE **2** : the discharge of a debt by setting against it a distinct claim in favor of the debtor; *also* : the claim itself **3** : OFFSET 7a

set off \(ˈ)set-ˈȯf\ *vt* (1596) **1** **a** : to put in relief : show up by contrast **b** : ADORN, EMBELLISH **c** : to set apart : make distinct or outstanding **2** **a** : OFFSET, COMPENSATE ⟨more variety in the Lancashire weather to *set off* its most disagreeable phases —*Geog. Jour.*⟩ **b** : to make a setoff of ⟨the respective totals shall be *set off* against one another —O. R. Hobson⟩ **3** **a** : to set in motion : cause to begin **b** : to cause to explode **4** : to measure off on a surface ~ *vi* : to start out on a course or a journey ⟨*set off* for home⟩

set on *vt* (1670) **1** : ATTACK **2** **a** *obs* : PROMOTE **b** : to urge (as a dog) to attack or pursue **c** : to incite to action : INSTIGATE **d** : to set to work ~ *vi* : GO ON, ADVANCE

se·tose \ˈsē-ˌtōs\ *adj* [L *saetosus*, fr. *saeta*] (1661) : SETACEOUS, BRISTLY

set·out \ˈset-ˌau̇t\ *n* (1806) **1** **a** (1) : ARRAY, DISPLAY (2) : ARRANGEMENT, LAYOUT **b** : BUFFET, SPREAD **c** : TURNOUT 5 **2** : PARTY, ENTERTAINMENT **3** : BEGINNING, OUTSET

set out \(ˈ)set-ˈau̇t\ *vt* (1540) **1** : to state, describe, or recite at length ⟨distributed copies of a pamphlet *setting out* his ideas in full —S. F. Mason⟩ **2** **a** : to arrange and present graphically or systematically **b** : to mark out (as a design) : lay out the plan of **3** : to begin with a definite purpose : INTEND, UNDERTAKE ~ *vi* : to start out on a course, a journey, or a career

set piece *n* (ca. 1909) **1** : a realistic piece of stage scenery standing by itself **2** : a composition (as in literature or music) executed in a fixed or ideal form often with studied artistry and brilliant effect **3** : a precisely planned and conducted military operation

set point *n* (1928) : a situation (as in tennis) in which one player will win the set by winning the next point; *also* : the point won

set·screw \ˈset-ˌskrü\ *n* (1855) **1** : a screw screwed through one part tightly upon or into another part to prevent relative movement **2** : a screw for regulating a valve opening or a spring tension

sett *var of* SET

set·tee \se-ˈtē\ *n* [alter. of *settle*] (1716) **1** : a long seat with a back **2** : a medium-sized sofa with arms and a back

set·ter \ˈset-ər\ *n* (15c) **1** : one that sets **2** : a large bird dog of a type trained to point on finding game

set theory *n* (1936) : a branch of mathematics or of symbolic logic that deals with the nature and relations of sets — **set theoretic** *adj*

set·ting \ˈset-iŋ\ *n* (15c) **1** : the manner, position, or direction in which something is set **2** : the frame or bed in which a gem is set; *also* : style of mounting **3** **a** : BACKGROUND, ENVIRONMENT **b** : the time and place of the action of a literary, dramatic, or cinematic work **c** : the scenery used in a theatrical or film production **4** : the music composed for a text (as a poem) **5** : the articles of tableware for setting a place at table ⟨two ~s of sterling silver⟩ **6** : a batch of eggs for incubation

setting circle *n* (ca. 1899) : a graduated scale or wheel on the mounting of an equatorial telescope for indicating right ascension or declination

setting–up exercise *n* (ca. 1900) : any of a series of gymnastic exercises used to give an erect carriage, supple muscles, and easy control of the limbs

¹set·tle \ˈset-ᵊl\ *n* [ME, place for sitting, seat, chair, fr. OE *setl*; akin to OHG *sezzal* seat, L *sella* seat, chair, saddle, OE *sittan* to sit] (bef. 12c) : a wooden bench with arms, a high solid back, and an enclosed foundation which can be used as a chest

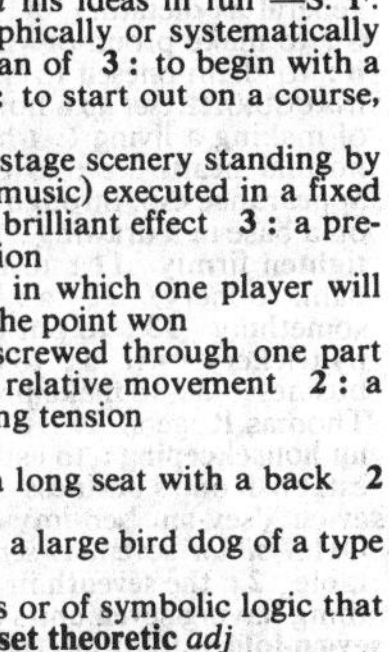

settle

²set·tle *vb* **set·tled; set·tling** \ˈset-liŋ, -ᵊl-iŋ\ [ME *settlen* to seat, bring to rest, come to rest, fr. OE *setlan*, fr. *setl* seat] *vt* (bef. 12c) **1** : to place so as to stay **2** **a** : to establish in residence **b** : to furnish with inhabitants : COLONIZE **3** **a** : to cause to pack down

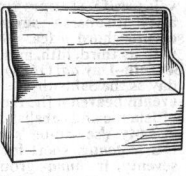

b : to clarify by causing dregs or impurities to sink 4 : to make quiet or orderly 5 a : to fix or resolve conclusively ⟨~ the question⟩ b : to establish or secure permanently ⟨~ the order of royal succession⟩ 6 : to arrange in a desired position 7 : to make or arrange for final disposition of ⟨*settled* his affairs⟩ 8 *of an animal* : IMPREGNATE ~ *vi* 1 : to come to rest 2 a : to sink gradually or to the bottom b : to become clear by the deposit of sediment or scum c : to become compact by sinking 3 a : to become fixed, resolved, or established ⟨a cold *settled* in his chest⟩ b : to establish a residence or colony ⟨*settled* in Europe for a few years⟩ — often used with *down* 4 a : to become quiet or orderly b : to take up an ordered or stable life — often used with *down* ⟨marry and ~ down⟩ 5 : to adjust differences or accounts 6 *of an animal* : CONCEIVE ***syn*** see DECIDE — **set·tle·able** \'set-ᵊl-ə-bəl, 'set-lə-bəl\ *adj* — **settle for** : to be content with — **settle one's hash** : to silence or subdue someone by decisive action — **settle the stomach** : to remove or relieve the distress or nausea of indigestion

set·tle·ment \'set-ᵊl-mənt\ *n* (1648) 1 : the act or process of settling 2 a : an act of bestowing or giving possession under legal sanction b : the sum, estate, or income secured to one by such a settlement 3 a : a place or region newly settled b : a small village 4 : an institution providing various community services esp. to large city populations 5 : an agreement composing differences

settlement house *n* (1907) : SETTLEMENT 4

set·tler \'set-lər, -ᵊl-ər\ *n* (1696) : one that settles (as a new region)

set·tling \'set-liŋ, -ᵊl-iŋ\ *n* (1594) : SEDIMENT, DREGS — usu. used in pl.

set·tlor \'set-,lȯ(ə)r, -ᵊl-,ȯ(ə)r\ *n* (1818) : one that makes a settlement or creates a trust of property

set–to \'set-,tü\ *n, pl* **set–tos** (1743) : a usu. brief and vigorous contest

set to \(')set-'tü\ *vi* (15c) 1 : to begin actively and earnestly 2 : to begin fighting

set·up \'set-,əp\ *n* (1890) 1 a : carriage of the body; *esp* : erect and soldierly bearing b : CONSTITUTION, MAKEUP 2 a : the assembly and arrangement of the tools and apparatus required for the performance of an operation b : the preparation and adjustment of machines for an assigned task 3 a : a table setting b : glass, ice, and mixer served to patrons who supply their own liquor 4 a : a camera position from which a scene is filmed; *also* : the footage taken from one camera position b : the final arrangement of the scenery and properties for a scene of a theatrical or cinematic production 5 a : a position of the balls in billiards or pool from which it is easy to score b : a task or contest purposely made easy c : something easy to get or accomplish 6 a : the manner in which the elements or components of a machine, apparatus, or mechanical, electrical, or hydraulic system are arranged, designed, or assembled b : the patterns within which political, social, or administrative forces operate : customary or established practice 7 : PROJECT, PLAN

set up \(')set-'əp\ *vt* (13c) 1 a : to raise to and place in a high position b : to place in view : POST c : to put forward (as a plan) for acceptance 2 a : to place upright : ERECT ⟨*set up* a statue⟩ b : to assemble the parts of and erect in position ⟨*set up* a printing press⟩ c : to put (a machine) in readiness or adjustment for a tooling operation 3 : CAUSE, CREATE ⟨*set up* a clamor⟩ 4 : to place in power or in office ⟨*set up* the general as dictator⟩ 5 a : to raise from depression : ELATE, GRATIFY b : to make proud or vain 6 a : to put forward or extol as a model b : to claim oneself to be ⟨*sets* himself *up* as an authority⟩ 7 : FOUND, INAUGURATE ⟨*set up* a home for orphans⟩ 8 a : to provide with means of making a living ⟨*set* him *up* in business⟩ b : to bring or restore to normal health c : to cause (one) to take on a soldierly or athletic appearance esp. through drill 9 : to erect (a perpendicular or a figure) on a base in a drawing 10 a : to make taut (a stay or hawser) b : to tighten firmly 11 : to make carefully worked out plans for ⟨*set up* a bank robbery⟩ 12 a : to pay for (drinks) b : to treat (someone) to something 13 : to put in a compromising or dangerous position usu. by trickery ~ *vi* 1 : to come into active operation or use 2 : to begin business 3 : to make pretensions ⟨has never *set up* to be a wise man — Thomas Rogers⟩ 4 : to become firm or consolidated : HARDEN — **set up housekeeping** : to establish one's living quarters — **set up shop** : to establish one's business

sev·en \'sev-ən, 'seb-ᵊm\ *n* [ME, fr. *seven*, adj., fr. OE *seofon;* akin to OHG *sibun* seven, L *septem*, Gk *hepta*] (bef. 12c) 1 — see NUMBER table 2 : the seventh in a set or series ⟨the ~ of diamonds⟩ 3 : something having seven units or members — **seven** *adj or pron*

sev·en·fold \-,fōld\ *adj* (bef. 12c) 1 : having seven units or members 2 : being seven times as great or as many — **sevenfold** *adv*

seven seas *n pl* (1872) : all the waters or oceans of the world

sev·en·teen \,sev-ən-'tēn, ,seb-ᵊm-\ *n* [*seventeen*, adj., fr. ME *seventene*, fr. OE *seofontēne;* akin to OE *tīen* ten] (bef. 12c) — see NUMBER table — **seventeen** *adj or pron* — **sev·en·teenth** \-'tēn(t)th\ *adj or n*

seventeen–year locust *n* (1817) : a cicada (*Magicicada septendecim*) of the U.S. that has in the North a life of seventeen years and in the South of thirteen years of which most is spent underground as a nymph and only a few weeks as a winged adult

sev·enth \'sev-ən(t)th, 'seb-ᵊm(t)th\ *n, pl* **sevenths** \'sev-ən(t)s, -ən(t)ths; 'seb-ᵊm(t)s, -ᵊm(t)ths\ (bef. 12c) 1 — see NUMBER table 2 a : a musical interval embracing seven diatonic degrees b : a tone at this interval; *specif* : LEADING TONE c : the harmonic combination of two tones a seventh apart — **seventh** *adj or adv*

seventh chord *n* (ca. 1909) : a chord comprising a fundamental tone with its third, fifth, and seventh

Seventh–Day *adj* (1684) : advocating or practicing observance of Saturday as the Sabbath

seventh heaven *n* [fr. the seventh being the highest of the seven heavens of Islamic and cabalist doctrine] (1818) : a state of extreme joy

sev·en·ty \'sev-ən-tē, 'seb-ᵊm-, -dē\ *n, pl* **-ties** [*seventy*, adj., fr. ME, fr. OE *seofontig*, short for *hundseofontig*, fr. *hundseofontig*, n., group of seventy, fr. *hund-* group of ten (akin to Goth *taihun* ten) + *seofon* seven + *-tig* group of ten — more at TEN] (bef. 12c) 1 — see NUMBER table 2 *pl* : the numbers 70 to 79; *specif* : the years 70 to 79 in a lifetime or century 3 *cap* : a Mormon elder ordained for missionary work under the apostles — **sev·en·ti·eth** \-tē-əth, -dē-\ *adj or n* — **seventy** *adj or pron*

sev·en·ty–eight \,sev-ən-tē-'āt, ,seb-ᵊm-, -dē-'āt\ *n* (bef. 12c) 1 — see NUMBER table 2 : a phonograph record designed to be played at 78 revolutions per minute — usu. written 78 — **seventy–eight** *adj or pron*

sev·en–up \,sev-ə-'nəp, ,seb-ᵊm-'əp\ *n* (1830) : an American variety of all fours in which a total of seven points constitutes game

sev·er \'sev-ər\ *vb* **sev·ered; sev·er·ing** \-(ə-)riŋ\ [ME *severen*, fr. MF *severer*, fr. L *separare* — more at SEPARATE] *vt* (14c) : to put or keep apart : DIVIDE; *esp* : to remove (as a part) by or as if by cutting ~ *vi* : to become separated ***syn*** see SEPARATE

sev·er·able \'sev-(ə-)rə-bəl\ *adj* (1548) : capable of being severed; *esp* : capable of being divided into legally independent rights or obligations — **sev·er·abil·i·ty** \,sev-(ə-)rə-'bil-ət-ē\ *n*

[1]**sev·er·al** \'sev-(ə-)rəl\ *adj* [ME, fr. AF, fr. ML *separalis*, fr. L *separ* separate, back-formation fr. *separare* to separate] (15c) 1 a : separate or distinct from one another ⟨federal union of the ~ states⟩ b (1) : individually owned or controlled : EXCLUSIVE ⟨a ~ fishery⟩ — compare COMMON (2) : of or relating separately to each individual involved ⟨a ~ judgment⟩ c : being separate and distinctive : RESPECTIVE ⟨specialists in their ~ fields⟩ 2 a : more than one ⟨~ pleas⟩ b : more than two but fewer than many ⟨moved ~ inches⟩ c *chiefly dial* : being a great many ***syn*** see DISTINCT — **sev·er·al·ly** \-ē\ *adv*

[2]**several** *pron, pl in constr* (1686) : an indefinite number more than two and fewer than many ⟨~ of the guests⟩

sev·er·al·fold \,sev-(ə-)rəl-'fōld\ *adj* (1738) 1 : having several parts or aspects 2 : being several times as large, as great, or as many as some understood size, degree, or amount ⟨a ~ increase⟩ — **severalfold** *adv*

sev·er·al·ty \'sev-(ə-)rəl-tē\ *n* [MF *severalte*, fr. AF *severalté*, fr. *several*] (1664) 1 : the quality or state of being several : DISTINCTNESS, SEPARATENESS 2 a : a sole, separate, and exclusive possession, dominion, or ownership : one's own right without a joint interest in any other person ⟨tenants in ~⟩ b : the quality or state of being individual or particular 3 a : land owned in severalty b : the quality or state of being held in severalty

sev·er·ance \'sev-(ə-)rən(t)s\ *n* (15c) : the act or process of severing : the state of being severed

severance pay *n* (1943) : an allowance usu. based on length of service that is payable to an employee on termination of employment

severance tax *n* (1928) : a tax levied by a state on the extractor of oil, gas, or minerals intended for consumption in other states — compare ROYALTY 5a

se·vere \sə-'vi(ə)r\ *adj* **se·ver·er; -est** [MF or L; MF, fr. L *severus*] (1548) 1 a : strict in judgment, discipline, or government b : of a strict or stern bearing or manner : AUSTERE 2 : rigorous in restraint, punishment, or requirement : STRINGENT, RESTRICTIVE 3 : strongly critical or condemnatory : CENSORIOUS ⟨a ~ critic⟩ 4 a : maintaining a scrupulously exacting standard of behavior or self-discipline b : establishing exacting standards of accuracy and integrity in intellectual processes ⟨a ~ logician⟩ 5 : sober or restrained in decoration or manner : PLAIN 6 a : inflicting physical discomfort or hardship : HARSH ⟨~ winters⟩ b : inflicting pain or distress : GRIEVOUS ⟨a ~ wound⟩ 7 : requiring great effort : ARDUOUS ⟨a ~ test⟩ 8 : of a great degree : SERIOUS ⟨~ depression⟩ — **se·vere·ly** *adv* — **se·vere·ness** *n* — **se·ver·i·ty** \sə-'ver-ət-ē\ *n*

syn SEVERE, STERN, AUSTERE, ASCETIC mean given to or marked by strict discipline and firm restraint. SEVERE implies standards enforced without indulgence or laxity and may suggest harshness; STERN stresses inflexibility and inexorability of temper or character; AUSTERE stresses absence of warmth, color, or feeling and may apply to rigorous restraint, simplicity, or self-denial; ASCETIC implies abstention from pleasure and comfort or self-indulgence as spiritual discipline.

se·vi·che \sə-'vē-(,)chā, -chē\ *n* [AmerSp] (1952) : a dish of raw fish marinated in lime or lemon juice often with oil, onions, peppers, and seasonings and served esp. as an appetizer

Sev·in \'sev-ən\ *trademark* — used for an insecticide consisting of a preparation of carbaryl

Sevres \'sev-rə, 'sev(rᵊ)\ *n* [*Sèvres*, France] (1764) : an often elaborately decorated French porcelain

sew \'sō\ *vb* **sewed; sewn** \'sōn\ *or* **sewed; sew·ing** [ME *sewen*, fr. OE *sīwian;* akin to OHG *siuwen* to sew, L *suere*] *vt* (bef. 12c) 1 : to unite or fasten by stitches 2 : to close or enclose by sewing ⟨~ the money in a bag⟩ ~ *vi* : to practice or engage in sewing — **sew·abil·i·ty** \,sō-ə-'bil-ət-ē\ *n* — **sew·able** \,sō-ə-bəl\ *adj*

sew·age \'sü-ij\ *n* [[3]*sewer*] (1834) : refuse liquids or waste matter carried off by sewers

[1]**sew·er** \'sü-ər, 'sü(-ə)r\ *n* [ME, fr. AF *asseour*, lit., seater, fr. OF *asseoir* to seat — more at ASSIZE] (14c) : a medieval household officer often of high rank in charge of serving the dishes at table and sometimes of seating and tasting

[2]**sew·er** \'sō(-ə)r\ *n* (14c) : one that sews

[3]**sew·er** \'sü-ər, 'sü(-ə)r\ *n* [ME, fr. MF *esseweur, seweur*, fr. *essewer* to drain, fr. (assumed) VL *exaquare*, fr. L *ex-* + *aqua* water — more at ISLAND] (15c) : an artificial usu. subterranean conduit to carry off sewage and sometimes surface water (as from rainfall)

sew·er·age \'sü-ə-rij, 'sü(-ə)r-ij\ *n* (1834) 1 : the removal and disposal of sewage and surface water by sewers 2 : a system of sewers 3 : SEWAGE

sew·ing \'sō-iŋ\ *n* (13c) 1 : the act, method, or occupation of one that sews 2 : material that has been or is to be sewed

sew up *vt* (15c) 1 : to mend completely by sewing 2 : to get exclusive use or control of 3 : to make certain of : ASSURE

[1]**sex** \'seks\ *n* [ME, fr. L *sexus*] (14c) 1 : either of two divisions of organisms distinguished respectively as male or female 2 : the sum of the structural, functional, and behavioral characteristics of living beings that subserve reproduction by two interacting parents and that distinguish males and females 3 a : sexually motivated phenomena or behavior b : SEXUAL INTERCOURSE 4 : GENITALIA

[2]**sex** *vt* (1884) 1 : to identify the sex of ⟨~ chicks⟩ 2 a : to increase the sexual appeal of b : to arouse the sexual desires of

sex- *or* **sexi-** *comb form* [L *sex* — more at SIX] : six ⟨*sex*partite⟩ ⟨*sexi*valent⟩

sex·a·ge·nar·i·an \,sek-sə-jə-'ner-ē-ən, (,)sek-,saj-ə-\ *n* [L *sexagenarius* of or containing sixty, sixty years old, fr. *sexageni* sixty each, fr. *sexaginta* sixty, irreg. fr. *sex* six + *-ginta* (akin to L *viginti* twenty) — more at SIX, VIGESIMAL] (1738) : a person whose age is in the sixties — **sexagenarian** *adj*

Sex·a·ges·i·ma \ˌsek-sə-ˈjes-ə-mə, -ˈjā-zə-\ *n* [LL, fr. L, fem. of *sexagesimus* sixtieth; fr. its being approximately 60 days before Easter] (15c) : the second Sunday before Lent

1sex·a·ges·i·mal \-ˈjes-ə-məl\ *adj* [L *sexagesimus* sixtieth, fr. *sexaginta* sixty] (1685) : of, relating to, or based on the number 60

2sexagesimal *n* (1685) : a sexagesimal fraction

sex appeal *n* (1924) **1** : personal appeal or physical attractiveness for members of the opposite sex **2** : general attractiveness

sex cell *n* (1889) : GAMETE; *also* : its cellular precursor

sex chromatin *n* (ca. 1952) : BARR BODY

sex chromosome *n* (1924) : a chromosome that is inherited differently in the two sexes, that is or is held to be concerned directly with the inheritance of sex, and that is the seat of factors governing the inheritance of various sex-linked and sex-limited characters

sex·de·cil·lion \ˌseks-di-ˈsil-yən\ *n, often attrib* [L *sedecim, sexdecim* sixteen (fr. *sex* six + *decem* ten) + E *-illion* (as in *million*) — more at TEN] (ca. 1939) — see NUMBER table

sexed \ˈsekst\ *adj* (ca. 1891) **1** : having sex or sexual instincts **2** : having sex appeal

sex gland *n* (1935) : GONAD

sex hormone *n* (1917) : a hormone (as from the gonads or adrenal cortex) that affects the growth or function of the reproductive organs or the development of secondary sex characteristics

sex·ism \ˈsek-ˌsiz-əm\ *n* [1*sex* + *-ism* (as in *racism*)] (1970) **1** : prejudice or discrimination based on sex; *esp* : discrimination against women **2** : behavior, conditions, or attitudes that foster stereotypes of social roles based on sex — **sex·ist** \ˈsek-sǝst\ *adj or n*

sex kitten *n* (1958) : a woman with conspicuous sex appeal

sex·less \ˈsek-sləs\ *adj* (1598) **1** : lacking sex : NEUTER **2** : devoid of sexual interest or activity ⟨a ~ relationship⟩ — **sex·less·ly** *adv* — **sex·less·ness** *n*

sex–lim·it·ed \ˈsek-ˈslim-ət-əd\ *adj* (1909) : expressed in the phenotype of only one sex

sex–link·age \ˈsek-ˌsliŋ-kij\ *n* (1914) : the quality or state of being sex-linked

sex–linked \ˈsek-ˌsliŋ(k)t\ *adj* (1913) **1** : located in a sex chromosome ⟨a ~ gene⟩ **2** : mediated by a sex-linked gene ⟨a ~ character⟩

sex object *n* (1911) : a person regarded esp. exclusively as an object of sexual interest

sex·ol·o·gy \sek-ˈsäl-ə-jē\ *n* (1902) : the study of sex or of the interaction of the sexes esp. among human beings — **sex·ol·o·gist** \-jəst\ *n*

sex·ploi·ta·tion \ˌsek-ˌsplȯi-ˈtā-shən\ *n* [blend of *sex* and *exploitation*] (ca. 1942) : the exploitation of sex in the media and esp. in film

sex·pot \ˈsek-ˌspät\ *n* (1948) : a conspicuously sexy woman

sex symbol *n* (ca. 1911) : a usu. renowned person (as an entertainer) noted and admired for conspicuous sex appeal

sext \ˈsekst\ *n, often cap* [ME *sexte*, fr. LL *sexta*, fr. L, sixth hour of the day, fr. fem. of *sextus* sixth, fr. *sex* six] (15c) : the fourth of the canonical hours

Sex·tans \ˈsek-ˌstanz\ *n* [NL (gen. *Sextantis*), lit., sextant] : a constellation on the equator south of Leo

sex·tant \ˈsek-stənt\ *n* [NL *sextant-, sextans* sixth part of a circle, fr. L, sixth part, fr. *sextus* sixth] (1628) : an instrument for measuring angular distances used esp. in navigation to observe altitudes of celestial bodies (as in ascertaining latitude and longitude)

sextant

sex·tet \sek-ˈstet\ *n* [alter. of *sestet*] (1841) **1** : a musical composition for six instruments or voices **2** : a group or set of six: as **a** : the performers of a sextet **b** : a hockey team

sex·til·lion \sek-ˈstil-yən\ *n, often attrib* [F, irreg. fr. *sex-* (fr. L *sex*) + *-illion* (as in *million*)] (1690) — see NUMBER table

sex·to \ˈsek-(ˌ)stō\ *n, pl* **sextos** [L *sexto*, abl. of *sextus* sixth] (1847) : SIXMO

sex·to·dec·i·mo \ˌsek-stə-ˈdes-ə-ˌmō\ *n, pl* **-mos** [L, abl. of *sextus decimus* sixteenth, fr. *sextus* sixth + *decimus* tenth — more at DIME] (1688) : SIXTEENMO

sex·ton \ˈsek-stən\ *n* [ME *secresteyn, sexteyn*, fr. MF *secrestain*, fr. ML *sacristanus* — more at SACRISTAN] (14c) : a church officer or employee who takes care of the church property and at some churches rings the bell for services and digs graves

1sex·tu·ple \sek-ˈst(y)üp-əl, -ˈstəp-; ˈsek-stəp-\ *adj* [prob. fr. ML *sextuplus*, fr. L *sextus* sixth + *-plus* multiplied by (akin to L *-plex* -plex) — more at -FOLD] (1626) **1** : having six units or members **2** : being six times as great or as many **3** : marked by six beats per measure of music ⟨~ time⟩ — **sextuple** *n*

2sextuple *vb* **sex·tu·pled; sex·tu·pling** \-(ə-)liŋ\ *vt* (1632) : to make six times as much or as many ~ *vi* : to become six times as much or as numerous

sex·tu·plet \sek-ˈstəp-lət, -ˈst(y)üp-; ˈsek-st(y)əp-\ *n* (1852) **1** : a combination of six of a kind **2** : one of six offspring born at one birth **3** : a group of six equal musical notes performed in the time ordinarily given to four of the same value

1sex·tu·pli·cate \sek-ˈst(y)ü-pli-kət\ *adj* [blend of *sextuple* and *-plicate* (as in *duplicate*)] (1657) **1** : repeated six times **2** : SIXTH ⟨file the ~ copy⟩ — **sextuplicate** *n*

2sex·tu·pli·cate \-plə-ˌkāt\ *vt* **-cat·ed; -cat·ing** (ca. 1934) **1** : SEXTUPLE **2** : to provide in sextuplicate

sex·u·al \ˈseksh-(ə-)wəl, ˈsek-shəl\ *adj* [LL *sexualis*, fr. L *sexus* sex] (1651) **1** : of, relating to, or associated with sex or the sexes ⟨~ differentiation⟩ ⟨~ conflict⟩ **2** : having or involving sex ⟨~ reproduction⟩ — **sex·u·al·ly** \ˈseksh-(ə-)wə-lē, ˈseksh-(ə-)lē\ *adv*

sexual generation *n* (1880) : the generation of an organism with alternation of generations that reproduces sexually

sexual intercourse *n* (1799) **1** : heterosexual intercourse involving penetration of the vagina by the penis : COITUS **2** : intercourse involving genital contact between individuals other than penetration of the vagina by the penis

sex·u·al·i·ty \ˌsek-shə-ˈwal-ət-ē\ *n* (1800) : the quality or state of being sexual: **a** : the condition of having sex **b** : sexual activity **c** : expression of sexual receptivity or interest esp. when excessive

sex·u·al·ize \ˈseksh-(ə-)wə-ˌlīz, ˈsek-shə-ˌlīz\ *vt* **-ized; -iz·ing** (1839) : to make sexual : endow with a sexual character or cast

sexual relations *n pl* (1950) : COITUS

sexy \ˈsek-sē\ *adj* **sex·i·er; -est** (1925) **1** : sexually suggestive or stimulating : EROTIC **2** : generally attractive or interesting : APPEALING ⟨big ~ matters of secrecy and national defense — Taylor Branch⟩ — **sex·i·ly** \-sə-lē\ *adv* — **sex·i·ness** \-sē-nəs\ *n*

Sey·fert galaxy \ˌsē-fərt- *also* ˌsī-\ *n* [Carl K. *Seyfert* †1960 Am. astronomer] (1959) : any of a class of spiral galaxies that have small compact bright nuclei characterized by variability in light intensity, emission of radio waves, and spectra which indicate hot gases in rapid motion

sfer·ics \ˈsfi(ə)r-iks, ˈsfer-\ *n pl* [by shortening & alter.] (1945) **1** : ATMOSPHERICS **2** *sing in constr* : an electronic detector of storms

1sfor·zan·do \sfȯrt-ˈsän-(ˌ)dō, -ˈsan-\ *adj or adv* [It, verbal of *sforzare* to force, fr. *s-* (fr. L *ex-* ex-) + *forzare* to force, fr. (assumed) VL *fortiare*, fr. L *fortis* strong] (ca. 1801) : played with prominent stress or accent — used as a direction in music

2sforzando *n, pl* **-dos** *or* **-di** \-(ˌ)dē\ (1952) : an accented tone or chord

sfu·ma·to \sfü-ˈmä-(ˌ)tō\ *n* [It, fr. pp. of *sfumare* to evaporate, fr. *s-* + *fumare* to smoke, fr. L, fr. *fumus* smoke — more at FUME] (1847) : the definition of form without abrupt outline by the blending of one tone into another

sgraf·fi·to \zgra-ˈfē-(ˌ)tō, skra-\ *n, pl* **-ti** \-(ˌ)tē\ [It, fr. pp. of *sgraffire* to scratch, produce sgraffito] (1730) **1** : decoration by cutting away parts of a surface layer (as of plaster or clay) to expose a different colored ground — compare GRAFFITO **2** : something (as traditional Pennsylvania Dutch pottery) decorated with sgraffito

sh \sh *often prolonged*\ *interj* (1847) — used often in prolonged or reduplicated form to urge or command silence or less noise

Sha'·ban \shə-ˈbän\ *n* [Ar *sha'bān*] (ca. 1769) : the 8th month of the Islamic year — see MONTH table

Shab·bat \shə-ˈbät, ˈshäb-əs\ *n* [Heb *shabbāth*] (ca. 1905) : the Jewish Sabbath

shab·by \ˈshab-ē\ *adj* **shab·bi·er; -est** [obs. E *shab* (a low fellow)] (1669) **1** : clothed with worn or seedy garments ⟨a ~ hobo⟩ **2 a** : threadbare and faded from wear ⟨a ~ sofa⟩ **b** : ill-kept : DILAPIDATED ⟨a ~ neighborhood⟩ **3 a** : MEAN, DESPICABLE, CONTEMPTIBLE ⟨must feel ~ . . . because of his compromises —Nat Hentoff⟩ **b** : UNGENEROUS, UNFAIR ⟨laments the ~ way in which this country often treated a poet —Paul Engle⟩ **c** : inferior in quality : SLOVENLY ⟨~ reasoning⟩ — **shab·bi·ly** \ˈshab-ə-lē\ *adv* — **shab·bi·ness** \ˈshab-ē-nəs\ *n*

Sha·bu·oth \shə-ˈvü-ˌōt(h), -ˌōs, -əs\ *n* [Heb *shābhū'ōth*, lit., weeks] (ca. 1903) : a Jewish holiday observed on the 6th and 7th of Sivan in commemoration of the revelation of the Ten Commandments at Mt. Sinai — called also *Pentecost*

shack \ˈshak\ *n* [prob. back-formation fr. E dial. *shackly* (rickety)] (1878) **1** : HUT, SHANTY **2** : a room or similar enclosed structure for a particular person or use ⟨a radio ~⟩

1shack·le \ˈshak-əl\ *n* [ME *schakel*, fr. OE *sceacul*; akin to ON *skǫkull* pole of a cart] (bef. 12c) **1** : something (as a manacle or fetter) that confines the legs or arms **2** : something that checks or prevents free action as if by fetters — usu. used in pl. **3** : a usu. U-shaped fastening device secured by a bolt or pin through holes in the end of the two arms **4** : a length of cable or anchor chain usu. 15 fathoms

2shackle *vt* **shack·led; shack·ling** \-(ə-)liŋ\ (15c) **1 a** : to bind with shackles : FETTER **b** : to make fast with or as if with a shackle **2** : to deprive of freedom esp. of action by means of restrictions or handicaps : IMPEDE *syn* see HAMPER — **shack·ler** \-(ə-)lər\ *n*

shack·le·bone \ˈshak-əl-ˌbōn, ˈshāk-\ *n, Scot* (1571) : WRIST

shack up \(ˈ)shak-ˈəp\ *vi* (1935) : to sleep or live together as unmarried sexual partners

shad \ˈshad\ *n, pl* **shad** [(assumed) ME, fr. OE *sceadd*; akin to L *scatēre* to bubble] (bef. 12c) : any of several clupeid fishes (genus *Alosa*) that differ from the typical herrings in having a relatively deep body and in being anadromous and that are extremely important food fishes of Europe and No. America

shad·ber·ry \-ˌber-ē\ *n* (1861) **1** : the fruit of the serviceberry **2** : SERVICEBERRY

shad·blow \ˈshad-ˌblō\ *n* (1846) : SERVICEBERRY

shad·bush \-ˌbu̇sh\ *n* (ca. 1817) : SERVICEBERRY

shad·dock \ˈshad-ək\ *n* [Captain *Shaddock*, 17th cent. Eng. ship commander] (1707) : a very large thick-rinded usu. pear-shaped citrus fruit differing from the closely related grapefruit esp. in its loose rind and often coarse dry pulp; *also* : the tree (*Citrus grandis*) that bears it

1shade \ˈshād\ *n* [ME, fr. OE *sceadu*; akin to OHG *scato* shadow, Gk *skotos* darkness] (bef. 12c) **1 a** : comparative darkness or obscurity owing to interception of the rays of light **b** : relative obscurity or retirement **2 a** : shelter (as by foliage) from the heat and glare of sunlight **b** : a place sheltered from the sun **3** : an evanescent or unreal appearance **4** *pl* **a** : the shadows that gather as darkness comes on **b** : NETHERWORLD, HADES **5 a** : a disembodied spirit : GHOST **b** — used to signal the similarity between a previously encountered person or situation and one at hand; usu. used in pl. ⟨~s of my childhood⟩ **6** : something that intercepts or shelters from light, sun, or heat: as **a** : a device partially covering a lamp so as to reduce glare **b** : a flexible screen usu. mounted on a roller for regulating the light or the view through a window **c** *pl* : SUNGLASSES **7 a** : the reproduction of the effect of shade in painting or drawing **b** : a subdued or somber feature **8 a** : a color produced by a pigment or dye mixture having some black in it **b** : a color slightly different from the one under consideration **9 a** : a minute difference or variation : NUANCE **b** : a minute degree or quantity **10** : a facial expression of sadness or displeasure — **shade·less** \-ləs\ *adj*

2shade *vb* **shad·ed; shad·ing** *vt* (15c) **1 a** : to shelter or screen by intercepting radiated light or heat **b** : to cover with a shade **2** : to hide partly by or as if by a shadow **3** : to darken with or as if with a shadow **4** : to better or exceed by a shade : SURPASS, ECLIPSE **5 a** : to represent the effect of shade or shadow on **b :** to add shading to **c :** to color so that the shades pass gradually from one to another **6 :** to change by gradual transition or qualification **7 :** to reduce slightly (as a price) **8 :** SLANT, BIAS ~ *vi* **1 :** to pass by slight changes or imperceptible degrees **2 :** to undergo or exhibit minute difference or variation — **shad·er** *n*

shade–grown \ˈshād-ˌgrōn\ *adj* (1922) **:** grown in the shade; *specif* **:** grown under cloth ⟨~ tobacco⟩

shade tree *n* (1806) **:** a tree grown primarily to produce shade

shad·ing \ˈshād-iŋ\ *n* (1663) **1 :** the use of marking made within outlines to suggest three-dimensionality, shadow, or degrees of light and dark in a picture or drawing **2 :** an interpretative effect in music gained esp. by subtle changes in dynamics

sha·doof *also* **sha·duf** \shə-ˈdüf, sha-\ *n* [Ar *shādūf*] (1836) **:** a counterbalanced sweep used since ancient times esp. in Egypt for raising water (as for irrigation)

[1]shad·ow \ˈshad-(ˌ)ō, -ə(-w)\ *n* [ME *shadwe*, fr. OE *sceaduw-*, *sceadu* shade, shadow] (bef. 12c) **1 :** partial darkness or obscurity within a part of space from which rays from a source of light are cut off by an interposed opaque body **2 :** a reflected image **3 :** shelter from danger or observation **4 a :** an imperfect and faint representation **b :** an imitation of something **:** COPY **5 :** the dark figure cast upon a surface by a body intercepting the rays from a source of light **6 :** PHANTOM **7** *pl* **:** DARK 1a **8 :** a shaded or darker portion of a picture **9 :** an attenuated form or a vestigial remnant **10 a :** an inseparable companion or follower **b :** one (as a spy or detective) that shadows **11 :** a small degree or portion **:** TRACE **12 :** a source of gloom or unhappiness **13 a :** an area near an object **:** VICINITY **b :** pervasive and dominant influence **14 :** a state of ignominy or obscurity — **shad·ow·less** \ˈshad-ō-ləs, -ə-ləs\ *adj* — **shad·ow·like** \-ˌlīk\ *adj*

[2]shadow *vt* (bef. 12c) **1** *archaic* **:** SHELTER, PROTECT **2 :** to cast a shadow upon **:** CLOUD **3** *obs* **:** to shelter from the sun **4** *obs* **:** CONCEAL **5 :** to represent or indicate obscurely or faintly — often used with *forth* or *out* **6 :** to follow esp. secretly **:** TRAIL **7** *archaic* **:** SHADE 5 ~ *vi* **1 :** to pass gradually or by degrees **2 :** to become overcast with or as if with shadows — **shad·ow·er** \-ə-wər\ *n*

[3]shadow *adj* (1906) **1 :** of, relating to, or resembling a shadow cabinet ⟨~ minister of defense⟩ **2 a :** having an indistinct pattern ⟨~ plaid⟩ **b :** having darker sections of design ⟨~ lace⟩

shadow band *n* (ca. 1900) **:** one of a series of dark narrow parallel bands that appear to rush swiftly across the landscape just before or after totality in a solar eclipse

shad·ow·box \ˈshad-ō-ˌbäks, -ə-ˌbäks\ *vi* (1919) **:** to box with an imaginary opponent esp. as a form of training

shadow box *n* (ca. 1909) **:** a shallow enclosing case usu. with a glass front in which something is set for protection and display

shadow cabinet *n* (1906) **:** a group of leaders of a parliamentary opposition who constitute the probable membership of the cabinet when their party is returned to power

shadow dance *n* (ca. 1909) **:** a dance shown by throwing the shadows of dancers on a screen

shad·ow·graph \ˈshad-ō-ˌgraf, -ə-ˌgraf\ *n* (1888) **1 :** SHADOW PLAY **2 :** a photographic image resembling a shadow — **shad·ow·gra·phy** \-graf-ē\ *n*

shadow mask *n* (1951) **:** a metal plate in a color television tube that contains minute apertures permitting passage of electron beams to specific phosphors on the screen during a scan

shadow play *n* (1895) **:** a drama exhibited by throwing shadows of puppets or actors on a screen — called also *shadow show*

shad·owy \ˈshad-ə-wē\ *adj* (14c) **1 a :** of the nature of or resembling a shadow **:** UNSUBSTANTIAL **b :** faintly perceptible **:** INDISTINCT, VAGUE **2 :** being in or obscured by shadow ⟨deep ~ interiors⟩ **3 :** SHADY 1 — **shad·ow·i·ly** \-wə-lē\ *adv* — **shad·ow·i·ness** \-wē-nəs\ *n*

shady \ˈshād-ē\ *adj* **shad·i·er; -est** (1579) **1 :** producing or affording shade **2 :** sheltered from the sun's rays **3 a :** of questionable merit **:** UNCERTAIN, UNRELIABLE **b :** DISREPUTABLE — **shad·i·ly** \ˈshād-ᵊl-ē\ *adv* — **shad·i·ness** \ˈshād-ē-nəs\ *n*

[1]shaft \ˈshaft\ *n, pl* **shafts** \ˈshaf(t)s, *for 1b usu* ˈshavz\ [ME, fr. OE *sceaft*; akin to OHG *scaft* shaft, L *scapus* shaft, stalk, Gk *skēptron* staff, L *capo* capon — more at CAPON] (bef. 12c) **1 a (1) :** the long handle of a spear or similar weapon **(2) :** SPEAR, LANCE **b** *or pl* **shaves** \ˈshavz\ **:** POLE; *specif* **:** either of two long pieces of wood between which a horse is hitched to a vehicle **c (1) :** an arrow esp. for a longbow **(2) :** the body or stem of an arrow extending from the nock to the head **2 :** a sharply delineated beam of light shining through an opening **3 :** something suggestive of the shaft of a spear or arrow esp. in long slender cylindrical form: as **a :** the trunk of a tree **b :** the cylindrical pillar between the capital and the base **c :** the handle or helve of a tool or instrument (as a hammer or golf club) **d :** a commonly cylindrical bar used to support rotating pieces or to transmit power or motion by rotation **e :** the stem or midrib of a feather **f :** the upright member of a cross esp. below the arms **g :** a small architectural column (as at each side of a doorway) **h :** a column, obelisk, or other spire-shaped or columnar monument **i :** a vertical or inclined opening of uniform and limited cross section made for finding or mining ore, raising water, or ventilating underground workings (as in a cave) **j :** a vertical opening or passage through the floors of a building **4 a :** a projectile thrown like a spear or shot like an arrow **b :** a scornful, satirical, or pithily critical remark or attack **c :** harsh or unfair treatment — usu. used with *the*

[2]shaft *vt* (1611) **1 :** to fit with a shaft **2 :** to treat unfairly or harshly

shaft horsepower *n* (1908) **:** horsepower transmitted by an engine shaft

shaft·ing \ˈshaf-tiŋ\ *n* (1825) **:** shafts or material for shafts

[1]shag \ˈshag\ *n* [(assumed) ME *shagge*, fr. OE *sceacga*; akin to ON *skegg* beard, OSlav *skokŭ* leap] (bef. 12c) **1 a :** a shaggy tangled mass or covering (as of hair) **b :** long coarse or matted fiber or nap **2 :** tobacco cut into fine shreds **3 :** CORMORANT 1

[2]shag *vb* **shagged; shag·ging** *vi* (1596) **:** to fall or hang in shaggy masses ~ *vt* **:** to make rough or shaggy

[3]shag *adj* (1808) **:** SHAGGY

[4]shag *vt* **shagged; shag·ging** [origin unknown] (1904) **1 a :** to chase after; *esp* **:** to chase after and return (a ball) hit usu. out of play **b :** to catch (a fly) in baseball practice **2 :** to chase away

[5]shag *vi* **shagged; shag·ging** [perh. alter. of *shack* (to lumber along)] (1914) **1 :** to move or lope along **2 :** to dance the shag

[6]shag *n* (1938) **:** a dance step executed by hopping livelily on each foot in turn

shag·bark \ˈshag-ˌbärk\ *n* (1777) **:** SHAGBARK HICKORY

shagbark hickory *n* (1751) **:** a hickory (*Carya ovata*) with sweet edible nuts and a gray shaggy outer bark that peels off in long strips; *also* **:** its wood

shag·gy \ˈshag-ē\ *adj* **shag·gi·er; -est** (1590) **1 a :** covered with or consisting of long, coarse, or matted hair **b :** covered with or consisting of thick, tangled, or unkempt vegetation **c :** having a rough nap, texture, or surface **d :** having hairlike processes **2 a :** UNKEMPT **b :** confused or unclear in conception or thinking — **shag·gi·ly** \ˈshag-ə-lē\ *adv* — **shag·gi·ness** \ˈshag-ē-nəs\ *n*

shag·gy–dog story \ˌshag-ē-ˈdȯg-\ *n* (1946) **:** a long-drawn-out circumstantial story concerning an inconsequential happening that impresses the teller as humorous but the hearer as boring and pointless; *also* **:** a similar humorous story whose humor lies in the pointlessness or irrelevance of the punch line

shag·gy·mane \ˈshag-ē-ˌmān\ *n* (ca. 1909) **:** a common edible mushroom (*Coprinus comatus*) having an elongated shaggy white pileus and black spores — called also *shaggy cap*

sha·green \sha-ˈgrēn, shə-\ *n* [by folk etymology fr. F *chagrin*, fr. Turk *sağrı*] (1611) **1 :** an untanned leather covered with small round granulations and usu. dyed green **2 :** the rough skin of various sharks and rays when covered with small close-set tubercles — **shagreen** *adj*

shah \ˈshä, ˈshȯ\ *n, often cap* [Per *shāh* king — more at CHECK] (1566) **:** a sovereign of Iran — **shah·dom** \ˈshäd-əm, ˈshȯd-\ *n*

Sha·hap·ti·an \shə-ˈhap-tē-ən\ *n, pl* **Shahaptian** *or* **Shahaptians** (1845) **1 :** a member of an American Indian people of a large territory along the Columbia river and its tributaries **2 :** the language of the Shahaptian people including Nez Percé and Yakima

shai·tan \shā-ˈtän, shī-\ *n* [Ar *shayṭān*] (1638) **:** an evil spirit; *specif* **:** an evil jinni

[1]shake \ˈshāk\ *vb* **shook** \ˈshu̇k\; **shak·en** \ˈshā-kən\; **shak·ing** [ME *shaken*, fr. OE *sceacan*; akin to ON *skaka* to shake, Skt *khajati* he agitates] *vi* (bef. 12c) **1 :** to move irregularly to and fro **2 :** to vibrate esp. as the result of a blow or shock **3 :** to tremble as a result of physical or emotional disturbance **4 :** to experience a state of instability **:** TOTTER **5 :** to briskly move something to and fro or up and down esp. in order to mix **6 :** to clasp hands **7 :** TRILL ~ *vt* **1 :** to brandish, wave, or flourish often in a threatening manner **2 :** to cause to move in a usu. quick jerky manner **3 :** to cause to quake, quiver, or tremble **4 a :** to free oneself from ⟨~ a habit⟩ ⟨~ off a cold⟩ **b :** to get away from **:** get rid of ⟨can you ~ your friend? I want to talk to you alone —Elmer Davis⟩ **5 :** to lessen the stability of **:** WEAKEN ⟨~ one's faith⟩ **6 :** to bring to a specified condition by or as if by repeated quick jerky movements ⟨*shook* himself loose from the man's grasp⟩ **7 :** to dislodge or eject by quick jerky movements of the support or container ⟨*shook* the dust from the cloth⟩ **8 :** to clasp (hands) in greeting or farewell or as a sign of goodwill or agreement **9 :** to stir the feelings of **:** UPSET ⟨*shook* her up⟩ **10 :** TRILL — **shak·able** *or* **shake·able** \ˈshā-kə-bəl\ *adj*

syn SHAKE, AGITATE, ROCK, CONVULSE mean to move up and down or to and fro with some violence. SHAKE often carries a further implication of a particular purpose; AGITATE suggests a violent and prolonged tossing or stirring; ROCK suggests a swinging or swaying motion resulting from violent impact or upheaval; CONVULSE suggests a violent pulling or wrenching as of a body in a paroxysm.

— **shake a leg 1 :** DANCE **2 :** to hurry up

[2]shake *n* (1581) **1 :** an act of shaking: as **a :** an act of shaking hands **b :** an act of shaking oneself **2 a :** a blow or shock that upsets the equilibrium or disturbs the balance of something **b :** EARTHQUAKE **3** *pl* **a :** a condition of trembling or nervousness; *specif* **:** DELIRIUM TREMENS **b :** MALARIA 2a **4 :** something produced by shaking: as **a :** a fissure separating annual rings of growth in timber **b :** MILK SHAKE **5 :** a wavering, quivering, or alternating motion caused by a blow or shock **6 :** TRILL **7 :** a very brief period of time **8** *pl* **:** one that is exceptional esp. in importance, ability, or merit — usu. used in the phrase *no great shakes* **9 :** a shingle split from a piece of log usu. three or four feet long **10 :** [3]DEAL 3 ⟨a fair ~⟩

shake·down \ˈshāk-ˌdau̇n\ *n* (1730) **1 :** an improvised bed (as one made up on the floor) **2 :** a boisterous dance **3 :** an act or instance of shaking someone down; *esp* **:** EXTORTION **4 :** a thorough search **5 :** a process or period of adjustment **6 :** a testing under operating conditions of something new (as a ship) for possible faults and defects and for familiarizing the operators with it

shake down \(ˈ)shāk-ˈdau̇n\ *vi* (1858) **1 a :** to take up temporary quarters **b :** to occupy an improvised or makeshift bed **2 a :** to become accustomed esp. to new surroundings or duties **b :** to settle down ~ *vt* **1 :** to obtain money from in a dishonest or illegal manner **2 :** to make a thorough search of **3 :** to bring about a reduction of **4 :** to give a shakedown test to

shake·out \ˈshā-ˌkau̇t\ *n* (1895) **:** the failure or retrenchment of a significant number of firms in the economy or a sector or an industry that usu. results in a depressed market

shak·er \ˈshā-kər\ *n* (15c) **1 :** one that shakes: as **a :** a utensil or machine used in shaking ⟨cocktail ~⟩ **b :** one that incites, promotes, or directs action **2** *cap* [fr. a dance with shaking movements performed as part of worship] **:** a member of a millenarian sect originating in England in 1747 and practicing celibacy and an ascetic communal life — **Shaker** *adj* — **Shak·er·ism** \-kə-ˌriz-əm\ *n*

[1]Shake·spear·ean *or* **Shake·spear·ian** *also* **Shak·sper·ean** *or* **Shak·sper·ian** \shāk-ˈspir-ē-ən\ *adj* (1817) **:** of, relating to, or having the characteristics of Shakespeare or his writings

[2]Shakespearean *or* **Shakespearian** *also* **Shaksperean** *or* **Shaksperian** *n* (1837) **:** an authority on or devotee of Shakespeare

Shake·spear·eana *or* **Shake·spear·iana** \(ˌ)shāk-ˌspir-ē-ˈan-ə, -ˈän-ə, -ˈā-nə\ *n pl* (1718) **:** collected items by, about, or relating to Shakespeare

Shakespearean sonnet *n* (1903) **:** ENGLISH SONNET

shake–up \ˈshā-ˌkəp\ *n* (1847) **:** an act or instance of shaking up; *specif* **:** an extensive and often drastic reorganization

shake up \(')shā-'kəp\ *vt* (1553) 1 *obs* : CHIDE, SCOLD 2 : to jar by or as if by a physical shock ⟨the collision *shook up* both drivers⟩ 3 : to effect an extensive and often drastic reorganization of
shaking palsy *n* (1615) : PARKINSON'S DISEASE
sha·ko \'shak-(,)ō, 'shāk-, 'shäk-\ *n, pl* **shakos** *or* **shakoes** [F, fr. Hung *csákó*] (1815) : a stiff military hat with a high crown and plume
Shak·ta \'s(h)äk-tə\ *n or adj* [Skt *śākta*, fr. *Śakti*] (ca. 1895) : an adherent of Shaktism
Shak·ti \-tē\ *n* [Skt *Śakti*] (ca. 1895) : the dynamic energy of a Hindu god personified as his female consort; *broadly* : cosmic energy as conceived in Hindu thought
Shak·tism \-,tiz-əm\ *n* (1901) : a Hindu sect worshiping Shakti under various names (as Kali or Durga) in a cult of devotion to the female principle often with magical or orgiastic rites
shaky \'shā-kē\ *adj* **shak·i·er; -est** (1703) 1 : characterized by shakes ⟨~ timber⟩ 2 a : lacking stability : PRECARIOUS b : lacking in firmness (as of beliefs or principles) c : lacking in authority or reliability : QUESTIONABLE 3 a : somewhat unsound in health b : characterized by shaking 4 : likely to give way or break down — **shak·i·ly** \-kə-lē\ *adv* — **shak·i·ness** \-kē-nəs\ *n*
shale \'shā(ə)l\ *n* [ME, shell, scale, fr. OE *scealu* — more at SHELL] (1747) : a fissile rock that is formed by the consolidation of clay, mud, or silt, has a finely stratified or laminated structure, and is composed of minerals essentially unaltered since deposition — **shal·ey** \'shā-lē\ *adj*
shale oil *n* (1857) : a crude dark oil obtained from oil shale by heating
shall \shəl, (')shal\ *vb, past* **should** \shəd, (')shůd\; *pres sing & pl* **shall** [ME *shal* (1st & 3d sing. pres. indic.), fr. OE *sceal*; akin to OHG *scal* (1st & 3d sing. pres. indic.) ought to, must, Lith *skola* debt] *verbal auxiliary* (bef. 12c) 1 *archaic* a : will have to : MUST b : will be able to : CAN 2 a — used to express a command or exhortation ⟨you ~ go⟩ b — used in laws, regulations, or directives to express what is mandatory ⟨it ~ be unlawful to carry firearms⟩ 3 a — used to express what is inevitable or seems likely to happen in the future ⟨we ~ have to be ready⟩ ⟨we ~ see⟩ b — used to express simple futurity ⟨when ~ we expect you⟩ 4 — used to express determination ⟨they ~ not pass⟩ ~ *vi, archaic* : will go ⟨he to England ~ along with you — Shak.⟩
usage From the reams of pronouncements written about the distinction between *shall* and *will* — dating back as far as the 17th century — it is clear that the rules laid down have never very accurately reflected actual usage. The nationalistic statements of 18th and 19th century British grammarians, who commonly cited the misuses of the Irish, the Scots, and occas. the Americans, suggest that the traditional rules may have come closest to the usage of southern England. Some modern commentators believe that English usage is still the closest to the traditionally prescribed norms. Most modern commentators allow that *will* is more common in nearly all uses. The entries for *shall* and *will* in this dictionary show current usage.
shal·loon \shə-'lün, sha-\ *n* [*Châlons*-sur-Marne, France] (1678) : a lightweight twilled fabric of wool or worsted used chiefly for the linings of coats and uniforms
shal·lop \'shal-əp\ *n* [MF *chaloupe*] (1578) 1 : a usu. 2-masted ship with lugsails 2 : a small open boat propelled by oars or sails and used chiefly in shallow waters
shal·lot \shə-'lät *also* 'shal-ət\ *n* [modif. of F *échalote*, deriv. of (assumed) VL *escalonia* — more at SCALLION] (1664) 1 : a bulbous perennial herb (*Allium ascalonicum*) that resembles an onion and produces small clustered bulbs used in seasoning 2 : GREEN ONION
1shal·low \'shal-(,)ō, -ə(-w)\ *adj* [ME *schalowe*] (15c) 1 : having little depth ⟨~ water⟩ 2 : having little extension inward or backward ⟨office buildings have taken the form of ~ slabs —Lewis Mumford⟩ 3 a : penetrating only the easily or quickly perceived ⟨~ generalizations⟩ b : lacking in depth of knowledge, thought, or feeling ⟨a ~ demagogue⟩ 4 : displacing comparatively little air : WEAK ⟨~ breathing⟩ *syn* see SUPERFICIAL — **shal·low·ly** \-ō-lē, -ə-lē\ *adv* — **shal·low·ness** *n*
2shallow *vt* (1510) : to make shallow ~ *vi* : to become shallow
3shallow *n* (1571) : a shallow place or area in a body of water — usu. used in pl. but sing. or pl. in constr.
sha·lom \shä-'lōm, shə-\ *interj* [Heb *shālōm* peace] (1904) — used as a Jewish greeting and farewell
sha·lom alei·chem \,shȯ-lə-mə-'lā-kəm, ,shō-, -kəm\ *interj* [Heb *shālōm ʽalēkhem* peace unto you] (1904) — used as a traditional Jewish greeting
shalt \shəlt, (')shalt\ *archaic pres 2d sing of* SHALL
1sham \'sham\ *n* [perh. fr. E dial. *sham* shame, alter. of E *shame*] (1677) 1 : a trick that deludes : HOAX 2 : cheap falseness : HYPOCRISY 3 : a decorative piece of cloth made to simulate an article of personal or household linen and used in place of or over it 4 : an imitation or counterfeit purporting to be genuine 5 : a person who shams *syn* see IMPOSTURE
2sham *vb* **shammed; sham·ming** *vt* (1677) : to go through the external motions necessary to counterfeit ~ *vi* : to act intentionally so as to give a false impression : FEIGN — **sham·mer** \'sham-ər\ *n* *syn* see ASSUME
3sham *adj* (1681) 1 : not genuine : FALSE ⟨~ pearls⟩ 2 : having such poor quality as to seem false
sha·man \'shäm-ən, 'shā-mən *also* shə-'män\ *n* [Russ or Tungus; Russ, fr. Tungus *šaman*] (1698) : a priest who uses magic for the purpose of curing the sick, divining the hidden, and controlling events — **sha·man·ic** \shə-'man-ik, -'män-\ *adj*
sha·man·ism \-,iz-əm\ *n* (1780) : a religion of the Ural-Altaic peoples of northern Asia and Europe characterized by belief in an unseen world of gods, demons, and ancestral spirits responsive only to the shamans; *also* : any similar religion — **sha·man·ist** \-əst\ *n* — **sha·man·is·tic** \,shäm-ən-'is-tik, ,shā-mən-\ *adj*
sham·ble \'sham-bəl\ *vi* **sham·bled; sham·bling** \-b(ə-)liŋ\ [*shamble* (bowed, malformed)] (1681) : to walk awkwardly with dragging feet : SHUFFLE — **shamble** *n*
sham·bles \'sham-bəlz\ *n pl but sing or pl in constr* [*shamble* (meat market) & obs. E *shamble* (table for exhibition of meat for sale)] (15c) 1 *archaic* : a meat market 2 : SLAUGHTERHOUSE 3 a : a place of mass slaughter or bloodshed b : a scene or a state of great destruction : WRECKAGE c (1) : a scene or a state of great disorder or confusion (2) : great confusion : MESS
sham·bling *adj* (1690) : characterized by slow awkward movement
1shame \'shām\ *n* [ME, fr. OE *scamu*; akin to OHG *scama* shame] (bef. 12c) 1 a : a painful emotion caused by consciousness of guilt, shortcoming, or impropriety b : the susceptibility to such emotion 2 : a condition of humiliating disgrace or disrepute : IGNOMINY 3 a : something that brings strong regret, censure, or reproach b : a cause of feeling shame
2shame *vt* **shamed; sham·ing** (13c) 1 : to bring shame to : DISGRACE 2 : to put to shame by outdoing 3 : to cause to feel shame 4 : to force by causing to feel guilty ⟨*shamed* into confessing⟩
shame·faced \'shām-'fāst\ *adj* [alter. of *shamefast*] (1593) 1 : showing modesty : BASHFUL 2 : showing shame : ASHAMED — **shame·faced·ly** \-'fā-səd-lē, -'fāst-lē\ *adv* — **shame·faced·ness** \-'fā-səd-nəs, -'fās(t)-nəs\ *n*
shame·fast \'shām-,fast\ *adj* [ME, fr. OE *scamfæst*, fr. *scamu* + *fæst* fixed, fast] *archaic* (bef. 12c) : SHAMEFACED
shame·ful \'shām-fəl\ *adj* (14c) 1 a : bringing shame : DISGRACEFUL b : arousing the feeling of shame : INDECENT 2 *archaic* : full of the feeling of shame : ASHAMED — **shame·ful·ly** \-fə-lē\ *adv* — **shame·ful·ness** *n*
shame·less \'shām-ləs\ *adj* (bef. 12c) 1 : having no shame : insensible to disgrace 2 : showing lack of shame : DISGRACEFUL — **shame·less·ly** *adv* — **shame·less·ness** *n*
sham·mes \'shäm-əs\ *n, pl* **sham·mo·sim** \shä-'mȯ-səm\ [Yiddish *shames*, fr. LHeb *shāmmāsh*] (1948) 1 : the sexton of a synagogue 2 : the candle or taper used to light the other candles in a Hanukkah menorah
sham·my \'sham-ē\ *var of* CHAMOIS
1sham·poo \sham-'pü\ *vt* [Hindi *cāpo*, imper. of *cāpnā* to press, shampoo] (1762) 1 *archaic* : MASSAGE 2 a : to wash (as the hair) with soap and water or with a special preparation b : to wash the hair of — **sham·poo·er** *n*
2shampoo *n, pl* **shampoos** (1838) 1 : an act or instance of shampooing 2 : a preparation used in shampooing
sham·rock \'sham-,räk\ *n* [IrGael *seamrōg*] (1571) : a trifoliolate plant used as a floral emblem by the Irish: as a : a yellow-flowered clover (*Trifolium dubium*) often regarded as the true shamrock b : WOOD SORREL c : WHITE CLOVER
sha·mus \'shäm-əs, 'shā-məs\ *n* [prob. fr. Yiddish *shames* shammes; prob. fr. a jocular comparison of the duties of a sexton and those of a store detective] (1929) 1 *slang* : POLICEMAN 2 *slang* : a private detective
Shan \'shän, 'shan\ *n, pl* **Shan** *or* **Shans** (1795) 1 a : a group of Mongoloid peoples of southeastern Asia b : a member of any of these peoples 2 : the Thai languages of the Shan
shan·dry·dan \'shan-drē-,dan\ *n* [origin unknown] (1820) 1 : a chaise with a hood 2 : a rickety vehicle
shan·dy \'shan-dē\ *n, pl* **shandies** (1888) 1 : SHANDYGAFF 2 : a drink consisting of beer and lemonade
shan·dy·gaff \'shan-dē-,gaf\ *n* [origin unknown] (1853) : beer diluted with a nonalcoholic drink (as ginger beer)
shang·hai \shaŋ-'hī\ *vt* **shang·haied; shang·hai·ing** [*Shanghai*, China; fr. the formerly widespread use of this method to secure sailors for voyages to the Orient] (1871) 1 a : to put aboard a ship by force often with the help of liquor or a drug b : to put by force or threat of force into or as if into a place of detention 2 : to put by trickery into an undesirable position — **shang·hai·er** \-'hī(-ə)r\ *n*
Shan·gri-la \,shaŋ-gri-'lä\ *n* [*Shangri-La*, imaginary land depicted in the novel *Lost Horizon* (1933) by James Hilton] (1940) 1 : a remote beautiful imaginary place where life approaches perfection : UTOPIA 2 : a remote usu. idyllic hideaway
1shank \'shaŋk\ *n* [ME *shanke*, fr. OE *scanca*; akin to ON *skakkr* crooked, Gk *skazein* to limp] (bef. 12c) 1 a : the part of the leg between the knee and the ankle in man or the corresponding part in various other vertebrates b : LEG c : a cut of beef, veal, mutton, or lamb from the upper or the lower part of the leg : SHIN — see BEEF illustration 2 : a straight narrow usu. essential part of an object: as a : the straight part of a nail or pin b : a straight part of a plant : STEM, STALK c : the part of an anchor between the ring and the crown d : the part of a fishhook between the eye and the bend e : the part of a key between the handle and the bit f : the stem of a tobacco pipe or the part between the stem and the bowl g : TANG 1 h (1) : the narrow part of the sole of a shoe beneath the instep (2) : SHANKPIECE 3 : a part of an object by which it can be attached: as a (1) : a projection on the back of a solid button (2) : a short stem of thread that holds a sewn button away from the cloth b : the projecting part of a knob handle that contains the spindle socket c : the end (as of a drill) that is gripped in a chuck 4 a : the latter part of a period of time b : the early or main part of a period of time — **shanked** \'shaŋ(k)t\ *adj*
2shank *vt* (1924) : to hit (a golf ball or shot) with the extreme heel of the club so that the ball goes off in an unintended direction
shank·piece \'shaŋk-,pēs\ *n* (1885) : a support for the arch of the foot inserted in the shank of a shoe
shan't \(')shant, (')shänt\ : shall not
shantey *or* **shanty** *var of* CHANTEY
shan·tung \(')shan-'təŋ\ *n* [*Shantung*, China] (ca. 1882) : a fabric in plain weave having a slightly irregular surface due to uneven slubbed filling yarns
shan·ty \'shant-ē\ *n, pl* **shanties** [CanF *chantier*, fr. F, gantry, fr. L *cantherius* trellis] (1820) : a small crudely built dwelling or shelter usu. of wood
shan·ty·man \-ē-mən, -,man\ *n* (ca. 1858) : one who lives in a shanty
shan·ty·town \-,taůn\ *n* (1888) : a usu. poor town or section of a town consisting mostly of shanties
shap·able *or* **shape·able** \'shā-pə-bəl\ *adj* (1647) 1 : capable of being shaped 2 : SHAPELY

\ə\ abut \ᵊ\ kitten, F table \ər\ further \a\ ash \ā\ ace \ä\ cot, cart \aů\ out \ch\ chin \e\ bet \ē\ easy \g\ go \i\ hit \ī\ ice \j\ job \ŋ\ sing \ō\ go \ȯ\ law \ȯi\ boy \th\ thin \t͟h\ the \ü\ loot \ů\ foot \y\ yet \zh\ vision \à, k̲, ⁿ, œ, œ̄, ue, ue̅, ʸ\ see Guide to Pronunciation

¹**shape** \'shāp\ vb **shaped; shap·ing** [ME shapen, alter. of OE scieppan; akin to OHG skepfen to shape] vt (bef. 12c) **1** : FORM, CREATE **b** : to give a particular form or shape to **2** obs : ORDAIN, DECREE **3** : to adapt in shape so as to fit neatly and closely ⟨a dress shaped to her figure⟩ **4 a** : DEVISE, PLAN **b** : to embody in definite form ⟨shaping a folktale into an epic⟩ **5 a** : to make fit for (as a particular use or purpose) : ADAPT **b** : to determine or direct the course or character of (as life) **c** : to modify (behavior) by rewarding changes that tend toward a desired response ∼ vi **1** : HAPPEN, BEFALL ⟨if things ∼ right⟩ **2** : to take on or approach a mature or definite form — often used with up   syn see MAKE — **shap·er** n

²**shape** n (bef. 12c) **1 a** : the visible makeup characteristic of a particular item or kind of item **b** (1) : spatial form (2) : a standard or universally recognized spatial form **2** : the appearance of the body as distinguished from that of the face : FIGURE **3 a** : PHANTOM, APPARITION **b** : assumed appearance : GUISE **4** : form of embodiment **5 a** : mode of existence or form of being having identifying features **6** : something having a particular form **7** : the condition in which someone or something exists at a particular time ⟨in excellent ∼ for his age⟩   syn see FORM — **shaped** \'shāpt\ adj — **in shape** : in an original, normal, or fit condition ⟨exercises to keep in shape⟩

shape·less \'shā-pləs\ adj (14c) **1** : having no definite shape **2 a** : deprived of usual or normal shape : MISSHAPEN ⟨a ∼ old hat⟩ **b** : not shapely — **shape·less·ly** adv — **shape·less·ness** n

shape·ly \'shā-plē\ adj **shape·li·er; -est** (14c) **1** : having a regular or pleasing shape **2** : orderly and consistent in arrangement or plan — **shape·li·ness** n

shap·en \'shā-pən\ adj [archaic pp. of shape] (14c) : fashioned in or provided with a definite shape — usu. used in combination ⟨an ill-shapen body⟩

shape note n (ca. 1933) : one of a system of seven notes showing the musical scale degree by the shape of the note head

shape-up \'shā-ˌpəp\ n (1942) : a system of hiring workers and esp. longshoremen by the day or shift by having applicants gather usu. in a semicircle for selection by a union-appointed hiring boss; also : an instance of such hiring practice

shape up \(ˈ)shā-ˈpəp\ vi (ca. 1920) : to improve to a good or acceptable condition or standard of behavior ∼ vt : to bring to a good or acceptable condition or standard of behavior

¹**shard** \'shärd\ also **sherd** \'shərd\ n [ME, fr. OE sceard; akin to OE sceran to cut — more at SHEAR] (bef. 12c) **1 a** : a piece or fragment of a brittle substance; broadly : a small piece or part **b** : SHELL, SCALE; esp : ELYTRON **2** usu **sherd** : fragments of pottery vessels found on sites and in refuse deposits where pottery-making peoples have lived **3** : highly angular curved glass fragments of tuffaceous sediments

¹**share** \'she(ə)r, 'sha(ə)r\ n [ME, fr. OE scearu cutting, tonsure; akin to OE scieran to cut — more at SHEAR] (bef. 12c) **1 a** : a portion belonging to, due to, or contributed by an individual or group **b** : one's full or fair portion **2 a** : the part allotted to or belonging to one of a number owning together property or interest **b** : any of the equal portions into which property or invested capital is divided; specif : any of the equal interests or rights into which the entire capital stock of a corporation is divided and ownership of which is regularly evidenced by one or more certificates **c** pl, chiefly Brit : STOCK 7c(1)

²**share** vb **shared; shar·ing** vt (1590) **1** : to divide and distribute in shares : APPORTION — usu. used with out or with **2 a** : to partake of, use, experience, occupy, or enjoy with others **b** : to have in common **3** : to grant or give a share in ∼ vi **1** : to have a share — used with in **2** : to apportion and take shares of something — **shar·er** n
  syn SHARE, PARTICIPATE, PARTAKE mean to have, get, or use in common with another or others. SHARE implies that one as the original holder grants to another the partial use, enjoyment, or possession of a thing though it may merely imply a mutual use or possession; PARTICIPATE implies a having or taking part in an undertaking, activity, or discussion; PARTAKE implies accepting or acquiring a share esp. of food or drink.

³**share** n [ME schare, fr. OE scear; akin to OHG scaro plowshare, OE scieran to cut] (bef. 12c) : PLOWSHARE

share·able or **shar·able** \'sher-ə-bəl, 'shar-\ adj (1920) : capable of being shared — **share·abil·i·ty** \ˌsher-ə-ˈbil-ət-ē, ˌshar-\ n

share·crop \'she(ə)r-ˌkräp, 'sha(ə)r-\ vb [back-formation fr. sharecropper] vi (1937) : to farm as a sharecropper ∼ vt : to farm (land) or produce (a crop) as a sharecropper

share·crop·per \-ˌkräp-ər\ n (1923) : a tenant farmer esp. in the southern U.S. who is provided with credit for seed, tools, living quarters, and food, who works the land, and who receives an agreed share of the value of the crop minus charges

share·hold·er \-ˌhōl-dər\ n (ca. 1828) : one that holds or owns a share in property; esp : STOCKHOLDER

sha·rif \shə-ˈrēf\ n [Ar sharif, lit., illustrious] (1599) : a descendant of the prophet Muhammad through his daughter Fatima; broadly : one of noble ancestry or political preeminence in predominantly Islamic countries — **sha·rif·ian** \-ˈrē-fē-ən\ adj

¹**shark** \'shärk\ n [origin unknown] (1569) : any of numerous mostly marine elasmobranch fishes of medium to large size that have a fusiform body, lateral branchial clefts, and a tough usu. dull gray skin roughened by minute tubercles, are typically active predators sometimes dangerous to humans, and are of economic importance esp. for their large livers which are a source of oil and for their hides from which leather is made — **shark·like** \'shär-ˌklīk\ adj

²**shark** n [prob. modif. of G schurke scoundrel] (1599) **1** : a rapacious crafty person who preys upon others through usury, extortion, or trickery **2** : one who excels greatly esp. in a particular field

³**shark** vt (1602) **1** archaic : to gather hastily **2** archaic : to obtain by some irregular means ∼ vi **1** archaic : to practice fraud or trickery **2** archaic : SNEAK

shark·skin \'shärk-ˌskin\ n (1851) **1** : the hide of a shark or leather made from it **2 a** : a smooth durable woolen or worsted suiting in twill or basket weave with small woven designs **b** : a smooth crisp fabric with a dull finish made usu. of rayon in basket weave

shark sucker n (ca. 1850) : REMORA 1

¹**sharp** \'shärp\ adj [ME, fr. OE scearp; akin to OE scieran to cut — more at SHEAR] (bef. 12c) **1** : adapted to cutting or piercing: as **a**

shark: 1 mako, 2 tiger, 3 thresher, 4 hammerhead, 5 white

: having a thin keen edge or fine point **b** : briskly or bitingly cold : NIPPING ⟨a ~ wind⟩ **2 a** : keen in intellect : QUICK-WITTED **b** : keen in perception : ACUTE ⟨~ sight⟩ **c** : keen in attention : VIGILANT ⟨keep a ~ lookout⟩ **d** : keen in attention to one's own interest sometimes to the point of being unethical ⟨a ~ trader⟩ **3** : keen in spirit or action: as **a** : full of activity or energy : BRISK ⟨~ blows⟩ **b** : capable of acting or reacting strongly; *esp* : CAUSTIC **4** : SEVERE, HARSH: as **a** : inclined to or marked by irritability or anger ⟨a ~ temper⟩ **b** : causing intense mental or physical distress ⟨a ~ pain⟩ **c** : cutting in language or import ⟨a ~ rebuke⟩ **5** : affecting the senses or sense organs intensely: as **a** (1) : having a strong odor or flavor ⟨~ cheese⟩ (2) : ACRID **b** : having a strong piercing sound **c** : having the effect of or involving a sudden brilliant display of light ⟨a ~ flash⟩ **6 a** : terminating in a point or edge ⟨~ features⟩ **b** : involving an abrupt or marked change esp. in direction ⟨a ~ turn⟩ **c** : clear in outline or detail : DISTINCT ⟨a ~ image⟩ **d** : set forth with clarity and distinctness ⟨~ contrast⟩ **7 a** *of a tone* : raised a half step in pitch **b** : higher than the proper pitch **c** : MAJOR, AUGMENTED — used of an interval in music **8** : STYLISH, DRESSY — **sharp·ly** *adv* — **sharp·ness** *n*

syn SHARP, KEEN, ACUTE mean having or showing alert competence and clear understanding. SHARP implies quick perception, clever resourcefulness, or sometimes questionable trickiness ⟨*sharp* traders⟩ KEEN suggests quickness, enthusiasm, and a penetrating mind ⟨a *keen* observer of the political scene⟩ ACUTE implies a power to penetrate and may suggest subtlety and sharpness of discrimination ⟨*acute* mathematical reasoning⟩

[2]**sharp** *adv* (bef. 12c) **1** : in a sharp manner : SHARPLY **2** : EXACTLY, PRECISELY ⟨4 o'clock ~⟩

[3]**sharp** *n* (14c) : one that is sharp: as **a** : a sharp edge or point **b** (1) : a musical note or tone one half step higher than a note or tone named **b** (2) : a character on a line or space of the musical staff indicating a pitch a half step higher than the degree would indicate without it **c** : a long sewing needle with sharp point **d** : a real or self-styled expert; *also* : SHARPER

[4]**sharp** *vt* (1662) : to raise (as a musical tone) in pitch; *esp* : to raise in pitch by a half step ~ *vi* : to sing or play above the proper pitch

sharp·en \ˈshär-pən\ *vb* **sharp·ened; sharp·en·ing** \ˈshärp-(ə-)niŋ\ *vt* (15c) : to make sharp or sharper; *esp* : IMPROVE, HONE ~ *vi* : to grow or become sharp or sharper — **sharp·en·er** \ˈshärp-(ə-)nər\ *n*

sharp·er \ˈshär-pər\ *n* (1681) : CHEAT, SWINDLER; *esp* : a cheating gambler

sharp–eyed \ˈshär-ˈpīd\ *adj* (1670) : having keen sight; *also* : keen in observing or penetrating

sharp–freeze \-ˈfrēz\ *vt* (1942) : QUICK-FREEZE

sharp·ie *or* **sharpy** \ˈshär-pē\ *n, pl* **sharp·ies** [[1]*sharp*] (1860) **1** : a long narrow shallow-draft boat with flat or slightly V-shaped bottom and one or two masts that bear a triangular sail **2 a** : SHARPER **b** : an exceptionally keen or alert person

sharp–nosed \ˈshärp-ˈnōzd\ *adj* (1675) **1** : having a pointed nose or snout **2** : keen in smelling

sharp practice *n* (1847) : the act of dealing in which advantage is taken or sought unscrupulously

sharp–set \ˈshärp-ˈset\ *adj* (1540) **1** : eager in appetite or desire **2** : set at a sharp angle or so as to present a sharp edge — **sharp–set·ness** *n*

sharp–shinned hawk \ˌshärp-ˌshind-\ *n* (ca. 1812) : a common widely distributed No. American bird-eating hawk (*Accipiter striatus*) having short rounded wings and a tail with a notched or square tip when folded

sharp·shoot·er \ˈshärp-ˌshüt-ər\ *n* (1802) : a good marksman

sharp·shoot·ing \-ˌshüt-iŋ\ *n* (1806) **1** : shooting with great precision **2** : accurate and usu. unexpected attack (as in words)

sharp–sight·ed \-ˈsīt-əd\ *adj* (1571) **1** : having acute sight **2** : mentally keen or alert — **sharp–sight·ed·ly** *adv* — **sharp–sight·ed·ness** *n*

sharp–tongued \-ˈtəŋd\ *adj* (1837) : having a sharp tongue : harsh or bitter in speech or language ⟨a ~ shrew⟩

sharp–wit·ted \-ˈwit-əd\ *adj* (1586) : having or showing an acute mind

shash·lik *also* **shash·lick** *or* **shas·lik** \shäsh-ˈlik, ˈshäsh-lik\ *n* [Russ *shashlyk*, of Turkic origin; akin to Kazan Tatar *šyšlyk* kabob] (1926) : KABOB

shat *past and past part of* SHIT

[1]**shat·ter** \ˈshat-ər\ *vb* [ME *schateren*] *vt* (14c) **1** : to cause to drop or be dispersed **2 a** : to break at once into pieces **b** : to damage badly : RUIN **3** : to cause the disruption or annihilation of : DEMOLISH ~ *vi* **1** : to break apart : DISINTEGRATE **2** : to drop off parts (as leaves, petals, or fruit) ⟨the wheat ~*ed* in the fields⟩ — **shat·ter·ing·ly** \-ə-riŋ-lē\ *adv*

[2]**shatter** *n* (1640) **1** : FRAGMENT, SHRED — usu. used in pl. ⟨the broken vase lay in ~*s*⟩ **2** : an act of shattering : the state of being shattered **3** : a result of shattering : SHOWER

shatter cone *n* (1947) : a conical fragment of rock that has striations radiating from the apex and that is formed by high pressure (as from volcanism or meteorite impact)

shat·ter·proof \ˌshat-ər-ˈprüf\ *adj* (1930) : proof against shattering

[1]**shave** \ˈshāv\ *vb* **shaved; shaved** *or* **shav·en** \ˈshā-vən\; **shav·ing** [ME *shaven*, fr. OE *scafan*; akin to L *scabere* to shave, *capo* capon] *vt* (bef. 12c) **1 a** : to remove a thin layer from **b** : to cut off in thin layers or shreds : SLICE **c** : to cut off closely **2 a** : to sever the hair from (the head or another part of the body) close to the roots **b** : to cut off (hair or beard) close to the skin **3 a** : to discount (a note) at an exorbitant rate **b** : DEDUCT, REDUCE **4** : to come close to or touch lightly in passing ~ *vi* **1** : to cut off hair or beard close to the skin **2** : to proceed with difficulty : SCRAPE

[2]**shave** *n* (1604) **1** : SHAVER 3 **2** : a thin slice : SHAVING **3** : an act or process of shaving

shave·ling \ˈshāv-liŋ\ *n* (1529) **1** : a tonsured clergyman : PRIEST — usu. used disparagingly **2** : YOUTH 2a, STRIPLING

shav·er \ˈshā-vər\ *n* (15c) **1** : a person who shaves **2** *archaic* : one who swindles **3** : a tool or machine for shaving; *specif* : an electric-powered razor **4** : BOY, YOUNGSTER

shaves *pl of* SHAFT

shave·tail \ˈshāv-ˌtāl\ *n* [fr. the practice of shaving the tails of newly broken mules to distinguish them from seasoned ones] (1846) **1** : a pack mule esp. when newly broken in **2** : SECOND LIEUTENANT — usu. used disparagingly

Sha·vi·an \ˈshā-vē-ən\ *n* [NL *Shavius*, Latinized form of George Bernard *Shaw*] (1907) : an admirer or devotee of G. B. Shaw, his writings, or his social and political theories — **Shavian** *adj*

shav·ie \ˈshā-vē\ *n* [*shave* (swindle) + *-ie*] *Scot* (1737) : PRANK

shav·ing \ˈshā-viŋ\ *n* (14c) **1** : the act of one that shaves **2** : something shaved off ⟨wood ~*s*⟩

[1]**shaw** \ˈshȯ\ *n* [ME, fr. OE *sceaga*; akin to ON *skegg* beard — more at SHAG] *dial* (bef. 12c) : COPPICE, THICKET

[2]**shaw** *n* [prob. alter. of *show*] *chiefly Brit* (1726) : the tops and stalks of a cultivated crop (as potatoes or turnips)

[1]**shawl** \ˈshȯl\ *n* [Per *shāl*] (1662) : a square or oblong usu. fabric garment or wrapper used esp. as a covering for the head or shoulders

[2]**shawl** *vt* (1812) : to wrap in or as if in a shawl

shawl collar *n* (ca. 1908) : an attached collar rolled back in a continuous tapering line that follows the surplice neckline of a garment

shawm \ˈshȯm\ *n* [ME *schalme*, fr. MF *chalemie*, modif. of LL *calamellus*, dim. of L *calamus* reed — more at CALAMUS] (14c) : an early double-reed woodwind instrument

Shaw·nee \shȯ-ˈnē, shä-\ *n, pl* **Shawnee** *or* **Shawnees** [back-formation fr. obs. E *Shawnese*, fr. Shawnee *Shaawanwaaki*] (1769) **1** : a member of an American Indian people orig. of the central Ohio valley **2** : the language of the Shawnee people

Shaw·wal \shə-ˈwäl\ *n* [Ar *shawwāl*] (ca. 1769) : the 10th month of the Islamic year — see MONTH table

shay \ˈshā\ *n* [back-formation fr. *chaise*, taken as pl.] *chiefly dial* (1717) : CHAISE 1

[1]**she** \(ˈ)shē\ *pron* [ME, prob. alter. of *hye* alter. of OE *hēo* she — more at HE] (12c) **1** : that female one who is neither speaker nor the one addressed ⟨~ is my wife⟩ — compare HE, HER, HERS, IT, THEY **2** — used to refer to one regarded as feminine (as by personification) ⟨~ was a fine ship⟩

[2]**she** \ˈshē\ *n* (1538) : a female person or animal — often used in combination ⟨*she*-cat⟩ ⟨*she*-cousin⟩

shea butter \ˈshē-, ˈshā-\ *n* (1847) : a pale solid fat from the seeds of the shea tree used in food, soap, and candles

sheaf \ˈshēf\ *n, pl* **sheaves** \ˈshēvz\ [ME *sheef*, fr. OE *scēaf*; akin to OHG *scoub* sheaf, Russ *chub* forelock] (bef. 12c) **1** : a quantity of the stalks and ears of a cereal grass or sometimes other plant material bound together **2** : something resembling a sheaf of grain ⟨a ~ of papers⟩ — **sheaf·like** \ˈshē-ˌflīk\ *adj*

shea nut *n* (1919) : the seed of the shea tree

[1]**shear** \ˈshi(ə)r\ *vb* **sheared; sheared** *or* **shorn** \ˈshō(ə)rn, ˈshȯ(ə)rn\; **shear·ing** [ME *sheren*, fr. OE *scieran*; akin to ON *skera* to cut, L *curtus* shortened, Gk *keirein* to cut, shear] *vt* (bef. 12c) **1 a** : to cut off the hair from ⟨with crown *shorn*⟩ **b** : to cut or clip (as hair or wool) from someone or something; *also* : to cut something from ⟨~ a lawn⟩ **c** *chiefly Scot* : to reap with a sickle **d** : to cut or trim with shears or a similar instrument **2** : to cut with something sharp **3** : to deprive of something as if by cutting **4 a** : to subject to a shear force **b** : to cause (as a rock mass) to move along the plane of contact ~ *vi* **1** : to cut through something with or as if with a sharp instrument **2** *chiefly Scot* : to reap crops with a sickle **3** : to become divided under the action of a shear ⟨the bolt may ~ off⟩ — **shear·er** *n*

[2]**shear** *n* (bef. 12c) **1 a** (1) : a cutting implement similar or identical to a pair of scissors but typically larger — usu. used in pl. (2) : one blade of a pair of shears **b** : any of various cutting tools or machines operating by the action of opposed cutting edges of metal — usu. used in pl. **c** (1) : something resembling a shear or a pair of shears (2) : a hoisting apparatus consisting of two or sometimes more upright spars fastened together at their upper ends and having tackle for masting or dismasting ships or lifting heavy loads (as guns) — usu. used in pl. but sing. or pl. in constr. **2** *chiefly Brit* : the action or process or an instance of shearing — used in combination to indicate the approximate age of sheep in terms of shearings undergone **3 a** : internal force tangential to the section on which it acts — called also *shearing force* **b** : an action or stress resulting from applied forces that causes or tends to cause two contiguous parts of a body to slide relatively to each other in a direction parallel to their plane of contact

sheared *adj* (1616) : formed or finished by shearing; *esp* : cut to uniform length ⟨a ~ raccoon coat⟩

shearing force *n* (ca. 1902) : SHEAR 3a

shear·ling \ˈshi(ə)r-liŋ\ (15c) : skin from a recently sheared sheep or lamb that has been tanned and dressed with the wool left on

shear pin *n* (ca. 1931) : an easily replaceable pin inserted at a critical point in a machine and designed to break when subjected to excess stress

shear·wa·ter \ˈshi(ə)r-ˌwȯt-ər, -ˌwät-\ *n* (1671) : any of numerous oceanic birds (esp. genus *Puffinus*) that are related to the petrels and albatrosses and usu. skim close to the waves in flight

sheath \ˈshēth\ *n, pl* **sheaths** \ˈshē*th*z, ˈshēths\ [ME *shethe*, fr. OE *scēath*; akin to OHG *sceida* sheath, L *scindere* to cut — more at SHED] (bef. 12c) **1** : a case for a blade (as of a knife) **2** : an investing cover or case of a plant or animal body or body part: as **a** : the tubular fold of skin into which the penis of many mammals is retracted **b** (1) : the lower part of a leaf (as of a grass) when surrounding the stem (2) : an ensheathing spathe **3** : any of various covering or supporting structures that are applied like or resemble the sheath of a blade: as **a** : SHEATHING 2 **b** : a woman's close-fitting dress usu. worn without a belt

sheath·bill \ˈshēth-ˌbil\ *n* (ca. 1781) : any of several white shore birds (family Chionididae) of colder parts of the southern hemisphere that have a horny sheath over the base of the upper mandible and suggest the pigeons in general appearance

sheathe \ˈshē*th*\ *also* **sheath** \ˈshēth\ *vt* **sheathed; sheath·ing** [ME *shethen*, fr. *shethe* sheath] (15c) **1** : to put into or furnish with a

\ə\ **abut** \ᵊ\ **kitten**, F **table** \ər\ **further** \a\ **ash** \ā\ **ace** \ä\ **cot, cart**
\au̇\ **out** \ch\ **chin** \e\ **bet** \ē\ **easy** \g\ **go** \i\ **hit** \ī\ **ice** \j\ **job**
\ŋ\ **sing** \ō\ **go** \ȯ\ **law** \ȯi\ **boy** \th\ **thin** *th*\ **the** \ü\ **loot** \u̇\ **foot**
\y\ **yet** \zh\ **vision** \à, k̲, ⁿ, œ, œ̄, ue, ue̅, ʸ\ *see* Guide to Pronunciation

sheath **2 :** to plunge or bury (as a sword) in flesh **3 :** to withdraw (a claw) into a sheath **4 :** to case or cover with something (as sheets of metal) that protects — **sheath·er** \'shē-t͟hər, -thər\ *n*

sheath·ing \'shē-t͟hiŋ, -thiŋ\ *n* (15c) **1 :** the action of one that sheathes something **2 :** material used to sheathe something; *esp* **:** the first covering of boards or of waterproof material on the outside wall of a frame house or on a timber roof

sheath knife *n* (1837) **:** a knife having a fixed blade and designed to be carried in a sheath

shea tree \'shē-, 'shā-\ *n* [Bambara *si*] (1799) **:** a tropical African tree (*Butyrospermum parkii*) of the sapodilla family with fatty nuts that yield shea butter

[1]sheave \'shiv, 'shēv\ *n* [ME *sheve;* akin to OE *scēath* sheath] (14c) **:** a grooved wheel or pulley (as of a pulley block)

[2]sheave \'shēv\ *vt* **sheaved; sheav·ing** [*sheaf*] (ca. 1598) **:** to gather and bind into a sheaf

she·bang \shi-'baŋ\ *n* [perh. alter. of *shebeen*] (1869) **:** CONTRIVANCE, AFFAIR, CONCERN ⟨in charge of the whole ~⟩

She·bat \shə-'bät, -'vät\ *n* [Heb *shĕbhāṭ*] (ca. 1769) **:** the 5th month of the civil year or the 11th month of the ecclesiastical year in the Jewish calendar — see MONTH table

she·been \shə-'bēn\ *n* [IrGael *sibín* bad ale] *chiefly Irish* (1787) **:** an unlicensed or illegally operated drinking establishment

She·chi·nah \shə-'kē-nə, -'kē-nə, -'kī-nə\ *n* [Heb *shĕkhīnāh*] (1663) **:** the presence of God in the world as conceived in Jewish theology

[1]shed \'shed\ *vb* **shed; shed·ding** [ME *sheden* to divide, separate, fr. OE *scēadan;* akin to OHG *skeidan* to separate, L *scindere* to cut, split, Gk *schizein* to split] *vt* (bef. 12c) **1** *chiefly dial* **:** to set apart **:** SEGREGATE **2 :** to cause to be dispersed without penetrating ⟨duck's plumage ~*s* water⟩ **3 a :** to cause (blood) to flow by cutting or wounding **b :** to pour forth in drops ⟨~ tears⟩ **c :** to give off in a stream ⟨fish *shedding* their eggs in spawning⟩ **d :** to give off or out ⟨his book ~*s* some light on this subject⟩ **4 a** (1) **:** to cast off (as a body covering) **:** MOLT (2) **:** to let fall (as leaves) (3) **:** to eject (as seed or spores) from a natural receptacle **b :** to rid oneself of temporarily or permanently as superfluous or unwanted ~ *vi* **1 :** to pour out **:** SPILL **2 :** to become dispersed **:** SCATTER **3 :** to cast off some natural covering ⟨the cat is *shedding*⟩ ***syn*** see DISCARD — **shed blood :** to cause death by violence

[2]shed *n* (bef. 12c) **1** *obs* **:** DISTINCTION, DIFFERENCE **2 :** something (as the skin of a snake) that is discarded in shedding **3 :** a divide of land

[3]shed *n* [alter. of earlier *shadde,* prob. fr. ME *shade*] (15c) **1 a :** a slight structure built for shelter or storage; *esp* **:** a single-storied building with one or more sides unenclosed **b :** a building that resembles a shed **2** *archaic* **:** HUT

[4]shed *vt* **shed·ded; shed·ding** (1850) **:** to put or house in a shed

she'd \(,)shēd\ **:** she had **:** she would

shed·der \'shed-ər\ *n* (14c) **:** one that sheds something: as **a :** a crab or lobster about to molt **b :** a newly molted crab

shed dormer *n* (1948) **:** a dormer with a roof sloping in the same direction as the roof from which the dormer projects

[1]sheen \'shēn\ *adj* [ME *shene,* fr. OE *sciene;* akin to OE *scēawian* to look — more at SHOW] (bef. 12c) **1** *archaic* **:** BEAUTIFUL **2** *archaic* **:** SHINING, RESPLENDENT

[2]sheen *vi* (14c) **:** to be bright **:** show a sheen

[3]sheen *n* (1602) **1 a :** a bright or shining condition **:** BRIGHTNESS **b :** a subdued glitter approaching but short of optical reflection **c :** a lustrous surface imparted to textiles through finishing processes or use of shiny yarns **2 :** a textile exhibiting notable sheen — **sheeny** \'shē-nē\ *adj*

sheep \'shēp\ *n, pl* **sheep** *often attrib* [ME, fr. OE *scēap;* akin to OHG *scāf* sheep] (bef. 12c) **1 :** any of numerous ruminant mammals (genus *Ovis*) related to the goats but stockier and lacking a beard in the male; *specif* **:** one (*O. aries*) long domesticated esp. for its flesh and wool **2 a :** a timid defenseless creature **b :** a timid docile person; *esp* **:** one easily influenced or led **3 :** leather prepared from the skins of sheep **:** SHEEPSKIN

sheep·ber·ry \-,ber-ē\ *n* (ca. 1814) **:** an often shrubby No. American viburnum (*Viburnum lentago*) with white flowers in flat cymes

sheep·cote \-,kōt, -,kät\ *n, chiefly Brit* (15c) **:** SHEEPFOLD

sheep–dip \-,dip\ *n* (1865) **:** a liquid preparation of toxic chemicals into which sheep are plunged esp. to destroy parasitic arthropods

sheep·dog \-,dȯg\ *n* (1774) **:** a dog used to tend, drive, or guard sheep

sheep fescue *n* (1945) **:** a hardy fine-foliaged European perennial grass (*Festuca ovina*) widely used as a lawn grass

sheep·fold \'shēp-,fōld\ *n* (15c) **:** a pen or shelter for sheep

sheep·herd·er \'shēp-,hərd-ər\ *n* (ca. 1871) **:** a worker in charge of sheep esp. on open range

sheep·herd·ing \-,hərd-iŋ\ *n* (1891) **:** the activities of a worker engaged in tending sheep

sheep·ish \'shē-pish\ *adj* (13c) **1 :** resembling a sheep in meekness, stupidity, or timidity **2 :** embarrassed by consciousness of a fault ⟨a ~ look⟩ — **sheep·ish·ly** *adv* — **sheep·ish·ness** *n*

sheep ked \'shēp-,ked\ *n* [*sheep* + *ked* (sheep ked), of unknown origin] (1925) **:** a wingless bloodsucking dipterous fly (*Melophagus ovinus*) that feeds chiefly on sheep and is a vector of sheep trypanosomiasis — called also *sheep tick*

sheep laurel *n* (1810) **:** a No. American dwarf shrub (*Kalmia angustifolia*) that is poisonous to young stock and resembles mountain laurel but has narrower leaves and smaller bright red flowers — called also *lambkill*

sheep's eye *n* (1529) **:** a shy longing usu. amorous glance — usu. used in pl.

sheep·shank \'shēp-,shaŋk\ *n* (ca. 1627) **1 :** a knot for shortening a line — see KNOT illustration **2** *Scot* **:** something of no worth or importance

sheeps·head \'shēps-,hed\ *n* (1643) **1 :** a marine percoid food fish (*Archosargus probatocephalus* of the family Sparidae) of the Atlantic and Gulf coasts of the U.S. with broad incisor teeth **2 :** FRESHWATER DRUM **3 :** a common largely red or rose California wrasse (*Semicossyphus pulcher*)

sheep·shear·er \'shēp-,shir-ər\ *n* (1539) **:** one that shears sheep

sheep·shear·ing \'shēp-,shi(ə)r-iŋ\ *n* (1607) **1 :** the act of shearing sheep **2 :** the time or season for shearing sheep

sheep·skin \-,skin\ *n* (13c) **1 a :** the skin of a sheep; *also* **:** leather prepared from it **b :** PARCHMENT **c :** a garment made of or lined with sheepskin **2 :** DIPLOMA

sheep sorrel *n* (1806) **:** a small acid dock (*Rumex acetosella*)

sheep walk *n, chiefly Brit* (1586) **:** a pasture or range for sheep

[1]sheer \'shi(ə)r\ *adj* [ME *schere* freed from guilt, prob. alter. of *skere,* fr. ON *skærr* pure; akin to OE *scīnan* to shine] (1568) **1** *obs* **:** BRIGHT, SHINING **2 :** of very thin or transparent texture **:** DIAPHANOUS **3 a :** UNQUALIFIED, UTTER ⟨~ folly⟩ ⟨~ ignorance⟩ **b :** being free from an adulterant **:** PURE, UNMIXED **c :** viewed or acting in dissociation from all else ⟨won through by ~ determination⟩ **4 :** marked by great steepness ***syn*** see STEEP — **sheer·ly** *adv* — **sheer·ness** *n*

[2]sheer *adv* (1600) **1 :** in a complete manner **:** ALTOGETHER **2 :** straight up or down without a break **:** PERPENDICULARLY

[3]sheer *n* (ca. 1920) **:** a sheer fabric; *also* **:** a garment of such a fabric

[4]sheer *vb* [perh. alter. of [1]*shear*] *vi* (1635) **:** to deviate from a course **:** SWERVE ~ *vt* **:** to cause to sheer

[5]sheer *n* (1670) **1 :** a turn, deviation, or change in a course (as of a ship) **2 :** the position of a ship riding to a single anchor and heading toward it

[6]sheer *n* [perh. alter. of [2]*shear*] (1691) **:** the fore-and-aft curvature from bow to stern of a ship's deck as shown in side elevation

sheer·legs \'shi(ə)r-,legz, -,lāgz\ *n pl but sing or pl in constr* (1900) **:** SHEAR 1c(2)

[1]sheet \'shēt\ *n* [ME *shete,* fr. OE *scȳte;* akin to OE *scēotan* to shoot — more at SHOOT] (bef. 12c) **1 a :** a broad piece of cloth; *esp* **:** an oblong of usu. linen or cotton cloth used as an article of bedding **b :** SAIL 1a(1) **2 a** (1) **:** a usu. rectangular piece of paper; *esp* **:** one manufactured for printing (2) **:** a rectangular piece of heavy paper with a plant specimen mounted on it ⟨an herbarium of 100,000 ~*s*⟩ **b :** a printed signature for a book esp. before it has been folded, cut, or bound — usu. used in pl. **c :** a newspaper, periodical, or occasional publication ⟨a gossip ~⟩ **d :** the unseparated postage stamps printed by one impression of a plate on a single piece of paper; *also* **:** a pane of stamps **3 :** a broad stretch or surface of something ⟨a ~ of ice⟩ **4 :** a suspended or moving expanse (as of fire or rain) **5 a :** a portion of something that is thin in comparison to its length and breadth **b :** a flat baking utensil of tinned metal ⟨a cookie ~⟩ **6 :** a surface or part of a surface in which it is possible to pass from any one point of it to any other without leaving the surface ⟨a hyperboloid of two ~*s*⟩ — **sheet·like** \-,līk\ *adj*

[2]sheet *adj* (1582) **1 :** rolled or spread out in a sheet **2 :** of, relating to, or concerned with the making of sheet metal

[3]sheet *vt* (1606) **1 :** to cover with a sheet **:** SHROUD **2 :** to furnish with sheets **3 :** to form into sheets ~ *vi* **:** to fall, spread, or flow in a sheet ⟨the rain ~*ed* against the windows⟩ — **sheet·er** *n* — **sheet home 1 :** to extend (a sail) and set as flat as possible by hauling upon the sheets **2 :** to fix the responsibility for **:** bring home to one

[4]sheet *n* [ME *shete,* fr. OE *scēata* lower corner of a sail; akin to OE *scȳte* sheet] (14c) **1 :** a rope or chain that regulates the angle at which a sail is set in relation to the wind **2** *pl* **:** the spaces at either end of an open boat not occupied by thwarts **:** foresheets and stern sheets together — **three sheets in the wind** *or* **three sheets to the wind :** DRUNK

sheet anchor *n* (15c) **1 :** a large strong anchor formerly carried in the waist of a ship and used as a spare in an emergency **2 :** something that constitutes a main support or dependence esp. in danger

sheet bend *n* (ca. 1823) **:** a bend or hitch used for temporarily fastening a rope to the bight of another rope or to an eye — see KNOT illustration

sheet·fed \'shēt-,fed\ *adj* (1888) **:** of, relating to, or printed by a press that prints on paper in sheet form

sheet glass *n* (1805) **:** glass made in large sheets directly from the furnace or by making a cylinder and then flattening it

sheet·ing \'shēt-iŋ\ *n* (1711) **1 :** material in the form of sheets or suitable for forming into sheets **2 :** a lining (as wood or steel) used to support an embankment or the walls of an excavation

sheet lightning *n* (1794) **:** lightning in diffused or sheet form due to reflection and diffusion by the clouds and sky

sheet metal *n* (ca. 1909) **:** metal in the form of a sheet

sheet music *n* (1857) **:** music printed on large unbound sheets of paper

Sheet·rock \'shēt-,räk\ *trademark* — used for plasterboard

sheikh *or* **sheik** \'shēk, *also* 'shāk *for 1*\ *n* [Ar *shaykh*] (1577) **1 :** an Arab chief **2** *usu* **sheik :** a man held to be irresistibly attractive to romantic young women

sheikh·dom *or* **sheik·dom** \-dəm, -təm\ *n* (1845) **:** a region under the rule of a sheikh

shek·el \'shek-əl\ *n* [Heb *sheqel*] (15c) **1 a :** any of various ancient units of weight; *esp* **:** a Hebrew unit equal to about 252 grains troy **b :** a unit of value based on a shekel weight of gold or silver **2 :** a coin weighing one shekel **3** *pl* **:** MONEY **4** — see MONEY table

Shekinah *var of* SHECHINAH

shel·drake \'shel-,drāk\ *n* [ME, fr. *sheld-* (akin to MD *schillede* parti-colored) + *drake*] (14c) **1 :** SHELDUCK **2 :** MERGANSER

shel·duck \-,dək\ *n* [*shel-* (as in *sheldrake*) + *duck*] (1707) **:** any of various Old World ducks (genus *Tadorna*); *esp* **:** a common mostly black-and-white European duck (*T. tadorna*) slightly larger than the mallard

shelf \'shelf\ *n, pl* **shelves** \'shelvz\ [ME, prob. fr. OE *scylfe;* akin to L *scalpere, sculpere* to carve, OE *sciell* shell] (bef. 12c) **1 a :** a thin flat usu. long and narrow piece of material (as wood) fastened horizontally (as on a wall) at a distance from the floor to hold objects **b :** one of several similar pieces in a closet, bookcase, or similar structure **c :** the contents of a shelf **2 :** something resembling a shelf in form or position: as **a :** a sandbank or ledge of rocks usu. partially submerged **b :** a stratum with a shelflike surface **c :** a flat projecting layer of rock **d :** the submerged gradually sloping border of a continent or island **:** CONTINENTAL SHELF — **shelf·ful** \'shelf-,fu̇l\ *n* — **shelf·like** \'shel-,flīk\ *adj* — **off the shelf :** available from stock **:** not made to order ⟨*off the shelf* equipment⟩ — **on the shelf :** in a state of inactivity or uselessness

shelf ice *n* (1910) **:** an extensive ice sheet originating on land but continuing out to sea beyond the depths at which it rests on the sea bottom

shelf life *n* (1927) **:** the period of time during which a material may be stored and remain suitable for use

[1]shell \'shel\ *n* [ME, fr. OE *sciell;* akin to OE *scealu* shell, ON *skel,* L *silex* pebble, flint, Gk *skallein* to hoe] (bef. 12c) **1 a :** a hard rigid usu. largely calcareous covering of an animal **b :** the hard or tough outer covering of an egg esp. of a bird — see EGG illustration **2 :** the covering or outside part of a fruit or seed esp. when hard or fibrous **3 :** shell material (as of mollusks or turtles) or their substance **4 :** something that resembles a shell: as **a :** a framework or exterior structure; *esp* **:** a building with an unfinished interior **b :** an external case or outside covering ⟨the ~ of a ship⟩ **c :** a casing without substance ⟨mere effigies and ~*s* of men —Thomas Carlyle⟩ **d :** an edible case for holding a filling ⟨a pastry ~⟩ **e :** a reinforced concrete arched or domed roof that is used primarily over large areas **f :** a small beer glass **5 :** a thin hard layer of rock **6 :** a shell-bearing mollusk **7 :** an impersonal attitude or manner that conceals the presence or absence of feeling **8 :** a narrow light racing boat propelled by one or more persons pulling oars or sculls **9 :** any of the spaces occupied by the orbits of a group of electrons of approximately equal energy surrounding the nucleus of an atom **10 a :** a projectile for cannon containing an explosive bursting charge **b :** a metal or paper case which holds the charge of powder and shot or bullet used with breech-loading small arms **11 :** a plain usu. sleeveless blouse or sweater — **shell** *adj* — **shelly** \'shel-ē\ *adj*

[2]**shell** *vt* (1562) **1 a :** to take out of a natural enclosing cover (as a shell, husk, pod, or capsule) ⟨~ peanuts⟩ **b :** to separate the kernels of (as an ear of Indian corn, wheat, or oats) from the cob, ear, or husk **2 :** to throw shells at, upon, or into **:** BOMBARD **3 :** to score heavily against (as an opposing pitcher in baseball) ~ *vi* **1 :** to fall or scale off in thin pieces **2 :** to cast the shell or exterior covering **:** fall out of the pod or husk ⟨nuts which ~ in falling⟩ **3 :** to gather shells (as from a beach) **:** collect shells

she'll \(,)shē(ə)l, shil\ **:** she will **:** she shall

[1]**shel·lac** \shə-'lak\ *n* [[1]*shell* + *lac*] (1713) **1 :** purified lac usu. prepared in thin orange or yellow flakes by heating and filtering and often bleached white **2 :** a preparation of lac dissolved usu. in alcohol and used chiefly as a wood filler and finish **3 a :** a composition containing shellac used for making phonograph records **b :** an old 78 rpm phonograph record

[2]**shellac** *vt* **shel·lacked; shel·lack·ing** (1882) **1 :** to coat or otherwise treat with shellac or a shellac varnish **2 :** to defeat decisively

shel·lack·ing *n* (1938) **:** a decisive defeat **:** DRUBBING

shell·back \'shel-,bak\ *n* (1883) **:** an old or veteran sailor

shell bean *n* (1868) **1 :** a bean grown primarily for its edible seeds — compare SNAP BEAN **2 :** the edible seed of a bean

shell·crack·er \'shel-,krak-ər\ *n* (1891) **:** REDEAR

shelled \'sheld\ *adj* (1577) **1 :** having a shell esp. of a specified kind — often used in combination ⟨pink-*shelled*⟩ ⟨thick-*shelled*⟩ **2 a :** having the shell removed ⟨~ oysters⟩ ⟨~ nuts⟩ **b :** removed from the cob ⟨~ corn⟩

shell·er \'shel-ər\ *n* (1694) **1 :** one that shells ⟨a peanut ~⟩ **2 :** one that collects seashells

shell·fish \-,fish\ *n* (bef. 12c) **:** an aquatic invertebrate animal with a shell; *esp* **:** an edible mollusk or crustacean

shell·fish·ery \-,fish-(ə-)rē\ *n* (1971) **:** a commercially exploited population of shellfish

shell game *n* (1890) **1 :** thimblerig played esp. with three walnut shells **2 :** FRAUD; *esp* **:** a swindle involving the substitution of something of little or no value for a valuable item

shell jacket *n* (1840) **1 :** a short tight military jacket worn buttoned up the front **2 :** MESS JACKET

shell out *vb* (1801) **:** PAY

shell pink *n* (1887) **:** a variable color averaging a light yellowish pink

shell·proof \'shel-'prüf\ *adj* (ca. 1864) **:** capable of resisting shells or bombs

shell shock *n* (1916) **:** any of numerous often hysterical psychoneurotic conditions appearing in soldiers under fire in modern warfare

shell–shocked *adj* (1918) **1 :** affected with shell shock **2 :** mentally confused, upset, or exhausted as a result of excessive stress

shell steak *n* (1971) **:** the part of a short loin of beef that contains no tenderloin

shell·work \'shel-,wərk\ *n* (ca. 1611) **:** work adorned with shells or composed of a pattern of shells

[1]**shel·ter** \'shel-tər\ *n* [origin unknown] (1585) **1 :** something that covers or affords protection ⟨a bomb ~⟩ **2 :** a position or the state of being covered and protected ⟨took ~⟩ — **shel·ter·less** \-ləs\ *adj*

[2]**shelter** *vb* **shel·tered; shel·ter·ing** \-t(ə-)riŋ\ *vt* (1590) **1 :** to constitute or provide a shelter for **:** PROTECT ⟨has led a ~*ed* life⟩ **2 :** to place under shelter or protection ⟨~*ed* himself in a mountain cave⟩ ~ *vi* **:** to take shelter — **shel·ter·er** \-tər-ər\ *n*

shel·ter·belt \'shel-tər-,belt\ *n* (1868) **:** a barrier of trees and shrubs that protects (as crops) from wind and storm and lessens erosion

shelter half *n* (1942) **:** one of the halves of a shelter tent

shelter tent *n* (ca. 1875) **:** a small tent usu. consisting of two interchangeable pieces of waterproof cotton duck packed separately and fitted together for use

shel·ty *or* **shel·tie** \'shel-tē\ *n, pl* **shelties** [prob. of Scand origin; akin to ON *Hjalti* Shetlander] (1654) **1 :** SHETLAND PONY **2 :** SHETLAND SHEEPDOG

shelve \'shelv\ *vb* **shelved; shelv·ing** [*shelf*] *vt* (1598) **1 :** to furnish with shelves **2 :** to place on a shelf **3 a :** to remove from active service **b :** to put off or aside ⟨~ a project⟩ ~ *vi* **:** to slope in a formation like a shelf — **shelv·er** *n*

[1]**shelv·ing** \'shel-viŋ\ *n* (1687) **1 :** the state or degree of sloping **2 :** a sloping surface or place

[2]**shelving** *n* (1844) **1 :** material for shelves **2 :** SHELVES

Shem \'shem\ *n* [Heb *Shēm*] **:** the eldest son of Noah held to be the progenitor of the Semitic peoples

She·ma \shə-'mä\ *n* [Heb *shĕma'* hear, first word of Deut 6:4] (1864) **:** the Jewish confession of faith made up of Deut 6:4–9 and 11:13–21 and Num 15:37–41

She·mi·ni Atze·reth \shə-,mē-nē-ät-'ser-ət(h), -əs\ *n* [Heb *shĕmīnī 'ăṣereth,* fr. Heb *shĕmīnī* eighth + *'ăṣereth* assembly] (ca. 1905) **:** a Jewish festival following the seventh day of Sukkoth and marked by a special prayer for seasonal rain

Shem·ite \'shem-,īt\ *n* [*Shem*] (1659) **:** SEMITE — **She·mit·ic** \shə-'mit-ik\ *or* **Shem·it·ish** \'shem-,īt-ish\ *adj*

she·nan·i·gan \shə-'nan-i-gən\ *n* [origin unknown] (1855) **1 :** a devious trick used esp. for an underhand purpose **2 a :** tricky or questionable practices or conduct — usu. used in pl. **b :** high-spirited or mischievous activity — usu. used in pl.

shend \'shend\ *vt* **shent** \'shent\; **shend·ing** [ME *shenden,* fr. OE *scendan;* akin to OE *scamu* shame — more at SHAME] (bef. 12c) **1** *archaic* **:** to put to shame or confusion **2** *archaic* **:** REPROVE, REVILE **3** *chiefly dial* **a :** INJURE, MAR **b :** RUIN, DESTROY

she–oak \'shē-,ōk\ *n* (1792) **:** any of several casuarinas

She·ol \shē-'ōl, 'shē-,\ *n* [Heb *Shĕ'ōl*] (1599) **:** the abode of the dead in early Hebrew thought

[1]**shep·herd** \'shep-ərd\ *n* [ME *sheepherde,* fr. OE *scēaphyrde,* fr. *scēap* sheep + *hierde* herdsman; akin to OE *heord* herd] (bef. 12c) **1 :** one who tends sheep **2 :** PASTOR

[2]**shepherd** *vt* (1790) **1 :** to tend as a shepherd **2 :** to guide or guard in the manner of a shepherd ⟨~*ed* the children onto the train⟩

shepherd dog *n* (15c) **:** SHEEPDOG

shep·herd·ess \'shep-ərd-əs\ *n* (14c) **:** a woman or girl who tends sheep; *also* **:** a rural girl or woman

shepherd's check *n* (1896) **:** a pattern of small even black-and-white checks; *also* **:** a fabric woven in this pattern — called also *shepherd's plaid*

shepherd's pie *n* (1896) **:** a meat pie with a mashed potato crust

shepherd's purse *n* (15c) **:** a white-flowered weedy annual herb (*Capsella bursa-pastoris*) of the mustard family with flat heart-shaped pods

Sher·a·ton \'sher-ət-ᵊn\ *adj* [Thomas *Sheraton*] (1883) **:** of, relating to, or being a style of furniture that originated in England around 1800 and is characterized by straight lines and graceful proportions

sher·bet \'shər-bət\ *n* [Turk & Per; Turk *şerbet,* fr. Per *sharbat,* fr. Ar *sharbah* drink] (1603) **1 :** a cold drink of sweetened and diluted fruit juice **2** *or* **sher·bert** \-bərt\ **:** an ice with milk, egg white, or gelatin added

sherd *var of* SHARD

she·rif \shə-'rēf\ *var of* SHARIF

sher·iff \'sher-əf\ *n* [ME *shirreve,* fr. OE *scīrgerēfa,* fr. *scīr* shire + *gerēfa* reeve — more at SHIRE, REEVE] (bef. 12c) **:** an important official of a shire or county charged primarily with judicial duties (as executing the processes and orders of courts and judges) — **sher·iff·dom** \-əf-dəm, -əf-təm\ *n*

sher·lock \'shər-,läk, 'she(ə)r-\ *n, often cap* [*Sherlock* Holmes, detective in stories by Sir Arthur Conan Doyle] (1926) **:** DETECTIVE

Sher·pa \'she(ə)r-pə, 'shər-\ *n* (1924) **:** a member of a Tibetan people living on the high southern slopes of the Himalayas and skilled in mountain climbing

sher·ris \'sher-is\ *archaic var of* SHERRY

sher·ry \'sher-ē\ *n, pl* **sherries** [alter. of earlier *sherris* (taken as pl.), fr. *Xeres* (now *Jerez*), Spain] (1597) **:** a Spanish fortified wine with a distinctive nutty flavor; *also* **:** a similar wine produced elsewhere

she's \(,)shēz\ **:** she is **:** she has

Shet·land \'shet-lənd\ *n* (1857) **1 a :** SHETLAND PONY **b :** SHETLAND SHEEPDOG **2** *often not cap* **a :** a lightweight loosely twisted yarn of Shetland wool used for knitting and weaving **b :** a fabric or a garment made from Shetland wool

Shet·land pony \,shet-lən(d)-\ *n* (1801) **:** any of a breed of small stocky hardy ponies that originated in the Shetland islands

Shetland sheepdog *n* (ca. 1931) **:** any of a breed of small heavy-coated dogs developed in the Shetland islands that resemble miniature collies

Shetland wool *n* (1790) **:** fine wool from sheep raised in the Shetland islands; *also* **:** yarn spun from this

sheugh \'shük\ *n* [ME *sough,* fr. *swoughen* to sough — more at SOUGH] *chiefly Scot* (1501) **:** DITCH, TRENCH

shew \'shō\ *Brit var of* SHOW

shew·bread \'shō-,bred\ *n* [trans. of G *schaubrot*] (1530) **:** consecrated unleavened bread ritually placed by the Jewish priests of ancient Israel on a table in the sanctuary of the Tabernacle on the Sabbath

Shia \'shē-(,)ä\ *n* [Ar *shī'ah* sect] (1626) **1 :** the Muslims of the branch of Islam comprising sects believing in Ali and the Imams as the only rightful successors of Muhammad and in the concealment and messianic return of the last recognized Imam — compare SUNNI **2 :** SHIITE **3 :** the branch of Islam formed by the Shia

shi·at·su *also* **shi·at·zu** \shē-'ät-(,)sü\ *n, often cap* [short for Jp *shiatsuryōhō,* lit., finger-pressure therapy, fr. *shi* finger + *atsu-* pressure + *ryōhō* treatment] (1968) **:** a massage with the fingers applied to those specific areas of the body used in acupuncture — called also *acupressure*

shib·bo·leth \'shib-ə-ləth *also* -,leth\ *n* [Heb *shibbōleth* stream; fr. the use of this word in Judg 12:6 as a test to distinguish Gileadites from Ephraimites, who pronounced it *sibbōleth*] (1658) **1 a :** CATCHWORD, SLOGAN **b :** a use of language regarded as distinctive of a particular group **c :** a commonplace idea or saying **2 :** a custom or usage regarded as a criterion for distinguishing members of one group

shiel \'shē(ə)l\ *n* [ME (northern dial.) *schele*] *chiefly Scot* (13c) **:** SHIELING

[1]**shield** \'shē(ə)ld\ *n* [ME *sheld,* fr. OE *scield;* akin to OE *sciell* shell] (bef. 12c) **1 :** a broad piece of defensive armor carried on the arm **2 :** one that protects or defends **:** DEFENSE **3 :** DRESS SHIELD **4 :** a fixture designed to protect persons from injury from moving parts of machinery or parts carrying electricity **5 :** ESCUTCHEON; *esp* **:** one that is wide at the top and rounds to a point at the bottom **6 :** an armored screen protecting an otherwise exposed gun **7 :** an iron or steel framework moved forward in excavating to support the ground ahead of the lining **8 :** a protective structure (as a carapace, scale, or plate) of some animals **9 :** the Precambrian nuclear mass of a continent that is surrounded and sometimes covered by sedimentary rocks **10 :** something resembling a shield: as **a :** APOTHECIUM **b :** a policeman's badge **c :** a decorative or identifying emblem

[2]**shield** *vt* (bef. 12c) **1 a :** to protect with or as if with a shield **:** provide with a protective cover or shelter **b :** to cut off from observation **:** HIDE **2** *obs* **:** FORBID **syn** see DEFEND — **shield·er** *n*

shield law *n* (1971) : a law that protects journalists from forced disclosure of confidential news sources

shield volcano *n* (1911) : a broad rounded volcano that is built up by successive outpourings of very fluid lava

shiel·ing \'shē-lən, -liŋ\ *n* (1585) **1** *Brit* : a mountain hut used as a shelter by shepherds **2** *dial Brit* : a summer pasture in the mountains

shier *comparative of* SHY

shiest *superlative of* SHY

1shift \'shift\ *vb* [ME *shiften,* fr. OE *sciftan* to divide, arrange; akin to OE *scēadan* to divide — more at SHED] *vt* (13c) **1** : to exchange for or replace by another : CHANGE **2 a** : to change the place, position, or direction of : MOVE **b** : to make a change in (place) **3** : to change phonetically ~ *vi* **1 a** : to change place or position **b** : to change direction ⟨the wind ~*ed*⟩ **c** : to change the gear rotating the transmission shaft of an automobile **d** : to depress the shift key (as on a typewriter) **2 a** : to assume responsibility ⟨had to ~ for themselves⟩ **b** : to resort to expedients **3 a** : to go through a change **b** : to change one's clothes **c** : to become changed phonetically — **shift·able** \'shif-tə-bəl\ *adj* — **shift·er** *n* — **shift gears** : to make a change

2shift *n* (1523) **1 a** : a means or device for effecting an end **b** (1) : a deceitful or underhand scheme : DODGE (2) : an expedient tried in difficult circumstances : EXTREMITY **2 a** *chiefly dial* : a change of clothes **b** (1) *chiefly dial* : SHIRT (2) : a woman's slip or chemise (3) : a woman's usu. loose-fitting or semifitted dress **3 a** : a change in direction ⟨a ~ in the wind⟩ **b** : a change in emphasis, judgment, or attitude **4 a** : a group of people who work or occupy themselves in turn with other groups **b** (1) : a change of one group of people (as workers) for another in regular alternation (2) : a scheduled period of work or duty **5** : a change in place or position: as **a** : a change in the position of the hand on a fingerboard (as of a violin) **b** (1) : FAULT 5 (2) : the relative displacement of rock masses on opposite sides of a fault or fault zone **c** (1) : a simultaneous change of position in football by two or more players from one side of the line to the other (2) : a change of positions made by one or more players in baseball to provide better defense against a particular hitter **d** : a change in frequency resulting in a change in position of a spectral line or band — compare DOPPLER EFFECT **e** : a movement of bits in a computer register a specified number of places to the right or left **6** : a removal from one person or thing to another : TRANSFER **7** : CONSONANT SHIFT **8** : a bid in bridge in a suit other than the suit one's partner has bid — compare JUMP **9** : GEARSHIFT ***syn*** see RESOURCE

shift key *n* (1893) : a key on a keyboard (as of a typewriter) that when pressed enables an alternate set of characters to be printed

shift·less \'shif(t)-ləs\ *adj* [*shift* (resourcefulness)] (1584) **1** : lacking in resourcefulness : INEFFICIENT **2** : lacking in ambition or incentive : LAZY — **shift·less·ly** *adv* — **shift·less·ness** *n*

shifty \'shif-tē\ *adj* **shift·i·er; -est** (ca. 1570) **1** : full of or ready with expedients : RESOURCEFUL **2 a** : given to deception, evasion, or fraud : TRICKY **b** : capable of evasive movement : ELUSIVE ⟨a ~ boxer⟩ **3** : indicative of a tricky nature ⟨~ eyes⟩ — **shift·i·ly** \-tə-lē\ *adv* — **shift·i·ness** \-tē-nəs\ *n*

shi·gel·la \shi-'gel-ə\ *n, pl* **-gel·lae** \-'gel-(,)ē, -(,)ī\ *also* **-gellas** [NL, fr. Kiyoshi *Shiga* †1957 Jp bacteriologist] (ca. 1934) : any of a genus (*Shigella*) of nonmotile aerobic bacteria that form acid but no gas on many carbohydrates and cause dysenteries in animals and esp. man

shig·el·lo·sis \,shig-ə-'lō-səs\ *n, pl* **-lo·ses** \-'lō-,sēz\ [NL] (1944) : infection with a dysentery caused by shigellae

Shih Tzu \'shēd-'zü\ *n* [Chin (Pek) *shih1 tzu kou3* Pekingese dog, fr. *shih1 tzu* lion + *kou3* dog] (1921) : a small short-legged dog of an ancient Chinese breed that has a short muzzle and a long dense coat

Shi·ism \'shē-,iz-əm\ *n* (ca. 1883) : Islam as taught by the Shia

shii·ta·ke \shē-'tä-kē\ *n* [Jp] (1877) : a large dark Oriental mushroom (*Lentinus edodes* of the family Agaricaceae) widely cultivated on woods of the beech family for its edible flavorful cap

Shi·ite \'shē-,īt\ *n* (1728) : a Muslim of the Shia branch of Islam

1shi·kar \shi-'kär\ *n* [Hindi *shikār,* fr. Per] *India* (1609) : HUNTING

2shikar *vb* **shi·karred; shi·kar·ring** *India* (1872) : HUNT

shi·ka·ri \shi-'kär-ē, -'kar-\ *n* [Hindi *shikārī,* fr. Per, fr. *shikār*] *India* (1822) : a big game hunter; *esp* : a professional hunter or guide

shik·sa *or* **shik·se** \'shik-sə\ *n* [Yiddish *shikse,* fem. of *sheykets, sheygets* non-Jewish boy, fr. Heb *sheqes* blemish, abomination] (1892) **1** : a non-Jewish girl — often used disparagingly **2** : a Jewish girl who does not observe Jewish precepts — used esp. by Orthodox Jews

shi·lingi \shil-'iŋ-ē\ *n, pl* **shilingi** [Swahili, fr. E *shilling*] (1966) : the shilling of Tanzania

shill \'shil\ *n* [prob. short for *shillaber,* of unknown origin] (ca. 1916) : one who acts as a decoy (as for a pitchman or gambler) — **shill** *vi*

shil·le·lagh *also* **shil·la·lah** \shə-'lā-lē\ *n* [*Shillelagh,* town in Ireland famed for its oak trees] (1772) : CUDGEL

shil·ling \'shil-iŋ\ *n* [ME, fr. OE *scilling;* akin to OHG *skilling,* a gold coin, OE *scield* shield] (bef. 12c) **1 a** : a former monetary unit of the United Kingdom equal to 12 pence or 1/20 pound **b** : a former monetary unit equal to 1/20 pound of any of various countries in or formerly in the Commonwealth **2** : a coin representing one shilling **3** : any of several early American coins **4** — see MONEY table

Shil·luk \shil-'ük\ *n, pl* **Shilluk** *or* **Shilluks** (1790) **1** : a member of a Nilotic Negro people of the Sudan dwelling mainly on the west bank of the White Nile **2** : the language of the Shilluk people

1shilly–shally \'shil-ē-,shal-ē\ *adv* [irreg. redupl. of *shall I*] (1700) : in an irresolute, undecided, or hesitating manner

2shilly–shally *adj* (1734) : IRRESOLUTE, VACILLATING

3shilly–shally *n* (1755) : INDECISION, IRRESOLUTION

4shilly–shally *vi* **shilly–shall·ied; shilly–shally·ing** (1782) **1** : to show hesitation or lack of decisiveness or resolution **2** : DAWDLE

shil·pit \'shil-pət\ *adj* [origin unknown] (1802) **1** *Scot* : pinched and starved in appearance **2** *Scot* : WEAK, INSIPID — used of drink

1shim \'shim\ *n* [origin unknown] (1860) : a thin often tapered piece of material (as wood, metal, or stone) used to fill in space between things (as for support, leveling, or adjustment of fit)

2shim *vt* **shimmed; shim·ming** (ca. 1891) : to fill out or level up by the use of a shim

1shim·mer \'shim-ər\ *vb* **shim·mered; shim·mer·ing** \-(ə-)riŋ\ [ME *schimeren,* fr. OE *scimerian;* akin to OE *scīnan* to shine — more at SHINE] *vi* (bef. 12c) **1** : to shine with a soft tremulous or fitful light : GLIMMER **2** : to reflect a wavering sometimes distorted visual image ~ *vt* : to cause to shimmer ***syn*** see FLASH

2shimmer *n* (1821) **1** : a light that shimmers : subdued sparkle or sheen : GLIMMER **2** : a wavering sometimes distorted visual image usu. resulting from heat-induced changes in atmospheric refraction — **shim·mery** \'shim-(ə-)rē\ *adj*

1shim·my \'shim-ē\ *n, pl* **shimmies** (1837) **1** [by alter.] : CHEMISE **2** [short for *shimmy-shake*] : a jazz dance characterized by a shaking of the body from the shoulders down **3** : an abnormal vibration esp. in the front wheels of a motor vehicle

2shimmy *vi* **shim·mied; shim·my·ing** (1919) **1** : to shake, quiver, or tremble in or as if in dancing a shimmy **2** : to vibrate abnormally — used esp. of automobiles

1shin \'shin\ *n* [ME *shine,* fr. OE *scinu;* akin to OHG *scina* shin, OE *scēadan* to divide — more at SHED] (bef. 12c) : the front part of the vertebrate leg below the knee

2shin *vb* **shinned; shin·ning** *vi* (1829) **1** : to move oneself up or down something vertical (as a pole) esp. by alternately hugging it with the arms or hands and the legs **2** : to move forward rapidly on foot ~ *vt* **1** : to kick or strike on the shins **2** : to climb by shinning

3shin \'shēn, 'shin\ *n* [Heb *shīn*] (1823) : the 22d letter of the Hebrew alphabet — see ALPHABET table

Shin \'shin, 'shēn\ *n* [Jp, lit., truth] (1877) : a major Japanese Buddhist sect that emphasizes salvation by faith in exclusive worship of Amida Buddha

Shi·na \'shē-nə\ *n* (1854) : the Dard language of Gilgit in northern Kashmir

shin·bone \'shin-'bōn, -,bōn\ *n* (bef. 12c) : TIBIA 1

shin·dig \'shin-,dig\ *n* [prob. alter. of *shindy*] (1871) **1 a** : a social gathering with dancing **b** : a usu. large or lavish party **2** : SHINDY 2

shin·dy \'shin-dē\ *n, pl* **shindys** *or* **shindies** [prob. alter. of *shinny*] (1821) **1** : SHINDIG 1 **2** : FRACAS, UPROAR

1shine \'shīn\ *vb* **shone** \'shōn, *esp Canad & Brit* 'shän\ *or* **shined; shin·ing** [ME *shinen,* fr. OE *scīnan;* akin to OHG *skīnan* to shine, Gk *skia* shadow] *vi* (bef. 12c) **1** : to emit rays of light **2** : to be bright by reflection of light **3** : to be eminent, conspicuous, or distinguished ⟨she always ~*s* in math class⟩ **4** : to have a bright glowing appearance ⟨his face *shone* with enthusiasm⟩ **5** : to be conspicuously evident or clear ~ *vt* **1 a** : to cause to emit light **b** : to throw or direct the light of **2** *past & past part* **shined** : to make bright by polishing ⟨*shined* his shoes⟩

2shine *n* (1529) **1** : brightness caused by the emission of light **2** : brightness caused by the reflection of light : LUSTER **3** : BRILLIANCE, SPLENDOR **4** : fair weather : SUNSHINE ⟨rain or ~⟩ **5** : TRICK, CAPER — usu. used in pl. **6** : LIKING, FANCY ⟨took a ~ to him⟩ **7 a** : a polish or gloss given to shoes **b** : a single polishing of a pair of shoes

shin·er \'shī-nər\ *n* (14c) **1** : one that shines **2** : a silvery fish; *esp* : any of numerous small freshwater American cyprinid fishes (esp. genus *Notropis*) — compare GOLDEN SHINER **3** : BLACK EYE 1

1shin·gle \'shiŋ-gəl\ *n* [ME *schingel*] (13c) **1** : a small thin piece of building material often with one end thicker than the other for laying in overlapping rows as a covering for the roof or sides of a building **2** : a small signboard esp. designating a professional office — used chiefly in the phrase *hang out one's shingle* **3** : a woman's haircut with the hair trimmed short from the back of the head to the nape

2shingle *vt* **shin·gled; shin·gling** \-g(ə-)liŋ\ (1562) **1** : to cover with or as if with shingles **2** : to bob and shape (the hair) in a shingle **3** : to lay out or arrange so as to overlap

3shingle *n* [prob. of Scand origin; akin to Norw *singel* coarse gravel] (1513) **1** : a place strewn with shingle **2** : coarse rounded detritus or alluvial material esp. on the seashore that differs from ordinary gravel only in the larger size of the stones — **shin·gly** \-g(ə-)lē\ *adj*

4shingle *vt* **shin·gled; shin·gling** \-g(ə-)liŋ\ [F dial. *chingler,* lit., to whip, fr. MF dial., fr. *chingle* strap, fr. L *cingula,* fr. *cingere* to gird — more at CINCTURE] (1674) : to subject (as iron) to the process of expelling cinder and impurities by hammering and squeezing

shin·gler \-g(ə-)lər\ *n* (1832) : one that shingles

shin·gles \'shiŋ-gəlz\ *n pl but sing in constr* [ME *schingles,* by folk etymology fr. ML *cingulus,* fr. L *cingulum* girdle — more at CINGULUM] (14c) : HERPES ZOSTER

Shin·gon \'shin-,gän, 'shēn-\ *n* [Jp, fr. *shin* truth, reality + *gen, gon* word, speech] (1727) : an esoteric Japanese Buddhist sect claiming the achievement of Buddhahood in this life through prescribed rituals

shin·ing \'shī-niŋ\ *adj* (bef. 12c) **1** : emitting or reflecting light **2** : bright and often splendid in appearance : RESPLENDENT **3** : possessing a distinguished quality : ILLUSTRIOUS **4** : full of sunshine

shin·leaf \'shin-,lēf\ *n, pl* **shinleafs** (ca. 1817) : any of several pyrolas (esp. *Pyrola elliptica*) with lustrous evergreen basal leaves and racemose white or pinkish flowers

shin·nery \'shin-ə-rē\ *n, pl* **-ner·ies** [modif. of LaF *chênière,* fr. F *chêne* oak] (1901) : a dense growth of small trees or an area of such growth; *esp* : one of scrub oak in the West and Southwest

1shin·ny *also* **shin·ney** \'shin-ē\ *n* [perh. fr. *1shin*] (1672) : a variation of hockey played by schoolboys with a curved stick and a ball or block of wood; *also* : the stick used

2shinny *vi* **shin·nied; shin·ny·ing** [alter. of *2shin*] (1851) : SHIN 1

shin·plas·ter \'shin-,plas-tər\ *n* (1824) **1** : a piece of privately-issued paper currency; *esp* : one poorly secured and depreciated in value **2** : a piece of fractional currency

shin·splints \'shin-,splin(t)s\ *n pl but sing in constr* (ca. 1930) : injury to and inflammation of the tibial and toe extensor muscles or their fasciae that is caused by repeated minimal traumas (as by running on a wood or cement floor)

Shin·to \'shin-(,)tō\ *n* [Jp *shintō* alter. of *shin* god, deity + *dō* province, prefecture] (1727) : the indigenous religion of Japan consisting chiefly in the cultic devotion to deities of natural forces and veneration of the Emperor as a descendant of the sun-goddess — **Shinto** *adj* — **Shin·to·ism** \-(,)tō-,iz-əm\ *n* — **Shin·to·ist** \-,tō-əst\ *n or adj* — **Shin·to·is·tic** \,shin-tō-'is-tik\ *adj*

shiny \'shī-nē\ *adj* **shin·i·er; -est** (1590) **1 a** : bright with the rays of the sun : SUNSHINY **b** : filled with light **2** : bright in appearance : POLISHED ⟨~ new shoes⟩ **3** : rubbed or worn smooth **4** : lustrous with natural secretions ⟨a ~ nose⟩ — **shin·i·ness** *n*

[1]ship \ˈship\ *n, often attrib* [ME, fr. OE *scip;* akin to OHG *skif* ship, OE *scēadan* to divide — more at SHED] (bef. 12c) **1 a :** a large seagoing vessel **b :** a sailing vessel having a bowsprit and usu. three masts each composed of a lower mast, a topmast, and a topgallant mast **2 :** BOAT; *esp* **:** one propelled by power or sail **3 :** a ship's crew **4 :** FORTUNE ⟨when their ~ comes in they'll be able to live in better style⟩ **5 :** AIRSHIP, AIRPLANE, SPACECRAFT

[2]ship *vb* **shipped; ship·ping** *vt* (14c) **1 a :** to place or receive on board a ship for transportation by water **b :** to cause to be transported ⟨*shipped* him off to prep school⟩ **2** *obs* **:** to provide with a ship **3 :** to put in place for use ⟨~ the tiller⟩ **4 :** to take into a ship or boat ⟨~ the gangplank⟩ **5 :** to engage for service on a ship **6 :** to take (as water) over the side — used of a boat or a ship ~ *vi* **1 :** to embark on a ship **2 :** to go or travel by ship **3 :** to engage to serve on shipboard — **ship·pa·ble** \ˈship-ə-bəl\ *adj*

-ship \ˌship\ *n suffix* [ME, fr. OE *-scipe;* akin to OHG *-scaft* -ship, OE *sceppan* to shape — more at SHAPE] **1 :** state **:** condition **:** quality ⟨friend*ship*⟩ **2 :** office **:** dignity **:** profession ⟨clerk*ship*⟩ **3 :** art **:** skill ⟨horseman*ship*⟩ **4 :** something showing, exhibiting, or embodying a quality or state ⟨town*ship*⟩ **5 :** one entitled to a (specified) rank, title, or appellation ⟨his Lord*ship*⟩ **6 :** the body of persons participating in a specified activity ⟨reader*ship*⟩ ⟨listener*ship*⟩

ship biscuit *n* (1799) **:** HARDTACK — called also *ship bread*

[1]ship·board \ˈship-ˌbō(ə)rd, -ˌbȯ(ə)rd\ *n* (13c) **1 :** the side of a ship **2 :** SHIP ⟨met on ~⟩

[2]shipboard *adj* (1857) **:** existing or taking place on board a ship

ship·borne \ˈship-ˌbō(ə)rn, -ˌbȯ(ə)rn\ *adj* (1835) **:** transported or designed to be transported by ship ⟨~ aircraft⟩

ship·build·er \ˈship-ˌbil-dər\ *n* (1700) **:** one who designs or constructs ships — **ship·build·ing** \-diŋ\ *n*

ship·fit·ter \ˈship-ˌfit-ər\ *n* (1941) **1 :** one that fits together the structural members of ships and puts them into position for riveting or welding **2 :** a naval enlisted man who works in sheet metal and performs the work of a plumber aboard ship

ship·lap \-ˌlap\ *n* (ca. 1854) **:** wooden sheathing in which the boards are rabbeted so that the edges of each board lap over the edges of adjacent boards to make a flush joint

ship·load \-ˈlōd, -ˌlōd\ *n* (1706) **1 :** as much or as many as will fill or load a ship **2 :** an indefinitely large amount or number

ship·man \-mən\ *n* (bef. 12c) **1 :** SAILOR, SEAMAN **2 :** SHIPMASTER

ship·mas·ter \-ˌmas-tər\ *n* (14c) **:** the master or commander of a ship other than a warship

ship·mate \-ˌmāt\ *n* (1748) **:** a fellow sailor

ship·ment \-mənt\ *n* (1802) **1 :** the act or process of shipping **2 :** the goods shipped

ship of the line (1706) **:** a warship large enough to have a place in the line of battle

ship·own·er \ˈship-ˌō-nər\ *n* (ca. 1530) **:** the owner of a ship or of a share in a ship

ship·per \ˈship-ər\ *n* (1755) **:** one that sends goods by any form of conveyance

ship·ping \ˈship-iŋ\ *n* (14c) **1 a :** passage on a ship **b :** SHIPS **c :** the body of ships in one place or belonging to one port or country **2 :** the act or business of one that ships

shipping clerk *n* (ca. 1858) **:** one who is employed in a shipping room to assemble, pack, and send out or receive goods

ship·shape \ˈship-ˈshāp\ *adj* [short for earlier *shipshapen,* fr. *ship* + *shapen,* archaic pp. of *shape*] (1644) **:** TRIM, TIDY

ship·side \-ˌsīd\ *n* (15c) **:** the area adjacent to a ship; *specif* **:** a dock at which a ship loads or unloads passengers and freight

ship's papers *n pl* **:** the papers a ship is legally required to carry for due inspection to show the character of the ship and cargo

ship·way \ˈship-ˌwā\ *n* (1834) **1 :** the ways on which a ship is built **2 :** a ship canal

ship·worm \-ˌwərm\ *n* (ca. 1778) **:** any of various elongated marine clams (esp. family Teredinidae) that resemble worms, burrow in submerged wood, and damage wharf piles and wooden ships

[1]ship·wreck \-ˌrek\ *n* [alter. of earlier *shipwrack,* fr. ME *schipwrak,* fr. OE *scipwræc,* fr. *scip* ship + *wræc* something driven by the sea — more at WRACK] (12c) **1 :** a wrecked ship or its parts **2 :** the destruction or loss of a ship **3 :** an irretrievable loss or failure

[2]shipwreck *vt* (1589) **1 a :** to cause to experience shipwreck **b :** RUIN **2 :** to destroy (a ship) by grounding or foundering

ship·wright \ˈship-ˌrīt\ *n* (bef. 12c) **:** a carpenter skilled in ship construction and repair

ship·yard \-ˌyärd\ *n* (1700) **:** a yard, place, or enclosure where ships are built or repaired

shire \ˈshī(ə)r, *in place-name compounds* ˌshi(ə)r, shər\ *n* [ME, fr. OE *scīr* office, shire; akin to OHG *scīra* care] (bef. 12c) **1 :** an administrative subdivision; *esp* **:** a county in England **2 :** any of a British breed of large heavy draft horses with heavily feathered legs

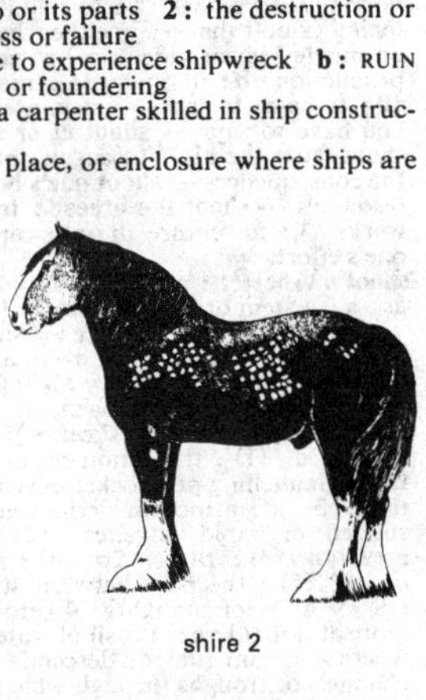

shire 2

shire town *n* (15c) **1** *Brit* **:** a town that is the seat of the government of a shire **2** *NewEng* **:** a town where a court of superior jurisdiction (as a circuit court or a court with a jury) sits

shirk \ˈshərk\ *vb* [origin unknown] *vi* (1681) **1 :** to go stealthily **:** SNEAK **2 :** to evade the performance of an obligation ~ *vt* **:** AVOID, EVADE ⟨~ one's duty⟩ — **shirk·er** *n*

shirr \ˈshər\ *vt* [origin unknown] (1891) **1 :** to draw (as cloth) together in a shirring **2 :** to bake (eggs removed from the shell) until set

shirr·ing \ˈshər-iŋ\ *n* (1882) **:** a decorative gathering (as of cloth) made by drawing up the material along two or more parallel lines of stitching

shirt \ˈshərt\ *n* [ME *shirte,* fr. OE *scyrte;* akin to ON *skyrta* shirt, OE *scort* short] (bef. 12c) **1 :** a garment for the upper part of the body: as **a :** a cloth garment usu. having a collar, sleeves, a front opening, and a tail long enough to be tucked inside trousers or a skirt **b :** UNDERSHIRT **2 :** all or a large part of one's money or resources ⟨lost his ~ on that business deal⟩

shirt·dress \-ˌdres\ *n* (1949) **:** a tailored dress patterned after a shirt and having buttons down the front

shirt·front \-ˌfrənt\ *n* (1838) **:** the front of a shirt; *also* **:** the part of a man's shirt not covered by coat or vest

shirt·ing \-iŋ\ *n* (1604) **:** fabric suitable for shirts

shirt jacket *n* (1879) **:** a jacket designed in the style of a shirt — called also *shirt-jac*

shirt·mak·er \ˈshərt-ˌmā-kər\ *n* (ca. 1858) **:** one that makes shirts

[1]shirt·sleeve \-ˌslēv\ *n* (1566) **:** the sleeve of a shirt — **in shirtsleeves :** wearing a shirt but no coat

[2]shirtsleeve *also* **shirt·sleeves** \-ˌslēvz\ *or* **shirt·sleeved** \-ˌslēvd\ *adj* (1864) **1 a :** being without a coat ⟨a ~ spectator⟩ **b :** calling for the removal of coats for the sake of comfort or efficiency ⟨~ weather⟩ **2 :** marked by informality and directness ⟨~ diplomacy⟩

[1]shirt·tail \ˈshərt-ˌtāl\ *n* (1873) **1 :** the part of a shirt that reaches below the waist esp. in the back **2 :** something small or inadequate

[2]shirttail *adj* (1900) **1 :** very young **:** IMMATURE ⟨~ boys fishing in the creek⟩ **2 :** distantly and indefinitely related ⟨a ~ cousin on her father's side⟩ **3 :** small, trivial, or short typically to the point of inadequacy ⟨has a gullied ~ ranch in the hills⟩

shirt·waist \ˈshərt-ˌwāst\ *n* (1879) **:** a woman's tailored garment (as a blouse or dress) with details copied from men's shirts

shirty \ˈshərt-ē\ *adj, chiefly Brit* (ca. 1859) **:** ANGRY, IRRITATED

shish ke·bab \ˈshish-kə-ˌbäb\ *n* [Arm *shish kabab*] (1936) **:** kabob cooked on skewers

[1]shit \ˈshit\ *vb* **shit** *or* **shat** \ˈshat\; **shit·ting** [alter. (influenced by [2]*shit* and the past and pp. forms) of earlier *shite,* fr. ME *shiten,* fr. OE *-scītan;* akin to MLG & MD *schiten* to defecate, OHG *scīzan,* ON *skīta* to defecate, OE *scēadan* to divide, separate — more at SHED] *vi* (bef. 12c) **:** DEFECATE — usu. considered vulgar ~ *vt* **:** to defecate in — usu. considered vulgar

[2]shit *n* [fr. (assumed) ME, fr. OE *scite* (attested only in place names); akin to MD *schit, schitte* excrement, OE *scītan* to defecate] (bef. 12c) **1 :** EXCREMENT — usu. considered vulgar **2 :** an act of defecation — usu. considered vulgar **3 :** NONSENSE, FOOLISHNESS — usu. considered vulgar **4 :** any of several intoxicating or narcotic drugs; *esp* **:** HEROIN — usu. considered vulgar

shit·tah \ˈshit-ə\ *n, pl* **shittahs** *or* **shit·tim** \ˈshit-əm\ [Heb *shiṭṭāh*] (1611) **:** a tree of uncertain identity but prob. an acacia (as *Acacia seyal*) from the wood of which the ark and fittings of the Hebrew tabernacle were made

shit·tim·wood \ˈshit-əm-ˌwu̇d\ *also* **shittim** *n* [Heb *shiṭṭīm* (pl. of *shiṭṭāh*) + E *wood*] (1588) **1 :** the wood of the shittah tree **2 :** any of several trees (genus *Bumelia,* esp. *B. lanuginosa*) of the sapodilla family of the southern U.S.; *also* **:** their hard heavy dense wood

shiv \ˈshiv\ *n* [prob. fr. Romany *chiv* blade] *slang* (1674) **:** KNIFE

Shi·va \ˈshiv-ə, ˈshē-və\ *var of* SIVA

shiv·a·ree \ˌshiv-ə-ˈrē, ˈshiv-ə-ˌ\ *n* [modif. of F *charivari* — more at CHARIVARI] (1843) **:** a noisy mock serenade to a newly married couple — **shivaree** *vt*

[1]shiv·er \ˈshiv-ər\ *n* [ME; akin to OE *scēadan* to divide — more at SHED] (13c) **:** one of the small pieces into which a brittle thing is broken by sudden violence

[2]shiver *vb* **shiv·ered; shiv·er·ing** \-(ə-)riŋ\ (13c) **:** to break into many small pieces **:** SHATTER

[3]shiver *vb* **shiv·ered; shiv·er·ing** \-(ə-)riŋ\ [ME *shiveren,* alter. of *chiveren*] *vi* (13c) **1 :** to undergo trembling **:** QUIVER **2 :** to tremble in the wind as it strikes first one and then the other side (of a sail) ~ *vt* **:** to cause (a sail) to shiver by steering close to the wind

[4]shiver *n* (1727) **:** an instance of shivering **:** TREMBLE

[1]shiv·ery \ˈshiv-(ə-)rē\ *adj* (1683) **:** easily broken into shivers

[2]shivery *adj* (1747) **1 :** characterized by shivers **2 :** causing shivers

shlemiehl *var of* SCHLEMIEL

shlep, shlepp *var of* SCHLEPP

shlock *var of* SCHLOCK

shm- — see SCHM-

[1]shoal \ˈshōl\ *adj* [alter. of ME *shold,* fr. OE *sceald* — more at SKELETON] (1554) **:** SHALLOW

[2]shoal *n* (1555) **1 :** SHALLOW **2 :** a sandbank or sandbar that makes the water shallow; *specif* **:** an elevation which is not rocky and on which there is a depth of water of six fathoms or less

[3]shoal *vi* (1574) **:** to become shallow ~ *vt* **1 :** to come to a shallow or less deep part of **2 :** to cause to become shallow or less deep

[4]shoal *n* [(assumed) ME *shole,* fr. OE *scolu* multitude — more at SCHOOL] (1579) **:** a large group or number **:** CROWD ⟨a ~ of fish⟩

[5]shoal *vi* (1610) **:** THRONG, SCHOOL

shoat \ˈshōt\ *n* [ME *shote;* akin to Flem *schote* shoat] (15c) **:** a young hog usu. less than one year old

[1]shock \ˈshäk\ *n* [ME; akin to MHG *schoc* heap, OE *hēah* high — more at HIGH] (14c) **:** a pile of sheaves of grain or stalks of Indian corn set up in a field with the butt ends down

[2]shock *vt* (15c) **:** to collect into shocks

[3]shock *n, often attrib* [MF *choc,* fr. *choquer* to strike against, fr. OF *choquier,* prob. of Gmc origin; akin to MD *schocken* to jolt] (ca. 1565) **1 :** the impact or encounter of individuals or groups in combat **2 a :** a violent shake or jar **:** CONCUSSION **b :** an effect of such violence **3 a (1) :** a disturbance in the equilibrium or permanence of something **(2) :** a sudden or violent mental or emotional disturbance **b :** something that causes such disturbance **c :** a state of being so disturbed **4 :** a state of profound depression of the vital processes associated with reduced blood volume and pressure and caused usu. by severe esp. crushing injuries, hemorrhage, or burns **5 :** sudden stimulation of the nerves and convulsive contraction of the muscles caused by the dis-

charge of electricity through the animal body **6 a** : STROKE 5 **b** : CORONARY THROMBOSIS **7** : SHOCK ABSORBER
⁴shock *vt* (1576) **1 a** : to strike with surprise, terror, horror, or disgust **b** : to cause to undergo a physical or nervous shock **c** : to subject to the action of an electrical discharge **2** : to drive by or as if by a shock ~ *vi* **1** : to meet with a shock : COLLIDE **2** : to cause surprise or shock — **shockable** *adj*
⁵shock *adj* [perh. fr. ¹*shock*] (1681) : BUSHY, SHAGGY
⁶shock *n* (1819) : a thick bushy mass (as of hair)
shock absorber *n* (1906) : any of several devices for absorbing the energy of sudden impulses or shocks in machinery or structures
shock·er \ˈshäk-ər\ *n* (ca. 1889) : one that shocks; *esp* : something horrifying or offensive (as a sensational film or work of fiction)
shock front *n* (1950) : the advancing edge of a shock wave
shock·ing *adj* (1703) : extremely startling, distressing, or offensive — **shock·ing·ly** \-iŋ-lē\ *adv*
shocking pink *n* (1938) : a striking, vivid, bright, or intense pink
shock·proof \ˈshäk-ˈprüf\ *adj* (1911) **1** : incapable of being shocked **2 a** : resistant to damage by shock **b** : unlikely to cause shock : protectively insulated ⟨a ~ switch⟩
shock therapy *n* (1937) : the treatment of mental disorder by the artificial induction of coma or convulsions through use of drugs or electricity — called also *shock treatment*
shock troops *n pl* (1917) **1** : troops esp. suited and chosen for offensive work because of their high morale, training, and discipline **2** : a group of people militant in pressing for a cause
shock tube *n* (1949) : a usu. enclosed tube in which experimental shock waves are produced as a result of the rupturing of a diaphragm separating two chambers containing a gas or gases at differential pressure
shock wave *n* (1947) **1** : BLAST 5c **2** : a compressional wave formed whenever the speed of a body or fluid relative to a medium exceeds that at which the medium can transmit sound **3** : a violent often pulsating disturbance or reaction ⟨*shock waves* of rebellion⟩
shod \ˈshäd\ *adj* [ME, fr. pp. of *shoen* to shoe, fr. OE *scōgan,* fr. *scōh* shoe — more at SHOE] (13c) **1 a** : wearing footgear (as shoes) **b** : equipped with tires **2** : furnished or equipped with a shoe
¹shod·dy \ˈshäd-ē\ *n* [origin unknown] (1832) **1 a** : a reclaimed wool from materials that are not felted that is of better quality and longer staple than mungo **b** : a fabric often of inferior quality manufactured wholly or partly from reclaimed wool **2 a** : inferior, imitative, or pretentious articles or matter **b** : pretentious vulgarity
²shoddy *adj* **shod·di·er; -est** (1847) **1** : made wholly or partly of shoddy **2 a** : cheaply imitative : vulgarly pretentious **b** : hastily or poorly done : INFERIOR **c** : SHABBY — **shod·di·ly** \ˈshäd-ᵊl-ē\ *adv* — **shod·di·ness** \ˈshäd-ē-nəs\ *n*
¹shoe \ˈshü\ *n* [ME *shoo,* fr. OE *scōh;* akin to OHG *scuoh* shoe, OE *hӯd* hide] (bef. 12c) **1 a** : an outer covering for the human foot usu. made of leather with a thick or stiff sole and an attached heel **b** : a metal plate or rim for the hoof of an animal **2** : something resembling a shoe: as **a** : a metal band on the runner of a sled **b** : the casing of a pneumatic tire; *broadly* : TIRE **3** *pl* : another's place, function, or viewpoint ⟨steps from assistant stage manager into the star's ~ *s* —Steven Fuller⟩ **4** : a device that retards, stops, or controls the motion of an object; *esp* : the part of a brake that presses on the brake drum **5 a** : any of various devices that are inserted in or run along a track or groove to guide a movement, provide a contact or friction grip, or protect against wear, damage, or slipping **b** : a device (as a clip or track) on a camera that permits attachment of accessory items — called also *accessory shoe* **6** : a dealing box designed to hold several decks of playing cards — **shoe·less** *adj*
²shoe *vt* **shod** \ˈshäd\ *also* **shoed** \ˈshüd\; **shoe·ing** \ˈshü-iŋ\ (bef. 12c) **1** : to furnish with a shoe **2** : to cover for protection, strength, or ornament
shoe·bill \ˈshü-ˌbil\ *n* (1874) : a large broad-billed wading bird (*Balaeniceps rex*) of the valley of the White Nile that is related to the storks and herons
shoe·black \-ˌblak\ *n* (1778) : BOOTBLACK
¹shoe·horn \-ˌhȯ(ə)rn\ *n* (1589) : a curved piece (as of horn, wood, or metal) used in putting on a shoe
²shoehorn *vt* (1926) : to force into a small, narrow, or insufficient space : SQUEEZE ⟨~ the past, present, and future into about 500 pages —Otis Port⟩
shoe·lace \ˈshü-ˌlās\ *n* (1647) : a lace or string for fastening a shoe
shoe·mak·er \-ˌmā-kər\ *n* (14c) : one whose occupation is making or repairing shoes
shoe·pac *or* **shoe·pack** \ˈshü-ˌpak\ *n* [by folk etymology fr. Del *shipak*] (1755) : a waterproof laced boot worn esp. over heavy socks in cold weather
¹shoe·string \ˈshü-ˌstriŋ\ *n* (1616) **1** : SHOELACE **2** [fr. shoestrings being a typical item sold by itinerant vendors] : a small sum of money : capital inadequate or barely adequate to the needs of a transaction ⟨start a business on a ~⟩
²shoestring *adj* (1897) **1** : narrow and long like a shoestring ⟨a ~ tie⟩ **2** : operating on, accomplished by, or consisting of a small amount of capital ⟨a ~ budget⟩
shoestring catch *n* (ca. 1929) : a catch (as in baseball) made very close to the ground
shoe tree *n* (1862) : a foot-shaped device for inserting in a shoe to preserve its shape
sho·far \ˈshō-ˌfär, -fər\ *n, pl* **sho·froth** \shō-ˈfrōt(h), -ˈfrōs\ [Heb *shōphār*] (1864) : a ram's-horn trumpet blown by the ancient Hebrews in battle and high religious observances and used in synagogues before and during Rosh Hashanah and at the conclusion of Yom Kippur
¹shog \ˈshäg\ *vi* **shogged; shog·ging** [ME *shoggen*] *chiefly dial* (15c) : to move along
²shog *n, chiefly dial* (1611) : SHAKE, JOLT
sho·gun \ˈshō-gən\ *n* [Jp *shōgun* general] (1615) : one of a line of military governors ruling Japan until the revolution of 1867–68 — **sho·gun·ate** \ˈshō-gə-nət, -ˌnāt\ *n*
sho·ji \ˈshō-(ˌ)jē\ *n, pl* **shoji** *also* **shojis** [Jp *shōji*] (1880) : a paper screen serving as a wall, partition, or sliding door
sho·lom \shä-ˈlōm, shə-\ *var of* SHALOM
shone *past and past part of* SHINE

¹shoo \ˈshü\ *interj* [ME *schowe*] (15c) — used in frightening away an animal (as a hen)
²shoo *vt* (1622) : to scare, drive, or send away by or as if by crying *shoo*
shoo·fly \ˈshü-ˌflī\ *n* [¹*shoo* + *fly*] (1902) **1** : a child's rocker having the seat built on or usu. between supports representing an animal figure **2** : any of several plants held to repel flies
shoofly pie *n* (1926) : a rich pie of Pennsylvania-Dutch origin made of molasses or brown sugar sprinkled with a crumbly mixture of flour, sugar, and butter
shoo–in \ˈshü-ˌin\ *n* (ca. 1950) : one that is a certain and easy winner
¹shook *past or chiefly dial past part of* SHAKE
²shook \ˈshu̇k\ *n* [origin unknown] (1768) **1 a** : a set of staves and headings for one hogshead, cask, or barrel **b** : a bundle of parts (as of boxes) ready to be put together **2** : ¹ SHOCK
shook–up \(ˈ)shu̇k-ˈəp\ *adj* [*shook,* substandard pp. of *shake*] (1897) : nervously upset : AGITATED
shoon \ˈshün, ˈshōn\ *chiefly dial pl of* SHOE
¹shoot \ˈshüt\ *vb* **shot** \ˈshät\; **shoot·ing** [ME *sheten, shuten,* fr. OE *scēotan;* akin to ON *skjōta* to shoot, Lith *skudrus* quick] *vt* (bef. 12c) **1 a** (1) : to eject or impel or cause to be ejected or impelled by a sudden release of tension (as of a bowstring or slingshot or by a flick of a finger) ⟨~ an arrow⟩ ⟨~ a spitball⟩ ⟨~ a marble⟩ (2) : to drive forth or cause to be driven forth by an explosion (as of a powder charge in a firearm or of ignited fuel in a rocket) (3) : to drive forth or cause to be driven forth by a sudden release of gas or air ⟨~ darts from a blowgun⟩ ⟨a steam catapult ~*s* planes from a carrier⟩ (4) : to propel (as a ball or puck) toward a goal by striking or pushing with the arm or hand or with an implement; *also* : to score by so doing ⟨~ the winning goal⟩ ⟨~ a basket⟩ (5) : to throw or cast off or out often with force ⟨~ dice⟩ ⟨the horse *shot* his rider out of the saddle⟩ **b** (1) : to utter (as words or sounds) rapidly or suddenly or with force ⟨~ out a stream of invective⟩ (2) : to emit (as light, flame, or fumes) suddenly and rapidly (3) : to send forth with suddenness or intensity ⟨*shot* a look of anger at them⟩ **c** : to discharge, dump, or empty esp. by overturning, upending, or directing into a slide **2** : to affect by shooting: as **a** : to strike with a missile esp. from a bow or gun; *esp* : to wound or kill with a missile discharged from a bow or firearm **b** : to remove or destroy by use of firearms ⟨*shot* out the light⟩; *also* : WRECK, EXPLODE **3 a** : to push or slide (as the bolt of a door or lock) into or out of a fastening **b** : to pass (a shuttle) through the warp threads in weaving **c** : to push or thrust forward : stick out ⟨toads ~*ing* out their tongues⟩ **d** : to put forth in growing **e** : to place, send, or bring into position abruptly **4 a** : to engage in (a sport or game or a portion of a game that involves shooting) : PLAY ⟨~ pool⟩ ⟨~ a round of golf⟩ ⟨~ craps⟩ **b** (1) : to place or offer (a bet) on the result of casting dice ⟨~ $5⟩ (2) : to use up by or as if by betting : EXHAUST ⟨*shot* his whole wad on a shady deal⟩ **5 a** : to engage in the hunting and killing of (as game) with firearms esp. as a sport ⟨~ woodcock⟩ **b** : to hunt over ⟨~ a tract of woodland⟩ **6 a** : to cause to move suddenly or swiftly forward ⟨*shot* the car onto the highway⟩ **b** : to send or carry quickly : DISPATCH ⟨~ the letter on to me as soon as you receive it⟩ **7** : to variegate as if by sprinkling color in streaks, flecks, or patches **8** : to pass swiftly by, past, or along ⟨~*ing* rapids⟩ **9** : to plane (as the edge of a board) straight or true **10 a** : to set off : DETONATE, IGNITE ⟨~ a charge of dynamite⟩ **b** : to effect by blasting **11** : to determine the altitude of **12** : to take a picture or series of pictures or television images of : PHOTOGRAPH, FILM **13 a** : to give an injection to **b** : to inject (an illicit drug) esp. into the bloodstream ~ *vi* **1 a** : to go or pass rapidly and precipitately ⟨sparks ~*ing* all over⟩ ⟨his feet *shot* out from under him⟩ **b** : to move ahead by force of momentum **c** : to stream out suddenly : SPURT **d** : to dart in or as if in rays from a source of light **e** : to dart with a piercing sensation ⟨pain *shot* up my arm⟩ **2 a** : to cause an engine or weapon to discharge a missile **b** : to use a firearm or bow esp. for sport (as in hunting) **3** : to propel a missile ⟨guns that ~ many miles⟩ **4** : PROTRUDE, PROJECT **5 a** : to grow or sprout by or as if by putting forth shoots **b** : DEVELOP, MATURE **c** : to spring or rise rapidly or suddenly — often used with *up* ⟨in a burst of growth he *shot* up to six feet tall⟩ ⟨prices *shot* up⟩ **6 a** : to propel an object (as a ball) in a particular way **b** : to drive the ball or puck toward a goal **7** : to cast dice **8** : to slide into or out of a fastening ⟨a bolt that ~*s* in either direction⟩ **9 a** : to record visually (as on movie film or videotape) a scene of a motion picture or television production **b** : to operate a camera or set cameras in operation : FILM **10** : to begin to speak — usu. used as an imperative ⟨OK, ~, what do you have to say⟩ — **shoot at** *or* **shoot for** : to aim at : strive for — **shoot from the hip** : to act or speak hastily without consideration of the consequences — **shoot one's bolt** : to exhaust one's capabilities and resources — **shoot the breeze** : to converse idly : GOSSIP — **shoot the works 1** : to venture all one's capital on one play **2** : to put forth all one's efforts
²shoot *n* (15c) **1** : a sending out of new growth or the growth sent out: as **a** : a stem or branch with its leaves and appendages esp. when not yet mature **b** : OFFSHOOT **c** : a similar formation of crystal **2 a** : an act of shooting (as with a bow or a firearm): (1) : SHOT (2) : the firing of a missile esp. by artillery **b** (1) : a hunting trip or party (2) : the right to shoot game in a particular area or land over which it is held **c** (1) : a shooting match ⟨skeet ~⟩ (2) : a round of shots in a shooting match **d** (1) : the action or an instance of shooting with a camera (2) : a launching of a rocket device or a guided missile esp. experimentally **3 a** : a motion or movement of rapid thrusting: as (1) : a sudden or rapid advance (2) : a momentary darting sensation : TWINGE (3) : THRUST 2b (4) : a falling of a detached mass of earth or ice (5) : the pace between strokes in rowing **b** : a bar of rays : BEAM ⟨a ~ of sunlight⟩ **4** [prob. by folk etymology fr. F *chute* — more at CHUTE] **a** : a rush of water down a steep or rapid **b** : a place where a stream runs or descends swiftly **c** : any of various inclined channels or troughs through which something (as water, logs, or grain) is moved **5** : an elongated usu. vertical body of ore in a vein
³shoot *interj* [euphemism for *shit*] (1876) — used to express annoyance or surprise
shoot down *vt* (1845) **1** : to bring down by shooting ⟨*shot* him *down* in cold blood⟩ ⟨enemy aircraft *shot down* the helicopter⟩ **2** : to put an end to : DEFEAT **3** : DEFLATE, RIDICULE **4** : DISCREDIT 2 ⟨*shoot down* a theory⟩

shoot–'em–up \'shüt-ə-,məp\ *n* (1947) **:** a movie or television show with much shooting and bloodshed

shoot·er \'shüt-ər\ *n* (13c) **1 :** one that shoots: as **a :** a person who fires a missile-discharging device (as a rifle or bow) **b :** the person who is shooting or whose turn it is to shoot **2 :** something that is used in shooting: as **a :** a marble shot from the hand **b :** REVOLVER — usu. used in combination ⟨six-*shooter*⟩

shooting gallery *n* (1836) **1 :** a usu. covered range equipped with targets for practice with firearms **2** *slang* **:** a place where one can obtain narcotics and shoot up

shooting iron *n* (1787) **:** FIREARM

shooting script *n* (ca. 1930) **1 :** the final completely detailed version of a motion-picture script in which scenes are grouped in the order most convenient for shooting **2 :** the final version of a television script used in the production of a program

shooting star *n* (1593) **1 :** a visual meteor appearing as a temporary streak of light in the night sky **2 :** any of several No. American perennial herbs (genus *Dodecatheon,* esp. *D. meadia*) of the primrose family that have entire oblong leaves and showy flowers with reflexed petals

shooting stick *n* (1683) **:** a spiked stick with a top that opens into a seat

shoot–out \'shüt-,au̇t\ *n* (1948) **1 :** a battle fought with handguns or rifles **2 :** something resembling a shoot-out; *broadly* **:** SHOWDOWN

shoot–the–chutes \,shüt-t͟hə-'shüts\ *n pl but sing in constr* (1923) **:** an amusement ride consisting of a steep incline down which boats slide into a pool at the bottom

shoot up \(')shüt-'əp\ *vt* (1577) **1 :** to shoot or shoot at esp. indiscriminately or recklessly ⟨cowboys *shooting up* the town⟩ **2 :** to inject (a narcotic drug) into a vein **~** *vi* **:** to inject a narcotic into a vein — **shoot–up** \'shüt-,əp\ *n*

[1]shop \'shäp\ *n, often attrib* [ME *shoppe,* fr. OE *sceoppa* booth; akin to OHG *scopf* shed] (bef. 12c) **1 :** a handicraft establishment **:** ATELIER **2 a :** a building or room stocked with merchandise for sale **:** STORE **b** *or* **shoppe** \'shäp\ **:** a small retail establishment or a department in a large one offering a specified line of goods or services ⟨a millinery ~⟩ ⟨a sandwich ~⟩ **3 :** FACTORY, MILL **4 a :** a school laboratory equipped for manual training **b :** the art or science of working with tools and machinery **5 a :** a business establishment; *esp* **:** OFFICE **b :** SHOPTALK

[2]shop *vb* **shopped; shop·ping** *vi* (1764) **1 a :** to examine goods or services with intent to buy **b :** to hunt through a market in search of the best buy **2 :** to make a search **:** HUNT **~** *vt* **:** to examine the stock or offerings of ⟨~ the stores for Christmas gift ideas⟩

shop·keep·er \'shäp-,kē-pər\ *n* (ca. 1530) **:** STOREKEEPER 2

shop·lift \-,lift\ *vb* [back-formation fr. *shoplifter*] *vt* (1698) **:** to steal (goods on display) from a store **~** *vi* **:** to steal displayed goods from a store

shop·lift·er \-,lif-tər\ *n* (1680) **:** one who shoplifts

shop·per \'shäp-ər\ *n* (1862) **1 :** one that shops **2 :** one whose occupation is shopping as an agent for customers or for an employer **3 :** a usu. free paper carrying advertising and sometimes local news

shopping bag *n* (1926) **:** a bag (as of strong paper) that has handles and is intended for carrying purchases

shopping–bag lady *n* (1976) **:** a homeless woman who roams the streets of a large city carrying her possessions in a shopping bag

shopping center *n* (1939) **:** a group of retail stores and service establishments usu. with ample parking facilities and usu. designed to serve a community or neighborhood — called also *shopping plaza*

shopping list *n* (1970) **:** a list of items to be purchased; *broadly* **:** a list of related items ⟨the biggest possible *shopping list* of budget cuts —Leonard Silk⟩

shopping mall *n* (1959) **1 :** a pedestrian mall lined by shops **2 :** a shopping center with stores facing an enclosed mall

shop steward *n* (1915) **:** a union member elected as the union representative of a shop or department in dealings with the management

shop·talk \'shäp-,tȯk\ *n* (1881) **:** the jargon or subject matter peculiar to an occupation or a special area of interest

shop·worn \-,wō(ə)rn, -,wȯ(ə)rn\ *adj* (1871) **1 :** faded, soiled, or otherwise impaired by remaining too long in a store **2 :** stale from excessive use or familiarity ⟨~ clichés⟩ **3 :** WORN-OUT ⟨think of himself as a ~ Hollywood cynic —A.H. Johnston⟩

sho·ran \'shō(ə)r-,an, 'shȯ(ə)r-\ *n* [*short-range navigation*] (ca. 1932) **:** a system of short-range navigation in which two radar signals transmitted by an airplane are intercepted and rebroadcast to the airplane by two ground stations of known position so as to determine the position of the airplane

[1]shore \'shō(ə)r, 'shȯ(ə)r\ *n, often attrib* [ME, fr. (assumed) OE *scor;* akin to OE *scieran* to cut — more at SHEAR] (14c) **1 :** the land bordering a usu. large body of water; *specif* **:** COAST **2 :** a boundary or the country or place that it bounds ⟨hold him accountable for difficulties beyond our ~*s* that he could do nothing about—Dorothy Fosdick⟩ **3 :** land as distinguished from the sea ⟨shipboard and ~ duty⟩

[2]shore *vt* **shored; shor·ing** [ME *shoren;* akin to ON *skortha* to prop] (14c) **1 :** to support by a shore **:** PROP **2 :** to give support to **:** BRACE — usu. used with *up*

[3]shore *n* (15c) **:** a prop for preventing sinking or sagging

shore·bird \'shō(ə)r-,bərd, 'shȯ(ə)r-\ *n* (1672) **:** any of a suborder (Charadrii) of birds (as a plover or snipe) that frequent the seashore

shore dinner *n* (1892) **:** a dinner consisting chiefly of seafoods

shore·front \-,frənt\ *n* (1919) **:** land along a shore; *specif* **:** BEACHFRONT

shore leave *n* (ca. 1909) **:** a leave of absence to go on shore granted to a sailor or naval officer

shore·line \-,līn\ *n* (1852) **:** the line where a body of water and the shore meet; *also* **:** the strip of land along this line

shore patrol *n* (ca. 1942) **1 :** a branch of a navy that exercises guard and police functions — compare MILITARY POLICE **2 :** petty officers detailed to perform police duty while a ship is in port

shore·side \-,sīd\ *adj* (1571) **:** situated at or near a shore

shore·ward \-wərd\ *or* **shore·wards** \-wərdz\ *adv* (1582) **:** toward the shore

shor·ing \'shōr-iŋ, 'shȯr-\ *n* (15c) **1 :** the act of supporting with or as if with a prop **2 :** a system or group of shores

shorn *past part of* SHEAR

[1]short \'shȯ(ə)rt\ *adj* [ME, fr. OE *scort*] (bef. 12c) **1 a :** having little length **b :** not tall or high **:** LOW **2 a :** not extended in time **:** BRIEF ⟨a ~ vacation⟩ **b :** not retentive ⟨a ~ memory⟩ **c :** EXPEDITIOUS, QUICK ⟨made ~ work of the problem⟩ **d :** seeming to pass quickly ⟨made great progress in just a few ~ years⟩ **3 a** *of a speech sound* **:** having a relatively short duration **b :** being the member of a pair of similarly spelled vowel or vowel-containing sounds that is descended from a vowel that was short in duration but is no longer so and that does not necessarily have duration as its chief distinguishing feature ⟨~ *i* in *sin*⟩ **c** *of a syllable in prosody* **(1) :** of relatively brief duration **(2) :** UNSTRESSED **4 :** limited in distance ⟨a ~ trip⟩ **5 a :** not coming up to a measure or requirement **:** INSUFFICIENT ⟨in ~ supply⟩ **b :** not reaching far enough ⟨the throw to first was ~⟩ **c :** enduring privation **d :** insufficiently supplied ⟨~ of cash⟩ ⟨~ on brains⟩ **6 a :** ABRUPT, CURT **b :** quickly provoked **7 :** [3]CHOPPY 1 **8 :** payable at an early date **9 a :** containing or cooked with shortening; *also* **:** FLAKY ⟨~ pastry⟩ **b** *of metal* **:** brittle under certain conditions **10 a :** not lengthy or drawn out **b :** made briefer **:** ABBREVIATED **11 a :** not having goods or property that one has sold in anticipation of a fall in prices **b :** consisting of or relating to a sale of securities or commodities that the seller does not possess or has not contracted for at the time of the sale ⟨~ sale⟩ **12 :** near the end of a tour of duty ***syn*** see BRIEF — **short·ish** \'shȯrt-ish\ *adj* — **in short order :** with dispatch **:** QUICKLY

[2]short *adv* (14c) **1 :** in a curt manner **2 :** for or during a brief time ⟨*short*-lasting⟩ **3 :** at a disadvantage **:** UNAWARES ⟨caught ~⟩ **4 :** in an abrupt manner **:** SUDDENLY ⟨the car stopped ~⟩ **5 :** at some point or degree before a goal or limit aimed at or under consideration ⟨the shells fell ~⟩ ⟨quit a month ~ of graduation⟩ **6 :** clean across ⟨the axle was snapped ~⟩ **7 :** by or as if by a short sale

[3]short *n* (1586) **1 :** the sum and substance **:** UPSHOT **2 a :** a short syllable **b :** a short sound or signal **3** *pl* **a :** a by-product of wheat milling that includes the germ, fine bran, and some flour **b :** refuse, clippings, or trimmings discarded in various manufacturing processes **4 a :** knee-length or less than knee-length trousers — usu. used in pl. **b** *pl* **:** short drawers **c :** a size in clothing for short men **5 a :** one who operates on the short side of the market **b** *pl* **:** short-term bonds **6** *pl* **:** DEFICIENCIES **7 :** SHORT CIRCUIT **8 :** SHORTSTOP **9 :** SHORT SUBJECT — **in short :** by way of summary **:** BRIEFLY

[4]short *vt* (1952) **1 :** SHORTCHANGE, CHEAT **2 :** SHORT-CIRCUIT

short account *n* (ca. 1902) **:** the total of open short sales in a given subject of trade or in the market as a whole

short·age \'shȯrt-ij\ *n* (1868) **:** LACK, DEFICIT

short ballot *n* (ca. 1911) **:** a ballot limiting the number of elective offices to the most important legislative and executive posts and leaving minor positions to be filled by appointment

short·bread \'shȯrt-,bred\ *n* (1801) **:** a thick cookie made of flour, sugar, and a large amount of shortening

short·cake \-,kāk\ *n* (1594) **1 :** a crisp and often unsweetened biscuit or cookie **2 a :** a dessert made typically of very short baking-powder-biscuit dough spread with sweetened fruit **b :** a dish consisting of a rich biscuit split and covered with a meat mixture

short·change \-'chānj\ *vt* (1903) **1 :** to give less than the correct amount of change to **2 :** to deprive of or give less than something due **:** CHEAT — **short·chang·er** *n*

short–cir·cuit *vt* (1873) **1 :** to apply a short circuit to or establish a short circuit in **2 :** BYPASS **3 :** FRUSTRATE, IMPEDE

short circuit *n* (1876) **:** a connection of comparatively low resistance accidentally or intentionally made between points on a circuit between which the resistance is normally much greater

short·com·ing \'shȯrt-,kəm-iŋ, (')shȯrt-'\ *n* (1680) **:** DEFICIENCY, DEFECT

[1]short·cut \'shȯrt-,kət, -'kət\ *n* (1796) **1 :** a route more direct than the one ordinarily taken **2 :** a method of doing something more directly and quickly than and often not so thoroughly as by ordinary procedure

[2]shortcut *vt* (1917) **:** to shorten (as a route or procedure) by use of a shortcut; *also* **:** CIRCUMVENT **~** *vi* **:** to take or use a shortcut

short–day \'shȯrt-,dā\ *adj* (ca. 1929) **:** responding to or relating to a short photoperiod — used esp. of a plant; compare DAY-NEUTRAL, LONG-DAY

short division *n* (ca. 1897) **:** mathematical division in which the successive steps are performed without writing out the remainders

short·en \'shȯrt-ᵊn\ *vb* **short·ened; short·en·ing** \'shȯrt-niŋ, -ᵊn-iŋ\ *vt* (1513) **1 a :** to reduce the length or duration of **b :** to cause to seem short **2 a :** to reduce in power or efficiency ⟨is my hand ~*ed,* that it cannot redeem —Isa 50:2 (RSV)⟩ **b** *obs* **:** to deprive of effect **3 :** to add fat to (pastry dough) in order to make tender and flaky **~** *vi* **:** to become short or shorter — **short·en·er** \-nər, -ᵊn-ər\ *n*

syn SHORTEN, CURTAIL, ABBREVIATE, ABRIDGE, RETRENCH mean to reduce in extent. SHORTEN implies reduction in length or duration; CURTAIL adds an implication of cutting that in some way deprives of completeness or adequacy; ABBREVIATE implies a making shorter usu. by omitting some part; ABRIDGE implies a reduction in compass or scope with retention of essential elements and a relative completeness in the result; RETRENCH suggests a reduction in extent or costs of something felt to be excessive.

short·en·ing \'shȯrt-niŋ, -ᵊn-iŋ\ *n* (1542) **1 :** the action or process of making or becoming short; *specif* **:** the dropping of the latter part of a word so as to produce a new and shorter word of the same meaning **2 :** an edible fat used to shorten baked goods

short·fall \'shȯrt-,fȯl\ *n* (1895) **:** a failure to come up to expectation or need; *also* **:** the amount of such failure

short·grass \-,gras\ *n* (1844) **:** any of various drought-resistant grasses of short stature that form the dominant feature of dry upland plains (as those just east of the Rocky Mountains) and include important range grasses ⟨~ prairies⟩

short·hair \-,ha(ə)r, -,he(ə)r\ *n* (1903) **:** a domestic cat with a short thick coat; *esp* **:** one of either of two breeds of muscular medium-sized cats with a short plushy coat — **short·haired** *adj*

short·hand \-ˌhand\ *n* (1636) **1 :** a method of writing rapidly by substituting characters, abbreviations, or symbols for letters, sounds, words, or phrases : STENOGRAPHY **2 :** a system or instance of rapid or abbreviated communication — **shorthand** *adj*
short·hand·ed \-ˈhan-dəd\ *adj* (1794) **:** having, working with, or done with fewer than the regular or necessary number of people
short–haul \-ˌhȯl\ *adj* (1895) **:** traveling or involving a short distance ⟨~ flights⟩
short·horn \-ˌhȯ(ə)rn\ *n, often cap* (1826) **:** any of a breed of red, roan, or white beef cattle originating in the north of England and including good milk-producing strains — called also *Durham*

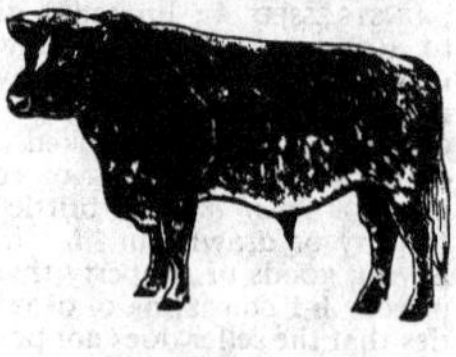
shorthorn

short–horned grasshopper \ˌshȯrt-ˌhȯrn(d)-\ *n* (ca. 1890) **:** any of a family (Acrididae) of grasshoppers with short antennae
short hundredweight *n* (1924) **:** HUNDREDWEIGHT 1
short·leaf pine \ˌshȯrt-ˌlēf-\ *n* (1796) **:** a pine (*Pinus echinata*) of the southern U.S. that has short flexible leaves and cinnamon-colored bark; *also* **:** its yellow wood
short line *n* (1917) **:** a transportation system (as a railroad) operating over a relatively short distance
short·list \ˈshȯrt-ˌlist\ *n, Brit* (1927) **:** a list of candidates for final consideration (as for a position or a prize) — **short–list** *vt, Brit*
short–lived \ˈshȯrt-ˈlīvd, -ˈlivd\ *adj* (1588) **:** not living or lasting long ⟨~ insects⟩ ⟨~ joy⟩
short loin *n* (ca. 1934) **:** a portion of the hindquarter of beef immediately behind the ribs that is usu. cut into steaks — see BEEF illustration
short·ly \ˈshȯrt-lē\ *adv* (bef. 12c) **1 a :** in a few words **:** BRIEFLY **b :** in an abrupt manner **2 a :** in a short time ⟨we will be there ~⟩ **b :** at a short interval ⟨~ after sunset⟩
short·ness \-nəs\ *n* (bef. 12c) **:** the quality or state of being short
short–nosed cattle louse \ˌshȯrt-ˌnōz(d)-\ *n* (1942) **:** a large bluish broad-bodied and short-headed sucking louse (*Haematopinus eurysternus*) that attacks domestic cattle
short order *n* (1906) **:** an order for food that can be quickly cooked — **short–order** *adj*
short–range \ˈshȯrt-ˈrānj\ *adj* (1869) **1 :** involving or taking into account a short period of time ⟨~ plans⟩ **2 :** relating to or fit for short distances
short ribs *n pl* (1912) **:** a cut of beef consisting of rib ends between the rib roast and the plate — see BEEF illustration
short run *n* (1879) **:** a relatively brief period of time — often used in the phrase *in the short run* — **short–run** *adj*
short shrift *n* (1594) **1 :** barely adequate time for confession before execution **2 a :** little or no attention or consideration **b :** quick work — usu. used in the phrase *make short shrift of*
short sight *n* (ca. 1822) **:** MYOPIA
short·sight·ed \ˈshȯrt-ˈsīt-əd\ *adj* (1649) **1 :** NEARSIGHTED **2 :** lacking foresight — **short·sight·ed·ly** *adv* — **short·sight·ed·ness** *n*
short–spo·ken \-ˈspō-kən\ *adj* (1865) **:** CURT
short·stop \-ˌstäp\ *n* (1857) **1 :** the player position in baseball for defending the infield area on the third-base side of second base **2 :** the player stationed in the shortstop position
short–stop \-ˌstäp\ *n* (1936) **:** STOP BATH
short story *n* (1877) **:** an invented prose narrative shorter than a novel usu. dealing with a few characters and aiming at unity of effect and often concentrating on the creation of mood rather than plot
short subject *n* (1944) **:** a brief often documentary or educational film
short–tem·pered \ˈshȯrt-ˈtem-pərd\ *adj* (1900) **:** having a quick temper
short–term \-ˈtərm\ *adj* (1901) **1 :** occurring over or involving a relatively short period of time **2 a :** of, relating to, or constituting a financial operation or obligation based on a brief term and esp. one of less than a year **b :** generated by assets held for less than six months
short ton *n* (1881) — see WEIGHT table
short·wave \ˈshȯrt-ˈwāv\ *n, often attrib* (1902) **1 :** a radio wave having a wavelength between 10 and 100 meters **2 :** a radio transmitter using shortwaves **3 :** electromagnetic radiation having a wavelength equal to or less than that of visible light
short–weight \(ˈ)shȯrt-ˈwāt\ *vt* (1926) **:** to defraud with short weight
short weight \ˈshȯrt-ˈwāt\ *n* (1789) **:** weight less than the stated weight or less than one is charged for
short–wind·ed \-ˈwin-dəd\ *adj* (15c) **1 :** affected with or characterized by shortness of breath **2 a :** BRIEF **b :** broken up into short units
shorty *or* **short·ie** \ˈshȯrt-ē\ *n, pl* **short·ies** (1888) **:** one that is short
Sho·shone \shə-ˈshōn(-ē), ˈshō-ˌshōn\ *or* **Sho·sho·ni** \shə-ˈshō-nē\ *n, pl* **Shoshones** *or* **Shoshoni** *also* **Shoshone** *or* **Shoshonis** (1805) **1 :** a group of American Indian peoples orig. ranging through California, Colorado, Idaho, Nevada, Utah, and Wyoming **2 :** a member of any of the Shoshone peoples
Sho·sho·ne·an \-nē-ən\ *n* (1892) **:** a language family of the Uto-Aztecan phylum comprising the languages of most of the Uto-Aztecan peoples in the U.S.
¹shot \ˈshät\ *n* [ME, fr. OE *scot;* akin to ON *skot* shot, OHG *scuz,* OE *scēotan* to shoot — more at SHOOT] (bef. 12c) **1 a :** an action of shooting **b :** a directed propelling of a missile; *specif* **:** a directed discharge of a firearm **c :** a stroke or throw in an attempt to score points in a game (as tennis, pool, or basketball); *also* **:** HOME RUN **d :** BLAST **e :** a medical or narcotics injection **2 a** *pl* **shot :** something propelled by shooting; *esp* **:** small lead or steel pellets esp. forming a charge for a shotgun **b :** a metal sphere of iron or brass that is heaved in the shot-put **3 a :** the distance that a missile is or can be thrown **b :** RANGE, REACH **4 :** a charge to be paid **:** SCOT **5 :** one that shoots; *esp* **:** MARKSMAN **6 a :** ATTEMPT, TRY **b :** GUESS, CONJECTURE **c :** CHANCE **d :** a single appearance as an entertainer ⟨did a guest ~ for the program⟩ **7 :** an effective remark **8 a :** a single photographic exposure; *esp* **:** SNAPSHOT **b :** a single sequence of a motion picture or a television program shot by one camera without interruption **9 :** a charge of explosives **10 a :** a small measure or serving (as one ounce) of undiluted liquor **b :** a small amount applied at one time **:** DOSE **11 :** THROW 7 **12 shot** *pl* **:** SPRINKLE 3, JIMMIES — **like a shot :** very rapidly — **shot in the arm :** STIMULUS, BOOST — **shot in the dark 1 :** a wild guess **2 :** an attempt that has little chance of success
²shot *past and past part of* SHOOT
³shot *adj* (1763) **1 a** *of a fabric* **:** having contrasting and changeable color effects **:** IRIDESCENT **b :** suffused or streaked with a color ⟨hair ~ with gray⟩ **c :** infused or permeated with a quality or element ⟨~ through with wit⟩ **2 :** having the form of pellets resembling shot **3 :** reduced to a state of ruin, prostration, or uselessness ⟨his nerves are ~⟩
¹shot·gun \ˈshät-ˌgən\ *n* (1776) **1 :** a smoothbore shoulder weapon for firing shot at short ranges **2 :** an offensive football formation in which the quarterback plays a few yards behind the line of scrimmage and the other backs are scattered as flankers or slotbacks — **shotgun** *vt* — **shot·gun·ner** \-ər\ *n*
²shotgun *adj* (1892) **1 :** of, relating to, or using a shotgun **2 :** involving coercion **3 :** covering a wide field with hit-or-miss effectiveness
shotgun house *n* (1940) **:** a house in which all the rooms are in direct line with each other usu. front to back — called also *shotgun cottage;* compare RAILROAD FLAT
shotgun marriage *n* (1929) **1 :** a marriage forced or required because of pregnancy — called also *shotgun wedding* **2 :** a forced union ⟨a spate of brokerage mergers . . . hastily arranged *shotgun marriages* —John Brooks⟩
shot hole *n* (1875) **1 :** a drilled hole in which a charge of dynamite is exploded **2 :** the dropping out of small rounded fragments of leaves that produces a shot-riddled appearance and is caused esp. by parasitic action
shot put *n* (1898) **:** a field event in which a shot is heaved for distance — **shot–put·ter** \ˈshät-ˌpu̇t-ər\ *n*
shott *var of* CHOTT
shot·ten \ˈshät-ᵊn\ *adj* [ME *shotyn,* fr. pp. of *shuten* to shoot] (15c) **:** having ejected the spawn and so of inferior food value ⟨~ herring⟩
should \shəd, (ˈ)shu̇d\ [ME *sholde,* fr. OE *sceolde* owed, was obliged to; akin to OHG *scolta* owed, was obliged to] *past of* SHALL (bef. 12c) **1 —** used in auxiliary function to express condition ⟨if he ~ leave his father, his father would die —Gen 44:22 (RSV)⟩ **2 —** used in auxiliary function to express obligation, propriety, or expediency ⟨'tis commanded I ~ do so —Shak.⟩ ⟨this is as it ~ be —H. L. Savage⟩ ⟨you ~ brush your teeth after each meal⟩ **3 —** used in auxiliary function to express futurity from a point of view in the past ⟨realized that she ~ have to do most of her farm work before sunrise —Ellen Glasgow⟩ **4 —** used in auxiliary function to express what is probable or expected ⟨with an early start, they ~ be here by noon⟩ **5 —** used in auxiliary function to express a request in a polite manner or to soften direct statement ⟨I ~ suggest that a guide . . . is the first essential —L. D. Reddick⟩
¹shoul·der \ˈshōl-dər\ *n* [ME *sholder,* fr. OE *sculdor;* akin to OHG *scultra* shoulder, OE *sciell* shell — more at SHELL] (bef. 12c) **1 a :** the laterally projecting part of the human body formed of the bones and joints by which the arm is connected with the trunk and the muscles covering them **b :** the region of the body of a lower vertebrate that corresponds to the shoulder but is less projecting **2 a :** the two shoulders and the upper part of the back — usu. used in pl. **b** *pl* **:** capacity for bearing a task or blame ⟨placed the guilt squarely on his ~*s*⟩ **3 :** a cut of meat including the upper joint of the foreleg and adjacent parts — see LAMB illustration **4 :** the part of a garment at the wearer's shoulder **5 :** an area adjacent to or along the edge of a higher, more prominent, or more important part: as **a** (1) **:** the part of a hill or mountain near the top (2) **:** a lateral protrusion or extension of a hill or mountain **b :** either edge of a roadway; *specif* **:** the part of a roadway outside of the traveled way **6 :** a rounded or sloping part (as of a stringed instrument or a bottle) where the neck joins the body — **shouldered** \-dərd\ *adj*
²shoulder *vb* **shoul·dered; shoul·der·ing** \-d(ə-)riŋ\ *vt* (14c) **1 :** to push or thrust with or as if with the shoulder **:** JOSTLE ⟨~*ed* his way through the crowd⟩ **2 a :** to place or bear on the shoulder ⟨~*ed* his knapsack and took off⟩ **b :** to assume the burden or responsibility of ⟨~ the blame⟩ ~ *vi* **:** to push with or as if with the shoulders aggressively
shoulder bag *n* (1912) **:** a usu. woman's handbag looped over the shoulder by a strap
shoulder belt *n* (1967) **:** an automobile safety belt worn across the torso and over the shoulder — called also *shoulder harness*
shoulder blade *n* (14c) **:** SCAPULA
shoulder board *n* (1945) **:** one of a pair of broad pieces of stiffened cloth worn on the shoulders of a military uniform and carrying insignia
shoulder girdle *n* (1868) **:** PECTORAL GIRDLE
shoulder knot *n* (1676) **1 :** an ornamental knot of ribbon or lace worn on the shoulder in the 17th and 18th centuries **2 :** a detachable ornament of braided wire cord worn on ceremonial occasions on the shoulders of a uniform by a commissioned officer
shoulder mark *n* (ca. 1909) **:** SHOULDER BOARD
shoulder patch *n* (1945) **:** a cloth patch bearing an identifying mark and worn on one sleeve of a uniform below the shoulder
shoulder strap *n* (1688) **:** a strap that passes across the shoulder and holds up an article or garment
should·est \ˈshu̇d-əst\ *archaic past 2d sing of* SHALL
shouldn't \ˈshu̇d-ᵊnt, -ᵊn, *dial also* ˈshu̇t-ᵊn(t) *or* (ˈ)shu̇nt\ **:** should not
shouldst \shədst, (ˈ)shu̇dst, shətst, (ˈ)shu̇tst\ *archaic past 2d sing of* SHALL
¹shout \ˈshau̇t\ *vb* [ME *shouten*] *vi* (14c) **1 :** to utter a sudden loud cry **2 :** to command attention as if by shouting ⟨a quality that ~*s* from good novels—John Gardner⟩ ~ *vt* **1 :** to utter in a loud voice **2 :** to cause to be, come, or stop by or as if by shouting ⟨~*ed* himself hoarse⟩ ⟨the proponents ~*ed* down the opposition⟩ — **shout·er** *n*
²shout *n* (14c) **:** a loud cry or call
shouting distance *n* (1930) **:** a short distance **:** easy reach — usu. used with *within* ⟨lived within *shouting distance* of his cousins⟩
shout song *n* (1925) **:** a rhythmic religious song used esp. by Negroes and characterized by responsive singing or shouting between leader and congregation
¹shove \ˈshəv\ *vb* **shoved; shov·ing** [ME *shoven,* fr. OE *scūfan* to thrust away; akin to OHG *scioban* to push, OSlav *skubati* to tear] *vt* (bef. 12c) **1 :** to push along **2 :** to push or put in a rough, careless, or hasty manner **:** THRUST **3 :** to force by other than physical means **:** COMPEL

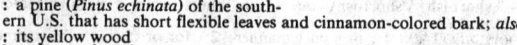

⟨~ a bill through the legislature⟩ ~ *vi* **1 :** to move by forcing a way ⟨bargain hunters *shoving* up to the counter⟩ **2 a :** to move something by exerting force **b :** LEAVE ⟨put on his hat and *shoved* off for home⟩ ***syn*** see PUSH — **shov·er** *n*

2**shove** *n* (14c) **:** an act or instance of shoving **:** a forcible push

1**shov·el** \ˈshəv-əl\ *n* [ME, fr. OE *scofl;* akin to OHG *scūfla* shovel, OE *scūfan* to thrust away] (bef. 12c) **1 a :** a hand implement consisting of a broad scoop or a more or less hollowed out blade with a handle used to lift and throw material **b :** something that resembles a shovel **c :** an excavating machine; *esp* **:** an hydraulic diesel-engine driven power shovel **2 :** SHOVELFUL

2**shovel** *vb* **-eled** *or* **-elled; -el·ing** *or* **-el·ling** \-(ə-)liŋ\ *vt* (15c) **1 :** to take up and throw with a shovel **2 :** to dig or clean out with a shovel **3 :** to throw or convey roughly or in a mass as if with a shovel ⟨~*ed* his food into his mouth⟩ ~ *vi* **:** to use a shovel

shov·el·er *or* **shov·el·ler** \ˈshəv-(ə-)lər\ *n* (15c) **1 :** one that shovels **2 :** any of several river ducks (genus *Anas*) having a large and very broad bill

shov·el·ful \ˈshəv-əl-ˌfu̇l\ *n, pl* **shovelfuls** \-ˌfu̇lz\ *also* **shov·els·ful** \-əlz-ˌfu̇l\ (1533) **:** as much as a shovel will hold

shovel hat *n* (1829) **:** a shallow-crowned hat with a wide brim curved up at the sides that is worn by some clergymen

shov·el·man \-ˌman, -mən\ *n* (1559) **:** one who works with a shovel or a power shovel

shov·el·nose \-ˌnōz\ *n* (1709) **:** a shovel-nosed animal and esp. a fish

shov·el–nosed \ˌshəv-əl-ˈnōzd\ *adj* (1707) **:** having a broad flat head, nose, or beak

1**show** \ˈshō\ *vb* **showed** \ˈshōd\; **shown** \ˈshōn\ *or* **showed; show·ing** [ME *shewen, showen,* fr. OE *scēawian* to look, look at, see; akin to OHG *scouwōn* to look, look at, and prob. to L *cavēre* to be on one's guard] *vt* (bef. 12c) **1 :** to cause or permit to be seen **:** EXHIBIT ⟨~*ed* every mark of extreme agitation⟩ **2 :** to offer for sale ⟨stores were ~*ing* new spring suits⟩ **3 :** to present as a public spectacle **:** PERFORM **4 :** to display for the notice of others **5 :** to reveal by one's condition, nature, or behavior **6 :** to give indication or record of ⟨an anemometer ~*s* wind speed⟩ **7 a :** to point out to someone ⟨~*ed* him the house⟩ **b :** CONDUCT, USHER ⟨~*ed* me to an aisle seat⟩ **8 :** ACCORD, BESTOW **9 a :** to set forth **:** DECLARE **b :** ALLEGE, PLEAD — used esp. in law ⟨~ cause⟩ **10 a :** to demonstrate or establish by argument or reasoning ⟨~ a plan to be faulty⟩ **b :** INFORM, INSTRUCT ⟨~*ed* me how to solve the problem⟩ **11 :** to present (an animal) for judging in a show ~ *vi* **1 a :** to be or come in view ⟨anger ~*ed* in his face⟩ **b :** to put in an appearance ⟨failed to ~⟩ **2 a :** to appear in a particular way ⟨her nature ~*ed* strong in adversity⟩ **b :** SEEM, APPEAR **3 a :** to give a theatrical performance **b :** to be staged or presented **4 :** to finish third or at least third (as in a horse race)

syn SHOW, EXHIBIT, DISPLAY, EXPOSE, PARADE, FLAUNT mean to present so as to invite notice or attention. SHOW implies no more than enabling another to see or examine ⟨*showed* her snapshots to the whole group⟩ EXHIBIT stresses putting forward prominently or openly ⟨*exhibit* paintings at a gallery⟩ DISPLAY emphasizes putting in a position where others may see to advantage ⟨*display* sale items⟩ EXPOSE suggests bringing forth from concealment and displaying ⟨sought to *expose* the hypocrisy of the town fathers⟩ PARADE implies an ostentatious or arrogant displaying ⟨*parading* their piety for all to see⟩ FLAUNT suggests a shameless, boastful, often offensive parading ⟨nouveaux riches *flaunting* their wealth⟩

syn SHOW, MANIFEST, EVIDENCE, EVINCE, DEMONSTRATE mean to reveal outwardly or make apparent. SHOW is the general term but sometimes implies that what is revealed must be gained by inference from acts, looks, or words; MANIFEST implies a plainer, more immediate revelation; EVIDENCE suggests serving as proof of the actuality or existence of something; EVINCE implies a showing by outward marks or signs; DEMONSTRATE implies showing by action or by display of feeling.

— **show one's hand 1 :** to display one's cards faceup **2 :** to declare one's intentions or reveal one's resources — **show one the door :** to tell someone to get out

2**show** *n* (14c) **1 :** a demonstrative display ⟨a ~ of strength⟩ **2 a** *archaic* **:** outward appearance **b :** a false semblance **:** PRETENSE ⟨made a ~ of friendship⟩ **c :** a more or less true appearance of something **:** SIGN **d :** an impressive display **e :** OSTENTATION **3 :** CHANCE ⟨gave him a ~ in spite of his background⟩ **4 :** something exhibited esp. for wonder or ridicule **:** SPECTACLE **5 a :** a large display or exhibition arranged to arouse interest or stimulate sales ⟨the national auto ~⟩ **b :** a competitive exhibition of animals (as dogs) to demonstrate quality in breeding **6 a :** a theatrical presentation **b :** a radio or television program **c :** ENTERTAINMENT 3a **7 :** ENTERPRISE, AFFAIR ⟨they ran the whole ~⟩ **8 :** an indication of metal in a mine or of gas or oil in a well **9 :** third place at the finish (as a horse race)

show–and–tell \ˈshō-ən-ˈtel\ *n* (1952) **1 :** a classroom exercise in which children display an item and talk about it **2 :** a public display or demonstration

show bill *n* (1801) **:** an advertising poster

show biz \-ˌbiz\ *n* [by shortening & alter.] (1946) **:** SHOW BUSINESS; *also* **:** RAZZLE-DAZZLE 3

1**show·boat** \ˈshō-ˌbōt\ *n* (1869) **:** a river steamship containing a theater and carrying a troupe of actors to give plays at river communities

2**showboat** *vi* (1952) **:** to behave in a conspicuous or ostentatious manner **:** SHOW OFF

showbread *var of* SHEWBREAD

show business *n* (1926) **:** the arts, occupations, and businesses (as theater, motion pictures, and television) that comprise the entertainment industry

1**show·case** \ˈshō-ˌkās\ *n* (1839) **1 :** a glazed case, box, or cabinet for displaying and protecting wares in a store or articles in a museum **2 a :** a setting or framework for exhibiting something esp. at its best **b :** a medium or vehicle for exhibiting a tentative offering or tryout of something

2**showcase** *vt* **show·cased; show·cas·ing** (1952) **:** EXHIBIT

show·down \ˈshō-ˌdau̇n\ *n* (1884) **1 :** the placing of poker hands faceup on the table to determine the winner of a pot **2 :** the final settlement of a contested issue or the test of strength that settles it

1**show·er** \ˈshau̇(-ə)r\ *n* [ME *shour,* fr. OE *scūr;* akin to OHG *scūr* shower, L *caurus* northwest wind] (bef. 12c) **1 a :** a fall of rain of short duration **b :** a similar fall of sleet, hail, or snow **2 :** something resembling a rain shower **3 :** a party given by friends who bring gifts often of a particular kind **4 :** a bath in which water is showered on the body; *also* **:** the apparatus that provides a shower — **show·ery** \-ē\ *adj* — **to the showers :** out of the ball game

2**shower** *vi* (1573) **1 :** to rain or fall in or as if in a shower ⟨letters ~*ed* on him in praise and protest⟩ **2 :** to bathe in a shower ~ *vt* **1 a :** to wet (as with water) in a spray, fine stream, or drops **b** (1) **:** to cause to fall in a shower ⟨factory chimneys ~*ed* soot on the district⟩ (2) **:** to cause a shower to fall on ⟨~*ed* the newlyweds with rice⟩ **2 :** to give in abundance ⟨~*ed* him with honors⟩

3**show·er** \ˈshō(-ə)r\ *n* (14c) **:** one that shows **:** EXHIBITOR

shower bath *n* (1785) **:** SHOWER 4

show·ing \ˈshō-iŋ\ *n* (bef. 12c) **1 :** an act of putting something on view **:** DISPLAY **2 :** PERFORMANCE, RECORD ⟨made a good ~ in competition⟩ **3 a :** a statement or presentation of a case **b :** APPEARANCE, EVIDENCE

show·man \ˈshō-mən\ *n* (1734) **1 :** the producer of a play or theatrical show **2 :** an individual having a sense or knack for dramatically effective presentation — **show·man·ship** \-ˌship\ *n*

show–me \ˈshō-mē\ *adj* (1909) **:** insistent on proof or evidence

show–off \ˈshō-ˌȯf\ *n* (1856) **1 :** the act of showing off **2 :** one that shows off **:** EXHIBITIONIST

show off \(ˈ)shō-ˈȯf\ *vt* (1793) **:** to display proudly ⟨wanted to *show* his new car *off*⟩ ~ *vi* **:** to seek to attract attention by conspicuous behavior ⟨boys *showing off* for the girls⟩

show·piece \ˈshō-ˌpēs\ *n* (1885) **:** a prime or outstanding example used for exhibition

show·place \-ˌplās\ *n* (1817) **:** a place (as an estate or building) that is regarded as an example of beauty or excellence

show·room \-ˌrüm, -ˌru̇m\ *n* (1616) **:** a room where merchandise is exhibited for sale or where samples are displayed

show·stop·per \-ˌstäp-ər\ *n* (1946) **1 :** an act, song, or performer that wins applause so prolonged as to interrupt a performance **2 :** something or someone exceptionally arresting or attractive ⟨the gold crown was ~ of the exhibition⟩

show trial *n* (1950) **:** a trial (as of political opponents) in which the verdict is rigged and a public confession is often extracted

show up *vt* (1874) **1 :** to expose or discredit esp. by revealing faults ⟨*showed* them *up* as frauds⟩ **2 :** to embarrass or cause to look bad esp. by comparison ⟨trying to *show up* the boss⟩ **3 :** REVEAL ⟨*showed up* my ignorance⟩ ~ *vi* **1 :** ARRIVE, APPEAR ⟨*showed up* late for his own wedding⟩ **2 :** to be plainly evident

show window *n* (1840) **1 :** an outside display window in which a store exhibits merchandise **2 :** a sample or setting used to exhibit or illustrate something at its best

showy \ˈshō-ē\ *adj* **show·i·er; -est** (1712) **1 :** making an attractive show **:** STRIKING **2 :** given to or marked by a flashy often meretricious display **:** GAUDY — **show·i·ly** \ˈshō-ə-lē\ *adv* — **show·i·ness** \ˈshō-ē-nəs\ *n*

syn SHOWY, PRETENTIOUS, OSTENTATIOUS mean given to excessive outward display. SHOWY implies an imposing or striking appearance but usu. suggests cheapness or poor taste; PRETENTIOUS implies an appearance of importance not justified by the thing's value or the person's standing; OSTENTATIOUS stresses vainglorious display or parade.

sho·yu \ˈshō(ˌ)yü\ *n* [Jp *shōyu* — more at SOY] (1900) **:** SOY 1

shrank *past of* SHRINK

shrap·nel \ˈshrap-nᵊl, *esp Southern* ˈsrap-\ *n, pl* **shrapnel** [Henry *Shrapnel* †1842 Eng. artillery officer] (1806) **1 :** a projectile that consists of a case provided with a powder charge and a large number of usu. lead balls and that is exploded in flight **2 :** bomb, mine, or shell fragments

1**shred** \ˈshred, *esp Southern* ˈsred\ *n* [ME *shrede,* fr. OE *scrēade;* akin to OHG *scrōt* piece cut off, L *scrupus* sharp stone, OE *scieran* to cut — more at SHEAR] (bef. 12c) **:** a long narrow strip cut or torn off; *also* **:** PARTICLE, SCRAP

2**shred** *vb* **shred·ded; shred·ding** *vt* (bef. 12c) **1** *archaic* **:** to cut off **2 :** to cut or tear into shreds ~ *vi* **:** to come apart in or break up into shreds — **shred·der** *n*

shredded wheat *n* (1898) **:** a breakfast cereal made from cooked partially dried wheat that is shredded and molded into biscuits which are then oven-baked and toasted

1**shrew** \ˈshrü, *esp Southern* ˈsrü\ *n* [ME *shrewe* evil or scolding person, fr. OE *scrēawa* shrew (animal)] (bef. 12c) **1 :** any of numerous small chiefly nocturnal mammals (family Soricidae) related to the moles and distinguished by a long pointed snout, very small eyes, and velvety fur **2 :** an ill-tempered scolding woman

2**shrew** *vt, obs* (14c) **:** CURSE

shrewd \ˈshrüd, *esp Southern* ˈsrüd\ *adj* [ME *shrewe* + *-ed*] (14c) **1** *archaic* **:** MISCHIEVOUS **2** *obs* **:** ABUSIVE, SHREWISH **3** *obs* **:** OMINOUS, DANGEROUS **4 a :** SEVERE, HARD ⟨a ~ knock⟩ **b :** SHARP, PIERCING ⟨a ~ wind⟩ **5 a :** marked by clever discerning awareness and hardheaded acumen ⟨~ common sense⟩ **b :** given to wily and artful ways or dealing ⟨a ~ operator⟩ — **shrewd·ly** *adv* — **shrewd·ness** *n*

syn SHREWD, SAGACIOUS, PERSPICACIOUS, ASTUTE mean acute in perception and sound in judgment. SHREWD stresses practical, hardheaded cleverness and judgment; SAGACIOUS suggests wisdom, penetration, and farsightedness; PERSPICACIOUS implies unusual power to see through and understand what is puzzling or hidden; ASTUTE suggests shrewdness, perspicacity, and diplomatic skill.

shrew·ish \ˈshrü-ish, *esp Southern* ˈsrü-\ *adj* (1565) **:** ILL-NATURED, INTRACTABLE — **shrew·ish·ly** *adv* — **shrew·ish·ness** *n*

shri \ˈs(h)rē\ *var of* SRI

1**shriek** \ˈshrēk, *esp Southern* ˈsrēk\ *vb* [prob. irreg. fr. ME *shriken* to shriek; akin to ME *scremen* to scream] *vi* (1567) **1 :** to utter a sharp shrill sound **2 a :** to cry out in a high-pitched voice **:** SCREECH **b :** to suggest such a cry (as by vividness of expression) ~ *vt* **1 :** to utter with a shriek or sharply and shrilly ⟨~ an alarm⟩ **2 :** to express in a manner suggestive of a shriek

\ə\ abut \ᵊ\ kitten, F table \ər\ further \a\ ash \ā\ ace \ä\ cot, cart \au̇\ out \ch\ chin \e\ bet \ē\ easy \g\ go \i\ hit \ī\ ice \j\ job \ŋ\ sing \ō\ go \ȯ\ law \ȯi\ boy \th\ thin \th\ the \ü\ loot \u̇\ foot \y\ yet \zh\ vision \à, k, ⁿ, œ, œ̄, ue, ue̅, ʸ\ *see* Guide to Pronunciation

[2]shriek *n* (1590) **1 :** a shrill usu. wild or involuntary cry **2 :** a sound resembling a shriek ⟨the ~ of chalk on the blackboard⟩
shrie•val \ˈshrē-vəl, *esp Southern* ˈsrē-\ *adj* [obs. *shrieve* sheriff, fr. ME *shirreve* — more at SHERIFF] (1681) **:** of or relating to a sheriff
shrie•val•ty \-vəl-tē\ *n* (1502) **1** *chiefly Brit* **:** the office of a sheriff; *also* **:** the term of office of a sheriff **2** *chiefly Brit* **:** the jurisdiction of a sheriff
shrieve \ˈshrēv, *esp Southern* ˈsrēv\ *archaic var of* SHRIVE
shrift \ˈshrift, *esp Southern* ˈsrift\ *n* [ME, fr. OE *scrift,* fr. *scrīfan* to shrive — more at SHRIVE] (bef. 12c) **1** *archaic* **a :** the act of shriving **:** CONFESSION **b :** a remission of sins pronounced by a priest in the sacrament of penance **2** *obs* **:** CONFESSIONAL
shrike \ˈshrīk, *esp Southern* ˈsrīk\ *n* [perh. fr. (assumed) ME *shrik,* fr. OE *scrīc* thrush; akin to ME *shriken* to shriek] (1544) **:** any of numerous usu. largely gray or brownish oscine birds (family Laniidae) that have a strong notched bill hooked at the tip, feed chiefly on insects, and often impale their prey on thorns
[1]shrill \ˈshril, *esp Southern* ˈsril\ *vb* [ME *shrillen*] *vi* (14c) **:** to utter or emit an acute piercing sound ⟨alarm clocks ~ at five a.m. —Lucy Cook⟩ ~ *vt* **:** SCREAM
[2]shrill *adj* (14c) **1 a :** having or emitting a sharp high-pitched tone or sound **:** PIERCING **b :** accompanied by sharp high-pitched sounds or cries ⟨~ gaiety⟩ **2 :** having a sharp or vivid effect on the senses ⟨~ light⟩ **3 :** STRIDENT, INTEMPERATE ⟨~ anger⟩ — **shrill** *adv* — **shrill•ness** *n* — **shril•ly** \ˈs(h)ril-lē\ *adv*
[3]shrill *n* (1591) **:** a shrill sound ⟨the ~ of the ship's whistle⟩
[1]shrimp \ˈshrimp, *esp Southern* ˈsrimp\ *n, pl* **shrimps** *or* **shrimp** [ME *shrimpe;* akin to ON *skorpna* to shrivel up, L *curvus* curved — more at CROWN] (14c) **1 :** any of numerous mostly small and marine decapod crustaceans (suborder Natantia) having a slender elongated body, compressed abdomen, long legs, and a long spiny rostrum; *also* **:** a small crustacean (as an amphipod or a branchiopod) resembling the true shrimps **2 :** a very small or puny person or thing — **shrimpy** \ˈs(h)rim-pē\ *adj*
[2]shrimp *vi* (ca. 1934) **:** to fish for or catch shrimps
shrimp•er \-pər\ *n* (1851) **:** one that shrimps: **a :** a shrimp fisherman **b :** a boat engaged in shrimping
shrimp pink *n* (1882) **:** a variable color averaging a deep pink
[1]shrine \ˈshrīn, *esp Southern* ˈsrīn\ *n* [ME, fr. OE *scrīn,* fr. L *scrinium* case, chest] (bef. 12c) **1 a :** a case, box, or receptacle; *esp* **:** one in which sacred relics (as the bones of a saint) are deposited **b :** a place in which devotion is paid to a saint or deity **:** SANCTUARY **c :** a niche containing a religious image **2 :** a receptacle (as a tomb) for the dead **3 :** a place or object hallowed by its associations
[2]shrine *vt* (13c) **:** ENSHRINE
Shrin•er \ˈshrī-nər, *esp Southern* ˈsrī-\ *n* [Ancient Arabic Order of Nobles of the Mystic *Shrine*] (1889) **:** a member of a secret fraternal society that is non-Masonic but admits only Knights Templars and 32d-degree Masons to membership
[1]shrink \ˈshriŋk, *esp Southern* ˈsriŋk\ *vb* **shrank** \ˈs(h)raŋk\ *also* **shrunk** \ˈs(h)rəŋk\; **shrunk** *or* **shrunk•en** \ˈs(h)rəŋ-kən\ [ME *shrinken,* fr. OE *scrincan;* akin to MD *schrinken* to draw back, L *curvus* curved — more at CROWN] *vi* (bef. 12c) **1 :** to contract or curl up the body or part of it **:** HUDDLE, COWER **2 a :** to contract to less extent or compass **b :** to become smaller or more compacted **c :** to lose substance or weight **d :** to lessen in value **:** DWINDLE **3 :** to recoil instinctively (as from something painful or horrible) ~ *vt* **:** to cause to contract or shrink; *specif* **:** to compact (cloth) by causing to contract when subjected to washing, boiling, steaming, or other processes ***syn*** see CONTRACT, RECOIL — **shrink•able** \ˈs(h)riŋ-kə-bəl\ *adj* — **shrink•er** *n*
[2]shrink *n* (1590) **1 :** the act of shrinking **2 :** SHRINKAGE **3 :** HEADSHRINKER 2 ⟨regaling us with all the stories he never told his ~ —*Rolling Stone*⟩
shrink•age \ˈshriŋ-kij, *esp Southern* ˈsriŋ-\ *n* (1800) **1 :** the act or process of shrinking **2 :** the loss in weight of livestock during shipment and in the process of preparing the meat for consumption **3 :** the amount lost by shrinkage
shrinking violet *n* (1927) **:** a bashful or retiring person
shrink–wrap \ˈshriŋk-ˌrap, *esp Southern* ˈsriŋk-\ *vt* (1966) **:** to wrap (as a book or meat) in tough clear plastic film that is then shrunk (as by heating) to form a tightly fitting package
shrive \ˈshrīv, *esp Southern* ˈsrīv\ *vb* **shrived** *or* **shrove** \ˈs(h)rōv\; **shriv•en** \ˈs(h)riv-ən\ *or* **shrived; shriv•ing** [ME *shriven,* fr. OE *scrīfan* to shrive, prescribe fr. L *scribere* to write — more at SCRIBE] *vt* (bef. 12c) **1 :** to administer the sacrament of penance to **2 :** to free from guilt ~ *vi, archaic* **:** to confess one's sins esp. to a priest
shriv•el \ˈshriv-əl, *esp Southern* ˈsriv-\ *vb* **-eled** *or* **-elled; -el•ing** *or* **-el•ling** \-(ə-)liŋ\ [origin unknown] *vi* (1612) **1 :** to draw into wrinkles esp. with a loss of moisture **2 a :** to become reduced to inanition, helplessness, or inefficiency **b :** DWINDLE ~ *vt* **:** to cause to shrivel
shroff \ˈshräf, ˈshrȯf, *esp Southern* ˈsräf, ˈsrȯf\ *n* [Hindi *ṣarrāf,* fr. Ar] (1618) **:** a banker or money changer in the Far East; *esp* **:** one who tests and evaluates coin
Shrop•shire \ˈshräp-ˌshi(ə)r, -shər, *esp US* -ˌshī(ə)r, *esp Southern* ˈsräp-\ *n* [*Shropshire,* England] (1803) **:** any of an English breed of dark-faced hornless sheep that are raised primarily for mutton
[1]shroud \ˈshrau̇d, *esp Southern* ˈsrau̇d\ *n* [ME, garment, fr. OE *scrūd;* akin to OE *scrēade* shred — more at SHRED] (14c) **1** *obs* **:** SHELTER, PROTECTION **2 :** something that covers, screens, or guards: as **a :** one of two flanges that give peripheral support to turbine or fan bedding **b :** a usu. fiberglass guard that protects a spacecraft from the heat of launching **3 :** burial garment **:** WINDING-SHEET, CEREMENT **4 a :** one of the ropes leading usu. in pairs from a ship's mastheads to give lateral support to the masts **b :** one of the cords that suspend the harness of a parachute from the canopy

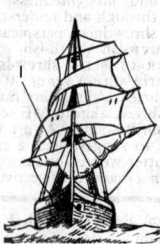

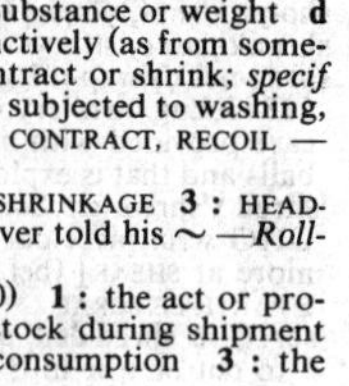
[1]shroud 4a

[2]shroud *vt* (14c) **1 a** *archaic* **:** to cover for protection **b** *obs* **:** CONCEAL **2 a :** to cut off from view **:** OBSCURE ⟨trees ~*ed* by a heavy fog⟩ **b :** to veil under another appearance (as by obscuring or disguising) ⟨~*ed* the decision in a series of formalities⟩ **3 :** to dress for burial ~ *vi, archaic* **:** to seek shelter
shroud–laid \-ˌlād\ *adj, of a rope* (1800) **:** composed of four strands and laid right-handed with a core
Shrove•tide \ˈshrōv-ˌtīd, *esp Southern* ˈsrōv-\ *n* [ME *schroftide,* fr. *schrof-* (fr. *shriven* to shrive) + *tide*] (15c) **:** the period usu. of three days immediately preceding Ash Wednesday
Shrove Tuesday \ˈshrōv-, *esp Southern* ˈsrōv-\ *n* [ME *schroftewesday,* fr. *schrof-* (as in *schroftide*) + *tewesday* Tuesday] (15c) **:** the Tuesday before Ash Wednesday
[1]shrub \ˈshrəb, *esp Southern* ˈsrəb\ *n* [ME *schrobbe,* fr. OE *scrybb* brushwood; akin to Norw *skrubbebær* a cornel of a dwarf species] (bef. 12c) **:** a low usu. several-stemmed woody plant
[2]shrub *n* [Ar *sharāb* beverage] (1747) **1 :** an aged blend of fruit juice, sugar, and spirits served chilled and diluted with water **2 :** a beverage made by adding acidulated fruit juice to iced water
shrub•bery \ˈshrəb-(ə-)rē, *esp Southern* ˈsrəb-\ *n, pl* **-ber•ies** (1748) **:** a planting or growth of shrubs
shrub•by \ˈshrəb-ē, *esp Southern* ˈsrəb-\ *adj* **shrub•bi•er; -est** (1540) **1 :** consisting of or covered with shrubs **2 :** resembling a shrub
[1]shrug \ˈshrəg, *esp Southern* ˈsrəg\ *vb* **shrugged; shrug•ging** [ME *schruggen*] *vi* (15c) **:** to raise or draw in the shoulders esp. to express aloofness, indifference, or aversion ~ *vt* **:** to lift or contract (the shoulders) esp. to express aloofness, indifference, or aversion
[2]shrug *n* (1594) **1 :** an act of shrugging **2 :** a woman's small waist-length or shorter jacket
shrug off *vt* (ca. 1909) **1 :** to brush aside **:** MINIMIZE ⟨*shrugs off* the problem⟩ **2 :** to shake off ⟨*shrugging off* sleep⟩ **3 :** to remove (a garment) by wriggling out
shtetl *also* **shte•tel** \ˈshtet-ᵊl, ˈshtāt-\ *n, pl* **shtet•lach** \ˈshtet-ˌläk, ˈshtāt-\ *also* **shtetels** [Yiddish, fr. MHG *stetel,* dim. of *stat* place, town, city, fr. OHG, place — more at STEAD] (1950) **:** a small Jewish town or village formerly found in Eastern Europe
shtick *also* **shtik** \ˈshtik\ *n* [Yiddish *shtik,* lit., piece, fr. MHG *stücke,* fr. OHG *stucki;* akin to OE *stycce* piece, OHG *stoc* stick — more at STOCK] (1959) **1 :** a show-business routine, gimmick, or gag **:** BIT **2 :** one's special trait, interest, or activity **:** BAG ⟨he's alive and well and now doing his ~ out in Hollywood —Robert Daley⟩
[1]shuck \ˈshək\ *n* [origin unknown] (1674) **1 :** SHELL, HUSK; as **a :** the outer covering of a nut or of Indian corn **b :** the shell of an oyster or clam **2 :** something of little value — usu. used in pl. often interjectionally ⟨not worth ~*s*⟩ ⟨~*s,* it was nothing⟩
[2]shuck *vt* (1754) **1 :** to strip of shucks **2 a :** to peel off (as clothing) — often used with *off* **b :** to lay aside — usu. used with *off* ⟨bad habits are being ~*ed off* —A. W. Smith⟩ — **shuck•er** *n*
[1]shud•der \ˈshəd-ər\ *vi* **shud•dered; shud•der•ing** \-(ə-)riŋ\ [ME *shoddren;* akin to OHG *skutten* to shake, Lith *kutėti* to shake up] (14c) **1 :** to tremble convulsively **:** SHIVER **2 :** QUIVER
[2]shudder *n* (1607) **:** an act of shuddering — **shud•dery** \-(ə-)rē\ *adj*
[1]shuf•fle \ˈshəf-əl\ *vb* **shuf•fled; shuf•fling** \-(ə-)liŋ\ [perh. irreg. fr. [1]*shove*] *vt* (ca. 1570) **1 :** to mix in a mass confusedly **:** JUMBLE **2 :** to put or thrust aside or under cover ⟨*shuffled* the whole matter out of his mind⟩ **3 a :** to rearrange (as playing cards, dominoes, or tiles) to produce a random order **b :** to move about, back and forth, or from one place to another **:** SHIFT ⟨~ funds among various accounts⟩ **4 a :** to move (as the feet) by sliding along or back and forth without lifting **b :** to perform (as a dance) with a dragging, sliding step ~ *vi* **1 :** to work into or out of trickily **:** WORM ⟨*shuffled* out of the difficulty somehow⟩ **2 :** to act or speak in a shifty or evasive manner **3 a :** to move or walk in a sliding dragging manner without lifting the feet **b :** to dance in a lazy nonchalant manner with sliding and tapping motions of the feet **c :** to execute in a perfunctory or clumsy manner **4 :** to mix playing cards or counters by shuffling — **shuf•fler** \-(ə-)lər\ *n*
[2]shuffle *n* (1628) **1 :** an evasion of the issue **:** EQUIVOCATION **2 a :** an act of shuffling (as of cards) **b :** a right or turn to shuffle ⟨was reminded that it was his ~⟩ **c :** JUMBLE ⟨lost in the ~ of papers⟩ **3 a :** a dragging sliding movement; *specif* **:** a sliding or scraping step in dancing **b :** a dance characterized by such a step
shuf•fle•board \ˈshəf-əl-ˌbō(ə)rd, -ˌbȯ(ə)rd\ *n* [alter. of obs. E *shove-board*] (1532) **1 :** a game in which players use long-handled cues to shove disks into scoring areas of a diagram marked on a smooth surface **2 :** a diagram on which shuffleboard is played
shul \ˈshül\ *n* [Yiddish, fr. MHG *schuol,* lit., school] (1903) **:** SYNAGOGUE
shun \ˈshən\ *vt* **shunned; shun•ning** [ME *shunnen,* fr. OE *scunian*] (bef. 12c) **:** to avoid deliberately and esp. habitually ***syn*** see ESCAPE — **shun•ner** *n*
shun•pike \ˈshən-ˌpīk\ *n* (1853) **:** a side road used to avoid the toll on or the speed and traffic of a superhighway — **shun•pik•er** \-ˌpī-kər\ *n* — **shun•pik•ing** \-kiŋ\ *n*
[1]shunt \ˈshənt\ *vb* [ME *shunten* to flinch] *vt* (13c) **1 a :** to turn off to one side **:** SHIFT ⟨was ~*ed* aside⟩ **b :** to switch (as a train) from one track to another **2 :** to provide with or divert by means of an electrical shunt **3 :** to divert (blood) from one part to another by a surgical shunt **4 :** SHUTTLE ⟨missiles ~*ed* quickly from shelter to shelter⟩ ~ *vi* **1 :** to move to the side **2 :** to travel back and forth ⟨~*ed* between the two towns⟩ — **shunt•er** *n*
[2]shunt *n* (1863) **1 :** a means or mechanism for turning or thrusting aside: as **a** *chiefly Brit* **:** a railroad switch **b :** a conductor joining two points in an electrical circuit so as to form a parallel or alternative path through which a portion of the current may pass (as for regulating the amount passing in the main circuit) **c :** a surgical passage created between two blood vessels to divert blood from one part to another **2 :** an accident (as a collision between two cars) in auto racing
shunt winding *n* (ca. 1909) **:** a winding so arranged as to divide the armature current and lead a portion of it around the field-magnet coils — **shunt–wound** \ˈshənt-ˈwau̇nd\ *adj*
shush \ˈshəsh, ˈshu̇sh\ *vt* [imit.] (1928) **:** to urge to be quiet **:** HUSH — **shush** *n*
[1]shut \ˈshət\ *vb* **shut; shut•ting** [ME *shutten,* fr. OE *scyttan;* akin to OE *scēotan* to shoot — more at SHOOT] *vt* (bef. 12c) **1 a :** to move into position to close an opening ⟨~ the lid⟩ **b :** to prevent entrance to or passage to or from **2 :** to confine by or as if by enclosure ⟨~ herself in her study⟩ **3 :** to fasten with a lock or bolt **4 :** to close by bringing

enclosing or covering parts together ⟨~ the eyes⟩ **5 :** to cause to cease or suspend operation — often used with *down* ~ *vi* **1 :** to close itself or become closed ⟨flowers that ~ at night⟩ **2 :** to cease or suspend an operation — often used with *down*

[2]shut *adj* (15c) **1 :** closed, fastened, or folded together **2 :** RID, CLEAR, FREE — usu. used with *of*

[3]shut *n* (1667) **:** the act of shutting

shut·down \ˈshət-ˌdau̇n\ *n* (1888) **:** the cessation or suspension of an operation

shut down \ˈshət-ˈdau̇n, ˌshət-\ *vi* (1807) **:** to settle so as to obscure vision **:** CLOSE IN ⟨the night *shut down* early⟩

shute *var of* CHUTE

shut–eye \ˈshət-ˌī\ *n* (1899) **:** SLEEP

[1]shut–in \ˈshət-ˌin\ *n* (1903) **1 :** an invalid confined to his home, room, or bed **2 :** a narrow gorge-shaped part of an otherwise wide valley **3 :** available oil or gas which is not being produced from an existing well

[2]shut–in \ˌshət-ˌin\ *adj* (1904) **1 :** confined to one's home or an institution by illness or incapacity **2 a :** SECRETIVE, BROODING ⟨a bitter, ~ face —Claudia Cassidy⟩ **b :** tending to avoid social contact **:** WITHDRAWN ⟨the ~ personality type —S. K. Weinberg⟩

shut in \ˌshət-ˈin\ *vt* (14c) **1 :** CONFINE, ENCLOSE **2 :** to prevent production of (oil or gas) by closing down a well

shut·off \ˈshət-ˌȯf\ *n* (1869) **1 :** something (as a valve) that shuts off **2 :** STOPPAGE, INTERRUPTION

shut off \ˌshət-ˈȯf\ *vt* (1824) **1 a :** to cut off (as flow or passage) **:** STOP ⟨*shuts off* the oxygen supply⟩ **b :** to stop the operation of (as a machine) ⟨*shut* the motor *off*⟩ **2 :** to close off **:** SEPARATE — usu. used with *from* ⟨*shut off* from the rest of the world⟩ ~ *vi* **:** to cease operating **:** STOP ⟨*shuts off* automatically⟩

shut·out \ˈshət-ˌau̇t\ *n* (1889) **1 :** a game or contest in which one side fails to score **2 :** a preemptive bid in bridge

shut out \ˌshət-ˈau̇t\ *vt* (14c) **1 :** EXCLUDE **2 :** to prevent (an opponent) from scoring in a game or contest **3 :** to forestall the bidding of (bridge opponents) by making a high or preemptive bid

[1]shut·ter \ˈshət-ər\ *n* (1542) **1 :** one that shuts **2 :** a usu. movable cover or screen for a window or door **3 :** a mechanical device that limits the passage of light; *esp* **:** a camera attachment that exposes the film or plate by opening and closing an aperture **4 :** the movable louvers in a pipe organ by which the swell box is opened — **shut·ter·less** \-ləs\ *adj*

[2]shutter *vt* (1826) **1 :** to close by or as if by shutters **2 :** to furnish with shutters

shut·ter·bug \ˈshət-ər-ˌbəg\ *n* (1940) **:** a photography enthusiast

[1]shut·tle \ˈshət-ᵊl\ *n* [ME *shittle,* prob. fr. OE *scytel* bar, bolt; akin to ON *skutill* bolt, OE *scēotan* to shoot — more at SHOOT] (14c) **1 a :** a device used in weaving for passing the thread of the woof between the threads of the warp **b :** a spindle-shaped device holding the thread in tatting, knotting, or netting **c :** a sliding thread holder for the lower thread of a sewing machine that carries the lower thread through a loop of the upper thread to make a stitch **2 :** SHUTTLECOCK **3 a :** a going back and forth regularly over an often short route by a vehicle **b :** an established route used in a shuttle; *also* **:** a vehicle used in a shuttle **c :** SPACE SHUTTLE — **shut·tle·less** *adj*

[2]shuttle *vb* **shut·tled; shut·tling** \ˈshət-liŋ, -ᵊl-iŋ\ *vt* (1550) **1 :** to cause to move or travel back and forth frequently **2 :** to transport in, by, or as if by a shuttle ~ *vi* **1 :** to move or travel back and forth frequently **2 :** to move by or as if by a shuttle

[1]shut·tle·cock \ˈshət-ᵊl-ˌkäk\ *n* (1522) **:** a lightweight conical object with a rounded often rubber-covered nose that is used in badminton

[2]shuttlecock *vt* (1687) **:** to send or toss to and fro **:** BANDY

shuttle diplomacy *n* (1974) **:** negotiations esp. between nations carried on by an intermediary who shuttles back and forth between the disputants

shut up *vt* (1814) **:** to cause (a person) to stop talking ~ *vi* **:** to cease writing or speaking

[1]shy \ˈshī\ *adj* **shi·er** *or* **shy·er** \ˈshī(-ə)r\; **shi·est** *or* **shy·est** \ˈshī-əst\ [ME *schey,* fr. OE *scēoh;* akin to OHG *sciuhen* to frighten off, OSlav *šcuti* to chase] (bef. 12c) **1 :** easily frightened **:** TIMID **2 :** disposed to avoid a person or thing ⟨publicity ~⟩ ⟨book-*shy* children⟩ **3 :** hesitant in committing oneself **:** CIRCUMSPECT **4 :** sensitively diffident or retiring **:** RESERVED ⟨a ~ seclusive person⟩; *also* **:** expressive of such a state or nature ⟨spoke in a ~ voice⟩ **5 :** SECLUDED, HIDDEN **6 :** having less than the full or specified amount or number **:** SHORT ⟨just ~ of six feet tall⟩ ⟨stew is a little ~ of seasoning⟩ **7 :** DISREPUTABLE ⟨gambling hells and ~ saloons —*Blackwood's*⟩ — **shy·ly** *adv* — **shy·ness** *n*

syn SHY, BASHFUL, DIFFIDENT, MODEST, COY mean not inclined to be forward. SHY implies a timid reserve and a shrinking from familiarity or contact with others; BASHFUL implies a frightened or hesitant shyness characteristic of childhood and adolescence; DIFFIDENT stresses a distrust of one's own ability or opinion that causes hesitation in acting or speaking; MODEST suggests absence of undue confidence or conceit; COY implies an assumed or affected shyness.

[2]shy *vi* **shied; shy·ing** (1650) **1 :** to develop or show a dislike or distaste **:** RECOIL **2 :** to start suddenly aside through fright or alarm

[3]shy *n, pl* **shies** (1791) **:** a sudden start aside (as from fright)

[4]shy *vb* **shied; shy·ing** [perh. fr. [1]*shy*] *vt* (1787) **:** to throw (an object) with a jerk **:** FLING ~ *vi* **:** to make a sudden throw

[5]shy *n, pl* **shies** (1791) **1 :** the act of shying **:** TOSS, THROW **2 :** a verbal fling or attack **3 :** COCKSHY

[1]shy·lock \ˈshī-ˌläk\ *n* **1** *cap* **:** the Jewish usurer and antagonist of Antonio in Shakespeare's *The Merchant of Venice* **2 :** an extortionate creditor **:** LOAN SHARK

[2]shylock *vi* (ca. 1934) **:** to lend money at high rates of interest ⟨exposé of systematic thievery . . . ~*ing,* and murder —*Current Biog.*⟩

shy·ster \ˈshī-stər\ *n* [prob. alter. of earlier *shicer* contemptible fellow, fr. G *scheisser,* lit., defecator] (1843) **:** one who is professionally unscrupulous esp. in the practice of law or politics **:** PETTIFOGGER

si \ˈsē\ *n* [It] (1728) **:** [2]TI

sial- *or* **sialo-** *comb form* [NL, fr. Gk *sialon;* akin to L *spuere* to spit — more at SPEW] **:** saliva ⟨*sialogenic*⟩ ⟨*sialoprotein*⟩

si·al·a·gogue \sī-ˈal-ə-ˌgäg\ *n* [NL *sialagogus* promoting the expulsion of saliva, fr. *sial-* + *-agogus* -agogue] (ca. 1783) **:** an agent that promotes the flow of saliva

si·al·ic \sī-ˈal-ik\ *adj* [ISV *si*licon + *al*uminum] (1924) **:** of, relating to, or being relatively light rock that is rich in silica and alumina and is typical of the outer layers of the earth

si·al·ic acid \(ˌ)sī-ˌal-ik-\ *n* [*sial-* + *-ic*] (ca. 1958) **:** any of a group of reducing amido acids that are essentially carbohydrates and are found esp. as components of blood glycoproteins and mucoproteins

si·a·mang \ˈsē-ə-ˌmaŋ, ˈsī-\ *n* [Malay] (1822) **:** a black gibbon (*Symphalangus syndactylus*) of Sumatra and the Malay peninsula that is the largest of the gibbons

[1]Si·a·mese \ˌsī-ə-ˈmēz, -ˈmēs\ *adj* [*Siam* (Thailand); in senses 2 & 3, fr. *Siamese twin*] (1693) **1 :** of, relating to, or characteristic of Thailand, the Thais, or their language **2 :** exhibiting great resemblance **:** very like **3** *not cap* **:** connecting two or more pipes or hose so as to permit discharge in a single stream

[2]Siamese *n, pl* **Siamese** (1693) **1 :** THAI 1 **2 :** THAI 2 **3 :** SIAMESE CAT

Siamese cat *n* (ca. 1909) **:** a slender blue-eyed shorthaired domestic cat of a breed of oriental origin with pale fawn or gray body and darker ears, paws, tail, and face — see CAT illustration

Siamese fighting fish *n* (1933) **:** a brightly colored highly aggressive betta (*Betta splendens*) that is a popular aquarium fish

Siamese twin *n* [fr. Chang †1874 and Eng †1874 congenitally united twins born in Siam] (1829) **:** one of a pair of congenitally united twins in man or lower animals

[1]sib \ˈsib\ *adj* [ME, fr. OE *sibb,* fr. *sibb* kinship; akin to OHG *sippa* kinship, family, L *sodalis* comrade, Gk *ethos* custom, character, L *suus* one's own — more at SUICIDE] (bef. 12c) **:** related by blood **:** AKIN

[2]sib *n* (bef. 12c) **1 a :** KINDRED, RELATIVES **b :** a blood relation **:** KINSMAN **2 :** a brother or sister considered irrespective of sex; *broadly* **:** any plant or animal of a group sharing a degree of genetic relationship corresponding to that of human sibs **3 :** a group of persons unilaterally descended from a real or supposed ancestor

Si·be·ri·an husky \sī-ˌbir-ē-ən-\ *n* (ca. 1934) **:** a medium-sized compact dog of a breed that was developed in Siberia for use as a sled dog

sib·i·lance \ˈsib-ə-lən(t)s\ *n* (1823) **:** a sibilant quality or sound

[1]sib·i·lant \ˈsib-ə-lənt\ *adj* [L *sibilant-, sibilans,* prp. of *sibilare* to hiss, whistle, of imit. origin] (1669) **:** having, containing, or producing the sound of or a sound resembling that of the *s* or the *sh* in *sash* ⟨a ~ affricate⟩ ⟨a ~ snake⟩ — **sib·i·lant·ly** *adv*

[2]sibilant *n* (1822) **:** a sibilant speech sound (as English \s\, \z\, \sh\, \zh\, \ch(=tsh)\, or \j(=dzh)\)

sib·i·late \ˈsib-ə-ˌlāt\ *vb* **-lat·ed; -lat·ing** [L *sibilatus,* pp. of *sibilare*] *vi* (ca. 1656) **1 :** HISS **2 :** to utter an initial sibilant **:** prefix an \s\-sound ~ *vt* **1 :** HISS **2 :** to pronounce with an initial sibilant **:** prefix an \s\-sound to — **sib·i·la·tion** \ˌsib-ə-ˈlā-shən\ *n*

sib·ling \ˈsib-liŋ\ *n* (bef. 12c) **:** SIB 2; *also* **:** one of two or more individuals having one common parent

sibling species *n* (1948) **:** one of two or more species that are nearly indistinguishable morphologically

sib·yl \ˈsib-əl\ *n, often cap* [ME *sibile, sybylle,* fr. MF & L; MF *sibile,* fr. L *sibylla,* fr. Gk] (14c) **1 :** any of several prophetesses usu. accepted as 10 in number and credited to widely separate parts of the ancient world (as Babylonia, Egypt, Greece, and Italy) **2 a :** a female prophet **b :** FORTUNE-TELLER — **si·byl·ic** *or* **si·byl·lic** \sə-ˈbil-ik\ *adj* — **sib·yl·line** \ˈsib-ə-ˌlīn, -ˌlēn\ *adj*

[1]sic \(ˈ)sik\ *chiefly Scot var of* SUCH

[2]sic *or* **sick** \ˈsik\ *vt* **sicced** *or* **sicked** \ˈsikt\; **sic·cing** *or* **sick·ing** [alter. of *seek*] (1845) **1 :** CHASE, ATTACK — usu. used as a command esp. to a dog ⟨~ 'em⟩ **2 :** to incite or urge to an attack, pursuit, or harassment **:** SET

[3]sic \ˈsik, ˈsēk\ *adv* [L, so, thus — more at SO] (ca. 1859) **:** intentionally so written — used after a printed word or passage to indicate that it is intended exactly as printed or to indicate that it exactly reproduces an original ⟨said he seed [~] it all⟩

sic·ca·tive \ˈsik-ət-iv\ *n* [LL *siccativus* making dry, fr. L *siccatus,* pp. of *siccare* to dry, fr. *siccus* dry — more at SACK] (1825) **:** DRIER 2

Sichuan *var of* SZECHUAN

sick \ˈsik\ *adj* [ME *sek, sik,* fr. OE *sēoc;* akin to OHG *sioh* sick, MIr *socht* depression] (bef. 12c) **1 a (1) :** affected with disease or ill health **:** AILING **(2) :** of, relating to, or intended for use in sickness ⟨~ pay⟩ ⟨a ~ ward⟩ **b :** QUEASY, NAUSEATED ⟨~ to one's stomach⟩ ⟨was ~ in the car⟩ **c :** undergoing menstruation **2 :** spiritually or morally unsound or corrupt **3 a :** sickened by strong emotion ⟨~ with fear⟩ ⟨worried ~⟩ **b :** having a strong distaste from surfeit **:** SATIATED ⟨~ of flattery⟩ **c :** filled with disgust or chagrin ⟨gossip makes me ~⟩ **d :** depressed and longing for something ⟨~ for one's home⟩ **4 a :** mentally or emotionally unsound or disordered **:** MORBID ⟨~ thoughts⟩ **b :** MACABRE, SADISTIC ⟨~ jokes⟩ **5 :** lacking vigor **:** SICKLY: as **a :** badly outclassed ⟨looked ~ in the contest⟩ **b :** incapable of yielding a profitable crop esp. because of buildup of disease organisms ⟨clover-*sick* soils⟩

sick and tired *adj* (1883) **:** thoroughly fatigued or bored

sick bay *n* (1813) **:** a compartment in a ship used as a dispensary and hospital; *broadly* **:** a place for the care of the sick or injured

sick·bed \ˈsik-ˌbed\ *n* (15c) **:** the bed on which one lies sick

sick call *n* (1836) **:** a scheduled time at which individuals (as soldiers) may report as sick to the medical officer

sick·en \ˈsik-ən\ *vb* **sick·ened; sick·en·ing** \-(ə-)niŋ\ *vi* (13c) **1 :** to become sick **2 :** to become weary or satiated ~ *vt* **1 :** to make sick **2 :** to cause revulsion in as a result of weariness or satiety — **sick·en·er** \ˈsik-(ə-)nər\ *n*

sick·en·ing \-niŋ\ *adj* (1789) **:** causing sickness or disgust ⟨a ~ odor⟩ ⟨a ~ display⟩ — **sick·en·ing·ly** \-niŋ-lē\ *adv*

sick·er \ˈsik-ər\ *adj* [ME *siker,* fr. OE *sicor,* fr. L *securus* secure] *chiefly Scot* (bef. 12c) **:** SECURE, SAFE; *also* **:** DEPENDABLE — **sicker** *adv, chiefly Scot* — **sick·er·ly** *adv, chiefly Scot*

sick headache *n* (1778) **:** MIGRAINE

sick·ie \'sik-ē\ *n* [*sick* + *-ie*] (1967) : a person who is mentally or morally sick
sick·ish \'sik-ish\ *adj* (1581) **1** *archaic* : somewhat ill : SICKLY **2** : somewhat nauseated : QUEASY **3** : somewhat sickening ⟨a ~ odor⟩ — **sick·ish·ly** *adv* — **sick·ish·ness** *n*
[1]**sick·le** \'sik-əl\ *n* [ME *sikel,* fr. OE *sicol,* fr. L *secula* sickle — more at SAW] (bef. 12c) **1 a** : an agricultural implement consisting of a curved metal blade with a short handle fitted on a tang **b** : the cutting mechanism (as of a reaper, combine, or mower) consisting of a bar with a series of cutting elements **2** *cap* : a group of six stars in the constellation Leo
[2]**sickle** *adj* (1607) : having the form of a sickle blade : having a curve similar to that of a sickle blade ⟨the ~ moon⟩
[3]**sickle** *vb* **sick·led; sick·ling** \'sik-(ə-)liŋ\ *vt* (1765) **1** : to mow or reap with a sickle **2** : to form (a red blood cell) into a crescent ~ *vi* : to form into a crescent ⟨the ability of red blood cells to ~⟩
sick leave *n* (1840) **1** : an absence from work permitted because of illness **2** : the number of days per year for which an employer agrees to pay employees who are sick
sickle cell *n* (1926) : an abnormal red blood cell of crescent shape
sickle–cell anemia *n* (1926) : a chronic inherited anemia in which a large proportion or the majority of the red blood cells tend to sickle, which occurs primarily in individuals of Negro ancestry, and which results from homozygosity for a semidominant gene — called also *sickle-cell disease*
sickle–cell trait *n* (1948) : an inherited blood condition in which some red blood cells tend to sickle but usu. not enough to produce anemia, which occurs primarily in individuals of Negro ancestry, and which results from heterozygosity for a semidominant gene
sickl·emia \,sik-ə-'lē-mē-ə\ *n* [NL, fr. E *sickle* (cell) + NL *-emia*] (1949) : SICKLE-CELL TRAIT
[1]**sick·ly** \'sik-lē\ *adj* (14c) **1** : somewhat unwell; *also* : habitually ailing **2** : produced by or associated with sickness ⟨a ~ complexion⟩ ⟨a ~ appetite⟩ **3** : producing or tending to produce disease : UNWHOLESOME ⟨a ~ climate⟩ **4** : appearing as if sick : **a** : LANGUID, PALE ⟨a ~ flame⟩ **b** : WRETCHED, UNEASY ⟨a ~ smile⟩ **c** : lacking in vigor : WEAK ⟨a ~ plant⟩ ⟨~ beer⟩ **5** : SICKENING ⟨a ~ odor⟩ ⟨a ~ green⟩ — **sick·li·ness** *n* — **sickly** *adv*
[2]**sickly** *vt* **sick·lied; sick·ly·ing** (1763) : to make sick or sickly
sick·ness \'sik-nəs\ *n* (bef. 12c) **1 a** : ill health : ILLNESS **b** : a disordered, weakened, or unsound condition **2** : a specific disease **3** : NAUSEA, QUEASINESS
sicko \'sik-(,)ō\ *n, pl* **sick·os** (1963) : SICKIE
sick–out \'sik-,au̇t\ *n* (1951) : an organized absence from work by workers on the pretext of sickness
sick pay *n* (1887) : salary or wages paid to an employee while on sick leave
sick·room \'sik-,rüm, -,ru̇m\ *n* (1749) : a room in which a person is confined by sickness
sic pas·sim \'sik-'pas-əm, 'sēk-'päs-im\ *adv* [L] (1921) : so throughout — used of a word or idea to be found throughout a book or a writer's work
sid·dur \'sid-ər, -,u̇(ə)r\ *n, pl* **sid·du·rim** \sə-'du̇r-əm\ [LHeb *siddūr,* lit., order, arrangement] (1903) : a Jewish prayer book containing both Hebrew and Aramaic prayers used in the Ashkenazic daily liturgy
[1]**side** \'sīd\ *n* [ME, fr. OE *sīde;* akin to OHG *sīta* side, OE *sīd* ample, wide, *sāwan* to sow — more at SOW] (bef. 12c) **1 a** : the right or left part of the wall or trunk of the body ⟨a pain in the ~⟩ **b** (1) : one of the halves of the animal body on either side of the mesial plane (2) : a cut of meat including that about the ribs of one half of the body — used chiefly of smoked pork products **c** : one longitudinal half of a hide **2** : a place, space, or direction with respect to a center or to a line of division (as of an aisle, river, or street) **3 a** : one of the longer bounding surfaces or lines of an object esp. contrasted with the ends ⟨the ~ of a barn⟩ **b** : a line or surface forming a border or face of an object ⟨a die has six ~*s*⟩ ⟨the back ~ of the moon⟩ **c** : either surface of a thin object ⟨one ~ of a record⟩ ⟨right ~ of the cloth⟩ **d** : a bounding line of a geometric figure ⟨~ of a triangle⟩ **4 a** : the space beside one ⟨stood by my ~⟩ **b** : an area next to something — usu. used in combination ⟨a pool*side* interview⟩ **5** : a slope or declivity of a hill or ridge **6 a** : the attitude or activity of one person or group with respect to another : PART ⟨there was no malice on my ~⟩ **b** : a position that is opposite to or contrasted with another ⟨two ~*s* to every question⟩ ⟨came down on the ~ of law and order⟩ **c** : a body of partisans or contestants ⟨victory for neither ~⟩ **d** : TEAM ⟨11 players on each ~⟩ **7** : a line of descent traced through one's parent ⟨grandfather on his mother's ~⟩ **8** : an aspect or part of something contrasted with some other real or implied aspect or part ⟨the better ~ of his nature⟩ ⟨the sales ~ of the business⟩ ⟨the seasoning is a bit on the heavy ~⟩ **9** *Brit* : sideways spin imparted to a billiard ball **10** : a sheet containing the lines and cues for a single theatrical role **11** : RECORDING — **on the side 1** : in addition to the main portion **2** : in addition to a principal occupation — **this side of** : short of : ALMOST ⟨an attitude just *this side of* scandalous⟩
[2]**side** *adj* (14c) **1 a** : of or relating to the side **b** : situated on the side ⟨~ window⟩ **2 a** : directed toward or from the side ⟨~ thrust⟩ ⟨~ wind⟩ **b** : INCIDENTAL, INDIRECT ⟨~ issue⟩ ⟨~ remark⟩ **c** : made on the side ⟨~ payment⟩ **d** : additional to the main portion ⟨~ order of french fries⟩
[3]**side** *vb* **sid·ed; sid·ing** *vt* (1591) **1** : to agree with : SUPPORT **2** : to be side by side with **3** : to set or put aside : clear away ⟨~ dishes⟩ **4** : to furnish with sides or siding ⟨~ a house⟩ ~ *vi* : to take sides : join or form sides ⟨*sided* with the rebels⟩
[4]**side** *n* [obs. E *side* (proud, boastful)] (1878) : swaggering or arrogant manner : PRETENTIOUSNESS
side·arm \'sīd-,ärm\ *adj* (ca. 1929) : of, relating to, or constituting a baseball pitching style in which the arm is not raised above the shoulder and the ball is thrown with a sideways sweep of the arm between shoulder and hip ⟨~ delivery⟩ — **sidearm** *adv*
side arm *n* (1689) : a weapon (as a sword, revolver, or bayonet) worn at the side or in the belt
side·band \-,band\ *n* (1922) : the band of frequencies (as of radio waves) on either side of the carrier frequency produced by modulation
side·bar \-,bär\ *n* (1945) : a short news story accompanying and presenting sidelights of a major story
side bearing *n* (1924) : the space provided at each side of a typeset letter to prevent its touching adjoining letters
side·board \'sīd-,bō(ə)rd, -,bȯ(ə)rd\ *n* (1671) : a piece of dining-room furniture having compartments and shelves for holding articles of table service

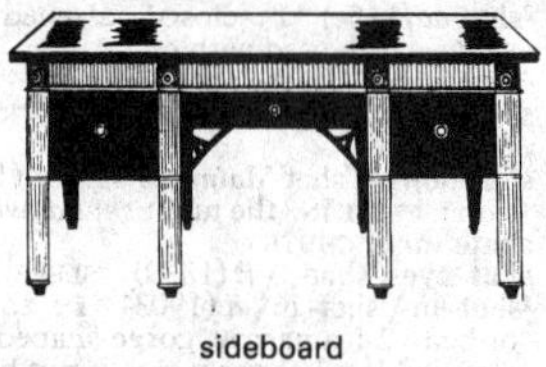

sideboard

side·burns \-,bərnz\ *n pl* [anagram of *burnsides*] (1887) **1** : SIDE-WHISKERS **2** : continuations of the hairline in front of the ears — **side·burned** \-,bərnd\ *adj*
side by side *adv* (13c) **1** : beside one another **2** : in the same place, time, or circumstance ⟨lived peacefully *side by side* for many years⟩ — **side–by–side** *adj*
side·car \'sīd-,kär\ *n* (1904) **1** : a car attached to the side of a motorcycle for a passenger **2** : a cocktail consisting of a liqueur with lemon juice and brandy
side chain *n* (1886) : a shorter chain of atoms attached to the principal chain or to a ring in a molecule
side chair *n* (1925) : a chair without arms used usu. in a dining room
sid·ed \'sīd-əd\ *adj* (15c) : having sides often of a specified number or kind ⟨one-*sided*⟩ ⟨glass-*sided*⟩ — **sid·ed·ness** *n*
side dish *n* (1725) : a food served separately along with the main course
side·dress \'sīd-,dres\ *n* (1966) **1** : plant nutrients placed on or in the soil near the roots of a growing crop often by means of a cultivator having a fertilizer-distributing attachment **2** : the act or process of applying sidedress to a crop — **side–dress** \'sīd-,dres\ *vt*
side–dress·ing *n* (1935) : SIDEDRESS
side drum *n* (ca. 1800) : SNARE DRUM
side effect *n* (1884) : a secondary and usu. adverse effect (as of a drug) ⟨toxic *side effects*⟩ — called also *side reaction*
side–glance \'sīd-,glan(t)s\ *n* (1611) **1** : a glance directed to the side **2** : a passing allusion : an indirect or slight reference
side·hill \-,hil\ *n* (1674) : HILLSIDE — **sidehill** *adj*
side horse *n* (ca. 1934) : POMMEL HORSE
side·kick \'sīd-,kik\ *n* (1916) : a person closely associated with another as subordinate or partner
side·light \-,līt\ *n* (1610) **1 a** : light coming or produced from the side **b** : incidental light or information **2** : the red light on the port bow or the green light on the starboard bow carried by ships under way at night
[1]**side·line** \-,līn\ *n* (1862) **1** : a line at right angles to a goal line or end line and marking a side of a court or field of play for athletic games **2 a** : a line of goods sold in addition to one's principal line **b** : a business or activity pursued in addition to one's regular occupation **3 a** : the space immediately outside the lines along either side of an athletic field or court **b** : the standpoint of persons not immediately participating — usu. used in pl.
[2]**sideline** *vt* (1943) : to put out of action : put on the sidelines
side·lin·er \'sīd-,lī-nər\ *n* (1947) : one that remains on the sidelines during an activity : one that does not participate
[1]**side·ling** \'sīd-liŋ\ *adv* [ME *sidling,* fr. [1]*side* + *-ling*] (14c) : in a sidelong direction : SIDEWAYS
[2]**sideling** *adj* (1611) **1** : directed toward one side : OBLIQUE **2** : having an inclination : SLOPING ⟨~ ground⟩
[1]**side·long** \'sīd-,lȯŋ\ *adv* [alter. of [1]*sideling*] (1580) **1** : SIDEWAYS, OBLIQUELY **2** : on the side
[2]**sidelong** \,sīd-\ *adj* (1597) **1** : lying or inclining to one side : SLANTING **2 a** : directed to one side ⟨~ looks⟩ **b** : indirect rather than straightforward
side·man \'sīd-,man\ *n* (1947) : a member of a band or orchestra and esp. of a jazz or swing orchestra
side·piece \-,pēs\ *n* (1802) : a piece forming or contained in the side of something ⟨the ~ of a carriage⟩
sider- *or* **sidero-** *comb form* [MF, fr. L, fr. Gk *sidēr-, sidēro-,* fr. *sidēros*] : iron ⟨*sidero*lite⟩ ⟨*sider*osis⟩
-sid·er \'sīd-ər\ *comb form* : one placed or living in a usu. specified side (as a section of the city) ⟨an east-*sider*⟩
si·de·re·al \sī-'dir-ē-əl, sə-\ *adj* [L *sidereus,* fr. *sider-, sidus* star, constellation; akin to Lith *svidus* shining] (1647) : of, relating to, or expressed in relation to stars or constellations : ASTRAL
sidereal day *n* (1794) : the interval between two successive transits of a point on the celestial sphere (as the vernal equinox) over the upper meridian of a place : 23 hours, 56 minutes, 4.09 seconds of mean time
sidereal hour *n* (ca. 1891) : the 24th part of a sidereal day
sidereal minute *n* (ca. 1909) : the 60th part of a sidereal hour
sidereal month *n* (1868) : the mean time of the moon's revolution in its orbit with reference to a star's position : 27 days, 7 hours, 43 minutes, 11.5 seconds of mean time
sidereal second *n* (ca. 1909) : the 60th part of a sidereal minute
sidereal time *n* (1812) **1** : time based on the sidereal day **2** : the hour angle of the vernal equinox at a place
sidereal year *n* (1681) : the time in which the earth completes one revolution in its orbit around the sun measured with respect to the fixed stars : 365 days, 6 hours, 9 minutes, and 9.54 seconds of solar time
[1]**sid·er·ite** \'sid-ə-,rīt\ *n* [G *siderit,* fr. Gk *sidēros* iron] (1850) : a native ferrous carbonate $FeCO_3$ that is a valuable iron ore
[2]**siderite** *n* (1875) : a nickel-iron meteorite
sid·er·it·ic \,sid-ə-'rit-ik\ *adj* (1796) : of, relating to, or containing siderite
si·de·ro·lite \sī-'dir-ə-,līt, 'sid-ə-rə-\ *n* (1863) : a stony iron meteorite
side·sad·dle \'sīd-,sad-ᵊl\ *n* (15c) : a saddle for women in which the rider sits with both legs on the same side of the horse — **sidesaddle** *adv*
side·show \-,shō\ *n* (1846) **1** : a minor show offered in addition to a main exhibition (as of a circus) **2** : an incidental diversion or spectacle
side·slip \-,slip\ *vi* (1887) **1** : to skid or slide sideways **2** : to slide sideways through the air in a downward direction in an airplane along an inclined lateral axis
side·spin \-,spin\ *n* [[1]*side* + *spin*] (1926) : a rotary motion that causes a ball to revolve horizontally

side·split·ting \-ˌsplit-iŋ\ *adj* (1856) **:** extremely funny — **side·split·ting·ly** *adv*
side·step \ˈsīd-ˌstep\ *vi* (1901) **1 :** to take a side step **2 :** to avoid an issue or decision ~ *vt* **1 :** to move out of the way of **:** AVOID ⟨~ a blow⟩ **2 :** BYPASS, EVADE ⟨~ a question⟩ — **side·step·per** *n*
side step *n* (1847) **1 :** a step aside (as in boxing to avoid a blow) **2 :** a step taken sideways (as when climbing on skis)
side–strad·dle hop \ˌsīd-ˌstrad-ᵊl-\ *n* (1952) **:** JUMPING JACK 2
side street *n* (1617) **:** a street joining and often terminated by a main thoroughfare
side·stroke \ˈsīd-ˌstrōk\ *n* (1867) **:** a swimming stroke which is executed on the side and in which the arms are swept backward and downward and the legs do a scissors kick
[1]**side·swipe** \-ˌswīp\ *vt* (1904) **:** to strike with a glancing blow along the side ⟨*sideswiped* a parked car⟩
[2]**sideswipe** *n* (1926) **1 a :** the action of sideswiping **b :** an instance of sideswiping **:** a glancing blow **2 :** an incidental deprecatory remark, allusion, or reference
side table *n* (14c) **:** a table designed to be placed against a wall
[1]**side·track** \ˈsīd-ˌtrak\ *n* (1835) **1 :** SIDING 2 **2 :** a position or condition of secondary importance to which one may be diverted
[2]**sidetrack** *vt* (1881) **1 :** to transfer to a railroad siding **2 a :** to turn aside from a purpose **:** DEFLECT **b :** to prevent action on by diversionary tactics ⟨~ an issue⟩
side·walk \ˈsīd-ˌwȯk\ *n* (1739) **:** a usu. paved walk for pedestrians at the side of a street
sidewalk superintendent *n* (1950) **:** a spectator at a building or demolition job
side·wall \ˈsīd-ˌwȯl\ *n* (14c) **1 :** a wall forming the side of something **2 :** the side of an automotive tire between the tread shoulder and the rim bead
side·ward \ˈsīd-wərd\ *or* **side·wards** \-wərdz\ *adv* (15c) **:** toward a side
side·way \ˈsīd-ˌwā\ *adv or adj* (1612) **:** SIDEWAYS
side·ways \-ˌwāz\ *adv or adj* (1577) **1 :** from one side **2 :** with one side forward ⟨turn ~⟩ **3 :** obliquely or downward to one side; *also* **:** ASKANCE ⟨look ~ at someone⟩
side–wheel \ˈsīd-ˌhwēl, ˈsīd-ˌwēl\ *adj* (1857) **:** of or being a steamer having a paddle wheel on each side — **side–wheel·er** \-ər\ *n*
side–whiskers \ˈsīd-ˌhwis-kərz, ˈsīd-ˌwis-\ *n pl* (1888) **:** whiskers on the side of the face usu. worn long — **side–whis·kered** \-kərd\ *adj*
side·wind·er \ˈsīd-ˌwīn-dər\ *n* (1840) **1 :** a heavy swinging blow from the side **2 :** a small pale-colored desert rattlesnake (*Crotalus cerastes*) of the southwestern U.S. that moves by thrusting its body diagonally forward in a series of flat S-shaped loops
side·wise \ˈsīd-ˌwīz\ *adv* (1571) **:** SIDEWAYS
sid·ing \ˈsīd-iŋ\ *n* (1603) **1** *archaic* **:** the taking of sides **:** PARTISANSHIP **2 :** a short railroad track connected with the main track **3 :** material (as boards or metal pieces) forming the exposed surface of outside walls of frame buildings
si·dle \ˈsīd-ᵊl\ *vb* **si·dled; si·dling** \ˈsīd-liŋ, -ᵊl-iŋ\ [prob. back-formation fr. [2]*sideling*] *vi* (1697) **:** to go or move with one side foremost esp. in a furtive advance ~ *vt* **:** to cause to move or turn sideways — **sidle** *n*
sid·ling \ˈsīd-liŋ\ *var of* SIDELING
siege \ˈsēj *also* ˈsēzh\ *n* [ME *sege,* fr. OF, seat, blockade, fr. (assumed) VL *sedicum,* fr. *sedicare,* to settle, fr. L *sedēre* to sit — more at SIT] (13c) **1** *obs* **:** a seat of distinction **:** THRONE **2 a :** a military blockade of a city or fortified place to compel it to surrender **b :** a persistent attack (as of illness) — **siege** *vt* — **lay siege to 1 :** to besiege militarily **2 :** to pursue diligently or persistently
Siege Perilous *n* **:** a seat at King Arthur's Round Table reserved for the knight destined to achieve the quest of the Holy Grail and fatal to any other occupying it
Sieg·fried \ˈsig-ˌfrēd, ˈsēg-\ *n* [G] **:** a hero in Germanic legend who slays a dragon guarding a gold hoard and wakes Brunhild from her enchanted sleep
Siegfried line *n* [*Siegfried*] (1918) **:** a line of German defensive fortifications facing the Maginot Line
sie·mens \ˈsē-mənz, ˈzē-\ *n, pl* **siemens** [Werner von *Siemens* †1892 Ger. electrical engineer and inventor] (ca. 1933) **:** a unit of conductance in the meter-kilogram-second system equivalent to one ampere per volt
si·en·na \sē-ˈen-ə\ *n* [It *terra di Siena,* lit., Siena earth, fr. *Siena,* Italy] (1787) **:** an earthy substance containing oxides of iron and usu. of manganese that is brownish yellow when raw and orange red or reddish brown when burnt and is used as a pigment
si·ero·zem \sē-ˌer-ə-ˈzhȯm\ *n* [Russ *serozem,* fr. *seryĭ* gray + *zemlya* earth; akin to L *humus* earth — more at HUMBLE] (1941) **:** any of a group of zonal soils brownish gray at the surface and lighter below, based in a carbonate or hardpan layer, and characteristic of temperate to cool arid regions
si·er·ra \sē-ˈer-ə\ *n* [Sp, lit., saw, fr. L *serra*] (1600) **1 a :** a range of mountains esp. with a serrated or irregular outline **b :** the country about a sierra **2 :** any of several large fishes (genus *Scomberomorus*) related to the mackerel
Sierra (ca. 1952) — a communications code word for the letter *s*
si·er·ran \sē-ˈer-ən\ *adj* (1873) **1 :** of or relating to a sierra ⟨~ foothills⟩ **2** *cap* **:** of or relating to the Sierra Nevada mountains of the western U.S.
Sierran *n* (1906) **:** a native or inhabitant of the region around the Sierra Nevada mountains
si·es·ta \sē-ˈes-tə\ *n* [Sp, fr. L *sexta (hora)* noon, lit., sixth hour — more at SEXT] (1655) **:** an afternoon nap or rest
sie·va bean \ˈsē-və-, ˈsiv-ē-\ *n* [origin unknown] (ca. 1891) **:** any of several small-seeded beans closely related to and sometimes classed as lima beans; *also* **:** the seed of a sieva bean
[1]**sieve** \ˈsiv\ *n* [ME *sive,* fr. OE *sife;* akin to OHG *sib* sieve, Serb *sípiti* to drizzle] (bef. 12c) **:** a device with meshes or perforations through which finer particles of a mixture (as of ashes, flour, or sand) of various sizes are passed to separate them from coarser ones, through which the liquid is drained from liquid-containing material, or through which soft materials are forced for reduction to fine particles
[2]**sieve** *vb* **sieved; siev·ing** (15c) **:** SIFT
sieve of Er·a·tos·the·nes \-ˌer-ə-ˈtäs-thə-ˌnēz\ (ca. 1928) **:** a procedure for finding prime numbers that involves writing down the odd numbers from 2 up in succession and drawing a line through every third number after 3, every fifth after 5 including those already lined out, every seventh after 7, and so on with each successive number which has not been lined out, every number that is not lined out being prime
sieve plate *n* (1875) **:** a perforated wall or part of a wall at the end of one of the individual cells making up a sieve tube
sieve tube *n* (1875) **:** a tube consisting of an end-to-end series of thin-walled living cells characteristic of the phloem and held to function chiefly in translocation of organic solutes
si·fa·ka \sə-ˈfak-ə\ *n* [Malagasy] (ca. 1845) **:** any of several diurnal mostly black and white lemurs (genus *Propithecus*) with a long tail and silky fur
sift \ˈsift\ *vb* [ME *siften,* fr. OE *siftan;* akin to OE *sife* sieve] *vt* (bef. 12c) **1 a :** to put through a sieve ⟨~ flour⟩ **b :** to separate or separate out by or as if by putting through a sieve **2 :** to go through esp. to sort out what is useful or valuable ⟨~*ed* the evidence⟩ — often used with *through* ⟨~ through a pile of old letters⟩ **3 :** to scatter by or as if by sifting ⟨~ sugar on a cake⟩ ~ *vi* **1 :** to use a sieve **2 :** to pass or fall as if through a sieve — **sift·er** *n*
sift·ing *n* (15c) **1 :** the act or process of sifting **2** *pl* **:** sifted material
[1]**sigh** \ˈsī\ *vb* [ME *sihen,* alter. of *sichen,* fr. OE *sīcan;* akin to MD *versiken* to sigh] *vi* (bef. 12c) **1 :** to take a deep audible breath (as in weariness or grief) **2 :** to make a sound like sighing ⟨wind ~*ing* in the branches⟩ **3 :** GRIEVE, YEARN ⟨~*ing* for days gone by⟩ ~ *vt* **1 :** to express by sighs **2** *archaic* **:** to utter sighs over **:** MOURN — **sigh·er** \ˈsī(-ə)r\ *n*
[2]**sigh** *n* (14c) **1 :** an act of sighing esp. when involuntary and expressing an emotion or feeling (as weariness or relief) **2 :** the sound of gently moving or escaping air ⟨~*s* of the summer breeze⟩
[1]**sight** \ˈsīt\ *n* [ME, fr. OE *gesiht* faculty or act of sight, thing seen; akin to OHG *gisiht* sight, OE *sēon* to see] (bef. 12c) **1 :** something that is seen **:** SPECTACLE **2 a :** a thing regarded as worth seeing — usu. used in pl. ⟨the ~*s* of the city⟩ **b :** something ludicrous or disorderly in appearance ⟨you look a ~⟩ **3 a** *chiefly dial* **:** a great number or quantity **b :** a good deal **:** LOT ⟨a far ~ better⟩ ⟨not by a damn ~⟩ **4 a :** the process, power, or function of seeing; *specif* **:** the animal sense of which the end organ is the eye and by which the position, shape, and color of objects are perceived **b :** mental or spiritual perception **c :** mental view; *specif* **:** JUDGMENT **5 a :** the act of looking at or beholding **b :** INSPECTION, PERUSAL **c :** VIEW, GLIMPSE **d :** an observation to determine direction or position (as by a navigator) **6 a :** a perception of an object by or as if by the eye ⟨never lost ~ of the objective⟩ **b :** the range of vision **7 :** presentation of a note or draft to the maker or draftee **:** DEMAND **8 a :** a device for guiding the eye (as in aiming a firearm or bomb) **b :** a device with a small aperture through which objects are to be seen and by which their direction is ascertained **c** *pl* **:** ASPIRATION ⟨set her ~*s* on a medical career⟩ — **in sight :** at or within a reasonable distance or time — **on sight :** as soon as seen — **out of sight 1 :** beyond comparison **2 :** beyond all expectation or reason **3** — used as a generalized expression of approval — **sight for sore eyes :** one whose appearance or arrival is an occasion for joy or relief
[2]**sight** *vt* (1602) **1 :** to get or catch sight of ⟨several whales were ~*ed*⟩ **2 :** to look at through or as if through a sight; *esp* **:** to test for straightness **3 :** to aim by means of sights **4 a :** to equip with sights **b :** to adjust the sights of ~ *vi* **1 :** to take aim **2 :** to look carefully in a particular direction
[3]**sight** *adj* (1801) **1 :** based on recognition or comprehension without previous study ⟨a ~ translation⟩ **2 :** payable on presentation
sight draft *n* (1850) **:** a draft payable on presentation
sight·ed \ˈsīt-əd\ *adj* (1552) **:** having sight ⟨clear-*sighted*⟩
sight gag *n* (1949) **:** a comic bit or episode whose effect is produced by pantomime or camera shot rather than by words
sight·less \ˈsīt-ləs\ *adj* (13c) **1 :** lacking sight **:** BLIND **2 :** INVISIBLE — **sight·less·ly** *adv* — **sight·less·ness** *n*
sight·ly \-lē\ *adj* (1562) **1 :** pleasing to the sight **:** ATTRACTIVE **2 :** affording a fine view — **sight·li·ness** *n* — **sightly** *adv*
sight–read \-ˌrēd\ *vb* **-read** \-ˌred\; **-read·ing** \-ˌrēd-iŋ\ [back-formation fr. *sight reader*] *vt* (1903) **:** to read (as a foreign language) or perform (music) without previous preparation or study ~ *vi* **:** to read at sight; *esp* **:** to perform music at sight — **sight reader** *n*
sight rhyme *n* (ca. 1936) **:** EYE RHYME
sight·see \ˈsīt-ˌsē\ *vi* [back-formation fr. *sight-seeing*] (1835) **:** to go about seeing sights of interest — **sight·se·er** \-ˌsē-ər, -ˌsi(-ə)r\ *n*
sight–see·ing \ˈsīt-ˌsē-iŋ\ *adj* (1863) **:** devoted to or used for seeing sights — **sight–seeing** *n*
sight unseen *adv* (1892) **:** without inspection or appraisal
sig·il \ˈsij-əl, ˈsig-ˌil\ *n* [L *sigillum* — more at SEAL] (1610) **1 :** SEAL, SIGNET **2 :** a sign, word, or device of supposed occult power in astrology or magic
sig·ma \ˈsig-mə\ *n* [Gk] (1607) **1 :** the 18th letter of the Greek alphabet — see ALPHABET table **2 :** an unstable subatomic particle of the baryon family existing in positive, negative, and neutral charge states with masses respectively 2328, 2343, and 2333 times the mass of an electron — called also *sigma particle* **3 :** STANDARD DEVIATION
sig·moid \ˈsig-ˌmȯid\ *also* **sig·moi·dal** \sig-ˈmȯid-ᵊl\ *adj* [Gk *sigmoeidēs,* fr. *sigma;* fr. a common form of sigma shaped like the Roman letter C] (1670) **1 a :** curved like the letter C **b :** curved in two directions like the letter S **2 :** of, relating to, or being the sigmoid flexure of the intestine — **sig·moi·dal·ly** \sig-ˈmȯid-ᵊl-ē\ *adv*
sigmoid flexure *n* (1786) **:** the contracted and crooked part of the colon immediately above the rectum — called also *sigmoid colon*
[1]**sign** \ˈsīn\ *n* [ME *signe,* fr. OF, fr. L *signum* mark, token, sign, image, seal; prob. akin to L *secare* to cut — more at SAW] (13c) **1 a :** a motion or gesture by which a thought is expressed or a command or wish made known **b :** SIGNAL 2a **c :** a fundamental linguistic unit that designates an object or relation or has a purely syntactic function **d :** one of a set of gestures used to represent language; *also* **:** SIGN LANGUAGE **2 :** a mark having a conventional meaning and used in place of

words or to represent a complex notion **3 :** one of the 12 divisions of the zodiac **4 a** (1) **:** a character (as a flat or sharp) used in musical notation (2) **:** SEGNO **b :** a character (as ÷) indicating a mathematical operation; *also* **:** one of two characters + and − that form part of the symbol of a number and characterize it as positive or negative **5 a :** a lettered board or other display used to identify or advertise a place of business **b :** a posted command, warning, or direction **c :** SIGNBOARD **6 a :** something material or external that stands for or signifies something spiritual **b :** something indicating the presence or existence of something else ⟨~*s* of success⟩ ⟨a ~ of the times⟩ **c :** PRESAGE, PORTENT ⟨~*s* of an early spring⟩ **d :** an objective evidence of plant or animal disease **7** *pl usu* **sign :** traces of a usu. wild animal ⟨red fox ~⟩ — **signed** *adj*

syn SIGN, MARK, TOKEN, NOTE, SYMPTOM mean a discernible indication of what is not itself directly perceptible. SIGN applies to any indication to be perceived by the senses or the reason; MARK suggests something impressed on or inherently characteristic of a thing often in contrast to general outward appearance; TOKEN applies to something that serves as a proof of something intangible; NOTE suggests a distinguishing mark or characteristic; SYMPTOM suggests an outward indication of an internal change or condition.

[2]sign *vb* [ME *signen,* fr. MF *signer,* fr. L *signare* to mark, sign, seal, fr. *signum*] *vt* (14c) **1 a :** to place a sign on **b :** CROSS 2 **c :** to represent or indicate by a sign **2 a :** to affix a signature to **:** ratify or attest by hand or seal ⟨~ a bill into law⟩ ⟨the prisoner ~*ed* a confession⟩ **b :** to assign or convey formally ⟨~*ed* over his property to his brother⟩ **c :** to write down (one's name) **3 :** to communicate by making a sign or by sign language **4 :** to engage or hire by securing the signature of on a contract of employment — often used with *up* or *on* ~ *vi* **1 :** to write one's name in token of assent, responsibility, or obligation **2 a :** to make a sign or signal **b :** to use sign language — **sign·ee** \ˌsī-ˈnē\ *n* — **sign·er** \ˈsī-nər\ *n*

[1]sig·nal \ˈsig-nᵊl\ *n* [ME, fr. MF, fr. ML *signale,* fr. LL, neut. of *signalis* of a sign, fr. L *signum*] (14c) **1 :** SIGN, INDICATION **2 a :** an act, event, or watchword that has been agreed on as the occasion of concerted action **b :** something that incites to action **3 :** something (as a sound, gesture, or object) that conveys notice or warning **4 :** an object (as a flag on a pole) centered over a point so as to be observed from other positions in surveying **5 a :** an object used to transmit or convey information beyond the range of human voice **b :** the sound or image conveyed in telegraphy, telephony, radio, radar, or television **c :** a detectable physical quantity or impulse (as a voltage, current, or magnetic field strength) by which messages or information can be transmitted

[2]signal *vb* **sig·naled** *or* **sig·nalled; sig·nal·ing** *or* **sig·nal·ling** \-nə-liŋ\ *vt* (1805) **1 :** to notify by a signal ⟨~*ed* the fleet to turn back⟩ **2 a :** to communicate by signals **b :** to constitute a characteristic feature of (a meaningful linguistic form) ~ *vi* **:** to make or send a signal — **sig·nal·er** *or* **sig·nal·ler** *n*

[3]signal *adj* [modif. of F *signalé,* pp. of *signaler* to distinguish, fr. OIt *segnalare* to signal, distinguish, fr. *segnale* signal, fr. ML *signale*] (1641) **1 :** distinguished from the ordinary ⟨~ achievement⟩ **2 :** used in signaling ⟨~ beacon⟩ ***syn*** see NOTICEABLE

sig·nal·ize \ˈsig-nə-ˌlīz\ *vt* **-ized; -iz·ing** [[3]*signal*] (1654) **1 :** to make conspicuous **:** DISTINGUISH **2 :** to point out carefully or distinctly **3 :** to make signals to **:** SIGNAL; *also* **:** INDICATE **4 :** to place traffic signals at or on — **sig·nal·iza·tion** \ˌsig-nə-lə-ˈzā-shən\ *n*

sig·nal·ly \ˈsig-nə-lē\ *adv* (1641) **:** in a signal manner **:** NOTABLY

sig·nal·man \ˈsig-nᵊl-mən, -ˌman\ *n* (1737) **:** one who signals or works with signals

sig·nal·ment \-mənt\ *n* [F *signalement,* fr. *signaler*] (1778) **:** description by peculiar, appropriate, or characteristic marks; *specif* **:** the systematic description of a person for purposes of identification

sig·na·to·ry \ˈsig-nə-ˌtōr-ē, -ˌtȯr-\ *n, pl* **-ries** [L *signatorius* of sealing, fr. *signatus,* pp.] (1866) **:** a signer with another or others ⟨*signatories* to a petition⟩; *esp* **:** a government bound with others by a signed convention — **signatory** *adj*

sig·na·ture \ˈsig-nə-ˌchu̇(ə)r, -chər, -ˌt(y)u̇(ə)r\ *n* [MF or ML; MF, fr. ML *signatura,* fr. L *signatus,* pp. of *signare* to sign, seal] (1580) **1 a :** the name of a person written with his own hand **b :** the act of signing one's name **2 :** a feature in the appearance or qualities of a natural object formerly held to indicate its utility in medicine **3 a :** a letter or figure placed usu. at the bottom of the first page on each sheet of printed pages (as of a book) as a direction to the binder in arranging and gathering the sheets **b :** a folded sheet that is one unit of a book **4 a :** KEY SIGNATURE **b :** TIME SIGNATURE **5 :** the part of a medical prescription that contains the directions to the patient **6 :** something (as a tune, musical number, or logo) that serves to identify; *also* **:** a characteristic mark

sign·board \ˈsīn-ˌbō(ə)rd, -ˌbȯ(ə)rd\ *n* (1632) **:** a board bearing a notice or sign

[1]sig·net \ˈsig-nət\ *n* [ME, fr. MF, dim. of *signe* sign, seal] (14c) **1 :** a seal used officially to give personal authority to a document in lieu of signature **2 :** the impression made by or as if by a signet **3 :** a small intaglio seal (as in a finger ring)

[2]signet *vt* (15c) **:** to stamp or authenticate with a signet

signet ring *n* (1681) **:** a finger ring engraved with a signet, seal, or monogram **:** SEAL RING

sig·nif·i·cance \sig-ˈnif-i-kən(t)s\ *n* (15c) **1 a :** something that is conveyed as a meaning often obscurely or indirectly **b :** the quality of conveying or implying **2 a :** the quality of being important **:** MOMENT **b :** the quality of being statistically significant ***syn*** see IMPORTANCE

significance level *n* (1947) **:** LEVEL OF SIGNIFICANCE

sig·nif·i·can·cy \sig-ˈnif-i-kən-sē\ *n* (1595) **:** SIGNIFICANCE

sig·nif·i·cant \-kənt\ *adj* [L *significant-, significans,* prp. of *significare* to signify] (1579) **1 :** having meaning; *esp* **:** SUGGESTIVE ⟨a ~ glance⟩ **2 a :** having or likely to have influence or effect **:** IMPORTANT ⟨a ~ piece of legislation⟩; *also* **:** of a noticeably or measurably large amount ⟨a ~ number of layoffs⟩ ⟨producing ~ profits ⟩ **b :** probably caused by something other than mere chance ⟨statistically ~ correlation between vitamin deficiency and disease⟩ — **sig·nif·i·cant·ly** *adv*

significant digit *n* (1923) **:** one of the digits of a number beginning with the digit farthest to the left that is not zero and ending with the last digit farthest to the right that is not zero or is a zero considered to be exact — called also *significant figure*

sig·ni·fi·ca·tion \ˌsig-nə-fə-ˈkā-shən\ *n* (14c) **1 a :** the act or process of signifying by signs or other symbolic means **b :** a formal notification **2 :** PURPORT; *esp* **:** the meaning that a term, symbol, or character regularly conveys or is intended to convey **3** *chiefly dial* **:** IMPORTANCE, CONSEQUENCE

sig·nif·i·ca·tive \sig-ˈnif-ə-ˌkāt-iv\ *adj* (15c) **1 :** SIGNIFICANT, SUGGESTIVE **2 :** INDICATIVE ⟨symptoms ~ of malaria⟩

sig·nif·ics \sig-ˈnif-iks\ *n pl but sing or pl in constr* [*signify*] (1896) **:** SEMIOTIC, SEMANTICS

sig·ni·fy \ˈsig-nə-ˌfī\ *vb* **-fied; -fy·ing** [ME *signifien,* fr. OF *signifier,* fr. L *significare* to indicate, signify, fr. *signum* sign] *vt* (13c) **1 a :** MEAN, DENOTE **b :** IMPLY **2 :** to show esp. by a conventional token (as word, signal, or gesture) ~ *vi* **:** to have significance **:** MATTER — **sig·ni·fi·er** \ˈsig-nə-ˌfī(-ə)r\ *n*

sign in *vi* (1949) **:** to make a record of arrival by signing a register or punching a time clock ~ *vt* **:** to record arrival of (a person) or receipt of (an article) by signing

sign language *n* (1847) **1 :** a system of hand gestures used for communication (as by the deaf) **2 :** an unsystematic method of communicating chiefly by manual gestures used by people speaking different languages

sign of aggregation (1942) **:** any of various conventional devices (as braces, brackets, parentheses, or vinculums) used in mathematics to indicate that two or more terms are to be treated as one quantity

sign off \(ˈ)sī-ˈnȯf\ *vi* (1926) **1 :** to announce the end of something (as a message or broadcast) **2 :** to approve or acknowledge something by or as if by a signature ⟨*sign off* on a memo⟩ — **sign–off** \ˈsī-ˌnȯf\ *n*

sign of the cross (13c) **:** a gesture of the hand forming a cross esp. on forehead, breast, and shoulders to profess Christian faith or invoke divine protection or blessing

sign on \(ˈ)sī-ˈnȯn, -ˈnän\ *vi* (1885) **1 :** to engage oneself by or as if by a signature **2 :** to announce the start of broadcasting for the day — **sign–on** \ˈsī-ˌnȯn, -ˌnän\ *n*

si·gnor *also* **si·gnior** \sēn-ˈyȯ(ə)r, -ˈyō(ə)r\ *n, pl* **signors** *or* **si·gno·ri** \sēn-ˈyōr-(ˌ)ē, -ˈyȯr-\ *also* **signiors** [It *signore, signor,* fr. ML *senior* superior, lord — more at SENOR] (1582) **:** an Italian man usu. of rank or gentility — used as a title equivalent to *Mister*

si·gno·ra \sēn-ˈyōr-ə, -ˈyȯr-\ *n, pl* **signoras** *or* **si·gno·re** \-ˈyōr-(ˌ)ā, -ˈyȯr-\ [It, fem. of *signore, signor*] (1763) **:** a married Italian woman usu. of rank or gentility — used as a title equivalent to *Mrs.*

si·gno·re \sēn-ˈyōr-(ˌ)ā, -ˈyȯr-\ *n, pl* **si·gno·ri** \-ˈyōr-(ˌ)ē, -ˈyȯr-\ [It] (1594) **:** SIGNOR

si·gno·ri·na \ˌsē-nyə-ˈrē-nə\ *n, pl* **-nas** *or* **-ne** \-(ˌ)nā\ [It, fr. dim. of *signora*] (1820) **:** an unmarried Italian woman — used as a title equivalent to *Miss*

si·gnory *or* **si·gniory** \ˈsē-nyə-rē\ *n, pl* **si·gnor·ies** *or* **si·gnior·ies** [ME *signorie,* fr. MF *seigneurie*] (14c) **:** SEIGNIORY

sign out \(ˈ)sī-ˈnau̇t\ *vi* (1948) **:** to indicate departure by signing a register ~ *vt* **:** to record or approve the release or departure of — **sign–out** \ˈsī-ˌnau̇t\ *n or adj*

[1]sign·post \ˈsīn-ˌpōst\ *n* (1620) **1 :** a post (as at the fork of a road) with signs on it to direct travelers **2 :** GUIDE, BEACON

[2]signpost *vt* (1923) **:** to provide with signposts or guides

sign up \(ˈ)sī-ˈnəp\ *vi* (1903) **:** to sign one's name (as to a contract) in order to obtain or do something ⟨*sign up* for insurance⟩ ⟨*sign up* for classes⟩ — **sign–up** \ˈsī-ˌnəp\ *n or adj*

Sig·urd \ˈsig-u̇(ə)rd, ˈsig-ərd\ *n* [ON *Sigurthr*] **:** a hero in Norse mythology who slays the dragon Fafnir

sike \ˈsīk\ *n* [ME, fr. OE *sīc;* akin to ON *sīk* sike, OE *sicerian* to trickle] (bef. 12c) **1** *dial chiefly Brit* **:** a small stream; *esp* **:** one that dries up in summer **2** *dial chiefly Brit* **:** DITCH

[1]Sikh \ˈsēk\ *n* [Hindi, lit., disciple] (1756) **:** an adherent of a monotheistic religion of India founded about 1500 by a Hindu under Islamic influence and marked by rejection of idolatry and caste — **Sikh·ism** \-ˌiz-əm\ *n*

[2]Sikh *adj* (1845) **:** of or relating to Sikhs or Sikhism

si·lage \ˈsī-lij\ *n* [short for *ensilage*] (1884) **:** fodder converted into succulent feed for livestock through processes of anaerobic acid fermentation (as in a silo)

si·lane \ˈsil-ˌān, ˈsī-ˌlān\ *n* [ISV *sil*icon + meth*ane*] (1916) **:** any of various compounds of hydrogen and silicon that have the general formula Si_nH_{2n+2} and are analogous to alkanes

Si·las·tic \sə-ˈlas-tik, sī-\ *trademark* — used for a soft pliable plastic

sild \ˈsil(d)\ *n, pl* **sild** *or* **silds** [Norw] (1928) **:** a young herring other than a brisling that is canned as a sardine in Norway

[1]si·lence \ˈsī-lən(t)s\ *n* [ME, fr. OF, fr. L *silentium,* fr. *silent-, silens*] (13c) **1 :** forbearance from speech or noise **:** MUTENESS — often used interjectionally **2 :** absence of sound or noise **:** STILLNESS **3 :** absence of mention: **a :** OBLIVION, OBSCURITY **b :** SECRECY ⟨weapons research was conducted in ~⟩

[2]silence *vt* **si·lenced; si·lenc·ing** (1603) **1 :** to compel or reduce to silence **:** STILL **2 :** to restrain from expression **:** SUPPRESS **3 :** to cause to cease hostile firing or criticism

si·lenc·er \ˈsī-lən-sər\ *n* (1635) **:** one that silences: as **a** *chiefly Brit* **:** the muffler of an internal-combustion engine **b :** a silencing device for small arms

si·lent \ˈsī-lənt\ *adj* [L *silent-, silens,* fr. prp. of *silēre* to be silent; akin to Goth *anasilan* to subside, L *sinere* to let go, lay — more at SITE] (ca. 1565) **1 a :** making no utterance **:** MUTE, SPEECHLESS **b :** indisposed to speak **:** not loquacious **2 :** free from sound or noise **:** STILL **3 :** performed or borne without utterance **:** UNSPOKEN ⟨~ prayer⟩ ⟨~ grief⟩ **4 a :** making no mention ⟨history is ~ about this person⟩ **b :** not widely or generally known or appreciated ⟨the ~ pressures on a person in public office⟩ **c :** making no protest or outcry ⟨the ~ majority⟩ **5 :** UNPRONOUNCED ⟨~ *b* in *doubt*⟩ **6 :** not exhibiting the usual signs or symptoms of presence ⟨a ~ infection⟩ **7 :** made without spoken dialogue ⟨~ movies⟩ — **si·lent·ly** *adv* — **si·lent·ness** *n*

syn SILENT, TACITURN, RETICENT, RESERVED, SECRETIVE mean showing restraint in speaking. SILENT implies a habit of saying no more than is needed ⟨a stern, *silent* man, long a widower —Willa Cather⟩ TACITURN implies a temperamental disinclination to speech and usu. connotes unsociability ⟨the farmer was *taciturn* and drove them speechlessly to the house —Pearl Buck⟩ RETICENT implies a reluctance to speak out or at length, esp. about one's own affairs ⟨had been . . . *reticent* regarding the details of his own financial affairs —J. P. Marquand⟩ RESERVED implies reticence and suggests the restraining influence of caution or formality in checking easy informal conversational exchange ⟨a certain vulgar gusto . . . divided him from the *reserved,* watchful rest of the family —D. H. Lawrence⟩ SECRETIVE, too, implies reticence but usu. carries a suggestion of deviousness and lack of frankness or of an often ostentatious will to conceal ⟨the king was a *secretive* child, and showed little of his mind —Edith Sitwell⟩

silent butler *n* (1937) **:** a receptacle with hinged lid for collecting table crumbs and the contents of ashtrays

silent partner *n* (1828) **1 :** a partner who is known to the public but has no voice in the conduct of a firm's business **2 :** SECRET PARTNER

si·lents \ˈsī-lən(t)s\ *n pl* (1929) **:** motion pictures without spoken dialogue

silent service *n* (1929) **1 :** NAVY — used with *the* **2 :** the submarine service — used with *the*

silent treatment *n* (1947) **:** an act of completely ignoring a person or thing by resort to silence esp. as a means of expressing contempt or disapproval

si·le·nus \sī-ˈlē-nəs\ *n, pl* **-ni** \-ˌnī\ [L, fr. Gk *silēnos,* fr. *Silēnos* foster father of Dionysus] **:** a minor woodland deity and companion of Dionysus in Greek mythology with a horse's ears and tail

si·lex \ˈsī-ˌleks\ *n* [L *silic-, silex* flint, quartz — more at SHELL] (1592) **:** silica or a siliceous material (as powdered tripoli) esp. for use as a filler in paints or wood

¹sil·hou·ette \ˌsil-ə-ˈwet\ *n* [F, fr. Étienne de *Silhouette* †1767 Fr. controller general of finances; prob. fr. his ephemeral tenure] (1783) **1 :** a likeness cut from dark material and mounted on a light ground or one sketched in outline and solidly colored in **2 :** the outline of a body viewed as circumscribing a mass ⟨the ~ of an airplane⟩ ***syn*** see OUTLINE

²silhouette *vt* **-ett·ed; -ett·ing** (1876) **:** to represent by a silhouette; *also* **:** to project on a background like a silhouette

silic- *or* **silico-** *comb form* [*silicon*] **:** silicon ⟨*silicone*⟩

sil·i·ca \ˈsil-i-kə\ *n* [NL, fr. L *silic-, silex* flint, quartz] (ca. 1801) **:** silicon dioxide SiO_2 occurring in crystalline, amorphous, and impure forms (as in quartz, opal, and sand respectively)

silica gel *n* (1919) **:** colloidal silica resembling coarse white sand in appearance but possessing many fine pores and therefore extremely adsorbent

sil·i·cate \ˈsil-ə-ˌkāt, ˈsil-i-kət\ *n* [*silicic (acid)*] (1811) **:** a salt or ester derived from a silicic acid; *esp* **:** any of numerous insoluble often complex metal salts that contain silicon and oxygen in the anion, constitute the largest class of minerals, and are used in building materials (as cement, bricks, and glass)

si·li·ceous *or* **si·li·cious** \sə-ˈlish-əs\ *adj* [L *siliceus* of flint, fr. *silic-, silex* flint, quartz] (ca. 1656) **:** of, relating to, or containing silica or a silicate ⟨~ limestone⟩

silici- *comb form* [NL *silica*] **:** silica ⟨*siliciferous*⟩

si·lic·ic \sə-ˈlis-ik\ *adj* [NL *silica* & NL *silicium* silicon (fr. *silica*)] (1817) **:** of, relating to, or derived from silica or silicon

silicic acid *n* (1817) **:** any of various weakly acid substances obtained as gelatinous masses by treating silicates with acids

sil·i·cide \ˈsil-ə-ˌsīd\ *n* [ISV *silic-* + *-ide*] (1868) **:** a binary compound of silicon usu. with a more electropositive element or radical

si·lic·i·fi·ca·tion \sə-ˌlis-ə-fə-ˈkā-shən\ *n* (1830) **:** the action or process of silicifying **:** the state of being silicified

si·lic·i·fy \sə-ˈlis-ə-ˌfī\ *vb* **-fied; -fy·ing** *vt* (1830) **:** to convert into or impregnate with silica ~ *vi* **:** to become silicified

sil·i·con \ˈsil-i-kən, ˈsil-ə-ˌkän\ *n* [NL *silica* + E *-on* (as in *carbon*)] (1817) **:** a tetravalent nonmetallic element that occurs combined as the most abundant element next to oxygen in the earth's crust and is used esp. in alloys and electronic devices — see ELEMENT table

silicon carbide *n* (1893) **:** a very hard dark crystalline compound SiC of silicon and carbon that is used as an abrasive and as a refractory and in electric resistors

sil·i·cone \ˈsil-ə-ˌkōn\ *n* [*silic-* + *-one*] (1943) **:** any of various polymeric organic silicon compounds obtained as oils, greases, or plastics and used esp. for water-resistant and heat-resistant lubricants, varnishes, binders, and electric insulators

silicone rubber *n* (1944) **:** rubber made from silicone elastomers and noted for its retention of flexibility, resilience, and tensile strength over a wide temperature range

sil·i·con·ized \ˈsil-ə-kə-ˌnīzd, -ˌkō-\ *adj* (1949) **:** treated or coated with a silicone ⟨~ glassware⟩

sil·i·co·sis \ˌsil-ə-ˈkō-səs\ *n* [NL] (1881) **:** a condition of massive fibrosis of the lungs marked by shortness of breath and caused by prolonged inhalation of silica dusts — **sil·i·cot·ic** \-ˈkät-ik\ *adj or n*

si·lique \sə-ˈlēk\ *n* [F, fr. NL *siliqua,* fr. L, pod, husk; akin to L *silic-, silex* flint — more at SHELL] (1785) **:** a narrow elongated two-valved usu. many-seeded capsule that is characteristic of the mustard family, opens by sutures at either margin, and has two parietal placentas

¹silk \ˈsilk\ *n, often attrib* [ME, fr. OE *seolc;* prob. of Baltic or Slav origin; akin to OPruss *silkas* silk, OSlav *shelkŭ*] (bef. 12c) **1 :** a fine continuous protein fiber produced by various insect larvae usu. for cocoons; *esp* **:** a lustrous tough elastic fiber produced by silkworms and used for textiles **2 :** thread, yarn, or fabric made from silk filaments **3 a :** a garment of silk **b** (1) **:** a distinctive silk gown worn by a King's or Queen's Counsel (2) **:** a King's or Queen's Counsel **c** *pl* **:** the colored cap and blouse of a jockey or harness horse driver made in the registered racing color of his stable **4 a :** a filament resembling silk (as that produced by a spider) **b :** silky material ⟨milkweed ~⟩; *esp* **:** the styles of an ear of Indian corn **5 :** PARACHUTE

²silk *vi, of corn* (1783) **:** to develop the silk

silk·aline *or* **silk·oline** \ˌsil-kə-ˈlēn\ *n* [¹*silk* + *-oline* (as in *crinoline*)] (1896) **:** a soft light cotton fabric with a smooth lustrous finish like that of silk

silk cotton *n* (1697) **:** the silky or cottony covering of seeds of various silk-cotton trees; *esp* **:** KAPOK

silk–cotton tree *n* (1712) **:** any of various tropical trees (family Bombacaceae, the silk-cotton family) with palmate leaves and large fruits with the seeds enveloped by silk cotton; *esp* **:** CEIBA 1

silk·en \ˈsil-kən\ *adj* (bef. 12c) **1 :** made or consisting of silk **2 :** resembling silk: as **a :** SOFT, LUSTROUS **b** (1) **:** agreeably smooth **:** HARMONIOUS (2) **:** INGRATIATING **3 a :** dressed in silk ⟨~ ankles⟩ **b :** LUXURIOUS ***syn*** see SLEEK

silk gland *n* (1870) **:** a gland that produces a viscid fluid which is extruded in filaments and hardens into silk on exposure to air: as **a :** either of a pair of greatly enlarged and modified salivary glands of an insect larva that produce a compound filament from which a larval or pupal cover (as a cocoon) is spun **b :** any of two or more abdominal glands of a spider that open through spinnerets and produce a filament used chiefly in the spinning of webs

silk hat *n* (1834) **:** a hat with a tall cylindrical crown and a silk-plush finish worn by men as a dress hat

silk oak *n* (1866) **:** any of various Australian timber trees (family Proteaceae and esp. genus *Grevillea*) with mottled wood used in cabinetmaking and veneering — called also *silky oak*

silk screen *n* (1930) **:** a stencil process in which coloring matter is forced onto the material to be printed through the meshes of a silk or organdy screen so prepared as to have pervious printing areas and impervious nonprinting areas; *also* **:** a print made by this process — **silk–screen** *vt*

silk–stock·ing \ˈsilk-ˈstäk-iŋ\ *adj* (1798) **1 :** ARISTOCRATIC, WEALTHY ⟨a ~ district⟩ **2 :** fashionably dressed ⟨a ~ audience⟩ **3 :** of or relating to the American Federalist party

silk stocking *n* (1891) **1 :** an aristocratic or wealthy person **2 :** a fashionably dressed person **3 :** FEDERALIST 2

silk tree *n* (ca. 1852) **:** an Asian tree (*Albizzia julibrissin*) having flowers with long silky stamens

silk·weed \ˈsil-ˌkwēd\ *n* (1784) **:** MILKWEED

silk·worm \ˈsil-ˌkwərm\ *n* (bef. 12c) **:** a moth whose larva spins a large amount of strong silk in constructing its cocoon; *esp* **:** an Asian moth (*Bombyx mori*) whose rough wrinkled hairless yellowish caterpillar produces the silk of commerce

silky \ˈsil-kē\ *adj* **silk·i·er; -est** (ca. 1611) **1 a :** resembling or consisting of silk **b :** INGRATIATING ⟨~ insinuations⟩ **2 :** having or covered with fine soft hairs, plumes, or scales — **silk·i·ly** \-kə-lē\ *adv* — **silk·i·ness** \-kē-nəs\ *n*

silky terrier *n* (1959) **:** a low-set toy terrier that has a flat silky glossy coat colored blue with tan on the head, chest, and legs — called also *silky*

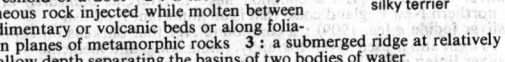

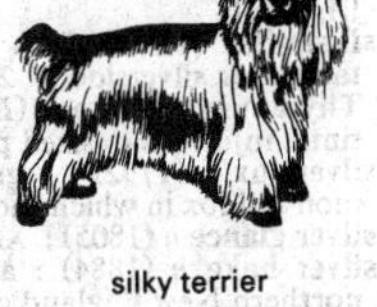
silky terrier

sill \ˈsil\ *n* [ME *sille,* fr. OE *syll;* akin to OHG *swelli* beam, threshold, Gk *selis* crossbeam] (bef. 12c) **1 :** a horizontal piece (as a timber) that forms the lowest member or one of the lowest members of a framework or supporting structure: as **a :** the horizontal member at the base of a window **b :** the threshold of a door **2 :** a tabular body of igneous rock injected while molten between sedimentary or volcanic beds or along foliation planes of metamorphic rocks **3 :** a submerged ridge at relatively shallow depth separating the basins of two bodies of water

sillabub *var of* SYLLABUB

sil·li·man·ite \ˈsil-ə-mə-ˌnīt\ *n* [Benjamin *Silliman* †1864 Am. geologist] (ca. 1830) **:** a brown, grayish, or pale green mineral Al_2SiO_5 that consists of an aluminum silicate in orthorhombic crystals often occurring in fibrous or columnar forms

sil·ly \ˈsil-ē\ *adj* **sil·li·er; -est** [ME *sely, silly* happy, innocent, pitiable, feeble, fr. OE *sǣlig,* fr. OE *sǣl* happiness; akin to OHG *sālig* happy, L *solari* to console, Gk *hilaros* cheerful] (ca. 1547) **1 a :** RUSTIC, PLAIN **b** *obs* **:** lowly in station **:** HUMBLE **2** *archaic* **:** HELPLESS, WEAK **3 a :** weak in intellect **:** FOOLISH **b :** exhibiting or indicative of a lack of common sense or sound judgment ⟨a very ~ mistake⟩ **c :** TRIFLING, FRIVOLOUS **4 :** being stunned or dazed ⟨scared ~⟩ ⟨knocked me ~⟩ ***syn*** see SIMPLE — **sil·li·ly** \ˈsil-ə-lē\ *adv* — **sil·li·ness** \ˈsil-ē-nəs\ *n* — **silly** *n or adv*

silly season *n* (1861) **:** a period (as late summer) when newspapers must resort to minor or fantastic matters for lack of major news stories

si·lo \ˈsī-(ˌ)lō\ *n, pl* **silos** [Sp] (1881) **1 :** a trench, pit, or esp. a tall cylinder (as of wood or concrete) usu. sealed to exclude air and used for making and storing silage **2 a :** a deep bin for storing material (as cement or coal) **b :** an underground structure for housing a guided missile

si·lox·ane \sə-ˈläk-ˌsān, sī-\ *n* [*sil*icon + *ox*ygen + meth*ane*] (1917) **:** any of various compounds containing alternate silicon and oxygen atoms in either a linear or cyclic arrangement usu. with one or two organic groups attached to each silicon atom

¹silt \ˈsilt\ *n* [ME *cylte,* prob. of Scand origin; akin to Dan *sylt* salt marsh; akin to OHG *sulza* salt marsh, OE *sealt* salt] (15c) **1 :** loose sedimentary material with rock particles usu. $^1/_{20}$ millimeter or less in diameter; *also* **:** soil containing 80 percent or more of such silt and less than 12 percent of clay **2 :** a deposit of sediment (as by a river) — **silty** \ˈsil-tē\ *adj*

²silt *vi* (1799) **:** to become choked or obstructed with silt — often used with *up* ⟨the channel ~*ed* up⟩ ~ *vt* **:** to choke, fill, cover, or obstruct with silt or mud ⟨the beaver had ~*ed* the creek —Hugh Fosburgh⟩ — **silt·ation** \sil-ˈtā-shən\ *n*

silt·stone \ˈsilt-ˌstōn\ *n* (1920) **:** a rock composed chiefly of indurated silt

Sil·u·res \ˈsil-yə-ˌrēz\ *n* [L] (ca. 1895) **:** a people of ancient Britain described by Tacitus as occupying chiefly southern Wales

Si·lu·ri·an \sī-ˈlu̇r-ē-ən, sə-\ *adj* [L *Silures*] (1708) **1 :** of or relating to the Silures or their place of habitation **2 :** of, relating to, or being a period of the Paleozoic era between the Ordovician and Devonian or the corresponding system of rocks marked by the beginning of coral=

reef building and the appearance of numerous eurypterid crustaceans — **Silurian** *n*

sil·va \'sil-və\ *n* [NL, fr. L, wood, forest] (1846) : the forest trees of a region or country

silvan *var of* SYLVAN

[1]**sil·ver** \'sil-vər\ *n* [ME, fr. OE *seolfor;* akin to OHG *silbar* silver] (bef. 12c) **1** : a white metallic element that is sonorous, ductile, very malleable, capable of a high degree of polish, and chiefly univalent in compounds, and that has the highest thermal and electric conductivity of any substance — see ELEMENT table **2** : silver as a commodity ⟨the value of ~ has risen⟩ **3** : coin made of silver **4** : articles (as hollowware or table flatware) made of or plated with silver; *also* : similar articles and esp. flatware of other metals (as stainless steel) **5** : a nearly neutral slightly brownish medium gray

[2]**silver** *adj* (bef. 12c) **1** : made of silver **2** : resembling silver: as **a** : having a white lustrous sheen **b** : giving a soft resonant sound : dulcet in tone **c** : eloquently persuasive **3** : consisting of or yielding silver **4** : of, relating to, or characteristic of silver **5** : advocating the use of silver as a standard of currency

[3]**silver** *vt* **sil·vered; sil·ver·ing** \'silv-(ə-)riŋ\ (15c) **1 a** : to cover with silver (as by electroplating) **b** : to coat with a substance (as a metal) resembling silver **2 a** : to give a silvery luster to **b** : to make white like silver — **sil·ver·er** \'sil-vər-ər\ *n*

silver age *n* (1565) : an historical period of achievement secondary to that of a golden age

silver bell *n* (1785) : a medium-sized tree (*Halesia carolina*) of the storax family of the southeastern U.S. cultivated for its bell-shaped white flowers

sil·ver·ber·ry \'sil-vər-,ber-ē\ *n* (1856) : a silvery No. American shrub (*Elaeagnus argentea*) related to the buffalo berry

silver bromide *n* (ca. 1878) : a compound AgBr that is extremely sensitive to light and is much used in the preparation of sensitive emulsion coatings for photographic materials

silver certificate *n* (1882) : a certificate formerly issued against the deposit of silver coin as legal tender in the U.S. and its possessions

silver chloride *n* (1897) : a compound AgCl sensitive to light and used esp. for photographic materials

silver cord *n* [*The Silver Cord* (1926), play by Sidney Howard] (1926) : the emotional tie between mother and child and esp. son

silver fir *n* (1707) : any of various firs (genus *Abies*) with leaves that are white or silvery white beneath; *esp* : a valuable European timber tree (*A. alba*)

sil·ver·fish \'sil-vər-,fish\ *n* (1703) **1** : any of various silvery fishes (as a tarpon or silversides) **2** : any of various small wingless insects (order Thysanura); *esp* : one (*Lepisma saccharina*) found in houses and sometimes injurious to sized papers or starched clothes

silver fox *n* (1792) : a genetically determined color phase of the common red fox in which the pelt is black tipped with white

silver glance *n* (1805) : ARGENTITE

silver hake *n* (1884) : a common hake (*Merluccius bilinearis*) of the northern New England coast that is an important food fish

silver iodide *n* (ca. 1909) : a compound AgI that darkens on exposure to light and is used in photography, rainmaking, and medicine

silver lining *n* [fr. the phrase "every cloud has a *silver lining*"] (1871) : a consoling or hopeful prospect

sil·ver·ly \'sil-vər-lē\ *adv* (1595) : with silvery appearance or sound

silver maple *n* (1765) **1** : a common No. American maple (*Acer saccharinum*) with deeply cut leaves that are light green above and silvery white below **2** : the hard close-grained but brittle light brown wood of the silver maple

sil·vern \'sil-vərn\ *adj* (bef. 12c) **1** : made of silver **2** : resembling or characteristic of silver : SILVERY

silver nitrate *n* (1885) : an irritant compound $AgNO_3$ that in contact with organic matter turns black and is used as a chemical reagent, in photography, and in medicine esp. as an antiseptic

silver paper *n* (ca. 1875) : a metallic paper with a coating or lamination resembling silver — called also *tinfoil*

silver perch *n* (1820) : any of various somewhat silvery fishes that resemble perch: as **a** : a drum (*Bairdiella chrysura*) that occurs along the more southern Atlantic coast of the U.S. — called also *mademoiselle, yellowtail* **b** : WHITE PERCH 1

silver plate *n* (1797) **1** : a plating of silver **2** : domestic flatware and hollowware of silver or of a silver-plated base metal

silver protein *n* (1928) : any of several colloidal light-sensitive preparations of silver and protein used in aqueous solution on mucous membranes as antiseptics

silver screen *n* (1918) **1** : a motion-picture screen **2** : MOTION PICTURES

sil·ver·side \'sil-vər-,sīd\ *n* (1820) : SILVERSIDES

sil·ver·sides \'sil-vər-,sīdz\ *n pl but sing or pl in constr* (1851) : any of various small fishes (family Atherinidae) with a silvery stripe along each side of the body

sil·ver·smith \-,smith\ *n* (bef. 12c) : an artisan who makes articles of silverware

silver spoon *n* [fr. the phrase "born with a *silver spoon* in one's mouth" (born wealthy)] (1801) : WEALTH; *esp* : inherited wealth

silver standard *n* (1896) : a monetary standard under which the currency unit is defined by a stated quantity of silver

Silver Star Medal *n* (1932) : a U.S. military decoration awarded for gallantry in action

sil·ver–tongued \,sil-vər-'təŋd\ *adj* (1592) : ELOQUENT

sil·ver·ware \'sil-vər-,wa(ə)r, -,we(ə)r\ *n* (1860) : SILVER PLATE, FLATWARE

sil·ver·weed \-,wēd\ *n* (1578) : any of several potentillas with leaves silvery or white-tomentose beneath; *esp* : one (*Potentilla anserina*) with silky hairs over the entire plant that is native to Europe but introduced elsewhere

sil·very \'silv-(ə-)rē\ *adj* (1600) **1** : having a soft clear musical tone : RESONANT ⟨a ~ voice⟩ **2** : having the luster of silver **3** : containing or consisting of silver — **sil·ver·i·ness** *n*

sil·vex \'sil-,veks\ *n* [prob. fr. L *silva* wood + E *exterminator*] (1961) : a selective herbicide $C_9H_7Cl_3O_3$ esp. effective in controlling woody plants but toxic to animals

sil·vi·cul·ture \'sil-və-,kəl-chər\ *n* [F, fr. L *silva, sylva* forest + *cultura* culture] (1880) : a branch of forestry dealing with the development and care of forests — **sil·vi·cul·tur·al** \,sil-və-'kəlch(-ə)-rəl\ *adj* — **sil·vi·cul·tur·al·ly** \-rə-lē\ *adv* — **sil·vi·cul·tur·ist** \,sil-və-'kəlch-(ə-)rəst\ *n*

si·ma·zine \'sī-mə-,zēn\ *n* [*sim-* (prob. alter. of *sym-* symmetrical, prefix used in names of organic compounds) + *triazine*] (1961) : a selective herbicide $C_7H_{12}N_5Cl$ used to control weeds among crop plants

Sim·chas To·rah \,sim-kə-'stōr-ə, -'stȯr-\ *n* [Heb *śimḥath tōrāh* rejoicing of the Torah] (ca. 1905) : a Jewish holiday observed on the 23d of Tishri in celebration of the completion of the annual reading of the Torah

Sim·e·on \'sim-ē-ən\ *n* [LL, fr. Gk *Symeōn,* fr. Heb *Shim'ōn*] **1** : a son of Jacob and the traditional eponymous ancestor of one of the tribes of Israel **2** : a devout man of Jerusalem held to have uttered the Nunc Dimittis on seeing the infant Jesus in the temple

[1]**sim·i·an** \'sim-ē-ən\ *adj* [L *simia* ape, fr. *simus* snub-nosed, fr. Gk *simos*] (1607) : of, relating to, or resembling monkeys or apes

[2]**simian** *n* (1880) : MONKEY, APE

sim·i·lar \'sim-(ə-)lər\ *adj* [F *similaire,* fr. L *similis* like, similar — more at SAME] (ca. 1611) **1** : having characteristics in common : strictly comparable **2** : alike in substance or essentials : CORRESPONDING ⟨no two animal habitats are exactly ~ —W. H. Dowdeswell⟩ **3** : not differing in shape but only in size or position ⟨~ triangles⟩ ⟨~ polygons⟩ — **sim·i·lar·ly** *adv*

syn SIMILAR, ANALOGOUS, PARALLEL mean closely resembling each other. SIMILAR implies the possibility of being mistaken for each other ⟨all the houses in the development are *similar*⟩ ANALOGOUS applies to things belonging in essentially different categories but nevertheless having many similarities ⟨*analogous* political systems⟩ PARALLEL suggests a marked likeness in the development of two things ⟨the *parallel* careers of two movie stars⟩

sim·i·lar·i·ty \,sim-ə-'lar-ət-ē\ *n, pl* **-ties** (1664) **1** : the quality or state of being similar : RESEMBLANCE **2** : a comparable aspect : CORRESPONDENCE ***syn*** see LIKENESS

sim·i·le \'sim-ə-(,)lē\ *n* [L, comparison, fr. neut. of *similis*] (14c) : a figure of speech comparing two unlike things that is often introduced by *like* or *as* (as in *cheeks like roses*) — compare METAPHOR

si·mil·i·tude \sə-'mil-ə-,t(y)üd\ *n* [ME, fr. MF, resemblance, likeness, fr. L *similitudo,* fr. *similis*] (14c) **1 a** : COUNTERPART, DOUBLE **b** : a visible likeness : IMAGE **2** : an imaginative comparison : SIMILE **3 a** : correspondence in kind or quality **b** : a point of comparison ***syn*** see LIKENESS

Sim·men·tal *also* **Sim·men·thal** \'zim-ən-,täl\ *n* [*Simmental,* valley of the Simme river in Switzerland] (1906) : any of a breed of large buff or dull red and white cattle of Swiss origin that are used widely throughout the world for meat and milk

[1]**sim·mer** \'sim-ər\ *vb* **sim·mered; sim·mer·ing** \-(ə-)riŋ\ [alter. of E dial. *simper,* fr. ME *simperen*] *vi* (1653) **1** : to stew gently below or just at the boiling point **2 a** : to be in a state of incipient development : FERMENT ⟨ideas ~*ing* in the back of my mind⟩ **b** : to be in inward turmoil : SEETHE ~ *vt* : to cook slowly in a liquid just below the boiling point

[2]**simmer** *n* (1809) : the state of simmering

simmer down *vi* (1889) **1** : to become calm or peaceful **2** : to become reduced by or as if by simmering

sim·nel \'sim-nᵊl\ *n* [ME *simenel,* fr. MF, fr. L *simila* fine wheat flour] (14c) **1** : a bun or bread of fine wheat flour **2** *Brit* : a rich fruitcake sometimes coated with almond paste and baked for mid-Lent, Easter, and Christmas

si·mo·le·on \sə-'mō-lē-ən\ *n* [origin unknown] *slang* (1896) : DOLLAR

Si·mon \'sī-mən\ *n* [Gk *Simōn,* fr. Heb *Shim'ōn*] **1** : PETER — called also *Simon Peter* **2** : one of the twelve disciples of Jesus — called also *Simon the Zealot* **3** : a kinsman of Jesus **4** : a Cyrenian constrained to help Jesus bear his cross to his place of crucifixion — called also *Simon the Cyrenian* **5** : SIMON MAGUS

si·mo·ni·ac \sī-'mō-nē-,ak, sə-\ *n* [ME, fr. MF or ML; MF *simoniaque,* fr. ML *simoniacus,* fr. LL *simonia* simony] (14c) : one who practices simony — **simoniac** *or* **si·mo·ni·a·cal** \,sī-mə-'nī-ə-kəl, ,sim-ə-\ *adj* — **si·mo·ni·a·cal·ly** \-k(ə-)lē\ *adv*

si·mo·nize \'sī-mə-,nīz\ *vt* **-nized; -niz·ing** [fr. *Simoniz,* a trademark] (1938) : to polish with or as if with wax

Si·mon Le·gree \,sī-mən-lə-'grē\ *n* : a slave owner who has Tom flogged to death in Harriet B. Stowe's novel *Uncle Tom's Cabin*

Simon Ma·gus \-'mā-gəs\ *n* : a Samaritan sorcerer converted by the apostle Philip and severely rebuked by Peter for offering money for the gifts of the Holy Ghost

si·mon–pure \,sī-mən-'pyu̇(ə)r\ *adj* [fr. *the real Simon Pure,* alluding to a character impersonated by another in the play *A Bold Stroke for a Wife* (1718) by Susanna Centlivre †1723 Eng. dramatist and actress] (1840) : of untainted purity or integrity; *also* : pretentiously or hypocritically pure

si·mo·ny \'sī-mə-nē, 'sim-ə-\ *n* [ME *symonie,* fr. LL *simonia,* fr. *Simon Magus*] (13c) : the buying or selling of a church office or ecclesiastical preferment

si·moom \sə-'müm, sī-\ *or* **si·moon** \-'mün\ *n* [Ar *samūm*] (1790) : a hot dry violent dust-laden wind from Asian and African deserts

simp \'simp\ *n* (1909) : SIMPLETON

sim·pa·ti·co \sim-'pät-i-,kō, -'pat-\ *adj* [It *simpatico* & Sp *simpático,* deriv. of L *sympathia* sympathy] (1864) : CONGENIAL, LIKABLE

[1]**sim·per** \'sim-pər\ *vb* **sim·pered; sim·per·ing** \-p(ə-)riŋ\ [perh. of Scand origin; akin to Dan dial. *simper* affected, coy] *vi* (1563) : to smile in a silly manner ~ *vt* : to say with a simper ⟨~*ed* an apology⟩ — **sim·per·er** \-pər-ər\ *n*

[2]**simper** *n* (1599) : a silly smile : SMIRK

[1]**sim·ple** \'sim-pəl\ *adj* **sim·pler** \-p(ə-)lər\; **sim·plest** \-p(ə-)ləst\ [ME, fr. OF, plain, uncomplicated, artless, fr. L *simplus, simplex,* lit., single; L *simplus* fr. *sem-, sim-* one + *-plus* multiplied by; L *simplic-, simplex* fr. *sem-, sim-* + *-plic-, -plex* -fold — more at SAME, -FOLD] (13c) **1** : free from guile : INNOCENT **2 a** : free from vanity : MODEST **b** : free from ostentation or display **3** : of humble origin or modest position ⟨a ~ farmer⟩ **4 a** : lacking in knowledge or expertise ⟨a ~ amateur of the arts⟩ **b** : STUPID; *esp* : mentally retarded **c** : not socially or culturally sophisticated : NAIVE; *also* : CREDULOUS **5 a** : SHEER, UNMIXED ⟨~ honesty⟩ **b** : free of secondary complications ⟨a ~ fracture⟩

c (1) **:** having only one main clause and no subordinate clauses ⟨a ~ sentence⟩ (2) *of a subject or predicate* **:** having no modifiers, complements, or objects **d :** constituting a basic element **:** FUNDAMENTAL **e :** not made up of many like units ⟨a ~ eye⟩ **6 :** free from elaboration or figuration ⟨~ harmony⟩ **7 a** (1) **:** not subdivided into branches ⟨a ~ stem⟩ (2) **:** consisting of a single carpel (3) **:** developing from a single ovary ⟨a ~ fruit⟩ **b :** controlled by a single gene ⟨~ inherited characters⟩ **8 :** not limited or restricted **:** UNCONDITIONAL ⟨a ~ obligation⟩ **9 :** readily understood or performed ⟨a ~ statement⟩ ⟨the adjustment was ~ to make⟩ **10** *of a statistical hypothesis* **:** specifying exact values for one or more statistical parameters — compare COMPOSITE 3 — **sim·ple·ness** \-pəl-nəs\ *n*

syn SIMPLE, FOOLISH, SILLY, FATUOUS, ASININE mean actually or apparently deficient in intelligence. SIMPLE implies a degree of intelligence inadequate to cope with anything complex or involving mental effort; FOOLISH implies the character of being or seeming unable to use judgment, discretion, or good sense; SILLY suggests failure to act as a rational being esp. by ridiculous behavior; FATUOUS implies foolishness, inanity, and disregard of reality; ASININE suggests utter and contemptible failure to use normal rationality or perception. ***syn*** see in addition EASY

[2]**simple** *n* (14c) **1 a :** a person of humble birth **:** COMMONER ⟨thought very little of anybody, ~s or gentry —Virginia Woolf⟩ **b** (1) **:** a rude or credulous person **:** IGNORAMUS (2) **:** a mentally retarded person **2 a :** a medicinal plant **b :** a vegetable drug having only one ingredient **3 :** one component of a complex; *specif* **:** an unanalyzable constituent

simple closed curve *n* (ca. 1968) **:** a closed plane curve (as a circle or an ellipse) that does not intersect itself — called also *Jordan curve*

simple equation *n* (1798) **:** a linear equation

simple fraction *n* (1910) **:** a fraction having whole numbers for the numerator and denominator — compare COMPLEX FRACTION

simple interest *n* (ca. 1798) **:** interest paid or computed on the original principal only of a loan or on the amount of an account

simple machine *n* (1902) **:** any of various elementary mechanisms formerly considered as the elements of which all machines are composed and including the lever, the wheel and axle, the pulley, the inclined plane, the wedge, and the screw

sim·ple·mind·ed \ˌsim-pəl-ˈmīn-dəd\ *adj* (1744) **:** devoid of subtlety **:** UNSOPHISTICATED; *also* **:** FOOLISH — **sim·ple·mind·ed·ly** *adv* — **sim·ple·mind·ed·ness** *n*

simple motion *n* (ca. 1909) **:** a motion in a straight line, circle or circular arc, or helix

simple protein *n* (1921) **:** a protein (as a globulin) that yields amino acids as the chief or only products of complete hydrolysis — compare CONJUGATED PROTEIN

simple sugar *n* (1942) **:** MONOSACCHARIDE

sim·ple·ton \ˈsim-pəl-tən\ *n* [[1]*simple* + *-ton* (as in surnames such as *Washington*)] (1650) **:** a person lacking in common sense

simple vow *n* (1901) **:** a public vow taken by a religious in the Roman Catholic Church under which retention of property by the individual is permitted and marriage though illicit is valid under canon law

[1]**sim·plex** \ˈsim-ˌpleks\ *adj* [L *simplic-, simplex* — more at SIMPLE] (1594) **1 :** SIMPLE, SINGLE **2 :** allowing telecommunication in only one direction at a time ⟨~ system⟩

[2]**simplex** *n, pl* **sim·plex·es** (1892) **1** *or pl* **sim·pli·ces** \-plə-ˌsēz\ *or* **sim·pli·cia** \sim-ˈplish-(ē-)ə\ **:** a simple word **2 :** a spatial configuration of *n* dimensions determined by $n + 1$ points in a space of dimension equal to or greater than *n* ⟨a triangle together with its interior determined by its three vertices is a two-dimensional ~ in the plane or any space of higher dimension⟩

sim·pli·cial \sim-ˈplish-əl\ *adj* (1957) **:** of or relating to simplexes — **sim·pli·cial·ly** \-ə-lē\ *adv*

sim·plic·i·ty \sim-ˈplis-ət-ē, -ˈplis-tē\ *n* [ME *simplicite*, fr. MF *simplicité*, fr. L *simplicitat-, simplicitas*, fr. *simplic-, simplex*] (14c) **1 :** the state of being simple or uncompounded **2 a :** lack of subtlety or penetration **:** INNOCENCE, NAIVETÉ **b :** FOLLY, SILLINESS **3 :** freedom from pretense or guile **:** CANDOR **4 a :** directness of expression **:** CLARITY **b :** restraint in ornamentation **:** AUSTERITY

sim·pli·fy \ˈsim-plə-ˌfī\ *vt* **-fied; -fy·ing** [F *simplifier*, fr. ML *simplificare*, fr. L *simplus* simple] (1759) **:** to make simple or simpler: as **a :** to reduce to basic essentials **b :** to diminish in scope or complexity **:** STREAMLINE ⟨was urged to ~ management procedures⟩ **c :** to make more intelligible **:** CLARIFY — **sim·pli·fi·ca·tion** \ˌsim-plə-fə-ˈkā-shən\ *n* — **sim·pli·fi·er** \ˈsim-plə-ˌfī(-ə)r\ *n*

sim·plism \ˈsim-ˌpliz-əm\ *n* (1882) **:** the act or an instance of oversimplifying; *esp* **:** the reduction of a problem to a false simplicity by ignoring complicating factors — **sim·plis·tic** \sim-ˈplis-tik\ *adj* — **sim·plis·ti·cal·ly** \-ti-k(ə-)lē\ *adv*

sim·ply \ˈsim-plē, *for 1 also* -pə-lē\ *adv* (13c) **1 a :** without ambiguity **:** CLEARLY **b :** without embellishment **:** PLAINLY **c :** DIRECTLY, CANDIDLY **2 a :** SOLELY, MERELY ⟨eats ~ to keep alive⟩ **b :** REALLY, LITERALLY ⟨the concert was ~ marvelous⟩

simply connected *adj* (ca. 1933) **:** being or characterized by a surface which is divided into two separate parts by every closed curve it contains

simply ordered *adj* (ca. 1909) **:** having any two elements connected by a relationship that is reflexive, antisymmetric, and transitive

Simp·son's rule \ˈsim(p)-sənz-\ *n* [Thomas *Simpson* †1761 Eng. mathematician] (ca. 1898) **:** a method for approximating the area under a curve over a given interval that involves partitioning the interval by an odd number $n + 1$ of equally spaced ordinates and adding the areas of the $n/2$ figures formed by pairs of successive odd-numbered ordinates and the parabolas which they determine with their included even-numbered ordinates

sim·u·la·cre \ˈsim-yə-ˌlāk-ər, -ˌlak-\ *n* [ME, fr. MF, fr. L *simulacrum*] *archaic* (14c) **:** SIMULACRUM

sim·u·la·crum \ˌsim-yə-ˈlak-rəm, -ˈlāk-\ *n, pl* **-cra** \-rə\ *also* **-crums** [L, fr. *simulare*] (1599) **1 :** IMAGE, REPRESENTATION ⟨a reasonable ~ of reality —Martin Mayer⟩ **2 :** an insubstantial form or semblance of something **:** TRACE

[1]**sim·u·lar** \ˈsim-yə-lər, -ˌlär\ *n* [irreg. fr. L *simulare* to simulate] *archaic* (1526) **:** one that simulates **:** DISSEMBLER

[2]**simular** *adj, archaic* (1611) **:** COUNTERFEIT, PRETENDED

sim·u·late \ˈsim-yə-ˌlāt\ *vt* **-lat·ed; -lat·ing** [L *simulatus*, pp. of *simulare* to copy, represent, feign, fr. *similis* like — more at SAME] (1652) **1 :** to assume the outward qualities or appearance of often with the intent to deceive **:** IMITATE **2 :** to make a simulation of (as a physical system) ***syn*** see ASSUME — **sim·u·la·tive** \-ˌlāt-iv\ *adj*

sim·u·lat·ed *adj* (1622) **:** made to look genuine **:** FAKE ⟨~ pearls⟩

sim·u·la·tion \ˌsim-yə-ˈlā-shən\ *n* [ME *simulacion*, fr. MF, fr. L *simulation-, simulatio*, fr. *simulare*] (14c) **1 :** the act or process of simulating **:** FEIGNING **2 :** a sham object **:** COUNTERFEIT **3 a :** the imitative representation of the functioning of one system or process by means of the functioning of another ⟨a computer ~ of an industrial process⟩ **b :** examination of a problem often not subject to direct experimentation by means of a simulating device

sim·u·la·tor \ˈsim-yə-ˌlāt-ər\ *n* (1835) **:** one that simulates; *esp* **:** a device that enables the operator to reproduce or represent under test conditions phenomena likely to occur in actual performance

si·mul·cast \ˈsī-məl-ˌkast *also* ˈsim-əl-\ *vb* [*simul*taneous broad*cast*] *vi* (1948) **:** to broadcast simultaneously by AM and FM radio or by radio and television ~ *vt* **:** to broadcast (a program) by simulcasting — **simulcast** *n*

si·mul·ta·neous \ˌsī-məl-ˈtā-nē-əs, -nyəs *also* ˌsim-əl-\ *adj* [(assumed) ML *simultaneus*, fr. L *simul* at the same time — more at SAME] (1660) **1 :** existing or occurring at the same time **:** exactly coincident **2 :** satisfied by the same values of the variables ⟨~ equations⟩ ***syn*** see CONTEMPORARY — **si·mul·ta·ne·ity** \-tə-ˈnē-ət-ē, -ˈnā-\ *n* — **si·mul·ta·neous·ly** \-ˈtā-nē-ə-slē, -nyə-\ *adv* — **si·mul·ta·neous·ness** *n*

[1]**sin** \ˈsin\ *n* [ME *sinne*, fr. OE *synn*; akin to OHG *sunta* sin] (bef. 12c) **1 a :** an offense against religious or moral law **b :** an action that is or is felt to be highly reprehensible ⟨it's a ~ to waste food⟩ **2 a :** transgression of the law of God **b :** a vitiated state of human nature in which the self is estranged from God ***syn*** see OFFENSE

[2]**sin** *vi* **sinned; sin·ning** (bef. 12c) **1 :** to commit a sin **2 :** to commit an offense or fault

[3]**sin** \ˈsēn, ˈsin\ *n* [Heb *sīn*] (ca. 1899) **:** the 21st letter of the Hebrew alphabet — see ALPHABET table

Sin·an·thro·pus \sī-ˈnan(t)-thrə-pəs, sə-; ˌsīn-ˌan-ˈthrō-, ˌsin-\ *n* [NL, fr. LL *Sinae*, pl., Chinese + Gk *anthrōpos* man — more at SINO-] (1929) **:** PEKING MAN

sin·a·pism \ˈsin-ə-ˌpiz-əm\ *n* [LL *sinapismus*, deriv. of Gk *sinapi* mustard] (1601) **:** MUSTARD PLASTER

[1]**since** \(ˈ)sin(t)s\ *adv* [ME *sins*, contr. of *sithens*, fr. *sithen*, fr. OE *siththan*, fr. *sith tham* since that, fr. *sith* since + *tham*, dat. of *thæt* that; akin to OHG *sīd* since, L *serus* late, OE *sāwan* to sow] (bef. 12c) **1 :** from a definite past time until now ⟨has stayed there ever ~⟩ **2 :** before the present time **:** AGO ⟨long ~ dead⟩ **3 :** after a time in the past **:** SUBSEQUENTLY ⟨has ~ become rich⟩

[2]**since** *conj* (15c) **1 :** at a time in the past after or later than ⟨has held two jobs ~ he graduated⟩ **:** from the time in the past when ⟨ever ~ I was a child⟩ **2** *obs* **:** WHEN **3 :** in view of the fact that **:** BECAUSE ⟨~ it was raining she took an umbrella⟩

[3]**since** *prep* (1530) **:** in the period after a specified time in the past **:** from a specified time in the past

sin·cere \sin-ˈsi(ə)r, sən-\ **sin·cer·er; sin·cer·est** *adj* [MF, fr. L *sincerus*] (1533) **1 a :** free of dissimulation **:** HONEST ⟨~ interest⟩ **b :** free from adulteration **:** PURE ⟨a ~ doctrine⟩ ⟨~ wine⟩ **2 :** marked by genuineness **:** TRUE — **sin·cere·ly** *adv* — **sin·cere·ness** *n*

syn SINCERE, WHOLEHEARTED, HEARTFELT, HEARTY, UNFEIGNED mean genuine in feeling. SINCERE stresses absence of hypocrisy, feigning, or any falsifying embellishment or exaggeration; WHOLEHEARTED suggests sincerity and earnest devotion without reservation or misgiving; HEARTFELT suggests depth of genuine feeling outwardly expressed; HEARTY suggests honesty, warmth, and exuberance in displaying feeling; UNFEIGNED stresses spontaneity and absence of pretense.

sin·cer·i·ty \-ˈser-ət-ē, -ˈsir-\ *n* (1557) **:** the quality or state of being sincere **:** honesty of mind **:** freedom from hypocrisy

sin·cip·i·tal \sin-ˈsip-ət-ᵊl\ *adj* (1653) **:** of or relating to the sinciput

sin·ci·put \ˈsin(t)-sə-(ˌ)pət\ *n, pl* **sinciputs** *or* **sin·cip·i·ta** \sin-ˈsip-ət-ə\ [L *sincipit-, sinciput*, fr. *semi-* + *caput* head — more at HEAD] (1578) **1 :** FOREHEAD **2 :** the upper half of the skull

Sind·bad \ˈsin-ˌbad\ *n* **:** a citizen of Baghdad whose adventures at sea are told in the *Arabian Nights' Entertainments*

Sind·hi \ˈsin-dē\ *n, pl* **Sindhi** *or* **Sindhis** [Ar *Sindī*] (ca. 1900) **1 :** a member of a mostly Muslim people of Sind **2 :** the Indic language of Sind

sine \ˈsīn\ *n* [ML *sinus*, fr. L, curve] (1593) **:** the trigonometric function that for an acute angle is the ratio between the leg opposite the angle when it is considered part of a right triangle and the hypotenuse

si·ne·cure \ˈsī-ni-ˌkyu̇(ə)r, ˈsin-i-\ *n* [ML *sine cura* without cure of souls] (1662) **1** *archaic* **:** an ecclesiastical benefice without cure of souls **2 :** an office or position that requires little or no work and that usu. provides an income

sine curve *n* (1902) **:** the graph in rectangular coordinates of the equation $y = a \sin bx$ where *a* and *b* are constants

si·ne die \ˌsī-ni-ˈdī(-ˌē), ˌsin-ā-ˈdē-ˌā\ *adv* [L, without day] (1607) **:** without any future date being designated (as for resumption) **:** INDEFINITELY ⟨the meeting adjourned *sine die*⟩

si·ne qua non \ˌsin-i-ˌkwä-ˈnän, -ˈnōn *also* ˌsēn-; *also* ˌsī-ni-ˌkwā-ˈnän\ *n* [LL, without which not] (1588) **:** an absolutely indispensable or essential thing

[1]**sin·ew** \ˈsin-(ˌ)yü, -yə(-w) *also* ˈsin-(ˌ)ü\ *n* [ME *sinewe*, fr. OE *seono*; akin to OHG *senawa* sinew, L *saeta* bristle] (bef. 12c) **1 :** TENDON; *esp* **:** one dressed for use as a cord or thread **2** *obs* **:** NERVE **3 a :** solid resilient strength **:** POWER ⟨intellectual and moral ~ —G. K. Chalmers⟩ **b :** the chief supporting force **:** MAINSTAY — usu. used in pl. ⟨providing the ~s of better living —Sam Pollock⟩

[2]**sinew** *vt* (1614) **:** to strengthen as if with sinews

sine wave *n* (1907) **:** a waveform that represents periodic oscillations in which the amplitude of displacement at each point is proportional to the sine of the phase angle of the displacement and that is visualized as a sine curve : SINE CURVE; *also* **:** a wave so represented
sin·ewy \'sin-yə-wē *also* 'sin-ə-\ *adj* (14c) **1 :** full of sinews : TOUGH, STRINGY ⟨~ meat⟩ **2 :** STRONG ⟨~ arms⟩
sin·fo·nia \ˌsin-fə-'nē-ə\ *n, pl* **-nie** \-'nē-ˌā\ [It, fr. L *symphonia* symphony] (1884) **1 :** an orchestral musical composition serving as an introduction to choral works (as opera) esp. in the 18th century : OVERTURE **2 :** SYMPHONY 2a, 2c
sinfonia con·cer·tante \-ˌkän(t)-sər-'tänt(-ē), -ˌkän-cher-'tän-ˌtā\ *n* [It, lit., symphony in concerto style] (1903) **:** a concerto for more than one solo instrument
sin·fo·niet·ta \ˌsin-fən-'yet-ə, -fōn-\ *n* [It, dim. of *sinfonia*] (ca. 1924) **1 :** a symphony of less than standard length or for fewer instruments **2 :** a small symphony orchestra; *esp* **:** an orchestra of strings only
sin·ful \'sin-fəl\ *adj* (bef. 12c) **:** tainted with, marked by, or full of sin : WICKED — **sin·ful·ly** \-fə-lē\ *adv* — **sin·ful·ness** *n*
[1]**sing** \'siŋ\ *vb* **sang** \'saŋ\ *or* **sung** \'səŋ\; **sung; sing·ing** \'siŋ-iŋ\ [ME *singen*, fr. OE *singan;* akin to OHG *singan* to sing, Gk *omphē* voice] *vi* (bef. 12c) **1 a :** to produce musical tones by means of the voice **b :** to utter words in musical tones and with musical inflections and modulations **c :** to deliver songs as a trained or professional singer **2 :** to make a shrill whining or whistling sound **3 a :** to relate or celebrate something in verse **b :** to compose poetry **4 :** to produce musical or harmonious sounds **5 :** BUZZ, RING **6 :** to make a cry : CALL **7 :** to give information or evidence ~ *vt* **1 :** to utter with musical inflections; *esp* **:** to interpret in musical tones produced by the voice **2 :** to relate or celebrate in verse **3 :** CHANT, INTONE **4 :** to bring or accompany to a place or state by singing ⟨~s the child to sleep⟩ — **sing·able** \'siŋ-ə-bəl\ *adj*
[2]**sing** *n* (1850) **:** a session of group singing
sing–along \'siŋ-ə-ˌlȯŋ\ *n* (1966) **:** SONGFEST
[1]**singe** \'sinj\ *vt* **singed; singe·ing** \'sin-jiŋ\ [ME *sengen*, fr. OE *sengan;* akin to OHG *bisengan* to singe, OSlav *isęčiti* to dry] (bef. 12c) **:** to burn superficially or lightly : SCORCH; *esp* **:** to remove the hair, down, or fuzz from usu. by passing rapidly over a flame
[2]**singe** *n* (1658) **:** a slight burn : SCORCH
[1]**sing·er** \'siŋ-ər\ *n* (14c) **:** one that sings
[2]**sing·er** \'sin-jər\ *n* (ca. 1875) **:** one that singes
singing game *n* (1923) **:** a children's game in which the players accompany their actions with the singing of a narrative song
[1]**sin·gle** \'siŋ-gəl\ *adj* [ME, fr. MF, fr. L *singulus* one only; akin to L *sem-* one — more at SAME] (14c) **1 a :** not married **b :** of or relating to celibacy **2 :** unaccompanied by others : LONE, SOLE ⟨the ~ survivor of the disaster⟩ **3 a** (1) **:** consisting of or having only one part, feature, or portion ⟨~ consonants⟩ (2) **:** consisting of one as opposed to or in contrast with many : UNIFORM ⟨a ~ standard for men and women⟩ (3) **:** consisting of only one in number ⟨holds to a ~ ideal⟩ **b :** having but one whorl of petals or ray flowers ⟨a ~ rose⟩ **4 a :** consisting of a separate unique whole : INDIVIDUAL ⟨every ~ citizen⟩ **b :** of, relating to, or involving only one person **5 a :** FRANK, HONEST ⟨a ~ devotion⟩ **b :** exclusively attentive ⟨an eye ~ to the truth⟩ **6 :** UNBROKEN, UNDIVIDED **7 :** having no equal or like : SINGULAR **8 :** designed for the use of one person only ⟨a ~ room⟩ ⟨~ bed⟩
[2]**single** *vb* **sin·gled; sin·gling** \-g(ə-)liŋ\ *vt* (1628) **1 :** to select or distinguish from a number or group — usu. used with *out* **2 a :** to advance or score (a base runner) by a single **b :** to bring about the scoring of (a run) by a single ~ *vi* **:** to make a single in baseball
[3]**single** *n* (1646) **1 a :** a separate individual person or thing **b :** a young unmarried adult **c :** a phonograph record (as a 45) having one short tune on each side **2 :** a base hit that allows the batter to reach first base **3 a** *pl* **:** a tennis match or similar game with one player on each side **b :** a golf match between two players — usu. used in pl. **4 :** a room (as in a hotel) for one guest — compare DOUBLE 7
sin·gle–ac·tion \'siŋ-gəl-'ak-shən\ *adj, of a revolver* (ca. 1900) **:** that can be cocked only by manually retracting the hammer
sin·gle–blind \ˌsiŋ-gəl-'blīnd\ *adj* (1965) **:** of, relating to, or being an experimental procedure in which the experimenters but not the subjects know the makeup of the test and control groups during the actual course of the experiments — compare DOUBLE-BLIND
single bond *n* (1927) **:** a chemical bond in which one pair of electrons is shared by two atoms in a molecule esp. when the atoms can share more than one pair of electrons
sin·gle–breast·ed \-'bres-təd\ *adj* (1796) **:** having a center closing with one row of buttons and no lap ⟨a ~ coat⟩
sin·gle–cell protein \ˌsiŋ-gəl-ˌsel-\ *n* (ca. 1967) **:** protein produced by microorganisms cultured on organic material and used esp. as a source of food
single combat *n* (1610) **:** combat between two persons
single cross *n* (1940) **:** a first-generation hybrid between two selected and usu. inbred lines — compare DOUBLE CROSS
single entry *n* (1826) **:** a method of bookkeeping that recognizes only one side of a business transaction and usu. consists only of a record of cash and personal accounts with debtors and creditors
single file *n* (1670) **:** [6]FILE 1 — **single file** *adv*
[1]**sin·gle–foot** \'siŋ-gəl-ˌfu̇t\ *n, pl* **single–foots** (1867) **:** [7]RACK b
[2]**single–foot** *vi, of a horse* (1890) **:** to go at a rack — **sin·gle–foot·er** *n*
[1]**sin·gle–hand·ed** \ˌsiŋ-gəl-'han-dəd\ *adj* (1709) **1 :** managed or done by one person or with one on a side **2 :** working alone or unassisted by others — **sin·gle–hand·ed·ly** *adv* — **sin·gle–hand·ed·ness** *n*
[2]**single–handed** *adv* (1815) **:** in a single-handed manner
sin·gle–hand·er \-'han-dər\ *n* (1946) **:** a person who sails single-handed
sin·gle–heart·ed \ˌsiŋ-gəl-'härt-əd\ *adj* (1577) **:** characterized by sincerity and unity of purpose or dedication — **sin·gle–heart·ed·ly** *adv* — **sin·gle–heart·ed·ness** *n*
single knot *n* (ca. 1930) **:** OVERHAND KNOT
single–lens reflex \ˌsiŋ-gəl-ˌlenz-\ *n* (1958) **:** a camera having a single lens that forms an image which is either reflected to the viewfinder or recorded on film
sin·gle–mind·ed \ˌsiŋ-gəl-'mīn-dəd\ *adj* (1860) **:** having one driving purpose or resolve : DETERMINED, DEDICATED — **sin·gle–mind·ed·ly** *adv* — **sin·gle–mind·ed·ness** *n*
sin·gle·ness \'siŋ-gəl-nəs\ *n* (1560) **:** the quality or state of being single
sin·gle–phase \ˌsiŋ-gəl-'fāz\ *adj* (ca. 1900) **:** of or relating to a circuit energized by a single alternating electromotive force
sin·gle–space \-'spās\ *vt* (ca. 1939) **:** to type or print with no blank lines between lines of text
sin·gle·stick \'siŋ-gəl-ˌstik\ *n* (1771) **:** fighting or fencing with a wooden stick or sword held in one hand; *also* **:** the weapon used
sin·glet \'siŋ-glət\ *n* (1746) **1** [fr. its having only one thickness of cloth] *chiefly Brit* **:** an athletic jersey : UNDERSHIRT **2 :** an atom or molecule that has no net electronic magnetic moment
single tax *n* (1879) **:** a tax to be levied on a single item (as real estate) as the sole source of public revenue
sin·gle·ton \'siŋ-gəl-tən\ *n* [F, fr. E *single*] (1876) **1 :** a card that is the only one of its suit orig. held in a hand **2 :** an individual member or thing distinct from others grouped with it
sin·gle–track \ˌsiŋ-gəl-ˌtrak\ *adj* (1849) **1 :** having only one track **2 :** lacking intellectual range, receptiveness, or flexibility : ONE-TRACK
sin·gle·tree \'siŋ-gəl-(ˌ)trē\ *n* (1841) **:** WHIFFLETREE
sin·gle–val·ued \ˌsiŋ-gəl-'val-(ˌ)yüd, -yəd\ *adj* (1879) **:** having one and only one value of the range associated with each value of the domain ⟨a ~ function⟩ — compare MULTIPLE-VALUED
single wing *n* (ca. 1949) **:** an offensive football formation in which one back plays as a flanker and two backs line up four or five yards behind the line in position to receive a direct snap from center
sin·gly \'siŋ-g(ə-)lē\ *adv* (14c) **1 :** without the company of others : INDIVIDUALLY **2 :** SINGLE-HANDED
[1]**sing·song** \'siŋ-ˌsȯŋ\ *n* (1609) **1 :** verse with marked and regular rhythm and rhyme **2 :** a voice delivery marked by a narrow range or monotonous pattern of pitch — **sing·songy** \-ˌsȯŋ-ē\ *adj*
[2]**singsong** *adj* (1734) **:** having a monotonous cadence or rhythm
sing·spiel \'siŋ-ˌspēl, 'ziŋ-ˌshpēl\ *n* [G, fr. *singen* to sing + *spiel* play; akin to G *spielen* to play — more at SPIEL] (1883) **:** a musical work popular in Germany esp. in the latter part of the 18th century characterized by spoken dialogue interspersed with popular or folk songs
[1]**sin·gu·lar** \'siŋ-gyə-lər\ *adj* [ME *singuler*, fr. MF, fr. L *singularis*, fr. *singulus* only one — more at SINGLE] (14c) **1 a :** of or relating to a separate person or thing : INDIVIDUAL **b :** of, relating to, or being a word form denoting one person, thing, or instance **c :** of or relating to a single instance or to something considered by itself **2 :** distinguished by superiority : EXCEPTIONAL ⟨an artist of ~ attainments⟩ **3 :** being out of the ordinary : UNUSUAL ⟨on the way home we had a ~ adventure⟩ **4 :** departing from general usage or expectation : PECULIAR, ODD ⟨the air had a ~ chill⟩ **5 a** *of a matrix* **:** having a determinant equal to zero **b** *of a linear transformation* **:** having the property that the matrix of coefficients of the new variables has a determinant equal to zero ***syn*** see STRANGE — **sin·gu·lar·ly** *adv*
[2]**singular** *n* (14c) **1 :** the singular number, the inflectional form denoting it, or a word in that form **2 :** a singular term
sin·gu·lar·i·ty \ˌsiŋ-gyə-'lar-ət-ē\ *n, pl* **-ties** [ME *singularite*, fr. MF *singularité*, fr. LL *singularitat-, singularitas*, fr. L *singularis*] (14c) **1 :** something that is singular: as **a :** a separate unit **b :** unusual or distinctive manner or behavior : PECULIARITY **2 :** the quality or state of being singular **3 :** a point at which the derivative of a given function of a complex variable does not exist but every neighborhood of which contains points for which the derivative exists **4 :** a point at which space and time are infinitely distorted by gravitational forces and which is held to be the final state of matter falling into a black hole
sin·gu·lar·ize \'siŋ-gyə-lə-ˌrīz\ *vt* **-ized; -iz·ing** (1589) **:** to make singular
singular point *n* (1886) **:** SINGULARITY 3
Sin·ha·lese *or* **Sin·gha·lese** \ˌsin-gə-'lēz, ˌsin-(h)ə-, -'lēs\ *n, pl* **Sinhalese** *or* **Singhalese** [Skt *Siṁhala* Ceylon] (1598) **1 :** a member of a people that inhabit Sri Lanka and form a major part of its population **2 :** the Indic language of the Sinhalese people — **Sinhalese** *or* **Singhalese** *adj*
si·ni·cize \'sī-nə-ˌsīz, 'sin-ə-\ *vt* **-cized; -ciz·ing** *often cap* [ML *sinicus* Chinese, fr. LL *Sinae*, pl., Chinese — more at SINO-] (1889) **:** to modify by Chinese influence
sin·is·ter \'sin-əs-tər, *archaic* sə-'nis-\ *adj* [ME *sinistre*, fr. L *sinistr-, sinister* on the left side, unlucky, inauspicious] (15c) **1** *archaic* **:** UNFAVORABLE, UNLUCKY **2** *archaic* **:** FRAUDULENT **3 :** singularly evil or productive of evil **4 a :** of, relating to, or situated to the left or on the left side of something; *esp* **:** being or relating to the side of a heraldic shield at the left of the person bearing it **b :** of ill omen by reason of being on the left **5 :** presaging ill fortune or trouble **6 :** accompanied by or leading to disaster — **sin·is·ter·ly** *adv* — **sin·is·ter·ness** *n*
syn SINISTER, BALEFUL, MALIGN mean seriously threatening evil or disaster. SINISTER suggests a general or vague feeling of fear or apprehension on the part of the observer; BALEFUL imputes perniciousness or destructiveness to something whether working openly or covertly; MALIGN applies to what is inherently evil or harmful.
si·nis·tral \'sin-əs-trəl, sə-'nis-\ *adj* (1803) **:** of, relating to, or inclined to the left: as **a :** LEFT-HANDED **b** *of a gastropod shell* **:** having the whorls coiling counterclockwise down the spire when viewed with the apex toward the observer and having the aperture situated on the left of the axis when held with the spire uppermost and with the aperture opening toward the observer
si·nis·trous \'sin-əs-trəs, sə-'nis-\ *adj, archaic* (1575) **:** SINISTER
Si·nit·ic \sī-'nit-ik, sə-\ *adj* [LL *Sinae*, pl., Chinese + E *-itic* (as in *Semitic*) — more at SINO-] (ca. 1895) **:** of or relating to the Chinese, their language, or their culture
[1]**sink** \'siŋk\ *vb* **sank** \'saŋk\ *or* **sunk** \'səŋk\; **sunk; sink·ing** [ME *sinken*, fr. OE *sincan;* akin to OHG *sinkan* to sink, Arm *ankanim* I fall] *vi* (bef. 12c) **1 a :** to go to the bottom : SUBMERGE **b :** to become partly buried (as in mud) **c :** to become engulfed **2 a** (1) **:** to fall or drop to a lower place or level (2) **:** to flow at a lower depth or level (3) **:** to burn with lower intensity (4) **:** to fall to a lower pitch or volume ⟨his voice *sank* to a whisper⟩ **b :** to subside gradually : SETTLE **c :** to disappear from view **d :** to slope gradually : DIP **3 a :** to soak or become absorbed : PENETRATE **b :** to become impressively known or felt ⟨the lesson had *sunk* in⟩ **4 :** to become deeply absorbed ⟨*sank* into reverie⟩ **5 a :** to go downward in quality, state, or condition **b :** to grow less in amount or worth **6 a :** to fall or drop slowly for lack of strength **b :** to become depressed **c :** to fail in health or strength ~ *vt* **1 a :** to cause to sink ⟨~ a battleship⟩ **b :** to force down esp. below the earth's surface **c :** to cause (something) to penetrate **2 :** to

engage deeply the attention of : IMMERSE **3 a :** to dig or bore (a well or shaft) in the earth : EXCAVATE **b :** to form by cutting or excising ⟨~ words in stone⟩ **4 :** to cast down or bring to a low condition or state : OVERWHELM, DEFEAT **5 :** to lower in standing or reputation : ABASE **6 a :** to lessen in value or amount **b :** to lower or soften (the voice) in speaking **7 :** RESTRAIN, SUPPRESS ⟨~*s* her pride and approaches the despised neighbor —Richard Harrison⟩ **8 :** to pay off (as a debt) : LIQUIDATE **9 :** INVEST — **sink·able** \ˈsiŋ-kə-bəl\ *adj*

[2]**sink** *n* (15c) **1 a :** a pool or pit for the deposit of waste or sewage : CESSPOOL **b :** a ditch or tunnel for carrying off sewage : SEWER **c :** a stationary basin connected with a drain and usu. a water supply for washing and drainage **2 :** a place where vice, corruption, or evil collects **3 :** SUMP **4 a :** a depression in the land surface; *esp* **:** one having a saline lake with no outlet **b :** SINKHOLE **5 :** a body or process that acts as a storage device or disposal mechanism: as **a :** HEAT SINK; *broadly* **:** a device that collects or dissipates energy (as radiation) **b :** a reactant with or absorber of a substance ⟨soil is a ~ for carbon dioxide⟩

sink·age \ˈsiŋ-kij\ *n* (1883) **1 :** the process or degree of sinking **2 :** DEPRESSION, INDENTATION **3 :** the distance from the top line of a full page to the first line of sunk matter

sink·er \ˈsiŋ-kər\ *n* (1844) **1 :** one that sinks; *specif* **:** a weight for sinking a fishing line, seine, or sounding line **2 :** DOUGHNUT **3 :** a fastball that sinks as it reaches the plate — called also *sinker ball*

sink·hole \ˈsiŋk-ˌhōl\ *n* (15c) **1 :** a hollow place or depression in which drainage collects **2 :** a hollow in a limestone region that communicates with a cavern or passage **3 :** SINK 2

sinking fund *n* (1724) **:** a fund set up and accumulated by usu. regular deposits for paying off the principal of a debt when it falls due

sin·less \ˈsin-ləs\ *adj* (bef. 12c) **:** free from sin : IMPECCABLE — **sin·less·ly** *adv* — **sin·less·ness** *n*

sin·ner \ˈsin-ər\ *n* (14c) **1 :** one that sins **2 :** REPROBATE, SCAMP

Si·no- *comb form* [F, fr. LL *Sinae,* pl., Chinese, fr. Gk *Sinai,* fr. Ar *Sīn* China] **1 :** Chinese ⟨*Sino*phile⟩ **2** \ˌsī-(ˌ)nō, ˈsī-\ **:** Chinese and ⟨*Sino*-Tibetan⟩

si·no·atri·al \ˌsī-nō-ˈā-trē-əl\ *adj* [NL *sinus* + *atrium*] (1913) **:** of, involving, or being the sinoatrial node ⟨~ block⟩

sinoatrial node *n* (1913) **:** a small mass of tissue that is embedded in the musculature of the right atrium of higher vertebrates and that originates the impulses stimulating the heartbeat

si·no·logue \ˈsīn-ᵊl-ˌȯg, ˈsin-, -ˌäg\ *n* [F, fr. LL *Sinae* + F *-logue*] (1853) **:** a specialist in sinology

si·nol·o·gy \sī-ˈnäl-ə-jē, sə-\ *n* [prob. fr. F *sinologie,* fr. *sino-* + *-logie* -logy] (ca. 1882) **:** the study of the Chinese and esp. their language, literature, history, and culture — **si·no·log·i·cal** \ˌsīn-ᵊl-ˈäj-i-kəl, ˌsin-\ *adj* — **si·nol·o·gist** \sī-ˈnäl-ə-jəst, sə-\ *n*

si·no·pia \sə-ˈnō-pē-ə\ *n, pl* **-pi·as** *or* **-pie** \-pē-ˌā\ [It, fr. L *sinopis,* fr. Gk *sinōpis,* fr. *Sinōpē* Sinop, ancient seaport in Asia Minor] (1844) **1 :** a red to reddish brown earth pigment used by the ancients that depends for its color on its content of red ferric oxide **2 :** a preliminary drawing for a fresco done in sinopia

Si·no–Ti·bet·an \ˌsī-nō-tə-ˈbet-ᵊn, ˈsī-\ *n* (1920) **:** a language group comprising Tibeto-Burman and Chinese

sin·syne \ˈsin-ˌsīn\ *adv* [ME (Sc) *sensyne,* fr. *sen* since (contr. of ME *sithen*) + *syne* since — more at SINCE, SYNE] *chiefly Scot* (14c) **:** since that time

[1]**sin·ter** \ˈsint-ər\ *n* [G, fr. OHG *sintar* slag — more at CINDER] (1780) **:** a deposit formed by the evaporation of spring or lake water

[2]**sinter** *vt* (1871) **:** to cause to become a coherent mass by heating without melting ~ *vi* **:** to undergo sintering — **sin·ter·abil·i·ty** \ˌsint-ə-rə-ˈbil-ət-ē\ *n*

sin·u·ate \ˈsin-yə-wət, -ˌwāt\ *adj* [L *sinuatus,* pp. of *sinuare* to bend, fr. *sinus* curve] (1688) **:** having the margin wavy with strong indentations ⟨~ leaves⟩

sin·u·os·i·ty \ˌsin-yə-ˈwäs-ət-ē\ *n, pl* **-ties** (1598) **1 :** the quality or state of being sinuous **2 :** something that is sinuous

sin·u·ous \ˈsin-yə-wəs\ *adj* [L *sinuosus,* fr. *sinus*] (1578) **1 a :** of a serpentine or wavy form : WINDING **b :** marked by strong lithe movements **2 :** INTRICATE, COMPLEX — **sin·u·ous·ly** *adv* — **sin·u·ous·ness** *n*

si·nus \ˈsī-nəs\ *n* [NL, fr. L, curve, fold, hollow] (1597) **:** CAVITY, HOLLOW: as **a :** a narrow elongated tract extending from a focus of suppuration and serving for the discharge of pus **b (1) :** a cavity in the substance of a bone of the skull that usu. communicates with the nostrils and contains air **(2) :** a channel for venous blood **(3) :** a dilatation in a bodily canal or vessel **c :** a cleft or indentation between adjoining lobes (as of a leaf or corolla)

si·nus·itis \ˌsī-n(y)ə-ˈsīt-əs\ *n* (1896) **:** inflammation of a sinus of the skull

si·nu·soid \ˈsī-n(y)ə-ˌsȯid\ *n* [ML *sinus* sine] (1823) **1 :** SINE CURVE, SINE WAVE **2** [NL *sinus*] **:** a minute endothelium-lined space or passage for blood in the tissues of an organ (as the liver)

si·nu·soi·dal \ˌsī-n(y)ə-ˈsȯid-ᵊl\ *adj* (1878) **:** of, relating to, shaped like, or varying according to a sine curve or sine wave ⟨~ motion⟩ ⟨~ alternating current⟩ ⟨~ grooves⟩ — **si·nu·soi·dal·ly** \-ᵊl-ē\ *adv*

sinusoidal projection *n* (1944) **:** an equal-area map projection capable of showing the entire surface of the earth with all parallels as straight lines evenly spaced, the central meridian as one half the length of the equator, and all other meridians as curved lines

si·nus ve·no·sus \ˌsī-nəs-vi-ˈnō-səs\ *n* [NL, venous sinus] (ca. 1836) **:** an enlarged pouch that adjoins the heart, is formed by the union of the large systemic veins, and is the passage through which venous blood enters the heart in lower vertebrates and in embryos of higher forms

Si·on \ˈsī-ən\ *var of* ZION

Siou·an \ˈsü-ən\ *n* (1889) **1 :** a language stock of central and eastern No. America **2 :** a member of any of the peoples speaking Siouan languages

Sioux \ˈsü\ *n, pl* **Sioux** \ˈsü(z)\ [F, short for *Nadowessioux,* fr. Ojibwa *Nadoweisiw*] (1761) **1 :** DAKOTA **2 :** SIOUAN

[1]**sip** \ˈsip\ *vb* **sipped; sip·ping** [ME *sippen;* akin to LG *sippen* to sip] *vi* (14c) **:** to take a sip of something esp. repeatedly ~ *vt* **1 :** to drink in small quantities **2 :** to take sips from — **sip·per** *n*

[2]**sip** *n* (1631) **1 :** a small draft taken with the lips **2 :** the act of sipping

[1]**si·phon** \ˈsī-fən\ *n* [F *siphon,* fr. L *siphon-, sipho* tube, pipe, siphon, fr. Gk *siphōn*] (1659) **1 a :** a tube bent to form two legs of unequal length by which a liquid can be transferred to a lower level over an intermediate elevation by the pressure of the atmosphere in forcing the liquid up the shorter branch of the tube immersed in it while the excess of weight of the liquid in the longer branch when once filled causes a continuous flow **b** *usu* **syphon :** a bottle for holding aerated water that is driven out through a bent tube in its neck by the pressure of the gas when a valve in the tube is opened **2 :** any of various tubular organs in animals and esp. mollusks or arthropods that are used for drawing in or ejecting fluids — see CLAM illustration

[2]**siphon** *vb* **si·phoned; si·phon·ing** \ˈsīf-(ə-)niŋ\ *vt* (1859) **:** to convey, draw off, or empty by or as if by a siphon ~ *vi* **:** to pass by or as if by a siphon

si·pho·no·phore \sī-ˈfän-ə-ˌfō(ə)r, ˈsī-fə-nə-, -ˌfȯ(ə)r\ *n* [deriv. of Gk *siphōn* + *pherein* to carry — more at BEAR] (1883) **:** any of an order (Siphonophora) of compound free-swimming or floating pelagic hydrozoans that are mostly delicate, transparent, and colored and have specialized zooids

si·pho·no·stele \sī-ˈfän-ə-ˌstēl, ˌsī-fə-nə-ˈstē-lē\ *n* [Gk *siphōn* tube, siphon] (1902) **:** a stele consisting of vascular tissue surrounding a central core of pith parenchyma

sip·pet \ˈsip-ət\ *n* [alter. of *sop*] *chiefly Brit* (ca. 1530) **:** a small bit of toast or fried bread esp. for garnishing

sir \(ˈ)sər\ *n* [ME, fr. *sire*] (13c) **1 a :** a man of rank or position **b :** a man entitled to be addressed as *sir* — used as a title before the given name of a knight or baronet and formerly sometimes before the given name of a priest **2 a —** used as a usu. respectful form of address **b** *cap* — used as a conventional form of address in the salutation of a letter

sir·dar \ˈsər-ˌdär, sər-ˈ\ *n* [Hindi *sardār,* fr. Per] (1615) **1 a :** a person of high rank (as an hereditary noble) esp. in India **b :** the commander of the Anglo-Egyptian army **2 :** one (as a foreman) holding a responsible position esp. in India

[1]**sire** \ˈsī(ə)r\ *n* [ME, fr. OF, fr. L *senior* older — more at SENIOR] (13c) **1 a :** FATHER **b** *archaic* **:** male ancestor : FOREFATHER **c :** AUTHOR, ORIGINATOR **2 a** *archaic* **:** a man of rank or authority; *esp* **:** LORD — used formerly as a form of address and as a title **b** *obs* **:** an elderly man : SENIOR **3 :** the male parent of an animal and esp. of a domestic animal

[2]**sire** *vt* **sired; sir·ing** (1611) **1 :** BEGET — used esp. of male domestic animals **2 :** to bring into being : ORIGINATE

[1]**si·ren** \ˈsī-rən, *for 3 also* sī-ˈrēn\ *n* [ME, fr. MF & L; MF *sereine,* fr. LL *sirena,* fr. L *siren,* fr. Gk *seirēn*] (14c) **1** *often cap* **:** any of a group of female and partly human creatures in Greek mythology that lured mariners to destruction by their singing **2 a :** a woman who sings with bewitching sweetness **b :** a temptingly beautiful woman; *esp* **:** one who is insidiously seductive : TEMPTRESS **3 a :** an apparatus producing musical tones esp. in acoustical studies by the rapid interruption of a current of air, steam, or fluid by a perforated rotating disk **b :** a device often electrically operated for producing a penetrating warning sound ⟨ambulance ~⟩ ⟨air-raid ~⟩ **4** [NL, fr. L] **:** any of a genus (*Siren*) of eel-shaped amphibians with small forelimbs but neither hind legs nor pelvis and with permanent external gills as well as lungs

[2]**si·ren** \ˈsī-rən\ *adj* (1568) **:** resembling that of a siren : ENTICING

si·re·ni·an \sī-ˈrē-nē-ən\ *n* [NL *Sirenia* fr. L *siren*] (1883) **:** any of an order (Sirenia) of aquatic herbivorous mammals including the manatee and dugong

siren song *n* (1568) **:** an alluring utterance or appeal; *esp* **:** one that is seductive or deceptive

Sir·i·us \ˈsir-ē-əs\ *n* [ME, fr. L, fr. Gk *Seirios,* lit., glowing] **:** a star of the constellation Canis Major that is the brightest star in the heavens — called also *Dog Star*

sir·loin \ˈsər-ˌlȯin\ *n* [alter. of earlier *surloin,* modif. of MF *surlonge,* fr. *sur* over (fr. L *super*) + *loigne, longe* loin — more at OVER, LOIN] (1554) **:** a cut of meat and esp. of beef from the part of the hindquarter just in front of the round — see BEEF illustration

si·roc·co \sə-ˈräk-(ˌ)ō\ *n, pl* **-cos** [It *scirocco, sirocco,* fr. Ar *sharq* east] (1617) **1 a :** a hot dust-laden wind from the Libyan deserts that blows on the northern Mediterranean coast chiefly in Italy, Malta, and Sicily **b :** a warm moist oppressive southeast wind in the same regions **2 :** a hot or warm wind of cyclonic origin from an arid or heated region

sir·rah *also* **sir·ra** \ˈsir-ə\ *n* [alter. of *sir*] *obs* (1526) — used as a form of address implying inferiority in the person addressed

sir·ree *also* **sir·ee** \(ˌ)sər-ˈē\ *n* [by alter.] (1823) **:** SIR — used as an emphatic form usu. after *yes* or *no*

sir–reverence *n* [prob. alter. of *save-reverence,* trans. of ML *salva reverentia* saving (your) reverence] (1575) **1** *obs* — used as an expression of apology before a statement that might be taken as offensive **2** *obs* **:** human feces; *also* **:** a lump of human feces

Sir Rog·er de Cov·er·ley \sə(r)-ˌräj-ər-di-ˈkəv-ər-lē\ *n* [alter. (influenced by *Sir Roger de Coverley,* fictitious country gentleman appearing in many of the *Spectator* papers by Joseph Addison and Sir Richard Steele, fr. *roger of coverley*) of *roger of coverley,* prob. fr. *Roger,* the name + *of* + *Coverley,* a fictitious place name] (1804) **:** an English country-dance that resembles the Virginia reel

sirup, sirupy *var of* SYRUP, SYRUPY

sir·vente \sir-ˈvänt\ *or* **sir·ven·tes** \-ˈvent-əs\ *n, pl* **sir·ventes** \-ˈvänt, -ˈvän(t)s, -ˈvent-əs\ [F, fr. Prov *sirventes,* lit., servant's song, fr. *sirvent* servant, fr. L *servient-, serviens,* prp. of *servire* to serve] (1819) **:** a usu. moral or religious song of the Provençal troubadours satirizing social vices

sis \ˈsis\ *n* (1835) **:** SISTER — usu. used in direct address

-sis \səs\ *n suffix, pl* **-ses** \ˌsēz\ [L, fr. Gk, fem. suffix of action] **:** process : action ⟨peristal*sis*⟩

si·sal \'sī-səl, -zəl\ *n* [MexSp, fr. *Sisal,* Yucatán, Mexico] (1843) **1 a** : a strong durable white fiber used esp. for hard fiber cordage and twine — called also *sisal hemp* **b** : a widely cultivated West Indian agave (*Agave sisalana*) whose leaves yield sisal **2** : any of several fibers similar to true sisal

sis·kin \'sis-kən\ *n* [G dial. *sisschen,* dim. of MHG *zise* siskin, of Slav origin; akin to Czech *čížek* siskin] (1562) : a small sharp-billed chiefly greenish and yellowish finch (*Carduelis spinus*) of temperate Europe and Asia related to the goldfinch — compare PINE SISKIN, RED SISKIN

sis·si·fied \'sis-i-,fīd\ *adj* (ca. 1903) : of, relating to, or having the characteristics of a sissy

sis·sy \'sis-ē\ *n, pl* **sissies** [*sis*] (1891) : an effeminate man or boy; *also* : a timid or cowardly person — **sissy** *adj*

sis·ter \'sis-tər\ *n* [ME *suster, sister,* partly fr. OE *sweostor* and partly of Scand origin; akin to ON *systir* sister; akin to L *soror* sister] (bef. 12c) **1 a (1)** : a female human being having the same parents as another person **(2)** : HALF SISTER **(3)** : SISTER-IN-LAW **b** : a female of a lower animal having a parent in common with another **2** *often cap* **a** : a member of a women's religious order (as of nuns or deaconesses); *esp* : one of a Roman Catholic congregation under simple vows **b** : a female member of a Christian church **3 a** : a woman related to another person by a common tie or interest **b** : one having similar characteristics to another ⟨~ ships⟩ **4** *chiefly Brit* : NURSE **5 a** : GIRL, WOMAN **b** : PERSON — usu. used in the phrase *weak sister*

sis·ter·hood \-,hu̇d\ *n* (14c) **1 a** : the state of being a sister **b** : sisterly relationship **2** : a community or society of sisters; *esp* : a society of women religious

sis·ter-in-law \'sis-t(ə-)rən-,lȯ, -tərn-,lȯ\ *n, pl* **sis·ters-in-law** \-tər-zən-\ (15c) **1** : the sister of one's spouse **2 a** : the wife of one's brother **b** : the wife of one's spouse's brother

sis·ter·ly \'sis-tər-lē\ *adj* (ca. 1570) : of, relating to, or having the characteristics of a sister — **sisterly** *adv*

Sis·tine \'sis-,tēn, sis-'\ *adj* [It *sistino,* fr. NL *sixtinus,* fr. *Sixtus,* name of some popes] (ca. 1864) **1** : of or relating to any of the popes named Sixtus **2** [fr. Pope *Sixtus* IV †1484] : of or relating to the Sistine chapel in the Vatican

Sis·y·phe·an \,sis-ə-'fē-ən\ *or* **Si·syph·i·an** \sis-'if-ē-ən\ *adj* (1635) : of, relating to, or suggestive of the labors of Sisyphus

Sis·y·phus \'sis-ə-fəs\ *n* [L, fr. Gk *Sisyphos*] : a legendary king of Corinth condemned to roll a heavy rock up a hill in Hades only to have it roll down again as it nears the top

[1]**sit** \'sit\ *vb* **sat** \'sat\; **sit·ting** [ME *sitten,* fr. OE *sittan;* akin to OHG *sizzen* to sit, L *sedēre,* Gk *hezesthai* to sit, *hedra* seat] *vi* (bef. 12c) **1 a** : to rest on the buttocks or haunches ⟨~ in a chair⟩ **b** : PERCH, ROOST **2** : to occupy a place as a member of an official body ⟨~ in Congress⟩ **3** : to hold a session : be in session for official business **4** : to cover eggs for hatching : BROOD **5 a** : to take a position for having one's portrait painted or for being photographed **b** : to serve as a model **6** *archaic* : to have one's dwelling place : DWELL **7 a** : to lie or hang relative to a wearer ⟨the collar ~s awkwardly⟩ **b** : to affect one with or as if with weight ⟨the food *sat* heavily on his stomach⟩ **8** : LIE, REST ⟨a kettle *sitting* on the stove⟩ **9 a** : to have a location ⟨the house ~s well back from the road⟩ **b** *of wind* : to blow from a certain direction **10** : to remain inactive or quiescent ⟨the car ~s in the garage⟩ **11** : to take an examination **12** : BABY-SIT ~ *vt* **1** : to cause to be seated : place on or in a seat **2** : to sit on (eggs) **3** : to keep one's seat on ⟨~ a horse⟩ **4** : to provide seats or seating room for ⟨the car will ~ six people⟩ — **sit on 1** : to hold deliberations concerning **2** : REPRESS, SQUELCH **3** : to delay action or decision concerning — **sit pretty** : to be in a highly favorable situation — **sit tight 1** : to maintain one's position without change **2** : to remain quiet in or as if in hiding — **sit under** : to attend religious service under the instruction or ministrations of; *also* : to attend the classes or lectures of

[2]**sit** *n* (1776) **1** : an act or period of sitting **2** : the manner in which a garment fits

si·tar \si-'tär, 'si-,\ *n* [Hindi *sitār,* fr. Per, a three-stringed guitar, fr. *sih* three + *tār* string, thread] (1845) : an Indian lute with a long neck and a varying number of strings — **si·tar·ist** \-əst\ *n*

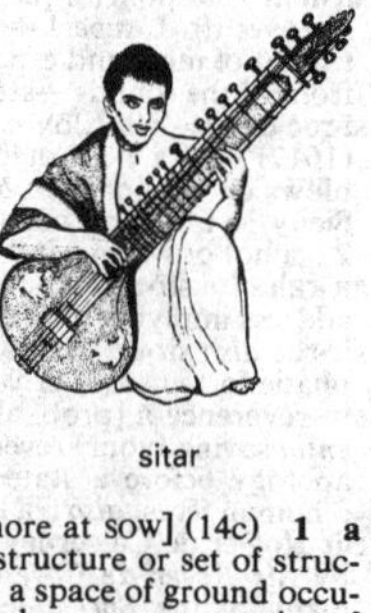
sitar

sit·com \'sit-,käm\ *n* [*situation comedy*] (1965) : SITUATION COMEDY

sit-down \'sit-,dau̇n, 'sid-,au̇n\ *n* (1936) **1** : a cessation of work by employees while maintaining continuous occupation of their place of employment as a protest and means toward forcing compliance with demands **2** : a mass obstruction of an activity by sitting down to demonstrate a grievance or to get the activity modified or halted

[1]**site** \'sīt\ *n* [ME, place, position, fr. MF or L; MF, fr. L *situs,* fr. *situs,* pp. of *sinere* to leave, place, lay; akin to L *serere* to sow — more at sow] (14c) **1 a** : the spatial location of an actual or planned structure or set of structures (as a building, town, or monuments) **b** : a space of ground occupied or to be occupied by a building **2** : the place, scene, or point of something

[2]**site** *vt* **sit·ed; sit·ing** (1598) : to place on a site or in position : LOCATE

sith \(')sith\ *or* **sith·ence** \'sith-ən(t)s\ *or* **sith·ens** \'sith-ənz\ *archaic var of* SINCE

sit-in \'sit-,in\ *n* (1937) **1** : SIT-DOWN 1 **2 a** : an act of occupying seats in a racially segregated establishment in organized protest against discrimination **b** : an act of sitting in the seats or on the floor of an establishment as a means of organized protest

sit in \sit-'in\ *vi* (1868) **1** : to take part in or be present at a session of music or discussion as a visitor **2** : to participate in a sit-in

Sit·ka spruce \,sit-kə-\ *n* [*Sitka,* Alaska] (1895) : a tall spruce (*Picea sitchensis*) of the northern Pacific coast that has thin reddish brown bark and flat needles

si·tos·ter·ol \sī-'täs-tə-,rōl, sə-, -,rȯl\ *n* [Gk *sitos* grain + E *sterol*] (1919) : any of several sterols that are widespread esp. in plant products (as wheat germ or soy bean oil) and are used as starting materials for the synthesis of steroid hormones

sit out *vt* (1659) : to refrain from participating in ⟨*sit out* the next dance⟩

sit·ter \'sit-ər\ *n* (14c) : one that sits; *esp* : one who baby-sits children

[1]**sit·ting** \'sit-iŋ\ *n* (13c) **1 a** : the act of one that sits **b** : a single occasion of continuous sitting (as for a portrait or meal) **2 a** : a brooding over eggs for hatching **b** : SETTING 6 **3** : SESSION ⟨a ~ of the legislature⟩

[2]**sitting** *adj* (ca. 1611) **1** : that is setting ⟨a ~ hen⟩ **2** : occupying a judicial or legislative seat : being in office **3** : easily hit or played ⟨a ~ target⟩ **4 a** : used in or for sitting ⟨a ~ position⟩ **b** : performed while sitting ⟨a ~ shot⟩

sitting duck *n* (1942) : an easy or defenseless target for attack or criticism or unscrupulous dealings

sitting room *n* (1771) : LIVING ROOM 1

[1]**sit·u·ate** \'sich-(ə-)wət, -ə-,wāt\ *adj* [ML *situatus,* pp. of *situare* to place, fr. L *situs*] (1501) : having a site : LOCATED

[2]**sit·u·ate** \'sich-ə-,wāt\ *vt* **-at·ed; -at·ing** (ca. 1532) : to place in a site, situation, or category : LOCATE

sit·u·at·ed *adj* (1560) **1** : having a site, situation, or location : LOCATED **2** : provided with money or possessions ⟨comfortably ~⟩

sit·u·a·tion \,sich-ə-'wā-shən\ *n* (15c) **1 a** : the way in which something is placed in relation to its surroundings **b** : SITE **c** *archaic* : LOCALITY **2** *archaic* : state of health **3 a** : position or place of employment : POST, JOB **b** : position in life : STATUS **4** : position with respect to conditions and circumstances ⟨the military ~ remains obscure⟩ **5 a** : relative position or combination of circumstances at a certain moment **b** : a critical, trying, or unusual state of affairs : PROBLEM **c** : a particular or striking complex of affairs at a stage in the action of a narrative or drama

sit·u·a·tion·al \-shnəl, -shən-ᵊl\ *adj* (1903) **1** : of, relating to, or appropriate to a situation **2** : of or relating to situation ethics — **sit·u·a·tion·al·ly** \-ē\ *adv*

situation comedy *n* (1946) : a radio or television comedy series that involves a continuing cast of characters in a succession of episodes

situation ethics *n* (1966) : a system of ethics by which acts are judged within their contexts instead of by categorical principles

sit-up \'sit-,əp\ *n* (1938) : a conditioning exercise performed from a supine position by raising the trunk to a sitting position without lifting the feet and returning to the original position

sit up \sit-'əp\ *vi* (13c) **1 a** : to rise from a lying to a sitting position **b** : to sit with the back erect **2** : to show interest, alertness, or surprise ⟨*sit up* and take notice⟩ **3** : to stay up after the usual time for going to bed ⟨*sat up* late to watch the movie⟩

si·tus \'sīt-əs\ *n* [L — more at SITE] (1701) : the place where something exists or originates; *specif* : the place where something (as a right) is held to be located in law

sitz bath \'sits-\ *n* [part trans. of G *sitzbad,* fr. *sitz* act of sitting (fr. MHG *siz,* fr. *sitzen* to sit, fr. OHG *sizzen*) + *bad* bath, fr. OHG — more at SIT, BATH] (1849) : a tub in which one bathes in a sitting posture; *also* : a bath so taken esp. therapeutically

sitz·krieg \'sit-,skrēg, 'zit-\ *n* [G, fr. *sitz* + *krieg* war] (1940) : static or nonaggressive warfare

sitz·mark \'sit-,smärk, 'zit-\ *n* [part trans. of G *sitzmarke,* fr. *sitz* + *marke* mark] (ca. 1939) : a depression left in the snow by a skier falling backward

Si·va \'s(h)iv-ə, 's(h)ē-və\ *n* [Skt *Śiva*] : the god of destruction and regeneration in the Hindu sacred triad — compare BRAHMA, VISHNU

Si·van \'siv-ən\ *n* [Heb *Sīwān*] (14c) : the 9th month of the civil year or the 3d month of the ecclesiastical year in the Jewish calendar — see MONTH table

Si·wash \'sī-,wȯsh, -,wäsh\ *n* [*Siwash,* fictional college in stories by George Fitch †1915 Am. author] (1936) : a small usu. inland college that is notably provincial in outlook ⟨cheer for dear old *Siwash*⟩

six \'siks\ *n* [ME, fr. *six,* adj., fr. OE *siex;* akin to OHG *sehs* six, L *sex,* Gk *hex*] (bef. 12c) **1** — see NUMBER table **2** : the sixth in a set or series ⟨the ~ of spades⟩ **3** : something having six units or members: as **a** : an ice-hockey team **b** : a 6-cylinder engine or automobile — **six** *adj or pron* — **at sixes and sevens** : being in disorder

six·fold \'siks-,fōld, -'fōld\ *adj* (bef. 12c) **1** : having six units or members **2** : being six times as great or as many — **six·fold** \-'fōld\ *adv*

six-gun \'siks-,gən\ *n* (1912) : a 6-chambered revolver

six·mo \'sik-(,)smō\ *n, pl* **sixmos** (1924) : the size of a piece of paper cut six from a sheet; *also* : a book, a page, or paper of this size

six-o-six *or* **606** \,sik-,sō-'siks\ *n* [fr. its having been the 606th compound tested and introduced by Paul Ehrlich †1915] (ca. 1910) : ARSPHENAMINE

six-pack \'sik-,spak\ *n* (1952) **1** : six bottles or cans (as of beer) packaged and purchased as a unit **2** : the contents of a six-pack

six·pence \'sik-spən(t)s, *US also* -,spen(t)s\ *n* (14c) **1** : a former British monetary unit equal to six pennies **2** *pl* **sixpence** *or* **six·penc·es** : a coin worth sixpence

six·pen·ny \'sik-spə-nē, *US also* -,spen-ē\ *adj* (15c) : costing or worth sixpence

sixpenny bit *n* (ca. 1911) : SIXPENCE 2

six·pen·ny nail \,sik-,spen-ē-\ *n* (15c) : a nail about two inches long

six-shoot·er \'sik(s)-'shüt-ər\ *n* (1844) : SIX-GUN

six·teen \(')sik-'stēn\ *n* [ME *sixtene,* fr. OE *sixtȳne,* adj., fr. *six* six + *-tȳne* (akin to OE *tīen* ten) — more at TEN] (bef. 12c) — see NUMBER table — **sixteen** *adj or pron* — **six·teenth** \-'tēn(t)th\ *adj or n*

six·teen·mo \sik-'stēn-(,)mō\ *n, pl* **-mos** (1847) : the size of a piece of paper cut 16 from a sheet; *also* : a book, a page, or paper of this size

sixteenth note *n* (ca. 1861) : a musical note with the time value of $^{1}/_{16}$ of a whole note

sixteenth rest *n* (ca. 1891) : a musical rest corresponding in time value to a sixteenth note

sixth \'siks(t)th, 'siks(t)\ *n, pl* **sixths** \'siks(ts), 'siks(t)ths\ (bef. 12c) **1** — see NUMBER table **2 a** : a musical interval embracing six diatonic degrees **b** : a tone at this interval; *specif* : SUBMEDIANT **c** : the harmonic combination of two tones a sixth apart — **sixth** *adj or adv* — **sixth·ly** \'sikst(h)-lē\ *adv*

sixth chord *n* (ca. 1909) : a musical chord consisting of a tone with its third and its sixth above and usu. being the first inversion of a triad

sixth sense *n* (1837) : a power of perception like but not one of the five senses : a keen intuitive power

Six·tine \'sik-,stīn, -,stēn\ *var of* SISTINE

six·ty \ˈsik-stē\ *n, pl* **sixties** [ME, fr. *sixty*, adj., fr. OE *siextig*, n., group of sixty, fr. *siex* six + *-tig* group of ten — more at TEN] (bef. 12c) **1** — see NUMBER table **2** *pl* **:** the numbers 60 to 69; *specif* **:** the years 60 to 69 in a lifetime or century — **six·ti·eth** \ˈsik-stē-əth\ *adj or n* — **sixty** *adj or pron*

sixty–fourth note \ˌsik-stē-ˈfōrth-, -ˈfȯrth-\ *n* (ca. 1891) **:** a musical note with the time value of $^{1}/_{64}$ of a whole note

sixty–fourth rest *n* (ca. 1924) **:** a musical rest corresponding in time value to a sixty-fourth note

six·ty–nine \ˌsik-stē-ˈnīn\ *n* (bef. 12c) **1** — see NUMBER table **2 :** mutual cunnilingus and fellatio **:** mutual fellatio **:** mutual cunnilingus

siz·able *or* **size·able** \ˈsī-zə-bəl\ *adj* (1613) **:** fairly large **:** CONSIDERABLE — **siz·able·ness** *n* — **siz·ably** \-blē\ *adv*

siz·ar *also* **siz·er** \ˈsī-zər\ *n* [*sizar* alter. of *sizer*, fr. [1]*size*] (1588) **:** a student (as in the university of Cambridge) who receives an allowance toward his college expenses and who orig. acted as a servant to other students in return for this allowance

[1]**size** \ˈsīz\ *n* [ME *sise* assize, fr. MF, fr. OF, short for *assise* — more at ASSIZE] (14c) **1** *dial Brit* **:** ASSIZE 5a — usu. used in pl. **2** *obs* **:** a fixed portion of food or drink **3 a :** physical magnitude, extent, or bulk **:** relative or proportionate dimensions **b :** relative aggregate amount or number **c :** considerable proportions **:** BIGNESS **4 :** one of a series of graduated measures esp. of manufactured articles (as of clothing) conventionally identified by numbers or letters ⟨a ~ 7 hat⟩ **5 :** character, quality, or status of a person or thing esp. with reference to importance, relative merit, or correspondence to needs ⟨try this idea on for ~⟩ **6 :** actual state of affairs ⟨that's about the ~ of it⟩

[2]**size** *vb* **sized; siz·ing** *vt* (1609) **1 :** to make a particular size **:** bring to proper or suitable size **2 :** to arrange, grade, or classify according to size or bulk **3 :** to form a judgment of — usu. used with *up* ~ *vi* **:** to equal in size or other particular characteristic **:** COMPARE — usu. used with *up* and often with *to* or *with*

[3]**size** \ˈsīz, ˌsīz\ *adj* (ca. 1924) **:** SIZED — usu. used in combination ⟨bite-size⟩

[4]**size** \ˈsīz\ *n* [ME *sise*] (15c) **:** any of various glutinous materials (as preparations of glue, flour, varnish, or resins) used for filling the pores in surfaces (as of paper, textiles, leather, or plaster) or for applying color or metal leaf (as to book edges or covers)

[5]**size** *vt* **sized; siz·ing** (1667) **:** to cover, stiffen, or glaze with or as if with size

sized \ˈsīzd, ˌsīzd\ *adj* (1582) **1 :** having a specified size or bulk — usu. used in combination ⟨a small-*sized* house⟩ **2 :** arranged or adjusted according to size

siz·ing \ˈsī-ziŋ\ *n* (1825) **:** [4]SIZE

[1]**siz·zle** \ˈsiz-əl\ *vb* **siz·zled; siz·zling** \-(ə-)liŋ\ [perh. freq. of *siss* (to hiss)] *vt* (1603) **:** to burn up or sear with or as if with a hissing sound ~ *vi* **1 :** to make a hissing sound in or as if in burning or frying **2 :** to seethe with deep anger or resentment

[2]**sizzle** *n* (ca. 1823) **:** a hissing sound (as of something frying over a fire)

siz·zler \ˈsiz-(ə-)lər\ *n* (1848) **:** one that sizzles; *esp* **:** SCORCHER

skag *var of* SCAG

skald \ˈskȯld, ˈskäld\ *n* [ON *skāld* — more at SCOLD] (1763) **:** an ancient Scandinavian poet; *broadly* **:** BARD — **skald·ic** \-ik\ *adj*

skat \ˈskät, ˈskat\ *n* [G, modif. of It *scarto* discard, fr. *scartare* to discard, fr. *s-* (fr. L *ex-*) + *carta* card — more at CARD] (1864) **1 :** a three-handed card game played with 32 cards in which players bid for the privilege of attempting any of several contracts **2 :** a widow of two cards in skat that may be used by the winner of the bid

[1]**skate** \ˈskāt\ *n, pl* **skates** *also* **skate** [ME *scate*, fr. ON *skata*] (14c) **:** any of a family (Rajidae, esp. genus *Raja*) of rays with the pectoral fins greatly developed giving the organism a rhomboidal shape

[2]**skate** *n* [modif. of D *schaats* stilt, skate, fr. (assumed) ONF *escache* stilt; akin to OF *eschace* stilt] (1684) **1 a :** a metal frame that can be fitted to the sole of a shoe and to which is attached a runner or a set of wheels for gliding over ice or a surface other than ice **b :** ROLLER SKATE **c :** ICE SKATE **2 :** a period of skating

[3]**skate** *vb* **skat·ed; skat·ing** *vi* (1696) **1 :** to glide along on skates propelled by the alternate action of the legs **2 :** to slip or glide as if on skates **3 :** to proceed in a superficial manner ~ *vt* **:** to go along or through by skating

[4]**skate** *n* [prob. alter. of E dial. *skite* (an offensive person)] (1894) **1 :** a thin awkward-looking or decrepit horse **:** NAG **2 :** FELLOW 4c

skate·board \ˈskāt-ˌbō(ə)rd, -ˌbȯ(ə)rd\ *n* (1965) **:** a narrow board about two feet long mounted on roller-skate wheels — **skate·board·er** \-ˌbōrd-ər, -ˌbȯrd-\ *n* — **skate·board·ing** \-iŋ\ *n*

skat·er \ˈskāt-ər\ *n* (1700) **1 :** one that skates **2 :** WATER STRIDER

skat·ing \ˈskāt-iŋ\ *n* (1723) **:** the act, art, or sport of gliding on skates

ska·tole \ˈskat-ˌōl, ˈskāt-\ *also* **ska·tol** \-ˌȯl, -ˌōl\ *n* [ISV, fr. Gk *skat-*, *skōr* excrement — more at SCAT-] (1879) **:** a foul-smelling compound C_9H_9N found in the intestines and feces, in civet, and in several plants or made synthetically and used in perfumes as a fixative

[1]**skean** *or* **skeane** *var of* SKEIN

[2]**skean** *or* **skene** \ˈskē(-ə)n\ *n* [IrGael *scian* & ScGael *sgian*] (1527) **:** DAGGER, DIRK

ske·dad·dle \ski-ˈdad-ᵊl\ *vi* **ske·dad·dled; ske·dad·dling** \-ˈdad-liŋ, -ᵊl-iŋ\ [origin unknown] (1861) **:** RUN AWAY; *esp* **:** to flee in a panic — **ske·dad·dler** \-ˈdad-lər, -ᵊl-ər\ *n*

skeet \ˈskēt\ *n* [alter. of *shoot*] (1926) **:** trapshooting in which clay targets are thrown in such a way as to simulate the angles of flight of birds

[1]**skee·ter** \ˈskēt-ər\ *n* [by shortening & alter.] (1839) **1 :** MOSQUITO **2 :** an iceboat 16 or more feet in length equipped with a single sail

[2]**skeet·er** \ˈskēt-ər\ *n* (1926) **:** a skeet shooter

skeg \ˈskeg\ *also* **skag** \ˈskag\ *n* [D *scheg*; akin to OSlav *skokŭ* leap — more at SHAG] (ca. 1625) **1 :** the stern of the keel of a ship near the sternpost; *esp* **:** the part connecting the keel with the bottom of the rudderpost in a single-screw ship **2 :** a fin situated on the rear bottom of a surfboard that is used for steering and stability

skeigh \ˈskēk\ *adj* [perh. of Scand origin; akin to Sw *skygg* shy; akin to OE *scēoh* shy — more at SHY] *chiefly Scot* (1508) **:** proudly spirited **:** SKITTISH

[1]**skein** \ˈskān\ *n* [ME *skeyne*, fr. MF *escaigne*] (15c) **1** *or* **skean** *or* **skeane** \ˈskān\ **:** a loosely coiled length of yarn or thread wound on a reel **2 :** something suggesting the twists or coils of a skein **:** TANGLE **3 :** a flock of wildfowl (as geese or ducks) in flight

[2]**skein** *vt* (ca. 1775) **:** to wind into skeins ⟨~ yarn⟩

skel·e·tal \ˈskel-ət-ᵊl\ *adj* (1854) **:** of, relating to, forming, attached to, or resembling a skeleton — **skel·e·tal·ly** \-ᵊl-ē\ *adv*

[1]**skel·e·ton** \ˈskel-ət-ᵊn\ *n* [NL, fr. Gk, neut. of *skeletos* dried up; akin to Gk *skellein* to dry up, *sklēros* hard, OE *scealds* shallow] (1578) **1 :** a usu. rigid supportive or protective structure or framework of an organism; *esp* **:** the bony or more or less cartilaginous framework supporting the soft tissues and protecting the internal organs of a vertebrate (as a fish or man) **2 :** something reduced to its minimum form or essential parts **3 :** an emaciated person or animal **4 a :** something forming a structural framework **b :** the straight or branched chain or ring of atoms that forms the basic structure of an organic molecule **5 :** something shameful and kept secret (as in a family) — often used in the phrase *skeleton in the closet*

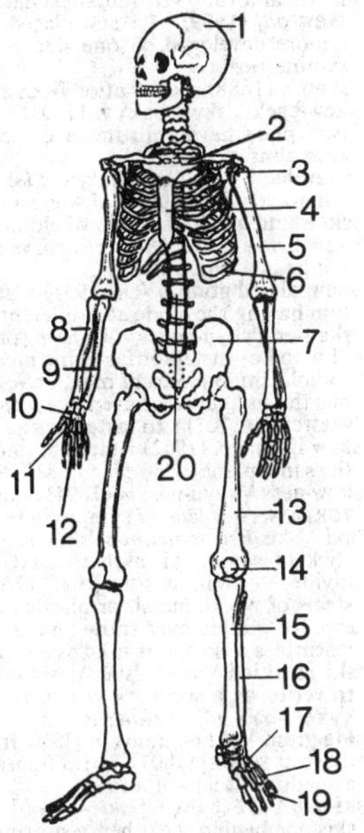

skeleton 1: *1* skull, *2* clavicle, *3* scapula, *4* sternum, *5* humerus, *6* rib, *7* pelvis, *8* radius, *9* ulna, *10* carpus, *11* metacarpal bones, *12* phalanges (fingers), *13* femur, *14* patella, *15* tibia, *16* fibula, *17* tarsus, *18* metatarsal bones, *19* phalanges (toes), *20* spinal column

[2]**skeleton** *adj* (1778) **:** of, consisting of, or resembling a skeleton

skel·e·ton·ize \-ˌīz\ *vt* **-ized; -iz·ing** (1644) **:** to produce in or reduce to skeleton form ⟨~ a leaf⟩ ⟨~ a news story⟩ ⟨~ a regiment⟩

skel·e·ton·iz·er \-ˌī-zər\ *n* (ca. 1891) **:** any of various lepidopterous larvae that eat the parenchyma of leaves reducing them to a skeleton of veins

skeleton key *n* (1810) **:** a key with a large part of the bit filed away to enable it to open low quality locks as a master key

skel·lum \ˈskel-əm\ *n* [D *schelm*, fr. LG; akin to OHG *skelmo* person deserving death] *chiefly Scot* (1611) **:** SCOUNDREL, RASCAL

[1]**skelp** \ˈskelp\ *vb* **skelped** \ˈskelpt\ *also* **skel·pit** \ˈskel-pət\; **skelp·ing** [ME *skelpen*] *vt, dial Brit* (15c) **:** STRIKE, SLAP, BEAT ~ *vi* **:** to step lively **:** HUSTLE

[2]**skelp** *n, dial Brit* (15c) **:** a smart blow **:** SLAP

skel·ter \ˈskel-tər\ *vi* **skel·tered; skel·ter·ing** \-t(ə-)riŋ\ [fr. *-skelter* (in *helter-skelter*)] (1852) **:** SCURRY

Skel·ton·ics \skel-ˈtän-iks\ *n pl* [John *Skelton*] (1898) **:** short verses of an irregular meter with two or three stresses sometimes in falling and sometimes in rising rhythm and usu. with rhymed couplets

skep \ˈskep\ *n* [ME *skeppe* basket, basketful, fr. OE *sceppe*, fr. ON *skeppa* bushel; akin to OE *scieppan* to form, create — more at SHAPE] (15c) **:** BEEHIVE; *esp* **:** a domed hive made of twisted straw

skep·sis \ˈskep-səs\ *n* [NL, fr. Gk *skepsis* examination, doubt, skeptical philosophy, fr. *skeptesthai*] (ca. 1864) **:** philosophic doubt as to the objective reality of phenomena; *broadly* **:** a skeptical outlook or attitude

skep·tic \ˈskep-tik\ *n* [L or Gk; L *scepticus*, fr. Gk *skeptikos*, fr. *skeptikos* thoughtful, fr. *skeptesthai* to look, consider — more at SPY] (1589) **1 :** an adherent or advocate of skepticism **2 :** a person disposed to skepticism esp. regarding religion or religious principles

skep·ti·cal \-ti-kəl\ *adj* (1639) **:** relating to, characteristic of, or marked by skepticism ⟨a ~ listener⟩ — **skep·ti·cal·ly** \-k(ə-)lē\ *adv*

skep·ti·cism \ˈskep-tə-ˌsiz-əm\ *n* (1646) **1 :** an attitude of doubt or a disposition to incredulity either in general or toward a particular object **2 a :** the doctrine that true knowledge or knowledge in a particular area is uncertain **b :** the method of suspended judgment, systematic doubt, or criticism characteristic of skeptics **3 :** doubt concerning basic religious principles (as immortality, providence, and revelation) ***syn*** see UNCERTAINTY

sker·ry \ˈsker-ē\ *n, pl* **skerries** [of Scand origin; akin to ON *sker* skerry and to ON *ey* island; akin to L *aqua* water — more at SCAR, ISLAND] (1612) **:** a rocky isle **:** REEF

[1]**sketch** \ˈskech\ *n* [D *schets*, fr. It *schizzo*, fr. *schizzare* to splash] (1668) **1 a :** a rough drawing representing the chief features of an object or scene and often made as a preliminary study **b :** a tentative draft (as for a literary work) **2 :** a brief description (as of a person) or outline **3 a :** a short literary composition somewhat resembling the short story and the essay but intentionally slight in treatment, discursive in style, and familiar in tone **b :** a short instrumental composition usu. for piano **c :** a slight theatrical piece having a single scene; *esp* **:** a comic variety act

[2]**sketch** *vt* (1694) **:** to make a sketch, rough draft, or outline of ~ *vi* **:** to draw or paint a sketch — **sketch·er** *n*

sketch·book \ˈskech-ˌbu̇k\ *n* (1820) **:** a book of or for sketches

sketchy \ˈskech-ē\ *adj* **sketch·i·er; -est** (1805) **1 :** of the nature of a sketch **:** roughly outlined **2 :** wanting in completeness, clearness, or substance **:** SLIGHT, SUPERFICIAL — **sketch·i·ly** \ˈskech-ə-lē\ *adv* — **sketch·i·ness** \ˈskech-ē-nəs\ *n*

[1]**skew** \'skyü\ *vb* [ME *skewen* to escape, skew, fr. ONF *escuer* to shun, of Gmc origin; akin to OHG *sciuhen* to frighten off — more at SHY] *vi* (15c) **1 :** to take an oblique course **2 :** to look askance ~ *vt* **1 :** to make, set, or cut on the skew **2 :** to distort from a true value or symmetrical form ⟨~*ed* statistical data⟩
[2]**skew** *adj* (1609) **1 :** set, placed, or running obliquely **:** SLANTING **2 :** more developed on one side or in one direction than another **:** not symmetrical
[3]**skew** *n* (1688) **:** a deviation from a straight line **:** SLANT
skew·back \'skyü-ˌbak\ *n* (1703) **:** a course of masonry, a stone, or an iron plate having an inclined face against which the voussoirs of an arch abut
[1]**skew·bald** \-ˌbȯld\ *adj* [*skewed* (skewbald) + *bald*] *of an animal* (1654) **:** marked with patches of white and any other color but black
[2]**skewbald** *n* (1863) **:** a skewbald horse
skew curve *n* (ca. 1890) **:** a curve in three-dimensional space that does not lie in a single plane
skew distribution *n* (ca. 1931) **:** an unsymmetrical frequency distribution having the mode at a different value from the mean
[1]**skew·er** \'skyü-ər, 'skyu̇(-ə)r\ *n* [prob. alter. of *skiver*] (1679) **1 :** a pin of wood or metal for fastening meat to keep it in form while roasting or to hold small pieces of meat or vegetables for broiling **2 :** any of various things shaped or used like a meat skewer
[2]**skewer** *vt* (1701) **:** to fasten or pierce with or as if with a skewer
skew lines *n pl* (1952) **:** straight lines that do not intersect and are not in the same plane
skew·ness \'skyü-nəs\ *n* (1894) **:** lack of straightness or symmetry **:** DISTORTION; *esp* **:** lack of symmetry in a frequency distribution
[1]**ski** \'skē *Brit sometimes* 'shē\ *n, pl* **skis** *also* **ski** [Norw, fr. ON *skīth* stick of wood, ski; akin to OHG *skīt* stick of wood, OE *scēadan* to divide — more at SHED] (ca. 1755) **1 a :** one of a pair of narrow strips of wood, metal, or plastic curving upward in front that are used esp. for gliding over snow **b :** WATER SKI **2 :** a piece of material that resembles a ski and is used as a runner on a vehicle
[2]**ski** *vb* **skied** \'skēd, 'shēd\; **ski·ing** *vi* (ca. 1890) **:** to glide on skis in travel or as a sport ~ *vt* **:** to travel or pass over on skis — **ski·able** \'skē-ə-bəl\ *adj* — **ski·er** *n*
skia·gram \'skī-ə-ˌgram\ *n* [ISV, fr. Gk *skia* shadow + ISV *-gram* — more at SCENE] (1801) **1 :** a figure formed by shading in the outline of a shadow **2 :** RADIOGRAPH
ski·bob \'skē-ˌbäb\ *n* [[1]*ski* + [7]*bob*] (1966) **:** a vehicle that has two short skis one behind the other, a steering handle attached to the forward ski, and a low upholstered seat over the rear ski and that is used for gliding downhill over snow by a rider wearing miniature skis for balance — **ski·bob·ber** \-ˌbäb-ər\ *n* — **ski·bob·bing** \-ˌbäb-iŋ\ *n*
ski boot *n* (ca. 1949) **:** a rigid padded shoe usu. of leather or plastic that extends just above the ankle, is securely fastened to the foot (as with laces, buckles, or hinges), and is locked into position in a ski binding
[1]**skid** \'skid\ *n* [perh. of Scand origin; akin to ON *skīth* stick of wood — more at SKI] (1609) **1 :** one of a group of objects (as planks or logs) used to support or elevate a structure or object **2 :** a wooden fender hung over a ship's side to protect it in handling cargo **3 :** a usu. iron shoe or clog attached to a chain and placed under a wheel to prevent its turning when descending a steep hill **:** DRAG **4 :** a timber, bar, rail, pole, or log used in pairs or sets to form a slideway (as for an incline from a truck to the sidewalk) **5 :** the act of skidding **:** SLIP, SIDESLIP **6 :** a runner used as a member of the landing gear of an airplane or helicopter **7** *pl* **:** a route to defeat or downfall ⟨on the ~*s*⟩ **8 :** a low platform mounted (as on wheels) on which material is set for handling and moving
[2]**skid** *vb* **skid·ded; skid·ding** *vt* (1674) **1 :** to apply a brake or skid to **:** slow or halt by a skid **2 :** to haul along, slide, hoist, or store on skids ~ *vi* **1 :** to slide without rotating (as a wheel held from turning while a vehicle moves onward) **2 a :** to fail to grip the roadway; *esp* **:** to slip sideways on the road **b** *of an airplane* **:** to slide sidewise away from the center of curvature when turning **c :** SLIDE, SLIP **3 :** to fall rapidly, steeply, or far
skid·der \'skid-ər\ *n* (1870) **:** one that skids or uses a skid
skid·doo *or* **ski·doo** \skid-'ü\ *vi* [prob. alter. of *skedaddle*] (1903) **:** to go away **:** DEPART
skid·dy \'skid-ē\ *adj* **skid·di·er; -est** (1920) **:** likely to skid or cause skidding ⟨a wet ~ road⟩
skid road *n* (1880) **1 :** a road along which logs are skidded **2 a** *West* **:** the part of a town frequented by loggers **b :** SKID ROW
skid row \-'rō\ *n* [alter. of *skid road*] (ca. 1941) **:** a district of cheap saloons and flophouses frequented by vagrants and alcoholics
ski·ey *var of* SKYEY
skiff \'skif\ *n* [MF or OIt; MF *esquif,* fr. OIt *schifo,* of Gmc origin; akin to OE *scip* ship] (1575) **1 :** a small light sailing ship **2 :** a light rowboat **3 :** a boat with centerboard and spritsail light enough to be rowed **4 :** a small fast motorboat
skif·fle \'skif-əl\ *n* [origin unknown] (1956) **:** jazz or folk music played by a group all or some of whose members play nonstandard instruments or noisemakers (as jugs, washboards, or Jew's harps)
ski·ing *n* (1893) **:** the art or sport of sliding and jumping on skis
ski·jor·ing \'skē-ˌjōr-iŋ, -ˌjȯr-, (ˌ)skē-'\ *n* [modif. of Norw *skikjøring,* fr. *ski* + *kjøring* driving] (1910) **:** a winter sport in which a person wearing skis is drawn over snow or ice by a horse or vehicle
ski jump *n* (1925) **:** a jump made by a person wearing skis; *also* **:** a course or track esp. prepared for such jumping — **ski jump** *vi*
ski lift *n* (1939) **:** a motor-driven conveyor consisting usu. of a series of bars or seats suspended from an overhead moving cable and used for transporting skiers or sightseers up a long slope
[1]**skill** \'skil\ *vi* [ME *skilen,* fr. ON *skilja* to separate, divide; akin to ON *skil* distinction] *archaic* (13c) **:** to make a difference **:** MATTER, AVAIL
[2]**skill** *n* [ME *skil,* fr. ON, distinction, knowledge; akin to OE *scylian* to separate, *sciell* shell — more at SHELL] (14c) **1** *obs* **:** CAUSE, REASON **2 a :** the ability to use one's knowledge effectively and readily in execution or performance **b :** dexterity or coordination esp. in the execution of learned physical tasks **3 :** a learned power of doing something competently **:** a developed aptitude or ability ⟨language ~*s*⟩ *syn* see ART — **skill–less** *or* **skil·less** \'skil-ləs\ *adj* — **skill–less·ness** *or* **skil·less·ness** *n*
skilled \'skild\ *adj* (1552) **1 :** having acquired mastery of or skill in something (as a technique or a trade) **2 :** of, relating to, or requiring workers or labor with skill and training in a particular occupation, craft, or trade *syn* see PROFICIENT
skil·let \'skil-ət\ *n* [ME *skelet*] (15c) **1** *chiefly Brit* **:** a small kettle or pot usu. having three or four often long feet and used for cooking on the hearth **2 :** FRYING PAN
skill·ful *or* **skil·ful** \'skil-fəl\ *adj* (14c) **1 :** possessed of or displaying skill **:** EXPERT **2 :** accomplished with skill *syn* see PROFICIENT — **skill·ful·ly** \-fə-lē\ *adv* — **skill·ful·ness** *n*
skil·ling \'skil-iŋ, 'shil-\ *n* [Sw, Norw, & Dan, fr. ON *skillingr,* a gold coin; akin to OE *scilling* shilling] (1793) **:** any of various old Scandinavian units of value or the coins representing them
[1]**skim** \'skim\ *vb* **skimmed; skim·ming** [ME *skimmen*] *vt* (15c) **1 a :** to clear (a liquid) of scum or floating substance ⟨~ boiling syrup⟩ **b :** to remove (as film or scum) from the surface of a liquid **c :** to remove cream from by skimming **d :** to remove the best or most easily obtainable contents from **2 :** to read, study, or examine superficially and rapidly; *esp* **:** to glance through (as a book) for the chief ideas or the plot **3 :** to throw in a gliding path; *esp* **:** to throw so as to ricochet along the surface of water **4 :** to cover with or as if with a film, scum, or coat **5 :** to pass swiftly or lightly over ~ *vi* **1 a :** to pass lightly or hastily **:** glide or skip along, above, or near a surface **b :** to give a cursory glance or consideration **2 :** to become coated with a thin layer of film or scum **3 :** to put on a finishing coat of plaster
[2]**skim** *n* (1539) **1 :** a thin layer, coating, or film **2 :** the act of skimming **3 :** something skimmed; *specif* **:** SKIM MILK
[3]**skim** *adj* (1596) **1 :** having the cream removed by skimming **2 :** made of skim milk ⟨~ cheese⟩
ski mask *n* (1966) **:** a knit fabric mask that covers the head, has openings for the eyes, mouth, and sometimes the nose, and is worn esp. by skiers for protection from the cold
skim·ble–skam·ble \ˌskim-bəl-'skam-bəl\ *adj* [redupl. of E dial. *scamble* to stumble along] (1596) **:** rambling and confused **:** SENSELESS
skim·mer \'skim-ər\ *n* (14c) **1 :** one that skims; *specif* **:** a flat perforated scoop or spoon used for skimming **2 a :** any of several long-winged marine birds (genus *Rhynchops*) related to the terns **b :** WATER STRIDER **3 :** a usu. straw flat-crowned hat with a wide straight brim **4 :** a fitted sleeveless usu. flaring dress
skim milk *n* (1596) **:** milk from which the cream has been taken — called also *skimmed milk*
skim·ming *n* (15c) **1 :** that which is skimmed from a liquid **2 :** the practice of fraudulently reporting gambling income (as of a casino) so as to avoid full tax payments
ski·mo·bile \'skē-mō-ˌbēl\ *n* (1944) **:** SNOWMOBILE
[1]**skimp** \'skimp\ *adj* [perh. alter. of *scrimp*] (1775) **:** SCANTY, MEAGER
[2]**skimp** *vt* (ca. 1879) **:** to give insufficient or barely sufficient attention or effort to or funds for ~ *vi* **:** to save by or as if by skimping
skimpy \'skim-pē\ *adj* **skimp·i·er; -est** (1842) **:** deficient in supply or execution esp. through skimping **:** SCANTY *syn* see MEAGER — **skimp·i·ly** \-pə-lē\ *adv* — **skimp·i·ness** \-pē-nəs\ *n*
[1]**skin** \'skin\ *n, often attrib* [ME, fr. ON *skinn;* akin to OE *scinn* skin, MHG *schint* fruit peel, W *ysgythru* to cut] (13c) **1 a (1) :** the integument of an animal (as a fur-bearing mammal or a bird) separated from the body usu. with its hair or feathers **(2) :** a usu. unmounted specimen of a vertebrate (as in a museum) **b :** the hide or pelt of a game or domestic animal **c (1) :** the pelt of an animal prepared for use as a trimming or in a garment ⟨it took 40 ~*s* to make the coat⟩ — compare [4]HIDE **(2) :** a sheet of parchment or vellum made from a hide **(3) :** BOTTLE 1b **2 a :** the external limiting layer of an animal body esp. when forming a tough but flexible cover relatively impermeable from without while intact **b :** any of various outer or surface layers (as a rind, husk, or pellicle) ⟨a sausage ~⟩ **3 :** the life or physical well-being of a person ⟨made sure to save his ~⟩ **4 :** a sheathing or casing forming the outside surface of a structure (as a ship or airplane) — **skin·less** \-ləs\ *adj* — **by the skin of one's teeth :** by a very narrow margin — **under one's skin :** so deeply penetrative as to irritate, stimulate, provoke thought, or otherwise excite — **under the skin :** beneath apparent or surface differences **:** at heart
[2]**skin** *vb* **skinned; skin·ning** *vt* (1547) **1 a :** to cover with or as if with skin **b :** to heal over with skin **2 a :** to strip, scrape, or rub off an outer covering (as the skin or rind) of **b :** to strip or peel off **c :** to cut, chip, or damage the surface of ⟨fell and *skinned* my knee⟩ **3 a :** to strip of money or property **:** FLEECE **b :** DEFEAT **c :** CENSURE, CASTIGATE **4 :** to urge on and direct the course of (as a draft animal) ~ *vi* **1 :** to become covered with or as if with skin **2 a :** SHIN **b :** to pass or get by with scant room to spare
[3]**skin** *adj* (1966) **:** involving subjects who are nude ⟨expected to conduct ~ searches for weapons —Diane K. Shah⟩; *esp* **:** devoted to showing nudes ⟨~ magazines⟩
skin–deep \'skin-'dēp\ *adj* (1613) **1 :** as deep as the skin **2 :** not thorough or lasting in impression **:** SUPERFICIAL
skin–dive \'skin-ˌdīv\ *vi* (1952) **:** to engage in skin diving — **skin diver** *n*
skin diving *n* (1949) **:** the sport of swimming under water with a face mask and flippers and esp. without a portable breathing device
skin effect *n* (ca. 1900) **:** an effect characteristic of current distribution in a conductor at high frequencies by virtue of which the current density is greater near the surface of the conductor than in its interior
skin·flint \'skin-ˌflint\ *n* (ca. 1700) **:** a person who would save, gain, or extort money by any means **:** MISER, NIGGARD
skin·ful \-ˌfu̇l\ *n* (1802) **1 :** the contents of a skin bottle **2 :** a large or satisfying quantity esp. of liquor
skin game *n* (1868) **:** a swindling game or trick
skin graft *n* (ca. 1891) **:** a piece of skin that is taken from a donor area to replace skin in a defective or denuded area (as one that has been burned) — **skin grafting** *n*
skin·head \'skin-ˌhed\ *n* (1956) **1 :** one whose hair is cut very short **2 :** a young short-haired working-class British hoodlum
[1]**skink** \'skiŋk\ *vt* [ME *skinken,* fr. MD *schenken;* akin to OE *scencan* to pour out drink, *scanca* shank] *chiefly dial* (14c) **:** to draw, pour out, or serve (drink)
[2]**skink** *n* [L *scincus,* fr. Gk *skinkos*] (1590) **:** any of a family (Scincidae) of mostly small pleurodont lizards that have small scales
skink·er \'skiŋ-kər\ *n* (1586) **:** one that serves liquor **:** TAPSTER

skinned \ˈskind\ *adj* (15c) **:** having skin esp. of a specified kind — usu. used in combination ⟨dark-*skinned*⟩
skin·ner \ˈskin-ər\ *n* (14c) **1 a :** one that deals in skins, pelts, or hides **b :** one that removes, cures, or dresses skins **2 :** SHARPER **3 :** a driver of draft animals **:** TEAMSTER
Skin·ner box \ˌskin-ər-ˈbäks\ *n* [B. F. *Skinner*] (1942) **:** a laboratory apparatus in which an animal is caged for experiments in operant conditioning and which typically contains a lever that must be pressed by the animal to gain reward or avoid punishment
skin·ny \ˈskin-ē\ *adj* **skin·ni·er; -est** (1573) **1 :** resembling skin **:** MEMBRANOUS **2 a :** lacking sufficient flesh **:** very thin **:** EMACIATED **b :** lacking usual or desirable bulk, quantity, qualities, or significance *syn* see LEAN — **skin·ni·ness** *n*
skin·ny–dip \ˈskin-ē-ˌdip\ *vi* (1964) **:** to swim in the nude — **skinny–dip** *n* — **skin·ny–dip·per** \-ˌdip-ər\ *n* — **skin·ny–dip·ping** \-ˌdip-iŋ\ *n*
skin–pop \ˈskin-ˈpäp\ *vi* (ca. 1952) **:** to inject a drug subcutaneously rather than into a vein ~ *vt* **:** to inject (a drug) by skin-popping — **skin–pop·per** \-ər\ *n*
skint \ˈskint\ *adj* [alter. of *skinned,* pp. of [2]*skin*] *Brit* (ca. 1931) **:** PENNILESS
skin test *n* (ca. 1930) **:** a test (as a scratch test) performed on the skin and used in detecting allergic hypersensitivity
skin·tight \ˈskin-ˈtīt\ *adj* (1885) **:** closely fitted to the figure
ski·ör·ing \ˈskē-ˌər-iŋ, (ˌ)skē-ˈ\ *var of* SKIJORING
[1]**skip** \ˈskip\ *vb* **skipped; skip·ping** [ME *skippen,* perh. of Scand origin; akin to Sw dial. *skopa* to hop] *vi* (14c) **1 a :** to move or proceed with leaps and bounds **:** CAPER **b :** to bound off one point after another **:** RICOCHET **2 :** to leave hurriedly or secretly ⟨*skipped* out without paying their bill⟩ **3 a :** to pass over or omit an interval, item, or step **b :** to omit a grade in school in advancing to the next **c :** MISFIRE 1 ~ *vt* **1 a :** to pass over without notice or mention **:** OMIT **b :** to pass by or leave out (a step in a progression or series) **2 a :** to cause to skip (a grade in school) **b :** to cause to bound or skim over a surface ⟨~ a stone across a pond⟩ **3 :** to leap over lightly and nimbly **4 a :** to depart from quickly and secretly ⟨*skipped* town⟩ **b :** to fail to attend ⟨~ the meeting⟩ — **skip·pa·ble** \ˈskip-ə-bəl\ *adj* — **skip bail :** to jump bail — **skip rope :** to jump rope
[2]**skip** *n* (15c) **1 a :** a light bounding step **b :** a gait composed of alternating hops and steps **2 :** an act of omission or the thing omitted
[3]**skip** *n* [short for [2]*skipper*] (1830) **1 :** the captain of a side in a game (as curling or lawn bowling) who advises his men as to the play and controls the action **2 :** SKIPPER
[4]**skip** *vt* **skipped; skip·ping** (1900) **:** to act as skipper of
skip bomb *vt* (1943) **:** to attack by releasing delayed-action bombs from a low-flying airplane so that they skip along a land or water surface and strike a target
skip·jack \ˈskip-ˌjak\ *n, pl* **skipjacks** *or* **skipjack** (1703) **1 :** any of various fishes (as a tenpounder or bluefish) that jump above or play at the surface of the water; *esp* **:** SKIPJACK TUNA **2 :** a small sailboat with the bottom similar to a flat V and sides vertical
skipjack tuna *n* (1950) **:** a relatively small but important scombroid food and sport fish (*Euthynnus pelamis*) that is bluish above and silvery below with oblique dark stripes on the sides and belly
ski pole *n* (1925) **:** one of a pair of lightweight usu. metal poles that have a handgrip and a wrist strap at one end and an encircling disk set a little above the point at the other end and that are used in skiing
[1]**skip·per** \ˈskip-ər\ *n* (13c) **1 :** any of various erratically active insects (as a click beetle or a water strider) **2 :** one that skips **3 :** SAURY **4 :** any of numerous small stout-bodied lepidopterous insects (superfamily Hesperioidea) that differ from the typical butterflies esp. in wing venation and the form of the antennae
[2]**skipper** *n* [ME, fr. MD *schipper,* fr. *schip* ship; akin to OE *scip* ship — more at SHIP] (14c) **1 :** the master of a ship; *esp* **:** the master of a fishing, small trading, or pleasure boat **2 :** the captain or first pilot of an airplane
[3]**skip·per** *vt* **skip·pered; skip·per·ing** \ˈskip-(ə-)riŋ\ (1893) **1 :** to act as skipper of (as a boat) **2 :** to act as coach of (as a team)
[1]**skirl** \ˈskər(-ə)l, ˈskir(-ə)l\ *vb* [ME (Sc) *skrillen, skirlen,* of Scand origin; akin to OSw *skrælla* to rattle; akin to OE *scrallettan* to sound loudly] *vi, of a bagpipe* (1665) **:** to emit the high shrill tone of the chanter; *also* **:** to give forth music ~ *vt* **:** to play (music) on the bagpipe
[2]**skirl** *n* (1856) **:** a high shrill sound produced by the chanter of a bagpipe
[1]**skir·mish** \ˈskər-mish\ *n* [ME *skyrmissh,* alter. of *skarmish,* fr. MF *escarmouche,* fr. OIt *scaramuccia,* of Gmc origin; akin to OHG *skirmen* to defend, OE *scieran* to cut — more at SHEAR] (14c) **1 :** a minor fight in war usu. incidental to larger movements **2 a :** a brisk preliminary verbal conflict **b :** a minor dispute or contest between opposing parties
[2]**skirmish** *vi* (15c) **1 :** to engage in a skirmish **2 :** to search about (as for supplies) **:** scout around — **skir·mish·er** *n*
skirr \ˈskər, ˈski(ə)r\ *vb* [perh. alter. of [1]*scour*] *vi* (1548) **1 :** to leave hastily **:** FLEE ⟨birds ~*ed* off from the bushes —D. H. Lawrence⟩ **2 :** to run, fly, sail, or move along rapidly ~ *vt* **1 :** to search about in ⟨~ the country round —Shak.⟩ **2 a :** to pass rapidly over **:** SKIM **b** *dial* **:** to cause to skim
[2]**skirr** *n* [prob. imit.] (1870) **:** WHIR, ROAR
[1]**skirt** \ˈskərt\ *n* [ME, fr. ON *skyrta* shirt, kirtle — more at SHIRT] (14c) **1 a** (1) **:** a free-hanging part of an outer garment or undergarment extending from the waist down (2) **:** a separate free-hanging outer garment or undergarment for women and girls covering the body from the waist down **b :** either of two usu. leather flaps on a saddle covering the bars on which the stirrups are hung **c :** a cloth facing that hangs loosely and usu. in folds or pleats from the bottom edge or across the front of a piece of furniture **d :** the lower branches of a tree when near the ground **2 a :** the rim, periphery, or environs of an area **b** *pl* **:** outlying parts (as of a town or city) **3 :** a part or attachment serving as a rim, border, or edging **4 :** GIRL, WOMAN — **skirt·ed** *adj*
[2]**skirt** *vt* (1602) **1 :** to form or run along the border or edge of **:** BORDER **2 a :** to provide a skirt for **b :** to furnish a border or shield for **3 a :** to go or pass around or about; *specif* **:** to go around or keep away from in order to avoid danger or discovery **b :** to avoid because of difficulty or fear of controversy ⟨~*ed* the important issues⟩ **c :** to evade or miss by a narrow margin ⟨having ~*ed* disaster —Edith Wharton⟩ ~ *vi* **:** to be, lie, or move along an edge, border, or margin — **skirt·er** *n*
skirt·ing \ˈskərt-iŋ\ *n* (1764) **1 :** something that skirts: as **a :** BORDER, EDGING **b** *Brit* **:** BASEBOARD **2 :** fabric suitable for skirts
skirt steak *n* (ca. 1909) **:** a boneless strip of beef cut from the plate
ski run *n* (1925) **:** a slope or trail suitable for skiing
skit \ˈskit\ *n* [origin unknown] (1727) **1 :** a jeering or satirical remark **:** TAUNT **2 a :** a satirical or humorous story or sketch **b** (1) **:** a brief burlesque or comic sketch included in a dramatic performance (as a revue) (2) **:** a short serious dramatic piece; *esp* **:** one done by amateurs
ski touring *n* (1935) **:** cross-country skiing for pleasure
ski tow *n* (1935) **1 :** a motor-driven conveyor that is used for pulling skiers up a slope and that consists usu. of an endless moving rope which a skier grasps **2 :** SKI LIFT
skit·ter \ˈskit-ər\ *vb* [prob. freq. of E dial. *skite* to move quickly] *vi* (1845) **1 :** to glide or skip lightly or quickly **2 :** to twitch the hook of a fishing line through or along the surface of water ~ *vt* **:** to cause to skitter
skit·tery \ˈskit-ə-rē\ *adj* (1944) **:** SKITTISH
skit·tish \ˈskit-ish\ *adj* [ME] (15c) **1 a :** lively or frisky in action **:** CAPRICIOUS **b :** VARIABLE, FLUCTUATING **2 :** easily frightened **:** RESTIVE ⟨a ~ horse⟩ **3 a :** COY, BASHFUL **b :** marked by extreme caution **:** WARY — **skit·tish·ly** *adv* — **skit·tish·ness** *n*
skit·tle \ˈskit-ᵊl\ *n* [perh. of Scand origin; akin to ON *skutill* bolt — more at SHUTTLE] (1634) **1** *pl but sing in constr* **:** English ninepins played with a wooden disk or ball **2 :** one of the pins used in skittles
skive \ˈskīv\ *vt* **skived; skiv·ing** [of Scand origin; akin to ON *skifa* to slice; akin to OE *scēadan* to divide — more at SHED] (1825) **:** to cut off (as leather or rubber) in thin layers or pieces **:** PARE
skiv·er \ˈskī-vər\ *n* (1800) **1 :** a thin soft leather made of the grain side of a split sheepskin, usu. tanned in sumac and dyed **2 :** one that skives something (as leather)
[1]**skiv·vy** \ˈskiv-ē\ *n, pl* **skivvies** [origin unknown] *Brit* (1914) **:** a female domestic servant
[2]**skivvy** *n, pl* **skivvies** [origin unknown] (1927) **:** men's underwear; *esp* **:** a T-shirt and briefs or shorts — usu. used in pl.
ski·wear \ˈskē-ˌwa(ə)r, -ˌwe(ə)r\ *n* (1964) **:** clothing suitable for wear while skiing
sklent \ˈsklent\ *vb* [ME *sclenten* to strike obliquely, alter. of *slenten* — more at SLANT] *vi* (1805) **1** *chiefly Scot* **:** to look askance **2** *chiefly Scot* **:** to cast aspersions ~ *vt, Scot* **:** to direct sideways **:** SLANT
skoal \ˈskōl\ *n* [Dan *skaal,* lit., cup; akin to ON *skāl* bowl — more at SCALE] (1600) **:** TOAST, HEALTH — often used interjectionally
skua \ˈskyü-ə\ *n* [NL, fr. Faeroese *skūgvur;* akin to ON *skūfr* tassel, skua, OE *scēaf* sheaf — more at SHEAF] (1678) **:** JAEGER 2; *esp* **:** GREAT SKUA
skul·dug·gery *or* **skull·dug·gery** \ˌskəl-ˈdəg-(ə-)rē, ˈskəl-ˌ\ *n, pl* **-ger·ies** [origin unknown] (1856) **:** a devious device or trick; *also* **:** underhanded or unscrupulous behavior
[1]**skulk** \ˈskəlk\ *vi* [ME *skulken,* of Scand origin; akin to Dan *skulke* to shirk, play truant] (13c) **1 :** to move in a stealthy or furtive manner **2 a :** to hide or conceal something (as oneself) often out of cowardice or fear or with sinister intent **b** *chiefly Brit* **:** MALINGER *syn* see LURK — **skulk·er** *n*
[2]**skulk** *n* (14c) **1 :** one that skulks **2 :** a group of foxes
skull \ˈskəl\ *n* [ME *skulle,* of Scand origin; akin to Sw *skulle* skull] (13c) **1 :** the skeleton of the head of a vertebrate forming a bony or cartilaginous case that encloses and protects the brain and chief sense organs and supports the jaws **2 :** the seat of understanding or intelligence **:** MIND — **skulled** \ˈskəld\ *adj*
skull and cross·bones \-ˈkrós-ˌbōnz\ *n, pl* **skulls and crossbones** (1826) **:** a representation of a human skull over crossbones usu. used as a warning of danger to life
skull·cap \ˈskəl-ˌkap\ *n* (1682) **1 :** a close-fitting cap; *esp* **:** a light cap without brim for indoor wear **2 :** any of various mints (genus *Scutellaria*) having a calyx that when inverted resembles a helmet
skull session *n* (1937) **1 :** a strategy class for an athletic team **2 :** a meeting for consultation, discussion, or the interchange of ideas or information — called also *skull practice*
[1]**skunk** \ˈskəŋk\ *n, pl* **skunks** *also* **skunk** [of Algonquian origin; akin to Abnaki *segākw* skunk] (1634) **1 a :** any of various common omnivorous black-and-white New World mammals (esp. genus *Mephitis*) related to the weasels and having a pair of perineal glands from which a secretion of pungent and offensive odor is ejected **b :** the fur of a skunk **2 :** an obnoxious person
[2]**skunk** *vt* (1846) **1 a :** DEFEAT **b :** to shut out in a game **2 :** to fail to pay; *also* **:** CHEAT
skunk cabbage *n* (1751) **:** an eastern No. American perennial herb (*Symplocarpus foetidus*) of the arum family that sends up in early spring a cowl-shaped brownish purple spathe having an unpleasant odor; *also* **:** a related plant (*Lysichitum americanum*) of the Pacific coast region with a large yellow spathe
[1]**sky** \ˈskī\ *n, pl* **skies** [ME, cloud, sky, fr. ON *sky̅* cloud; akin to OE *scēo* cloud, L *cutis* skin — more at HIDE] (14c) **1 :** the upper atmosphere that constitutes an apparent great vault or arch over the earth **2 :** HEAVEN 2 **3**

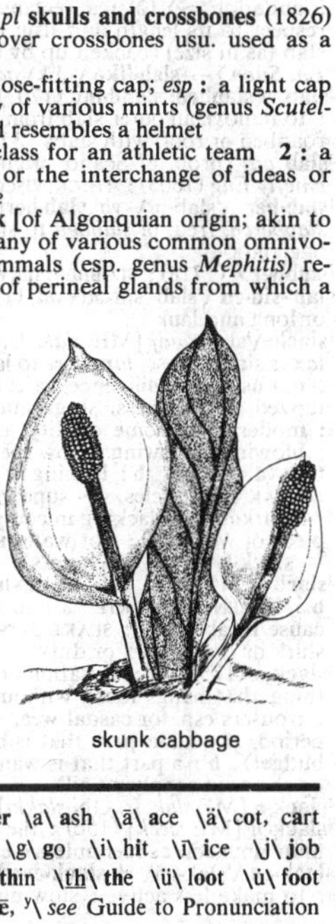
skunk cabbage

\ə\ abut \ᵊ\ kitten, F table \ər\ further \a\ ash \ā\ ace \ä\ cot, cart \aů\ out \ch\ chin \e\ bet \ē\ easy \g\ go \i\ hit \ī\ ice \j\ job \ŋ\ sing \ō\ go \ó\ law \ói\ boy \th\ thin \th\ the \ü\ loot \ů\ foot \y\ yet \zh\ vision \á, k̲, ⁿ, œ, œ̄, ue, ue̅, ʸ\ see Guide to Pronunciation

a : weather in the upper atmosphere **b** : CLIMATE ⟨temperate English *skies* —G. G. Coulton⟩

[2]**sky** *vt* **skied** *or* **skyed; sky·ing** (1802) **1** *chiefly Brit* : to throw or toss up : FLIP **2** : to hang (as a painting) above the line of vision

sky blue *n* (1738) : a variable color averaging a pale to light blue

sky·borne \'skī-,bō(ə)rn, -,bȯ(ə)rn\ *adj* (1589) : AIRBORNE ⟨~ troops⟩

sky·cap \-,kap\ *n* [[1]*sky* + *-cap* (as in *redcap*)] (1941) : one employed to carry hand luggage at an airport — compare REDCAP

sky·div·ing \-,dī-viŋ\ *n* (1957) : the sport of jumping from an airplane at a moderate altitude (as 6000 feet) and executing various body maneuvers before pulling the rip cord of a parachute — **sky diver** *n*

Skye terrier \'skī-\ *n* [*Skye*, Scotland] (1847) : any of a Scottish breed of terriers with a long low body and long straight coat

sky·ey \'skī-ē\ *adj* (1603) : of or resembling the sky : ETHEREAL

[1]**sky–high** \'skī-'hī\ *adv* (1818) **1 a** : high into the air **b** : to a high level or degree **2** : in an enthusiastic manner **3** : to bits : APART ⟨blown ~⟩

[2]**sky–high** *adj* (1945) : excessively expensive : EXORBITANT

sky·hook \-,hu̇k\ *n* (1915) : a hook conceived as being suspended from the sky

sky·jack \'skī-,jak\ *vt* [[1]*sky* + *jack* (as in *hijack*)] (1961) : to commandeer (an airplane in flight) by the threat of violence — **sky·jack·er** \-ər\ *n* — **sky·jack·ing** \-iŋ\ *n*

[1]**sky·lark** \'skī-,lärk\ *n* (1686) **1** : a common largely brown Old World lark (*Alauda arvensis*) noted for its song esp. as uttered in vertical flight **2** : any of various birds resembling the skylark

[2]**skylark** *vi* (1809) **1** : to run up and down the rigging of a ship in sport **2** : FROLIC, SPORT — **sky·lark·er** *n*

sky·light \'skī-,līt\ *n* (1679) **1** : the diffused and reflected light of the sky **2** : an opening in a house roof or ship's deck that is covered with translucent or transparent material and that is designed to admit light

sky·light·ed \-,līt-əd\ *also* **sky·lit** \-,lit\ *adj* (1849) : having a skylight

sky·line \-,līn\ *n* (1824) **1** : the apparent juncture of earth and sky : HORIZON **2** : an outline (as of buildings or a mountain range) against the background of the sky

sky·lounge \-,lau̇nj\ *n* (1966) : a vehicle that picks up passengers and is then carried by helicopter between a downtown terminal and an airport

sky marshal *n* (1968) : an armed federal plainclothesman assigned to prevent skyjackings

sky pilot *n* (ca. 1887) : CLERGYMAN; *specif* : CHAPLAIN

[1]**sky·rock·et** \'skī-,räk-ət\ *n* (1688) : [2]ROCKET 1a

[2]**skyrocket** *vt* (1851) **1** : to cause to rise or increase abruptly and rapidly **2** : CATAPULT ~ *vi* : to shoot up abruptly ⟨prices are ~*ing*⟩

sky·sail \'skī-,sāl, -səl\ *n* (1829) : the sail above the royal

sky·scrap·er \-,skrā-pər\ *n* (1883) : a very tall building

sky·walk \-,wȯk\ *n* (1953) : a usu. enclosed aerial walkway connecting two buildings

sky·ward \-wərd\ *adv* (1582) **1** : toward the sky **2** : UPWARD

sky wave *n* (1928) : a radio wave that is propagated by means of the ionosphere

sky·way \'skī-,wā\ *n* (1919) **1** : a route used by airplanes : AIR LANE **2** : an elevated highway

sky·write \-,rīt\ *vb* **-wrote** \-,rōt\; **-writ·ten** \-,rit-ᵊn\; **-writ·ing** \-,rīt-iŋ\ [back-formation from *skywriting*] *vt* (1926) : to letter by skywriting ~ *vi* : to do skywriting — **sky·writ·er** *n*

sky·writ·ing \-,rīt-iŋ\ *n* (1922) : writing formed in the sky by means of a visible substance (as smoke) emitted from an airplane

[1]**slab** \'slab\ *n* [ME *slabbe*] (13c) **1** : a thick plate or slice (as of stone, wood, or bread): as **a** : the outside piece cut from a log in squaring it **b** : concrete pavement (as of a road); *specif* : a strip of concrete pavement laid as a single unjointed piece **c** (1) : a flat rectangular architectural element that is usu. formed of a single piece or mass ⟨a concrete foundation ~⟩ (2) : a rectangular building having little width with respect to its length and usu. height **2** : something that resembles a slab (as in size) ⟨backed up by a solid ~ of reference material —*Times Lit. Supp.*⟩ — **slab·like** \-,līk\ *adj*

[2]**slab** *vt* **slabbed; slab·bing** (1703) **1 a** : to divide or form into slabs **b** : to remove an outer slab from (as a log) **2** : to cover or support (as a roadbed or roof) with slabs **3** : to put on thickly

[3]**slab** *adj* [prob. of Scand origin; akin to obs. Dan *slab* slippery] *dial chiefly Eng* (1605) : THICK, VISCOUS

[1]**slab·ber** \'slab-ər\ *vb* **slab·bered; slab·ber·ing** \-(ə-)riŋ\ [prob. fr. D *slabberen*, freq. of *slabben* to slaver — more at SLAVER] (1542) : SLOBBER, DROOL

[2]**slabber** *n* (1718) : SLOBBER, SLAVER

slab–sid·ed \'slab-'sīd-əd\ *adj* (1817) : having flat sides; *also* : being tall or long and lank

[1]**slack** \'slak\ *adj* [ME *slak*, fr. OE *sleac*; akin to OHG *slah* slack, L *laxus* slack, loose, *languēre* to languish, Gk *lēgein* to stop] (bef. 12c) **1** : not using due diligence, care, or dispatch : NEGLIGENT **2 a** : characterized by slowness, sluggishness, or lack of energy ⟨a ~ pace⟩ **b** : moderate in some quality; *esp* : moderately warm ⟨a ~ oven⟩ **c** : blowing or flowing at low speed ⟨the tide was ~⟩ **3 a** : not tight or taut ⟨a ~ rope⟩ **b** : lacking in usual or normal firmness and steadiness : WEAK ⟨~ muscles⟩ ⟨~ supervision⟩ **4** : wanting in activity : DULL ⟨a ~ market⟩ **5** : lacking in completeness, finish, or perfection ⟨a very ~ piece of work⟩ **6** : not watertight ⟨~ cooperage⟩ *syn* see NEGLIGENT — **slack·ly** *adv* — **slack·ness** *n*

[2]**slack** *vt* (1530) **1 a** : to be slack or negligent in performing or doing **b** : LESSEN, MODERATE **2** : to release tension on : LOOSEN **3 a** : to cause to abate **b** : SLAKE 3 ~ *vi* **1** : to be or become slack **2** : to shirk or evade work or duty

[3]**slack** *n* (1756) **1** : cessation in movement or flow **2** : a part of something that hangs loose without strain ⟨take up the ~ of a rope⟩ **3** : trousers esp. for casual wear — usu. used in pl. **4** : a dull season or period **5 a** : a part that is available but not used ⟨some ~ in the budget⟩ **b** : a part that is wanted but not supplied : SHORTFALL ⟨take up the ~ in supplying oil⟩

[4]**slack** *n* [ME *slak*, fr. ON *slakki*] *dial Eng* (14c) : a pass between hills

[5]**slack** *n* [ME *sleck*] (15c) : the finest screenings of coal produced at a mine unusable as fuel unless cleaned

slack·en \'slak-ən\ *vb* **slack·ened; slack·en·ing** \-(ə-)niŋ\ *vt* (ca. 1580) **1** : to make less active : slow up ⟨~ speed at a crossing⟩ **2** : to make slack (as by lessening tension or firmness) ⟨~ sail⟩ ~ *vi* **1** : to become slack or slow or negligent : slow down **2** : to become less active : SLACK *syn* see DELAY

slack·er \'slak-ər\ *n* (1898) : a person who shirks work or obligation; *esp* : one who evades military service in time of war

slack water *n* (ca. 1769) : the period at the turn of the tide when there is little or no horizontal motion of tidal water — called also *slack tide*

slag \'slag\ *n* [MLG *slagge*] (1552) **1** : the dross or scoria of a metal : CINDER **2** : the scoriaceous lava from a volcano

slain *past part of* SLAY

slake \'slāk, *vi* 2 & *vt* 3 *are also* 'slak\ *vb* **slaked; slak·ing** [ME *slaken*, fr. OE *slacian*, fr. *sleac* slack] *vi* (13c) **1** *archaic* : SUBSIDE, ABATE **2** : to become slaked : CRUMBLE ⟨lime may ~ spontaneously in moist air⟩ ~ *vt* **1** *archaic* : to lessen the force of : MODERATE **2** : SATISFY, QUENCH ⟨~ your thirst⟩ ⟨the newspaper account will ~ your curiosity⟩ **3** : to cause (as lime) to heat and crumble by treatment with water : HYDRATE

[1]**sla·lom** \'släl-əm\ *n* [Norw, lit., sloping track] (1921) **1** : skiing in a zigzag or wavy course between upright obstacles (as flags) **2** : a timed race (as on skis or in an automobile or kayak) over a winding or zigzag course past a series of flags or markers; *broadly* : movement over a zigzag route

[2]**slalom** *vi* (1932) : to move over a zigzag course in or as if in a slalom

[1]**slam** \'slam\ *n* [origin unknown] (1660) **1** : GRAND SLAM **2** : LITTLE SLAM

[2]**slam** *n* [prob. of Scand origin; akin to Icel *slæma* to slam] (1672) **1** : a heavy blow or impact **2 a** : a noisy violent closing **b** : a banging noise; *esp* : one made by the slam of a door **3** : a cutting or violent criticism **4** : SLAMMER

[3]**slam** *vb* **slammed; slam·ming** *vt* (ca. 1691) **1** : to strike or beat hard : KNOCK **2** : to shut forcibly and noisily : BANG **3 a** : to set or slap down violently or noisily ⟨*slammed* his fist on the table⟩ **b** : to propel, thrust, or produce by or as if by striking hard ⟨~ on the brakes⟩ **4** : to criticize harshly ~ *vi* **1** : to make a banging noise **2** : to function (as in moving) with emphatic and usu. noisy vigor ⟨the hurricane *slammed* into the coast⟩ **3** : to utter verbal abuse or harsh criticism

slam–bang \'slam-'baŋ\ *adj* (ca. 1823) **1** : unduly loud or violent ⟨a ~ clatter⟩ **2** : notably vigorous often with nonstop action ⟨made a ~ effort to win⟩ ⟨a ~ adventure novel⟩

slam dunk *n* (1972) : DUNK SHOT — **slam–dunk** *vb*

slam·mer \'slam-ər\ *n* (1952) : JAIL, PRISON

[1]**slan·der** \'slan-dər\ *n* [ME *sclaundre*, *slaundre*, fr. OF *esclandre*, fr. LL *scandalum* stumbling block, offense — more at SCANDAL] (13c) **1** : the utterance of false charges or misrepresentations which defame and damage another's reputation **2** : a false and defamatory oral statement about a person — compare LIBEL — **slan·der·ous** \-d(ə-)rəs\ *adj* — **slan·der·ous·ly** *adv* — **slan·der·ous·ness** *n*

[2]**slander** *vt* **slan·dered; slan·der·ing** \-d(ə-)riŋ\ (14c) : to utter slander against : DEFAME *syn* see MALIGN — **slan·der·er** \-dər-ər\ *n*

[1]**slang** \'slaŋ\ *n* [origin unknown] (1756) **1** : language peculiar to a particular group: as **a** : ARGOT **b** : JARGON 2 **2** : an informal nonstandard vocabulary composed typically of coinages, arbitrarily changed words, and extravagant, forced, or facetious figures of speech — **slang** *adj* — **slang·i·ly** \'slaŋ-ə-lē\ *adv* — **slang·i·ness** \'slaŋ-ē-nəs\ *n* — **slangy** \'slaŋ-ē\ *adj*

[2]**slang** *vi* (1828) : to use slang or vulgar abuse ~ *vt* : to abuse with harsh or coarse language

slan·guage \'slaŋ-gwij\ *n* [blend of *slang* and *language*] (1879) : slangy speech or writing

[1]**slant** \'slant\ *n* (1655) **1** : a slanting direction, line, or plane : SLOPE **2 a** : something that slants **b** : DIAGONAL 3 **c** : a football running play in which the ballcarrier runs obliquely toward the line of scrimmage **3 a** : a peculiar or personal point of view, attitude, or opinion **b** : a slanting view : GLANCE — **slant** *adj* — **slant·ways** \-,wāz\ *adv* — **slant·wise** \-,wīz\ *adv or adj* — **slanty** \-ē\ *adj*

[2]**slant** *vb* [ME *slenten* to fall obliquely, of Scand origin; akin to Sw *slinta* to slide; akin to OE *slīdan* to slide] *vi* (1698) **1** : to turn or incline from a right line or a level : SLOPE **2** : to take a diagonal course, direction, or path ~ *vt* **1** : to give an oblique or sloping direction to **2** : to interpret or present in line with a special interest : ANGLE ⟨stories ~*ed* toward youth⟩; *esp* : to maliciously or dishonestly distort or falsify — **slant·ing·ly** \-iŋ-lē\ *adv*

slant height *n* (1798) **1** : the length of an element of a right circular cone **2** : the altitude of a side of a regular pyramid

[1]**slap** \'slap\ *n* [ME *slop*, fr. MD; akin to MD *slippen* to slip] *dial Brit* (14c) : OPENING, BREACH

[2]**slap** *vt* **slapped; slap·ping** [LG *slapp*, n.] (ca. 1632) **1 a** : to strike sharply with or as if with the open hand **b** : to cause to strike with a motion or sound like that of a blow with the open hand ⟨~ your feet on the floor⟩ **2** : to put, place, or throw with careless haste or force **3** : to assail verbally : INSULT

[3]**slap** *n* (1648) **1 a** : a blow with the open hand **b** : a quick sharp blow **2** : a noise like that of a slap; *esp* : a noise resulting from play or slackness between parts of a machine **3** : REBUFF, INSULT

[4]**slap** *adv* [prob. fr. LG *slapp*, fr. *slapp*, n.] (1672) : DIRECTLY, SMACK

slap·dash \'slap-'dash, -,dash\ *adj* (1792) : HAPHAZARD, SLIPSHOD

slap down *vt* (1842) **1** : to prohibit or restrain usu. abruptly and with censure from acting in a specified way : SQUELCH **2** : to put an abrupt stop to : SUPPRESS

slap·hap·py \'slap-,hap-ē\ *adj* (1936) **1** : PUNCH-DRUNK **2** : buoyantly or recklessly carefree or foolish : HAPPY-GO-LUCKY

slap·jack \-,jak\ *n* [[2]*slap* + *-jack* (as in *flapjack*)] (1796) **1** : PANCAKE **2** : a card game in which each player tries to be the first to slap his hand on any jack that appears faceup

slap shot *n* (1942) : a shot in ice hockey made with a swinging stroke

slap·stick \'slap-,stik\ *n* (1896) **1** : a device made of two flat pieces of wood fastened at one end so as to make a loud noise when used by an actor to strike a person **2** : comedy stressing farce and horseplay — **slapstick** *adj*

slap–up \'slap-,əp\ *adj*, *chiefly Brit* (ca. 1823) : FIRST-RATE, BANG-UP

[1]**slash** \'slash\ *vb* [ME *slaschen*] *vt* (14c) **1** : to cut with or as if with rough sweeping strokes **2** : CANE, LASH **3** : to cut slits in (as a garment) so as to reveal a color beneath **4** : to criticize cuttingly **5** : to

reduce sharply : CUT ~ *vi* : to lash out, cut, or thrash about with or as if with an edged blade — **slash·er** *n*
[2]**slash** *n* (1576) **1 :** the act of slashing; *also* **:** a long cut or stroke made by or as if by slashing **2 :** an ornamental slit in a garment **3 a :** an open tract in a forest strewn with debris (as from logging) **b :** the debris in such a tract **4 :** DIAGONAL 3 — called also *slash mark*
[3]**slash** *n* [prob. alter. of *plash* (marshy pool)] (1652) **:** a low swampy area often overgrown with brush
slash–and–burn *adj* (1939) **:** characterized or developed by girdling, felling, and burning trees to make land arable usu. for a temporary purpose
[1]**slash·ing** \ˈslash-iŋ\ *n* (1596) **1 :** the act or process of slashing **2 :** an insert or layer of contrasting color revealed by a slash (as in a garment) **3 :** SLASH 3
[2]**slashing** *adj* (1735) **1 :** incisively satiric or critical **2 :** DRIVING, PELTING **3 :** VIVID, BRILLIANT — **slash·ing·ly** \-iŋ-lē\ *adv*
slash pine *n* [[3]*slash*] (1882) **:** a southern pine (*Pinus elliottii*) that is an important source of turpentine and lumber
slash pocket *n* (1942) **:** a pocket suspended on the wrong side of a garment from a finished slit on the right side that serves as its opening
[1]**slat** \ˈslat\ *vt* **slat·ted; slat·ting** [prob. of Scand origin; akin to ON *sletta* to slap, throw] (13c) **1 :** to hurl or throw smartly **2 :** STRIKE, PUMMEL
[2]**slat** *n* [ME, slate, fr. MF *esclat* splinter, fr. OF, fr. *esclater* to burst, splinter] (1764) **1 :** a thin narrow flat strip esp. of wood or metal: as **a :** LATH **b :** LOUVER **c :** STAVE **d :** one of the thin flat members in the back of a ladder-back chair **2** *pl, slang* **:** RIBS — **slat** *adj*
[3]**slat** *vt* **slat·ted; slat·ting** (1886) **:** to make or equip with slats
[1]**slate** \ˈslāt\ *n* [ME, fr. MF *esclat* splinter] (15c) **1 :** a piece of construction material (as laminated rock) prepared as a shingle for roofing and siding **2 :** a dense fine-grained metamorphic rock produced by the compression of various sediments (as clay or shale) so as to develop a characteristic cleavage **3 :** a tablet of material (as slate) used for writing on **4 a :** a written or unwritten record (as of deeds) **b :** a list of candidates for nomination or election **5 a :** a dark purplish gray **b :** any of various grays similar in color to common roofing slates — **slate** *adj* — **slate·like** \-ˌlīk\ *adj*
[2]**slate** *vt* **slat·ed; slat·ing** (1530) **1 :** to cover with slate or a slatelike substance ⟨~ a roof⟩ **2 :** to register, schedule, or designate for action or appointment
[3]**slate** *vt* **slat·ed; slat·ing** [prob. alter. of [1]*slat*] (1825) **1 :** to thrash or pummel severely **2** *chiefly Brit* **:** to criticize or censure severely
slate black *n* (1889) **:** a nearly neutral slightly purplish black
slate blue *n* (1796) **:** a variable color averaging a grayish blue
slat·er \ˈslāt-ər\ *n* (15c) **1 :** one that slates **2** [[1]*slate;* fr. its color] **a :** WOOD LOUSE **b :** any of various marine isopods
[1]**slath·er** \ˈslat͟h-ər\ *n* [origin unknown] (1876) **:** a great quantity — often used in pl.
[2]**slather** *vt* **slath·ered; slath·er·ing** \-(ə-)riŋ\ (1881) **1 a :** to spread thickly or lavishly **b :** to spread something thickly or lavishly on **2 :** to use or spend in a wasteful or lavish manner **:** SQUANDER
slat·ing \ˈslāt-iŋ\ *n* (1579) **:** the work of a slater
[1]**slat·tern** \ˈslat-ərn\ *n* [prob. fr. G *schlottern* to hang loosely, slouch; akin to D *slodderen* to hang loosely, *slodder* slut] (ca. 1639) **:** an untidy slovenly woman; *also* **:** SLUT, PROSTITUTE
[2]**slattern** *adj* (1716) **:** SLATTERNLY
slat·tern·ly \ˈslat-ərn-lē\ *adj* (1830) **1 :** untidy and dirty through habitual neglect; *also* **:** CARELESS, DISORDERLY **2 :** of, relating to, or characteristic of a slut or prostitute — **slat·tern·li·ness** *n*
slaty *also* **slat·ey** \ˈslāt-ē\ *adj* (1529) **:** of, containing, or characteristic of slate; *also* **:** gray like slate
[1]**slaugh·ter** \ˈslȯt-ər\ *n* [ME, of Scand origin; akin to ON *slātra* to slaughter; akin to OE *sleaht* slaughter, *slēan* to slay — more at SLAY] (14c) **1 :** the act of killing; *specif* **:** the butchering of livestock for market **2 :** killing of great numbers of human beings (as in battle or a massacre) **:** CARNAGE
[2]**slaughter** *vt* (1535) **1 :** to kill (animals) for food **:** BUTCHER **2 a :** to kill in a bloody or violent manner **:** SLAY **b :** to kill in large numbers **:** MASSACRE — **slaugh·ter·er** \-ər-ər\ *n*
slaugh·ter·house \ˈslȯt-ər-ˌhau̇s\ *n* (14c) **:** an establishment where animals are butchered
slaugh·ter·ous \ˈslȯt-ə-rəs\ *adj* (1582) **:** of or relating to slaughter **:** MURDEROUS — **slaugh·ter·ous·ly** *adv*
Slav \ˈsläv, ˈslav\ *n* [ME *Sclav,* fr. ML *Sclavus,* fr. LGk *Sklabos,* fr. *Sklabēnoi* Slavs, of Slav origin; akin to OSlav *Slověne,* a Slavic people in the area of Salonika] (14c) **:** a person who speaks a Slavic language as his native tongue — **Slav** *adj*
[1]**slave** \ˈslāv\ *n* [ME *sclave,* fr. OF or ML; OF *esclave,* fr. ML *sclavus,* fr. *Sclavus* Slav; fr. the reduction to slavery of many Slavic peoples of central Europe] (13c) **1 :** a person held in servitude as the chattel of another **:** BONDMAN **2 :** one that is completely subservient to a dominating influence **3 :** a device (as the typewriter unit of a computer) that is directly responsive to another **4 :** DRUDGE, TOILER — **slave** *adj*
[2]**slave** *vb* **slaved; slav·ing** *vt* (1602) **1** *archaic* **:** ENSLAVE **2 :** to make directly responsive to another mechanism ~ *vi* **1 :** to work like a slave **:** DRUDGE **2 :** to traffic in slaves
slave driver *n* (1807) **1 :** a supervisor of slaves at work **2 :** a harsh taskmaster
slave·hold·er \ˈslāv-ˌhōl-dər\ *n* (1776) **:** an owner of slaves — **slave·hold·ing** \-diŋ\ *adj or n*
slave–mak·ing ant \ˈslāv-ˌmā-kiŋ-\ *n* (1817) **:** an ant that attacks the colonies of ants of other species and carries off the larvae and pupae to be reared in its own nest as slaves
[1]**sla·ver** \ˈslav-ər, ˈslāv-, ˈsläv-\ *vb* **sla·vered; sla·ver·ing** \-(ə-)riŋ\ [ME *slaveren,* of Scand origin; akin to ON *slafra* to slaver; akin to MD *slabben* to slaver, L *labi* to slip — more at SLEEP] *vi* (14c) **:** DROOL, SLOBBER ~ *vt, archaic* **:** to smear with or as if with saliva
[2]**slaver** *n* (14c) **:** saliva dribbling from the mouth
[3]**slav·er** \ˈslā-vər\ *n* [[1]*slave*] (1827) **1 a :** a person engaged in the slave trade **b :** a ship used in the slave trade **2 :** WHITE SLAVER
slav·ery \ˈslāv-(ə-)rē\ *n* (1551) **1 :** DRUDGERY, TOIL **2 :** submission to a dominating influence **3 a :** the state of a person who is a chattel of another **b :** the practice of slaveholding
slave state *n* (1809) **1 :** a state of the U.S. in which Negro slavery was legal until the Civil War **2 :** a nation subjected to totalitarian rule
slave trade *n* (1734) **:** traffic in slaves; *esp* **:** the buying and selling of Negroes for profit prior to the American Civil War
slav·ey \ˈslā-vē\ *n, pl* **slaveys** (ca. 1812) **:** DRUDGE; *esp* **:** a household servant who does general housework
[1]**Slav·ic** \ˈslav-ik, ˈsläv-\ *adj* (1813) **:** of, relating to, or characteristic of the Slavs or their languages
[2]**Slavic** *n* (1866) **:** a branch of the Indo-European language family containing Belorussian, Bulgarian, Czech, Polish, Serbo-Croatian, Slovene, Russian, and Ukrainian — see INDO-EUROPEAN LANGUAGES table
Slav·i·cist \ˈslav-ə-səst, ˈsläv-\ *n* (1943) **:** a specialist in the Slavic languages or literatures
slav·ish \ˈslā-vish\ *adj* (1565) **1 a :** of or characteristic of a slave; *esp* **:** basely or abjectly servile **b** *archaic* **:** DESPICABLE, LOW **2** *archaic* **:** OPPRESSIVE, TYRANNICAL **3 :** copying obsequiously or without originality **:** IMITATIVE ***syn*** see SUBSERVIENT — **slav·ish·ly** *adv* — **slav·ish·ness** *n*
Slav·ist \ˈsläv-əst, ˈslav-\ *n* (1863) **:** SLAVICIST
slav·oc·ra·cy \slā-ˈväk-rə-sē\ *n* (1840) **:** a faction of slaveholders and advocates of slavery in the South before the Civil War
[1]**Sla·vo·ni·an** \slə-ˈvō-nē-ən\ *n* [*Slavonia,* region of southeast Europe, fr. ML *Sclavonia, Slavonia* land of the Slavs, fr. *Sclavus* Slav] (1601) **:** SLOVENE 1b
[2]**Slavonian** *adj* (1605) **1 :** SLOVENE **2** *archaic* **:** SLAVIC
[1]**Sla·von·ic** \slə-ˈvän-ik\ *adj* [NL *slavonicus,* fr. ML *Sclavonia, Slavonia*] (1645) **:** SLAVIC
[2]**Slavonic** *n* (1668) **1 :** SLAVIC **2 :** OLD CHURCH SLAVONIC
Slav·o·phile \ˈslav-ə-ˌfīl, ˈsläv-\ *or* **Slav·o·phil** \-ˌfil\ *n* (1877) **:** an admirer of the Slavs **:** an advocate of Slavophilism
Slav·oph·i·lism \slə-ˈväf-ə-ˌliz-əm, ˈslav-ə-ˌfi-ˌliz-\ *n* (1877) **:** advocacy of Slavic and specif. Russian culture over western European culture esp. as practiced among some members of the Russian intelligentsia in the middle 19th century
slaw \ˈslȯ\ *n* (1861) **:** COLESLAW
slay \ˈslā\ *vb* **slew** \ˈslü\; **slain** \ˈslān\; **slay·ing** [ME *slen,* fr. OE *slēan* to strike, slay; akin to OHG *slahan* to strike, MIr *slacaim* I beat] *vt* (bef. 12c) **1 :** to kill violently, wantonly, or in great numbers **2** *slang* **:** to affect overpoweringly **:** OVERWHELM ~ *vi* **:** KILL, MURDER ***syn*** see KILL — **slay·er** *n*
[1]**sleave** \ˈslēv\ *n, archaic* (1605) **:** SKEIN ⟨sleep that knits up the raveled ~ of care —Shak.⟩
[2]**sleave** *vt* [(assumed) ME *sleven,* fr. OE *-slǣfan* to cut — more at SLIVER] *obs* (1628) **:** to separate (silk thread) into filaments
sleave silk *n, obs* (1588) **:** floss silk that is easily separated into filaments for embroidery
sleaze \ˈslēz *also* ˈslāz\ *n* [back-formation fr. *sleazy*] (1954) **:** a sleazy quality or appearance
slea·zy \ˈslē-zē *also* ˈslā-\ *adj* **slea·zi·er; -est** [origin unknown] (ca. 1670) **1 a :** lacking firmness of texture **:** FLIMSY **b :** carelessly made of inferior materials **:** SHODDY **2 :** marked by cheapness of character or quality **:** TAWDRY — **slea·zi·ly** \-zə-lē\ *adv* — **slea·zi·ness** \-zē-nəs\ *n*
[1]**sled** \ˈsled\ *n* [ME *sledde,* fr. MD; akin to OE *slīdan* to slide] (14c) **1 :** a vehicle on runners for transportation esp. on snow or ice; *esp* **:** a small steerable one used esp. by children for coasting down snow-covered hills **2 :** ROCKET SLED
[2]**sled** *vb* **sled·ded; sled·ding** *vt* (1706) **:** SLEDGE ~ *vi* **:** to ride on a sled or sleigh — **sled·der** *n*
sled·ding *n* (1682) **1 a :** the use of a sled **b :** the conditions under which one may use a sled **2 :** GOING 4
sled dog *n* (1692) **:** a dog trained to draw a sledge esp. in the Arctic regions — called also *sledge dog*
[1]**sledge** \ˈslej\ *n* [ME *slegge,* fr. OE *slecg;* akin to ON *sleggja* sledgehammer, OE *slēan* to strike — more at SLAY] (bef. 12c) **:** SLEDGEHAMMER
[2]**sledge** *vb* **sledged; sledg·ing** (1654) **:** SLEDGEHAMMER
[3]**sledge** *n* [D dial. *sleedse;* akin to MD *sledde* sled] (1617) **1** *Brit* **:** SLEIGH **2 :** a vehicle with low runners that is used for transporting loads esp. over snow or ice
[4]**sledge** *vb* **sledged; sledg·ing** *vi* (1853) **1** *Brit* **:** to ride in a sleigh **2 :** to travel with a sledge ~ *vt* **:** to transport on a sledge
[1]**sledge·ham·mer** \ˈslej-ˌham-ər\ *n* [[1]*sledge*] (15c) **:** a large heavy hammer that is wielded with both hands; *also* **:** something that resembles a sledgehammer in action
[2]**sledgehammer** *vt* (1834) **:** to strike with or as if with a sledgehammer ~ *vi* **:** to strike blows with or as if with a sledgehammer
[3]**sledgehammer** *adj* (1844) **:** marked by heavy-handed directness or the unsubtle use of force ⟨trusting in ~ warfare —C.J. Rolo⟩
[1]**sleek** \ˈslēk\ *vb* [ME *sleken,* alter. of *sliken*] *vt* (15c) **1 :** SLICK **2 :** to cover up **:** gloss over ~ *vi* **:** SLICK
[2]**sleek** *adj* [alter. of [2]*slick*] (1589) **1 a :** smooth and glossy as if polished ⟨~ dark hair⟩ **b :** having a smooth well-groomed look ⟨~ cattle grazing⟩ **c :** healthy-looking **2 :** SLICK 3 **3 a :** having a prosperous air **:** THRIVING **b :** having slender graceful lines **:** ELEGANT, STYLISH — **sleek·ly** *adv* — **sleek·ness** *n*
syn SLEEK, SLICK, GLOSSY, SILKEN mean having a smooth bright surface or appearance. SLEEK suggests a smoothness or brightness resulting from attentive grooming or physical conditioning ⟨a *sleek* racehorse⟩ SLICK suggests extreme smoothness that results in a slippery surface ⟨slipped and fell on the *slick* floor⟩ GLOSSY suggests a surface that is smooth and highly polished ⟨photographs having a *glossy* finish⟩ SILKEN implies the smoothness and luster as well as the softness of silk ⟨*silken* hair⟩
sleek·en \ˈslē-kən\ *vt* **sleek·ened; sleek·en·ing** \ˈslēk-(ə-)niŋ\ (1621) **:** to make sleek
sleek·it \ˈslē-kət\ *adj* [Sc, fr. pp. of [1]*sleek*] (1513) **1** *chiefly Scot* **:** SLEEK, SMOOTH **2** *chiefly Scot* **:** CRAFTY, DECEITFUL
[1]**sleep** \ˈslēp\ *n* [ME *slepe,* fr. OE *slǣp;* akin to OHG *slāf* sleep, L *labi* to slip, slide] (bef. 12c) **1 :** the natural periodic suspension of consciousness during which the powers of the body are restored **2 :** a state

\ə\ abut \ᵊ\ kitten, F table \ər\ further \a\ ash \ā\ ace \ä\ cot, cart \au̇\ out \ch\ chin \e\ bet \ē\ easy \g\ go \i\ hit \ī\ ice \j\ job \ŋ\ sing \ō\ go \ȯ\ law \ȯi\ boy \th\ thin \t͟h\ the \ü\ loot \u̇\ foot \y\ yet \zh\ vision \ȧ, k̲, ⁿ, œ, œ̄, ue, ue̅, ʸ\ see Guide to Pronunciation

resembling sleep: as **a :** a state of torpid inactivity **b :** DEATH ⟨put a pet cat to ~⟩; *also* **:** TRANCE, COMA **c :** the closing of leaves or petals esp. at night **d :** a state marked by a diminution of feeling followed by tingling ⟨my foot's gone to ~⟩ **e :** the state of an animal during hibernation ⟨the groundhog's winter ~⟩ **3 a :** a period spent sleeping **b :** NIGHT **c :** a day's journey — **sleep·like** \'slē-ˌplīk\ *adj*

[2]sleep *vb* **slept** \'slept\; **sleep·ing** *vi* (bef. 12c) **1 :** to rest in a state of sleep **2 :** to be in a state (as of quiescence or death) resembling sleep **3 :** to have sexual relations ~ *vt* **1 :** to be slumbering in ⟨*slept* the sleep of the dead⟩ **2 :** to get rid of or spend in or by sleep ⟨~ away the hours⟩ ⟨~ off a drunk⟩ **3 :** to provide sleeping accommodations for ⟨the boat ~s six⟩

sleep around *vi* (ca. 1964) **:** to engage in sex promiscuously

sleep·er \'slē-pər\ *n* (13c) **1 :** one that sleeps **2 :** a piece of timber, stone, or steel on or near the ground to support a superstructure, keep railroad rails in place, or receive floor joists **:** STRINGPIECE **3 :** SLEEPING CAR **4 :** someone or something unpromising or unnoticed that suddenly attains prominence or value **5** *pl* **:** children's pajamas usu. with feet

sleep–in \ˌslē-ˌpin\ *adj* (1951) **:** that lives at the place of employment ⟨a ~ maid⟩

sleep in \'slē-'pin\ *vi* (ca. 1912) **1 :** to sleep where one is employed **2 a :** OVERSLEEP **b :** to sleep late intentionally

sleeping bag *n* (1856) **:** a bag that is warmly lined or padded for sleeping outdoors or in a camp or tent

Sleeping Beauty *n* **:** a princess of a fairy tale who is wakened from an enchanted sleep by the kiss of a prince

sleeping car *n* (1839) **:** a railroad passenger car having berths for sleeping

sleeping partner *n* (ca. 1785) **:** SECRET PARTNER

sleeping pill *n* (1945) **:** a drug and esp. a barbiturate that is taken as a tablet or capsule to induce sleep — called also *sleeping tablet*

sleeping porch *n* (1920) **:** a porch or room having open sides or many windows arranged to permit sleeping in the open air

sleeping sickness *n* (1875) **1 :** a serious disease that is prevalent in much of tropical Africa, is marked by fever, protracted lethargy, tremors, and loss of weight, is caused by either of two trypanosomes (*Trypanosoma gambiense* and *T. rhodesiense*), and is transmitted by tsetse flies **2 :** any of various viral encephalitides or encephalomyelitides of which lethargy or somnolence is a prominent feature

sleep·less \'slē-pləs\ *adj* (15c) **1 :** not able to sleep **:** INSOMNIAC **2 :** affording no sleep **3 :** unceasingly active — **sleep·less·ly** *adv* — **sleep·less·ness** *n*

sleep out *vi* (1912) **:** to sleep outdoors

sleep·walk·er \'slēp-ˌwȯ-kər\ *n* (1747) **:** one that walks in or as if in his sleep **:** SOMNAMBULIST — **sleep·walk** \-ˌwȯk\ *vi*

sleep·wear \-ˌwa(ə)r, -ˌwe(ə)r\ *n* (1951) **:** NIGHTCLOTHES

sleepy \'slē-pē\ *adj* **sleep·i·er; -est** (13c) **1 a :** ready to fall asleep **b :** of, relating to, or characteristic of sleep **2 :** sluggish as if from sleep **:** LETHARGIC; *also* **:** INACTIVE **3 :** sleep-inducing — **sleep·i·ly** \-pə-lē\ *adv* — **sleep·i·ness** \-pē-nəs\ *n*

sleepy·head \'slē-pē-ˌhed\ *n* (1577) **:** a sleepy person

[1]sleet \'slēt\ *n* [ME *slete;* akin to MHG *slōz* hailstone, ME *sloor* mud — more at SLUR] (14c) **1 :** frozen or partly frozen rain **2 :** GLAZE 1 — **sleety** \-ē\ *adj*

[2]sleet *vi* (14c) **:** to shower sleet

sleeve \'slēv\ *n* [ME *sleve,* fr. OE *slīefe;* akin to OE *slēfan* to slip (clothes) on, *slūpan* to slip, OHG *sliofan,* L *lubricus* slippery] (bef. 12c) **1 a :** a part of a garment covering an arm **b :** SLEEVELET **2 a :** a tubular part (as a hollow axle or a bushing) designed to fit over another part **b :** an open-ended flat or tubular packaging or cover; *esp* **:** JACKET 3c(2) — **sleeved** \'slēvd\ *adj* — **sleeve·less** \'slēv-ləs\ *adj* — **up one's sleeve :** held secretly in reserve

sleeve·let \'slēv-lət\ *n* (ca. 1912) **:** a covering for the forearm to protect clothing from wear or dirt

[1]sleigh \'slā\ *n* [D *slee,* alter. of *slede;* akin to MD *sledde* sled] (1703) **:** a vehicle on runners used for transporting persons or goods on snow or ice

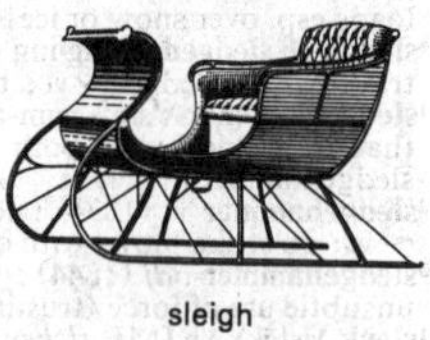
sleigh

[2]sleigh *vi* (1728) **:** to drive or travel in a sleigh

sleigh bed *n* (1926) **:** a bed common esp. in the first half of the 19th century having a solid headboard and footboard that roll outward at the top

sleigh bell *n* (1772) **:** any of various bells commonly attached to a sleigh or to the harness of a horse drawing a sleigh: as **a :** CASCABEL 2 **b :** a hemispherical bell with an attached clapper

sleight \'slīt\ *n* [ME, fr. ON *slœgth,* fr. *slœgr* sly — more at SLY] (13c) **1 :** deceitful craftiness; *also* **:** STRATAGEM **2 :** DEXTERITY, SKILL

sleight of hand (1605) **1 a :** a conjuring trick requiring sleight of hand **b :** a cleverly executed trick or deception **2 a :** skill and dexterity in conjuring tricks **b :** adroitness in deception

slen·der \'slen-dər\ *adj* [ME *sclendre, slendre*] (14c) **1 a :** spare in frame or flesh; *esp* **:** gracefully slight **b :** small or narrow in circumference or width in proportion to length or height **2 :** limited or inadequate in amount or scope **:** MEAGER *syn* see THIN — **slen·der·ly** *adv* — **slen·der·ness** *n*

slen·der·ize \-də-ˌrīz\ *vt* **-ized; -iz·ing** (1923) **:** to make slender

[1]sleuth \'slüth\ *n* [short for *sleuthhound*] (1901) **:** DETECTIVE

[2]sleuth *vi* (1903) **:** to act as a detective ~ *vt* **:** to search for and discover

sleuth·hound \'slüth-ˌhau̇nd\ *n* [ME, fr. *sleuth* track of an animal or person (fr. ON *slōth*) + *hound*] (1856) **:** DETECTIVE

[1]slew \'slü\ *past of* SLAY

[2]slew *var of* SLOUGH

[3]slew *vb* [origin unknown] *vt* (ca. 1769) **1 :** to turn (as a telescope or a ship's spar) about a fixed point that is usu. the axis **2 :** to cause to skid **:** VEER ⟨~ a car around a turn⟩ ~ *vi* **1 :** to turn, twist, or swing about **:** PIVOT **2 :** SKID

[4]slew *n* [IrGael *sluagh*] (1840) **:** a large number

[1]slice \'slīs\ *n* [ME, fr. MF *esclice* splinter, fr. OF, fr. *esclicier* to splinter, of Gmc origin; akin to OHG *slīzan* to tear apart — more at SLIT] (15c) **1 a :** a thin flat piece cut from something **b :** a wedge-shaped piece (as of pie or cake) **2 :** a spatula for spreading paint or ink **3 :** a serving knife with wedge-shaped blade ⟨a fish ~⟩ **4 :** a flight of a ball that deviates from a straight course in the direction of the dominant hand of the player propelling it; *also* **:** a ball following such a course — compare HOOK **5 :** PORTION, SHARE ⟨a ~ of the profits⟩

[2]slice *vb* **sliced; slic·ing** *vt* (15c) **1 :** to cut with or as if with a knife **2 :** to stir or spread with a slice **3 :** to hit (a ball) so that a slice results ~ *vi* **1 :** to slice something **2 :** to move with a cutting action ⟨the ship *sliced* through the waves⟩ — **slic·er** *n*

slice bar *n* (1846) **:** a steel bar with a broad flat blade for chipping or scraping (as in breaking up clinkers)

slice–of–life *adj* [fr. the n. phrase *slice of life,* trans. of F *tranche de vie*] (ca. 1934) **:** of, relating to, or marked by the accurate transcription (as into drama) of a segment of actual life experience

[1]slick \'slik\ *vb* [ME *sliken;* akin to OHG *slīhhan* to glide, Gk *leios* smooth] *vt* (13c) **:** to make sleek or smooth ~ *vi* **:** SPRUCE — usu. used with *up*

[2]slick *adj* (14c) **1 a :** having a smooth surface **:** SLIPPERY **b :** having surface plausibility or appeal **:** GLIB, GLOSSY **c :** based on stereotype **:** TRITE **2** *archaic* **:** SLEEK 1 **3 a :** characterized by subtlety or nimble wit **:** CLEVER; *esp* **:** WILY **b :** DEFT, SKILLFUL **4 :** extremely good **:** FIRST-RATE *syn* see SLEEK — **slick** *adv* — **slick·ly** *adv* — **slick·ness** *n*

[3]slick *n* (1849) **1 a :** something that is smooth or slippery; *esp* **:** a smooth patch of water covered with a film of oil **b :** a film of oil **2 :** an implement for producing a slick surface: as **a :** a flat paddle usu. of steel for smoothing a sample of flour **b :** a foundry tool for smoothing the surface of a sand mold or unbaked core **3 :** a popular magazine printed on coated stock **4 :** an automobile tire made without a tread for maximum traction (as in drag racing)

slick–ear \'slik-ˌi(ə)r\ *n* (1926) **:** a range animal lacking an earmark

slick·en·side \'slik-ən-ˌsīd\ *n* [E dial. *slicken* smooth (alter. of E [2]*slick*) + E *side*] (1822) **:** a smooth often striated surface produced on rock by movement along a fault or a subsidiary fracture — usu. used in pl.

slick·er \'slik-ər\ *n* (1881) **1** [[2]*slick*] **:** OILSKIN; *broadly* **:** RAINCOAT **2** [*slick* (to defraud cleverly)] **a :** a clever crook **:** SWINDLER **b :** a city dweller esp. of natty appearance or sophisticated mannerisms

[1]slide \'slīd\ *vb* **slid** \'slid\; **slid·ing** \'slīd-iŋ\ [ME *sliden,* fr. OE *slīdan;* akin to MHG *slīten* to slide, Gk *leios* smooth — more at LIME] *vi* (bef. 12c) **1 a :** to move smoothly along a surface **:** SLIP **b :** to coast over snow or ice **c :** to approach a base in baseball by gliding along the ground usu. feetfirst with the weight of the body supported esp. on one hip **2 a :** to slip or fall by loss of footing **b :** to change position or become dislocated **:** SHIFT **3 a :** to slither along the ground **:** CRAWL **b :** to stream along **:** FLOW **4 :** to take a natural course **:** DRIFT ⟨let his affairs ~⟩ **5 a :** to pass unobtrusively **:** STEAL **b :** to pass by gradations esp. downward ⟨the economy *slid* from recession to depression⟩ ~ *vt* **1 a :** to cause to glide or slip **b :** to traverse in a sliding manner **2 :** to put unobtrusively or stealthily ⟨*slid* the bill into his hand⟩

[2]slide *n* (1570) **1 a :** an act or instance of sliding **b (1) :** a musical grace of two or more small notes **(2) :** PORTAMENTO **2 :** a sliding part or mechanism: as **a (1) :** a U-shaped section of tube in the trombone that is pushed out and in to produce the tones between the fundamental and its harmonics **(2) :** a short U-shaped section of tube in brass instruments that is used to adjust the pitch of the instrument or of individual valves **b (1) :** a moving piece (as the ram of a punch press) that is guided by a part along which it slides **(2) :** a guiding surface (as a feeding mechanism) along which something slides **c :** SLIDING SEAT **3 a :** the descent of a mass of earth, rock, or snow down a hill or mountainside **b :** a dislocation in which one rock mass in a mining lode has slid on another **:** FAULT **4 a (1) :** a slippery surface for coasting **(2) :** a chute with a slippery bed down which children slide in play **b :** a channel or track on which something is slid **c :** a sloping trough down which objects are carried by gravity ⟨a log ~⟩ **5 a :** a flat piece of glass on which an object is mounted for microscopic examination **b :** a photographic transparency on a small plate or film arranged for projection **6 :** BOTTLENECK 3

slide fastener *n* (1939) **:** ZIPPER

slid·er \'slīd-ər\ *n* (1530) **1 :** one that slides **2 :** a fast baseball pitch that breaks slightly in the same direction as a curve

slide rule *n* (1663) **:** an instrument used for calculation that consists in its simple form of a ruler and a medial slide that are graduated with similar logarithmic scales labeled with the corresponding antilogarithms

slide valve *n* (1802) **:** a valve that opens and closes a passageway by sliding over a port; *specif* **:** such a valve often used in steam engines for admitting steam to the piston and releasing it

slide·way \'slīd-ˌwā\ *n* (1856) **:** a way along which something slides

sliding scale *n* (1842) **1 :** a wage scale geared to the selling price of the product or to the consumer price index but usu. guaranteeing a minimum below which the wage will not fall **2 a :** a system for raising or lowering tariffs in accord with price changes **b :** a flexible scale (as of fees or subsidies) adjusted to the needs or income of individuals ⟨the *sliding scale* of medical fees⟩

sliding seat *n* (1874) **:** a rower's seat (as in a racing shell) that slides fore and aft — called also *slide*

slier *comparative of* SLY

sliest *superlative of* SLY

[1]slight \'slīt\ *adj* [ME, smooth, slight, prob. fr. MD *slicht;* akin to OHG *slīhhan* to glide — more at SLICK] (14c) **1 a :** having a slim or delicate build **:** not stout or massive in body **b :** lacking in strength or substance **:** FLIMSY, FRAIL **c :** deficient in weight, solidity, or importance **:** TRIVIAL **2 :** small of its kind or in amount **:** SCANTY, MEAGER *syn* see THIN — **slight·ly** *adv* — **slight·ness** *n*

[2]slight *vt* (1597) **1 :** to treat as slight or unimportant **:** make light of **2 :** to treat with disdain or indifference **3 :** to perform or attend to carelessly and inadequately **4 :** [1]SLUR 3 *syn* see NEGLECT

[3]slight *n* (1701) **1 :** an act or an instance of slighting **2 :** an instance of being slighted **:** a humiliating discourtesy

slight·ing *adj* (1632) **:** characterized by disregard or disrespect **:** DISPARAGING ⟨a ~ remark⟩ — **slight·ing·ly** \-iŋ-lē\ *adv*

sli·ly *var of* SLYLY

[1]slim \'slim\ *adj* **slim·mer; slim·mest** [D, bad, inferior, fr. MD *slimp* crooked, bad; akin to MHG *slimp* awry] (1657) **1 :** of small diameter or thickness in proportion to the height or length **:** SLENDER **2 a**

: MEAN, WORTHLESS **b** : ADROIT, CRAFTY **3 a** : inferior in quality or amount : SLIGHT **b** : SCANTY, SMALL ⟨a ~ chance⟩ ***syn*** see THIN — **slim·ly** *adv* — **slim·ness** *n*

2**slim** *vb* **slimmed; slim·ming** *vt* (1862) : to make slender : decrease the size of ~ *vi* : to become slender

1**slime** \ˈslīm\ *n* [ME, fr. OE *slīm;* akin to OHG *slīmen* to smooth, L *lima* file — more at LIME] (bef. 12c) **1** : soft moist earth or clay; *esp* : viscous mud **2** : a viscous or glutinous substance: as **a** : a mucous or mucoid secretion of various animals (as slugs and catfishes) **b** : a product of wet crushing consisting of ore ground so fine as to pass a 200-mesh screen **3** : one that is odious

2**slime** *vb* **slimed; slim·ing** *vt* (1628) **1** : to smear or cover with slime **2** : to remove slime from (as fish for canning) **3** : to crush or grind (ore) to a slime ~ *vi* : to become slimy

slime mold *n* (1880) : any of a group (Myxomycetes or Mycetozoa) of organisms usu. held to be lower fungi but sometimes considered protozoans that exist vegetatively as mobile plasmodia and reproduce by spores

slim–jim \ˈslim-ˈjim, -ˌjim\ *adj* [1*slim* + *Jim,* nickname for *James*] (1921) : notably slender

slim·sy *or* **slimp·sy** \ˈslim-zē, ˈslim(p)-sē\ *adj* [blend of *slim* and *flimsy*] (1845) : FLIMSY, FRAIL

slimy \ˈslī-mē\ *adj* **slim·i·er; -est** (14c) **1** : of, relating to, or resembling slime : VISCOUS; *also* : covered with or yielding slime **2** : VILE, OFFENSIVE — **slim·i·ly** \-mə-lē\ *adv* — **slim·i·ness** \-mē-nəs\ *n*

1**sling** \ˈsliŋ\ *vt* **slung** \ˈsləŋ\; **sling·ing** \ˈsliŋ-iŋ\ [ME *slingen,* prob. fr. ON *slyngva* to hurl; akin to OE & OHG *slingan* to worm, twist, Lith *slinkti*] (13c) **1** : to cast with a sudden and usu. sweeping or swirling motion ⟨*slung* the sweater over her shoulder⟩ **2** : to throw with a sling ***syn*** see THROW — **sling·er** \ˈsliŋ-ər\ *n*

2**sling** *n* (14c) **1 a** : an instrument for throwing stones that usu. consists of a short strap with strings fastened to its ends and is whirled round to discharge its missile by centrifugal force **b** : SLINGSHOT 1 **2 a** : a usu. looped line (as of strap, chain, or rope) used to hoist, lower, or carry something; *esp* : a hanging bandage suspended from the neck to support an arm or hand **b** : a chain or rope attached to a lower yard at the middle and passing around a mast near the masthead to support a yard **c** : a chain hooked at the bow and stern of a boat for lowering or hoisting **d** : a device (as a rope net) for enclosing material to be hoisted by a tackle or crane **3** : a slinging or hurling of or as if of a missile

3**sling** *vt* **slung** \ˈsləŋ\; **sling·ing** \ˈsliŋ-iŋ\ (1522) : to place in a sling for hoisting or lowering

4**sling** *n* [origin unknown] (1768) : an alcoholic drink that is served hot or cold and that usu. consists of liquor, sugar, lemon juice, and plain or carbonated water ⟨gin ~⟩ ⟨rum ~⟩

sling·shot \ˈsliŋ-ˌshät\ *n* (1895) **1** : a forked stick with an elastic band attached for shooting small stones **2 a** : a maneuver in auto racing in which a drafting car accelerates past the car in front by taking advantage of reserve power **b** : a dragster in which the driver sits behind the rear wheels

1**slink** \ˈsliŋk\ *vb* **slunk** \ˈsləŋk\ *also* **slinked** \ˈsliŋ(k)t\; **slink·ing** [ME *slinken,* fr. OE *slincan* to creep; akin to OE *slingan* to worm, twist] *vi* (14c) **1** : to go or move stealthily or furtively (as in fear or shame) : STEAL **2** : to move in a sinuous provocative manner ~ *vt* : to give premature birth to — used esp. of a domestic animal ⟨a cow that ~*s* her calf⟩ ***syn*** see LURK

2**slink** *n* (1607) : the young of an animal (as a calf) brought forth prematurely; *also* : the flesh or skin of such an animal

3**slink** *adj* (1750) : born prematurely or abortively ⟨a ~ calf⟩

slinky \ˈsliŋ-kē\ *adj* **slink·i·er; -est** (1918) **1** : characterized by slinking : stealthily quiet ⟨~ movements⟩ **2** : sleek and sinuous in movement or outline; *esp* : following the lines of the figure in a gracefully flowing manner ⟨a ~ evening gown⟩ — **slink·i·ly** \-kə-lē\ *adv* — **slink·i·ness** \-kē-nəs\ *n*

1**slip** \ˈslip\ *vb* **slipped; slip·ping** [ME *slippen,* fr. MD or MLG; akin to Gk *olibros* slippery, *leios* smooth — more at LIME] *vi* (14c) **1 a** : to move with a smooth sliding motion **b** : to move quietly and cautiously : STEAL **c** : ELAPSE, PASS **2 a** (1) : to escape from memory or consciousness (2) : to become uttered through inadvertence **b** : to pass quickly or easily away : become lost ⟨let an opportunity ~⟩ **3** : to fall into error or fault : LAPSE **4 a** : to slide out of place or away from a support or one's grasp **b** : to slide on or down a slippery surface ⟨~ on the stairs⟩ **c** : to flow smoothly **5** : to get speedily into or out of clothing ⟨*slipped* into his coat⟩ **6** : to fall off from a standard or accustomed level by degrees : DECLINE **7** : SIDESLIP ~ *vt* **1** : to cause to move easily and smoothly : SLIDE **2 a** : to get away from : ELUDE, EVADE ⟨*slipped* his pursuers⟩ **b** : to free oneself from ⟨the dog *slipped* its collar⟩ **c** : to escape from (one's memory or notice) ⟨her name ~*s* my mind⟩ **3** : SHED, CAST ⟨the snake *slipped* its skin⟩ **4** : to put on (a garment) hurriedly — usu. used with *on* ⟨~ on a coat⟩ **5 a** : to let loose from a restraining leash or grasp **b** : to cause to slip open : RELEASE, UNDO ⟨~ a lock⟩ **c** : to let go of **d** : to disengage from (an anchor) instead of hauling **6 a** : to insert, place, or pass quietly or secretly **b** : to give or pay on the sly **7** : SLINK, ABORT **8** : DISLOCATE ⟨*slipped* his shoulder⟩ **9** : to transfer (a stitch) from one needle to another without working a stitch **10** : to avoid (a punch) by moving the body or head quickly to one side

2**slip** *n* (15c) **1 a** : a sloping ramp extending out into the water to serve as a place for landing or repairing ships **b** : a ship's or boat's berth between two piers **2** : the act or an instance of departing secretly or hurriedly ⟨gave his pursuer the ~⟩ **3 a** : a mistake in judgment, policy, or procedure **b** : an unintentional and trivial mistake or fault : LAPSE **4** : a leash so made that it can be quickly slipped **5 a** : the act or an instance of slipping down or out of a place ⟨a ~ on the ice⟩; *also* : a sudden mishap **b** : a movement dislocating parts (as of a rock or soil mass); *also* : the result of such movement **c** : a fall from some level or standard : DECLINE ⟨a ~ in stock prices⟩ **6 a** : an undergarment made in dress length with shoulder straps **b** : a case into which something is slipped; *specif* : PILLOWCASE **7 a** : the motion of the center of resistance of the float of a paddle wheel or the blade of an oar through the water horizontally **b** : retrograde movement of a belt on a pulley **c** : the amount of leakage past the piston of a pump or the impellers of a blower **8** : a disposition or tendency to slip easily **9** : the action of sideslipping : an instance of sideslipping ***syn*** see ERROR

3**slip** *adj* (1681) **1 a** : operating by slipping ⟨~ bar⟩ **b** : capable of being detached ⟨~ compartment⟩ **2** : having a slipknot ⟨~ cord⟩ **3** : capable of being released quickly ⟨~ bolt⟩

4**slip** *n* [ME *slippe,* prob. fr. MD or MLG *slippe* cut, slit, flap] (15c) **1 a** : a small shoot or twig cut for planting or grafting : SCION **b** : DESCENDANT, OFFSPRING **2 a** : a long narrow strip of material **b** : a small piece of paper **3** : a young and slender person ⟨a ~ of a girl⟩ **4** : a long seat or narrow pew

5**slip** *vt* **slipped; slip·ping** (1530) : to take cuttings from (a plant) : divide into slips ⟨~ a geranium⟩

6**slip** *n* [ME *slyp* slime, fr. OE *slypa* slime, paste; akin to OE *slūpan* to slip — more at SLEEVE] (1640) : a mixture of finely divided clay and water used by potters (as for casting or decorating wares or in cementing separately formed parts)

slip·case \ˈslip-ˌkās\ *n* (ca. 1925) : a protective container with one open end for books — **slip·cased** \-ˌkāst\ *adj*

slip·cov·er \ˈslip-ˌkəv-ər\ *n* (ca. 1890) : a cover that may be slipped off and on; *specif* : a removable protective covering for an article of furniture

slip·form \ˈslip-ˌfȯrm\ *vt* (1962) : to construct with the use of a slip form

slip form *n* (1949) : a form that is moved slowly as concrete is placed during construction (as of a building or pavement)

slip·knot \ˈslip-ˌnät\ *n* (1659) : a knot that slips along the rope or line around which it is made; *esp* : one made by tying an overhand knot around the standing part of a rope — see KNOT illustration

slip noose *n* (1847) : a noose with a slipknot

slip–on \ˈslip-ˌȯn, -ˌän\ *n* (1915) : an article of clothing that is easily slipped on or off: as **a** : a glove or shoe without fastenings **b** : a garment (as a girdle) that one steps into and pulls up **c** : PULLOVER

slip·over \-ˌō-vər\ *n* (1917) : a garment or cover that slips on and off easily; *specif* : a pullover sweater

slip·page \ˈslip-ij\ *n* (1850) **1** : an act, instance, or process of slipping **2** : a loss in transmission of power; *also* : the difference between theoretical and actual output (as of power)

slipped disk *n* (1942) : a protrusion of one of the cartilage disks between vertebrae with pressure on spinal nerves resulting in low back pain or sciatic pain

1**slip·per** \ˈslip-ər\ *adj* [ME] *chiefly dial* (13c) : SLIPPERY

2**slipper** *n* [ME, fr. *slippen* to slip] (15c) : a light low-cut shoe that is easily slipped on the foot — **slip·pered** \-ərd\ *adj*

slip·pery \ˈslip-(ə-)rē\ *adj* **slip·peri·er; -est** [alter. of ME *slipper,* fr. OE *slipor;* akin to MLG *slipper* slippery, *slippen* to slip] (1535) **1 a** : causing or tending to cause something to slide or fall ⟨~ roads⟩ **b** : tending to slip from the grasp **2** : not firmly fixed : UNSTABLE **3** : not to be trusted : TRICKY — **slip·peri·ness** *n*

slip·py \ˈslip-ē\ *adj* **slip·pi·er; -est** (1548) : SLIPPERY

slip ring *n* [2*slip*] (ca. 1903) : one of two or more continuous conducting rings from which the brushes take or to which they deliver current in a dynamo or motor

slip–sheet \ˈslip-ˌshēt\ *vt* (ca. 1909) : to insert slip sheets between (newly printed sheets)

slip sheet *n* [1*slip*] (1903) : a sheet of paper placed between newly printed sheets to prevent offsetting

slip·shod \ˈslip-ˈshäd\ *adj* [1*slip*] (1580) **1 a** : wearing loose shoes or slippers **b** : down at the heel : SHABBY **2** : CARELESS, SLOVENLY

slip·slop \-ˌsläp\ *n* [redupl. of 2*slop*] (1675) **1** *archaic* : watery food : SLOPS **2** *archaic* : shallow talk or writing : TWADDLE — **slip–slop** *adj*

slip·sole \-ˌsōl\ *n* (ca. 1908) **1** : a thin insole **2** : a half sole inserted between the insole or welt and the outsole of a shoe to give additional height — called also *slip tap*

slip·stick \-ˌstik\ *n* (ca. 1932) : SLIDE RULE

slip stitch *n* (ca. 1882) **1** : a concealed stitch for sewing folded edges (as hems) made by alternately running the needle inside the fold and picking up a thread or two from the body of the article **2** : an unworked stitch; *esp* : a knitting stitch that is shifted from one needle to another without knitting it

1**slip·stream** \ˈslip-ˌstrēm\ *n* (1916) **1** : a stream of fluid (as air or water) driven aft by a propeller **2** : an area of reduced air pressure and forward suction immediately behind a rapidly moving racing car

2**slipstream** *vi* (1971) : to drive in the slipstream of a racing car

slip·up \ˈslip-ˌəp\ *n* (1854) **1** : MISTAKE **2** : MISCHANCE

slip up \slip-ˈəp\ *vi* (1909) : to make a mistake : BLUNDER

slip·ware \ˈslip-ˌwa(ə)r, -ˌwe(ə)r\ *n* (ca. 1909) : pottery coated with slip to improve or decorate the surface

slip·way \-ˌwā\ *n* (1840) : an inclined usu. concrete surface for a ship being built or repaired; *also* : a space between docks

1**slit** \ˈslit\ *vt* **slit; slit·ting** [ME *slitten;* akin to MHG *slitzen* to slit, OHG *slīzan* to tear apart, OE *sciell* shell — more at SHELL] (13c) **1 a** : to make a slit in **b** : to cut off or away : SEVER **c** : to form into a slit **2** : to cut into long narrow strips — **slit·ter** *n*

2**slit** *n* (13c) : a long narrow cut or opening — **slit** *adj* — **slit·less** \ˈslit-ləs\ *adj*

slith·er \ˈslith-ər\ *vb* [ME *slideren,* fr. OE *slidrian,* freq. of *slīdan* to slide] *vi* (13c) **1** : to slide on or as if on a loose gravelly surface **2** : to slip or slide like a snake ~ *vt* : to cause to slide

slith·ery \ˈslith-ə-rē\ *adj* (ca. 1825) : having a slippery surface, texture, or quality

slit trench *n* (1942) : a narrow trench esp. for shelter in battle from bomb and shell fragments

1**sliv·er** \ˈsliv-ər, *2 is usu* ˈslīv-\ *n* [ME *slivere,* fr. *sliven* to slice off, fr. OE *-slīfan;* akin to OE *-slǣfan* to cut] (14c) **1 a** : a long slender piece cut or torn off : SPLINTER **b** : a small and narrow portion ⟨a ~ of land⟩ **c** : PARTICLE, SCRAP ⟨not a ~ of evidence⟩ **2** : an untwisted strand or rope of textile fiber produced by a carding or combing machine and ready for drawing, roving, or spinning

²sliv·er \'sliv-ər\ *vb* **sliv·ered; sliv·er·ing** \-(ə-)riŋ\ *vt* (1605) **:** to cut into slivers **:** SPLINTER ~ *vi* **:** to become split into slivers

sliv·o·vitz \'sliv-ə-,vits, 'slēv-, -,wits\ *n* [Serbo-Croatian *šljivovica,* fr. *šljiva, sliva* plum; akin to Russ *sliva* plum — more at LIVID] (1885) **:** a dry usu. colorless plum brandy made esp. in the Balkan countries

slob \'släb\ *n* [IrGael *slab* mud] (1861) **1 :** a slovenly or boorish person **2 :** a heavy sludge of sea ice — **slob·bish** \'släb-ish\ *adj*

¹slob·ber \'släb-ər\ *vb* **slob·bered; slob·ber·ing** \-(ə-)riŋ\ [ME *sloberen;* akin to LG *slubberen* to sip, Lith *lūpa* lip] *vi* (1733) **1 :** to let saliva dribble from the mouth **:** DROOL **2 :** to indulge the feelings effusively and without restraint ~ *vt* **:** to smear with or as if with dribbling saliva or food — **slob·ber·er** \-ər-ər\ *n*

²slobber *n* (ca. 1755) **1 :** saliva drooled from the mouth **2 :** driveling, sloppy, or incoherent utterance — **slob·bery** \'släb-(ə-)rē\ *adj*

sloe \'slō\ *n* [ME *slo,* fr. OE *slāh* — more at LIVID] (bef. 12c) **:** the small dark globose astringent fruit of the blackthorn; *also* **:** BLACKTHORN 1

sloe–eyed \'slō-'īd\ *adj* (1867) **1 :** having soft dark bluish or purplish black eyes **2 :** having slanted eyes

sloe gin *n* (1895) **:** a sweet reddish liqueur consisting of grain spirits flavored chiefly with sloes

¹slog \'släg\ *vb* **slogged; slog·ging** [origin unknown] *vt* (1824) **1 :** to hit hard **:** BEAT **2 :** to plod (one's way) perseveringly esp. against difficulty ~ *vi* **1 :** to plod heavily **:** TRAMP ⟨*slogged* through the snow⟩ **2 :** to work hard and steadily **:** PLUG — **slog·ger** *n*

²slog *n* (1888) **1 :** hard persistent work **2 :** a hard dogged march or tramp

slo·gan \'slō-gən\ *n* [alter. of earlier *slogorn,* fr. ScGael *sluagh-ghairm* army cry] (1513) **1 a :** a war cry or rallying cry esp. of a Scottish clan **b :** a word or phrase used to express a characteristic position or stand or a goal to be achieved **2 :** a brief attention-getting phrase used in advertising or promotion

slo·gan·eer \,slō-gə-'ni(ə)r\ *n* (1922) **:** a maker or user of slogans — **sloganeer** *vi*

slo·gan·ize \'slō-gə-,nīz\ *vt* **-ized; -iz·ing** (1926) **:** to express as a slogan

sloop \'slüp\ *n* [D *sloep*] (1629) **:** a fore-and-aft rigged boat with one mast and a single headsail jib

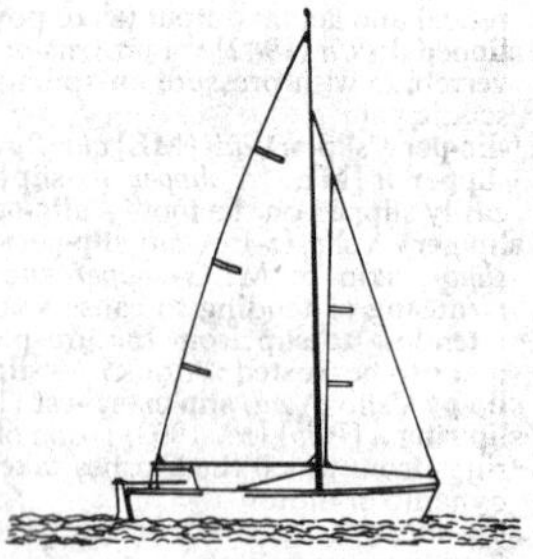

sloop

sloop of war (1704) **1 :** a warship rigged as a ship, brig, or schooner mounting from 10 to 32 guns **2 :** a warship larger than a gunboat with guns on one deck only

¹slop \'släp\ *n* [ME *sloppe,* prob. fr. MD *slop;* akin to OE *oferslop* slop] (14c) **1 :** a loose smock or overall **2** *pl* **:** short full breeches worn by men in the 16th century **3** *pl* **:** articles (as clothing) sold to sailors

²slop *n* [ME *sloppe*] (15c) **1 :** soft mud **:** SLUSH **2 :** thin tasteless drink or liquid food — usu. used in pl. **3 :** liquid spilled or splashed **4 a :** food waste (as garbage) fed to animals **:** SWILL 2a **b :** excreted body waste — usu. used in pl. **5 :** sentimental effusiveness in speech or writing **:** GUSH

³slop *vb* **slopped; slop·ping** *vt* (1557) **1 a :** to spill from a container **b :** to splash or spill liquid on **c :** to cause (a liquid) to splash **2 :** to dish out messily **3 :** to eat or drink greedily or noisily **4 :** to feed slop to ⟨~ the hogs⟩ ~ *vi* **1 :** to tramp in mud or slush **2 :** to become spilled or splashed **3 :** to be effusive **:** GUSH **4 :** to pass beyond or exceed a boundary or limit

slop basin *n, Brit* (1731) **:** SLOP BOWL

slop bowl *n* (1810) **:** a bowl for receiving the leavings of tea or coffee cups at table

slop chest *n* ['slop] (1840) **:** a store of clothing and personal requisites (as tobacco) carried on merchant ships for issue to the crew usu. as a charge against their wages

¹slope \'slōp\ *adj* [ME *slope,* adv., obliquely] (1502) **:** that slants **:** SLOPING — often used in combination ⟨*slope*-sided⟩

²slope *vb* **sloped; slop·ing** *vi* (1591) **1 :** to take an oblique course **2 :** to lie or fall in a slant **:** INCLINE **3 :** GO, TRAVEL ⟨~*s* off into the night — Wolcott Gibbs⟩ ~ *vt* **:** to cause to incline or slant — **slop·er** *n*

³slope *n* (ca. 1611) **1 :** upward or downward slant or inclination or degree of slant **2 :** ground that forms a natural or artificial incline **3 :** the part of a continent draining to a particular ocean **4 a :** the tangent of the angle made by a straight line with the x-axis **b :** the slope of the line tangent to a plane curve at a point

slope–intercept form *n* (ca. 1942) **:** the equation of a straight line in the form $y = mx + b$ where m is the slope of the line and b is the point on the y-axis through which the line passes

slo–pitch \'slō-'pich, -,pich\ *n* [alter. of *slow pitch*] (1967) **:** SLOW-PITCH

slop jar *n* (1855) **:** a large pail used as a chamber pot or to receive waste water from a washbowl or the contents of chamber pots

slop pail *n* (1864) **:** a pail for toilet or household slops

slop·py \'släp-ē\ *adj* **slop·pi·er; -est** (1707) **1 a :** wet so as to spatter easily **:** SLUSHY ⟨a ~ racetrack⟩ **b :** wet or smeared with or as if with something slopped over **2 :** SLOVENLY, CARELESS ⟨she's a ~ dresser⟩ ⟨did ~ work⟩ **3 :** disagreeably effusive ⟨~ sentimentalism⟩ — **slop·pi·ly** \'släp-ə-lē\ *adv* — **slop·pi·ness** *n*

sloppy joe \-'jō\ *n* [prob. fr. the name *Joe,* nickname for *Joseph*] (1968) **:** ground beef cooked in a seasoned sauce (as chili) and usu. served on a bun

slop·work \'släp-,wərk\ *n* (1849) **1 :** the manufacture of cheap ready-made clothing **2 :** hastily slovenly work

¹slosh \'släsh, 'slȯsh\ *n* [prob. blend of *slop* and *slush*] (1814) **1 :** SLUSH **2 :** the slap or splash of liquid

²slosh *vi* (1844) **1 :** to flounder or splash through water, mud, or slush **2 :** to move with a splashing motion ⟨the water ~*ed* around him —Bill Alcine⟩ ~ *vt* **1 :** to splash about in liquid **2 :** to splash (a liquid) about or on something **3 :** to splash with liquid

sloshed \'släsht, 'slȯsht\ *adj, slang* (ca. 1946) **:** DRUNK, INTOXICATED

¹slot \'slät\ *n* [ME, the hollow running down the middle of the breast, fr. MF *esclot*] (1523) **1 a :** a narrow opening or groove **:** SLIT, NOTCH ⟨a mail ~ in a door⟩ **b :** a narrow passage or enclosure **c :** a passage through the wing of an airplane or of a missile that is located usu. near the leading edge and formed between a main and an auxiliary airfoil for improving flow conditions over the wing so as to increase lift and delay stalling of the wing **2 :** a place or position in an organization or sequence **:** NICHE **3 :** SLOT MACHINE **4 :** a gap between an end and a tackle in an offensive football line

²slot *vt* **slot·ted; slot·ting** (1747) **1 :** to cut a slot in **2 :** to place in or assign to a slot

³slot *n, pl* **slot** [MF *esclot* track] (1575) **:** the track of an animal (as a deer)

slot·back \'slät-,bak\ *n* (1959) **:** an offensive football halfback who lines up just behind the slot between an offensive end and tackle

slot car *n* (1966) **:** an electric toy racing automobile that has an arm underneath to fit into a groove for guidance and metal strips alongside the groove to supply electricity and that is remotely controlled by the operator's hand-held rheostat

sloth \'slȯth, 'slōth\ *n, pl* **sloths** *with* ths *or* thz\ [ME *slouthe,* fr. *slow*] (12c) **1 a :** disinclination to action or labor **:** INDOLENCE **b :** spiritual apathy and inactivity ⟨the deadly sin of ~⟩ **2 :** any of several slow-moving arboreal edentate mammals that inhabit tropical forests of So. and Central America, hang from the branches back downward, and feed on leaves, shoots, and fruits

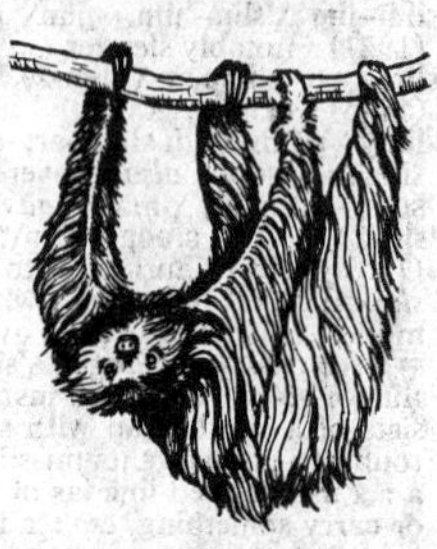

sloth 2

sloth·ful \'slȯth-fəl, 'slōth-\ *adj* (15c) **:** inclined to sloth **:** INDOLENT ***syn*** see LAZY — **sloth·ful·ly** \-fə-lē\ *adv* — **sloth·ful·ness** *n*

slot machine *n* (ca. 1891) **1 :** a machine whose operation is begun by dropping a coin into a slot **2 :** a coin-operated gambling machine that pays off according to the matching of symbols on wheels spun by a handle — called also *one-armed bandit*

slot racing *n* (1965) **:** the racing of slot cars — **slot racer** *n*

¹slouch \'slau̇ch\ *n* [origin unknown] (1515) **1 a :** an awkward fellow **:** LOUT **b :** a lazy or incompetent person ⟨was no ~ at cooking⟩ **2 :** a gait or posture characterized by ungainly stooping of head and shoulders or excessive relaxation of body muscles

²slouch *vi* (1754) **1 :** to walk, stand, or sit with a slouch **:** assume a slouch **2 :** DROOP ~ *vt* **:** to cause to droop ⟨~*ed* his shoulders⟩ — **slouch·er** *n*

slouch hat *n* (1837) **:** a soft usu. felt hat with a wide flexible brim

slouchy \'slau̇-chē\ *adj* **slouch·i·er; -est** (1693) **:** lacking erectness or stiffness esp. in gait or posture — **slouch·i·ly** \-chə-lē\ *adv* — **slouch·i·ness** \-chē-nəs\ *n*

¹slough \'slü, 'slau̇; *in the US (exc NewEng)* 'slü *is usual for sense 1 with those to whom the sense is familiar; Brit usu* 'slau̇ *for both senses*\ *n* [ME *slogh,* fr. OE *slōh;* akin to MHG *slouche* ditch] (bef. 12c) **1 a :** a place of deep mud or mire **b (1) :** SWAMP **(2) :** an inlet on a river; *also* **:** BACKWATER **(3) :** a creek in a marsh or tide flat **2 :** a state of moral degradation or spiritual dejection

²slough *vt* (1846) **:** to engulf in a slough ~ *vi* **:** to plod through or as if through mud **:** SLOG

³slough \'sləf\ *or* **sluff** *n* [ME *slughe;* akin to MHG *slūch* snakeskin, Lith *šliaužti* to crawl] (14c) **1 :** the cast-off skin of a snake **2 :** a mass of dead tissue separating from an ulcer **3 :** something that may be shed or cast off

⁴slough \'sləf\ *or* **sluff** *vi* (1720) **1 a :** to become shed or cast off **b :** to cast off one's skin **c :** to separate in the form of dead tissue from living tissue **2 :** to crumble slowly and fall away ~ *vt* **1 :** to cast off **2 a :** to get rid of or discard as irksome, objectionable, or disadvantageous — usu. used with *off* **b :** to dispose of (a losing card in bridge) by discarding ***syn*** see DISCARD

slough of de·spond \,slau̇-əv-di-'spänd, ,slü-\ [fr. the *Slough of Despond,* deep bog into which Christian falls on the way from the City of Destruction and from which Help saves him in the allegory *Pilgrim's Progress* (1678) by John Bunyan] (1776) **:** a state of extreme depression

slough over \,sləf-\ *vt* (1955) **:** to treat as slight or unimportant

sloughy \'slü-ē, 'slau̇- — *see* ¹SLOUGH\ *adj* (1704) **:** full of sloughs **:** MIRY

Slo·vak \'slō-,väk, -,vak\ *n* [Slovak *Slovák*] (1829) **1 :** a member of a Slavic people of eastern Czechoslovakia **2 :** the Slavic language of the Slovak people — **Slovak** *adj* — **Slo·va·ki·an** \slō-'väk-ē-ən, -'vak-\ *adj or n*

¹slov·en \'sləv-ən\ *n* [ME *sloveyn* rascal, perh. fr. Flem *sloovin* woman of low character] (1530) **:** one habitually negligent of neatness or cleanliness esp. in personal appearance

²sloven *adj* (1815) **:** SLOVENLY

Slo·vene \'slō-,vēn\ *n* [G, fr. Slovene *Sloven*] (1883) **1 a :** a member of a southern Slavic group of people usu. classed with the Serbs and Croats and living in Yugoslavia **b :** a native or inhabitant of Slovenia **2 :** the language of the Slovenes — **Slovene** *adj* — **Slo·ve·nian** \slō-'vē-nē-ən, -nyən\ *adj or n*

slov·en·ly \'sləv-ən-lē\ *adj* (1583) **1 a :** untidy esp. in personal appearance **b :** lazily slipshod ⟨~ in thought⟩ **2 :** characteristic of a sloven ⟨~ workmanship⟩ — **slo·ven·li·ness** *n* — **slovenly** *adv*

¹slow \'slō\ *adj* [ME, fr. OE *slāw;* akin to OHG *slēo* dull, Skt *srēvayati* he causes to fail] (bef. 12c) **1 a :** mentally dull **:** STUPID ⟨a ~ student⟩ **b :** naturally inert or sluggish **2 a :** lacking in readiness, promptness, or willingness **b :** not hasty or precipitate ⟨was ~ to anger⟩ **3 a :** moving, flowing, or proceeding without speed or at less than usual speed ⟨traffic was ~⟩ **b :** exhibiting or marked by retarded speed ⟨he moved with ~ deliberation⟩ **c :** not acute ⟨a ~ disease⟩ **d :** LOW, GENTLE ⟨~ fire⟩ **4 :** requiring a long time **:** GRADUAL ⟨a ~ convalescence⟩ **5 :** having qualities that hinder or stop rapid progress or action **6 a :** registering behind or below what is correct ⟨his clock is ~⟩ **b :** less than the time indicated by another method of reckoning **c :** that is behind the time at a specified time or place **7 a :** lacking in life, animation, or gaiety : BORING **b :** marked by reduced sales or patronage ⟨business was ~⟩ — **slow·ish** \ˈslō-ish\ *adj* — **slow·ness** *n*

[2]**slow** *adv* (1500) : SLOWLY

usage Some commentators claim that careful writers avoid the adverb *slow,* in spite of the fact that it has over four centuries of usage behind it ⟨have a continent forbearance till the speed of his rage goes *slower* —Shak.⟩ In actual practice, *slow* and *slowly* are not used in quite the same way. *Slow* is almost always used with verbs that denote movement or action, and it regularly follows the verb it modifies ⟨beans . . . are best cooked long and *slow* —Louise Prothro⟩ *Slowly* is used before the verb ⟨a sense of outrage, which *slowly* changed to shame —Paul Horgan⟩ and with participial adjectives ⟨a *slowly* dawning awareness . . . of the problem —*Amer. Labor*⟩ *Slowly* is used after verbs where *slow* might also be used ⟨burn *slow* or *slowly*⟩ and after verbs where *slow* would be unidiomatic ⟨the leadership turned *slowly* toward bombing as a means of striking back —David Halberstam⟩

[3]**slow** *vt* (1557) : to make slow or slower : slacken the speed of ⟨~ a car⟩ — often used with *down* or *up* ~ *vi* : to go or become slower ⟨production of new cars ~*ed* sharply⟩ ***syn*** see DELAY

slow·down \ˈslō-ˌdau̇n\ *n* (1897) : a slowing down ⟨a business ~⟩

slow–foot·ed \-ˈfu̇t-əd\ *adj* (1642) : moving at a very slow pace : PLODDING ⟨a ~ novel⟩ ⟨a ~ ship⟩ — **slow–foot·ed·ness** *n*

slow·ly \-lē\ *adv* (14c) : in a slow manner : not quickly, fast, early, rashly, or readily

slow match *n* (ca. 1802) : a match or fuse made so as to burn slowly and evenly and used for firing (as of blasting charges)

slow–motion \ˈslō-ˈmō-shən\ *adj* (1923) : of, relating to, or being motion-picture or video photography in which the action that has been photographed is made to appear to occur slower than it actually occurred ⟨a ~ replay⟩; *also* : slowly moving ⟨a ~ dance⟩

slow motion *n* (1923) : slow-motion photography

slow–pitch \ˈslō-ˈpich, -ˌpich\ *n* (1967) : softball which is played with 10 players on each side and in which each pitch must have an arc 3 to 10 feet high and base stealing is not allowed

slow·poke \ˈslō-ˌpōk\ *n* [[1]*slow* + *poke* (annoyingly stupid person)] (1848) : a very slow person

slow virus *n* (1954) : a virus with a long incubation period between infection and development of the degenerative disease (as multiple sclerosis, rheumatoid arthritis, or kuru) associated with it

slow–wit·ted \-ˈwit-əd\ *adj* (1571) : mentally slow : DULL

slow·worm \-ˌwərm\ *n* [ME *sloworm,* fr. OE *slāwyrm,* fr. *slā-* (akin to Sw *slå* earthworm) + *wyrm* worm] (bef. 12c) : any of several small burrowing limbless lizards with minute eyes; *esp* : a European lizard (*Anguis fragilis*) popularly believed to be blind — called also *blindworm*

[1]**slub** \ˈsləb\ *vt* **slubbed; slub·bing** [back-formation fr. *slubbing*] (1834) : to draw out and twist (as slivers of wool) slightly

[2]**slub** *n* (1851) : SLUBBING

slub·ber \ˈsləb-ər\ *vt* **slub·bered; slub·ber·ing** \-(ə-)riŋ\ [prob. fr. obs. D *slubberen*] (1530) **1** *dial chiefly Eng* : STAIN, SULLY **2 :** to perform in a slipshod fashion

slub·bing \ˈsləb-iŋ\ *n* [origin unknown] (1779) : slightly twisted roving

sludge \ˈsləj\ *n* [prob. alter. of *slush*] (1649) **1 :** MUD, MIRE; *esp* : a muddy deposit (as on a riverbed) : OOZE **2 :** a muddy or slushy mass, deposit, or sediment: as **a :** precipitated solid matter produced by water and sewage treatment processes **b :** muddy sediment in a steam boiler **c :** a precipitate or settling (as a mixture of impurities and acid) from a mineral oil **3 :** new sea ice forming in thin detached crystals **4 :** SLUSH 6

sludgy \ˈsləj-ē\ *adj* **sludg·i·er; -est** (1782) : containing or full of sludge

[1]**slue** \ˈslü\ *var of* SLOUGH

[2]**slue** *var of* [3]SLEW

[3]**slue** *n* (1860) **1 :** position or inclination after sluing **2 :** SKID 5

[1]**slug** \ˈsləg\ *n* [ME *slugge,* of Scand origin; akin to Norw dial. *slugga* to walk sluggishly; akin to ME *sloor* mud — more at SLUR] (15c) **1 :** SLUGGARD **2 :** a lump, disk, or cylinder of material (as plastic or metal): as **a** (1) : a musket ball (2) : BULLET **b :** a piece of metal roughly shaped for subsequent processing **c :** a $50 gold piece **d :** a disk for insertion in a slot machine; *esp* : one used illegally instead of a coin **3 :** any of numerous chiefly terrestrial pulmonate gastropods (family Limacidae) that are found in most parts of the world where there is a reasonable supply of moisture and are closely related to the land snails but are long and wormlike and have only a rudimentary shell often buried in the mantle or entirely absent **4 :** a smooth soft larva of a sawfly or moth that creeps like a mollusk **5 a :** a quantity of liquor drunk in one swallow : SHOT **b :** a detached mass of fluid (as water vapor or oil) that causes impact (as in a circulating system) **6 a :** a strip of metal thicker than a printer's lead **b :** a line of type cast as one piece **c :** a usu. temporary type line serving to instruct or identify **7 :** the gravitational unit of mass in the foot-pound-second system to which a pound force can impart an acceleration of one foot per second per second

[2]**slug** *vt* **slugged; slug·ging** (1912) : to add a printer's slug to

[3]**slug** *n* [perh. fr. *slug* (to load with slugs)] (1830) : a heavy blow esp. with the fist

[4]**slug** *vt* **slugged; slug·ging** (1861) **1 :** to strike heavily with or as if with the fist or a bat **2 :** FIGHT 4b — usu. used in the phrase *slug it out*

slug·abed \ˈsləg-ə-ˌbed\ *n* (1592) : one who stays in bed after his usual or proper time of getting up; *broadly* : SLUGGARD

slug·fest \ˈsləg-ˌfest\ *n* (ca. 1916) : a fight marked by the exchange of heavy blows; *also* : a heated dispute ⟨a vocal ~⟩

[1]**slug·gard** \ˈsləg-ərd\ *n* [ME *sluggart*] (14c) : an habitually lazy person

[2]**sluggard** *adj* (1593) : SLUGGARDLY — **slug·gard·ness** *n*

slug·gard·ly \ˈsləg-ərd-lē\ *adj* (1865) : lazily inactive

slug·ger \ˈsləg-ər\ *n* (1877) : one that strikes hard or with heavy blows: as **a :** a prizefighter who punches hard but has usu. little defensive skill **b :** a hard-hitting batter in baseball

slugging average *n* (1969) : the ratio (as a rate per thousand) of the total number of bases reached on base hits to official times at bat for a baseball player — called also *slugging percentage*

slug·gish \ˈsləg-ish\ *adj* (15c) **1 :** averse to activity or exertion : INDOLENT; *also* : TORPID **2 :** slow to respond (as to stimulation or treatment) **3 a :** markedly slow in movement, flow, or growth **b :** economically inactive or slow — **slug·gish·ly** *adv* — **slug·gish·ness** *n*

[1]**sluice** \ˈslüs\ *n* [alter. of ME *scluse,* fr. MF *escluse,* fr. LL *exclusa,* fr. L, fem. of *exclusus,* pp. of *excludere* to exclude] (14c) **1 a :** an artificial passage for water (as in a millstream) fitted with a valve or gate for stopping or regulating flow **b :** a body of water pent up behind a floodgate **2 :** a dock gate : FLOODGATE **3 a :** a stream flowing through a floodgate **b :** a channel to drain or carry off surplus water **4 :** a long inclined trough usu. on the ground (as for floating logs); *esp* : such a contrivance paved usu. with riffles to hold quicksilver for catching gold

[2]**sluice** *vb* **sluiced; sluic·ing** *vt* (1593) **1 :** to draw off by or through a sluice **2 a :** to wash with or in water running through or from a sluice **b :** to drench with a sudden flow : FLUSH **3 :** to transport (as logs) in a sluice ~ *vi* : to pour as if from a sluice

sluice·way \ˈslü-ˌswā\ *n* (1779) : an artificial channel into which water is let by a sluice

sluicy \ˈslü-sē\ *adj* (1697) : falling copiously or in streams : STREAMING

[1]**slum** \ˈsləm\ *n, often attrib* [origin unknown] (1825) : a densely populated usu. urban area marked by crowding, dirty run-down housing, poverty, and social disorganization

[2]**slum** *vi* **slummed; slum·ming** (1884) : to visit slums esp. out of curiosity; *broadly* : to go somewhere or do something that might be considered beneath one's station — **slum·mer** *n*

[1]**slum·ber** \ˈsləm-bər\ *vi* **slum·bered; slum·ber·ing** \-b(ə-)riŋ\ [ME *slumberen,* freq. of *slumen* to doze, prob. fr. *slume* slumber, fr. OE *slūma;* perh. akin to Lith *slugti* to diminish] (13c) **1 a :** to sleep lightly : DOZE **b :** SLEEP **2 a :** to be in a torpid, slothful, or negligent state **b :** to lie dormant or latent — **slum·ber·er** \-bər-ər\ *n*

[2]**slumber** *n* (14c) **1 a :** SLEEP **b :** a light sleep **2 :** LETHARGY, TORPOR

slum·ber·ous *or* **slum·brous** \ˈsləm-b(ə-)rəs\ *adj* (15c) **1 :** heavy with sleep : SLEEPY **2 :** inducing slumber : SOPORIFIC **3 :** marked by or suggestive of a state of sleep or lethargy ⟨a ~ peace pervaded every province —Pearl Buck⟩

slumber party *n* (1925) : an overnight gathering esp. of teenage girls usu. at one of their homes

slum·bery \ˈsləm-b(ə-)rē\ *adj, archaic* (14c) : SLUMBEROUS

slum·gul·lion \ˈsləm-ˌgəl-yən, ˌsləm-ˈ\ *n* [perh. fr. *slum* (slime) + E dial. *gullion* (mud, cesspool)] (1902) : a meat stew

slum·lord \ˈsləm-ˌlȯ(ə)rd\ *n* [[1]*slum* + land*lord*] (ca. 1954) : a landlord who receives unusually large profits from substandard properties

slum·my \ˈsləm-ē\ *adj* **slum·mi·er; -est** (1873) : of, relating to, or suggestive of a slum ⟨~ streets⟩

[1]**slump** \ˈsləmp\ *vi* [prob. of Scand origin; akin to Norw *slumpa* to fall; akin to L *labi* to slide — more at SLEEP] (1677) **1 a :** to fall or sink suddenly **b :** to drop or slide down suddenly : COLLAPSE ⟨~*ed* to the floor⟩ **2 :** to assume a drooping posture or carriage : SLOUCH **3 :** to go into a slump ⟨sales ~*ed*⟩

[2]**slump** *n* (1887) **1 a :** a marked or sustained decline esp. in economic activity or prices **b :** a period of poor or losing play by a team or individual ⟨one spring I was in a batting ~ —Ted Williams⟩ **2 :** a downward slide of a mass of rock or land

slump·fla·tion \ˌsləmp-ˈflā-shən\ *n* [[2]*slump* + in*flation*] (1974) : a state or period of combined economic decline and rising inflation

slung *past and past part of* SLING

slung·shot \ˈsləŋ-ˌshät\ *n* (1842) : a striking weapon consisting of a small mass of metal or stone fixed on a flexible handle or strap

slunk *past and past part of* SLINK

[1]**slur** \ˈslər\ *n* [obs. E dial. *slur* thin mud, fr. ME *sloor;* akin to MHG *slier* mud, Lith *slugti* to diminish] (1609) **1 a :** an insulting or disparaging remark or innuendo : ASPERSION **b :** a shaming or degrading effect : STAIN, STIGMA **2 :** a blurred spot in printed matter : SMUDGE

[2]**slur** *vb* **slurred; slur·ring** *vt* (1660) **1 :** to cast aspersions on : DISPARAGE **2 :** to make indistinct : OBSCURE ~ *vi* : to slip so as to cause a slur — used of a sheet being printed

[3]**slur** *vb* **slurred; slur·ring** [prob. fr. LG *slurrn* to shuffle; akin to ME *sloor* mud] *vt* (1660) **1 a :** to slide or slip over without due mention, consideration, or emphasis ⟨*slurred* over certain facts⟩ **b :** to perform hurriedly : SKIMP ⟨let him not ~ his lesson —R. W. Emerson⟩ **2 :** to perform (successive tones of different pitch) in a smooth or connected manner **3 a :** to reduce, make a substitution for, or omit (sounds that would normally occur in an utterance) **b :** to utter with such reduction, substitution, or omission of sounds ⟨his speech was *slurred* to an indistinct murmur⟩ ~ *vi* **1** *dial chiefly Eng* : SLIP, SLIDE **2 :** DRAG, SHUFFLE

[4]**slur** *n* (ca. 1801) **1 a :** a curved line connecting notes to be sung to the same syllable or performed without a break **b :** the combination of two or more slurred tones **2 :** a slurring manner of speech

slurp \ˈslərp\ *vb* [D *slurpen;* akin to MLG *slorpen* to slurp] *vi* (1648) : to make a sucking noise while eating or drinking ~ *vt* : to eat or drink noisily or with a sucking sound — **slurp** *n*

[1]**slur·ry** \ˈslər-ē, ˈslə-rē\ *n, pl* **slur·ries** [ME *slory*] (15c) : a watery mixture of insoluble matter (as mud, lime, or plaster of paris)

[2]**slurry** *vt* **slur·ried; slur·ry·ing** (1947) : to convert into a slurry

[1]**slush** \ˈsləsh\ *n* [perh. of Scand origin; akin to Norw *slusk* slush] (1641) **1 a :** partly melted or watery snow **b :** loose ice crystals formed during the early stages of freezing of salt water **2 a :** soft mud : MIRE **b :** grout made of portland cement, sand, and water **3 :** refuse grease and fat from cooking esp. on shipboard **4 :** a soft mixture of grease or oil and other materials for protecting the surface of metal parts against corrosion; *esp* : a mixture of white lead and lime for painting the bright parts of machines to preserve them from oxidation **5 :** paper pulp in water suspension **6 :** trashy and usu. cheaply sentimental material **7 :** unsolicited writings submitted (as to a magazine) for publication

[2]**slush** *vt* (1807) **1 :** to wet, splash, or paint with slush **2 :** to fill in (as joints) with slush or grout ~ *vi* **1 :** to make one's way through slush **2 :** to make a splashing sound

\ə\ abut \ᵊ\ kitten, F table \ər\ further \a\ ash \ā\ ace \ä\ cot, cart \au̇\ out \ch\ chin \e\ bet \ē\ easy \g\ go \i\ hit \ī\ ice \j\ job \ŋ\ sing \ō\ go \ȯ\ law \ȯi\ boy \th\ thin \t͟h\ the \ü\ loot \u̇\ foot \y\ yet \zh\ vision \à, k̲, ⁿ, œ, œ̅, ue, ue̅, ʸ\ *see* Guide to Pronunciation

slush fund *n* (1864) **1 :** a fund raised from the sale of refuse to obtain small luxuries or pleasures for a warship's crew **2 :** a fund for bribing public officials or carrying on corruptive propaganda

slushy \'sləsh-ē\ *adj* **slush·i·er; -est** (1791) **:** being, involving, or resembling slush: as **a :** full of or covered with slush ⟨~ streets⟩ **b :** made up of or having the consistency of slush ⟨~ snow⟩ ⟨a ~ mixture⟩ **c :** having a cheaply sentimental quality **:** TRASHY ⟨a ~ novel⟩ — **slush·i·ness** *n*

slut \'slət\ *n* [ME *slutte*] (15c) **1 :** a slovenly woman **:** SLATTERN **2 a :** a lewd woman; *esp* **:** PROSTITUTE **b :** a saucy girl **:** MINX — **slut·tish** \'slət-ish\ *adj* — **slut·tish·ly** *adv* — **slut·tish·ness** *n*

sly \'slī\ *adj* **sli·er** *also* **sly·er** \'slī(-ə)r\; **sli·est** *also* **sly·est** \'slī-əst\ [ME *sli*, fr. ON *slœgr;* akin to OE *slēan* to strike — more at SLAY] (13c) **1** *chiefly dial* **a :** wise in practical affairs **b :** displaying cleverness **:** INGENIOUS **2 a :** clever in concealing one's aims or ends **:** FURTIVE ⟨the ~ fox⟩ **b :** lacking in straightforwardness and candor **:** DISSEMBLING ⟨a ~ scheme⟩ **3 :** lightly mischievous **:** ROGUISH ⟨a ~ jest⟩ — **sly·ly** *adv* — **sly·ness** *n*

syn SLY, CUNNING, CRAFTY, TRICKY, FOXY, ARTFUL mean attaining or seeking to attain one's ends by devious means. SLY implies furtiveness, lack of candor, and skill in concealing one's aims and methods ⟨with knowing leer and words of *sly* import —Washington Irving⟩ CUNNING suggests the inventive use of sometimes limited intelligence in overreaching or circumventing ⟨every man wishes to be wise, and they who cannot be wise are almost always *cunning* —Samuel Johnson⟩ CRAFTY implies cleverness and subtlety of method ⟨as a *crafty* envoy does his country's business by dint of flirting and conviviality —C. E. Montague⟩ TRICKY is more likely to suggest shiftiness and unreliability than skill in deception and maneuvering ⟨he avoided the mean and *tricky:* he was always an honorable foe —W. C. Ford⟩ FOXY implies a shrewd and wary craftiness usu. involving devious dealing ⟨this *foxy* publicity man turned fumbling poet —Sherwood Anderson⟩ ARTFUL implies alluring indirectness in dealing and often connotes sophistication or coquetry or cleverness ⟨being *artful*, she cajoled him with . . . flattery until his suspicion was quieted —John Bennett⟩

— **on the sly :** in a manner intended to avoid notice

sly·boots \'slī-ˌbüts\ *n pl but sing in constr* (1680) **:** a sly tricky person; *esp* **:** one who is cunning or mischievous in an engaging way

slype \'slīp\ *n* [prob. fr. Flem *slijpe* place for slipping in and out] (1861) **:** a narrow passage; *specif* **:** one between the transept and chapter house or deanery in an English cathedral

[1]smack \'smak\ *n* [ME, fr. OE *smæc;* akin to OHG *smac* taste, Lith *smaguriauti* to nibble] (bef. 12c) **1 :** characteristic taste or flavor; *also* **:** a perceptible taste or tincture **2 :** a small quantity

[2]smack *vi* (14c) **1 :** to have a taste or flavor **2 :** to have a trace, vestige, or suggestion ⟨a proposal that ~*s* of treason⟩

[3]smack *vb* [akin to MD *smacken* to strike] *vt* (1557) **1 :** to close and open (lips) noisily and in rapid succession esp. in eating **2 a :** to kiss with or as if with a smack **b :** to strike so as to produce a smack ~ *vi* **:** to make or give a smack

[4]smack *n* (1570) **1 :** a quick sharp noise made by rapidly compressing and opening the lips **2 :** a loud kiss **3 :** a sharp slap or blow

[5]smack *adv* (1782) **:** squarely and sharply **:** DIRECTLY ⟨~ in the middle⟩

[6]smack *n* [D *smak* or LG *smack*] (1611) **:** a sailing ship (as a sloop or cutter) used chiefly in coasting and fishing

[7]smack *n* [perh. fr. Yiddish *shmek* sniff, whiff, pinch (of snuff)] *slang* (1965) **:** HEROIN

smack–dab \'smak-'dab\ *adv* (ca. 1892) **:** EXACTLY, SQUARELY

smack·er \'smak-ər\ *n* (1611) **1 :** one that smacks **2** *slang* **:** DOLLAR

smack·ing \'smak-iŋ\ *adj* (1820) **:** BRISK, LIVELY ⟨a ~ breeze⟩

[1]small \'smȯl\ *adj* [ME *smal*, fr. OE *smæl;* akin to OHG *smal* small, L *malus* bad] (bef. 12c) **1 a :** having comparatively little size or slight dimensions **b :** LOWERCASE **2 a :** minor in influence, power, or rank **b :** operating on a limited scale **3 :** lacking in strength ⟨a ~ voice⟩ **4 a :** little or close to zero in an objectively measurable aspect (as quantity, amount, or value) **b :** made up of few or little units **5 a :** of little consequence **:** TRIVIAL, INSIGNIFICANT **b :** HUMBLE, MODEST ⟨a ~ beginning⟩ **6 :** limited in degree **7 a :** MEAN, PETTY **b :** reduced to a humiliating position — **small·ish** \'smȯ-lish\ *adj* — **small·ness** \'smȯl-nəs\ *n*

syn SMALL, LITTLE, DIMINUTIVE, MINUTE, TINY, MINIATURE mean noticeably below average in size. SMALL and LITTLE are often interchangeable, but SMALL applies more to relative size determined by capacity, value, number; LITTLE is more absolute in implication often carrying the idea of petiteness, pettiness, insignificance, or immaturity; DIMINUTIVE implies abnormal smallness; MINUTE implies extreme smallness; TINY is an informal equivalent to MINUTE; MINIATURE applies to an exactly proportioned reproduction on a very small scale.

[2]small *adv* (bef. 12c) **1 :** in or into small pieces **2 :** without force or loudness ⟨speak as ~ as you will —Shak.⟩ **3 :** in a small manner

[3]small *n* (15c) **1 :** a part smaller and esp. narrower than the remainder ⟨the ~ of the back⟩ **2 a** *pl* **:** small-sized products **b** *pl, Brit* **:** SMALLCLOTHES; *esp* **:** UNDERWEAR

small arm *n* (1689) **:** a hand-held firearm (as a handgun or shoulder arm)

small beer *n* (1568) **1 :** weak or inferior beer **2 :** something of small importance **:** TRIVIA — **small–beer** *adj*

small calorie *n* (ca. 1890) **:** CALORIE 1a

small capital *n* (1770) **:** a letter having the form of but smaller than a capital letter (as in THESE WORDS)

small change *n* (1819) **1 :** coins of low denomination **2 :** something trifling or petty

small–claims court *n* (1925) **:** a special court intended to simplify and expedite the handling of small claims on debts — called also *small-debts court*

small·clothes \'smȯl-ˌklō(th)z\ *n pl* (1796) **1 :** close-fitting knee breeches worn in the 18th century **2 :** small articles of clothing (as underclothing or handkerchiefs)

smaller *comparative of* SMALL

smaller European elm bark beetle *n* (ca. 1945) **:** ELM BARK BEETLE b

small–fry \'smȯl-ˌfrī\ *adj* (1897) **1 :** MINOR, UNIMPORTANT ⟨a ~ politician⟩ **2 :** of, relating to, or intended for children **:** CHILDISH

small·hold·er \-ˌhōl-dər\ *n, chiefly Brit* (1915) **:** an owner or operator of a smallholding

small·hold·ing \-diŋ\ *n, chiefly Brit* (ca. 1892) **:** a piece of land that is detached from a cottage, is hired or owned by a laboring man, and is cultivated to supplement his main income

small hours *n pl* (1836) **:** the early morning hours

small intestine *n* (1767) **:** the part of the intestine that lies between the stomach and colon, consists of duodenum, jejunum, and ileum, secretes digestive enzymes, and is the chief site of the absorption of digested nutrients

small–mind·ed \'smȯl-'mīn-dəd\ *adj* (1847) **1 :** having narrow interests, sympathies, or outlook **2 :** typical of a small-minded person **:** marked by pettiness, narrowness, or meanness ⟨~ conduct⟩ — **small–mind·ed·ly** *adv* — **small–mind·ed·ness** *n*

small·mouth bass \ˌsmȯl-ˌmau̇th-\ *n* (1882) **:** a black bass (*Micropterus dolomieui*) of clear rivers and lakes that is bronzy green above and lighter below and has the vertex of the angle of the jaw falling below the eye — called also *smallmouth, smallmouth black bass*

small octave *n* (ca. 1890) **:** the musical octave that begins on the first C below middle C — see PITCH illustration

small potato *n* (1831) **:** one that is of trivial importance or worth — usu. used in pl. but sing. or pl. in constr.

small·pox \'smȯl-ˌpäks\ *n* (1518) **:** an acute contagious febrile disease caused by a pox virus and characterized by skin eruption with pustules, sloughing, and scar formation

small–scale \-'skā(ə)l\ *adj* (1852) **1 :** small in scope; *esp* **:** small in output or operation **2** *of a map* **:** having a scale (as one inch to 25 miles) that permits plotting of comparatively little detail

small screen *n* (1966) **:** TELEVISION

small stuff *n* (ca. 1867) **:** small rope (as spun yarn or marline) usu. identified by the number of threads or yarns which it contains

small·sword \'smȯl-ˌsō(ə)rd, -ˌsȯ(ə)rd\ *n* (1687) **:** a light tapering sword for thrusting used chiefly in dueling and fencing

small talk *n* (1751) **:** light or casual conversation **:** CHITCHAT

small–time \'smȯl-'tīm\ *adj* (1917) **:** insignificant in performance, scope, or standing **:** PETTY ⟨~ hoodlums⟩ — **small–tim·er** \-'tī-mər\ *n*

smalt \'smȯlt\ *n* [MF, fr. OIt *smalto*, of Gmc origin; akin to OHG *smelzan* to melt — more at SMELT] (1558) **:** a deep blue pigment used esp. as a ceramic color and prepared by fusing together silica, potash, and oxide of cobalt and grinding to powder the resultant glass

smalt·ite \'smȯl-ˌtīt\ *n* [alter. of *smaltine*, fr. F, fr. *smalt*, fr. MF] (1868) **:** a bluish white or gray isometric mineral of metallic luster that is essentially an arsenide of cobalt and nickel

smal·to \'smäl-(ˌ)tō, 'smȯl-\ *n, pl* **smal·ti** \-(ˌ)tē\ [It, smalt, smalto] (1705) **:** colored glass or enamel or a piece of either used in mosaic work

sma·ragd \smə-'ragd, 'smar-ˌagd\ *n* [ME *smaragde*, fr. L *smaragdus*] (13c) **:** EMERALD — **sma·rag·dine** \smə-'rag-dən, 'smar-əg-ˌdīn\ *adj*

sma·rag·dite \smə-'rag-ˌdīt, 'smar-əg-ˌdīt\ *n* [F, fr. L *smaragdus* emerald — more at EMERALD] (1804) **:** a green foliated amphibole

smarmy \'smär-mē\ *adj* [*smarm* (to gush, slobber)] (1924) **:** revealing or marked by a smug, ingratiating, or false earnestness ⟨a tone of ~ self-satisfaction — *New Yorker*⟩

[1]smart \'smärt\ *vi* [ME *smerten*, fr. OE *smeortan;* akin to OHG *smerzan* to pain, L *mordēre* to bite, Gk *marainein* to waste away] (bef. 12c) **1 :** to cause or be the cause or seat of a sharp poignant pain; *also* **:** to feel or have such a pain **2 a :** to feel or endure distress, remorse, or embarrassment ⟨~*ing* from wounded vanity —W. L. Shirer⟩ **b :** to pay a heavy or stinging penalty ⟨would have to ~ for this foolishness⟩

[2]smart *adj* (bef. 12c) **1 :** making one smart **:** causing a sharp stinging **2 :** marked by often sharp forceful activity or vigorous strength ⟨a ~ pull of the starter cord⟩ **3 :** BRISK, SPIRITED **4 a :** mentally alert **:** BRIGHT **b :** KNOWLEDGEABLE **c :** SHREWD ⟨a ~ investment⟩ **5 a :** WITTY, CLEVER **b :** PERT, SAUCY ⟨was fired for being ~ with the boss⟩ **6 a :** NEAT, TRIM **b :** stylish or elegant in dress or appearance **c (1) :** SOPHISTICATED **(2) :** characteristic of or patronized by fashionable society **7 a :** being a guided missile ⟨a laser-guided ~ bomb⟩ **b :** operating by automation ⟨a ~ machine tool⟩ **c** *of a computer terminal* **:** having part of the processing done by a microcomputer — **smart·ly** *adv* — **smart·ness** *n*

[3]smart *n* (13c) **1 :** a smarting pain; *esp* **:** a stinging local pain **2 :** poignant grief or remorse ⟨was not the sort to get over ~*s* —Sir Winston Churchill⟩ **3 :** an affectedly witty or fashionable person **4** *pl, slang* **:** INTELLIGENCE, KNOW-HOW

[4]smart *adv* (14c) **:** in a smart manner **:** SMARTLY

smart al·eck *also* **smart alec** \'smärt-ˌal-ik, -ˌel-\ *n* [*Aleck*, nickname for *Alexander*] (1865) **:** an obnoxiously conceited and self-assertive person with pretensions to smartness or cleverness — **smart–al·ecky** \-ˌal-ə-kē, -ˌel-\ *or* **smart–aleck** \-ik\ *adj*

smart·en \'smärt-ᵊn\ *vb* **smart·ened; smart·en·ing** \'smärt-niŋ, -ᵊn-iŋ\ *vt* (1815) **:** to make smart or smarter; *esp* **:** SPRUCE — usu. used with *up* ~ *vi* **:** to smarten oneself — used with *up*

[1]smart money \'smärt-ˌmən-ē\ *n* [[3]*smart*] (1693) **:** PUNITIVE DAMAGES

[2]smart money \-'mən-ē, -ˌmən-\ *n* [[2]*smart*] (1926) **1 :** money ventured by one having inside information or much experience **2 :** well-informed bettors or speculators

smart set *n* (1890) **:** ultrafashionable society

smart·weed \'smärt-ˌwēd\ *n* (ca. 1787) **:** any of various polygonums with strong acid juice

smarty *or* **smart·ie** \'smärt-ē\ *n, pl* **smart·ies** (1861) **:** SMART ALECK

smarty–pants \-ˌpan(t)s\ *n pl but sing in constr* (1941) **:** SMART ALECK

[1]smash \'smash\ *n* (1754) **1 :** the condition of being smashed **2 a :** a smashing blow or attack **b :** a hard overhand stroke (as in tennis or badminton) **3 a :** the action or sound of smashing; *esp* **:** a wreck due to collision **:** CRASH **b :** utter collapse **:** RUIN; *esp* **:** BANKRUPTCY **4 :** a fruit beverage made with crushed or squeezed fruit **5 :** a striking success **:** HIT

[2]smash *vb* [perh. blend of *smack* and *mash*] *vt* (1778) **1 :** to break in pieces by violence **:** SHATTER **2 a :** to drive or throw violently esp. with a shattering or battering effect; *also* **:** to effect in this way **b :** to hit violently **:** BATTER **c (1) :** to hit (as a tennis ball) with a hard overhand stroke **(2) :** to drive (a ball) with a forceful stroke **3 :** to destroy utterly **:** WRECK ~ *vi* **1 :** to move or become propelled with violence or crashing effect ⟨~*ed* into a tree⟩ **2 :** to become wrecked **3 :** to go to pieces suddenly under collision or pressure — **smash·er** *n*

[3]smash *adv* (1823) **:** with a resounding crash

4smash *adj* (1923) **:** being a smash **:** OUTSTANDING ⟨a ~ hit⟩

smashed \ˈsmasht\ *adj, slang* (ca. 1959) **:** DRUNK, INTOXICATED

smash·ing \ˈsmash-iŋ\ *adj* (1833) **1 :** that smashes **:** CRUSHING ⟨a ~ defeat⟩ **2 :** extraordinarily impressive or effective ⟨a ~ performance⟩ — **smash·ing·ly** \-iŋ-lē\ *adv*

smash–up \ˈsmash-ˌəp\ *n* (1856) **1 :** a complete collapse **2 :** a motor vehicle collision

1smat·ter \ˈsmat-ər\ *vb* [ME *smateren*] *vi* (15c) **:** to talk superficially **:** BABBLE ~ *vt* **1 :** to speak with spotty or superficial knowledge ⟨~*s* French⟩ **2 :** to dabble in — **smat·ter·er** \-ər-ər\ *n*

2smatter *n* (1668) **:** SMATTERING

smat·ter·ing \ˈsmat-ə-riŋ\ *n* (1538) **1 :** superficial piecemeal knowledge ⟨a ~ of carpentry, house painting, bricklaying —Alva Johnston⟩ **2 :** a small scattered number or amount ⟨a ~ of spectators⟩

smaze \ˈsmāz\ *n* [*sm*oke + h*aze*] (1953) **:** a combination of haze and smoke similar to smog in appearance but less damp in consistency

1smear \ˈsmi(ə)r\ *n* [ME *smere,* fr. OE *smeoru;* akin to OHG *smero* grease, Gk *smyris* emery, *myron* unguent] (bef. 12c) **1 a :** a viscous or sticky substance **b :** a spot made by or as if by an unctuous or adhesive substance **2 :** material smeared on a surface (as of a microscopic slide); *also* **:** a preparation made by smearing material on a surface ⟨a vaginal ~⟩ **3 :** a usu. unsubstantiated charge or accusation against a person or organization

2smear *vt* (bef. 12c) **1 a :** to overspread with something unctuous, viscous, or adhesive **:** DAUB **b :** to spread over a surface **2 a :** to stain, smudge, or dirty by or as if by smearing **b :** SULLY, BESMIRCH; *specif* **:** to vilify esp. by secretly and maliciously spreading grave charges and imputations **3 :** to obliterate, obscure, blur, blend, wipe out, or defeat by or as if by smearing — **smear·er** *n*

smear·case *also* **smier·case** \ˈsmi(ə)r-ˌkās\ *n* [modif. of G *schmierkäse,* fr. *schmieren* to smear + *käse* cheese] *chiefly Midland* (1829) **:** COTTAGE CHEESE

smeary \ˈsmi(ə)r-ē\ *adj* (1529) **1 :** marked by or covered with smears **2 :** liable to cause smears ⟨~ lipstick⟩

smec·tic \ˈsmek-tik\ *adj* [L *smecticus* cleansing, having the properties of soap, fr. Gk *smēktikos,* fr. *smēchein* to clean] (1923) **:** of, relating to, or being the phase of a liquid crystal characterized by arrangement of molecules in layers with the long molecular axes in a given layer being parallel to one another and those of other layers and perpendicular or slightly inclined to the plane of the layer — compare CHOLESTERIC, NEMATIC

smeg·ma \ˈsmeg-mə\ *n* [NL, fr. L, detergent, soap, fr. Gk *smēgma,* fr. *smēchein* to wash off, clean] (ca. 1819) **:** the secretion of a sebaceous gland; *specif* **:** the cheesy sebaceous matter that collects between the glans penis and the foreskin or around the clitoris and labia minora

1smell \ˈsmel\ *vb* **smelled** \ˈsmeld\ *or* **smelt** \ˈsmelt\; **smell·ing** [ME *smellen;* akin to MD *smölen* to scorch, Russ *smalit'*] *vt* (12c) **1 :** to perceive the odor or scent of through stimuli affecting the olfactory nerves **:** get the odor or scent of with the nose **2 :** to detect or become aware of as if by the sense of smell **3 :** to emit the odor of ~ *vi* **1 :** to exercise the sense of smell **2 a** (1) **:** to have an odor or scent (2) **:** to have a characteristic aura or atmosphere **:** SMACK ⟨the accounts . . . seemed to me to ~ of truth —R. S. Bourne⟩; *also* **:** SEEM, APPEAR ⟨the story didn't ~ right⟩ **b** (1) **:** to have an offensive odor **:** STINK (2) **:** to appear evil, dishonest, or ugly ⟨all this from the moral point of view ~*s* —A.F. Wills⟩ — **smell·er** *n* — **smell a rat :** to have a suspicion of something wrong

2smell *n* (12c) **1 :** the property of a thing that affects the olfactory organs **:** ODOR **2 a :** the process, function, or power of smelling **b :** the special sense concerned with the perception of odor **3 :** a very small amount **:** TRACE ⟨add only a ~ of garlic⟩ **b :** a pervading or characteristic quality **:** AURA ⟨the ~ of affluence, of power —Harry Hervey⟩ **4 :** an act or instance of smelling

syn SMELL, SCENT, ODOR, AROMA mean the quality that makes a thing perceptible to the olfactory sense. SMELL implies solely the sensation without suggestion of quality or character; SCENT applies to the characteristic smell given off by a substance, an animal, or a plant; ODOR may imply a stronger or more readily distinguished scent or it may be equivalent to SMELL; AROMA suggests a somewhat penetrating usu. pleasant odor.

smelling salts *n pl but sing or pl in constr* (1840) **:** a usu. scented aromatic preparation of ammonium carbonate and ammonia water used as a stimulant and restorative

smelly \ˈsmel-ē\ *adj* **smell·i·er; -est** (1862) **:** having a smell; *esp* **:** MALODOROUS

1smelt \ˈsmelt\ *n, pl* **smelts** *or* **smelt** [ME, fr. OE; akin to Norw *smelte* whiting] (bef. 12c) **:** any of various small salmonoid fishes (family Osmeridae and esp. genus *Osmerus*) that closely resemble the trouts in general structure, live along coasts and ascend rivers to spawn or are landlocked, and have delicate oily flesh with a distinctive odor and taste

2smelt *vt* [D or LG *smelten;* akin to OHG *smelzan* to melt, OE *meltan* —more at MELT] (1543) **1 :** to melt or fuse (as ore) often with an accompanying chemical change usu. to separate the metal **2 :** REFINE, REDUCE

smelt·er \ˈsmel-tər\ *n* (15c) **:** one that smelts: **a :** a worker who smelts ore **b :** an owner or operator of a smeltery **c** *or* **smelt·ery** \-t(ə-)rē\ **:** an establishment for smelting

smew \ˈsmyü\ *n* [akin to MHG *smiehe* smew] (1674) **:** a merganser (*Mergus albellus*) of northern Europe and Asia the male of which is white-crested

smid·gen *also* **smid·geon** *or* **smid·gin** \ˈsmij-ən\ *n* [prob. alter. of E dial. *smitch* (soiling mark)] (1845) **:** a small amount **:** BIT

smi·lax \ˈsmī-ˌlaks\ *n* [L, bindweed, yew, fr. Gk] (1601) **1 :** GREENBRIER **2 :** a tender twining plant (*Asparagus asparagoides*) that has ovate bright green cladophylls and is often grown in greenhouses

1smile \ˈsmī(ə)l\ *vb* **smiled; smil·ing** [ME *smilen;* akin to OE *smerian* to laugh, L *mirari* to wonder, Skt *smayate* he smiles] *vi* (14c) **1 :** to have, produce, or exhibit a smile **2 a :** to look or regard with amusement or ridicule ⟨*smiled* at his own folly —Martin Gardner⟩ **b :** to bestow approval ⟨feeling that Heaven *smiled* on his labors —Sheila Rowlands⟩ **c :** to appear pleasant or agreeable ~ *vt* **1 :** to affect with or by smiling **2 :** to express by a smile — **smil·er** *n* — **smil·ey** \ˈsmī-lē\ *adj* — **smil·ing·ly** \ˈsmī-liŋ-lē\ *adv*

2smile *n* (1562) **1 :** a facial expression in which the eyes brighten and the corners of the mouth curve slightly upward and which expresses esp. amusement, pleasure, approval, or sometimes scorn **2 :** a pleasant or encouraging appearance — **smile·less** \ˈsmī(ə)l-ləs\ *adj*

smirch \ˈsmərch\ *vt* [ME *smorchen*] (15c) **1 a :** to make dirty, stained, or discolored **:** SULLY **b :** to smear with something that stains or dirties **2 :** to bring discredit or disgrace on — **smirch** *n*

smirk \ˈsmərk\ *vi* [ME *smirken,* fr. OE *smearcian* to smile; akin to OE *smerian* to laugh] (bef. 12c) **:** to smile in an affected or smug manner **:** SIMPER — **smirk** *n*

smirky \ˈsmər-kē\ *adj* (1728) **1 :** that smirks **:** SMIRKING **2 :** SNIDE, INSINUATING

smite \ˈsmīt\ *vb* **smote** \ˈsmōt\; **smit·ten** \ˈsmit-ᵊn\ *or* **smote; smit·ing** \ˈsmīt-iŋ\ [ME *smiten,* fr. OE *smītan;* akin to OHG *bismīzan* to defile] *vt* (bef. 12c) **1 :** to strike sharply or heavily esp. with the hand or an implement held in the hand **2 a :** to kill or severely injure by smiting **b :** to attack or afflict suddenly and injuriously ⟨*smitten* by disease⟩ **3 :** to cause to strike **4 :** to affect as if by striking ⟨children *smitten* with the fear of hell —V. L. Parrington⟩ ~ *vi* **:** to deliver or deal a blow with or as if with the hand or something held — **smit·er** \ˈsmīt-ər\ *n*

smith \ˈsmith\ *n* [ME, fr. OE; akin to OHG *smid* smith, Gk *smilē* wood-carving knife] (bef. 12c) **1 :** a worker in metals **:** BLACKSMITH **2 :** MAKER — often used in combination ⟨gun*smith*⟩ ⟨tune*smith*⟩

smith·er·eens \ˌsmith-ə-ˈrēnz\ *n pl* [IrGael *smidirīn*] (1829) **:** FRAGMENTS, BITS ⟨the house was blown to ~ by the explosion⟩

smith·ery \ˈsmith-ə-rē\ *n, pl* **-er·ies** (1625) **1 :** the work, art, or trade of a smith **2 :** SMITHY 1

smith·son·ite \ˈsmith-sə-ˌnīt\ *n* [James *Smithson*] (1835) **1 :** a mineral $Zn_4Si_2O_7OH \cdot H_2O$ that is a silicate of zinc and constitutes an ore of zinc **2 :** a usu. white or nearly white native zinc carbonate $ZnCO_3$

smithy \ˈsmith-ē *also* ˈsmith-\ *n, pl* **smith·ies** (13c) **1 :** the workshop of a smith **2 :** BLACKSMITH

1smock \ˈsmäk\ *n* [ME *smok,* fr. OE *smoc;* akin to OHG *smocco* adornment] (bef. 12c) **1** *archaic* **:** a woman's undergarment; *esp* **:** CHEMISE **2 :** a light loose garment worn esp. for protection of clothing while working

2smock *vt* (1888) **:** to embroider or shirr with smocking

smock frock *n* (ca. 1800) **:** a loose outer garment worn by workmen esp. in Europe

smock·ing \ˈsmäk-iŋ\ *n* (1888) **:** a decorative embroidery or shirring made by gathering cloth in regularly spaced round tucks

smog \ˈsmäg *also* ˈsmȯg\ *n* [blend of *smoke* and *fog*] (1905) **:** a fog made heavier and darker by smoke and chemical fumes; *also* **:** a photochemical haze caused by the action of solar ultraviolet radiation on atmosphere polluted with hydrocarbons and oxides of nitrogen from automobile exhaust — **smog·less** \-ləs\ *adj*

smog·gy \-ē\ *adj* **smog·gi·er; -est** (1905) **:** characterized by or abounding in smog

smok·able *or* **smoke·able** \ˈsmō-kə-bəl\ *adj* (1839) **:** fit for smoking

1smoke \ˈsmōk\ *n* [ME, fr. OE *smoca;* akin to MHG *smouch* smoke, Gk *smychein* to smolder] (bef. 12c) **1 a :** the gaseous products of burning carbonaceous materials made visible by the presence of small particles of carbon **b :** a suspension of particles in a gas **2 a :** a mass or column of smoke **b :** SMUDGE **3 :** fume or vapor often resulting from the action of heat on moisture **4 :** something of little substance, permanence, or value **5 :** something that obscures **6 a** (1) **:** something (as a cigarette) to smoke (2) **:** MARIJUANA 2 **b :** an act or spell of smoking tobacco **7 a :** a pale blue **b :** any of the colors of smoke **8 :** pitches that are fastballs ⟨if a guy's going to hit you . . . he certainly isn't going to throw a spitter — he gives you ~ —Tony Conigliaro⟩ — **smoke·less** \ˈsmō-kləs\ *adj* — **smoke·like** \-ˌklīk\ *adj*

2smoke *vb* **smoked; smok·ing** *vi* (bef. 12c) **1 a :** to emit or exhale smoke **b :** to emit excessive smoke **2** *archaic* **:** to undergo punishment **:** SUFFER **3 :** to spread or rise like smoke **4 :** to inhale and exhale the fumes of burning plant material and esp. tobacco; *esp* **:** to smoke tobacco habitually ~ *vt* **1 a :** FUMIGATE **b :** to drive (as mosquitoes) away by smoke **c :** to blacken or discolor with smoke ⟨*smoked* glasses⟩ **d :** to cure by exposure to smoke **e :** to stupefy (as bees) by smoke **2** *archaic* **:** SUSPECT **3 :** to inhale and exhale the smoke of **4** *archaic* **:** RIDICULE

smoke detector *n* (ca. 1927) **:** an alarm that activates automatically when it detects smoke

smoke–filled room \ˌsmōk-ˌfil-ˈdrüm\ *n* (1920) **:** a room (as in a hotel) in which a small group of politicians carry on negotiations

smoke·house \ˈsmōk-ˌhau̇s\ *n* (1746) **:** a building where meat or fish is cured by means of dense smoke

smoke·jack \-ˌjak\ *n* (1675) **:** a device for turning a spit by a fly or wheel moved by rising gases in a chimney

smoke jumper *n* (1927) **:** a forest fire fighter who parachutes to locations otherwise difficult to reach

smokeless powder *n* (1890) **:** any of a class of explosive propellants that produce comparatively little smoke on explosion and consist mostly of gelatinized cellulose nitrates

smoke out *vt* (1605) **1 :** to drive out by or as if by smoke **2 :** to bring to public view or knowledge

smoke pipe *n* (1815) **:** a usu. thin metal pipe that connects a source of smoke to a chimney

smoke·proof \ˈsmōk-ˈprüf\ *adj* (1901) **:** impermeable to smoke; *specif* **:** designed to restrict the spread of smoke through a building

smok·er \ˈsmō-kər\ *n* (1599) **1 :** one that smokes **2 :** a railroad car or compartment in which smoking is allowed **3 :** an informal social gathering for men

smoke screen *n* (1915) **1 :** a screen of smoke to hinder enemy observation of a military force, area, or activity **2 :** something designed to obscure, confuse, or mislead

smoke·stack \ˈsmōk-ˌstak\ *n* (1859) **:** a pipe or funnel through which smoke and gases are discharged

\ə\ abut \ᵊ\ kitten, F table \ər\ further \a\ ash \ā\ ace \ä\ cot, cart \au̇\ out \ch\ chin \e\ bet \ē\ easy \g\ go \i\ hit \ī\ ice \j\ job \ŋ\ sing \ō\ go \ȯ\ law \ȯi\ boy \th\ thin \t͟h\ the \ü\ loot \u̇\ foot \y\ yet \zh\ vision \à, k̲, ⁿ, œ, œ̄, ue, u̅e̅, ʸ\ *see* Guide to Pronunciation

smoke tree *n* (1846) : either of two small shrubby trees (genus *Cotinus*) of the sumac family often grown for their large panicles of minute flowers that suggest a cloud of smoke

smoking gun *n* (ca. 1974) : something that serves as conclusive evidence or proof esp. of a crime

smoking jacket *n* (1878) : a man's loose-fitting jacket for wear at home

smoking lamp *n* (ca. 1881) : a lamp on a ship kept lighted during the hours when smoking is allowed

smoking–room *adj* (1886) : marked by indecency or obscenity : SMUTTY

smoking room *n* (1689) : a room (as in a hotel or club) set apart for smokers

smoky *also* **smok·ey** \'smō-kē\ *adj* **smok·i·er; -est** (14c) **1** : emitting smoke esp. in large quantities **2 a** : having the characteristics of or resembling smoke **b** : suggestive of smoke esp. in flavor or odor **3 a** : filled with smoke **b** : made dark or black by smoke — **smok·i·ly** \-kə-lē\ *adv* — **smok·i·ness** \-kē-nəs\ *n*

smoky quartz *n* (1837) : CAIRNGORM

smoky topaz *n* (1797) : CAIRNGORM

[1]**smol·der** *or* **smoul·der** \'smōl-dər\ *n* [ME *smolder;* akin to ME *smellen* to smell] (14c) **1** : SMOKE, SMUDGE **2** : a smoldering fire

[2]**smolder** *or* **smoulder** *vi* **smol·dered** *or* **smoul·dered; smol·der·ing** *or* **smoul·der·ing** \-d(ə-)riŋ\ (1529) **1 a** : to burn sluggishly, without flame, and often with much smoke **b** : to be consumed by smoldering — often used with *out* **2** : to exist in a state of suppressed activity ⟨resentment ~*ed* in her⟩ **3** : to show suppressed anger, hate, or jealousy ⟨eyes ~*ing* with hate⟩

smolt \'smōlt\ *n* [ME (Sc)] (14c) : a young salmon or sea trout that is about two years old and that is at the stage of development when it assumes the silvery color of the adult

[1]**smooch** \'smüch\ *n* (1578) : KISS

[2]**smooch** *vi* [alter. of *smouch* (to kiss loudly)] (1588) : KISS, PET

[3]**smooch** *vt* [prob. alter. of *smutch*, vb.] (ca. 1825) : SMUDGE, SMEAR

[4]**smooch** *n* (1825) : SMUDGE, SMEAR — **smoochy** \'smü-chē\ *adj*

[1]**smooth** \'smüth\ *adj* [ME *smothe,* fr. OE *smōth;* akin to OS *smōthi* smooth] (bef. 12c) **1 a** (1) : having a continuous even surface (2) *of a curve* : being the representation of a function with a continuous first derivative **b** : being without hair **c** : GLABROUS ⟨a ~ leaf⟩ **d** : causing no resistance to sliding **2** : free from difficulties or impediments ⟨the ~ course of his life⟩ **3** : even and uninterrupted in flow or flight **4** : excessively and often artfully suave : INGRATIATING **5 a** : SERENE, EQUABLE ⟨a ~ disposition⟩ **b** : AMIABLE, COURTEOUS **6 a** : not sharp or harsh ⟨a ~ sherry⟩ **b** : free from lumps ***syn*** see LEVEL, EASY, SUAVE — **smooth** *adv* — **smooth·ly** *adv* — **smooth·ness** *n*

[2]**smooth** *vt* (14c) **1 a** : to free from what is harsh or disagreeable : POLISH ⟨~*ed* out his style⟩ **b** : SOOTHE **2** : to make smooth **3** : to minimize (as a fault) esp. in order to allay anger or ill will ⟨his main job is to ~ over the friction that so often arises —Brian Crozier⟩ **4** : to free from obstruction or difficulty **5 a** : to press flat **b** : to remove expression from (one's face) : COMPOSE **6** : to cause to lie evenly and in order : PREEN **7** : to free (as a graph or data) from irregularities by ignoring random variations ~ *vi* : to become smooth — **smooth·er** *n*

[3]**smooth** *n* (15c) **1** : a smooth part **2** : the act of smoothing **3** : a smoothing implement

smooth·bore \'smüth-'bō(ə)r, -'bȯ(ə)r\ *adj, of a firearm* (1799) : having a barrel with an unrifled bore — **smoothbore** \-,bō(ə)r, -,bȯ(ə)r\ *n*

smooth breathing *n* (ca. 1888) **1** : a mark ʼ placed over some initial vowels in Greek to show that they are not aspirated (as in ἐκεῖ pronounced \e-'kā\) **2** : the absence of aspiration indicated by a mark ʼ

smooth·en \'smü-thən\ *vb* **smooth·ened; smooth·en·ing** \'smüth-(ə-)niŋ\ *vt* (1635) : to make smooth ~ *vi* : to become smooth

smooth hound *n* [fr. the absence of a spine in front of the dorsal fin] (1603) : any of several dogfishes (genus *Mustelus*) closely related to or included with the requiem sharks

smooth muscle *n* (ca. 1890) : muscle tissue that lacks cross striations, that is made up of elongated spindle-shaped cells having a central nucleus, and that is found in vertebrate visceral structures (as the stomach and bladder) as thin sheets performing functions not subject to conscious control by the mind and in all or most of the musculature of invertebrates other than arthropods — compare STRIATED MUSCLE

smooth–tongued \'smüth-'təŋd\ *adj* (1592) : ingratiating in speech

smoothy *or* **smooth·ie** \'smü-thē\ *n, pl* **smooth·ies** (1904) **1** : a smooth-tongued person **2 a** : a person with polished manners **b** : one who behaves or performs with deftness, assurance, and easy competence; *esp* : a man with an ingratiating manner toward women

smor·gas·bord \'smȯr-gəs-,bō(ə)rd, -,bȯ(ə)rd\ *n* [Sw *smörgåsbord,* fr. *smörgås* open sandwich + *bord* table] (ca. 1919) **1** : a luncheon or supper buffet offering a variety of foods and dishes (as hors d'oeuvres, hot and cold meats, smoked and pickled fish, cheeses, salads, and relishes) **2** : a heterogeneous mixture : MÉLANGE

smote *past of* SMITE

[1]**smoth·er** \'sməth-ər\ *n* [ME, alter. of *smorther,* fr. *smoren* to smother, fr. OE *smorian* to suffocate; akin to MD *smoren* to suffocate] (12c) **1 a** : thick stifling smoke or smudge **b** : a state of being stifled or suppressed **2** : a dense cloud of fog, foam, spray, snow, or dust **3** : a confused multitude of things : WELTER — **smoth·ery** \-(ə-)rē\ *adj*

[2]**smother** *vb* **smoth·ered; smoth·er·ing** \-(ə-)riŋ\ *vi* (1520) : to be overcome or killed through or as if through lack of air ~ *vt* **1** : to overcome or kill with smoke or fumes **2 a** : to destroy the life of by depriving of air **b** : to overcome or discomfit through or as if through lack of air **c** : to suppress (a fire) by excluding oxygen **3 a** : to cause to smolder **b** : to suppress expression or knowledge of ⟨~*ed* his rage⟩ **c** : to stop or prevent the growth or activity of ⟨~ a child with too much care⟩; *also* : OVERWHELM **d** : to cover thickly : BLANKET ⟨snow ~*ed* the trails⟩ **e** : to overcome or vanquish quickly or decisively **4** : to cook in a covered pan or pot with little liquid over low heat

[1]**smudge** \'sməj\ *vb* **smudged; smudg·ing** [ME *smogen*] *vt* (15c) **1 a** : to make a smudge on **b** : to soil as if by smudging **2 a** : to rub, daub, or wipe in a smeary manner **b** : to make indistinct : BLUR **3** : to smoke or protect by means of a smudge ~ *vi* **1** : to make a smudge **2** : to become smudged

[2]**smudge** *n* (1768) **1 a** : a blurry spot or streak **b** : an immaterial stain ⟨cleanse him of every last ~ of impropriety —Richard Hanser⟩ **c** : an indistinct mass : BLUR **2** : a smoldering mass placed on the windward side (as to protect from frost) **3** : a bid of 4 in pitch that if made wins the game — **smudg·i·ly** \'sməj-ə-lē\ *adv* — **smudg·i·ness** \'sməj-ē-nəs\ *n* — **smudgy** \-ē\ *adj*

smug \'sməg\ *adj* **smug·ger; smug·gest** [prob. modif. of LG *smuck* neat, fr. MLG, fr. *smucken* to dress; akin to OE *smoc* smock] (1551) **1** : trim or smart in dress : SPRUCE **2** : scrupulously clean, neat, or correct : TIDY **3** : highly self-satisfied — **smug·ly** *adv* — **smug·ness** *n*

smug·gle \'sməg-əl\ *vb* **smug·gled; smug·gling** \-(ə-)liŋ\ [LG *smuggeln* & D *smokkelen;* akin to OE *smoc* smock] *vt* (1687) **1** : to import or export secretly contrary to the law and esp. without paying duties imposed by law **2** : to convey or introduce surreptitiously ~ *vi* : to import or export something in violation of the customs laws — **smuggler** \'sməg-lər\ *n*

[1]**smut** \'smət\ *vb* **smut·ted; smut·ting** [prob. alter. of earlier *smot* to stain, fr. ME *smotten;* akin to MHG *smutzen* to stain] *vt* (1587) **1** : to stain or taint with smut **2** : to affect (a crop or plant) with smut ~ *vi* : to become affected by smut

[2]**smut** *n* (1664) **1** : matter that soils or blackens; *specif* : a particle of soot **2** : any of various destructive diseases esp. of cereal grasses caused by parasitic fungi (order Ustilaginales) and marked by transformation of plant organs into dark masses of spores; *also* : a fungus causing a smut **3** : obscene language or matter

smutch \'sməch\ *n* [prob. irreg. fr. [1]*smudge*] (1530) : a dark stain : SMUDGE — **smutch** *vt* — **smutchy** \-ē\ *adj*

smut·ty \'smət-ē\ *adj* **smut·ti·er; -est** (1597) **1** : soiled or tainted with smut; *esp* : affected with smut fungus **2** : OBSCENE, INDECENT **3** : resembling smut in appearance : SOOTY — **smut·ti·ly** \'smət-ᵊl-ē\ *adv* — **smut·ti·ness** \'smət-ē-nəs\ *n*

[1]**snack** \'snak\ *n* (1757) : a light meal : food eaten between regular meals; *also* : food suitable for snacking

[2]**snack** *vi* [ME *snaken* to bite] (1807) : to eat a snack

snack bar *n* (1930) : a public eating place where snacks are served usu. at a counter

[1]**snaf·fle** \'snaf-əl\ *n* [origin unknown] (1533) : a simple usu. jointed bit for a bridle

[2]**snaffle** *vt* **snaf·fled; snaf·fling** \'snaf-(ə-)liŋ\ [origin unknown] (1724) : to obtain esp. by devious or irregular means

[1]**sna·fu** \sna-'fü\ *n* [*s*ituation *n*ormal *a*ll *f*ucked *u*p (*f*ouled *u*p)] (ca. 1940) : CONFUSION, MUDDLE

[2]**snafu** *adj* (1943) : snarled or stalled in confusion : AWRY

[3]**snafu** *vt* (1944) : to bring into a state of confusion

[1]**snag** \'snag\ *n* [of Scand origin; akin to ON *snagi* clothes peg] (1577) **1 a** : a tree or branch embedded in a lake or stream bed and constituting a hazard to navigation **b** : a standing dead tree **2** : a rough sharp or jagged projecting part : PROTUBERANCE: as **a** : a projecting tooth; *also* : a stump of a tooth **b** : one of the secondary branches of an antler **3** : a concealed or unexpected difficulty or obstacle **4** : a jagged tear made by or as if by catching on a snag ⟨a ~ in her stocking⟩ — **snag·gy** \'snag-ē\ *adj*

[2]**snag** *vt* **snagged; snag·ging** (1807) **1 a** : to catch and usu. damage on or as if on a snag **b** : to halt or impede as if by catching on a snag **2** : to hew, trim, or cut roughly or jaggedly **3** : to clear (as a river) of snags **4** : to catch or obtain by quick action

snag·gle·tooth \'snag-əl-,tüth\ *n* [E dial. *snaggle* (irregularly shaped tooth) + E *tooth*] (ca. 1825) : an irregular, broken, or projecting tooth — **snag·gle·toothed** \,snag-əl-'tütht\ *adj*

[1]**snail** \'snā(ə)l\ *n* [ME, fr. OE *snægl;* akin to OHG *snecko* snail, *snahhan* to creep, Lith *snãke* snail] (bef. 12c) **1** : a gastropod mollusk esp. when having an external enclosing spiral shell **2** : a slow-moving or sluggish person or thing — **snail·like** \'snā(ə)l-,līk\ *adj*

[2]**snail** *vi* (1582) : to move, act, or go slowly or lazily

snail fever *n* [fr. the snails which serve as intermediate hosts to the schistosomes causing the disease] (1947) : SCHISTOSOMIASIS

snail–paced \'snā(ə)l-'pāst\ *adj* (1594) : moving very slowly

[1]**snake** \'snāk\ *n* [ME, fr. OE *snaca;* akin to OE *snægl* snail] (bef. 12c) **1** : any of numerous limbless scaled reptiles (suborder Serpentes or Ophidia) with a long tapering body and with salivary glands often modified to produce venom which is injected through grooved or tubular fangs **2** : a worthless or treacherous fellow **3** : something (as a plumber's snake) resembling a snake — **snake·like** \'snā-,klīk\ *adj*

[2]**snake** *vb* **snaked; snak·ing** *vt* (1653) **1** : to wind (as one's way) in the manner of a snake **2** : to move (as logs) by dragging ~ *vi* : to crawl, move, or extend silently, secretly, or sinuously

snake·bird \'snāk-,bərd\ *n* (1791) : ANHINGA

snake·bite \-,bīt\ *n* (1839) : the bite of a snake and esp. a venomous snake

snake charmer *n* (1836) : an entertainer who exhibits his professed power to charm or fascinate venomous snakes

snake–dance *vi* (1931) : to engage in a snake dance

snake dance *n* (1772) **1** : a ceremonial dance in which snakes or their images are handled, invoked, or symbolically imitated by individual sinuous actions **2** : a group progression in a single-file serpentine path (as in celebration of an athletic victory)

snake doctor *n* (1862) **1** : DRAGONFLY **2** : HELLGRAMMITE

snake fence *n* (1805) : WORM FENCE

snake in the grass (1696) : a secretly faithless friend

snake oil *n* (1927) **1** : any of various substances or mixtures sold (as by a traveling medicine show) as medicine usu. without regard to their medical worth or properties **2** : POPPYCOCK, BUNKUM

snake pit *n* (1946) **1** : a hospital for mental diseases **2** : a place or state of chaotic disorder and distress

snake·root \'snā-,krüt, -,krůt\ *n* (1635) : any of numerous plants most of which have roots sometimes believed to cure snakebites; *also* : the root of such a plant — compare SENECA SNAKEROOT

snake·skin \'snāk-,skin\ *n* (1825) : leather prepared from the skin of a snake

snake·weed \'snā-,kwēd\ *n* (1597) : any of various plants popularly associated with snakes (as in appearance, habitat, or the treatment of snakebite); *esp* : any of an American genus (*Gutierrezia*) of composite herbs or low shrubs with alternate linear entire leaves and clustered yellow flower heads

snaky *also* **snak·ey** \'snā-kē\ *adj* (1567) **1** : of, formed of, or entwined with snakes ⟨the Gorgon with ~ hair —Joseph Addison⟩ **2** : SERPENTINE, SNAKELIKE ⟨~ coils⟩ **3** : suggestive of a snake ⟨the oiliness and

~ insinuation of his demeanor — Thomas DeQuincy⟩ **4 :** abounding in snakes — **snak·i·ly** \-kə-lē\ *adv*

1snap \'snap\ *vb* **snapped; snap·ping** [D or LG *snappen;* akin to MHG *snappen* to snap] *vi* (1530) **1 a :** to make a sudden closing of the jaws : seize something sharply with the mouth ⟨fish *snapping* at the bait⟩ **b :** to grasp at something eagerly : make a pounce or snatch ⟨~ at any chance⟩ **2 :** to utter sharp biting words : bark out irritable or peevish retorts **3 a :** to break suddenly with a sharp sound ⟨the twig *snapped*⟩ **b :** to give way suddenly under strain **4 :** to make a sharp or crackling sound **5 :** to close or fit in place with an abrupt movement or sharp sound ⟨the lock *snapped* shut⟩ **6 a :** to move briskly or sharply ⟨~*s* to attention⟩ **b :** to undergo a sudden and rapid change (as from one condition to another) ⟨~ out of it⟩ ⟨*snapped* awake⟩ **7 :** SPARKLE, FLASH ⟨eyes *snapping* with fury⟩ ~ *vt* **1 :** to seize with or as if with a snap of the jaws **2 :** to take possession or advantage of suddenly or eagerly — usu. used with *up* ⟨shoppers *snapping* up bargains⟩ **3 a :** to retort to or interrupt curtly and irritably **b :** to utter curtly or abruptly **4 :** to break suddenly : break short or in two **5 a :** to cause to make a snapping sound ⟨~ a whip⟩ **b :** to put into or remove from a particular position by a sudden movement or with a sharp sound ⟨~ the lock shut⟩ **6 a :** to project with a snap **b :** to put (a football) in play with a snap **c** (1) **:** to take photographically ⟨*snapping* exclusive news pictures — *Current Biog.*⟩ (2) **:** to take a snapshot of

2snap *n* (1555) **1 :** an abrupt closing (as of the mouth in biting or of scissors in cutting) **2 a** *archaic* **:** a share of profits or booty **b :** something that brings quick and easy profit or advantage **c :** something that is easy and presents no problems : CINCH **3 :** a small amount : BIT **4 a :** an act or instance of seizing abruptly : a sudden snatching at something **b :** a quick short movement ⟨lithe ~*s* of its body —Barbara Taylor⟩ **c :** a sudden sharp breaking **5 a :** a sound made by snapping something ⟨shut the book with a ~⟩ **b :** a brief sharp and usu. irritable speech or retort **6 :** a sudden spell of weather ⟨a cold ~⟩ **7 :** a catch or fastening that closes or locks with a click ⟨the ~ of a bracelet⟩ **8 :** a flat brittle cookie — compare GINGERSNAP **9 :** SNAPSHOT **10 a :** the condition of being vigorous in body, mind, or spirit : ALERTNESS, ENERGY **b :** a pleasing vigorous quality **11 :** the act of a center's putting the football in play from its position on the ground by quickly passing it between his legs to a teammate (as a quarterback) standing behind him

3snap *adv* (1583) **:** with a snap

4snap *adj* (1739) **1 :** done, made, or carried through suddenly or without deliberation ⟨a ~ judgment⟩ **2 :** called or taken without prior warning ⟨a ~ test⟩ **3 :** shutting or fastening with a click or by means of a device that snaps ⟨a ~ lock⟩ **4 :** unusually easy or simple ⟨a ~ course⟩

snap·back \'snap-,bak\ *n* (1887) **1 :** a football snap **2 :** a sudden rebound or recovery ⟨a ~ of prices on the stock exchange⟩

snap back \(')snap-'bak\ *vi* (1945) **:** to make a quick or vigorous recovery

snap bean *n* (1770) **:** a bean grown primarily for its pods that are usu. broken in pieces and cooked as a vegetable while young and tender and before the seeds have become enlarged — compare SHELL BEAN

snap–brim \,snap-,brim\ *n* (ca. 1908) **:** a usu. felt hat with brim turned up in back and down in front and with a dented crown

snap·drag·on \'snap-,drag-ən\ *n* [fr. the fancied resemblance of the flowers to the face of a dragon] (1593) **:** any of several garden plants (genus *Antirrhinum* and esp. *A. majus*) of the figwort family having showy white, crimson, or yellow bilabiate flowers

snap fastener *n* (1926) **:** a metal fastener consisting essentially of a ball and a socket attached to opposed parts of an article and used to hold meeting edges together

snap–on \'snap-,ȯn, -,än\ *adj* (1925) **:** designed to snap into position and fit tightly ⟨~ cuffs⟩

snap·per \'snap-ər\ *n, pl* **snappers** (1577) **1 :** one that snaps: as **a :** something (as a remark) that gives new orientation to a situation or utterance **b** (1) **:** SNAPPING TURTLE (2) **:** CLICK BEETLE **2** *pl also* **snapper a :** any of numerous active carnivorous fishes (family Lutjanidae) of warm seas important as food and often as sport fishes **b :** any of several immature fishes (as the young of the bluefish) that resemble a snapper

snap·per–back \-ər-,bak\ *n* (1887) **:** a football center

snapping turtle *n* (1784) **:** either of two large edible American aquatic turtles (family Chelydridae) with powerful jaws and a strong musky odor: **a :** a turtle (*Chelydra serpentina*) that has the head covered with smooth skin, has large plates in a double row on the underside of the tail, and is distributed from eastern Canada to Central America and Ecuador **b :** ALLIGATOR SNAPPER

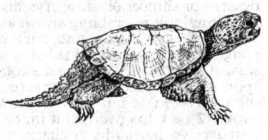

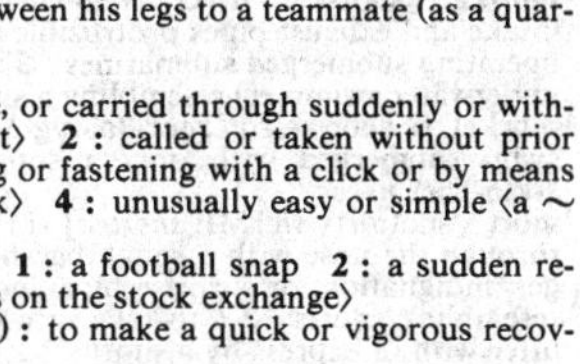
snapping turtle a

snap·pish \'snap-ish\ *adj* (1542) **1 a :** given to curt irritable speech **b :** arising from annoyance or irascibility **2 :** inclined to bite ⟨a ~ dog⟩ — **snap·pish·ly** *adv* — **snap·pish·ness** *n*

snap·py \'snap-ē\ *adj* **snap·pi·er; -est** (1746) **1 :** SNAPPISH 1 **2 a :** quickly made or done **b :** marked by vigor or liveliness **c :** briskly cold **d :** STYLISH, SMART ⟨a ~ dresser⟩ — **snap·pi·ly** \'snap-ə-lē\ *adv* — **snap·pi·ness** \'snap-ē-nəs\ *n*

snap roll *n* (ca. 1934) **:** a maneuver in which an airplane is made by quick movement of the controls to complete a full revolution about its longitudinal axis while maintaining an approximately level line of flight

snap·shoot·er \'snap-,shüt-ər\ *n* (1896) **:** a person who takes snapshots

snap·shot \'snap-,shät\ *n* (1890) **1 :** a casual photograph made typically by an amateur with a small hand-held camera and without regard to technique **2 :** an impression or view of something brief or transitory

1snare \'sna(ə)r, 'sne(ə)r\ *n* [ME, fr. OE *sneare,* fr. ON *snara;* akin to OHG *snuor* cord and prob. to Gk *narkē* numbness] (bef. 12c) **1 a** (1) **:** a contrivance often consisting of a noose for entangling birds or mammals (2) **:** TRAP, GIN **b** (1) **:** something by which one is entangled, involved in difficulties, or impeded (2) **:** something deceptively attractive **2** [prob. fr. D *snaar,* lit., cord; akin to OHG *snuor*] **:** one of the catgut strings or metal spirals of a snare drum **3 :** a surgical instrument consisting usu. of a wire loop constricted by a mechanism in the handle and used for removing tissue masses (as tonsils)

2snare *vt* **snared; snar·ing** (14c) **1 a :** to capture by or as if by use of a snare **b :** to win or attain by artful or skillful maneuvers **2 :** to entangle or hold as if in a snare ⟨any object that *snared* his eye —*Current Biog.*⟩ ***syn*** see CATCH — **snar·er** *n*

snare drum *n* (1873) **:** a small double-headed drum with one or more snares stretched across its lower head — see DRUM illustration

1snarl \'snär(-ə)l\ *n* [ME *snarle,* prob. dim. of *snare*] (14c) **1 :** a tangle esp. of hairs or thread : KNOT **2 :** a tangled situation ⟨traffic ~*s*⟩ — **snarly** \'snär-lē\ *adj*

2snarl *vt* (14c) **1 :** to cause to become knotted and intertwined : TANGLE **2 :** to make excessively complicated ~ *vi* **:** to become snarled — **snarl·er** *n*

3snarl *vb* [freq. of obs. E *snar* (to growl)] *vi* (1589) **1 :** to growl with a snapping or gnashing of teeth **2 :** to give vent to anger in surly language ~ *vt* **:** to utter or express with a snarl or by snarling — **snarl·er** *n*

4snarl *n* (1613) **:** a surly angry growl — **snarly** \'snär-lē\ *adj*

1snatch \'snach\ *vb* [ME *snacchen* to give a sudden snap, seize; akin to MD *snacken* to snap at] *vi* (13c) **:** to attempt to seize something suddenly ~ *vt* **:** to take or grasp abruptly or hastily; *also* **:** to seize or grab suddenly without permission, ceremony, or right ***syn*** see TAKE — **snatch·er** *n*

2snatch *n* (1563) **1 a :** a brief period ⟨caught ~*es* of sleep⟩ **b :** a brief, fragmentary, or hurried part : BIT ⟨caught ~*es* of the conversation⟩ **2 a :** a snatching at or of something **b** *slang* **:** an act or instance of kidnapping **3 :** a lift in weight lifting in which the weight is raised from the floor directly to an overhead position in a single motion — compare CLEAN AND JERK, PRESS

snatch block *n* (ca. 1625) **:** a block that can be opened on one side to receive the bight of a rope

snath \'snath, 'sneth\ *or* **snathe** \'snāth, 'snāth\ *n* [ME *snede,* fr. OE *snǣd;* akin to OHG *snīdan* to cut, Czech *snět* branch] (1574) **:** the handle of a scythe

snaz·zy \'snaz-ē\ *adj* **snaz·zi·er; -est** [origin unknown] (1932) **:** conspicuously or flashily attractive : FANCY

1sneak \'snēk\ *vb* **sneaked** \'snēkt\ *or* **snuck** \'snək\; **sneak·ing** [akin to OE *snīcan* to sneak along, OHG *snahhan* to creep — more at SNAIL] *vi* (1596) **1 :** to go stealthily or furtively : SLINK **2 :** to act in or as if in a furtive manner **3 :** to carry the football on a quarterback sneak ~ *vt* **:** to put, bring, or take in a furtive or artful manner ⟨~ a smoke⟩ ***syn*** see LURK — **sneak up on :** to approach or act on stealthily

2sneak *n* (1643) **1 :** a person who acts in a stealthy, furtive, or shifty manner **2 a :** a stealthy or furtive move **b :** an unobserved departure or escape **3 :** SNEAKER 2 **4 :** QUARTERBACK SNEAK

3sneak *adj* (ca. 1859) **1 :** carried on secretly : CLANDESTINE **2 :** occurring without warning : SURPRISE ⟨a ~ attack⟩

sneak·er \'snē-kər\ *n* (1598) **1 :** one that sneaks **2 :** a usu. canvas sports shoe with a pliable rubber sole — **sneak·ered** \-kərd\ *adj*

sneak·ing \'snē-kiŋ\ *adj* (1582) **1 :** MEAN, CONTEMPTIBLE **2 :** characteristic of a sneak : FURTIVE, UNDERHANDED **3 a :** not openly expressed or acknowledged ⟨he has a ~ respect for culture —H. A. Burton⟩ **b :** that is a persistent conjecture ⟨a ~ suspicion⟩ — **sneak·ing·ly** \-kiŋ-lē\ *adv*

sneak preview *n* (1937) **:** a special advance showing of a motion picture usu. announced but not named

sneak thief *n* (ca. 1859) **:** a thief who steals whatever he can without using violence or forcibly breaking into buildings

sneaky \'snē-kē\ *adj* **sneak·i·er; -est** (1833) **:** marked by stealth, furtiveness, or shiftiness — **sneak·i·ly** \-kə-lē\ *adv* — **sneak·i·ness** \-kē-nəs\ *n*

1sneap \'snēp\ *vt* [ME *snaipen,* prob. of Scand origin; akin to Icel *sneypa* to scold — more at SNUB] (14c) **1** *archaic* **:** to blast or blight with cold : NIP **2** *dial Eng* **:** CHIDE

2sneap *n, archaic* (1597) **:** REBUKE, SNUB

sneck \'snek\ *n* [ME *snekke*] *chiefly dial* (15c) **:** LATCH

1sneer \'sni(ə)r\ *vb* [prob. akin to MHG *snerren* to chatter, gossip — more at SNORE] *vi* (1680) **1 :** to smile or laugh with facial contortions that express scorn or contempt **2 :** to speak or write in a scornfully jeering manner ~ *vt* **:** to utter with a sneer ***syn*** see SCOFF — **sneer·er** *n*

2sneer *n* (1707) **:** the act of sneering; *also* **:** a sneering expression or remark

sneesh \'snēsh\ *n* [short for E dial. *sneeshing,* alter. of obs. E *sneezing,* fr. E, gerund of *sneeze*] *dial Brit* (1685) **:** 5SNUFF 1

1sneeze \'snēz\ *vi* **sneezed; sneez·ing** [ME *snesen,* alter. of *fnesen,* fr. OE *fnēosan;* akin to MHG *pfnūsen* to snort, sneeze, Gk *pnein* to breathe] (15c) **:** to make a sudden violent spasmodic audible expiration of breath through the nose and mouth esp. as a reflex act — **sneez·er** *n* — **sneeze at :** to make light of

2sneeze *n* (1646) **:** an act or instance of sneezing

sneeze·weed \'snēz-,wēd\ *n* (ca. 1837) **:** any of several composite plants; *esp* **:** a No. American yellow-flowered perennial herb (*Helenium autumnale*) whose odor is held to cause sneezing

sneezy \'snē-zē\ *adj* (1839) **:** given to or causing sneezing

1snell \'snel\ *adj* [ME, fr. OE; akin to OHG *snel* bold, agile] (bef. 12c) **1** *chiefly Scot* **:** QUICK, ACUTE **2** *chiefly Scot* **:** KEEN, PIERCING ⟨a ~ wind smote us —*Scotsman*⟩ **3** *chiefly Scot* **:** GRIEVOUS, SEVERE

2snell *n* [origin unknown] (1846) **:** a short line (as of gut) by which a fishhook is attached to a longer line

1snick \'snik\ *vb* [prob. fr. obs. *snick or snee* to engage in cut-and-thrust fighting — more at SNICKERSNEE] *vt* (ca. 1560) **1** *archaic* **:** to cut through **2 :** to cut slightly : NICK ~ *vi* **:** to perform a light cutting action

2snick *n* (ca. 1775) **:** a small cut : NICK

\ə\ abut \ᵊ\ kitten, F table \ər\ further \a\ ash \ā\ ace \ä\ cot, cart \au̇\ out \ch\ chin \e\ bet \ē\ easy \g\ go \i\ hit \ī\ ice \j\ job \ŋ\ sing \ō\ go \ȯ\ law \ȯi\ boy \th\ thin \t͟h\ the \ü\ loot \u̇\ foot \y\ yet \zh\ vision \à, k̲, ⁿ, œ, ᵫ, ue, ᵫ, ʸ\ see Guide to Pronunciation

[3]**snick** *vb* [imit.] (1828) : CLICK

[4]**snick** *n* (1886) : a slight often metallic sound : CLICK

[1]**snick·er** \'snik-ər\ *vi* **snick·ered; snick·er·ing** \-(ə-)riŋ\ [origin unknown] (1694) : to laugh in a covert or partly suppressed manner : TITTER — **snick·er·er** \-ər-ər\ *n* — **snick·ery** \-(ə-)rē\ *adj*

[2]**snicker** *n* (1835) : an act or sound of snickering

snick·er·snee \'snik-ə(r)-,snē\ *n* [obs. *snick or snee* to engage in cut-and-thrust fighting, alter. of earlier *steake or snye,* fr. D *steken of snijden* to thrust or cut] (ca. 1775) : a large knife

snide \'snīd\ *adj* [origin unknown] (ca. 1859) **1 a :** FALSE, COUNTERFEIT **b :** practicing deception : DISHONEST ⟨a ~ merchant⟩ **2 :** unworthy of esteem : LOW ⟨a ~ trick⟩ **3 :** slyly disparaging : INSINUATING ⟨~ remarks⟩ — **snide·ly** *adv* — **snide·ness** *n*

[1]**sniff** \'snif\ *vb* [ME *sniffen*] *vi* (14c) **1 :** to draw air audibly up the nose esp. for smelling ⟨~*ed* at the flowers⟩ **2 :** to show or express disdain or scorn ~ *vt* **1 :** to smell or take by inhalation through the nose **2 :** to utter contemptuously **3 :** to recognize or detect by or as if by smelling ⟨~ out trouble⟩

[2]**sniff** *n* (1767) **1 :** an act or sound of sniffing **2 :** a quantity that is sniffed

sniff·er *n* (1864) : one that sniffs; *esp* : one who takes drugs illicitly by sniffing

sniff·ish \'snif-ish\ *adj* (1923) : having or expressing a haughty attitude : DISDAINFUL, SUPERCILIOUS — **sniff·ish·ly** *adv* — **sniff·ish·ness** *n*

[1]**snif·fle** \'snif-əl\ *vi* **snif·fled; snif·fling** \-(ə-)liŋ\ [freq. of *sniff*] (ca. 1632) **1 :** to sniff repeatedly : SNUFFLE **2 :** to speak with or as if with sniffling — **snif·fler** \-(ə-)lər\ *n*

[2]**sniffle** *n* (ca. 1825) **1** *pl* **:** a head cold marked by nasal discharge **2 :** an act or sound of sniffling

sniffy \'snif-ē\ *adj* (1871) : SNIFFISH, SUPERCILIOUS — **sniff·i·ly** \'snif-ə-lē\ *adv* — **sniff·i·ness** \'snif-ē-nəs\ *n*

snif·ter \'snif-tər\ *n* [E dial., sniff, snort, fr. ME *snifteren* to sniff, snort] (1844) **1 :** a small drink of distilled liquor **2 :** a short-stemmed goblet with a bowl narrowing toward the top

[1]**snig·ger** \'snig-ər\ *vi* **snig·gered; snig·ger·ing** \-(ə-)riŋ\ [by alter.] (ca. 1706) : SNICKER — **snig·ger·er** \-ər-ər\ *n*

[2]**snigger** *n* (1823) : SNICKER

snig·gle \'snig-əl\ *vb* **snig·gled; snig·gling** \-(ə-)liŋ\ [E dial. *snig* small eel, fr. ME *snygge*] *vi* (1653) : to fish for eels by thrusting a baited hook or needle into their hiding places ~ *vt* : to catch (an eel) by sniggling

[1]**snip** \'snip\ *n* [fr. or akin to D & LG *snip*] (1558) **1 a :** a small piece that is snipped off; *also* : FRAGMENT, BIT **b :** a cut or notch made by snipping **c :** an act or sound of snipping **2 :** a white or light mark (as on a horse) **3 :** a presumptuous or impertinent person; *esp* : an impertinent or saucy girl **4** *Brit* **:** BARGAIN, BUY

[2]**snip** *vb* **snipped; snip·ping** *vt* (1586) : to cut or cut off with or as if with shears or scissors; *specif* : to clip suddenly or by bits ~ *vi* : to make a short quick cut with or as if with shears or scissors — **snip·per** *n*

[1]**snipe** \'snīp\ *n, pl* **snipes** [ME, of Scand origin; akin to ON *snīpa* snipe; akin to OHG *snepfa* snipe] (14c) **1** *or pl* **snipe :** any of various usu. slender-billed birds (suborder Charadrii); *esp* : any of several game birds (genera *Capella* and *Gallinago*) that occur esp. in marshy areas and resemble the related woodcocks **2 :** a contemptible person

[2]**snipe** *vi* **sniped; snip·ing** (1832) **1 :** to shoot at exposed individuals (as of an enemy's forces) from a usu. concealed point of vantage **2 :** to aim a carping or snide attack — **snip·er** *n*

snip·er·scope \'snī-pər-,skōp\ *n* (1918) : a snooperscope for use on a rifle or carbine

snip·per·snap·per \'snip-ər-,snap-ər\ *n* [origin unknown] (1590) : WHIPPERSNAPPER

snip·pet \'snip-ət\ *n* [[1]*snip*] (1664) : a small part, piece, or thing; *esp* : a brief quotable passage

snip·pety \-ət-ē\ *adj* (1864) **1 :** made up of snippets **2** [prob. fr. [2]*snip* + *-ety* (as in *pernickety*)] **:** SNIPPY

snip·py \'snip-ē\ *adj* **snip·pi·er; -est** [[2]*snip*] (ca. 1848) **1 :** SHORT-TEMPERED, SNAPPISH **2 :** unduly brief or curt **3 :** putting on airs : SNIFFY

snips \'snips\ *n pl but sing or pl in constr* (ca. 1846) : hand shears used esp. for cutting sheet metal

snit \'snit\ *n* [origin unknown] (1939) : a state of agitation

[1]**snitch** \'snich\ *n* [origin unknown] (1785) : one that snitches : TATTLETALE

[2]**snitch** *vi* [origin unknown] (1801) : INFORM, TATTLE ~ *vt* [prob. alter. of *snatch*] : to take by stealth : PILFER — **snitch·er** *n*

[1]**sniv·el** \'sniv-əl\ *vi* **-eled** *or* **-elled; -el·ing** *or* **-el·ling** \-(ə-)liŋ\ [ME *snivelen,* fr. (assumed) OE *snyflan;* akin to D *snuffelen* to snuffle, *snuffen* to sniff, Gk *nan* to flow — more at NOURISH] (14c) **1 :** to run at the nose **2 :** to snuff mucus up the nose audibly : SNUFFLE **3 :** to cry or whine with snuffling **4 :** to speak or act in a whining, sniffling, tearful, or weakly emotional manner — **sniv·el·er** \-(ə-)lər\ *n*

[2]**snivel** *n* (1600) **1** *pl, dial* **:** HEAD COLD **2 :** an act or instance of sniveling

snob \'snäb\ *n* [obs. *snob* member of the lower classes, fr. E dial., shoemaker] (1781) **1** *Brit* **:** COBBLER **2 :** one who blatantly imitates, fawningly admires, or vulgarly seeks association with those he regards as his superiors **3 a :** one who tends to rebuff, avoid, or ignore those he regards as inferior **b :** one who has an offensive air of superiority in matters of knowledge or taste

snob appeal *n* (1933) : qualities in a product that appeal to the snobbery in a purchaser

snob·bery \'snäb-(ə-)rē\ *n, pl* **-ber·ies** (1843) **1 :** snobbish conduct or character : SNOBBISHNESS **2 :** an instance of snobbery

snob·bish \'snäb-ish\ *adj* (1840) : being, characteristic of, or befitting a snob — **snob·bish·ly** *adv* — **snob·bish·ness** *n*

snob·bism \'snäb-,iz-əm\ *n* (1845) : SNOBBERY

snob·by \'snäb-ē\ *adj* **snob·bi·er; -est** (1846) : characterized by snobbery

Sno–Cat \'snō-,kat\ *trademark* — used for a tracklaying vehicle designed for travel on snow

sno–cone *var of* SNOW CONE

snol·ly·gos·ter \'snäl-ē-,gäs-tər\ *n* [prob. alter. of *snallygaster* (a mythical creature that preys on poultry and children)] (ca. 1860) : a shrewd unprincipled person

[1]**snood** \'snüd\ *n* [(assumed) ME, fr. OE *snōd;* akin to OIr *snáth* thread, OE *nǣdl* needle] (bef. 12c) **1 a** *Scot* **:** a fillet or band for a woman's hair **b :** a net or fabric bag pinned or tied on at the back of a woman's head for holding the hair **2 :** SNELL

[2]**snood** *vt* (1714) : to secure with a snood

[1]**snook** \'snu̇k, 'snük\ *n, pl* **snook** *or* **snooks** [D *snoek* pike, snook] (1697) **1 :** a large vigorous percoid sport and food fish (*Centropomus undecimalis*) of warm seas resembling a pike **2 :** any of various marine fishes other than the snook of the same family (Centropomidae)

[2]**snook** *n* [origin unknown] (1879) : a gesture of derision made by thumbing the nose

[1]**snook·er** \'snu̇k-ər\ *n* [origin unknown] (1889) : a variation of pool played with 15 red balls and 6 variously colored balls

[2]**snooker** *vt* (1925) : to make a dupe of : HOODWINK

[1]**snoop** \'snüp\ *vi* [D *snoepen* to buy or eat on the sly; akin to D *snappen* to snap] (1832) : to look or pry esp. in a sneaking or meddlesome manner — **snoop·er** *n*

[2]**snoop** *n* (ca. 1890) : one that snoops

snoop·er·scope \'snü-pər-,skōp\ *n* (1946) : a device utilizing infrared radiation for enabling a person to see an object that is obscured (as by darkness)

snoopy \'snü-pē\ *adj* (ca. 1895) : given to snooping esp. for personal information about others — **snoop·i·ly** \-pə-lē\ *adv*

[1]**snoot** \'snüt\ *n* [ME *snute*] (1861) **1 a :** SNOUT **b :** NOSE **2 :** a grimace expressive of contempt **3 :** a snooty person : SNOB

[2]**snoot** *vt* (1931) : to treat with disdain : look down one's nose at

snooty \'snüt-ē\ *adj* **snoot·i·er; -est** (ca. 1920) **1 :** looking down the nose : showing disdain ⟨~ people who won't speak to their neighbors⟩ **2 :** characterized by snobbery ⟨a ~ store⟩ — **snoot·i·ly** \'snüt-ᵊl-ē\ *adv* — **snoot·i·ness** \'snüt-ē-nəs\ *n*

[1]**snooze** \'snüz\ *vi* **snoozed; snooz·ing** [origin unknown] (1788) : to take a nap : DOZE — **snooz·er** *n*

[2]**snooze** *n* (1793) : NAP

snoo·zle \'snü-zəl\ *vb* **snoo·zled; snoo·zling** \'snüz-(ə-)liŋ\ [perh. blend of *snooze* and *nuzzle*] *chiefly dial* (1831) : NUZZLE

[1]**snore** \'snō(ə)r, 'snȯ(ə)r\ *vb* **snored; snor·ing** [ME *snoren;* akin to MLG *snorren* to drone, MHG *snerren* to chatter] *vi* (15c) : to breathe during sleep with a rough hoarse noise due to vibration of the soft palate ~ *vt* : to spend (time) in snoring or sleeping — **snor·er** *n*

[2]**snore** *n* (1605) **1 :** an act of snoring **2 :** a noise of or as if of snoring

[1]**snor·kel** \'snȯr-kəl\ *n* [G *schnorchel*] (1944) **1 :** a tube housing air intake and exhaust pipes protrusible above the surface of the water for operating submerged submarines **2 :** any of various devices (as for an underwater swimmer) resembling a snorkel in function

[2]**snorkel** *vi* **snor·keled; snor·kel·ing** \-k(ə-)liŋ\ (1949) : to operate or swim submerged with only a snorkel above water — **snor·kel·er** \-k(ə-)lər\ *n*

[1]**snort** \'snȯ(ə)rt\ *vb* [ME *snorten*] *vi* (14c) **1 a :** to force air violently through the nose with a rough harsh sound **b :** to express scorn, anger, indignation, or surprise by a snort **2 :** to emit explosive sounds resembling snorts **3 :** to take in a drug by inhalation ~ *vt* **1 :** to utter with or express by a snort **2 :** to expel or emit with or as if with snorts **3 :** to take in (a drug) by inhalation

[2]**snort** *n* (1808) **1 :** an act or sound of snorting **2 :** a drink of usu. straight liquor taken in one draft

snort·er \'snȯrt-ər\ *n* (1601) **1 :** one that snorts **2 :** something that is extraordinary or prominent : HUMDINGER **3 :** SNORT 2

snot \'snät\ *n* [ME, fr. OE *gesnot;* akin to OHG *snuzza* nasal mucus, Gk *nan* to flow — more at NOURISH] (bef. 12c) **1 :** nasal mucus **2 :** a snotty person

snot·ty \'snät-ē\ *adj* **snot·ti·er; -est** (ca. 1570) **1 :** foul with nasal mucus **2 :** annoyingly or spitefully unpleasant — **snot·ti·ly** \'snät-ᵊl-ē\ *adv* — **snot·ti·ness** \'snät-ē-nəs\ *n*

snout \'snau̇t\ *n* [ME *snute;* akin to G *schnauze* snout] (13c) **1 a** (1) **:** a long projecting nose (as of a swine) (2) **:** an anterior prolongation of the head of various animals (as a weevil) : ROSTRUM **b :** the human nose esp. when large or grotesque **2 :** something resembling an animal's snout in position, function, or shape: as **a :** PROW **b :** NOZZLE **c :** the terminal face of a glacier — **snout·ed** \-əd\ *adj* — **snout·ish** \-ish\ *adj* — **snouty** \-ē\ *adj*

snout beetle *n* (1862) : WEEVIL

[1]**snow** \'snō\ *n, often attrib* [ME, fr. OE *snāw;* akin to OHG *snēo* snow, L *niv-, nix,* Gk *nipha* (acc.)] (bef. 12c) **1 a :** precipitation in the form of small tabular and columnar white ice crystals formed directly from the water vapor of the air at a temperature of less than 32°F **b** (1) **:** a descent or shower of snow crystals (2) **:** a mass of fallen snow crystals **2 :** something resembling snow: as **a :** a dessert made of stiffly beaten whites of eggs, sugar, and fruit pulp ⟨apple ~⟩ **b :** any of various congealed or crystallized substances resembling snow in appearance **c** *slang* (1) **:** COCAINE (2) **:** HEROIN **d :** small transient light or dark spots on a television or radar screen — **snow·less** \-ləs\ *adj*

[2]**snow** *vi* (14c) : to fall in or as snow ~ *vt* **1 :** to cause to fall like or as snow **2 a :** to cover, shut in, or imprison with or as if with snow **b :** to deceive, persuade, or charm glibly **3 :** to whiten like snow

[1]**snow·ball** \'snō-,bȯl\ *n* (15c) **1 a :** a round mass of snow pressed or rolled together **b :** shaved ice molded into a ball and flavored with a syrup **2 :** any of several cultivated shrubs (genus *Viburnum*) with clusters of white sterile flowers — called also *snowball bush*

[2]**snowball** *vt* (1854) **1 :** to throw snowballs at **2 :** to cause to increase or multiply at a rapidly accelerating rate ~ *vi* **1 :** to engage in throwing snowballs **2 :** to increase, accumulate, expand, or multiply at a rapidly accelerating rate

snow·bank \'snō-,baŋk\ *n* (1779) : a mound or slope of snow

snow·belt \-,belt\ *n, often cap* (1874) : a region that receives an appreciable amount of annual snowfall

snow·ber·ry \-,ber-ē\ *n* (1760) : any of several white-berried shrubs (esp. genus *Symphoricarpos* of the honeysuckle family); *esp* : a low-growing No. American shrub (*S. albus*) with pink flowers in small axillary clusters

snow·bird \-,bərd\ *n* (1674) **1 :** any of several small birds (as a junco or fieldfare) seen chiefly in winter **2 :** one who travels to warm climes for the winter

snow–blind \-,blīnd\ *or* **snow–blind·ed** \-,blīn-dəd\ *adj* (1748) : affected with snow blindness

snow blindness *n* (1748) : inflammation and photophobia caused by exposure of the eyes to ultraviolet rays reflected from snow or ice

snow·blink \'snō-ˌbliŋk\ *n* (1863) **:** a white glare in the sky over a snowfield
snow·blow·er \-ˌblō(-ə)r\ *n* (1950) **1 :** a machine using blasts of air to remove snow (as from a railroad) **2 :** SNOW THROWER
snow·bound \-'baůnd\ *adj* (1814) **:** shut in or blockaded by snow
snow·brush \'snō-ˌbrəsh\ *n* (ca. 1923) **:** any of several white-flowered shrubs (genus *Ceanothus*) of the buckthorn family; *esp* **:** a spreading western No. American shrub (*C. velutinus*) with scented leaves and panicles of small flowers
snow·cap \-ˌkap\ *n* (1871) **:** a covering cap of snow (as on a mountain peak) — **snow·capped** \-'kapt\ *adj*
snow cone *n* (1964) **:** SNOWBALL 1b
snow·drift \-ˌdrift\ *n* (14c) **:** a bank of drifted snow
snow·drop \-ˌdräp\ *n* (1664) **:** a bulbous European herb (*Galanthus nivalis*) of the amaryllis family bearing nodding white flowers that often appear while the snow is on the ground
snow·fall \-ˌfȯl\ *n* (1821) **:** a fall of snow; *specif* **:** the amount of snow that falls in a single storm or in a given period
snow fence *n* (1872) **:** a usu. slatted fence placed across the path of prevailing winds to protect (as a building, road, or railroad track) from drifting snow by disrupting the flow of wind and causing the snow to be deposited on the lee side of the fence
snow·field \'snō-ˌfēld\ *n* (1845) **:** a broad level expanse of snow; *esp* **:** a mass of perennial snow at the head of a glacier
snow·flake \-ˌflāk\ *n* (1734) **1 :** a flake or crystal of snow **2 :** any of a genus (*Leucojum*) of bulbous plants of the amaryllis family; *esp* **:** one (*L. vernum*) resembling the snowdrop
snow job *n* (1945) **:** an intensive effort at persuasion or deception
snow leopard *n* (1866) **:** a showily marked large cat (*Felis uncia*) of upland central Asia with a long heavy pelt that is grayish white irregularly blotched with brownish black in summer and almost pure white in winter

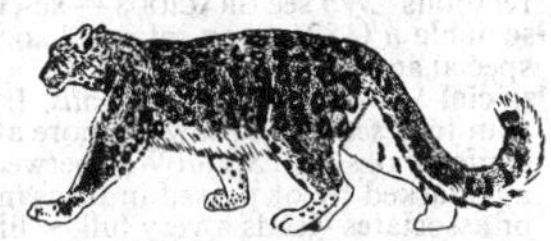
snow leopard

snow line *n* (ca. 1835) **:** the lower margin of a perennial snowfield
snow·mak·er \'snō-ˌmā-kər\ *n* (1954) **:** a device for making snow artificially
snow·mak·ing \-ˌmā-kiŋ\ *adj* (1953) **:** used for the production of artificial snow usu. for ski slopes ⟨~ machines⟩
snow·man \-ˌman, -'man\ *n* (1827) **:** snow shaped to resemble a human figure
snow·melt \-ˌmelt\ *n* (ca. 1946) **:** runoff produced by the melting of snow
snow·mo·bile \'snō-mō-ˌbēl\ *n* [¹*snow* + auto*mobile*] (1923) **:** any of various automotive vehicles for travel on snow
snow·mo·bil·ing \-ˌbē-liŋ\ *n* (1967) **:** the sport of driving a snowmobile — **snow·mo·bil·er** \-lər\ *also* **snow·mo·bil·ist** \-ləst\ *n*
snow–on–the–mountain *n* (1878) **:** a spurge (*Euphorbia marginata*) of the western U.S. that has showy white-bracted flower clusters and is grown as an ornamental
snow·pack \'snō-ˌpak\ *n* (ca. 1946) **:** a seasonal accumulation of slow-melting packed snow
snow pea *n* (1954) **:** any of a variety (*Pisum sativum macrocarpon*) of the cultivated pea with edible pods — called also *sugar pea*
snow plant *n* (1846) **:** a fleshy bright-red saprophytic California herb (*Sarcodes sanguinea*) of the wintergreen family that grows in coniferous woods at high altitudes and often appears before the snow melts
¹snow·plow \'snō-ˌplaů\ *n* (1792) **1 :** any of various devices used for clearing away snow **2 :** a stemming with both skis used for coming to a stop, slowing down, or descending slowly
²snowplow *vi* (ca. 1939) **:** to execute a snowplow ⟨~*ed* to a stop⟩
snow pudding *n* (ca. 1885) **:** a pudding made very fluffy and light by the addition of whipped egg whites and gelatin
snow·scape \'snō-ˌskāp\ *n* (1886) **:** a landscape covered with snow
snow·shed \-ˌshed\ *n* (1868) **:** a shelter against snowslides
¹snow·shoe \-ˌshü\ *n* (1666) **:** a light oval wooden frame that is strengthened by two crosspieces, strung with thongs, and attached to the foot and that is used to enable a person to walk on soft snow without sinking
²snowshoe *vi* **snow·shoed; snow·shoe·ing** (1880) **:** to travel on snowshoes — **snow·sho·er** \-ˌshü-ər\ *n*
snowshoe rabbit *n* (ca. 1889) **:** a rather large rabbit (*Lepus americanus*) of northern No. America with heavy fur on the hind feet and a coat that in most populations is brown in the summer but usu. white in the winter — called also *snowshoe hare, varying hare*
snow·slide \'snō-ˌslīd\ *n* (1841) **:** an avalanche of snow
snow·storm \-ˌstȯrm\ *n* (1771) **1 :** a storm of or with snow **2 :** something that resembles a snowstorm
snow·suit \-ˌsüt\ *n* (1937) **:** a one-piece or two-piece lined garment for winter wear by children
snow thrower *n* (1954) **:** a snowplow in which a rotating device picks up and propels snow aside
snow tire *n* (1943) **:** an automotive tire with a tread designed to give added traction on snow or ice
snow under *vt* (1880) **1 :** to overwhelm esp. in excess of capacity to absorb or deal with something **2 :** to defeat by a large margin
snow–white \'snō-'hwīt, -'wīt\ *adj* (bef. 12c) **:** white as snow
snowy \'snō-ē\ *adj* **snow·i·er; -est** (bef. 12c) **1 a :** composed of snow or melted snow **b :** marked by or covered with snow **2 a :** whitened by snow **b :** SNOW-WHITE — **snow·i·ly** \'snō-ə-lē\ *adv* — **snow·i·ness** \'snō-ē-nəs\ *n*
¹snub \'snəb\ *vt* **snubbed; snub·bing** [ME *snubben,* of Scand origin; akin to ON *snubba* to scold; akin to Icel *sneypa* to scold] (14c) **1 :** to check or stop with a cutting retort **:** REBUKE **2 a :** to check (as a line) suddenly while running out esp. by turning around a fixed object (as a post); *also* **:** to check the motion of by snubbing a line **b :** to restrain the action of **:** SUPPRESS ⟨~ a vibration⟩ **3 :** to treat with contempt or neglect **4 :** to extinguish by stubbing ⟨~ out a cigarette⟩
²snub *n* (1537) **:** an act or an instance of snubbing; *esp* **:** SLIGHT
³snub *adj* (1724) **1** *or* **snubbed** \'snəbd\ **:** BLUNT, STUBBY ⟨a ~ nose⟩ **2 :** used in snubbing ⟨~ line⟩ — **snub·ness** *n*
snub·ber \'snəb-ər\ *n* (1853) **1 :** one that snubs **2 :** SHOCK ABSORBER
snub·by \'snəb-ē\ *adj* (1828) **1 :** SNUB **2 :** SNUB-NOSED — **snub·bi·ness** *n*
snub–nosed \'snəb-'nōzd\ *adj* (1725) **1 :** having a stubby and usu. slightly turned-up nose **2 :** having a very short barrel ⟨a ~ revolver⟩
snuck *past and past part of* SNEAK
¹snuff \'snəf\ *n* [ME *snoffe*] (14c) **1 :** the charred part of a candlewick **2 a** *obs* **:** UMBRAGE, OFFENSE **b** *chiefly Scot* **:** HUFF
²snuff *vt* (1527) **1 :** to crop the snuff of (a candle) by pinching or by the use of snuffers so as to brighten the light **2 a :** to extinguish by the use of a snuffer **b :** to make extinct **:** put an end to — usu. used with *out* ⟨an accident that ~*ed* out a life⟩
³snuff *vb* [akin to D *snuffen* to sniff, snuff — more at SNIVEL] *vt* (1527) **1 :** to draw forcibly through or into the nostrils **2 :** SCENT, SMELL **3 :** to sniff at in order to examine — used of an animal ~ *vi* **1 :** to inhale through the nose noisily and forcibly; *also* **:** to sniff or smell inquiringly **2** *obs* **:** to sniff loudly in or as if in disgust **3 :** to take snuff
⁴snuff *n* (1570) **:** the act of snuffing **:** SNIFF
⁵snuff *n* [D *snuf,* short for *snuftabak,* fr. *snuffen* to snuff + *tabak* tobacco] (1671) **1 :** a preparation of pulverized tobacco to be inhaled through the nostrils, chewed, or placed against the gums **2 :** the amount of snuff taken at one time — **up to snuff :** of sufficient quality **:** meeting an applicable standard
snuff·box \'snəf-ˌbäks\ *n* (ca. 1687) **:** a small box for holding snuff usu. carried about the person
¹snuff·er \'snəf-ər\ *n* (15c) **1 :** a device somewhat like a pair of scissors for cropping and holding the snuff of a candle — usu. used in pl. but sing. or pl. in constr. **2 :** a device for extinguishing candles
²snuffer *n* (1610) **:** one that snuffs or sniffs
¹snuf·fle \'snəf-əl\ *vb* **snuf·fled; snuf·fling** \-(ə-)liŋ\ [akin to D *snuffelen* to snuffle — more at SNIVEL] *vi* (1583) **1 :** to snuff or sniff usu. audibly and repeatedly **2 :** to breathe through an obstructed nose with a sniffing sound **3 :** to speak through or as if through the nose **:** WHINE ~ *vt* **:** to seek or test by or as if by repeated sniffs — **snuf·fler** \-(ə-)lər\ *n*
²snuffle *n* (1764) **1 :** the act or sound of snuffling **2 :** a nasal twang **3** *pl* **:** SNIFFLES
¹snuffy \'snəf-ē\ *adj* [³*snuff*] (1678) **1 :** quick to become annoyed or take offense **2 :** marked by snobbery
²snuffy *adj* [⁵*snuff*] (1787) **1 :** resembling snuff **2 a :** addicted to the use of snuff **b :** having unpleasant habits **3 :** soiled with snuff
¹snug \'snəg\ *vb* **snugged; snug·ging** *vi* (1583) **:** SNUGGLE ~ *vt* **1 :** to cause to fit closely **2 :** to make snug **3 :** HIDE **4 :** to secure by fastening or lashing down
²snug *adj* **snug·ger; snug·gest** [perh. of Scand origin; akin to Sw *snygg* tidy; akin to ON *snøggr* shorn, bald, L *novacula* razor] (1595) **1 a** *of a ship* **:** manifesting seaworthiness **:** TAUT **b :** TRIM, NEAT **c :** fitting closely and comfortably ⟨a ~ coat⟩ **2 a :** enjoying or affording warm secure shelter or cover and opportunity for ease and contentment **b :** marked by cordiality and secure privacy **3 :** affording a degree of comfort and ease **4 :** offering safe concealment ⟨a ~ hideout⟩ ***syn*** see COMFORTABLE — **snug** *adv* — **snug·ly** *adv* — **snug·ness** *n*
³snug *n* [short for *snuggery*] *Brit* (1864) **:** a small private room in a pub
snug·gery \'snəg-(ə-)rē\ *n, pl* **-ger·ies** *chiefly Brit* (1812) **:** a snug cozy place; *esp* **:** a small room
snug·gle \'snəg-əl\ *vb* **snug·gled; snug·gling** \-(ə-)liŋ\ [freq. of ¹*snug*] *vi* (ca. 1687) **:** to curl up comfortably or cozily ~ *vt* **1 :** to draw close esp. for comfort or in affection **2 :** to make snug
¹so \(ˈ)sō, *esp before adj or adv followed by "that"* sə\ *adv* [ME, fr. OE *swā;* akin to OHG *sō* so, L *sic* so, thus, *si* if, Gk *hōs* so, thus, L *suus* one's own — more at SUICIDE] (bef. 12c) **1 a :** in a manner or way indicated or suggested ⟨do you really think ~⟩ — often used as a substitute for a preceding clause ⟨are you ready? I think ~⟩ ⟨I didn't like it and I told her ~⟩ **b :** in the same manner or way **:** ALSO ⟨worked hard and ~ did she⟩ **c :** THUS ⟨for ~ the Lord said —Isa 18:4 (AV)⟩ **d :** THEN, SUBSEQUENTLY ⟨and ~ home and to bed⟩ **2 a :** to an indicated or suggested extent or degree ⟨had never been ~ happy⟩ **b :** to a great extent or degree **:** VERY, EXTREMELY ⟨loves her ~⟩ **c :** to a definite but unspecified extent or degree ⟨can only do ~ much in a day⟩ **d :** most certainly **:** INDEED ⟨you did ~ do it⟩ **3 :** THEREFORE, CONSEQUENTLY ⟨the witness is biased and ~ unreliable⟩
usage The intensive use of *so* (sense 2b) has been condemned as overworked at least since 1917 but nonetheless continues to thrive esp. in speech. In writing it is more common in informal contexts but is not limited to them ⟨the international rules, which *so* favor an aggressive offense —Frank Deford⟩ ⟨the cephalopod eye is an example of a remarkable evolutionary parallel because it is *so* like the eye of a vertebrate —Sarah F. Robbins⟩ ⟨the kind of sterile over-ingenuity which afflicts *so* many academic efforts —*Times Lit. Supp.*⟩ There is no stigma attached to its use in negative contexts and when qualified by a dependent clause ⟨not *so* long ago⟩ ⟨was *so* good in mathematics that he began to consider engineering —*Current Biog.*⟩ The denotation in these uses is, of course, slightly different (see sense 2a).
²so \(ˈ)sō\ *conj* (bef. 12c) **1 a :** with the result that ⟨the acoustics are good, ~ every note is clear⟩ **b :** in order that ⟨be quiet ~ he can sleep⟩ **2** *archaic* **:** provided that **3 a :** for that reason **:** THEREFORE ⟨don't want to go, ~ I won't⟩ **b** (1) — used as an introductory particle ⟨~ here we are⟩ often to belittle a point under discussion ⟨~ what?⟩ (2) — used interjectionally to indicate awareness of a discovery ⟨~, that's who did it⟩ or surprised dissent
usage Although occas. condemned, use of *so* to introduce clauses of result (sense 1a) and purpose (sense 1b) is standard. In sense 1b *so that* is more common in formal contexts than *so* alone.
³so \'sō\ *adj* (bef. 12c) **1 :** conforming with actual facts **:** TRUE ⟨said things that were not ~⟩ **2 :** marked by a desired order ⟨his books are always just ~⟩ **3** — used to replace a preceding adjective ⟨was witty by adult standards and of course doubly ~ by mine —Sally Kempton⟩
⁴so \ˌsō, 'sō\ *pron* (bef. 12c) **1 :** such as has been specified or suggested **:** the same ⟨if you have to file a claim, do ~ as soon as possible⟩ **2** —

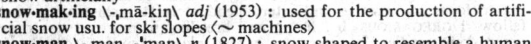

used in the phrase *or so* to indicate an estimate, approximation, or conjecture ⟨stayed a week or ∼⟩ ⟨cost $15 or ∼⟩

⁵**so** \'sō\ *var of* SOL

¹**soak** \'sōk\ *vb* [ME *soken,* fr. OE *socian;* akin to OE *sūcan* to suck] *vi* (bef. 12c) **1 :** to lie immersed in liquid (as water) **2 a :** to enter or pass through something by or as if by pores or interstices **:** PERMEATE **b :** to penetrate or affect the mind or feelings — usu. used with *in* or *into* **3 :** to drink alcoholic beverages intemperately ∼ *vt* **1 :** to permeate so as to wet, soften, or fill thoroughly **2 :** to place in a surrounding element (as liquid) to wet or permeate thoroughly **3 :** to extract by or as if by steeping ⟨∼ the dirt out⟩ **4 a :** to draw in by or as if by suction or absorption ⟨∼ed up the sunshine⟩ **b :** to intoxicate (oneself) by drinking alcoholic beverages **5 :** to cause to pay an exorbitant amount — **soak·er** *n*

syn SOAK, SATURATE, DRENCH, STEEP, IMPREGNATE mean to permeate or be permeated with a liquid. SOAK implies usu. prolonged immersion as for softening or cleansing; SATURATE implies a resulting effect of complete absorption until no more liquid can be held; DRENCH implies a thorough wetting by something that pours down or is poured; STEEP suggests either the extraction of an essence (as of tea leaves) by the liquid or the imparting of a quality (as a color) to the thing immersed; IMPREGNATE implies a thorough interpenetration of one thing by another.

²**soak** *n* (1598) **1 a :** the act or process of soaking **:** the state of being soaked **b :** that (as liquid) in which something is soaked **2 :** DRUNKARD **3** *slang* **:** ²PAWN 2

soak·age \'sō-kij\ *n* (1766) **1 :** liquid gained by absorption or lost by seepage **2 :** the act or process of soaking **:** the state of being soaked

¹**so-and-so** \'sō-ən-,sō\ *n, pl* **so-and-sos** *or* **so-and-so's** \-,sōz\ (1596) **1 :** an unnamed or unspecified person, thing, or action **2 :** BASTARD 3

²**so-and-so** *adv* (1631) **1 :** to an unspecified amount or degree **2 :** in an unspecified manner or fashion

¹**soap** \'sōp\ *n* [ME *sope,* fr. OE *sāpe;* akin to OHG *seifa* soap, L *sebum* tallow] (bef. 12c) **1 a :** a cleansing and emulsifying agent made usu. by action of alkali on fat or fatty acids and consisting essentially of sodium or potassium salts of such acids **b :** a salt of a fatty acid and a metal **2 :** SOAP OPERA

²**soap** *vt* (1585) **1 :** to rub soap over or into **2 :** FLATTER

soap·bark \'sōp-,bärk\ *n* (1861) **:** a Chilean tree (*Quillaja saponaria*) of the rose family with shining leaves and terminal white flowers; *also* **:** its saponin-rich bark used in cleaning and in emulsifying oils

soap·ber·ry \-,ber-ē\ *n* (1693) **:** any of a genus (*Sapindus* of the family Sapindaceae, the soapberry family) of chiefly tropical woody plants; *also* **:** the fruit of a soapberry and esp. of a tree (*S. saponaria*) that is saponin-rich and used as a soap substitute

soap·box \-,bäks\ *n* (1917) **:** an improvised platform used by a self-appointed, spontaneous, or informal orator — **soapbox** *adj*

soap bubble *n* (1815) **:** a hollow iridescent globe formed by blowing a film of soapsuds (as from a pipe)

soap·er \'sō-pər\ *n* (1946) **:** SOAP OPERA

soap opera *n* [fr. its frequently being sponsored by soap manufacturers] (1939) **:** a serial drama performed usu. on a daytime radio or television program and chiefly characterized by tangled interpersonal situations and melodramatic or sentimental treatment

soap plant *n* (1844) **:** a plant having a part (as a root or fruit) that may be used in place of soap; *esp* **:** a California plant (*Chlorogalum pomeridianum*) of the lily family

soap·stone \'sōp-,stōn\ *n* (ca. 1681) **:** a soft stone having a soapy feel and composed essentially of talc, chlorite, and often some magnetite

soap·suds \-,sədz\ *n pl* (1611) **:** SUDS 1

soap·wort \-,wərt, -,wȯ(ə)rt\ *n* (1548) **:** BOUNCING BET

soapy \'sō-pē\ *adj* **soap·i·er; -est** (1610) **1 :** smeared with soap **:** LATHERED **2 :** containing or combined with soap or saponin **3 a :** resembling or having the qualities of soap; *esp* **:** being smooth and slippery **b :** UNCTUOUS, SUAVE **4 :** of, relating to, or having the characteristics of soap opera — **soap·i·ly** \-pə-lē\ *adv* — **soap·i·ness** \-pē-nəs\ *n*

¹**soar** \'sō(ə)r, 'sȯ(ə)r\ *vi* [ME *soren,* fr. MF *essorer* to air, soar, fr. (assumed) VL *exaurare* to air, fr. L *ex-* + *aura* air — more at AURA] (14c) **1 a :** to fly aloft or about **b** (1) **:** to sail or hover in the air often at a great height **:** GLIDE (2) *of a glider* **:** to fly without engine power and without loss of altitude **2 :** to rise or increase dramatically (as in position, value, or price) **3 :** to ascend to a higher or more exalted level **4 :** to rise to majestic stature — **soar·er** *n*

²**soar** *n* (1596) **1 :** the range, distance, or height attained in soaring **2 :** the act of soaring **:** upward flight

soar·ing *n* (1575) **:** the act or process of soaring; *specif* **:** the act or sport of flying a heavier-than-air craft without power by utilizing ascending air currents

Soa·ve \'swäv-(,)ā, sə-'wäv-\ *n* [Soave, village near Verona, Italy] (1943) **:** a dry white Italian wine

¹**sob** \'säb\ *vb* **sobbed; sob·bing** [ME *sobben*] *vi* (13c) **1 a :** to catch the breath audibly in a spasmodic contraction of the throat **b :** to cry or weep with convulsive catching of the breath **2 :** to make a sound like that of a sob or sobbing ∼ *vt* **1 :** to bring (as oneself) to a specified state by sobbing ⟨*sobbed* himself to sleep⟩ **2 :** to utter with sobs ⟨*sobbed* out her grief⟩

²**sob** *n* (14c) **1 :** an act of sobbing **2 :** a sound like that of a sob

SOB \,es-,ō-'bē\ *n* [son of a bitch] (ca. 1925) **:** BASTARD 3, SON OF A BITCH

¹**so·ber** \'sō-bər\ *adj* **so·ber·er** \-bər-ər\; **so·ber·est** \-b(ə-)rəst\ [ME *sobre,* fr. MF, fr. L *sobrius;* akin to L *ebrius* drunk] (14c) **1 a :** sparing in the use of food and drink **:** ABSTEMIOUS **b :** not addicted to intoxicating drink **c :** not drunk **2 :** marked by sedate or gravely or earnestly thoughtful character or demeanor **3** *archaic* **:** UNHURRIED, CALM **4 :** marked by temperance, moderation, or seriousness **5 :** subdued in tone or color **6 :** showing no excessive or extreme qualities of fancy, emotion, or prejudice *syn* see SERIOUS — **so·ber·ly** \-bər-lē\ *adv* — **so·ber·ness** *n*

²**sober** *vb* **so·bered; so·ber·ing** \-b(ə-)riŋ\ *vt* (14c) **:** to make sober ∼ *vi* **:** to become sober — usu. used with *up*

so·ber·ing *adj* (1831) **:** tending to make one thoughtful or sober

so·ber·ize \'sō-bə-,rīz\ *vt* **-ized; -iz·ing** *archaic* (1706) **:** to make sober

so·ber·sid·ed \,sō-bər-'sīd-əd\ *adj* (1847) **:** solemn or serious in nature or appearance

so·ber·sides \'sō-bər-,sīdz\ *n pl but sing or pl in constr* (1705) **:** one who is sobersided

so·bri·ety \sə-'brī-ət-ē, sō-\ *n* [ME *sobrietie,* fr. MF *sobrieté,* fr. L *sobrietat-, sobrietas,* fr. *sobrius*] (14c) **:** the quality or state of being sober

so·bri·quet \'sō-bri-,kā, -,ket, ,sō-bri-'\ *n* [F] (1646) **:** a descriptive name or epithet **:** NICKNAME

sob sister *n* (1912) **1 :** a journalist who specializes in writing or editing sob stories or other material of a sentimental type **2 :** a sentimental and often impractical person usu. engaged in good works

sob story *n* (1916) **:** a sentimental story or account intended chiefly to evoke sympathy or sadness

so·cage \'säk-ij, 'sōk-\ *also* **soc·cage** \'säk-\ *n* [ME, fr. *soc* soke] (14c) **:** a tenure of land by agricultural service fixed in amount and kind or by payment of money rent only and not burdened with any military service — **so·cag·er** \-ij-ər\ *n*

so-called \'sō-'kȯld\ *adj* (1657) **1 :** commonly named **:** popularly so termed ⟨the ∼ pocket veto⟩ **2 :** falsely or improperly so named ⟨deceived by a ∼ friend⟩

soc·cer \'säk-ər\ *n* [by shortening & alter. fr. *association football*] (1891) **:** a game played on a field between two teams of 11 players each with the object to propel a round ball into the opponent's goal by kicking or by hitting it with any part of the body except the hands and arms — called also *association football*

so·cia·bil·i·ty \,sō-shə-'bil-ət-ē\ *n, pl* **-ties** (15c) **:** the quality or state of being sociable; *also* **:** the act or an instance of being sociable

¹**so·cia·ble** \'sō-shə-bəl\ *adj* [MF or L; MF, fr. L *sociabilis,* fr. *sociare* to join, associate, fr. *socius*] (1553) **1 :** inclined by nature to companionship with others of the same species **:** SOCIAL **2 a :** inclined to seek or enjoy companionship **b :** conducive to friendliness or pleasant social relations *syn* see GRACIOUS — **so·cia·ble·ness** *n* — **so·cia·bly** \-blē\ *adv*

²**sociable** *n* (1826) **:** an informal social gathering frequently involving a special activity or interest

¹**so·cial** \'sō-shəl\ *adj* [L *socialis,* fr. *socius* companion, ally, associate; akin to L *sequi* to follow — more at SUE] (1665) **1 :** involving allies or confederates ⟨the *Social* War between the Athenians and their allies⟩ **2 a :** marked by or passed in pleasant companionship with one's friends or associates ⟨leads a very full ∼ life⟩ **b :** SOCIABLE **c :** of, relating to, or designed for sociability ⟨a ∼ club⟩ **3 :** of or relating to human society, the interaction of the individual and the group, or the welfare of human beings as members of society ⟨∼ institutions⟩ **4 a :** tending to form cooperative and interdependent relationships with one's fellows **:** GREGARIOUS **b :** living and breeding in more or less organized communities ⟨∼ insects⟩ **c** *of a plant* **:** tending to grow in groups or masses so as to form a pure stand **5 a :** of, relating to, or based on rank or status in a particular society ⟨a member of our ∼ set⟩ **b :** of, relating to, or characteristic of the upper classes **c :** FORMAL

²**social** *n* (1870) **:** SOCIABLE

social climber *n* (1924) **:** one who attempts to gain a higher social position or acceptance in fashionable society — **social climbing** *n*

social contract *n* [trans. of F *contrat social*] (1849) **:** an actual or hypothetical agreement among individuals forming an organized society or between the community and the ruler that defines and limits the rights and duties of each

social Darwinism *n* (1939) **:** an extension of Darwinism to social phenomena; *specif* **:** a theory in sociology: sociocultural advance is the product of intergroup conflict and competition and the socially elite classes (as those possessing wealth and power) possess biological superiority in the struggle for existence

social democracy *n* (ca. 1890) **:** a political movement advocating a gradual and peaceful transition from capitalism to socialism by democratic means — **social democrat** *n* — **social democratic** *adj*

social disease *n* (1918) **1 :** VENEREAL DISEASE **2 :** a disease (as tuberculosis) whose incidence is directly related to social and economic factors

social engineering *n* (1925) **:** management of human beings in accordance with their place and function in society **:** applied social science — **social engineer** *n*

social gospel *n* (1920) **1 :** the application of Christian principles to social problems **2** *cap S&G* **:** a movement in American Protestant Christianity esp. in the first part of the 20th century to bring the social order into conformity with Christian principles

social insurance *n* (1917) **:** protection of the individual against economic hazards (as unemployment, old age, or disability) in which the government participates or enforces the participation of employers and affected individuals

so·cial·ism \'sō-shə-,liz-əm\ *n* (1839) **1 :** any of various economic and political theories advocating collective or governmental ownership and administration of the means of production and distribution of goods **2 a :** a system of society or group living in which there is no private property **b :** a system or condition of society in which the means of production are owned and controlled by the state **3 :** a stage of society in Marxist theory transitional between capitalism and communism and distinguished by unequal distribution of goods and pay according to work done

so·cial·ist \'sō-sh(ə-)ləst\ *n* (1833) **1 :** one who advocates or practices socialism **2** *cap* **:** a member of a socialist party or political group — **socialist** *adj, often cap* — **so·cial·is·tic** \,sō-shə-'lis-tik\ *adj* — **so·cial·is·ti·cal·ly** \-ti-k(ə-)lē\ *adv*

socialist realism *n* (ca. 1943) **:** a Marxist aesthetic theory calling for the didactic use of literature, art, and music to develop social consciousness in an evolving socialist state — **socialist realist** *n*

so·cial·ite \'sō-shə-,līt\ *n* (1929) **:** a socially prominent person

so·cial·i·ty \,sō-shē-'al-ət-ē\ *n, pl* **-ties** (1649) **1 a :** SOCIABILITY **b :** an instance of social intercourse or sociability **2 :** the tendency to associate in or form social groups

so·cial·ize \'sō-shə-,līz\ *vb* **-ized; -iz·ing** *vt* (1836) **1 :** to make social; *esp* **:** to fit or train for a social environment **2 a :** to constitute on a socialistic basis ⟨∼ industry⟩ **b :** to adapt to social needs or uses ⟨∼ science⟩ **3 :** to organize group participation in ⟨∼ a recitation⟩ ∼ *vi* **:** to participate actively in a social group — **so·cial·iza·tion** \,sōsh-(ə-)lə-'zā-shən\ *n* — **so·cial·iz·er** \'sō-shə-,lī-zər\ *n*

socialized medicine *n* (1938) **:** medical and hospital services for the members of a class or population administered by an organized group (as a state agency) and paid for from funds obtained usu. by assessments, philanthropy, or taxation

so·cial·ly \ˈsōsh-(ə-)lē\ *adv* (1763) **1 :** in a social manner **2 :** with respect to society **3 :** by or through society
so·cial–mind·ed \ˌsō-shəl-ˈmīn-dəd\ *adj* (1927) **:** having an interest in society; *specif* **:** actively interested in social welfare or the well-being of society as a whole
social psychology *n* (ca. 1909) **:** the study of the manner in which the personality, attitudes, motivations, and behavior of the individual influence and are influenced by social groups — **social psychologist** *n*
social science *n* (1785) **1 :** a branch of science that deals with the institutions and functioning of human society and with the interpersonal relationships of individuals as members of society **2 :** a science (as economics or political science) dealing with a particular phase or aspect of human society — **social scientist** *n*
social secretary *n* (1903) **:** a personal secretary employed to handle social correspondence and appointments
social security *n* (1935) **:** the principle or practice or a program of public provision (as through social insurance or assistance) for the economic security and social welfare of the individual and his family; *specif, often cap* **:** a U.S. government program established in 1935 to include old-age and survivors insurance, contributions to state unemployment insurance, and old-age assistance
social service *n* (1851) **:** an activity designed to promote social welfare; *specif* **:** organized philanthropic assistance of the sick, destitute, or unfortunate **:** WELFARE WORK
social studies *n pl* (1927) **:** a part of a school or college curriculum concerned with the study of social relationships and the functioning of society and usu. made up of courses in history, government, economics, civics, sociology, geography, and anthropology
social welfare *n* (1917) **:** organized public or private social services for the assistance of disadvantaged groups; *specif* **:** SOCIAL WORK
social work *n* (1920) **:** any of various professional services, activities, or methods concretely concerned with the investigation, treatment, and material aid of the economically underprivileged and socially maladjusted — **social worker** *n*
so·ci·etal \sə-ˈsī-ət-ᵊl\ *adj* (1898) **:** of or relating to society **:** SOCIAL ⟨~ forces⟩ — **so·ci·etal·ly** \-ᵊl-ē\ *adv*
[1]**so·ci·ety** \sə-ˈsī-ət-ē\ *n, pl* **-et·ies** [MF *societé*, fr. L *societat-, societas*, fr. *socius* companion — more at SOCIAL] (1531) **1 :** companionship or association with one's fellows **:** friendly or intimate intercourse **:** COMPANY **2 :** a voluntary association of individuals for common ends; *esp* **:** an organized group working together or periodically meeting because of common interests, beliefs, or profession **3 a :** an enduring and cooperating social group whose members have developed organized patterns of relationships through interaction with one another **b :** a community, nation, or broad grouping of people having common traditions, institutions, and collective activities and interests **4 a :** a part of a community that is a unit distinguishable by particular aims or standards of living or conduct **:** a social circle or a group of social circles having a clearly marked identity ⟨move in polite ~⟩ ⟨literary ~⟩ **b :** a part of the community that sets itself apart as a leisure class and that regards itself as the arbiter of fashion and manners **5 a :** a natural group of plants usu. of a single species or habit within an association **b :** the progeny of a pair of insects when constituting a social unit (as a hive of bees); *broadly* **:** an interdependent system of organisms or biological units
[2]**society** *adj* (1693) **:** of, relating to, or characteristic of fashionable society
So·cin·i·an \sə-ˈsin-ē-ən, sō-\ *n* [NL *socinianus*, fr. Faustus *Socinus*] (1645) **:** an adherent of a 16th and 17th century theological movement professing belief in God and adherence to the Christian Scriptures but denying the divinity of Christ and consequently denying the Trinity — **Socinian** *adj* — **So·cin·i·an·ism** \-ē-ə-ˌniz-əm\ *n*
socio- *comb form* [F, fr. L *socius* companion] **1 :** society ⟨*sociography*⟩ **:** social ⟨*sociogram*⟩ **2 :** social and ⟨*sociopolitical*⟩ **3 :** sociological and ⟨*sociopsychiatric*⟩
so·cio·bi·ol·o·gy \ˌsō-sē-ō-bī-ˈäl-ə-jē, ˌsō-shē-\ *n* (1956) **:** the comparative study of social organization in animals and man esp. with regard to its genetic basis and evolutionary history — **so·cio·bio·log·i·cal** \-ˌbī-ə-ˈläj-i-kəl\ *adj* — **so·cio·bi·ol·o·gist** \-bī-ˈäl-ə-jəst\ *n*
so·cio·cul·tur·al \ˌsō-sē-ō-ˈkəlch(-ə)-rəl, ˌsō-shē-\ *adj* (1928) **:** of, relating to, or involving a combination of social and cultural factors — **so·cio·cul·tur·al·ly** \-rə-lē\ *adv*
so·cio·eco·nom·ic \-ˌek-ə-ˈnäm-ik, -ˌē-kə-\ *adj* (1883) **:** of, relating to, or involving a combination of social and economic factors — **so·cio·eco·nom·i·cal·ly** \-i-k(ə-)lē\ *adv*
so·cio·gram \ˈsō-sē-ə-ˌgram, ˈsō-shē-\ *n* (1937) **:** a sociometric chart plotting the structure of interpersonal relations in a group situation
so·cio·lin·guis·tic \ˌsō-sē-ō-liŋ-ˈgwis-tik, ˌsō-shē-\ *adj* (ca. 1951) **1 :** of or relating to the social aspects of language **2 :** of or relating to sociolinguistics
so·cio·lin·guis·tics \-tiks\ *n pl but sing in constr* (1965) **:** the study of linguistic behavior as determined by sociocultural factors
so·ci·ol·o·gese \ˌsō-sē-ˌäl-ə-ˈjēz, ˌsō-shē-, -ˈjēs\ *n* [*sociology* + [2]*-ese*] (1952) **:** a style of writing held to be characteristic of sociologists
so·cio·log·i·cal \ˌsō-sē-ə-ˈläj-i-kəl, ˌsō-sh(ē-)ə-\ *also* **so·cio·log·ic** \-ik\ *adj* (1843) **1 :** of or relating to sociology or to the methodological approach of sociology **2 :** oriented or directed toward social needs and problems — **so·cio·log·i·cal·ly** \-i-k(ə-)lē\ *adv*
so·ci·ol·o·gy \ˌsō-sē-ˈäl-ə-jē, ˌsō-shē-\ *n* [F *sociologie*, fr. *socio-* + *-logie* -logy] (1843) **1 :** the science of society, social institutions, and social relationships; *specif* **:** the systematic study of the development, structure, interaction, and collective behavior of organized groups of human beings **2 :** the scientific analysis of a social institution as a functioning whole and as it relates to the rest of society **3 :** SYNECOLOGY — **so·ci·ol·o·gist** \-jəst\ *n*
so·ci·om·e·try \-ˈäm-ə-trē\ *n* [ISV] (1935) **:** the study and measurement of interpersonal relationships in a group of people — **so·cio·met·ric** \ˌsō-sē-ə-ˈme-trik, ˌsō-shē-\ *adj*
so·cio·path \ˈsō-sē-ə-ˌpath, ˈsō-sh(ē-)ə-\ *n* (ca. 1944) **:** PSYCHOPATH
so·cio·path·ic \ˌsō-sē-ə-ˈpath-ik, ˌsō-sh(ē-)ə-\ *adj* (1944) **:** of, relating to, or characterized by asocial or antisocial behavior or a psychopathic personality
so·cio·po·lit·i·cal \ˌsō-sē-ō-pə-ˈlit-i-kəl, ˌsō-shē-\ *adj* (1884) **:** of, relating to, or involving a combination of social and political factors
so·cio·psy·cho·log·i·cal \-ˌsī-kə-ˈläj-i-kəl\ *adj* (1924) **1 :** of, relating to, or involving a combination of social and psychological factors **2 :** of or relating to social psychology
so·cio·re·li·gious \-ri-ˈlij-əs\ *adj* (1889) **:** involving a combination of social and religious factors
so·cio·sex·u·al \-ˈseksh-(ə-)wəl, -ˈsek-shəl\ *adj* (1940) **:** of or relating to the interpersonal aspects of sexuality
[1]**sock** \ˈsäk\ *n, pl* **socks** [ME *socke*, fr. OE *socc*, fr. L *soccus*] (bef. 12c) **1** *archaic* **:** a low shoe or slipper **2** *or pl* **sox** \ˈsäks\ **:** a knitted or woven covering for the foot usu. extending above the ankle and sometimes to the knee **3 a :** a shoe worn by actors in Greek and Roman comedy **b :** comic drama — **sock·less** *adj*
[2]**sock** *vb* [prob. of Scand origin; akin to ON *søkkva* to sink; akin to OE *sincan* to sink] *vt* (ca. 1700) **:** to hit, strike, or apply forcefully ~ *vi* **:** to deliver a blow **:** HIT — **sock it to** *slang* **:** to subject to vigorous assault ⟨they may let you off the first time . . . but the second time they'll *sock it to* you —James Jones⟩
[3]**sock** *n* (ca. 1700) **:** a vigorous or violent blow **:** PUNCH
sock away *vt* [fr. the practice of concealing savings in the toe of a sock] (1949) **:** to put away (money) as savings or investment
sock·dol·a·ger *or* **sock·dol·o·ger** \säk-ˈdäl-i-jər\ *n* [perh. alter. of *doxology*] (ca. 1830) **1 :** something that settles a matter **:** a decisive blow or answer **:** FINISHER **2 :** something outstanding or exceptional
[1]**sock·et** \ˈsäk-ət\ *n* [ME *soket*, fr. AF, dim. of OF *soc* plowshare, of Celt origin; akin to MIr *soc* plowshare, lit., snout of a hog; akin to OE *sugu* sow — more at SOW] (15c) **:** an opening or hollow that forms a holder for something ⟨an electric bulb ~⟩ ⟨the eye ~⟩
[2]**socket** *vt* (1533) **:** to provide with or support in or by a socket
socket wrench *n* (ca. 1890) **:** a wrench usu. in the form of a bar and removable socket made to fit a bolt or nut
sock·eye \ˈsäk-ˌī\ *n* [by folk etymology fr. Salish dial. *suk-kegh*] (1869) **:** a small but commercially important Pacific salmon (*Oncorhynchus nerka*) that ascends rivers chiefly from the Columbia northward to spawn in late summer or fall — called also *red salmon, sockeye salmon*
sock in *vt* [(*wind*) *sock*] (1944) **1 :** to close to takeoffs or landings by aircraft **2 :** to restrict from flying
socko \ˈsäk-(ˌ)ō\ *adj* [[2]*sock*] *slang* (1938) **:** strikingly impressive, effective, or successful **:** OUTSTANDING
so·cle \ˈsō-kəl, ˈsäk-əl\ *n* [F, fr. It *zoccolo* sock, socle, fr. L *socculus*, dim. of *soccus* sock] (ca. 1704) **:** a projecting usu. molded member at the foot of a wall or pier or beneath the base of a column, pedestal, or superstructure
[1]**So·crat·ic** \sə-ˈkrat-ik, sō-\ *adj* (1637) **:** of or relating to Socrates, his followers, or his philosophical method of systematic doubt and questioning of another to reveal his hidden ignorance or to elicit a clear expression of a truth supposed to be implicitly known by all rational beings — **So·crat·i·cal·ly** \-i-k(ə-)lē\ *adv*
[2]**Socratic** *n* (1678) **:** a follower of Socrates
Socratic irony *n* (ca. 1871) **:** IRONY 1
[1]**sod** \ˈsäd\ *n* [ME, fr. MD or MLG *sode*; akin to OFris *sātha* sod] (15c) **1 :** TURF 1; *also* **:** the grass- and forb-covered surface of the ground **2 :** one's native land
[2]**sod** *vt* **sod·ded; sod·ding** (1653) **:** to cover with sod or turfs
[3]**sod** *n* [short for *sodomite*] *chiefly Brit* (1818) **:** BUGGER ⟨he's not a bad little ~ taken by and large —Noel Coward⟩
so·da \ˈsōd-ə\ *n* [It, barilla plant, soda, fr. (assumed) ML, barilla plant] (1558) **1 a :** SODIUM CARBONATE **b :** SODIUM BICARBONATE **c :** sodium oxide Na_2O **d :** SODIUM — used in combination ⟨~ alum⟩ **2 a :** SODA WATER 2a **b :** SODA POP **c :** a sweet drink consisting of soda water, flavoring, and often ice cream **3 :** the faro card that shows faceup in the dealing box before play begins
soda ash *n* (1839) **:** commercial anhydrous sodium carbonate
soda biscuit *n* (1830) **1 :** a biscuit leavened with baking soda and sour milk or buttermilk **2 :** SODA CRACKER
soda cracker *n* (1830) **:** a cracker leavened with bicarbonate of soda and cream of tartar
soda fountain *n* (1824) **1 :** an apparatus with delivery tube and faucets for drawing soda water **2 :** the equipment and counter for the preparation and serving of sodas, sundaes, and ice cream
soda jerk \-ˌjərk\ *n* (1927) **:** a person who dispenses carbonated drinks and ice cream at a soda fountain — called also *soda jerker*
soda lime *n* (1862) **:** a mixture of sodium hydroxide and slaked lime used esp. to absorb moisture and gases
so·da·list \ˈsōd-ᵊl-əst, sō-ˈdal-\ *n* (1794) **:** a member of a sodality
so·da·lite \ˈsōd-ᵊl-ˌīt\ *n* [*soda*] (1810) **:** a transparent to translucent mineral $Na_4Al_3Si_3O_{12}Cl$ that consists of a sodium aluminum silicate with some chlorine, has a vitreous or greasy luster, and is found in various igneous rocks
so·dal·i·ty \sō-ˈdal-ət-ē\ *n, pl* **-ties** [L *sodalitat-, sodalitas* comradeship, club, fr. *sodalis* comrade — more at SIB] (1600) **1 :** BROTHERHOOD, COMMUNITY **2 :** an organized society or fellowship; *specif* **:** a devotional or charitable association of Roman Catholic laity
soda pop *n* (ca. 1906) **:** a beverage consisting of soda water, flavoring, and a sweet syrup
soda water *n* (1802) **1 :** a weak solution of sodium bicarbonate with some acid added to cause effervescence **2 a :** a beverage consisting of water highly charged with carbon dioxide **b :** SODA POP
sod·bust·er \ˈsäd-ˌbəs-tər\ *n* (ca. 1918) **:** one (as a farmer or a plow) that breaks the sod
[1]**sod·den** \ˈsäd-ᵊn\ *adj* [ME *soden*, fr. pp. of *sethen* to seethe] (1599) **1 a :** dull or expressionless esp. from continued indulgence in alcoholic beverages ⟨his ~ features⟩ **b :** TORPID, SLUGGISH ⟨~ minds⟩ **2 a :** heavy with or as if with moisture or water ⟨the ~ ground⟩ **b :** heavy or doughy because of imperfect cooking ⟨~ biscuits⟩ — **sod·den·ly** *adv* — **sod·den·ness** \-ᵊn-(n)əs\ *n*
[2]**sodden** *vb* **sod·dened; sod·den·ing** \ˈsäd-niŋ, -ᵊn-iŋ\ *vt* (1812) **:** to make sodden ~ *vi* **:** to become soaked or saturated

\ə\ abut \ᵊ\ kitten, F table \ər\ further \a\ ash \ā\ ace \ä\ cot, cart
\au̇\ out \ch\ chin \e\ bet \ē\ easy \g\ go \i\ hit \ī\ ice \j\ job
\ŋ\ sing \ō\ go \ȯ\ law \ȯi\ boy \th\ thin \t͟h\ the \ü\ loot \u̇\ foot
\y\ yet \zh\ vision \à, k̲, ⁿ, œ, œ̄, ue, ue̅, ʸ\ *see* Guide to Pronunciation

so·dic \'sōd-ik\ *adj* (1859) : of, relating to, or containing sodium
so·di·um \'sōd-ē-əm\ *n* [NL, fr. E *soda*] (1807) : a silver white soft waxy ductile element of the alkali metal group that occurs abundantly in nature in combined form and is very active chemically — see ELEMENT table
sodium azide *n* (ca. 1937) : a poisonous crystalline salt NaN_3 used esp. to make lead azide
sodium benzoate *n* (ca. 1900) : a crystalline or granular salt $C_7H_5O_2Na$ used chiefly as a food preservative
sodium bicarbonate *n* (ca. 1885) : a white crystalline weakly alkaline salt $NaHCO_3$ used esp. in baking powders, fire extinguishers, and medicine — called also *baking soda, saleratus*
sodium bo·ro·hy·dride \-ˌbōr-ə-'hī-ˌdrīd, -ˌbȯr-\ *n* [*sodium* + *boron* + *hydride*] (1946) : a crystalline compound $NaBH_4$ used in various industrial applications and esp. as a reducing agent in organic chemistry
sodium carbonate *n* (1868) : a sodium salt of carbonic acid used esp. in making soaps and chemicals, in water softening, in cleaning and bleaching, and in photography: as **a** : a hygroscopic crystalline anhydrous strongly alkaline salt Na_2CO_3 **b** : SAL SODA
sodium chlorate *n* (ca. 1885) : a colorless crystalline salt $NaClO_3$ used esp. as an oxidizing agent and weed killer
sodium chloride *n* (1868) : SALT 1a
sodium cyanide *n* (ca. 1885) : a white deliquescent poisonous salt NaCN used esp. in electroplating, in fumigating, and in treating steel
sodium dichromate *n* (ca. 1903) : a red crystalline salt $Na_2Cr_2O_7$ used esp. in tanning leather, in cleaning metals, and as an oxidizing agent
sodium fluoride *n* (ca. 1903) : a poisonous crystalline salt NaF that is used in trace amounts in the fluoridation of water, in metallurgy, as a flux, and as a pesticide
sodium fluoroacetate *n* (1945) : a poisonous powdery compound $C_2H_2FO_2Na$ used as a rodent poison
sodium hydroxide *n* (ca. 1885) : a white brittle solid NaOH that is a strong caustic base used esp. in making soap, rayon, and paper
sodium hypochlorite *n* (ca. 1885) : an unstable salt NaOCl produced usu. in aqueous solution and used as a bleaching and disinfecting agent
sodium hyposulfite *n* (1868) : SODIUM THIOSULFATE
sodium meta·sil·i·cate \-ˌmet-ə-'sil-ə-ˌkāt, -'sil-i-kət\ *n* (ca. 1926) : a toxic corrosive crystalline salt Na_2SiO_3 used esp. as a detergent or as a substitute for phosphates in detergent formulations
sodium nitrate *n* (ca. 1885) : a deliquescent crystalline salt $NaNO_3$ used as a fertilizer and an oxidizing agent and in curing meat
sodium nitrite *n* (ca. 1903) : a salt $NaNO_2$ used esp. in dye manufacture and as a meat preservative
sodium pump *n* (1962) : a molecular mechanism by which sodium ions are actively transported across a cell membrane; *esp* : the one by which the appropriate internal and external concentrations of sodium and potassium ions are maintained in a nerve fiber and which involves the active transport of sodium ions outward with movement of potassium ions to the interior
sodium salicylate *n* (ca. 1904) : a crystalline salt $NaC_7H_5O_3$ that has a sweetish saline taste and is used chiefly as an analgesic, antipyretic, and antirheumatic
sodium sulfate *n* (ca. 1885) : a bitter salt Na_2SO_4 used esp. in detergents, in the manufacture of wood pulp and rayon, in dyeing and finishing textiles, and in its hydrated form as a cathartic — compare GLAUBER'S SALT
sodium thiosulfate *n* (ca. 1885) : a hygroscopic crystalline salt $Na_2S_2O_3$ used esp. as a photographic fixing agent and a reducing or bleaching agent — called also *hypo, sodium hyposulfite*
sodium tri·poly·phos·phate \-ˌtrī-ˌpäl-i-'fäs-ˌfāt\ *n* (ca. 1945) : a crystalline salt $Na_5P_3O_{10}$ that is a major component of many detergents and a major contributor to water pollution
sodium–vapor lamp *n* (1936) : an electric lamp that contains sodium vapor and electrodes between which a luminous discharge takes place and that is used esp. for lighting highways
Sod·om \'säd-əm\ *n* [*Sodom*, city of ancient Palestine destroyed by God for its wickedness in Gen 18:20, 21; 19:24–28] (1649) : a place notorious for vice or corruption
sod·om·ite \'säd-ə-ˌmīt\ *n* (14c) : one who practices sodomy
sod·om·ize \'säd-ə-ˌmīz\ *vt* **-ized; -iz·ing** (1951) : to perform sodomy on
sod·omy \'säd-ə-mē\ *n* [ME, fr. OF *sodomie*, fr. LL *Sodoma* Sodom; fr. the homosexual proclivities of the men of the city in Gen 19:1–11] (13c) **1** : copulation with a member of the same sex or with an animal **2** : noncoital and esp. anal or oral copulation with a member of the opposite sex — **sod·omit·ic** \ˌsäd-ə-'mit-ik\ *or* **sod·omit·i·cal** \-i-kəl\ *adj*
so·ev·er \sō-'ev-ər\ *adv* [*-soever* (as in *howsoever*)] (1557) **1** : to any possible or known extent — used after an adjective preceded by *how* or a superlative preceded by *the* ⟨how fair ~ she may be⟩ ⟨the most selfish ~ in this world⟩ **2** : of any or every kind that may be specified — used after a noun modified esp. by *any, no,* or *what* ⟨he gives no information ~⟩
so·fa \'sō-fə\ *n* [Ar *ṣuffah* long bench] (1717) : a long upholstered seat usu. with arms and a back and often convertible into a bed
sofa bed *n* (1816) : a sofa that can be made to serve as a bed by lowering its hinged upholstered back to horizontal position or by pulling out a concealed mattress
so·far \'sō-ˌfär\ *n* [*sound fixing and ranging*] (1946) : a system for locating an underwater explosion at sea by triangulation based on the reception of the sound by three widely separated stations
so far as *conj* (1565) : INSOFAR AS
sof·fit \'säf-ət\ *n* [F *soffite*, fr. It *soffitto*, fr. (assumed) VL *suffictus*, pp. of L *suffigere* to fasten underneath — more at SUFFIX] (1613) : the underside of a part or member of a building (as of an overhang or staircase); *esp* : the intrados of an arch
[1]**soft** \'sȯft\ *adj* [ME, fr. OE *sōfte*, alter. of *sēfte*; akin to OHG *semfti* soft] (bef. 12c) **1 a** : pleasing or agreeable to the senses : bringing ease, comfort, or quiet ⟨the ~ influences of home⟩ **b** : having a bland or mellow rather than a sharp or acid taste **c (1)** : not bright or glaring : SUBDUED **(2)** : having or producing little contrast or a relatively short range of tones ⟨a ~ photographic print⟩ **d** : quiet in pitch or volume **e** *of the eyes* : having a liquid or gentle appearance **f** : smooth or delicate in texture, grain, or fiber ⟨~ cashmere⟩ ⟨~ fur⟩ **g (1)** : balmy, mild, or clement in weather or temperature **(2)** : moving or falling with slight force or impact : not violent ⟨~ breezes⟩ **2** : demanding little work or effort : EASY, IDLE ⟨a ~ job⟩ **3 a** : sounding as in *ace* and *gem* respectively — used of *c* and *g* or their sound **b** *of a consonant* : VOICED **c** : constituting a vowel before which there is a \y\ sound or a \y\-like modification of a consonant or constituting a consonant in whose articulation there is a \y\-like modification or which is followed by a \y\ sound (as in Russian) **4** *archaic* : moving in a leisurely manner **5** : rising gradually ⟨a ~ slope⟩ **6** : having curved or rounded outline : not harsh or jagged ⟨~ hills against the horizon⟩ **7** : marked by a gentleness, kindness, or tenderness: as **a (1)** : not being or involving harsh or onerous terms : EASY ⟨a policy of ~ competition⟩ **(2)** : based on negotiation and conciliation rather than on a show of power or on threats ⟨took a ~ line toward the enemy⟩ **b** : tending to ingratiate or disarm : ENGAGING, KIND ⟨a ~ answer turns away wrath —Prov 15:1 (RSV)⟩ **c** : marked by mildness : UNASSUMING, LOW-KEY **8 a** : emotionally suggestible or responsive : IMPRESSIONABLE **b** : unduly susceptible to influence : COMPLIANT **c** : lacking firmness or strength of character : FEEBLE, UNMANLY **d** : amorously attracted or emotionally involved — used with *on* ⟨has been ~ on her for years⟩ **9 a** : lacking robust strength, stamina, or endurance esp. because of living in ease or luxury **b** : weak or deficient mentally **10 a** : yielding to physical pressure **b** : permitting someone or something to sink in — used of wet ground **c (1)** : of a consistency that may be shaped or molded **(2)** : capable of being spread **d** : easily magnetized and demagnetized **e** : lacking relatively or comparatively in hardness ⟨~ iron⟩ **11** : deficient in or free from substances (as calcium and magnesium salts) that prevent lathering of soap ⟨~ water⟩ **12** : having relatively low energy ⟨~ X rays⟩ **13** : occurring at such a speed and under such circumstances as to avoid destructive impact ⟨~ landing of a spacecraft on the moon⟩ **14** : not protected against enemy attack ⟨a ~ aboveground launching site⟩ **15** : BIODEGRADABLE ⟨a ~ detergent⟩ ⟨~ pesticides⟩ **16** *of a drug* : considered less detrimental than a hard narcotic ⟨marijuana is usually regarded as a ~ drug⟩ **17** : easily polarized — used of acids and bases **18 a** *of currency* : not readily convertible **b** *of a loan* : not secured by collateral **19 a** : being low due to sluggish market conditions ⟨~ prices⟩ **b** : SLUGGISH, SLOW ⟨a ~ market⟩ **20** : not firmly committed : UNDECIDED ⟨~ voters⟩ **21** : SOFT-CORE **22 a** : being or based on interpretive or speculative data ⟨~ evidence⟩ **b** : utilizing or based on soft data ⟨~ science⟩ **23** : being or using renewable sources of energy (as solar radiation, wind, tides, biomass conversion) ⟨~ technologies⟩ — **soft·ish** \'sȯf-tish\ *adj* — **soft·ly** \'sȯf(t)-lē\ *adv* — **soft·ness** \'sȯf(t)-nəs\ *n*
[2]**soft** *adv* (bef. 12c) : in a soft or gentle manner : SOFTLY
[3]**soft** *n* (1593) : a soft object, material, or part ⟨the ~ of the thumb⟩
soft·back \'sȯf(t)-ˌbak\ *adj* (1967) : SOFTCOVER — **softback** *n*
soft·ball \-ˌbȯl\ *n* (1927) : baseball played on a small diamond with a ball that is larger than a baseball and that is pitched underhand; *also* : the ball used in this game
soft–boiled \-'bȯi(ə)ld\ *adj* (ca. 1902) **1** *of an egg* : boiled to a soft consistency **2** : SENTIMENTAL
soft·bound \-ˌbau̇nd\ *adj* (1953) : SOFTCOVER
soft chancre *n* (1859) : CHANCROID
soft coal *n* (1789) : BITUMINOUS COAL
soft–coated wheaten terrier *n* [*wheaten*; fr. its color] (1948) : a compact medium-sized terrier of a breed developed in Ireland and having a soft abundant light fawn coat
soft–core \'sȯf(t)-'kō(ə)r\ *adj* [[1]*soft* + *-core* (as in *hard-core*)] *of pornography* (ca. 1966) : containing descriptions or scenes of sex acts that are less explicit than hard-core material
soft·cov·er \-'kəv-ər\ *adj* (1952) : bound in flexible covers : not bound in hard covers; *specif* : PAPERBACK ⟨~ books⟩ — **softcover** *n*
soft drink *n* (1880) : a usu. carbonated nonalcoholic beverage; *esp* : SODA POP
soft·en \'sȯ-fən\ *vb* **soft·ened; soft·en·ing** \'sȯf-(ə-)niŋ\ *vt* (14c) **1** : to make soft or softer **2 a** : to weaken the military resistance or the morale of esp. by harassment (as preliminary bombardment) — often used with *up* **b** : to impair the strength or resistance of — often used with *up* ⟨~ up a sales prospect⟩ ~ *vi* : to become soft or softer — **soft·en·er** \'sȯf-(ə-)nər\ *n*
soft–finned \'sȯf(t)-'find\ adj (ca. 1890) : having fins in which the membrane is supported entirely or mostly by soft or articulated rays — used of higher teleost fishes; compare SPINY-FINNED
soft–fo·cus \'sȯf(t)-'fō-kəs\ *adj* (1916) **1** *of a photographic image* : having unsharp outlines **2** *of a lens* : producing an image having unsharp outlines
soft goods *n pl* (1894) : goods that are not durable — used esp. of textile products
soft hail *n* (1894) : GRAUPEL
soft·head \'sȯft-ˌhed\ *n* (1650) : a silly or feebleminded person
soft·head·ed \-'hed-əd\ *adj* (1667) : having a weak, unrealistic, or uncritical mind — **soft·head·ed·ly** *adv* — **soft·head·ed·ness** *n*
soft·heart·ed \-'härt-əd\ *adj* (1593) : emotionally responsive : SYMPATHETIC — **soft·heart·ed·ly** *adv* — **soft·heart·ed·ness** *n*
soft–land \-'land\ *vb* [back-formation fr. *soft landing*] *vt* (1960) : to cause to make a soft landing on a celestial body (as the moon) ~ *vi* : to make a soft landing — **soft–lander** *n*
soft–lin·er \-'lī-nər\ *n* [[1]*soft* + *-liner* (as in *hard-liner*)] (1966) : an advocate of a flexible course of action
soft palate *n* (ca. 1811) : the fold at the back of the hard palate that partially separates the mouth and pharynx
soft–ped·al \'sȯf(t)-'ped-ᵊl\ *vt* (1925) **1** : to play down : OBSCURE, MUFFLE ⟨~ the issue⟩ **2** : to use the soft pedal in playing
soft pedal *n* (1854) **1** : a foot pedal on a piano that reduces the volume of sound **2** : something that muffles, deadens, or reduces effect
soft rock *n* (1967) : rock music that is less driving and gentler sounding than hard rock
soft rot *n* (ca. 1902) : a mushy, watery, or slimy decay of plants or their parts caused by bacteria or fungi
soft scale *n* (ca. 1895) : a scale insect more or less active in all stages
soft sell *n* (1954) : the use of suggestion or gentle persuasion in selling rather than aggressive pressure — compare HARD SELL
soft–shell \'sȯf(t)-ˌshel\ *or* **soft–shelled** \-'sheld\ *adj* (1805) : having a soft or fragile shell esp. as a result of recent shedding

soft–shell clam *n* (1796) : an elongated clam (*Mya arenaria*) of the east coast of No. America that has a thin friable shell and long siphons and is used esp. for steaming — called also *soft-shelled clam, steamer*

soft–shelled turtle *n* (1771) : any of numerous aquatic turtles (family Trionychidae) that have sharp claws and mandibles and a flat shell covered with soft leathery skin instead of with horny plates

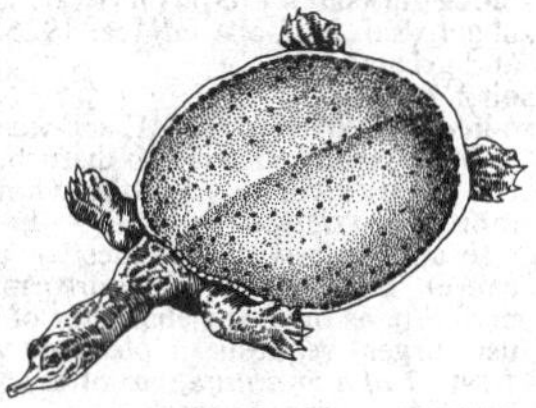

soft-shelled turtle

soft–shoe \'sȯf(t)-'shü\ *adj* (1920) : of or relating to tap dancing done in soft-soled shoes without metal taps

soft–soap \'sȯf(t)-'sōp\ *vt* (1840) : to soothe or persuade with flattery or blarney — **soft–soap·er** \-'sō-pər\ *n*

soft soap *n* (1634) **1** : a semifluid soap **2** : FLATTERY

soft–spo·ken \-'spō-kən\ *adj* (1609) : having a mild or gentle voice; *also* : SUAVE

soft spot *n* (1845) **1** : a sentimental weakness ⟨has a *soft spot* for him⟩ **2** : a vulnerable point ⟨a *soft spot* in the defense system⟩

soft touch *n* (1939) : one who is easily imposed on or taken advantage of

soft·ware \'sȯf-,twa(ə)r, -,twe(ə)r\ *n* (1960) **1** : the entire set of programs, procedures, and related documentation associated with a system and esp. a computer system; *specif* : computer programs **2** : something used or associated with and usu. contrasted with hardware; *esp* : materials for use with audiovisual equipment

soft wheat *n* (1812) : a wheat with soft starchy kernels high in starch but usu. low in gluten

[1]**soft·wood** \'sȯf-,twu̇d\ *n* (1832) **1** : the wood of a coniferous tree (as a fir or pine) whether hard or soft as distinguished from that of an angiospermous tree **2** : a tree that yields softwood

[2]**softwood** *adj* (1905) : having or made of softwood

soft–wood·ed \'sȯf-'twu̇d-əd\ *adj* (1827) **1** : having soft wood that is easy to work or finish **2** : SOFTWOOD

softy *or* **soft·ie** \'sȯf-tē\ *n, pl* **soft·ies** [[1]*soft*] (1863) **1** : a weak, effeminate, or foolish person **2** : an excessively sentimental or susceptible person

Sog·di·an \'säg-dē-ən\ *n* [L *Sogdiani,* pl., fr. pl. of *sogdianus* adj., Sogdian, fr. OPers *Sughuda* Sogdiana] (1553) **1** : a native or inhabitant of Sogdiana **2** : an Iranian language of the Sogdians — see INDO-EUROPEAN LANGUAGES table — **Sogdian** *adj*

sog·gy \'säg-ē, 'sȯg-\ *adj* **sog·gi·er; -est** [E dial. *sog* (to soak)] (1599) **1** : saturated or heavy with water or moisture: as **a** : WATERLOGGED, SOAKED ⟨a ~ lawn⟩ **b** : heavy or doughy because of imperfect cooking ⟨~ bread⟩ **2** : heavily dull ⟨~ prose⟩ — **sog·gi·ly** \'säg-ə-lē, 'sȯg-\ *adv* — **sog·gi·ness** \'säg-ē-nəs, 'sȯg-\ *n*

soi–di·sant \,swäd-ē-'zäⁿ\ *adj* [F, lit., saying oneself] (1752) : SELF-STYLED, SO-CALLED — usu. used disparagingly ⟨a ~ artist⟩

soi·gné *or* **soi·gnée** \swän-'yā\ *adj* [F, fr. pp. of *soigner* to take care of, fr. ML *soniare*] (1821) **1** : WELL-GROOMED, SLEEK **2** : elegantly maintained or designed ⟨a ~ restaurant⟩ ⟨a ~ black dress⟩

[1]**soil** \'sȯi(ə)l\ *vb* [ME *soilen,* fr. OF *soiller* to wallow, soil, fr. *soil* pigsty, perh. fr. L *suile,* fr. *sus* pig — more at SOW] *vt* (13c) **1** : to stain or defile morally : CORRUPT, POLLUTE **2** : to make unclean esp. superficially : DIRTY **3** : to blacken or besmirch (as a person's reputation) by word or deed ~ *vi* : to become soiled or dirty

[2]**soil** *n* (1501) **1 a** : [1]SOILAGE, STAIN ⟨protect a dress from ~⟩ **b** : moral defilement : CORRUPTION **2** : something that spoils or pollutes: as **a** : REFUSE **b** : SEWAGE **c** : DUNG, EXCREMENT

[3]**soil** *n* [ME, fr. AF, prob. fr. L *solium* seat; prob. akin to L *sedēre* to sit — more at SIT] (14c) **1** : firm land : EARTH **2 a** : the upper layer of earth that may be dug or plowed and in which plants grow **b** : the superficial unconsolidated and usu. weathered part of the mantle of a planet and esp. of the earth **3** : COUNTRY, LAND ⟨our native ~⟩ **4** : the agricultural life or calling **5** : a medium in which something takes hold and develops

[4]**soil** *vt* [origin unknown] (1605) : to feed (livestock) in the barn or an enclosure with fresh grass or green food; *also* : to purge (livestock) by feeding on green food

[1]**soil·age** \'sȯi-lij\ *n* [[1]*soil*] (1926) : the act of soiling : the condition of being soiled

[2]**soilage** *n* [[4]*soil*] (1928) : green crops for feeding confined animals

soil bank *n* (1955) : acreage retired from crop cultivation and planted with soil-building plants under a plan sponsored by the U.S. government that provides subsidies to farmers for the retired land

soil·borne \'sȯil-,bō(ə)rn, -,bȯ(ə)rn\ *adj* (1944) : transmitted by or in soil ⟨~ fungi⟩ ⟨~ diseases⟩

soil·less \'sȯi(ə)l-ləs\ *adj* (1939) : having, containing, or utilizing no soil ⟨~ agriculture⟩

soil pipe *n* (1833) : a pipe for carrying off wastes from toilets

soil science *n* (1915) : a science dealing with soils — called also *pedology* — **soil scientist** *n*

soil series *n* (ca. 1922) : a group of soils with similar profiles developed from similar parent materials under comparable climatic and vegetational conditions

soil·ure \'sȯil-yər\ *n* [ME, fr. OF *soilleure,* fr. *soiller* to soil] (13c) **1** : the act of soiling : the condition of being soiled **2** : STAIN, SMUDGE

soi·ree *or* **soi·rée** \swä-'rā\ *n* [F *soirée* evening period, evening party, fr. MF, fr. *soir* evening, fr. L *sero* at a late hour, fr. *serus* late — more at SINCE] (1802) : a party or reception held in the evening

soi·xante–neuf \swȧ-säⁿt-nœf\ *n* [F] (ca. 1920) : SIXTY-NINE 2

[1]**so·journ** \'sō-jərn, sō-'\ *n* [ME *sojorn,* fr. OF, fr. *sojorner*] (13c) : a temporary stay ⟨a ~ in the country⟩

[2]**sojourn** *vi* [ME *sojornen,* fr. OF *sojorner,* fr. (assumed) VL *subdiurnare,* fr. L *sub* under, during + LL *diurnum* day — more at SUB-, JOURNEY] (13c) : to stay as a temporary resident : STOP ⟨~*ed* for a month at a resort⟩ — **so·journ·er** *n*

soke \'sōk\ *n* [ME *soc, soke,* fr. ML *soca,* fr. OE *sōcn* inquiry, jurisdiction; akin to OE *sēcan* to seek] (bef. 12c) **1** : the right in Anglo-Saxon and early English law to hold court and administer justice with the franchise to receive certain fees or fines arising from it : jurisdiction over a territory or over people **2** : the district included in a soke jurisdiction or franchise

soke·man \'sōk-mən\ *n* (1579) : a man who is under the soke of another

[1]**sol** \'sōl\ *also* **so** \'sō\ *n* [ML *sol;* fr. the syllable sung to this note in a medieval hymn to St. John the Baptist] (14c) : the 5th tone of the diatonic scale in solmization

[2]**sol** \'säl, 'sȯl\ *n* [MF — more at SOU] (1583) : an old French coin equal to 12 deniers; *also* : a corresponding unit of value

[3]**sol** \'säl, 'sȯl\ *n, pl* **so·les** \'sō-(,)lās\ [AmerSp, fr. Sp, sun, fr. L] (ca. 1883) : the former basic monetary unit of Peru replaced in 1985 by the inti

[4]**sol** \'säl, 'sȯl\ *n* [*-sol* (as in *hydrosol*), fr. *solution*] (1899) : a fluid colloidal system; *esp* : one in which the continuous phase is a liquid

Sol \'säl\ *n* [ME, fr. L] **1** : the Roman god of the sun — compare HELIOS **2** : SUN

sola *pl of* SOLUM

[1]**so·lace** \'säl-əs *also* 'sōl-\ *n* [ME *solas,* fr. OF, fr. L *solacium,* fr. *solari* to console — more at SILLY] (13c) **1** : alleviation of grief or anxiety **2** : a source of relief or consolation

[2]**solace** *vt* **so·laced; so·lac·ing** (13c) **1** : to give solace to : CONSOLE **2 a** : to make cheerful **b** : AMUSE **3** : ALLAY, SOOTHE ⟨~ grief⟩ — **so·lace·ment** \-ə-smənt\ *n* — **so·lac·er** *n*

so·la·na·ceous \,sō-lə-'nā-shəs\ *adj* [NL *Solanaceae,* group name, fr. *Solanum*] (1804) : of or relating to the nightshade family of plants

so·lan goose \,sō-lən-\ *n* [ME *soland,* fr. ON *súla* pillar, gannet (akin to OE *sȳl* pillar) + *ǫnd* duck; akin to OHG *anut* duck, L *anas*] (1536) : a very large white gannet (*Sula bassana* or *Morus bassanus*) with black wing tips

so·la·nine *or* **so·la·nin** \'sō-lə-,nēn, -nən\ *n* [F *solanine,* fr. L *solanum*] (1838) : a bitter poisonous crystalline alkaloid $C_{45}H_{72}NO_{15}$ from several plants (as some potatoes or tomatoes) of the nightshade family

so·la·num \sə-'lān-əm, -'län-, -'lan-\ *n* [NL, fr. L, nightshade] (1621) : any of a genus (*Solanum*) of herbs, shrubs, or trees of the nightshade family that have often prickly-veined leaves, cymose white, purple, or yellow flowers, and a fruit that is a berry

so·lar \'sō-lər, -,lär\ *adj* [ME, fr. L *solaris,* fr. *sol* sun; akin to OE & ON *sōl* sun, Gk *hēlios*] (15c) **1** : of, derived from, or relating to the sun esp. as affecting the earth **2** : measured by the earth's course in relation to the sun ⟨~ time⟩ ⟨~ year⟩; *also* : relating to or reckoned by solar time **3 a** : produced or operated by the action of the sun's light or heat ⟨~ energy⟩ ⟨~ cooker⟩ **b** : utilizing the sun's rays esp. to produce heat or electricity ⟨a ~ house⟩; *also* : of or relating to such utilization ⟨~ design⟩ ⟨~ subsidies⟩

solar battery *n* (1954) : an array of solar cells

solar cell *n* (1958) : a photovoltaic cell (as one including a junction between two types of silicon semiconductors) that is able to convert sunlight into electrical energy and is used as a power source

solar collector *n* (1955) : any of various devices for the absorption of solar radiation for the heating of water or buildings or the production of electricity

solar constant *n* (1869) : the quantity of radiant solar heat received normally at the outer layer of the earth's atmosphere and having an average value of about 1.94 gram calories per square centimeter per minute

solar day *n* (ca. 1764) : the interval between transits of the apparent or mean sun across the meridian at any place

solar flare *n* (1938) : a sudden temporary outburst of energy from a small area of the sun's surface

so·lar·i·um \sō-'lar-ē-əm, sə-, -'ler-\ *n, pl* **-ia** \-ē-ə\ *also* **-ums** [L, fr. *sol*] (ca. 1823) : a glass-enclosed porch or room; *also* : a room (as in a hospital) used esp. for sunbathing or therapeutic exposure to light

so·lar·iza·tion \,sō-lə-rə-'zā-shən\ *n* (1853) **1** : a reversal of gradation in a photographic image obtained by intense or continued exposure **2** : an act or process of solarizing

so·lar·ize \'sō-lə-,rīz\ *vt* **-ized; -iz·ing** (1855) **1 a** : to expose to sunlight **b** : to affect by the action of the sun's rays **2** : to subject (photographic materials) to solarization

solar panel *n* (1961) : a battery of solar cells (as in a spacecraft)

solar plexus \'sō-lər-\ *n* [fr. the radiating nerve fibers] (1771) **1** : a nerve plexus in the abdomen that is situated behind the stomach and in front of the aorta and the crura of the diaphragm and contains several ganglia distributing nerve fibers to the viscera **2** : the pit of the stomach

solar pond *n* (1961) : a pool of salt water heated by the sun and used either as a direct source of heat or to provide power for an electric generator

solar sail *n* (1958) : a propulsive device that consists of a flat material (as aluminized plastic) designed to receive thrust from solar radiation pressure and that can be attached to a spacecraft

solar system *n* (1704) : a star with the group of celestial bodies that are gravitationally bound to it; *esp* : the sun with the planets, moons, asteroids, and comets that orbit it

solar wind *n* (1958) : plasma continuously ejected from the sun's surface into and through interplanetary space

sol·ate \'säl-,āt, 'sȯl-\ *vi* **sol·at·ed; sol·at·ing** [[4]*sol*] (1915) : to change to a sol — **sol·ation** \sä-'lā-shən, sȯ-\ *n*

so·la·ti·um \sō-'lā-shē-əm\ *n, pl* **-tia** \-shē-ə\ [LL *solacium, solatium,* fr. L, solace] (1817) : a compensation (as money) given as solace for suffering, loss, or injured feelings

sold *past and past part of* SELL

sol·dan \'säl-dən, 'sōl-\ *n* [ME, fr. OF, fr. Ar *sulṭān*] *archaic* (13c) : SULTAN; *esp* : the sultan of Egypt

[1]**sol·der** \'säd-ər, 'sȯd-, *Brit also* 'säl-dər, 'sōl-\ *n* [ME *soudure,* fr. MF, fr. *souder* to solder, fr. L *solidare* to make solid, fr. *solidus* solid] (15c) **1** : a metal or metallic alloy used when melted to join metallic surfaces; *esp* : an alloy of lead and tin so used **2** : something that unites

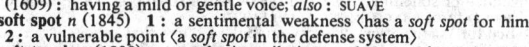

[2]solder *vb* **soldered; sol·der·ing** \-(ə-)riŋ\ *vt* (15c) **1 :** to unite or make whole by solder **2 :** to bring into or restore to firm union ⟨a friendship ~*ed* by common interests⟩ ~ *vi* **1 :** to use solder **2 :** to become united or repaired by or as if by solder — **sol·der·abil·i·ty** \ˌsäd-ə-rə-ˈbil-ət-ē, ˌsȯd-\ *n* — **sol·der·er** \ˈsäd-ər-ər, ˈsȯd-\ *n*
soldering iron *n* (1688) **:** a pointed or wedge-shaped device that is usu. electrically heated and that is used for soldering
[1]sol·dier \ˈsōl-jər\ *n* [ME *soudier,* fr. MF, fr. *soulde* pay, fr. LL *solidus* solidus] (14c) **1 a :** one engaged in military service and esp. in the army **b :** an enlisted man or woman **c :** a skilled warrior **2 :** a militant leader, follower, or worker **3 a :** one of a caste of wingless sterile termites usu. differing from workers in larger size and head and long jaws **b :** one of a type of worker ants distinguished by exceptionally large head and jaws **4 :** one who shirks his work — **sol·dier·ly** \-lē\ *adj or adv* — **sol·dier·ship** \-ˌship\ *n*
[2]soldier *vi* **sol·diered; sol·dier·ing** \ˌsōlj-(ə-)riŋ\ (1647) **1 a :** to serve as a soldier **b :** to behave in a soldierly manner **c :** to push doggedly forward — usu. used with *on* ⟨didn't know whether to quit or ~ on⟩ **2 :** to make a pretense of working while really loafing
sol·dier·ing *n* (1643) **:** the life, service, or practice of one who soldiers
soldier of fortune (1661) **:** one who follows a military career wherever there is promise of profit, adventure, or pleasure
soldiers' home *n* (1861) **:** an institution maintained (as by the federal or a state government) for the care and relief of military veterans
soldier's medal *n* (1926) **:** a U.S. military decoration awarded for heroism not involving combat
sol·diery \ˈsōlj-(ə-)rē\ *n* (ca. 1570) **1 a :** a body of soldiers **b :** SOLDIERS, MILITARY **2 :** the profession or technique of soldiering
sol·do \ˈsȯl-(ˌ)dō\ *n, pl* **sol·di** \-(ˌ)dē\ [It, fr. LL *solidus* solidus] (1599) **:** an old Italian coin worth five centesimi
sold–out \ˈsōl-ˈdau̇t\ *adj* (1907) **:** having all available tickets or accommodations sold completely and esp. in advance
[1]sole \ˈsōl\ *n* [ME, fr. MF, fr. L *solea* sandal; akin to L *solum* base, ground, soil] (14c) **1 a :** the undersurface of a foot **b :** the part of an item of footwear on which the sole rests and upon which the wearer treads **2 :** the usu. flat or flattened bottom or lower part of something or the base on which something rests — **soled** \ˈsōld\ *adj*
[2]sole *vt* **soled; sol·ing** (ca. 1570) **1 :** to furnish with a sole ⟨~ a shoe⟩ **2 :** to place the sole of (a golf club) on the ground
[3]sole *n* [ME, fr. MF, fr. L *solea* sandal, a flatfish] (14c) **:** a flatfish (family Soleidae) having a small mouth, small or rudimentary fins, and small eyes placed close together and including superior food fishes (as *Solea solea* of Europe); *also* **:** any of various mostly market flatfishes of other families
[4]sole *adj* [ME, alone, fr. MF *seul,* fr. L *solus*] (14c) **1 :** not married — used chiefly of women **2** *archaic* **:** having no companion **:** SOLITARY **3 a :** having no sharer **b :** being the only one ⟨she was her mother's ~ support⟩ **4 :** functioning independently and without assistance or interference ⟨let conscience be the ~ judge⟩ **5 :** belonging exclusively or otherwise limited to one usu. specified individual, unit, or group — **sole·ness** \ˈsōl-nəs\ *n*
so·le·cism \ˈsäl-ə-ˌsiz-əm, ˈsō-lə-\ *n* [L *soloecismus,* fr. Gk *soloikismos,* fr. *soloikos* speaking incorrectly, lit., inhabitant of Soloi, fr. *Soloi,* city in ancient Cilicia where a substandard form of Attic was spoken] (1577) **1 :** an ungrammatical combination of words in a sentence; *also* **:** a minor blunder in speech **2 :** something deviating from the proper, normal, or accepted order **3 :** a breach of etiquette or decorum — **so·le·cis·tic** \ˌsäl-ə-ˈsis-tik, ˌsō-lə-\ *adj*
sole·ly \ˈsō(l)-lē\ *adv* (15c) **1 :** without another **:** SINGLY ⟨went ~ on her way⟩ **2 :** to the exclusion of all else ⟨done ~ for money⟩
sol·emn \ˈsäl-əm\ *adj* [ME *solemne,* fr. MF, fr. L *sollemnis* regularly appointed, solemn] (14c) **1 :** marked by the invocation of a religious sanction ⟨a ~ oath⟩ **2 :** marked by the observance of established form or ceremony; *specif* **:** celebrated with full liturgical ceremony **3 a :** awe-inspiring **:** SUBLIME **b :** marked by grave sedateness and earnest sobriety **c :** SOMBER, GLOOMY ***syn*** see SERIOUS — **sol·emn·ly** *adv* — **sol·emn·ness** *n*
so·lem·ni·fy \sə-ˈlem-nə-ˌfī\ *vt* **-fied; -fy·ing** (1882) **:** to make solemn
so·lem·ni·ty \sə-ˈlem-nət-ē\ *n, pl* **-ties** [ME *solempnite, solemnite,* fr. OF, fr. LL *solemnitat-, solemnitas,* fr. *solemnis*] (13c) **1 :** formal or ceremonious observance of an occasion or event **2 :** a solemn event or occasion **3 :** a solemn condition or quality ⟨the ~ of his words⟩
sol·em·nize \ˈsäl-əm-ˌnīz\ *vb* **-nized; -niz·ing** *vt* (14c) **1 :** to observe or honor with solemnity **2 :** to perform with pomp or ceremony; *esp* **:** to celebrate (a marriage) with religious rites **3 :** to make solemn **:** DIGNIFY ~ *vi* **:** to speak or act with solemnity — **sol·em·ni·za·tion** \ˌsäl-əm-nə-ˈzā-shən\ *n*
solemn mass *n* (15c) **:** a mass marked by the use of incense and by the presence of a deacon and a subdeacon in attendance on the celebrant
solemn vow *n* (14c) **:** an absolute and irrevocable public vow taken by a religious in the Roman Catholic Church under which ownership of property by the individual is prohibited and marriage is invalid under canon law
so·le·noid \ˈsō-lə-ˌnȯid, ˈsäl-ə-\ *n* [F *solénoïde,* fr. Gk *sōlēnoeidēs* pipe-shaped, fr. Gk, *sōlēn* pipe — more at SYRINGE] (ca. 1832) **:** a coil of wire commonly in the form of a long cylinder that when carrying a current resembles a bar magnet so that a movable core is drawn into the coil when a current flows — **so·le·noi·dal** \ˌsō-lə-ˈnȯid-ᵊl, ˌsäl-ə-\ *adj*
sole·plate \ˈsōl-ˌplāt\ *n* (1844) **1 :** the lower plate of a studded partition on which the bases of the studs butt **2 :** the undersurface of a flatiron
soles *pl of* SOL
so·le·us \ˈsō-lē-əs\ *n, pl* **so·lei** \-lē-ˌī\ [NL, fr. L *solea* sandal — more at SOLE] (1676) **:** a broad flat muscle of the calf of the leg lying immediately below the gastrocnemius
[1]sol–fa \(ˈ)sōlˈfä\ *vi* (14c) **:** to sing the sol-fa syllables ~ *vt* **:** to sing (as a melody) to sol-fa syllables
[2]sol–fa *n* (1548) **1 :** SOL-FA SYLLABLES **2 :** SOLMIZATION; *also* **:** an exercise thus sung **3 :** TONIC SOL-FA — **sol-fa·ist** \-ˈfä-(ə)st, -ˈfä-ˌist\ *n*
sol–fa syllables *n pl* (ca. 1913) **:** the syllables *do, re, mi, fa, sol, la, ti,* used in singing the tones of the scale
sol·fa·ta·ra \ˌsōl-fə-ˈtär-ə\ *n* [It, sulfur mine, fr. *solfo* sulfur, fr. L *sulfur*] (1777) **:** a volcanic area or vent that yields only hot vapors and sulfurous gases
sol·fège \säl-ˈfezh\ *n* [F, fr. It *solfeggio*] (ca. 1903) **1 :** the application of the sol-fa syllables to a musical scale or to a melody **2 :** a singing exercise esp. using sol-fa syllables; *also* **:** practice in sight-reading vocal music using the sol-fa syllables
sol·feg·gio \säl-ˈfej-(ē-ˌ)ō\ *n* [It, fr. *sol-fa*] (1774) **:** SOLFÈGE
sol·gel \ˈsäl-ˌjel, ˈsȯl-\ *adj* (ca. 1925) **:** involving alternation between sol and gel states
soli *pl of* SOLO
so·lic·it \sə-ˈlis-ət\ *vb* [ME *soliciten* to disturb, take charge of, fr. MF *solliciter,* fr. L *sollicitare* to disturb, fr. *sollicitus* anxious, fr. *sollus* whole (fr. Oscan; akin to Gk *holos* whole) + *citus,* pp. of *ciēre* to move — more at SAFE, HIGHT] *vt* (1509) **1 a :** to make petition to **:** ENTREAT **b :** to approach with a request or plea **2 :** to strongly urge (as one's cause) **3 a :** to entice or lure esp. into evil **b :** to proposition (someone) esp. as or in the character of a prostitute **4 :** to try to obtain by usu. urgent requests or pleas ~ *vi* **1 :** to make solicitation **:** IMPORTUNE **2** *of a prostitute* **:** to offer to have sexual relations with someone for money ***syn*** see ASK
so·lic·i·tant \sə-ˈlis-ət-ənt\ *n* (1802) **:** one who solicits
so·lic·i·ta·tion \sə-ˌlis-ə-ˈtā-shən\ *n* (1500) **1 :** the practice or act or an instance of soliciting; *esp* **:** ENTREATY, IMPORTUNITY **2 :** a moving or drawing force **:** INCITEMENT, ALLUREMENT
so·lic·i·tor \sə-ˈlis-ət-ər, -ˈlis-tər\ *n* (15c) **1 :** one that solicits; *esp* **:** an agent that solicits (as contributions to charity) **2 :** a British lawyer who advises clients, represents them in the lower courts, and prepares cases for barristers to try in higher courts **3 :** the chief law officer of a municipality, county, or government department — **so·lic·i·tor·ship** \-ˌship\ *n*
solicitor general *n, pl* **solicitors general** (1647) **:** a law officer appointed primarily to assist an attorney general
so·lic·i·tous \sə-ˈlis-ət-əs, -ˈlis-təs\ *adj* [L *sollicitus*] (1563) **1 :** manifesting or expressing solicitude ⟨a ~ inquiry about his health⟩ **2 :** full of concern or fears **:** APPREHENSIVE ⟨~ about the future⟩ **3 :** meticulously careful ⟨~ in matters of dress⟩ **4 :** full of desire **:** EAGER — **so·lic·i·tous·ly** *adv* — **so·lic·i·tous·ness** *n*
so·lic·i·tude \sə-ˈlis-ə-ˌt(y)üd\ *n* (15c) **1 a :** the state of being solicitous **:** ANXIETY **b :** attentive care and protectiveness; *also* **:** an attitude of solicitous concern or attention **2 :** a cause of care or concern — usu. used in pl. ***syn*** see CARE
[1]sol·id \ˈsäl-əd\ *adj* [ME *solide,* fr. MF, fr. L *solidus;* akin to Gk *holos* whole — more at SAFE] (14c) **1 a :** being without an internal cavity ⟨a ~ ball of rubber⟩ **b (1) :** printed with minimum space between lines **(2) :** joined without a hyphen ⟨a ~ compound⟩ **c :** not interrupted by a break or opening ⟨a ~ wall⟩ **2 :** having, involving, or dealing with three dimensions or with solids ⟨~ configuration⟩ **3 a :** of uniformly close and coherent texture **:** not loose or spongy **:** COMPACT **b :** neither gaseous nor liquid **4 :** of good substantial quality or kind ⟨~ comfort⟩: as **a :** SOUND ⟨~ reasons⟩ **b :** made firmly and well ⟨~ furniture⟩ **5 a :** having no break or interruption ⟨waited three ~ hours⟩ **b :** UNANIMOUS ⟨had the ~ support of his party⟩ **c :** intimately friendly or associated ⟨~ with his boss⟩ **6 a :** PRUDENT; *also* **:** well-established financially **b :** serious in purpose or character **7 :** of one substance or character: as **a :** entirely of one metal or containing the minimum of alloy necessary to impart hardness ⟨~ gold⟩ **b :** of a single color ***syn*** see FIRM — **sol·id·ly** *adv* — **sol·id·ness** *n*
[2]solid *n* (15c) **1 :** a geometrical figure or element (as a cube or sphere) having three dimensions **2 a :** a substance that does not flow perceptibly under moderate stress **b :** the part of a solution or suspension that when freed from solvent or suspending medium has the qualities of a solid — usu. used in pl. ⟨milk ~*s*⟩ **3 :** something that is solid: as **a :** a solid color **b :** a compound word whose members are joined together without a hyphen
[3]solid *adv* (1651) **:** in a solid manner; *also* **:** UNANIMOUSLY
sol·i·da·go \ˌsäl-ə-ˈdā-(ˌ)gō, -ˈdäg-(ˌ)ō\ *n, pl* **-gos** [NL, fr. ML *soldago,* an herb reputed to heal wounds, fr. *soldare* to make whole, fr. L *solidare,* fr. *solidus* solid] (1771) **:** any of a genus (*Solidago*) of chiefly No. American composite herbs including the typical goldenrods
solid angle *n* (ca. 1704) **:** the three-dimensional angular spread at the vertex of a cone measured by the area intercepted by the cone on a unit sphere whose center is the vertex of the cone
sol·i·da·rism \ˈsäl-əd-ə-ˌriz-əm\ *n* [*solidarity* + *-ism*] (ca. 1931) **:** SOLIDARITY — **sol·i·da·rist** \-rəst\ *n* — **sol·i·da·ris·tic** \ˌsäl-əd-ə-ˈris-tik\ *adj*
sol·i·dar·i·ty \ˌsäl-ə-ˈdar-ət-ē\ *n* [F *solidarité,* fr. *solidaire* characterized by solidarity, fr. L *solidum* whole sum, fr. neut. of *solidus* solid] (1848) **:** unity (as of a group or class) that produces or is based on community of interests, objectives, and standards
solid geometry *n* (1733) **:** a branch of geometry that deals with figures of three-dimensional space
so·lid·i·fy \sə-ˈlid-ə-ˌfī\ *vb* **-fied; -fy·ing** *vt* (1799) **1 :** to make solid, compact, or hard **2 :** to make secure, substantial, or firmly fixed ⟨factors that ~ public opinion⟩ ~ *vi* **:** to become solid, compact, or hard — **so·lid·i·fi·ca·tion** \-ˌlid-ə-fə-ˈkā-shən\ *n*
so·lid·i·ty \sə-ˈlid-ət-ē\ *n, pl* **-ties** (1532) **1 :** the quality or state of being solid **2 :** something solid
sol·id–look·ing \ˌsäl-əd-ˈlu̇k-iŋ\ *adj* (1883) **:** giving an impression of solid worth or substance ⟨~ well-fed citizens⟩
solid of revolution (1816) **:** a mathematical solid conceived as formed by the revolution of a plane figure about an axis in its plane
solid–state *adj* (1950) **1 :** relating to the properties, structure, or reactivity of solid material; *esp* **:** relating to the arrangement or behavior of ions, molecules, nucleons, electrons, and holes in the crystals of a substance (as a semiconductor) or to the effect of crystal imperfections on the properties of a solid substance ⟨~ physics⟩ **2 :** utilizing the electric, magnetic, or photic properties of solid materials **:** not utilizing electron tubes ⟨a ~ stereo system⟩
sol·i·dus \ˈsäl-əd-əs\ *n, pl* **-i·di** \-ə-ˌdī, -ˌdē\ [ME, fr. LL, fr. L, solid] (14c) **1 :** an ancient Roman gold coin introduced by Constantine and used to the fall of the Byzantine Empire **2** [ML, shilling, fr. LL; fr. its use as a symbol for shillings] **:** DIAGONAL 3
sol·i·fluc·tion \ˈsō-lə-ˌflək-shən\ *n* [L *solum* soil + *-i-* + *fluction-, fluctio* act of flowing, fr. *fluctus,* pp. of *fluere* to flow — more at FLUID] (ca. 1916) **:** the slow creeping of saturated fragmental material (as soil) down a slope that usu. occurs in regions of perennial frost
so·lil·o·quist \sə-ˈlil-ə-kwəst\ *n* (1804) **:** one who soliloquizes

so·lil·o·quize \-ˌkwīz\ *vi* **-quized; -quiz·ing** (1759) **:** to utter a soliloquy **:** talk to oneself — **so·lil·o·quiz·er** *n*

so·lil·o·quy \sə-ˈlil-ə-kwē\ *n, pl* **-quies** [LL *soliloquium,* fr. L *solus* alone + *loqui* to speak] (ca. 1604) **1 :** the act of talking to oneself **2 :** a dramatic monologue that gives the illusion of being a series of unspoken reflections

so·lip·sism \ˈsō-ləp-ˌsiz-əm, ˈsäl-əp-\ *n* [L *solus* alone + *ipse* self] (1874) **:** a theory holding that the self can know nothing but its own modifications and that the self is the only existent thing — **so·lip·sist** \ˈsō-ləp-səst, ˈsäl-əp-, sə-ˈlip-\ *n* — **so·lip·sis·tic** \ˌsō-ləp-ˈsis-tik, ˌsäl-əp-\ *adj* — **so·lip·sis·ti·cal·ly** \-ti-k(ə-)lē\ *adv*

sol·i·taire \ˈsäl-ə-ˌta(ə)r, -ˌte(ə)r\ *n* [F, fr. *solitaire,* adj., solitary, fr. L *solitarius*] (1727) **1 :** a single gem (as a diamond) set alone **2 :** any of various card games that can be played by one person

[1]**sol·i·tary** \ˈsäl-ə-ˌter-ē\ *adj* [ME, fr. L *solitarius,* fr. *solitas* aloneness, fr. *solus* alone] (14c) **1 a :** being, living, or going alone or without companions **b :** saddened by isolation **2 :** UNFREQUENTED, DESOLATE **3 :** taken, passed, or performed without companions ⟨a ~ ramble⟩ **4 :** being at once single and isolated ⟨a ~ example⟩ **5 a :** occurring singly and not as part of a group or cluster ⟨flowers terminal and ~⟩ **b :** not gregarious, colonial, social, or compound ⟨~ bees⟩ ***syn*** see ALONE — **sol·i·tari·ly** \ˌsäl-ə-ˈter-ə-lē\ *adv* — **sol·i·tari·ness** \ˈsäl-ə-ˌter-ē-nəs\ *n*

[2]**solitary** *n, pl* **-tar·ies** (15c) **1 :** one who lives or seeks to live a solitary life **:** RECLUSE **2 :** solitary confinement in prison

sol·i·tons \ˈsäl-ə-ˌtänz\ *n pl* [*solitary* + [2]*-on*] (ca. 1975) **:** solitary waves (as in a gaseous plasma) that retain their shape and speed after colliding with each other

sol·i·tude \ˈsäl-ə-ˌt(y)üd\ *n* [ME, fr. MF, fr. L *solitudin-, solitudo,* fr. *solus*] (14c) **1 :** the quality or state of being alone or remote from society **:** SECLUSION **2 :** a lonely place (as a desert)

syn SOLITUDE, ISOLATION, SECLUSION mean the state of one who is alone. SOLITUDE may imply a condition of being apart from all human beings or of being cut off by wish or compulsion from one's usual associates; ISOLATION stresses detachment from others often involuntarily; SECLUSION suggests a shutting away or keeping apart from others often connoting deliberate withdrawal from the world or retirement to a quiet life.

sol·i·tu·di·nar·i·an \ˌsäl-ə-ˌt(y)üd-ᵊn-ˈer-ē-ən\ *n* [L *solitudin-, solitudo* + E *-arian*] (1691) **:** RECLUSE

sol·ler·et \ˌsäl-ə-ˈret\ *n* [F] (1826) **:** a flexible steel shoe forming part of a medieval suit of armor — see ARMOR illustration

sol·mi·za·tion \ˌsäl-mə-ˈzā-shən\ *n* [F *solmisation,* fr. *solmiser* to sol-fa, fr. *sol* (fr. ML) + *mi* (fr. ML) + *-iser* -ize] (1730) **:** the act, practice, or system of using syllables to denote the tones of a musical scale

[1]**so·lo** \ˈsō-(ˌ)lō\ *n, pl* **solos** [It, fr. *solo* alone, fr. L *solus*] (1695) **1** *or pl* **so·li** \ˈsō-(ˌ)lē\ **a :** a musical composition for a single voice or instrument with or without accompaniment **b :** the featured part of a concerto or similar work **2 :** a performance in which the performer has no partner or associate **3 :** any of several card games in which a player elects to play without a partner against the other players

[2]**solo** *adv* (1712) **:** without a companion **:** ALONE ⟨fly ~⟩

[3]**solo** *adj* (1776) **:** of, relating to, or being a solo ⟨a ~ performance⟩

[4]**solo** *vi* **so·loed; so·lo·ing** \-(ˌ)lō-iŋ, -lə-wiŋ\ (1886) **:** to perform by oneself; *esp* **:** to fly an airplane without one's instructor

so·lo·ist \ˈsō-lə-wəst, -(ˌ)lō-əst\ *n* (1864) **:** one who performs a solo

Sol·o·mon \ˈsäl-ə-mən\ *n* [LL, fr. Heb *Shĕlōmōh*] **:** a son of David and 10th century B.C. king of Israel proverbial for his wisdom

Sol·o·mon·ic \ˌsäl-ə-ˈmän-ik\ *adj* (1857) **:** marked by notable wisdom, reasonableness, or discretion esp. under trying circumstances

Solomon's seal *also* **Sol·o·mon·seal** \ˌsäl-ə-mən-ˈsē(ə)l, ˈsäl-ə-mən-ˌ\ *n* (1543) **1 :** any of a genus (*Polygonatum*) of perennial herbs of the lily family with gnarled rhizomes **2 :** an emblem consisting of two interlaced triangles forming a 6-pointed star and formerly used as an amulet esp. against fever

so·lon \ˈsō-lən, -ˌlän\ *n* [*Solon*] (1625) **1 :** a wise and skillful lawgiver **2 :** a member of a legislative body

sol·on·chak \ˌsäl-ən-ˈchak\ *n* [Russ, salt marsh] (1936) **:** any of a group of intrazonal strongly saline usu. pale soils found esp. in poorly drained arid or semiarid areas

sol·o·netz *also* **sol·o·nets** \ˌsäl-ə-ˈnets\ *n* [Russ *solonets* salt not extracted by decoction] (1936) **:** any of a group of intrazonal dark hard alkaline soils evolved by leaching and alkalizing from solonchak — **sol·o·netz·ic** \-ˈnet-sik\ *adj*

so long \sō-ˈlȯŋ, sə-\ *interj* [origin unknown] (ca. 1850) — used to express farewell

so long as *conj* (15c) **1 :** during and up to the end of the time that **:** WHILE **2 :** provided that

sol·stice \ˈsäl-stəs, ˈsōl-, ˈsȯl-\ *n* [ME, fr. OF, fr. L *solstitium,* fr. *sol* sun + *status,* pp. of *sistere* to come to a stop, cause to stand; akin to L *stare* to stand — more at SOLAR, STAND] (13c) **1 :** one of the two points on the ecliptic at which its distance from the celestial equator is greatest and which is reached by the sun each year about June 22d and December 22d **2 :** the time of the sun's passing a solstice which occurs about June 22d to begin summer in the northern hemisphere and about December 22d to begin winter in the northern hemisphere

sol·sti·tial \säl-ˈstish-əl, sōl-, sȯl-\ *adj* [L *solstitialis,* fr. *solstitium*] (1559) **1 :** of, relating to, or characteristic of a solstice and esp. the summer solstice **2 :** happening or appearing at or associated with a solstice

sol·u·bil·i·ty \ˌsäl-yə-ˈbil-ət-ē\ *n* (1661) **1 :** the quality or state of being soluble **2 :** the amount of a substance that will dissolve in a given amount of another substance

sol·u·bi·lize \ˈsäl-yə-bə-ˌlīz\ *vt* **-lized; -liz·ing** (ca. 1926) **:** to make soluble or increase the solubility of — **sol·u·bi·li·za·tion** \ˌsäl-yə-bə-lə-ˈzā-shən\ *n*

sol·u·ble \ˈsäl-yə-bəl\ *adj* [ME, fr. MF, capable of being loosened or dissolved, fr. LL *solubilis,* fr. L *solvere* to loosen, dissolve — more at SOLVE] (15c) **1 a :** susceptible of being dissolved in or as if in a fluid **b :** capable of being emulsified **:** EMULSIFIABLE ⟨a ~ oil⟩ **2 :** subject to being solved or explained ⟨~ questions⟩

soluble glass *n* (1875) **:** WATER GLASS 4

soluble RNA *n* (ca. 1961) **:** TRANSFER RNA

so·lum \ˈsō-ləm\ *n, pl* **so·la** \-lə\ *or* **solums** [NL, fr. L, ground, soil] (1935) **:** the altered layer of soil above the parent material that includes the A- and B-horizons

so·lus \ˈsō-ləs\ *adv or adj* [L] (1599) **:** ALONE — often used in stage directions

sol·ute \ˈsäl-ˌyüt\ *n* [L *solutus,* pp.] (1902) **:** a dissolved substance

so·lu·tion \sə-ˈlü-shən\ *n* [ME, fr. MF, fr. L *solution-, solutio,* fr. *solutus,* pp. of *solvere* to loosen, solve] (14c) **1 a :** an action or process of solving a problem **b :** an answer to a problem **:** EXPLANATION; *specif* **:** a set of values of the variables that satisfies an equation **2 a :** an act or the process by which a solid, liquid, or gaseous substance is homogeneously mixed with a liquid or sometimes a gas or solid **b :** a homogeneous mixture formed by this process; *esp* **:** a single-phase liquid system **c :** the condition of being dissolved **3 :** a bringing or coming to an end or into a state of discontinuity

solution set *n* (1959) **:** the set of values that satisfy an equation; *also* **:** TRUTH SET

So·lu·tre·an \sə-ˈlü-trē-ən\ *adj* [*Solutré,* village in France] (1888) **:** of or relating to an upper Paleolithic culture characterized by leaf-shaped finely flaked stone implements

solv·able \ˈsäl-və-bəl, ˈsȯl-\ *adj* (1676) **:** susceptible of solution or of being solved, resolved, or explained — **solv·abil·i·ty** \ˌsäl-və-ˈbil-ət-ē, ˌsȯl-\ *n*

[1]**sol·vate** \ˈsäl-ˌvāt, ˈsȯl-\ *n* [*solvent* + *-ate*] (1904) **:** an aggregate that consists of a solute ion or molecule with one or more solvent molecules; *also* **:** a substance (as a hydrate) containing such ions

[2]**solvate** *vt* **sol·vat·ed; sol·vat·ing** (1917) **:** to make part of a solvate — **sol·va·tion** \säl-ˈvā-shən, sȯl-\ *n*

Sol·vay process \ˈsäl-ˌvā-\ *n* [Ernest *Solvay* †1922 Belg. chemist] (1888) **:** a process for making soda from common salt by passing carbon dioxide into ammoniacal brine resulting in precipitation of sodium bicarbonate which is then calcined to carbonate

solve \ˈsälv, ˈsȯlv\ *vb* **solved; solv·ing** [ME *solven* to loosen, fr. L *solvere* to loosen, solve, dissolve, fr. *sed-, se-* apart + *luere* to release — more at SECEDE, LOSE] *vt* (1533) **1 :** to find a solution for ⟨~ a problem⟩ **2 :** to pay (as a debt) in full ~ *vi* **:** to solve something ⟨substitute the known values of the constants and ~ for *x*⟩ — **solv·er** *n*

sol·ven·cy \ˈsäl-vən-sē, ˈsȯl-\ *n* (ca. 1727) **:** the quality or state of being solvent

[1]**sol·vent** \-vənt\ *adj* [L *solvent-, solvens,* prp. of *solvere* to dissolve, pay] (1630) **1 :** able to pay all legal debts **2 :** that dissolves or can dissolve ⟨~ fluids⟩ ⟨~ action of water⟩ — **sol·vent·ly** *adv*

[2]**solvent** *n* (1671) **1 :** a usu. liquid substance capable of dissolving or dispersing one or more other substances **2 :** something that provides a solution **3 :** something that eliminates or attenuates something esp. unwanted — **sol·vent·less** \-ləs\ *adj*

sol·vol·y·sis \säl-ˈväl-ə-səs, sȯl-\ *n* [NL, fr. E *solvent* + *-o-* + *-lysis*] (ca. 1924) **:** a chemical reaction (as hydrolysis) of a solvent and solute that results in the formation of new compounds — **sol·vo·lyt·ic** \ˌsäl-və-ˈlit-ik, ˌsȯl-\ *adj*

[1]**so·ma** \ˈsō-mə\ *n* [Skt; akin to Av *haoma,* a Zoroastrian ritual drink, Gk *hyein* to rain — more at SUCK] (1827) **1 :** an East Indian leafless vine (*Sarcostemma acidum*) of the milkweed family with a milky acid juice **2 :** an intoxicating plant juice of ancient India used as an offering to the gods and as a drink of immortality by worshipers in Vedic ritual and worshiped as a Vedic god

[2]**soma** *n, pl* **so·ma·ta** \ˈsō-mət-ə\ *or* **somas** [NL *somat-, soma,* fr. Gk *sōmat-, sōma* body] (ca. 1885) **1 :** the body of an organism **2 :** all of an organism except the germ cells **3 :** CELL BODY

So·ma·li \sō-ˈmäl-ē, sə-\ *n, pl* **Somali** *or* **Somalis** (1850) **1 :** a member of a people of Somaliland apparently of mixed Mediterranean and Negroid stock **2 :** the Cushitic language of the Somali people

so many *adj* (1533) **1 :** constituting an unspecified number ⟨read *so many* chapters each night⟩ **2 :** constituting a group or pack ⟨behaved like *so many* animals⟩

somat- *or* **somato-** *comb form* [NL, fr. Gk *sōmat-, sōmato-,* fr. *sōmat-, sōma* body; akin to L *tumēre* to swell — more at THUMB] **:** body ⟨*somato*logy⟩

so·mat·ic \sō-ˈmat-ik, sə-\ *adj* [Gk *sōmatikos,* fr. *sōmat-, sōma*] (ca. 1775) **1 :** of, relating to, or affecting the body esp. as distinguished from the germ plasm or the psyche **2 :** of or relating to the wall of the body **:** PARIETAL — **so·mat·i·cal·ly** \-i-k(ə-)lē\ *adv*

somatic cell *n* (1888) **:** one of the cells of the body that compose the tissues, organs, and parts of that individual other than the germ cells

so·ma·tol·o·gy \ˌsō-mə-ˈtäl-ə-jē\ *n* [NL *somatologia,* fr. *somat-* + *-logia* -logy] (ca. 1878) **:** a branch of anthropology primarily concerned with the comparative study of human evolution, variation, and classification esp. through measurement and observation — **so·ma·to·log·i·cal** \ˌsō-mət-ᵊl-ˈäj-i-kəl, sō-ˌmat-\ *adj*

so·mato·me·din \sō-ˌmat-ə-ˈmēd-ᵊn\ *n* [*somat-* + *-medin* (perh. as in *intermedin*)] (1972) **:** any of several endogenous peptides produced esp. in the liver and dependent on and mediating growth hormone activity (as in sulfate uptake by epiphyseal cartilage)

so·mato·pleure \sō-ˈmat-ə-ˌplu̇(ə)r\ *n* [NL *somatopleura,* fr. *somat-* + Gk *pleura* side] (1874) **:** a complex layer in the embryo of a craniate vertebrate consisting of the outer of the two layers into which the lateral plate of the mesoderm splits together with the ectoderm that sheathes it externally and giving rise to the body wall

so·mato·sen·so·ry \sō-ˌmat-ə-ˈsen(t)s-(ə-)rē\ *adj* (1960) **:** of, relating to, or being sensory activity having its origin elsewhere than in the special sense organs (as eyes and ears) and conveying information about the state of the body proper and its immediate environment

so·mato·stat·in \sō-ˌmat-ə-ˈstat-ᵊn\ *n* [*somat-* + *-stat* + *-in*] (ca. 1973) **:** a polypeptide neurohormone that is found esp. in the hypothalamus and inhibits the secretion of several other hormones (as growth hormone, insulin, and gastrin)

\ə\ abut \ᵊ\ kitten, F table \ər\ further \a\ ash \ā\ ace \ä\ cot, cart \au̇\ out \ch\ chin \e\ bet \ē\ easy \g\ go \i\ hit \ī\ ice \j\ job \ŋ\ sing \ō\ go \ȯ\ law \ȯi\ boy \th\ thin \t͟h\ the \ü\ loot \u̇\ foot \y\ yet \zh\ vision \à, k̲, ⁿ, œ, œ̄, ue, ue̅, ʸ\ see Guide to Pronunciation

so·mato·tro·pic hormone \-ˌtrō-pik-\ *n* [*somat-* + *-tropic*] (ca. 1943) : GROWTH HORMONE 1
so·mato·tro·pin \-ˈtrō-pən\ *also* **so·mato·tro·phin** \-fən\ *n* [*somatotropic* + *-in*] (1941) : GROWTH HORMONE 1
so·mato·type \sō-ˈmat-ə-ˌtīp\ *n* (1940) : body type : PHYSIQUE
som·ber *or* **som·bre** \ˈsäm-bər\ *adj* [F *sombre*] (1760) **1** : so shaded as to be dark and gloomy **2 a** : of a serious mien : GRAVE **b** : of a dismal or depressing character : MELANCHOLY **c** : conveying gloomy suggestions or ideas **3** : of a dull or heavy cast or shade : dark colored — **som·ber·ly** *adv* — **som·ber·ness** *n*
som·bre·ro \səm-ˈbre(ə)r-(ˌ)ō, säm-\ *n, pl* **-ros** [Sp, fr. *sombra* shade] (1598) : a high-crowned hat of felt or straw with a very wide brim worn esp. in the Southwest and Mexico

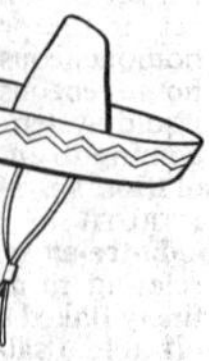
sombrero

som·brous \ˈsäm-brəs\ *adj* [F *sombre*] *archaic* (1730) : SOMBER
[1]some \ˈsəm, *for 2 without stress*\ *adj* [ME *som,* adj. & pron., fr. OE *sum;* akin to OHG *sum* some, Gk *hamē* somehow, *homos* same — more at SAME] (bef. 12c) **1** : being an unknown, undetermined, or unspecified unit or thing ⟨~ person knocked⟩ **2 a** : being one, a part, or an unspecified number of something (as a class or group) named or implied ⟨~ gems are hard⟩ **b** : being of an unspecified amount or number ⟨give me ~ water⟩ ⟨have ~ apples⟩ **3** : REMARKABLE, STRIKING ⟨that was ~ party⟩ **4** : being at least one — used to indicate that a logical proposition is asserted only of a subclass or certain members of the class denoted by the term which it modifies
[2]some \ˈsəm\ *pron, sing or pl in constr* (bef. 12c) **1** : one indeterminate quantity, portion, or number as distinguished from the rest **2** : an indefinite additional amount ⟨ran a mile and then ~⟩
[3]some \ˈsəm, ˌsəm\ *adv* (1817) **1 a** : in some degree : SOMEWHAT ⟨felt ~ better⟩ **b** : to some degree or extent : a little ⟨the cut bled ~⟩ ⟨I need to work on it ~ more⟩ **c** — used as a mild intensive ⟨that's going ~⟩ **2** : ABOUT ⟨~ 80 houses⟩ ⟨twenty-*some* people⟩
usage When *some* is used to modify a number, it is almost always a round number ⟨a community of *some* 150,000 inhabitants⟩ but because *some* is slightly more emphatic than *about* or *approximately* it is occas. used with a more exact number in an intensive function ⟨an expert parachutist, he has *some* 115 jumps to his credit — *Current Biog.*⟩ When *some* is used without a number, most commentators feel that *somewhat* is to be preferred. Their advice is an oversimplification, however; only when *some* modifies an adjective, usu. a comparative, will *somewhat* always substitute smoothly. When *some* modifies a verb or adverb, and esp. when it follows a verb, substitution of *somewhat* may prove awkward ⟨Italy forced me to grow up *some* —E.W. Brooke⟩ ⟨I'm not a prude; I've been around *some* in my day —Roy Rogers⟩ ⟨here in Newport, both Southern Cross and Courageous practiced *some* more —W.N. Wallace⟩
[1]-some \səm\ *adj suffix* [ME *-som,* fr. OE *-sum;* akin to OHG *-sam* -some, OE *sum* some] : characterized by a (specified) thing, quality, state, or action ⟨awe*some*⟩ ⟨burden*some*⟩ ⟨cuddle*some*⟩
[2]-some *n suffix* [ME (northern dial.) *-sum,* fr. ME *sum,* pron., one, some] : group of (so many) members and esp. persons ⟨four*some*⟩
[3]-some \ˌsōm\ *n comb form* [NL *-somat-, -soma,* fr. Gk *sōmat-, sōma* — more at SOMAT-] **1** : body ⟨chromo*some*⟩ **2** : chromosome ⟨mono*some*⟩
[1]some·body \ˈsəm-ˌbäd-ē, -bəd-\ *pron* (14c) : one or some person of unspecified or indefinite identity ⟨~ will come in⟩
[2]somebody *n* (1566) : a person of position or importance
some·day \ˈsəm-ˌdā\ *adv* (14c) : at some future time
some·deal \ˈsəm-ˌdēl\ *adv, archaic* (bef. 12c) : SOMEWHAT
some·how \ˈsəm-ˌhau̇\ *adv* (1664) : in one way or another not known or designated : by some means
some·one \-(ˌ)wən\ *pron* (14c) : some person : SOMEBODY
some·place \-ˌplās\ *adv* (14c) : SOMEWHERE
som·er·sault \ˈsəm-ər-ˌsȯlt\ *n* [MF *sombresaut* leap, deriv. of L *super* over + *saltus* leap, fr. *saltus,* pp. of *salire* to jump — more at OVER, SALLY] (ca. 1530) : a leap or roll in which a person turns forward or backward in a complete revolution bringing the feet over the head and finally landing on the feet — **somersault** *vi*
som·er·set \-ˌset\ *n or vi* [by alter.] (1591) : SOMERSAULT
[1]some·thing \ˈsəm(p)-thiŋ, *esp in rapid speech or for 2* ˈsəmp-ᵊm\ *pron* (bef. 12c) **1** : some indeterminate or unspecified thing **2** : a person or thing of consequence **3** : one having more or less the character, qualities, or nature of something different ⟨is ~ of a bore⟩ — **something else** : something or someone special or extraordinary
[2]something *adv* (13c) **1** : in some degree : SOMEWHAT **2** : to an extreme degree ⟨swears ~ awful⟩
[1]some·time \ˈsəm-ˌtīm\ *adv* (13c) **1** *archaic* : in the past : FORMERLY **2** *archaic* : once in a while : OCCASIONALLY **3** : at some time in the future ⟨I'll do it ~⟩ **4** : at some not specified or definitely known point of time ⟨~ last night⟩
[2]sometime *adj* (15c) **1** : having been formerly : FORMER, LATE **2** : being so occasionally or in only some respects ⟨a ~ . . . father who appears and disappears —Evelyn Shelby⟩
[1]some·times \ˈsəm-ˌtīmz *also* (ˌ)səm-ˈ\ *adv* (1526) : at times : now and then : OCCASIONALLY
[2]sometimes *adj* (1593) : SOMETIME
some·way \ˈsəm-ˌwā\ *also* **some·ways** \-ˌwāz\ *adv* (13c) : SOMEHOW
[1]some·what \-(ˌ)(h)wät, -ˌ(h)wət, (ˌ)səm-ˈ\ *pron* (13c) : SOMETHING
[2]somewhat *adv* (13c) : in some degree or measure : SLIGHTLY
some·when \ˈsəm-ˌ(h)wen\ *adv* (13c) : SOMETIME
[1]some·where \-ˌ(h)we(ə)r, -ˌ(h)wa(ə)r, -(ˌ)(h)wər\ *adv* (13c) **1** : in, at, from, or to a place unknown or unspecified ⟨makes reference to it ~⟩ **2** : to a place symbolizing positive accomplishment or progress ⟨at last we're getting ~⟩ **3** : in the vicinity of : APPROXIMATELY ⟨~ about nine o'clock⟩
[2]somewhere *n* (1647) : an undetermined or unnamed place
some·wheres \-ˌ(h)we(ə)rz, -ˌ(h)wa(ə)rz, -(ˌ)(h)wərz\ *adv* (1815) : SOMEWHERE
some·whith·er \-ˌ(h)wit͟h-ər\ *adv, archaic* (14c) : to some place : SOMEWHERE

-so·mic \ˈsō-mik\ *adj comb form* [ISV [3]*-some* + *-ic*] : having or being a body of chromosomes of which one or more but not all members exhibit (such) a degree of reduplication of chromosomes or genomes ⟨mono*somic*⟩
so·mite \ˈsō-ˌmīt\ *n* [ISV, fr. Gk *sōma* body — more at SOMAT-] (1869) : one of the longitudinal series of segments into which the body of many animals (as articulate animals and vertebrates) is divided : METAMERE
som·me·lier \ˌsəm-əl-ˈyā\ *n, pl* **sommeliers** \-ˈyā(z)\ [F, fr. MF, court official charged with transportation of supplies, pack animal driver, fr. OProv *saumalier* pack animal driver, fr. *sauma* pack animal, load of a pack animal, fr. LL *sagma* packsaddle — more at SUMPTER] (1921) : a waiter in a restaurant who has charge of wines and their service : a wine steward
somnambul- *comb form* [NL, fr. *somnambulus* somnambulist, fr. L *somnus* sleep + *-ambulus* (as in *funambulus* funambulist) — more at SOMNOLENT] : somnambulism : somnambulist ⟨*somnambul*ant⟩
som·nam·bu·lant \säm-ˈnam-byə-lənt\ *adj* (1866) : walking or addicted to walking while asleep
som·nam·bu·late \-ˌlāt\ *vi* **-lat·ed; -lat·ing** (1833) : to walk when asleep — **som·nam·bu·la·tion** \(ˌ)säm-ˌnam-byə-ˈlā-shən\ *n*
som·nam·bu·lism \säm-ˈnam-byə-ˌliz-əm\ *n* (ca. 1797) **1** : an abnormal condition of sleep in which motor acts (as walking) are performed **2** : actions characteristic of somnambulism — **som·nam·bu·list** \-ləst\ *n* — **som·nam·bu·lis·tic** \(ˌ)säm-ˌnam-byə-ˈlis-tik\ *adj* — **som·nam·bu·lis·ti·cal·ly** \-ti-k(ə-)lē\ *adv*
som·ni·fa·cient \ˌsäm-nə-ˈfā-shənt\ *adj* [L *somnus* sleep + E *-facient*] (ca. 1890) : HYPNOTIC 1 — **somnifacient** *n*
som·nif·er·ous \säm-ˈnif-(ə-)rəs\ *adj* [L *somnifer* somniferous, fr. *somnus* + *-fer* -ferous] (1602) : SOPORIFIC
som·no·lence \ˈsäm-nə-lən(t)s\ *n* (14c) : the quality or state of being drowsy : SLEEPINESS
som·no·len·cy \-lən-sē\ *n* (ca. 1623) : SOMNOLENCE
som·no·lent \-lənt\ *adj* [ME *sompnolent,* fr. MF, fr. L *somnolentus,* fr. *somnus* sleep; akin to OE *swefn* sleep, Gk *hypnos*] (15c) **1** : of a kind likely to induce sleep ⟨a ~ sermon⟩ **2** : inclined to or heavy with sleep : DROWSY — **som·no·lent·ly** *adv*
[1]so much *adv* (13c) : by the amount indicated or suggested ⟨if they lose their way, *so much* the better for us⟩
[2]so much *pron* (14c) **1** : something (as an amount or price) unspecified or undetermined ⟨charge *so much* a mile⟩ **2** : all that can be or is to be said or done ⟨*so much* for the history of the case⟩
[3]so much *adj* (1695) — used as an intensive ⟨the house burned like *so much* paper⟩ ⟨sounded like *so much* nonsense⟩
so much as *adv* (15c) : EVEN
son \ˈsən\ *n* [ME *sone,* fr. OE *sunu;* akin to OHG *sun* son, Gk *hyios*] (bef. 12c) **1 a** : a male offspring esp. of human beings **b** : a male adopted child **c** : a male descendant **2** *cap* : the second person of the Trinity **3** : a person closely associated with or deriving from a formative agent (as a nation, school, or race) — **son·hood** \-ˌhu̇d\ *n*
so·nant \ˈsō-nənt\ *adj* [L *sonant-, sonans,* prp. of *sonare* to sound — more at SOUND] (1846) **1** : VOICED 2 **2** : SYLLABIC 1a — **sonant** *n*
so·nar \ˈsō-ˌnär\ *n* [*so*und *na*vigation *r*anging] (1945) : an apparatus that detects the presence and location of a submerged object (as a submarine) by means of sonic and supersonic waves reflected back from or produced by an object; *also* : any of various devices using such waves for locating or measuring the distance to other objects
so·na·ta \sə-ˈnät-ə\ *n* [It, fr. *sonare* to sound, fr. L] (1694) : an instrumental musical composition typically of three or four movements in contrasting forms and keys
sonata form *n* (1873) : a musical form that consists basically of an exposition, a development, and a recapitulation and that is used esp. for the first movement of a sonata
son·a·ti·na \ˌsän-ə-ˈtē-nə\ *n* [It, dim. of *sonata*] (ca. 1724) : a short usu. simplified sonata
sonde \ˈsänd\ *n* [F, lit., sounding line — more at SOUND] (ca. 1923) : any of various devices for testing physical conditions (as at high altitudes, below the earth's surface, or inside the body)
sone \ˈsōn\ *n* [ISV, fr. L *sonus* sound — more at SOUND] (1948) : a subjective unit of loudness for an average listener equal to the loudness of a 1000-cycle sound that has an intensity 40 decibels above the listener's own threshold of hearing
son et lu·mière \ˌsōⁿ-(n)ā-lüm-ˈye(ə)r\ *n* [F, lit., sound and light] (1957) : an outdoor spectacle at an historic site consisting of recorded narration with light and sound effects
song \ˈsȯŋ\ *n* [ME, fr. OE *sang;* akin to OE *singan* to sing] (bef. 12c) **1** : the act or art of singing **2** : poetical composition **3 a** : a short musical composition of words and music **b** : a collection of such compositions **4** : a distinctive or characteristic sound or series of sounds (as of a bird or insect) **5 a** : a melody for a lyric poem or ballad **b** : a poem easily set to music **6 a** : a habitual or characteristic manner **b** : a violent, abusive, or noisy reaction ⟨put up quite a ~⟩ **7** : a small amount ⟨sold for a ~⟩ — **song·like** \-ˌlīk\ *adj*
song and dance *n* (1872) **1** : a theatrical performance (as a vaudeville performance) combining singing and dancing **2** : a long and often familiar statement or explanation that is not necessarily true or pertinent
song·bird \ˈsȯŋ-ˌbərd\ *n* (1774) **1 a** : a bird that utters a succession of musical tones **b** : a passerine bird **2** : a female singer
song·book \-ˈbu̇k\ *n* (bef. 12c) : a collection of songs; *specif* : a book containing vocal music (as hymns)
song cycle *n* (1899) : a group of related songs designed to form a musical entity
song·fest \ˈsȯŋ-ˌfest\ *n* (ca. 1917) : an informal session of group singing of popular or folk songs
song·ful \-fəl\ *adj* (15c) : given to or suggestive of singing : MELODIOUS — **song·ful·ly** \-fə-lē\ *adv* — **song·ful·ness** *n*
song·less \-ləs\ *adj* (1805) : lacking in, incapable of, or not given to song — **song·less·ly** *adv*
Song of Sol·o·mon \-ˈsäl-ə-mən\ [fr. the opening verse: "The song of songs, which is Solomon's"] : a collection of love poems forming a book in the Protestant canon of the Old Testament — see BIBLE table
Song of Songs [trans. of Heb *shir hashshirim*] : a collection of love poems forming a book in the canonical Jewish Scriptures and correspond-

ing to the Song of Solomon in the Protestant canon of the Old Testament — see BIBLE table
song·smith \'sȯŋ-ˌsmith\ *n* (1795) : a composer of songs
song sparrow *n* (1810) : a common No. American sparrow (*Melospiza melodia*) that is brownish above and white below and that is noted for its melodious song
song·ster \'sȯŋ(k)-stər\ *n* [ME, fr. OE *sangestre* woman singer, fr. *sang* song + *-estre* female agent — more at -STER] (14c) **1 :** one that sings with skill **2 :** SONGBOOK
song·stress \'sȯŋ(k)-strəs\ *n* [*songster* + *-ess*] (1703) : a female singer
song thrush *n* (1668) : an Old World thrush (*Turdus ericetorum*) largely brown above and white below — called also *mavis, throstle*
song·writ·er \'sȯŋ-ˌrīt-ər\ *n* (1821) : a person who composes words or music or both esp. for popular songs — **song·writ·ing** \-ˌrīt-iŋ\ *n*
son·ic \'sän-ik\ *adj* [L *sonus* sound — more at SOUND] (1923) **1 :** utilizing, produced by, or relating to sound waves ⟨~ altimeter⟩ **2 :** having a frequency within the audibility range of the human ear — used of waves and vibrations **3 :** of, relating to, or being the speed of sound in air or about 741 miles per hour at sea level **4 :** capable of uttering sounds — **son·i·cal·ly** \-i-k(ə-)lē\ *adv*
son·i·cate \'sän-ə-ˌkāt\ *vt* **-cat·ed; -cat·ing** [*sonic* + *-ate*] (1961) : to disrupt (as bacteria) by treatment with high-frequency sound waves — **son·i·ca·tion** \ˌsän-ə-'kā-shən\ *n*
sonic barrier *n* (1947) : a sudden large increase in aerodynamic drag that occurs as the speed of an aircraft approaches the speed of sound
sonic boom *n* (1952) : a sound resembling an explosion produced when a shock wave formed at the nose of an aircraft traveling at supersonic speed reaches the ground — called also *sonic bang*
son–in–law \'sən-ən-ˌlȯ\ *n, pl* **sons–in–law** (14c) : the husband of one's daughter
son·less \'sən-ləs\ *adj* (14c) : not possessing or never having had a son
son·ly \-lē\ *adj* (15c) : FILIAL
son·net \'sän-ət\ *n* [It *sonetto,* fr. OProv *sonet* little song, fr. *son* sound, song, fr. L *sonus* sound] (1557) : a fixed verse form of Italian origin consisting of fourteen lines that are typically five-foot iambics rhyming according to a prescribed scheme; *also* : a poem in this pattern
son·ne·teer \ˌsän-ə-'ti(ə)r\ *n* (1588) **1 :** a minor or insignificant poet **2 :** a composer of sonnets
son·net·ize \'sän-ə-ˌtīz\ *vb* **-ized; -iz·ing** *vi* (1798) : to compose a sonnet ~ *vt* : to compose a sonnet on or to
sonnet sequence *n* (1881) : a series of sonnets often having a unifying theme
son·ny \'sən-ē\ *n* (1850) : a young boy — usu. used in address
so·no·buoy \'sō-nō-ˌbü-ē, 'sän-ō-, -ˌbȯi\ *n* [L *sonus* sound + E *-o-* + *buoy* — more at SOUND] (1945) : a buoy equipped for detecting underwater sounds and transmitting them by radio
son of a bitch \'sən-ə-və-ˌbich; *as an interj* ˌsən-ə-və-'bich\ *n, pl* **sons of bitch·es** \ˌsən-zə-'bich-əz\ (1712) : BASTARD 3 — sometimes considered vulgar; sometimes used interjectionally to express surprise or disappointment
son of God (bef. 12c) **1** *often cap S* **:** a superhuman or divine being (as an angel) **2** *cap S* **:** MESSIAH 1 **3 :** a person established in the love of God by divine promise
son of man (bef. 12c) **1 :** a human being **2** *often cap S* **:** God's messiah destined to preside over the final judgment of mankind
so·nor·i·ty \sə-'nȯr-ət-ē, -'när-\ *n, pl* **-ties** (1623) **1 :** the quality or state of being sonorous : RESONANCE **2 :** a sonorous tone or speech
so·no·rous \sə-'nōr-əs, -'nȯr-; 'sän-ə-rəs\ *adj* [L *sonorus;* akin to L *sonus* sound] (ca. 1611) **1 :** producing sound (as when struck) **2 :** full or loud in sound **3 :** imposing or impressive in effect or style **4 :** having a high or an indicated degree of sonority ⟨~ sounds like \ä\ and \ȯ\⟩ — **so·no·rous·ly** *adv* — **so·no·rous·ness** *n*
so·no·vox \'sō-nə-ˌväks, 'sän-ə-\ *n* [L *sonus* + *vox* voice — more at VOICE] (1939) : an electronic sound effects device held against the throat to give the effect of speech to recorded nonhuman sounds (as of a waterfall or train whistle) that are transmitted through the larynx and formed into words by the mouth
son·ship \'sən-ˌship\ *n* (1587) : the relationship of son to father
sonsy *or* **sons·ie** \'sän(t)-sē\ *adj* [Sc *sons* health] *chiefly dial* (1725) : BUXOM, COMELY
soon \'sün, *esp NewEng* 'sůn\ *adv* [ME *soone,* fr. OE *sōna;* akin to OHG *sān* immediately] (bef. 12c) **1 a** *obs* **:** at once : IMMEDIATELY **b :** before long : without undue time lapse ⟨~ after sunrise⟩ **2 :** in a prompt manner : SPEEDILY ⟨as ~ as possible⟩ ⟨the ~*er* the better⟩ **3** *archaic* **:** before the usual time **4 :** in agreement with one's choice or preference : WILLINGLY ⟨I'd ~*er* walk than drive⟩
soon·er \'sü-nər\ *n* [*sooner,* compar. of *soon*] (1890) **1 :** a person settling on land in the early West before its official opening to settlement in order to gain the prior claim allowed by law to the first settler after official opening **2** *cap* **:** a native or resident of Oklahoma — used as a nickname
sooner or later *adv* (1577) : at some uncertain future time : SOMETIME
[1]**soot** \'sůt, 'sət, 'süt\ *n* [ME, fr. OE *sōt;* akin to OIr *súide* soot, OE *sittan* to sit] (bef. 12c) : a black substance formed by combustion or separated from fuel during combustion, rising in fine particles, and adhering to the sides of the chimney or pipe conveying the smoke; *esp* : the fine powder consisting chiefly of carbon that colors smoke
[2]**soot** *vt* (1602) : to coat or cover with soot
[1]**sooth** \'süth\ *adj* [ME, fr. OE *sōth;* akin to OHG *sand* true, Gk *eteos,* L *esse* to be] (bef. 12c) **1** *archaic* **:** TRUE **2** *archaic* **:** SOFT, SWEET
[2]**sooth** *n* (bef. 12c) **1** *archaic* **:** TRUTH, REALITY **2** *obs* **:** BLANDISHMENT
soothe \'süṯẖ\ *vb* **soothed; sooth·ing** [ME *sothen* to prove the truth, fr. OE *sōthian,* fr. *sōth*] *vt* (1573) **1 :** to please by or as if by attention or concern : PLACATE **2 :** RELIEVE, ALLEVIATE **3 :** to bring comfort, solace, or reassurance to ~ *vi* : to bring peace, composure, or quietude — **sooth·er** *n*
sooth·fast \'süth-ˌfast\ *adj* (bef. 12c) **1** *archaic* **:** TRUE **2** *archaic* **:** TRUTHFUL
sooth·ing \'sü-ṯẖiŋ\ *adj* (1599) : tending to soothe; *also* : having a sedative effect ⟨~ syrup⟩ — **sooth·ing·ly** \-ṯẖiŋ-lē\ *adv* — **sooth·ing·ness** *n*
sooth·ly \'süth-lē\ *adv, archaic* (bef. 12c) : in truth : TRULY
sooth·say \-ˌsā\ *vi* (1606) : to practice soothsaying — **sooth·say·er** *n*
sooth·say·ing \-ˌsā-iŋ\ *n* (1535) **1 :** the act of foretelling events **2 :** PREDICTION, PROPHECY

sooty \'sůt-ē, 'sət-, 'süt-\ *adj* **soot·i·er; -est** (13c) **1 a :** of, relating to, or producing soot **b :** soiled with soot **2 :** of the color of soot — **soot·i·ly** \-ᵊl-ē\ *adv* — **soot·i·ness** \-ē-nəs\ *n*
sooty mold *n* (1903) : a dark growth of fungus mycelium growing in insect honeydew on plants; *also* : a fungus producing such growth
sooty tern *n* (1785) : a widely distributed tern (*Sterna fuscata*) of tropical oceans that is blackish above and white below — called also *wide-awake*
[1]**sop** \'säp\ *n* [ME *soppe,* fr. OE *sopp;* akin to OE *sūpan* to swallow — more at SUP] (bef. 12c) **1** *chiefly dial* **:** a piece of food dipped or steeped in a liquid **2 :** a conciliatory or propitiatory bribe, gift, or advance
[2]**sop** *vt* **sopped; sop·ping** (bef. 12c) **1 a :** to steep or dip in or as if in liquid **b :** to wet thoroughly : SOAK **2 :** to mop up (as water) **3 :** to give a bribe or conciliatory gift to
so·pai·pil·la \ˌsō-pī-'pē(l)-yə\ *also* **so·pa·pil·la** \'sō-pə-\ *n* [Sp *sopaipilla,* dim. of *sopaipa* fritter soaked in honey, fr. *sopa* sop, food soaked in milk, of Gmc origin; akin to OE *sūpan* to swallow] (ca. 1940) : a square of deep-fried dough often sweetened and eaten as dessert
soph·ism \'säf-ˌiz-əm\ *n* (14c) **1 :** an argument apparently correct in form but actually invalid; *esp* : such an argument used to deceive **2 :** SOPHISTRY 1
soph·ist \'säf-əst\ *n* [L *sophista,* fr. Gk *sophistēs,* lit., expert, wise man, fr. *sophizesthai* to become wise, deceive, fr. *sophos* clever, wise] (ca. 1542) **1** *cap* **:** any of a class of ancient Greek teachers of rhetoric, philosophy, and the art of successful living prominent about the middle of the 5th century B.C. for their adroit subtle and allegedly often specious reasoning **2 :** PHILOSOPHER, THINKER **3 :** a captious or fallacious reasoner
so·phis·tic \sä-'fis-tik, sə-\ *or* **so·phis·ti·cal** \-ti-kəl\ *adj* (1549) **1 :** of or relating to sophists, sophistry, or the ancient Sophists ⟨~ rhetoric⟩ ⟨~ subtleties⟩ **2 :** plausible but fallacious ⟨~ reasoning⟩ — **so·phis·ti·cal·ly** \-ti-k(ə-)lē\ *adv*
[1]**so·phis·ti·cate** \sə-'fis-tə-ˌkāt\ *vt* **-cat·ed; -cat·ing** [ME *sophisticaten,* fr. ML *sophisticatus,* pp. of *sophisticare,* fr. L *sophisticus* sophistic, fr. Gk *sophistikos,* fr. *sophistēs* sophist] (15c) **1 :** to alter deceptively; *esp* : ADULTERATE **2 :** to deprive of genuineness, naturalness, or simplicity; *esp* : to deprive of naiveté and make worldly-wise : DISILLUSION **3 :** to make complicated or complex
[2]**so·phis·ti·cate** \-ti-kət, -tə-ˌkāt\ *n* (1923) : a sophisticated person
so·phis·ti·cat·ed \-tə-ˌkāt-əd\ *adj* [ML *sophisticatus*] (1603) **1 :** not in a natural, pure, or original state : ADULTERATED ⟨a ~ oil⟩ **2 :** deprived of native or original simplicity: as **a :** highly complicated or developed : COMPLEX ⟨~ electronic devices⟩ **b :** WORLDLY-WISE, KNOWING ⟨a ~ adolescent⟩ **3 :** devoid of grossness: as **a :** finely experienced and aware ⟨a ~ columnist⟩ **b :** intellectually appealing ⟨a ~ novel⟩ — **so·phis·ti·cat·ed·ly** *adv*
syn SOPHISTICATED, WORLDLY-WISE, BLASÉ mean experienced in the ways of the world. SOPHISTICATED often implies refinement, urbanity, cleverness, and cultivation ⟨guests at her salon were usu. rich and *sophisticated*⟩ WORLDLY-WISE suggests a close and practical knowledge of the affairs and manners of society and an inclination toward materialism ⟨a *worldly-wise* woman with a philosophy of personal independence⟩ BLASÉ implies a lack of responsiveness to common joys as a result of a real or affected surfeit of experience and cultivation ⟨*blasé* travelers who claimed to have been everywhere⟩
so·phis·ti·ca·tion \sə-ˌfis-tə-'kā-shən\ *n* (15c) **1 a :** the use of sophistry : sophistic reasoning **b :** SOPHISM, QUIBBLE **2 :** the process of making impure or weak : ADULTERATION **3 :** the process or result of becoming cultured, knowledgeable, or disillusioned; *esp* : CULTIVATION, URBANITY **4 :** the process or result of becoming more complex, developed, or subtle
soph·ist·ry \'säf-ə-strē\ *n* (14c) **1 :** subtly deceptive reasoning or argumentation **2 :** SOPHISM 1
soph·o·more \'säf-ˌmō(ə)r, -ˌmȯ(ə)r; 'säf-ᵊm-ˌō(ə)r, -ˌȯ(ə)r; *also* 'sȯf-\ *n* [prob. fr. Gk *sophos* wise + *mōros* foolish — more at MORON] (1684) : a student in the second year at college or secondary school
soph·o·mor·ic \ˌsäf-ə-'mōr-ik, -'mȯr-, -'mär-\ *adj* (1873) **1 :** conceited and overconfident of knowledge but poorly informed and immature **2 :** of, relating to, or characteristic of a sophomore
So·pho·ni·as \ˌsäf-ə-'nī-əs, ˌsō-fə-\ *n* [LL, fr. Gk, fr. Heb *Sĕphanyāh*] : ZEPHANIAH
so·phy \'sō-fē\ *n* [Per *Safī*] *archaic* (1539) : a sovereign of Persia
-so·phy \sə-fē\ *n comb form* [ME *-sophie,* fr. OF, fr. L *-sophia,* fr. Gk, fr. *sophia* wisdom, fr. *sophos*] : knowledge : wisdom : science ⟨anthropo*sophy*⟩
so·pite \sō-'pīt\ *vt* **so·pit·ed; so·pit·ing** [L *sopitus,* pp. of *sopire* to put to sleep, fr. *sopor*] (1542) **1** *archaic* **:** to put to sleep : LULL **2** *archaic* **:** to put an end to (as a claim) : SETTLE
so·po·rif·er·ous \ˌsäp-ə-'rif-(ə-)rəs, ˌsō-pə-\ *adj* [L *soporifer* soporiferous, fr. *sopor* + *-fer* -ferous] (1590) : SOPORIFIC — **so·po·rif·er·ous·ness** *n*
[1]**so·po·rif·ic** \-'rif-ik\ *adj* [prob. fr. F *soporifique,* fr. L *sopor* deep sleep; akin to L *somnus* sleep — more at SOMNOLENT] (1665) **1 a :** causing or tending to cause sleep **b :** tending to dull awareness or alertness **2 :** of, relating to, or marked by sleepiness or lethargy
[2]**soporific** *n* (ca. 1772) : a soporific agent; *specif* : HYPNOTIC 1
sop·ping \'säp-iŋ\ *adj* (1877) : wet through : SOAKING
sop·py \'säp-ē\ *adj* **sop·pi·er; -est** (1823) **1 a :** soaked through : SATURATED **b :** very wet **2 :** SENTIMENTAL, MAWKISH
so·pra·ni·no \ˌsō-prə-'nē-(ˌ)nō, ˌsäp-rə-\ *n, pl* **-nos** [It, dim. of *soprano*] (1905) : a musical instrument (as a recorder or saxophone) higher in pitch than the soprano
[1]**so·pra·no** \sə-'pran-(ˌ)ō, -'prän-\ *adj* [It, adj. & n., fr. *sopra* above, fr. L *supra* — more at SUPRA-] (1730) : relating to or having the range or part of a soprano
[2]**soprano** *n, pl* **-nos** (1738) **1 :** the highest singing voice of women, boys, or castrati; *also* : a person having this voice **2 :** the highest voice part

in a 4-part chorus **3 :** a member of a family of instruments having the highest range

so·ra \'sōr-ə, 'sór-\ *n* [origin unknown] (1705) **:** a small short-billed No. American rail (*Porzana carolina*) common in marshes

[1]**sorb** \'só(ə)rb\ *n* [F *sorbe* fruit of the service tree, fr. L *sorbum*] (1530) **1 :** the fruit of a sorb **2 :** any of several Old World trees related to the apples and pears (as a service or rowan tree)

[2]**sorb** *vt* [back-formation fr. *absorb* & *adsorb*] (1926) **:** to take up and hold by either adsorption or absorption — **sorb·abil·i·ty** \ˌsórb-ə-'bil-ət-ē\ *n* — **sorb·able** \'sórb-ə-bəl\ *adj*

Sorb \'só(ə)rb\ *n* [G *Sorbe*, fr. Sorbian *Serb*] (1843) **1 :** a member of a Slavic people whose present representatives are the Wends living in Saxony and Brandenburg **2 :** WENDISH — **Sor·bi·an** \'sór-bē-ən\ *adj or n*

sor·bate \'só(ə)r-ˌbāt, 'sór-bət\ *n* (1926) **:** a sorbed substance

sor·bent \'sór-bənt\ *n* [L *sorbent-, sorbens*, prp. of *sorbēre* to suck up — more at ABSORB] (ca. 1890) **:** a substance that sorbs

sor·bet \'sór-bət\ *n* [MF, fr. OIt *sorbetto*, fr. Turk *şerbet* — more at SHERBET] (1766) **:** a fruit-flavored ice typically served between courses as a palate refresher

sor·bic acid \ˌsór-bik-\ *n* [[1]*sorb*] (1815) **:** a crystalline acid $C_6H_8O_2$ obtained from the unripe fruits of the mountain ash or synthesized and used as a fungicide and food preservative

sor·bi·tol \'sór-bə-ˌtól, -ˌtōl\ *n* [[1]*sorb* + *-itol*] (ca. 1895) **:** a faintly sweet alcohol $C_6H_{14}O_6$ that occurs esp. in mountain ash fruits, is made synthetically, and is used esp. as a humectant and softener and in making ascorbic acid

sor·cer·er \'sórs-(ə-)rər\ *n* (1526) **:** a person who practices sorcery **:** WIZARD — **sor·cer·ess** \-(ə-)rəs\ *n*

sor·cer·ous \'sórs-(ə-)rəs\ *adj* (1546) **:** of or relating to sorcery **:** MAGICAL

sor·cery \'sórs-(ə-)rē\ *n* [ME *sorcerie*, fr. MF, fr. *sorcier* sorcerer, fr. (assumed) VL *sortiarius*, fr. L *sort-, sors* chance, lot — more at SERIES] (14c) **1 :** the use of power gained from the assistance or control of evil spirits esp. for divining **:** NECROMANCY **2 :** MAGIC 2a

sor·did \'sórd-əd\ *adj* [L *sordidus*, fr. *sordes* dirt — more at SWART] (1597) **1 a :** DIRTY, FILTHY **b :** WRETCHED, SQUALID **2 :** marked by baseness or grossness **:** VILE ⟨~ motives⟩ **3 :** meanly avaricious **:** COVETOUS **4 :** of a dull or muddy color ***syn*** see MEAN — **sor·did·ly** *adv* — **sor·did·ness** *n*

sor·di·no \sór-'dē-(ˌ)nō\ *n, pl* **-di·ni** \-(ˌ)nē\ [It, fr. *sordo* silent, fr. L *surdus* — more at SURD] (1801) **:** MUTE 3

[1]**sore** \'sō(ə)r, 'só(ə)r\ *adj* **sor·er; sor·est** [ME *sor*, fr. OE *sār*; akin to OHG *sēr* sore, L *saevus* fierce] (bef. 12c) **1 a :** causing pain or distress **b :** painfully sensitive **:** TENDER ⟨~ muscles⟩ **c :** hurt or inflamed so as to be or seem painful ⟨~ runny eyes⟩ ⟨a dog limping on a ~ leg⟩ **2 :** attended by difficulties, hardship, or exertion **3 :** ANGRY, VEXED — **sore·ness** *n*

[2]**sore** *n* (bef. 12c) **1 :** a localized sore spot on the body; *esp* **:** one (as an ulcer) with the tissues ruptured or abraded and usu. with infection **2 :** a source of pain or vexation **:** AFFLICTION

[3]**sore** *adv* (bef. 12c) **:** SORELY

sore·head \'sō(ə)r-ˌhed, 'só(ə)r-\ *n* (1848) **:** a person easily angered or disgruntled — **sorehead** *or* **sore·head·ed** \-'hed-əd\ *adj*

sore·ly \'sō(ə)r-lē, 'só(ə)r-\ *adv* (bef. 12c) **1 :** in a sore manner **:** PAINFULLY **2 :** VERY, EXTREMELY ⟨~ needed changes⟩

sore throat *n* (1686) **:** painful throat due to inflammation of the fauces and pharynx

sor·ghum \'sór-gəm\ *n* [NL, fr. It *sorgo*, perh. fr. (assumed) VL *Syricum (granum)*, lit., Syrian grain] (1597) **1 :** any of an economically important genus (*Sorghum*) of Old World tropical grasses similar to Indian corn in habit but with the spikelets in pairs on a hairy rachis; *esp* **:** a cultivated plant (as a grain sorghum or sorgo) derived from a common species (*S. vulgare*) **2 :** syrup from the juice of a sorgo that resembles cane syrup **3 :** something cloyingly sentimental

sor·go \'só(ə)r-(ˌ)gō\ *n* [It] (ca. 1760) **:** a sorghum cultivated primarily for the sweet juice in its stems from which sugar and syrup are made but also used for fodder and silage — called also *sweet sorghum*

so·ri·tes \sə-'rīt-(ˌ)ēz\ *n, pl* **sorites** [L, fr. Gk *sōritēs*, fr. *sōros* heap — more at THUMB] (1551) **:** an argument consisting of propositions so arranged that the predicate of any one forms the subject of the next and the conclusion unites the subject of the first proposition with the predicate of the last

So·rop·ti·mist \sə-'räp-tə-məst, sò-\ *n* [*Soroptomist* (club)] (ca. 1924) **:** a member of a service club composed of professional women and women business executives

so·ro·ral \sə-'rōr-əl, -'ròr-\ *adj* [L *soror* sister — more at SISTER] (1858) **:** of, relating to, or characteristic of a sister **:** SISTERLY

so·ro·rate \sə-'rōr-ət, -'ròr-\ *n* [L *soror*] (1910) **:** the marriage of one man to two or more sisters usu. successively and after the first wife has been found to be barren or after her death

so·ror·i·ty \sə-'ròr-ət-ē, -'rär-\ *n, pl* **-ties** [ML *sororitas* sisterhood, fr. L *soror* sister] (1532) **:** a club of women; *specif* **:** a women's student organization (as at a college) that is formed chiefly for social purposes and has a name consisting of Greek letters

sorp·tion \'sórp-shən\ *n* [back-formation fr. *absorption* & *adsorption*] (1909) **:** the process of sorbing **:** the state of being sorbed — **sorp·tive** \'sórp-tiv\ *adj*

[1]**sor·rel** \'sòr-əl, 'sär-\ *n* [ME *sorelle*, fr. MF *sorel*, n. & adj., fr. *sor* reddish brown] (15c) **1 :** a sorrel-colored animal; *esp* **:** a light bright chestnut horse often with white mane and tail — compare [1]CHESTNUT 4, [2]BAY 1 **2 :** a brownish orange to light brown

[2]**sorrel** *n* [ME *sorel*, fr. MF *surele*, fr. OF, fr. *sur* sour, of Gmc origin; akin to OHG *sūr* sour — more at SOUR] (15c) **:** any of various plants with sour juice: as **a :** [1]DOCK 1 **b :** WOOD SORREL

sorrel tree *n* (1687) **:** SOURWOOD

[1]**sor·row** \'sär-(ˌ)ō, 'sòr-, -ə(-w)\ *n* [ME *sorow*, fr. OE *sorg*; akin to OHG *sorga* sorrow, OSlav *sraga* sickness] (bef. 12c) **1 :** deep distress and regret (as over the loss of something loved) **2 :** a cause of grief or sadness **3 :** a display of grief or sadness

syn SORROW, GRIEF, ANGUISH, WOE, REGRET mean distress of mind. SORROW implies a sense of loss or a sense of guilt and remorse; GRIEF implies poignant sorrow for an immediate cause; ANGUISH suggests torturing grief or dread; WOE is deep or inconsolable grief or misery; REGRET implies pain caused by deep disappointment, fruitless longing, or unavailing remorse.

[2]**sorrow** *vi* (bef. 12c) **:** to feel or express sorrow — **sor·row·er** \-ə-wər\ *n*

sor·row·ful \-ō-fəl, -ə-fəl\ *adj* (bef. 12c) **1 :** full of or marked by sorrow **2 :** expressive of or inducing sorrow — **sor·row·ful·ly** \-f(ə-)lē\ *adv* — **sor·row·ful·ness** \-fəl-nəs\ *n*

sor·ry \'sär-ē, 'sòr-\ *adj* **sor·ri·er; -est** [ME *sory*, fr. OE *sārig*, fr. *sār* sore] (bef. 12c) **1 :** feeling sorrow, regret, or penitence **2 :** MOURNFUL, SAD **3 :** inspiring sorrow, pity, scorn, or ridicule ***syn*** see CONTEMPTIBLE — **sor·ri·ly** \-ə-lē\ *adv* — **sor·ri·ness** \-ē-nəs\ *n*

[1]**sort** \'só(ə)rt\ *n* [ME, fr. MF *sorte*, prob. fr. ML *sort-, sors*, fr. L, chance, lot — more at SERIES] (14c) **1 a :** a group set up on the basis of any characteristic in common **:** CLASS, KIND **b :** an instance of a kind ⟨a ~ of black Paul Bunyan, towering 6′10″ —Jack Olsen⟩ **c :** PERSON, INDIVIDUAL ⟨he's not a bad ~⟩ **2** *archaic* **:** GROUP, COMPANY **3 a :** method or manner of acting **:** WAY, MANNER **b :** CHARACTER, NATURE ⟨people of an evil ~⟩ **4 a :** a letter or character that is one element of a font **b :** a character or piece of type that is not part of a regular font ***syn*** see TYPE — **after a sort :** in a rough or haphazard way — **of sorts** *or* **of a sort :** of an inconsequential or mediocre quality ⟨a poet *of sorts*⟩ — **out of sorts 1 :** somewhat ill **2 :** GROUCHY, IRRITABLE

[2]**sort** *vt* (15c) **1 a :** to put in a certain place or rank according to kind, class, or nature ⟨~ the good apples from the bad⟩ **b :** to arrange according to characteristics **:** CLASSIFY ⟨~ out colors⟩ **2** *chiefly Scot* **:** to put to rights **:** put in order **3 a :** to examine in order to clarify ⟨~*ing* out his problems⟩ **b :** to free of confusion **:** CLARIFY ⟨waited until things ~*ed* themselves out⟩ ~ *vi* **1 :** to join or associate with others esp. of the same kind ⟨~ with thieves⟩ **2 :** SUIT, AGREE — **sort·able** \'sórt-ə-bəl\ *adj* — **sort·er** *n*

sor·tie \'sórt-ē, sór-'tē\ *n* [F, fr. MF, fr. *sortir* to escape, prob. fr. L *sortiri* to cast lots] (1795) **1 :** a sudden issuing of troops from a defensive position against the enemy **2 :** one mission or attack by a single plane **3 :** FORAY, RAID — **sortie** *vi*

sor·ti·lege \'sórt-ᵊl-ij, -ˌej\ *n* [ME, fr. ML *sortilegium*, fr. L *sortilegus* foretelling, fr. *sort-, sors* lot + *-i-* + *legere* to gather — more at LEGEND] (14c) **1 :** divination by lots **2 :** SORCERY

sor·ti·tion \sór-'tish-ən\ *n* [L *sortition-, sortitio*, fr. *sortitus*, pp. of *sortiri* to cast or draw lots, fr. *sort-, sors* lot — more at SERIES] (1597) **:** the act or an instance of casting lots

sort of \ˌsórt-ə(v), -ər\ *adv* (1790) **:** to a moderate degree **:** RATHER

so·rus \'sōr-əs, 'sòr-\ *n, pl* **so·ri** \'sō(ə)r-ˌī, 'só(ə)r-, -ˌē\ [NL, fr. Gk *sōros* heap — more at THUMB] (1832) **:** a cluster of plant reproductive bodies: as **a :** one of the dots on the underside of a fertile fern frond consisting of a cluster of spores **b :** a mass of spores bursting through the epidermis of the host plant of a parasitic fungus **c :** a cluster of gemmae on the thallus of a lichen

SOS \ˌes-(ˌ)ō-'es, ˌes-ə-'wes\ *n* (1910) **1 :** an internationally recognized signal of distress in radio code ••• ––– ••• used esp. by ships calling for help **2 :** a call or request for help or rescue

[1]**so–so** \'sō-'sō\ *adv* (ca. 1530) **:** moderately well **:** TOLERABLY, PASSABLY

[2]**so–so** *adj* (1542) **:** neither very good nor very bad **:** MIDDLING

[1]**so·ste·nu·to** \ˌsō-stə-'nüt-(ˌ)ō, ˌsò-\ *adj or adv* [It, fr. pp. of *sostenere* to sustain, fr. L *sustinēre*] (ca. 1724) **:** sustained to or beyond the note's full value — used as a direction in music

[2]**sostenuto** *n* (1757) **:** a movement or passage whose notes are markedly prolonged

sot \'sät\ *n* [ME, fool, fr. OE *sott*] (1592) **:** a habitual drunkard

so·te·ri·ol·o·gy \sō-ˌtir-ē-'äl-ə-jē\ *n* [Gk *sōtērion* salvation (fr. *sōtēr* savior, fr. *sōzein* to save) + E *-logy*; akin to Gk *sōma* body — more at SOMAT-] (1768) **:** theology dealing with salvation esp. as effected by Jesus Christ — **so·te·ri·o·log·i·cal** \-ē-ə-'läj-i-kəl\ *adj*

so that *conj* (bef. 12c) **:** THAT 2a(1)

So·thic cycle \ˌsō-thik-, ˌsäth-ik-\ *n* (1860) **:** a cycle of 1460 Sothic years

Sothic year *n* [Gk *Sōthis* Sirius] (1828) **:** an ancient Egyptian year of 365¼ days

So·tho \'sō-(ˌ)tō\ *n* (1930) **1 :** any one of the Sotho languages and esp. the language of Lesotho **2 :** a group of closely related Bantu languages of Lesotho, Botswana, and northern So. Africa

so·tol \'sō-ˌtōl\ *n* [AmerSp, fr. Nahuatl *tzotolli*] (1881) **:** a plant (genus *Dasylirion*) of the lily family of the southwestern U.S. and Mexico that resembles a yucca

sot·tish \'sät-ish\ *adj* (1566) **:** resembling a sot **:** DRUNKEN; *also* **:** DOLTISH, STUPID — **sot·tish·ly** *adv* — **sot·tish·ness** *n*

sot·to vo·ce \ˌsät-ō-'vō-chē\ *adv or adj* [It *sottovoce*, lit., under the voice] (1737) **1 :** under the breath **:** in an undertone; *also* **:** in a private manner **2 :** very softly — used as a direction in music

sou \'sü\ *n, pl* **sous** \'süz\ [F, fr. OF *sol*, fr. LL *solidus* solidus] (1512) **1 :** [2]SOL **2 :** a 5-centime piece

sou·bise \sü-'bēz\ *n* [F, fr. Charles de Rohan, Prince de *Soubise* †1787 Fr. nobleman] (1822) **:** a garnish or white sauce containing onions or onion purée

sou·brette \sü-'bret\ *n* [F, fr. Prov *soubreto*, fem. of *soubret* coy, fr. *soubra* to surmount, exceed, fr. L *superare* — more at SUPERABLE] (1753) **1 a :** a coquettish maid or frivolous young woman in comedies **b :** an actress who plays such a part **2 :** a soprano who sings supporting roles in comic opera

sou·bri·quet \'sō-, ˌsō-, 'sü-, ˌsü-\ *var of* SOBRIQUET

sou·chong \'sü-ˌchòŋ, -ˌshòŋ\ *n* [Chin (Pek) *hsiao*³ *chung*³, lit., small sort] (1760) **:** a tea made from the larger leaves of the shoot

[1]**souf·flé** \sü-'flā, 'sü-ˌ\ *n* [F, fr. *soufflé*, pp. of *souffler* to blow, puff up, fr. L *sufflare*, fr. *sub-* + *flare* to blow — more at BLOW] (1813) **:** a dish that is made from a sauce, egg yolks, beaten egg whites, and a flavoring or purée (as of seafood, fruit, or vegetables) and baked until puffed up

[2]**soufflé** *or* **souf·fléed** \-'flād, -ˌflād\ *adj* (1888) **:** puffed up by or in cooking

sough \'saù, 'səf\ *vi* [ME *swoughen*, fr. OE *swōgan*; akin to Goth *gaswogjan* to groan, Lith *svagėti* to sound] (bef. 12c) **:** to make a moaning or sighing sound — **sough** *n*

sought *past and past part of* SEEK

souk \'sük\ *n* [Ar *sūq* market] (1899) **:** a marketplace in northern Africa or the Middle East; *also* **:** one of the stalls in such a marketplace

[1]**soul** \'sōl\ *n* [ME *soule*, fr. OE *sāwol*; akin to OHG *sēula* soul] (bef. 12c) **1 :** the immaterial essence, animating principle, or actuating

cause of an individual life 2 a : the spiritual principle embodied in human beings, all rational and spiritual beings, or the universe b *cap, Christian Science* : GOD 1b 3 : a person's total self 4 a : an active or essential part b : a moving spirit : LEADER 5 a : man's moral and emotional nature b : the quality that arouses emotion and sentiment c : spiritual or moral force : FERVOR 6 : PERSON 7 : EXEMPLIFICATION, PERSONIFICATION ⟨he is the ~ of integrity⟩ 8 a : a strong positive feeling (as of intense sensitivity and emotional fervor) conveyed esp. by black American performers b : NEGRITUDE c : SOUL MUSIC d : SOUL FOOD e : SOUL BROTHER

[2]soul *adj* (1958) 1 : of, relating to, or characteristic of black Americans or their culture 2 : designed for or controlled by blacks ⟨~ radio stations⟩

soul brother *n* (1959) : a black male

souled \ˈsōld\ *adj* (15c) : having a soul : possessing soul and feeling — usu. used in combination ⟨whole-*souled* repentance⟩

soul food *n* (1964) : food (as chitterlings, ham hocks, and collard greens) traditionally eaten by southern black Americans

soul·ful \ˈsōl-fəl\ *adj* (1860) : full of or expressing feeling or emotion — **soul·ful·ly** \-fə-lē\ *adv* — **soul·ful·ness** *n*

soul kiss *n* (ca. 1948) : FRENCH KISS

soul·less \ˈsōl-ləs\ *adj* (1553) : having no soul or no greatness or warmth of mind or feeling — **soul·less·ly** *adv* — **soul·less·ness** *n*

soul mate *n* (1822) : a person temperamentally suited to another

soul music *n* (1961) : music that originated in black American gospel singing, is closely related to rhythm and blues, and is characterized by intensity of feeling and earthiness

soul–search·ing \ˈsōl-ˌsər-chiŋ\ *n* (1924) : examination of one's conscience esp. with regard to motives and values

[1]sound \ˈsau̇nd\ *adj* [ME, fr. OE *gesund;* akin to OHG *gisunt* healthy] (bef. 12c) 1 a : free from injury or disease : exhibiting normal health b : free from flaw, defect, or decay ⟨~ timber⟩ 2 : SOLID, FIRM; *also* : STABLE 3 a : free from error, fallacy, or misapprehension ⟨~ reasoning⟩ b : exhibiting or based on thorough knowledge and experience ⟨~ scholarship⟩ c : legally valid ⟨a ~ title⟩ d : logically valid and having true premises e : agreeing with accepted views : ORTHODOX 4 a : THOROUGH b : deep and undisturbed ⟨a ~ sleep⟩ c : HARD, SEVERE ⟨a ~ whipping⟩ 5 : showing good judgment or sense *syn* see HEALTHY, VALID — **sound·ly** \ˈsau̇n-(d)lē\ *adv* — **sound·ness** \ˈsau̇n(d)-nəs\ *n*

[2]sound *adv* (15c) : to the full extent : THOROUGHLY ⟨~ asleep⟩

[3]sound *n* [ME *soun,* fr. OF *son,* fr. L *sonus;* akin to OE *swinn* melody, L *sonare* to sound, Skt *svanati* it sounds] (13c) 1 a : the sensation perceived by the sense of hearing b : a particular auditory impression : TONE c : mechanical radiant energy that is transmitted by longitudinal pressure waves in a material medium (as air) and is the objective cause of hearing 2 a : a speech sound ⟨a peculiar *r-sound*⟩ b : value in terms of speech sounds ⟨*-cher* of *teacher* and *-ture* of *creature* have the same ~⟩ 3 *archaic* : RUMOR, FAME 4 a : meaningless noise b *obs* : MEANING c : the impression conveyed : IMPORT 5 : hearing distance : EARSHOT 6 : recorded auditory material 7 : a particular musical style characteristic of an individual, a group, or an area ⟨the Nashville ~⟩

[4]sound *vi* (14c) 1 a : to make a sound b : RESOUND c : to give a summons by sound ⟨the bugle ~*s* to battle⟩ 2 : to make or convey an impression : SEEM ⟨his story ~*s* incredible⟩ ~ *vt* 1 a : to cause to sound ⟨~ a trumpet⟩ b : PRONOUNCE 3a 2 : to put into words : VOICE 3 a : to make known : PROCLAIM b : to order, signal, or indicate by a sound ⟨~ the alarm⟩ 4 : to examine by causing to emit sounds ⟨~ the lungs⟩ — **sound·able** \ˈsau̇n-də-bəl\ *adj*

[5]sound *n* [ME, fr. OE *sund* swimming, sea & ON *sund* swimming, strait; akin to OE *swimman* to swim] (14c) 1 a : a long broad inlet of the ocean generally parallel to the coast b : a long passage of water connecting two larger bodies (as a sea with the ocean) or separating a mainland and an island 2 : the air bladder of a fish

[6]sound *vb* [ME *sounden,* fr. MF *sonder,* fr. *sonde* sounding line, prob. of Gmc origin; akin to OE *sundline* sounding line, *sund* sea] *vt* (15c) 1 : to measure the depth of : FATHOM 2 : to try to find out the views or intentions of : PROBE — often used with *out* 3 : to explore or examine (a body cavity) with a sound ~ *vi* 1 a : to ascertain the depth of water esp. with a sounding line b : to look into or investigate the possibility ⟨sent commissioners . . . to ~ for peace —Thomas Jefferson⟩ 2 : to dive down suddenly — used of a fish or whale

[7]sound *n* [F *sonde,* fr. MF, lit., sounding line] (1739) : an elongated instrument for exploring or sounding body cavities

sound·alike \ˈsau̇n-də-ˌlīk\ *n* (1970) : one that sounds like another

sound–and–light show *n* (1967) : SON ET LUMIÈRE

sound barrier *n* (1939) : SONIC BARRIER

sound bite *n* (1972) : a brief videotaped statement (as by a public official) that is telecast on a news program

sound·board \ˈsau̇n(d)-ˌbō(ə)rd, -ˌbȯ(ə)rd\ *n* (1504) 1 : a thin resonant board (as the belly of a violin) so placed in an instrument as to reinforce its tones by sympathetic vibration — see VIOLIN illustration 2 : SOUNDING BOARD 1a

sound bow *n* (ca. 1688) : the thick part of a bell against which the clapper strikes

sound box *n* (ca. 1875) 1 : a hollow chamber in a musical instrument for increasing its sonority 2 : a device in a phonograph using vibrating needle and thin diaphragm to convert phonograph record groove undulations into sound

sound effects *n pl* (1909) : effects that are imitative of sounds called for in the script of a play, radio or television program, or motion picture and are produced by various means

sound·er \ˈsau̇n-dər\ *n* (1575) : one that sounds; *specif* : a device for making soundings

sound hole *n* (ca. 1611) : an opening in the top surface of a stringed instrument (as a violin) to enhance vibration and resonance

[1]sound·ing \ˈsau̇n-diŋ\ *adj* (14c) 1 : RESONANT, SONOROUS 2 a : POMPOUS b : IMPOSING — **sound·ing·ly** \-diŋ-lē\ *adv*

[2]sounding *n* (15c) 1 a : measurement of depth esp. with a sounding line b : the depth so ascertained c *pl* : a place or part of a body of water where a hand sounding line will reach bottom 2 : measurement of atmospheric conditions at various heights 3 : a probe, test, or sampling of opinion or intention

sounding board *n* (1766) 1 a : a structure behind or over a pulpit, rostrum, or platform to give distinctness and sonority to sound b : a device or agency that helps propagate opinions or utterances c : a person or group on whom one tries out an idea or opinion as a means of evaluating it 2 : SOUNDBOARD 1

sounding line *n* (1627) : a line or wire weighted at one end for sounding

sounding rocket *n* (ca. 1945) : a rocket used to obtain information concerning atmospheric conditions at various altitudes

[1]sound·less \ˈsau̇n-(d)ləs\ *adj* [[6]*sound*] (1586) : incapable of being sounded : UNFATHOMABLE

[2]soundless *adj* [[3]*sound*] (1601) : making no sound : SILENT — **sound·less·ly** *adv*

sound off *vi* (1909) 1 : to play three chords before and after marching up and down a line of troops during a ceremonial parade or formal guard mount 2 : to count cadence while marching 3 a : to speak up in a loud voice b : to voice one's opinions freely and vigorously

sound pollution *n* (1967) : NOISE POLLUTION

sound pressure *n* (1893) : the difference between the actual pressure at any point in the field of a sound wave at any instant and the average pressure at that point

[1]sound·proof \ˈsau̇n(d)-ˈprüf\ *adj* (ca. 1878) : impervious to sound

[2]soundproof *vt* (1919) : to insulate so as to obstruct the passage of sound

sound·stage \ˈsau̇n(d)-ˌstāj\ *n* (1931) : the part of a motion-picture studio in which a production is filmed

sound track *n* (ca. 1929) 1 : the area on a motion-picture film that carries the sound record 2 : the sound recorded on a sound track; *esp* : the music on a sound track

sound truck *n* (1938) : a truck equipped with a loudspeaker

sound wave *n* (1867) 1 : [3]SOUND 1b 2 *pl* : longitudinal pressure waves in any material medium regardless of whether they constitute audible sound ⟨earthquake waves and ultrasonic waves are sometimes called *sound waves*⟩

[1]soup \ˈsüp\ *n* [F *soupe* sop, soup, of Gmc origin; akin to ON *soppa* soup, OE *sopp* sop — more at SUP] (1653) 1 : a liquid food esp. with a meat, fish, or vegetable stock as a base and often containing pieces of solid food 2 : something (as a heavy fog or nitroglycerine) having or suggesting the consistency or nutrient qualities of soup 3 : an unfortunate predicament

[2]soup *vt* [E slang *soup* (dope injected into a racehorse to improve its performance)] (1931) : to increase the power or efficiency of ⟨~ up an engine⟩

soup·çon \süp-ˈsōⁿ, ˈsüp-ˌsän\ *n* [F, lit., suspicion, fr. (assumed) VL *suspection-, suspectio,* fr. L *suspectus,* pp. of *suspicere* to suspect — more at SUSPECT] (1766) : a little bit : TRACE

soup du jour \ˌsüp-də-ˈzhu̇(ə)r\ *n* [part trans. of F *soupe du jour* soup of the day] (ca. 1945) : a soup that is offered by a restaurant on a particular day

soup kitchen *n* (1839) : an establishment dispensing minimum dietary essentials (as soup and bread) to the needy

soup·spoon \ˈsüp-ˌspün\ *n* (1705) : a spoon with a large or rounded bowl for eating soup

soupy \ˈsü-pē\ *adj* **soup·i·er; -est** (1869) 1 : having the consistency of soup 2 : densely foggy or cloudy 3 : overly sentimental

[1]sour \ˈsau̇(ə)r\ *adj* [ME, fr. OE *sūr;* akin to OHG *sūr* sour, Lith *suras* salty] (bef. 12c) 1 : causing or characterized by the one of the four basic taste sensations that is produced chiefly by acids ⟨~ pickles⟩ — compare BITTER, SALT, SWEET 2 a (1) : having the acid taste or smell of or as if of fermentation : TURNED ⟨~ milk⟩ (2) : of or relating to fermentation b : smelling or tasting of decay : RANCID, ROTTEN ⟨~ breath⟩ c (1) : BAD, WRONG ⟨a project gone ~⟩ (2) : HOSTILE, DISENCHANTED ⟨went ~ on Marxism⟩ 3 a : UNPLEASANT, DISTASTEFUL b : CROSS, SULLEN c : not up to the usual, expected, or standard quality or pitch 4 : acid in reaction — used esp. of soil 5 : containing malodorous sulfur compounds — used esp. of petroleum products — **sour·ish** \ˈsau̇(ə)r-ish\ *adj* — **sour·ly** *adv* — **sour·ness** *n*

[2]sour *n* (bef. 12c) 1 a : something sour b : the primary taste sensation produced by acid stimuli 2 : a cocktail consisting of a liquor (as whiskey), lemon or lime juice, sugar, and sometimes ice

[3]sour *vi* (14c) : to become sour ~ *vt* : to make sour

sour ball *n* (ca. 1909) : a spherical piece of hard candy having a tart flavor

[1]source \ˈsō(ə)rs, ˈsȯ(ə)rs\ *n* [ME *sours,* fr. MF *sors, sourse,* fr. OF, fr. pp. of *sourdre* to rise, spring forth, fr. L *surgere* — more at SURGE] (14c) 1 a : a generative force : CAUSE b (1) : a point of origin or procurement : BEGINNING (2) : one that initiates : AUTHOR; *also* : PROTOTYPE, MODEL (3) : one that supplies information 2 a : the point of origin of a stream of water : FOUNTAINHEAD b *archaic* : SPRING, FOUNT 3 : a firsthand document or primary reference work *syn* see ORIGIN — **source·less** \-ləs\ *adj*

[2]source *vt* **sourced; sourc·ing** (1957) : to specify the source of (as quoted material)

source·book \-ˌbu̇k\ *n* (1899) : a fundamental document or record (as of history, literature, art, or religion) on which subsequent writings, compositions, opinions, beliefs, or practices are based; *also* : a collection of such documents

source language *n* (1953) : a language which is to be translated into another language — compare TARGET LANGUAGE

sour cherry *n* (15c) : a round-headed Eurasian tree (*Prunus cerasus*) widely grown for its bright red to almost black soft-fleshed acid fruits; *also* : its fruit

sour cream *n* (1855) : a commercial cream product produced by the use of lactobacilli

sour·dough \ˈsau̇(ə)r-ˌdō, *1 is also* -ˈdō\ *n* (14c) 1 : a leaven consisting of dough in which fermentation is active 2 [fr. the use of sourdough for making bread in prospectors' camps] : a veteran inhabitant and esp. an old time prospector of Alaska or northwestern Canada

sour grapes *n pl* [fr. the fable ascribed to Aesop of the fox who after finding himself unable to reach some grapes he had desired disparaged them as sour] (1760) **:** disparagement of something that has proven unattainable
sour gum *n* (1785) **:** BLACK GUM
sour mash *n* (1885) **:** grain mash for brewing or distilling whose initial acidity has been adjusted to optimum condition for yeast fermentation by mash from a previous run
sour orange *n* (1748) **:** a citrus tree (*Citrus aurantium*) that is used esp. as a stock in grafting citrus; *also* **:** its bitter fruit
sour·puss \ˈsau̇(ə)r-ˌpu̇s\ *n* [[2]*puss*] (1937) **:** GROUCH, KILLJOY
sour·sop \ˈsau̇(ə)r-ˌsäp\ *n* (1667) **1 :** the large edible fruit of the soursop that has fleshy spines and a slightly acid fibrous pulp **2 :** a small tropical American tree (*Annona muricata*) of the custard-apple family that has spicy odoriferous leaves
sour·wood \-ˌwu̇d\ *n* (1709) **:** a small tree (*Oxydendrum arboreum*) of the heath family with white flowers and sour-tasting leaves
sous \ˈsü\ *adj* [F, prep., lit., under, fr. L *subtus*, adv., below, under; akin to L *sub* under — more at UP] (1687) **:** being an assistant — used chiefly in titles ⟨a *sous*-chef⟩
sou·sa·phone \ˈsü-zə-ˌfōn, -sə-\ *n* [John Philip *Sousa*] (1925) **:** a large circular tuba that has a flared adjustable bell — compare HELICON

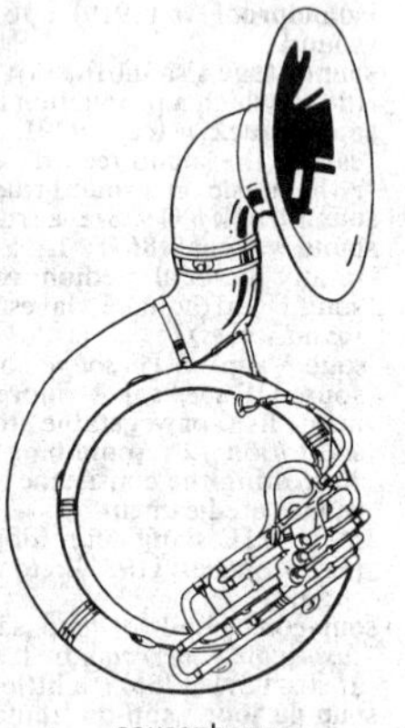
sousaphone

[1]**souse** \ˈsau̇s\ *vb* **soused; sous·ing** [ME *sousen*, fr. MF *souz*, *souce* pickling solution, of Gmc origin; akin to OHG *sulza* brine, OE *sealt* salt] *vt* (14c) **1 :** PICKLE **2 a :** to plunge in liquid **:** IMMERSE **b :** DRENCH, SATURATE **3 :** to make drunk **:** INEBRIATE ~ *vi* **:** to become immersed or drenched
[2]**souse** *n* (15c) **1 :** something pickled; *esp* **:** seasoned and chopped pork trimmings, fish, or shellfish **2 :** an act of sousing **:** WETTING **3 a :** a habitual drunkard **b :** a drinking spree **:** BINGE
[3]**souse** *vb* **soused; sous·ing** [ME *souce*, n., start of a bird's flight, alter. of *sours*, fr. MF *sourse* source — more at SOURCE] *vi*, *archaic* (1583) **:** to swoop down **:** PLUNGE ~ *vt*, *archaic* **:** to swoop down on
sou·tache \sü-ˈtash\ *n* [F, fr. Hung *sujtás*] (ca. 1856) **:** a narrow braid with herringbone pattern used as trimming
sou·tane \sü-ˈtän, -ˈtan\ *n* [F, fr. It *sottana*, lit., undergarment, fr. fem. of *sottano* being underneath, fr. ML *subtanus*, fr. L *subtus* underneath — more at SOUS] (1838) **:** CASSOCK
sou·ter \ˈsüt-ər\ *n* [ME, fr. OE *sūtere*, fr. L *sutor*, fr. *sutus*, pp. of *suere* to sew — more at SEW] *chiefly Scot* (bef. 12c) **:** SHOEMAKER
[1]**south** \ˈsau̇th\ *adv* [ME, fr. OE *sūth*; akin to OHG *sund*- south, OE *sunne* sun] (bef. 12c) **:** to, toward, or in the south
[2]**south** *adj* (bef. 12c) **1 :** situated toward or at the south ⟨the ~ entrance⟩ **2 :** coming from the south ⟨a ~ wind⟩
[3]**south** *n* (bef. 12c) **1 a :** the direction of the south terrestrial pole **:** the direction to the right of one facing east **b :** the compass point directly opposite to north **2** *cap* **:** regions or countries lying to the south of a specified or implied point of orientation; *esp* **:** the southeastern part of the U.S. **3 :** the right side of a church looking toward the altar from the nave **4** *often cap* **a :** the one of four positions at 90-degree intervals that lies to the south or at the bottom of a diagram **b :** a person (as a bridge player) occupying this position in the course of a specified activity; *specif* **:** the declarer in bridge
South African *n* (ca. 1909) **:** a native or inhabitant of the Republic of South Africa; *esp* **:** AFRIKANER — **South African** *adj*
south·bound \ˈsau̇th-ˌbau̇nd\ *adj* (1885) **:** traveling or heading south
south by east (ca. 1682) **:** a compass point that is one point east of due south **:** S11°15′E
south by west (ca. 1682) **:** a compass point that is one point west of due south **:** S11°15′W
South·down \ˈsau̇th-ˌdau̇n\ *n* [*South Downs*, England] (1787) **:** any of an English breed of small medium-wooled hornless mutton-type sheep
[1]**south·east** \sau̇-ˈthēst, *naut* sau̇-ˈēst\ *adv* (bef. 12c) **:** to, toward, or in the southeast
[2]**southeast** *n* (bef. 12c) **1 a :** the general direction between south and east **b :** the point midway between the south and east compass points **2** *cap* **:** regions or countries lying to the southeast of a specified or implied point of orientation
[3]**southeast** *adj* (1548) **1 :** coming from the southeast ⟨a ~ wind⟩ **2 :** situated toward or at the southeast ⟨the ~ corner⟩
southeast by east (ca. 1682) **:** a compass point that is one point east of due southeast **:** S56°15′E
southeast by south (ca. 1682) **:** a compass point that is one point south of due southeast **:** S33°45′E
south·east·er \sau̇-ˈthē-stər, sau̇-ˈē-\ *n* (1797) **1 :** a strong southeast wind **2 :** a storm with southeast winds
south·east·er·ly \-stər-lē\ *adv or adj* [[2]*southeast* + *-erly* (as in *easterly*)] (ca. 1708) **1 :** from the southeast **2 :** toward the southeast
south·east·ern \-stərn\ *adj* [[2]*southeast* + *-ern* (as in *eastern*)] (1577) **1** *often cap* **:** of, relating to, or characteristic of a region conventionally designated southeast **2 :** lying toward or coming from the southeast — **south·east·ern·most** \-ˌmōst\ *adj*
South·east·ern·er \-stə(r)-nər\ *n* (1919) **:** a native or inhabitant of the Southeast; *esp* **:** a native or resident of the southeastern part of the U.S.
[1]**south·east·ward** \sau̇-ˈthēs-twərd, sau̇-ˈēs-\ *adv or adj* (1528) **:** toward the southeast — **south·east·wards** \-twərdz\ *adv*
[2]**southeastward** *n* (1555) **:** SOUTHEAST
south·er \ˈsau̇-thər\ *n* (1862) **:** a southerly wind
[1]**south·er·ly** \ˈsəth-ər-lē\ *adj or adv* [[3]*south* + *-erly* (as in *easterly*)] (1551) **1 :** situated toward or belonging to the south ⟨the ~ shore of the lake⟩ **2 :** coming from the south ⟨a ~ wind⟩
[2]**southerly** *n, pl* **-lies** (1944) **:** a wind from the south
south·ern \ˈsəth-ərn\ *adj* [ME *southern*, *southren*, fr. OE *sūtherne*; akin to OHG *sundrōni* southern, OE *sūth* south] (bef. 12c) **1** *cap* **:** of, relating to, or characteristic of a region conventionally designated South **2 a :** lying toward the south **b :** coming from the south ⟨a ~ breeze⟩ — **south·ern·most** \-ˌmōst\ *adj* — **south·ern·ness** \-ərn-nəs\ *n, often cap*
Southern *n* (1948) **:** the dialect of English spoken in most of the Chesapeake Bay area, the coastal plain and the greater part of the upland plateau in Virginia, No. Carolina, So. Carolina, and Georgia, and the Gulf states at least as far west as the valley of the Brazos in Texas and sometimes taken to include the south Midland area
southern corn rootworm *n* (1918) **:** SPOTTED CUCUMBER BEETLE
Southern Cross *n* **:** four bright stars in the southern hemisphere, situated as if at the extremities of a Latin cross; *also* **:** the constellation of which these four stars are the brightest
Southern Crown *n* **:** CORONA AUSTRALIS
Southern English *n* (14c) **1 :** the English spoken esp. by cultivated people native to or educated in the South of England **2 :** SOUTHERN
South·ern·er \ˈsəth-ə(r)-nər\ *n* (1828) **:** a native or inhabitant of the South; *esp* **:** a native or resident of the southern part of the U.S.
southern hemisphere *n, often cap S&H* (ca. 1771) **:** the half of the earth that lies south of the equator
South·ern·ism \ˈsəth-ər-ˌniz-əm\ *n* (1861) **1 :** an attitude or trait characteristic of the South or Southerners esp. in the U.S. **2 :** a locution or pronunciation characteristic of the southern U.S.
southern lights *n pl* (1775) **:** AURORA AUSTRALIS
south·ern·wood \ˈsəth-ərn-ˌwu̇d\ *n* (bef. 12c) **:** a shrubby fragrant European wormwood (*Artemisia abrotanum*) with bitter foliage
south·ing \ˈsau̇-thiŋ, -thiŋ\ *n* (1669) **1 :** difference in latitude to the south from the last preceding point of reckoning **2 :** southerly progress
south·land \ˈsau̇th-ˌland, -lənd\ *n, often cap* (bef. 12c) **:** land in the south **:** the south of a country
south·paw \-ˌpȯ\ *n* (1891) **:** LEFT-HANDER; *specif* **:** a left-handed baseball pitcher — **southpaw** *adj*
south pole *n* (1594) **1 a** *often cap S & P* **:** the southernmost point of the earth **b :** the zenith of the heavens as viewed from the south terrestrial pole **2** *of a magnet* **:** the pole that points toward the south
[1]**South·ron** \ˈsəth-rən\ *adj* [ME (Sc), fr. ME *southren*] *chiefly Scot* (15c) **:** SOUTHERN; *specif* **:** ENGLISH
[2]**Southron** *n* (15c) **:** SOUTHERNER: as **a** *chiefly Scot* **:** ENGLISHMAN **b** *chiefly Southern* **:** a native or inhabitant of the southern U.S.
south–seek·ing pole *n* (ca. 1922) **:** SOUTH POLE 2
south–southeast *n* (14c) **:** a compass point that is two points east of due south **:** S22°30′E
south–southwest *n* (14c) **:** a compass point that is two points west of due south **:** S22°30′W
[1]**south·ward** \ˈsau̇th-wərd\ *adv or adj* (bef. 12c) **:** toward the south — **south·wards** \-wərdz\ *adv*
[2]**southward** *n* (1555) **:** southward direction or part ⟨sail to the ~⟩
[1]**south·west** \sau̇th-ˈwest, *naut* sau̇-ˈwest\ *adv* (bef. 12c) **:** to, toward, or in the southwest
[2]**southwest** *n* (bef. 12c) **1 a :** the general direction between south and west **b :** the point midway between the south and west compass points **2** *cap* **:** regions or countries lying to the southwest of a specified or implied point of orientation
[3]**southwest** *adj* (14c) **1 :** coming from the southwest ⟨a ~ wind⟩ **2 :** situated toward or at the southwest ⟨the ~ corner⟩
southwest by south (ca. 1682) **:** a compass point that is one point south of due southwest **:** S33°45′W
southwest by west (ca. 1682) **:** a compass point that is one point west of due southwest **:** S56°15′W
south·west·er \sau̇(th)-ˈwes-tər\ *n* (1833) **1 :** a strong southwest wind **2 :** a storm with southwest winds
south·west·er·ly \-tər-lē\ *adv or adj* [[2]*southwest* + *-erly* (as in *westerly*)] (ca. 1708) **1 :** from the southwest **2 :** toward the southwest
south·west·ern \-tərn\ *adj* [[2]*southwest* + *-ern* (as in *western*)] (bef. 12c) **1 :** lying toward or coming from the southwest **2** *often cap* **:** of, relating to, or characteristic of a region conventionally designated Southwest — **south·west·ern·most** \-ˌmōst\ *adj*
southwestern corn borer *n* (ca. 1943) **:** a pyralid moth (*Diatraea grandiosella*) whose larva causes serious damage esp. to corn crops by boring in the stalks
South·west·ern·er \sau̇(th)-ˈwes-tə(r)-nər\ *n* (1860) **:** a native or inhabitant of the Southwest; *esp* **:** a native or resident of the southwestern U.S.
[1]**south·west·ward** \sau̇(th)-ˈwes-twərd\ *adv or adj* (1548) **:** toward the southwest — **south·west·wards** \-wərdz\ *adv*
[2]**southwestward** *n* (1775) **:** SOUTHWEST
sou·ve·nir \ˈsü-və-ˌni(ə)r, ˌsü-və-ˈ\ *n* [F, lit., act of remembering, fr. MF, fr. (*se*) *souvenir* to remember, fr. L *subvenire* to come up, come to mind — more at SUBVENTION] (1775) **:** something that serves as a reminder **:** MEMENTO
souvenir sheet *n* (1940) **:** a block or set of postage stamps or a single stamp printed on a single sheet of paper often without gum or perforations and with margins containing lettering or design that identifies some notable event being commemorated
sou·vla·kia \süv-ˈläk-ē-ə\ *or* **sou·vla·ki** \-ˈläk-ē\ *n* [NGk *souvlakia*, fr. *souvla* spit, skewer, fr. Gk *soublizein* to pierce] (1950) **:** SHISH KEBAB
sou'·west·er \sau̇-ˈwes-tər\ *n* (1837) **1 a :** a long oilskin coat worn esp. at sea during stormy weather **b :** a waterproof hat with wide slanting brim longer in back than in front **2 :** SOUTHWESTER
[1]**sov·er·eign** *also* **sov·ran** \ˈsäv-(ə-)rən, ˈsäv-ərn, ˈsəv-\ *n* [ME *soverain*, fr. OF, fr. *soverain*, adj.] (13c) **1 a :** one possessing or held to possess sovereignty **b :** one that exercises supreme authority within a limited sphere **c :** an acknowledged leader **:** ARBITER **2 :** a coin of the United Kingdom containing 113 grains of fine gold
[2]**sovereign** *also* **sovran** *adj* [ME *soverain*, fr. MF, fr. OF, fr. (assumed) VL *superanus*, fr. L *super* over, above — more at OVER] (14c) **1 a :** of the most exalted kind **:** SUPREME ⟨~ virtue⟩ **b :** superlative in quality **:** EXCELLENT **c :** having generalized curative powers ⟨a ~ remedy⟩ **d :** of an unqualified nature **:** UNMITIGATED ⟨~ contempt⟩ **e :** having undisputed ascendancy **:** PARAMOUNT **2 a :** possessed of supreme power ⟨~ ruler⟩ **b :** unlimited in extent **:** ABSOLUTE **c :** enjoying autonomy **:** INDEPENDENT ⟨~ state⟩ **3 :** relating to, characteristic of, or befitting a sovereign ***syn*** see DOMINANT, FREE — **sov·er·eign·ly** *adv*

sov•er•eign•ty *also* **sov•ran•ty** \-tē\ *n, pl* **-ties** [ME *soverainte,* fr. MF *soveraineté,* fr. OF, fr. *soverain*] (14c) **1** *obs* **:** supreme excellence or an example of it **2 a :** supreme power esp. over a body politic **b :** freedom from external control **:** AUTONOMY **c :** controlling influence **3 :** one that is sovereign; *esp* **:** an autonomous state

so•vi•et \'sō-vē-,et, 'säv-, -ē-ət\ *n* [Russ *sovet* council, soviet] (1917) **1 :** an elected governmental council in a Communist country **2** *pl, cap* **a :** BOLSHEVIKS **b :** the people and esp. the political and military leaders of the U.S.S.R. — **soviet** *adj, often cap* — **so•vi•et•ism** \-,iz-əm\ *n, often cap*

so•vi•et•ize \'sō-vē-,et-,īz, 'säv-, -ē-ət-\ *vt* **-ized; -iz•ing** *often cap* (1919) **1 :** to bring under Soviet control **2 :** to force into conformity with Soviet cultural patterns or governmental policies — **so•vi•et•iza•tion** \,sō-vē-,et-ə-'zā-shən, -ē-ət-\ *n, often cap*

So•vi•et•ol•o•gist \,sō-vē-,et-'äl-ə-jəst, ,säv-, -ē-ət-\ *n* (1955) **:** one who studies the policies and practices of the Soviet government **:** KREMLINOLOGIST

sov•khoz \säf-'kȯz, -'kȯs\ *n, pl* **sov•kho•zy** \-'kȯ-zē\ *or* **sov•khoz•es** [Russ, short for *sovetskoe khozyaĭstvo* soviet farm] (1926) **:** a state-owned farm of the U.S.S.R. paying wages to the workers

¹sow \'sau̇\ *n* [ME *sowe,* fr. OE *sugu;* akin to OE & OHG *sū* sow, L *sus* pig, swine, hog, Gk *hys*] (bef. 12c) **1 :** an adult female swine; *also* **:** the adult female of various other animals (as a bear) **2 a :** a channel that conducts molten metal to molds in a pig bed **b :** a mass of metal solidified in such a mold **:** INGOT

²sow \'sō\ *vb* **sowed; sown** \'sōn\ *or* **sowed; sow•ing** [ME *sowen,* fr. OE *sāwan;* akin to OHG *sāwen* to sow, L *serere*] *vi* (bef. 12c) **1 :** to plant seed for growth esp. by scattering **2 :** to set something in motion **:** begin an enterprise ~ *vt* **1 a :** to scatter (as seed) upon the earth for growth; *broadly* **:** PLANT 1a **b :** to strew with or as if with seed **c :** to introduce into a selected environment **:** IMPLANT **2 :** to set in motion **:** FOMENT ⟨~ suspicion⟩ **3 :** to spread abroad **:** DISPERSE — **sow•er** \'sō(-ə)r\ *n*

sow•bel•ly \'sau̇-,bel-ē\ *n* (1867) **:** fat salt pork or bacon

sow bug \'sau̇-\ *n* (1750) **:** WOOD LOUSE

sow•ens \'sü-ənz, 'sō-\ *n pl but sing or pl in constr* [ScGael *sūghan*] (1582) **:** porridge from oat husks and siftings

sow thistle \'sau̇-\ *n* (13c) **:** any of a genus (*Sonchus*) of spiny weedy European composite herbs widely naturalized

sox *pl of* SOCK

soy \'sȯi\ *n* [Jp *shōyu,* fr. Chin (Cant) *shi-yau,* lit., soybean oil] (1679) **1 :** an oriental brown liquid sauce made by subjecting beans (as soybeans) to long fermentation and to digestion in brine **2** *also* **soya** \'sȯi-(y)ə\ **:** SOYBEAN

soy•bean \'sȯi-'bēn, -,bēn\ *also* **soya bean** \'sȯi-(y)ə-\ *n* (1802) **:** a hairy annual Asian legume (*Glycine max*) widely grown for its oil-rich proteinaceous seeds and for forage and soil improvement; *also* **:** its seed

soybean oil *also* **soya–bean oil** *n* (ca. 1916) **:** a pale yellow drying or semidrying oil that is obtained from soybeans and is used chiefly as a food, in paints, varnishes, linoleum, printing ink, and soap, and as a source of phospholipids, fatty acids, and sterols

soz•zled \'säz-əld\ *adj* [pp. of *sozzle* to splash, intoxicate, fr. earlier *sossle,* prob. freq. of Brit. dial. *soss* to mess] (ca. 1880) **:** DRUNK, INTOXICATED

spa \'spä, 'spȯ\ *n* [*Spa,* watering place in Belgium] (1610) **1 a :** a mineral spring **b :** a resort with mineral springs **2 :** a fashionable resort or hotel **3** *NewEng* **:** SODA FOUNTAIN **4 :** a commercial establishment with facilities for exercising and bathing

¹space \'spās\ *n, often attrib* [ME, fr. OF *espace,* fr. L *spatium* area, room, interval of space or time — more at SPEED] (14c) **1 :** a period of time; *also* **:** its duration **2 a :** a limited extent in one, two, or three dimensions **:** DISTANCE, AREA, VOLUME **b :** an extent set apart or available ⟨parking ~⟩ ⟨floor ~⟩ **3 :** one of the degrees between or above or below the lines of a musical staff **4 a :** a boundless three-dimensional extent in which objects and events occur and have relative position and direction **b :** physical space independent of what occupies it — called also *absolute space* **5 :** the region beyond the earth's atmosphere or beyond the solar system **6 a :** a blank area separating words or lines **b :** material used to produce such blank area; *specif* **:** a piece of type less than one en in width **7 :** a set of mathematical elements and esp. of abstractions of all the points on a line, in a plane, or in physical space; *esp* **:** a set of mathematical entities with a set of axioms of geometric character — compare METRIC SPACE, TOPOLOGICAL SPACE, VECTOR SPACE **8 :** an interval in operation during which a telegraph key is not in contact **9 a :** LINAGE **b :** broadcast time available esp. to advertisers **10 :** accommodations on a public vehicle

²space *vb* **spaced; spac•ing** *vt* (1703) **:** to place at intervals or arrange with space between — often used with *out* ~ *vi* **:** to leave one or more blank spaces (as in a line of typing) — **spac•er** *n*

space–age \'spā-,sāj\ *adj* (1957) **:** of, relating to, or befitting the age of space exploration; *esp* **:** MODERN ⟨~ technology⟩

space•band \'spās-,band\ *n* (1904) **:** a device on a linecaster that provides variable but even spacing between words in a justified line

space charge *n* (1913) **:** an electric charge distributed throughout a three-dimensional region

space•craft \'spā-,skraft\ *n* (1958) **:** a manned or unmanned device that is designed to orbit the earth or to travel beyond the earth's atmosphere

spaced–out \(')spā-'stau̇t\ *adj* (ca. 1967) **1** *or* **spaced** \'spāst\ **:** dazed or stupefied by or as if by a narcotic substance **:** HIGH **2 :** of very strange or weird character ⟨a ~ fantasy⟩

space•flight \'spās-,flīt\ *n* (1949) **:** flight beyond the earth's atmosphere

space heater *n* (1925) **:** a device for heating an enclosed space; *esp* **:** an often portable device that heats the space in which it is located and has no external heating ducts or connection to a chimney

space heating *n* (ca. 1942) **:** heating of spaces esp. for human comfort by any means (as fuel, electricity, or solar radiation) with the heater either within the space or external to it

space lattice *n* (ca. 1909) **:** the geometrical arrangement of the atoms in a crystal

space•less \'spā-sləs\ *adj* (1606) **1 :** having no limits **:** BOUNDLESS **2 :** occupying no space

space•man \'spā-,sman, -smən\ *n* (1938) **1 a :** one who travels outside the earth's atmosphere **b :** one engaged in any of various fields bearing on flight through outer space **2 :** a visitor to earth from outer space

space mark *n* (ca. 1890) **:** the symbol #

space medicine *n* (1951) **:** a branch of medicine that deals with the physiological and biological effects on the human body of rocket or jet flight beyond the earth's atmosphere

space opera *n* (1949) **:** a futuristic melodramatic fantasy involving space travelers and extraterrestrial beings

space•port \'spā-,spō(ə)rt, -,spȯ(ə)rt\ *n* (1952) **:** an installation for testing and launching spacecraft

space•ship \'spās(h)-,ship\ *n* (1942) **:** a vehicle designed to operate in free space outside the earth's atmosphere

space shuttle *n* (1969) **:** a reusable rocket-launched vehicle that is designed to go into earth orbit, to shuttle people and cargo to and from an orbiting spacecraft, and to glide to a landing

space station *n* (1945) **:** a usu. manned artificial satellite designed for a fixed orbit about the earth and to serve as a base (as for scientific observation) — called also *space platform*

space suit *n* (1938) **1 :** a suit equipped with life supporting provisions to make life in space possible for its wearer **2 :** G SUIT

space–time \'spā-'stīm, 'spā-,\ *n* (1915) **1 :** a system of one temporal and three spatial coordinates by which any physical object or event can be located — called also *space-time continuum* **2 :** the whole or a portion of physical reality determinable by a four-dimensional coordinate system; *also* **:** the properties characteristic of such an order

space walk *n* (1965) **:** an extravehicular venture made by an astronaut in space — **space walk** *vi* — **space•walk•er** \'spā-,swȯ-kər\ *n* — **space•walk•ing** \-kiŋ\ *n*

space•ward \'spā-swərd\ *adv* (1958) **:** toward space

spac•ey *also* **spacy** \'spā-sē\ *adj* **spac•i•er; -est** (1970) **:** SPACED-OUT

spa•cial *var of* SPATIAL

spac•ing \'spā-siŋ\ *n* (1683) **1 a :** the act of providing with spaces or placing at intervals **b :** an arrangement in space **2 a :** a limited extent **:** SPACE **b :** the distance between any two objects in a usu. regularly arranged series

spa•cious \'spā-shəs\ *adj* [ME, fr. MF *spacieux,* fr. L *spatiosus,* fr. *spatium* space, room — more at SPEED] (14c) **1 :** vast or ample in extent **:** ROOMY ⟨a ~ residence⟩ **2 :** large or magnificent in scale **:** EXPANSIVE ⟨a more ~ and stimulating existence than the farm could offer —H. L. Mencken⟩ — **spa•cious•ly** *adv* — **spa•cious•ness** *n*

syn SPACIOUS, COMMODIOUS, CAPACIOUS, AMPLE mean larger in extent or capacity than the average. SPACIOUS implies great length and breadth ⟨a mansion with a *spacious* front lawn⟩ COMMODIOUS stresses roominess and comfortableness ⟨a *commodious* and airy penthouse apartment⟩ CAPACIOUS stresses the ability to hold, contain, or retain more than the average ⟨a *capacious* suitcase⟩ AMPLE implies having a greater size, expanse, or amount than that deemed adequate ⟨we have *ample* means to buy the house⟩

spack•le \'spak-əl\ *vt* **spack•led; spack•ling** \-(ə-)liŋ\ [*Spackle*] (1954) **:** to apply Spackle paste to

Spackle *trademark* — used for a powder mixed with water to form a paste and used as a filler for cracks in a surface before painting

¹spade \'spād\ *n* [ME, fr. OE *spadu;* akin to Gk *spathē* blade of a sword or oar, OHG *spān* chip of wood — more at SPOON] (bef. 12c) **1 :** a digging implement adapted for being pushed into the ground with the foot **2 :** a spade-shaped instrument — **spade•ful** \-,fu̇l\ *n* — **call a spade a spade 1 :** to call a thing by its right name however coarse **2 :** to speak frankly

²spade *vb* **spad•ed; spad•ing** *vt* (1647) **:** to dig up or out or shape with or as if with a spade ~ *vi* **:** to use a spade — **spad•er** *n*

³spade *n* [It *spada* or Sp *espada* broad sword; both fr. L *spatha,* fr. Gk *spathē* blade] (1598) **1 a :** a black figure that resembles a stylized spearhead on each playing card of one of the four suits; *also* **:** a card marked with this figure **b** *pl but sing or pl in constr* **:** the suit comprising cards marked with a spade **2 :** NEGRO — usu. taken to be offensive — **in spades :** to an unusually great degree **:** in the extreme

spade beard *n* [¹*spade*] (1598) **1 :** an oblong beard with square ends **2 :** a beard rounded off at the top and pointed at the bottom — **spade–beard•ed** \'spād-'bird-əd\ *adj*

spade•fish \'spād-,fish\ *n* (1805) **:** a deep-bodied spiny-finned food fish (*Chaetodipterus faber*) found in the warmer parts of the western Atlantic

spade•work \-,wərk\ *n* (1778) **1 :** work done with the spade **2 :** the hard plain preliminary drudgery in an undertaking

spa•dille \spə-'dil, -'dē\ *n* [F, fr. Sp *espadilla,* dim. of *espada* broad sword, spade (in cards) — more at SPADE] (1728) **:** the highest trump in various card games (as ombre)

spa•dix \'spād-iks\ *n, pl* **spa•di•ces** \'spād-ə-,sēz\ [NL *spadic-, spadix,* fr. L, frond torn from a palm tree, fr. Gk *spadik-, spadix,* fr. *span* to draw, pull — more at SPAN] (ca. 1760) **:** a floral spike with a fleshy or succulent axis usu. enclosed in a spathe

spae \'spā\ *vt* **spaed; spae•ing** [ME *span,* fr. ON *spā;* akin to OHG *spehōn* to watch, spy — more at SPY] *chiefly Scot* (14c) **:** FORETELL

spa•ghet•ti \spə-'get-ē\ *n* [It, fr. pl. of *spaghetto,* dim. of *spago* cord, string] (1888) **1 :** pasta made in thin solid strings **2 :** electrically insulating tubing typically of varnished cloth or of plastic for covering bare wire or holding insulated wires together — **spa•ghet•ti•like** \-,līk\ *adj*

spa•ghet•ti•ni \spə-,ge-'tē-nē\ *n* [It, dim. of *spaghetti*] (1923) **:** a pasta thinner than spaghetti but thicker than vermicelli

spaghetti western *n, often cap W* (1971) **:** a western motion picture produced by Italians

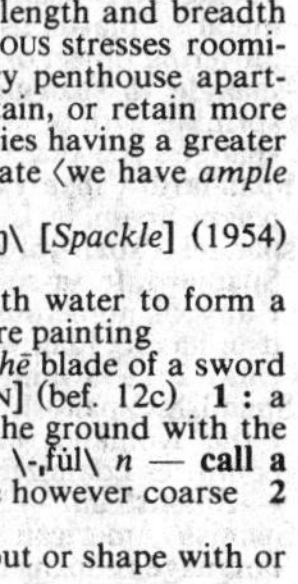

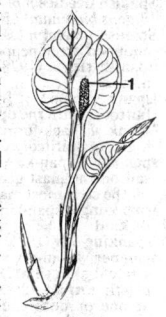

1 spadix

spa·hi \'spä-,hē\ *n* [MF, fr. Turk *sipahi*, fr. Per *sipāhī* cavalryman] (1562) **1 :** one of a former corps of irregular Turkish cavalry **2 :** one of a former corps of Algerian native cavalry in the French army

spake \'spāk\ *archaic past of* SPEAK

1spall \'spȯl\ *n* [ME *spalle*] (15c) **:** a small fragment or chip esp. of stone

2spall *vt* (1758) **:** to break up or reduce by or as if by chipping with a hammer ~ *vi* **1 :** to break off chips, scales, or slabs **:** EXFOLIATE **2 :** to undergo spallation — **spall·able** \'spȯ-lə-bəl\ *adj*

spall·ation \spȯ-'lā-shən\ *n* [2*spall*] (1947) **1 :** the process of spalling **2 :** a nuclear reaction in which light particles are ejected as the result of bombardment (as by high-energy protons)

spal·peen \spal-'pēn, spȯl-\ *n* [IrGael *spailpín* migratory laborer, rascal] *chiefly Irish* (1815) **:** RASCAL

1span \'span\ *archaic past of* SPIN

2span *n* [ME, fr. OE *spann;* akin to OHG *spanna* span, MD *spannen* to stretch, hitch up] (bef. 12c) **1 :** the distance from the end of the thumb to the end of the little finger of a spread hand; *also* **:** an English unit of length equal to 9 inches (22.9 centimeters) **2 :** an extent, stretch, reach, or spread between two limits: as **a :** a limited space (as of time); *esp* **:** an individual's lifetime **b :** spread or extent between abutments or supports (as of a bridge); *also* **:** a portion thus supported **c :** the maximum distance laterally from tip to tip of an airplane

3span *vt* **spanned; span·ning** (1560) **1 a :** to measure by or as if by the hand with fingers and thumb extended **b :** MEASURE **2 a :** to extend across ⟨his career *spanned* four decades⟩ **b :** to form an arch over ⟨a small bridge *spanned* the pond⟩ **c :** to place or construct a span over **3 :** to be capable of expressing any element of under given operations ⟨a set of vectors that ~*s* a vector space⟩

4span *n* [D, fr. MD, fr. *spannen* to hitch up] (1769) **:** a pair of animals (as mules) usu. matched in appearance and action and driven together

span·dex \'span-,deks\ *n* [anagram of *expand*] (ca. 1959) **:** any of various elastic textile fibers made chiefly of polyurethane

span·drel *or* **span·dril** \'span-drəl\ *n* [ME *spandrell*, fr. AF *spaundre*, fr. OF *espandre* to spread out — more at SPAWN] (15c) **1 :** the sometimes ornamented space between the right or left exterior curve of an arch and an enclosing right angle **2 :** the triangular space beneath the string of a stair

spang \'spaŋ\ *adv* [Sc *spang* to leap, cast, bang] (1843) **1 :** to a complete degree **2 :** in an exact or direct manner **:** SQUARELY

1span·gle \'spaŋ-gəl\ *n* [ME *spangel*, dim. of *spang* shiny ornament, prob. of Scand origin; akin to ON *spǫng* spangle; akin to OE *spang* buckle, MD *spannen* to stretch] (15c) **1 :** a small plate of shining metal or plastic used for ornamentation esp. on clothing **2 :** a small glittering object or particle

2spangle *vb* **span·gled; span·gling** \'spaŋ-g(ə-)liŋ\ *vt* (1598) **:** to set or sprinkle with or as if with spangles ~ *vi* **:** to glitter as if covered with spangles **:** SPARKLE

Span·iard \'span-yərd\ *n* [ME *Spaignard*, fr. MF *Espaignart*, fr. *Espaigne* Spain, fr. L *Hispania*] (15c) **:** a native or inhabitant of Spain

span·iel \'span-yəl *also* 'span-ᵊl\ *n* [ME *spaniell*, fr. MF *espaignol*, lit., Spaniard, fr. (assumed) VL *Hispaniolus*, fr. L *Hispania* Spain] (14c) **1 :** any of numerous small or medium-sized mostly short-legged dogs usu. having long wavy hair, feathered legs and tail, and large drooping ears **2 :** a fawning servile person

Span·ish \'span-ish\ *n* [*Spanish*, adj., fr. ME *Spainish*, fr. *Spain*] (15c) **1 :** the Romance language of the largest part of Spain and of the countries colonized by Spaniards **2** *pl in constr* **:** the people of Spain — **Spanish** *adj* — **Span·ish·ness** *n*

Spanish American *n* (1811) **1 :** a resident of the U.S. whose native language is Spanish and whose culture is of Spanish origin **2 :** a native or inhabitant of one of the countries of America in which Spanish is the national language — **Spanish–American** *adj*

Spanish bayonet *n* (1843) **:** any of several yuccas; *esp* **:** one (*Yucca aloifolia*) with a short trunk and rigid spine-tipped leaves

Spanish chestnut *n* (1699) **:** MARRON

Spanish fly *n* (1634) **1 :** a green blister beetle (*Lytta vesicatoria*) of southern Europe **2 :** CANTHARIS 2

Spanish mackerel *n* (1666) **:** any of various usu. large fishes (esp. genus *Scomberomorus*) chiefly of warm seas that resemble or are related to the common mackerel; *esp* **:** one (*S. maculatus*) that is bluish above with oval brown spots on the sides and is found off the American Atlantic coast from Cape Ann to Brazil

Spanish moss *n* (1823) **:** an epiphytic plant (*Tillandsia usneoides*) of the pineapple family forming pendent tufts of grayish green filaments on trees in the southern U.S. and the West Indies

Spanish needles *n pl but sing or pl in constr* (1743) **:** a bur marigold (esp. *Bidens bipinnata*) of the eastern U.S.

Spanish omelet *n* (ca. 1909) **:** an omelet served with a sauce containing chopped green pepper, onion, and tomato

Spanish rice *n* (1928) **:** rice cooked with onions, green pepper, and tomatoes

1spank \'spaŋk\ *vt* [origin unknown] (ca. 1727) **:** to strike esp. on the buttocks with the open hand — **spank** *n*

2spank *vi* [back-formation fr. *spanking*] (1807) **:** to move quickly, dashingly, or spiritedly ⟨~*ing* along in his new car⟩

span·ker \'spaŋ-kər\ *n* [origin unknown] (1794) **1 :** the fore-and-aft sail on the mast nearest the stern of a square-rigged ship **2 :** the sail on the sternmost mast in a schooner of four or more masts

1spank·ing \'spaŋ-kiŋ\ *adj* [origin unknown] (1666) **1 :** remarkable of its kind **2 :** being fresh and strong **:** BRISK

2spanking *adv* (1925) **:** VERY ⟨a ~ clean floor⟩ ⟨a ~ white gown⟩

span·ner \'span-ər\ *n* [G, instrument for winding springs, fr. *spannen* to stretch; akin to MD *spannen* to stretch — more at SPAN] (ca. 1790) **1** *chiefly Brit* **:** WRENCH **2 :** a wrench that has a hole, projection, or hook at one or both ends of the head for engaging with a corresponding device on the object that is to be turned

span–new \'span-'n(y)ü\ *adj* [ME, part trans. of ON *spánnýr*, fr. *spánn* chip of wood + *nýr* new] (14c) **:** BRAND-NEW

span·worm \'span-,wərm\ *n* [3*span*] (1820) **:** LOOPER 1

1spar \'spär\ *n* [ME *sparre;* akin to OE *spere* spear — more at SPEAR] (14c) **1 :** a stout pole **2 a :** a stout rounded wood or metal piece (as a mast, boom, gaff, or yard) used to support rigging **b** (1) **:** one of the main longitudinal members of the wing of an airplane that carry the ribs (2) **:** LONGERON

2spar *vi* **sparred; spar·ring** [prob. alter. of 2*spur*] (1537) **1 :** SKIRMISH, WRANGLE **2 :** to strike or fight with feet or spurs in the manner of a gamecock **3 a :** BOX; *esp* **:** to gesture without landing a blow to draw one's opponent or create an opening **b :** to engage in a practice or exhibition bout of boxing

3spar *n* (1814) **1 :** a movement of offense or defense in boxing **2 :** a sparring match or session

4spar *n* [LG; akin to OE *spærstān* gypsum, *spæren* of plaster] (1581) **:** any of various nonmetallic usu. cleavable and lustrous minerals

SPAR \'spär\ *n* [Semper *Par*atus, motto of the U.S. Coast Guard, fr. NL, always ready] (1942) **:** a member of the women's reserve of the U.S. Coast Guard

1spare \'spa(ə)r, 'spe(ə)r\ *vb* **spared; spar·ing** [ME *sparen*, fr. OE *sparian;* akin to OHG *sparōn* to spare, OE *spær*, adj., scant] *vt* (bef. 12c) **1 :** to forbear to destroy, punish, or harm **2 :** to refrain from attacking or reprimanding with necessary or salutary severity **3 :** to relieve of the necessity of doing or undergoing something ⟨~ yourself the trouble⟩ **4 :** to refrain from **:** AVOID ⟨*spared* no expense⟩ **5 :** to use or dispense frugally — used chiefly in the negative ⟨don't ~ the syrup⟩ **6 a :** to give up as not strictly needed ⟨do you have any cash to ~⟩ **b :** to have left over or as margin ⟨time to ~⟩ ~ *vi* **1 :** to be frugal **2 :** to refrain from doing harm **:** be lenient — **spare·able** \-ə-bəl\ *adj* — **spar·er** *n*

2spare *adj* **spar·er; spar·est** [ME; akin to OSlav *sporŭ* abundant, OE *spēd* prosperity — more at SPEED] (14c) **1 :** not being used; *esp* **:** held for emergency use ⟨a ~ tire⟩ **2 :** being over and above what is needed **:** SUPERFLUOUS ⟨~ time⟩ **3 :** not liberal or profuse **:** SPARING ⟨a ~ prose style⟩ **4 :** healthily lean **5 :** not abundant or plentiful ***syn*** see LEAN, MEAGER — **spare·ly** *adv* — **spare·ness** *n*

3spare *n* (1642) **1 a :** a spare tire **b :** a duplicate (as a key or shirt) kept in reserve **2 :** the knocking down of all 10 pins with the first 2 balls in a frame in bowling

spare·ribs \'spa(ə)r-,(r)ibz, 'spe(ə)r-, -əbz\ *n pl* [by folk etymology fr. LG *ribbesper* pickled pork ribs roasted on a spit, fr. MLG, fr. *ribbe* rib + *sper* spear, spit] (1596) **:** a cut of pork ribs separated from the bacon strip

sparge \'spärj\ *vt* **sparged; sparg·ing** [prob. fr. MF *espargier*, fr. L *spargere* to scatter] (1785) **1 :** SPRINKLE, BESPATTER; *esp* **:** SPRAY **2 :** to agitate (a liquid) by means of compressed air or gas entering through a pipe — **sparge** *n* — **sparg·er** *n*

spar·ing \'spa(ə)r-iŋ, 'spe(ə)r-\ *adj* (14c) **1 :** marked by or practicing careful restraint (as in the use of resources) **2 :** MEAGER, BARE ⟨the map is ~ of information⟩ — **spar·ing·ly** \-iŋ-lē\ *adv*

syn SPARING, FRUGAL, THRIFTY, ECONOMICAL mean careful in the use of one's money or resources. SPARING stresses abstention and restraint; FRUGAL implies absence of luxury and simplicity of life-style; THRIFTY stresses good management and industry; ECONOMICAL stresses prudent management, lack of wastefulness, and use of things to their best advantage.

1spark \'spärk\ *n* [ME *sparke*, fr. OE *spearca;* akin to MD *sparke* spark, L *spargere* to scatter, Gk *spargan* to swell] (bef. 12c) **1 a :** a small particle of a burning substance thrown out by a body in combustion or remaining when combustion is nearly completed **b :** a hot glowing particle struck from a larger mass; *esp* **:** one heated by friction **2 a :** a luminous disruptive electrical discharge of very short duration between two conductors separated by a gas (as air) **b :** the discharge in a spark plug **c :** the mechanism controlling the discharge in a spark plug **3 :** SPARKLE, FLASH **4 :** something that sets off a sudden force ⟨provided the ~ that helped the team to rally⟩ **5 :** a latent particle capable of growth or developing **:** GERM ⟨still retains a ~ of decency⟩ **6** *pl but sing in constr* **:** a radio operator on a ship

2spark *vi* (14c) **1 a :** to throw out sparks **b :** to flash or fall like sparks **2 :** to produce sparks; *specif* **:** to have the electric ignition working **3 :** to respond with enthusiasm ~ *vt* **1 :** to set off in a burst of activity **:** ACTIVATE ⟨the question ~*ed* a lively discussion⟩ — often used with *off* **2 :** to stir to activity **:** INCITE ⟨a player can ~ his team to victory⟩ — **spark·er** *n*

3spark *n* [perh. of Scand origin; akin to ON *sparkr* sprightly] (1600) **1 :** a foppish young man **2 :** LOVER, BEAU — **spark·ish** \'spär-kish\ *adj*

4spark *vb* (1787) **:** WOO, COURT — **spark·er** *n*

spark chamber *n* (1961) **:** a device usu. used to detect the path of a high-energy particle that consists of a series of charged metal plates or wires separated by a gas (as neon) in which observable electric discharges follow the path of the particle

spark coil *n* (1896) **:** an induction coil for producing the spark for an internal-combustion engine

spark gap *n* (1889) **:** a space between two high-potential terminals (as of an induction coil) through which pass discharges of electricity; *also* **:** a device having a spark gap

sparking plug *n, Brit* (1902) **:** SPARK PLUG

1spar·kle \'spär-kəl\ *vb* **spar·kled; spar·kling** \-k(ə-)liŋ\ [ME *sparklen*, freq. of *sparken* to spark] *vi* (13c) **1 a :** to throw out sparks **b :** to give off or reflect bright moving points of light **c :** to perform brilliantly **2 :** EFFERVESCE ⟨wine that ~*s*⟩ **3 :** to become lively or animated ⟨the dialogue ~*s* with wit⟩ ⟨eyes *sparkling* with anger⟩ ~ *vt* **:** to cause to glitter or shine ***syn*** see FLASH

2sparkle *n* [ME, dim. of *sparke*] (14c) **1 :** a little spark **:** SCINTILLATION **2 :** the quality of sparkling **3 a :** ANIMATION, LIVELINESS **b :** the quality or state of being effervescent

spar·kler \'spär-klər\ *n* (1713) **:** one that sparkles: as **a :** DIAMOND **b :** a firework that throws off brilliant sparks on burning

sparkling wine *n* (1697) **:** an effervescent table wine

spark plug *n* (1903) **1 :** a part that fits into the cylinder head of an internal-combustion engine and carries two electrodes separated by an air gap across which the current from the ignition system discharges to form the spark for combustion **2 :** one that initiates or gives impetus to an undertaking — **spark-plug** \'spärk-,pləg\ *vt*

spark transmitter *n* (1916) **:** a radio transmitter that utilizes the discharge of a condenser through a spark gap as a source of its alternating-current power

sparky \'spär-kē\ *adj* **spark·i·er; -est** (ca. 1865) **:** marked by animation **:** LIVELY — **spark·i·ly** \-kə-lē\ *adv*

sparring partner *n* (1908) **:** a boxer's companion for practice in sparring during training

spar·row \'spar-(,)ō, -ə(-w)\ *n* [ME *sparow,* fr. OE *spearwa;* akin to OHG *sparo* sparrow, Gk *psar* starling] (bef. 12c) **1 :** any of several small dull singing birds (genus *Passer* of the family Ploceidae) related to the finches; *esp* **:** ENGLISH SPARROW **2 :** any of various finches (as of the genera *Spizella* or *Melospiza*) resembling the true sparrows — **spar·row-like** \-ō-,līk, -ə-,līk\ *adj*

sparrow hawk *n* (15c) **:** any of various small hawks or falcons (as the Old World *Accipiter nisus* or the No. American *Falco sparverius*)

sparse \'spärs\ *adj* **spars·er; spars·est** [L *sparsus* spread out, fr. pp. of *spargere* to scatter — more at SPARK] (1753) **:** of few and scattered elements; *esp* **:** not thickly grown or settled ***syn*** see MEAGER — **sparse·ly** *adv* — **sparse·ness** *n* — **spar·si·ty** \'spär-sət-ē, -stē\ *n*

Spar·ta·cist \'spärt-ə-səst\ *n* [G *Spartakist,* fr. *Spartakusbund,* lit., league of Spartakus, a revolutionary organization, fr. *Spartakus,* pen name of Karl Liebknecht, its cofounder] (1919) **:** a member of a revolutionary political group organized in Germany in 1918 and advocating extreme socialistic doctrines

¹Spar·tan \'spärt-ᵊn\ *n* (15c) **1 :** a native or inhabitant of ancient Sparta **2 :** a person of great courage and self-discipline — **Spar·tan·ism** \-,iz-əm\ *n*

²Spartan *adj* (1582) **1 :** of or relating to Sparta in ancient Greece **2 a :** marked by strict self-discipline or self-denial ⟨a ~ athlete⟩ **b :** marked by simplicity, frugality, or avoidance of luxury and comfort **c :** LACONIC **d :** undaunted by pain or danger — **Spar·tan·ly** *adv*

spar·te·ine \'spärt-ē-ən, 'spär-,tēn\ *n* [L *spartum* esparto, broom + ISV *-eine* — more at ESPARTO] (1851) **:** a liquid alkaloid $C_{15}H_{26}N_2$ extracted from the Scotch broom and used in medicine in the form of its sulfate

spar varnish *n* [¹*spar*] (ca. 1909) **:** an exterior waterproof varnish

spasm \'spaz-əm\ *n* [ME *spasme,* fr. MF, fr. L *spasmus,* fr. Gk *spasmos,* fr. *span* to draw, pull — more at SPAN] (15c) **1 :** an involuntary and abnormal muscular contraction **2 :** a sudden violent and temporary effort or emotion ⟨a ~ of creativity⟩

spas·mod·ic \spaz-'mäd-ik\ *adj* [NL *spasmodicus,* fr. Gk *spasmōdēs,* fr. *spasmos*] (ca. 1681) **1 a :** relating to or affected or characterized by spasm **b :** resembling a spasm esp. in sudden violence ⟨a ~ jerk⟩ **2 :** acting or proceeding fitfully **:** INTERMITTENT **3 :** subject to outbursts of emotional excitement **:** EXCITABLE ***syn*** see FITFUL — **spas·mod·i·cal·ly** \-ik(ə-)lē\ *adv*

spas·mo·lyt·ic \,spaz-mə-'lit-ik\ *adj* [ISV *spasmo-* (fr. Gk *spasmos* spasm) + *-lytic*] (ca. 1935) **:** tending or having the power to relieve spasms or convulsions — **spasmolytic** *n*

¹spas·tic \'spas-tik\ *adj* [L *spasticus,* fr. Gk *spastikos* drawing in, fr. *span*] (1753) **1 :** of, relating to, or characterized by spasm ⟨a ~ colon⟩ **2 :** suffering from spastic paralysis ⟨a ~ child⟩ **3 :** SPASMODIC ⟨a ~ influx of data⟩ — **spas·ti·cal·ly** \-ti-k(ə-)lē\ *adv* — **spas·tic·i·ty** \spa-'stis-ət-ē\ *n*

²spastic *n* (1939) **:** one suffering from spastic paralysis

spastic paralysis *n* (1879) **:** paralysis with tonic spasm of the affected muscles and with increased tendon reflexes — compare CEREBRAL PALSY

¹spat \'spat\ *past and past part of* SPIT

²spat *n, pl* **spat** *or* **spats** [origin unknown] (1667) **:** a young bivalve (as an oyster)

³spat *n* [short for *spatterdash* (legging)] (ca. 1802) **:** a cloth or leather gaiter covering the instep and ankle

⁴spat *n* [origin unknown] (1804) **1 :** a brief petty quarrel or angry outburst **2** *chiefly dial* **:** SLAP **3 :** a sound like that of rain falling in large drops ⟨the ~ of bullets⟩

⁵spat *vb* **spat·ted; spat·ting** *vt, chiefly dial* (ca. 1848) **:** SLAP ~ *vi* **1 :** to quarrel pettily or briefly **2 :** to strike with a sound like that of rain falling in large drops

spate \'spāt\ *n* [ME] (15c) **1 :** FRESHET, FLOOD **2 a :** a large number or amount ⟨a ~ of books on gardening⟩ **b :** a sudden or strong outburst **:** RUSH ⟨a ~ of anger⟩

spathe \'spāth\ *n* [NL *spatha,* fr. L, broad sword — more at SPADE] (1785) **:** a sheathing bract or pair of bracts enclosing an inflorescence and esp. a spadix on the same axis ⟨the ~ of the calla⟩

spath·ic \'spath-ik\ *adj* [G *spath, spat* spar; akin to OHG *spān* chip — more at SPOON] (1831) **:** resembling spar **:** FOLIATED

spath·u·late \'spath-yə-lət\ *adj* [LL *spathula, spatula* spatula] (1821) **:** SPATULATE ⟨~ petals of a flower⟩

spa·tial \'spā-shəl\ *adj* [L *spatium* space — more at SPEED] (1847) **:** relating to, occupying, or having the character of space — **spa·ti·al·i·ty** \,spā-shē-'al-ət-ē\ *n* — **spa·tial·ly** \'spāsh-(ə-)lē\ *adv*

spatial summation *n* (1968) **:** sensory summation that involves stimulation of several spatially separated neurons at the same time

spa·tio·tem·po·ral \,spā-shē-ō-'tem-p(ə-)rəl\ *adj* [L *spatium* + *tempor-, tempus* time — more at TEMPORAL] (1926) **1 :** having both spatial and temporal qualities **2 :** of or relating to space-time — **spa·tio·tem·po·ral·ly** \-ē\ *adv*

¹spat·ter \'spat-ər\ *vb* [akin to Flem *spetteren* to spatter] *vi* (1600) **:** to spurt forth in scattered drops ⟨blood *~ing* everywhere⟩ ~ *vt* **1 :** to splash with or as if with a liquid; *also* **:** to soil in this way ⟨his coat was *~ed* with mud⟩ **2 :** to scatter by or as if by splashing ⟨~ water⟩ **3 :** to cover with or as if with splashes or spots **4 :** to injure by aspersion **:** DEFAME ⟨~ his good reputation⟩

²spatter *n* (1797) **1 a :** the act or process of spattering **:** the state of being spattered **b :** the noise of spattering **2 a :** a drop or splash spattered on something or a spot or stain due to spattering **b :** a small amount or number **:** SPRINKLE ⟨a ~ of applause⟩

spat·ter·dock \'spat-ər-,däk\ *n* (1813) **:** a common yellow No. American water lily (*Nuphar advenum*); *also* **:** a congeneric plant

spat·u·la \'spach-(ə-)lə\ *n* [LL, spoon, spatula — more at EPAULET] (1525) **:** a flat thin usu. metal implement used esp. for spreading or mixing soft substances, scooping, or lifting

spat·u·late \'spach-ə-lət\ *adj* (1760) **:** shaped like a spatula ⟨a ~ leaf⟩ ⟨~ spines of a caterpillar⟩ ⟨a ~ tool⟩

spav·in \'spav-ən\ *n* [ME *spavayne,* fr. MF *espavain*] (15c) **:** SWELLING; *esp* **:** a bony enlargement of the hock of a horse associated with strain — **spav·ined** \-ənd\ *adj*

¹spawn \'spȯn, 'spän\ *vb* [ME *spawnen,* fr. AF *espaundre,* fr. OF *espandre* to spread out, expand, fr. L *expandere*] *vi* (15c) **1 :** to deposit spawn **2 :** to produce young esp. in large numbers ~ *vt* **1 a :** to produce or deposit (eggs) — used of an aquatic animal **b :** to induce (fish) to spawn **c :** to plant with mushroom spawn **2 :** BRING FORTH, GENERATE — **spawn·er** *n*

²spawn *n* (15c) **1 :** the eggs of aquatic animals (as fishes or oysters) that lay many small eggs **2 :** PRODUCT, OFFSPRING; *also* **:** numerous issue **3 :** the seed, germ, or source of something **4 :** mycelium esp. prepared (as in bricks) for propagating mushrooms

spay \'spā, *substand* 'spād\ *vt* **spayed** \'spād, *substand* 'spād-əd\; **spay·ing** \'spā-iŋ, *substand* 'spād-iŋ\ [ME *spayen,* fr. MF *espeer* to cut with a sword, fr. OF, fr. *espee* sword, fr. L *spatha* sword — more at SPADE] (15c) **:** to remove the ovaries of (a female animal)

speak \'spēk\ *vb* **spoke** \'spōk\; **spo·ken** \'spō-kən\; **speak·ing** [ME *speken,* fr. OE *sprecan, specan;* akin to OHG *sprehhan* to speak, Gk *spharageisthai* to crackle] *vi* (bef. 12c) **1 a :** to utter words or articulate sounds with the ordinary voice **:** TALK **b** (1) **:** to express thoughts, opinions, or feelings orally (2) **:** to extend a greeting (3) **:** to be on speaking terms ⟨still were not *~ing* after the dispute⟩ **c** (1) **:** to express oneself before a group (2) **:** to address one's remarks ⟨~ to the issue⟩ **2 a :** to make a written statement ⟨his diaries . . . *spoke* . . . of his entrancement with death —Sy Kahn⟩ **b :** to use such an expression — often used in the phrase *so to speak* ⟨he was at the enemy's gates, so to ~ —C. S. Forester⟩ **c :** to serve as spokesman ⟨*spoke* for the whole group⟩ **3 a :** to express feelings by other than verbal means ⟨actions ~ louder than words⟩ **b :** SIGNAL **c :** to be interesting or attractive **:** APPEAL ⟨great music . . . *~s* directly to the emotions —A. N. Whitehead⟩ **4 :** to make a request **:** ASK ⟨*spoke* for the remaining piece of pie⟩ **5 :** to make a characteristic or natural sound ⟨all at once the thunder *spoke* —George Meredith⟩ **6 a :** TESTIFY **b :** to be indicative or suggestive ⟨his gold . . . *spoke* of riches in the land —Julian Dana⟩ ~ *vt* **1 a** (1) **:** to utter with the speaking voice **:** PRONOUNCE (2) **:** to give a recitation of **:** DECLAIM **b :** to express orally **:** DECLARE ⟨free to ~ their minds⟩ **c :** ADDRESS, ACCOST; *esp* **:** HAIL **2 :** to make known in writing **:** STATE **3 :** to use or be able to use in speaking ⟨*~s* Spanish⟩ **4 :** to indicate by other than verbal means **5** *archaic* **:** DESCRIBE, DEPICT — **speak·able** \'spē-kə-bəl\ *adj* — **to speak of :** worthy of mention or notice — usu. used in negative constructions

speak·easy \'spē-,kē-zē\ *n, pl* **-eas·ies** (1889) **:** a place where alcoholic beverages are illegally sold

speak·er \'spē-kər\ *n* (14c) **1 a :** one that speaks **b :** one who makes a public speech **c :** one who acts as a spokesman **2 :** the presiding officer of a deliberative assembly ⟨*Speaker* of the House of Representatives⟩ **3 :** LOUDSPEAKER — **speak·er·ship** \-,ship\ *n*

speak·er·phone \'spē-kər-,fōn\ *n* (1955) **:** a combination microphone and loudspeaker device for two-way communication by telephone lines

speak·ing \'spē-kiŋ\ *adj* (13c) **1 a :** that speaks **:** capable of speech **b :** having a population that speaks a specified language — usu. used in combination ⟨English-*speaking* countries⟩ **c :** that involves talking or giving speeches ⟨a ~ role⟩ ⟨a ~ tour⟩ **2 :** highly significant or expressive **:** ELOQUENT **3 :** resembling a living being or a real object

speaking tube *n* (1833) **:** a pipe through which conversation may be conducted (as between different parts of a building)

speak out *vi* (1530) **1 :** to speak loud enough to be heard **2 :** to speak boldly **:** express an opinion frankly ⟨*spoke out* on the issues⟩

speak up *vi* (1705) **1 :** to express an opinion freely ⟨*speak up* for truth and justice —Clive Bell⟩ **2 :** to speak loudly and distinctly

spean \'spēn\ *vt* [MD *spenen*] *chiefly Scot* (1595) **:** WEAN

¹spear \'spi(ə)r\ *n* [ME *spere,* fr. OE; akin to OHG *sper* spear, L *sparus,* Gk *sparos* gilthead] (bef. 12c) **1 :** a thrusting or throwing weapon with long shaft and sharp head or blade **2 :** a sharp-pointed instrument with barbs used in spearing fish **3 :** SPEARMAN

²spear *adj* [¹*spear*] (bef. 12c) **:** PATERNAL, MALE ⟨the ~ side of the family⟩ — compare DISTAFF

³spear *vt* (ca. 1755) **1 :** to pierce, strike, or take with or as if with a spear ⟨~ salmon⟩ ⟨*~ed* a chop from the platter⟩ **2 :** to catch (as a baseball) with a sudden thrust of the arm ~ *vi* **:** to thrust at or wound something with or as if with a spear — **spear·er** *n*

⁴spear *vi* [alter. of ²*spire*] *of a plant* (1573) **:** to thrust a spear upward

⁵spear *n* (1647) **:** a usu. young blade, shoot, or sprout (as of grass)

spear–car·ri·er \'spi(ə)r-,kar-ē-ər\ *n* (1953) **1 a :** a member of an opera chorus **b :** a bit actor in a play **2 :** a person whose actions are of little significance or value in an event or organization

¹spear·fish \'spi(ə)r-,fish\ *n* (ca. 1882) **:** any of several large powerful pelagic fishes (genus *Tetrapturus*) related to the marlins and sailfishes

²spearfish *vi* (ca. 1949) **:** to fish with a spear

¹spear·head \'spi(ə)r-,hed\ *n* (15c) **1 :** the sharp-pointed head of a spear **2 :** a leading element, force, or influence in an undertaking or development

²spearhead *vt* (1937) **:** to serve as leader or leading element of

spear·man \'spi(ə)r-mən\ *n* (13c) **:** one armed with a spear

spear·mint \-,mint, -mənt\ *n* (1562) **:** a common mint (*Mentha spicata*) grown for flavoring and esp. for its aromatic oil

spear·wort \-,wərt, -,wȯ(ə)rt\ *n* (14c) **:** any of several crowfoots (esp. *Ranunculus flammula*) with spear-shaped leaves

spec \'spek\ *vt* **specced** *or* **spec'd** \'spekt\; **spec·cing** [²*specs*] (1965) **:** to write specifications for

¹spe·cial \'spesh-əl\ *adj* [ME, fr. OF or L; OF *especial,* fr. L *specialis* individual, particular, fr. *species* species — more at SPY] (13c) **1 :** distinguished by some unusual quality; *esp* **:** being in some way superior **2 :** held in particular esteem ⟨a ~ friend⟩ **3 a :** readily distinguishable from others of the same category **:** UNIQUE ⟨they set it apart as a ~ day of thanksgiving⟩ **b :** of, relating to, or constituting a species **:** SPECIFIC **4 :** being other than the usual **:** ADDITIONAL, EXTRA **5 :** designed for a particular purpose or occasion — **spe·cial·ly** \-(ə-)lē\ *adv* — **spe·cial·ness** *n*

syn SPECIAL, ESPECIAL, SPECIFIC, PARTICULAR, INDIVIDUAL mean of or relating to one thing or class. SPECIAL stresses having a quality, character, identity, or use of its own; ESPECIAL may add implications of preeminence or preference; SPECIFIC implies a quality or character distinguishing a kind or a species; PARTICULAR stresses the distinctness of something as an individual; INDIVIDUAL implies unequivocal reference to one of a class or group

[2]special *n* (1867) **1 :** something (as a television program) that is not part of a regular series **2 :** one that is used for a special service or occasion ⟨caught the commuter ~ to work⟩

special assessment *n* (1875) **:** a specific tax levied on private property to meet the cost of public improvements that enhance the value of the property

special delivery *n* (1886) **:** expedited messenger delivery of mail matter for an extra fee

special district *n* (1950) **:** a political subdivision of a state established to provide a single public service (as water supply or sanitation) within a specific geographical area

special drawing rights *n* (1967) **:** a means of exchange used by governments to settle their international indebtedness

special education *n* (1921) **:** classes for students (as the handicapped) with special educational needs

special effects *n pl* (1937) **:** visual or sound effects introduced into a motion picture or a taped television production during laboratory processing

Special Forces *n pl* (1962) **:** a branch of the army composed of men specially trained in guerrilla warfare

special handling *n* (1928) **:** the handling of parcel-post or fourth-class mail as first-class but not as special-delivery matter for an extra postal fee

special interest *n* (1910) **:** a person or group seeking to influence legislative or government policy to further often narrowly defined interests; *esp* **:** LOBBY

spe·cial·ism \ˈspesh-ə-ˌliz-əm\ *n* (1856) **1 :** specialization in an occupation or branch of learning **2 :** a field of specialization **:** SPECIALTY

spe·cial·ist \ˈspesh-(ə-)ləst\ *n* (1856) **1 :** one who devotes himself to a special occupation or branch of learning **2 :** any of four enlisted ranks in the army corresponding to the grades of corporal through sergeant first class — **specialist** *or* **spe·cial·is·tic** \ˌspesh-ə-ˈlis-tik\ *adj*

spe·ci·al·i·ty \ˌspesh-ē-ˈal-ət-ē\ *n, pl* **-ties** (15c) **1 :** a special mark or quality **2 :** a special object or class of objects **3 a :** a special aptitude or skill **b :** a particular occupation or branch of learning

spe·cial·iza·tion \ˌspesh-(ə-)lə-ˈzā-shən\ *n* (1843) **1 :** a making or becoming specialized **2 a :** structural adaptation of a body part to a particular function or of an organism for life in a particular environment **b :** a body part or an organism adapted by specialization

spe·cial·ize \ˈspesh-ə-ˌlīz\ *vb* **-ized; -iz·ing** *vt* (1613) **1 :** to make particular mention of **:** PARTICULARIZE **2 :** to apply or direct to a specific end or use ⟨*specialized* his study⟩ ~ *vi* **1 :** to concentrate one's efforts in a special activity or field **2 :** to undergo specialization; *esp* **:** to change adaptively

specialized *adj* (1853) **1 :** designed or fitted for one particular purpose or occupation ⟨~ personnel⟩ **2 :** characterized by or exhibiting biological specialization; *esp* **:** highly differentiated esp. in a particular direction or for a particular end

special jury *n* (1730) **:** a jury chosen by the court on request from a list of better educated or presumably more intelligent prospective jurors for a case involving complicated issues of fact or serious felonies — called also *blue-ribbon jury*

special pleading *n* (1684) **1 :** the allegation of special or new matter to offset the effect of matter pleaded by the opposite side and admitted, as distinguished from a direct denial of the matter pleaded **2 :** misleading argument that presents one point or phase as if it covered the entire question at issue

special theory of relativity (1920)**:** RELATIVITY 3a

spe·cial·ty \ˈspesh-əl-tē\ *n, pl* **-ties** [ME *specialte,* fr. MF *especialté,* fr. LL *specialitat-, specialitas,* fr. L *specialis* special] (14c) **1 :** a distinctive mark or quality **2 a :** a special object or class of objects: as (1) **:** a legal agreement embodied in a sealed instrument (2) **:** a product of a special kind or of special excellence ⟨fried chicken was father's ~⟩ **b :** the state of being special, distinctive, or peculiar **3 :** something in which one specializes

spe·ci·a·tion \ˌspē-s(h)ē-ˈā-shən\ *n* (1906) **:** the process of biological species formation — **spe·ci·ate** \ˈspē-s(h)ē-ˌāt\ *vi* — **spe·ci·a·tion·al** \ˌspē-s(h)ē-ˈā-shnəl, -shənᵊl\ *adj*

[1]spe·cie \ˈspē-shē, -sē\ *n* [fr. *in specie,* fr. L, in kind] (1617) **:** money in coin — **in specie :** in the same or like form or kind ⟨ready to return insult *in specie*⟩; *also* **:** in coin

[2]specie *n* [back-formation fr. *species* (taken as a pl.)] *substand* (1711) **:** SPECIES

[1]spe·cies \ˈspē-(ˌ)shēz, -(ˌ)sēz\ *n, pl* **species** [L, appearance, kind, species — more at SPY] (1551) **1 a :** a class of individuals having common attributes and designated by a common name; *specif* **:** a logical division of a genus or more comprehensive class **b :** KIND, SORT **c :** the human race **:** human beings — often used with *the* ⟨survival of the ~ in the nuclear age⟩ **d** (1) **:** a category of biological classification ranking immediately below the genus or subgenus, comprising related organisms or populations potentially capable of interbreeding, and being designated by a binomial that consists of the name of a genus followed by a Latin or latinized uncapitalized noun or adjective agreeing grammatically with the genus name (2) **:** an individual or kind belonging to a biological species **e :** a particular kind of atomic nucleus, atom, molecule, or ion **2 :** the consecrated eucharistic elements of the Roman Catholic or Eastern Orthodox Eucharist **3 a :** a mental image; *also* **:** a sensible object **b :** an object of thought correlative with a natural object

[2]species *adj* (1899) **:** belonging to a biological species as distinguished from a horticultural variety ⟨a ~ rose⟩

spe·cies·ism \ˈspē-shē-ˌziz-əm, -sē-\ *n* [[1]*species* + *-ism* (as in *racism*)] (1973) **:** prejudice or discrimination based on species; *esp* **:** discrimination against animals

[1]spe·cif·ic \spi-ˈsif-ik\ *adj* [LL *specificus,* fr. L *species*] (1631) **1 a :** constituting or falling into a specifiable category **b :** sharing or being those properties of something that allow it to be referred to a particular category **2 a :** restricted to a particular individual, situation, relation, or effect ⟨a disease ~ to horses⟩ **b :** exerting a distinctive influence (as on a body part or a disease) ⟨~ antibodies⟩ **3 :** free from ambiguity **:** ACCURATE ⟨a ~ statement of faith⟩ **4 :** of, relating to, or constituting a species and esp. a biologic species **5 a :** being any of various arbitrary physical constants and esp. one relating a quantitative attribute to unit mass, volume, or area **b :** imposed at a fixed rate per unit (as of weight or count) ⟨~ import duties⟩ — compare AD VALOREM ***syn*** see SPECIAL, EXPLICIT — **spe·cif·i·cal·ly** \-i-k(ə-)lē\ *adv*

[2]specific *n* (1661) **1 a :** something peculiarly adapted to a purpose or use **b :** a drug or remedy having a specific mitigating effect on a disease **2 a :** a characteristic quality or trait **b :** DETAILS, PARTICULARS — usu. used in pl. ⟨haggling over the legal and financial ~*s* of independence —*Time*⟩ **c** *pl* **:** SPECIFICATION 2a

spec·i·fi·ca·tion \ˌspes-(ə-)fə-ˈkā-shən\ *n* (1615) **1 :** the act or process of specifying **2 a :** a detailed precise presentation of something or of a plan or proposal for something — usu. used in pl. **b :** a statement of legal particulars (as of charges or of contract terms); *also* **:** a single item of such statement **c :** a written description of an invention for which a patent is sought

specific epithet *n* (1906) **:** the Latin or latinized noun or adjective that follows the genus name in a taxonomic binomial

specific gravity *n* (1666) **:** the ratio of the density of a substance to the density of some substance (as pure water or hydrogen) taken as a standard when both densities are obtained by weighing in air

specific heat *n* (1832) **1 :** the ratio of the quantity of heat required to raise the temperature of a body one degree to that required to raise the temperature of an equal mass of water one degree **2 :** the heat in calories required to raise the temperature of one gram of a substance one degree Celsius

specific impulse *n* (1947) **:** the thrust produced per unit rate of consumption of the propellant that is usu. expressed in pounds of thrust per pound of propellant used per second and that is a measure of the efficiency of a rocket engine

spec·i·fic·i·ty \ˌspes-ə-ˈfis-ət-ē\ *n* (1876) **:** the quality or condition of being specific: as **a :** the condition of being peculiar to a particular individual or group of organisms ⟨host ~ of a parasite⟩ **b :** the condition of participating in or catalyzing only one or a few chemical reactions ⟨the ~ of an enzyme⟩

specific performance *n* (1873) **1 :** the performance of a legal contract strictly or substantially according to its terms **2 :** an equitable remedy enjoining specific performance

spec·i·fy \ˈspes-ə-ˌfī\ *vt* **-fied; -fy·ing** [ME *specifien,* fr. MF *specifier,* fr. LL *specificare,* fr. *specificus*] (14c) **1 :** to name or state explicitly or in detail **2 :** to include as an item in a specification — **spec·i·fi·able** \-ˌfī-ə-bəl\ *adj* — **spec·i·fi·er** \-ˌfī(-ə)r\ *n*

spec·i·men \ˈspes-(ə-)mən\ *n* [L, fr. *specere* to look at, look — more at SPY] (1610) **1 :** an item or part typical of a group or whole **2 a :** something that obviously belongs to a particular category but is noticed by reason of an individual distinguishing characteristic **b :** PERSON, INDIVIDUAL ⟨he's a tough ~⟩ ***syn*** see INSTANCE

spe·ci·os·i·ty \ˌspē-shē-ˈäs-ət-ē\ *n* (1608) **:** the quality or state of being specious **:** SPECIOUSNESS

spe·cious \ˈspē-shəs\ *adj* [ME, fr. L *speciosus* beautiful, plausible, fr. *species*] (15c) **1** *obs* **:** SHOWY **2 :** having deceptive attraction or allure **3 :** having a false look of truth or genuineness **:** SOPHISTIC — **spe·cious·ly** *adv* — **spe·cious·ness** *n*

[1]speck \ˈspek\ *n* [ME *specke,* fr. OE *specca*] (bef. 12c) **1 :** a small discoloration or spot esp. from stain or decay **2 :** a very small amount **:** BIT **3 :** something marked or marred with specks — **specked** \ˈspekt\ *adj*

[2]speck *vt* (1580) **:** to produce specks on or in

[1]speck·le \ˈspek-əl\ *n* [ME; akin to OE *specca*] (15c) **:** a little speck (as of color)

[2]speckle *vt* **speck·led; speck·ling** \-(ə-)liŋ\ (ca. 1570) **1 :** to mark with speckles **2 :** to be distributed in or on like speckles

speckled perch *n* (1877) **:** BLACK CRAPPIE

speckled trout *n* (1805) **1 :** BROOK TROUT **2 :** SPOTTED SEA TROUT

[1]specs \ˈspeks\ *n pl* [contr. of *spectacles*] (1807) **:** EYEGLASSES

[2]specs *n pl* [by contr.] (1942) **:** SPECIFICATIONS

spec·ta·cle \ˈspek-ti-kəl *also* -ˌtik-əl\ *n* [ME, fr. MF, fr. L *spectaculum,* fr. *spectare* to watch, fr. *spectus,* pp. of *specere* to look, look at — more at SPY] (14c) **1 a :** something exhibited to view as unusual, notable, or entertaining; *esp* **:** an eye-catching or dramatic public display **b :** an object of curiosity or contempt ⟨made a ~ of herself⟩ **2** *pl* **:** GLASSES **3 :** something (as natural markings on an animal) suggesting a pair of glasses

spec·ta·cled \-ti-kəld, -ˌtik-əld\ *adj* (1607) **1 :** having or wearing spectacles **2 :** having markings suggesting a pair of spectacles ⟨a ~ alligator⟩

[1]spec·tac·u·lar \spek-ˈtak-yə-lər, spək-\ *adj* [L *spectaculum*] (1682) **:** of, relating to, or constituting a spectacle **:** STRIKING, SENSATIONAL ⟨a ~ display of fireworks⟩ — **spec·tac·u·lar·ly** *adv*

[2]spectacular *n* (1890) **:** something that is spectacular

spec·tate \ˈspek-ˌtāt\ *vi* **spec·tat·ed; spec·tat·ing** [back-formation fr. *spectator*] (1709) **:** to be present as a spectator (as at a sports event)

spec·ta·tor \ˈspek-ˌtāt-ər, spek-ˈ\ *n* [L, fr. *spectatus,* pp. of *spectare* to watch] (1586) **:** one who looks on or watches — **spectator** *adj*

spec·ter *or* **spec·tre** \ˈspek-tər\ *n* [F *spectre,* fr. L *spectrum* appearance, specter, fr. *specere* to look, look at — more at SPY] (1605) **1 :** a visible disembodied spirit **:** GHOST **2 :** something that haunts or perturbs the mind **:** PHANTASM ⟨the ~ of hunger⟩

spec·ti·no·my·cin \ˌspek-tə-nō-ˈmīs-ᵊn\ *n* [NL, fr. *spectabilis* + *-in* + *-o-* + *-mycin*] (1964) **:** a white crystalline broad-spectrum antibiotic $C_{14}H_{24}N_2O_7$ produced by a bacterium (*Streptomyces spectabilis*) that is used clinically esp. in the form of its hydrochloride to treat gonorrhea

spec·tral \ˈspek-trəl\ *adj* (1815) **1 :** of, relating to, or suggesting a specter **:** GHOSTLY **2 :** of, relating to, or made by a spectrum — **spec·tral·ly** \ˈspek-trə-lē\ *adv*

spectral line *n* (1902) **:** one of a series of linear images of the narrow slit of a spectrograph or similar instrument corresponding to a component of the spectrum of the radiation emitted by a particular source

spectro- *comb form* [NL *spectrum*] **:** spectrum ⟨*spectroscope*⟩

spec·tro·flu·o·rom·e·ter \ˌspek-(ˌ)trō-ˌflu̇(-ə)r-ˈäm-ət-ər\ *also* **spec·tro·flu·o·rim·e·ter** \-ˈim-\ *n* [*spectr-* + *fluorometer*] (1957) **:** a device for measuring and recording fluorescence spectra — **spec·tro·flu·o·ro·met·ric**

\-ˌflü(-ə)r-ə-ˈme-trik\ *adj* — **spec·tro·flu·o·rom·e·try** \-ˌflü(-ə)r-ˈäm-ə-trē\ *n*
spec·tro·gram \ˈspek-t(r)ə-ˌgram\ *n* [ISV] (1892) **:** a photograph or diagram of a spectrum
spec·tro·graph \-ˌgraf\ *n* [ISV] (1884) **:** an instrument for dispersing radiation (as electromagnetic radiation or sound waves) into a spectrum and photographing or mapping the spectrum — **spec·tro·graph·ic** \ˌspek-t(r)ə-ˈgraf-ik\ *adj* — **spec·tro·graph·i·cal·ly** \-i-k(ə-)lē\ *adv* — **spec·trog·ra·phy** \spek-ˈträg-rə-fē\ *n*
spec·tro·he·lio·gram \ˌspek-trō-ˈhē-lē-ə-ˌgram\ *n* (ca. 1909) **:** a photograph of the sun that is made by monochromatic light and shows the sun's faculae and prominences
spec·tro·he·lio·graph \-ˌgraf\ *n* [ISV] (1892) **:** an apparatus for making spectroheliograms — **spec·tro·he·li·og·ra·phy** \-ˌhē-lē-ˈäg-rə-fē\ *n*
spec·tro·he·lio·scope \-ˈhē-lē-ə-ˌskōp\ *n* [ISV] (1926) **1 :** SPECTROHELIOGRAPH **2 :** an instrument similar to a spectroheliograph used for visual as distinguished from photographic observations
spec·trom·e·ter \spek-ˈträm-ət-ər\ *n* [ISV] (1874) **1 :** an instrument used in determining the index of refraction of a transparent solid in the form of a prism **2 :** a spectroscope that can measure the spectra produced ⟨mass ~⟩ ⟨nuclear magnetic resonance ~⟩ — **spec·tro·met·ric** \ˌspek-trə-ˈme-trik\ *adj* — **spec·trom·e·try** \spek-ˈträm-ə-trē\ *n*
spec·tro·pho·tom·e·ter \ˌspek-trō-fə-ˈtäm-ət-ər\ *n* [ISV] (1881) **:** a photometer for measuring the relative intensities of the light in different parts of a spectrum — **spec·tro·pho·to·met·ric** \-trə-ˌfōt-ə-ˈme-trik\ *or* **spec·tro·pho·to·met·ri·cal** \-tri-kəl\ *adj* — **spec·tro·pho·to·met·ri·cal·ly** \-tri-k(ə-)lē\ *adv* — **spec·tro·pho·tom·e·try** \ˌspek-(ˌ)trō-fə-ˈtäm-ə-trē\ *n*
spec·tro·scope \ˈspek-trə-ˌskōp\ *n* [ISV] (1861) **:** an instrument that produces spectra which result from the use or production of, or which relate to electromagnetic radiation or closely associated phenomena — **spec·tro·scop·ic** \ˌspek-trə-ˈskäp-ik\ *adj* — **spec·tro·scop·i·cal·ly** \-i-k(ə-)lē\ *adv* — **spec·tros·co·pist** \spek-ˈträs-kə-pəst\ *n*
spec·tros·co·py \spek-ˈträs-kə-pē\ *n* (1870) **1 a :** the production and investigation of a spectra **b :** the process or technique of using a spectroscope **2 :** physics that deals with the theory and interpretation of interactions between matter and radiation (as electromagnetic radiation)
spec·trum \ˈspek-trəm\ *n, pl* **spec·tra** \-trə\ *or* **spectrums** [NL, fr. L, appearance — more at SPECTER] (1671) **1 a :** an array of the components of an emission or wave separated and arranged in the order of some varying characteristic (as wavelength, mass, or energy): as (1) **:** a series of images formed when a beam of radiant energy is subjected to dispersion and brought to focus so that the component waves are arranged in the order of their wavelengths (as when a beam of sunlight that is refracted and dispersed by a prism forms a display of colors) (2) **:** ELECTROMAGNETIC SPECTRUM (3) **:** RADIO SPECTRUM (4) **:** the range of frequencies of sound waves (5) **:** MASS SPECTRUM **b :** the representation (as a plot) of a spectrum **2 a :** a continuous sequence or range ⟨a wide ~ of interests⟩ **b :** kinds of organisms associated with a particular situation (as an environment) or susceptible to an agent (as an antibiotic)
spec·u·lar \ˈspek-yə-lər\ *adj* [L *specularis* of a mirror, fr. *speculum*] (1661) **:** of, relating to, or having the qualities of a mirror — **spec·u·lar·i·ty** \ˌspek-yə-ˈlar-ət-ē\ *n* — **spec·u·lar·ly** \ˈspek-yə-lər-lē\ *adv*
spec·u·late \ˈspek-yə-ˌlāt\ *vb* **-lat·ed; -lat·ing** [L *speculatus,* pp. of *speculari* to spy out, examine, fr. *specula* watchtower, fr. *specere* to look, look at — more at SPY] *vi* (1599) **1 a :** to meditate on or ponder a subject **:** REFLECT **b :** to review something idly or casually and often inconclusively **2 :** to assume a business risk in hope of gain; *esp* **:** to buy or sell in expectation of profiting from market fluctuations ~ *vt* **1 :** to take to be true on the basis of insufficient evidence **:** ASSUME ⟨*speculated* that a virus caused the disease⟩ **2 :** to be curious or doubtful about **:** WONDER ⟨~*s* whether it will rain for his vacation⟩ ***syn*** see THINK — **spec·u·la·tor** \-ˌlāt-ər\ *n*
spec·u·la·tion \ˌspek-yə-ˈlā-shən\ *n* (14c) **:** an act or instance of speculating: as **a :** assumption of unusual business risk in hopes of obtaining commensurate gain **b :** a transaction involving such speculation
spec·u·la·tive \ˈspek-yə-lət-iv, -ˌlāt-\ *adj* (14c) **1 :** involving, based on, or constituting intellectual speculation; *also* **:** theoretical rather than demonstrable ⟨~ knowledge⟩ **2 :** marked by questioning curiosity ⟨gave him a ~ glance⟩ **3 :** of, relating to, or being a financial speculation ⟨~ stocks⟩ ⟨~ venture⟩ — **spec·u·la·tive·ly** *adv*
spec·u·lum \ˈspek-yə-ləm\ *n, pl* **-la** \-lə\ *also* **-lums** [L, mirror, fr. *specere*] (1597) **1 :** an instrument inserted into a body passage for inspection or medication **2 a :** an ancient mirror usu. of bronze or silver **b :** a reflector in an optical instrument **3 :** a medieval compendium of all knowledge **4 :** a drawing or table showing the relative positions of all the planets (as in an astrological nativity) **5 :** a patch of color on the secondaries of most ducks and some other birds
speech \ˈspēch\ *n* [ME *speche,* fr. OE *spræc, spæc;* akin to OE *sprecan* to speak — more at SPEAK] (bef. 12c) **1 a :** the communication or expression of thoughts in spoken words **b :** exchange of spoken words **:** CONVERSATION **2 a :** something that is spoken **:** UTTERANCE **b :** a public discourse **:** ADDRESS **3 a :** LANGUAGE, DIALECT **b :** an individual manner or style of speaking **4 :** the power of expressing or communicating thoughts by speaking
speech community *n* (1894) **:** a group of people sharing characteristic patterns of vocabulary, grammar, and pronunciation
speech form *n* (1863) **:** LINGUISTIC FORM
speech·ify \ˈspē-chə-ˌfī\ *vi* **-ified; -ify·ing** (1723) **:** to make a speech
speech·less \ˈspēch-ləs\ *adj* (bef. 12c) **1 :** unable to speak **:** DUMB **2 :** not speaking **:** SILENT **3 :** not capable of being expressed in words — **speech·less·ly** *adv* — **speech·less·ness** *n*
[1]**speed** \ˈspēd\ *n* [ME *spede,* fr. OE *spēd;* akin to OHG *spuot* prosperity, speed, L *spes* hope, *spatium* space] (bef. 12c) **1** *archaic* **:** prosperity in an undertaking **:** SUCCESS **2 a :** the act or state of moving swiftly **:** SWIFTNESS **b :** rate of motion: as (1) **:** VELOCITY 1,3a (2) **:** the magnitude of a velocity irrespective of direction **c :** IMPETUS **3 :** swiftness or rate of performance or action **4 a :** the sensitivity of a photographic film, plate, or paper expressed numerically **b :** the light-gathering power of a lens or optical system **c :** the time during which a camera shutter is open **5 :** a transmission gear in automotive vehicles or bicycles **6 :** someone or something that appeals to one's taste **7 :** METHAMPHETAMINE; *also* **:** a related drug ***syn*** see HASTE
[2]**speed** *vb* **sped** \ˈsped\ *or* **speed·ed; speed·ing** *vi* (bef. 12c) **1 a** *archaic* **:** to prosper in an undertaking **b** *archaic* **:** GET ALONG, FARE **2 a :** to make haste ⟨*sped* to her bedside⟩ **b :** to go or drive at excessive or illegal speed **3 :** to move, work, or take place faster **:** ACCELERATE ⟨the heart ~*s* up⟩ ~ *vt* **1 a** *archaic* **:** to cause or help to prosper **:** AID **b :** to further the success of **2 a :** to cause to move quickly **:** HASTEN **b :** to wish Godspeed to **c :** to increase the speed of **:** ACCELERATE ⟨~*ed* up the engine⟩ **3 :** to send out ⟨~ an arrow⟩ — **speed·er** *n* — **speed·ster** \ˈspēd-stər\ *n*
[1]**speed·ball** \ˈspēd-ˌbȯl\ *n, slang* (1909) **:** cocaine mixed with heroin or morphine or an amphetamine and usu. taken by injection
[2]**speedball** *n* (1923) **:** a game which resembles soccer but in which a ball that is caught in the air may be passed with the hands and in which scoring is accomplished by kicking or heading the ball between the goalposts or by a successful forward pass over the goal line
speed·boat \-ˌbōt\ *n* (1911) **:** a fast launch or motorboat — **speed·boat·ing** \-iŋ\ *n*
speed bump *n* (1972) **:** a low raised ridge across a roadway (as in a parking lot) to limit vehicle speed
speed freak *n* (1967) **:** one who habitually misuses amphetamines and esp. methamphetamine
speed·light \ˈspēd-ˌlīt\ *n* (1898) **:** STROBOTRON
speed limit *n* (1893) **:** the maximum or minimum speed permitted by law in a given area under specified circumstances
speedo \ˈspēd-(ˌ)ō\ *n, pl* **speed·os** [by shortening] *chiefly Brit* (1934) **:** SPEEDOMETER
speed·om·e·ter \spi-ˈdäm-ət-ər\ *n* (1903) **1 :** an instrument for indicating speed **:** TACHOMETER **2 :** an instrument for indicating distance traversed as well as speed of travel; *also* **:** ODOMETER
speed–read·ing \ˈspēd-ˌrēd-iŋ\ *n* (1962) **:** a method of reading rapidly by skimming — **speed–read** *vt*
speed shop *n* (1953) **:** a shop that sells custom automotive equipment esp. to hot-rodders
speed trap *n* (1925) **:** a stretch of road policed by often concealed officers or devices (as radar) so as to catch speeders
speed·up \ˈspēd-ˌəp\ *n* (1921) **1 :** ACCELERATION **2 :** an employer's demand for accelerated output without increased pay
speed·way \ˈspēd-ˌwā\ *n* (1894) **1 :** a public road on which fast driving is allowed; *specif* **:** EXPRESSWAY **2 :** a racecourse for automobiles or motorcycles **3 :** a sprint race for motorcycles
speed·well \ˈspēd-ˌwel\ *n* (1578) **1 :** a perennial European herb (*Veronica officinalis*) of the figwort family with small bluish flowers in axillary racemes **2 :** a plant congeneric with the speedwell
speedy \ˈspēd-ē\ *adj* **speed·i·er; -est** (14c) **:** marked by swiftness of motion or action ***syn*** see FAST — **speed·i·ly** \ˈspēd-ᵊl-ē\ *adv* — **speed·i·ness** \ˈspēd-ē-nəs\ *n*
speel \ˈspē(ə)l\ *vb* [origin unknown] *chiefly Scot* (1752) **:** CLIMB
speer *or* **speir** \ˈspi(ə)r\ *vb* [ME (Sc) *speren,* fr. OE *spyrian* to seek after; akin to OE *spor* spoor] *chiefly Scot* (bef. 12c) **:** ASK, INQUIRE
speiss \ˈspīs\ *n* [G *speise,* lit., food, fr. OHG *spīsa,* prob. fr. ML *spensa* storehouse, fr. LL *expensa* expense — more at EXPENSE] (1797) **:** a mixture of impure metallic arsenides produced as a regulus in smelting certain ores
spe·le·ol·o·gy \ˌspē-lē-ˈäl-ə-jē, ˌspel-ē-\ *n* [L *speleum* cave (fr. Gk *spēlaion*) + ISV *-o-* + *-logy* — more at SPELUNKER] (1895) **:** the scientific study or exploration of caves — **spe·le·o·log·i·cal** \ˌspē-lē-ə-ˈläj-i-kəl, ˌspel-ē-\ *adj* — **spe·le·ol·o·gist** \ˌspē-lē-ˈäl-ə-jəst, ˌspel-ē-\ *n*
[1]**spell** \ˈspel\ *n* [ME, talk, tale, fr. OE; akin to OHG *spel* talk, tale] (bef. 12c) **1 a :** a spoken word or form of words held to have magic power **:** INCANTATION **b :** a state of enchantment **2 :** a strong compelling influence or attraction
[2]**spell** *vt* **spelled** \ˈspeld\; **spell·ing** (1623) **:** to put under a spell
[3]**spell** *vb* **spelled** \ˈspeld\; **spell·ing** [ME *spelen,* fr. OE *spelian;* akin to OE *spala* substitute] *vt* (bef. 12c) **1 :** to take the place of for a time **:** RELIEVE ⟨he and the other assistant . . . ~*ed* each other —Mary McCarthy⟩ **2 :** REST ~ *vi* **1 :** to work in turns **2** *chiefly Austral* **:** to rest from work or activity for a time
[4]**spell** *vb* **spelled** \ˈspeld, ˈspelt\; **spell·ing** [ME *spellen,* fr. MF *espeller,* of Gmc origin; akin to OE *spell* talk] *vt* (14c) **1 :** to read slowly and with difficulty — often used with *out* **2 :** to find out by study **:** come to understand — often used with *out* ⟨it requires some pains to ~ out those decorations —F. J. Mather⟩ **3 a :** to name the letters of in order; *also* **:** to write or print the letters of in order **b :** to make up (a word) ⟨what word do these letters ~⟩ **4 :** to add up to **:** MEAN ⟨crop failure was likely to ~ stark famine —Stringfellow Barr⟩ ~ *vi* **:** to form words with letters
[5]**spell** *n* [prob. alter. (influenced by ME *spelen* to substitute) of ME *spale* substitute, fr. OE *spala*] (1593) **1 a** *archaic* **:** a shift of workers **b :** one's turn at work **2 a :** a period spent in a job or occupation **b** *chiefly Austral* **:** a period of rest from work, activity, or use **3 a :** an indeterminate period of time ⟨waited a ~ before advancing⟩ **b :** a stretch of a specified type of weather **4 :** a period of bodily or mental distress or disorder ⟨a ~ of coughing⟩ ⟨fainting ~*s*⟩
spell·bind \ˈspel-ˌbīnd\ *vt* **-bound** \-ˌbau̇nd\; **-bind·ing** [back-formation fr. *spellbound*] (1808) **:** to bind or hold by or as if by a spell or charm **:** FASCINATE
spell·bind·er \-ˌbīn-dər\ *n* (1888) **:** a speaker of compelling eloquence
spell·bound \-ˌbau̇nd\ *adj* (1799) **:** held by or as if by a spell
spell·er \ˈspel-ər\ *n* (15c) **1 :** one who spells words **2 :** a book with exercises for teaching spelling
spell·ing \ˈspel-iŋ\ *n* (15c) **1 :** the forming of words from letters according to accepted usage **:** ORTHOGRAPHY **2 :** a sequence of letters composing a word
spelling bee *n* (1872) **:** a spelling contest in which each contestant is eliminated as soon as he misspells a word
spell out *vt* (1943) **:** to make plain ⟨*spelled out* his orders in detail⟩

\ə\ abut \ᵊ\ kitten, F table \ər\ further \a\ ash \ā\ ace \ä\ cot, cart \au̇\ out \ch\ chin \e\ bet \ē\ easy \g\ go \i\ hit \ī\ ice \j\ job \ŋ\ sing \ō\ go \ȯ\ law \ȯi\ boy \th\ thin \t͟h\ the \ü\ loot \u̇\ foot \y\ yet \zh\ vision \à, k̲, ⁿ, œ, ᵫ, ue, ᵾ, ʸ\ see Guide to Pronunciation

[1]spelt \'spelt\ *n* [ME, fr. OE, fr. LL *spelta,* of Gmc origin; akin to MHG *spelte* split piece of wood, OHG *spaltan* to split — more at SPILL] (bef. 12c) : a wheat (*Triticum spelta*) with lax spikes and spikelets containing two light red kernels
[2]spelt \'spelt\ *chiefly Brit past and past part of* SPELL
spel·ter \'spel-tər\ *n* [prob. alter. of MD *speauter*] (1661) : ZINC; *esp* : zinc cast in slabs for commercial use
spe·lunk·er \spi-'ləŋ-kər, 'spē-ˌ\ *n* [L *spelunca* cave, fr. Gk *spēlynx;* akin to Gk *spēlaion* cave] (1944) : one who makes a hobby of exploring and studying caves
spe·lunk·ing \-kiŋ\ *n* (1944) : the hobby or practice of exploring caves
spence \'spen(t)s\ *n* [ME, fr. MF *despense,* fr. ML *dispensa,* fr. L, fem. of *dispensus,* pp. of *dispendere* to weigh out — more at DISPENSE] *dial Brit* (14c) : PANTRY
[1]spen·cer \'spen(t)-sər\ *n* [George John, 2d earl *Spencer* †1834 Eng. politician] (1796) : a short waist-length jacket
[2]spencer *n* [prob. fr. the name *Spencer*] (1840) : a trysail abaft the foremast or mainmast
Spen·ce·ri·an \spen-'sir-ē-ən\ *adj* [Platt R. *Spencer* †1864 Am. calligrapher] (1878) : of or relating to a form of slanting handwriting
Spen·ce·ri·an·ism \spen-'sir-ē-ə-ˌniz-əm\ *n* (1880) : the synthetic philosophy of Herbert Spencer that has as its central idea the mechanistic evolution of the cosmos from relative simplicity to relative complexity
spend \'spend\ *vb* **spent** \'spent\; **spend·ing** [ME *spenden,* fr. OE & OF; OE *spendan,* fr. L *expendere* to expend; OF *despendre,* fr. L *dispendere* to weigh out — more at DISPENSE] *vt* (12c) **1** : to use up or pay out : EXPEND **2 a** : EXHAUST, WEAR OUT ⟨the hurricane gradually *spent* itself⟩ **b** : to consume wastefully : SQUANDER ⟨the waters are not ours to ~ —J. R. Ellis⟩ **3** : to cause or permit to elapse : PASS ⟨*spent* the summer at the beach⟩ **4** : GIVE UP, SACRIFICE ~ *vi* **1** : to expend or waste wealth or strength **2** : to become expended or consumed — **spend·er** *n*
spend·able \'spen-də-bəl\ *adj* (1500) : available for spending
spending money *n* (1598) : POCKET MONEY
spend·thrift \'spen(d)-ˌthrift\ *n* (1601) : one who spends improvidently or wastefully — **spendthrift** *adj*
Spen·gle·ri·an \s(h)peŋ-'(g)lir-ē-ən\ *adj* (1926) : of or relating to the theory of world history developed by Oswald Spengler which holds that all major cultures undergo similar cyclical developments from birth to maturity to decay — **Spenglerian** *n*
Spen·se·ri·an stanza \spen-ˌsir-ē-ən-\ *n* [Edmund *Spenser*] (1818) : a stanza consisting of eight verses of iambic pentameter and an alexandrine with a rhyme scheme *ababbcbcc*
spent \'spent\ *adj* [ME, fr. pp. of *spenden* to spend] (15c) **1 a** : used up : CONSUMED **b** : exhausted of active or required components or qualities often for a particular purpose ⟨~ grain that remains from wort production is a useful livestock feed⟩ **2** : drained of energy or effectiveness : EXHAUSTED **3** : exhausted of spawn or sperm ⟨a ~ salmon⟩
sperm \'spərm\ *n, pl* **sperm** *or* **sperms** [ME, fr. MF *esperme,* fr. LL *spermat-, sperma,* fr. Gk, lit., seed; akin to Gk *speirein* to sow — more at SPROUT] (14c) **1 a** : the male fecundating fluid : SEMEN **b** : a male gamete **2** : a product (as spermaceti or oil) of the sperm whale
sperm- *or* **spermo-** *or* **sperma-** *or* **spermi-** *comb form* [Gk *sperm-, spermo-,* fr. *sperma*] : seed : germ : sperm ⟨*sperma*theca⟩ ⟨*sperm*ary⟩ ⟨*spermi*cidal⟩
sper·ma·ce·ti \ˌspər-mə-'sēt-ē, -'set-\ *n* [ME *sperma cete,* fr. ML *sperma ceti* whale sperm] (15c) : a waxy solid obtained from the oil of cetaceans and esp. sperm whales and used in ointments, cosmetics, and candles
sper·ma·go·ni·um \ˌspər-mə-'gō-nē-əm\ *n, pl* **-nia** \-nē-ə\ [NL, fr. *sperm-* + *gon-* + *-ium*] (1897) : a flask-shaped or depressed receptacle in which spermatia are produced in some fungi and lichens
sper·ma·ry \'spərm-(ə-)rē\ *n, pl* **-ries** [NL *spermarium,* fr. Gk *sperma*] (ca. 1864) : an organ in which male gametes are developed
spermat- *or* **spermato-** *comb form* [MF, fr. LL, fr. Gk, fr. *spermat-, sperma*] : seed : spermatozoon ⟨*spermat*id⟩ ⟨*spermato*cyte⟩
sper·ma·the·ca \ˌspər-mə-'thē-kə\ *n* [NL] (1826) : a sac for sperm storage in the female reproductive tract of many lower animals
sper·mat·ic \(ˌ)spər-'mat-ik\ *adj* (1539) **1** : relating to sperm or a spermary **2** : resembling, carrying, or full of sperm
spermatic cord *n* (1797) : a cord that suspends the testis within the scrotum and contains the vas deferens and vessels and nerves of the testis
sper·ma·tid \'spər-mət-əd\ *n* (1889) : one of the cells that are formed by division of the secondary spermatocytes and that differentiate into spermatozoa
sper·ma·ti·um \(ˌ)spər-'mā-sh(ē-)əm\ *n, pl* **-tia** \-sh(ē-)ə\ [NL, fr. Gk *spermation,* dim. of *spermat-, sperma*] (1856) : a nonmotile cell functioning or held to function as a male gamete in some lower plants — **sper·ma·tial** \-sh(ē-)əl\ *adj*
sper·mato·cyte \(ˌ)spər-'mat-ə-ˌsīt\ *n* (1886) : a cell giving rise to sperm cells; *esp* : a cell of the last generation or next to the last generation preceding the spermatozoon
sper·mato·gen·e·sis \(ˌ)spər-ˌmat-ə-'jen-ə-səs\ *n* [NL] (1881) : the process of male gamete formation including meiosis and transformation of the four resulting spermatids into spermatozoa — **sper·mato·gen·ic** \-'jen-ik\ *adj*
sper·mato·go·ni·um \-'gō-nē-əm\ *n, pl* **-nia** \-nē-ə\ [NL, fr. *spermat-* + *gon-* + *-ium*] (1861) : a primitive male germ cell — **sper·mato·go·ni·al** \-nē-əl\ *adj*
sper·mato·phore \(ˌ)spər-'mat-ə-ˌfō(ə)r, -ˌfȯ(ə)r\ *n* [ISV] (1847) : a capsule, packet, or mass enclosing spermatozoa extruded by the male and conveyed to the female in the insemination of various lower animals
sper·mato·phyte \-ˌfīt\ *n* [deriv. of NL *spermat-* + Gk *phyton* plant — more at PHYT-] (1897) : any of a group (Spermatophyta) of higher plants comprising those that produce seeds and including the gymnosperms and angiosperms — **sper·mato·phyt·ic** \-ˌmat-ə-'fit-ik\ *adj*
sper·ma·to·zo·an \(ˌ)spər-ˌmat-ə-'zō-ən, ˌspər-mət-\ *n* (ca. 1900) : SPERMATOZOON — **spermatozoan** *adj*
sper·ma·to·zo·id \-'zō-əd\ *n* [ISV, fr. NL *spermatozoa*] (1857) : a male gamete of a plant motile by anterior cilia and usu. produced in an antheridium
sper·ma·to·zo·on \-'zō-ˌän, -'zō-ən\ *n, pl* **-zoa** \-'zō-ə\ [NL] (1836) **1** : a motile male gamete of an animal usu. with rounded or elongate head and a long posterior flagellum **2** : SPERMATOZOID — **sper·ma·to·zo·al** \-'zō-əl\ *adj*
sperm cell *n* (1851) : a male gamete : a male germ cell
sper·mi·cid·al \ˌspər-mə-'sīd-ᵊl\ *adj* (1935) : killing sperm ⟨~ jelly⟩ — **sper·mi·cide** \'spər-mə-ˌsīd\ *n*
sper·mio·gen·e·sis \ˌspər-mē-ō-'jen-ə-səs\ *n* [NL, fr. *spermium* spermatozoon + *-o-* + L *genesis*] (1916) **1** : SPERMATOGENESIS **2** : transformation of a spermatid into a spermatozoon
sperm nucleus *n* (1887) : either of two nuclei that derive from the generative nucleus of a pollen grain and function in the fertilization of a seed plant
sperm oil *n* (1839) : a pale yellow oil from the sperm whale
sper·mo·phile \'spər-mə-ˌfīl\ *n* [deriv. of Gk *sperma* seed + *philos* loving] (1824) : GROUND SQUIRREL
sperm whale \'spərm-\ *n* [short for *spermaceti* + *whale*] (1839) : a large toothed whale (*Physeter catodon*) with a large closed cavity in the head containing a fluid mixture of spermaceti and oil

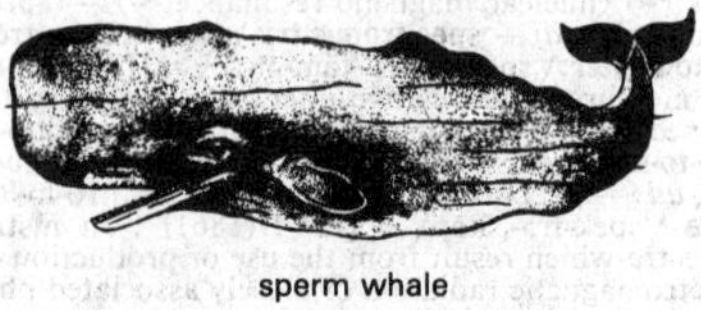

sperm whale

-sper·my \ˌspər-mē\ *n comb form* [Gk *sperma* seed, sperm] : state of exhibiting or resulting from (such) a fertilization ⟨agamo*spermy*⟩
sper·ry·lite \'sper-i-ˌlīt\ *n* [Francis L. *Sperry,* 19th cent. Canad. chemist + E *-lite*] (ca. 1909) : a mineral $PtAs_2$ consisting of a platinum arsenide occurring near Sudbury, Ontario, in grains and minute isometric crystals of a bluish white color
spes·sar·tite \'spes-ər-ˌtīt\ *also* **spes·sar·tine** \-ˌtēn\ *n* [F, fr. *Spessart* mountain range, Germany] (ca. 1887) : a manganese aluminum garnet usu. containing other elements (as iron and magnesium) in minor amounts
[1]spew \'spyü\ *vb* [ME *spewen,* fr. OE *spīwan;* akin to OHG *spīwan* to spit, L *spuere,* Gk *ptyein*] *vi* (bef. 12c) **1** : VOMIT **2** : to come forth in a flood or gush ⟨pornography ~*ing* from the presses⟩ **3** : to ooze out as if under pressure : EXUDE ~ *vt* **1** : VOMIT **2** : to send or cast forth with vigor or violence or in great quantity — **spew·er** *n*
[2]spew *n* (1609) **1** : matter that is vomited : VOMIT **2** : material that exudes or is extruded
sphag·nous \'sfag-nəs\ *adj* (ca. 1828) : of, relating to, or abounding in sphagnum
sphag·num \'sfag-nəm\ *n* [NL, fr. L *sphagnos,* a moss, fr. Gk] (1753) **1** : any of a large genus (*Sphagnum,* coextensive with the order Sphagnales) of atypical mosses that grow only in wet acid areas where their remains become compacted with other plant debris to form peat **2** : a mass of sphagnum plants
sphal·er·ite \'sfal-ə-ˌrīt\ *n* [G *sphalerit,* fr. Gk *sphaleros* deceitful, fr. *sphallein* to cause to fall; fr. its often being mistaken for galena — more at SPILL] (ca. 1868) : a widely distributed ore of zinc composed essentially of zinc sulfide ZnS
S phase *n* (1945) : the period in the cell cycle during which DNA replication takes place — compare G_1 PHASE, G_2 PHASE, M PHASE
sphene \'sfēn\ *n* [F *sphène,* fr. Gk *sphēn* wedge — more at SPOON] (ca. 1815) : a mineral $CaTiSiO_5$ that is a silicate of calcium and titanium and often contains other elements
sphen·odon \'sfē-nə-ˌdän, 'sfen-ə-\ *n* [NL, deriv. of Gk *sphēn* wedge + *odōn* tooth — more at TOOTH] (1878) : TUATARA — **sphen·odont** \-ˌdänt\ *adj*
[1]sphe·noid \'sfē-ˌnȯid\ *or* **sphe·noi·dal** \sfi-'nȯid-ᵊl\ *adj* [NL *sphenoides,* fr. Gk *sphēnoeidēs* wedge-shaped, fr. *sphēn* wedge] (1732) **1** : of, relating to, or being a winged compound bone of the base of the cranium **2** *usu sphenoidal* : wedge-shaped
[2]sphenoid *n* (1828) : a sphenoid bone
sphe·nop·sid \sfi-'näp-səd\ *n* [deriv. of Gk *sphēn* wedge + NL *-opsis*] (1957) : any of a subdivision (Sphenopsida) of the tracheophytes characterized by jointed stems, small leaves usu. in whorls at distinct stem nodes, and sporangia in sporangiophores and made up of the equisetums and extinct related forms
spher- *or* **sphero-** *also* **sphaer-** *or* **sphaero-** *comb form* [L *sphaer-,* fr. Gk *sphair-, sphairo-,* fr. *sphaira* sphere] : sphere ⟨*spher*ule⟩ ⟨*sphero*meter⟩
spher·al \'sfir-əl\ *adj* (1571) **1** : SPHERICAL **2** : of or relating to the spheres of ancient astronomy
[1]sphere \'sfi(ə)r\ *n* [ME *spere* globe, celestial sphere, fr. MF *espere,* fr. L *sphaera,* fr. Gk *sphaira,* lit., ball] (14c) **1 a** (1) : the apparent surface of the heavens of which half forms the dome of the visible sky (2) : one of the concentric and eccentric revolving spherical transparent shells in which according to ancient astronomy stars, sun, planets, and moon are set **b** : a globe depicting such a sphere; *broadly* : GLOBE **a 2 a** : a globular body : BALL **b** : PLANET, STAR **c** (1) : a solid that is bounded by a surface consisting of all points at a given distance from a point constituting its center — see VOLUME table (2) : the bounding surface of a sphere **3** : natural, normal, or proper place; *esp* : social order or rank **4 a** *obs* : ORBIT **b** : a field or range of influence or significance — **spher·ic** \'sfi(ə)r-ik, 'sfer-\ *adj* — **sphe·ric·i·ty** \sfir-'is-ət-ē\ *n*
[2]sphere *vt* **sphered; spher·ing** (1607) **1** : to place in a sphere or among the spheres : ENSPHERE **2** : to form into a sphere
sphere of influence (1885) : a territorial area within which the political influence or the interests of one nation are held to be more or less paramount
spher·i·cal \'sfir-i-kəl, 'sfer-\ *adj* (1523) **1** : having the form of a sphere or of one of its segments **2** : relating to or dealing with a sphere or its properties — **spher·i·cal·ly** \-k(ə-)lē\ *adv*

spherical aberration *n* (1868) : aberration that is caused by the spherical form of a lens or mirror and that gives different foci for central and marginal rays
spherical angle *n* (1678) : the angle between two intersecting arcs of great circles of a sphere measured by the plane angle formed by the tangents to the arcs at the point of intersection
spherical coordinate *n* (ca. 1864) : one of three coordinates that are used to locate a point in space and that comprise the radius of the sphere on which the point lies in a system of concentric spheres, the angle formed by the point, the center, and a given axis of the sphere, and the angle between the plane of the first angle and a reference plane through the given axis of the sphere
spherical geometry *n* (1728) : the geometry of figures on a sphere
spherical polygon *n* (ca. 1824) : a figure analogous to a plane polygon that is formed on a sphere by arcs of great circles
spherical triangle *n* (1585) : a spherical polygon of three sides
spherical trigonometry *n* (1728) : trigonometry applied to spherical triangles and polygons
spherics *var of* SFERICS
sphe·roid \'sfi(ə)r-,ȯid, 'sfe(ə)r-\ *n* (1664) : a figure resembling a sphere — **sphe·roi·dal** \sfir-'ȯid-ᵊl\ *also* **spheroid** *adj* — **sphe·roi·dal·ly** \-ᵊl-ē\ *adv*
sphe·rom·e·ter \sfir-'äm-ət-ər\ *n* [ISV] (1827) : an instrument for measuring the curvature of a surface
sphe·ro·plast \'sfir-ə-,plast, 'sfer-\ *n* (ca. 1920) : a modified gram-negative bacterium that is characterized by major alteration and partial loss of the cell wall and by increased osmotic sensitivity and that can result from various nutritional or environmental factors or be induced artificially by use of a lysozyme
spher·ule \'sfi(ə)r-(,)(y)ü(ə)l, 'sfe(ə)r-\ *n* (1665) : a little sphere or spherical body
spher·u·lite \'sfir-(y)ə-,līt, 'sfer-\ *n* (1823) : a usu. spherical crystalline body of radiating crystal fibers often found in vitreous volcanic rocks — **spher·u·lit·ic** \,sfir-(y)ə-'lit-ik, ,sfer-\ *adj*
sphery \'sfi(ə)r-ē\ *adj* (1590) **1** : of, relating to, or suggestive of the celestial bodies **2** : ROUND, SPHERICAL
sphinc·ter \'sfiŋ(k)-tər\ *n* [LL, fr. Gk *sphinktēr*, lit., band, fr. *sphingein* to bind tight] (1578) : an annular muscle surrounding and able to contract or close a bodily opening — **sphinc·ter·al** \-t(ə-)rəl\ *adj*
sphin·gid \'sfin-jəd\ *n* [deriv. of Gk *sphing-, sphinx* sphinx] (ca. 1909) : HAWKMOTH
sphin·go·sine \'sfiŋ-gə-,sēn\ *n* [Gk *sphingos* (gen. of *sphinx*) + E *-ine*; fr. riddles it posed to its first investigators] (1884) : a long-chain unsaturated amino alcohol $C_{18}H_{37}O_2N$ found esp. in nervous tissue and cell membranes
sphinx \'sfiŋ(k)s\ *n, pl* **sphinx·es** *or* **sphin·ges** \'sfin-,jēz\ [L, fr. Gk; akin to Gk *sphinktēr* sphincter] (15c) **1 a** *cap* : a winged female monster in Greek mythology having a woman's head and a lion's body and noted for killing anyone unable to answer its riddle **b** : an enigmatic or mysterious person **2** : an ancient Egyptian image in the form of a recumbent lion having a man's head, a ram's head, or a hawk's head **3** : HAWKMOTH
sphyg·mo·graph \'sfig-mə-,graf\ *n* [Gk *sphygmos* pulse + ISV *-graph*] (ca. 1859) : an instrument that records graphically the movements or character of the pulse — **sphyg·mo·graph·ic** \,sfig-mə-'graf-ik\ *adj* — **sphyg·mog·ra·phy** \sfig-'mäg-rə-fē\ *n*
sphyg·mo·ma·nom·e·ter \,sfig-mō-mə-'näm-ət-ər\ *n* [Gk *sphygmos* pulse (akin to Gk *asphyxia* stopping of the pulse) + ISV *manometer* — more at ASPHYXIA] (ca. 1891) : an instrument for measuring blood pressure and esp. arterial blood pressure — **sphyg·mo·ma·nom·e·try** \-mə-'näm-ə-trē\ *n*
spi·ca \'spī-kə\ *n, pl* **spi·cae** \-,kē\ *or* **spicas** [L, spike of grain — more at SPINE] (ca. 1731) : a bandage that is applied in successive V-shaped crossings and is used to immobilize a limb esp. at a joint
Spi·ca \'spī-kə\ *n* [L, lit., spike of grain] : a star of the first magnitude in the constellation Virgo
spi·cate \'spī-,kāt\ *adj* [L *spicatus*, pp. of *spicare* to arrange in the shape of heads of grain, fr. *spica*] (1668) : arranged in the form of a spike ⟨a ~ inflorescence⟩
¹spic·ca·to \spi-'kät-(,)ō\ *adj* [It, pp. of *spiccare* to detach, pick off] (ca. 1724) : performed with springing bow — used as a direction in music
²spiccato *n, pl* **-tos** (ca. 1903) : a spiccato technique, performance, or passage
¹spice \'spīs\ *n* [ME, fr. OF *espice*, fr. LL *species* spices, fr. L, species — more at SPY] (13c) **1** : any of various aromatic vegetable products (as pepper or nutmeg) used to season or flavor foods **2 a** *archaic* : a small portion, quantity, or admixture : DASH **b** : something that gives zest or relish ⟨variety's the very ~ of life —William Cowper⟩ **3** : a pungent or fragrant odor : PERFUME
²spice *vt* **spiced; spic·ing** (14c) **1** : to season with spices **2** : to add zest or relish to ⟨cynicism *spiced* with humor —J. W. Dawson⟩
spice·bush \'spīs-,bu̇sh\ *n* (1770) : an aromatic shrub (*Lindera benzoin*) of the laurel family that bears dense clusters of small yellow flowers followed by scarlet or yellow berries
spic·ery \'spīs-(ə-)rē\ *n, pl* **-er·ies** (13c) **1** : SPICES **2** *archaic* : a repository of spices **3** : a spicy quality
spick *or* **spic** *or* **spik** \'spik\ *n* [alter. of earlier *spiggoty*, of unknown origin] (1916) : SPANISH AMERICAN — usu. taken to be offensive
spick–and–span *or* **spic–and–span** \,spik-ən-'span, ,spik-ᵊŋ-\ *adj* [short for *spick-and-span-new*, fr. obs. E *spick* (spike) + E *and* + *span-new* (brand-new)] (1665) **1** : FRESH, BRAND-NEW **2** : spotlessly clean
spic·ule \'spik-(,)yü(ə)l\ *n* [NL *spicula* & L *spiculum*] (1785) **1** : a minute slender pointed usu. hard body; *esp* : one of the minute calcareous or siliceous bodies that support the tissue of various invertebrates (as a sponge) **2** : a spikelike short-lived prominence appearing close to the chromosphere of the solar atmosphere — **spic·u·lar** \'spik-yə-lər\ *adj* — **spic·u·la·tion** \,spik-yə-'lā-shən\ *n*
spicy \'spī-sē\ *adj* **spic·i·er; -est** (1562) **1** : having the quality, flavor, or fragrance of spice **2** : producing or abounding in spices **3** : LIVELY, SPIRITED **4** : PIQUANT, RACY; *esp* : somewhat scandalous or salacious ⟨~ gossip⟩ — **spic·i·ly** \-sə-lē\ *adv* — **spic·i·ness** \-sē-nəs\ *n*
spi·der \'spīd-ər\ *n* [ME, alter. of *spithre*; akin to OE *spinnan* to spin] (14c) **1** : any of an order (Araneida) of arachnids having a body with two main divisions, four pairs of walking legs, and two or more pairs of abdominal spinnerets for spinning threads of silk used in making cocoons for their eggs, nests for themselves, or webs to catch prey **2** : a cast-iron frying pan orig. made with short feet to stand among coals on the hearth **3** : any of various devices consisting of a frame or skeleton with radiating arms or members
spider crab *n* (ca. 1710) : any of numerous crabs (esp. family Majidae) with extremely long legs and nearly triangular bodies which they often cover with kelp
spider mite *n* (1870) : RED SPIDER
spider monkey *n* (1764) : any of a genus (*Ateles*) of New World monkeys with long slender limbs, the thumb absent or rudimentary, and a very long prehensile tail
spider plant *n* (1944) : a widely grown houseplant (*Chlorophytum comosum* var. *variegatum*) of the lily family having long green leaves usu. striped with white or ivory and producing white flowers and tufts of plantlets on long hanging stems
spi·der·web \'spīd-ər-,web\ *n* (1535) : the silken web spun by most spiders and used as a resting place and as a trap for small prey
spi·der·wort \-,wərt, -,wȯ(ə)rt\ *n* (1629) : any of a genus (*Tradescantia* of the family Commelinaceae, the spiderwort family) of monocotyledonous plants with ephemeral usu. blue or violet flowers
spi·dery \'spīd-ə-rē\ *adj* (1837) **1 a** : resembling a spider in form or manner **b** : resembling a spiderweb; *esp* : composed of fine threads or lines in a weblike arrangement ⟨~ lace⟩ **2** : infested with spiders
spie·gel·ei·sen \'spē-gə-,līz-ᵊn\ *also* **spie·gel** \'spē-gəl\ *n* [G *spiegeleisen*, fr. *spiegel* mirror (fr. OHG *spiagal*, fr. L *speculum*) + *eisen* iron, fr. OHG *isarn* — more at SPECULUM, IRON] (1868) : a composition of iron that contains 15 to 30 percent manganese and 4.5 to 6.5 percent carbon
¹spiel \'spē(ə)l\ *vb* [G *spielen* to play, fr. OHG *spilōn*; akin to OHG *spil* play, OE *spilian* to revel] *vi* (1870) **1** : to play music **2** : to talk volubly or extravagantly ~ *vt* : to utter, express, or describe volubly or extravagantly — **spiel·er** \'spē-lər\ *n*
²spiel *n* (1896) : a voluble line of often extravagant talk : PITCH
¹spi·er \'spī(-ə)r\ *n* (13c) : SPY
²spier \'spi(ə)r\ *chiefly Scot var of* SPEER
spiffy \'spif-ē\ *adj* **spiff·i·er; -est** [E dial. *spiff* dandified] (1853) : fine looking : SMART ⟨a ~ sports jacket⟩
spig·ot \'spig-ət, 'spik-ət\ *n* [ME] (14c) **1** : SPILE 2 **2** : the plug of a faucet or cock **3** : FAUCET **4** : something resembling a spigot esp. in regulating availability or flow (as of money)
¹spike \'spīk\ *n* [ME, prob. fr. MD] (14c) **1** : a very large nail **2 a** : one of a row of pointed irons placed (as on the top of a wall) to prevent passage **b** (1) : one of several metal projections set in the sole and heel of a shoe to improve traction (2) *pl* : a pair of shoes having spikes attached to the soles or soles and heels **3** : something resembling a spike: as **a** : a young mackerel not over six inches (15.2 centimeters) long **b** : an unbranched antler of a young deer **4** *pl* : shoes with spike heels **5** : the act or an instance of spiking (as in volleyball) **6 a** : a pointed element in a graph or tracing **b** : an unusually high and sharply defined maximum (as of amplitude in a wave train) **7** *slang* : HYPODERMIC NEEDLE **8** : a momentary sharp increase and fall in the record of an electric potential; *also* : ACTION POTENTIAL — **spike·like** \'spī-,klīk\ *adj*
²spike *vt* **spiked; spik·ing** (1624) **1** : to fasten or furnish with spikes **2 a** : to disable (a muzzle-loading cannon) temporarily by driving a spike into the vent **b** : to suppress or block completely ⟨*spiked* the rumor⟩ **3** : to pierce or impale with or on a spike **4 a** : to add an alcoholic beverage to (a drink) **b** : to add something highly reactive (as a radioactive tracer) to **5** : to drive (as a volleyball) sharply downward with a hard blow; *also* : to throw down sharply ⟨*spiked* the ball in the end zone⟩ — **spik·er** *n*
³spike *n* [ME *spik* head of grain, fr. L *spica* — more at SPINE] (14c) **1** : an ear of grain **2** : an elongated inflorescence similar to a raceme but having the flowers sessile on the main axis — see INFLORESCENCE illustration
spiked \'spīkt, 'spī-kəd\ *adj* (1681) **1** : having an inflorescence that is a spike **2** : having a sharp projecting point
spike heel *n* (1926) : a very high tapering heel used on women's shoes
spike lavender \'spīk-\ *n* [alter. of E dial. *spick* (lavender)] (ca. 1891) : a European mint (*Lavandula latifolia*) related to true lavender
spike·let \'spī-klət\ *n* (1851) : a small or secondary spike; *specif* : one of the small few-flowered bracted spikes that make up the compound inflorescence of a grass or sedge
spike·nard \'spīk-,närd\ *n* [ME, fr. MF or ML; MF *spicanarde*, fr. ML *spica nardi*, lit., spike of nard] (14c) **1 a** : a fragrant ointment of the ancients **b** : an East Indian aromatic plant (*Nardostachys jatamansi*) of the valerian family from which spikenard is believed to have been derived **2** : an American herb (*Aralia racemosa*) of the ginseng family with aromatic root and panicled umbels
spike–tooth harrow \,spīk-,tüth-\ *n* (1926) : a harrow with straight steel teeth set in horizontal bars
spiky \'spī-kē\ *adj* **spik·i·er; -est** (1720) **1** : of, relating to, or characterized by spikes **2** : sharply irritating or acerbic (as in temper or manner) **3** [fr. the alleged harshness of such views] *Brit* : strongly favoring Anglo-Catholic teaching or practice
¹spile \'spī(ə)l\ *n* [prob. fr. D *spijl* stake; akin to L *spina* thorn — more at SPINE] (1513) **1** : ¹PILE 1 **2** : a small plug used to stop the vent of a cask : BUNG **3** : a spout inserted in a tree to draw off sap
²spile *vt* **spiled; spil·ing** (1691) **1** : to plug with a spile **2** : to supply with a spile
spil·ing \'spī-liŋ\ *n* (1841) : a set of piles : PILING
¹spill \'spil\ *vb* **spilled** \'spild, 'spilt\ *also* **spilt** \'spilt\; **spill·ing** [ME *spillen*, fr. OE *spillan*; akin to OHG *spaltan* to split, L *spolia* spoils, Gk *sphallein* to cause to fall] *vt* (bef. 12c) **1 a** *archaic* : KILL, DESTROY **b** : to cause (blood) to flow **2** : to cause or allow esp. accidentally or unintentionally to fall, flow, or run out so as to be lost or wasted **3 a** : to relieve (a sail) from the pressure of the wind so as to reef or furl it

\ə\ abut \ᵊ\ kitten, F table \ər\ further \a\ ash \ā\ ace \ä\ cot, cart \au̇\ out \ch\ chin \e\ bet \ē\ easy \g\ go \i\ hit \ī\ ice \j\ job \ŋ\ sing \ō\ go \ȯ\ law \ȯi\ boy \th\ thin \t͟h\ the \ü\ loot \u̇\ foot \y\ yet \zh\ vision \á, k̲, ⁿ, œ, œ̄, ue, ue̅, ʸ\ *see* Guide to Pronunciation

b : to relieve the pressure of (wind) on a sail by coming about or by adjusting the sail with lines **4 :** to throw off or out ⟨a horse ~*ed* him⟩ **5 :** to let out : DIVULGE ⟨~ a secret⟩ ~ *vi* **1 a :** to flow, run, or fall out, over, or off and become wasted, scattered, or lost **b :** to cause or allow something to spill **2 :** to spread profusely or beyond bounds ⟨crowds ~*ed* into the streets⟩ **3 :** to fall from one's place (as on a horse) — **spill·able** \ˈspil-ə-bəl\ *adj* — **spill·er** *n* — **spill the beans :** to divulge information indiscreetly

²spill *n* (1845) **1 :** the act or an instance of spilling; *esp* **:** a fall from a horse or vehicle or an erect position **2 :** something spilled **3 :** SPILLWAY

³spill *n* [ME *spille*] (14c) **1 :** a wooden splinter **2 :** a slender piece: as **a :** a metallic rod or pin **b** (1) **:** a small roll or twist of paper or slip of wood for lighting a fire (2) **:** a roll or cone of paper serving as a container **c :** a peg or pin for plugging a hole : SPILE

spill·age \ˈspil-ij\ *n* (1924) **1 :** the act or process of spilling **2 :** the quantity that spills : material lost or scattered by spilling

spil·li·kin \ˈspil-i-kən\ *n* [prob. alter. of obs. D *spelleken* small peg] (1734) **1 :** JACKSTRAW 1 **2** *pl* **:** JACKSTRAW 2

spill·over \ˈspil-ˌō-vər\ *n* (1944) **1 :** the act or an instance of spilling over **2 :** a quantity that spills over

spill·way \-ˌwā\ *n* (1889) **:** a passage for surplus water to run over or around an obstruction (as a dam)

spi·lo·site \ˈspī-lə-ˌsīt\ *n* [G *spilosit,* fr. Gk *spilos* spot; akin to L *spina* thorn — more at SPINE] (1882) **:** a spotted schistose rock produced by the metamorphism of clay slate by magma

spilth \ˈspilth\ *n* (1607) **1 :** the act or an instance of spilling **2 a :** something spilled **b :** REFUSE, RUBBISH

¹spin \ˈspin\ *vb* **spun** \ˈspən\; **spin·ning** [ME *spinnen,* fr. OE *spinnan;* akin to OHG *spinnan* to spin, L *sponte* voluntarily, *pendere* to weigh] *vi* (bef. 12c) **1 :** to draw out and twist fiber into yarn or thread **2 :** to form a thread by extruding a viscous rapidly hardening fluid — used esp. of a spider or insect **3 a :** to revolve rapidly : GYRATE **b :** to feel as if in a whirl : REEL ⟨my head is *spinning*⟩ **4 :** to move swiftly esp. on wheels or in a vehicle **5 :** to fish with spinning bait : TROLL **6 a** *of an airplane* **:** to fall in a spin **b :** to plunge helplessly and out of control ~ *vt* **1 a :** to draw out and twist into yarns or threads **b :** to produce by drawing out and twisting a fibrous material **2 :** to form (as a web or cocoon) by spinning **3 a :** to stretch out or extend (as a story) lengthily : PROTRACT — usu. used with *out* **b :** to evolve, express, or fabricate by processes of mind or imagination ⟨~ a yarn⟩ **4 :** to cause to whirl : TWIRL ⟨~ a top⟩ **5 :** to shape into threadlike form in manufacture; *also* **:** to manufacture by a whirling process

²spin *n* (1831) **1 a :** the act of spinning or twirling something **b :** the whirling motion imparted (as to a ball or top) by spinning **c :** an excursion in a vehicle esp. on wheels **2 a :** an aerial maneuver or flight condition consisting of a combination of roll and yaw with the longitudinal axis of the airplane inclined steeply downward **b :** a plunging descent or downward spiral **c :** a state of mental confusion ⟨in a ~⟩ **3 a :** the rotation of an elementary particle on its axis or of a system of such particles in orbital motion that is responsible for measurable angular momentum and magnetic moment **b :** the angular momentum associated with such rotation — **spin·less** \ˈspin-ləs\ *adj*

spi·na bi·fi·da \ˌspī-nə-ˈbī-fəd-ə\ *n* [NL, lit., spine split in two] (1720) **:** a congenital cleft of the vertebral column with hernial protrusion of the meninges

spin·ach \ˈspin-ich\ *n* [MF *espinache, espinage,* fr. OSp *espinaca,* fr. Ar *isfānākh,* fr. Per] (1530) **1 :** a potherb (*Spinacia oleracea*) of the goosefoot family cultivated for its edible leaves **2 a :** something unwanted, insubstantial, or spurious **b :** an untidy overgrowth

¹spi·nal \ˈspīn-ᵊl\ *adj* (1578) **1 :** of, relating to, or situated near the backbone **2 a :** of, relating to, or affecting the spinal cord ⟨~ reflexes⟩ **b :** having the spinal cord functionally isolated (as by surgical section) from the brain ⟨experiments on ~ animals⟩ **3 :** of, relating to, or resembling a spine

²spinal *n* (1944) **:** a spinal anesthetic

spinal canal *n* (1845) **:** a canal that contains the spinal cord and is delimited by the arches on the dorsal side of the vertebrae

spinal column *n* (1836) **:** the axial skeleton of the trunk and tail of a vertebrate consisting of an articulated series of vertebrae and protecting the spinal cord — called also *backbone*

spinal cord *n* (1836) **:** the cord of nervous tissue that extends from the brain lengthwise along the back in the spinal canal, gives off the pairs of spinal nerves, carries impulses to and from the brain, and serves as a center for initiating and coordinating many reflex acts — see BRAIN illustration

spinal ganglion *n* (ca. 1860) **:** a ganglion on the dorsal root of each spinal nerve that is one of a series of ganglia lodging cell bodies of sensory neurons

spi·nal·ly \ˈspīn-ᵊl-ē\ *adv* (1885) **:** with respect to or along the spine

spinal nerve *n* (1793) **:** any of the paired nerves which leave the spinal cord of a craniate vertebrate, supply muscles of the trunk and limbs, and connect with the nerves of the sympathetic nervous system, which arise by a short motor ventral root and a short sensory dorsal root, and of which there are 31 pairs in man classified according to the part of the spinal cord from which they arise into 8 cervical pairs, 12 thoracic pairs, 5 lumbar pairs, 5 sacral pairs, and one coccygeal pair

¹spin·dle \ˈspin-dᵊl\ *n* [ME *spindel,* fr. OE *spinel;* akin to OE *spinnan* to spin] (bef. 12c) **1 a :** a round stick with tapered ends used to form and twist the yarn in hand spinning **b :** the long slender pin by which the thread is twisted in a spinning wheel **c :** any of various rods or pins holding a bobbin in a textile machine (as a spinning frame) **d :** the pin in a loom shuttle **e :** a device usu. consisting of an upright spike in a base on which papers can be stuck for filing — called also *spindle file* **2 :** something shaped like a spindle: as **a :** a spindle-shaped achromatic figure along which the chromosomes are distributed during mitosis and meiosis **b :** MUSCLE SPINDLE **3 a :** the bar or shaft usu. of square section that carries the knobs and actuates the latch or bolt of a lock **b** (1) **:** a turned often decorative piece (as in a baluster) (2) **:** NEWEL **c** (1) **:** a revolving piece esp. if less in size than a shaft (2) **:** a horizontal or vertical axle revolving on pin or pivot ends (3) **:** a rod attached to a valve to move or guide it **d :** the part of an axle on which a vehicle wheel turns

²spindle *vb* **spin·dled; spin·dling** \-(d)liŋ, -dᵊl-iŋ\ *vi* (1577) **1 :** to shoot or grow into a long slender stalk **2 :** to grow to stalk or stem rather than to flower or fruit ~ *vt* **1 :** to impale, thrust, or perforate on the spike of a spindle file **2 :** to make or equip (as a piece of furniture) with spindles — **spin·dler** \-(d)lər, -dᵊl-ər\ *n*

spindle cell *n* (1878) **:** a fusiform cell (as in some tumors)

spin·dle–legged \ˌspin-dᵊl-ˈ(l)eg(-ə)d, -ˈ(l)āg(-ə)d\ *adj* (1710) **:** having long slender legs

spin·dle–shanked \-ˈshaŋ(k)t\ *adj* (1600) **:** SPINDLE-LEGGED

spindle tree *n* (1548) **:** any of a genus (*Euonymus*) of often evergreen shrubs, small trees, or vines of the staff-tree family

spin·dling \ˈspin-(d)liŋ, -(d)lən, -dᵊl-iŋ, -dᵊl-ən\ *adj* (1750) **:** SPINDLY

spin·dly \ˈspin-(d)lē, -dᵊl-ē\ *adj* (1651) **1 :** of a disproportionately tall or long and thin appearance that often suggests physical weakness ⟨~ legs⟩ **2 :** frail or flimsy in appearance or structure

spin·drift \ˈspin-ˌdrift\ *n* [alter. of Sc *speendrift,* fr. *speen* to drive before a strong wind + E *drift*] (1823) **:** sea spray : SPOONDRIFT

spine \ˈspīn\ *n* [ME, thorn, spinal column, fr. L *spina;* akin to L *spica* spike of grain, OE *spitu* ¹spit, Latvian *spina* twig] (15c) **1 a :** SPINAL COLUMN **b :** something resembling a spinal column or constituting a central axis or chief support **c :** the backbone of a book **2 :** a stiff pointed plant process; *esp* **:** one that is a modified leaf or leaf part **3 :** a sharp rigid process on an animal: as **a :** SPICULE **b :** a stiff unsegmented fin ray of a fish **c :** a pointed prominence on a bone — **spined** \ˈspīnd\ *adj* — **spine·like** \-ˌlīk\ *adj*

spi·nel *or* **spi·nelle** \spə-ˈnel\ *n* [It *spinella,* dim. of *spina* thorn, fr. L] (1528) **1 :** a hard crystalline mineral $MgAl_2O_4$ consisting of an oxide of magnesium and aluminum that varies from colorless to ruby-red to black and is used as a gem **2 :** any of a group of minerals that are essentially oxides of magnesium, ferrous iron, zinc, or manganese

spine·less \ˈspīn-ləs\ *adj* (1827) **1 :** free from spines, thorns, or prickles **2 a :** having no spinal column : INVERTEBRATE **b :** lacking strength of character — **spine·less·ly** *adv* — **spine·less·ness** *n*

spin·et \ˈspin-ət *also* spin-ˈet\ *n* [It *spinetta,* deriv. of L *spina* thorn; fr. the manner of plucking its strings] (1664) **1 :** an early harpsichord having a single keyboard and only one string for each note **2 a :** a compactly built small upright piano **b :** a small electronic organ

spin fishing *n* (1950) **:** SPINNING

spi·ni·fex \ˈspī-nə-ˌfeks\ *n* [NL, genus name, fr. L *spina* + *facere* to make — more at DO] (1846) **:** any of several Australian grasses (genera *Spinifex* or *Triodia*) with spiny seeds or stiff sharp leaves

spin·na·ker \ˈspin-i-kər\ *n* [origin unknown] (1866) **:** a large triangular sail set on a long light pole and used when running before the wind

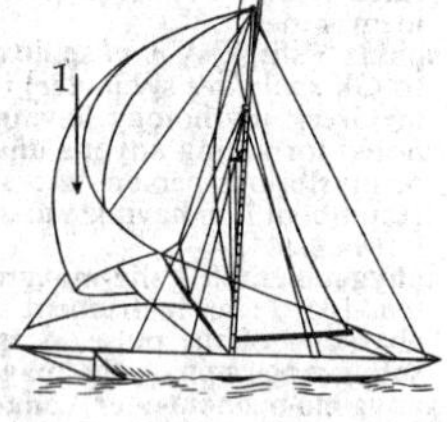

1 spinnaker

spin·ner \ˈspin-ər\ *n* (13c) **1 :** one that spins **2 :** a fisherman's lure consisting of a spoon, blade, or set of wings that revolves when drawn through the water **3 :** a conical sheet metal fairing that is attached to an airplane propeller boss and revolves with it **4 :** a movable arrow that is spun on its dial to indicate the number or kind of moves a player may make in a board game

spin·ner·et \ˌspin-ə-ˈret\ *n* (1826) **1 :** an organ (as of a spider or caterpillar) for producing threads of silk from the secretion of silk glands **2** *or* **spin·ner·ette :** a small metal plate, thimble, or cap with fine holes through which a chemical solution (as of cellulose) is forced in the spinning of man-made filaments (as of rayon or nylon)

spin·ney \ˈspin-ē\ *n, pl* **spinneys** [MF *espinaye* thorny thicket, fr. *espine* thorn, fr. L *spina*] *Brit* (1597) **:** a small wood with undergrowth

spin·ning \ˈspin-iŋ\ *n* (1855) **:** a method of fishing in which a lure is cast by use of a light flexible rod, a spinning reel, and a light line

spinning frame *n* (1825) **:** a machine that draws, twists, and winds yarn

spinning jen·ny \-ˌjen-ē\ *n* [*Jenny,* nickname for *Jane*] (1783) **:** an early multiple-spindle machine for spinning wool or cotton

spinning reel *n* (1950) **:** a fishing reel with a nonmoving spool on which the line is wound by means of a revolving arm which can be disengaged to allow the line to spiral freely off the spool during casting

spinning rod *n* (1870) **:** a light flexible fishing rod used with a spinning reel

spinning wheel *n* (15c) **:** a small domestic hand-driven or foot-driven machine for spinning yarn or thread

spin–off \ˈspin-ˌȯf\ *n* (1950) **1 :** the distribution by a business to its stockholders of particular assets and esp. of stock of another company; *also* **:** the new company created by such a distribution **2 :** a collateral or derived product or effect : BY-PRODUCT ⟨household products that are ~*s* of missile research⟩ **3 :** something that is imitative or derivative of an earlier work; *esp* **:** a television show starring a character popular in a secondary role of an earlier show

spin off \(ˈ)spin-ˈȯf\ *vt* (1950) **:** to establish or produce as a spin-off ⟨the company *spun off* its computer division⟩ ⟨*spin off* a new TV series⟩

spin·or \ˈspin-ər, -ˌȯ(ə)r\ *n* [ISV *spin* + *-or* (as in *vector*)] (1933) **:** a vector whose components are complex numbers in a two-dimensional or four-dimensional space and which is used esp. in the mathematics of the theory of relativity

spi·nose \ˈspī-ˌnōs\ *adj* (1660) **:** SPINY 1 ⟨a fly with black ~ legs⟩ — **spi·nos·i·ty** \spī-ˈnäs-ət-ē\ *n*

spi·nous \ˈspī-nəs\ *adj* (1638) **1 :** difficult or unpleasant to handle or meet : THORNY **2 :** SPINY 1, 3 ⟨~ appendages⟩ ⟨a ~ larva⟩

spin·out \ˈspin-ˌau̇t\ *n* (1955) **:** a rotational skid by an automobile that usu. causes it to leave the roadway

spin out \spin-ˈau̇t\ *vi* (1951) **:** to make a rotational skid in an automobile

Spi·no·zism \spin-ˈō-ˌziz-əm\ *n* (1728) **:** the philosophy of Baruch Spinoza who taught that reality is one substance with an infinite number of attributes of which only thought and extension are capable of being apprehended by the human mind — **Spi·no·zist** \-zest\ *n* — **Spi·no·zis·tic** \ˌspin-ō-ˈzis-tik, spin-ˌō-\ *adj*

spin·ster \ˈspin(t)-stər\ *n* (14c) **1 :** a woman whose occupation is to spin **2 a** *archaic* **:** an unmarried woman of gentle family **b :** an unmarried woman and esp. one past the common age for marrying **3** : a woman who seems unlikely to marry — **spin·ster·hood** \-ˌhu̇d\ *n* — **spin·ster·ish** \-st(ə-)rish\ *adj* — **spin·ster·ly** *adj*

spin·thari·scope \spin-ˈthar-ə-ˌskōp\ *n* [Gk *spintharis* spark + E *-scope*] (1903) : an instrument for visual detection of alpha rays that consists of a fluorescent screen and a magnifying lens system

spin the bottle *n* (1955) : a kissing game in which one has as a partner the person a bottle points to when it stops spinning

spin·to \ˈspēn-(ˌ)tō, ˈspin-\ *n, pl* **spin·tos** [It, lit., pushed, fr. pp. of *spingere* to push, fr. (assumed) VL *expingere,* fr. L *ex-* + *pangere* to fasten — more at PACT] (1944) : a singing voice having both lyric and dramatic qualities — **spinto** *adj*

spi·nule \ˈspī-(ˌ)nyü(ə)l\ *n* [L *spinula,* dim. of *spina* thorn — more at SPINE] (1752) : a minute spine — **spi·nu·lose** \ˈspī-nyə-ˌlōs\ *adj*

spiny \ˈspī-nē\ *adj* **spin·i·er; -est** (1615) **1** : covered or armed with spines; *broadly* : bearing spines, prickles, or thorns **2** : abounding with difficulties, obstacles, or annoyances : THORNY ⟨~ problems⟩ **3** : slender and pointed like a spine — **spin·i·ness** *n*

spiny anteater *n* (1827) : ECHIDNA

spiny–finned \ˌspī-nē-ˈfind\ *adj* (1881) : having fins with one or more stiff unbranched rays without transverse segmentation — used of acanthopterygian fishes; compare SOFT-FINNED

spiny–head·ed worm \ˌspī-nē-ˌhed-əd-\ *n* (1946) : any of a small phylum (Acanthocephala) of unsegmented parasitic worms that have a proboscis bearing hooks by which attachment is made to the intestinal wall of the host

spiny lobster *n* (1819) : an edible crustacean (family Palinuridae) distinguished from the true lobster by the simple unenlarged first pair of legs and the spiny carapace

spi·ra·cle \ˈspir-i-kəl, ˈspī-ri-\ *n* [L *spiraculum,* fr. *spirare* to breathe — more at SPIRIT] (1620) **1** : a breathing hole : VENT **2** : a breathing orifice: as **a** : BLOWHOLE 2 **b** : an external tracheal aperture of a terrestrial arthropod that in an insect is usu. one of a series of small apertures located along each side of the thorax and abdomen — see INSECT illustration — **spi·rac·u·lar** \spə-ˈrak-yə-lər, spī-\ *adj*

[1]**spi·ral** \ˈspī-rəl\ *adj* [ML *spiralis,* fr. L *spira* coil — more at SPIRE] (1551) **1 a** : winding around a center or pole and gradually receding from or approaching it ⟨the ~ curve of a watch spring⟩ **b** : HELICAL **2** : of or relating to the advancement to higher levels through a series of cyclical movements — **spi·ral·ly** \-rə-lē\ *adv*

[2]**spiral** *n* (1656) **1 a** : the path of a point in a plane moving around a central point while continuously receding from or approaching it **b** : a three-dimensional curve (as a helix) with one or more turns about an axis **2** : a single turn or coil in a spiral object **3 a** : something having a spiral form **b** (1) : a spiral flight (2) : a kick or pass in which a football rotates on its long axis while moving through the air **4** : a continuously spreading and accelerating increase or decrease ⟨wage ~*s*⟩

[3]**spiral** *vb* **-raled** *or* **-ralled; -ral·ing** *or* **-ral·ling** *vi* (1834) : to go and esp. to rise or fall in a spiral course ⟨costs ~*ed* upward⟩ ~ *vt* **1** : to form into a spiral **2** : to cause to spiral

spiral binding *n* (1944) : a book or notebook binding in which a continuous spiral wire or plastic strip is passed through holes along one edge

spi·ral–bound \ˌspī-rəl-ˈbau̇nd\ *adj* (1941) : having a spiral binding

spiral galaxy *n* (1943) : a galaxy exhibiting a central nucleus or barred structure from which extend concentrations of matter forming curved arms — called also *spiral nebula*

spiral of Ar·chi·me·des \-ˌär-kə-ˈmēd-ēz\ [*Archimedes*] (ca. 1856) : a plane curve that is generated by a point moving away from or toward a fixed point at a constant rate while the radius vector from the fixed point rotates at a constant rate and that has the equation $\rho = a\,\theta$ in polar coordinates

spiral spring *n* (1690) : a spring consisting of a wire coiled usu. in a flat spiral or in a helix

spi·rant \ˈspī-rənt\ *n* [ISV, fr. L *spirant-, spirans,* prp. of *spirare* to breathe — more at SPIRIT] (1866) : a consonant (as \f\, \s\, \sh\) uttered with friction of the breath against some part of the oral passage : FRICATIVE — **spirant** *adj*

[1]**spire** \ˈspī(ə)r\ *n* [ME, fr. OE *spīr;* akin to MD *spier* blade of grass, L *spina* thorn — more at SPINE] (bef. 12c) **1** : a slender tapering blade or stalk (as of grass) **2** : the upper tapering part of something (as a tree or antler) : PINNACLE **3 a** : a tapering roof or analogous pyramidal construction surmounting a tower **b** : STEEPLE

[2]**spire** *vi* **spired; spir·ing** (14c) : to rise like a spire

[3]**spire** *n* [L *spira* coil, fr. Gk *speira;* akin to Gk *sparton* rope, esparto, Lith *springti* to choke in swallowing] (1572) **1 a** : SPIRAL **b** : COIL **2** : the inner or upper part of a spiral gastropod shell consisting of all the whorls except the whorl in contact with the body

[4]**spire** *vi* **spired; spir·ing** (1607) : to rise in or as if in a spiral

spi·rea *or* **spi·raea** \spī-ˈrē-ə\ *n* [NL *Spiraea,* fr. L, a plant, fr. Gk *speiraia*] (1669) **1** : any of a genus (*Spiraea*) of shrubs of the rose family with small perfect white or pink flowers in dense racemes, corymbs, cymes, or panicles **2** : any of several garden plants resembling spireas; *esp* : a shrub (*Astilbe japonica*) of the saxifrage family

spired \ˈspī(ə)rd\ *adj* (1610) **1** : having a spire ⟨a ~ church⟩ **2** : tapering usu. to a sharp point ⟨~ cedars⟩

spi·reme \ˈspī-ˌrēm\ *n* [G *spirem,* fr. Gk *speirama, speirēma* convolution, fr. *speirasthai* to be coiled, fr. *speira*] (1889) : a continuous thread observed in fixed preparations of the prophase of mitosis that appears to be a strand of chromatin but is generally held to be an artifact

spi·ril·lum \spī-ˈril-əm\ *n, pl* **-ril·la** \-ˈril-ə\ [NL, fr. dim. of L *spira* coil] (1875) : any of a genus (*Spirillum*) of long curved flagellate bacteria; *broadly* : a spiral filamentous bacterium (as a spirochete)

[1]**spir·it** \ˈspir-ət\ *n* [ME, fr. OF or L; OF, fr. L *spiritus,* lit., breath; akin to L *spirare* to blow, breathe, ON *fīsa* to break wind] (13c) **1** : an animating or vital principle held to give life to physical organisms **2** : a supernatural being or essence: as **a** *cap* : HOLY SPIRIT **b** : SOUL 2a **c** : an often malevolent being that is bodiless but can become visible; *specif* : GHOST 2 **d** : a malevolent being that enters and possesses a human being **3** : temper or disposition of mind or outlook esp. when vigorous or animated ⟨in high ~*s*⟩ **4** : the immaterial intelligent or sentient part of a person **5 a** : the activating or essential principle influencing a person ⟨acted in a ~ of helpfulness⟩ **b** : an inclination, impulse, or tendency of a specified kind : MOOD **6 a** : a special attitude or frame of mind ⟨the money-making ~ was for a time driven back —J. A. Froude⟩ **b** : the feeling, quality, or disposition characterizing something ⟨undertaken in a ~ of fun⟩ **7** : a lively or brisk quality in a person or his actions **8** : a person having a character or disposition of a specified nature **9** : a mental disposition characterized by firmness or assertiveness ⟨denied the charge with ~⟩ **10 a** : DISTILLATE 1: as (1) : the liquid containing ethyl alcohol and water that is distilled from an alcoholic liquid or mash — often used in pl. (2) : any of various volatile liquids obtained by distillation or cracking (as of petroleum, shale, or wood) — often used in pl. (3) : ALCOHOL 1 **b** : a usu. volatile organic solvent (as an alcohol, ester, or hydrocarbon) **11 a** : prevailing tone or tendency ⟨~ of the age⟩ **b** : general intent or real meaning ⟨~ of the law⟩ **12** : an alcoholic solution of a volatile substance ⟨~ of camphor⟩ **13** : enthusiastic loyalty ⟨school ~⟩ **14** *cap, Christian Science* : GOD 1b ***syn*** see COURAGE

[2]**spirit** *vt* (1608) **1** : to infuse with spirit; *esp* : ANIMATE ⟨hope and apprehension of feasibleness ~*s* all industry —John Goodman⟩ **2** : to carry off usu. secretly or mysteriously ⟨was hustled into a . . . motorcar and ~*ed* off to the country —W.L. Shirer⟩

spir·it·ed \ˈspir-ət-əd\ *adj* (1599) : full of energy, animation, or courage ⟨a ~ discussion⟩ — **spir·it·ed·ly** *adv* — **spir·it·ed·ness** *n*

spirit gum *n* (ca. 1891) : a solution (as of gum arabic in ether) used esp. for attaching false hair to the skin

spir·it·ism \ˈspir-ət-ˌiz-əm\ *n* (1864) : SPIRITUALISM 2a — **spir·it·ist** \-ət-əst\ *n* — **spir·it·is·tic** \ˌspir-ət-ˈis-tik\ *adj*

spir·it·less \ˈspir-ət-ləs\ *adj* (1597) : lacking animation, cheerfulness, or courage — **spir·it·less·ly** *adv* — **spir·it·less·ness** *n*

spirit level *n* (1768) : LEVEL 1

spirit of hartshorn *or* **spirits of hartshorn** (1683) : AMMONIA WATER

spir·i·to·so \ˌspir-ə-ˈtō-(ˌ)sō, -(ˌ)zō\ *adj* [It, fr. *spirito* spirit, fr. L *spiritus*] (ca. 1724) : ANIMATED — used as a direction in music

spir·it·ous \ˈspir-ət-əs\ *adj* (1605) **1** *archaic* : PURE, REFINED **2** : SPIRITUOUS

spirit rapping *n* (1852) : communication by raps held to be from the spirits of the dead

spirits of turpentine (1792) : TURPENTINE 2a — called also *spirit of turpentine*

spirits of wine (1753) : rectified spirit : ALCOHOL 1 — called also *spirit of wine*

[1]**spir·i·tu·al** \ˈspir-ich-(ə-)wəl, -ich-əl\ *adj* [ME, fr. MF & LL; MF *spirituel,* fr. LL *spiritualis,* fr. L, of breathing, of wind, fr. *spiritus*] (14c) **1** : of, relating to, consisting of, or affecting the spirit : INCORPOREAL ⟨man's ~ needs⟩ **2 a** : of or relating to sacred matters ⟨~ songs⟩ **b** : ecclesiastical rather than lay or temporal ⟨~ authority⟩ ⟨lords ~⟩ **3** : concerned with religious values **4** : related or joined in spirit ⟨our ~ home⟩ ⟨his ~ heir⟩ **5 a** : of or relating to supernatural beings or phenomena **b** : of, relating to, or involving spiritualism : SPIRITUALISTIC — **spir·i·tu·al·ly** \-ē\ *adv* — **spir·i·tu·al·ness** *n*

[2]**spiritual** *n* (1582) **1** *pl* : things of a spiritual, ecclesiastical, or religious nature **2** : a religious song usu. of a deeply emotional character that was developed esp. among blacks in the southern U.S. **3** *cap* : any of a party of 13th and 14th century Franciscans advocating strict observance of a rule of poverty for their order

spiritual bouquet *n* (1926) : a card notifying the recipient of a number of devotional acts performed by a Roman Catholic on behalf of a person on special occasions (as name days or anniversaries) or for the soul of someone recently deceased esp. as an expression of sympathy

spir·i·tu·al·ism \ˈspir-ich-(ə-)wə-ˌliz-əm, -ich-ə-ˌliz-\ *n* (1836) **1** : the view that spirit is a prime element of reality **2 a** : a belief that spirits of the dead communicate with the living usu. through a medium **b** *cap* : a movement comprising religious organizations emphasizing spiritualism — **spir·i·tu·al·ist** \-ləst\ *n, often cap* — **spir·i·tu·al·is·tic** \ˌspir-ich-(ə-)wə-ˈlis-tik, -ich-ə-ˈlis-\ *adj*

spir·i·tu·al·i·ty \ˌspir-ich-ə-ˈwal-ət-ē\ *n, pl* **-ties** (15c) **1** : something that in ecclesiastical law belongs to the church or to a cleric as such **2** : CLERGY **3** : sensitivity or attachment to religious values **4** : the quality or state of being spiritual

spir·i·tu·al·ize \ˈspir-ich-(ə-)wə-ˌlīz, -ich-ə-ˌlīz\ *vt* **-ized; -iz·ing** (1631) **1** : to make spiritual; *esp* : to purify from the corrupting influences of the world **2** : to give a spiritual meaning to or understand in a spiritual sense — **spir·i·tu·al·iza·tion** \ˌspir-ich-(ə-)wə-lə-ˈzā-shən, -ich-ə-lə-\ *n*

spir·i·tu·al·ty \ˈspir-ich-(ə-)wəl-tē, -ich-əl-\ *n* [ME *spiritualte,* fr. MF *spiritualté,* fr. ML *spiritualitat-, spiritualitas,* fr. LL *spiritualis* spiritual] (14c) : SPIRITUALITY 1, 2

spi·ri·tu·el *or* **spi·ri·tu·elle** \ˌspir-i-chə-ˈwel, spē-rē-tw(ʸ)el\ *adj* [*spirituel* fr. F, lit., spiritual; *spirituelle* fr. F, fem. of *spirituel*] (1673) : having or marked by a refined and esp. sprightly or witty nature

spir·i·tu·ous \ˈspir-ich-(ə-)wəs, -ich-əs, ˈspir-ət-əs\ *adj* [prob. fr. F *spiritueux,* fr. L *spiritus* spirit] (1681) : containing or impregnated with alcohol obtained by distillation ⟨~ liquors⟩

spirit varnish *n* (1850) : a varnish in which a volatile liquid (as alcohol) is the solvent

spirit writing *n* (1871) : automatic writing held to be produced under the influence of spirits

spiro- *comb form* [ISV, fr. L *spirare* to breathe — more at SPIRIT] : respiration ⟨*spiro*graph⟩

spi·ro·chet·al \ˌspī-rə-ˈkēt-ᵊl\ *adj* (1915) : caused by spirochetes

spi·ro·chete *also* **spi·ro·chaete** \ˈspī-rə-ˌkēt\ *n* [NL *Spirochaeta,* genus of bacteria, fr. Gk *speira* coil + *chaitē* long hair — more at SPIRE] (ca. 1877) : any of an order (Spirochaetales) of slender spirally undulating bacteria including those causing syphilis and relapsing fever

spi·ro·chet·osis \ˌspī-rə-ˌkēt-ˈō-səs\ *n, pl* **-oses** \-ˌsēz\ (1922) : infection with or a disease caused by spirochetes

spi·ro·gy·ra \ˌspī-rə-ˈjī-rə\ *n* [NL, fr. Gk *speira* + *gyros* ring, circle — more at SPIRE, COWER] (ca. 1900) : any of a genus (*Spirogyra*) of freshwater green algae with spiral chlorophyll bands

spi·rom·e·ter \spī-ˈräm-ət-ər\ *n* [ISV] (1846) : an instrument for measuring the air entering and leaving the lungs — **spi·ro·met·ric** \ˌspī-rə-ˈme-trik\ *adj* — **spi·rom·e·try** \spī-ˈräm-ə-trē\ *n*

spirt *var of* SPURT

spiry \ˈspī(ə)r-ē\ *adj* (1602) : resembling a spire; *esp* : being tall, slender, and tapering ⟨~ trees⟩

[1]**spit** \ˈspit\ *n* [ME, fr. OE *spitu* — more at SPINE] (bef. 12c) **1** : a slender pointed rod for holding meat over a fire **2** : a small point of land esp. of sand or gravel running into a body of water

[2]**spit** *vt* **spit·ted; spit·ting** (13c) : to fix on or as if on a spit : IMPALE

[3]**spit** *vb* **spit** *or* **spat** \ˈspat\; **spit·ting** [ME *spitten*, fr. OE *spittan*] *vt* (bef. 12c) **1 a** : to eject (as saliva) from the mouth : EXPECTORATE **b** (1) : to express (unpleasant or malicious feelings) by or as if by spitting (2) : to utter with a spitting sound or scornful expression ⟨*spat* out his words⟩ **c** : to emit as if by spitting; *esp* : to emit (precipitation) in driving particles or in flurries ⟨~ rain⟩ **2** : to set to burning ⟨~ a fuse⟩ ~ *vi* **1 a** (1) : to eject saliva as an expression of aversion or contempt (2) : to exhibit contempt **b** : to eject saliva from the mouth : EXPECTORATE **2** : to rain or snow slightly or in flurries **3** : to make a noise suggesting expectoration : SPUTTER — **spit it out** : to say what is in the mind without further delay

[4]**spit** *n* (14c) **1 a** (1) : SPITTLE, SALIVA (2) : the act or an instance of spitting **b** (1) : a frothy secretion exuded by spittlebugs (2) : SPITTLEBUG **2** : perfect likeness **3** : a sprinkle of rain or flurry of snow

spit·al \ˈspit-ᵊl\ *n* [ME *spitel*, modif. of ML *hospitale* — more at HOSPITAL] (1634) : LAZARETTO, HOSPITAL

spit and polish *n* [fr. the practice of polishing objects such as shoes by spitting on them and then rubbing them with a cloth] (1895) : extreme attention to cleanliness, orderliness, smartness of appearance, and ceremonial esp. at the expense of operational efficiency — **spit–and–polish** *adj*

spit·ball \ˈspit-ˌbȯl\ *n* (1846) **1** : paper chewed and rolled into a ball to be thrown or shot as a missile **2** : a baseball pitch delivered after the ball has been moistened with saliva or sweat

spit curl *n* [prob. fr. its being sometimes plastered down with saliva] (1858) : a spiral curl that is usu. plastered on the forehead, temple, or cheek

[1]**spite** \ˈspīt\ *n* [ME, short for *despite*] (14c) **1** : petty ill will or hatred with the disposition to irritate, annoy, or thwart **2** : an instance of spite ***syn*** see MALICE — **in spite of** : in defiance or contempt of : without being prevented by

[2]**spite** *vt* **spit·ed; spit·ing** (1592) **1** : to treat maliciously (as by shaming or thwarting) **2 a** : to fill with spite **b** : ANNOY, OFFEND

spite·ful \ˈspīt-fəl\ *adj* (15c) : filled with or showing spite : MALICIOUS — **spite·ful·ly** \-fə-lē\ *adv* — **spite·ful·ness** *n*

spit·fire \ˈspit-ˌfī(ə)r\ *n* (1680) : a quick-tempered or highly emotional person

[1]**spit·ter** \ˈspit-ər\ *n* (14c) : one that spits

[2]**spitter** *n* (1911) : SPITBALL 2

spitting cobra *n* (1910) : either of two venomous African elapid snakes (*Naja nigricollis* and *Haemachates haemachatus*) that eject their venom toward the victim without striking

spitting image *n* [alter. of *spit and image*] (1929) : IMAGE 3b

spit·tle \ˈspit-ᵊl\ *n* [ME *spetil*, fr. OE *spǣtl*; akin to OE *spittan*] (bef. 12c) **1** : SALIVA **2** : [4]SPIT 1b(1)

spit·tle·bug \-ˌbəg\ *n* (1882) : any of numerous leaping homopterous insects (family Cercopidae) whose larvae secrete froth

spittle insect *n* (1891) : SPITTLEBUG

spit·toon \spi-ˈtün, spə-\ *n* [[4]*spit* + *-oon* (as in *balloon*)] (1823) : a receptacle for spit — called also *cuspidor*

spit up *vb* (1779) : REGURGITATE, VOMIT

spitz \ˈspits\ *n* [G, fr. *spitz* pointed; akin to OE *spitu* spit; fr. the shape of its ears and muzzle — more at SPINE] (1845) : any of several stocky heavy-coated dogs of northern origin with erect ears and a heavily furred tail carried over the back

spiv \ˈspiv\ *n* [alter. of E dial. *spiff* flashy dresser, fr. *spiff* dandified] (1936) **1** *Brit* : one who lives by his wits without regular employment **2** *Brit* : SLACKER

splanch·nic \ˈsplaŋk-nik\ *adj* [NL *splanchnicus*, fr. Gk *splanchnikos*, fr. *splanchna*, pl., viscera; akin to Gk *splēn* spleen] (1681) : of or relating to the viscera : VISCERAL

[1]**splash** \ˈsplash\ *vb* [alter. of *plash*] *vi* (1722) **1 a** : to strike and dash about a liquid or semiliquid substance **b** : to move in or into a liquid or semiliquid substance and cause it to spatter **2 a** (1) : to become spattered about (2) : to spread or scatter in the manner of splashed liquid **b** : to fall, strike, or move with a splashing sound ⟨a brook ~*ing* over rocks⟩ ~ *vt* **1 a** (1) : to dash a liquid or thinly viscous substance upon or against (2) : to soil or stain with splashed liquid **b** : to mark or overlay with patches of contrasting color or texture **c** : to display prominently **2 a** : to cause (a liquid or thinly viscous substance) to spatter about esp. with force **b** : to scatter in the manner of a splashed liquid — **splash·er** *n*

[2]**splash** *n* (1736) **1 a** (1) : splashed liquid or semiliquid substance; *also* : impounded water released suddenly (2) : a spot or daub from or as if from splashed liquid ⟨a mud ~ on the fender⟩ **b** : a colored patch **2 a** : the action of splashing **b** : a short plunge **3** : a sound produced by or as if by a liquid falling, moving, being hurled, or oscillating **4 a** : a vivid impression created esp. by ostentatious activity or appearance **b** : ostentatious display **5** : a small amount : SPRINKLING

splash·board \ˈsplash-ˌbō(ə)rd, -ˌbȯ(ə)rd\ *n* (1826) **1 a** : DASHBOARD 1 **b** : a panel to protect against splashes **2** : a plank used to close a sluice or spillway of a dam

splash·down \ˈsplash-ˌdau̇n\ *n* (1959) : the landing of a manned spacecraft in the ocean — **splash down** \(ˈ)splash-ˈdau̇n\ *vi*

splash guard *n* (1926) : a flap suspended behind a rear wheel to prevent tire splash from muddying windshields of following vehicles

splashy \ˈsplash-ē\ *adj* **splash·i·er; -est** (1856) **1** : that can be easily splashed about **2** : moving or being moved with a splash or splashing sounds **3** : tending to or exhibiting ostentatious display **4** : consisting of, being, or covered with colored splashes — **splash·i·ly** \ˈsplash-ə-lē\ *adv* — **splash·i·ness** \ˈsplash-ē-nəs\ *n*

[1]**splat** \ˈsplat\ *n* [obs. *splat* (to spread flat)] (1833) : a single flat thin often ornamental member of a back of a chair

[2]**splat** *n* [imit.] (1897) : a splattering or slapping sound

[1]**splat·ter** \ˈsplat-ər\ *vb* [prob. blend of *splash* and *spatter*] *vt* (1785) : SPATTER ~ *vi* : to scatter or fall in or as if in drops

[2]**splatter** *n* (1819) : SPATTER, SPLASH

[1]**splay** \ˈsplā\ *vb* [ME *splayen*, short for *displayen* — more at DISPLAY] *vt* (14c) **1** : to cause to spread outward **2** : to make (as the jamb of a door) oblique : BEVEL ~ *vi* **1** : to become splayed **2** : SLOPE, SLANT

[2]**splay** *n* (1507) **1** : a slope or bevel esp. of the sides of a door or window **2** : SPREAD, EXPANSION

[3]**splay** *adj* (1767) **1** : turned outward ⟨~ knees⟩ **2** : AWKWARD, UNGAINLY

splay·foot \ˈsplā-ˌfu̇t, -ˈfu̇t\ *n* (1548) : a foot abnormally flattened and spread out; *specif* : FLATFOOT — **splay·foot·ed** \-ˈfu̇t-əd\ *adj*

spleen \ˈsplēn\ *n* [ME *splen*, fr. MF or L; MF *esplen*, fr. L *splen*, fr. Gk *splēn*; akin to L *lien* spleen] (14c) **1** : a highly vascular ductless organ near the stomach or intestine of most vertebrates concerned with final destruction of blood cells, storage of blood, and production of lymphocytes **2** *obs* : the seat of emotions or passions **3** *archaic* : MELANCHOLY **4** : mingled ill will and bad temper **5** *obs* : a sudden impulse or whim : CAPRICE ***syn*** see MALICE

spleen·ful \-fəl\ *adj* (1594) : full of or affected with spleen : SPLENETIC

spleen·wort \-ˌwərt, -ˌwȯ(ə)rt\ *n* [fr. the belief in its power to cure disorders of the spleen] (1578) : any of a genus (*Asplenium*) of ferns having linear or oblong sori borne obliquely on the upper side of a veinlet

spleeny \ˈsplē-nē\ *adj* (1604) **1** : full of or displaying spleen **2** *NewEng* : peevish and irritable with hypochondriac inclinations

splen- *or* **spleno-** *comb form* [L, fr. Gk *splēn-*, *splēno-*, fr. *splēn*] : spleen ⟨*splen*ectomy⟩ ⟨*spleno*megaly⟩

splen·dent \ˈsplen-dənt\ *adj* [ME, fr. LL *splendent-*, *splendens*, fr. L, prp. of *splendēre*] (15c) **1** : SHINING, GLOSSY ⟨~ luster⟩ **2** : ILLUSTRIOUS, BRILLIANT ⟨~ genius⟩

splen·did \ˈsplen-dəd\ *adj* [L *splendidus*, fr. *splendēre* to shine; akin to Gk *splēdos* ashes, Skt *sphuliṅga* spark] (1634) **1** : possessing or displaying splendor: as **a** : SHINING, BRILLIANT **b** : SHOWY, MAGNIFICENT **2** : ILLUSTRIOUS, GRAND **3** : EXCELLENT ⟨a ~ opportunity⟩ — **splen·did·ly** *adv* — **splen·did·ness** *n*

syn SPLENDID, RESPLENDENT, GORGEOUS, GLORIOUS, SUBLIME, SUPERB mean extraordinarily or transcendently impressive. SPLENDID implies outshining the usual or customary; RESPLENDENT suggests a glowing or blazing splendor; GORGEOUS implies a rich splendor esp. in display of color; GLORIOUS suggests radiance that heightens beauty or distinction; SUBLIME implies an exaltation or elevation almost beyond human comprehension; SUPERB suggests a magnificence or excellence reaching the highest conceivable degree.

splen·dif·er·ous \splen-ˈdif-(ə-)rəs\ *adj* [*splendor* + *-i-* + *-ferous*] (15c) **1** : SPLENDID **2** : deceptively splendid — **splen·dif·er·ous·ly** *adv* — **splen·dif·er·ous·ness** *n*

splen·dor \ˈsplen-dər\ *n* [ME *splendure*, fr. AF *splendur*, fr. L *splendor*, fr. *splendēre*] (15c) **1 a** : great brightness or luster : BRILLIANCY **b** : MAGNIFICENCE, POMP **2** : something splendid — **splen·dor·ous** *also* **splen·drous** \-d(ə-)rəs\ *adj*

splen·dour \-dər\ *chiefly Brit var of* SPLENDOR

sple·nec·to·my \spli-ˈnek-tə-mē\ *n, pl* **-mies** [ISV] (ca. 1859) : surgical removal of the spleen — **sple·nec·to·mized** \-ˌmīzd\ *adj*

sple·net·ic \spli-ˈnet-ik, *archaic* ˈsplen-ə-(ˌ)tik\ *adj* [LL *spleneticus*, fr. L *splen* spleen] (1697) **1** *archaic* : given to melancholy **2** : marked by bad temper, malevolence, or spite — **splenetic** *n* — **sple·net·i·cal·ly** \spli-ˈnet-i-k(ə-)lē\ *adv*

splen·ic \ˈsplen-ik\ *adj* [L *splenicus*, fr. Gk *splēnikos*, fr. *splēn* spleen] (1619) : of, relating to, or located in the spleen ⟨~ blood flow⟩

sple·ni·us \ˈsplē-nē-əs\ *n, pl* **-nii** \-nē-ˌī\ [NL, fr. L *splenium* plaster, compress, fr. Gk *splēnion*, fr. *splēn*] (1732) : a flat oblique muscle of each side of the back of the neck

spleno·meg·a·ly \ˌsplen-ō-ˈmeg-ə-lē\ *n, pl* **-lies** [ISV *splen-* + Gk *megal-*, *megas* large — more at MUCH] (ca. 1900) : enlargement of the spleen

spleu·chan \ˈsplü-kən, ˈsplüe̅-k-\ *n* [ScGael *spliūcan* & IrGael *spliūchān*] *Scot & Irish* (1785) : a pouch esp. for tobacco or money

[1]**splice** \ˈsplīs\ *vt* **spliced; splic·ing** [obs. D *splissen*; akin to MD *splitten* to split] (1524) **1 a** : to unite (as two ropes) by interweaving the strands **b** : to unite (as spars, timbers, or rails) by lapping two ends together or by applying a piece that laps upon two ends and making fast **2** : to unite or insert as if by splicing **3** : to combine (genetic information) from two or more organisms ⟨use enzymes to cut and ~ genes⟩ — **splic·er** *n*

[2]**splice** *n* (1627) **1** : a joining or joint made by splicing something **2** : MARRIAGE, WEDDING

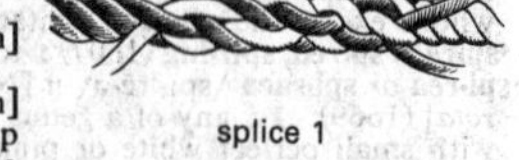

splice 1

spliff \ˈsplif\ *n* [origin unknown] (1969) : JOINT 4

spline \ˈsplīn\ *n* [origin unknown] (1756) **1** : a thin wood or metal strip used in building construction **2** : a key that is fixed to one of two connected mechanical parts and fits into a keyway in the other; *also* : a keyway for such a key

[1]**splint** \ˈsplint\ *also* **splent** \ˈsplent\ *n* [ME, fr. MLG *splinte*, *splente*; akin to OHG *spaltan* to split — more at SPILL] (14c) **1** : a small plate or strip of metal used in making armor **2 a** : a thin strip of wood suitable for interweaving (as into baskets) **b** : SPLINTER **c** : material or a device used to protect and immobilize a body part (as a broken arm) **3** : a bony enlargement on the upper part of the cannon bone of a horse usu. on the inside of the leg

[2]**splint** *vt* (1543) **1** : to support and immobilize (as a broken bone) with a splint **2** : to brace with or as if with splints

splint bone *n* (1704) : one of the slender rudimentary metacarpal or metatarsal bones on either side of the cannon bone in the limbs of the horse and related animals

[1]**splin·ter** \ˈsplint-ər\ *n* [ME, fr. MD; akin to MLG *splinte* splint] (14c) **1** : a thin piece split or rent off lengthwise : SLIVER **2** : a group or faction broken away from a parent body — **splinter** *adj* — **splin·tery** \ˈsplint-ə-rē, ˈsplin-trē\ *adj*

[2]**splinter** *vb* **splin·tered; splin·ter·ing** \ˈsplint-ə-riŋ, ˈsplin-triŋ\ *vt* (1582) **1** : to split or rend into long thin pieces : SHIVER **2** : to split into fragments, parts, or factions ~ *vi* : to become splintered

1split \ˈsplit\ *vb* **split; split·ting** [D *splitten,* fr. MD; akin to OHG *spaltan* to split — more at SPILL] *vt* (1593) **1 a :** to divide lengthwise usu. along a grain or seam or by layers **b :** to affect as if by cleaving or forcing apart ⟨the river ~*s* the town in two⟩ **2 a** (1) **:** to tear or rend apart **:** BURST (2) **:** to subject (an atom or atomic nucleus) to artificial disintegration esp. by fission **b :** to affect as if by breaking up or tearing apart **:** SHATTER ⟨a roar that ~ the air⟩ **3 :** to divide into parts or portions: as **a :** to divide between persons **:** SHARE **b :** to divide into factions, parties, or groups **c :** to mark (a ballot) or cast or register (a vote) so as to vote for candidates of different parties **d** (1) **:** to divide or break down (a chemical compound) into constituents ⟨~ a fat into glycerol and fatty acids⟩ (2) **:** to remove by such separation ⟨~ off carbon dioxide⟩ **e :** to divide (stock) by issuing a larger number of shares to existing shareholders usu. without increase in total par value **4 :** to separate (the parts of a whole) by interposing something ⟨~ an infinitive⟩ **5 :** LEAVE ⟨~ the party⟩ ⟨~ town⟩ ~ *vi* **1 a :** to become split lengthwise or into layers **b :** to break apart **:** BURST **2 a :** to become divided up or separated off ⟨~ into factions⟩ **b :** to sever relations or connections **c :** LEAVE; *esp* **:** to leave without delay **3 :** to apportion shares ***syn*** see TEAR — **split·ter** *n* — **split hairs :** to make oversubtle or trivial distinctions — **split one's sides :** to laugh heartily

2split *n* (1597) **1 a :** a narrow break made by or as if by splitting **b :** a position of bowling pins left standing with space for pins between them **2 :** a piece split off or made thin by splitting **3 a :** a division into or between divergent or antagonistic elements or forces **b :** a faction formed in this way **4 a :** the act or process of splitting **b :** the act of lowering oneself to the floor or leaping into the air with legs extended at right angles to the trunk **5 :** a product of division by or as if by splitting **6 :** a wine bottle holding one quarter the usual amount or about .1875 liters (6 to 6.5 ounces) **7 :** a sweet composed of sliced fruit (as banana), ice cream, syrup, and often nuts and whipped cream

3split *adj* (1648) **1 :** DIVIDED, FRACTURED **2 :** prepared for use by splitting ⟨~ bamboo⟩ ⟨~ hides⟩ **3 :** HETEROZYGOUS — used esp. by breeders of cage birds sometimes with *for* **4 :** widely spaced

split–brain \ˌsplit-ˌbrān\ *adj* (1963) **:** having the optic chiasma and corpus callosum severed ⟨behavior in ~ animals⟩

split decision *n* (1952) **:** a decision in a boxing match reflecting a division of opinion among the referee and judges

split end *n* (1962) **:** an offensive football end who lines up usu. several yards to the side of the formation

split infinitive *n* (1897) **:** an infinitive with *to* having a modifier between the *to* and the verbal (as in "to really start")

usage The split infinitive was discovered and named in the 19th century. 19th century writers seem to have made greater use of this construction than earlier writers; the frequency of occurrence attracted the disapproving attention of grammarians, many of whom thought it to be a modern corruption (one commentator blamed it on Byron). In fact *to* was orig. limited to use with the gerund and not until the 12th century did it become attached to the infinitive. By the 14th century writers were occas. separating *to* and the verb with an adverb; the practice went unnoticed until the 19th century. Modern commentators do not consider the split infinitive a vice, merely advising writers to avoid trying to crowd too long an adverbial phrase between *to* and the infinitive.

split–lev·el \ˈsplit-ˈlev-əl\ *adj* (1946) **:** divided vertically so that the floor level of rooms in one part is approximately midway between the levels of two successive stories in an adjoining part ⟨a ~ house⟩ — **split–lev·el** \-ˌlev-əl\ *n*

split pea *n* (1736) **:** a dried hulled pea in which the cotyledons usu. split apart

split personality *n* (1927) **:** SCHIZOPHRENIA; *also* **:** MULTIPLE PERSONALITY

split rail *n* (1826) **:** a fence rail split from a log

split second *n* (1912) **:** a fractional part of a second **:** FLASH

split shift *n* (1943) **:** a shift of working hours divided into two or more working periods at times (as mornings and evening) separated by more than normal periods of time off (as for lunch or rest)

split ticket *n* (1836) **:** a ballot cast by a voter who votes for candidates of more than one party

split·ting \ˈsplit-iŋ\ *adj* (1593) **:** that splits or causes to split: as **a :** causing a piercing sensation ⟨a ~ headache⟩ **b :** very fast or quick **c :** SIDESPLITTING ⟨a ~ laugh⟩

splore \ˈsplō(ə)r, ˈsplȯ(ə)r\ *n* [origin unknown] (1785) **1** *Scot* **:** FROLIC, CAROUSAL **2** *Scot* **:** COMMOTION

1splotch \ˈspläch\ *n* [perh. blend of *spot* and *blotch*] (1601) **:** SPOT, BLOTCH — **splotchy** \-ē\ *adj*

2splotch *vt* (1654) **:** to mark with a splotch **:** cover with splotches

1splurge \ˈsplərj\ *n* [perh. blend of *splash* and *surge*] (1830) **:** an ostentatious effort, display, or expenditure

2splurge *vb* **splurged; splurg·ing** *vi* (1843) **1 :** to make a splurge **2 :** to indulge oneself extravagantly — often used with *on* ⟨~ on a new dress⟩ ~ *vt* **:** to spend extravagantly or ostentatiously

1splut·ter \ˈsplət-ər\ *n* [prob. alter. of *sputter*] (1677) **1 :** a confused noise (as of hasty speaking) **2 :** a splashing or sputtering sound

2splutter *vi* (1818) **1 :** to make a noise as if spitting **2 :** to speak hastily and confusedly ~ *vt* **:** to utter hastily or confusedly **:** STAMMER — **splut·ter·er** \ˈsplət-ər-ər\ *n*

splut·tery \ˈsplət-ə-rē\ *adj* (1866) **:** marked by spluttering

Spode \ˈspōd\ *n* (1869) **:** ceramic ware (as bone china, stone china, or Parian ware) made at the works established by Josiah Spode in 1770 at Stoke in Staffordshire, England

spod·u·mene \ˈspäj-ə-ˌmēn\ *n* [prob. fr. F *spodumène,* fr. G *spodumen,* fr. Gk *spodoumenos,* prp. of *spodousthai* to be burnt to ashes, fr. *spodos* ashes] (1893) **:** a white to yellowish, purplish, or emerald-green monoclinic mineral $LiAlSi_2O_6$ that is a lithium aluminum silicate and occurs in prismatic crystals often of great size

1spoil \ˈspȯi(ə)l\ *n* [ME *spoile,* fr. MF *espoille,* fr. L *spolia,* pl. of *spolium* — more at SPILL] (14c) **1 a :** plunder taken from an enemy in war or a victim in robbery **:** LOOT **b :** public offices made the property of a successful party — usu. used in pl. **c :** something gained by special effort or opportune timing — usu. used in pl. **2 a :** SPOLIATION, PLUNDERING **b :** the act of damaging **:** HARM, IMPAIRMENT **3 :** an object of plundering **:** PREY **4 :** earth and rock excavated or dredged **5 :** an object damaged or flawed in the making

syn SPOIL, PILLAGE, PLUNDER, BOOTY, PRIZE, LOOT mean something taken from another by force or craft. SPOIL, more commonly SPOILS, applies to what belongs by right or custom to the victor in war or political contest; PILLAGE stresses more open violence or lawlessness; PLUNDER applies to what is taken not only in war but in robbery, banditry, grafting, or swindling; BOOTY implies plunder to be shared among confederates; PRIZE applies to spoils captured on the high seas or territorial waters of the enemy; LOOT applies esp. to what is taken from victims of a catastrophe.

2spoil *vb* **spoiled** \ˈspȯi(ə)ld, ˈspȯi(ə)lt\ *or* **spoilt** \ˈspȯi(ə)lt\; **spoil·ing** [ME *spoilen,* fr. MF *espoillier,* fr. L *spoliare,* fr. *spolium*] *vt* (14c) **1 a** *archaic* **:** DESPOIL, STRIP **b :** PILLAGE, ROB **2** *archaic* **:** to seize by force **3 a :** to damage seriously **:** RUIN **b :** to impair the quality or effect of ⟨a quarrel ~*ed* the celebration⟩ **4 a :** to impair the disposition or character of by overindulgence or excessive praise **b :** to pamper excessively **:** CODDLE ~ *vi* **1 :** to practice plunder and robbery **2 :** to lose valuable or useful qualities usu. as a result of decay **3 :** to have an eager desire ⟨~*ing* for a fight⟩ ***syn*** see DECAY, INDULGE — **spoil·able** \ˈspȯi-lə-bəl\ *adj*

spoil·age \ˈspȯi-lij\ *n* (1597) **1 :** the act or process of spoiling **2 :** something spoiled or wasted **3 :** loss by spoilage

spoil·er \ˈspȯi-lər\ *n* (1535) **1 :** one that spoils **2 :** a long narrow plate along the upper surface of an airplane wing that may be raised for reducing lift and increasing drag — see AIRPLANE illustration **3 :** an air deflector on the front or on the rear deck of an automobile and esp. a racer to reduce the tendency to lift off the road at high speeds

spoils·man \ˈspȯi(ə)lz-mən\ *n* (1846) **:** one who serves a party for a share of the spoils; *also* **:** one who sanctions such practice

spoil·sport \ˈspȯi(ə)l-ˌspō(ə)rt, -ˌspȯ(ə)rt\ *n* (1821) **:** one who spoils the sport or pleasure of others

spoils system *n* (1838) **:** a practice of regarding public offices and their emoluments as plunder to be distributed to members of the victorious party

1spoke \ˈspōk\ *past & archaic past part of* SPEAK

2spoke *n* [ME, fr. OE *spāca;* akin to MD *spike* spike — more at SPIKE] (bef. 12c) **1 a :** one of the small radiating bars inserted in the hub of a wheel to support the rim **b :** something resembling the spoke of a wheel **2 :** a rung of a ladder **3 :** one of the projecting handles of a steering wheel of a boat

3spoke *vt* **spoked; spok·ing** (bef. 12c) **:** to furnish with or as if with spokes

spo·ken \ˈspō-kən\ *adj* [pp. of *speak*] (1595) **1 :** delivered by word of mouth **:** ORAL **2 :** characterized by speaking in (such) a manner — used in combination ⟨soft-*spoken*⟩ ⟨plain*spoken*⟩

spoke·shave \ˈspōk-ˌshāv\ *n* [2*spoke*] (1510) **:** a drawknife or small transverse plane with end handles for planing convex or concave surfaces

spokes·man \ˈspōk-smən\ *n* [prob. irreg. fr. *spoke,* obs. pp. of *speak*] (1540) **:** one who speaks as the representative of another or others — **spokes·man·ship** \-smən-ˌship\ *n*

spokes·per·son \-ˌspərs-ᵊn\ *n* (1972) **:** SPOKESMAN

spokes·wom·an \-ˌswu̇m-ən\ *n* (1654) **:** a woman who speaks as the representative of another or others

spo·li·ate \ˈspō-lē-ˌāt\ *vt* **-at·ed; -at·ing** [L *spoliatus,* pp.] (ca. 1722) **:** DESPOIL — **spo·li·a·tor** \-ˌāt-ər\ *n*

spo·li·a·tion \ˌspō-lē-ˈā-shən\ *n* [ME, fr. L *spoliation-, spoliatio,* fr. *spoliatus,* pp. of *spoliare* to plunder — more at SPOIL] (15c) **1 a :** the act of plundering **b :** the state of having been plundered esp. in war **2 :** the act of injuring esp. beyond reclaim

spon·dee \ˈspän-ˌdē\ *n* [ME *sponde,* fr. MF or L; MF *spondee,* fr. L *spondeum,* fr. Gk *spondeios,* fr. *spondeios* of a libation, fr. *spondē* libation; fr. its use in music accompanying libations — more at SPOUSE] (14c) **:** a metrical foot consisting of two long or stressed syllables — **spon·da·ic** \spän-ˈdā-ik\ *adj or n*

spon·dy·li·tis \ˌspän-də-ˈlīt-əs\ *n* [NL, fr. Gk *sphondylos, spondylos* vertebra, lit., whorl; akin to Gk *sphadazein* to jerk, *sphendonē* sling] (ca. 1849) **:** inflammation of the vertebrae

1sponge \ˈspənj\ *n* [ME, fr. OE, fr. L *spongia,* fr. Gk] (bef. 12c) **1 a** (1) **:** an elastic porous mass of interlacing horny fibers that forms the internal skeleton of various marine animals (phylum Porifera) and is able when wetted to absorb water (2) **:** a piece of sponge (as for scrubbing and cleaning) (3) **:** a porous rubber or cellulose product used similarly to a sponge **b :** any of a phylum (Porifera) of aquatic lower invertebrate animals that are essentially double-walled cell colonies and permanently attached as adults **2 :** a pad (as of folded gauze) used in surgery and medicine (as to remove discharge or apply medication) **3 :** one who lives on others **:** SPONGER **4 a :** raised dough (as for yeast bread) **b :** a whipped dessert usu. containing whites of eggs or gelatin **c :** a metal (as platinum) obtained in porous form usu. by reduction without fusion ⟨titanium ~⟩ **d :** the egg mass of a crab ***syn*** see PARASITE

2sponge *vb* **sponged; spong·ing** *vt* (14c) **1 :** to cleanse, wipe, or moisten with or as if with a sponge **2 :** to erase or destroy with or as if with a sponge — often used with *out* ⟨whole paragraphs had been *sponged* out⟩ **3 :** to get by sponging on another **4 :** to absorb with or as if with or in the manner of a sponge ~ *vi* **1 :** to absorb, soak up, or imbibe like a sponge **2 :** to get something from or live on another by imposing on hospitality or good nature **3 :** to dive or dredge for sponges — **spong·er** *n*

sponge cake *n* (1805) **:** a light cake made without shortening

sponge cloth *n* (1862) **:** any of various soft porous fabrics esp. in a loose honeycomb weave

sponge rubber *n* (1886) **:** cellular rubber resembling a natural sponge in structure used esp. for cushions, vibration dampeners, weather stripping, and gaskets

sponge·ware \ˈspənj-ˌwa(ə)r, -ˌwe(ə)r\ *n* (1943) **:** a typically 19th century earthenware with background color spattered or dabbed (as with a sponge) and usu. a freehand central design

\ə\ abut \ᵊ\ kitten, F table \ər\ further \a\ ash \ā\ ace \ä\ cot, cart \au̇\ out \ch\ chin \e\ bet \ē\ easy \g\ go \i\ hit \ī\ ice \j\ job \ŋ\ sing \ō\ go \ȯ\ law \ȯi\ boy \th\ thin \t͟h\ the \ü\ loot \u̇\ foot \y\ yet \zh\ vision \á, k̲, ⁿ, œ, œ̄, ue, u̅e̅, ʸ\ *see* Guide to Pronunciation

spon·gin \ˈspən-jən\ *n* [G, fr. L *spongia* sponge] (ca. 1868) **:** a scleroprotein that is the chief constituent of flexible fibers in sponge skeletons

spongy \ˈspən-jē\ *adj* **spong·i·er; -est** (1539) **1 :** resembling a sponge: **a :** soft and full of cavities ⟨~ ice⟩ **b :** elastic, porous, and absorbent **2 a :** not firm or solid **b :** being in the form of a metallic sponge ⟨~ iron⟩ **3 :** moist and soft like a sponge full of water ⟨a ~ moor⟩ — **spong·i·ness** *n*

spongy parenchyma *n* (1884) **:** a spongy layer of irregular chlorophyll-bearing cells interspersed with air spaces that fills the part of a leaf between the palisade parenchyma and the lower epidermis — called also *spongy layer, spongy tissue*

spon·son \ˈspän(t)-sən\ *n* [prob. by shortening & alter. fr. *expansion*] (1835) **1 a :** a projection (as a gun platform) from the side of a ship or a tank **b :** an air chamber along a canoe to increase stability and buoyancy **2 :** a light air-filled structure or a winglike part protruding from the hull of a seaplane to steady it on water

¹spon·sor \ˈspän(t)-sər\ *n* [LL, fr. L, guarantor, surety, fr. *sponsus,* pp. of *spondēre* to promise — more at SPOUSE] (1651) **1 :** one who presents a candidate for baptism or confirmation and undertakes responsibility for his religious education or spiritual welfare **2 :** one who assumes responsibility for some other person or thing **3 :** a person or an organization that pays for or plans and carries out a project or activity; *esp* **:** one that pays the cost of a radio or television program usu. in return for limited advertising time during its course — **spon·so·ri·al** \spän-ˈsōr-ē-əl, -ˈsȯr-\ *adj* — **spon·sor·ship** \ˈspän(t)-sər-ˌship\ *n*

²sponsor *vt* **spon·sored; spon·sor·ing** \ˈspän(t)s-(ə-)riŋ\ (1884) **:** to be or stand sponsor for

spon·ta·ne·ity \ˌspänt-ən-ˈē-ət-ē, ˌspänt-ᵊn-, -ˈā-ət-\ *n* (1651) **1 :** the quality or state of being spontaneous **2 :** voluntary or undetermined action or movement; *also* **:** its source

spon·ta·ne·ous \spän-ˈtā-nē-əs\ *adj* [LL *spontaneus,* fr. L *sponte* of one's free will, voluntarily — more at SPIN] (1656) **1 :** proceeding from natural feeling or native tendency without external constraint **2 :** arising from a momentary impulse **3 :** controlled and directed internally **:** SELF-ACTING ⟨~ movement characteristic of living things⟩ **4 :** produced without being planted or without human labor **:** INDIGENOUS **5 :** developing without apparent external influence, force, cause, or treatment **6 :** not apparently contrived or manipulated **:** NATURAL — **spon·ta·ne·ous·ly** *adv* — **spon·ta·ne·ous·ness** *n*

syn SPONTANEOUS, IMPULSIVE, INSTINCTIVE, AUTOMATIC, MECHANICAL mean acting or activated without deliberation. SPONTANEOUS implies lack of prompting and connotes naturalness ⟨a *spontaneous* burst of applause⟩ IMPULSIVE implies acting under stress of emotion or spirit of the moment ⟨*impulsive* acts of violence⟩ INSTINCTIVE stresses spontaneous action involving neither judgment nor will ⟨blinking is an *instinctive* reaction⟩ AUTOMATIC implies action engaging neither the mind nor the emotions and connotes a predictable response ⟨his denial was *automatic*⟩ MECHANICAL stresses the lifeless, often perfunctory character of the response ⟨over the years her style of teaching became *mechanical*⟩

spontaneous combustion *n* (1809) **:** self-ignition of combustible material through chemical action (as oxidation) of its constituents — called also *spontaneous ignition*

spontaneous generation *n* (1665) **:** ABIOGENESIS

spontaneous recovery *n* (1943) **:** reappearance of an extinguished conditioned response without positive reinforcement

spon·toon \spän-ˈtün\ *n* [F *sponton,* fr. It *spuntone,* fr. *punta* sharp point, fr. (assumed) VL *puncta* — more at POINT] (1598) **:** a short pike formerly borne by subordinate officers of infantry

¹spoof \ˈspüf\ *vt* [*Spoof,* a hoaxing game invented by Arthur Roberts †1933 Eng. comedian] (1895) **1 :** DECEIVE, HOAX **2 :** to make good-natured fun of

²spoof *n* (1897) **1 :** HOAX, DECEPTION **2 :** a light humorous parody — **spoof·ery** \ˈspü-f(ə)rē\ *n* — **spoofy** \ˈspü-fē\ *adj*

¹spook \ˈspük\ *n* [D; akin to MLG *spōk* ghost] (1801) **1 :** GHOST, SPECTER **2 :** an undercover agent **:** SPY — **spook·ery** \ˈspü-k(ə-)rē\ *n* — **spook·ish** \ˈspü-kish\ *adj*

²spook *vt* (1867) **1 :** HAUNT 3 **2 :** to make frightened or frantic **:** SCARE; *esp* **:** to startle into violent activity (as stampeding) ~ *vi* **:** to become spooked ⟨cattle ~*ing* at shadows⟩

spooky \ˈspü-kē\ *adj* **spook·i·er; -est** (1854) **1 :** relating to, resembling, or suggesting spooks **2 :** NERVOUS, SKITTISH ⟨a ~ horse⟩ — **spook·i·ly** \-kə-lē\ *adv* — **spook·i·ness** \-kē-nəs\ *n*

¹spool \ˈspül\ *n* [ME *spole,* fr. MF or MD; MF *espole,* fr. MD *spoele;* akin to OHG *spuola* spool; akin to OHG *spaltan* to split — more at SPILL] (14c) **1 :** a cylindrical device which has a rim or ridge at each end and an axial hole for a pin or spindle and on which material (as thread, wire, or tape) is wound **2 :** material or the amount of material wound on a spool

²spool *vt* (1603) **1 :** to wind on a spool **2 :** WIND ⟨~ the thread off the bobbin⟩ ~ *vi* **1 :** to wind itself on a spool **2 :** WIND

¹spoon \ˈspün\ *n* [ME, fr. OE *spōn* splinter, chip; akin to OHG *spān* splinter, chip, Gk *sphēn* wedge] (14c) **1 :** an eating or cooking implement consisting of a small shallow bowl with a handle **2 :** something that resembles a spoon in shape (as a usu. metal or shell fishing lure)

²spoon *vt* (1715) **1 :** to take up and usu. transfer in a spoon **2 :** to propel (a ball) by a weak lifting stroke ~ *vi* **1** [perh. fr. the Welsh custom of an engaged man's presenting his fiancée with an elaborately carved wooden spoon] **:** to make love by caressing, kissing, and talking amorously **:** NECK **2 :** to spoon a ball

spoon·bill \ˈspün-ˌbil\ *n* (ca. 1678) **1 :** any of several wading birds (family Plataleidae) related to the ibises that have the bill greatly expanded and flattened at the tip **2 :** any of several broad-billed ducks (as the shoveler)

spoonbill cat *n* (ca. 1882) **:** a paddlefish (*Polyodon spathula*)

spoon–billed \ˈspün-ˈbild\ *adj* (1668) **:** having the bill or snout expanded and spatulate at the end

spoon bread *n* (1916) **:** soft bread made of cornmeal mixed with milk, eggs, and shortening and served with a spoon

spoon·drift \ˈspün-ˌdrift\ *n* [alter. of Sc *speendrift* — more at SPINDRIFT] (ca. 1769) **:** spray blown from waves during a gale at sea

spoo·ner·ism \ˈspü-nə-ˌriz-əm\ *n* [William A. *Spooner* †1930 Eng. clergyman & educator] (1900) **:** a transposition of usu. initial sounds of two or more words (as in *tons of soil* for *sons of toil*)

spoon–feed \ˈspün-ˌfēd\ *vt* **-fed** \-ˌfed\; **-feed·ing** (1615) **1 :** to feed by means of a spoon **2 a :** to present (information) so completely as to preclude independent thought ⟨~ material to students⟩ **b :** to present information to in this manner

spoon·ful \ˈspün-ˌfu̇l\ *n, pl* **spoonfuls** \-ˌfu̇lz\ *also* **spoons·ful** \ˈspünz-ˌfu̇l\ (13c) **:** as much as a spoon will hold; *specif* **:** TEASPOONFUL

spoony *or* **spoon·ey** \ˈspü-nē\ *adj* **spoon·i·er; -est** [E slang *spoon* (simpleton)] (ca. 1812) **1 :** SILLY, FOOLISH; *esp* **:** unduly sentimental **2 :** being sentimentally in love

¹spoor \ˈspu̇(ə)r, ˈspō(ə)r, ˈspȯ(ə)r\ *n, pl* **spoor** *or* **spoors** [Afrik, fr. MD; akin to OE *spor* footprint, spoor, *spurnan* to kick — more at SPURN] (1823) **:** a track, a trail, a scent, or droppings esp. of a wild animal

²spoor *vt* (1850) **:** to track by a spoor ~ *vi* **:** to track something by its spoor

spor- *or* **spori-** *or* **sporo-** *comb form* [NL *spora*] **:** seed **:** spore ⟨*sporocyst*⟩ ⟨*sporangium*⟩ ⟨*sporicidal*⟩

spo·rad·ic \spə-ˈrad-ik\ *adj* [ML *sporadicus,* fr. Gk *sporadikos,* fr. *sporadēn* here and there, fr. *sporad-, sporas* scattered; akin to Gk *speirein* to sow, OE *sprǣdan* to spread — more at SPREAD] (1689) **:** occurring occasionally, singly, or in scattered instances ***syn*** see INFREQUENT — **spo·rad·i·cal·ly** \-i-k(ə-)lē\ *adv*

sporadic E layer *n* (1957) **:** a layer of ionization occurring irregularly within the E region of the ionosphere

spo·ran·gio·phore \spə-ˈran-jē-ə-ˌfō(ə)r, -ˌfȯ(ə)r\ *n* (1875) **:** a stalk or receptacle bearing sporangia

spo·ran·gi·um \spə-ˈran-jē-əm\ *n, pl* **-gia** \-jē-ə\ [NL, fr. *spor-* + Gk *angeion* vessel — more at ANGI-] (1821) **:** a case within which usu. asexual spores are produced whether a cell (as in bacteria or algae) producing spores endogenously or a complex structure (as in a fern) — **spo·ran·gial** \-j(ē-)əl\ *adj*

¹spore \ˈspō(ə)r, ˈspȯ(ə)r\ *n* [NL *spora* seed, spore, fr. Gk, act of sowing, seed, fr. *speirein* to sow — more at SPROUT] (1836) **:** a primitive usu. unicellular resistant or reproductive body produced by plants and some invertebrates and capable of development into a new individual in some cases unlike the parent either directly or after fusion with another spore — **spored** \ˈspō(ə)rd, ˈspȯ(ə)rd\ *adj*

²spore *vi* **spored; spor·ing** (1903) **:** to produce or reproduce by spores

spore case *n* (1836) **:** a case containing spores **:** SPORANGIUM

spo·ri·cid·al \ˌspōr-ə-ˈsīd-ᵊl, ˌspȯr-\ *adj* (1939) **:** tending to kill spores — **spo·ri·cide** \ˈspōr-ə-ˌsīd, ˈspȯr-\ *n*

spo·ro·carp \ˈspōr-ə-ˌkärp, ˈspȯr-\ *n* [ISV *spor-* + Gk *karpos* fruit — more at HARVEST] (1849) **:** a structure (as in red algae, fungi, or mosses) in or on which spores are produced

spo·ro·cyst \-ˌsist\ *n* [ISV] (1861) **1 :** a case or cyst secreted by some sporozoans preliminary to sporogony; *also* **:** a sporozoan encysted in such a case **2 :** a saccular body that is the first asexual reproductive form of a digenetic trematode and buds off cells from its inner surface which develop into rediae

spo·ro·gen·e·sis \ˌspōr-ə-ˈjen-ə-səs, ˌspȯr-\ *n* [NL] (ca. 1890) **1 :** reproduction by spores **2 :** spore formation — **spo·rog·e·nous** \spə-ˈräj-ə-nəs, spō-\ *also* **spo·ro·gen·ic** \ˌspōr-ə-ˈjen-ik, ˌspȯr-\ *adj*

spo·ro·go·ni·um \ˌspōr-ə-ˈgō-nē-əm, ˌspȯr-\ *n, pl* **-nia** \-nē-ə\ [NL, fr. *spor-* + *-gonium* (as in *archegonium*)] (1875) **:** the sporophyte of a moss or liverwort consisting typically of a stalk bearing a capsule in which spores are produced and remaining permanently attached to the gametophyte

spo·rog·o·ny \spə-ˈräg-ə-nē, spō-\ *n* [ISV] (1888) **:** reproduction by spores; *specif* **:** spore formation in a sporozoan by encystment and subsequent division of a zygote — **spo·ro·gon·ic** \ˌspōr-ə-ˈgän-ik, ˌspȯr-\ *also* **spo·rog·o·nous** \spə-ˈräg-ə-nəs, spō-\ *adj*

spo·ro·phore \ˌspōr-ə-ˌfō(ə)r, ˈspȯr-ə-ˌfȯ(ə)r\ *n* [ISV] (1849) **:** the part (as a fruiting body of a fungus or the placenta of a seed plant) of a sporophyte that develops spores

spo·ro·phyll \-ˌfil\ *n* [ISV] (1888) **:** a spore-bearing and usu. greatly modified leaf

spo·ro·phyte \-ˌfīt\ *n* [ISV] (1886) **:** the individual or generation of a plant exhibiting alternation of generations that bears asexual spores — compare GAMETOPHYTE — **spo·ro·phyt·ic** \ˌspōr-ə-ˈfit-ik, ˌspȯr-\ *adj*

spo·ro·pol·len·in \ˌspōr-ə-ˈpäl-ə-nən, ˌspȯr-\ *n* [ISV *spor-* + *pollen* + *-in*] (ca. 1948) **:** a relatively chemically inert polymer that makes up the outer layer of pollen grains and spores of higher plants

spo·ro·tri·cho·sis \spə-ˌrä-trik-ˈō-səs; ˌspōr-ə-trik-, ˌspȯr-\ *n* [NL, fr. *sporotrichum,* fr. *spor-* + Gk *trich-, thrix* hair — more at TRICH-] (ca. 1909) **:** infection with or disease caused by fungi (genus *Sporotrichum*) that is characterized by nodules and abscesses in the superficial lymph nodes, skin, and subcutaneous tissues, that occurs esp. in man and horses, and that is usu. transmitted by entry of the fungus through a skin abrasion or wound (as from the prick of a thorn)

-spo·rous \ˈspōr-əs, ˈspȯr-; s-pə-rəs\ *adj comb form* [NL *spora* spore] **:** having (such or so many) spores ⟨homo*sporous*⟩

spo·ro·zo·an \ˌspōr-ə-ˈzō-ən, ˌspȯr-\ *n* [NL *Sporozoa,* fr. *spor-* + *-zoa*] (1888) **:** any of a large class (Sporozoa) of strictly parasitic protozoans that have a complicated life cycle usu. involving both asexual and sexual generations often in different hosts and include important pathogens (as malaria parasites, coccidia, and piroplasms) — **sporozoan** *adj*

spo·ro·zo·ite \-ˈzō-ˌīt\ *n* [NL *Sporozoa* + ISV *-ite*] (1888) **:** a usu. motile infective form of some sporozoans that is a product of sporogony and initiates an asexual cycle in the new host

spor·ran \ˈspȯr-ən, ˈspär-\ *n* [ScGael *sporan*] (1752) **:** a pouch of skin with the hair or fur on that is worn in front of the kilt with Scots Highland dress

¹sport \ˈspō(ə)rt, ˈspȯ(ə)rt\ *vb* [ME *sporten* to divert, disport, short for *disporten*] *vi* (15c) **1 a :** to amuse oneself **:** FROLIC ⟨lambs ~*ing* in the meadow⟩ **b :** to engage in a sport **2 a :** to mock or ridicule something **b :** to speak or act in jest **:** TRIFLE **3** [²*sport*] **:** to deviate or vary abruptly from type (as by bud variation) **:** MUTATE ~ *vt* **1 :** to display or wear usu. ostenta-

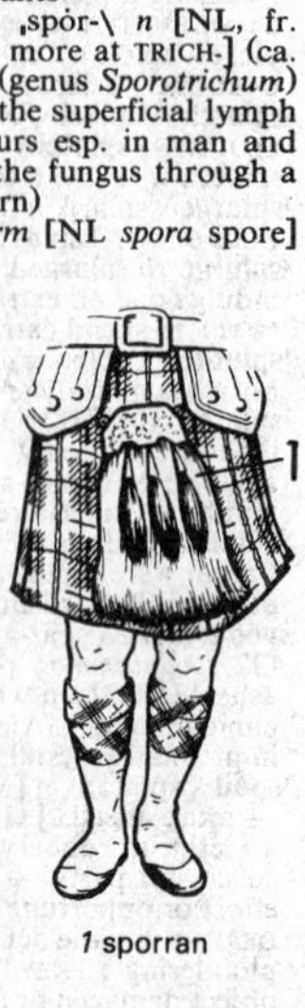

1 sporran

tiously : BOAST 2 [[2]sport] : to put forth as a sport or bud variation

[2]**sport** *n* (15c) **1 a :** a source of diversion : RECREATION **b :** sexual play **c** (1) **:** physical activity engaged in for pleasure (2) **:** a particular activity (as an athletic game) so engaged in **2 a :** PLEASANTRY, JEST **b :** MOCKERY, DERISION **3 a :** something tossed or driven about in or as if in play **b :** LAUGHINGSTOCK **4 a :** SPORTSMAN **b :** a person living up to the ideals of sportsmanship ⟨a good ~ about losing⟩ **c :** a companionable person **5 :** an individual exhibiting a sudden deviation from type beyond the normal limits of individual variation usu. as a result of mutation esp. of somatic tissue ***syn*** see FUN

[3]**sport** *or* **sports** *adj* (1582) **:** of, relating to, or suitable for sports; *esp* **:** styled in a manner suitable for casual or informal wear ⟨~ coats⟩

sport fish *n* (1944) **:** a fish important for the sport it affords anglers

sport·fish·er·man \'spōrt-ˌfish-ər-mən, 'spȯrt-\ *n* (1954) **:** a motorboat equipped for sportfishing

sport·fish·ing \-ˌfish-iŋ\ *n* (1946) **:** fishing done with a rod and reel for sport or recreation

sport·ful \-fəl\ *adj* (15c) **1 a :** productive of sport or amusement **:** ENTERTAINING, DIVERTING **b :** PLAYFUL, FROLICSOME **2 :** done in sport — **sport·ful·ly** \-fə-lē\ *adv* — **sport·ful·ness** *n*

sport·ing \'spōrt-iŋ, 'spȯrt-\ *adj* (1867) **1 a :** used or suitable for sport **b :** marked by or calling for sportsmanship **c :** involving such risk as a sports contender may expect to take or encounter ⟨a ~ chance⟩ **2 :** of or relating to dissipation and esp. gambling **3 :** tending to mutate freely — **sport·ing·ly** \-iŋ-lē\ *adv*

sporting house *n* (1891) **:** BROTHEL

sport·ive \-iv\ *adj* (1590) **1 a :** FROLICSOME, PLAYFUL **b :** ARDENT, WANTON **2 :** of or relating to sports and esp. field sports — **sport·ive·ly** *adv* — **sport·ive·ness** *n*

sports car *n* (1932) **:** a low small usu. 2-passenger automobile designed for quick response, easy maneuverability, and high-speed driving

sports·cast \'spō(ə)rt-ˌskast, 'spȯ(ə)rt-\ *n* [*sport* + broad*cast*] (1941) **:** a radio or television broadcast of a sports event or of information about sports — **sports·cast·er** \-ˌskas-tər\ *n*

sports·man \'spō(ə)rt-smən, 'spȯ(ə)rt-\ *n* (1706) **1 :** one who engages in sports and esp. in hunting and fishing **2 :** a person who is fair, generous, a good loser, and a gracious winner — **sports·man·like** \-ˌlīk\ *adj* — **sports·man·ly** \-lē\ *adj*

sports·man·ship \-ˌship\ *n* (1745) **:** conduct becoming to a sportsman

sports·wear \'spō(ə)rt-ˌswa(ə)r, 'spȯ(ə)rt-, -ˌswe(ə)r\ *n* (1912) **:** clothing suitable for recreation

sports·wom·an \-ˌswu̇m-ən\ *n* (1754) **:** a woman who engages in sports

sports·writ·er \'spō(ə)rts-ˌrīt-ər, 'spȯ(ə)rts-\ *n* (1901) **:** one who writes about sports esp. for a newspaper — **sports·writ·ing** \-iŋ\ *n*

sporty \'spōrt-ē, 'spȯrt-\ *adj* **sport·i·er; -est** (1889) **1 :** characteristic of a sport or sportsman : SPORTSMANLIKE **2 a :** notably loose or dissipated : FAST **b :** FLASHY, SHOWY ⟨~ clothes⟩ **3 :** capable of giving good sport ⟨a ~ boat⟩ **4 :** SPORT — **sport·i·ly** \'spōrt-^{ə}l-ē, 'spȯrt-\ *adv* — **sport·i·ness** \'spōrt-ē-nəs, 'spȯrt-\ *n*

spor·u·late \'spȯr-(y)ə-ˌlāt, 'spȯr-\ *vi* **-lat·ed; -lat·ing** [back-formation fr. *sporulation*] (ca. 1891) **:** to undergo sporulation

spor·u·la·tion \ˌspōr-(y)ə-'lā-shən, ˌspȯr-\ *n* [ISV, fr. NL *sporula*, dim. of *spora* spore] (1876) **:** the formation of spores; *esp* **:** division into many small spores (as after encystment) — **spor·u·la·tive** \'spōr-(y)ə-ˌlāt-iv, 'spȯr-\ *adj*

-spo·ry \ˌspōr-ē, ˌspȯr-; s-pə-rē\ *n comb form* [*-sporous* + *-y*] **:** quality or state of having (such) spores ⟨homo*spory*⟩

[1]**spot** \'spät\ *n* [ME; akin to MD *spotte* stain, speck, ON *spotti* small piece] (13c) **1 :** a taint on character or reputation : FAULT ⟨the only ~ on the family name⟩ **2 a :** a small area visibly different (as in color, finish, or material) from the surrounding area **b** (1) **:** an area marred or marked (as by dirt) (2) **:** a circumscribed surface lesion of disease (as measles) or decay ⟨~*s* of rot⟩ ⟨rust ~*s* on a leaf⟩ **c :** a conventionalized design used on playing cards to distinguish suits and indicate values **3 :** an object having a specified number of spots or a specified numeral on its surface **4 :** a small quantity or amount : BIT **5 a :** a particular place, area, or part **b :** a small extent of space **6** *pl usu* **spot :** a small croaker (*Leiostomus xanthurus*) of the Atlantic coast with a black spot behind the shoulders **7 a :** a particular position (as in an organization or a hierarchy) **b :** a place or appearance on an entertainment program **8 :** SPOTLIGHT **9 :** a position usu. of difficulty or embarrassment **10 :** a brief announcement or advertisement broadcast between scheduled radio or television programs **11 :** a brief segment or report on a broadcast esp. of news — **on the spot 1 :** at once : IMMEDIATELY **2 :** at the place of action **3 a :** in a responsible or accountable position **b :** in a difficult or trying situation

[2]**spot** *vb* **spot·ted; spot·ting** *vt* (15c) **1 :** to stain the character or reputation of : DISGRACE **2 :** to mark in or with a spot : STAIN **3 :** to locate or identify by a spot **4 a :** to single out : IDENTIFY; *esp* **:** to note as a known criminal or a suspicious person **b :** DETECT, NOTICE ⟨~ a mistake⟩ **c** (1) **:** to locate accurately ⟨~ an enemy position⟩ (2) **:** to cause to strike accurately ⟨~ the battery's fire⟩ **5 a :** to lie at intervals in or over : STUD **b :** to place at intervals or in a desired spot ⟨~ field telephones⟩ **c :** to fix in or as if in the beam of a spotlight **d :** to schedule in a particular spot or at a particular time **6 :** to remove a spot from **7 :** to allow as a handicap ~ *vi* **1 :** to become stained or discolored in spots **2 :** to cause a spot **3 :** to act as a spotter; *esp* **:** to locate targets — **spot·ta·ble** \'spät-ə-bəl\ *adj*

[3]**spot** *adj* (1881) **1 a :** being, originating, or done on the spot or in or for a particular spot ⟨~ coverage of the news⟩ **b :** available for immediate delivery after sale ⟨~ commodities⟩ **c** (1) **:** paid out upon delivery ⟨~ cash⟩ (2) **:** involving immediate cash payment ⟨~ transaction⟩ **d** (1) **:** broadcast between scheduled programs ⟨~ announcements⟩ (2) **:** originating in a local station for a national advertiser **e :** performing occasionally when needed ⟨chance of making the . . . varsity as a ~ starter and relief pitcher —*N.Y. Times*⟩ **2 :** made at random or restricted to a few places or instances ⟨a ~ check⟩; *also* **:** selected at random or as a sample

spot–check \'spät-ˌchek\ *vt* (1943) **:** to sample or investigate quickly or at random ~ *vi* **:** to make a spot check

spot·less \'spät-ləs\ *adj* (14c) **:** having no spot: **a :** free from impurity : IMMACULATE ⟨~ kitchens⟩ **b :** PURE, UNBLEMISHED ⟨~ reputation⟩ — **spot·less·ly** *adv* — **spot·less·ness** *n*

[1]**spot·light** \'spät-ˌlīt\ *n* (1912) **1 a :** a projected spot of light used to illuminate brilliantly a person, object, or group on a stage **b :** conspicuous public notice ⟨held the political ~⟩ **2 a :** a light designed to direct a narrow intense beam of light on a small area **b :** something that illuminates brilliantly

[2]**spotlight** *vt* **-light·ed** *or* **-lit; -light·ing** (1922) **:** to illuminate with or as if with a spotlight

spot pass *n* (ca. 1948) **:** a pass (as in football or basketball) made to a predetermined spot on the field or court rather than directly to a player

spot·ted \'spät-əd\ *adj* (13c) **1 :** marked with spots **2 :** being sullied : TARNISHED **3 :** characterized by the appearance of spots

spotted alfalfa aphid *n* (1958) **:** a highly destructive Old World aphid (*Therioaphis maculata*) that is established in the U.S. from coast to coast in warmer areas and that injects a toxic saliva in feeding esp. on alfalfa and causes yellowing and stunting of affected plants

spotted cucumber beetle *n* (1923) **:** a rather slender greenish yellow beetle (*Diabrotica undecimpunctata howardi*) that feeds as an adult on various ornamental and crop plants and is a vector of wilt disease esp. of cucumbers and melons

spotted fever *n* (1650) **:** any of various eruptive fevers: as **a :** TYPHUS **b :** ROCKY MOUNTAIN SPOTTED FEVER

spotted salamander *n* (ca. 1922) **:** a common No. American salamander (*Ambystoma maculatum*) with glossy black skin spotted with yellow or orange on the back

spotted sea trout *n* (ca. 1902) **:** a weakfish (*Cynoscion nebulosus*) that is a valuable food and sport fish of the southern Atlantic and Gulf coasts of the U.S. — called also *sea trout, speckled trout, spotted weakfish*

spot·ter \'spät-ər\ *n* (ca. 1611) **1 :** one that makes or applies a spot (as for identification) **2 :** one that looks or keeps watch: as **a :** one that locates enemy targets **b :** a civilian who watches for approaching airplanes **3 :** one that removes spots **4 :** one that places something on or in a desired spot

spot test *n* (ca. 1928) **1 :** a test conducted on the spot to yield immediate results **2 :** a test limited to a few key or sample points or a relatively small percentage of random spots

spot·ty \'spät-ē\ *adj* **spot·ti·er; -est** (14c) **1 :** marked with spots : SPOTTED **2 :** lacking uniformity esp. in quality ⟨the performance was ~⟩; *also* **:** irregularly or sparsely distributed ⟨~ attendance⟩ ⟨~ data⟩ — **spot·ti·ly** \'spät-^{ə}l-ē\ *adv* — **spot·ti·ness** \'spät-ē-nəs\ *n*

spou·sal \'spau̇-zəl, -səl\ *n* [ME *spousaille*, fr. MF *espousailles* espousal] (14c) **:** NUPTIALS — usu. used in pl.

[1]**spouse** \'spau̇s *also* 'spau̇z\ *n* [ME, fr. OF *espous* (masc.) & *espouse* (fem.), fr. L *sponsus* betrothed man, groom & *sponsa* betrothed woman, bride, both fr. *sponsus*, pp. of *spondēre* to promise, betroth; akin to Gk *spendein* to make a libation, promise, *spondē* libation (pl., treaty)] (13c) **:** married person : HUSBAND, WIFE — **spou·sal** \'spau̇-zəl, -səl\ *adj*

[2]**spouse** \'spau̇z, 'spau̇s\ *vt* **spoused; spous·ing** *archaic* (13c) **:** WED

[1]**spout** \'spau̇t\ *vb* [ME *spouten*; akin to MD *spoiten* to spout, OE *spīwan* to spew] *vt* (14c) **1 :** to eject (as liquid) in a stream ⟨wells ~*ing* oil⟩ **2 a :** to speak or utter readily, volubly, and at length **b :** to speak or utter in a pompous or oratorical manner : DECLAIM ~ *vi* **1 :** to issue with force or in a jet : SPURT **2 :** to eject material (as liquid) in a jet **3 :** DECLAIM — **spout·er** *n*

[2]**spout** *n* (14c) **1 :** a pipe or conductor through which a liquid is discharged or conveyed in a stream: as **a :** a pipe for carrying rainwater from a roof **b :** a projecting tube or lip from which water issues **2 :** a discharge or jet of liquid from or as if from a pipe; *esp* **:** WATERSPOUT **3** *archaic* **:** PAWNSHOP — **spout·ed** \'spau̇t-əd\ *adj*

sprach·ge·fühl \'shpräk-gə-ˌfu̅e̅l\ *n* [G, fr. *sprache* language (fr. OHG *sprāhha*; akin to OE *sprǣc* speech) + *gefühl* feeling — more at SPEECH] (1894) **1 :** sensibility to conformity with or divergence from the established usage of a language **2 :** a feeling for what is linguistically effective or appropriate

sprad·dle \'sprad-^{ə}l\ *vb* **sprad·dled; sprad·dling** \'sprad-liŋ -^{ə}l-iŋ\ [perh. irreg. fr. *straddle* and *sprawl* or *spread*] *vi* (1632) **1 :** SPRAWL **2 :** to go or walk with a straddling gait : STRADDLE ~ *vt* **1 :** SPRAWL **2 :** to spread (the legs) in walking : STRADDLE

sprag \'sprag\ *n* [perh. of Scand origin; akin to Sw dial. *spragge* branch] (1878) **:** a pointed stake or steel bar let down from a halted vehicle (as a wagon) to prevent it from rolling

[1]**sprain** \'sprān\ *n* [origin unknown] (1601) **1 :** a sudden or violent twist or wrench of a joint with stretching or tearing of ligaments **2 :** a sprained condition

[2]**sprain** *vt* (1622) **:** to injure by a sudden or severe twist

[1]**sprang** \'spraŋ\ *past of* SPRING

[2]**sprang** *n* [prob. fr. Norw, tatting, fr. ON, lace-weaving, fr. MD *sprank* ornament; akin to OE *spranca* twig and prob. to OE *springan* to spring] (1951) **:** a weaving technique in which threads or cords are intertwined and twisted over one another to form an openwork mesh

sprat \'sprat\ *n* [alter. of ME *sprot*, fr. OE *sprott*] (1597) **1 :** a small European herring (*Clupea sprattus*) closely related to the common herring; *also* **:** a small or young herring or similar fish (as an anchovy) **2 :** a young, small, or insignificant person

sprawl \'sprȯl\ *vb* [ME *sprawlen*, fr. OE *sprēawlian*; akin to OE *-sprūtan* to sprout — more at SPROUT] *vi* (bef. 12c) **1 a** *archaic* **:** to lie thrashing or tossing about **b :** to creep or clamber awkwardly **2 :** to lie or sit with arms and legs spread out **3 :** to spread or develop irregularly ~ *vt* **:** to cause to spread out carelessly or awkwardly — **sprawl** *n*

[1]**spray** \'sprā\ *n* [ME] (13c) **1 :** a usu. flowering branch or shoot **2 :** a decorative flat arrangement of flowers and foliage (as on a coffin) **3 :** something (as a jeweled pin) resembling a spray

[2]**spray** *n* [obs. E *spray* (to sprinkle), fr. MD *sprayen*; akin to Gk *speirein* to scatter — more at SPROUT] (1621) **1 :** water flying in small drops or particles blown from waves or thrown up by a waterfall **2 a :** a jet of vapor or finely divided liquid **b :** a device (as an atomizer or sprayer) by which a spray is dispersed or applied **c** (1) **:** an application of a

spray or by spraying (2) : a substance (as paint) so applied

3spray *vt* (1829) **1** : to disperse or apply as a spray **2** : to project spray on or into ~ *vi* **1** : to break up into spray **2** : to disperse or apply a spray — **spray·er** *n*

spray can *n* (1958) : a pressurized container from which aerosols are dispensed

spray gun *n* (1920) : an apparatus resembling a gun for applying a substance (as paint or insecticide) in the form of a spray

1spread \'spred\ *vb* **spread; spread·ing** [ME *spreden,* fr. OE *sprǣdan;* akin to OHG *spreiten* to spread, OE *-sprūtan* to sprout — more at SPROUT] *vt* (bef. 12c) **1 a** : to open or expand over a larger area ⟨~ out the map⟩ **b** : to stretch out : EXTEND ⟨~ its wings for flight⟩ **2 a** : to distribute over an area ⟨~ fertilizer⟩ **b** : to distribute over a period or among a group ⟨~ the work over a few weeks⟩ **c** : to apply on a surface ⟨~ butter on bread⟩ **d** (1) : to cover or overlay something with ⟨~ the cloth on the table⟩ (2) *archaic* : to cover completely **e** (1) : to prepare or furnish for dining : SET ⟨~ the table⟩ (2) : SERVE ⟨~ the afternoon tea⟩ **3 a** : to make widely known ⟨~ the news⟩ **b** : to extend the range or incidence of ⟨~ a disease⟩ **c** : DIFFUSE, EMIT ⟨flowers ~*ing* their fragrance⟩ **4** : to push apart by weight or force ~ *vi* **1 a** : to become dispersed, distributed, or scattered **b** : to become known or disseminated ⟨panic ~ rapidly⟩ **2** : to grow in length or breadth : EXPAND **3** : to move apart (as from pressure or weight) : SEPARATE — **spread·abil·i·ty** \ˌspred-ə-'bil-ət-ē\ *n* — **spread·able** \'spred-ə-bəl\ *adj*

2spread *n* (1626) **1 a** : the act or process of spreading **b** : extent of spreading **2** : something spread out: as **a** : a surface area : EXPANSE **b** *West* (1) : RANCH (2) : a herd of animals **c** (1) : a prominent display in a periodical (2) : two facing pages (as of a newspaper) usu. with matter running across the fold; *also* : the matter occupying these pages **3** : something spread on or over a surface: as **a** : a food to be spread (as on bread or crackers) ⟨a cheese ~⟩ **b** : a sumptuous meal : FEAST **c** : a cloth cover for a table or bed **4** : distance between two points : GAP **5** : a commodities market transaction in which a participant hedges with simultaneous long and short options in different commodities or different delivery dates in the same commodity

1spread–ea·gle \'spred-ˌē-gəl\ *vb* **–ea·gled; –ea·gling** \-ˌē-g(ə-)liŋ\ *vi* (1826) **1** : to execute a spread eagle (as in skating) **2** : to stand or move with arms and legs stretched out : SPRAWL ~ *vt* **1** : to stretch out into the position of a spread eagle **2** : to spread over

2spread–eagle *adj* [fr. the spread eagle on the Great Seal of the U.S.] (1858) : marked by bombast and boastful exaggeration esp. of the greatness of the U.S. ⟨~ oratory⟩

spread eagle *n* (1570) **1** : a representation of an eagle with wings raised and legs extended **2** : something resembling or suggestive of a spread eagle; *specif* : a skating figure executed with the skates heel to heel in a straight line

spread·er \'spred-ər\ *n* (15c) : one that spreads: as **a** : an implement for scattering material **b** : a small knife for spreading butter **c** : WETTING AGENT **d** : a device (as a bar) holding two linear elements (as lines, guys, rails) apart and usu. taut

spread formation *n* (ca. 1949) : an offensive football formation in which the ends are positioned three to five yards outside the tackles, the tailback plays seven to eight yards behind the line, and the other three backs are in flanking position close to the line

spreading factor *n* (1932) : HYALURONIDASE

spread·sheet \'spred-ˌshēt\ *n* [fr. *spreadsheet* outsize page used by accountants] (1982) : an accounting program for a computer; *also* : the ledger layout modeled by such a program

spree \'sprē\ *n* [perh. alter. of Sc *spreath* cattle raid, foray, fr. ScGael *sprēidh* cattle, fr. L *praeda* booty — more at PREY] (1804) : an unrestrained indulgence in or outburst of an activity ⟨went on a buying ~⟩; *esp* : BINGE, CAROUSAL

sprent \'sprent\ *adj* [fr. pp. of obs. *sprenge* (to sprinkle)] *archaic* (15c) : sprinkled over

sprier *comparative of* SPRY

spriest *superlative of* SPRY

1sprig \'sprig\ *n* [ME *sprigge*] (15c) **1 a** : a small shoot : TWIG **b** : a small division of grass used for propagation **2 a** : HEIR **b** : YOUTH **c** : a small specimen **3** : an ornament resembling a sprig, stemmed flower, or leaf **4** : a small headless nail : BRAD

2sprig *vt* **sprigged; sprig·ging** (1713) **1** : to drive sprigs or brads into **2** : to mark or adorn with the representation of plant sprigs **3** : to propagate (a grass) by means of stolons or small divisions

spright·ful \'sprīt-fəl\ *adj* [obs. *spright*] (1595) : full of life or spirit : SPRIGHTLY — **spright·ful·ly** \-fə-lē\ *adv* — **spright·ful·ness** *n*

spright·ly \-lē\ *adj* **spright·li·er; -est** [obs. *spright* (sprite), alter. of *sprite*] (1596) : marked by a gay lightness and vivacity : SPIRITED *syn* see LIVELY — **spright·li·ness** *n* — **sprightly** *adv*

1spring \'spriŋ\ *vb* **sprang** \'spraŋ\ *or* **sprung** \'sprəŋ\; **sprung; spring·ing** \'spriŋ-iŋ\ [ME *springen,* fr. OE *springan;* akin to OHG *springan* to jump, Gk *sperchesthai* to hasten] *vi* (bef. 12c) **1 a** (1) : DART, SHOOT (2) : to be resilient or elastic; *also* : to move by elastic force ⟨the lid *sprang* shut⟩ **b** : to become warped **2** : to issue with speed and force or as a stream **3 a** : to grow as a plant **b** : to issue by birth or descent **c** : to come into being : ARISE **d** *archaic* : DAWN **e** : to begin to blow — used with *up* ⟨a breeze quickly *sprang* up⟩ **4 a** : to make a leap or series of leaps **b** : to leap or jump up suddenly **5** : to stretch out in height : RISE **6** : PAY — used with *for* ⟨I'll ~ for the drinks⟩ ~ *vt* **1** : to cause to spring **2 a** : to undergo or bring about the splitting or cracking of ⟨wind *sprang* the mast⟩ **b** : to undergo the opening of (a leak) **3 a** : to cause to operate suddenly ⟨~ a trap⟩ **b** : to apply or insert by bending **c** : to bend by force **4** : to leap over **5** : to produce or disclose suddenly or unexpectedly **6** : to make lame **7** : to release or cause to be released from confinement or custody

syn SPRING, ARISE, RISE, ORIGINATE, DERIVE, FLOW, ISSUE, EMANATE, PROCEED, STEM mean to come up or out of something into existence. SPRING implies rapid or sudden emerging; ARISE and RISE may both convey the fact of coming into existence or notice but RISE often stresses gradual growth or ascent; ORIGINATE implies a definite source or starting point; DERIVE implies a prior existence in another form; FLOW adds to SPRING a suggestion of abundance or ease of inception; ISSUE suggests emerging from confinement through an outlet; EMANATE applies to the coming of something immaterial (as a thought) from a source; PROCEED stresses place of origin, derivation, parentage, or logical cause; STEM implies originating by dividing or branching off from something as an outgrowth or subordinate development.

2spring *n, often attrib* (bef. 12c) **1 a** : a source of supply; *esp* : a source of water issuing from the ground **b** : an ultimate source esp. of action or motion **2** : SPRING TIDE **3** : a time or season of growth or development; *specif* : the season between winter and summer comprising in the northern hemisphere usu. the months of March, April, and May or as reckoned astronomically extending from the March equinox to the June solstice **4** : an elastic body or device that recovers its original shape when released after being distorted **5 a** : the act or an instance of leaping up or forward : BOUND **b** (1) : capacity for springing : RESILIENCE (2) : ENERGY, BOUNCE **6** : the point or plane at which an arch or vault curve springs from its impost

3spring *vt* **sprung** \'sprəŋ\; **spring·ing** \'spriŋ-iŋ\ (1884) : to fit with springs

spring·ald \'spriŋ-əld\ *or* **spring·al** \-əl\ *n* [prob. fr. ME, a kind of catapult, fr. MF *espringale*] (15c) : a young man : STRIPLING

spring beauty *n* (1821) : any of a genus (*Claytonia*) of plants of the purslane family; *esp* : one (*C. virginica*) that sends up in early spring a 2-leaved stem bearing delicate pink flowers

spring·board \'spriŋ-ˌbō(ə)rd, -ˌbȯ(ə)rd\ *n* (1799) **1** : a flexible board usu. secured at one end and used for gymnastic stunts or diving **2** : a point of departure : JUMPING-OFF PLACE

spring·bok \'spriŋ-ˌbäk\ *n, pl* **springbok** *or* **springboks** [Afrik, fr. *spring* to jump (akin to OE *springan*) + *bok* male goat, fr. MD; akin to OHG *boc* he-goat — more at BUCK] (1775) : a swift and graceful southern African gazelle (*Antidorcas euchore*) noted for its habit of springing lightly and suddenly into the air

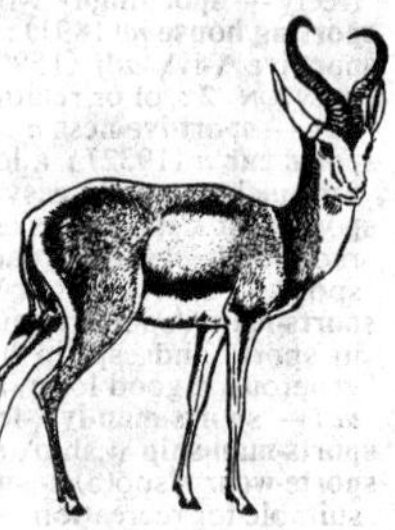

springbok

spring bolt *n* (1634) : a bolt retracted by pressure and shot by a spring when the pressure is released

spring chicken *n* (1879) : a young person

spring–clean·ing \'spriŋ-'klē-niŋ\ *n* [*2spring*] (1857) : the act or process of doing a thorough cleaning of a place

springe \'sprinj\ *n* [ME *sprenge, springe;* akin to OE *springan* to spring] (13c) **1** : a noose fastened to an elastic body to catch small game **2** : SNARE, TRAP

spring·er \'spriŋ-ər\ *n* (1611) **1** : a stone or other solid laid at the impost of an arch — see ARCH illustration **2** : one that springs; *esp* : SPRINGER SPANIEL **3** : a cow nearly ready to calve

springer spaniel *n* (1885) : a medium-sized sporting dog of either of two breeds that is used chiefly for finding and flushing small game: **a** : ENGLISH SPRINGER SPANIEL **b** : WELSH SPRINGER SPANIEL

spring fever *n* (1843) : a lazy or restless feeling often associated with the onset of spring

Spring·field rifle \ˌspriŋ-ˌfēl(d)-\ *n* [*Springfield,* Mass.] (1888) : a .30 caliber bolt-action rifle used by U.S. troops esp. in World War I

spring·form pan \'spriŋ-ˌfȯrm-\ *n* [fr. the spring by which the rim is attached to the bottom] (1927) : a pan or mold with an upright detachable rim fastened to the bottom of the pan with a clamp or spring

spring·head \'spriŋ-ˌhed\ *n* (1561) : FOUNTAINHEAD

spring·house \-ˌhau̇s\ *n* (1755) : a small building situated over a spring and used for cool storage (as of dairy products or meat)

spring·ing \'spriŋ-iŋ\ *n* (1590) **1** : SPRING 5 **2** : a point where an arch rises from its support

springing bow *n* (ca. 1903) : a method of bowing a stringed instrument so that the bow rebounds from the string

spring–load \'spriŋ-'lōd\ *vt* (1944) : to load or secure by means of spring tension or compression

spring peeper *n* (1906) : a small brown tree toad (*Hyla crucifer*) of the eastern U.S. and Canada that has a shrill piping call and breeds in ponds and streams in the spring

spring·tail \'spriŋ-ˌtāl\ *n* (ca. 1797) : COLLEMBOLAN

spring·tide \-ˌtīd\ *n* (1530) : SPRINGTIME

spring tide *n* (1548) : a tide of greater-than-average range around the times of new and full moon

spring·time \'spriŋ-ˌtīm\ *n* (15c) **1** : the season of spring **2** : YOUTH **3** : an early or flourishing stage of development

spring wagon *n* (1794) : a light farm wagon equipped with springs

spring·wa·ter \'spriŋ-ˌwȯt-ər, -ˌwät-\ *n* (15c) : water from a spring

spring·wood \-ˌwu̇d\ *n* (1884) : the softer more porous portion of an annual ring of wood that develops early in the growing season — compare SUMMERWOOD

springy \'spriŋ-ē\ *adj* **spring·i·er; -est** (1641) **1** : having an elastic quality : RESILIENT **2** : having or showing a lively and energetic movement ⟨walks with a ~ step⟩ *syn* see ELASTIC — **spring·i·ly** \'spriŋ-ə-lē\ *adv* — **spring·i·ness** \'spriŋ-ē-nəs\ *n*

1sprin·kle \'spriŋ-kəl\ *vb* **sprin·kled; sprin·kling** \-k(ə-)liŋ\ [ME *sprenklen, sprinclen;* akin to MHG *spreckel, sprenkel* spot, OE *spearca* spark] *vt* (15c) **1** : to scatter in drops or particles **2 a** : to scatter over **b** : to scatter at intervals in or among : DOT **c** : to wet lightly ~ *vi* **1** : to scatter a liquid in fine drops **2** : to rain lightly in scattered drops — **sprin·kler** \-k(ə-)lər\ *n*

2sprinkle *n* (1641) **1** : the act or an instance of sprinkling; *esp* : a light rain **2** : SPRINKLING **3** *pl* : small particles of candy used as a topping (as on ice cream) : JIMMIES

sprin·klered \'spriŋ-klərd\ *adj* (1927) : having a sprinkler system

sprinkler system *n* (ca. 1909) : a system for protecting a building against fire by means of overhead pipes which convey an extinguishing fluid (as water) to heat-activated outlets

sprin·kling \'spriŋ-kliŋ\ *n* (1594) **1** : a limited quantity or amount : MODICUM **2** : a small quantity falling in scattered drops or particles **3** : a small number distributed at random : SCATTERING

1sprint \'sprint\ *vi* [of Scand origin; akin to Sw dial. *sprinta* to jump, hop; akin to OHG *sprinzan* to jump up and perh. to Gk *spyrthizein*] (ca. 1864) : to run at top speed esp. for a short distance — **sprint·er** *n*

²**sprint** n (ca. 1865) **1 :** the act or an instance of sprinting **2 a :** DASH **6 b :** a burst of speed

sprit \'sprit\ n [ME *spret, sprit,* fr. OE *sprēot* pole, spear; akin to OE *-sprūtan* to sprout] (14c) **:** a spar that crosses a fore-and-aft sail diagonally

sprite \'sprit\ n [ME *sprit,* fr. MF *esprit,* fr. L *spiritus* spirit — more at SPIRIT] (14c) **1 a** *archaic* **:** SOUL **b :** a disembodied spirit **:** GHOST **2 a :** ELF, FAIRY **b :** an elfish person

sprit·sail \'sprit-ˌsāl, -səl\ n (15c.) **:** a sail extended by a sprit

spritz \'s(h)prits\ vi (1902) **:** SPRAY ~ vi **:** to disperse or apply a spray

spritz·er \'s(h)prit-sər\ n [G, fr. *spritzen* to squirt, spray] (1945) **:** a beverage of usu. white wine and soda water

sprock·et \'spräk-ət\ n [origin unknown] (1750) **1 :** a tooth or projection (as on a wheel) shaped so as to engage with a chain **2 :** a toothed cylinder or wheel that engages the perforations of something (as motion-picture film) to move it through a mechanism (as a projector)

sprocket wheel n (1769) **:** a wheel with cogs or sprockets to engage the links of a chain

¹**sprout** \'spraut\ vb [ME *sprouten,* fr. OE *-sprūtan;* akin to OHG *spriozan* to sprout, Gk *speirein* to scatter, sow] vi (13c) **1 :** to grow, spring up, or come forth as or as if a sprout **2 :** to send out new growth ~ vt **:** to send forth or up **:** cause to develop **:** GROW

²**sprout** n (14c) **1 a :** SHOOT 1a; *esp* **:** a young shoot (as from a seed or root) **b** *pl* (1) **:** edible shoots esp. of a crucifer (2) **:** a plant (as brussels sprouts) producing sprouts **2 :** something resembling a sprout: as **a :** a young person **b :** SCION

sprouting broccoli n (1852) **:** BROCCOLI 2

¹**spruce** \'sprüs\ vb **spruced; spruc·ing** vt (1594) **:** to make spruce — often used with *up* ~ vi **:** to make oneself spruce ⟨~ up a bit⟩

²**spruce** adj **spruc·er; spruc·est** [perh. fr. obs. E *Spruce leather* leather imported from Prussia] (1599) **:** neat or smart in appearance **:** TRIM — **spruce·ly** adv — **spruce·ness** n

³**spruce** n [obs. *Spruce* Prussia, fr. ME, alter. of *Pruce,* fr. OF] (1670) **1 a :** any of a genus (*Picea*) of evergreen trees of the pine family with a conical head of dense foliage and soft light wood **b :** any of several coniferous trees (as Douglas fir) of similar habit **2 :** the wood of a spruce

spruce beer n (1500) **:** a beverage flavored with spruce; *esp* **:** one made from spruce twigs and leaves boiled with molasses or sugar and fermented with yeast

spruce budworm n (1884) **:** a tortricid moth (*Choristoneura fumiferana*) whose larva feeds on evergreen trees (as spruce and balsam fir) in the northern U.S. and Canada

spruce pine n (1684) **:** an American tree (as some pines and spruces or the common eastern hemlock) of the pine family with light, soft, or weak wood

sprucy \'sprü-sē\ adj **spruc·i·er; -est** (1774) **:** SPRUCE

¹**sprue** \'sprü\ n [origin unknown] (1880) **1 :** the hole through which metal or plastic is poured into the gate and thence into a mold **2 :** the waste piece cast in a sprue

²**sprue** n [D *spruw;* akin to MLG *sprūwe,* a kind of tumor] (1888) **:** a chronic disease marked esp. by fatty diarrhea and deficiency symptoms

sprung past and past part of SPRING

sprung rhythm n (1877) **:** a poetic rhythm designed to approximate the natural rhythm of speech and characterized by the frequent juxtaposition of single accented syllables and the occurrence of mixed types of feet

spry \'sprī\ adj **spri·er** or **spry·er** \'sprī(-ə)r\; **spri·est** or **spry·est** \'sprī-əst\ [perh. of Scand origin; akin to Sw dial. *sprygg* spry] (1746) **:** NIMBLE 1 ⟨a ~ 75-year-old woman⟩ — **spry·ly** adv — **spry·ness** n

¹**spud** \'spəd\ vb **spud·ded; spud·ding** vt (1652) **1 :** to dig with a spud **2 :** to begin to drill (an oil well) ~ vi **:** to use a spud

²**spud** n [ME *spudde* dagger] (1667) **1 :** a tool or device (as for digging, lifting, or cutting) having the characteristics of a spade and a chisel **2 :** POTATO

¹**spume** \'spyüm\ n [ME, fr. MF, fr. L *spuma* — more at FOAM] (14c) **:** frothy matter on liquids **:** FOAM, SCUM — **spu·mous** \'spyü-məs\ adj — **spumy** \-mē\ adj

²**spume** vi **spumed; spum·ing** (14c) **:** FROTH, FOAM

spu·mo·ni or **spu·mo·ne** \spü-'mō-nē\ n [It *spumone,* aug. of *spuma* foam, fr. L] (1924) **:** ice cream in layers of different colors, flavors, and textures often with candied fruits and nuts

spun past and past part of SPIN

spun-bond·ed \'spən-ˌbän-dəd\ adj (1961) **:** of or relating to a nonwoven polymeric material that resembles cloth or fabric

spun glass n (1779) **1 :** blown glass that has slender threads of glass incorporated in it **2 :** FIBERGLASS

¹**spunk** \'spəŋk\ n [ScGael *spong* sponge, tinder, fr. L *spongia* sponge] (1665) **1 a :** a woody tinder **:** PUNK **b :** any of various fungi used to make tinder **2 :** METTLE, PLUCK **3 :** SPIRIT, LIVELINESS

²**spunk** vi, dial (1840) **:** to show spirit — usu. used with *up*

spunk·ie \'spəŋ-kē\ n, Scot (1727) **:** IGNIS FATUUS

spunky \'spəŋ-kē\ adj **spunk·i·er; -est** (1786) **:** full of spunk **:** SPIRITED — **spunk·i·ly** \-kə-lē\ adv — **spunk·i·ness** \-kē-nəs\ n

spun rayon n (1926) **:** a rayon-staple yarn or fabric

spun sugar n (1846) **:** sugar boiled to long threads and gathered up and shaped or heaped on a stick as a candy

spun yarn n (1860) **1 :** a textile yarn spun from staple-length fiber **2 :** a small rope or stuff formed of two or more rope yarns loosely twisted and used for seizings esp. on board ship

¹**spur** \'spər\ n [ME *spure,* fr. OE *spura;* akin to OE *spurnan* to kick — more at SPURN] (bef. 12c) **1 a :** a pointed device secured to a rider's heel and used to urge on the horse **b** *pl* [fr. the acquisition of spurs by a person achieving knighthood] **:** recognition and reward for achievement ⟨won his academic ~s as the holder of a chair in a university — James Mountford⟩ **2 :** a goad to action **:** STIMULUS **3 :** something projecting like or suggesting a spur: as **a :** a projecting root or branch of a tree **b** (1) **:** a stiff sharp spine (as on the wings or legs of a bird or insect); *esp* **:** one on a cock's leg — see COCK illustration (2) **:** a gaff for a gamecock **c :** a hollow projecting appendage of a corolla or calyx (as in larkspur or columbine) **d :** CLIMBING IRON **4 :** an angular projection, offshoot, or branch extending out beyond or away from a main body or formation; *esp* **:** a ridge or lesser elevation that extends laterally from a mountain or mountain range **5 :** a short wooden brace of a post **6 :** a reinforcing buttress of masonry in a fortification **syn** see MOTIVE — **on the spur of the moment :** on impulse **:** SUDDENLY

²**spur** vb **spurred; spur·ring** vt (13c) **1 :** to urge (a horse) on with spurs **2 :** to incite to action or accelerated growth or development **:** STIMULATE **3 :** to put spurs on ~ vi **:** to spur one's horse on

spurge \'spərj\ n [ME, fr. MF, purge, spurge, fr. *espurgier* to purge, fr. L *expurgare* — more at EXPURGATE] (14c) **:** any of various mostly shrubby plants (family Euphorbiaceae, the spurge family, and esp. genus *Euphorbia*) with a bitter milky juice

spur gear n (1823) **:** a gear wheel with radial teeth parallel to its axis — called also *spur wheel*

spurge laurel n (1597) **:** a low Eurasian shrub (*Daphne laureola*) with oblong evergreen leaves and axillary racemes of yellowish flowers

spu·ri·ous \'spyùr-ē-əs\ adj [LL & L; LL *spurius* false, fr. L, of illegitimate birth, fr. *spurius,* n., bastard] (1598) **1 :** of illegitimate birth **:** BASTARD **2 a :** outwardly similar or corresponding to something without having its genuine qualities **:** FALSE **b :** superficially like but morphologically unlike ⟨a ~ fruit⟩ **3 a :** of falsified or erroneously attributed origin **:** FORGED **b :** of a deceitful nature or quality — **spu·ri·ous·ly** adv — **spu·ri·ous·ness** n

¹**spurn** \'spərn\ vb [ME *spurnen,* fr. OE *spurnan;* akin to OHG *spurnan* to kick, L *spernere* to spurn, Gk *spairein* to quiver] vi (bef. 12c) **1 a :** STUMBLE **b :** KICK **2** *archaic* **:** to reject something disdainfully ~ vt **1 :** to tread sharply or heavily upon **:** TRAMPLE **2 :** to reject with disdain or contempt **:** SCORN **syn** see DECLINE — **spurn·er** n

²**spurn** n (14c) **1 a :** KICK **b** *obs* **:** STUMBLE **2 a :** disdainful rejection **b :** contemptuous treatment

spur-of-the-moment adj (1806) **:** occurring or developing without premeditation **:** hastily extemporized ⟨a ~ decision⟩

spurred \'spərd\ adj (15c) **1 :** wearing spurs **2 :** having one or more spurs ⟨a ~ violet⟩

spur·rey or **spur·ry** \'spər-ē, 'spə-rē\ n, pl **spurreys** or **spurries** [D *spurrie,* fr. ML *spergula*] (1577) **:** a small white-flowered European weed (*Spergula arvensis*) of the pink family with whorled filiform leaves; *also* **:** any of several related and similar herbs

¹**spurt** \'spərt\ vb [perh. akin to MHG *spürzen* to spit, OE *-sprūtan* to sprout — more at SPROUT] vi (1570) **:** to gush forth **:** SPOUT ~ vt **:** to expel in a stream or jet **:** SQUIRT

²**spurt** n (ca. 1775) **:** a sudden gush **:** JET

³**spurt** n [origin unknown] (1591) **1 :** a short period of time **:** MOMENT **2 a :** a sudden brief burst of effort or activity **:** a sharp or sudden increase in business activity

⁴**spurt** vi (1664) **:** to make a spurt

spur·tle \'spərt-ᵊl\ n [origin unknown] *chiefly Scot* (1572) **:** a wooden stick for stirring porridge

spur track n (1884) **:** a track that diverges from a main line **:** SIDING

sput·nik \'spüt-nik, 'spət-, 'spüt-\ n [Russ, lit., traveling companion, fr. *s, so* with ⟨akin to Gk *hama* together⟩ + *put'* path ⟨akin to Skt *patha* way⟩ — more at SAME, FIND] (1957) **:** SATELLITE 2b

¹**sput·ter** \'spət-ər\ vb [akin to D *sputteren* to sputter, OE *-sprūtan* to sprout] vt (1598) **1 :** to spit or squirt from the mouth with explosive sounds **2 :** to utter hastily or explosively in confusion or excitement **3 :** to dislodge (atoms) from the surface of a material by collision with high energy particles; *also* **:** to deposit (a metallic film) by such a process ~ vi **1 :** to spit or squirt particles of food or saliva noisily from the mouth **2 :** to speak explosively or confusedly in anger or excitement **3 :** to make explosive popping sounds — **sput·ter·er** n

²**sputter** n (1673) **1 :** confused and excited speech or discussion **2 :** the act or sound of sputtering

spu·tum \'sp(y)üt-əm\ n, pl **spu·ta** \-ə\ [L, fr. neut. of *sputus,* pp. of *spuere* to spit — more at SPEW] (ca. 1693) **:** expectorated matter made up of saliva and often discharges from the respiratory passages

¹**spy** \'spī\ vb **spied; spy·ing** [ME *spien,* fr. OF *espier* fr. of Gmc origin; akin to OHG *spehōn* to spy; akin to L *specere* to look, look at, *species* appearance, species, Gk *skeptesthai* & *skopein* to watch, look at, consider] vt (13c) **1 :** to watch secretly usu. for hostile purposes **2 :** to catch sight of **:** SEE **3 :** to search or look for intensively ~ vi **1 :** to observe or search for something **:** LOOK **2 :** to watch secretly as a spy

²**spy** n, pl **spies** (13c) **1 :** one that spies: **a :** one who keeps secret watch on a person or thing to obtain information **b :** one who acts in a clandestine manner or on false pretenses to obtain information in the zone of operations of a belligerent with the intention of communicating it to the hostile party **2 :** an act of spying

spy·glass \'spī-ˌglas\ n (1706) **:** a small telescope

squab \'skwäb\ n, pl **squabs** [prob. of Scand origin; akin to Sw dial. *skvabb* anything soft and thick] (1682) **1** or *pl* **squab :** a fledgling bird; *specif* **:** a fledgling pigeon about four weeks old **2 :** a short fat person **3 a :** COUCH **b :** a cushion for a chair or couch — **squab** adj

¹**squab·ble** \'skwäb-əl\ n [prob. of Scand origin; akin to Sw dial. *skvabbel* dispute] (1602) **:** a noisy altercation or quarrel usu. over trifles

²**squabble** vi **squab·bled; squab·bling** \-(ə-)liŋ\ (1604) **:** to quarrel noisily and to no purpose **:** WRANGLE — **squab·bler** \-(ə-)lər\ n

¹**squad** \'skwäd\ n [MF *esquade,* fr. OSp & OIt; OSp *escuadra* & OIt *squadra* derivs. of (assumed) VL *exquadrare* to make square — more at SQUARE] (1649) **1 :** a small organized group of military personnel; *esp* **:** a tactical unit that can be easily directed in the field **2 :** a small group engaged in a common effort or occupation

²**squad** vt **squad·ded; squad·ding** (ca. 1802) **:** to arrange in squads

squad car n (ca. 1939) **:** a police automobile connected by a two-way radio with headquarters — called also *cruiser, prowl car*

squad·ron \'skwäd-rən\ n [It *squadrone,* aug. of *squadra* squad, fr. OIt] (1562) **:** a unit of military organization: **a :** a cavalry unit higher than a troop and lower than a regiment **b :** a naval unit consisting of two or more divisions and sometimes additional vessels **c** (1) **:** a unit of the U.S. Air Force higher than a flight and lower than a group (2) **:** a military flight formation

\ə\ abut \ᵊ\ kitten, F table \ər\ further \a\ ash \ā\ ace \ä\ cot, cart \aù\ out \ch\ chin \e\ bet \ē\ easy \g\ go \i\ hit \ī\ ice \j\ job \ŋ\ sing \ō\ go \ò\ law \òi\ boy \th\ thin \t͟h\ the \ü\ loot \ù\ foot \y\ yet \zh\ vision \a, k, ⁿ, œ, œ̄, ᵫ, ᵫ̄, �\ see Guide to Pronunciation

squadron leader *n* (1919) **:** a commissioned officer in the British air force who ranks with a major in the army
squad room *n* (1943) **1 :** a room in a barracks used to billet soldiers **2 :** a room in a police station where members of the force assemble
squa·lene \'skwā-,lēn\ *n* [ISV, fr. L *squalus,* a sea fish — more at WHALE] (1916) **:** an acyclic hydrocarbon $C_{30}H_{50}$ that is widely distributed in nature (as a major component of sebum and in shark-liver oils) and is a precursor of sterols (as cholesterol)
squal·id \'skwäl-əd\ *adj* [L *squalidus* — more at SQUALOR] (1596) **1 :** marked by filthiness and degradation from neglect or poverty **2 :** SORDID *syn* see DIRTY — **squal·id·ly** *adv* — **squal·id·ness** *n*
[1]**squall** \'skwȯl\ *vb* [prob. of Scand origin; akin to ON *skval* useless chatter] *vi* (1631) **:** to cry out raucously **:** SCREAM ~ *vt* **:** to utter in a strident voice — **squall·er** *n*
[2]**squall** *n* (1709) **:** a raucous cry
[3]**squall** *n* [prob. of Scand origin; akin to Sw *skval* rushing water] (ca. 1699) **1 :** a sudden violent wind often with rain or snow **2 :** a short-lived commotion
[4]**squall** *vi* (ca. 1891) **:** to blow a squall
squally \'skwȯ-lē\ *adj* **squall·i·er; -est** (1719) **1 :** marked by squalls **2 :** GUSTY
squa·lor \'skwäl-ər *also* 'skwāl- *or* 'skwȯl-\ *n* [L; akin to L *squalidus* squalid] (1621) **:** the quality or state of being squalid
squam- *or* **squamo-** *comb form* [NL, fr. L *squama*] **:** scale **:** squama ⟨*squam*ation⟩
squa·ma \'skwā-mə, 'skwä-\ *n, pl* **squa·mae** \'skwā-,mē, 'skwä-,mī\ [L] (1706) **:** SCALE; *also* **:** a structure resembling a scale
squa·mate \-,māt\ *adj* (1826) **:** SCALY ⟨~ reptiles⟩
squa·ma·tion \skwə-'mā-shən\ *n* (1881) **1 :** the state of being scaly **2 :** the arrangement of scales on an animal
[1]**squa·mo·sal** \skwə-'mō-səl, -zəl\ *n* (1848) **:** a squamosal bone
[2]**squamosal** *adj* (1849) **1 :** SQUAMOUS **2 :** of, relating to, or being a membrane bone of the skull of many vertebrates corresponding to the squamous portion of the temporal bone of man
squa·mous \'skwā-məs *also* 'skwä-\ *adj* [L *squamosus,* fr. *squama* scale] (1541) **1 a :** covered with or consisting of scales **:** SCALY **b :** of, relating to, or being a stratified epithelium that consists at least in its outer layers of small scalelike cells **2 :** of, relating to, or being the anterior upper portion of the temporal bone of various mammals (as man)
squamous cell *n* (ca. 1947) **:** a cell of or derived from squamous epithelium
squa·mu·lose \'skwā-myə-,lōs, 'skwä-\ *adj* [L *squamula,* dim. of *squama*] (1846) **:** being or having a thallus made up of small leafy lobes
[1]**squan·der** \'skwän-dər\ *vb* **squan·dered; squan·der·ing** \-d(ə-)riŋ\ [origin unknown] *vt* (1596) **1 :** to cause to disperse **:** SCATTER **2 :** to spend extravagantly or foolishly **:** DISSIPATE ~ *vi* **:** DISPERSE, SCATTER — **squan·der·er** \-dər-ər\ *n*
[2]**squander** *n* (1709) **:** an act of squandering
[1]**square** \'skwa(ə)r, 'skwe(ə)r\ *n* [ME, fr. MF *esquarre,* fr. (assumed) VL *exquadra,* fr. *exquadrare* to square, fr. L *ex-* + *quadrare* to square — more at QUADRATE] (14c) **1 :** an instrument having at least one right angle and two straight edges used to lay out or test right angles **2 :** a rectangle with all four sides equal **3 :** any of the quadrilateral spaces marked out on a board for playing games **4 :** the product of a number multiplied by itself **5 a :** an open place or area formed at the meeting of two or more streets **b :** BLOCK 6c **6 :** a solid object or piece approximating a cube or having a square as its largest face **7 :** an unopened cotton flower with its enclosing bracts **8 :** a person who is overly conventional or conservative in taste or way of life — **on the square 1 :** at right angles **2 :** in a fair open manner **:** HONESTLY — **out of square :** not at an exact right angle
[2]**square** *adj* **squar·er; squar·est** (14c) **1 a :** having four equal sides and four right angles **b :** forming a right angle ⟨~ corner⟩ **c :** having a square base ⟨a ~ pyramid⟩ **2 :** raised to the second power **3 a :** being approximately a cube ⟨~ cabinet⟩ **b :** having a shape that is broad for the height and a rectangular rather than a curving outline ⟨~ shoulders⟩ ⟨a ~, thick, hard-working man —Maria Edgeworth⟩ **c :** rectangular and equilateral in section ⟨~ tower⟩ **4 a :** being or converted to a unit of area equal in measure to a square each side of which measures one unit of a specified unit of length ⟨a ~ foot⟩ — see METRIC SYSTEM table, WEIGHT table **b :** being of a specified length in each of two equal dimensions ⟨10 feet ~⟩ **5 a :** exactly adjusted **:** precisely constructed or aligned **b :** JUST, FAIR ⟨~ in all his dealings⟩ **c :** leaving no balance **:** SETTLED **d :** EVEN, TIED **e :** SUBSTANTIAL, SATISFYING ⟨~ meal⟩ **f :** being unsophisticated, conservative, or conventional **6 :** set at right angles with the mast and keel — used of the yards of a square-rigged ship — **square·ness** *n*
[3]**square** *vb* **squared; squar·ing** *vt* (14c) **1 a :** to make square or rectangular ⟨~ a building stone⟩ **b :** to test for deviation from a right angle, straight line, or plane surface **2 :** to bring approximately to a right angle ⟨*squared* his shoulders⟩ **3 a :** to multiply (a number) by itself **:** raise to the second power **b :** to find a square equal in area to ⟨~ a circle⟩ **4 :** to regulate or adjust by or to some standard or principle ⟨~ our actions by the opinions of others —John Milton⟩ **5 a :** BALANCE, SETTLE ⟨~ an account⟩ **b :** to even the score of **6 :** to mark off into squares **7 a :** to set right **:** bring into agreement **b :** BRIBE, FIX ~ *vi* **1 :** to agree with exactness **:** match precisely **2 :** to settle matters; *esp* **:** to pay the bill **3 :** to take a fighting stance — **squar·er** *n*
[4]**square** *adv* (1577) **1 :** in a straightforward or honest manner **2 a :** so as to face or be face to face **b :** at right angles **3 :** with nothing intervening **:** DIRECTLY ⟨ran ~ into him⟩ **4 :** in a firm manner ⟨looked him ~ in the eye⟩ **5 :** in a square shape
square away *vi* (1894) **1 :** to square the yards so as to sail before the wind **2 :** to put everything in order or in readiness **3 :** to take up a fighting stance ~ *vt* **:** to put in order or in readiness
square bracket *n* (ca. 1888) **:** BRACKET 3a
square dance *n* (1870) **:** a dance for four couples who form a hollow square — **square dancer** *n* — **square dancing** *n*
square deal *n* (1876) **:** an honest and fair transaction or trade
square knot *n* (ca. 1867) **:** a knot made of two reverse half-knots and typically used to join the ends of two cords — see KNOT illustration
square·ly \'skwa(ə)r-lē, 'skwe(ə)r-\ *adv* (1564) **1 :** in a straightforward or honest manner ⟨we must ~ face the issue⟩ **2 a :** EXACTLY, PRECISELY ⟨~ in the middle⟩ **b :** so as to make solid contact ⟨hit the ball ~⟩ ⟨feet ~ planted⟩ **3 :** in a square form or manner **:** so as to be square ⟨a ~ cut dress⟩ **4 :** in a plain or unequivocal manner ⟨the responsibility lies ~ with us⟩ ⟨a ~ commercial hotel⟩ ⟨align ourselves ~ with our allies⟩
square matrix *n* (ca. 1934) **:** a mathematical matrix with the same number of rows and columns
square measure *n* (1728) **:** a unit or system of units for measuring area — see METRIC SYSTEM table, WEIGHT table
square of opposition (ca. 1909) **:** a square figure on which may be demonstrated the logical relationships of contraries, contradictories, subcontraries, and subalterns and superalterns
square one *n* [fr. the use of numbered squares in some board games] (1960) **:** the initial stage or starting point
square rig *n* (ca. 1875) **:** a sailing-ship rig in which the principal sails are extended on yards fastened to the masts horizontally and at their center
square–rigged \'skwa(ə)r-'rigd, 'skwe(ə)r-\ *adj* (1769) **:** having or equipped with a square rig
square–rig·ger \-'rig-ər\ *n* (1855) **:** a square-rigged craft

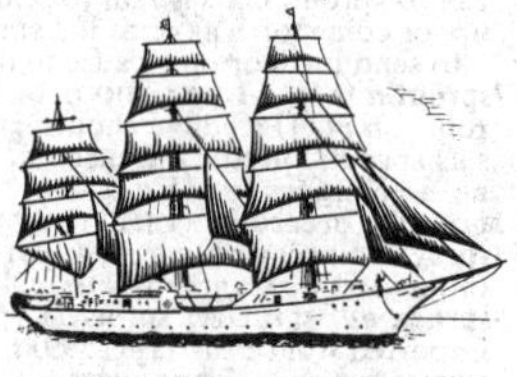
square-rigger

square root *n* (1557) **:** a factor of a number that when squared gives the number ⟨the *square root* of 9 is ± 3⟩
square sail \'skwa(ə)r-,sāl, 'skwe(ə)r-səl\ *n* (1600) **:** a 4-sided sail extended on a yard suspended at the middle from a mast
square shooter *n* (ca. 1914) **:** a just or honest person
square–shoul·dered \'skwa(ə)r-'shōl-dərd, 'skwe(ə)r-\ *adj* (1825) **:** having shoulders of a rectangular outline that are straight across the back
square–toed \-'tōd\ *adj* (1785) **1 :** having a toe that is square **2 :** OLD-FASHIONED, CONSERVATIVE — **square–toed·ness** *n*
square wave *n* (1932) **:** the rectangular waveform of a quantity that varies periodically and abruptly from one to the other of two uniform values
squar·ish \'skwa(ə)r-ish, 'skwe(ə)r-\ *adj* (1742) **:** somewhat square in form or appearance — **squar·ish·ly** *adv* — **squar·ish·ness** *n*
[1]**squash** \'skwäsh, 'skwȯsh\ *vb* [MF *esquasser,* fr. (assumed) VL *exquassare,* fr. L *ex-* + *quassare* to shake — more at QUASH] *vt* (1565) **1 :** to press or beat into a pulp or a flat mass **:** CRUSH **2 :** PUT DOWN, SUPPRESS ⟨~ a revolt⟩ ~ *vi* **1 :** to flatten out under pressure or impact **2 :** to proceed with a splashing or squelching sound **3 :** SQUEEZE, PRESS — **squash·er** *n*
[2]**squash** *n* (1590) **1** *obs* **:** something soft and easily crushed; *specif* **:** an unripe pod of peas **2 :** the sudden fall of a heavy soft body or the sound of such a fall **3 :** a squelching sound made by walking on oozy ground or in water-soaked boots **4 :** a crushed mass **5** *Brit* **:** sweetened citrus fruit juice usu. with added soda water **6 :** SQUASH RACQUETS
[3]**squash** *adv* (1766) **:** with a squash or a squashing sound
[4]**squash** *n, pl* **squash·es** *or* **squash** [by shortening & alter. fr. earlier *isquoutersquash,* fr. Natick & Narraganset *askútasquash*] (1634) **:** any of various fruits of plants (genus *Cucurbita*) of the gourd family widely cultivated as vegetables and for livestock feed; *also* **:** a plant and esp. a vine that bears squashes
squash bug *n* (ca. 1846) **:** a large black American bug (*Anasa tristis* of the family Coreidae) injurious to squash vines
squash racquets *n pl but sing in constr* (1886) **:** a singles or doubles game played in a 4-wall court with a long-handled racket and a rubber ball that can be caromed off any number of walls
squash tennis *n* (1920) **:** a singles racket game resembling squash racquets played with an inflated ball the size of a tennis ball
squashy \'skwäsh-ē, 'skwȯsh-\ *adj* **squash·i·er; -est** (1698) **1 :** easily squashed **:** very soft ⟨~ cushions⟩ **2 :** softly wet **:** BOGGY **3 :** soft because overripe ⟨~ melons⟩ — **squash·i·ly** \-ə-lē\ *adv* — **squash·i·ness** \-ē-nəs\ *n*
[1]**squat** \'skwät\ *vb* **squat·ted; squat·ting** [ME *squatten,* fr. MF *esquatir,* fr. *es-* ex- (fr. L *ex-*) + *quatir* to press, fr. (assumed) VL *coactire* to press together, fr. L *coactus,* pp. of *cogere* to drive together — more at COGENT] *vt* (15c) **1 :** to cause (oneself) to crouch or sit on the ground **2 :** to occupy as a squatter ~ *vi* **1 :** to crouch close to the ground as if to escape observation ⟨a hare *squatting* in the grass⟩ **2 :** to assume or maintain a position in which the body is supported on the feet and the knees are bent so that the buttocks rest on or near the heels **3 :** to become a squatter
[2]**squat** *adj* **squat·ter; squat·test** (15c) **1 :** sitting with the haunches close above the heels **2 a :** low to the ground **b :** marked by disproportionate shortness or thickness — **squat·ly** *adv* — **squat·ness** *n*
[3]**squat** *n* (1580) **1 a :** the act of squatting **b :** the posture of one that squats **2 a :** a place where one squats **b :** the lair of a small animal ⟨~ of a hare⟩
[1]**squat·ter** \'skwät-ər\ *vi* [prob. of Scand origin; akin to Dan *skvatte* to sprinkle] (1785) **:** to go along through or as if through water
[2]**squatter** *n* (1788) **:** one that squats: as **a :** one that settles on property without right or title or payment of rent **b :** one that settles on public land under government regulation with the purpose of acquiring title
squatter sovereignty *n* (1854) **:** POPULAR SOVEREIGNTY 2
squat·ty \'skwät-ē\ *adj* **squat·ti·er; -est** (1881) **1 :** low to the ground **2 :** DUMPY, THICKSET
squaw \'skwȯ\ *n* [of Algonquian origin; akin to Natick *squáas* woman] (1634) **1 :** an American Indian woman **2 :** WOMAN, WIFE — usu. used disparagingly
squaw·fish \-,fish\ *n* (1881) **:** any of several large cyprinid fishes (genus *Ptychocheilus*) of western No. America
[1]**squawk** \'skwȯk\ *vi* [prob. blend of *squall* and *squeak*] (1821) **1 :** to utter a harsh abrupt scream **2 :** to complain or protest loudly or vehemently — **squawk·er** *n*
[2]**squawk** *n* (1850) **1 :** a harsh abrupt scream **2 :** a noisy complaint
squawk box *n* (1946) **:** an intercom speaker

squaw man *n* (1866) : a white man married to an Indian woman and usu. living as one of her tribe

squaw·root \ˈskwȯ-ˌrüt, -ˌru̇t\ *n* (1815) : a No. American scaly herb (*Conopholis americana*) of the broomrape family parasitic on oak and hemlock roots

¹**squeak** \ˈskwēk\ *vb* [ME *squeken*] *vi* (14c) **1** : to utter or make a short shrill cry or noise **2** : SQUEAL 2a **3** : to pass, succeed, or win by a narrow margin ~ *vt* : to utter in a shrill piping tone

²**squeak** *n* (1700) **1** : a sharp shrill cry or sound **2** : ESCAPE ⟨a close ~⟩ — **squeaky** \ˈskwē-kē\ *adj*

squeak·er \ˈskwē-kər\ *n* (1671) **1** : one that squeaks **2** : a contest (as an election) won by a small margin : a close game

squeaky–clean *adj* (1968) **1** : completely clean ⟨~ hair⟩ **2** : completely free from moral taint of any kind ⟨a ~ reputation⟩

¹**squeal** \ˈskwē(ə)l\ *vb* [ME *squelen*] *vi* (14c) **1** : to make a shrill cry or noise **2 a** : to turn informer **b** : COMPLAIN, PROTEST ~ *vt* **1** : to utter or express with or as if with a squeal **2** : to cause to make a loud shrill noise ⟨~*ing* the tires⟩ — **squeal·er** *n*

²**squeal** *n* (1747) : a shrill sharp cry or noise

squea·mish \ˈskwē-mish\ *adj* [ME *squaymisch*, modif. of AF *escoymous*] (15c) **1 a** : easily nauseated : QUEASY **b** : affected with nausea **2 a** : excessively fastidious or scrupulous in conduct or belief **b** : easily offended or disgusted — **squea·mish·ly** *adv* — **squea·mish·ness** *n*

¹**squee·gee** \ˈskwē-ˌjē\ *n* [origin unknown] (1844) : a blade of leather or rubber set on a handle and used for spreading, pushing, or wiping liquid material on, across, or off a surface (as a window); *also* : a smaller similar device or a small rubber roller with handle used by a photographer or lithographer

²**squeegee** *vt* **squee·geed; squee·gee·ing** (1883) : to smooth, wipe, or treat with a squeegee

¹**squeeze** \ˈskwēz\ *vb* **squeezed; squeez·ing** [alter. of obs. E *quease*, fr. ME *queysen*, fr. OE *cwȳsan*; akin to Icel *kveisa* stomach cramps] *vt* (1601) **1 a** : to exert pressure esp. on opposite sides of : COMPRESS **b** : to extract or emit under pressure **c** : to force or thrust by compression **2 a** (1) : to get by extortion (2) : to deprive by extortion **b** : to cause economic hardship to **c** : to reduce the amount of ⟨~*s* profits⟩ **3** : to crowd into a limited area **4** : to gain or win by a narrow margin **5** : to force (another player) to discard in bridge so as to unguard a suit **6** : to score by means of a squeeze play ~ *vi* **1** : to give way before pressure **2** : to exert pressure; *also* : to practice extortion or oppression **3** : to force one's way ⟨~ through a door⟩ **4** : to pass, win, or get by narrowly — **squeez·abil·i·ty** \ˌskwē-zə-ˈbil-ət-ē\ *n* — **squeez·able** \ˈskwē-zə-bəl\ *adj* — **squeez·er** *n*

²**squeeze** *n* (1611) **1 a** : an act or instance of squeezing : COMPRESSION **b** : HANDCLASP; *also* : EMBRACE **2 a** : a quantity squeezed out from something ⟨a ~ of lemon⟩ **b** : a group crowded together : CROWD **3** : a profit taken by a middleman on goods or transactions **4** : a financial pressure caused by narrowing margins or by shortages **5** : a forced discard in bridge **6** : SQUEEZE PLAY

squeeze bottle *n* (1950) : a bottle of flexible plastic that dispenses its contents by being pressed

squeeze off *vt* (ca. 1949) : to fire (a round) by squeezing the trigger ~ *vi* : to fire a weapon by squeezing the trigger

squeeze play *n* (1905) **1** : a baseball play in which a runner on third base starts for home plate as the ball is being pitched and the batter attempts to bunt to give the runner a chance to score **2** : the exertion of pressure in order to extort a concession or gain a goal

squeg \ˈskweg, ˈskwāg\ *vi* **squegged; squeg·ging** [back-formation fr. *squegger* (tube in which the valve oscillates)] (1933) : to oscillate in a highly irregular fashion — used of an electronic system

¹**squelch** \ˈskwelch\ *n* [origin unknown] (1620) **1** : the act of suppressing; *esp* : a retort that silences an opponent **2** : a sound of or as if of semiliquid matter under suction ⟨the ~ of mud⟩ — **squelchy** *adj*

²**squelch** *vt* (1624) **1 a** : to fall or stamp on so as to crush **b** (1) : to completely suppress : QUELL (2) : SILENCE **2** : to emit or move with a sucking sound ~ *vi* **1** : to emit a sucking sound **2** : to splash through water, slush, or mire — **squelch·er** *n*

sque·teague \skwi-ˈtēg\ *n, pl* **squeteague** [Narraganset *pesukwiteaug*, pl.] (1803) : any of several weakfishes (esp. *Cynoscion regalis*)

¹**squib** \ˈskwib\ *n* [origin unknown] (1530) **1 a** : a small firecracker **b** : a broken firecracker in which the powder burns with a fizz **2** : a small electric or pyrotechnic device used to ignite a charge; *also* : a similar device used to fire an igniter in a rocket **3 a** : a short humorous or satiric writing or speech **b** : a short news item; *esp* : FILLER

²**squib** *vb* **squibbed; squib·bing** *vi* (1579) **1** : to speak, write, or publish squibs **2** : to fire a squib ~ *vt* **1 a** : to utter in an offhand manner **b** : to make squibs against : LAMPOON **2** : to shoot off : FIRE **3** : to kick (a football) just far enough on a kickoff to be legally recoverable by the kicking team

squib kick *n* (ca. 1956) : ONSIDE KICK

¹**squid** \ˈskwid\ *n, pl* **squid** *or* **squids** [origin unknown] (1613) : any of numerous 10-armed cephalopods (esp. of the genera *Loligo* and *Ommastrephes*) having a long tapered body, a caudal fin on each side, and usu. a slender internal chitinous support

²**squid** *vi* **squid·ded; squid·ding** (1859) : to fish with or for squid

squiffed \ˈskwift\ *or* **squif·fy** \ˈskwif-ē\ *adj* [origin unknown] (1874) : INTOXICATED, DRUNK

¹**squig·gle** \ˈskwig-əl\ *vb* **squig·gled; squig·gling** \-(ə-)liŋ\ [blend of *squirm* and *wriggle*] *vi* (ca. 1816) **1** : SQUIRM, WRIGGLE **2** : to write or paint hastily : SCRIBBLE ~ *vt* **1** : SCRIBBLE **2** : to form or cause to form in squiggles

²**squiggle** *n* (1900) : a short wavy twist or line : CURLICUE; *esp* : an illegible scrawl — **squig·gly** \-(ə-)lē\ *adj*

squil·gee \ˈskwē-ˌjē, ˈskwil-ˌjē\ *var of* SQUEEGEE

squill \ˈskwil\ *n* [ME, fr. L *squilla, scilla*, fr. Gk *skilla*] (15c) **1 a** : a Mediterranean bulbous herb (*Urginea maritima*) of the lily family — called also *sea onion;* compare RED SQUILL 1 **b** (1) : the dried sliced bulb scales of a squill used as an expectorant, cardiac stimulant, and diuretic (2) : RED SQUILL 2 **2** : SCILLA

squil·la \ˈskwil-ə\ *n, pl* **squillas** *or* **squil·lae** \ˈskwil-ˌē, -ˌī\ [NL, fr. L, squill, prawn] (1658) : any of various stomatopod crustaceans (esp. genus *Squilla*) that burrow in mud or beneath stones in shallow water along the seashore

¹**squinch** \ˈskwinch\ *n* [alter. of earlier *scunch* (back part of the side of an opening)] (ca. 1840) : a support (as an arch, lintel, or corbeling) carried across the corner of a room under a superimposed mass

²**squinch** *vb* [prob. blend of *squint* and *pinch*] *vt* (1840) **1** : to screw up (the eyes or face) : SQUINT **2 a** : to make more compact **b** : to cause to crouch down or draw together ~ *vi* **1** : FLINCH **2** : to crouch down or draw together **3** : SQUINT

¹**squin·ny** \ˈskwin-ē\ *vb* **squin·nied; squin·ny·ing** [prob. fr. obs. E *squin* asquint, fr. ME *skuin*] (1605) : SQUINT

²**squinny** *n* (1881) : SQUINT — **squinny** *adj*

¹**squint** \ˈskwint\ *adj* [ME *asquint*] (1579) **1** *of an eye* : looking or tending to look obliquely or askance (as with envy or disdain) **2** *of the eyes* : not having the visual axes parallel : CROSSED

²**squint** *vi* (1599) **1 a** : to have an indirect bearing, reference, or aim **b** : to deviate from a true line **2 a** : to look in a squint-eyed manner **b** : to be cross-eyed **c** : to look or peer with eyes partly closed ~ *vt* : to cause (an eye) to squint — **squint·er** *n* — **squint·ing·ly** \-iŋ-lē\ *adv*

³**squint** *n* (1652) **1** : STRABISMUS **2** : an instance of squinting **3** : HAGIOSCOPE — **squinty** \ˈskwint-ē\ *adj*

squint–eyed \ˈskwint-ˈīd\ *adj* (1589) **1** : having eyes that squint; *specif* : affected with cross-eye **2** : looking askance (as in envy)

squinting modifier *n* (1924) : a modifier (as *often* in "getting dressed often is a nuisance") so placed in a sentence that it can be interpreted as modifying either what precedes or what follows

¹**squire** \ˈskwī(ə)r\ *n* [ME *squier*, fr. OF *esquier* — more at ESQUIRE] (13c) **1** : a shield bearer or armor-bearer of a knight **2 a** : a male attendant esp. on a great personage **b** : a man who devotedly attends a lady : GALLANT **3 a** : a member of the British gentry ranking below a knight and above a gentleman **b** : an owner of a country estate; *esp* : the principal landowner in a village or district **c** (1) : JUSTICE OF THE PEACE (2) : LAWYER (3) : JUDGE — **squir·ish** \ˈskwī(ə)r-ish\ *adj*

²**squire** *vt* **squired; squir·ing** (14c) : to attend as a squire : ESCORT

squire·ar·chy *or* **squir·ar·chy** \ˈskwī(ə)r-ˌär-kē\ *n, pl* **-chies** (ca. 1796) : the class of landed gentry or landed proprietors

squirm \ˈskwərm\ *vi* [origin unknown] (1691) : to twist about like a worm : FIDGET — **squirm** *n* — **squirmy** \ˈskwər-mē\ *adj*

¹**squir·rel** \ˈskwər(-ə)l, ˈskwə-rəl, *chiefly Brit* ˈskwir-əl\ *n, pl* **squirrels** *also* **squirrel** [ME *squirel*, fr. MF *esquireul*, fr. (assumed) VL *scuriolus*, dim. of *scurius*, alter. of L *sciurus*, fr. Gk *skiouros*, fr. *skia* shadow + *oura* tail — more at SHINE, ASS] (14c) **1** : any of various small or medium-sized rodents (family Sciuridae): as **a** : any of numerous New or Old World arboreal forms having a long bushy tail and strong hind legs **b** : GROUND SQUIRREL **2** : the fur of a squirrel

²**squirrel** *vt* **-reled** *or* **-relled; -rel·ing** *or* **-rel·ling** [fr. the squirrel's habit of storing up gathered nuts and seeds for winter use] (1925) : to store up for future use — often used with *away*

squirrel cage *n* (1831) **1** : a cage for a small animal (as a squirrel) that contains a rotatable cylinder for exercising **2** : something resembling the working of a squirrel cage in repetitiveness or endlessness

squirrel corn *n* (1843) : a No. American herb (*Dicentra canadensis*) of the fumitory family with much-divided leaves and a scapose raceme of cream-colored flowers

squir·rel·ly \ˈskwər(-ə)-lē, ˈskwə-rə-\ *adj* (1928) : NUTTY 3

squirrel monkey *n* (1773) : a small soft-haired So. American monkey (*Saimiri sciureus*) that has a long tail not used for grasping and is colored chiefly yellowish gray with a white face and black nose

squirrel rifle *n* [fr. its being suitable only for small game] (1834) : a small-bore rifle — called also *squirrel gun*

¹**squirt** \ˈskwərt\ *vb* [ME *squirten;* akin to LG *swirtjen* to squirt] *vi* (15c) : to come forth in a sudden rapid stream from a narrow opening : SPURT ~ *vt* : to cause to squirt — **squirt·er** *n*

²**squirt** *n* (ca. 1530) **1 a** : an instrument (as a syringe) for squirting a liquid **b** : a small quick stream : JET **c** : the action or an instance of squirting **2 a** : an impudent youngster **b** : KID

squirt gun *n* (1803) : WATER PISTOL

squirting cucumber *n* (1802) : a Mediterranean plant (*Ecballium elaterium*) of the gourd family with oblong fruit that bursts from the peduncle when ripe and forcibly ejects the seeds

squish \ˈskwish\ *vb* [alter. of *squash*] *vt* (ca. 1647) **1** : SQUASH **2** : SQUELCH, SUCK ~ *vi* : SQUELCH, SUCK ⟨their wet tennis shoes ~*ed* — Frank Noel⟩ — **squish** *n*

squishy \-ē\ *adj* **squish·i·er; -est** (ca. 1847) : being soft, yielding, and damp — **squish·i·ness** *n*

squoosh \ˈskwu̇sh, ˈskwüsh\ *vb* [by alter.] (1942) : SQUASH

squush \ˈskwəsh\ *vb* [by alter.] (1837) : SQUASH

sri \ˈs(h)rē\ *n* [Skt *śrī*, lit., majesty, holiness; akin to Gk *kreiōn* ruler, master] (ca. 1885) — used as a conventional title of respect when addressing or speaking of a distinguished Indian

sRNA \ˈes-ˌär-ˌen-ˈā\ *n* [*soluble RNA*] (1963) : TRANSFER RNA

SS \(ˈ)es-ˈes\ *n* [G, abbr. for *Schutzstaffel* elite guard] (1935) : a unit of Nazis created to serve as bodyguard to Hitler and later expanded to take charge of intelligence, central security, policing action, and extermination of undesirables

SST \ˌes-ˌes-ˈtē\ *n* [*supersonic transport*] (1964) : SUPERSONIC TRANSPORT

¹**-st** — see -EST

²**-st** *symbol* — used after the figure 1 to indicate the ordinal number *first* ⟨1*st*⟩ ⟨91*st*⟩

¹**stab** \ˈstab\ *n* [ME *stabbe*] (15c) **1** : a wound produced by a pointed weapon **2 a** : a thrust of a pointed weapon **b** : a jerky thrust **3** : EFFORT, TRY

²**stab** *vb* **stabbed; stab·bing** *vt* (1530) **1** : to wound or pierce by the thrust of a pointed weapon **2** : THRUST, DRIVE ~ *vi* : to thrust or give a wound with or as if with a pointed weapon — **stab·ber** *n*

¹**sta·bile** \ˈstā-ˌbīl, -ˌbil\ *adj* [L *stabilis* — more at STABLE] (1896) **1** : STATIONARY, STABLE **2** : resistant to chemical change

\ə\ abut \ᵊ\ kitten, F table \ər\ further \a\ ash \ā\ ace \ä\ cot, cart \au̇\ out \ch\ chin \e\ bet \ē\ easy \g\ go \i\ hit \ī\ ice \j\ job \ŋ\ sing \ō\ go \ȯ\ law \ȯi\ boy \th\ thin \t͟h\ the \ü\ loot \u̇\ foot \y\ yet \zh\ vision \à, k̲, ⁿ, œ, œ̄, ue, ue̅, ʸ\ *see* Guide to Pronunciation

²sta·bile \-ˌbēl\ *n* [prob. F, fr. L *stabilis,* adj.] (1937) **:** an abstract sculpture or construction similar in appearance to a mobile but made to be stationary

sta·bil·i·ty \stə-ˈbil-ət-ē\ *n, pl* **-ties** [ME, fr. MF *estabilité,* fr. L *stabilitat-, stabilitas,* fr. *stabilis*] (15c) **1 :** the quality, state, or degree of being stable: as **a :** the strength to stand or endure **:** FIRMNESS **b :** the property of a body that causes it when disturbed from a condition of equilibrium or steady motion to develop forces or moments that restore the original condition **c :** resistance to chemical change or to physical disintegration **2 :** residence for life in one monastery

sta·bi·lize \ˈstā-bə-ˌlīz\ *vb* **-lized; -liz·ing** *vt* (1861) **1 :** to make stable, steadfast, or firm **2 :** to hold steady: as **a :** to maintain the stability of (as an airplane) by means of a stabilizer **b :** to limit fluctuations of (as prices) **c :** to establish a minimum price for **~** *vi* **:** to become stable, firm, or steadfast — **sta·bi·li·za·tion** \ˌstā-bə-lə-ˈzā-shən\ *n*

sta·bi·liz·er \ˈstā-bə-ˌlī-zər\ *n* (ca. 1909) **:** one that stabilizes something: as **a :** a substance added to another substance (as an explosive or plastic) or to a system (as an emulsion) to prevent or retard an unwanted alteration of physical state **b :** a gyroscope device to keep ships steady in a heavy sea **c :** an airfoil providing stability for an airplane; *specif* **:** the fixed horizontal member of the tail assembly — see AIRPLANE illustration

¹sta·ble \ˈstā-bəl\ *n* [ME, fr. OF *estable,* fr. L *stabulum,* fr. *stare* to stand — more at STAND] (13c) **1 :** a building in which domestic animals are sheltered and fed; *esp* **:** such a building having stalls or compartments ⟨horse ~⟩ **2 a :** the racehorses of one owner **b :** a group of athletes (as boxers) or performers under one management **c :** the racing cars of one owner **d :** GROUP, COLLECTION — **sta·ble·man** \-mən, -ˌman\ *n*

²stable *vb* **sta·bled; sta·bling** \-b(ə-)liŋ\ *vt* (14c) **:** to put or keep in a stable **~** *vi* **:** to dwell in or as if in a stable

³stable *adj* **sta·bler** \-b(ə-)lər\; **sta·blest** \-b(ə-)ləst\ [ME, fr. MF *estable,* fr. L *stabilis,* fr. *stare* to stand] (14c) **1 a :** firmly established **:** FIXED, STEADFAST **b :** not changing or fluctuating **:** UNVARYING **c :** PERMANENT, ENDURING **2 a :** steady in purpose **:** firm in resolution **b :** not subject to insecurity or emotional illness **:** SANE, RATIONAL ⟨a ~ personality⟩ **3 a (1) :** placed so as to resist forces tending to cause motion or change of motion **(2) :** designed so as to develop forces that restore the original condition when disturbed from a condition of equilibrium or steady motion **b (1) :** not readily altering in chemical makeup or physical state ⟨~ emulsions⟩ **(2) :** not spontaneously radioactive ***syn*** see LASTING — **sta·ble·ness** \-bəl-nəs\ *n* — **sta·bly** \-b(ə-)lē\ *adv*

stable fly *n* (1862) **:** a two-winged fly (*Stomoxys calcitrans*) that bites severely, is abundant about stables, and often enters dwellings esp. in autumn

sta·ble·mate \ˈstā-bəl-ˌmāt\ *n* (1926) **1 :** a horse stabled with another **2 :** a member of a stable

sta·bler \-b(ə-)lər\ *n* (15c) **:** one who keeps a stable

sta·bling \-b(ə-)liŋ\ *n* (15c) **:** accommodation for animals in a building; *also* **:** the building for this

stab·lish \ˈstab-lish\ *vb* [by shortening] *archaic* (14c) **:** ESTABLISH — **stab·lish·ment** \-mənt\ *n, archaic*

stac·ca·to \stə-ˈkät-(ˌ)ō\ *adj* [It, fr. pp. of *staccare* to detach, deriv. of OF *destachier* — more at DETACH] (ca. 1724) **1 a :** cut short or apart in performing **:** DISCONNECTED ⟨~ notes⟩ **b :** marked by short clear-cut playing or singing of tones or chords ⟨a ~ style⟩ **2 :** ABRUPT, DISJOINTED — **staccato** *adv* — **staccato** *n*

staccato mark *n* (ca. 1903) **:** a pointed vertical stroke or a dot placed over or under a musical note to be produced staccato

¹stack \ˈstak\ *n* [ME *stak,* fr. ON *stakkr;* akin to OE *staca* stake] (14c) **1 :** a large usu. conical pile (as of hay, straw, or grain in the sheaf) left standing in the field for storage **2 a :** an orderly pile or heap **b :** a large quantity or number **3 :** an English unit of measure esp. for firewood that is equal to 108 cubic feet **4 a :** a number of flues embodied in one structure rising above a roof **b :** a vertical pipe (as to carry off smoke) **c :** the exhaust pipe of an internal-combustion engine **5 :** a pyramid of three rifles interlocked **6 :** a structure of bookshelves for compact storage of books — usu. used in pl. **7 :** a pile of chips sold to or won by a poker player **8 a :** a memory or a section of memory in a computer for temporary storage ⟨a push-down ~⟩ **b :** a computer memory consisting of arrays of memory elements stacked one on top of another

²stack *vt* (14c) **1 a :** to arrange in a stack **:** PILE **b :** to pile in or on ⟨~*ed* the table with books⟩ ⟨~ the dishwasher⟩ **2 a :** to arrange secretly for cheating ⟨~ a deck of cards⟩ **b :** to arrange or fix so as to make a particular result likely ⟨the odds are ~*ed* against us⟩ ⟨will ~ juries to suit themselves —Patrice Horn⟩ **3 a :** to assign (an airplane) by radio to a particular altitude and position within a group circling before landing **b :** to put into a queue ⟨another dozen rigs are ~*ed* up and waiting their turns to refuel —P.H. Hutchins, Jr.⟩ **4 :** COMPARE — used with *against* ⟨such a crime is nothing when ~*ed* against a murder —Pete Censky⟩ **~** *vi* **:** to form a stack — **stack·er** *n*

stack·able \ˈstak-ə-bəl\ *adj* (1964) **:** easily stacked

stacked \ˈstakt\ *adj, slang, of a woman* (1950) **:** being shapely and having large breasts

stack up *vi* (ca. 1934) **1 :** to add up **:** TOTAL **2 :** MEASURE UP, COMPARE — usu. used with *against*

stac·te \ˈstak-tē\ *n* [ME *stacten,* fr. L, fr. Gk *staktē,* fr. fem. of *staktos* oozing out in drops, fr. *stazein* to drip — more at STAGNATE] (14c) **:** a sweet spice used by the ancient Jews in preparing incense

stad·dle \ˈstad-ᵊl\ *n* [ME *stathel* base, support, fr. OE *stathol;* akin to OE *stede* place — more at STEAD] (bef. 12c) **1 :** a base (as of piling) for a stack of hay or straw **2 :** a supporting framework

stade \ˈstād\ *n* [MF *estade,* fr. L *stadium*] (1537) **:** STADIUM 1a

sta·dia \ˈstād-ē-ə\ *n* [It, prob. fr. L, pl. of *stadium*] (1865) **:** a surveying method for determination of distances and differences of elevation by means of a telescopic instrument having two horizontal lines through which the marks on a graduated rod are observed; *also* **:** the instrument or rod

sta·di·um \ˈstād-ē-əm\ *n, pl* **-dia** \-ē-ə\ *or* **-di·ums** [ME, fr. L, fr. Gk *stadion,* perh. alter. of *spadion,* fr. *span* to pull — more at SPAN] (14c) **1 a :** any of various ancient Greek units of length ranging in value from 607 to 738 English feet **b :** an ancient Roman unit of length equal to 606.95 English feet **2 a :** a course for footraces in ancient Greece orig. one stadium in length **b :** a tiered structure with seats for spectators surrounding an ancient Greek running track **c :** a large usu. unroofed building with tiers of seats for spectators at sports events **3** [NL, fr. L] **:** a stage in a life history; *esp* **:** one between successive molts

stadt·hold·er \ˈstat-ˌhōl-dər\ *n* [part trans. of D *stadhouder,* fr. *stad* place (akin to OHG *stat* place) + *houder* holder, fr. *houden* to hold, fr. MD; akin to OHG *haltan* to hold — more at STEAD, HOLD] (1668) **1 :** a viceroy in a province of the Netherlands **2 :** a chief executive officer of the provinces that formed a union leading to establishment of the Netherlands — **stadt·hold·er·ate** \-də-rət\ *n* — **stadt·hold·er·ship** \-dər-ˌship\ *n*

¹staff \ˈstaf\ *n, pl* **staffs** \ˈstafs, ˈstavz\ *or* **staves** \ˈstavz, ˈstāvz\ [ME *staf,* fr. OE *stæf;* akin to OHG *stab* staff, *stampfōn* to stamp — more at STAMP] (bef. 12c) **1 a :** a long stick carried in the hand for support in walking **b :** a supporting rod: as **(1)** *archaic* **:** SHAFT 1a(1) **(2) :** a crosspiece in a ladder or chair **:** RUNG **(3) :** FLAGSTAFF **(4) :** a pivoted arbor **c :** CLUB, CUDGEL **2 a :** CROSIER **b :** a rod carried as a symbol of office or authority **3 :** the horizontal lines with their spaces on which music is written — called also *stave* **4 :** any of various graduated sticks or rules used for measuring **:** ROD **5** *pl* ***staffs*** **a :** the officers chiefly responsible for the internal operations of an institution or business **b :** a group of officers appointed to assist a civil executive or commanding officer **c :** military or naval officers not eligible for operational command **d :** the personnel who assist a director in carrying out an assigned task **e** *pl* **staff :** a member of a staff — **staff** *adj*

²staff *vt* (1859) **1 :** to supply with a staff or with workers **2 :** to serve as a staff member of

³staff *n* [prob. fr. G *staffieren* to trim] (1892) **:** a building material having a plaster of Paris base and used in exterior wall coverings of temporary buildings

staff·er \ˈstaf-ər\ *n* (1941) **:** a member of a staff (as of a newspaper)

staff officer *n* (1777) **:** a commissioned officer assigned to a military commander's staff — compare LINE OFFICER

staff of life (1638) **:** a staple of diet; *esp* **:** BREAD

Staf·ford·shire bull terrier \ˌstaf-ərd-ˌshi(ə)r-, -shər-\ *n* [*Staffordshire,* England] (1936) **:** any of a breed of compact muscular terriers that have a short stiff glossy coat

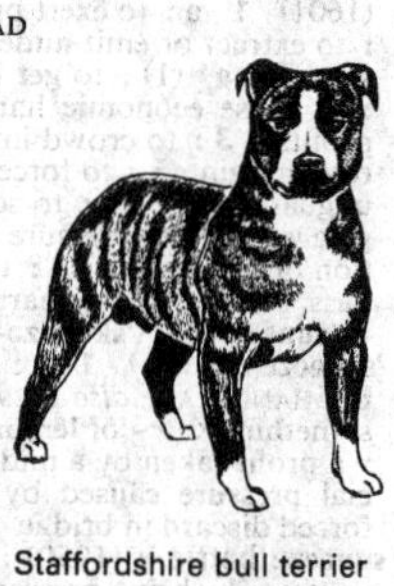

Staffordshire bull terrier

staff sergeant *n* (1851) **:** a noncommissioned officer ranking in the army above a sergeant and below a platoon sergeant or sergeant first class, in the air force above a sergeant and below a technical sergeant, and in the marine corps above a sergeant and below a gunnery sergeant

staff sergeant major *n* (1967) **:** a noncommissioned officer in the army ranking above a master sergeant

staff tree *n* (ca. 1633) **:** any of a genus (*Celastrus* of the family Celastraceae, the staff-tree family) of mostly twining shrubby plants including the common bittersweet

¹stag \ˈstag\ *n, pl* **stags** [ME *stagge,* fr. OE *stagga;* akin to ON *andarsteggi* drake, OE *stingan* to sting] (bef. 12c) **1** *or pl* **stag :** an adult male red deer; *broadly* **:** the male of various deer (esp. genus *Cervus*) **2** *chiefly Scot* **:** a young horse; *esp* **:** a young unbroken stallion **3 :** a male animal castrated after maturity — compare STEER 1 **4 :** a young adult male domestic fowl **5 a :** a social gathering of men only **b :** a man who attends a dance or party unaccompanied by a woman

²stag *vb* **stagged; stag·ging** *vt* [*stag* (informer)] *Brit* (ca. 1823) **:** to spy on **~** *vi* **:** to attend a dance or party without a woman companion

³stag *adj* (1843) **1 a :** restricted to men ⟨a ~ party⟩ **b :** intended or suitable for a gathering of men only; *esp* **:** PORNOGRAPHIC ⟨~ movies⟩ **2 :** unaccompanied by someone of the opposite sex ⟨~ women⟩ — **stag** *adv*

stag beetle *n* (1681) **:** any of numerous mostly large lamellicorn beetles (family Lucanidae) having males with long and often branched mandibles suggesting the antlers of a stag

¹stage \ˈstāj\ *n* [ME, fr. MF *estage,* fr. (assumed) VL *staticum,* fr. L *stare* to stand — more at STAND] (14c) **1 a :** one of a series of positions or stations one above the other **:** STEP **b :** the height of the surface of a river above an arbitrary zero point **2 a (1) :** a raised platform **(2) :** the part of a theater between the proscenium and the rear wall including the acting area, wings, and storage space **(3) :** the acting profession **:** the theater as an occupation or activity **(4) :** SOUNDSTAGE **b :** a center of attention or scene of action **3 a :** a scaffold for workmen **b :** the small platform of a microscope on which an object is placed for examination **4 a :** a place of rest formerly provided for those traveling by stagecoach **:** STATION **b :** the distance between two stopping places on a road **c :** STAGECOACH **5 a :** a period or step in a progress, activity, or development; *esp* **:** one of the distinguishable periods of growth and development of a plant or animal ⟨the larval ~ of an insect⟩ **b :** one passing through a (specified) stage **6 :** an element or part in a complex electronic contrivance; *specif* **:** a single tube with its associated components in an amplifier **7 :** a propulsion unit of a rocket with its own fuel and container — **stage·ful** \-ˌfu̇l\ *n* — **on the stage :** in or into the acting profession

²stage *vt* **staged; stag·ing** (1879) **1 :** to produce (as a play) on a stage **2 :** to produce for public view ⟨~ a track meet⟩ — **stage·able** \ˈstā-jə-bəl\ *adj*

stage business *n* (1825) **:** BUSINESS 5

stage·coach \ˈstāj-ˌkōch\ *n* (1658) **:** a horse-drawn passenger and mail coach running on a regular schedule between established stops

stage·craft \-ˌkraft\ *n* (1882) **:** the effective management of theatrical devices or techniques

stage direction *n* (1790) **:** a description (as of a character or setting) or direction (as to indicate stage business) provided in the text of a play

stage director *n* (ca. 1909) **1 :** DIRECTOR c **2 :** STAGE MANAGER

stage fright *n* (1878) **:** nervousness felt at appearing before an audience

stage·hand \ˈstāj-ˌhand\ *n* (ca. 1902) **:** a stage worker who handles scenery, properties, or lights

stage left *n* (1931) **:** the left part of a stage from the viewpoint of one who faces the audience

stage–man·age \-ˌman-ij\ *vt* [back-formation fr. *stage manager*] (1879) **1 a** : to arrange or exhibit so as to achieve a desired effect **b** : to arrange or direct from behind the scenes **2** : to act as stage manager for — **stage management** *n*

stage manager *n* (1817) : one who supervises the physical aspects of a stage production, assists the director during rehearsals, and is in charge of the stage during a performance

stag·er \ˈstā-jər\ *n* (1570) : an experienced person : VETERAN

stage right *n* (1931) : the right part of a stage from the viewpoint of one who faces the audience

stage set *n* (1917) : scenery and properties designed and arranged for a particular scene in a play

stage·struck \ˈstāj-ˌstrək\ *adj* (1813) : fascinated by the stage; *esp* : having an ardent desire to become an actor

stage whisper *n* (ca. 1865) **1** : a loud whisper by an actor that is audible to the spectators but is supposed for dramatic effect not to be heard by one or more of the actors **2** : an audible whisper — **stage–whisper** *vb*

stag·fla·tion \ˌstag-ˈflā-shən\ *n* [blend of *stagnation* and *inflation*] (1970) : persistent inflation combined with stagnant consumer demand and relatively high unemployment — **stag·fla·tion·ary** \-shə-ˌner-ē\ *adj*

1stag·ger \ˈstag-ər\ *vb* **stag·gered; stag·ger·ing** \-(ə-)riŋ\ [alter. of earlier *stacker,* fr. ME *stakeren,* fr. ON *stakra,* freq. of *staka* to push — more at STAKE] *vi* (15c) **1 a** : to reel from side to side : TOTTER **b** : to move on unsteadily **2** : to waver in purpose or action : HESITATE **3** : to rock violently : SHAKE ⟨the ship ~*ed*⟩ ~ *vt* **1** : to cause to doubt or hesitate : PERPLEX **2** : to cause to reel or totter **3** : to arrange in any of various zigzags, alternations, or overlappings of position or time ⟨~ work shifts⟩ ⟨~ teeth on a cutter⟩ **4** : to adjust (as the wings of a biplane) so that the leading edge of one wing projects beyond the leading edge of another wing — **stag·ger·er** \-ər-ər\ *n*

2stagger *n* (1577) **1** *pl but sing or pl in constr* : an abnormal condition of domestic mammals and birds associated with damage to the central nervous system and marked by incoordination and a reeling unsteady gait **2** : a reeling or unsteady gait or stance **3** : the amount by which the leading edge of an upper wing of a biplane is advanced over that of a lower expressed as percentage of gap

3stagger *adj* (1928) : marked by an alternating or overlapping arrangement

stag·ger·bush \ˈstag-ər-ˌbu̇sh\ *n* (1847) : a shrubby heath (*Lyonia mariana*) of the eastern U.S. that is poisonous to livestock

stag·ger·ing *adj* (1530) : so great as to cause one to stagger : ASTONISHING, OVERWHELMING ⟨a ~ feat⟩ ⟨~ medical bills⟩ — **stag·ger·ing·ly** \ˈstag-(ə-)riŋ-lē\ *adv*

stag·gery \ˈstag-(ə-)rē\ *adj* (1778) : UNSTEADY

stag·gy \ˈstag-ē\ *adj* (1918) : having the appearance of a mature male — used of female or castrated male domestic animals

stag·horn sumac \ˌstag-ˌhȯrn-\ *n* (ca. 1868) : a small tree or shrub (*Rhus typhina*) of eastern No. America with velvety-pubescent branches and flower stalks, leaves that turn brilliant red in fall, and dense panicles of greenish yellow flowers followed by bright crimson fruits

stag·hound \ˈstag-ˌhau̇nd\ *n* (1707) : a hound formerly used in hunting the stag and other large animals; *specif* : a large heavy hound resembling the English foxhound

stag·ing \ˈstā-jiŋ\ *n* (14c) **1** : SCAFFOLDING **2 a** : the business of running stagecoaches **b** : the act of journeying in stagecoaches **3** : the putting of a play on the stage **4 a** : the moving of troops or matériel forward in several stages **b** : the assembling of troops or matériel in transit in a particular place **5** : the disengaging and discarding of a burned-out rocket unit from a space vehicle during flight

staging area *n* (1943) : an area in which participants in a new operation or mission are assembled and readied

Stag·i·rite \ˈstaj-ə-ˌrīt\ *n* [Gk *Stagiritēs,* fr. *Stagira,* city in ancient Macedonia] (1620) : a native or resident of Stagira ⟨Aristotle the ~⟩

stag·nant \ˈstag-nənt\ *adj* (1666) **1 a** : not flowing in a current or stream : MOTIONLESS ⟨~ water⟩ **b** : STALE ⟨long disuse had made the air ~ and foul —Bram Stoker⟩ **2** : not advancing or developing : INACTIVE — **stag·nan·cy** \-nən-sē\ *n* — **stag·nant·ly** *adv*

stag·nate \ˈstag-ˌnāt\ *vi* **stag·nat·ed; stag·nat·ing** [L *stagnatus,* pp. of *stagnare,* fr. *stagnum* body of standing water; akin to Gk *stazein* to drip] (1669) : to become or remain stagnant — **stag·na·tion** \stag-ˈnā-shən\ *n*

stagy \ˈstā-jē\ *or* **stag·ey** *adj* **stag·i·er; -est** (1860) : of or characteristic of the stage; *esp* : marked by pretense or artificiality : THEATRICAL — **stag·i·ly** \-jə-lē\ *adv* — **stag·i·ness** \-jē-nəs\ *n*

1staid \ˈstād\ *adj* [fr. pp. of 3*stay*] (1557) : marked by settled sedateness and often prim self-restraint : SOBER, GRAVE ***syn*** see SERIOUS — **staid·ly** *adv* — **staid·ness** *n*

2staid *past and past part of* STAY

1stain \ˈstān\ *vb* [ME *steynen,* partly fr. MF *desteindre* to discolor & partly of Scand origin; akin to ON *steina* to paint — more at DISTAIN] *vt* (14c) **1** : DISCOLOR, SOIL **2** : to suffuse with color **3 a** : to taint with guilt, vice, or corruption **b** : to bring reproach on **4** : to color (as wood, glass, or cloth) by processes affecting chemically or otherwise the material itself ~ *vi* : to receive a stain — **stain·able** \ˈstā-nə-bəl\ *adj*

2stain *n* (1583) **1 a** : a soiled or discolored spot **b** : a natural spot of color contrasting with the ground **2** : a taint of guilt : STIGMA **3 a** : a preparation (as of dye or pigment) used in staining; *esp* : one capable of penetrating the pores of wood **b** : a dye or mixture of dyes used in microscopy to make visible minute and transparent structures, to differentiate tissue elements, or to produce specific chemical reactions — **stain·proof** \-ˌprüf\ *adj*

stain·abil·i·ty \ˌstā-nə-ˈbil-ət-ē\ *n* (1890) : the capacity of cells and cell parts to stain specifically and consistently with particular dyes and stains

stained glass *n* (1791) : glass colored or stained for use in windows: **a** : glass colored throughout by metallic oxides fused into it **b** : clear glass cased with colored glass **c** : clear glass into whose surface the pigments have been burned

stain·er \ˈstā-nər\ *n* (14c) : one that stains: as **a** : a worker who applies a coloring or finishing stain to wood or leather **b** : a pigment used merely to give color to a paint as distinguished from the base

1stain·less \ˈstān-ləs\ *adj* (1586) **1 a** : free from stain or stigma **b** : highly resistant to stain or corrosion **2** : made from materials resistant to stain — **stain·less·ly** *adv*

2stainless *n* (1953) : tableware made of stainless steel

stainless steel *n* (1920) : an alloy of steel with chromium and sometimes another element (as nickel or molybdenum) that is practically immune to rusting and ordinary corrosion

stair \ˈsta(ə)r, ˈste(ə)r\ *n* [ME *steir,* fr. OE *stǣger;* akin to OE & OHG *stīgan* to rise, Gk *steichein* to walk] (bef. 12c) **1** : a series of steps or flights of steps for passing from one level to another — often used in pl. but sing. or pl. in constr. ⟨a narrow private ~*s* —Lewis Mumford⟩ **2** : a single step of a stairway

stair·case \-ˌkās\ *n* (1624) **1** : the structure containing a stairway **2** : a flight of stairs with the supporting framework, casing, and balusters

stair·way \-ˌwā\ *n* (1767) : one or more flights of stairs usu. with landings to pass from one level to another

stair·well \-ˌwel\ *n* (1920) : a vertical shaft in which stairs are located

1stake \ˈstāk\ *n* [ME, fr. OE *staca;* akin to MLG *stake* stake, L *tignum* beam, ON *stāka* to push] (bef. 12c) **1** : a pointed piece of wood or other material driven or to be driven into the ground as a marker or support **2 a** : a post to which a person is bound for execution by burning **b** : execution by burning at a stake **3 a** : something that is staked for gain or loss **b** : the prize in a contest **c** : an interest or share in an undertaking (as a commercial venture) **4** : a Mormon territorial jurisdiction comprising a group of wards **5** : an upright stick at the side or end of a vehicle to retain the load **6** : GRUBSTAKE — **at stake** : at issue : in jeopardy

2stake *vt* **staked; stak·ing** (14c) **1** : to mark the limits of by or as if by stakes **2** : to tether to a stake **3** : BET, HAZARD **4** : to fasten up or support (as plants) with stakes **5** : to back financially **6** : GRUBSTAKE — **stake a claim** : to assert a title or right to something by or as if by placing stakes to satisfy a legal requirement

stake body *n* (ca. 1931) : an open motortruck body consisting of a platform with stakes inserted along the outside edges to retain a load

stake·hold·er \ˈstāk-ˌhōl-dər\ *n* (1708) : a person entrusted with the stakes of bettors

stake·out \ˈstā-ˌkau̇t\ *n* (1943) : a surveillance maintained by the police of an area or a person suspected of criminal activity

stake out \stā-ˈkau̇t\ *vt* (1951) **1** : to assign (as a police officer) to an area usu. to conduct a surveillance **2** : to maintain a stakeout of

stake race *n* (ca. 1909) : a horse race in which the prize offered is made up at least in part of money (as entry fees) put up by the owners of the horses entered

stake truck *n* (1926) : a truck having a stake body

Sta·kha·nov·ite \stə-ˈkän-ə-ˌvīt\ *n* [Alexei G. *Stakhanov b*1905 Russ. miner] (1936) : a Soviet industrial worker awarded recognition and special privileges for output beyond production norms — **Sta·kha·nov·ism** \-ˌviz-əm\ *n*

sta·lac·tite \stə-ˈlak-ˌtīt *also* ˈstal-ək-\ *n* [NL *stalactites,* fr. Gk *stalaktos* dripping, fr. *stalassein* to let drip — more at STALE] (1677) : a deposit of calcium carbonate (as calcite) resembling an icicle hanging from the roof or sides of a cavern — **sta·lac·tit·ic** \ˌstal-ˌak-ˈtit-ik, -ək-; stə-ˌlak-\ *adj*

sta·lag \ˈstäl-ˌäg\ *n* [G, short for *stammlager* base camp, fr. *stamm* base + *lager* camp] (1943) : a German prison camp for noncommissioned officers or enlisted men

sta·lag·mite \stə-ˈlag-ˌmīt *also* ˈstal-əg-\ *n* [NL *stalagmites,* fr. Gk *stalagma* drop or *stalagmos* dripping; akin to Gk *stalassein* to let drip] (1681) : a deposit of calcium carbonate like an inverted stalactite formed on the floor of a cave by the drip of calcareous water — **sta·lag·mit·ic** \ˌstal-ˌag-ˈmit-ik, -əg-; stə-, -lag-\ *adj*

1stale \ˈstā(ə)l\ *vb* **staled; stal·ing** *vt* (15c) **1** : to make stale **2** *archaic* : to make common : CHEAPEN ~ *vi* : to become stale

2stale *adj* **stal·er; stal·est** [ME, aged (of ale); akin to MD *stel* stale] (1530) **1** : tasteless or unpalatable from age **2** : tedious from familiarity **3** : impaired in legal force or effect by reason of being allowed to rest without timely use, action, or demand ⟨a ~ affidavit⟩ ⟨a ~ debt⟩ **4** : impaired in vigor or effectiveness — **stale·ly** \ˈstā(ə)l-lē\ *adv* — **stale·ness** *n*

3stale *n* [ME; akin to MLG *stal* horse urine, Gk *stalassein* to let drip] (15c) : urine of a domestic animal (as a horse)

4stale *vi* **staled; stal·ing** (15c) : URINATE — used chiefly of camels and horses

1stale·mate \ˈstā(ə)l-ˌmāt\ *n* [obs. E *stale* (stalemate) + E 1*mate*] (1765) **1** : a drawing position in chess in which only the king can move and although not in check can move only into check **2** : a drawn contest : DEADLOCK; *also* : the state of being stalemated

2stalemate *vt* (1765) : to bring into a stalemate

Sta·lin·ism \ˈstäl-ə-ˌniz-əm, ˈstal-\ *n* (1927) : the political, economic, and social principles and policies associated with Stalin; *esp* : the theory and practice of communism developed by Stalin from Marxism-Leninism and characterized esp. by rigid authoritarianism, widespread use of terror, and often by emphasis on Russian nationalism — **Sta·lin·ist** \-nəst\ *n or adj* — **Sta·lin·ize** \-ˌnīz\ *vt* — **Sta·lin·oid** \-ˌnȯid\ *n or adj*

1stalk \ˈstȯk\ *n* [ME *stalke;* akin to OE *stealc* lofty] (14c) **1 a** : the main stem of an herbaceous plant often with its dependent parts **b** : a part of a plant (as a petiole, stipe, or peduncle) that supports another **2** : a slender upright object or supporting or connecting part; *esp* : PEDUNCLE ⟨the ~ of a crinoid⟩ — **stalked** \ˈstȯkt\ *adj* — **stalk·less** \ˈstȯk-ləs\ *adj* — **stalky** \ˈstȯ-kē\ *adj*

2stalk *vb* [ME *stalken,* fr. OE *bestealcian;* akin to OE *stealc* lofty, *stelan* to steal — more at STEAL] *vi* (15c) **1** : to pursue quarry or prey stealthily **2** : to walk stiffly or haughtily ~ *vt* **1** : to pursue by stalking **2** : to go through (an area) in search of prey or quarry ⟨~ the woods for deer⟩ — **stalk·er** *n*

3stalk *n* (15c) **1** : the act of stalking **2** : a stalking gait

stalk·ing–horse \'stȯ-kiŋ-ˌhȯ(ə)rs\ *n* (1519) **1 :** a horse or a figure like a horse behind which a hunter stalks game **2 :** something used to mask a purpose **3 :** a candidate put forward to divide the opposition or to conceal someone's real candidacy

[1]**stall** \'stȯl\ *n* [ME, fr. OE *steall;* akin to OHG *stal* place, stall, L *locus* (OL *stlocus*) place, Gk *stellein* to set up, place, send] (bef. 12c) **1 a :** a compartment for a domestic animal in a stable or barn **b :** a space marked off for parking a motor vehicle **2 a :** a seat in the chancel of a church with back and sides wholly or partly enclosed **b :** a church pew **c** *Brit* **:** a front orchestra seat in a theater **3 :** a booth, stand, or counter at which articles are displayed for sale **4 :** a protective sheath for a finger or toe : COT **5 :** a small compartment ⟨a shower ~⟩

[2]**stall** *vt* (14c) **1 :** to put into or keep in a stall **2** *obs* **:** to install in office **3 a :** to bring to a standstill : BLOCK; *esp* **:** MIRE **b :** to cause (an engine) to stop usu. inadvertently **c :** to cause (an airplane or airfoil) to go into a stall ~ *vi* **1 :** to come to a standstill (as from mired wheels or engine failure) **2 :** to experience a stall in flying

[3]**stall** *n* (ca. 1918) **:** the condition of an airfoil or airplane operating so that there is a flow breakdown and loss of lift with a tendency to drop

[4]**stall** *n* [alter. of *stale* (lure)] (1914) **:** a ruse to deceive or delay

[5]**stall** *vi* (1917) **:** to play for time : DELAY ~ *vt* **:** to hold off, divert, or delay by evasion or deception

stall–feed \'stȯl-ˌfēd\ *vt* **-fed** \-ˌfed\; **-feed·ing** (1763) **:** to feed in a stall esp. so as to fatten ⟨~ an ox⟩

stal·lion \'stal-yən\ *n* [ME *stalion,* fr. MF *estalon,* of Gmc origin; akin to OHG *stal* stall] (14c) **:** an uncastrated male horse : a male horse kept for breeding; *also* **:** a male animal (as a dog or a sheep) kept primarily as a stud

[1]**stal·wart** \'stȯl-wərt\ *adj* [ME, alter. of *stalworth,* fr. OE *stǣlwierthe* serviceable] (15c) **:** marked by outstanding strength and vigor of body, mind, or spirit ⟨~ common sense⟩ ***syn*** see STRONG — **stal·wart·ly** *adv* — **stal·wart·ness** *n*

[2]**stalwart** *n* (15c) **1 :** a stalwart person **2 :** an unwavering partisan

stal·worth \'stȯl-(ˌ)wərth\ *archaic var of* STALWART

sta·men \'stā-mən\ *n, pl* **stamens** *also* **sta·mi·na** \'stā-mə-nə, 'stam-ə-\ [L, warp, thread; akin to Gk *stēmōn* thread, *histanai* to cause to stand — more at STAND] (1668) **:** a microsporophyll of a seed plant; *specif* **:** the organ of a flower that produces the male gamete, consists of an anther and a filament, and is morphologically a spore-bearing leaf — see FLOWER illustration

stamin- *or* **stamini-** *comb form* [L *stamin-, stamen*] **:** stamen ⟨*stamini*ferous⟩

stam·i·na \'stam-ə-nə\ *n* [L, pl. of *stamen* warp, thread of life spun by the Fates] (1691) **:** STAYING POWER, ENDURANCE

sta·mi·nal \'stā-mən-ᵊl, 'stam-ən-\ *adj* (1845) **:** of, relating to, or consisting of a stamen

sta·mi·nate \'stā-mə-nət, 'stam-ə-, -ˌnāt\ *adj* (ca. 1845) **1 :** having or producing stamens **2** *of a diclinous flower* **:** having stamens but no pistils

sta·mi·no·di·um \ˌstā-mə-'nōd-ē-əm, ˌstam-ə-\ *n, pl* **-dia** \-ē-ə\ [NL, fr. *stamin-* + *-odium* thing resembling, fr. Gk *-ōdēs* like] (ca. 1821) **:** an abortive or sterile stamen

stam·mel \'stam-əl\ *n* [prob. fr. *stamin* (a woolen fabric)] (1530) **1** *obs* **:** a coarse woolen clothing fabric usu. dyed red and used sometimes for undershirts of penitents **2** *archaic* **:** the bright red color of stammel

stam·mer \'stam-ər\ *vb* **stam·mered; stam·mer·ing** \-(ə-)riŋ\ [ME *stameren,* fr. OE *stamerian;* akin to OHG *stamalōn* to stammer, Lith *stumti* to push] *vi* (bef. 12c) **:** to make involuntary stops and repetitions in speaking : HALT — compare STUTTER ~ *vt* **:** to utter with involuntary stops or repetitions — **stammer** *n* — **stam·mer·er** \-ər-ər\ *n*

[1]**stamp** \'stamp; *vt2a & vi2 are also* 'stämp *or* 'stȯmp\ *vb* [ME *stampen;* akin to OHG *stampfōn* to stamp, L *temnere* to despise, Gk *stembein* to shake up] *vt* (bef. 12c) **1 :** to pound or crush with a pestle or a heavy instrument **2 a (1) :** to strike or beat forcibly with the bottom of the foot **(2) :** to bring down (the foot) forcibly **b :** to extinguish or destroy by or as if by stamping with the foot — usu. used with *out* ⟨~ out cancer⟩ **3 a :** IMPRESS, IMPRINT ⟨~ "paid" on the bill⟩ **b :** to attach a stamp to **4 :** to cut out, bend, or form with a stamp or die **5 a :** to provide with a distinctive character ⟨~*ed* with a dreary, institutionalized look —Bernard Taper⟩ **b :** CHARACTERIZE ~ *vi* **1 :** POUND **2 :** to strike or thrust the foot forcibly or noisily downward

[2]**stamp** *n* (15c) **1 :** a device or instrument for stamping **2 :** the impression or mark made by stamping or imprinting **3 a :** a distinctive character, indication, or mark **b :** a lasting imprint **4 :** the act of stamping **5 :** a stamped or printed paper affixed in evidence that a tax has been paid; *also* **:** POSTAGE STAMP — **stamp·less** *adj*

[1]**stam·pede** \stam-'pēd\ *n* [AmerSp *estampida,* fr. Sp, crash, fr. *estampar* to stamp, of Gmc origin; akin to OHG *stampfōn* to stamp] (1834) **1 :** a wild headlong rush or flight of frightened animals **2 :** a mass movement of people at a common impulse **3 :** an extended festival combining a rodeo with exhibitions, contests, and social events

[2]**stampede** *vb* **stam·ped·ed; stam·ped·ing** *vt* (1843) **1 :** to cause to run away in headlong panic **2 :** to cause (a group of people) to act on mass impulse ~ *vi* **1 :** to flee headlong in panic **2 :** to act on mass impulse — **stam·ped·er** *n*

stamp·er \'stam-pər, 'stäm-, 'stȯm-; *compare* [1]STAMP\ *n* (14c) **:** one that stamps: as **a :** a worker who performs an industrial stamping operation **b :** an implement for pounding or stamping **c :** any of various stamping machines

stamping ground \'stamp-, 'stämp-, 'stȯmp-\ *n* (1786) **:** a favorite or habitual resort

stamp·ing mill \'stam-piŋ-\ *n* (1749) **:** STAMP MILL

stamp mill \'stamp-\ *n* (1749) **:** a mill in which ore is crushed with stamps; *also* **:** a machine for stamping ore

stamp tax *n* (1797) **:** a tax collected by means of a stamp purchased and affixed (as to a deck of playing cards); *specif* **:** such a tax on a document (as a deed or promissory note) — called also *stamp duty*

stance \'stan(t)s\ *n* [MF *estance* position, posture, stay, fr. (assumed) VL *stantia,* fr. L *stant-, stans,* prp. of *stare* to stand] (1532) **1** *chiefly Scot* **a :** STATION **b :** SITE **2 a :** a way of standing or being placed : POSTURE **b :** intellectual or emotional attitude ⟨took an antiwar ~⟩ **3 a :** the position of the feet of a golfer or batter preparatory to making a swing **b :** the position of both body and feet from which an athlete starts or operates

[1]**stanch** \'stȯnch, 'stänch\ *vt* [ME *staunchen,* fr. MF *estancher,* fr. (assumed) VL *stanticare,* fr. L *stant-, stans,* prp.] (15c) **1 :** to check or stop the flowing of ⟨~*ed* her tears⟩; *also* **:** to stop the flow of blood from (a wound) **2** *archaic* **:** ALLAY, EXTINGUISH **3 a :** to stop or check in its course ⟨trying to ~ the crime wave⟩ **b :** to make watertight : stop up — **stanch·er** *n*

[2]**stanch** *var of* STAUNCH

[1]**stan·chion** \'stan-chən\ *n* [ME *stanchon,* fr. MF *estanchon,* fr. OF, aug. of *estance* stay, prop] (15c) **1 :** an upright bar, post, or support (as for a roof) **2 :** a device that fits loosely around a cow's neck and limits forward and backward motion (as in a stall)

[2]**stanchion** *vt* **stan·chioned; stan·chion·ing** \'stanch-(ə-)niŋ\ (1528) **1 a :** to provide with stanchions **b :** to support or brace with or as if with a stanchion **2 :** to secure (as a cow) by a stanchion

[1]**stand** \'stand\ *vb* **stood** \'stu̇d\; **stand·ing** [ME *standen,* fr. OE *standan;* akin to OHG *stantan, stān* to stand, L *stare,* Gk *histanai* to cause to stand, set, *histasthai* to stand, be standing] *vi* (bef. 12c) **1 a :** to support oneself on the feet in an erect position **b :** to be a specified height when fully erect ⟨~*s* six feet two⟩ **c :** to rise to an erect position **2 a :** to take up or maintain a specified position or posture ⟨~ aside⟩ ⟨can you ~ on your head⟩ **b :** to maintain one's position ⟨~ firm⟩ **3 :** to be in a particular state or situation ⟨~*s* accused⟩ **4 :** to hold a course at sea **5** *obs* **:** HESITATE **6 a :** to have or maintain a relative position in or as if in a graded scale ⟨~*s* first in the class⟩ **b :** to be in a position to gain or lose because of an action taken or a commitment made ⟨~*s* to make quite a profit⟩ **7** *chiefly Brit* **:** to be a candidate : RUN **8 a :** to rest or remain upright on a base or lower end ⟨a clock *stood* on the mantle⟩ **b :** to occupy a place or location ⟨the house ~*s* on a knoll⟩ **9 a :** to remain stationary or inactive ⟨the car *stood* in the garage for a week⟩ **b :** to gather slowly and remain ⟨tears ~*ing* in her eyes⟩ **10 :** AGREE, ACCORD — used chiefly in the expression *it stands to reason* **11 a :** to exist in a definite written or printed form ⟨copy a passage exactly as it ~*s*⟩ **b :** to remain valid or efficacious ⟨the order given last week still ~*s*⟩ **12** *of a male animal* **:** to be available as a sire — used esp. of horses ~ *vt* **1 a :** to endure or undergo successfully ⟨this book will ~ the test of time⟩ **b :** to tolerate without flinching : bear courageously ⟨~*s* pain well⟩ **c :** to endure the presence or personality of ⟨can't ~ the boss⟩ **d :** to derive benefit or enjoyment from ⟨you look like you could ~ a drink⟩ **2 :** to remain firm in the face of ⟨~ a siege⟩ **3 :** to submit to ⟨~ trial⟩ **4 a :** to perform the duty of ⟨~ guard⟩ **b :** to participate in (a military formation) **5 :** to pay the cost of (a treat) : pay for ⟨I'll ~ you a dinner⟩ ⟨~ drinks⟩ **6 :** to cause to stand : set upright ***syn*** see BEAR — **stand·er** *n* — **stand a chance :** to have a chance — **stand for 1 :** to be a symbol for : REPRESENT **2 :** to put up with : PERMIT — **stand on 1 :** to depend on **2 :** to insist on ⟨never *stands on* ceremony⟩ — **stand one's ground :** to maintain one's position — **stand on one's own feet :** to think or act independently — **stand treat :** to pay the cost of food, drink, or entertainment for others in a group

[2]**stand** *n* (1592) **1 :** an act of stopping or staying in one place **2 a :** a halt for defense or resistance **b :** an often defensive effort of some duration or degree of success ⟨a goal-line ~⟩ **c (1) :** a stop made to give a performance ⟨a 6-game ~ at home⟩ **(2) :** a town where such a stop is made **3 a :** a place or post where one stands **b :** a strongly or aggressively held position esp. on a debatable issue **4 a :** the place taken by a witness for testifying in court **b** *pl* **(1) :** a section of the tiered seats for spectators of a sport or spectacle **(2) :** the occupants of such seats **c :** a raised platform (as for a speaker) serving as a point of vantage **5 a :** a small often open-air structure for a small retail business ⟨a vegetable ~⟩ ⟨a hot dog ~⟩ **b :** a site fit for business opportunity **6 :** a place where a passenger vehicle stops or parks ⟨a taxi ~⟩ **7 :** [1]HIVE 2 **8 :** a frame on or in which something may be placed for support **9 :** a group of plants growing in a continuous area **10 :** a standing posture

stand–alone \ˌstan-də-ˌlōn\ *adj* (1969) **:** operating or capable of operating independent of a computer ⟨a ~ word processing system⟩

[1]**stan·dard** \'stan-dərd\ *n* [ME, fr. OF *estandard* rallying point, standard, of Gmc origin; akin to OE *standan* to stand and to OE *ord* point — more at ODD] (12c) **1 :** a conspicuous object (as a banner) formerly carried at the top of a pole and used to mark a rallying point esp. in battle or to serve as an emblem **2 a :** a long narrow tapering flag that is personal to an individual or corporation and bears heraldic devices **b :** the personal flag of the head of a state or of a member of a royal family **c :** an organization flag carried by a mounted or motorized military unit **d :** BANNER **3 :** something established by authority, custom, or general consent as a model or example : CRITERION **4 :** something set up and established by authority as a rule for the measure of quantity, weight, extent, value, or quality **5 a :** the fineness and legally fixed weight of the metal used in coins **b :** the basis of value in a monetary system **6 :** a structure built for or serving as a base or support **7 a :** a shrub or herb grown with an erect main stem so that it forms or resembles a tree **b :** a fruit tree grafted on a stock that does not induce dwarfing **8 a :** the large odd upper petal of a papilionaceous flower (as the pea) **b :** one of the three inner usu. erect and incurved petals of an iris **9 :** a musical composition (as a song) that has become a part of the standard repertoire — **stan·dard·less** *adj*

syn STANDARD, CRITERION, GAUGE, YARDSTICK, TOUCHSTONE mean a means of determining what a thing should be. STANDARD applies to any definite rule, principle, or measure established by authority; CRITERION may apply to anything used as a test of quality whether formulated as a rule or principle or not; GAUGE applies to a means of testing a particular dimension (as thickness, depth, diameter) or figuratively a particular quality or aspect; YARDSTICK is an informal substitute for CRITERION that suggests quantity more often than quality; TOUCHSTONE suggests a simple test of the authenticity or value of something intangible.

[2]**standard** *adj* (1622) **1 a :** constituting or conforming to a standard esp. as established by law or custom ⟨~ weight⟩ **b :** sound and usable but not of top quality ⟨~ beef⟩ **2 a :** regularly and widely used, available, or supplied ⟨~ automobile equipment⟩ **b :** well-established and very familiar ⟨the ~ opera⟩ **3 :** having recognized and permanent value ⟨a ~ reference work⟩ **4 :** substantially uniform and well established by usage in the speech and writing of the educated and widely

recognized as acceptable ⟨~ pronunciation is subject to regional variations⟩ — **stan·dard·ly** *adv*

stan·dard–bear·er \ˈstan-dərd-ˌbar-ər, -ˌber-\ *n* (15c) **1 :** one that bears a standard or banner **2 :** the leader of an organization, movement, or party

stan·dard·bred \-ˌbred\ *n, often cap* (ca. 1891) **:** any of an American breed of trotting and pacing horses bred for speed and noted for stamina

standard candle *n* (1879) **:** CANDLE 3

standard deviation *n* (1925) **1 :** a measure of the dispersion of a frequency distribution that is the square root of the arithmetic mean of the squares of the deviation of each of the class frequencies from the arithmetic mean of the frequency distribution; *also* **:** a similar quantity found by dividing by one less than the number of squares in the sum of squares instead of taking the arithmetic mean **2 :** a parameter that indicates the way in which a probability function or a probability density function is centered around its mean and that is equal to the square root of the moment in which the deviation from the mean is squared

Standard English *n* (1873) **:** the English that with respect to spelling, grammar, pronunciation, and vocabulary is substantially uniform though not devoid of regional differences, that is well established by usage in the formal and informal speech and writing of the educated, and that is widely recognized as acceptable wherever English is spoken and understood

standard error *n* (1939) **:** the standard deviation of the probability function or probability density function of a random variable and esp. of a statistic; *specif* **:** the standard error of the mean of a sample from a population with a normal distribution that is equal to the standard deviation of the normal distribution divided by the square root of the sample size

standard gauge *n* (1871) **:** a railroad gauge of 4 feet 8½ inches

stan·dard·ize \ˈstan-dərd-ˌīz\ *vt* **-ized; -iz·ing** (1873) **1 :** to compare with a standard **2 :** to bring into conformity with a standard — **stan·dard·iza·tion** \ˌstan-dərd-ə-ˈzā-shən\ *n*

standard of living (1902) **1 :** the necessities, comforts, and luxuries enjoyed or aspired to by an individual or group **2 :** a minimum of necessities, comforts, or luxuries held essential to maintaining a person or group in customary or proper status or circumstances

standard operating procedure *n* (1952) **:** established or prescribed methods to be followed routinely for the performance of designated operations or in designated situations — called also *standing operating procedure*

standard position *n* (1950) **:** the position of an angle with its vertex at the origin of a rectangular-coordinate system and its initial side coinciding with the positive x-axis

standard schnauzer *n* (ca. 1934) **:** a schnauzer of a breed that attains a height at the highest point of the shoulder blades of 18 to 20 inches (45.7 to 50.8 centimeters) in the male and 17 to 19 inches (43.2 to 48.3 centimeters) in the female

standard score *n* (1928) **:** an individual test score expressed as the deviation from the mean score of the group in units of standard deviation

standard time *n* (1904) **:** the time of a region or country that is established by law or general usage as civil time; *specif* **:** the mean solar time of a meridian that is a multiple of 15 arbitrarily applied to a local area or to one of the 24 time zones and designated as a number of hours earlier or later than Greenwich time

stand·away \ˌstan-də-ˌwā\ *adj* (1948) **:** standing out from the body ⟨a ~ skirt⟩

[1]**stand·by** \ˈstan(d)-ˌbī\ *n, pl* **stand·bys** \-ˌbīz\ (1796) **1 a :** one to be relied on esp. in emergencies **b :** a favorite or reliable choice or resource **2 :** one that is held in reserve ready for use **:** SUBSTITUTE — **on standby :** ready or available for immediate action or use

[2]**stand·by** \ˌstan(d)-ˌbī\ *adj* (1909) **1 :** held near at hand and ready for use ⟨a ~ power plant⟩ ⟨~ equipment⟩ **2 :** relating to the act or condition of standing by ⟨~ duty⟩ ⟨a ~ period⟩ **3 :** of, relating to, or traveling by an airline service in which the passenger must wait for an available unreserved seat ⟨~ passengers⟩ ⟨a ~ ticket⟩

[3]**stand·by** \ˈstan(d)-ˌbī\ *adv* (1971) **:** on a standby basis ⟨fly ~⟩

stand by \(ˌ)stan(d)-ˈbī\ *vi* (14c) **1 :** to be present; *also* **:** to remain apart or aloof **2 :** to be or to get ready to act ~ *vt* **:** to remain loyal or faithful to **:** DEFEND

stand down *vi* (1681) **1 :** to leave the witness stand **2** *chiefly Brit* **a :** to go off duty **b :** to withdraw from a contest or from a position of leadership

stand·ee \stan-ˈdē\ *n* (ca. 1880) **:** one who occupies standing room

stand–in \ˈstan-ˌdin\ *n* (ca. 1934) **1 :** someone employed to occupy an actor's place while lights and camera are readied **2 :** SUBSTITUTE

stand in \(ˌ)stan-ˈdin\ *vi* (ca. 1945) **:** to act as a stand-in — **stand in with :** to be in a specially favored position with

[1]**stand·ing** \ˈstan-diŋ\ *adj* (15c) **1 a :** upright on the feet or base **:** ERECT ⟨the ~ audience⟩ **b :** not yet cut or harvested ⟨~ timber⟩ ⟨~ grain⟩ **2 a :** not being used or operated ⟨a ~ factory⟩ **b :** not flowing **:** STAGNANT ⟨~ water⟩ **3 a :** remaining at the same level, degree, or amount for an indeterminate period ⟨a ~ offer⟩ **b :** continuing in existence or use indefinitely **4 :** established by law or custom **5 :** not movable **6 :** done from a standing position ⟨a ~ jump⟩ ⟨a ~ ovation⟩

[2]**standing** *n* (15c) **1 a :** a place to stand in **:** LOCATION **b :** a position from which one may assert or enforce legal rights and duties **2 a :** length of service or experience esp. as determining rank, pay, or privilege **b :** position or condition in society or in a profession; *esp* **:** good reputation **c :** position relative to a standard of achievement or to achievements of competitors **3 :** maintenance of position or condition **:** DURATION ⟨a custom of long ~⟩

standing army *n* (1603) **:** a permanent army of paid soldiers

standing committee *n* (1902) **:** a permanent committee esp. of a legislative body

standing crop *n* (ca. 1925) **:** the total amount or number of living things or of one kind of living thing (as an uncut farm crop, the fish in a pond, or organisms in an ecosystem) in a particular situation at any given time

standing order *n* (1737) **:** an instruction or prescribed procedure in force permanently or until specifically changed or canceled; *esp* **:** any of the rules for the guidance and government of parliamentary procedure which endure through successive sessions until vacated or repealed

standing room *n* (1603) **:** space for standing; *esp* **:** accommodation available for spectators or passengers after all seats are filled

standing wave *n* (ca. 1909) **:** a single-frequency mode of vibration of a body or physical system in which the amplitude varies from place to place, is constantly zero at fixed points, and has maxima at other points

stan·dish \ˈstan-dish\ *n* [origin unknown] (15c) **:** a stand for writing materials **:** INKSTAND

[1]**stand·off** \ˈstan-ˌdȯf\ *adj* (1837) **1 :** STANDOFFISH **2 :** used for holding something at a distance from a surface ⟨a ~ insulator⟩

[2]**standoff** *n* (1883) **1 :** the act of standing off **2 a :** a counterbalancing effect **b :** TIE, DRAW ⟨the two teams played to a ~⟩

stand off \(ˈ)stan-ˈdȯf\ *vi* (1601) **1 :** to stay at a distance from something **2 :** to sail away from the shore ~ *vt* **1 :** to keep from advancing **:** REPEL **2 :** PUT OFF, STALL

stand·off·ish \stan-ˈdȯ-fish\ *adj* (1860) **:** somewhat cold and reserved — **stand·off·ish·ly** *adv* — **stand·off·ish·ness** *n*

stand oil *n* (1924) **:** a thickened drying oil; *esp* **:** linseed oil heated to about 600° F

stand·out \ˈstan-ˌdau̇t\ *n* (1540) **:** one that is prominent or conspicuous esp. because of excellence

stand out \(ˈ)stan-ˈdau̇t\ *vi* (1928) **1 a :** to appear as if in relief **:** PROJECT **b :** to be prominent or conspicuous **2 :** to steer away from shore **3 :** to be stubborn in resolution or resistance

stand·pat \ˌstan(d)-ˌpat\ *adj* [*stand pat*] (1904) **:** stubbornly conservative **:** resisting or opposing change

stand pat \ˈstan(d)-ˈpat\ *vi* [[4]*pat*] (1882) **1 :** to play one's hand as dealt in draw poker without drawing **2 :** to oppose or resist change — **stand·pat·ter** \ˈstan(d)-ˌpat-ər, -ˈpat-\ *n* — **stand·pat·tism** \-ˌpat-ˌiz-əm\ *n*

stand·pipe \ˈstan(d)-ˌpīp\ *n* (ca. 1850) **:** a high vertical pipe or reservoir that is used to secure a uniform pressure in a water-supply system

stand·point \-ˌpȯint\ *n* (1829) **:** a position from which objects or principles are viewed and according to which they are compared and judged

stand·still \-ˌstil\ *n* (1702) **:** a state characterized by absence of motion or of progress **:** STOP

stand–up \ˌstan-ˌdəp\ *adj* (1812) **1 a :** ERECT, UPRIGHT **b :** stiffened to stay upright without folding over ⟨a ~ collar⟩ **2 :** performed in, performing in, or requiring a standing position ⟨a ~ bar⟩

stand up \(ˈ)stan-ˈdəp\ *vi* (bef. 12c) **1 :** to rise to a standing position **2 :** to remain sound and intact under stress, attack, or close scrutiny ~ *vt* **:** to fail to keep an appointment with — **stand up for :** to defend against attack or criticism — **stand up to 1 :** to meet fairly and fully **2 :** to face boldly — **stand up with :** to be best man or maid of honor for at a wedding ceremony

stand–up comedian *n* (1966) **:** a comedian whose act consists of a monologue of jokes, gags, or satirical comments performed usu. while standing alone on a stage or in front of a camera

stand–up·per \ˈstan-ˈdəp-ər\ *n* (1973) **:** a television news report or interview by an on-camera reporter standing usu. at the scene of an occurrence

stane \ˈstān\ *Scot var of* STONE

Stan·ford–Bi·net test \ˌstan-fərd-bi-ˈnā-\ *n* [*Stanford* University + Alfred *Binet* †1911 Fr. psychologist] (1924) **:** an intelligence test prepared at Stanford University as a revision of the Binet-Simon scale and commonly used with children — called also *Stanford-Binet*

[1]**stang** \ˈstaŋ\ *vt* [ME *stangen*, fr. ON *stanga* to prick; akin to ON *stinga* to sting] *chiefly Scot* (14c) **:** STING

[2]**stang** *n, chiefly Scot* (1513) **:** PANG

[3]**stang** *var of* SATANG

stan·hope \ˈstan-əp\ *n* [Fitzroy *Stanhope* †1864 Brit. clergyman] (1825) **:** a gig, buggy, or phaeton typically having a high seat and closed back

sta·nine \ˈstā-ˌnīn\ *n* [*sta*ndard (score) + *nine*] (ca. 1942) **:** one of the nine classes into which a set of normalized standard scores arranged according to rank in educational testing are divided, which include the bottom 4% and the top 4% of the scores in the first and ninth classes and the middle 20% in the fifth, and which have a standard deviation of 2 and a mean of 5

Sta·ni·slav·ski method \ˌstan-ə-ˈslaf-ski-, -ˈslav-\ *n* [Konstantin *Stanislavski*] (1941) **:** a technique in acting by which an actor strives to empathize with the character he is portraying so as to effect a realistic interpretation

[1]**stank** \ˈstaŋk\ *past of* STINK

[2]**stank** *n* [ME, fr. MF *estanc*] (14c) **1** *dial Brit* **a :** POND, POOL **b :** a ditch containing water **2** *Brit* **:** a small dam **:** WEIR

stan·na·ry \ˈstan-ə-rē\ *n, pl* **-ries** [ML *stannaria* tin mine, fr. LL *stannum* tin] (15c) **:** one of the regions in England containing tinworks — usu. used in pl.

stan·nic \ˈstan-ik\ *adj* [prob. fr. F *stannique*, fr. LL *stannum* tin, fr. L, an alloy of silver and lead, prob. of Celt origin; akin to Corn *stēn* tin] (1790) **:** of, relating to, or containing tin esp. with a valence of four

stan·nite \ˈstan-ˌīt\ *n* [LL *stannum*] (1896) **:** a mineral Cu_2FeSnS_4 that is a steel-gray or iron-black sulfide of copper, iron, and tin with a metallic luster and occurs in granular masses

stan·nous \ˈstan-əs\ *adj* [ISV, fr. LL *stannum*] (1849) **:** of, relating to, or containing tin esp. when bivalent

stan·za \ˈstan-zə\ *n* [It, stay, abode, room, stanza, fr. (assumed) VL *stantia* stay — more at STANCE] (1588) **:** a division of a poem consisting of a series of lines arranged together in a usu. recurring pattern of meter and rhyme **:** STROPHE — **stan·za·ic** \stan-ˈzā-ik\ *adj*

sta·pe·dec·to·my \ˌstā-pi-ˈdek-tə-mē\ *n, pl* **-mies** [ISV, fr. NL *staped-, stapes*] (1894) **:** surgical removal and prosthetic replacement of the stapes to relieve deafness — **sta·pe·dec·to·mized** \-ˌmīzd\ *adj*

sta·pe·di·al \stā-ˈpēd-ē-əl, stə-\ *adj* (1875) **:** of, relating to, or located near the stapes

sta·pe·lia \stə-ˈpēl-yə\ *n* [NL, fr. J. B. van *Stapel* †1636 Du. botanist] (ca. 1785) **:** any of a genus (*Stapelia*) of African plants of the milkweed family with succulent leafless toothed stems like cactus joints and showy but putrid-smelling flowers

sta·pes \'stā-(,)pēz\ *n, pl* **stapes** *or* **sta·pe·des** \'stā-pə-,dēz\ [NL *staped-, stapes*, fr. ML, stirrup, alter. of LL *stapia*] (1670) **:** the innermost ossicle of the ear of mammals — called also *stirrup;* see EAR illustration

staph \'staf\ *n* (ca. 1935) **:** STAPHYLOCOCCUS

staph·y·li·nid \,staf-ə-'lī-nəd\ *n* [NL *Staphylinidae*, deriv. of Gk *staphylē* bunch of grapes; akin to OE *stæf* staff] (ca. 1891) **:** any of a family (Staphylinidae) of beetles that have a long body and very short wing covers beneath which the wings are folded transversely — **staphylinid** *adj*

staph·y·lo·coc·cal \,staf-(ə-)lō-'käk-əl\ *also* **staph·y·lo·coc·cic** \-'käk-(s)ik\ *adj* (1900) **:** of, relating to, caused by, or being a staphylococcus

staph·y·lo·coc·cus \-'käk-əs\ *n, pl* **-coc·ci** \-'käk-,(s)ī, -(,)(s)ē\ [NL, fr. Gk *staphylē* bunch of grapes + NL *-coccus*] (1887) **:** any of various nonmotile gram-positive spherical bacteria (esp. genus *Staphylococcus*) that occur singly, in pairs or tetrads, or in irregular clusters and include parasites of skin and mucous membranes

[1]**sta·ple** \'stā-pəl\ *n* [ME *stapel* post, staple, fr. OE *stapol* post; akin to MD *stapel* step, heap, emporium, OE *steppan* to step] (13c) **1 :** a U-shaped metal loop both ends of which are driven into a surface to hold the hook, hasp, or bolt of a lock, secure a rope, or fix a wire in place **2 :** a small U-shaped wire both ends of which are driven through layers of thin and easily penetrable material (as paper) and usu. clinched to hold the layers together

[2]**staple** *vt* **sta·pled; sta·pling** \-p(ə-)liŋ\ (14c) **:** to provide with or secure by staples

[3]**staple** *n* [ME, fr. MD *stapel* emporium] (15c) **1 :** a town used as a center for the sale or exportation of commodities in bulk **2 :** a place of supply **:** SOURCE **3 :** a chief commodity or production of a place **4 a :** a commodity for which the demand is constant **b :** something having widespread and constant use or appeal **c :** the sustaining or principal element **:** SUBSTANCE **5 :** RAW MATERIAL **6 a :** textile fiber (as wool or rayon) of relatively short length that when spun and twisted forms a yarn rather than a filament **b :** the length of a piece of such textile fiber

[4]**staple** *adj* (1615) **1 :** used, needed, or enjoyed constantly usu. by many individuals **2 :** produced regularly or in large quantities ⟨~ crops such as wheat and rice⟩ **3 :** PRINCIPAL, CHIEF

[1]**sta·pler** \'stā-p(ə-)lər\ *n* (1513) **:** one that deals in staple goods or in staple fiber

[2]**stapler** *n* (ca. 1909) **:** one that inserts staples; *esp* **:** a small usu. hand-operated device for inserting wire staples

[1]**star** \'stär\ *n, often attrib* [ME *sterre*, fr. OE *steorra;* akin to OHG *sterno* star, L *stella*, Gk *astēr, astron*] (bef. 12c) **1 a :** a natural luminous body visible in the sky esp. at night **b :** a self-luminous gaseous celestial body of great mass whose shape is usu. spheroidal and whose size may be as small as the earth or larger than the earth's orbit **2 a** (1) **:** a planet or a configuration of the planets that is held in astrology to influence one's destiny or fortune — usu. used in pl. (2) **:** a waxing or waning fortune or fame ⟨her ~ was rising⟩ **b** *obs* **:** DESTINY **3 a :** a conventional figure with five or more points that represents a star; *esp* **:** ASTERISK **b :** an often star-shaped ornament or medal worn as a badge of honor, authority, or rank or as the insignia of an order **c :** one of a group of conventional stars used to place something in a scale of value **4 :** something resembling a star ⟨was hit on the head and saw ~*s*⟩ **5 a :** the principal member of a theatrical or operatic company who usu. plays the chief roles **b :** a highly publicized theatrical or motion-picture performer **c :** an outstandingly talented performer ⟨a track ~⟩ **d :** a person who is preeminent in a particular field — **star·less** \-ləs\ *adj* — **star·like** \-,līk\ *adj*

[2]**star** *vb* **starred; star·ring** *vt* (1718) **1 :** to sprinkle or adorn with stars **2 a :** to mark with a star as being preeminent **b :** to mark with an asterisk **3 :** to advertise or display prominently **:** FEATURE ⟨the movie ~*s* a famous stage personality⟩ ~ *vi* **1 :** to play the most prominent or important role **2 :** to perform outstandingly

[3]**star** *adj* (1824) **1 :** of, relating to, or being a star ⟨received ~ billing⟩ **2 :** of outstanding excellence **:** PREEMINENT ⟨a ~ athlete⟩

star apple *n* (1683) **:** a tropical American tree (*Chrysophyllum cainito*) of the sapodilla family grown in warm regions for ornament or fruit; *also* **:** the apple-shaped edible fruit

[1]**star·board** \'stär-bərd\ *n* [ME *sterbord*, fr. OE *stēorbord*, fr. *stēor-* steering oar + *bord* ship's side — more at STEER, BOARD] (bef. 12c) **:** the right side of a ship or aircraft looking forward — compare PORT

[2]**starboard** *adj* (15c) **:** of, relating to, or situated to starboard

[3]**starboard** *vt* (1598) **:** to turn or put (a helm or rudder) to the right

[1]**starch** \'stärch\ *vt* [ME *sterchen*, prob. fr. (assumed) OE *stercan* to stiffen; akin to OE *stearc* stiff — more at STARK] (15c) **:** to stiffen with or as if with starch

[2]**starch** *n* (15c) **1 :** a white odorless tasteless granular or powdery complex carbohydrate $(C_6H_{10}O_5)_x$ that is the chief storage form of carbohydrate in plants, is an important foodstuff, and is used also in adhesives and sizes, in laundering, and in pharmacy and medicine **2 :** a stiff formal manner **:** FORMALITY **3 :** resolute vigor

star–cham·ber \'stär-'chām-bər\ *adj* [*Star Chamber*, a court existing in England from the 15th century until 1641] (1598) **:** characterized by secrecy and often being irresponsibly arbitrary and oppressive

starchy \'stär-chē\ *adj* **starch·i·er; -est** (1802) **1 :** containing, consisting of, or resembling starch **2 :** consisting of or marked by formality or stiffness — **starch·i·ly** \-chə-lē\ *adv* — **starch·i·ness** \-chē-nəs\ *n*

star–crossed \'stär-,kröst\ *adj* (1592) **:** not favored by the stars **:** ILL-FATED ⟨a pair of ~ lovers take their life —Shak.⟩

star·dom \'stärd-əm\ *n* (1865) **:** the status or position of a star ⟨the actress quickly reached ~⟩

star·dust \'stär-,dəst\ *n* (1927) **:** a feeling or impression of romance, magic, or ethereality

[1]**stare** \'sta(ə)r, 'ste(ə)r\ *vb* **stared; star·ing** [ME *staren*, fr. OE *starian;* akin to OHG *starēn* to stare, L *strenuus* strenuous, Gk *stereos* solid, Lith *starinti* to stiffen] *vi* (bef. 12c) **1 :** to look fixedly often with wide-open eyes **2 :** to show oneself conspicuously ⟨the error *stared* from the page⟩ **3** *of hair* **:** to stand on end **:** BRISTLE; *also* **:** to appear rough and lusterless ~ *vt* **1 :** to have an effect on by staring **2 :** to look at with a searching or earnest gaze ***syn*** see GAZE — **star·er** *n* — **stare one in the face :** to be undeniably and forcefully evident or apparent

[2]**stare** *n* (15c) **:** the act or an instance of staring ⟨a blank ~⟩

sta·re de·ci·sis \,ster-ē-di-'sī-səs, ,star-\ *n* [L, to stand by decided matters] (ca. 1860) **:** a doctrine or policy of following rules or principles laid down in previous judicial decisions unless they contravene the ordinary principles of justice

stare down *vt* (ca. 1934) **:** to cause to waver or submit by or as if by staring

sta·rets \'stär-(y)əts\ *n, pl* **star·tsy** \'stärt-sē\ [Russ, lit., old man, fr. *staryĭ* old — more at STOUR] (1917) **:** a spiritual director or religious teacher in the Eastern Orthodox Church; *specif* **:** a spiritual adviser who is not necessarily a priest, who is recognized for his piety, and who is turned to by monks or laymen for spiritual guidance

star facet *n* (1813) **:** one of the eight small triangular facets which abut on the table in the bezel of a brilliant — see BRILLIANT illustration

star·fish \'stär-,fish\ *n* (1538) **:** any of a class (Asteroidea) of echinoderms having a body of usu. five radially disposed arms about a central disk and feeding largely on mollusks (as oysters)

star·flow·er \-,flau̇(-ə)r\ *n* (1629) **:** any of several plants having star-shaped pentamerous flowers; *esp* **:** any of a genus (*Trientalis*, esp. *T. americana*) of plants of the primrose family

star·gaze \-,gāz\ *vi* [back-formation fr. *stargazer*] (1626) **1 :** to gaze at stars **2 :** to gaze raptly or contemplatively

star·gaz·er \-,gā-zər\ *n* (1560) **1 :** one who gazes at the stars: as **a :** ASTROLOGER **b :** ASTRONOMER **2 :** any of several marine percoid fishes (family Uranoscopidae) with the eyes on top of the head

star·gaz·ing \-,gā-ziŋ\ *n* (1576) **1 :** the act or practice of a stargazer **2 a :** absorption in chimerical or impractical ideas **:** WOOLGATHERING **b :** the quality or state of being absentminded

star grass *n* (1687) **:** any of various grassy plants with stellate flowers or arrangement of leaves: as **a :** any of a genus (*Hypoxis*) of herbs of the amaryllis family **b :** either of two colicroots (*Aletris farinosa* and *A. aurea*) **c :** a perennial grass (*Cynodon plectostachyum*) that has stems attaining a height of 3 to 4 feet and that is used esp. in Africa and India for pasture and hay

[1]**stark** \'stärk\ *adj* [ME, stiff, strong, fr. OE *stearc;* akin to OHG *starc* strong, Lith *starinti* to stiffen — more at STARE] (bef. 12c) **1** *archaic* **:** STRONG, ROBUST **2 a :** rigid in or as if in death **b :** rigidly conforming (as to a pattern or doctrine) **:** ABSOLUTE ⟨~ discipline⟩ **3 :** UTTER, SHEER ⟨~ nonsense⟩ **4 a :** BARREN, DESOLATE **b** (1) **:** having few or no ornaments **:** BARE ⟨a ~ white room⟩ (2) **:** HARSH, BLUNT ⟨the ~ realities of death⟩ **5 :** sharply delineated ⟨a ~ contrast⟩ ***syn*** see STIFF — **stark·ly** *adv* — **stark·ness** *n*

[2]**stark** *adv* (13c) **1 :** in a stark manner **2 :** to an absolute or complete degree **:** WHOLLY ⟨~ naked⟩ ⟨~ mad⟩

stark·ers \'stär-kərz\ *adj* [alter. of [1]*stark*] *chiefly Brit* (ca. 1923) **:** completely unclothed **:** NAKED

star·let \'stär-lət\ *n* (1920) **:** a young movie actress being coached and publicized for starring roles

star·light \-,līt\ *n* (14c) **:** the light given by the stars

star·ling \'stär-liŋ\ *n* [ME, fr. OE *stærlinc*, fr. *stær* starling + *-ling*, *-linc* -ling; akin to OHG *stara* starling, L *sturnus*] (bef. 12c) **:** any of a family (Sturnidae, esp. genus *Sturnus*) of usu. dark gregarious passerine birds; *esp* **:** a dark brown or in summer glossy greenish black European bird (*S. vulgaris*) naturalized in No. America, Australia, and New Zealand and often a pest

star·lit \'stär-,lit\ *adj* (1827) **:** lighted by the stars

star–nosed mole \,stär-,nōz(d)-\ *n* (1826) **:** a common black long-tailed semiaquatic No. American mole (*Condylura cristata*) distinguished by a series of pink fleshy projections surrounding the nostrils

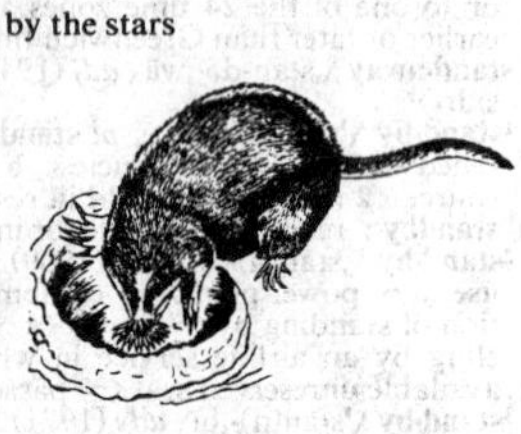

star-nosed mole

star–of–Beth·le·hem \-'beth-li-,hem, -lē-(h)əm\ *n* (1573) **:** any of a genus (*Ornithogalum*) of bulbous herbs (as the chincherinchee) of the lily family with basal leaves resembling grass; *esp* **:** one (*O. umbellatum*) with greenish flowers that is naturalized in the eastern U.S.

star of Bethlehem : a star which according to Christian tradition guided the Magi to the infant Jesus in Bethlehem

Star of Da·vid \-'dā-vəd\ (ca. 1936) **:** MAGEN DAVID

star route *n* [so called fr. the asterisk used to designate such routes in postal publications] (1880) **:** a mail-delivery route in a rural or thinly populated area served by a private carrier under contract who takes mail from one post office to another or from a railroad station to a post office and usu. also delivers mail to private mailboxes along the route

star·ry \'stär-ē\ *adj* **star·ri·er; -est** (14c) **1 a :** adorned or studded with stars **b :** of, relating to, or consisting of stars **:** STELLAR **c :** shining like stars **:** SPARKLING **d :** having parts arranged like the rays of a star **:** STELLATE **2 :** as high as or seemingly as high as the stars ⟨~ speculations⟩ **3 :** STARRY-EYED

star·ry–eyed \,stär-ē-'īd\ *adj* (1904) **:** regarding an object or a prospect in an overly favorable light; *specif* **:** characterized by dreamy, impractical, or utopian thinking **:** VISIONARY

Stars and Bars *n pl but sing in constr* (1861) **:** the first flag of the Confederate States of America having three bars of red, white, and red respectively and a blue union with white stars in a circle representing the seceded states

Stars and Stripes *n pl but sing in constr* (1777) **:** the flag of the United States having 13 alternately red and white horizontal stripes and a blue union with white stars representing the states

star sapphire *n* (ca. 1805) **:** a sapphire that when cut with a convex surface and polished exhibits asterism

star shell *n* (ca. 1876) **1 :** a shell that on bursting releases a shower of brilliant stars and is used for signaling **2 :** a shell with an illuminating projectile

star·ship \'stär-,ship\ *n* (1934) **:** a spacecraft designed for interstellar travel

star–span·gled \'stär-,spaŋ-gəld\ *adj* (1591) **:** STAR-STUDDED

star–stud·ded \'stär-,stəd-əd\ *adj* (1955) **:** abounding in or covered with stars ⟨a ~ cast⟩ ⟨a ~ uniform⟩

star system *n* (1902) **:** the practice of casting famous performers in principal roles (as in motion pictures or the theater) esp. in order to exploit their popular appeal

[1]**start** \ˈstärt\ *vb* [ME *sterten;* akin to MHG *sterzen* to stand up stiffly, move quickly, Lith *starinti* to stiffen — more at STARE] *vi* (13c) **1 a :** to move suddenly and violently **:** SPRING ⟨~*ed* angrily to his feet⟩ **b :** to react with a sudden brief involuntary movement ⟨~*ed* when a shot rang out⟩ **2 a :** to issue with sudden force ⟨blood ~*ing* from the wound⟩ **b :** to come into being, activity, or operation ⟨when does the movie ~⟩ **3 :** to protrude or seem to protrude ⟨his eyes ~*ing* from their sockets⟩ **4 :** to become loosened or forced out of place ⟨one of the planks has ~*ed*⟩ **5 a :** to begin a course or journey ⟨~*ed* toward the door⟩ ⟨~*ed* north⟩ **b :** to range from a specified initial point ⟨the rates ~ at $10⟩ **6 :** to begin an activity or undertaking; *esp* **:** to begin work **7 :** to be a participant in a game or contest; *esp* **:** to be in the starting lineup ~ *vt* **1 :** to cause to leave a place of concealment **:** FLUSH ⟨~ a rabbit⟩ **2** *archaic* **:** STARTLE, ALARM **3 :** to bring up for consideration or discussion **4 :** to bring into being ⟨~ a rumor⟩ **5 :** to cause to become loosened or displaced **6 :** to begin the use or employment of ⟨~ a fresh loaf of bread⟩ **7 a :** to cause to move, act, or operate ⟨~ the motor⟩ **b :** to cause to enter a game or contest; *esp* **:** to put in the starting lineup **c :** to care for during early stages **8 :** to do or experience the first stages or actions of ⟨~*ed* studying music at the age of five⟩ *syn* see BEGIN — **start something :** to make trouble — **to start with 1 :** at the beginning **:** INITIALLY **2 :** in any event

[2]**start** *n* (14c) **1 a :** a sudden involuntary bodily movement or reaction **b :** a brief and sudden action or movement **c :** a sudden capricious impulse or outburst **2 :** a beginning of movement, activity, or development **3 :** a lead or handicap at the beginning of a race or competition **4 :** a place of beginning **5 :** the act or an instance of being a competitor in a race or a member of a starting lineup in a game ⟨undefeated in six ~*s* —*Current Biog.*⟩

start·er \ˈstärt-ər\ *n* (1622) **1 :** one who initiates or sets going: as **a :** an official who gives the signal to begin a race **b :** one who dispatches vehicles **2 a :** one that enters a competition; *esp* **:** a member of a starting lineup **b :** one that begins to engage in an activity or process **3 :** one that causes something to begin operating: as **a :** SELF-STARTER **b :** material containing microorganisms used to induce a desired fermentation **4 :** something that is the beginning of a process, activity, or series; *esp* **:** APPETIZER — **for starters :** to begin with

star thistle *n* (1578) **1 :** a widely naturalized spiny European weed (*Centaurea calcitrapa*) with purple flowers — called also *caltrops* **2 :** any of various knapweeds related to the star thistle

starting block *n* (ca. 1949) **:** a device that consists of two blocks mounted on either side of an adjustable frame which is usu. anchored to the ground and that provides a runner with a rigid surface against which to brace his feet at the start of a race

starting gate *n* (1898) **1 :** a mechanically operated barrier used as a starting device for a race **2 :** a barrier that when knocked aside by a competitor (as a skier) starts an electronic timing device

[1]**star·tle** \ˈstärt-ᵊl\ *vb* **star·tled; star·tling** \ˈstärt-liŋ, -ᵊl-iŋ\ [ME *stertlen,* freq. of *sterten* to start] *vi* (1530) **:** to move or jump suddenly (as in surprise or alarm) ⟨the baby ~*s* easily⟩ ~ *vt* **:** to frighten or surprise suddenly and usu. not seriously — **star·tle·ment** \-mənt\ *n*

[2]**startle** *n* (1714) **:** a sudden mild shock (as of surprise or alarm)

star·tling *adj* (1714) **:** causing momentary fright, surprise, or astonishment — **star·tling·ly** \ˈstärt-liŋ-lē, -ᵊl-iŋ-\ *adv*

start–up \ˈstärt-ˌəp\ *n* (1845) **:** the act or an instance of setting in operation or motion

star turn *n, chiefly Brit* (ca. 1909) **:** the featured skit or number in a theatrical production; *broadly* **:** the most widely publicized person or item in a group

star·va·tion \stär-ˈvā-shən\ *n* (1778) **1 :** the act or an instance of starving **2 :** the state of being starved

starvation wages *n* (1898) **:** wages insufficient to provide the ordinary necessities of life

starve \ˈstärv\ *vb* **starved; starv·ing** [ME *sterven* to die, fr. OE *steorfan;* akin to OHG *sterban* to die, Lith *starinti* to stiffen — more at STARE] *vi* (bef. 12c) **1 a :** to perish from lack of food **b :** to suffer extreme hunger **2** *archaic* **a :** to die of cold **b :** to suffer greatly from cold **3 :** to suffer or perish from deprivation ⟨*starved* for affection⟩ ~ *vt* **1 a :** to kill with hunger **b :** to deprive of nourishment **c :** to cause to capitulate by or as if by depriving of nourishment **2 :** to destroy by or cause to suffer from deprivation **3** *archaic* **:** to kill with cold

starve·ling \ˈstärv-liŋ\ *n* (1546) **:** one that is thin from or as if from lack of food

[1]**stash** \ˈstash\ *vt* [origin unknown] (1785) **1 :** to store in a usu. secret place for future use **2** *chiefly Brit* **:** to put an end to **:** STOP, QUIT

[2]**stash** *n* (ca. 1929) **1 :** hiding place **:** CACHE **2 :** something stored or hidden away ⟨a ~ of narcotics⟩

sta·sis \ˈstā-səs, ˈstas-əs\ *n, pl* **sta·ses** \ˈstā-ˌsēz, ˈstas-ˌēz\ [NL, fr. Gk, act or condition of standing, stopping, fr. *histasthai* to stand — more at STAND] (1745) **1 :** a slowing or stoppage of the normal flow of a bodily fluid or semifluid: as **a :** slowing of the current of circulating blood **b :** reduced motility of the intestines with retention of feces **2 :** a state of static balance or equilibrium **:** STAGNATION

-sta·sis \ˈstā-səs\ *n comb form, pl* **-sta·ses** \ˈstā-ˌsēz\ [NL, fr. Gk *stasis*] **1 :** stoppage **:** slowing ⟨hemo*stasis*⟩ ⟨bacterio*stasis*⟩ **2 :** stable state ⟨homeo*stasis*⟩

stat \ˈstat\ *n* (1968) **:** STATISTIC

-stat \ˌstat\ *n comb form* [NL *-stata,* fr. Gk *-statēs* one that stops or steadies, fr. *histanai* to cause to stand — more at STAND] **1 :** stabilizing agent or device ⟨gyro*stat*⟩ ⟨thermo*stat*⟩ **2 :** instrument for reflecting (something specified) constantly in one direction ⟨helio*stat*⟩ **3 :** agent causing inhibition of growth without destruction ⟨bacterio*stat*⟩

sta·tant \ˈstāt-ᵊnt\ *adj* [L *status,* pp. + E *-ant*] (ca. 1500) **:** standing in profile with all feet on the ground — used of a heraldic animal

[1]**state** \ˈstāt\ *n, often attrib* [ME *stat,* fr. OF & L; OF *estat,* fr. L *status,* fr. *status,* pp. of *stare* to stand — more at STAND] (13c) **1 a :** mode or condition of being ⟨a ~ of readiness⟩ **b (1) :** condition of mind or temperament ⟨in a highly nervous ~⟩ **(2) :** a condition of abnormal tension or excitement **2 a :** a condition or stage in the physical being of something ⟨insects in the larval ~⟩ ⟨the gaseous ~ of water⟩ **b :** any of various conditions characterized by definite quantities (as of energy, angular momentum, or magnetic moment) in which an atomic system may exist **3 a :** social position; *esp* **:** high rank **b (1) :** elaborate or luxurious style of living **(2) :** formal dignity **:** POMP — usu. used with *in* **4 a :** a body of persons constituting a special class in a society **:** ESTATE 3 **b** *pl* **:** the members or representatives of the governing classes assembled in a legislative body **c** *obs* **:** a person of high rank (as a noble) **5 a :** a politically organized body of people usu. occupying a definite territory; *esp* **:** one that is sovereign **b :** the political organization of such a body of people **6 :** the operations or concerns of the government of a country **7 a :** one of the constituent units of a nation having a federal government ⟨the fifty *states*⟩ **b** *pl, cap* **:** The United States of America **8 :** the territory of a state

[2]**state** *vt* **stat·ed; stat·ing** (1590) **1 :** to set by regulation or authority **2 :** to express the particulars of esp. in words **:** REPORT; *broadly* **:** to express in words — **stat·able** *or* **state·able** \ˈstāt-ə-bəl\ *adj*

state aid *n* (1856) **:** public monies appropriated by a state government for the partial support or improvement of a public local institution

state bank *n* (1815) **1 :** CENTRAL BANK **2 :** a bank chartered by and operating under the laws of a state of the U.S.

state bird *n* (1910) **:** a bird selected (as by the legislature) as an emblem of a state of the U.S.

state capitalism *n* (1903) **:** an economic system in which private capitalism is modified by a varying degree of government ownership and control

state church *n, often cap S&C* (1726) **:** ESTABLISHED CHURCH

state college *n* (1831) **:** a college that is financially supported by a state government, often specializes in a branch of technical or professional education, and often forms part of the state university

state·craft \ˈstāt-ˌkraft\ *n* (1642) **:** the art of conducting state affairs

stat·ed \ˈstāt-əd\ *adj* (1641) **1 :** FIXED, REGULAR ⟨the president shall, at ~ times, receive . . . a compensation —*U.S. Constitution*⟩ **2 :** set down explicitly **:** DECLARED — **stat·ed·ly** *adv*

stated clerk *n* (ca. 1909) **:** an executive officer of a Presbyterian general assembly, synod, or presbytery ranking below the moderator

state flower *n* (1898) **:** a flowering plant selected (as by the legislature) as an emblem of a state of the U.S.

state·hood \ˈstāt-ˌhu̇d\ *n* (1868) **:** the condition of being a state; *esp* **:** the status of being one of the states of the U.S.

state·house \-ˌhau̇s\ *n* (1638) **:** the building in which a state legislature sits

state·less \ˈstāt-ləs\ *adj* (1609) **1 :** having no state **2 :** lacking the status of a national ⟨a ~ person⟩ — **state·less·ness** *n*

state·ly \ˈstāt-lē\ *adj* **state·li·er; -est** (15c) **1 a :** HAUGHTY, UNAPPROACHABLE **b :** marked by lofty or imposing dignity **2 :** impressive in size or proportions *syn* see GRAND — **state·li·ness** *n* — **stately** *adv*

state medicine *n* (ca. 1922) **:** administration and control by the national government of medical and hospital services provided to the whole population and paid for out of funds raised by taxation

state·ment \ˈstāt-mənt\ *n* (1789) **1 :** the act or process of stating or presenting orally or on paper **2 :** something stated: as **a :** a report of facts or opinions **b :** a single declaration or remark **:** ASSERTION **3 :** PROPOSITION 2a **4 :** the presentation of a theme in a musical composition **5 :** a summary of a financial account showing the balance due **6 :** an opinion or message conveyed indirectly and usu. nonverbally **7 :** an instruction in a computer program

state of the art (1910) **:** the level of development (as of a device, procedure, process, technique, or science) reached at any particular time usu. as a result of modern methods — **state–of–the–art** *adj*

state of war (1948) **1 a :** a state of actual armed hostilities regardless of a formal declaration of war **b :** a legal state created and ended by official declaration regardless of actual armed hostilities and usu. characterized by operation of the rules of war **2 :** the period of time during which a state of war is in effect

sta·ter \ˈstāt-ər, stä-ˈte(ə)r\ *n* [ME, fr. LL, fr. Gk *statēr,* lit., a unit of weight, fr. *histanai* to cause to stand, weigh — more at STAND] (14c) **:** an ancient gold or silver coin of the Greek city-states of any of numerous standards

state·room \ˈstāt-ˌrüm, -ˌru̇m\ *n* (1774) **1 :** CABIN 1a **2 :** a private room on a railroad car with one or more berths and a toilet

state's attorney *n* (1779) **:** a legal officer (as a district attorney) appointed or elected to represent a state in court proceedings within a district — called also *state attorney*

state's evidence *n, often cap S* (1796) **:** a participant in a crime or an accomplice who gives evidence for the prosecution esp. in return for a reduced sentence; *also* **:** the evidence given — used chiefly in the phrase *turn state's evidence*

States General *n pl* (1585) **1 :** the assembly of the three orders of clergy, nobility, and third estate in France before the Revolution **2 :** the legislature of the Netherlands from the 15th century to 1796

[1]**state·side** \ˈstāt-ˌsīd\ *adj, often cap* [*(United) States* + *side*] (1944) **:** being in, going to, coming from, or characteristic of the 48 conterminous states of the U.S. ⟨transferred from Europe to ~ duty⟩

[2]**stateside** *adv, often cap* (1946) **:** in or to the continental U.S.

states·man \ˈstāt-smən\ *n* (1592) **1 :** one versed in the principles or art of government; *esp* **:** one actively engaged in conducting the business of a government or in shaping its policies **2 :** one who exercises political leadership wisely and without narrow partisanship — **states·man·like** \-ˌlīk\ *adj* — **states·man·ly** \-lē\ *adj* — **states·man·ship** \-ˌship\ *n*

state socialism *n* (1879) **:** an economic system with limited socialist characteristics introduced by usu. gradual political action

states' right·er \ˈstāts-ˈrīt-ər\ *n* (1945) **:** one who advocates strict interpretation of the U.S. constitutional guarantee of states' rights

states' rights *n pl* (1798) **:** all rights not vested by the Constitution of the U.S. in the federal government nor forbidden by it to the separate states

state tree *n* (1917) **:** a tree selected (as by the legislature) as an emblem of a state of the U.S.

\ə\ abut \ᵊ\ kitten, F table \ər\ further \a\ ash \ā\ ace \ä\ cot, cart \au̇\ out \ch\ chin \e\ bet \ē\ easy \g\ go \i\ hit \ī\ ice \j\ job \ŋ\ sing \ō\ go \ȯ\ law \ȯi\ boy \th\ thin \t͟h\ the \ü\ loot \u̇\ foot \y\ yet \zh\ vision \á, k̲, ⁿ, œ, œ̄, ue, ue̅, ʸ\ *see* Guide to Pronunciation

state university *n* (1831) **:** a university maintained and administered by one of the states of the U.S. as part of the state public educational system

[1]**state·wide** \'stāt-'wīd\ *adj* (1913) **:** affecting or extending throughout all parts of a state

[2]**statewide** *adv* (ca. 1934) **:** throughout the state

[1]**stat·ic** \'stat-ik\ *adj* [NL *staticus,* fr. Gk *statikos* causing to stand, skilled in weighing, fr. *histanai* to cause to stand, weigh — more at STAND] (1638) **1 :** exerting force by reason of weight alone without motion **2 :** of or relating to bodies at rest or forces in equilibrium **3 :** showing little change ⟨a ~ population⟩ **4 a :** characterized by a lack of movement, animation, or progression **b :** producing an effect of repose or quiescence ⟨a ~ design⟩ **5 a :** standing or fixed in one place **:** STATIONARY **b** *of water* **:** stored in a tank but not under pressure **6 :** of, relating to, or producing stationary charges of electricity **:** ELECTROSTATIC **7 :** of, relating to, or caused by radio static — **stat·i·cal** \-i-kəl\ *adj* — **stat·i·cal·ly** \-i-k(ə-)lē\ *adv*

[2]**static** *n* [*static electricity*] (1913) **1 :** disturbing effects produced in a radio or television receiver by atmospheric or various natural or man-made electrical disturbances; *also* **:** the electrical disturbances producing these effects **2 :** heated opposition or criticism

stat·i·ce \'stat-ə-(,)sē\ *n* [NL, genus of herbs, fr. L, an astringent plant, fr. Gk *statikē,* fr. fem. of *statikos* causing to stand, astringent] (ca. 1731) **:** SEA LAVENDER, THRIFT

static line *n* (1942) **:** a cord attached to a parachute pack and to an airplane to open the parachute after a jumper clears the plane

stat·ics \'stat-iks\ *n pl but sing or pl in constr* (ca. 1656) **:** mechanics dealing with the relations of forces that produce equilibrium among material bodies

static tube *n* (ca. 1934) **:** a tube used for indicating static as distinct from impact pressure in a stream of fluid

[1]**sta·tion** \'stā-shən\ *n* [ME *stacioun,* fr. MF *station,* fr. L *station-, statio,* fr. *status,* pp. — more at STATE] (15c) **1 :** the place or position in which something or someone stands or is assigned to stand or remain **2 :** the act or manner of standing **:** POSTURE **3 :** a stopping place: as **a** (1) **:** a regular stopping place in a transportation route (2) **:** the building connected with such a stopping place **:** DEPOT 3 **b :** one of the stations of the cross **4 a :** a post or sphere of duty or occupation **b :** a stock farm or ranch of Australia or New Zealand **5 :** STANDING, RANK ⟨a woman of high ~⟩ **6 :** a place for specialized observation and study of scientific phenomena ⟨a seismological ~⟩ ⟨a marine biological ~⟩ **7 :** a place established to provide a public service: as **a** (1) **:** FIRE STATION (2) **:** POLICE STATION **b :** a branch post office **8 a :** a complete assemblage of radio or television equipment for transmitting or receiving **b :** the place in which such a station is located

[2]**station** *vt* **sta·tioned; sta·tion·ing** \'stā-sh(ə-)niŋ\ (1748) **:** to assign to or set in a station or position **:** POST

sta·tion·al \'stā-shnəl, -shən-ᵊl\ *adj* (1902) **:** of, relating to, or being a mass formerly celebrated by the pope at designated churches in Rome on appointed holy days

sta·tion·ary \'stā-shə-,ner-ē\ *adj* (1648) **1 :** fixed in a station, course, or mode **:** IMMOBILE **2 :** unchanging in condition

stationary front *n* (ca. 1940) **:** the boundary between two air masses neither of which is replacing the other

stationary wave *n* (1900) **:** STANDING WAVE — called also *stationary vibration*

station break *n* (1937) **:** a pause in a radio or television broadcast for announcement of the identity of the network or station; *also* **:** an announcement or advertisement during this pause

sta·tio·ner \'stā-sh(ə-)nər\ *n* [ME *staciouner,* fr. ML *stationarius,* fr. *station-, statio* shop, fr. L, station] (14c) **1** *archaic* **a :** BOOKSELLER **b :** PUBLISHER **2 :** one that sells stationery

sta·tio·nery \'stā-shə-,ner-ē\ *n* [*stationer*] (ca. 1727) **1 :** materials (as paper, pens, and ink) for writing or typing **2 :** letter paper usu. accompanied with matching envelopes

station house *n* (1833) **:** a house at a post or station; *specif* **:** POLICE STATION

sta·tion·mas·ter \'stā-shən-,mas-tər\ *n* (1856) **:** an official in charge of the operation of a railroad station

stations of the cross *often cap S&C* (ca. 1890) **1 :** a series of usu. 14 images or pictures esp. in a church that represent the stages of Christ's passion **2 :** a devotion involving commemorative meditation before the stations of the cross

station wagon *n* (1904) **:** an automobile that has an interior longer than a sedan's, has one or more rear seats readily lifted out or folded to facilitate light trucking, has no separate luggage compartment, and often has an adjustable rear window and a tailgate

stat·ism \'stāt-,iz-əm\ *n* (1880) **:** concentration of economic controls and planning in the hands of a highly centralized government

stat·ist \'stāt-əst\ *n* (1941) **:** an advocate of statism — **statist** *adj*

sta·tis·tic \stə-'tis-tik\ *n* [back-formation fr. *statistics*] (1898) **1 :** a single term or datum in a collection of statistics **2 a :** a quantity (as the mean of a sample) that is computed from a sample; *specif* **:** ESTIMATE 3b **b :** a random variable that takes on the possible values of a statistic

sta·tis·ti·cal \-ti-kəl\ *adj* (1787) **:** of, relating to, or employing the principles of statistics — **sta·tis·ti·cal·ly** \-k(ə-)lē\ *adv*

statistical mechanics *n pl but usu sing in constr* (ca. 1909) **:** a branch of mechanics dealing with the application of the principles of statistics to the mechanics of a system consisting of a large number of parts having motions that differ by small steps over a large range

stat·is·ti·cian \,stat-ə-'stish-ən\ *n* (1825) **:** one versed in or engaged in compiling statistics

sta·tis·tics \stə-'tis-tiks\ *n pl but sing or pl in constr* [G *statistik* study of political facts and figures, fr. NL *statisticus* of politics, fr. L *status* state] (1787) **1 :** a branch of mathematics dealing with the collection, analysis, interpretation, and presentation of masses of numerical data **2 :** a collection of quantitative data

sta·tive \'stāt-iv\ *adj* (1874) **:** expressing a bodily or mental state — compare ACTIVE 3b

stato- *comb form* [ISV, fr. Gk *statos* stationary, fr. *histasthai* to stand — more at STAND] **1 :** resting ⟨*stato*blast⟩ **2 :** equilibrium ⟨*stato*cyst⟩

stato·blast \'stat-ə-,blast\ *n* [ISV] (1855) **1 :** a bud in a freshwater bryozoan that overwinters in a chitinous envelope and develops into a new individual in spring **2 :** GEMMULE b

stato·cyst \-,sist\ *n* [ISV] (1902) **:** an organ of equilibrium occurring esp. among invertebrate animals and consisting usu. of a fluid-filled vesicle in which are suspended calcareous particles

stat·ol·a·try \stāt-'äl-ə-trē\ *n* [[1]*state* + *-o-* + *-latry*] (1853) **:** advocacy of a highly centralized and all-powerful national government

stato·lith \'stat-ᵊl-,ith\ *n* [ISV] (1900) **1 :** the calcareous body in a statocyst **2 :** any of various starch grains or other solid bodies in the plant cytoplasm that are held to be responsible by changes in their position for changes in orientation of a part or organ

sta·tor \'stāt-ər\ *n* [NL, fr. L, one that stands, fr. *status,* pp. — more at STATE] (1902) **:** a stationary part in a machine in or about which a rotor revolves

stato·scope \'stat-ə-,skōp\ *n* [ISV] (ca. 1900) **1 :** a sensitive aneroid barometer for recording small changes in atmospheric pressure **2 :** an instrument for indicating small changes in the altitude of an aircraft

[1]**stat·u·ary** \'stach-ə-,wer-ē\ *n, pl* **-ar·ies** (1542) **1 :** SCULPTOR **2 a :** the art of making statues **b :** a collection of statues

[2]**statuary** *adj* (1627) **:** of, relating to, or suitable for statues

stat·ue \'stach-(,)ü, 'stach-ə(-w)\ *n* [ME, fr. MF, fr. L *statua,* fr. *statuere* to set up — more at STATUTE] (14c) **:** a three-dimensional representation usu. of a person, animal, or mythical being that is produced by sculpturing, modeling, or casting

Statue of Liberty (ca. 1900) **1 :** a large copper statue of a woman holding a torch aloft in her right hand located on Liberty Island in New York harbor **2 :** a trick play in football in which the ballcarrier takes the ball from the raised hand of a teammate who is faking a pass

stat·u·esque \,stach-ə-'wesk\ *adj* (1834) **:** resembling a statue esp. in dignity or shapeliness — **stat·u·esque·ly** *adv* — **stat·u·esque·ness** *n*

stat·u·ette \,stach-ə-'wet\ *n* (1843) **:** a small statue

stat·ure \'stach-ər\ *n* [ME, fr. MF, fr. L *statura,* fr. *status,* pp. — more at STATE] (14c) **1 :** natural height (as of a person) in an upright position **2 :** quality or status gained by growth, development, or achievement

sta·tus \'stāt-əs, 'stat-\ *n, pl* **sta·tus·es** [L — more at STATE] (1791) **1 :** the condition of a person or thing in the eyes of the law **2 a :** position or rank in relation to others ⟨the ~ of a father⟩ **b :** relative rank in a hierarchy of prestige; *esp* **:** high prestige **3 :** state of affairs

status offender *n* (ca. 1976) **:** a young offender (as a runaway or a truant) who is under the jurisdiction of a court for repeated offenses that are not crimes

sta·tus quo \,stāt-ə-'skwō, ,stat-\ *n* [L, state in which] (1833) **:** the existing state of affairs ⟨seeks to preserve the *status quo*⟩

status quo an·te \-'ant-ē\ *n* [prob. *status quo,* fr. L + *ante* before, fr. *ante-*] (1877) **:** the state of affairs that existed previously

stat·ut·able \'stach-ət-ə-bəl, 'stach-,üt-\ *adj* (1636) **:** made, regulated, or imposed by or in conformity to statute **:** STATUTORY ⟨~ tonnage⟩

stat·ute \'stach-(,)üt, -ət\ *n* [ME, fr. OF *statut,* fr. LL *statutum* law, regulation, fr. L, neut. of *statutus,* pp. of *statuere* to set up, station, fr. *status* position, condition, state] (13c) **1 :** a law enacted by the legislative branch of a government **2 :** an act of a corporation or of its founder intended as a permanent rule **3 :** an international instrument setting up an agency and regulating its scope or authority ***syn*** see LAW

statute book *n* (1593) **:** the whole body of legislation of a given jurisdiction whether or not published as a whole — usu. used in pl.

statute mile *n* (1862) **:** MILE 1a

statute of limitations (1768) **:** a statute assigning a certain time after which rights cannot be enforced by legal action or offenses cannot be punished

stat·u·to·ry \'stach-ə-,tōr-ē, -,tȯr-\ *adj* (1766) **1 :** of or relating to statutes **2 :** enacted, created, or regulated by statute ⟨a ~ age limit⟩ — **stat·u·to·ri·ly** \,stach-ə-'tōr-ə-lē, -'tȯr-\ *adv*

statutory offense *n* (ca. 1934) **:** a crime created by statute; *esp* **:** STATUTORY RAPE

statutory rape *n* (ca. 1934) **:** sexual intercourse with a female who is below the statutory age of consent

[1]**staunch** \'stȯnch, 'stänch\ *var of* STANCH

[2]**staunch** *adj* [ME, fr. MF *estanche,* fem. of *estanc,* fr. OF, fr. *estancher* to stanch — more at STANCH] (15c) **1 a :** WATERTIGHT, SOUND **b :** strongly built **:** SUBSTANTIAL **2 :** steadfast in loyalty or principle ***syn*** see FAITHFUL — **staunch·ly** *adv* — **staunch·ness** *n*

stau·ro·lite \'stȯr-ə-,līt\ *n* [F, fr. Gk *stauros* cross + F *-lite* — more at STEER] (ca. 1815) **:** a mineral $(Fe,Mg)_2Al_9Si_4O_{23}(OH)$ consisting of basic iron aluminum silicate in prismatic orthorhombic crystals often twinned so as to resemble a cross — **stau·ro·lit·ic** \,stȯr-ə-'lit-ik\ *adj*

[1]**stave** \'stāv\ *n* [back-formation fr. *staves*] (12c) **1 :** RUNG 1b **2 :** [1]STAFF 1, 2 **3 :** any of the narrow strips of wood or narrow iron plates placed edge to edge to form the sides, covering, or lining of a vessel (as a barrel) or structure **4 :** STANZA **5 :** [1]STAFF 3

[2]**stave** *vb* **staved** *or* **stove** \'stōv\; **stav·ing** *vt* (1595) **1 :** to break in the staves of (a cask) **2 :** to smash a hole in ⟨~ in a boat⟩; *also* **:** to crush or break inward ⟨*staved* in several ribs⟩ **3 :** to drive or thrust away ~ *vi* **1 :** to become stove in — used of a boat or ship **2 :** to walk or move rapidly

stave off *vt* (1624) **1 :** to fend off ⟨*staving off* creditors⟩ **2 :** to ward off (as something adverse) **:** FORESTALL ⟨trying to *stave off* disaster⟩

staves *pl of* STAFF

staves·acre \'stāv-,zā-kər\ *n* [by folk etymology fr. ME *staphisagre,* fr. ML *staphis agria,* fr. Gk, lit., wild raisin] (15c) **:** a Eurasian larkspur (*Delphinium staphisagria*); *also* **:** its violently emetic and cathartic seeds

[1]**stay** \'stā\ *n* [ME, fr. OE *stæg;* akin to ON *stag* stay, OE *stēle* steel] (bef. 12c) **1 :** a large strong rope usu. of wire used to support a mast **2 :** a guy rope

[2]**stay** *vt* (1627) **1 :** to fasten (as a smokestack) with or as if with stays **2 :** to incline (a mast) forward, aft, or to one side by the stays ~ *vi* **:** to go about **:** TACK

[3]**stay** *vb* **stayed** \'stād\ *also* **staid** \'stād\; **stay·ing** [ME *stayen,* fr. MF *ester* to stand, stay, fr. L *stare* — more at STAND] *vi* (15c) **1 :** to stop going forward **:** PAUSE **2 :** to stop doing something **:** CEASE **3 :** to continue in a place or condition **:** REMAIN ⟨~*ed* up all night⟩ ⟨went for a short vacation but ~*ed* on for weeks⟩ **4 :** to stand firm **5 :** to take up residence **:** LODGE **6 :** to keep even in a contest or rivalry ⟨~ with the leaders⟩ **7 :** to call a poker bet without raising **8** *obs* **:** to be in

waiting or attendance ~ *vt* **1 :** to wait for : AWAIT **2 :** to last out (as a race or a trial of endurance) **3 :** to remain during ⟨~*ed* the whole time⟩ **4 a :** to stop or delay the proceeding or advance of by or as if by interposing an obstacle : HALT ⟨~ an execution⟩ **b :** to check the course of (as a disease) **c :** ALLAY, PACIFY ⟨~*ed* the civil war⟩ **d :** to quiet the hunger of temporarily ***syn*** see DEFER — **stay put :** to be or remain firmly fixed, attached, or established

4stay *n* (1537) **1 a :** the action of halting : the state of being stopped **b :** a stopping or suspension of procedure or execution by judicial or executive order **2** *obs* **:** SELF-CONTROL, MODERATION **3 :** a residence or sojourn in a place **4 :** capacity for endurance

5stay *n* [MF *estaie,* of Gmc origin; akin to OHG *stān* to stand — more at STAND] (1515) **1 :** one that serves as a prop : SUPPORT **2 :** a corset stiffened with bones — usu. used in pl.

6stay *vt* (1548) **1 :** to provide physical or moral support for : SUSTAIN **2 :** to fix on something as a foundation

stay–at–home \ˌstā-ət-ˌhōm\ *adj* (1806) **:** remaining habitually in one's residence, locality, or country — **stay–at–home** \'stā-\ *n*

stay·er \'stā-ər\ *n* (1579) **:** one that stays; *esp* **:** one that upholds or supports

staying power *n* (1859) **:** capacity for endurance : STAMINA

stay·sail \'stā-ˌsāl, -səl\ *n* (1669) **:** a fore-and-aft sail hoisted on a stay — see SAIL illustration

1stead \'sted\ *n* [ME *stede,* fr. OE; akin to OHG *stat* place, OE *standan* to stand — more at STAND] (bef. 12c) **1** *obs* **:** LOCALITY, PLACE **2 :** ADVANTAGE, SERVICE — used chiefly in the phrase *to stand one in good stead* **3 :** the office, place, or function ordinarily occupied or carried out by someone or something else ⟨acted in his brother's ~⟩

2stead *vt* (12c) **:** to be of avail to : HELP

stead·fast \'sted-ˌfast *also* -fəst\ *adj* [ME *stedefast,* fr. OE *stedefæst,* fr. *stede* + *fæst* fixed, fast] (bef. 12c) **1 a :** firmly fixed in place : IMMOVABLE **b :** not subject to change ⟨the ~ doctrine of original sin —Ellen Glasgow⟩ **2 :** firm in belief, determination, or adherence : LOYAL ***syn*** see FAITHFUL — **stead·fast·ly** *adv* — **stead·fast·ness** \-ˌfas(t)-nəs, -fəs(t)-\ *n*

stead·ing \'sted-ᵊn, 'stēd-, -iŋ\ *n* [ME *steding,* fr. *stede* place, farm] (15c) **1 :** a small farm **2** *chiefly Scot* **:** the service buildings or area of a farm

1steady \'sted-ē\ *adj* **steadi·er; -est** [1*stead*] (1530) **1 a :** firm in position : FIXED **b :** direct or sure in movement : UNFALTERING **c :** keeping nearly upright in a seaway ⟨a ~ ship⟩ **2 :** showing little variation or fluctuation : STABLE, UNIFORM ⟨a ~ breeze⟩ ⟨~ prices⟩ **3 a :** not easily disturbed or upset ⟨~ nerves⟩ **b (1) :** constant in feeling, principle, purpose, or attachment **(2) :** DEPENDABLE **c :** not given to dissipation : SOBER — **steadi·ly** \'sted-ᵊl-ē\ *adv* — **steadi·ness** \'sted-ē-nəs\ *n*

syn STEADY, EVEN, EQUABLE mean not varying throughout a course or extent. STEADY implies lack of fluctuation or interruption of movement; EVEN suggests a lack of variation in quality or character; EQUABLE implies lack of extremes or of sudden sharp changes.

2steady *vb* **stead·ied; steady·ing** *vt* (1530) **:** to make or keep steady ~ *vi* **:** to become steady — **steadi·er** *n*

3steady *adv* (1605) **1 :** in a steady manner : STEADILY **2 :** on the course set — used as a direction to the helmsman of a ship

4steady *n, pl* **stead·ies** (1792) **:** one that is steady; *specif* **:** a boyfriend or girlfriend with whom one goes steady

steady state *n* (ca. 1928) **:** a state or condition of a system or process (as one of the energy states of an atom) that does not change in time; *broadly* **:** a condition that changes only negligibly over a specified time

steady state theory *n* (1954) **:** a theory in astronomy: the universe has always existed and has always been expanding with hydrogen being created continuously — compare BIG BANG THEORY

steak \'stāk\ *n* [ME *steke,* fr. ON *steik;* akin to ON *steikja* to roast on a stake, *stik* stick, stake — more at STICK] (15c) **1 a :** a slice of meat cut from a fleshy part of a beef carcass **b :** a similar slice of a specified meat other than beef ⟨ham ~⟩ **c :** a cross-section slice of a large fish ⟨swordfish ~⟩ **2 :** ground beef prepared for cooking or for serving in the manner of a steak ⟨hamburger ~⟩

steak house *n* (1946) **:** a restaurant whose specialty is beefsteak

steak knife *n* (1928) **:** a table knife with a sharp often serrated blade

steak tar·tare \-tär-'tär\ *n* [F *tartare* Tartar] (1955) **:** highly seasoned ground beef eaten raw

1steal \'stē(ə)l\ *vb* **stole** \'stōl\; **sto·len** \'stō-lən\; **steal·ing** [ME *stelen,* fr. OE *stelan;* akin to OHG *stelan* to steal] *vi* (bef. 12c) **1 :** to take the property of another wrongfully and esp. as an habitual or regular practice **2 :** to come or go secretly, unobtrusively, gradually, or unexpectedly **3 :** to steal a base ~ *vt* **1 a :** to take or appropriate without right or leave and with intent to keep or make use of wrongfully ⟨*stole* a car⟩ **b :** to take away by force or unjust means ⟨they've *stolen* our liberty⟩ **c :** to take surreptitiously or without permission ⟨~ a kiss⟩ **d :** to appropriate entirely to oneself or beyond one's proper share ⟨~ the show⟩ **2 a :** to move, convey, or introduce secretly : SMUGGLE **b :** to accomplish in a concealed or unobserved manner ⟨~ a visit⟩ **3 a :** to seize, gain, or win by trickery, skill, or daring ⟨a basketball player adept at ~*ing* the ball⟩ **b** *of a base runner* **:** to gain (a base) solely by running and usu. catching the opposing team off guard — **steal·able** \'stē-lə-bəl\ *adj* — **steal·er** *n*

syn STEAL, PILFER, FILCH, PURLOIN mean to take from another without right or without detection. STEAL may apply to any surreptitious taking of something and differs from the other terms by commonly applying to intangibles as well as material things; PILFER implies stealing repeatedly in small amounts; FILCH adds a suggestion of snatching quickly and surreptitiously; PURLOIN stresses removing or carrying off for one's own use or purposes.

— **steal a march on :** to gain an advantage on unobserved — **steal one's thunder :** to grab attention from another esp. by anticipating an idea, plan, or presentation; *also* **:** to claim credit for another's idea

2steal *n* (ca. 1825) **1 :** the act or an instance of stealing **2 :** a fraudulent or questionable political deal **3 :** BARGAIN 2 ⟨it's a ~ at that price⟩

stealth \'stelth\ *n* [ME *stelthe;* akin to OE *stelan* to steal] (13c) **1 a** *archaic* **:** THEFT **b** *obs* **:** something stolen **2 :** the act or action of proceeding furtively, secretly, or imperceptibly ⟨the state moves by ~ to gather information —Nat Hentoff⟩ **3 :** the state of being furtive or unobtrusive ⟨his leopard ~ and grace —James Purdy⟩

stealthy \'stel-thē\ *adj* **stealth·i·er; -est** (1605) **1 :** slow, deliberate, and secret in action or character **2 :** intended to escape observation : FURTIVE ***syn*** see SECRET — **stealth·i·ly** \-thə-lē\ *adv* — **stealth·i·ness** \-thē-nəs\ *n*

1steam \'stēm\ *n* [ME *stem,* fr. OE *stēam;* akin to D *stoom* steam] (bef. 12c) **1 :** a vapor arising from a heated substance **2 a :** the invisible vapor into which water is converted when heated to the boiling point **b :** the mist formed by the condensation on cooling of water vapor **3 a :** water vapor kept under pressure so as to supply energy for heating, cooking, or mechanical work; *also* **:** the power so generated **b :** driving force : POWER ⟨got there under his own ~⟩ **c :** emotional tension ⟨needed to let off a little ~ after exams⟩ **4 a :** STEAMER 2a **b :** travel by or a trip in a steamer

2steam *vi* (1582) **1 :** to rise or pass off as vapor **2 :** to give off steam or vapor **3 :** to move or travel by or as if by the agency of steam **4 :** to be angry : BOIL ⟨~*ing* over the insult he had received⟩ ~ *vt* **1 :** to give out as fumes : EXHALE **2 :** to apply steam to; *esp* **:** to expose to the action of steam (as for softening or cooking)

steam·boat \'stēm-ˌbōt\ *n* (1785) **:** a boat driven by steam power

steamboat Gothic *n* [fr. its use in homes of retired steamboat captains in imitation of the style of river steamboats] (1941) **:** an elaborately ornamented architectural style used in homes built in the middle 19th century in the Ohio and Mississippi river valleys

steam boiler *n* (1805) **:** a boiler for producing steam

steam chest *n* (1797) **:** the chamber from which steam is distributed to a cylinder of a steam engine

steam engine *n* (1751) **:** an engine driven or worked by steam; *specif* **:** a reciprocating engine having a piston driven in a closed cylinder by steam

steam·er \'stē-mər\ *n* (1814) **1 :** a vessel in which articles are subjected to steam **2 a :** a ship propelled by steam **b :** an engine, machine, or vehicle operated or propelled by steam **3 :** one that steams **4 :** SOFT-SHELL CLAM

steamer rug *n* (1890) **:** a warm covering for the lap and feet esp. of a person sitting on a ship's deck

steamer trunk *n* (1891) **:** a trunk suitable for use in a stateroom of a steamer; *esp* **:** a shallow trunk that may be stowed beneath a berth

steam·fit·ter \'stēm-ˌfit-ər\ *n* (ca. 1890) **:** one that installs or repairs equipment (as steam pipes) for heating, ventilating, or refrigerating systems — **steam fitting** *n*

steam heating *n* (ca. 1879) **:** a system of heating (as for a building) in which steam generated in a boiler is piped to radiators

steam iron *n* (ca. 1943) **:** a pressing iron with a compartment holding water that is converted to steam by the iron's heat and emitted through the soleplate onto the fabric being pressed

1steam·roll·er \'stēm-'rō-lər\ *n* (1866) **1 :** a steam-driven road roller; *broadly* **:** ROAD ROLLER **2 :** a crushing force esp. when ruthlessly applied to overcome opposition

2steam·roll·er \-'rō-lər\ *also* **steam·roll** \-ˌrōl\ *vt* (1879) **1 :** to crush or consolidate with a steamroller **2 a :** to overwhelm usu. by greatly superior force ⟨~ the opposition⟩ **b :** to bring by overwhelming force or pressure ⟨~*ed* the bill through the legislature⟩ ~ *vi* **:** to move or proceed with irresistible force

steam·ship \'stēm-ˌship\ *n* (1790) **:** STEAMER 2a

steam shovel *n* (1879) **:** a power shovel operated by steam; *broadly* **:** POWER SHOVEL

steam table *n* (1862) **:** a table having openings to hold containers of cooked food over steam or hot water circulating beneath them

steam turbine *n* (1900) **:** a turbine that is driven by the pressure of steam discharged at high velocity against the turbine vanes

steam up *vt* (ca. 1934) **:** to make angry or excited : AROUSE

steamy \'stē-mē\ *adj* **steam·i·er; -est** (1644) **1 :** consisting of, characterized by, or full of steam **2 :** EROTIC ⟨a ~ love scene⟩ — **steam·i·ly** \-mə-lē\ *adv* — **steam·i·ness** \-mē-nəs\ *n*

ste·ap·sin \stē-'ap-sən\ *n* [Gk *stear* hard fat + E *-psin* (as in *pepsin*) — more at STONE] (1896) **:** the lipase in pancreatic juice

stea·rate \'stē-ə-ˌrāt, 'sti(ə)r-ˌāt\ *n* (1841) **:** a salt or ester of stearic acid

stea·ric acid \stē-ˌar-ik-, ˌsti(ə)r-ik-\ *n* (1831) **:** a white crystalline fatty acid $C_{18}H_{36}O_2$ obtained by saponifying tallow or other hard fats containing stearin; *also* **:** a commercial mixture of stearic and palmitic acids

stea·rin \'stē-ə-rən, 'sti(ə)r-ən\ *n* [F *stéarine,* fr. Gk *stear*] (1817) **1 :** an ester of glycerol and stearic acid **2** *also* **stea·rine** *same or* 'stē-ə-ˌrēn, 'sti(ə)r-ˌēn\ **:** the solid portion of a fat

steat- *or* **steato-** *comb form* [Gk, fr. *steat-, stear* — more at STONE] **:** fat ⟨*steato*rrhea⟩

ste·atite \'stē-ə-ˌtīt\ *n* [L *steatitis,* a precious stone, fr. Gk, fr. *steat-*] (1758) **1 :** a massive talc having a grayish green or brown color : SOAPSTONE **2 :** an electrically insulating porcelain composed largely of steatite — **ste·atit·ic** \ˌstē-ə-'tit-ik\ *adj*

ste·ato·py·gia \(ˌ)stē-ˌat-ə-'pī-j(ē-)ə\ *n* [NL, fr. *steat-* + Gk *pygē* rump, buttocks; akin to Latvian *pauga* cushion, Gk *physan* to blow — more at FOG] (ca. 1860) **:** an excessive development of fat on the buttocks esp. of females that is common among the Hottentots and some Negro peoples — **ste·ato·py·gic** \-'pī-jik\ *or* **ste·ato·py·gous** \-'pī-gəs\ *adj*

ste·at·or·rhea \(ˌ)stē-ˌat-ə-'rē-ə\ *n* [NL] (ca. 1860) **:** an excess of fat in the stools

stedfast *var of* STEADFAST

steed \'stēd\ *n* [ME *stede,* fr. OE *stēda* stallion; akin to OE *stōd* stud — more at STUD] (bef. 12c) **:** HORSE; *esp* **:** a spirited horse for state or war

steek \'stēk\ *vb* [ME *steken* to pierce, fix, enclose; akin to OE *stician* to pierce — more at STICK] *chiefly Scot* (14c) **:** SHUT, CLOSE

1steel \'stē(ə)l\ *n* [ME *stele,* fr. OE *stȳle, stēle;* akin to OHG *stahal* steel, Skt *stakati* he resists] (bef. 12c) **1 :** commercial iron that contains carbon in any amount up to about 1.7 percent as an essential alloying constituent, is malleable when under suitable conditions, and is distinguished from cast iron by its malleability and lower carbon content **2**

: an instrument or implement of or characteristically of steel: as **a** : a thrusting or cutting weapon **b** : an instrument (as a fluted round rod with a handle) for sharpening knives **c** : a piece of steel for striking sparks from flint **d** : a strip of steel used for stiffening **3** : a quality (as hardness of mind or spirit) that suggests steel ⟨nerves of ∼⟩ **4 a** : the steel manufacturing industry **b** *pl* : shares of stock in steel companies

[2]steel *vt* (13c) **1** : to overlay, point, or edge with steel **2 a** : to cause to resemble steel (as in looks or hardness) **b** : to fill with resolution or determination

[3]steel *adj* (14c) **1** : made of steel **2** : of or relating to the production of steel **3** : resembling steel

steel band *n* (1950) : a band orig. developed in Trinidad and composed of tuned percussion instruments cut out of oil barrels

steel blue *n* (1817) **1** : a variable color averaging a grayish blue **2** : any of the blue colors assumed by steel at various temperatures in tempering

steel engraving *n* (1824) **1** : the art or process of engraving on steel **2** : an impression taken from an engraved steel plate

steel guitar *n* (1925) **1** : HAWAIIAN GUITAR **2** : PEDAL STEEL

steel·head \ˈstē(ə)l-ˌhed\ *n, pl* **steelhead** *also* **steelheads** (ca. 1882) : a large-sized western No. American silvery anadromous trout usu. held to be a race of the rainbow trout (*Salmo gairdneri*) — called also *steelhead trout*

steel·ie *also* **steely** \ˈstē-lē\ *n, pl* **steel·ies** (1922) : a steel playing marble

steel–trap \ˌstē(ə)l-ˌtrap\ *adj* (1945) : extremely quick and incisive

steel wool *n* (ca. 1900) : an abrasive material composed of long fine steel shavings and used esp. for scouring and burnishing

steel·work \ˈstē(ə)l-ˌwərk\ *n* (1681) **1** : work in steel **2** *pl but sing or pl in constr* : an establishment where steel is made

steel·work·er \-ˌwər-kər\ *n* (1884) : one that works in steel and esp. in the manufacturing of it

steely \ˈstē-lē\ *adj* **steel·i·er; -est** (1586) **1** : made of steel **2** : resembling steel — **steel·i·ness** *n*

steel·yard \ˈstē(ə)l-ˌyärd, ˈstil-yərd\ *n* [prob. fr. [3]*steel* + *yard* (rod)] (1639) : a balance in which an object to be weighed is suspended from the shorter arm of a lever and the weight determined by moving a counterpoise along a graduated scale on the longer arm until equilibrium is attained

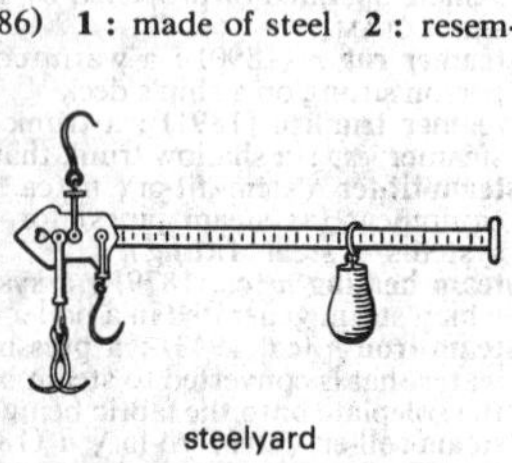
steelyard

steen·bok \ˈstēn-ˌbäk, ˈstān-\ *or* **stein·bok** \ˈstīn-, ˈstān-\ *n* [Afrik *steenbok;* akin to OE *stānbucca* ibex, *stān* stone and *bucca* buck] (1775) : any of a genus (*Raphicerus*) of small plains antelopes of southern and eastern Africa

[1]steep \ˈstēp\ *adj* [ME *stepe,* fr. OE *stēap* high, steep, deep; akin to MHG *stief* steep, ON *staup* lump, knoll, cup, L *stupēre* to be benumbed — more at TYPE] (bef. 12c) **1** : LOFTY, HIGH — used chiefly of a sea **2** : making a large angle with the plane of the horizon **3 a** : mounting or falling precipitously ⟨the stairs were very ∼⟩ **b** : being or characterized by a rapid and intensive decline or increase **4** : difficult to accept, meet, or perform : EXCESSIVE — **steep·ly** *adv* — **steep·ness** *n*

syn STEEP, ABRUPT, PRECIPITOUS, SHEER mean having an incline approaching the perpendicular. STEEP implies such sharpness of pitch that ascent or descent is very difficult; ABRUPT implies a sharper pitch and a sudden break in the level; PRECIPITOUS applies to an incline approaching the vertical; SHEER suggests an unbroken perpendicular expanse.

[2]steep *n* (13c) : a precipitous place

[3]steep *vb* [ME *stepen;* akin to Sw *stöpa* to steep, and prob. to ON *staup* cup] *vt* (14c) **1** : to soak in a liquid at a temperature under the boiling point (as for softening, bleaching, or extracting an essence) **2** : to cover with or plunge into a liquid (as in bathing, rinsing, or soaking) **3** : to saturate with or subject thoroughly to (some strong or pervading influence) ∼ *vi* : to undergo the process of soaking in a liquid ***syn*** see SOAK — **steep·er** *n*

[4]steep *n* (15c) **1** : the state or process of being steeped **2** : a bath or solution in which something is steeped **3** : a tank in which a material is steeped

steep·en \ˈstē-pən, ˈstēp-ᵊm\ *vb* **steep·ened; steep·en·ing** \ˈstēp-(ə-)niŋ\ *vi* (1847) : to become steeper ∼ *vt* : to make steeper

stee·ple \ˈstē-pəl\ *n* [ME *stepel,* fr. OE *stēpel* tower; akin to OE *stēap* steep] (bef. 12c) : a tall structure usu. having a small spire at the top and surmounting a church tower; *broadly* : a whole church tower — **stee·pled** \-pəld\ *adj*

stee·ple·bush \ˈstē-pəl-ˌbu̇sh\ *n* (ca. 1817) : HARDHACK

stee·ple·chase \-ˌchās\ *n* [perh. fr. the use of church steeples as landmarks to guide the riders] (1793) **1 a** : a horse race across country **b** : a horse race over a closed course with obstacles (as hedges and walls) **2** : a footrace of usu. 3000 meters over hurdles and a water jump — **stee·ple·chas·er** \-ˌchā-sər\ *n*

stee·ple·jack \-ˌjak\ *n* (ca. 1881) : one whose work is building smokestacks, towers, or steeples or climbing up the outside of such structures to paint and make repairs

[1]steer \ˈsti(ə)r\ *n* [ME, fr. OE *stēor* young ox; akin to OHG *stior* young ox, Skt *sthavira, sthūra* stout, thick, broad] (bef. 12c) **1** : a male bovine animal castrated before sexual maturity — compare STAG 3 **2** : an ox less than four years old

[2]steer *vb* [ME *steren,* fr. OE *stīeran;* akin to OE *stēor-* steering oar, Gk *stauros* stake, cross, *stylos* pillar, Skt *sthavira, sthūra* stout, thick, L *stare* to stand — more at STAND] *vt* (bef. 12c) **1** : to direct the course of; *esp* : to guide by mechanical means (as a rudder) **2** : to set and hold to (a course) ∼ *vi* **1** : to direct the course (as of a ship or automobile) **2** : to pursue a course of action **3** : to be subject to guidance or direction ⟨an automobile that ∼*s* well⟩ ***syn*** see GUIDE — **steer·able** \ˈstir-ə-bəl\ *adj* — **steer·er** *n* — **steer clear** : to keep entirely away — often used with *of*

[3]steer *n* (1894) : a hint as to procedure : TIP

[4]steer *dial Brit var of* STIR

steer·age \ˈsti(ə)r-ij\ *n* (15c) **1** : the act or practice of steering; *broadly* : DIRECTION **2** [fr. its orig. being located near the rudder] : a section in a passenger ship for passengers paying the lowest fares and given inferior accommodations

steer·age·way \-ˌwā\ *n* (1769) : a rate of motion sufficient to make a ship or boat respond to movements of the rudder

steering column *n* (1903) : the column that encloses the connections to the steering gear of a vehicle (as an automobile)

steering committee *n* (1887) : a managing or directing committee; *specif* : a committee that determines the order in which business will be taken up in a U.S. legislative body

steering gear *n* (1869) : a mechanism by which something is steered

steering wheel *n* (1750) : a handwheel by means of which one steers

steers·man \ˈsti(ə)rz-mən\ *n* [ME *steresman,* fr. OE *stēoresman,* fr. *stēores-* (gen. of *stēor-* rudder, steering oar) + *man*] (bef. 12c) : one who steers : HELMSMAN

[1]steeve \ˈstēv\ *vt* **steeved; steev·ing** [ME *steven,* prob. fr. Sp *estibar* or Pg *estivar* to pack tightly, fr. L *stipare* to press together — more at STIFF] (15c) : to stow esp. in a ship's hold

[2]steeve *vb* **steeved; steev·ing** [origin unknown] *vi, of a bowsprit* (ca. 1644) : to incline upward at an angle with the horizon or the line of the keel ∼ *vt* : to set (a bowsprit) at an upward inclination

[3]steeve *n* (1794) : the angle that a bowsprit makes with the horizon or with the keel

stego·saur \ˈsteg-ə-ˌsȯr\ *n* [NL *Stegosauria,* fr. *Stegosaurus*] (1901) : any of a suborder (Stegosauria) of dinosaurs with strongly developed dorsal bony armor

stego·sau·rus \ˌsteg-ə-ˈsȯr-əs\ *n* [NL *Stegosaurus,* fr. Gk *stegos* roof + *sauros* lizard — more at THATCH, SAURIAN] (1892) : any of a genus (*Stegosaurus*) of large armored dinosaurs of the Upper Jurassic rocks of Colorado and Wyoming

stein \ˈstīn\ *n* [prob. fr. G *steingut* stoneware, fr. *stein* stone + *gut* goods] (1855) : a large mug (as of earthenware) used esp. for beer; *also* : the quantity of beer that a stein holds

ste·la \ˈstē-lə\ *or* **ste·le** \ˈstē-lē\ *n, pl* **ste·lae** \-(ˌ)lē\ [L & Gk; L *stela,* fr. Gk *stēlē;* akin to Gk *stellein* to set up — more at STALL] (1776) : a usu. carved or inscribed stone slab or pillar used for commemorative purposes

ste·lar \ˈstē-lər, -ˌlär\ *adj* (1901) : of, relating to, or constituting a stele

Stel·a·zine \ˈstel-ə-ˌzēn\ *trademark* — used for trifluoperazine

stele \ˈstē(ə)l, ˈstē-lē\ *n* [NL, fr. Gk *stēlē* stela, pillar] (1895) : the usu. cylindrical central vascular portion of the axis of a vascular plant

stel·la \ˈstel-ə\ *n* [L, star; fr. the star on the reverse] (1879) : an experimental international coin based on the metric system that was issued by the U.S. in 1879 and 1880 and was worth about four dollars

stel·lar \ˈstel-ər\ *adj* [LL *stellaris,* fr. L *stella* star — more at STAR] (ca. 1656) **1 a** : of or relating to the stars : ASTRAL **b** : composed of stars **2** : of or relating to a theatrical or film star ⟨∼ names⟩ **3 a** : PRINCIPAL, LEADING ⟨a ∼ role⟩ **b** : OUTSTANDING

stellar wind *n* (ca. 1965) : plasma ejected at varying rates from a star's surface into interstellar space

stel·late \ˈstel-ˌāt\ *adj* [L *stella*] (1661) : resembling a star (as in shape) ⟨a ∼ leaf⟩

stel·li·form \ˈstel-ə-ˌfȯrm\ *adj* [NL *stelliformis,* fr. L *stella* + *-iformis* -iform] (1796) : shaped like a star ⟨a starfish is a ∼ echinoderm⟩

[1]stem \ˈstem\ *n* [ME, fr. OE *stefn, stemn* stem of a plant or ship; akin to OE *stæf* staff — more at STAFF] (bef. 12c) **1 a** : the main trunk of a plant; *specif* : a primary plant axis that develops buds and shoots instead of roots **b** : a plant part (as a branch, petiole, or stipe) that supports another (as a leaf or fruit) **c** : the complete fruiting stalk of a banana plant with its bananas **2** : the bow or prow of a ship — compare STERN **3** : a line of ancestry : STOCK; *esp* : a fundamental line from which others have arisen **4** : the part of an inflected word that remains unchanged except by phonetic changes or variations throughout an inflection **5** : something held to resemble a plant stem: as **a** : a main or heavy stroke of a letter **b** : the short perpendicular line extending from the head of a musical note **c** : the part of a tobacco pipe from the bowl outward **d** : the cylindrical support of a piece of stemware (as a goblet) **e** : a shaft of a watch used for winding — **from stem to stern** : THROUGHOUT, THOROUGHLY

[2]stem *vb* **stemmed; stem·ming** *vi* (1577) : to occur or develop as a consequence : have or trace an origin ⟨her success ∼*s* from hard work⟩ ∼ *vt* **1** : to remove the stem from **2** : to make stems for (as artificial flowers) ***syn*** see SPRING — **stem·mer** *n*

[3]stem *vt* **stemmed; stem·ming** (1593) **1** : to make headway against (as an adverse tide, current, or wind) **2** : to check or go counter to (something adverse) — **stem·mer** *n*

[4]stem *vb* **stemmed; stem·ming** [ME *stemmen* to dam up, fr. ON *stemma;* akin to OE *stamerian* to stammer] *vt* (15c) **1 a** : to stop or dam up (as a river) **b** : to stop or check by or as if by damming; *esp* : STANCH ⟨∼ a flow of blood⟩ **2** : to turn (skis) in stemming ∼ *vi* **1** : to restrain or check oneself; *also* : to become checked or stanched **2** : to retard oneself by forcing the heel of one ski or of both skis outward from the line of progress

[5]stem *n* (1700) **1** : CHECK, DAM **2** : an act or instance of stemming on skis

stem cell *n* (1885) : an unspecialized cell that gives rise to differentiated cells ⟨hematopoietic *stem cells* in bone marrow⟩

stem christie *n, often cap C* (1936) : a turn in skiing begun by stemming one ski and completed by bringing the skis parallel into a christie

stem·less \ˈstem-ləs\ *adj* (1796) : having no stem : ACAULESCENT

stem·ma \ˈstem-ə\ *n, pl* **stem·ma·ta** \-ət-ə\ [L, wreath, pedigree (fr. the wreaths placed on ancestral images), fr. Gk, wreath, fr. *stephein* to crown, enwreathe] (1826) **1** : a simple eye present in some insects **2** : a scroll (as among the ancient Romans) containing a genealogical list **3** : a tree showing the relationships of the manuscripts of a literary work

stemmed \ˈstemd\ *adj* (1576) : having a stem — usu. used in combination ⟨long-*stemmed* roses⟩

stem·my \ˈstem-ē\ *adj* **stem·mi·er; -est** (1863) : abounding in stems

stem rust *n* (1899) **1** : a rust attacking the stem of a plant; *esp* : a destructive disease esp. of wheat caused by a rust fungus (*Puccinia graminis*) which produces reddish brown lesions in the uredostage and black lesions in the teliospore stage and has any of several plants of the barberry family as an alternate host **2 :** the fungus causing stem rust

stem·son \'stem(p)-sən\ *n* [*stem* + *-son* (as in *keelson*)] (ca. 1769) **:** a piece of curved timber bolted to the stem, keelson, and apron in a ship's frame near the bow

stem turn *n* (1935) **:** a skiing turn executed by stemming an outside ski

stem·ware \'stem-ˌwa(ə)r, -ˌwe(ə)r\ *n* (1926) **:** glass hollowware mounted on a stem

stem–wind·er \-'wīn-dər\ *n* (1875) **1 :** a stem-winding watch **2** [fr. the superiority of the stem-winding watch over the older key-wound watch] **:** one that is first-rate of its kind; *esp* **:** a stirring speech

stem–wind·ing \-diŋ\ *adj* (1867) **:** wound by an inside mechanism turned by the knurled knob at the outside end of the stem ⟨a ~ watch⟩

Sten \'sten\ *n* [Major *S*heppard, 20th cent. Eng. army officer + Mr. *T*urpin, 20th cent. Eng. civil servant + *En*gland] (1942) **:** a light simple 9-millimeter British submachine gun

sten- *or* **steno-** *comb form* [Gk, fr. *stenos*] **:** close **:** narrow **:** little ⟨*steno*bathic⟩

stench \'stench\ *n* [ME, fr. OE *stenc;* akin to OE *stincan* to emit a smell — more at STINK] (bef. 12c) **:** STINK — **stench·ful** \-fəl\ *adj* — **stenchy** \'sten-chē\ *adj*

[1]**sten·cil** \'sten(t)-səl\ *n* [ME *stanselen* to ornament with sparkling colors, fr. MF *estanceler,* fr. *estancele* spark, fr. (assumed) VL *stincilla,* fr. L *scintilla*] (1707) **1 :** an impervious material (as a sheet of paper, thin wax, or woven fabric) perforated with lettering or a design through which a substance (as ink, paint, or metallic powder) is forced onto a surface to be printed **2 :** something (as a pattern, design, or print) that is produced by means of a stencil **3 :** a printing process that uses a stencil

[2]**stencil** *vt* **sten·ciled** *or* **sten·cilled; sten·cil·ing** *or* **sten·cil·ling** \-s(ə-)liŋ\ (1833) **1 :** to mark or paint with a stencil **2 :** to produce by stencil — **sten·cil·er** *or* **sten·cil·ler** \-s(ə-)lər\ *n*

stencil paper *n* (1868) **:** strong tissue paper impregnated or coated (as with paraffin) for stencils

steno \'sten-(ˌ)ō\ *n, pl* **sten·os** (1913) **1 :** STENOGRAPHER **2 :** STENOGRAPHY

steno·bath·ic \ˌsten-ə-'bath-ik\ *adj* [*sten-* + Gk *bathos* depth — more at BATH-] *of a pelagic organism* (1902) **:** living within narrow limits of depth

ste·nog·ra·pher \stə-'näg-rə-fər\ *n* (1809) **1 :** a writer of shorthand **2 :** one employed chiefly to take and transcribe dictation

ste·nog·ra·phy \-fē\ *n* (1602) **1 :** the art or process of writing in shorthand **2 :** shorthand esp. written from dictation or oral discourse **3 :** the making of shorthand notes and subsequent transcription of them — **steno·graph·ic** \ˌsten-ə-'graf-ik\ *adj* — **steno·graph·i·cal·ly** \-i-k(ə-)lē\ *adv*

steno·ha·line \ˌsten-ō-'hā-ˌlīn, -'hal-ˌīn\ *adj* [ISV *sten-* + Gk *halinos* of salt, fr. *hals* salt — more at SALT] *of an aquatic organism* (ca. 1920) **:** unable to withstand wide variation in salinity of the surrounding water

ste·nosed \stə-'nōzd, -'nōst\ *adj* [fr. pp. of *stenose* (to affect with stenosis)] (1897) **:** affected with stenosis

ste·no·sis \stə-'nō-səs\ *n, pl* **-no·ses** \-ˌsēz\ [NL, fr. Gk *stenōsis* act of narrowing, fr. *stenoun* to narrow, fr. *stenos* narrow] (ca. 1860) **:** a narrowing or constriction of the diameter of a bodily passage or orifice — **ste·not·ic** \-'nät-ik\ *adj*

steno·ther·mal \ˌsten-ə-'thər-məl\ *adj* (1881) **:** capable of surviving over only a narrow range of temperatures ⟨~ fish⟩ — **steno·therm** \'sten-ə-ˌthərm\ *n*

steno·top·ic \ˌsten-ə-'täp-ik\ *adj* [prob. fr. G *stenotop* stenotopic, fr. *sten-* + Gk *topos* place — more at TOPIC] (1945) **:** having a narrow range of adaptability to changes in environmental conditions

steno·type \'sten-ə-ˌtīp\ *n* [*steno-* (as in *stenography*) + *type*] (1922) **:** a small machine somewhat like a typewriter used to record speech by means of phonograms — **stenotype** *vt* — **steno·typ·ist** \-ˌtī-pəst\ *n* — **ste·no·ty·py** \'sten-ə-ˌtī-pē, stə-'nät-ə-pē\ *n*

sten·tor \'sten-ˌtȯ(ə)r, 'stent-ər\ *n* [L, fr. Gk *Stentōr* Stentor, a Greek herald in the Trojan War noted for his loud voice] (1609) **1 :** a person having a loud voice **2 :** any of a widely distributed genus (*Stentor*) of ciliate protozoans that have a trumpet-shaped body attached to the substrate by the smaller end with the mouth at the larger end

sten·to·ri·an \sten-'tōr-ē-ən, -'tȯr-\ *adj* (1605) **:** extremely loud ***syn*** see LOUD

[1]**step** \'step\ *n* [ME, fr. OE *stæpe;* akin to OHG *stapfo* step, *stampfōn* to stamp] (bef. 12c) **1 :** a rest for the foot in ascending or descending: as **a :** STAIR **b :** a ladder rung **2 a** (1) **:** an advance or movement made by raising the foot and bringing it down elsewhere (2) **:** a combination of foot or foot and body movements constituting a unit or a repeated pattern ⟨a dance ~⟩ (3) **:** manner of walking **:** STRIDE **b :** FOOTPRINT **c :** the sound of a footstep ⟨heard his ~s in the hall⟩ **3 a :** the space passed over in one step **b :** a short distance ⟨a store located just a ~ from the bank⟩ **c :** the height of one stair **4** *pl* **:** COURSE, WAY ⟨directed his ~s toward the river⟩ **5 a :** a degree, grade, or rank in a scale **b :** a stage in a process ⟨was guided through every ~ of my career⟩ **6 :** a frame on a ship designed to receive an upright shaft; *esp* **:** a block supporting the heel of a mast **7 :** an action, proceeding, or measure often occurring as one in a series ⟨is taking ~s to improve the situation⟩ **8 :** a steplike offset or part usu. occurring in a series **9 :** a musical scale degree — **step·like** \-ˌlīk\ *adj* — **stepped** \'stept\ *adj* — **in step 1 :** with each foot moving to the same time as the corresponding foot of others or in time to music **2 :** in harmony or agreement — **out of step :** not in step ⟨*out of step* with the times⟩

[2]**step** *vb* **stepped; step·ping** *vi* (bef. 12c) **1 a :** to move by raising the foot and bringing it down elsewhere or by moving each foot in succession **b :** DANCE **2 a :** to go on foot **:** WALK **b** *obs* **:** ADVANCE, PROCEED **c :** to be on one's way **:** LEAVE — often used with *along* **d :** to move briskly ⟨kept us *stepping*⟩ **3 :** to press down with the foot ⟨~ on the brake⟩ **4 :** to come as if at a single step ⟨*stepped* into a good job⟩ ~ *vt* **1 :** to take by moving the feet in succession ⟨~ three paces⟩ **2 a :** to move (the foot) in any direction **:** SET ⟨the first man to ~ foot on the moon⟩ **b :** to traverse on foot **3 :** to go through the steps of **:** PERFORM ⟨~ a minuet⟩ **4 :** to make erect by fixing the lower end in a step ⟨~ the mast⟩ **5 :** to measure by steps ⟨~ off 50 yards⟩ **6 a :** to provide with steps **b :** to make steps in ⟨~ a key⟩ **7 :** to construct or arrange in or as if in steps ⟨craggy peaks with terraces *stepped* up the sides —*Time*⟩ — **step on it :** to increase one's speed **:** hurry up

step- *comb form* [ME, fr. OE *stēop-;* akin to OHG *stiof-* step-] **:** related by virtue of a remarriage (as of a parent) and not by blood ⟨*step*parent⟩ ⟨*step*sister⟩

step·broth·er \'step-ˌbrət͟h-ər\ *n* (15c) **:** a son of one's stepparent by a former marriage

step–by–step \ˌstep-bə-'step, -bī-\ *adj or adv* (1701) **:** marked by successive degrees usu. of limited extent **:** GRADUAL

step·child \'step-ˌchīld\ *n* (bef. 12c) **1 :** a child of one's wife or husband by a former marriage **2 :** one that fails to receive proper care or attention ⟨is no longer a ~ in the family of nations —F. R. Smith⟩

step dance *n* (1888) **:** a dance in which steps are emphasized rather than gesture or posture

step·daugh·ter \'step-ˌdȯt-ər\ *n* (bef. 12c) **:** a daughter of one's wife or husband by a former marriage

step–down \'step-ˌdau̇n\ *n* (1943) **:** a decrease or reduction in size or amount ⟨a ~ in dosage⟩

step down \(ˈ)step-'dau̇n\ *vt* (1903) **:** to lower the voltage of (a current) by means of a transformer ~ *vi* **:** RETIRE, RESIGN ⟨*stepped down* as chairman of the board —*Current Biog.*⟩

step·fa·ther \'step-ˌfät͟h-ər\ *n* (bef. 12c) **:** the husband of one's mother by a subsequent marriage

step function *n* (ca. 1929) **:** a mathematical function of a single real variable that remains constant within each of a series of adjacent intervals but changes in value from one interval to the next

steph·a·no·tis \ˌstef-ə-'nōt-əs\ *n* [NL, fr. Gk *stephanōtis* fit for a crown, fr. *stephanos* crown, fr. *stephein* to crown] (1870) **:** any of a genus (*Stephanotis*) of Old World tropical woody vines of the milkweed family with fragrant white flowers the corolla of which has a cylindrical dilated tube and spreading limb

step–in \'step-ˌin\ *n* (1921) **:** an article of clothing put on by being stepped into: as **a :** a shoe resembling but usu. having a higher vamp than a pump and concealed elastic to adjust the fit **b :** a woman's short panties — usu. used in pl. — **step–in** *adj*

step in \(ˈ)step-'in\ *vi* (15c) **1 :** to intervene in an affair or dispute **2 :** to make a brief informal visit

step·lad·der \'step-ˌlad-ər\ *n* (1751) **:** a portable set of steps with a hinged frame for steadying

step·moth·er \-ˌmət͟h-ər\ *n* (bef. 12c) **:** the wife of one's father by a subsequent marriage

step out \(ˈ)step-'au̇t\ *vi* (1533) **1 :** to go away from a place usu. for a short distance and for a short time ⟨*stepped out* for a smoke⟩ **2 :** to go or march at a vigorous or increased pace **3 :** DIE **4 :** to lead an active social life **5 :** to be unfaithful — usu. used with *on*

step·par·ent \'step-ˌpar-ənt, -ˌper-\ *n* (ca. 1890) **:** the spouse of one's mother or father by a subsequent marriage

steppe \'step\ *n* [Russ *step'*] (1671) **1 :** one of the vast usu. level and treeless tracts in southeastern Europe or Asia **2 :** arid land with xerophilous vegetation found usu. in regions of extreme temperature range and loess soil

stepped–up \'step-'təp\ *adj* (ca. 1902) **:** increased in intensity **:** ACCELERATED, INTENSIFIED ⟨a ~ advertising program⟩

step·per \'step-ər\ *n* (1835) **:** one (as a fast horse or a dancer) that steps

step·ping–off place \ˌstep-iŋ-'ȯf-\ *n* (1893) **1 :** the outbound end of a transportation line **2 :** a place from which one departs for unknown territory

step·ping–stone \'step-iŋ-ˌstōn\ *n* (14c) **1 :** a stone on which to step (as in crossing a stream) **2 :** a means of progress or advancement

step·sis·ter \'step-ˌsis-tər\ *n* (15c) **:** a daughter of one's stepparent by a former marriage

step·son \-ˌsən\ *n* (bef. 12c) **:** a son of one's husband or wife by a former marriage

step stool *n* (1946) **:** a stool with one or two steps that often fold away beneath the seat

step turn *n* (1941) **:** a skiing turn executed in a downhill traverse by lifting the upper ski from the ground, placing it in the desired direction, weighting it, and bringing the other ski parallel

step–up \'step-ˌəp\ *n* (1925) **:** an increase or advance in size or amount

step up \(ˈ)step-'əp\ *vt* (1902) **1 :** to increase the voltage of (a current) by means of a transformer **2 :** to increase, augment, or advance by one or more steps ⟨*step up* production⟩ ~ *vi* **1 :** to come forward **2 :** to undergo an increase ⟨business is *stepping up*⟩ **3 :** to receive a promotion — **step–up** \'step-ˌəp\ *adj*

step·wise \-ˌwīz\ *adj* (1902) **1 :** marked by or proceeding in steps **2 :** moving by step to adjacent musical tones

-ster \stər\ *n comb form* [ME, fr. OE *-estre* female agent; akin to MD *-ster*] **1 :** one that does or handles or operates ⟨spin*ster*⟩ ⟨tap*ster*⟩ ⟨team*ster*⟩ **2 :** one that makes or uses ⟨song*ster*⟩ ⟨pun*ster*⟩ **3 :** one that is associated with or participates in ⟨game*ster*⟩ ⟨gang*ster*⟩ **4 :** one that is ⟨young*ster*⟩

ster·co·ra·ceous \ˌstər-kə-'rā-shəs\ *adj* [L *stercor-, stercus* excrement; akin to MHG *drec* filth] (1731) **:** relating to, being, or containing feces

ster·cu·lia gum \ˌstər-ˌk(y)ül-yə-\ *n* [NL *Sterculia,* genus of trees] (ca. 1943) **:** KARAYA GUM

stere- *or* **stereo-** *comb form* [NL, fr. Gk, fr. *stereos* solid — more at STARE] **1 :** solid **:** solid body ⟨*stereo*taxis⟩ **2 a :** stereoscopic ⟨*stere*opsis⟩ **b :** having or dealing with three dimensions of space ⟨*stereo*chemistry⟩

[1]**ste·reo** \'ster-ē-ˌō, 'stir-\ *n, pl* **ste·re·os** (1823) **1 :** STEREOTYPE **2** [short for *stereoscopy*] **a :** a stereoscopic method, system, or effect **b :** a stereoscopic photograph **3** [by shortening] **a :** stereophonic reproduction **b :** a stereophonic sound system

[2]**stereo** *adj* (1876) **1 a :** STEREOSCOPIC **b :** STEREOTYPED **2 :** STEREOPHONIC

\ə\ abut \ᵊ\ kitten, F table \ər\ further \a\ ash \ā\ ace \ä\ cot, cart \au̇\ out \ch\ chin \e\ bet \ē\ easy \g\ go \i\ hit \ī\ ice \j\ job \ŋ\ sing \ō\ go \ȯ\ law \ȯi\ boy \th\ thin \t͟h\ the \ü\ loot \u̇\ foot \y\ yet \zh\ vision \à, k̲, ⁿ, œ, œ̄, ue, ue̅, ʸ\ *see* Guide to Pronunciation

ste·reo·bate \'ster-ē-ə-,bāt, 'stir-\ *n* [F or L; F *stéréobate*, fr. L *stereobata* foundation, fr. Gk *stereobatēs*, fr. *stere-* + *bainein* to step, go — more at COME] (ca. 1836) : a substructure of masonry visible above the ground level

ste·reo·chem·is·try \,ster-ē-ō-'kem-ə-strē, ,stir-\ *n* [ISV] (1890) **1** : a branch of chemistry that deals with the spatial arrangement of atoms and groups in molecules **2** : the spatial arrangement of atoms and groups in a compound and its relation to the properties of the compound — **ste·reo·chem·i·cal** \-'kem-i-kəl\ *adj*

ste·reo·gram \'ster-ē-ə-,gram, 'stir-\ *n* [ISV] (1868) **1** : a diagram or picture representing objects with an impression of solidity or relief **2** : STEREOGRAPH

ste·reo·graph \-,graf\ *n* [ISV] (1859) : a pair of stereoscopic pictures or a picture composed of two superposed stereoscopic images that gives a three-dimensional effect when viewed with a stereoscope or special spectacles — **stereograph** *vt*

ste·re·og·ra·phy \,ster-ē-'äg-rə-fē, ,stir-\ *n* (ca. 1700) **1** : the art, process, or technique of delineating the forms of solid bodies on a plane **2** : stereoscopic photography — **ste·reo·graph·ic** \,ster-ē-ə-'graf-ik\ *adj* — **ste·reo·graph·i·cal·ly** \-i-k(ə-)lē\ *adv*

ste·reo·iso·mer \,ster-ē-ō-'ī-sə-mər, ,stir-\ *n* [ISV] (1900) : any of a group of isomers in which atoms are linked in the same order but differ in their spatial arrangement — **ste·reo·iso·mer·ic** \-,ī-sə-'mer-ik\ *adj* — **ste·reo·isom·er·ism** \-ī-'säm-ə-,riz-əm\ *n*

ste·re·ol·o·gy \,ster-ē-'äl-ə-jē, ,stir-\ *n* [ISV] (1967) : a branch of science concerned with inferring the three-dimensional properties of objects or matter ordinarily observed two-dimensionally — **ste·reo·log·i·cal** \-ē-ə-'läj-i-kəl\ *adj* — **ste·reo·log·i·cal·ly** \-i-k(ə-)lē\ *adv*

ste·reo·met·ric \,ster-ē-ō-'me-trik, ,stir-\ *adj* [NL *stereometricus*, fr. Gk *stereometrikos*, fr. *stereometria* measurement of solids, fr. *stere-* + *-metria* -metry] (1862) : having or representing a simple readily measurable solid form

ste·reo·mi·cro·scope \-'mī-krə-,skōp\ *n* (1948) : a microscope having a set of optics for each eye to make an object appear in three dimensions — **ste·reo·mi·cro·scop·ic** \-,mī-krə-'skäp-ik\ *adj* — **ste·reo·mi·cro·scop·i·cal·ly** \-i-k(ə-)lē\ *adv*

ste·reo·phon·ic \,ster-ē-ə-'fän-ik, ,stir-\ *adj* [ISV] (1937) : giving, relating to, or constituting a three-dimensional effect of auditory perspective — **ste·reo·phon·i·cal·ly** \-i-k(ə-)lē\ *adv* — **ste·reo·pho·ny** \,ster-ē-'äf-ə-nē, ,stir-; 'ster-ē-ə-,fō-nē, 'stir-\ *n*

ste·reo·pho·tog·ra·phy \,ster-ē-ō-fə-'täg-rə-fē, ,stir-\ *n* [ISV] (1903) : stereoscopic photography — **ste·reo·pho·to·graph·ic** \-,fōt-ə-'graf-ik\ *adj*

ste·re·op·sis \,ster-ē-'äp-səs, ,stir-\ *n* [NL, fr. *stere-* + Gk *opsis* vision — more at OPTIC] (1926) : stereoscopic vision

ste·re·op·ti·con \-'äp-ti-kən\ *n* [NL, fr. *stere-* + Gk *optikon*, neut. of *optikos* optic] (1863) : a projector for transparent slides often made double so as to produce dissolving views

ste·reo·reg·u·lar \,ster-ē-ō-'reg-yə-lər, ,stir-\ *adj* (1958) : of, relating to, or involving stereochemical regularity in the repeating units of a polymeric structure — **ste·reo·reg·u·lar·i·ty** \-,reg-yə-'lar-ət-ē\ *n*

ste·reo·scope \'ster-ē-ə-,skōp, 'stir-\ *n* (1838) : an optical instrument with two eyeglasses for helping the observer to combine the images of two pictures taken from points of view a little way apart and thus to get the effect of solidity or depth

ste·reo·scop·ic \,ster-ē-ə-'skäp-ik, ,stir-\ *adj* (1855) **1** : of or relating to stereoscopy or the stereoscope **2** : characterized by stereoscopy ⟨~ vision⟩ — **ste·reo·scop·i·cal·ly** \-i-k(ə-)lē\ *adv*

ste·re·os·co·py \,ster-ē-'äs-kə-pē, ,stir-; 'ster-ē-ə-,skō-pē, 'stir-\ *n* [ISV] (1861) **1** : a science that deals with stereoscopic effects and methods **2** : the seeing of objects in three dimensions

ste·reo·spe·cif·ic \,ster-ē-ō-spi-'sif-ik, ,stir-\ *adj* (1950) : being, produced by, or involved in a stereochemically specific process ⟨many enzymes act as ~ catalysts in biological reactions⟩ ⟨~ plastics⟩ — **ste·reo·spe·cif·i·cal·ly** \-i-k(ə-)lē\ *adv* — **ste·reo·spec·i·fic·i·ty** \-,spes-ə-'fis-ət-ē\ *n*

ste·reo·tac·tic \,ster-ē-ə-'tak-tik, ,stir-\ *adj* [NL *stereotaxis*, after such pairs as NL *hypotaxis*: E *hypotactic*] (1950) : STEREOTAXIC

ste·reo·tape \'ster-ē-ō-,tāp, 'stir-\ *n* (1957) : a stereophonic magnetic tape

ste·reo·tax·ic \,ster-ē-ə-'tak-sik, ,stir-\ *adj* [NL *stereotaxis* stereotaxic technique (fr. *stere-* + *taxis*) + E *-ic*] (1919) : of, relating to, or being a technique or apparatus used in neurological research or surgery for directing the tip of a delicate instrument (as a needle or an electrode) in three planes in attempting to reach a specific locus in the brain — **ste·reo·tax·i·cal·ly** \-si-k(ə-)lē\ *adv*

[1]**ste·reo·type** \'ster-ē-ə-,tīp, 'stir-\ *vt* (1804) **1** : to make a stereotype from **2** **a** : to repeat without variation : make hackneyed **b** : to develop a mental stereotype about — **ste·reo·typ·er** *n*

[2]**stereotype** *n* [F *stéréotype*, fr. *stéré-* stere- + *type*] (1817) **1** : a plate cast from a printing surface **2** : something conforming to a fixed or general pattern; *esp* : a standardized mental picture that is held in common by members of a group and that represents an oversimplified opinion, affective attitude, or uncritical judgment — **ste·reo·typ·i·cal** \,ster-ē-ə-'tip-i-kəl\ *also* **ste·reo·typ·ic** \-ik\ *adj*

ste·reo·typed *adj* (1849) : lacking originality or individuality ***syn*** see TRITE

ste·reo·ty·py \'ster-ē-ə-,tī-pē, 'stir-\ *n*, *pl* **-pies** (ca. 1864) **1** : the art or process of making or of printing from stereotype plates **2** : frequent almost mechanical repetition of the same posture, movement, or form of speech (as in schizophrenia)

ste·ric \'ster-ik, 'sti(ə)r-\ *adj* [ISV] (1898) : relating to or involving the arrangement of atoms in space : SPATIAL — **ste·ri·cal·ly** \'ster-i-k(ə-)lē, 'stir-\ *adv*

ste·rig·ma \stə-'rig-mə\ *n*, *pl* **-ma·ta** \-mət-ə\ *also* **-mas** [NL, fr. Gk *stērigma* support, fr. *stērizein* to prop; akin to Gk *stereos* solid — more at STARE] (ca. 1866) : one of the slender stalks at the top of the basidium of some fungi from the tips of which the basidiospores are abstricted; *broadly* : a stalk or filament that bears conidia or spermatia

ster·il·ant \'ster-ə-lənt\ *n* (1941) : a sterilizing agent

ster·ile \'ster-əl, *chiefly Brit* -,īl\ *adj* [L *sterilis*; akin to Goth *stairo* sterile, Gk *steira*] (1558) **1** **a** : failing to produce or incapable of producing offspring ⟨a ~ hybrid⟩ **b** : failing to bear or incapable of producing fruit or spores **c** : incapable of germinating ⟨~ spores⟩ **d** *of a flower* : neither perfect nor pistillate **2** **a** : unproductive of vegetation ⟨a ~ arid region⟩ **b** : free from living organisms and esp. microorganisms **c** : lacking in stimulating emotional or intellectual quality : LIFELESS ⟨a ~ work of art⟩ — **ster·ile·ly** \-əl-(l)ē\ *adv* — **ste·ril·i·ty** \stə-'ril-ət-ē\ *n*

ster·il·ize \'ster-ə-,līz\ *vt* **-ized; -iz·ing** (1695) : to make sterile: as **a** : to cause (land) to become unfruitful **b** (1) : to deprive of the power of reproducing (2) : to make incapable of germination **c** : to make powerless or useless usu. by restraining from a normal function, relation, or participation ⟨capital *sterilized* by hoarders⟩ **d** : to free from living microorganisms — **ster·il·iza·tion** \,ster-ə-lə-'zā-shən\ *n* — **ster·il·iz·er** \'ster-ə-,lī-zər\ *n*

[1]**ster·ling** \'stər-liŋ\ *n* [ME, silver penny] (13c) **1** : British money **2** : sterling silver or articles of it

[2]**sterling** *adj* (15c) **1** **a** : of, relating to, or calculated in terms of British sterling **b** : payable in sterling **2** **a** *of silver* : having a fixed standard of purity usu. defined legally as represented by an alloy of 925 parts of silver with 75 parts of copper **b** : made of sterling silver **3** : conforming to the highest standard ⟨~ character⟩ — **ster·ling·ly** \-liŋ-lē\ *adv* — **ster·ling·ness** *n*

sterling area *n* (1943) : a group of countries whose currencies are tied to the British pound sterling — called also *sterling bloc*

[1]**stern** \'stərn\ *adj* [ME *sterne*, fr. OE *styrne*; akin to OE *starian* to stare] (bef. 12c) **1** **a** : having a definite hardness or severity of nature or manner : AUSTERE **b** : expressive of severe displeasure : HARSH **2** : forbidding or gloomy in appearance **3** : INEXORABLE ⟨~ necessity⟩ **4** : STURDY, STOUT ⟨a ~ resolve⟩ ***syn*** see SEVERE — **stern·ly** *adv* — **stern·ness** \'stərn-nəs\ *n*

[2]**stern** *n* [ME, rudder, prob. of Scand origin; akin to ON *stjōrn* act of steering; akin to OE *stīeran* to steer — more at STEER] (14c) **1** : the rear end of a boat **2** : a hinder or rear part : the last or latter part

ster·nal \'stərn-ᵊl\ *adj* (1756) : of or relating to the sternum

stern chase *n* [[2]*stern*] (1627) : a chase in which a pursuing ship follows in the path of another

stern chaser *n* (1815) : a gun so placed as to be able to fire astern at a pursuing ship

stern·fore·most \'stərn-'fō(ə)r-,mōst, -'fȯ(ə)r-\ *adv* (1840) : with the stern in advance : BACKWARD

ster·nite \'stər-,nīt\ *n* [ISV, fr. Gk *sternon* chest] (1868) : the ventral part or shield of a somite of an arthropod; *esp* : the chitinous plate that forms the ventral surface of an abdominal or occas. a thoracic segment of an insect

stern·most \'stərn-,mōst\ *adj* (1622) : farthest astern

ster·no·cos·tal \,stər-nō-'käs-tᵊl\ *adj* [NL *sternum* + E *-o-* + *costal*] (1785) : of, relating to, or situated between the sternum and ribs

stern·post \'stərn-,pōst\ *n* (1580) : the principal member at the stern of a ship extending from keel to deck

stern sheets *n pl* (1568) : the space in the stern of an open boat not occupied by the thwarts

stern·son \'stərn(t)-sən\ *n* [*stern* + *keelson*] (ca. 1846) : the end of a keelson to which the sternpost is bolted

ster·num \'stər-nəm\ *n*, *pl* **sternums** *or* **ster·na** \-nə\ [NL, fr. Gk *sternon* chest, breastbone; akin to OHG *stirna* forehead, L *sternere* to spread out — more at STREW] (1667) : a compound ventral bone or cartilage of most vertebrates above fishes that connects the ribs or the shoulder girdle or both and in man consists of the manubrium, gladiolus, and xiphoid process — called also *breastbone*

ster·nu·ta·tion \,stər-nyə-'tā-shən\ *n* [L *sternutation-*, *sternutatio*, fr. *sternutatus*, pp. of *sternutare* to sneeze, fr. *sternutus*, pp. of *sternuere* to sneeze; akin to Gk *ptarnysthai* to sneeze] (1545) : the act, fact, or noise of sneezing

ster·nu·ta·tor \'stər-nyə-,tāt-ər\ *n* (1923) : an agent that induces sneezing and often lacrimation and vomiting

stern·ward \'stərn-wərd\ *or* **stern·wards** \-wərdz\ *adv* (1832) : AFT

stern·way \'stərn-,wā\ *n* (1769) : movement of a ship backward or with stern foremost

stern–wheel·er \-'hwē-lər, -'wē-\ *n* (1855) : a paddle-wheel steamer having a stern wheel instead of side wheels

ste·roid \'sti(ə)r-,ȯid *also* 'ste(ə)r-\ *n* [ISV *sterol* + *-oid*] (ca. 1926) : any of numerous compounds containing a 17-carbon 4-ring system and including the sterols and various hormones and glycosides — **steroid** *or* **ste·roi·dal** \stə-'rȯid-ᵊl\ *adj*

ste·roido·gen·e·sis \stə-,rȯid-ə-'jen-ə-səs; ,stir-,ȯid- *also* ,ster-\ *n* [NL] (1962) : synthesis of steroids

ste·roido·gen·ic \-'jen-ik\ *adj* (ca. 1967) : of, relating to, or involved in steroidogenesis ⟨~ cells⟩ ⟨~ response of ovarian tissue⟩

ste·rol \'sti(ə)r-,ōl, 'ste(ə)r-, -,ȯl\ *n* [ISV, fr. *-sterol* (as in *cholesterol*)] (1913) : any of various solid steroid alcohols (as cholesterol) widely distributed in animal and plant lipids

ster·tor \'stərt-ər, 'stər-,tȯ(ə)r\ *n* [NL, fr. L *stertere* to snore; akin to *sternuere* to sneeze] (1804) : the act or fact of producing a snoring sound : SNORING

ster·to·rous \'stərt-ə-rəs\ *adj* (1802) : characterized by a harsh snoring or gasping sound — **ster·to·rous·ly** *adv*

stet \'stet\ *vt* **stet·ted; stet·ting** [L, let it stand, fr. *stare* to stand — more at STAND] (1821) : to direct retention of (a word or passage previously ordered to be deleted or omitted from a manuscript or printer's proof) by annotating usu. with the word *stet*

stetho·scope \'steth-ə-,skōp *also* 'steth-\ *n* [F *stéthoscope*, fr. Gk *stēthos* chest + F *-scope*] (1820) : an instrument used to detect and study sounds produced in the body — **stetho·scop·ic** \,steth-ə-'skäp-ik *also* ,steth-\ *adj*

Stet·son \'stet-sən\ *trademark* — used for a broad-brimmed high-crowned felt hat

[1]**ste·ve·dore** \'stēv(-ə)-,dō(ə)r, -,dȯ(ə)r\ *n* [Sp *estibador*, fr. *estibar* to pack, fr. L *stipare* to press together — more at STIFF] (1788) : one who works at or is responsible for loading and unloading ships in port

[2]**stevedore** *vb* **-dored; -dor·ing** *vt* (1862) : to handle (cargo) as a stevedore; *also* : to load or unload the cargo of (a ship) in port ~ *vi* : to work as a stevedore

stevedore knot *n* (ca. 1863) : a stopper knot similar to a figure eight knot but with one or more extra turns — called also *stevedore's knot*; see KNOT illustration

Ste·ven·graph \'stē-vən-,graf\ *or* **Ste·vens·graph** \-vənz-\ *n* [Thomas *Stevens*, 19th cent. Am. weaver] (1961) : a woven silk picture

[1]**stew** \'st(y)ü\ *n* [ME *stu*, fr. MF *estuve*, fr. (assumed) VL *extufa*, fr. *extufare* to stew] (14c) **1** *obs* : a utensil used for boiling **2** : a hot

bath **3 a :** WHOREHOUSE **b :** a district of brothels — usu. used in pl. **4 a :** fish or meat usu. with vegetables prepared by stewing **b** (1) : a heterogeneous mixture (2) : a state of heat and congestion **5 :** a state of excitement, worry, or confusion

2stew *vt* (15c) **:** to boil slowly or with simmering heat ~ *vi* **1 :** to become cooked by stewing **2 :** to swelter esp. from confinement in a hot or stuffy atmosphere **3 :** to become agitated or worried

3stew *n* [short for *stewardess*] (1973) **:** an airline stewardess

1stew·ard \ˈst(y)ü-ərd, ˈst(y)u̇(-ə)rd\ *n* [ME, fr. OE *stīweard*, fr. *stī* hall, sty + *weard* ward — more at WARD] (bef. 12c) **1 :** one employed in a large household or estate to manage domestic concerns (as the supervision of servants, collection of rents, and keeping of accounts) **2 :** SHOP STEWARD **3 :** a fiscal agent **4 a :** an employee on a ship, airplane, bus, or train who manages the provisioning of food and attends passengers **b :** one appointed to supervise the provision and distribution of food and drink in an institution **5 :** one who actively directs affairs **:** MANAGER

2steward *vt* (1621) **:** to act as a steward for **:** MANAGE ~ *vi* **:** to perform the duties of a steward

stew·ard·ess \-əs\ *n* (1631) **:** a woman who performs the duties of a steward; *esp* **:** one who attends passengers (as on an airplane)

stew·ard·ship \-ˌship\ *n* (15c) **:** the office, duties, and obligations of a steward; *also* **:** the individual's responsibility to manage his life and property with proper regard to the rights of others

stewed \ˈst(y)üd\ *adj* (1917) **:** DRUNK

stew·pan \ˈst(y)ü-ˌpan\ *n* (1651) **:** a saucepan used for stewing

sthen·ic \ˈsthen-ik\ *adj* [NL *sthenicus*, fr. Gk *sthenos* strength] (ca. 1788) **1 :** notably or excessively vigorous or energetic ⟨~ fever⟩ ⟨~ emotions⟩ **2 :** PYKNIC

stib·ine \ˈstib-ˌēn\ *n* [ISV, fr. L *stibium* antimony, fr. Gk *stibi*, fr. Egypt *stm*] (1852) **:** a colorless poisonous flammable gas SbH_3 of antimony and hydrogen with a disagreeable odor

stib·nite \ˈstib-ˌnīt\ *n* [alter. of obs. E *stibine* stibnite, fr. F, fr. L *stibium*] (ca. 1854) **:** a mineral Sb_2S_3 consisting of antimony trisulfide that occurs in orthorhombic lead-gray crystals of metallic luster and that is also massive in form

sticho·myth·ia \ˌstik-ə-ˈmith-ē-ə\ *also* **sti·chom·y·thy** \stik-ˈäm-ə-thē\ *n* [Gk *stichomythia*, fr. *stichomythein* to speak dialogue in alternate lines, fr. *stichos* row, verse + *mythos* speech, myth; akin to Gk *steichein* to walk, go — more at STAIR] (1861) **:** dialogue esp. of altercation or dispute delivered by two actors in alternating lines (as in classical Greek drama) — **sticho·myth·ic** \ˌstik-ə-ˈmith-ik\ *adj*

1stick \ˈstik\ *n* [ME *stik*, fr. OE *sticca*; akin to ON *stik* stick, OE *stician* to stick] (bef. 12c) **1 :** a woody piece or part of a tree or shrub: as **a :** a usu. dry or dead severed shoot, twig, or slender branch **b :** a cut or broken branch or piece of wood gathered for fuel or construction material **2 a :** a long slender piece of wood: as (1) **:** a club or staff used as a weapon (2) **:** WALKING STICK **b :** an implement used for striking or propelling an object in a game **c :** something used to force compliance **d :** a baton symbolizing an office or dignity; *also* **:** a person entitled to bear such a baton **3 :** a piece of the materials composing something (as a building) **4 a :** any of various implements resembling a stick in shape, origin, or use: as (1) **:** COMPOSING STICK (2) **:** an airplane lever operating the elevators and ailerons (3) **:** the gearshift lever of an automobile **b :** STICKFUL **5 :** something prepared (as by cutting, molding, or rolling) in a relatively long and slender often cylindrical form ⟨a ~ of candy⟩ ⟨a ~ of butter⟩ **6 a :** PERSON, CHAP **b :** a dull, inert, stiff, or spiritless person **7** *pl* **:** wooded or rural districts **8 :** an herbaceous stalk resembling a woody stick ⟨celery ~s⟩ **9 :** 1MAST 1; *also* **:** 1YARD 3 **10 :** a piece of furniture **11 a :** a number of bombs arranged for release from a bombing plane in a series across a target **b :** a number of parachutists dropping together **12** *slang* **:** a marijuana cigarette — **stick·like** \-ˌlīk\ *adj*

2stick *vt* (1573) **1 :** to arrange (lumber) in stacks **2 :** to provide a stick as a support for

3stick *vb* **stuck** \ˈstək\; **stick·ing** [ME *stikken*, fr. OE *stician*; akin to OHG *sticken* to prick, L *instigare* to urge on, goad, Gk *stizein* to tattoo] *vt* (bef. 12c) **1 a :** to pierce with something pointed **:** STAB **b :** to kill by piercing **2 :** to push or thrust so as or as if to pierce **3 a :** to fasten by thrusting in **b :** IMPALE **c :** PUSH, THRUST **4 :** to put or set in a specified place or position **5 :** to furnish with things fastened on by or as if by piercing **6 :** to attach by or as if by causing to adhere to a surface **7 a :** to compel to pay esp. by trickery **b :** OVERCHARGE **8 a :** to halt the movement or action of **b :** BAFFLE, STUMP **9 a :** CHEAT, DEFRAUD **b :** to saddle with something disadvantageous or disagreeable ~ *vi* **1 :** to hold to something firmly by or as if by adhesion: **a :** to become fixed in place by means of a pointed end **b :** to become fast by or as if by miring or by gluing or plastering ⟨*stuck* in the mud⟩ **2 a :** to remain in a place, situation, or environment **b :** to hold fast or adhere resolutely **:** CLING **c :** to remain effective **d :** to keep close in a chase or competition **3 :** to become blocked, wedged, or jammed **4 a :** BALK, SCRUPLE **b :** to find oneself baffled **c :** to be unable to proceed **5 :** PROJECT, PROTRUDE

syn STICK, ADHERE, COHERE, CLING, CLEAVE mean to become closely attached. STICK implies attachment by affixing or by being glued together; ADHERE is often interchangeable with *stick* but sometimes implies a growing together; COHERE suggests a sticking together of parts so that they form a unified mass; CLING implies attachment by hanging on with arms or tendrils; CLEAVE stresses strength of attachment.

— **stick it to :** to treat harshly or unfairly — **stick one's neck out :** to make oneself vulnerable by taking a risk — **stick to one's guns :** to maintain one's position esp. in face of opposition — **stuck on :** infatuated with

4stick *n* (1633) **1 :** a thrust with a pointed instrument **:** STAB **2 a :** DELAY, STOP **b :** IMPEDIMENT **3 :** adhesive quality or substance

stick around *vi* (ca. 1927) **:** to stay or wait about **:** LINGER

stick·ball \ˈstik-ˌbȯl\ *n* (1939) **:** baseball adapted for play in streets or small areas and using a broomstick and a lightweight ball

stick·er \ˈstik-ər\ *n* (1585) **1 :** one that pierces with a point **2 a :** one that adheres or causes adhesion **b :** a slip of paper with adhesive back that can be fastened to a surface

stick figure *n* (1949) **1 :** a drawing showing the head of a human being or animal as a circle and all other parts as straight lines **2 :** a fictional character lacking depth and believability

stick·ful \ˈstik-ˌfu̇l\ *n* (1683) **:** as much set type as fills a composing stick

stick·han·dle \ˈstik-ˌhan-dᵊl\ *vi* (ca. 1949) **:** to maneuver a puck (as in hockey) or a ball (as in lacrosse) with a stick — **stick·han·dler** \-ˌhan(d)lər, -dᵊl-ər\ *n*

sticking plaster *n* (1655) **:** an adhesive plaster esp. for closing superficial wounds

sticking point *n* (1826) **:** an item (as in negotiations) resulting or likely to result in an impasse

stick insect *n* (ca. 1854) **:** any of various usu. wingless insects (esp. family Phasmatidae) with a long round body resembling a stick

stick–in–the–mud \ˈstik-ən-thə-ˌməd\ *n* (1733) **:** one who is slow, old-fashioned, or unprogressive; *esp* **:** an old fogy

stick·it \ˈstik-ət\ *adj* [Sc, fr. pp. of E 3*stick*] (1787) **1** *Scot* **:** UNFINISHED **2** *chiefly Scot* **:** having failed esp. in an intended profession

stick·le \ˈstik-əl\ *vi* **stick·led; stick·ling** \-(ə-)liŋ\ [ME *stightlen*, freq. of *stighten* to arrange, fr. OE *stihtan*; akin to OE *stǣger* stair — more at STAIR] (1642) **1 :** to contend esp. stubbornly and usu. on insufficient grounds **2 :** to feel scruples **:** SCRUPLE

stick·le·back \ˈstik-əl-ˌbak\ *n* [ME *stykylbak*, fr. OE *sticel* goad + ME *bak* back; akin to OE *stician* to stick] (15c) **:** any of numerous small scaleless fishes (family Gasterosteidae) having two or more free spines in front of the dorsal fin

stick·ler \ˈstik-(ə-)lər\ *n* (1644) **1 :** one who insists on exactness or completeness in the observance of something ⟨a ~ for the rules⟩ **2 :** something that baffles or puzzles **:** POSER, STICKER

stick·man \ˈstik-ˌman, -mən\ *n* (ca. 1931) **:** one who handles a stick: as **a :** one who supervises the play at a dice table, calls the decisions, and retrieves the dice **b :** a player in any of various games (as hockey or lacrosse) played with a stick

stick out *vi* (1567) **1 a :** to jut out **:** PROJECT **b :** to be prominent or conspicuous **2 :** to be persistent (as in a demand or an opinion) ~ *vt* **:** ENDURE, LAST — often used with *it* ⟨*stuck* it *out* to the end⟩

stick·pin \ˈstik-ˌpin\ *n* (1903) **:** an ornamental pin; *esp* **:** one worn in a necktie

stick·seed \-ˌsēd\ *n* (ca. 1843) **:** any of various weedy herbs (genera *Lappula* and *Hackelia*) of the borage family with bristly adhesive fruit

stick shift *n* (1959) **:** a manually operated gearshift mounted on the steering column or floor of an automobile

stick·tight \ˈstik-ˌtīt\ *n* (ca. 1884) **:** BUR MARIGOLD

stick–to–it·ive·ness \stik-ˈtü-ət-iv-nəs\ *n* [fr. the phrase *stick to it*] (1867) **:** dogged perseverance **:** TENACITY

stick·um \ˈstik-əm\ *n* [3*stick* + *-um* (prob. alter. of *'em* them)] (ca. 1909) **:** a substance that adheres or causes adhesion

stick·up \ˈstik-ˌəp\ *n* (1920) **:** a robbery at gunpoint **:** HOLDUP

stick up \(ˈ)stik-ˈəp\ *vi* (15c) **:** to stand upright or on end **:** PROTRUDE ~ *vt* **:** to rob at gunpoint — **stick up for :** to speak or act in defense of **:** SUPPORT

stick·weed \ˈstik-ˌwēd\ *n* (ca. 1743) **:** any of several plants (as a beggar's-lice) with adhesive seeds

stick·work \-ˌwərk\ *n* (1903) **:** the use (as in hockey) of one's stick in offensive and defensive techniques

sticky \ˈstik-ē\ *adj* **stick·i·er; -est** (ca. 1735) **1 a :** ADHESIVE **b** (1) **:** VISCOUS, GLUEY (2) **:** coated with a sticky substance **2 :** HUMID, MUGGY; *also* **:** CLAMMY **3 :** tending to stick **4 a :** DISAGREEABLE, UNPLEASANT **b :** AWKWARD, STIFF **c :** DIFFICULT, PROBLEMATIC — **stick·i·ly** \ˈstik-ə-lē\ *adv* — **stick·i·ness** \ˈstik-ē-nəs\ *n*

sticky wicket *n* (1926) **:** a difficult or delicate problem or situation

stic·tion \ˈstik-shən\ *n* [*st*atic + fr*iction*] (ca. 1948) **:** the force required to cause one body in contact with another to begin to move

1stiff \ˈstif\ *adj* [ME *stif*, fr. OE *stīf*; akin to MD *stijf* stiff, L *stipare* to press together, Gk *steibein* to tread on] (bef. 12c) **1 a :** not easily bent **:** RIGID **b :** lacking in suppleness or responsiveness ⟨~ muscles⟩ **c :** impeded in movement — used of a mechanism **d :** DRUNK **2 a :** FIRM, RESOLUTE **b :** STUBBORN, UNYIELDING **c :** PROUD **d** (1) **:** marked by reserve or decorum (2) **:** lacking in ease or grace **:** STILTED **3 :** hard fought **:** PUGNACIOUS, SHARP **4 a** (1) **:** exerting great force ⟨a ~ wind⟩ (2) **:** FORCEFUL, VIGOROUS **b :** POTENT ⟨a ~ dose⟩ **5 :** of a dense or glutinous consistency **:** THICK **6 a :** HARSH, SEVERE ⟨a ~ penalty⟩ **b :** ARDUOUS, RUGGED ⟨~ terrain⟩ **7 :** not easily heeled over by an external force (as the wind) ⟨a ~ ship⟩ **8 :** EXPENSIVE, STEEP ⟨paid a ~ price⟩ — **stiff·ish** \-ish\ *adj* — **stiff·ly** *adv* — **stiff·ness** *n*

syn STIFF, RIGID, INFLEXIBLE mean difficult to bend. STIFF may apply to any degree of this condition; RIGID applies to something so stiff that it cannot be bent without breaking; INFLEXIBLE stresses lack of suppleness or pliability.

2stiff *adv* (15c) **1 :** in a stiff manner **:** STIFFLY **2 :** to an extreme degree **:** SEVERELY ⟨scared ~⟩ ⟨bored ~⟩

3stiff *n* (ca. 1859) **1 :** CORPSE **2 a :** TRAMP, BUM **b :** HAND, LABORER **3 :** FLOP, FAILURE

4stiff *vt* (1950) **:** to treat harshly or unfairly; *esp* **:** to refrain from tipping ⟨~ a waiter⟩

stiff–arm \ˈstif-ˌärm\ *vb or n* (1922) **:** STRAIGHT-ARM

stiff·en \ˈstif-ən\ *vb* **stiff·ened; stiff·en·ing** \-(ə-)niŋ\ *vt* (1500) **:** to make stiff or stiffer ~ *vi* **:** to become stiff or stiffer — **stiff·en·er** \-(ə-)nər\ *n*

stiff–necked \-ˈnekt\ *adj* (1526) **1 :** HAUGHTY, STUBBORN **2 :** STILTED

stiff upper lip *n* [fr. the phrase *keep a stiff upper lip*] (1837) **:** a steady and determined attitude or manner in the face of trouble

1sti·fle \ˈstī-fəl\ *n* [ME] (14c) **:** the joint next above the hock in the hind leg of a quadruped (as a horse) corresponding to the knee in man — see HORSE illustration

2stifle *vb* **sti·fled; sti·fling** \-f(ə-)liŋ\ [alter. of ME *stuflen*] *vt* (14c) **1 a :** to kill by depriving of oxygen **:** SUFFOCATE **b** (1) **:** SMOTHER (2) **:** MUFFLE **2 a :** to cut off (as the voice or breath) **b :** to withhold from circulation or expression **:** REPRESS ⟨~*ed* our anger⟩ **c :** DETER, DISCOURAGE ~ *vi* **:** to become suffocated by or as if by lack of oxygen **:** SMOTHER — **sti·fler** \-f(ə-)lər\ *n* — **sti·fling·ly** \-f(ə-)liŋ-lē\ *adv*

\ə\ abut \ᵊ\ kitten, F table \ər\ further \a\ ash \ā\ ace \ä\ cot, cart \au̇\ out \ch\ chin \e\ bet \ē\ easy \g\ go \i\ hit \ī\ ice \j\ job \ŋ\ sing \ō\ go \ȯ\ law \ȯi\ boy \th\ thin \th\ the \ü\ loot \u̇\ foot \y\ yet \zh\ vision \à, k, ⁿ, œ, œ̄, ue, ue̅, ʸ\ *see* Guide to Pronunciation

stig·ma \'stig-mə\ *n, pl* **stig·ma·ta** \stig-'mät-ə, 'stig-mət-ə\ *or* **stigmas** [L *stigmat-, stigma* mark, brand, fr. Gk, fr. *stizein* to tattoo — more at STICK] (ca. 1588) **1 a** *archaic* **:** a scar left by a hot iron **:** BRAND **b :** a mark of shame or discredit **:** STAIN **c :** an identifying mark or characteristic; *specif* **:** a specific diagnostic sign of a disease **2 a** *stigmata pl* **:** bodily marks or pains resembling the wounds of the crucified Christ and sometimes accompanying religious ecstasy **b :** PETECHIA **3 a :** a small spot, scar, or opening on a plant or animal **b :** the part of the pistil of a flower which receives the pollen grains and on which they germinate — see FLOWER illustration — **stig·mal** \'stig-məl\ *adj*

stig·mas·ter·ol \stig-'mas-tə-,ról, -,rōl\ *n* [NL *Physostigma* (genus including the Calabar bean) + ISV *sterol*] (ca. 1924) **:** a crystalline sterol $C_{29}H_{48}O$ obtained esp. from the oils of Calabar beans and soybeans

[1]**stig·mat·ic** \stig-'mat-ik\ *n* (1594) **:** one marked with stigmata

[2]**stigmatic** *adj* (1602) **1 :** having or conveying a social stigma **2 :** of or relating to supernatural stigmata **3 :** ANASTIGMATIC — used esp. of a bundle of light rays intersecting at a single point — **stig·mat·i·cal·ly** \-i-k(ə-)lē\ *adv*

stig·ma·tist \'stig-mət-əst, stig-'mät-\ *n* (1607) **:** STIGMATIC

stig·ma·tize \'stig-mə-,tīz\ *vt* **-tized; -tiz·ing** (1585) **1 a** *archaic* **:** BRAND **b :** to describe or identify in opprobrious terms **2 :** to mark with stigmata — **stig·ma·ti·za·tion** \,stig-mət-ə-'zā-shən\ *n*

stil·bene \'stil-,bēn\ *n* [ISV, fr. Gk *stilbein* to glitter] (ca. 1868) **1 :** an aromatic hydrocarbon $C_{14}H_{12}$ used as a phosphor and in making dyes **2 :** substituted stilbene

stil·bes·trol \stil-'bes-,tról, -,trōl\ *n* [*stilbene* + *estrus* + *-ol*] (ca. 1939) **1 :** a crystalline synthetic derivative $C_{14}H_{12}O_2$ of stilbene that differs from the related diethylstilbestrol in lack of the ethyl groups and in possession of but slight estrogenic activity **2 :** DIETHYLSTILBESTROL

stil·bite \'stil-,bīt\ *n* [F, fr. Gk *stilbein*] (1815) **:** a mineral $NaCa_2Al_5Si_{13}O_{36}{\cdot}14H_2O$ consisting of a hydrous silicate of aluminum, calcium, and sodium and often occurring in sheaflike aggregations of crystals

[1]**stile** \'stī(ə)l\ *n* [ME, fr. OE *stigel;* akin to OE *stǣger* stair — more at STAIR] (bef. 12c) **:** a step or set of steps for passing over a fence or wall; *also* **:** TURNSTILE

[2]**stile** *n* [prob. fr. D *stijl* post] (1678) **:** one of the vertical members in a frame or panel into which the secondary members are fitted

sti·let·to \stə-'let-(,)ō\ *n, pl* **-tos** *or* **-toes** [It, dim. of *stilo* stylus, dagger, fr. L *stilus* stylus — more at STYLE] (1611) **1 :** a slender dagger with a blade thick in proportion to its breadth **2 :** a pointed instrument for piercing holes for eyelets or embroidery

[1]**still** \'stil\ *adj* [ME *stille,* fr. OE; akin to OHG *stilli* still, OE *steall* stall — more at STALL] (bef. 12c) **1 a :** devoid of or abstaining from motion **b** *archaic* **:** SEDENTARY **c :** not carbonated ⟨~ wine⟩ **d** (1) **:** of, relating to, or being a static photograph as contrasted with a motion picture (2) **:** designed for taking still photographs ⟨a ~ camera⟩ (3) **:** engaged in taking still photographs ⟨a ~ photographer⟩ **2 a :** uttering no sound **:** QUIET **b :** SUBDUED, MUTED **3 a :** CALM, TRANQUIL **b :** free from noise or turbulence — **still·ness** *n*

[2]**still** *vt* (bef. 12c) **1 a :** ALLAY, CALM **b :** to put an end to **:** SETTLE **2 :** to arrest the motion of **3 :** SILENCE ~ *vi* **:** to become motionless or silent **:** QUIET

[3]**still** *adv* (bef. 12c) **1 :** without motion ⟨sit ~⟩ **2** *archaic* **a :** ALWAYS, CONTINUALLY **b :** in a progressive manner **:** INCREASINGLY **3** — used as a function word to indicate the continuance of an action or condition ⟨~ lived there⟩ ⟨drink it while it's ~ hot⟩ ⟨will ~ be rich⟩ **4 :** in spite of that **:** NEVERTHELESS ⟨those who take the greatest care ~ make mistakes⟩ **5 a :** EVEN 2c ⟨a ~ more difficult problem⟩ **b :** YET 1a

[4]**still** *n* (13c) **1 :** QUIET, SILENCE **2 :** a static photograph; *specif* **:** a photograph of actors or scenes of a motion picture for publicity or documentary purposes

[5]**still** *vb* [ME *stillen,* short for *distillen* to distill] (14c) **:** DISTILL

[6]**still** *n* (1533) **1 :** DISTILLERY **2 :** apparatus used in distillation comprising either the chamber in which the vaporization is carried out or the entire equipment

still alarm *n* (1875) **:** a fire alarm transmitted (as by telephone call) without sounding the signal apparatus

still and all *adv* (1917) **:** NEVERTHELESS, STILL

still·birth \'stil-,bərth, -'bərth\ *n* (1788) **:** the birth of a dead fetus

still·born \-'bó(ə)rn\ *adj* (1597) **1 :** failing from the start **:** ABORTIVE **2 :** dead at birth — **still·born** \-,bó(ə)rn\ *n*

still–hunt \-,hənt\ *vi* (1858) **:** to ambush or stalk a quarry; *esp* **:** to pursue game noiselessly usu. without a dog ~ *vt* **:** to lie in wait for **:** approach by stealth

still hunt *n* (1834) **:** a quiet pursuing or ambushing of game

still life *n, pl* **still lifes** \-'līfs, -'līvz\ (1695) **1 :** a picture consisting predominantly of inanimate objects **2 :** the category of graphic arts concerned with inanimate subject matter

still·man \'stil-mən\ *n* (1864) **1 :** one who owns or operates a still **2 :** one who tends distillation equipment (as in an oil refinery)

still·room \'stil-,rüm, -,rům\ *n* [[6]*still*] *Brit* (1710) **:** a room connected with the kitchen where liqueurs, preserves, and cakes are kept and beverages (as tea) are prepared

still water *n* (1832) **:** a part of a stream where the gradient is so gentle that no current is visible

[1]**stil·ly** \'stil-lē\ *adv* (bef. 12c) **:** in a calm manner **:** QUIETLY

[2]**stilly** \'stil-ē\ *adj* [[4]*still* + *-y*] (1776) **:** STILL, QUIET

[1]**stilt** \'stilt\ *n* [ME *stilte;* akin to OHG *stelza* stilt, OE *steall* position, stall — more at STALL] (15c) **1 a :** one of two poles each with a rest or strap for the foot used to elevate the wearer above the ground in walking **b :** a pile or post serving as one of the supports of a structure above ground or water level **2** *pl also* **stilt :** any of various notably long-legged 3-toed limicoline birds (genera *Himantopus* and *Cladorhynchus*) that are related to the avocets, frequent inland ponds and marshes, and nest in small colonies

[2]**stilt** *vt* (1649) **:** to raise on or as if on stilts

stilt·ed \'stil-təd\ *adj* (1820) **1 a :** POMPOUS, LOFTY **b :** FORMAL, STIFF **2 :** having the curve beginning at some distance above the impost ⟨a ~ arch⟩ — **stilt·ed·ly** *adv* — **stilt·ed·ness** *n*

Stil·ton \'stilt-ᵊn\ *n* [*Stilton,* Huntingdonshire, England] (1835) **:** a blue-veined cheese with wrinkled rind made of whole cows' milk enriched with cream

stime \'stīm\ *n* [ME (northern dial.)] *chiefly Scot & Irish* (14c) **:** GLIMMER; *also* **:** GLIMPSE

stim·u·lant \'stim-yə-lənt\ *n* (1728) **1 :** an agent (as a drug) that produces a temporary increase of the functional activity or efficiency of an organism or any of its parts **2 :** STIMULUS **3 :** an alcoholic beverage — not used technically — **stimulant** *adj*

stim·u·late \-,lāt\ *vb* **-lat·ed; -lat·ing** [L *stimulatus,* pp. of *stimulare,* fr. *stimulus* goad; akin to L *stilus* stake, stylus — more at STYLE] *vt* (1619) **1 :** to excite to activity or growth or to greater activity **:** ANIMATE, AROUSE **2 a :** to function as a physiological stimulus to **b :** to arouse or affect by a stimulant (as a drug) ~ *vi* **:** to act as a stimulant or stimulus *syn* see PROVOKE — **stim·u·la·tion** \,stim-yə-'lā-shən\ *n* — **stim·u·la·tive** \'stim-yə-,lāt-iv\ *adj* — **stim·u·la·tor** \-,lāt-ər\ *n* — **stim·u·la·to·ry** \-lə-,tōr-ē, -,tór-\ *adj*

stim·u·lus \'stim-yə-ləs\ *n, pl* **-li** \-,lī, -,lē\ [L] (1684) **:** something that rouses or incites to activity: as **a :** INCENTIVE **b :** STIMULANT 1 **c :** an agent (as an environmental change) that directly influences the activity of living protoplasm (as by exciting a sensory organ or evoking muscular contraction or glandular secretion)

[1]**sting** \'stiŋ\ *vb* **stung** \'stəŋ\; **sting·ing** \'stiŋ-iŋ\ [ME *stingen,* fr. OE *stingan;* akin to ON *stinga* to sting, Gk *stachys* spike of grain, *stochos* target, aim] *vt* (bef. 12c) **1 :** to prick painfully: as **a :** to pierce or wound with a poisonous or irritating process **b :** to affect with sharp quick pain or smart ⟨hail *stung* their faces⟩ **2 :** to cause to suffer acutely ⟨*stung* with remorse⟩ **3 :** OVERCHARGE, CHEAT ~ *vi* **1 :** to use a sting **2 :** to feel a keen burning pain or smart — **sting·ing·ly** \-iŋ-lē\ *adv*

[2]**sting** *n* (bef. 12c) **1 a :** the act of stinging; *specif* **:** the thrust of a stinger into the flesh **b :** a wound or pain caused by or as if by stinging **2 :** STINGER 2 **3 :** a sharp or stinging element, force, or quality **4 :** an elaborate confidence game; *specif* **:** such a game worked by undercover police in order to trap criminals

sting·a·ree \'stiŋ-ə-rē *also* 'stiŋ-rē\ *n* [by alter.] (1836) **:** STINGRAY

sting·er \'stiŋ-ər\ *n* (ca. 1552) **1 :** one that stings; *specif* **:** a sharp blow or remark **2 :** a sharp organ (as of a bee, scorpion, or stingray) of offense and defense usu. connected with a poison gland or otherwise adapted to wound by piercing and inoculating a poisonous secretion **3 :** a cocktail consisting of brandy, white crème de menthe, and sometimes lime juice

sting·less \'stiŋ-ləs\ *adj* (1554) **:** having no sting or stinger

sting·ray \-,rā *also* -rē\ *n* (1624) **:** any of numerous rays (as of the family Dasyatidae) with one or more large sharp barbed dorsal spines near the base of the whiplike tail capable of inflicting severe wounds

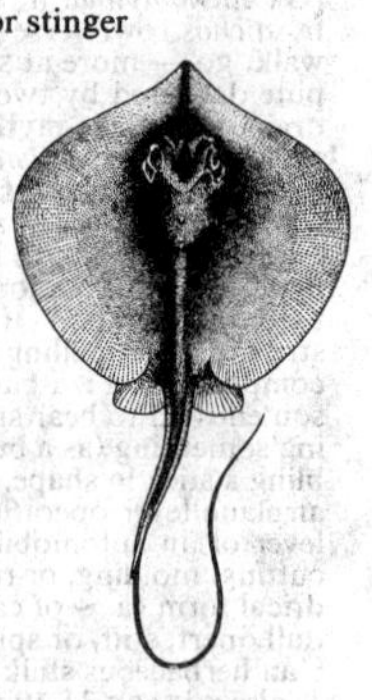
stingray

stin·gy \'stin-jē\ *adj* **stin·gi·er; -est** [prob. fr. (assumed) E dial. *stinge,* n., sting; akin to OE *stingan* to sting] (1659) **1 :** not generous or liberal **:** sparing or scant in giving or spending **2 :** meanly scanty or small — **stin·gi·ly** \-jə-lē\ *adv* — **stin·gi·ness** \-jē-nəs\ *n*

syn STINGY, CLOSE, NIGGARDLY, PARSIMONIOUS, PENURIOUS, MISERLY mean being unwilling or showing unwillingness to share with others. STINGY implies a marked lack of generosity; CLOSE suggests keeping a tight grip on one's money and possessions; NIGGARDLY implies giving or spending the very smallest amount possible; PARSIMONIOUS suggests a frugality so extreme as to lead to stinginess; PENURIOUS implies niggardliness that gives an appearance of actual poverty; MISERLY suggests a sordid avariciousness and a morbid pleasure in hoarding.

[1]**stink** \'stiŋk\ *vi* **stank** \'staŋk\ *or* **stunk** \'stəŋk\; **stunk; stink·ing** [ME *stinken,* fr. OE *stincan;* akin to OHG *stinkan* to emit a smell] (bef. 12c) **1 :** to emit a strong offensive odor **2 :** to be offensive; *also* **:** to be in bad repute **3 :** to possess something to an offensive degree ⟨~*ing* with wealth⟩ **4 :** to be extremely bad in quality — **stinky** \'stiŋ-kē\ *adj*

[2]**stink** *n* (13c) **1 :** a strong offensive odor **:** STENCH **2 :** a public outcry against something offensive

stink·ard \'stiŋ-kərd\ *n* (1600) **:** a mean or contemptible person

stink·bug \'stiŋk-,bəg\ *n* (ca. 1877) **:** any of various true bugs (order Hemiptera) that emit a disagreeable odor

stink·er \'stiŋ-kər\ *n* (1607) **1 a :** one that stinks **b :** an offensive or contemptible person **c :** something of very poor quality **2 :** any of several large petrels that have an offensive odor **3** *slang* **:** something extremely difficult ⟨the examination was a real ~⟩

stink·horn \'stiŋk-,hó(ə)rn\ *n* (ca. 1724) **:** an ill-smelling fungus (order Phallales, esp. *Phallus impudicus*)

[1]**stink·ing** *adj* (bef. 12c) **1 :** strong and offensive to the sense of smell **2** *slang* **:** offensively drunk *syn* see MALODOROUS — **stink·ing·ly** \'stiŋ-kiŋ-lē\ *adv*

[2]**stinking** *adv* (1589) **:** to an extreme degree ⟨got ~ drunk⟩

stink·ing rog·er \,stiŋ-kiŋ-'räj-ər, -kən-\ *n* [fr. the name *Roger*] (ca. 1900) **:** any of various fetid plants (as a figwort or henbane)

stinking smut *n* (ca. 1891) **:** [4]BUNT

stink·pot \'stiŋk-,pät\ *n* (1669) **1 :** an earthen jar charged with materials of an offensive and suffocating smell formerly sometimes thrown on an enemy's deck **2 :** STINKER 1

stink·stone \-,stōn\ *n* (ca. 1804) **:** a stone that emits a fetid smell on being struck or rubbed owing to decomposition of organic matter

stink up *vt* (1941) **:** to cause to stink or be filled with a stench

stink·weed \'stiŋ-,kwēd\ *n* (1753) **:** any of various strong-scented or fetid plants; *esp* **:** PENNYCRESS

stink·wood \-,kwůd\ *n* (1731) **1 :** any of several trees with a wood of unpleasant odor; *esp* **:** a southern African tree (*Ocotea bullata*) of the laurel family yielding a valued cabinet wood **2 :** the wood of a stinkwood

[1]**stint** \'stint\ *vb* [ME *stinten,* fr. OE *styntan* to blunt, dull; akin to ON *stuttr* scant, L *tundere* to beat, OE *stocc* stock] *vi* (13c) **1** *archaic* **:** STOP, DESIST **2 :** to be sparing or frugal ~ *vt* **1** *archaic* **:** to put an end to **:** STOP **2 a :** to restrain within certain limits **:** CONFINE **b :** to restrict with respect to a share or allowance **3 :** to assign a task to (a person) — **stint·er** *n*

[2]**stint** *n* (14c) **1 :** RESTRAINT, LIMITATION **2 a :** a definite quantity of work assigned **b :** a period of time spent at a particular activity ⟨served a brief ~ as a waiter⟩ ***syn*** see TASK

[3]**stint** *n, pl* **stints** *also* **stint** [ME *stynte*] (15c) **:** any of several small sandpipers

stipe \'stīp\ *n* [NL *stipes,* fr. L, tree trunk; akin to L *stipare* to press together — more at STIFF] (1785) **:** a usu. short plant stalk: as **a :** the stem supporting the cap of a fungus **b :** a part that is similar to a stipe and connects the holdfast and blade of a frondose alga **c :** the petiole of a fern frond **d :** a prolongation of the receptacle beneath the ovary of a seed plant — **stiped** \'stīpt\ *adj*

sti·pend \'stī-,pend, -pənd\ *n* [alter. of ME *stipendy,* fr. L *stipendium,* fr. *stip-, stips* gift + *pendere* to weigh, pay — more at SPIN] (15c) **:** a fixed sum of money paid periodically for services or to defray expenses

[1]**sti·pen·di·ary** \stī-'pen-dē-,er-ē\ *adj* (1545) **1 :** receiving or compensated by wages or salary ⟨a ~ curate⟩ **2 :** of or relating to a stipend

[2]**stipendiary** *n, pl* **-ar·ies** (1584) **:** one who receives a stipend

sti·pes \'stī-,pēz\ *n, pl* **stip·i·tes** \'stip-ə-,tēz\ [NL *stipit-, stipes,* fr. L, tree trunk — more at STIPE] (ca. 1760) **:** PEDUNCLE; *esp* **:** the second basal segment of a maxilla of an insect or crustacean — **stip·i·tate** \'stip-ə-,tāt\ *adj*

[1]**stip·ple** \'stip-əl\ *vt* **stip·pled; stip·pling** \-(ə-)liŋ\ [D *stippelen* to spot, dot; akin to L *stipare* to press together — more at STIFF] (1760) **1 :** to engrave by means of dots and flicks **2 a :** to make by small short touches (as of paint or ink) that together produce an even or softly graded shadow **b :** to apply (as paint) by repeated small touches **3 :** SPECKLE, FLECK — **stip·pler** \-(ə-)lər\ *n*

[2]**stipple** *n* (1837) **:** production of gradation of light and shade in graphic art by stippling small points, larger dots, or longer strokes; *also* **:** an effect produced in this way

stip·u·lar \'stip-yə-lər\ *adj* (ca. 1793) **:** of, resembling, or provided with stipules ⟨~ glands⟩

[1]**stip·u·late** \'stip-yə-,lāt\ *vb* **-lat·ed; -lat·ing** [L *stipulatus,* pp. of *stipulari* to demand some term in an agreement] *vi* (1624) **1 :** to make an agreement or covenant to do or forbear something **:** CONTRACT **2 :** to demand an express term in an agreement — used with *for* ~ *vt* **1 :** to specify as a condition or requirement of an agreement or offer **2 :** to give a guarantee of — **stip·u·la·tor** \-,lāt-ər\ *n*

[2]**stip·u·late** \'stip-yə-lət\ *adj* [NL *stipula*] (ca. 1776) **:** having stipules

stip·u·la·tion \,stip-yə-'lā-shən\ *n* [L *stipulation-, stipulatio,* fr. *stipulatus,* pp.] (ca. 1552) **1 :** an act of stipulating **2 :** something stipulated; *esp* **:** a condition, requirement, or item specified in a legal instrument — **stip·u·la·to·ry** \'stip-yə-lə-,tōr-ē, -,tȯr-\ *adj*

stip·ule \'stip-(,)yü(ə)l\ *n* [NL *stipula,* fr. L, stalk; akin to L *stipes* tree trunk] (ca. 1793) **:** either of a pair of appendages borne at the base of the leaf in many plants

[1]**stir** \'stər\ *vb* **stirred; stir·ring** [ME *stiren,* fr. OE *styrian;* akin to MHG *stürn* to incite] *vt* (bef. 12c) **1 a :** to cause an esp. slight movement or change of position of **b :** to disturb the quiet of **:** AGITATE **2 a :** to disturb the relative position of the particles or parts of esp. by a continued circular movement **b :** to mix by or as if by stirring **3 :** BESTIR, EXERT **4 :** to bring into notice or debate **:** RAISE **5 a :** to rouse to activity **:** evoke strong feelings in **b :** to call forth (as a memory) **:** EVOKE **c :** PROVOKE ~ *vi* **1 a :** to make a slight movement **b :** to begin to move (as in rousing) **2 :** to begin to be active **3 :** to be active or busy **4 :** to pass an implement through a substance with a circular movement **5 :** to be able to be stirred ⟨the mixture *stirred* easily⟩ — **stir·rer** *n*

[2]**stir** *n* (14c) **1 a :** a state of disturbance, agitation, or brisk activity **b :** widespread notice and discussion **:** IMPRESSION ⟨the book caused quite a ~⟩ **2 :** a slight movement **3 :** a stirring movement

[3]**stir** *n* [origin unknown] *slang* (1851) **:** PRISON

stir·about \'stər-ə-,bau̇t\ *n* (1682) **:** a porridge of Irish origin consisting of oatmeal or cornmeal boiled in water or milk and stirred

stir–cra·zy \'stər-'krā-zē\ *adj* [[3]*stir*] *slang* (1938) **:** distraught because of prolonged confinement

stir–fry \-'frī\ *vt* (1958) **:** to fry quickly over high heat in a lightly oiled pan (as a wok) while stirring continuously

stirk \'stərk\ *n* [ME, fr. OE *stirc;* akin to L *sterilis* sterile] *Brit* (bef. 12c) **:** a young bull or cow esp. between one and two years old

Stir·ling engine \'stər-liŋ-\ *n* [Robert *Stirling* †1878 Scot. engineer] (ca. 1896) **:** an external-combustion engine having an enclosed working fluid (as helium) that is alternately compressed and expanded to operate a piston

Stir·ling's formula \'stər-liŋz-\ *n* [James *Stirling* †1770 Scot. mathematician] (ca. 1929) **:** the formula

$$\sqrt{2\pi n}\, n^n e^{-n}$$

that gives the approximate value of the factorial of a very large number *n*

stirp \'stərp\ *n* [L *stirp-, stirps* — more at TORPID] (1502) **:** a line descending from a common ancestor **:** STOCK, LINEAGE

stirps \'sti(ə)rps, 'stərps\ *n, pl* **stir·pes** \'sti(ə)r-,pās, 'stər-(,)pēz\ [L, lit., stem, stock] (1771) **1 :** a branch of a family or the person from whom it is descended **2 a :** a group of animals equivalent to a superfamily **b :** a race or fixed variety of plants

stir·ring \'stər-iŋ\ *adj* (bef. 12c) **1 :** ACTIVE, BUSTLING **2 :** ROUSING, INSPIRING ⟨a ~ speech⟩

stir·rup \'stər-əp *also* 'stir-əp *or* 'stə-rəp\ *n* [ME *stirop,* fr. OE *stigrāp,* fr. *stig-* (akin to OHG *stīgan* to go up) + *rāp* rope — more at STAIR, ROPE] (bef. 12c) **1 :** either of a pair of small light frames or rings for receiving the foot of a rider that are attached by a strap to a saddle and used to aid in mounting and as a support while riding **2 :** a piece resembling a stirrup (as a support or clamp in carpentry and machinery) **3 :** a rope secured to a yard and attached to a thimble in its lower end for supporting a footrope **4 :** STAPES

stirrup cup *n* (1681) **1 :** a cup of drink (as wine) taken by a rider about to depart **2 :** a farewell cup

stirrup leather *n* (14c) **:** the strap suspending a stirrup

stirrup pump *n* (1940) **:** a portable hand pump held in position by a foot bracket and used for throwing a jet or spray of liquid

[1]**stitch** \'stich\ *n* [ME *stiche,* fr. OE *stice;* akin to OE *stician* to stick] (bef. 12c) **1 :** a local sharp and sudden pain esp. in the side **2 a :** one in-and-out movement of a threaded needle in sewing, embroidering, or suturing **b :** a portion of thread left in the material or suture left in the tissue after one stitch **3 :** a least part esp. of clothing **4 :** a single loop of thread or yarn around an implement (as a knitting needle or crochet hook) **5 :** a stitch or series of stitches formed in a particular way ⟨a basting ~⟩ — **in stitches :** in a state of uncontrollable laughter

[2]**stitch** *vt* (13c) **1 a :** to fasten, join, or close with or as if with stitches **b :** to make, mend, or decorate with or as if with stitches **2 :** to unite by means of staples ~ *vi* **:** SEW — **stitch·er** *n*

stitch·ery \'stich-(ə-)rē\ *n* (1607) **:** NEEDLEWORK

stitch·wort \'stich-,wərt, -,wȯ(ə)rt\ *n* (13c) **:** any of several chickweeds (genus *Stellaria*)

stithy \'stith-ē, 'stith-\ *n, pl* **stith·ies** [ME, fr. ON *stethi;* akin to OE *stede* stead] (13c) **1 :** ANVIL **2 :** SMITHY 1

sti·ver \'stī-vər\ *n* [D *stuiver*] (1502) **1 :** a unit of value and coin of the Netherlands equal to 1/20 gulden **2 :** something of little value

stoa \'stō-ə\ *n* [Gk; akin to Gk *stylos* pillar — more at STEER] (1603) **:** an ancient Greek portico usu. walled at the back with a front colonnade designed to afford a sheltered promenade

stoat \'stōt\ *n, pl* **stoats** *also* **stoat** [ME *stote*] (15c) **:** ERMINE 1a; *broadly* **:** a weasel with a black-tipped tail — used esp. of an animal in the brown summer coat

stob \'stäb\ *n* [ME, stump; akin to ME *stubb* stub] *chiefly dial* (15c) **:** STAKE, POST

stoc·ca·do \stə-'käd-(,)ō\ *n, pl* **-dos** [It *stoccata*] *archaic* (1582) **:** a thrust with a rapier

sto·chas·tic \stə-'kas-tik, stō-\ *adj* [Gk *stochastikos* skillful in aiming, fr. *stochazesthai* to aim at, guess at, fr. *stochos* target, aim, guess — more at STING] (1662) **1 :** RANDOM; *specif* **:** involving a random variable ⟨a ~ process⟩ **2 :** involving chance or probability **:** PROBABILISTIC ⟨a ~ model of radiation-induced mutation⟩ — **sto·chas·ti·cal·ly** \-ti-k(ə-)lē\ *adv*

[1]**stock** \'stäk\ *n* [ME *stok,* fr. OE *stocc;* akin to OHG *stoc* stick, MIr *tūag* bow — more at STINT] (bef. 12c) **1 a :** STUMP **b** *archaic* **:** a log or block of wood **c (1) :** something without life or consciousness **(2) :** a dull, stupid, or lifeless person **2 :** a supporting framework or structure: as **a** *pl* **:** the frame or timbers holding a ship during construction **b** *pl* **:** a device for publicly punishing offenders consisting of a wooden frame with holes in which the feet or feet and hands can be locked **c (1) :** the wooden part by which a shoulder arm is held during firing **(2) :** the butt of an implement (as a whip or fishing rod) **(3) :** BITSTOCK, BRACE **d (1) :** a long beam on a field gun forming the third support point in firing **(2) :** the beam of a plow to which handles, share, colter, and moldboard are secured **3 a :** the main stem of a plant **:** TRUNK **b (1) :** a plant or plant part united with a scion in grafting and supplying mostly underground parts to a graft **(2) :** a plant from which slips or cuttings are taken **4 :** the crosspiece of an anchor **5 a :** the original (as a man, race, or language) from which others derive **:** SOURCE **b (1) :** the descendants of one individual **:** FAMILY, LINEAGE **(2) :** a compound organism — compare CLONE **c :** an infraspecific group usu. having unity of descent **d (1) :** a related group of languages **(2) :** a language family **6 a (1) :** the equipment, materials, or supplies of an establishment **(2) :** LIVESTOCK **b :** a store or supply accumulated; *esp* **:** the inventory of goods of a merchant or manufacturer **7 a** *archaic* **:** a supply of capital **:** FUNDS; *esp* **:** money or capital invested or available for investment or trading **b (1) :** the part of a tally formerly given to the creditor in a transaction **(2) :** a debt or fund due (as from a government) for money loaned at interest; *also, Brit* **:** capital or a debt or fund bearing interest in perpetuity and not ordinarily redeemable as to principal **c (1) :** the proprietorship element in a corporation usu. divided into shares and represented by transferable certificates **(2) :** a portion of such stock of one or more companies **(3) :** STOCK CERTIFICATE **8 :** any of a genus (*Matthiola*) of herbs or subshrubs of the mustard family with racemes of usu. sweet-scented flowers **9 :** a wide band or scarf worn about the neck esp. by some clergymen **10 a :** liquid in which meat, fish, or vegetables have been simmered that is used as a basis for soup, gravy, or sauce **b :** raw material from which something is manufactured **c :** the portion of a pack of cards not distributed to the players at the beginning of a game **11 a (1) :** an estimate or evaluation of something ⟨take ~ of the situation⟩ **(2) :** the estimation in which someone or something is held ⟨his ~ with the electorate remains high —*Newsweek*⟩ **b :** confidence or faith placed in someone or something ⟨put little ~ in his testimony⟩ **12 :** the production and presentation of plays by a stock company **13 :** STOCK CAR 1 — **in stock :** on hand **:** in the store and ready for delivery — **out of stock :** having no more on hand **:** sold out

[2]**stock** *vt* (15c) **1 :** to make (a domestic animal) pregnant **2 :** to fit to or with a stock **3 :** to provide with stock or a stock **:** SUPPLY ⟨~ a stream with trout⟩ **4 :** to procure or keep a stock of **5 :** to graze (livestock) on land ~ *vi* **1 :** to send out new shoots **2 :** to put in stock or supplies ⟨~ up on canned goods⟩

[3]**stock** *adj* (1625) **1 a :** kept regularly in stock ⟨comes in ~ sizes⟩ ⟨a ~ model⟩ **b :** commonly used or brought forward **:** STANDARD ⟨the ~ answer⟩ **2 a :** kept for breeding purposes **:** BROOD ⟨a ~ mare⟩ **b :** devoted to the breeding and rearing of livestock ⟨a ~ farm⟩ **c :** used or intended for livestock ⟨a ~ train⟩ **3 :** of or relating to a stock company **4 :** employed in handling, checking, or taking care of the stock of merchandise on hand ⟨a ~ boy⟩

[1]**stock·ade** \stä-'kād\ *n* [Sp *estacada,* fr. *estaca* stake, pale, of Gmc origin; akin to OE *staca* stake] (1614) **1 :** a line of stout posts set firmly to form a defense **2 a :** an enclosure or pen made with posts and stakes **b :** an enclosure in which prisoners are kept

[2]**stockade** *vt* **stock·ad·ed; stock·ad·ing** (1677) **:** to fortify or surround with a stockade

stock·breed·er \'stäk-,brēd-ər\ *n* (1815) **:** one who is engaged in the breeding and care of livestock for the market, for show purposes, or for racing

stock·bro·ker \-,brō-kər\ *n* (ca. 1706) **:** a broker who executes orders to buy and sell securities and often also acts as a security dealer — **stock·bro·ker·age** \-k(ə-)rij\ *n* — **stock·brok·ing** \-,brō-kiŋ\ *n*

stock car *n* (1858) **1 :** a latticed railroad boxcar for carrying livestock **2 :** a racing car having the basic chassis of a commercially produced assembly-line model **3 :** an automotive vehicle of a model and type kept in stock for regular sales

stock certificate *n* (1863) **:** an instrument evidencing ownership of one or more shares of the capital stock of a corporation

stock company *n* (1827) **1 :** a corporation or joint-stock company of which the capital is represented by stock **2 :** a theatrical company attached to a repertory theater; *esp* **:** one without outstanding stars

stock dividend *n* (ca. 1902) **1 :** the payment by a corporation of a dividend in the form of shares usu. of its own stock without change in par value — compare STOCK SPLIT **2 :** the stock distributed in a stock dividend

stock·er \'stäk-ər\ *n* (1881) **1 :** a young animal (as a steer or heifer) suitable for being fed and fattened for market **2 :** an animal (as a heifer) suitable for use in a breeding establishment **3 :** STOCK CAR 2

stock exchange *n* (1773) **1 :** a place where security trading is conducted on an organized system **2 :** an association of people organized to provide an auction market among themselves for the purchase and sale of securities

stock·fish \-,fish\ *n* [ME *stokfish,* fr. MD *stocvisch,* fr. *stoc* stick + *visch* fish; akin to OHG *fisc* fish — more at FISH] (13c) **:** fish (as cod, haddock, or hake) dried hard in the open air without salt

stock·hold·er \'stäk-,hōl-dər\ *n* (ca. 1776) **:** an owner of corporate stock

stock·i·nette *or* **stock·i·net** \,stäk-ə-'net\ *n* [alter. of earlier *stocking net*] (1784) **:** a soft elastic usu. cotton fabric used esp. for bandages and infants' wear

stock·ing \'stäk-iŋ\ *n* [obs. *stock* to cover with a stocking] (1583) **1 a :** a usu. knit close-fitting covering for the foot and leg **b :** SOCK **2 :** something resembling a stocking; *esp* **:** a ring of distinctive color on the lower part of the leg of an animal — **stock·inged** \-iŋd\ *adj* — **in one's stocking feet :** having on stockings but no shoes

stocking cap *n* (ca. 1897) **:** a long knitted cone-shaped cap with a tassel or pom-pom worn esp. for winter sports or play

stock–in–trade \,stäk-ən-'trād, 'stäk-ən-,\ *n* (1762) **1 :** the equipment necessary to or used in a trade or business **2 :** something that resembles the standard equipment of a tradesman or business ⟨the light and frivolous charm which was her stage ~ —S. H. Adams⟩

stock·ish \'stäk-ish\ *adj* (1596) **:** like a stock **:** STUPID

stock·ist \'stäk-əst\ *n, Brit* (1910) **:** one (as a retailer) that stocks goods

stock·job·ber \'stäk-,jäb-ər\ *n* (1676) **:** STOCKBROKER — usu. used disparagingly

stock·job·bing \-,jäb-iŋ\ *n* (1692) **:** speculative exchange dealings

stock·keep·er \'stäk-,kē-pər\ *n* (1806) **1 :** one (as a herdsman or shepherd) having the charge or care of livestock **2 :** one that keeps and records stock (as in a warehouse) **:** one that keeps an inventory of goods on hand, shipped, or received

stock·man \-mən, -,man\ *n* (1806) **:** one occupied as an owner or worker in the raising of livestock (as cattle or sheep)

stock market *n* (1809) **1 :** STOCK EXCHANGE 1 **2 a :** a market for particular stocks **b :** the market for stocks throughout a country

stock option *n* (1945) **:** a right granted by a corporation to officers or employees as a form of compensation that allows purchase of corporate stock at a fixed price at a specified time with reimbursement derived from the difference between purchase and market prices

1**stock·pile** \'stäk-,pīl\ *n* (1920) **:** a storage pile: as **a :** a reserve supply of something essential accumulated within a country for use during a shortage **b :** a gradually accumulated reserve of something ⟨avert ~s of unsold cars —Bert Pierce⟩

2**stockpile** *vt* (1924) **1 :** to place or store in or on a stockpile **2 :** to accumulate a stockpile of ⟨~ war materials in Europe —A. O. Wolfers⟩ — **stock·pil·er** *n*

stock·pot \'stäk-,pät\ *n* (1853) **1 :** a pot in which soup stock is prepared **2 :** an abundant supply **:** REPOSITORY

stock·proof \-'prüf\ *adj* (1928) **:** proof against livestock

stock·room \-,rüm, -,ru̇m\ *n* (1825) **:** a storage place for supplies or goods used in a business

stock saddle *n* (1886) **:** a deep-seated saddle with a high pommel and broad skirts and fenders used orig. by cattlemen — called also *western saddle;* see SADDLE illustration

stock split *n* (1950) **:** a division of corporate stock by the issuance to existing shareholders of a specified number of new shares with a corresponding lowering of par value for each outstanding share — compare STOCK DIVIDEND

stock–still \'stäk-'stil\ *adj* (15c) **:** very still **:** MOTIONLESS ⟨stood ~⟩

stock·tak·ing \'stäk-,tā-kiŋ\ *n* (ca. 1858) **1 :** INVENTORY 3 **2 :** the action of estimating a situation at a given moment

stocky \'stäk-ē\ *adj* **stock·i·er; -est** (1622) **:** compact, sturdy, and relatively thick in build — **stock·i·ly** \'stäk-ə-lē\ *adv* — **stock·i·ness** \'stäk-ē-nəs\ *n*

stock·yard \'stäk-,yärd\ *n* (1802) **:** a yard for stock; *specif* **:** one in which transient cattle, sheep, swine, or horses are kept temporarily for slaughter, market, or shipping

1**stodge** \'stäj\ *vt* **stodged; stodg·ing** [origin unknown] (1674) **:** to stuff full esp. with food

2**stodge** *n* (ca. 1841) **:** a thick filling food (as oatmeal or stew)

stodgy \'stäj-ē\ *adj* **stodg·i·er; -est** [2*stodge*] (ca. 1823) **1 :** having a thick gluey consistency **:** HEAVY ⟨~ bread⟩ **2 :** moving in a slow plodding way esp. as a result of physical bulkiness **3 :** BORING, DULL ⟨out on a peaceful rather ~ Sunday boat trip —Edna Ferber⟩ **4 :** extremely old-fashioned **:** HIDEBOUND ⟨received a pompously Victorian letter from his ~ father —E.E.S. Montagu⟩ **5 a :** DRAB **b :** DOWDY — **stodg·i·ly** \'stäj-ə-lē\ *adv* — **stodg·i·ness** \'stäj-ē-nəs\ *n*

sto·gie *or* **sto·gy** \'stō-gē\ *n, pl* **stogies** [*Conestoga,* Pa.] (1853) **1 :** a stout coarse shoe **:** BROGAN **2 :** an inexpensive slender cylindrical cigar; *broadly* **:** CIGAR

1**sto·ic** \'stō-ik\ *n* [ME, fr. L *stoicus,* fr. Gk *stōïkos,* lit., of the portico, fr. *Stoa* (*Poikilē*) the Painted Portico, portico at Athens where Zeno taught] (14c) **1** *cap* **:** a member of a school of philosophy founded by Zeno of Citium about 300 B.C. holding that the wise man should be free from passion, unmoved by joy or grief, and submissive to natural law **2 :** one apparently or professedly indifferent to pleasure or pain

2**stoic** *or* **sto·i·cal** \-i-kəl\ *adj* (15c) **1** *cap* **:** of, relating to, or resembling the Stoics or their doctrines ⟨*Stoic* logic⟩ **2 :** not affected by or showing passion or feeling; *esp* **:** firmly restraining response to pain or distress ⟨a ~ indifference to cold⟩ ***syn*** see IMPASSIVE — **sto·i·cal·ly** \-i-k(ə-)lē\ *adv*

stoi·chio·met·ric \,stȯi-kē-ō-'me-trik\ *adj* (1892) **:** of, relating to, used in, or marked by stoichiometry — **stoi·chio·met·ri·cal·ly** \-tri-k(ə-)lē\ *adv*

stoi·chi·om·e·try \,stȯi-kē-'äm-ə-trē\ *n* [Gk *stoicheion* element + E *-metry;* akin to Gk *stichos* row, *steichein* to walk, go — more at STAIR] (1807) **1 :** a branch of science that deals with the application of the laws of definite proportions and of the conservation of matter and energy to chemical activity **2 a :** the quantitative relationship between constituents in a chemical substance **b :** the quantitative relationship between two or more substances esp. in processes involving physical or chemical change

sto·icism \'stō-ə-,siz-əm\ *n* (1626) **1** *cap* **:** the philosophy of the Stoics **2 :** indifference to pleasure or pain **:** IMPASSIVENESS

stoke \'stōk\ *vb* **stoked; stok·ing** [D *stoken;* akin to MD *stuken* to push] *vt* (1683) **1 :** to poke or stir up (as a fire) **:** supply with fuel **2 :** to feed abundantly ~ *vi* **:** to stir up or tend a fire (as in a furnace) **:** supply a furnace with fuel

stoked \'stōkt\ *adj, slang* (1965) **:** being in an enthusiastic or exhilarated state

stoke·hold \'stōk-,hōld\ *n* (1887) **1 :** a room containing a ship's boilers — called also *fireroom* **2 :** one of the spaces in front of the boilers of a ship from which the furnaces are fed

stoke·hole \-,hōl\ *n* (1660) **1 :** the mouth to the grate of a furnace **2 :** STOKEHOLD

stok·er \'stō-kər\ *n* (1660) **1 :** one employed to tend a furnace and supply it with fuel; *specif* **:** one that tends a marine steam boiler **2 :** a machine for feeding a fire

Stokes' aster \'stōk-,sas-tər, ,stōk-sə-'zas-\ *n* [Jonathan *Stokes* †1831 Eng. botanist] (ca. 1890) **:** a perennial composite herb (*Stokesia laevis*) of the southern U.S. often grown for its large showy heads of blue flowers

1**stole** \'stōl\ *past of* STEAL

2**stole** *n* [ME, fr. OE, fr. L *stola,* fr. Gk *stolē* equipment, robe, fr. *stellein* to set up, make ready — more at STALL] (bef. 12c) **1 :** a long loose garment **:** ROBE **2 :** an ecclesiastical vestment consisting of a long usu. silk band worn traditionally around the neck by bishops and priests and over the left shoulder by deacons — see VESTMENT illustration **3 :** a long wide scarf or similar covering worn by women usu. across the shoulders

stolen *past part of* STEAL

stol·id \'stäl-əd\ *adj* [L *stolidus* dull, stupid; akin to OHG *stal* place — more at STALL] (1600) **:** having or expressing little or no sensibility **:** UNEMOTIONAL ***syn*** see IMPASSIVE — **sto·lid·i·ty** \stä-'lid-ət-ē, stə-\ *n* — **stol·id·ly** \'stäl-əd-lē\ *adv*

stol·len \'s(h)tō-lən, 's(h)tȯ-; 'stəl-ə(n)\ *n, pl* **stollen** *or* **stollens** [G, pl. of *stolle,* lit., post, support, fr. OHG *stollo;* akin to OHG *stal* place] (1926) **:** a sweet yeast bread of German origin containing fruit and nuts

sto·lon \'stō-lən, -,län\ *n* [NL *stolon-, stolo,* fr. L, branch, sucker; akin to Arm *steɫn* branch, OHG *stal* place] (1601) **1 a :** a horizontal branch from the base of a plant that produces new plants from buds at its tip or nodes (as in the strawberry) — called also *runner* **b :** a hypha (as of rhizopus) produced on the surface and connecting a group of conidiophores **2 :** an extension of the body wall (as of a hydrozoan) that develops buds giving rise to new zooids which usu. remain united by the stolon

sto·lon·if·er·ous \,stō-lə-'nif-(ə-)rəs\ *adj* (ca. 1777) **:** bearing or developing stolons

stom- *or* **stomo-** *comb form* [Gk & NL *stoma*] **:** mouth **:** stoma ⟨*stomo*daeum⟩

sto·ma \'stō-mə\ *n, pl* **sto·ma·ta** \-mət-ə\ *also* **stomas** [NL, fr. Gk *stomat-, stoma* mouth] (ca. 1684) **1 :** any of various small simple bodily openings esp. in a lower animal **2 :** one of the minute openings in the epidermis of a plant organ (as a leaf) through which gaseous interchange takes place; *also* **:** the opening with its associated cellular structures **3 :** an artificial permanent opening esp. in the abdominal wall made in surgical procedures

1**stom·ach** \'stəm-ək, -ik\ *n* [ME *stomak,* fr. MF *estomac,* fr. L *stomachus* gullet, esophagus, stomach, fr. Gk *stomachos,* fr. *stoma* mouth; akin to MBret *staffn* mouth, Av *staman-*] (14c) **1 a** (1) **:** a dilatation of the alimentary canal of a vertebrate communicating anteriorly with the esophagus and posteriorly with the duodenum (2) **:** one of the compartments of a ruminant stomach ⟨the abomasum is the fourth ~ of a ruminant⟩ **b :** a cavity in an invertebrate animal that is analogous to a stomach **c :** the part of the body that contains the stomach **:** BELLY, ABDOMEN **2 a :** desire for food caused by hunger **:** APPETITE **b :** INCLINATION, DESIRE ⟨had no ~ for an argument⟩ **3** *obs* **a :** SPIRIT, VALOR **b :** PRIDE **c :** SPLEEN, RESENTMENT

2**stomach** *vt* (1523) **1** *archaic* **:** to take offense at **2 :** to bear without overt reaction or resentment **:** BROOK ⟨couldn't ~ her attitude⟩

stom·ach·ache \-,āk\ *n* (1763) **:** pain in or in the region of the stomach

stom·ach·er \'stəm-i-kər, -i-chər\ *n* (15c) **:** the center front section of a waist or underwaist or a usu. heavily embroidered or jeweled separate piece for the center front of a bodice worn by men and women in the 15th and 16th centuries

1**sto·mach·ic** \stə-'mak-ik\ *adj* (ca. 1656) **:** of or relating to the stomach ⟨~ vessels⟩

2**stomachic** *n* (1735) **:** a stimulant or tonic for the stomach

stom·achy \'stəm-ək-ē, -ik-\ *adj* (ca. 1825) **1** *dial Brit* **:** IRASCIBLE, IRRITABLE **2 :** having a large stomach

sto·mal \'stō-məl\ *adj* (ca. 1941) **:** of, relating to, or situated near a surgical stoma ⟨a ~ ulcer⟩

stomat- *or* **stomato-** *comb form* [NL, fr. Gk, fr. *stomat-, stoma*] **:** mouth **:** stoma ⟨*stomat*itis⟩ ⟨*stomato*logy⟩

sto·ma·tal \'stōm-ət-ᵊl\ *adj* (1861) **:** of, relating to, or constituting plant stomata ⟨~ openings⟩ ⟨~ transpiration⟩

sto·mate \ˈstō-ˌmāt\ *n* [irreg. fr. NL *stomat-, stoma*] (1835) : STOMA 2

sto·ma·ti·tis \ˌstō-mə-ˈtīt-əs\ *n, pl* **-tit·i·des** \-ˈtit-ə-ˌdēz\ *or* **-ti·tis·es** \-ˈtīt-ə-səz\ [NL] (1859) : any of numerous inflammatory diseases of the mouth

sto·mato·pod \stō-ˈmat-ə-ˌpäd\ *n* [NL *Stomatopoda*, fr. *stomat-* + *-poda*] (1877) : any of an order (Stomatopoda) of marine crustaceans (as a squilla) that have gills on the abdominal appendages — **stomatopod** *adj*

sto·mo·dae·um *or* **sto·mo·de·um** \ˌstō-mə-ˈdē-əm\ *n, pl* **-daea** \-ˈdē-ə\ *or* **-dea** [NL, fr. *stom-* + Gk *hodaion*, neut. of *hodaios* being on the way, fr. *hodos* way — more at CEDE] (1876) : the anterior ectodermal part of the alimentary canal or tract — **sto·mo·dae·al** *or* **sto·mo·de·al** \-ˈdē-əl\ *adj*

[1]**stomp** \ˈstämp, ˈstȯmp\ *vb* (ca. 1828) : STAMP

[2]**stomp** *n* (ca. 1899) **1** : STAMP 4 **2** : a jazz dance marked by heavy stamping

-s·to·my \s-tə-mē\ *n comb form* [ISV, fr. Gk *stoma* mouth, opening] : surgical operation establishing a usu. permanent opening into (such) a part ⟨entero*stomy*⟩

[1]**stone** \ˈstōn\ *n* [ME, fr. OE *stān;* akin to OHG *stein* stone, Gk *stear* hard fat] (bef. 12c) **1** : a concretion of earthy or mineral matter: **a** (1) : such a concretion of indeterminate size or shape (2) : ROCK **b** : a piece of rock for a specified function: as (1) : a building block (2) : a paving block (3) : a precious stone : GEM (4) : GRAVESTONE (5) : GRINDSTONE (6) : WHETSTONE (7) : a surface upon which a drawing, text, or design to be lithographed is drawn or transferred **2** : something resembling a small stone: as **a** : CALCULUS 3a **b** : the hard central portion of a drupaceous fruit (as a peach) **c** : a hard stony seed (as of a date) **3** *pl usu* **stone** : any of various units of weight; *esp* : an official British unit equal to 14 pounds (6.3 kilograms) **4 a** : CURLING STONE **b** : a round playing piece used in various games (as backgammon or go) **5** : a stand or table with a smooth flat top on which to impose or set type

[2]**stone** *adj* (bef. 12c) **1** : of, relating to, or made of stone **2** : ABSOLUTE, UTTER ⟨pure ~ craziness—Edwin Shrake⟩

[3]**stone** *vt* **stoned; ston·ing** (13c) **1** : to hurl stones at; *esp* : to kill by pelting with stones **2** *archaic* : to make hard or insensitive to feeling **3** : to face, pave, or fortify with stones **4** : to remove the stones or seeds of (a fruit) **5 a** : to rub, scour, or polish with a stone **b** : to sharpen with a whetstone — **ston·er** *n*

[4]**stone** *adv* (13c) : ENTIRELY, UTTERLY — used as an intensive; often used in combination ⟨*stone*-broke⟩ ⟨*stone*-cold soup⟩ ⟨*stone*-dead⟩

Stone Age *n* (1864) : the first known period of prehistoric human culture characterized by the use of stone tools

stone–blind \ˈstōn-ˈblīnd\ *adj* (14c) : totally blind

stone canal *n* (1887) : a tube in many echinoderms that contains calcareous deposits and leads from the ring of the water-vascular system surrounding the mouth to the madreporite

stone cell *n* (1884) : a more or less spherical sclereid

stone·chat \-ˌchat\ *n* [[2]*chat*] (ca. 1783) : a common European songbird (*Saxicola torquata*); *also* : any of various related birds (genus *Saxicola*)

stone china *n* (1823) : a hard dense opaque feldspathic pottery developed in England; *broadly* : IRONSTONE CHINA

stone–cold \ˌstōn-ˌkōld\ *adv* (1592) : ABSOLUTELY, COMPLETELY ⟨~ sober⟩

stone crab *n* (1709) : a large edible crab (*Menippe mercenaria*) found on the southern coast of the U.S. and in the Caribbean area

stone·crop \ˈstōn-ˌkräp\ *n* (bef. 12c) **1** : SEDUM; *esp* : a mossy evergreen creeping sedum (*Sedum acre*) with pungent fleshy leaves **2** : any of various plants of the orpine family related to the sedums

stone·cut·ter \-ˌkət-ər\ *n* (1540) **1** : one that cuts, carves, or dresses stone **2** : a machine for dressing stone — **stone·cut·ting** \-ˌkət-iŋ\ *n*

stoned \ˈstōnd\ *adj* (1952) **1** : DRUNK **2** : being under the influence of a drug (as marijuana) taken esp. for pleasure : HIGH

stone–deaf \-ˈdef\ *adj* (1837) : totally deaf

stone·fish \ˈstōn-ˌfish\ *n* (1896) : any of several small spiny venomous scorpion fishes (esp. genus *Synanceja*) common about coral reefs of the tropical Indo-Pacific

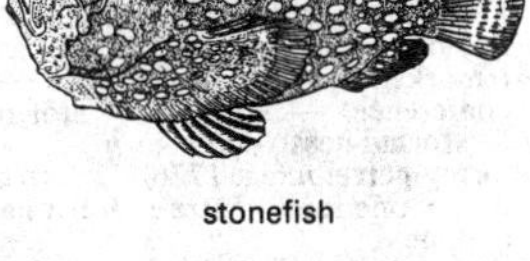

stonefish

stone fly *n* (15c) : an insect (order Plecoptera) with an aquatic carnivorous nymph having gills and an adult used by anglers for bait

stone fruit *n* (1523) : a fruit with a stony endocarp : DRUPE

stone–ground \ˈstōn-ˈgrau̇nd\ *adj* (1905) : ground in a buhrstone mill ⟨~ flour⟩

stone·ma·son \ˈstōn-ˌmās-ᵊn\ *n* (1758) : a mason who builds with stone — **stone·ma·son·ry** \-rē\ *n*

stone parsley *n* (1548) : a slender herb (*Sison amomum*) of the carrot family with aromatic seeds that are used as a condiment

stone roller *n* (1882) **1** : HOG SUCKER **2** : a common cyprinid fish (*Campostoma anomalum*) found esp. in clear streams of the central U.S.

stone's throw *n* (1581) : a short distance ⟨lives within a *stone's throw* of town⟩

stone·wall \ˈstōn-ˈwȯl, -ˌwȯl\ *vi* (1889) **1** *chiefly Brit* : to engage in obstructive parliamentary debate or delaying tactics **2** : to be uncooperative, obstructive, or evasive ~ *vt* : to refuse to comply or cooperate with — **stone·wall·er** *n*

stone wall *n* (bef. 12c) **1** : a fence made of stones; *esp* : one built of rough stones without mortar to enclose a field **2** : an immovable block or obstruction (as in public affairs)

stone·ware \-ˌwa(ə)r, -ˌwe(ə)r\ *n* (1683) : a strong opaque ceramic ware that is high-fired, well vitrified, and nonporous

stone·work \-ˌwərk\ *n* (bef. 12c) **1** : a structure or part built of stone : MASONRY **2** : the shaping, preparation, or setting of stone

stone·wort \-ˌwərt, -ˌwȯ(ə)rt\ *n* (ca. 1816) : any of a family (Characeae) of freshwater green algae resembling the horsetails and often encrusted with calcareous deposits

stony *also* **ston·ey** \ˈstō-nē\ *adj* **ston·i·er; -est** (bef. 12c) **1** : abounding in or having the nature of stone : ROCKY **2 a** : insensitive to pity or human feeling **b** : manifesting no movement or reaction : DUMB, EXPRESSIONLESS **c** : fearfully gripping : PETRIFYING **3** *archaic* : consisting of or made of stones **4** : stone-broke — **ston·i·ly** \ˈstōn-ᵊl-ē\ *adv* — **ston·i·ness** \ˈstōn-ē-nəs\ *n*

stony·heart·ed \ˌstō-nē-ˈhärt-əd\ *adj* (1569) : UNFEELING, CRUEL

stood *past and past part of* STAND

[1]**stooge** \ˈstüj\ *n* [origin unknown] (ca. 1913) **1 a** : one who plays a subordinate or compliant role to a principal **b** : PUPPET 3 **2** : STRAIGHT MAN **3** : STOOL PIGEON

[2]**stooge** *vi* **stooged; stoog·ing** (1946) : to act as a stooge ⟨congressmen who ~ for the oil and mineral interests —*New Republic*⟩

[1]**stool** \ˈstül\ *n* [ME, fr. OE *stōl;* akin to OHG *stuol* chair, OSlav *stolŭ* seat, throne, OE *standan* to stand] (bef. 12c) **1 a** : a seat usu. without back or arms supported by three or four legs or by a central pedestal **b** : a low bench or portable support for the feet or knees : FOOTSTOOL **2** : a seat used as a symbol of office or authority; *also* : the rank, dignity, office, or rule of a chieftain **3 a** : a seat used while defecating or urinating **b** : a discharge of fecal matter **4 a** : a stump or group of stumps of a tree esp. when producing suckers **b** : a plant crown from which shoots grow out **c** : a shoot or growth from a stool **5** : STOOL PIGEON

[2]**stool** *vi* (1770) : to throw out shoots in the manner of a stool

stool·ie \ˈstü-lē\ *n* (1937) : STOOL PIGEON 2

stool pigeon *n* [prob. fr. the early practice of fastening the decoy bird to a stool] (1836) **1** : a pigeon used as a decoy to draw others within a net **2** : a person acting as a decoy or informer; *esp* : a spy sent into a group to report (as to the police) on its activities

[1]**stoop** \ˈstüp\ *vb* [ME *stoupen*, fr. OE *stūpian;* akin to OE *stēap* steep, deep — more at STEEP] *vi* (bef. 12c) **1 a** : to bend the body forward and downward sometimes simultaneously bending the knees **b** : to stand or walk with a forward inclination of the head, body, or shoulders **2** : YIELD, SUBMIT **3 a** : to descend from a superior rank, dignity, or status **b** : to lower oneself morally **4 a** *archaic* : to move down from a height : ALIGHT **b** : to fly or dive down swiftly usu. to attack prey ~ *vt* **1** : DEBASE, DEGRADE **2** : to bend (a part of the body) forward and downward

[2]**stoop** *n* (1571) **1 a** : an act of bending the body forward **b** : a temporary or habitual forward bend of the back and shoulders **2** : the descent of a bird esp. on its prey **3** : a lowering of oneself

[3]**stoop** *n* [D *stoep;* akin to OE *stæpe* step — more at STEP] (1755) : a porch, platform, entrance stairway, or small veranda at a house door

stoop·ball \ˈstüp-ˌbȯl\ *n* (1945) : a variation of baseball in which a player throws a ball against a stoop or building and runs to base while other players attempt to retrieve the rebound and put him out

stoop labor *n* (1949) : the hard labor done or required to plant, cultivate, and harvest a crop and esp. a crop of vegetables

[1]**stop** \ˈstäp\ *vb* **stopped; stop·ping** [ME *stoppen*, fr. OE *-stoppian*, fr. (assumed) VL *stuppare* to stop with tow, fr. L *stuppa* tow, fr. Gk *styppē*] *vt* (bef. 12c) **1 a** : to close by filling or obstructing **b** : to hinder or prevent the passage of **c** : to get in the way of : be wounded or killed by ⟨easy to ~ a bullet along a lonely . . . road —Harvey Fergusson⟩ **2 a** : to close up or block off (an opening) : PLUG **b** : to make impassable : CHOKE, OBSTRUCT **c** : to cover over or fill in (a hole or crevice) **3 a** : to cause to give up or change a course of action **b** : HOLD BACK, RESTRAIN, PREVENT **4 a** : to cause to cease : CHECK, SUPPRESS **b** : DISCONTINUE **5 a** : to deduct or withhold (a sum due) **b** : to instruct one's bank to refuse (payment) or refuse payment of (as a check) **6 a** : to arrest the progress or motion of : cause to halt ⟨*stopped* the car⟩ **b** : PARRY **c** : to check by means of a weapon : BRING DOWN, KILL **d** : to beat in a boxing match by a knockout; *broadly* : DEFEAT **e** : BAFFLE, NONPLUS **7** : to change the pitch of (as a violin string) by pressing with the finger or (as a wind instrument) by closing one or more finger holes or by thrusting the hand or a mute into the bell **8** : to hold an honor card and enough protecting cards to be able to block (a bridge suit) before an opponent can run many tricks ~ *vi* **1 a** : to cease activity or operation **b** : to come to an end esp. suddenly : CLOSE, FINISH **2 a** : to cease to move on : HALT **b** : PAUSE, HESITATE **3 a** : to break one's journey : STAY **b** *chiefly Brit* : REMAIN **c** : to make a brief call : drop in **4** : to become choked : CLOG — **stop·pa·ble** \ˈstäp-ə-bəl\ *adj*

syn STOP, CEASE, QUIT, DISCONTINUE, DESIST mean to suspend or cause to suspend activity. STOP applies to action or progress or to what is operating or progressing and may imply suddenness or definiteness ⟨*stopped* at the red light⟩ CEASE applies to states, conditions, or existence and may add a suggestion of gradualness and a degree of finality ⟨by nightfall the fighting had *ceased*⟩ QUIT may stress either finality or abruptness in stopping or ceasing ⟨the engine faltered, sputtered, then *quit* altogether⟩ DISCONTINUE applies to the stopping of an accustomed activity or practice ⟨we have *discontinued* the manufacture of that item⟩ DESIST implies forbearance or restraint as a motive for stopping or ceasing ⟨*desisted* from further efforts to persuade them⟩

[2]**stop** *n* (15c) **1 a** : CESSATION, END **b** : a pause or breaking off in speech **2 a** (1) : a graduated set of organ pipes of similar design and tone quality (2) : a corresponding set of vibrators or reeds of a reed organ (3) : STOP KNOB **b** : a means of regulating the pitch of a musical instrument **3 a** : something that impedes, obstructs, or brings to a halt : IMPEDIMENT, OBSTACLE **b** : the aperture of a camera lens; *also* : a marking of a series (as of f-numbers) on a camera for indicating settings of the diaphragm **c** : a drain plug : STOPPER **4** : a device for arresting or limiting motion **5** : the act of stopping : the state of being stopped : CHECK **6 a** : a halt in a journey : STAY ⟨made a brief ~ to refuel⟩ **b** : a stopping place ⟨a bus ~⟩ **7 a** *chiefly Brit* : any of several punctuation marks **b** — used in telegrams and cables to indicate a period **c** : a pause or break in a verse that marks the end of a grammatical unit **8 a** : an order stopping payment (as of a check or note) by a bank **b** : STOP ORDER **9** : a consonant in the articulation of which there is a stage (as in the *p* of *apt* or the *g* of *tiger*) when the breath passage is

completely closed **10 :** a depression in the face of an animal at the junction of forehead and muzzle — see DOG illustration

[3]**stop** *adj* (1594) **:** serving to stop **:** designed to stop ⟨~ line⟩ ⟨~ signal⟩

stop–and–go \ˌstäp-ən-ˈgō, -ᵊm-, *attributively* -ˌgō\ *adj* (1925) **:** of, relating to, or involving frequent stops; *esp* **:** controlled or regulated by traffic lights ⟨~ driving⟩

stop bath *n* (ca. 1918) **:** an acid bath used to check photographic development of a negative or print

stop·cock \ˈstäp-ˌkäk\ *n* (1584) **:** a cock for stopping or regulating flow (as through a pipe)

stop down *vt* (ca. 1891) **:** to reduce the effective aperture of (a lens) by means of a diaphragm

[1]**stope** \ˈstōp\ *n* [prob. fr. LG *stope,* lit., step; akin to OE *stæpe* step — more at STEP] (1747) **:** a usu. steplike excavation underground for the removal of ore that is formed as the ore is mined in successive layers

[2]**stope** *vb* **stoped; stop·ing** *vi* (1778) **:** to mine by means of a stope ~ *vt* **:** to extract (ore) from a stope — **stop·er** *n*

stop·gap \ˈstäp-ˌgap\ *n* (1684) **:** something that serves as a temporary expedient **:** MAKESHIFT ***syn*** see RESOURCE

stop knob *n* (1887) **:** one of the handles by which an organist draws or shuts off a particular stop

stop·light \ˈstäp-ˌlīt\ *n* (1926) **1 :** a light on the rear of a motor vehicle that is illuminated when the driver presses the brake pedal **2 :** TRAFFIC SIGNAL

stop order *n* (ca. 1891) **:** an order to a broker to buy or sell respectively at the market when the price of a security advances or declines to a designated level

stop out \(ˈ)stäp-ˈau̇t\ *vi* [ˈ*stop* + *out* (as in *drop out*)] (1973) **:** to withdraw temporarily from enrollment at a college or university — **stop–out** \ˈstäp-ˌau̇t\ *n*

stop·over \ˈstäp-ˌō-vər\ *n* (1885) **1 :** a stop at an intermediate point in one's journey **2 :** a stopping place on a journey

stop·page \ˈstäp-ij\ *n* (15c) **:** the act of stopping **:** the state of being stopped **:** HALT, OBSTRUCTION

stop payment *n* (ca. 1919) **:** a depositor's order to a bank to refuse to honor a specified check drawn by him

[1]**stop·per** \ˈstäp-ər\ *n* (15c) **1 :** one that brings to a halt or causes to stop operating or functioning **:** CHECK: as **a :** a playing card that will stop the running of a suit **b :** a baseball pitcher depended on to win important games or to stop a losing streak; *also* **:** an effective relief pitcher **2 :** one that closes, shuts, or fills up; *specif* **:** something (as a bung or cork) used to plug an opening

[2]**stopper** *vt* **stop·pered; stop·per·ing** \-(ə-)riŋ\ (ca. 1769) **:** to close or secure with or as if with a stopper

stopper knot *n* (1860) **:** a knot used to prevent a rope from passing through a hole or opening

[1]**stop·ple** \ˈstäp-əl\ *n* [ME *stoppell,* fr. *stoppen* to stop] (14c) **:** something that closes an aperture **:** STOPPER, PLUG

[2]**stopple** *vt* **stop·pled; stop·pling** \-(ə-)liŋ\ (1795) **:** STOPPER

stop street *n* (ca. 1930) **:** a street on which a vehicle must stop just before entering a through street

stop·watch \ˈstäp-ˌwäch\ *n* (1737) **:** a watch having a component (as a hand) that can be started and stopped at will for exact timing (as of a race)

stor·age \ˈstōr-ij, ˈstȯr-\ *n* (1612) **1 a :** space or a place for storing **b :** an amount stored **c :** MEMORY 4 **2 a :** the act of storing **:** the state of being stored; *esp* **:** the safekeeping of goods in a depository (as a warehouse) **b :** the price charged for keeping goods in a storehouse **3 :** the production by means of electric energy of chemical reactions that when allowed to reverse themselves generate electricity again without serious loss

storage cell *n* (1881) **:** a cell or connected group of cells that converts chemical energy into electrical energy by reversible chemical reactions and that may be recharged by passing a current through it in the direction opposite to that of its discharge — called also *storage battery*

sto·rax \ˈstō(ə)r-ˌaks, ˈstȯ(ə)r-\ *n* [ME, fr. LL, alter. of L *styrax,* fr. Gk] (14c) **1 a :** a fragrant balsam obtained from the bark of an Asian tree (*Liquidambar orientalis*) of the witch-hazel family that is used as an expectorant and sometimes in perfumery — called also *Levant storax* **b :** a balsam from the sweet gum that is similar to storax **2 :** any of a genus (*Styrax* of the family Styracaceae, the storax family) of trees or shrubs with usu. hairy leaves and flowers in drooping racemes — compare BENZOIN

[1]**store** \ˈstō(ə)r, ˈstȯ(ə)r\ *vt* **stored; stor·ing** [ME *storen,* fr. OF *estorer* to construct, restore, store, fr. L *instaurare* to renew, restore, fr. *in-* + *-staurare* (akin to Gk *stauros* stake) — more at STEER] (13c) **1 :** FURNISH, SUPPLY: *esp* **:** to stock against a future time ⟨~ a ship with provisions⟩ **2 :** LAY AWAY, ACCUMULATE ⟨~ vegetables for winter use⟩ ⟨an organism that absorbs and ~s DDT⟩ **3 :** to place or leave in a location (as a warehouse, library, or computer memory) for preservation or later use or disposal **4 :** to provide storage room for **:** HOLD ⟨elevators for *storing* surplus wheat⟩ — **stor·able** \ˈstōr-ə-bəl, ˈstȯr-\ *adj*

[2]**store** *n* (13c) **1 a :** something that is stored or kept for future use **b** *pl* **:** articles (as of food) accumulated for some specific object and drawn upon as needed **:** STOCK, SUPPLIES **c :** something that is accumulated **d :** a source from which things may be drawn as needed **:** a reserve fund **2 :** STORAGE — usu. used with *in* ⟨when placing eggs in ~ —*Dublin Sunday Independent*⟩ **3 :** VALUE, IMPORTANCE ⟨set great ~ by a partner's opinion⟩ **4 :** a large quantity, supply, or number **:** ABUNDANCE **5 a :** STOREHOUSE, WAREHOUSE **b** *chiefly Brit* **:** MEMORY 4 **6 :** a business establishment where usu. diversified goods are kept for retail sale ⟨grocery ~⟩ — compare SHOP — **in store :** in a state of imminence

[3]**store** *adj* (1602) **1** *or* **stores :** of, relating to, kept in, or used for a store **2 :** purchased from a store as opposed to being natural or homemade **:** MANUFACTURED, READY-MADE ⟨~ clothes⟩ ⟨~ bread⟩

store–bought \ˈstō(ə)r-ˌbȯt, ˈstȯ(ə)r-\ *adj* (1905) **:** STORE 2

store cheese *n* [fr. its being a staple article stocked in grocery stores] (1863) **:** CHEDDAR

[1]**store·front** \ˈstō(ə)r-ˌfrənt, ˈstȯ(ə)r-\ *adj* (1937) **1 :** of, relating to, or characteristic of a storefront church ⟨a ~ evangelist⟩ **2 :** occupying a room or suite of rooms in a store building at street level and immediately behind a storefront ⟨a ~ school⟩ **3 :** of, relating to, or being outreach professional services ⟨~ lawyers⟩ ⟨~ day-care center⟩ ⟨~ hospitals⟩

[2]**storefront** *n* (1943) **1 :** the front side of a store or store building facing a street **2 :** a building, room, or suite of rooms having a storefront

storefront church *n* (1937) **:** a city church that utilizes storefront quarters as a meeting place and that usu. holds services of a highly emotional nature

store·house \ˈstō(ə)r-ˌhau̇s, ˈstȯ(ə)r-\ *n* (14c) **1 :** a building for storing goods (as provisions) **:** MAGAZINE, WAREHOUSE **2 :** an abundant supply or source **:** REPOSITORY

store·keep·er \-ˌkē-pər\ *n* (1618) **1 :** one that has charge of supplies (as military stores) **2 :** one that operates a retail store

store·room \-ˌrüm, -ˌru̇m\ *n* (1746) **1 :** a room or space for the storing of goods or supplies **2 :** STOREHOUSE 2

store·ship \-ˌship\ *n* (ca. 1693) **:** a ship used to carry supplies

store·wide \-ˈwīd\ *adj* (ca. 1937) **:** including all or most merchandise in a store ⟨a ~ sale⟩

[1]**sto·ried** \ˈstōr-ēd, ˈstȯr-\ *adj* (15c) **1 :** decorated with designs representing scenes from story or history ⟨a ~ frieze⟩ ⟨a ~ tapestry⟩ **2 :** having an interesting history **:** celebrated in story or history

[2]**storied** *or* **sto·reyed** \ˈstōr-ēd, ˈstȯr-\ *adj* (1624) **:** having stories ⟨a two-*storied* house⟩

stork \ˈstȯ(ə)rk\ *n* [ME, fr. OE *storc;* akin to OHG *storah* stork, OE *stearc* stiff — more at STARK] (bef. 12c) **:** any of various large mostly Old World wading birds (family Ciconiidae) that have long stout bills and are related to the ibises and herons

storks·bill \ˈstȯrks-ˌbil\ *n* (ca. 1562) **:** any of several plants of the geranium family with elongate beaked fruits: **a :** PELARGONIUM **b :** ALFILARIA: *also* **:** a related plant (genus *Erodium*)

[1]**storm** \ˈstȯ(ə)rm\ *n, often attrib* [ME, fr. OE; akin to OHG *sturm* storm, OE *styrian* to stir] (bef. 12c) **1 a :** a disturbance of the atmosphere marked by wind and usu. by rain, snow, hail, sleet, or thunder and lightning **b :** a heavy fall of rain, snow, or hail **c** (1) **:** wind having a speed of 64 to 72 miles (103 to 116 kilometers) per hour (2) **:** WHOLE GALE — see BEAUFORT SCALE table **d :** a serious disturbance of any element of nature **2 :** a disturbed or agitated state **:** a sudden or violent commotion **3 :** a heavy discharge of objects (as missiles) **4 :** a tumultuous outburst **5 a :** PAROXYSM, CRISIS **b :** a sudden heavy influx or onset **6 :** a violent assault on a defended position — **by storm :** by or as if by employing a bold swift frontal movement esp. with the intent of defeating or winning over quickly

[2]**storm** *vi* (15c) **1 a :** to blow with violence **b :** to rain, hail, snow, or sleet **2 :** to attack by storm ⟨~*ed* ashore at zero hour⟩ **3 :** to be in or to exhibit a violent passion **:** RAGE ⟨~*ing* at the unusual delay⟩ **4 :** to rush about or move impetuously, violently, or angrily ⟨the mob ~*ed* through the streets⟩ ~ *vt* **:** to attack, take, or win over by storm ⟨~ a fort⟩ ***syn*** see ATTACK

storm and stress *n, often cap both Ss* (1855) **:** STURM UND DRANG

storm boat *n* (1942) **:** a light fast craft used to transport attacking troops across streams

storm·bound \ˈstȯ(ə)rm-ˈbau̇nd\ *adj* (1830) **:** cut off from outside communication by a storm or its effects **:** stopped or delayed by storms

storm cellar *n* (ca. 1902) **:** CYCLONE CELLAR

storm door *n* (1878) **:** an additional door placed outside an ordinary outside door for protection against severe weather

storm petrel *n* (ca. 1833) **:** any of various small petrels; *esp* **:** a small sooty black white-marked petrel (*Hydrobates pelagicus*) frequenting the north Atlantic and Mediterranean

storm trooper *n* (1935) **1 :** a member of a private Nazi army notorious for aggressiveness, violence, and brutality **2 :** one that resembles a Nazi storm trooper

storm window *n* (ca. 1888) **:** a sash placed outside an ordinary window as a protection against severe weather — called also *storm sash*

stormy \ˈstȯr-mē\ *adj* **storm·i·er; -est** (13c) **1 :** relating to, characterized by, or indicative of a storm ⟨a ~ day⟩ ⟨a ~ autumn⟩ **2 :** marked by turmoil or fury ⟨a ~ life⟩ ⟨a ~ conference⟩ — **storm·i·ly** \ˈstȯr-mə-lē\ *adv* — **storm·i·ness** \-mē-nəs\ *n*

stormy petrel *n* (ca. 1776) **1 :** STORM PETREL **2 a :** one fond of strife **b :** a harbinger of trouble

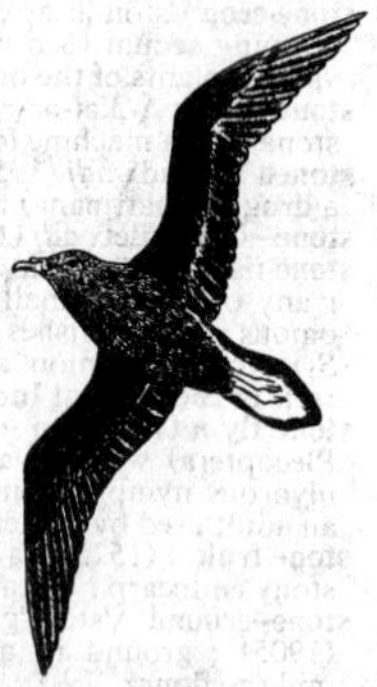

storm petrel

[1]**sto·ry** \ˈstōr-ē, ˈstȯr-\ *n, pl* **stories** [ME *storie,* fr. OF *estorie,* fr. L *historia* — more at HISTORY] (13c) **1** *archaic* **:** HISTORY 1,3 **2 a :** an account of incidents or events **b :** a statement regarding the facts pertinent to a situation in question **c :** ANECDOTE; *esp* **:** an amusing one **3 a :** a fictional narrative shorter than a novel; *specif* **:** SHORT STORY **b :** the intrigue or plot of a narrative or dramatic work **4 :** a widely circulated rumor **5 :** LIE, FALSEHOOD **6 :** LEGEND, ROMANCE **7 :** a news article or broadcast

[2]**story** *vt* **sto·ried; sto·ry·ing** (15c) **1** *archaic* **:** to narrate or describe in story **2 :** to adorn with a story or a scene from history

[3]**story** *also* **sto·rey** \ˈstōr-ē, ˈstȯr-ē\ *n, pl* **stories** *also* **storeys** [ME *storie,* fr. ML *historia* picture, story of a building, fr. L, history, tale; prob. fr. pictures adorning the windows of medieval buildings] (15c) **1 a :** the space in a building between two adjacent floor levels or between a floor and the roof **b :** a set of rooms in such a space **c :** a unit of measure equal to the height of the story of a building ⟨one ~ high⟩ **2 :** a horizontal division of a building's exterior not necessarily corresponding exactly with the stories within

sto·ry·board \-ˌbō(ə)rd, -ˌbȯ(ə)rd\ *n* (ca. 1946) **:** a panel or series of panels on which is tacked a set of small rough drawings depicting consecutively the important changes of scene and action in a planned film or television show or act

[1]**sto·ry·book** \-ˌbu̇k\ *n* (1711) **:** a book of stories ⟨~*s* for children⟩

[2]**storybook** *adj* (1910) **:** FAIRY-TALE

story line *n* (1946) **:** the plot of a story or play

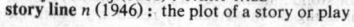

sto·ry·tell·er \ˈstōr-ē-ˌtel-ər, ˈstȯr-\ *n* (1709) **:** a teller of stories: as **a :** a relater of anecdotes **b :** a reciter of tales (as in a children's library) **c :** LIAR, FIBBER **d :** a writer of stories

stoss \ˈstäs, ˈstȯs, ˈs(h)tōs\ *adj* [G *stoss-*, fr. *stossen* to push, fr. OHG *stōzen;* akin to L *tundere* to beat — more at STINT] (ca. 1880) **:** facing toward the direction from which an overriding glacier impinges ⟨the ~ slope of a hill⟩

sto·tin·ka \stō-ˈtiŋ-kə, stə-\ *n, pl* **-tin·ki** \-kē\ [Bulg] (ca. 1909) — see *lev* at MONEY table

stound \ˈstau̇nd, ˈstünd\ *n* [ME, fr. OE *stund;* akin to OHG *stunta* time, hour, OE *standan* to stand] *archaic* (bef. 12c) **:** TIME, WHILE

stoup \ˈstüp\ *n* [ME *stowp*, prob. of Scand origin; akin to ON *staup* cup — more at STEEP] (14c) **1 a :** a beverage container (as a glass or tankard) **b :** FLAGON **2 :** a basin for holy water at the entrance of a church

[1]**stour** \ˈstu̇(ə)r\ *adj* [ME *stor*, fr. OE *stōr;* akin to OHG *stuori* large, Russ *staryĭ* old, OE *standan* to stand] (bef. 12c) **1** *chiefly Scot* **:** STRONG, HARDY **2** *chiefly Scot* **:** STERN, HARSH

[2]**stour** *n* [ME, fr. MF *estour*, of Gmc origin; akin to OHG *sturm* storm, battle — more at STORM] (14c) **1 a** *archaic* **:** BATTLE, CONFLICT **b** *dial Brit* **:** TUMULT, UPROAR **2** *chiefly Scot* **:** DUST, POWDER

[1]**stout** \ˈstau̇t\ *adj* [ME, fr. MF *estout*, of Gmc origin; akin to OHG *stolz* proud; akin to OHG *stelza* stilt — more at STILT] (14c) **1 :** strong of character: as **a :** BRAVE, BOLD **b :** FIRM, DETERMINED; *also* **:** OBSTINATE, UNCOMPROMISING **2 :** physically or materially strong: **a :** STURDY, VIGOROUS **b :** STAUNCH, ENDURING **c :** SOLID, SUBSTANTIAL **3 :** FORCEFUL ⟨a ~ attack⟩; *also* **:** VIOLENT ⟨a ~ wind⟩ **4 :** bulky in body **:** FAT *syn* see STRONG — **stout·ish** \-ish\ *adj* — **stout·ly** *adv* — **stout·ness** *n*

[2]**stout** *n* (1677) **1 :** a very dark full-bodied ale with a distinctive malty flavor **2 a :** a fat person **b :** a clothing size designed for the large figure

stout·en \ˈstau̇t-ᵊn\ *vb* **stout·ened; stout·en·ing** \ˈstau̇t-niŋ, -ᵊn-iŋ\ *vt* (1834) **:** to make stout ⟨~ a resolve⟩ ~ *vi* **:** to become stout

stout·heart·ed \ˈstau̇t-ˈhärt-əd\ *adj* (ca. 1652) **:** having a stout heart or spirit: **a :** COURAGEOUS **b :** STUBBORN — **stout·heart·ed·ly** *adv* — **stout·heart·ed·ness** *n*

[1]**stove** \ˈstōv\ *n* [ME, fr. MD or MLG, heated room, steam room, fr. (assumed) VL *extufa*, deriv. of L *ex-* + Gk *typhein* to smoke — more at DEAF] (1591) **1 a :** a portable or fixed apparatus that burns fuel or uses electricity to provide heat (as for cooking or heating) **b :** a device that generates heat for special purposes (as for heating tools or heating air for a hot blast) **c :** KILN **2** *chiefly Brit* **:** a hothouse esp. for the cultivation of tropical exotics; *broadly* **:** GREENHOUSE

[2]**stove** *past and past part of* STAVE

stove·pipe \ˈstōv-ˌpīp\ *n* (1699) **1 :** pipe of large diameter usu. of sheet steel used as a stove chimney or to connect a stove with a flue **2 :** SILK HAT

sto·ver \ˈstō-vər\ *n* [ME, modif. of AF *estovers* necessary supplies, fr. OF *estoveir* to be necessary, fr. L *est opus* there is need] (14c) **1** *chiefly dial Eng* **:** FODDER **2 :** mature cured stalks of grain with the ears removed that are used as feed for livestock

stow \ˈstō\ *vt* [ME *stowen* to place, fr. *stowe* place, fr. OE *stōw;* akin to OFris *stō* place, Gk *stylos* pillar — more at STEER] (14c) **1 :** HOUSE, LODGE **2 a :** to put away for future use **:** STORE **b** *obs* **:** to lock up for safekeeping **:** CONFINE **3 a :** to dispose in an orderly fashion **:** ARRANGE, PACK **b :** LOAD **4** *slang* **:** to put aside **:** STOP **5 a** *archaic* **:** CROWD **b :** to eat or drink up **:** CONSUME — usu. used with *away* ⟨~*ed* away a huge dinner⟩

stow·age \-ij\ *n* (14c) **1 a :** an act or process of stowing **b :** goods in storage or to be stowed **2 a :** storage capacity **b :** a place or receptacle for storage **3 :** the state of being stored

stow·away \ˈstō-ə-ˌwā\ *n* (1854) **:** one that stows away

stow away \ˌstō-ə-ˈwā\ *vi* (1879) **:** to secrete oneself aboard a vehicle as a means of obtaining transportation

STP \ˌes-ˌtē-ˈpē\ *n* [serenity, tranquillity, and peace] (1967) **:** a psychedelic drug chemically related to mescaline and amphetamine

stra·bis·mus \strə-ˈbiz-məs\ *n* [NL, fr. Gk *strabismos* condition of squinting, fr. *strabizein* to squint, fr. *strabos* squint-eyed; akin to Gk *strephein* to twist — more at STROPHE] (ca. 1684) **:** inability of one eye to attain binocular vision with the other because of imbalance of the muscles of the eyeball — called also *squint* — **stra·bis·mic** \-mik\ *adj*

[1]**strad·dle** \ˈstrad-ᵊl\ *vb* **strad·dled; strad·dling** \ˈstrad-liŋ, -ᵊl-iŋ\ [irreg. fr. *stride*] *vi* (ca. 1565) **1 :** to stand, sit, or walk with the legs wide apart; *esp* **:** to sit astride **2 :** to spread out irregularly **:** SPRAWL **3 :** to be noncommittal **:** favor or seem to favor two apparently opposite sides **4 :** to execute a commodities market spread ~ *vt* **1 :** to stand, sit, or be astride of ⟨~ a horse⟩ **2 :** to be noncommittal in regard to ⟨~ an issue⟩ — **strad·dler** \-lər, -ᵊl-ər\ *n* — **straddle the fence :** to be in a position of neutrality or indecision

[2]**straddle** *n* (1611) **1 :** the act or position of one who straddles **2 :** a noncommittal or equivocal position **3 :** [2]SPREAD 5

Stra·di·va·ri \ˌstrad-ə-ˈvär-ē, -ˈvar-, -ˈver-\ *n* (ca. 1903) **:** STRADIVARIUS

Strad·i·var·i·us \ˌstrad-ə-ˈvar-ē-əs, -ˈver-\ *n, pl* **-var·ii** \-ē-ˌī\ [latinized form of *Stradivari*] (1833) **:** a stringed instrument (as a violin) made by Antonio Stradivari of Cremona

strafe \ˈstrāf, *esp Brit* ˈsträf\ *vt* **strafed; straf·ing** [G *Gott strafe England* God punish England, slogan of the Germans in World War I] (ca. 1916) **:** to rake (as ground troops) with fire at close range and esp. with machine-gun fire from low-flying aircraft — **strafe** *n* — **straf·er** *n*

[1]**strag·gle** \ˈstrag-əl\ *vi* **strag·gled; strag·gling** \-(ə-)liŋ\ [ME *straglen*] (15c) **1 :** to wander from the direct course or way **:** ROVE, STRAY **2 :** to trail off from others of its kind ⟨little cabins *straggling* off into the woods⟩ — **strag·gler** \-(ə-)lər\ *n*

[2]**straggle** *n* (1865) **:** a straggling group (as of persons or objects)

strag·gly \ˈstrag-(ə-)lē\ *adj* **strag·gli·er; -est** (1866) **:** spread out or scattered irregularly ⟨a ~ beard⟩

[1]**straight** \ˈstrāt\ *adj* [ME *streght, straight*, fr. pp. of *strecchen* to stretch — more at STRETCH] (14c) **1 a :** free from curves, bends, angles, or irregularities ⟨~ hair⟩ ⟨~ timber⟩ ⟨a ~ stream⟩ **b :** generated by a point moving continuously in the same direction and expressed by a linear equation ⟨a ~ line⟩ ⟨the ~ segment of a curve⟩ **2 :** DIRECT, UNINTERRUPTED: as **a :** lying along or holding to a direct or proper course or method ⟨a ~ thinker⟩ **b :** CANDID, FRANK ⟨gave me a ~ answer⟩ **c :** coming directly from a trustworthy source ⟨a ~ tip on the horses⟩ **d** (1) **:** having the elements in an order ⟨the ~ sequence of events⟩ (2) **:** CONSECUTIVE ⟨12 ~ days⟩ **e :** having the cylinders arranged in a single straight line ⟨a ~ 8-cylinder engine⟩ **f :** PLUMB, VERTICAL ⟨the picture isn't quite ~⟩ **3 a :** exhibiting honesty and fairness ⟨~ dealing⟩ **b :** properly ordered or arranged ⟨set the kitchen ~⟩ ⟨set us ~ on that issue⟩; *also* **:** CORRECT ⟨get the facts ~⟩ **c :** free from extraneous matter **:** UNMIXED ⟨~ gin⟩ **d :** marked by no exceptions or deviations in support of a principle or party ⟨a ~ Republican⟩ ⟨votes a ~ Democratic ticket⟩ **e :** having a fixed price for each regardless of the number sold ⟨cigars 20 cents ~⟩ **f :** not deviating from the general norm or prescribed pattern ⟨wrote ~ biography with no fictional passages⟩ **g** (1) **:** exhibiting no deviation from what is established or accepted as usual, normal, or proper **:** CONVENTIONAL; *also* **:** SQUARE 5f (2) **:** not using or under the influence of drugs or alcohol **h :** HETEROSEXUAL **4 :** being the only form of remuneration ⟨a salesman on ~ commission⟩ — **straight·ish** \-ish\ *adj* — **straight·ly** *adv* — **straight·ness** *n*

[2]**straight** *adv* (14c) **:** in a straight manner

[3]**straight** *vt, chiefly Scot* (1530) **:** STRAIGHTEN

[4]**straight** *n* (1645) **1 :** something that is straight: as **a :** a straight line or arrangement **b :** STRAIGHTAWAY; *esp* **:** HOMESTRETCH **c :** a true or honest report or course **2 a :** a sequence (as of shots, strokes, or moves) resulting in a perfect score in a game or contest **b :** first place at the finish of a horse race **:** WIN **3 :** a poker hand containing five cards in sequence but not of the same suit — see POKER illustration **4 :** a person who adheres to conventional attitudes and mores

straight A \ˌstrāt-ˌā\ *adj* (1949) **:** having or constituting a first-class record of achievement ⟨a *straight A* student⟩

straight and narrow *n* [prob. alter. of *strait and narrow;* fr. the admonition of Mt 7:14 (AV), "strait is the gate and narrow is the way which leadeth unto life"] (1946) **:** the way of propriety and rectitude — used with *the*

straight angle *n* (1601) **:** an angle whose sides lie in opposite directions from the vertex in the same straight line and which equals two right angles

[1]**straight–arm** \ˈstrāt-ˌärm\ *n* (1925) **:** an act or instance of warding off a football tackler with the arm fully extended from the shoulder, elbow locked, and the palm of the hand placed firmly against any part of his body — called also *stiff-arm*

[2]**straight–arm** *vt* (1928) **:** to ward off with or as if with a straight-arm ~ *vi* **:** to use a straight-arm in warding off an opponent

straight–arrow \-ˈar-(ˌ)ō, -ˈar-ə-(-w)\ *adj* [fr. the expression *straight as an arrow*] (ca. 1969) **:** rigidly proper and conventional

[1]**straight·away** \ˈstrāt-ə-ˌwā\ *adj* (1874) **1 :** proceeding in a straight line **:** continuous in direction **2 :** IMMEDIATE

[2]**straightaway** *n* (1895) **:** a straight course: as **a :** the straight part of a closed racecourse **:** STRETCH **b :** a straight and unimpeded stretch of road or way

[3]**straight·away** \ˌstrāt-ə-ˈwā\ *adv* (1903) **:** without hesitation or delay

straight·bred \ˈstrāt-ˈbred\ *adj* (1901) **:** produced by breeding a single breed, strain, or type ⟨a ~ Angus heifer⟩ — compare CROSSBRED — **straight·bred** \-ˌbred\ *n*

straight chain *n* (ca. 1930) **:** an open chain of atoms having no side chains

straight·edge \ˈstrāt-ˌej\ *n* (ca. 1812) **:** a bar or piece of material (as of wood, metal, or plastic) with a straight edge for testing straight lines and surfaces or drawing straight lines

straight·en \ˈstrāt-ᵊn\ *vb* **straight·ened; straight·en·ing** \ˈstrāt-niŋ, -ᵊn-iŋ\ *vt* (1542) **:** to make straight — usu. used with *up* or *out* ~ *vi* **:** to become straight — usu. used with *up* or *out* — **straight·en·er** \ˈstrāt-nər, -ᵊn-ər\ *n*

straight face *n* (ca. 1891) **:** a face giving no evidence of emotion and esp. of merriment — **straight–faced** \ˈstrāt-ˈfāst\ *adj* — **straight–faced·ly** \-ˈfā-səd-lē, -ˈfās-tlē\ *adv*

straight flush *n* (1864) **:** a poker hand containing five cards of the same suit in sequence — see POKER illustration

[1]**straight·for·ward** \(ˈ)strāt-ˈfȯr-wərd\ *adj* (1806) **1 a :** free from evasiveness or obscurity **:** EXACT, CANDID ⟨a ~ account⟩ **b :** CLEAR-CUT, PRECISE **2 :** proceeding in a straight course or manner **:** DIRECT, UNDEVIATING — **straight·for·ward·ly** *adv* — **straight·for·ward·ness** *n*

[2]**straightforward** *also* **straight·for·wards** \-wərdz\ *adv* (1809) **:** in a straightforward manner

straight–line \ˌstrāt-ˌlīn\ *adj* (1843) **1 :** being a mechanical linkage or equivalent device designed to produce or copy motion in a straight line **2 :** having the principal parts arranged in a straight line **3 :** marked by a uniform spread and esp. in equal segments over a given term ⟨~ amortization⟩ ⟨~ depreciation⟩ **4 :** occurring, measured, or made in or along a straight line ⟨~ motion⟩ ⟨~ extrapolation⟩

straight man *n* (ca. 1926) **:** a member of a comedy team who feeds lines to his partner who in turn replies with usu. humorous quips

straight off *adv* (1873) **:** at once **:** IMMEDIATELY

straight–out \ˌstrāt-ˌau̇t\ *adj* (1848) **1 :** FORTHRIGHT, BLUNT ⟨gave him a ~ answer⟩ **2 :** OUTRIGHT, THOROUGHGOING

straight poker *n* (1864) **:** poker in which the players bet on the five cards dealt to them and then have a showdown without drawing — compare DRAW POKER, STUD POKER

straight razor *n* (1938) **:** a razor with a rigid steel cutting blade hinged to a case that forms a handle when the razor is open for use

[1]**straight·way** \ˈstrāt-ˈwā, -ˌwā\ *adv* (15c) **1 :** in a direct course **:** DIRECTLY ⟨fell ~ to the bottom of the stairs⟩ **2 :** RIGHT AWAY, IMMEDIATELY, FORTHWITH ⟨~ the clouds began to part⟩

[2]**straight·way** \ˌstrāt-ˌwā\ *adj* (ca. 1896) **:** having or affording a straight way ⟨a ~ valve⟩

[1]**strain** \ˈstrān\ *n* [ME *streen* progeny, lineage, fr. OE *strēon* gain, acquisition; akin to OHG *gistriuni* gain, L *struere* to heap up — more at STREW] (13c) **1 a :** LINEAGE, ANCESTRY **b :** a group of presumed common ancestry with clear-cut physiological but usu. not morpholog-

ical distinctions ⟨a high-yielding ~ of winter wheat⟩; *broadly* **:** a specified infraspecific group (as a stock, line, or ecotype) **c :** KIND, SORT ⟨discussions of a lofty ~⟩ **2 a :** inherited or inherent character, quality, or disposition ⟨a ~ of madness in the family⟩ **b :** TRACE, STREAK ⟨a ~ of fanaticism⟩ **3 a :** TUNE, AIR **b :** a passage of verbal or musical expression **c :** a stream or outburst of forceful or impassioned speech **4 a :** the tenor, pervading note, burden, or tone of an utterance or of a course of action or conduct **b :** MOOD, TEMPER

[2]**strain** *vb* [ME *strainen,* fr. MF *estraindre,* fr. L *stringere* to bind or draw tight, press together; akin to Gk *strang-, stranx* drop squeezed out, *strangalē* halter] *vt* (14c) **1 a :** to draw tight **:** cause to fit firmly ⟨~ the bandage over the wound⟩ **b :** to stretch to maximum extension and tautness ⟨~ a canvas over a frame⟩ **2 a :** to exert (as oneself) to the utmost **b :** to injure by overuse, misuse, or excessive pressure ⟨~*ed* his heart⟩ **c :** to cause a change of form or size in (a body) by application of external force **3 :** to squeeze or clasp tightly: as **a :** HUG **b :** to compress painfully **:** CONSTRICT **4 a :** to cause to pass through a strainer **:** FILTER **b :** to remove by straining ⟨~ lumps out of the gravy⟩ **5 :** to stretch beyond a proper limit ⟨that story ~*s* my credulity⟩ **6** *obs* **:** to squeeze out **:** EXTORT **~** *vi* **1 a :** to make violent efforts **:** STRIVE ⟨has to ~ to reach the high notes⟩ **b :** to sustain a strain, wrench, or distortion **c :** to contract the muscles forcefully in attempting to defecate — often used in the phrase *strain at stool* **2 :** to pass through or as if through a strainer ⟨the liquid ~*s* readily⟩ **3 :** to make great difficulty or resistance **:** BALK — **strain a point :** to go beyond a usual, accepted, or proper limit or rule

[3]**strain** *n* (1532) **1 :** an act of straining or the condition of being strained: as **a :** excessive physical or mental tension; *also* **:** a force, influence, or factor causing such tension ⟨her responsibilities were a constant ~⟩ **b :** excessive or difficult exertion or labor **c :** bodily injury from excessive tension, effort, or use ⟨heart ~⟩; *esp* **:** one resulting from a wrench or twist and involving undue stretching of muscles or ligaments ⟨back ~⟩ **d :** deformation of a material body under the action of applied forces **2 :** an unusual reach, degree, or intensity **:** PITCH **3** *archaic* **:** a strained interpretation of something said or written

strained \'strānd\ *adj* (1542) **1 :** done or produced with excessive effort **2 :** pushed by antagonism near to open conflict ⟨~ relations⟩

strain·er \'strā-nər\ *n* (14c) **:** one that strains: as **a :** a device (as a sieve) to retain solid pieces while a liquid passes through **b :** any of various devices for stretching or tightening something

strain gauge *n* (1920) **:** EXTENSOMETER

[1]**strait** \'strāt\ *adj* [ME, fr. OF *estreit,* fr. L *strictus* strait, strict, fr. pp. of *stringere*] (13c) **1** *archaic* **a :** NARROW **b :** limited in space or time **c :** closely fitting **:** CONSTRICTED, TIGHT **2** *archaic* **:** STRICT, RIGOROUS **3 a :** causing distress **:** DIFFICULT **b :** limited as to means or resources — **strait·ly** *adv* — **strait·ness** *n*

[2]**strait** *adv, obs* (13c) **:** in a close or tight manner

[3]**strait** *n* (14c) **1 a** *archaic* **:** a narrow space or passage **b :** a comparatively narrow passageway connecting two large bodies of water — often used in pl. but sing. in constr. **c :** ISTHMUS **2 :** a situation of perplexity or distress — often used in pl. ***syn*** see JUNCTURE

strait·en \'strāt-ᵊn\ *vt* **strait·ened; strait·en·ing** \'strāt-niŋ, -ᵊn-iŋ\ (ca. 1552) **1 a :** to make strait or narrow **b :** to hem in **:** CONFINE **2** *archaic* **:** to restrict in freedom or scope **:** HAMPER **3 :** to subject to distress, privation, or deficiency ⟨in ~*ed* circumstances⟩

[1]**strait·jack·et** *or* **straight·jack·et** \'strāt-,jak-ət\ *n* (1814) **1 :** a cover or overgarment of strong material (as canvas) used to bind the body and esp. the arms closely in restraining a violent prisoner or patient **2 :** something that restricts or confines like a straitjacket

[2]**straitjacket** *or* **straightjacket** *vt* (1863) **:** to confine in or as if in a straitjacket

strait·laced *or* **straight·laced** \'strāt-'lāst\ *adj* (1554) **1 :** excessively strict in manners, morals, or opinion **2 :** wearing or having a bodice or stays tightly laced — **strait·laced·ly** \-'lā-səd-lē, -'lās-tlē\ *adv* — **strait·laced·ness** \-'lās(t)-nəs, -'lā-səd-nəs\ *n*

Straits dollar \'strāts-\ *n* [*Straits* Settlements, former British crown colony] (1908) **:** a dollar formerly issued by British Malaya and used in much of southern and eastern Asia and the East Indies

strake \'strāk\ *n* [ME; akin to OE *streccan* to stretch — more at STRETCH] (14c) **1 :** STREAK, STRIPE **2 :** a continuous band of hull planking or plates on a ship; *also* **:** the width of such a band

stra·mash \strə-'mash\ *n* [origin unknown] *chiefly Scot* (1803) **1 :** DISTURBANCE, RACKET **2 :** CRASH, SMASHUP

stra·mo·ni·um \strə-'mō-nē-əm\ *n* [NL] (1665) **1 :** the dried leaves of the jimsonweed or of a related plant (genus *Datura*) used in medicine similarly to belladonna esp. in the treatment of asthma **2 :** JIMSONWEED

[1]**strand** \'strand\ *n* [ME, fr. OE; akin to ON *strǫnd* strand, L *sternere* to spread out — more at STREW] (bef. 12c) **:** the land bordering a body of water **:** SHORE, BEACH

[2]**strand** *vt* (1621) **1 :** to run, drive, or cause to drift onto a strand **:** run aground **2 :** to leave in a strange or an unfavorable place esp. without funds or means to depart **3 :** to leave (a base runner) on base at the end of an inning in baseball **~** *vi* **:** to become stranded

[3]**strand** *n* [ME *stronde, strande*] (13c) **1** *Scot & dial Eng* **:** STREAM **2** *Scot & dial Eng* **:** SEA

[4]**strand** *n* [ME *strond*] (15c) **1 a :** fibers or filaments twisted, plaited, or laid parallel to form a unit for further twisting or plaiting into yarn, thread, rope, or cordage **b :** one of the wires twisted together or laid parallel to form a wire rope or cable **c :** something (as a molecular chain) resembling a strand **2 :** an element (as a yarn or thread) of a woven or plaited material **3 :** an elongated or twisted and plaited body resembling a rope ⟨a ~ of pearls⟩ **4 :** one of the elements interwoven in a complex whole

[5]**strand** *vt* (1780) **1 :** to break a strand of (a rope) accidentally **2 a :** to form (as a rope) from strands **b :** to play out, twist, or arrange in a strand

strand·ed \'stran-dəd\ *adj* (1875) **:** having a strand or strands esp. of a specified kind or number — usu. used in combination ⟨the double-stranded molecule of DNA⟩ — **strand·ed·ness** *n*

strand·er \'stran-dər\ *n* (1919) **:** a machine that makes strands into cable or rope

strand·line \'stran-,(d)līn\ *n* (1903) **:** SHORELINE; *esp* **:** a shoreline above the present water level

strange \'strānj\ *adj* **strang·er; strang·est** [ME, fr. OF *estrange,* fr. L *extraneus,* lit., external, fr. *extra* outside — more at EXTRA-] (13c) **1 a** *archaic* **:** of, relating to, or characteristic of another country **:** FOREIGN **b :** not native to or naturally belonging in a place **:** of external origin, kind, or character **2 a :** not before known, heard, or seen **:** NEW, UNFAMILIAR **b :** exciting wonder or awe **:** EXTRAORDINARY, QUEER **3 a :** discouraging familiarities **:** RESERVED, DISTANT **b :** ILL AT EASE **4 :** UNACCUSTOMED, UNVERSED ⟨she was ~ to his ways⟩ **5 :** of, relating to, or being a particle (as the kaon) having a strangeness quantum number different from zero ⟨~ quark⟩ — **strange·ly** *adv*

syn STRANGE, SINGULAR, UNIQUE, PECULIAR, ECCENTRIC, ERRATIC, ODD, QUEER, QUAINT, OUTLANDISH mean departing from what is ordinary, usual, or to be expected. STRANGE stresses unfamiliarity and may apply to the foreign, the unnatural, the unaccountable; SINGULAR suggests individuality or puzzling strangeness; UNIQUE implies singularity and the fact of being without a known parallel; PECULIAR implies a marked distinctiveness; ECCENTRIC suggests a wide divergence from the usual or normal esp. in behavior; ERRATIC stresses a capricious and unpredictable wandering or deviating; ODD applies to a departure from the regular or expected; QUEER suggests a dubious sometimes sinister oddness; QUAINT suggests an old-fashioned but pleasant oddness; OUTLANDISH applies to what is uncouth, bizarre, or barbaric.

strange·ness \'strānj-nəs\ *n* (14c) **1 :** the quality or state of being strange **2 :** a quantum characteristic of a quark or strongly interacting fundamental particle that is conserved in strong interactions with other fundamental particles

[1]**strang·er** \'strān-jər\ *n* [ME, fr. MF *estrangier* foreign, foreigner, fr. *estrange*] (14c) **1 :** one who is strange: as **a** (1) **:** FOREIGNER (2) **:** a resident alien **b :** one in the house of another as a guest, visitor, or intruder **c :** a person or thing that is unknown or with whom one is unacquainted **d :** one who does not belong to or is kept from the activities of a group **e :** one not privy or party to an act, contract, or title **:** one that interferes without right **2 :** one ignorant of or unacquainted with someone or something

[2]**stranger** *adj* (15c) **:** of, relating to, or being a stranger **:** FOREIGN

[3]**stranger** *vt, obs* (1605) **:** ESTRANGE, ALIENATE

strange woman *n* [fr. the expression frequently used in Prov (AV)] (1535) **:** PROSTITUTE

stran·gle \'straŋ-gəl\ *vb* **stran·gled; stran·gling** \-g(ə-)liŋ\ [ME *stranglen,* fr. MF *estrangler,* fr. L *strangulare,* fr. Gk *strangalan,* fr. *strangalē* halter — more at STRAIN] *vt* (14c) **1 a :** to choke to death by compressing the throat with something (as a hand or rope) **:** THROTTLE **b :** to obstruct seriously or fatally the normal breathing of ⟨the bone wedged in his throat and *strangled* him⟩ **c :** STIFLE **2 :** to suppress or hinder the rise, expression, or growth of **~** *vi* **1 :** to become strangled **2 :** to die from or as if from interference with breathing — **stran·gler** \-g(ə-)lər\ *n*

stran·gle·hold \'straŋ-gəl-,hōld\ *n* (1893) **1 :** an illegal wrestling hold by which one's opponent is choked **2 :** a force or influence that chokes or suppresses freedom of movement or expression

stran·gles \'straŋ-gəlz\ *n pl but sing or pl in constr* [pl. of obs. *strangle* (act of strangling)] (1706) **:** an infectious febrile disease of horses caused by a bacterium (*Streptococcus equi*) and marked by inflammation and congestion of mucous membranes

stran·gu·late \'straŋ-gyə-,lāt\ *vb* **-lat·ed; -lat·ing** [L *strangulatus,* pp. of *strangulare*] *vt* (1665) **:** STRANGLE, CONSTRICT **~** *vi* **:** to become constricted so as to stop circulation ⟨the hernia will ~ and become necrotic⟩

stran·gu·la·tion \,straŋ-gyə-'lā-shən\ *n* [L *strangulation-, strangulatio,* fr. *strangulatus,* pp.] (1542) **1 :** the action or process of strangling or strangulating **2 :** the state of being strangled or strangulated; *esp* **:** excessive or pathological constriction or compression of a bodily tube (as a blood vessel or a loop of intestine) that interrupts its ability to act as a passage

stran·gu·ry \'straŋ-gyə-rē, -,gyu̇r-ē\ *n, pl* **-ries** [ME, fr. L *stranguria,* fr. Gk *strangouria,* fr. *strang-, stranx* drop squeezed out + *ourein* to urinate, fr. *ouron* urine — more at STRAIN, URINE] (15c) **:** a slow and painful discharge of urine drop by drop

[1]**strap** \'strap\ *n* [alter. of *strop,* fr. ME, band or loop of leather or rope, fr. OE, thong for securing an oar, fr. L *struppus* band, strap, fr. Gk *strophos* twisted band — more at STROPHE] (1573) **1 :** a band, plate, or loop of metal for binding objects together or for clamping an object in position **2 a :** a narrow usu. flat strip or thong of a flexible material and esp. leather used for securing, holding together, or wrapping **b :** something made of a strap forming a loop ⟨a boot ~⟩ **c :** a strip of leather used for flogging **d :** STROP **3 :** a shoe fastened with a usu. buckled strap **4** *Irish* **:** TROLLOP

[2]**strap** *vt* **strapped; strap·ping** (1711) **1 a** (1) **:** to secure with or attach by means of a strap (2) **:** to support (as a sprained joint) with overlapping strips of adhesive plaster **b :** BIND, CONSTRICT **2 :** to beat or punish with a strap **3 :** STROP **4 :** to cause to suffer from an extreme scarcity ⟨is often *strapped* for cash⟩

strap·hang·er \'strap-,haŋ-ər\ *n* (1905) **:** a standing passenger in a subway, streetcar, bus, or train who clings for support to one of the short straps or similar devices placed along the aisle — **strap·hang** \-,haŋ\ *vi*

strap·less \-ləs\ *adj* (1846) **:** having no strap; *specif* **:** made or worn without shoulder straps ⟨a ~ evening gown⟩ — **strapless** *n*

strap·pa·do \strə-'pād-(,)ō, -'päd-\ *n* [modif. of It *strappata,* lit., sharp pull] (1560) **:** a former punishment or torture consisting of hoisting the subject by a rope and letting him fall to the length of the rope; *also* **:** a machine used to inflict this torture

strap·per \'strap-ər\ *n* (1675) **:** one that is unusually large or robust

[1]**strap·ping** \'strap-iŋ\ *adj* (1657) **:** having a vigorously sturdy constitution

[2]**strapping** *n* (1818) **1 :** material for a strap **2 :** STRAPS

strass \'stras\ *n* [F *stras, strass*] (1820) **:** PASTE 3

strat·a·gem \'strat-ə-jəm, -,jem\ *n* [It *stratagemma,* fr. L *strategema,* fr. Gk *stratēgēma,* fr. *stratēgein* to be a general, maneuver, fr. *stratēgos* general, fr. *stratos* army (akin to L *stratus,* pp., spread out) + *agein* to lead — more at STRATUM, AGENT] (15c) **1 a :** an artifice or trick in war for deceiving and outwitting the enemy **b :** a cleverly contrived trick or scheme for gaining an end **2 :** skill in ruses or trickery ***syn*** see TRICK

stra·te·gic \strə-'tē-jik\ *adj* (1825) **1 :** of, relating to, or marked by strategy ⟨a ~ retreat⟩ **2 a :** necessary to or important in the initiation, conduct, or completion of a strategic plan **b :** required for the conduct of war and not available in adequate quantities domestically ⟨~ materials⟩ **c :** of great importance within an integrated whole or to a planned effect ⟨emphasized ~ points⟩ **3 :** designed or trained to strike an enemy at the sources of his military, economic, or political power ⟨a ~ bomber⟩ — **stra·te·gi·cal** \-ji-kəl\ *adj* — **stra·te·gi·cal·ly** \-ji-k(ə-)lē\ *adv*

strat·e·gist \'strat-ə-jəst\ *n* (1838) **:** one skilled in strategy

strat·e·gy \-jē\ *n, pl* **-gies** [Gk *stratēgia* generalship, fr. *stratēgos*] (1810) **1 a** (1) **:** the science and art of employing the political, economic, psychological, and military forces of a nation or group of nations to afford the maximum support to adopted policies in peace or war (2) **:** the science and art of military command exercised to meet the enemy in combat under advantageous conditions **b :** a variety of or instance of the use of strategy **2 a :** a careful plan or method **:** a clever stratagem **b :** the art of devising or employing plans or stratagems toward a goal **3 :** an adaptation or complex of adaptations (as of behavior, metabolism, or structure) that serves or appears to serve an important function in achieving evolutionary success ⟨foraging *strategies* of insects⟩

strath \'strath\ *n* [ScGael *srath*] (ca. 1639) **:** a flat wide river valley or the low-lying grassland along it

strath·spey \(')strath-'spā\ *n, pl* **strathspeys** [*Strath Spey,* district of Scotland] (1653) **:** a Scottish dance that is similar to but slower than the reel; *also* **:** the music for this dance

strati- *comb form* [NL *stratum*] **:** stratum ⟨*strati*form⟩

stra·tic·u·late \strə-'tik-yə-lət, stra-\ *adj* [(assumed) NL *straticulum,* dim. of *stratum*] (ca. 1880) **:** characterized by thin parallel strata

strat·i·fi·ca·tion \,strat-ə-fə-'kā-shən\ *n* (ca. 1617) **1 a :** the act or process of stratifying **b :** the state of being stratified **2 :** a stratified formation

strat·i·fi·ca·tion·al grammar \,strat-ə-fə-'kā-shnəl-, -shən-ᵊl-\ *n* (1962) **:** a grammar based on the theory that language consists of a series of hierarchically related strata linked together by representational rules

stratified charge engine *n* (1962) **:** an internal-combustion engine in whose cylinders the combustion of fuel in a layer of rich fuel-air mixture promotes ignition in a greater volume of lean mixture

strat·i·form \'strat-ə-,fȯrm\ *adj* (1805) **:** having a stratified formation

strat·i·fy \'strat-ə-,fī\ *vb* **-fied; -fy·ing** [NL *stratificare,* fr. *stratum* + L *-ificare* -ify] *vt* (1661) **1 :** to form, deposit, or arrange in strata **2 a :** to divide or arrange into classes, castes, or social strata **b :** to divide into a series of graded statuses ~ *vi* **:** to become arranged in strata

strati·graph·ic \,strat-ə-'graf-ik\ *adj* (1877) **:** of, relating to, or determined by stratigraphy

stra·tig·ra·phy \strə-'tig-rə-fē, stə-\ *n* [ISV] (1865) **1 :** geology that deals with the origin, composition, distribution, and succession of strata **2 :** the arrangement of strata

strato- *comb form* [NL *stratus*] **:** stratus and ⟨*strato*cumulus⟩

stra·toc·ra·cy \strə-'täk-rə-sē\ *n, pl* **-cies** [Gk *stratos* army — more at STRATAGEM] (1652) **:** a military government

stra·to·cu·mu·lus \,strāt-ō-'kyü-myə-ləs, ,strat-\ *n* [NL] (ca. 1891) **:** stratified cumulus consisting of large balls or rolls of dark cloud which often cover the whole sky esp. in winter — see CLOUD illustration

strato·sphere \'strat-ə-,sfi(ə)r\ *n* [F *stratosphère,* fr. NL *stratum* + *-o-* + F *sphère* sphere, fr. L *sphaera*] (ca. 1909) **1 :** an upper portion of the atmosphere which is above approximately 7 miles (11 kilometers) depending on latitude, season, and weather and extends to about 31 miles (50 kilometers) and in which temperature changes little with changing altitude and clouds of water are rare **2 :** a very high or the highest region on a graded scale ⟨executive ~⟩ — **strato·spher·ic** \,strat-ə-'sfi(ə)r-ik, -'sfer-\ *adj*

stra·to·vol·ca·no \,strat-ō-väl-'kā-(,)nō, ,strāt-, -vȯl-\ *n* [NL *stratum* + E *-o-* + *volcano*] (1937) **:** a volcano composed of explosively erupted cinders and ash with occasional lava flows

stra·tum \'strāt-əm 'strat-\ *n, pl* **stra·ta** \'strāt-ə, 'strat-\ [NL, fr. L, spread, bed, fr. neut. of *stratus,* pp. of *sternere* to spread out — more at STREW] (1599) **1 :** a bed or layer artificially made **2 a :** a sheetlike mass of sedimentary rock or earth of one kind lying between beds of other kinds **b :** a region of the sea or atmosphere that is analogous to a stratum of the earth **c :** a layer of tissue ⟨deep ~ of the skin⟩ **d :** a layer in which archaeological material (as artifacts, skeletons, and dwelling remains) is found on excavation **3 a :** a part of a historical or sociological series representing a period or a stage of development **b :** a socioeconomic level of society comprising persons of the same or similar status esp. with regard to education or culture **4 :** one of a series of layers, levels, or gradations in an ordered system ⟨*strata* of thought⟩ **5 :** a statistical subpopulation

usage The plural *strata* is sometimes used as a singular and is occas. given the plural *stratas* ⟨there was a *strata* of Paris which mere criticism of books fails to get hold of —Ezra Pound⟩ ⟨a Roman burial ground suggests *stratas* of corruption and decay —Connie Fletcher, *Booklist*⟩ Current evidence shows senses 2, 3b, and 4 so used, with 3b the most common. Most commentators consider such use erroneous, and in fact it has not yet established itself as reputable. But *strata,* along with *criteria* and *phenomena,* may eventually become established as a singular like *candelabra* or *agenda.*

stra·tus \'strāt-əs, 'strat-\ *n, pl* **stra·ti** \'strāt-,ī, 'strat-\ [NL, fr. L, pp. of *sternere*] (ca. 1803) **:** a cloud form of greater horizontal extension and comparatively lower altitude (2000 to 7000 feet) than the cumulostratus or cirrostratus — see CLOUD illustration

stra·vage *or* **stra·vaig** \strə-'vāg\ *vi* [prob. by shortening and alter. fr. *extravagate*] *chiefly Scot* (1773) **:** ROAM

[1]straw \'strȯ\ *n* [ME, fr. OE *strēaw;* akin to OHG *strō* straw, OE *strewian* to strew] (bef. 12c) **1 a :** stalks of grain after threshing; *broadly* **:** dry stalky plant residue used like grain straw (as for bedding or packing) **b :** a natural or artificial heavy fiber used for weaving, plaiting, or braiding **2 :** a dry coarse stem esp. of a cereal grass **3 a** (1) **:** something of small worth or significance (2) **:** something too insubstantial to provide support or help in a desperate situation ⟨clutching at ~*s*⟩ **b :** CHAFF 2 **4 a :** something (as a hat) made of straw **b :** a tube (as of paper, plastic, or glass) for sucking up a beverage — **strawy** \'strȯ(-)i\ *adj* — **straw in the wind :** a slight fact that is an indication of a coming event

[2]straw *adj* (15c) **1 :** made of straw ⟨a ~ rug⟩ **2 :** of, relating to, or used for straw ⟨a ~ barn⟩ **3 :** of the color of straw ⟨~ hair⟩ **4 :** of little or no value **:** WORTHLESS **5 :** of, relating to, resembling, or being a straw man **6 :** of, relating to, or concerned with the discovery of preferences by means of a straw vote

straw·ber·ry \'strȯ-,ber-ē, -b(ə-)rē\ *n, often attrib* [ME, fr. OE *strēawberige,* fr. *strēaw* straw + *berige* berry; perh. fr. the appearance of the achenes on the surface] (bef. 12c) **:** the juicy edible usu. red fruit of a plant (genus *Fragaria*) of the rose family that is technically an enlarged pulpy receptacle bearing numerous achenes; *also* **:** a plant whose fruits are strawberries

strawberry bush *n* (ca. 1856) **1 :** a No. American euonymus (*Euonymus americanus*) with crimson pods and seeds with a scarlet aril **2 :** [2]WAHOO

strawberry mark *n* (1847) **:** a tumor of the skin filled with small blood vessels and appearing usu. as a red and elevated birthmark

strawberry roan *n* (ca. 1934) **:** a roan horse with a light red ground color

strawberry shrub *n* (ca. 1890) **:** any of a genus (*Calycanthus* of the family Calycanthaceae, the strawberry-shrub family) of shrubs with fragrant brownish red flowers

strawberry tomato *n* (ca. 1847) **:** GROUND-CHERRY; *esp* **:** a stout hairy annual herb (*Physalis pruinosa*) of eastern No. America with sweet globular yellow fruits

strawberry tree *n* (15c) **:** a small European evergreen tree (*Arbutus unedo*) of the heath family with racemose white flowers and fruits like strawberries

straw boss *n* (1894) **1 :** an assistant to a foreman in charge of supervising and expediting the work of a small gang of workers **2 :** a member of a group of workers who supervises the work of the others in addition to doing his own job

straw·flow·er \'strȯ-,flau̇(-ə)r\ *n* (ca. 1922) **:** any of several everlasting flowers; *esp* **:** an Australian annual herb (*Helichrysum bracteatum*) that is much grown for its heads of chaffy brightly colored long-keeping flowers

straw·hat \,strȯ-,hat\ *adj* [fr. the former fashion of wearing straw hats in summer] (1937) **:** of, relating to, or being summer theater

straw man *n* (ca. 1900) **1 :** a weak or imaginary opposition (as an argument or adversary) set up only to be easily confuted **2 :** a person set up to serve as a cover for a usu. questionable transaction

straw vote *n* (1887) **:** an unofficial vote taken (as at a chance gathering) to indicate the relative strength of opposing candidates or issues — called also *straw poll*

straw wine *n* (ca. 1824) **:** a sweet wine produced by partially drying the grapes on beds of straw prior to vinification

straw yellow *n* (ca. 1796) **:** a pale yellow

[1]stray \'strā\ *n* [ME, fr. OF *estraié,* pp. of *estraier*] (13c) **1 a :** a domestic animal that is wandering at large or is lost **b :** a person or thing that strays **2** [ME, fr. *straien* to stray] *archaic* **:** the act of going astray **3 :** a disturbing electrical effect in radio reception not produced by a transmitting station **4 :** an unexpected formation encountered in drilling an oil or gas well

[2]stray *vi* [ME *straien,* fr. MF *estraier,* fr. (assumed) VL *extragare,* fr. L *extra-* outside + *vagari* to wander — more at EXTRA-, VAGARY] (14c) **:** WANDER: as **a :** to wander from company, restraint, or proper limits **b :** to roam about without fixed direction or purpose **c :** to move in a winding course **:** MEANDER **d :** to move without conscious or intentional effort ⟨eyes ~*ing* absently around the room⟩ **e :** to become distracted from an argument or chain of thought ⟨~*ed* from the point⟩ **f :** to wander accidentally from a fixed or chosen route **g :** ERR, SIN — **stray·er** *n*

[3]stray *adj* (15c) **1 :** having strayed **:** WANDERING ⟨a ~ cow⟩ **2 :** occurring at random or sporadically ⟨a few ~ hairs⟩ **3 :** not serving any useful purpose **:** UNWANTED ⟨~ light⟩

[1]streak \'strēk\ *n* [ME *streke,* fr. OE *strica;* akin to OHG *strich* line, L *striga* row — more at STRIKE] (bef. 12c) **1 :** a line or mark of a different color or texture from the ground **:** STRIPE **2 a :** the color of the fine powder of a mineral obtained by scratching or rubbing against a hard white surface and constituting an important distinguishing character **b :** inoculum implanted in a line on a solid medium **c :** any of several virus diseases of plants (as the potato, tomato, or raspberry) resembling mosaic but usu. producing at least some linear markings **3 a :** a narrow band of light **b :** a lightning bolt **4 a :** a slight admixture **:** TRACE ⟨had a mean ~ in him⟩ **b :** a brief run (as of luck) **c :** a consecutive series ⟨was on a winning ~⟩ **5 :** a narrow layer (as of ore)

[2]streak *vt* (1545) **:** to make streaks on or in ⟨tears ~*ing* her face⟩ ~ *vi* **1 :** to move swiftly **:** RUSH ⟨a jet ~*ing* across the sky⟩ **2 :** to have a streak (as of winning or outstanding performances)

streaked \'strēkt, 'strē-kəd\ *adj* (1596) **1 :** marked with stripes or linear discolorations **2 :** physically or mentally disturbed **:** UPSET

streak·ing \'strē-kiŋ\ *n* (ca. 1964) **:** the lightening (as by chemicals) of a few long strands of hair to produce a streaked effect

streaky \'strē-kē\ *adj* **streak·i·er; -est** (1745) **1 :** marked with streaks ⟨~ bacon⟩ **2 :** APPREHENSIVE ⟨nervous and ~⟩ **3 :** apt to vary (as in effectiveness) **:** UNRELIABLE — **streak·i·ness** *n*

[1]stream \'strēm\ *n* [ME *streme,* fr. OE *strēam;* akin to OHG *stroum* stream, Gk *rhein* to flow, Skt *sarati* it flows — more at SERUM] (bef. 12c) **1 :** a body of running water (as a river or brook) flowing on the earth; *also* **:** any body of flowing fluid (as water or gas) **2 a :** a steady succession (as of words or events) ⟨kept up an endless ~ of chatter⟩ **b :** a constantly renewed supply **c :** a continuous moving procession ⟨a ~ of traffic⟩ **3 :** an unbroken flow (as of gas or particles of matter) **4 :** a ray of light **5 a :** a prevailing attitude or group ⟨has always run against the ~ of current fashion⟩ **b :** a dominant influence or line of development 6 *Brit* : TRACK 3c — **on stream** : in or into production

²**stream** *vi* (13c) 1 a : to flow in or as if in a stream b : to leave a bright trail ⟨a meteor ~*ed* through the sky⟩ 2 a : to exude a bodily fluid profusely ⟨her eyes were ~*ing* from the onions⟩ b : to become wet with a discharge of bodily fluid ⟨~*ing* with perspiration⟩ 3 : to trail out at full length ⟨her hair ~*ing* back as she ran⟩ 4 : to pour in large numbers ⟨complaints came ~*ing* in⟩ ~ *vt* 1 : to emit freely or in a stream ⟨his eyes ~*ed* tears⟩ 2 : to display (as a flag) by waving

stream·bed \'strēm-,bed\ *n* (1857) : the channel occupied or formerly occupied by a stream

stream·er \'strē-mər\ *n* (13c) 1 a : a flag that streams in the wind; *esp* : PENNANT b : any long narrow wavy strip resembling or suggesting a banner floating in the wind c : BANNER 2 2 a : a long extension of the solar corona visible only during a total solar eclipse b *pl* : AURORA BOREALIS

stream·ing \'strē-miŋ\ *n* (14c) 1 : an act or instance of flowing; *specif* : CYCLOSIS 2 *Brit* : TRACKING

stream·let \'strēm-lət\ *n* (1552) : a small stream

¹**stream·line** \'strēm-,līn, -'līn\ *n* (ca. 1873) 1 : the path of a particle in a fluid relative to a solid body past which the fluid is moving in smooth flow without turbulence 2 a : a contour designed to minimize resistance to motion through a fluid (as air) b : a smooth or flowing line designed as if for decreasing air resistance

²**streamline** *vt* (1913) 1 : to design or construct with a streamline 2 : to bring up to date : MODERNIZE 3 a : ORGANIZE b : to make simpler or more efficient

stream·lined \-,līnd, -'līnd\ *adj* (1913) 1 a : contoured to reduce resistance to motion through a fluid (as air) b : stripped of nonessentials : COMPACT c : effectively integrated : ORGANIZED 2 : having flowing lines 3 : brought up to date : MODERNIZED 4 : of or relating to streamline flow

streamline flow *n* (ca. 1907) : an uninterrupted flow (as of air) past a solid body in which the direction at every point remains unchanged with the passage of time

stream·lin·er \'strēm-'lī-nər\ *n* (1934) : one that is streamlined; *esp* : a streamlined train

stream of consciousness (1890) 1 : the continuous unedited chronological flow of conscious experience through the mind 2 : INTERIOR MONOLOGUE

stream·side \'strēm-,sīd\ *n* (1844) : the land bordering on a stream

streek \'strēk\ *vt* [ME (northern dial.) *streken*; akin to OE *streccan* to stretch] (13c) 1 *chiefly Scot* : STRETCH, EXTEND 2 *chiefly Scot* : to lay out (a dead body)

¹**street** \'strēt\ *n* [ME *strete*, fr. OE *strǣt*, fr. LL *strata* paved road, fr. L, fem. of *stratus*, pp. — more at STRATUM] (bef. 12c) 1 a : a thoroughfare esp. in a city, town, or village that is wider than an alley or lane and that usu. includes sidewalks b : the part of a street reserved for vehicles c : a thoroughfare with abutting property ⟨lives on a fashionable ~⟩ 2 : the people occupying property on a street ⟨the whole ~ knew about the accident⟩ 3 : a promising line of development or a channeling of effort 4 *cap* : a district (as Wall Street or Fleet Street) identified with a particular profession 5 : an environment (as in a depressed neighborhood or section of a city) of prostitution, poverty, dereliction, or crime — **on the street** *or* **in the street** 1 : idle, homeless, or out of a job 2 : out of prison : at liberty — **up one's street** *or* **down one's street** : suited to one's abilities or taste

²**street** *adj* (15c) 1 a : adjoining or giving access to a street ⟨the ~ door⟩ b : carried on or taking place in the street ⟨~ fighting⟩ c : living or working on the streets ⟨a ~ peddler⟩ d : located in, used for, or serving as a guide to the streets ⟨a ~ map⟩ e : performing in or heard on the street ⟨a ~ band⟩ f : suitable for wear or use on the street ⟨~ clothes⟩ g : not touching the ground — used of a woman's dress in lengths reaching the knee, calf, or ankle 2 : caused by a street virus ⟨~ distemper⟩

street arab \-'ar-əb, -'ā-,rab\ *n, often cap A* (1865) : a homeless vagabond and esp. an outcast boy or girl in the streets of a city : GAMIN

street·car \'strēt-,kär\ *n* (1862) : a vehicle on rails used primarily for transporting passengers and typically operating on city streets

street·light \-,līt\ *n* (1906) : a light usu. mounted on a pole and constituting one of a series spaced at intervals along a public street or highway

street railway *n* (1861) : a line operating streetcars or buses

streets \'strēts\ *adv, chiefly Brit* (1898) : by a considerable margin ⟨a nice woman, ~ above these other callers —Katherine Mansfield⟩

street theater *n* (1967) : drama dealing with controversial social and political issues that is usu. performed outdoors (as on streets or in parks)

street virus *n* (ca. 1911) : virulent or natural virus (as that causing rabies) as distinguished from virus attenuated in the laboratory

street·walk·er \'strēt-,wȯ-kər\ *n* (1592) : PROSTITUTE; *esp* : one who solicits in the streets — compare CALL GIRL — **street·walk·ing** \-kiŋ\ *n*

street·wise \-,wīz\ *adj* (ca. 1965) : possessing the skills and attitudes necessary to survive in an often violent urban environment

strength \'streŋ(k)th, 'stren(t)th\ *n, pl* **strengths** \'streŋ(k)ths, 'stren(t)ths, 'streŋks\ [ME *strengthe*, fr. OE *strengthu*; akin to OHG *strengi* strong — more at STRONG] (bef. 12c) 1 : the quality or state of being strong : capacity for exertion or endurance 2 : power to resist force : SOLIDITY, TOUGHNESS 3 : power of resisting attack : IMPREGNABILITY 4 a : legal, logical, or moral force b : a strong attribute or inherent asset ⟨the ~*s* and the weaknesses of the book are evident⟩ 5 a : degree of potency of effect or of concentration b : intensity of light, color, sound, or odor c : vigor of expression 6 : force as measured in numbers : effective numbers of any body or organization ⟨an army at full ~⟩ 7 : one regarded as embodying or affording force or firmness : SUPPORT 8 : maintenance of or a rising tendency in a price level : firmness of prices 9 : BASIS — used in the phrase *on the strength of* ***syn*** see POWER — **from strength to strength** : vigorously forward : from one high point to the next

strength·en \'streŋ(k)-thən, 'stren(t)-\ *vb* **strength·ened; strength·en·ing** \'streŋ(k)th-(ə-)niŋ, 'stren(t)th-\ *vt* (15c) : to make stronger ~ *vi* : to become stronger — **strength·en·er** \'streŋ(k)th-(ə-)nər, 'stren(t)th-\ *n*

stren·u·ous \'stren-yə-wəs\ *adj* [L *strenuus* — more at STARE] (1599) 1 a : vigorously active : ENERGETIC b : FERVENT, ZEALOUS 2 : marked by or calling for energy or stamina : ARDUOUS ***syn*** see VIGOROUS — **stren·u·os·i·ty** \,stren-yə-'wäs-ət-ē\ *n* — **stren·u·ous·ly** \'stren-yə-wəs-lē\ *adv* — **stren·u·ous·ness** *n*

strep \'strep\ *adj* (1938) : STREPTOCOCCAL

strep throat *n* (ca. 1927) : SEPTIC SORE THROAT

strepto- *comb form* [NL, fr. Gk, fr. *streptos* twisted, fr. *strephein* to twist — more at STROPHE] 1 : twisted : twisted chain ⟨*strepto*coccus⟩ 2 : streptococcus ⟨*strepto*kinase⟩

strep·to·ba·cil·lus \,strep-tō-bə-'sil-əs\ *n* [NL] (1897) : any of various nonmotile gram-negative bacilli in which the individual cells are joined in a chain; *esp* : one (*Streptobacillus moniliformis*) that is the causative agent of one form of rat-bite fever

strep·to·coc·cal \,strep-tə-'käk-əl\ *also* **strep·to·coc·cic** \-'käk-(s)ik\ *adj* (1877) : of, relating to, or caused by streptococci ⟨a ~ sore throat⟩ ⟨~ organisms⟩

strep·to·coc·cus \-'käk-əs\ *n, pl* **-coc·ci** \-'käk-,(s)ī, -'käk-(,)(s)ē\ [NL] (ca. 1946) : any of a genus (*Streptococcus*) of nonmotile chiefly parasitic gram-positive bacteria that divide only in one plane, occur in pairs or chains but not in packets, and include important pathogens of man and domestic animals; *broadly* : a coccus occurring in chains

strep·to·ki·nase \,strep-tō-'kī-,nās, -,nāz\ *n* (ca. 1946) : a proteolytic enzyme from hemolytic streptococci active in promoting dissolution of blood clots

strep·to·ly·sin \,strep-tə-'līs-ᵊn\ *n* (1904) : an antigenic hemolysin produced by streptococci

strep·to·my·ces \-'mī-,sēz\ *n, pl* **streptomyces** [NL, fr. *strepto-* + Gk *mykēs* fungus; akin to L *mucus* mucus] (1951) : any of a genus (*Streptomyces*) of mostly soil actinomycetes including some that form antibiotics as by-products of their metabolism

strep·to·my·cete \-'mī-,sēt, -,mī-'sēt\ *n* [NL *Streptomycet-*, *Streptomyces*, genus name] (1948) : any of a family (Streptomycetaceae) of actinomycetes (as a streptomyces) that form vegetative mycelia which rarely break up into bacillary forms, have conidia borne on sporophores, and are typically aerobic soil saprophytes but include a few parasites of plants and animals

strep·to·my·cin \-'mīs-ᵊn\ *n* (1946) : an antibiotic organic base $C_{21}H_{39}N_7O_{12}$ produced by a soil actinomycete (*Streptomyces griseus*), active against many bacteria, and used esp. in the treatment of infections (as tuberculosis) by gram-negative bacteria

strep·to·thri·cin \-'thrīs-ᵊn, -'thris-\ *n* [NL *Streptothric-*, *Streptothrix*, genus of bacteria, fr. *strepto-* + Gk *trich-*, *thrix* hair — more at TRICH-] (1926) : a basic antibiotic produced by a soil actinomycete (*Streptomyces lavendulae*) and active against bacteria and to some degree against fungi

¹**stress** \'stres\ *n* [ME *stresse* stress, distress, fr. *destresse* — more at DISTRESS] (14c) 1 : constraining force or influence: as a : a force exerted when one body or body part presses on, pulls on, pushes against, or tends to compress or twist another body or body part; *esp* : the intensity of this mutual force commonly expressed in pounds per square inch b : the deformation caused in a body by such a force c : a physical, chemical, or emotional factor that causes bodily or mental tension and may be a factor in disease causation d : a state resulting from a stress; *esp* : one of bodily or mental tension resulting from factors that tend to alter an existent equilibrium e : STRAIN, PRESSURE ⟨the environment is under ~ to the point of collapse —Joseph Shoben⟩ 2 : EMPHASIS, WEIGHT ⟨lay ~ on a point⟩ 3 *archaic* : intense effort or exertion 4 : intensity of utterance given to a speech sound, syllable, or word producing relative loudness 5 a : relative force or prominence of sound in verse b : a syllable having relative force or prominence 6 : ACCENT 6a, 6b(2)

²**stress** *vt* (1545) 1 : to subject to physical or psychological stress 2 : to subject to phonetic stress : ACCENT 3 : to lay stress on : EMPHASIZE

stress·ful \'stres-fəl\ *adj* (1853) : full of or tending to induce stress — **stress·ful·ly** \-fə-lē\ *adv*

stress·less \-ləs\ *adj* (1885) : having no stress; *specif* : having no accent ⟨a ~ syllable⟩ — **stress·less·ness** *n*

stress mark *n* (ca. 1961) : a mark used with (as before, after, or over) a written syllable in the respelling of a word to show that this syllable is to be stressed when spoken : ACCENT MARK

stress·or \'stres-ər, -,ȯ(ə)r\ *n* (1952) : a stimulus that causes stress

stress–verse \'stres-,vərs\ *n* (1921) : verse whose rhythm is produced by recurrence of stresses without regard to number of syllables or any fixed distribution of unstressed elements

¹**stretch** \'strech\ *vb* [ME *strecchen*, fr. OE *streccan*; akin to OHG *strecchan* to stretch, OE *starian* to stare] *vt* (bef. 12c) 1 : to extend (as one's limbs or body) in a reclining position 2 : to reach out : EXTEND ⟨~*ed* forth his arm⟩ 3 : to extend in length ⟨~*ed* her neck to see what was going on⟩ 4 : to fell with or as if with a blow 5 : to cause the limbs of (a person) to be pulled esp. in torture 6 : to draw up (one's body) from a cramped, stooping, or relaxed position 7 : to pull taut ⟨canvas ~*ed* on a frame⟩ 8 a : to enlarge or distend esp. by force b : to extend or expand as if by physical force ⟨~ one's mind with a good book⟩ c : STRAIN ⟨~*ed* his already thin patience⟩ 9 : to cause to reach or continue (as from one point to another or across a space) ⟨~ a wire between two posts⟩ 10 a : to amplify or enlarge beyond natural or proper limits ⟨the rules can be ~*ed* this once⟩ b : to expand (as by improvisation) to fulfill a larger function ⟨~*ing* a dollar⟩ ~ *vi* 1 a : to become extended in length or breadth or both : SPREAD ⟨broad plains ~*ing* to the sea⟩ b : to extend over a continuous period 2 : to become extended without breaking 3 a : to extend one's body or limbs b : to lie down at full length — **stretch·abil·i·ty** \,strech-ə-'bil-ət-ē\ *n* — **stretch·able** \'strech-ə-bəl\ *adj* — **stretchy** \-ē\ *adj* — **stretch a point** : to go beyond what is strictly warranted in making a claim or concession — **stretch one's legs** 1 : to extend the legs 2 : to take a walk in order to relieve stiffness caused by prolonged sitting

²**stretch** *n* (1541) 1 a : an exercise of something (as the understanding or the imagination) beyond ordinary or normal limits b : an extension of the scope or application of something ⟨a ~ of language⟩ 2 : the extent to which something may be stretched 3 : the act of stretching : the state of being stretched 4 a : an extent in length or area ⟨a ~ of woods⟩ b : a continuous period of time ⟨can write for eight hours at a ~⟩ 5 : a walk to relieve fatigue 6 : a term of imprisonment 7

a : either of the straight sides of a racecourse; *esp* : HOMESTRETCH **b** : a final stage **8** : the capacity for being stretched : ELASTICITY
³stretch *adj* (1954) : easily stretched : ELASTIC ⟨a ~ wig⟩
stretch·er \'strech-ər\ *n* (15c) **1** : one that stretches; *esp* : a device or machine for stretching or expanding something **2 a** : a brick or stone laid with its length parallel to the face of the wall **b** : a timber or rod used esp. when horizontal as a tie in framed work **3** : a litter (as of canvas) for carrying a disabled or dead person **4** : a rod or bar extending between two legs of a chair or table
stretch·er–bear·er \-ˌbar-ər, -ˌber-\ *n* (ca. 1876) : one who carries one end of a stretcher
stretch limo *n* (1971) : a long usu. six-passenger limousine that is luxuriously furnished (as with a TV or bar) — called also *stretch limousine*
stretch–out \'strech-ˌau̇t\ *n* (1930) **1** : a system of industrial operation in which workers are required to do extra work and esp. to operate more machines than formerly either with slight or with no additional pay **2 a** : the act of stretching out : the state of being stretched out **b** : an economizing measure that spreads a limited quantity over a larger field than orig. intended
stretch receptor *n* (1936) : MUSCLE SPINDLE
stretch runner *n* (1922) : a racehorse that makes a strong bid in the homestretch
stret·to \'stret-(ˌ)ō\ *also* **stret·ta** \-ə\ *n, pl* **stret·ti** \-(ˌ)ē\ *or* **strettos** [*stretto* fr. It, fr. *stretto* narrow, close, fr. L *strictus,* pp.; *stretta* fr. It, fr. fem. of *stretto* — more at STRICT] (1854) **1 a** : the overlapping of answer with subject in a musical fugue **b** : the part of a fugue characterized by this overlapping **2** : a concluding passage performed in a quicker tempo
streu·sel \'strü-səl, -zəl, 's(h)trȯi-\ *n* [G, lit., something strewn, fr. MHG *ströusel,* fr. *ströuwen* to strew, fr. OHG *strewen*] (1909) : a crumbly mixture of fat, sugar, and flour and sometimes nuts and spices that is used as topping or filling for cake
strew \'strü\ *vt* **strewed; strewed** *or* **strewn** \'strün\; **strew·ing** [ME *strewen, strowen,* fr. OE *strewian, strēowian;* akin to OHG *strewen* to strew, L *struere* to heap up, *sternere* to spread out, Gk *stornynai*] (bef. 12c) **1** : to spread by scattering **2** : to cover by or as if by scattering something ⟨~*ing* the highways with litter⟩ **3** : to become dispersed over as if scattered **4** : to spread abroad : DISSEMINATE
strew·ment \'strü-mənt\ *n, archaic* (1602) : something (as flowers) strewed or designed for strewing
stria \'strī-ə\ *n, pl* **stri·ae** \'strī-ˌē\ [L, furrow, channel — more at STRIKE] (1563) **1** : STRIATION 2 **2** : a stripe or line (as in the skin) distinguished from surrounding tissue by color, texture, or elevation ⟨the *striae* of pregnancy resulting from stretching and rupture of elastic fibers⟩
¹stri·ate \'strī-ət, -ˌāt\ *adj* (1670) : STRIATED
²stri·ate \-ˌāt\ *vt* **stri·at·ed; stri·at·ing** (1709) : to mark with striations or striae
stri·at·ed \'strī-ˌāt-əd\ *adj* (1646) **1** : marked with striations or striae **2** : of, relating to, or being striated muscle
striated muscle *n* (1866) : muscle tissue that is marked by transverse dark and light bands, that is made up of elongated multinuclear fibers, and that is found in the muscles under voluntary control clothing the vertebrate skeleton and in all or most of the musculature of arthropods — compare SMOOTH MUSCLE
stri·a·tion \strī-'ā-shən\ *n* (ca. 1847) **1 a** : the fact or state of being striated **b** : arrangement of striations or striae **2** : a minute groove, scratch, or channel esp. when one of a parallel series **3** : any of the alternate dark and light cross bands of a myofibril of striated muscle
strick \'strik\ *n* [ME *stric, strik,* prob. of LG or D origin; akin to MLG *strik* rope, MD *stric*] (15c) : a bunch of hackled flax, jute, or hemp
strick·en \'strik-ən\ *adj* [fr. pp. of *strike*] (15c) **1** : hit or wounded by or as if by a missile **2 a** : afflicted or overwhelmed by or as if by disease, misfortune, or sorrow **b** : made incapable or unfit
strick·le \'strik-əl\ *n* [ME *strikell;* akin to OE *strīcan* to stroke — more at STRIKE] (15c) : a foundry tool for smoothing the surface of a core or mold — **strickle** *vt*
strict \'strikt\ *adj* [L *strictus,* fr. pp. of *stringere* to bind tight — more at STRAIN] (1578) **1 a** : stringent in requirement or control ⟨under ~ orders⟩ **b** : severe in discipline ⟨a ~ teacher⟩ **2 a** : inflexibly maintained or adhered to ⟨~ secrecy⟩ **b** : rigorously conforming to principle or a norm or condition **3** *archaic* **a** : TIGHT, CLOSE; *also* : INTIMATE **b** : NARROW **4** : EXACT, PRECISE ⟨in the ~ sense of the word⟩ **5** : of narrow erect habit of growth ⟨a ~ inflorescence⟩ ***syn*** see RIGID — **strict·ly** \'strik-(t)lē\ *adv* — **strict·ness** \'strik(t)-nəs\ *n*
stric·ture \'strik-chər\ *n* [ME, fr. LL *strictura,* fr. L *strictus,* pp.] (15c) **1** : an abnormal narrowing of a bodily passage; *also* : the narrowed part **2** : something that closely restrains or limits : RESTRICTION ⟨moral ~*s*⟩ **3** : an adverse criticism : CENSURE
¹stride \'strīd\ *vb* **strode** \'strōd\; **strid·den** \'strid-ᵊn\; **strid·ing** \'strīd-iŋ\ [ME *striden,* fr. OE *strīdan;* akin to MLG *striden* to straddle, OE *starian* to stare — more at STARE] *vi* (bef. 12c) **1** : to stand astride **2** : to move with or as if with long steps **3** : to take a very long step ~ *vt* **1** : BESTRIDE, STRADDLE **2** : to step over **3** : to move over or along with or as if with long measured steps — **strid·er** \'strīd-ər\ *n*
²stride *n* (bef. 12c) **1** : a long step **2** : an act of striding **3** : a stage of progress : ADVANCE **4 a** : a cycle of locomotor movements (as of a horse) completed when the feet regain the initial relative positions; *also* : the distance traversed in a stride **b** : the most effective natural pace : maximum competence or capability **5** : a manner of striding — **in stride 1** : without interference with regular activities **2** : without becoming upset
stri·dence \'strīd-ᵊn(t)s\ *n* (1890) : STRIDENCY
stri·den·cy \'strīd-ᵊn-sē\ *n* (1865) : the quality or state of being strident
stri·dent \'strīd-ᵊnt\ *adj* [L *strident-, stridens,* prp. of *stridere, stridēre* to make a harsh noise; akin to Gk & L *strix* owl] (ca. 1656) : characterized by harsh, insistent, and discordant sound ⟨a ~ voice⟩; *also* : commanding attention by a loud or obtrusive quality ⟨~ slogans⟩ ***syn*** see LOUD, VOCIFEROUS — **stri·dent·ly** *adv*
stride piano *n* [fr. *stride bass* (left hand part consisting of large skips)] (1952) : a style of jazz piano playing in which the right hand plays the melody while the left hand alternates between a single note and a chord played an octave or more higher
stri·dor \'strīd-ər, 'strī-ˌdȯ(ə)r\ *n* [L, fr. *stridere, stridēre*] (1632) **1** : a harsh, shrill, or creaking noise **2** : a harsh vibrating sound heard during respiration in cases of obstruction of the air passages
strid·u·late \'strij-ə-ˌlāt\ *vi* **-lat·ed; -lat·ing** [back-formation fr. *stridulation,* fr. F, high-pitched sound, fr. L *stridulus* shrill] (1838) : to make a shrill creaking noise by rubbing together special bodily structures — used esp. of male insects (as crickets or grasshoppers) — **strid·u·la·tion** \ˌstrij-ə-'lā-shən\ *n* — **strid·u·la·to·ry** \'strij-ə-lə-ˌtōr-ē, -ˌtȯr-\ *adj*
strid·u·lous \'strij-ə-ləs\ *adj* [L *stridulus,* fr. pp. of *stridere, stridēre*] (1611) : making a shrill creaking sound — **strid·u·lous·ly** *adv*
strife \'strīf\ *n* [ME *strif,* fr. OF *estrif,* prob. fr. *estriver* to struggle — more at STRIVE] (13c) **1 a** : bitter sometimes violent conflict or dissension ⟨political ~⟩ **b** : an act of contention : FIGHT, STRUGGLE **2** : exertion or contention for superiority **3** *archaic* : earnest endeavor ***syn*** see DISCORD — **strife·less** \'strī-fləs\ *adj*
strig·il \'strij-əl\ *n* [L *strigilis;* akin to L *stringere* to touch lightly] (1581) : an instrument used by ancient Greeks and Romans for scraping moisture off the skin after a bath or exercising
stri·gose \'strī-ˌgōs\ *adj* [NL *strigosus,* fr. *striga* bristle, fr. L, furrow] (ca. 1793) : having appressed bristles or scales ⟨a ~ leaf⟩
¹strike \'strīk\ *vb* **struck** \'strək\; **struck** *also* **strick·en** \'strik-ən\; **strik·ing** \'strī-kiŋ\ [ME *striken,* fr. OE *strīcan* to stroke, go; akin to OHG *strīhhan* to stroke, L *stringere* to touch lightly, *striga, stria* furrow] *vi* (bef. 12c) **1** : to take a course : GO ⟨*struck* off through the brush⟩ **2** : to aim and usu. deliver a blow or thrust (as with the hand, a weapon, or a tool) **3** : to come into contact forcefully ⟨two ships *struck* in mid channel⟩ **4** : to delete something **5** : to lower a flag usu. in surrender **6 a** : to become indicated by a clock, bell, or chime ⟨the hour had just *struck*⟩ **b** : to make known the time by sounding ⟨the clock *struck* as they entered⟩ **7** : PIERCE, PENETRATE ⟨the wind seemed to ~ through our clothes⟩ **8 a** : to engage in battle **b** : to make a military attack **9** : to become ignited **10** : to discover something ⟨he *struck* on a new plan of attack⟩ **11 a** : to pull on a fishing rod in order to set the hook **b** *of a fish* : to seize the bait **12** : DART, SHOOT **13 a** *of a plant cutting* : to take root **b** *of a seed* : GERMINATE **14** : to make an impression **15** : to stop work in order to force an employer to comply with demands **16** : to make a beginning ⟨the need to ~ vigorously for success⟩ **17** : to thrust oneself forward ⟨he *struck* into the midst of the argument⟩ **18** : to work diligently : STRIVE ~ *vt* **1 a** : to strike at : HIT **b** : to drive or remove by or as if by a blow **c** : to attack or seize with a sharp blow (as of fangs or claws) ⟨*struck* by a snake⟩ **d** : INFLICT ⟨~ a blow⟩ **e** : to produce by or as if by a blow or stroke ⟨Moses *struck* water from the rock⟩ **f** : to separate by a sharp blow ⟨~ off flints⟩ **2 a** : to haul down : LOWER ⟨~ the sails⟩ **b** : to dismantle and take away **c** : to strike the tents of (a camp) **3** : to afflict suddenly ⟨*stricken* by a heart attack⟩ **4 a** : to engage in (a battle) : FIGHT **b** : to make a military attack on **5** : DELETE, CANCEL ⟨~ the last paragraph⟩ **6 a** : to penetrate painfully : PIERCE **b** : to cause to penetrate **c** : to send down or out ⟨trees *struck* roots deep into the soil⟩ **7 a** : to level (as a measure of grain) by scraping off what is above the rim **b** : to smooth or form with a strickle **8** : to indicate by sounding **9 a** (1) : to bring into forceful contact (2) : to shake (hands) in confirming an agreement (3) : to thrust suddenly **b** : to come into contact or collision with **c** *of light* : to fall on **d** *of a sound* : to become audible to **10 a** : to affect with a mental or emotional state or a strong emotion ⟨*struck* with horror at the sight⟩ **b** : to affect a person with (a strong emotion) ⟨his words *struck* fear in the listeners⟩ **c** : to cause to become by or as if by a sudden blow ⟨*struck* him dead⟩ **11 a** : to produce by stamping **b** (1) : to produce (as fire) by or as if by striking (2) : to cause to ignite by friction **12** : to make and ratify the terms of ⟨~ a bargain⟩ **13 a** : to play or produce by stroking keys or strings ⟨*struck* a series of chords on the piano⟩ **b** : to produce as if by playing an instrument ⟨his voice *struck* a note of concern⟩ **14 a** : to hook (a fish) by a sharp pull on the line **b** *of a fish* : to snatch at (a bait) **15 a** : to occur to ⟨the answer *struck* him suddenly⟩ **b** : to appear to esp. as a revelation or as remarkable : IMPRESS **16** : BEWITCH **17** : to arrive at by computation ⟨~ a balance⟩ **18 a** : to come to : ATTAIN **b** : to come upon : DISCOVER ⟨~ gold⟩ **19** : to engage in a strike against (an employer) **20** : TAKE ON, ASSUME ⟨~ a pose⟩ **21 a** : to place (a plant cutting) in a medium for growth and rooting **b** : to so propagate (a plant) **22** : to make one's way along **23** : to cause (an arc) to form (as between electrodes of an arc lamp) **24** *of an insect* : to oviposit on or in ***syn*** see HIT, AFFECT
²strike *n* (15c) **1** : STRICKLE **2** : an act or instance of striking **3 a** : a work stoppage by a body of workers to enforce compliance with demands made on an employer **b** : a temporary stoppage of activities in protest against an act or condition **4** : the direction of the line of intersection of a horizontal plane with an uptilted geological stratum **5 a** : a pull on a fishing rod to strike a fish **b** : a pull on a line by a fish in striking **6** : a stroke of good luck; *esp* : a discovery of a valuable mineral deposit **7 a** : a pitched ball that is in the strike zone or is swung at and is not hit fair **b** : a perfectly thrown ball **8** : DISADVANTAGE, HANDICAP **9** : an act or instance of knocking down all the bowling pins with the first bowl **10** : establishment of roots and plant growth **11** : cutaneous myiasis (as of sheep) ⟨body ~⟩ **12 a** : a military attack; *esp* : an air attack on a single objective **b** : a group of airplanes taking part in such an attack
strike·bound \'strīk-ˌbau̇nd\ *adj* (1943) : subjected to a strike
strike·break·er \-ˌbrā-kər\ *n* (1904) : one hired to replace a striking worker
strike·break·ing \-kiŋ\ *n* (1905) : action designed to break up a strike
strike off *vt* (1821) **1** : to produce in an effortless manner **2** : to depict clearly and exactly
strike·out \'strīk-ˌau̇t\ *n* (1887) : an out in baseball resulting from a batter's being charged with three strikes
strike out \(ˈ)strīk-'au̇t\ *vi* (1712) **1** : to enter upon a course of action **2** : to set out vigorously **3** : to make an out in baseball by a strikeout

\ə\ abut \ᵊ\ kitten, F table \ər\ further \a\ ash \ā\ ace \ä\ cot, cart \au̇\ out \ch\ chin \e\ bet \ē\ easy \g\ go \i\ hit \ī\ ice \j\ job \ŋ\ sing \ō\ go \ȯ\ law \ȯi\ boy \th\ thin \t͟h\ the \ü\ loot \u̇\ foot \y\ yet \zh\ vision \à, k̲, ⁿ, œ, œ̄, ue, ue̅, ʸ\ *see* Guide to Pronunciation

4 : to finish bowling a string with consecutive strikes; *specif* : to bowl three strikes in the last frame ~ *vt, of a baseball pitcher* : to retire (a batter) by a strikeout

strike·over \'strīk-,ō-vər\ *n* (ca. 1938) : an act or instance of striking a typewriter character on a spot occupied by another character

strik·er \'strī-kər\ *n* (15c) **1** : one that strikes: as **a** : a player in any of several games who is striking or attempting to strike a ball **b** : the hammer of the striking mechanism of a clock or watch **c** : a blacksmith's helper who swings the sledgehammer **d** : a worker on strike **2** : an enlisted man working for a petty officer's rate

strike up *vi* (1549) : to begin to sing or play or to be sung or played ~ *vt* **1** : to cause to begin singing or playing ⟨*strike up* the band⟩ **2** : to cause to begin ⟨*strike up* a conversation⟩

strike zone *n* (1948) : the area (as between the armpits and tops of the knees of a batter in his natural stance) over home plate through which a pitched baseball must pass to be called a strike

strik·ing \'strī-kiŋ\ *adj* (1752) : attracting attention or notice through unusual or conspicuous qualities ⟨a woman of ~ beauty⟩ *syn* see NOTICEABLE — **strik·ing·ly** \-kiŋ-lē\ *adv*

striking price *n* (1961) : an agreed-upon price at which an option contract can be exercised

[1]**string** \'striŋ\ *n* [ME, fr. OE *streng;* akin to L *stringere* to bind tight — more at STRAIN] (bef. 12c) **1** : a small cord used to bind, fasten, or tie **2** **a** *archaic* : a cord (as a tendon or ligament) of an animal body **b** : a plant fiber (as a leaf vein) **3** **a** : the gut, wire, or nylon cord of a musical instrument **b** *pl* (1) : the stringed instruments of an orchestra (2) : the players of such instruments **4** **a** : a group of objects threaded on a string ⟨a ~ of fish⟩ **b** (1) : a series of things arranged in or as if in a line ⟨a ~ of cars⟩ (2) : a sequence of like items (as bits, characters, or words) **c** : a group of business properties scattered geographically ⟨a ~ of newspapers⟩ **d** : the animals and esp. horses belonging to or used by one individual **5** **a** : a means of recourse : EXPEDIENT **b** : a group of players ranked according to skill or proficiency **6** : SUCCESSION 3a ⟨a ~ of successes⟩ **7** **a** : one of the inclined sides of a stair supporting the treads and risers **b** : STRINGCOURSE **8** **a** : BALKLINE 1 **b** : the action of lagging for break in billiards **9** : LINE 13 **10** *pl* **a** : contingent conditions or obligations **b** : CONTROL, DOMINATION — **string·less** \'striŋ-ləs\ *adj* — **on the string** : subject to one's influences

[2]**string** *vb* **strung** \'strəŋ\; **string·ing** \'striŋ-iŋ\ *vt* (15c) **1** **a** : to equip with strings **b** : to tune the strings of **2** : to make tense : key up **3** **a** : to thread on or as if on a string **b** : to thread with objects **c** : to tie, hang, or fasten with string **d** : to put together (as words or ideas) like objects threaded on a string **4** : to hang by the neck **5** : to remove the strings of ⟨~ beans⟩ **6** **a** : to extend or stretch like a string ⟨~ wires from tree to tree⟩ **b** : to set out in a line or series **7** : FOOL, HOAX ⟨cowboys ~*ing* tenderfeet with tall tales —Carl Van Doren⟩ — often used with *along* ~ *vi* **1** : to move, progress, or lie in a string **2** : to form into strings **3** : LAG 3

string along *vt* (1914) : to keep waiting ~ *vi* : GO ALONG, AGREE

string bass *n* (ca. 1927) : DOUBLE BASS

string bean *n* (1759) **1** : a bean of one of the older varieties of kidney bean that have stringy fibers on the lines of separation of the pods; *broadly* : SNAP BEAN **2** : a very tall thin person

string·board \'striŋ-,bō(ə)rd, -,bȯ(ə)rd\ *n* (1703) : a board or built-up facing used in stair building to cover the ends of the steps and hide the true string

string·course \-,kō(ə)rs, -,kȯ(ə)rs\ *n* (ca. 1825) : a horizontal band (as of bricks) in a building forming a part of the design

stringed \'striŋd\ *adj* (bef. 12c) **1** : having strings ⟨~ instruments⟩ **2** : produced by strings

strin·gen·cy \'strin-jən-sē\ *n* (1844) : the quality or state of being stringent

strin·gen·do \strin-'jen-(,)dō\ *adv* [It, verbal of *stringere* to press, fr. L, to bind tight — more at STRAIN] (1853) : with quickening of tempo (as to a climax) — used as a direction in music

strin·gent \'strin-jənt\ *adj* [L *stringent-, stringens,* prp. of *stringere* to bind tight] (1736) **1** : TIGHT, CONSTRICTED **2** : marked by rigor, strictness, or severity esp. with regard to rule or standard **3** : marked by money scarcity and credit strictness *syn* see RIGID — **strin·gent·ly** *adv*

string·er \'striŋ-ər\ *n* (15c) **1** : one that strings **2** : a string, wire, or chain often with snaps on which fish are strung by a fisherman **3** : a narrow vein or irregular filament of mineral traversing a rock mass of different material **4** **a** : a long horizontal timber to connect uprights in a frame or to support a floor **b** : STRING 7a **c** : a tie in a truss **5** **a** : a longitudinal member extending from bent to bent of a railroad bridge and carrying the track **b** : a longitudinal member (as in an airplane fuselage or wing) to reinforce the skin **6** **a** : a news correspondent who is paid space rates **b** : a reporter who works for a publication or news agency on a part-time basis; *broadly* : CORRESPONDENT **7** : one estimated to be of specified excellence or efficiency — usu. used in combination ⟨first-*stringer*⟩ ⟨second-*stringer*⟩

string·halt \'striŋ-,hȯlt\ *n* (1523) : a condition of lameness in a horse's hind legs caused by muscular spasms — **string·halt·ed** \-,hȯl-təd\ *adj*

string·ing \'striŋ-iŋ\ *n* (1873) : the material with which a racket is strung

string line *n* (1867) : BALKLINE 1

string·piece \'striŋ-,pēs\ *n* (1802) : the heavy squared timber lying along the top of the piles forming a dock front or timber pier

string quartet *n* (1875) **1** : a composition for string quartet **2** : a quartet of performers on stringed instruments usu. including a first and second violin, a viola, and a cello

string tie *n* (1916) : a narrow necktie

stringy \'striŋ-ē\ *adj* **string·i·er; -est** (1669) **1** **a** : containing, consisting of, or resembling fibrous matter or string ⟨~ hair⟩ **b** : lean and sinewy in build : WIRY **2** : capable of being drawn out to form a string : ROPY ⟨a ~ precipitate⟩ — **string·i·ness** *n*

stringy·bark \'striŋ-ē-,bärk\ *n* (1802) **1** : any of several Australian eucalypti with fibrous inner bark **2** : the bark of a stringybark

[1]**strip** \'strip\ *vb* **stripped** \'stript\ *also* **stript; strip·ping** [ME *strippen,* fr. OE *-strīpan;* akin to OHG *stroufen* to strip] *vt* (bef. 12c) **1** **a** : to remove clothing, covering, or surface matter from **b** : to deprive of possessions **c** : to divest of honors, privileges, or functions **2** **a** : to remove extraneous or superficial matter from ⟨a prose style *stripped* to the bones⟩ **b** : to remove furniture, equipment, or accessories from ⟨~ a ship for action⟩ **3** : to make bare or clear (as by cutting or grazing) **4** : to finish a milking of by pressing the last available milk from the teats ⟨~ a cow⟩ **5** **a** : to remove cured leaves from the stalks of (tobacco) **b** : to remove the midrib from (tobacco leaves) **6** : to tear or damage the thread of (a separable part or fitting) **7** : to separate (components) from a mixture or solution **8** : to press eggs or milt out of (a fish) ~ *vi* **1** **a** : to take off clothes **b** : to perform a striptease **2** : PEEL 1 — **strip·pa·ble** \'strip-ə-bəl\ *adj*

[2]**strip** *n* [perh. fr. MLG *strippe* strap] (15c) **1** **a** : a long narrow piece of a material **b** : a long narrow area of land or water **2** : AIRSTRIP **3** : a commercially developed area esp. along a highway

strip chart *n* (1950) : a device used for the continuous graphic recording of time-dependent data

strip–crop·ping \'strip-,kräp-iŋ\ *n* (1936) : the growing of a cultivated crop (as corn) in strips alternating with strips of a sod-forming crop (as hay) arranged to follow an approximate contour of the land and minimize erosion — **strip–crop** \'strip-,kräp\ *vb*

[1]**stripe** \'strīp\ *n* [ME; akin to MD *stripe*] (15c) : a stroke or blow with a rod or lash

[2]**stripe** *vt* **striped** \'strīpt; *see* STRIPED *adj*\; **strip·ing** [prob. fr. MD; akin to OE *strica* streak — more at STREAK] (15c) : to make stripes on or variegate with stripes

[3]**stripe** *n* (1626) **1** **a** : a line or long narrow section differing in color or texture from parts adjoining **b** (1) : a textile design consisting of lines or bands against a plain background (2) : a fabric with a striped design **2** : a narrow strip of braid or embroidery usu. in the shape of a bar, arc, or chevron that is worn (as on the sleeve of a military uniform) to indicate rank or length of service **3** : a distinct variety or sort : TYPE ⟨persons of the same political ~⟩ — **stripe·less** \'strī-pləs\ *adj*

striped \'strīpt, 'strī-pəd\ *adj* (1616) : having stripes or streaks

striped bass *n* (1818) : a large anadromous food and sport fish (*Morone saxatilis* of the family Percichthyidae) that occurs along the Atlantic coast of the U.S. and has been introduced along the Pacific coast — called also *rock bass, rockfish*

striped skunk *n* (ca. 1882) : a common No. American skunk (*Mephitis mephitis*) usu. with white on the top of the head that extends posteriorly in two narrowly separated stripes

strip·er \'strī-pər\ *n* (ca. 1914) **1** : one that wears stripes (as on a sleeve) to indicate rank or length of service **2** : STRIPED BASS

strip·film \'strip-,film\ *n* (1927) : FILMSTRIP

strip·ing \'strī-piŋ\ *n* (1677) **1** **a** : the stripes marked or painted on something **b** : a design of stripes **2** : the act or process of marking with stripes

strip·ling \'strip-liŋ\ *n* [ME] (14c) : YOUTH 2a

strip mine *n* (1926) : a mine that is worked from the earth's surface by the stripping of overburden; *esp* : a coal mine situated along the outcrop of a flat dipping bed — **strip–mine** *vb* — **strip miner** *n*

stripped–down \(')strip(t)-'daủn\ *adj* (1928) : lacking any extra features

strip·per \'strip-ər\ *n* (1581) **1** : one that strips **2** : STRIPTEASER **3** : a machine that separates a desired part of an agricultural crop **4** : an oil well that has fallen off in production to 10 barrels or less per day

strip poker *n* (1919) : a poker game in which players pay their losses by removing articles of clothing

strip search *n* (1973) : a search for something concealed on a person made after removal of the person's clothing — **strip–search** *vb*

strip·tease \'strip-,tēz\ *n* (1936) : a burlesque act in which a performer removes his or her clothing piece by piece

strip·teas·er \-,tē-zər\ *n* (1930) : one who performs a striptease

stripy \'strī-pē\ *adj* **strip·i·er; -est** (1513) : marked by stripes or streaks

strive \'strīv\ *vi* **strove** \'strōv\ *also* **strived** \'strīvd\; **striv·en** \'striv-ən\ *or* **strived; striv·ing** \'strī-viŋ\ [ME *striven,* fr. OF *estriver,* of Gmc origin; akin to MHG *streben* to endeavor, OE *strīdan* to stride] (13c) **1** : to struggle in opposition : CONTEND **2** : to devote serious effort or energy : ENDEAVOR *syn* see ATTEMPT — **striv·er** \'strī-vər\ *n*

strobe \'strōb\ *n* [by shortening & alter.] (1942) **1** : STROBOSCOPE **2** : a device that utilizes a flashtube for high-speed illumination (as in photography) **3** : STROBOTRON

strobe light *n* (1947) : STROBE

stro·bi·la \strō-'bī-lə, 'strō-bə-\ *n, pl* **-lae** \-(,)lē\ [NL, fr. Gk *strobilē* plug of lint shaped like a pinecone, fr. *strobilos* pinecone] (1855) : a linear series of similar animal structures (as the segmented body of a tapeworm) produced by budding

stro·bi·la·tion \,strō-bə-'lā-shən\ *n* [NL *strobila*] (1878) : asexual reproduction by transverse division of the body into segments which develop into separate individuals, zooids, or proglottids in many coelenterates and worms

stro·bile \'strō-,bīl, -bəl\ *n* [NL *strobilus*] (1836) : a spike with persistent overlapping bracts that resembles a cone and is the pistillate inflorescence of the hop

stro·bi·lus \strō-'bī-ləs, 'strō-bə-\ *n, pl* **-li** \-,lī\ [NL, fr. LL, pinecone, fr. Gk *strobilos* twisted object, top, pinecone, fr. *strobos* action of whirling — more at STROPHE] (1771) **1** : an aggregation of sporophylls resembling a cone (as in the club mosses and horsetails) **2** : the cone of a gymnosperm

stro·bo·scope \'strō-bə-,skōp\ *n* [Gk *strobos* whirling + ISV *-scope*] (1896) : an instrument for determining the speed of cyclic motion (as rotation or vibration) that causes the motion to appear slowed or stopped: as **a** : a revolving disk with holes around the edge through which an object is viewed **b** : a device that uses a flashtube to intermittently illuminate a moving object **c** : a cardboard disk with marks to be viewed under intermittent light

stro·bo·scop·ic \,strō-bə-'skäp-ik\ *adj* (ca. 1846) : of, utilizing, or relating to a stroboscope or a strobe — **stro·bo·scop·i·cal·ly** \-i-k(ə-)lē\ *adv*

stro·bo·tron \'strō-bə-,trän\ *n* [*strobo*scope + *-tron*] (1937) : a gas-filled electron tube used esp. as a source of bright flashes of light for a stroboscope

strode *past of* STRIDE

[1]**stroke** \'strōk\ *vt* **stroked; strok·ing** [ME *stroken,* fr. OE *strācian;* akin to OHG *strīhhan* to stroke — more at STRIKE] (bef. 12c) **1** : to rub gently in one direction; *also* : CARESS **2** : to flatter or pay attention to in a manner designed to reassure or persuade — **strok·er** *n*

[2]**stroke** *n* [ME; akin to OE *strican* to stroke — more at STRIKE] (13c) **1** : the act of striking; *esp* : a blow with a weapon or implement **2** : a

single unbroken movement; *esp* : one of a series of repeated or to-and-fro movements 3 a : a controlled swing intended to hit a ball or shuttlecock; *also* : a striking of the ball b : such a stroke charged to a player as a unit of scoring in golf 4 a : a sudden action or process producing an impact ⟨~ of lightning⟩ b : an unexpected result ⟨~ of luck⟩ 5 : sudden diminution or loss of consciousness, sensation, and voluntary motion caused by rupture or obstruction (as by a clot) of an artery of the brain — called also *apoplexy* 6 a : one of a series of propelling beats or movements against a resisting medium ⟨a ~ of the oar⟩ b : a rower who sets the pace for a crew 7 a : a vigorous or energetic effort ⟨a ~ of genius⟩ b : a delicate or clever touch in a narrative, description, or construction 8 : HEARTBEAT 9 : the movement or the distance of the movement in either direction of a mechanical part (as a piston rod) having a reciprocating motion 10 : the sound of a bell being struck ⟨at the ~ of twelve⟩ 11 [[1]*stroke*] : an act of stroking or caressing 12 a : a mark or dash made by a single movement of an implement b : one of the lines of a letter of the alphabet

[3]stroke *vb* **stroked; strok·ing** *vt* (1597) 1 a : to mark with a short line ⟨~ the *t's*⟩ b : to cancel by drawing a line through ⟨*stroked* out his name⟩ 2 : to set the stroke for (a rowing crew); *also* : to set the stroke for the crew of (a rowing boat) 3 : HIT; *esp* : to propel (a ball) with a controlled swinging blow ~ *vi* 1 : to execute a stroke 2 : to row at a certain number of strokes a minute

stroke play *n* (1910) : golf competition scored by total number of strokes

stroll \ˈstrōl\ *vb* [prob. fr. G dial. *strollen*] *vi* (1603) 1 : to walk in a leisurely or idle manner : RAMBLE 2 : to go from place to place in search of occupation or profit ⟨~*ing* players⟩ ⟨~*ing* musicians⟩ ~ *vt* : to walk at leisure along or about — **stroll** *n*

stroll·er \ˈstrō-lər\ *n* (1608) 1 : one that strolls 2 a : VAGRANT, TRAMP b : an itinerant actor 3 : a carriage designed as a chair in which a baby may be pushed

stro·ma \ˈstrō-mə\ *n, pl* **stro·ma·ta** \-mət-ə\ [NL *stromat-, stroma,* fr. L, bed covering, fr. Gk *strōmat-, strōma,* fr. *stornynai* to spread out — more at STREW] (ca. 1832) 1 a : a compact mass of fungous hyphae producing perithecia or pycnidia b : the colorless proteinaceous matrix of a chloroplast in which the chlorophyll-containing lamellae are embedded 2 a : the supporting framework of an animal organ typically consisting of connective tissue b : the spongy protoplasmic framework of some cells (as a red blood cell) — **stro·mal** \-məl\ *adj*

stro·mat·o·lite \strō-ˈmat-ᵊl-ˌīt\ *n* [L *stromat-, stroma* bed covering + E *-o-* + *-lite*] (1943) : a laminated sedimentary fossil formed from layers of blue-green algae — **stro·mat·o·lit·ic** \-ˌmat-ᵊl-ˈit-ik\ *adj*

stro·mey·er·ite \ˈstrō-ˌmī(ə)r-ˌīt, strō-ˈ\ *n* [G *stromeyerit,* fr. Friedrich *Strohmeyer* †1835 Ger. chemist] (ca. 1835) : a steel-gray mineral CuAgS consisting of silver copper sulfide of metallic luster

strong \ˈstrȯŋ\ *adj* **stron·ger** \ˈstrȯŋ-gər *also* -ər\; **stron·gest** \ˈstrȯŋ-gəst *also* -əst\ [ME, fr. OE *strang;* akin to OHG *strengi* strong, L *stringere* to bind tight — more at STRAIN] (bef. 12c) 1 : having or marked by great physical power : ROBUST 2 : having moral or intellectual power 3 : having great resources (as of wealth or talent) 4 : of a specified number ⟨an army ten thousand ~⟩ 5 a : striking or superior of its kind ⟨a ~ resemblance⟩ b : effective or efficient esp. in a specified direction 6 : FORCEFUL, COGENT ⟨~ evidence⟩ 7 : not mild or weak : EXTREME, INTENSE: as a : rich in some active agent ⟨~ beer⟩ b *of a color* : high in chroma c : ionizing freely in solution ⟨~ acids and bases⟩ d : magnifying by refracting greatly ⟨~ lens⟩ 8 *obs* : FLAGRANT 9 : moving with rapidity or force ⟨~ wind⟩ 10 : ARDENT, ZEALOUS ⟨a ~ supporter⟩ 11 a : not easily injured or disturbed : SOLID b : not easily subdued or taken ⟨a ~ fort⟩ 12 : well established : FIRM ⟨~ beliefs⟩ 13 : not easily upset or nauseated ⟨a ~ stomach⟩ 14 : having an offensive or intense odor or flavor : RANK 15 : tending to steady or higher prices ⟨a ~ market⟩ 16 : of, relating to, or constituting a verb or verb conjugation that forms the past tense by a change in the root vowel and the past participle usu. by the addition of no suffix or a suffix containing *n* with or without change of the root vowel (as *strive, strove, striven* or *drink, drank, drunk*) — **strong** *adv* — **strong·ish** \ˈstrȯŋ-ish\ *adj* — **strong·ly** \ˈstrȯŋ-lē\ *adv*

syn STRONG, STOUT, STURDY, STALWART, TOUGH, TENACIOUS mean showing power to resist or to endure. STRONG may imply power derived from muscular vigor, large size, structural soundness, intellectual or spiritual resources; STOUT suggests an ability to endure stress, pain, or hard use without giving way; STURDY implies strength derived from vigorous growth, determination of spirit, solidity of construction; STALWART suggests an unshakable dependability and connotes great physical strength; TOUGH implies great firmness and resiliency; TENACIOUS suggests strength in seizing, retaining, clinging to, or holding together.

[1]strong–arm \ˈstrȯŋ-ˈärm\ *adj* (1901) : having or using undue force

[2]strong–arm *vt* (ca. 1903) 1 : to use force on : ASSAULT 2 : to rob by force

strong·box \ˈstrȯŋ-ˌbäks\ *n* (1684) : a strongly made chest or case for money or valuables

strong breeze *n* (1805) : wind having a speed of 25 to 31 miles (40 to 50 kilometers) per hour

strong drink *n* (14c) : intoxicating liquor

strong gale *n* (ca. 1805) : wind having a speed of 47 to 54 miles (76 to 87 kilometers) per hour

strong·hold \ˈstrȯŋ-ˌhōld\ *n* (15c) 1 : a fortified place 2 a : a place of security or survival ⟨one of the last ~*s* of the ancient Gaelic language —George Holmes⟩ b : a place dominated by a particular group or marked by a particular characteristic ⟨a Republican ~⟩ ⟨~*s* of snobbery —Lionel Trilling⟩

strong interaction *n* (ca. 1961) : a fundamental interaction experienced by elementary particles (as hadrons) that is more powerful than any other known force and is responsible for the binding together of neutrons and protons in the atomic nucleus and for processes of particle creation in high-energy collisions — called also *strong force*

strong·man \ˈstrȯŋ-ˌman\ *n* (1859) : one who leads or controls by force of will and character or by military methods

strong–mind·ed \ˈstrȯŋ-ˈmīn-dəd\ *adj* (1791) : having a vigorous mind; *esp* : marked by independence of thought and judgment — **strong–mind·ed·ly** *adv* — **strong-mind·ed·ness** *n*

strong room *n* (1761) : a room for money or valuables specially constructed to be fireproof and burglarproof

strong side *n* (ca. 1951) : the side of a football formation having the greater number of players; *specif* : the side on which the tight end plays

strong suit *n* (1865) 1 : a long suit containing high cards 2 : something in which one excels : FORTE

stron·gyle \ˈsträn-ˌjīl, -jəl\ *n* [deriv. of Gk *strongylos* round, compact; akin to L *stringere* to bind tight — more at STRAIN] (ca. 1847) : any of various roundworms (family Strongylidae) related to the hookworms and mostly parasitic in the alimentary tract and tissues of the horse

stron·gy·loi·di·a·sis \ˌsträn-jə-ˌlȯi-ˈdī-ə-səs\ *also* **stron·gy·loi·do·sis** \-ˈdō-səs\ *n* (ca. 1905) : infestation with or disease caused by any of a genus (*Strongyloides*) of strongyles that sometimes parasitize the intestines of vertebrates including man

stron·tian·ite \ˈsträn-chə-ˌnīt\ *n* (ca. 1794) : a mineral $SrCO_3$ consisting of strontium carbonate and occurring in various forms and colors

stron·tium \ˈsträn-ch(ē-)əm, ˈstränt-ē-əm\ *n* [NL, fr. *strontia,* fr. obs. E *strontian,* fr. *Strontian,* village in Scotland] (ca. 1808) : a soft malleable ductile metallic element of the alkaline-earth group occurring only in combination and used esp. in color TV tubes, in crimson fireworks, and in the production of some ferrites — see ELEMENT table

strontium 90 *n* (1952) : a heavy radioactive isotope of strontium having the mass number 90 that is present in the fallout from nuclear explosions and is hazardous because like calcium it can be assimilated in biological processes and deposited in the bones of human beings and animals — called also *radiostrontium*

[1]strop \ˈsträp\ *n* [ME — more at STRAP] (bef. 12c) : STRAP: a : a short rope with its ends spliced to form a circle b : a usu. leather band for sharpening a razor

[2]strop *vt* **stropped; strop·ping** (1841) : to sharpen (a razor) on a strop

stro·phan·thin \strō-ˈfan(t)-thən\ *n* [ISV, fr. NL *Strophanthus,* fr. Gk *strophos* twisted band + *anthos* flower] (ca. 1877) : any of several glycosides or mixtures of glycosides from African plants (genera *Strophanthus* and *Acocanthera*) of the dogbane family; *esp* : a bitter toxic glycoside $C_{36}H_{54}O_{14}$ from a woody vine (*Strophanthus kombé*) used similarly to digitalis

stro·phe \ˈstrō-fē, -ˌfē\ *n* [Gk *strophē,* lit., act of turning, fr. *strephein* to turn, twist; akin to Gk *strobos* action of whirling, *strophos* twisted band] (1603) 1 a : a rhythmic system composed of two or more lines repeated as a unit; *esp* : such a unit recurring in a series of strophic units b : STANZA c : the part of a Greek choral ode sung during the strophe of the dance 2 : the movement of the classical Greek chorus while turning from one side to the other of the orchestra

stro·phic \ˈstrō-fik, ˈsträf-ik\ *adj* (1848) 1 : relating to, containing, or consisting of strophes 2 *of a song* : using the same music for successive stanzas — compare THROUGH-COMPOSED

strop·py \ˈsträp-ē\ *adj* [by shortening & alter. of *obstreperous*] *Brit* (1970) : TOUCHY, BELLIGERENT

stroud \ˈstraủd\ *n* [prob. fr. *Stroud,* town in England] (1683) 1 *also* **stroud·ing** \-iŋ\ : a coarse woolen cloth formerly used in trade with No. American Indians 2 : a blanket or garment of stroud

strove *past & chiefly dial past part of* STRIVE

strow \ˈstrō\ *vt* **strowed; strown** \ˈstrōn\ *or* **strowed; strow·ing** [ME *strowen* — more at STREW] *archaic* (bef. 12c) : SCATTER

stroy *vb* [ME *stroyen,* short for *destroyen*] *obs* (13c) : DESTROY

struck \ˈstrək\ *adj* [pp. of *strike*] (1921) : closed by or subjected to a labor strike ⟨a ~ factory⟩ ⟨a ~ employer⟩

struc·tur·al \ˈstrək-chə-rəl, ˈstrək-shrəl\ *adj* (1835) 1 : of or relating to the physical makeup of a plant or animal body 2 a : of, relating to, or affecting structure ⟨~ stability⟩ b : used in building structures ⟨~ clay⟩ c : involved in or caused by structure esp. of the economy ⟨~ unemployment⟩ 3 : of, relating to, or resulting from the effects of folding or faulting of the earth's crust : TECTONIC 4 : concerned with or relating to structure rather than history or comparison ⟨~ linguistics⟩ — **struc·tur·al·ly** \-ē\ *adv*

structural formula *n* (ca. 1890) : an expanded molecular formula showing the arrangement within the molecule of atoms and of bonds

structural gene *n* (1962) : a gene that determines the amino acid sequence of a protein (as an enzyme) through a specific messenger RNA

structural iron *n* (1895) : iron worked or cast in structural shapes

struc·tur·al·ism \ˈstrək-chə-rə-ˌliz-əm, ˈstrək-shrə-\ *n* (ca. 1948) 1 : psychology concerned esp. with resolution of the mind into structural elements 2 : structural linguistics 3 : an anthropological movement associated esp. with Claude Lévi-Strauss that seeks to analyze social relationships in terms of highly abstract relational structures often expressed in a logical symbolism 4 : a method of analysis (as of a literary text or a political system) that is related to cultural anthropology and that focuses on recurring patterns of thought and behavior — **struc·tur·al·ist** \-ləst\ *n or adj*

structural isomerism *n* (ca. 1929) : isomerism in which atoms are linked in a different order

struc·tur·al·ize \ˈstrək-chə-rə-ˌlīz, ˈstrək-shrə-ˌlīz\ *vt* **-ized; -iz·ing** (ca. 1931) : to organize or incorporate into a structure — **struc·tur·al·iza·tion** \ˌstrək-chə-rə-lə-ˈzā-shən, ˌstrək-shrə-\ *n*

structural steel *n* (1895) 1 : rolled steel in structural shapes 2 : steel suitable for structural shapes

[1]struc·ture \ˈstrək-chər\ *n* [ME, fr. L *structura,* fr. *structus,* pp. of *struere* to heap up, build — more at STREW] (15c) 1 : the action of building : CONSTRUCTION 2 a : something (as a building) that is constructed b : something arranged in a definite pattern of organization ⟨a rigid totalitarian ~ —J. L. Hess⟩ ⟨leaves and other plant ~*s*⟩ 3 : manner of construction : MAKEUP ⟨Gothic in ~⟩ 4 a : the arrangement of particles or parts in a substance or body ⟨soil ~⟩ ⟨molecular ~⟩ b : organization of parts as dominated by the general character of the whole ⟨economic ~⟩ ⟨personality ~⟩ 5 : the aggregate of elements of an entity in their relationships to each other

[2]structure *vt* **struc·tured; struc·tur·ing** \ˈstrək-chə-riŋ, ˈstrək-shriŋ\ (1693) **1 :** to form into or according to a structure **2 :** CONSTRUCT

struc·tured *adj* (1966) **:** of, relating to, or being a method of computer programming in which each step of the solution to a problem is contained in a separate subprogram

struc·ture·less \ˈstrək-chər-ləs\ *adj* (1847) **:** lacking structure; *esp* **:** devoid of cells ⟨a ∼ membrane⟩ — **struc·ture·less·ness** *n*

stru·del \ˈs(h)trüd-ᵊl\ *n* [G, lit., whirlpool] (ca. 1893) **:** a pastry made from a thin sheet of dough rolled up with filling and baked ⟨apple ∼⟩

[1]strug·gle \ˈstrəg-əl\ *vi* **strug·gled; strug·gling** \-(ə-)liŋ\ [ME *struglen*] (14c) **1 :** to make strenuous or violent efforts against opposition **:** CONTEND **2 :** to proceed with difficulty or with great effort ⟨*struggled* through the agenda⟩ — **strug·gler** \-(ə-)lər\ *n*

[2]struggle *n* (1692) **1 :** CONTEST, STRIFE **2 :** a violent effort or exertion **:** an act of strongly motivated striving

struggle for existence (1832) **:** the automatic competition (as for food, space, or light) of members of a natural population that tends to eliminate less efficient individuals and thereby increase the chance of the more efficient to pass on inherited adaptive traits

[1]strum \ˈstrəm\ *vb* **strummed; strum·ming** [imit.] *vt* (1777) **1 a :** to brush the fingers over the strings of (a musical instrument) in playing ⟨∼ a guitar⟩; *also* **:** [3]THRUM 1 **b :** to play (music) on a stringed instrument ⟨∼ a tune⟩ **2 :** to cause to sound vibrantly ⟨winds *strummed* the rigging — H.A. Chippendale⟩ ∼ *vi* **1 :** to strum a stringed instrument **2 :** to sound vibrantly — **strum·mer** *n*

[2]strum *n* (1793) **:** an act, instance, or sound of strumming

stru·ma \ˈstrü-mə\ *n, pl* **stru·mae** \-(ˌ)mē, -ˌmī\ *or* **strumas** (1565) **1** [L — more at STRUT] **:** GOITER **2** [NL, fr. L] **:** a swelling at the base of the capsule in many mosses — **stru·mose** \-ˌmōs\ *adj*

strum·pet \ˈstrəm-pət\ *n* [ME] (14c) **:** PROSTITUTE

strung \ˈstrəŋ\ *past and past part of* STRING

strung out *adj* (ca. 1959) **1 :** physically debilitated (as from long-term drug addiction) **2 :** addicted to a drug **3 :** intoxicated or stupefied from drug use

strunt \ˈstrənt\ *vi* [by alter.] *Scot* (1789) **:** STRUT

[1]strut \ˈstrət\ *vb* **strut·ted; strut·ting** [ME *strouten,* fr. OE *strūtian* to exert oneself; akin to L *struma* goiter, OE *starian* to stare] *vi* (14c) **1 :** to become turgid **:** SWELL **2 a :** to walk with a proud gait **b :** to walk with a pompous and affected air ∼ *vt* **:** to parade (as clothes) with a show of pride — **strut·ter** *n*

[2]strut *n* (1587) **1 :** a structural piece designed to resist pressure in the direction of its length **2 :** a pompous step or walk

[3]strut *vt* **strut·ted; strut·ting** (ca. 1828) **:** to provide, stiffen, support, or hold apart with or as if with a strut

stru·thi·ous \ˈstrü-thē-əs, -thē-\ *adj* [LL *struthio* ostrich, irreg. fr. Gk *strouthos*] (1773) **:** of or relating to the ostriches and related birds **:** RATITE

strych·nine \ˈstrik-ˌnīn, -nən, -ˌnēn\ *n* [F, fr. NL *Strychnos,* fr. L, nightshade, fr. Gk] (1819) **:** a bitter poisonous alkaloid $C_{21}H_{22}N_2O_2$ that is obtained from nux vomica and related plants (genus *Strychnos*) and is used as a poison (as for rodents) and medicinally as a stimulant to the central nervous system

Stu·art \ˈst(y)ü-ərt, ˈst(y)u̇(-ə)rt\ *adj* [Robert *Stewart* (Robert II of Scotland) †1390] (ca. 1894) **:** of or relating to the Scottish royal house to which belonged the rulers of Scotland from 1371 to 1603 and of Great Britain from 1603 to 1649 and from 1660 to 1714 — **Stuart** *n*

[1]stub \ˈstəb\ *n* [ME *stubb,* fr. OE *stybb;* akin to Gk *stypos* stem, *typtein* to beat — more at TYPE] (bef. 12c) **1 a :** STUMP 2 **b :** a short piece remaining on a stem or trunk where a branch has been lost **2 :** something made or worn to a short or blunt shape; *esp* **:** a pen with a short blunt nib **3 :** a short blunt part left after a larger part has been broken off or used up ⟨pencil ∼⟩ **4 :** something cut short or stunted **5 a :** a small part of a leaf (as of a checkbook) attached to the backbone for memoranda of the contents of the part torn away **b :** the part of a ticket returned to the user

[2]stub *vt* **stubbed; stub·bing** (15c) **1 a :** to grub up by the roots **b :** to clear (land) by grubbing out rooted growth **c :** to hew or cut down (a tree) close to the ground **2 :** to extinguish (as a cigarette) by crushing **3 :** to strike (one's foot or toe) against an object

stub·ble \ˈstəb-əl\ *n, often attrib* [ME *stuble,* fr. OF *estuble,* fr. L *stupula* stalk, straw, alter. of *stipula* — more at STIPULE] (13c) **1 :** the basal part of herbaceous plants and esp. cereal grasses remaining attached to the soil after harvest **2 :** a rough surface or growth resembling stubble; *esp* **:** a short growth of beard — **stub·bly** \-(ə-)lē\ *adj*

stubble mulch *n* (1942) **:** a lightly tilled mulch of plant residue used to prevent erosion, conserve moisture, and add organic matter to the soil

stub·born \ˈstəb-ərn\ *adj* [ME *stuborn*] (14c) **1 a (1) :** unreasonably or perversely unyielding **:** MULISH **(2) :** justifiably unyielding **:** RESOLUTE **b :** suggestive or typical of a strong stubborn nature ⟨a ∼ jaw⟩ **2 :** performed or carried on in an unyielding, obstinate, or persistent manner ⟨∼ effort⟩ **3 :** difficult to handle, manage, or treat ⟨a ∼ cold⟩ **4 :** LASTING ⟨∼ facts⟩ ***syn*** see OBSTINATE — **stub·born·ly** *adv* — **stub·born·ness** \-ərn-(n)əs\ *n*

stub·by \ˈstəb-ē\ *adj* (1572) **1 a :** resembling a stub **:** being short and thick ⟨∼ fingers⟩ **b :** being short and thickset **:** SQUAT **c :** being short, broad, or blunt (as from use or wear) **2 :** abounding with stubs

[1]stuc·co \ˈstək-(ˌ)ō\ *n, pl* **stuccos** *or* **stuccoes** [It, of Gmc origin; akin to OHG *stucki* piece, crust, OE *stocc* stock — more at STINT] (1598) **1 a :** a fine plaster used in the decoration and ornamentation of interior walls **b :** a material usu. made of portland cement, sand, and a small percentage of lime and applied in a plastic state to form a hard covering for exterior walls **2 :** STUCCOWORK

[2]stucco *vt* (1726) **:** to coat or decorate with stucco

stuc·co·work \ˈstək-ō-ˌwərk\ *n* (1686) **:** work done in stucco

stuck *past and past part of* STICK

stuck–up \ˈstək-ˈəp\ *adj* (1829) **:** superciliously self-important

[1]stud \ˈstəd\ *n, often attrib* [ME *stod,* fr. OE *stōd;* akin to OE *standan* to stand] (bef. 12c) **1 a :** a group of animals and esp. horses kept primarily for breeding **b :** a place (as a farm) where a stud is kept **2 a :** STUDHORSE; *broadly* **:** a male animal kept for breeding **b :** a young man; *esp* **:** one who is virile and promiscuous — **at stud :** for breeding as a stud ⟨retired racehorses are *at stud*⟩

[2]stud *n* [ME *stode,* fr. OE *studu;* akin to OE *stōw* place — more at STOW] (bef. 12c) **1 a :** one of the smaller uprights in the framing of the walls of a building to which sheathing, paneling, or laths are fastened **:** SCANTLING **b :** height from floor to ceiling **2 a :** a boss, rivet, or nail with a large head used (as on a shield or belt) for ornament or protection **b :** a solid button with a shank or eye on the back inserted (as through an eyelet in a garment) as a fastener or ornament **3 a :** any of various infixed pieces (as a rod or pin) projecting from a machine and serving chiefly as a support or axis **b :** one of the metal cleats inserted in a snow tire to increase traction

[3]stud *vt* **stud·ded; stud·ding** (1505) **1 :** to furnish (as a building or wall) with studs **2 :** to adorn, cover, or protect with studs **3 :** to set or mark (a place or thing) with a number of prominent objects

stud·book \ˈstəd-ˌbu̇k\ *n* (1803) **:** an official record (as in a book) of the pedigree of purebred animals (as horses or dogs)

stud·ding \ˈstəd-iŋ\ *n* (1588) **1 :** the studs of a building or wall **2 :** material for studs

stud·ding sail \ˈstəd-iŋ-ˌsāl, ˈstən(t)-səl\ *n* [origin unknown] (1549) **:** a light sail set at the side of a principal square sail of a ship in free winds

stu·dent \ˈst(y)üd-ᵊnt, *chiefly Southern* -ənt\ *n, often attrib* [ME, fr. L *student-, studens,* fr. prp. of *studēre* to study — more at STUDY] (14c) **1 :** SCHOLAR, LEARNER; *esp* **:** one who attends a school **2 :** one who studies **:** an attentive and systematic observer

student body *n* (1906) **:** the students at an educational institution

student government *n* (1948) **:** the organization and management of student life by various student organizations

student lamp *n* (1873) **:** a desk reading lamp with a tubular shaft, one or two arms for a shaded light, and orig. an oil reservoir

stu·dent·ship \ˈst(y)üd-ᵊnt-ˌship, -ənt-\ *n* (1782) **1** *Brit* **:** a grant for university study **2 :** the state of being a student

stu·dent's t distribution \ˈst(y)üd-ᵊn(t)s-, -ən(t)s-\ *n, often cap S* [*Student,* pen name of W. S. Gossett †1937 Brit. statistician] (1929) **:** T DISTRIBUTION

Student's t–test *n* [*Student,* pen name of W.S. Gossett] (1935) **:** T-TEST

student teacher *n* (1909) **:** a student who is engaged in practice teaching

student teaching *n* (1929) **:** PRACTICE TEACHING

student union *n* (1949) **:** a building on a college campus that is devoted to student activities and that usu. contains lounges, auditoriums, offices, and game rooms

stud·horse \ˈstəd-ˌhȯ(ə)rs\ *n* (bef. 12c) **:** a stallion kept esp. for breeding

stud·ied \ˈstəd-ēd\ *adj* (15c) **1 :** carefully considered or prepared **:** THOUGHTFUL **2 :** KNOWLEDGEABLE, LEARNED **3 :** produced or marked by conscious design or premeditation ⟨∼ indifference⟩ — **stud·ied·ly** *adv* — **stud·ied·ness** *n*

stu·dio \ˈst(y)üd-ē-ˌō\ *n, pl* **-dios** [It, lit., study, fr. L *studium*] (1810) **1 a :** the working place of a painter, sculptor, or photographer **b :** a place for the study of an art (as dancing, singing, or acting) **2 :** a place where motion pictures are made **3 :** a place maintained and equipped for the transmission of radio or television programs **4 :** a place where audio recordings are made

studio apartment *n* (1925) **:** a small apartment consisting typically of a main room, kitchenette, and bathroom

studio couch *n* (1936) **:** an upholstered usu. backless couch that can be made to serve as a double bed by sliding from underneath it the frame of a single cot

stu·di·ous \ˈst(y)üd-ē-əs\ *adj* (14c) **1 :** assiduous in the pursuit of learning **2 a :** of, relating to, or concerned with study **b :** favorable to study ⟨a ∼ environment⟩ **3 a :** diligent or earnest in intent ⟨made a ∼ effort⟩ **b :** marked by or suggesting purposefulness or diligence ⟨a ∼ expression on his face⟩ **c :** deliberately or consciously planned ⟨spoke with a ∼ accent⟩ — **stu·di·ous·ly** *adv* — **stu·di·ous·ness** *n*

stud poker *n* [[1]*stud*] (1864) **:** poker in which each player is dealt his first card facedown and his other four cards faceup with a round of betting taking place after each of the last four rounds of dealing

[1]study \ˈstəd-ē\ *n, pl* **stud·ies** [ME *studie,* fr. OF *estudie,* fr. L *studium;* akin to L *studēre* to study, *tundere* to beat — more at STINT] (14c) **1 :** a state of contemplation **:** REVERIE **2 a :** application of the mental faculties to the acquisition of knowledge ⟨years of ∼⟩ **b :** such application in a particular field or to a specific subject ⟨the ∼ of Latin⟩ **c :** careful or extended consideration ⟨the proposal is under ∼⟩ **d (1) :** a careful examination or analysis of a phenomenon, development, or question **(2) :** the published report of such a study **3 :** a building or room devoted to study or literary pursuits **4 :** PURPOSE, INTENT **5 a :** a branch or department of learning **:** SUBJECT **b :** the activity or work of a student ⟨returning to his *studies* after vacation⟩ **c :** an object of study or deliberation ⟨every gesture a careful ∼ —Marcia Davenport⟩ **d :** something attracting close attention or examination **6 :** one who memorizes something (as a part in a play) — usu. used with a qualifying adjective ⟨he's a fast ∼⟩ **7 :** a literary or artistic production intended as a preliminary outline, an experimental interpretation, or an exploratory analysis of specific features or characteristics **8 :** a musical composition for the practice of a point of technique

[2]study *vb* **stud·ied; study·ing** *vi* (14c) **1 a :** to engage in study **b :** to undertake formal study of a subject **2** *dial* **:** MEDITATE, REFLECT **3 :** ENDEAVOR, TRY ∼ *vt* **1 :** to read in detail esp. with the intention of learning **2 :** to engage in the study of ⟨∼ biology⟩ **3 :** PLOT, DESIGN **4 :** to consider attentively or in detail ***syn*** see CONSIDER — **studi·er** \ˈstəd-ē-ər\ *n*

study hall *n* (1846) **1 :** a room in a school set aside for study **2 :** a period in a student's day set aside for study and homework

[1]stuff \ˈstəf\ *n* [ME, fr. MF *estoffe,* fr. OF, fr. *estoffer* to equip, stock] (15c) **1 :** materials, supplies, or equipment used in various activities: as **a** *obs* **:** military baggage **b :** bullets or shells fired from a gun **c :** PERSONAL PROPERTY **2 :** material to be manufactured, wrought, or used in construction ⟨clear half-inch pine ∼ —Emily Holt⟩ **3 :** a finished textile suitable for clothing; *esp* **:** wool or worsted material **4 a :** literary or artistic production **b :** writing, discourse, or ideas of little value **:** TRASH **5 a :** an aggregate of matter ⟨volcanic rock is curious ∼⟩ **b (1) :** matter of a particular and often unspecified kind ⟨sold tons of the ∼⟩ **(2) :** something (as a drug or food) consumed or introduced into the body by humans **(3) :** a matter to be considered ⟨the truth was heady ∼⟩ ⟨long-term policy∼⟩ **c :** a group or scattering of miscellaneous objects or articles ⟨pick that ∼ up off the floor⟩ **6 a :** fundamental material **:** SUBSTANCE ⟨∼ of greatness⟩ ⟨∼ of manhood⟩ **b :** subject matter ⟨a teacher who knows his ∼⟩ **7 a :** actions or talk in specific circumstances ⟨don't give me any of that ∼⟩ **b**

: special knowledge or capability ⟨showing their ~⟩ **8 a :** spin imparted to a thrown or hit ball to make it curve or change course **b :** the movement of a baseball pitch out of its apparent line of flight **:** the liveliness of a pitch ⟨greatest pitcher of my time . . . had tremendous ~ —Ted Williams⟩ — **stuff·less** *adj*

[2]stuff *vt* (15c) **1 a :** to fill by packing things in **:** CRAM ⟨the child ~*ed* his pockets with candy⟩ **b :** to fill to satiety **:** SURFEIT ⟨~*ed* himself with turkey⟩ **c :** to prepare (meat or vegetables) by filling or lining with a stuffing **d :** to fill (as a cushion) with a soft material **e :** to fill out the skin of (an animal) for mounting **2 :** to fill by intellectual effort ⟨~*ing* their heads with facts⟩ **3 :** to choke or block up (as nasal passages) **4 a :** to cause to enter or fill **:** THRUST ⟨~*ed* a lot of clothing into a laundry bag⟩ **b :** to put (as a ball or puck) into a goal forcefully from close range

stuffed shirt *n* (1913) **:** a smug, conceited, and usu. pompous person often with an inflexibly conservative or reactionary attitude

stuff·er \'stəf-ər\ *n* (ca. 1611) **1 :** one that stuffs **2 :** an enclosure (as a leaflet) inserted in an envelope in addition to a bill, statement, or notice **3 :** a series of extra threads or yarn running lengthwise in a fabric to add weight and bulk and to form a backing esp. for carpets

stuff·ing \'stəf-iŋ\ *n* (ca. 1530) **:** material used to stuff; *esp* **:** a seasoned mixture used to stuff food (as meat, vegetables, or eggs)

stuffing box *n* (1798) **:** a device that prevents leakage along a moving part (as a piston rod) passing through a hole in a vessel (as a cylinder) containing steam, water, or oil and that consists of a box or chamber made by enlarging the hole and a gland to compress the contained packing

stuff shot *n* (1970) **:** DUNK SHOT

stuffy \'stəf-ē\ *adj* **stuff·i·er; -est** (1825) **1 :** ILL-NATURED, ILL-HUMORED **2 a :** oppressive to the breathing **:** CLOSE **b :** stuffed up ⟨a ~ nose⟩ **3 :** lacking in vitality or interest **:** STODGY, DULL **4 :** narrowly inflexible in standards of conduct **:** SELF-RIGHTEOUS — **stuff·i·ly** \'stəf-ə-lē\ *adv* — **stuff·i·ness** \'stəf-ē-nəs\ *n*

stull \'stəl\ *n* [perh. modif. of G *stolle* post, support — more at STOLLEN] (1898) **1 :** a round timber used to support the sides or back of a mine **2 :** one of a series of props wedged between the walls of a stope to hold up a platform

stul·ti·fi·ca·tion \,stəl-tə-fə-'kā-shən\ *n* (1832) **:** the act or process of stultifying **:** the state of being stultified

stul·ti·fy \'stəl-tə-,fī\ *vt* **-fied; -fy·ing** [LL *stultificare* to make foolish, fr. L *stultus* foolish; akin to L *stolidus* stolid] (1766) **1 :** to allege or prove to be of unsound mind and hence not responsible **2 :** to cause to appear or be stupid, foolish, or absurdly illogical **3 a :** to impair, invalidate, or make ineffective **:** NEGATE **b :** to have a dulling or inhibiting effect on

[1]stum·ble \'stəm-bəl\ *vb* **stum·bled; stum·bling** \-b(ə-)liŋ\ [ME *stumblen,* prob. of Scand origin; akin to Norw dial. *stumle* to stumble; akin to OE *stamerian* to stammer] *vi* (14c) **1 a :** to fall into sin or waywardness **b :** to make an error **:** BLUNDER **c :** to come to an obstacle to belief **2 :** to trip in walking or running **3 a :** to walk unsteadily or clumsily **b :** to speak or act in a hesitant or faltering manner **4 a :** to come unexpectedly or by chance ⟨~ onto the truth⟩ **b :** to fall or move carelessly ~ *vt* **1 :** to cause to stumble **:** TRIP **2 :** BEWILDER, CONFOUND — **stum·bler** \-b(ə-)lər\ *n* — **stum·bling·ly** \-b(ə-)liŋ-lē\ *adv*

[2]stumble *n* (1547) **:** an act or instance of stumbling

stum·ble·bum \'stəm-bəl-,bəm\ *n* (1939) **:** a clumsy or inept person; *specif* **:** an inept boxer

stumbling block \'stəm-bliŋ-\ *n* (1588) **1 :** an impediment to belief or understanding **:** PERPLEXITY **2 :** an obstacle to progress

[1]stump \'stəmp\ *n* [ME *stumpe;* akin to OHG *stumpf* stump, ME *stampen* to stamp] (14c) **1 a :** the basal portion of a bodily part remaining after the rest is removed **b :** a rudimentary or vestigial bodily part **2 :** the part of a plant and esp. a tree remaining attached to the root after the trunk is cut **3 :** a remaining part **:** STUB **4 :** a place or occasion for political public speaking

[2]stump *vt* (1596) **1 :** to reduce to a stump **:** TRIM **2 a :** DARE, CHALLENGE **b :** to frustrate the progress or efforts of **:** BAFFLE **3 :** to clear (land) of stumps **4 :** to travel over (a region) making political speeches or supporting a cause **5 a :** to walk over heavily or clumsily **b :** STUB 3 ~ *vi* **1 :** to walk heavily or noisily **2 :** to go about making political speeches or supporting a cause — **stump·er** *n*

[3]stump *n* [F or Flem; F *estompe,* fr. Flem *stomp,* lit., stub, fr. MD; akin to OHG *stumpf* stump] (1778) **:** a short thick roll of leather, felt, or paper usu. pointed at both ends and used for shading or blending a drawing in crayon, pencil, charcoal, pastel, or chalk

[4]stump *vt* (1807) **:** to tone or treat (a drawing) with a stump

stump·age \'stəm-pij\ *n* (1835) **1 :** the value of standing timber **2 :** uncut marketable timber; *also* **:** the right to cut it

stump–tailed macaque \,stəmp-,tāl(d)-\ *n* (1893) **:** a dark reddish brown pink-faced short-tailed macaque (*Macaca speciosa*) that is found in eastern Asia — called also *stump-tailed monkey*

stump work *n* (1904) **:** embroidery with intricate padded designs or scenes in high relief popular esp. in the 17th century

stumpy \'stəm-pē\ *adj* (1600) **1 :** being short and thick **:** STUBBY **2 :** full of stumps

[1]stun \'stən\ *vt* **stunned; stun·ning** [ME *stunen,* modif. of MF *estoner* — more at ASTONISH] (14c) **1 :** to make senseless, groggy, or dizzy by or as if by a blow **:** DAZE **2 :** to shock with noise **3 :** to overcome esp. with paralyzing astonishment or disbelief

[2]stun *n* (1727) **:** the effect of something that stuns **:** SHOCK

stung *past and past part of* STING

stun gun *n* (1967) **:** a weapon designed to stun or immobilize rather than kill or injure a victim; *esp* **:** a gun used by riot-control forces that shoots large pellets or sand- or shot-filled bags

stunk *past and past part of* STINK

stun·ner \'stən-ər\ *n* (1847) **:** one that stuns or is stunning

stun·ning \'stən-iŋ\ *adj* (1856) **:** strikingly impressive esp. in beauty or excellence — **stun·ning·ly** \-iŋ-lē\ *adv*

[1]stunt \'stənt\ *vt* [E dial. *stunt* stubborn, stunted, abrupt, prob. of Scand origin; akin to ON *stuttr* scant — more at STINT] (1659) **:** to hinder the normal growth, development, or progress of — **stunt·ed·ness** *n*

[2]stunt *n* (1725) **1 :** one (as an animal) that is stunted **2 :** a check in growth **3 :** a plant disease in which dwarfing occurs

[3]stunt *n* [prob. alter. of *stump* (challenge)] (ca. 1895) **1 :** an unusual or difficult feat requiring great skill or daring; *esp* **:** one performed or undertaken chiefly to gain attention or publicity **2 :** a shifting or switching of the positions by defensive players at the line of scrimmage in football to disrupt the opponent's blocking efforts

[4]stunt *vi* (1917) **:** to perform or engage in a stunt

stunt·man \'stənt-,man\ *n* (1927) **:** a man who performs stunts; *esp* **:** one who doubles for an actor during the filming of stunts and dangerous scenes

stunt·wom·an \-,wu̇m-ən\ *n* (1948) **:** a woman who doubles for an actress during the filming of stunts and dangerous scenes

stu·pa \'stü-pə\ *n* [Skt *stūpa*] (1876) **:** a usu. dome-shaped mound or tower serving as a Buddhist shrine

[1]stupe \'st(y)üp\ *n* [ME, fr. L *stuppa* coarse part of flax, tow, fr. Gk *styppē*] (15c) **:** a hot wet often medicated cloth applied externally (as to stimulate circulation)

[2]stupe *n* [short for *stupid*] (1762) **:** a stupid person **:** DOLT

stu·pe·fac·tion \,st(y)ü-pə-'fak-shən\ *n* [NL *stupefaction-, stupefactio,* fr. L *stupefactus,* pp. of *stupefacere*] (1543) **:** the act of stupefying **:** the state of being stupefied

stu·pe·fy \'st(y)ü-pə-,fī\ *vt* **-fied; -fy·ing** [MF *stupefier,* modif. of L *stupefacere,* fr. *stupēre* to be astonished + *facere* to make, do — more at DO] (1596) **1 :** ASTONISH **2 :** to make stupid, groggy, or insensible

stu·pen·dous \st(y)u̇-'pen-dəs\ *adj* [L *stupendus,* gerundive of *stupēre*] (1666) **1 :** causing astonishment or wonder **:** AWESOME, MARVELOUS **2 :** of amazing size or greatness **:** TREMENDOUS ***syn*** see MONSTROUS — **stu·pen·dous·ly** *adv* — **stu·pen·dous·ness** *n*

[1]stu·pid \'st(y)ü-pəd\ *adj* [MF *stupide,* fr. L *stupidus,* fr. *stupēre* to be benumbed, be astonished — more at TYPE] (1541) **1 a :** slow of mind **:** OBTUSE **b :** given to unintelligent decisions or acts **:** acting in an unintelligent or careless manner **c :** lacking intelligence or reason **:** BRUTISH **2 :** dulled in feeling or sensation **:** TORPID ⟨still ~ from the sedative⟩ **3 :** marked by or resulting from unreasoned thinking or acting **:** SENSELESS **4 a :** lacking interest or point **b :** VEXATIOUS, EXASPERATING ⟨this ~ flashlight won't work⟩ — **stu·pid·ly** *adv* — **stu·pid·ness** *n*

syn STUPID, DULL, DENSE, CRASS, DUMB mean lacking in power to absorb ideas or impressions. STUPID implies a slow-witted or dazed state of mind that may be either congenital or temporary; DULL suggests a slow or sluggish mind such as results from disease, depression, or shock; DENSE implies a thickheaded imperviousness to ideas; CRASS suggests a grossness of mind precluding discrimination or delicacy; DUMB applies to an exasperating obtuseness or lack of comprehension.

[2]stupid *n* (1712) **:** a stupid person

stu·pid·i·ty \st(y)u̇-'pid-ət-ē\ *n, pl* **-ties** (1541) **1 :** the quality or state of being stupid **2 :** a stupid idea or act

stu·por \'st(y)ü-pər\ *n* [ME, fr. L, fr. *stupēre*] (14c) **1 :** a condition of greatly dulled or completely suspended sense or sensibility ⟨drunken ~⟩ **2 :** a state of extreme apathy or torpor resulting often from stress or shock **:** DAZE ***syn*** see LETHARGY

stu·por·ous \'st(y)ü-p(ə-)rəs\ *adj* (1892) **:** marked or affected by or as if by stupor

stur·dy \'stərd-ē\ *adj* **stur·di·er; -est** [ME, brave, stubborn, fr. MF *estourdi* stunned, fr. pp. of *estourdir* to stun, fr. (assumed) VL *exturdire* to be dizzy as a thrush, fr. L *ex-* + *turdus* thrush — more at THRUSH] (14c) **1 a :** firmly built or constituted **:** STOUT **b :** HARDY **c :** sound in design or execution **:** SUBSTANTIAL **2 a :** marked by or reflecting physical strength or vigor **b :** FIRM, RESOLUTE **c :** RUGGED, STABLE ***syn*** see STRONG — **stur·di·ly** \'stərd-ᵊl-ē\ *adv* — **stur·di·ness** \'stərd-ē-nəs\ *n*

stur·geon \'stər-jən\ *n* [ME, fr. MF *estourjon,* of Gmc origin; akin to OE *styria* sturgeon] (14c) **:** any of various usu. large elongate edible ganoid fishes (as of the genus *Acipenser*) which are widely distributed in the north temperate zone and whose roe is made into caviar

sturgeon

Sturm und Drang \,s(h)tu̇r-mu̇nt-'dräŋ, -mənt-\ *n* [G, lit., storm and stress, fr. *Sturm und Drang* (1776), drama by Friedrich von Klinger †1831 Ger. novelist and dramatist] (1845) **1 :** a late 18th century German literary movement characterized by works containing rousing action and high emotionalism that often deal with the individual's revolt against society **2 :** TURMOIL

sturt \'stərt\ *n* [ME, contention, alter. of *strut;* akin to OE *strūtian* to exert oneself — more at STRUT] *chiefly Scot* (14c) **:** CONTENTION

[1]stut·ter \'stət-ər\ *vb* [freq. of E dial. *stut* to stutter, fr. ME *stutten;* akin to D *stotteren* to stutter, L *tundere* to beat — more at STINT] *vi* (ca. 1570) **1 :** to speak with involuntary disruption or blocking of speech (as by spasmodic repetition or prolongation of vocal sounds) **2 :** to move or act in a halting or spasmodic manner ⟨the old jalopy bucks and ~*s* uphill —William Cleary⟩ ~ *vt* **:** to say, speak, or sound with or as if with a stutter — **stut·ter·er** \-ər-ər\ *n*

[2]stutter *n* (ca. 1847) **1 :** an act or instance of stuttering **2 :** a speech disorder involving stuttering accompanied by fear and anxiety

[1]sty \'stī\ *n, pl* **sties** *also* **styes** [ME, fr. OE *stig;* akin to ON *-stī* sty] (bef. 12c) **1 :** a pen or enclosed housing for swine **2 :** an unkempt filthy place ⟨this house is a ~⟩

[2]sty *vb* **stied** *or* **styed; sty·ing** *vt* (12c) **:** to lodge or keep in a sty ~ *vi* **:** to live in a sty

[3]**sty** *or* **stye** \'stī\ *n, pl* **sties** *or* **styes** [short for obs. E *styan,* fr. (assumed) ME, alter. of OE *stīgend,* fr. *stīgan* to go up, rise — more at STAIR] (1617) **:** an inflamed swelling of a sebaceous gland at the margin of an eyelid

sty·gian \'stij-(ē-)ən\ *adj, often cap* [L *stygius,* fr. Gk *stygios,* fr. *Styg-, Styx* Styx] (1566) **1 :** of or relating to the river Styx **2 :** extremely dark, gloomy, or forbidding

[1]**styl-** *or* **stylo-** *comb form* [L, fr. Gk, fr. *stylos* — more at STEER] **:** pillar ⟨*stylo*lite⟩

[2]**styl-** *or* **styli-** *or* **stylo-** *comb form* [L *stilus* stake, stalk — more at STYLE] **:** style **:** styloid process ⟨*styl*ate⟩ ⟨*styli*ferous⟩ ⟨*stylo*graphic⟩

sty·lar \'stī-lər, -,lär\ *adj* [[1]*style*] (ca. 1928) **:** of or relating to the style of a plant ovary

-sty·lar \'stī-lər, -,lär\ *adj comb form* [Gk *stylos* pillar — more at STEER] **:** having (such or so many) pillars **:** having (such) columniation ⟨am-phi*stylar*⟩

[1]**style** \'stī(ə)l\ *n* [ME *stile, style,* fr. L *stilus* stake, stylus, style of writing; akin to OE *stician* to stick] (14c) **1 :** DESIGNATION, TITLE **2 a :** a distinctive manner of expression (as in writing or speech) ⟨writes with more attention to ~ than to content⟩ ⟨the flowery ~ of 18th century prose⟩ **b :** a distinctive manner or custom of behaving or conducting oneself ⟨the formal ~ of the court⟩ ⟨his ~ is abrasive⟩; *also* **:** a particular mode of living ⟨has bought an expensive home and intends to live in grand ~⟩ **c :** a particular manner or technique by which something is done, created, or performed ⟨a unique ~ of horseback riding⟩ ⟨the classical ~ of dance⟩ **3 a :** STYLUS **b :** the shadow-producing pin of a sundial **c :** a filiform prolongation of a plant ovary bearing a stigma at its apex — see FLOWER illustration **d :** a slender elongated process (as a bristle) on an animal **4 :** a distinctive quality, form, or type of something ⟨a new dress ~⟩ ⟨the Greek ~ of architecture⟩ **5 a :** the state of being popular **:** FASHION ⟨clothes that are always in ~⟩ **b :** fashionable elegance **c :** beauty, grace, or ease of manner or technique ⟨an awkward moment she handled with ~⟩ **6 :** a convention with respect to spelling, punctuation, capitalization, and typographic arrangement and display followed in writing or printing ***syn*** see FASHION — **style·less** \'stī(ə)l-ləs\ *adj* — **style·less·ness** *n*

[2]**style** *vt* **styled; styl·ing** (1563) **1 :** to call or designate by an identifying term **:** NAME **2 a :** to give a particular style to **b :** to design, make, or arrange in accord with the prevailing mode — **styl·er** *n*

-style \,stīl\ *adj or adv comb form* **:** being in a particular style

style·book *n* (1708) **:** a book explaining, describing, or illustrating a prevailing, accepted, or authorized style

sty·let \stī-'let, 'stī-lət\ *n* [F, fr. MF *stilet* stiletto, fr. OIt *stiletto*] (1697) **1 a :** a slender surgical probe **b :** a thin wire inserted into a catheter to maintain rigidity or into a hollow needle to maintain patency **c :** a pointed instrument (as for graving) **2 :** a relatively rigid elongated organ or appendage (as a piercing mouthpart) of an animal **3 :** STILETTO

sty·li·form \'stī-lə-,fȯrm\ *adj* [NL *stiliformis,* fr. L *stilus* + *-formis* -form] (1578) **:** resembling a style **:** bristle-shaped ⟨a ~ copulatory organ⟩

styl·ing \'stī-liŋ\ *n* (1932) **:** the way in which something is styled

styl·ish \'stī-lish\ *adj* (1785) **:** having style; *specif* **:** conforming to current fashion — **styl·ish·ly** *adv* — **styl·ish·ness** *n*

styl·ist \'stī-ləst\ *n* (1795) **1 a :** a master or model of style; *esp* **:** a writer or speaker in matters of style **b :** one (as a writer or singer) noted for a distinctive style **2 :** one who develops, designs, or advises on styles

sty·lis·tic \stī-'lis-tik\ *adj* (1860) **:** of or relating esp. to literary or artistic style — **sty·lis·ti·cal·ly** \-ti-k(ə-)lē\ *adv*

sty·lis·tics \stī-'lis-tiks\ *n pl but sing or pl in constr* (1882) **1 :** an aspect of literary study that emphasizes the analysis of various elements of style (as metaphor and diction) **2 :** the study of the devices in a language that produce expressive value

sty·lite \'stī-,līt\ *n* [LGk *stylitēs,* fr. Gk *stylos* pillar — more at STEER] (1638) **:** a Christian ascetic living atop a pillar — **sty·lit·ic** \stī-'lit-ik\ *adj*

styl·ize \'stī(ə)l-,īz\ *vt* **styl·ized; styl·iz·ing** (1898) **:** to conform to a conventional style; *specif* **:** to represent or design according to a style or stylistic pattern rather than according to nature — **styl·iza·tion** \,stī-lə-'zā-shən\ *n*

sty·lo·bate \'stī-lə-,bāt\ *n* [L *stylobates,* fr. Gk, *stylobatēs,* fr. *stylos* pillar + *bainein* to walk, go — more at COME] (1563) **:** a continuous flat coping or pavement on which a row of architectural columns is supported

sty·log·ra·phy \stī-'läg-rə-fē\ *n* (ca. 1840) **:** a mode of writing or tracing lines by means of a style or similar instrument

sty·loid \'stī(ə)l-,ȯid\ *adj* (1709) **:** resembling a style **:** STYLIFORM — used esp. of slender pointed skeletal processes (as on the ulna)

sty·lo·lite \'stī-lə-,līt\ *n* [ISV] (1866) **:** a small longitudinally grooved column of the same material as the rock in which it occurs

sty·lo·po·di·um \,stī-lə-'pōd-ē-əm\ *n, pl* **-dia** \-ē-ə\ [NL, fr. [2]*styl-* + Gk *podion* small foot, base — more at PEW] (ca. 1832) **:** a disk-shaped or conical expansion at the base of the style in plants of the carrot family

sty·lus \'stī-ləs\ *n, pl* **sty·li** \'stī(ə)l-,ī\ *also* **sty·lus·es** \'stī-lə-səz\ [modif. of L *stilus* stake, stylus — more at STYLE] (1807) **:** an instrument for writing, marking, or incising: as **a :** an instrument used by the ancients in writing on clay or waxed tablets **b :** a hard-pointed pen-shaped instrument for marking on stencils used in a reproducing machine **c** (1) **:** NEEDLE 3c (2) **:** a cutting tool used to produce an original record groove during disc recording

sty·mie \'stī-mē\ *vt* **sty·mied; sty·mie·ing** [Sc *stimie, stymie* to obstruct a golf shot by interposition of the opponent's ball] (1857) **:** to present an obstacle to **:** stand in the way of

styp·tic \'stip-tik\ *adj* [ME *stiptik,* fr. L *stypticus,* fr. Gk *styptikos,* fr. *styphein* to contract] (15c) **:** tending to contract or bind **:** ASTRINGENT; *esp* **:** tending to check bleeding — **styptic** *n*

styptic pencil *n* (ca. 1933) **:** a stick of a medicated styptic substance for use esp. in shaving to stop the bleeding from small cuts

sty·rax \'stī-,raks\ *n* [L — more at STORAX] (1558) **:** STORAX

sty·rene \'stī-,rēn\ *n* [ISV, fr. L *styrax*] (ca. 1885) **:** a fragrant liquid unsaturated hydrocarbon C_8H_8 used chiefly in making synthetic rubber, resins, and plastics and in improving drying oils

Sty·ro·foam \'stī-rə-,fōm\ *trademark* — used for an expanded rigid polystyrene plastic

Styx \'stiks\ *n* [L *Styg-, Styx,* fr. Gk] **:** the principal river of the underworld in Greek mythology

su·able \'sü-ə-bəl\ *adj* (1623) **:** liable to be sued in court — **su·abil·i·ty** \,sü-ə-'bil-ət-ē\ *n* — **su·ably** \-blē\ *adv*

sua·sion \'swā-zhən\ *n* [ME, fr. L *suasion-, suasio,* fr. *suasus,* pp. of *suadēre* to urge, persuade — more at SWEET] (14c) **:** the act of influencing or persuading — **sua·sive** \'swā-siv, -ziv\ *adj* — **sua·sive·ly** *adv* — **sua·sive·ness** *n*

suave \'swäv\ *adj* **suav·er; -est** [MF, pleasant, sweet, fr. L *suavis* — more at SWEET] (1847) **1 :** smoothly though often superficially gracious and sophisticated **2 :** smooth in texture, performance, or finish — **suave·ly** *adv* — **suave·ness** *n* — **sua·vi·ty** \'swäv-ət-ē\ *n*

syn SUAVE, URBANE, DIPLOMATIC, BLAND, SMOOTH, POLITIC mean pleasantly tactful and well-mannered. SUAVE suggests a specific ability to deal with others easily and without friction; URBANE implies high cultivation and poise coming from wide social experience; DIPLOMATIC stresses an ability to deal with ticklish situations tactfully; BLAND emphasizes mildness of manner and absence of irritating qualities; SMOOTH suggests often a deliberately assumed suavity; POLITIC implies shrewd as well as tactful and suave handling of people.

[1]**sub** \'səb\ *n* (1830) **:** SUBSTITUTE

[2]**sub** *vb* **subbed; sub·bing** *vi* (1853) **:** to act as a substitute ~ *vt* **1** *Brit* **:** SUBEDIT **2 :** SUBCONTRACT 1

[3]**sub** *n* (1916) **:** SUBMARINE

sub- *prefix* [ME, fr. L, under, below, secretly, from below, up, near, fr. *sub* under, close to — more at UP] **1 :** under **:** beneath **:** below ⟨*sub*soil⟩ ⟨*sub*aqueous⟩ **2 a :** subordinate **:** secondary **:** next lower than or inferior to ⟨*sub*station⟩ ⟨*sub*editor⟩ **b :** subordinate portion of **:** subdivision of ⟨*sub*committee⟩ ⟨*sub*species⟩ **c :** with repetition (as of a process) so as to form, stress, or deal with subordinate parts or relations ⟨*sub*let⟩ ⟨*sub*contract⟩ **3 a :** less than completely, perfectly, or normally **:** somewhat ⟨*sub*dominant⟩ ⟨*sub*ovate⟩ **b :** containing less than the usual or normal amount of (such) an element or group ⟨*sub*oxide⟩ **4 a :** almost **:** nearly ⟨*sub*erect⟩ **b :** falling nearly in the category of and often adjoining **:** bordering on ⟨*sub*arctic⟩

sub·ad·o·les·cent	**sub·econ·o·my**	**sub·pro·le·tar·i·at**
sub·agen·cy	**sub·erect**	**sub·ra·tio·nal**
sub·agent	**sub·et·y·mol·o·gy**	**sub·sa·line**
sub·al·lo·ca·tion	**sub·file**	**sub·sat·u·rat·ed**
sub·ar·ea	**sub·frame**	**sub·sat·u·ra·tion**
sub·au·di·ble	**sub·gen·er·a·tion**	**sub·scale**
sub·av·er·age	**sub·genre**	**sub·science**
sub·base·ment	**sub·goal**	**sub·sea**
sub·ba·sin	**sub·gov·ern·ment**	**sub·sec·re·tary**
sub·block	**sub·hu·mid**	**sub·sec·tor**
sub·branch	**sub·im·print**	**sub·sei·zure**
sub·caste	**sub·in·dus·try**	**sub·sense**
sub·cat·e·go·ri·za·tion	**sub·in·hib·i·to·ry**	**sub·sen·tence**
sub·cat·e·go·rize	**sub·lan·guage**	**sub·se·ries**
sub·cat·e·go·ry	**sub·lev·el**	**sub·site**
sub·ceil·ing	**sub·li·brar·i·an**	**sub·so·cial**
sub·cel·lar	**sub·li·cense**	**sub·so·ci·ety**
sub·chap·ter	**sub·lot**	**sub·spe·cial·ist**
sub·chief	**sub·man·ag·er**	**sub·spe·cial·ize**
sub·clan	**sub·mar·ket**	**sub·spe·cial·ty**
sub·clus·ter	**sub·min·i·mal**	**sub·state**
sub·code	**sub·min·i·mum**	**sub·sys·tem**
sub·col·lec·tion	**sub·min·is·ter**	**sub·task**
sub·col·lege	**sub·na·tion·al**	**sub·tax·on**
sub·col·le·giate	**sub·net·work**	**sub·test**
sub·col·o·ny	**sub·niche**	**sub·theme**
sub·com·mis·sion	**sub·op·ti·mal**	**sub·ther·a·peu·tic**
sub·com·po·nent	**sub·op·ti·mi·za·tion**	**sub·top·ic**
sub·con·den·sa·tion	**sub·op·ti·mize**	**sub·trea·sury**
sub·cor·date	**sub·op·ti·mum**	**sub·trend**
sub·co·ri·a·ceous	**sub·or·ga·ni·za·tion**	**sub·tribe**
sub·coun·ty	**sub·pan·el**	**sub·type**
sub·cu·ra·tive	**sub·par**	**sub·unit**
sub·dean	**sub·para·graph**	**sub·va·ri·ety**
sub·de·ci·sion	**sub·par·al·lel**	**sub·vas·sal**
sub·de·part·ment	**sub·part**	**sub·ver·bal**
sub·de·vel·op·ment	**sub·phase**	**sub·vil·lain**
sub·di·a·lect	**sub·po·lit·i·cal**	**sub·vis·i·ble**
sub·di·rec·tor	**sub·pri·mate**	**sub·vi·su·al**
sub·dis·ci·pline	**sub·pro·cess**	**sub·writ·er**
sub·dis·trict	**sub·prod·uct**	**sub·ze·ro**
sub·eco·nom·ic	**sub·proj·ect**	**sub·zone**

sub·ac·id \,səb-'as-əd, 'səb-\ *adj* [L *subacidus,* fr. *sub-* + *acidus* acid] (1669) **:** somewhat acrimonious **:** CUTTING ⟨~ comments⟩ — **sub·ac·id·ly** *adv* — **sub·ac·id·ness** *n*

sub·acute \,səb-ə-'kyüt\ *adj* (1822) **1 :** having a tapered but not sharply pointed form ⟨~ leaves⟩ **2 a :** falling between acute and chronic in character esp. when closer to acute ⟨~ endocarditis⟩ **b :** less marked in severity or duration than a corresponding acute state ⟨~ pain⟩ — **sub·acute·ly** *adv*

subacute scle·ros·ing pan·en·ceph·a·li·tis \-sklə-'rō-siŋ-,pan-in-,sef-ə-'līt-əs\ *n* [*sclerosing* (prp. of *sclerose*) + *pan-* + *encephalitis*] (1968) **:** a central nervous system disease of children and young adults caused by infection of the brain by measles virus or a closely related virus and marked by intellectual deterioration, convulsions, and paralysis

sub·adult \,səb-ə-'dəlt; ,səb-'ad-,əlt, 'səb-\ *n* (1923) **:** an individual that has passed through the juvenile period but not yet attained typical adult characteristics — **subadult** *adj*

sub·aer·i·al \,səb-'ar-ē-əl, 'səb-, -'er-; ,səb-ā-'ir-ē-əl\ *adj* (1833) **:** situated, formed, or occurring on or immediately adjacent to the surface of the earth ⟨~ erosion⟩ ⟨~ roots⟩ — **sub·aer·i·al·ly** \-ē-ə-lē\ *adv*

su·bah·dar *or* **su·ba·dar** \,sü-bə-'där\ *n* [Per *sūbadār*] (1673) **1 :** a governor of a province **2 :** the chief native officer of a native company in the former British Indian army

sub·al·pine \ˌsəb-ˈal-ˌpīn, ˈsəb-\ *adj* (ca. 1656) **1 :** of or relating to the region about the foot and lower slopes of the Alps **2 :** of, relating to, or growing on high upland slopes

¹sub·al·tern \sə-ˈbȯl-tərn, *esp Brit* ˈsəb-əl-tərn\ *adj* [LL *subalternus,* fr. L *sub-* + *alternus* alternate, fr. *alter* other (of two) — more at ALTER] (1581) **1 :** SUBORDINATE **2 :** particular with reference to a related universal proposition ⟨"some S is P" is a ~ proposition to "all S is P"⟩

²subaltern *n* (1605) **1 :** a person holding a subordinate position; *specif* **:** a junior officer (as in the British army) **2 :** a particular proposition that follows immediately from a universal

¹sub·al·ter·nate \sə-ˈbȯl-tər-nət\ *adj* (15c) **:** SUBALTERN 1 — **sub·al·ter·nate·ly** *adv*

²subalternate *n* (1826) **:** SUBALTERN 2

sub·al·ter·na·tion \sə-ˌbȯl-tər-ˈnā-shən\ *n* (1650) **:** the relation of a subaltern to a superaltern

sub·ant·arc·tic \ˌsəb-ant-ˈärk-tik, -ˈärt-ik\ *adj* (1897) **:** of, relating to, characteristic of, or being a region just outside the antarctic circle

sub·api·cal \ˌsəb-ˈā-pi-kəl, ˈsəb- *also* -ˈap-i-\ *adj* (1846) **:** situated below or near an apex

sub·aquat·ic \ˌsəb-ə-ˈkwät-ik, -ˈkwat-\ *adj* [ISV] (1844) **:** somewhat aquatic ⟨a marginal ~ flora⟩

sub·aque·ous \ˌsəb-ˈā-kwē-əs, ˈsəb-, -ˈak-wē-\ *adj* (ca. 1677) **:** existing, formed, or taking place in or under water

sub·arach·noid \ˌsəb-ə-ˈrak-ˌnȯid\ *also* **sub·arach·noid·al** \-rak-ˈnȯid-ᵊl\ *adj* (1839) **:** of, relating to, or situated under the arachnoid membrane

sub·arc·tic \ˌsəb-ˈärk-tik, ˈsəb-ˈärt-ik\ *adj* [ISV] (1854) **:** of, relating to, characteristic of, or being regions immediately outside of the arctic circle or regions similar to these in climate or conditions of life — **subarctic** *n*

sub·as·sem·bly \ˌsəb-ə-ˈsem-blē\ *n* (1926) **:** an assembled unit designed to be incorporated with other units in a finished product

sub·at·mo·spher·ic \ˌsəb-ˌat-mə-ˈsfi(ə)r-ik, ˈsəb-, -ˈsfer-\ *adj* (1941) **:** less or lower than that of the atmosphere ⟨~ temperatures⟩

sub·atom·ic \ˌsəb-ə-ˈtäm-ik\ *adj* (1903) **:** of or relating to the inside of the atom or to particles smaller than atoms

sub·au·di·tion \ˌsəb-ȯ-ˈdish-ən\ *n* [LL *subaudition-, subauditio,* fr. *subauditus,* pp. of *subaudire* to understand, fr. L *sub-* + *audire* to hear — more at AUDIBLE] (1798) **1 :** the act of understanding or supplying something not expressed **2 :** something that is understood or supplied in comprehending a text

sub·base \ˈsəb-ˌbās\ *n* (1826) **:** underlying support placed below what is normally construed as a base: as **a :** the lowest member horizontally of an architectural base or of a baseboard or pedestal **b :** pervious fill (as crushed stone) placed under a roadbed

sub·bi·tu·mi·nous \ˌsəb-bə-ˈt(y)ü-mə-nəs, -bī-\ *adj* (ca. 1908) **:** of, relating to, or being coal of lower rank than bituminous coal but higher than lignite

sub·cab·i·net \ˌsəb-ˈkab-(ə-)nət, ˈsəb-\ *adj* (1954) **:** of, relating to, or being a high administrative position in the U.S. government that ranks below the cabinet level

sub·cap·su·lar \ˌsəb-ˈkap-sə-lər, ˈsəb-\ *adj* (1889) **:** situated or occurring beneath or within a capsule ⟨~ cataracts⟩

sub·ce·les·tial \ˌsəb-sə-ˈles(h)-chəl\ *adj* (1561) **:** situated beneath the heavens; *specif* **:** MUNDANE

sub·cel·lu·lar \ˌsəb-ˈsel-yə-lər, ˈsəb-\ *adj* (1948) **:** of less than cellular scope or level of organization ⟨~ particles⟩ ⟨~ studies⟩

sub·cen·ter \ˌsəb-ˌsent-ər\ *n* (ca. 1925) **:** a secondary center; *esp* **:** a center (as for shopping) located outside the main business area of a city

sub·cen·tral \ˌsəb-ˈsen-trəl, ˈsəb-\ *adj* (1822) **1 :** nearly but not quite central **2 :** located under a center — **sub·cen·tral·ly** \-trə-lē\ *adv*

sub·chas·er \ˈsəb-ˌchā-sər\ *n* (1919) **:** SUBMARINE CHASER

sub·class \ˈsəb-ˌklas\ *n* (1819) **:** a primary division of a class: as **a :** a biological taxonomic category below a class and above an order **b :** SUBSET

sub·clas·si·fi·ca·tion \ˌsəb-ˌklas-ə-fə-ˈkā-shən\ *n* (1894) **1 :** a primary division of a classification **2 :** arrangement into or assignment to subclassifications — **sub·clas·si·fy** \-ˈklas-ə-ˌfī\ *vt*

¹sub·cla·vi·an \ˌsəb-ˈklā-vē-ən\ *adj* [NL *subclavius,* fr. *sub-* + *clavicula* clavicle] (1646) **1 :** of or relating to a subclavian part (as an artery, vein, or nerve) **2 :** located under the clavicle

²subclavian *n* (1719) **:** a subclavian part (as an artery, vein, or nerve)

subclavian artery *n* (1688) **:** the proximal part of the main artery of the arm or forelimb

subclavian vein *n* (1770) **:** the proximal part of the main vein of the arm or forelimb

sub·cli·max \ˌsəb-ˈklī-ˌmaks, ˈsəb-\ *n* (1935) **:** a stage or community in an ecological succession immediately preceding a climax; *esp* **:** one held in relative stability throughout edaphic or biotic influences or by fire

sub·clin·i·cal \-ˈklin-i-kəl\ *adj* (ca. 1935) **:** not detectable or producing effects that are not detectable by the usual clinical tests ⟨a ~ infection⟩ ⟨~ cancer⟩ — **sub·clin·i·cal·ly** \-k(ə-)lē\ *adv*

sub·com·mit·tee \ˈsəb-kə-ˌmit-ē, ˌsəb-kə-ˈ\ *n* (1607) **:** a subdivision of a committee usu. organized for a specific purpose

sub·com·mu·ni·ty \ˌsəb-kə-ˈmyü-nət-ē\ *n* (1966) **:** a distinct grouping within a community

sub·com·pact \ˈsəb-ˈkäm-ˌpakt\ *n* (1967) **:** an automobile smaller than a compact

¹sub·con·scious \ˌsəb-ˈkän-chəs, ˈsəb-\ *adj* (1832) **:** existing in the mind but not immediately available to consciousness ⟨his ~ motive⟩ — **sub·con·scious·ly** *adv* — **sub·con·scious·ness** *n*

²subconscious *n* (1923) **:** the mental activities just below the threshold of consciousness

sub·con·ti·nent \ˈsəb-ˈkänt-ᵊn-ənt, -ˈkänt-nənt, -ˌkänt-\ *n* (1863) **1 :** a landmass (as Greenland) of great size but smaller than any of the usu. recognized continents **2 :** a vast subdivision of a continent — **sub·con·ti·nen·tal** \ˌsəb-ˌkänt-ᵊn-ˈent-ᵊl\ *adj*

¹sub·con·tract \ˈsəb-ˈkän-ˌtrakt, -ˌkän-\ *n* (1817) **:** a contract between a party to an original contract and a third party; *esp* **:** one to provide all or a specified part of the work or materials required in the original contract

²sub·con·tract \ˌsəb-ˈkän-ˌtrakt, ˈsəb-; ˌsəb-kən-ˈ\ *vi* (ca. 1842) **:** to let out or undertake work under a subcontract ~ *vt* **1 :** to engage a third party to perform under a subcontract all or part of (work included in an original contract) **2 :** to undertake (work) under a subcontract

sub·con·trac·tor \ˌsəb-ˈkän-ˌtrak-tər, ˈsəb-; ˌsəb-kən-ˈ\ *n* (1842) **:** an individual or business firm contracting to perform part or all of another's contract

sub·con·tra·oc·tave \ˌsəb-ˌkän-trə-ˈäk-tiv, ˈsəb-, -təv, -ˌtāv\ *n* (ca. 1902) **:** the musical octave that begins on the fourth C below middle C — see PITCH illustration

sub·con·tra·ri·ety \ˌsəb-ˌkän-trə-ˈrī-ət-ē\ *n* (1697) **:** the relation existing between subcontrary propositions in logic

sub·con·trary \ˌsəb-ˈkän-ˌtrer-ē, ˈsəb-\ *n* (1685) **:** a proposition so related to another that though both may be true they cannot both be false — **subcontrary** *adj*

sub·cool \-ˈkül\ *vt* (1916) **:** SUPERCOOL

sub·cor·ti·cal \-ˈkȯrt-i-kəl\ *adj* (1887) **:** of, relating to, involving, or being nerve centers below the cerebral cortex ⟨~ lesions⟩

sub·crit·i·cal \-ˈkrit-i-kəl\ *adj* (ca. 1944) **1 :** less or lower than critical in respect to a specified factor **2 a :** of insufficient size to sustain a chain reaction ⟨a ~ mass of fissionable material⟩ **b :** designed for use with fissionable material of subcritical mass ⟨a ~ reactor⟩

sub·crust·al \-ˈkrəs-tᵊl\ *adj* (1897) **:** situated or occurring below a crust and esp. the crust of the earth

sub·cul·ture \ˈsəb-ˌkəl-chər\ *n* (1899) **1 a :** a culture (as of bacteria) derived from another culture **b :** an act or instance of producing a subculture **2 :** an ethnic, regional, economic, or social group exhibiting characteristic patterns of behavior sufficient to distinguish it from others within an embracing culture or society ⟨a criminal ~⟩ — **sub·cul·tur·al** \-ˈkəlch-(ə-)rəl\ *adj* — **sub·cul·tur·al·ly** \-ē\ *adv* — **subculture** *vt*

sub·cu·ta·ne·ous \ˌsəb-kyu̇-ˈtā-nē-əs\ *adj* [LL *subcutaneus,* fr. L *sub-* + *cutis* skin — more at HIDE] (1651) **:** being, living, used, or made under the skin ⟨~ parasites⟩ — **sub·cu·ta·ne·ous·ly** *adv*

sub·cu·tis \ˌsəb-ˈkyüt-əs, ˈsəb-\ *n* [NL, fr. LL, beneath the skin, fr. L *sub-* + *cutis*] (ca. 1900) **:** the deeper part of the dermis

sub·dea·con \-ˈdē-kən\ *n* [ME *subdecon,* fr. LL *subdiaconus,* fr. L *sub-* + LL *diaconus* deacon — more at DEACON] (14c) **:** a cleric ranking below a deacon: as **a :** a cleric in the lowest of the former major orders of the Roman Catholic Church **b :** an Eastern Orthodox or Armenian cleric in minor orders **c :** a clergyman performing the liturgical duties of a subdeacon

sub·deb \ˈsəb-ˌdeb\ *n* (1920) **:** SUBDEBUTANTE

sub·deb·u·tante \ˌsəb-ˈdeb-yu̇-ˌtänt, ˈsəb-\ *n* (1919) **:** a young girl who is about to become a debutante; *broadly* **:** a girl in her middle teens

sub·di·vide \ˌsəb-də-ˈvīd, ˈsəb-də-ˌ\ *vb* [ME *subdividen,* fr. LL *subdividere,* fr. L *sub-* + *dividere* to divide] *vt* (15c) **1 :** to divide the parts of into more parts **2 :** to divide into several parts; *esp* **:** to divide (a tract of land) into building lots ~ *vi* **:** to separate or become separated into subdivisions — **sub·di·vid·able** \-ˈvīd-ə-bəl, -ˌvīd-\ *adj* — **sub·di·vid·er** *n* — **sub·di·vi·sion** \-ˈvizh-ən, -ˌvizh-\ *n*

sub·dom·i·nant \ˌsəb-ˈdäm(-ə)-nənt, ˈsəb-\ *n* (1793) **:** something dominant to an inferior or partial degree: as **a :** the fourth tone of a diatonic scale **b :** an ecologically important life form subordinate in influence to the dominants of a community — **subdominant** *adj*

sub·duc·tion \(ˌ)səb-ˈdək-shən\ *n* [LL *subduction-, subductio* withdrawal, fr. L *subductus,* pp. of *subducere* to withdraw, fr. *sub-* + *ducere* to draw — more at TOW] (1970) **:** the action or process of the edge of one crustal plate descending below the edge of another — **sub·duct** \(ˌ)səb-ˈdəkt\ *vb*

sub·due \səb-ˈd(y)ü\ *vt* **sub·dued; sub·du·ing** [ME *sodewen, subduen* (influenced in form and meaning by L *subdere* to subject), fr. MF *soduire* to seduce (influenced in meaning by L *seducere* to seduce), fr. L *subducere*] (14c) **1 :** to conquer and bring into subjection **:** VANQUISH **2 :** to bring under control esp. by an exertion of the will **:** CURB ⟨*subdued* my foolish fears⟩ **3 :** to bring under cultivation **4 :** to reduce the intensity or degree of **:** tone down *syn* see CONQUER — **sub·du·er** *n*

sub·dued \-ˈd(y)üd\ *adj* (1604) **:** lacking in force, intensity, or strength ⟨~ colors⟩ — **sub·dued·ly** \-ˈd(y)ü(-ə)d-lē\ *adv*

sub·dur·al \ˌsəb-ˈd(y)u̇r-əl, ˈsəb-ˌ\ *adj* [*sub-* + *dura* mater + *-al*] (1875) **:** situated or occurring beneath the dura mater or between the dura mater and the arachnoid membrane ⟨~ space⟩ ⟨~ hematomas⟩

sub·ed·it \ˌsəb-ˈed-ət, ˈsəb-\ *vt* [back-formation fr. *subeditor*] *chiefly Brit* (1862) **:** to read and edit as a copy editor

sub·ed·i·tor \-ˈed-ət-ər\ *n, chiefly Brit* (1835) **:** COPY EDITOR — **sub·ed·i·to·ri·al** \ˌsəb-ˌed-ə-ˈtōr-ē-əl, -ˈtȯr-\ *adj*

sub·em·ployed \ˌsəb-im-ˈplȯid\ *adj* (1967) **:** UNDEREMPLOYED

sub·em·ploy·ment \-ˈplȯi-mənt\ *n* (1967) **:** a condition of inadequate employment in a labor force including unemployment and underemployment

sub·en·try \ˈsəb-ˌen-trē\ *n* (ca. 1891) **:** an entry (as in a catalog or an account) made under a more general entry

sub·epi·der·mal \ˌsəb-ˌep-ə-ˈdər-məl\ *adj* (1853) **:** lying beneath or constituting the innermost part of the epidermis

su·ber·in \ˈsü-bə-rən\ *n* [F *subérine,* fr. L *suber* cork tree, cork] (1830) **:** a complex fatty substance that is the basis of cork

su·ber·iza·tion \ˌsü-bə-rə-ˈzā-shən\ *n* (1882) **:** conversion of the cell walls into corky tissue by infiltration with suberin — **su·ber·ized** \ˈsü-bə-ˌrīzd\ *adj*

sub·fam·i·ly \ˈsəb-ˌfam-(ə-)lē\ *n* [ISV] (1833) **1 :** a taxonomic category next below a family **2 :** a subgroup of languages within a language family

sub·field \-ˌfēld\ *n* (ca. 1949) **:** a subset of a mathematical field that is itself a field

sub·fix \-ˌfiks\ *n* [*sub-* + *-fix* (as in *prefix*)] (ca. 1894) **:** a subscript sign, letter, or character

sub·fos·sil \-ˌfäs-əl\ *adj* [ISV] (1832) **:** of less than typical fossil age but partially fossilized — **subfossil** *n*

sub·freez·ing \-ˈfrē-ziŋ\ *adj* (1949) **:** being or marked by temperature below the freezing point (as of water) ⟨~ weather⟩

sub·fusc \(ˌ)səb-ˈfəsk, ˈsəb-ˌ\ *adj* [L *subfuscus* brownish, dusky, fr. *sub-* + *fuscus* dark brown — more at DUSK] (1710) : DRAB, SOMBER
sub·ge·nus \ˈsəb-ˌjē-nəs\ *n* [NL] (1813) : a category in biological taxonomy below a genus and above a species
sub·gla·cial \ˌsəb-ˈglā-shəl, ˈsəb-\ *adj* (1820) : of or relating to the bottom of a glacier or the area immediately underlying a glacier — **sub·gla·cial·ly** \-shə-lē\ *adv*
sub·grade \ˈsəb-ˌgrād\ *n* (ca. 1898) : a surface of earth or rock leveled off to receive a foundation (as of a road)
sub·graph \ˈsəb-ˌgraf\ *n* (1963) : a graph all of whose points and lines are contained in a larger graph
sub·group \-ˌgrüp\ *n* (ca. 1879) **1** : a subordinate group whose members usu. share some common differential quality **2** : a subset of a mathematical group that is itself a group
sub·gum \ˈsəb-ˈgəm\ *n* [Chin (Cant) *shāp kám,* lit., mixture] (1938) : a dish of Chinese origin prepared with a mixture of vegetables (as peppers, water chestnuts, and mushrooms)
sub·head \-ˌhed\ *n* (1673) **1** : a heading of a subdivision (as in an outline) **2** : a subordinate caption, title, or headline
sub·head·ing \-ˌhed-iŋ\ *n* (1889) : SUBHEAD
[1]**sub·hu·man** \ˌsəb-ˈhyü-mən, ˈsəb-, -ˈyü-\ *adj* (1793) : less than human: as **a** : failing to attain the level (as of morality or intelligence) associated with normal human beings **b** : unsuitable to or unfit for human beings ⟨~ living conditions⟩ **c** : of or relating to an infrahuman taxonomic group ⟨the ~ primates⟩
[2]**subhuman** *n* (1937) : a subhuman individual
sub·in·dex \ˌsəb-ˈin-ˌdeks, ˈsəb-\ *n* (1923) : an index to a division of a main classification
sub·in·feu·da·tion \ˌsəb-ˌin-fyü-ˈdā-shən\ *n* [*sub-* + *infeudation* (enfeoffment)] (ca. 1730) : the subdivision of a feudal estate by a vassal who in turn becomes feudal lord over his tenants — **sub·in·feu·date** *vt*
sub·in·ter·val \ˌsəb-ˈint-ər-vəl, ˈsəb-\ *n* (1927) : an interval that is a subdivision or a subset of an interval
sub·ir·ri·ga·tion \ˌsəb-ˌir-ə-ˈgā-shən\ *n* (1880) : irrigation below the surface (as by a periodic rise of the water table or by a system of underground porous pipes) — **sub·ir·ri·gate** \ˌsəb-ˈir-ə-ˌgāt, ˈsəb-\ *vt*
su·bi·to \ˈsü-bi-ˌtō\ *adv* [It, fr. L, suddenly, fr. *subitus* sudden — more at SUDDEN] (ca. 1724) : IMMEDIATELY, SUDDENLY — used as a direction in music
sub·ja·cen·cy \ˌsəb-ˈjās-ᵊn-sē\ *n* (ca. 1891) : the quality or state of being subjacent
sub·ja·cent \-ᵊnt\ *adj* [L *subjacent-, subjacens,* prp. of *subjacēre* to lie under, fr. *sub-* + *jacēre* to lie — more at ADJACENT] (1597) : lying under or below; *also* : lower than though not directly below ⟨hills and ~ valleys⟩ — **sub·ja·cent·ly** *adv*
[1]**sub·ject** \ˈsəb-jikt, -(ˌ)jekt\ *n* [ME, fr. MF, fr. L *subjectus* one under authority & *subjectum* subject of a proposition, fr. masc. & neut. respectively of *subjectus,* pp. of *subicere* to subject, lit., to throw under, fr. *sub-* + *jacere* to throw — more at JET] (14c) **1** : one that is placed under authority or control: as **a** : VASSAL **b** (1) : one subject to a monarch and governed by his law (2) : one who lives in the territory of, enjoys the protection of, and owes allegiance to a sovereign power or state **2 a** : that of which a quality, attribute, or relation may be affirmed or in which it may inhere **b** : SUBSTRATUM; *esp* : material or essential substance **c** : the mind, ego, or agent of whatever sort that sustains or assumes the form of thought or consciousness **3 a** : a department of knowledge or learning **b** : MOTIVE, CAUSE **c** (1) : one that is acted on ⟨the helpless ~ of their cruelty⟩ (2) : an individual whose reactions or responses are studied (3) : a dead body for anatomical study and dissection **d** (1) : something concerning which something is said or done (2) : something represented or indicated in a work of art **e** (1) : the term of a logical proposition that denotes the entity of which something is affirmed or denied; *also* : the entity denoted (2) : a word or word group denoting that of which something is predicated **f** : the principal melodic phrase on which a musical composition or movement is based ***syn*** see CITIZEN — **sub·ject·less** \-ləs\ *adj*
[2]**subject** *adj* (14c) **1** : owing obedience or allegiance to the power or dominion of another **2 a** : suffering a particular liability or exposure ⟨~ to temptation⟩ **b** : having a tendency or inclination : PRONE ⟨~ to colds⟩ **3** : contingent on or under the influence of some later action ⟨the plan is ~ to discussion⟩
[3]**sub·ject** \səb-ˈjekt, ˈsəb-ˌjekt\ *vt* (14c) **1 a** : to bring under control or dominion : SUBJUGATE **b** : to make (as oneself) amenable to the discipline and control of a superior **2** : to make liable : PREDISPOSE **3** : to cause or force to undergo or endure (something unpleasant, inconvenient, or trying) ⟨was ~*ed* to constant verbal abuse⟩ — **sub·jec·tion** \səb-ˈjek-shən\ *n*
[1]**sub·jec·tive** \(ˌ)səb-ˈjek-tiv\ *adj* (15c) **1** : of, relating to, or constituting a subject: as **a** *obs* : of, relating to, or characteristic of one that is a subject esp. in lack of freedom of action or in submissiveness **b** : being or relating to a grammatical subject; *esp* : NOMINATIVE **2** : of or relating to the essential being of that which has substance, qualities, attributes, or relations **3 a** : relating to or determined by the mind as the subject of experience ⟨~ reality⟩ **b** : characteristic of or belonging to reality as perceived rather than as independent of mind : PHENOMENAL — compare OBJECTIVE 1b **c** : relating to or being experience or knowledge as conditioned by personal mental characteristics or states **4 a** : peculiar to a particular individual : PERSONAL ⟨~ judgments⟩ **b** : arising from conditions within the brain or sense organs and not directly caused by external stimuli ⟨~ sensations⟩ **c** : arising out of or identified by means of one's perception of one's own states and processes ⟨a ~ symptom of disease⟩ — compare OBJECTIVE 1c **5** : lacking in reality or substance : ILLUSORY — **sub·jec·tive·ly** *adv* — **sub·jec·tive·ness** *n* — **sub·jec·tiv·i·ty** \-ˌjek-ˈtiv-ət-ē\ *n*
[2]**subjective** *n* (1817) : something that is subjective; *also* : NOMINATIVE
subjective complement *n* (1923) : a grammatical complement relating to the subject of an intransitive verb ⟨in "he had fallen sick" *sick* is a *subjective complement*⟩
sub·jec·tiv·ism \(ˌ)səb-ˈjek-tiv-ˌiz-əm\ *n* (ca. 1857) **1 a** : a theory that limits knowledge to subjective experience **b** : a theory that stresses the subjective elements in experience **2 a** : a doctrine that the supreme good is the realization of a subjective experience or feeling (as pleasure) **b** : a doctrine that individual feeling or apprehension is the ultimate criterion of the good and the right — **sub·jec·tiv·ist** \-əst\ *n* — **sub·jec·tiv·is·tic** \-ˌjek-tiv-ˈis-tik\ *adj*
sub·jec·tiv·ize \-tiv-ˌīz\ *vt* **-ized; -iz·ing** (1868) : to make subjective — **sub·jec·tiv·iza·tion** \-ˌjek-tiv-ə-ˈzā-shən\ *n*
subject matter *n* (1598) : matter presented for consideration in discussion, thought, or study
sub·join \(ˌ)səb-ˈjȯin\ *vt* [MF *subjoindre,* fr. L *subjungere* to join beneath, add, fr. *sub-* + *jungere* to join — more at YOKE] (1573) : ANNEX, APPEND ⟨~*ed* a statement of expenses to his report⟩
sub ju·di·ce \(ˈ)su̇b-ˈyüd-i-ˌkā, ˈsəb-ˈjüd-ə-(ˌ)sē\ *adv* [L] (1613) : before a judge or court : not yet judicially decided
sub·ju·gate \ˈsəb-ji-ˌgāt\ *vt* **-gat·ed; -gat·ing** [ME *subjugaten,* fr. L *subjugatus,* pp. of *subjugare,* lit., to bring under the yoke, fr. *sub-* + *jugum* yoke — more at YOKE] (15c) **1** : to bring under control and governance as a subject : CONQUER **2** : to make submissive : SUBDUE — **sub·ju·ga·tion** \ˌsəb-ji-ˈgā-shən\ *n* — **sub·ju·ga·tor** \ˈsəb-ji-ˌgāt-ər\ *n*
sub·junc·tion \(ˌ)səb-ˈjəŋ(k)-shən\ *n* (1633) **1** : an act of subjoining or the state of being subjoined **2** : something subjoined
[1]**sub·junc·tive** \səb-ˈjəŋ(k)-tiv\ *adj* [LL *subjunctivus,* fr. L *subjunctus,* pp. of *subjungere* to join beneath, subordinate] (1530) : of, relating to, or constituting a verb form or set of verb forms that represents a denoted act or state not as fact but as contingent or possible or viewed emotionally (as with doubt or desire) ⟨the ~ mood⟩
[2]**subjunctive** *n* (1622) **1** : the subjunctive mood of a language **2** : a form of verb or verbal in the subjective mood
sub·king·dom \ˈsəb-ˌkiŋ-dəm\ *n* (1825) : a primary division of a taxonomic kingdom
sub·late \ˌsəb-ˈlāt\ *vt* **sub·lat·ed; sub·lat·ing** [L *sublatus* (pp. of *tollere* to take away, lift up), fr. *sub-* up + *latus,* pp. of *ferre* to carry — more at SUB-, TOLERATE, BEAR] (1838) **1** : NEGATE, DENY **2** : to negate or eliminate (as an element in a dialectic process) but preserve as a partial element in a synthesis — **sub·la·tion** \-ˈlā-shən\ *n*
[1]**sub·lease** \ˈsəb-ˈlēs, -ˌlēs\ *n* (1826) : a lease by a tenant or lessee of part or all of leased premises to another person but with the original tenant retaining some right or interest under the original lease
[2]**sublease** *vt* (1828) : to make or obtain a sublease of
[1]**sub·let** \ˈsəb-ˈlet\ *vb* **-let; -let·ting** *vt* (1766) **1** : SUBLEASE **2** : SUBCONTRACT 1 ~ *vi* : to lease or rent all or part of a leased or rented property
[2]**sub·let** \-ˌlet\ *n* (ca. 1906) : property and esp. housing obtained by or available through a sublease
sub·le·thal \ˌsəb-ˈlē-thəl, ˈsəb-\ *adj* (ca. 1895) : less than but usu. only slightly less than lethal ⟨a ~ dose⟩ — **sub·le·thal·ly** \-thə-lē\ *adv*
sub·lieu·ten·ant \ˌsəb-lü-ˈten-ənt, *Brit* -le(f)-ˈten-\ *n* (1804) : a commissioned officer in the British navy ranking immediately below lieutenant
[1]**sub·li·mate** \ˈsəb-lə-ˌmāt, -mət\ *n* [ML *sublimatus,* pp. of *sublimare*] (ca. 1543) **1** : MERCURIC CHLORIDE **2** : a chemical product obtained by sublimation
[2]**sub·li·mate** \ˈsəb-lə-ˌmāt\ *vt* **-mat·ed; -mat·ing** (ca. 1591) **1 a** : SUBLIME 1 **b** *archaic* : to improve or refine as if by subliming **2** : to divert the expression of (an instinctual desire or impulse) from its primitive form to one that is considered more socially or culturally acceptable — **sub·li·ma·tion** \ˌsəb-lə-ˈmā-shən\ *n*
[1]**sub·lime** \sə-ˈblīm\ *vb* **sub·limed; sub·lim·ing** [ME *sublimen,* fr. MF *sublimer,* fr. ML *sublimare* to refine, sublime, fr. L, to elevate, fr. *sublimis*] *vt* (14c) **1** : to cause to pass directly from the solid to the vapor state and condense back to solid form **2** [F *sublimer,* fr. L *sublimare*] **a** (1) : to elevate or exalt esp. in dignity or honor (2) : to render finer (as in purity or excellence) **b** : to convert (something inferior) into something of higher worth ~ *vi* : to pass directly from the solid to the vapor state — **sub·lim·able** \-ˈblī-mə-bəl\ *adj* — **sub·lim·er** *n*
[2]**sublime** *adj* [L *sublimis,* lit., to or in a high position, fr. *sub* under, up to + *limen* threshold, lintel — more at UP, LIMB] (1586) **1 a** : lofty, grand, or exalted in thought, expression, or manner **b** : of outstanding spiritual, intellectual, or moral worth **c** : tending to inspire awe usu. because of elevated quality (as of beauty, nobility, or grandeur) or transcendent excellence **2 a** *archaic* : high in place **b** *obs* : lofty of mien : HAUGHTY **c** *cap* : SUPREME — used in a style of address **d** : COMPLETE, UTTER ⟨~ ignorance⟩ ***syn*** see SPLENDID — **sub·lime·ly** *adv* — **sub·lime·ness** *n*
sub·lim·i·nal \(ˌ)səb-ˈlim-ən-ᵊl, ˈsəb-\ *adj* [*sub-* + L *limin-, limen* threshold] (1886) **1** : inadequate to produce a sensation or a perception **2** : existing or functioning below the threshold of conscious awareness ⟨the ~ mind⟩ ⟨~ advertising⟩ — **sub·lim·i·nal·ly** \-ē\ *adv*
sub·lim·i·ty \sə-ˈblim-ət-ē\ *n, pl* **-ties** (1526) **1** : the quality or state of being sublime **2** : something sublime or exalted
sub·line \ˈsəb-ˌlīn\ *n* (1942) : an inbred line within a strain
sub·lin·gual \ˌsəb-ˈliŋ-g(yə-)wəl, ˈsəb-\ *adj* [NL *sublingualis,* fr. L *sub-* + *lingua* tongue — more at TONGUE] (1661) : situated or administered under the tongue ⟨~ tablets⟩ ⟨~ glands⟩
sub·lit·er·ary \-ˈlit-ə-ˌrer-ē\ *adj* (1936) : relating to or being subliterature
sub·lit·er·ate \ˌsəb-ˈlit-ə-rət, ˈsəb-, -ˈli-trət\ *adj* (1949) : less than completely literate ⟨the popular narrative art in the ~ culture will be TV, movies, comic books —Herbert Kubly⟩
sub·lit·er·a·ture \(ˈ)səb-ˈlit-ə-rə-ˌchu̇(ə)r, -ˈli-trə-ˌchu̇(ə)r, -ˈlit-ə(r)-ˌchu̇(ə)r, -chər, -ˌt(y)u̇(ə)r\ *n* (1952) : popular writing (as mystery or adventure stories) considered inferior to standard literature
[1]**sub·lit·to·ral** \(ˈ)səb-ˈlit-ə-rəl; ˌsəb-ˌlit-ə-ˈral, -ˈräl\ *adj* (1846) **1** : situated, occurring, or formed on the aquatic side of a shoreline or littoral zone **2** : constituting the sublittoral
[2]**sublittoral** *n* (ca. 1935) : the deeper part of the littoral portion of a body of water: **a** : the region in a lake between the deepest-growing rooted vegetation and the part of the lake below the thermocline **b** : the region in an ocean between the lowest point exposed by a low-low tide and the margin of the continental shelf
sub·lu·na·ry \ˌsəb-ˈlü-nə-rē, ˈsəb-; ˈsəb-lu̇-ˌner-ē\ *also* **sub·lu·nar** \ˌsəb-ˈlü-nər, ˈsəb- *also* -ˌnär\ *adj* [modif. of LL *sublunaris,* fr. L *sub-* + *luna* moon — more at LUNAR] (1592) : of, relating to, or characteristic of the terrestrial world ⟨dull ~ lovers —John Donne⟩
sub·lux·a·tion \ˌsəb-ˌlək-ˈsā-shən\ *n* (ca. 1688) : partial dislocation (as of one of the bones in a joint)
sub·ma·chine gun \ˌsəb-mə-ˈshēn-ˌgən\ *n* (1920) : a portable automatic firearm that uses pistol-type ammunition and is fired from the shoulder or hip
sub·man·dib·u·lar \ˌsəb-man-ˈdib-yə-lər\ *adj* (1875) : SUBMAXILLARY

sub·mar·gin·al \ˌsəb-ˈmär-jnəl, ˈsəb-, -jən-ᵊl\ *adj* (1829) **1 :** adjacent to a margin or a marginal part or structure ⟨~ spots on an insect wing⟩ **2 :** falling below a necessary minimum ⟨~ economic conditions⟩ — **sub·mar·gin·al·ly** \-ē\ *adv*

1**sub·ma·rine** \ˈsəb-mə-ˌrēn, ˌsəb-mə-ˈ\ *adj* (1648) **:** UNDERWATER; *esp* **:** UNDERSEA ⟨~ plants⟩ ⟨~ minerals⟩

2**submarine** *n* (1703) **1 :** something (as a vessel or explosive mine) that functions or operates underwater; *specif* **:** a warship that can operate on the surface or underwater **2 :** a large sandwich on a long split roll with any of a variety of fillings (as meatballs or cold cuts, cheese, lettuce, and tomato) — called also *grinder, hero, hoagie, Italian sandwich, poor boy, sub, torpedo*

3**submarine** *vb* **-rined; -rin·ing** *vt* (1914) **:** to attack or sink by means of a submarine ~ *vi* **:** to dive or slide under something

submarine chaser *n* (ca. 1920) **:** a highly maneuverable patrol or escort vessel fitted to attack submarines

sub·ma·ri·ner \ˌsəb-ˈmar-ə-nər, -mə-ˈrē-nər; ˈsəb-mə-ˌrē-nər\ *n* (1914) **:** a member of a submarine crew

sub·max·il·la \ˌsəb-mak-ˈsil-ə\ *n, pl* **-lae** \-(ˌ)ē, -ˌī\ *also* **-las** [NL] (ca. 1900) **:** the lower jaw or inferior maxillary bone; *specif* **:** the human mandible

1**sub·max·il·lary** \ˌsəb-ˈmak-sə-ˌler-ē, ˈsəb-, *chiefly Brit* ˌsəb-mak-ˈsil-ə-rē\ *adj* (1787) **1 :** of, relating to, or situated below the lower jaw **2 :** of, relating to, or associated with the submaxillary salivary gland of either side

2**submaxillary** *n, pl* **-lar·ies** (ca. 1900) **:** a submaxillary part (as an artery or bone)

sub·me·di·ant \ˌsəb-ˈmēd-ē-ənt, ˈsəb-\ *n* (1806) **:** the sixth tone of a diatonic scale midway between the subdominant and the upper tonic

sub·merge \səb-ˈmərj\ *vb* **sub·merged; sub·merg·ing** [L *submergere,* fr. *sub-* + *mergere* to plunge — more at MERGE] *vt* (ca. 1611) **1 :** to put under water **2 :** to cover or overflow with water **3 :** to make obscure or subordinate **:** SUPPRESS ⟨personal lives *submerged* by professional responsibilities⟩ ~ *vi* **:** to go under water — **sub·mer·gence** \-ˈmər-jən(t)s\ *n* — **sub·merg·ible** \-ˈmər-jə-bəl\ *adj*

sub·merged *adj* (1799) **1 :** covered with water **2 :** SUBMERSED b **3 :** sunk in poverty and misery ⟨the ~ masses⟩ ⟨the ~ tenth of the population⟩ **4 :** HIDDEN, SUPPRESSED ⟨~ emotions⟩

sub·merse \səb-ˈmərs\ *vt* **sub·mersed; sub·mers·ing** [L *submersus,* pp. of *submergere*] (1837) **:** SUBMERGE — **sub·mer·sion** \-ˈmər-zhən, -shən\ *n*

sub·mersed *adj* (ca. 1727) **:** SUBMERGED: as **a :** covered with water **b :** growing or adapted to grow underwater ⟨~ weeds⟩

1**sub·mers·ible** \səb-ˈmər-sə-bəl\ *adj* (1866) **:** capable of being submerged

2**submersible** *n* (1900) **:** something that is submersible; *esp* **:** SUBMARINE

sub·meta·cen·tric \ˌsəb-ˌmet-ə-ˈsen-trik\ *adj, of a chromosome* (1962) **:** having arms of unequal length because the centromere is closer to one end than the other — **submetacentric** *n*

sub·mi·cro·gram \ˌsəb-ˈmī-krə-ˌgram, ˈsəb-\ *adj* (1946) **:** relating to or having a mass of less than one microgram ⟨~ quantities of a chemical⟩

sub·mi·cron \-ˌkrän\ *adj* (ca. 1948) **1 :** being less than a micron in a (specified) measurement and esp. in diameter ⟨a ~ particle⟩ **2 :** having or consisting of submicron particles ⟨a ~ metal powder⟩

sub·mi·cro·scop·ic \ˌsəb-ˌmī-krə-ˈskäp-ik\ *adj* [ISV] (1917) **1 :** too small to be seen in an ordinary light microscope **2 :** of, relating to, or dealing with the very minute ⟨the ~ world⟩ — **sub·mi·cro·scop·i·cal·ly** \-i-k(ə-)lē\ *adv*

sub·mil·li·me·ter \ˌsəb-ˈmil-ə-ˌmēt-ər\ *adj* (1968) **:** being less than a millimeter in diameter or wavelength ⟨a ~ particle⟩ ⟨a ~ radio wave⟩

sub·min·ia·ture \ˌsəb-ˈmin-ē-ə-ˌchü(ə)r, ˈsəb-, -ˈmin-i-ˌchü(ə)r, -ˈmin-yə-, -chər, -ˌt(y)ü(ə)r\ *adj* [ISV] (1948) **:** very small — used esp. of a very compact assembly of electronic equipment

sub·miss \səb-ˈmis\ *adj* [L *submissus,* fr. pp. of *submittere*] *archaic* (1570) **:** SUBMISSIVE, HUMBLE

sub·mis·sion \səb-ˈmish-ən\ *n* [ME, fr. MF, fr. L *submission-, submissio* act of lowering, fr. *submissus,* pp. of *submittere*] (15c) **1 a :** a legal agreement to submit to the decision of arbitrators **b :** an act of submitting something (as for consideration or inspection); *also* **:** something submitted (as a manuscript) **2 :** the condition of being submissive, humble, or compliant **3 :** an act of submitting to the authority or control of another

sub·mis·sive \-ˈmis-iv\ *adj* (1586) **:** submitting to others — **sub·mis·sive·ly** *adv* — **sub·mis·sive·ness** *n*

sub·mit \səb-ˈmit\ *vb* **sub·mit·ted; sub·mit·ting** [ME *submitten,* fr. L *submittere* to lower, submit, fr. *sub-* + *mittere* to send] *vt* (14c) **1 a :** to yield to governance or authority **b :** to subject to a condition, treatment, or operation ⟨the metal was *submitted* to analysis⟩ **2 :** to present or propose to another for review, consideration, or decision ⟨~ a question to the court⟩ ⟨~ a bid on a contract⟩ ⟨~ a report⟩; *also* **:** to deliver formally ⟨*submitted* my resignation⟩ **3 :** to put forward as an opinion or contention ⟨we ~ that the charge is not proved⟩ ~ *vi* **1 a :** to yield oneself to the authority or will of another **:** SURRENDER **b :** to permit oneself to be subjected to something ⟨had to ~ to surgery⟩ **2 :** to defer to or consent to abide by the opinion or authority of another *syn* see YIELD — **sub·mit·tal** \-ˈmit-ᵊl\ *n*

sub·mi·to·chon·dri·al \ˌsəb-ˌmīt-ə-ˈkän-drē-əl\ *adj* (1963) **:** relating to, composed of, or being parts and esp. fragments of mitochondria ⟨~ membranes⟩ ⟨~ particles⟩

sub·mu·co·sa \ˌsəb-myü-ˈkō-zə\ *n* [NL] (1885) **:** a supporting layer of loose connective tissue directly under a mucous membrane — **sub·mu·co·sal** \-zəl\ *adj*

sub·mul·ti·ple \-ˈməl-tə-pəl\ *n* (1758) **:** an exact divisor of a number ⟨8 is a ~ of 72⟩

sub·nor·mal \-ˈnȯr-məl\ *adj* [ISV] (ca. 1890) **1 :** lower or smaller than normal **2 :** having less of something and esp. of intelligence than is normal — **sub·nor·mal·i·ty** \ˌsəb-nȯr-ˈmal-ət-ē\ *n* — **sub·nor·mal·ly** \ˌsəb-ˈnȯr-mə-lē, ˈsəb-\ *adv*

sub·nu·cle·ar \ˌsəb-ˈn(y)ü-klē-ər, ˈsəb-, ÷-kyə-lər\ *adj* (1937) **:** of, relating to, or being a particle smaller than the atomic nucleus

sub·oce·an·ic \ˌsəb-ˌō-shē-ˈan-ik\ *adj* (1858) **:** situated, taking place, or formed beneath the ocean or its bottom ⟨~ oil resources⟩

sub·or·bic·u·lar \ˌsəb-ȯr-ˈbik-yə-lər\ *adj* [ISV] (1753) **:** approximately circular ⟨~ leaves⟩

sub·or·bit·al \ˌsəb-ˈȯr-bət-ᵊl, ˈsəb-\ *adj* (1822) **1 :** situated beneath the eye or the orbit of the eye **2 :** being or involving less than one orbit (as of the earth or moon) ⟨a spacecraft's ~ flight⟩; *also* **:** intended for suborbital flight ⟨a ~ rocket⟩

sub·or·der \ˈsəb-ˌȯrd-ər\ *n* (1826) **:** a subdivision of an order ⟨a soil ~⟩; *esp* **:** a taxonomic category ranking between an order and a family

1**sub·or·di·nate** \sə-ˈbȯrd-ᵊn-ət, -ˈbȯrd-nət\ *adj* [ME *subordinat,* fr. ML *subordinatus,* pp. of *subordinare* to subordinate, fr. L *sub-* + *ordinare* to order — more at ORDAIN] (15c) **1 :** placed in or occupying a lower class, rank, or position **:** INFERIOR **2 :** submissive to or controlled by authority **3 a :** of, relating to, or constituting a clause that functions as a noun, adjective, or adverb **b :** SUBORDINATING — **sub·or·di·nate·ly** *adv* — **sub·or·di·nate·ness** *n*

2**subordinate** *n* (1640) **:** one that is subordinate

3**sub·or·di·nate** \sə-ˈbȯrd-ᵊn-ˌāt\ *vt* **-nat·ed; -nat·ing** [ML *subordinatus,* pp.] (1597) **1 :** to make subject or subservient **2 :** to treat as of less value or importance ⟨stylist . . . whose crystalline prose ~s content to form —Susan Heath⟩ — **sub·or·di·na·tion** \-ˌbȯrd-ᵊn-ˈā-shən\ *n* — **sub·or·di·na·tive** \-ˈbȯrd-ᵊn-ˌāt-iv\ *adj*

sub·or·di·nat·ing \sə-ˈbȯrd-ᵊn-ˌāt-iŋ\ *adj* (1857) **:** introducing and linking a subordinate clause to a main clause ⟨~ conjunction⟩

sub·or·di·na·tor \-ˌāt-ər\ *n* (1959) **:** one that subordinates; *esp* **:** a subordinating conjunction

sub·orn \sə-ˈbȯ(ə)rn\ *vt* [MF *suborner,* fr. L *subornare,* fr. *sub-* secretly + *ornare* to furnish, equip — more at ORNATE] (1534) **1 :** to induce secretly to do an unlawful thing **2 :** to induce to commit perjury; *also* **:** to obtain (perjured testimony) from a witness — **sub·or·na·tion** \ˌsəb-ˌȯr-ˈnā-shən\ *n* — **sub·orn·er** *n*

sub·ox·ide \ˌsəb-ˈäk-ˌsīd\ *n* [ISV] (1801) **:** an oxide containing a relatively small proportion of oxygen

sub·phy·lum \ˈsəb-ˌfī-ləm\ *n* [NL] (ca. 1934) **:** a primary division of a phylum

sub·plot \ˈsəb-ˌplät\ *n* (1916) **1 :** a subordinate plot in fiction or drama **2 :** a subdivision of an experimental plot of land

1**sub·poe·na** \sə-ˈpē-nə, ÷-nē\ *n* [ME *suppena,* fr. L *sub poena* under penalty] (15c) **:** a writ commanding a person designated in it to appear in court under a penalty for failure

2**subpoena** *vt* **-naed; -na·ing** (1640) **:** to serve or summon with a writ of subpoena

subpoena ad tes·ti·fi·can·dum \-ˌad-ˌtes-tə-fi-ˈkan-dəm\ *n* [NL, under penalty to give testimony] (ca. 1765) **:** a writ commanding a person to appear in court to testify as a witness

subpoena du·ces te·cum \-ˌdü-sə-ˈstē-kəm\ *n* [NL, under penalty you shall bring with you] (ca. 1765) **:** a writ commanding a person to produce in court certain designated documents or evidence

sub·po·lar \ˌsəb-ˈpō-lər, ˈsəb-\ *adj* (1826) **:** SUBANTARCTIC, SUBARCTIC

sub·pop·u·la·tion \ˈsəb-ˌpäp-yə-ˈlā-shən\ *n* (1890) **:** an identifiable fraction or subdivision of a population

sub·po·tent \ˌsəb-ˈpōt-ᵊnt, ˈsəb-\ *adj* (ca. 1909) **:** less potent than normal ⟨~ drugs⟩ — **sub·po·ten·cy** \-ˈpōt-ᵊn-sē\ *n*

sub·prin·ci·pal \-ˈprin(t)-s(ə-)pəl, ˈsəb-, -sə-bəl\ *n* (1597) **1 :** an assistant principal (as of a school) **2 :** a secondary or bracing rafter

sub·prob·lem \ˈsəb-ˌpräb-ləm\ *n* (1906) **:** a problem that is contingent on or forms a part of another more inclusive problem

sub·pro·fes·sion·al \ˌsəb-prə-ˈfesh-nəl, -ən-ᵊl\ *adj* (ca. 1941) **:** functioning or qualified to function below the professional level but distinctly above the clerical or labor level and usu. under the supervision of a professionally trained person — **subprofessional** *n*

sub·pro·gram \ˈsəb-ˈprō-ˌgram, -grəm\ *n* (1958) **:** a semi-independent portion of a program (as for a computer)

sub·re·gion \ˈsəb-ˌrē-jən\ *n* [ISV] (1864) **:** a subdivision of a region; *esp* **:** one of the primary divisions of a biogeographic region — **sub·re·gion·al** \-ˌrēj-nəl, -ən-ᵊl\ *adj*

sub·rep·tion \(ˌ)səb-ˈrep-shən\ *n* [LL *subreption-, subreptio,* fr. L, act of stealing, fr. *subreptus,* pp. of *subripere, surripere* to take away secretly — more at SURREPTITIOUS] (1600) **:** a deliberate misrepresentation; *also* **:** an inference drawn from it — **sub·rep·ti·tious** \ˌsəb-ˌrep-ˈtish-əs\ *adj* — **sub·rep·ti·tious·ly** *adv*

sub·ring \ˈsəb-ˌriŋ\ *n* (ca. 1955) **:** a subset of a mathematical ring which is itself a ring

sub·ro·gate \ˈsəb-rō-ˌgāt\ *vt* **-gat·ed; -gat·ing** [L *subrogatus,* pp. of *subrogare, surrogare* — more at SURROGATE] (ca. 1538) **:** to put in the place of another **:** SUBSTITUTE

sub·ro·ga·tion \ˌsəb-rō-ˈgā-shən\ *n* (ca. 1710) **:** the act of subrogating; *specif* **:** the assumption by a third party (as a second creditor or an insurance company) of another's legal right to collect a debt or damages

sub–rosa *adj* (1654) **:** SECRETIVE, PRIVATE

sub ro·sa \ˌsəb-ˈrō-zə\ *adv* [NL, lit., under the rose; fr. the ancient association of the rose with secrecy] (1923) **:** in confidence **:** SECRETLY

sub·rou·tine \ˌsəb-(ˌ)rü-ˈtēn\ *n* [ISV] (1949) **:** a subordinate routine; *esp* **:** a sequence of computer instructions for performing a specified task that can be used repeatedly

sub–Sa·ha·ran \ˌsəb-sə-ˈhar-ən, ˈsəb-, -ˈher-, -ˈhär-\ *adj* (1962) **:** of, relating to, or being the part of Africa south of the Sahara

1**sub·sam·ple** \ˈsəb-ˌsam-pəl, -ˈsam-\ *vt* (ca. 1899) **:** to draw samples from (a previously selected group or population) **:** sample a sample of

2**subsample** *n* (ca. 1899) **:** a sample or specimen obtained by subsampling

sub·sat·el·lite \ˈsəb-ˈsat-ᵊl-ˌīt\ *n* (1957) **:** an object carried into orbit in and subsequently released from a satellite or spacecraft

sub·scribe \səb-ˈskrīb\ *vb* **sub·scribed; sub·scrib·ing** [ME *subscriben,* fr. L *subscribere,* lit., to write beneath, fr. *sub-* + *scribere* to write — more at SCRIBE] *vt* (15c) **1 :** to write (one's name) underneath **:** SIGN **2 a :** to sign (as a document) with one's own hand in token of consent or obligation **b :** to attest by signing **c :** to pledge (a gift or contribution) by writing one's name with the amount **3 :** to assent to **:** SUP-

PORT ~ *vi* **1 :** to sign one's name to a document **2 a :** to give consent or approval to something written by signing ⟨found him unwilling to ~ to the agreement⟩ **b :** to set one's name to a paper in token of promise to give something (as a sum of money); *also* **:** to give something in accordance with such a promise **c :** to enter one's name for a publication or service; *also* **:** to receive a periodical or service regularly on order **d :** to agree to purchase and pay for securities esp. of a new offering ⟨*subscribed* for 1000 shares⟩ **3 :** to feel favorably disposed ⟨I ~ to your sentiments⟩ ***syn*** see ASSENT — **sub·scrib·er** *n*

sub·script \'səb-ˌskript\ *n* [L *subscriptus,* pp. of *subscribere*] (1895) **:** a distinguishing symbol (as a letter or numeral) written immediately below or below and to the right or left of another character — **subscript** *adj*

sub·scrip·tion \səb-'skrip-shən\ *n* [ME *subscripcioun* signature, fr. L *subscription-, subscriptio,* fr. *subscriptus,* pp.] (15c) **1 a :** the act of signing one's name (as in attesting or witnessing a document) **b :** the acceptance (as of ecclesiastical articles of faith) attested by the signing of one's name **2 :** something that is subscribed: as **a :** an autograph signature; *also* **:** a paper to which a signature is attached **b :** a sum subscribed **3 :** an arrangement for providing, receiving, or making use of something of a continuing or periodic nature on a prepayment plan: as **a :** a purchase by prepayment for a certain number of issues (as of a periodical) **b :** application to purchase securities of a new issue **c :** a method of offering or presenting a series of public performances

subscription TV *n* (ca. 1954) **:** pay-TV that broadcasts programs directly over the air to customers provided with a special receiver — called also *subscription television;* compare PAY-CABLE

sub·sec·tion \'səb-ˌsek-shən\ *n* (1621) **1 :** a subdivision or a subordinate division of a section **2 :** a subordinate part or branch

¹sub·se·quence \'səb-sə-ˌkwen(t)s, -si-kwən(t)s\ *n* (1500) **:** the quality or state of being subsequent; *also* **:** a subsequent event

²sub·se·quence \'səb-'sē-kwən(t)s, -ˌsē-, -ˌkwen(t)s\ *n* (ca. 1942) **:** a mathematical sequence that is part of another sequence

sub·se·quent \'səb-si-kwənt, -sə-ˌkwent\ *adj* [ME, fr. L *subsequent-, subsequens,* prp. of *subsequi* to follow close, fr. *sub-* near + *sequi* to follow — more at SUB-, SUE] (15c) **:** following in time, order, or place **:** SUCCEEDING — **subsequent** *n* — **sub·se·quent·ly** \-ˌkwent-lē, -kwənt-\ *adv* — **sub·se·quent·ness** \-ˌkwent-, -kwənt-\ *n*

sub·serve \(ˌ)səb-'sərv\ *vt* [L *subservire* to serve, be subservient, fr. *sub-* + *servire* to serve] (1661) **1 :** to promote the welfare or purposes of **2 :** to serve as an instrument or means in carrying out

sub·ser·vi·ence \səb-'sər-vē-ən(t)s\ *n* (1676) **1 :** a subservient or subordinate place or function **2 :** obsequious servility

sub·ser·vi·en·cy \-ən-sē\ *n* (1651) **:** SUBSERVIENCE

sub·ser·vi·ent \-ənt\ *adj* [L *subservient-, subserviens,* prp. of *subservire*] (1632) **1 :** serving to promote some end **2 :** useful in an inferior capacity **:** SUBORDINATE **3 :** obsequiously submissive **:** TRUCKLING — **sub·ser·vi·ent·ly** *adv*

syn SUBSERVIENT, SERVILE, SLAVISH, OBSEQUIOUS mean showing or characterized by extreme compliance or abject obedience. SUBSERVIENT implies the cringing manner of one very conscious of a subordinate position ⟨domestic help was expected to be properly *subservient*⟩ SERVILE suggests the mean or fawning behavior of a slave ⟨a political boss and his entourage of *servile* hangers-on⟩ SLAVISH suggests abject or debased servility ⟨the *slavish* status of migrant farm workers⟩ OBSEQUIOUS implies fawning or sycophantic compliance and exaggerated deference of manner ⟨waiters who are *obsequious* in the presence of celebrities⟩

sub·set \'səb-ˌset\ *n* (1902) **:** a set each of whose elements is an element of an inclusive set

sub·shrub \-ˌshrəb, *esp Southern* -ˌsrəb\ *n* (1851) **:** a perennial plant having woody stems except for the terminal part of the new growth which is killed back annually; *also* **:** a low shrub

sub·side \səb-'sīd\ *vi* **sub·sid·ed; sub·sid·ing** [L *subsidere,* fr. *sub-* + *sidere* to sit down, sink; akin to L *sedēre* to sit — more at SIT] (1646) **1 :** to sink or fall to the bottom **:** SETTLE **2 :** to tend downward **:** DESCEND; *esp* **:** to flatten out so as to form a depression **3 :** to let oneself settle down **:** SINK ⟨*subsided* into a chair⟩ **4 :** to become quiet or less ⟨as the fever ~*s*⟩ ⟨my anger *subsided*⟩ ***syn*** see ABATE — **sub·si·dence** \səb-'sīd-ᵊn(t)s, 'səb-səd-ən(t)s\ *n*

¹sub·sid·iary \səb-'sid-ē-ˌer-ē, -'sid-ə-rē\ *adj* [L *subsidiarius,* fr. *subsidium* reserve troops] (1543) **1 a :** furnishing aid or support **:** AUXILIARY ⟨~ details⟩ **b :** of secondary importance **:** TRIBUTARY ⟨a ~ stream⟩ **2 :** of, relating to, or constituting a subsidy ⟨a ~ payment to an ally⟩ — **sub·sid·iari·ly** \-ˌsid-ē-'er-ə-lē\ *adv*

²subsidiary *n, pl* **-iar·ies** (1603) **:** one that is subsidiary; *esp* **:** a company wholly controlled by another

sub·si·dize \'səb-sə-ˌdīz, -zə-\ *vt* **-dized; -diz·ing** (1795) **:** to furnish with a subsidy: as **a :** to purchase the assistance of by payment of a subsidy **b :** to aid or promote (as a private enterprise) with public money ⟨~ a steamship line⟩ — **sub·si·di·za·tion** \ˌsəb-səd-ə-'zā-shən, -zəd-\ *n* — **sub·si·diz·er** *n*

sub·si·dy \'səb-səd-ē, -zəd-\ *n, pl* **-dies** [ME, fr. L *subsidium* reserve troops, support, assistance, fr. *sub-* near + *sedēre* to sit — more at SUB-, SIT] (14c) **:** a grant or gift of money: as **a :** a sum of money formerly granted by the British Parliament to the crown and raised by special taxation **b :** money granted by one state to another **c :** a grant by a government to a private person or company to assist an enterprise deemed advantageous to the public

sub·sist \səb-'sist\ *vb* [LL *subsistere* to exist, fr. L, to come to a halt, remain, fr. *sub-* + *sistere* to come to a stand; akin to L *stare* to stand — more at STAND] *vi* (1549) **1 a :** to have existence **:** BE **b :** PERSIST, CONTINUE **2 :** to have or acquire the necessities of life (as food and clothing); *esp* **:** to nourish oneself ⟨~*ing* on roots, berries and grubs⟩ **3 a :** to hold true **b :** to be logically conceivable as the subject of true statements ~ *vt* **:** to support with provisions

sub·sis·tence \səb-'sis-tən(t)s\ *n* [ME, fr. LL *subsistentia,* fr. *subsistent-, subsistens,* prp. of *subsistere*] (15c) **1 a** (1) **:** real being **:** EXISTENCE ⟨an abstraction without real ~⟩ (2) **:** the condition of remaining in existence **:** CONTINUATION, PERSISTENCE **b :** an essential characteristic quality of something that exists **c :** the character possessed by whatever is logically conceivable **2 :** means of subsisting: as **a :** the minimum (as of food and shelter) necessary to support life **b :** a source or means of obtaining the necessities of life — **sub·sis·tent** \-tənt\ *adj*

subsistence farming *n* (1937) **1 :** farming or a system of farming that provides all or almost all the goods required by the farm family usu. without any significant surplus for sale **2 :** farming or a system of farming that produces a minimum and often inadequate return to the farmer — called also *subsistence agriculture* — **subsistence farmer** *n*

sub·so·cial \ˌsəb-'sō-shəl, 'səb-\ *adj* (ca. 1909) **:** incompletely social; *esp* **:** tending to associate gregariously but lacking fixed or complex social organization ⟨~ insects⟩

¹sub·soil \'səb-ˌsȯil\ *n* (1799) **:** the stratum of weathered material that underlies the surface soil

²subsoil *vt* (1840) **:** to turn, break, or stir the subsoil of — **sub·soil·er** *n*

sub·so·lar point \ˌsəb-ˌsō-lər-\ *n* (1908) **:** the point on the surface of the earth or a planet at which the sun is at the zenith

sub·son·ic \ˌsəb-'sän-ik, 'səb-\ *adj* [ISV] (1942) **1 :** of, relating to, or being a speed less than that of sound in air **2 :** moving, capable of moving, or utilizing air currents moving at a subsonic speed **3 :** INFRASONIC 1 — **sub·son·i·cal·ly** \-i-k(ə-)lē\ *adv*

sub·space \'səb-ˌspās\ *n* (1927) **:** a subset of a space; *esp* **:** one that has the essential properties (as those of a vector space or topological space) of the including space

sub·spe·cial·ty \ˌsəb-'spesh-əl-tē, 'səb-\ *n* (1926) **:** a subordinate field within a specialty (as in medicine)

sub spe·cie ae·ter·ni·ta·tis \sub-'spek-ē-ˌā-ˌī-ˌter-nə-'tät-əs\ *adv* [NL, lit., under the aspect of eternity] (1895) **:** in its essential or universal form or nature

sub·spe·cies \'səb-ˌspē-shēz, -sēz\ *n* [NL] (1699) **:** a subdivision of a species: as **a :** a taxonomic category that ranks immediately below a species and designates a morphologically or physiologically distinguishable and geographically isolated group whose members interbreed successfully with those of other subspecies of the same species where their ranges overlap **b :** a named subdivision (as a race or variety) of a taxonomic species — **sub·spe·cif·ic** \ˌsəb-spi-'sif-ik\ *adj*

sub·stage \'səb-ˌstāj\ *n* (1888) **:** an attachment to a microscope by means of which accessories (as mirrors, diaphragms, or condensers) are held in place beneath the stage of the instrument

sub·stance \'səb-stən(t)s\ *n* [ME, fr. MF, fr. L *substantia,* fr. *substant-, substans,* prp. of *substare* to stand under, fr. *sub-* + *stare* to stand — more at STAND] (14c) **1 a :** essential nature **:** ESSENCE **b :** a fundamental or characteristic part or quality **c** *Christian Science* **:** GOD 1b **2 a :** ultimate reality that underlies all outward manifestations and change **b :** practical importance **:** MEANING, USEFULNESS ⟨the . . . bill — which will be without ~ in the sense that it will authorize nothing more than a set of ideas —Richard Reeves⟩ **3 a :** physical material from which something is made or which has discrete existence **b :** matter of particular or definite chemical constitution **4 :** material possessions **:** PROPERTY ⟨a man of ~⟩ — **sub·stance·less** \-ləs\ *adj* — **in substance :** in respect to essentials **:** FUNDAMENTALLY

substance P *n* (1942) **:** a protein present esp. in the gastrointestinal tract and pituitary gland that causes reduction in blood pressure and contraction of smooth muscle and that is thought to function as a neurotransmitter

sub·stan·dard \ˌsəb-'stan-dərd, 'səb-\ *adj* (1897) **:** deviating from or falling short of a standard or norm: as **a :** of a quality lower than that prescribed by law **b :** conforming to a pattern of linguistic usage existing within a speech community but not that of the prestige group in that community — compare NONSTANDARD **c :** constituting a greater than normal risk to an insurer

sub·stan·tial \səb-'stan-chəl\ *adj* (14c) **1 a :** consisting of or relating to substance **b :** not imaginary or illusory **:** REAL, TRUE **c :** IMPORTANT, ESSENTIAL **2 :** ample to satisfy and nourish **:** FULL ⟨a ~ meal⟩ **3 a :** possessed of means **:** WELL-TO-DO **b :** considerable in quantity **:** significantly large ⟨earned a ~ wage⟩ **4 :** firmly constructed **:** STURDY **5 :** being largely but not wholly that which is specified ⟨a ~ lie⟩ — **substantial** *n* — **sub·stan·ti·al·i·ty** \-ˌstan-chē-'al-ət-ē\ *n* — **sub·stan·tial·ly** \-'stanch-(ə-)lē\ *adv* — **sub·stan·tial·ness** \-'stan-chəl-nəs\ *n*

sub·stan·tia ni·gra \səb-ˌstan-chē-ə-'nī-grə, -'nig-rə\ *n, pl* **sub·stan·ti·ae ni·grae** \-chē-ˌē-'nī-(ˌ)grē, -'nig-(ˌ)rē\ [NL, lit., black substance] (ca. 1885) **:** a layer of deeply pigmented gray matter situated in the midbrain and containing the cell bodies of a tract of dopamine-producing nerve cells whose secretion tends to be deficient in Parkinson's disease

sub·stan·ti·ate \səb-'stan-chē-ˌāt\ *vt* **-at·ed; -at·ing** (1657) **1 :** to give substance or form to **:** EMBODY **2 :** to establish by proof or competent evidence **:** VERIFY ⟨~ a charge⟩ ***syn*** see CONFIRM — **sub·stan·ti·a·tion** \-ˌstan-chē-'ā-shən\ *n* — **sub·stan·ti·a·tive** \-'stan-chē-ˌāt-iv\ *adj*

sub·stan·ti·val \ˌsəb-stən-'tī-vəl\ *adj* (1832) **:** of, relating to, or serving as a substantive — **sub·stan·ti·val·ly** \-və-lē\ *adv*

¹sub·stan·tive \'səb-stən-tiv\ *n* [ME *substantif,* fr. MF, fr. *substantif,* adj., having or expressing substance, fr. LL *substantivus*] (14c) **:** NOUN; *broadly* **:** a word or word group functioning syntactically as a noun — **sub·stan·tiv·ize** \-tiv-ˌīz\ *vt*

²sub·stan·tive \'səb-stən-tiv; *2c & 3 also* səb-'stant-iv\ *adj* [ME, fr. LL *substantivus* having substance, fr. L *substantia*] (15c) **1 :** being a totally independent entity **2 a :** real rather than apparent **:** FIRM; *also* **:** PERMANENT, ENDURING **b :** belonging to the substance of a thing **:** ESSENTIAL **c :** expressing existence ⟨the ~ verb is the verb *to be*⟩ **d :** requiring or involving no mordant ⟨a ~ dyeing process⟩ **3 a :** having the nature or function of a grammatical substantive ⟨a ~ phrase⟩ **b :** relating to or having the character of a noun or pronominal term in logic **4 :** considerable in amount or numbers **:** SUBSTANTIAL **5 :** creating and defining rights and duties ⟨~ law⟩ **6 :** having substance **:** involving matters of major or practical importance to all concerned ⟨~ discussions among world leaders⟩ — **sub·stan·tive·ly** *adv* — **sub·stan·tive·ness** *n*

substantive right *n* (1939) **:** a right (as of life, liberty, property, or reputation) held to exist for its own sake and to constitute part of the normal legal order of society

sub·sta·tion \'səb-ˌstā-shən\ *n* (1890) **1 :** a branch post office **2 :** a subsidiary station in which electric current is transformed

sub·stit·u·ent \səb-'stich-(ə-)wənt\ *n* [L *substituent-, substituens,* prp. of *substituere*] (1895) **:** an atom or group that replaces another atom or group in a molecule — **substituent** *adj*

sub·sti·tut·able \'səb-stə-ˌt(y)üt-ə-bəl\ *adj* (1805) **:** capable of being substituted — **sub·sti·tut·abil·i·ty** \ˌsəb-stə-ˌt(y)üt-ə-'bil-ət-ē\ *n*

¹sub·sti·tute \ˈsəb-stə-ˌt(y)üt\ *n* [ME, fr. L *substitutus*, pp. of *substituere* to put in place of, fr. *sub-* + *statuere* to set up, place — more at STATUTE] (15c) **:** a person or thing that takes the place or function of another — **substitute** *adj*

²substitute *vb* **-tut·ed; -tut·ing** *vt* (1555) **1 a :** to put or use in the place of another **b :** to introduce (an atom or group) as a substituent; *also* **:** to alter (as a compound) by introduction of a substituent ⟨a *substituted* benzene ring⟩ **2 :** to take the place of **:** REPLACE ~ *vi* **:** to serve as a substitute

sub·sti·tu·tion \ˌsəb-stə-ˈt(y)ü-shən\ *n* [ME *substitucion*, fr. MF *substitution*, fr. LL *substitution-*, *substitutio*, fr. *substitutus*, pp.] (14c) **1 a :** the act, process, or result of substituting one thing for another **b :** replacement of one mathematical entity by another of equal value **2 :** one that is substituted for another — **sub·sti·tu·tion·al** \-shnəl, -shən-ᵊl\ *adj* — **sub·sti·tu·tion·al·ly** \-ē\ *adv* — **sub·sti·tu·tion·ary** \-shə-ˌner-ē\ *adj*

substitution cipher *n* (1936) **:** a cipher in which the letters of the plaintext are systematically replaced by substitute letters — compare TRANSPOSITION CIPHER

sub·sti·tu·tive \ˈsəb-stə-ˌt(y)üt-iv\ *adj* (1668) **:** serving or suitable as a substitute — **sub·sti·tu·tive·ly** *adv*

sub·strate \ˈsəb-ˌstrāt\ *n* [ML *substratum*] (1807) **1 :** SUBSTRATUM **2 :** the base on which an organism lives ⟨the soil is the ~ of most seed plants⟩ **3 :** a substance acted upon (as by an enzyme)

sub·strato·sphere \ˌsəb-ˈstrat-ə-ˌsfi(ə)r, ˈsəb-\ *n* [ISV] (1916) **:** the region of the atmosphere just below the stratosphere — **sub·strato·spher·ic** \-ˌstrat-ə-ˈsfi(ə)r-ik, -ˈsfer-\ *adj*

sub·stra·tum \ˈsəb-ˌstrāt-əm, -ˌstrat-, ˈsəb-ˈ\ *n, pl* **-stra·ta** \-ə\ [ML, fr. L, neut. of *substratus*, pp. of *substernere* to spread under, fr. *sub-* + *sternere* to spread — more at STREW] (1631) **:** an underlying support **:** FOUNDATION: as **a :** substance that is a permanent subject of qualities or phenomena **b :** the material of which something is made and from which it derives its special qualities **c :** a layer beneath the surface soil; *specif* **:** SUBSOIL **d :** SUBSTRATE 2

sub·struc·ture \ˈsəb-ˌstrək-chər\ *n* (1726) **:** an underlying or supporting part of a structure — **sub·struc·tur·al** \-chə-rəl, -shrəl\ *adj*

sub·sume \səb-ˈsüm\ *vt* **sub·sumed; sub·sum·ing** [NL *subsumere*, fr. L *sub-* + *sumere* to take up — more at CONSUME] (1535) **:** to include or place within something larger or more comprehensive **:** encompass as a subordinate or component element ⟨red, green, and yellow are *subsumed* under the term "color"⟩ — **sub·sum·able** \-ˈsü-mə-bəl\ *adj*

sub·sump·tion \səb-ˈsəm(p)-shən\ *n* [NL *subsumption-*, *subsumptio*, fr. *subsumptus*, pp. of *subsumere*] (1651) **:** the act or process of subsuming

¹sub·sur·face \ˈsəb-ˌsər-fəs\ *n* (1778) **:** earth material (as rock) near but not exposed at the surface of the ground

²sub·sur·face \(ˌ)səb-ˈsər-fəs\ *adj* (1875) **:** of, relating to, or being something located beneath a surface and esp. underground

sub·teen \ˈsəb-ˈtēn\ *n* (1951) **:** a preadolescent child

sub·tem·per·ate \ˌsəb-ˈtem-p(ə-)rət, ˈsəb-\ *adj* (1852) **:** less than typically temperate ⟨a ~ climate⟩; *also* **:** of or relating to the colder parts of the temperate zones

sub·ten·an·cy \-ˈten-ən-sē\ *n* (1861) **:** the state of being a subtenant

sub·ten·ant \-ˈten-ənt\ *n* (15c) **:** one who rents from a tenant

sub·tend \səb-ˈtend\ *vt* [L *subtendere* to stretch beneath, fr. *sub-* + *tendere* to stretch — more at THIN] (1570) **1 a :** to be opposite to and extend from one side to the other of ⟨a hypotenuse ~*s* a right angle⟩ **b :** to fix the angular extent of with respect to a fixed point or object taken as the vertex ⟨the angle ~*ed* at the eye by an object of given width and a fixed distance away⟩ ⟨a central angle ~*ed* by an arc⟩ **c :** to determine the measure of by marking off the endpoints of ⟨a chord ~*s* an arc⟩ **2 a :** to underlie so as to include **b :** to occupy an adjacent and usu. lower position to and often so as to embrace or enclose ⟨a bract that ~*s* a flower⟩

sub·ter·fuge \ˈsəb-tər-ˌfyüj\ *n* [LL *subterfugium*, fr. L *subterfugere* to escape, evade, fr. *subter-* secretly (fr. *subter* underneath; akin to L *sub* under) + *fugere* to flee — more at UP, FUGITIVE] (1573) **1 :** deception by artifice or stratagem in order to conceal, escape, or evade **2 :** a deceptive device or stratagem ***syn*** see DECEPTION

sub·ter·mi·nal \ˌsəb-ˈtərm-nəl, -ən-ᵊl, ˈsəb-\ *adj* (1828) **:** situated or occurring near but not precisely at an end ⟨a ~ band of color on the tail feathers⟩

sub·ter·ra·nean \ˌsəb-tə-ˈrā-nē-ən, -nyən\ *also* **sub·ter·ra·neous** \-nē-əs, -nyəs\ *adj* [L *subterraneus*, fr. *sub-* + *terra* earth — more at TERRACE] (1603) **1 :** being, lying, or operating under the surface of the earth **2 :** existing or working in secret **:** HIDDEN — **sub·ter·ra·nean·ly** *also* **sub·ter·ra·neous·ly** *adv*

sub·text \ˈsəb-ˌtekst\ *n* (1726) **:** the implicit or metaphorical meaning (as of a literary text) — **sub·tex·tu·al** \ˌsəb-ˈteks-chə(-wə)l\ *adj*

sub·thresh·old \ˌsəb-ˈthresh-ˌ(h)ōld, ˈsəb-\ *adj* (1942) **:** inadequate to produce a response ⟨a ~ dosage⟩ ⟨a ~ stimulus⟩

sub·tile \ˈsət-ᵊl, ˈsəb-tᵊl\ *adj* **sub·til·er** \ˈsət-lər, -ᵊl-ər; ˈsəb-tə-lər\; **sub·til·est** \ˈsət-ləst, -ᵊl-əst; ˈsəb-tə-ləst\ [ME, fr. L *subtilis*] (14c) **1 :** SUBTLE, ELUSIVE ⟨a ~ aroma⟩ **2 a :** CUNNING, CRAFTY **b :** SAGACIOUS, DISCERNING — **sub·tile·ly** \ˈsət-lē, -ᵊl-(l)ē; ˈsəb-tə-lē\ *adv* — **sub·tile·ness** \ˈsət-ᵊl-nəs, ˈsəb-tᵊl-\ *n*

sub·til·i·sin \ˌsəb-ˈtil-ə-sən\ *n* [NL *subtilis*, specific epithet of *Bacillus subtilis*, species to which *Bacillus amyloliquefaciens* was once thought to belong] (1953) **:** an extracellular protease produced by a soil bacillus (*Bacillus amyloliquefaciens*)

sub·til·ize \ˈsət-ᵊl-ˌīz, ˈsəb-tə-ˌlīz\ *vb* **-ized; -iz·ing** *vi* (1592) **:** to act or think subtly ~ *vt* **:** to make subtile — **sub·til·iza·tion** \ˌsət-ᵊl-ə-ˈzā-shən, ˌsəb-tə-lə-\ *n*

sub·til·ty \ˈsət-ᵊl-tē, ˈsəb-tᵊl-\ *n, pl* **-ties** (14c) **:** SUBTLETY

¹sub·ti·tle \ˈsəb-ˌtīt-ᵊl\ *n* (1878) **1 :** a secondary or explanatory title **2 :** a printed statement or fragment of dialogue appearing on the screen between the scenes of a silent motion picture or appearing as a translation at the bottom of the screen during the scenes

²subtitle *vt* (1891) **:** to give a subtitle to

sub·tle \ˈsət-ᵊl\ *adj* **sub·tler** \ˈsət-lər, -ᵊl-ər\; **sub·tlest** \ˈsət-ləst, -ᵊl-əst\ [ME *sutil*, *sotil*, fr. MF *soutil*, fr. L *subtilis*, lit., finely woven, fr. *sub-* + *tela* web; akin to L *texere* to weave — more at TECHNICAL] (14c) **1 a :** DELICATE, ELUSIVE ⟨a ~ fragrance⟩ **b :** difficult to understand or distinguish **:** OBSCURE ⟨~ differences in sound⟩ **2 a :** PERCEPTIVE, REFINED ⟨a writer's sharp and ~ moral sense⟩ **b :** having or marked by keen insight and ability to penetrate deeply and thoroughly ⟨a ~ scholar⟩ **3 a :** highly skillful **:** EXPERT ⟨a ~ craftsman⟩ **b :** cunningly made or contrived **:** INGENIOUS **4 :** ARTFUL, CRAFTY ⟨a ~ rogue⟩ **5 :** operating insidiously ⟨~ poisons⟩ — **sub·tle·ness** \ˈsət-ᵊl-nəs\ *n* — **sub·tly** \ˈsət-lē, ˈsət-ᵊl-(l)ē\ *adv*

sub·tle·ty \ˈsət-ᵊl-tē\ *n, pl* **-ties** [ME *sutilte*, fr. MF *sutilté*, fr. L *subtilitat-*, *subtilitas*, fr. *subtilis*] (14c) **1 :** the quality or state of being subtle **2 :** something subtle

sub·ton·ic \ˌsəb-ˈtän-ik, ˈsəb-\ *n* [fr. its being a half tone below the upper tonic] (1833) **:** LEADING TONE

¹sub·to·tal \ˈsəb-ˌtōt-ᵊl\ *n* (1909) **:** the sum of part of a series of figures

²sub·to·tal \ˌsəb-ˈtōt-ᵊl\ *adj* (1926) **:** somewhat less than complete **:** nearly total ⟨~ thyroidectomy⟩ — **sub·to·tal·ly** \-ᵊl-ē\ *adv*

sub·tract \səb-ˈtrakt\ *vb* [L *subtractus*, pp. of *subtrahere* to draw from beneath, withdraw, fr. *sub-* + *trahere* to draw — more at DRAW] *vt* (1557) **:** to take away by deducting ⟨~ 5 from 9⟩ ~ *vi* **:** to perform a subtraction — **sub·tract·er** *n*

sub·trac·tion \səb-ˈtrak-shən\ *n* [ME *subtraccion*, fr. LL *subtraction-*, *subtractio*, fr. L *subtractus*, pp.] (15c) **:** an act, operation, or instance of subtracting: as **a :** the withdrawing or withholding from one of a right to which he is entitled **b :** the operation of deducting one number from another

sub·trac·tive \-ˈtrak-tiv\ *adj* (1690) **1 :** tending to subtract **2 :** constituting or involving subtraction

sub·tra·hend \ˈsəb-trə-ˌhend\ *n* [L *subtrahendus*, gerundive of *subtrahere*] (ca. 1674) **:** a number that is to be subtracted from a minuend

sub·trop·i·cal \ˌsəb-ˈträp-i-kəl, ˈsəb-\ *also* **sub·trop·ic** \-ik\ *adj* [ISV] (1842) **:** of, relating to, or being the regions bordering on the tropical zone

sub·trop·ics \-iks\ *n pl* (1886) **:** subtropical regions

su·bu·late \ˈsü-byə-lət, ˈsəb-yə-, -ˌlāt\ *adj* [NL *subulatus*, fr. L *subula* awl; akin to OHG *siula* awl, L *suere* to sew — more at SEW] (ca. 1760) **:** linear and tapering to a fine point ⟨a ~ leaf⟩

sub·um·brel·la \ˌsəb-(ˌ)əm-ˈbrel-ə\ *n* (1878) **:** the concave undersurface of a jellyfish

sub·urb \ˈsəb-ˌərb\ *n* [ME, fr. L *suburbium*, fr. *sub-* near + *urbs* city — more at SUB-] (14c) **1 a :** an outlying part of a city or town **b :** a smaller community adjacent to or within commuting distance of a city **c** *pl* **:** the residential area on the outskirts of a city or large town **2** *pl* **:** the near vicinity **:** ENVIRONS — **sub·ur·ban** \sə-ˈbər-bən\ *adj or n* — **sub·ur·ban·ite** \-bə-ˌnīt\ *n*

sub·ur·ban·ize \sə-ˈbər-bə-ˌnīz\ *vt* **-ized; -iz·ing** (1893) **:** to make suburban **:** give a suburban character to — **sub·ur·ban·iza·tion** \-ˌbərb-ə-nə-ˈzā-shən\ *n*

sub·ur·bia \sə-ˈbər-bē-ə\ *n* [NL, fr. E *suburb* + L *-ia* -y] (1895) **1 :** the suburbs of a city **2 :** people who live in the suburbs **3 :** suburban life

sub·ven·tion \səb-ˈven-chən\ *n* [LL *subvention-*, *subventio* assistance, fr. L *subventus*, pp. of *subvenire* to come up, come to the rescue, fr. *sub-* up + *venire* to come — more at SUB-, COME] (1535) **:** the provision of assistance or financial support: as **a :** ENDOWMENT **b :** a subsidy from a government or foundation — **sub·ven·tion·ary** \-chə-ˌner-ē\ *adj*

sub·ver·sion \səb-ˈvər-zhən, -shən\ *n* [ME, fr. MF, fr. LL *subversion-*, *subversio*, fr. L *subversus*, pp. of *subvertere*] (14c) **1 :** the act of subverting **:** the state of being subverted; *esp* **:** a systematic attempt to overthrow or undermine a government or political system by persons working secretly from within **2** *obs* **:** a cause of overthrow or destruction — **sub·ver·sion·ary** \-zhə-ˌner-ē, -shə-\ *adj* — **sub·ver·sive** \-ˈvər-siv, -ziv\ *adj or n* — **sub·ver·sive·ly** *adv* — **sub·ver·sive·ness** *n*

sub·vert \səb-ˈvərt\ *vt* [ME *subverten*, fr. MF *subvertir*, fr. L *subvertere*, lit., to turn from beneath, fr. *sub-* + *vertere* to turn — more at WORTH] (14c) **1 :** to overturn or overthrow from the foundation **:** RUIN **2 :** to pervert or corrupt by an undermining of morals, allegiance, or faith — **sub·vert·er** *n*

sub·vi·ral \ˌsəb-ˈvī-rəl, ˈsəb-\ *adj* (1963) **:** relating to, being, or caused by a piece or a structural part (as a protein) of a virus ⟨~ infection⟩

sub·vo·cal \-ˈvō-kəl\ *adj* (1924) **:** characterized by the occurrence in the mind of words in speech order with or without inaudible articulation of the speech organs — **sub·vo·cal·ly** \-kə-lē\ *adv*

sub·vo·cal·iza·tion \ˌsəb-ˌvō-kə-lə-ˈzā-shən\ *n* (1947) **:** the act or process of inaudibly articulating speech with the speech organs — **sub·vo·cal·ize** \ˌsəb-ˈvō-kə-ˌlīz, ˈsəb-\ *vb*

sub·way \ˈsəb-ˌwā\ *n* (1825) **:** an underground way: as **a :** a passage under a street (as for pedestrians, power cables, or water or gas mains) **b :** a usu. electric underground railway **c :** UNDERPASS — **subway** *vi*

suc·ce·da·ne·um \ˌsək-sə-ˈdā-nē-əm\ *n, pl* **-ne·ums** *or* **-nea** \-nē-ə\ [NL, fr. L, neut. of *succedaneus* substituted, fr. *succedere* to follow after] (1641) **:** SUBSTITUTE — **suc·ce·da·ne·ous** \-nē-əs\ *adj*

suc·ce·dent \sək-ˈsēd-ᵊnt\ *adj* [L *succedent-*, *succedens*, prp. of *succedere*] (15c) **:** coming next **:** SUCCEEDING, SUBSEQUENT

suc·ceed \sək-ˈsēd\ *vb* [ME *succeden*, fr. L *succedere* to go up, follow after, succeed, fr. *sub-* near + *cedere* to go — more at SUB-, CEDE] *vi* (14c) **1 a :** to come next after another in office or position or in possession of an estate; *esp* **:** to inherit sovereignty, rank, or title **b :** to follow after another in order **2 a :** to turn out well **b :** to attain a desired object or end **3** *obs* **:** to pass to a person by inheritance ~ *vt* **1 :** to follow in sequence and esp. immediately **2 :** to come after as heir or successor ***syn*** see FOLLOW — **suc·ceed·er** *n*

suc·cès de scan·dale \sək-ˌsā-də-skäⁿ-ˈdäl, (ˌ)sük-\ *n* [F, lit., success of scandal] (1896) **:** something (as a work of art) that wins popularity or notoriety because of its scandalous nature; *also* **:** the reception accorded such a piece

suc·cès d'es·time \-ˌdes-ˈtēm\ *n* [F, lit., success of esteem] (1859) **:** something (as a work of art) that wins critical respect but not popular success; *also* **:** the reception accorded such a piece

suc·cès fou \-ˈfü\ *n* [F, lit., mad success] (1878) **:** an extraordinary success

suc·cess \sək-'ses\ *n* [L *successus,* fr. *successus,* pp. of *succedere*] (1537) **1** *obs* **:** OUTCOME, RESULT **2 a :** degree or measure of succeeding **b :** favorable or desired outcome; *also* **:** the attainment of wealth, favor, or eminence **3 :** one that succeeds

suc·cess·ful \-fəl\ *adj* (1588) **1 :** resulting or terminating in success **2 :** gaining or having gained success — **suc·cess·ful·ly** \-fə-lē\ *adv* — **suc·cess·ful·ness** *n*

suc·ces·sion \sək-'sesh-ən\ *n* [ME, fr. MF or L; MF, fr. L *succession-, successio,* fr. *successus,* pp.] (14c) **1 a :** the order in which or the conditions under which one person after another succeeds to a property, dignity, title, or throne **b :** the right of a person or line to succeed **c :** the line having such a right **2 a :** the act or process of following in order **:** SEQUENCE **b (1) :** the act or process of one person's taking the place of another in the enjoyment of or liability for his rights or duties or both **(2) :** the act or process of a person's becoming beneficially entitled to a property or property interest of a deceased person **c :** the continuance of corporate personality **d :** unidirectional change in the composition of an ecosystem as the available competing organisms and esp. the plants respond to and modify the environment ⟨the highlights of the ~ were the weed, grass, and forest communities developed in that order⟩ **3 a :** a number of persons or things that follow each other in sequence **b :** a group, type, or series that succeeds or displaces another — **suc·ces·sion·al** \-'sesh-nəl, -ən-ᵊl\ *adj* — **suc·ces·sion·al·ly** \-ē\ *adv*

succession duty *n, chiefly Brit* (1853) **:** INHERITANCE TAX

suc·ces·sive \sək-'ses-iv\ *adj* (15c) **1 :** following in order **:** following each other without interruption **2 :** characterized by or produced in succession — **suc·ces·sive·ly** *adv* — **suc·ces·sive·ness** *n*

suc·ces·sor \sək-'ses-ər\ *n* [ME *successour,* fr. OF, fr. L *successor,* fr. *successus,* pp.] (13c) **:** one that follows; *esp* **:** one who succeeds to a throne, title, estate, or office

suc·ci·nate \'sək-sə-ˌnāt\ *n* (1790) **:** a salt or ester of succinic acid

suc·cinct \(ˌ)sək-'siŋ(k)t, sə-'siŋ(k)t\ *adj* [ME, fr. L *succinctus,* pp. of *succingere* to gird from below, tuck up, fr. *sub-* + *cingere* to gird — more at CINCTURE] (13c) **1** *archaic* **a :** being girded **b :** close-fitting **2 :** marked by compact precise expression without wasted words ***syn*** see CONCISE — **suc·cinct·ly** \-'siŋ(k)-tlē, -'siŋ-klē\ *adv* — **suc·cinct·ness** \-'siŋt-nəs, -'siŋk-nəs\ *n*

suc·cin·ic acid \(ˌ)sək-ˌsin-ik-\ *n* [F *succinique,* fr. L *succinum* amber + F *-ique* -ic] (ca. 1790) **:** a crystalline dicarboxylic acid $C_4H_6O_4$ found widely in nature and active in energy-yielding metabolic reactions

succinic dehydrogenase *n* (1942) **:** an iron-containing flavoprotein enzyme that catalyzes often reversibly the dehydrogenation of succinic acid to fumaric acid in the presence of a hydrogen acceptor and that is widely distributed esp. in animal tissues, bacteria, and yeast — called also *succinate dehydrogenase*

suc·ci·nyl \'sək-sən-ᵊl, -sə-ˌnil\ *n* [ISV] (ca. 1868) **:** either of two groups of succinic acid: **a :** a bivalent group $OCCH_2CH_2CO$ **b :** a univalent group $HOOCCH_2CH_2CO$

suc·ci·nyl·cho·line \ˌsək-sən-ᵊl-'kō-ˌlēn, -sə-ˌnil-\ *n* (1952) **:** a basic compound that acts similarly to curare and is used intravenously chiefly in the form of a hydrated chloride $C_{14}H_{30}Cl_2N_2O_4 \cdot 2H_2O$ as a muscle relaxant in surgery

1suc·cor \'sək-ər\ *n* [ME *succur,* fr. earlier *sucurs,* taken as pl., fr. OF *sucors,* fr. ML *succursus,* fr. L *succursus,* pp. of *succurrere* to run up, run to help, fr. *sub-* up + *currere* to run — more at CURRENT] (13c) **1 :** RELIEF; *also* **:** AID, HELP **2 :** something that furnishes relief

2succor *vt* **suc·cored; suc·cor·ing** \'sək-(ə-)riŋ\ (13c) **:** to go to the aid of **:** RELIEVE — **suc·cor·er** \'sək-ər-ər\ *n*

suc·co·ry \'sək-(ə-)rē\ *n* [alter. of ME *cicoree*] (1533) **:** CHICORY

suc·co·tash \'sək-ə-ˌtash\ *n* [of Algonquian origin; akin to Narraganset *msakwatas* succotash] (1751) **:** lima or shell beans and green corn cooked together

suc·cour \'sək-ər\ *chiefly Brit var of* SUCCOR

suc·cu·ba \'sək-yə-bə\ *n, pl* **-bae** \-ˌbē, -ˌbī\ [LL, prostitute] (1559) **:** SUCCUBUS

suc·cu·bus \-bəs\ *n, pl* **-bi** \-ˌbī, -ˌbē\ [ME, fr. ML, alter. of LL *succuba* prostitute, fr. L *succubare* to lie under, fr. *sub-* + *cubare* to lie, recline — more at HIP] (14c) **:** a demon assuming female form to have sexual intercourse with men in their sleep — compare INCUBUS

suc·cu·lence \'sək-yə-lən(t)s\ *n* (1787) **1 :** the state of being succulent **2 :** succulent feed ⟨wild game subsisting on ~⟩

1suc·cu·lent \-lənt\ *adj* [L *suculentus,* fr. *sucus* juice, sap; akin to L *sugere* to suck — more at SUCK] (1601) **1 a :** full of juice **:** JUICY **b :** moist and tasty **:** TOOTHSOME **c** *of a plant* **:** having fleshy tissues designed to conserve moisture **2 :** rich in interest — **suc·cu·lent·ly** *adv*

2succulent *n* (1825) **:** a succulent plant (as a cactus)

suc·cumb \sə-'kəm\ *vi* [F & L; F *succomber,* fr. L *succumbere,* fr. *sub-* + *-cumbere* to lie down — more at HIP] (1604) **1 :** to yield to superior strength or force or overpowering appeal or desire **2 :** to be brought to an end (as death) by the effect of destructive or disruptive forces ***syn*** see YIELD

1such \(ˈ)səch, (ˌ)sich\ *adj* [ME, fr. OE *swilc;* akin to OHG *sulīh* such, OE *swā* so — more at SO] (bef. 12c) **1 a :** of a kind or character to be indicated or suggested ⟨a bag ~ as a doctor carries⟩ **b :** having a quality to a degree to be indicated ⟨his excitement was ~ that he shouted⟩ **2 :** of the character, quality, or extent previously indicated or implied ⟨in the past few years many ~ women have shifted to full-time jobs⟩ **3 :** of so extreme a degree or quality ⟨never heard ~ a hubbub⟩ **4 :** of the same class, type, or sort ⟨other ~ clinics throughout the state⟩ **5 :** not specified

2such *pron* (bef. 12c) **1 :** such a person or thing **2 :** someone or something stated, implied, or exemplified ⟨~ was the result⟩ **3 :** someone or something similar **:** similar persons or things ⟨tin and glass and ~⟩
usage For reasons that are hard to understand, commentators on usage disapprove of *such* used as a pronoun. Dictionaries, however, recognize it as standard; all of the citations upon which our definitions of this word are based are clearly standard.
— **as such :** intrinsically considered **:** in itself ⟨*as such* the gift was worth little⟩

3such *adv* (bef. 12c) **1 a :** to such a degree **:** SO ⟨~ tall buildings⟩ ⟨~ a fine person⟩ **b :** VERY, ESPECIALLY ⟨hasn't been in ~ good spirits lately⟩ **2 :** in such a way

1such and such *adj* (15c) **:** not named or specified

2such and such *pron* (1560) **:** something not specified

1such·like \'səch-ˌlīk\ *adj* (15c) **:** of like kind **:** SIMILAR

2suchlike *pron* (15c) **:** SUCH 3

1suck \'sək\ *vb* [ME *souken,* fr. OE *sūcan;* akin to OHG *sūgan* to suck, L *sugere,* Gk *hyein* to rain] *vt* (bef. 12c) **1 a :** to draw (as liquid) into the mouth through a suction force produced by movements of the lips and tongue ⟨~*ed* milk from his mother's breast⟩ **b :** to draw something from or consume by such movements ⟨~ an orange⟩ ⟨~ a lollipop⟩ **c :** to apply the mouth to in order to or as if to suck out a liquid ⟨~*ed* his burned finger⟩ **2 a :** to draw by or as if by suction ⟨when a receding wave ~*s* the sand from under your feet —Kenneth Brower⟩ ⟨inadvertently ~*ed* into the . . . intrigue —Martin Levin⟩ **b :** to take in and consume by or as if by suction ⟨a vacuum cleaner ~*ing* up dirt⟩ ⟨~ up a few beers⟩ ⟨opponents say that malls ~ the life out of downtown areas —Michael Knight⟩ ~ *vi* **1 :** to draw something in by or as if by exerting a suction force; *esp* **:** to draw milk from a breast or udder with the mouth **2 :** to make a sound or motion associated with or caused by suction ⟨his pipe ~*ed* wetly⟩ ⟨flanks ~*ed* in and out, the long nose resting on his paws —Virginia Woolf⟩ **3 :** to act in an obsequious manner ⟨when they want votes . . . the candidates come ~*ing* around —W. G. Hardy⟩ ⟨~*ed* up to the boss⟩ **4** *slang* **:** to be extremely objectionable or inadequate ⟨our lifestyle ~*s* —*Playboy*⟩ ⟨people who went said it ~*ed* —H.S. Thompson⟩

2suck *n* (13c) **1 :** a sucking movement or force **2 :** the act of sucking

1suck·er \'sək-ər\ *n* (14c) **1 a :** one that sucks esp. a breast or udder **:** SUCKLING **b :** a device for creating or regulating suction (as a piston or valve in a pump) **c :** a pipe or tube through which something is drawn by suction **d (1) :** an organ in various animals for adhering or holding **(2) :** a mouth (as of a leech) adapted for sucking or adhering **2 :** a shoot from the roots or lower part of the stem of a plant **3 :** any of numerous freshwater fishes (family Catostomidae) closely related to the carps but distinguished from them esp. by the structure of the mouth which usu. has thick soft lips **4 :** LOLLIPOP **5 a :** a person easily cheated or deceived **b :** a person irresistibly attracted by something specified ⟨a ~ for ghost stories⟩ **c** — used as generalized term of reference ⟨see if you can get that ~ working again⟩

2sucker *vb* **suck·ered; suck·er·ing** \'sək-(ə-)riŋ\ *vt* (1661) **1 :** to remove suckers from ⟨~ tobacco⟩ **2 :** HOODWINK ~ *vi* **:** to send out suckers

suck in *vt* (15c) **1 :** to contract, flatten, and tighten (the abdomen) esp. by inhaling deeply **2 :** DUPE, HOODWINK

suck·ing *adj* (bef. 12c) **:** not yet weaned; *broadly* **:** very young

sucking louse *n* (ca. 1907) **:** any of an order (Anoplura) of wingless insects comprising the true lice with mouthparts adapted to sucking body fluids

suck·le \'sək-əl\ *vt* **suck·led; suck·ling** \-(ə-)liŋ\ [prob. back-formation fr. *suckling*] (15c) **1 a :** to give milk to from the breast or udder ⟨a mother *suckling* her child⟩ **b :** to nurture as if by giving milk from the breast ⟨was *suckled* on pulp magazines⟩ **2 :** to draw milk from the breast or udder of ⟨lambs *suckling* the ewes⟩

suck·ling \'sək-liŋ\ *n* (15c) **:** a young unweaned animal

su·crase \'sü-ˌkrās, -ˌkrāz\ *n* [ISV, fr. F *sucre* sugar, fr. MF — more at SUGAR] (ca. 1900) **:** INVERTASE

su·cre \'sü-(ˌ)krā\ *n* [Sp, fr. Antonio José de *Sucre*] (1886) — see MONEY table

su·crose \'sü-ˌkrōs, -ˌkrōz\ *n* [ISV, fr. F *sucre* sugar] (1862) **:** a sweet crystalline dextrorotatory disaccharide sugar $C_{12}H_{22}O_{11}$ that occurs naturally in most land plants, is obtained from sugarcane or sugar beets, and unlike glucose and galactose does not reduce Fehling's solution to produce a colored precipitate

suc·tion \'sək-shən\ *n* [LL *suction-, suctio,* fr. L *suctus,* pp. of *sugere* to suck — more at SUCK] (1626) **1 :** the act or process of sucking **2 a :** the act or process of exerting a force upon a solid, liquid, or gaseous body by reason of reduced air pressure over part of its surface **b :** force so exerted **3 :** a device (as a pipe or fitting) used in a machine that operates by suction — **suc·tion·al** \-shən-ᵊl, -shnəl\ *adj*

suction pump *n* (1825) **:** a common pump in which the liquid to be raised is pushed by atmospheric pressure into the partial vacuum under a retreating valved piston on the upstroke and reflux is prevented by a check valve in the pipe

suction stop *n* (1887) **:** a voice stop in the formation of which air behind the articulation is rarefied with consequent inrush of air when articulation is broken

suc·to·ri·al \ˌsək-'tōr-ē-əl, -'tȯr-\ *adj* [NL *suctorius,* fr. L *suctus,* pp.] (1833) **:** adapted for sucking; *esp* **:** serving to draw up fluid or to adhere by suction ⟨~ mouths⟩

suc·to·ri·an \-ē-ən\ *n* [NL *Suctoria,* fr. neut. pl. of *suctorius* suctorial] (ca. 1842) **:** any of a class (Suctoria) of complex protozoans which have cilia only early in development and in which the mature form is fixed to the substrate, lacks locomotor organelles or a mouth, and obtains food through specialized suctorial tentacles

Su·dan grass \sü-'dan-, -'dän-\ *n* [the *Sudan,* region in Africa] (1911) **:** a vigorous tall-growing annual grass (*Sorghum vulgare sudanensis*) widely grown for hay and fodder

Su·dan·ic \sü-'dan-ik\ *n* [the *Sudan*] (1925) **:** the languages neither Bantu nor Hamitic spoken in a belt extending from Senegal to southern Sudan — **Sudanic** *adj*

su·da·to·ri·um \ˌsüd-ə-'tōr-ē-əm, -'tȯr-\ *n* [L, fr. *sudatus,* pp. of *sudare* to sweat — more at SWEAT] (1756) **:** a sweat room in a bath

su·da·to·ry \'süd-ə-ˌtōr-ē, -ˌtȯr-\ *n, pl* **-ries** (1615) **:** SUDATORIUM

sudd \'səd\ *n* [Ar, lit., obstruction] (1874) **:** floating vegetable matter that forms obstructive masses in the upper White Nile

1sud·den \'səd-ᵊn\ *adj* [ME *sodain,* fr. MF, fr. L *subitaneus,* fr. *subitus* sudden, fr. pp. of *subire* to come up, fr. *sub-* up + *ire* to go — more at SUB-, ISSUE] (14c) **1 a :** happening or coming unexpectedly ⟨a ~ shower⟩ **b :** changing angle or character all at once **2 :** marked by or manifesting abruptness or haste **3 :** made or brought about in a short time **:** PROMPT ***syn*** see PRECIPITATE — **sud·den·ly** *adv* — **sud·den·ness** \'səd-ᵊn-(n)əs\ *n*

2sudden *n, obs* (1558) **:** an unexpected occurrence **:** EMERGENCY — **all of a sudden** *or* **on a sudden :** sooner than was expected **:** at once

sudden death *n* (1548) **1 :** unexpected death that is instantaneous or occurs within minutes from any cause other than violence ⟨*sudden death* following coronary occlusion⟩ **2 :** extra play to break a tie in a sports contest in which the first to go ahead wins

sudden infant death syndrome *n* (ca. 1971) **:** death due to unknown causes of an infant in apparently good health that occurs usu. before one year of age — called also *crib death*
su·do·rif·er·ous \ˌsüd-ə-ˈrif-(ə-)rəs\ *adj* [LL *sudorifer,* fr. L *sudor* sweat + *-ifer* -iferous — more at SWEAT] (1597) **:** producing or conveying sweat ⟨~ glands⟩ ⟨a ~ duct⟩
su·do·rif·ic \-ˈrif-ik\ *adj* [NL *sudorificus,* fr. L *sudor*] (1626) **:** causing or inducing sweat **:** DIAPHORETIC ⟨~ herbs⟩ — **sudorific** *n*
Su·dra \ˈs(h)ü-drə\ *n* [Skt *śūdra*] (1630) **:** a Hindu of a lower caste traditionally assigned to menial occupations — **Sudra** *adj*
[1]**suds** \ˈsədz\ *n pl but sing or pl in constr* [prob. fr. MD *sudse* marsh; akin to OE *sēothan* to seethe — more at SEETHE] (1581) **1 :** water impregnated with soap or a synthetic detergent compound and worked up into froth; *also* **:** the lather or froth on such water **2 a :** FOAM, FROTH **b :** BEER — **suds·less** \-ləs\ *adj*
[2]**suds** *vt* (1893) **:** to wash in suds ~ *vi* **:** to form suds — **suds·er** *n*
sudsy \ˈsəd-zē\ *adj* **suds·i·er; -est** (1866) **1 :** full of suds **:** FROTHY, FOAMY **2 :** SOAPY 4
sue \ˈsü\ *vb* **sued; su·ing** [ME *suen,* fr. MF *suivre,* fr. (assumed) VL *sequere,* fr. L *sequi* to follow, come or go after; akin to Gk *hepesthai* to follow and prob. to OHG *sehan* to see — more at SEE] *vt* (14c) **1** *obs* **:** to make petition to or for **2 :** to pay court or suit to **:** WOO **3 a :** to seek justice or right from (a person) by legal process; *specif* **:** to bring an action against **b :** to proceed with and follow up (a legal action) to proper termination ~ *vi* **1 :** to make a request or application **:** PLEAD — usu. used with *for* or *to* **2 :** to pay court **:** WOO **3 :** to take legal proceedings in court — **su·er** *n*
[1]**suede** *or* **suède** \ˈswād\ *n* [F *gants de Suède* Swedish gloves] (1884) **1 :** leather with a napped surface **2 :** a fabric finished with a nap to simulate suede
[2]**suede** *vb* **sued·ed; sued·ing** *vt* (1921) **:** to give a suede finish or nap to (a fabric or leather) ~ *vi* **:** to give cloth or leather a suede finish
su·et \ˈsü-ət\ *n* [ME *sewet,* fr. (assumed) AF, dim. of AF *sue,* fr. L *sebum* tallow, suet — more at SOAP] (14c) **:** the hard fat about the kidneys and loins in beef and mutton that yields tallow
suf·fer \ˈsəf-ər\ *vb* **suf·fered; suf·fer·ing** \-(ə-)riŋ\ [ME *suffren,* fr. OF *souffrir,* fr. (assumed) VL *sufferire,* fr. L *sufferre,* fr. *sub-* up + *ferre* to bear — more at SUB-, BEAR] *vt* (13c) **1 a :** to submit to or be forced to endure ⟨~ martyrdom⟩ **b :** to feel keenly **:** labor under ⟨~ thirst⟩ **2 :** UNDERGO, EXPERIENCE **3 :** to put up with esp. as inevitable or unavoidable **4 :** to allow esp. by reason of indifference ⟨the eagle ~*s* little birds to sing —Shak.⟩ ~ *vi* **1 :** to endure death, pain, or distress **2 :** to sustain loss or damage **3 :** to be subject to disability or handicap ***syn*** see BEAR — **suf·fer·able** \ˈsəf-(ə-)rə-bəl\ *adj* — **suf·fer·able·ness** *n* — **suf·fer·ably** \-blē\ *adv* — **suf·fer·er** \ˈsəf-ər-ər\ *n*
suf·fer·ance \ˈsəf-(ə-)rən(t)s\ *n* (14c) **1 :** patient endurance **:** LONGSUFFERING **2 :** PAIN, MISERY **3 :** consent or sanction implied by a lack of interference or failure to enforce a prohibition **4 :** power or ability to withstand **:** ENDURANCE
suf·fer·ing *n* (14c) **1 :** the state or experience of one that suffers **2 :** PAIN ***syn*** see DISTRESS
suf·fice \sə-ˈfīs *also* -ˈfīz\ *vb* **suf·ficed; suf·fic·ing** [ME *sufficen,* fr. MF *suffis-,* stem of *suffire,* fr. L *sufficere,* lit., to put under, fr. *sub-* + *facere* to make, do — more at DO] *vi* (14c) **1 :** to meet or satisfy a need **:** be sufficient ⟨a brief note will ~⟩ — often used with an impersonal *it* ⟨~ it to say that they are dedicated, serious personalities —Cheryl Aldridge⟩ **2 :** to be competent or capable ~ *vt* **:** to be enough for — **suf·fic·er** *n*
suf·fi·cien·cy \sə-ˈfish-ən-sē\ *n* (15c) **1 :** sufficient means to meet one's needs **:** COMPETENCY; *also* **:** a modest but adequate scale of living **2 :** the quality or state of being sufficient **:** ADEQUACY
suf·fi·cient \sə-ˈfish-ənt\ *adj* [ME, fr. L *sufficient-, sufficiens,* fr. prp. of *sufficere*] (14c) **1 a :** enough to meet the needs of a situation or a proposed end ⟨~ provisions for a month⟩ **b :** being a sufficient condition **2** *archaic* **:** QUALIFIED, COMPETENT — **suf·fi·cient·ly** *adv*
syn SUFFICIENT, ENOUGH, ADEQUATE, COMPETENT mean being what is necessary or desirable. SUFFICIENT suggests a close meeting of a need; ENOUGH is less exact in suggestion than SUFFICIENT; ADEQUATE may imply barely meeting a requirement; COMPETENT suggests measuring up to all requirements without question or being adequately adapted to an end.
sufficient condition *n* (1914) **1 :** a proposition whose truth assures the truth of another proposition **2 :** a state of affairs whose existence assures the existence of another state of affairs
[1]**suf·fix** \ˈsəf-ˌiks\ *n* [NL *suffixum,* fr. L, neut. of *suffixus,* pp. of *suffigere* to fasten underneath, fr. *sub-* + *figere* to fasten — more at DIKE] (1778) **:** an affix occurring at the end of a word, base, or phrase — compare PREFIX — **suf·fix·al** \ˈsəf-ˌik-səl, (ˌ)sə-ˈfik-səl\ *adj*
[2]**suf·fix** \ˈsəf-iks, (ˌ)sə-ˈfiks\ *vt* (1778) **:** to attach as a suffix — **suf·fix·ation** \ˌsəf-ˌik-ˈsā-shən\ *n*
suf·fo·cate \ˈsəf-ə-ˌkāt\ *vb* **-cat·ed; -cat·ing** [L *suffocatus,* pp. of *suffocare* to choke, stifle, fr. *sub-* + *fauces* throat] *vt* (15c) **1 a :** to stop the respiration of (as by strangling or asphyxiation) **b :** to deprive of oxygen **c :** to make uncomfortable by want of cool fresh air **2 :** to impede or stop the development of ~ *vi* **1 :** to become suffocated: **a :** to die from being unable to breathe **b :** to be uncomfortable through lack of air **2 :** to become checked in development — **suf·fo·cat·ing·ly** \-ˌkāt-iŋ-lē\ *adv* — **suf·fo·ca·tion** \ˌsəf-ə-ˈkā-shən\ *n* — **suf·fo·ca·tive** \ˈsəf-ə-ˌkāt-iv\ *adj*
Suf·folk \ˈsəf-ək, -ˌōk\ *n* [*Suffolk,* England] (1831) **1 :** any of an English breed of chestnut-colored draft horses — called also *Suffolk punch* **2 :** any of an English breed of black-faced hornless mutton-type sheep
[1]**suf·fra·gan** \ˈsəf-ri-gən, ˈsəf-ri-jən\ *n* [ME, fr. MF, fr. ML *suffraganeus,* fr. *suffragium* support, prayer] (14c) **1 :** a diocesan bishop (as in the Roman Catholic Church and the Church of England) subordinate to a metropolitan **2 :** an Anglican or Episcopal bishop assisting a diocesan bishop and not having the right of succession
[2]**suffragan** *adj* (15c) **1 :** of or being a suffragan **2 :** subordinate to a metropolitan or archiepiscopal see
suf·frage \ˈsəf-rij, *sometimes* -ə-rij\ *n* [in sense 1, fr. ME, fr. MF, fr. ML *suffragium,* fr. L, vote, political support; in other senses, fr. L *suffragium*] (14c) **1 :** a short intercessory prayer usu. in a series **2 :** a vote given in deciding a controverted question or in the choice of a person for an office or trust **3 :** the right of voting **:** FRANCHISE; *also* **:** the exercise of such right
suf·frag·ette \ˌsəf-ri-ˈjet\ *n* (1906) **:** a woman who advocates suffrage for her sex
suf·frag·ist \ˈsəf-ri-jəst\ *n* (1822) **:** one who advocates extension of suffrage esp. to women
suf·fuse \sə-ˈfyüz\ *vt* **suf·fused; suf·fus·ing** [L *suffusus,* pp. of *suffundere,* lit., to pour beneath, fr. *sub-* + *fundere* to pour — more at FOUND] (1590) **:** to spread over or through in the manner of fluid or light **:** FLUSH, FILL ***syn*** see INFUSE — **suf·fu·sion** \-ˈfyü-zhən\ *n* — **suf·fu·sive** \-ˈfyü-siv, -ziv\ *adj*
Su·fi \ˈsü-(ˌ)fē\ *n* [Ar *ṣūfīy,* lit., (man) of wool] (1653) **:** a Muslim mystic — **Sufi** *adj* — **Su·fic** \-fik\ *adj* — **Su·fism** \-ˌfiz-əm\ *n*
[1]**sug·ar** \ˈshu̇g-ər\ *n* [ME *sucre,* fr. MF, fr. ML *zuccarum,* fr. OIt *zucchero,* fr. Ar *sukkar,* fr. Per *shakar,* fr. Skt *śarkarā;* akin to Skt *śarkara* pebble] (13c) **1 a :** a sweet crystallizable material that consists wholly or essentially of sucrose, is colorless or white when pure tending to brown when less refined, is obtained commercially from sugarcane or sugar beet and less extensively from sorghum, maples, and palms, and is nutritionally important as a source of dietary carbohydrate and as a sweetener and preservative of other foods **b :** any of various water-soluble compounds that vary widely in sweetness and include the oligosaccharides (as sucrose) **2 :** a unit (as a spoonful, cube, or lump) of sugar **3 :** a sugar bowl
[2]**sugar** *vb* **sug·ared; sug·ar·ing** \ˈshu̇g-(ə-)riŋ\ *vt* (15c) **1 :** to make palatable or attractive **:** SWEETEN **2 :** to sprinkle or mix with sugar ~ *vi* **1 :** to form or be converted into sugar **2 :** to become granular **:** GRANULATE **3 :** to make maple syrup or maple sugar
sugar apple *n* (1738) **:** SWEETSOP
sugar beet *n* (1817) **:** a white-rooted beet grown for the sugar in its roots

sugar beet

sug·ar·ber·ry \ˈshu̇g-ər-ˌber-ē\ *n* (ca. 1837) **:** any of several hackberries (esp. *Celtis laevigata* and *C. occidentalis*) with sweet edible fruits
sugar bush *n* (1823) **:** a woods in which sugar maples predominate
sug·ar·cane \ˈshu̇g-ər-ˌkān\ *n* (1568) **:** a stout tall perennial grass (*Saccharum officinarum*) that has a large terminal panicle and is widely grown in warm regions as a source of sugar
sug·ar·coat \ˌshu̇g-ər-ˈkōt\ *vt* [back-formation fr. *sugarcoated*] (1870) **1 :** to coat with sugar **2 :** to make superficially attractive or palatable ⟨tried to ~ an unpleasant truth⟩
sugar daddy *n* (1926) **1 :** a well-to-do usu. older man who supports or spends lavishly on a mistress or girlfriend **2 :** a generous benefactor of a cause
sug·ar·house \ˈshu̇g-ər-ˌhau̇s\ *n* (1600) **:** a building where sugar is made or refined; *specif* **:** one where maple sap is boiled and maple syrup and maple sugar are made
sugaring off *n* (1836) **1 :** the act or process of converting maple syrup into sugar **2 :** a party held at the time of sugaring off
sug·ar·loaf \ˈshu̇g-ər-ˌlōf\ *n* (15c) **1 :** refined sugar molded into a cone **2 :** a hill or mountain shaped like a sugarloaf — **sugar–loaf** *adj*
sugar maple *n* (1731) **:** a maple with a sweet sap; *specif* **:** one (*Acer saccharum*) of eastern No. America with 3- to 5-lobed leaves, hard close-grained wood much used for cabinetwork, and sap that is the chief source of maple syrup and maple sugar
sugar off *vi* (1836) **1 :** to complete the process of boiling down the syrup in making maple sugar until it is thick enough to crystallize **2 :** to approach or reach the state of granulation
sugar of lead (1661) **:** LEAD ACETATE
sugar orchard *n, chiefly NewEng* (1833) **:** SUGAR BUSH
sugar pea *n* (1707) **:** SNOW PEA
sug·ar·plum \ˈshu̇g-ər-ˌpləm\ *n* (1668) **:** a small candy in the shape of a ball or disk **:** SWEETMEAT
sug·ary \ˈshu̇g-(ə-)rē\ *adj* (1591) **1 a :** exaggeratedly sweet **:** HONEYED ⟨his ~ deprecating voice —D. H. Lawrence⟩ **b :** cloyingly sweet **:** SENTIMENTAL **2 :** containing, resembling, or tasting of sugar
sug·gest \sə(g)-ˈjest\ *vt* [L *suggestus,* pp. of *suggerere* to put under, furnish, suggest, fr. *sub-* + *gerere* to carry — more at CAST] (1526) **1 a** *obs* **:** to seek to influence **:** SEDUCE **b :** to call forth **:** EVOKE **c :** to mention or imply as a possibility ⟨~*ed* that he might bring his family⟩ **d :** to propose as desirable or fitting ⟨~ a stroll⟩ **e :** to offer for consideration or as a hypothesis ⟨~ a solution to a problem⟩ **2 a :** to call to mind by thought or association ⟨the explosion . . . ~*ed* sabotage —F. L. Paxson⟩ **b :** to serve as a motive or inspiration for ⟨a play ~*ed* by a historic incident⟩ — **sug·gest·er** *n*
syn SUGGEST, IMPLY, HINT, INTIMATE, INSINUATE mean to convey an idea indirectly. SUGGEST may stress putting into the mind by association of ideas, awakening of a desire, or initiating a train of thought ⟨he can *suggest* in his work the immobility of a plain or the extreme action of a bolt of lightning, without showing either —Dale Nichols⟩ IMPLY is close to SUGGEST but may indicate a more definite or logical relation of the unexpressed idea to the expressed ⟨the philosophy of Nature which is *implied* in Chinese art —Laurence Binyon⟩ HINT implies the use of slight or remote suggestion with a minimum of overt statement ⟨the soft *hinted* green in the branches —Shirley Jackson⟩ ⟨as thou with wary speech . . . hast *hinted* —John Keats⟩ INTIMATE stresses delicacy of suggestion without connoting any lack of candor ⟨had *intimated* to the President that he wanted to go back to teaching —*Current Biog.*⟩ INSINUATE applies to the conveying of a usually unpleasant idea in a sly underhanded manner ⟨the *insinuated* scoff of coward tongues —William Wordsworth⟩

\ə\ abut \ᵊ\ kitten, F table \ər\ further \a\ ash \ā\ ace \ä\ cot, cart \au̇\ out \ch\ chin \e\ bet \ē\ easy \g\ go \i\ hit \ī\ ice \j\ job \ŋ\ sing \ō\ go \ȯ\ law \ȯi\ boy \th\ thin \t͟h\ the \ü\ loot \u̇\ foot \y\ yet \zh\ vision \à, k̲, ⁿ, œ, œ̄, ue, ue̅, ʸ\ see Guide to Pronunciation

sug·gest·ible \sə(g)-ˈjes-tə-bəl\ *adj* (1890) **:** easily influenced by suggestion — **sug·gest·ibil·i·ty** \-ˌjes-tə-ˈbil-ət-ē\ *n*

sug·ges·tion \sə(g)-ˈjes(h)-chən\ *n* (14c) **1 a :** the act or process of suggesting **b :** something suggested **2 a :** the process by which one thought leads to another esp. through association of ideas **b :** a means or process of influencing attitudes and behavior hypnotically **3 :** a slight indication **:** TRACE ⟨a ~ of a smile⟩

sug·ges·tive \sə(g)-ˈjes-tiv\ *adj* (1631) **1 a :** giving a suggestion **:** INDICATIVE ⟨~ of a past era⟩ **b :** full of suggestions **:** stimulating thought ⟨provided a ~ . . . commentary on the era —Lloyd Morris⟩ **c :** stirring mental associations **:** EVOCATIVE **2 :** suggesting or tending to suggest something improper or indecent **:** RISQUÉ— **sug·ges·tive·ly** *adv* — **sug·ges·tive·ness** *n*

sui·cid·al \ˌsü-ə-ˈsīd-ᵊl\ *adj* (1777) **1 a :** dangerous esp. to life **b :** destructive to one's own interests **2 :** relating to or of the nature of suicide **3 :** marked by an impulse to commit suicide — **sui·cid·al·ly** \-ᵊl-ē\ *adv*

¹**sui·cide** \ˈsü-ə-ˌsīd\ *n* [L *sui* (gen.) of oneself + E *-cide;* akin to OE & OHG *sīn* his, L *suus* one's own, Skt *sva* oneself, one's own] (1651) **1 a :** the act or an instance of taking one's own life voluntarily and intentionally esp. by a person of years of discretion and of sound mind **b :** ruin of one's own interests ⟨political ~⟩ **2 :** one that commits or attempts suicide

²**suicide** *vb* **sui·cid·ed; sui·cid·ing** *vi* (1841) **:** to commit suicide ~ *vt* **:** to put (oneself) to death **:** KILL

suicide squad *n* [fr. the fact that kickoffs and punts are more dangerous than other plays] (1966) **:** a special squad used on kickoffs in football

sui ge·ner·is \ˌsü-ˌī-ˈjen-ə-rəs; ˌsü-ē-ˈjen-, -ˈgen-\ *adj* [L, of its own kind] (1787) **:** constituting a class alone **:** UNIQUE, PECULIAR

sui ju·ris \ˌsü-ˌī-ˈju̇r-əs, ˌsü-ē-ˈyu̇r-\ *adj* [L, of one's own right] (1614) **:** having full legal rights or capacity

su·int \ˈsü-ənt, ˈswint\ *n* [F, fr. MF, fr. *suer* to sweat, fr. L *sudare* — more at SWEAT] (1791) **:** dried perspiration of sheep deposited in the wool and rich in potassium salts

¹**suit** \ˈsüt\ *n* [ME *siute* act of following, retinue, sequence, set, fr. OF, act of following, retinue, fr. (assumed) VL *sequita,* fr. fem. of *sequitus,* pp. of *sequere* to follow — more at SUE] (13c) **1** *archaic* **:** SUITE 1 **2 a :** recourse or appeal to a feudal superior for justice or redress **b :** an action or process in a court for the recovery of a right or claim **3 :** an act or instance of suing or seeking by entreaty **:** APPEAL; *specif* **:** COURTSHIP **4 :** SUITE 2 — used chiefly of armor, sails, and counters in games **5 :** a set of garments: as **a :** an outer costume of two or more pieces **b :** a costume to be worn for a special purpose or under particular conditions ⟨gym ~⟩ **6 a :** all the playing cards in a pack bearing the same symbol **b :** all the dominoes bearing the same number **c :** all the cards or counters in a particular suit held by one player ⟨a 5-card ~⟩ **d :** the suit led ⟨follow ~⟩

²**suit** *vt* (1577) **1 :** to outfit with clothes **:** DRESS **2 :** ACCOMMODATE, ADAPT ⟨~ the action to the word⟩ **3 a :** to be proper for **:** BEFIT **b :** to be becoming to **4 :** to meet the needs or desires of **:** PLEASE ⟨~*s* me fine⟩ ~ *vi* **1 :** to be in accordance **:** AGREE ⟨the position ~*s* with his abilities⟩ **2 :** to be appropriate or satisfactory ⟨these prices don't ~⟩ **3 :** to put on specially required clothing (as a uniform or protective garb) — usu. used with *up*

suit·able \ˈsüt-ə-bəl\ *adj* (1582) **1** *obs* **:** SIMILAR, MATCHING **2 a :** adapted to a use or purpose **b :** satisfying propriety **:** PROPER **c :** ABLE, QUALIFIED ***syn*** see FIT — **suit·abil·i·ty** \ˌsüt-ə-ˈbil-ət-ē\ *n* — **suit·able·ness** *n* — **suit·ably** \-blē\ *adv*

suit·case \ˈsüt-ˌkās\ *n* (1902) **:** TRAVELING BAG; *esp* **:** a rigid flat rectangular one

suite \ˈswēt, *2d is also* ˈsüt\ *n* [F, alter. of OF *siute* — more at SUIT] (1673) **1 :** RETINUE; *esp* **:** the personal staff accompanying a ruler, diplomat, or dignitary on official business **2 :** a group of things forming a unit or constituting a collection **:** SET: as **a :** a group of rooms occupied as a unit **:** APARTMENT **b (1) :** a 17th and 18th century instrumental musical form consisting of a series of dances in the same or related keys **(2) :** a modern instrumental composition in several movements of different character **(3) :** a long orchestral concert arrangement in suite form of material drawn from a longer work (as a ballet) **c :** a collection of minerals or rocks having some characteristic in common (as type or origin) **d :** a set of matched furniture for a room

suit·er \ˈsüt-ər\ *n* (1952) **:** a suitcase for holding a specified number of suits — usu. used in combination ⟨a two-*suiter*⟩

suit·ing \ˈsüt-iŋ\ *n* (1883) **1 :** fabric for suits **2 :** a suit of clothes

suit·or \ˈsüt-ər\ *n* [ME, follower, pleader, fr. AF, fr. L *secutor* follower, fr. *secutus,* pp. of *sequi* to follow — more at SUE] (15c) **1 :** one that petitions or entreats **:** PETITIONER **2 :** a party to a suit at law **3 :** one who courts a woman or seeks to marry her

su·ki·ya·ki \skē-ˈ(y)äk-ē; ˌsu̇k-ē-ˈ, ˌsük-\ *n* [Jp, fr. *suki-* (as in *sukimi* slices of fish) + *yaki* roast] (1924) **:** a dish consisting of thin slices of meat, bean curd, and vegetables cooked in soy sauce, sake, and sugar

suk·kah \ˈsu̇k-ə\ *n* [Heb *sukkāh*] (ca. 1902) **:** a booth or shelter with a roof of branches and leaves that is used esp. for meals during the Sukkoth

Suk·koth *or* **Suk·kot** \ˈsu̇k-əs, -ˌōt(h), -ˌōs\ *n* [Heb *sukkōth,* pl. of *sukkāh*] (ca. 1905) **:** a Jewish harvest festival beginning on the 15th of Tishri and commemorating the temporary shelters used by the Jews during their wandering in the wilderness

sul·cate \ˈsəl-ˌkāt\ *adj* [L *sulcatus,* pp. of *sulcare* to furrow, fr. *sulcus*] (1760) **:** scored with usu. longitudinal furrows ⟨a ~ seedpod⟩

sul·cus \ˈsəl-kəs\ *n, pl* **sul·ci** \-ˌkī, -ˌkē, -ˌsī\ [L; akin to OE *sulh* plow, Gk *holkos* furrow, *helkein* to pull] (1662) **:** FURROW, GROOVE; *esp* **:** a shallow furrow on the surface of the brain separating adjacent convolutions

sulf- *or* **sulfo-** *or* **sulph-** *or* **sulpho-** *comb form* [F *sulf-, sulfo-,* fr. L *sulfur*] **:** sulfur **:** containing sulfur ⟨*sulfo*chloride⟩

sul·fa \ˈsəl-fə\ *adj* [short for *sulfanilamide*] (1940) **1 :** related chemically to sulfanilamide **2 :** of, relating to, or containing sulfa drugs

sul·fa·di·a·zine \ˌsəl-fə-ˈdī-ə-ˌzēn\ *n* (1940) **:** a sulfa drug $C_{10}H_{10}N_4O_2S$ that is used esp. in the treatment of meningitis, pneumonia, and intestinal infections

sulfa drug *n* (1940) **:** any of various synthetic organic bacteria-inhibiting drugs that are sulfonamides closely related chemically to sulfanilamide

sul·fa·nil·amide \ˌsəl-fə-ˈnil-ə-ˌmīd, -məd\ *n* [*sulfanil*ic + *amide*] (1937) **:** a crystalline sulfonamide $C_6H_8N_2O_2S$ that is the amide of sulfanilic acid and the parent compound of most of the sulfa drugs

sul·fa·nil·ic acid \ˌsəl-fə-ˌnil-ik-\ *n* [ISV *sulf-* + *anil*ine + *-ic*] (1856) **:** a crystalline acid $C_6H_7NO_3S$ obtained from aniline and used esp. in making dyes

sul·fa·tase \ˈsəl-fə-ˌtās, -ˌtāz\ *n* [¹*sulfate*] (ca. 1934) **:** any of various esterases that accelerate the hydrolysis of sulfuric esters and that are found in animal tissues and in microorganisms

¹**sul·fate** \ˈsəl-ˌfāt\ *n* [F, fr. L *sulfur*] (1790) **1 :** a salt or ester of sulfuric acid **2 :** a bivalent group or anion SO_4 characteristic of sulfuric acid and the sulfates

²**sulfate** *vt* **sul·fat·ed; sul·fat·ing** (ca. 1802) **1 a :** to treat or combine with sulfuric acid or a sulfate **b :** to convert into a sulfate **2 :** to form a deposit of a whitish scale of sulfate of lead on (the plates of a storage battery)

sulf·hy·dryl \ˌsəlf-ˈ(h)ī-drəl\ *n* [ISV *sulf-* + *hydr-* + *-yl*] (ca. 1934) **:** a functional group SH that is characteristic of mercaptans and is present in many biologically active compounds (as various proteins, coenzymes, and enzyme inhibitors)

sul·fide \ˈsəl-ˌfīd\ *n* (1836) **1 :** any of various organic compounds characterized by a sulfur atom attached to two carbon atoms **2 :** a binary compound (as CuS) of sulfur usu. with a more electropositive element or group **:** a salt of hydrogen sulfide

sul·fin·py·ra·zone \ˌsəl-fən-ˈpī-rə-ˌzōn\ *n* [*sulfin* (containing the group SO_2H) + *pyr-* + *azole* + *-one*] (ca. 1960) **:** a uricosuric drug $C_{23}H_{20}N_2O_3S$ used in long-term treatment of chronic gout

sul·fi·nyl \ˈsəl-fə-ˌnil\ *n* [*sulfin*ic acid (RSO_2H) + *-yl*] (ca. 1934) **:** the bivalent group SO

sul·fite \ˈsəl-ˌfīt\ *n* [F *sulfite,* alter. of *sulfate*] (ca. 1790) **:** a salt or ester of sulfurous acid — **sul·fit·ic** \ˌsəl-ˈfit-ik\ *adj*

sulfon- *comb form* [ISV *sulfonic*] **:** sulfonic ⟨*sulfon*amide⟩

sul·fon·amide \ˌsəl-ˈfän-ə-ˌmīd, -məd; -ˈfō-nə-ˌmīd\ *n* (ca. 1903) **:** an amide (as sulfanilamide) of a sulfonic acid; *also* **:** SULFA DRUG

¹**sul·fo·nate** \ˈsəl-fə-ˌnāt\ *n* (1876) **:** a salt or ester of a sulfonic acid

²**sulfonate** *vt* **-nat·ed; -nat·ing** (1890) **:** to introduce the SO_3H group into; *broadly* **:** to treat (an organic substance) with sulfuric acid — **sul·fo·na·tion** \ˌsəl-fə-ˈnā-shən\ *n*

sul·fone \ˈsəl-ˌfōn\ *n* (1872) **:** any of various compounds containing the sulfonyl group with its sulfur atom having two bonds with carbon

sul·fon·ic \ˌsəl-ˈfän-ik, -ˈfōn-\ *adj* (1873) **:** of, relating to, being, or derived from the univalent acid group SO_3H

sulfonic acid *n* (1873) **:** any of numerous acids that contain the SO_3H group and may be derived from sulfuric acid by replacement of a hydroxyl group by either an inorganic anion or a univalent organic group

sul·fo·ni·um \ˌsəl-ˈfō-nē-əm\ *n* [NL, fr. *sulf-* + *ammonium*] (1885) **:** a univalent group or cation SH_3 or derivative SR_3

sul·fo·nyl \ˈsəl-fə-ˌnil\ *n* (ca. 1930) **:** the bivalent group SO_2

sul·fo·nyl·urea \ˌsəl-fə-ˌnil-ˈ(y)u̇r-ē-ə\ *n* [NL, fr. ISV *sulfonyl* + NL *urea*] (1956) **:** any of several hypoglycemic compounds related to the sulfonamides and used in the oral treatment of diabetes

sulf·ox·ide \ˌsəl-ˈfäk-ˌsīd\ *n* [ISV] (1894) **:** any of a class of organic compounds characterized by a sulfinyl group with its sulfur atom having two bonds with carbon

sul·fur *or* **sul·phur** \ˈsəl-fər\ *n* [ME *sulphur* brimstone, fr. L *sulpur, sulphur, sulfur*] (14c) **1 :** a nonmetallic element that occurs either free or combined esp. in sulfides and sulfates, is a constituent of proteins, exists in several allotropic forms including yellow orthorhombic crystals, resembles oxygen chemically but is less active and more acidic, and is used esp. in the chemical and paper industries, in rubber vulcanization, and in medicine for treating skin diseases — see ELEMENT table **2 :** something (as scathing language) that suggests sulfur

sulfur bacterium *n* (ca. 1903) **:** any of various bacteria (esp. genus *Thiobacillus*) capable of reducing sulfur compounds

sulfur dioxide *n* (1869) **:** a heavy pungent toxic gas SO_2 that is easily condensed to a colorless liquid, is used esp. in making sulfuric acid, in bleaching, as a preservative, and as a refrigerant, and is a major air pollutant esp. in industrial areas

sul·fu·re·ous \ˌsəl-ˈfyu̇r-ē-əs\ *adj* (1552) **:** SULFUROUS

sul·fu·ric \ˌsəl-ˈfyu̇(ə)r-ik\ *adj* (1794) **:** of, relating to, or containing sulfur esp. with a higher valence than sulfurous compounds ⟨~ esters⟩

sulfuric acid *n* (1790) **:** a heavy corrosive oily dibasic strong acid H_2SO_4 that is colorless when pure and is a vigorous oxidizing and dehydrating agent — called also *oil of vitriol*

sul·fu·rize \ˈsəl-f(y)ə-ˌrīz\ *vt* **-rized; -riz·ing** (1794) **:** to treat with sulfur or a sulfur compound

sul·fu·rous \ˈsəl-f(y)ə-rəs, *also esp for 1b* ˌsəl-ˈfyu̇r-əs\ *adj* (ca. 1530) **1 a :** of, relating to, or containing sulfur esp. with a lower valence than sulfuric compounds ⟨~ esters⟩ **b :** resembling or emanating from sulfur and esp. burning sulfur **2** *or* **sul·phu·rous a :** of, relating to, or dealing with the fire of hell **:** INFERNAL **b :** SCATHING, VIRULENT ⟨~ denunciations⟩ **c :** PROFANE, BLASPHEMOUS ⟨~ language⟩ — **sul·fu·rous·ly** *adv* — **sul·fu·rous·ness** *n*

sulfurous acid *n* (1885) **:** a weak unstable dibasic acid H_2SO_3 known in solution and through its salts and used as a reducing and bleaching agent

sul·fu·ryl \ˈsəl-f(y)ə-ˌril\ *n* [ISV] (1867) **:** SULFONYL — used esp. in names of inorganic compounds

¹**sulk** \ˈsəlk\ *vi* [back-formation fr. *sulky*] (1781) **:** to be moodily silent

²**sulk** *n* (1804) **1 :** the state of one sulking — often used in pl. ⟨had a case of the ~*s*⟩ **2 :** a sulky mood or spell ⟨in a ~⟩

¹**sulky** \ˈsəl-kē\ *adj* [prob. alter. of obs. *sulke* (sluggish)] (1744) **1 :** sulking or given to spells of sulking **2** [²*sulky*] **:** having wheels and usu. a seat for the driver ⟨a ~ plow⟩ ***syn*** see SULLEN — **sulk·i·ly** \-kə-lē\ *adv* — **sulk·i·ness** \-kē-nəs\ *n*

²**sulky** *n, pl* **sulkies** [prob. fr. ¹*sulky;* fr. its having room for only one person] (1756) **:** a light 2-wheeled vehicle having a seat for the driver only and usu. no body

sul·lage \ˈsəl-ij\ *n* [prob. fr. MF *soiller, souiller* to soil — more at SOIL] (1553) **:** REFUSE, SEWAGE

sul·len \ˈsəl-ən\ *adj* [ME *solain* solitary, prob. fr. (assumed) MF, fr. L *solus* alone] (1573) **1 a :** gloomily or resentfully silent or repressed **b :** suggesting a sullen state **:** LOWERING **2 :** dull or somber in sound or color **3 :** DISMAL, GLOOMY **4 :** moving sluggishly — **sul·len·ly** *adv* — **sul·len·ness** \'səl-ən-(n)əs\ *n*

syn SULLEN, GLUM, MOROSE, SURLY, SULKY, CRABBED, SATURNINE, GLOOMY mean showing a forbidding or disagreeable mood. SULLEN implies a silent ill humor and a refusal to be sociable; GLUM suggests a silent dispiritedness; MOROSE adds to GLUM an element of bitterness or misanthropy; SURLY implies gruffness and sullenness of speech or manner; SULKY suggests childish resentment expressed in peevish sullenness; CRABBED applies to a forbidding morose harshness of manner; SATURNINE describes a heavy forbidding aspect or suggests a bitter disposition; GLOOMY implies a depression in mood making for seeming sullenness or glumness.

¹sul·ly \'səl-ē\ *vt* **sul·lied; sul·ly·ing** [prob. fr. MF *soiller* to soil] (1591) **:** to make soiled or tarnished **:** DEFILE

²sully *n, pl* **sullies** *archaic* (1602) **:** SOIL, STAIN

sulph- *or* **sulpho-** — see SULF-

sulphur butterfly *n* (1879) **:** any of numerous butterflies (esp. *Colias* and related genera of the family Pieridae) having the wings usu. yellow or orange with a black border — called also *sulphur*

sulphur yellow *n* (1816) **:** a variable color averaging a brilliant greenish yellow

Sul·pi·cian \ˌsəl-'pish-ən\ *n* [F *sulpicien*, fr. Compagnie de Saint-*Sulpice* Society of St. Sulpice] (1786) **:** a member of the Society of Priests of St. Sulpice founded by Jean Jacques Olier in Paris, France, in 1642 and dedicated to the teaching of seminarians

sul·tan \'səlt-ᵊn\ *n* [MF, fr. Ar *sulṭān*] (1555) **:** a king or sovereign esp. of a Muslim state

sul·ta·na \(ˌ)səl-'tan-ə\ *n* [It, fem. of *sultano* sultan, fr. Ar *sulṭān*] (1585) **1 :** a female member of a sultan's family; *esp* **:** a sultan's wife **2 a :** a pale yellow seedless grape grown for raisins and wine **b :** the raisin of a sultana

sul·tan·ate \'səlt-ᵊn-ˌāt\ *n* (1822) **1 :** a state or country governed by a sultan **2 :** the office, dignity, or power of a sultan

sul·tan·ess \'səlt-ᵊn-əs\ *n, archaic* (ca. 1611) **:** SULTANA

sul·try \'səl-trē\ *adj* **sul·tri·er; -est** [obs. E *sulter* to swelter, alter. of E *swelter*] (1594) **1 a :** very hot and humid **:** SWELTERING ⟨a ~ day⟩ **b :** burning hot **:** TORRID **2 a :** hot with passion or anger **b :** exciting or capable of exciting strong sexual desire ⟨~ glances⟩ — **sul·tri·ly** \-trə-lē\ *adv* — **sul·tri·ness** \-trē-nəs\ *n*

¹sum \'səm\ *n* [ME *summe*, fr. OF, fr. L *summa*, fr. fem. of *summus* highest; akin to L *super* over — more at OVER] (13c) **1 :** an indefinite or specified amount of money **2 :** the whole amount **:** AGGREGATE **3 :** the utmost degree **:** SUMMIT ⟨reached the ~ of human happiness⟩ **4 a :** a summary of the chief points or thoughts **:** SUMMATION ⟨the ~ of this criticism follows —C. W. Hendel⟩ **b :** GIST ⟨the ~ and substance of an argument⟩ **5 a (1) :** the result of adding numbers ⟨~ of 5 and 7 is 12⟩ **(2) :** the limit of the sum of the first *n* terms of an infinite series as *n* increases indefinitely **b :** numbers to be added; *broadly* **:** a problem in arithmetic **c (1) :** DISJUNCTION 2 **(2) :** UNION 2d — **sum·ma·bil·i·ty** \ˌsəm-ə-'bil-ət-ē\ *n* — **sum·ma·ble** \'səm-ə-bəl\ *adj* — **in sum :** in short **:** BRIEFLY

²sum *vb* **summed; sum·ming** *vt* (14c) **1 :** to calculate the sum of **:** TOTAL **2 :** SUMMARIZE ~ *vi* **:** to reach a sum **:** AMOUNT

su·mac *also* **su·mach** \'s(h)ü-ˌmak\ *n* [ME *sumac*, fr. MF, fr. Ar *summāq*] (15c) **1 :** a material used in tanning and dyeing that consists of dried powdered leaves and flowers of various sumacs **2 :** any of a genus (*Rhus* of the family Anacardiaceae, the sumac family) of trees, shrubs, and woody vines that have pinnately compound leaves turning to brilliant colors in the autumn, dioecious flowers, spikes or loose clusters of red or whitish berries, and in some cases foliage poisonous to the touch — compare POISON IVY, POISON OAK

Su·me·ri·an \sü-'mer-ē-ən, -'mir-\ *n* (1878) **1 :** a native of Sumer **2 :** the agglutinative language of the Sumerians that has no known linguistic affinities — **Sumerian** *adj*

sum·ma \'sům-ə, 'süm-, 'səm-\ *n, pl* **sum·mae** \'sům-ˌī, 'süm-, -ˌā; 'səm-ˌē, -ˌī\ [ML, fr. L, sum] (1725) **:** a comprehensive treatise; *esp* **:** one by a scholastic philosopher

sum·ma cum lau·de \ˌsům-ə-(ˌ)kům-'laů-də, ˌsüm-, -'laů-dē; ˌsəm-ə-ˌkəm-'lȯd-ē\ *adv or adj* [L, with highest praise] (1900) **:** with highest distinction ⟨graduated *summa cum laude*⟩ — compare CUM LAUDE, MAGNA CUM LAUDE

sum·mand \'səm-ˌand, ˌsə-'mand\ *n* [ML *summandus*, gerund of *summare* to sum, fr. *summa*] (1893) **:** a term in a summation **:** ADDEND

sum·ma·ri·za·tion \ˌsəm-(ə-)rə-'zā-shən\ *n* (1865) **1 :** the act of summarizing **2 :** SUMMARY

sum·ma·rize \'səm-ə-ˌrīz\ *vb* **-rized; -riz·ing** *vt* (1871) **:** to tell in or reduce to a summary ~ *vi* **:** to make a summary — **sum·ma·riz·er** *n*

¹sum·ma·ry \'səm-ə-rē *also* 'səm-rē *or* -ˌer-ē\ *adj* [ME, fr. ML *summarius*, fr. L *summa* sum] (15c) **1 :** COMPREHENSIVE; *esp* **:** covering the main points succinctly **2 a :** done without delay or formality **:** quickly executed ⟨a ~ dismissal⟩ **b :** of, relating to, or using a summary proceeding ⟨a ~ trial⟩ *syn* see CONCISE — **sum·mari·ly** \(ˌ)sə-'mer-ə-lē\ *adv*

²sum·ma·ry \'səm-ə-rē *also* 'səm-rē\ *n, pl* **-ries** (1509) **:** an abstract, abridgment, or compendium esp. of a preceding discourse

sum·mate \'səm-ˌāt\ *vb* **sum·mat·ed; sum·mat·ing** [back-formation fr. *summation*] *vt* (1900) **:** to add together **:** SUM UP ~ *vi* **:** to form a sum or cumulative effect

sum·ma·tion \(ˌ)sə-'mā-shən\ *n* (1760) **1 :** the act or process of forming a sum **:** ADDITION **2 :** SUM, TOTAL **3 :** cumulative action or effect; *esp* **:** the process by which a sequence of stimuli that are individually inadequate to produce a response are cumulatively able to induce a nerve impulse **4 :** a final part of an argument reviewing points made and expressing conclusions — **sum·ma·tion·al** \-shnəl, -shən-ᵊl\ *adj*

sum·ma·tive \'səm-ət-iv, -ˌāt-\ *adj* (1881) **:** ADDITIVE, CUMULATIVE

¹sum·mer \'səm-ər\ *n* [ME *sumer*, fr. OE *sumor*; akin to OHG & ON *sumer* summer, Skt *samā* year, season] (bef. 12c) **1 :** the season between spring and autumn comprising in the northern hemisphere usu. the months of June, July, and August or as reckoned astronomically extending from the June solstice to the September equinox **2 :** the warmer half of the year **3 :** YEAR ⟨a girl of seventeen ~*s*⟩ **4 :** a period of maturing powers

²summer *adj* (14c) **1 :** of, relating to, or suitable for summer ⟨~ vacation⟩ ⟨a ~ home⟩ **2 :** sown in the spring and harvested in the same year as sown ⟨~ wheat⟩ — compare WINTER

³summer *vb* **sum·mered; sum·mer·ing** \'səm-(ə-)riŋ\ *vi* (15c) **:** to pass the summer ~ *vt* **:** to keep or carry through the summer; *esp* **:** to provide (as cattle or sheep) with pasture during the summer

⁴summer *n* [ME, packhorse, beam, fr. MF *somier*, fr. (assumed) VL *sagmarius*, fr. LL *sagma* packsaddle —more at SUMPTER] (14c) **:** a large horizontal beam or stone used esp. in building: as **a :** the lintel of a door or window **b :** a stone forming the cap of a pier (as to support a lintel or arch)

summer cypress *n* (ca. 1767) **:** a densely branched Eurasian herb (*Kochia scoparia*) of the goosefoot family grown for its foliage which turns red in autumn

sum·mer·house \'səm-ər-ˌhaůs\ *n* (15c) **:** a covered structure in a garden or park designed to provide a shady resting place in summer

summer kitchen *n* (1874) **:** a small building or shed that is usu. adjacent to a house and is used as a kitchen in warm weather

sum·mer·sault *var of* SOMERSAULT

summer savory *n* (ca. 1573) **:** an annual European herb (*Satureia hortensis*) used in cookery — compare WINTER SAVORY

summer school *n* (1871) **:** a school or school session conducted in summer enabling students to accelerate progress toward a degree, to make up credits lost through absence or failure, or to round out professional education

summer squash *n* (1815) **:** any of various garden squashes derived from a variety (*Cucurbita pepo* var. *melopepo*) and used as a vegetable while immature and before hardening of the seeds and rind

summer stock *n* (1927) **:** theatrical productions of stock companies presented during the summer

summer theater *n* (1946) **:** a theater that presents several different plays or musicals during the summer

sum·mer·time \'səm-ər-ˌtīm\ *n* (14c) **:** the summer season or a period like summer

summer time *n, chiefly Brit* (1916) **:** DAYLIGHT SAVING TIME

sum·mer·wood \'səm-ər-ˌwůd\ *n* (1902) **:** the harder less porous portion of an annual ring of wood that develops late in the growing season — compare SPRINGWOOD

sum·mery \'səm-(ə-)rē\ *adj* (1824) **:** of, resembling, or fit for summer

sum·ming–up \ˌsəm-iŋ-'əp\ *n* (1790) **:** the act or statement of one who sums up

sum·mit \'səm-ət\ *n* [ME *somete*, fr. MF, fr. OF, dim. of *sum* top, fr. L *summum*, neut. of *summus* highest — more at SUM] (15c) **1 :** TOP, APEX; *esp* **:** the highest point **:** PEAK **2 :** the topmost level attainable ⟨the ~ of human fame⟩ **3 a :** the highest level of officials; *esp* **:** the diplomatic level of heads of government **b :** a conference of highest-level officials (as heads of government)

syn SUMMIT, PEAK, PINNACLE, CLIMAX, APEX, ACME, CULMINATION mean the highest point attained or attainable. SUMMIT implies the topmost level attainable; PEAK suggests the highest among other high points; PINNACLE suggests a dizzying and often insecure height; CLIMAX implies the highest point in an ascending series; APEX implies the point where all ascending lines converge; ACME implies a level of quality representing the perfection of a thing; CULMINATION suggests the outcome of a growth or development representing an attained objective.

sum·mit·eer \ˌsəm-ə-'ti(ə)r\ *n* (1958) **:** one who takes part in a summit

sum·mit·ry \'səm-ə-trē\ *n* (1958) **:** the use of a summit conference for international negotiation

sum·mon \'səm-ən\ *vt* **sum·moned; sum·mon·ing** \-(ə-)niŋ\ [ME *somonen*, fr. OF *somondre*, fr. (assumed) VL *summonere*, alter. of L *summonēre* to remind secretly, fr. *sub-* secretly + *monēre* to warn — more at SUB-, MENTAL] (13c) **1 :** to issue a call to convene **:** CONVOKE **2 :** to command by service of a summons to appear in court **3 :** to call upon for specified action ⟨~ one to be in readiness⟩ **4 :** to bid to come **:** send for ⟨~ a physician⟩ **5 :** to call forth **:** EVOKE — **sum·mon·er** \-(ə-)nər\ *n*

syn SUMMON, CALL, CITE, CONVOKE, CONVENE, MUSTER mean to demand the presence of. SUMMON specif. implies the exercise of authority; CALL may be used less formally for SUMMON; CITE implies a summoning to court usu. to answer a charge; CONVOKE implies a summons to assemble for deliberative or legislative purposes; CONVENE is somewhat less formal than CONVOKE; MUSTER suggests a calling up of a number of things that form a group in order that they may be exhibited, displayed, or utilized as a whole.

¹sum·mons \'səm-ənz\ *n, pl* **sum·mons·es** [ME *somouns*, fr. OF *somonse*, fr. pp. of *somondre*] (13c) **1 :** the act of summoning; *esp* **:** a call by authority to appear at a place named or to attend to a duty **2 :** a warning or citation to appear in court: as **a :** a written notification to be served on a person warning him to appear in court at a day specified to answer to the plaintiff **b :** a subpoena to appear as a witness **3 :** something (as a call) that summons

²summons *vt* (1711) **:** SUMMON 2

sum·mum bo·num \ˌsům-əm-'bō-nəm, ˌsüm-, ˌsəm-\ *n* [L] (1563) **:** the supreme good from which all others are derived

summum ge·nus \-'gen-əs, -'gā-nəs; -'jē-nəs\ *n, pl* **sum·ma ge·nera** \ˌsům-ə-'gen-ə-rə, ˌsüm-, -'gān-; ˌsəm-ə-'jen-ə-rə\ [NL, lit., highest genus] (1592) **:** a logical genus that cannot be classed as a species of a higher genus

su·mo \'sü-(ˌ)mō\ *n* [Jp *sumō*] (1898) **:** a Japanese form of wrestling in which a contestant loses if he is forced out of the ring or if any part of his body except the soles of his feet touches the ground

sump \'səmp\ *n* [ME *sompe* swamp — more at SWAMP] (1653) **1 :** a pit or reservoir serving as a drain or receptacle for liquids: as **a :** CESSPOOL **b :** a pit at the lowest point in a circulating or drainage system (as the oil-circulating system of an internal-combustion engine) **c** *chiefly Brit* **:** OIL PAN **2** *Brit* **:** CRANKCASE **3** [G *sumpf*, lit., marsh, fr. MHG — more at SWAMP] **a :** the lowest part of a mine shaft into

\ə\ abut \ᵊ\ kitten, F table \ər\ further \a\ ash \ā\ ace \ä\ cot, cart \aů\ out \ch\ chin \e\ bet \ē\ easy \g\ go \i\ hit \ī\ ice \j\ job \ŋ\ sing \ō\ go \ȯ\ law \ȯi\ boy \th\ thin \t͟h\ the \ü\ loot \ů\ foot \y\ yet \zh\ vision \á, k̲, ⁿ, œ, ǣ, ue, ue̅, ʸ\ *see* Guide to Pronunciation

which water drains **b :** an excavation ahead of regular work in driving a mine tunnel or sinking a mine shaft
sump pump *n* (ca. 1899) **:** a pump (as in a basement) to remove accumulations of liquid from a sump pit
sump·ter \ˈsəm(p)-tər\ *n* [short for *sumpter horse,* fr. ME *sumpter* driver of a packhorse, fr. MF *sometier,* fr. (assumed) VL *sagmatarius,* fr. LL *sagmat-, sagma* packsaddle, fr. Gk] (15c) **:** a pack animal
sump·tu·ary \ˈsəm(p)-chə-ˌwer-ē\ *adj* [L *sumptuarius,* fr. *sumptus* expense, fr. *sumptus,* pp. of *sumere* to take, spend — more at CONSUME] (1600) **1 :** designed to regulate personal expenditures and esp. to prevent extravagance and luxury ⟨conservative ~ tastes —John Cheever⟩ **2 :** designed to regulate habits on moral or religious grounds ⟨~ laws⟩ ⟨~ tax⟩
sump·tu·ous \ˈsəm(p)-ch(ə-w)əs, ˈsəm(p)sh-wəs\ *adj* [MF *sumptueux,* fr. L *sumptuosus,* fr. *sumptus*] (15c) **:** excessively costly, rich, luxurious, or magnificent ⟨~ banquets⟩ — **sump·tu·ous·ly** *adv* — **sump·tu·ous·ness** *n*
sum total *n* (14c) **1 :** a total arrived at through the counting of sums **2 :** total result **:** TOTALITY
sum–up \ˈsəm-ˌəp\ *n* (1894) **:** SUMMARY
sum up \ˌsəm-ˈəp\ *vt* (15c) **1 :** to be the sum of **:** bring to a total ⟨10 victories *summed up* his record⟩ **2 a :** to state succinctly **:** SUMMARIZE ⟨*sum up* the evidence presented⟩ **b :** to assess and then describe briefly **:** size up ~ *vi* **:** to present a summary or recapitulation
[1]**sun** \ˈsən\ *n* [ME *sunne,* fr. OE; akin to OHG *sunna* sun, L *sol* — more at SOLAR] (bef. 12c) **1 a :** the luminous celestial body around which the earth and other planets revolve, from which they receive heat and light, and which has a mean distance from earth of 93,000,000 miles (150,000,000 kilometers), a linear diameter of 864,000 miles (1,390,000 kilometers), a mass 332,000 times greater than earth, and a mean density about one fourth that of earth **b :** a celestial body like the sun **2 :** the heat or light radiated from the sun **3 :** one resembling the sun usu. in brilliance **4 :** the rising or setting of the sun ⟨from ~ to ~⟩ **5 :** GLORY, SPLENDOR — **in the sun :** in the public eye — **under the sun :** in the world **:** on earth
[2]**sun** *vb* **sunned; sun·ning** *vt* (1519) **:** to expose to or as if to the rays of the sun ~ *vi* **:** to sun oneself
sun·baked \ˈsən-ˌbākt\ *adj* (1628) **1 :** heated, parched, or compacted esp. by excessive sunlight **2 :** baked by exposure to sunshine
sun·bath \ˈsən-ˌbath, -ˌbàth\ *n* (1866) **:** an exposure to sunlight or a sunlamp
sun·bathe \-ˌbāth\ *vi* [back-formation fr. *sunbather*] (1600) **:** to take a sunbath — **sun·bath·er** \-ˌbā-thər\ *n*
sun·beam \-ˌbēm\ *n* (bef. 12c) **:** a ray of sunlight
sun·belt \-ˌbelt\ *n, often cap* (1952) **:** the southern and southwestern states of the U.S. — compare FROSTBELT
sun·bird \-ˌbərd\ *n* (ca. 1826) **:** any of numerous small brilliantly colored singing birds (family Nectariniidae) of the tropical Old World somewhat resembling hummingbirds
sun·bon·net \-ˌbän-ət\ *n* (1824) **:** a woman's bonnet with a wide brim framing the face and usu. having a ruffle at the back to protect the neck from the sun
sun·bow \-ˌbō\ *n* (1816) **:** an arch resembling a rainbow made by the sun shining through vapor or mist
[1]**sun·burn** \-ˌbərn\ *vb* **-burned** \-ˌbərnd\ *or* **-burnt** \-ˌbərnt\; **-burn·ing** [back-formation fr. *sunburned,* fr. *sun* + *burned*] *vt* (ca. 1530) **:** to burn or discolor by the sun ~ *vi* **:** to become sunburned
[2]**sunburn** *n* (1652) **:** inflammation of the skin caused by overexposure to sunlight

sunbonnet

sun·burst \ˈsən-ˌbərst\ *n* (1816) **1 :** a flash of sunlight esp. through a break in clouds **2 :** a jeweled brooch representing a sun surrounded by rays
sun·dae \ˈsən-dē\ *n* [prob. alter. of *Sunday*] (ca. 1903) **:** ice cream served with topping (as crushed fruit, syrup, nuts, or whipped cream)
sun dance *n* (1849) **:** a solo or group solstice rite of American Indians
[1]**Sun·day** \ˈsən-dē, -(ˌ)dā\ *n* [ME, fr. OE *sunnandæg* (akin to OHG *sunnūntag*), fr. *sunne* sun + *dæg* day] (bef. 12c) **:** the first day of the week **:** the Christian analogue of the Jewish Sabbath — **Sun·days** \-dēz\ *adv*
[2]**Sunday** *adj* (12c) **1 :** of, relating to, or associated with Sunday **2** [fr. the practice of wearing one's best clothes on Sunday to attend church] **:** BEST ⟨~ suit⟩ **3 :** AMATEUR ⟨~ painters⟩
Sun·day–go–to–meet·ing \ˈsən-de-ˌgōt-ə-ˈmēt-iŋ\ *adj* (1841) **:** appropriate for Sunday churchgoing
Sunday punch *n* (1929) **1 :** a powerful or devastating blow; *esp* **:** a knockout punch **2 :** something capable of delivering a powerful or devastating blow to the opposition ⟨saving his *Sunday punch* for the end of the campaign —*Newsweek*⟩
Sunday school *n* (1783) **:** a school held on Sunday for religious education; *also* **:** the teachers and pupils of such a school
sun deck *n* (1909) **1 :** the usu. upper deck of a ship that is exposed to the most sun **2 :** a roof or terrace used for sunning
sun·der \ˈsən-dər\ *vt* **sun·dered; sun·der·ing** \-d(ə-)riŋ\ [ME *sunderen,* fr. OE *gesundrian, syndrian;* akin to OHG *suntarōn* to sunder, L *sine* without, OE *syndrig* sundry] (bef. 12c) **:** to break apart or in two **:** sever finally and completely or with violence ***syn*** see SEPARATE
sun·dew \ˈsən-(ˌ)d(y)ü\ *n* (1578) **:** any of a genus (*Drosera* of the family Droseraceae, the sundew family) of bog-inhabiting insectivorous herbs having viscid glands on the leaves
sun·di·al \-ˌdī(-ə)l\ *n* (ca. 1579) **:** an instrument to show the time of day by the shadow of a gnomon on a usu. horizontal plate or on a cylindrical surface
sun disk *n* (1877) **:** an ancient Near Eastern symbol consisting of a disk with conventionalized wings emblematic of the sun-god (as Ra in Egypt)
sun dog *n* (1635) **1 :** PARHELION **2 :** a small nearly round halo on the parhelic circle most frequently just outside the halo of 22 degrees
sun·down \ˈsən-ˌdau̇n\ *n* (1620) **:** SUNSET 2
sun·down·er \-ˌdau̇-nər\ *n* (1868) **1** [fr. his habit of arriving at a place where he hopes to obtain food and lodging too late to do any work] *Austral* **:** HOBO, TRAMP **2** *chiefly Brit* **:** a drink taken at sundown
sun·dress \-ˌdres\ *n* (1944) **:** a dress with an abbreviated bodice usu. exposing the shoulders, arms, and back
sun·dries \ˈsən-drēz\ *n pl* [[1]*sundry*] (1755) **:** miscellaneous small articles, details, or items
sun·drops \ˈsən-ˌdräps\ *n pl but sing or pl in constr* (ca. 1784) **:** any of several day-flowering herbs (genus *Oenothera*) — compare EVENING PRIMROSE
[1]**sun·dry** \ˈsən-drē\ *adj* [ME, different for each, fr. OE *syndrig* — more at SUNDER] (13c) **:** MISCELLANEOUS, VARIOUS ⟨~ articles⟩
[2]**sundry** *pron, pl in constr* (15c) **:** an indeterminate number ⟨recommended for reading by all and ~ —Edward Huberman⟩
sun·fish \-ˌfish\ *n* (1629) **1 :** a large marine bony fish (*Mola mola* of the order Tetraodontiformes) having high dorsal and anal fins and a body nearly oval in outline due to a sharply truncated posterior extremity and attaining a length of 10 feet (3 meters) and a weight in excess of 2 tons (1.8 metric tons) — called also *ocean sunfish* **2 :** any of numerous American percoid freshwater fishes (family Centrarchidae, esp. genus *Lepomis*) usu. with a deep compressed body and metallic luster
Sunfish *trademark* — used for a light sailboat that has one sail and is designed for use by no more than two people
sun·flow·er \-ˌflau̇(-ə)r\ *n* (ca. 1597) **:** any of a genus (*Helianthus*) of composite plants with large yellow-rayed flower heads bearing seeds that serve as stock food and yield an edible oil
sung \ˈsəŋ\ *past and past part of* SING
Sung \ˈsu̇ŋ\ *n* [Chin (Pek) *Sung*[4]] (1738) **:** a Chinese dynasty dated A.D. 960–1280 and marked by cultural refinement and achievements in philosophy, literature, and art — **Sung** *adj*
sun·glass \ˈsən-ˌglas\ *n* (1804) **1 :** a convex lens for converging the sun's rays **2** *pl* **:** glasses to protect the eyes from the sun
sung mass *n* (ca. 1931) **:** HIGH MASS
sun–god \ˈsən-ˌgäd\ *n* (1592) **:** a god that represents or personifies the sun in various religions — **sun–god·dess** \-ˌgäd-əs\ *n*
sun–grebe \-ˌgrēb\ *n* (ca. 1919) **:** any of several tropical American and African birds (family Heliornithidae) related to the cranes and herons
sunk *past and past part of* SINK
sunk·en \ˈsəŋ-kən\ *adj* [fr. obs. pp. of *sink*] (14c) **1 :** SUBMERGED; *esp* **:** lying at the bottom of a body of water **2 a :** HOLLOW, RECESSED ⟨~ cheeks⟩ **b :** lying in a depression ⟨a ~ garden⟩ **c :** settled below the normal level **d :** constructed below the normal floor level ⟨a ~ living room⟩
sunk fence *n* (1761) **:** a ditch with a retaining wall used to divide lands without defacing a landscape — called also *ha-ha*
sun·lamp \ˈsən-ˌlamp\ *n* (1885) **:** an electric lamp designed to emit radiation of wavelengths from ultraviolet to infrared
sun·less \-ləs\ *adj* (1589) **:** lacking sunshine **:** DARK, CHEERLESS
sun·light \-ˌlīt\ *n* (13c) **:** the light of the sun **:** SUNSHINE
sun·lit \-ˌlit\ *adj* (1822) **:** lighted by or as if by the sun
sunn \ˈsən\ *n* [Hindi *san,* fr. Skt *śaṇa*] (ca. 1590) **:** an East Indian leguminous plant (*Crotalaria juncea*) with slender branches, simple leaves, and yellow flowers; *also* **:** its valuable fiber resembling hemp that is lighter and stronger than jute
sun·na \ˈsu̇n-(ˌ)n(ə), ˈsən-\ *n, often cap* [Ar *sunnah*] (1626) **:** the body of Islamic custom and practice based on Muhammad's words and deeds
sunn hemp *n* (1800) **:** SUNN
Sun·ni \ˈsu̇n-(ˌ)n(ē\ *n* [Ar *sunnīy,* fr. *sunnah*] (1590) **1 :** the Muslims of the branch of Islam that adheres to the orthodox tradition and acknowledges the first four caliphs as rightful successors of Muhammad — compare SHIA **2 :** SUNNITE — **Sunni** *adj*
Sun·nism \ˈsu̇n-(n)iz-əm\ *n* (1902) **:** the religious system or distinctive tenets of the Sunni
Sun·nite \-(ˌ)n)īt\ *n* (1718) **:** a Sunni Muslim
sun·ny \ˈsən-ē\ *adj* **sun·ni·er; -est** (14c) **1 :** marked by brilliant sunlight **:** full of sunshine **2 :** MERRY, OPTIMISTIC ⟨a ~ disposition⟩ **3 :** exposed to, brightened, or warmed by the sun ⟨a ~ room⟩ — **sun·ni·ly** \ˈsən-ᵊl-ē\ *adv* — **sun·ni·ness** \ˈsən-ē-nəs\ *n*
sun·ny–side up \ˌsən-ē-ˌsīd-ˈəp\ *adj, of an egg* (ca. 1901) **:** fried on one side only
sun parlor *n* (1917) **:** a glass-enclosed porch or living room with a sunny exposure — called also *sun porch, sun-room*
sun·rise \ˈsən-ˌrīz\ *n* (15c) **1 :** the apparent rising of the sun above the horizon; *also* **:** the accompanying atmospheric effects **2 :** the time when the upper limb of the sun appears above the sensible horizon as a result of the diurnal rotation of the earth
sun·roof \-ˌrüf, -ˌru̇f\ *n* (1952) **:** an automobile roof having a panel that can be opened
sun·scald \-ˌskȯld\ *n* (1851) **:** an injury of woody plants (as fruit or forest trees) characterized by localized death of the tissues and sometimes by cankers and caused when it occurs in the summer by the combined action of both the heat and light of the sun and in the winter by the combined action of sun and low temperature to produce freezing of bark and underlying tissues
sun·screen \-ˌskrēn\ *n* (1845) **:** a screen to protect against sun; *esp* **:** a substance (as para-aminobenzoic acid) used in suntan preparations to protect the skin from excessive ultraviolet radiation — **sun·screen·ing** *adj*
sun·seek·er \-ˌsē-kər\ *n* (1954) **:** a person who travels to an area of warmth and sun esp. in winter
[1]**sun·set** \-ˌset\ *n* (14c) **1 :** the apparent descent of the sun below the horizon; *also* **:** the accompanying atmospheric effects **2 :** the time when the upper limb of the sun disappears below the sensible horizon as a result of the diurnal rotation of the earth **3 :** a period of decline; *esp* **:** old age
[2]**sunset** *adj* (1976) **:** stipulating the periodic review of government agencies and programs in order to continue their existence ⟨~ law⟩
sun·shade \ˈsən-ˌshād\ *n* (1842) **:** something used as a protection from the sun's rays: as **a :** PARASOL **b :** AWNING
[1]**sun·shine** \-ˌshīn\ *n* (13c) **1 a :** the sun's light or direct rays **b :** the warmth and light given by the sun's rays **c :** a spot or surface on which the sun's light shines **2 :** something (as a person, condition, or

influence) that radiates warmth, cheer, or happiness — **sun·shiny** \-ˌshī-nē\ *adj*

[2]sunshine *adj* (1972) **:** forbidding or restricting closed meetings of legislative or executive bodies and sometimes providing for public access to records ⟨~ law⟩

sun·spot \-ˌspät\ *n* (1868) **:** one of the dark spots that appear from time to time on the sun's surface consisting commonly of a blue-black umbra with a surrounding penumbra of lighter shade and usu. visible only with the telescope

sun·stroke \-ˌstrōk\ *n* (1851) **:** heatstroke caused by direct exposure to the sun

sun·struck \-ˌstrək\ *adj* (1794) **:** affected or touched by the sun

sun·suit \-ˌsüt\ *n* (1929) **:** an outfit (as of halter and shorts) worn usu. for sunbathing and play

sun·tan \-ˌtan\ *n* (1904) **1 :** a browning of the skin from exposure to the rays of the sun **2** *pl* **:** a tan-colored summer uniform — **sun·tanned** \-ˌtand\ *adj*

sun·up \-ˌəp\ *n* (1712) **:** SUNRISE

[1]sun·ward \ˈsən-wərd\ *or* **sun·wards** \-wərdz\ *adv* (1611) **:** toward the sun

[2]sunward *adj* (1769) **:** facing the sun

sun·wise \ˈsən-ˌwīz\ *adv* (ca. 1864) **:** CLOCKWISE

[1]sup \ˈsəp\ *vb* **supped; sup·ping** [ME *suppen,* fr. OE *sūpan, suppan;* akin to OHG *sūfan* to drink, sip, OE *sopp* sop, *sūcan* to suck — more at SUCK] *vt* (bef. 12c) **:** to take or drink in swallows or gulps **~** *vi, chiefly dial* **:** to take food and esp. liquid food into the mouth a little at a time either by drinking or with a spoon

[2]sup *n* (ca. 1570) **:** a mouthful esp. of liquor or broth **:** SIP; *also* **:** a small quantity of liquid ⟨a ~ of tea⟩

[3]sup *vi* **supped; sup·ping** [ME *soupen, suppen,* fr. OF *souper,* fr. *soupe* sop, soup — more at SOUP] (13c) **1 :** to eat the evening meal **2 :** to make one's supper — used with *on* or *off* ⟨~ on roast beef⟩

[1]su·per \ˈsü-pər\ *adj* [*super-*] (1837) **1** [by shortening of *superfine*] **a** —used as a generalized term of approval ⟨a ~ cook⟩ **b :** of high grade or quality **2 :** very large or powerful ⟨a ~ atom bomb⟩ **3 :** exhibiting the characteristics of its type to an extreme or excessive degree ⟨~ secrecy⟩

[2]super *n* (1838) **1** [by shortening] **a :** SUPERNUMERARY; *esp* **:** a supernumerary actor **b :** SUPERINTENDENT, SUPERVISOR; *esp* **:** the superintendent of an apartment building **2** [short for obs. *superhive*] **:** a removable upper story of a beehive **3** [[1]*super*] **:** a superfine grade or extra large size **4** [origin unknown] **:** a thin loosely woven open-meshed starched cotton fabric used esp. for reinforcing books

[3]super *vt* **su·pered; su·per·ing** \-p(ə-)riŋ\ (1914) **:** to reinforce (as a book backbone) with super

[4]super *adv* [*super-*] (1944) **1 :** VERY, EXTREMELY ⟨a ~ fast car⟩ **2 :** to an excessive degree

super- *prefix* [L, over, above, in addition, fr. *super* over, above, on top of — more at OVER] **1 a** (1) **:** over and above **:** higher in quantity, quality, or degree than **:** more than ⟨*super*human⟩ (2) **:** in addition **:** extra ⟨*super*tax⟩ **b** (1) **:** exceeding or so as to exceed a norm ⟨*super*heat⟩ (2) **:** in or to an extreme or excessive degree or intensity ⟨*super*subtle⟩ **c :** surpassing all or most others of its kind ⟨*super*highway⟩ **2 a :** situated or placed above, on, or at the top of ⟨*super*lunary⟩; *specif* **:** situated on the dorsal side of **b :** next above or higher ⟨*super*tonic⟩ **3 :** having the (specified) ingredient present in a large or unusually large proportion ⟨*super*phosphate⟩ **4 :** constituting a more inclusive category than that specified ⟨*super*family⟩ **5 :** superior in status, title, or position ⟨*super*power⟩

su·per·achiev·er
su·per·ac·tiv·i·ty
su·per·add
su·per·ad·di·tion
su·per·ad·min·is·tra·tor
su·per·agent
su·per·am·bi·tious
su·per·ath·lete
su·per·bad
su·per·bank
su·per·bear
su·per·bil·lion·aire
su·per·bitch
su·per·black
su·per·board
su·per·bomb
su·per·bomb·er
su·per·bright
su·per·bu·reau·crat
su·per·cab·i·net
su·per·car
su·per·car·ri·er
su·per·cau·tious
su·per·cen·ter
su·per·chic
su·per·chip
su·per·church
su·per·civ·i·li·za·tion
su·per·civ·i·lized
su·per·clean
su·per·club
su·per·co·los·sal
su·per·com·fort·able
su·per·com·pet·i·tive
su·per·con·fi·dent
su·per·con·glom·er·ate
su·per·con·ser·va·tive
su·per·con·ve·nient
su·per·cop
su·per·cor·po·ra·tion
su·per·coun·try
su·per·crim·i·nal
su·per·cute
su·per·de·luxe
su·per·dip·lo·mat
su·per·ef·fec·tive
su·per·ef·fi·cien·cy
su·per·ef·fi·cient
su·per·ego·ist
su·per·elite
su·per·em·i·nence
su·per·em·i·nent
su·per·em·i·nent·ly
su·per·ex·press
su·per·fan
su·per·fast
su·per·firm
su·per·flack
su·per·fund
su·per·good
su·per·gov·ern·ment
su·per·group
su·per·growth
su·per·he·ro
su·per·her·o·ine
su·per·hit
su·per·hype
su·per·in·tel·lec·tu·al
su·per·in·tel·li·gence
su·per·in·tel·li·gent
su·per·in·ten·si·ty
su·per·jock
su·per·joint
su·per·jum·bo
su·per·large
su·per·life
su·per·light
su·per·lob·by·ist
su·per·loy·al·ist
su·per·lux·u·ri·ous
su·per·lux·u·ry
su·per·ma·cho
su·per·male
su·per·mas·cu·line
su·per·mil·i·tant
su·per·mil·lion·aire
su·per·mind
su·per·min·is·ter
su·per·mod·el
su·per·mod·ern
su·per·mom
su·per·na·tion
su·per·na·tion·al
su·per·nu·tri·tion
su·per·op·ti·mis·tic
su·per·or·gan·ic
su·per·or·gasm
su·per·park
su·per·pa·tri·ot
su·per·pa·tri·ot·ic
su·per·pa·tri·o·tism
su·per·per·son
su·per·per·son·al
su·per·phe·nom·e·non
su·per·pimp
su·per·plane
su·per·play·er
su·per·po·lite
su·per·port
su·per·pow·er·ful
su·per·prize
su·per·pro
su·per·qual·i·ty
su·per·race
su·per·real
su·per·re·al·ism
su·per·re·al·ist
su·per·re·gion·al
su·per·rich
su·per·road
su·per·ro·man·tic
su·per·ro·man·ti·cism
su·per·safe
su·per·sales·man
su·per·scale
su·per·school
su·per·scout
su·per·se·cre·cy
su·per·se·cret
su·per·sell
su·per·sell·er
su·per·sex·u·al·i·ty
su·per·sharp
su·per·show
su·per·sing·er
su·per·size
su·per·sized
su·per·sleuth
su·per·slick
su·per·smooth
su·per·soft
su·per·so·phis·ti·cat·ed
su·per·spe·cial
su·per·spe·cial·ist
su·per·spe·cial·iza·tion
su·per·spe·cial·ized
su·per·spec·ta·cle
su·per·spec·tac·u·lar
su·per·spec·u·la·tion
su·per·spy
su·per·state
su·per·sta·tion
su·per·stim·u·late
su·per·stock
su·per·store
su·per·stra·tum
su·per·strength
su·per·strike
su·per·strong
su·per·stud
su·per·sub·tle
su·per·sub·tle·ty
su·per·sur·geon
su·per·tank·er
su·per·ter·rif·ic
su·per·thick
su·per·thin
su·per·thril·ler
su·per·tight
su·per·trick
su·per·vir·ile
su·per·vir·tu·o·so
su·per·wave
su·per·weap·on
su·per·wide
su·per·wife
su·per·wom·an

su·per·a·ble \ˈsü-p(ə-)rə-bəl\ *adj* [L *superabilis,* fr. *superare* to surmount — more at INSUPERABLE] (1629) **:** capable of being overcome or conquered — **su·per·a·ble·ness** *n* — **su·per·a·bly** \-blē\ *adv*

su·per·abound \ˌsü-pə-rə-ˈbau̇nd\ *vi* [ME *superabounden,* fr. LL *superabundare,* fr. L *super-* + *abundare* to abound] (15c) **:** to abound or prevail in greater measure or to excess

su·per·abun·dant \-ˈbən-dənt\ *adj* [ME, fr. LL *superabundant-, superabundans,* fr. prp. of *superabundare*] (15c) **:** more than ample **:** EXCESSIVE — **su·per·abun·dance** \-dən(t)s\ *n* — **su·per·abun·dant·ly** *adv*

su·per·agen·cy \ˈsü-pə-ˌrā-jən-sē\ *n* (1943) **:** a large complex governmental agency esp. when set up to supervise other agencies

su·per·al·loy \ˌsü-pə-ˈral-ˌȯi, -rə-ˈlȯi\ *n* (1948) **:** any of various high-strength often complex alloys having resistance to high temperature

su·per·al·tern \ˌsü-pə-ˈrȯl-tərn\ *n* [*super-* + *-altern* (as in *subaltern*)] (1921) **:** a universal proposition in traditional logic that is a ground for the immediate inference of a corresponding subaltern

su·per·an·nu·ate \ˌsü-pə-ˈran-yə-ˌwāt\ *vb* **-at·ed; -at·ing** [back-formation fr. *superannuated*] *vt* (1649) **1 :** to make, declare, or prove obsolete or out-of-date **2 :** to retire and pension because of age or infirmity **~** *vi* **1 :** to become retired **2 :** to become antiquated — **su·per·an·nu·a·tion** \-ˌran-yə-ˈwā-shən\ *n*

su·per·an·nu·at·ed *adj* [ML *superannuatus,* pp. of *superannuari* to be too old, fr. L *super-* + *annus* year — more at ANNUAL] (1633) **:** incapacitated or disqualified for active duty by advanced age

su·perb \su̇-ˈpərb\ *adj* [L *superbus* excellent, proud, fr. *super* above + *-bus* (akin to OE *bēon* to be) — more at OVER, BE] (1549) **:** marked to the highest degree by grandeur, excellence, brilliance, or competence ***syn*** see SPLENDID — **su·perb·ly** *adv* — **su·perb·ness** *n*

su·per·block \ˈsü-pər-ˌbläk\ *n* (1928) **:** a very large commercial or residential block barred to through traffic, crossed by pedestrian walks and sometimes access roads, and often spotted with grassed malls

[1]su·per·cal·en·der \-ˌkal-ən-dər\ *vt* (1888) **:** to process (paper) in a supercalender

[2]supercalender *n* (1894) **:** a stack of highly polished calender rolls used to give an extra finish to paper

su·per·car·go \ˌsü-pər-ˈkär-(ˌ)gō, ˈsü-pər-ˌ\ *n* [Sp *sobrecargo,* fr. *sobre-* over (fr. L *super-*) + *cargo* cargo] (1697) **:** an officer on a merchant ship in charge of the commercial concerns of the voyage

supercede *var of* SUPERSEDE

su·per·charge \ˈsü-pər-ˌchärj\ *vt* (1876) **1 :** to charge greatly or excessively (as with vigor or tension) **2 :** to supply a charge to the intake of (as an engine) at a pressure higher than that of the surrounding atmosphere **3 :** PRESSURIZE 1 — **supercharge** *n*

su·per·charg·er \-ˌchär-jər\ *n* (1921) **:** a device (as a blower or compressor) for pressurizing the cabin of an airplane or for increasing the volume air charge of an internal-combustion engine over that which would normally be drawn in through the pumping action of the pistons

su·per·cil·i·ary \ˌsü-pər-ˈsil-ē-ˌer-ē\ *adj* [NL *superciliaris,* fr. L *supercilium*] (1732) **:** of, relating to, or adjoining the eyebrow

su·per·cil·ious \-ˈsil-ē-əs, -ˈsil-yəs\ *adj* [L *superciliosus,* fr. *supercilium* eyebrow, haughtiness, fr. *super-* + *-cilium* (akin to *celare* to hide) — more at HELL] (1598) **:** coolly and patronizingly haughty ***syn*** see PROUD — **su·per·cil·ious·ly** *adv* — **su·per·cil·ious·ness** *n*

su·per·city \ˈsü-pər-ˌsit-ē\ *n* (1925) **:** MEGALOPOLIS

su·per·class \-ˌklas\ *n* (ca. 1891) **:** a category in taxonomy ranking between a phylum or division and a class

su·per·clu·ster \ˈsü-pər-ˌkləs-tər\ *n* (1926) **:** a group of gravitationally associated clusters of galaxies

su·per·coil \-ˌkȯi(ə)l\ *n* (1967) **:** SUPERHELIX — **supercoil** *vb*

su·per·com·put·er \-kəm-ˌpyüt-ər\ *n* (1968) **:** a large very fast mainframe used esp. for scientific computations

su·per·con·duct \ˌsü-pər-kən-ˈdəkt\ *vi* (1952) **:** to exhibit superconductivity

su·per·con·duc·tive \-ˈdək-tiv\ *adj* (1929) **:** exhibiting superconductivity

su·per·con·duc·tiv·i·ty \-ˌkän-ˌdək-ˈtiv-ət-ē, -kən-\ *n* (1916) **:** a complete disappearance of electrical resistance in a substance at temperatures near absolute zero — **su·per·con·duc·tor** \-kən-ˈdək-tər\ *n*

su·per·con·ti·nent \ˈsü-pər-ˌkänt-ᵊn-ənt, -ˌkänt-nənt\ *n* (1960) **:** a hypothetical former large continent from which other continents broke off and drifted away

su·per·cool \ˌsü-pər-ˈkül\ *vt* (1906) **:** to cool below the freezing point without solidification or crystallization **~** *vi* **:** to become supercooled

su·per·cur·rent \-ˌkər-ənt, -ˌkə-rənt\ *n* (1948) **:** a current of electricity flowing in a superconductor

su·per·dom·i·nant \-ˈdäm-(ə-)nənt\ *n* (1833) **:** SUBMEDIANT

su·per–du·per \ˈsü-pər-ˈdü-pər\ *adj* [redupl. of [1]*super*] (1940) **:** of the greatest excellence, size, effectiveness, or impressiveness

su·per·ego \ˌsü-pə-ˈrē-(ˌ)gō *also* -ˈreg-(ˌ)ō\ *n* [NL, trans. of G *über-ich,* fr. *über* over + *ich* I] (1919) **:** the one of the three divisions of the psyche in psychoanalytic theory that is only partly conscious, represents internalization of parental conscience and the rules of society, and functions to reward and punish through a system of moral attitudes, conscience, and a sense of guilt — compare EGO, ID

su·per·el·e·vate \ˌsü-pə-ˈrel-ə-ˌvāt\ *vt* (ca. 1945) : BANK 1c

su·per·el·e·va·tion \-ˌrel-ə-ˈvā-shən\ *n* (1889) **1** : the vertical distance between the heights of inner and outer edges of highway pavement or railroad rails **2** : additional elevation

su·per·em·pir·i·cal \ˌsü-pə-rim-ˈpir-i-kəl, -(ˌ)rem-\ *adj* (1947) : experienced or experiencing by more than empirical means : TRANSCENDENT, TRANSCENDENTAL

su·per·en·ci·pher \-rin-ˈsī-fər\ *vt* (ca. 1962) : to encipher what is already a cryptogram — **su·per·en·ci·pher·ment** \-mənt\ *n*

su·per·er·o·ga·tion \ˌsü-pə-ˌrer-ə-ˈgā-shən\ *n* [ML *supererogation-, supererogatio,* fr. *supererogatus,* pp. of *supererogare* to perform beyond the call of duty, fr. LL, to expend in addition, fr. L *super-* + *erogare* to expend public funds after asking the consent of the people, fr. *e-* + *rogare* to ask — more at RIGHT] (1526) : the act of performing more than is required by duty, obligation, or need

su·per·erog·a·to·ry \ˌsü-pə-ri-ˈräg-ə-ˌtōr-ē, -ˌtȯr-\ *adj* (1593) **1** : observed or performed to an extent not enjoined or required **2** : SUPERFLUOUS, NONESSENTIAL

su·per·fam·i·ly \ˈsü-pər-ˌfam-(ə-)lē\ *n* (ca. 1872) : a category of taxonomic classification ranking next above a family

su·per·fe·cun·da·tion \ˌsü-pər-ˌfek-ən-ˈdā-shən, -ˌfē-kən-\ *n* (ca. 1855) **1** : successive fertilization of two or more ova from the same ovulation esp. by different sires **2** : fertilization at one time of a number of ova excessive for the species

su·per·fe·ta·tion \-fē-ˈtā-shən\ *n* [ML *superfetation-, superfetatio,* fr. L *superfetatus,* pp. of *superfetare* to conceive while already pregnant, fr. *super-* + *fetus* act of bearing young, offspring — more at FETUS] (1603) **1** : successive fertilization of two or more ova of different ovulations resulting in the presence of embryos of unlike ages in the same uterus **2** : a progressive accumulation or accretion reaching an extreme or excessive degree

su·per·fi·cial \ˌsü-pər-ˈfish-əl\ *adj* [ME, fr. LL *superficialis,* fr. L *superficies*] (15c) **1 a** (1) : of or relating to a surface (2) : lying on, not penetrating below, or affecting only the surface ⟨~ wounds⟩ **b** *of a unit of measure* : SQUARE ⟨~ foot⟩ **2 a** : concerned only with the obvious or apparent : SHALLOW **b** : lying on the surface : EXTERNAL **c** : presenting only an appearance without substance or significance — **su·per·fi·cial·ly** \-ˈfish-(ə-)lē\ *adv*

syn SUPERFICIAL, SHALLOW, CURSORY mean lacking in depth or solidity. SUPERFICIAL implies a concern only with surface aspects; SHALLOW is more generally derogatory in implying lack of depth in knowledge, reasoning, emotions, or character; CURSORY suggests a lack of thoroughness or a neglect of details.

superficial fascia *n* (1876) : the thin layer of loose fatty connective tissue underlying the skin and binding it to the parts beneath — called also *hypodermis*

su·per·fi·ci·al·i·ty \ˌsü-pər-ˌfish-ē-ˈal-ət-ē\ *n, pl* **-ties** (ca. 1530) **1** : the quality or state of being superficial **2** : something superficial

su·per·fi·cies \-ˈfish-(ˌ)ēz, -ē-ˌēz\ *n, pl* **superficies** [L, surface, fr. *super-* + *facies* face, aspect — more at FACE] (1530) **1** : a surface of a body or a region of space **2** : the external aspects or appearance of a thing

su·per·fine \ˌsü-pər-ˈfīn\ *adj* (1575) **1** : overly refined or nice **2** : of extremely fine size or texture ⟨~ toothbrush bristles⟩ ⟨~ sugar⟩ **3** : of high quality or grade — used esp. of merchandise

su·per·fix \ˈsü-pər-ˌfiks\ *n* [*super-* + *-fix* (as in *prefix*)] (ca. 1948) : a recurrent predictable pattern of stress that characterizes small stretches of speech whose constituents are parallel in relationship

su·per·flu·id \ˌsü-pər-ˈflü-əd\ *n* (1942) **1** : a peculiar state of matter noted only in liquid helium cooled to near absolute zero and characterized by apparently frictionless flow (as through fine holes) **2** : the electron gas in a superconducting metal; *also* : a condensed state of matter (as in a neutron star) in which neutrons are held to behave frictionlessly — **su·per·flu·id·i·ty** \-flü-ˈid-ət-ē\ *n*

su·per·flu·ity \ˌsü-pər-ˈflü-ət-ē\ *n, pl* **-ities** [ME *superfluitee,* fr. MF *superfluité,* fr. LL *superfluitat-, superfluitas,* fr. L *superfluus*] (14c) **1 a** : EXCESS, OVERSUPPLY **b** : something unnecessary or superfluous **2** : immoderate and esp. luxurious living, habits, or desires

su·per·flu·ous \sü-ˈpər-flə-wəs\ *adj* [ME, fr. L *superfluus,* lit., running over, fr. *superfluere* to overflow, fr. *super-* + *fluere* to flow — more at FLUID] (15c) **1** : exceeding what is sufficient or necessary : EXTRA **2** *obs* : marked by wastefulness : EXTRAVAGANT — **su·per·flu·ous·ly** *adv* — **su·per·flu·ous·ness** *n*

su·per·gal·axy \ˈsü-pər-ˌgal-ək-sē\ *n* (1926) : a large cluster of galaxies

su·per·gene \ˈsü-pər-ˌjēn\ *n* (ca. 1949) : a group of linked genes acting as an allelomorphic unit esp. when due to the suppression of crossing over

su·per·gi·ant \-ˌjī-ənt\ *n* (1926) : a star of very great intrinsic luminosity and enormous size

su·per·graph·ics \-ˌgraf-iks\ *n pl but sing or pl in constr* (1969) : billboard-sized graphic shapes usu. of bright color and simple design

[1]**su·per·heat** \ˌsü-pər-ˈhēt\ *vt* (1859) **1 a** : to heat (a vapor not in contact with its own liquid) so as to cause to remain free from suspended liquid droplets ⟨~*ed* steam⟩ **b** : to heat (a liquid) above the boiling point without converting into vapor **2** : OVERHEAT ⟨~*ed* protest⟩ — **su·per·heat·er** *n*

[2]**su·per·heat** \ˈsü-pər-ˌhēt, ˌsü-pər-ˈ\ *n* (1884) : the extra heat imparted to a vapor in superheating it from a dry and saturated condition; *also* : the corresponding rise of temperature

su·per·he·lix \ˈsü-pər-ˌhē-liks\ *n* (1965) : a helix (as of DNA) which has its axis arranged in a helical coil — **su·per·he·li·cal** \ˌsü-pər-ˈhel-i-kəl, ˈsü-, -ˈhē-li-\ *adj*

[1]**su·per·het·ero·dyne** \ˌsü-pər-ˈhet-ə-rə-ˌdīn, -ˈhe-trə-\ *adj* [*supersonic* + *heterodyne*] (1922) : of or relating to a form of beat reception in which beats are produced of a frequency above audibility but below that of the received signals and the current of the beat frequency is then rectified, amplified, and finally rectified again so as to reproduce the sound

[2]**superheterodyne** *n* (1922) : a radio set for superheterodyne reception

su·per·high frequency \ˈsü-pər-ˌhī-\ *n* (ca. 1945) : a radio frequency in the next to the highest range of the radio spectrum — see RADIO FREQUENCY table

su·per·high·way \ˌsü-pər-ˈhī-ˌwā, ˈsü-pər-ˌ\ *n* (ca. 1926) : a broad arterial highway (as an expressway or turnpike) designed for high-speed traffic

su·per·hu·man \ˌsü-pər-ˈhyü-mən, -ˈyü-\ *adj* (1633) **1** : being above the human : DIVINE ⟨~ beings⟩ **2** : exceeding normal human power, size, or capability : HERCULEAN ⟨a ~ effort⟩ — **su·per·hu·man·i·ty** \-hyü-ˈman-ət-ē, -yü-\ *n* — **su·per·hu·man·ly** \-ˈhyü-mən-lē, -ˈyü-\ *adv* — **su·per·hu·man·ness** \-mən-nəs\ *n*

su·per·im·pose \ˌsü-pə-rim-ˈpōz\ *vt* (1794) : to place or lay over or above something — **su·per·im·pos·able** \-ˈpō-zə-bəl\ *adj* — **su·per·im·po·si·tion** \-ˌrim-pə-ˈzish-ən\ *n*

su·per·in·cum·bent \-rin-ˈkəm-bənt\ *adj* [L *superincumbent-, superincumbens,* prp. of *superincumbere* to lie on top of, fr. *super-* + *incumbere* to lie down on — more at INCUMBENT] (1664) : lying or resting and usu. exerting pressure on something else — **su·per·in·cum·bent·ly** *adv*

su·per·in·di·vid·u·al \ˌsü-pə-ˌrin-də-ˈvij-(ə-)wəl, -ˈvij-əl\ *adj* (1916) : of, relating to, or being an organism, entity, or complex of more than individual complexity or nature

su·per·in·duce \-rin-ˈd(y)üs\ *vt* [L *superinducere,* fr. *super-* + *inducere* to lead in — more at INDUCE] (1555) **1** : to introduce as an addition over or above something already existing **2** : BRING ON, INDUCE — **su·per·in·duc·tion** \-ˈdək-shən\ *n*

su·per·in·fec·tion \-rin-ˈfek-shən\ *n* (ca. 1923) : reinfection or a second infection with the same type of microbial agent (as a bacterium, fungus, or virus) — **su·per·in·fect** \-ˈfekt\ *vt*

su·per·in·tend \ˌsü-p(ə-)rin-ˈtend, ˌsü-pərn-\ *vt* [LL *superintendere,* fr. L *super-* + *intendere* to attend, direct attention to — more at INTEND] (1615) : to have or exercise the charge and oversight of : DIRECT

su·per·in·ten·dence \-ˈten-dən(t)s\ *n* (1603) : the act or function of superintending or directing : SUPERVISION

su·per·in·ten·den·cy \-dən-sē\ *n, pl* **-cies** (1598) : the office, post, or jurisdiction of a superintendent; *also* : SUPERINTENDENCE

su·per·in·ten·dent \-dənt\ *n* [ML *superintendent-, superintendens,* fr. LL, prp. of *superintendere*] (1554) : one who has executive oversight and charge — **superintendent** *adj*

[1]**su·pe·ri·or** \sü-ˈpir-ē-ər\ *adj* [ME, fr. MF *superieur,* fr. L *superior,* compar. of *superus* upper, fr. *super* over, above — more at OVER] (14c) **1** : situated higher up : UPPER **2** : of higher rank, quality, or importance **3** : courageously or serenely indifferent (as to something painful or disheartening) **4 a** : greater in quantity or numbers ⟨escaped by ~ speed⟩ **b** : excellent of its kind : BETTER ⟨her ~ memory⟩ **5** : being a superscript **6 a** *of an animal structure* : situated above or anterior or dorsal to another and esp. a corresponding part ⟨a ~ artery⟩ **b** *of a plant structure* : situated above or near the top of another part: as (1) *of a calyx* : attached to and apparently arising from the ovary (2) *of an ovary* : free from the calyx or other floral envelope **7** : more comprehensive ⟨a genus is ~ to a species⟩ **8** : affecting or assuming an air of superiority : SUPERCILIOUS — **su·pe·ri·or·ly** *adv*

[2]**superior** *n* (15c) **1** : one who is above another in rank, station, or office; *esp* : the head of a religious house or order **2** : one that surpasses another in quality or merit **3** : SUPERSCRIPT

superior conjunction *n* (1833) : a conjunction in which a lesser or secondary celestial body passes farther from the observer than the primary body around which it revolves

superior court *n* (1686) **1** : a court of general jurisdiction intermediate between the inferior courts (as a justice of the peace court) and the higher appellate courts **2** : a court with juries having original jurisdiction

superior general *n, pl* **superiors general** (1775) : the superior of a religious order or congregation

su·pe·ri·or·i·ty \sü-ˌpir-ē-ˈȯr-ət-ē, ˌsü-, -ˈär-\ *n, pl* **-ties** (1526) : the quality or state of being superior; *also* : a superior characteristic

superiority complex *n* (1924) : an exaggerated opinion of oneself

superior planet *n* (1583) : a planet whose orbit lies outside that of the earth

superior vena cava *n* (ca. 1909) : the branch of the vena cava of a vertebrate that brings blood back from the head and anterior part of the body to the heart

su·per·ja·cent \ˌsü-pər-ˈjās-ᵊnt\ *adj* [L *superjacent-, superjacens,* prp. of *superjacēre* to lie over or upon, fr. *super-* + *jacēre* to lie; akin to L *jacere* to throw — more at JET] (1610) : lying above or upon : OVERLYING ⟨~ rocks⟩

su·per·jet \ˈsü-pər-ˌjet\ *n* (1963) : a supersonic jet airplane

[1]**su·per·la·tive** \sü-ˈpər-lət-iv\ *adj* [ME *superlatif,* fr. MF, fr. LL *superlativus,* fr. L *superlatus* (pp. of *superferre* to carry over, raise high), fr. *super-* + *latus,* pp. of *ferre* to carry — more at TOLERATE, BEAR] (14c) **1** : of, relating to, or constituting the degree of grammatical comparison that denotes an extreme or unsurpassed level or extent **2 a** : surpassing all others : SUPREME **b** : of very high quality : EXCELLENT **3** : EXCESSIVE, EXAGGERATED — **su·per·la·tive·ly** *adv* — **su·per·la·tive·ness** *n*

[2]**superlative** *n* (1530) **1 a** : the superlative degree of comparison in a language **b** : a superlative form of an adjective or adverb **2** : the superlative or utmost degree of something : ACME **3** : a superlative person or thing **4** : an exaggerated expression esp. of praise

su·per·lin·er \ˈsü-pər-ˌlī-nər\ *n* (1919) : a fast luxurious passenger liner of great size

su·per·lu·na·ry \ˌsü-pər-ˈlü-nə-rē\ *also* **su·per·lu·nar** \-nər, -ˌnär\ *adj* [L *super-* + *luna* moon — more at LUNAR] (1614) : being above the moon : CELESTIAL

su·per·man \ˈsü-pər-ˌman\ *n* [trans. of G *übermensch,* fr. *über* over, super- + *mensch* man] (1903) **1** : a superior man that according to Nietzsche has learned to forgo fleeting pleasures and attain happiness and dominance through the exercise of creative power **2** : a person of extraordinary or superhuman power or achievements

su·per·mar·ket \-ˌmär-kət\ *n* (1937) **1** : a self-service retail market selling foods and household merchandise **2** : something resembling a supermarket esp. in the variety, abundance, or accessibility of its goods or services

su·per·nal \sü-ˈpərn-ᵊl\ *adj* [ME, fr. MF, fr. L *supernus,* fr. *super* over, above — more at OVER] (15c) **1 a** : being or coming from on high **b** : HEAVENLY, ETHEREAL ⟨~ melodies⟩ **2** : located in or belonging to the sky — **su·per·nal·ly** \-ᵊl-ē\ *adv*

su·per·na·tant \ˌsü-pər-ˈnāt-ᵊnt\ *n* [L *supernatant-, supernatans,* prp. of *supernatare* to float, fr. *super-* + *natare* to swim — more at NATANT] (1661) : the usu. clear liquid overlying material deposited by settling, precipitation, or centrifugation — **supernatant** *adj*

su·per·nat·u·ral \ˌsü-pər-ˈnach-(ə-)rəl\ *adj* [ML *supernaturalis,* fr. L *super-* + *natura* nature] (1526) **1 :** of or relating to an order of existence beyond the visible observable universe; *esp* **:** of or relating to God or a god, demigod, spirit, or devil **2 a :** departing from what is usual or normal esp. so as to appear to transcend the laws of nature **b :** attributed to an invisible agent (as a ghost or spirit) — **supernatural** *n* — **su·per·nat·u·ral·ly** \-ˈnach-(ə-)rə-lē, -ˈnach-ər-lē\ *adv* — **su·per·nat·u·ral·ness** \-ˈnach-(ə-)rəl-nəs\ *n*

su·per·nat·u·ral·ism \ˌsü-pər-ˈnach-(ə-)rə-ˌliz-əm\ *n* (1799) **1 :** the quality or state of being supernatural **2 :** belief in a supernatural power and order of existence — **su·per·nat·u·ral·ist** \-ləst\ *n or adj* — **su·per·nat·u·ral·is·tic** \-ˌnach-(ə-)rə-ˈlis-tik\ *adj*

su·per·na·ture \ˈsü-pər-ˌnā-chər\ *n* [fr. *supernatural,* after such E pairs as *natural: nature*] (1844) **:** the realm of the supernatural

su·per·nor·mal \ˌsü-pər-ˈnȯr-məl\ *adj* (1868) **1 :** exceeding the normal or average **2 :** being beyond normal human powers **:** PARANORMAL — **su·per·nor·mal·i·ty** \-nȯr-ˈmal-ət-ē\ *n* — **su·per·nor·mal·ly** \-ˈnȯr-mə-lē\ *adv*

su·per·no·va \ˌsü-pər-ˈnō-və\ *n* [NL] (1926) **:** the explosion of a very large star in which the star may reach a maximum intrinsic luminosity one billion times that of the sun

[1]**su·per·nu·mer·ary** \ˌsü-pər-ˈn(y)ü-mə-ˌrer-ē, -ˈn(y)üm-(ə-)rē\ *adj* [LL *supernumerarius,* fr. L *super-* + *numerus* number — more at NIMBLE] (1605) **1 a :** exceeding the usual, stated, or prescribed number ⟨a ~ tooth⟩ **b :** not enumerated among the regular components of a group and esp. of a military organization **2 :** exceeding what is necessary, required, or desired **3 :** more numerous

[2]**supernumerary** *n, pl* **-ar·ies** (1639) **1 :** a supernumerary person or thing **2 :** an actor employed to play a walk-on

su·per·or·der \ˈsü-pə-ˌrȯrd-ər\ *n* (ca. 1890) **:** a taxonomic category between an order and a class or a subclass

su·per·or·di·nate \ˌsü-pə-ˈrȯrd-nət, -ᵊn-ət, -ᵊn-ˌāt\ *adj* [*super-* + *-ordinate* (as in *subordinate*)] (1620) **:** superior in rank, class, or status

su·per·or·gan·ism \-ˈrȯr-gə-ˌniz-əm\ *n* (1899) **:** an organized society (as of a social insect) that functions as an organic whole

su·per·ovu·la·tion \-ˌräv-yə-ˈlā-shən, -ˌrōv-\ *n* (ca. 1935) **:** production of exceptional numbers of eggs at one time — **su·per·ovu·late** \-ˈräv-yə-ˌlāt, -ˈrōv-\ *vb*

su·per·ox·ide \-ˈräk-ˌsīd\ *n* (ca. 1847) **:** the univalent anion O_2^- or a compound containing it ⟨potassium ~ KO_2⟩

su·per·par·a·sit·ism \ˌsü-pər-ˈpar-ə-ˌsīt-ˌiz-əm, -sə-ˌtiz-\ *n* (ca. 1899) **:** parasitization of a host by more than one parasitic individual usu. of one kind — used esp. of parasitic insects

su·per·phos·phate \ˌsü-pər-ˈfäs-ˌfāt\ *n* (1797) **1 :** an acid phosphate **2 :** a soluble mixture of phosphates used as fertilizer and made from insoluble mineral phosphates by treatment with sulfuric acid

su·per·phys·i·cal \-ˈfiz-i-kəl\ *adj* (1603) **:** being above or beyond the physical world or explanation on physical principles

su·per·plas·tic \-ˈplas-tik\ *adj* (1947) **1 :** capable of plastic deformation under low stress at an elevated temperature — used of metals and alloys **2 :** of or relating to superplastic materials ⟨~ forming⟩ — **su·per·plas·tic·i·ty** \-pla-ˈstis-ət-ē\ *n*

su·per·pose \ˌsü-pər-ˈpōz\ *vt* **-posed; -pos·ing** [prob. fr. F *superposer,* back-formation fr. *superposition,* fr. LL *superposition-, superpositio,* fr. L *superpositus,* pp. of *superponere* to superpose, fr. *super-* + *ponere* to place — more at POSITION] (1823) **1 :** to place or lay over or above whether in or not in contact **:** SUPERIMPOSE **2 :** to lay (as a geometric figure) upon another so as to make all like parts coincide — **su·per·pos·able** \-ˈpō-zə-bəl\ *adj* — **su·per·po·si·tion** \-pə-ˈzish-ən\ *n*

su·per·posed \-ˈpōzd\ *adj* (1823) **:** situated vertically over another layer or part

su·per·pow·er \ˈsü-pər-ˌpau̇(-ə)r\ *n* (1923) **1 :** excessive or superior power **2 a :** an extremely powerful nation; *specif* **:** one of a very few dominant states in an era when the world is divided politically into these states and their satellites **b :** an international governing body able to enforce its will upon the most powerful states — **su·per·pow·ered** \-ˌpau̇(-ə)rd\ *adj*

su·per·sat·u·rate \ˌsü-pər-ˈsach-ə-ˌrāt\ *vt* (1788) **:** to add to (a solution) beyond saturation

su·per·sat·u·rat·ed *adj* (1854) **:** containing an amount of a substance greater than that required for saturation as a result of having been cooled from a higher temperature to a temperature below that at which saturation occurs ⟨a ~ solution⟩ ⟨air ~ with water vapor⟩

su·per·sat·u·ra·tion \-ˌsach-ə-ˈrā-shən\ *n* (1904) **:** the state of being supersaturated

su·per·scribe \ˈsü-pər-ˌskrīb, ˌsü-pər-ˈ\ *vt* **-scribed; -scrib·ing** [L *superscribere,* fr. *super-* + *scribere* to write — more at SCRIBE] (1598) **1 :** to write (as a name or address) on the outside or cover of **:** ADDRESS **2 :** to write or engrave on the top or outside

su·per·script \ˈsü-pər-ˌskript\ *n* [L *superscriptus,* pp. of *superscribere*] (ca. 1909) **:** a distinguishing symbol (as a numeral or letter) written immediately above or above and to the right or left of another character — **superscript** *adj*

su·per·scrip·tion \ˌsü-pər-ˈskrip-shən\ *n* [ME, fr. MF, fr. LL *superscription-, superscriptio,* fr. L *superscriptus*] (14c) **1 :** something written or engraved on the surface of, outside, or above something else **:** INSCRIPTION; *also* **:** ADDRESS **2 :** the act of superscribing

su·per·sede \ˌsü-pər-ˈsēd\ *vt* **-sed·ed; -sed·ing** [ME *superceden,* fr. MF *superseder* to refrain from, fr. L *supersedēre* to be superior to, refrain from, fr. *super-* + *sedēre* to sit — more at SIT] (15c) **1 a :** to cause to be set aside **b :** to force out of use as inferior **2 :** to take the place, room, or position of **3 :** to displace in favor of another **:** SUPPLANT *syn* see REPLACE — **su·per·sed·er** *n*

su·per·se·de·as \-ˈsēd-ē-əs\ *n, pl* **supersedeas** [ME, fr. L, you shall refrain, fr. *supersedēre*] (14c) **1 :** a common-law writ commanding a stay of legal proceedings issued under various conditions and esp. to stay an officer from proceeding under another writ **2 :** an order staying proceedings of an inferior court

su·per·se·dure \-ˈsē-jər\ *n* (1788) **:** the act or process of superseding; *esp* **:** the replacement of an old or inferior queen bee by a young or superior queen

su·per·sen·si·ble \ˌsü-pər-ˈsen(t)-sə-bəl\ *adj* (1798) **:** being above or beyond that which is apparent to the senses **:** SPIRITUAL

su·per·sen·si·tive \-ˈsen(t)-sət-iv, -ˈsen(t)-stiv\ *adj* (1839) **1 :** HYPERSENSITIVE ⟨a ~ palate⟩ **2 :** specially treated to increase sensitivity ⟨a ~ photographic emulsion⟩ — **su·per·sen·si·tive·ly** *adv* — **su·per·sen·si·tiv·i·ty** \-ˌsen(t)-sə-ˈtiv-ət-ē\ *n*

su·per·sen·so·ry \-ˈsen(t)s-(ə-)rē\ *adj* (1883) **:** SUPERSENSIBLE

su·per·ser·vice·able \-ˈsər-və-sə-bəl\ *adj* (1605) **:** offering unwanted services **:** OFFICIOUS

su·per·ses·sion \ˌsü-pər-ˈsesh-ən\ *n* [ML *supersession-, supersessio,* fr. L *supersessus,* pp. of *supersedēre*] (1790) **:** the act of superseding **:** the state of being superseded

[1]**su·per·son·ic** \-ˈsän-ik\ *adj* [L *super-* + *sonus* sound — more at SOUND] (1919) **1 :** ULTRASONIC **2 :** of, being, or relating to speeds from one to five times the speed of sound in air — compare SONIC **3 :** moving, capable of moving, or utilizing air currents moving at supersonic speed **4 :** relating to supersonic airplanes or missiles ⟨the ~ age⟩ — **su·per·son·i·cal·ly** \-i-k(ə-)lē\ *adv*

[2]**supersonic** *n* (ca. 1924) **1 :** a supersonic wave or frequency **2 :** a supersonic airplane

su·per·son·ics \ˌsü-pər-ˈsän-iks\ *n pl but sing in constr* (1926) **:** the science of supersonic phenomena

supersonic transport *n* (1966) **:** a supersonic transport airplane

su·per·star \ˈsü-pər-ˌstär\ *n* (1924) **:** a star (as in sports or the movies) who is considered extremely talented, has great public appeal, and can usu. command a high salary; *broadly* **:** one that is very prominent or is a prime attraction — **su·per·star·dom** \-dəm\ *n*

su·per·sti·tion \ˌsü-pər-ˈstish-ən\ *n* [ME *supersticion,* fr. MF, fr. L *superstition-, superstitio,* fr. *superstit-, superstes* standing over (as witness or survivor), fr. *super-* + *stare* to stand — more at STAND] (15c) **1 a :** a belief or practice resulting from ignorance, fear of the unknown, trust in magic or chance, or a false conception of causation **b :** an irrational abject attitude of mind toward the supernatural, nature, or God resulting from superstition **2 :** a notion maintained despite evidence to the contrary

su·per·sti·tious \-ˈstish-əs\ *adj* [ME *supersticious,* fr. MF *supersticieux,* fr. L *superstitiosus,* fr. *superstitio*] (14c) **:** of, relating to, or swayed by superstition — **su·per·sti·tious·ly** *adv*

su·per·struc·ture \-ˌstrək-chər\ *n* (1641) **1 a :** an entity, concept, or complex based on a more fundamental one **b :** social institutions (as the law or politics) that are in Marxist theory erected upon the economic base **2 :** a structure built as a vertical extension of something else: as **a :** all of a building above the basement **b :** the structural part of a ship above the main deck **c :** the ties, rails, and fastenings of a railroad track as distinct from the roadbed — **su·per·struc·tur·al** \ˌsü-pər-ˈstrək-chə-rəl, -ˈstrək-shrəl\ *adj*

su·per·sub·stan·tial \ˌsü-pər-səb-ˈstan-chəl\ *adj* [LL *supersubstantialis,* fr. L *super-* + *substantia* substance] (1534) **:** being above material substance **:** of a transcending substance

su·per·sys·tem \ˈsü-pər-ˌsis-təm\ *n* (ca. 1928) **:** a system that is made up of systems

su·per·tax \-ˌtaks\ *n* (1906) **1 :** SURTAX **2 :** a graduated income tax imposed in the United Kingdom in addition to the normal income tax

su·per·ton·ic \ˌsü-pər-ˈtän-ik\ *n* (1806) **:** the second tone of a diatonic scale

su·per·vene \ˌsü-pər-ˈvēn\ *vi* **-vened; -ven·ing** [L *supervenire,* fr. *super-* + *venire* to come — more at COME] (1647) **:** to follow or result as an additional, adventitious, or unlooked-for development *syn* see FOLLOW — **su·per·ven·tion** \-ˈven-chən\ *n*

su·per·ve·nient \-ˈvē-nyənt\ *adj* [L *supervenient-, superveniens,* prp. of *supervenire*] (1594) **:** coming or occurring as something additional, extraneous, or unexpected

su·per·vise \ˈsü-pər-ˌvīz\ *vt* **-vised; -vis·ing** [ML *supervisus,* pp. of *supervidēre,* fr. L *super-* + *vidēre* to see — more at WIT] (1588) **:** SUPERINTEND, OVERSEE

su·per·vi·sion \ˌsü-pər-ˈvizh-ən\ *n* (1640) **:** the action, process, or occupation of supervising; *esp* **:** a critical watching and directing (as of activities or a course of action)

su·per·vi·sor \ˈsü-pər-ˌvī-zər\ *n* (15c) **:** one that supervises; *esp* **:** an administrative officer in charge of a business, government, or school unit or operation — **su·per·vi·so·ry** \ˌsü-pər-ˈvīz-(ə-)rē\ *adj*

su·pi·nate \ˈsü-pə-ˌnāt\ *vb* **-nat·ed; -nat·ing** [L *supinatus,* pp. of *supinare* to lay backward or on the back, fr. *supinus*] *vt* (1831) **:** to cause to undergo supination ~ *vi* **:** to undergo supination

su·pi·na·tion \ˌsü-pə-ˈnā-shən\ *n* (1666) **1 :** rotation of the forearm and hand so that the palm faces forward or upward and the radius lies parallel to the ulna; *also* **:** a corresponding movement of the foot and leg **2 :** the position resulting from supination

su·pi·na·tor \ˈsü-pə-ˌnāt-ər\ *n* [NL, fr. L *supinatus,* pp.] (1615) **:** a muscle that produces the motion of supination

[1]**su·pine** \sü-ˈpīn, *attrib also* ˌsü-ˌpīn\ *adj* [L *supinus;* akin to L *sub* under, up to — more at UP] (1500) **1 a :** lying on the back or with the face upward **b :** marked by supination **2 :** exhibiting indolent or apathetic inertia or passivity; *esp* **:** mentally or morally slack **3** *archaic* **:** leaning or sloping backward *syn* see PRONE, INACTIVE — **su·pine·ly** \sü-ˈpīn-lē\ *adv* — **su·pine·ness** \-ˈpīn-nəs\ *n*

[2]**su·pine** \ˈsü-ˌpīn\ *n* [LL *supinum,* fr. L, neut. of *supinus,* adj.] (1522) **1 :** a Latin verbal noun having an accusative of purpose in *-um* and an ablative of specification in *-u* **2 :** an English infinitive with *to*

sup·per \ˈsəp-ər\ *n* [ME, fr. OF *souper,* fr. *souper* to sup — more at SUP] (13c) **1 a :** the evening meal esp. when dinner is taken at midday **b :** a social affair featuring a supper; *esp* **:** an evening social esp. for raising funds ⟨a church ~⟩ **2 :** the food served as a supper ⟨eat your ~⟩ **3 :** a light meal served late in the evening

supper club *n* (1925) **:** NIGHTCLUB

sup·plant \sə-ˈplant\ *vt* [ME *supplanten,* fr. MF *supplanter,* fr. L *supplantare* to overthrow by tripping up, fr. *sub-* + *planta* sole of the foot — more at PLACE] (14c) **1 :** to supersede (another) esp. by force or treachery **2 a** (1) *obs* **:** UPROOT (2) **:** to eradicate and supply a substitute for ⟨efforts to ~ the vernacular⟩ **b :** to take the place of and serve as a substitute for esp. by reason of superior excellence or power ***syn*** see REPLACE — **sup·plan·ta·tion** \(ˌ)sə-ˌplan-ˈtā-shən\ *n* — **sup·plant·er** \sə-ˈplant-ər\ *n*

¹sup·ple \ˈsəp-əl *also* ˈsüp-\ *adj* **sup·pler** \-(ə-)lər\; **sup·plest** \-(ə-)ləst\ [ME *souple,* fr. MF, fr. L *supplic-, supplex* submissive, suppliant, lit., bending under, fr. *sub-* + *plic-* (akin to *plicare* to fold) — more at PLY] (14c) **1 a :** compliant often to the point of obsequiousness **b :** readily adaptable or responsive to new situations **2 a :** capable of being bent or folded without creases, cracks, or breaks **:** PLIANT ⟨~ leather⟩ **b :** able to perform bending or twisting movements with ease and grace **:** LIMBER ⟨~ legs of a dancer⟩ **c :** easy and fluent without stiffness or awkwardness ⟨sang with a lively, ~ voice —Douglas Watt⟩ ***syn*** see ELASTIC — **sup·ple·ly** \-ə(l)-lē\ *or* **sup·ply** \-(ə-)lē\ *adv* — **sup·ple·ness** \-əl-nəs\ *n*

²supple *vb* **sup·pled; sup·pling** \-(ə-)liŋ\ *vt* (14c) **1 :** to make pacific or complaisant ⟨~ the tempers of your race —Laurence Sterne⟩ **2 :** to alleviate with a salve **3 :** to make flexible or pliant ~ *vi* **:** to become soft and pliant

sup·ple·jack \ˈsəp-əl-ˌjak *also* ˈsüp-\ *n* (ca. 1725) **:** any of various woody climbers having tough pliant stems; *esp* **:** a southern U.S. vine (*Berchemia scandens*) of the buckthorn family

¹sup·ple·ment \ˈsəp-lə-mənt\ *n* [ME, fr. L *supplementum,* fr. *supplēre* to fill up, complete — more at SUPPLY] (14c) **1 :** something that completes or makes an addition ⟨dietary ~*s*⟩ **2 :** a part added to or issued as a continuation of a book or periodical to correct errors or make additions **3 :** an angle or arc that when added to a given angle or arc equals 180°

²sup·ple·ment \ˈsəp-lə-ˌment\ *vt* (1829) **:** to add a supplement to ⟨does odd jobs to ~ his income⟩ — **sup·ple·men·ta·tion** \ˌsəp-lə-ˌmen-ˈtā-shən, -mən-\ *n* — **sup·ple·ment·er** \ˈsəp-lə-ˌment-ər\ *n*

sup·ple·men·tal \ˌsəp-lə-ˈment-ᵊl\ *adj* (1605) **1 :** serving to supplement **2 :** NONSCHEDULED ⟨a ~ airline⟩ — **supplemental** *n*

sup·ple·men·ta·ry \ˌsəp-lə-ˈment-ə-rē, -ˈmen-trē\ *adj* (1667) **1 :** added or serving as a supplement **:** ADDITIONAL ⟨~ reading⟩ **2 :** being or relating to a supplement or a supplementary angle

supplementary angle *n* (ca. 1924) **:** one of two angles or arcs whose sum is 180° — usu. used in pl.

sup·ple·tion \sə-ˈplē-shən\ *n* [ML *suppletion-, suppletio* act of supplementing, fr. L *suppletus,* pp. of *supplēre*] (1914) **:** the occurrence of phonemically unrelated allomorphs of the same morpheme (as *went* as the past tense of *go* or *better* as the comparative form of *good*) — **sup·ple·tive** \sə-ˈplēt-iv, ˈsəp-lət-\ *adj*

sup·ple·to·ry \ˈsəp-lə-ˌtōr-ē; ˈsəp-lə-ˌtōr-ē, -ˌtȯr-\ *adj* [L *suppletus,* pp.] (1628) **:** supplying deficiencies **:** SUPPLEMENTARY

sup·pli·ance \ˈsəp-lē-ən(t)s\ *n* (1611) **:** ENTREATY, SUPPLICATION

¹sup·pli·ant \-ənt\ *n* [ME, fr. MF, fr. prp. of *supplier* to supplicate, fr. L *supplicare*] (15c) **:** one who supplicates

²suppliant *adj* [MF, prp.] (1586) **1 :** humbly imploring **:** ENTREATING ⟨a ~ sinner seeking forgiveness —O. J. Baab⟩ **2 :** expressing supplication ⟨upraised to the heavens . . . ~ arms —William Styron⟩ — **sup·pli·ant·ly** *adv*

¹sup·pli·cant \ˈsəp-li-kənt\ *adj* (1597) **:** SUPPLIANT

²supplicant *n* (1597) **:** SUPPLIANT

sup·pli·cate \ˈsəp-lə-ˌkāt\ *vb* **-cat·ed; -cat·ing** [ME *supplicaten,* fr. L *supplicatus,* pp. of *supplicare,* fr. *supplic-, supplex* suppliant — more at SUPPLE] *vi* (15c) **:** to make a humble entreaty; *esp* **:** to pray to God ~ *vt* **1 :** to ask humbly and earnestly of **2 :** to ask for earnestly and humbly ***syn*** see BEG — **sup·pli·ca·tion** \ˌsəp-lə-ˈkā-shən\ *n*

sup·pli·ca·to·ry \ˈsəp-li-kə-ˌtōr-ē, -ˌtȯr-\ *adj* (15c) **:** expressing supplication **:** SUPPLIANT ⟨a ~ prayer⟩

¹sup·ply \sə-ˈplī\ *vb* **sup·plied; sup·ply·ing** [ME *supplien,* fr. MF *soupleier,* fr. L *supplēre* to fill up, supplement, supply, fr. *sub-* up + *plēre* to fill — more at SUB-, FULL] *vt* (14c) **1 :** to add as a supplement **2 a :** to provide for **:** SATISFY ⟨laws by which the material wants of men are *supplied* —*Bull. of Bates Coll.*⟩ **b :** to make available for use **:** PROVIDE ⟨*supplied* the necessary funds⟩ **c :** to satisfy the needs or wishes of **3 :** to substitute for another in; *specif* **:** to serve as a supply in (a church or pulpit) ~ *vi* **:** to serve as a supply or substitute — **sup·pli·er** \-ˈplī(-ə)r\ *n*

²supply *n, pl* **supplies** (15c) **1** *obs* **:** ASSISTANCE, SUCCOR **2 a** *obs* **:** REINFORCEMENTS — often used in pl. **b :** a clergyman filling a vacant pulpit temporarily **c :** the quantity or amount (as of a commodity) needed or available ⟨beer was in short ~ in that hot weather —Nevil Shute⟩ **d :** PROVISIONS, STORES — usu. used in pl. **3 :** the act or process of filling a want or need ⟨engaged in the ~ of raw materials to industry⟩ **4 :** the quantities of goods or services offered for sale at a particular time or at one price **5 :** something that maintains or constitutes a supply

sup·ply–side \sə-ˈplī-ˈsīd\ *adj* (1979) **:** of, relating to, or being an economic theory that reduction of tax rates encourages more earnings, savings, and investment and thereby expands economic activity and the total taxable national income — **sup·ply–sid·er** \-ˈsīd-ər\ *n*

¹sup·port \sə-ˈpō(ə)rt, -ˈpȯ(ə)rt\ *vt* [ME *supporten,* fr. MF *supporter,* fr. LL *supportare,* fr. L, to carry, fr. *sub-* + *portare* to carry — more at FARE] (14c) **1 :** to endure bravely or quietly **:** BEAR **2 a** (1) **:** to promote the interests or cause of (2) **:** to uphold or defend as valid or right **:** ADVOCATE (3) **:** to argue or vote for **b** (1) **:** ASSIST, HELP (2) **:** to act with (a star actor) (3) **:** to bid in bridge so as to show support for **c :** to provide with substantiation **:** CORROBORATE ⟨~ an alibi⟩ **3 a :** to pay the costs of **:** MAINTAIN **b :** to provide a basis for the existence or subsistence of ⟨the island could probably ~ three —A. B. C. Whipple⟩ **4 a :** to hold up or serve as a foundation or prop for **b :** to maintain (a price) at a desired level by purchases or loans; *also* **:** to maintain the price of by purchases or loans **5 :** to keep from fainting, yielding, or losing courage **:** COMFORT **6 :** to keep (something) going — **sup·port·abil·i·ty** \sə-ˌpōrt-ə-ˈbil-ət-ē, -ˌpȯrt-\ *n* — **sup·port·able** \-ˈpōrt-ə-bəl, -ˈpȯrt-\ *adj* — **sup·port·ive** \-ˈpōrt-iv, -ˈpȯrt-\ *adj* — **sup·port·ive·ness** \-nəs\ *n*

syn SUPPORT, UPHOLD, ADVOCATE, BACK, CHAMPION mean to favor actively one that meets opposition. SUPPORT is least explicit about the nature of the assistance given; UPHOLD implies extended support given to something attacked; ADVOCATE stresses urging or pleading; BACK suggests supporting by lending assistance to one failing or falling; CHAMPION suggests publicly defending one unjustly attacked or too weak to advocate his own cause.

²support *n* (14c) **1 :** the act or process of supporting **:** the condition of being supported **2 :** one that supports

sup·port·er *n* (15c) **:** one that supports or acts as a support: as **a :** ADHERENT, PARTISAN **b :** one of two figures (as of men or animals) placed one on each side of an escutcheon and exterior to it **c :** GARTER 1 **d :** ATHLETIC SUPPORTER

support hose *n* (1963) **:** elastic stockings

support level *n* (1953) **:** a price level on a declining market at which a security resists further decline due to increased attractiveness to traders and investors — called also *support area*

sup·pos·able \sə-ˈpō-zə-bəl\ *adj* (1643) **:** capable of being supposed **:** CONCEIVABLE — **sup·pos·ably** \-blē\ *adv*

sup·pos·al \-ˈpō-zəl\ *n* (14c) **1 :** the act or process of supposing **2 :** something supposed **:** HYPOTHESIS, SUPPOSITION

sup·pose \sə-ˈpōz, *oftenest after* "*I*" ˈspōz\ *vb* **sup·posed; sup·pos·ing** [ME *supposen,* fr. MF *supposer,* fr. ML *supponere* (perf. indic. *supposui*), fr. L, to put under, substitute, fr. *sub-* + *ponere* to put — more at POSITION] *vt* (14c) **1 a :** to lay down tentatively as a hypothesis, assumption, or proposal ⟨~ a fire broke out⟩ ⟨~ you bring the salad⟩ **b** (1) **:** to hold as an opinion **:** BELIEVE ⟨they *supposed* they were early⟩ (2) **:** to think probable or in keeping with the facts ⟨seems reasonable to ~ that he would profit⟩ **2 a :** CONCEIVE, IMAGINE **b :** to have a suspicion of **3 :** PRESUPPOSE ~ *vi* **:** CONJECTURE, OPINE

sup·posed \sə-ˈpōzd; *1b & 2a usu* -ˈpō-zəd, *3 & 4 often* -ˈpōst\ *adj* (1566) **1 a :** PRETENDED ⟨twelve hours are ~ to elapse between Acts I and II —A. S. Sullivan⟩ **b :** ALLEGED ⟨trusted my ~ friends⟩ **2 a :** held as an opinion **:** BELIEVED; *also* **:** mistakenly believed **:** IMAGINED ⟨the sight which makes ~ terror true —Shak.⟩ **b :** considered probable or certain **:** EXPECTED ⟨it was not ~ that everybody could master the technical aspects —J. C. Murray⟩ **c :** UNDERSTOOD ⟨you will be ~ to refer to my grandaunt —G. B. Shaw⟩ **3 :** made or fashioned by intent or design ⟨what's that button ~ to do⟩ ⟨pills that are ~ to kill pain⟩ **4 a :** required by or as if by authority ⟨soldiers are ~ to obey their commanding officers⟩ **b :** given permission **:** PERMITTED ⟨was not ~ to have visitors⟩ — **sup·pos·ed·ly** \-ˈpō-zəd-lē *also* -ˈpōz-dlē\ *adv*

sup·pos·ing \sə-ˈpō-ziŋ\ *conj* (ca. 1843) **:** if by way of hypothesis **:** on the assumption that

sup·po·si·tion \ˌsəp-ə-ˈzish-ən\ *n* [ME, fr. LL *supposition-, suppositio,* fr. L, act of placing beneath, fr. *suppositus,* pp. of *supponere*] (15c) **1 :** something that is supposed **:** HYPOTHESIS **2 :** the act of supposing — **sup·po·si·tion·al** \-ˈzish-nəl, -ən-ᵊl\ *adj*

sup·po·si·tious \-ˈzish-əs\ *adj* [by contr.] (1624) **:** SUPPOSITITIOUS

sup·pos·i·ti·tious \sə-ˌpäz-ə-ˈtish-əs\ *adj* [L *supposititius,* fr. *suppositus,* pp. of *supponere* to substitute] (1611) **1 a :** fraudulently substituted **:** SPURIOUS **b** *of a child* (1) **:** falsely presented as a genuine heir (2) **:** ILLEGITIMATE **2** [influenced in meaning by *supposition*] **a :** IMAGINARY **b :** of the nature of or based on a supposition **:** HYPOTHETICAL — **sup·pos·i·ti·tious·ly** *adv*

sup·pos·i·to·ry \sə-ˈpäz-ə-ˌtōr-ē, -ˌtȯr-\ *n, pl* **-ries** [ML *suppositorium,* fr. LL, neut. of *suppositorius* placed beneath, fr. L *suppositus,* pp. of *supponere* to put under] (15c) **:** a solid but readily meltable cone or cylinder of usu. medicated material for insertion into a bodily passage or cavity (as the rectum)

sup·press \sə-ˈpres\ *vt* [ME *suppressen,* fr. L *suppressus,* pp. of *supprimere,* fr. *sub-* + *premere* to press — more at PRESS] (14c) **1 :** to put down by authority or force **:** SUBDUE **2 :** to keep from public knowledge: as **a :** to keep secret **b :** to stop or prohibit the publication or revelation of **3 a :** to exclude from consciousness **b :** to keep from giving vent to **:** CHECK **4** *obs* **:** to press down **5 a :** to restrain from a usual course or action **:** ARREST ⟨~ a cough⟩ **b :** to inhibit the growth or development of **:** STUNT **6 :** to inhibit the genetic expression of ⟨~ a mutation⟩ — **sup·press·ibil·i·ty** \-ˌpres-ə-ˈbil-ət-ē\ *n* — **sup·press·ible** \-ˈpres-ə-bəl\ *adj* — **sup·pres·sive** \-ˈpres-iv\ *adj* — **sup·pres·sive·ness** \-nəs\ *n*

sup·pres·sant \sə-ˈpres-ᵊnt\ *n* (1942) **:** an agent (as a drug) that tends to suppress or reduce in intensity rather than eliminate something (as appetite)

sup·pres·sion \sə-ˈpresh-ən\ *n* (15c) **1 :** an act or instance of suppressing **:** the state of being suppressed **2 :** the conscious intentional exclusion from consciousness of a thought or feeling

sup·pres·sor \-ˈpres-ər\ *n* (1560) **:** one that suppresses; *esp* **:** a gene that suppresses the expression of another nonallelic gene when both are present

sup·pu·rate \ˈsəp-yə-ˌrāt\ *vi* **-rat·ed; -rat·ing** [L *suppuratus,* pp. of *suppurare,* fr. *sub-* + *pur-, pus* pus — more at FOUL] (1656) **:** to form or discharge pus — **sup·pu·ra·tion** \ˌsəp-yə-ˈrā-shən\ *n* — **sup·pu·ra·tive** \ˈsəp-yə-rət-iv, -ˌrāt-; ˈsəp-rət-iv\ *adj*

su·pra \ˈsü-prə, -ˌprä\ *adv* [L] (1592) **:** earlier in this writing **:** ABOVE

supra- *prefix* [L, fr. *supra* above, beyond, earlier; akin to L *super* over — more at OVER] **1 :** SUPER- 2a ⟨*supra*orbital⟩ **2 :** transcending ⟨*supra*molecular⟩

su·pra·lim·i·nal \ˌsü-prə-ˈlim-ən-ᵊl, -ˌprä-\ *adj* [*supra-* + L *limin-, limen* threshold — more at LIMB] (1892) **1 :** existing above the threshold of consciousness **2 :** adequate to evoke a response or induce a sensation ⟨~ stimulus⟩

su·pra·mo·lec·u·lar \-mə-ˈlek-yə-lər\ *adj* (ca. 1909) **:** more complex than a molecule; *also* **:** composed of many molecules

su·pra·na·tion·al \-ˈnash-nəl, -ən-ᵊl\ *adj* (1908) **:** transcending national boundaries, authority, or interests ⟨a ~ authority, regulating ocean usage —N. H. Jacoby⟩ ⟨taking a ~ view of economic problems⟩ — **su·pra·na·tion·al·ism** \-ˌiz-əm\ *n* — **su·pra·na·tion·al·ist** \-əst\ *n* — **su·pra·na·tion·al·i·ty** \-ˌnash-ə-ˈnal-ət-ē\ *n*

su·pra·op·tic \-ˈäp-tik\ *adj* (1948) **:** situated above the optic chiasma; *also* **:** being a small nucleus of closely packed neurons overlying the optic chiasma and intimately connected with the neurohypophysis

su·pra·or·bit·al \-ˈȯr-bət-ᵊl\ *adj* [NL *supraorbitalis,* fr. L *supra-* + ML *orbita* orbit] (1828) **:** situated or occurring above the orbit of the eye

su·pra·pro·test \-ˈprō-ˌtest\ *n* [modif. of It *sopra protesto* upon protest] (ca. 1860) **:** an acceptance or payment of a bill by a third person for the honor of the drawer after protest for nonacceptance or nonpayment by the drawee

su·pra·ra·tio·nal \-'rash-nəl, -ən-ᵊl\ *adj* (1894) : transcending the rational : based on or involving factors not to be comprehended by reason alone ⟨the stars inspire ~ dreams —R. J. Dubos⟩

¹su·pra·re·nal \-'rēn-ᵊl\ *adj* [NL *suprarenalis*, fr. L *supra-* + *renes* kidneys] (1828) : situated above or anterior to the kidneys; *specif* : ADRENAL

²suprarenal *n* (1841) : a suprarenal part; *esp* : ADRENAL GLAND

suprarenal gland *n* (1876) : ADRENAL GLAND

su·pra·seg·men·tal \ˌsü-prə-seg-'ment-ᵊl, -ˌprä-\ *adj* (1941) : of or relating to significant features (as stress, pitch, or juncture) that occur simultaneously with vowels and consonants in an utterance

su·pra·vi·tal \-'vīt-ᵊl\ *adj* [ISV] (ca. 1919) : constituting or relating to the staining of living tissues or cells surviving after removal from a living body by dyes that penetrate living substance but induce more or less rapid degenerative changes — compare INTRAVITAL 2 — **su·pra·vi·tal·ly** \-ᵊl-ē\ *adv*

su·prem·a·cist \sə-'prem-ə-səst, sü-\ *n* (1949) **1** : an advocate or adherent of group supremacy **2** : WHITE SUPREMACIST

su·prem·a·cy \sə-'prem-ə-sē, sü-\ *also* -'prēm-\ *n, pl* **-cies** [*supreme* + *-acy* (as in *primacy*)] (1547) : the quality or state of being supreme; *also* : supreme authority or power

su·preme \sə-'prēm, sü-; *in rapid speech also* 'sprēm; *attrib also* 'süˌprēm\ *adj* [L *supremus*, superl. of *superus* upper — more at SUPERIOR] (1520) **1** : highest in rank or authority ⟨the ~ commander⟩ **2** : highest in degree or quality ⟨~ endurance in war and in labour —R. W. Emerson⟩ **3** : ULTIMATE, FINAL ⟨the ~ sacrifice⟩ — **su·preme·ly** *adv* — **su·preme·ness** *n*

Supreme Being *n* (1699) : GOD 1

supreme court *n* (1709) **1** : the highest judicial tribunal in a political unit (as a nation or state) **2** : a court of original jurisdiction in New York state that is subordinate to a final court of appeals

Supreme Soviet *n* (1943) : the highest legislative body of the Soviet Union consisting of two chambers one of which represents the overall population and the other the constituent republics

su·pre·mo \su-'prē-(ˌ)mō, sü-\ *n, pl* **-mos** [Sp & It, fr. *supremo*, adj., supreme, fr. L *supremus*] *Brit* (1937) : one who is highest in rank or authority

sur- *prefix* [ME, fr. OF, fr. L *super-*] **1** : over : SUPER- ⟨*surprint*⟩ ⟨*surtax*⟩ **2** : above : up ⟨*surbase*⟩

su·ra \'sur-ə\ *n* [Ar *sūrah*, lit., row] (1661) : a chapter of the Koran

su·rah \'sur-ə\ *n* [prob. alter. of *surat* (a cotton produced in Surat, India)] (1881) : a soft twilled fabric of silk or rayon

sur·base \'sər-ˌbās\ *n* (1678) : a molding just above the base of a wall, pedestal, or podium

¹sur·cease \(ˌ)sər-'sēs, 'sər-ˌ\ *vb* **sur·ceased; sur·ceas·ing** [ME *sursesen*, *surcesen*, fr. MF *sursis*, pp. of *surseoir*, fr. L *supersedēre* — more at SUPERSEDE] *vi* (15c) : to desist from action; *also* : to come to an end : CEASE ~ *vt* : to put an end to : DISCONTINUE

²sur·cease \'sər-ˌsēs, (ˌ)sər-'\ *n* (1586) : CESSATION; *esp* : a temporary respite or end

¹sur·charge \'sər-ˌchärj\ *vt* [ME *surchargen*, fr. MF *surchargier*, fr. *sur-* + *chargier* to charge, fr. OF — more at CHARGE] (15c) **1 a** : OVERCHARGE **b** : to charge an extra fee **c** : to show an omission (in an account) for which credit ought to have been given **2** *Brit* : OVERSTOCK **3** : to fill or load to excess ⟨the atmosphere . . . was *surcharged* with war hysteria —H. A. Chippendale⟩ **4 a** : to mark a new denomination figure or a surcharge on (a stamp) **b** : OVERPRINT ⟨~ a banknote⟩

²surcharge *n* (1601) **1 a** : an additional tax, cost, or impost **b** : an extra fare ⟨a sleeping car ~⟩ **c** : an instance of surcharging an account **2** : an excessive load or burden **3** : the action of surcharging : the state of being surcharged **4 a** (1) : an overprint on a stamp; *specif* : one that alters the denomination (2) : a stamp bearing such an overprint **b** : an overprint on a currency note

sur·cin·gle \'sər-ˌsin-gəl\ *n* [ME *sursengle*, fr. MF *surcengle*, fr. *sur-* + *cengle* girdle, fr. L *cingulum* — more at CINGULUM] (15c) **1** : a belt, band, or girth passing around the body of a horse to bind a saddle or pack fast to the horse's back **2** *archaic* : the cincture of a cassock

sur·coat \'sər-ˌkōt\ *n* [ME *surcote*, fr. MF, fr. *sur-* + *cote* coat] (14c) : an outer coat or cloak; *specif* : a tunic worn over armor

¹surd \'sərd\ *adj* [L *surdus* deaf, silent, stupid; akin to L *susurrus* hum — more at SWARM] (1551) **1** : lacking sense : IRRATIONAL ⟨the ~ mystery and the strange forces of existence —D. C. Williams⟩ **2** : VOICELESS — used of speech sounds

²surd *n* (1557) **1 a** : an irrational root (as √3) **b** : IRRATIONAL NUMBER **2** : a surd speech sound

¹sure \'shu̇(ə)r, *esp Southern* 'shō(ə)r\ *adj* **sur·er; sur·est** [ME, fr. MF *sur*, fr. L *securus* secure] (14c) **1** *obs* : safe from danger or harm **2** : firmly established : STEADFAST ⟨a ~ hold⟩ **3** : RELIABLE, TRUSTWORTHY **4** : marked by or given to feelings of confident certainty ⟨he was ~ he was right⟩ **5** : admitting of no doubt : INDISPUTABLE ⟨~ disaster⟩ **6 a** : bound to happen : INEVITABLE ⟨~ disaster⟩ **b** : BOUND, DESTINED ⟨he is ~ to win⟩ **7** : careful to remember, attend to, or find out something ⟨be ~ to lock the door⟩ ⟨make ~ you give them our regards⟩ — **sure·ness** *n*

syn SURE, CERTAIN, POSITIVE, COCKSURE mean having no doubt or uncertainty. SURE usu. stresses the subjective or intuitive feeling of assurance; CERTAIN may apply to a basing of a conclusion or conviction on definite grounds or indubitable evidence; POSITIVE intensifies sureness or certainty and may imply opinionated conviction or forceful expression of it; COCKSURE implies presumptuous or careless positiveness.

— **for sure** : without doubt or question : CERTAINLY — **to be sure** : it must be acknowledged : ADMITTEDLY

²sure *adv* (15c) : SURELY

usage Most commentators consider the adverb *sure* to be something less than completely standard; *surely* is usu. recommended as a substitute. Our current evidence shows, however, that *sure* and *surely* have become differentiated in use. *Sure* is used in much more informal contexts than *surely*. It is used as a simple intensive ⟨I can never know how much I bored her, but, be certain, she *sure* amused me —Norman Mailer⟩ and, because it connotes strong affirmation, it is used when the speaker or writer expects to be agreed with ⟨it's a moot point whether politicians are less venal than in Twain's day. But they're *sure* as the devil more intrusive —Alan Abelson⟩ ⟨he *sure* gets them to play

—D.S. Looney⟩ *Surely*, like *sure*, is used as a simple intensive ⟨I *surely* don't want to leave the impression that I had an unhappy childhood —E.C. Welsh⟩ but it occurs in more formal contexts than *sure*. Unlike *sure* it may be used neutrally — the reader or hearer may or may not agree ⟨it would *surely* be possible, within a few years, to program a computer to construct a grammar —Noam Chomsky⟩ and it is often used when the writer is trying to persuade ⟨*surely* a book on the avant-garde cannot be so conventional —Karl Shapiro⟩

sure–enough \ˌshu̇r-ə-ˌnəf\ *adj* (1846) : ACTUAL, GENUINE, REAL

sure enough *adv* (1545) : as one might confidently expect : CERTAINLY

sure–fire \ˌshu̇r-ˌfī(ə)r\ *adj* (1917) : certain to get successful or expected results ⟨a ~ recipe⟩

sure–foot·ed \'shu̇(ə)r-ˈfu̇t-əd\ *adj* (1633) : not liable to stumble, fall, or err — **sure–foot·ed·ly** *adv* — **sure–foot·ed·ness** *n*

sure–hand·ed \-'han-dəd\ *adj* (1946) : proficient and confident in performance esp. using the hands — **sure–hand·ed·ness** *n*

sure·ly \'shu̇(ə)r-lē, *esp Southern* 'shō(ə)r-\ *adv* (14c) **1** : in a sure manner: **a** *archaic* : without danger or risk of injury or loss : SAFELY **b** (1) : with assurance : CONFIDENTLY ⟨answered quickly and ~⟩ (2) : without doubt : CERTAINLY ⟨they will ~ be heard from in the future —R. J. Lifton⟩ **2** : INDEED, REALLY — often used as an intensive ⟨you ~ don't believe that⟩ *usage* see ²SURE

sure thing *n* (1836) : one that is certain to succeed : a sure bet

sure·ty \'shu̇r-ət-ē, 'shu̇(ə)rt-ē\ *n, pl* **-ties** [ME *surte*, fr. L *securitat-*, *securitas* security, fr. *securus*] (14c) **1** : the state of being sure: as **a** : sure knowledge : CERTAINTY **b** : confidence in manner or behavior : ASSURANCE **2 a** : a formal engagement (as a pledge) given for the fulfillment of an undertaking : GUARANTEE **b** : ground of confidence or security **3** : one who has become legally liable for the debt, default, or failure in duty (as appearance in court) of another — **sure·ty·ship** \-ˌship\ *n*

surety bond *n* (1911) : a bond guaranteeing performance of a contract or obligation

¹surf \'sərf\ *n* [origin unknown] (1685) **1** : the swell of the sea that breaks upon the shore **2** : the foam, splash, and sound of breaking waves

²surf *vi* (1926) : to ride the surf (as on a surfboard) — **surf·er** *n*

¹sur·face \'sər-fəs\ *n* [F, fr. *sur-* + *face* face, fr. OF — more at FACE] (ca. 1611) **1** : the exterior or upper boundary of an object or body **2** : a plane or curved two-dimensional locus of points (as the boundary of a three-dimensional region) ⟨plane ~⟩ ⟨~ of a sphere⟩ **3 a** : the external or superficial aspect of something **b** : an external part or layer ⟨sand down the damaged ~⟩ — **on the surface** : to all outward appearances

²surface *adj* (1664) **1 a** : of, located on, or designed for use at the surface of something **b** : situated, transported, or employed on the surface of the earth ⟨~ mail⟩ ⟨~ vehicles⟩ **2** : appearing on the surface only : SUPERFICIAL ⟨~ friendships⟩

³surface *vb* **sur·faced; sur·fac·ing** *vt* (1778) **1** : to give a surface to: as **a** : to plane or make smooth **b** : to apply the surface layer to ⟨~ a highway⟩ **2** : to bring to the surface ~ *vi* **1** : to work on or at the surface **2** : to come to the surface **3** : to come into public view : SHOW UP — **sur·fac·er** *n*

surface–active *adj* (1920) : altering the properties and esp. lowering the tension at the surface of contact between phases ⟨soaps and wetting agents are typical ~ substances⟩

surface feeder *n* (1907) : DABBLER b

surface of revolution (1840) : a surface formed by the revolution of a plane curve about a line in its plane

sur·face–rip·ened \'sər-fəs-ˌrī-pənd, -ˌrip-ᵊmd\ *adj, of cheese* (1945) : ripened by the action of microorganisms (as molds or bacteria) on the surface

surface structure *n* (1964) : a formal representation of the phonetic form of a sentence; *also* : the structure which such a representation describes

surface tension *n* (1876) : the attractive force exerted upon the surface molecules of a liquid by the molecules beneath that tends to draw the surface molecules into the bulk of the liquid and makes the liquid assume the shape having the least surface area

surface–to–air missile *n* (1949) : a usu. guided missile launched from the ground against a target in the air

sur·fac·ing *n* (1882) : material forming or used to form a surface

sur·fac·tant \(ˌ)sər-'fak-tənt, 'sər-ˌ\ *n* [*surface-active* + *-ant*] (1950) : a surface-active substance (as a detergent) — **surfactant** *adj*

surf·bird \'sərf-ˌbərd\ *n* (1839) : a shorebird (*Aphriza virgata*) of the Pacific coasts of America that is related to the turnstones and has the tail blackish at the tip and white at the base

surf·board \-ˌbō(ə)rd, -ˌbȯ(ə)rd\ *n* (1826) : a long narrow buoyant board (as of lightweight wood or fiberglass-covered foam) used in the sport of surfing — **surfboard** *vi* — **surf·board·er** *n*

surf·boat \-ˌbōt\ *n* (1856) : a boat for use in heavy surf

surf casting *n* (1935) : a method of fishing in which artificial or natural bait is cast into the open ocean or in a bay where waves break on a beach — **surf caster** *n*

surf clam *n* (ca. 1883) : any of various typically rather large surf-dwelling edible clams (family Mactridae)

¹sur·feit \'sər-fət\ *n* [ME *surfait*, fr. MF, fr. *surfaire* to overdo, fr. *sur-* + *faire* to do, fr. L *facere* — more at DO] (14c) **1** : an overabundant supply : EXCESS **2** : an intemperate or immoderate indulgence in something (as food or drink) **3** : disgust caused by excess

²surfeit *vt* (14c) : to feed, supply, or give to surfeit ~ *vi, archaic* : to indulge to satiety in a gratification (as indulgence of the appetite or senses) *syn* see SATIATE — **sur·feit·er** *n*

surf fish *n* (ca. 1882) : SURFPERCH

sur·fi·cial \ˌsər-'fish-əl\ *adj* [*surface* + *-icial* (as in *superficial*)] (1892) : of or relating to a surface ⟨~ geologic processes⟩

\ə\ abut \ᵊ\ kitten, F table \ər\ further \a\ ash \ā\ ace \ä\ cot, cart
\au̇\ out \ch\ chin \e\ bet \ē\ easy \g\ go \i\ hit \ī\ ice \j\ job
\ŋ\ sing \ō\ go \ȯ\ law \ȯi\ boy \th\ thin \t̲h̲\ the \ü\ loot \u̇\ foot
\y\ yet \zh\ vision \à, ᴋ, ⁿ, œ, œ̄, ᵫ, ᵫ̄, �\ see Guide to Pronunciation

surf·ing \ˈsər-fiŋ\ *n* (1917) **:** the sport of riding the surf esp. on a surfboard
surf·perch \ˈsərf-ˌpərch\ *n* (1885) **:** any of a family (Embiotocidae) of small or medium-sized viviparous fishes of shallow water along the Pacific coast of No. America
[1]**surge** \ˈsərj\ *vb* **surged; surg·ing** [MF *sourge-,* stem of *sourdre* to rise, surge, fr. L *surgere* to go straight up, rise, fr. *sub-* up + *regere* to lead straight — more at SUB-, RIGHT] *vi* (1511) **1 :** to rise and fall actively **:** TOSS ⟨a ship *surging* in heavy seas⟩ **2 :** to rise and move in waves or billows **:** SWELL **3 :** to slip around a windlass, capstan, or bitts — used esp. of a rope **4 :** to rise suddenly to an excessive or abnormal value — used esp. of current or voltage **5 :** to move with a surge or in surges ⟨felt the blood *surging* into his face —Harry Hervey⟩ ∼ *vt* **:** to let go or slacken gradually (as a rope) ⟨∼ a hawser to prevent its parting⟩
[2]**surge** *n* (1520) **1 :** a swelling, rolling, or sweeping forward like that of a wave or series of waves ⟨a ∼ of interest⟩ **2 a :** a large wave or billow **:** SWELL **b** (1) **:** a series of such swells or billows (2) **:** the resulting elevation of water level **3 :** the tapered part of a windlass barrel or a capstan **4 a :** a movement (as a slipping or slackening) of a rope or cable **b :** a sudden jerk or strain caused by such a movement **5 :** a transient sudden rise of current in an electrical circuit
sur·geon \ˈsər-jən\ *n* [ME *surgien,* fr. AF, fr. OF *cirurgien,* fr. *cirurgie* surgery] (14c) **:** a medical specialist who practices surgery
surgeon general *n, pl* **surgeons general** (1777) **:** the chief medical officer of a branch of the armed services or of a federal or state public health service
surgeon's knot *n* (1813) **:** any of several knots used in tying ligatures or surgical stitches; *esp* **:** a reef knot in which the first knot has two turns — see KNOT illustration
sur·gery \ˈsərj-(ə-)rē\ *n, pl* **-ger·ies** [ME *surgerie,* fr. MF *cirurgie, surgerie,* fr. L *chirurgia,* fr. Gk *cheirourgia,* fr. *cheirourgos* surgeon, fr. *cheirourgos* working with the hand, fr. *cheir* hand + *ergon* work — more at CHIR-, WORK] (14c) **1 :** a branch of medicine concerned with diseases and conditions requiring or amenable to operative or manual procedures **2 :** alterations made as if by surgery ⟨literary ∼⟩ **3 a** *Brit* **:** a physician's or dentist's office **b :** a room or area where surgery is performed **4 a :** the work done by a surgeon **b :** OPERATION
sur·gi·cal \ˈsər-ji-kəl\ *adj* [*surg*eon + *-ical*] (1770) **1 a :** of or relating to surgeons or surgery ⟨∼ skills⟩ **b :** used in or in connection with surgery ⟨a ∼ stocking⟩ **2 :** following or resulting from surgery ⟨∼ fevers⟩ — **sur·gi·cal·ly** \-k(ə-)lē\ *adv*
sur·jec·tion \(ˌ)sər-ˈjek-shən\ *n* [prob. fr. F *sur* over, on, onto + E *-jection* (as in *projection*) — more at SUR-] (1964) **:** a mathematical function that is an onto mapping — compare BIJECTION, INJECTION 3
sur·jec·tive \-ˈjek-tiv\ *adj* (1965) **:** ONTO ⟨a set of ∼ functions⟩
sur·ly \ˈsər-lē\ *adj* **sur·li·er; -est** [alter. of ME *sirly* lordly, imperious, fr. *sir*] (1573) **1** *obs* **:** ARROGANT, IMPERIOUS **2 :** irritably sullen and churlish in mood or manner **:** CRABBED **3 :** menacing or threatening in appearance ⟨∼ weather⟩ ***syn*** see SULLEN — **sur·li·ly** \-lə-lē\ *adv* — **sur·li·ness** \-lē-nəs\ *n* — **surly** *adv*
[1]**sur·mise** \sər-ˈmīz, ˈsər-ˌ\ *n* (1569) **:** a thought or idea based on scanty evidence **:** CONJECTURE
[2]**sur·mise** \sər-ˈmīz\ *vt* **sur·mised; sur·mis·ing** [ME *surmisen* to accuse, fr. MF *surmis,* pp. of *surmetre,* fr. L *supermittere* to throw on, fr. *super-* + *mittere* to send] (1700) **:** to imagine or infer on slight grounds
sur·mount \sər-ˈmau̇nt\ *vt* [ME *surmounten,* fr. MF *surmonter,* fr. *sur-* + *monter* to mount] (14c) **1** *obs* **:** to surpass in quality or attainment **:** EXCEL **2 :** to rise superior to **:** OVERCOME ⟨∼ an obstacle⟩ **3 :** to get to the top of **:** CLIMB **4 :** to stand or lie at the top of — **sur·mount·able** \-ə-bəl\ *adj*
sur·mul·let \ˌsər-ˈməl-ət, ˈsər-ˌ\ *n, pl* **surmullets** *also* **surmullet** [F *surmulet*] (ca. 1672) **:** MULLET 2
[1]**sur·name** \ˈsər-ˌnām\ *n* [ME, fr. *sur-* + *name*] (14c) **1 :** an added name derived from occupation or other circumstance **:** NICKNAME 1 **2 :** the name borne in common by members of a family
[2]**surname** *vt* (1512) **:** to give a surname to
sur·pass \sər-ˈpas\ *vt* [MF *surpasser,* fr. *sur-* + *passer* to pass] (1555) **1 :** to become better, greater, or stronger than **:** EXCEED **2 :** to go beyond **:** OVERSTEP **3 :** to transcend the reach, capacity, or powers of ***syn*** see EXCEED — **sur·pass·able** \-ə-bəl\ *adj*
sur·pass·ing *adj* (1580) **:** greatly exceeding others **:** of a very high degree — **sur·pass·ing·ly** \-iŋ-lē\ *adv*
[1]**sur·plice** \ˈsər-pləs\ *n* [ME *surplis,* fr. OF *surpliz,* fr. ML *superpellicium,* fr. *super-* + *pellicium* coat of skins, fr. L, neut. of *pellicius* made of skins, fr. *pellis* skin — more at FELL] (13c) **:** a loose white outer ecclesiastical vestment usu. of knee length with large open sleeves
[2]**surplice** *adj* (ca. 1897) **:** having a diagonally overlapping neckline or closing ⟨a ∼ collar⟩ ⟨∼ sweaters⟩
sur·plus \ˈsər-(ˌ)pləs\ *n* [ME, fr. MF, fr. ML *superplus,* fr. L *super-* + *plus* more — more at PLUS] (14c) **1 a :** the amount that remains when use or need is satisfied **b :** an excess of receipts over disbursements **2 :** the excess of a corporation's net worth over the par or stated value of its capital stock — **surplus** *adj*
sur·plus·age \-(ˌ)pləs-ij\ *n* (15c) **1 :** SURPLUS 1a **2 a :** excessive or nonessential matter **b :** matter introduced in legal pleading which is not necessary or relevant to the case
surplus value *n* (1887) **:** the difference in Marxist theory between the value of work done or of commodities produced by labor and the usu. subsistence wages paid by the employer
sur·print \ˈsər-ˌprint\ *vt or n* (ca. 1917) **:** OVERPRINT
sur·pris·al \sə(r)-ˈprī-zəl\ *n* (1591) **:** the action of surprising **:** the state of being surprised
[1]**sur·prise** \sə(r)-ˈprīz\ *n* [ME, fr. MF, fr. fem. of *surpris,* pp. of *surprendre* to take over, surprise, fr. *sur-* + *prendre* to take — more at PRIZE] (15c) **1 a :** an attack made without warning **b :** a taking unawares **2 :** something that surprises **3 :** the state of being surprised **:** ASTONISHMENT
[2]**surprise** *also* **sur·prize** *vb* **sur·prised; sur·pris·ing** *vt* (15c) **1 :** to attack unexpectedly; *also* **:** to capture by an unexpected attack **2 a :** to take unawares **b :** to detect or elicit by a taking unawares **3 :** to strike with wonder or amazement esp. because unexpected ∼ *vi* **:** to cause astonishment or surprise ⟨nothing he might do with a basketball would ∼ —*Current Biog.*⟩ — **sur·pris·er** *n*

syn SURPRISE, ASTONISH, ASTOUND, AMAZE, FLABBERGAST mean to impress forcibly through unexpectedness. SURPRISE stresses causing an effect through being unexpected at a particular time or place rather than by being essentially unusual or novel; ASTONISH implies surprising so greatly as to seem incredible; ASTOUND stresses the shock of astonishment; AMAZE suggests an effect of bewilderment; FLABBERGAST may suggest thorough astonishment and bewilderment or dismay.
sur·pris·ing *adj* (1645) **:** of a nature that excites surprise — **sur·pris·ing·ly** \-ˈprī-ziŋ-lē\ *adv*
sur·ra \ˈsu̇r-ə\ *n* [Marathi *sūra* wheezing sound] (ca. 1890) **:** a severe Old World febrile and hemorrhagic disease of domestic animals that is caused by a flagellate protozoan (*Trypanosoma evansi*) and is transmitted by biting insects
sur·re·al \sə-ˈrē(-ə)l, -ˈri-əl *also* -ˈrā-əl\ *adj* [back-formation fr. *surrealism*] (1943) **1 :** having the intense irrational reality of a dream **2 :** SURREALISTIC — **sur·re·al·ly** \-ē\ *adv*
sur·re·al·ism \sə-ˈrē-ə-ˌliz-əm, -ˈri- *also* -ˈrā-\ *n* [F *surréalisme,* fr. *sur-* + *réalisme* realism] (1925) **:** the principles, ideals, or practice of producing fantastic or incongruous imagery or effects in art, literature, film, or theater by means of unnatural juxtapositions and combinations — **sur·re·al·ist** \-ləst\ *n or adj*
sur·re·al·is·tic \-ˌrē-ə-ˈlis-tik, -ˌri- *also* -ˌrā-\ *adj* (1925) **1 :** of or relating to surrealism **2 :** having a strange dreamlike atmosphere or quality like that of a surrealist painting — **sur·re·al·is·ti·cal·ly** \-ti-k(ə-)lē\ *adv*
sur·re·but·ter \ˌsər-(r)i-ˈbət-ər\ *n* (1601) **:** the reply in common law pleading of a plaintiff to a defendant's rebutter
sur·re·join·der \-(r)i-ˈjȯin-dər\ *n* (1542) **:** the reply in common law pleading of a plaintiff to a defendant's rejoinder
[1]**sur·ren·der** \sə-ˈren-dər\ *vb* **-dered; -der·ing** \-d(ə-)riŋ\ [ME *surrenderen,* fr. MF *surrendre,* fr. *sur-* + *rendre* to give back, yield — more at RENDER] *vt* (15c) **1 a :** to yield to the power, control, or possession of another upon compulsion or demand ⟨∼*ed* the fort⟩ **b :** to give up completely or agree to forgo esp. in favor of another **2 a :** to give (oneself) up into the power of another esp. as a prisoner **b :** to give (oneself) over to something (as an influence or course of action) ∼ *vi* **:** to give oneself up into the power of another **:** YIELD ***syn*** see RELINQUISH
[2]**surrender** *n* (15c) **1 a :** the action of yielding one's person or giving up the possession of something esp. into the power of another **b :** the relinquishment by a patentee of his rights or claims under a patent **c :** the delivery of a principal into lawful custody by his bail — called also *surrender by bail* **d :** the voluntary cancellation of the legal liability of an insurance company by the insured and beneficiary for a consideration **e :** the delivery of a fugitive from justice by one government to another **2 :** an instance of surrendering
sur·rep·ti·tious \ˌsər-əp-ˈtish-əs, ˌsə-rəp-, sə-ˌrep-\ *adj* [ME, fr. L *surrepticius,* fr. *surreptus,* pp. of *surripere* to snatch secretly, fr. *sub-* + *rapere* to seize — more at RAPID] (15c) **1 :** done, made, or acquired by stealth **:** CLANDESTINE **2 :** acting or doing something clandestinely **:** STEALTHY ***syn*** see SECRET — **sur·rep·ti·tious·ly** *adv*
sur·rey \ˈsər-ē, ˈsə-rē\ *n, pl* **surreys** [*Surrey,* England] (ca. 1891) **:** a four-wheel two-seated horse-drawn pleasure carriage

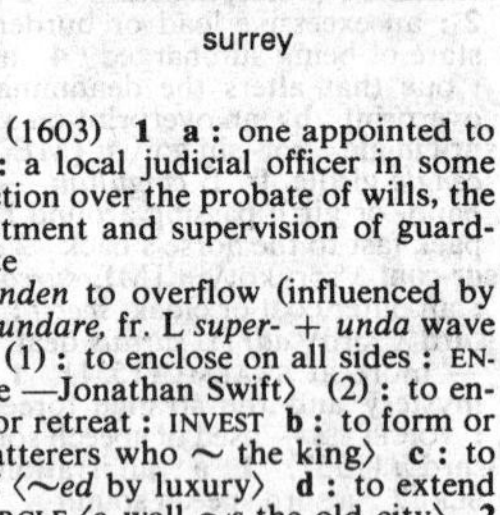
surrey

[1]**sur·ro·gate** \ˈsər-ə-ˌgāt, ˈsə-rə-\ *vt* **-gat·ed; -gat·ing** [L *surrogatus,* pp. of *surrogare* to choose in place of another, substitute, fr. *sub-* + *rogare* to ask — more at RIGHT] (1533) **:** to put in the place of another: **a :** to appoint as successor, deputy, or substitute for oneself **b :** SUBSTITUTE
[2]**sur·ro·gate** \-ˌgāt, -gət\ *n, often attrib* (1603) **1 a :** one appointed to act in place of another **:** DEPUTY **b :** a local judicial officer in some states (as New York) who has jurisdiction over the probate of wills, the settlement of estates, and the appointment and supervision of guardians **2 :** one that serves as a substitute
[1]**sur·round** \sə-ˈrau̇nd\ *vt* [ME *surrounden* to overflow (influenced by [6]*round*), fr. MF *suronder,* fr. LL *superundare,* fr. L *super-* + *unda* wave — more at WATER] (ca. 1616) **1 a** (1) **:** to enclose on all sides **:** ENVELOP ⟨was ∼*ed* by a crowd of people —Jonathan Swift⟩ (2) **:** to enclose so as to cut off communication or retreat **:** INVEST **b :** to form or be a member of the entourage of ⟨flatterers who ∼ the king⟩ **c :** to constitute part of the environment of ⟨∼*ed* by luxury⟩ **d :** to extend around the margin or edge of **:** ENCIRCLE ⟨a wall ∼*s* the old city⟩ **2 :** to cause to be surrounded by something ⟨he ∼*ed* himself with able advisers⟩
[2]**surround** *n* (ca. 1891) **:** something (as a border or ambient environment) that surrounds ⟨from urban centre to rural ∼ —Emrys Jones⟩
sur·round·ings \sə-ˈrau̇n-diŋz\ *n pl* (1861) **:** the circumstances, conditions, or objects by which one is surrounded **:** ENVIRONMENT
sur·roy·al \ˈsər-ˌrȯi(-ə)l\ *n* [ME *surryal,* fr. *sur-* + *royal* royal antler] (15c) **:** one of the terminal tines above the royal antler of a large deer (as a stag) usu. grown by four years of age
sur·sum cor·da \ˌsu̇(ə)r-səm-ˈkȯrd-ə, -ˈkō(ə)r-ˌdä\ *n* [LL, (lift) up (your) hearts; fr. the opening words] (1559) **1** *often cap S&C* **:** a versicle that in traditional eucharistic liturgies exhorts the faithful to enthusiastic worship **2 :** something inspiriting
sur·tax \ˈsər-ˌtaks\ *n* (1881) **1 :** an extra tax or charge **2 :** a graduated income tax in addition to the normal income tax imposed on the amount by which one's net income exceeds a specified sum
sur·tout \(ˌ)sər-ˈtü, ˈsər-ˌ\ *n* [F, fr. *sur* over (fr. L *super*) + *tout* all, fr. L *totus* whole — more at OVER] (1686) **:** a man's long close-fitting overcoat
sur·veil \sər-ˈvā(ə)l\ *vt* **sur·veilled; sur·veil·ling** [back-formation fr. *surveillance*] (1966) **:** to subject to surveillance
sur·veil·lance \sər-ˈvā-lən(t)s *also* -ˈvāl-yən(t)s *or* -ˈvā-ən(t)s\ *n* [F, fr. *surveiller* to watch over, fr. *sur-* + *veiller* to watch, fr. L *vigilare,* fr. *vigil* watchful — more at VIGIL] (1802) **:** close watch kept over someone or something (as by a detective); *also* **:** SUPERVISION
sur·veil·lant \-ˈvā-lənt *also* -ˈvāl-yənt *or* -ˈvā-ənt\ *n* (1819) **:** one that exercises surveillance

[1]**sur·vey** \sər-ˈvā, ˈsər-ˌ\ *vb* **sur·veyed; sur·vey·ing** [ME *surveyen,* fr. MF *surveeir* to look over, fr. *sur-* + *veeir* to see — more at VIEW] *vt* (15c) **1 a :** to examine as to condition, situation, or value : APPRAISE **b :** to query (someone) in order to collect data for the analysis of some aspect of a group or area **2 :** to determine and delineate the form, extent, and position of (as a tract of land) by taking linear and angular measurements and by applying the principles of geometry and trigonometry **3 :** to view or consider comprehensively **4 :** INSPECT, SCRUTINIZE ⟨he ~*ed* us in a lordly way —Alan Harrington⟩ ~ *vi* **:** to make a survey

[2]**sur·vey** \ˈsər-ˌvā, sər-ˈ\ *n, pl* **surveys** (1535) **:** the act or an instance of surveying; *also* **:** something that is surveyed

survey course \ˈsər-ˌvā-\ *n* (1916) **:** a course treating briefly the chief topics of a broad field of knowledge

sur·vey·ing \sər-ˈvā-iŋ\ *n* (1682) **:** a branch of applied mathematics that teaches the art of determining the area of any portion of the earth's surface, the lengths and directions of the bounding lines, and the contour of the surface and of accurately delineating the whole on paper

sur·vey·or \sər-ˈvā-ər\ *n* (15c) **:** one that surveys; *esp* **:** one whose occupation is surveying land

sur·viv·able \sər-ˈvī-və-bəl\ *adj* (1955) **:** resulting in or permitting survival — **sur·viv·abil·i·ty** \-ˌvī-və-ˈbil-ət-ē\ *n*

sur·viv·al \sər-ˈvī-vəl\ *n, often attrib* (1598) **1 a :** a living or continuing longer than another person or thing **b :** the continuation of life or existence ⟨problems of ~ in arctic conditions⟩ **2 :** one that survives

sur·viv·al·ist \-və-ləst\ *n* (1970) **:** one who views survival of a catastrophic event as a primary objective — **survivalist** *adj*

survival of the fittest (1864) **:** NATURAL SELECTION

sur·viv·ance \sər-ˈvī-vən(t)s\ *n* (1623) **:** SURVIVAL

sur·vive \sər-ˈvīv\ *vb* **sur·vived; sur·viv·ing** [ME *surviven,* fr. MF *survivre* to outlive, fr. L *supervivere,* fr. *super-* + *vivere* to live — more at QUICK] *vi* (15c) **1 :** to remain alive or in existence **:** live on **2 :** to continue to function or prosper ~ *vt* **1 :** to remain alive after the death of ⟨his son *survived* him⟩ **2 :** to continue to exist or live after ⟨*survived* the earthquake⟩ **3 :** to continue to function or prosper despite **:** WITHSTAND — **sur·vi·vor** \-ˈvī-vər\ *n*

sur·vi·ver \-ˈvī-vər\ *n, archaic* (1602) **:** one that survives **:** SURVIVOR

sur·vi·vor·ship \-ˈvī-vər-ˌship\ *n* (1625) **1 :** the legal right of the survivor of persons having joint interests in property to take the interest of the person who has died **2 :** the state of being a survivor

Su·san B. An·tho·ny Day \ˌsüz-ᵊn-ˌbē-ˈan(t)-thə-nē-\ *n* (ca. 1951) **:** February 15 observed to commemorate the birth of Susan B. Anthony

sus·cep·ti·bil·i·ty \sə-ˌsep-tə-ˈbil-ət-ē\ *n, pl* **-ties** (ca. 1644) **1 :** the quality or state of being susceptible; *esp* **:** lack of ability to resist some extraneous agent (as a pathogen or drug) **:** SENSITIVITY **2 a :** a susceptible temperament or constitution **b** *pl* **:** FEELINGS, SENSIBILITIES **3 a :** the ratio of the magnetization in a substance to the corresponding magnetizing force **b :** the ratio of the electric polarization to the electric intensity in a polarized dielectric

sus·cep·ti·ble \sə-ˈsep-tə-bəl\ *adj* [LL *susceptibilis,* fr. L *susceptus,* pp. of *suscipere* to take up, admit, fr. *sub-, sus-* up + *capere* to take — more at SUB-, HEAVE] (1605) **1 :** capable of submitting to an action, process, or operation ⟨a theory ~ to proof⟩ **2 :** open, subject, or unresistant to some stimulus, influence, or agency **3 :** IMPRESSIONABLE, RESPONSIVE *syn* see LIABLE — **sus·cep·ti·ble·ness** *n* — **sus·cep·ti·bly** \-blē\ *adv*

sus·cep·tive \-tiv\ *adj* (1548) **1 :** RECEPTIVE **2 :** SUSCEPTIBLE — **sus·cep·tive·ness** *n* — **sus·cep·tiv·i·ty** \sə-ˌsep-ˈtiv-ət-ē\ *n*

su·shi \ˈsü-shē, ˈsu̇sh-ē\ *n* [Jp] (ca. 1898) **:** cold rice dressed with vinegar, shaped into small cakes, and topped or wrapped with garnishes (as of raw fish)

sus·lik \ˈsü-slik\ *n* [Russ] (ca. 1774) **1 :** any of several rather large short-tailed ground squirrels (genus *Citellus*) of eastern Europe or northern Asia **2 :** the mottled grayish black fur of a suslik

[1]**sus·pect** \ˈsəs-ˌpekt, sə-ˈspekt\ *adj* [ME, fr. MF, fr. L *suspectus,* fr. pp. of *suspicere*] (14c) **:** regarded or deserving to be regarded with suspicion **:** SUSPECTED

[2]**sus·pect** \ˈsəs-ˌpekt\ *n* (1591) **:** one who is suspected; *esp* **:** one suspected of a crime

[3]**sus·pect** \sə-ˈspekt\ *vb* [ME *suspecten,* fr. L *suspectare,* fr. *suspectus,* pp. of *suspicere* to look up at, regard with awe, suspect, fr. *sub-, sus-* up, secretly + *specere* to look at — more at SUB-, SPY] *vt* (15c) **1 :** to imagine (one) to be guilty or culpable on slight evidence or without proof ⟨~ him of giving false information⟩ **2 :** to have doubts of **:** DISTRUST **3 :** to imagine to exist or be true, likely, or probable ~ *vi* **:** to imagine something to be true or likely

sus·pend \sə-ˈspend\ *vb* [ME *suspenden,* fr. OF *suspendre* to hang up, interrupt, fr. L *suspendere,* fr. *sub-, sus-* up + *pendere* to cause to hang, weigh — more at PENDANT] *vt* (13c) **1 :** to debar temporarily from a privilege, office, or function ⟨~ a student from school⟩ **2 a :** to cause to stop temporarily ⟨~ bus service⟩ **b :** to set aside or make temporarily inoperative ⟨~ the rules⟩ **3 :** to defer to a later time on specified conditions ⟨~ sentence⟩ **4 :** to hold in an undetermined or undecided state awaiting further information ⟨~ judgment⟩ **5 a :** HANG; *esp* **:** to hang so as to be free on all sides except at the point of support ⟨~ a ball by a thread⟩ **b :** to keep from falling or sinking by some invisible support (as buoyancy) ⟨dust ~*ed* in the air⟩ **6 a :** to keep fixed or lost (as in wonder or contemplation) **b :** to keep waiting in suspense or indecision **7 :** to hold (a musical note) over into the following chord ~ *vi* **1 :** to cease operation temporarily **2 :** to stop payment or fail to meet obligations **3 :** HANG *syn* see DEFER

suspended animation *n* (ca. 1820) **:** temporary suspension of the vital functions (as in persons nearly drowned)

sus·pend·er \sə-ˈspen-dər\ *n* (1524) **1 :** one that suspends **2 :** a device by which something may be suspended: as **a :** one of two supporting bands worn across the shoulders to support trousers, skirt, or belt — usu. used in pl. and often with *pair* **b** *Brit* **:** a fastener attached to a garment or garter to hold up a stocking or sock; *also* **:** a device consisting of garter and fastener

sus·pense \sə-ˈspen(t)s\ *n* [ME, fr. MF, fr. *suspendre*] (15c) **1 :** the state of being suspended **:** SUSPENSION **2 a :** mental uncertainty **:** ANXIETY **b :** pleasant excitement as to a decision or outcome ⟨a novel of ~⟩ **3 :** the state or character of being undecided or doubtful **:** INDECISIVENESS — **sus·pense·ful** \-fəl\ *adj*

suspense account *n* (ca. 1879) **:** an account for the temporary entry of charges or credits or esp. of doubtful accounts receivable pending determination of their ultimate disposition

sus·pen·sion \sə-ˈspen-chən\ *n* [LL *suspension-, suspensio,* fr. L *suspensus,* pp. of *suspendere*] (1528) **1 :** the act of suspending **:** the state or period of being suspended: as **a :** temporary removal from office or privileges **b :** temporary withholding (as of belief or decision) **c :** temporary abrogation of a law or rule **d** (1) **:** the holding over of one or more musical tones of a chord into the following chord producing a momentary discord and suspending the concord which the ear expects; *specif* **:** such a dissonance which resolves downward — compare RETARDATION (2) **:** the tone thus held over **e :** stoppage of payment of business obligations **:** FAILURE — used esp. of a business or a bank **f :** a rhetorical device whereby the principal idea is deferred to the end of a sentence or longer unit **2 a :** the act of hanging **:** the state of being hung **b** (1) **:** the state of a substance when its particles are mixed with but undissolved in a fluid or solid (2) **:** a substance in this state (3) **:** a system consisting of a solid dispersed in a solid, liquid, or gas usu. in particles of larger than colloidal size — compare EMULSION **3 :** something suspended **4 a :** a device by which something (as a magnetic needle) is suspended **b :** the system of devices (as springs) supporting the upper part of a vehicle on the axles **c :** the act, process, or manner in which the pendulum or torsion balance of a timepiece is suspended

suspension bridge *n* (1821) **:** a bridge that has its roadway suspended from two or more cables usu. passing over towers and securely anchored at the ends — see BRIDGE illustration

suspension points *n pl* (1919) **:** usu. three spaced periods used to show the omission of a word or word group from a written context

sus·pen·sive \sə-ˈspen(t)-siv\ *adj* (1550) **1 :** stopping temporarily **:** SUSPENDING **2 :** characterized by suspense, suspended judgment, or indecisiveness **3 :** characterized by suspension — **sus·pen·sive·ly** *adv*

sus·pen·soid \sə-ˈspen(t)-ˌsȯid\ *n* [ISV *suspension* + *colloid*] (1922) **1 :** a colloidal system in which the dispersed particles are solid **2 :** a lyophobic sol (as a gold sol)

sus·pen·sor \sə-ˈspen(t)-sər\ *n* [NL, fr. *suspensus,* pp.] (1832) **:** a suspending part or structure: as **a :** a group or chain of cells that is produced from the zygote of a heterosporous plant and serves to push the embryo which arises at its extremity deeper into the embryo sac and into contact with the food supply of the megaspore **b :** one of the two hyphae in fungi (order Mucorales) that bear gametangia at their tips and later support the zygospore

[1]**sus·pen·so·ry** \sə-ˈspen(t)s-(ə-)rē\ *adj* (1541) **1 :** held in suspension; *also* **:** fitted or serving to suspend **2 :** temporarily leaving undetermined **:** SUSPENSIVE 1

[2]**suspensory** *n, pl* **-ries** (ca. 1656) **:** something that suspends or holds up; *esp* **:** a fabric supporter for the scrotum

suspensory ligament *n* (1831) **:** a ligament or fibrous membrane suspending an organ or part; *esp* **:** a ringlike fibrous membrane connecting the ciliary body and the lens of the eye and holding the lens in place — see EYE illustration

[1]**sus·pi·cion** \sə-ˈspish-ən\ *n* [ME, fr. L *suspicion-, suspicio,* fr. *suspicere* to suspect — more at SUSPECT] (13c) **1 a :** the act or an instance of suspecting something wrong without proof or on slight evidence **:** MISTRUST **b :** a state of mental uneasiness and uncertainty **:** DOUBT **2 :** a slight touch or trace ⟨just a ~ of garlic⟩ *syn* see UNCERTAINTY

[2]**suspicion** *vt* **sus·pi·cioned; sus·pi·cion·ing** \-ˈspish-(ə-)niŋ\ *chiefly substand* (1637) **:** SUSPECT

sus·pi·cious \sə-ˈspish-əs\ *adj* (14c) **1 :** tending to arouse suspicion **:** QUESTIONABLE **2 :** disposed to suspect **:** DISTRUSTFUL ⟨~ of strangers⟩ **3 :** expressing or indicative of suspicion ⟨a ~ glance⟩ — **sus·pi·cious·ly** *adv* — **sus·pi·cious·ness** *n*

sus·pi·ra·tion \ˌsəs-pə-ˈrā-shən\ *n* (15c) **:** a long deep breath **:** SIGH

sus·pire \sə-ˈspī(ə)r\ *vi* **sus·pired; sus·pir·ing** [ME *suspiren,* fr. L *suspirare,* fr. *sub-* + *spirare* to breathe — more at SPIRIT] (15c) **:** to draw a long deep breath **:** SIGH

Sus·sex spaniel \ˌsəs-ik(s)-, -ˌek(s)-\ *n* [*Sussex,* England] (1856) **:** any of a British breed of short-legged short-necked long-bodied spaniels with a flat or slightly wavy golden liver-colored coat

suss out \(ˈ)səs-ˈau̇t\ *vt* [perh. short for *suspect*] (1966) **1** *Brit* **:** FIGURE OUT **2** *Brit* **:** STUDY

sus·tain \sə-ˈstān\ *vt* [ME *sustenen,* fr. OF *sustenir,* fr. L *sustinēre* to hold up, sustain, fr. *sub-, sus-* up + *tenēre* to hold — more at SUB-, THIN] (13c) **1 :** to give support or relief to **2 :** to supply with sustenance **:** NOURISH **3 :** KEEP UP, PROLONG **4 :** to support the weight of **:** PROP; *also* **:** to carry or withstand (a weight or pressure) **5 :** to buoy up ⟨~*ed* by hope⟩ **6 a :** to bear up under **b :** SUFFER, UNDERGO ⟨~*ed* heavy losses⟩ **7 a :** to support as true, legal, or just **b :** to allow or admit as valid ⟨the court ~*ed* the motion⟩ **8 :** to support by adequate proof **:** CONFIRM ⟨testimony that ~*s* our contention⟩ — **sus·tain·able** \-ˈstā-nə-bəl\ *adj* — **sus·tain·er** *n*

sustained yield *n* (ca. 1905) **:** production of a biological resource (as timber or fish) under management procedures which insure replacement of the part harvested by regrowth or reproduction before another harvest occurs — **sustained–yield** *adj*

sus·tain·ing *adj* (1605) **1 a :** serving to sustain **b :** aiding in the support of an organization through a special fee ⟨a ~ member⟩ **2 :** of or relating to a sustaining program

sustaining program *n* (1931) **:** a radio or television program that is paid for by a station or network and has no commercial sponsor

sus·te·nance \ˈsəs-tə-nən(t)s\ *n* [ME, fr. OF, fr. *sustenir*] (13c) **1 a :** means of support, maintenance, or subsistence **:** LIVING **b :** FOOD, PROVISIONS; *also* **:** NOURISHMENT **2 a :** the act of sustaining **:** the state of being sustained **b :** a supplying or being supplied with the necessaries of life **3 :** something that gives support, endurance, or strength

sus·ten·tac·u·lar cell \ˌsəs-tən-ˈtak-yə-lər-, -ˌten-\ *n* [NL *sustentaculum* supporting part, fr. L, prop, fr. *sustentare*] (1901) **:** a supporting epithelial cell (as a Sertoli cell or a cell of the olfactory epithelium) that lacks a specialized function (as nerve-impulse conduction)

sus·ten·ta·tion \-'tā-shən\ *n* [ME, fr. MF, fr. L *sustentation-, sustentatio* act of holding up, fr. *sustentatus,* pp. of *sustentare* to hold up, fr. *sustentus,* pp. of *sustinēre* to sustain] (14c) **1 :** the act of sustaining : the state of being sustained: as **a :** MAINTENANCE, UPKEEP **b :** PRESERVATION, CONSERVATION **c :** maintenance of life, growth, or morale **d :** provision with sustenance **2 :** something that sustains : SUPPORT — **sus·ten·ta·tive** \'səs-tən-,tāt-iv, sə-'stent-ət-\ *adj*

sus·ten·tion \sə-'sten-chən\ *n* [fr. *sustain,* after such pairs as E *retain : retention*] (1868) : SUSTENTATION

Su·su \'sü-(,)sü\ *n, pl* **Susu** *or* **Susus** (1920) **1 :** a member of a West African people of Mali, Guinea, and the area along the northern border of Sierra Leone **2 :** the language of the Susu people

su·sur·ra·tion \,sü-sə-'rā-shən\ *n* (15c) : a whispering sound : MURMUR

su·sur·rous \sü-'sər-əs, -'sə-rəs\ *adj* (1859) : full of whispering sounds

su·sur·rus \sü-'sər-əs, -'sə-rəs\ *n* [L, hum, whisper — more at SWARM] (1831) : a whispering or rustling sound — **su·sur·rant** \-'sər-ənt, -'sə-rənt\ *adj*

sut·ler \'sət-lər\ *n* [obs. D *soeteler,* fr. LG *suteler* sloppy worker, camp cook; akin to OE *besūtian* to dirty, Gk *hyein* to rain — more at SUCK] (1599) : a civilian provisioner to an army post often with a shop on the post

su·tra \'sü-trə\ *n* [Skt *sūtra* thread, string of precepts, sutra; akin to L *suere* to sew — more at SEW] (1801) **1 :** a precept summarizing Vedic teaching; *also* **:** a collection of these precepts **2 :** a discourse of the Buddha

sut·tee \(,)sə-'tē, 'sə-,tē\ *n* [Skt *satī* wife who performs suttee, lit., good woman, fr. fem. of *sat* true, good; akin to OE *sōth* true — more at SOOTH] (1786) : the act or custom of a Hindu widow willingly being cremated on the funeral pyre of her husband as an indication of her devotion to him; *also* **:** a woman cremated in this way

[1]**su·ture** \'sü-chər\ *n* [MF & L; MF, fr. L *sutura* seam, suture, fr. *sutus,* pp. of *suere* to sew — more at SEW] (1541) **1 a :** a stitch made with a suture **b :** a strand or fiber used to sew parts of the living body **c :** the act or process of sewing with sutures **2 a :** a uniting of parts **b :** the seam or seamlike line along which two things or parts are sewed or united **3 a :** the line of union in an immovable articulation (as between the bones of the skull); *also* **:** such an articulation **b :** a furrow at the junction of adjacent bodily parts; *esp* **:** a line of dehiscence (as on a fruit) — **su·tur·al** \'süch(-ə)-rəl\ *adj* — **su·tur·al·ly** \-rə-lē\ *adv*

[2]**suture** *vt* **su·tured; su·tur·ing** \'süch-(ə-)riŋ\ (1777) : to unite, close, or secure with sutures ⟨~ a wound⟩

su·zer·ain \'süz-(ə-)rən, -ə-,rān\ *n* [F, fr. (assumed) MF *suserain,* fr. MF *sus* up (fr. L *sursum,* fr. *sub-* up + *versum* -ward, fr. neut. of *versus,* pp. of *vertere* to turn) + *-erain* (as in *soverain* sovereign) — more at SUB-, WORTH] (1807) **1 :** a superior feudal lord to whom fealty is due : OVERLORD **2 :** a dominant state controlling the foreign relations of a vassal state but allowing it sovereign authority in its internal affairs

su·zer·ain·ty \-tē\ *n* [F *suzeraineté,* fr. MF *susereneté,* fr. (assumed) MF *suserain*] (1822) : the dominion of a suzerain : OVERLORDSHIP

sved·berg \'sfed-,bərg, -,ber-ē\ *n* [The *Svedberg*] (1939) : a unit of time amounting to 10^{-13} second that is used to measure the sedimentation velocity of a colloidal solution (as of a protein) in an ultracentrifuge and to determine molecular weight by substitution in an equation — called also *svedberg unit*

svelte \'sfelt\ *adj* [F, fr. It *svelto,* fr. pp. of *svellere* to pluck out, modif. of L *evellere,* fr. *e-* + *vellere* to pluck — more at VULNERABLE] (1817) **1 a :** SLENDER, LITHE **b :** having clean lines : SLEEK **2 :** URBANE, SUAVE — **svelte·ly** *adv* — **svelte·ness** *n*

Sven·ga·li \sfen-'gäl-ē\ *n* [*Svengali,* maleficent hypnotist in the novel *Trilby* (1894) by George du Maurier] (ca. 1945) : one who attempts usu. with evil intentions to persuade or force another to do his bidding

[1]**swab** \'swäb\ *n* [prob. fr. obs. D *swabbe;* akin to LG *swabber* mop] (1653) **1 a :** MOP; *esp* **:** a yarn mop **b (1) :** a wad of absorbent material usu. wound around one end of a small stick and used for applying medication or for removing material from an area **(2) :** a specimen taken with a swab **c :** a sponge or cloth patch attached to a long handle and used to clean the bore of a firearm **2 a :** a useless or contemptible person **b :** SAILOR, GOB

[2]**swab** *vt* **swabbed; swab·bing** [back-formation fr. *swabber*] (1719) **1 :** to clean with or as if with a swab **2 :** to apply medication to with a swab ⟨*swabbed* the wound with iodine⟩

swab·ber \'swäb-ər\ *n* [akin to LG *swabber* mop, ME *swabben* to sway] (1592) **1 :** one that swabs **2 :** SWAB 2a

swab·bie *also* **swab·by** \-ē\ *n, pl* **swabbies** *slang* (1944) : SWAB 2b

swad·dle \'swäd-ᵊl\ *vt* **swad·dled; swad·dling** \'swäd-liŋ, -ᵊl-iŋ\ [ME *swadelen, swathelen,* prob. alter. of *swedelen, swethelen,* fr. *swethel* swaddling band, fr. OE; akin to OE *swathian* to swathe] (14c) **1 a :** to wrap (an infant) with swaddling clothes **b :** ENVELOP, SWATHE **2 :** RESTRAIN, RESTRICT

swaddling clothes *n pl* (1535) **1 :** narrow strips of cloth wrapped around an infant to restrict movement **2 :** limitations or restrictions imposed on the immature or inexperienced

[1]**swag** \'swag\ *vi* **swagged; swag·ging** [prob. of Scand origin; akin to ON *sveggja* to cause to sway; akin to OHG *swingan* to swing] (ca. 1530) **1 :** SWAY, LURCH **2 :** SAG

[2]**swag** *n* (1660) **1 :** SWAY **2 a :** something (as a decoration) hanging in a curve between two points : FESTOON **b :** a suspended cluster (as of evergreen branches) **3 a :** goods acquired by unlawful means : LOOT **b :** SPOILS, PROFITS **4 :** a depression in the earth **5** *chiefly Austral* **:** a pack of personal belongings

[1]**swage** \'swāj, 'swej\ *n* [ME, ornamental border, fr. MF *souage*] (ca. 1812) : a tool used by metalworkers for shaping their work by holding it on the work or the work on it and striking with a hammer or sledge

[2]**swage** *vt* **swaged; swag·ing** (1831) : to shape by or as if by means of a swage

swage block *n* (1843) : a perforated cast-iron or steel block with grooved sides that is used in heading bolts and swaging bars by hand

[1]**swag·ger** \'swag-ər\ *vb* **swag·gered; swag·ger·ing** \-(ə-)riŋ\ [prob. fr. [1]*swag* + *-er* (as in *chatter*)] *vi* (1590) **1 :** to conduct oneself in an arrogant or superciliously pompous manner; *esp* **:** to walk with an air of overbearing self-confidence **2 :** BOAST, BRAG ~ *vt* **:** to force by argument or threat : BULLY — **swag·ger·er** \-ər-ər\ *n* — **swag·ger·ing·ly** \-(ə-)riŋ-lē\ *adv*

[2]**swagger** *adj* (1725) : marked by elegance or showiness : POSH

[3]**swagger** *n* (1879) **1 a :** an act or instance of swaggering **b :** arrogant or conceitedly self-assured behavior **c :** ostentatious display or bravado **2 :** a self-confident outlook : COCKINESS

swagger stick *n* (1887) : a short light stick usu. covered with leather and tipped with metal at each end and intended for carrying in the hand (as by military officers)

swag·man \'swag-mən\ *n, chiefly Austral* (1879) : WANDERER; *esp* **:** one who carries a swag when traveling

Swa·hi·li \swä-'hē-lē\ *n, pl* **Swahili** *or* **Swahilis** [Ar *sawāhil,* pl. of *sāḥil* coast] (1814) **1 :** a member of a Bantu-speaking people of Zanzibar and the adjacent coast **2 :** a Bantu language that is a trade and governmental language over much of East Africa and in the Congo region

swain \'swān\ *n* [ME *swein* boy, servant, fr. ON *sveinn;* akin to OE *swān* swain, L *suus* one's own — more at SUICIDE] (1579) **1 :** RUSTIC, PEASANT; *specif* **:** SHEPHERD **2 :** a male admirer or suitor — **swain·ish** \'swā-nish\ *adj* — **swain·ish·ness** *n*

swale \'swā(ə)l\ *n* [ME, shade, prob. of Scand origin; akin to ON *svalr* cool; akin to OE *swelan* to burn — more at SWELTER] (1584) : a low-lying or depressed and often wet stretch of land

[1]**swal·low** \'swäl-(,)ō, -ə(-w)\ *n* [ME *swalowe,* fr. OE *swealwe;* akin to OHG *swalawa* swallow, Russ *solovei* nightingale] (bef. 12c) **1 :** any of numerous small long-winged passerine birds (family Hirundinidae) that are noted for their graceful flight and regular migrations, have a short bill with a wide gape, small weak feet, and often a deeply forked tail, occur in all parts of the world except New Zealand and polar regions, and feed on insects caught on the wing **2 :** any of several swifts that superficially resemble swallows

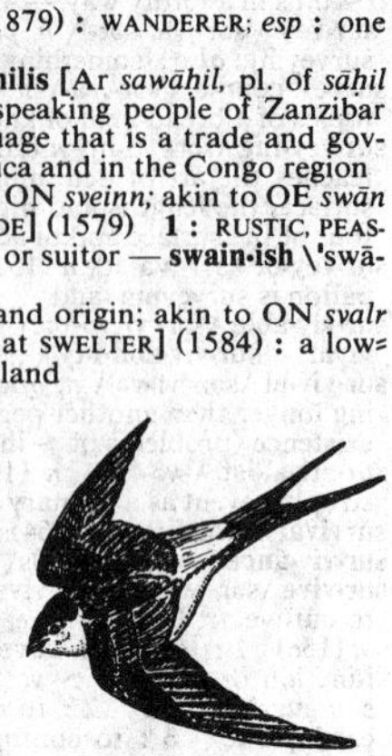
swallow 1

[2]**swallow** *vb* [ME *swalowen,* fr. OE *swelgan;* akin to OHG *swelgan* to swallow] *vt* (bef. 12c) **1 :** to take through the mouth and esophagus into the stomach **2 :** to envelop or take in as if by swallowing : ABSORB **3 :** to accept without question, protest, or resentment ⟨~ an insult⟩ ⟨a hard story to ~⟩ **4 :** TAKE BACK, RETRACT ⟨had to ~ my words⟩ **5 :** to keep from expressing or showing : REPRESS ⟨~*ed* my anger⟩ **6 :** to utter (as words) indistinctly ~ *vi* **1 :** to receive something into the body through the mouth and esophagus **2 :** to perform the action characteristic of swallowing something esp. under emotional stress — **swal·low·able** \'swäl-ō-ə-bəl\ *adj* — **swal·low·er** \'swäl-ə-wər\ *n*

[3]**swallow** *n* (14c) **1 :** the passage connecting the mouth to the stomach **2 :** a capacity for swallowing **3 a :** an act of swallowing **b :** an amount that can be swallowed at one time **4 :** an aperture in a block on a ship between the sheave and frame through which the rope reeves

swal·low·tail \'swäl-ō-,tāl, -ə-\ *n* (1703) **1 :** a deeply forked and tapering tail (as of a swallow) **2 :** TAILCOAT **3 :** any of various large butterflies (esp. genus *Papilio*) with the hind wing produced into a process resembling a tail — **swal·low–tailed** \,swäl-ō-'tāld, -ə-\ *adj*

swal·low·wort \'swäl-ō-,wərt, -ə-, -,wȯ(ə)rt\ *n* [fr. the shape of the pods] (1578) : CELANDINE 1

swam *past of* SWIM

swa·mi \'swäm-ē\ *n* [Hindi *svāmī,* fr. Skt *svāmin* owner, lord, fr. *sva* one's own — more at SUICIDE] (1895) **1 :** a Hindu ascetic or religious teacher; *specif* **:** a senior member of a religious order — used as a title **2 :** one that resembles or emulates a swami : PUNDIT, SEER

[1]**swamp** \'swämp, 'swȯmp\ *n* [alter. of ME *sompe,* fr. MD *somp* morass; akin to MHG *sumpf* marsh, Gk *somphos* spongy] (1624) **1 :** wet spongy land saturated and sometimes partially or intermittently covered with water **2 :** a tract of swamp — **swamp** *adj*

[2]**swamp** *vt* (1772) **1 a :** to fill with or as if with water : INUNDATE, SUBMERGE **b :** to overwhelm numerically or by an excess of something : FLOOD ⟨~*ed* with work⟩ **2 :** to open by removing underbrush and debris ~ *vi* **:** to become submerged

swamp buggy *n* (1941) : a vehicle designed to travel over swampy terrain; *esp.* **:** a four-wheel motor vehicle with oversize tires

swamp·er \'swäm-pər, 'swȯm-\ *n* (1735) **1 a :** an inhabitant of swamps or lowlands **b :** one familiar with swampy terrain **2 :** a general assistant : HANDYMAN, HELPER

swamp·land \-,pland\ *n* (1663) : SWAMP 1

swampy \'swäm-pē, 'swȯm-\ *adj* **swamp·i·er; -est** (1649) : consisting of or resembling swamp : MARSHY — **swamp·i·ness** *n*

[1]**swan** \'swän\ *n, pl* **swans** [ME, fr. OE; akin to MHG *swan,* L *sonus* sound — more at SOUND] (bef. 12c) **1** *pl also* **swan :** any of various heavy-bodied long-necked mostly pure white aquatic birds (family Anatidae) that are related to but larger than the geese, walk awkwardly, fly strongly when once started, and are graceful swimmers **2 :** one that resembles or is likened to a swan **3** *cap* **:** the constellation Cygnus

[2]**swan** *vi* **swanned; swan·ning** (ca. 1940) : to wander aimlessly : DALLY

[3]**swan** *vi* **swanned; swan·ning** [perh. euphemism for *swear*] *dial* (1784) : DECLARE, SWEAR

swan boat *n* (1953) : a small boat usu. for children or sightseers pedaled by an operator who sits aft in a large model of a swan

swan dive *n* (1898) : a front dive executed with the head back, back arched, and arms spread sideways and then brought together above the head to form a straight line with the body as the diver enters the water

[1]**swank** \'swaŋk\ *adj* [MLG or MD *swanc* supple; akin to OHG *swingan* to swing] *Scot* (1773) : full of life or energy : ACTIVE

[2]**swank** *vi* [perh. fr. MHG *swanken* to sway; akin to MD *swanc* supple] (ca. 1809) : SHOW OFF, SWAGGER

[3]**swank** *or* **swanky** \'swaŋ-kē\ *adj* **swank·er** *or* **swank·i·er; -est** (ca. 1842) **1 :** characterized by showy display : OSTENTATIOUS ⟨a ~ limousine⟩ **2 :** fashionably elegant : SMART ⟨a ~ restaurant⟩ — **swank·i·ly** \-kə-lē\ *adv* — **swank·i·ness** \-kē-nəs\ *n*

[4]**swank** *n* (ca. 1854) **1 :** arrogance or ostentation of dress or manner : PRETENTIOUSNESS, SWAGGER **2 :** ELEGANCE

swan·nery \'swän-(ə-)rē\ *n, pl* **-ner·ies** (1754) **:** a place where swans are bred or kept

swans·down \'swänz-ˌdau̇n\ *n* (1606) **1 :** the soft downy feathers of the swan often used as trimming on articles of dress **2 :** a heavy cotton flannel that has a thick nap on the face and is made with sateen weave

swan·skin \'swän-ˌskin\ *n* (1610) **1 :** the skin of a swan with the down or feathers on it **2 :** fabric resembling flannel and having a soft nap or surface

swan song *n* (1831) **1 :** a song of great sweetness said to be sung by a dying swan **2 :** a farewell appearance or final act or pronouncement

[1]**swap** \'swäp\ *vb* **swapped; swap·ping** [ME *swappen* to strike; fr. the practice of striking hands in closing a business deal] *vt* (14c) **:** to give in exchange **:** BARTER ~ *vi* **:** to make an exchange — **swap·per** *n*

[2]**swap** *n* (1625) **:** the act or process of exchanging one thing for another

swap meet *n* (1965) **:** a gathering for the sale or barter of secondhand objects

swa·raj \swə-'räj\ *n* [Skt *svarāj* self-ruling, fr. *sva* one's self + *rājya* rule — more at SUICIDE, RAJ] (1908) **:** national or local self-government in India — **swa·raj·ist** \-əst\ *n*

sward \'swȯ(ə)rd\ *n* [ME, fr. OE *sweard, swearth* skin, rind; akin to MHG *swart* skin, hide] (15c) **1 :** a portion of ground covered with grass **2 :** the grassy surface of land — **sward·ed** \'swȯrd-əd\ *adj*

swarf \'swȯ(ə)rf\ *n* [of Scand origin; akin to ON *svarf* file dust; akin to OE *sweorfan* to file away — more at SWERVE] (1587) **:** material (as metallic particles and abrasive fragments) removed by a cutting or grinding tool

[1]**swarm** \'swȯ(ə)rm\ *n* [ME, fr. OE *swearm;* akin to OHG *swaram* swarm and prob. to L *susurrus* hum] (bef. 12c) **1 a** (1) **:** a great number of honeybees emigrating together from a hive in company with a queen to start a new colony elsewhere (2) **:** a colony of honeybees settled in a hive **b :** an aggregation of free-floating or free-swimming unicellular organisms — usu. used of zoospores **2 a :** a large number of animate or inanimate things massed together and usu. in motion **:** THRONG ⟨~s of sightseers⟩ ⟨a ~ of meteors⟩ **b :** a number of similar geological features or phenomena close together in space or time ⟨a ~ of dikes⟩ ⟨an earthquake ~⟩

[2]**swarm** *vi* (14c) **1 a :** to form and depart from a hive in a swarm **b :** to escape in a swarm (as from a sporangium) **2 a :** to move or assemble in a crowd **:** THRONG **b :** to hover about in the manner of a bee in a swarm **3 :** to contain a swarm **:** TEEM ~ *vt* **:** to fill with a swarm — **swarm·er** *n*

[3]**swarm** *vb* [origin unknown] *vi* (15c) **:** to climb with the hands and feet; *specif* **:** SHIN ⟨~ up a pole⟩ ~ *vt* **:** to climb up **:** MOUNT

swarm spore *n* (1859) **:** any of various minute motile sexual or asexual spores; *esp* **:** ZOOSPORE

swart \'swȯ(ə)rt\ *adj* [ME, fr. OE *sweart;* akin to OHG *swarz* black, L *sordes* dirt] (bef. 12c) **1 a :** SWARTHY **b** *archaic* **:** producing a swarthy complexion **2 :** BANEFUL, MALIGNANT — **swart·ness** *n*

swar·thy \'swȯr-t͟hē, -thē\ *adj* **swar·thi·er; -est** [alter. of obs. *swarty,* fr. *swart*] (1587) **:** of a dark color, complexion, or cast — **swar·thi·ness** *n*

[1]**swash** \'swäsh, 'swȯsh\ *vb* [prob. imit.] *vi* (1565) **1 :** BLUSTER, SWAGGER **2 :** to make violent noisy movements **3 :** to move with a splashing sound ~ *vt* **:** to cause to splash

[2]**swash** *n* (1593) **1 :** SWAGGER **2 a :** a body of splashing water **b :** a narrow channel of water lying within a sandbank or between a sandbank and the shore **3 :** a dashing of water against or on something

[3]**swash** *adj* [obs. E *swash* slanting] (1683) **:** having one or more strokes ending in an extended flourish ⟨~ capitals⟩

swash·buck·le \'swäsh-ˌbək-əl, 'swȯsh-\ *vi* **-led; -ling** \-ˌbək-(ə-)liŋ\ [back-formation fr. *swashbuckler*] (1897) **:** to act the part of a swashbuckler

swash·buck·ler \-ˌbək-lər\ *n* [[1]*swash* + *buckler*] (1560) **1 :** a boasting soldier or blustering daredevil **:** BRAVO **2 :** a novel or drama dealing with a swashbuckler

swash·buck·ling \-ˌbək-(ə-)liŋ\ *adj* [*swashbuckler*] (1693) **1 :** acting in the manner of a swashbuckler **2 :** characteristic of, marked by, or done by swashbucklers

swash·er \'swäsh-ər, 'swȯsh-\ *n* (1589) **:** SWASHBUCKLER

swas·ti·ka \'swäs-ti-kə *also* swä-'stē-\ *n* [Skt *svastika,* fr. *svasti* welfare, fr. *su-* well + *asti* he is; akin to OE *is;* fr. its being regarded as a good luck symbol] (1854) **1 :** a symbol or ornament in the form of a Greek cross with the ends of the arms extended at right angles all in the same rotary direction **2 :** a swastika used as a symbol of anti-Semitism or of Nazism

[1]**swat** \'swät\ *vt* **swat·ted; swat·ting** [E dial., to squat, alter. of E *squat*] (1796) **:** to hit with a sharp slapping blow usu. with an instrument (as a bat or swatter)

[2]**swat** *n* (ca. 1800) **1 :** a powerful or crushing blow **2 :** a long hit in baseball; *esp* **:** HOME RUN

swatch \'swäch\ *n* [origin unknown] (1647) **1 a :** a sample piece (as of fabric) or a collection of samples **b :** a characteristic specimen **2 :** PATCH **3 :** a small collection **4 :** SWATH 2

swath \'swäth, 'swȯth, *or* **swathe** \'swät͟h, 'swȯt͟h, 'swāt͟h\ *n* [ME, fr. OE *swæth* footstep, trace; akin to MHG *swade* swath] (14c) **1 a :** a row of cut grain or grass left by a scythe or mowing machine **b :** the sweep of a scythe or a machine in mowing or the path cut in one course **2 :** a long broad strip or belt **3 :** a stroke of or as if of a scythe **4 :** a space devastated as if by a scythe

[1]**swathe** \'swät͟h, 'swȯt͟h, 'swāt͟h\ *vt* **swathed; swath·ing** [ME *swathen,* fr. OE *swathian;* akin to ON *svatha* to swathe, OE *swāpan* to sweep, Lith *svaigti* to become dizzy] (bef. 12c) **1 :** to bind, wrap, or swaddle with or as if with a bandage **2 :** ENVELOP

[2]**swathe** \'swät͟h, 'swȯt͟h, 'swāt͟h\ *or* **swath** \'swät͟h, 'swäth, 'swȯt͟h, 'swȯth\ *n* (bef. 12c) **1 :** a band used in swathing **2 :** an enveloping medium

swath·er \'swäth-ər, 'swät͟h-\ *n* (ca. 1875) **:** a harvesting machine that cuts and windrows grain and seed crops; *also* **:** a mower attachment that windrows the swath

swathing clothes *n pl* [ME] *obs* (14c) **:** SWADDLING CLOTHES

swats \'swäts\ *n pl* [prob. fr. OE *swātan,* pl., beer] *Scot* (1508) **:** DRINK; *esp* **:** new ale

swat·ter \'swät-ər\ *n* (1912) **:** one that swats; *esp* **:** FLYSWATTER

[1]**sway** \'swā\ *n* (14c) **1 :** the action or an instance of swaying or of being swayed **:** an oscillating, fluctuating, or sweeping motion **2 :** an inclination or deflection caused by or as if by swaying **3 a :** a controlling influence **b :** sovereign power **:** DOMINION **c :** the ability to exercise influence or authority **:** DOMINANCE ***syn*** see POWER

[2]**sway** *vb* [alter. of earlier *swey* to fall, swoon, fr. ME *sweyen,* prob. of Scand origin; akin to ON *sveigja* to sway; akin to OE *swathian* to swathe] *vi* (1500) **1 a :** to swing slowly and rhythmically back and forth from a base or pivot **b :** to move gently from an upright to a leaning position **2 :** to hold sway **:** act as ruler or governor **3 :** to fluctuate or veer between one point, position, or opinion and another ~ *vt* **1 a :** to cause to sway **:** set to swinging, rocking, or oscillating **b :** to cause to bend downward to one side **c :** to cause to turn aside **:** DEFLECT, DIVERT **2** *archaic* **a :** WIELD **b :** GOVERN, RULE **3 a :** to cause to vacillate **b :** to exert a guiding or controlling influence on **4 :** to hoist in place ⟨~ up a mast⟩ ***syn*** see SWING, AFFECT — **sway·er** *n*

sway-backed \'swā-ˌbakt\ *also* **sway·back** \-ˌbak\ *adj* (1680) **:** having an abnormally hollow or sagging back ⟨a ~ mare⟩ — **sway·back** *n*

sway bar *n* (1949) **:** a bar that torsionally couples the right and left front-wheel suspensions of an automobile to reduce roll and sway

Swa·zi \'swäz-ē\ *n, pl* **Swazi** *or* **Swazis** (ca. 1901) **1 :** a member of a Bantu people of southeastern Africa **2 :** a Bantu language of the Swazi people

[1]**swear** \'swa(ə)r, 'swe(ə)r\ *vb* **swore** \'swō(ə)r, 'swȯ(ə)r\; **sworn** \'swō(ə)rn, 'swȯ(ə)rn\; **swear·ing** [ME *sweren,* fr. OE *swerian;* akin to OHG *swerien* to swear, Russ *svara* altercation] *vt* (bef. 12c) **1 :** to utter or take solemnly (an oath) **2 a :** to assert as true or promise under oath ⟨a *sworn* affidavit⟩ **b :** to assert or promise emphatically or earnestly ⟨*swore* to uphold the Constitution⟩ **3 a :** to put to an oath **:** administer an oath to **b :** to bind by an oath ⟨*swore* him to secrecy⟩ **4** *obs* **:** to invoke the name of (a sacred being) in an oath **5 :** to bring into a specified state by swearing ⟨*swore* his life away⟩ ~ *vi* **1 :** to take an oath **2 :** to use profane or obscene language **:** CURSE — **swear·er** *n* — **swear by :** to place great confidence in — **swear for :** to give assurance for **:** GUARANTEE — **swear off :** to vow to abstain from **:** RENOUNCE ⟨*swear off* smoking⟩

[2]**swear** *n* (1643) **:** OATH, SWEARWORD

swear in *vt* (1700) **:** to induct into office by administration of an oath

swear out *vt* (1895) **:** to procure (a warrant for arrest) by making a sworn accusation

swear·word \'swa(ə)r-ˌwərd, 'swe(ə)r-\ *n* (1883) **:** a profane or obscene oath or word

[1]**sweat** \'swet\ *vb* **sweat** *or* **sweat·ed; sweat·ing** [ME *sweten,* fr. OE *swǣtan,* fr. *swāt* sweat; akin to OHG *sweiz* sweat, L *sudor* sweat, *sudare* to sweat, Gk *hidrōs* sweat] *vi* (bef. 12c) **1 a :** to excrete moisture in visible quantities through the openings of the sweat glands **:** PERSPIRE **b :** to labor so as to cause perspiration **:** work hard **2 a :** to emit or exude moisture ⟨cheese ~s in ripening⟩ **b :** to gather surface moisture in beads as a result of condensation ⟨stones ~ at night⟩ **c** (1) **:** FERMENT (2) **:** PUTREFY **3 :** to undergo anxiety or mental or emotional distress **4 :** to become exuded through pores or a porous surface **:** OOZE ~ *vt* **1 :** to emit or seem to emit from pores **:** EXUDE **2 :** to manipulate or produce by hard work or drudgery **3 :** to get rid of or lose (weight) by or as if by sweating or being sweated **4 :** to make wet with perspiration **5 a :** to cause to excrete moisture from the skin **b :** to drive hard **:** OVERWORK **c :** to exact work from at low wages and under unfair or unhealthful conditions **d** *slang* **:** to give the third degree to **6 :** to cause to exude or lose moisture; *esp* **:** to subject (as tobacco leaves) to fermentation **7 a :** to extract something valuable from by unfair or dishonest means **:** FLEECE **b :** to remove particles of metal from (a coin) by abrasion **8 a :** to heat (as solder) so as to melt and cause to run esp. between surfaces to unite them; *also* **:** to unite by such means ⟨~ a pipe joint⟩ **b :** to heat so as to extract an easily fusible constituent ⟨~ bismuth ore⟩ **c :** to apply heat to **:** STEAM — **sweat blood :** to work or worry intensely ⟨in preparing speeches each *sweats blood* in his own way —Stewart Cockburn⟩

[2]**sweat** *n* (14c) **1 :** hard work **:** DRUDGERY **2 :** the fluid excreted from the sweat glands of the skin **:** PERSPIRATION **3 :** moisture issuing from or gathering in drops on a surface **4 a :** the condition of one sweating or sweated **b :** a spell of sweating **5 :** a state of anxiety or impatience — **no sweat** *slang* **:** with little or no difficulty

sweat·band \'swet-ˌband\ *n* (1891) **1 :** a usu. leather band lining the inner edge of a hat or cap to prevent sweat damage **2 :** a band of material worn around the head or wrist to absorb sweat

sweat·box \-ˌbäks\ *n* (1864) **1 :** a place in which one is made to sweat; *esp* **:** a narrow box or cell in which a prisoner is placed for punishment **2 :** a device for sweating something (as hides in tanning or dried figs)

sweat·ed \'swet-əd\ *adj* (1882) **:** of, subjected to, or produced under sweatshop conditions ⟨~ labor⟩ ⟨~ goods⟩

sweat equity *n* (1966) **:** an owner's labor on improvements that increase the value of the property

sweat·er \'swet-ər\ *n* (1529) **1 :** one that sweats or causes sweating **2 :** a knitted or crocheted jacket or pullover

sweater girl *n* (1940) **:** a woman with a shapely bust

sweat gland *n* (1845) **:** a simple tubular gland of the skin that secretes perspiration, in man is widely distributed in nearly all parts of the skin, and consists typically of an epithelial tube extending spirally from a minute pore on the surface of the skin into the dermis or subcutaneous tissues where it ends in a convoluted tuft

sweat out *vt* (1589) **1 :** to work one's way painfully through or to **2 :** to endure or wait through the course of

sweat·pants \'swet-ˌpan(t)s\ *n pl* (1925) **:** pants having a drawstring waist and elastic cuffs at the ankle that are worn esp. by athletes in warming up

sweat·shirt \-ˌshərt\ *n* (1925) **:** a loose collarless pullover of heavy cotton jersey

sweat·shop \-ˌshäp\ *n* (ca. 1867) **:** a shop or factory in which workers are employed for long hours at low wages and under unhealthy conditions

sweat suit *n* (1930) **:** an exercise suit that consists of a sweatshirt and sweatpants

sweaty \'swet-ē\ *adj* **sweat·i·er; -est** (14c) **1 :** causing sweat ⟨a ~ day⟩ ⟨~ work⟩ **2 :** wet or stained with or smelling of sweat — **sweat·i·ly** \'swet-ᵊl-ē\ *adv* — **sweat·i·ness** \'swet-ē-nəs\ *n*

swede \'swēd\ *n* [LG or obs. D] (1589) **1** *cap* **a :** a native or inhabitant of Sweden **b :** a person of Swedish descent **2 :** RUTABAGA

Swe·den·bor·gian \ˌswēd-ᵊn-'bȯr-j(ē-)ən, -'bȯr-gē-ən\ *adj* (1807) **:** of or relating to the teachings of Emanuel Swedenborg or the Church of the New Jerusalem based on his teachings — **Swedenborgian** *n* — **Swe·den·bor·gian·ism** \-ˌiz-əm\ *n*

Swed·ish \'swēd-ish\ *n* (1605) **1 :** the North Germanic language spoken in Sweden and a part of Finland **2** *pl in constr* **:** the people of Sweden — **Swedish** *adj*

Swedish massage *n* (1911) **:** massage with Swedish movements

Swedish movements *n pl* (1886) **:** a system of active and passive exercise of muscles and joints

1**sweep** \'swēp\ *vb* **swept** \'swept\; **sweep·ing** [ME *swepen;* akin to OE *swāpan* to sweep — more at SWATHE] *vt* (14c) **1 a :** to remove from a surface with or as if with a broom or brush ⟨*swept* the crumbs from the table⟩ **b :** to destroy completely **:** WIPE OUT — usu. used with *away* ⟨everything she cherished, might be *swept* away overnight —Louis Bromfield⟩ **c :** to remove or take with a single continuous forceful action ⟨*swept* the books off the desk⟩ **d :** to drive or carry along with irresistible force ⟨a wave of protest that *swept* the opposition into office⟩ **2 a :** to clean with or as if with a broom or brush **b :** to clear by repeated and forcible action **c :** to move across or along swiftly, violently, or overwhelmingly ⟨fire *swept* the business district —*Amer. Guide Series: Md.*⟩ **d :** to win an overwhelming victory in or on ⟨~ the elections⟩ **e :** to win all the games of ⟨~ a double-header⟩ ⟨~ a series⟩ **3 :** to touch in passing with a swift continuous movement **4 :** to trace or describe the locus or extent of (as a line, circle, or angle) **5 :** to cover the entire range of ⟨his eyes *swept* the horizon⟩ ~ *vi* **1 a :** to clean a surface with or as if with a broom **b :** to move swiftly, forcefully, or devastatingly ⟨the wind *swept* through the treetops⟩ **2 :** to go with stately or sweeping movements ⟨his formidable wife *swept* past him to greet us —Maurice Cranston⟩ **3 :** to move or extend in a wide curve or range — **sweep·er** *n* — **sweep one off one's feet :** to gain immediate and unquestioning support, approval, or acceptance by a person — **sweep the board** *or* **sweep the table 1 :** to win all the bets on the table **2 :** to win everything **:** excel all competitors

2**sweep** *n* (1548) **1 :** something that sweeps or works with a sweeping motion: as **a :** a long pole or timber pivoted on a tall post and used to raise and lower a bucket in a well **b :** a triangular cultivator blade that cuts off weeds under the soil surface **c :** a windmill sail **2 a :** an instance of sweeping; *specif* **:** a clearing out or away with or as if with a broom **b :** the removal from the table in one play in casino of all the cards by pairing or combining **c :** an overwhelming victory **d :** a winning of all the contests or prizes in a competition **3 a :** a movement of great range and force **b :** a curving or circular course or line **c :** the compass of a sweeping movement **:** SCOPE **d :** a broad extent **e :** an end run in football in which one or more linemen pull back and run interference for the ballcarrier **4 :** CHIMNEY SWEEP **5 :** SWEEPSTAKES **6 :** obliquity with respect to a reference line ⟨~ of an airplane wing⟩; *esp* **:** SWEEPBACK ***syn*** see RANGE

sweep·back \'swēp-ˌbak\ *n* (ca. 1916) **:** the backward slant of an airplane wing in which the outer portion of the wing is downstream from the inner portion

sweep hand *n* (1943) **:** SWEEP-SECOND HAND

1**sweep·ing** *n* (15c) **1 :** the act or action of one that sweeps ⟨gave the room a good ~⟩ **2** *pl* **:** things collected by sweeping **:** REFUSE

2**sweeping** *adj* (1610) **1 a :** moving or extending in a wide curve or over a wide area **b :** having a curving line or form **2 a :** EXTENSIVE ⟨~ reforms⟩ **b :** marked by wholesale and indiscriminate inclusion ⟨~ generalities⟩ — **sweep·ing·ly** \'swē-piŋ-lē\ *adv* — **sweep·ing·ness** *n*

sweep–sec·ond hand \'swēp-ˌsek-ənd-, -ənt-\ *n* (ca. 1940) **:** a hand marking seconds on a timepiece mounted concentrically with the other hands and read from the same dial as the minute hand

sweep·stakes \-ˌstāks\ *n pl but sing or pl in constr, also* **sweep–stake** \-ˌstāk\ [ME *swepestake* one who wins all the stakes in a game, fr. *swepen* to sweep + *stake*] (1785) **1 a :** a race or contest in which the entire prize may be awarded to the winner; *specif* **:** STAKE RACE **b :** CONTEST, COMPETITION **2 :** any of various lotteries

sweepy \'swē-pē\ *adj* **sweep·i·er; -est** (1697) **:** sweeping in motion, line, or force

1**sweet** \'swēt\ *adj* [ME *swete,* fr. OE *swēte;* akin to OHG *suozi* sweet, L *suadēre* to urge, *suavis* sweet, Gk *hēdys*] (bef. 12c) **1 a (1) :** pleasing to the taste **(2) :** being or inducing the one of the four basic taste sensations that is typically induced by disaccharides and is mediated esp. by receptors in taste buds at the front of the tongue — compare BITTER, SALT, SOUR **b (1)** *of a beverage* **:** containing a sweetening ingredient **:** not dry **(2)** *of wine* **:** retaining a portion of natural sugar **2 a :** pleasing to the mind or feelings **:** AGREEABLE — often used as a generalized term of approval **b :** marked by gentle good humor or kindliness **c :** FRAGRANT **d (1) :** delicately pleasing to the ear or eye **(2) :** played in a straightforward melodic style ⟨~ jazz⟩ **e :** SACCHARINE, CLOYING **3 :** much loved **:** DEAR **4 a :** not sour, rancid, decaying, or stale **:** WHOLESOME ⟨~ milk⟩ **b :** not salt or salted **:** FRESH ⟨~ butter⟩ **c** *of land* **:** free from excessive acidity **d :** free from noxious gases and odors **e :** free from excess of acid, sulfur, or corrosive salts ⟨~ crude oil⟩ **5 :** FINE, GREAT — used as an intensive — **sweet·ly** *adv* — **sweet·ness** *n* — **sweet on :** in love with

2**sweet** *adv* (13c) **:** in a sweet manner

3**sweet** *n* (14c) **1 :** something that is sweet to the taste: as **a :** a food (as a candy or preserve) having a high sugar content ⟨fill up on ~*s*⟩ **b** *Brit* **:** DESSERT **c** *Brit* **:** HARD CANDY **2 :** a sweet taste sensation **3 :** a pleasant or gratifying experience, possession, or state **4 :** DARLING, SWEETHEART **5 a** *archaic* **:** FRAGRANCE **b** *pl, archaic* **:** things having a sweet smell

sweet alyssum *n* (1822) **:** a perennial European herb (*Lobularia maritima*) of the mustard family having clusters of small fragrant usu. white flowers

sweet–and–sour \ˌswēt-ᵊn-'saů(ə)r\ *adj* (ca. 1928) **:** seasoned with a sauce containing sugar and vinegar or lemon juice ⟨~ shrimp⟩

sweet basil *n* (ca. 1647) **:** a common basil (*Ocimum basilicum*) that has white flowers tinged with purple and is used esp. as a seasoning

sweet bay *n* (ca. 1716) **1 :** LAUREL 1 **2 :** an American magnolia (*Magnolia virginiana*) abundant along the Atlantic coast and in the southern states that has glaucous leaves and rather small globose fragrant white flowers

sweet birch *n* (ca. 1785) **:** a common birch (*Betula lenta*) of the eastern U.S. that has hard dark-colored wood and spicy brown bark containing a volatile oil

sweet·bread \'swēt-ˌbred\ *n* (ca. 1565) **:** the thymus or pancreas of a young animal (as a calf) used for food

sweet·bri·er *also* **sweet·bri·ar** \-ˌbrī(-ə)r\ *n* (ca. 1548) **:** an Old World rose (esp. *Rosa eleganteria*) with stout recurved prickles and white to deep rosy pink single flowers — called also *eglantine*

sweet cherry *n* (ca. 1901) **:** a white-flowered Eurasian cherry (*Prunus avium*) widely grown for its large sweet-flavored fruits; *also* **:** its fruit

sweet chocolate *n* (1897) **:** chocolate that contains added sugar

sweet cic·e·ly \-'sis-(ə-)lē\ *n* [*cicely* fr. L *seselis,* fr. Gk] (1668) **:** any of various herbs of an American genus (*Osmorhiza*) that typically have thick fleshy roots and grow in moist woodlands

sweet clover *n* (1868) **:** any of a genus (*Melilotus*) of erect legumes widely grown for soil improvement or hay

sweet corn *n* (1646) **:** an Indian corn (esp. *Zea mays saccharata*) with kernels containing a high percentage of sugar and adapted for table use when in the milk stage

sweet·en \'swēt-ᵊn\ *vb* **sweet·ened; sweet·en·ing** \'swēt-niŋ, -ᵊn-iŋ\ *vt* (ca. 1552) **1 :** to make sweet **2 :** to soften the mood or attitude of **3 :** to make less painful or trying **4 :** to free from a harmful or undesirable quality or substance; *esp* **:** to remove sulfur compounds from ⟨~ natural gas⟩ **5 :** to make more valuable or attractive: as **a :** to increase (a pot not won on the previous deal) by anteing prior to another deal **b :** to place additional securities as collateral for (a loan) ~ *vi* **:** to become sweet — **sweet·en·er** \'swēt-nər, -ᵊn-ər\ *n*

sweet·en·ing *n* (13c) **:** something that sweetens

sweet fern *n* (1654) **:** a small No. American shrub (*Comptonia peregrina*) of the wax-myrtle family with sweet-scented or aromatic leaves

sweet flag *n* (ca. 1784) **:** a perennial marsh herb (*Acorus calamus*) of the arum family with long leaves and a pungent rootstock — called also *calamus*

sweet gum *n* (1700) **1 :** a No. American tree (*Liquidambar styraciflua*) with palmately lobed leaves, corky branches, and hard wood **2 :** heartwood of the sweet gum or reddish brown lumber sawed from it

sweet gum 1

sweet·heart \'swēt-ˌhärt\ *n* (13c) **1 :** DARLING **2 :** one who is loved

sweetheart contract *n* (1946) **:** an agreement between an employer and a labor union on terms favorable to the employer and often arranged by a union official without the participation or approval of the union members — called also *sweetheart agreement*

sweetheart neckline *n* (1941) **:** a neckline for women's clothing that is high in back and low in front where it is scalloped to resemble the top of a heart

sweet·ie \'swēt-ē\ *n* (1705) **1** *pl, Brit* **:** SWEET 1a **2 :** SWEETHEART

sweetie pie *n* (1940) **:** SWEETHEART

sweet·ing \'swēt-iŋ\ *n* (14c) **1** *archaic* **:** SWEETHEART **2 :** a sweet apple

sweet·ish \-ish\ *adj* (ca. 1580) **1 :** somewhat sweet **2 :** unpleasantly sweet — **sweet·ish·ly** *adv*

sweet marjoram *n* (ca. 1565) **:** an aromatic European herb (*Majorana hortensis*) with dense spikelike flower clusters

sweet·meat \'swēt-ˌmēt\ *n* (15c) **:** a food rich in sugar: as **a :** a candied or crystallized fruit **b :** CANDY, CONFECTION

sweetness and light *n* (1704) **1 :** a harmonious combination of beauty and intelligence **2 :** amiable reasonableness of disposition

sweet orange *n* (ca. 1796) **:** an orange (*Citrus sinensis*) that is prob. native to southeastern Asia, has a fruit with a pithy central axis, and is the source of the widely cultivated oranges of commerce; *also* **:** a cultivated orange derived from the sweet orange and usu. having fruit with a relatively thin skin and sweet juicy edible pulp

sweet pea *n* (ca. 1732) **1 :** a garden plant (*Lathyrus odoratus*) having slender climbing stems and large fragrant flowers **2 :** the flower of a sweet pea

sweet pepper *n* (1836) **:** a large mild thick-walled capsicum fruit; *also* **:** a pepper plant bearing this fruit

sweet potato *n* (1750) **1 :** a tropical vine (*Ipomoea batatas*) related to the morning glory with variously shaped leaves and purplish flowers; *also* **:** its large thick sweet and nutritious tuberous root that is cooked and eaten as a vegetable **2 :** OCARINA

sweet·shop \'swēt-ˌshäp\ *n, chiefly Brit* (1877) **:** a candy store

sweet·sop \-ˌsäp\ *n* (ca. 1756) **:** a tropical American tree (*Annona squamosa*) of the custard-apple family; *also* **:** its edible sweet pulpy fruit with thick green scaly rind and shining black seeds

sweet sorghum *n* (1867) **:** SORGO

sweet spot *n* (ca. 1949) **:** the area around the center of mass of a bat, racket, or head of a club that is the most effective part with which to hit a ball

sweet–talk \'swēt-ˌtȯk\ *vt* (1926) **:** BLANDISH, COAX ~ *vi* **:** to use flattery

sweet talk *n* (1928) **:** FLATTERY

sweet tooth *n* (14c) **:** a craving or fondness for sweet food

sweet wil·liam \swēt-'wil-yəm\ *n, often cap W* [fr. the name *William*] (1573) **:** a widely cultivated Eurasian pink (*Dianthus barbatus*) with small white to deep red or purple flowers often showily spotted, banded, or mottled and borne in flat bracteate heads on erect stalks

1**swell** \'swel\ *vb* **swelled; swelled** *or* **swol·len** \'swō-lən\; **swell·ing** [ME *swellen,* fr. OE *swellan;* akin to OHG *swellan* to swell] *vi* (bef. 12c) **1 a :** to expand (as in size, volume, or numbers) gradually beyond a normal or original limit ⟨the population ~*ed*⟩ **b :** to become distended or puffed up ⟨her ankle is badly *swollen*⟩ **c :** to form a bulge or rounded elevation **2 a :** to become filled with pride and arrogance **b :** to behave or speak in a pompous, blustering, or self-important manner **c**

: to play the swell **3** : to become distended with emotion ~ *vt* **1** : to affect with a powerful or expansive emotion **2** : to increase the size, number, or intensity of **syn** see EXPAND

²swell *n* (13c) **1 a** : a rounded elevation **b** : the condition of being protuberant **2** : a long often massive and crestless wave or succession of waves often continuing beyond or after its cause (as a gale) **3 a** : the act or process of swelling **b** (1) : a gradual increase and decrease of the loudness of a musical sound; *also* : a sign indicating a swell (2) : a device used in an organ for governing loudness **4 a** *archaic* : an impressive, pompous, or fashionable air or display **b** : a person dressed in the height of fashion **c** : a person of high social position or outstanding competence

³swell *adj* (1785) **1 a** : STYLISH **b** : socially prominent **2** : EXCELLENT — used as a generalized term of enthusiasm

swell box *n* (ca. 1801) : a chamber in an organ containing a set of pipes and having shutters that open or shut to regulate the volume of tone

swelled head *n* (1891) : an exaggerated opinion of oneself : SELF-CONCEIT — **swelled–head·ed** \'sweld-'hed-əd\ *adj* — **swelled–head·ed·ness** *n*

swell·fish \'swel-,fish\ *n* (1807) : PUFFER 2a

swell–front \'swel-,frənt\ *adj* (1914) : BOWFRONT 1

swell·head \-,hed\ *n* (1845) : one who has a swelled head — **swell·head·ed** \-'hed-əd\ *adj* — **swell·head·ed·ness** *n*

swell·ing \'swel-iŋ\ *n* (bef. 12c) **1** : something that is swollen; *specif* : an abnormal bodily protuberance or localized enlargement **2** : the condition of being swollen

¹swel·ter \'swel-tər\ *vb* **swel·tered; swel·ter·ing** \-t(ə-)riŋ\ [ME *sweltren,* freq. of *swelten* to die, be overcome by heat, fr. OE *sweltan* to die; akin to OHG *swelzan* to burn up and prob. to OE *swelan* to burn] *vi* (15c) : to suffer, sweat, or be faint from heat ~ *vt* **1** : to oppress with heat **2** *archaic* : EXUDE ⟨~*ed* venom —Shak.⟩

²swelter *n* (1851) **1** : a state of oppressive heat **2** : WELTER **3** : an excited or overwrought state of mind : SWEAT ⟨in a ~⟩

swel·ter·ing *adj* (1586) : oppressively hot — **swel·ter·ing·ly** \-t(ə-)riŋ-lē\ *adv*

swept \'swept\ *adj* [*swept,* pp. of *sweep*] (1903) : slanted backward

swept–back \'swep(t)-'bak\ *adj* (1916) : possessing sweepback

¹swerve \'swərv\ *vb* **swerved; swerv·ing** [ME *swerven,* fr. OE *sweorfan* to wipe, file away; akin to OHG *swerban* to wipe off, Gk *syrein* to drag] *vi* (14c) : to turn aside abruptly from a straight line or course : DEVIATE ~ *vt* : to cause to turn aside or deviate

syn SWERVE, VEER, DEVIATE, DEPART, DIGRESS, DIVERGE mean to turn aside from a straight course. SWERVE may suggest a physical, mental, or moral turning away from a given course, often with abruptness; VEER implies a major change in direction; DEVIATE implies a turning from a customary or prescribed course; DEPART suggests a deviation from a traditional or conventional course or type; DIGRESS applies to a departing from the subject of one's discourse; DIVERGE may equal DEPART but usu. suggests a branching of a main path into two or more leading in different directions.

²swerve *n* (1741) : an act or instance of swerving

swev·en \'swev-ən\ *n* [ME, fr. OE *swefn* sleep, dream, vision — more at SOMNOLENT] *archaic* (bef. 12c) : DREAM, VISION

swid·den \'swid-ᵊn\ *n* [E dial., burned clearing, prob. fr. ON *svithinn,* pp. of *svitha* to burn, singe] (1951) : a temporary agricultural plot produced by cutting back and burning off vegetative cover

¹swift \'swift\ *adj* [ME, fr. OE; akin to OE *swifan* to revolve — more at SWIVEL] (bef. 12c) **1** : moving or capable of moving with great speed **2** : occurring suddenly or within a very short time **3** : quick to respond : READY **syn** see FAST

²swift *adv* (14c) : SWIFTLY ⟨*swift*-flowing⟩

³swift *n* (1530) **1** : any of several lizards (esp. of the genus *Sceloporus*) that run swiftly **2 a** : a reel for winding yarn or thread **b** : one of the large cylinders that carry forward the material in a carding machine; *also* : a comparable cylinder in another machine **3** : any of numerous small plainly colored birds (family Apodidae) that are related to the hummingbirds and goatsuckers but superficially much resemble swallows

swift·ly *adv* (bef. 12c) : in a swift manner : with speed : QUICKLY

swift·ness \'swif(t)-nəs\ *n* (bef. 12c) **1** : the quality or state of being swift : CELERITY **2** : the fact of being swift

¹swig \'swig\ *n* [origin unknown] (1621) : a quantity drunk at one time

²swig *vb* **swigged; swig·ging** *vi* (1650) : to take a swig : DRINK ~ *vt* : to drink in long drafts ⟨~ cider⟩ — **swig·ger** *n*

¹swill \'swil\ *vb* [ME *swilen,* fr. OE *swillan*] *vt* (bef. 12c) **1** : WASH, DRENCH **2** : to drink great drafts of : GUZZLE **3** : to feed (as a pig) with swill ~ *vi* **1** : to drink or eat freely, greedily, or to excess **2** : SWASH — **swill·er** *n*

²swill *n* (1553) **1** : something suggestive of slop or garbage : REFUSE **2 a** : a semiliquid food for animals (as swine) composed of edible refuse mixed with water or skimmed or sour milk **b** : GARBAGE

¹swim \'swim\ *vb* **swam** \'swam\; **swum** \'swəm\; **swim·ming** [ME *swimmen,* fr. OE *swimman;* akin to OHG *swimman* to swim] *vi* (bef. 12c) **1 a** : to propel oneself in water by natural means (as movements of the limbs, fins, or tail) **b** : to play in the water (as at a beach or swimming pool) **2** : to move with a motion like that of swimming : GLIDE ⟨a cloud *swam* slowly across the moon⟩ **3 a** : to float on a liquid : not sink **b** : to surmount difficulties : not go under ⟨sink or ~, live or die, survive or perish —Daniel Webster⟩ **4** : to become immersed or flooded with or as if with a liquid **5** : to have a floating or reeling appearance or sensation ~ *vt* **1 a** : to cross by propelling oneself through water ⟨~ a stream⟩ **b** : to execute in swimming **2** : to cause to swim or float — **swim·mer** *n* — **swim against the stream** : to move counter to or work against the prevailing or popular trend

²swim *n* (1599) **1** : a smooth gliding motion **2** : an act or period of swimming **3** : a temporary dizziness or unconsciousness **4 a** : an area frequented by fish **b** : the main current of activity ⟨be in the ~⟩

³swim *adj* (1837) : of, relating to, or used in or for swimming ⟨a ~ meet⟩

swim bladder *n* (1837) : the air bladder of a fish

swim fin *n* (1947) : FLIPPER 1b

swim·ma·ble \'swim-ə-bəl\ *adj* (1852) : that can be swum

swim·mer·et \,swim-ə-'ret, 'swim-ə-,\ *n* (1840) : one of a series of small unspecialized appendages under the abdomen of many crustaceans that are best developed in some decapods and are used in some cases for swimming but usu. for carrying eggs

swimmer's itch *n* (1942) : a severe urticarial reaction to the presence in the skin of schistosomes that are not normally parasites of man

¹swim·ming *adj* (bef. 12c) **1** [prp. of *swim*] : that swims ⟨a ~ bird⟩ **2** [gerund of *swim*] : adapted to or used in or for swimming

²swimming *n* (14c) : the act, art, or sport of one that swims and dives

swim·ming·ly \'swim-iŋ-lē\ *adv* (1622) : very well : SPLENDIDLY

swimming pool *n* (1899) : a pool suitable for swimming; *esp* : a tank (as of concrete or plastic) made for swimming

swim·my \'swim-ē\ *adj* **swim·mi·er; -est** (1836) **1** : verging on, causing, or affected by dizziness or giddiness **2** *of vision* : UNSTEADY, BLURRED — **swim·mi·ly** \'swim-ə-lē\ *adv*

swim·suit \'swim-,süt\ *n* (1926) : a suit for swimming or bathing

¹swin·dle \'swin-dᵊl\ *vb* **swin·dled; swin·dling** \-(d)liŋ, -dᵊl-iŋ\ [back-formation fr. *swindler,* fr. G *schwindler* giddy person, fr. *schwindeln* to be dizzy, fr. OHG *swintilōn,* freq. of *swintan* to diminish, vanish; akin to OE *swindan* to vanish, OIr *a-sennad* finally] *vi* (ca. 1782) : to obtain money or property by fraud or deceit ~ *vt* : to take money or property from by fraud or deceit **syn** see CHEAT — **swin·dler** \-(d)lər, -dᵊl-ər\ *n*

²swindle *n* (1852) : an act or instance of swindling : FRAUD

swine \'swīn\ *n, pl* **swine** [ME, fr. OE *swīn;* akin to OHG *swīn* swine, L *sus* — more at SOW] (bef. 12c) **1** : any of various stout-bodied short-legged omnivorous mammals (family Suidae) with a thick bristly skin and a long mobile snout; *esp* : a domesticated member of the species (*Sus scrofa*) that includes the European wild boar **2** : a contemptible person

swine·herd \-,hərd\ *n* (12c) : one who tends swine

¹swing \'swiŋ\ *vb* **swung** \'swəŋ\; **swing·ing** \'swiŋ-iŋ\ [ME *swingen* to beat, fling, hurl, rush, fr. OE *swingan* to beat, fling oneself, rush; akin to OHG *swingan* to fling, rush] *vt* (14c) **1 a** : to cause to move vigorously through a wide arc or circle ⟨~ an ax⟩ **b** : to cause to sway to and fro **c** (1) : to cause to turn on an axis (2) : to cause to face or move in another direction ⟨~ the car into a side road⟩ **2** : to suspend so as to permit swaying or turning **3** : to convey by suspension ⟨huge cranes that ~ cargo up over the ship's side and into the hold⟩ **4 a** (1) : to influence decisively ⟨~ a lot of votes⟩ (2) : to bring around by influence **b** : to handle successfully : MANAGE ⟨wasn't able to ~ a new car on his income⟩ **5** : to play or sing (as a melody) in the style of swing music ~ *vi* **1** : to move freely to and fro esp. in suspension from an overhead support **2 a** : to die by hanging **b** : to hang freely from a support **3** : to move in or describe a circle or arc: **a** : to turn on a hinge or pivot **b** : to turn in place **c** : to convey oneself by grasping a fixed support ⟨~ aboard the train⟩ **4 a** : to have a steady pulsing rhythm **b** : to play or sing with a lively compelling rhythm; *specif* : to play swing music **5** : to shift or fluctuate from one condition, form, position, or object of attention or favor to another ⟨~ constantly from optimism to pessimism and back —Sinclair Lewis⟩ **6 a** : to move along rhythmically **b** : to start up in a smooth vigorous manner ⟨ready to ~ into action⟩ **7** : to hit or aim at something with a sweeping arm movement **8 a** : to be lively and up-to-date **b** : to engage freely in sex — **swing·able** \'swiŋ-ə-bəl\ *adj* — **swing·ably** \-blē\ *adv*

syn SWING, WAVE, FLOURISH, BRANDISH, THRASH mean to wield or cause to move to and fro or up and down. SWING implies regular or uniform movement; WAVE usu. implies smooth or continuous motion; FLOURISH suggests vigorous, ostentatious, graceful movement; BRANDISH implies threatening or menacing motion; THRASH suggests vigorous, abrupt, violent movement.

syn SWING, SWAY, OSCILLATE, VIBRATE, FLUCTUATE, WAVER, UNDULATE mean to move from one direction to its opposite. SWING implies a movement of something attached at one end or one side; SWAY implies a slow swinging or teetering movement; OSCILLATE stresses a usu. rapid alternation of direction; VIBRATE suggests the rapid oscillation of an elastic body under stress or impact; FLUCTUATE suggests constant irregular changes of level, intensity, or value; WAVER stresses irregular motion suggestive of reeling or tottering; UNDULATE suggests a gentle wavelike motion.

²swing *n* (14c) **1** : an act or instance of swinging : swinging movement: as **a** (1) : a stroke or blow delivered with a sweeping arm movement ⟨a batter with a powerful ~⟩ (2) : a sweeping or rhythmic movement of the body or a bodily part (3) : a dance figure in which two dancers revolve with joined arms or hands (4) : jazz dancing in moderate tempo with a lilting syncopation **b** (1) : the regular movement of a freely suspended object (as a pendulum) along an arc and back (2) : back and forth sweep ⟨the ~ of the tides⟩ **c** (1) : steady pulsing rhythm (as in poetry or music) (2) : a steady vigorous movement characterizing an activity or creative work **d** (1) : a trend toward a high or low point in a fluctuating cycle (as of business activity) (2) : an often periodic shift from one condition, form, position, or object of attention or favor to another **2 a** : liberty of action : free scope **b** (1) : the driving power of something swung or hurled (2) : steady vigorous advance : driving speed ⟨a train approaching at full ~⟩ **3** : the progression of an activity, process, or phase of existence ⟨the work is in full ~⟩ **4** : the arc or range through which something swings **5** : something that swings freely from or on a support; *esp* : a seat suspended by a rope or chains for swinging to and fro on for pleasure **6 a** : a curving course or outline **b** : a course from and back to a point : a circular tour **7** : jazz played usu. by a large dance band and characterized by a steady lively rhythm, simple harmony, and a basic melody often submerged in improvisation **8** : a short pass in football thrown to a back running to the outside — **swing** *adj*

swing–by \'swiŋ-,bī\ *n, pl* **swing–bys** [²*swing* + *-by* (as in *fly-by*)] (1965) : an interplanetary mission in which a space vehicle utilizes the gravitational field of a planet near which it passes for changing course

¹swinge \'swinj\ *vt* **swinged; swinge·ing** [ME *swengen* to shake, fr. OE *swengan;* akin to OE *swingan*] *chiefly dial* (13c) : BEAT, SCOURGE

\ə\ abut \ᵊ\ kitten, F table \ər\ further \a\ ash \ā\ ace \ä\ cot, cart \au̇\ out \ch\ chin \e\ bet \ē\ easy \g\ go \i\ hit \ī\ ice \j\ job \ŋ\ sing \ō\ go \ȯ\ law \ȯi\ boy \th\ thin \th\ the \ü\ loot \u̇\ foot \y\ yet \zh\ vision \à, k, ⁿ, œ, œ̄, ue, ue̅, ʸ\ see Guide to Pronunciation

2swinge *vt* **swinged; swinge·ing** [alter. of *singe*] *dial* (1590) : SINGE, SCORCH
1swinge·ing *or* **swing·ing** \'swin-jiŋ\ *adj* [fr. prp. of *1swinge*] *chiefly Brit* (1590) : superlative in size, amount, or character
2swingeing *or* **swinging** *adv, chiefly Brit* (1690) : VERY, SUPERLATIVELY
1swing·er \'swiŋ-ər\ *n* (1543) : one that swings: as **a** : a lively up-to-date person who indulges in what is considered fashionable **b** : one who engages freely in sex
2swing·er \'swin-jər\ *n* [*1swinge*] (1599) : WHOPPER 1
swing·ing \'swiŋ-iŋ\ *adj* [prp. of *1swing*] (1956) : being lively and up-to-date ⟨~ moderns⟩; *also* : abounding in swingers and swinging entertainment ⟨a ~ coffeehouse⟩
1swing·ing·ly \'swin-jiŋ-lē\ *adv, chiefly Brit* (1672) : VERY, EXTREMELY
2swing·ing·ly \'swiŋ-iŋ-lē\ *adv* (1882) : in a swinging manner : with a swinging movement
swin·gle·tree \'swiŋ-gəl-(,)trē\ *n* [*swingle* (cudgel) + *tree*] (15c) : WHIFFLETREE
swing shift *n* (1940) **1** : the work shift between the day and night shifts (as from 4 P.M. to midnight) **2** : a group of workers in a factory operating seven days a week that work as needed to permit the regular shift workers to have one or more free days per week
swingy \'swiŋ-ē\ *adj* **swing·i·er; -est** (1915) : marked by swing
swin·ish \'swī-nish\ *adj* (13c) : of, suggesting, or characteristic of swine : BEASTLY — **swin·ish·ly** *adv* — **swin·ish·ness** *n*
1swink \'swiŋk\ *vi* [ME *swinken,* fr. OE *swincan;* akin to OHG *swingan* to rush — more at SWING] *archaic* (bef. 12c) : TOIL, SLAVE
2swink *n, archaic* (12c) : LABOR, DRUDGERY
1swipe \'swīp\ *vb* **swiped; swip·ing** [prob. alter. of *sweep*] *vt* (13c) **1** : to strike or wipe with a sweeping motion **2** : STEAL, PILFER ~ *vi* : to strike or move with a sweeping motion
2swipe *n* (1739) **1** : a strong sweeping blow **2** : a sharp often critical remark
swipes \'swīps\ *n pl* [origin unknown] *Brit* (ca. 1786) : poor, thin, or spoiled beer; *also* : BEER
1swirl \'swər(-ə)l\ *n* [ME (Sc)] (15c) **1 a** : a whirling mass or motion : EDDY **b** : whirling confusion ⟨a ~ of events⟩ **2** : a twisting shape, mark, or pattern **3** : an act or instance of swirling
2swirl *vi* (ca. 1513) **1 a** : to move with an eddying or whirling motion **b** : to pass in whirling confusion **2** : to have a twist or convolution ~ *vt* : to cause to swirl — **swirl·ing·ly** \'swər-liŋ-lē\ *adv*
swirly \'swər-lē\ *adj* **swirl·i·er; -est** (1785) **1** *Scot* : KNOTTED, TWISTED **2** : that swirls : SWIRLING ⟨the ~ water of the rapids⟩
1swish \'swish\ *vb* [imit.] *vi* (1756) : to move, pass, swing, or whirl with the sound of a swish ~ *vt* : to move, cut, or strike with a swish ⟨the horse ~*ed* its tail⟩ — **swish·er** *n* — **swish·ing·ly** \-iŋ-lē\ *adv*
2swish *n* (1820) **1 a** : a prolonged hissing sound (as of a whip cutting the air) **b** : a light sweeping or brushing sound (as of a full silk skirt in motion) **2** : a swishing movement **3** : an effeminate homosexual — often used disparagingly
3swish *adj* [origin unknown] (1879) : SMART, FASHIONABLE
swishy \'swish-ē\ *adj* **swish·i·er; -est** (1828) **1** : producing a swishing sound **2** : characterized by effeminate behavior
1Swiss \'swis\ *n* [MF *Suisse,* fr. MHG *Swizer,* fr. *Swīz* Switzerland] (1515) **1** *pl* **Swiss a** : a native or inhabitant of Switzerland **b** : one that is of Swiss descent **2** *often not cap* : any of various fine sheer fabrics of cotton orig. made in Switzerland; *esp* : DOTTED SWISS **3** : SWISS CHEESE
2Swiss *adj* (ca. 1538) : of, relating to, or characteristic of Switzerland or the Swiss
Swiss chard *n* (1832) : CHARD
Swiss cheese *n* (1822) : a hard cheese characterized by elastic texture, mild nutlike flavor, and large holes that form during ripening
Swiss steak *n* (ca. 1924) : a slice of steak pounded with flour and braised usu. with vegetables and seasonings
1switch \'swich\ *n* [perh. fr. MD *swijch* twig] (1592) **1** : a slender flexible whip, rod, or twig ⟨a riding ~⟩ **2** : an act of switching: as **a** : a blow with a switch **b** : a shift from one to another **3** : a tuft of long hairs at the end of the tail of an animal (as a cow) — see COW illustration **4 a** : a device made usu. of two movable rails and necessary connections and designed to turn a locomotive or train from one track to another **b** : a railroad siding **5** : a device for making, breaking, or changing the connections in an electrical circuit **6** : a heavy strand of hair used in addition to a person's own hair for some coiffures
2switch *vt* (1611) **1** : to strike or beat with or as if with a switch **2** : WHISK, LASH ⟨a cat ~*ing* his tail⟩ **3 a** (1) : to turn from one railroad track to another : SHUNT (2) : to move (cars) to different positions on the same track within terminal areas **b** : to make a shift in or exchange of ⟨~ the talk to another subject⟩ **4 a** : to shift to another electrical circuit by means of a switch **b** : to operate an electrical switch so as to turn (as a light) off or on ~ *vi* **1** : to lash from side to side **2** : to make a shift or exchange — **switch·able** \-ə-bəl\ *adj* — **switch·er** *n*
switch·back \'swich-,bak\ *n* (1863) : a zigzag road in a mountainous region; *esp* : an arrangement of zigzag railroad tracks for surmounting the grade of a steep hill
switch·blade \-,blād\ *n* (1936) : a pocketknife having the blade spring-operated so that pressure on a release catch causes it to fly open — called also *switchblade knife*
switch·board \-,bō(ə)rd, -,bȯ(ə)rd\ *n* (1873) : an apparatus consisting of a panel or a frame on which are mounted insulated switching, measuring, controlling, and protective devices with connections so arranged that a number of circuits may be connected, combined, controlled, measured, and protected
switch cane *n* (1845) : an important forage grass (*Arundinaria tecta*) of moist locations esp. in the southern U.S.
switch engine *n* (1867) : a railroad engine used in switching cars
switch·er·oo \,swich-ə-'rü\ *n, pl* **-oos** [alter. of *switch*] *slang* (1933) : a surprising variation : REVERSAL
switch·grass \'swich-,gras\ *n* (ca. 1839) : a panic grass (*Panicum virgatum*) of the western U.S. that is used for hay
switch–hit \-'hit\ *vi* **-hit; -hit·ting** [back-formation fr. *switch-hitter*] *of a baseball player* (1953) : to bat either left-handed or right-handed
switch–hit·ter \-'hit-ər\ *n* (ca. 1949) **1** : a baseball player who switch-hits **2** *slang* : BISEXUAL
switch knife *n* (1950) : SWITCHBLADE
switch·man \'swich-mən\ *n* (1843) : one who attends a switch (as in a railroad yard)
switch·yard \-,yärd\ *n* (1888) **1** : a place where railroad cars are switched from one track to another and trains are made up **2** : a usu. enclosed area for the switching facilities of a power station
swith \'swith\ *adv* [ME, strongly, quickly, fr. OE *swīthe* strongly, fr. *swīth* strong; akin to OE *gesund* sound — more at SOUND] *chiefly dial* (bef. 12c) : INSTANTLY, QUICKLY
1swith·er \'swith-ər\ *vi* [origin unknown] *dial chiefly Brit* (1501) : DOUBT, WAVER
2swither *n, dial chiefly Brit* (1719) : DOUBT, AGITATION
Swit·zer \'swit-sər\ *n* [MHG *Swizer*] (1549) : SWISS
1swiv·el \'swiv-əl\ *n, often attrib* [ME; akin to OE *swīfan* to revolve, ON *sveigja* to sway — more at SWAY] (15c) : a device joining two parts so that one or both can pivot freely (as on a bolt or pin)
2swivel *vb* **-eled** *or* **-elled; -el·ing** *or* **-el·ling** \-(ə-)liŋ\ *vt* (1794) : to turn on or as if on a swivel ⟨~*ed* his eyes in various directions⟩ ~ *vi* : to swing or turn on or as if on a swivel
swivel chair *n* (1860) : a chair that swivels on its base
swiv·el–hipped \,swiv-əl-'hipt\ *adj* (1947) : moving with or characterized by movement with a twisting motion of the hips
swiv·et \'swiv-ət\ *n* [origin unknown] (1881) : a state of extreme agitation
1swiz·zle \'swiz-əl\ *n* [origin unknown] (1813) : an iced sour churned with a swizzle stick until the glass or pitcher becomes frosted
2swizzle *vb* **swiz·zled; swiz·zling** \-(ə-)liŋ\ *vi* (ca. 1847) : to drink esp. to excess : GUZZLE ~ *vt* : to mix or stir with or as if with a swizzle stick — **swiz·zler** \-(ə-)lər\ *n*
swizzle stick *n* (1879) : a stick used to stir mixed drinks
swob *var of* SWAB
swollen *past part of* SWELL
1swoon \'swün\ *vi* [ME *swounen*] (13c) **1 a** : FAINT **b** : to become enraptured ⟨the ladies were ~*ing* with joy —Frederick Way⟩ **2** : FLOAT, FADE — **swoon·er** *n* — **swoon·ing·ly** \'swü-niŋ-lē\ *adv*
2swoon *n* (14c) **1 a** : a partial or total loss of consciousness **b** : a state of bewilderment or ecstasy : DAZE, RAPTURE **2** : a state of suspended animation : TORPOR
1swoop \'swüp\ *vb* [alter. of ME *swopen* to sweep, fr. OE *swāpan* — more at SWATHE] *vi* (1566) : to move with a sweep; *specif* : to make a sudden attack — usu. used with *down* ⟨the eagle ~*ed* down on its prey⟩ ~ *vt* : to carry off abruptly : SWEEP, SNATCH — **swoop·er** *n*
2swoop *n* (1605) : an act or instance of swooping
swoop·stake \'swüp-,stāk\ *adv* [fr. alter. of *sweepstake*] *obs* (1602) : in an indiscriminate manner
1swoosh \'swüsh, 'swu̇sh\ *vb* [imit.] *vi* (1867) **1** : to make or move with a rushing sound ⟨a car ~*ed* by⟩ **2** : GUSH, SWIRL ~ *vt* : to discharge or transport with a rushing sound
2swoosh *n* (1885) : an act or instance of swooshing
swop *var of* SWAP
sword \'sō(ə)rd, 'sȯ(ə)rd\ *n, often attrib* [ME, fr. OE *sweord;* akin to OHG *swert* sword, Av *xvara* wound] (bef. 12c) **1** : a weapon (as a cutlass or rapier) with a long blade for cutting or thrusting often used as a symbol of honor or authority **2 a** : an agency or instrument of destruction or combat **b** : the use of force (as in war) ⟨the pen is mightier than the ~ —E. G. Bulwer-Lytton⟩ **3** : coercive power **4** : something that resembles a sword — **sword·like** \-,līk\ *adj* — **at swords' points** : mutually antagonistic : ready to fight
sword cane *n* (1837) : a cane in which a sword blade is concealed
sword dance *n* (1604) **1** : a dance performed by men in a circle holding a sword in the right hand and grasping the tip of a neighbor's sword in the left hand **2** : a dance performed over or around swords — **sword dancer** *n*
sword fern *n* (ca. 1829) : any of several ferns with long narrow more or less sword-shaped fronds: as **a** : a tropical fern (*Nephrolepis exaltata*) from which the Boston fern has been developed **b** : a fern (*Polystichum munitum*) of western No. America with a large fleshy rhizome
sword·fish \'sō(ə)rd-,fish, 'sȯ(ə)rd-\ *n* (15c) : a very large oceanic food fish (*Xiphias gladius*) having a long swordlike beak formed by the bones of the upper jaw

swordfish

sword grass *n* (1598) : any of various grasses or sedges having leaves with a sharp or toothed edge
sword knot *n* (1694) : an ornamental cord or tassel tied to the hilt of a sword
sword of Dam·o·cles \-'dam-ə-,klēz\ *often cap S* (1820) : an impending disaster
sword·play \'sō(ə)rd-,plā, 'sȯ(ə)rd-\ *n* (bef. 12c) **1** : the art or skill of wielding a sword esp. in fencing **2** : an exhibition of swordplay — **sword·play·er** *n*
swords·man \'sō(ə)rdz-mən, 'sȯ(ə)rdz-\ *n* (1680) **1** : one skilled in swordplay; *esp* : a saber fencer **2** *archaic* : a soldier armed with a sword
swords·man·ship \-,ship\ *n* (1851) : SWORDPLAY
sword·tail \'sō(ə)rd-,tāl, 'sȯ(ə)rd-\ *n* (ca. 1928) : a small brightly marked Central American live-bearer (*Xiphophorus helleri* of the family Poeciliidae) often kept in the tropical aquarium and bred in many colors
swore *past of* SWEAR
sworn *past part of* SWEAR

¹swot \'swät\ *n* [E dial., sweat, fr. ME *swot,* fr. OE *swāt* — more at SWEAT] *Brit* (1850) **:** GRIND 2b
²swot *vi* **swot·ted; swot·ting** *Brit* (ca. 1859) **:** GRIND 4
¹swound \'swau̇nd, 'swünd\ *n* [ME, alter. of *swoun* swoon, fr. *swounen* to swoon] *archaic* (15c) **:** SWOON 1a
²swound *vi, archaic* (ca. 1530) **:** SWOON
swum *past part of* SWIM
swung *past and past part of* SWING
swung dash *n* (1951) **:** a character ~ used in printing to conserve space by representing part or all of a previously spelled-out word
Syb·a·rite \'sib-ə-ˌrīt\ *n* (ca. 1597) **1 :** a native or resident of the ancient city of Sybaris **2** [fr. the notorious luxury of the Sybarites] *often not cap* **:** VOLUPTUARY, SENSUALIST — **syb·a·rit·ic** \ˌsib-ə-'rit-ik\ *adj* — **syb·a·rit·i·cal·ly** \-i-k(ə-)lē\ *adv* — **Syb·a·rit·ism** \'sib-ə-ˌrīt-ˌiz-əm\ *n*
syc·a·mine \'sik-ə-ˌmīn, -mən\ *n* [L *sycaminus,* fr. Gk *sykaminos,* of Sem origin; akin to Heb *shiqmāh* mulberry tree, sycamore] (1526) **:** MULBERRY 1
syc·a·more \'sik-ə-ˌmō(ə)r, -ˌmȯ(ə)r\ *n* [ME *sicamour,* fr. MF *sicamor,* fr. L *sycomorus,* fr. Gk *sykomoros,* prob. modif. of a Sem word akin to Heb *shiqmāh* sycamore] (14c) **1 :** a tree (*Ficus sycomorus*) of Egypt and Asia Minor that is the sycamore of Scripture, is useful as a shade tree, and has sweet and edible fruit similar but inferior to the common fig **2 :** a Eurasian maple (*Acer pseudoplatanus*) with long racemes of showy yellowish green flowers that is widely planted as a shade tree **3 :** ²PLANE; *esp* **:** a very large spreading tree (*Platanus occidentalis*) of eastern and central No. America with 3- to 5-lobed broadly ovate leaves
syce \'sīs\ *n* [Hindi *sā'is,* fr. Ar] (1653) **:** an attendant (as a groom) esp. in India
sy·cee \'sī-ˌsē\ *n* [Chin (Cant) *sai sz,* lit., fine silk] (1711) **:** silver money made in the form of ingots and formerly used in China
sy·co·ni·um \sī-'kō-nē-əm\ *n, pl* **-nia** \-nē-ə\ [NL, fr. Gk *sykon* fig + NL *-ium*] (ca. 1856) **:** a multiple fleshy fruit in which the ovaries are borne within an enlarged succulent concave or hollow receptacle
sy·co·phan·cy \'sik-ə-fən-sē *also* 'sīk- & -ˌfan(t)-sē\ *n* (1672) **:** obsequious flattery; *also* **:** the character or behavior of a sycophant
sy·co·phant \-fənt *also* -ˌfant\ *n* [L *sycophanta* informer, swindler, sycophant, fr. Gk *sykophantēs* informer] (1575) **:** a servile self-seeking flatterer *syn* see PARASITE — **sycophant** *adj*
sy·co·phan·tic \ˌsik-ə-'fant-ik *also* ˌsīk-\ *adj* (1676) **:** of, relating to, or characteristic of a sycophant **:** FAWNING, OBSEQUIOUS — **sy·co·phan·ti·cal·ly** \-'fant-i-k(ə-)lē\ *adv*
sy·co·phant·ish \ˌsik-ə-'fant-ish *also* ˌsīk-\ *adj* (1840) **:** SYCOPHANTIC — **sy·co·phant·ish·ly** *adv*
sy·co·phant·ism \'sik-ə-fənt-ˌiz-əm *also* 'sīk- & -ˌfant-\ *n* (1821) **:** SYCOPHANCY
sy·co·phant·ly \-lē\ *adv* (1672) **:** in a sycophantic manner
sy·co·sis \sī-'kō-səs\ *n* [NL, fr. Gk *sykōsis,* fr. *sykon* fig] (1822) **:** a chronic inflammatory disorder of the hair follicles marked by papules, pustules, and tubercles with crusting
sy·enite \'sī-ə-ˌnīt\ *n* [L *Syenites* (*lapis*) stone of Syene, fr. *Syene,* ancient city in Egypt] (ca. 1796) **:** an igneous rock composed chiefly of feldspar — **sy·enit·ic** \ˌsī-ə-'nit-ik\ *adj*
sy·li \'sē-lē\ *n, pl* **sylis** [native name in Guinea] (1974) **:** the monetary unit of Guinea from 1972 to 1986
syl·la·bar·i·um \ˌsil-ə-'ber-ē-əm\ *n, pl* **-ia** \-ē-ə\ [NL] (1850) **:** SYLLABARY
syl·la·bary \'sil-ə-ˌber-ē\ *n, pl* **-bar·ies** [NL *syllabarium,* fr. L *syllaba* syllable] (1586) **:** a table or listing of syllables; *specif* **:** a series or set of written characters each one of which is used to represent a syllable
¹syl·lab·ic \sə-'lab-ik\ *adj* [LL *syllabicus,* fr. Gk *syllabikos,* fr. *syllabē* syllable] (1728) **1 :** constituting a syllable or the nucleus of a syllable: **a :** not accompanied in the same syllable by a vowel ⟨\n\ is ~ in \'bät-ᵊn-ē\ *botany,* nonsyllabic in \'bät-nē\⟩ **b :** having vowel quality more prominent than that of another vowel in the syllable ⟨the first vowel of a falling diphthong, as \ȯ\ in \ȯi\, is ~⟩ **2 :** of, relating to, or denoting syllables ⟨~ accent⟩ **3 :** characterized by distinct enunciation or separation of syllables **4 :** of, relating to, or constituting a type of verse distinguished primarily by count of syllables rather than by rhythmical arrangement of accents or quantities — **syl·lab·i·cal·ly** \-i-k(ə-)lē\ *adv*
²syllabic *n* (ca. 1880) **:** a syllabic character or sound
syl·lab·i·cate \sə-'lab-ə-ˌkāt\ *vt* **-cat·ed; -cat·ing** (ca. 1775) **:** SYLLABIFY
syl·lab·i·ca·tion \sə-ˌlab-ə-'kā-shən\ *n* (15c) **:** the act, process, or method of forming or dividing words into syllables
syl·la·bic·i·ty \ˌsil-ə-'bis-ət-ē\ *n* (1933) **:** the state of being or the power of forming a syllable
syl·lab·i·fi·ca·tion \sə-ˌlab-ə-fə-'kā-shən\ *n* (1838) **:** SYLLABICATION
syl·lab·i·fy \sə-'lab-ə-ˌfī\ *vt* **-fied; -fy·ing** [L *syllaba* syllable] (ca. 1859) **:** to form or divide into syllables
¹syl·la·ble \'sil-ə-bəl\ *n* [ME, fr. MF *sillabe,* fr. L *syllaba,* fr. Gk *syllabē,* fr. *syllambanein* to gather together, fr. *syn-* + *lambanein* to take — more at LATCH] (14c) **1 :** a unit of spoken language that is next bigger than a speech sound and consists of one or more vowel sounds alone or of a syllabic consonant alone or of either with one or more consonant sounds preceding or following **2 :** one or more letters (as *syl, la,* and *ble*) in a word (as *syl·la·ble*) usu. set off from the rest of the word by a centered dot or a hyphen and roughly corresponding to the syllables of spoken language and treated as helps to pronunciation or as guides to placing hyphens at the end of a line **3 :** the smallest conceivable expression or unit of something **:** JOT **4 :** SOL-FA SYLLABLES
²syllable *vt* **syl·la·bled; syl·la·bling** \-b(ə-)liŋ\ (15c) **1 :** to give a number or arrangement of syllables to (a word or verse) **2 :** to express or utter in or as if in syllables
syl·la·bub \'sil-ə-ˌbəb\ *n* [origin unknown] (1537) **1 :** a drink made by curdling milk or cream with an acid beverage (as wine or cider) **2 :** a sweetened drink or topping made of milk or cream beaten with wine or liquor and sometimes further thickened with gelatin and served as a dessert
syl·la·bus \-bəs\ *n, pl* **-bi** \-ˌbī, -ˌbē\ *or* **-bus·es** [LL, alter. of L *sillybus* label for a book, fr. Gk *sillybos*] (ca. 1656) **1 :** a summary outline of a discourse, treatise, or course of study or of examination requirements **2 :** HEADNOTE 2
syl·lep·sis \sə-'lep-səs\ *n, pl* **-lep·ses** \-ˌsēz\ [L, fr. Gk *syllēpsis,* fr. *syllambanein*] (ca. 1577) **1 :** the use of a word to modify or govern syntactically two or sometimes more words with only one of which it formally agrees in gender, number, or case **2 :** the use of a word in the same grammatical relation to two adjacent words in the context with one literal and the other metaphorical in sense — **syl·lep·tic** \-'lep-tik\ *adj*
syl·lo·gism \'sil-ə-ˌjiz-əm\ *n* [ME *silogisme,* fr. MF, fr. L *syllogismus,* fr. Gk *syllogismos,* fr. *syllogizesthai* to syllogize, fr. *syn-* + *logizesthai* to calculate, fr. *logos* reckoning, word — more at LEGEND] (14c) **1 :** a deductive scheme of a formal argument consisting of a major and a minor premise and a conclusion (as in "every virtue is laudable; kindness is a virtue; therefore kindness is laudable") **2 :** a subtle, specious, or crafty argument **3 :** deductive reasoning — **syl·lo·gis·tic** \ˌsil-ə-'jis-tik\ *adj* — **syl·lo·gis·ti·cal·ly** \-ti-k(ə-)lē\ *adv*
syl·lo·gist \'sil-ə-jəst\ *n* (1799) **:** one who applies or is skilled in syllogistic reasoning
syl·lo·gize \'sil-ə-ˌjīz\ *vb* **-gized; -giz·ing** [ME *sylogysen,* fr. LL *syllogizare,* fr. Gk *syllogizesthai*] *vi* (15c) **:** to reason by means of syllogisms ~ *vt* **:** to deduce by syllogism ⟨~s his moral laws⟩
sylph \'silf\ *n* [NL *sylphus*] (1657) **1 :** an elemental being in the theory of Paracelsus that inhabits air **2 :** a slender graceful woman or girl — **sylph·like** \'sil-ˌflīk\ *adj*
sylph·id \'sil-fəd\ *n* (1680) **:** a young or diminutive sylph
sylva, sylviculture *var of* SILVA, SILVICULTURE
¹syl·van \'sil-vən\ *n* (1565) **:** one that frequents groves or woods
²sylvan *adj* [ML *silvanus, sylvanus,* fr. L *silva, sylva* wood] (1580) **1 a :** living or located in the woods or forest **b :** of, relating to, or characteristic of the woods or forest **2 a :** made, shaped, or formed of woods or trees **b :** abounding in woods, groves, or trees **:** WOODED
syl·va·nite \'sil-və-ˌnīt\ *n* [F *sylvanite,* fr. NL *sylvanium* tellurium, fr. *Transylvania,* region in Romania] (1796) **:** a mineral (Au, Ag)Te_2 that is a gold silver telluride and often occurs in crystals resembling written characters
syl·vat·ic \sil-'vat-ik\ *adj* [L *silvaticus* of the woods, wild — more at SAVAGE] (1661) **1 :** SYLVAN ⟨~ rodents⟩ **2 :** occurring in or affecting wild animals ⟨~ diseases⟩
syl·vite \'sil-ˌvīt\ *also* **syl·vine** \-ˌvēn\ *n* [F *sylvine,* fr. NL *sal digestivus Sylvii* digestive salt of Sylvius, fr. *Sylvius* latinized name of Jacques Dubois †1555 Fr. physician] (ca. 1868) **:** a mineral KCl that is a natural potassium chloride and occurs in colorless cubes or crystalline masses
sym- — see SYN-
sym·bi·ont \'sim-bē-ˌänt\ *n* [prob. fr. G, modif. of Gk *symbiount-, symbiōn,* prp. of *symbioun*] (1887) **:** an organism living in symbiosis; *esp* **:** the smaller member of a symbiotic pair — **sym·bi·on·tic** \ˌsim-ˌbī-'änt-ik, -bē-\ *adj*
sym·bi·o·sis \ˌsim-bē-'ō-səs, -ˌbī-\ *n, pl* **-bi·o·ses** \-ˌsēz\ [NL, fr. G *symbiose,* fr. Gk *symbiōsis* state of living together, fr. *symbioun* to live together, fr. *symbios* living together, fr. *sym-* + *bios* life — more at QUICK] (1622) **1 :** the living together in more or less intimate association or close union of two dissimilar organisms **2 :** the intimate living together of two dissimilar organisms in a mutually beneficial relationship; *esp* **:** MUTUALISM **3 :** a cooperative relationship (as between two persons or groups) ⟨the ~ . . . between the resident population and the immigrants —John Geipel⟩ — **sym·bi·ot·ic** \-'ät-ik\ *adj* — **sym·bi·ot·i·cal·ly** \-i-k(ə-)lē\ *adv*
sym·bi·ote \'sim-bē-ˌōt, -ˌbī-\ *n* [F, fr. Gk *symbiōtēs* companion, fr. *symbioun* to live together] (ca. 1909) **:** SYMBIONT
¹sym·bol \'sim-bəl\ *n* [in sense 1, fr. LL *symbolum,* fr. LGk *symbolon,* fr. Gk, token, sign; in other senses fr. L *symbolum* token, sign, symbol, fr. Gk *symbolon,* lit., token of identity verified by comparing its other half, fr. *symballein* to throw together, compare, fr. *syn-* + *ballein* to throw — more at DEVIL] (15c) **1 :** an authoritative summary of faith or doctrine **:** CREED **2 :** something that stands for or suggests something else by reason of relationship, association, convention, or accidental resemblance; *esp* **:** a visible sign of something invisible ⟨the lion is a ~ of courage⟩ **3 :** an arbitrary or conventional sign used in writing or printing relating to a particular field to represent operations, quantities, elements, relations, or qualities **4 :** an object or act representing something in the unconscious mind that has been repressed ⟨phallic ~s⟩ **5 :** an act, sound, or object having cultural significance and the capacity to excite or objectify a response
²symbol *vb* **-boled** *or* **-bolled; -bol·ing** *or* **-bol·ling** (1832) **:** SYMBOLIZE
sym·bol·ic \sim-'bäl-ik\ *also* **sym·bol·i·cal** \-i-kəl\ *adj* (1656) **1 a :** using, employing, or exhibiting a symbol **b :** consisting of or proceeding by means of symbols **2 :** of, relating to, or constituting a symbol **3 :** characterized by or terminating in symbols ⟨~ thinking⟩ **4 :** characterized by symbolism ⟨a ~ dance⟩ — **sym·bol·i·cal·ly** \-i-k(ə-)lē\ *adv*
symbolic logic *n* (1856) **:** a science of developing and representing logical principles by means of a formalized system consisting of primitive symbols, combinations of these symbols, axioms, and rules of inference
sym·bol·ism \'sim-bə-ˌliz-əm\ *n* (1654) **1 :** the art or practice of using symbols esp. by investing things with a symbolic meaning or by expressing the invisible or intangible by means of visible or sensuous representations: as **a :** artistic imitation or invention that is a method of revealing or suggesting immaterial, ideal, or otherwise intangible truth or states **b :** the use of conventional or traditional signs in the representation of divine beings and spirits **2 :** a system of symbols or representations
sym·bol·ist \'sim-bə-ləst\ *n* (1812) **1 :** one who employs symbols or symbolism **2 :** one skilled in the interpretation or explication of symbols **3 :** one of a group of writers and artists in France after 1880 reacting against realism, concerning themselves with general truths instead of actualities, exalting the metaphysical and the mysterious, and aiming to unify and blend the arts and the functions of the senses — **symbolist** *adj*
sym·bol·is·tic \ˌsim-bə-'lis-tik\ *adj* (ca. 1864) **:** SYMBOLIC

sym·bol·iza·tion \ˌsim-bə-lə-ˈzā-shən\ *n* (1603) **1 :** an act or instance of symbolizing **2 :** man's capacity to develop a system of meaningful symbols

sym·bol·ize \ˈsim-bə-ˌlīz\ *vb* **-ized; -iz·ing** *vt* (1603) **1 :** to serve as a symbol of **2 :** to represent, express, or identify by a symbol ~ *vi* **:** to use symbols or symbolism — **sym·bol·iz·er** *n*

sym·bol·o·gy \sim-ˈbäl-ə-jē\ *n, pl* **-gies** [*symbol* + *-logy*] (1840) **1 :** a system of symbols **2 :** the art of expression by symbols **3 :** the study or interpretation of symbols

sym·met·al·lism \(ˈ)sim-ˈ(m)et-ᵊl-ˌiz-əm\ *n* [*syn-* + *-metallism* (as in *bimetallism*)] (ca. 1895) **:** a system of coinage in which the unit of currency consists of a particular weight of an alloy of two or more metals

sym·met·ri·cal \sə-ˈme-tri-kəl\ *or* **sym·met·ric** \-trik\ *adj* (1751) **1 :** having, involving, or exhibiting symmetry **2 :** having corresponding points whose connecting lines are bisected by a given point or perpendicularly bisected by a given line or plane ⟨~ curves⟩ **3** *symmetric* **:** being such that the terms or variables may be interchanged without altering the value, character, or truth ⟨*symmetric* equations⟩ ⟨R is a *symmetric* relation if *a*R*b* implies *b*R*a*⟩ **4 a :** capable of division by a longitudinal plane into similar halves ⟨~ plant parts⟩ **b :** having the same number of members in each whorl of floral leaves ⟨~ flowers⟩ **5 :** affecting corresponding parts simultaneously and similarly ⟨~ rash⟩ **6 :** exhibiting symmetry in a structural formula; *esp* **:** being a derivative with groups substituted symmetrically in the molecule — **sym·met·ri·cal·ly** \-tri-k(ə-)lē\ *adv* — **sym·met·ri·cal·ness** \-kəl-nəs\ *n*

symmetric group *n* (ca. 1909) **:** a permutation group that is composed of all of the permutations of *n* things

symmetric matrix *n* (ca. 1949) **:** a matrix that is its own transpose

sym·me·trize \ˈsim-ə-ˌtrīz\ *vt* **-trized; -triz·ing** (1796) **:** to make symmetrical — **sym·me·tri·za·tion** \ˌsim-ə-trə-ˈzā-shən\ *n*

sym·me·try \ˈsim-ə-trē\ *n, pl* **-tries** [L *symmetria,* fr. Gk, fr. *symmetros* symmetrical, fr. *syn-* + *metron* measure — more at MEASURE] (1541) **1 :** balanced proportions; *also* **:** beauty of form arising from balanced proportions **2 :** the property of being symmetrical; *esp* **:** correspondence in size, shape, and relative position of parts on opposite sides of a dividing line or median plane or about a center or axis — compare BILATERAL SYMMETRY, RADIAL SYMMETRY **3 :** a rigid motion of a geometric figure that determines a one-to-one mapping onto itself **4 :** the property of remaining invariant under certain changes (as of orientation in space, of the sign of the electric charge, of parity, or of the direction of time flow) — used of physical phenomena and of equations describing them

sym·pa·thec·to·my \ˌsim-pə-ˈthek-tə-mē\ *n, pl* **-mies** [ISV *sympath-* (fr. ²*sympathetic*) + *-ectomy*] (1900) **:** surgical interruption of sympathetic nerve pathways — **sym·pa·thec·to·mized** \-ˌmīzd\ *adj*

¹**sym·pa·thet·ic** \ˌsim-pə-ˈthet-ik\ *adj* [NL *sympatheticus,* fr. L *sympathia* sympathy] (1644) **1 :** existing or operating through an affinity, interdependence, or mutual association **2 a :** not discordant or antagonistic **b :** appropriate to one's mood, inclinations, or disposition **c :** marked by kindly or pleased appreciation **3 :** given to, marked by, or arising from sympathy, compassion, friendliness, and sensitivity to others' emotions ⟨a ~ gesture⟩ **4 :** favorably inclined **:** APPROVING ⟨not ~ to the idea⟩ **5 a :** showing empathy **b :** arousing sympathy or compassion ⟨a ~ role in the play⟩ **6 a :** of or relating to the sympathetic nervous system **b :** mediated by or acting on the sympathetic nerves **7 :** relating to musical tones produced by sympathetic vibration or to strings so tuned as to sound by sympathetic vibration — **sym·pa·thet·i·cal·ly** \-i-k(ə-)lē\ *adv*

²**sympathetic** *n* (1808) **:** a sympathetic structure; *esp* **:** SYMPATHETIC NERVOUS SYSTEM

sympathetic nervous system *n* (ca. 1891) **:** the part of the autonomic nervous system that contains chiefly adrenergic fibers and tends to depress secretion, decrease the tone and contractility of smooth muscle, and cause the contraction of blood vessels

sympathetic strike *n* (1895) **:** SYMPATHY STRIKE

sympathetic vibration *n* (1898) **:** a vibration produced in one body by the vibrations of exactly the same period in a neighboring body

sym·pa·thin \ˈsim-pə-thən\ *n* [ISV, fr. ²*sympathetic*] (ca. 1932) **:** a substance (as norepinephrine) that is secreted by sympathetic nerve endings and acts as a chemical mediator

sym·pa·thize \ˈsim-pə-ˌthīz\ *vi* **-thized; -thiz·ing** (1591) **1 :** to be in keeping, accord, or harmony **2 :** to react or respond in sympathy **3 :** to share in suffering or grief **:** COMMISERATE ⟨~ with a friend in trouble⟩; *also* **:** to express such sympathy **4 :** to be in sympathy intellectually ⟨~ with a proposal⟩ — **sym·pa·thiz·er** *n*

sym·pa·tho·lyt·ic \ˌsim-pə-thō-ˈlit-ik\ *adj* [ISV *sympath*etic + *-o-* + *-lytic*] (1943) **:** tending to oppose the physiological results of sympathetic nervous activity or of sympathomimetic drugs — **sympatholytic** *n*

sym·pa·tho·mi·met·ic \-mə-ˈmet-ik, -(ˌ)mī-\ *adj* [ISV *sympath*etic + *-o-* + *mimetic*] (1926) **:** simulating sympathetic nervous action in physiological effect — **sympathomimetic** *n*

sym·pa·thy \ˈsim-pə-thē\ *n, pl* **-thies** [L *sympathia,* fr. Gk *sympatheia,* fr. *sympathēs* having common feelings, sympathetic, fr. *syn-* + *pathos* feelings, emotion, experience — more at PATHOS] (1579) **1 a :** an affinity, association, or relationship between persons or things wherein whatever affects one similarly affects the other **b :** mutual or parallel susceptibility or a condition brought about by it **c :** unity or harmony in action or effect **2 a :** inclination to think or feel alike **:** emotional or intellectual accord **b :** feeling of loyalty **:** tendency to favor or support ⟨republican *sympathies*⟩ **3 a :** the act or capacity of entering into or sharing the feelings or interests of another **b :** the feeling or mental state brought about by such sensitivity ⟨have ~ for the poor⟩ **4 :** the correlation existing between bodies capable of communicating their vibrational energy to one another through some medium *syn* see ATTRACTION

sympathy strike *n* (1912) **:** a strike in which the strikers have no direct grievance against their own employer but attempt to support or aid usu. another group of workers on strike

sym·pat·ric \sim-ˈpa-trik\ *adj* [*syn-* + Gk *patra* fatherland, fr. *patēr* father — more at FATHER] (ca. 1904) **:** occurring in the same area; *specif* **:** occupying the same range without loss of identity from interbreeding ⟨~ species⟩ — compare ALLOPATRIC — **sym·pat·ri·cal·ly** \-tri-k(ə-)lē\ *adv* — **sym·pat·ry** \ˈsim-ˌpa-trē\ *n*

sym·pet·al·ous \(ˈ)sim-ˈpet-ᵊl-əs\ *adj* (ca. 1877) **:** GAMOPETALOUS — **sym·pet·aly** \-ᵊl-ē, ˈsim-ˌ\ *n*

sym·phon·ic \sim-ˈfän-ik\ *adj* (1856) **1 :** HARMONIOUS, SYMPHONIOUS **2 :** relating to or having the form or character of a symphony ⟨~ music⟩ **3 :** suggestive of a symphony esp. in form, interweaving of themes, or harmonious arrangement ⟨a ~ drama⟩ — **sym·phon·i·cal·ly** \-i-k(ə-)lē\ *adv*

symphonic poem *n* (1873) **:** an extended programmatic composition for symphony orchestra usu. freer in form than a symphony

sym·pho·ni·ous \sim-ˈfō-nē-əs\ *adj* (1652) **:** agreeing esp. in sound **:** HARMONIOUS — **sym·pho·ni·ous·ly** *adv*

sym·pho·nist \ˈsim(p)-fə-nəst\ *n* (1767) **1 :** a member of a symphony orchestra **2 :** a composer of symphonies

sym·pho·ny \-nē\ *n, pl* **-nies** [ME *symphonie,* fr. MF, fr. L *symphonia,* fr. Gk *symphōnia,* fr. *symphōnos* concordant in sound, fr. *syn-* + *phōnē* voice, sound — more at BAN] (15c) **1 :** consonance of sounds **2 a :** RITORNELLO 1 **b :** SINFONIA 1 **c** (1) **:** a usu. long and complex sonata for symphony orchestra (2) **:** a musical composition (as for organ) resembling such a symphony in complexity or variety **3 :** consonance or harmony of color (as in a painting) **4 a :** SYMPHONY ORCHESTRA **b :** a symphony orchestra concert **5 :** something that in its harmonious complexity or variety suggests a symphonic composition

symphony orchestra *n* (ca. 1881) **:** a large orchestra of winds, strings, and percussion that plays symphonic works

sym·phy·se·al \ˌsim(p)-fə-ˈsē-əl\ *also* **sym·phys·i·al** \sim-ˈfiz-ē-əl\ *adj* [Gk *symphyse-, symphysis* symphysis] (1835) **:** of, relating to, or constituting a symphysis

sym·phy·sis \ˈsim(p)-fə-səs\ *n, pl* **-phy·ses** \-ˌsēz\ [NL, fr. Gk, state of growing together, fr. *symphyesthai* to grow together, fr. *syn-* + *phyein* to make grow, bring forth — more at BE] (ca. 1578) **1 :** an immovable or more or less movable articulation of various bones in the median plane of the body **2 :** an articulation in which the bony surfaces are connected by pads of fibrous cartilage without a synovial membrane

sym·po·di·al \sim-ˈpōd-ē-əl\ *adj* [NL *sympodium* apparent main axis formed from secondary axes, fr. Gk *syn-* + *podion* base — more at -PODIUM] (1875) **:** having or involving the formation of an apparent main axis from successive secondary axes ⟨~ branching of a cyme⟩

sym·po·si·arch \sim-ˈpō-zē-ˌärk\ *n* [Gk *symposiarchos,* fr. *symposion* symposium + *-archos* -arch] (1603) **:** one who presides over a symposium

sym·po·si·ast \-zē-ˌast, -əst\ *n* [Gk *symposiazein* to take part in a symposium, fr. *symposion*] (ca. 1656) **:** one who contributes to a symposium

sym·po·sium \sim-ˈpō-zē-əm *also* -zh(ē-)əm\ *n, pl* **-sia** \-zē-ə, -zh(ē-)ə\ *or* **-siums** [L, fr. Gk *symposion,* fr. *sympinein* to drink together, fr. *syn-* + *pinein* to drink — more at POTABLE] (1603) **1 a :** a convivial party (as after a banquet in ancient Greece) with music and conversation **b :** a social gathering at which there is free interchange of ideas **2 a :** a formal meeting at which several specialists deliver short addresses on a topic or on related topics — compare COLLOQUIUM **b :** a collection of opinions on a subject; *esp* **:** one published by a periodical **c :** DISCUSSION

symp·tom \ˈsim(p)-təm\ *n* [LL *symptomat-, symptoma,* fr. Gk *symptōmat-, symptōma* happening, attribute, symptom, fr. *sympiptein* to happen, fr. *syn-* + *piptein* to fall — more at FEATHER] (14c) **1 a :** subjective evidence of disease or physical disturbance; *broadly* **:** something that indicates the presence of bodily disorder **b :** an evident reaction by a plant to a pathogen **2 a :** something that indicates the existence of something else ⟨imagination is thought to be a ~ of indirection —Richard Poirier⟩ **b :** a slight indication **:** TRACE *syn* see SIGN — **symp·tom·less** \-ləs\ *adj*

symp·tom·at·ic \ˌsim(p)-tə-ˈmat-ik\ *adj* (1698) **1 a :** being a symptom of a disease **b :** having the characteristics of a particular disease but arising from another cause **2 :** concerned with or affecting symptoms **3 :** CHARACTERISTIC, INDICATIVE ⟨his behavior was ~ of his character⟩ — **symp·tom·at·i·cal·ly** \-i-k(ə-)lē\ *adv*

symp·tom·atol·o·gy \ˌsim(p)-tə-mə-ˈtäl-ə-jē\ *n* (1798) **1 :** the symptom complex of a disease **2 :** a branch of medical science concerned with symptoms of diseases — **symp·tom·at·o·log·i·cal** \-ˌmat-ᵊl-ˈäj-i-kəl\ *or* **symp·tom·at·o·log·ic** \-ˈäj-ik\ *adj* — **symp·tom·at·o·log·i·cal·ly** \-i-k(ə-)lē\ *adv*

syn- *or* **sym-** *prefix* [ME, fr. OF, fr. L, fr. Gk, fr. *syn* with, together with] **1 :** with **:** along with **:** together ⟨*syn*clinal⟩ ⟨*sym*petalous⟩ **2 :** at the same time ⟨*syn*esthesia⟩

syn·ae·re·sis *var of* SYNERESIS

syn·aes·the·sia, syn·aes·thet·ic *var of* SYNESTHESIA, SYNESTHETIC

syn·aes·the·sis \ˌsin-əs-ˈthē-səs\ *n* [Gk *synaisthēsis* joint perception, fr. *synaisthanesthai* to perceive simultaneously, fr. *syn-* + *aisthanesthai* to perceive — more at AUDIBLE] (ca. 1939) **:** harmony of different or opposing impulses produced by a work of art

syn·a·gogue *or* **syn·a·gog** \ˈsin-ə-ˌgäg\ *n* [ME *synagoge,* fr. OF, fr. LL *synagoga,* fr. Gk *synagōgē* assembly, synagogue, fr. *synagein* to bring together, fr. *syn-* + *agein* to lead — more at AGENT] (12c) **1 :** a Jewish congregation **2 :** the house of worship and communal center of a Jewish congregation — **syn·a·gog·al** \ˌsin-ə-ˈgäg-əl\ *adj*

syn·a·loe·pha *or* **syn·a·le·pha** \ˌsin-ə-ˈlē-fə\ *n* [NL, fr. Gk *synaloiphē,* fr. *synaleiphein* to clog up, coalesce, unite two syllables into one, fr. *syn-* + *aleiphein* to anoint; akin to Gk *lipos* fat — more at LEAVE] (1540) **:** the reduction to one syllable of two vowels of adjacent syllables (as in *th' army* for *the army*)

¹**syn·apse** \ˈsin-ˌaps, sə-ˈnaps\ *n* [NL *synapsis,* fr. Gk, juncture, fr. *synaptein* to fasten together, fr. *syn-* + *haptein* to fasten] (1899) **:** the point at which a nervous impulse passes from one neuron to another

²**synapse** *vi* **syn·apsed; syn·aps·ing** (1910) **:** to form a synapse or come together in synapsis

syn·ap·sis \sə-ˈnap-səs\ *n, pl* **-ap·ses** \-ˌsēz\ [NL] (ca. 1892) **:** the association of homologous chromosomes with chiasma formation that is characteristic of the first meiotic prophase and is held to be the mechanism for genetic crossing-over — **syn·ap·tic** \-ˈnap-tik\ *adj* — **syn·ap·ti·cal·ly** \-ti-k(ə-)lē\ *adv*

syn·ap·to·ne·mal complex \sə-ˌnap-tə-ˌnē-məl-\ *or* **syn·ap·ti·ne·mal complex** *same*\ *n* [*synaptic* + *-o-* or *-i-* + Gk *nēma* thread + ¹*-al* — more at NEMAT-] (1965) **:** a complex tripartite protein structure that spans the region between synapsed chromosomes in meiotic prophase

syn·ap·to·some \sə-ˈnap-tə-ˌsōm\ *n* [*synaptic* + *-o-* + ³*-some*] (1964) **:** a nerve ending that is isolated from homogenized nerve tissue — **syn·ap·to·som·al** \-ˌnap-tə-ˈsō-məl\ *adj*

syn·ar·thro·di·al \ˌsin-är-ˈthrōd-ē-əl\ *adj* [NL *synarthrodia* synarthrosis] (1830) **:** of, relating to, or being a synarthrosis

syn·ar·thro·sis \-ˈthrō-səs\ *n, pl* **-thro·ses** \-ˌsēz\ [Gk *synarthrōsis,* fr. *syn-* + *arthrōsis* arthrosis] (1578) **:** an immovable articulation in which the bones are united by intervening fibrous connective tissues

¹**sync** *also* **synch** \ˈsiŋk\ *vt* **synced** *also* **synched** \ˈsiŋ(k)t\; **sync·ing** *also* **synch·ing** \ˈsiŋ-kiŋ\ (ca. 1931) **:** SYNCHRONIZE

²**sync** *also* **synch** *n* (1937) **:** SYNCHRONIZATION, SYNCHRONISM — **sync** *adj*

syn·car·pous \(ˌ)sin-ˈkär-pəs\ *adj* (ca. 1830) **:** having the carpels of the gynoecium united in a compound ovary — **syn·car·py** \ˈsin-ˌkär-pē\ *n*

¹**syn·chro** \ˈsiŋ-(ˌ)krō, ˈsin-\ *n, pl* **synchros** [*synchronous*] (1943) **:** SELSYN

²**synchro** *adj* [*synchro-*] (1947) **:** adapted to synchronization

synchro- *comb form* [*synchronized* & *synchronous*] **:** synchronized **:** synchronous ⟨*synchro*flash⟩ ⟨*synchro*mesh⟩

syn·chro·cy·clo·tron \ˌsiŋ-(ˌ)krō-ˈsī-klə-ˌträn, ˌsin-\ *n* (1947) **:** a modified cyclotron that achieves greater energies for the charged particles by compensating for the variation in mass that the particles experience with increasing velocity

syn·chro·flash \ˈsiŋ-krō-ˌflash, ˈsin-\ *adj* (1939) **:** employing or produced with a mechanism for synchronizing the firing or peak brilliance of a flash lamp with the opening of a camera shutter

syn·chro·mesh \-ˌmesh\ *adj* (1928) **:** designed for effecting synchronized shifting of gears — **synchromesh** *n*

syn·chro·nal \ˈsiŋ-krən-ᵊl, ˈsin-\ *adj* (1660) **:** SYNCHRONOUS

syn·chro·ne·ity \ˌsiŋ-krə-ˈnē-ət-ē, ˌsin-, -ˈnā-\ *n* [*synchronous* + *-eity* (as in *spontaneity*)] (ca. 1909) **:** the state of being synchronous

syn·chron·ic \sin-ˈkrän-ik, siŋ-\ *adj* (1833) **1 :** SYNCHRONOUS **2 a :** DESCRIPTIVE 4 ⟨~ linguistics⟩ **b :** concerned with the complex of events existing in a limited time period and ignoring historical antecedents — **syn·chron·i·cal** \-i-kəl\ *adj* — **syn·chron·i·cal·ly** \-i-k(ə-)lē\ *adv* — **syn·chro·nic·i·ty** \ˌsiŋ-krə-ˈnis-ət-ē, ˌsin-\ *n*

syn·chro·nism \ˈsiŋ-krə-ˌniz-əm, ˈsin-\ *n* (1588) **1 :** the quality or state of being synchronous **:** SIMULTANEOUSNESS **2 :** chronological arrangement of historical events and personages so as to indicate coincidence or coexistence; *also* **:** a table showing such concurrences — **syn·chro·nis·tic** \ˌsiŋ-krə-ˈnis-tik, ˌsin-\ *adj*

syn·chro·ni·za·tion \ˌsiŋ-krə-nə-ˈzā-shən, ˌsin-\ *n* (1828) **1 :** the act or result of synchronizing **2 :** the state of being synchronous

syn·chro·nize \ˈsiŋ-krə-ˌnīz, ˈsin-\ *vb* **-nized; -niz·ing** *vi* (1624) **:** to happen at the same time ~ *vt* **1 :** to represent or arrange (events) to indicate coincidence or coexistence **2 :** to make synchronous in operation **3 :** to make (motion picture sound) exactly simultaneous with the action — **syn·chro·niz·er** *n*

synchronized swimming *n* (1950) **:** exhibition swimming in which the movements of one or more swimmers are synchronized with a musical accompaniment so as to form changing patterns

syn·chro·nous \ˈsiŋ-krə-nəs, ˈsin-\ *adj* [LL *synchronos,* fr. Gk, fr. *syn-* + *chronos* time] (1669) **1 :** happening, existing, or arising at precisely the same time **2 :** recurring or operating at exactly the same periods **3 :** involving or indicating synchronism **4 a :** having the same period; *also* **:** having the same period and phase **b :** GEOSTATIONARY *syn* see CONTEMPORARY — **syn·chro·nous·ly** *adv* — **syn·chro·nous·ness** *n*

synchronous motor *n* (ca. 1897) **:** an electric motor having a speed strictly proportional to the frequency of the operating current

syn·chro·ny \ˈsiŋ-krə-nē, ˈsin-\ *n, pl* **-nies** [*synchronous* + *-y*] (1848) **:** synchronistic occurrence, arrangement, or treatment

syn·chro·scope \-ˌskōp\ *n* (ca. 1907) **:** any of several devices for showing whether two associated machines or moving parts are operating in synchronism with each other

syn·chro·tron \ˈsiŋ-k(r)ə-ˌträn, ˈsin-\ *n* (1945) **1 :** an apparatus for imparting very high speeds to charged particles by means of a combination of a high-frequency electric field and a low-frequency magnetic field **2 :** SYNCHROTRON RADIATION

synchrotron radiation *n* [fr. its having been first observed in a synchrotron] (1956) **:** radiation emitted by high-energy charged relativistic particles (as electrons) when they are accelerated by a magnetic field (as in a nebula)

syn·cli·nal \(ˌ)sin-ˈklīn-ᵊl\ *adj* [Gk *syn-* + *klinein* to lean — more at LEAN] (1833) **1 :** inclined down from opposite directions so as to meet **2 :** having or relating to a folded rock structure in which the sides dip toward a common line or plane

syn·cline \ˈsin-ˌklīn\ *n* [back-formation fr. *synclinal*] (1873) **:** a trough of stratified rock in which the beds dip toward each other from either side — compare ANTICLINE

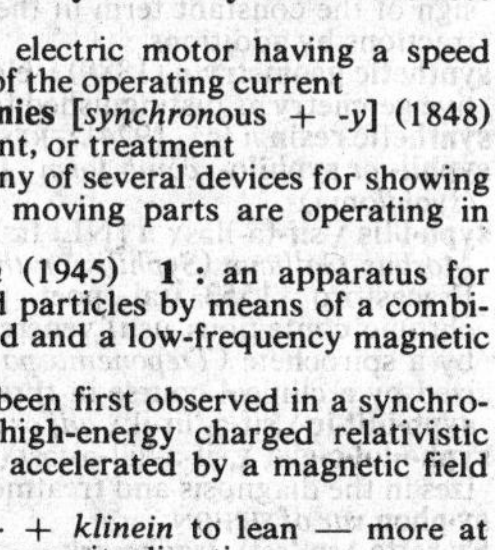

syncline

syn·co·pate \ˈsiŋ-kə-ˌpāt, ˈsin-\ *vt* **-pat·ed; -pat·ing** (1605) **1 a :** to shorten or produce by syncope ⟨~ *suppose* to *s'pose*⟩ **b :** to cut short **:** CLIP, ABBREVIATE **2 :** to modify or affect (musical rhythm) by syncopation — **syn·co·pa·tor** \-ˌpāt-ər\ *n*

syn·co·pat·ed *adj* (1665) **1 :** cut short **:** ABBREVIATED **2 :** marked by or exhibiting syncopation ⟨~ rhythm⟩

syn·co·pa·tion \ˌsiŋ-kə-ˈpā-shən, ˌsin-\ *n* [ML *syncopation-, syncopatio,* fr. *syncopatus,* pp. of *syncopare* to syncopate, fr. LL *syncope*] (1597) **1 :** a temporary displacement of the regular metrical accent in music caused typically by stressing the weak beat **2 :** a syncopated rhythm, passage, or dance step — **syn·co·pa·tive** \ˈsiŋ-kə-ˌpāt-iv, ˈsin-\ *adj*

syn·co·pe \ˈsiŋ-kə-(ˌ)pē, ˈsin-\ *n* [LL, fr. Gk *synkopē,* lit., cutting short, fr. *synkoptein* to cut short, fr. *syn-* + *koptein* to cut — more at CAPON] (15c) **1 :** a partial or complete temporary suspension of respiration and circulation due to cerebral ischemia **:** FAINT **2 :** the loss of one or more sounds or letters in the interior of a word (as in *fo'c'sle* for *forecastle*) — **syn·co·pal** \-kə-pəl\ *adj*

syn·cret·ic \sin-ˈkret-ik, siŋ-\ *adj* (1840) **:** characterized or brought about by syncretism **:** SYNCRETISTIC

syn·cre·tism \ˈsiŋ-krə-ˌtiz-əm, ˈsin-\ *n* [NL *syncretismus,* fr. Gk *synkrētismos* federation of Cretan cities, fr. *syn-* + *Krēt-, Krēs* Cretan] (1618) **1 :** the combination of different forms of belief or practice **2 :** the fusion of two or more orig. different inflectional forms — **syn·cre·tist** \-təst\ *n or adj* — **syn·cre·tis·tic** \ˌsiŋ-krə-ˈtis-tik, ˌsin-\ *adj*

syn·cre·tize \ˈsiŋ-krə-ˌtīz, ˈsin-\ *vt* **-tized; -tiz·ing** (ca. 1891) **:** to attempt to unite and harmonize esp. without critical examination or logical unity

syn·cy·tium \sin-ˈsish-(ē-)əm\ *n, pl* **-tia** \-(ē-)ə\ [NL, fr. *syn-* + *cyt-* + *-ium*] (ca. 1877) **1 :** a multinucleate mass of protoplasm (as in the plasmodium of a slime mold) resulting from fusion of cells **2 :** COENOCYTE 1 — **syn·cy·tial** \-ˈsish-(ē-)əl\ *adj*

syn·dac·ty·lism \(ˈ)sin-ˈdak-tə-ˌliz-əm\ *n* (1889) **:** SYNDACTYLY

syn·dac·ty·ly \-lē\ *n* [NL *syndactylia,* fr. *syn-* + Gk *daktylos* finger] (1864) **:** a union of two or more digits that is normal in many birds (as kingfishers) and in some lower mammals (as the kangaroos) and occurs in man as a familial anomaly marked by webbing of two or more fingers or toes

syn·des·mo·sis \ˌsin-ˌdez-ˈmō-səs, -ˌdes-\ *n, pl* **-mo·ses** \-ˌsēz\ [NL, fr. Gk *syndesmos* fastening, ligament, fr. *syndein*] (1726) **:** an articulation in which the contiguous surfaces of the bones are rough and are bound together by a ligament

syn·det·ic \sin-ˈdet-ik\ *adj* [Gk *syndetikos,* fr. *syndein* to bind together — more at ASYNDETON] (1621) **:** CONNECTIVE, CONNECTING ⟨~ pronoun⟩; *also* **:** marked by a conjunctive ⟨~ relative clause⟩ — **syn·det·i·cal·ly** \-i-k(ə-)lē\ *adv*

syn·dic \ˈsin-dik\ *n* [F, fr. LL *syndicus* representative of a corporation, fr. Gk *syndikos* assistant at law, advocate, representative of a state, fr. *syn-* + *dikē* judgment, case at law — more at DICTION] (1621) **1 :** a municipal magistrate in some countries **2 :** an agent of a university or corporation

syn·di·cal \-di-kəl\ *adj* (1864) **1 :** of or relating to a syndic or to a committee that assumes the powers of a syndic **2 :** of or relating to syndicalism

syn·di·cal·ism \ˈsin-di-kə-ˌliz-əm\ *n* [F *syndicalisme,* fr. *chambre syndicale* trade union] (1907) **1 :** a revolutionary doctrine by which workers seize control of the economy and the government by direct means (as a general strike) **2 :** a system of economic organization in which industries are owned and managed by the workers **3 :** a theory of government based on functional rather than territorial representation — **syn·di·cal·ist** \-ləst\ *adj or n*

¹**syn·di·cate** \ˈsin-di-kət\ *n* [F *syndicat,* fr. *syndic*] (ca. 1624) **1 a :** a council or body of syndics **b :** the office or jurisdiction of a syndic **2 :** an association of persons officially authorized to undertake a duty or negotiate business **3 a :** a group of persons or concerns who combine to carry out a particular transaction **b :** CARTEL 2 **c :** a loose association of racketeers in control of organized crime **4 :** a business concern that sells materials for publication in a number of newspapers or periodicals simultaneously **5 :** a group of newspapers under one management

²**syn·di·cate** \ˈsin-də-ˌkāt\ *vb* **-cat·ed; -cat·ing** *vt* (1882) **1 :** to subject to or manage as a syndicate **2 a :** to sell (as a cartoon) to a syndicate or for publication in many newspapers or periodicals at once **b :** to sell (as a series of television programs) directly to local stations ~ *vi* **:** to unite to form a syndicate — **syn·di·ca·tion** \ˌsin-də-ˈkā-shən\ *n* — **syn·di·ca·tor** \ˈsin-də-ˌkāt-ər\ *n*

syn·drome \ˈsin-ˌdrōm *also* -drəm\ *n* [NL, fr. Gk *syndromē* combination, syndrome, fr. *syn-* + *dramein* to run — more at DROMEDARY] (1541) **1 :** a group of signs and symptoms that occur together and characterize a particular abnormality **2 :** a set of concurrent things (as emotions or actions) that usu. form an identifiable pattern

¹**syne** \(ˈ)sīn\ *adv* [ME (northern), prob. fr. ON *sīthan;* akin to OE *siththan* since — more at SINCE] *chiefly Scot* (15c) **:** since then **:** AGO

²**syne** *conj or prep, Scot* (15c) **:** SINCE

syn·ec·do·che \sə-ˈnek-də-(ˌ)kē\ *n* [L, fr. Gk *synekdochē,* fr. *syn-* + *ekdochē* sense, interpretation, fr. *ekdechesthai* to receive, understand, fr. *ex* from + *dechesthai* to receive; akin to Gk *dokein* to seem good — more at EX-, DECENT] (14c) **:** a figure of speech by which a part is put for the whole (as *fifty sail* for *fifty ships*), the whole for a part (as *society* for *high society*), the species for the genus (as *cutthroat* for *assassin*), the genus for the species (as *a creature* for *a man*), or the name of the material for the thing made (as *boards* for *stage*) — **syn·ec·doch·ic** \ˌsin-ˌek-ˈdäk-ik\ *adj* — **syn·ec·doch·i·cal** \-ˈdäk-i-kəl\ *adj* — **syn·ec·doch·i·cal·ly** \-i-k(ə-)lē\ *adv*

syn·ecol·o·gy \ˌsin-i-ˈkäl-ə-jē, ˌsin-e-ˈkäl-\ *n* [G *synökologie,* fr. *syn-* syn- + *ökologie* ecology] (1910) **;** a branch of ecology that deals with the structure, development, and distribution of ecological communities — **syn·eco·log·i·cal** \ˌsin-ˌē-kə-ˈläj-i-kəl, -ˌek-ə-\ *adj*

syn·ec·tics \sə-ˈnek-tiks\ *n pl but usu sing in constr* [perh. fr. Gk *synektiktein* to bring forth together (fr. *syn-* + *ektiktein* to bring forth, fr. *ex-* out + *tiktein* to beget) + E *-s* (as in *dialectics*) — more at EX-, THANE] (1961) **:** a theory or system of problem-stating and problem-solution based on creative thinking that involves free use of metaphor and analogy in informal interchange within a carefully selected small group of individuals of diverse personality and areas of specialization — **syn·ec·tic** \-tik\ *adj* — **syn·ec·ti·cal·ly** \-ti-k(ə-)lē\ *adv*

syn·er·e·sis \sə-ˈner-ə-səs, -ˈnir-, *esp for 2* ˌsin-ə-ˈrē-\ *n* [LL *synaeresis,* fr. Gk *synairesis,* fr. *synairein* to contract, fr. *syn-* + *hairein* to take] (ca. 1577) **1 :** SYNIZESIS **2 :** the separation of liquid from a gel caused by contraction

syn·er·get·ic \ˌsin-ər-ˈjet-ik\ *adj* [Gk *synergētikos,* fr. *synergein* to work with, cooperate, fr. *synergos* working together, fr. *syn-* + *ergon* work — more at WORK] (ca. 1836) **:** SYNERGIC

syn·er·gic \sə-ˈnər-jik\ *adj* (ca. 1859) **:** working together **:** COOPERATING — **syn·er·gi·cal·ly** \-ji-k(ə-)lē\ *adv*

\ə\ **abut** \ᵊ\ **kitten,** F **table** \ər\ **further** \a\ **ash** \ā\ **ace** \ä\ **cot, cart**
\au̇\ **out** \ch\ **chin** \e\ **bet** \ē\ **easy** \g\ **go** \i\ **hit** \ī\ **ice** \j\ **job**
\ŋ\ **sing** \ō\ **go** \ȯ\ **law** \ȯi\ **boy** \th\ **thin** \t͟h\ **the** \ü\ **loot** \u̇\ **foot**
\y\ **yet** \zh\ **vision** \á, k̲, ⁿ, œ, œ̄, ue, ue̅, ʸ\ *see* Guide to Pronunciation

syn·er·gid \sə-'nər-jəd, 'sin-ər-\ *n* [NL *synergida*, fr. Gk *synergos* working together] (1898) : one of two small cells lying near the micropyle of the embryo sac of a seed plant

syn·er·gism \'sin-ər-ˌjiz-əm\ *n* [NL *synergismus*, fr. Gk *synergos*] (1924) : interaction of discrete agencies (as industrial firms) or agents (as drugs) such that the total effect is greater than the sum of the individual effects

syn·er·gist \-jəst\ *n* (1876) : something (as a chemical or a muscle) that enhances the effectiveness of an active agent; *broadly* : either member of a synergistic pair

syn·er·gis·tic \ˌsin-ər-'jis-tik\ *adj* (ca. 1841) **1** : having the capacity to act in synergism ⟨~ drugs⟩ **2** : of, relating to, or resembling synergism ⟨a ~ reaction⟩ ⟨a ~ effect⟩ — **syn·er·gis·ti·cal·ly** \-ti-k(ə-)lē\ *adv*

syn·er·gy \'sin-ər-jē\ *n* [NL *synergia*, fr. Gk *synergos* working together] (1660) : SYNERGISM; *broadly* : combined action or operation

syn·e·sis \'sin-ə-səs\ *n* [NL, fr. Gk, understanding, sense, fr. *synienai* to bring together, understand, fr. *syn-* + *hienai* to send — more at JET] (ca. 1891) : a grammatical construction in which agreement or reference is according to sense rather than strict syntax (as *anyone* and *them* in "if anyone calls, tell them I am out")

syn·es·the·sia \ˌsin-əs-'thē-zh(ē-)ə\ *n* [NL, fr. *syn-* + *-esthesia* (as in *anesthesia*)] (ca. 1891) : a concomitant sensation; *esp* : a subjective sensation or image of a sense (as of color) other than the one (as of sound) being stimulated — **syn·es·thet·ic** \-'thet-ik\ *adj*

syn·fu·el \'sin-ˌfyü(-ə)l\ *n* [*syn*thetic + *fuel*] (ca. 1975) : a liquid or gaseous fuel derived from a fossil fuel that is a solid (as coal) or part of a solid (as tar sand or oil shale) or from fermentation (as of grain)

syn·ga·my \'siŋ-gə-mē\ *n* [ISV] (ca. 1904) : sexual reproduction by union of gametes

syn·gas \'sin-ˌgas\ *n* (ca. 1975) : SYNTHESIS GAS

syn·ge·ne·ic \ˌsin-jə-'nē-ik\ *adj* [Gk *syngeneia* kinship (fr. *syn-* + *genos* kind, kin) + E *-ic* — more at KIN] (1963) : genetically identical esp. with respect to antigens or immunological reactions ⟨~ tumor cells⟩ ⟨grafts between ~ mice⟩

syn·i·ze·sis \ˌsin-ə-'zē-səs\ *n* [LL, fr. Gk *synizēsis*, fr. *synizein* to sit down together, collapse, blend, fr. *syn-* + *hizein* to sit down; akin to L *sidere* to sit down — more at SUBSIDE] (1846) : contraction of two syllables into one by uniting in pronunciation two adjacent vowels

syn·kary·on \sin-'kar-ē-ˌän, -ē-ən\ *n* [NL, fr. Gk *syn-* + *karyon* nut] (1908) : a cell nucleus formed by the fusion of two preexisting nuclei

syn·od \'sin-əd *also* -ˌäd\ *n* [LL *synodus*, fr. LGk *synodos*, fr. Gk, meeting, assembly, fr. *syn-* + *hodos* way, journey — more at CEDE] (14c) **1** : an ecclesiastical governing or advisory council: as **a** : the governing assembly of an Episcopal province **b** : a Presbyterian governing body ranking between the presbytery and the general assembly **c** : a regional or national organization of Lutheran congregations **2** : the ecclesiastical district governed by a synod — **syn·od·al** \-əd-ᵊl *also* -ˌäd-ᵊl\ *adj*

syn·od·ic \sə-'näd-ik\ *or* **syn·od·i·cal** \-i-kəl\ *adj* (1561) **1** : of or relating to a synod : SYNODAL **2** *usu synodic* [Gk *synodikos*, fr. *synodos* meeting, conjunction] : relating to conjunction; *esp* : relating to the period between two successive conjunctions of the same celestial bodies (as the moon and the sun)

synodic month *n* (1654) : a lunar month

syn·onym \'sin-ə-ˌnim\ *n* [ME *sinonyme*, fr. L *synonymum*, fr. Gk *synōnymon*, fr. neut. of *synōnymos* synonymous, fr. *syn-* + *onyma* name — more at NAME] (15c) **1** : one of two or more words or expressions of the same language that have the same or nearly the same meaning in some or all senses **2** : a symbolic or figurative name : METONYM **3** : a taxonomic name rejected as being incorrectly applied or incorrect in form — compare HOMONYM — **syn·onym·ic** \ˌsin-ə-'nim-ik\ *also* **syn·onym·i·cal** \-i-kəl\ *adj* — **syn·onym·i·ty** \-'nim-ət-ē\ *n*

syn·on·y·mist \sə-'nän-ə-məst\ *n* (ca. 1753) : one who lists, studies, or discriminates synonyms

syn·on·y·mize \-ˌmīz\ *vt* **-mized; -miz·ing** (1595) **1 a** : to give or analyze the synonyms of (a word) **b** : to provide (as a dictionary) with synonymies **2** : to demonstrate (a taxonomic name) to be a synonym

syn·on·y·mous \-məs\ *adj* (1610) **1** : having the character of a synonym; *also* : alike in meaning or significance **2** : having the same connotations, implications, or reference ⟨to runners, Boston is ~ with marathon —*Runners World*⟩ — **syn·on·y·mous·ly** *adv*

syn·on·y·my \-mē\ *n, pl* **-mies** (1683) **1 a** : the study or discrimination of synonyms **b** : a list or collection of synonyms often defined and discriminated from each other **2** : the scientific names that have been used in different publications to designate a taxonomic group (as a species); *also* : a list of these **3** : the quality or state of being synonymous

syn·op·sis \sə-'näp-səs\ *n, pl* **-op·ses** \-ˌsēz\ [LL, fr. Gk, lit., comprehensive view, fr. *synopsesthai* to be going to see together, fr. *syn-* + *opsesthai* to be going to see — more at OPTIC] (1611) **1** : a condensed statement or outline (as of a narrative or treatise) : ABSTRACT **2** : the abbreviated conjugation of a verb in one person only

syn·op·size \-ˌsīz\ *vt* **-sized; -siz·ing** (1882) **1** : EPITOMIZE **2** : to make a synopsis of (as a novel)

syn·op·tic \sə-'näp-tik\ *also* **syn·op·ti·cal** \-ti-kəl\ *adj* [Gk *synoptikos*, fr. *synopsesthai*] (1763) **1** : affording a general view of a whole **2** : manifesting or characterized by comprehensiveness or breadth of view **3** : presenting or taking the same or common view; *specif, often cap* : of or relating to the first three Gospels of the New Testament **4** : relating to or displaying conditions (as of the atmosphere or weather) as they exist simultaneously over a broad area — **syn·op·ti·cal·ly** \-ti-k(ə-)lē\ *adv*

syn·os·to·sis \ˌsin-ˌäs-'tō-səs\ *n, pl* **-to·ses** \-ˌsēz\ [NL] (ca. 1848) : union of two or more separate bones to form a single bone

sy·no·via \sə-'nō-vē-ə, sī-\ *n* [NL] (ca. 1650) : a transparent viscid lubricating fluid secreted by a membrane of an articulation, bursa, or tendon sheath

sy·no·vi·al \-vē-əl\ *adj* (1756) : of, relating to, or secreting synovia ⟨~ membranes⟩

sy·no·vi·tis \ˌsī-nə-'vīt-əs\ *n* (1835) : inflammation of a synovial membrane

syn·tac·tic \sin-'tak-tik\ *or* **syn·tac·ti·cal** \-ti-kəl\ *adj* [NL *syntacticus*, fr. Gk *syntaktikos* arranging together, fr. *syntassein*] (1577) : of, relating to, or according to the rules of syntax or syntactics — **syn·tac·ti·cal·ly** \-ti-k(ə-)lē\ *adv*

syn·tac·tics \-tiks\ *n pl but sing or pl in constr* (1938) : a branch of semiotic that deals with the formal relations between signs or expressions in abstraction from their signification and their interpreters

syn·tag·ma \sin-'tag-mə\ *n, pl* **-mas** *or* **-ma·ta** \-mət-ə\ [Gk, fr. *syntassein*] (1946) : a syntactic element — **syn·tag·mat·ic** \ˌsin-ˌtag-'mat-ik\ *adj*

syn·tax \'sin-ˌtaks\ *n* [F or LL; F *syntaxe*, fr. LL *syntaxis*, fr. Gk, fr. *syntassein* to arrange together, fr. *syn-* + *tassein* to arrange — more at TACTICS] (1574) **1** : a connected or orderly system : harmonious arrangement of parts or elements **2 a** : the way in which words are put together to form phrases, clauses, or sentences **b** : the part of grammar dealing with this **3** : syntactics esp. as dealing with the formal properties of languages or calculi

syn·the·sis \'sin(t)-thə-səs\ *n, pl* **-the·ses** \-ˌsēz\ [Gk, fr. *syntithenai* to put together, fr. *syn-* + *tithenai* to put, place — more at DO] (1589) **1 a** : the composition or combination of parts or elements so as to form a whole **b** : the production of a substance by the union of chemical elements, groups, or simpler compounds or by the degradation of a complex compound **c** : the combining of often diverse conceptions into a coherent whole; *also* : the complex so formed **2 a** : deductive reasoning **b** : the dialectic combination of thesis and antithesis into a higher stage of truth **3** : the frequent and systematic use of inflected forms as a characteristic device of a language — **syn·the·sist** \-səst\ *n*

synthesis gas *n* (ca. 1941) : a mixture of carbon monoxide and hydrogen used esp. in chemical synthesis

syn·the·size \-ˌsīz\ *vb* **-sized; -siz·ing** *vt* (1830) **1** : to combine or produce by synthesis **2** : to make a synthesis of ~ *vi* : to make a synthesis

syn·the·siz·er \-ˌsī-zər\ *n* (1869) **1** : one that synthesizes ⟨I am an expert ~ of diverse views⟩ **2** : a usu. computerized electronic apparatus for the production and control of sound (as for producing music)

syn·the·tase \'sin-thə-ˌtās, -ˌtāz\ *n* [*synthetic* + *-ase*] (ca. 1948) : an enzyme that catalyzes the linking together of two molecules usu. with concurrent splitting off of a pyrophosphate group from a triphosphate (as ATP) — called also *ligase*

[1]**syn·thet·ic** \sin-'thet-ik\ *adj* [Gk *synthetikos* of composition, component, fr. *syntithenai* to put together] (1697) **1** : relating to or involving synthesis : not analytic **2** : attributing to a subject something determined by observation rather than analysis of the nature of the subject and not resulting in self-contradiction if negated — compare ANALYTIC **3** : characterized by frequent and systematic use of inflected forms to express grammatical relationships **4 a** (1) : of, relating to, or produced by chemical or biochemical synthesis; *esp* : produced artificially or man-made ⟨~ drugs⟩ ⟨~ dyes⟩ ⟨~ silk⟩ (2) : of or relating to a synfuel **b** : devised, arranged, or fabricated for special situations to imitate or replace usual realities **c** : FACTITIOUS, BOGUS — **syn·thet·i·cal·ly** \-i-k(ə-)lē\ *adv*

[2]**synthetic** *n* (1946) : something resulting from synthesis rather than occurring naturally; *esp* : a product (as a drug or plastic) of chemical synthesis

synthetic division *n* (ca. 1904) : a simplified method for dividing a polynomial by another polynomial of the first degree by writing down only the coefficients of the several powers of the variable and changing the sign of the constant term in the divisor so as to replace the usual subtractions by additions

synthetic geometry *n* (1889) : elementary euclidean geometry or projective geometry as distinguished from analytic geometry

synthetic resin *n* (ca. 1924) : RESIN 2

syphil- *or* **syphilo-** *comb form* [NL, fr. *syphilis*] : syphilis ⟨*syphilo*logy⟩ ⟨*syphil*oma⟩

syph·i·lis \'sif-(ə-)ləs\ *n* [NL, fr. *Syphilus*, hero of the poem *Syphilis sive Morbus Gallicus* (*Syphilis or the French disease*) (1530) by Girolamo Fracastoro †1553 Ital. poet, physician, and astronomer] (1718) : a chronic contagious usu. venereal and often congenital disease caused by a spirochete (*Treponema pallidum*) and if left untreated characterized by a clinical course in three stages continued over many years — **syph·i·lit·ic** \ˌsif-ə-'lit-ik\ *adj or n*

syph·i·lol·o·gist \ˌsif-ə-'läl-ə-jəst\ *n* (ca. 1890) : a physician who specializes in the diagnosis and treatment of syphilis — **syph·i·lol·o·gy** \-jē\ *n*

sy·phon *var of* SIPHON

Sy·rette \sə-'ret\ *trademark* — used for a small collapsible tube fitted with a hypodermic needle for injecting a single dose of a medicinal agent

Syr·i·ac \'sir-ē-ˌak\ *n* [L *syriacus* Syrian, fr. Gk *syriakos*, fr. *Syria*, ancient country in Asia] (1611) **1** : a literary language based on an eastern Aramaic dialect and used as the literary and liturgical language by several eastern Christian churches **2** : Aramaic spoken by Christian communities — **Syriac** *adj*

Syr·i·an hamster \ˌsir-ē-ən-\ *n* (ca. 1949) : GOLDEN HAMSTER

sy·rin·ga \sə-'riŋ-gə\ *n* [NL, genus name, fr. Gk *syring-*, *syrinx* panpipe] (1664) : PHILADELPHUS

[1]**sy·ringe** \sə-'rinj *also* 'sir-inj\ *n* [ME *syring*, fr. ML *syringa*, fr. LL, injection, fr. Gk *syring-*, *syrinx* panpipe, tube; akin to Gk *sōlēn* pipe, Skt *tūnava* flute] (15c) : a device used to inject fluids into or withdraw them from something (as the body or its cavities): as **a** : a device that consists of a nozzle of varying length and a compressible rubber bulb and is used for injection or irrigation **b** : an instrument (as for the injection of medicine or the withdrawal of bodily fluids) that consists of a hollow barrel fitted with a plunger and a hollow needle **c** : a gravity device consisting of a reservoir fitted with a long rubber tube ending with an exchangeable nozzle that is used for irrigation of the vagina or bowel

[2]**syringe** *vt* **sy·ringed; sy·ring·ing** (1610) : to irrigate or spray with or as if with a syringe

sy·rin·go·my·elia \sə-ˌriŋ-gō-mī-'ē-lē-ə\ *n* [NL, fr. Gk *syring-*, *syrinx* tube, fistula + NL *myel-* + *-ia*] (ca. 1879) : a chronic progressive disease of the spinal cord associated with sensory disturbances, muscle atrophy, and spasticity — **sy·rin·go·my·el·ic** \-'el-ik\ *adj*

syr·inx \'sir-iŋ(k)s\ *n, pl* **sy·rin·ges** \sə-'riŋ-ˌgēz, -'rin-ˌjēz\ *or* **syr·inx·es** (1606) **1** [LL, fr. Gk] : PANPIPE **2** [NL, fr. Gk] : the vocal organ of birds that is a special modification of the lower part of the trachea or of the bronchi or of both

syr·phid \'sər-fəd, 'sir-\ *n* [NL *Syrphidae,* fr. *Syrphus,* genus of flies, fr. Gk *syrphos* gnat] (ca. 1891) : any of a family (Syrphidae) of dipterous flies which frequent flowers and some of whose larvae prey on plant lice — **syrphid** *adj*

syr·up \'sər-əp, 'sir-əp, 'sə-rəp\ *n* [ME *sirup,* fr. MF *sirop,* fr. ML *syrupus,* fr. Ar *sharāb*] (14c) **1 a** : a thick sticky solution of sugar and water often flavored or medicated **b** : the concentrated juice of a fruit or plant **2** : cloying sweetness or sentimentality — **syr·upy** \-ē\ *adj*

sys·tal·tic \sis-'tȯl-tik, -'tal-\ *adj* [Gk *systaltos,* (assumed) verbal of *systellein* to contract — more at SYSTOLE] (1676) : marked by regular contraction and dilatation : PULSING

sys·tem \'sis-təm\ *n* [LL *systemat-, systema,* fr. Gk *systēmat-, systēma,* fr. *synistanai* to combine, fr. *syn-* + *histanai* to cause to stand — more at STAND] (1619) **1 a** : a regularly interacting or interdependent group of items forming a unified whole ⟨a number ∼⟩: as **a** (1) : a group of interacting bodies under the influence of related forces ⟨a gravitational ∼⟩ (2) : an assemblage of substances that is in or tends to equilibrium ⟨a thermodynamic ∼⟩ **b** (1) : a group of body organs that together perform one or more vital functions ⟨the digestive ∼⟩ (2) : the body considered as a functional unit **c** : a group of related natural objects or forces ⟨a river ∼⟩ **d** : a group of devices or artificial objects or an organization forming a network esp. for distributing something or serving a common purpose ⟨a telephone ∼⟩ ⟨a heating ∼⟩ ⟨a highway ∼⟩ ⟨a data processing ∼⟩ **e** : a major division of rocks usu. larger than a series and including all formed during a period or era **f** : a form of social, economic, or political organization or practice ⟨the capitalist ∼⟩ **2** : an organized set of doctrines, ideas, or principles usu. intended to explain the arrangement or working of a systematic whole ⟨the Newtonian ∼ of mechanics⟩ **3 a** : an organized or established procedure ⟨the touch ∼ of typing⟩ **b** : a manner of classifying, symbolizing, or schematizing ⟨a taxonomic ∼⟩ ⟨the decimal ∼⟩ **4** : harmonious arrangement or pattern : ORDER ⟨bring ∼ out of confusion —Ellen Glasgow⟩ **5** : an organized society or social situation regarded as stultifying : ESTABLISHMENT 2 — usu. used with *the* *syn* see METHOD — **sys·tem·less** \-ləs\ *adj*

sys·tem·at·ic \sis-tə-'mat-ik\ *also* **sys·tem·at·i·cal** \-i-kəl\ *adj* [LL *systematicus,* fr. Gk *systēmatikos,* fr. *systēmat-, systēma*] (1680) **1** : relating to or consisting of a system ⟨∼ thought⟩ **2** : presented or formulated as a system : SYSTEMATIZED **3 a** : methodical in procedure or plan ⟨∼ investigation⟩ ⟨a ∼ scholar⟩ **b** : marked by thoroughness and regularity ⟨∼ efforts⟩ **4** : of, relating to, or concerned with classification; *specif* : TAXONOMIC — **sys·tem·at·i·cal·ly** \-i-k(ə-)lē\ *adv* — **sys·tem·at·ic·ness** \-ik-nəs\ *n*

systematic error *n* (1891) : an error that is not determined by chance but by a bias

sys·tem·at·ics \sis-tə-'mat-iks\ *n pl but sing in constr* (1888) **1** : the science of classification **2 a** : a system of classification **b** : the classification and study of organisms with regard to their natural relationships : TAXONOMY

systematic theology *n* (1836) : a branch of theology concerned with summarizing the doctrinal traditions of a religion (as Christianity) esp. with a view to relating the traditions convincingly to the religion's present-day setting

sys·tem·atism \'sis-tə-mə-ˌtiz-əm, sis-'tem-ə-\ *n* (1846) : the practice of forming intellectual systems

sys·tem·atist \'sis-tə-mət-əst, sis-'tem-ət-\ *n* (1700) **1** : a maker or follower of a system **2** : a specialist in taxonomy : TAXONOMIST

sys·tem·atize \'sis-tə-mə-ˌtīz\ *vt* **-atized; -atiz·ing** (1764) : to arrange in accord with a definite plan or scheme : order systematically ⟨the need to ∼ their work⟩ *syn* see ORDER — **sys·tem·ati·za·tion** \ˌsis-tə-mət-ə-'zā-shən, sis-ˌtem-ət-\ *n* — **sys·tem·atiz·er** *n*

¹sys·tem·ic \sis-'tem-ik\ *adj* (ca. 1803) : of, relating to, or common to a system: as **a** : affecting the body generally **b** : supplying those parts of the body that receive blood through the aorta rather than through the pulmonary artery **c** : acting through the bodily systems after absorption or ingestion to make the organism toxic to a pest (as a mite or insect) — **sys·tem·i·cal·ly** \-i-k(ə-)lē\ *adv*

²systemic *n* (1951) : a systemic pesticide

systemic lupus er·y·the·ma·to·sus \-ˌer-ə-ˌthē-mə-'tō-səs\ *n* (1951) : a systemic disease of unknown cause and unpredictable course that is characterized esp. by fever, skin rash, and arthritis, often by acute hemolytic anemia, by small hemorrhages in the skin and mucous membranes, by inflammation of the pericardium, and in serious cases by involvement of the kidneys and central nervous system

sys·tem·ize \'sis-tə-ˌmīz\ *vt* **-ized; -iz·ing** (1778) : SYSTEMATIZE — **sys·tem·iza·tion** \ˌsis-tə-mə-'zā-shən\ *n*

systems analysis *n* (1950) : the act, process, or profession of studying an activity (as a procedure, a business, or a physiological function) typically by mathematical means in order to define its goals or purposes and to discover operations and procedures for accomplishing them most efficiently — **systems analyst** *n*

sys·to·le \'sis-tə-(ˌ)lē\ *n* [Gk *systolē,* fr. *systellein* to contract, fr. *syn-* + *stellein* to send — more at STALL] (1578) : a rhythmically recurrent contraction; *esp* : the contraction of the heart by which the blood is forced onward and the circulation kept up — **sys·tol·ic** \sis-'täl-ik\ *adj*

syz·y·gy \'siz-ə-jē\ *n, pl* **-gies** [LL *syzygia* conjunction, fr. Gk, fr. *syzygos* yoked together, fr. *syn-* + *zygon* yoke — more at YOKE] (ca. 1847) : the nearly straight-line configuration of three celestial bodies (as the sun, moon, and earth during a solar or lunar eclipse) in a gravitational system

Szech·uan *or* **Szech·wan** \'sech-ˌwän\ *adj* [*Szechwan* or *Szechuan,* province in China] (1971) : of, relating to, or being a style of Chinese cooking that is spicy, oily, and esp. peppery

---

T

t \'tē\ *n, pl* **t's** *or* **ts** \'tēz\ *often cap, often attrib* **1 a** : the 20th letter of the English alphabet **b** : a graphic representation of this letter **c** : a speech counterpart of orthographic *t* **2** : a graphic device for reproducing the letter *t* **3** : one designated *t* esp. as the 20th in order or class **4** : something shaped like the letter T **5** : T FORMATION — **to a T** [short for *to a tittle*] : to perfection

't \t\ *pron* : IT ⟨my country, 'tis of thee —S. F. Smith⟩

ta \'tä\ *n baby talk* *Brit* (1772) : THANKS

Taal \'täl\ *n* [Afrik, fr. D, language; akin to OE *talu* talk — more at TALE] (1896) : AFRIKAANS — usu. used with *the*

¹tab \'tab\ *n, often attrib* [origin unknown] (1607) **1 a** : a short projecting device: as (1) : a small flap or loop by which something may be grasped or pulled (2) : a projection from a card used as an aid in filing **b** : a small insert, addition, or remnant ⟨license plate ∼⟩ **c** : APPENDAGE, EXTENSION; *esp* : one of a series of small pendants forming a decorative border or edge of a garment **d** : a small auxiliary airfoil hinged to a control surface (as a trailing edge) to help stabilize an airplane in flight — see AIRPLANE illustration **2** [partly short for ¹*table;* partly fr. sense 1] **a** : close surveillance : WATCH ⟨keep ∼s on him⟩ **b** : a creditor's statement : BILL, CHECK **c** : COST ⟨the ∼ for the new program⟩ **3** [by shortening] **a** : TABLOID **b** : TABULATOR **c** : TABLET

²tab *vt* **tabbed; tab·bing** (1872) **1** : to furnish or ornament with tabs **2** : to single out : DESIGNATE **3** : TABULATE

ta·ba·nid \'ta-bä-nəd, -'ban-əd\ *n* [deriv. of L *tabanus* horsefly] (ca. 1891) : HORSEFLY

tab·ard \'tab-ərd *also* -ˌärd\ *n* [ME, fr. MF *tabart*] (14c) **1** : a short loose-fitting sleeveless or short-sleeved coat or cape: as **a** : a tunic worn by a knight over his armor and emblazoned with his arms **b** : a herald's official cape or coat emblazoned with his lord's arms

Ta·bas·co \tə-'bas-(ˌ)kō\ *trademark* — used for a pungent condiment sauce made from hot peppers

tab·bou·leh \tə-'bü-lə, -lē\ *n* [Ar *tabbūla;* akin to Ar *taubala* to spice, season] (1955) : a Lebanese salad consisting chiefly of cracked wheat, tomatoes, parsley, mint, onions, lemon juice, and olive oil

¹tab·by \'tab-ē\ *n, pl* **tabbies** [F *tabis,* fr. ML *attabi,* fr. Ar *'attābī,* fr. Al-*'Attābīya,* quarter in Baghdad] (1638) **1 a** *archaic* : a plain silk taffeta esp. with moiré finish **b** : a plain-woven fabric **2** [²*tabby*] **a** : a domestic cat with a striped and mottled coat — see CAT illustration **b** : a domestic cat; *esp* : a female cat

²tabby *adj* (1638) **1** : of, relating to, or made of tabby **2** : striped and mottled with darker color : BRINDLED ⟨a ∼ cat⟩

¹tab·er·na·cle \'tab-ər-ˌnak-əl\ *n* [ME, fr. OF, fr. LL *tabernaculum,* fr. L, tent, dim. of *taberna* hut — more at TAVERN] (13c) **1 a** *often cap* : a tent sanctuary used by the Israelites during the Exodus **b** *archaic* : a dwelling place **c** *archaic* : a temporary shelter : TENT **2** : a receptacle for the consecrated elements of the Eucharist; *esp* : an ornamental locked box fixed to the middle of the altar and used for reserving the host **3** : a house of worship; *specif* : a large building or tent used for evangelistic services — **tab·er·nac·u·lar** \ˌtab-ər-'nak-yə-lər\ *adj*

²tabernacle *vi* **tab·er·na·cled; tab·er·na·cling** \-ˌnak-(ə-)liŋ\ (1653) **1** : to take up temporary residence; *esp* : to inhabit a physical body

ta·bes \'tā-(ˌ)bēz\ *n, pl* **tabes** [L — more at THAW] (1651) : wasting accompanying a chronic disease — **ta·bet·ic** \tə-'bet-ik\ *adj or n*

tabes dor·sa·lis \-ˌdȯr-'sal-əs, -'säl-, -'sal-\ *n* [NL, dorsal tabes] (ca. 1681) : a syphilitic disorder of the nervous system marked by wasting, pain, lack of coordination of voluntary movements and reflexes, and disorders of sensation, nutrition, and vision — called also *locomotor ataxia*

ta·bla \'täb-lə\ *n* [Hindi *tabla,* fr. Ar *tablā*] (ca. 1903) : a pair of small different-sized hand drums used esp. in Indian music

tab·la·ture \'tab-lə-ˌchu̇(ə)r, -chər, -ˌt(y)u̇(ə)r\ *n* [MF, fr. ML *tabulatus* tablet, fr. L *tabula*] (1574) : an instrumental notation indicating the string, fret, key, or finger to be used instead of the tone to be sounded

tabla

¹ta·ble \'tā-bəl\ *n, often attrib* [ME, fr. OE *tabule* & OF *table;* both fr. L *tabula* board, tablet, list] (bef. 12c) **1** : TABLET 1a **2 a** *pl* : BACKGAM-

MON **b** : one of the two leaves of a backgammon board or either half of a leaf **3 a** : a piece of furniture consisting of a smooth flat slab fixed on legs **b** (1) : a supply or source of food (2) : an act or instance of assembling to eat : MEAL ⟨sit down to ~⟩ ⟨father mentioned the matter at ~⟩ **c** (1) : a group of people assembled at or as if at a table ⟨a famous poker ~, which challenged all comers —Harvey Fergusson⟩ (2) : a legislative or negotiating session ⟨bring the warring nations to the peace ~⟩ **4** : STRINGCOURSE **5 a** : a systematic arrangement of data usu. in rows and columns for ready reference **b** : a condensed enumeration : LIST ⟨a ~ of contents⟩ **6** : something that resembles a table esp. in having a plane surface: as **a** : the upper flat surface of a precious stone — see BRILLIANT illustration **b** (1) : TABLELAND (2) : a horizontal stratum ⟨water ~⟩ — **under the table 1** : into a stupor ⟨can drink you *under the table*⟩ **2** : made or done in a covert manner ⟨*under the table* payoffs⟩

²table *adj* (15c) : suitable for a table or for table use ⟨a ~ radio⟩

³table *vt* **ta·bled; ta·bling** \-b(ə-)liŋ\ (15c) **1** : to enter in a table **2 a** *Brit* : to place on the agenda **b** : to remove (a parliamentary motion) from consideration indefinitely **c** : to put on a table

tab·leau \ˈtab-ˌlō, ta-ˈblō\ *n, pl* **tab·leaux** \-ˌlōz, -ˈblōz\ *also* **tableaus** [F, fr. MF *tablel,* dim. of *table,* fr. OF] (1699) **1** : a graphic description or representation : PICTURE ⟨winsome *tableaux* of old-fashioned literary days —J. D. Hart⟩ **2** : a striking or artistic grouping **3** [short for *tableau vivant* (fr. F, lit., living picture)] : a depiction of a scene usu. presented on a stage by silent and motionless costumed participants

tableau curtain *n* (1949) : a stage curtain that opens in the center and has its sections drawn upward as well as to the side in order to produce a draped effect

ta·ble·cloth \ˈtā-bəl-ˌklȯth\ *n* (15c) : a covering spread over a dining table before the tableware is set

ta·ble d'hôte \ˌtäb-əl-ˈdōt, ˌtab-\ *n* [F, lit., host's table] (ca. 1617) **1** : a meal served to all guests at a stated hour and fixed price **2** : a complete meal of several courses offered at a fixed price

ta·ble·ful \ˈtā-bəl-ˌfu̇l\ *n* (1535) : as much or as many as a table can hold or accommodate

ta·ble–hop \ˈtā-bəl-ˌhäp\ *vi* (1942) : to move from table to table (as in a restaurant) in order to chat with friends — **ta·ble–hop·per** *n*

ta·ble·land \-bəl-ˌ(l)and\ *n* (1697) : a broad level elevated area : PLATEAU

table linen *n* (1680) : linen (as tablecloths and napkins) for the table

ta·ble·mate \ˈtā-bəl-ˌmāt\ *n* (1624) : a dining companion

table of organization (ca. 1918) : a table listing the number and duties of personnel and the major items of equipment authorized for a military unit

table salt *n* (1878) : salt suitable for use at the table and in cooking : refined sodium chloride

ta·ble·spoon \ˈtā-bəl-ˌspün\ *n* (1763) **1** : a large spoon used for serving **2** : TABLESPOONFUL

ta·ble·spoon·ful \ˌtā-bəl-ˈspün-ˌfu̇l, ˈtā-bəl-ˌ\ *n, pl* **tablespoonfuls** \-ˌfu̇lz\ *also* **ta·ble·spoons·ful** \-ˈspünz-ˌfu̇l, -ˌspünz-\ (1772) **1** : enough to fill a tablespoon **2** : a unit of measure used esp. in cookery equal to 4 fluidrams (or ½ fluidounce)

table sugar *n* (1958) : SUGAR 1a; *esp* : granulated white sugar

tab·let \ˈtab-lət\ *n* [ME *tablett,* fr. MF *tablete,* dim. of *table* table] (14c) **1 a** : a flat slab or plaque suited for or bearing an inscription **b** : a thin slab or one of a set of portable sheets used for writing **c** : PAD 4 **2 a** : a compressed or molded block of a solid material **b** : a small mass of medicated material (as in the shape of a disk)

table talk *n* (1569) : informal conversation at or as if at a dining table; *esp* : the social talk of a celebrity recorded for publication

table tennis *n* (1901) : a game resembling tennis that is played on a tabletop with wooden paddles and a small hollow plastic ball

ta·ble·top \ˈtā-bəl-ˌtäp\ *n* (1807) **1** : the top of a table **2** : a photograph of small objects or a miniature scene arranged on a table — **table·top** *adj*

ta·ble·ware \-ˌwa(ə)r, -ˌwe(ə)r\ *n* (1832) : utensils (as of china, glass, or silver) for table use

table wine *n* (ca. 1827) : an unfortified wine averaging 12 percent alcohol by volume and usu. suitable for serving with food

¹tab·loid \ˈtab-ˌlȯid\ *adj* [fr. *Tabloid,* a trademark] (1901) **1** : compressed or condensed into small scope ⟨~ criticism⟩ **2** : of, relating to, or characteristic of tabloids ⟨~ journalism⟩

²tabloid *n* (1906) **1** : DIGEST, SUMMARY **2** : a newspaper that is about half the page size of an ordinary newspaper and that contains news in condensed form and much photographic matter

¹ta·boo *also* **ta·bu** \tə-ˈbü, ta-\ *adj* [Tongan *tabu*] (1777) **1** : forbidden to profane use or contact because of supposedly dangerous supernatural powers **2 a** : banned on grounds of morality or taste **b** : banned as constituting a risk ⟨the area beyond is ~, still alive with explosives —Robert Leckie⟩

²taboo *also* **tabu** *n, pl* **taboos** *also* **tabus** (1777) **1** : a prohibition against touching, saying, or doing something for fear of immediate harm from a mysterious superhuman force **2** : a prohibition imposed by social custom or as a protective measure **3** : belief in taboos

³taboo *also* **tabu** *vt* (1779) **1** : to set apart as taboo esp. by marking with a ritualistic symbol **2** : to avoid or ban as taboo

ta·bor *also* **ta·bour** \ˈtā-bər\ *n* [ME, fr. OF] (13c) : a small drum with one head of soft calfskin used to accompany a pipe or fife played by the same person

ta·bor·er *also* **ta·bour·er** \-bər-ər\ *n* (15c) : one that plays on the tabor

tab·o·ret *or* **tab·ou·ret** \ˌtab-ə-ˈret, -ˈrā\ *n* [F *tabouret,* lit., small drum, fr. MF, dim. of *tabor, tabour* drum] (1656) **1** : a cylindrical seat or stool without arms or back **2** : a small portable stand

Ta·briz \tə-ˈbrēz\ *n* [*Tabriz,* Iran] (1904) : a Persian rug usu. having a cotton warp, firm wool pile, and a medallion design

tab·u·lar \ˈtab-yə-lər\ *adj* [L *tabularis* of boards, fr. *tabula* board, tablet] (ca. 1656) **1** : having a flat surface : LAMINAR ⟨a ~ crystal⟩ **2 a** : of, relating to, or arranged in a table; *specif* : set up in rows and columns **b** : computed by means of a table

ta·bu·la ra·sa \ˌtab-yə-lə-ˈräz-ə, -ˈräs-\ *n, pl* **ta·bu·lae ra·sae** \-ˌlī-ˈräz-ˌī, -ˈräs-\ [L, smoothed or erased tablet] (1607) **1** : the mind in its hypothetical primary blank or empty state before receiving outside impressions **2** : something existing in its original pristine state

tab·u·late \ˈtab-yə-ˌlāt\ *vt* **-lat·ed; -lat·ing** [L *tabula* tablet] (1734) : to put into tabular form — **tab·u·la·tion** \ˌtab-yə-ˈlā-shən\ *n*

tab·u·la·tor \ˈtab-yə-ˌlāt-ər\ *n* (1885) : one that tabulates: as **a** : a business machine that sorts and selects information from marked or perforated cards **b** : a device (as on a typewriter) for arranging data in columns

tac·a·ma·hac \ˈtak-ə-mə-ˌhak\ *n* [Sp *tacamahaca,* fr. Nahuatl *tecamaca*] (1739) : BALSAM POPLAR

tace \ˈtas, ˈtās\ *var of* TASSE

ta·cet \ˈtäk-ˌet; ˈtās-ət, ˈtas-\ [L, lit., (it) is silent, fr. *tacēre* to be silent — more at TACIT] (ca. 1724) — used as a direction in music to indicate that an instrument is not to play during a movement or long section

tach \ˈtak\ *n* (ca. 1930) : TACHOMETER

tach·i·nid \ˈtak-ə-nəd, -ˌnid\ *n* [NL *Tachinidae,* fr. *Tachina,* genus of flies, fr. Gk *tachinos* fleet, fr. *tachos* speed; akin to Gk *tachys* swift] (ca. 1891) : any of a family (Tachinidae) of bristly usu. grayish or black flies whose parasitic larvae are often important in the biological control of insect pests — **tachinid** *adj*

tach·ism \ˈtash-ˌiz-əm\ *n, often cap* [F *tachisme,* fr. *tache* stain, spot, blob, fr. MF *teche, tache,* of Gmc origin; akin to OS *tēkan* sign — more at TOKEN] (1955) : ACTION PAINTING — **tach·ist** \ˈtash-əst\ *also* **ta·chiste** \ta-ˈshēst\ *adj or n, often cap*

ta·chis·to·scope \tə-ˈkis-tə-ˌskōp, ta-\ *n* [Gk *tachistos* (superl. of *tachys* swift) + ISV *-scope*] (ca. 1901) : an apparatus for the brief exposure of visual stimuli that is used in the study of learning, attention, and perception — **ta·chis·to·scop·ic** \-ˌkis-tə-ˈskäp-ik\ *adj* — **ta·chis·to·scop·i·cal·ly** \-i-k(ə-)lē\ *adv*

ta·chom·e·ter \ta-ˈkäm-ət-ər, tə-\ *n* [Gk *tachos* speed + E *-meter*] (1810) : a device for indicating speed of rotation

tachy- *comb form* [Gk, fr. *tachys*] : rapid : accelerated ⟨*tachy*cardia⟩

tachy·car·dia \ˌtak-i-ˈkärd-ē-ə\ *n* [NL] (1889) : relatively rapid heart action whether physiological (as after exercise) or pathological — compare BRADYCARDIA

tachy·lyte *also* **tachy·lite** \ˈtak-ə-ˌlīt\ *n* [G *tachylyt,* fr. Gk *tachy-* + *lyein* to dissolve — more at LOSE] (ca. 1864) : black glossy basalt

ta·chym·e·ter \ta-ˈkim-ət-ər, tə-\ *n* [ISV] (ca. 1860) **1** : a surveying instrument (as a transit) for determining quickly the distances, bearings, and elevations of distant objects **2** : a speed indicator

tachy·on \ˈtak-ē-ˌän\ *n* [*tachy-* + ²*-on*] (1967) : a hypothetical particle held to travel faster than light

tac·it \ˈtas-ət\ *adj* [F or L; F *tacite,* fr. L *tacitus* silent, fr. pp. of *tacēre* to be silent; akin to OHG *dagēn* to be silent] (1605) **1** : expressed or carried on without words or speech **2 a** : implied or indicated but not actually expressed ⟨~ consent⟩ **b** (1) : arising without express contract or agreement (2) : arising by operation of law ⟨~ mortgage⟩ — **tac·it·ly** *adv* — **tac·it·ness** *n*

tac·i·turn \ˈtas-ə-ˌtərn\ *adj* [F or L; F *taciturne,* fr. L *taciturnus,* fr. *tacitus*] (1771) : temperamentally disinclined to talk ***syn*** see SILENT — **tac·i·tur·ni·ty** \ˌtas-ə-ˈtər-nət-ē\ *n*

¹tack \ˈtak\ *vt* (14c) **1** : ATTACH; *esp* : to fasten or affix with tacks **2** : to join in a slight or hasty manner **3 a** : to add as a supplement **b** : to add (a rider) to a parliamentary bill **4** : to change the direction of (a sailing ship) when sailing close-hauled by turning the bow to the wind and shifting the sails so as to fall off on the other side at about the same angle as before ~ *vi* **1 a** : to tack a sailing ship **b** *of a ship* : to change to an opposite tack by turning the bow to the wind **2 a** : to follow a zigzag course **b** : to modify one's policy or attitude abruptly — **tack·er** *n*

²tack *n* [ME *tak* something that attaches; akin to MD *tac* sharp point] (15c) **1 a** : a rope to hold in place the forward lower corner of a course on a sailing ship **b** : a rope for hauling the outer lower corner of a studding sail to the end of the boom **c** : the lower forward corner of a fore-and-aft sail **d** : the corner of a sail to which a tack is fastened **2** : a small short sharp-pointed nail usu. having a broad flat head **3 a** : the direction of a ship with respect to the trim of her sails ⟨starboard ~⟩ **b** : the run of a sailing ship on one tack **c** : a change when close-hauled from the starboard to the port tack or vice versa **d** : a zigzag movement on land **e** : a course or method of action; *esp* : one sharply divergent from that previously followed **4** : any of various usu. temporary stitches **5** : a sticky or adhesive quality or condition

³tack *n* [origin unknown] (1841) : HARDTACK 1

⁴tack *n* [perh. short for *tackle*] (ca. 1935) : stable gear; *esp* : articles of harness (as saddle and bridle) for use on a saddle horse

tack·board \ˈtak-ˌbō(ə)rd, -ˌbȯ(ə)rd\ *n* (ca. 1909) : a board (as of cork) for tacking up notices and display materials

tack claw *n* (ca. 1876) : a small hand tool for removing tacks

tacki·fy \ˈtak-ə-ˌfī\ *vt* **-fied; -fy·ing** (1942) : to make (as a resin adhesive) tacky or more tacky — **tacki·fi·er** \-ˌfī(-ə)r\ *n*

tacki·ly \ˈtak-ə-lē\ *adv* (1952) : in a tacky manner : so as to be tacky

tacki·ness \ˈtak-ē-nəs\ *n* (1883) : the quality or state of being tacky

¹tack·le \ˈtak-əl, *naut often* ˈtāk-\ *n* [ME *takel;* akin to MD *takel* ship's rigging] (13c) **1** : a set of the equipment used in a particular activity : GEAR ⟨fishing ~⟩ **2 a** : a ship's rigging **b** : an assemblage of ropes and pulleys arranged to gain mechanical advantage for hoisting and pulling **3 a** : the act or an instance of tackling **b** (1) : one of two offensive football players positioned on each side of the center and between guard and end (2) : one of two football players positioned on the inside of a defensive line

²tackle *vb* **tack·led; tack·ling** \-(ə-)liŋ\ *vt* (1714) **1** : to attach or secure with or as if with tackle **2 a** : to seize, take hold of, or grapple with esp. with the intention of stopping or subduing **b** : to seize and throw down or stop (an opposing player with the ball) in football **3** : to set about dealing with ⟨~ the problem⟩ ~ *vi* : to tackle an opposing player in football — **tack·ler** \-(ə-)lər\ *n*

tack·ling \ˈtak-liŋ, *naut often* ˈtāk-\ *n* (15c) : TACKLE, GEAR

¹tacky \ˈtak-ē\ *adj* **tack·i·er; -est** [²*tack*] (1788) : somewhat sticky to the touch ⟨~ varnish⟩; *also* : characterized by tack : ADHESIVE

²tacky *adj* **tacki·er; -est** [*tacky* (a low-class person)] (1883) **1 a** : characterized by lack of good breeding : COMMON ⟨a poor-white and untidy person . . . he, in short, was ~ —J. B. Cabell⟩ **b** : SHABBY, SEEDY **2 a** : marked by lack of style or good taste : DOWDY **b** : marked by cheap showiness : GAUDY

ta·co \'täk-(,)ō\ *n, pl* **tacos** \-(,)ōz, -(,)ōs\ [MexSp] (1934) **:** a usu. fried tortilla that is folded or rolled and stuffed with a mixture (as of seasoned meat, cheese, and lettuce)
tac·o·nite \'tak-ə-,nīt\ *n* [*Taconic* mountain range, U.S.] (1892) **:** a flintlike rock high enough in iron content to constitute a low-grade iron ore
tact \'takt\ *n* [F, sense of touch, fr. L *tactus*, fr. *tactus*, pp. of *tangere* to touch — more at TANGENT] (1797) **1 :** sensitive mental or aesthetic perception ⟨converted the novel into a play with remarkable skill and ~⟩ **2 :** a keen sense of what to do or say in order to maintain good relations with others or avoid offense
syn TACT, ADDRESS, POISE, SAVOIR FAIRE mean skill and grace in dealing with others. TACT implies delicate and considerate perception of what is appropriate ⟨without the *tact* to perceive when remarks were untimely —Thomas Hardy⟩ ADDRESS stresses dexterity and grace in dealing with new and trying situations and may imply success in attaining one's ends ⟨to bring the thing off as well as Mike has done requires *address* —Herman Wouk⟩ POISE may imply both tact and address but stresses self-possession and ease in meeting difficult situations ⟨the . . . *poise* that comes from an habitual attention to what is graceful and becoming —D. C. Hodges⟩ SAVOIR FAIRE is likely to stress worldly experience and a sure awareness of what is proper or expedient ⟨the inexperience and want of *savoir faire* in high matters of diplomacy —C. C. F. Greville⟩
tact·ful \'takt-fəl\ *adj* (1864) **:** having or showing tact — **tact·ful·ly** \-fə-lē\ *adv* — **tact·ful·ness** *n*
1tac·tic \'tak-tik\ *n* [NL *tactica*, fr. Gk *taktikē*, fr. fem. of *taktikos*] (1766) **1 :** a device for accomplishing an end **2 :** a method of employing forces in combat
2tactic *adj* [NL *tacticus*, fr. Gk *taktikos*] (1871) **:** of or relating to arrangement or order
-tac·tic \'tak-tik\ *adj comb form* [Gk *taktikos*] **1 :** of, relating to, or having (such) an arrangement or pattern ⟨para*tactic*⟩ **2 :** showing orientation or movement directed by a (specified) force or agent ⟨geo*tactic*⟩
tac·ti·cal \'tak-ti-kəl\ *adj* (1570) **1 :** of or relating to combat tactics: as **a :** involving actions or means of less magnitude or at a shorter distance from a base of operations than those of strategy **b** *of an air force* **:** of, relating to, or designed for air attack in close support of friendly ground forces **2 a :** of or relating to tactics: as **(1) :** of or relating to small-scale actions serving a larger purpose **(2) :** made or carried out with only a limited or immediate end in view **b :** adroit in planning or maneuvering to accomplish a purpose — **tac·ti·cal·ly** \-k(ə-)lē\ *adv*
tac·ti·cian \tak-'tish-ən\ *n* (1798) **:** one versed in tactics
tac·tics \'tak-tiks\ *n pl but sing or pl in constr* [NL *tactica*, pl., fr. Gk *taktika*, fr. neut. pl. of *taktikos* of order, of tactics, fit for arranging, fr. *tassein* to arrange, place in battle formation; akin to Lith *patogus* comfortable] (1626) **1 a :** the science and art of disposing and maneuvering forces in combat **b :** the art or skill of employing available means to accomplish an end **2 :** a system or mode of procedure **3 :** the study of the grammatical relations within a language including morphology and syntax
tac·tile \'tak-tᵊl, -,tīl\ *adj* [F or L; F, fr. L *tactilis*, fr. *tactus*, pp. of *tangere* to touch — more at TANGENT] (1615) **1 :** perceptible by touch **:** TANGIBLE **2 :** of or relating to the sense of touch — **tac·tile·ly** \-tə-lē, -,tīl-lē\ *adv*
tactile corpuscle *n* (1873) **:** an end organ of touch
tac·til·i·ty \tak-'til-ət-ē\ *n* (1659) **1 :** the capability of being felt or touched **2 :** responsiveness to stimulation of the sense of touch
tac·tion \'tak-shən\ *n* [L *taction-*, *tactio*, fr. *tactus*, pp.] (ca. 1623) **:** TOUCH
tact·less \'takt-ləs\ *adj* (ca. 1847) **:** marked by lack of tact — **tact·less·ly** *adv* — **tact·less·ness** *n*
tac·tu·al \'tak-ch(ə-w)əl\ *adj* [L *tactus* sense of touch — more at TACT] (1642) **:** TACTILE 2 — **tac·tu·al·ly** \-ē\ *adv*
tad \'tad\ *n* [prob. fr. E dial., toad, fr. ME *tode* — more at TOAD] (ca. 1877) **1 :** a small child; *esp* **:** BOY **2 :** a small or insignificant amount or degree **:** BIT ⟨might give him some water and a ~ to eat —C.T. Walker⟩ — **a tad :** SOMEWHAT, RATHER ⟨looked a ~ bigger than me —Larry Hodgson⟩
tad·pole \'tad-,pōl\ *n* [ME *taddepol*, fr. *tode* toad + *polle* head] (15c) **:** a larval amphibian; *specif* **:** a frog or toad larva that has a rounded body with a long tail bordered by fins and external gills soon replaced by internal gills and that undergoes a metamorphosis to the adult

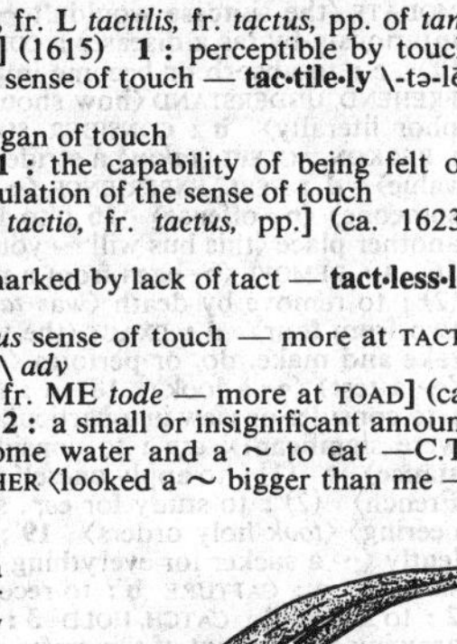

tadpole

tae·di·um vi·tae \,tēd-ē-əm-'vī-,tē, ,tīd-ē-əm-'wē-,tī\ *n* [L] (ca. 1811) **:** weariness or loathing of life
tae kwon do \'tī-'kwän-'dō\ *n, often cap T&K&D* [Korean] (1970) **:** a Korean martial art resembling karate
tael \'tā(ə)l\ *n* [Pg, fr. Malay *tahil*] (1588) **1 :** any of various units of weight of eastern Asia; *esp* **:** LIANG **2 :** any of various Chinese units of value based on the value of a tael weight of silver
tae·nia \'tē-nē-ə\ *n, pl* **-ni·ae** \-nē-,ī, -,ē\ *or* **-nias** [L, fr. Gk *tainia*; akin to Gk *teinein* to stretch — more at THIN] (1563) **1 :** a band on a Doric order separating the frieze from the architrave **2 :** TAPEWORM **3 :** an ancient Greek fillet **4** [NL, fr. L, fillet, band] **:** a band of nervous tissue or muscle
tae·ni·a·sis *or* **te·ni·a·sis** \tē-'nī-ə-səs\ *n* [NL, fr. L *taenia* tapeworm] (ca. 1890) **:** infestation with or disease caused by tapeworms
taf·fe·ta \'taf-ət-ə\ *n* [ME, fr. MF *taffetas*, fr. OIt *taffettà*, fr. Turk *tafta*, fr. Per *tāftah* woven] (14c) **:** a crisp plain-woven lustrous fabric of various fibers used esp. for women's clothing
taf·fe·tized \'taf-ə-,tīzd\ *adj, of cloth* (1949) **:** having a crisp finish
taff·rail \'taf-,rāl, -rəl\ *n* [modif. of D *tafereel*, fr. MD, picture, fr. OF *tablel* — more at TABLEAU] (ca. 1704) **1 :** the upper part of the stern of a wooden ship **2 :** a rail around the stern of a ship
taf·fy \'taf-ē\ *n, pl* **taffies** [origin unknown] (ca. 1817) **1 :** a boiled candy usu. of molasses or brown sugar that is pulled until porous and light-colored **2 :** insincere flattery
1tag \'tag\ *n* [ME *tagge*, prob. of Scand origin; akin to Sw *tagg* barb] (15c) **1 :** a loose hanging piece of cloth **:** TATTER **2 :** a metal or plastic binding on an end of a shoelace **3 :** a piece of hanging or attached material; *specif* **:** a loop, knot, or tassel on a garment **4 a :** a brief quotation used for rhetorical emphasis or sententious effect **b :** a recurrent or characteristic verbal expression **c :** TAG LINE 1 **5 a :** a cardboard, plastic, or metal marker used for identification or classification ⟨license ~*s*⟩ **b :** a descriptive or identifying epithet **c :** something used for identification or location **:** FLAG **d :** LABEL 3d **e :** PRICE TAG **6 :** a small piece of tinsel or bright material around the shank of the hook at the end of the body of an artificial fly **7 :** a detached fragmentary piece **:** BIT
2tag *vb* **tagged; tag·ging** *vt* (15c) **1 :** to provide or mark with or as if with a tag: as **a :** to supply with an identifying marker or price ⟨*tagged* every item in the store⟩ ⟨was *tagged* at $4.95⟩ **b :** to provide with a name or epithet **:** LABEL, BRAND ⟨*tagged* him a has-been⟩ **c :** to put a ticket on (a motor vehicle) for a traffic violation **2 :** to attach as an addition **:** APPEND **3 :** to follow closely and persistently **4 :** to hold to account; *esp* **:** to charge with violating the law ⟨was *tagged* for . . . assault —Burt Woolis⟩ **5 :** LABEL 2 ~ *vi* **:** to keep close ⟨*tagging* at their heels —Corey Ford⟩
3tag *n* [origin unknown] (1738) **1 :** a game in which one player chases others and tries to make one of them it by touching him **2 :** an act or instance of tagging a runner in baseball
4tag *vt* **tagged; tag·ging** (1878) **1 a :** to touch in or as if in a game of tag **b :** to put out (a runner) in baseball by a touch with the ball or the gloved hand containing the ball **2 :** to hit solidly **3 :** to choose usu. for a special purpose **:** SELECT **4 :** to make a hit or run off (a pitcher) in baseball
Ta·ga·log \tə-'gäl-əg, -,ȯg\ *n, pl* **Tagalog** *or* **Tagalogs** [Tag] (ca. 1808) **1 :** a member of a people of central Luzon **2 :** an Austronesian language of the Tagalog people
tag·along \'tag-ə-,lȯŋ\ *n* (ca. 1935) **:** one that persistently and often annoyingly follows the lead of another
tag along \,tag-ə-'lȯŋ\ *vi* (1951) **:** to follow another's lead esp. in going from one place to another
tag·board \'tag-,bō(ə)rd, -,bȯ(ə)rd\ *n* (1904) **:** strong cardboard used esp. for making shipping tags
tag end *n* (1818) **1 :** the last part **2 :** a miscellaneous or random bit
tag line *n* (ca. 1937) **1 :** a final line (as in a play or joke); *esp* **:** one that serves to clarify a point or create a dramatic effect **2 :** a reiterated phrase identified with an individual, group, or product **:** SLOGAN
tag question *n* (1964) **:** a question (as *isn't it* in "it's fine, isn't it?") added to a statement or command to gain the assent of the person addressed
tag, rag, and bobtail *or* **tagrag and bobtail** \,tag-,rag-ən-'bäb-,tāl, -,rag-ᵊŋ-\ *n* (1645) **:** RABBLE
tag sale *n* [fr. the price tag on each item] (1955) **:** GARAGE SALE
tag team *n* [4*tag*] (1952) **:** a team of two or more professional wrestlers who spell each other during a match
tag up *vi* (1947) **:** to touch a base in baseball before running after a fly ball is caught
ta·hi·ni \tə-'hē-nē, tä-\ *n* [Turk *tāhin* sesame flour or oil] (ca. 1899) **:** a smooth paste of sesame seeds
Ta·hi·tian \tə-'hē-shən\ *n* (1825) **1 :** a native or inhabitant of Tahiti **2 :** the Polynesian language of the Tahitians — **Tahitian** *adj*
tah·sil \tä-'sē(ə)l\ *n* [Hindi *taḥsīl*, fr. Ar, collection of revenue] (1849) **:** a district administration or revenue subdivision in India
Tai \'tī\ *n, pl* **Tai** (ca. 1895) **:** a widespread group of peoples in southeast Asia associated ethnically with valley paddy-rice culture
t'ai chi ch'uan *or* **tai chi chuan** \'tī-'jē-chü-'än, 'tī-'chē-\ *n, often cap T & both Cs* [Chin (Pek) *t'ai4 chi2 ch'uan2* Chinese shadowboxing, prob. fr. *t'ai4 chi2* the Absolute in Chinese cosmology + *ch'uan2* boxing] (1961) **:** an ancient Chinese discipline of meditative movements practiced as a system of exercises — called also *t'ai chi*
tai·ga \'tī-gə\ *n* [Russ *taĭga*] (1888) **:** a moist subarctic coniferous forest that begins where the tundra ends and is dominated by spruces and firs
1tail \'tā(ə)l\ *n, often attrib* [ME, fr. OE *tægel*; akin to OHG *zagal* tail, OIr *dúal* lock of hair] (bef. 12c) **1 :** the rear end or a process or prolongation of the rear end of the body of an animal **2 :** something (as the luminous train of a comet) resembling an animal's tail in shape or position **3 :** RETINUE **4** *pl* **a :** TAILCOAT **b :** full evening dress for men **5 a :** BUTTOCKS **b :** a female sexual partner — usu. considered vulgar **6 :** the back, last, lower, or inferior part of something **7 :** TAILING 1 — usu. used in pl. **8 :** the reverse of a coin — usu. used in pl. ⟨~*s*, I win⟩ **9 :** one (as a detective) who follows or keeps watch on someone **10 :** the blank space at the bottom of a page **11 :** the rear part of an airplane consisting of horizontal and vertical stabilizing surfaces with attached control surfaces **12 :** the trail of a fugitive in flight ⟨had a posse on his ~⟩ — **tailed** \'tā(ə)ld\ *adj* — **tail·less** \'tā(ə)l-ləs\ *adj* — **tail·like** \-,līk\ *adj*
2tail *vt* (1523) **1 :** to connect end to end **2 :** to remove the tail of (an animal) **:** DOCK **3 a :** to make or furnish with a tail **b :** to follow or be drawn behind like a tail **4 :** to fasten an end of (a tile, brick, or timber) into a wall or other support **5 :** to follow for purposes of surveillance ~ *vi* **1 :** to form or move in a straggling line **2 :** to grow progressively smaller, fainter, or more scattered **:** ABATE — usu. used with *off* ⟨productivity is ~*ing* off —Tom Nicholson⟩ **3 :** to hold by the end — used of a timber, tile, or brick built into a support **4 :** to swing or lie with the stern in a named direction — used of a ship at anchor **5 :** 2TAG — **tail·er** *n*

3**tail** *n* [ME, fr. MF, fr. OF, fr. *taillier*] (14c) : ENTAIL 1a

4**tail** *adj* [ME *taille,* fr. AF *taylé,* fr. OF *taillié,* pp. of *taillier* to cut, limit — more at TAILOR] (15c) : limited as to tenure : ENTAILED

tail·back \ˈtā(ə)l-ˌbak\ *n* (1940) : the offensive football back farthest from the line of scrimmage

tail·board \-ˌbō(ə)rd, -ˌbȯ(ə)rd\ *n* (1805) : TAILGATE 1

tail·bone \-ˈbōn, -ˌbōn\ *n* (1548) **1** : a caudal vertebra **2** : COCCYX

tail·coat \-ˈkōt\ *n* (1847) : a coat with tails; *esp* : a man's full-dress coat with two long tapering skirts at the back — **tail·coat·ed** \-əd\ *adj*

tail covert *n* (1815) : one of the coverts of the tail quills

tail end *n* (14c) **1** : BUTTOCKS, RUMP **2** : the hindmost end **3** : the concluding period ⟨the *tail end* of the session⟩

tail fin *n* (1681) **1** : the terminal fin of a fish or whale **2** : FIN 2b

1**tail·gate** \ˈtā(ə)l-ˌgāt\ *n* (1868) **1** : a board or gate at the rear of a vehicle that can be removed or let down (as for loading) **2** [fr. the custom of seating trombonists at the rear of trucks carrying jazz bands in parades] : a jazz trombone style marked by much use of slides to and from long sustained tones

2**tailgate** *adj* (1941) : relating to or being a picnic set up on the tailgate esp. of a station wagon

3**tailgate** *vb* **tail·gat·ed; tail·gat·ing** *vi* (1949) **1** : to drive dangerously close behind another vehicle **2** : to hold a tailgate picnic ~ *vt* : to drive dangerously close behind — **tail·gat·er** *n*

tail·ing \ˈtā-liŋ\ *n* (1764) **1** : residue separated in the preparation of various products (as grain or ores) — usu. used in pl. **2** : the part of a projecting stone or brick inserted in a wall

tail lamp *n* (ca. 1891) : TAILLIGHT

taille \ˈtä-yə, ˈtī-, ˈtā(ə)l\ *n* [F, fr. OF, fr. *taillier* to cut, tax] (1553) : a tax formerly levied by a French king or seigneur on his subjects or on lands held of him

tail·light \ˈtā(ə)l-ˌlīt\ *n* (1844) : a usu. red warning light mounted at the rear of a vehicle

1**tai·lor** \ˈtā-lər\ *n* [ME *taillour,* fr. OF *tailleur,* fr. *taillier* to cut, fr. LL *taliare,* fr. L *talea* twig, cutting; akin to Gk *tēlis* fenugreek] (13c) : one whose occupation is making or altering outer garments

2**tailor** *vi* (1662) : to do the work of a tailor ~ *vt* **1 a** : to make or fashion as the work of a tailor **b** : to make or adapt to suit a special need or purpose **2** : to fit with clothes **3** : to style with trim straight lines and finished handwork

tai·lor·bird \ˈtā-lər-ˌbərd\ *n* (ca. 1769) : any of a genus (*Orthotomus* of the family Sylviidae) of numerous Asian, East Indian, and African warblers that stitch leaves together to support and hide their nests

tai·lored \ˈtā-lərd\ *adj* (1856) **1** : fashioned or fitted to resemble a tailor's work **2** : CUSTOM-MADE **3** : having the look of one fitted by a custom tailor

tai·lor·ing \ˈtā-lə-riŋ\ *n* (1662) **1 a** : the business or occupation of a tailor **b** : the work or workmanship of a tailor **2** : the making or adapting of something to suit a particular purpose

1**tai·lor–made** \ˌtā-lər-ˈmād\ *adj* (1832) **1** : made by a tailor or with a tailor's care and style **2** : made or fitted esp. to a particular use or purpose **3** : factory made rather than hand-rolled ⟨~ cigarettes⟩

2**tailor–made** *n* (1892) : one that is tailor-made; *specif* : a woman's garment styled for a trim fit and with stiff straight lines

tail·piece \ˈtā(ə)l-ˌpēs\ *n* (1601) **1** : a piece added at the end **2** : a device from which the strings of a stringed instrument are stretched to the pegs — see VIOLIN illustration **3** : a short beam or rafter tailed in a wall and supported by a header **4** : an ornament placed below the text matter of a page

tail pipe *n* (ca. 1932) **1** : the pipe discharging the exhaust gases from the muffler of an automotive engine **2** : the part of a jet engine that carries the exhaust gases rearward and discharges them through a nozzle

tail plane *n* (ca. 1909) : the horizontal tail surfaces of an airplane including the stabilizer and the elevator

tail·race \ˈtā(ə)l-ˌrās\ *n* (1776) **1** : a lower millrace **2** : a channel in which mine tailings are floated off

tail·spin \ˈtā(ə)l-ˌspin\ *n* (ca. 1917) **1** : SPIN 2a **2** : a mental or emotional letdown or collapse **3** : a sharp downturn : SLUMP

tail·wa·ter \-ˌwȯt-ər, -ˌwät-\ *n* (1759) **1** : water below a dam or water-power development **2** : excess surface water draining esp. from a field under cultivation

tail wind *n* (1897) : a wind having the same general direction as the course of a moving airplane or ship

Tai·no \ˈtī-(ˌ)nō\ *n, pl* **Taino** *or* **Tainos** [Sp] (ca. 1895) **1** : a member of an extinct aboriginal Arawakan people of the Greater Antilles and the Bahamas **2** : the language of the Taino people

1**taint** \ˈtānt\ *vb* [ME *tainten* to color & *taynten* to attaint; ME *tainten,* fr. AF *teinter,* fr. MF *teint,* pp. of *teindre,* fr. L *tingere;* ME *taynten,* fr. MF *ataint,* pp. of *ataindre* — more at TINGE, ATTAIN] *vt* (1573) **1** : to contaminate morally : CORRUPT ⟨scholarship ~*ed* by envy⟩ **2** : to affect with putrefaction : SPOIL **3** : to touch or affect slightly with something bad ⟨persons ~*ed* with prejudice⟩ ~ *vi* **1** *obs* : to become weak **2** : to become affected with putrefaction : SPOIL ***syn*** see CONTAMINATE

2**taint** *n* (1601) : a contaminating mark or influence — **taint·less** \-ləs\ *adj*

'tain't \ˈtānt\ : it ain't

1**tai·pan** \ˈtī-ˌpan, ˈtī-ˈpän\ *n* [Chin (Pek) *tai⁴ pan¹*] (ca. 1898) : a powerful businessman and esp. formerly a foreigner living and operating in Hong Kong or China

2**tai·pan** \ˈtī-ˌpan\ *n* [native name in Australia] (1937) : an exceedingly venomous elapid snake (*Oxyuranus scutellatus*) of northern Australia and New Guinea

Ta·jik \tä-ˈjik, tə-, -ˈjēk\ *n* (1815) : a member of a people of Iranian blood and speech who resemble Europeans and are dispersed among the populations of Afghanistan and Turkestan

Ta·jiki \-ˈjik-ē, -ˈjē-kē\ *n* (ca. 1902) : the Iranian language of the Tajik people

ta·ka \ˈtäk-ə, -(ˌ)ä\ *n* [Bengali *tākā* rupee, taka, fr. Skt *ṭaṅka,* a stamped coin] (ca. 1972) — see MONEY table

1**take** \ˈtāk\ *vb* **took** \ˈtu̇k\; **tak·en** \ˈtā-kən\; **tak·ing** [ME *taken,* fr. OE *tacan,* fr. ON *taka;* akin to MD *taken* to take] *vt* (bef. 12c) **1** : to get into one's hands or into one's possession, power, or control: as **a** : to seize or capture physically ⟨*took* them as prisoners⟩ **b** : to get possession of (as fish or game) by killing or capturing **c** (1) : to move against (as an opponent's piece in chess) and remove from play (2) : to win in a card game ⟨able to ~ 12 tricks⟩ **d** : to acquire by eminent domain **2** : GRASP, GRIP ⟨~ the ax by the handle⟩ **3 a** : to catch or attack through the effect of a sudden force or influence ⟨*taken* with a fit of laughing⟩ ⟨*taken* ill⟩ **b** : to catch or come upon in a particular situation or action ⟨was *taken* unawares⟩ **c** : to gain the approval or liking of : CAPTIVATE, DELIGHT ⟨was quite *taken* with her at their first meeting⟩ **4 a** : to receive into one's body (as by eating, drinking, or inhaling) ⟨~ a glass of water⟩ **b** : to expose oneself to (as sun or air) for pleasure or physical benefit **c** : to partake of : EAT ⟨~*s* dinner about seven⟩ **5 a** : to bring or receive into a relation or connection ⟨~*s* just four students a year⟩ ⟨it's time he *took* a wife⟩ **b** : to copulate with **6** : to transfer into one's own keeping: **a** : APPROPRIATE **b** : to obtain or secure for use (as by lease or purchase) ⟨~ a cottage for the summer⟩ ⟨I'll ~ the red one⟩ ⟨*took* an ad in the paper⟩ **7 a** : ASSUME ⟨gods often *took* the likeness of a human being⟩ ⟨when the college *took* its present form⟩ **b** : to enter into or undertake the duties of ⟨~ a job⟩ ⟨~ office⟩ ⟨*took* command of the fleet⟩ **c** : to bind oneself by ⟨~ the oath of office⟩ **d** : to impose upon oneself ⟨~ the trouble to do good work⟩ **e** (1) : to adopt as one's own ⟨~ a stand on the issue⟩ ⟨~ an interest⟩ (2) : to align or ally oneself with ⟨mother *took* his side⟩ **f** : to adopt or advance as one's fundamental point of argument or defense ⟨a point well *taken*⟩ **g** : to assume as if rightfully one's own or as if granted ⟨~ the credit⟩ **h** : to have or assume as a proper part of or accompaniment to itself ⟨transitive verbs ~ an object⟩ **8 a** : to secure by winning in competition ⟨*took* first place⟩ **b** : DEFEAT **9** : to pick out : CHOOSE, SELECT **10** : to adopt, choose, or avail oneself of for use: as **a** : to have recourse to as an instrument for doing something ⟨~ a scythe to the weeds⟩ **b** : to use as a means of transportation or progression ⟨~ the bus⟩ **c** : to have recourse to for safety or refuge ⟨~ shelter⟩ **d** : to go along, into, or through ⟨*took* a different route⟩ **e** (1) : to proceed to occupy ⟨~ a seat in the rear⟩ (2) : to use up (as space or time) ⟨~*s* a long time to dry⟩ (3) : NEED, REQUIRE ⟨~*s* a size nine shoe⟩ ⟨it ~*s* two to start a fight⟩ **11 a** : to obtain by deriving from a source : DRAW ⟨~*s* its title from the name of the hero⟩ **b** (1) : to obtain as the result of a special procedure : ASCERTAIN ⟨~ the temperature⟩ ⟨~ a census⟩ (2) : to get in or as if in writing ⟨~ notes⟩ ⟨~ an inventory⟩ (3) : to get by drawing or painting or by photography ⟨~ a snapshot⟩ (4) : to get by transference from one surface to another ⟨~ a proof⟩ ⟨~ fingerprints⟩ **12** : to receive or accept whether willingly or reluctantly ⟨~ a bribe⟩ ⟨~ a bet⟩: as **a** (1) : to submit to : ENDURE ⟨*took* a lot of heat from angry constituents⟩ ⟨~ a cut in pay⟩ (2) : WITHSTAND ⟨it will ~ a lot of punishment⟩ (3) : SUFFER ⟨*took* a direct hit⟩ ⟨~ a loss⟩ **b** (1) : to accept as true : BELIEVE ⟨I'll ~ your word for it⟩ (2) : FOLLOW ⟨~ my advice⟩ (3) : to accept with the mind in a specified way ⟨~ things as they come⟩ ⟨*took* the news hard⟩ **c** : to indulge in and enjoy ⟨was *taking* his ease on the porch⟩ **d** : to receive or accept as a return (as in payment, compensation, or reparation) **e** : to refrain from hitting at (a pitched ball) **13 a** (1) : to let in : ADMIT ⟨the boat was ~*ing* water fast⟩ (2) : ACCOMMODATE ⟨the suitcase wouldn't ~ another thing⟩ **b** : to be affected injuriously by (as a disease) : CONTRACT ⟨~ cold⟩ : be seized by ⟨~ a fit⟩ **c** : to absorb or become impregnated with (as dye) **14 a** : APPREHEND, UNDERSTAND ⟨how should I ~ your remark⟩ ⟨*took* the metaphor literally⟩ **b** : CONSIDER, SUPPOSE ⟨I ~ it you're not going⟩ **c** : RECKON, ACCEPT ⟨*taking* a stride at 30 inches⟩ ⟨*took* the report at face value⟩ **d** : FEEL, EXPERIENCE ⟨~ pleasure⟩ ⟨~ an instant dislike to someone⟩ ⟨~ offense⟩ **15** : to lead, carry, or cause to go along to another place ⟨this bus will ~ you into town⟩ ⟨*took* the children home⟩ **16 a** : REMOVE ⟨~ eggs from a nest⟩ **b** (1) : to put an end to (life) (2) : to remove by death ⟨was *taken* in his prime⟩ **c** : SUBTRACT ⟨~ two from four⟩ **d** : EXACT ⟨the weather *took* its toll⟩ **17** : to undertake and make, do, or perform ⟨~ a walk⟩ ⟨~ aim⟩ ⟨~ legal action⟩ ⟨~ a test⟩ ⟨~ a look⟩ **18 a** : to deal with ⟨~ first things first⟩ **b** : to consider or view in a particular relation ⟨*taken* together, the details were significant⟩; *esp* : to consider as an example ⟨~ style, for instance⟩ **c** (1) : to apply oneself to the study of ⟨~ music lessons⟩ ⟨~ French⟩ (2) : to study for esp. successfully ⟨*taking* a degree in engineering⟩ ⟨*took* holy orders⟩ **19** : to obtain money from esp. fraudulently ⟨~ a sucker for everything he's got⟩ ~ *vi* **1** : to obtain possession: as **a** : CAPTURE **b** : to receive property under law as one's own **2** : to lay hold : CATCH, HOLD **3** : to establish a take esp. by uniting or growing ⟨90 percent of the grafts ~⟩ **4 a** : to betake oneself : set out : GO ⟨~ after a purse snatcher⟩ **b** *chiefly dial* — used as an intensifier or redundantly with a following verb ⟨*took* and swung at the ball⟩ **5 a** : to take effect : ACT, OPERATE ⟨hoped the lesson he taught would ~⟩ **b** : to show the natural or intended effect ⟨dry fuel ~*s* readily⟩ **6** : CHARM, CAPTIVATE **7** : DETRACT **8** : to be seized or attacked in a specified way : BECOME ⟨*took* sick⟩ — **tak·er** *n*

syn TAKE, SEIZE, GRASP, CLUTCH, SNATCH, GRAB mean to get hold of by or as if by catching up with the hand. TAKE is a general term applicable to any manner of getting something into one's possession or control; SEIZE implies a sudden and forcible movement in getting hold of something tangible or an apprehending of something fleeting or elusive when intangible; GRASP stresses a laying hold so as to have firmly in possession; CLUTCH suggests avidity or anxiety in seizing or grasping and may imply less success in holding; SNATCH suggests more suddenness or quickness but less force than SEIZE; GRAB implies more roughness or rudeness than SNATCH.

— **take a bath** : to suffer a heavy financial loss — **take account of** : to take into account — **take advantage of 1** : to use to advantage : profit by **2** : to impose on : EXPLOIT — **take after** : to resemble in features, build, character, or disposition — **take apart** : to treat roughly or harshly : tear into — **take a powder** : to leave hurriedly — **take care** : to be careful or watchful : exercise caution or prudence — **take care of** : to attend to or provide for the needs, operation, or treatment of — **take charge** : to assume care, custody, command, or control — **take effect 1** : to become operative **2** : to be effective — **take exception** : OBJECT — **take five** *or* **take ten** : to take a brief intermission — **take for** : to suppose to be; *esp* : to suppose mistakenly to be — **take for granted 1** : to assume as true, real, or expected **2** : to value too lightly — **take heart** : to gain courage or confidence — **take hold 1** : GRASP, GRIP, SEIZE **2** : to become attached or established : take effect — **take into account** : to make allowance for — **take in vain** : to use (a name) profanely or without proper respect — **take issue** : DISAGREE — **take it on the chin** : to suffer from the results of a situation — **take kindly to** : to show an inclination to accept or approve — **take notice of** : to observe or treat with special attention — **take one's time** : to be leisurely about doing something — **take part** : JOIN, PARTICIPATE, SHARE — **take place** : HAPPEN, OCCUR — **take root** 1 : to become rooted 2 : to become fixed or established — **take shape** : to assume a definite or distinctive form — **take stock** : INVENTORY, ASSESS — **take the cake** : to carry off the prize : rank first — **take the count** 1 *of a boxer* : to be counted out 2 : to go down in defeat — **take the floor** : to rise (as in a meeting or a legislative assembly) to make a formal address — **take to** 1 : to go to or into ⟨*take to* the woods⟩ 2 : to apply or devote oneself to (as a practice, habit, or occupation) ⟨*take to* begging⟩ 3 : to adapt oneself to : respond to ⟨*takes to* water like a duck⟩ 4 : to conceive a liking for — **take to task** : to call to account for a shortcoming — **take turns** : ALTERNATE

2take *n* (1654) 1 : something that is taken: **a** : the amount of money received : PROCEEDS, RECEIPTS, INCOME **b** : SHARE, CUT ⟨wanted a bigger ~⟩ **c** : the number or quantity (as of animals, fish, or pelts) taken at one time : CATCH, HAUL **d** : a section or installment done as a unit or at one time **e** (1) : a scene filmed or televised at one time without stopping the camera (2) : a sound recording made during a single recording period; *esp* : a trial recording 2 : an act or the action of taking (as by seizing, accepting, or otherwise coming into possession): as **a** : the action of killing, capturing, or catching (as game or fish) **b** (1) : the uninterrupted photographing or televising of a scene (2) : the making of a sound recording 3 **a** : a local or systemic reaction indicative of successful vaccination against smallpox **b** : a successful union (as of a graft) 4 : mental response or reaction ⟨a delayed ~⟩ — **on the take** : illegally paid for favors

take back *vt* (1775) : to make a retraction of : WITHDRAW

1take·down \ˈtāk-ˌdau̇n\ *n* (1893) 1 : the action or an act of taking down 2 : something (as a rifle or shotgun) having takedown construction

2take·down \ˌtāk-ˌdau̇n\ *adj* (ca. 1907) : constructed so as to be readily taken apart ⟨a ~ rifle⟩

take down \(ˈ)tāk-ˈdau̇n\ *vt* (15c) 1 : to lower without removing ⟨*took down* his pants⟩ 2 **a** : to pull to pieces ⟨*take down* a building⟩ **b** : DISASSEMBLE ⟨*take* a rifle *down*⟩ 3 : to lower the spirit or vanity of 4 **a** : to write down **b** : to record by mechanical means ~ *vi* : to become seized or attacked esp. by illness

take–home pay \ˌtāk-ˌhōm-\ *n* (1943) : income remaining from salary or wages after deductions (as for income-tax withholding)

take–in \ˈtā-ˌkin\ *n* (1778) : an act of taking in esp. by deceiving

take in \(ˈ)tā-ˈkin\ *vt* (1515) 1 : to draw into a smaller compass ⟨*take in* the slack of a line⟩: **a** : FURL **b** : to make (a garment) smaller by enlarging seams or tucks 2 **a** : to receive as a guest or lodger **b** : to give shelter to **c** : to take to a police station as a prisoner 3 : to receive as payment or proceeds ⟨the store *took in* a lot of money today⟩ 4 : to receive (work) into one's house to be done for pay ⟨*take in* washing⟩ 5 : to encompass within its limits 6 **a** : to include in an itinerary **b** : ATTEND ⟨*take in* a movie⟩ 7 : to receive into the mind : PERCEIVE 8 : DECEIVE, DUPE

taken *past part of* TAKE

take·off \ˈtā-ˌkȯf\ *n* (1846) 1 : an imitation esp. in the way of caricature 2 **a** : a spot at which one takes off **b** : a starting point : point of departure 3 **a** : a rise or leap from a surface in making a jump or flight or an ascent in an aircraft or in the launching of a rocket **b** : an action of starting out 4 : an action of removing something 5 : a mechanism for transmission of the power of an engine or vehicle to operate some other mechanism

take off \(ˈ)tā-ˈkȯf\ *vt* (14c) 1 : REMOVE ⟨*take* your shoes *off*⟩ 2 **a** : RELEASE ⟨*take* the brake *off*⟩ **b** : DISCONTINUE, WITHDRAW ⟨*took off* the morning train⟩ **c** : to take or allow as a discount : DEDUCT ⟨*took* 10 percent *off*⟩ 3 *slang* : ROB ~ *vi* 1 : to take away : DETRACT 2 **a** : to start off or away : SET OUT, DEPART **b** (1) : to branch off (as from a main stream or stem) (2) : to take a point of origin **c** : to begin a leap or spring **d** : to leave the surface : begin flight **e** : to embark on rapid activity, development, or growth **f** : to spring into wide use or popularity

take on *vt* (15c) 1 **a** : to begin to perform or deal with : UNDERTAKE ⟨*took on* new responsibilities⟩ **b** : to contend with as an opponent ⟨*took on* the neighborhood bully⟩ 2 : ENGAGE, HIRE 3 **a** : to assume or acquire as or as if one's own ⟨the city's plaza *takes on* a carnival air —W. T. LeViness⟩ **b** : to have as a mathematical domain or range ⟨what values does the function *take on*⟩ ~ *vi* : to show one's feelings esp. of grief or anger in a demonstrative way ⟨they cried and *took on* something terrible —Bob Hope⟩

take·out \ˈtā-ˌkau̇t\ *n* (ca. 1917) 1 : the action or an act of taking out 2 **a** : something taken out or prepared to be taken out **b** (1) : an article (as in a newspaper) printed on consecutive pages so as to be conveniently removed (2) : an intensive study or report

take–out \ˌtā-ˌkau̇t\ *adj* (1965) : designed for the sale of or being food not to be consumed on the premises ⟨~ counter⟩ ⟨a ~ supper⟩

take out \(ˈ)tā-ˈkau̇t\ *vt* (13c) 1 **a** (1) : DEDUCT, SEPARATE (2) : EXCLUDE, OMIT (3) : WITHDRAW, WITHHOLD **b** : to find release for : VENT ⟨*take out* their resentments on one another —J. W. Aldridge⟩ **c** (1) : ELIMINATE (2) : KILL, DESTROY (3) : KNOCK OUT 2 : to take as an equivalent in another form ⟨*took* the debt *out* in trade⟩ 3 **a** : to obtain from the proper authority ⟨*take out* a charter⟩ **b** : to arrange for (insurance) 4 : to overcall (a bridge partner) in a different suit ~ *vi* : to start on a course : SET OUT — **take it out on** : to expend anger, vexation, or frustration in harassment of

take·out double \ˌtā-ˌkau̇t-\ *n* (ca. 1944) : a double made in bridge to convey information to one's partner and to invite a bid from him

take·over \ˈtā-ˌkō-vər\ *n* (1942) : the action or an act of taking over

take over \(ˈ)tā-ˈkō-vər\ *vt* (1884) : to assume control or possession of or responsibility for ⟨military leaders *took over* the government⟩ ~ *vi* 1 : to assume control or possession 2 : to become dominant

take–up \ˈtā-ˌkəp\ *n* (1838) : the action of taking up

take up \(ˈ)tā-ˈkəp\ *vt* (14c) 1 : to pick up 2 **a** : to begin to occupy (land) **b** : to gather from a number of sources ⟨*took up* a collection⟩ 3 **a** : to accept or adopt for the purpose of assisting **b** : to accept or adopt as one's own ⟨*took up* the life of a farmer⟩ ⟨*took up* Irish citizenship⟩ **c** : to absorb or incorporate into itself ⟨plants *taking up* nutrients⟩ 4 **a** : to enter upon (as a business, practice, or subject of study) ⟨*took up* a second career⟩ ⟨*take up* skiing⟩ ⟨*took up* the trumpet⟩ ⟨had *taken up* Marxism⟩ **b** : to proceed to consider or deal with ⟨*take up* one problem at a time⟩ 5 : to establish oneself in ⟨*took up* residence in town⟩ 6 : to occupy entirely or exclusively : fill up ⟨the meeting was *taken up* with old business⟩ 7 : to make tighter or shorter ⟨*take up* the slack⟩ 8 : to respond favorably to (as a person offering a bet, challenge, or proposal) ⟨*took* me *up* on it⟩ 9 : to begin again or take over from another ⟨we must *take* the good work *up* again⟩ ~ *vi* 1 : to make a beginning where another has left off 2 : to become shortened : draw together : SHRINK — **take up the cudgels** : to engage vigorously in a defense — **take up with** 1 : to become interested or absorbed in 2 : to begin to associate with : CONSORT

ta·kin \ˈtäk-ˌēn\ *n* [Mishmi] (1850) : a large heavily built ruminant (*Budorcas taxicolor*) of Tibet that is related to the goats but in some respects resembles the antelopes

takin

tak·ings \ˈtā-kiŋz\ *n pl* (14c) : receipts esp. of money

1ta·la \ˈtäl-ə\ *n* [Skt *tāla,* lit., handclapping] (ca. 1945) : one of the ancient traditional rhythmic patterns of Indian music — compare RAGA

2ta·la \ˈtäl-ə, -(ˌ)ä\ *n, pl* **tala** [Samoan, fr. E *dollar*] (1967) — see MONEY table

Tal·bot \ˈtȯl-bət, ˈtal-\ *n* [prob. fr. *Talbot,* name of a Norman family in England] (1562) : a large heavy mostly white hound with pendulous ears and drooping flews held to be ancestral to the bloodhound

talc \ˈtalk\ *n* [MF *talc* mica, fr. ML *talk,* fr. Ar *ṭalq*] (1610) : a soft mineral $Mg_3Si_4O_{10}(OH)_2$ that is a basic magnesium silicate, is usu. whitish, greenish, or grayish with a soapy feel, and occurs in foliated, granular, or fibrous masses (hardness 1, sp. gr. 2.6–2.9) — **talc·ose** \ˈtal-ˌkōs\ *adj*

tal·cum powder \ˈtal-kəm-\ *n* [ML *talcum* mica, alter. of earlier *talk*] (ca. 1890) 1 : powdered talc 2 : a toilet powder composed of perfumed talc or talc and a mild antiseptic

tale \ˈtā(ə)l\ *n* [ME, fr. OE *talu;* akin to ON *tala* talk, and prob. to L *dolus* guile, deceit, Gk *dolos*] (bef. 12c) 1 *obs* : DISCOURSE, TALK 2 **a** : a series of events or facts told or presented : ACCOUNT **b** (1) : a report of a private or confidential matter ⟨dead men tell no ~*s*⟩ (2) : a libelous report or piece of gossip 3 **a** : a usu. imaginative narrative of an event : STORY **b** : an intentionally untrue report : FALSEHOOD ⟨always preferred the ~ to the truth —Sir Winston Churchill⟩ 4 **a** : COUNT, TALLY **b** : TOTAL

tale·bear·er \-ˌbar-ər, -ˌber-\ *n* (15c) : one that spreads gossip or rumors; *also* : TATTLETALE — **tale·bear·ing** \-iŋ\ *adj or n*

tal·ent \ˈtal-ənt\ *n* [ME, fr. OE *talente,* fr. L *talenta,* pl. of *talentum* unit of weight or money, fr. Gk *talanton;* akin to L *tollere* to lift up; in senses 2–5, fr. the parable of the talents in Mt 25:14–30 — more at TOLERATE] (bef. 12c) 1 **a** : any of several ancient units of weight (as a unit of Palestine and Syria equal to 3000 shekels or a Greek unit equal to 6000 drachmas) **b** : a unit of value equal to the value of a talent of gold or silver 2 *archaic* : a characteristic feature, aptitude, or disposition of a person or animal 3 : the natural endowments of a person 4 **a** : a special often creative or artistic aptitude **b** : general intelligence or mental power : ABILITY 5 : a person of talent or a group of persons of talent in a field or activity ***syn*** see GIFT — **tal·ent·ed** \-ən-təd\ *adj* — **tal·ent·less** \-ənt-ləs\ *adj*

talent scout *n* (1941) : a person engaged in discovering and recruiting people of talent for a specialized field or activity

talent show *n* (1953) : a show consisting of a series of individual performances (as singing) by amateurs who may be selected for special recognition as performing talent

ta·ler \ˈtäl-ər\ *n* [G — more at DOLLAR] (ca. 1905) : any of numerous silver coins issued by various German states from the 15th to the 19th centuries

tales·man \ˈtā(ə)lz-mən, ˈtā-lēz-\ *n* [ME *tales* talesmen, fr. ML *tales de circumstantibus* such (persons) of the bystanders; fr. the wording of the writ summoning them] (1679) 1 : a person added to a jury usu. from among bystanders to make up a deficiency in the available number of jurors 2 : a member of a large pool of persons called for jury duty from which jurors are selected

tale–tell·er \ˈtā(ə)l-ˌtel-ər\ *n* (14c) 1 : one who tells tales or stories 2 : TALEBEARER — **tale–tell·ing** \-ˌtel-iŋ\ *adj or n*

tali *pl of* TALUS

tali·pes \ˈtal-ə-ˌpēz\ *n* [NL, fr. L *talus* ankle + *pes* foot — more at FOOT] (ca. 1841) : CLUBFOOT

tal·is·man \ˈtal-ə-smən, -əz-mən\ *n, pl* **-mans** [F *talisman* or Sp *talismán* or It *talismano;* all fr. Ar *ṭilsam,* fr. MGk *telesma,* fr. Gk, consecration, fr. *telein* to initiate into the mysteries, complete, fr. *telos* end — more at WHEEL] (1638) 1 : an object held to act as a charm to avert evil and bring good fortune 2 : something producing apparently magical or miraculous effects — **tal·is·man·ic** \ˌtal-ə-ˈsman-ik, -əz-ˈman-\ *adj* — **tal·is·man·i·cal·ly** \-i-k(ə-)lē\ *adv*

1talk \ˈtȯk\ *vb* [ME *talken;* akin to OE *talu* tale] *vt* (13c) 1 : to deliver or express in speech : UTTER 2 : to make the subject of conversation or discourse : DISCUSS ⟨~ business⟩ 3 : to influence, affect, or cause by talking ⟨~*ed* them into agreeing⟩ 4 : to use (a language) for conversing or communicating : SPEAK ~ *vi* 1 **a** : to express or exchange ideas by means of spoken words **b** : to convey information or communicate in any way (as with signs or sounds) ⟨can make a trumpet ~⟩ 2 : to use speech : SPEAK 3 **a** : to speak idly : PRATE **b** : GOSSIP **c**

: to reveal secret or confidential information 4 : to give a talk : LECTURE — **talk·er** *n* — **talk back** : to answer impertinently — **talk sense** : to voice rational, logical, or sensible thoughts — **talk through one's hat** : to voice irrational, illogical, or erroneous ideas — **talk turkey** : to speak frankly or bluntly

[2]talk *n* (15c) **1** : the act or an instance of talking : SPEECH **2** : a way of speaking : LANGUAGE **3** : pointless or fruitless discussion : VERBIAGE **4** : a formal discussion, negotiation, or exchange of views : CONFERENCE **5 a** : MENTION, REPORT **b** : RUMOR, GOSSIP **6** : the topic of interested comment, conversation, or gossip **7 a** : ADDRESS, LECTURE **b** : written analysis or discussion presented in an informal or conversational manner **8** : communicative sounds or signs resembling or functioning as talk ⟨bird ~⟩

talk·athon \'tȯ-kə-,thän\ *n* [*talk* + *marathon*] (ca. 1934) : a long session of discussion or speech-making

talk·ative \'tȯ-kət-iv\ *adj* (15c) : given to talking; *also* full of talk — **talk·ative·ly** *adv* — **talk·ative·ness** *n*

syn TALKATIVE, LOQUACIOUS, GARRULOUS, VOLUBLE mean given to talk or talking. TALKATIVE may imply a readiness to engage in talk or a disposition to enjoy conversation; LOQUACIOUS suggests the power of expressing oneself articulately, fluently, or glibly; GARRULOUS implies prosy, rambling, or tedious loquacity; VOLUBLE suggests a free, easy, and unending loquacity.

talk down *vi* (1901) : to speak in a condescending or oversimplified fashion ~ *vt* : to disparage or belittle by talking

talk·ie \'tȯ-kē\ *n* [*talk* + *-ie*] (1913) : a motion picture with a synchronized sound track

talking book *n* (1932) : a phonograph or tape recording of a reading of a book or magazine designed chiefly for the use of the blind

talking head *n* (1968) : the televised head and shoulders shot of a person talking

talking machine *n* (1890) : PHONOGRAPH

talking point *n* (ca. 1914) : something that lends support to an argument

talk·ing–to \'tȯ-kiŋ-,tü\ *n* (1884) : REPRIMAND, LECTURE

talk out *vt* (1954) : to clarify or settle by oral discussion

talk over *vt* (1734) : to review or consider in conversation : DISCUSS

talk show *n* (1965) : a radio or television program in which usu. well-known persons engage in discussions or are interviewed

talk up *vt* (1722) : to discuss favorably : ADVOCATE, PROMOTE ~ *vi* : to speak up plainly or directly

talky \'tȯ-kē\ *adj* (1815) **1** : TALKATIVE **2** : containing too much talk

tall \'tȯl\ *adj* [ME, prob. fr. OE *getæl* quick, ready; akin to OHG *gizal* quick, OE *talu* tale] (15c) **1** *obs* : BRAVE, COURAGEOUS **2 a** : high in stature **b** : of a specified height ⟨five feet ~⟩ **3 a** : of considerable height ⟨~ trees⟩ **b** : long from bottom to top ⟨a ~ book⟩ **c** : of a higher growing variety or species of plant **4 a** : large or formidable in amount, extent, or degree ⟨a ~ order to fill⟩ **b** : POMPOUS, HIGH-FLOWN ⟨~ talk about the vast mysteries of life —W. A. White⟩ **c** : highly exaggerated : INCREDIBLE, IMPROBABLE ⟨a ~ story⟩ ***syn*** see HIGH — **tall** *adv* — **tall·ish** \'tȯ-lish\ *adj* — **tall·ness** \'tȯl-nəs\ *n*

tal·lage \'tal-ij\ *n* [ME *taillage, tallage*, fr. OF *taillage*, fr. *taillier* to cut, limit, tax — more at TAILOR] (13c) : an impost or due levied by a lord upon his tenants

tall·boy \'tȯl-,bȯi\ *n* (1769) **1 a** : HIGHBOY **b** : a double chest of drawers usu. with the upper section slightly smaller than the lower **2** *Brit* : CLOTHESPRESS

tall fescue *n* (ca. 1762) : a fescue of a variety (*Festuca elatior* var. *arundinacea*) of meadow fescue with erect smooth stems 3 to 4 feet high — called also *tall fescue grass*; compare FESCUE FOOT

tal·lith \'täl-əs, 'tal-, -ət(h)\ *n, pl* **tal·li·thim** \,täl-ə-'sēm, -'t(h)ēm\ *or* **ta·ley·sim** \tə-'lā-səm\ [Heb *tallīth* cover, cloak] (1613) : a shawl with fringed corners traditionally worn over the head or shoulders by Jewish men during morning prayers

tall oil \'täl-, 'tȯl-\ *n* [part trans. of G *tallöl*, part trans. of Sw *tallolja*, fr. *tall* pine + *olja* oil] (ca. 1926) : a resinous by-product from the manufacture of chemical wood pulp used esp. in making soaps, coatings, and oils

[1]tal·low \'tal-(,)ō, -ə(-w)\ *n* [ME *talgh, talow*; akin to MD *talch* tallow] (14c) : the white nearly tasteless solid rendered fat of cattle and sheep used chiefly in soap, margarine, candles, and lubricants — **tal·lowy** \'tal-ə-wē\ *adj*

[2]tallow *vt* (15c) : to grease or smear with tallow

[1]tal·ly \'tal-ē\ *n, pl* **tallies** [ME *talye*, fr. ML *talea, tallia* fr. L *talea* twig, cutting — more at TAILOR] (15c) **1** : a device (as a notched rod or mechanical counter) for visibly recording or accounting esp. business transactions **2 a** : a recorded reckoning or account (as of items or charges) ⟨keep a daily ~ of accidents⟩ **b** : a score or point made (as in a game) **3 a** : a part that corresponds to an opposite or companion member : COMPLEMENT **b** : a state of correspondence or agreement

[2]tally *vb* **tal·lied; tal·ly·ing** *vt* (15c) **1 a** : to record on or as if on a tally : TABULATE **b** : to list or check off (as a cargo) by items **c** : to register (as a score) in a contest **2** : to make a count of : RECKON **3** : to cause to correspond ~ *vi* **1 a** : to make a tally by or as if by tabulating **b** : to register a point in a contest : SCORE **2** : CORRESPOND, MATCH

tal·ly·ho \,tal-ē-'hō\ *n, pl* **-hos** [prob. fr. F *taïaut*, a cry used to excite hounds in deer hunting] (1772) **1** : a call of a huntsman at sight of the fox **2** [*Tally-ho*, name of a coach formerly plying between London and Birmingham] : a four-in-hand coach

tal·ly·man \'tal-ē-mən, -,man\ *n* (1654) **1** *Brit* : one who sells goods on the installment plan **2** : one who tallies, checks, or keeps an account or record (as of receipt of goods)

Tal·mud \'täl-,mu̇d, 'tal-məd\ *n* [LHeb *talmūdh*, lit., instruction] (1532) : the authoritative body of Jewish tradition comprising the Mishnah and Gemara — **Tal·mu·dic** \tal-'m(y)üd-ik, -'məd-; täl-'mu̇d-\ *adj* — **tal·mud·ism** \'täl-,mu̇d-,iz-əm, 'tal-məd-\ *n, often cap*

Tal·mud·ist \'täl-,mu̇d-əst, 'tal-məd-\ *n* (1569) : a specialist in Talmudic studies

tal·on \'tal-ən\ *n* [ME, fr. MF, heel, spur, fr. (assumed) VL *talon-, talo*, fr. L *talus* ankle, anklebone] (15c) **1 a** : the claw of an animal and esp. of a bird of prey **b** : a finger or hand of a human being **2** : a part or object shaped like or suggestive of a heel or claw: as **a** : an ogee molding **b** : the shoulder of the bolt of a lock on which the key acts to shoot the bolt **3 a** : cards laid aside in a pile in solitaire **b** : STOCK 10c — **tal·oned** \-ənd\ *adj*

[1]ta·lus \'tā-ləs, 'tal-əs\ *n* [F, fr. L *talutium* slope indicating presence of gold under the soil] (1645) **1** : a slope formed esp. by an accumulation of rock debris **2** : rock debris at the base of a cliff

[2]ta·lus \'tā-ləs\ *n, pl* **ta·li** \'tā-,lī\ [NL, fr. L] (ca. 1693) **1** : the astragalus of man bearing the weight of the body and with the tibia and fibula forming the ankle joint **2** : the entire ankle

tam \'tam\ *n* (1895) : TAM-O'-SHANTER

ta·ma·le \tə-'mäl-ē\ *n* [MexSp *tamales*, pl. of *tamal* tamale, fr. Nahuatl *tamalli*] (ca. 1854) : ground meat seasoned usu. with chili, rolled in cornmeal dough, wrapped in corn husks, and steamed

ta·man·dua \tə-'man-də-wə, -,man-də-'wä\ *n* [Pg *tamanduá*, fr. Tupi] (1691) : an arboreal anteater (*Tamandua tetradactyla*) of Central and So. America

tam·a·rack \'tam-(ə-),rak\ *n* [origin unknown] (1805) **1** : any of several American larches; *esp* : a larch (*Larix laricina*) of the northern U.S., Canada, and Alaska **2** : the wood of a tamarack

tam·a·rau \,tam-ə-'rau̇\ *n* [Tag *tamaráw*] (1898) : a small dark sturdily built buffalo (*Bubalus mindorensis*) native to Mindoro

tam·a·rin \'tam-ə-rən, -,ran\ *n* [F, fr. Galibi] (ca. 1780) : any of numerous small So. American marmosets (genera *Saguinus* and *Leontideus*) with silky fur, a long tail, and lower canine teeth that are longer than the incisors

tam·a·rind \'tam-ə-rənd, -,rind\ *n* [Sp & Pg *tamarindo*, fr. Ar *tamr hindī*, lit., Indian date] (1533) : a tropical leguminous tree (*Tamarindus indica*) with hard yellowish wood, pinnate leaves, and red-striped yellow flowers; *also* : its fruit which has an acid pulp used for preserves or in a cooling laxative drink

tam·a·risk \'tam-ə-,risk\ *n* [ME *tamarisc*, fr. LL *tamariscus*, fr. L *tamaric-, tamarix*] (15c) : any of a genus (*Tamarix* of the family Tamaricaceae, the tamarisk family) of chiefly desert shrubs and trees having tiny narrow leaves and masses of minute flowers with five stamens and a one-celled ovary

tam·ba·la \täm-'bäl-ə\ *n, pl* **-la** *or* **-las** [native name in Malawi, lit., cockerel] (1970) — see *kwacha* at MONEY table

[1]tam·bour \'tam-,bu̇(ə)r, tam-'\ *n* [F, drum, fr. Ar *ṭanbūr*, modif. of Per *tabīr*] (15c) **1** : [1]DRUM 1 **2 a** : an embroidery frame; *esp* : a set of two interlocking hoops between which cloth is stretched before stitching **b** : embroidery made on a tambour frame **3** : a shallow metallic cup or drum with a thin elastic membrane supporting a writing lever used to transmit and register slight motions (as arterial pulsations) **4** : a rolling top or front (as of a desk) of narrow strips of wood glued on canvas

[2]tambour *vt* (1774) : to embroider (cloth) with tambour ~ *vi* : to work at a tambour frame — **tam·bour·er** *n*

tam·bou·ra *or* **tam·bu·ra** \tam-'bu̇r-ə\ *n* [Per *ṭambūra*] (1585) : an Asian musical instrument resembling a lute in construction but without frets and used to produce a drone accompaniment to singing

tam·bou·rine \,tam-bə-'rēn\ *n* [MF *tambourin*, dim. of *tambour*] (1579) : a small drum; *esp* : a shallow one-headed drum with loose metallic disks at the sides played by shaking, striking with the hand, or rubbing with the thumb

tam·bu·rit·za \,tam-bə-'rit-sə\ *n* [Serb *tamburica*, prob. fr. Turk *tambur*, *tambura* tamboura, fr. Per *ṭambūra*] (ca. 1929) : one of a family of plucked stringed instruments of Yugoslavia similar to the guitar in shape and the mandolin in sound

[1]tame \'tām\ *adj* **tam·er; tam·est** [ME, fr. OE *tam*; akin to OHG *zam* tame, L *domare* to tame, Gk *damnanai*] (bef. 12c) **1** : reduced from a state of native wildness esp. so as to be tractable and useful to man : DOMESTICATED ⟨~ animals⟩ **2** : made docile and submissive : SUBDUED **3** : lacking spirit, zest, interest, or the capacity to excite : INSIPID ⟨a ~ campaign⟩ — **tame·ly** *adv* — **tame·ness** *n*

[2]tame *vb* **tamed; tam·ing** *vt* (14c) **1 a** : to reduce from a wild to a domestic state **b** : to subject to cultivation **c** : to bring under control : HARNESS **2** : to deprive of spirit : HUMBLE, SUBDUE ⟨the once revolutionary ... party, long since *tamed* —*Times Lit. Supp.*⟩ **3** : to tone down : SOFTEN ⟨*tamed* the language in the play⟩ ~ *vi* : to become tame — **tam·able** *or* **tame·able** \'tā-mə-bəl\ *adj* — **tam·er** *n*

tame·less \'tām-ləs\ *adj* (1597) : not tamed or not capable of being tamed

Tam·il \'tam-əl, 'tām-\ *n* (1734) **1** : a Dravidian language of Tamil Nadu state and of northern and eastern Ceylon **2** : a Tamil-speaking person or a descendant of Tamil-speaking ancestors

Tam·ma·ny \'tam-ə-nē\ *adj* [*Tammany Hall*, headquarters of the Tammany Society, political organization in New York City] (1887) : of, relating to, or constituting a group or organization exercising or seeking municipal political control by methods often associated with corruption and bossism — **Tam·ma·ny·ism** \-,iz-əm\ *n*

Tam·muz \'täm-,u̇z\ *n* [Heb *Tammūz*] (ca. 1769) : the 10th month of the civil year or the 4th month of the ecclesiastical year in the Jewish calendar — see MONTH table

Tam o' Shan·ter *n* **1** \,tam-ə-'shant-ər\ : the hero of Burns's poem *Tam o' Shanter* **2** *usu* **tam–o'–shanter** \'tam-ə-,\ : a woolen cap of Scottish origin with a tight headband, wide flat circular crown, and usu. a pompon in the center

[1]tamp \'tamp\ *vt* [prob. back-formation fr. obs. *tampion, tampin* (plug), fr. ME, fr. MF *tapon, tampon*, fr. (assumed) OF *taper* to plug, of Gmc origin; akin to OE *tæppa* tap] (1819) **1** : to fill up (a drill hole above a blasting charge) with material (as clay) to confine the force of the explosion **2** : to drive in or down by a succession of light or medium blows ⟨~ wet concrete⟩ **3** : to put a check on : REDUCE, LESSEN — **tamp·er** *n*

[2]tamp *n* (1920) : a tool for tamping

tam·per \'tam-pər\ *vi* **tam·pered; tam·per·ing** \-p(ə-)riŋ\ [prob. fr. MF *temprer* to temper, mix, meddle — more at TEMPER] (1567) **1** : to carry on underhand or improper negotiations (as by bribery) **2 a** : to interfere so as to weaken or change for the worse — used with *with* **b** : to try foolish or dangerous experiments — used with *with* — **tam·per·er** \-pər-ər\ *n* — **tam·per·proof** \,tam-pər-'prüf\ *adj*

tam·pi·on \'tam-pē-ən, 'täm-\ *n* [obs. *tampion, tampin* plug — more at TAMP] (1625) : a wooden plug or a metal or canvas cover for the muzzle of a gun

[1]tam·pon \ˈtam-ˌpän\ *n* [F, lit., plug, fr. MF — more at TAMP] (ca. 1860) **:** a plug (as of cotton) introduced into a cavity usu. to arrest hemorrhage or absorb secretions

[2]tampon *vt* (1860) **:** to plug with a tampon

tam–tam \ˈtam-ˌtam, ˈtäm-ˌtäm\ *n* [Hindi *ṭamṭam*] (1782) **1 :** TOM-TOM **2 :** GONG; *esp* **:** one of a tuned set in a gamelan orchestra

[1]tan \ˈtan\ *vb* **tanned; tan·ning** [ME *tannen,* fr. MF *tanner,* fr. ML *tannare,* fr. *tanum, tannum* tanbark] *vt* (15c) **1 a :** to convert (hide) into leather by treatment with an infusion of tannin-rich bark or other agent of similar effect **b :** to convert (protein) to leather or a similar substance **2 :** to make (skin) tan esp. by exposure to the sun **3 :** THRASH, WHIP ~ *vi* **:** to get or become tanned

[2]tan *adj* **tan·ner; tan·nest** (1586) **1 :** of, relating to, or used for tan or tanning **2 :** of the color tan

[3]tan *n* [F, tanbark, fr. OF, fr. ML *tanum*] (1674) **1 :** a tanning material or its active agent (as tannin) **2 :** a brown color imparted to the skin by exposure to the sun or wind **3 :** a variable color averaging a light yellowish brown **4** *pl* **:** tan-colored articles of clothing

tan·a·ger \ˈtan-i-jər\ *n* [NL *tanagra,* fr. Pg *tangará,* fr. Tupi] (1688) **:** any of numerous American passerine birds (family Thraupidae) having brightly colored males, being mainly unmusical, and chiefly inhabiting woodlands

tan·bark \ˈtan-ˌbärk\ *n* (1799) **1 :** a bark rich in tannin bruised or cut into small pieces and used in tanning **2 :** a surface (as a circus ring) covered with spent tanbark

[1]tan·dem \ˈtan-dəm\ *n* [L, at last, at length (taken to mean "lengthwise"), fr. *tam* so; akin to OE *thæt* that] (1785) **1 a** (1) **:** a 2-seated carriage drawn by horses harnessed one before the other (2) **:** a team so harnessed **b :** TANDEM BICYCLE **c :** a vehicle (as a motortruck) having close-coupled pairs of axles **2 :** a group of two or more arranged one behind the other or used or acting in conjunction — **in tandem 1 :** in a tandem arrangement **2 :** in partnership or conjunction

[2]tandem *adv* (ca. 1795) **:** one after or behind another ⟨ride ~⟩

[3]tandem *adj* (1815) **1 :** consisting of things or having parts arranged one behind the other **2 :** working or occurring in conjunction with each other

tandem bicycle *n* (ca. 1890) **:** a bicycle for two or more persons sitting tandem

tan·door \tän-ˈdu̇(ə)r\ *n, pl* **tan·doori** \-ˈdu̇(ə)r-ē\ [Punjabi *tandoor* clay oven; akin to Turk *tandir* oven] (1662) **:** a cylindrical clay oven in which food is cooked over charcoal

tan·doori \tän-ˈdu̇(ə)r-ē\ *adj* (ca. 1968) **:** cooked in a tandoor ⟨~ chicken⟩

[1]tang \ˈtaŋ\ *n* [ME, of Scand origin; akin to ON *tangi* point of land, tang] (15c) **1 :** a projecting shank, prong, fang, or tongue (as on a knife, file, or sword) to connect with the handle **2 a :** a sharp distinctive often lingering flavor **b :** a pungent odor **c :** something having the effect of a tang (as in stimulation of the senses) ⟨treated murder as a joke with a ~ to it —Graham Greene⟩ **3 a :** a faint suggestion **:** TRACE **b :** a distinguishing characteristic that sets apart or gives a special individuality — **tanged** \ˈtaŋd\ *adj*

[2]tang *vt* (1566) **1 :** to furnish with a tang **2 :** to affect with a tang

[3]tang *vb* [imit.] (1556) **:** CLANG, RING

[4]tang *n* (1669) **:** a sharp twanging sound

Tang \ˈtäŋ\ *n* [Chin (Pek) *t'ang²*] (ca. 1899) **:** a Chinese dynasty dated A.D. 618–907 and marked by wide contacts with other cultures and by the development of printing and the flourishing of poetry and art

tan·ge·lo \ˈtan-jə-ˌlō\ *n, pl* **-los** [blend of *tangerine* and *pomelo*] (ca. 1904) **:** a hybrid between a tangerine or mandarin orange and either a grapefruit or pomelo; *also* **:** its fruit

tan·gen·cy \ˈtan-jən-sē\ *n* (1819) **:** the quality or state of being tangent

[1]tan·gent \-jənt\ *adj* [L *tangent-, tangens,* prp. of *tangere* to touch; akin to OE *thaccian* to touch gently, stroke] (1594) **1 a :** meeting a curve or surface in a single point if a sufficiently small interval is considered ⟨straight line ~ to a curve⟩ **b** (1) **:** having a common tangent line at a point ⟨~ curves⟩ (2) **:** having a common tangent plane at a point ⟨~ surfaces⟩ **2 :** diverging from an original purpose or course **:** IRRELEVANT ⟨~ remarks⟩

[2]tangent *n* [NL *tangent-, tangens,* fr. *linea tangens* tangent line] (1594) **1 :** the trigonometric function that for an acute angle is the ratio between the leg opposite to the angle when it is considered part of a right triangle and the leg adjacent **2 :** a line that is tangent; *specif* **:** a straight line that is the limiting position of a secant of a curve through a fixed point and a variable point on the curve as the variable point approaches the fixed point **3 :** an abrupt change of course **:** DIGRESSION ⟨the speaker went off on a ~⟩ **4 :** a small upright flat-ended metal pin at the inner end of a clavichord key that strikes the string to produce the tone **5 :** a straight section of a road or railroad

tan·gen·tial \tan-ˈjen-chəl\ *adj* (1630) **1 :** of, relating to, or of the nature of a tangent **2 :** acting along or lying in a tangent ⟨~ forces⟩ **3 a :** DIVERGENT, DIGRESSIVE **b :** touching lightly **:** INCIDENTAL, PERIPHERAL ⟨~ comment⟩ — **tan·gen·tial·ly** \-ˈjench-(ə-)lē\ *adv*

tangent line *n* (1713) **:** TANGENT 2

tangent plane *n* (ca. 1890) **:** the plane through a point of a surface that contains the tangent lines to all the curves on the surface through the same point

tan·ger·ine \ˈtan-jə-ˌrēn, ˌtan-jə-ˈ\ *n* [F *Tanger* Tangier, Morocco] (ca. 1841) **1 a :** any of various mandarins that have deep orange to almost scarlet skin and pulp and are grown in the U.S. and southern Africa; *broadly* **:** MANDARIN 3b **b :** a tree producing tangerines **2 :** a moderate to strong reddish orange

[1]tan·gi·ble \ˈtan-jə-bəl\ *adj* [LL *tangibilis,* fr. L *tangere* to touch] (1589) **1 a :** capable of being perceived esp. by the sense of touch **:** PALPABLE **b :** substantially real **:** MATERIAL **2 :** capable of being precisely identified or realized by the mind **3 :** capable of being appraised at an actual or approximate value ⟨~ assets⟩ ***syn*** see PERCEPTIBLE — **tan·gi·bil·i·ty** \ˌtan-jə-ˈbil-ət-ē\ *n* — **tan·gi·ble·ness** \ˈtan-jə-bəl-nəs\ *n* — **tan·gi·bly** \-blē\ *adv*

[2]tangible *n* (1873) **:** something tangible; *esp* **:** a tangible asset

[1]tan·gle \ˈtaŋ-gəl\ *vb* **tan·gled; tan·gling** \-g(ə-)liŋ\ [ME *tangilen,* prob. of Scand origin; akin to Sw dial. *taggla* to tangle] *vt* (14c) **1 :** to involve so as to hamper, obstruct, or embarrass **2 :** to seize and hold in or as if in a snare **:** ENTRAP **3 :** to unite or knit together in intricate confusion ~ *vi* **1 :** to interact in a contentious or conflicting way **2 :** to become entangled

[2]tangle *n* (1615) **1 :** a tangled twisted mass (as of vines) **:** SNARL **2 a :** a complicated or confused state or condition **b :** a state of perplexity or complete bewilderment **3 :** a serious altercation **:** DISPUTE

[3]tangle *n* [of Scand origin; akin to ON *thǫngull* tangle, *thang* kelp] (1536) **:** a large seaweed

tan·gled \ˈtaŋ-gəld\ *adj* (1590) **1 :** existing in or giving the appearance of a state of utter disorder **2 :** very involved ⟨~ relationships⟩

tan·gle·ment \-gəl-mənt\ *n* (1831) **:** ENTANGLEMENT

tan·gly \ˈtaŋ-g(ə-)lē\ *adj* (1813) **:** full of tangles or knots **:** INTRICATE

[1]tan·go \ˈtaŋ-(ˌ)gō\ *n, pl* **tangos** [AmerSp] (1913) **:** a ballroom dance of Latin-American origin in $^2/_4$ time with a basic pattern of step-step-step-step-close and characterized by long pauses and stylized body positions; *also* **:** the music for this dance

[2]tango *vi* (1913) **:** to dance the tango

Tan·go (1952) — a communications code word for the letter *t*

tan·gram \ˈtaŋ-grəm, ˈtan-\ *n* [perh. fr. Chin (Pek) *t'ang²* Chinese + E *-gram*] (ca. 1864) **:** a Chinese puzzle made by cutting a square of thin material into five triangles, a square, and a rhomboid which are capable of being recombined in many different figures

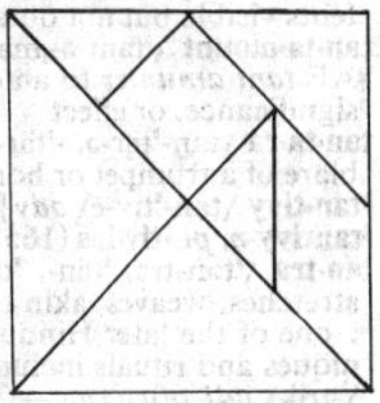

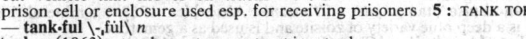

tangram

tangy \ˈtaŋ-ē\ *adj* **tang·i·er; -est** (1875) **:** having or suggestive of a tang

[1]tank \ˈtaŋk\ *n* [Pg *tanque,* alter. of *estanque,* fr. *estancar* to stanch, fr. (assumed) VL *stanticare* — more at STANCH] (1616) **1** *dial* **:** POND, POOL; *esp* **:** one built as a water supply **2 :** a usu. large receptacle for holding, transporting, or storing liquids **3 :** an enclosed heavily armed and armored combat vehicle that moves on tracks **4 :** a prison cell or enclosure used esp. for receiving prisoners **5 :** TANK TOP — **tank·ful** \-ˌfu̇l\ *n*

[2]tank *vt* (1863) **:** to place, store, or treat in a tank

tan·ka \ˈtäŋ-kə\ *n* [Jp] (1917) **:** an unrhymed Japanese verse form of five lines containing 5, 7, 5, 7, and 7 syllables respectively; *also* **:** a poem in this form — compare HAIKU

tank·age \ˈtaŋ-kij\ *n* (1866) **1 a :** the capacity or contents of a tank **b :** the aggregate of tanks required for a purpose **2 :** dried animal residues usu. freed from the fat and gelatin and used as fertilizer and feedstuff **3 a :** the act or process of putting or storing in tanks

tan·kard \ˈtaŋ-kərd\ *n* [ME] (15c) **:** a tall one-handled drinking vessel; *esp* **:** a silver or pewter mug with a lid

tank destroyer *n* (1941) **:** a highly mobile lightly armored vehicle usu. on a half-track or a tank chassis and mounting a cannon

tanked \ˈtaŋ(k)t\ *adj, slang* (1897) **:** DRUNK

tank·er \ˈtaŋ-kər\ *n* (1900) **1 a :** a cargo ship fitted with tanks for carrying liquid in bulk **b :** a vehicle on which a tank is mounted to carry fluids; *also* **:** a cargo airplane for transporting fuel **2 :** a member of a military tank crew

tank farm *n* (1923) **:** an area with tanks for storage of oil

tank suit *n* (1940) **:** a one-piece bathing suit with shoulder straps

tank top *n* (ca. 1950) **:** a sleeveless collarless shirt with shoulder straps and no front opening

tank town *n* [fr. the fact that formerly trains stopped at such towns only to take on water] (1913) **:** a small town

tank trailer *n* (1942) **:** a truck-drawn trailer equipped as a tanker

tan·nage \ˈtan-ij\ *n* (1662) **:** the act, process, or result of tanning

tan·nate \ˈtan-ˌāt\ *n* [F, fr. *tannin*] (1802) **:** a compound of a tannin

[1]tan·ner \ˈtan-ər\ *n* (bef. 12c) **:** one that tans hides

[2]tanner *n* [origin unknown] *Brit* (ca. 1811) **:** SIXPENCE

tan·nery \ˈtan-(ə-)rē\ *n, pl* **-ner·ies** (1736) **:** a place where tanning is carried on

tan·nic \ˈtan-ik\ *adj* [F *tannique,* fr. *tannin*] (ca. 1864) **1 :** of, resembling, or derived from tan or a tannin **2** *of wine* **:** containing an abundance of tannins **:** markedly astringent

tannic acid *n* (1836) **:** TANNIN 1

tan·nin \ˈtan-ən\ *n* [F, fr. *tanner* to tan] (1802) **1 :** any of various soluble astringent complex phenolic substances of plant origin used in tanning, dyeing, the making of ink, and in medicine **2 :** a substance that has a tanning effect

tan·ning \ˈtan-iŋ\ *n* (15c) **1 :** the art or process by which a skin is tanned **2 :** a browning of the skin by exposure to sun **3 :** a sound spanking **4 :** a natural darkening and hardening of the cuticle of an insect immediately after molting

tan·nish \ˈtan-ish\ *adj* (ca. 1938) **:** somewhat tan

tan oak *n* (ca. 1923) **:** an evergreen oak (*Lithocarpus densiflora*) of the Pacific coast area that yields tanbark and differs from the typical oaks esp. in having erect staminate catkins

Ta·no·an \ˈtän-ə-wən\ *n* [*Tano,* a group of former pueblos in New Mexico] (1946) **:** a language family of New Mexico — **Tanoan** *adj*

tan·sy \ˈtan-zē\ *n, pl* **tansies** [ME *tanesey,* fr. MF *tanesie,* fr. ML *athanasia,* fr. Gk, immortality, fr. *athanatos* immortal, fr. *a-* + *thanatos* death — more at THANATOS] (15c) **:** a common weedy composite herb (*Tanacetum vulgare*) with an aromatic odor, very bitter taste, and finely divided leaves; *broadly* **:** a plant of the same genus

tansy ragwort *n* (ca. 1900) **:** a common ragwort (*Senecio jacobaea*) that has yellow flower heads, is a troublesome weed in some areas, and is toxic to cattle

tan·ta·late \ˈtant-ᵊl-ˌāt\ *n* (1849) **:** a salt of a tantalic acid

tan·tal·ic \tan-ˈtal-ik\ *adj* (1842) **:** of, relating to, or derived from tantalum; *esp* **:** being one of the weak acids derived from the pentoxide of tantalum and known chiefly in salts

tantalise *Brit var of* TANTALIZE

tan·ta·lite \ˈtant-ᵊl-ˌīt\ *n* (1805) : a mineral $(FeMn)(TaNb)_2O_6$ consisting of a heavy dark lustrous oxide of iron, manganese, tantalum, and niobium

tan·ta·lize \ˈtant-ᵊl-ˌīz\ *vb* **-lized; -liz·ing** [*Tantalus*] *vt* (1597) : to tease or torment by or as if by presenting something desirable to the view but continually keeping it out of reach ~ *vi* : to cause one to be tantalized — **tan·ta·liz·er** *n*

tan·ta·liz·ing *adj* (1657) : possessing a quality that arouses or stimulates desire or interest; *also* : mockingly or teasingly out of reach — **tan·ta·liz·ing·ly** \-ˌī-ziŋ-lē\ *adv*

tan·ta·lum \ˈtant-ᵊl-əm\ *n* [NL, fr. L *Tantalus;* fr. its inability to absorb acid] (ca. 1809) : a hard ductile gray-white acid-resisting metallic element of the vanadium family found combined in rare minerals (as tantalite and columbite) — see ELEMENT table

Tan·ta·lus \ˈtant-ᵊl-əs\ *n* [L, fr. Gk *Tantalos*] **1** : a legendary king of Lydia condemned to stand up to the chin in a pool of water in Hades and beneath fruit-laden boughs only to have the water or fruit recede at each attempt to drink or eat **2** *not cap* : a locked cellarette with contents visible but not obtainable without a key

tan·ta·mount \ˈtant-ə-ˌmau̇nt\ *adj* [obs. *tantamount,* n. (equivalent), fr. AF *tant amunter* to amount to as much] (1641) : equivalent in value, significance, or effect

tan·ta·ra \tan-ˈtar-ə, -ˈtär-\ *n* [L *taratantara,* of imit. origin] (1537) : the blare of a trumpet or horn

[1]tan·tivy \tan-ˈtiv-ē\ *adv* [origin unknown] (1641) : at a gallop

[2]tantivy *n, pl* **-tiv·ies** (1658) **1** : a rapid gallop or ride **2** : TANTARA

tan·tra \ˈtən-trə, ˈtän-, ˈtan-\ *n, often cap* [Skt, lit., warp, fr. *tanoti* he stretches, weaves; akin to Gk *teinein* to stretch — more at THIN] (1799) : one of the later Hindu or Buddhist scriptures dealing esp. with techniques and rituals including meditative and sexual practices — **tan·tric** \-trik\ *adj, often cap* — **Tan·trism** \-ˌtriz-əm\ *n* — **Tan·trist** \-trəst\ *n*

tan·trum \ˈtan-trəm\ *n* [origin unknown] (1748) : a fit of bad temper

tan·yard \ˈtan-ˌyärd\ *n* (1666) : the section or part of a tannery housing tanning vats

tan·za·nite \ˈtan-zə-ˌnīt\ *n* [*Tanzania,* Africa] (ca. 1968) : a mineral that is a deep blue variety of zoisite and is used as a gemstone

Tao \ˈdau̇, ˈtau̇\ *n* [Chin (Pek) *tao⁴*, lit., way] (1736) **1** : the creative principle that orders the universe as conceived by Taoists **2** *often not cap* : the path of virtuous conduct as conceived by Confucians

Tao·ism \-ˌiz-əm\ *n* [*Tao*] (1838) **1** : a Chinese mystical philosophy traditionally founded by Lao-tzu in the 6th century B.C. that teaches conformity to the Tao by unassertive action and simplicity **2** : a religion developed from Taoist philosophy and folk and Buddhist religion and concerned with obtaining long life and good fortune often by magical means — **Tao·ist** \-əst\ *adj or n* — **Tao·is·tic** \dau̇-ˈis-tik, tau̇-\ *adj*

[1]tap \ˈtap\ *n* [ME *tappe,* fr. OE *tæppa;* akin to OHG *zapho* tap] (bef. 12c) **1 a** : a plug for a hole (as in a cask) : SPIGOT **b** : a device consisting of a spout and valve attached to the end of a pipe to control the flow of a fluid : COCK **2 a** : liquor drawn through a tap **b** : the procedure of removing fluid (as from a body cavity) **3** : a tool for forming an internal screw thread **4** : an intermediate point in an electric circuit where a connection may be made **5** : the action or an instance of wiretapping — **on tap 1** : ready to be drawn from a large container (as a cask or keg) ⟨ale *on tap*⟩ **2** : broached or furnished with a tap **3** : on hand : AVAILABLE ⟨other sports and entertainment facilities are *on tap* —Richard Joseph⟩

[2]tap *vt* **tapped; tap·ping** (15c) **1** : to let out or cause to flow by piercing or by drawing a plug from the containing vessel ⟨~ wine from a cask⟩ **2 a** : to pierce so as to let out or draw off a fluid ⟨~ maple trees⟩ **b** : to draw out, from, or upon ⟨~ new sources of revenue⟩: as **(1)** : to cut in on (a telephone or telegraph wire) to get information **(2)** : to cut in (an electrical circuit) on another circuit **3** : to form a female screw in by means of a tap **4** : to get money from as a loan or gift **5** : to connect (a street gas or water main) with a local supply — **tap·per** *n*

[3]tap *vb* **tapped; tap·ping** [ME *tappen,* fr. MF *taper* to strike with the flat of the hand, of Gmc origin; akin to MHG *tāpe* paw, blow dealt with the paw] *vt* (13c) **1** : to strike lightly esp. with a slight sound **2** : to give a light blow with ⟨~ a pencil on the table⟩ **3** : to bring about by repeated light blows ⟨~ out a by-line on the typewriter⟩ **4** : to repair by putting a tap on **5** : SELECT, DESIGNATE ⟨was *tapped* for police commissioner⟩; *specif* : to elect to membership (as in a fraternity) ~ *vi* **1** : to strike a light audible blow : RAP **2** : to walk with light audible steps **3** : TAP-DANCE — **tap·per** *n*

[4]tap *n* (14c) **1 a** : a light usu. audible blow; *also* : its sound **b** : one of several usu. rapid drumbeats on a snare drum **2** : HALF SOLE **3** : a small metal plate for the sole or heel of a shoe **4** : TAP DANCE

ta·pa \ˈtäp-ə, ˈtap-\ *n* [Marquesan & Tahitian] (1823) : a coarse cloth made in the Pacific islands from the pounded bark esp. of the paper mulberry and usu. decorated with geometric patterns

tap dance *n* (1928) : a step dance tapped out audibly by means of shoes with hard soles or soles and heels to which taps have been added — **tap–dance** *vi* — **tap dancer** *n* — **tap dancing** *n*

[1]tape \ˈtāp\ *n* [ME, fr. OE *tæppe*] (bef. 12c) **1** : a narrow woven fabric **2** : a string stretched breast-high above the finishing line of a race **3** : a narrow flexible strip or band; *esp* : MAGNETIC TAPE **4** : TAPE RECORDING

[2]tape *vb* **taped; tap·ing** *vt* (1609) **1** : to fasten, tie, bind, cover, or support with tape **2** : to measure with a tape measure **3** : to record on tape and esp. magnetic tape ⟨~ an interview⟩ ~ *vi* : to record something on tape and esp. magnetic tape

[3]tape *adj* (1952) **1** : recorded on tape ⟨~ music⟩ **2** : intended for use with recording (as magnetic) tape ⟨a ~ cartridge⟩

tape deck *n* (1949) : a device used to play back and often to record on magnetic tape that usu. has to be connected to an audio system

tape grass *n* (1817) : a submerged aquatic plant (*Vallisneria spiralis* of the family Vallisneriaceae) with long ribbonlike leaves

tape measure *n* (1845) : a narrow strip (as of a limp cloth or steel tape) marked off in units (as inches or centimeters) for measuring

tape player *n* (1954) : a self-contained device for the playback of recorded magnetic tapes

[1]ta·per \ˈtā-pər\ *n* [ME, fr. OE, prob. fr. L *papyrus*] (bef. 12c) **1 a** : a slender candle **b** : a long waxed wick used esp. for lighting candles, lamps, pipes, or fires **c** : a feeble light **2 a** : a tapering form or figure **b** : gradual diminution of thickness, diameter, or width in an elongated object **c** : a gradual decrease

[2]taper *adj* (15c) **1** : progressively narrowed toward one end **2** : furnished with or adjusted to a scale : GRADUATED ⟨~ freight rates⟩

[3]taper *vb* **ta·pered; ta·per·ing** \ˈtā-p(ə-)riŋ\ *vi* (1610) **1** : to become progressively smaller toward one end **2** : to diminish gradually ~ *vt* : to cause to taper

[4]tap·er \ˈtā-pər\ *n* [[1]*tape*] (ca. 1920) : one that applies or dispenses tape

tape–re·cord \ˌtā-pri-ˈkȯ(ə)rd, ˈtā-pri-ˌ\ *vt* [back-formation fr. *tape recording*] (1950) : to make a recording of on magnetic tape

tape recorder *n* (1932) : a device for recording on and playing back magnetic tape

tape recording *n* (1940) : magnetic recording on magnetic tape; *also* : a recording made by this process

ta·per·er \ˈtā-pər-ər\ *n* (15c) : one who bears a taper in a religious procession

taper off *vb* (1848) : TAPER ⟨business growth had *tapered off* seriously while the unemployment rate had climbed — *Current Biog.*⟩

ta·per·stick \ˈtā-pər-ˌstik\ *n* (1546) : a candlestick for holding small tapers

tap·es·tried \ˈtap-ə-strēd\ *adj* (1630) **1** : covered or decorated with or as if with tapestry **2** : woven or depicted in tapestry

tap·es·try \ˈtap-ə-strē\ *n, pl* **-tries** [ME *tapistry,* modif. of MF *tapisserie,* fr. *tapisser* to carpet, cover with tapestry, fr. OF *tapis* carpet, fr. Gk *tapēs* rug, carpet] (15c) **1** : a heavy handwoven reversible textile used for hangings, curtains, and upholstery and characterized by complicated pictorial designs **2** : a nonreversible imitation of tapestry used chiefly for upholstery **3** : embroidery on canvas resembling woven tapestry ⟨needlepoint ~⟩ **4** : something resembling tapestry (as in complexity or richness of design)

tapestry carpet *n* (1852) : a carpet in which the designs are printed in colors on the threads before the fabric is woven

ta·pe·tum \tə-ˈpēt-əm\ *n, pl* **ta·pe·ta** \-ˈpēt-ə\ [NL, fr. L *tapete* carpet, tapestry, fr. Gk *tapēt-, tapēs* rug, carpet] (1713) **1** : any of various membranous layers or areas esp. of the choroid coat and retina of the eye **2** : a layer of nutritive cells that invests the sporogenous tissue in the sporangium of higher plants

tape·worm \ˈtāp-ˌwərm\ *n* [fr. its shape] (1752) : any of numerous cestode worms (as of the genus *Taenia*) parasitic when adult in the intestine of man or other vertebrates

tap·hole \ˈtap-ˌhōl\ *n* (1594) : a hole for a tap; *specif* : a hole at or near the bottom of a furnace or ladle through which molten metal, matte, or slag can be tapped

tap·i·o·ca \ˌtap-ē-ˈō-kə\ *n* [Sp & Pg, fr. Tupi *typyóca*] (1707) **1** : a usu. granular preparation of cassava starch used esp. in puddings and as a thickening in liquid food; *also* : a dish (as pudding) containing tapioca **2** : a cassava plant — called also *tapioca plant*

ta·pir \ˈtā-pər *also* ˈtā-ˌpi(ə)r *or* tə-ˈpi(ə)r\ *n, pl* **tapir** *or* **tapirs** [Tupi *tapiíra*] (1774) : any of several large inoffensive chiefly nocturnal ungulates (family Tapiridae) of tropical America, Malaya, and Sumatra related to the horses and rhinoceroses

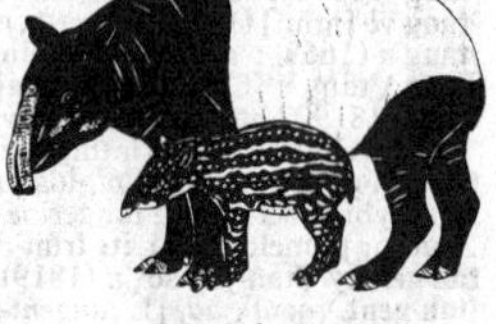
tapir

tapis *n* [ME, fr. MF — more at TAPESTRY] *obs* (15c) : tapestry or similar material used for hangings and floor and table coverings — **on the ta·pis** \-ˈtap-ˌē, -ta-ˈpē\ : under consideration

tap–off \ˈtap-ˌȯf\ *n* (ca. 1932) : [1]TIP-OFF

tap pants *n pl* (1979) : a loose-fitting woman's undergarment of a style similar to pants formerly worn for tap dancing

tap·pet \ˈtap-ət\ *n* [irreg. fr. [3]*tap*] (1745) : a lever or projection moved by some other piece (as a cam) or intended to tap or touch something else to cause a particular motion

tap·ping *n* (1597) : the act, process, or means by which something is tapped

tap·pit hen \ˈtap-ət-\ *n* [Sc *tappit,* alter. of E *topped*] *Scot* (1721) : a drinking vessel with a knob on the lid

tap·room \ˈtap-ˌrüm, -ˌru̇m\ *n* (1807) : BARROOM

tap·root \-ˌrüt, -ˌru̇t\ *n* [[1]*tap*] (1601) **1** : a primary root that grows vertically downward and gives off small lateral roots **2** : the central element or position in a line of growth or development

taps \ˈtaps\ *n pl but sing or pl in constr* [prob. alter. of earlier *taptoo* tattoo — more at TATTOO] (1824) : the last bugle call at night blown as a signal that lights are to be put out; *also* : a similar call blown at military funerals and memorial services

tap·sal–tee·rie \ˌtap-səl-ˈtē-rē\ *adv* [by alter.] *Scot* (1623) : TOPSY-TURVY

tap·ster \ˈtap-stər\ *n* [ME, fr. OE *tæppestre* female tapster, barmaid, fr. *tæppere* barkeeper (fr. *tæppa* tap) + *-estre* -ster] (bef. 12c) : one employed to dispense liquors in a barroom

[1]tar \ˈtär\ *n* [ME *terr, tarr,* fr. OE *teoru;* akin to OE *trēow* tree — more at TREE] (bef. 12c) **1 a** : a dark brown or black bituminous usu. odorous viscous liquid obtained by destructive distillation of organic material (as wood, coal, or peat) **b** : a substance in some respects resembling tar; *esp* : a condensable residue present in smoke from burning tobacco that contains combustion by-products (as resins, acids, phenols, and essential oils) **2** [short for *tarpaulin*] : SAILOR

[2]tar *vt* **tarred; tar·ring** (13c) : to smear with or as if with tar — **tar and feather** : to smear (a person) with tar and cover with feathers as a punishment or indignity

[3]tar *or* **tarre** \ˈtär\ *vt* **tarred; tar·ring; tars** *or* **tarres** [ME *terren, tarren,* fr. OE *tyrwan*] (bef. 12c) : to urge to action — usu. used with *on*

Tara·ca·hi·tian \ˌtar-ə-kə-ˈhē-shən\ *adj* [*Tara*humara (a Mexican people) + *Cahita* (a Mexican people)] (ca. 1940) : of, relating to, or constituting a language family of the Uto-Aztecan phylum

tar·a·did·dle *or* **tar·ra·did·dle** \ˌtar-ə-ˈdid-ᵊl, ˈtar-ə-ˌ\ *n* [origin unknown] (ca. 1796) **1** : a minor falsehood : FIB **2** : pretentious nonsense

tar·an·tel·la \ˌtar-ən-'tel-ə\ *n* [It, fr. *Taranto,* Italy] (ca. 1782) : a vivacious folk dance of southern Italy in 6/8 time

tar·an·tism \'tar-ən-ˌtiz-əm\ *n* [NL *tarantismus,* fr. *Taranto,* Italy] (1638) : a dancing mania or malady of late medieval Europe

ta·ran·tu·la \tə-'ranch-(ə-)lə, -'rant-ᵊl-ə\ *n, pl* **ta·ran·tu·las** *also* **ta·ran·tu·lae** \-'ran-chə-ˌlē, -'rant-ᵊl-ˌē\ [ML, fr. OIt *tarantola,* fr. *Taranto*] (1561) **1 :** a European wolf spider (*Lycosa tarentula*) popularly held to be the cause of tarantism **2 :** any of various large hairy spiders (family Theraphosidae) that are typically rather sluggish and though capable of biting sharply are not significantly poisonous to man

ta·rax·a·cum \tə-'rak-si-kəm\ *n* [NL, fr. Ar *ṭarakhshaqūn* wild chicory] (1845) : the dried rhizome and roots of a dandelion (*Taraxacum officinale*) used as a diuretic, a tonic, and an aperient

tar baby *n* [fr. the tar baby which confounded Brer Rabbit in a story in *Uncle Remus: His Songs and His Stories* (1880) by Joel Chandler Harris] (1926) : something from which it is nearly impossible to extricate oneself

tar·boosh *also* **tar·bush** \tär-'büsh, 'tär-ˌ\ *n* [Ar *ṭarbūsh*] (ca. 1702) : a red hat similar to the fez worn esp. by Muslim men

tar·di·grade \'tärd-ə-ˌgrād\ *n* [deriv. of L *tardigradus* slow-moving, fr. *tardus* slow + *gradi* to step, go — more at GRADE] (1847) : any of a division (Tardigrada) of microscopic arthropods with four pairs of legs that live usu. in water or damp moss — **tardigrade** *adj*

tar·di·ly \'tärd-ᵊl-ē\ *adv* (1597) **1 :** at a slow pace **2 :** LATE

tar·dive dyskinesia \ˌtärd-iv-\ *n* [*tardive* tending toward late development (fr. F, fem. of *tardif,* fr. MF) + *dyskinesia*] (1964) : a central nervous system disorder characterized by twitching of the face and tongue and involuntary motor movements of the trunk and limbs and occurring esp. as a side effect of prolonged use of antipsychotic drugs (as phenothiazine)

tar·do \'tärd-(ˌ)ō\ *adj* [It, fr. L *tardus*] (ca. 1847) : SLOW — used as a direction in music

1tar·dy \'tärd-ē\ *adj* **tar·di·er; -est** [alter. of earlier *tardif,* fr. MF, fr. (assumed) VL *tardivus,* fr. L *tardus*] (15c) **1 :** moving slowly : SLUGGISH **2 :** delayed beyond the expected or proper time : LATE — **tar·di·ness** \'tärd-ē-nəs\ *n*

2tardy *n, pl* **tardies** (1960) : an instance of being tardy (as to a class)

1tare \'ta(ə)r, 'te(ə)r\ *n* [ME] (14c) **1 a :** the seed of a vetch **b :** any of several vetches (esp. *Vicia sativa* and *V. hirsuta*) **2 :** a weed of grainfields usu. held to be the darnel **3** *pl* **:** an undesirable element

2tare *n* [ME, fr. MF, fr. OIt *tara,* fr. Ar *ṭarḥa,* lit., that which is removed] (15c) **1 :** a deduction from the gross weight of a substance and its container made in allowance for the weight of the container **2 :** COUNTERWEIGHT; *esp* **:** an empty vessel similar to a container used to counterpoise change in weight of the container due to conditions (as temperature or moisture)

3tare *vt* **tared; tar·ing** (1812) : to ascertain or mark the tare of; *esp* **:** to weigh so as to determine the tare

targe \'tärj\ *n* [ME, fr. OF] (13c) : a light shield

1tar·get \'tär-gət\ *n, often attrib* [ME, fr. MF *targette,* dim. of *targe* light shield, of Gmc origin; akin to ON *targa* shield] (15c) **1 :** a small round shield **2 a :** a mark to shoot at **b :** a target marked by shots fired at it **c :** something fired at **3 a :** an object of ridicule or criticism **b :** something or someone to be affected by an action or development **c :** a goal to be achieved **4 a :** a railroad day signal that is attached to a switch stand and indicates whether the switch is open or closed **b :** a sliding sight on a surveyor's leveling rod **5 a :** the metallic surface usu. of platinum or tungsten upon which the stream of cathode rays within an X-ray tube is focused and from which the X rays are emitted **b :** a body, surface, or material bombarded with nuclear particles or electrons; *esp* **:** fluorescent material on which desired visual effects are produced in electronic devices (as in radar) — **off target :** not valid : INACCURATE — **on target :** precisely correct or valid esp. in interpreting or addressing a problem or vital issue

2target *vt* (1837) **1 :** to make a target of; *esp* **:** to set as a goal **2 :** to direct or use toward a target

tar·get·able \'tär-gət-ə-bəl\ *adj* (1964) : capable of being aimed at a target ⟨missiles with ~ warheads⟩

target date *n* (1945) : the date set for an event or for the completion of a project, goal, or quota

target language *n* (1953) : a language into which another language is to be translated — compare SOURCE LANGUAGE

Tar·gum \'tär-ˌgüm, -ˌgüm\ *n* [LHeb *targūm,* fr. Aram, translation] (1587) : an Aramaic translation or paraphrase of a portion of the Old Testament

Tar·heel \'tär-ˌhēl\ *n* (1864) : a native or resident of North Carolina — used as a nickname

1tar·iff \'tar-əf\ *n* [It *tariffa,* fr. Ar *ta'rīf* notification] (1592) **1 a :** a schedule of duties imposed by a government on imported or in some countries exported goods **b :** a duty or rate of duty imposed in such a schedule **2 :** a schedule of rates or charges of a business or a public utility **3 :** PRICE, CHARGE

2tariff *vt* (ca. 1828) : to subject to a tariff

tar·la·tan \'tär-lət-ᵊn\ *n* [F *tarlatane*] (1727) : a sheer cotton fabric in open plain weave usu. heavily sized for stiffness

tar·mac \'tär-ˌmak\ *n* [fr. *Tarmac,* a trademark] (1905) : a tarmacadam road, apron, or runway

Tarmac *trademark* — used for a bituminous binder for roads

tar·mac·ad·am \ˌtär-mə-'kad-əm\ *n* (1882) **1 :** a pavement constructed by spraying or pouring a tar binder over layers of crushed stone and then rolling **2 :** a material of tar and aggregates mixed in a plant and shaped on the roadway

tarn \'tärn\ *n* [ME *terne,* of Scand origin; akin to ON *tjǫrn* small lake] (14c) : a small steep-banked mountain lake or pool

1tar·nish \'tär-nish\ *vb* [MF *terniss-,* stem of *ternir*] *vt* (1598) **1 :** to dull or destroy the luster of by or as if by air, dust, or dirt : SOIL, STAIN **2 a :** to detract from the good quality of : VITIATE ⟨his fine dreams now slightly ~*ed*⟩ **b :** to bring disgrace on : SULLY ~ *vi* **:** to become tarnished — **tar·nish·able** \-ə-bəl\ *adj*

2tarnish *n* (1738) : something that tarnishes; *esp* **:** a film of chemically altered material on the surface of a metal (as silver)

tarnished plant bug *n* (ca. 1890) : a common and widespread destructive bug (*Lygus oblineatus*) that causes injury to plants by sucking sap from buds, leaves, and fruits and that carries plant diseases

ta·ro \'tär-(ˌ)ō, 'tar-, 'ter-\ *n, pl* **taros** [Tahitian & Maori] (1769) : a plant (*Colocasia esculenta*) of the arum family grown throughout the tropics for its edible starchy tuberous rootstocks and in temperate regions for ornament; *also* **:** its rootstock

tar·ok \'tar-ˌäk\ *n* [It *tarocchi* tarots] (1739) : an old card game popular in central Europe and played with a pack containing 40, 52, or 56 cards equivalent to modern playing cards plus the 22 tarots

tar·ot \'tar-(ˌ)ō\ *n* [MF, fr. It *tarocchi* (pl.)] (1673) : any of a set of 22 pictorial playing cards used for fortune-telling and serving as trumps in tarok

tarp \'tärp\ *n* (1906) : TARPAULIN

tar paper *n* (1891) : a heavy paper coated or impregnated with tar for use esp. in building

tar·pau·lin \tär-'pò-lən, 'tär-pə-; ÷tär-'pōl-yən\ *n* [prob. fr. 1*tar* + *-palling, -pauling* (fr. *pall*)] (1605) **1 :** a piece of material (as waterproofed canvas) used for protecting exposed objects **2 :** SAILOR

tar pit *n* (1839) : an area in which natural bitumens collect and are exposed at the earth's surface and which tends to trap animals and preserve their hard parts

tar·pon \'tär-pən\ *n, pl* **tarpon** *or* **tarpons** [origin unknown] (1685) : a large silvery elongate teleost sport fish (*Megalops atlanticus* syn *Tarpon atlanticus* of the family Elopidae) that occurs esp. in warm coastal waters of the Atlantic and on the Pacific side of Central America and reaches a length of about six feet

tar·ra·gon \'tar-ə-gən\ *n* [MF *targon,* fr. ML *tarchon,* fr. Ar *ṭarkhūn*] (ca. 1538) : a small European perennial wormwood (*Artemisia dracunculus*) grown for its pungent aromatic foliage which is used as a flavoring (as in making pickles and vinegar); *also* **:** its foliage

tarre *var of* TAR

tar·ri·ance \'tar-ē-ən(t)s\ *n* (15c) : the act or an instance of tarrying

1tar·ry \'tar-ē\ *vi* **tar·ried; tar·ry·ing** [ME *tarien*] (14c) **1 a :** to delay or be tardy in acting or doing **b :** to linger in expectation : WAIT **2 :** to abide or stay in or at a place

2tarry *n, pl* **tarries** (14c) : STAY, SOJOURN

3tar·ry \'tär-ē\ *adj* (1552) : of, resembling, or covered with tar

1tar·sal \'tär-səl\ *adj* (1817) **1 :** of or relating to the tarsus **2 :** being or relating to plates of dense connective tissue that serve to stiffen the eyelids

2tarsal *n* (1881) : a tarsal part (as a bone or cartilage)

tar sand *n* (1899) : a natural impregnation of sand or sandstone with petroleum from which the lighter portions have escaped

tar·si·er \'tär-sē-ər, -sē-ˌā\ *n* [F, fr. *tarse* tarsus, fr. NL *tarsus*] (ca. 1774) : any of several small nocturnal arboreal mammals (genus *Tarsius*) related to the lemurs and found in parts of the Malay archipelago

tar·so·meta·tar·sus \ˌtär-(ˌ)sō-ˌmet-ə-ˌtär-səs\ *n* [NL, fr. *tarsus* + -o- + *metatarsus*] (1854) : the large compound bone of the tarsus of a bird; *also* **:** the segment of the limb it supports

tar·sus \'tär-səs\ *n, pl* **tar·si** \-ˌsī, -ˌsē\ [NL, fr. Gk *tarsos* wickerwork mat, flat of the foot, ankle, edge of the eyelid; akin to Gk *tersesthai* to become dry — more at THIRST] (1676) **1 :** the part of the foot of a vertebrate between the metatarsus and the leg; *also* **:** the small bones that support this part of the limb **2 :** the tarsal plate of the eyelid **3 :** the distal part of the limb of an arthropod **4 :** TARSOMETATARSUS

1tart \'tärt\ *adj* [ME, fr. OE *teart* sharp, severe; akin to MHG *traz* spite] (14c) **1 :** agreeably sharp or acid to the taste **2 :** marked by a biting, acrimonious, or cutting quality — **tart·ish** \'tärt-ish\ *adj* — **tart·ly** *adv* — **tart·ness** *n*

2tart *n* [ME *tarte,* fr. MF] (15c) **1 a :** a small pie or pastry shell containing jelly, custard, or fruit **b** *Brit* **:** PIE **2 :** PROSTITUTE

tar·tan \'tärt-ᵊn\ *n* [prob. fr. MF *tiretaine* linsey-woolsey] (1550) **1 :** a plaid textile design of Scottish origin consisting of stripes of varying width and color usu. patterned to designate a distinctive clan **2 a :** a twilled woolen fabric with tartan design **b :** a fabric with tartan design **3 :** a garment of tartan design

1tar·tar \'tärt-ər\ *n* [ME, fr. ML *tartarum*] (14c) **1 :** a substance consisting essentially of cream of tartar that is derived from the juice of grapes and deposited in wine casks together with yeast and other suspended matters as a pale or dark reddish crust or sediment; *esp* **:** a recrystallized product yielding cream of tartar on further purification **2 :** an incrustation on the teeth consisting of salivary secretion, food residue, and various salts (as calcium carbonate)

2tartar *n* [ME *Tartre,* fr. MF *Tartare,* prob. fr. ML *Tartarus,* modif. of Per *Tātār* — more at TATAR] (14c) **1** *cap* **:** a native or inhabitant of Tatary **2** *cap* **:** TATAR 2 **3** *often cap* **:** a person of irritable or violent temper **4 :** one that proves to be unexpectedly formidable — **Tartar** *adj* — **Tar·tar·i·an** \tär-'tar-ē-ən, -'ter-\ *adj*

Tar·tar·e·an \tär-'tar-ē-ən, -'ter-\ *adj* [L *tartareus,* fr. Gk *tartareios,* fr. *Tartaros*] (ca. 1623) : of, relating to, or resembling Tartarus : INFERNAL

tartar emetic *n* (1704) : a poisonous efflorescent crystalline salt $KSbOC_4H_4O_6 \cdot {}^1/_2H_2O$ of sweetish metallic taste that is used in dyeing as a mordant and in medicine esp. in the treatment of amebiasis

tar·tar·ic acid \(ˌ)tär-ˌtar-ik-\ *n* (1810) : a strong dicarboxylic acid $C_4H_6O_6$ of plant origin that occurs in four optically isomeric crystalline forms, is usu. obtained from tartar, and is used esp. in food and medicines, in photography, and in making salts and esters

tar·tar sauce *or* **tar·tare sauce** \ˌtärt-ər-\ *n* [F *sauce tartare*] (1855) : a sauce made with mayonnaise and chopped pickles

Tar·ta·rus \'tärt-ə-rəs\ *n* [L, fr. Gk *Tartaros*] : a section of Hades reserved for punishment of the wicked

tart·let \'tärt-lət\ *n* (15c) : a small tart

tar·trate \'tär-ˌtrāt\ *n* [ISV, fr. F *tartre* tartar, fr. ML *tartarum*] (1794) : a salt or ester of tartaric acid

Tar·tuffe \tär-'tu̇f, -'tüf\ *n* [F *Tartufe*] : a religious hypocrite and protagonist in Molière's play *Tartuffe*

---

tart up *vt, chiefly Brit* (1947) : DRESS UP, FANCY UP ⟨*tarted up* pubs and restaurants for the spenders —Arnold Ehrlich⟩
Tar·via \ˈtär-vē-ə\ *trademark* — used for a viscid surfacing and binding material for roads
Tar·zan \ˈtärz-ᵊn, ˈtär-ˌzan\ *n* [*Tarzan*, hero of adventure stories by Edgar Rice Burroughs] (1945) : a well-built, agile, and very strong man
[1]task \ˈtask\ *n* [ME *taske*, fr. ONF *tasque*, fr. ML *tasca* tax or service imposed by a feudal superior, fr. *taxare* to tax] (14c) **1 a :** a usu. assigned piece of work often to be finished within a certain time **b :** something hard or unpleasant that has to be done **c :** DUTY, FUNCTION **2 :** subjection to adverse criticism : REPRIMAND —used in the expressions *to take, call,* or *bring to task*
syn TASK, DUTY, JOB, CHORE, STINT, ASSIGNMENT mean a piece of work to be done. TASK implies work imposed by a person in authority or an employer or by circumstance; DUTY implies an obligation to perform or responsibility for performance; JOB applies to a piece of work voluntarily performed; it may sometimes suggest difficulty or importance; CHORE implies a minor routine activity necessary for maintaining a household or farm; STINT implies a carefully allotted or measured quantity of assigned work or service; ASSIGNMENT implies a definite limited task assigned by one in authority.
[2]task *vt* (15c) **1** *obs* : to impose a tax on **2 :** to assign a task to **3 :** to oppress with great labor ⟨~*s* his mind with petty details⟩
task force *n* (1941) : a temporary grouping under one leader for the purpose of accomplishing a definite objective
task·mas·ter \ˈtask-ˌmas-tər\ *n* (1530) : one that imposes a task or burdens another with labor
task·mis·tress \-ˌmis-trəs\ *n* (1630) : a female taskmaster
Tas·ma·nian devil \(ˌ)taz-ˌmā-nē-ən-, -nyən-\ *n* (ca. 1890) : a powerful carnivorous burrowing Tasmanian marsupial (*Sarcophilus ursinus*) that is about the size of a large cat or badger and has a black coat marked with white on the chest
Tasmanian wolf *n* (ca. 1890) : a carnivorous marsupial (*Thylacinus cynocephalus*) that was formerly common in Australia but is now limited to the remoter parts of Tasmania and that somewhat resembles a dog — called also *Tasmanian tiger*

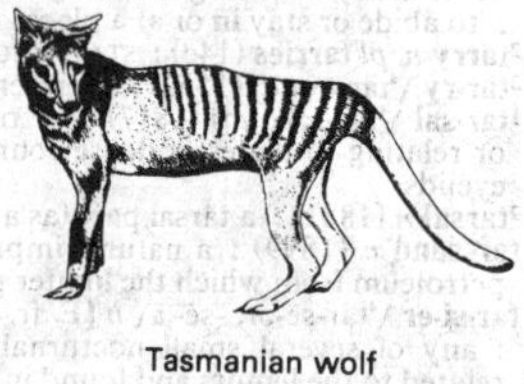
Tasmanian wolf

tasse \ˈtas\ *n* [perh. fr. MF *tasse* purse, pouch] (1548) : one of a series of overlapping metal plates in a suit of armor that form a short skirt over the body below the waist
[1]tas·sel \ˈtas-əl, *oftenest of corn* ˈtäs-, ˈtȯs-\ *n* [ME, clasp, tassel, fr. MF, fr. (assumed) VL *tassellus*, fr. L *taxillus* small die; akin to L *talus* anklebone, die] (14c) **1 :** a dangling ornament made by laying parallel a bunch of cords or threads of even length and fastening them at one end **2 :** something resembling a tassel; *esp* : the terminal male inflorescence of some plants and esp. Indian corn
[2]tassel *vb* **-seled** *or* **-selled; -sel·ing** *or* **-sel·ling** \-(ə-)liŋ\ *vt* (14c) : to adorn with tassels ~ *vi* : to put forth tassel inflorescences
[1]taste \ˈtāst\ *vb* **tast·ed; tast·ing** [ME *tasten* to touch, test, taste, fr. MF *taster*, fr. (assumed) VL *taxitare*, freq. of L *taxare* to touch — more at TAX] *vt* (14c) **1 :** to become acquainted with by experience ⟨has *tasted* the frustration of defeat⟩ **2 :** to ascertain the flavor of by taking a little into the mouth **3 :** to eat or drink esp. in small quantities ⟨the first food I've *tasted* in days⟩ **4 :** to perceive or recognize as if by the sense of taste **5** *archaic* : APPRECIATE, ENJOY ~ *vi* **1 :** to eat or drink a little **2 :** to test the flavor of something by taking a small part into the mouth **3 :** to have perception, experience, or enjoyment : PARTAKE — often used with *of* **4 :** to have a specific flavor ⟨the milk ~*s* sour⟩
[2]taste *n* (14c) **1** *obs* : TEST **2 a** *obs* : the act of tasting **b :** a small amount tasted **c :** a small amount : BIT; *esp* : a sample of experience ⟨her first ~ of success⟩ **3 :** the one of the special senses that perceives and distinguishes the sweet, sour, bitter, or salty quality of a dissolved substance and is mediated by taste buds on the tongue **4 :** the objective sweet, sour, bitter, or salty quality of a dissolved substance as perceived by the sense of taste **5 a :** a sensation obtained from a substance in the mouth that is typically produced by the stimulation of the sense of taste combined with those of touch and smell : FLAVOR **b :** the distinctive quality of an experience ⟨the attempt to cheat left a bad ~ in my mouth⟩ **6 :** individual preference : INCLINATION **7 a :** critical judgment, discernment, or appreciation **b :** manner or aesthetic quality indicative of such discernment or appreciation
taste bud *n* (ca. 1890) : an end organ mediating the sensation of taste and lying chiefly in the epithelium of the tongue
taste·ful \ˈtāst-fəl\ *adj* (1611) **1 :** TASTY 1a **2 :** having, exhibiting, or conforming to good taste — **taste·ful·ly** \-fə-lē\ *adv* — **taste·ful·ness** *n*
taste·less \ˈtāst-ləs\ *adj* (1603) **1 a :** having no taste : INSIPID ⟨~ vegetables⟩ **b :** arousing no interest : DULL **2 :** not having or exhibiting good taste — **taste·less·ly** *adv* — **taste·less·ness** *n*
taste·mak·er \-ˌmā-kər\ *n* (1954) : one who sets the standards of what is currently popular or fashionable
tast·er \ˈtā-stər\ *n* (15c) **1 :** one that tastes; *esp* : one that tests (as tea) for quality by tasting **2 :** a device for tasting or sampling
tasty \ˈtā-stē\ *adj* **tast·i·er; -est** (1617) **1 a :** having a marked and appetizing flavor **b :** strikingly attractive or interesting ⟨a ~ bit of gossip⟩ **2 :** TASTEFUL ***syn*** see PALATABLE — **tast·i·ly** \-stə-lē\ *adv* — **tast·i·ness** \-stē-nəs\ *n*
tat \ˈtat\ *vb* **tat·ted; tat·ting** [back-formation fr. *tatting*] *vi* (1882) : to work at tatting ~ *vt* : to make by tatting
ta·ta·mi \tä-ˈtäm-ē, ta-\ *n, pl* **-mi** *or* **-mis** [Jp] (ca. 1898) : straw matting used as a floor covering in a Japanese home
Ta·tar \ˈtät-ər\ *n* [Per *Tātār*, of Turkic origin; akin to Turk *Tatar*] (1811) **1 :** a member of any of numerous chiefly Turkic peoples found mainly in the Tatar Republic of the U.S.S.R., the north Caucasus, Crimea, and parts of Siberia **2 :** the Turkic language of any of the Tatar peoples
ta·ter \ˈtāt-ər\ *n* [by shortening & alter.] *dial* (1759) : POTATO
[1]tat·ter \ˈtat-ər\ *vt* (14c) : to make ragged ~ *vi* : to become ragged
[2]tatter *n* [ME, of Scand origin; akin to ON *tǫturr* tatter; akin to OHG *zotta* matted hair, tuft, OE *tætteca* rag] (15c) **1 a :** a part torn and left hanging : SHRED **2** *pl* : tattered clothing : RAGS
[1]tat·ter·de·ma·lion \ˌtat-ərd-i-ˈmāl-yən, -ˈmal-, -ē-ən\ *n* [origin unknown] (1611) : a person dressed in ragged clothing : RAGAMUFFIN
[2]tatterdemalion *adj* (1614) **1 a :** ragged or disreputable in appearance **b :** being in a decayed state or condition : DILAPIDATED **2 :** BEGGARLY, DISREPUTABLE
tat·tered \ˈtat-ərd\ *adj* (14c) **1 :** wearing ragged clothes ⟨a ~ barefoot boy⟩ **2 :** torn into shreds : RAGGED **3 a :** broken down : DILAPIDATED **b :** being in a shattered condition : DISRUPTED
tat·ter·sall \ˈtat-ər-ˌsȯl, -səl\ *n* [*Tattersall's* horse market, London, England] (1904) **1 :** a pattern of colored lines forming squares of solid background **2 :** a fabric woven or printed in a tattersall pattern
tat·ting \ˈtat-iŋ\ *n* [origin unknown] (1842) **1 :** a delicate handmade lace formed usu. by looping and knotting with a single cotton thread and a small shuttle **2 :** the act or process of making tatting
[1]tat·tle \ˈtat-ᵊl\ *n* (1529) **1 :** idle talk : CHATTER **2 :** GOSSIP
[2]tattle *vb* **tat·tled; tat·tling** \ˈtat-liŋ, -ᵊl-iŋ\ [MD *tatelen;* akin to ME *tateren* to tattle] *vi* (1547) **1 :** CHATTER, PRATE **2 :** to tell secrets : BLAB ~ *vt* : to utter or disclose in gossip or chatter
tat·tler \ˈtat-lər, -ᵊl-ər\ *n* (1550) **1 :** TATTLETALE **2 :** any of various slender long-legged shorebirds (as the willet, yellowlegs, and redshank) with a loud and frequent call
tat·tle·tale \ˈtat-ᵊl-ˌtāl\ *n* (1888) : one that tattles : INFORMER
tattletale gray *n* [fr. the suggestion made by a soap advertiser that such a color observed in clothes hanging out to dry betrays inefficient laundering] (1943) : a grayish white
[1]tat·too \ta-ˈtü\ *n, pl* **tattoos** [alter. of earlier *taptoo*, fr. D *taptoe*, fr. the phrase *tap toe!* taps shut!] (1627) **1 a :** a call sounded shortly before taps as notice to go to quarters **b :** outdoor military exercise given by troops as evening entertainment **2 :** a rapid rhythmic rapping
[2]tattoo *vt* (1780) : to beat or rap rhythmically on : drum on ~ *vi* : to give a series of rhythmic taps
[3]tattoo *vt* [Tahitian *tatau*, n., tattoo] (1769) **1 :** to mark or color (the skin) with tattoos **2 :** to mark the skin with (a tattoo) ⟨~*ed* a flag on his chest⟩ — **tat·too·er** *n* — **tat·too·ist** \-ˈtü-əst\ *n*
[4]tattoo *n, pl* **tattoos** (1777) **1 :** the act of tattooing : the fact of being tattooed **2 :** an indelible mark or figure fixed upon the body by insertion of pigment under the skin or by production of scars
tat·ty \ˈtat-ē\ *adj* **tat·ti·er; -est** [perh. akin to OE *tætteca* rag — more at TATTER] (1513) : rather worn or frayed : SHABBY
tau \ˈtau̇, ˈtȯ\ *n* [Gk, of Sem origin; akin to Heb *tāw* taw] (14c) : the 19th letter of the Greek alphabet — see ALPHABET table
tau cross *n* (15c) : a T-shaped cross sometimes having expanded ends and foot — see CROSS illustration
taught *past and past part of* TEACH
[1]taunt \ˈtȯnt, ˈtänt\ *n* (1529) : a sarcastic challenge or insult
[2]taunt *vt* [perh. fr. MF *tenter* to try, tempt — more at TEMPT] (1560) : to reproach or challenge in a mocking or insulting manner : jeer at ***syn*** see RIDICULE — **taunt·er** *n* — **taunt·ing·ly** \-iŋ-lē\ *adv*
[3]taunt *adj* [origin unknown] (1622) : very tall — used of a ship's mast
tau particle *n* (1972) : a short-lived elementary particle of the lepton family that exists in positive and negative charge states and has a mass about 3500 times heavier than an electron
taupe \ˈtōp\ *n* [F, lit., mole, fr. L *talpa*] (ca. 1909) : a brownish gray
Tau·re·an \ˈtȯr-ē-ən\ *n* (1914) : TAURUS 2b
[1]tau·rine \ˈtȯ-ˌrīn\ *adj* [L *taurinus*, fr. *taurus* bull; akin to Gk *tauros* bull, MIr *tarb*] (1613) **1 :** of or relating to a bull : BOVINE **2 :** of or relating to the common ox (*Bos taurus*) as distinguished from the zebu (*B. indicus*)
[2]tau·rine \ˈtȯ-ˌrēn\ *n* [ISV, fr. L *taurus;* fr. its having been discovered in ox bile] (1845) : a colorless crystalline compound $C_2H_7NO_3S$ of neutral reaction found in the juices of muscle esp. in invertebrates and obtained as a cleavage product of taurocholic acid
tau·ro·cho·lic acid \ˌtȯr-ə-ˌkō-lik-, -ˌkäl-ik-\ *n* [L *taurus* + ISV *-o-* + *cholic (acid)*] (1857) : a deliquescent acid $C_{26}H_{45}NO_7S$ occurring as the sodium salt in the bile of man, the ox, and various carnivores
Tau·rus \ˈtȯr-əs\ *n* [ME, fr. L (gen. *Tauri*), lit., bull] **1 :** a zodiacal constellation that contains the Pleiades and Hyades and is represented pictorially by a bull's forequarters **2 a :** the 2d sign of the zodiac in astrology **b :** one born under this sign — see ZODIAC table
[1]taut \ˈtȯt\ *adj* [ME *tought*] (14c) **1 a :** having no give or slack : tightly drawn **b :** HIGH-STRUNG, TENSE ⟨~ nerves⟩ **2 a :** kept in proper order or condition ⟨a ~ ship⟩ **b (1) :** not loose or flabby **(2) :** marked by economy of structure and detail ⟨a ~ story⟩ — **taut·ly** *adv* — **taut·ness** *n*
[2]taut *vt* [origin unknown] *Scot* (1782) : MAT, TANGLE
taut- *or* **tauto-** *comb form* [LL, fr. Gk, fr. *tauto* the same, contr. of *to auto*] : same ⟨*tautomerism*⟩ ⟨*tautonym*⟩
taut·en \ˈtȯt-ᵊn\ *vb* **taut·ened; taut·en·ing** \ˈtȯt-niŋ, -ᵊn-iŋ\ *vt* (1814) : to make taut ~ *vi* : to become taut
tau·tog \ˈtȯ-ˌtȯg, -ˌtäg, tȯ-ˈ\ *n* [Narraganset *tautauog*, pl.] (1643) : an edible fish (*Tautoga onitis*) of the wrasse family found along the Atlantic coast of the U.S. — called also *blackfish*
tau·to·log·i·cal \ˌtȯt-ᵊl-ˈäj-i-kəl\ *adj* (1620) : TAUTOLOGOUS — **tau·to·log·i·cal·ly** \-k(ə-)lē\ *adv*
tau·tol·o·gous \tȯ-ˈtäl-ə-gəs\ *adj* [Gk *tautologos*, fr. *taut-* + *legein* to say — more at LEGEND] (1714) **1 :** involving or containing rhetorical tautology : REDUNDANT **2 :** true by virtue of its logical form alone — **tau·tol·o·gous·ly** *adv*
tau·tol·o·gy \tȯ-ˈtäl-ə-jē\ *n, pl* **-gies** [LL *tautologia*, fr. Gk, fr. *tautologos*] (1579) **1 a :** needless repetition of an idea, statement, or word **b :** an instance of tautology **2 :** a tautologous statement
tau·to·mer \ˈtȯt-ə-mər\ *n* [ISV, fr. *tautomeric*] (1903) : one of the forms of a tautomeric compound
tau·to·mer·ic \ˌtȯt-ə-ˈmer-ik\ *adj* [ISV] (ca. 1890) : of, relating to, or marked by tautomerism
tau·tom·er·ism \tȯ-ˈtäm-ə-ˌriz-əm\ *n* (ca. 1890) : isomerism in which the isomers change into one another with great ease so that they ordinarily exist together in equilibrium
taut·onym \ˈtȯt-ə-ˌnim\ *n* [*taut-* + *-onym*] (1899) : a taxonomic binomial in which the generic name and specific epithet are alike and which is common in zoology esp. to designate a typical form but is forbidden

to botany under the International Code of Botanical Nomenclature — **tau·ton·y·my** \-mē\ *n*

tav·ern \'tav-ərn\ *n* [ME *taverne,* fr. OF, fr. L *taberna,* lit., hut, shop, prob. fr. *trabs* beam] (13c) **1 :** an establishment where alcoholic beverages are sold to be drunk on the premises **2 :** INN

ta·ver·na \tä-'ve(ə)r-nə\ *n* [NGk, fr. L *taberna*] (1946) : a café in Greece

tav·ern·er \'tav-ə(r)-nər\ *n* (14c) : one who keeps a tavern

¹taw \'tȯ\ *vt* [ME *tawen* to prepare for use, fr. OE *tawian;* akin to L *bonus* good] (bef. 12c) : to dress (skins) usu. by a dry process (as with alum or salt)

²taw *n* [origin unknown] (1709) **1 a :** a marble used as a shooter **b :** RINGTAW **2 :** the line from which players shoot at marbles **3 :** a square-dance partner

³taw *vi* (1863) : to shoot a marble

⁴taw \'täf, 'tȯf, 'täv, 'tȯv\ *n* [Heb *tāw,* lit., mark, cross] (1701) : the 23d letter of the Hebrew alphabet — see ALPHABET table

¹taw·dry \'tȯd-rē, 'täd-\ *adj* **taw·dri·er; -est** [*tawdry lace* (a tie of lace for the neck), fr. *St. Audrey* (St. Etheldreda) †679 queen of Northumbria] (1676) : cheap and gaudy in appearance or quality; *also* : IGNOBLE *syn* see GAUDY — **taw·dri·ly** \-rə-lē\ *adv* — **taw·dri·ness** \-rē-nəs\ *n*

²tawdry *n* (1680) : cheap showy finery

¹taw·ny \'tȯ-nē, 'tän-ē\ *adj* **taw·ni·er; -est** [ME, fr. MF *tanné,* pp. of *tanner* to tan] (14c) **1 :** of the color tawny **2 :** of a warm sandy color like that of well-tanned skin ⟨the lion's ~ coat⟩ — **taw·ni·ness** *n*

²tawny *n, pl* **tawnies** (15c) : a brownish orange to light brown color

taw·pie \'tȯ-pē\ *n* [of Scand origin; akin to Norw *tåpe* simpleton] *chiefly Scot* (1728) : a foolish or awkward young person

tawse *also* **taws** \'tȯz\ *n pl but sing or pl in constr* [prob. fr. pl. of obs. *taw* (tawed leather)] *Brit* (1585) : a leather strap slit into strips at the end

¹tax \'taks\ *vt* [ME *taxen* to estimate, assess, tax, fr. OF *taxer,* fr. ML *taxare,* fr. L, to feel, estimate, censure, freq. of *tangere* to touch — more at TANGENT] (13c) **1 :** to assess or determine judicially the amount of (costs in a court action) **2 :** to levy a tax on **3** *obs* **:** to enter (a name) in a list ⟨there went out a decree . . . that all the world should be ~*ed* —Lk 2:1 (AV)⟩ **4 :** CHARGE, ACCUSE ⟨~*ed* him with neglect of his duty⟩; *also* : CENSURE **5 :** to make onerous and rigorous demands on ⟨the job ~*ed* her strength⟩ — **tax·able** \'tak-sə-bəl\ *adj* — **tax·er** *n*

²tax *n, often attrib* (14c) **1 a :** a charge usu. of money imposed by authority on persons or property for public purposes **b :** a sum levied on members of an organization to defray expenses **2 :** a heavy demand

tax- *or* **taxo-** *also* **taxi-** *comb form* [Gk *taxi-,* fr. *taxis*] : arrangement ⟨*taxeme*⟩ ⟨*taxidermy*⟩

taxa *pl of* TAXON

tax·a·tion \tak-'sā-shən\ *n* (14c) **1 :** the action of taxing; *esp* **:** the imposition of taxes **2 :** revenue obtained from taxes **3 :** the amount assessed as a tax

tax base *n* (ca. 1943) : the wealth (as real estate or income) within a jurisdiction that is liable to taxation

tax·eme \'tak-,sēm\ *n* [*tax-*] (1933) : a minimum grammatical feature of selection, order, stress, pitch, or phonetic modification — **tax·e·mic** \tak-'sē-mik\ *adj*

tax–ex·empt \,tak-sig-'zem(p)t\ *adj* (1923) **1 :** exempted from a tax **2 :** bearing interest that is free from federal or state income tax

¹taxi \'tak-sē\ *n, pl* **tax·is** \-sēz\ *also* **tax·ies** (1913) : TAXICAB; *also* : a similarly operated boat or airplane

²taxi *vb* **tax·ied; taxi·ing** *or* **taxy·ing; tax·is** *or* **tax·ies** *vi* (1916) **1 a** *of an airplane* **:** to go at low speed along the surface of the ground or water **b :** to operate an airplane on the ground under its own power **2 :** to ride in a taxicab ~ *vt* **1 :** to transport by or as if by taxi **2 :** to cause (an airplane) to taxi

taxi·cab \'tak-sē-,kab\ *n* [*taximeter cab*] (ca. 1907) : an automobile that carries passengers for a fare usu. determined by the distance traveled

taxi dancer *n* (ca. 1927) : a girl employed by a dance hall, café, or cabaret to dance with patrons who pay a certain amount for each dance

taxi·der·my \'tak-sə-,dər-mē\ *n* [*tax-* + *derm-* + *-y*] (1820) : the art of preparing, stuffing, and mounting the skins of animals and esp. vertebrates — **taxi·der·mic** \,tak-sə-'dər-mik\ *adj* — **taxi·der·mist** \'tak-sə-,dər-məst\ *n*

taxi·man \'tak-sē-mən\ *n, chiefly Brit* (1923) : the operator of a taxi

taxi·me·ter \'tak-sē-,mēt-ər\ *n* [F *taximètre,* modif. of G *taxameter,* fr. ML *taxa* tax, charge (fr. *taxare* to tax) + G *-meter*] (1894) : an instrument for use in a hired vehicle (as a taxicab) for automatically showing the fare due

tax·ing \'tak-siŋ\ *adj* (1946) : ONEROUS, WEARING ⟨a ~ operatic role⟩ — **tax·ing·ly** \-siŋ-lē\ *adv*

tax·is \'tak-səs\ *n, pl* **tax·es** \-,sēz\ [Gk, lit., arrangement, order, fr. *tassein* to arrange — more at TACTICS] (1758) **1 :** reflex translational or orientational movement by a freely motile and usu. simple organism in relation to a source of stimulation (as a light or a temperature or chemical gradient) **2 :** a reflex reaction involving a taxis

-tax·is \'tak-səs\ *n comb form, pl* **-tax·es** \-,sēz\ [NL, fr. Gk, fr. *taxis*] **1 :** arrangement : order ⟨homo*taxis*⟩ **2 :** physiological taxis ⟨chemo*taxis*⟩

taxi squad *n* (1964) : a group of professional football players under contract who practice with a team but are ineligible to participate in official games

taxi stand *n* (1937) : a place where taxis may park while awaiting hire

taxi·way \'tak-sē-,wā\ *n* (ca. 1934) : a usu. paved strip for taxiing (as from the terminal to a runway) at an airport

tax·on \'tak-,sän\ *n, pl* **taxa** \-sə\ *also* **tax·ons** [NL, back-formation fr. ISV *taxonomy*] (ca. 1948) **1 :** a taxonomic group or entity **2 :** the name applied to a taxonomic group in a formal system of nomenclature

tax·on·o·my \tak-'sän-ə-mē\ *n* [F *taxonomie,* fr. *tax-* + *-nomie* -nomy] (ca. 1828) **1 :** the study of the general principles of scientific classification : SYSTEMATICS **2 :** CLASSIFICATION; *specif* **:** orderly classification of plants and animals according to their presumed natural relationships — **tax·o·nom·ic** \,tak-sə-'näm-ik\ *adj* — **tax·o·nom·i·cal·ly** \-i-k(ə-)lē\ *adv* — **tax·on·o·mist** \tak-'sän-ə-məst\ *n*

tax·pay·er \'taks-,pā-ər\ *n* (1816) : one that pays or is liable for a tax

tax·pay·ing \-,pā-iŋ\ *adj* (1832) : of, relating to, or subject to the paying of a tax

tax selling *n* (1963) : concerted selling of securities late in the year to establish gains and losses for income-tax purposes

tax shelter *n* (1952) : a strategy, investment, or tax code provision that reduces one's tax liability — **tax–shel·tered** \'taks-,shel-tərd, 'tak-,shel-\ *adj*

tax stamp *n* (ca. 1929) : a stamp marked on or affixed to a taxable item as evidence that the tax has been paid

tax·us \'tak-səs\ *n, pl* **tax·us** \-səs\ [NL, genus comprising the yews, fr. L, yew] (ca. 1945) : YEW 1a

Tay·lor's series \'tā-lərz-\ *n* [Brook *Taylor* †1731 Eng. mathematician] (ca. 1909) : a power series that gives the expansion of a function $f(x)$ in the neighborhood of a point *a* provided that in the neighborhood the function is continuous, all its derivatives exist, and the series converges to the function in which case it has the form

$$f(x) = f(a) + \frac{f^{[1]}(a)}{1!}(x-a) + \frac{f^{[2]}(a)}{2!}(x-a)^2 + \ldots + \frac{f^{[n]}(a)}{n!}(x-a)^n + \ldots$$

where $f^{[n]}(a)$ is the derivative of nth order of $f(x)$ evaluated at *a* — called also *Taylor series*

Tay–Sachs disease \'tā-'saks-\ *n* [Waren *Tay* †1927 Brit. physician & Bernard P. *Sachs* †1944 Am. neurologist] (ca. 1923) : a fatal hereditary disorder of lipid metabolism characterized by the accumulation of lipids esp. in nervous tissue due to an enzyme deficiency — called also *Tay-Sachs*

taz·za \'tät-sə\ *n* [It, cup, fr. Ar *ṭassah*] (1841) : a shallow cup or vase on a pedestal

TB \(')tē-'bē\ *n* [*TB* (abbr. for *tubercle bacillus*)] (1916) : TUBERCULOSIS

T–bar lift \,tē-,bär-\ *n* (1954) : a ski lift having a series of T-shaped bars each of which pulls two skiers

T–bill \'tē-,bil\ *n* [*Treasury*] (1973) a U.S. treasury note

T–bone \'tē-,bōn\ *n* (1925) : a small beefsteak from the thin end of the short loin containing a T-shaped bone and a small piece of tenderloin — see BEEF illustration

TCDD \,tē-,sē-,dē-'dē\ *n* [*tetra-* + *chlor-* + *dibenzo-* (containing two benzene rings) + *dioxin*] (1971) : a carcinogenic dioxin $C_{12}H_4O_2Cl_4$ found esp. as a contaminant in 2,4,5-T

T cell *n* [*thymus-derived cell*] (ca. 1970) : a lymphocyte differentiated in the thymus, characterized by specific surface antigens, and specialized esp. for cell-mediated immunity (as in the defense against viruses and the rejection of foreign tissues) or for cooperation with B cells in immunoglobulin synthesis

t distribution *n* (ca. 1957) : a probability density function that is used esp. in testing hypotheses concerning means of normal distributions whose standard deviations are unknown and that is the distribution of a random variable

$$t = \frac{u\sqrt{n}}{v}$$

where *u* and *v* are themselves independent random variables and *u* has a normal distribution with mean 0 and a standard deviation of 1 and v^2 has a chi-square distribution with *n* degrees of freedom — called also *student's t distribution*

tea \'tē\ *n* [Chin (Amoy) *t'e*] (ca. 1655) **1 a :** a shrub (*Camellia sinensis* of the family Theaceae, the tea family) cultivated esp. in China, Japan, and the East Indies **b :** the leaves, leaf buds, and internodes of the tea plant prepared and cured for the market, classed according to method of manufacture into one set of types (as green tea, black tea, or oolong), and graded according to leaf size into another (as congou, orange pekoe, pekoe, or souchong) **2 :** an aromatic beverage prepared from tea leaves by infusion with boiling water **3 :** any of various plants somewhat resembling tea in properties; *also* : an infusion of their leaves used medicinally or as a beverage **4 a :** refreshments usu. including tea with sandwiches, crackers, or cookies served in late afternoon **b :** a reception at which tea is served **5** *slang* **:** MARIJUANA — **tea·like** \-,līk\ *adj*

tea bag *n* (ca. 1935) : a bag usu. of filter paper holding enough tea for an individual serving

tea ball *n* (1902) : a perforated metal ball that holds tea leaves and is used in brewing tea in a pot or cup

tea·ber·ry \'tē-,ber-ē\ *n* [fr. the use of its leaves as a substitute for tea] (ca. 1837) : CHECKERBERRY

tea caddy *n* (1790) : CADDY

tea cake *n* (1829) **1** *Brit* **:** a light flat cake **2 :** COOKIE

tea cart *n* (1926) : TEA WAGON

teach \'tēch\ *vb* **taught** \'tȯt\; **teach·ing** [ME *techen* to show, instruct, fr. OE *tǣcan;* akin to OE *tācn* sign — more at TOKEN] *vt* (bef. 12c) **1 a :** to cause to know a subject ⟨*taught* his sons a trade⟩ **b :** to cause to know how ⟨is ~*ing* me to drive⟩ **c :** to accustom to some action or attitude ⟨~ students to think for themselves⟩ **d :** to make to know the disagreeable consequences of some action ⟨I'll ~ you to come home late⟩ **2 :** to guide the studies of **3 :** to impart the knowledge of ⟨~ algebra⟩ **4 a :** to instruct by precept, example, or experience **b :** to seek to make known and accepted ⟨experience ~*es* us our limitations⟩ **5 :** to conduct instruction regularly in ⟨~ school⟩ ~ *vi* **:** to provide instruction : act as a teacher

syn TEACH, INSTRUCT, EDUCATE, TRAIN, DISCIPLINE, SCHOOL mean to cause to acquire knowledge or skill. TEACH applies to any manner of imparting information or skill so that others may learn; INSTRUCT suggests methodical or formal teaching; EDUCATE implies attempting to bring out latent capabilities; TRAIN stresses instruction and drill with a specific end in view; DISCIPLINE implies subordinating to a master for the sake of controlling; SCHOOL implies training or disciplining esp. in what is hard to master or to bear.

teach·able \'tē-chə-bəl\ *adj* (15c) **1 a :** capable of being taught **b :** apt and willing to learn **2 :** favorable to teaching — **teach·able·ness** *n* — **teach·ably** \-blē\ *adv*

teach·er \'tē-chər\ *n* (14c) **1** : one that teaches; *esp* : one whose occupation is to instruct **2** : a Mormon ranking above a deacon in the Aaronic priesthood

teachers college *n* (ca. 1910) : a college for the training of teachers usu. offering a full 4-year course and granting a bachelor's degree

teacher's pet *n* (ca. 1930) **1** : a pupil who has won his teacher's special favor **2** : one who has ingratiated himself with an authority

teach–in \'tē-ˌchin\ *n* [*teach* + *-in* (as in *sit-in*)] (1965) : an extended meeting usu. held on a college campus for lectures, debates, and discussions on an important and often controversial topic (as U.S. foreign policy)

[1]**teach·ing** *n* (12c) **1** : the act, practice, or profession of a teacher **2** : something taught; *esp* : DOCTRINE ⟨the ~*s* of Confucius⟩

[2]**teaching** *adj* (1642) : of, relating to, used for, or engaged in teaching ⟨a ~ aid⟩ ⟨the ~ profession⟩ ⟨a ~ assistant⟩ ⟨a ~ hospital⟩

tea·cup \'tē-ˌkəp\ *n* (1700) : a cup usu. of less than 8-ounce capacity used with a saucer for hot beverages — **teacupful** *n*

tea dance *n* (1920) : a dance held in the late afternoon

tea garden *n* (1802) **1** : a public garden where tea and light refreshments are served **2** : a tea plantation

tea gown *n* (1888) : a semiformal gown of fine materials in graceful flowing lines worn esp. for afternoon entertaining at home

tea·house \'tē-ˌhau̇s\ *n* (1689) : a public house or restaurant where tea and light refreshments are sold

teak \'tēk\ *n* [Pg *teca*, fr. Malayalam *tēkka*] (1675) **1** : a tall East Indian timber tree (*Tectona grandis*) of the vervain family **2** : the hard yellowish brown wood of teak used esp. for furniture and shipbuilding

tea·ket·tle \'tē-ˌket-ᵊl, -ˌkit-\ *n* (1705) : a covered kettle with a handle and spout for boiling water

teak·wood \'tē-ˌkwu̇d\ *n* (1783) : TEAK 2

teal \'tē(ə)l\ *n, pl* **teal** *or* **teals** [ME *tele;* akin to MD *teling* teal] (14c) : any of several small short-necked river ducks (esp. genus *Anas*) of Europe and America

teal blue *n* (1938) : a variable color averaging a dark greenish blue

[1]**team** \'tēm\ *n* [ME *teme*, fr. OE *tēam* offspring, lineage, group of draft animals; akin to OE *tēon* to draw, pull — more at TOW] (bef. 12c) **1 a** : two or more draft animals harnessed to the same vehicle or implement; *also* : these with their harness and attached vehicle **b** : a draft animal often with harness and vehicle **c** : a drawn vehicle (as a wagon) **2** *obs* : LINEAGE, RACE **3** : a group of animals: as **a** : a brood esp. of young pigs or ducks **b** : a matched group of animals for exhibition **4** : a number of persons associated together in work or activity: as **a** : a group on one side (as in football or a debate) **b** : CREW, GANG

[2]**team** *vt* (1552) **1** : to yoke or join in a team **2** : to convey or haul with a team ~ *vi* **1** : to drive a team or motortruck **2** : to form a team or association : COLLABORATE ⟨~*ed* up to write a book⟩

[3]**team** *adj* (14c) : of or performed by a team ⟨a ~ effort⟩

team foul *n* (1966) : one of a designated number of personal fouls the players on a basketball team may commit during a given period of play before the opposing team begins receiving bonus free throws

team handball *n* (1971) : a game developed from soccer which is played between two teams of seven players each and in which the ball is thrown, caught, and dribbled with the hands

team·mate \'tēm-ˌmāt\ *n* (1915) : a fellow member of a team

team play *n* (1890) **1** : collective play with mutual assistance of team members ⟨skillful *team play* in hockey⟩ **2** : cooperative effort ⟨need for *team play* in time of war —Christopher La Farge⟩ — **team player** *n*

team·ster \'tēm(p)-stər\ *n* (1777) : one who drives a team or motortruck esp. as an occupation

team·work \'tēm-ˌwərk\ *n* (1886) : work done by several associates with each doing a part but all subordinating personal prominence to the efficiency of the whole

tea party *n* (1778) **1** : an afternoon social gathering at which tea is served **2** [fr. the Boston Tea Party, name facetiously applied to the occasion in 1773 when a group of citizens threw a shipment of tea into Boston harbor in protest against the tax on imports] : an exciting disturbance or proceeding

tea·pot \'tē-ˌpät\ *n* (1705) : a vessel with a spout in which tea is brewed and from which it is served

tea·poy \'tē-ˌpȯi\ *n* [Hindi *tipāī*] (1828) **1** : a 3-legged ornamental stand **2** [influenced by *tea*] : a stand for a tea service

[1]**tear** \'ti(ə)r\ *n* [ME, fr. OE *tæhher, tēar;* akin to OHG *zahar* tear, Gk *dakry*] (bef. 12c) **1 a** : a drop of clear saline fluid secreted by the lacrimal gland and diffused between the eye and eyelids to moisten the parts and facilitate their motion **b** *pl* : a secretion of profuse tears that overflow the eyelids and dampen the face **2** : a transparent drop of fluid or hardened fluid matter (as resin) **3** *pl* : an act of weeping or grieving ⟨broke into ~*s*⟩ — **tear·less** *adj*

[2]**tear** *vi* (bef. 12c) : to fill with tears : shed tears ⟨eyes ~*ing* in the November wind —Saul Bellow⟩

[3]**tear** \'ta(ə)r, 'te(ə)r\ *vb* **tore** \'tō(ə)r, 'tȯ(ə)r\; **torn** \'tō(ə)rn, 'tȯ(ə)rn\; **tear·ing** [ME *teren*, fr. OE *teran;* akin to OHG *zeran* to destroy, Gk *derein* to skin] *vt* (bef. 12c) **1 a** : to separate parts of or pull apart by force : REND **b** : to wound by or as if by tearing : LACERATE ⟨~ the skin⟩ **2** : to divide or disrupt by the pull of contrary forces ⟨a mind *torn* with doubts⟩ **3** : to remove by force : WRENCH ⟨~ a cover off a box⟩ **4** : to make or effect by or as if by tearing ⟨~ a hole in the wall⟩ ~ *vi* **1** : to separate on being pulled : REND ⟨this cloth ~*s* easily⟩ **2** : to move or act with violence, haste, or force ⟨went ~*ing* down the street⟩ — **tear·er** *n*

syn TEAR, RIP, REND, SPLIT, CLEAVE, RIVE mean to separate forcibly. TEAR implies pulling apart by force and leaving jagged edges; RIP implies a pulling apart in one rapid uninterrupted motion often along a seam or joint; REND implies very violent or ruthless severing or sundering; SPLIT implies a cutting or breaking apart in a continuous, straight, and usu. lengthwise direction or in the direction of grain or layers; CLEAVE implies very forceful splitting or cutting with a blow; RIVE suggests action rougher and more violent than SPLIT or CLEAVE.

— **tear at** : to cause anguish to : DISTRESS ⟨her grief *tore at* his heart⟩ — **tear into** : to attack without restraint or caution — **tear one's hair** : to pull one's hair as an expression of grief, rage, frustration, desperation, or anxiety

[4]**tear** \'ta(ə)r, 'te(ə)r\ *n* (1611) **1 a** : the act of tearing **b** : damage from being torn; *esp* : a hole or flaw made by tearing **2 a** : a tearing pace : HURRY **b** : SPREE ⟨go on a ~⟩

tear around *vi* (1844) : to lead a wild or disorderly life

tear away *vt* (1699) : to remove (as oneself) reluctantly

tear·down \'ta(ə)r-ˌdau̇n, 'te(ə)r-\ *n* (1926) : the act or process of disassembling

tear down \(ˈ)ta(ə)r-'dau̇n, (ˌ)te(ə)r-\ *vt* (1614) **1 a** : to cause to decompose or disintegrate **b** : VILIFY, DENIGRATE **2** : to take apart : DISASSEMBLE ⟨*tear* an engine *down* for an overhaul⟩

tear·drop \'ti(ə)r-ˌdräp\ *n* (1799) **1** : [1]TEAR 1a **2** : something shaped like a dropping tear; *specif* : a pendent gem (as on an earring)

tear·ful \'ti(ə)r-fəl\ *adj* (1586) **1** : flowing with or accompanied by tears ⟨~ entreaties⟩ **2** : causing tears : TEARY — **tear·ful·ly** \-fə-lē\ *adv* — **tear·ful·ness** *n*

tear·gas \-ˌgas\ *vt* (1946) : to use tear gas on

tear gas *n* (1917) : a solid, liquid, or gaseous substance that on dispersion in the atmosphere blinds the eyes with tears and is used chiefly in dispelling mobs

tear·ing \'ta(ə)r-iŋ, 'te(ə)r-\ *adj* (1606) **1** : causing continued or repeated pain or distress **2** : HASTY, VIOLENT **3** *chiefly Brit* : SPLENDID

tear·jerk·er \'ti(ə)r-ˌjər-kər\ *n* (1936) : an extravagantly pathetic story, song, play, film, or broadcast — **tear–jerk·ing** \-kiŋ\ *adj*

tea·room \'tē-ˌrüm, -ˌru̇m\ *n* (1778) : a small restaurant with service and decor designed primarily for a female clientele

tea rose *n* (1850) : any of numerous tender or half-hardy hybrid garden bush roses descended chiefly from a Chinese rose (*Rosa odorata*) and valued esp. for their abundant large usu. tea-scented blossoms — compare HYBRID TEA ROSE

tear sheet *n* (ca. 1924) : a sheet torn from a publication

tear·stain \'ti(ə)r-ˌstān\ *n* (1922) : a spot or streak left by tears — **tear·stained** \-ˌstānd\ *adj*

tear tape *n* (1954) : a strong tape glued to the inside of a shipping container with one end protruding so that the container is readily opened by pulling out the tape

tear up *vt* (1699) : to damage, remove, or effect an opening in ⟨*tore up* the street to lay a new water main⟩

teary \'ti(ə)r-ē\ *adj* **tear·i·er; -est** (14c) **1 a** : wet or stained with tears : TEARFUL **b** : consisting of tears or drops resembling tears **2** : causing tears : PATHETIC ⟨a ~ story⟩

[1]**tease** \'tēz\ *vt* **teased; teas·ing** [ME *tesen*, fr. OE *tǣsan;* akin to OHG *zeisan* to tease] (bef. 12c) **1 a** : to disentangle and lay parallel by combing or carding ⟨~ wool⟩ **b** : TEASEL **2** : to tear in pieces; *esp* : to shred (a tissue or specimen) for microscopic examination **3 a** : to disturb or annoy by persistent irritating or provoking **b** : to attempt to provoke to anger, resentment, or confusion : GOAD **c** : to annoy with petty persistent requests : PESTER; *also* : to obtain by repeated coaxing **d** : to persuade to acquiesce esp. by persistent small efforts : COAX **e** : to manipulate or influence as if by teasing **4** : to comb (hair) by taking hold of a strand and pushing the short hairs toward the scalp with the comb **5** : to tantalize esp. by arousing desire or curiosity without intending to satisfy it ***syn*** see WORRY — **teas·er** *n* — **teas·ing·ly** \'tē-ziŋ-lē\ *adv*

[2]**tease** *n* (1693) **1** : the act of teasing : the state of being teased **2** : one that teases

[1]**tea·sel** *also* **tea·zel** *or* **tea·zle** \'tē-zəl\ *n* [ME *tesel*, fr. OE *tǣsel;* akin to OE *tǣsan* to tease] (bef. 12c) **1 a** : an Old World prickly herb (*Dipsacus fullonum* of the family Dipsacaceae, the teasel family) with flower heads that are covered with stiff hooked bracts and are used in the woolen industry — called also *fuller's teasel* **b** : a plant of the same genus as the teasel **2 a** : a flower head of the fuller's teasel used when dried to raise a nap on woolen cloth **b** : a wire substitute for the teasel

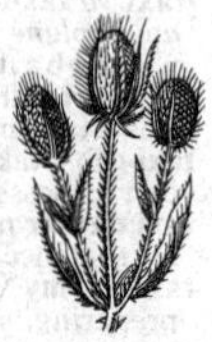
teasel 1a

[2]**teasel** *vt* **tea·seled** *or* **tea·selled; tea·sel·ing** *or* **tea·sel·ling** \'tēz-(ə-)liŋ\ (1543) : to nap (cloth) with teasels

tease out *vt* (1828) : to obtain by or as if by disentangling or freeing with a pointed instrument

tea service *n* (ca. 1858) : a set of china or metalware for service at table: **a** : a set of china consisting of a teapot, sugar bowl, creamer, sometimes a coffeepot, and usu. plates, cups, and saucers **b** : a set of metalware consisting of a teapot, sugar bowl, creamer, sometimes a coffeepot, and usu. waste bowl, kettle, and tray

tea set *n* (1849) **1** : TEA SERVICE b **2** : a china set consisting of a teapot, sugar bowl, creamer, cups and saucers and plates

tea shop *n* (1856) **1** *chiefly Brit* : TEAROOM **2** *Brit* : RESTAURANT

tea·spoon \'tē-ˌspün, -ˌspün\ *n* (1686) **1** : a small spoon that is used esp. for eating soft foods and stirring beverages and that holds one third of a tablespoon **2** : TEASPOONFUL

tea·spoon·ful \-ˌfu̇l\ *n, pl* **teaspoonfuls** \-ˌfu̇lz\ *also* **tea·spoons·ful** \-ˌspünz-ˌfu̇l, -ˌspünz-\ (1731) **1** : as much as a teaspoon can hold **2** : a unit of measure used esp. in cooking equal to 1$\frac{1}{3}$ fluidrams or $\frac{1}{3}$ tablespoon : $\frac{1}{3}$ tablespoon

teat \'tit, 'tēt\ *n* [ME *tete*, fr. OF, of Gmc origin; akin to OE *tit* teat, MHG *zitze*] (13c) **1** : the protuberance through which milk is drawn from an udder or breast : NIPPLE **2** : a small projection or a nib (as on a mechanical part) — **teat·ed** \-əd\ *adj*

tea table *n* (1688) : a table used or spread for tea; *specif* : a small table for serving afternoon tea

tea·time \'tē-ˌtīm\ *n* (1756) : the customary time for tea : late afternoon or early evening

tea towel *n* (1871) : a cloth for drying dishes

tea tray *n* (1773) : a tray that accommodates a tea service

tea wagon *n* (ca. 1922) : a small table on wheels used in serving tea

Te·bet \tā-'vāt(h), 'tā-ˌves\ *n* [Heb *Ṭēbhēth*] (14c) : the 4th month of the civil year or the 10th month of the ecclesiastical year in the Jewish calendar — see MONTH table

teched \'techt\ *adj* [alter. of *touched*] (1921) : mentally unbalanced

tech·ne·tium \tek-'nē-sh(ē-)əm\ *n* [NL, fr. Gk *technētos* artificial, fr. *technasthai* to devise by art, fr. *technē*] (ca. 1946) : a metallic element obtained by bombarding molybdenum with deuterons or neutrons and in the fission of uranium — see ELEMENT table

tech·ne·tron·ic \ˌtek-nə-ˈträn-ik\ *adj* [*technological* + *electronic*] (1967) : shaped or influenced by the changes wrought by advances in technology and communications ⟨our modern ~ society⟩

tech·nic \ˈtek-nik, *for 1 also* tek-ˈnēk\ *n* (1855) **1** : TECHNIQUE 1 **2** *pl but sing or pl in constr* : TECHNOLOGY 2a

tech·ni·cal \ˈtek-ni-kəl\ *adj* [Gk *technikos* of art, skillful, fr. *technē* art, craft, skill; akin to Gk *tektōn* builder, carpenter, L *texere* to weave, OHG *dahs* badger] (1617) **1 a** : having special and usu. practical knowledge esp. of a mechanical or scientific subject ⟨a ~ consultant⟩ **b** : marked by or characteristic of specialization ⟨~ language⟩ **2 a** : of or relating to a particular subject **b** : of or relating to a practical subject organized on scientific principles ⟨a ~ school⟩ **c** : TECHNOLOGICAL 1 **3 a** : based on or marked by a strict or legal interpretation **b** : LEGAL 6 **4** : of or relating to technique **5** : of, relating to, or produced by ordinary commercial processes without being subjected to special purification ⟨~ sulfuric acid⟩ **6** : relating to or caused by the functioning of the market as a discrete mechanism not influenced by macroeconomic factors ⟨~ rally⟩ ⟨~ analysis⟩ — **tech·ni·cal·ly** \-k(ə-)lē\ *adv*

technical foul *n* (ca. 1929) : a foul (as in basketball) that involves no physical contact with an opponent and that usu. is incurred by unsportsmanlike conduct —compare PERSONAL FOUL

tech·ni·cal·i·ty \ˌtek-nə-ˈkal-ət-ē\ *n, pl* **-ties** (1814) **1** : something technical; *esp* : a detail meaningful only to a specialist ⟨a legal ~⟩ **2** : the quality or state of being technical

tech·ni·cal·ize \ˈtek-ni-kə-ˌlīz\ *vt* **-ized; -iz·ing** (1852) : to give a technical slant to — **tech·ni·cal·iza·tion** \ˌtek-ni-kə-lə-ˈzā-shən\ *n*

technical knockout *n* (1949) : the termination of a boxing match when a boxer is unable or is declared by the referee to be unable (as because of injuries) to continue the fight

technical sergeant *n* (ca. 1956) : a noncommissioned officer in the air force ranking above a staff sergeant and below a master sergeant

tech·ni·cian \tek-ˈnish-ən\ *n* (1833) **1** : a specialist in the technical details of a subject or occupation ⟨a medical ~⟩ **2** : one who has acquired the technique of an art or other area of specialization ⟨a superb ~ and a musician of integrity —Irving Kolodin⟩

Tech·ni·col·or \ˈtek-ni-ˌkəl-ər\ *trademark* — used for color motion pictures

tech·nique \tek-ˈnēk\ *n* [F, fr. *technique* technical, fr. Gk *technikos*] (1817) **1** : the manner in which technical details are treated (as by a writer) or basic physical movements are used (as by a dancer); *also* : ability to treat such details or use such movements ⟨good piano ~⟩ **2 a** : a body of technical methods (as in a craft or in scientific research) **b** : a method of accomplishing a desired aim

techno- *comb form* [Gk, fr. *technē*] **1** : art : craft ⟨*techno*graphy⟩ **2** : technical : technological ⟨*techno*cracy⟩

tech·noc·ra·cy \tek-ˈnäk-rə-sē\ *n* (ca. 1919) : government by technicians; *specif* : management of society by technical experts

tech·no·crat \ˈtek-nə-ˌkrat\ *n* (1932) **1** : an adherent of technocracy **2** : a technical expert; *esp* : one exercising managerial authority

tech·no·crat·ic \ˌtek-nə-ˈkrat-ik\ *adj* (1932) : of, relating to, or suggestive of a technocrat or a technocracy

tech·no·log·i·cal \ˌtek-nə-ˈläj-i-kəl\ *also* **tech·no·log·ic** \-ˈläj-ik\ *adj* (1800) **1** : of, relating to, or characterized by technology ⟨~ advances⟩ **2** : resulting from improvements in technical processes that increases productivity of machines and eliminates manual operations or operations done by older machines ⟨~ unemployment⟩ — **tech·no·log·i·cal·ly** \-i-k(ə-)lē\ *adv*

tech·nol·o·gist \tek-ˈnäl-ə-jəst\ *n* (1859) : a specialist in technology

tech·nol·o·gize \-ˌjīz\ *vt* **-gized; -giz·ing** (1954) : to make technological

tech·nol·o·gy \-jē\ *n, pl* **-gies** [Gk *technologia* systematic treatment of an art, fr. *techno-* + *-logia* -logy] (1658) **1** : technical language **2 a** : applied science **b** : a scientific method of achieving a practical purpose **3** : the totality of the means employed to provide objects necessary for human sustenance and comfort

tech·no·struc·ture \ˈtek-nō-ˌstrək-chər\ *n* (1967) : the network of professionally skilled managers (as scientists, engineers, and administrators) that increasingly tends to control the economy both within and beyond individual corporate groups

techy *var of* TETCHY

tec·ton·ic \tek-ˈtän-ik\ *adj* [LL *tectonicus*, fr. Gk *tektonikos* of a builder, fr. *tektōn* builder — more at TECHNICAL] (ca. 1656) : of or relating to the deformation of the crust of a moon or planet (as earth), the forces involved in or producing such deformation, and the resulting forms — **tec·ton·i·cal·ly** \-i-k(ə-)lē\ *adv*

tec·ton·ics \-iks\ *n pl but sing or pl in constr* (1634) **1** : geological structural features as a whole **2 a** : a branch of geology concerned with structure esp. with folding and faulting **b** : DIASTROPHISM

tec·to·nism \ˈtek-tə-ˌniz-əm\ *n* [ISV *tecton-* (fr. *tectonic*) + *-ism*] (1948) : DIASTROPHISM

tec·tum \ˈtek-təm\ *n, pl* **tec·ta** \-tə\ [NL, fr. L, roof, dwelling, fr. neut. of *tectus*, pp. of *tegere* to cover — more at THATCH] (ca. 1901) : a bodily structure resembling or serving as a roof; *esp* : the dorsal part of the midbrain — **tec·tal** \ˈtek-tᵊl\ *adj*

ted \ˈted\ *vt* **ted·ded; ted·ding** [(assumed) ME *tedden*; akin to Gk *daiesthai* to divide, distribute — more at TIDE] (15c) : to spread or turn from the swath and scatter (as new-mown grass) for drying

ted·der \ˈted-ər\ *n* (15c) : one that teds; *specif* : a machine for stirring and spreading hay to hasten drying and curing

ted·dy \ˈted-ē\ *n, pl* **teddies** [origin unknown] (1924) : CHEMISE 1

ted·dy bear \ˈted-ē-ˌ, ˌted-ē-ˈ\ *n* [*Teddy*, nickname of Theodore Roosevelt fr. a cartoon depicting the president sparing the life of a bear cub while hunting] (1907) : a stuffed toy bear

ted·dy boy \ˈted-ē-ˌ\ *n* [*Teddy*, nickname for Edward] (1954) : a young British hoodlum who affects Edwardian dress

Te De·um \(ˌ)tā-ˈdā-əm, (ˌ)tē-ˈdē-\ *n, pl* **Te Deums** [ME, fr. LL *te deum laudamus* thee, God, we praise; fr. the opening words of the hymn] (bef. 12c) : a liturgical Christian hymn of praise to God

te·dious \ˈtēd-ē-əs, ˈtē-jəs\ *adj* [ME, fr. LL *taediosus*, fr. L *taedium*] (15c) : tiresome because of length or dullness : BORING ⟨a ~ public ceremony⟩ — **te·dious·ly** *adv* — **te·dious·ness** *n*

te·di·um \ˈtēd-ē-əm\ *n* [L *taedium* disgust, irksomeness, fr. *taedēre* to disgust, weary] (1662) **1** : the quality or state of being tedious : TEDIOUSNESS; *also* : BOREDOM **2** : a tedious period of time ⟨long ~s of strained anxiety —H. G. Wells⟩

¹tee \ˈtē\ *n* [ME] (15c) **1** : the letter *t* **2** : something shaped like a capital T **3** : a mark aimed at in various games (as curling) — **to a tee** : EXACTLY, PRECISELY

²tee *n* [origin unknown] (1673) **1 a** : a small mound or a peg on which a golf ball is placed before the beginning of play on a hole **b** : a device for holding a football in position for kicking **2** : the area from which a golf ball is struck at the beginning of play on a hole

³tee *vt* **teed; tee·ing** (1673) : to place (a ball) on a tee — often used with *up*

teed off \(ˈ)tēd-ˈóf\ *adj* [prob. fr. *tee off* (on)] (1951) : ANGRY, ANNOYED

¹teem \ˈtēm\ *vb* [ME *temen*, fr. OE *tīman*, *tǣman*; akin to OE *tēam* offspring — more at TEAM] *vt, archaic* (bef. 12c) : BRING FORTH : give birth to : PRODUCE ~ *vi* **1** *obs* : to become pregnant : CONCEIVE **2 a** : to become filled to overflowing : ABOUND ⟨lakes ~ with fish⟩ **b** : to be present in large quantity — **teem·ing·ly** \ˈtē-miŋ-lē\ *adv* — **teem·ing·ness** *n*

²teem *vt* [ME *temen*, fr. ON *tœma*; akin to OE *tōm* empty] (14c) : EMPTY, POUR ⟨~ molten metal into a mold⟩

¹teen \ˈtēn\ *n* [ME *tene*, fr. OE *tēona* injury, grief; akin to ON *tjōn* loss, damage] *archaic* (13c) : MISERY, AFFLICTION

²teen *n* (1820) : TEENAGER

³teen *adj* (1926) : TEENAGE

teen·age \ˈtē-ˌnāj\ *or* **teen·aged** \-ˌnājd\ *adj* (1925) : of, being, or relating to people in their teens

teen·ag·er \-ˌnā-jər\ *n* (1939) : a teenage person

teen·er \ˈtē-nər\ *n* (1894) : TEENAGER

teens \ˈtēnz\ *n pl* [*-teen* (as in *thirteen*)] (1604) : the numbers 13 to 19 inclusive; *specif* : the years 13 to 19 in a lifetime or century

teen·sy \ˈtēn(t)-sē\ *adj* **teen·si·er; -est** [baby-talk alter. of *teeny*] (ca. 1899) : TINY

teen·sy–ween·sy \ˌtēn(t)-sē-ˈwēn(t)-sē\ *adj* [baby-talk alter. of *teeny-weeny*] (ca. 1906) : TINY

tee·ny \ˈtē-nē\ *adj* **tee·ni·er; -est** [by alter. (influenced by *weeny*)] (1825) : TINY

teeny·bop \ˈtē-nē-ˌbäp\ *adj* [back-formation fr. *teenybopper*] (1967) : of, relating to, or being a teenybopper

teeny·bop·per \-ˌbäp-ər\ *n* [²*teen* + *-y* + *bopper*] (1966) **1** : a teenage girl **2** : a young teenager who rejects middle-class mores, dresses in mod styles, enthusiastically listens to rock music, and is interested in the illicit use of drugs

tee·ny–wee·ny \ˌtē-nē-ˈwē-nē\ *adj* [*teeny* + *weeny*] (ca. 1879) : TINY

tee off *vi* (1895) **1** : to drive from a tee **2** : BEGIN, START **3** : to hit hard **4** : to make an angry denunciation — often used with *on*

tee·pee *var of* TEPEE

tee shirt *var of* T-SHIRT

¹tee·ter \ˈtēt-ər\ *vi* [ME *titeren* to totter, reel; akin to OHG *zittarōn* to shiver, Gk *dramein* to run] (1843) **1 a** : to move unsteadily : WOBBLE **b** : WAVER, VACILLATE ⟨a passive type who ~s between conformity and revolt —R. N. Denney⟩ **2** : SEESAW

²teeter *n* (1863) : SEESAW 2b

tee·ter·board \-ˌbō(ə)rd, -ˌbó(ə)rd\ *n* (1855) **1** : SEESAW 2b **2** : a board placed on a raised support in such a way that a person standing on one end of the board is thrown into the air if another person jumps on the opposite end

tee·ter–tot·ter \ˈtēt-ər-ˌtät-ər\ *n* (ca. 1790) : SEESAW 2b

teeth *pl of* TOOTH

teethe \ˈtēth\ *vi* **teethed; teeth·ing** [back-formation fr. *teething*] (15c) : to cut one's teeth : grow teeth

teeth·er \ˈtē-thər\ *n* (1946) : an object (as a teething ring) designed for a baby to bite on during teething

teeth·ing \ˈtē-thiŋ\ *n* [*teeth*] (1732) **1** : the first growth of teeth **2** : the phenomena accompanying growth of teeth through the gums

teething ring *n* (1872) : a usu. rubber or plastic ring for a teething infant to bite on

teeth·ridge \ˈtē-ˌthrij\ *n* (1928) : the inner surface of the gums of the upper front teeth

tee·to·tal \ˈtē-ˈtōt-ᵊl, -ˌtōt-\ *adj* [*total* + *total* (abstinence)] (1834) **1** : of, relating to, or practicing teetotalism **2** : TOTAL, COMPLETE — **tee·to·tal·ly** \-ᵊl-ē\ *adv*

tee·to·tal·er *or* **tee·to·tal·ler** \-ˈtōt-ᵊl-ər\ *n* (1834) : one who practices or advocates teetotalism

tee·to·tal·ism \-ᵊl-ˌiz-əm\ *n* (1834) : the principle or practice of complete abstinence from alcoholic drinks — **tee·to·tal·ist** \-ᵊl-əst\ *n*

tee·to·tum \ˈtē-ˈtōt-əm\ *n* [¹*tee* + L *totum* all, fr. neut. of *totus* whole; fr. the letter *T* inscribed on one side as an abbr. of *totum* (take) all] (1720) : a small top usu. inscribed with letters and used in put-and-take

teff \ˈtef\ *n* [Amharic *ṭēf*] (1790) : an economically important African cereal grass (*Eragrostis abyssinica*) that is grown for its grain which yields a white flour and as a forage and hay crop — called also *teff grass*

te·fil·lin \tə-ˈfil-ən *also* -əm\ *n pl but sometimes sing in constr* [LHeb *tĕphīlīn*, fr. Aram, attachments] (1895) : the phylacteries worn by Jews

Tef·lon \ˈtef-ˌlän\ *trademark* — used for synthetic fluorine-containing resins used esp. for molding articles and for coatings to prevent sticking (as of food in cooking utensils)

teg·men \ˈteg-mən\ *n, pl* **teg·mi·na** \-mə-nə\ [NL *tegmin-*, *tegmen*, fr. L, covering, fr. *tegere* to cover — more at THATCH] (1807) : a superficial layer or cover usu. of a plant or animal part

teg·men·tal \teg-ˈment-ᵊl\ *adj* (ca. 1890) : of, relating to, or associated with an integument or a tegmentum

teg·men·tum \teg-ˈment-əm\ *n, pl* **-men·ta** \-ˈment-ə\ [NL, fr. L *tegumentum*, *tegmentum*, covering, fr. *tegere*] (1832) : an anatomical covering : TEGMEN; *esp* : the part of the ventral midbrain above the substantia nigra formed of longitudinal white fibers with arched transverse fibers and gray matter

teg·u·ment \ˈteg-yə-mənt\ *n* [ME, fr. L *tegumentum*] (15c) : INTEGUMENT

te·iid \ˈtē-(y)əd, ˈtī-əd\ *n* [NL *Teiidae*, fr. *Teius*, genus of lizards, fr. Pg *teiu*, a lizard, fr. Tupi *tejú*] (1956) : any of a family (Teiidae) of mostly tropical American lizards (as the race runner) with a flat elongate scaly tongue that ends in two long smooth points — **teiid** *adj*

tek·tite \ˈtek-ˌtīt\ *n* [ISV, fr. Gk *tēktos* molten, fr. *tēkein* to melt — more at THAW] (ca. 1922) : a glassy body of probably meteoritic origin and of rounded but indefinite shape found esp. in Czechoslovakia, Australia, and the U.S. — **tek·tit·ic** \tek-ˈtit-ik\ *adj*

tel- *or* **telo-** *comb form* [ISV, fr. Gk *telos* — more at WHEEL] : end ⟨*tel*angiectasia⟩

tel·a·mon \ˈtel-ə-ˌmän\ *n, pl* **tel·a·mo·nes** \ˌtel-ə-ˈmō-(ˌ)nēz\ [L, fr. Gk *telamōn* bearer, supporter; akin to Gk *tlēnai* to bear — more at TOLERATE] (ca. 1706) : a male figure used like a caryatid as a supporting column or pilaster

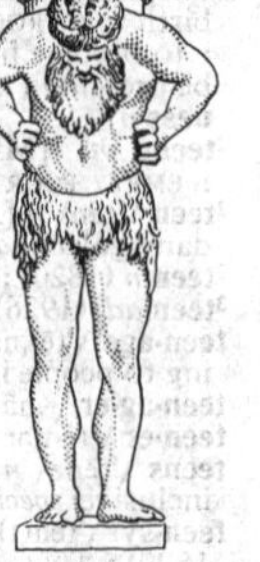

telamon

tel·an·gi·ec·ta·sia \ˌtel-ˌan-jē-ˌek-ˈtā-zh(ē-)ə, ˌtēl-, təl-\ *or* **tel·an·gi·ec·ta·sis** \-ˈek-tə-səs\ *n, pl* **-ta·sias** *or* **-ta·ses** \-tə-ˌsēz\ [NL, fr. *tel-* + *angi-* + *ectasia*, *ectasis* (as in *atelectasis*)] (1831) : an abnormal dilatation of capillary vessels and arterioles that often forms an angioma — **tel·an·gi·ec·tat·ic** \-ˌek-ˈtat-ik\ *adj*

tele \ˈtel-ē\ *n* (1946) : TELEVISION

tele- *or* **tel-** *comb form* [NL, fr. Gk *tēle-*, *tēl-*, fr. *tēle* far off — more at PALE-] **1** : distant : at a distance : over a distance ⟨*tele*gram⟩ ⟨*tel*esthesia⟩ **2** **a** : telegraph ⟨*tele*typewriter⟩ **b** : television ⟨*tele*cast⟩ **c** : telecommunication ⟨*tele*man⟩

tele·cam·era \ˈtel-i-ˌkam-(ə-)rə\ *n* (1937) : a television camera

tele·cast \ˈtel-i-ˌkast\ *vb* **-cast** *also* **-cast·ed; -cast·ing** [*tele-* + *broadcast*] *vt* (1937) : to broadcast by television ~ *vi* : to broadcast a television program — **telecast** *n* — **tele·cast·er** *n*

tele·com·mu·ni·ca·tion \ˌtel-i-kə-ˌmyü-nə-ˈkā-shən\ *n* [ISV] (1932) **1** : communication at a distance (as by telephone or television) **2** : a science that deals with telecommunication — usu. used in pl.

tele·con·fer·ence \ˈtel-i-ˌkän-f(ə-)rən(t)s, -fərn(t)s\ *n* (1953) : a conference among people remote from one another who are linked by telecommunication devices (as telephones, televisions, or computer terminals) — **tele·con·fer·enc·ing** \-f(ə-)rən(t)-siŋ, -fərn(t)-siŋ\ *n*

Tele·copi·er \ˈtel-ə-ˌkäp-ē-ər\ *trademark* — used for transmitting and receiving equipment for producing facsimile copies of documents

tele·course \ˈtel-i-ˌkō(ə)rs, -ˌkȯ(ə)rs\ *n* (1950) : a course of study conducted over television

tele·fac·sim·i·le \ˌtel-i-fak-ˈsim-ə-(ˌ)lē\ *n* (1952) : a system of transmitting and reproducing fixed graphic material (as printing) by means of signals transmitted over telephone lines

tele·film \ˈtel-i-ˌfilm\ *n* (1939) : a motion picture produced for televising

tele·ge·nic \ˌtel-ə-ˈjen-ik, -ˈjēn-\ *adj* (1939) : having an appearance and manner that are markedly attractive to television viewers

[1]**tele·gram** \ˈtel-ə-ˌgram, *Southern also* -grəm\ *n* (ca. 1852) : a telegraphic dispatch

[2]**tele·gram** \-ˌgram\ *vt* **-grammed; -gram·ming** (1864) : TELEGRAPH

[1]**tele·graph** \-ˌgraf\ *n* [F *télégraphe*, fr. *télé-* tele- (fr. Gk *tēle-*) + *-graphe* -graph] (1794) **1** : an apparatus for communication at a distance by coded signals; *esp* : an apparatus, system, or process for communication at a distance by electric transmission over wire **2** : TELEGRAM

[2]**telegraph** *vt* (1805) **1** **a** : to send or communicate by or as if by telegraph **b** : to send a telegram to **c** : to send by means of a telegraphic order ⟨~ flowers to a sick friend⟩ **2** : to make known by signs esp. unknowingly and in advance ⟨~ a punch⟩ — **te·leg·ra·pher** \tə-ˈleg-rə-fər\ *n* — **te·leg·ra·phist** \-fəst\ *n*

tele·graph·ese \ˌtel-ə-graf-ˈēz, -ˈēs\ *n* (1885) : language characterized by the terseness and ellipses that are common in telegrams

tele·graph·ic \ˌtel-ə-ˈgraf-ik\ *adj* (1794) **1** : of or relating to the telegraph **2** : CONCISE, TERSE ⟨with ~ economy of words —F. S. Mitchell⟩ — **tele·graph·i·cal·ly** \-i-k(ə-)lē\ *adv*

te·leg·ra·phy \tə-ˈleg-rə-fē\ *n* (1795) : the use or operation of a telegraph apparatus or system for transmitting or receiving communications

tele·ki·ne·sis \ˌtel-i-kə-ˈnē-səs, -kī-\ *n* [NL, fr. Gk *tēle-* + *kinēsis* motion — more at -KINESIS] (1890) : the apparent production of motion in objects (as by a spiritualistic medium) without contact or other physical means — **tele·ki·net·ic** \-ˈnet-ik\ *adj* — **tele·ki·net·i·cal·ly** \-i-k(ə-)lē\ *adv*

Te·lem·a·chus \tə-ˈlem-ə-kəs\ *n* [L, fr. Gk *Tēlemachos*] : the son of Odysseus and Penelope who contrived with his father to slay his mother's suitors

tel·e·mark \ˈtel-ə-ˌmärk\ *n, often cap* [Norw, fr. *Telemark*, region in Norway] (1910) : a turn in skiing in which the outside ski is advanced considerably ahead of the other ski and then turned inward at a steadily widening angle until the turn is completed

tele·mar·ket·ing \ˌtel-ə-ˈmär-kət-iŋ\ *n* (1982) : the marketing of goods or services by telephone

[1]**tele·me·ter** \ˈtel-ə-ˌmēt-ər\ *n* [ISV] (ca. 1860) **1** : an instrument for measuring the distance of an object from an observer **2** : an electrical apparatus for measuring a quantity (as pressure, speed, or temperature), transmitting the result esp. by radio to a distant station, and there indicating or recording the quantity measured

[2]**telemeter** *vt* (1925) : to transmit (as the measurement of a quantity) by telemeter ~ *vi* : to telemeter the measurement of a quantity

te·lem·e·try \tə-ˈlem-ə-trē\ *n* (ca. 1891) **1** : the science or process of telemetering data **2** : data transmitted by telemetry **3** : BIOTELEMETRY — **tele·met·ric** \ˌtel-ə-ˈme-trik\ *adj* — **tele·met·ri·cal·ly** \-tri-k(ə-)lē\ *adv*

tel·en·ceph·a·lon \ˌtel-en-ˈsef-ə-ˌlän, -lən\ *n* [NL, fr. *tel-* + *encephalon*] (ca. 1909) : the anterior subdivision of the forebrain comprising the cerebral hemispheres and associated structures — **tel·en·ce·phal·ic** \-ˌen-sə-ˈfal-ik\ *adj*

te·le·o·log·i·cal \ˌtel-ē-ə-ˈläj-i-kəl, ˌtēl-\ *also* **te·le·o·log·ic** \-ˈläj-ik\ *adj* (1798) : exhibiting or relating to design or purpose esp. in nature — **te·le·o·log·i·cal·ly** \-i-k(ə-)lē\ *adv*

te·le·ol·o·gy \ˌtel-ē-ˈäl-ə-jē, ˌtēl-\ *n* [NL *teleologia*, fr. Gk *tele-*, *telos* end, purpose + *-logia* -logy — more at WHEEL] (1740) **1** **a** : the study of evidences of design in nature **b** : a doctrine (as in vitalism) that ends are immanent in nature **c** : a doctrine explaining phenomena by final causes **2** : the fact or character attributed to nature or natural processes of being directed toward an end or shaped by a purpose **3** : the use of design or purpose as an explanation of natural phenomena — **te·le·ol·o·gist** \-jəst\ *n*

te·le·ost \ˈtel-ē-ˌäst, ˈtē-lē-\ *n* [deriv. of Gk *teleios* complete, perfect (fr. *telos* end) + *osteon* bone — more at OSSEOUS] (1862) : any of a group (Teleostei or Teleostomi) of fishes comprising the fishes with a bony rather than a cartilaginous skeleton and including all jawed fishes with the exception of the elasmobranchs and sometimes the ganoids and dipnoans — **teleost** *adj* — **te·le·os·te·an** \ˌtel-ē-ˈäs-tē-ən, ˌtēl-\ *adj*

te·lep·a·thy \tə-ˈlep-ə-thē\ *n* (ca. 1882) : apparent communication from one mind to another by extrasensory means — **tele·path·ic** \ˌtel-ə-ˈpath-ik\ *adj* — **tele·path·i·cal·ly** \-i-k(ə-)lē\ *adv*

[1]**tele·phone** \ˈtel-ə-ˌfōn\ *n, often attrib* (1849) : an instrument for reproducing sounds at a distance; *specif* : one in which sound is converted into electrical impulses for transmission by wire

[2]**telephone** *vb* **-phoned; -phon·ing** *vi* (1879) : to communicate by telephone ~ *vt* **1** : to send by telephone **2** : to speak to by telephone — **tele·phon·er** *n*

telephone booth *n* (ca. 1895) : an enclosure within which one may stand or sit while making a telephone call

telephone box *n, Brit* (1904) : a public telephone booth

telephone directory *n* (1907) : a book listing names, addresses, and telephone numbers of telephone subscribers — called also *telephone book*

telephone number *n* (1885) : a number assigned to a telephone and used by a person to call that telephone

telephone receiver *n* (1906) : a device (as in a telephone) for converting electric impulses or varying current into sound

tele·phon·ic \ˌtel-ə-ˈfän-ik\ *adj* (1834) **1** : conveying sound to a distance **2** : of, relating to, or conveyed by telephone — **tele·phon·i·cal·ly** \-i-k(ə-)lē\ *adv*

te·le·pho·nist \tə-ˈlef-ə-nist, ˈtel-ə-ˌfō-nist\ *n, Brit* (1884) : a telephone switchboard operator

te·le·pho·ny \tə-ˈlef-ə-nē *also* ˈtel-ə-ˌfō-\ *n* (ca. 1835) : the use or operation of an apparatus for transmission of sounds between widely removed points with or without connecting wires

[1]**tele·pho·to** \ˌtel-ə-ˈfōt-(ˌ)ō\ *adj* (ca. 1895) : being a camera lens system designed to give a large image of a distant object; *also* : relating to or being photography in which a telephoto lens is used

[2]**telephoto** *n, pl* **-tos** (ca. 1909) **1** : a telephoto lens **2** : a photograph taken with a camera having a telephoto lens

Telephoto *trademark* — used for an apparatus for transmitting photographs electrically or for a photograph so transmitted

tele·pho·to·graph·ic \ˌtel-ə-ˌfōt-ə-ˈgraf-ik\ *adj* (1892) : of, relating to, or being the photographic process of telephotography

tele·pho·tog·ra·phy \-fə-ˈtäg-rə-fē\ *n* [ISV] (1881) **1** : FACSIMILE 2 **2** : the photography of distant objects (as by a camera provided with a telephoto lens)

tele·play \ˈtel-i-ˌplā\ *n* (1952) : a play written for television

tele·por·ta·tion \ˌtel-ə-ˌpōr-ˈtā-shən, -ˌpȯr-, -pər-\ *n* [*tele-* + *-portation* (as in *transportation*)] (1931) : the act or process of moving an object or person without physical contact by psychokinesis — **tele·port** \ˈtel-ə-ˌpō(ə)rt, -ˌpȯ(ə)rt\ *vt*

tele·print·er \ˈtel-ə-ˌprint-ər\ *n* (1929) : a device capable of producing hard copy from signals received over a communications circuit; *esp* : TELETYPEWRITER

tele·pro·cess·ing \-ˈpräs-ˌes-iŋ, -ˈprōs-, -əs-\ *n* (1962) : computer processing via remote terminals

Tele·Promp·Ter \ˈtel-ə-ˌpräm(p)-tər\ *trademark* — used for a device for unrolling a magnified script in front of a speaker on television

tele·ran \ˈtel-ə-ˌran\ *n* [*tele*vision-*ra*dar *n*avigation] (1946) : a system of aerial navigation that utilizes a combination of television and radar for the guidance of aircraft

[1]**tele·scope** \ˈtel-ə-ˌskōp\ *n, often attrib* [NL *telescopium*, fr. Gk *tēleskopos* farseeing, fr. *tēle-* tele- + *skopos* watcher; akin to Gk *skopein* to look — more at SPY] (1648) **1** : a usu. tubular optical instrument for viewing distant objects by means of the refraction of light rays through a lens or the reflection of light rays by a concave mirror — compare REFLECTOR, REFRACTOR **2** : any of various tubular magnifying optical instruments **3** : RADIO TELESCOPE **4** : an expandable traveling bag having a top half that slips over the bottom half and is fastened with straps — called also *telescope bag*

[2]**telescope** *vb* **-scoped; -scop·ing** *vi* (1867) **1** : to force a way into or enter another lengthwise as the result of collision **2** : to slide or pass one within another like the cylindrical sections of a hand telescope **3** : to become telescoped ~ *vt* **1** : to cause to telescope **2** : COMPRESS, CONDENSE ⟨the book arbitrarily ~*s* time and space, and as arbitrarily extends them —Phoebe Adams⟩

tele·scop·ic \ˌtel-ə-ˈskäp-ik\ *adj* (1705) **1** **a** : of, relating to, or performed with a telescope **b** : suitable for seeing or magnifying distant objects **2** : seen or discoverable only by a telescope ⟨~ stars⟩ **3** : able to discern objects at a distance **4** : having parts that telescope — **tele·scop·i·cal·ly** \-i-k(ə-)lē\ *adv*

tel·e·sis \ˈtel-ə-səs\ *n, pl* **-e·ses** \-ˌsēz\ [NL, fr. Gk, fulfillment, fr. *telein* to complete, fr. *telos* end — more at WHEEL] (1898) : progress that is intelligently planned and directed : the attainment of desired ends by the application of intelligent human effort to the means

tele·text \ˈtel-ə-ˌtekst\ *n* (1974) : an electronic system in which printed matter is broadcast by a television station and displayed on a subscriber's television set having a decoder

tele·thon \ˈtel-ə-ˌthän\ *n* [*tele-* + *-thon* (as in *marathon*)] (1949) : a long television program usu. to solicit funds esp. for a charity

Tele·type \ˈtel-ə-ˌtīp\ *trademark* — used for a teletypewriter

Tele·type·set·ter \ˌtel-ə-ˈtīp-ˌset-ər\ *trademark* — used for a telegraphic apparatus for the automatic operation of a keyboard typesetting machine

tele·type·writ·er \-ˌrīt-ər\ *n* (1903) : a printing device resembling a typewriter that is used to send and receive telephonic signals

te·leu·to·spore \tə-ˈlüt-ə-ˌspō(ə)r, -ˌspȯ(ə)r\ *n* [Gk *teleutē* end (akin to Gk *telos* end) + ISV *spore* — more at WHEEL] (ca. 1847) : TELIOSPORE

tel·evan·ge·list \ˌtel-i-ˈvan-jə-ləst\ *n* (1973) : an evangelist who conducts regularly televised religious services — **tel·evan·ge·lism** \-ˌliz-əm\ *n*

tele·view \ˈtel-i-ˌvyü\ *vi* (1935) : to observe or watch by means of a television receiver — **tele·view·er** *n*

tele·vise \ˈtel-ə-ˌvīz\ *vb* **-vised; -vis·ing** [back-formation fr. *television*] *vt* (1927) : to pick up and usu. broadcast (as a baseball game) by television ~ *vi* : to broadcast by television

tele·vi·sion \ˈtel-ə-ˌvizh-ən *esp Brit* ˌtel-ə-ˈ\ *n* [F *télévision,* fr. *télé-* tele- (fr. Gk *tēle-*) + *vision*] (1907) **1 :** an electronic system of transmitting transient images of fixed or moving objects together with sound over a wire or through space by apparatus that converts light and sound into electrical waves and reconverts them into visible light rays and audible sound **2 :** a television receiving set **3 a :** the television broadcasting industry **b :** television as a medium of communication

television tube *n* (1937) : PICTURE TUBE

tele·vi·sor \ˈtel-ə-ˌvī-zər\ *n* (1926) **1 :** a transmitting or receiving apparatus for television **2 :** a television broadcaster : TELECASTER

tele·vi·su·al \ˌtel-ə-ˈvizh-(ə-)wəl, -ˈvizh-əl\ *adj, chiefly Brit* (1926) : of, relating to, or suitable for broadcast by television

tel·ex \ˈtel-ˌeks\ *n* [*teleprinter* + *exchange*] (1932) : a communication service involving teletypewriters connected by wire through automatic exchanges — **telex** *vt*

te·lic \ˈtel-ik, ˈtēl-\ *adj* [Gk *telikos,* fr. *telos* end — more at WHEEL] (ca. 1846) : tending toward an end — **te·li·cal·ly** \-i-k(ə-)lē\ *adv*

te·lio·spore \ˈtē-lē-ə-ˌspō(ə)r, -ˌspȯ(ə)r\ *n* [Gk *teleios* complete (fr. *telos* end) + E *spore*] (1905) : a thick-walled chlamydospore that is the final stage in the life cycle of a rust fungus and that after nuclear fusion gives rise to the basidium

te·li·um \ˈtē-lē-əm\ *n, pl* **te·lia** \-lē-ə\ [NL, fr. Gk *teleios* complete] (ca. 1905) : a teliospore-containing sorus or pustule on the host plant of a rust fungus — **te·li·al** \ˈtē-lē-əl\ *adj*

[1]**tell** \ˈtel\ *vb* **told** \ˈtōld\; **tell·ing** [ME *tellen,* fr. OE *tellan;* akin to OHG *zellen* to count, tell, OE *talu* tale] *vt* (bef. 12c) **1 :** COUNT, ENUMERATE ⟨all *told* there were 27 public schools —C. L. Jones⟩ **2 a :** to relate in detail : NARRATE **b :** to give utterance to : SAY ⟨who dares think one thing, and another ~ —Alexander Pope⟩ **3 a :** to make known : DIVULGE, REVEAL **b :** to express in words ⟨she never *told* her love —Shak.⟩ **4 a :** to report to : INFORM **b :** to assure emphatically ⟨they did not do it, I ~ you⟩ **5 :** ORDER, DIRECT ⟨*told* me to wait⟩ **6 :** to ascertain by observing : FIND OUT ~ *vi* **1 :** to give an account **2 :** to act as an informer — often used with *on* ⟨I'll get even with you if you ever ~ on me —*Inside Detective*⟩ **3 :** to take effect : have a marked effect **4 :** to serve as evidence or indication ***syn*** see REVEAL

[2]**tell** *n* [Ar *tall*] (1864) : HILL, MOUND; *specif* : an ancient mound in the Middle East composed of remains of successive settlements

tell·er \ˈtel-ər\ *n* (14c) **1 :** one that relates or communicates ⟨a ~ of stories⟩ **2 :** one that reckons or counts: as **a :** one appointed to count votes **b :** a member of a bank's staff concerned with the direct handling of money received or paid out

tell·ing \ˈtel-iŋ\ *adj* (1851) : carrying great weight and producing a marked effect : EFFECTIVE, EXPRESSIVE ⟨the most ~ evidence⟩ ***syn*** see VALID — **tell·ing·ly** \-iŋ-lē\ *adv*

tell off *vt* (1827) **1 :** to number and set apart; *esp* : to assign to a special duty ⟨*told off* a detail and put them to opening a trench —J. F. Dobie⟩ **2 :** REPRIMAND, SCOLD ⟨*tell off* the big shots⟩

tell·tale \ˈtel-ˌtāl\ *n* (1548) **1 a :** TALEBEARER, INFORMER **b :** an outward sign : INDICATION **2 :** a device for indicating or recording something: as **a :** a device for keeping a check on employees; *esp* : TIME CLOCK **b :** a device that shows the position of the helm or rudder **c :** a strip of metal on the front wall of a racquets or squash court usu. to a height of from 2 to 2½ feet above the ground over which the ball must be hit **d :** a railroad warning device (as a row of long strips hanging over tracks at the approach to a low overhead bridge) — **telltale** *adj*

tellur- *or* **telluro-** *comb form* [L *tellur-, tellus* — more at THILL] **1 :** earth ⟨*tellur*ian⟩ **2** [NL *tellurium*] : tellurium ⟨*tellur*ic⟩

tel·lu·ri·an \tə-ˈlu̇r-ē-ən, te-\ *adj* (1846) : of, relating to, or characteristic of the earth

tel·lu·ric \tə-ˈlu̇(ə)r-ik, te-\ *adj* (1800) **1 :** of, relating to, or containing tellurium esp. with a higher valence than in tellurous compounds **2 :** of or relating to the earth : TERRESTRIAL **3 :** being or relating to a usu. natural electric current flowing near the earth's surface

tel·lu·ride \ˈtel-yə-ˌrīd\ *n* [ISV] (1849) : a binary compound of tellurium usu. with a more electropositive element or group

tel·lu·ri·um \tə-ˈlu̇r-ē-əm, te-\ *n* [NL, fr. L *tellur-, tellus* earth] (1800) : a semimetallic element related to selenium and sulfur that occurs in a silvery white brittle crystalline form of metallic luster, in a dark amorphous form, or combined with metals and that is used esp. in alloys — see ELEMENT table

tel·lu·rom·e·ter \ˌtel-yə-ˈräm-ət-ər\ *n* (1957) : a device that measures distance by means of microwaves

tel·lu·rous \ˈtel-yə-rəs; tə-ˈlu̇r-əs, te-\ *adj* [ISV] (1842) : of, relating to, or containing tellurium esp. with a lower valence than in telluric compounds

tel·ly \ˈtel-ē\ *n, pl* **tellys** *also* **tellies** [by shortening & alter.] *chiefly Brit* (1939) : TELEVISION

telo- — see TEL-

telo·cen·tric \ˌtel-ə-ˈsen-trik, ˌtēl-\ *adj* [ISV *tel-* + *centromere* + *-ic*] (1939) : having the form of a straight rod due to the terminal position of the centromere ⟨a ~ chromosome⟩ — **telocentric** *n*

te·lome \ˈtē-ˌlōm\ *n* [ISV] (ca. 1935) : a basic structural unit of the vascular plant consisting typically of a terminal branchlet with distal sporangium and vascular supply

telo·mere \ˈtel-ə-ˌmi(ə)r, ˈtēl-\ *n* [ISV] (1940) : the natural end of a chromosome

telo·phase \ˈtel-ə-ˌfāz, ˈtēl-\ *n* [ISV] (1895) **1 :** the final stage of mitosis in which the spindle disappears and two new nuclei appear each with a set of chromosomes **2 :** a stage in meiosis that is usu. the final stage in the first and second meiotic divisions but may be missing in the first and that is characterized by formation of the nuclear membrane and by changes in coiling and arrangement of the chromosomes

te·los \ˈtel-ˌäs, ˈtē-ˌläs\ *n* [Gk — more at WHEEL] (1904) : an ultimate end

telo·tax·is \ˌtel-ə-ˈtak-səs, ˌtēl-\ *n* [NL] (1934) : a taxis in which an organism orients itself in respect to a stimulus (as a light source) as though that were the only stimulus acting on it

tel·pher \ˈtel-fər\ *n* [irreg. fr. Gk *tēle-* tele- + *pherein* to bear — more at BEAR] (ca. 1901) : a light car suspended from and running on aerial cables; *esp* : one propelled by electricity

tel·son \ˈtel-sən\ *n* [NL, fr. Gk, end of a plowed field; prob. akin to Gk *telos* end] (ca. 1855) : the terminal segment of the body of an arthropod or segmented worm; *esp* : that of a crustacean forming the middle lobe of the tail

Tel·u·gu \ˈtel-ə-ˌgü\ *n, pl* **Telugu** *or* **Telugus** (1789) **1 :** a member of the largest group of people in Andhra Pradesh, India **2 :** the Dravidian language of the Telugu people

tem·blor \ˈtem-blər; ˈtem-ˌblō(ə)r, -ˌblȯ(ə)r, tem-ˈ\ *n* [Sp, lit., trembling, fr. *temblar* to tremble, fr. ML *tremulare* — more at TREMBLE] (1876) : EARTHQUAKE

tem·er·ar·i·ous \ˌtem-ə-ˈrer-ē-əs, -ˈrar-\ *adj* [L *temerarius,* fr. *temere*] (1532) : marked by temerity : rashly or presumptuously daring — **tem·er·ar·i·ous·ly** *adv* — **tem·er·ar·i·ous·ness** *n*

te·mer·i·ty \tə-ˈmer-ət-ē\ *n, pl* **-ties** [ME *temeryte,* fr. L *temeritas,* fr. *temere* at random, rashly, lit., in the dark; akin to OHG *demar* darkness, L *tenebrae,* Skt *tamas*] (15c) **1 :** unreasonable or foolhardy contempt of danger or opposition : RASHNESS, RECKLESSNESS **2 :** an act or instance of temerity

syn TEMERITY, AUDACITY, HARDIHOOD, EFFRONTERY, NERVE, CHEEK, GALL, CHUTZPAH mean conspicuous or flagrant boldness. TEMERITY suggests boldness arising from rashness and contempt of danger; AUDACITY implies a disregard of restraints commonly imposed by convention or prudence; HARDIHOOD suggests firmness in daring and defiance; EFFRONTERY implies shameless, insolent disregard of propriety or courtesy; NERVE, CHEEK, GALL, and CHUTZPAH are informal equivalents for EFFRONTERY.

temp \ˈtemp\ *n* (ca. 1931) : a temporary worker

tem·peh \ˈtem-ˌpā\ *n* [Indonesian *tempé*] (1961) : an Asian food prepared by fermenting soybeans with a rhizopus

[1]**tem·per** \ˈtem-pər\ *vb* **tem·pered; tem·per·ing** \-p(ə-)riŋ\ [ME *temperen,* fr. OE & OF; OE *temprian* & OF *temprer,* fr. L *temperare* to moderate, mix, temper; prob. akin to L *tempor-, tempus* time — more at TEMPORAL] *vt* (bef. 12c) **1 :** to adjust to the needs of a situation by a counterbalancing or mitigating addition : MODERATE ⟨~ justice with mercy⟩ **2** *archaic* **a :** to exercise control over : GOVERN, RESTRAIN **b :** to cause to be well disposed : MOLLIFY ⟨~*ed* and reconciled them both —Richard Steele⟩ **3 :** to bring to a suitable state by mixing in or adding a usu. liquid ingredient: as **a :** to mix (clay) with water or a modifier (as grog) and knead to a uniform texture **b :** to mix oil with (colors) in making paint ready for use **4 a** (1) **:** to soften (hardened steel or cast iron) by reheating at a lower temperature (2) **:** to harden (steel) by reheating and cooling in oil **b :** to anneal or toughen (glass) by a process of gradually heating and cooling **5 :** to make stronger and more resilient through hardship : TOUGHEN ⟨troops ~*ed* in battle⟩ **6 a :** to put in tune with something : ATTUNE **b :** to adjust the pitch of (a note, chord, or instrument) to a temperament ~ *vi* : to produce satisfactory temper (as in a metal) — **tem·per·able** \-p(ə-)rə-bəl\ *adj* — **tem·per·er** \-pər-ər\ *n*

[2]**temper** *n* (14c) **1 a** *archaic* : a suitable proportion or balance of qualities : a middle state between extremes : MEAN, MEDIUM ⟨virtue is . . . a just ~ between propensities —T. B. Macaulay⟩ **b** *archaic* : CHARACTER, QUALITY ⟨the ~ of the land you design to sow —John Mortimer⟩ **c :** characteristic tone : TREND, TENDENCY ⟨the ~ of the times⟩ **d :** high quality of mind or spirit : COURAGE, METTLE **2 :** the state of a substance with respect to certain desired qualities (as hardness, elasticity, or workability): as **a** (1) **:** the degree of hardness or resiliency given steel by tempering (2) **:** the color of steel after tempering **b :** the feel and relative solidity of leather **3 a :** a characteristic cast of mind or state of feeling : DISPOSITION **b :** calmness of mind : COMPOSURE, EQUANIMITY **c :** state of feeling or frame of mind at a particular time usu. dominated by a single strong emotion **d :** heat of mind or emotion : proneness to anger : PASSION **4 :** a substance added to or mixed with something else to modify the properties of the latter: as **a :** any of various mixtures of metals added to another metal in making an alloy **b :** the carbon content of steel that affects its hardening properties ***syn*** see DISPOSITION

tem·pera \ˈtem-pə-rə\ *n* [It *tempera,* lit., temper, fr. *temperare* to temper, fr. L] (1832) **1 :** a process of painting in which an albuminous or colloidal medium (as egg yolk) is employed as a vehicle instead of oil; *also* : a painting done in tempera **2 :** POSTER COLOR

tem·per·a·ment \ˈtem-p(ə-)rə-mənt, -pər-mənt\ *n* [ME, fr. L *temperamentum,* fr. *temperare* to mix, temper] (15c) **1** *obs* **a :** constitution of a substance, body, or organism with respect to the mixture or balance of its elements, qualities, or parts : MAKEUP **b :** COMPLEXION 1 **2** *obs* **a :** CLIMATE **b :** TEMPERATURE 2 **3 a :** the peculiar or distinguishing mental or physical character determined by the relative proportions of the humors according to medieval physiology **b :** characteristic or habitual inclination or mode of emotional response ⟨a nervous ~⟩ **c :** extremely high sensibility; *esp* : excessive sensitiveness or irritability **4 a :** the act or process of tempering or modifying : ADJUSTMENT, COMPROMISE **b :** middle course : MEAN **5 :** the process of slightly modifying the musical intervals of the pure scale to produce a set of 12 equally spaced tones to the octave which enables a keyboard instrument to play in all keys ***syn*** see DISPOSITION

tem·per·a·men·tal \ˌtem-p(ə-)rə-ˈment-ᵊl\ *adj* (1646) **1 :** of, relating to, or arising from temperament : CONSTITUTIONAL ⟨~ peculiarities⟩ **2 a :** marked by excessive sensitivity and impulsive changes of mood ⟨a ~ opera singer⟩ **b :** unpredictable in behavior or performance — **tem·per·a·men·tal·ly** \-ᵊl-ē\ *adv*

tem·per·ance \'tem-p(ə-)rən(t)s, -pərn(t)s\ *n* [ME, fr. L *temperantia,* fr. *temperant-, temperans,* prp. of *temperare* to moderate, be moderate] (14c) **1 :** moderation in action, thought, or feeling : RESTRAINT **2 :** habitual moderation in the indulgence of the appetites or passions; *specif* : moderation in or abstinence from the use of intoxicating drink

tem·per·ate \'tem-p(ə-)rət\ *adj* [ME *temperat,* fr. L *temperatus,* fr. pp. of *temperare*] (14c) **1 :** marked by moderation: as **a :** keeping or held within limits : not extreme or excessive : MILD **b :** moderate in indulgence of appetite or desire **c :** moderate in the use of intoxicating liquors **d :** marked by an absence or avoidance of extravagance, violence, or extreme partisanship : RESTRAINED **2 a :** having a moderate climate **b :** found in or associated with a moderate climate ⟨~ insects⟩ **3 :** existing as a prophage in infected cells and rarely causing lysis ⟨~ bacteriophages⟩ — **tem·per·ate·ly** *adv* — **tem·per·ate·ness** *n*

temperate rain forest *n* (ca. 1930) **:** woodland of temperate but usu. rather mild climatic areas with heavy rainfall usu. including numerous kinds of trees and distinguished from tropical rain forest by the presence of a dominant tree

temperate zone *n, often cap T&Z* (1551) **:** the area or region between the tropic of Cancer and the arctic circle or between the tropic of Capricorn and the antarctic circle

tem·per·a·ture \'tem-pə(r)-,chu̇(ə)r, -p(ə-)rə-, chər, -,t(y)u̇(ə)r; *in rapid speech* 'tem(p)-chər\ *n* [L *temperatura* mixture, moderation, fr. *temperatus,* pp. of *temperare*] (1533) **1** *archaic* **a :** COMPLEXION 1 **b :** TEMPERAMENT 3b **2 a :** degree of hotness or coldness measured on a definite scale — compare THERMOMETER **b :** the degree of heat that is natural to the body of a living being **c :** abnormally high body heat **d :** relative state of emotional warmth ⟨aware of a change in the ~ of our friendship —Christopher Isherwood⟩

temperature gradient *n* (1882) **:** the rate of change of temperature with displacement in a given direction (as with increase of height)

tem·pered \'tem-pərd\ *adj* (14c) **1 a :** having the elements mixed in satisfying proportions : TEMPERATE **b :** qualified, lessened, or diluted by the mixture or influence of an additional ingredient : MODERATED ⟨a pale gleam of ~ sunlight fell through the leaves —W. H. Hudson †1922⟩ **2 :** treated by tempering **3 :** having a specified temper — used in combination ⟨short-*tempered*⟩ **4 :** conforming to adjustment by temperament — used of a musical interval, intonation, semitone, or scale

[1]**tem·pest** \'tem-pəst\ *n* [ME, fr. OF *tempeste,* fr. (assumed) VL *tempesta,* alter. of L *tempestas* season, weather, storm, fr. *tempus* time — more at TEMPORAL] (13c) **1 :** an extensive violent wind esp. when accompanied by rain, hail, or snow **2 :** TUMULT, UPROAR

[2]**tempest** *vt* (14c) **:** to raise a tempest in or around

tem·pes·tu·ous \tem-'pes(h)-chə-wəs\ *adj* [LL *tempestuosus,* fr. OL *tempestus* season, weather, storm, fr. *tempus*] (15c) **:** of, relating to, or resembling a tempest : TURBULENT, STORMY ⟨~ weather⟩ ⟨a ~ debate⟩ — **tem·pes·tu·ous·ly** *adv* — **tem·pes·tu·ous·ness** *n*

Tem·plar \'tem-plər\ *n* [ME *templer,* fr. OF *templier,* fr. ML *templarius,* fr. L *templum* temple] (13c) **1 :** a knight of a religious military order established in the early 12th century in Jerusalem for the protection of pilgrims and the Holy Sepulcher **2** *not cap* **:** a barrister or student of law in London **3 :** KNIGHT TEMPLAR 2

tem·plate *or* **tem·plet** \'tem-plət\ *n* [prob. fr. F *templet,* dim. of *temple,* part of a loom, prob. fr. L *templum*] (1677) **1 :** a short piece or block placed horizontally in a wall under a beam to distribute its weight or pressure (as over a door) **2 a** (1) **:** a gauge, pattern, or mold (as a thin plate or board) used as a guide to the form of a piece being made (2) **:** a molecule (as of DNA) that serves as a pattern for the generation of another macromolecule (as messenger RNA) **b :** OVERLAY c

[1]**tem·ple** \'tem-pəl\ *n* [ME, fr. OE & OF; OE *tempel* & OF *temple,* both fr. L *templum* space marked out for observation of auguries, temple, small timber; prob. akin to L *tempus* time] (bef. 12c) **1 :** an edifice for religious exercises: as **a** *often cap* **:** one of three successive national sanctuaries in ancient Jerusalem **b :** a building for Mormon sacred ordinances **c :** a Reform or Conservative synagogue **2 :** a local lodge of any of various fraternal orders; *also* **:** the building housing it **3 :** a place devoted to a special purpose — **tem·pled** \-pəld\ *adj*

[2]**temple** *n* [ME, fr. MF, fr. (assumed) VL *tempula,* alter. of L *tempora* (pl.) temples; prob. akin to L *tempor-, tempus* time] (14c) **1 :** the flattened space on each side of the forehead of some mammals (as man) **2 :** one of the side supports of a pair of glasses jointed to the bows and passing on each side of the head

tem·po \'tem-(,)pō\ *n, pl* **tem·pi** \-(,)pē\ *or* **tempos** [It, lit., time, fr. L *tempus*] (ca. 1724) **1 :** the rate of speed of a musical piece or passage indicated by one of a series of directions (as largo, presto, or allegro) and often by an exact metronome marking **2 :** rate of motion or activity : PACE **3 :** a turn to move in chess in relation to the number of moves required to gain an objective

[1]**tem·po·ral** \'tem-p(ə-)rəl\ *adj* [ME, fr. L *temporalis,* fr. *tempor-, tempus* time; akin to Lith *tempti* to stretch, and prob. to L *tendere* to stretch — more at THIN] (14c) **1 a :** of or relating to time as opposed to eternity **b :** of or relating to earthly life **c :** lay or secular rather than clerical or sacred : CIVIL ⟨lords ~⟩ **2 :** of or relating to grammatical tense or a distinction of time **3 a :** of or relating to time as distinguished from space **b :** of or relating to the sequence of time or to a particular time : CHRONOLOGICAL — **tem·po·ral·ly** \-ē\ *adv*

[2]**temporal** *n* [MF, fr. *temporal,* adj.] (1541) **:** a temporal part (as a bone or muscle)

[3]**temporal** *adj* [MF, fr. LL *temporalis,* fr. L *tempora* temples] (1597) **:** of or relating to the temples or the sides of the skull behind the orbits

temporal bone *n* (1771) **:** a compound bone of the side of the skull of some mammals including man

tem·po·ral·i·ty \,tem-pə-'ral-ət-ē\ *n, pl* **-ties** (14c) **1 a :** civil or political as distinguished from spiritual or ecclesiastical power or authority **b :** an ecclesiastical property or revenue — often used in pl. **2 :** the quality or state of being temporal

tem·po·ral·ize \'tem-p(ə-)rə-,līz\ *vt* **-ized; -iz·ing** (1828) **1 :** SECULARIZE **2 :** to place or define in time relations

temporal lobe *n* (ca. 1891) **:** a large lobe of each cerebral hemisphere that is situated in front of the occipital lobe and contains a sensory area associated with the organ of hearing

temporal summation *n* (ca. 1950) **:** sensory summation that involves the addition of single stimuli over a short period of time

tem·po·rari·ly \,tem-pə-'rer-ə-lē\ *adv* (1694) **:** during a limited time

[1]**tem·po·rary** \'tem-pə-,rer-ē\ *adj* [L *temporarius,* fr. *tempor-, tempus* time] (1547) **:** lasting for a limited time — **tem·po·rari·ness** *n*

[2]**temporary** *n, pl* **-rar·ies** (1848) **:** one serving for a limited time ⟨adding several *temporaries* as typists during the summer⟩

temporary duty *n* (1945) **:** temporary military service away from one's permanent duty station

tem·po·rize \'tem-pə-,rīz\ *vi* **-rized; -riz·ing** [MF *temporiser,* fr. ML *temporizare* to pass the time, fr. L *tempor-, tempus*] (1579) **1 :** to act to suit the time or occasion : yield to current or dominant opinion : COMPROMISE **2 :** to draw out discussions or negotiations so as to gain time ⟨you'd have to ~ until you found out how she wanted to be advised —Mary Austin⟩ — **tem·po·ri·za·tion** \,tem-pə-rə-'zā-shən\ *n* — **tem·po·riz·er** *n*

tem·po·ro·man·dib·u·lar \'tem-pə-rō-man-'dib-yə-lər\ *adj* [*temporal* + *-o-* + *mandibular*] (ca. 1890) **:** relating to, being, or affecting the joint between the temporal bone and the mandible ⟨~ dysfunction⟩

tempt \'tem(p)t\ *vt* [ME *tempten,* fr. OF *tempter, tenter,* fr. L *temptare, tentare* to feel, try, tempt; akin to L *tendere* to stretch — more at THIN] (13c) **1 :** to entice to do wrong by promise of pleasure or gain **2 a** *obs* **:** to make trial of : TEST **b :** to try presumptuously : PROVOKE **c :** to risk the dangers of **3 a :** to induce to do something **b :** to cause to be strongly inclined ⟨was ~*ed* to call it quits⟩ ***syn*** see LURE — **tempt·able** \'tem(p)-tə-bəl\ *adj*

temp·ta·tion \tem(p)-'tā-shən\ *n* (13c) **1 :** the act of tempting or the state of being tempted esp. to evil : ENTICEMENT **2 :** something tempting : a cause or occasion of enticement

tempt·er \'tem(p)-tər\ *n* (14c) **:** one that tempts or entices

tempt·ing *adj* (1596) **:** having an appeal : ENTICING ⟨a ~ offer⟩ — **tempt·ing·ly** \-tiŋ-lē\ *adv*

tempt·ress \'tem(p)-trəs\ *n* (1594) **:** a woman who tempts or entices

tem·pu·ra \'tem-pə-rə, -,rä; tem-'pu̇r-ə\ *n* [Jp *tenpura*] (ca. 1937) **:** seafood or vegetables dipped in batter and fried in deep fat

ten \'ten\ *n* [ME, fr. OE *tīene,* fr. *tīen,* adj., ten; akin to OHG *zehan* ten, L *decem,* Gk *deka,* OE *-tig* group of ten] (bef. 12c) **1** — see NUMBER table **2 :** the 10th in a set or series ⟨wears a ~⟩ **3 :** something having 10 units or members **4 :** a 10-dollar bill — **ten** *adj or pron*

ten·a·ble \'ten-ə-bəl\ *adj* [MF, fr. OF, fr. *tenir* to hold, fr. L *tenēre* — more at THIN] (1579) **:** capable of being held, maintained, or defended : DEFENSIBLE, REASONABLE — **ten·a·bil·i·ty** \,ten-ə-'bil-ət-ē\ *n* — **ten·a·ble·ness** *n* — **ten·a·bly** \'ten-ə-blē\ *adv*

ten·ace \'ten-,ās, te-'nās, 'ten-əs\ *n* [modif. of Sp *tenaza,* lit., forceps, prob. fr. L *tenacia,* neut. pl. of *tenax*] (1655) **:** a combination of two high or relatively high cards (as ace and queen) of the same suit in one hand with one ranking two degrees below the other

te·na·cious \tə-'nā-shəs\ *adj* [L *tenac-, tenax* tending to hold fast, fr. *tenēre* to hold] (1607) **1 a :** not easily pulled apart : COHESIVE, TOUGH ⟨a ~ metal⟩ **b :** tending to adhere or cling esp. to another substance : STICKY ⟨~ burs⟩ ⟨~ clay⟩ **2 a :** persistent in maintaining or adhering to something valued as habitual ⟨a man very ~ of his rights⟩ **b :** RETENTIVE ⟨a ~ memory⟩ ***syn*** see STRONG — **te·na·cious·ly** *adv* — **te·na·cious·ness** *n*

te·nac·i·ty \tə-'nas-ət-ē\ *n* (1526) **:** the quality or state of being tenacious ***syn*** see COURAGE

te·nac·u·lum \tə-'nak-yə-ləm\ *n, pl* **-la** \-lə\ *or* **-lums** [NL, fr. LL, instrument for holding, fr. L *tenēre*] (ca. 1693) **1 :** a slender sharp-pointed hook attached to a handle and used mainly in surgery for seizing and holding parts (as arteries) **2 :** an adhesive animal structure

ten·an·cy \'ten-ən-sē\ *n, pl* **-cies** (1590) **:** a holding of an estate or a mode of holding an estate : the temporary possession or occupancy of something (as a house) that belongs to another; *also* **:** the period of a tenant's occupancy or possession

[1]**ten·ant** \'ten-ənt\ *n* [ME, fr. MF, fr. prp. of *tenir* to hold] (14c) **1 a :** one who holds or possesses real estate or sometimes personal property (as an annuity) by any kind of right **b :** one who has the occupation or temporary possession of lands or tenements of another; *specif* **:** one who rents or leases (as a house) from a landlord **2 :** OCCUPANT, DWELLER — **ten·ant·less** \-ləs\ *adj*

[2]**tenant** *vt* (1634) **:** to hold or occupy as a tenant : INHABIT — **ten·ant·able** \-ən-tə-bəl\ *adj*

tenant farmer *n* (1860) **:** a farmer who works land owned by another and pays rent either in cash or in shares of produce

ten·ant·ry \'ten-ən-trē\ *n, pl* **-ries** (14c) **1 :** TENANCY **2 :** a body of tenants

ten–cent store \ten-'sent-\ *n* (1901) **:** FIVE-AND-TEN

tench \'tench\ *n, pl* **tench** *or* **tench·es** [ME, fr. MF *tenche,* fr. LL *tinca*] (14c) **:** a Eurasian freshwater fish (*Tinca tinca*) related to the dace and noted for its ability to survive outside water

Ten Commandments *n pl* (13c) **:** the ethical commandments of God given according to biblical accounts to Moses by voice and by writing on stone tablets on Mount Sinai

[1]**tend** \'tend\ *vb* [ME *tenden,* short for *attenden* to attend] *vi* (14c) **1** *archaic* **:** LISTEN **2 :** to pay attention : apply oneself ⟨~ to your own affairs⟩ **3 :** to act as an attendant : SERVE **4** *obs* **:** AWAIT **~** *vt* **1** *archaic* **:** to attend as a servant **2 a :** to apply oneself to the care of : watch over **b :** to have or take charge of as a caretaker or overseer **c :** CULTIVATE, FOSTER **d :** to manage the operations of : MIND ⟨~ a store⟩ **3 :** to stand by (as a rope) in readiness to prevent mischance (as fouling)

[2]**tend** *vi* [ME *tenden,* fr. MF *tendre* to stretch, fr. L *tendere* — more at THIN] (14c) **1 :** to move, direct, or develop one's course in a particular direction ⟨cannot tell where society is ~*ing*⟩ **2 :** to exhibit an inclination or tendency : CONDUCE ⟨she ~*s* to be optimistic⟩

ten·dance \'ten-dən(t)s\ *n* [short for *attendance*] (1573) **1 :** watchful care **2** *archaic* **:** persons in attendance : RETINUE

ten·den·cy \'ten-dən-sē\ *n, pl* **-cies** [ML *tendentia,* fr. L *tendent-, tendens,* prp. of *tendere*] (1628) **1 a :** direction or approach toward a place, object, effect, or limit **b :** a proneness to a particular kind of thought or action **2 a :** the purposeful trend of something written or said : AIM **b :** deliberate but indirect advocacy

syn TENDENCY, TREND, DRIFT, TENOR, CURRENT mean movement in a particular direction. TENDENCY implies an inclination sometimes amounting to an impelling force ⟨the whole *tendency* of evolution is towards a diminishing birthrate —Havelock Ellis⟩ TREND applies to the general direction maintained by a winding or irregular course ⟨the long-term *trend* of the stock market is upward⟩ DRIFT may apply to a tendency determined by external forces ⟨the *drift* of the population away from large cities⟩ or it may apply to an underlying or obscure trend of meaning or discourse ⟨I see the whole *drift* of your argument —Oliver Goldsmith⟩ TENOR stresses a clearly perceptible direction and a continuous, undeviating course ⟨along the cool sequestered vale of life they kept the noiseless *tenor* of their way —Thomas Gray⟩ CURRENT implies a clearly defined but not necessarily unalterable course ⟨he has not . . . changed the *current* of our constitutional law —M.R. Cohen⟩

ten·den·tious *also* **ten·den·cious** \ten-ˈden-chəs\ *adj* (1900) **:** marked by a tendency in favor of a particular point of view **:** BIASED — **ten·den·tious·ly** *adv* — **ten·den·tious·ness** *n*

[1]**ten·der** \ˈten-dər\ *adj* [ME, fr. OF *tendre,* fr. L *tener*] (13c) **1 a :** having a soft or yielding texture **:** easily broken, cut, or damaged **:** DELICATE, FRAGILE ⟨~ feet⟩ **b :** easily chewed **:** SUCCULENT **2 a :** physically weak **:** not able to endure hardship **b :** IMMATURE, YOUNG ⟨children of ~ years⟩ **c :** incapable of resisting cold **:** not hardy **3 :** marked by, responding to, or expressing the softer emotions **:** FOND, LOVING ⟨a ~ lover⟩ **4 a :** showing care **:** CONSIDERATE, SOLICITOUS ⟨~ regard⟩ **b :** highly susceptible to impressions or emotions **:** IMPRESSIONABLE ⟨a ~ conscience⟩ **5 a :** appropriate or conducive to a delicate or sensitive constitution or character **:** GENTLE, MILD ⟨~ breeding⟩ ⟨~ irony⟩ **b :** delicate or soft in quality or tone ⟨never before heard the piano sound so ~ —Elva S. Daniels⟩ **6** *obs* **:** DEAR, PRECIOUS **7 a :** sensitive to touch or palpation ⟨~ skin⟩ **b :** sensitive to injury or insult **:** TOUCHY ⟨~ pride⟩ **c :** demanding careful and sensitive handling **:** TICKLISH ⟨a ~ situation⟩ **d** *of a ship* **:** inclined to heel over easily under sail — **ten·der·ly** *adv* — **ten·der·ness** *n*

[2]**tender** *vb* **ten·dered; ten·der·ing** \-d(ə-)riŋ\ *vt* (14c) **1 :** to make tender **:** SOFTEN, WEAKEN **2** *archaic* **:** to regard or treat with tenderness ~ *vi* **:** to become tender

[3]**tender** *n* [MF *tendre* to stretch, stretch out, offer — more at TEND] (1542) **1 :** an unconditional offer of money or service in satisfaction of a debt or obligation made to save a penalty or forfeiture for nonpayment or nonperformance **2 :** an offer or proposal made for acceptance: as **a :** an offer of a bid for a contract **b :** a public expression of willingness to buy not less than a specified number of shares of a stock at a fixed price from stockholders usu. in an attempt to gain control of the issuing company **3 :** something that may be offered in payment; *specif* **:** MONEY

[4]**tender** *vb* **ten·dered; ten·der·ing** \-d(ə-)riŋ\ *vt* (1542) **1 :** to make a tender of **2 :** to present for acceptance **:** PROFFER ⟨~*ed* my resignation⟩ ~ *vi* **:** to make a bid ⟨the nuclear consortia ~ for and build . . . power stations —Christopher Hinton⟩

[5]**tender** *n* [[1]*tender*] *obs* (1596) **:** CONSIDERATION, REGARD

[6]**tend·er** \ˈten-dər\ *n* (1675) **:** one that tends: as **a** (1) **:** a ship employed to attend other ships (as to supply provisions) (2) **:** a boat or small steamer for communication between shore and a larger ship (3) **:** a warship that provides logistic support **b :** a vehicle attached to a locomotive for carrying a supply of fuel and water

ten·der·foot \ˈten-dər-ˌfu̇t\ *n, pl* **ten·der·feet** \-ˌfēt\ *also* **ten·der·foots** \-ˌfu̇ts\ (1849) **1 :** a newcomer in a comparatively rough or newly settled region; *esp* **:** one not hardened to frontier or outdoor life **2 :** an inexperienced beginner **:** NOVICE ⟨a political ~⟩

ten·der·heart·ed \ˌten-dər-ˈhärt-əd\ *adj* (1539) **:** easily moved to love, pity, or sorrow **:** COMPASSIONATE, IMPRESSIONABLE — **ten·der·heart·ed·ly** *adv* — **ten·der·heart·ed·ness** *n*

ten·der·ize \ˈten-də-ˌrīz\ *vt* **-ized; -iz·ing** (1930) **:** to make (meat or meat products) tender by applying a process or substance that breaks down connective tissue — **ten·der·iza·tion** \ˌten-d(ə-)rə-ˈzā-shən\ *n* — **ten·der·iz·er** \ˈten-də-ˌrī-zər\ *n*

ten·der·loin \ˈten-dər-ˌlȯin\ *n* (ca. 1828) **1 :** a strip of tender meat consisting of a large internal muscle of the loin on each side of the vertebral column **2** [fr. its making possible a luxurious diet for a corrupt policeman] **:** a district of a city largely devoted to vice

ten·der–mind·ed \ˌten-dər-ˈmīn-dəd\ *adj* (1605) **:** marked by idealism, optimism, and dogmatism

ten·der·om·e·ter \ˌten-də-ˈräm-ət-ər\ *n* (1939) **:** a device for determining the maturity and tenderness of samples of fruits and vegetables

ten·di·ni·tis *or* **ten·don·itis** \ˌten-də-ˈnīt-əs\ *n* [*tendinitis* fr. NL, fr. *tendin, tendo* + *-itis; tendonitis* fr. *tendon* + *-itis*] (ca. 1901) **:** inflammation of a tendon

ten·di·nous \ˈten-də-nəs\ *adj* [NL *tendinosus,* fr. *tendin-, tendo* tendon, alter. of ML *tendon-, tendo*] (1658) **1 :** consisting of tendons **:** SINEWY ⟨~ tissue⟩ **2 :** of, relating to, or resembling a tendon

ten·don \ˈten-dən\ *n* [ML *tendon-, tendo,* fr. L *tendere* to stretch — more at THIN] (1541) **:** a tough cord or band of dense white fibrous connective tissue that unites a muscle with some other part and transmits the force which the muscle exerts

tendon of Achil·les \-ə-ˈkil-ēz\ (ca. 1885) **:** ACHILLES TENDON

ten·dresse \täⁿ-dres\ *n* [ME, fr. MF, fr. *tendre* tender] (14c) **:** FONDNESS

ten·dril \ˈten-drəl\ *n* [perh. modif. of MF *tendron,* alter. of *tendon,* lit., tendon, fr. ML *tendon-, tendo*] (1538) **1 :** a leaf, stipule, or stem modified into a slender spirally coiling sensitive organ serving to attach a plant to its support **2 :** something (as a ringlet of hair) that curls like a tendril — **ten·driled** *or* **ten·drilled** \-drəld\ *adj* — **ten·dril·ous** \-drə-ləs\ *adj*

[1]**-tene** \ˌtēn\ *adj comb form* [L *taenia* ribbon, band — more at TAENIA] **:** having (such or so many) chromosomal filaments ⟨poly*tene*⟩ ⟨pachy*tene*⟩

[2]**-tene** *n comb form* **:** stage of meiotic prophase characterized by (such) chromosomal filaments ⟨diplo*tene*⟩ ⟨pachy*tene*⟩

Ten·e·brae \ˈten-ə-ˌbrā, -ˌbrī, -ˌbrē\ *n pl but sing or pl in constr* [ML, fr. L, darkness — more at TEMERITY] (1651) **:** the office of matins and lauds for the last three days of Holy Week commemorating the sufferings and death of Christ

ten·e·brif·ic \ˌten-ə-ˈbrif-ik\ *adj* [L *tenebrae* darkness] (1785) **1 :** GLOOMY **2 :** causing gloom or darkness

te·ne·bri·o·nid \tə-ˈneb-rē-ə-nəd, ˌten-ə-ˈbrī-ə-nəd\ *n* [NL *Tenebrionidae,* fr. *Tenebrion-, Tenebrio,* type genus, fr. L, one that shuns the light, fr. *tenebrae* darkness — more at TEMERITY] (ca. 1902) **:** any of a family (Tenebrionidae) of firm-bodied mostly dark-colored vegetable-feeding beetles which often have the hind wings vestigial and functionless and whose larvae are usu. hard cylindrical worms — **tenebrionid** *adj*

te·neb·ri·ous \tə-ˈneb-rē-əs\ *adj* [by alter.] (1594) **:** TENEBROUS

ten·e·brism \ˈten-ə-ˌbriz-əm\ *n, often cap* [L *tenebrae* darkness] (1954) **:** a style of painting esp. associated with the Italian painter Caravaggio and his followers in which most of the figures are engulfed in shadow but some are dramatically illuminated by a concentrated beam of light usu. from an identifiable source — **ten·e·brist** \-brəst\ *n or adj, often cap*

ten·e·brous \ˈten-ə-brəs\ *adj* [ME, fr. MF *tenebreus,* fr. L *tenebrosus,* fr. *tenebrae*] (15c) **1 :** shut off from the light **:** DARK, MURKY **2 :** hard to understand **:** OBSCURE **3 :** causing gloom

1080 *also* **ten-eighty** \te-ˈnāt-ē\ *n* [fr. its laboratory serial number] (1945) **:** a poisonous compound sodium fluoroacetate $C_2H_2FNaO_2$ that is used as a rodenticide and pesticide

ten·e·ment \ˈten-ə-mənt\ *n* [ME, fr. MF, fr. ML *tenementum,* fr. L *tenēre* to hold — more at THIN] (14c) **1 :** land or any of various forms of incorporeal property treated like land that is held by one person from another **:** HOLDING **2 a :** a house used as a dwelling **:** RESIDENCE **b :** APARTMENT, FLAT **c :** TENEMENT HOUSE **3 :** DWELLING

ten·e·men·ta·ry \ˌten-ə-ˈment-ə-rē, -ˈmen-trē\ *adj* (1641) **:** consisting of tenements

tenement house *n* (ca. 1859) **:** APARTMENT HOUSE; *esp* **:** one meeting minimum standards of sanitation, safety, and comfort and occupied by poorer families usu. in a city

te·nes·mus \tə-ˈnez-məs\ *n* [L, fr. Gk *teinesmos,* fr. *teinein* to stretch, strain — more at THIN] (ca. 1527) **:** a distressing but ineffectual urge to evacuate the rectum or bladder

te·net \ˈten-ət *also* ˈtē-nət\ *n* [L, he holds, fr. *tenēre* to hold] (1600) **:** a principle, belief, or doctrine generally held to be true; *esp* **:** one held in common by members of an organization, group, movement, or profession

ten·fold \ˈten-ˌfōld, -ˈfōld\ *adj* [ME, fr. OE *tienfald, tienfeald,* fr. *tien* ten + *-fald, -feald* -fold] (bef. 12c) **1 :** being 10 times as great or as many **2 :** having 10 units or members — **ten·fold** \-ˈfōld\ *adv*

ten–gallon hat *n* [fr. its great size] (1927) **:** COWBOY HAT

te·nia, te·ni·a·sis *var of* TAENIA, TAENIASIS

ten·ner \ˈten-ər\ *n* [alter. of *ten*] (1861) **1 :** a 10-pound note **2 :** a 10-dollar bill

Ten·nes·see walking horse \ˈten-ə-ˌsē-\ *n* [*Tennessee,* state of U.S.] (ca. 1944) **:** any of an American breed of large easy-gaited saddle horses largely of Standardbred and Morgan ancestry — called also *Tennessee walker*

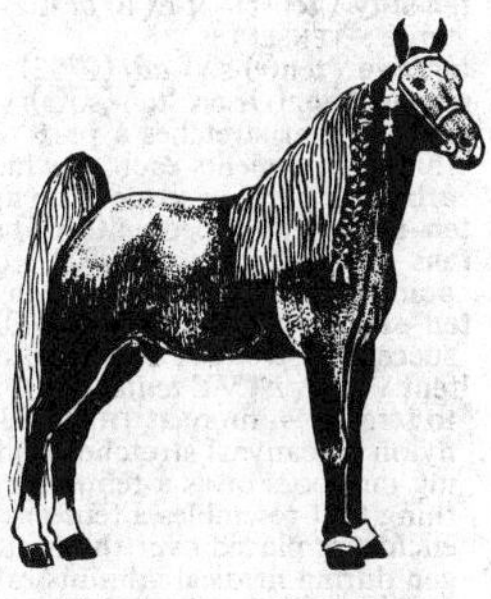

Tennessee walking horse

ten·nis \ˈten-əs\ *n, often attrib* [ME *tenetz, tenys*] (15c) **1 :** COURT TENNIS **2 :** a typically outdoor game that is played with rackets and a light elastic ball by two players or pairs of players on a level court (as of clay or grass) divided by a low net

tennis elbow *n* (1883) **:** inflammation and pain over the outer side of the elbow usu. resulting from excessive twisting of the hand

tennis shoe *n* (1892) **:** a lightweight low-cut sneaker

ten·nist \ˈten-əst\ *n* [blend of *tennis* and *-ist*] (ca. 1932) **:** a tennis player

[1]**ten·on** \ˈten-ən\ *n* [ME, fr. MF, fr. *tenir* to hold — more at TENABLE] (15c) **:** a projecting member in a piece of wood or other material for insertion into a mortise to make a joint — see DOVETAIL illustration

[2]**tenon** *vt* (1626) **1 :** to unite by a tenon **2 :** to cut or fit for insertion in a mortise

[1]**ten·or** \ˈten-ər\ *n* [ME, fr. MF, fr. L *tenor* uninterrupted course, fr. *tenēre* to hold — more at THIN] (14c) **1 a :** the drift of something spoken or written **:** PURPORT **b :** an exact copy of a writing **:** TRANSCRIPT **c :** the concept, object, or person meant in a metaphor **2 a :** the melodic line usu. forming the cantus firmus in medieval music **b :** the voice part next to the lowest in a 4-part chorus **c :** the highest natural adult male singing voice; *also* **:** a person having this voice **d :** a member of a family of instruments having a range next higher than that of the bass **3 :** a continuance in a course, movement, or activity **4 :** habitual condition **:** CHARACTER ***syn*** see TENDENCY

[2]**tenor** *adj* (1522) **:** relating to or having the range or part of a tenor

ten·or·ist \ˈten-ə-rəst\ *n* (1865) **:** one who sings tenor or plays a tenor instrument

te·no·syn·o·vi·tis \ˈten-ō-ˌsin-ə-ˈvīt-əs, ˌtē-nō-\ *n* [NL, fr. Gk *tenōn* tendon (akin to Gk *teinein* to stretch) + NL *synovitis* — more at THIN] (ca. 1860) **:** inflammation of a tendon sheath

ten·our \ˈten-ər\ *chiefly Brit var of* TENOR

ten·pen·ny \ˌten-ˌpen-ē, *Brit* -pə-nē\ *adj* (1592) **:** amounting to, worth, or costing 10 pennies

tenpenny nail *n* [fr. its original price per hundred] (15c) **:** a nail three inches long

ten·pin \ˈten-ˌpin\ *n* (1807) **1 :** a bottle-shaped bowling pin 15 inches high **2** *pl but sing in constr* **:** a bowling game using 10 tenpins and a large ball 27 inches in circumference and allowing each player to bowl 2 balls in each of 10 frames

ten·pound·er \ˈten-ˈpau̇n-dər\ *n* (1699) **:** LADYFISH 2

ten·rec \ˈten-ˌrek\ *n* [F, fr. Malagasy *tàndraka*] (ca. 1729) **:** any of numerous small often spiny insectivorous mammals (family Tenrecidae) of Madagascar

tens digit \ˈtenz-\ *n* (1955) **:** a numeral (as 5 in 456) occupying the tens place in a number expressed in the Arabic system of writing numbers

[1]tense \'ten(t)s\ *n* [ME *tens* time, tense, fr. MF, fr. L *tempus* — more at TEMPORAL] (14c) **1 :** a distinction of form in a verb to express distinctions of time or duration of the action or state it denotes **2 a :** a set of inflectional forms of a verb that express distinctions of time **b :** an inflectional form of a verb expressing a specific time distinction

[2]tense *adj* **tens·er; tens·est** [L *tensus,* fr. pp. of *tendere* to stretch — more at THIN] (1670) **1 :** stretched tight : made taut : RIGID **2 a :** feeling or showing nervous tension **b :** marked by strain or suspense **3 :** produced with the muscles involved in a relatively tense state ⟨the vowels \ē\ and \ü\ in contrast with the vowels \i\ and \u̇\ are ~⟩ ***syn*** see STIFF — **tense·ly** *adv* — **tense·ness** *n*

[3]tense *vb* **tensed; tens·ing** *vt* (1676) **:** to make tense ~ *vi* **:** to become tense

ten·sile \'ten(t)-səl *also* 'ten-ˌsīl\ *adj* [NL *tensilis,* fr. L *tensus,* pp. + *-ilis* -ile] (1626) **1 :** capable of tension : DUCTILE **2 :** of, relating to, or involving tension ⟨~ stress⟩ — **ten·sil·i·ty** \ten-'sil-ət-ē\ *n*

tensile strength *n* (ca. 1864) **:** the greatest longitudinal stress a substance can bear without tearing apart

ten·sim·e·ter \ten-'sim-ət-ər\ *n* [*tension* + *-meter*] (1904) **:** an instrument for measuring differences of vapor pressure between two liquids

ten·si·om·e·ter \ˌten(t)-sē-'äm-ət-ər\ *n* [*tension*] (1912) **1 :** a device for measuring tension (as of structural material) **2 :** an instrument for determining the moisture content of soil **3 :** an instrument for measuring the surface tension of liquids — **ten·sio·met·ric** \-sē-ō-'me-trik\ *adj* — **ten·si·om·e·try** \-sē-'äm-ə-trē\ *n*

[1]ten·sion \'ten-chən\ *n* [MF or L; MF, fr. L *tension-, tensio,* fr. *tensus,* pp.] (1533) **1 a :** the act or action of stretching or the condition or degree of being stretched to stiffness : TAUTNESS **b :** STRESS 1b **2 a :** either of two balancing forces causing or tending to cause extension **b :** the stress resulting from the elongation of an elastic body **c** *archaic* **:** PRESSURE **3 a :** inner striving, unrest, or imbalance often with physiological indication of emotion **b :** a state of latent hostility or opposition between individuals or groups **c :** a balance maintained in an artistic work between opposing forces or elements **4 :** electrical potential **5 :** a device to produce a desired tension (as in a loom) — **ten·sion·al** \'tench-nəl, -ən-ᵊl\ *adj* — **ten·sion·less** \'ten-chən-ləs\ *adj*

[2]tension *vt* **ten·sioned; ten·sion·ing** \'tench-(ə-)niŋ\ (1872) **:** to subject to tension; *esp* **:** to tighten to a desired or appropriate degree — **ten·sion·er** \-(ə-)nər\ *n*

ten·si·ty \'ten(t)-sət-ē\ *n, pl* **-ties** (ca. 1658) **:** the quality or state of being tense : TENSENESS

ten·sive \'ten(t)-siv\ *adj* (1702) **:** of, relating to, or causing tension

ten·sor \'ten(t)-sər, 'ten-ˌsȯ(ə)r\ *n* [NL, fr. L *tensus,* pp.] (1704) **1 :** a muscle that stretches a part **2 :** a generalized vector with more than three components each of which is a function of the coordinates of an arbitrary point in space of an appropriate number of dimensions

ten–speed \'ten-ˌspēd\ *n* (1973) **:** a bicycle with a 10-speed derailleur

tens place \'tenz-\ *n* (1937) **:** the place two to the left of the decimal point in a number expressed in the Arabic system of writing numbers

ten–strike \'ten-ˌstrīk\ *n* (1840) **1 :** a strike in tenpins **2 :** a highly successful stroke or achievement

[1]tent \'tent\ *n* [ME *tente,* fr. OF, fr. L *tenta,* fem. of *tentus,* pp. of *tendere* to stretch — more at THIN] (13c) **1 :** a collapsible shelter of fabric (as nylon or canvas) stretched and sustained by poles and used for camping outdoors or as a temporary building **2 :** DWELLING **3 a :** something that resembles a tent or that serves as a shelter; *esp* **:** a canopy or enclosure placed over the head and shoulders to retain vapors or oxygen during medical administration **b :** the web of a tent caterpillar — **tent·less** \'tent-ləs\ *adj*

[2]tent *vi* (1607) **1 :** to reside for the time being : LODGE **2 :** to live in a tent ~ *vt* **1 :** to cover with or as if with a tent **2 :** to lodge in tents

[3]tent *vt* [ME *tenten,* fr. *tent* attention, short for *attent,* fr. OF *attente,* fr. *attendre* to attend] *chiefly Scot* (14c) **:** to attend to

ten·ta·cle \'tent-i-kəl\ *n* [NL *tentaculum,* fr. L *tentare* to feel, touch — more at TEMPT] (1762) **1 :** any of various elongate flexible usu. tactile or prehensile processes borne by animals chiefly on the head or about the mouth **2 a :** something that resembles a tentacle esp. in grasping or feeling out **b :** a sensitive hair or emergence on a plant (as the sundew) — **ten·ta·cled** \-kəld\ *adj*

ten·tac·u·lar \ten-'tak-yə-lər\ *adj* [NL *tentaculum*] (1828) **1 :** of, relating to, or resembling tentacles **2 :** equipped with tentacles

tent·age \'tent-ij\ *n* (1603) **:** a collection of tents : tent equipment

ten·ta·tive \'tent-ət-iv\ *adj* [ML *tentativus,* fr. L *tentatus,* pp. of *tentare* to feel, try — more at TEMPT] (1626) **1 :** not fully worked out or developed ⟨~ plans⟩ **2 :** HESITANT, UNCERTAIN ⟨a ~ smile⟩ — **tentative** *n* — **ten·ta·tive·ly** *adv* — **ten·ta·tive·ness** *n*

tent caterpillar *n* (1854) **:** any of several destructive gregarious caterpillars (genus *Malacosoma* and esp. *M. americanum* of the family Lasiocampidae) that construct large silken webs on trees

tent·ed \'tent-əd\ *adj* (1604) **1 :** covered with a tent or tents **2 :** shaped like a tent

ten·ter \'tent-ər\ *n* [ME *teyntur, tentowre*] (14c) **1 :** a frame or endless track with hooks or clips along two sides that is used for drying and stretching cloth **2** *archaic* **:** TENTERHOOK

ten·ter·hook \'tent-ər-ˌhu̇k\ *n* (15c) **:** a sharp hooked nail used esp. for fastening cloth on a tenter — **on tenterhooks :** in a state of uneasiness, strain, or suspense

tenth \'ten(t)th\ *n, pl* **tenths** \'ten(t)s, 'ten(t)ths\ — see NUMBER table — **tenth** *adj or adv*

tenth–rate \'ten-'thrāt\ *adj* (1834) **:** of the lowest character or quality

tent stitch *n* (1639) **:** a short stitch slanting to the right that is used in embroidery and canvas work to form even lines of solid background

tenty *also* **tent·ie** \'tent-ē\ *adj* [[3]tent] *Scot* (1555) **:** ATTENTIVE, WATCHFUL

ten·u·is \'ten-yə-wəs\ *n, pl* **-u·es** \-yə-ˌwēz, -ˌwās\ [ML, fr. L, thin, slight] (1650) **:** an unaspirated voiceless stop

te·nu·i·ty \te-'n(y)ü-ət-ē, tə-\ *n* [L *tenuitas,* fr. *tenuis* thin, tenuous] (1535) **1 :** lack of substance or strength **2 :** lack of thickness : SLENDERNESS, THINNESS **3 :** lack of density : rarefied quality or state

ten·u·ous \'ten-yə-wəs\ *adj* [L *tenuis* thin, slight, tenuous — more at THIN] (1597) **1 :** not dense : RARE ⟨a ~ fluid⟩ **2 :** not thick : SLENDER ⟨a ~ rope⟩ **3 :** having little substance or strength : FLIMSY, WEAK ⟨~ influences⟩ ***syn*** see THIN — **ten·u·ous·ly** *adv* — **ten·u·ous·ness** *n*

ten·ure \'ten-yər *also* -ˌyu̇(ə)r\ *n* [ME, fr. MF *teneüre, tenure,* fr. ML *tenitura,* fr. (assumed) VL *tenitus,* pp. of L *tenēre* to hold — more at THIN] (15c) **1 :** the act, right, manner, or term of holding something (as a landed property, a position, or an office); *esp* **:** a status granted after a trial period to a teacher protecting him from summary dismissal **2 :** GRASP, HOLD — **te·nur·ial** \te-'nyu̇r-ē-əl\ *adj* — **te·nur·ial·ly** \-ə-lē\ *adv*

ten·ured \'ten-yərd\ *adj* (1963) **:** having tenure ⟨~ faculty members⟩

te·nu·to \tā-'nüt-(ˌ)ō\ *adv or adj* [It, fr. pp. of *tenere* to hold, fr. L *tenēre*] (ca. 1891) **:** in a manner so as to hold a tone or chord to its full value — used as a direction in music

te·o·cal·li \ˌtē-ə-'kal-ē, ˌtā-ə-'käl-\ *n* [Nahuatl, fr. *teotl* god + *calli* house] (1613) **:** an ancient temple of Mexico or Central America usu. built upon the summit of a truncated pyramidal mound; *also* **:** the mound itself

te·o·sin·te \ˌtā-ō-'sint-ē\ *n* [MexSp, fr. Nahuatl *teocentli,* fr. *teotl* god + *centli* ear of corn] (ca. 1877) **:** a large annual grass (*Euchlaena mexicana*) of Mexico and Central America closely related to maize

te·pa \'tē-pə\ *n* [*tri-* + *ethylene* + *phosphor-* + *amide*] (1953) **:** a soluble crystalline compound $C_6H_{12}N_3OP$ that is used esp. as a chemical sterilizing agent of insects, a palliative in some kinds of cancer, and in finishing and flame-proofing textiles

te·pa·ry bean \'tep-ə-rē-\ *n* [origin unknown] (1912) **:** an annual twining bean (*Phaseolus acutifolius* var. *latifolius*) that is prob. native to the southwestern U.S. and northern Mexico and is cultivated for its roundish white, yellow, brown, or bluish black edible seeds

te·pee \'tē-(ˌ)pē\ *n* [Dakota *tipi,* fr. *ti* to dwell + *pi* to use for] (1835) **:** an American Indian conical tent usu. consisting of skins and used esp. by the Plains peoples

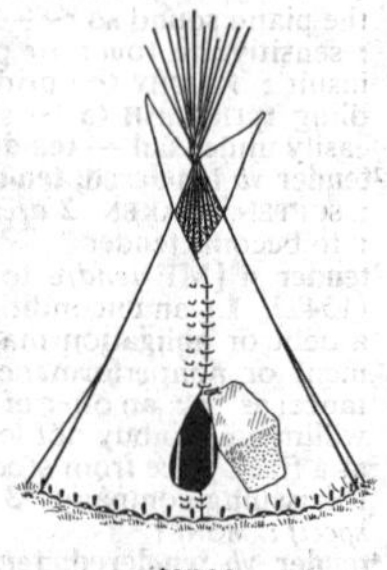

tepee

teph·ra \'tef-rə\ *n* [NL, fr. Gk, ashes; akin to L *febris* fever — more at FEVER] (1965) **:** solid material ejected during the eruption of a volcano and transported through the air

tep·id \'tep-əd\ *adj* [L *tepidus,* fr. *tepēre* to be moderately warm; akin to Skt *tapati* it gives out heat, OIr *tess* heat] (15c) **1 :** moderately warm : LUKEWARM ⟨a ~ bath⟩ **2 a :** lacking in passion, force, or zest ⟨~ prose⟩ **b :** marked by an absence of enthusiasm or conviction ⟨a ~ interest⟩ — **te·pid·i·ty** \tə-'pid-ət-ē, te-\ *n* — **tep·id·ly** \'tep-əd-lē\ *adv* — **tep·id·ness** *n*

TEPP \ˌtē-ˌē-ˌpē-'pē\ *n* [*tetraethyl pyrophosphate*] (1948) **:** a mobile hygroscopic corrosive liquid organophosphate $C_8H_{20}O_7P_2$ that is a powerful anticholinesterase and is used as an insecticide and parasympathomimetic agent

te·qui·la \tə-'kē-lə, tā-\ *n* [Sp, fr. *Tequila,* district of Mexico] (1849) **:** a Mexican liquor distilled from pulque

ter- *comb form* [L, fr. *ter;* akin to Gk & Skt *tris* three times, L *tres* three — more at THREE] **:** three times : threefold : three ⟨*ter*centenary⟩

tera- *comb form* [ISV, fr. Gk *terat-, teras* monster] **:** trillion ⟨*tera*ton⟩ ⟨*tera*hertz⟩

te·rai \tə-'rī\ *n* [*Tarai,* lowland belt of India] (1921) **:** a wide-brimmed double felt sun hat worn esp. in subtropical regions

ter·aph \'ter-əf\ *n, pl* **ter·a·phim** \'ter-ə-ˌfim\ [Heb *tĕrāphīm* (pl. in form but sing. in meaning)] (14c) **:** an image of a Semitic household god

terat- *or* **terato-** *comb form* [Gk, *terat-, teras* marvel, portent, monster; akin to Lith *keras* enchantment] **:** monster ⟨*terato*genic⟩

te·rato·car·ci·no·ma \ˌter-ət-ō-ˌkärs-ᵊn-'ō-mə\ *n* (ca. 1943) **:** a malignant teratoma; *esp* **:** one involving germinal cells of the testis

te·rato·gen \tə-'rat-ə-jən\ *n* (1903) **:** a teratogenic agent

ter·a·to·gen·e·sis \ˌter-ə-tə-'jen-ə-səs\ *n* [NL] (1901) **:** production of monstrous growths or fetuses

ter·a·to·gen·ic \-'jen-ik\ *adj* (1879) **:** of, relating to, or causing developmental malformations and monstrosities ⟨~ substances⟩ ⟨~ effects⟩ — **ter·a·to·ge·nic·i·ty** \-jə-'nis-ət-ē\ *n*

ter·a·to·log·i·cal \ˌter-ət-ᵊl-'äj-i-kəl\ *or* **ter·a·to·log·ic** \-ik\ *adj* (1857) **1 :** abnormal in growth or structure **2 :** of or relating to teratology

ter·a·tol·o·gy \ˌter-ə-'täl-ə-jē\ *n* (1842) **:** the study of malformations, monstrosities, or serious deviations from the normal type in organisms — **ter·a·tol·o·gist** \-jəst\ *n*

ter·a·to·ma \ˌter-ə-'tō-mə\ *n* [NL] (ca. 1890) **:** a tumor made up of a heterogeneous mixture of tissues

ter·bi·um \'tər-bē-əm\ *n* [NL, fr. *Ytterby,* Sweden] (1843) **:** a usu. trivalent metallic element of the rare-earth group — see ELEMENT table

terce \'tərs\ *n* [ME, third, terce — more at TIERCE] *often cap* (14c) **:** the third of the canonical hours

ter·cel \'tər-səl\ *var of* TIERCEL

ter·cen·te·na·ry \ˌtər-(ˌ)sen-'ten-ə-rē, (ˌ)tər-'sent-ᵊn-ˌer-ē\ *n, pl* **-ries** (1855) **:** a 300th anniversary or its celebration — **tercentenary** *adj*

ter·cen·ten·ni·al \ˌtər-(ˌ)sen-'ten-ē-əl\ *adj or n* (1872) **:** TERCENTENARY

ter·cet \'tər-sət\ *n* [It *terzetto,* fr. dim. of *terzo* third, fr. L *tertius* — more at THIRD] (1598) **:** a unit or group of three lines of verse: **a :** one of the 3-line stanzas in terza rima **b :** one of the two groups of three lines forming the sestet in an Italian sonnet

ter·e·bene \'ter-ə-ˌbēn\ *n* [F *térébène,* fr. *térébinthe* terebinth] (ca. 1890) **:** a mixture of terpenes from oil of turpentine

ter·e·binth \'ter-ə-ˌbin(t)th\ *n* [ME *terebynt,* fr. MF *terebinthe,* fr. L *terebinthus* — more at TURPENTINE] (14c) **:** a small European tree (*Pistacia terebinthus*) of the sumac family yielding Chian turpentine

ter·e·bin·thine \ˌter-ə-'bin(t)-thən, -'bin-ˌthīn\ *adj* [L *terebinthinus* of the terebinth] (ca. 1656) **:** consisting of or resembling turpentine

te·re·do \tə-'rēd-(ˌ)ō, -'rād-\ *n, pl* **teredos** *or* **te·red·i·nes** \-'red-ᵊn-ˌēz\ [L *teredin-, teredo,* fr. Gk *terēdōn;* akin to Gk *tetrainein* to bore — more at THROW] (14c) **:** SHIPWORM

tere·phthal·ate \ˌter-ə(f)-'thal-ˌāt\ *n* (1868) **:** a salt or ester of terephthalic acid; *esp* **:** a dimethyl-ester that is a major starting material for polyester fibers and coatings

tere·phthal·ic acid \ˌter-ə(f)-ˌthal-ik-\ *n* [ISV *terebene* + *phthalic acid*] (1857) **:** a *p*-dicarboxylic acid $C_8H_6O_4$ that is obtained esp. by oxidation of xylene and is used chiefly in the synthesis of polyesters

te·rete \tə-'rēt, te-\ *adj* [L *teret-, teres* well turned, rounded; akin to L *terere* to rub — more at THROW] (1619) **:** approximately cylindrical but usu. tapering at both ends ⟨a ~ seedpod⟩

Te·reus \'tir-,yüs, 'tē-,rüs\ *n* [L, fr. Gk *Tēreus*] **:** the husband of Procne who rapes his sister-in-law Philomela
ter·gite \'tər-,gīt\ *n* [ISV *terg-* (fr. L *tergum* back) + *-ite*] (1885) **:** the dorsal plate or dorsal portion of the covering of a metameric segment of an articulate animal; *esp* **:** one on the abdomen
ter·gi·ver·sate \,tər-'jiv-ər-,sāt, -'giv-; ,tər-jə-'vər-\ *vi* **-sat·ed; -sat·ing** [L *tergiversatus*, pp. of *tergiversari* to turn the back, shuffle, fr. *tergum* back + *versare* to turn, fr. *versus*, pp. of *vertere* to turn — more at WORTH] (1654) **1 :** to become a renegade **:** APOSTATIZE **2 :** to use subterfuges **:** EQUIVOCATE — **ter·gi·ver·sa·tor** \-,sāt-ər\ *n*
ter·gi·ver·sa·tion \,tər-,jiv-ər-'sā-shən, -,giv-; ,tər-ji-(,)vər-\ *n* (1570) **1 :** evasion of straightforward action or clear-cut statement **:** EQUIVOCATION **2 :** desertion of a cause, party, or faith
ter·gum \'tər-gəm\ *n, pl* **ter·ga** \-gə\ [NL, fr. L, back] (ca. 1826) **:** the dorsal part or plate of a segment of an arthropod **:** TERGITE, NOTUM — **ter·gal** \-gəl\ *adj*
ter·i·ya·ki \,ter-ē-'(y)äk-ē\ *n* [Jp, fr. *teri* sunshine + *yaki* roast] (1963) **:** a Japanese dish of meat, chicken, or shellfish that is grilled or broiled after being soaked in a spicy soy sauce marinade
¹term \'tərm\ *n* [ME *terme* boundary, end, fr. OF, fr. L *terminus;* akin to Gk *termōn* boundary, end, Skt *tarati* he crosses over — more at THROUGH] (13c) **1 a :** END, TERMINATION; *also* **:** a point in time assigned to something (as a payment) **b :** the time at which a pregnancy of normal length terminates ⟨had her baby at full ~⟩ **2 a :** a limited or definite extent of time; *esp* **:** the time for which something lasts **:** DURATION, TENURE ⟨~ of office⟩ **b :** the whole period for which an estate is granted; *also* **:** the estate or interest held by one for a term **c :** the time during which a court is in session **3** *pl* **:** provisions that are stated or offered for acceptance and that determine the nature and scope of an agreement **:** CONDITIONS ⟨~*s* of sale⟩ ⟨liberal credit ~*s*⟩ **4 a :** a word or expression that has a precise meaning in some uses or is peculiar to a science, art, profession, or subject ⟨legal ~*s*⟩ **b** *pl* **:** diction of a specified kind ⟨described in glowing ~*s*⟩ **5 a :** a unitary or compound expression connected with another by a plus or minus sign **b :** an element of a fraction or proportion or of a series or sequence **6** *pl* **a :** mutual relationship ⟨on good ~*s*⟩ **b :** AGREEMENT, CONCORD ⟨come to ~*s*⟩ **7 :** any of the three substantive elements of a syllogism **8 :** a quadrangular pillar often tapering downward and adorned on the top with the figure of a head or the upper part of the body **9 :** division in a school year during which instruction is regularly given to students — **in terms of :** with respect to or in relation to ⟨thinks of everything *in terms of* money⟩ — **on one's own terms :** in accordance with one's wishes **:** in one's own way ⟨prefers to live *on his own terms*⟩
²term *vt* (1557) **:** to apply a term to **:** CALL, NAME
¹ter·ma·gant \'tər-mə-gənt\ *n* [ME] **1** *cap* **:** a legendary Muslim deity represented in early English drama as a boisterous character **2 :** an overbearing or nagging woman **:** SHREW
²termagant *adj* (1667) **:** OVERBEARING, SHREWISH
term·er \'tər-mər\ *n* (1634) **:** a person serving for a specified term (as in a political office or in prison) ⟨a first ~⟩
ter·mi·na·ble \'tərm-(ə-)nə-bəl\ *adj* [ME, fr. *terminen* to terminate, fr. MF *terminer*, fr. L *terminare*] (15c) **:** capable of being terminated — **ter·mi·na·ble·ness** *n* — **ter·mi·na·bly** \-blē\ *adv*
¹ter·mi·nal \'tərm-nəl, -ən-ᵊl\ *adj* [L *terminalis*, fr. *terminus*] (1744) **1 a :** of or relating to an end, extremity, boundary, or terminus ⟨a ~ pillar⟩ **b :** growing at the end of a branch or stem ⟨a ~ bud⟩ **2 a :** of, relating to, or occurring in a term or each term ⟨~ payments⟩ **b :** leading ultimately to death **:** FATAL ⟨~ cancer⟩ **c :** extremely or hopelessly severe ⟨~ boredom⟩ **3 a :** occurring at or constituting the end of a period or series **:** CONCLUDING ⟨the ~ moments of life⟩ **b :** not intended as preparation for further academic work ⟨a ~ curriculum⟩ ***syn*** see LAST — **ter·mi·nal·ly** \-ē\ *adv*
²terminal *n* (1831) **1 :** a part that forms the end **:** EXTREMITY, TERMINATION **2 :** a terminating usu. ornamental detail **:** FINIAL **3 :** a device attached to the end of a wire or cable or to an electrical apparatus for convenience in making connections **4 a :** either end of a carrier line (as a railroad, trucking or shipping line, or airline) with classifying yards, dock and lighterage facilities, management offices, storage sheds, and freight and passenger stations **b :** a freight or passenger station that is central to a considerable area or serves as a junction at any point with other lines **c :** a town or city at the end of a carrier line **:** TERMINUS **5 :** a device (as a video display unit) by which data can enter or leave a communication network
terminal leave *n* (1944) **:** a final leave consisting of accumulated unused leave granted to a member of the armed forces just prior to his separation or discharge from service
terminal side *n* (ca. 1927) **:** a straight line that has been rotated around a point on another line to form an angle measured in a clockwise or counterclockwise direction — compare INITIAL SIDE
¹ter·mi·nate \'tər-mə-nət\ *adj* [ME, fr. L *terminatus*, pp. of *terminare*, fr. *terminus*] (15c) **:** coming to an end or capable of ending
²ter·mi·nate \-,nāt\ *vb* **-nat·ed; -nat·ing** *vi* (1613) **1 :** to extend only to a limit (as a point or line); *esp* **:** to reach a terminus **2 :** to form an ending **3 :** to come to an end in time ~ *vt* **1 a :** to bring to an end **:** CLOSE ⟨~ a marriage by divorce⟩ ⟨~ a transmission line⟩ **b :** to form the conclusion of ⟨review questions ~ each chapter⟩ **c :** to discontinue the employment of ⟨workers *terminated* because of slow business⟩ **2 :** to serve as an ending, limit, or boundary of ***syn*** see CLOSE
terminating decimal *n* (ca. 1909) **:** a decimal which can be expressed in a finite number of figures or for which all figures to the right of some place are zero — compare REPEATING DECIMAL
ter·mi·na·tion \,tər-mə-'nā-shən\ *n* (1500) **1 :** end in time or existence **:** CONCLUSION ⟨the ~ of life⟩ **2 :** the last part of a word; *esp* **:** an inflectional ending **3 :** the act of terminating **4 :** a limit in space or extent **:** BOUND **5 :** OUTCOME, RESULT ***syn*** see END — **ter·mi·na·tion·al** \-shnəl, -shən-ᵊl\ *adj*
ter·mi·na·tive \'tər-mə-,nāt-iv\ *adj* (15c) **:** tending or serving to terminate **:** ENDING — **ter·mi·na·tive·ly** *adv*
ter·mi·na·tor \-,nāt-ər\ *n* (1770) **1 :** the dividing line between the illuminated and the unilluminated part of the moon's or a planet's disk **2 :** one that terminates
ter·mi·nol·o·gy \,tər-mə-'näl-ə-jē\ *n* [ML *terminus* term, expression (fr. L, boundary, limit) + E *-o-* + *-logy*] (1801) **1 :** the technical or special terms used in a business, art, science, or special subject **2 :** nomenclature as a field of study — **ter·mi·no·log·i·cal** \-mən-ᵊl-'äj-i-kəl\ *adj* — **ter·mi·no·log·i·cal·ly** \-i-k(ə-)lē\ *adv*
term insurance *n* (1897) **:** insurance for a specified period that provides for no payment to the insured except on losses during the period and that becomes void upon its expiration
ter·mi·nus \'tər-mə-nəs\ *n, pl* **-ni** \-,nī, -,nē\ *or* **-nus·es** [L, boundary, end — more at TERM] (1617) **1 :** a final goal **:** a finishing point **2 :** a post or stone marking a boundary **3 :** either end of a transportation line or travel route; *also* **:** the station, town, or city at such a place **:** TERMINAL **4 :** an extreme point or element **:** TIP ⟨the ~ of a glacier⟩ ***syn*** see END
terminus ad quem \-,äd-'kwem\ *n* [NL, lit., limit to which] (1551) **1 :** a goal, object, or course of action **:** DESTINATION, PURPOSE **2 :** a final limiting point in time
terminus a quo \-,ä-'kwō\ *n* [NL, lit., limit from which] (1551) **1 :** a point of origin **2 :** the first of two limiting points in time
ter·mi·tar·i·um \,tər-mə-'ter-ē-əm, -,mī-\ *n, pl* **-ia** \-ē-ə\ [NL] (1863) **:** a termites' nest
ter·mi·tary \'tər-mə-,ter-ē, -,mīt-,er-ē\ *n, pl* **-tar·ies** (1826) **:** TERMITARIUM
ter·mite \'tər-,mīt\ *n* [NL *Termit-*, *Termes*, genus of termites, fr. LL, a worm that eats wood, alter. of L *tarmit-*, *tarmes;* akin to Gk *tetrainein* to bore — more at THROW] (1781) **:** any of numerous pale-colored soft-bodied social insects (order Isoptera) that live in colonies consisting of winged sexual forms, wingless sterile workers, and often soldiers, feed on wood, and include some which are very destructive to wooden structures and trees — called also *white ant*
term·less \'tərm-ləs\ *adj* (1536) **1 :** having no term or end **:** BOUNDLESS, UNENDING **2 :** UNCONDITIONED, UNCONDITIONAL
term paper *n* (1926) **:** a major written assignment in a school or college course representative of a student's achievement during a term
tern \'tərn\ *n* [of Scand origin; akin to Dan *terne* tern] (1678) **:** any of numerous sea gulls (*Sterna* and related genera) that are smaller and slenderer in body and bill than typical gulls and have narrower wings, often forked tails, black cap, and white body
ter·na·ry \'tər-nə-rē\ *adj* [ME, fr. L *ternarius*, fr. *terni* three each; akin to L *tres* three — more at THREE] (15c) **1 a :** of, relating to, or proceeding by threes **b :** having three elements, parts, or divisions **:** THREEFOLD **c :** arranged in threes ⟨~ petals⟩ **2 :** using three as the base ⟨a ~ logarithm⟩ **3 a :** being or consisting of an alloy of three elements **b :** of, relating to, or containing three different elements, atoms, radicals, or groups ⟨sulfuric acid is a ~ acid⟩ **4 :** third in order or rank
ter·nate \'tər-,nāt, -nət\ *adj* [NL *ternatus*, fr. ML, pp. of *ternare* to treble, fr. L *terni*] (1760) **:** arranged in threes or in subdivisions so arranged ⟨a ~ leaf⟩ — **ter·nate·ly** *adv*
terne \'tərn\ *n* [*terneplate*] (1891) **1 :** an alloy of lead and tin typically in a ratio of four to one that is used as a coating in producing terneplate **2 :** TERNEPLATE
terne·plate \-,plāt\ *n* [prob. fr. F *terne* dull (fr. MF, fr. *ternir* to tarnish) + E *plate*] (ca. 1858) **:** sheet iron or steel coated with an alloy of about four parts lead to one part tin
ter·pene \'tər-,pēn\ *n* [ISV *terp-* (fr. G *terpentin* turpentine, fr. ML *terbentina*) + *-ene* — more at TURPENTINE] (1873) **:** any of various isomeric hydrocarbons $C_{10}H_{16}$ found present in essential oils (as from conifers) and used esp. as solvents and in organic synthesis; *broadly* **:** any of numerous hydrocarbons $(C_5H_8)_n$ found esp. in essential oils, resins, and balsams — **ter·pene·less** \-ləs\ *adj* — **ter·pe·noid** \'tər-pə-,nȯid, ,tər-'pē-\ *adj or n*
ter·pin·e·ol \,tər-'pin-ē-,ȯl, -,ōl\ *n* [ISV, fr. *terpine* $(C_{10}H_{18}(OH)_2)$] (ca. 1848) **:** any of three fragrant isomeric alcohols $C_{10}H_{17}OH$ found in essential oils or made artificially and used esp. in perfume or as solvents
ter·poly·mer \,tər-'päl-ə-mər\ *n* (1947) **:** a polymer (as a complex resin) that results from copolymerization of three discrete monomers
Terp·sich·o·re \,tərp-'sik-ə-(,)rē\ *n* [L, fr. Gk *Terpsichorē*] **:** the Greek Muse of dancing and choral song
terp·si·cho·re·an \,tərp-(,)sik-ə-'rē-ən; -sə-'kōr-ē-, -'kȯr-\ *adj* (1825) **:** of or relating to dancing
ter·ra \'ter-ə\ *n, pl* **ter·rae** \-(,)ē, -,ī\ [NL, fr. L, land] (1946) **:** any of the relatively light-colored highland areas on the surface of the moon or a planet
ter·ra al·ba \,ter-ə-'al-bə, -'ȯl-\ *n* [NL, lit., white earth] (ca. 1871) **:** any of several white mineral substances: as **a :** a pigment consisting of ground gypsum; *broadly* **:** GYPSUM **b :** kaolin used esp. as an adulterant of paints
¹ter·race \'ter-əs\ *n* [MF, pile of earth, platform, terrace, fr. OProv *terrassa*, fr. *terra* earth, fr. L, earth, land — more at THIRST] (1515) **1 a :** a colonnaded porch or promenade **b :** a flat roof or open platform **c :** a relatively level paved or planted area adjoining a building **2 :** a raised embankment with the top leveled **3 :** a level ordinarily narrow plain usu. with steep front bordering a river, lake, or sea; *also* **:** a similar undersea feature **4 a :** a row of houses or apartments on raised ground or a sloping site **b :** a group of row houses **c :** a strip of park in the middle of a street often planted with trees or shrubs **d :** STREET
²terrace *vt* **ter·raced; ter·rac·ing** (1615) **1 :** to provide (as a building) with a terrace **2 :** to make into a terrace
ter·ra–cot·ta \,ter-ə-'kät-ə\ *n* [It *terra cotta*, lit., baked earth] (1722) **1 :** a glazed or unglazed fired clay used esp. for statuettes and vases and architectural purposes (as roofing, facing, and relief ornamentation) **2 :** a brownish orange
terra fir·ma \-'fər-mə *also* -'fir-\ *n* [NL, lit., solid land] (ca. 1693) **:** dry land **:** solid ground
ter·rain \tə-'rān *also* te-\ *n* [F, land, ground, fr. L *terrenum*, fr. neut. of *terrenus* of earth — more at TERRENE] (1766) **1 a** (1) **:** a geographical area (2) **:** a piece of land **:** GROUND **b :** the physical features of a tract of land **2 :** TERRANE 1 **3 a :** a field of knowledge or interest **:** TERRITORY **b :** ENVIRONMENT, MILIEU

ter·ra in·cog·ni·ta \ˈter-ə-ˌin-ˌkäg-ˈnēt-ə, -in-ˈkäg-nət-ə\ *n, pl* **ter·rae in·cog·ni·tae** \ˈte(ə)r-ˌī-ˌin-ˌkäg-ˈnē-ˌtī, -in-ˈkäg-nə-ˌtī\ [L] (1616) **:** unknown territory **:** an unexplored country or field of knowledge

Ter·ra·my·cin \ˌter-ə-ˈmīs-ᵊn\ *trademark* — used for oxytetracycline

ter·rane \tə-ˈrān, te-\ *n* [alter. of *terrain*] (1823) **1 :** the area or surface over which a particular rock or group of rocks is prevalent **2 :** TERRAIN 1a

ter·ra·pin \ˈter-ə-pən, ˈtar-\ *n* [of Algonquian origin; akin to Delaware *torope* turtle] (1613) **:** any of various edible No. American turtles (family Testudinidae) living in fresh or brackish water

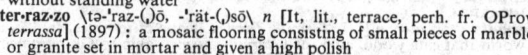

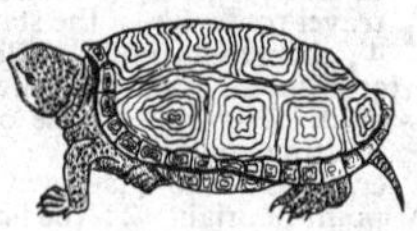
terrapin

ter·raque·ous \te-ˈrā-kwē-əs, tə-, -ˈrak-wē-\ *adj* [L *terra* land + E *aqueous*] (ca. 1658) **:** consisting of land and water

ter·rar·i·um \tə-ˈrar-ē-əm, -ˈrer-\ *n, pl* **-ia** \-ē-ə\ *or* **-i·ums** [NL, fr. L *terra* + *-arium* (as in *aquarium*)] (1890) **:** a vivarium without standing water

ter·raz·zo \tə-ˈraz-(ˌ)ō, -ˈrät-(ˌ)sō\ *n* [It, lit., terrace, perh. fr. OProv *terrassa*] (1897) **:** a mosaic flooring consisting of small pieces of marble or granite set in mortar and given a high polish

1**ter·rene** \te-ˈrēn, tə-; ˈte(ə)r-ˌēn\ *adj* [ME, fr. L *terrenus* of earth, fr. *terra* earth] (14c) **:** MUNDANE, EARTHLY

2**terrene** *n* (1667) **:** a land area **:** EARTH, TERRAIN

ter·re·plein \ˈter-ə-ˌplān\ *n* [MF, fr. OIt *terrapieno,* fr. ML *terraplenum,* fr. *terra plenus* filled with earth] (1591) **:** the level space behind a parapet of a rampart where guns are mounted

ter·res·tri·al \tə-ˈres-t(r)ē-əl, -ˈres(h)-chəl\ *adj* [ME, fr. L *terrestris,* fr. *terra* earth — more at TERRACE] (15c) **1 a :** of or relating to the earth or its inhabitants ⟨~ magnetism⟩ **b :** mundane in scope or character **:** PROSAIC **2 a :** of or relating to land as distinct from air or water ⟨~ transportation⟩ **b (1) :** living on or in or growing from land ⟨~ plants⟩ **(2) :** of or relating to terrestrial organisms ⟨~ habits⟩ **3 :** belonging to the class of planets that are like the earth (as in density and silicate composition) ⟨the ~ planets Mercury, Venus, and Mars⟩ — **terrestrial** *n* — **ter·res·tri·al·ly** \-ē\ *adv*

ter·ret \ˈter-ət\ *n* [ME *teret,* alter. of *toret,* fr. MF, fr. OF, dim. of *tour* circuit, ring — more at TURN] (15c) **:** one of the rings on the top of a harness pad through which the reins pass

ter·ri·ble \ˈter-ə-bəl\ *adj* [ME, fr. MF, fr. L *terribilis,* fr. *terrēre* to frighten — more at TERROR] (15c) **1 a :** exciting extreme alarm or intense fear **:** TERRIFYING **b :** formidable in nature **:** AWESOME ⟨a ~ responsibility⟩ **c :** DIFFICULT **2 :** EXTREME, GREAT **3 :** extremely bad: as **a :** strongly repulsive **:** OBNOXIOUS ⟨a ~ smell⟩ **b :** notably unattractive or objectionable ⟨~ sentimentality⟩ **c :** of very poor quality ⟨a ~ movie⟩ — **ter·ri·ble·ness** *n* — **ter·ri·bly** \-blē\ *adv*

ter·ric·o·lous \te-ˈrik-ə-ləs, tə-\ *adj* [L *terricola* earth dweller, fr. *terra* earth + *colere* to inhabit — more at WHEEL] (1835) **:** living on or in the ground

ter·ri·er \ˈter-ē-ər\ *n* [ME, fr. MF *(chien) terrier,* lit., earth dog, fr. *terrier* of earth, fr. ML *terrarius,* fr. L *terra*] (15c) **:** any of various usu. small dogs orig. used by hunters to dig for small furred game and engage the quarry underground or drive it out

ter·rif·ic \tə-ˈrif-ik\ *adj* [L *terrificus,* fr. *terrēre* to frighten] (1667) **1 a :** exciting or fit to excite fear or awe **b :** very bad **:** FRIGHTFUL **2 :** EXTRAORDINARY ⟨~ speed⟩ **3 :** unusually fine **:** MAGNIFICENT ⟨~ weather⟩ — **ter·rif·i·cal·ly** \-i-k(ə-)lē\ *adv*

ter·ri·fy \ˈter-ə-ˌfī\ *vt* **-fied; -fy·ing** [L *terrificare,* fr. *terrificus*] (1575) **1 a :** to drive or impel by menacing **:** SCARE **b :** DETER, INTIMIDATE **2 :** to fill with terror

ter·ri·fy·ing \-ˌfī-iŋ\ *adj* (1586) **1 :** causing terror or apprehension **2 :** of a formidable nature — **ter·ri·fy·ing·ly** \-iŋ-lē\ *adv*

ter·rig·e·nous \te-ˈrij-ə-nəs, tə-\ *adj* [L *terrigena* earthborn, fr. *terra* earth + *gignere* to beget — more at KIN] (1882) **:** being or relating to oceanic sediment derived directly from the destruction of rocks on the earth's surface

ter·rine \tə-ˈrēn, ter-ˈēn\ *n* [F — more at TUREEN] (ca. 1706) **1 a :** TUREEN 1 **b :** a usu. earthenware dish in which foods are cooked and served **2 :** a mixture of chopped meat, fish, or vegetables cooked and served in a terrine

1**ter·ri·to·ri·al** \ˌter-ə-ˈtōr-ē-əl, -ˈtȯr-\ *adj* (1625) **1 a :** NEARBY, LOCAL **b :** serving outlying areas **:** REGIONAL **2 a :** of or relating to a territory ⟨~ government⟩ **b :** of or relating to or organized chiefly for home defense ⟨a ~ army⟩ **c :** of or relating to private property **3 a :** of or relating to an assigned or preempted area ⟨~ commanders⟩ **b :** exhibiting territoriality ⟨~ birds⟩ — **ter·ri·to·ri·al·ly** \-ē-ə-lē\ *adv*

2**territorial** *n* (1907) **:** a member of a territorial military unit

territorial court *n* (1857) **:** a court in a U.S. territory that has jurisdiction over local and federal cases

ter·ri·to·ri·al·ism \ˌter-ə-ˈtōr-ē-ə-ˌliz-əm, -ˈtȯr-\ *n* (1881) **1 :** LANDLORDISM **2 :** the principle established in 1555 requiring the inhabitants of a territory of the Holy Roman Empire to conform to the religion of their ruler or to emigrate **3** *often cap* **:** a theory or movement proposing an autonomous territory for the Jews — **ter·ri·to·ri·al·ist** \-ləst\ *n*

ter·ri·to·ri·al·i·ty \-ˌtōr-ē-ˈal-ət-ē, -ˌtȯr-\ *n* (1894) **1 :** territorial status **2 a :** persistent attachment to a specific territory **b :** the pattern of behavior associated with the defense of a territory

ter·ri·to·ri·al·ize \-ˈtōr-ē-ə-ˌlīz, -ˈtȯr-\ *vt* **-ized; -iz·ing** (1818) **:** to organize on a territorial basis — **ter·ri·to·ri·al·iza·tion** \-ˌtōr-ē-ə-lə-ˈzā-shən, -ˌtȯr-\ *n*

territorial waters *n pl* (ca. 1875) **:** the waters under the sovereign jurisdiction of a nation or state including both marginal sea and inland waters

ter·ri·to·ry \ˈter-ə-ˌtōr-ē, -ˌtȯr-\ *n, pl* **-ries** [ME, fr. L *territorium,* lit., land around a town, prob. fr. *terra* land + *-torium* (as in *praetorium*) — more at TERRACE] (15c) **1 a :** a geographical area belonging to or under the jurisdiction of a governmental authority **b :** an administrative subdivision of a country **c :** a part of the U.S. not included within any state but organized with a separate legislature **d :** a geographical area (as a colonial possession) dependent on an external government but having some degree of autonomy **2 a :** an indeterminate geographical area **b :** a field of knowledge or interest **3 a :** an assigned area; *esp* **:** one in which a salesman or distributor operates **b :** an area often including a nesting or denning site and a variable foraging range that is occupied and defended by an animal or group of animals

ter·ror \ˈter-ər\ *n* [ME, fr. MF *terreur,* fr. L *terror,* fr. *terrēre* to frighten; akin to Gk *trein* to be afraid, flee, *tremein* to tremble — more at TREMBLE] (14c) **1 :** a state of intense fear **2 a :** one that inspires fear **:** SCOURGE **b :** a frightening aspect ⟨the ~*s* of invasion⟩ **c :** a cause of anxiety **:** WORRY **d :** an appalling person or thing; *esp* **:** BRAT **3 :** REIGN OF TERROR **4 :** violence (as bomb-throwing) committed by groups in order to intimidate a population or government into granting their demands ⟨insurrection and revolutionary ~⟩ ***syn*** see FEAR — **ter·ror·less** \-ləs\ *adj*

ter·ror·ism \ˈter-ər-ˌiz-əm\ *n* (1795) **:** the systematic use of terror esp. as a means of coercion — **ter·ror·ist** \-ər-əst\ *adj or n* — **ter·ror·is·tic** \ˌter-ər-ˈis-tik\ *adj*

ter·ror·ize \ˈter-ər-ˌīz\ *vt* **-ized; -iz·ing** (1823) **1 :** to fill with terror or anxiety **:** SCARE **2 :** to coerce by threat or violence — **ter·ror·iza·tion** \ˌter-ər-ə-ˈzā-shən\ *n*

ter·ry \ˈter-ē\ *n, pl* **terries** [perh. modif. of F *tiré,* pp. of *tirer* to draw — more at TIRADE] (1784) **1 :** the loop forming the pile in uncut pile fabrics **2 :** an absorbent fabric with such loops — called also *terry cloth*

terse \ˈtərs\ *adj* **ters·er; ters·est** [L *tersus* clean, neat, fr. pp. of *tergēre* to wipe off; akin to Gk *trōgein* to gnaw, L *terere* to rub — more at THROW] (1601) **1 :** smoothly elegant **:** POLISHED **2 :** devoid of superfluity ⟨a ~ reply⟩ ***syn*** see CONCISE — **terse·ly** *adv* — **terse·ness** *n*

1**ter·tian** \ˈtər-shən\ *adj* [ME *tercian,* fr. L *tertianus,* lit., of the third, fr. *tertius* third — more at THIRD] (14c) **:** recurring at approximately 48-hour intervals — used of malaria

2**tertian** *n* (14c) **:** a tertian fever (as vivax malaria)

1**ter·tia·ry** \ˈtər-shē-ˌer-ē, -shə-rē\ *n, pl* **-ries** (1550) **1** [ML *tertiarius,* fr. L, of a third] **:** a member of a monastic third order esp. of lay people **2** *cap* **:** the Tertiary period or system of rocks

2**tertiary** *adj* [L *tertiarius* of or containing a third, fr. *tertius* third] (1656) **1 a :** of third rank, importance, or value **b :** of, relating to, or constituting the third strongest of the three or four degrees of stress recognized by most linguists ⟨the third syllable of *basketball team* carries ~ stress⟩ **2** *cap* **:** of, relating to, or being the first period of the Cenozoic era or the corresponding system of rocks marked by the formation of high mountains (as the Alps, Caucasus, and Himalayas) and the dominance of mammals on land **3 a :** involving or resulting from the substitution of three atoms or groups ⟨a ~ salt⟩ ⟨~ amine⟩ **b :** being or containing a carbon atom with three valences linked to other carbon atoms ⟨an acid containing a ~ carbon⟩ ⟨~ alcohols⟩ **4 :** occurring in or being a third stage: as **a :** being or relating to the recovery of oil and gas from old wells by means of the underground application of heat and chemicals **b :** being or relating to the purification of wastewater by removal of fine particles, nitrates, and phosphates

tertiary color *n* (ca. 1864) **:** a color produced by mixing two secondary colors

tertiary syphilis *n* (1875) **:** the third stage of syphilis that develops after the disappearance of the secondary symptoms and is marked by ulcers in and gummas under the skin and commonly by involvement of the skeletal, cardiovascular, and nervous systems

ter·ti·um quid \ˌtər-shē-əm-ˈkwid, ˌtərt-ē-\ *n* [LL, lit., third something; fr. its failing to fit into a dichotomy] (ca. 1724) **1 :** a middle course or an intermediate component ⟨where there are two systems of law and two orders of courts, there must . . . be some *tertium quid* to deal with conflicts of law and jurisdiction —Ernest Baker⟩ **2 :** a third party of ambiguous status ⟨there was a man and his wife and a *tertium quid* —Rudyard Kipling⟩

ter·va·lent \ˌtər-ˈvā-lənt, ˈtər-\ *adj* (ca. 1903) **:** TRIVALENT

ter·za ri·ma \ˌtert-sə-ˈrē-mə\ *n* [It, lit., third rhyme] (1819) **:** a verse form consisting of tercets usu. in iambic pentameter in English poetry with an interlaced rhyme scheme (as *aba, bcb, cdc*)

tes·la \ˈtes-lə\ *n* [Nikola *Tesla*] (1958) **:** a unit of magnetic flux density in the mks system equivalent to one weber per square meter

tes·sel·late \ˈtes-ə-ˌlāt\ *vt* **-lat·ed; -lat·ing** [LL *tessellatus,* pp. of *tessellare* to pave with tesserae, fr. L *tessella,* dim. of *tessera*] (1791) **:** to form into or adorn with mosaic

tes·sel·lat·ed \-ˌlāt-əd\ *adj* (1695) **:** having a checkered appearance

tes·sel·la·tion \ˌtes-ə-ˈlā-shən\ *n* (1660) **1 :** MOSAIC; *esp* **:** a covering of an infinite geometric plane without gaps or overlaps by congruent plane figures of one type or a few types **2 :** an act of tessellating **:** the state of being tessellated

tes·sera \ˈtes-ə-rə\ *n, pl* **-ser·ae** \-ˌrē, -ˌrī\ [L, prob. deriv. of Gk *tessares* four; fr. its having four corners — more at FOUR] (ca. 1656) **1 :** a small tablet (as of wood, bone, or ivory) used by the ancient Romans as a ticket, tally, voucher, or means of identification **2 :** a small piece (as of marble, glass, or tile) used in mosaic work

tes·ser·act \ˈtes-ə-ˌrakt\ *n* [Gk *tessares* four + *aktis* ray — more at ACTIN-] (ca. 1888) **:** the four-dimensional analogue of a cube

tes·si·tu·ra \ˌtes-ə-ˈtu̇r-ə\ *n* [It, lit., texture, fr. L *textura*] (ca. 1891) **:** the general range of a melody or voice part; *specif* **:** the part of the register in which most of the tones of a melody or voice part lie

1**test** \ˈtest\ *n* [ME, vessel in which metals were assayed, cupel, fr. MF, fr. L *testum* earthen vessel; akin to L *testa* earthen pot, shell, *texere* to weave — more at TECHNICAL] (14c) **1 a** *chiefly Brit* **:** CUPEL **b (1) :** a critical examination, observation, or evaluation **:** TRIAL; *specif* **:** the procedure of submitting a statement to such conditions or operations as will lead to its proof or disproof or to its acceptance or rejection ⟨a ~ of a statistical hypothesis⟩ **(2) :** a basis for evaluation **:** CRITERION **c :** an ordeal or oath required as proof of conformity with a set of beliefs **2 a :** a means of testing: as **(1) :** a procedure, reaction, or reagent used to identify or characterize a substance or constituent **(2) :** something (as a series of questions or exercises) for measuring the skill, knowledge, intelligence, capacities, or aptitudes of an individual or group **b :** a positive result in such a test **3 :** a result or value determined by testing

2**test** *vt* (1689) **1 :** to require a doctrinal oath of **2 :** to put to test or proof **:** TRY ~ *vi* **1 a :** to undergo a test **b :** to achieve a rating on the basis of tests **2 :** to apply a test as a means of analysis or diagnosis — used with *for* ⟨~ for mechanical aptitude⟩ — **test·abil·i·ty** \ˌtes-tə-ˈbil-ət-ē\ *n* — **test·able** \ˈtes-tə-bəl\ *adj*

[3]**test** *n* [L *testa* shell] (ca. 1842) **:** an external hard or firm covering (as a shell) of many invertebrates (as a foraminifer or a mollusk)
tes·ta \ˈtes-tə\ *n, pl* **tes·tae** \-ˌtē, -ˌtī\ [NL, fr. L, shell] (1796) **:** the hard external coating or integument of a seed
tes·ta·ceous \tes-ˈtā-shəs\ *adj* [L *testaceus,* fr. *testa* shell, earthen pot, brick] (1646) **1 a :** having a shell ⟨a ~ protozoan⟩ **b :** consisting of shell or calcareous material ⟨stone of ~ composition⟩ **2 :** of any of the several light colors of bricks
tes·ta·cy \ˈtes-tə-sē\ *n, pl* **-cies** (ca. 1864) **:** the state of being testate
tes·ta·ment \ˈtes-tə-mənt\ *n* [ME, fr. LL & L; LL *testamentum* covenant with God, holy scripture, fr. L, last will, fr. *testari* to be a witness, call to witness, make a will, fr. *testis* witness; akin to L *tres* three & to L *stare* to stand; fr. the witness's standing by as a third party in a litigation — more at THREE, STAND] (14c) **1 a** *archaic* **:** a covenant between God and man **b** *cap* **:** either of two main divisions of the Bible **2 a :** a tangible proof or tribute **b :** an expression of conviction **:** CREDO **3 a :** an act by which a person determines the disposition of his property after his death **b :** WILL — **tes·ta·men·ta·ry** \ˌtes-tə-ˈment-ə-rē, -ˈmen-trē\ *adj*
tes·tate \ˈtes-ˌtāt, -tət\ *adj* [ME, fr. L *testatus,* pp. of *testari* to make a will] (15c) **:** having left a valid will ⟨he died ~⟩
tes·ta·tor \ˈtes-ˌtāt-ər, tes-ˈ\ *n* [ME *testatour,* fr. AF, fr. LL *testator,* fr. L *testatus,* pp.] (15c) **:** a person who dies leaving a will or testament in force
tes·ta·trix \ˈtes-ˌtā-triks, tes-ˈ\ *n* [LL, fem. of *testator*] (1591) **:** a female testator
test ban *n* (1958) **:** a self-imposed ban on the atmospheric testing of nuclear weapons that is mutually agreed to by countries possessing such weapons
test case *n* (1894) **1 :** a representative case whose outcome is likely to serve as a precedent **2 :** a proceeding brought by agreement or on an understanding of the parties to obtain a decision as to the constitutionality of a statute
test·cross \ˈtes(t)-ˌkrȯs\ *n* (1934) **:** a genetic cross between a homozygous recessive individual and a corresponding suspected heterozygote to determine the genotype of the latter — **testcross** *vt*
test–drive \ˈtes(t)-ˌdrīv\ *vt* **-drove** \-ˌdrōv\; **-driv·en** \-ˌdriv-ən\; **-driv·ing** \-ˌdrī-viŋ\ (1950) **:** to drive (a motor vehicle) in order to evaluate performance
test·ed \ˈtes-təd\ *adj* (1748) **:** subjected to or qualified through testing — often used in combination ⟨time-*tested* principles⟩
test·ee \tes-ˈtē\ *n* (1930) **:** one who takes an examination
[1]**tes·ter** \ˈtēs-tər, ˈtes-\ *n* [ME, fr. MF *testiere* headpiece, head covering, fr. *teste* head, fr. LL *testa* skull, fr. L, shell — more at TEST] (14c) **:** the canopy over a bed, pulpit, or altar
[2]**tes·ter** \ˈtes-tər\ *n* [modif. of MF *testart,* fr. *teston*] (1546) **:** TESTON b
[3]**test·er** \ˈtes-tər\ *n* (1661) **:** one that tests
test–fly \-ˌflī\ *vt* **-flew** \-ˌflü\; **-flown** \-ˌflōn\; **-fly·ing** (1936) **:** to subject to a flight test ⟨~ an experimental plane⟩
tes·ti·cle \ˈtes-ti-kəl\ *n* [ME *testicule,* fr. L *testiculus,* dim. of *testis*] (15c) **:** a male genital gland usu. with its enclosing structures **:** TESTIS — **tes·tic·u·lar** \tes-ˈtik-yə-lər\ *adj*
tes·ti·fi·er \ˈtes-tə-ˌfī(-ə)r\ *n* (1611) **:** one that testifies **:** WITNESS
tes·ti·fy \ˈtes-tə-ˌfī\ *vb* **-fied; -fy·ing** [ME *testifien,* fr. L *testificari,* fr. *testis* witness] *vi* (14c) **1 a :** to make a statement based on personal knowledge or belief **:** bear witness **b :** to serve as evidence or proof **2 :** to express a personal conviction **3 :** to make a solemn declaration under oath for the purpose of establishing a fact (as in a court) ~ *vt* **1 a :** to bear witness to **:** ATTEST **b :** to serve as evidence of **:** PROVE **2** *archaic* **a :** to make known (a personal conviction) **b :** to give evidence of **:** SHOW **3 :** to declare under oath before a tribunal or officially constituted public body
[1]**tes·ti·mo·ni·al** \ˌtes-tə-ˈmō-nē-əl, -nyəl\ *adj* (15c) **1 :** of, relating to, or constituting testimony **2 :** expressive of appreciation or esteem ⟨a ~ dinner⟩
[2]**testimonial** *n* (15c) **1 :** EVIDENCE, TESTIMONY **2 a :** a statement testifying to benefits received **b :** a character reference **:** letter of recommendation **3 :** an expression of appreciation **:** TRIBUTE
tes·ti·mo·ny \ˈtes-tə-ˌmō-nē\ *n, pl* **-nies** [ME, fr. LL & L; LL *testimonium* Decalogue, fr. L, evidence, witness, fr. *testis* witness — more at TESTAMENT] (14c) **1 a (1) :** the tablets inscribed with the Mosaic law **(2) :** the ark containing the tablets **b :** a divine decree attested in the Scriptures **2 a :** firsthand authentication of a fact **:** EVIDENCE **b :** an outward sign **c :** a solemn declaration usu. made orally by a witness under oath in response to interrogation by a lawyer or authorized public official **3 a :** an open acknowledgment **b :** a public profession of religious experience
test·ing *adj* (1878) **:** requiring maximum effort or ability ⟨a most difficult and ~ problem —Ernest Bevin⟩
tes·tis \ˈtes-təs\ *n, pl* **tes·tes** \ˈtes-ˌtēz\ [L, witness, testis] (ca. 1704) **:** a typically paired male reproductive gland that produces sperm
test match *n* (1862) **1 :** any of a series of championship cricket matches played between teams representing Australia and England **2 :** a championship game or series (as of cricket) played between teams representing different countries
tes·ton \ˈtes-ˌtän\ *or* **tes·toon** \tes-ˈtün\ *n* [MF, fr. OIt *testone,* aug. of *testa* head, fr. LL, skull — more at TESTER] (1543) **:** any of several old European coins: as **a :** a French silver coin of the 16th century worth between 10 and $14\frac{1}{2}$ sous **b :** a shilling of Henry VIII of England decreasing in value to ninepence and then to sixpence in Shakespeare's time
tes·tos·ter·one \te-ˈstäs-tə-ˌrōn\ *n* [*testis* + *-o-* + *sterol* + *-one*] (1935) **:** a male hormone that is produced by the testes or made synthetically, is responsible for inducing and maintaining male secondary sex characters, and is a crystalline hydroxy steroid ketone $C_{19}H_{28}O_2$
test pattern *n* (ca. 1946) **:** a fixed picture broadcast by a television station to assist viewers in adjusting their receivers
test pilot *n* (1917) **:** a pilot who specializes in putting new or experimental airplanes through maneuvers designed to test them (as for strength) by producing strains in excess of normal
test–tube *adj* (1935) **:** produced by fertilization in laboratory apparatus and implantation in the uterus, by fertilization and growth in laboratory apparatus, or sometimes by artificial insemination ⟨~ babies⟩
test tube *n* (1846) **:** a plain or lipped tube usu. of thin glass closed at one end and used esp. in chemistry and biology
tes·tu·do \tes-ˈt(y)üd-(ˌ)ō\ *n, pl* **-dos** [L *testudin-, testudo,* lit., tortoise, tortoise shell; akin to L *testa* shell — more at TEST] (1609) **:** a cover of overlapping shields or a shed wheeled up to a wall used by the ancient Romans to protect an attacking force
tes·ty \ˈtes-tē\ *adj* **tes·ti·er; -est** [ME *testif,* fr. AF, headstrong, fr. OF *teste* head — more at TESTER] (1526) **1 :** easily annoyed **:** IRRITABLE **2 :** marked by impatience or ill humor ⟨~ remarks⟩ — **tes·ti·ly** \-tə-lē\ *adv* — **tes·ti·ness** \-tē-nəs\ *n*
Tet \ˈtet\ *n* [Vietnamese *tết*] (1885) **:** the Vietnamese New Year observed for three days beginning at the first new moon after January 20
tet·a·nal \ˈtet-ᵊn-əl\ *adj* (1939) **:** of, relating to, or derived from tetanus ⟨~ toxin⟩
te·tan·ic \te-ˈtan-ik\ *adj* (ca. 1727) **:** of, relating to, being, or tending to produce tetany or tetanus — **te·tan·i·cal·ly** \-i-k(ə-)lē\ *adv*
tet·a·nize \ˈtet-ᵊn-ˌīz\ *vt* **-nized; -niz·ing** (1849) **:** to induce tetanus in ⟨~ a muscle⟩ — **tet·a·ni·za·tion** \ˌtet-ᵊn-ə-ˈzā-shən, ˌtet-nə-\ *n*
tet·a·nus \ˈtet-ᵊn-əs, ˈtet-nəs\ *n* [ME, fr. L, fr. Gk *tetanos,* fr. *tetanos* stretched, rigid; akin to Gk *teinein* to stretch — more at THIN] (14c) **1 a :** an acute infectious disease characterized by tonic spasm of voluntary muscles esp. of the jaw and caused by the specific toxin of a bacillus (*Clostridium tetani*) which is usu. introduced through a wound **b :** the bacterium that causes tetanus **2 :** prolonged contraction of a muscle resulting from rapidly repeated motor impulses
tet·a·ny \ˈtet-ᵊn-ē, ˈtet-nē\ *n* [ISV, fr. L *tetanus*] (ca. 1885) **:** a condition of physiologic mineral imbalance marked by tonic spasm of muscles and associated usu. with deficient parathyroid secretion
te·tar·to·he·dral \te-ˌtärt-ə-ˈhē-drəl\ *adj* [Gk *tetartos* fourth; akin to Gk *tettares* four — more at FOUR] *of a crystal* (ca. 1858) **:** having one fourth the number of planes required by complete symmetry — compare HEMIHEDRAL, HOLOHEDRAL
tetched *var of* TECHED
tetchy \ˈtech-ē\ *adj* **tetchi·er; -est** [perh. fr. obs. *tetch* (habit)] (1592) **:** irritably or peevishly sensitive **:** TOUCHY ⟨the ~ manner of two women living in the same house —Elizabeth Taylor⟩ — **tetchi·ness** \-nəs\ *n*
[1]**tête–à–tête** \ˌtet-ə-ˈtet, ˌtāt-ə-ˈtāt, *2 is also* ˈtēt-ə-ˌtēt\ *n* [F, lit., head to head] (1697) **1 :** a private conversation between two persons **2 :** a short piece of furniture (as a sofa) intended to seat two persons esp. facing each other
[2]**tête–à–tête** \ˌtet-ə-ˈtet, ˌtāt-ə-ˈtāt\ *adv* (1700) **:** in private
[3]**tête–à–tête** \ˌtet-ə-ˌtet, ˌtāt-ə-ˌtāt\ *adj* (1728) **:** FACE-TO-FACE, PRIVATE
tête–bêche \ˈtet-ˈbesh\ *adj* [F, n., pair of inverted stamps, fr. *tête* head + *-bêche,* alter. of MF *bechevet* head against foot] (1921) **:** of or relating to a pair of stamps inverted in relation to one another either through a printing error or intentionally
teth \ˈtāt(h), ˈtās\ *n* [Heb *ṭēth*] (1823) **:** the 9th letter of the Hebrew alphabet — see ALPHABET table
[1]**teth·er** \ˈteth-ər\ *n* [ME *tethir,* prob. of Scand origin; akin to ON *tjōthr* tether; akin to OHG *zeotar* pole of a wagon] (14c) **1 :** something (as a rope or chain) by which an animal is fastened so that it can range only within a set radius **2 :** the limit of one's strength or resources **:** SCOPE ⟨at the end of my ~⟩
[2]**tether** *vt* **teth·ered; teth·er·ing** \-(ə-)riŋ\ (15c) **:** to fasten or restrain by or as if by a tether
teth·er·ball \ˈteth-ər-ˌbȯl\ *n* (ca. 1900) **:** a game played with a ball suspended by a string from an upright pole with the object for each contestant to wrap the string around the pole by striking the ball in a direction opposite to that of the other contestant; *also* **:** the ball used in this game
Te·thys \ˈtē-thəs\ *n* [L, fr. Gk *Tēthys*] **:** a Titaness and wife of Oceanus
tet·ra \ˈte-trə\ *n* [by shortening fr. NL *Tetragonopterus,* former genus name, fr. LL *tetragonum* quadrangle + Gk *pteron* wing — more at TETRAGONAL, FEATHER] (1931) **:** any of numerous small brightly colored So. American characin fishes often bred in tropical aquariums
tetra- *or* **tetr-** *comb form* [ME, fr. L, fr. Gk; akin to Gk *tettares* four — more at FOUR] **1 :** four **:** having four **:** having four parts ⟨*tetra*tomic⟩ **2 :** containing four atoms or groups (of a specified kind) ⟨*tetra*chloride⟩
tet·ra·caine \ˈte-trə-ˌkān\ *n* [*tetra-* + *procaine*] (ca. 1935) **:** a crystalline basic ester $C_{15}H_{24}N_2O_2$ that is closely related chemically to procaine and is used chiefly in the form of its hydrochloride as a local anesthetic
tet·ra·chlo·ride \ˌte-trə-ˈklō(ə)r-ˌīd, -ˈklȯ(ə)r-\ *n* (1866) **:** a chloride containing four atoms of chlorine
tet·ra·chord \ˈte-trə-ˌkȯ(ə)rd\ *n* [Gk *tetrachordon,* fr. neut. of *tetrachordos* of four strings, fr. *tetra-* + *chordē* string — more at YARN] (1603) **:** a diatonic series of four tones with an interval of a perfect fourth between the first and last
tet·ra·cy·cline \ˌte-trə-ˈsī-ˌklēn\ *n* [ISV *tetracyclic* + *-ine*] (1952) **:** a yellow crystalline broad-spectrum antibiotic $C_{22}H_{24}N_2O_8$ produced by a soil actinomycete (*Streptomyces viridifaciens*) or synthetically
tet·rad \ˈte-ˌtrad\ *n* [Gk *tetrad-, tetras,* fr. *tetra-*] (1653) **:** a group or arrangement of four: as **a :** a group of four cells arranged usu. in the form of a tetrahedron and produced by the successive divisions of a mother cell ⟨a ~ of spores⟩ **b :** a group of four synapsed chromatids that become visibly evident in the pachytene stage of meiotic prophase and are produced by the longitudinal splitting of each of two paired homologous chromosomes — **te·trad·ic** \te-ˈtrad-ik\ *adj*
tet·ra·drachm \ˈte-trə-ˌdram\ *n* [Gk *tetradrachmon,* fr. *tetra-* + *drachmē* drachma] (1579) **:** an ancient Greek silver coin worth four drachmas
te·trad·y·mite \te-ˈtrad-ə-ˌmīt\ *n* [LGk *tetradymos* fourfold, fr. Gk *tetra-* + *-dymos* (as in *didymos* didymous); fr. its occurrence in compound twin crystals] (1850) **:** a pale steel-gray mineral Bi_2Te_2S consisting essentially of a telluride and sulfide of bismuth and having a metallic luster

tet·ra·dy·na·mous \ˌte-trə-ˈdī-nə-məs\ *adj* [ISV *tetra-* + Gk *dynamis* power — more at DYNAMIC] (ca. 1847) **:** having six stamens four of which are longer than the others ⟨~ plants of the mustard family⟩

tet·ra·eth·yl lead \ˌte-trə-ˌeth-əl-ˈled\ *n* (1925) **:** a heavy oily poisonous liquid $Pb(C_2H_5)_4$ used as an antiknock agent

tet·ra·flu·o·ride \ˌte-trə-ˈflu̇(-ə)r-ˌīd\ *n* (ca. 1909) **:** a fluoride containing four atoms of fluorine

te·trag·o·nal \te-ˈtrag-ən-ᵊl\ *adj* [LL *tetragonalis* having four angles and four sides, fr. *tetragonum* quadrangle, fr. Gk *tetragōnon,* fr. neut. of *tetragōnos* tetragonal, fr. *tetra-* + *gōnia* angle — more at -GON] (1868) **:** of, relating to, or characteristic of the tetragonal system — **te·trag·o·nal·ly** \-ᵊl-ē\ *adv*

tetragonal system *n* (1879) **:** a crystal system characterized by three axes at right angles of which only the two lateral axes are equal

tet·ra·gram·ma·ton \ˌte-trə-ˈgram-ə-ˌtän\ *n* [ME, fr. Gk, fr. neut. of *tetragrammatos* having four letters, fr. *tetra-* + *grammat-, gramma* letter — more at GRAM] (15c) **:** the four Hebrew letters usu. transliterated YHWH or JHVH that form a biblical proper name of God — compare YAHWEH

tet·ra·he·dral \ˌte-trə-ˈhē-drəl\ *adj* (1794) **1 :** being a polyhedral angle with four faces **2 :** relating to, forming, or having the form of a tetrahedron — **tet·ra·he·dral·ly** \-drə-lē\ *adv*

tet·ra·he·drite \-ˌdrīt\ *n* [G *tetraëdrit,* fr. LGk *tetraedros* having four faces] (1868) **:** a fine-grained gray mineral $(Cu,Fe)_{12}Sb_4S_{13}$ that consists essentially of a sulfide of copper, iron, and antimony, often contains other elements (as silver), occurs in tetrahedral crystals and also in massive form, and is often a valuable ore of silver

tet·ra·he·dron \ˌte-trə-ˈhē-drən\ *n, pl* **-drons** *or* **-dra** \-drə\ [NL, fr. LGk *tetraedron,* neut. of *tetraedros* having four faces, fr. Gk *tetra-* + *hedra* seat, face — more at SIT] (ca. 1570) **:** a polyhedron that has four faces

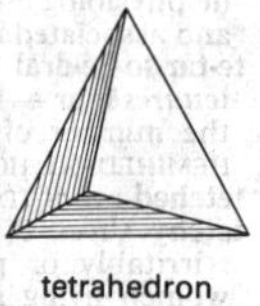
tetrahedron

tet·ra·hy·dro·can·nab·i·nol \-ˌhī-drə-kə-ˈnab-ə-ˌnȯl, -ˌnōl\ *n* [*tetrahydro-* (combined with four atoms of hydrogen) + *cannabin* + *-ol*] (1966) **:** THC

tet·ra·hy·dro·fu·ran \-ˈfyu̇(ə)r-ˌan, -fyu̇-ˈran\ *n* [*tetrahydro-* + *furan*] (ca. 1943) **:** a flammable liquid heterocyclic ether C_4H_8O that is derived from furan and used as a solvent and as an intermediate in organic synthesis

tet·ra·hy·me·na \ˌte-trə-ˈhī-mə-nə\ *n* [NL, fr. *tetra-* + Gk *hymēn* membrane] (1962) **:** any of a genus (*Tetrahymena*) of ciliate protozoans

te·tral·o·gy \te-ˈträl-ə-jē, -ˈtral-\ *n, pl* **-gies** [Gk *tetralogia,* fr. *tetra-* + *-logia* -logy] (1656) **1 :** a group of four dramatic pieces presented consecutively on the Attic stage at the Dionysiac festival **2 :** a series of four connected works (as operas or novels)

tet·ra·mer \ˈte-trə-mər\ *n* (1936) **:** a molecule (as an enzyme or a polymer) that consists of four structural subunits (as peptide chains or condensed monomers) — **tet·ra·mer·ic** \ˌte-trə-ˈmer-ik\ *adj*

te·tram·er·ous \te-ˈtram-ə-rəs\ *adj* [NL *tetramerus,* fr. Gk *tetramerēs,* fr. *tetra-* + *meros* part — more at MERIT] (1826) **:** having or characterized by the presence of four parts or of parts arranged in sets or multiples of four ⟨~ flowers⟩

te·tram·e·ter \te-ˈtram-ət-ər\ *n* [Gk *tetrametron,* fr. neut. of *tetrametros* having four measures, fr. *tetra-* + *metron* measure — more at MEASURE] (1612) **:** a line of verse consisting either of four dipodies (as in classical iambic, trochaic, and anapestic verse) or four metrical feet (as in modern English verse)

tet·ra·meth·yl·lead \ˌte-trə-ˌmeth-əl-ˈled\ *n* (1964) **:** a volatile poisonous liquid $Pb(CH_3)_4$ used as an antiknock agent

[1]**tet·ra·ploid** \ˈte-trə-ˌplȯid\ *adj* [ISV] (1912) **:** having or being a chromosome number four times the monoploid number ⟨a ~ cell⟩ — **tet·ra·ploi·dy** \-ˌplȯid-ē\ *n*

[2]**tetraploid** *n* (1926) **:** a tetraploid individual

tet·ra·pod \ˈte-trə-ˌpäd\ *n* [NL *tetrapodus,* fr. Gk *tetrapod-, tetrapous* four-footed, fr. *tetra-* + *pod-, pous* foot — more at FOOT] (ca. 1891) **:** a vertebrate (as a frog, bird, or cat) with two pairs of limbs

tet·ra·pyr·role \ˌte-trə-ˈpi(ə)r-ˌōl\ *n* (ca. 1928) **:** a chemical group consisting of four pyrrole rings joined either in a straight chain or in a ring (as in chlorophyll)

te·trarch \ˈte-ˌträrk, ˈtē-\ *n* [ME, fr. L *tetrarcha,* fr. Gk *tetrarchēs,* fr. *tetra-* + *-archēs* -arch] (14c) **1 :** a governor of the fourth part of a province **2 :** a subordinate prince — **te·trar·chic** \te-ˈträr-kik, tē-\ *adj*

te·trar·chy \ˈte-ˌträr-kē, ˈtē-\ *n, pl* **-chies** (1630) **:** government by four persons ruling jointly

tet·ra·spore \ˈte-trə-ˌspō(ə)r, -ˌspȯ(ə)r\ *n* [ISV] (1857) **:** one of the haploid asexual spores developed meiotically in the red algae usu. in groups of four — **tet·ra·spor·ic** \ˌte-trə-ˈspōr-ik, -ˈspȯr-\ *adj*

tet·ra·va·lent \ˌte-trə-ˈvā-lənt\ *adj* [ISV] (1868) **:** having a valence of four

te·traz·zi·ni \ˌte-trə-ˈzē-nē\ *adj* [Luisa *Tetrazzini* †1940 Ital. opera singer] (1951) **:** prepared with pasta and a white sauce seasoned with sherry and served au gratin ⟨chicken ~⟩

tet·ra·zo·li·um \ˌte-trə-ˈzō-lē-əm\ *n* [NL, fr. ISV *tetrazole* (CH_2N_4) + NL *-ium* (as in *ammonium*)] (ca. 1909) **:** a univalent cation or group CH_3N_4 that is analogous to ammonium; *also* **:** any of several of its derivatives used esp. as electron acceptors to test for metabolic activity in living cells

tet·rode \ˈte-ˌtrōd\ *n* (ca. 1902) **:** a vacuum tube with four electrodes, a cathode, an anode, a control grid, and an additional grid or other electrode

te·tro·do·tox·in \te-ˌtrōd-ə-ˈtäk-sən\ *n* [ISV *tetrodo-* (fr. NL *Tetrodon,* genus of tropical marine fishes) + *toxin*] (ca. 1923) **:** a poisonous compound $C_{11}H_{17}N_3O_8$ that has been isolated from a Japanese globefish and a newt and that blocks nerve conduction by suppressing permeability of the nerve fiber to sodium ions

te·trox·ide \te-ˈträk-ˌsīd\ *n* [ISV] (1866) **:** a compound of an element or group with four atoms of oxygen

tet·ryl \ˈte-trəl\ *n* [ISV] (ca. 1918) **:** a pale yellow crystalline explosive $C_7H_5N_5O_8$ used esp. as a detonator

tet·ter \ˈtet-ər\ *n* [ME *teter,* fr. OE; akin to OE *teran* to tear] (bef. 12c) **:** any of various vesicular skin diseases (as ringworm, eczema, and herpes)

Teu·ton \ˈt(y)üt-ᵊn\ *n* [L *Teutoni,* pl.] (1727) **1 :** a member of an ancient prob. Germanic or Celtic people **2 :** a member of a people speaking a language of the Germanic branch of the Indo-European language family; *esp* **:** GERMAN

[1]**Teu·ton·ic** \t(y)ü-ˈtän-ik\ *n* (1612) **:** GERMANIC

[2]**Teutonic** *adj* (1617) **:** of, relating to, or characteristic of the Teutons — **Teu·ton·i·cal·ly** \-i-k(ə-)lē\ *adv*

Teu·ton·ism \ˈt(y)üt-ᵊn-ˌiz-əm\ *n* (1854) **:** GERMANISM

Teu·ton·ist \-ᵊn-əst\ *n* (1882) **:** GERMANIST

teu·ton·ize \-ᵊn-ˌīz\ *vt* **-ized; -iz·ing** *often cap* (1845) **:** GERMANIZE

tex·as \ˈtek-səs, -siz\ *n* [*Texas,* state of U.S.; fr. the naming of cabins on Mississippi steamboats after states, the officers' cabins being the largest] (1857) **:** a structure on the awning deck of a steamer that contains the officers' cabins and has the pilothouse in front or on top

Texas fever *n* (1866) **:** an infectious disease of cattle transmitted by the cattle tick and caused by a protozoan (*Babesia bigemina*) that multiplies in the blood and destroys the red blood cells

Texas Independence Day *n* (ca. 1928) **:** March 2 observed as the anniversary of the declaration of independence of Texas from Mexico in 1836 and also as the birthday of Sam Houston

texas leaguer *n* [*Texas League,* a baseball minor league] (1900) **:** a fly in baseball that falls too far out to be caught by an infielder and too close in to be caught by an outfielder

Texas Ranger *n* (1911) **:** a member of a formerly mounted police force in Texas

Tex–Mex \ˈtek-ˈsmeks\ *adj* [*Texas* + *Mexico*] (1949) **:** of, relating to, or being the Mexican-American culture or cuisine existing or originating in esp. southern Texas ⟨~ cooking⟩ ⟨~ music⟩

text \ˈtekst\ *n* [ME, fr. MF *texte,* fr. ML *textus,* fr. L, texture, context, fr. *textus,* pp. of *texere* to weave — more at TECHNICAL] (14c) **1 a** (1) **:** the original words and form of a written or printed work (2) **:** an edited or emended copy of an original work **b :** a work containing such text **2 a :** the main body of printed or written matter on a page **b :** the principal part of a book exclusive of front and back matter **c :** the printed score of a musical composition **3 a** (1) **:** a verse or passage of Scripture chosen esp. for the subject of a sermon or for authoritative support (as for a doctrine) (2) **:** a passage from an authoritative source providing an introduction or basis (as for a speech) **b :** a source of information or authority **4 :** THEME, TOPIC **5 a :** the words of something (as a poem) set to music **b :** matter chiefly in the form of words captured by computer-based equipment ⟨a *text*-editing typewriter⟩ **6 :** a type suitable for printing running text **7 :** TEXTBOOK

[1]**text·book** \ˈteks(t)-ˌbu̇k\ *n* (1779) **:** a book used in the study of a subject: as **a :** one containing a presentation of the principles of a subject **b :** a literary work relevant to the study of a subject

[2]**textbook** *adj* (1905) **:** of, suggesting, or suitable to a textbook; *esp* **:** CLASSIC ⟨a ~ example of bureaucratic waste⟩

text·book·ish \-ish\ *adj* (1927) **:** of, relating to, or having the characteristics of a textbook ⟨the style is heavy and ~ —*Nation*⟩

text edition *n* (1895) **:** an edition of a book prepared for use esp. in schools and colleges — compare TRADE EDITION

tex·tile \ˈtek-ˌstīl, ˈteks-tᵊl\ *n* [L, fr. neut. of *textilis* woven, fr. *textus,* pp. of *texere*] (1626) **1 :** CLOTH 1a; *esp* **:** a woven or knit cloth **2 :** a fiber, filament, or yarn used in making cloth

tex·tu·al \ˈteks-chə(-wə)l\ *adj* [ME, fr. ML *textus* text] (15c) **:** of, relating to, or based on a text — **tex·tu·al·ly** \-ē\ *adv*

textual critic *n* (1938) **:** a practitioner of textual criticism

textual criticism *n* (1875) **1 :** the study of a literary work that aims to establish the original text **2 :** a critical study of literature emphasizing a close reading and analysis of the text

[1]**tex·tu·ary** \ˈteks-chə-ˌwer-ē\ *n, pl* **-ar·ies** [ML *textus*] (1608) **:** one who is well informed in the Bible or in biblical scholarship

[2]**textuary** *adj* (1646) **:** TEXTUAL

[1]**tex·ture** \ˈteks-chər\ *n* [L *textura,* fr. *textus,* pp. of *texere* to weave — more at TECHNICAL] (1578) **1 a :** something composed of closely interwoven elements; *specif* **:** a woven cloth **b :** the structure formed by the threads of a fabric **2 a :** essential part **:** SUBSTANCE **b :** identifying quality **:** CHARACTER **3 a :** the disposition or manner of union of the particles of a body or substance **b :** the visual or tactile surface characteristics and appearance of something ⟨the ~ of an oil painting⟩ **4 a :** a composite of the elements of prose or poetry ⟨all these words . . . meet violently to form a ~ impressive and exciting —John Berryman⟩ **b :** a pattern of musical sound created by tones or lines played or sung together **5 a :** basic scheme or structure **b :** overall structure — **tex·tur·al** \-chə-rəl\ *adj* — **tex·tur·al·ly** \-ē\ *adv* — **textured** \-chərd\ *adj*

[2]**texture** *vt* **tex·tured; tex·tur·ing** (1694) **:** to give a particular texture to

tex·tur·ize \ˈteks-chə-ˌrīz\ *vt* **-ized; -iz·ing** (ca. 1950) **:** TEXTURE ⟨~ a polyester yarn⟩

tex·tus re·cep·tus \ˌtek-stəs-ri-ˈsep-təs\ *n* [NL, lit., received text] (ca. 1856) **:** the generally accepted text of a literary work (as the Greek New Testament)

T formation *n* (1937) **:** an offensive football formation in which the fullback lines up behind the center and quarterback with one halfback stationed on each side of the fullback

T–group \ˈtē-ˌgrüp\ *n* [*training group*] (1964) **:** a group of people under the leadership of a trainer who seek to develop self-awareness and sensitivity to others by verbalizing feelings uninhibitedly at group sessions — compare ENCOUNTER GROUP

[1]**-th** — see -ETH

[2]**-th** *or* **-eth** *adj suffix* [ME *-the, -te,* fr. OE *-tha, -ta;* akin to OHG *-do* -th, L *-tus,* Gk *-tos,* Skt *-tha*] — used in forming ordinal numbers ⟨hundred*th*⟩ ⟨fortie*th*⟩

[3]**-th** *n suffix* [ME, fr. OE; akin to OHG *-ida,* suffix forming abstract nouns, L *-ta,* Gk *-tē,* Skt *-tā*] **1 :** act or process ⟨spil*th*⟩ **2 :** state or condition ⟨dear*th*⟩

Thai \ˈtī\ *n, pl* **Thai** *or* **Thais** (ca. 1904) **1 a :** a native or inhabitant of Thailand **b :** one who is descended from a Thai **2 :** the official language of Thailand **3 :** a group of languages including Thai held by some to belong to the Sino-Tibetan language group

tha·lam·ic \thə-ˈlam-ik\ *adj* (1860) **:** of, relating to, or involving the thalamus

thal·a·mus \ˈthal-ə-məs\ *n, pl* **-mi** \-ˌmī, -ˌmē\ [NL, fr. Gk *thalamos* chamber] (1756) **:** the largest subdivision of the diencephalon consisting chiefly of an ovoid mass of nuclei in each lateral wall of the third ventricle — see BRAIN illustration

thal·as·se·mia \ˌthal-ə-ˈsē-mē-ə\ *n* [NL, fr. Gk *thalassa* sea + NL *-emia*] (ca. 1936) **:** any of a group of inherited hypochromic anemias controlled by a series of allelic genes which cause reduction in or failure of synthesis of one of the globin chains making up hemoglobin resulting in its deficiency and some of which occur with relatively high frequencies in Negro, Mediterranean, or Oriental populations; *esp* **:** COOLEY'S ANEMIA — **thal·as·se·mic** \-mik\ *adj or n*

tha·las·sic \thə-ˈlas-ik\ *adj* [F *thalassique,* fr. Gk *thalassa* sea] (1860) **:** of, relating to, or situated or developed about inland seas ⟨~ civilizations of the Aegean⟩

thal·as·soc·ra·cy \ˌthal-ə-ˈsäk-rə-sē\ *n* [Gk *thalassokratia,* fr. *thalassa* + *-kratia* -cracy] (1846) **:** maritime supremacy

tha·las·so·crat \thə-ˈlas-ə-ˌkrat\ *n* (1846) **:** one who has maritime supremacy

tha·ler \ˈtäl-ər\ *var of* TALER

Tha·lia \thə-ˈlī-ə\ *n* [L, fr. Gk *Thaleia*] **1 :** the Greek Muse of comedy **2 :** one of the three Graces

tha·lid·o·mide \thə-ˈlid-ə-ˌmīd, -məd\ *n* [ph*thal*ic acid + *-id-* (fr. *imide*) + *-o-* + *imide*] (1962) **:** a sedative and hypnotic drug $C_{13}H_{10}N_2O_4$ that has been the cause of malformation of infants born to mothers using it during pregnancy

thall- *or* **thallo-** *comb form* [NL, fr. Gk, fr. *thallos* — more at THALLUS] **1 a :** a young shoot ⟨*thall*ium⟩ **b :** thallus ⟨*thall*oid⟩ **2 :** thallium ⟨*thall*ic⟩

thal·lic \ˈthal-ik\ *adj* (1868) **:** of, relating to, or containing thallium esp. with a valence of three

thal·li·um \ˈthal-ē-əm\ *n* [NL, fr. Gk *thallos* green shoot; fr. the bright green line in its spectrum] (ca. 1861) **:** a sparsely but widely distributed poisonous metallic element that resembles lead in physical properties and is used chiefly in the form of compounds in photoelectric cells or as a pesticide — see ELEMENT table

thal·loid \ˈthal-ˌȯid\ *adj* (1857) **:** of, relating to, resembling, or consisting of a thallus ⟨~ liverworts⟩

thal·lo·phyte \ˈthal-ə-ˌfīt\ *n* [deriv. of Gk *thallos* + *phyton* plant — more at PHYT-] (ca. 1864) **:** any of a primary division (Thallophyta) of the plant kingdom comprising plants with single-celled sex organs or with many-celled sex organs of which all cells give rise to gametes, including the algae, fungi, and lichens, and usu. held to be a heterogeneous assemblage — **thal·lo·phyt·ic** \ˌthal-ə-ˈfit-ik\ *adj*

thal·lous \ˈthal-əs\ *adj* (1888) **:** of, relating to, or containing thallium with a valence of one

thal·lus \ˈthal-əs\ *n, pl* **thal·li** \ˈthal-ˌī, -ˌē\ *or* **thal·lus·es** [NL, fr. Gk *thallos,* fr. *thallein* to sprout; akin to Alb *dal* I come forth] (1829) **:** a plant body that is characteristic of thallophytes, lacks differentiation into distinct members (as stem, leaves, and roots), and does not grow from an apical point

¹than \thən, (ˈ)than\ *conj* [ME *than, then* then, than — more at THEN] (bef. 12c) **1 a** — used as a function word to indicate the second member or the member taken as the point of departure in a comparison expressive of inequality; used with comparative adjectives and comparative adverbs ⟨older ~ I am⟩ ⟨easier said ~ done⟩ **b** — used as a function word to indicate difference of kind, manner, or identity; used esp. with some adjectives and adverbs that express diversity ⟨anywhere else ~ at home⟩ **2 :** rather than — usu. used only after *prefer, preferable,* and *preferably* **3 :** other than **4 :** WHEN — used esp. after *scarcely* and *hardly*

²than *prep* (1560) **:** in comparison with ⟨you are older ~ me⟩
usage After about 200 years of innocent if occasional use, the preposition *than* was called into question by 18th century grammarians. Some 200 years of elaborate and sometimes tortuous reasoning have led to these present-day inconsistent conclusions: *than whom* is standard but clumsy ⟨Beelzebub . . . *than* whom, Satan except, none higher sat —John Milton⟩ ⟨T.S. Eliot, *than* whom nobody could have been more insularly English —Anthony Burgess⟩; *than me* may be acceptable in speech ⟨a man no mightier *than* thyself or me —Shak.⟩ ⟨Macmillan was nine or ten years older *than* me —Lord Butler of Saffron Walden, in a BBC interview⟩; *than* followed by a third-person objective pronoun (*her, him, them*) is usu. frowned upon. Surveyed opinion tends to agree with these conclusions. Our evidence shows that the conjunction is more common than the preposition, that *than whom* is chiefly limited to writing, that *than me* is more common than *than* with a third-person objective pronoun, and that both of these last are more common in speech than in edited prose. Some handbooks go into considerable detail discussing more complicated constructions and their possible ambiguities; our evidence indicates that these are relatively uncommon in edited prose.

than·a·tol·o·gy \ˌthan-ə-ˈtäl-ə-jē\ *n* [Gk *thanatos* + E *-logy*] (ca. 1842) **:** the description or study of the phenomena of death and of psychological mechanisms for coping with them — **than·a·to·log·i·cal** \ˌthan-ət-ᵊl-ˈäj-i-kəl\ *adj* — **than·a·tol·o·gist** \-ə-ˈtäl-ə-jəst\ *n*

Than·a·tos \ˈthan-ə-ˌtäs\ *n* [Gk, death; akin to Skt *adhvanīt* it vanished, L *fumus* smoke] (ca. 1939) **:** DEATH INSTINCT

thane \ˈthān\ *n* [ME *theyn,* fr. OE *thegn;* akin to OHG *thegan* thane, Gk *tiktein* to bear, beget] (bef. 12c) **1 :** a free retainer of an Anglo-Saxon lord; *esp* **:** one resembling a feudal baron by holding lands of and performing military service for the king **2 :** a Scottish feudal lord — **thane·ship** \-ˌship\ *n*

thank \ˈthaŋk\ *vt* [ME *thanken,* fr. OE *thancian;* akin to OE *thanc* gratitude — more at THANKS] (bef. 12c) **1 :** to express gratitude to ⟨~*ed* her for the present⟩ — used in the phrase *thank you* usu. without a subject to politely express gratitude ⟨~ you for the loan⟩; used in such phrases as *thank God, thank heaven* usu. without a subject to express gratitude or more often only the speaker's or writer's pleasure or satisfaction in something **2 :** to hold responsible ⟨had only himself to ~ for his loss⟩ — **thank·er** *n*

thank·ful \ˈthaŋk-fəl\ *adj* (bef. 12c) **1 :** conscious of benefit received ⟨for what we are about to receive make us truly ~⟩ **2 :** expressive of thanks ⟨~ service⟩ **3 :** well pleased **:** GLAD ⟨was ~ that it didn't rain⟩ — **thank·ful·ly** \-fə-lē\ *adv* — **thank·ful·ness** *n*

thank·less \ˈthaŋ-kləs\ *adj* (1536) **1 :** not expressing or feeling gratitude **:** UNGRATEFUL ⟨how sharper than a serpent's tooth it is to have a ~ child —Shak.⟩ **2 :** not likely to obtain thanks **:** UNAPPRECIATED ⟨a ~ task⟩ — **thank·less·ly** *adv* — **thank·less·ness** *n*

thanks \ˈthaŋ(k)s\ *n pl* [pl. of ME *thank,* fr. OE *thanc* thought, gratitude; akin to OHG *dank* gratitude, L *tongēre* to know] (bef. 12c) **1 :** kindly or grateful thoughts **:** GRATITUDE **2 :** an expression of gratitude ⟨return ~ before the meal⟩ — often used in an utterance containing no verb and serving as a courteous and somewhat informal expression of gratitude ⟨many ~⟩ — **no thanks to :** not as a result of any benefit conferred by ⟨he feels better now, *no thanks to* you⟩ — **thanks to :** with the help of **:** owing to ⟨arrived early, *thanks to* good weather⟩

thanks·giv·ing \thaŋ(k)s-ˈgiv-iŋ\ *n* (1533) **1 :** the act of giving thanks **2 :** a prayer expressing gratitude **3 a :** a public acknowledgment or celebration of divine goodness **b** *cap* **:** THANKSGIVING DAY

Thanksgiving Day *n* (1674) **:** a day appointed for giving thanks for divine goodness: as **a :** the fourth Thursday in November observed as a legal holiday in the U.S. **b :** the second Monday in October observed as a legal holiday in Canada

thank·wor·thy \ˈthaŋ-ˌkwər-t͟hē\ *adj* (14c) **:** worthy of thanks or gratitude **:** MERITORIOUS

thank–you \ˈthaŋ-ˌkyü\ *n* [fr. the phrase *thank you* used in expressing gratitude] (15c) **:** a polite expression of one's gratitude

thank–you–ma'am \ˈthaŋk-yü-ˌmam, -(y)ē-\ *n* [prob. fr. its causing a nodding of the head] (1849) **:** a bump or depression in a road; *esp* **:** a ridge or hollow made across a road on a hillside to cause water to run off

¹that \(ˈ)t͟hat\ *pron, pl* **those** \(ˈ)t͟hōz\ [ME, fr. OE *thæt,* neut. demonstrative pron. & definite article; akin to OHG *daz,* neuter demonstrative pron. & definite article, Gk *to,* L *istud,* neut. demonstrative pron.] (bef. 12c) **1 a :** the person, thing, or idea indicated, mentioned, or understood from the situation ⟨~ is my father⟩ **b :** the time, action, or event specified ⟨after ~ I went to bed⟩ **c :** the kind or thing specified as follows ⟨the purest water is ~ produced by distillation⟩ **d :** one or a group of the indicated kind ⟨~'s a cat — quick and agile⟩ **2 a :** the one farther away or less immediately under observation or discussion ⟨*those* are maples and these are elms⟩ **b :** the former one **3 a** — used as a function word after *and* to indicate emphatic repetition of the idea expressed by a previous word or phrase ⟨he was helpful, and ~ to an unusual degree⟩ **b** — used as a function word immediately before or after a word group consisting of a verbal auxiliary or a form of the verb *be* preceded by *there* or a personal pronoun subject to indicate emphatic repetition of the idea expressed by a previous verb or predicate noun or predicate adjective ⟨is she capable? She is ~⟩ **4 a :** the one **:** the thing **:** the kind **:** SOMETHING, ANYTHING ⟨the truth of ~ which is true⟩ ⟨the senses are ~ whereby we experience the world⟩ ⟨what's ~ you say⟩ **b** *pl* **:** some persons ⟨*those* who think the time has come⟩ — **all that :** everything of the kind indicated ⟨tact, discretion, and *all that*⟩ — **at that 1 :** in spite of what has been said or implied **2 :** in addition **:** ²BESIDES

²that *adj, pl* **those** (bef. 12c) **1 a :** being the person, thing, or idea specified, mentioned, or understood **b :** so great a **:** SUCH **2 :** the farther away or less immediately under observation or discussion ⟨this chair or ~ one⟩

³that \t͟hət, (ˌ)t͟hat\ *conj* (bef. 12c) **1 a** (1) — used as a function word to introduce a noun clause that is usu. the subject or object of a verb or a predicate nominative ⟨said ~ he was afraid⟩ (2) — used as a function word to introduce a subordinate clause that is anticipated by the expletive *it* occurring as subject of the verb ⟨it is unlikely ~ he'll be in⟩ (3) — used as a function word to introduce a subordinate clause that is joined as complement to a noun or adjective ⟨we are certain ~ this is true⟩ ⟨the fact ~ you are here⟩ (4) — used as a function word to introduce a subordinate clause modifying an adverb or adverbial expression ⟨will go anywhere ~ he is invited⟩ **b** — used as a function word to introduce an exclamatory clause expressing a strong emotion esp. of surprise, sorrow, or indignation ⟨~ it should come to this!⟩ **2 a** (1) — used as a function word to introduce a subordinate clause expressing purpose or desired result ⟨cutting down expenses ~ her son might inherit an unencumbered estate —W. B. Yeats⟩ (2) — used as a function word to introduce a subordinate clause expressing a reason or cause ⟨rejoice ~ you are lightened of a load —Robert Browning⟩ (3) — used as a function word to introduce a subordinate clause expressing consequence, result, or effect ⟨are of sufficient importance ~ they cannot be neglected —Hannah Wormington⟩ **b** — used as a function word to introduce an exclamatory clause expressing a wish ⟨oh, ~ he would come⟩ **3** — used as a function word after a subordinating conjunction without modifying its meaning ⟨if ~ thy bent of love be honorable —Shak.⟩

⁴that \t͟hət, (ˌ)t͟hat\ *pron* [ME, fr. OE *thæt,* neut. rel. pron., fr. *thæt,* neut. demonstrative pron.] (bef. 12c) **1** — used as a function word to introduce a restrictive relative clause and to serve as a substitute within that clause for the substantive modified by that clause ⟨the house ~ Jack built⟩ **2 a :** at which **:** in which **:** on which **:** by which **:** with which **:** to which ⟨each year ~ the lectures are given⟩ **b :** according to what **:** to the extent of what — used after a negative ⟨has never been here ~ I know of⟩ **3 a** *archaic* **:** that which **b** *obs* **:** the person who

⁵that \ˈt͟hat\ *adv* (15c) **1 :** to such an extent ⟨a nail about ~ long⟩ **2 :** VERY, EXTREMELY — usu. used with the negative ⟨did not take the festival ~ seriously —Eric Goldman⟩

¹thatch \ˈthach\ *vt* [ME *thecchen,* fr. OE *theccan* to cover; akin to OHG *decchen* to cover, L *tegere,* Gk *stegein* to cover, *stegos* roof, Skt *sthagati* he covers] (14c) **:** to cover with or as if with thatch — **thatch·er** *n*

²thatch *n* (14c) **1 a :** a plant material (as straw) used as a sheltering cover esp. of a house **b :** a sheltering cover (as a house roof) made of such material **c :** a mat of undecomposed plant material (as grass clippings) accumulated next to the soil in a grassy area (as a lawn) **2 :** something resembling the thatch of a house; *esp* **:** the hair of one's head

thau·ma·turge \ˈthȯ-mə-ˌtərj\ *n* [F, fr. NL *thaumaturgus,* fr. Gk *thaumatourgos* working miracles, fr. *thaumat-, thauma* miracle + *ergon* work — more at THEATER, WORK] (1715) **:** THAUMATURGIST

\ə\ abut \ᵊ\ kitten, F table \ər\ further \a\ ash \ā\ ace \ä\ cot, cart
\au̇\ out \ch\ chin \e\ bet \ē\ easy \g\ go \i\ hit \ī\ ice \j\ job
\ŋ\ sing \ō\ go \ȯ\ law \ȯi\ boy \th\ thin \t͟h\ the \ü\ loot \u̇\ foot
\y\ yet \zh\ vision \a̅, k̲, ⁿ, œ, œ̄, ue, ue̅, ʸ\ *see* Guide to Pronunciation

thau·ma·tur·gic \ˌthȯ-mə-'tər-jik\ *adj* (1680) **1** : performing miracles **2** : of, relating to, or dependent on thaumaturgy

thau·ma·tur·gist \'thȯ-mə-ˌtər-jəst\ *n* (1829) : a performer of miracles; *esp* : MAGICIAN

thau·ma·tur·gy \-jē\ *n* (ca. 1727) : the performance of miracles; *specif* : MAGIC

[1]**thaw** \'thȯ\ *vb* [ME *thawen,* fr. OE *thawian;* akin to OHG *douwen* to thaw, Gk *tēkein* to melt, L *tabes* wasting disease] *vt* (bef. 12c) : to cause to thaw ~ *vi* **1 a** : to go from a frozen to a liquid state : MELT **b** : to become free of the effect (as stiffness, numbness, or hardness) of cold as a result of exposure to warmth **2** : to be warm enough to melt ice and snow — used with *it* in reference to the weather **3** : to abandon aloofness, reserve, or hostility : UNBEND **4** : to become mobile, active, or susceptible to change

[2]**thaw** *n* (15c) **1** : the action, fact, or process of thawing **2** : a period of weather warm enough to thaw ice ⟨the January ~⟩ **3** : the action or process of becoming less aloof, less hostile, or more genial ⟨a ~ in international relations⟩

THC \ˌtē-ˌāch-'sē\ *n* [*t*etra*h*ydro*c*annabinol] (1967) : a physiologically active chemical from hemp plant resin that is the chief intoxicant in marijuana — called also *tetrahydrocannabinol*

[1]**the** \thə (*before consonant & esp Southern sometimes vowel sounds*), thē (*before vowel sounds*); *1k is often* 'thē\ *definite article* [ME, fr. OE *thē,* masc. demonstrative pron. & definite article, alter. (influenced by oblique cases — as *thæs,* gen. — & neut., *thæt*) of *sē;* akin to Gk *ho,* masc. demonstrative pron. & definite article — more at THAT] (bef. 12c) **1 a** — used as a function word to indicate that a following noun or noun equivalent is definite or has been previously specified by context or by circumstance ⟨put ~ cat out⟩ **b** — used as a function word to indicate that a following noun or noun equivalent is a unique or a particular member of its class ⟨~ President⟩ ⟨~ Lord⟩ **c** — used as a function word before nouns that designate natural phenomena or points of the compass ⟨~ night is cold⟩ **d** — used as a function word before a noun denoting time to indicate reference to what is present or immediate or is under consideration ⟨in ~ future⟩ **e** — used as a function word before names of some parts of the body or of the clothing as an equivalent of a possessive adjective ⟨how's ~ arm today⟩ **f** — used as a function word before the name of a branch of human endeavor or proficiency ⟨~ law⟩ **g** — used as a function word in prepositional phrases to indicate that the noun in the phrase serves as a basis for computation ⟨sold by ~ dozen⟩ **h** — used as a function word before a proper name (as of a ship or a well-known building) ⟨~ Mayflower⟩ **i** — used as a function word before the plural form of a numeral that is a multiple of ten to denote a particular decade of a century or of a person's life ⟨life in ~ twenties⟩ **j** — used as a function word before the name of a commodity or any familiar appurtenance of daily life to indicate reference to the individual thing, part, or supply thought of as at hand ⟨talked on ~ telephone⟩ **k** — used as a function word to designate one of a class as the best, most typical, or most worth singling out ⟨this is ~ life⟩; sometimes used before a personal name to denote the most prominent bearer of that name **2 a** (1) — used as a function word with a noun modified by an adjective or by an attributive noun to limit the application of the modified noun to that specified by the adjective or by the attributive noun ⟨~ right answer⟩ ⟨Peter ~ Great⟩ (2) — used as a function word before an absolute adjective ⟨nothing but ~ best⟩ **b** — used as a function word before a noun to limit its application to that specified by a succeeding element in the sentence ⟨~ poet Wordsworth⟩ ⟨~ days of our youth⟩ ⟨didn't have ~ time to write⟩ **3 a** — used as a function word before a singular noun to indicate that the noun is to be understood generically ⟨~ dog is a domestic animal⟩ **b** — used as a function word before a singular substantivized adjective to indicate an abstract idea ⟨an essay on ~ sublime⟩ **4** — used as a function word before a noun or a substantivized adjective to indicate reference to a group as a whole ⟨~ elite⟩

[2]**the** *adv* [ME, fr. OE *thȳ* by that, instrumental of *thæt* that] (bef. 12c) **1** : than before : than otherwise — used before a comparative ⟨none ~ wiser for attending⟩ **2 a** : to what extent ⟨~ sooner the better⟩ **b** : to that extent ⟨the sooner ~ better⟩ **3** : beyond all others ⟨likes this ~ best⟩

[3]**the** *prep* [[1]the] (15c) : PER 2

the- *or* **theo-** *comb form* [ME *theo-,* fr. L, fr. Gk *the-, theo-,* fr. *theos*] : god : God ⟨*the*ism⟩ ⟨*theo*centric⟩

[1]**the·ater** *or* **the·atre** \'thē-ət-ər, 'thi-ət-, *oftenest in Southern* 'thē-ˌāt- *also* thē-'āt-\ *n* [ME *theatre,* fr. MF, fr. L *theatrum,* fr. Gk *theatron,* fr. *theasthai* to view, fr. *thea* act of seeing; akin to Gk *thauma* miracle] (bef. 12c) **1 a** : an outdoor structure for dramatic performances or spectacles in ancient Greece and Rome **b** : a building for dramatic performances **c** : a building or area for showing motion pictures **2** : a place of enactment of significant events or action ⟨the ~ of public life⟩ **3 a** : a place rising by steps or gradations ⟨a woody ~ of stateliest view —John Milton⟩ **b** : a room often with rising tiers of seats for assemblies (as for lectures or surgical demonstrations) **4 a** : dramatic literature : PLAYS **b** : dramatic representation as an art or profession : DRAMA **5** : dramatic or theatrical quality or effectiveness

[2]**theater** *adj* (1978) : TACTICAL ⟨~ nuclear weapons⟩

the·ater·go·er \'thē-ət-ər-ˌgō(-ə)r\ *n* (1874) : one who frequently goes to the theater — **the·ater·go·ing** \-ˌgō-iŋ, -gō(-)iŋ\ *n or adj*

theater–in–the–round *n* (1948) : ARENA THEATER

theater of operations (ca. 1879) : the part of a theater of war in which active operations are conducted

theater of the absurd (ca. 1963) : theater that seeks to represent the absurdity of man's existence in a meaningless universe by bizarre or fantastic means

theater of war (ca. 1890) : the entire land, sea, and air area that is or may become involved directly in war operations

The·atine \'thē-ə-ˌtīn, -ˌtēn\ *n* [NL *Theatinus,* fr. L *Teatinus* inhabitant of Chieti, fr. *Teate* Chieti, Italy] (1597) : a priest of the Order of Clerks Regular founded in 1524 in Italy by St. Cajetan and Gian Pietro Caraffa to reform Catholic morality and combat Lutheranism — **Theatine** *adj*

[1]**the·at·ri·cal** \thē-'a-tri-kəl\ *also* **the·at·ric** \-trik\ *adj* (1558) **1** : of or relating to the theater or the presentation of plays ⟨a ~ costume⟩ **2** : marked by pretense or artificiality of emotion **3 a** : HISTRIONIC ⟨a ~ gesture⟩ **b** : marked by extravagant display or exhibitionism ***syn*** see DRAMATIC — **the·at·ri·cal·ism** \-kə-ˌliz-əm\ *n* — **the·at·ri·cal·i·ty** \-ˌa-trə-'kal-ət-ē\ *n* — **the·at·ri·cal·ly** \-'a-tri-k(ə-)lē\ *adv*

[2]**theatrical** *n* (1657) **1** *pl* **a** : the performance of plays **b** : DRAMATICS **2** *Brit* : a professional actor **3** *pl* : showy or extravagant gestures

the·at·ri·cal·ize \thē-'a-tri-kə-ˌlīz\ *vt* **-ized; -iz·ing** (1778) **1** : to adapt to the theater : DRAMATIZE **2** : to display in showy fashion — **the·at·ri·cal·iza·tion** \-ˌa-tri-kə-lə-'zā-shən\ *n*

the·at·rics \thē-'a-triks\ *n pl* (1807) **1** : THEATRICAL 1 **2** : staged or contrived effects

the·be \'thā-(ˌ)bā\ *n, pl* **thebe** [native name in Botswana] (1967) — see *pula* at MONEY table

the·ca \'thē-kə\ *n, pl* **the·cae** \'thē-ˌsē, -ˌkē\ [NL, fr. Gk *thēkē* case — more at TICK] (1829) **1** : an urn-shaped spore-containing upper part of a moss capsule **2** : an enveloping sheath or case of an animal or animal part — **the·cal** \'thē-kəl\ *adj*

-the·ci·um \'thē-s(h)ē-əm\ *n comb form, pl* **-the·cia** \-s(h)ē-ə\ [NL, fr. Gk *thēkion,* dim. of *thēkē* case] : small containing structure ⟨endo*thecium*⟩

[1]**thec·odont** \'thē-kə-ˌdänt\ *adj* [ISV *thec-* (fr. NL *theca*) + *-odont*] (1840) : having the teeth inserted in sockets

[2]**thecodont** *n* (1840) : a thecodont animal; *esp* : any of an order (Thecodontia) of Triassic diapsid thecodont reptiles that were presumably on the common ancestral line of the dinosaurs, birds, and crocodiles

thé dan·sant \tā-dän-sän\ *n, pl* **thés dansants** *same*\ [F] (ca. 1845) : TEA DANCE

thee \(')thē\ *pron, objective case of* THOU **1 a** — used esp. in ecclesiastical or literary language and by Friends esp. among themselves in contexts where the objective case form would be expected **b** — used by Friends esp. among themselves in contexts where the subjective case form would be expected **2** *archaic* : THYSELF

thee·lin \'thē-(ə-)lən\ *n* [irreg. fr. Gk *thēlys* female; akin to Gk *thēlē* nipple — more at FEMININE] (1932) : ESTRONE

theft \'theft\ *n* [ME *thiefthe,* fr. OE *thīefth;* akin to OE *thēof* thief] (bef. 12c) **1 a** : the act of stealing; *specif* : the felonious taking and removing of personal property with intent to deprive the rightful owner of it **b** : an unlawful taking (as by embezzlement or burglary) of property **2** *obs* : something stolen **3** : a stolen base in baseball

thegn \'thān\ *n* [OE — more at THANE] (bef. 12c) : THANE 1

thegn·ly \-lē\ *adj* (bef. 12c) : of, relating to, or befitting a thegn

their \thər, (ˌ)the(ə)r, (ˌ)tha(ə)r\ *adj* [ME, fr. *their,* pron., fr. ON *theirra,* gen. pl. demonstrative & personal pron.; akin to OE *thæt* that] (13c) **1** : of or relating to them or themselves esp. as possessors, agents, or objects of an action ⟨~ furniture⟩ ⟨~ verses⟩ ⟨~ being seen⟩ **2** : his or her : HIS, HER, ITS — used with an indefinite third person singular antecedent ⟨anyone in ~ senses —W. H. Auden⟩

theirs \'the(ə)rz, 'tha(ə)rz\ *pron, sing or pl in constr* (14c) **1** : that which belongs to them — used without a following noun as a pronoun equivalent in meaning to the adjective *their* **2** : his or hers : HIS, HERS — used with an indefinite third person singular antecedent ⟨I will do my part if everybody else will do ~⟩

the·ism \'thē-ˌiz-əm\ *n* (1678) : belief in the existence of a god or gods; *specif* : belief in the existence of one God viewed as the creative source of man and the world who transcends yet is immanent in the world — **the·ist** \-əst\ *n or adj* — **the·is·tic** \thē-'is-tik\ *adj* — **the·is·ti·cal** \-ti-kəl\ *adj* — **the·is·ti·cal·ly** \-ti-k(ə-)lē\ *adv*

-theism *n comb form* [MF *-théisme,* fr. Gk *theos* god] : belief in (such) a god or (such or so many) gods ⟨mono*theism*⟩

-theist *n comb form* : believer in (such) a god or (such or so many) gods ⟨pan*theist*⟩

[1]**them** \(th)əm, (')them, *after* p, b, v, f, *also* ᵊm\ *pron, objective case of* THEY

[2]**them** \(')them\ *adj, substand* (1594) : THOSE

the·mat·ic \thi-'mat-ik\ *adj* [Gk *thematikos,* fr. *themat-, thema* theme] (1861) **1 a** : of or relating to the stem of a word **b** *of a vowel* : being the last part of a word stem before an inflectional ending **2** : of, relating to, or constituting a theme — **the·mat·i·cal·ly** \-i-k(ə-)lē\ *adv*

thematic apperception test *n* (1941) : a projective technique that is widely used in clinical psychology to make personality, psychodynamic, and diagnostic assessments based on the subject's verbal responses to a series of black and white pictures

theme \'thēm\ *n* [ME *teme, theme,* fr. MF & L; MF *teme,* fr. L *thema,* fr. Gk, lit., something laid down, fr. *tithenai* to place — more at DO] (14c) **1 a** : a subject or topic of discourse or of artistic representation **b** : a specific and distinctive quality, characteristic, or concern ⟨the campaign has lacked a ~⟩ **2** : STEM 4 **3** : a written exercise : COMPOSITION ⟨a research ~⟩ **4** : a melodic subject of a musical composition or movement

theme park *n* (1967) : an amusement park in which the structures and settings are based on a central theme

theme song *n* (ca. 1931) **1** : a melody recurring so often in a musical play that it characterizes the production or one of its characters **2** : a song used as a signature

them·selves \thəm-'selvz, them-\ *pron pl* (14c) **1 a** : those identical ones that are they — compare THEY 1a; used reflexively, for emphasis, or in absolute constructions ⟨nations that govern ~⟩ ⟨they ~ were present⟩ ⟨~ busy, they disliked idleness in others⟩ **b** : himself or herself : HIMSELF, HERSELF — used with an indefinite third person singular antecedent ⟨nobody can call ~ oppressed —Leonard Wibberley⟩ **2** : their normal, healthy, or sane condition ⟨were ~ again after a night's rest⟩

[1]**then** \(')then\ *adv* [ME *than, then* then, than, fr. OE *thonne, thænne;* akin to OHG *denne* then, than, OE *thæt* that] (bef. 12c) **1** : at that time **2 a** : soon after that : next in order of time ⟨walked to the door, ~ turned⟩ **b** : following next after in order of position, narration, or enumeration : being next in a series ⟨first came the clowns, ~ came the elephants⟩ **c** : in addition : BESIDES ⟨~ there is the interest to be paid⟩ **3 a** (1) : in that case ⟨take it, ~, if you want it so much⟩ (2) — used after *but* to qualify or offset a preceding statement ⟨she lost the race, but ~ she never really expected to win⟩ **b** : according to that : as may be inferred ⟨your mind is made up, ~⟩ **c** : as it appears : by way of summing up ⟨the cause of the accident, ~, is established⟩ **d** : as a necessary consequence ⟨if the angles are equal, ~ the complements are equal⟩ — **and then some** : with much more in addition ⟨would require all his strength *and then some*⟩

[2]**then** \ˈthen\ *n* (14c) : that time ⟨since ~, he's been more cautious⟩
[3]**then** \ˈthen\ *adj* (1584) : existing or acting at or belonging to the time mentioned ⟨the ~ secretary of state⟩
then and there *adv* (15c) : on the spot : IMMEDIATELY ⟨wanted the money right *then and there*⟩
the·nar \ˈthē-ˌnär, -nər\ *adj* [NL, fr. Gk — more at DEN] (ca. 1857) : of, relating to, involving, or constituting the ball of the thumb or the intrinsic musculature of the thumb ⟨~ muscles⟩
thence \ˈthen(t)s *also* ˈthen(t)s\ *adv* [ME *thannes,* fr. *thanne* from that place, fr. OE *thanon;* akin to OHG *thanan* from that place, OE *thænne* then — more at THEN] (13c) **1** : from that place **2** *archaic* : from that time : THENCEFORTH **3** : from that fact or circumstance : THEREFROM
thence·forth \-ˌfō(ə)rth, -ˌfȯ(ə)rth\ *adv* (14c) : from that time forward
thence·for·ward \then(t)s-ˈfȯr-wərd *also* then(t)s-\ *also* **thence·for·wards** \-wərdz\ *adv* (15c) : onward from that place or time
theo- — see THE-
theo·bro·mine \ˌthē-ə-ˈbrō-ˌmēn, -mən\ *n* [NL *Theobroma,* genus of trees, fr. *the-* + Gk *brōma* food, fr. *bibrōskein* to devour — more at VORACIOUS] (1842) : a bitter alkaloid $C_7H_8N_4O_2$ closely related to caffeine that occurs esp. in cacao beans and has stimulant and diuretic properties
theo·cen·tric \-ˈsen-trik\ *adj* (1886) : having God as the central interest and ultimate concern ⟨a ~ culture⟩ — **theo·cen·tric·i·ty** \-ˌsen-ˈtris-ət-ē\ *n* — **theo·cen·trism** \-ˈsen-ˌtriz-əm\ *n*
the·oc·ra·cy \thē-ˈäk-rə-sē\ *n, pl* **-cies** [Gk *theokratia,* fr. *the-* + *-kratia* -cracy] (1622) **1** : government of a state by immediate divine guidance or by officials who are regarded as divinely guided **2** : a state governed by a theocracy
theo·crat \ˈthē-ə-ˌkrat\ *n* (1827) **1** : one who rules in or lives under a theocratic form of government **2** : one who favors a theocratic form of government
theo·crat·ic \ˌthē-ə-ˈkrat-ik\ *also* **theo·crat·i·cal** \-i-kəl\ *adj* (1690) : of, relating to, or being a theocracy — **theo·crat·i·cal·ly** \-i-k(ə-)lē\ *adv*
the·od·i·cy \thē-ˈäd-ə-sē\ *n, pl* **-cies** [modif. of F *théodicée,* fr. *théo-* the- (fr. L *theo-*) + Gk *dikē* judgment, right — more at DICTION] (ca. 1797) : defense of God's goodness and omnipotence in view of the existence of evil
the·od·o·lite \thē-ˈäd-ᵊl-ˌīt\ *n* [NL *theodelitus*] (1571) : a surveyor's instrument for measuring horizontal and usu. also vertical angles — **the·od·o·lit·ic** \-ˌäd-ᵊl-ˈit-ik\ *adj*
the·og·o·ny \thē-ˈäg-ə-nē\ *n, pl* **-nies** [Gk *theogonia,* fr. *the-* + *-gonia* -gony] (1612) : an account of the origin and descent of the gods — **theo·gon·ic** \ˌthē-ə-ˈgän-ik\ *adj*
theo·lo·gian \ˌthē-ə-ˈlō-jən\ *n* (15c) : a specialist in theology
theo·log·i·cal \-ˈläj-i-kəl\ *also* **theo·log·ic** \-ik\ *adj* (15c) **1** : of or relating to theology **2** : preparing for a religious vocation ⟨a ~ student⟩ — **theo·log·i·cal·ly** \-i-k(ə-)lē\ *adv*
theological virtue *n* (1526) : one of the three spiritual graces faith, hope, and charity drawing the soul to God according to scholastic theology
the·ol·o·gize \thē-ˈäl-ə-ˌjīz\ *vb* **-gized; -giz·ing** *vi* (1649) : to theorize theologically ~ *vt* : to make theological : give a religious significance to — **the·ol·o·giz·er** *n*

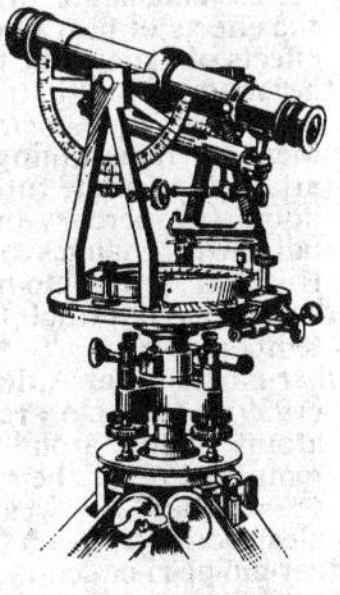
theodolite

theo·logue *or* **theo·log** \ˈthē-ə-ˌlȯg, -ˌläg\ *n* [L *theologus* theologian, fr. Gk *theologos,* fr. *the-* + *legein* to speak — more at LEGEND] (1663) : a theological student or specialist
the·ol·o·gy \thē-ˈäl-ə-jē\ *n, pl* **-gies** [ME *theologie,* fr. L *theologia,* fr. Gk, fr. *the-* + *-logia* -logy] (14c) **1** : the study of religious faith, practice, and experience; *esp* : the study of God and his relation to the world **2** **a** : a theological theory or system ⟨Thomist ~⟩ ⟨a ~ of atonement⟩ **b** : a distinctive body of theological opinion ⟨Catholic ~⟩ **3** : a usu. 4-year course of specialized religious training in a Roman Catholic major seminary
the·on·o·mous \thē-ˈän-ə-məs\ *adj* [*the-* + *-nomous* (as in *autonomous*)] (1947) : governed by God : subject to God's authority
the·on·o·my \-mē\ *n* [G *theonomie,* fr. *theo-* the- (fr. L) + *-nomie* -nomy] (1890) : the state of being theonomous : government by God
the·oph·a·ny \thē-ˈäf-ə-nē\ *n, pl* **-nies** [ML *theophania,* fr. LGk *theophaneia,* fr. Gk *the-* + *-phaneia* (as in *epiphaneia* appearance) — more at EPIPHANY] (1633) : a visible manifestation of a deity — **theo·phan·ic** \ˌthē-ə-ˈfan-ik\ *adj*
the·oph·yl·line \thē-ˈäf-ə-lən\ *n* [ISV *theo-* (fr. NL *thea* tea) + *phyll-* + *-ine*] (ca. 1894) : a feebly basic bitter crystalline compound $C_7H_8N_4O_2$ from tea leaves that is isomeric with theobromine and is used in medicine esp. as a muscle relaxant and vasodilator
the·or·bo \thē-ˈȯr-(ˌ)bō\ *n pl* **-bos** [modif. of It *tiorba, teorba*] (1605) : a stringed instrument of the 17th century resembling a large lute but having an extra set of long bass strings
the·o·rem \ˈthē-ə-rəm, ˈthi(-ə)r-əm\ *n* [LL *theorema,* fr. Gk *theōrēma,* fr. *theōrein* to look at, fr. *theōros* spectator, fr. *thea* act of seeing — more at THEATER] (1551) **1** : a formula, proposition, or statement in mathematics or logic deduced or to be deduced from other formulas or propositions **2** : an idea accepted or proposed as a demonstrable truth often as a part of a general theory : PROPOSITION ⟨the ~ that the best defense is offense⟩ **3** : STENCIL **4** : a painting produced esp. on velvet by the use of stencils for each color — **the·o·rem·at·ic** \ˌthē-ə-rə-ˈmat-ik, ˌthi(-ə)r-ə-\ *adj*
the·o·ret·i·cal \ˌthē-ə-ˈret-i-kəl, ˌthi(-ə)r-ˈet-\ *also* **the·o·ret·ic** \-ik\ *adj* [LL *theoreticus,* fr. Gk *theōrētikos,* fr. *theōrein* to look at] (1652) **1** **a** : relating to or having the character of theory : ABSTRACT **b** : confined to theory or speculation : SPECULATIVE ⟨~ mechanics⟩ **2** : given to or skilled in theorizing ⟨a brilliant ~ physicist⟩ **3** : existing only in theory : HYPOTHETICAL ⟨gave as an example a ~ situation⟩
the·o·ret·i·cal·ly \-i-k(ə-)lē\ *adv* (1701) **1** : in a theoretical way **2** : according to an ideal or assumed set of facts or principles : in theory
the·o·re·ti·cian \ˌthē-ə-rə-ˈtish-ən, -re-; ˌthi(-ə)r-ə-\ *n* (1886) : THEORIST
the·o·rist \ˈthē-ə-rəst, ˈthi(-ə)r-əst\ *n* (1646) : a person that theorizes
the·o·rize \ˈthē-ə-ˌrīz\ *vb* **-rized; -riz·ing** *vi* (1638) : to form a theory : SPECULATE ~ *vt* **1** : to form a theory about **2** : to propose as a theory — **the·o·ri·za·tion** \ˌthē-ə-rə-ˈzā-shən, ˌthi(-ə)r-ə-\ *n* — **the·o·riz·er** *n*
the·o·ry \ˈthē-ə-rē, ˈthi(-ə)r-ē\ *n, pl* **-ries** [LL *theoria,* fr. Gk *theōria,* fr. *theōrein*] (1597) **1** : the analysis of a set of facts in their relation to one another **2** : abstract thought : SPECULATION **3** : the general or abstract principles of a body of fact, a science, or an art ⟨music ~⟩ **4** **a** : a belief, policy, or procedure proposed or followed as the basis of action ⟨her method is based on the ~ that all children want to learn⟩ **b** : an ideal or hypothetical set of facts, principles, or circumstances — often used in the phrase *in theory* ⟨in ~, we have always advocated freedom for all⟩ **5** : a plausible or scientifically acceptable general principle or body of principles offered to explain phenomena ⟨wave ~ of light⟩ **6** **a** : a hypothesis assumed for the sake of argument or investigation **b** : an unproved assumption : CONJECTURE **c** : a body of theorems presenting a concise systematic view of a subject ⟨~ of equations⟩ ***syn*** see HYPOTHESIS
theory of games (1951) : GAME THEORY
theory of numbers (1811) : NUMBER THEORY
the·os·o·phist \thē-ˈäs-ə-fəst\ *n* (1656) **1** : an adherent of theosophy **2** *cap* : a member of a theosophical society
the·os·o·phy \-fē\ *n* [ML *theosophia,* fr. LGk, fr. Gk *the-* + *sophia* wisdom — more at -SOPHY] (1650) **1** : teaching about God and the world based on mystical insight **2** *often cap* : the teachings of a modern movement originating in the U.S. in 1875 and following chiefly Buddhist and Brahmanic theories esp. of pantheistic evolution and reincarnation — **theo·soph·i·cal** \ˌthē-ə-ˈsäf-i-kəl\ *adj* — **theo·soph·i·cal·ly** \-k(ə-)lē\ *adv*
ther·a·peu·sis \ˌther-ə-ˈpyü-səs\ *n* [NL, fr. Gk, treatment, fr. *therapeuein*] (ca. 1857) : THERAPEUTICS
ther·a·peu·tic \-ˈpyüt-ik\ *adj* [Gk *therapeutikos,* fr. *therapeuein* to attend, treat, fr. *theraps* attendant] (1646) **1** : of or relating to the treatment of disease or disorders by remedial agents or methods ⟨a ~ rather than a diagnostic specialty⟩ **2** : CURATIVE, MEDICINAL ⟨~ diets⟩ — **ther·a·peu·ti·cal·ly** \-i-k(ə-)lē\ *adv*
therapeutic index *n* (1926) : a measure of the relative desirability of a drug for the attaining of a particular medical end that is usu. expressed as the ratio of the largest dose producing no toxic symptoms to the smallest dose routinely producing cures
ther·a·peu·tics \ˌther-ə-ˈpyüt-iks\ *n pl but sing or pl in constr* (1671) : a branch of medical science dealing with the application of remedies to diseases
ther·a·peu·tist \-ˈpyüt-əst\ *n* (1816) : one skilled in therapeutics
ther·a·pist \ˈther-ə-pəst\ *n* (1886) : one specializing in therapy; *esp* : a person trained in methods of treatment and rehabilitation other than the use of drugs or surgery ⟨a speech ~⟩
the·rap·sid \thə-ˈrap-səd\ *n* [NL *Therapsida,* perh. fr. Gk *theraps* attendant] (1912) : any of an order (Therapsida) of Permian and Triassic reptiles that are considered ancestors of the mammals — **therapsid** *adj*
ther·a·py \ˈther-ə-pē\ *n, pl* **-pies** [NL *therapia,* fr. Gk *therapeia,* fr. *therapeuein*] (ca. 1846) : therapeutic treatment: as **a** : remedial treatment of bodily disorder **b** : PSYCHOTHERAPY **c** : an agency (as treatment) designed or serving to bring about social adjustment
Ther·a·va·da \ˌther-ə-ˈväd-ə\ *n* [Pali *theravāda,* lit., doctrine of the elders] (1882) : a conservative branch of Buddhism comprising sects chiefly in Sri Lanka, Myanmar, Thailand, Laos, and Cambodia and adhering to the original Pali scriptures alone and to the nontheistic ideal of nirvana for a limited select number — compare MAHAYANA
[1]**there** \ˈtha(ə)r, ˈthe(ə)r\ *adv* [ME, fr. OE *thǣr;* akin to OHG *dār* there, OE *thæt* that] (bef. 12c) **1** : in or at that place ⟨stand over ~⟩ — often used interjectionally **2** : to or into that place : THITHER ⟨went ~ after church⟩ **3** : at that point or stage ⟨stop right ~ before you say something you'll regret⟩ **4** : in that matter, respect, or relation ⟨~ is where I disagree with you⟩ **5** — used interjectionally to express satisfaction, approval, encouragement or sympathy, or defiance ⟨~, it's finished⟩
[2]**there** \(ˌ)tha(ə)r, (ˌ)the(ə)r, *1 is also* thər\ *pron* (bef. 12c) **1** — used as a function word to introduce a sentence or clause ⟨~ shall come a time⟩ **2** — used as an indefinite substitute for a name ⟨hi ~⟩
[3]**there** *like* \ *n* (1588) **1** : that place or position ⟨there is no here and no ~ . . . in pure space —James Ward⟩ **2** : that point ⟨you take it from ~⟩
[4]**there** *like* \ *adj* (1590) **1** — used for emphasis esp. after a demonstrative pronoun or a noun modified by a demonstrative adjective ⟨those men ~ can tell you⟩ **2** *substand* — used for emphasis after a demonstrative adjective but before the noun modified ⟨I bet I cussed that ~ blamed mule five hundred times —Elizabeth M. Roberts⟩
there·abouts *or* **there·about** \ˌthar-ə-ˈbau̇t(s), ˈthar-ə-ˌ, ˌther-ə-ˈbau̇t(s) ˈther-ə-ˌ\ *adv* (15c) **1** : near that place or time **2** : near that number, degree, or quantity ⟨a boy of 18 or ~⟩
there·af·ter \tha-ˈraf-tər, the-\ *adv* (bef. 12c) **1** : after that **2** *archaic* : according to that : ACCORDINGLY
there·at \-ˈrat\ *adv* (bef. 12c) **1** : at that place **2** : at that occurrence
there·by \tha(ə)r-ˈbī, the(ə)r-, ˈtha(ə)r-ˌ, ˈthe(ə)r-ˌ\ *adv* (bef. 12c) **1** : by that : by that means ⟨~ lost his chance to win⟩ **2** : connected with or with reference to that ⟨~ hangs a tale —Shak.⟩
there·for \tha(ə)r-ˈfō(ə)r, the(ə)r-\ *adv* (12c) : for or in return for that ⟨ordered a change and gave his reasons ~⟩
there·fore \ˈtha(ə)r-ˌfō(ə)r, ˈthe(ə)r-, -ˌfȯ(ə)r\ *adv* (15c) **1** **a** : for that reason : CONSEQUENTLY **b** : because of that **c** : on that ground **2** : to that end
there·from \tha(ə)r-ˈfrəm, the(ə)r-, -ˈfräm\ *adv* (13c) : from that or it
there·in \tha-ˈrin, the-\ *adv* (bef. 12c) **1** : in or into that place, time, or thing **2** : in that particular or respect ⟨~ lies the problem⟩
there·in·af·ter \ˌthar-in-ˈaf-tər, ˌther-\ *adv* (1818) : in the following part of that matter (as writing, document, or speech)
there·in·to \tha-ˈrin-(ˌ)tü, the-\ *adv, archaic* (14c) : into that or it

there·min \ˈther-ə-mən\ *n* [Leo *Theremin b*1896 Russ. engineer & inventor] (1929) **:** a purely melodic electronic musical instrument typically played by moving a hand between two projecting electrodes
there·of \t͟hа-ˈrəv, -ˈräv, t͟he-\ *adv* (bef. 12c) **1 :** of that or it **2 :** from that cause or particular **:** THEREFROM
there·on \-ˈrȯn, -ˈrän\ *adv* (bef. 12c) **1 :** on that ⟨a text with a commentary ~⟩ **2** *archaic* **:** THEREUPON
there·to \t͟ha(ə)r-ˈtü, t͟he(ə)r-\ *adv* (bef. 12c) **:** to that ⟨a text and the notes ~⟩
there·to·fore \ˈt͟hart-ə-ˌfō(ə)r, ˈthert-, -ˌfȯ(ə)r; ˌt͟hart-ə-ˈ, ˌt͟hert-\ *adv* (14c) **:** up to that time ⟨a ~ unknown author⟩
there·un·der \t͟ha-ˈrən-dər, t͟he-\ *adv* (bef. 12c) **:** under that
there·un·to \-ˈrən-(ˌ)tü; ˌt͟har-ən-ˈtü, ˌt͟her-\ *adv, archaic* (14c) **:** THERETO
there·up·on \ˈt͟har-ə-ˌpȯn, ˈt͟her-, -ˌpän; ˌt͟har-ə-ˈ, ˌt͟her-\ *adv* (12c) **1 :** on that matter **2 :** THEREFORE **3 :** immediately after that
there·with \t͟ha(ə)r-ˈwit͟h, t͟he(ə)r-, -ˈwith\ *adv* (bef. 12c) **1 :** with that **2** *archaic* **:** THEREUPON, FORTHWITH
there·with·al \ˈt͟ha(ə)r-wit͟h-ˌȯl, ˈt͟he(ə)r-, -with-\ *adv* (14c) **1** *archaic* **:** BESIDES **2 :** THEREWITH
the·ri·ac \ˈthir-ē-ˌak\ *n* [NL *theriaca*] (15c) **1 :** THERIACA **2 :** CURE-ALL
the·ri·a·ca \thi-ˈrī-ə-kə\ *n* [NL, fr. L, antidote against poison — more at TREACLE] (1562) **:** a mixture of many drugs and honey formerly held to be an antidote to poison — **the·ri·a·cal** \-kəl\ *adj*
the·rio·mor·phic \ˌthir-ē-ō-ˈmȯr-fik\ *adj* [Gk *thēriomorphos,* fr. *thērion* beast + *morphē* form — more at TREACLE] (1882) **:** having an animal form ⟨~ gods⟩
therm \ˈthərm\ *n* [Gk *thermē* heat; akin to Gk *thermos* hot — more at WARM] (ca. 1888) **:** any of several units of quantity of heat: as **a :** CALORIE 1b **b :** CALORIE 1a **c :** 1000 kilogram calories **d :** 100,000 British thermal units
therm- *or* **thermo-** *comb form* [Gk, fr. *thermē*] **1 :** heat ⟨*thermion*⟩ ⟨*thermostat*⟩ **2 :** thermoelectric ⟨*thermopile*⟩
-therm \ˌthərm\ *n comb form* [Gk *thermē* heat] **:** animal having a (specified) body temperature ⟨ecto*therm*⟩
[1]**ther·mal** \ˈthər-məl\ *adj* [L *thermae* public baths, fr. Gk *thermai,* pl. of *thermē* heat] (1756) **:** of, relating to, or marked by the presence of hot springs ⟨~ waters⟩
[2]**thermal** *adj* [Gk *thermē*] (1837) **1 a :** of, relating to, or caused by heat ⟨~ stress⟩ ⟨~ insulation⟩ **b :** being or involving a state of matter dependent upon temperature ⟨~ conductivity⟩ ⟨~ agitation of molecular structure⟩ **2 :** designed (as with insulating air spaces) to prevent the dissipation of body heat ⟨~ underwear⟩ — **ther·mal·ly** \-mə-lē\ *adv*
[3]**thermal** *n* (ca. 1936) **:** a rising body of warm air
thermal barrier *n* (1951) **:** a limit to unlimited increase in aircraft or rocket speeds imposed by aerodynamic heating
ther·mal·ize \ˈthər-mə-ˌlīz\ *vt* **-ized; -iz·ing** (1948) **:** to change the effective speed of (a particle) to a thermal value ⟨~ a neutron⟩ — **ther·mal·iza·tion** \ˌthər-mə-lə-ˈzā-shən\ *n*
thermal pollution *n* (1966) **:** the discharge of heated liquid (as wastewater from a factory) into natural waters at a temperature harmful to the environment
thermal spring *n* (1800) **:** a spring whose water issues at a temperature higher than the mean temperature of the locality where the spring is situated
ther·mic \ˈthər-mik\ *adj* (1846) **:** [2]THERMAL 1 ⟨~ energy⟩ — **ther·mi·cal·ly** \-mi-k(ə-)lē\ *adv*
therm·ion \ˈthər-ˌmī-ən, -ˌmī-ˌän\ *n* [ISV *therm-* + *ion*] (1912) **:** an electrically charged particle emitted by an incandescent substance — **therm·ion·ic** \ˌthər-(ˌ)mī-ˈän-ik\ *adj*
thermionic current *n* (1915) **:** an electric current due to the directed movements of thermions (as in the electric discharge through a vacuum tube with the cathode incandescent)
therm·ion·ics \ˌthər-(ˌ)mī-ˈän-iks\ *n pl but sing in constr* (ca. 1927) **:** physics dealing with thermionic phenomena
thermionic tube *n* (1926) **:** an electron tube in which electron emission is produced by the heating of an electrode
therm·is·tor \ˈthər-ˌmis-tər\ *n* [*therm*al res*istor*] (ca. 1940) **:** an electrical resistor making use of a semiconductor whose resistance varies sharply in a known manner with the temperature
Ther·mit \ˈthər-mət, -ˌmīt\ *trademark* —used for thermite
ther·mite \ˈthər-ˌmīt\ *n* [*therm-* + *-ite*] (1900) **:** a mixture of aluminum powder and a metal oxide (as iron oxide) that when ignited evolves a great deal of heat and is used in welding and in incendiary bombs
ther·mo·chem·is·try \ˌthər-mō-ˈkem-ə-strē\ *n* (1844) **:** a branch of chemistry that deals with the interrelation of heat with chemical reaction or physical change of state — **ther·mo·chem·i·cal** \-ˈkem-i-kəl\ *adj* — **ther·mo·chem·ist** \-ˈkem-əst\ *n*
ther·mo·cline \ˈthər-mə-ˌklīn\ *n* (1898) **:** a layer in a thermally stratified body of water that separates an upper warmer lighter oxygen-rich zone from a lower colder heavier oxygen-poor zone; *specif* **:** a stratum in which temperature declines at least one degree centigrade with each meter increase in depth
ther·mo·co·ag·u·la·tion \ˌthər-mō-kō-ˌag-yə-ˈlā-shən\ *n* (ca. 1923) **:** surgical coagulation of tissue by the application of heat
ther·mo·cou·ple \ˈthər-mə-ˌkəp-əl\ *n* (1890) **:** a device for measuring temperature in which a pair of wires of dissimilar metals (as copper and iron) are joined and the free ends of the wires are connected to an instrument (as a voltmeter) that measures the difference in potential created at the junction of the two metals
ther·mo·du·ric \ˌthər-mō-ˈd(y)u̇(ə)r-ik\ *adj* [*therm-* + L *durare* to last — more at DURING] (ca. 1932) **:** able to survive high temperatures; *specif* **:** able to survive pasteurization — used of microorganisms
ther·mo·dy·nam·ic \ˌthər-mō-dī-ˈnam-ik, -də-\ *also* **ther·mo·dy·nam·i·cal** \-i-kəl\ *adj* (1849) **1 :** of or relating to thermodynamics **2 :** being or relating to a system of atoms, molecules, colloidal particles, or larger bodies considered as an isolated group in the study of thermodynamic processes — **ther·mo·dy·nam·i·cal·ly** \-i-k(ə-)lē\ *adv*
ther·mo·dy·nam·ics \-iks\ *n pl but sing or pl in constr* (1854) **1 :** physics that deals with the mechanical action or relations of heat **2 :** thermodynamic processes and phenomena — **ther·mo·dy·nam·i·cist** \-ˈnam-ə-səst\ *n*
ther·mo·elec·tric \ˌthər-mō-i-ˈlek-trik\ *adj* (1823) **:** of, relating to, or dependent on phenomena that involve relations between the temperature and the electrical condition in a metal or in contacting metals
ther·mo·elec·tric·i·ty \ˌthər-mō-i-ˌlek-ˈtris-ət-ē, -ˈtris-tē\ *n* (1823) **:** electricity produced by the direct action of heat (as by the unequal heating of a circuit composed of two dissimilar metals)
ther·mo·elec·tron \-i-ˈlek-ˌträn\ *n* (1926) **:** an electron released in thermionic emission
ther·mo·el·e·ment \-ˈel-ə-mənt\ *n* [*thermo*couple + *element*] (1920) **:** a device for measuring small currents consisting of a wire heating element and a thermocouple in electrical contact with it
ther·mo·form \ˈthər-mə-ˌfȯrm\ *vt* (1956) **:** to give a final shape to (as a plastic) with the aid of heat and usu. pressure — **ther·mo·form·able** \-ˌfȯr-mə-bəl\ *adj*
ther·mo·gram \-ˌgram\ *n* (1883) **1 :** the record made by a thermograph **2 :** a photographic record made by thermography
ther·mo·graph \-ˌgraf\ *n* [ISV] (1840) **1 :** the apparatus used in thermography **2 :** THERMOGRAM **3 :** a self-recording thermometer
ther·mog·ra·phy \(ˌ)thər-ˈmäg-rə-fē\ *n* (1840) **1 :** a process of writing or printing involving the use of heat; *esp* **:** a raised-printing process in which matter printed by letterpress is dusted with powder and heated to make the lettering rise **2 :** a technique for detecting and measuring variations in the heat emitted by various regions of the body and transforming them into visible signals that can be recorded photographically (as for diagnosing abnormal or diseased underlying conditions); *also* **:** a similar technique used elsewhere (as on buildings) — **ther·mo·graph·ic** \ˌthər-mə-ˈgraf-ik\ *adj* — **ther·mo·graph·i·cal·ly** \-i-k(ə-)lē\ *adv*
ther·mo·ha·line \ˌthər-mō-ˈhā-ˌlīn, -ˈhal-ˌīn\ *adj* [*therm-* + Gk *hal-, hals* salt — more at SALT] (ca. 1946) **:** involving or dependent upon the conjoint effect of temperature and salinity ⟨~ circulation in the eastern Pacific⟩
ther·mo·junc·tion \ˌthər-mō-ˈjəŋ(k)-shən\ *n* (1889) **:** a junction of two dissimilar conductors used to produce a thermoelectric current
ther·mo·la·bile \-ˈlā-ˌbīl, -bəl\ *adj* [ISV] (1904) **:** unstable when heated; *specif* **:** subject to loss of characteristic properties on being heated to or above 55°C ⟨many immune bodies, enzymes, and vitamins are ~⟩ — **ther·mo·la·bil·i·ty** \-lā-ˈbil-ət-ē\ *n*
ther·mo·lu·mi·nes·cence \-ˌlü-mə-ˈnes-ᵊn(t)s\ *n* [ISV] (ca. 1897) **:** phosphorescence developed in a previously excited substance upon gentle heating — **ther·mo·lu·mi·nes·cent** \-ᵊnt\ *adj*
ther·mo·mag·net·ic \ˌthər-mō-mag-ˈnet-ik\ *adj* (1823) **:** of or relating to the effects of heat upon the magnetic properties of substances or to the effects of a magnetic field upon thermal conduction
ther·mom·e·ter \thə(r)-ˈmäm-ət-ər\ *n* [F *thermomètre,* fr. Gk *thermē* heat + F *-o-* + *-mètre* -meter — more at THERM] (ca. 1633) **:** an instrument for determining temperature consisting typically of a glass bulb attached to a fine tube of glass with a numbered scale and containing a liquid (as mercury or colored alcohol) that is sealed in and rises and falls with changes of temperature — **ther·mo·met·ric** \ˌthər-mə-ˈme-trik\ *adj* — **ther·mo·met·ri·cal·ly** \-tri-k(ə-)lē\ *adv*
ther·mom·e·try \thə(r)-ˈmäm-ə-trē\ *n* [ISV] (1858) **:** the measurement of temperature
ther·mo·nu·cle·ar \ˌthər-mō-ˈn(y)ü-klē-ər, ÷-ˈn(y)ü-kyə-lər\ *adj* [ISV] (1939) **1 :** of or relating to the transformations in the nucleus of atoms of low atomic weight (as hydrogen) that require a very high temperature for their inception (as in the hydrogen bomb or in the sun) ⟨~ reaction⟩ ⟨~ weapon⟩ **2 :** of, utilizing, or relating to a thermonuclear bomb ⟨~ war⟩ ⟨~ attack⟩
ther·mo·pe·ri·od·ic·i·ty \-ˌpir-ē-ə-ˈdis-ət-ē\ *n* (1944) **:** THERMOPERIODISM
ther·mo·pe·ri·od·ism \ˌthər-mō-ˈpir-ē-ə-ˌdiz-əm\ *n* (ca. 1937) **:** the sum of the responses of an organism and esp. a plant to appropriately fluctuating temperatures
ther·mo·phil·ic \ˌthər-mə-ˈfil-ik\ *also* **ther·moph·i·lous** \(ˌ)thər-ˈmäf-ə-ləs\ *or* **ther·mo·phile** \ˈthər-mə-ˌfīl\ *adj* (ca. 1896) **:** of, relating to, or being an organism growing at a high temperature ⟨~ fermentation⟩ ⟨~ bacteria⟩ — **thermophile** *n*
ther·mo·pile \ˈthər-mə-ˌpīl\ *n* [[3]*pile*] (1849) **:** an apparatus that consists of a number of thermocouples combined so as to multiply the effect and is used for generating electric currents or for determining intensities of radiation
ther·mo·plas·tic \ˌthər-mə-ˈplas-tik\ *adj* (1883) **:** capable of softening or fusing when heated and of hardening again when cooled ⟨~ synthetic resins⟩ — compare THERMOSETTING — **thermoplastic** *n* — **ther·mo·plas·tic·i·ty** \-ˌplas-ˈtis-ət-ē\ *n*
ther·mo·re·cep·tor \ˌthər-mō-ri-ˈsep-tər\ *n* (1946) **:** a sensory end organ that is stimulated by heat or cold
ther·mo·reg·u·la·tion \-ˌreg-yə-ˈlā-shən\ *n* [ISV] (1927) **:** the maintenance or regulation of temperature; *specif* **:** the maintenance of a particular temperature of the living body — **ther·mo·reg·u·late** \-ˈreg-yə-ˌlāt\ *vb*
ther·mo·reg·u·la·tor \-ˈreg-yə-ˌlāt-ər\ *n* [ISV] (1875) **:** a device (as a thermostat) for the regulation of temperature
ther·mo·reg·u·la·to·ry \-ˈreg-yə-lə-ˌtōr-ē, -ˌtȯr-\ *adj* (1941) **:** tending to maintain a body at a particular temperature whatever its environmental temperature ⟨~ adjustments⟩
ther·mo·rem·a·nent \-ˈrem-ə-nənt\ *adj* (1953) **:** being or relating to magnetic remanence (as in a rock cooled from a molten state or in a baked clay object containing magnetic minerals) that indicates the strength and direction of the earth's magnetic field at a former time — **ther·mo·rem·a·nence** \-nən(t)s\ *n*
ther·mos \ˈthər-məs\ *n* [fr. *Thermos,* a trademark] (1907) **:** VACUUM BOTTLE
ther·mo·scope \ˈthər-mə-ˌskōp\ *n* [NL *thermoscopium,* fr. *therm-* + *-scopium* -scope] (1860) **:** an instrument for indicating changes of temperature by accompanying changes in volume (as of a gas)
ther·mo·set \ˈthər-mō-ˌset\ *n* (1936) **:** a thermosetting resin or plastic
ther·mo·set·ting \-ˌset-iŋ\ *adj* (1936) **:** capable of becoming permanently rigid when heated or cured ⟨a ~ resin⟩ — compare THERMOPLASTIC
ther·mo·sphere \ˈthər-mə-ˌsfi(ə)r\ *n* [ISV] (ca. 1951) **:** the part of the earth's atmosphere that begins at about 50 miles above the earth's surface, extends to outer space, and is characterized by steadily increasing temperature with height — **ther·mo·spher·ic** \ˌthər-mə-ˈsfi(ə)r-ik, -ˈsfe(ə)r-\ *adj*
ther·mo·sta·ble \ˌthər-mō-ˈstā-bəl\ *adj* (1904) **:** stable when heated; *specif* **:** retaining characteristic properties on being moderately heated ⟨a ~ bacterial proteinase⟩ — **ther·mo·sta·bil·i·ty** \-stə-ˈbil-ət-ē\ *n*

1ther·mo·stat \ˈthər-mə-ˌstat\ *n* (ca. 1831) **:** an automatic device for regulating temperature (as by controlling the supply of gas or electricity to a heating apparatus); *also* **:** a similar device for actuating fire alarms or for controlling automatic sprinklers — **ther·mo·stat·ic** \ˌthər-mə-ˈstat-ik\ *adj* — **ther·mo·stat·i·cal·ly** \-i-k(ə-)lē\ *adv*

2thermostat *vt* **-stat·ed** \-ˌstat-əd\ *also* **-stat·ted; -stat·ing** *also* **-stat·ting** (1924) **:** to provide with or control the temperature of by a thermostat

ther·mo·tac·tic \ˌthər-mə-ˈtak-tik\ *adj* (1896) **:** of, relating to, or exhibiting thermotaxis

ther·mo·tax·is \-ˈtak-səs\ *n* [NL] (1891) **1 :** the regulation of body temperature **2 :** a taxis in which a temperature gradient constitutes the directive factor

ther·mo·trop·ic \-ˈträp-ik\ *adj* [ISV] (1885) **:** of, relating to, or exhibiting thermotropism

ther·mot·ro·pism \(ˌ)thər-ˈmä-trə-ˌpiz-əm\ *n* [ISV] (ca. 1890) **:** a tropism in which a temperature gradient determines the orientation

-ther·my \ˌthər-mē\ *n comb form* [NL *-thermia,* fr. Gk *thermē* heat — more at THERM] **1 :** state of heat ⟨homoio*thermy*⟩ **2 :** generation of heat ⟨dia*thermy*⟩

Ther·si·tes \(ˌ)thər-ˈsīt-(ˌ)ēz\ *n* [L, fr. Gk *Thersitēs*] **:** a Greek warrior at Troy known as a carping critic and slain by Achilles for mocking him

the·sau·rus \thi-ˈsȯr-əs\ *n, pl* **-sau·ri** \-ˈsȯ(ə)r-ˌī, -ˌē\ *or* **-sau·rus·es** \-ˈsȯr-ə-səz\ [NL, fr. L, treasure, collection, fr. Gk *thēsauros*] (ca. 1823) **1 :** TREASURY, STOREHOUSE **2 a :** a book of words or of information about a particular field or set of concepts; *esp* **:** a book of words and their synonyms **b :** a list of subject headings or descriptors usu. with a cross-reference system for use in the organization of a collection of documents for reference and retrieval — **the·sau·ral** \-ˈsȯr-əl\ *adj*

these *pl of* THIS

The·seus \ˈthē-ˌsüs, -sē-əs\ *n* [L, fr. Gk *Thēseus*] **:** a king of Athens in Greek mythology who kills Procrustes and the Minotaur before defeating the Amazons and marrying their queen

the·sis \ˈthē-səs, *Brit esp for 1* ˈthes-is\ *n, pl* **the·ses** \ˈthē-ˌsēz\ [in sense 1, ME, fr. LL & Gk; LL, lowering of the voice, fr. Gk, downbeat, more important part of a foot, lit., act of laying down; in other senses, L, fr. Gk, lit., act of laying down, fr. *tithenai* to put, lay down — more at DO] (14c) **1 a (1) :** the unstressed part of a poetic foot esp. in accentual verse **(2) :** the longer part of a poetic foot esp. in quantitative verse **b :** the accented part of a musical measure **:** DOWNBEAT — compare ARSIS **2 a :** a position or proposition that a person (as a candidate for scholastic honors) advances and offers to maintain by argument **b :** a proposition to be proved or one advanced without proof **:** HYPOTHESIS **3 :** the first and least adequate stage of dialectic — compare SYNTHESIS **4 :** a dissertation embodying results of original research and esp. substantiating a specific view; *esp* **:** one written by a candidate for an academic degree

1thes·pi·an \ˈthes-pē-ən\ *adj* (1675) **1** *cap* **:** of or relating to Thespis **2** *often cap* [fr. the tradition that Thespis was the originator of the actor's role] **:** relating to the drama **:** DRAMATIC

2thespian *n* (1827) **:** ACTOR

Thes·sa·lo·nians \ˌthes-ə-ˈlō-nyənz, -nē-ənz\ *n pl but sing in constr* [*Thessalonian* (inhabitant of ancient Thessalonica), irreg. fr. *Thessalonica*] **:** either of two letters written by St. Paul to the Christians of Thessalonica and included as books in the New Testament — see BIBLE table

the·ta \ˈthāt-ə, *chiefly Brit* ˈthēt-ə\ *n* [Gk *thēta,* of Sem origin; akin to Heb *ṭēth* teth] (1603) **:** the 8th letter of the Greek alphabet — see ALPHABET table

theta rhythm *n* (1947) **:** a relatively high amplitude brain wave pattern between approximately 4 and 9 hertz that is characteristic esp. of the hippocampus but occurs in many regions of the brain including the cortex — called also *theta, theta wave*

thet·ic \ˈthet-ik, ˈthēt-\ *adj* [Gk *thetikos* of a proposition, fr. *tithenai* to lay down — more at DO] (1815) **:** constituting or beginning with a poetic thesis ⟨a ~ syllable⟩ — **thet·i·cal·ly** \-i-k(ə-)lē\ *adv*

The·tis \ˈthēt-əs\ *n* [L, fr. Gk] **:** a sea goddess who marries Peleus and becomes the mother of Achilles

the·ur·gist \ˈthē-(ˌ)ər-jəst\ *n* (1652) **:** WONDER-WORKER, MAGICIAN

the·ur·gy \ˈthē-(ˌ)ər-jē\ *n* [LL *theurgia,* fr. LGk *theourgia,* fr. *theourgos* miracle worker, fr. Gk *the-* + *ergon* work — more at WORK] (1569) **:** the art or technique of compelling or persuading a god or beneficent or supernatural power to do or refrain from doing something — **the·ur·gic** \thē-ˈər-jik\ *or* **the·ur·gi·cal** \-ji-kəl\ *adj*

thew \ˈth(y)ü\ *n* [ME, personal quality, virtue, fr. OE *thēaw;* akin to OHG *kathau* discipline] (15c) **1 a :** muscular power or development **b :** STRENGTH, VITALITY **2 :** MUSCLE, SINEW — usu. used in pl.

they \(ˈ)thā\ *pron, pl in constr* [ME, fr. ON *their,* masc. pl. demonstrative & personal pron.; akin to OE *thæt* that] (13c) **1 a :** those ones — used as third person pronoun serving as the plural of *he, she,* or *it* or referring to a group of two or more individuals not all of the same sex ⟨~ dance well⟩ **b :** 1HE 2 — often used with an indefinite third person singular antecedent ⟨everyone knew where ~ stood —E. L. Doctorow⟩ ⟨nobody has to go to school if ~ don't want to —*N.Y. Times*⟩ **2 :** PEOPLE 2 — used in a generic sense ⟨as lazy as ~ come⟩

usage *They* used as an indefinite subject (sense 2) is sometimes objected to on the grounds that it does not have an antecedent. Not every pronoun requires an antecedent, however. The indefinite *they* is used in all varieties of contexts and is standard.

they'd \(ˌ)thād\ **:** they had **:** they would

they'll \(ˌ)thā(ə)l, thel\ **:** they will **:** they shall

they're \thər, (ˌ)the(ə)r\ **:** they are

they've \(ˌ)thāv\ **:** they have

thi- *or* **thio-** *comb form* [ISV, fr. Gk *thei-, theio-* sulfur, fr. *theion*] **:** containing sulfur ⟨*thi*amine⟩ ⟨*thio*cyanate⟩

thia·ben·da·zole \ˌthī-ə-ˈben-də-ˌzōl\ *n* [*thiazole* + *benz-* + imide + *azole*] (1961) **:** a drug $C_{10}H_7N_3S$ used in the control of parasitic roundworms and in the treatment of fungus infections and as an agricultural fungicide

thi·ami·nase \thī-ˈam-ə-ˌnās, ˈthī-ə-mə-, -ˌnāz\ *n* [ISV] (1938) **:** an enzyme that promotes the breakdown of thiamine

thi·a·mine \ˈthī-ə-mən, -ˌmēn\ *also* **thi·a·min** \-mən\ *n* [*thiamine* alter. of *thiamin,* fr. *thi-* + *-amin* (as in *vitamin*)] (1937) **:** a vitamin $(C_{12}H_{17}N_4OS)Cl$ of the B complex that is essential to normal metabolism and nerve function and is widespread in plants and animals — called also *vitamin* B_1

thi·a·zide \ˈthī-ə-ˌzīd, -zəd\ *n* [*thia-* + di*azine* + diox*ide*] (1959) **:** any of several drugs used as oral diuretics esp. in the control of high blood pressure

thi·a·zine \ˈthī-ə-ˌzēn\ *n* [ISV] (1900) **:** any of various compounds that are characterized by a ring composed of four carbon atoms, one sulfur atom, and one nitrogen atom and include some important as dyes and others as tranquilizers

thi·a·zole \ˈthī-ə-ˌzōl\ *n* [ISV] (1888) **1 :** a colorless basic liquid C_3H_3NS consisting of a 5-membered ring and having an odor like pyridine **2 :** any of various thiazole derivatives including some used in medicine and others important as chemical accelerators

1thick \ˈthik\ *adj* [ME *thikke,* fr. OE *thicce;* akin to OHG *dicki* thick, OIr *tiug*] (bef. 12c) **1 a :** having or being of relatively great depth or extent from one surface to its opposite ⟨a ~ plank⟩ **b :** heavily built **:** THICKSET **2 a :** close-packed with units or individuals ⟨the air was ~ with snow⟩ **b :** occurring in large numbers **:** NUMEROUS **c :** viscous in consistency ⟨~ syrup⟩ **d :** SULTRY, STUFFY **e :** marked by haze, fog, or mist ⟨~ weather⟩ **f :** impenetrable to the eye **:** PROFOUND ⟨~ darkness⟩ **g :** extremely intense ⟨~ silence⟩ **3 :** measuring in thickness ⟨12 inches ~⟩ **4 a :** imperfectly articulated **:** INDISTINCT ⟨~ speech⟩ **b :** plainly apparent **:** DECIDED ⟨a ~ French accent⟩ **c :** producing inarticulate speech ⟨a ~ tongue⟩ **5 :** OBTUSE, STUPID **6 :** associated on close terms **:** INTIMATE ⟨was quite ~ with his pastor⟩ **7 :** exceeding bounds of propriety or fitness **:** EXCESSIVE ⟨called it a bit ~ to be fired without warning⟩ — **thick·ish** \-ish\ *adj* — **thick·ly** *adv*

2thick *adv* (bef. 12c) **:** in a thick manner **:** THICKLY

3thick *n* (13c) **1 :** the most crowded or active part ⟨in the ~ of the battle⟩ **2 :** the part of greatest thickness ⟨the ~ of the thumb⟩

thick and thin *n* (14c) **:** every difficulty and obstacle — used esp. in the phrase *through thick and thin*

thick·en \ˈthik-ən\ *vb* **thick·ened; thick·en·ing** \-(ə-)niŋ\ *vt* (15c) **1 a :** to make thick, dense, or viscous in consistency ⟨~ gravy with flour⟩ **b :** to make close or compact **2 :** to increase the depth or diameter of **3 :** to make inarticulate **:** BLUR ⟨alcohol ~*ed* his speech⟩ ~ *vi* **1 a :** to become dense ⟨the mist ~*ed*⟩ **b :** to become concentrated in numbers, mass, or frequency **2 :** to grow blurred or obscure **3 :** to grow broader or bulkier **4 :** to grow complicated or keen ⟨the plot ~*s*⟩ — **thick·en·er** \-(ə-)nər\ *n*

thick·en·ing *n* (ca. 1580) **1 :** the act of making or becoming thick **2 :** a thickened part or place **3 :** something used to thicken (as flour in a gravy)

thick·et \ˈthik-ət\ *n* [(assumed) ME *thikket,* fr. OE *thiccet,* fr. *thicce* thick] (bef. 12c) **1 :** a dense growth of shrubbery or small trees **:** COPPICE **2 :** something resembling a thicket in density or impenetrability **:** TANGLE — **thick·ety** \-ē\ *adj*

thick·et·ed \ˈthik-ət-əd\ *adj* (1624) **:** dotted or covered with thickets

thick·head \ˈthik-ˌhed\ *n* (ca. 1864) **:** a stupid person **:** BLOCKHEAD

thick·head·ed \-ˈhed-əd\ *adj* (1707) **1 :** having a thick head **2 :** sluggish and obtuse of mind

thick·ness \-nəs\ *n* (bef. 12c) **1 :** the quality or state of being thick **2 :** the smallest of three dimensions ⟨length, width, and ~⟩ **3 a :** viscous consistency ⟨boiled to the ~ of honey⟩ **b :** the condition of being smoky, foul, or foggy **4 :** the thick part of something **5 :** CONCENTRATION, DENSITY **6 :** STUPIDITY, DULLNESS **7 :** LAYER, PLY, SHEET ⟨a single ~ of canvas⟩

thick·set \-ˈset\ *adj* (14c) **1 :** closely placed; *also* **:** growing thickly ⟨a ~ wood⟩ **2 :** having a thick body **:** BURLY

thick–skinned \-ˈskind\ *adj* (1545) **1 :** having a thick skin **:** PACHYDERMATOUS **2 :** CALLOUS, INSENSITIVE

thick–wit·ted \-ˈwit-əd\ *adj* (1634) **:** dull or slow of mind **:** STUPID

thief \ˈthēf\ *n, pl* **thieves** \ˈthēvz\ [ME *theef,* fr. OE *thēof;* akin to OHG *diob* thief, Lith *tupėti* to crouch] (bef. 12c) **:** one that steals esp. stealthily or secretly; *also* **:** one who commits theft or larceny

thieve \ˈthēv\ *vb* **thieved; thiev·ing** (bef. 12c) **:** STEAL, ROB

thiev·ery \ˈthēv-(ə-)rē\ *n, pl* **-er·ies** (1568) **:** the act or practice or an instance of stealing **:** THEFT

thiev·ish \ˈthē-vish\ *adj* (15c) **1 :** of, relating to, or characteristic of a thief **2 :** given to stealing — **thiev·ish·ly** *adv* — **thiev·ish·ness** *n*

thigh \ˈthī\ *n* [ME, fr. OE *thēoh;* akin to OHG *dioh* thigh, L *tumēre* to swell — more at THUMB] (bef. 12c) **1 a :** the proximal segment of the vertebrate hind limb extending from the hip to the knee and supported by a single large bone **b :** the segment of the leg immediately distal to the thigh in a bird or in a quadruped in which the true thigh is obscured **c :** the femur of an insect **2 :** something resembling or covering a thigh — **thighed** \ˈthīd\ *adj*

thigh·bone \ˈthī-ˈbōn, -ˌbōn\ *n* (15c) **:** FEMUR 1

thig·mo·tax·is \ˌthig-mə-ˈtak-səs\ *n* [NL, fr. Gk *thigma* touch (fr. *thinganein* to touch) + NL *-taxis;* akin to L *fingere* to shape — more at DOUGH] (1897) **:** a taxis in which contact esp. with a solid body is the directive factor

thig·mot·ro·pism \thig-ˈmä-trə-ˌpiz-əm\ *n* [Gk *thigma* + ISV *-o-* + *-tropism*] (ca. 1900) **:** a tropism in which contact esp. with a solid or a rigid surface is the orienting factor

thill \ˈthil\ *n* [ME *thille,* perh. fr. OE, plank; akin to OHG *dili* plank, L *tellus* earth] (14c) **:** a shaft of a vehicle

thim·ble \ˈthim-bəl\ *n* [ME *thymbyl,* prob. alter. of OE *thȳmel* thumbstall, fr. *thūma* thumb] (15c) **1 :** a pitted cap or cover worn on the finger to push the needle in sewing **2 :** a thimble-shaped cup, appendage, or fixture: as **a :** a grooved ring of thin metal used to fit in a spliced loop in a rope as protection from chafing **b :** a fixed or movable ring, tube, or lining in a hole

thim·ble·ber·ry \-ˌber-ē\ *n* (1788) **:** any of several American raspberries or blackberries (esp. *Rubus occidentalis, R. parviflorus,* and *R. argutus*) having thimble-shaped fruit

thim·ble·ful \-ˌfu̇l\ *n* (1607) **1 :** as much as a thimble will hold **2 :** a very small quantity

[1]**thim·ble·rig** \-ˌrig\ *n* (1826) **1 :** a swindling trick in which a small ball or pea is quickly shifted from under one to another of three small cups to fool the spectator guessing its location **2 :** one who manipulates the cup in thimblerig : THIMBLERIGGER

[2]**thimblerig** *vt* (1839) **1 :** to cheat by trickery **2 :** to swindle by thimblerig — **thim·ble·rig·ger** *n*

thim·ble·weed \ˈthim-bəl-ˌwēd\ *n* (1833) **:** any of various anemones (as *Anemone virginiana*)

thi·mer·o·sal \thī-ˈmer-ə-ˌsal\ *n* [prob. fr. *thi-* + *mer*cury + *-o-* + *sal*icylate] (1949) **:** a crystalline organic mercurial $C_9H_9HgNaO_2S$ used as an antiseptic and germicide — compare MERTHIOLATE

[1]**thin** \ˈthin\ *adj* **thin·ner; thin·nest** [ME *thinne,* fr. OE *thynne;* akin to OHG *dunni* thin, L *tenuis* thin, *tenēre* to hold, *tendere* to stretch, Gk *teinein*] (bef. 12c) **1 a :** having little extent from one surface to its opposite ⟨~ paper⟩ **b :** measuring little in cross section or diameter ⟨~ rope⟩ **2 :** not dense in arrangement or distribution ⟨~ hair⟩ **3 :** not well fleshed : LEAN **4 a :** more fluid or rarefied than normal ⟨~ air⟩ **b :** having less than the usual number : SCANTY ⟨~ attendance⟩ **c :** few in number : SCARCE **d :** scantily supplied **e :** characterized by a paucity of bids or offerings ⟨a ~ market⟩ **5 a :** lacking substance or strength ⟨~ broth⟩ ⟨a ~ plot⟩ **b** *of a soil* **:** INFERTILE, POOR **6 a :** FLIMSY, UNCONVINCING ⟨a ~ disguise⟩ **b :** disappointingly poor or hard ⟨had a ~ time of it⟩ **7 :** somewhat feeble, shrill, and lacking in resonance ⟨a ~ voice⟩ **8 :** lacking in intensity or brilliance ⟨~ light⟩ **9 :** lacking sufficient photographic density or contrast — **thin·ly** *adv* — **thin·ness** \ˈthin-nəs\ *n* — **thin·nish** \ˈthin-ish\ *adj*

syn THIN, SLENDER, SLIM, SLIGHT, TENUOUS mean not thick, broad, abundant, or dense. THIN implies comparatively little extension between surfaces or in diameter, or it may imply lack of substance, richness, or abundance; SLENDER implies leanness or spareness often with grace and good proportion; SLIM applies to slenderness that suggests fragility or scantiness; SLIGHT implies smallness as well as thinness; TENUOUS implies extreme thinness, sheerness, or lack of substance and firmness.

[2]**thin** *vb* **thinned; thin·ning** *vt* (bef. 12c) **:** to make thin or thinner: **a :** to reduce in thickness or depth : ATTENUATE **b :** to make less dense or viscous **c :** DILUTE, WEAKEN **d :** to cause to lose flesh ⟨*thinned* by weeks of privation⟩ **e :** to reduce in number or bulk ~ *vi* **1 :** to become thin or thinner **2 :** to become weak

[3]**thin** *adv* **thin·ner; thin·nest** (13c) **:** in a thin manner : THINLY — used esp. in combinations ⟨*thin*-clad⟩

thin·clad \ˈthin-ˌklad\ *n* (1952) **:** a runner on a track team

[1]**thine** \(ˈ)thīn\ *adj* [ME *thin,* fr. OE *thīn*] *archaic* (bef. 12c) **:** THY — used esp. before a word beginning with a vowel or *h*

[2]**thine** \ˈthīn\ *pron, sing or pl in constr* [ME *thin,* fr. OE *thīn,* fr. *thīn* thy — more at THY] (bef. 12c) **:** that which belongs to thee — used without a following noun as a pronoun equivalent in meaning to the adjective *thy;* used esp. in ecclesiastical or literary language and still surviving in the speech of Friends esp. among themselves

thing \ˈthiŋ\ *n* [ME, fr. OE, thing, assembly; akin to OHG *ding* thing, assembly, Goth *theihs* time] (bef. 12c) **1 a :** a matter of concern : AFFAIR ⟨many ~*s* to do⟩ **b** *pl* **:** state of affairs in general or within a specified or implied sphere ⟨~*s* are improving⟩ **c :** a particular state of affairs : SITUATION ⟨look at this ~ another way⟩ **d :** EVENT, CIRCUMSTANCE ⟨that shooting was a terrible ~⟩ **2 a :** DEED, ACT, ACCOMPLISHMENT ⟨do great ~*s*⟩ **b :** a product of work or activity ⟨likes to build ~*s*⟩ **c :** the aim of effort or activity ⟨the ~ is to get well⟩ **3 a :** a separate and distinct individual quality, fact, idea, or usu. entity **b :** the concrete entity as distinguished from its appearances **c :** a spatial entity **d :** an inanimate object distinguished from a living being **4 a** *pl* **:** POSSESSIONS, EFFECTS ⟨pack your ~*s*⟩ **b :** whatever may be possessed or owned or be the object of a right **c :** an article of clothing ⟨not a ~ to wear⟩ **d** *pl* **:** equipment or utensils esp. for a particular purpose ⟨bring the tea ~*s*⟩ **5 :** an object or entity not precisely designated or capable of being designated ⟨use this ~⟩ **6 a :** DETAIL, POINT ⟨checks every little ~⟩ **b :** a material or substance of a specified kind ⟨avoid starchy ~*s*⟩ **7 a :** a spoken or written observation or point **b :** IDEA, NOTION ⟨says the first ~ he thinks of⟩ **c :** a piece of news or information ⟨couldn't get a ~ out of him⟩ **8 :** INDIVIDUAL ⟨not a living ~ in sight⟩ **9 :** the proper or fashionable way of behaving, talking, or dressing — used with *the* **10 a :** a mild obsession or phobia ⟨has a ~ about driving⟩; *also* **:** the object of such an obsession or phobia **b :** something (as an activity) that makes a strong appeal to the individual : FORTE ⟨letting students do their own ~ —*Newsweek*⟩

thing·am·a·bob \ˈthiŋ-ə-mə-ˌbäb\ *n* (1751) **:** THINGAMAJIG

thing·am·a·jig *or* **thing·um·a·jig** \ˈthiŋ-ə-mə-ˌjig\ *n* [alter. of earlier *thingum,* fr. *thing*] (1873) **:** something that is hard to classify or whose name is unknown or forgotten

thing–in–itself *n, pl* **things–in–themselves** [trans. of G *ding an sich*] (1798) **:** NOUMENON

thing·ness \ˈthiŋ-nəs\ *n* (1896) **:** the quality or state of objective existence or reality

thing·um·my \ˈthiŋ-ə-mē\ *n, pl* **-mies** [alter. of earlier *thingum*] (1796) **:** THINGAMAJIG

[1]**think** \ˈthiŋk\ *vb* **thought** \ˈthȯt\; **think·ing** [ME *thenken,* fr. OE *thencan;* akin to OHG *denken* to think, L *tongēre* to know — more at THANK] *vt* (bef. 12c) **1 :** to form or have in the mind **2 :** to have as an intention ⟨*thought* to return early⟩ **3 a :** to have as an opinion ⟨~ it's so⟩ **b :** to regard as : CONSIDER ⟨~ the rule unfair⟩ **4 a :** to reflect on : PONDER ⟨~ the matter over⟩ **b :** to determine by reflecting ⟨~ what to do next⟩ **5 :** to call to mind : REMEMBER ⟨he never ~*s* to ask how we do⟩ **6 :** to devise by thinking — usu. used with *up* ⟨*thought* up a plan to escape⟩ **7 :** to have as an expectation : ANTICIPATE ⟨we didn't ~ we'd have any trouble⟩ **8 a :** to center one's thoughts on ⟨talks and ~*s* business⟩ **b :** to form a mental picture of **9 :** to subject to the processes of logical thought ⟨~ things out⟩ ~ *vi* **1 a :** to exercise the powers of judgment, conception, or inference : REASON **b :** to have in or call to mind a thought **2 a :** to have the mind engaged in reflection : MEDITATE **b :** to consider the suitability ⟨*thought* of him for president⟩ **3 :** to have a view or opinion ⟨~*s* of himself as a poet⟩ **4 :** to have concern — usu. used with *of* ⟨a man must ~ first of his family⟩ **5 :** to consider something likely : SUSPECT ⟨may happen sooner than you ~⟩ — **think·er** *n*

syn THINK, CONCEIVE, IMAGINE, FANCY, REALIZE, ENVISAGE, ENVISION mean to form an idea of. THINK implies the entrance of an idea into one's mind with or without deliberate consideration or reflection; CONCEIVE suggests the forming and bringing forth and usu. developing of an idea, plan, or design; IMAGINE stresses a visualization; FANCY suggests an imagining often unrestrained by reality but spurred by desires; REALIZE stresses a grasping of the significance of what is conceived or imagined; ENVISAGE and ENVISION imply a conceiving or imagining that is esp. clear or detailed.

syn THINK, COGITATE, REFLECT, REASON, SPECULATE, DELIBERATE mean to use one's powers of conception, judgment, or inference. THINK is general and may apply to any mental activity, but used alone often suggests attainment of clear ideas or conclusions; COGITATE implies deep or intent thinking; REFLECT suggests unhurried consideration of something recalled to the mind; REASON stresses consecutive logical thinking; SPECULATE implies reasoning about things theoretical or problematic; DELIBERATE suggests slow or careful reasoning before forming an opinion or reaching a conclusion or decision.

— **think better of :** to reconsider and make a wiser decision — **think much of :** to view with satisfaction : APPROVE — usu. used in negative constructions ⟨I didn't *think much of* the new car⟩

[2]**think** *n* (1834) **:** an act of thinking ⟨has another ~ coming⟩

[3]**think** *adj* (1906) **:** of or relating to thinking

think·able \ˈthiŋ-kə-bəl\ *adj* (1854) **1 :** capable of being comprehended or reasoned about ⟨the ultimate nature of Deity is scarcely ~⟩ **2 :** conceivably possible — **think·able·ness** *n* — **think·ably** \-blē\ *adv*

[1]**think·ing** *n* (14c) **1 :** the action of using one's mind to produce thoughts **2 a :** OPINION, JUDGMENT **b :** thought that is characteristic (as of a period, group, or person) ⟨the current student ~ on fraternities⟩

[2]**thinking** *adj* (1681) **:** marked by use of the intellect : RATIONAL ⟨~ citizens⟩ — **think·ing·ly** \ˈthiŋ-kiŋ-lē\ *adv* — **think·ing·ness** *n*

thinking cap *n* (1874) **:** a state or mood in which one thinks

think piece *n* (1941) **:** a piece of writing meant to be thought-provoking and speculative that consists chiefly of background material and personal opinion and analysis

think tank *n* (1959) **:** an institute, corporation, or group organized for interdisciplinary research (as in technological and social problems) — called also *think factory*

thin–layer chromatography *n* (1957) **:** chromatography in which the stationary phase is an absorbent medium (as alumina or silica gel) arranged as a thin layer on a rigid support (as a glass plate)

thin·ner \ˈthin-ər\ *n* (1832) **:** one that thins; *specif* **:** a volatile liquid (as turpentine) used esp. to thin paint

thin–skinned \ˈthin-ˈskind\ *adj* (1598) **1 :** having a thin skin or rind **2 :** unduly susceptible to criticism or insult : TOUCHY

thio- — see THI-

thio acid \ˈthī-ō-\ *n* [ISV, fr. *thi-*] (ca. 1891) **:** an acid in which oxygen is partly or wholly replaced by sulfur

thio·car·ba·mide \ˌthī-ō-ˈkär-bə-ˌmīd, -kär-ˈbam-ˌīd\ *n* [ISV] (1878) **:** THIOUREA

thio·cy·a·nate \-ˈsī-ə-ˌnāt, -nət\ *n* [ISV] (1877) **:** a compound that consists of the chemical group SCN bonded by the sulfur atom to a group or an atom other than a hydrogen atom

Thi·o·kol \ˈthī-ə-ˌkȯl, -ˌkōl\ *trademark* — used for polysulfide polymers or water-dispersed latices

thi·ol \ˈthī-ˌȯl, -ˌōl\ *n* [ISV *thi-* + [1]*-ol*] (ca. 1890) **1 :** MERCAPTAN **2 :** the group SH characteristic of mercaptans — **thi·o·lic** \thī-ˈō-lik\ *adj*

thion- *comb form* [ISV, fr. Gk *theion*] **:** sulfur ⟨*thion*ic⟩

thio·pen·tal \ˌthī-ō-ˈpen-ˌtal, -ˌtȯl\ *n* [*thio-* + *pento*barbit*al*] (1947) **:** a barbiturate $C_{11}H_{18}N_2O_2S$ used as the sodium derivative in intravenous anesthesia and in the treatment of some forms of mental illness — compare PENTOTHAL

thio·phene \ˈthī-ə-ˌfēn\ *n* [ISV *thi-* + *phene* (benzene)] (ca. 1883) **:** a heterocyclic liquid C_4H_4S from coal tar that resembles benzene

thi·o·rid·a·zine \ˌthī-ə-ˈrid-ə-ˌzēn, -zən\ *n* [*thio-* + pipe*ridine* + phenothi*azine*] (1960) **:** a phenothiazine tranquilizer used as the hydrochloride $C_{21}H_{26}N_2S_2{\cdot}HCl$ for relief of anxiety states and in the treatment of schizophrenia

thio·sul·fate \-ˈsəl-ˌfāt\ *n* [ISV] (1873) **:** a salt or ester of thiosulfuric acid

thio·sul·fu·ric \-ˌsəl-ˈfyu̇(ə)r-ik\ *adj* (1873) **:** of, relating to, or being an unstable acid $H_2S_2O_3$ derived from sulfuric acid by replacement of one oxygen atom by sulfur and known only in solution or in salts and esters

thio·te·pa \ˌthī-ə-ˈtē-pə\ *n* (1953) **:** a sulfur analogue of tepa $C_6H_{12}N_3PS$ that is used esp. as an antineoplastic agent and is less toxic than tepa

thio·ura·cil \ˌthī-ō-ˈyu̇r-ə-ˌsil\ *n* [ISV] (1905) **:** a bitter crystalline compound $C_4H_4N_2OS$ that depresses the function of the thyroid gland

thio·urea \-yu̇-ˈrē-ə\ *n* [NL] (1894) **:** a colorless crystalline bitter compound $CS(NH_2)_2$ analogous to and resembling urea that is used esp. as a photographic and organic chemical reagent; *also* **:** a substituted derivative of this compound

thir \thər, (ˈ)thi(ə)r, (ˈ)thu̇(ə)r\ *pron* [ME (northern), perh. irreg. fr. ME *this*] *dial Brit* (14c) **:** THESE

thi·ram \ˈthī-ˌram\ *n* [prob. by alter. fr. *thiuram* (the chemical group NH_2CS)] (ca. 1949) **:** a compound $C_6H_{12}N_2S_4$ used as a fungicide and seed disinfectant

[1]**third** \ˈthərd\ *adj* [ME *thridde, thirde,* fr. OE *thridda, thirdda;* akin to L *tertius* third, Gk *tritos, treis* three — more at THREE] (bef. 12c) **1 a :** being next to the second in place or time ⟨the ~ taxi in line⟩ **b :** ranking next to the second of a grade or degree in authority or precedence ⟨~ mate⟩ **c :** being the forward speed or gear next higher than second in a motor vehicle **2 a :** being one of three equal parts into which something is divisible **b :** being the last in each group of three in a series ⟨take out every ~ card⟩ — **third** *or* **third·ly** *adv*

[2]**third** *n* (14c) **1 :** one of three equal parts of something **2 a** — see NUMBER table **b :** one that is next after second in rank, position, authority, or precedence ⟨the ~ in line⟩ **3 a :** the musical interval embracing three diatonic degrees **b :** a tone at this interval; *specif* **:** MEDIANT **c :** the harmonic combination of two tones a third apart **4** *pl* **:** merchandise whose quality falls below the manufacturer's standard for seconds **5 :** THIRD BASE **6 :** the third forward gear or speed of a motor vehicle

third base *n* (1845) **1 :** the base that must be touched third by a base runner in baseball **2 :** the player position for defending the area around third base — **third baseman** *n*

third–class *adj* (1839) **:** of or relating to a class, rank, or grade next below the second — **third–class** *adv*

third class *n* (1845) **1 :** the third and usu. next below second class in a classification **2 :** the least expensive class of accommodations (as on a passenger ship) **3 a :** a class of U.S. mail comprising printed matter exclusive of regularly issued periodicals and merchandise less than 16 ounces in weight and not sealed against inspection **b :** a similar class of Canadian mail with different weight limits

third degree *n* (1900) **:** the subjection of a prisoner to mental or physical torture to wring a confession from him

third–degree burn *n* (1930) **:** a burn characterized by destruction of the skin through its deeper layers and possibly into underlying tissues, loss of fluid, and sometimes shock

third dimension *n* (1858) **1 :** THICKNESS, DEPTH; *also* **:** a dimension that adds the effect of solidity to a two-dimensional system **2 :** a quality that confers reality or lifelikeness ⟨night sounds that stick in the mind and give a *third dimension* to the memory —Adie Suehsdorf⟩ — **third–di·men·sion·al** \\ˌthərd-də-ˈmench-nəl, -(ˌ)dī-, -ən-ᵊl\\ *adj*

third estate *n, often cap T & E* (1604) **:** the third of the traditional political orders; *specif* **:** the commons

third force *n* [trans. of F *troisième force*] (1936) **:** a grouping (as of political parties or international powers) intermediate between two opposing political forces

third·hand \\ˈthərd-ˈhand\\ *adj* (1599) **1 :** received from or through two intermediaries ⟨~ information⟩ **2 a :** acquired after being used by two previous owners **b :** dealing in thirdhand merchandise

third house *n* (1852) **:** a legislative lobby

third market *n* (1964) **:** the over-the-counter market in listed securities

third order *n, often cap T & O* (1629) **1 :** an organization composed of lay people living in secular society under a religious rule and directed by a religious order **2 :** a congregation esp. of teaching or nursing sisters affiliated with a religious order

third party *n* (1801) **1 a :** a major political party operating over a limited period of time in addition to two other major parties in a nation or state normally characterized by a two-party system **b :** MINOR PARTY **2 :** a person other than the principals ⟨a *third party* to a divorce proceeding⟩

third person *n* (1586) **1 a :** a set of linguistic forms (as verb forms, pronouns, and inflectional affixes) referring to one that is neither the speaker or writer of the utterance in which they occur nor the one to whom that utterance is addressed **b :** a linguistic form belonging to such a set **2 :** reference of a linguistic form to one that is neither the speaker or writer of the utterance in which it occurs nor the one to whom that utterance is addressed

third rail *n* (1890) **:** a metal rail through which electric current is led to the motors of an electric locomotive

third–rate \\ˈthər-ˈdrāt\\ *adj* (1838) **:** of third quality or value; *specif* **:** worse than second-rate — **third–rat·er** \\-ˈdrāt-ər\\ *n*

third reading *n* (ca. 1934) **:** the final stage of the consideration of a legislative bill before a vote on its final disposition

third–stream *adj* (1963) **:** of, relating to, or being music that incorporates elements of classical music and jazz

third ventricle *n* (ca. 1860) **:** the median unpaired ventricle of the brain bounded by parts of the telencephalon and diencephalon

third world *n, often cap T&W* [trans. of F *tiers monde*] (1965) **1 :** a group of nations esp. in Africa and Asia that are not aligned with either the Communist or the non-Communist blocs **2 :** an aggregate of minority groups within a larger predominant culture **3 :** the aggregate of the underdeveloped nations of the world

¹thirl \\ˈthər(-ə)l\\ *n* [ME, fr. OE *thyrel,* fr. *thurh* through — more at THROUGH] *dial* (bef. 12c) **:** HOLE, PERFORATION, OPENING

²thirl *vt, dial Brit* (bef. 12c) **:** PIERCE, PERFORATE

¹thirst \\ˈthərst\\ *n* [ME, fr. OE *thurst;* akin to OHG *durst* thirst, L *terra* land, earth, *torrēre* to dry, parch, Gk *tersesthai* to become dry] (bef. 12c) **1 a :** a sensation of dryness in the mouth and throat associated with a desire for liquids; *also* **:** the bodily condition (as of dehydration) that induces this sensation **b :** a desire or need to drink **2 :** an ardent desire **:** CRAVING, LONGING

²thirst *vi* (bef. 12c) **1 :** to feel thirsty **:** suffer thirst **2 :** to crave vehemently and urgently ***syn*** see LONG — **thirst·er** *n*

thirst·i·ly \\ˈthər-stə-lē\\ *adv* (1549) **:** with or on account of thirst

thirsty \\ˈthər-stē\\ *adj* **thirst·i·er; -est** (bef. 12c) **1 a :** feeling thirst **b :** deficient in moisture **:** PARCHED ⟨~ land⟩ **c :** highly absorbent ⟨~ towels⟩ **2 :** having a strong desire **:** AVID ⟨~ for knowledge⟩ — **thirst·i·ness** \\-stē-nəs\\ *n*

thir·teen \\ˌthər(t)-ˈtēn, ˈthər(t)-\\ *n* [ME *thrittene,* fr. *thrittene,* adj., fr. OE *thrēotīne;* akin to OE *tien* ten — more at TEN] (bef. 12c) — see NUMBER table — **thirteen** *adj or pron* — **thir·teenth** \\-ˈtēn(t)th\\ *adj or n*

thir·ty \\ˈthərt-ē\\ *n, pl* **thirties** [ME *thritty,* fr. *thritty,* adj., fr. OE *thrītig,* fr. *thrītig* group of 30, fr. *thrie* three + *-tig* group of ten — more at TEN] (bef. 12c) **1** — see NUMBER table **2** *pl* **:** the numbers 30 to 39; *specif* **:** the years 30 to 39 in a lifetime or century **3 :** a sign of completion **:** END — usu. written 30 ⟨wrote ~ on the last page of the story⟩ **4 :** the second point scored by a side in a game of tennis **5 :** a .30 caliber machine gun or rifle — usu. written .30 — **thir·ti·eth** \\-ē-əth\\ *adj or n* — **thirty** *adj or pron*

thir·ty–eight \\ˌthərt-ē-ˈāt\\ *n* (bef. 12c) **1** — see NUMBER table **2 :** a handgun nominally of .38 caliber — usu. written .38 — **thirty–eight** *adj or pron*

thir·ty–sec·ond note \\-ˈsek-ən-ˌnōt\\ *n* (ca. 1890) **:** a musical note with the time value of $^1/_{32}$ of a whole note

thir·ty–sec·ond rest \\-ˌsek-ən-ˈ(d)rest\\ *n* (ca. 1903) **:** a musical rest corresponding in time value to a thirty-second note

thir·ty–thir·ty \\ˌthərt-ē-ˈthərt-ē\\ *n* (1929) **:** a rifle that fires a .30 caliber cartridge having a 30 grain powder charge — usu. written .30-30

thir·ty–three \\ˌthərt-ē-ˈthrē\\ *n* (bef. 12c) **1** — see NUMBER table **2 :** a microgroove phonograph record designed to be played at $33^1/_3$ revolutions per minute — usu. written 33 — **thirty–three** *adj or pron*

thir·ty–two \\-ˈtü\\ *n* (bef. 12c) **1** — see NUMBER table **2 :** a .32 caliber handgun — usu. written .32 — **thirty–two** *adj or pron*

thir·ty–two·mo \\-(ˌ)mō\\ *n, pl* **-mos** (ca. 1841) **:** the size of a piece of paper cut 32 from a sheet; *also* **:** a book, a page, or paper of this size

¹this \\(ˈ)t̲h̲is, t̲h̲əs\\ *pron, pl* **these** \\(ˈ)t̲h̲ēz\\ [ME, pron. & adj., fr. OE *thes* (masc.), *this* (neut.); akin to OHG *dese* this; akin to OE *thæt* that] (bef. 12c) **1 a** (1) **:** the person, thing, or idea that is present or near in place, time, or thought or that has just been mentioned ⟨*these* are my hands⟩ (2) **:** what is stated in the following phrase, clause, or discourse ⟨I can only say ~: it wasn't here yesterday⟩ **b :** this time or place ⟨expected to return before ~⟩ **2 a :** the one nearer or more immediately under observation or discussion ⟨~ is iron and that is tin⟩ **b :** the latter one

²this *adj, pl* **these** (bef. 12c) **1 a :** being the person, thing, or idea that is present or near in place, time, or thought or that has just been mentioned ⟨~ book is mine⟩ ⟨early ~ morning⟩ **b :** constituting the immediately following part of the present discourse **c :** constituting the immediate past or future ⟨friends all *these* years⟩ **d :** being one not previously mentioned — used esp. in narrative to give a sense of immediacy or vividness ⟨then ~ guy runs in⟩ **2 :** being the nearer at hand or more immediately under observation or discussion ⟨~ car or that one⟩

³this \\ˈt̲h̲is\\ *adv* (15c) **:** to the degree or extent indicated by something in the immediate context or situation ⟨didn't expect to wait ~ long⟩

This·be \\ˈthiz-bē\\ *n* [L, fr. Gk *Thisbē*] **:** a legendary young woman of Babylon who dies for love of Pyramus

this·tle \\ˈthis-əl\\ *n* [ME *thistel,* fr. OE; akin to OHG *distil* thistle] (bef. 12c) **:** any of various prickly composite plants (esp. genera *Carduus, Cirsium,* and *Onopordon*) with often showy heads of mostly tubular flowers; *also* **:** any of various other prickly plants — **this·tly** \\ˈthis-(ə-)lē\\ *adj*

this·tle·down \\ˈthis-əl-ˌdau̇n\\ *n* (1561) **:** the pappus from the ripe flower head of a thistle

thistle tube *n* (ca. 1891) **:** a funnel tube usu. of glass with a bulging top and flaring mouth

this–world·li·ness \\ˈt̲h̲is-ˈwərld-lē-nəs\\ *n* (1872) **:** interest in, concern with, or devotion to things of this world

this–world·ly \\-lē\\ *adj* (1883) **:** characterized by or manifesting this-worldliness

¹thith·er \\ˈthit̲h̲-ər *also* ˈt̲h̲ith-\\ *adv* [ME, fr. OE *thider;* akin to ON *thathra* there, OE *thæt* that] (bef. 12c) **:** to that place **:** THERE

²thither *adj* (1830) **:** being on the other and farther side **:** more remote

thith·er·to \\-ˌtü; ˌthit̲h̲-ər-ˈ, ˌt̲h̲ith-\\ *adv* (15c) **:** until that time

thith·er·ward \\ˈthit̲h̲-ər-wərd, ˈt̲h̲ith-\\ *also* **thith·er·wards** \\-wərdz\\ *adv* (bef. 12c) **:** toward that place **:** THITHER

thix·ot·ro·py \\thik-ˈsä-trə-pē\\ *n* [ISV *thixo-* (fr. Gk *thixis* act of touching, fr. *thinganein* to touch) + *-tropy* — more at THIGMOTAXIS] (ca. 1927) **:** the property of various gels of becoming fluid when disturbed (as by shaking) — **thixo·tro·pic** \\ˌthik-sə-ˈtrō-pik, -ˈträp-ik\\ *adj*

tho *var of* THOUGH

¹thole \\ˈthōl\\ *vb* **tholed; thol·ing** [ME *tholen,* fr. OE *tholian* — more at TOLERATE] *chiefly dial* (bef. 12c) **:** ENDURE

²thole *n* [ME *tholle,* fr. OE *thol;* akin to Gk *tylos* knob, callus, L *tumēre* to swell — more at THUMB] (bef. 12c) **1 :** one of a pair of pins set in the gunwale of a boat to hold an oar in place **2 :** PEG, PIN

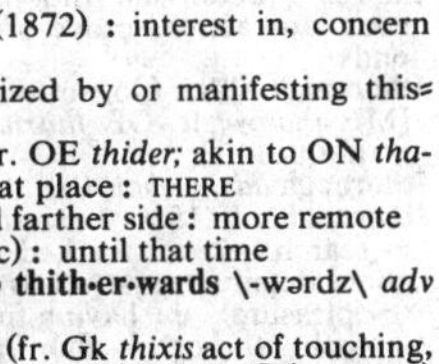

thole 1

tho·lei·ite \\ˈt(h)ō-lə-ˌīt\\ *n* [G *tholeiit,* fr. *Tholey,* village in Saarland, Germany + G *-it* -ite] (1866) **:** a basaltic rock that is rich in aluminum and low in potassium, typically underlies the depths of the sea, and is prob. derived from the earth's mantle — **tho·lei·it·ic** \\ˌt(h)ō-lə-ˈit-ik\\ *adj*

thole·pin \\ˈthōl-ˌpin\\ *n* (15c) **:** THOLE 1

Thom·as \\ˈtäm-əs\\ *n* [Gk *Thōmas,* fr. Heb *tʼōm* twin] **:** an apostle who demanded proof of Christ's resurrection

Thom·as Jef·fer·son's Birthday \\ˌtäm-əs-ˌjef-ər-sənz-\\ *n* (ca. 1928) **:** April 13 observed as a legal holiday in Alabama

Tho·mism \\ˈtō-ˌmiz-əm\\ *n* [prob. fr. (assumed) NL *thomismus,* fr. St. *Thomas* Aquinas] (ca. 1727) **:** the scholastic philosophical and theological system of St. Thomas Aquinas — **Tho·mist** \\-məst\\ *n or adj* — **Tho·mis·tic** \\tō-ˈmis-tik\\ *adj*

Thomp·son submachine gun \\ˈtäm(p)-sən-\\ *n* [John T. *Thompson* †1940 Am. army officer] (1920) **:** a .45 caliber submachine gun with a drum or stick magazine, a pistol grip, and a detachable buttstock — called also *tommy gun*

thong \\ˈthȯŋ\\ *n* [ME, fr. OE *thwong;* akin ON *thvengr* thong] (bef. 12c) **1 :** a strip esp. of leather or hide **2 :** a sandal held on the foot by a thong fitting between the toes and connected to a strap across the top or around the sides of the foot — **thonged** \\ˈthȯŋd\\ *adj*

Thor \\ˈthȯ(ə)r\\ *n* [ON *Thōrr*] **:** the Norse god of thunder, weather, and crops

tho·rac·ic \\thə-ˈras-ik\\ *adj* (ca. 1656) **:** of, relating to, located within, or involving the thorax — **tho·rac·i·cal·ly** \\-i-k(ə-)lē\\ *adv*

thoracic duct *n* (ca. 1727) **:** the main trunk of the system of lymphatic vessels that lies along the front of the spinal column and opens into the left subclavian vein

tho·ra·cot·o·my \\ˌthōr-ə-ˈkät-ə-mē, ˌthȯr-\\ *n, pl* **-mies** [L *thorac-, thorax* + ISV *-tomy*] (ca. 1857) **:** surgical incision of the chest wall

tho·rax \\ˈthō(ə)r-ˌaks, ˈthȯ(ə)r-\\ *n, pl* **tho·rax·es** *or* **tho·ra·ces** \\ˈthōr-ə-ˌsēz, ˈthȯr-\\ [ME, fr. L *thorac-, thorax* breastplate, thorax, fr. Gk *thōrak-, thōrax*] (15c) **1 :** the part of the mammalian body between the neck and the abdomen; *also* **:** its cavity in which the heart and lungs lie **2 :** the middle of the three chief divisions of the body of an insect; *also* **:** the corresponding part of a crustacean or an arachnid

Tho·ra·zine \\ˈthōr-ə-ˌzēn, ˈthȯr-\\ *trademark* — used for chlorpromazine

tho·ria \'thōr-ē-ə, 'thȯr-\ *n* [NL, fr. *thor*ium + *-a*] (ca. 1841) **:** a powdery white oxide of thorium ThO_2 used esp. as a catalyst and in crucibles and refractories and optical glass

tho·ri·a·nite \-ē-ə-,nīt\ *n* [irreg. fr. *thoria*] (ca. 1904) **:** a strongly radioactive mineral ThO_2 that is an oxide of thorium and often contains rare-earth metals

tho·rite \'thō(ə)r-,īt, 'thȯ(ə)r-\ *n* [Sw *thorit*, fr. NL *thorium*] (1832) **:** a rare mineral $ThSiO_4$ that is a brown to black or sometimes orange-yellow thorium silicate resembling zircon

tho·ri·um \'thōr-ē-əm, 'thȯr-\ *n* [NL, fr. ON *Thōrr* Thor] (1832) **:** a radioactive metallic element that occurs combined in minerals and is usu. associated with rare earths — see ELEMENT table

thorn \'thȯ(ə)rn\ *n, often attrib* [ME, fr. OE; akin to OHG *dorn* thorn, Skt *tṛṇa* grass, blade of grass] (bef. 12c) **1 :** a woody plant bearing sharp impeding processes (as briers, prickles, or spines); *esp* **:** HAWTHORN **2 a :** a sharp rigid process on a plant; *specif* **:** a short, indurated, sharp-pointed, and leafless branch **b :** any of various sharp spinose structures on an animal **3 :** the runic letter þ used in Old English, Middle English, and Icelandic to represent either of the fricatives \th\ or \t͟h\ **4 :** something that causes distress or irritation — **thorned** \'thȯ(ə)rnd\ *adj* — **thorn·less** \'thȯ(ə)rn-ləs\ *adj* — **thorn·like** \-,līk\ *adj*

thorn apple *n* (1578) **1 :** JIMSONWEED; *also* **:** any plant of the same genus **2 :** the fruit of a hawthorn; *also* **:** HAWTHORN

thorn·back \'thȯ(ə)rn-,bak\ *n* (14c) **:** any of various rays having spines on the back

thorn·bush \-,bu̇sh\ *n* (14c) **1 :** any of various spiny or thorny shrubs or small trees **2 :** a low growth of thorny shrubs esp. of dry tropical regions

thorny \'thȯr-nē\ *adj* **thorn·i·er; -est** (bef. 12c) **1 :** full of thorns **2 :** full of difficulties or controversial points **:** TICKLISH ⟨a ~ problem⟩ — **thorn·i·ness** *n*

thoro *nonstand var of* THOROUGH

tho·ron \'thō(ə)r-,än, 'thȯ(ə)r-\ *n* [NL, fr. *thorium*] (ca. 1926) **:** a gaseous radioactive isotope of radon that has a half-life of about 55 seconds

[1]**thor·ough** \'thər-(,)ō, -ə(-w), *sometimes* 'thȯr-; 'thə-(,)rō, -rə(-w)\ *prep* [ME *thorow*, fr. OE *thurh, thuruh*, prep. & adv.] *archaic* (bef. 12c) **:** THROUGH

[2]**thorough** *adv, archaic* (bef. 12c) **:** THROUGH

[3]**thorough** *adj* (15c) **1 :** carried through to completion **:** EXHAUSTIVE ⟨a ~ search⟩ **2 a :** marked by full detail ⟨a ~ description⟩ **b :** careful about detail **:** PAINSTAKING ⟨a ~ scholar⟩ **c :** complete in all respects ⟨~ pleasure⟩ **d :** having full mastery (as of an art) ⟨a ~ musician⟩ **3 :** passing through — **thor·ough·ly** *adv* — **thor·ough·ness** *n*

thor·ough·bass \'thər-ə-,bās, 'thə-rə-\ *n* (1662) **:** CONTINUO

thor·ough·brace \-,brās\ *n* (1837) **:** one of several leather straps supporting the body of a carriage and serving as springs

[1]**thor·ough·bred** \-,bred\ *adj* (1701) **1 :** thoroughly trained or skilled **2 :** bred from the best blood through a long line **:** PUREBRED ⟨~ dogs⟩ **3 a** *cap* **:** of, relating to, or being a member of the Thoroughbred breed of horses **b :** having characteristics resembling those of a Thoroughbred

[2]**thoroughbred** *n* (1842) **1** *cap* **:** any of an English breed of light speedy horses kept chiefly for racing that originated from crosses between English mares of uncertain ancestry and Arabian stallions **2 :** a purebred or pedigreed animal **3 :** one that has characteristics resembling those of a Thoroughbred

thor·ough·fare \-,fa(ə)r, -,fe(ə)r\ *n* (14c) **1 :** a way or place for passage: as **a :** a street open at both ends **b :** a main road **2 a :** PASSAGE, TRANSIT **b :** the conditions necessary for passing through

thor·ough·go·ing \,thər-ə-'gō-iŋ, ,thə-rə-, -'gȯ(-)iŋ\ *adj* (1819) **:** marked by thoroughness or zeal

thor·ough–paced \-'pāst\ *adj* (1646) **1 :** THOROUGH, COMPLETE **2 :** thoroughly trained **:** ACCOMPLISHED

thor·ough·pin \'thər-ə-,pin, 'thə-rə-\ *n* (1789) **:** a synovial dilatation just above the hock of a horse on both sides of the leg and slightly anterior to the hamstring tendon that is often associated with lameness

thor·ough·wort \-,wərt, -,wȯ(ə)rt\ *n* (1814) **:** BONESET

thorp \'thȯ(ə)rp\ *n* [ME, fr. OE, perh. fr. ON; akin to OHG *dorf* village, L *trabs* beam, roof] *archaic* (bef. 12c) **:** VILLAGE, HAMLET

those [ME, fr. *those* these, fr. OE *thās*, pl. of *thes* this — more at THIS] *pl of* THAT

[1]**thou** \(')t͟hau̇\ *pron* [ME, fr. OE *thū*; akin to OHG *dū* thou, L *tu*, Gk *sy*] (bef. 12c) **:** the one addressed ⟨~ shalt have no other gods before me —Exod 20:3 (AV)⟩ — used esp. in ecclesiastical or literary language and by Friends as the universal form of address to one person; compare THEE, THINE, THY, YE, YOU

[2]**thou** \'t͟hau̇\ *vt* (15c) **:** to address as *thou*

[3]**thou** \'thau̇\ *n, pl* **thou** [short for *thousand*] (1869) **:** a thousand of something (as dollars)

[1]**though** \'t͟hō\ *adv* [ME, adv. & conj., of Scand origin; akin to ON *thō* nevertheless; akin to OE *thēah* nevertheless, OHG *doh*] (bef. 12c) **:** HOWEVER, NEVERTHELESS ⟨It's hard work. I enjoy it ~⟩

[2]**though** \(,)t͟hō\ *conj* (bef. 12c) **1 :** in spite of the fact that **:** WHILE ⟨~ they know the war is lost, they continue to fight —Bruce Bliven †1977⟩ **2 :** in spite of the possibility that **:** even if ⟨~ they all may fail, they all will try⟩

[1]**thought** \'thȯt\ *past of* THINK

[2]**thought** *n* [ME, fr. OE *thōht*; akin to OE *thencan* to think — more at THINK] (bef. 12c) **1 a :** the action or process of thinking **:** COGITATION **b :** serious consideration **:** REGARD **c** *archaic* **:** RECOLLECTION, REMEMBRANCE **2 a :** reasoning power **b :** the power to imagine **:** CONCEPTION **3 :** something that is thought: as **a :** an individual act or product of thinking **b :** a developed intention or plan ⟨he had no ~ of leaving home⟩ **c :** something (as an opinion or belief) in the mind ⟨he spoke his ~s freely⟩ **d :** the intellectual product or the organized views and principles of a period, place, group, or individual ***syn*** see IDEA — **a thought :** a little **:** SOMEWHAT ⟨*a thought* too much seasoning in the stew⟩

thought·ful \'thȯt-fəl\ *adj* (13c) **1 a :** absorbed in thought **:** MEDITATIVE **b :** characterized by careful reasoned thinking **2 a :** having thoughts **:** HEEDFUL ⟨became ~ about his parents⟩ **b :** given to heedful anticipation of the needs and wants of others **:** SOLICITOUS — **thought·ful·ly** \-fə-lē\ *adv* — **thought·ful·ness** *n*

thought·less \-ləs\ *adj* (1592) **1 a :** insufficiently alert **:** CARELESS **b :** RECKLESS, RASH **2 :** devoid of thought **:** INSENSATE **3 :** lacking concern for others **:** INCONSIDERATE — **thought·less·ly** *adv* — **thought·less·ness** *n*

thought–out \-'au̇t\ *adj* (1870) **:** produced or arrived at through mental effort and esp. through careful and thorough consideration

thought·way \-,wā\ *n* (1943) **:** a way of thinking that is characteristic of a particular group, time, or culture

thou·sand \'thau̇z-ᵊn(d)\ *n, pl* **thousands** *or* **thousand** [ME, fr. OE *thūsend*; akin to OHG *dūsunt* thousand; both fr. a prehistoric Gmc compound whose constituents are respectively akin to Russ *tysyacha* thousand, Skt *tavas* strong, L *tumēre* to swell and to OE *hund* hundred — more at THUMB] (bef. 12c) **1** — see NUMBER table **2 :** a very large number ⟨~s of ants⟩ — **thousand** *adj* — **thou·sand·fold** \-ᵊn(d)-,fōld\ *adj or adv* — **thou·sandth** \-ᵊn(t)th\ *adj or n*

Thousand Island dressing *n* [*Thousand Islands*, islands in the St. Lawrence river] (1924) **:** mayonnaise with chili sauce and seasonings (as chopped pimientos and green peppers)

thou·sand–leg·ger \,thau̇z-ᵊn-'(d)leg-ər, -'(d)lāg-\ *n* (1914) **:** MILLIPEDE

thousands digit \'thau̇z-ᵊn(d)z-\ *n* (1969) **:** the numeral (as 1 in 1456) occupying the thousands place in a number expressed in the Arabic system of writing numbers

thousands place *n* (1937) **:** the place four to the left of the decimal point in a number expressed in the Arabic system of writing numbers

Thra·cian \'thrā-shən\ *n* (1569) **1 :** a native or inhabitant of Thrace **2 :** the language of the Thracians generally assumed to be Indo-European — see INDO-EUROPEAN LANGUAGES table — **Thracian** *adj*

Thra·co–Il·lyr·i·an \,thrā-(,)kō-il-'ir-ē-ən\ *adj* (1902) **:** of, relating to, or constituting a supposed subfamily of Indo-European languages comprising Thracian, Illyrian, and Albanian

[1]**thrall** \'thrȯl\ *n* [ME *thral*, fr. OE *thrǣl*, fr. ON *thrǣll*] (bef. 12c) **1 a :** a servant slave **:** BONDMAN; *also* **:** SERF **b :** a person in moral or mental servitude **2 a :** the state of a thrall **:** SLAVERY **b :** a state of complete absorption ⟨mountains could hold me in ~ with a subtle attraction of their own —Elyne Mitchell⟩ — **thrall** *adj*

[2]**thrall** *vt, archaic* (13c) **:** ENTHRALL, ENSLAVE

thrall·dom *or* **thral·dom** \'thrȯl-dəm\ *n* (12c) **:** the condition of a thrall

[1]**thrash** \'thrash\ *vb* [alter. of *thresh*] *vt* (1588) **1 :** to separate the seeds of from the husks and straw by beating **:** THRESH 1 **2 a :** to beat soundly with or as if with a stick or whip **:** FLOG **b :** to defeat decisively or severely ⟨~*ed* the visiting team⟩ **3 :** to swing, beat, or strike in the manner of a rapidly moving flail ⟨~*ing* his arms⟩ **4 a :** to go over again and again ⟨~ the matter over inconclusively⟩ **b :** to hammer out **:** FORGE ⟨~ out a plan⟩ ~ *vi* **1 :** THRESH 1 **2 :** to deal blows or strokes like one using a flail or whip **3 :** to move or stir about violently **:** toss about ⟨~ in bed with a fever⟩ ***syn*** see SWING

[2]**thrash** *n* (1840) **:** an act of thrashing esp. in swimming

[1]**thrash·er** \'thrash-ər\ *n* (1632) **:** one that thrashes or threshes

[2]**thrash·er** \'thrash-ər\ *n* [prob. alter. of *thrush*] (1810) **:** any of numerous long-tailed American singing birds (family Mimidae and esp. genus *Toxostoma*) that resemble thrushes and include notable singers and mimics

thra·son·i·cal \thrā-'sän-i-kəl, thrə-\ *adj* [L *Thrason-, Thraso* Thraso, braggart soldier in the comedy *Eunuchus* by Terence] (1564) **:** of, relating to, resembling, or characteristic of Thraso **:** BRAGGING, BOASTFUL — **thra·son·i·cal·ly** \-k(ə-)lē\ *adv*

[1]**thraw** \'thrȧ\ *vb* [ME *thrawen* — more at THROW] *vt* (bef. 12c) **1** *chiefly Scot* **:** to cause to twist or turn **2** *chiefly Scot* **:** CROSS, THWART ~ *vi* **1** *chiefly Scot* **:** TWIST, TURN **2** *chiefly Scot* **:** to be in disagreement

[2]**thraw** *n* (1585) **1** *chiefly Scot* **:** TWIST, TURN **2** *chiefly Scot* **:** ill humor

thra·wart \'thrȧ-wərt\ *adj* [ME (Sc), alter. of ME *fraward, froward* froward] (15c) **1** *chiefly Scot* **:** STUBBORN **2** *Scot* **:** CROOKED

thrawn \'thrȧn\ *adj* [ME (Sc) *thrawin*, fr. pp. of ME *thrawen* to twist] *chiefly Scot* (15c) **:** lacking in pleasing or attractive qualities: as **a :** PERVERSE, RECALCITRANT **b :** CROOKED, MISSHAPEN — **thrawn·ly** *adv, chiefly Scot*

[1]**thread** \'thred\ *n* [ME *thred*, fr. OE *thrǣd*; akin to OHG *drāt* wire, OE *thrāwan* to cause to twist or turn — more at THROW] (bef. 12c) **1 a :** a filament, a group of filaments twisted together, or a filamentous length formed by spinning and twisting short textile fibers into a continuous strand **b :** a piece of thread **2 a :** any of various natural filaments ⟨the ~s of a spider web⟩ **b :** a slender stream (as of water) **c :** a streak of light or color **d :** a projecting helical rib (as in a fitting or on a pipe) by which parts can be screwed together **:** SCREW THREAD **3 :** something continuous or drawn out: as **a :** a train of thought **b :** a continuing element ⟨a ~ of melancholy marked all his writing⟩ **4 :** a tenuous or feeble support **5** *pl* **:** CLOTHING — **thread·less** \-ləs\ *adj* — **thread·like** \-,līk\ *adj*

[2]**thread** *vt* (14c) **1 a :** to pass a thread through the eye of (a needle) **b :** to arrange a thread, yarn, or lead-in piece in working position for use in (a machine) **2 a** (1) **:** to pass something through in the manner of a thread ⟨~ a pipe with wire⟩ (2) **:** to pass (as a tape, line, or film) into or through something ⟨~*ed* a fresh film into the camera⟩ **b :** to make one's way through or between ⟨~*ing* narrow alleys⟩ **3 :** to put together on or as if on a thread **:** STRING ⟨~ beads⟩ **4 :** to interweave with or as if with threads **:** INTERSPERSE ⟨dark hair ~*ed* with silver⟩ **5 :** to form a screw thread on or in ~ *vi* **1 :** to make one's way **2 :** to form a thread when poured from a spoon — **thread·er** *n*

thread·bare \'thred-,ba(ə)r, -,be(ə)r\ *adj* (14c) **1 :** having the nap worn off so that the thread shows **:** SHABBY **2 :** HACKNEYED ⟨~ phrases⟩ ***syn*** see TRITE — **thread·bare·ness** *n*

thread·fin \-,fin\ *n* (ca. 1890) **:** any of a family (Polynemidae) of fishes related to the mullets and having filamentous rays on the lower part of the pectoral fin

thread·worm \-,wərm\ *n* (1802) **:** a long slender nematode worm

thready \-ē\ *adj* (15c) **1 :** consisting of or bearing fibers or filaments ⟨a ~ bark⟩ **2 a :** resembling a thread **:** FILAMENTOUS **b :** tending to form or draw out into strands **:** ROPY **3 :** lacking in fullness, body, or vigor **:** THIN ⟨a ~ voice⟩ — **thread·i·ness** *n*

threap \'thrēp\ *vt* [ME *threpen*, fr. OE *thrēapian*] (bef. 12c) **1** *chiefly Scot* **:** SCOLD, CHIDE **2** *chiefly Scot* **:** to maintain persistently

[1]**threat** \'thret\ *n* [ME *thret* coercion, threat, fr. OE *thrēat* threat, coercion; akin to MHG *drōz* annoyance, L *trudere* to push, thrust] (bef. 12c) **1 :** an expression of intention to inflict evil, injury, or damage **2**

: one that threatens 3 : an indication of something impending ⟨the air held a ~ of rain⟩

[2]**threat** *vb, archaic* (bef. 12c) : THREATEN

threat·en \ˈthret-ᵊn\ *vb* **threat·ened; threat·en·ing** \ˈthret-niŋ, -ᵊn-iŋ\ *vt* (13c) **1** : to utter threats against **2 a** : to give signs or warning of : PORTEND ⟨the clouds ~*ed* rain⟩ **b** : to hang over dangerously : MENACE **3** : to announce as intended or possible ⟨the workers ~*ed* a strike⟩ ~ *vi* **1** : to utter threats **2** : to portend evil — **threat·en·er** \ˈthret-nər, -ᵊn-ər\ *n* — **threat·en·ing·ly** \ˈthret-niŋ-lē, -ᵊn-iŋ-\ *adv*

three \ˈthrē\ *n* [ME, fr. *three,* adj., fr. OE *thrīe* (masc.), *thrēo* (fem. & neut.); akin to OHG *drī* three, L *tres,* Gk *treis*] (bef. 12c) **1** — see NUMBER table **2** : the third in a set or series ⟨the ~ of hearts⟩ **3** : something having three units or members — **three** *adj or pron*

three–bag·ger \-ˈbag-ər\ *n* (1881) : TRIPLE

three–ball \-ˌbȯl\ *adj* (ca. 1890) : relating to or being a golf match in which three players compete against one another with each playing his own ball

three–card monte \ˌthrē-ˌkärd-\ *n* (1854) : a gambling game in which the dealer shows three cards, shuffles them, places them face down, and invites spectators to bet they can identify the location of a particular card

three–col·or \ˈthrē-ˈkəl-ər\ *adj* (1893) : being or relating to a printing or photographic process wherein three primary colors are used to reproduce all the colors of the subject

3–D \ˈthrē-ˈdē\ *n* [*D,* abbr. of *dimensional*] (1951) : the three-dimensional form; *also* : an image or a picture produced in it — **3–D** *adj*

three–deck·er \ˈthrē-ˈdek-ər\ *n* (1795) **1 a** : a warship carrying guns on three decks **b** : a cargo or passenger ship with three full decks **2** : something made with three floors, tiers, or layers; *esp* : a sandwich made of three slices of bread and two fillings

three–dimensional *adj* (ca. 1891) **1** : of or relating to three dimensions **2** : giving the illusion of depth or varying distances — used of an image or a pictorial representation esp. when this illusion is enhanced by stereoscopic means **3** : describing or being described in well-rounded completeness ⟨a ~ analysis of multiple historical processes —L. L. Snyder⟩ **4** : true to life : LIFELIKE

three·fold \ˈthrē-ˌfōld, -ˈfōld\ *adj* (bef. 12c) **1** : having three units or members : TRIPLE **2** : being three times as great or as many — **three-fold** \-ˈfōld\ *adv*

three–gait·ed \-ˈgāt-əd\ *adj, of a horse* (1948) : trained to use the walk, trot, and canter

three–hand·ed \-ˈhan-dəd\ *adj* (1719) : played by three players ⟨~ bridge⟩

Three Hours *n* (ca. 1891) : a service of devotion between noon and three o'clock on Good Friday

three–legged \ˈthrē-ˈleg(-ə)d, -ˈlāg(-ə)d\ *adj* (1596) : having three legs ⟨a ~ stool⟩

three–legged race *n* (1903) : a race between pairs of competitors with each pair having their adjacent legs bound together

three–line octave *n* (ca. 1931) : the musical octave that begins on the second C above middle C — see PITCH illustration

three–mast·er \ˈthrē-ˈmas-tər\ *n* (1883) : a ship having three masts

three–mile limit *n* (ca. 1891) : the limit of the marginal sea of three miles included in the territorial waters of a state

three of a kind : three cards of the same rank in one hand — see POKER illustration

three·pence \ˈthrep-ən(t)s, ˈthrip-, ˈthrəp-, *US also* ˈthrē-pen(t)s\ *n* (1589) **1** *pl* **threepence** *or* **three·penc·es** : a coin worth threepence **2** : the sum of three British pennies

three·pen·ny \ˈthrep-(ə-)nē, ˈthrip-, ˈthrəp-, *US also* ˈthrē-ˌpen-ē\ *adj* (15c) **1** : costing or worth threepence **2** : POOR

three–phase *adj* (ca. 1900) : of, relating to, or operating by means of a combination of three circuits energized by alternating electromotive forces that differ in phase by one third of a cycle

three–piece *adj* (ca. 1909) : consisting of or made in three pieces ⟨a ~ suit⟩

three–point landing *n* (1926) : an airplane landing in which the two main wheels of the landing gear and the tail wheel or skid or nose wheel touch the ground simultaneously

three–quarter *adj* (1677) : extending to three-quarters of the normal full length ⟨a ~ sleeve⟩

three–quarter–bound *adj, of a book* (ca. 1951) : bound like a half-bound book but having the material on the spine extended to cover about one third of the boards — **three–quarter binding** *n*

three–ring circus *n* (ca. 1920) **1** : something wild, confusing, engrossing, or entertaining **2** : a circus with simultaneous performances in three rings

three R's *n pl* [fr. the facetiously used phrase *reading, 'riting, and 'rithmetic*] (1828) **1** : the fundamentals taught in elementary school; *esp* : reading, writing, and arithmetic **2** : the fundamental skills in a field of endeavor

three·score \ˈthrē-ˈskō(ə)r, -ˈskȯ(ə)r\ *adj* (14c) : being three times twenty : SIXTY

three·some \ˈthrē-səm\ *n* (14c) **1** : a group of three persons or things : TRIO **2** : a golf match in which one person plays his ball against the ball of two others playing each stroke alternately

three–spined stickleback \ˌthrē-ˌspīn(d)-\ *n* (ca. 1891) : a stickleback (*Gasterosteus aculeatus*) of fresh and brackish waters that typically has three dorsal spines

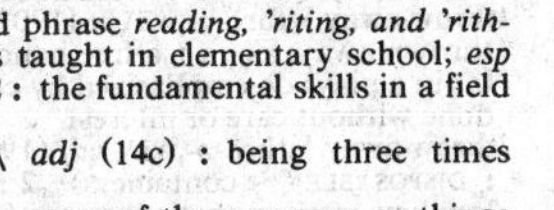

three-spined stickleback

thre·node \ˈthrē-ˌnōd, ˈthren-ˌōd\ *n* (1858) : THRENODY — **thre·nod·ic** \thri-ˈnäd-ik\ *adj* — **thren·o·dist** \ˈthren-əd-əst\ *n*

thren·o·dy \ˈthren-əd-ē\ *n, pl* **-dies** [Gk *thrēnōidia,* fr. *thrēnos* dirge (akin to Skt *dhraṇati* it sounds) + *aeidein* to sing — more at DRONE, ODE] (1634) : a song of lamentation for the dead : ELEGY

thre·o·nine \ˈthrē-ə-ˌnēn\ *n* [prob. fr. *threonic acid* ($C_4H_8O_5$)] (ca. 1938) : a colorless crystalline amino acid $C_4H_9NO_3$ that is essential to normal nutrition

thresh \ˈthrash, ˈthresh\ *vb* [ME *thresshen,* fr. OE *threscan;* akin to OHG *dreskan* to thresh, L *terere* to rub — more at THROW] *vt* (bef. 12c) **1** : to separate seed from (a harvested plant) mechanically; *also* : to separate (seed) in this way **2** : THRASH 4 **3** : to strike repeatedly ~ *vi* **1** : to thresh grain **2** : to strike with or as if with a flail or whip **3** : to toss about

thresh·er *n* (14c) **1** : one that threshes **2** : a large nearly cosmopolitan shark (*Alopias vulpinus*) having a greatly elongated curved upper lobe of its tail with which it is said to thresh the water to round up the fish on which it feeds — see SHARK illustration

threshing machine *n* (1775) : a machine for separating grain crops into grain or seeds and straw

thresh·old \ˈthresh-ˌ(h)ōld\ *n* [ME *thresshold,* fr. OE *threscwald;* akin to ON *threskjǫldr* threshold, OE *threscan* to thresh] (bef. 12c) **1** : the plank, stone, or piece of timber that lies under a door : SILL **2 a** : GATE, DOOR **b** (1) : END, BOUNDARY; *specif* : the end of a runway (2) : the place or point of entering or beginning : OUTSET ⟨on the ~ of a new age⟩ **3 a** : the point at which a physiological or psychological effect begins to be produced **b** : a level, point, or value above which something is true or will take place and below which it is not or will not

threw *past of* THROW

thrice \ˈthrīs\ *adv* [ME *thrie, thries,* alter. (influenced by ME *ones* once) of OE *thriga;* akin to OFris *thria* three times, OE *thrīe* three] (bef. 12c) **1** : three times **2 a** : in a threefold manner or degree **b** : to a high degree

thrift \ˈthrift\ *n* [ME, fr. ON, prosperity, fr. *thrīfask* to thrive] (13c) **1** : healthy and vigorous growth **2** : careful management esp. of money **3** *chiefly Scot* : gainful occupation **4** : any of a genus (*Armeria*) of the plumbago family of tufted acaulescent herbs; *esp* : a scapose herb (*A. maritima*) with pink or white flower heads **5** : a mutual savings bank or savings and loan association — called also *thrift institution*

thrift·less \ˈthrift-ləs\ *adj* (1568) **1** : lacking usefulness or worth **2** : careless, wasteful, or incompetent in handling money or resources : IMPROVIDENT — **thrift·less·ly** *adv* — **thrift·less·ness** *n*

thrift shop *n* (1944) : a shop that sells secondhand articles and esp. clothes and is often run for charitable purposes

thrifty \ˈthrif-tē\ *adj* **thrift·i·er; -est** (14c) **1** : thriving by industry and frugality : PROSPEROUS **2** : growing vigorously **3** : practicing economy and good management : PROVIDENT ***syn*** see SPARING — **thrift·i·ly** \-tə-lē\ *adv* — **thrift·i·ness** \-tē-nəs\ *n*

thrill \ˈthril\ *vb* [ME *thirlen, thrillen* to pierce, fr. OE *thyrlian,* fr. *thyrel* hole, fr. *thurh* through — more at THROUGH] *vt* (bef. 12c) **1 a** : to cause to experience a sudden sharp feeling of excitement **b** : to cause to have a shivering or tingling sensation **2** : to cause to vibrate or tremble perceptibly ~ *vi* **1** : to move or pass so as to cause thrills **2** : to become thrilled: **a** : to experience a sudden sharp excitement **b** : TINGLE, THROB **3** : TREMBLE, VIBRATE — **thrill** *n* — **thrill·ing·ly** \-iŋ-lē\ *adv*

thril·ler \ˈthril-ər\ *n* (1889) : one that thrills; *esp* : a work of fiction or drama designed to hold the interest by the use of a high degree of intrigue, adventure, or suspense

thrips \ˈthrips\ *n, pl* **thrips** [L, woodworm, fr. Gk] (1795) : any of an order (Thysanoptera) of small to minute sucking insects most of which feed often destructively on plant juices

thrive \ˈthrīv\ *vi* **throve** \ˈthrōv\ *or* **thrived; thriv·en** \ˈthriv-ən\ *also* **thrived; thriv·ing** \ˈthrī-viŋ\ [ME *thriven,* fr. ON *thrīfask,* prob. reflexive of *thrīfa* to grasp] (13c) **1** : to grow vigorously : FLOURISH **2** : to gain in wealth or possessions : PROSPER **3** : to progress toward or realize a goal — **thriv·er** \ˈthrī-vər\ *n*

thriv·ing *adj* (15c) : characterized by success or prosperity — **thriv·ing·ly** \ˈthrī-viŋ-lē\ *adv*

thro \(ˈ)thrü\ *prep, archaic* (15c) : THROUGH

[1]**throat** \ˈthrōt\ *n* [ME *throte,* fr. OE; akin to OHG *drozza* throat] (bef. 12c) **1 a** (1) : the part of the neck in front of the spinal column (2) : the passage through the neck to the stomach and lungs **b** (1) : VOICE (2) : the seat of the voice **2** : something resembling the throat esp. in being an entrance, a passageway, a constriction, or a narrowed part: as **a** : the orifice of a tubular organ esp. of a plant **b** : the opening in the vamp of a shoe at the instep **c** : the part of a tennis racket that connects the head with the shaft **3** : the curved part of an anchor's arm where it joins the shank — **at each other's throats** : in open and aggressive conflict

[2]**throat** *vt* (1611) **1** : to utter in the throat : MUTTER **2** : to sing or enunciate in a throaty voice

throat·ed \ˈthrōt-əd\ *adj* (ca. 1530) : having a throat esp. of a specified kind — usu. used in combination ⟨white-*throated*⟩

throat·latch \-ˌlach\ *n* (1794) **1** : a strap of a bridle or halter passing under a horse's throat **2** : the part of a horse's throat around which the throatlatch passes — see HORSE illustration

throaty \ˈthrōt-ē\ *adj* **throat·i·er; -est** (1645) **1** : uttered or produced from low in the throat ⟨a ~ voice⟩ **2** : heavy, thick, and deep as if from the throat ⟨~ notes of a horn⟩ — **throat·i·ly** \ˈthrōt-ᵊl-ē\ *adv* — **throat·i·ness** \ˈthrōt-ē-nəs\ *n*

[1]**throb** \ˈthräb\ *vi* **throbbed; throb·bing** [ME *throbben*] (14c) **1** : to pulsate or pound with abnormal force or rapidity **2** : to beat or vibrate rhythmically — **throb·ber** *n*

[2]**throb** *n* (1579) : BEAT, PULSE

throe \ˈthrō\ *n* [ME *thrawe, throwe,* fr. OE *thrawu, thrēa* threat, pang; akin to OHG *drawa* threat, Gk *trauma* wound, *tetrainein* to bore — more at THROW] (13c) **1** : PANG, SPASM ⟨death ~*s*⟩ ⟨~*s* of childbirth⟩ **2** *pl* : a hard or painful struggle ⟨the ~*s* of revolutionary social change —M. D. Geismar⟩

\ə\ abut \ᵊ\ kitten, F table \ər\ further \a\ ash \ā\ ace \ä\ cot, cart \au̇\ out \ch\ chin \e\ bet \ē\ easy \g\ go \i\ hit \ī\ ice \j\ job \ŋ\ sing \ō\ go \ȯ\ law \ȯi\ boy \th\ thin \t͟h\ the \ü\ loot \u̇\ foot \y\ yet \zh\ vision \à, k̲, ⁿ, œ, œ̄, ue, ue̅, ʸ\ see Guide to Pronunciation

thromb- *or* **thrombo-** *comb form* [Gk *thrombos* clot —more at ATROPHY] : blood clot : clotting of blood ⟨*thromb*in⟩ ⟨*thrombo*plastic⟩
throm·bin \ˈthräm-bən\ *n* [ISV] (1898) : a proteolytic enzyme that is formed from prothrombin and facilitates the clotting of blood by catalyzing conversion of fibrinogen to fibrin
throm·bo·cyte \-bə-ˌsīt\ *n* [ISV] (1893) : BLOOD PLATELET; *also* : an invertebrate cell with similar function — **throm·bo·cyt·ic** \ˌthräm-bə-ˈsit-ik\ *adj*
throm·bo·cy·to·pe·nia \ˌthräm-bə-ˌsīt-ə-ˈpē-nē-ə, -nyə\ *n* [NL, fr. ISV *thrombocyte* + Gk *penia* poverty, lack; perh. akin to L *sponte* voluntarily —more at SPIN] (1923) : persistent decrease in the number of blood platelets that is usu. associated with hemorrhagic conditions — **throm·bo·cy·to·pe·nic** \-nik\ *adj*
throm·bo·em·bo·lism \ˌthräm-bō-ˈem-bə-ˌliz-əm\ *n* (1907) : the blocking of a blood vessel by a particle that has broken away from a blood clot at its site of formation — **throm·bo·em·bol·ic** \-em-ˈbäl-ik\ *adj*
throm·bo·ki·nase \ˌthräm-bō-ˈkī-ˌnās, -ˌnāz\ *n* [ISV] (1908) : THROMBOPLASTIN
throm·bo·phle·bi·tis \-fli-ˈbīt-əs\ *n* [NL] (ca. 1890) : inflammation of a vein with formation of a thrombus
throm·bo·plas·tic \ˌthräm-bō-ˈplas-tik\ *adj* [ISV] (1911) : initiating or accelerating the clotting of blood
throm·bo·plas·tin \-ˈplas-tən\ *n* [ISV, fr. *thromboplastic*] (1911) : a complex enzyme found esp. in blood platelets that functions in the clotting of blood
throm·bo·sis \thräm-ˈbō-səs, thrəm-\ *n, pl* **-bo·ses** \-ˌsēz\ [NL, fr. Gk *thrombōsis* clotting, deriv. of *thrombos* clot — more at ATROPHY] (ca. 1860) : the formation or presence of a blood clot within a blood vessel during life — **throm·bot·ic** \-ˈbät-ik\ *adj*
throm·box·ane \thräm-ˈbäk-ˌsān\ *n* [*thromb-* + *ox-* + *-ane*] (1975) : any of several potent regulators of cellular function that were first isolated from thrombocytes
throm·bus \ˈthräm-bəs\ *n, pl* **throm·bi** \-ˌbī, -ˌbē\ [NL, fr. Gk *thrombos* clot] (ca. 1693) : a clot of blood formed within a blood vessel and remaining attached to its place of origin — compare EMBOLUS
1throne \ˈthrōn\ *n* [ME *trone, throne,* fr. OF *trone,* fr. L *thronus,* fr. Gk *thronos* — more at FIRM] (13c) **1 a :** the chair of state of a king, prince, or bishop **b :** the seat of a deity **2 :** royal power and dignity : SOVEREIGNTY **3** *pl* **:** an order of angels — see CELESTIAL HIERARCHY
2throne *vb* **throned; thron·ing** *vt* (14c) **1 :** to seat on a throne **2 :** to invest with kingly rank or power ~ *vi* **1 :** to sit on a throne **2 :** to hold kingly power
throne room *n* (1864) : a formal audience room containing the throne of a sovereign
1throng \ˈthrȯŋ\ *n* [ME *thrang, throng,* fr. OE *thrang, gethrang;* akin to OE *thringan* to press, crowd, OHG *dringan,* Lith *trenkti* to jolt, L *truncus* trunk, torso] (bef. 12c) **1 a :** a multitude of assembled persons **b :** a large number : HOST **2 a :** a crowding together of many persons **b :** PRESSURE ⟨this ~ of business —S. R. Crockett⟩ ***syn*** see CROWD
2throng *vb* **thronged; throng·ing** \ˈthrȯŋ-iŋ\ *vt* (1534) **1 :** to crowd upon : PRESS **2 :** to crowd into : PACK ⟨shoppers ~*ing* the streets⟩ ~ *vi* **:** to crowd together in great numbers
thros·tle \ˈthräs-əl\ *n* [ME, fr. OE — more at THRUSH] (bef. 12c) : 1THRUSH 1; *specif* : SONG THRUSH
1throt·tle \ˈthrät-ᵊl\ *vb* **throt·tled; throt·tling** \ˈthrät-liŋ, -ᵊl-iŋ\ [ME *throtlen,* fr. *throte* throat] *vt* (15c) **1 a (1) :** to compress the throat of : CHOKE **(2) :** to kill by such action **b :** to prevent or check expression or activity of : SUPPRESS **2 a :** to decrease the flow of (as steam or fuel to an engine) by a valve **b :** to regulate and esp. to reduce the speed of (as an engine) by such means **c :** to vary the thrust of (a rocket engine) during flight ~ *vi* **:** to throttle something (as an engine) — usu. used with *back* or *down* ⟨the pilot *throttled* back⟩ — **throt·tler** \-lər, -ᵊl-ər\ *n*
2throttle *n* [perh. alter. of E dial. *thropple* (throat)] (1547) **1 a :** THROAT 1a **b :** TRACHEA 1 **2 a :** a valve for regulating the supply of a fluid (as steam) to an engine; *esp* **:** the valve controlling the volume of vaporized fuel charge delivered to the cylinders of an internal-combustion engine **b :** the lever controlling this valve **c :** the condition of being throttled — **at full throttle :** at full speed
throt·tle·able \ˈthrät-ᵊl-ə-bəl\ *adj* (1963) : capable of having the thrust varied — used of a rocket engine
throt·tle·hold \ˈthrät-ᵊl-ˌhōld\ *n* (1935) : a vicious, strangling, or stultifying control
1through \(ˈ)thrü\ *prep* [ME *thurh, thruh, through,* fr. OE *thurh;* akin to OHG *durh* through, L *trans* across, beyond, Skt *tarati* he crosses over] (bef. 12c) **1 a (1)** — used as a function word to indicate movement into at one side or point and out at another and esp. the opposite side of ⟨drove a nail ~ the board⟩ **(2) :** by way of ⟨left ~ the door⟩ **(3)** — used as a function word to indicate passage from one end or boundary to another ⟨a highway ~ the forest⟩ ⟨a road ~ the desert⟩ **(4) :** without stopping for : PAST ⟨drove ~ a red light⟩ **b** — used as a function word to indicate passage into and out of a treatment, handling, or process ⟨the matter has already passed ~ his hands⟩ **2** — used as a function word to indicate means, agency, or intermediacy: as **a :** by means of : by the agency of **b :** because of ⟨failed ~ ignorance⟩ **c :** by common descent from or relationship with ⟨related ~ their grandfather⟩ **3 a :** over the whole surface or extent of : THROUGHOUT ⟨homes scattered ~ the valley⟩ **b** — used as a function word to indicate movement within a large expanse ⟨flew ~ the air⟩ **c** — used as a function word to indicate exposure to a specified set of conditions ⟨put her ~ hell⟩ **4** — used as a function word to indicate a period of time: as **a :** during the entire period of ⟨all ~ her life⟩ **b :** from the beginning to the end of ⟨the tower stood ~ the earthquake⟩ **c :** to and including ⟨Monday ~ Friday⟩ **5 a** — used as a function word to indicate completion or exhaustion ⟨got ~ the book⟩ ⟨went ~ a fortune in a year⟩ **b** — used as a function word to indicate acceptance or approval esp. by an official body ⟨got the bill ~ the legislature⟩
2through \ˈthrü\ *adv* (bef. 12c) **1 :** from one end or side to the other **2 a :** from beginning to end **b :** to completion, conclusion, or accomplishment ⟨see it ~⟩ **3 :** to the core : COMPLETELY ⟨soaked ~⟩ **4 :** into the open : OUT ⟨break ~⟩
3through \ˈthrü\ *adj* (1523) **1 a :** extending from one surface to another ⟨a ~ mortise⟩ **b :** admitting free or continuous passage : DIRECT ⟨a ~ road⟩ **2 a (1) :** going from point of origin to destination without change or reshipment ⟨a ~ train⟩ **(2) :** of or relating to such movement ⟨a ~ ticket⟩ **b :** initiated at and destined for points outside a local zone ⟨~ traffic⟩ **3 a :** arrived at completion or accomplishment ⟨he is ~ with the job⟩ **b :** WASHED-UP, FINISHED
through and through *adv* (15c) : in every way : THOROUGHLY
through–com·posed \ˌthrü-kəm-ˈpōzd\ *adj* [trans. of G *durchkomponiert*] *of a song* (ca. 1903) : having new music provided for each stanza — compare STROPHIC
through·ith·er *or* **through·oth·er** \ˈthrü-(ə-)t͟hər\ *adv* [ˈ*through* + *other*] *chiefly Scot* (1596) : in confusion : PROMISCUOUSLY
through·ly \ˈthrü-lē\ *adv, archaic* (15c) : in a thorough manner
1through·out \thrü-ˈau̇t\ *adv* (bef. 12c) **1 :** in or to every part : EVERYWHERE ⟨of one color ~⟩ **2 :** during the whole time or action : from beginning to end ⟨remained loyal ~⟩
2throughout *prep* (bef. 12c) **1 :** all the way from one end to the other of : in or to every part of ⟨cities ~ the United States⟩ **2 :** during the whole course or period of ⟨troubled him ~ his life⟩
through·put \ˈthrü-ˌpu̇t\ *n* (1922) : OUTPUT, PRODUCTION ⟨the ~ of a computer⟩
through street *n* (1930) : a street on which the through movement of traffic is given preference
through·way *var of* THRUWAY
throve *past of* THRIVE
1throw \ˈthrō\ *vb* **threw** \ˈthrü\; **thrown** \ˈthrōn\; **throw·ing** [ME *thrawen, throwen* to cause to twist, throw, fr. OE *thrāwan* to cause to twist or turn; akin to OHG *drāen* to turn, L *terere* to rub, Gk *tribein* to rub, *tetrainein* to bore, pierce] *vt* (14c) **1 a :** to propel through the air by a forward motion of the hand and arm ⟨~ a baseball⟩ **b :** to propel through the air in any manner ⟨a rifle that can ~ a bullet five miles⟩ **2 a :** to cause to fall ⟨*threw* his opponent⟩ **b :** to cause to fall off : UNSEAT ⟨the horse *threw* his rider⟩ **c :** to get the better of : OVERCOME ⟨the problem didn't ~ her⟩ **3 a :** to fling (oneself) precipitately ⟨*threw* himself down on the sofa⟩ **b :** to drive or impel violently : DASH ⟨the ship was *thrown* on a reef⟩ **4 a (1) :** to put in a particular position or condition ⟨*threw* her arms around him⟩ **(2) :** to put on or off hastily or carelessly ⟨*threw* on a coat⟩ **b :** to bring to bear : EXERT ⟨*threw* all his influence into the boy's defense⟩ **c :** BUILD, CONSTRUCT ⟨*threw* a pontoon bridge over the river⟩ **5 :** to form or shape on a potter's wheel **6 :** to deliver (a blow) in or as if in boxing **7 :** to twist two or more filaments of into a thread or yarn **8 a :** to make a cast of (dice or a specified number on dice) **b :** ROLL 1a ⟨~ a bowling ball⟩ **9 :** to give up : ABANDON **10 :** to send forth : PROJECT ⟨the setting sun *threw* long shadows⟩ **11 :** to make (oneself) dependent : commit (oneself) for help, support, or protection ⟨*threw* himself on the mercy of the court⟩ **12 :** to indulge in : give way to ⟨*threw* a temper tantrum⟩ **13 :** to bring forth : give birth to : SIRE, PRODUCE ⟨~s a good crop⟩ ⟨*threw* large litters⟩ **14 :** to lose intentionally ⟨~ a game⟩ **15 :** to move (a lever) so as to connect or disconnect parts of a clutch or switch; *also* **:** to make or break (a connection) with a lever **16 :** to give by way of entertainment ⟨~ a party⟩ ~ *vi* **:** CAST, HURL — **throw·er** \ˈthrō(-ə)r\ *n*

syn THROW, CAST, TOSS, FLING, HURL, PITCH, SLING mean to cause to move swiftly through space by a propulsive movement or a propelling force. THROW is general and interchangeable with the other terms but may specif. imply a distinctive motion with bent arm; CAST usu. implies lightness in the thing thrown and sometimes a scattering; TOSS suggests a light or careless or aimless throwing and may imply an upward motion; FLING stresses a violent throwing; HURL implies power as in throwing a massive weight; PITCH suggests throwing carefully at a target; SLING stresses either the use of whirling momentum in throwing or directness of aim.

— **throw one's weight around** *or* **throw one's weight about :** to exercise influence or authority esp. to an excessive degree or in an objectionable manner — **throw together 1 :** to put together in a hurried and usu. careless manner ⟨a bookshelf hastily *thrown together*⟩ **2 :** to bring into casual association ⟨different kinds of people are *thrown together* —Richard Sennett⟩
2throw *n* (ca. 1530) **1 a :** an act of throwing, hurling, or flinging **b (1) :** an act of throwing dice **(2) :** the number thrown with a cast of dice **c :** a method of throwing an opponent in wrestling or judo **2 :** the distance a missile may be thrown or light rays may be projected **3 :** an undertaking involving chance or danger : RISK, VENTURE **4 :** the amount of vertical displacement produced by a geological fault **5 a :** the extreme movement given to a pivoted or reciprocating piece by a cam, crank, or eccentric : STROKE **b :** the length of the radius of a crank or the virtual crank radius of an eccentric or cam **6 a :** a light coverlet (as for a bed) **b :** a woman's scarf or light wrap **7 :** an object or individual regarded as a distinct member of a kind or class : UNIT ⟨copies are to be sold at $5 a ~ —Harvey Breit⟩
1throw·away \ˈthrō-ə-ˌwā\ *n* (1903) **1 :** one that is or is designed to be thrown away: as **a :** a free handbill or circular **b :** a line of dialogue (as in a play) de-emphasized by casual delivery **2 :** something made or done without care or interest
2throw·away \ˌthrō-ə-ˌwā\ *adj* (1905) **1 :** designed to be thrown away : DISPOSABLE ⟨~ containers⟩ **2 :** written or spoken (as in a play) in a low-key or unemphatic manner ⟨~ lines⟩ **3 :** NONCHALANT, CASUAL
throw away \ˌthrō-ə-ˈwā\ *vt* (1530) **1 a :** to get rid of as worthless or unnecessary **b :** DISCARD 1b **2 a :** to use in a foolish or wasteful manner : SQUANDER **b :** to fail to take advantage of : WASTE **3 :** to make (as a line in a play) unemphatic by casual delivery
throw·back \ˈthrō-ˌbak\ *n* (1889) **1 a :** reversion to an earlier type or phase : ATAVISM **b :** an instance or product of atavistic reversion **c :** one that is suggestive of or suited to an earlier time or style ⟨his manners were a ~ to a more polite era⟩ **2 :** FLASHBACK
throw back \(ˈ)thrō-ˈbak\ *vt* (1840) **1 :** to delay the progress or advance of : CHECK **2 :** to cause to rely : make dependent ⟨they are *thrown back* upon . . . native intelligence —Michael Novak⟩ **3 :** REFLECT ~ *vi* **:** to revert to an earlier type or phase
throw down *vt* (14c) **1 :** to cause to fall : OVERTHROW **2 :** PRECIPITATE **3 :** to cast off : DISCARD
throw–in \ˈthrō-ˌin\ *n* (1898) : an act or instance of throwing a ball in: as **a :** a throw made from the touchline in soccer to put the ball back in play after it has gone into touch **b :** a throw made by an outfielder

to the infield in baseball **c** : a throw made from outside the boundaries in basketball to put the ball back in play after it has gone out of bounds

throw in \(ˈ)thrō-ˈin\ *vt* (1678) **1** : to add as a gratuity or supplement **2** : to introduce or interject in the course of something : CONTRIBUTE ⟨they *throw in* some . . . sound effects on several songs —Tom Phillips⟩ **3** : DISTRIBUTE 3b **4 a** : to cause (as gears) to mesh **b** : ENGAGE ⟨*throw in* the clutch⟩ ~ *vi* : to enter into association or partnership : JOIN ⟨agrees to *throw in* with a crooked ex-cop —*Newsweek*⟩ — **throw in the sponge** *or* **throw in the towel** : to abandon a struggle or contest : acknowledge defeat : GIVE UP

throw off *vt* (15c) **1 a** : to free oneself from : get rid of ⟨threw *off* his inhibitions⟩ **b** : to cast off often in a hurried or vigorous manner : ABANDON ⟨*threw off* all restraint⟩ **c** : DISTRACT, DIVERT ⟨dogs *thrown off* by a false scent⟩ **2** : EMIT, GIVE OFF ⟨stacks *throwing off* plumes of smoke⟩ **3** : to produce in an offhand manner : execute with speed or facility ⟨some little . . . tune that the composer had *thrown off* —James Hilton⟩ **4 a** : to cause to depart from an expected or desired course ⟨mistakes *threw* his calculations *off* a bit⟩ **b** : to cause to make a mistake : MISLEAD ~ *vi* **1** : to begin hunting **2** : to make derogatory comments

throw out \(ˈ)thrō-ˈau̇t\ *vt* (1526) **1 a** : to remove from a place, office, or employment usu. in a sudden or unexpected manner **b** : to get rid of as worthless or unnecessary **2** : to give expression to : UTTER ⟨*threw out* a remark . . . that utterly confounded him —Jean Stafford⟩ **3** : to dismiss from acceptance or consideration : REJECT ⟨the testimony was *thrown out*⟩ **4** : to make visible or manifest : DISPLAY ⟨the signal was *thrown out* for the . . . fleet to prepare for action —Archibald Duncan⟩ **5** : to leave behind : OUTDISTANCE **6** : to give forth from within : EMIT **7 a** : to send out **b** : to cause to project : EXTEND **8** : CONFUSE, DISCONCERT ⟨automobiles in line blocking the road . . . *threw* the whole schedule *out* —F. D. Roosevelt⟩ **9** : to cause to stand out : make prominent **10** : to make a throw that enables a teammate to put out (a base runner) **11** : DISENGAGE ⟨*throw out* the clutch⟩

throw over *vt* (1836) **1** : to forsake despite bonds of attachment or duty **2** : to refuse to accept : REJECT

throw pillow *n* (1956) : a small pillow used esp. as a decorative accessory

throw rug *n* (1928) : SCATTER RUG

throw·ster \ˈthrō-stər\ *n* (15c) : one who throws textile filaments

throw up *vt* (15c) **1** : to raise quickly **2** : GIVE UP, QUIT ⟨the urge . . . to *throw up* all intellectual work —Norman Mailer⟩ **3** : to build hurriedly ⟨new houses *thrown up* almost overnight⟩ **4** : VOMIT **5** : to bring forth : PRODUCE **6** : to make distinct esp. by contrast : cause to stand out **7** : to mention repeatedly by way of reproach ~ *vi* : VOMIT — **throw up one's hands** : to admit defeat ⟨in the end *throws up his hands* in despair —Frank Conroy⟩

thru *var of* THROUGH

[1]**thrum** \ˈthrəm\ *n* [ME, fr. OE *-thrum* (in *tungethrum* ligament of the tongue); akin to OHG *drum* fragment, L *terminus* boundary, end — more at TERM] (14c) **1 a** (1) : a fringe of warp threads left on the loom after the cloth has been removed (2) : one of these warp threads **b** : a tuft or short piece of rope yarn used in thrumming canvas — usu. used in pl. **c** : BIT, PARTICLE **2** : a hair, fiber, or threadlike leaf on a plant; *also* : a tuft or fringe of such structures — **thrum** *adj*

[2]**thrum** *vt* **thrummed; thrum·ming** (1525) **1** : to furnish with thrums : FRINGE **2** : to insert short pieces of rope yarn or spun yarn in (a piece of canvas) to make a rough surface or a mat which can be wrapped about rigging to prevent chafing

[3]**thrum** *vb* **thrummed; thrum·ming** [imit.] *vi* (1592) **1** : to play or pluck a stringed instrument idly : STRUM **2** : to sound with a monotonous hum ~ *vt* **1** : to play (as a stringed instrument) in an idle or relaxed manner **2** : to recite tiresomely or monotonously

[4]**thrum** *n* (1798) : the monotonous sound of thrumming

[1]**thrush** \ˈthrəsh\ *n* [ME *thrusche,* fr. OE *thrysce;* akin to OE *throstle* thrush, OHG *droscala,* L *turdus*] (bef. 12c) **1** : any of numerous small or medium-sized passerine birds (family Turdidae) which are mostly of a plain color often with spotted underparts and many of which are excellent singers **2** : a bird held to resemble a thrush

[2]**thrush** *n* [prob. of Scand origin; akin to Dan & Norw *trøske* thrush] (1665) **1** : a disease that is caused by a fungus (*Candida albicans*), occurs esp. in infants and children, and is marked by white patches in the oral cavity **2** : a suppurative disorder of the feet in various animals

[1]**thrust** \ˈthrəst\ *vb* **thrust; thrust·ing** [ME *thrusten, thristen,* fr. ON *thrȳsta*] *vt* (13c) **1** : to push or drive with force : SHOVE **2** : to cause to enter or pierce something by or as if by pushing ⟨~ a dagger into her heart⟩ **3** : EXTEND, SPREAD **4** : STAB, PIERCE **5 a** : to put (as an unwilling person) forcibly into a course of action or position ⟨was *thrust* into power⟩ **b** : to introduce often improperly into a position : INTERPOLATE **6** : to press, force, or impose the acceptance of upon someone ⟨~ new responsibilities upon him⟩ ~ *vi* **1 a** : to force an entrance or passage **b** : to push forward : press onward **c** : to push upward : PROJECT **2** : to make a thrust, stab, or lunge with or as if with a pointed weapon ⟨~ at her with a knife⟩ ***syn*** see PUSH

[2]**thrust** *n* (1586) **1 a** : a push or lunge with a pointed weapon **b** (1) : a verbal attack (2) : a military assault **2 a** : a strong continued pressure **b** : the sideways force or pressure of one part of a structure against another part (as of an arch against an abutment) **c** (1) : the force exerted endways through a propeller shaft to give forward motion (2) : the forward directed reaction force produced by a high-speed jet of fluid discharged rearward from a nozzle (as in a jet airplane) **d** : a nearly horizontal geological fault **3 a** : a forward or upward push **b** : a movement (as by a group of people) in a specified direction **4 a** : salient or essential element or meaning **b** : principal concern or objective

thrust·er *also* **thrust·or** \ˈthrəs-tər\ *n* (1597) : one that thrusts; *esp* : REACTION ENGINE

thrust·ful \ˈthrəst-fəl\ *adj, Brit* (1909) : characterized by thrust : AGGRESSIVE ⟨~ young man on the make —*Current Literature*⟩

thrust stage *n* [*thrust,* pp. of [1]*thrust*] (1965) : a stage surrounded on three sides by the audience; *also* : a forestage that is extended into the auditorium to increase the stage area

thru·way \ˈthrü-ˌwā\ *n* (1943) : EXPRESSWAY

[1]**thud** \ˈthəd\ *vi* **thud·ded; thud·ding** [prob. fr. ME *thudden* to thrust, fr. OE *thyddan*] (bef. 12c) : to move or strike so as to make a thud

[2]**thud** *n* (1787) **1** : BLOW **2** : a dull sound : THUMP

thug \ˈthəg\ *n* [Hindi *ṭhag,* lit., thief, fr. Skt *sthaga* rogue, fr. *sthagati* he covers, conceals — more at THATCH] (ca. 1810) : a brutal ruffian or assassin : GANGSTER, KILLER — **thug·gery** \ˈthəg(-ə)-rē\ *n* — **thug·gish** \ˈthəg-ish\ *adj*

thu·ja \ˈth(y)ü-jə\ *n* [NL *Thuja,* fr. ML *thuia,* a cedar, fr. Gk *thyia*] (ca. 1760) : any of a genus (*Thuja*) of evergreen shrubs and trees of the pine family; *esp* : ARBORVITAE

Thu·le \ˈth(y)ü-lē\ *n* [ME *Tyle,* fr. OE, fr. L *Thule, Thyle,* fr. Gk *Thoulē, Thylē*] (bef. 12c) : the northernmost part of the habitable ancient world

thu·li·um \ˈth(y)ü-lē-əm\ *n* [NL, fr. L *Thule*] (ca. 1879) : a trivalent metallic element of the rare-earth group — see ELEMENT table

[1]**thumb** \ˈthəm\ *n* [ME *thoume, thoumbe,* fr. OE *thūma;* akin to OHG *thūmo* thumb, L *tumēre* to swell, *tuber* swelling, hump, Gk *sōs* safe, whole, *sōros* heap] (bef. 12c) **1** : the digit of the human hand that is closest to the trunk when the hand extends forward with the palm down; *also* : a corresponding digit in lower animals **2** : the part of a glove or mitten that covers the thumb **3** : a convex molding : OVOLO — **all thumbs** : extremely awkward or clumsy — **under one's thumb** *or* **under the thumb** : under control : in a state of subservience ⟨her father did not have her that much *under his thumb* —Hamilton Basso⟩

[2]**thumb** *vt* (1644) **1 a** : to leaf through (pages) with the thumb : TURN **b** : to soil or wear by or as if by repeated thumbing ⟨a badly ~*ed* book⟩ **2** : to request or obtain (a ride) in a passing automobile by signaling with the thumb ~ *vi* **1** : to turn over pages ⟨~ through a book⟩ **2** : to travel by thumbing rides : HITCH-HIKE ⟨~*ed* across the country⟩ — **thumb one's nose 1** : to place the thumb at one's nose and extend the fingers as a gesture of scorn or defiance **2** : to express disdain or defiance ⟨*thumb their nose* at opulence —*Sales Management*⟩

thumb·hole \ˈthəm-ˌhōl\ *n* (1859) **1** : an opening in which to insert the thumb **2** : a hole in a wind musical instrument opened or closed by the thumb

thumb index *n* (1903) : a series of notches cut in the fore edge of a book to facilitate reference

[1]**thumb·nail** \ˈthəm-ˌnāl, -ˈnā(ə)l\ *n* (1604) : the nail of the thumb

[2]**thumb·nail** \ˌthəm-ˌnāl\ *adj* (1852) : CONCISE, BRIEF ⟨a ~ sketch⟩

thumb piano *n* (1949) : MBIRA

thumb·print \ˈthəm-ˌprint\ *n* (1900) : an impression made by the thumb; *esp* : a print made by the inside of the first joint

thumb·screw \-ˌskrü\ *n* (1794) **1** : a screw having a flat-sided or knurled head so that it may be turned by the thumb and forefinger **2** : an instrument of torture for compressing the thumb by a screw

thumbs–down \ˈthəmz-ˈdau̇n\ *n* (1889) : an instance or gesture of rejection, disapproval, or condemnation

thumbs–up \ˈthəm-ˈzəp\ *n* (ca. 1922) : an instance or gesture of approval or encouragement

[1]**thumb·tack** \ˈthəm-ˌtak\ *n* (1884) : a tack with a broad flat head for pressing into a surface with the thumb

[2]**thumbtack** *vt* (1914) : to fasten with a thumbtack

[1]**thump** \ˈthəmp\ *vb* [imit.] *vt* (1537) **1** : to strike or beat with or as if with something thick or heavy so as to cause a dull sound **2** : POUND, KNOCK **3** : WHIP, THRASH **4** : to produce (music) mechanically or in a mechanical manner — usu. used with *out* ⟨~*ed* out a tune on the piano⟩ ~ *vi* **1 a** : to inflict a thump **b** : to make a thumping sound **2** : to make a vigorous endorsement ⟨got a couple of . . . senators to ~ for him —*N.Y. Herald Tribune*⟩ — **thump·er** *n*

[2]**thump** *n* (ca. 1552) : a blow or knock with or as if with something blunt or heavy; *also* : the sound made by such a blow

thump·ing *adj* [*thumping,* prp. of [1]*thump*] (1576) : impressively large, great, or excellent ⟨a ~ majority⟩

[1]**thun·der** \ˈthən-dər\ *n* [ME *thoner, thunder,* fr. OE *thunor;* akin to OHG *thonar* thunder, L *tonare* to thunder] (bef. 12c) **1** : the sound that follows a flash of lightning and is caused by sudden expansion of the air in the path of the electrical discharge **2** : a loud utterance or threat **3** : BANG, RUMBLE ⟨the ~ of big guns⟩

[2]**thunder** *vb* **thun·dered; thun·der·ing** \-d(ə-)riŋ\ *vi* (bef. 12c) **1 a** : to produce thunder — usu. used impersonally ⟨it ~*ed*⟩ **b** : to give forth a sound that resembles thunder ⟨horses ~*ed* down the road⟩ **2** : ROAR, SHOUT ~ *vt* **1** : to utter loudly : ROAR **2** : to strike with a sound likened to thunder — **thun·der·er** \-dər-ər\ *n*

thun·der·bird \ˈthən-dər-ˌbərd\ *n* (ca. 1827) : a bird that causes lightning and thunder in American Indian myth

thun·der·bolt \-ˌbōlt\ *n* (15c) **1 a** : a single discharge of lightning with the accompanying thunder **b** : an imaginary elongated mass cast as a missile to earth in the lightning flash **2 a** : a person or thing that resembles lightning in suddenness, effectiveness, or destructive power **b** : a vehement threat or censure

thun·der·clap \-ˌklap\ *n* (14c) **1** : a clap of thunder **2** : something sharp, loud, or sudden like a clap of thunder

thun·der·cloud \-ˌklau̇d\ *n* (1697) : a cloud charged with electricity and producing lightning and thunder

thunder egg *n* (1941) : chalcedony in rounded concretionary nodules

thun·der·head \-ˌhed\ *n* (1853) : a rounded mass of cumulus cloud often appearing before a thunderstorm

thun·der·ing *adj* [*thundering,* prp. of [2]*thunder*] (1543) : awesomely great, intense, or unusual — **thun·der·ing·ly** \-d(ə-)riŋ-lē\ *adv*

thunder lizard *n* [trans. of NL *brontosaurus*] (ca. 1960) : BRONTOSAURUS

thun·der·ous \ˈthən-d(ə-)rəs\ *adj* (1582) : producing thunder; *also* : making or accompanied by a noise like thunder ⟨~ applause⟩ — **thun·der·ous·ly** *adv*

thun·der·peal \ˈthən-dər-ˌpēl\ *n* (1804) : THUNDERCLAP

thun·der·show·er \-ˌshau̇(-ə)r\ *n* (1699) : a shower accompanied by lightning and thunder

thun·der·stone \-ˌstōn\ *n* (1598) **1** *archaic* : THUNDERBOLT 1b **2** : any of various stones (as a meteorite or an ancient artifact) that are the probable source of the imaginary thunderbolt
thun·der·storm \-ˌstȯ(ə)rm\ *n* (1652) : a storm accompanied by lightning and thunder
thun·der·strike \-ˌstrīk\ *vt* **-struck** \-ˌstrək\; **-struck** *also* **-strick·en** \-ˌstrik-ən\; **-strik·ing** \-ˌstrī-kiŋ\ (1586) **1** : to strike dumb : ASTONISH **2** *archaic* : to strike by or as if by lightning
thun·der·stroke \-ˌstrōk\ *n* (1587) : a stroke of or as if of lightning with the attendant thunder
thunk \ˈthəŋk\ *n* [imit.] (1947) : a flat hollow sound
thu·ri·ble \ˈth(y)u̇r-ə-bəl, ˈthər-\ *n* [ME *turrible,* fr. MF *thurible,* fr. L *thuribulum,* fr. *thur-, thus* incense, fr. Gk *thyos* incense, sacrifice, fr. *thyein* to sacrifice — more at THYME] (15c) : CENSER
thu·ri·fer \-ə-fər\ *n* [NL, fr. L *thurifer,* adj., incense-bearing, fr. *thur-, thus* + *-ifer* -iferous] (1853) : one who carries a censer in a liturgical service
Thu·rin·ger \ˈth(y)u̇r-ən-jər\ *n* [G *thüringerwurst,* fr. *thüringer* Thuringian + *wurst* sausage] (1923) : a mildly seasoned fresh or smoked sausage
Thu·rin·gian \th(y)u̇-ˈrin-j(ē-)ən\ *n* (1618) **1** : a member of an ancient Germanic people whose kingdom was overthrown by the Franks in the 6th century **2** : a native or inhabitant of Thuringia — **Thuringian** *adj*
thurl \ˈthər(-ə)l\ *n* [perh. fr. E dial., gaunt] : the hip joint in cattle — see COW illustration
Thurs·day \ˈthərz-dē, -(ˌ)dā\ *n* [ME, fr. OE *thursdæg,* fr. ON *thōrsdagr;* akin to OE *thunresdæg* Thursday, ON *Thōrr* Thor, OE *thunor* thunder — more at THUNDER] (bef. 12c) : the fifth day of the week — **Thurs·days** \-dēz\ *adv*
thus \ˈt͟həs\ *adv* [ME, fr. OE; akin to MD *dus* thus, OE *thæt,* neut. demonstrative pron. — more at THAT] (bef. 12c) **1** : in this or that manner or way **2** : to this degree or extent : SO **3** : because of this or that : HENCE, CONSEQUENTLY **4** : as an example
thus·ly \-lē\ *adv* (1865) : in this manner : THUS
[1]**thwack** \ˈthwak\ *vt* [imit.] (1530) : to strike with or as if with something flat or heavy : WHACK
[2]**thwack** *n* (1587) : a heavy blow : WHACK
[1]**thwart** \ˈthwȯ(ə)rt\ *vt* [ME *thwerten,* fr. *thwert,* adv.] (13c) **1 a** : to run counter to so as to effectively oppose or baffle : CONTRAVENE **b** : to oppose successfully : defeat the hopes or aspirations of **2** : to pass through or across ***syn*** see FRUSTRATE — **thwart·er** *n*
[2]**thwart** \ˈthwȯ(ə)rt, *naut often* ˈthȯ(ə)rt\ *adv* [ME *thwert,* fr. ON *thvert,* fr. neut. of *thverr* transverse, oblique; akin to OHG *dwerah* transverse, oblique, L *torquēre* to twist — more at TORTURE] (14c) : ATHWART
[3]**thwart** *adj* (15c) : situated or placed across something else : TRANSVERSE — **thwart·ly** *adv*
[4]**thwart** *n* (ca. 1736) : a rower's seat extending athwart a boat
thwart·wise \-ˌwīz\ *adv or adj* (1589) : CROSSWISE
thy \(ˌ)t͟hī\ *adj* [ME *thin, thy,* fr. OE *thīn,* gen. of *thū* thou — more at THOU] *archaic* (12c) : of or relating to thee or thyself esp. as possessor or agent or as object of an action — used esp. in ecclesiastical or literary language and sometimes by Friends esp. among themselves
Thy·es·te·an \thī-ˈes-tē-ən\ *adj* [*Thyestes,* brother of Atreus who unwittingly ate the flesh of his children] (1667) : of or relating to the eating of human flesh : CANNIBAL
thy·la·cine \ˈthī-lə-ˌsīn\ *n* [NL *Thylacinus,* genus of marsupials, fr. Gk *thylakos* sack, pouch] (1838) : TASMANIAN WOLF
thy·la·koid \ˈthī-lə-ˌkȯid\ *n* [ISV *thylak-* (fr. Gk *thylakos* sack) + *-oid;* prob. orig. formed in G] (1966) : any of the membranous lamellae of plant chloroplasts that are composed of protein and lipid and are the sites of the photochemical reactions of photosynthesis
[1]**thym-** *or* **thymo-** *comb form* [ISV, fr. L *thymum*] : thyme ⟨thymol⟩
[2]**thym-** *or* **thymo-** *comb form* [NL *thymus*] : thymus ⟨*thymic*⟩ ⟨*thymocyte*⟩
thyme \ˈtīm *also* ˈthīm\ *n* [ME, fr. MF *thym,* fr. L *thymum,* fr. Gk *thymon,* fr. *thyein* to make a burnt offering, sacrifice; akin to L *fumus* smoke — more at FUME] (14c) : any of a genus (*Thymus*) of mints with small pungent aromatic leaves; *esp* : a garden herb (*T. vulgaris*) used in seasoning and formerly in medicine
thy·mec·to·my \thī-ˈmek-tə-mē\ *n, pl* **-mies** (ca. 1905) : excision of the thymus — **thy·mec·to·mize** \-ˌmīz\ *vt*
-thy·mia \ˈthī-mē-ə\ *n comb form* [NL, fr. Gk, fr. *thymos* mind — more at FUME] : condition of mind and will ⟨schizo*thymia*⟩
thy·mic \ˈthī-mik\ *adj* (1656) : of or relating to the thymus
thy·mi·dine \ˈthī-mə-ˌdēn\ *n* [*thymine* + *-idine*] (1944) : a nucleoside $C_{10}H_{14}N_2O_5$ that is composed of thymine and deoxyribose and occurs as a structural part of DNA
thy·mine \ˈthī-ˌmēn\ *n* [G *thymin,* fr. *thym-* [2]thym- + *-in* -ine] (1894) : a pyrimidine base $C_5H_6N_2O_2$ that is one of the four bases coding genetic information in the polynucleotide chain of DNA — compare ADENINE, CYTOSINE, GUANINE, URACIL
thy·mo·cyte \ˈthī-mə-ˌsīt\ *n* [ISV] (ca. 1923) : a cell of the thymus; *esp* : a thymic lymphocyte
thy·mol \ˈthī-ˌmȯl, -ˌmōl\ *n* [ISV] (1857) : a crystalline phenol $C_{10}H_{14}O$ of aromatic odor and antiseptic properties found esp. in thyme oil or made synthetically and used chiefly as a fungicide and preservative
thy·mo·sin \ˈthī-mə-sən\ *n* [fr. Gk *thymos* thymus + E *-in*] (1968) : a polypeptide thymic hormone that influences the maturation of T cells destined for an active role in cell-mediated immunity
thy·mus \ˈthī-məs\ *n* [NL, fr. Gk *thymos* warty excrescence, thymus] (ca. 1693) : a glandular structure of largely lymphoid tissue that functions esp. in the development of the body's immune system, is present in the young of most vertebrates typically in the upper anterior chest or at the base of the neck, and tends to disappear or become rudimentary in the adult
thymy *or* **thym·ey** \ˈtī-mē *also* ˈthī-\ *adj* (1727) : abounding in or fragrant with thyme
thyr- *or* **thyro-** *comb form* [*thyroid*] : thyroid ⟨*thyro*toxicosis⟩ ⟨*thyrox*ine⟩
thy·ra·tron \ˈthī-rə-ˌträn\ *n* [fr. *Thyratron,* a trademark] (ca. 1929) : a gas-filled 3-element hot-cathode electron tube in which the grid controls only the start of a continuous current thus giving the tube a trigger effect
thy·ris·tor \thī-ˈris-tər\ *n* [*thyra*tron + *transistor*] (1966) : any of several semiconductor devices that act as switches, rectifiers, or voltage regulators
thy·ro·cal·ci·to·nin \ˌthī-rō-ˌkal-sə-ˈtō-nən\ *n* (1965) : CALCITONIN
thy·ro·glob·u·lin \-ˈgläb-yə-lən\ *n* [ISV] (ca. 1905) : an iodine-containing protein of the thyroid gland that is the form in which hormones of the thyroid are stored
[1]**thy·roid** \ˈthī-ˌrȯid\ *also* **thy·roi·dal** \thī-ˈrȯid-ᵊl\ *adj* [NL *thyroides,* fr. Gk *thyreoeidēs* shield-shaped, thyroid, fr. *thyreos* shield shaped like a door, fr. *thyra* door — more at DOOR] (1726) **1 a** : of, relating to, or being a large endocrine gland of craniate vertebrates lying at the base of the neck and producing esp. the hormone thyroxine **b** : suggestive of a disordered thyroid ⟨a ~ personality⟩ **2** : of, relating to, or being the chief cartilage of the larynx
[2]**thyroid** *n* (1840) **1** : a thyroid gland or cartilage; *also* : a part (as an artery or nerve) associated with either of these **2** : a preparation of mammalian thyroid gland used in treating thyroid disorders
thy·roid·ec·to·my \ˌthī-ˌrȯid-ˈek-tə-mē, -rəd-\ *n, pl* **-mies** (1889) : surgical removal of thyroid gland tissue — **thy·roid·ec·to·mized** \-ˌmīzd\ *adj*
thy·roid·itis \ˌthī-ˌrȯid-ˈīt-əs, -rəd-\ *n* [NL] (ca. 1885) : inflammation of the thyroid gland
thyroid–stimulating hormone *n* (ca. 1956) : THYROTROPIN
thy·ro·tox·i·co·sis \ˈthī-rō-ˌtäk-sə-ˈkō-səs\ *n* [NL] (1916) : HYPERTHYROIDISM
thy·ro·tro·pic \ˌthī-rə-ˈtrō-pik, -ˈträp-ik\ *also* **thy·ro·tro·phic** \-ˈtrō-fik\ *adj* (ca. 1923) : exerting or characterized by a direct influence on the secretory activity of the thyroid gland ⟨~ functions⟩
thy·ro·tro·pin \ˌthī-rə-ˈtrō-pən\ *also* **thy·ro·tro·phin** \-fən\ *n* [*thyrotropic, thyrotrophic*] (1939) : a hormone secreted by the anterior pituitary that regulates the formation and secretion of thyroid hormone — called also *thyroid-stimulating hormone, thyrotropic hormone*
thyrotropin–releasing hormone *n* (1970) : a tripeptide hormone synthesized in the hypothalamus that stimulates secretion of thyrotropin by the anterior lobe of the pituitary gland — called also *thyrotropin-releasing factor*
thy·rox·ine *or* **thy·rox·in** \thī-ˈräk-ˌsēn, -sən\ *n* [ISV] (1919) : an iodine-containing hormone $C_{15}H_{11}I_4NO_4$ that is an amino acid produced by the thyroid gland, is a product of the cleavage of thyroglobulin, is made synthetically or obtained from animal thyroid glands, and is used to treat thyroid disorders
thyrse \ˈthərs\ *n* [NL *thyrsus,* fr. L, thyrsus] (1744) : an inflorescence (as in the lilac and horse chestnut) in which the main axis is racemose and the secondary and later axes are cymose
thyr·sus \ˈthər-səs\ *n, pl* **thyr·si** \-ˌsī, -ˌsē\ [L, fr. Gk *thyrsos*] (1591) : a staff surmounted by a pinecone or by a bunch of vine or ivy leaves with grapes or berries that is carried by Bacchus and by satyrs and others engaging in bacchic rites
thy·sa·nu·ran \ˌthī-sə-ˈn(y)u̇r-ən\ *n* [deriv. of Gk *thysanos* tassel + *oura* tail — more at ASS] (ca. 1864) : any of an order (Thysanura) of wingless insects having projecting caudal bristles and comprising the bristletails — **thysanuran** *adj*
thy·self \t͟hī-ˈself\ *pron, archaic* (bef. 12c) : YOURSELF — used esp. in ecclesiastical or literary language and sometimes by Friends esp. among themselves
[1]**ti** \ˈtē\ *n* [Tahitian, Marquesan, Samoan, & Maori] (ca. 1839) : any of several Asian and Pacific trees or shrubs (genus *Cordyline*) of the lily family with leaves in terminal tufts
[2]**ti** *n* [alter. of *si*] (ca. 1845) : the seventh tone of the diatonic scale in solmization
ti·ara \tē-ˈar-ə, -ˈer-, -ˈär-\ *n* [L, royal Persian headdress, fr. Gk] (1616) **1** : a 3-tiered crown worn by the pope **2** : a decorative jeweled or flowered headband or semicircle for formal wear by women
Ti·bet·an \tə-ˈbet-ᵊn\ *n* (1747) **1 a** : a member of the Mongoloid native race of Tibet **b** : a native or inhabitant of Tibet **2** : the Tibeto-Burman language of the Tibetan people — **Tibetan** *adj*
Tibetan terrier *n* (1905) : any of a breed of terriers resembling Old English sheepdogs but having a curled well-feathered tail

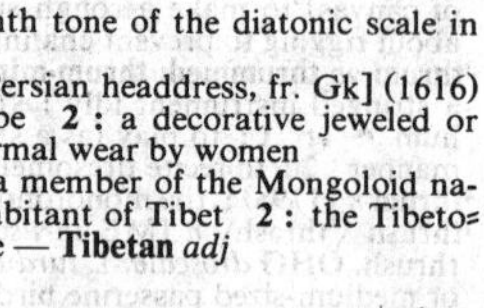
Tibetan terrier

Ti·beto–Bur·man \tə-ˌbet-ō-ˈbər-mən\ *n* (1901) **1** : a language family of Asia sometimes included in Sino-Tibetan **2** : a member of a people speaking a Tibeto-Burman language
tib·ia \ˈtib-ē-ə\ *n, pl* **-i·ae** \-ē-ˌē, -ē-ˌī\ *also* **-i·as** [L] (ca. 1706) **1** : the inner and usu. larger of the two bones of the vertebrate hind limb between the knee and ankle **2** : the fourth joint of the leg of an insect between the femur and tarsus — **tib·i·al** \-ē-əl\ *adj*
tib·io·fib·u·la \ˌtib-ē-ō-ˈfib-yə-lə\ *n* [NL] (ca. 1909) : a bone esp. in frogs and toads that is formed by fusion of the tibia and fibula
tic \ˈtik\ *n* [F] (ca. 1822) **1** : local and habitual spasmodic motion of particular muscles esp. of the face : TWITCHING **2** : a persistent trait of character or behavior ⟨"you know" is a verbal ~ of many inexperienced speakers⟩
ti·cal \ti-ˈkäl, ˈtik-əl\ *n, pl* **ticals** *or* **tical** [Thai, fr. Malay *tikal,* a monetary unit] (1662) : BAHT
tic dou·lou·reux \ˈtik-ˌdü-lə-ˈrü, -ˈrə(r)\ *n* [F, painful twitch] (1800) : TRIGEMINAL NEURALGIA
[1]**tick** \ˈtik\ *n* [ME *tyke, teke;* akin to MHG *zeche* tick, Arm *tiz*] (14c) **1** : any of numerous bloodsucking arachnids that form a superfamily (Ixodoidea of the order Acarina), are larger than the related mites, attach themselves to warm-blooded vertebrates to feed, and include important vectors of infectious diseases **2** : any of various usu. wingless parasitic dipterous insects — compare SHEEP KED
[2]**tick** *n* [ME *tike,* prob. fr. MD (akin to OHG *ziahha* tick), fr. L *theca* cover, fr. Gk *thēkē* case; akin to Gk *tithenai* to place — more at DO] (14c) **1** : the fabric case of a mattress, pillow, or bolster; *also* : a mattress consisting of a tick and its filling **2** : TICKING

[3]tick *n* [ME *tek;* akin to MHG *zic* light push] (15c) **1 a :** a light rhythmic audible tap or beat; *also* **:** a series of such ticks **b** *chiefly Brit* **:** the time taken by the tick of a clock **:** MOMENT **2 :** a small spot or mark; *esp* **:** one used to direct attention to something, to check an item on a list, or to represent a point on a scale

[4]tick *vi* (1721) **1 :** to make the sound of a tick or a series of ticks **2 :** to operate as a functioning mechanism **:** RUN ⟨tried to understand what made him ~⟩ ⟨the motor was ~*ing* over quietly⟩ ~ *vt* **1 :** to mark with a written tick **:** CHECK — usu. used with *off* ⟨~*ed* off each item in the list⟩ **2 :** to mark, count, or announce by or as if by ticking beats ⟨a meter ~*ing* off his cab fare⟩

[5]tick *n* [short for [1]*ticket*] (1642) **:** CREDIT, TRUST; *also* **:** a credit account

tick–borne \ˈtik-ˌbō(ə)rn, -ˌbȯ(ə)rn\ *adj* (1939) **:** capable of being transmitted by the bites of ticks ⟨~ encephalitis⟩

[1]ticked \ˈtikt\ *adj* (ca. 1688) **1 :** marked with ticks **:** FLECKED **2** *of a hair* **:** banded with two or more colors

[2]ticked *adj* [*tick off*] (ca. 1959) **:** ANGRY, UPSET

tick•er \ˈtik-ər\ *n* (1828) **:** something that ticks or produces a ticking sound: as **a :** WATCH **b :** a telegraphic receiving instrument that automatically prints off information (as stock quotations or news) on a paper ribbon **c** *slang* **:** HEART

ticker tape *n* (1902) **:** the paper ribbon on which a telegraphic ticker prints off its information

[1]tick•et \ˈtik-ət\ *n* [obs. F *etiquet* (now *étiquette*), notice attached to something, fr. MF *estiquet,* fr. *estiquier* to attach, fr. MD *steken* to stick; akin to OHG *sticken* to prick — more at STICK] (1529) **1 a :** a document that serves as a certificate, license, or permit; *esp* **:** a mariner's or airman's certificate **b :** TAG, LABEL **2 a :** a certificate or token showing that a fare or admission fee has been paid **b :** a means of access or passage ⟨education is the ~ to a good job⟩ **3 :** a list of candidates for nomination or election **:** SLATE **4 :** the correct or desirable thing ⟨cooperation, that's the ~ —K. E. Trombley⟩ **5 :** a slip or card recording a transaction or undertaking or giving instructions ⟨a savings deposit ~⟩ **6 :** a summons or warning issued to a traffic-law violator

[2]ticket *vt* (1611) **1 :** to attach a ticket to **:** LABEL; *also* **:** DESIGNATE **2 :** to furnish or serve with a ticket ⟨~*ed* for illegal parking⟩

ticket agency *n* (ca. 1934) **:** an agency selling transportation or theater and entertainment tickets

ticket agent *n* (1861) **1 :** one who acts as an agent of a transportation company to sell tickets for travel by train, boat, airplane, or bus **2 :** one who sells theater and entertainment tickets

ticket office *n* (1666) **:** an office of a transportation company, theatrical or entertainment enterprise, or ticket agency where tickets are sold and reservations made

tick•et–of–leave \ˌtik-ət-ə(v)-ˈlēv\ *n, pl* **tickets–of–leave** (1732) **:** a license or permit formerly given in the United Kingdom and the British Commonwealth to a convict under imprisonment to go at large and to labor for himself subject to certain specific conditions

tick fever *n* (ca. 1897) **1 :** TEXAS FEVER **2 :** a febrile disease (as Rocky Mountain spotted fever) transmitted by the bites of ticks

[1]tick•ing \ˈtik-iŋ\ *n* [[2]*tick*] (1649) **:** a strong linen or cotton fabric used in upholstering and as a covering for a mattress or pillow

[2]ticking *n* [[3]*tick*] (1885) **:** ticked marking on a bird or mammal or on individual hairs

[1]tick•le \ˈtik-əl\ *vb* **tick•led; tick•ling** \-(ə-)liŋ\ [ME *tikelen;* akin to OE *tinclian* to tickle] *vi* (14c) **1 :** to have a tingling or prickling sensation ⟨my back ~*s*⟩ **2 :** to excite the surface nerves to prickle ~ *vt* **1 a :** to excite or stir up agreeably **:** PLEASE ⟨music . . . does more than ~ our sense of rhythm —Edward Sapir⟩ **b :** to provoke to laughter or merriment **:** AMUSE ⟨were *tickled* by the clown's antics⟩ **2 :** to touch (as a body part) lightly so as to excite the surface nerves and cause uneasiness, laughter, or spasmodic movements

[2]tickle *n* (1801) **1 :** the act of tickling **2 :** a tickling sensation **3 :** something that tickles

tick•ler \ˈtik-(ə-)lər\ *n* (1680) **1 :** a person or device that tickles **2 :** a device for jogging the memory; *specif* **:** a file that serves as a reminder and is arranged to bring matters to timely attention

tickler coil *n* (1922) **:** small coil connected in series with the plate circuit of an electron tube and inductively coupled with its grid circuit to return a part of the amplified signal for repeated amplification

tick•lish \ˈtik-(ə-)lish\ *adj* (1581) **1 a :** TOUCHY, OVERSENSITIVE ⟨~ about his baldness⟩ **b :** easily overturned ⟨a canoe is a ~ craft⟩ **2 :** requiring delicate handling **:** CRITICAL ⟨a ~ subject⟩ **3 :** sensitive to tickling — **tick•lish•ly** *adv* — **tick•lish•ness** *n*

tick off *vt* [[4]*tick*] (ca. 1919) **1 :** REPRIMAND, REBUKE ⟨his father *ticked* him *off* for his impudence⟩ **2 :** to make angry or indignant ⟨the cancellation really *ticked* me *off*⟩

tick•seed \ˈtik-ˌsēd\ *n* [[1]*tick*] (ca. 1562) **:** COREOPSIS

tick•tack *or* **tic•tac** \ˈtik-ˌtak\ *n* [redupl. of *tick*] (1549) **1 :** a ticking or tapping beat like that of a clock or watch **2 :** a contrivance used by children to tap on a window from a distance

tick•tack•toe *also* **tic–tac–toe** \ˌtik-ˌtak-ˈtō\ *n* [*tic-tac-toe* (former game in which players with eyes shut brought a pencil down on a slate marked with numbers and scored the number hit)] (ca. 1866) **:** a game in which two players alternately put Xs and Os in compartments of a figure formed by two vertical lines crossing two horizontal lines and each tries to get a row of three Xs or three Os before the opponent does

tick•tock \ˈtik-ˈtäk, -ˌtäk\ *n* [imit.] (1848) **:** the ticking sound of a clock

tick trefoil *n* [[1]*tick*] (1857) **:** any of various leguminous plants (genus *Desmodium*) with trifoliolate leaves and rough sticky loments

[1]ticky–tacky \ˌtik-ē-ˈtak-ē\ *also* **ticky–tack** \-ˈtak\ *n, pl* **ticky–tackies** *also* **ticky–tacks** [redupl. of *tacky*] (1962) **:** sleazy or shoddy material used esp. in the construction of look-alike tract houses; *also* **:** something built of ticky-tacky

[2]ticky–tacky *also* **ticky–tack** *adj* (1964) **1 :** of an uninspired or monotonous sameness **2 :** TACKY **3 :** built of ticky-tacky

tid•al \ˈtīd-ᵊl\ *adj* (1807) **1 a :** of, relating to, caused by, or having tides ⟨~ cycles⟩ ⟨~ erosion⟩ **b :** periodically rising and falling or flowing and ebbing ⟨~ waters⟩ **2 :** dependent (as to the time of arrival or departure) upon the state of the tide ⟨a ~ steamer⟩ — **tid•al•ly** \-ᵊl-ē\ *adv*

tidal wave *n* (1830) **1 a :** an unusually high sea wave that sometimes follows an earthquake **b :** an unusual rise of water alongshore due to strong winds **2 :** something overwhelming (as a sweeping majority vote or an irresistible impulse)

tid•bit \ˈtid-ˌbit\ *n* [perh. fr. *tit-* (as in *titmouse*) + *bit*] (1640) **1 :** a choice morsel of food **2 :** a choice or pleasing bit (as of news)

tid•dle•dy•winks *or* **tid•dly•winks** \ˈtid-ᵊl-(d)ē-ˌwiŋ(k)s, ˈtid-lē-ˌwiŋ(k)s\ *n pl but sing in constr* [prob. fr. E dial. *tiddly* little] (1898) **:** a game whose object is to snap small disks from a flat surface into a small container

[1]tide \ˈtīd\ *n* [ME, time, fr. OE *tīd;* akin to OHG *zīt* time, Gk *daiesthai* to divide] (bef. 12c) **1 a** *obs* **:** a space of time **:** PERIOD **b :** a fit or opportune time **:** OPPORTUNITY **c :** an ecclesiastical anniversary or festival; *also* **:** its season — usu. used in combination ⟨Easter*tide*⟩ **2 a** (1) **:** the alternate rising and falling of the surface of the ocean and of water bodies (as gulfs and bays) connected with the ocean that occurs usu. twice a day and is caused by the gravitational attraction of the sun and moon occurring unequally on different parts of the earth (2) **:** a less marked rising and falling of an inland body of water (3) **:** a periodic movement in the earth's crust caused by the same forces that produce ocean tides (4) **:** a tidal distortion on one celestial body caused by the gravitational attraction of another (5) **:** one of the tidal movements of the atmosphere resembling those of the ocean and produced by gravitation or diurnal temperature changes — called also *atmospheric tide* **b :** FLOOD TIDE 1 **3 :** something that fluctuates like the tides of the sea ⟨the ~ of public opinion⟩ **4 a :** a flowing stream **:** CURRENT **b :** the waters of the ocean **c :** the overflow of a flooding stream — **tide•less** \-ləs\ *adj*

[2]tide *vb* **tid•ed; tid•ing** *vi* (1593) **1 :** to flow as or in a tide **:** SURGE **2 :** to drift with the tide esp. in navigating a ship into or out of an anchorage, harbor, or river ~ *vt* **1 :** to cause to float with or as if with the tide **2 :** to proceed along (one's way) by taking advantage of tides

[3]tide *vi* **tid•ed; tid•ing** [ME *tiden,* fr. OE *tīdan;* akin to MD *tiden* to go, come, OE *tīd* time] *archaic* (bef. 12c) **:** BETIDE, BEFALL

tide•land \ˈtīd-ˌland, -lənd\ *n* (1802) **1 :** land overflowed during flood tide **2 :** land underlying the ocean and lying beyond the low-water limit of the tide but being within the territorial waters of a nation — often used in pl.

tide•mark \-ˌmärk\ *n* (1799) **1 a :** a high-water or sometimes low-water mark left by tidal water or a flood **b :** a mark placed to indicate this point **2 :** the point to which something has attained or below which it has receded ⟨the ~ of tolerance has risen —*New Republic*⟩

tide over *vt* [[2]*tide*] (ca. 1909) **:** to enable to surmount or endure a difficulty ⟨money to *tide* us *over* the emergency⟩

tide table *n* (1594) **:** a table that indicates the height of the tide at one place at different times of day throughout one year

tide•wa•ter \-ˌwȯt-ər, -ˌwät-\ *n* (1772) **1 :** water overflowing land at flood tide; *also* **:** water affected by the ebb and flow of the tide **2 :** low-lying coastal land

tide•way \-ˌwā\ *n* (1798) **:** a channel in which the tide runs

tid•ing \ˈtīd-iŋ\ *n* [ME, fr. OE *tīdung,* fr. *tīdan* to betide] (bef. 12c) **:** a piece of news — usu. used in pl. ⟨good ~*s*⟩

[1]ti•dy \ˈtīd-ē\ *adj* **ti•di•er; -est** [ME, timely, in good condition, fr. *tide* time] (13c) **1 :** properly filled out **:** PLUMP **2 :** adequately satisfactory **:** ACCEPTABLE, FAIR ⟨a ~ solution to their problem⟩ **3 a :** neat and orderly in appearance or habits **:** well ordered and cared for **b :** METHODICAL, PRECISE ⟨a ~ mind⟩ **4 :** LARGE, SUBSTANTIAL ⟨a ~ profit⟩ — **ti•di•ly** \ˈtīd-ᵊl-ē\ *adv* — **ti•di•ness** \ˈtīd-ē-nəs\ *n*

[2]tidy *vb* **ti•died; ti•dy•ing** *vt* (1821) **:** to put in order ⟨~ up a room⟩ ~ *vi* **:** to make things tidy ⟨~*ing* up after supper⟩ — **ti•di•er** *n*

[3]tidy *n, pl* **tidies** (ca. 1828) **1 :** a receptacle for sewing materials or odds and ends **2 :** a piece of fancywork used to protect the back, arms, or headrest of a chair or sofa from wear or soil

ti•dy•tips \ˈtīd-ē-ˌtips\ *n pl but sing or pl in constr* (1888) **:** an annual California composite herb (*Layia platyglossa*) having yellow-rayed flower heads often tipped with white

[1]tie \ˈtī\ *n* [ME *teg, tye,* fr. OE *tēag;* akin to ON *taug* rope, OE *tēon* to pull — more at TOW] (bef. 12c) **1 a :** a line, ribbon, or cord used for fastening, uniting, or drawing something closed; *esp* **:** SHOELACE **b** (1) **:** a structural element (as a rod or angle iron) holding two pieces together **:** a tension member in a construction (2) **:** one of the transverse supports to which railroad rails are fastened to keep them in line **2 :** something that serves as a connecting link: as **a :** a moral or legal obligation to someone or something typically constituting a restraining power, influence, or duty **b :** a bond of kinship or affection **3 :** a curved line that joins two musical notes of the same pitch to denote a single tone sustained through the time value of the two **4 a :** an equality in number (as of votes or scores) **b :** equality in a contest; *also* **:** a contest that ends in a draw **5 :** a method or style of tying or knotting **6 :** something that is knotted or is to be knotted when worn: as **a :** NECKTIE **b :** a low laced shoe **:** OXFORD — **tie•less** \-ləs\ *adj*

[2]tie *vb* **tied; ty•ing** \ˈtī-iŋ\ *or* **tie•ing** *vt* (bef. 12c) **1 a :** to fasten, attach, or close by means of a tie **b :** to form a knot or bow in ⟨~ your scarf⟩ **c :** to make by tying constituent elements ⟨*tied* a wreath⟩ ⟨~ a fishing fly⟩ **2 a :** to place or establish in relationship **:** CONNECT **b :** to unite in marriage **c :** to unite (musical notes) by a tie **d :** to join (power systems) electrically **3 :** to restrain from independence or freedom of action or choice **:** constrain by or as if by authority, influence, agreement, or obligation **4 a** (1) **:** to make or have an equal score with in a contest (2) **:** to equalize (the score) in a game or contest (3) **:** to equalize the score of (a game) **b :** to provide or offer something equal to **:** EQUAL ~ *vi* **:** to make a tie: as **a :** to make a bond or connection **b :** to make an equal score **c :** to become attached **d :** to close by means of a tie — **tie into :** to attack with vigor — **tie one on** *slang* **:** to get drunk — **tie the knot :** to perform a marriage ceremony; *also* **:** to get married

tie–and–dye \ˈtī-ən-ˌdī\ *n* (1928) **:** TIE-DYEING

tie•back \ˈtī-ˌbak\ *n* (1926) **1 :** a decorative strip or device of cloth, cord, or metal for draping a curtain to the side of a window **2 :** a curtain with a tieback — usu. used in pl.

tie·break·er \'tī-ˌbrā-kər\ *n* (ca. 1932) : a contest used to select a winner from among contestants with tied scores at the end of a previous contest
tie–dye \'tī-ˌdī\ *n* (ca. 1939) : TIE-DYEING
tie–dyed *adj* (1943) : having patterns produced by tie-dyeing ⟨~ jeans⟩
tie–dye·ing *n* (1928) : a hand method of producing patterns in textiles by tying portions of the fabric or yarn so that they will not absorb the dye
tie–in \'tī-ˌin\ *n* (1925) **1** : something that ties in, relates, or connects esp. in a promotional campaign **2** : a book that inspired or was inspired by a motion picture or television program
tie in \(ˈ)tī-'in\ *vt* (1927) : to bring into connection with something relevant: as **a** : to make the final connection of ⟨*tied in* the new branch pipeline⟩ **b** : to coordinate in such a manner as to produce balance and unity ⟨the illustrations were *tied in* with the text⟩ **c** : to use as a tie-in esp. in advertising **~** *vi* : to become tied in
tie·mann·ite \'tē-mə-ˌnīt\ *n* [G *tiemannit,* fr. W. *Tiemann* †1899 Ger. scientist] (1868) : a mineral HgSe that consists of mercuric selenide and occurs in dark gray or nearly black masses of metallic luster
tie·pin \'tī-ˌpin\ *n* (1780) : an ornamental straight pin that has usu. an ornamental head and a sheath for the point and is used to hold the ends of a necktie in place
[1]**tier** \'ti(ə)r\ *n* [MF *tire* rank, fr. OF — more at ATTIRE] (1569) **1** : a row, rank, or layer of articles; *esp* : one of two or more rows or ranks arranged one above another **2** : CLASS, CATEGORY
[2]**tier** *vt* (1888) : to place or arrange in tiers **~** *vi* : to rise in tiers
[3]**ti·er** \'tī(-ə)r\ *n* (1633) : one that ties
[1]**tierce** \'ti(ə)rs\ *var of* TERCE
[2]**tierce** *n* [ME *terce, tierce,* fr. MF, fr. fem. of *terz,* adj., third, fr. L *tertius* — more at THIRD 2] (15c) **1** *obs* : THIRD 2 **2** : any of various units of liquid capacity equal to 1/3 pipe; *esp* : a unit equal to 42 gallons (159 liters) **3** : a sequence of three playing cards of the same suit
tier·cel \'ti(ə)r-səl\ *n* [ME *tercel,* fr. MF, fr. (assumed) VL *tertiolus,* fr. dim. of L *tertius* third] (14c) : a male hawk
tiered \'ti(ə)rd\ *adj* (1807) : having or arranged in tiers, rows, or layers — often used in combination ⟨triple-*tiered*⟩
tie–rod \'tī-ˌräd\ *n* (1839) : a rod (as of steel) used as a connecting member or brace
tie silk *n* (ca. 1915) : a silk fabric of firm resilient pliable texture used for neckties and for blouses and accessories
tie tack *or* **tie tac** \-ˌtak\ *n* (ca. 1954) : an ornamented pin with a receiving button or clasp that is used to attach the two ends of a necktie together or to attach a necktie to a shirt
tie–up \'tī-ˌəp\ *n* (1851) **1 a** : a mooring place for a boat **b** : a cow stable; *also* : a space for a single cow in a stable **2** : a slowdown or stoppage of traffic, business, or operation (as by a mechanical breakdown) **3** : CONNECTION, ASSOCIATION ⟨a helpful financial ~⟩
tie up \(ˈ)tī-'əp\ *vt* (1530) **1** : to attach, fasten, or bind securely; *also* : to wrap up and fasten **2 a** : to connect closely : JOIN ⟨*tie up* the loose ends⟩ **b** : to cause to be linked so as to depend on something **3 a** : to place or invest in such a manner as to make unavailable for other purposes ⟨his money was *tied up* in stocks⟩ **b** : to restrain from operation or progress ⟨traffic was *tied up* for miles⟩ **4 a** : to keep busy ⟨was *tied up* in conference all day⟩ **b** : to preempt the use of ⟨*tied up* the phone for an hour⟩ **~** *vi* **1** : DOCK ⟨the ferry *ties up* at the south slip⟩ **2** : to assume a definite relationship ⟨this *ties up* with what I told you before⟩
[1]**tiff** \'tif\ *vi* [origin unknown] (ca. 1727) : to have a minor quarrel
[2]**tiff** *n* (1754) : a petty quarrel
tif·fa·ny \'tif-ə-nē\ *n, pl* **-nies** [prob. fr. obs. F *tiphanie* Epiphany, fr. LL *theophania,* fr. LGk, deriv. of Gk *theos* god + *phainein* to show] (1601) **1** : a sheer silk gauze formerly used for clothing and trimmings **2** : a plain-woven open-mesh cotton fabric (as cheesecloth)
tif·fin \'tif-ən\ *n, chiefly Brit* [prob. alter. of *tiffing,* gerund of obs. E *tiff* (to eat between meals)] (1800) : a midday meal : LUNCHEON
ti·ger \'tī-gər\ *n, pl* **tigers** [ME *tigre,* fr. OE *tiger* & OF *tigre,* both fr. L *tigris,* fr. Gk, of Iranian origin; perh. akin to Av *tighra-* pointed; akin to Gk *stizein* to tattoo — more at STICK] (bef. 12c) **1** *pl also* **tiger a** : a large Asian carnivorous mammal (*Felis tigris*) of the cat family having a tawny coat transversely striped with black **b** : any of several large wildcats (as the jaguar or cougar) **c** : a domestic cat with striped pattern **d** *Austral* : TASMANIAN WOLF **2 a** : a fierce and bloodthirsty person or quality ⟨aroused the ~ in him⟩ **b** : a vigorously aggressive person ⟨a ~ for work⟩ **3** *Brit* : a groom in livery; *esp* : a young or small groom — **ti·ger·ish** \-g(ə-)rish\ *adj* — **ti·ger·ish·ly** *adv* — **ti·ger·ish·ness** *n* — **ti·ger·like** \-gər-ˌlīk\ *adj*

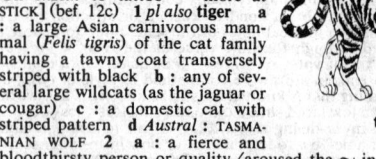

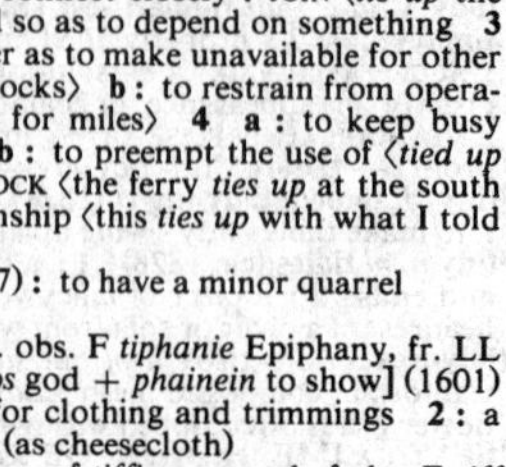
tiger 1a

tiger beetle *n* (1826) : any of numerous active carnivorous beetles (family Cicindelidae) having larvae that tunnel in the soil
tiger cat *n* (1699) **1** : any of various wildcats (as the serval, ocelot, or margay) of moderate size and variegated coloration **2** : a striped or sometimes blotched tabby cat
ti·ger·eye \'tī-gə-ˌrī\ *or* **ti·ger's–eye** \-gər-ˌzī\ *n* (ca. 1891) : a usu. yellowish to grayish brown chatoyant stone that is much used for ornament and is a silicified crocidolite
tiger lily *n* (1824) : a common Asian garden lily (*Lilium tigrinum*) having nodding orange-colored flowers densely spotted with black; *also* : any of various lilies with similar flowers
tiger moth *n* (1816) : any of a family (Arctiidae) of stout-bodied moths usu. with broad striped or spotted wings
tiger salamander *n* (ca. 1909) : a widely distributed No. American salamander (*Ambystoma tigrinum*) that is brown or black above with vertical yellowish lateral blotches often running together ventrally
tiger shark *n* (1784) : a large gray or brown stocky-bodied requiem shark (*Galeocerdo cuvieri*) that is a man-eater and is nearly cosmopolitan esp. in warm seas — see SHARK illustration
tiger swallowtail *n* (ca. 1890) : a large widely distributed swallowtail (*Papilio glaucus*) of eastern No. America that is largely yellow with black margins and black stripes on the wings
[1]**tight** \'tīt\ *adj* [alter. of earlier *thight* (close set, dense), of Scand origin; akin to ON *théttr* tight; akin to MHG *dīhte* thick, Skt *tanakti* it causes to coagulate] (1507) **1** : so close or substantial in structure as not to permit passage (as of a liquid or gas or light) ⟨a ~ roof⟩ — often used in combination ⟨a hog*tight* fence⟩ **2 a** : fixed very firmly in place ⟨loosen a ~ jar cover⟩ **b** : firmly stretched, drawn, or set ⟨a ~ drumhead⟩ ⟨a ~ knot⟩ **c** : fitting usu. too closely (as for comfort) ⟨~ shoes⟩ **3** : set close together : COMPACT ⟨a ~ defensive formation in football⟩ **4 a** : CAPABLE, ALERT, READY **b** (1) : trim and tidy in dress (2) : neat and orderly in arrangement or design : SNUG **5** : difficult to get through or out of : TRYING, EXACTING ⟨in a ~ situation⟩ **6 a** : firm in control ⟨kept a ~ hand on all his affairs⟩ **b** : characterized by firmness of control ⟨ran a ~ courtroom⟩ **c** : STINGY, MISERLY **7** : evenly contested : CLOSE ⟨a ~ tennis match⟩ **8** : packed or compressed to the limit : entirely full ⟨a ~ bale⟩ **9** : INTOXICATED, DRUNK **10 a** : highly condensed ⟨a ~ literary style⟩ **b** : closely spaced ⟨a ~ line of print⟩ **11** : scantily supplied or obtainable in proportion to demand ⟨~ money⟩; *also* : characterized by such a scarcity ⟨a ~ labor market⟩ **12** *of lumber* : sound and free from checks ⟨logs with ~ hearts⟩ **13** : INTIMATE, CLOSE **14** : being or performing music in a polished style with precise arrangements ⟨some favor ~ playing, with crisply articulated notes —Eleanor Blau⟩ — **tight·ly** *adv* — **tight·ness** *n*
[2]**tight** *adv* (1680) **1** : FAST, TIGHTLY, FIRMLY ⟨the door was shut ~⟩ **2** : in a sound manner : SOUNDLY ⟨sleep ~⟩
tight·en \'tīt-ᵊn\ *vb* **tight·ened; tight·en·ing** \'tīt-niŋ, -ᵊn-iŋ\ *vt* (ca. 1727) : to make tight or tighter **~** *vi* : to become tight or tighter — **tight·en·er** \-nər, -ᵊn-ər\ *n*
tight end *n* (1962) : an offensive football end who lines up within two yards of the tackle
tight·fist·ed \'tīt-'fis-təd\ *adj* (1844) : reluctant to part with money
tight–lipped \-'lipt\ *adj* (1876) **1** : having the lips closed tight (as in determination) **2** : reluctant to speak : TACITURN
tight–mouthed \-'mau̇thd, -'mau̇tht\ *adj* (1926) : CLOSEMOUTHED
tight·rope \'tīt-ˌrōp\ *n* (1801) **1** : a rope or wire stretched taut for acrobats to perform on **2** : a dangerously precarious situation
tights \'tīts\ *n pl* (1836) : a skintight garment covering the body from the neck down or from the waist down
tight·wad \'tīt-ˌwäd\ *n* (ca. 1900) : a close or miserly person
tight·wire \-ˌwī(ə)r\ *n* (1928) : a tightrope made of wire
ti·glon \'tī-glən\ *n* [*tiger* + *lion*] (1942) : a hybrid between a male tiger and a female lion
ti·gon \'tī-gən\ *n* [*tiger* + *lion*] (ca. 1926) : TIGLON
Ti·gre \ti-'grā\ *n* (ca. 1892) : a Semitic language of northern Ethiopia
ti·gress \'tī-grəs\ *n* (1611) : a female tiger; *also* : a tigerish woman
Ti·gri·nya \tə-'grē-nyə\ *n* (1905) : a Semitic language of northern Ethiopia
tike *var of* TYKE
ti·ki \'tē-kē\ *n* [Maori & Marquesan, fr. *Tiki,* first man or creator of first man] (1878) : a wood or stone image of a Polynesian supernatural power
til \'til\ *n* [Hindi, fr. Skt *tila*] (1840) : SESAME
ti·la·pia \tə-'läp-ē-ə, -'lāp-\ *n* [NL, genus name] (ca. 1923) : any of a genus (*Tilapia*) of African freshwater cichlid food fishes
til·bury \'til-ˌber-ē, -b(ə-)rē\ *n, pl* **-bur·ies** [*Tilbury,* 19th cent. Eng. coach builder] (1814) : a light 2-wheeled carriage : GIG
til·de \'til-də\ *n* [Sp, fr. ML *titulus* tittle] (ca. 1864) **1** : a mark ˜ placed esp. over the letter *n* (as in Spanish *señor* sir) to denote the sound \nʸ\ or over vowels (as in Portuguese *irmã* sister) to indicate nasality **2** : the mark ~ used in logic and mathematics to indicate negation
[1]**tile** \'tī(ə)l\ *n, often attrib* [ME, fr. OE *tigele,* fr. L *tegula* tile; akin to L *tegere* to cover — more at THATCH] (bef. 12c) **1** *pl* **tiles** *or* **tile a** : a flat or curved piece of fired clay, stone, or concrete used esp. for roofs, floors, or walls and often for ornamental work **b** : a hollow or a semicircular and open earthenware or concrete piece used in constructing a drain **c** : a hollow building unit made of fired clay or of shale or gypsum **2** : TILING **3** : HAT; *esp* : a high silk hat **4** : a thin piece of resilient material (as cork, linoleum, or rubber) used esp. for covering floors or walls
[2]**tile** *vt* **tiled; til·ing** (14c) **1** : to cover with tiles **2** : to install drainage tile in — **til·er** *n*
tile·fish \'tī(ə)l-ˌfish\ *n* [*tile-* modif. of NL *Lopholatilus*] (1881) : a large violet marine percoid food fish (*Lopholatilus chamaeleonticeps*) of deep waters with a fleshy appendage on the head and large round yellow spots
til·ing \'tī-liŋ\ *n* (15c) **1** : the action or work of one who tiles **2 a** : TILES **b** : a surface of tiles
[1]**till** \tᵊl, təl, (ˌ)til\ *prep* [ME, fr. OE *til;* akin to ON *til* to, till, OE *til* good] (bef. 12c) **1** *chiefly Scot* : TO **2** : UNTIL
[2]**till** *conj* (12c) : UNTIL
[3]**till** \'til\ *vt* [ME *tilien, tillen,* fr. OE *tilian;* akin to OE *til* good, suitable, OHG *zil* goal] (bef. 12c) : to work by plowing, sowing, and raising crops : CULTIVATE — **till·able** \-ə-bəl\ *adj*
[4]**till** \'til\ *n* [AF *tylle*] (15c) **1 a** : a box, drawer, or tray in a receptacle (as a cabinet or chest) used esp. for valuables **b** : a money drawer in a store or bank **2 a** : the money contained in a till **b** : a supply of esp. ready money
[5]**till** \'til\ *n* [origin unknown] (1842) : unstratified glacial drift consisting of clay, sand, gravel, and boulders intermingled
till·age \'til-ij\ *n* (15c) **1** : the operation of tilling land **2** : cultivated land
til·land·sia \tə-'lan(d)-zē-ə\ *n* [NL, fr. Elias *Tillands* †1693 Finn. botanist] (1759) : any of a very large genus (*Tillandsia*) of chiefly epiphytic plants of the pineapple family native to tropical and subtropical America
[1]**til·ler** \'til-ər\ *n* [fr. (assumed) ME, fr. OE *telgor, telgra* twig, shoot; akin to OHG *zelga* twig, Gk *daidalos* ingeniously formed — more at CONDOLE] (bef. 12c) : STALK, SPROUT; *esp* : one from the base of a plant or from the axils of its lower leaves
[2]**til·ler** *vi* **til·lered; til·ler·ing** \'til-(ə-)riŋ\ *of a plant* (1677) : to put forth tillers
[3]**till·er** \'til-ər\ *n* (13c) : one that tills : CULTIVATOR

[4]**til·ler** \'til-ər\ *n* [ME *tiler* stock of a crossbow, fr. MF *telier,* lit., beam of a loom, fr. ML *telarium,* fr. L *tela* web — more at TOIL] (1625) : a lever used to turn the rudder of a boat from side to side; *broadly* : a device or system that plays a part in steering something

til·ler·man \'til-ər-mən\ *n* (ca. 1934) : one in charge of a tiller : STEERSMAN

Til·sit \'til-sət\ *also* **Til·sit·er** \-sət-ər\ *n* [G *tilsiter,* fr. *Tilsit* (now Sovetsk, U.S.S.R.)] (ca. 1932) : a semisoft porous light yellow cheese with a flavor that ranges from mild to sharp

[1]**tilt** \'tilt\ *n* [ME *teld, telte* tent, canopy, fr. OE *teld;* akin to OHG *zelt* tent] (15c) : a canopy for a wagon, boat, or stall

[2]**tilt** *vt* (15c) : to cover or provide with a tilt

[3]**tilt** *n* [deriv. of ME *tulten, tilten*] (1511) **1 a :** a contest on horseback in which two combatants charging with lances or similar weapons try to unhorse each other : JOUST **b :** a tournament of tilts **2 a :** a verbal contest between disputants : CONTENTION **b :** SPEED — used in the phrase *at full tilt* **3 a :** the act of tilting : the state or position of being tilted **b :** a sloping surface **c :** SLANT, BIAS ⟨a ~ toward military involvement⟩ **4 :** any of various sports resembling or suggesting tilting with lances; *esp* : a water sport in which the contestants stand on logs or in canoes or boats and thrust with poles — **tilt** *adj*

[4]**tilt** *vb* [ME *tulten, tilten* to cause to fall; akin to Sw *tulta* to waddle] *vt* (1594) **1 :** to cause to slope : INCLINE ⟨don't ~ the boat⟩ **2 a :** to point or thrust in or as if in a tilt ⟨~ a lance⟩ **b :** to charge against ⟨~ an adversary⟩ ~ *vi* **1 a :** to move or shift so as to lean or incline : SLANT **b :** to incline, tend, or become drawn toward an opinion, course of action, or one side of a controversy **2 a :** to engage in a combat with lances : JOUST **b :** to make an impetuous attack ⟨~ at wrongs⟩ — **tilt·able** \'til-tə-bəl\ *adj* — **tilt·er** *n*

tilth \'tilth\ *n* [ME, fr. OE, fr. *tilian* to till] (bef. 12c) **1 :** cultivated land : TILLAGE **2 :** the state of aggregation of a soil esp. in relation to its suitability for crop growth

tilt·me·ter \'tilt-,mēt-ər\ *n* (1932) : an instrument to measure the tilting of the earth's surface

tilt·yard \'tilt-,yärd\ *n* (1528) : a yard or place for tilting contests

tim·bal \'tim-bəl\ *n* [F *timbale,* fr. MF, alter. of *tamballe,* modif. of OSp *atabal,* fr. Ar *at-tabl* the drum] (1680) : KETTLEDRUM

tim·bale \'tim-bəl; tim-'bäl, tam-\ *n* [F, lit., kettledrum] (1824) **1 :** a creamy mixture (as of meat or vegetables) baked in a mold; *also* : the mold in which it is baked **2 :** a small pastry shell filled with a cooked timbale mixture

[1]**tim·ber** \'tim-bər\ *n* [ME, fr. OE, building, wood; akin to OHG *zimbar* wood, room, L *domus* house, Gk *demein* to build, *domos* house] (bef. 12c) **1 a :** growing trees or their wood **b** — used interjectionally to warn of a falling tree **2 :** wood suitable for building or for carpentry **3 :** MATERIAL, STUFF; *esp* : personal qualification for a particular position or status **4 a :** a large squared or dressed piece of wood ready for use or forming part of a structure **b** *Brit* : [2]LUMBER 2a **c :** a curving frame branching outward from the keel of a ship and bending upward in a vertical direction that is usu. composed of several pieces united : RIB — **timber** *adj*

[2]**timber** *vt* **tim·bered; tim·ber·ing** \-b(ə-)riŋ\ (bef. 12c) : to frame, cover, or support with timbers

tim·ber·doo·dle \,tim-bər-'düd-ᵊl\ *n* [[1]*timber* + *doodle* (cock)] (1856) : the American woodcock

tim·bered \'tim-bərd\ *adj* (15c) **1 :** having walls framed by exposed timbers **2 :** having a specified structure or constitution **3 :** covered with growing timber : WOODED

tim·ber·head \'tim-bər-,hed\ *n* (1794) **1 :** the top end of a ship's timber used above the gunwale (as for belaying ropes) **2 :** a bollard bolted to the deck where the end of a timber would come

timber hitch *n* (ca. 1815) : a knot used to secure a line to a log or spar — see KNOT illustration

tim·ber·ing \'tim-b(ə-)riŋ\ *n* (15c) : a set or arrangement of timbers

tim·ber·land \-bər-,land\ *n* (1654) : wooded land esp. with marketable timber

tim·ber·line \-,līn\ *n* (1867) : the upper limit of arboreal growth in mountains or high latitudes — called also *tree line*

tim·ber·man \-mən\ *n* (15c) : LUMBERMAN

timber rattlesnake *n* (1893) : a moderate-sized rattlesnake (*Crotalus horridus horridus*) that is widely distributed through the eastern half of the U.S.

timber wolf *n* (1876) : a wolf (*Canis lupus lycaon*) formerly common over much of eastern No. America — called also *lobo*

tim·ber·work \'tim-bər-,wərk\ *n* (14c) : timber construction

tim·bre *also* **tim·ber** \'tam-bər, 'tim-; 'tam(brᵊ)\ *n* [F, fr. MF, bell struck by a hammer, fr. OF, drum, fr. MGk *tymbanon* kettledrum, fr. Gk *tympanon* — more at TYMPANUM] (1849) : the quality given to a sound by its overtones: as **a :** the resonance by which the ear recognizes and identifies a voiced speech sound **b :** the quality of tone distinctive of a particular singing voice or musical instrument — **tim·bral** \'tam-brəl, 'tim-\ *adj*

tim·brel \'tim-brəl\ *n* [dim. of obs. E *timbre* tambourine, fr. ME, fr. OF, drum] (1500) : a small hand drum or tambourine — **tim·brelled** \-brəld\ *adj*

[1]**time** \'tīm\ *n* [ME, fr. OE *tīma;* akin to ON *tīmi* time, OE *tīd* — more at TIDE] (bef. 12c) **1 a :** the measured or measurable period during which an action, process, or condition exists or continues : DURATION **b :** a continuum which lacks spatial dimensions and in which events succeed one another from past through present to future **c :** LEISURE ⟨~ for reading⟩ **2 :** the point or period when something occurs : OCCASION **3 :** an appointed, fixed, or customary moment or hour for something to happen, begin, or end ⟨arrived ahead of ~⟩ **4 a :** an historical period : AGE **b :** a division of geologic chronology **c :** conditions at present or at some specified period ⟨~*s* are hard⟩ ⟨move with the ~*s*⟩ **d :** the present time ⟨issues of the ~⟩ **5 a :** LIFETIME **b :** a period of apprenticeship **c :** a term of military service **d :** a prison sentence **6 :** SEASON ⟨very hot for this ~ of year⟩ **7 a :** rate of speed : TEMPO **b :** the grouping of the beats of music : RHYTHM **8 a :** a moment, hour, day, or year as indicated by a clock or calendar ⟨what ~ is it⟩ **b :** any of various systems (as sidereal or solar) of reckoning time **9 a :** one of a series of recurring instances or repeated actions ⟨you've been told many ~*s*⟩ **b** *pl* (1) : added or accumulated quantities or instances ⟨five ~*s* greater⟩ (2) : equal fractional parts of which an indicated number equal a comparatively greater quantity ⟨seven ~*s* smaller⟩ ⟨three ~*s* closer⟩ **c :** TURN ⟨three ~*s* at bat⟩ **10 :** finite as contrasted with infinite duration **11 :** a person's experience during a specified period or on a particular occasion ⟨a good ~⟩ **12 a :** the hours or days occupied by one's work ⟨make up ~⟩ **b :** an hourly pay rate ⟨straight ~⟩ **c :** wages paid at discharge or resignation ⟨pick up your ~ and get out⟩ **13 a :** the playing time of a game **b :** TIME-OUT — **at the same time :** HOWEVER, NEVERTHELESS ⟨glorify the equalitarian ideal and *at the same time* keep woman in the subordinate role —Vance Packard⟩ — **at times :** at intervals : OCCASIONALLY — **for the time being :** for the present — **from time to time :** once in a while : OCCASIONALLY — **in no time :** in the shortest possible time — **in time 1 :** sufficiently early **2 :** in the course of time : EVENTUALLY **3 :** in correct tempo ⟨learn to play *in time*⟩ — **on time 1 a :** at the appointed time **b :** on schedule **2 :** on the installment plan — **time and again :** FREQUENTLY, REPEATEDLY

[2]**time** *vb* **timed; tim·ing** *vt* (14c) **1 a :** to arrange or set the time of : SCHEDULE **b :** to regulate (a watch) to keep correct time **2 :** to set the tempo, speed, or duration of ⟨*timed* his leap perfectly —Neil Amdur⟩ **3 :** to cause to keep time with something **4 :** to determine or record the time, duration, or rate of ⟨~ a horse⟩ **5 :** to dispose (as a mechanical part) so that an action occurs at a desired instant or in a desired way ~ *vi* : to keep or beat time

[3]**time** *adj* (1711) **1 a :** of or relating to time **b :** recording time **2 :** timed to ignite or explode at a specific moment ⟨a ~ bomb⟩ **3 a :** payable on a specified future day or a certain length of time after presentation for acceptance **b :** based on installment payments ⟨a ~ sale⟩

time and a half *n* (1888) : payment of a worker (as for overtime or holiday work) at one and a half times his regular wage rate

time bill *n* (1831) : a bill of exchange payable at a definite future time

time bomb *n* (1893) **1 :** a bomb so made as to explode at a predetermined time **2 :** something with a potentially dangerous delayed reaction

time capsule *n* (1938) : a container holding historical records or objects representative of current culture that is deposited (as in a cornerstone) for preservation until discovery by some future age

time card *n* (ca. 1891) : a card used with a time clock to record an employee's starting and quitting times each day or on each job

time chart *n* (ca. 1830) **1 :** a chart showing the standard times in various parts of the world with reference to a specified time at a specified place **2 :** a table listing important events for successive years within a particular historical period

time clock *n* (1887) : a clock that stamps an employee's starting and quitting times on his time card

time–con·sum·ing \'tīm-kən-'sü-miŋ\ *adj* (1931) **1 :** using or taking up a great deal of time ⟨~ chores⟩ **2 :** wasteful of time ⟨~ tactics⟩

timed \'tīmd\ *adj* (ca. 1855) **1 :** made to occur at or in a set time ⟨a ~ explosion⟩ **2 :** done or taking place at a time of a specified sort ⟨an ill-*timed* arrival⟩

time deposit *n* (1851) : a bank deposit payable a specified number of days after deposit or on advance notice to the bank

time dilation *n* (1957) : a slowing of time on a system moving at a velocity approaching that of light relative to an observer as predicted by the theory of relativity — called also *time dilatation*

time draft *n* (1863) : a draft payable a specified number of days after date of the draft or presentation to the drawee

time exposure *n* (1893) : exposure of a photographic film for a definite time usu. of more than one half second; *also* : a photograph taken by such exposure

time frame *n* (1964) : a period of time esp. with respect to some action or project

time–hon·ored \'tī-,män-ərd\ *adj* (1593) : honored because of age or long usage ⟨~ traditions⟩

time immemorial *n* (1602) **1 :** a time antedating a period legally fixed as the basis for a custom or right **2 :** time so long past as to be indefinite in history or tradition — called also *time out of mind*

time·keep·er \'tīm-,kē-pər\ *n* (1686) **1 :** TIMEPIECE **2 :** a clerk who keeps records of the time worked by employees **3 :** one appointed to mark and announce the time in an athletic game or contest — **time·keep·ing** \-piŋ\ *n*

time killer *n* (1751) **1 :** a person with time on his hands **2 :** something that passes the time : DIVERSION

time lag *n* (1895) : an interval of time between two related phenomena (as a cause and its effect)

time–lapse \'tīm-,laps\ *adj* (1927) : of, relating to, or constituting a motion picture made so that when projected a slow action (as the opening of a flower bud) appears to be speeded up

time·less \'tīm-ləs\ *adj* (1560) **1** *archaic* : PREMATURE, UNTIMELY **2 a :** having no beginning or end : ETERNAL **b :** not restricted to a particular time or date ⟨the ~ themes of love, solitude, joy, and nature —*Writer*⟩ **3 :** not affected by time : AGELESS — **time·less·ly** *adv* — **time·less·ness** *n*

time loan *n* (1910) : a loan with a definite maturity date

time lock *n* (ca. 1877) : a lock controlled by clockwork to prevent its being opened before a set time

[1]**time·ly** \'tīm-lē\ *adv* (bef. 12c) **1** *archaic* : EARLY, SOON **2 :** in time : OPPORTUNELY ⟨the question was not . . . ~ raised in the state court —W. O. Douglas⟩

[2]**timely** *adj* **time·li·er; -est** (13c) **1 :** coming early or at the right time : OPPORTUNE **2 :** appropriate or adapted to the times or the occasion ⟨a ~ book⟩ — **time·li·ness** *n*

time machine *n* (1895) : a hypothetical device that permits travel into the past and future

time money *n* (ca. 1914) : money loaned or available to be loaned for a specified period of time

time note *n* (ca. 1909) : a note payable at a specified time

time·ous \'tī-məs\ *adj* (15c) : TIMELY — **time·ous·ly** *adv*
time–out \'tī-'maut\ *n* (1926) : a brief suspension of activity : BREAK; *esp* : a suspension of play in an athletic game
time out of mind (15c) : TIME IMMEMORIAL 2
time·piece \'tīm-,pēs\ *n* (1765) : a device (as a clock or watch) to measure or show progress of time
time·pleas·er \-,plē-zər\ *n, obs* (1601) : TIMESERVER
tim·er \'tī-mər\ *n* (1841) : one that times: as **a** : TIMEPIECE; *esp* : a stopwatch for timing races **b** : TIMEKEEPER **c** : a device in the ignition system of an internal-combustion engine that causes the spark to be produced in the cylinder at the correct time **d** : a device (as a clock) that indicates by a sound the end of an interval of time or that starts or stops a device at predetermined times
time reversal *n* (ca. 1963) : a formal operation in mathematical physics that reverses the order in which a sequence of events occurs
times \,tīmz, təmz\ *prep* (14c) : multiplied by ⟨two ~ two is four⟩
time·sav·ing \'tīm-,sā-viŋ\ *adj* (1865) : intended or serving to expedite something ⟨~ kitchen appliances⟩ — **time–sav·er** \-,sā-vər\ *n*
time·serv·er \-,sər-vər\ *n* (1584) : a person who fits his behavior and ideas to the pattern of his time or his superiors : TEMPORIZER
[1]**time·serv·ing** \-viŋ\ *n* (1621) : the behavior or practice of a timeserver
[2]**timeserving** *adj* (1630) : marked by or revealing a lack of independence or integrity ⟨a mean, ~ little man, grovelling odiously before the wealthy people —Peter Forster⟩
time–shar·ing \'tīm-,she(ə)r-iŋ, -,sha(ə)r-\ *n* (1967) **1** : simultaneous use of a central computer by many users at remote locations **2** *or* **time–share** \-,she(ə)r, -,sha(ə)r\ : joint ownership or rental of a vacation lodging (as a condominium) by several persons with each occupying the premises in turn for short periods — **time–share** *vt*
time sheet *n* (1893) **1** : a sheet for recording the time of arrival and departure of workers and for recording the amount of time spent on each job **2** : a sheet for summarizing hours worked by each worker during a pay period
time signature *n* (ca. 1875) : a fractional sign placed just after the key signature whose denominator indicates the kind of note (as a quarter note) taken as the time unit for the beat and whose numerator indicates the number of these to the measure
times sign \'tīm(z)-\ *n* (ca. 1948) : the symbol × used to indicate multiplication
time stamp *n* (1892) : a device for recording the date and time of day that letters or papers are received or sent out — **time–stamp** *vt*
time·ta·ble \'tīm-,tā-bəl\ *n* (1838) **1** : a table of departure and arrival times of trains, buses, or airplanes **2** : a schedule showing a planned order or sequence
time–test·ed \-,tes-təd\ *adj* (1945) : having effectiveness that has been proved over a long period of time ⟨~ methods⟩
time trial *n* (ca. 1949) : a competitive event (as in auto racing) in which individuals are successively timed over a set course or distance
time warp *n* (1971) : an anomaly, discontinuity, or suspension held to occur in the progress of time
time·work \'tīm-,wərk\ *n* (ca. 1829) : work paid for at a standard rate for the hour or the day — **time·work·er** \-,wər-kər\ *n*
time·worn \-,wō(ə)rn, -,wȯ(ə)rn\ *adj* (1729) **1** : worn or impaired by time ⟨~ mansions⟩ **2 a** : AGE-OLD, ANCIENT ⟨~ procedures⟩ **b** : HACKNEYED, STALE ⟨a ~ joke⟩
time zone *n* (1906) : a geographical region within which the same standard time is used

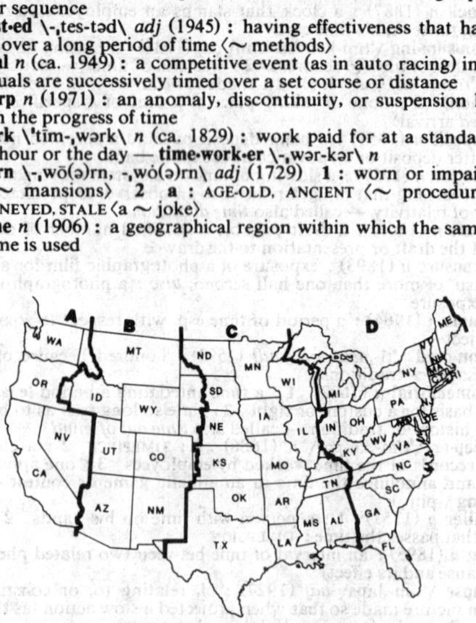

time zones in the conterminous United States: *A* Pacific time, *B* mountain time, *C* central time, *D* eastern time

tim·id \'tim-əd\ *adj* [L *timidus,* fr. *timēre* to fear] (1549) **1** : lacking in courage or self-confidence ⟨a ~ person⟩ **2** : lacking in boldness or determination ⟨a ~ policy⟩ — **ti·mid·i·ty** \tə-'mid-ət-ē\ *n* — **tim·id·ly** \'tim-əd-lē\ *adv* — **tim·id·ness** *n*
tim·ing \'tī-miŋ\ *n* (1597) **1** : selection for maximum effect of the precise moment for beginning or doing something **2** : observation and recording (as by a stopwatch) of the elapsed time of an act, action, or process
ti·moc·ra·cy \tī-'mäk-rə-sē\ *n* [MF *tymocracie,* fr. ML *timocratia,* fr. Gk *timokratia,* fr. *timē* price, value, honor + *-kratia* -cracy — more at PAIN] (1586) **1** : government in which a certain amount of property is necessary for office **2** : government in which love of honor is the ruling principle — **ti·mo·crat·ic** \,tī-mə-'krat-ik\ *or* **ti·mo·crat·i·cal** \-i-kəl\ *adj*
tim·o·rous \'tim-(ə-)rəs\ *adj* [ME, fr. MF *timoureus,* fr. ML *timorosus,* fr. L *timor* fear, fr. *timēre* to fear] (15c) **1** : of a timid disposition : FEARFUL **2** : expressing or suggesting timidity ⟨proceed with doubtful and ~ steps —Edward Gibbon⟩ — **tim·o·rous·ly** *adv* — **tim·o·rous·ness** *n*
tim·o·thy \'tim-ə-thē\ *n* [prob. after *Timothy* Hanson, 18th cent. Am. farmer said to have introduced it from New England to the southern states] (1747) : a European grass (*Phleum pratense*) that has long cylindrical spikes and is widely grown for hay
Tim·o·thy \'tim-ə-thē\ *n* [L *Timotheus,* fr. Gk *Timotheos*] **1** : a disciple of the apostle Paul **2** : either of two letters written with regard to pastoral care in the early Church and included as books in the New Testament — see BIBLE table
tim·pa·ni \'tim-pə-nē\ *n pl but sing or pl in constr* [It, pl. of *timpano* kettledrum, fr. L *tympanum* drum — more at TYMPANUM] (ca. 1854) : a set of two or three kettledrums played by one performer in an orchestra or band
tim·pa·nist \-nəst\ *n* (ca. 1905) : one who plays the timpani
Tim·u·cua \,tim-ə-'kü-ə\ *n* (ca. 1902) : an extinct American Indian language of northeastern Florida
[1]**tin** \'tin\ *n* [ME, fr. OE; akin to OHG *zin* tin] (bef. 12c) **1** : a soft faintly bluish white lustrous low-melting crystalline metallic element that is malleable and ductile at ordinary temperatures and that is used as a protective coating, in tinfoil, and in soft solders and alloys — see ELEMENT table **2 a** : a box, can, pan, vessel, or a sheet made of tinplate; *broadly* : such a container of any metal (as aluminum) **b** : a metal container and its contents ⟨a ~ of tomatoes⟩ — **tin** *adj* — **tin·ful** \-,fu̇l\ *n*
[2]**tin** *vt* **tinned; tin·ning** (14c) **1** : to cover or plate with tin or a tin alloy **2** : to put up or pack in tins : CAN
tin·a·mou \'tin-ə-,mü\ *n* [F, fr. Galibi *tinamu*] (ca. 1783) : any of a family (Tinamidae) of So. and Central American game birds that have a deeply keeled sternum and a rudimentary tail and that produce eggs with a surface resembling enamel
tin·cal \'tiŋ-kəl\ *n* [Malay *tingkal*] (ca. 1635) : crude native borax
tin can *n* (1770) **1** : a can made of tinplate; *broadly* : CAN 1c **2** *slang* : DESTROYER 2
[1]**tinct** \'tiŋ(k)t\ *adj* [L *tinctus,* pp.] (1579) : COLORED, TINGED
[2]**tinct** *n* (1602) : TINCTURE, TINGE
tinc·to·ri·al \tiŋ(k)-'tōr-ē-əl, -'tȯr-\ *adj* [L *tinctorius,* fr. *tinctus,* pp.] (1655) : of or relating to colors or to dyeing or staining; *also* : imparting color — **tinc·to·ri·al·ly** \-ē-ə-lē\ *adv*
[1]**tinc·ture** \'tiŋ(k)-chər\ *n* [ME, fr. L *tinctura* act of dyeing, fr. *tinctus,* pp. of *tingere* to tinge] (15c) **1 a** : a substance that colors, dyes, or stains **b** : COLOR, TINT **2 a** : a characteristic quality : CAST **b** : a slight admixture : TRACE **3** *obs* : an active principle or extract **4** : a heraldic metal, color, or fur **5** : a solution of a medicinal substance in an alcoholic menstruum
[2]**tincture** *vt* **tinc·tured; tinc·tur·ing** \'tiŋ(k)-chə-riŋ, -shriŋ\ (1616) **1** : to tint or stain with a color : TINGE **2 a** : to infuse or instill with a property or entity : IMPREGNATE **b** : to imbue with a quality : AFFECT ⟨writing *tinctured* with wit and wisdom⟩
tin·der \'tin-dər\ *n* [ME, fr. OE *tynder;* akin to OHG *zuntra* tinder, OE *tendan* to kindle] (bef. 12c) **1** : a very flammable substance adaptable for use as kindling **2** : something that serves to incite or inflame ⟨the . . . agreement could not possibly be more loaded with ~ —*Life*⟩
tin·der·box \'tin-dər-,bäks\ *n* (ca. 1530) **1 a** : a metal box for holding tinder and usu. a flint and steel for striking a spark **b** : a highly inflammable object or place **2** : a potentially explosive place or situation
[1]**tine** \'tīn\ *n* [ME *tind,* fr. OE; akin to OHG *zint* point, tine] (bef. 12c) **1** : a slender pointed projecting part : PRONG **2** : a pointed branch of an antler — **tined** \'tīnd\ *adj*
[2]**tine** *vb* **tined** \'tīnd\ *or* **tint** \'tint\; **tin·ing** \'tī-niŋ\ [ME *tinen,* of Scand origin; akin to ON *tȳna* to lose, destroy, *tjōn* injury — more at TEEN] *vt, dial Brit* (13c) : LOSE ~ *vi, dial Brit* : to become lost
tin·ea \'tin-ē-ə\ *n* [ME, fr. ML, fr. L, worm, moth] (14c) : any of several fungal diseases of the skin; *esp* : RINGWORM — **tin·e·al** \-ē-əl\ *adj*
tinea cru·ris \-'kru̇r-əs\ *n* [NL, lit., tinea of the leg] (ca. 1923) : a fungal infection involving esp. the groin and perineum
tin ear *n* (ca. 1920) : a deafened or insensitive ear
tin fish *n, slang* (ca. 1925) : TORPEDO
tin·foil \'tin-,fȯil\ *n* (15c) **1** : a paper-thin metal sheeting usu. of aluminum or tin-lead alloy **2** : SILVER PAPER
ting *n* [*ting,* vb., fr. ME *tingen*] (1602) : a high-pitched sound like that made by a light stroke on a crystal goblet — **ting** *vi*
[1]**tinge** \'tinj\ *vt* **tinged; tinge·ing** *or* **ting·ing** \'tin-jiŋ\ [ME *tingen,* fr. L *tingere* to dip, moisten, tinge; akin to OHG *dunkōn* to dip, Gk *tengein* to moisten] (15c) **1 a** : to color with a slight shade or stain : TINT **b** : to affect or modify with a slight odor or taste **2** : to affect or modify in character
[2]**tinge** *n* (1752) **1** : a slight staining or suffusing shade or color **2** : an affective or modifying property or influence : TOUCH
tin·gle \'tiŋ-gəl\ *vi* **tin·gled; tin·gling** \-g(ə-)liŋ\ [ME *tinglen,* alter. of *tinklen* to tinkle, tingle] (14c) **1 a** : to feel a ringing, stinging, prickling, or thrilling sensation **b** : to cause such a sensation **2** : TINKLE — **tingle** *n* — **tin·gling·ly** \-g(ə-)liŋ-lē\ *adv* — **tin·gly** \-g(ə-)lē\ *adj*
tin hat *n* (1917) : a metal helmet
tin·horn \'tin-,hȯ(ə)rn\ *n* (1885) : one (as a gambler) who pretends to have money, ability, or influence
[1]**tin·ker** \'tiŋ-kər\ *n* [ME *tinkere*] (13c) **1 a** : a usu. itinerant mender of household utensils **b** : an unskillful mender : BUNGLER **2** *chiefly Irish* : GYPSY
[2]**tinker** *vb* **tin·kered; tin·ker·ing** \-k(ə-)riŋ\ *vi* (1592) : to work in the manner of a tinker; *esp* : to repair, adjust, or work with something in an unskilled or experimental manner : FIDDLE ~ *vt* : to repair, adjust, or experiment with — **tin·ker·er** \-kər-ər\ *n*
tinker's damn *or* **tinker's dam** \-'dam\ *n* [prob. fr. the tinkers' reputation for blasphemy] (ca. 1876) : a minimum amount or degree (as of care) ⟨didn't give a *tinker's damn* about poetry —James Blish⟩
Tin·ker·toy \'tiŋ-kər-,tȯi\ *trademark* — used for a construction toy of fitting parts
[1]**tin·kle** \'tiŋ-kəl\ *vb* **tin·kled; tin·kling** \-k(ə-)liŋ\ [ME *tinklen,* freq. of *tinken* to tinkle, of imit. origin] *vi* (15c) : to make or emit a tinkle or a sound suggestive of a tinkle ~ *vt* **1** : to sound or make known (the time) by a tinkle **2 a** : to cause to make a tinkle **b** : to produce by tinkling ⟨~ a tune⟩
[2]**tinkle** *n* (1776) **1** : a jingling effect in verse or prose **2** : a series of short high ringing or clinking sounds
tin·kly \'tiŋ-k(ə-)lē\ *adj* (1892) : that tinkles : TINKLING
tin·ner \'tin-ər\ *n* (1512) **1** : a tin miner **2** : TINSMITH

tin·ni·tus \'tin-ət-əs\ *n* [L, ringing, tinnitus, fr. *tinnitus,* pp. of *tinnire* to ring, of imit. origin] (1843) **:** a sensation of noise (as a ringing or roaring) that is caused by a bodily condition (as wax in the ear or a perforated tympanic membrane) and can usu. be heard only by the one affected

tin·ny \'tin-ē\ *adj* **tin·ni·er; -est** (1552) **1 :** of, abounding in, or yielding tin **2 a :** resembling tin **b :** LIGHT, CHEAP **3 :** thin in tone ⟨a ~ voice⟩ — **tin·ni·ly** \'tin-ᵊl-ē\ *adv* — **tin·ni·ness** \'tin-ē-nəs\ *n*

Tin Pan Alley *n* (1899) **:** a district that is a center for composers and publishers of popular music; *also* **:** the body of such composers and publishers

tin·plate \'tin-'plāt\ *n* (1677) **:** thin sheet iron or steel coated with tin

tin–plate *vt* (1890) **:** to plate or coat (as a metal sheet) with tin

[1]**tin·sel** \'tin(t)-səl *also* 'tin-zəl\ *adj* (1575) **1 :** made of or covered with tinsel **2 a :** cheaply gaudy **:** TAWDRY **b :** SPECIOUS ⟨spent his life chasing ~ promises —Ved Mehta⟩

[2]**tinsel** *n* [MF *estincelle, estancele, etincelle* spark, glitter, spangle — more at STENCIL] (1593) **1 :** a thread, strip, or sheet of metal, paper, or plastic used to produce a glittering and sparkling appearance in fabrics, yarns, or decorations **2 :** something superficially attractive or glamorous but of little real worth ⟨disfigured by no gaudy ~ of rhetoric or declamation —Thomas Jefferson⟩

[3]**tinsel** *vt* **tin·seled** *or* **tin·selled; tin·sel·ing** *or* **tin·sel·ling** \'tin(t)-s(ə-)liŋ, 'tin-zə-liŋ\ (1594) **1 :** to interweave, overlay, or adorn with or as if with tinsel **2 :** to impart a specious brightness to

tin·sel·ly \'tin(t)-s(ə-)lē, 'tin-zə-lē\ *adj* (1811) **:** TINSEL

tin·smith \'tin-ˌsmith\ *n* (1812) **:** a worker who makes or repairs things of sheet metal (as tinplate) — **tin·smith·ing** \-iŋ\ *n*

tin·stone \'tin-ˌstōn\ *n* (1602) **:** CASSITERITE

[1]**tint** \'tint\ *n* [alter. of earlier *tinct,* fr. L *tinctus* act of dyeing, fr. *tinctus,* pp. of *tingere* to tinge] (1717) **1 a :** a usu. slight or pale coloration **:** HUE **b :** any of various lighter or darker shades of a color **:** TINGE **2 :** a variation of a color produced by adding white to it and characterized by a low saturation with relatively high lightness **3 :** a usu. slight modifying quality or characteristic **:** TOUCH **4 :** a shaded effect in engraving produced by fine parallel lines close together **5 :** a panel of light color serving as background **6 :** dye for the hair — **tint·er** *n*

[2]**tint** *vt* (1791) **:** to impart or apply a tint to **:** COLOR

tint·ing *n* (ca. 1841) **1 :** the act or process of one that tints **2 :** the engraved or colored tint produced by tinting

tin·tin·nab·u·lary \ˌtin-tə-'nab-yə-ˌler-ē\ *adj* [L *tintinnabulum* bell] (1787) **:** of, relating to, or characterized by bells or their sounds

tin·tin·nab·u·la·tion \ˌtin-tə-ˌnab-yə-'lā-shən\ *n* [L *tintinnabulum* bell, fr. *tintinnare* to ring, jingle, of imit. origin] (1831) **1 :** the ringing or sounding of bells **2 :** a jingling or tinkling sound as if of bells

tint·less \'tint-ləs\ *adj* (1789) **:** having no tints **:** lacking color

tin·type \-ˌtīp\ *n* (1864) **:** FERROTYPE 1

tin·ware \'tin-ˌwa(ə)r, -ˌwe(ə)r\ *n* (1758) **:** articles and esp. utensils made of tinplate

tin·work \-ˌwərk\ *n* (15c) **1 :** work in tin **2** *pl but sing or pl in constr* **:** an establishment where tin is smelted, rolled, or otherwise worked

ti·ny \'tī-nē\ *adj* **ti·ni·er; -est** [alter. of ME *tine*] (15c) **:** very small or diminutive **:** MINUTE ***syn*** see SMALL — **ti·ni·ly** \'tīn-ᵊl-ē\ *adv* — **ti·ni·ness** \'tī-nē-nəs\ *n*

[1]**tip** \'tip\ *vb* **tipped; tip·ping** [ME *tipen*] *vt* (14c) **1 :** OVERTURN, UPSET — usu. used with *over* **2 a :** CANT, TILT **b :** to raise and tilt forward in salute ⟨*tipped* his hat⟩ ~ *vi* **1 :** to become tipped **:** TOPPLE **2 :** LEAN, SLANT — **tip the scales 1 :** to register weight ⟨*tips the scales* at 285 pounds⟩ **2 :** to shift the balance of power or influence ⟨*tipped the scales* in favor of a declaration of war —S. F. Bemis⟩

[2]**tip** *n* (1673) **1 :** the act or an instance of tipping **:** TILT **2** *chiefly Brit* **:** a place for depositing something (as rubbish) by dumping

[3]**tip** *n* [ME; akin to MHG *zipf* tip, OE *tæppa* tap — more at TAP] (15c) **1 :** the usu. pointed end of something **2 :** a small piece or part serving as an end, cap, or point — **tipped** \'tipt\ *adj*

[4]**tip** *vt* **tipped; tip·ping** (15c) **1 a :** to furnish with a tip **b** (1) **:** to cover or adorn the tip of (2) **:** to blend (furs) for improved appearance by brushing the tips of the hair with dye **2 :** to affix (an insert) in a book — often used with *in* **3 :** to remove the ends of ⟨~ raspberries⟩

[5]**tip** *n* [ME *tippe;* akin to LG *tippen* to tap] (15c) **:** a light touch or blow

[6]**tip** *vb* **tipped; tip·ping** *vt* (1567) **1 :** to strike lightly **:** TAP **2 :** to give (a baseball) a glancing blow ~ *vi* **:** TIPTOE

[7]**tip** *n* [origin unknown] (1567) **1 :** an item of expert or authoritative information **2 :** a piece of advance or confidential information given by one thought to have access to special or inside sources

[8]**tip** *vt* **tipped; tip·ping** (1883) **1 :** to impart a piece of information or advice about or to — often used with *off* **2 :** to mention as a prospective winner or profitable investment ⟨industrials are being *tipped* in the forecasts⟩ — **tip one's hand** *also* **tip one's mitt :** to declare one's intentions or reveal one's resources ⟨the Justice Department wouldn't *tip its hand* by saying what its next move . . . would be —*Newsweek*⟩

[9]**tip** *vb* **tipped; tip·ping** [perh. fr. [6]*tip*] *vt* (ca. 1610) **1 :** GIVE, PRESENT **2 :** to give a gratuity to ~ *vi* **:** to bestow a gratuity

[10]**tip** *n* (1755) **:** a gift or a sum of money tendered for a service performed or anticipated **:** GRATUITY

tip·cart \'tip-ˌkärt\ *n* (ca. 1877) **:** a cart whose body can be tipped on the frame to empty its contents

tip·cat \-ˌkat\ *n* [[6]*tip*] (ca. 1801) **:** a game in which one player using a bat strikes lightly a tapered wooden peg and as it flies up strikes it again to drive it as far as possible while fielders try to recover it; *also* **:** the peg used in this game

ti·pi \'tē-(ˌ)pē\ *var of* TEPEE

tip–in \'tip-ˌin\ *n* [[6]*tip*] (1948) **:** a goal in basketball made by deflecting a rebound into the basket with the fingertips

[1]**tip–off** \'tip-ˌȯf\ *n* [[6]*tip*] (1922) **:** the act or an instance of putting the ball in play in basketball by a jump ball

[2]**tip–off** *n* [[8]*tip*] (1923) **:** WARNING, TIP

tip of the iceberg [fr. an iceberg being mostly submerged] (1969) **:** the earliest, most obvious, or most superficial manifestation of some phenomenon

tip·per \'tip-ər\ *n* (1819) **:** one that tips

tip·pet \'tip-ət\ *n* [ME *tipet*] (14c) **1 :** a long hanging end of cloth attached to a sleeve, cap, or hood **2 :** a shoulder cape of fur or cloth often with hanging ends **3 :** a long black scarf worn over the robe by Anglican clergymen during morning and evening prayer

[1]**tip·ple** \'tip-əl\ *vb* **tip·pled; tip·pling** \-(ə-)liŋ\ [back-formation fr. obs. *tippler* (barkeeper)] *vi* (1560) **:** to drink liquor esp. by habit or to excess ~ *vt* **:** to drink (liquor) esp. continuously in small amounts — **tip·pler** \-(ə-)lər\ *n*

[2]**tipple** *n* (1581) **:** an intoxicating beverage **:** DRINK

[3]**tipple** *n* [E dial. *tipple* to tip over, freq. of E *tip*] (1880) **1 :** a place where or an apparatus by which cars (as for coal) are loaded or emptied **2 :** a coal-screening plant

tip·py \'tip-ē\ *adj* **tip·pi·er; -est** (1886) **:** liable to tip ⟨a ~ boat⟩

tip·staff \'tip-ˌstaf\ *n, pl* **tip·staves** \-ˌstavz, -ˌstāvz\ [obs. *tipstaff* (staff tipped with metal)] (1570) **:** an officer (as a constable or bailiff) who bears a staff

tip·ster \'tip-stər\ *n* (1862) **:** one who gives or sells tips esp. for gambling or speculation

tip·sy \'tip-sē\ *adj* **tip·si·er; -est** [[1]*tip* + *-sy* (as in *tricksy*)] (1577) **1 :** unsteady, staggering, or foolish from the effects of liquor **:** FUDDLED **2 :** UNSTEADY, ASKEW ⟨a ~ angle⟩ — **tip·si·ly** \-sə-lē\ *adv* — **tip·si·ness** \-sē-nəs\ *n*

[1]**tip·toe** \'tip-ˌtō, -'tō\ *n* (14c) **:** the tip of a toe; *also* **:** the ends of the toes — **on tiptoe :** ALERT, AROUSED ⟨the contest of skill that puts one *on tiptoe* to win —*Deerfield (Wis.) Independent*⟩

[2]**tiptoe** *adv* (1592) **:** on or as if on tiptoe

[3]**tiptoe** *adj* (1593) **1 :** standing or walking on or as if on tiptoe **2 :** CAUTIOUS, STEALTHY

[4]**tiptoe** *vi* **tip·toed; tip·toe·ing** (1661) **1 :** to stand or raise oneself on tiptoe **2 :** to walk or proceed quietly or cautiously on or as if on tiptoe

[1]**tip–top** \'tip-'täp, -ˌtäp\ *n* [[3]*tip* + *top*] (1702) **:** the highest point

[2]**tip–top** *adj* (1732) **:** EXCELLENT, FIRST-RATE ⟨~ working conditions⟩

[3]**tip–top** *adv* (1882) **:** very well

ti·rade \tī-'rād, 'tī-ˌ\ *n* [F, shot, tirade, fr. MF, fr. OIt *tirata,* fr. *tirare* to draw, shoot; akin to Sp & Pg *tirar* to draw, shoot, OF *tirer*] (1802) **:** a protracted speech usu. marked by intemperate, vituperative, or harshly censorious language

[1]**tire** \'tī(ə)r\ *vb* **tired; tir·ing** [ME *tyren,* fr. OE *tēorian, tȳrian*] *vi* (bef. 12c) **:** to become weary ~ *vt* **1 :** to exhaust or greatly decrease the physical strength of **:** FATIGUE **2 :** to wear out the patience of **:** bore completely

syn TIRE, WEARY, FATIGUE, EXHAUST, JADE, FAG mean to make or become unable or unwilling to continue. TIRE implies a draining of one's strength or patience; WEARY stresses tiring until one is unable to endure more of the same thing; FATIGUE suggests causing great lassitude through excessive strain or undue effort; EXHAUST implies complete draining of strength by hard exertion; JADE suggests the loss of all freshness and eagerness; FAG implies a drooping with fatigue.

[2]**tire** *n* [ME, short for *attire*] (14c) **1** *obs* **:** ATTIRE **2** *archaic* **:** a woman's headband or hair ornament

[3]**tire** *vt* **tired; tir·ing** (14c) **1** *obs* **:** ATTIRE **2** *archaic* **:** to adorn (the hair) with an ornament

[4]**tire** *n, often attrib* [ME, prob. fr. [2]*tire*] (15c) **1 :** a metal hoop forming the tread of a wheel **2 a :** a continuous solid or pneumatic rubber cushion encircling a wheel and usu. consisting when pneumatic of an external rubber-and-fabric covering that contains and protects from injury an air-filled inner tube **b :** the external rubber-and-fabric covering of a pneumatic tire

tired \'tī(ə)rd\ *adj* (15c) **1 :** drained of strength and energy **:** fatigued often to the point of exhaustion **:** WEARY **2 :** obviously worn by hard use **:** RUN-DOWN **3 :** TRITE, HACKNEYED ⟨the same old ~ themes⟩ — **tired·ly** *adv* — **tired·ness** *n*

tire·less \'tī(ə)r-ləs\ *adj* (1591) **:** seemingly incapable of tiring **:** INDEFATIGABLE — **tire·less·ly** *adv* — **tire·less·ness** *n*

Ti·re·si·as \tī-'rē-sē-əs, -zē-\ *n* [L, fr. Gk *Teiresias*] **:** a blind seer of Thebes who in one Greek myth is changed into a woman for several years and then changed back to a man

tire·some \'tī(ə)r-səm\ *adj* (1500) **:** WEARISOME, TEDIOUS — **tire·some·ly** *adv* — **tire·some·ness** *n*

tir·ing–house \'tī-riŋ-ˌhau̇s\ *n* [[3]*tire*] (1590) **:** a section of a theater reserved for the actors and used esp. for dressing for stage entrances

tir·ing–room \-ˌrüm, -ˌru̇m\ *n* [[3]*tire*] (1623) **:** a dressing room esp. in a theater

tirl \'tərl\ *vb* [alter. of [1]*trill*] *vi, chiefly Scot* (1500) **:** to make a rattling sound (as with a door latch) ~ *vt, chiefly Scot* **:** TWIRL

tiro *chiefly Brit var of* TYRO

'tis \'tiz, (ˌ)tiz, təz\ [contr.] **:** it is

ti·sane \ti-'zan, -'zän\ *n* [ME, fr. MF, fr. L *ptisana,* fr. Gk *ptisanē,* lit., crushed barley] (14c) **:** an infusion (as of dried herbs) used as a beverage or for medicinal effects

Tish·ah–b'Ab \'tish-ə-ˌbäv, -ˌbȯv\ *n* [Heb *tish'āh bĕ Ābh* ninth in Ab] (ca. 1902) **:** a Jewish holiday observed with fasting on the 9th of Ab in commemoration of the destruction of the temples at Jerusalem

Tish·ri \'tish-rē\ *n* [Heb *tishrī*] (1769) **:** the 1st month of the civil year or the 7th month of the ecclesiastical year in the Jewish calendar — see MONTH table

tis·sue \'tish-(ˌ)ü, 'tish-ə(-w), *chiefly Brit* 'tis-(ˌ)yü\ *n* [ME *tissu,* a rich fabric, fr. OF, fr. pp. of *tistre* to weave, fr. L *texere* — more at TECHNICAL] (1711) **1 a :** a fine lightweight often sheer fabric **b :** MESH, NETWORK, WEB ⟨a ~ of lies⟩ **2 :** a piece of soft absorbent tissue paper used esp. as a handkerchief or for removing cosmetics **3 :** an aggregate of cells usu. of a particular kind together with their intercellular substance that form one of the structural materials of a plant or an animal — **tis·su·ey** \'tish-ə-wē\ *adj*

tissue culture *n* (ca. 1923) **:** the process or technique of making body tissue grow in a culture medium outside the organism; *also* **:** a culture of tissue (as epithelium)

\ə\ abut \ᵊ\ kitten, F table \ər\ further \a\ ash \ā\ ace \ä\ cot, cart \au̇\ out \ch\ chin \e\ bet \ē\ easy \g\ go \i\ hit \ī\ ice \j\ job \ŋ\ sing \ō\ go \ȯ\ law \ȯi\ boy \th\ thin \t͟h\ the \ü\ loot \u̇\ foot \y\ yet \zh\ vision \à, k̲, ⁿ, œ, œ̄, ue, ue̅, ʸ\ see Guide to Pronunciation

tissue fluid *n* (ca. 1916) **:** a fluid that permeates the spaces between individual cells, that is in osmotic contact with the blood and lymph, and that serves in interstitial transport of nutrients and waste
tissue paper *n* (1777) **:** a thin gauzy paper used esp. for protecting something (as by covering or wrapping)
tis·su·lar \ˈtish-ə-lər\ *adj* [*tissue* + *-lar* (as in *cellular*)] (ca. 1935) **:** of, relating to, or affecting organismic tissue ⟨~ grafts⟩ ⟨~ lesions⟩
1**tit** \ˈtit\ *n* [ME, fr. OE] (bef. 12c) **1 :** TEAT **2 :** BREAST — usu. used in pl.; usu. considered vulgar
2**tit** *n* (ca. 1706) **:** TITMOUSE; *broadly* **:** any of various small plump often long-tailed birds
ti·tan \ˈtīt-ᵊn\ *n* [Gk] (15c) **1** *cap* **:** any of a family of giants born of Uranus and Gaea and ruling the earth until overthrown by the Olympian gods **2 :** one that is gigantic in size or power **:** one that stands out for greatness of achievement
titan- *or* **titano-** *comb form* [NL *titanium*] **:** titanium ⟨*titanate*⟩
ti·ta·nate \ˈtīt-ᵊn-ˌāt\ *n* (1839) **1 :** any of various multiple oxides of titanium dioxide with other metallic oxides **2 :** a titanium ester of the general formula $Ti(OR)_4$
ti·tan·ess \ˈtīt-ᵊn-əs\ *n, often cap* (1596) **:** a female titan
ti·ta·nia \tī-ˈtān-ē-ə, tə-, -ˈtān-yə *also* -ˈtan-\ *n* (1922) **:** TITANIUM DIOXIDE; *esp* **:** a clear transparent rutile cut as a gemstone
Ti·ta·nia \tə-ˈtān-yə, -ˈtän-; tī-ˈtān-\ *n* **:** the wife of Oberon and queen of the fairies in Shakespeare's *A Midsummer Night's Dream*
1**ti·tan·ic** \tī-ˈtan-ik *also* tə-\ *adj* [Gk *titanikos* of the Titans] (1709) **:** having great magnitude, force, or power **:** COLOSSAL — **ti·tan·i·cal·ly** \-i-k(ə-)lē\ *adv*
2**ti·ta·nic** \tī-ˈtan-ik, tə-, -ˈtān-\ *adj* [NL *titanium*] (1826) **:** of, relating to, or containing titanium esp. when tetravalent
ti·ta·nif·er·ous \ˌtīt-ᵊn-ˈif-(ə-)rəs\ *adj* (ca. 1828) **:** containing or yielding titanium ⟨~ minerals⟩
ti·tan·ism \ˈtīt-ᵊn-ˌiz-əm\ *n, often cap* [fr. the Titans' rebellion against their father Uranus] (1867) **:** defiance of and revolt against social or artistic conventions
ti·ta·ni·um \tī-ˈtān-ē-əm, tə- *also* -ˈtan-\ *n* [NL, fr. Gk *Titan*] (ca. 1796) **:** a silvery gray light strong metallic element found combined in ilmenite and rutile and used esp. in alloys (as steel) and combined in refractory materials and in coatings — see ELEMENT table
titanium dioxide *n* (ca. 1924) **:** an oxide TiO_2 of titanium that occurs in rutile, anatase, or ilmenite and is used esp. as a pigment
titanium white *n* (ca. 1924) **:** TITANIUM DIOXIDE; *also* **:** a brilliant white lead-free pigment consisting of titanium dioxide often together with barium sulfate and zinc oxide
ti·ta·nous \tī-ˈtan-əs, tə-, -ˈtān-; ˈtīt-ᵊn-\ *adj* [ISV] (1866) **:** of, relating to, or containing titanium esp. when trivalent
tit·bit \ˈtit-ˌbit\ *var of* TIDBIT
ti·ter \ˈtīt-ər\ *n* [F *titre* title, proportion of gold or silver in a coin, fr. OF *title* inscription, title] (1888) **:** the strength of a solution or the concentration of a substance (as an antibody) in solution as determined by titration
tit·fer \ˈtit-fər\ *n* [by shortening & alter. fr. *tit for tat*, rhyming slang for *hat*] *Brit* (ca. 1945) **:** HAT
tit for tat \ˌtit-fər-ˈtat\ [alter. of earlier *tip for tap*, fr. *tip* (blow) + *for* + *tap*] (1556) **:** an equivalent given in return (as for an injury)
tith·able \ˈtī-t͟hə-bəl\ *adj* (15c) **:** subject or liable to payment of tithes
1**tithe** \ˈtīt͟h\ *vb* **tithed; tith·ing** [ME *tithen*, fr. OE *teogothian*, fr. *teogotha* tenth; akin to OE *tien* ten — more at TEN] *vt* (bef. 12c) **1 :** to pay or give a tenth part of esp. for the support of the church **2 :** to levy a tithe on ~ *vi* **:** to give a tenth of one's income as a tithe
2**tithe** *n* (bef. 12c) **1 :** a tenth part of something paid as a voluntary contribution or as a tax esp. for the support of a religious establishment **2 :** the obligation represented by individual tithes **3 :** TENTH; *broadly* **:** a small part **4 :** a small tax or levy
tith·er \ˈtī-t͟hər\ *n* (14c) **1 :** one that pays tithes **2 :** one that collects or advocates the payment of tithes
tith·ing \ˈtī-t͟hiŋ\ *n* [ME, fr. OE *tēothung*, fr. *teogothian*, *tēothian* to tithe, take one tenth] (bef. 12c) **:** a small administrative division preserved in parts of England apparently orig. made up of ten men with their families
ti·tho·nia \tə-ˈthō-nyə, tī-, -nē-ə\ *n* [NL, prob. fr. L *Tithonia*, poetical name of Aurora] (1940) **:** any of a genus (*Tithonia*) of tall composite herbs that have alternate leaves and flower heads resembling sunflowers and that are sometimes grown as annual ornamentals
1**ti·ti** \ˈtī-ˌtī\ *n* [prob. fr. Timucua] (1827) **:** a tree (*Cliftonia monophylla* of the family Cyrillaceae) of the southern U.S. with glossy leaves and racemes of fragrant white flowers; *also* **:** any of several trees of a related genus (*Cyrilla*)
2**ti·ti** \ti-ˈtē\ *n* [Sp *tití*, fr. Aymara *titi*, lit., little cat] (1832) **:** any of various small So. American monkeys (genus *Callicebus*) resembling squirrel monkeys — called also *titi monkey*

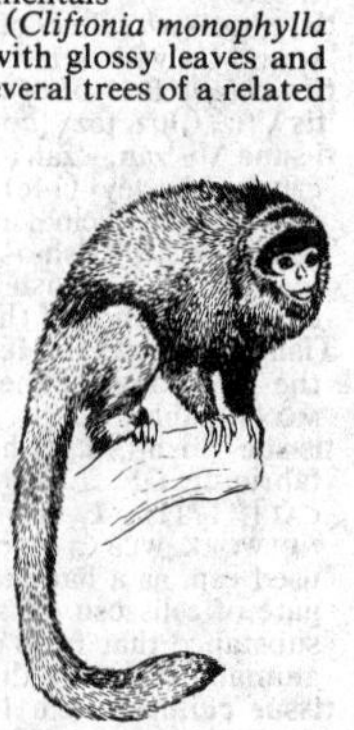
titi

ti·tian \ˈtish-ən\ *adj, often cap* [*Titian* (Tiziano Vecellio)] (1896) **:** of a brownish orange color
tit·il·late \ˈtit-ᵊl-ˌāt\ *vb* **-lat·ed; -lat·ing** [L *titillatus*, pp. of *titillare*] *vt* (1620) **1 :** to excite pleasurably **:** arouse by stimulation **2 :** TICKLE ~ *vi* **:** to act as a stimulant to pleasurable excitement — **tit·il·la·tion** \ˌtit-ᵊl-ˈā-shən\ *n* — **tit·il·la·tive** \ˈtit-ᵊl-ˌāt-iv\ *adj*
tit·il·lat·ing \ˈtit-ᵊl-ˌāt-iŋ\ *adj* (1712) **:** pleasantly stimulating or exciting ⟨~ reading⟩; *also* **:** EROTIC — **tit·il·lat·ing·ly** \-iŋ-lē\ *adv*
tit·i·vate *or* **tit·ti·vate** \ˈtit-ə-ˌvāt\ *vb* **-vat·ed; -vat·ing** [perh. fr. 1*tidy* + *-vate* (as in *renovate*)] *vt* (1824) **:** to make smart or spruce ~ *vi* **:** SMARTEN, SPRUCE — **tit·i·va·tion** \ˌtit-ə-ˈvā-shən\ *n*
tit·lark \ˈtit-ˌlärk\ *n* [*tit-* (as in *titmouse*) + *lark*] (1688) **:** PIPIT
1**ti·tle** \ˈtīt-ᵊl\ *n* [ME, fr. MF, fr. L *titulus* inscription, title] (14c) **1 a** *obs* **:** INSCRIPTION **b :** written material introduced into a motion picture or television program to give credits, explain an action, or represent dialogue — usu. used in pl. **2 a :** all the elements constituting legal ownership **b :** a legally just cause of exclusive possession **c :** the instrument (as a deed) that is evidence of a right **3 a :** something that justifies or substantiates a claim **b :** an alleged or recognized right **4 a :** a descriptive or general heading (as of a chapter in a book) **b :** the heading which names an act or statute **c :** the heading of a legal action or proceeding **5 a :** the distinguishing name of a written, printed, or filmed production **b :** a similar distinguishing name of a musical composition or a work of art **6 :** a descriptive name **:** APPELLATION **7 :** a division of an instrument, book, or bill; *esp* **:** one larger than a section or article **8 a :** an appellation of dignity, honor, distinction, or preeminence attached to a person or family by virtue of rank, office, precedent, privilege, attainment, or lands **b :** a person holding a title esp. of nobility **9 :** a written work as distinguished from a particular copy ⟨published 25 ~*s* last year⟩ **10 :** CHAMPIONSHIP 1 ⟨won the batting ~⟩
2**title** *vt* **ti·tled; ti·tling** \ˈtīt-liŋ, -ᵊl-iŋ\ (14c) **1 :** to provide a title for **2 :** to designate or call by a title **:** TERM, STYLE
3**title** *adj* (1886) **:** of or relating to a title: as **a :** having the same name as the title of a production ⟨did the ~ role in *Hamlet*⟩ **b :** having the same title as or providing the title for the collection or production of which it forms a part ⟨the ~ song⟩ **c :** of, relating to, or involving a championship ⟨a ~ match⟩ **d :** of, relating to, or used with the titles that introduce a motion picture or television program ⟨~ music⟩
ti·tled \ˈtīt-ᵊld\ *adj* (1746) **:** having a title esp. of nobility
title deed *n* (1768) **:** the deed constituting the evidence of a person's legal ownership
ti·tle·hold·er \ˈtīt-ᵊl-ˌhōl-dər\ *n* (1904) **:** one that holds a title; *specif* **:** CHAMPION
title page *n* (1613) **:** a page of a book bearing the title and usu. the names of the author and publisher and the place and sometimes date of publication
ti·tlist \ˈtīt-ᵊl-əst, ˈtīt-ləst\ *n* (1936) **:** TITLEHOLDER
tit·mouse \ˈtit-ˌmau̇s\ *n, pl* **tit·mice** \-ˌmīs\ [by folk etymology fr. ME *titmose*, fr. (assumed) ME *tit* any small object or creature + *mose* titmouse, fr. OE *māse;* akin to OHG *meisa* titmouse] (14c) **:** any of numerous small arboreal and insectivorous passerine birds (family Paridae and esp. genus *Parus*) that are related to the nuthatches but have longer tails
Ti·to·ism \ˈtēt-(ˌ)ō-ˌiz-əm\ *n* (1949) **:** the political, economic, and social policies associated with Tito; *specif* **:** nationalistic policies and practices followed by a communist state or group independently of and often in opposition to the U.S.S.R. — **Ti·to·ist** \-ˌō-əst\ *n or adj*
ti·trant \ˈtī-trənt\ *n* (1939) **:** a substance (as a reagent solution of precisely known concentration) that is added in titration
ti·trate \ˈtī-ˌtrāt\ *vb* **ti·trat·ed; ti·trat·ing** [*titer*] *vt* (1863) **:** to subject to titration ~ *vi* **:** to perform titration — **ti·trat·able** \-ˌtrāt-ə-bəl\ *adj* — **ti·tra·tor** \-ˌtrāt-ər\ *n*
ti·tra·tion \tī-ˈtrā-shən\ *n* (ca. 1859) **:** a method or the process of determining the concentration of a dissolved substance in terms of the smallest amount of a reagent of known concentration required to bring about a given effect in reaction with a known volume of the test solution
ti·tre \ˈtīt-ər\ *var of* TITER
ti·tri·met·ric \ˌtī-trə-ˈme-trik\ *adj* [*titration* + *-i-* + *-metric*] (1902) **:** employing or determined by titration — **ti·tri·met·ri·cal·ly** \-tri-k(ə-)lē\ *adv*
tit–tat–toe \ˌti-ˌta(t)-ˈtō\ *var of* TICKTACKTOE
tit·ter \ˈtit-ər\ *vi* [imit.] (1619) **:** to laugh in a nervous, affected, or partly suppressed manner **:** GIGGLE, SNICKER — **titter** *n*
tit·tie \ˈtit-ē\ *n* [prob. baby talk alter. of *sister*] *chiefly Scot* (1700) **:** SISTER
tit·tle \ˈtit-ᵊl\ *n* [ME *titel*, fr. ML *titulus*, fr. L, title] (14c) **1 :** a point or small sign used as a diacritical mark in writing or printing **2 :** a very small part
tit·tle–tat·tle \ˈtit-ᵊl-ˌtat-ᵊl\ *n* [redupl. of 1*tattle*] (1529) **:** GOSSIP, PRATTLE — **tittle–tattle** *vi*
1**tit·tup** \ˈtit-əp\ *n* [imit. of the sound of a horse's hooves] (1703) **:** lively, gay, or restless behavior **:** PRANCE, CAPER
2**tittup** *vi* **-tupped** *or* **-tuped; -tup·ping** *or* **-tup·ing** (1785) **:** to move in a lively manner often with an exaggerated or affected action
1**tit·u·lar** \ˈtich-(ə-)lər\ *adj* [L *titulus* title] (1611) **1 a :** existing in title only; *esp* **:** bearing a title derived from a defunct ecclesiastical jurisdiction (as an episcopal see) ⟨a ~ bishop⟩ **b :** having the title and usu. the honors belonging to an office or dignity without the duties, functions, or responsibilities ⟨the ~ head of a political party⟩ **2 :** bearing a title **:** TITLED **3 :** of, relating to, or constituting a title ⟨the ~ hero of the play⟩ — **tit·u·lar·ly** *adv*
2**titular** *n* (1613) **:** a person holding a title
Ti·tus \ˈtīt-əs\ *n* [LL, fr. Gk *Titos*] **1 :** an early Christian convert who assisted Paul in his missionary work **2 :** a letter written on the subject of pastoral care in the early Church and included as a book in the New Testament — see BIBLE table
Tiu \ˈtē-(ˌ)ü\ *n* [OE *Tīw* — more at DEITY] **:** an ancient Germanic god of war identified with Tyr
tiz·zy \ˈtiz-ē\ *n, pl* **tizzies** [origin unknown] (1935) **:** a highly excited and distracted state of mind
TKO \ˌtē-ˌkā-ˈō\ *n* [*technical knockout*] (1941) **:** TECHNICAL KNOCKOUT
Tlin·git \ˈtliŋ-(g)ət, ˈtliŋ-kət\ *n, pl* **Tlingit** *or* **Tlingits** (1881) **1 :** a member of a group of Indian peoples of the islands and coast of southern Alaska **2 :** a language stock of the Na-dene phylum
T lymphocyte *n* [*thymus-derived lymphocyte*] (1972) **:** T CELL
T–man \ˈtē-ˌman\ *n* [*Treasury man*] (1937) **:** a special agent of the U.S. Treasury Department
tme·sis \(tə-)ˈmē-səs\ *n* [LL, fr. Gk *tmēsis* act of cutting, fr. *temnein* to cut — more at TOME] (ca. 1586) **:** separation of parts of a compound word by the intervention of one or more words (as *what place soever* for *whatsoever place*)
TNT \ˌtē-ˌen-ˈtē\ *n* [*trinitrotoluene*] (1915) **:** TRINITROTOLUENE
1**to** \tə, tu̇, (ˈ)tü; *before vowels usu* tə *also* təw; *after* t (*as in "want"*) *often* ə; *sentence-final usu* (ˈ)tü\ *prep* [ME, fr. OE *tō;* akin to OHG *zuo* to, L *donec* as long as, until] (bef. 12c) **1 a** — used as a function word to indicate movement or an action or condition suggestive of movement toward a place, person, or thing reached ⟨drove ~ the city⟩ ⟨went back ~ his original idea⟩ **b** — used as a function word to indicate direction ⟨a mile ~ the south⟩ ⟨turned his back ~ the door⟩ ⟨a tendency ~ silli-

ness⟩ **c** — used as a function word to indicate contact or proximity ⟨applied polish ~ the table⟩ ⟨stood there with her hands ~ her eyes⟩ **d** (1) — used as a function word to indicate the place or point that is the far limit ⟨100 miles ~ the nearest town⟩ (2) — used as a function word to indicate the limit of extent ⟨stripped ~ the waist⟩ **e** — used as a function word to indicate relative position ⟨perpendicular ~ the floor⟩ **2 a** — used as a function word to indicate purpose, intention, tendency, result, or end ⟨came ~ our aid⟩ ⟨drink ~ his health⟩ **b** — used as a function word to indicate the result of an action or a process ⟨broken all ~ pieces⟩ ⟨go ~ seed⟩ ⟨~ their surprise, the train left on time⟩ **c** — used as a function word to indicate a determined condition or end ⟨sentenced ~ death⟩ **3** — used as a function word to indicate position or relation in time: as **a** : BEFORE ⟨five minutes ~ five⟩ **b** : TILL ⟨from eight ~ five⟩ **4** — used as a function word to indicate addition, attachment, connection, belonging, possession, accompaniment, or response ⟨the key ~ the door⟩ ⟨danced ~ live music⟩ ⟨comes ~ his call⟩ **5** — used as a function word (1) to indicate the extent or degree (as of completeness or accuracy) ⟨loyal ~ a man⟩ or the extent and result (as of an action or a condition) ⟨beaten ~ death⟩ (2) to indicate the last or an intermediate point of a series ⟨moderate ~ cool temperatures⟩ **6 a** — used as a function word (1) to indicate a relation to one that serves as a standard ⟨inferior ~ his earlier works⟩ (2) to indicate similarity, correspondence, dissimilarity, or proportion ⟨compared him ~ a god⟩ **b** — used as a function word to indicate agreement or conformity ⟨add salt ~ taste⟩ ⟨~ my knowledge⟩ **c** — used as a function word to indicate a proportion in terms of numbers or quantities ⟨400 ~ the box⟩ **7 a** — used as a function word (1) to indicate the application of an adjective or a noun ⟨agreeable ~ everyone⟩ ⟨attitude ~ friends⟩ ⟨title ~ the property⟩ (2) to indicate the relation of a verb to its complement or to a complementary element ⟨refers ~ the traditions⟩ ⟨refers him ~ the traditions⟩ (3) to indicate the receiver of an action or the one for which something is done or exists ⟨spoke ~ his father⟩ ⟨gives a dollar ~ the man⟩ ⟨the total effect was a gain ~ reading —Joseph Trenaman⟩ and often used with a reflexive pronoun to indicate exclusiveness (as of possession) or separateness ⟨had the house ~ themselves⟩ ⟨thought ~ himself⟩ **b** — used as a function word to indicate agency ⟨falls ~ his opponent's blows⟩ **8** — used as a function word to indicate that the following verb is an infinitive ⟨wants ~ go⟩ and often used by itself at the end of a clause in place of an infinitive suggested by the preceding context ⟨knows more than he seems ~⟩

2to \ˈtü\ *adv* (bef. 12c) **1 a** — used as a function word to indicate direction toward ⟨feathers wrong end ~⟩ ⟨run ~ and fro⟩ **b** : close to the wind ⟨the gale having gone over, we came ~ —R. H. Dana⟩ **2 a** : into contact esp. with the frame — used of a door or a window ⟨the door snapped ~⟩ **b** — used as a function word to indicate physical application or attachment ⟨set ~ his seal⟩ **3** — used as a function word to indicate application or attention ⟨will stand ~ —Shak.⟩ **4** : to a state of consciousness or awareness ⟨brings her ~ with smelling salts⟩ **5** : at hand : BY ⟨get to see 'em close ~ —Richard Llewellyn⟩

toad \ˈtōd\ *n* [ME *tode*, fr. OE *tāde, tādige*] (bef. 12c) **1** : any of numerous tailless leaping amphibians (esp. family Bufonidae) that as compared with the related frogs are generally more terrestrial in habit though returning to water to lay their eggs, squatter and shorter in build and with weaker hind limbs, and rough, dry, and warty rather than smooth and moist of skin **2** : a contemptible person or thing

toad·eat·er \-ˌē-tər\ *n, archaic* (1572) : TOADY

toad·fish \-ˌfish\ *n* (1612) : any of various marine fishes (family Batrachoididae) with jugular pelvic fins, a large thick head, a wide mouth, and scaleless slimy skin

toad·flax \-ˌflaks\ *n* (1578) : BUTTER-AND-EGGS; *also* : any of several related plants (esp. genus *Linaria*)

toad·stone \-ˌstōn\ *n* (1558) : a stone or similar object held to have formed in the head or body of a toad and formerly often worn as a charm or antidote to poison

toad·stool \-ˌstül\ *n* (14c) : a fungus having an umbrella-shaped pileus : MUSHROOM; *esp* : a poisonous or inedible one as distinguished from an edible mushroom

1toady \ˈtō-dē\ *n, pl* **toad·ies** (1826) : one who flatters in the hope of gaining favors : SYCOPHANT *syn* see PARASITE

2toady *vi* **toad·ied; toady·ing** (1861) : to behave as a toady : engage in sycophancy *syn* see FAWN — **toady·ism** \-ē-ˌiz-əm\ *n*

1to–and–fro \ˌtü-ən-ˈfrō\ *adj* (1839) : forward and backward ⟨~ motion⟩

2to–and–fro *n* (1847) : activity involving alternating movement in opposite directions ⟨the busy ~ of the holiday shoppers⟩

to and fro *adv* (14c) : from one place to another

1toast \ˈtōst\ *vb* [ME *tosten*, fr. MF *toster*, fr. LL *tostare* to roast, fr. L *tostus*, pp. of *torrēre* to dry, parch — more at THIRST] *vt* (14c) **1** : to warm thoroughly **2** : to make (as bread) crisp, hot, and brown by heat ~ *vi* : to become toasted; *esp* : to warm thoroughly

2toast *n* (15c) **1 a** : sliced bread browned on both sides by heat **b** : food prepared with toasted bread **2** [fr. the use of pieces of spiced toast to flavor drinks] **a** (1) : a person whose health is drunk (2) : something in honor of which persons usu. drink **b** : one that is highly admired ⟨she's the ~ of society⟩ **3** [3*toast*] : an act of proposing or of drinking in honor of a toast **4** : a rhyming narrative poem existing in oral tradition among black Americans

3toast *vt* (1700) : to propose or drink to as a toast

toast·er \ˈtō-stər\ *n* (1582) : one that toasts; *esp* : an electrical appliance for toasting

toaster oven *n* (1976) : a portable electrical appliance that can function as an oven or a toaster

toast·mas·ter \ˈtōs(t)-ˌmas-tər\ *n* (1749) : one that presides at a banquet and introduces the after-dinner speakers

toast·mis·tress \-ˌmis-trəs\ *n* (1923) : a female toastmaster

toasty \ˈtō-stē\ *adj* **toast·i·er; -est** (1953) : pleasantly or comfortably warm ⟨felt snug and ~ by the fire⟩

to·bac·co \tə-ˈbak-(ˌ)ō, -ˈbak-ə(-w)\ *n, pl* **-cos** [Sp *tabaco*, prob. fr. Taino, roll of tobacco leaves smoked by the Indians of the Antilles at the time of Columbus] (ca. 1565) **1** : any of a genus (*Nicotiana*) of chiefly American plants of the nightshade family with viscid foliage and tubular flowers; *esp* : a tall erect annual So. American herb (*N. tabacum*) cultivated for its leaves **2** : the leaves of cultivated tobacco prepared for use in smoking or chewing or as snuff **3** : manufactured products of tobacco (as cigars or cigarettes); *also* : smoking as a practice ⟨has sworn off ~⟩

tobacco budworm *n* (1918) : a noctuid moth (*Heliothis virescens*) whose small rusty often green-striped caterpillar feeds on buds and young leaves esp. of tobacco and cotton

tobacco hornworm *n* (ca. 1909) : a hawkmoth (*Manduca sexta*) whose large usu. green larva is a hornworm that feeds on tobacco

tobacco juice *n* (1833) : saliva colored brown by tobacco or snuff

tobacco mosaic *n* (1939) : any of a complex of virus diseases of plants of the nightshade family and esp. of tobacco

to·bac·co·nist \tə-ˈbak-ə-nəst\ *n* [irreg. fr. *tobacco* + *-ist*] (1657) : a dealer in tobacco esp. at retail

tobacco road *n, often cap T & R* [fr. *Tobacco Road*, novel (1932) by Erskine Caldwell and play (1933) by Jack Kirkland †1969 Am. playwright] (1947) : a squalid poverty-stricken rural area or community

to–be \tə-ˈbē\ *adj* (1600) : that is to be : FUTURE — usu. used postpositively and often in combination ⟨a bride-*to-be*⟩

To·bi·as \tə-ˈbī-əs\ *n* [Gk *Tobias*] **1** : a Jewish hero who with divine aid marries his kinswoman Sarah in spite of a jealous evil spirit and restores his father Tobit's sight **2** : a book of Scripture included in the Roman Catholic canon of the Old Testament and corresponding to the Book of Tobit in the Protestant Apocrypha — see BIBLE table

To·bit \ˈtō-bət\ *n* [Gk *Tōbit*] **1** : the elderly father of Tobias **2** : a book of Scripture in the Protestant Apocrypha — see BIBLE table

1to·bog·gan \tə-ˈbäg-ən\ *n* [CanF *tobogan*, of Algonquian origin; akin to Micmac *tobâgun* drag made of skin] (1829) **1** : a long flat-bottomed light sled made usu. of thin boards curved up at one end with usu. low handrails at the sides **2** : a downward course or a sharp decline

2toboggan *vi* (1863) **1** : to coast on a toboggan **2** : to decline suddenly and sharply — **to·bog·gan·er** *n* — **to·bog·gan·ist** \-ə-nəst\ *n*

to·bog·gan·ing *n* (1855) : the act, art, or sport of riding a toboggan

to·by \ˈtō-bē\ *n, pl* **tobies** *often cap* [*Toby*, nickname fr. the name *Tobias*] (1840) : a small jug, pitcher, or mug shaped somewhat like a stout man with a cocked hat for the brim — called also *toby jug*

toc·ca·ta \tə-ˈkät-ə\ *n* [It, fr. *toccare* to touch, fr. (assumed) VL] (ca. 1724) : a musical composition usu. for organ or harpsichord in a free style and characterized by full chords, rapid runs, and high harmonies

To·char·i·an \tō-ˈkar-ē-ən, -ˈker-, -ˈkär-\ *n* [L *Tochari* (pl.), fr. Gk *Tocharoi*] (ca. 1926) **1** : a member of a people of presumably European origin dwelling in central Asia during the first millennium of the Christian era **2 a** : a language of central Asia known from documents from the seventh century A.D. **b** : a branch of the Indo-European language family containing Tocharian — see INDO-EUROPEAN LANGUAGES table

Tocharian A *n* (ca. 1926) : the eastern dialect of Tocharian — see INDO-EUROPEAN LANGUAGES table

Tocharian B *n* (ca. 1926) : the western dialect of Tocharian — see INDO-EUROPEAN LANGUAGES table

toch·er \ˈtäk-ər\ *n* [ScGael *tochar*] *chiefly Scot* (15c) : DOWRY 2a, 3

to·coph·er·ol \tō-ˈkäf-ə-ˌrȯl, -ˌrōl\ *n* [ISV, deriv. of Gk *tokos* childbirth, offspring (akin to Gk *tiktein* to beget) + *pherein* to carry, bear — more at THANE, BEAR] (ca. 1936) : any of several fat-soluble oily phenolic compounds with varying degrees of antioxidant vitamin E activity; *esp* : one $C_{29}H_{50}O_2$ of high vitamin E potency obtained from germ oils or by synthesis

toc·sin \ˈtäk-sən\ *n* [MF *toquassen*, fr. OProv *tocasenh*, fr. *tocar* to touch, ring a bell (fr. assumed VL *toccare*) + *senh* sign, bell, fr. ML & L *signum*; ML, bell, fr. LL, ringing of a bell, fr. L, mark, sign — more at SIGN] (1586) **1** : an alarm bell or the ringing of it **2** : a warning signal

1tod \ˈtäd\ *n* [ME] *chiefly Scot* (12c) : FOX

2tod *n* [ME *todd, todde*; prob. akin to OHG *zotta* tuft of hair] (15c) **1** : any of various units of weight for wool; *esp* : one equal to 28 pounds (13 kilograms) **2** *Brit* : a bushy clump (as of ivy)

1to·day \tə-ˈdā\ *adv* (bef. 12c) **1** : on or for this day **2** : at the present time

2today *n* (1535) : the present day, time, or age ⟨the youth of ~⟩

3today *adj* (1966) : of or characteristic of today : NOW

tod·dle \ˈtäd-ᵊl\ *vi* **tod·dled; tod·dling** \ˈtäd-liŋ, -ᵊl-iŋ\ [origin unknown] (1600) **1** : to walk with short tottering steps in the manner of a young child **2** : to take a stroll : SAUNTER — **toddle** *n*

tod·dler \ˈtäd-lər, -ᵊl-ər\ *n* (1793) : one that toddles; *esp* : a young child — **tod·dler·hood** \-ˌhu̇d\ *n*

tod·dy \ˈtäd-ē\ *n, pl* **toddies** [Hindi *tāṛī* juice of the palmyra palm, fr. *tāṛ* palmyra palm, fr. Skt *tāla*] (1609) **1** : the fresh or fermented sap of various chiefly East Indian palms **2** : a usu. hot drink consisting of liquor (as rum), water, sugar, and spices

to–do \tə-ˈdü\ *n, pl* **to–dos** \-ˈdüz\ (1570) : BUSTLE, STIR

1toe \ˈtō\ *n* [ME *to*, fr. OE *tā*; akin to OHG *zēha* toe, L *digitus* finger, toe] (bef. 12c) **1 a** (1) : one of the terminal members of a vertebrate's foot (2) : the fore end of a foot or hoof **b** : a terminal segment of a limb of an invertebrate **c** : the forepart of something worn on the foot ⟨the ~ of a boot⟩ **2** : a part that by its position or form is felt to resemble a toe ⟨the ~ of Italy⟩: as **a** : a journal or pivot supported in a bearing **b** : a lateral projection at one end or between the ends of a piece (as a rod or bolt) by which it is moved **c** : the lowest part (as of an embankment, dam, or cliff) **3** : TOE DANCE — **on one's toes** : ALERT 2 — **toe to toe** : facing one another

2toe *vb* **toed; toe·ing** *vt* (1607) **1** : to furnish with a toe ⟨~ a sock⟩ **2** : to touch, reach, or drive with the toe ⟨~ a football⟩ **3** : to drive (as a nail) obliquely; *also* : to clinch or fasten by or with nails or rods so driven ~ *vi* **1** : TIPTOE **2** : to stand, walk, or be placed so that the toes assume an indicated position or direction ⟨~ in⟩ — **toe the line** *or* **toe the mark** : to conform rigorously to a rule or standard

\ə\ abut \ᵊ\ kitten, F table \ər\ further \a\ ash \ā\ ace \ä\ cot, cart \au̇\ out \ch\ chin \e\ bet \ē\ easy \g\ go \i\ hit \ī\ ice \j\ job \ŋ\ sing \ō\ go \ȯ\ law \ȯi\ boy \th\ thin \t͟h\ the \ü\ loot \u̇\ foot \y\ yet \zh\ vision \à, ḵ, ⁿ, œ, œ̄, ue, ue̅, ʸ\ *see* Guide to Pronunciation

toea \'tȯi-ə\ *n, pl* **toea** [native name in Papua New Guinea] (1975) — see *kina* at MONEY table

toe box *n* (ca. 1930) : a piece of material (as leather) placed between the toe cap and lining of a shoe and treated with a substance (as a gum) that hardens after the shoe is lasted permanently

toe cap *n* (1797) : a piece of leather covering the toe of a shoe and reinforcing or decorating it

toed \'tōd\ *adj* [[1]*toe*] (1611) **1 :** having a toe or toes esp. of a specified kind or number — usu. used in combination ⟨five-*toed*⟩ ⟨round-*toed* shoes⟩ **2** [fr. pp. of [2]*toe*] **:** driven obliquely ⟨a ~ nail⟩; *also* **:** secured by diagonal or oblique nailing

toe dance *n* (ca. 1931) **:** a dance executed on the tips of the toes by means of a ballet slipper with a reinforced toe — **toe–dance** *vi* — **toe dancer** *n* — **toe dancing** *n*

toe·hold \'tō-ˌhōld\ *n* (1880) **1 a :** a hold or place of support for the toes (as in climbing) **b** (1) **:** a means of progressing (as in surmounting barriers) (2) **:** a slight footing ⟨used his money to get a ~, then a foothold, then a near stranglehold on the political economy —R.W. Armstrong⟩ **2 :** a wrestling hold in which the aggressor bends or twists his opponent's foot

toe–in \'tō-ˌin\ *n* (1928) **1 :** CAMBER 3 **2 :** adjustment of the front wheels of an automotive vehicle so that they are closer together at the front than at the back

toe·less \'tō-ləs\ *adj* (ca. 1891) **:** lacking a toe ⟨a ~ shoe⟩

[1]**toe·nail** \'tō-ˌnāl, -'nā(ə)l\ *n* (1841) **:** a nail of a toe

[2]**toenail** *vt* (1900) **:** to fasten by toed nails **:** TOE

toe·piece \'tō-ˌpēs\ *n* (1879) **:** a piece designed to form a toe (as of a shoe) or cover the toes of the foot

toe·plate \-ˌplāt\ *n* (1898) **:** a tab attached to the toe of a shoe (as to prevent wear due to heavy use)

toe–to–toe *adj or adv* (1925) **:** slugging it out at or as if at close range ⟨a ~ confrontation over the new policy⟩

toff \'täf\ *n* [prob. alter. of *tuft* (titled college student)] *chiefly Brit* (1851) **:** DANDY, SWELL

tof·fee *or* **tof·fy** \'tȯ-fē, 'täf-ē\ *n, pl* **toffees** *or* **toffies** [alter. of *taffy*] (ca. 1783) **:** candy of brittle but tender texture made by boiling sugar and butter together

tof·fee–nosed \ˌtäf-ē-'nōzd\ *adj, chiefly Brit* (ca. 1923) **:** STUCK-UP

toft \'tȯft, 'täft\ *n* [ME, fr. OE, fr. ON *topt*] *Brit* (bef. 12c) **:** a site for a dwelling and its outbuildings; *also* **:** an entire holding comprising a homestead and additional land

to·fu \'tō-(ˌ)fü\ *n* [Jp *tōfu*] (1880) **:** BEAN CURD

tog \'täg, 'tȯg\ *vt* **togged; tog·ging** [*togs*] (ca. 1785) **:** to dress esp. in fine clothing — usu. used with *up* or *out*

to·ga \'tō-gə\ *n* [L; akin to L *tegere* to cover — more at THATCH] (1600) **:** the loose outer garment worn in public by citizens of ancient Rome; *also* **:** a similar loose wrap or a professional, official, or academic gown — **to·gaed** \-gəd\ *adj*

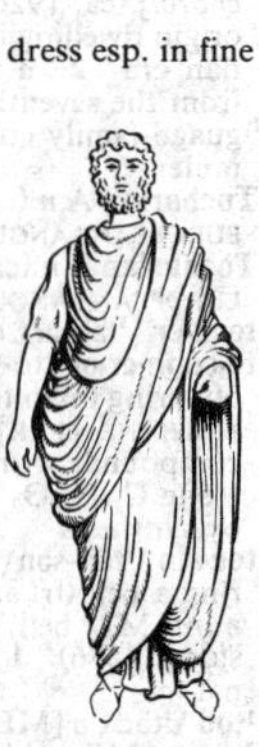
toga

to·ga vi·ri·lis \ˌtō-gə-və-'rēl-əs, -'ril-\ *n, pl* **to·gae vi·ri·les** \'tō-ˌgī-və-'rēl-ˌās, -'ril-\ [L, men's toga] (1600) **:** the white toga of manhood assumed by boys of ancient Rome at age 15

[1]**to·geth·er** \tə-'ge*th*-ər\ *adv* [ME *togedere*, fr. OE *togædere*, fr. *tō* to + *gædere* together; akin to MHG *gater* together, OE *gaderian* to gather] (bef. 12c) **1 a :** in or into one place, mass, collection, or group ⟨the men get ~ every Thursday for poker⟩ **b :** in a body **:** as a group ⟨students and faculty ~ presented the petition⟩ **2 a :** in or into contact (as connection, collision, or union) ⟨mix these ingredients ~⟩ **b :** in or into association or relationship ⟨colors that go well ~⟩ ⟨went to school ~⟩ **3 a :** at one time **:** SIMULTANEOUSLY ⟨events that happened ~⟩ **b :** in succession **:** without intermission ⟨was depressed for days ~⟩ **4 a :** by combined action **:** JOINTLY ⟨~ we forced the door⟩ **b :** in or into agreement or harmony ⟨the soloist and the orchestra weren't quite ~⟩ **c :** in or into a unified or coherent structure or an integrated whole ⟨can't even put a simple sentence ~⟩ ⟨pull yourself ~⟩ **5 a :** with each other — used pleonastically and as an intensive after certain verbs ⟨join ~⟩ ⟨add ~⟩ **b :** as a unit **:** in the aggregate ⟨these arguments taken ~ make a convincing case⟩ **c :** considered as a whole **:** counted or summed up ⟨all ~, there were 21 entries⟩ — **to·geth·er·ness** *n* — **together with :** in addition to **:** in association with

[2]**together** *adj* (1966) **1 :** appropriately prepared, organized, or balanced **2 :** composed in mind or manner **:** SELF-POSSESSED ⟨a warm, sensitive, reasonably ~ girl —*East Village Other*⟩

tog·gery \'täg-(ə-)rē, 'tȯg-\ *n* [*togs*] (ca. 1811) **:** CLOTHING

[1]**tog·gle** \'täg-əl\ *n* [origin unknown] (ca. 1769) **1 :** a piece or device for holding or securing: as **a :** a pin inserted in a nautical knot to make it more secure or easier to slip **b :** a crosspiece attached to the end of or to a loop in something (as a chain, rope, line, strap, or belt) usu. to prevent slipping, to serve in twisting or tightening, or to hold something attached **2 :** a device having a toggle joint

[2]**toggle** *vt* **tog·gled; tog·gling** \-(ə-)liŋ\ (ca. 1775) **1 :** to fasten with or as if with a toggle **2 :** to furnish with a toggle

toggle joint *n* (ca. 1847) **:** a device consisting of two bars jointed together end to end but not in line so that when a force is applied to the knee tending to straighten the arrangement the parts abutting or jointed to the ends of the bars will receive an endways pressure

toggle switch *n* (ca. 1924) **:** an electric switch that depends on a toggle joint with a spring to open or close the circuit when a projecting lever is pushed through a small arc

togs \'tägz, 'tȯgz\ *n pl* [pl. of E slang *tog* (coat), short for obs. E cant *togeman, togman*] (ca. 1809) **:** CLOTHING; *esp* **:** a set of clothes and accessories for a specified use ⟨riding ~⟩

togue \'tōg\ *n* [CanF] (1839) **:** LAKE TROUT

[1]**toil** \'tȯi(ə)l\ *n* [ME *toile*, fr. AF *toyl*, fr. OF *toeil* battle, confusion, fr. *toeillier*] (14c) **1** *archaic* **a :** STRUGGLE, BATTLE **b :** laborious effort **2 :** long strenuous fatiguing labor ***syn*** see WORK

[2]**toil** *vb* [ME *toilen* to argue, struggle, fr. AF *toiller*, fr. OF *toeillier* to stir, disturb, dispute, fr. L *tudiculare* to crush, grind, fr. *tudicula* machine for crushing olives, dim. of *tudes* hammer; akin to L *tundere* to beat — more at STINT] *vi* (14c) **1 :** to work hard and long **:** LABOR **2 :** to proceed with laborious effort **:** PLOD ⟨~*ing* wearily up the hill⟩ ~ *vt* **1** *archaic* **:** OVERWORK **2** *archaic* **:** to get or accomplish with great effort — **toil·er** \'tȯi-lər\ *n*

[3]**toil** *n* [MF *toile* cloth, net, fr. L *tela* web, fr. *texere* to weave, construct — more at TECHNICAL] (1529) **1 :** a net to trap game **2 :** something by which one is held fast or inextricably involved **:** SNARE, TRAP — usu. used in pl. ⟨caught in the ~*s* of the law⟩

toile \'twäl\ *n* [F, cloth, linen, fr. MF] (ca. 1858) **1 :** any of many plain or simple twill weave fabrics; *esp* **:** LINEN **2 :** a muslin model of a garment

toile de Jouy \ˌtwäl-dəzh-'wē\ *n* [F, lit., cloth of Jouy, fr. *Jouy*-en-Josas, France] (ca. 1920) **:** an 18th century French scenic pattern usu. printed on cotton, linen, or silk in one color on a light ground; *broadly* **:** a similar printed fabric

[1]**toi·let** \'tȯi-lət\ *n* [MF *toilette* cloth put over the shoulders while dressing the hair or shaving, dim. of *toile* cloth] (1695) **1** *archaic* **:** DRESSING TABLE **2 :** the act or process of dressing and grooming oneself **3 a** (1) **:** BATHROOM, LAVATORY 2 (2) **:** PRIVY **b :** a fixture that consists usu. of a water-flushed bowl and seat and is used for defecation and urination **4 :** cleansing in preparation for or in association with a medical or surgical procedure ⟨a pharyngeal ~⟩

[2]**toilet** *vi* (1840) **1 :** to dress and groom oneself **2 :** to use the toilet — usu. used of a child ~ *vt* **1 :** DRESS, GARB **2 :** to help (a child) use the toilet

toilet paper *n* (1884) **:** a thin sanitary absorbent paper for bathroom use chiefly after defecation and urination

toilet powder *n* (1895) **:** a fine powder usu. with soothing or antiseptic ingredients for sprinkling or rubbing (as after bathing) over the skin

toi·let·ry \'tȯi-lə-trē\ *n, pl* **-ries** (1892) **:** an article or preparation (as toothpaste, shaving cream, or cologne) used in making one's toilet — usu. used in pl.

toilet soap *n* (1839) **:** a mild soap that is often perfumed and colored and stabilized with preservatives

toi·lette \twä-'let\ *n* [F, fr. MF] (1681) **1 :** TOILET 2 **2 a :** formal or fashionable attire or style of dressing **b :** a particular costume or outfit

toilet training *n* (1948) **:** the process of training a child to control bladder and bowel movements and to use the toilet — **toilet train** *vt*

toilet water *n* (1855) **:** a perfumed liquid containing a high percentage of alcohol for use in or after a bath or as a skin freshener

toil·ful \'tȯi(ə)l-fəl\ *adj* (1596) **:** marked by or demanding toil **:** LABORIOUS — **toil·ful·ly** \-fə-lē\ *adv*

toil·some \-səm\ *adj* (1581) **:** marked by or full of toil or fatigue **:** LABORIOUS — **toil·some·ly** *adv* — **toil·some·ness** *n*

toil·worn \-ˌwō(ə)rn, -ˌwȯ(ə)rn\ *adj* (1751) **:** showing the effects of or worn out with toil ⟨~ hands⟩

to–ing and fro–ing \'tü-iŋ-ən(d)-'frō-iŋ\ *n, pl* **to–ings and fro–ings** [*to and fro*] (1847) **:** a passing back and forth

to·ka·mak *also* **to·ko·mak** \'tō-kə-ˌmak, 'täk-ə-\ *n* [Russ] (1965) **:** a toroidal device for producing controlled nuclear fusion that involves the confining and heating of a gaseous plasma by means of an electric current and magnetic field

To·kay \tō-'kā\ *n* (1710) **1 :** a naturally sweet wine from the area around Tokaj, Hungary **2 :** a blend of Angelica, port, and sherry made in California

toke \'tōk\ *n* [origin unknown] *slang* (1968) **:** a puff on a cigarette and esp. on a marijuana cigarette — **toke** *vi, slang*

[1]**to·ken** \'tō-kən\ *n* [ME, fr. OE *tācen, tācn* sign, token; akin to OHG *zeihhan* sign, Gk *deiknynai* to show — more at DICTION] (bef. 12c) **1 :** an outward sign or expression ⟨his tears were ~*s* of his grief⟩ **2 a :** SYMBOL, EMBLEM ⟨a white flag is a ~ of surrender⟩ **b :** an instance of a linguistic expression **3 :** a distinguishing feature **:** CHARACTERISTIC **4 a :** SOUVENIR, KEEPSAKE **b :** a small part representing the whole **:** INDICATION ⟨this is only a ~ of what he hopes to accomplish⟩ **c :** something given or shown as a guarantee (as of authority, right, or identity) **5 a :** a piece resembling a coin issued as money by some person or body other than a de jure government **b :** a piece resembling a coin issued for use (as for fare on a bus) by a particular group on specified terms **6 :** a token member of a group; *esp* **:** a token employee ***syn*** see SIGN — **by the same token :** for the same reason

[2]**token** *adj* (1547) **1 :** done or given as a token esp. in partial fulfillment of an obligation or engagement ⟨a ~ payment⟩ **2 a :** MINIMAL, PERFUNCTORY ⟨~ resistance⟩ ⟨~ integration⟩ **b :** serving or intended to show absence of discrimination ⟨a ~ female employee⟩

to·ken·ism \'tō-kə-ˌniz-əm\ *n* (1961) **:** the policy or practice of making only a token effort (as to desegregate)

token money *n* (1889) **:** money of regular government issue (as paper currency or coins) having a greater face value than intrinsic value

To·khar·i·an *var of* TOCHARIAN

to·ko·no·ma \ˌtō-kə-'nō-mə\ *n* [Jp] (1898) **:** a niche or recess opening from the living room of a Japanese house

tol- *or* **tolu-** *comb form* [ISV, fr. Sp *tolú*, fr. Santiago de *Tolú*, Colombia] **:** toluene ⟨*tolu*ic⟩ ⟨*tol*yl⟩ **:** toluic ⟨*tolu*ate⟩

to·la \'tō-lə, tō-'lä\ *n* [Hindi *tolā*, fr. Skt *tulā* weight; akin to L *tollere* to lift up] (1615) **:** a unit of weight of India equal to 180 grains troy or 0.4114 ounce (11.7 grams)

tol·booth \'tō(l)-ˌbüth, 'täl-, 'tōl-\ *n* [ME *tolbothe, tollbothe* tollbooth, town hall, jail] (15c) **1** *Scot* **:** a town or market hall **2** *Scot* **:** JAIL, PRISON

tol·bu·ta·mide \täl-'byüt-ə-ˌmīd\ *n* [*tol-* + butyric + *amide*] (ca. 1957) **:** a sulfonamide $C_{12}H_{18}N_2O_3S$ that lowers blood sugar level and is used in the treatment of diabetes

told *past and past part of* TELL

tole \'tōl\ *n* [F *tôle* sheet metal (esp. iron), fr. F dial. (Bordeaux area), table, slab, fr. L *tabula* board, tablet] (1927) **:** sheet metal and esp. tinplate for use in domestic and ornamental wares in which it is usu. japanned or painted and often elaborately decorated; *also* **:** objects made of tole

To·le·do \tə-'lēd-(ˌ)ō\ *n, pl* **-dos** (1596) **:** a finely tempered sword of a kind made in Toledo, Spain

tol·er·a·ble \'täl-(ə-)rə-bəl, 'täl-ər-bəl\ *adj* (15c) **1 :** capable of being borne or endured ⟨~ pain⟩ **2 :** moderately good or agreeable **:** PASS-

ABLE ⟨a ~ singing voice⟩ — **tol·er·a·bil·i·ty** \ˌtäl-(ə-)rə-ˈbil-ət-ē\ *n* — **tol·er·a·bly** \ˈtäl-(ə-)rə-blē, -ər-blē\ *adv*

tol·er·ance \ˈtäl(-ə)-rən(t)s\ *n* (15c) **1 :** capacity to endure pain or hardship : ENDURANCE, FORTITUDE, STAMINA **2 a :** sympathy or indulgence for beliefs or practices differing from or conflicting with one's own **b :** the act of allowing something : TOLERATION ⟨has a large ~ for uncertainty⟩ **3 :** the allowable deviation from a standard; *esp* **:** the range of variation permitted in maintaining a specified dimension in machining a piece **4 a** (1) **:** the ability to endure the effects of a drug or food or of a physiological insult without exhibiting the usu. unfavorable effects ⟨immunological ~ to a virus⟩ ⟨an addict's increasing ~ for a drug⟩ (2) **:** relative capacity of an organism to grow or thrive when subjected to an unfavorable environmental factor **b :** the maximum amount of a pesticide residue that may lawfully remain on or in food

tol·er·ant \-rənt\ *adj* (1784) **1 :** inclined to tolerate; *esp* **:** marked by forbearance or endurance **2 :** exhibiting tolerance (as for an environmental factor) — **tol·er·ant·ly** *adv*

tol·er·ate \ˈtäl-ə-ˌrāt\ *vt* **-at·ed; -at·ing** [L *toleratus,* pp. of *tolerare* to endure, put up with; akin to OE *tholian* to bear, OHG *dolēn,* L *tollere* to lift up, *latus* carried (suppletive pp. of *ferre*), Gk *tlēnai* to bear] (1531) **1 :** to endure or resist the action of (as a drug) without grave or lasting injury **2 :** to suffer to be or to be done without prohibition, hindrance, or contradiction ***syn*** see BEAR — **tol·er·a·tive** \-ˌrāt-iv\ *adj* — **tol·er·a·tor** \-ˌrāt-ər\ *n*

tol·er·a·tion \ˌtäl-ə-ˈrā-shən\ *n* (1531) **1 a :** the act or practice of tolerating something **b :** a government policy of permitting forms of religious belief and worship not officially established **2 :** TOLERANCE 4a(1)

tol·i·dine \ˈtäl-ə-ˌdēn\ *n* [ISV *tol-* + *-idine*] (1900) **:** any of several isomeric aromatic diamines $C_{14}H_{16}N_2$ that are homologues of benzidine and used esp. as dye intermediates

[1]**toll** \ˈtōl\ *n* [ME, fr. OE, fr. (assumed) VL *tolonium,* alter. of LL *telonium* customhouse, fr. Gk *tolōnion,* fr. *telōnēs* collector of tolls, fr. *telos* tax, toll; akin to Gk *tlēnai* to bear] (bef. 12c) **1 :** a tax or fee paid for some liberty or privilege (as of passing over a highway or bridge) **2 :** compensation for services rendered: as **a :** a charge for transportation **b :** a charge for a long-distance telephone call **3 :** a grievous or ruinous price; *esp* **:** cost in life or health ⟨fever had taken a heavy ~ of her —L. C. Douglas⟩

[2]**toll** *vi* (14c) **:** to take or levy toll ~ *vt* **1 a :** to exact part of as a toll **b :** to take as toll **2 :** to exact a toll from (someone)

[3]**toll** *or* **tole** \ˈtōl\ *vt* **tolled** *or* **toled; toll·ing** *or* **tol·ing** [ME *tollen, tolen;* akin to OE *talu* talk, narrative — more at TALE] (13c) **1 :** ALLURE, ENTICE **2 a :** to entice (game) to approach **b :** to attract (fish) with scattered bait **c :** to lead or attract (domestic animals) to a desired point

[4]**toll** *vb* [ME *tollen,* perh. fr. *tollen* to entice] *vt* (15c) **1 :** to sound (a bell) by pulling the rope **2 a :** to give signal or announcement of ⟨the clock *~ed* each hour⟩ **b :** to announce by tolling ⟨church bells *~ed* the death of the bishop⟩ **c :** to call to or from a place or occasion ⟨bells *~ed* the congregation to church⟩ ~ *vi* **:** to sound with slow measured strokes ⟨the bell *~s* solemnly⟩

[5]**toll** *n* (15c) **:** the sound of a tolling bell

toll·booth \ˈtōl-ˌbüth\ *n* [ME *tolbothe, tollbothe* tollbooth, town hall, jail, fr. *tol, toll* toll + *bothe* booth] (14c) **:** a booth (as on a highway or bridge) where tolls are paid

toll bridge *n* (1773) **:** a bridge at which a toll is charged for crossing

toll call *n* (1928) **:** a long-distance telephone call at charges above a local rate

toll·gate \ˈtōl-ˌgāt\ *n* (1773) **:** a point where the driver of a vehicle must pay a toll

toll·house \-ˌhau̇s\ *n* (15c) **:** a house or booth where tolls are taken

toll·way \-ˌwā\ *n* (1949) **:** a road for the use of which tolls are collected

Tol·tec \ˈtōl-ˌtek, ˈtäl-\ *n* [Sp *tolteca,* of AmerInd origin] (1814) **:** a member of a Nahuatlan people of central and southern Mexico — **Tol·tec·an** \-ən\ *adj*

tol·u·ene \-yə-ˌwēn\ *n* [ISV] (1871) **:** a liquid aromatic hydrocarbon C_7H_8 that resembles benzene but is less volatile, flammable, and toxic, is produced commercially from light oils from coke-oven gas and coal tar and from petroleum, and is used as a solvent, in organic synthesis, and as an antiknock agent for gasoline

to·lu·ic \tə-ˈlü-ik\ *adj* [ISV] (1857) **:** of, relating to, or being any of four isomeric acids $C_8H_8O_2$ derived from toluene

to·lu·idine \tə-ˈlü-ə-ˌdēn\ *n* [ISV] (1850) **:** any of three isomeric amino derivatives of toluene C_7H_9N that are analogous to aniline and are used as dye intermediates

toluidine blue *n* (ca. 1901) **:** a basic thiazine dye that is related to methylene blue and is used as a biological stain

tol·u·ol \ˈtäl-yə-ˌwȯl, -ˌwōl\ *n* (1845) **:** toluene esp. of commercial grade

tol·yl \ˈtäl-əl\ *n* [ISV] (ca. 1868) **:** any of three univalent groups $CH_3C_6H_4$ derived from toluene

tom \ˈtäm\ *n* [*Tom,* nickname for *Thomas*] (1762) **1 :** the male of various animals; *esp* **:** TOMCAT **2** *cap* **:** UNCLE TOM 2

[1]**tom·a·hawk** \ˈtäm-i-ˌhȯk\ *n* [*tomahack* (in some Algonquian language of Virginia)] (ca. 1612) **:** a light ax used as a missile and as a hand weapon esp. by No. American Indians

[2]**tomahawk** *vt* (ca. 1650) **:** to cut, strike, or kill with a tomahawk

to·mal·ley \tə-ˈmal-ē, ˈtäm-ˌal-ē\ *n, pl* **-leys** [of Cariban origin; akin to Galibi *tumali* sauce of lobster livers] (ca. 1666) **:** the liver of the lobster

Tom and Jer·ry \ˌtäm-ən-ˈjer-ē\ *n* [Corinthian *Tom* & *Jerry* Hawthorne, characters in *Life in London* (1821) by Pierce Egan †1849 Eng. sportswriter] (1845) **:** a hot drink that is a combination of a toddy and an eggnog

to·ma·til·lo \ˌtō-mə-ˈtē-(ˌ)(y)ō, -ˈtēl-(ˌ)yō\ *n, pl* **-los** [Sp, dim. of *tomate*] (ca. 1913) **:** a ground cherry (*Physalis ixocarpa*) of Mexico and the southern U.S. with an edible purplish viscid fruit

to·ma·to \tə-ˈmāt-(ˌ)ō, -ə(-w); *chiefly Brit, eNewEng, neVirginia, and sometimes elsewhere in cultivated speech* -ˈmàt- *or* -ˈmät-; *chiefly Northern* -ˈmat-\ *n, pl* **-toes** [alter. of earlier *tomate,* fr. Sp, fr. Nahuatl *tomatl*] (1604) **1 :** the usu. large rounded and red or yellow pulpy berry of a tomato **2 :** any of a genus (*Lycopersicon*) of So. American herbs of the nightshade family; *esp* **:** one (*L. esculentum*) that is more or less perennial in its native habitat but is widely cultivated as an annual for its edible fruit — **to·ma·to·ey** \-ə-wē\ *adj*

tomato fruitworm *n* (ca. 1891) **:** CORN EARWORM

tomato hornworm *n* (1921) **:** a hawkmoth (*Manduca quinquemaculata*) whose larva is a hornworm feeding on plants of the nightshade family and esp. tobacco and tomato

[1]**tomb** \ˈtüm\ *n* [ME *tombe,* fr. AF *tumbe,* fr. LL *tumba* sepulchral mound, fr. Gk *tymbos;* akin to L *tumēre* to be swollen — more at THUMB] (13c) **1 a :** an excavation in which a corpse is buried **:** GRAVE **b :** a place of interment **2 :** a house, chamber, or vault for the dead formed wholly or partly in the earth or entirely above ground **3 :** a building or structure resembling a tomb (as in appearance) — **tomb·less** \-ləs\ *adj*

[2]**tomb** *vt* (14c) **:** BURY, ENTOMB

tom·bac \ˈtäm-ˌbak\ *n* [F, fr. D *tombak,* fr. Malay *tĕmbaga* copper] (1602) **:** an alloy essentially of copper and zinc and sometimes tin or arsenic that is used esp. for cheap jewelry and gilding

tom·bo·lo \ˈtōm-bə-ˌlō, ˈtäm-\ *n, pl* **-los** [It, fr. L *tumulus* mound, tumulus] (ca. 1909) **:** a sand or gravel bar connecting an island with the mainland or another island

tom·boy \ˈtäm-ˌbȯi\ *n* (1592) **:** a girl of boyish behavior : HOYDEN — **tom·boy·ish** \-ish\ *adj* — **tom·boy·ish·ness** *n*

tomb·stone \ˈtüm-ˌstōn\ *n* (1565) **:** GRAVESTONE

tom·cat \ˈtäm-ˌkat\ *n* (1789) **:** a male cat

tom·cod \-ˌkäd\ *n* (1722) **:** any of several small fishes (genus *Microgadus*) resembling the related common codfish

Tom Col·lins \ˈtäm-ˈkäl-ənz\ *n* [fr. the name *Tom Collins*] (ca. 1909) **:** a collins with a base of gin

Tom, Dick, and Har·ry \ˌtäm-ˌdik-ən-ˈhar-ē\ *n* (1815) **:** the common man : ANYONE — often used with *every* ⟨helps every *Tom, Dick, and Harry* in need⟩

tome \ˈtōm\ *n* [MF or L; MF, fr. L *tomus,* fr. Gk *tomos* section, roll of papyrus, tome, fr. *temnein* to cut; akin to L *tondēre* to shear, Gk *tendein* to gnaw] (1519) **1 :** a volume forming part of a larger work **2 :** BOOK; *esp* **:** a large or scholarly book

-tome \ˌtōm\ *n comb form* [Gk *tomos*] **1 :** part : segment ⟨myo*tome*⟩ **2 :** cutting instrument ⟨pharyngo*tome*⟩

to·men·tose \tō-ˈmen-ˌtōs, ˈtō-mən-\ *adj* [NL *tomentosus,* fr. *tomentum*] (1698) **:** covered with densely matted hairs ⟨a ~ leaf⟩

to·men·tum \tō-ˈment-əm\ *n, pl* **-ta** \-ə\ [NL, fr. L, cushion stuffing; akin to L *tumēre* to be swollen — more at THUMB] (1699) **:** pubescence composed of densely matted woolly hairs

[1]**tom·fool** \ˈtäm-ˈfül\ *n* (14c) **:** a great fool : BLOCKHEAD

[2]**tom·fool** \ˌtäm-ˌfül\ *adj* (1819) **:** extremely foolish, stupid, or doltish

tom·fool·ery \täm-ˈfül-(ə-)rē\ *n* (1812) **:** foolish trifling : NONSENSE

Tom·my \ˈtäm-ē\ *n, pl* **Tommies** [*Thomas* Atkins, name used as model in official army forms] (1893) **:** a British soldier

Tommy At·kins \-ˈat-kənz\ *n* (1883) **:** TOMMY

tommy–gun *vt* (1948) **:** to shoot with a tommy gun

tom·my gun \ˈtäm-ē-ˌgən\ *n* [by shortening & alter.] (1929) **:** THOMPSON SUBMACHINE GUN; *broadly* **:** SUBMACHINE GUN

tom·my·rot \ˈtäm-ē-ˌrät\ *n* [E dial. *tommy* fool + E *rot*] (1884) **:** utter foolishness or nonsense

to·mo·gram \ˈtō-mə-ˌgram\ *n* (1940) **:** a roentgenogram made by tomography

to·mog·ra·phy \tō-ˈmäg-rə-fē\ *n* [Gk *tomos* section + ISV *-graphy* — more at TOME] (1937) **:** a diagnostic technique using X-ray photographs in which the shadows of structures before and behind the section under scrutiny do not show — compare COMPUTERIZED AXIAL TOMOGRAPHY — **to·mo·graph·ic** \ˌtō-mə-ˈgraf-ik\ *adj*

[1]**to·mor·row** \tə-ˈmär-(ˌ)ō, -ˈmȯr-, -ə(-w)\ *adv* [ME *to morgen,* fr. OE *tō morgen,* fr. *tō* to + *morgen* morrow, morning — more at MORN] (13c) **:** on or for the day after today ⟨will do it ~⟩

[2]**tomorrow** *n* (13c) **1 :** the day after the present ⟨the court will recess until ~⟩ **2 :** FUTURE 1a ⟨the world of ~⟩

tom·pi·on \ˈtäm-pē-ən\ *var of* TAMPION

Tom Thumb \ˈtäm-ˈthəm\ *n* **1 :** a legendary English dwarf **2 :** a dwarf type, race, or individual

tom·tit \ˈtäm-ˌtit, täm-ˈ\ *n* [prob. short for *tomtitmouse,* fr. the name *Tom* + *titmouse*] (1709) **:** any of various small active birds

tom–tom \ˈtäm-ˌtäm, ˈtəm-ˌtəm\ *n* [Hindi *ṭamṭam*] (1693) **1 :** a usu. long and narrow small-headed drum commonly beaten with the hands **2 :** a monotonous beating, rhythm, or rhythmical sound

-t·o·my \t-ə-mē\ *n comb form* [NL *-tomia,* fr. Gk, fr. *-tomos* that cuts, fr. *temnein* to cut — more at TOME] **:** incision : section ⟨laparo*tomy*⟩

[1]**ton** \ˈtən\ *n, pl* **tons** *also* **ton** [ME *tunne* unit of weight or capacity — more at TUN] (14c) **1 a :** a unit of internal capacity for ships equal to 100 cubic feet — called also *register ton* **b :** a unit approximately equal to the volume of a long ton weight of seawater used in reckoning the displacement of ships and equal to 35 cubic feet **c :** a unit of volume for cargo freight usu. reckoned at 40 cubic feet — called also *freight ton, measurement ton* **2 :** any of various units of weight: **a —** see WEIGHT table **b :** METRIC TON **3 :** a great quantity : LOT — often used in pl. ⟨ate *~s* of hamburgers⟩ ⟨has *~s* of money⟩

[2]**ton** \ˈtōⁿ\ *n* [F, lit., tone, fr. L *tonus*] (1765) **1 :** the prevailing fashion : VOGUE **2 :** the quality or state of being smart or fashionable

ton·al \ˈtōn-ᵊl\ *adj* (1776) **1 :** of or relating to tone, tonality, or tonicity **2 :** having tonality — **ton·al·ly** \-ᵊl-ē\ *adv*

to·nal·i·ty \tō-ˈnal-ət-ē\ *n, pl* **-ties** (1838) **1 :** tonal quality **2 a :** KEY 8 **b :** the organization of all the tones and chords of a piece of music in relation to a tonic **3 :** the arrangement or interrelation of the tones of a picture

ton·do \ˈtän-(ˌ)dō\ *n, pl* **ton·di** \-(ˌ)dē\ [It, fr. *tondo* round, short for *rotondo,* fr. L *rotundus* — more at ROUND] (1890) **1 :** a circular painting **2 :** a sculptured medallion

[1]**tone** \ˈtōn\ *n* [ME, fr. L *tonus* tension, tone, fr. Gk *tonos,* lit., act of stretching; akin to Gk *teinein* to stretch — more at THIN] (14c) **1 :** vo-

cal or musical sound of a specific quality ⟨spoke in low ~*s*⟩ ⟨masculine ~*s*⟩; *esp* : musical sound with respect to timbre and manner of expression **2** **a** : a sound of definite pitch and vibration **b** : WHOLE STEP **3** : accent or inflection expressive of a mood or emotion **4** : the pitch of a word often used to express differences of meaning **5** : a particular pitch or change of pitch constituting an element in the intonation of a phrase or sentence ⟨high ~⟩ ⟨low ~⟩ ⟨mid ~⟩ ⟨low-rising ~⟩ ⟨falling ~⟩ **6** : style or manner of expression in speaking or writing ⟨seemed wise to adopt a conciliatory ~⟩ **7** **a** (1) : color quality or value (2) : a tint or shade of color **b** : the color that appreciably modifies a hue or white or black ⟨gray walls of greenish ~⟩ **8** : the effect in painting of light and shade together with color **9** **a** : the state of a living body or of any of its organs or parts in which the functions are healthy and performed with due vigor **b** : normal tension or responsiveness to stimuli; *specif* : muscular tonus **10** **a** : healthy elasticity : RESILIENCY **b** : general character, quality, or trend ⟨a city's low moral ~⟩ **c** : frame of mind : MOOD

²**tone** *vb* **toned; ton·ing** *vt* (1660) **1** : INTONE **2** : to give a particular intonation or inflection to **3** **a** : to impart tone to : STRENGTHEN ⟨medicine to ~ up the system⟩ **b** : to soften in color, appearance, or sound : MELLOW — often used with *down* **c** : to change the normal silver image of (as a photographic print) into a colored image ~ *vi* **1** : to assume a pleasing color quality or tint **2** : to blend or harmonize in color

tone·arm \ˈtō-ˌnärm\ *n* (1913) : the movable part of a phonograph or record player that carries the pickup and permits the needle to follow the record groove

toned \ˈtōnd\ *adj* (15c) **1** : having tone or a specified tone : characterized or distinguished by a tone **2** *of paper* : having a slight tint

tone–deaf \ˈtōn-ˌdef\ *adj* (1894) : relatively insensitive to differences in musical pitch — **tone deafness** *n*

tone language *n* (ca. 1909) : a language (as Chinese, Sudanic, or Bantu) in which variations in tone distinguish words of different meaning that otherwise would sound alike

tone·less \ˈtōn-ləs\ *adj* (1773) : lacking in tone, modulation, or expression — **tone·less·ly** *adv* — **tone·less·ness** *n*

to·neme \ˈtō-ˌnēm\ *n* (ca. 1924) : an intonation phoneme in a tone language — **to·ne·mic** \tō-ˈnē-mik\ *adj*

tone poem *n* (1902) : SYMPHONIC POEM — **tone poet** *n*

ton·er \ˈtō-nər\ *n* (1888) : one that tones or is a source of tones: as **a** : a pure organic pigment **b** : a solution used to impart color to a silver photographic image **c** : a substance used to develop a latent xerographic image

tone row *n* [trans. of G *tonreihe*, fr. *ton* tone (fr. L *tonus*) + *reihe* row] (1944) : an arbitrary but fixed sequence in which a composer uses the tones of a musical work; *specif* : TWELVE-TONE ROW

to·net·ic \tō-ˈnet-ik\ *adj* (ca. 1924) **1** : relating to linguistic tones or to tone languages **2** : of or relating to intonation ⟨~ notation⟩ — **to·net·i·cal·ly** \-i-k(ə-)lē\ *adv*

to·net·ics \-iks\ *n pl but sing in constr* (1924) : the use or study of linguistic tones

to·nette \tō-ˈnet\ *n* [¹*tone* + *-ette*] (1939) : a simple fipple flute with a range somewhat larger than an octave that is often used in elementary music education

ton·ey *var of* TONY

¹**tong** \ˈtäŋ, ˈtȯŋ\ *n* [Chin (Cant) *t'ong* hall] (1883) : a secret society or fraternal organization esp. of Chinese in the U.S. formerly notorious for gang warfare

²**tong** *vb* [*tongs*] *vt* (1901) : to take, gather, hold, or handle with tongs ⟨~ oysters⟩ ~ *vi* : to use tongs esp. in taking or gathering something — **tong·er** \ˈtäŋ-ər, ˈtȯŋ-\ *n*

ton·ga \ˈtäŋ-gə\ *n* [Hindi *tāṅgā*] (1874) : a light 2-wheeled vehicle for two or four persons drawn by one horse and common in India

Ton·gan \ˈtäŋ-(g)ən\ *n* (ca. 1891) **1** : a member of a Polynesian people of the Tonga islands **2** : the Polynesian language of the Tongans — **Tongan** *adj*

tongs \ˈtäŋz, ˈtȯŋz\ *n pl but sing or pl in constr* [ME *tonges*, pl. of *tonge*, fr. OE *tang*; akin to OHG *zanga* tongs, Gk *daknein* to bite] (bef. 12c) : any of numerous grasping devices consisting commonly of two pieces joined at one end by a pivot or hinged like scissors

¹**tongue** \ˈtəŋ\ *n* [ME *tunge*, fr. OE; akin to OHG *zunga* tongue, L *lingua*] (bef. 12c) **1** **a** : a fleshy movable process of the floor of the mouths of most vertebrates that bears sensory end organs and small glands and functions esp. in taking and swallowing food and in man as a speech organ **b** : a part of various invertebrate animals that is analogous to the tongue **2** : the flesh of a tongue (as of the ox or sheep) used as food **3** : the power of communication through speech **4** **a** : LANGUAGE; *esp* : a spoken language **b** : manner or quality of utterance with respect to tone or sound, the sense of what is expressed, or the intention of the speaker ⟨she has a clever ~⟩ ⟨a sharp ~⟩ **c** : ecstatic usu. unintelligible utterance accompanying religious excitation — usu. used in pl. **d** : the cry of or as if of a hound pursuing or in sight of game — used esp. in the phrase *to give tongue* **5** : a tapering flame ⟨~*s* of fire⟩ **6** : a long narrow strip of land projecting into a body of water **7** : something resembling an animal's tongue in being elongated and fastened at one end only: as **a** : a movable pin in a buckle **b** : a metal ball suspended inside a bell so as to strike against the sides as the bell is swung **c** : the pole of a vehicle **d** : the flap under the lacing or buckles of a shoe at the throat of the vamp **8** **a** : the rib on one edge of a board that fits into a corresponding groove in an edge of another board to make a flush joint **b** : FEATHER 4 — **tongue·like** \-ˌlīk\ *adj* — **on the tip of one's tongue** **1** : about to be uttered ⟨it was *on the tip of my tongue* to tell him exactly what I thought⟩ **2** : just eluding recall

²**tongue** *vb* **tongued; tongu·ing** \ˈtəŋ-iŋ\ *vt* (14c) **1** *archaic* : SCOLD **2** : to touch or lick with or as if with the tongue **3** **a** : to cut a tongue on ⟨~ a board⟩ **b** : to join (as boards) by means of a tongue and groove ⟨~ flooring together⟩ **4** : to articulate (notes) by tonguing ~ *vi* **1** : to project in a tongue **2** : to articulate notes on a wind instrument by successively interrupting the stream of wind with the action of the tongue

tongue and groove *n* (ca. 1876) : a joint made by a tongue on one edge of a board fitting into a corresponding groove on the edge of another board

tongued \ˈtəŋd\ *adj* (14c) : having a tongue esp. of a specified kind — often used in combination ⟨sharp-*tongued*⟩

tongue–in–cheek *adj* (ca. 1934) : characterized by insincerity, irony, or whimsical exaggeration

tongue in cheek *adv* (ca. 1934) : with insincerity, irony, or whimsical exaggeration

tongue–lash \ˈtəŋ-ˌlash\ *vb* [back-formation fr. *tongue-lashing*] (1885) : CHIDE, SCOLD — **tongue–lash·ing** *n*

tongue·less \ˈtəŋ-ləs\ *adj* (14c) **1** : having no tongue **2** : lacking power of speech : MUTE

¹**tongue–tie** \ˈtəŋ-ˌtī\ *vt* [back-formation fr. *tongue-tied*] (1555) : to deprive of speech or the power of distinct articulation

²**tongue–tie** *n* (ca. 1849) : limited mobility of the tongue due to shortness of its frenum

tongue–tied \ˈtəŋ-ˌtīd\ *adj* (1529) **1** : unable or disinclined to speak freely (as from shyness) **2** : affected with tongue-tie

tongue twister *n* (1904) : a word, phrase, or sentence difficult to articulate because of a succession of similar consonantal sounds (as in "twin-screw steel cruiser")

-to·nia \ˈtō-nē-ə\ *n comb form* [NL, fr. *tonus*] : condition or degree of tonus ⟨my*otonia*⟩

¹**ton·ic** \ˈtän-ik\ *adj* [Gk *tonikos*, fr. *tonos* tension, tone] (1649) **1** **a** : characterized by tonus ⟨~ contraction of muscle⟩; *also* : marked by prolonged muscular contraction ⟨~ convulsions⟩ **b** : producing or adapted to produce healthy muscular condition and reaction of organs (as muscles) **2** **a** : increasing or restoring physical or mental tone : REFRESHING **b** : yielding a tonic substance **3** : relating to or based on the first tone of a scale ⟨~ harmony⟩ **4** *of a syllable* : bearing a principal stress or accent **5** : of or relating to speech tones or to languages using them to distinguish words otherwise identical — **ton·i·cal·ly** \ˈtän-i-k(ə-)lē\ *adv*

²**tonic** *n* (1799) **1** **a** : an agent (as a drug) that increases body tone **b** : one that invigorates, restores, refreshes, or stimulates ⟨a day in the country was a ~ for him⟩ **c** : a liquid preparation for the scalp or hair **d** *chiefly NewEng* : a carbonated flavored beverage **e** : QUININE WATER **2** : the first tone of a diatonic scale : KEYNOTE **3** : a voiced sound

tonic accent *n* (1867) **1** : relative phonetic prominence (as from greater stress or higher pitch) of a spoken syllable or word **2** : accent depending on pitch rather than stress

to·nic·i·ty \tō-ˈnis-ət-ē\ *n* (1824) **1** : the property of possessing tone; *esp* : healthy vigor of body or mind **2** : muscular tonus

tonic sol–fa *n* (1852) : a system of solmization based on key relationships that replaces the normal notation with sol-fa syllables or their initials

¹**to·night** \tə-ˈnīt\ *adv* (bef. 12c) : on this present night or the night following this present day ⟨will do it ~⟩

²**tonight** *n* (14c) : the present night or the night following this present day

ton·ka bean \ˈtäŋ-kə-\ *n* [prob. fr. Tupi *tonka*] (1796) : the seed of any of several leguminous trees (genus *Dipteryx*) that contains coumarin and is used in perfumes and as a flavoring; *also* : a tree bearing tonka beans

ton·nage \ˈtən-ij\ *n* (15c) **1** [ME, fr. MF *tonne* tun — more at TUNNEL] : a duty formerly levied on every tun of wine imported into England **2** **a** : a duty or impost on vessels based on cargo capacity **b** : a duty on goods per ton transported **3** : ships in terms of the total number of tons registered or carried or of their carrying capacity **4** **a** : the cubical content of a merchant ship in units of 100 cubic feet **b** : the displacement of a warship **5** **a** : total weight in tons shipped, carried, or produced **b** : impressively large amount or weight

tonne \ˈtən\ *n* [F, fr. *tonne* tun, fr. OF — more at TUNNEL] (ca. 1902) : METRIC TON

ton·neau \ˈtän-ˌō, tə-ˈnō\ *n, pl* **tonneaus** [F, lit., tun, fr. OF *tonel* — more at TUNNEL] (1901) **1** : the rear seating compartment of an automobile; *also* : the entire seating compartment **2** : a shape of watch case or dial resembling a barrel in profile

ton·ner \ˈtən-ər\ *n* (1851) : an object (as a ship) having a specified tonnage — used in combination ⟨a thousand-*tonner*⟩

to·nom·e·ter \tō-ˈnäm-ət-ər\ *n* [Gk *tonos* tone + E *-meter*] (1725) **1** : an instrument or device for determining the exact pitch or the vibration rate of tones **2** : an instrument for measuring tension (as of the eyeball) or pressure (as of blood or a gas) — **to·nom·e·try** \tō-ˈnäm-ə-trē\ *n*

to·no·plast \ˈtō-nə-ˌplast\ *n* [ISV *tono-* (fr. Gk *tonos* tension) + *-plast* — more at TONE] (ca. 1888) : a semipermeable protoplasmic membrane surrounding a plant-cell vacuole

ton·sil \ˈtän(t)-səl\ *n* [L *tonsillae*, pl., tonsils] (1601) **1** : either of a pair of prominent masses of lymphoid tissue that lie one on each side of the throat between the anterior and posterior pillars of the fauces **2** : any of various masses of lymphoid tissue that are similar to tonsils — **ton·sil·lar** \ˈtän(t)-s(ə-)lər\ *adj*

tonsill- *or* **tonsillo-** *comb form* [L *tonsillae*] : tonsil ⟨*tonsill*ectomy⟩ ⟨*tonsillo*tomy⟩

ton·sil·lec·to·my \ˌtän(t)-sə-ˈlek-tə-mē\ *n, pl* **-mies** (ca. 1901) : the surgical removal of the tonsils

ton·sil·li·tis \-ˈlīt-əs\ *n* [NL] (ca. 1801) : inflammation of the tonsils

ton·so·ri·al \tän-ˈsōr-ē-əl, -ˈsȯr-\ *adj* [L *tonsorius*, fr. *tonsus*, pp.] (1813) : of or relating to a barber or his work

¹**ton·sure** \ˈtän-chər\ *n* [ME, fr. ML *tonsura*, fr. L, act of shearing, fr. *tonsus*, pp. of *tondēre* to shear — more at TOME] (14c) **1** : the Roman Catholic or Eastern rite of admission to the clerical state by the clipping or shaving of a portion of the head **2** : the shaven crown or patch worn by monks and other clerics **3** : a bald spot resembling a tonsure

²**tonsure** *vt* **ton·sured; ton·sur·ing** \ˈtänch-(ə-)riŋ\ (1706) : to shave the head of; *esp* : to confer the tonsure upon

ton·tine \ˈtän-ˌtēn, tän-ˈ\ *n* [F, fr. Lorenzo *Tonti* †1695 Ital. banker] (1765) : a joint financial arrangement whereby the participants usu. contribute equally to a prize that is awarded entirely to the participant who survives all the others

to·nus \ˈtō-nəs\ *n* [NL, fr. L, tension, tone] (1876) : TONE 9a; *esp* : a state of partial contraction characteristic of normal muscle

tony \ˈtō-nē\ *adj* **ton·i·er; -est** (1877) : marked by an aristocratic or high-toned manner or style ⟨~ private schools⟩

To·ny \ˈtō-nē\ *n, pl* **Tonys** [*Tony,* nickname of Antoinette Perry †1946 Am. actress & producer] (1950) **:** a medallion awarded annually by a professional organization for notable achievement in the theater

too \(ˈ)tü\ *adv* [ME, fr. OE *tō* to, too — more at TO] (bef. 12c) **1 :** BESIDES, ALSO ⟨sell the house and furniture ~⟩ **2 a :** to an excessive degree **:** EXCESSIVELY ⟨~ large a house for us⟩ **b :** to such a degree as to be regrettable ⟨this time he has gone ~ far⟩ **c :** VERY **3 :** SO 2d ⟨"I didn't do it." "You did ~."⟩

took *past of* TAKE

[1]**tool** \ˈtül\ *n* [ME, fr. OE *tōl;* akin to OE *tawian* to prepare for use — more at TAW] (bef. 12c) **1 a :** an instrument (as a hammer) used or worked by hand **:** IMPLEMENT **b** (1) **:** the cutting or shaping part in a machine or machine tool (2) **:** a machine for shaping metal **:** MACHINE TOOL **2 a :** something (as an instrument or apparatus) used in performing an operation or necessary in the practice of a vocation or profession ⟨a scholar's books are his ~*s*⟩ **b :** a means to an end **3 :** one that is used or manipulated by another ***syn*** see IMPLEMENT

[2]**tool** *vt* (1812) **1 a :** to cause (a vehicle) to go **:** DRIVE **b :** to convey in a vehicle **2 :** to shape, form, or finish with a tool; *esp* **:** to letter or ornament (as leather) by means of hand tools **3 :** to equip (as a plant or industry) with tools, machines, and instruments for production ~ *vi* **1 :** DRIVE, RIDE **2 :** to equip a plant or industry with the means (as machines, machine tools, and instruments) of production — often used with *up*

[3]**tool** *n* (1881) **:** a design (as on the binding of a book) made by tooling

tool·box \ˈtül-ˌbäks\ *n* (1841) **:** a chest for tools

tool·head \ˈtül-ˌhed\ *n* (ca. 1932) **:** a part of a machine in which a tool or toolholder is clamped and which is provided with adjustments to bring the tool into the desired position

tool·hold·er \-ˌhōl-dər\ *n* (ca. 1876) **:** a short steel bar having a shank at one end to fit into the toolhead of a machine and a clamp at the other end to hold small interchangeable cutting bits

tool·house \-ˌhau̇s\ *n* (1818) **:** a building (as in a garden) for storing tools

tool·mak·er \ˈtül-ˌmā-kər\ *n* (1844) **:** a machinist who specializes in the construction, repair, maintenance, and calibration of the tools, jigs, fixtures, and instruments of a machine shop

tool·mak·ing \-kiŋ\ *n* (1893) **:** the action, process, or art of making tools; *also* **:** the trade of a toolmaker

tool·room \ˈtül-ˌrüm, -ˌru̇m\ *n* (1902) **:** a room where tools are kept; *esp* **:** a room in a machine shop in which tools are made, stored, and issued for use by workmen

tool·shed \-ˌshed\ *n* (1840) **:** TOOLHOUSE

tool subject *n* (1925) **:** a subject studied to gain competence in a skill used in other subjects

toom \ˈtüm\ *adj* [ME, fr. OE *tōm* — more at TEEM] *chiefly Scot* (bef. 12c) **:** EMPTY

toon \ˈtün\ *n* [Hindi *tūn,* fr. Skt *tunna*] (1810) **:** an East Indian and Australian tree (*Cedrela toona*) of the mahogany family with fragrant dark red wood and flowers that yield a dye; *also* **:** its wood

[1]**toot** \ˈtüt\ *vb* [prob. imit.] *vi* (1510) **1 a :** to sound a short blast ⟨the horn ~*ed*⟩ **b :** to sound a note or call suggesting the short blast of a wind instrument **2 :** to blow or sound an instrument (as a horn) esp. so as to produce short blasts ~ *vt* **:** to cause to sound ⟨~ a whistle⟩ — **toot·er** *n*

[2]**toot** *n* (1641) **:** a short blast (as on a horn); *also* **:** a sound resembling such a blast

[3]**toot** *n* [Sc *toot* to drink heavily] (ca. 1790) **:** a drinking bout **:** SPREE

[1]**tooth** \ˈtüth\ *n, pl* **teeth** \ˈtēth\ [ME, fr. OE *tōth;* akin to OHG *zand* tooth, L *dent-, dens,* Gk *odont-, odous*] (bef. 12c) **1 a :** one of the hard bony appendages that are borne on the jaws or in many of the lower vertebrates on other bones in the walls of the mouth or pharynx and serve esp. for the prehension and mastication of food and as weapons of offense and defense **b :** any of various usu. hard and sharp processes esp. about the mouth of an invertebrate **2 :** TASTE, LIKING **3 :** a projection resembling or suggesting the tooth of an animal in shape, arrangement, or action ⟨saw ~⟩**:** as **a :** one of the regular projections on the circumference or sometimes the face of a wheel that engage with corresponding projections on another wheel esp. to transmit force **:** COG **b :** a small sharp-pointed marginal lobe or process on a plant **4 a :** something that injures, tortures, devours, or destroys **b** *pl* **:** effective means of enforcement **5 :** a roughness of surface produced by mechanical or artificial means — **tooth·like** \ˈtüth-ˌlīk\ *adj* — **in the teeth of 1 :** in or into direct contact or collision with ⟨found themselves sailing *in the teeth of* a hurricane —*Current Biog.*⟩ **2 :** in direct opposition to ⟨rule had . . . been imposed by conquest *in the teeth of* obstinate resistance —A. J. Toynbee⟩ — **to the teeth :** FULLY, COMPLETELY ⟨armed *to the teeth*⟩

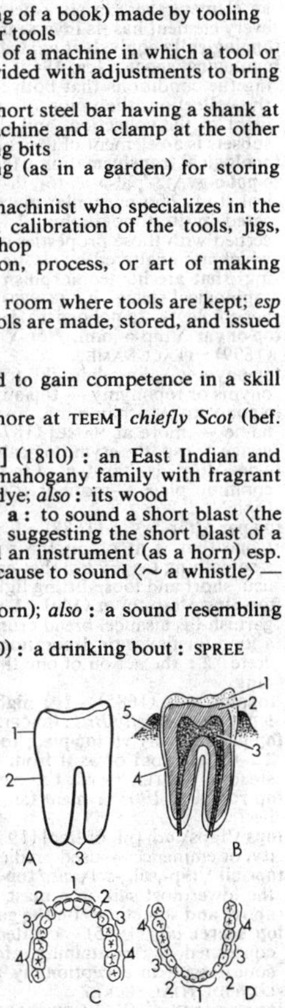

tooth 1a: *A* outside of a molar: *1* crown, *2* neck, *3* roots; *B* cross section of a molar: *1* enamel, *2* dentin, *3* pulp, *4* cementum, *5* gum; *C* dentition of adult human, upper; *D* dentition of adult human, lower: *1* incisors, *2* canines, *3* bicuspids, *4* molars

[2]**tooth** \ˈtüth, ˈtüth\ *vt* (15c) **1 :** to furnish with teeth esp. by cutting notches ⟨~ a saw⟩ **2 :** to roughen the surface of ⟨~ a cement floor to prevent slipping⟩

tooth·ache \ˈtü-ˌthāk\ *n* (14c) **:** pain in or about a tooth

tooth and nail *adv* (1550) **:** with every available means **:** ALL OUT ⟨fight *tooth and nail*⟩

tooth·brush \ˈtüth-ˌbrəsh\ *n* (1651) **:** a brush for cleaning the teeth

tooth·brush·ing \-iŋ\ *n* (1924) **:** the action of using a toothbrush to clean teeth

toothed \ˈtütht, *uncompounded also* ˈtü-thəd\ *adj* (14c) **:** having teeth esp. of a specified kind or number — often used in combination ⟨buck-*toothed*⟩

toothed whale \ˈtütht-, ˌtü-thəd-\ *n* (1843) **:** any of various whales (suborder Odontoceti) with numerous simple conical teeth — compare WHALEBONE WHALE

tooth fairy *n* (1962) **:** a fairy believed by children to leave money while they sleep in exchange for a tooth that has come out

tooth·less \ˈtüth-ləs\ *adj* (14c) **1 :** having no teeth **2 a :** lacking in sharpness or bite ⟨spoke in ~ generalities —Arthur Hepner⟩ **b :** lacking in means of enforcement or coercion **:** INEFFECTUAL

tooth·paste \-ˌpāst\ *n* (1832) **:** a paste for cleaning the teeth

tooth·pick \-ˌpik\ *n* (15c) **:** a pointed instrument (as a slender tapering piece of wood) used for removing food particles lodged between the teeth

tooth powder *n* (1542) **:** a powder for cleaning the teeth

tooth shell *n* (1711) **:** any of a class (Scaphopoda) of marine mollusks with a tapering tubular shell; *also* **:** this shell

tooth·some \ˈtüth-səm\ *adj* (1551) **1 a :** AGREEABLE, ATTRACTIVE **b :** sexually attractive ⟨a ~ blonde⟩ **2 :** of palatable flavor and pleasing texture **:** DELICIOUS ⟨crisp ~ fried chicken⟩ ***syn*** see PALATABLE — **tooth·some·ly** *adv* — **tooth·some·ness** *n*

tooth·wort \-ˌwərt, -ˌwȯ(ə)rt\ *n* (ca. 1597) **1 :** a European parasitic plant (*Lathraea squamaria*) of the broomrape family having a rootstock covered with tooth-shaped scales **2 :** any of various cresses (genus *Dentaria*) including several cultivated for their showy flowers

toothy \ˈtü-thē\ *adj* **tooth·i·er; -est** (1530) **1 :** having or showing prominent teeth ⟨~ grin⟩ **2 :** TOOTHSOME 2 — **tooth·i·ly** \-thə-lē\ *adv*

too·tle \ˈtüt-ᵊl\ *vb* **too·tled; too·tling** \ˈtüt-liŋ, -ᵊl-iŋ\ [freq. of [1]*toot*] *vi* (1820) **1 :** to toot gently, repeatedly, or continuously **2 :** to drive or move along in a leisurely manner ~ *vt* **:** to toot continuously on — **tootle** *n* — **too·tler** \ˈtüt-lər, -ᵊl-ər\ *n*

too–too \ˈtü-ˈtü\ *adj* (1533) **1 :** going beyond the bounds of convention, good taste, or common sense **:** EXTREME **2 :** LA-DI-DA

toot·sie \ˈtu̇t-sē\ *n* [origin unknown] (1905) **1 :** DEAR, SWEETHEART **2 :** PROSTITUTE

toot·sy *also* **toot·sie** \ˈtu̇t-sē\ *n, pl* **tootsies** [baby-talk alter. of *foot*] (1854) **:** FOOT

[1]**top** \ˈtäp\ *n* [ME, fr. OE; akin to OHG *zopf* tip, tuft of hair] (bef. 12c) **1 a** (1) **:** the highest point, level, or part of something **:** SUMMIT, CROWN (2) **:** the head or top of the head — used esp. in the phrase *top to toe* (3) **:** the head of a plant and esp. one with edible roots ⟨beet ~*s*⟩ (4) **:** a garment worn on the upper body **b** (1) **:** the highest or uppermost region or part (2) **:** the upper end, edge, or surface **2 :** a fitted, integral, or attached part or unit serving as an upper piece, lid, or covering **3 a :** a platform surrounding the head of a lower mast that serves to spread the topmast rigging, strengthen the mast, and furnish a standing place for men aloft **b :** a comparable part of the superstructure; *esp* **:** such a part on a warship used as a fire-control station or antiaircraft gun platform **4 :** the highest degree or pitch conceivable or attained **:** ACME, PINNACLE **5 a :** the part that is nearest in space or time to the source or beginning **b :** the first half of an inning in baseball **6 a** (1) **:** the highest position (as in rank or achievement) (2) **:** a person or thing at the top **b** *pl* **:** aces and kings in a hand or the three highest honors in a suit **7 :** the choicest part **:** CREAM, PICK **8 :** a forward spin given to a ball (as in golf or billiards) by striking it on or near the top or above the center; *also* **:** the stroke so given — **topped** \ˈtäpt\ *adj* — **off the top of one's head :** in an impromptu manner ⟨sat down and wrote the . . . story *off the top of his head* —Jerome Beatty, Jr.⟩ — **on top of 1 a :** in control of ⟨acted like a man *on top of* his job —*Newsweek*⟩ **b :** informed about ⟨tried to keep *on top of* new developments⟩ **2 :** in sudden and unexpected proximity to ⟨the deadline was *on top of* them⟩ **3 :** in addition to — **on top of the world :** in a position of eminent success, happiness, or fame

[2]**top** *vb* **topped; top·ping** *vt* (14c) **1 :** to remove or cut the top of: as **a :** to shorten or remove the top of (a plant) **:** PINCH 1b **b :** to remove the most volatile parts from (as crude petroleum) **2 a :** to cover with a top or on the top **:** provide, form, or serve as a top for **b :** to supply with a decorative or protective finish or final touch **c :** REFUEL, RESUPPLY — usu. used with *off* or *up* **d :** to complete the basic structure of (as a high-rise building) by putting on a cap or uppermost section — usu. used with *out* or *off* **3 a :** to be or become higher than **:** OVERTOP ⟨~*s* the previous record⟩ **b :** to be superior to **:** EXCEL, SURPASS **c :** to gain ascendancy over **:** DOMINATE **4 a :** to rise to, reach, or be at the top of **b :** to go over the top of **:** CLEAR, SURMOUNT **5 :** to strike (a ball) above the center thereby imparting topspin ~ *vi* **1 :** to make an end, finish, or conclusion **2 :** to reach a summit or crest — usu. used with *off* or *out*

[3]**top** *adj* (1593) **1 :** of, relating to, or being at the top **:** UPPERMOST **2 :** CHIEF, LEADING ⟨one of the world's ~ journalists⟩ **3 :** of the highest quality, amount, or degree ⟨~ value⟩ ⟨~ form⟩

[4]**top** *n* [ME, fr. OE] (bef. 12c) **:** a commonly cylindrical or conoidal device that has a tapering usu. steel-shod point on which it is made to spin and that is used esp. as a toy

top- *or* **topo-** *comb form* [ME, fr. LL, fr. Gk, fr. *topos* — more at TOPIC] **:** place **:** locality ⟨*topo*logy⟩ ⟨*top*onymy⟩

to·paz \ˈtō-ˌpaz\ *n* [ME *topace,* fr. OF, fr. L *topazus,* fr. Gk *topazos*] (13c) **1 a :** a mineral $Al_2SiO_4(F,OH)_2$ that is essentially a silicate of aluminum and usu. occurs in orthorhombic translucent or transparent crystals or in white translucent masses **b :** a usu. yellow to brownish yellow transparent mineral topaz used as a gem **c :** a yellow sapphire **d :** a yellow quartz (as cairngorm) **2 :** either of two large brilliantly colored So. American hummingbirds (*Topaza pella* and *T. pyra*)

top banana *n* [fr. a burlesque routine involving three comedians in which the one that gets the punch line also gets a banana] (1952) **:** the leading comedian in a burlesque show; *broadly* **:** KINGPIN 2

top billing *n* (1945) **1 :** prominent emphasis, featuring, or advertising **2 :** the position at the top of a theatrical bill usu. featuring the star's name

top boot *n* (1768) : a high boot often with light-colored leather bands around the upper part

top·coat \'täp-ˌkōt\ *n* (1819) : a lightweight overcoat

top·cross \-ˌkrȯs\ *n* (1890) : a cross between a superior or purebred male and inferior female stock to improve the average quality of the progeny; *also* : the product of such a cross

top dog *n* (1900) : a person or group in a position of authority esp. through victory in a hard-fought competition

top–down \ˌtäp-ˌdau̇n\ *adj* [fr. the phrase *from the top down*] (1941) **1** : controlled, directed, or instituted from the top level ⟨a ~ corporate structure⟩ **2** : proceeding by breaking large general aspects (as of a problem) into smaller more detailed constituents : working from the general to the specific ⟨~ programming⟩ ⟨~ design⟩

top drawer *n* (1905) : the highest level of society, authority, or excellence

top–dress \'täp-ˌdres\ *vt* (1733) : to apply material to (as land or a road) without working it in; *esp* : to scatter fertilizer over (land)

top·dress·ing \-iŋ\ *n* (1764) : a material used to top-dress soil

[1]tope \'tōp\ *vi* **toped; top·ing** [obs. E *tope* (interj. used to wish good health before drinking)] (1667) : to drink liquor to excess

[2]tope *n* [origin unknown] (1686) : a small cosmopolitan shark (*Galeorhinus galeus*) with a liver very rich in vitamin A

[3]tope *n* [Hindi *top,* perh. fr. Skt *stūpa*] (ca. 1815) : STUPA

to·pee *or* **to·pi** \tō-'pē, 'tō-(ˌ)pē\ *n* [Hindi *ṭopī*] (1835) : a lightweight helmet-shaped hat made of pith or cork

top·er \'tō-pər\ *n* (1673) : one that topes; *esp* : DRUNKARD

top flight *n* (1934) : the highest level of achievement, excellence, or eminence — **top·flight** *adj*

[1]Top 40 *n pl* (1966) : the forty best-selling phonograph records for a given period

[2]Top 40 *adj* (1966) : constituting, playing, listing, or relating to the Top 40 ⟨*Top 40* hits⟩ ⟨*Top 40* stations⟩ ⟨*Top 40* charts⟩

top·ful *or* **top·full** \'täp-'fu̇l\ *adj* (1553) : BRIMFUL

[1]top·gal·lant \(')täp-'gal-ənt, tə-'gal-\ *adj* [[1]*top* + *gallant,* adj.] (1514) **1** : of, relating to, or being a part next above the topmast and below the royal mast ⟨~ sails⟩ ⟨the ~ mast⟩ **2** : raised above adjoining parts or structures

[2]topgallant *n* (1514) **1** : a topgallant mast or sail **2** : the topmost point : SUMMIT ⟨the high ~ of my joy —Shak.⟩

top–ham·per \'täp-'ham-pər\ *n* (1791) **1** : matter or weight (as spars or rigging) in the upper part of a ship **2** : unnecessary cumbersome matter

top hat *n* (1822) : a man's tall-crowned hat usu. of beaver or silk

top–heavy \'täp-ˌhev-ē\ *adj* (1533) **1** : having the top part too heavy for the lower part **2** : capitalized beyond what is prudent or safe

To·phet \'tō-fət\ *n* [ME, shrine south of ancient Jerusalem where human sacrifices were performed to Moloch in Jer 7:31, Gehenna, fr. Heb *tōpheth*] (14c) : HELL, GEHENNA

top–hole \'täp-'hōl\ *adj, chiefly Brit* (1908) : EXCELLENT, FIRST-CLASS

to·phus \'tō-fəs\ *n, pl* **to·phi** \'tō-ˌfī, -ˌfē\ [L, tufa] (1607) : a deposit of urates in tissues (as cartilage) characteristic of gout

to·pi \'tō-pē\ *n* [of Mande origin; akin to Mande *ndopa, ndope* antelope] (ca. 1908) : an antelope (*Damaliscis korrigum*) of Central Africa having a glossy purplish brown coat

[1]to·pi·ary \'tō-pē-ˌer-ē\ *adj* [L *topiarius,* fr. *topia* ornamental gardening, irreg. fr. Gk *topos* place] (1592) : of, relating to, or being the practice or art of training, cutting, and trimming trees or shrubs into odd or ornamental shapes; *also* : characterized by such work

[2]topiary *n, pl* **-ar·ies** (1908) : topiary art or gardening; *also* : a topiary garden

top·ic \'täp-ik\ *n* [L *Topica* Topics (work by Aristotle), fr. Gk *Topika,* fr. *topika,* neut. pl. of *topikos* of a place, of a topos, fr. *topos* place, topos; akin to OE *thafian* to agree] (1634) **1 a** : one of the general forms of argument employed in probable reasoning **b** : ARGUMENT, REASON **2 a** : a heading in an outlined argument or exposition **b** : the subject of a discourse or of a section of a discourse

top·i·cal \-i-kəl\ *adj* (1588) **1** : designed for or involving local application and action (as on the body) ⟨a ~ anesthetic⟩ ⟨a ~ remedy⟩ **2 a** : of, relating to, or arranged by topics ⟨set down in ~ form⟩ **b** : referring to the topics of the day or place : of local or temporary interest — **top·i·cal·ly** \-k(ə-)lē\ *adv*

top·i·cal·i·ty \ˌtäp-ə-'kal-ət-ē\ *n, pl* **-ties** (1904) **1** : the quality or state of being topical **2** : an item of merely topical interest

topic sentence *n* (1919) : a sentence that states the main thought of a paragraph or of a larger unit of discourse and is usu. placed at or near the beginning

top·kick \'täp-'kik\ *n* (ca. 1926) : FIRST SERGEANT 1

top·knot \-ˌnät\ *n* (1686) **1** : an ornament (as a knot of ribbons or a pompom) forming a headdress or worn as part of a coiffure **2** : a crest of feathers or hair on the top of the head

top·less \-ləs\ *adj* (1589) **1** *archaic* : so high as to reach up beyond sight ⟨and burnt the ~ towers of Ilium —Christopher Marlowe⟩ **2** : being without a top **3 a** : wearing no clothing on the upper body **b** : featuring topless waitresses or entertainers

top lift *n* (ca. 1896) : the bottom layer of a heel

top·lofty \'täp-ˌlȯf-tē\ *also* **top·loft·i·cal** \täp-'lȯf-ti-kəl\ *adj* [prob. fr. the phrase *top loft*] (1823) : very superior in air or attitude — **top·loft·i·ly** \täp-'lȯf-tə-lē\ *adv* — **top·loft·i·ness** \'täp-ˌlȯf-tē-nəs\ *n*

top·mast \'täp-ˌmast, -məst\ *n* (15c) : the mast that is next above the lower mast and is topmost in a fore-and-aft rig

top milk *n* (1891) : the upper layer of milk in a container enriched by whatever cream has risen

top·min·now \'täp-ˌmin-(ˌ)ō, -ə(-w)\ *n* (1883) : any of several live-bearers (family Poeciliidae) or killifish (family Cyprinodontidae)

top·most \'täp-ˌmōst\ *adj* (1697) : highest of all : UPPERMOST

top–notch \-'näch\ *adj* (1910) : of the highest quality : FIRST-RATE — **top·notch·er** \-'näch-ər\ *n*

to·po·cen·tric \ˌtäp-ə-'sen-trik, ˌtōp-\ *adj* (ca. 1942) : relating to, measured from, or as if observed from a particular point on the earth's surface : having or relating to such a point as origin ⟨~ coordinates⟩ — compare GEOCENTRIC

to·pog·ra·pher \tə-'päg-rə-fər\ *n* (1603) : one skilled in topography

to·po·graph·ic \ˌtäp-ə-'graf-ik, ˌtōp-ə-\ *adj* (1632) : TOPOGRAPHICAL 1

to·po·graph·i·cal \-i-kəl\ *adj* (1570) **1** : of, relating to, or concerned with topography ⟨a ~ engineer⟩ **2** : of, relating to, or concerned with the artistic representation of a particular locality ⟨a ~ poem⟩ ⟨~ painting⟩ — **to·po·graph·i·cal·ly** \-k(ə-)lē\ *adv*

to·pog·ra·phy \tə-'päg-rə-fē\ *n* [ME *topographie,* fr. LL *topographia,* fr. Gk, fr. *topographein* to describe a place, fr. *topos* place + *graphein* to write — more at CARVE] (15c) **1 a** : the art or practice of graphic delineation in detail usu. on maps or charts of natural and man-made features of a place or region esp. in a way to show their relative positions and elevations **b** : topographical surveying **2 a** : the configuration of a surface including its relief and the position of its natural and man-made features **b** : the physical or natural features of an object or entity and their structural relationships

to·po·log·i·cal \ˌtäp-ə-'läj-i-kəl, ˌtōp-\ *adj* (1715) **1** : of or relating to topology **2** : being or involving properties unaltered under a homeomorphism ⟨continuity and connectedness are ~ properties⟩ — **to·po·log·i·cal·ly** \-k(ə-)lē\ *adv*

topological group *n* (ca. 1949) : a mathematical group which is also a topological space, whose multiplicative operation is continuous such that given any neighborhood of a product there exist neighborhoods of the elements composing the product with the property that any pair of elements representing each of these neighborhoods form a product belonging to the given neighborhood, and whose operation of taking inverses is continuous such that for any neighborhood of the inverse of an element there exists a neighborhood of the element itself in which every element has its inverse in the other neighborhood

topologically equivalent *adj* (ca. 1949) : related by a homeomorphism

topological space *n* (ca. 1949) : a set with a collection of subsets satisfying the conditions that both the empty set and the set itself belong to the collection, the union of any number of the subsets is also an element of the collection, and the intersection of a finite number of the subsets is an element of the collection

topological transformation *n* (ca. 1949) : HOMEOMORPHISM

to·pol·o·gy \tə-'päl-ə-jē, tō-, tä-\ *n, pl* **-gies** [ISV] (1850) **1** : topographical study of a particular place; *specif* : the history of a region as indicated by its topography **2 a (1)** : a branch of mathematics concerned with those properties of geometric configurations (as point sets) which are unaltered by elastic deformations (as a stretching or a twisting) that are homeomorphisms **(2)** : the set of all open subsets of a topological space **b** : CONFIGURATION ⟨~ of a molecule⟩ ⟨~ of a magnetic field⟩ — **to·pol·o·gist** \-jəst\ *n*

top·onym \'täp-ə-ˌnim, 'tōp-\ *n* [ISV, back-formation fr. *toponymy*] (1899) : PLACE-NAME

top·onym·ic \ˌtäp-ə-'nim-ik, ˌtōp-\ *adj* (ca. 1891) : of or relating to toponyms or toponymy — **top·onym·i·cal** \-i-kəl\ *adj*

to·pon·y·my \tə-'pän-ə-mē, tō-\ *n* [ISV, fr. *top-* + Gk *onyma, onoma* name — more at NAME] (1876) : the place-names of a region or language or esp. the etymological study of them

to·pos \'tō-ˌpäs, 'täp-\ *n, pl* **to·poi** \-ˌȯi\ [Gk, short for *koinos topos,* lit., common place —more at TOPIC] (1936) : a stock rhetorical theme or topic

top·per \'täp-ər\ *n* (1688) **1** : one that puts on or takes off tops **2** : one that is at or on the top **3 a** : SILK HAT **b** : OPERA HAT **4** : something (as a joke) that caps everything preceding **5** : a woman's usu. short and loose-fitting lightweight outer coat

[1]top·ping \'täp-iŋ\ *n* (14c) **1** : something that forms a top: as **a** : a garnish (as a sauce, bread crumbs, or whipped cream) placed on top of a food for flavor or decoration **b** : a finishing layer of mortar on concrete **2** : the action of one that tops **3** : something removed by topping

[2]topping *adj* (1685) **1** : highest in rank or eminence **2** *NewEng* : PROUD **3** *chiefly Brit* : EXCELLENT

top·ple \'täp-əl\ *vb* **top·pled; top·pling** \-(ə-)liŋ\ [freq. of [2]*top*] *vi* (1590) **1** : to fall from or as if from being top-heavy **2** : to be or seem unsteady : TOTTER ~ *vt* **1** : to cause to topple **2** : OVERTHROW 2

top round *n* (1903) : meat (as steak) from the inner part of a round of beef

tops \'täps\ *adj* [pl. of [1]*top*] (1936) : topmost in quality, ability, popularity, or eminence — used predicatively ⟨is ~ in his field⟩

top·sail \'täp-ˌsāl, -səl\ *also* **top·s'l** \-səl\ *n* (14c) **1** : the sail next above the lowermost sail on a mast in a square-rigged ship **2** : the sail set above and sometimes on the gaff in a fore-and-aft rigged ship

top secret *adj* (1945) **1** : demanding inviolate secrecy among those concerned **2** : containing information whose unauthorized disclosure could result in exceptionally grave danger to the nation — compare CONFIDENTIAL, SECRET

top sergeant *n* (1916) : FIRST SERGEANT 1

[1]top·side \'täp-'sīd\ *n* (1815) **1** *pl* : the top portion of the outer surface of a ship on each side above the waterline **2** : the highest level of authority **3** : the upper portion of the ionosphere

[2]topside *adv or adj* (1873) **1** : to or on the top or surface **2** : in a position of authority **3** : on deck

top·soil \'täp-ˌsȯil\ *n* (ca. 1864) : surface soil usu. including the organic layer in which plants have most of their roots and which the farmer turns over in plowing

top·spin \-ˌspin\ *n* [[1]*top*] (1902) : a rotary motion imparted to a ball that causes it to rotate forward in the direction it is traveling

top·stitch \'täp-ˌstich\ *vt* (1949) : to make a line of stitching on the outside of (a garment) close to a seam

top·sy–tur·vi·ness \ˌtäp-sē-'tər-vē-nəs\ *n* (1842) : the quality or state of being topsy-turvy

[1]top·sy–tur·vy \ˌtäp-sē-'tər-vē\ *adv* [prob. deriv. of *tops* (pl. of [1]*top*) + obs. E *terve* (to turn upside down)] (1528) **1** : in utter confusion or disorder **2** : with the top or head downward : upside down

[2]topsy–turvy *adj* (1612) : turned topsy-turvy : totally disordered — **top·sy–tur·vi·ly** \-'tər-və-lē\ *adv* — **top·sy–tur·vy·dom** \-vēd-əm\ *n*

[3]topsy–turvy *n* (1655) : TOPSY-TURVINESS

top·work \'täp-ˌwərk\ *vt* (1882) : to graft scions of another variety on the main branches of (as fruit trees) usu. to obtain more desirable fruit

toque \'tōk\ *n* [MF, soft hat with a narrow brim worn esp. in the 16th cent., fr. OSp *toca* headdress] (1505) **1** : a woman's small hat without a brim made in any of various soft close-fitting shapes **2** : TUQUE

tor \'tȯ(ə)r\ *n* [ME, fr. OE *torr*] (bef. 12c) : a high craggy hill

To·rah \'tōr-ə, 'tȯr-; 'tȯi-rə\ *n* [Heb *tōrāh*] (1577) **1 :** LAW 2b **2 :** the body of wisdom and law contained in Jewish Scripture and other sacred literature and oral tradition **3 :** a leather or parchment scroll of the Pentateuch used in a synagogue for liturgical purposes

[1]**torch** \'tȯ(ə)rch\ *n, often attrib* [ME *torche,* fr. OF, bundle of twisted straw or tow, torch, fr. (assumed) VL *torca;* akin to L *torquēre* to twist — more at TORTURE] (13c) **1 :** a burning stick of resinous wood or twist of tow used to give light and usu. carried in the hand : FLAMBEAU **2 :** something (as wisdom or knowledge) likened to a torch as giving light or guidance **3 :** any of various portable devices for emitting an unusually hot flame — compare BLOWTORCH **4** *chiefly Brit* **:** FLASHLIGHT **5 :** INCENDIARY 1a

[2]**torch** *vt* (1901) **:** to set fire to with or as if with a torch

torch·bear·er \-,bar-ər, -,ber-\ *n* (1538) **1 :** one that carries a torch **2 :** someone in the forefront of a campaign, crusade, or movement

torch·light \-,līt\ *n* (15c) **1 :** light given by torches **2 :** TORCH

tor·chon \'tȯr-,shän\ *n* [F, duster, fr. OF, bundle of twisted straw, fr. *torche*] (1879) **:** a coarse bobbin or machine-made lace made with fan-shaped designs forming a scalloped edge

torch singer *n* (ca. 1932) **:** a singer of torch songs

torch song *n* [fr. the phrase *to carry a torch for* (to be in love)] (1930) **:** a popular sentimental song of unrequited love

torch·wood \'tȯrch-,wu̇d\ *n* (1601) **1 :** a notably resinous or oily wood suitable for torches **2 a :** any of a genus (*Amyris*) usu. placed in the rue family of tropical American trees and shrubs with hard heavy fragrant resinous streaky yellowish brown wood **b :** the wood of a torchwood

tore *past of* TEAR

to·re·ador \'tȯr-ē-ə-,dȯ(ə)r, 'tōr-, 'tär-\ *n* [Sp, fr. *toreado,* pp. of *torear* to fight bulls, fr. *toro* bull, fr. L *taurus* — more at TAURINE] (1618) **:** TORERO, BULLFIGHTER

to·re·ro \tə-'re(ə)r-(,)ō\ *n, pl* **-ros** [Sp, fr. LL *taurarius,* fr. L *taurus*] (1728) **:** a matador or a member of his cuadrilla

to·reu·tics \tə-'rüt-iks\ *n pl but sing in constr* [*toreutic,* adj., fr. Gk *toreutikos,* fr. *toreuein* to bore through, chase, fr. *toreus* boring tool; akin to Gk *tetrainein* to bore — more at THROW] (1847) **:** the art or process of working in metal esp. by embossing or chasing — **to·reu·tic** \-'rüt-ik\ *adj*

tori *pl of* TORUS

to·ric \'tōr-ik, 'tȯr-\ *adj* (ca. 1898) **:** of, relating to, or shaped like a torus or segment of a torus ⟨a ~ lens⟩

to·rii \'tōr-ē-,ē, 'tȯr-\ *n, pl* **torii** [Jp] (1727) **:** a Japanese gateway of light construction commonly built at the approach to a Shinto shrine

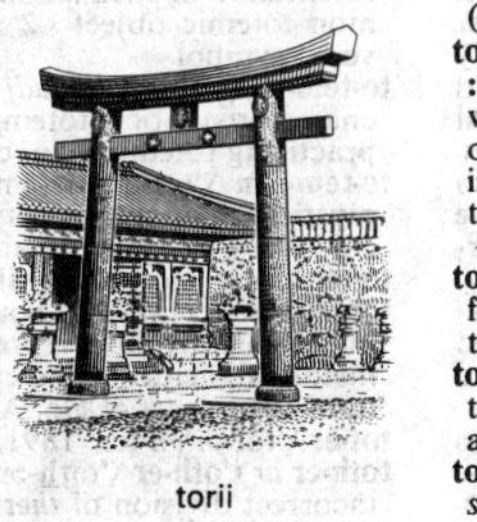
torii

[1]**tor·ment** \'tȯr-,ment\ *n* [ME, fr. OF, fr. L *tormentum* torture; akin to *torquēre* to twist — more at TORTURE] (13c) **1 :** the infliction of torture (as by rack or wheel) **2 :** extreme pain or anguish of body or mind : AGONY **3 :** a source of vexation or pain

[2]**tor·ment** \tȯr-'ment, 'tȯr-,\ *vt* (13c) **1 :** to cause severe usu. persistent or recurrent distress of body or mind to ⟨cattle ~*ed* by flies⟩ **2 :** DISTORT, TWIST ***syn*** see AFFLICT

tor·men·til \'tȯr-mən-,til\ *n* [ME *turmentill,* fr. ML *tormentilla,* fr. L *tormentum;* fr. its use in allaying pain] (15c) **:** a yellow-flowered Eurasian potentilla (*Potentilla tormentilla*) with a root used in tanning and dyeing

tor·men·tor *also* **tor·ment·er** \tȯr-'ment-ər, 'tȯr-,\ *n* (13c) **1 :** one that torments **2 :** a fixed curtain or flat on each side of a theater stage that prevents the audience from seeing into the wings

torn *past part of* TEAR

tor·na·dic \tȯr-'nād-ik, -'nad-\ *adj* (1884) **:** relating to, characteristic of, or constituting a tornado

tor·na·do \tȯr-'nād-(,)ō\ *n, pl* **-does** *or* **-dos** [modif. of Sp *tronada* thunderstorm, fr. *tronar* to thunder, fr. L *tonare* — more at THUNDER] (1556) **1** *archaic* **:** a tropical thunderstorm **2 a :** a squall accompanying a thunderstorm in Africa **b :** a violent destructive whirling wind accompanied by a funnel-shaped cloud that progresses in a narrow path over the land **3 :** a violent windstorm : WHIRLWIND

tor·nil·lo \tȯr-'nē-(,)(y)ō, -'nil-(,)ō\ *n, pl* **-los** [Sp, lit., small lathe, screw, dim. of *torno* lathe, fr. L *tornus* — more at TURN] (ca. 1844) **:** SCREWBEAN 1

to·roid \'tō(ə)r-,ȯid, 'tȯ(ə)r-\ *n* [NL *torus*] (ca. 1900) **1 :** a surface generated by a plane closed curve rotated about a line that lies in the same plane as the curve but does not intersect it **2 :** a body whose surface has the form of a toroid

to·roi·dal \tə-'rȯid-ᵊl\ *adj* (ca. 1889) **:** of, relating to, or shaped like a torus or toroid : doughnut-shaped ⟨a ~ resistance coil⟩ — **to·roi·dal·ly** \-ᵊl-ē\ *adv*

[1]**tor·pe·do** \tȯr-'pēd-(,)ō, -ə(-w)\ *n, pl* **-does** [L, lit., stiffness, numbness, fr. *torpēre* to be stiff or numb — more at TORPID] (1520) **1 :** ELECTRIC RAY **2 :** an engine or machine for destroying ships by blowing them up: as **a :** a submarine mine **b :** a dirigible self-propelling cigar-shaped submarine projectile filled with an explosive charge **3 a :** a charge of explosive enclosed in a container or case **b :** a small firework that explodes when thrown against a hard object **4 :** a professional gunman or assassin **5 :** SUBMARINE 2

[2]**torpedo** *vt* **tor·pe·doed; tor·pe·do·ing** \-'pēd-ə-wiŋ\ (ca. 1879) **1 :** to hit or sink (a ship) with a naval torpedo **:** strike or destroy by torpedo **2 :** to destroy or nullify altogether : WRECK ⟨~ a plan⟩

torpedo boat *n* (1810) **:** a boat designed for launching torpedoes; *specif* **:** a small very fast boat with one or more torpedo tubes

torpedo–boat destroyer *n* (ca. 1893) **:** a large, swift, and powerfully armed torpedo boat orig. intended principally for the destruction of torpedo boats but later used also as a formidable torpedo boat

torpedo bomber *n* (1939) **:** a military airplane designed to carry torpedoes

torpedo plane *n* (ca. 1918) **:** TORPEDO BOMBER

torpedo tube *n* (ca. 1891) **:** a tube from which torpedoes are fired

tor·pid \'tȯr-pəd\ *adj* [L *torpidus,* fr. *torpēre* to be stiff or numb; akin to L *stirps* trunk, stock, lineage, OE *starian* to stare — more at STARE] (1613) **1 a :** having lost motion or the power of exertion or feeling : DORMANT, NUMB **b :** sluggish in functioning or acting ⟨a ~ frog⟩ ⟨a ~ mind⟩ **2 :** lacking in energy or vigor : APATHETIC, DULL — **tor·pid·i·ty** \tȯr-'pid-ət-ē\ *n*

tor·por \'tȯr-pər\ *n* [L, fr. *torpēre*] (1607) **1 :** APATHY, DULLNESS **2 :** a state of mental and motor inactivity with partial or total insensibility **:** extreme sluggishness or stagnation of function ***syn*** see LETHARGY

[1]**torque** \'tȯ(ə)rk\ *n* [F, fr. L *torques,* fr. *torquēre* to twist — more at TORTURE] (1695) **:** a usu. metal collar or neck chain worn by the ancient Gauls, Germans, and Britons

[2]**torque** *n* [L *torquēre* to twist] (ca. 1884) **1 :** a force that produces or tends to produce rotation or torsion ⟨an automobile engine delivers ~ to the drive shaft⟩; *also* **:** a measure of the effectiveness of such a force that consists of the product of the force and the perpendicular distance from the line of action of the force to the axis of rotation **2 :** a turning or twisting force

[3]**torque** *vt* **torqued; torqu·ing** (1959) **:** to impart torque to **:** cause to twist (as about an axis) — **torqu·er** *n*

torque converter *n* (1927) **:** a device for transmitting and amplifying torque esp. by hydraulic means

torr \'tȯ(ə)r\ *n, pl* **torr** [Evangelista *Torricelli*] (ca. 1950) **:** a unit of pressure equal to $^1/_{760}$ of an atmosphere

[1]**tor·rent** \'tȯr-ənt, 'tär-\ *n* [F, fr. L *torrent-, torrens,* fr. *torrent-, torrens,* adj., burning, seething, rushing, fr. prp. of *torrēre* to parch, burn — more at THIRST] (1600) **1 :** a tumultuous outpouring : RUSH **2 :** a violent stream of a liquid (as water or lava) **3 :** a channel of a mountain stream

[2]**torrent** *adj* (1667) **:** TORRENTIAL

tor·ren·tial \tȯ-'ren-chəl, tə-\ *adj* (1849) **1 a :** relating to or having the character of a torrent ⟨~ rains⟩ **b :** caused by or resulting from action of rapid streams ⟨~ gravel⟩ **2 :** resembling a torrent in violence or rapidity of flow — **tor·ren·tial·ly** \-'rench-(ə-)lē\ *adv*

tor·rid \'tȯr-əd, 'tär-\ *adj* [L *torridus,* fr. *torridus,* pp. of *torrēre*] (1611) **1 a :** parched with heat esp. of the sun : HOT ⟨~ sands⟩ **b :** giving off intense heat : SCORCHING **2 :** ARDENT, PASSIONATE ⟨~ love letters⟩ — **tor·rid·i·ty** \tȯ-'rid-ət-ē\ *n* — **tor·rid·ly** \'tȯr-əd-lē, 'tär-\ *adv* — **tor·rid·ness** *n*

torrid zone *n* (1586) **:** the region of the earth between the tropic of Cancer and the tropic of Capricorn

tor·sade \tȯr-'säd, -'sād\ *n* [F, fr. obs. F *tors* twisted, fr. LL *torsus*] (1882) **:** a twisted cord or ribbon used esp. as a hat ornament

tor·sion \'tȯr-shən\ *n* [LL *torsus,* pp. of L *torquēre* to twist] (15c) **1 :** the twisting of a bodily organ on its own axis **2 :** the twisting or wrenching of a body by the exertion of forces tending to turn one end or part about a longitudinal axis while the other is held fast or turned in the opposite direction; *also* **:** the state of being twisted **3 :** the reactive torque that an elastic solid exerts by reason of being under torsion — **tor·sion·al** \'tȯr-shnəl, -shən-ᵊl\ *adj* — **tor·sion·al·ly** \-ē\ *adv*

torsion balance *n* (ca. 1828) **:** an instrument used to measure minute forces (as electrostatic or magnetic attraction and repulsion) by the torsion of a wire or filament

torsion bar *n* (1948) **:** a long metal element in an automobile suspension that has one end held rigidly to the frame end and the other twisted and connected to the axle and that acts as a spring

tor·so \'tȯr-(,)sō\ *n, pl* **torsos** *or* **tor·si** \'tȯr-,sē\ [It, lit., stalk, fr. L *thyrsus* stalk, thyrsus] (1722) **1 :** the trunk of a sculptured representation of a human body; *esp* **:** the trunk of a statue whose head and limbs are mutilated **2 :** something (as a piece of writing) that is mutilated or left unfinished **3 :** the human trunk

tort \'tȯ(ə)rt\ *n* [ME, injury, fr. MF, fr. ML *tortum,* fr. L, neut. of *tortus* twisted, fr. pp. of *torquēre*] (1586) **:** a wrongful act for which a civil action will lie except one involving a breach of contract

torte \'tȯrt-ə, 'tȯ(ə)rt\ *n, pl* **tor·ten** \'tȯrt-ᵊn\ *or* **tortes** [G, prob. fr. It *torta,* fr. LL, round loaf of bread] (1555) **:** a cake made with many eggs and often grated nuts or dry bread crumbs and usu. covered with a rich frosting

tor·tel·li·ni \,tȯrt-ᵊl-'ē-nē\ *n* [It, dim. of *tortelli* (pl.), a pasta, deriv. of LL *torta*] (ca. 1910) **:** pasta cut in rounds, filled, formed into rings, and boiled

tor·ti·col·lis \,tȯrt-ə-'käl-əs\ *n* [NL, fr. L *tortus* twisted + -*i*- + *collum* neck — more at COLLAR] (ca. 1811) **:** a more-or-less fixed twisting of the neck resulting in an abnormal carriage of the head — called also *wryneck*

tor·ti·lla \tȯr-'tē-(y)ə\ *n* [AmerSp, dim. of Sp *torta* cake, fr. LL, round loaf of bread] (ca. 1699) **:** a round thin cake of unleavened cornmeal or wheat flour bread usu. eaten hot with a topping or filling (as of ground meat or cheese)

tor·tious \'tȯr-shəs\ *adj* (1544) **:** implying or involving tort — **tor·tious·ly** *adv*

tor·toise \'tȯrt-əs\ *n* [ME *tortu, tortuce,* fr. MF *tortue* — more at TURTLE] (14c) **1 :** TURTLE; *esp* **:** a land turtle **2 :** someone or something regarded as slow or laggard

tortoise beetle *n* (1711) **:** any of a family (Chrysomelidae) of small tortoise-shaped beetles with larvae that feed on leaves

[1]**tor·toise·shell** \'tȯrt-ə-,shel, -əs(h)-,shel\ *n* (1632) **1 :** the mottled horny substance of the shell of some turtles (as the hawksbill turtle) used in inlaying and in making various ornamental articles **2 :** any of several showy nymphalid butterflies (genus *Nymphalis*)

[2]**tortoiseshell** *adj* (1651) **1 :** made of or resembling tortoiseshell esp. in mottled brown and yellow coloring **2 :** of, relating to, or being a color pattern of the domestic cat consisting of patches of black, orange, and cream

tor·to·ni \tȯr-'tō-nē\ *n* [prob. fr. It *Tortoni,* of or relating to Tortona, commune in northwestern Italy] (1922) **:** ice cream made of heavy cream often with minced almonds and chopped maraschino cherries and often flavored with rum

\ə\ abut \ᵊ\ kitten, F table \ər\ further \a\ ash \ā\ ace \ä\ cot, cart \au̇\ out \ch\ chin \e\ bet \ē\ easy \g\ go \i\ hit \ī\ ice \j\ job \ŋ\ sing \ō\ go \ȯ\ law \ȯi\ boy \th\ thin \th\ the \ü\ loot \u̇\ foot \y\ yet \zh\ vision \á, k̲, ⁿ, œ, œ̄, ue, ue̅, ʸ\ see Guide to Pronunciation

tor·tri·cid \'tȯr-trə-səd\ *n* [NL *Tortricidae*, fr. *Tortric-*, *Tortrix*] (ca. 1891) : any of a family (Tortricidae) of small stout-bodied moths many of whose larvae feed in fruits — **tortricid** *adj*

tor·trix \'tȯr-triks\ *n* [NL *Tortric-*, *Tortrix*, genus of moths, fr. L *tortus*, pp. of *torquēre* to twist; fr. the habit of twisting or rolling leaves to make a nest] (ca. 1797) : a tortricid moth

tor·tu·os·i·ty \ˌtȯr-chə-'wäs-ət-ē\ *n, pl* **-ties** (1603) **1 :** the quality or state of being tortuous **2 :** something winding or twisted : BEND

tor·tu·ous \'tȯrch-(ə-)wəs\ *adj* [ME, fr. MF *tortueux*, fr. L *tortuosus*, fr. *tortus* twist, fr. *tortus*, pp.] (15c) **1 :** marked by repeated twists, bends, or turns : WINDING **2 a :** marked by devious or indirect tactics : CROOKED, TRICKY **b :** CIRCUITOUS, INVOLVED — **tor·tu·ous·ly** *adv* — **tor·tu·ous·ness** *n*

[1]tor·ture \'tȯr-chər\ *n* [F, fr. LL *tortura*, fr. L *tortus*, pp. of *torquēre* to twist; akin to OHG *drāhsil* turner, Gk *atraktos* spindle] (1540) **1 a :** anguish of body or mind : AGONY **b :** something that causes agony or pain **2 :** the infliction of intense pain (as from burning, crushing, or wounding) to punish, coerce, or afford sadistic pleasure **3 :** distortion or overrefinement of a meaning or an argument : STRAINING

[2]torture *vt* **tor·tured; tor·tur·ing** \'tȯrch-(ə-)riŋ\ (1588) **1 :** to cause intense suffering to : TORMENT **2 :** to punish or coerce by inflicting excruciating pain **3 :** to twist or wrench out of shape : DISTORT, WARP ***syn*** see AFFLICT — **tor·tur·er** \'tȯr-chər-ər\ *n*

tor·tur·ous \'tȯrch-(ə-)rəs\ *adj* (15c) : causing torture : cruelly painful — **tor·tur·ous·ly** *adv*

tor·u·la \'tȯr-(y)ə-lə, 'tär-\ *n, pl* **-lae** \-ˌlē, -ˌlī\ *also* **-las** [NL, fr. L *torus* protuberance] (1861) : any of various fungi and esp. yeasts that lack sexual spores, do not produce alcoholic fermentations, and are typically acid formers — called also *torula yeast*

to·rus \'tȯr-əs, 'tȯr-\ *n, pl* **to·ri** \'tō(ə)r-ˌī, 'tȯ(ə)r-, -ˌē\ [NL, fr. L, protuberance, bulge, torus molding] (1563) **1 :** a large molding of convex profile commonly occurring as the lowest molding in the base of a column — see BASE illustration, MOLDING illustration **2 :** the thickening of a membrane closing a wood-cell pit (as of gymnosperm tracheids) having the secondary cell wall arched over the pit cavity **3 :** a doughnut-shaped surface generated by a circle rotated about an axis in its plane that does not intersect the circle; *broadly* : TOROID **4 :** a smooth rounded anatomical protuberance (as a bony ridge on the skull)

To·ry \'tōr-ē, 'tȯr-\ *n, pl* **Tories** [IrGael *tōraidhe* pursued man, robber, fr. MIr *tōir* pursuit] (1646) **1 :** an Irish papist or royalist outlaw chiefly of the 17th century **2** *obs* : BANDIT, OUTLAW **3 a :** a member or supporter of a major British political group of the 18th and early 19th centuries favoring at first the Stuarts and later royal authority and the established church and seeking to preserve the traditional political structure and defeat parliamentary reform — compare WHIG **b :** CONSERVATIVE 1b **4 :** an American upholding the cause of the British Crown against the supporters of colonial independence during the American Revolution : LOYALIST **5** *often not cap* : an extreme conservative esp. in political and economic principles — **Tory** *adj*

Tory Democracy *n* (1879) : a political philosophy advocating preservation of established institutions and traditional principles combined with political democracy and a social and economic program designed to benefit the common man

To·ry·ism \'tōr-ē-ˌiz-əm, 'tȯr-\ *n* (1682) **1 :** the principles and practices of or associated with Tories **2 :** the British Tory party or its members

tosh \'täsh\ *n* [origin unknown] (1528) : sheer nonsense : BOSH, TWADDLE

[1]toss \'tȯs, 'täs\ *vb* [prob. of Scand origin; akin to Sw dial. *tossa* to spread, scatter] *vt* (1506) **1 a :** to fling or heave continuously about, to and fro, or up and down ⟨a ship ~*ed* by waves⟩ **b :** BANDY 2b, c, d **c :** to mix lightly until well coated with a dressing ⟨~ a salad⟩ **2 :** to make uneasy : stir up : DISTURB **3 a :** to throw with a quick, light, or careless motion or with a sudden jerk ⟨~ a ball around⟩ **b :** to throw up in the air ⟨~*ed* by a bull⟩ **c :** [2]MATCH 5a **4 a :** to fling or lift with a sudden motion ⟨~*es* her head angrily⟩ **b :** to tilt suddenly so as to empty by drinking ⟨~*ed* his glass⟩ **5 :** to accomplish, provide, or dispose of readily or easily ⟨~ off a few verses⟩ ~ *vi* **1 a :** to move restlessly or turbulently; *esp* : to twist and turn repeatedly ⟨~*ed* sleeplessly all night⟩ **b :** to move with a quick or spirited gesture **2 :** to decide an issue by flipping a coin ***syn*** see THROW — **toss·er** *n*

[2]toss *n* (1634) **1 :** the state or fact of being tossed **2 :** an act or instance of tossing: as **a :** an abrupt tilting or upward fling **b :** a deciding by chance and esp. by flipping a coin **c :** THROW, PITCH

toss·pot \-ˌpät\ *n* (1568) : DRUNKARD, SOT

toss–up \-ˌəp\ *n* (1802) **1 :** TOSS 2b **2 :** an even chance **3 :** something that offers no clear basis for choice

tos·ta·da \tō-'städ-ə\ *also* **tos·ta·do** \-(ˌ)ō\ *n* [MexSp *tostada*, fem. of *tostado* fried, fr. Sp, toasted, fr. pp. of *tostar* to toast, roast, fr. LL *tostare* — more at TOAST] (1939) : a tortilla fried in deep fat

[1]tot \'tät\ *n* [origin unknown] (1725) **1 :** a small child : TODDLER **2 :** a small drink or allowance of liquor : SHOT

[2]tot *vb* **tot·ted; tot·ting** [*tot.*, abbr. of *total*] *vt* (1766) : to add together : TOTAL — usu. used with *up* ⟨~*s* up the score⟩ ~ *vi* : ADD

[1]to·tal \'tōt-ᵊl\ *adj* [ME, fr. MF, fr. ML *totalis*, fr. L *totus* whole, entire] (15c) **1 :** comprising or constituting a whole : ENTIRE ⟨the ~ amount⟩ **2 :** ABSOLUTE, UTTER ⟨a ~ failure⟩ **3 :** involving a complete and unified effort esp. to achieve a desired effect ⟨~ war⟩ ⟨~ theater⟩ ***syn*** see WHOLE

[2]total *n* (1557) **1 :** a product of addition : SUM **2 :** an entire quantity : AMOUNT

[3]total *adv* (1601) : TOTALLY

[4]total *vt* **to·taled** *or* **to·talled; to·tal·ing** *or* **to·tal·ling** (1716) **1 :** to add up : COMPUTE **2 :** to amount to : NUMBER **3 :** to make a total wreck of : DEMOLISH ⟨~*ed* the car⟩

total depravity *n* (1794) : a state of corruption due to original sin held in Calvinism to infect every part of man's nature and to make the natural man unable to know or obey God

total eclipse *n* (1671) : an eclipse in which one celestial body is completely obscured by the shadow or body of another

to·tal·ism \'tōt-ᵊl-ˌiz-əm\ *n* (1941) : TOTALITARIANISM — **to·tal·is·tic** \ˌtōt-ᵊl-'is-tik\ *adj*

[1]to·tal·i·tar·i·an \(ˌ)tō-ˌtal-ə-'ter-ē-ən\ *adj* [*total* + *-itarian* (as in *authoritarian*)] (1926) **1 a :** of or relating to centralized control by an autocratic leader or hierarchy : AUTHORITARIAN, DICTATORIAL; *esp* : DESPOTIC **b :** of or relating to a political regime based on subordination of the individual to the state and strict control of all aspects of the life and productive capacity of the nation esp. by coercive measures (as censorship and terrorism) **2 a :** advocating or characteristic of totalitarianism **b :** completely regulated by the state esp. as an aid to national mobilization in an emergency **c :** exercising autocratic powers : tending toward monopoly

[2]totalitarian *n* (ca. 1934) : an advocate or practitioner of totalitarianism

to·tal·i·tar·i·an·ism \(ˌ)tō-ˌtal-ə-'ter-ē-ə-ˌniz-əm\ *n* (1926) **1 :** centralized control by an autocratic authority **2 :** the political concept that the citizen should be totally subject to an absolute state authority

to·tal·i·tar·i·an·ize \-ˌnīz\ *vt* **-ized; -iz·ing** (1935) : to make totalitarian ⟨a society *totalitarianized* by the military-industrial complex —W. F. Buckley *b*1925⟩

to·tal·i·ty \tō-'tal-ət-ē\ *n, pl* **-ties** (1598) **1 :** an aggregate amount : SUM, WHOLE **2 a :** the quality or state of being total : WHOLENESS **b :** the phase of an eclipse during which it is total : state of total eclipse

to·tal·iza·tor *or* **to·tal·isa·tor** \'tōt-ᵊl-ə-ˌzāt-ər\ *n* (1879) : PARI-MUTUEL 2

to·tal·ize \'tōt-ᵊl-ˌīz\ *vt* **-ized; -iz·ing** (1818) **1 :** to add up : TOTAL **2 :** to express as a whole

to·tal·iz·er \-ˌī-zər\ *n* (1887) : one that totalizes: as **a :** PARI-MUTUEL 2 **b :** a device (as a meter) that records a remaining total (as of fuel)

to·tal·ly \'tōt-ᵊl-ē\ *adv* (1509) : in a total manner : to a total or complete degree : WHOLLY

total recall *n* (1926) : the faculty of remembering with complete clarity and in complete detail

[1]tote \'tōt\ *vt* **tot·ed; tot·ing** [origin unknown] (1677) **1 :** to carry by hand : bear on the person : LUG, PACK **2 :** HAUL, CONVEY

[2]tote *n* (1771) **1 :** BURDEN, LOAD **2 :** a large handbag — called also *tote bag*

[3]tote *vt* **tot·ed; tot·ing** [E dial. *tote*, n. (total)] (ca. 1888) : ADD, TOTAL — usu. used with *up* ⟨*toted* up his accomplishments —G. P. Morrill⟩

[4]tote *n* [short for *totalizator*] (1891) : PARI-MUTUEL 2

tote board *n* [[4]*tote*] (ca. 1949) : an electrically operated board (as at a racetrack) on which pertinent information (as betting odds and race results) is posted

to·tem \'tōt-əm\ *n* [Ojibwa *ototeman* his totem] (1760) **1 a :** an object (as an animal or plant) serving as the emblem of a family or clan and often as a reminder of its ancestry; *also* : a usu. carved or painted representation of such an object **b :** a family or clan identified by a common totemic object **2 :** something that serves as an emblem or revered symbol

to·tem·ic \tō-'tem-ik\ *adj* (1846) **1 :** of, relating to, suggestive of, or characteristic of a totem or totemism ⟨a ~ animal⟩ **2 :** based on or practicing totemism ⟨~ clan structure⟩

to·tem·ism \'tōt-ə-ˌmiz-əm\ *n* (1791) **1 :** belief in kinship with or a mystical relationship between a group or an individual and a totem **2 :** a system of social organization based on totemic affiliations

to·tem·is·tic \ˌtōt-ə-'mis-tik\ *adj* (1881) : TOTEMIC

totem pole *n* (1897) **1 :** a pole or pillar carved and painted with a series of totemic symbols representing family lineage and often mythical or historical incidents and erected before the houses of Indian tribes of the northwest coast of No. America **2 :** an order of rank : HIERARCHY

tot·er \'tōt-ər\ *n* (ca. 1891) : one that totes

toth·er *or* **t'oth·er** \'təth-ər\ *pron or adj* [ME *tother*, alter. (resulting from incorrect division of *thet other* the other, fr. *thet* the — fr. OE *thæt* — + *other*) of *other* — more at THAT] *chiefly dial* (13c) : the other

toti- *comb form* [L *totus* whole, entire] : whole : wholly ⟨*toti*potent⟩

to·ti·po·ten·cy \tō-'tip-ət-ən-sē, ˌtōt-ə-'pōt-ᵊn-\ *n* (1909) : ability to generate or regenerate a whole organism from a part

to·ti·po·tent \-ənt, -ᵊnt\ *adj* (ca. 1899) : capable of developing into a complete organism or differentiating into any of its cells or tissues ⟨~ blastomeres⟩

[1]tot·ter \'tät-ər\ *vi* [ME *toteren*] (15c) **1 a :** to tremble or rock as if about to fall : SWAY **b :** to become unstable : threaten to collapse **2 :** to move unsteadily : STAGGER, WOBBLE

[2]totter *n* (1747) : an unsteady gait : WOBBLE

tot·ter·ing *adj* (1534) **1 a :** being in an unstable condition ⟨a ~ building⟩ **b :** walking unsteadily **2 :** lacking firmness or stability : INSECURE ⟨a ~ regime⟩ — **tot·ter·ing·ly** \-ə-riŋ-lē\ *adv*

tot·tery \'tät-ə-rē\ *adj* (ca. 1755) : of an infirm or precarious nature

Toua·reg *var of* TUAREG

tou·can \'tü-ˌkan, -ˌkän, tü-'\ *n* [F, fr. Pg *tucano*, fr. Tupi] (1568) : any of a family (Ramphastidae) of fruit-eating birds of tropical America with brilliant coloring and a very large but light and thin-walled beak

[1]touch \'təch\ *vb* [ME *touchen*, fr. OF *tuchier*, fr. (assumed) VL *toccare* to knock, strike a bell, touch] *vt* (13c) **1 :** to bring a bodily part into contact with esp. so as to perceive through the tactile sense : handle or feel gently usu. with the intent to understand or appreciate ⟨loved to ~ the soft silk⟩ **2 :** to strike or push lightly esp. with the hand or foot or an implement **3 :** to lay hands upon (one afflicted with scrofula) with intent to heal — compare KING'S EVIL **4** *archaic* **a :** to play on (a stringed instrument) **b :** to perform (a melody) by playing or singing **5 a :** to take into the hands or mouth ⟨never ~*es* alcohol⟩ **b :** to put hands upon in any way or degree ⟨don't ~ anything before the police come⟩; *esp* : to commit violence upon ⟨swears he never ~*ed* the child⟩ **6 :** to concern oneself with **7 :** to induce to give or lend ⟨~*ed* him for ten dollars⟩ **8 :** to cause to be briefly in contact or conjunction with something ⟨~*ed* his spurs to his horse⟩ ⟨~ a match to the wick⟩ **9 a (1) :** to meet without overlapping or penetrating : ADJOIN **(2) :** to get to : REACH ⟨the speedometer needle ~*ed* 80⟩ **b :** to be tangent to **c :** to rival in quality or value ⟨nothing can ~ that cloth for durability⟩ **10 :** to speak or tell of esp. in passing ⟨barely ~*ed* on the incident in the speech⟩ **11 a :** to relate to : CONCERN **b :** to have an influence on : AFFECT **12 a :** to leave a mark or impression on ⟨few reagents will ~ gold⟩; *also* : TINGE **b :** to harm slightly by or as if by contact : TAINT, BLEMISH ⟨fruit ~*ed* by frost⟩ ⟨a horse ~*ed* in the wind⟩ **c :** to give a delicate tint, line, or expression to ⟨a smile ~*ed* her lips⟩ **13 :** to draw or delineate with light strokes **14 a :** to hurt the feelings of : WOUND **b :** to move to sympathetic feeling ~ *vi* **1 a :** to feel something with a body part (as the hand or foot) **b :** to lay hand or finger on a person to cure disease (as scrofula) **2 :** to be in contact **3 :** to come close : VERGE ⟨your actions ~ on treason⟩ **4 :** to have a bearing : RELATE — used with *on* or *upon* **5 a :** to make a brief or incidental stop on shore during a trip by water ⟨~*ed* at several ports⟩ **b :** to treat a topic in a brief or casual manner — used with *on* or *upon* ⟨~*ed* upon many points⟩ ***syn*** see AFFECT — **touch•able** \-ə-bəl\ *adj* — **touch•er** *n* — **touch base :** to come in contact or communication ⟨coming in from the cold to *touch base* with civilization —Carla Hunt⟩

[2]**touch** *n* (13c) **1 :** a light stroke, tap, or push **2 :** the act or fact of touching **3 :** the special sense by which pressure or traction exerted on the skin or mucous membrane is perceived **4 :** mental or moral sensitiveness, responsiveness, or tact ⟨has a wonderful ~ in dealing with children⟩ **5 :** a specified sensation that arises in response to stimulation of nerves sensitive to touch **6 a :** the act of rubbing gold or silver on a touchstone to test its quality **b :** TEST, TRIAL — used chiefly in the phrase *put to the touch* **7 a :** a visible effect : MARK ⟨a ~ of the tropical sun⟩ **b :** WEAKNESS, DEFECT **8 :** something slight of its kind: as **a :** a light attack ⟨a ~ of fever⟩ **b :** a small quantity or indication : HINT ⟨a ~ of spring in the air⟩ **c :** a transient emotion ⟨a momentary ~ of compunction⟩ **d :** a near approach : CLOSE CALL ⟨beaten in the championships by a mere ~⟩ **9 a** *archaic* **:** the playing of an instrument (as a lute or piano) with the fingers; *also* **:** musical notes or strains so produced **b :** particular action of a keyboard with reference to the resistance of its keys to pressure ⟨piano with a stiff ~⟩ **10 :** control of the hands: as **a :** a manner or method of touching or striking esp. the keys of a keyboard instrument **b :** ability to control the distance something (as a ball) is propelled ⟨developed his putting ~⟩ **11 :** a set of changes in change ringing that is less than a peal **12 a :** an effective and subtle detail ⟨applies the finishing ~*es* to the story⟩ **b :** distinctive manner or method ⟨the ~ of a master⟩ **c :** a characteristic or distinguishing trait or quality **13** *slang* **:** an act of soliciting or getting a gift or loan **14 :** the state or fact of being in contact or communication ⟨lost ~ with her cousin⟩ ⟨let's keep in ~⟩ ⟨out of ~ with modern times⟩ **15 :** the area outside of the touchlines in soccer or outside of and including the touchlines in rugby — **a touch :** SOMEWHAT, RATHER ⟨aimed *a touch* too low and missed⟩

touch and go *adj* (1815) **:** PRECARIOUS, UNPREDICTABLE

touch•back \ˈtəch-ˌbak\ *n* (ca. 1890) **:** a situation in football in which the ball is down behind the goal line after a kick or intercepted forward pass after which it is put in play by the team defending the goal on its own 20-yard line — compare SAFETY

touch•down \ˈtəch-ˌdau̇n\ *n* (1876) **1 :** the act of touching a football to the ground behind an opponent's goal; *specif* **:** the act of scoring six points in American football by being lawfully in possession of the ball on, above, or behind an opponent's goal line when the ball is declared dead **2 :** the act or moment of touching down (as with an airplane or spacecraft)

touch down \(ˈ)təch-ˈdau̇n\ *vt* (1864) **:** to place (the ball in rugby) by hand on the ground on or over an opponent's goal line in scoring a try or behind one's own goal line as a defensive measure ~ *vi* **:** to reach the ground : LAND

tou•ché \tü-ˈshā\ *interj* [F, fr. pp. of *toucher* to touch, fr. OF *tuchier*] (1921) — used to acknowledge a hit in fencing or the success of an argument, an accusation, or a witty point

touched \ˈtəcht\ *adj* (14c) **1 :** emotionally stirred (as with gratitude) **2 :** slightly unbalanced mentally

touch football *n* (1935) **:** football played informally and chiefly characterized by the substitution of touching for tackling

touch•hole \ˈtəch-ˌhōl\ *n* (1501) **:** the vent in muzzle-loading guns through which the charge is ignited

[1]**touch•ing** *prep* (14c) **:** in reference to : CONCERNING

[2]**touching** *adj* (1601) **:** capable of arousing emotions of tenderness or compassion ***syn*** see MOVING — **touch•ing•ly** \-iŋ-lē\ *adv*

touch•line \ˈtəch-ˌlīn\ *n* (1868) **:** either of the lines that bound the sides of the field of play in rugby and soccer

touch•mark \-ˌmärk\ *n* (1697) **:** an identifying maker's mark impressed on pewter

touch–me–not \ˈtəch-mē-ˌnät\ *n* [fr. the bursting of the ripe pods and scattering of their seeds when touched] (1659) **:** IMPATIENS

touch off *vt* (1758) **1 :** to describe or characterize with precision **2 a :** to cause to explode by or as if by touching with fire **b :** to release or initiate with sudden intensity ⟨the charges *touched off* a storm of protest —R. A. Billington⟩

touch•stone \ˈtəch-ˌstōn\ *n* (1530) **1 :** a black siliceous stone related to flint and formerly used to test the purity of gold and silver by the streak left on the stone when rubbed by the metal **2 :** a test or criterion for determining the quality or genuineness of a thing ***syn*** see STANDARD

touch system *n* (1918) **:** a method of typewriting that assigns a particular finger to each key and makes it possible to type without looking at the keyboard

touch–type \ˈtəch-ˌtīp\ *vi* (1943) **:** to type by the touch system

touch–up \ˈtəch-ˌəp\ *n* (1885) **:** an act or instance of touching up

touch up \(ˈ)təch-ˈəp\ *vt* (1715) **1 :** to improve or perfect by small additional strokes or alterations : make good the minor and usu. visible defects or damages of **2 :** to stimulate by or as if by a flick of a whip

touch•wood \ˈtəch-ˌwu̇d\ *n* (1579) **:** [3]PUNK

touchy \ˈtəch-ē\ *adj* **touch•i•er; -est** (1605) **1 :** marked by readiness to take offense on slight provocation **2 a** *of a body part* **:** acutely sensitive or irritable **b** *of a chemical* **:** highly explosive or inflammable **3 :** calling for tact, care, or caution in treatment ⟨a ~ subject⟩ — **touch•i•ly** \ˈtəch-ə-lē\ *adv* — **touch•i•ness** \ˈtəch-ē-nəs\ *n*

[1]**tough** \ˈtəf\ *adj* [ME, fr. OE *tōh;* akin to OHG *zāhi* tough] (bef. 12c) **1 a :** strong or firm in texture but flexible and not brittle **b :** not easily chewed **2 :** GLUTINOUS, STICKY **3 :** characterized by severity or uncompromising determination **4 :** capable of enduring strain, hardship, or severe labor **5 :** very hard to influence : STUBBORN **6 :** difficult to accomplish, resolve, or deal with ⟨a ~ question⟩ **7 :** stubbornly fought ⟨a ~ contest⟩ **8 :** UNRULY, ROWDYISH **9 :** marked by absence of softness or sentimentality **10** *slang* **:** EXCELLENT, GREAT ***syn*** see STRONG — **tough•ly** *adv* — **tough•ness** *n*

[2]**tough** *adv* (14c) **:** in a tough manner ⟨talks ~ and insensitively —A. E. Stevenson †1965⟩

[3]**tough** *vt* (1830) **:** to bear unflinchingly : ENDURE — used esp. in the phrase *tough it out*

[4]**tough** *n* (1866) **:** a tough person : ROWDY

tough•en \ˈtəf-ən\ *vb* **tough•ened; tough•en•ing** \-(ə-)niŋ\ *vt* (1582) **:** to make tough ~ *vi* **:** to become tough

tough•ie *also* **toughy** \ˈtəf-ē\ *n, pl* **tough•ies** (1921) **:** one that is tough: as **a :** a loud rough rowdy person **b :** a difficult problem or question

tough–mind•ed \ˈtəf-ˈmīn-dəd\ *adj* (1909) **:** realistic or unsentimental in temper or outlook — **tough–mind•ed•ness** *n*

tou•pee \tü-ˈpā\ *n* [F *toupet* forelock, fr. OF, dim. of *top, toup,* of Gmc origin; akin to OHG *zopf* tuft of hair — more at TOP] (1728) **1 :** a curl or lock of hair made into a topknot on a periwig or natural coiffure; *also* **:** a periwig with such a topknot **2 :** a wig or section of hair worn to cover a bald spot

[1]**tour** \ˈtu̇(ə)r, *1 is also* ˈtau̇(ə)r\ *n* [ME, fr. MF, fr. OF *tourn, tour* lathe, circuit, turn — more at TURN] (14c) **1 a :** one's turn in an orderly schedule : SHIFT **b :** a period during which an individual or unit is on a specific duty or at one place ⟨served a ~ of duty in Europe⟩ **2 a :** a journey for business, pleasure, or education in which one returns to the starting point; *also* **:** something resembling such a tour **b :** a brief turn : ROUND

[2]**tour** *vi* (1746) **:** to make a tour ~ *vt* **1 :** to make a tour of **2 :** to present (as a theatrical production) on a tour

tou•ra•co \ˈtu̇r-ə-ˌkō\ *n, pl* **-cos** [native name in western Africa] (ca. 1743) **:** any of a family (Musophagidae) of African birds that are related to the cuckoos and have a long tail, a short stout often colored bill, and red wing feathers

tour•bil•lion \tu̇r-ˈbil-yən\ *or* **tour•bil•lon** \tür-bē-(y)ōⁿ\ *n* [ME, fr. MF *tourbillon,* fr. L *turbin-, turbo* — more at TURBINE] (15c) **1 :** WHIRLWIND **2 :** a vortex esp. of a whirlwind or whirlpool **3 :** a firework having a spiral flight

tour de force \ˌtu̇(ə)rd-ə-ˈfō(ə)rs, -ˈfȯ(ə)rs\ *n, pl* **tours de force** *same*\ [F] (1805) **:** a feat of strength, skill, or ingenuity

tour•er \ˈtu̇r-ər\ *n* (1926) **1 :** TOURING CAR **2 :** one that tours

tour•ing \ˈtu̇(ə)r-iŋ\ *n* (1818) **1 :** participation in a tour **2 :** cross-country skiing for pleasure

touring car *n* (1903) **:** an automobile suitable for distance driving: as **a :** a vintage automobile with two cross seats, usu. four doors, and a folding top : PHAETON 2 **b :** a modern usu. 2-door sedan as distinguished from a sports car

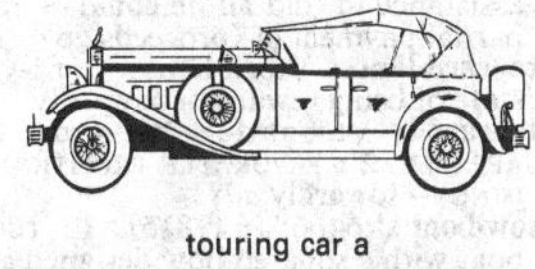

touring car a

tour•ism \ˈtu̇(ə)r-ˌiz-əm\ *n* (1811) **1 :** the practice of traveling for recreation **2 :** the guidance or management of tourists **3 a :** the promotion or encouragement of touring **b :** the accommodation of tourists

tour•ist \ˈtu̇r-əst\ *n* (1780) **1 :** one that makes a tour for pleasure or culture **2 :** TOURIST CLASS — **tourist** *adj or adv*

tourist card *n* (1948) **:** a citizenship identity card issued to a tourist usu. for a stated period of time in lieu of a passport or a visa

tourist class *n* (1935) **:** economy accommodations (as on a ship)

tourist court *n* (1937) **:** MOTEL

tour•is•tic \tu̇r-ˈis-tik\ *adj* (1848) **:** of or relating to a tour, tourism, or tourists — **tour•is•ti•cal•ly** \-ti-k(ə-)lē\ *adv*

tour•isty \ˈtu̇r-əs-tē\ *adj* (1906) **:** of or relating to tourists: as **a :** patronized by tourists **b :** of a type appealing to tourists

tour•ma•line \ˈtu̇r-mə-lən, -ˌlēn\ *n* [Sinhalese *toramalli* carnelian] (1759) **:** a mineral $(Na,Ca)(Li,Mg,Fe,Al)(Al,Fe)_6B_3Si_6O_{27}(O,OH,F)_4$ of variable color that consists of a complex silicate and makes a striking gem when transparent and cut

tour•na•ment \ˈtu̇r-nə-mənt *also* ˈtər- *or* ˈtȯr-\ *n* [ME *tornement,* fr. OF *torneiement,* fr. *torneier*[1] (13c) **1 a :** a knightly sport of the middle ages between mounted combatants armed with blunted lances or swords and divided into two parties contesting for a prize or favor bestowed by the lady of the tournament **b :** the whole series of knightly sports, jousts, and tilts occurring at one time and place **2 :** a championship series of games or athletic contests

tour•ne•dos \ˌtu̇r-nə-ˈdō\ *n, pl* **tour•ne•dos** \-ˈdō(z)\ [F, fr. *tourner* to turn (fr. OF) + *dos* back, fr. L *dorsum* — more at TURN] (ca. 1923) **:** a small fillet of beef usu. cut from the tip of the tenderloin

[1]**tour•ney** \ˈtu̇(ə)r-nē *also* ˈtər- *or* ˈtȯr-\ *vi* **tour•neyed; tour•ney•ing** [ME *tourneyen,* fr. MF *torneier,* fr. OF, fr. *torn, tourn* lathe, circuit] (14c) **:** to perform in a tournament

[2]**tourney** *n, pl* **tourneys** (14c) **:** TOURNAMENT

tour•ni•quet \ˈtu̇r-ni-kət, ˈtər-\ *n* [F, turnstile, tourniquet, fr. *tourner* to turn, fr. OF — more at TURN] (1695) **:** a device (as a bandage twisted tight with a stick) to check bleeding or blood flow

[1]**touse** \ˈtau̇z\ *vt* **toused; tous•ing** [ME *-tousen;* akin to OHG *zirzūsōn* to pull to pieces] (1598) **:** RUMPLE, TOUSLE

[2]**touse** *n* (1795) **:** a noisy disturbance

[1]**tou•sle** \ˈtau̇-zəl, -səl\ *vt* **tou•sled; tou•sling** \ˈtau̇z-(ə-)liŋ, ˈtau̇s-\ [ME *touselen,* freq. of *-tousen*] (15c) **:** DISHEVEL, RUMPLE

[2]**tou•sle** \ˈtau̇-zəl, *1 is also* ˈtü-\ *n* (1788) **1** *Scot* **:** rough dalliance : TUSSLE **2 :** a tangled mass (as of hair)

[1]**tout** \ˈtau̇t\ *vb* [ME *tuten* to peer; akin to OE *tōtian* to stick out, Norw *tyte*] *vi* (1731) **1 :** to solicit patronage **2 a** *chiefly Brit* **:** to spy on racehorses in training to gain information for betting **b :** to give a tip or solicit bets on a racehorse ~ *vt* **1 :** to spy on : WATCH **2 a** *Brit* **:** to spy out information about (as a racing stable or horse) **b :** to give a tip or solicit bets on (a racehorse) **3 :** to solicit, peddle, or persuade importunately ⟨not meant to ~ you off the movie —Russell Baker⟩

[2]**tout** *n* (1853) **:** one who touts: as **a :** one who solicits patronage **b** *chiefly Brit* **:** one who spies out racing information for betting purposes **c :** one who gives tips or solicits bets on a racehorse

[3]**tout** \ˈtau̇t, ˈtüt\ *vt* [alter. of [1]*toot*] (1926) **:** to praise or publicize loudly or extravagantly ⟨~*ed* as the . . . most elaborate suburban shopping development —*Wall Street Jour.*⟩

tout•er \ˈtau̇t-ər\ *n* (1754) **:** [2]TOUT

to·va·rich *or* **to·va·rish** \tə-ˈvär-ish, -ich\ *n* [Russ *tovarishch*] (ca. 1917) : COMRADE

[1]**tow** \ˈtō\ *vb* [ME *towen,* fr. OE *togian;* akin to OE *tēon* to draw, pull, OHG *ziohan* to draw, pull, L *ducere* to draw, lead] *vt* (bef. 12c) : to draw or pull along behind : HAUL ~ *vi* : to move in tow ⟨trailers that ~ behind the family auto —Bob Munger⟩

[2]**tow** *n* (1600) **1** : a rope or chain for towing **2 a** : the act or an instance of towing **b** : the fact or state of being towed **3 a** : something towed (as a boat or car) **b** : a group of barges lashed together and usu. pushed **4 a** : something (as a tugboat) that tows **b** : SKI TOW — **in tow 1** : under guidance or protection ⟨taken *in tow* by a friendly native⟩ **2** : in the position of a dependent or devoted follower or admirer

[3]**tow** *n* [ME, fr. OE *tow-* spinning; akin to ON *tō* tuft of wool for spinning, OE *tawian* to prepare for use — more at TAW] (14c) **1** : short or broken fiber (as of flax, hemp, or synthetic material) that is used esp. for yarn, twine, or stuffing **2 a** : yarn or cloth made of tow **b** : a loose essentially untwisted strand of synthetic fibers

[4]**tow** *n* [ME (Sc), prob. fr. OE *toh-* (in *tohlīne* towline); akin to OE *togian* to tow] *chiefly Scot & dial Eng* (15c) : ROPE

tow·age \ˈtō-ij\ *n* (14c) **1** : the act of towing **2** : a charge for towing

[1]**to·ward** \ˈtō(-ə)rd, ˈtȯ(-ə)rd\ *adj* [ME *toward,* fr. OE *tōweard* facing, imminent, fr. *tō,* prep., to + *-weard* -ward] (bef. 12c) **1** *also* **to·wards** \ˈtō(-ə)rdz, ˈtȯ(-ə)rdz\ [ME *towardes,* fr. OE *tōweardes,* prep., toward, fr. *tōweard,* adj.] **a** : coming soon : IMMINENT **b** : happening at the moment : AFOOT **2 a** *obs* : quick to learn : APT **b** : PROPITIOUS, FAVORING ⟨a ~ breeze⟩

[2]**to·ward** *or* **to·wards** \(ˈ)tō(-ə)rd(z), (ˈ)tȯ(-ə)rd(z), tə-ˈwȯrd(z), (ˈ)twȯrd(z), (ˈ)twōrd(z)\ *prep* (bef. 12c) **1** : in the direction of ⟨driving ~ town⟩ **2 a** : along a course leading to ⟨a long stride ~ disarmament⟩ **b** : in relation to ⟨an attitude ~ life⟩ **3 a** : at a point in the direction of : NEAR ⟨a cottage somewhere up ~ the lake⟩ **b** : in such a position as to be in the direction of ⟨your back was ~ me⟩ **4** : not long before ⟨~ the end of the afternoon⟩ **5 a** : in the way of help or assistance in ⟨did all he could ~ raising campaign funds⟩ **b** : for the partial payment of ⟨proceeds go ~ the establishment of a scholarship⟩

to·ward·li·ness \ˈtōrd-lē-nəs, ˈtȯrd-\ *n, archaic* (1566) : the quality or state of being toward or towardly

to·ward·ly \ˈtō(-ə)rd-lē, ˈtȯ(-ə)rd-\ *adj, archaic* (1513) **1** : PLEASANT, AFFABLE **2** : FAVORABLE, PROPITIOUS **3** : developing favorably : PROMISING — **towardly** *adv*

tow·boat \ˈtō-ˌbōt\ *n* (1815) **1** : TUGBOAT **2** : a compact shallow-draft boat with a squared bow designed and fitted for pushing tows of barges on inland waterways

[1]**tow·el** \ˈtau̇(-ə)l\ *n* [ME *towaille,* fr. OF *toaille,* of Gmc origin; akin to OHG *dwahila* towel; akin to OHG *dwahan* to wash, OPruss *twaxtan* bath cloth] (13c) : an absorbent cloth or paper for wiping or drying

[2]**towel** *vb* **-eled** *or* **-elled; -el·ing** *or* **-el·ling** *vt* (1836) : to rub or dry (as the body) with a towel ~ *vi* : to use a towel to dry oneself

tow·el·ette \ˌtau̇-(ə-)ˈlet\ *n* (1902) : a small usu. premoistened piece of material used for personal cleansing (as of the hands)

tow·el·ing *or* **tow·el·ling** \ˈtau̇-(ə-)liŋ\ *n* (1583) : a cotton or linen fabric often used for making towels

[1]**tow·er** \ˈtau̇(-ə)r\ *n* [ME *tour, tor,* fr. OE *torr* & OF *tor, tur,* both fr. L *turris,* fr. Gk *tyrsis*] (bef. 12c) **1** : a building or structure typically higher than its diameter and high relative to its surroundings that may stand apart (as a campanile), or be attached (as a church belfry) to a larger structure, and that may be fully walled in or of skeleton framework (as an observation or transmission tower) **2** : a towering citadel : FORTRESS **3** : one that provides support or protection : BULWARK ⟨a ~ of strength⟩ — **tow·ered** \ˈtau̇(-ə)rd\ *adj* — **tow·er·like** \ˈtau̇(-ə)r-ˌlīk\ *adj*

[2]**tower** *vi* (1582) **1** : to reach or rise to a great height **2** : to exhibit superior qualities : SURPASS ⟨her intellect ~*ed* over the others⟩

tower house *n* (1687) : a medieval fortified castle (as in Scotland)

tow·er·ing *adj* (1598) **1** : impressively high or great : IMPOSING ⟨~ pines⟩ **2** : reaching a high point of intensity : OVERWHELMING ⟨a ~ rage⟩ **3** : going beyond proper bounds : EXCESSIVE ⟨~ ambitions⟩ — **tow·er·ing·ly** \ˈtau̇-(ə-)r-iŋ-lē\ *adv*

Tower of Babel (ca. 1887) : BABEL 2

tow·head \ˈtō-ˌhed\ *n* (1830) **1** : a head of hair resembling tow esp. in being flaxen or tousled; *also* : a person having such a head of hair **2** : a low alluvial island or shoal in a river : SANDBAR — **tow·head·ed** \-ˌhed-əd\ *adj*

to·whee \ˈtō-ˌhē, ˈtō-(ˌ)ē, tō-ˈhē\ *n* [imit.] (1729) **1** : a common finch (*Pipilo erythrophthalmus*) of eastern No. America having the male black, white, and rufous — called also *chewink* **2** : any of numerous American finches (genera *Pipilo* and *Chlorura*) related to the towhee

to wit \tə-ˈwit\ *adv* [ME *to witen,* lit., to know — more at WIT] (14c) : that is to say : NAMELY

tow·line \ˈtō-ˌlīn\ *n* (1719) : a line used in towing

tow·mond \ˈtō-ˌmänd\ *n* [ME *towlmonyth,* fr. OE *twelf mōnath,* fr. *twelf* twelve + *mōnath* month] *Scot* (bef. 12c) : YEAR, TWELVEMONTH

town \ˈtau̇n\ *n* [ME, fr. OE *tūn* enclosure, village, town; akin to OHG *zūn* enclosure, OIr *dūn* fortress] (bef. 12c) **1** *dial Eng* : a cluster or aggregation of houses recognized as a distinct place with a place-name : HAMLET **2 a** : a compactly settled area as distinguished from surrounding rural territory **b** : a compactly settled area usu. larger than a village but smaller than a city **c** : a large densely populated urban area : CITY **d** : an English village having a periodic fair or market **3** : a neighboring city, capital city, or metropolis **4** : the city or urban life as contrasted with the country **5** : the inhabitants of a city or town **6** : a New England territorial and political unit usu. containing both rural and unincorporated urban areas under a single town government — called also *township; also* : a New England community governed by a town meeting — **town** *adj* — **on the town** : in usu. carefree pursuit of entertainment or amusement (as city nightlife) esp. as a relief from routine

town car *n* (1923) : a 4-door automobile with a permanently enclosed passenger compartment in the rear separated from the driver's compartment by a sliding glass partition

town clerk *n* (14c) : a public officer charged with recording the official proceedings and vital statistics of a town

town crier *n* (1602) : a town officer who makes public proclamations

town·ee \tau̇-ˈnē\ *n, chiefly Brit* (1897) : TOWNIE

town hall *n* (15c) : a public building used for town-government offices and meetings

town house *n* (1803) **1** : a house in town; *specif* : the city residence of one having a countryseat or having a chief residence elsewhere ⟨stayed at their *town house* during the social season⟩ **2** : a usu. single-family house of two or sometimes three stories that is usu. connected to a similar house by a common sidewall; *also* : ROW HOUSE

town·ie *or* **towny** \ˈtau̇-nē\ *n, pl* **townies** (1852) : TOWNSMAN; *esp* : a permanent inhabitant of a town as distinguished from a member of another group (as the academic community)

town·let \ˈtau̇n-lət\ *n* (1552) : a very small town

town manager *n* (1922) : an official appointed to direct the administration of a town government

town meeting *n* (1636) : a meeting of inhabitants or taxpayers constituting the legislative authority of a town

town·scape \-ˌskāp\ *n* (1880) **1** : a representation of an urban scene **2** : a town or city viewed as a scene

towns·folk \ˈtau̇nz-ˌfōk\ *n pl* (1737) : TOWNSPEOPLE

town·ship \ˈtau̇n-ˌship\ *n* (15c) **1** : an ancient unit of administration in England identical in area with or a division of a parish **2 a** : TOWN 6 **b** : a unit of local government in some northeastern and north central states usu. having a chief administrative officer or board **c** : an unorganized subdivision of the county in Maine, New Hampshire, and Vermont **d** : an electoral and administrative district of the county in the southern U.S. **3** : a division of territory in surveys of U.S. public land containing 36 sections or 36 square miles

towns·man \ˈtau̇nz-mən\ *n* (bef. 12c) **1 a** : a native or resident of a town or city **b** : an urban or urbane person **2** : a fellow citizen of a town

towns·peo·ple \-ˌpē-pəl\ *n pl* (1648) **1** : the inhabitants of a town or city : TOWNSMEN **2** : town-dwelling or town-bred persons

towns·wom·an \-ˌwu̇m-ən\ *n* (1684) **1** : a female native or resident of a town or city **2** : a woman born or residing in the same town or city as another

tow·path \ˈtō-ˌpath, -ˌpȧth\ *n* (1788) : a path (as along a canal) traveled by men or animals towing boats — called also *towing path*

tow·rope \-ˌrōp\ *n* (1743) : a line used in towing something (as a boat)

tow sack \ˈtō-ˌsak\ *n* [[3]*tow*] *Midland & Southern* (1926) : GUNNYSACK

tow truck *n* (1944) : WRECKER 1b

tox- *or* **toxi-** *or* **toxo-** *comb form* [LL, fr. L *toxicum* poison] : poisonous : poison ⟨*tox*emia⟩

tox·a·phene \ˈtäk-sə-ˌfēn\ *n* [fr. *Toxaphene,* a trademark] (1947) : an insecticide with the approximate empirical formula $C_{10}H_{10}Cl_8$ that is a complex mixture of chlorinated compounds

tox·emia \täk-ˈsē-mē-ə\ *n* [NL] (ca. 1860) : an abnormal condition associated with the presence of toxic substances in the blood — **tox·emic** \-mik\ *adj*

tox·ic \ˈtäk-sik\ *adj* [LL *toxicus,* fr. L *toxicum* poison, fr. Gk *toxikon* arrow poison, fr. neut. of *toxikos* of a bow, fr. *toxon* bow, arrow; prob. akin to L *taxus* yew] (1664) **1** : of, relating to, or caused by a poison or toxin **2** : affected by a poison or toxin ⟨~ pregnant women⟩ **3** : POISONOUS — **tox·ic·i·ty** \täk-ˈsis-ət-ē\ *n*

toxic- *or* **toxico-** *comb form* [NL, fr. L *toxicum*] : poison ⟨*toxico*logy⟩

tox·i·cant \ˈtäk-si-kənt\ *n* [ML *toxicant-, toxicans,* prp. of *toxicare* to poison, fr. L *toxicum*] (ca. 1882) : a toxic agent; *esp* : one for insect control that kills rather than repels

tox·i·co·log·i·cal \ˌtäk-si-kə-ˈläj-i-kəl\ *or* **tox·i·co·log·ic** \-ik\ *adj* (1839) : of or relating to toxicology or toxins — **tox·i·co·log·i·cal·ly** \-i-k(ə-)lē\ *adv*

tox·i·col·o·gy \-ˈkäl-ə-jē\ *n* (ca. 1799) : a science that deals with poisons and their effect and with the problems involved (as clinical, industrial, or legal) — **tox·i·col·o·gist** \-jəst\ *n*

tox·i·co·sis \ˌtäk-sə-ˈkō-səs\ *n, pl* **-co·ses** \-ˌsēz\ [NL] (ca. 1857) : a pathological condition caused by the action of a poison or toxin

toxic shock syndrome *n* (1978) : an acute disease that is characterized by fever, sore throat, and diffuse erythema, that is associated esp. with the presence of a bacterium (*Streptomyces aureus*), and that occurs esp. in menstruating females using tampons

toxi·gen·ic \ˌtäk-sə-ˈjen-ik\ *adj* (ca. 1923) : producing toxin ⟨~ bacteria and fungi⟩ — **toxi·ge·nic·i·ty** \ˌtäk-si-jə-ˈnis-ət-ē\ *n*

tox·in \ˈtäk-sən\ *n* [ISV] (1886) : a colloidal proteinaceous poisonous substance that is a specific product of the metabolic activities of a living organism and is usu. very unstable, notably toxic when introduced into the tissues, and typically capable of inducing antibody formation

tox·in–an·ti·tox·in \ˈtäk-sə-ˈnant-i-ˌtäk-sən\ *n* (1904) : a mixture of toxin and antitoxin used esp. formerly in immunizing against a disease (as diphtheria) for which they are specific

tox·oid \ˈtäk-ˌsȯid\ *n* [ISV] (ca. 1894) : a toxin of a pathogenic organism treated so as to destroy its toxicity but leave it capable of inducing the formation of antibodies on injection

tox·oph·i·lite \täk-ˈsäf-ə-ˌlīt\ *n* [Gk *toxon* bow, arrow + *philos* dear, loving] (1813) : one fond of or expert at archery — **toxophilite** *adj* — **tox·oph·i·ly** \-lē\ *n*

toxo·plas·ma \ˌtäk-sə-ˈplaz-mə\ *n* [NL] (1926) : any of a genus (*Toxoplasma*) of parasitic microorganisms that are usu. held to be protozoans related to the sporozoans and that are typically serious pathogens of vertebrates — **toxo·plas·mic** \-mik\ *adj*

toxo·plas·mo·sis \-ˌplaz-ˈmō-səs\ *n, pl* **-mo·ses** \-ˌsēz\ [NL] (1926) : infection of man, other mammals, or birds with disease caused by toxoplasmas that invade the tissues and may seriously damage the central nervous system esp. of infants

[1]**toy** \ˈtȯi\ *n* [ME *toye* dalliance] (1500) **1** *obs* **a** : flirtatious or seductive behavior **b** : PASTIME; *also* : a sportive or amusing act : ANTIC **2 a** : something (as a preoccupation) that is paltry or trifling **b** : a literary or musical trifle or diversion **c** : TRINKET, BAUBLE **3** : something for a child to play with **4** : something diminutive; *esp* : a diminutive animal (as of a small breed or variety) **5** : something that can be toyed with **6** *Scot* : a headdress of linen or woolen hanging down over the shoulders and formerly worn by old women of the lower classes — **toy·like** \-ˌlīk\ *adj*

[2]**toy** *vi* (1529) **1** : to engage in flirtation **2** : to act or deal with something lightly or without vigor or purpose **3** : to amuse oneself as if with a toy : PLAY ***syn*** see TRIFLE — **toy·er** \ˈtȯi-ər\ *n*

³toy *adj* (1806) **1 :** resembling a toy esp. in diminutive size **2 :** designed or made for use as a toy ⟨a ~ stove⟩

toy Man·ches·ter terrier \-ˌman-ˌches-tər-, -chə-stər-\ *n* (ca. 1935) **:** any of a variety of Manchester terrier having erect ears of moderate size and weighing not more than 12 pounds — called also *toy Manchester*

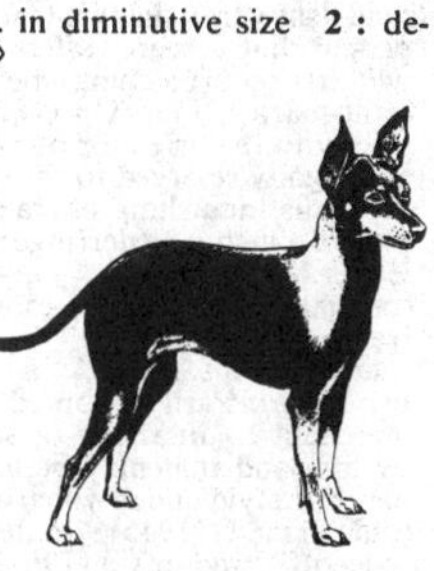

toy Manchester terrier

toy·on \ˈtȯi-ˌän\ *n* [AmerSp *tollon*] (1848) **:** an ornamental evergreen shrub (*Photinia arbutifolia*) of the rose family of the No. American Pacific coast having white flowers succeeded by persistent bright red berries

toy poodle *n* (ca. 1935) **:** a toy dog that was developed from the standard poodle and is not more than 10 inches high at the withers

TPN \ˌtē-ˌpē-ˈen\ *n* [*tri*phosphopyridine *n*ucleotide] (1938) **:** NADP

tra·be·at·ed \ˈtrā-bē-ˌāt-əd\ *also* **tra·be·ate** \-ˌāt\ *adj* [L *trabs, trabes* beam — more at THORP] (1843) **:** designed or constructed with horizontal beams or lintels — **tra·be·ation** \ˌtrā-bē-ˈā-shən\ *n*

tra·bec·u·la \trə-ˈbek-yə-lə\ *n, pl* **-lae** \-ˌlē, -ˌlī\ *also* **-las** [NL, fr. L, little beam, dim. of *trabs, trabes* beam — more at THORP] (ca. 1866) **1 :** a small bar, rod, bundle of fibers, or septal membrane in the framework of a body organ or part **2 :** a fold, ridge, or bar projecting into or extending from a plant part; *esp* **:** a row of cells bridging an intercellular space — **tra·bec·u·lar** \-lər\ *adj* — **tra·bec·u·late** \-lət\ *adj*

¹trace \ˈtrās\ *n* [ME, fr. MF, fr. *tracier* to trace] (14c) **1** *archaic* **:** a course or path that one follows **2 a :** a mark or line left by something that has passed; *also* **:** FOOTPRINT **b :** a path, trail, or road made by the passage of animals, people, or vehicles **3 a :** a sign or evidence of some past thing **:** VESTIGE **b :** ENGRAM **4 :** something (as a line) traced or drawn: as **a :** the marking made by a recording instrument (as a seismograph or kymograph) **b :** the ground plan of a military installation or position either on a map or on the ground **5 a :** the intersection of a line or plane with a plane **b :** the usu. bright line or spot that moves across the screen of a cathode-ray tube; *also* **:** the path taken by such a line or spot **6 a :** a minute and often barely detectable amount or indication ⟨a ~ of a smile⟩ **b :** an amount of a chemical constituent not always quantitatively determinable because of minuteness

syn TRACE, VESTIGE, TRACK mean a perceptible sign made by something that has passed. TRACE may suggest any line, mark, or discernible effect; VESTIGE applies to a tangible reminder such as a fragment or remnant of what is past and gone; TRACK implies a continuous line that can be followed.

²trace *vb* **traced; trac·ing** [ME *tracen*, fr. MF *tracier*, fr. (assumed) VL *tractiare* to drag, draw, fr. L *tractus*, pp. of *trahere* to pull, draw — more at DRAW] *vt* (14c) **1 a :** DELINEATE, SKETCH **b :** to form (as letters or figures) carefully or painstakingly **c :** to copy (as a drawing) by following the lines or letters as seen through a transparent superimposed sheet **d :** to impress or imprint (as a design or pattern) with a tracer **e :** to record a tracing of in the form of a curved, wavy, or broken line ⟨~ the heart action⟩ **f :** to adorn with linear ornamentation (as tracery or chasing) **2** *archaic* **:** to travel over **:** TRAVERSE **3 a :** to follow the footprints, track, or trail of **b :** to follow or study out in detail or step by step ⟨~ the history of the labor movement⟩ **c :** to discover by going backward over the evidence step by step ⟨~ one's ancestry⟩ **d :** to discover signs, evidence, or remains of **4 :** to lay out the trace of (a military installation) ~ *vi* **1 :** to make one's way; *esp* **:** to follow a track or trail **2 :** to be traceable historically — **trace·abil·i·ty** \ˌtrā-sə-ˈbil-ət-ē\ *n* — **trace·able** \ˈtrā-sə-bəl\ *adj*

³trace *n* [ME *trais*, pl., traces, fr. MF, pl. of *trait* pull, draft, trace — more at TRAIT] (14c) **1 :** either of two straps, chains, or lines of a harness for attaching a horse to something (as a vehicle) to be drawn **2 :** LEADER 1e(2) **3 :** one or more vascular bundles supplying a leaf or twig **4 :** a connecting bar or rod pivoted at each end to another piece and used for transmitting motion

trace element *n* (1937) **:** a chemical element present in minute quantities; *esp* **:** one used by organisms and held essential to their physiology

trace·less \ˈtrā-sləs\ *adj* (1651) **:** having or leaving no trace — **trace·less·ly** *adv*

trac·er \ˈtrā-sər\ *n* (ca. 1552) **1 :** one that traces, tracks down, or searches out: as **a :** a person who traces missing persons or property and esp. goods lost in transit **b :** an inquiry sent out in tracing a shipment lost in transit **2 :** one who traces designs, patterns, or markings **3 :** a device (as a stylus) used in tracing **4 a :** ammunition containing a chemical composition to mark the flight of projectiles by a trail of smoke or fire **b :** a substance and esp. a labeled element used to trace the course of a chemical or biological process

trac·ery \ˈtrās(-ə-)rē\ *n, pl* **-er·ies** (1669) **1 :** architectural ornamental work with branching lines; *esp* **:** decorative openwork in the head of a Gothic window **2 :** a decorative interlacing of lines suggestive of Gothic tracery — **trac·er·ied** \-rēd\ *adj*

trache- *or* **tracheo-** *comb form* [NL, fr. ML *trachea*] **1 :** trachea ⟨*tracheitis*⟩ ⟨*tracheotomy*⟩ **2 :** tracheal and ⟨*tracheo*bronchial⟩

tra·chea \ˈtrā-kē-ə\ *n, pl* **-che·ae** \-kē-ˌē, -kē-ˌī\ *also* **-che·as** [ME, fr. ML, fr. LL *trachia*, fr. Gk *tracheia* (*artēria*) rough (artery), fr. fem. of *trachys* rough; akin to Gk *thrassein* to trouble — more at DARK] (15c) **1 :** the main trunk of the system of tubes by which air passes to and from the lungs in vertebrates **2** [NL, fr. ML] **:** VESSEL 3b; *also* **:** one of its constituent cellular elements **3** [NL] **:** one of the air-conveying tubules forming the respiratory system of most insects and many other arthropods — **tra·che·al** \-kē-əl\ *adj*

tra·che·ary \ˈtrā-kē-ˌer-ē\ *adj* (1885) **:** of, relating to, or being plant tracheae ⟨~ elements⟩

tra·che·ate \-kē-ˌāt, -ət\ *or* **tra·che·at·ed** \-ˌāt-əd\ *adj* (1888) **:** having tracheae as breathing organs

tra·cheid \ˈtrā-kē-əd, -ˌkēd\ *n* [ISV] (1875) **:** a long tubular cell that is peculiar to xylem, functions in conduction and support, and has tapering closed ends and thickened lignified walls

tra·che·itis \ˌtrā-kē-ˈīt-əs\ *n* [NL] (ca. 1842) **:** inflammation of the trachea

tra·cheo·bron·chi·al \ˌtrā-kē-ō-ˈbräŋ-kē-əl\ *adj* (1896) **:** of or relating to both trachea and bronchi ⟨~ lesions⟩

tra·che·ole \ˈtrā-kē-ˌōl\ *n* [NL *tracheola*, dim. of *trachea*] (1901) **:** one of the minute delicate endings of a branched trachea of an insect — **tra·che·o·lar** \trā-ˈkē-ə-lər\ *adj*

tra·cheo·phyte \ˈtrā-kē-ə-ˌfīt\ *n* [NL *Tracheophyta*, fr. *trache-* + Gk *phyton* plant; akin to Gk *phyein* to bring forth — more at BE] (1937) **:** any of a division (Tracheophyta) comprising green plants (as ferns and seed plants) with a vascular system that contains tracheids or tracheary elements

tra·che·os·to·my \ˌtrā-kē-ˈäst-ə-mē\ *n, pl* **-mies** (ca. 1923) **:** the surgical formation of an opening into the trachea through the neck esp. to allow the passage of air

tra·che·ot·o·my \ˌtrā-kē-ˈät-ə-mē\ *n, pl* **-mies** (ca. 1726) **:** the surgical operation of cutting into the trachea esp. through the skin

tra·cho·ma \trə-ˈkō-mə\ *n* [NL, fr. Gk *trachōma*, fr. *trachys* rough] (ca. 1693) **:** a chronic contagious conjunctivitis marked by inflammatory granulations on the conjunctival surfaces, caused by a chlamydia (*Chlamydia trachomatis*), and commonly resulting in blindness if left untreated

tra·chyte \ˈtrak-ˌīt, ˈtrā-ˌkīt\ *n* [F, fr. Gk *trachys* rough] (1821) **:** a usu. light-colored volcanic rock consisting chiefly of potash feldspar

tra·chyt·ic \trə-ˈkit-ik\ *adj* (1827) **:** of or relating to a texture of igneous rocks in which lath-shaped feldspar crystals are in almost parallel lines

trac·ing \ˈtrā-siŋ\ *n* (15c) **1 :** the act of one that traces **2 :** something that is traced: as **a :** a copy made on a superimposed transparent sheet **b :** a graphic record made by an instrument (as a seismograph) that registers some movement

tracing paper *n* (1824) **:** a semitransparent paper for tracing drawings

¹track \ˈtrak\ *n* [ME *trak*, fr. MF *trac*, perh. of Gmc origin; akin to MD *tracken, trecken* to pull, haul — more at TREK] (15c) **1 a :** detectable evidence (as the wake of a ship, a line of footprints, or a wheel rut) that something has passed **b :** a path made by repeated footfalls **:** TRAIL **c :** a course laid out esp. for racing **d :** the parallel rails of a railroad; *also* **:** a metal way (as a groove) serving as a guide (as for a movable lighting fixture) **e** (1) **:** one of a series of parallel or concentric paths along which material (as music or information) is recorded (as on a phonograph record or magnetic tape) (2) **:** BAND 7 **2 :** a footprint whether recent or fossil ⟨the huge ~ of a dinosaur⟩ **3 a :** the course along which something moves **b :** a way of life, conduct, or action **c :** one of several curricula of study to which students are assigned according to their needs or levels of ability **d :** the projection on the earth's surface of the path along which something (as a missile or an airplane) has actually flown **4 a :** a sequence of events **:** a train of ideas **:** SUCCESSION **b :** an awareness of a fact, progression, or condition ⟨keep ~ of the costs⟩ ⟨lose ~ of the time⟩ **5 a :** the width of a wheeled vehicle from wheel to wheel and usu. from the outside of the rims **b :** the tread of an automobile tire **c :** either of two endless metal belts on which a tracklaying vehicle travels **6 :** track-and-field sports; *esp* **:** those performed on a running track *syn* see TRACE — **track·less** \ˈtrak-ləs\ *adj* — **in one's tracks :** where one stands or is at the moment **:** on the spot ⟨was stopped *in his tracks*⟩

²track *vt* (1565) **1 a :** to follow the tracks or traces of **:** TRAIL **b :** to pursue until caught up with ⟨~ down a criminal⟩ **c :** to search for until found ⟨~ down the source⟩ **2 a :** to follow by vestiges **:** TRACE **b :** to observe or plot the moving path of (as a spacecraft or missile) instrumentally **3 :** to travel over **:** TRAVERSE ⟨~ a desert⟩ **4 a :** to make tracks upon **b :** to carry (as mud) on the feet and deposit **5 :** to keep track of (as a trend) **:** FOLLOW ~ *vi* **1 :** TRAVEL ⟨comet ~*s* eastward⟩ ⟨camera ~*s* back⟩ **2 a** *of a phonograph needle* **:** to follow the groove undulations of a recording **b** *of a pair of wheels* (1) **:** to maintain a constant distance apart on the straightaway (2) **:** to fit a track or rails **c** *of a rear wheel of a vehicle* **:** to follow accurately the corresponding fore wheel on a straightaway **3 :** to leave tracks (as on a floor) — **track·er** *n*

track·age \ˈtrak-ij\ *n* (1880) **1 :** lines of railway track **2 a :** a right to use the tracks of another railroad line **b :** the charge for such right

track–and–field \ˌtrak-ən-ˈfē(ə)ld\ *adj* (ca. 1932) **:** of, relating to, or being any of various competitive athletic events (as running, jumping, and weight throwing) performed on a running track and on the adjacent field

tracked \ˈtrakt\ *adj* (ca. 1926) **1 :** traveling on endless metal belts instead of wheels **2 :** moving along a rail ⟨a ~ air-cushion vehicle⟩

track·ing \ˈtrak-iŋ\ *n* (1928) **:** the assigning of students to a curricular track

tracking shot *n* (1945) **:** a scene photographed from a moving dolly

track·lay·er \ˈtrak-ˌlā-ər, -ˌle(-ə)r\ *n* (1861) **1 :** a worker engaged in tracklaying **2 :** a tracklaying vehicle

¹track·lay·ing \-ˌlā-iŋ\ *n* (1861) **:** the laying of tracks on a railway line

²tracklaying *adj* (1884) **:** of, relating to, or being a vehicle that travels on two or more endless usu. metal belts

trackless trolley *n* (1921) **:** TROLLEYBUS

track lighting *n* (ca. 1972) **:** lighting provided by adjustable lamps mounted along an electrified metal track

track·man \ˈtrak-mən, -ˌman\ *n* (1922) **:** a runner on a track team

track record *n* [¹*track* (track-and-field sports)] (1952) **:** a record of accomplishments

track·side \ˌtrak-ˌsīd\ *adj* (1886) **:** of, relating to, or situated in the area immediately adjacent to a track — **trackside** *n*

track·suit \ˈtrak-ˌsüt\ *n* (1922) **:** a suit of clothing consisting usu. of a jacket and pants that is often worn by athletes when working out

track·walk·er \-ˌwȯ-kər\ *n* (1872) **:** a worker employed to walk over and inspect a section of railroad tracks

track·way \-ˌwā\ *n* (1818) **:** a beaten or trodden path

1tract \'trakt\ *n, often cap* [ME *tracte,* fr. ML *tractus,* fr. L, action of drawing, extension; fr. its being sung without a break by one voice] (14c) **:** verses of Scripture (as from the Psalms) used between the gradual and the Gospel at some masses (as during penitential seasons)

2tract *n* [L *tractus* action of drawing, extension, fr. *tractus,* pp. of *trahere* to pull, draw — more at DRAW] (15c) **1** *archaic* **:** extent or lapse of time **2 :** an area either large or small: as **a :** an indefinite stretch of land **b :** a defined area of land **3 :** a system of body parts or organs that collectively serve some special purpose ⟨the digestive ~⟩; *esp* **:** a bundle of nerve fibers having a common origin, termination, and function

3tract *n* [ME, treatise, modif. of L *tractatus* tractate] (1760) **:** a pamphlet or leaflet of political or religious propaganda

trac·ta·ble \'trak-tə-bəl\ *adj* [L *tractabilis,* fr. *tractare* to handle, treat] (1502) **1 :** capable of being easily led, taught, or controlled **:** DOCILE ⟨a ~ horse⟩ **2 :** easily handled, managed, or wrought **:** MALLEABLE *syn* see OBEDIENT — **trac·ta·bil·i·ty** \,trak-tə-'bil-ət-ē\ *n* — **trac·ta·ble·ness** \'trak-tə-bəl-nəs\ *n* — **trac·ta·bly** \-blē\ *adv*

Trac·tar·i·an \trak-'ter-ē-ən\ *n* [fr. *Tracts for the Times,* series of pamphlets expounding the Oxford movement] (ca. 1839) **:** a promoter or supporter of the Oxford movement

Trac·tar·i·an·ism \-ē-ə-,niz-əm\ *n* (1840) **:** a system of High Church principles set forth in a series of tracts at Oxford (1833–41)

trac·tate \'trak-,tāt\ *n* [L *tractatus,* fr. *tractatus,* pp. of *tractare* to draw out, handle, treat — more at TREAT] (15c) **:** TREATISE, DISSERTATION

tract house *n* (1956) **:** any of many similarly designed houses built on a tract of land

trac·tion \'trak-shən\ *n* [ML *traction-, tractio,* fr. L *tractus,* pp.] (1615) **1 :** the act of drawing **:** the state of being drawn; *also* **:** the force exerted in drawing **2 :** the drawing of a vehicle by motive power; *also* **:** the motive power employed **3 a :** the adhesive friction of a body on a surface on which it moves ⟨the ~ of a wheel on a rail⟩ **b :** a pulling force exerted on a skeletal structure (as in a fracture) by means of a special device ⟨a ~ splint⟩; *also* **:** a state of tension created by such a pulling force ⟨a leg in ~⟩ — **trac·tion·al** \-shnəl, -shən-ᵊl\ *adj*

trac·tive \'trak-tiv\ *adj* [L *tractus,* pp.] (1615) **1 :** serving to draw **2 :** of or relating to traction **:** TRACTIONAL

trac·tor \'trak-tər\ *n* [NL, fr. L *tractus,* pp.] (1900) **1 :** a steam-powered vehicle used to draw other vehicles or equipment (as a threshing rig) over roads or fields and sometimes to provide power (as for sawing or threshing) **2 a :** a 4-wheeled or tracklaying rider-controlled automotive vehicle used esp. for drawing implements (as agricultural) or for bearing and propelling such implements **b :** a smaller 2-wheeled apparatus controlled through handlebars by a walking operator **c :** a truck with short chassis and no body used in combination with a trailer for the highway hauling of freight **3 :** an airplane having the propeller forward of the main supporting surfaces

trad \'trad\ *adj, chiefly Brit* (1952) **:** TRADITIONAL

1trade \'trād\ *n* [ME, fr. MLG; akin to OHG *trata* track, course, OE *tredan* to tread] (14c) **1 a** *obs* **:** a path traversed **:** WAY **b** *archaic* **:** a track or trail left by a person or animal **:** TREAD 1 **2 :** a customary course of action **:** PRACTICE ⟨thy sin's not accidental, but a ~ —Shak.⟩ **3 a :** the business or work in which one engages regularly **:** OCCUPATION **b :** an occupation requiring manual or mechanical skill **:** CRAFT **c :** the persons engaged in an occupation, business, or industry **4 a** *obs* **:** dealings between persons or groups **b** (1) **:** the business of buying and selling or bartering commodities **:** COMMERCE (2) **:** BUSINESS, MARKET ⟨novelties for the tourist ~⟩ ⟨did a good ~ in small appliances⟩ **5 a :** an act or instance of trading **:** TRANSACTION; *also* **:** an exchange of property usu. without use of money **b :** a firm's customers **:** CLIENTELE **c :** the group of firms engaged in a business or industry **6 :** TRADE WIND *syn* see BUSINESS

2trade *vb* **trad·ed; trad·ing** *vi* (1553) **1** *obs* **:** to have dealings **:** NEGOTIATE **2 a :** to engage in the exchange, purchase, or sale of goods **b :** to make one's purchases **:** SHOP ⟨~s at his store⟩ **3 :** to give one thing in exchange for another **4 :** SELL 3 ~ *vt* **1** *archaic* **:** to do business with **2 a :** to give in exchange for another commodity **:** BARTER; *also* **:** to make an exchange of ⟨*traded* places⟩ **b :** to engage in frequent buying and selling of (as stocks or commodities) usu. in search of quick profits — **trad·able** *also* **trade·able** \'trād-ə-bəl\ *adj* — **trade on :** to take often unscrupulous advantage of **:** EXPLOIT ⟨*traded on* their influence . . . in securing special favors —T. C. Pease⟩

3trade *adj* (1633) **1 :** of, relating to, or used in trade **2 a :** intended for or limited to persons in a business or industry ⟨a ~ publication⟩ ⟨~ sales⟩ **b :** serving others in the same business rather than the ultimate user or consumer ⟨a ~ printing house⟩ **3** *also* **trades :** of, composed of, or representing the trades or trade unions ⟨a ~ committee⟩ **4 :** of or associated with a trade wind ⟨the ~ belts⟩

trade acceptance *n* (ca. 1916) **:** a time draft or bill of exchange for the amount of a specific purchase drawn by the seller on the buyer, bearing the buyer's acceptance, and often noting the place of payment (as a bank)

trade agreement *n* (ca. 1921) **1 :** an international agreement on conditions of trade in goods and services **2 :** an agreement resulting from collective bargaining

trade book *n* (ca. 1945) **1 :** a book intended for general readership **2 :** TRADE EDITION

trade discount *n* (1901) **:** a deduction from the list price of goods allowed by a manufacturer or wholesaler to a retailer

trade dollar *n* (1873) **:** a U.S. silver dollar weighing 420 grains .900 fine issued 1873–85 for use in oriental trade

trade down *vi* (1949) **1 :** to trade something in (as an automobile) for something less expensive or valuable of its kind **2 :** to stock or purchase lower-priced items **:** ECONOMIZE

trade edition *n* (ca. 1947) **:** an edition of a book intended for general distribution — compare TEXT EDITION

trade–in \'trād-,in\ *n* (1923) **:** an item of merchandise (as an automobile or refrigerator) taken as payment or part payment for a purchase

trade in \(')trād-'in\ *vt* (1923) **1 :** to turn in as payment or part payment for a purchase or bill ⟨*trade* an old car *in* for a new one⟩ **2 :** EXCHANGE 2

trade language *n* (1662) **:** a mongrel language (as a lingua franca or pidgin) used esp. in commercial communication

trade–last \'trād-,last\ *n* (ca. 1895) **:** a complimentary remark by a third person that a hearer offers to repeat to the person complimented if he will first report a compliment made about the hearer

1trade·mark \-,märk\ *n* (1838) **1 :** a device (as a word) pointing distinctly to the origin or ownership of merchandise to which it is applied and legally reserved to the exclusive use of the owner as maker or seller **2 :** a distinguishing characteristic or feature firmly associated with a person or thing ⟨derringers . . . became almost a ~ of gamblers —Elmer Keith⟩

2trademark *vt* (1906) **:** to secure trademark rights for **:** register the trademark of

1trade name *n* (1861) **1 a :** the name used for an article among traders **b :** an arbitrarily adopted name that is given by a manufacturer or merchant to an article or service to distinguish it as produced or sold by him and that may be used and protected as a trademark **2 :** the name or style under which a concern does business

2trade name *vt* (1945) **:** to designate with a trade name

trade–off \'trād-,ȯf\ *n* (1962) **1 :** a balancing of factors all of which are not attainable at the same time ⟨the education versus experience ~ which governs personnel practices —H. S. White⟩ **2 :** a giving up of one thing in return for another **:** EXCHANGE — **trade off** *vt*

trad·er \'trād-ər\ *n* (1585) **1 :** a person whose business is buying and selling or barter: as **a :** MERCHANT **b :** a person who buys and sells (as securities) for his own account in search of short-term profits **2 :** a ship engaged in the coastal or foreign trade

trade route *n* (1876) **1 :** a route followed by traders (as in caravans) **2 :** one of the sea-lanes ordinarily used by merchant ships

trad·es·can·tia \,trad-ə-'skan-ch(ē-)ə\ *n* [NL, genus name, fr. John *Tradescant* †1638 Eng. traveler & gardener] (ca. 1909) **:** SPIDERWORT

trade school *n* (1889) **:** a secondary school teaching the skilled trades

trade secret *n* (1903) **:** a formula, process, or device used in a business that is not published or divulged and that thereby gives an advantage over competitors

trades·man \'trādz-mən\ *n* (1597) **1 :** a worker in a skilled trade **:** CRAFTSMAN **2 :** one who runs a retail store **:** SHOPKEEPER

trades·peo·ple \-,pē-pəl\ *n pl* (1728) **:** people engaged in trade

trade union *also* **trades union** *n* (1835) **:** LABOR UNION — **trade unionism** *n* — **trade unionist** *n*

trade up *vi* (1926) **1 :** to trade something in (as an automobile) for something more expensive or valuable of its kind **2 :** to stock or purchase higher-priced items

tra·dev·man \trə-'dev-mən, 'trā-,\ *n* [*tr*aining *dev*ices *man*] (ca. 1947) **:** a petty officer in charge of naval training equipment

trade wind *n* (1650) **:** a wind blowing almost constantly in one direction; *esp* **:** a wind blowing almost continually toward the equator from the northeast in the belt between the northern horse latitudes and the doldrums and from the southeast in the belt between the southern horse latitudes and the doldrums

trading post *n* (1796) **1 :** a station of a trader or trading company established in a sparsely settled region where trade in products of local origin (as furs) is carried on **2 :** 6POST 3b

trading stamp *n* (1898) **:** a printed stamp of value given as a premium to a retail customer to be redeemed in merchandise when accumulated in numbers

tra·di·tion \trə-'dish-ən\ *n* [ME *tradicioun,* fr. MF & L; MF *tradition,* fr. L *tradition-, traditio* action of handing over, tradition — more at TREASON] (14c) **1 :** an inherited, established, or customary pattern of thought, action, or behavior (as a religious practice or a social custom) **2 :** the handing down of information, beliefs, and customs by word of mouth or by example from one generation to another without written instruction **3 :** cultural continuity in social attitudes and institutions **4 :** characteristic manner, method, or style — **tra·di·tion·al** \-'dish-nəl, -ən-ᵊl\ *adj* — **tra·di·tion·al·ly** \-ē\ *adv* — **tra·di·tion·less** \-'dish-ən-ləs\ *adj*

tra·di·tion·al·ism \trə-'dish-nə-,liz-əm, -ən-ᵊl-,iz-\ *n* (1860) **1 :** the doctrines or practices of those who follow or accept tradition **2 :** the beliefs of those opposed to modernism, liberalism, or radicalism — **tra·di·tion·al·ist** \-nə-ləst, -ən-ᵊl-əst\ *n or adj* — **tra·di·tion·al·is·tic** \-,dish-nə-'lis-tik, -ən-ᵊl-'is-\ *adj*

tra·di·tion·al·ize \trə-'dish-nə-,līz, -ən-ᵊl-,īz\ *vt* **-ized; -iz·ing** (1882) **:** to make traditional **:** imbue with traditions or traditionalism

tra·di·tion·ary \trə-'dish-ə-,ner-ē\ *adj* (1661) **:** TRADITIONAL

tra·duce \trə-'d(y)üs\ *vt* **tra·duced; tra·duc·ing** [L *traducere* to lead across, transfer, degrade, fr. *tra-, trans-* trans- + *ducere* to lead — more at TOW] (1592) **1 :** to expose to shame or blame by means of falsehood and misrepresentation **2 :** VIOLATE, BETRAY ⟨~ a principle of law⟩ *syn* see MALIGN — **tra·duce·ment** \-mənt\ *n* — **tra·duc·er** *n*

1traf·fic \'traf-ik\ *n, often attrib* [MF *trafique,* fr. OIt *traffico,* fr. *trafficare* to traffic] (1506) **1 a :** import and export trade **b :** the business of bartering or buying and selling **c :** illegal or disreputable usu. commercial activity ⟨the drug ~⟩ **2 a :** communication or dealings esp. between individuals or groups **b :** EXCHANGE ⟨a lively ~ in ideas —F. L. Allen⟩ **3** *archaic* **:** WARES, GOODS **4 a :** the movement (as of vehicles or pedestrians) through an area or along a route **b :** the vehicles, pedestrians, ships, or planes moving along a route **c :** the information or signals transmitted over a communications system **:** MESSAGES **5 a :** the passengers or cargo carried by a transportation system **b :** the business of transporting passengers or freight **6 :** the volume of customers visiting a business establishment *syn* see BUSINESS — **the traffic will bear :** existing conditions will allow or permit ⟨charge what *the traffic will bear*⟩

2traffic *vb* **traf·ficked; traf·fick·ing** *vi* (1540) **:** to carry on traffic ~ *vt* **1 :** to travel over ⟨heavily *trafficked* highways⟩ **2 :** TRADE, BARTER — **traf·fick·er** *n*

traf·fic·abil·i·ty \,traf-i-kə-'bil-ət-ē\ *n* (1899) **:** the quality of a terrain to permit passage (as of vehicles and troops) — **traf·fic·able** \'traf-i-kə-bəl\ *adj*

traffic circle *n* (ca. 1947) **:** ROTARY 2

traffic cone *n* (1953) **:** a conical marker used on a road or highway (as for indicating an area under repair)

traffic court *n* (1929) **:** a minor court for disposition of petty prosecutions for violations of statutes, ordinances, and local regulations governing the use of highways and motor vehicles

traffic engineering *n* (1956) : engineering dealing with the design of streets and control of traffic — **traffic engineer** *n*

traffic island *n* (1940) : a paved or planted island in a roadway designed to guide the flow of traffic

traffic light *n* (1926) : an electrically operated visual signal (as a system of colored lights) for controlling traffic

traffic manager *n* (1862) **1** : a supervisor of the traffic functions of a commercial or industrial organization **2** : the director of a large telegraph office

traffic signal *n* (1924) : a signal (as a traffic light) for controlling traffic

trag·a·canth \ˈtraj-ə-ˌkan(t)th, ˈtrag-, -kən(t)th; *also* ˈtrag-ə-ˌsan(t)th\ *n* [MF *tragacanthe,* fr. L *tragacantha,* fr. Gk *tragakantha,* fr. *tragos* goat + *akantha* thorn — more at ACANTH-] (1573) : a gum obtained from various Asian or East European leguminous plants (genus *Astragalus,* esp. *A. gummifer*) that swells in water and is used in the arts and in pharmacy

tra·ge·di·an \trə-ˈjēd-ē-ən\ *n* [ME *tragedien,* fr. MF, fr. *tragedie*] (14c) **1** : a writer of tragedies **2** : an actor specializing in tragic roles

tra·ge·di·enne \trə-ˌjēd-ē-ˈen\ *n* [F *tragédienne,* fr. MF, fr. *tragedie*] (1851) : an actress who plays tragic roles

trag·e·dy \ˈtraj-əd-ē\ *n, pl* **-dies** [ME *tragedie,* fr. MF, fr. L *tragoedia,* fr. Gk *tragōidia,* fr. *tragos* goat (akin to Gk *trōgein* to gnaw) + *aeidein* to sing — more at TERSE, ODE] (14c) **1** **a** : a medieval narrative poem or tale typically describing the downfall of a great man **b** : a serious drama typically describing a conflict between the protagonist and a superior force (as destiny) and having a sorrowful or disastrous conclusion that excites pity or terror **c** : the literary genre of tragic dramas **2** **a** : a disastrous event : CALAMITY **b** : MISFORTUNE **3** : tragic quality or element

trag·ic \ˈtraj-ik\ *also* **trag·i·cal** \-i-kəl\ *adj* [ME, fr. L *tragicus,* fr. Gk *tragikos,* irreg. fr. *tragōidia* tragedy] (15c) **1** : of, marked by, or expressive of tragedy ⟨the ~ significance of the atomic bomb —H. S. Truman⟩ **2** **a** : dealing with or treated in tragedy ⟨the ~ hero⟩ **b** : appropriate to or typical of tragedy **3** **a** : regrettably serious or unpleasant : DEPLORABLE, LAMENTABLE ⟨a ~ mistake⟩ **b** : marked by a sense of tragedy — **trag·i·cal·ly** \-i-k(ə-)lē\ *adv*

tragic flaw *n* (ca. 1951) : a flaw in the character of the hero of a tragedy that brings about his downfall

tragic irony *n* (1833) : IRONY 3b

tragi·com·e·dy \ˌtraj-i-ˈkäm-əd-ē\ *n* [MF *tragicomedie,* fr. OIt *tragicomedia,* fr. OSp, fr. L *tragicomoedia,* fr. *tragicus* + *comoedia* comedy] (1579) : a drama or a situation blending tragic and comic elements — **tragi·com·ic** \-ˈkäm-ik\ *also* **tragi·com·i·cal** \-i-kəl\ *adj*

tra·gus \ˈtrā-gəs\ *n, pl* **tra·gi** \-ˌgī, -ˌjī\ [NL, fr. Gk *tragos,* a part of the ear, lit., goat] (ca. 1693) : the prominence in front of the external opening of the ear

[1]trail \ˈtrā(ə)l\ *vb* [ME *trailen,* fr. MF *trailler* to tow, fr. (assumed) VL *tragulare,* fr. L *tragula* sledge, dragnet; akin to L *trahere* to pull — more at DRAW] *vi* (14c) **1** **a** : to hang down so as to drag along or sweep the ground **b** : to extend over a surface in a loose or straggling manner ⟨a vine that ~*s* over the ground⟩ **c** : to grow to such length as to droop over toward the ground ⟨~*ing* branches of a weeping birch⟩ **2** **a** : to walk or proceed draggingly, heavily, or wearily : PLOD, TRUDGE **b** : to lag behind : do poorly in relation to others **3** : to move, flow, or extend slowly in thin streams ⟨smoke ~*ing* from chimneys⟩ **4** **a** : to extend in an erratic or uneven course or line : STRAGGLE **b** : DWINDLE ⟨voice ~*ing* off⟩ **5** : to follow a trail : track game ~ *vt* **1** **a** : to draw or drag loosely along a surface : allow to sweep the ground **b** : HAUL, TOW **2** **a** : to drag (as a limb or the body) heavily or wearily **b** : to carry or bring along as an addition, burden, or encumbrance **c** : to draw along in one's wake **3** **a** : to follow upon the scent or trace of : TRACK **b** : to follow in the footsteps of : PURSUE **c** : to follow along behind **d** : to lag behind (as a competitor) ***syn*** see CHASE

[2]trail *n* (14c) **1** : something that trails or is trailed: as **a** : a trailing plant **b** : the train of a gown **c** : a trailing arrangement (as of flowers) : SPRAY **d** : the part of a gun carriage that rests on the ground when the piece is unlimbered **2** **a** : something that follows or moves along as if being drawn along : TRAIN ⟨a ~ of admirers⟩ **b** (1) : the streak produced by a meteor (2) : a continuous line produced photographically by permitting the image of a celestial body (as a star) to move over the plate **c** : a chain of consequences : AFTERMATH ⟨the . . . movement left a ~ of bitterness and prejudice behind it —Paul Blanshard⟩ **3** **a** : a trace or mark left by something that has passed or been drawn along : SCENT, TRACK ⟨a ~ of blood⟩ **b** (1) : a track made by passage esp. through a wilderness (2) : a marked or established path or route esp. through a forest or mountainous region **c** : a course followed or to be followed ⟨hit the campaign ~⟩ — **trail·less** \ˈtrā(ə)l-ləs\ *adj*

trail bike *n* (1966) : a small motorcycle designed for uses other than on highways and for easy transport (as on an automobile bumper)

trail·blaz·er \ˈtrā(ə)l-ˌblā-zər\ *n* (1908) **1** : one that blazes a trail to guide others : PATHFINDER **2** : PIONEER 2 ⟨a ~ in astrophysics⟩

trail·blaz·ing \-ziŋ\ *adj* (1951) : making or pointing a new way ⟨~ legislation⟩

trail·break·er \-ˌbrā-kər\ *n* (1925) : TRAILBLAZER

[1]trail·er \ˈtrā-lər\ *n* (1590) **1** : one that trails **2** : a trailing plant **3** **a** : a highway or industrial-plant vehicle designed to be hauled (as by a tractor) **b** : a usu. automobile-drawn highway vehicle designed to serve wherever parked as a dwelling or as a place of business **4** **a** : PREVIEW 2 **b** : a short blank strip of film attached to the end of a reel

[2]trailer *vt* (1938) : to transport (as a boat) by means of a trailer ~ *vi* **1** : to live or travel in a trailer **2** : to be transportable by trailer ⟨a light boat that ~*s* easily⟩ — **trail·er·able** \-lə-rə-bəl\ *adj* — **trail·er·ing** *n*

trail·er·ist \-ə-rəst\ *n* (1950) **1** : a person traveling or vacationing with a trailer **2** : TRAILERITE 1

trail·er·ite \-ˌrīt\ *n* (1936) **1** : a person living in a mobile home **2** : TRAILERIST 1

trailer park *n* (1942) : an area equipped to accommodate house trailers — called also *trailer camp, trailer court*

trail·er·ship \ˈtrā-lər-ˌship\ *n* (1949) : a ship designed to carry trucks and trailers

trail·head \ˈtrāl-ˌhed\ *n* (1948) : the point at which a trail begins

trailing arbutus *n* (1785) : ARBUTUS 2

trailing edge *n* (ca. 1910) : the rearmost edge of an object that moves and esp. of an airfoil

trail·side \ˌtrāl-ˌsīd\ *adj* (1923) : of, relating to, or situated in the area immediately adjacent to a trail

[1]train \ˈtrān\ *n* [ME *traine,* fr. MF, fr. OF, fr. *traïr* to betray, fr. L *tradere* — more at TRAITOR] *obs* (14c) : SCHEME, TRICK

[2]train *n* [ME, fr. MF, fr. OF, fr. *trainer* to draw, drag] (15c) **1** : a part of a gown that trails behind the wearer **2** **a** : RETINUE, SUITE **b** : a moving file of persons, vehicles, or animals **3** : the vehicles, men, and sometimes animals that furnish supply, maintenance, and evacuation services to a combat unit **4** **a** : order of occurrence designed to lead to some result **b** : an orderly succession ⟨a ~ of thought⟩ **c** : accompanying or resultant circumstances : AFTERMATH **5** : a line of combustible material laid to lead fire to a charge **6** : a series of moving mechanical parts (as gears) that transmit and modify motion **7** **a** : a connected line of railroad cars with or without a locomotive **b** : an automotive tractor with one or more trailer units **8** : a series of parts or elements that together constitute a system for producing a result and esp. for carrying on a process (as of manufacture) automatically — **train·ful** \ˈtrān-ˌfu̇l\ *n*

[3]train *vb* [ME *trainen,* fr. MF *trainer,* fr. OF, fr. (assumed) VL *traginare;* akin to L *trahere* to draw — more at DRAW] *vt* (15c) **1** : TRAIL, DRAG **2** : to direct the growth of (a plant) usu. by bending, pruning, and tying **3** **a** : to form by instruction, discipline, or drill **b** : to teach so as to make fit, qualified, or proficient **4** : to make prepared (as by exercise) for a test of skill **5** : to aim at an object or objective : DIRECT ⟨~*ed* his gaze at the deer⟩ ⟨~*ing* every effort toward success⟩ ~ *vi* **1** : to undergo instruction, discipline, or drill **2** : to go by train ***syn*** see TEACH — **train·abil·i·ty** \ˌtrā-nə-ˈbil-ət-ē\ *n* — **train·able** \ˈtrā-nə-bəl\ *adj*

train·band \ˈtrān-ˌband\ *n* [alter. of *trained band*] (1630) : a 17th or 18th century militia company in England or America

train·bear·er \ˈtrān-ˌbar-ər, -ˌber-\ *n* (1722) : an attendant who holds up (as on a ceremonial occasion) the train of a robe or gown

train case *n* (1948) : a small boxlike piece of luggage used esp. for toilet articles

train dispatcher *n* (1857) : a railroad employee who directs the movement of trains within a division and coordinates their movement from one division to another

train·ee \trā-ˈnē\ *n* (1861) : one who is being trained for a job — **train·ee·ship** \-ˈnē-ˌship\ *n*

train·er \ˈtrā-nər\ *n* (1598) **1** : one that trains **2** : one (as a machine or vehicle) used in training **3** : one who treats the ailments and minor injuries of the members of an athletic team

train·ing *n* (1539) **1** **a** : the act, process, or method of one who trains **b** : the knowledge or experience acquired by one who trains **2** : the state of being trained

training college *n, Brit* (ca. 1829) : TEACHERS COLLEGE

training school *n* (1829) **1** : a school preparing students for a particular occupation **2** : a correctional institution for the custody and reeducation of juvenile delinquents

training table *n* (1893) : a table where athletes under a training regimen eat meals planned to help in their conditioning

train·load \ˈtrān-ˈlōd, -ˌlōd\ *n* (1876) : the full freight or passenger capacity of a railroad train

train·man \ˈtrān-mən, -ˌman\ *n* (1877) : a member of a train crew supervised by a conductor

train oil \ˈtrān-\ *n* [obs. *train* (train oil), fr. ME *trane,* fr. MD *trane* or MLG *trān*] (1553) : oil from a marine animal (as a whale)

traipse \ˈtrāps\ *vb* **traipsed; traips·ing** [origin unknown] *vi* (1593) : to walk, tramp, or travel about : GAD ~ *vt* : TRAMP, WALK ***syn*** see WANDER — **traipse** *n*

trait \ˈtrāt, *Brit usu* ˈtrā\ *n* [MF, lit., act of drawing, fr. L *tractus* — more at TRACT] (1589) **1** **a** : a stroke of or as if of a pencil **b** : TOUCH, TRACE **2** **a** : a distinguishing quality (as of personal character) : PECULIARITY **b** : an inherited characteristic

trai·tor \ˈtrāt-ər\ *n* [ME *traitre,* fr. OF, fr. L *traditor,* fr. *traditus,* pp. of *tradere* to hand over, deliver, betray, fr. *trans-, tra-* trans- + *dare* to give — more at DATE] (13c) **1** : one who betrays another's trust or is false to an obligation or duty **2** : one who commits treason

trai·tor·ous \ˈtrāt-ə-rəs, ˈtrā-trəs\ *adj* (14c) **1** : guilty or capable of treason **2** : constituting treason ⟨~ activities⟩ ***syn*** see FAITHLESS — **trai·tor·ous·ly** *adv*

trai·tress \ˈtrā-trəs\ *or* **trai·tor·ess** \ˈtrāt-ə-rəs, ˈtrā-trəs\ *n* (14c) : a female traitor

tra·ject \trə-ˈjekt\ *vt* [L *trajectus,* pp.] (1657) : TRANSMIT — **tra·jec·tion** \-ˈjek-shən\ *n*

tra·jec·to·ry \trə-ˈjek-t(ə-)rē\ *n, pl* **-ries** [NL *trajectoria,* fr. fem. of *trajectorius* of passing, fr. L *trajectus,* pp. of *traicere* to cause to cross, cross, fr. *trans-, tra-* trans- + *jacere* to throw — more at JET] (1696) **1** : the curve that a body (as a planet or comet in its orbit or a rocket) describes in space **2** : a path, progression, or line of development resembling a physical trajectory

[1]tram \ˈtram\ *n* [E dial., shaft of a wheelbarrow, prob. fr. LG *traam,* lit., beam] (1516) **1** : any of various vehicles: as **a** : a boxlike wagon running on rails (as in a mine) **b** *chiefly Brit* : STREETCAR **c** : a carrier that travels on an overhead cable or rails **2** **a** *pl, chiefly Brit* : a streetcar line **b** : TRAMROAD

[2]tram *vt* **trammed; tram·ming** (1874) : to haul in a tram or over a tramway

tram·car \ˈtram-ˌkär\ *n* (1873) **1** *chiefly Brit* : STREETCAR **2** : TRAM 1a

tram·line \-ˌlīn\ *n, Brit* (1886) : a streetcar line

[1]tram·mel \ˈtram-əl\ *n* [ME *tramayle,* a kind of net, fr. MF *tremail,* fr. LL *tremaculum,* fr. L *tres* three + *macula* mesh, spot — more at THREE] (15c) **1** : a net for catching birds or fish; *esp* : one having three layers with the middle one finer-meshed and slack so that fish passing through carry some of the center net through the coarser opposite net and are trapped **2 :** an adjustable pothook for a fireplace crane **3 :** a shackle used for making a horse amble **4 :** something impeding activity, progress, or freedom **:** RESTRAINT — usu. used in pl. **5 a :** an instrument for drawing ellipses **b :** a compass for drawing large circles that consists of a beam with two sliding parts — usu. used in pl. **c :** any of various gauges used for aligning or adjusting machine parts

[2]trammel *vt* **-meled** *or* **-melled; -mel·ing** *or* **-mel·ling** \-(ə-)liŋ\ (1605) **1 :** to catch or hold in or as if in a net **:** ENMESH **2 :** to prevent or impede the free play of **:** CONFINE ***syn*** see HAMPER

[1]tra·mon·tane \trə-ˈmän-ˌtān, ˌtram-ən-ˈ\ *n* (1593) **:** one dwelling in a tramontane region; *broadly* **:** FOREIGNER

[2]tramontane *adj* [It *tramontano,* fr. L *transmontanus,* fr. *trans-* + *mont-, mons* mountain — more at MOUNT] (1596) **1 :** TRANSALPINE **2 :** lying on or coming from the other side of a mountain range

[1]tramp \ˈtramp, *vi 1 & vt 1 are also* ˈträmp, ˈtrȯmp\ *vb* [ME *trampen;* akin to MLG *trampen* to stamp, OE *treppan* to tread — more at TRAP] *vi* (14c) **1 :** to walk, tread, or step esp. heavily **2 a :** to travel about on foot **:** HIKE **b :** to journey as a tramp ∼ *vt* **1 :** to tread on forcibly and repeatedly **2 :** to travel or wander through on foot ⟨has ∼*ed* all the woods on his property⟩ — **tramp·er** *n*

[2]tramp \ˈtramp, *3, 4 are also* ˈträmp, ˈtrȯmp\ *n* (1664) **1 a :** a foot traveler **b :** a begging or thieving vagrant **c :** a woman of loose morals; *specif* **:** PROSTITUTE **2 :** a walking trip **:** HIKE **3 :** the succession of sounds made by the beating of feet on a surface (as a road, pavement, or floor) **4 :** an iron plate to protect the sole of a shoe **5 :** a ship not making regular trips but taking cargo when and where it offers and to any port — called also *tramp steamer*

[3]tramp \ˈtramp\ *adj* (1873) **:** having no fixed abode, connection, or destination ⟨a ∼ dog⟩

tram·ple \ˈtram-pəl\ *vb* **tram·pled; tram·pling** \-p(ə-)liŋ\ [ME *tramplen,* freq. of *trampen* to tramp] *vi* (14c) **1 :** TRAMP; *esp* **:** to tread heavily so as to bruise, crush, or injure **2 :** to inflict injury or destruction esp. contemptuously or ruthlessly — usu. used with *on, over,* or *upon* ⟨*trampling* on the rights of others⟩ ∼ *vt* **:** to crush, injure, or destroy by or as if by treading **:** STAMP — **trample** *n* — **tram·pler** \-p(ə-)lər\ *n*

tram·po·line \ˌtram-pə-ˈlēn, ˈtram-pə-ˌ\ *n* [Sp *trampolín,* fr. It *trampolino,* of Gmc origin; akin to MLG *trampen* to stamp] (1928) **:** a resilient canvas sheet or web supported by springs in a metal frame and used as a springboard and landing area in tumbling — **tram·po·lin·er** \-ˈlē-nər, -ˌlē-\ *n* — **tram·po·lin·ist** \-nəst\ *n*

tram·po·lin·ing *n* (1949) **:** the sport of jumping and tumbling on a trampoline

tram·road \ˈtram-ˌrōd\ *n* (1800) **:** a roadway for trams consisting of parallel tracks made usu. of metal-faced wooden beams, stone blocks, metal plates, or rails; *esp* **:** a railway in a mine

tram·way \-ˌwā\ *n* (1825) **:** a way for trams: as **a :** TRAMROAD **b** *Brit* **:** a streetcar line **c :** an overhead cable or rails for trams

[1]trance \ˈtran(t)s\ *n* [ME, fr. MF *transe,* fr. *transir* to pass away, swoon, fr. L *transire* to pass, pass away — more at TRANSIENT] (14c) **1 :** a state of partly suspended animation or inability to function **2 :** a somnolent state (as of deep hypnosis) **3 :** a state of profound abstraction or absorption — **trance·like** \-ˌlīk\ *adj*

[2]trance *vt* **tranced; tranc·ing** (1597) **:** ENTRANCE, ENRAPTURE

tranche \ˈtränsh\ *n* [F, fr. OF, fr. *trenchier, trancher* to cut] (1930) **:** a bond series issued for sale in a foreign country

tran·gam \ˈtraŋ-gəm\ *n* [origin unknown] *archaic* (1658) **:** TRINKET, GIMCRACK

tran·quil \ˈtraŋ-kwəl, ˈtran-\ *adj* [L *tranquillus;* akin to L *quies* quiet, rest — more at WHILE] (1604) **1 a :** free from agitation of mind or spirit ⟨∼ faith⟩ **b :** free from disturbance or turmoil ⟨a ∼ scene⟩ **2 :** unvarying in aspect **:** STEADY, STABLE ***syn*** see CALM — **tran·quil·ly** \-kwə-lē\ *adv* — **tran·quil·ness** *n*

tran·quil·ize *also* **tran·quil·lize** \ˈtraŋ-kwə-ˌlīz, ˈtran-\ *vb* **-ized** *also* **-lized; -iz·ing** *also* **-liz·ing** *vt* (1623) **:** to make tranquil or calm **:** PACIFY; *esp* **:** to relieve of mental tension and anxiety by means of drugs ∼ *vi* **1 :** to become tranquil **:** RELAX 1 **2 :** to make one tranquil

tran·quil·iz·er *also* **tran·quil·liz·er** \-ˌlī-zər\ *n* (1800) **1 :** one that tranquilizes **2 :** a drug used to reduce mental disturbance (as anxiety and tension) in people and animals

tran·quil·li·ty *or* **tran·quil·i·ty** \tran-ˈkwil-ət-ē, traŋ-\ *n* (14c) **:** the quality or state of being tranquil

trans \ˈtran(t)s, ˈtranz\ *adj* (1892) **:** having or characterized by certain atoms or groups on opposite sides of the molecule

trans- *prefix* [L *trans-, tra-* across, beyond, through, so as to change, fr. *trans* across, beyond — more at THROUGH] **1 :** on or to the other side of **:** across **:** beyond ⟨*trans*atlantic⟩ **2 a :** beyond (a specified chemical element) in the periodic table ⟨*trans*uranium⟩ **b** *usu ital* **:** characterized by having such atoms or groups on opposite sides of the molecule ⟨*trans*-dichloro-ethylene⟩ ⟨the isomer with *trans*-configuration⟩ — compare CIS- 2 **3 :** through ⟨*trans*cutaneous⟩ **4 :** so or such as to change or transfer ⟨*trans*literate⟩ ⟨*trans*location⟩ ⟨*trans*amination⟩ ⟨*trans*ship⟩

trans·act \tran(t)s-ˈakt, tranz-\ *vb* [L *transactus,* pp. of *transigere* to drive through, complete, transact, fr. *trans-* + *agere* to drive, do — more at AGENT] *vi* (1584) **:** to carry on business ∼ *vt* **:** CARRY OUT, PERFORM; *esp* **:** CARRY ON — **trans·ac·tor** \-ˈak-tər\ *n*

trans·ac·ti·nide \-ˈak-tə-ˌnīd\ *adj* (1969) **:** of, relating to, or being actual or hypothetical elements with atomic weights higher than those of the actinide series ⟨∼ chemistry⟩

trans·ac·tion \-ˈak-shən\ *n* (1647) **1 a :** something transacted; *esp* **:** a business deal **b** *pl* **:** the often published record of the meeting of a society or association **2 a :** an act, process, or instance of transacting **b :** a communicative action or activity involving two parties or things that reciprocally affect or influence each other — **trans·ac·tion·al** \-shnəl, -shən-ᵊl\ *adj*

trans·al·pine \tran(t)s-ˈal-ˌpīn, tranz-\ *adj* [L *transalpinus,* fr. *trans-* + *Alpes* the Alps] (1590) **:** situated on the north side of the Alps ⟨*Transalpine* Gaul⟩ — compare CISALPINE

trans·am·i·nase \tran(t)s-ˈam-ə-ˌnās, tranz-, -ˌnāz\ *n* (1940) **:** an enzyme promoting transamination — called also *aminotransferase*

trans·am·i·na·tion \ˌtran(t)s-ˌam-ə-ˈnā-shən, ˌtranz-\ *n* (1939) **:** a reversible oxidation-reduction reaction in which an amino group is transferred typically from an alpha-amino acid to the carbonyl carbon atom of an alpha-keto acid

trans·at·lan·tic \ˌtran(t)s-ət-ˈlant-ik, ˌtranz-\ *adj* (1779) **1 a :** crossing or extending across the Atlantic ocean ⟨a ∼ cable⟩ **b :** relating to or involving crossing the Atlantic ocean ⟨∼ air fares⟩ **2 :** situated or coming from beyond the Atlantic ocean

trans·ax·le \tran(t)s-ˈak-səl, tranz-\ *n* [*trans*mission + *axle*] (1958) **:** a unit that consists of a combination of transmission and front axle used in front-wheel-drive automobiles

trans·ceiv·er \tran(t)s-ˈē-vər, tranz-\ *n* [*trans*mitter + *receiver*] (ca. 1937) **:** a radio transmitter-receiver that uses many of the same components for both transmission and reception

tran·scend \tran(t)s-ˈend\ *vb* [L *transcendere* to climb across, transcend, fr. *trans-* + *scandere* to climb — more at SCAN] *vt* (14c) **1 a :** to rise above or go beyond the limits of **b :** to triumph over the negative or restrictive aspects of **:** OVERCOME **c :** to be prior to, beyond, and above (the universe or material existence) **2 :** to outstrip or outdo in some attribute, quality, or power ∼ *vi* **:** to rise above or extend notably beyond ordinary limits ***syn*** see EXCEED

tran·scen·dence \-ˈen-dən(t)s\ *n* (1601) **:** the quality or state of being transcendent

tran·scen·den·cy \-dən-sē\ *n* (1615) **:** TRANSCENDENCE

tran·scen·dent \-dənt\ *adj* [L *transcendent-, transcendens,* prp. of *transcendere*] (1598) **1 a :** exceeding usual limits **:** SURPASSING **b :** extending or lying beyond the limits of ordinary experience **c** *Kantianism* **:** being beyond the limits of all possible experience and knowledge **2 :** being beyond comprehension **3 :** transcending the universe or material existence — **tran·scen·dent·ly** *adv*

tran·scen·den·tal \ˌtran(t)s-ˌen-ˈdent-ᵊl, -ən-\ *adj* (1624) **1 a :** TRANSCENDENT 1b **b :** SUPERNATURAL **c :** ABSTRUSE, ABSTRACT **d :** of or relating to transcendentalism **2 a :** incapable of being the root of an algebraic equation with rational coefficients ⟨π is a ∼ number⟩ **b :** being, involving, or representing a function (as sin *x,* log *x,* e^x) that cannot be expressed by a finite number of algebraic operations ⟨∼ curves⟩ **3** *Kantianism* **a :** of or relating to experience as determined by the mind's makeup **b :** transcending experience but not human knowledge **4 :** TRANSCENDENT 1a — **tran·scen·den·tal·ly** \-ᵊl-ē\ *adv*

tran·scen·den·tal·ism \-ᵊl-ˌiz-əm\ *n* (1803) **1 :** a philosophy that emphasizes the a priori conditions of knowledge and experience or the unknowable character of ultimate reality or that emphasizes the transcendent as the fundamental reality **2 :** a philosophy that asserts the primacy of the spiritual and transcendental over the material and empirical **3 :** the quality or state of being transcendental; *esp* **:** visionary idealism — **tran·scen·den·tal·ist** \-ᵊl-əst\ *adj or n*

transcendental meditation *n* (1966) **:** a technique of meditation in which a mantra is chanted in order to foster calm, creativity, and spiritual well-being

trans·con·ti·nen·tal \ˌtran(t)s-ˌkänt-ᵊn-ˈent-ᵊl\ *adj* (1853) **:** extending or going across a continent ⟨a ∼ railroad⟩

tran·scribe \tran(t)s-ˈkrīb\ *vt* **tran·scribed; tran·scrib·ing** [L *transcribere,* fr. *trans-* + *scribere* to write — more at SCRIBE] (1552) **1 a :** to make a written copy of **b :** to make a copy of (dictated or recorded matter) in longhand or on a typewriter **c :** to paraphrase or summarize in writing **d :** WRITE DOWN, RECORD **2 a :** to represent (speech sounds) by means of phonetic symbols **b :** TRANSLATE 2a **c :** to transfer (data) from one recording form to another **d :** to record (as on magnetic tape) for later broadcast **3 :** to make a musical transcription of **4 :** to broadcast by electrical transcription **5 :** to cause (as DNA) to undergo genetic transcription — **tran·scrib·er** *n*

tran·script \ˈtran(t)s-ˌkript\ *n* [ME, fr. ML *transcriptum,* fr. L, neut. of *transcriptus,* pp. of *transcribere*] (13c) **1 a :** a written, printed, or typed copy; *esp* **:** a usu. typewritten copy of dictated or recorded material **b :** an official or legal and often published copy ⟨a court reporter's ∼⟩; *esp* **:** an official copy of a student's educational record **2 :** a representation (as of experience) in an art form **3 :** a sequence of RNA produced by transcription from a DNA template

tran·scrip·tase \tran-ˈskrip-ˌtās, -tāz\ *n* [*transcription* + *-ase*] (1963) **:** REVERSE TRANSCRIPTASE

tran·scrip·tion \tran(t)s-ˈkrip-shən\ *n* (1598) **1 :** an act, process, or instance of transcribing **2 :** COPY, TRANSCRIPT: as **a :** an arrangement of a musical composition for some instrument or voice other than the original **b :** a phonograph record made esp. for use in radiobroadcasting **3 :** the process of constructing a messenger RNA molecule using a DNA molecule as a template with resulting transfer of genetic information to the messenger RNA — compare TRANSLATION 2 — **tran·scrip·tion·al** \-shnəl, -shən-ᵊl\ *adj* — **tran·scrip·tion·al·ly** \-ē\ *adv* — **tran·scrip·tion·ist** \-shə-nəst\ *n*

trans·cu·ta·ne·ous \ˌtran(t)s-kyu̇-ˈtā-nē-əs\ *adj* (ca. 1941) **:** passing, entering, or made by penetration through the skin ⟨∼ infection⟩ ⟨∼ inoculation⟩

trans·duce \tran(t)s-ˈd(y)üs, tranz-\ *vt* **trans·duced; trans·duc·ing** [L *transducere* to lead across, transfer, fr. *trans-* + *ducere* to lead — more at TOW] (1947) **1 :** to convert (as energy or a message) into another form ⟨essentially sense organs ∼ physical energy into a nervous signal⟩ **2 :** to bring about the transfer of (as a gene) from one microorganism to another by means of a viral agent

trans·duc·er \-ˈd(y)ü-sər\ *n* (1924) **:** a device that is actuated by power from one system and supplies power usu. in another form to a second system (as a telephone receiver that is actuated by electric power and supplies acoustic power to the surrounding air)

trans·duc·tion \-ˈdək-shən\ *n* [L *transductus,* pp. of *transducere*] (1953) **:** the action or process of transducing; *esp* **:** the transfer of genetic determinants from one microorganism to another by a viral agent (as a bacteriophage) — **trans·duc·tant** \-tənt\ *n* — **trans·duc·tion·al** \-shnəl, -shən-ᵊl\ *adj*

[1]tran·sect \tran(t)s-ˈekt\ *vt* (1634) **:** to cut transversely — **tran·sec·tion** \-ˈek-shən\ *n*

[2]tran·sect \ˈtran(t)s-ˌekt\ *n* (ca. 1909) **:** a sample area (as of vegetation) usu. in the form of a long continuous strip

tran·sept \ˈtran(t)s-ˌept\ *n* [NL *transeptum,* fr. L *trans-* + *septum, saeptum* enclosure, wall — more at SEPTUM] (1538) **:** the part of a cruciform church that crosses at right angles to the greatest length between the nave and the apse or choir; *also* **:** either of the projecting ends of a transept — **tran·sep·tal** \tran(t)s-ˈep-tᵊl\ *adj*

trans·fec·tion \tran(t)s-'fek-shən, tranz-\ n [*trans-* + in*fection*] (1966) : infection of a cell with isolated viral nucleic acid followed by production of the complete virus in the cell — **trans·fect** \-'fekt\ vt

¹trans·fer \tran(t)s-'fər, 'tran(t)s-,\ vb **trans·ferred; trans·fer·ring** [ME *transferren*, fr. L *transferre*, fr. *trans-* + *ferre* to carry — more at BEAR] vt (14c) **1 a** : to convey from one person, place, or situation to another : TRANSPORT **b** : to cause to pass from one to another : TRANSMIT **c** : TRANSFORM, CHANGE **2** : to make over the possession or control of : CONVEY **3** : to print or otherwise copy from one surface to another by contact ~ vi **1** : to move to a different place, region, or situation; *esp* : to withdraw from one educational institution to enroll at another **2** : to change from one vehicle or transportation line to another — **trans·fer·abil·i·ty** \(,)tran(t)s-,fər-ə-'bil-ət-ē\ n — **trans·fer·able** also **trans·fer·ra·ble** \tran(t)s-'fər-ə-bəl\ adj — **trans·fer·al** \-əl\ n — **trans·fer·rer** \-ər\ n

²trans·fer \'tran(t)s-,fər\ n (1674) **1 a** : conveyance of right, title, or interest in real or personal property from one person to another **b** : removal or acquisition of property by mere delivery with intent to transfer title **2 a** : an act, process, or instance of transferring : TRANSFERENCE 2 **b** : the carryover or generalization of learned responses from one type of situation to another **3** : one that transfers or is transferred; *esp* : a graphic image transferred by contact from one surface to another **4** : a place where a transfer is made (as of trains to ferries or as where one form of power is changed to another) **5** : a ticket entitling a passenger on a public conveyance to continue his journey on another route

trans·fer·ase \'tran(t)s-(,)fər-,ās, -,āz\ n (1950) : an enzyme that promotes transfer of a group from one molecule to another

trans·fer·ee \,tran(t)s-(,)fər-'ē\ n (ca. 1736) **1** : a person to whom a conveyance is made **2** : one who is transferred

trans·fer·ence \tran(t)s-'fər-ən(t)s, 'tran(t)s-(,)\ n [NL *transferentia*, fr. L *transferent-, transferens*, prp. of *transferre*] (1681) **1** : an act, process, or instance of transferring : CONVEYANCE, TRANSFER **2** : the redirection of feelings and desires and esp. of those unconsciously retained from childhood toward a new object (as a psychoanalyst conducting therapy) — **trans·fer·en·tial** \,tran(t)s-fə-'ren-chəl\ adj

transfer factor n (1962) : a polypeptide that is produced and secreted by a lymphocyte functioning in cell-mediated immunity and that upon incorporation into a lymphocyte which has not been sensitized confers on it the same immunological specificity as the sensitized cell

trans·fer·or \,tran(t)s-(,)fər-'ò(ə)r\ n (1875) : one that conveys a title, right, or property

transfer payment n (ca. 1945) **1** : a public expenditure made for a purpose (as unemployment compensation) other than procuring goods or services — usu. used in pl. **2** pl : money (as welfare payments) that is received by individuals and that is neither compensation for goods or services currently supplied nor income from investments

trans·fer·rin \tran(t)s-'fer-ən\ n [*trans-* + L *ferrum* iron] (1948) : a beta globulin in blood plasma capable of combining with ferric ions and transporting iron in the body

transfer RNA \'tran(t)s-,fər-\ n (1961) : a relatively small RNA that transfers a particular amino acid to a growing polypeptide chain at the ribosomal site of protein synthesis during translation — compare MESSENGER RNA

trans·fig·u·ra·tion \(,)tran(t)s-,fig-(y)ə-'rā-shən\ n [ME, fr. MF, fr. ML *transfiguration-, transfiguratio*, fr. L *transfiguratus*, pp. of *transfigurare*] (14c) **1 a** : a change in form or appearance : METAMORPHOSIS **b** : an exalting, glorifying, or spiritual change **2** cap : August 6 observed as a Christian feast in commemoration of the transfiguration of Christ on a mountaintop in the presence of three disciples

trans·fig·ure \tran(t)s-'fig-yər, esp Brit -'fig-ər\ vt **-ured; -ur·ing** [ME *transfiguren*, fr. L *transfigurare*, fr. *trans-* + *figurare* to shape, fashion, fr. *figura* figure] (14c) **1** : to give a new and typically exalted or spiritual appearance to : transform outwardly and usu. for the better **syn** see TRANSFORM

trans·fi·nite \(')tran(t)s-'fī-,nīt\ adj [G *transfinit*, fr. *trans-* (fr. L) + *finit* finite, fr. L *finitus*] (1902) **1** : going beyond or surpassing any finite number, group, or magnitude **2** : being or relating to cardinal and ordinal numbers of which an infinite number of elements

trans·fix \tran(t)s-'fiks\ vt [L *transfixus*, pp. of *transfigere*, fr. *trans-* + *figere* to fasten, pierce — more at DIKE] (1590) **1** : to pierce through with or as if with a pointed weapon : IMPALE **2** : to hold motionless by or as if by piercing — **trans·fix·ion** \-'fik-shən\ n

¹trans·form \tran(t)s-'fó(ə)rm\ vb [ME *transformen*, fr. L *transformare*, fr. *trans-* + *formare* to form, fr. *forma* form] vt (14c) **1 a** : to change in composition or structure **b** : to change the outward form or appearance of **c** : to change in character or condition : CONVERT **2** : to subject to mathematical transformation **3** : to change (a current) in potential (as from high voltage to low) or in type (as from alternating to direct) **4** : to cause (a cell) to undergo genetic transformation ~ vi : to become transformed : CHANGE — **trans·form·able** \-'fór-mə-bəl\ adj — **trans·for·ma·tive** \-'fór-mət-iv\ adj

syn TRANSFORM, METAMORPHOSE, TRANSMUTE, CONVERT, TRANSMOGRIFY, TRANSFIGURE mean to change a thing into a different thing. TRANSFORM implies a major change in form, nature, or function; METAMORPHOSE suggests an abrupt or startling change induced by or as if by magic or a supernatural power; TRANSMUTE implies transforming into a higher element or thing; CONVERT implies a change fitting something for a new or different use or function; TRANSMOGRIFY suggests a grotesque or preposterous metamorphosis; TRANSFIGURE implies a change that exalts or glorifies.

²trans·form \'tran(t)s-,fórm\ n (1853) **1** : a mathematical element obtained from another by transformation **2** : TRANSFORMATION 3 **3** : a linguistic structure (as a sentence) produced by means of a transformation ("the duckling is killed by the farmer" is a ~ of "the farmer kills the duckling")

trans·for·ma·tion \,tran(t)s-fər-'mā-shən, -fór-\ n (15c) **1** : an act, process, or instance of transforming or being transformed **2 a** (1) : the operation of changing (as by rotation or mapping) one configuration or expression into another in accordance with a mathematical rule; *esp* : a change of variables or coordinates in which a function of new variables or coordinates is substituted for each original variable or coordinate (2) : the formula that effects a transformation **b** : FUNCTION 5a **3** : genetic modification of a bacterium by incorporation of free DNA from another ruptured bacterial cell — compare TRANSDUCTION **4** : one of an ordered set of rules that converts the deep structures of a language into surface structures; *also* : the process or relation specified by such a rule

trans·for·ma·tion·al \-shnəl, -shən-ᵊl\ adj (1894) : of, relating to, characterized by, or concerned with transformation and esp. linguistic transformation — **trans·for·ma·tion·al·ly** \-ē\ adv

transformational grammar n (1961) : a grammar that generates the deep structures of a language and converts these to the surface structures by means of transformations

trans·for·ma·tion·al·ist \,tran(t)s-fər-'mā-shnəl-əst, -shən-ᵊl-\ n (ca. 1964) : an exponent of transformational grammar

trans·form·er \tran(t)s-'fór-mər\ n (1601) : one that transforms; *specif* : a device employing the principle of mutual induction to convert variations of current in a primary circuit into variations of voltage and current in a secondary circuit

trans·fuse \tran(t)s-'fyüz\ vt **trans·fused; trans·fus·ing** [ME *transfusen*, fr. L *transfusus*, pp. of *transfundere*, fr. *trans-* + *fundere* to pour — more at FOUND] (15c) **1 a** : to cause to pass from one to another : TRANSMIT **b** : to diffuse into or through : PERMEATE (sunlight ~s the bay) **2 a** : to transfer (as blood) into a vein of a person or animal **b** : to subject (a patient) to transfusion — **trans·fus·ible** or **trans·fus·able** \-'fyü-zə-bəl\ adj

trans·fu·sion \tran(t)s-'fyü-zhən\ n (1578) **1** : an act, process, or instance of transfusing; *esp* : the process of transfusing fluid into a vein or artery **2** : something transfused — **trans·fu·sion·al** \-'fyüzh-nəl, -ən-ᵊl\ adj

trans·gress \tran(t)s-'gres, tranz-\ vb [F *transgresser*, fr. L *transgressus*, pp. of *transgredi* to step beyond or across, fr. *trans-* + *gradi* to step — more at GRADE] (1526) **1** : to go beyond limits set or prescribed by : VIOLATE (~ the divine law) **2** : to pass beyond or go over (a limit or boundary) ~ vi **1** : to violate a command or law : SIN **2** : to go beyond a boundary or limit — **trans·gres·sive** \-'gres-iv\ adj — **trans·gres·sor** \-'gres-ər\ n

trans·gres·sion \-'gresh-ən\ n (15c) : an act, process, or instance of transgressing: as **a** : infringement or violation of a law, command, or duty **b** : the spread of the sea over land areas and the consequent unconformable deposit of sediments on older rocks

tran·ship var of TRANSSHIP

trans·hu·mance \tran(t)s-'(h)yü-mən(t)s, tranz-\ n [F, fr. *transhumer* to practice transhumance, fr. Sp *trashumar*, fr. *tras-* trans- (fr. L *trans-*) + L *humus* earth — more at HUMBLE] (ca. 1901) : seasonal movement of livestock and esp. sheep between mountain and lowland pastures either under the care of herders or in company with the owners — **trans·hu·mant** \-mənt\ adj or n

tran·sience \'tranch-ən(t)s, 'tranz-ē-ən(t)s, 'tran(t)s-ē-, 'tranch-ē-; 'tranzh-ən(t)s, 'tranj-\ n (1745) : the quality or state of being transient

tran·sien·cy \-ən-sē\ n (1652) : TRANSIENCE

¹tran·sient \-ənt\ adj [L *transeunt-, transiens*, prp. of *transire* to go across, pass, fr. *trans-* + *ire* to go — more at ISSUE] (1599) **1 a** : passing esp. quickly into and out of existence : TRANSITORY **b** : passing through or by a place with only a brief stay or sojourn **2** : affecting something or producing results beyond itself — **tran·sient·ly** adv

syn TRANSIENT, TRANSITORY, EPHEMERAL, MOMENTARY, FUGITIVE, FLEETING, EVANESCENT mean lasting or staying only a short time. TRANSIENT applies to what is actually short in its duration or stay (a hotel catering primarily to *transient* guests) TRANSITORY applies to what is by its nature or essence bound to change, pass, or come to an end (fame in the movies is *transitory*) EPHEMERAL implies striking brevity of life or duration (many slang words are *ephemeral*) MOMENTARY suggests coming and going quickly and therefore being merely a brief interruption of a more enduring state (my feelings of guilt were only *momentary*) FUGITIVE and FLEETING imply passing so quickly as to make apprehending difficult (in winter the days are short and sunshine is *fugitive*) (a life with only *fleeting* moments of joy) EVANESCENT suggests a quick vanishing and an airy or fragile quality (the story has an *evanescent* touch of whimsy that is lost on stage)

²transient n (1652) **1** : one that is transient: as **a** : a transient guest **b** : a person traveling about usu. in search of work **2 a** : a temporary oscillation that occurs in a circuit because of a sudden change of voltage or of load **b** : a transient current or voltage

trans·il·lu·mi·nate \,tran(t)s-ə-'lü-mə-,nāt, ,tranz-\ vt (1900) : to cause light to pass through; *esp* : to pass light through (a body part) for medical examination — **trans·il·lu·mi·na·tion** \-,lü-mə-'nā-shən\ n — **trans·il·lu·mi·na·tor** \-'lü-mə-,nāt-ər\ n

tran·sis·tor \tranz-'is-tər, tran(t)s-\ n [¹*transfer* + *resistor*; fr. its transferring an electrical signal across a resistor] (1948) **1** : an electronic device that is similar to the electron tube in use (as amplification and rectification) and consists of a small block of a semiconductor (as germanium) with at least three electrodes **2** : a transistorized radio

tran·sis·tor·ize \-tə-,rīz\ vt **-ized; -iz·ing** (ca. 1952) : to equip (a device) with transistors — **tran·sis·tor·iza·tion** \-,is-tə-rə-'zā-shən\ n

¹tran·sit \'tran(t)s-ət, 'tranz-\ n [L *transitus*, fr. *transire* to go across, pass] (15c) **1 a** : an act, process, or instance of passing through or over : PASSAGE **b** : CHANGE, TRANSITION **c** (1) : conveyance of persons or things from one place to another (2) : usu. local transportation esp. of people by public conveyance; *also* : vehicles or a system engaged in such transportation **2 a** : passage of a celestial body over the meridian of a place or through the field of a telescope **b** : passage of a smaller body (as Venus) across the disk of a larger (as the sun) **3** : a theodolite with the telescope mounted so that it can be transited

²transit vi (15c) : to make a transit ~ vt **1 a** : to pass over or through : TRAVERSE **b** : to cause to pass over or through **2** : to pass across (a meridian, a celestial body, or the field of view of a telescope) **3** : to turn (a telescope) over about the horizontal transverse axis in surveying

---

\ə\ abut \ᵊ\ kitten, F table \ər\ further \a\ ash \ā\ ace \ä\ cot, cart \aú\ out \ch\ chin \e\ bet \ē\ easy \g\ go \i\ hit \ī\ ice \j\ job \ŋ\ sing \ō\ go \ó\ law \ói\ boy \th\ thin \th̲\ the \ü\ loot \ú\ foot \y\ yet \zh\ vision \à, ḳ, ⁿ, œ, œ̄, ᵫ, ᵫ̄, �\ see Guide to Pronunciation

tran·si·tion \tran(t)s-ˈish-ən, tranz-, *chiefly Brit* tran(t)s-ˈizh-\ *n* [L *transition-, transitio,* fr. *transitus,* pp.] (1551) **1 a :** passage from one state, stage, subject, or place to another : CHANGE **b :** a movement, development, or evolution from one form, stage, or style to another **2 a :** a musical modulation **b :** a musical passage leading from one section of a piece to another **3 :** an abrupt change in energy state or level (as of an atomic nucleus or a molecule) usu. accompanied by loss or gain of a single quantum of energy — **tran·si·tion·al** \-ˈish-nəl, -ˈizh-, -ən-ᵊl\ *adj* — **tran·si·tion·al·ly** \-ē\ *adv*

transition element *n* [fr. their being transitional between the more highly electropositive and the less highly electropositive elements] (1922) : any of various metallic elements (as chromium, iron, and nickel) that have valence electrons in two shells instead of only one — called also *transition metal*

tran·si·tive \ˈtran(t)s-ət-iv, ˈtranz-; ˈtran(t)s-tiv\ *adj* [LL *transitivus,* fr. L *transitus,* pp.] (1571) **1 :** characterized by having or containing a direct object ⟨a ~ verb⟩ ⟨a ~ construction⟩ **2 :** being or relating to a relation with the property that if the relation holds between a first element and a second and between the second element and a third, it holds between the first and third elements ⟨equality is a ~ relation⟩ **3 :** of, relating to, or characterized by transition — **tran·si·tive·ly** *adv* — **tran·si·tive·ness** *n* — **tran·si·tiv·i·ty** \ˌtran(t)s-ə-ˈtiv-ət-ē, ˌtranz-\ *n*

tran·si·to·ry \ˈtran(t)s-ə-ˌtōr-ē, ˈtranz-, -ˌtȯr-\ *adj* [ME *transitorie,* fr. MF *transitoire,* fr. LL *transitorius,* fr. L, of or allowing passage, fr. *transitus,* pp.] (14c) **1 :** tending to pass away : not persistent **2 :** of brief duration : TEMPORARY ***syn*** see TRANSIENT — **tran·si·to·ri·ly** \ˌtran(t)s-ə-ˈtōr-ə-lē, ˌtranz-, -ˈtȯr-\ *adv* — **tran·si·to·ri·ness** \ˌtran(t)s-ə-ˌtōr-ē-nəs, ˈtran(z)-, -ˌtȯr-\ *n*

trans·late \tran(t)s-ˈlāt, tranz-\ *vb* **trans·lat·ed; trans·lat·ing** [L *translatus* (pp. of *transferre* to transfer, translate), fr. *trans-* + *latus,* pp. of *ferre* to carry — more at TOLERATE, BEAR] *vt* (14c) **1 a :** to bear, remove, or change from one place, state, form, or appearance to another : TRANSFER, TRANSFORM ⟨a country boy *translated* to the city⟩ ⟨~ ideas into action⟩ **b :** to convey to heaven or to a nontemporal condition without death **c :** to transfer (a bishop) from one see to another **2 a :** to turn into one's own or another language **b :** to transfer or turn from one set of symbols into another : TRANSCRIBE **c (1) :** to express in different terms and esp. different words : PARAPHRASE **(2) :** to express in more comprehensible terms : EXPLAIN, INTERPRET **3 :** ENRAPTURE **4 :** to subject to mathematical translation **5 :** to subject (as genetic information) to translation in protein synthesis ~ *vi* **1 :** to practice translation or make a translation; *also* : to admit of or be adaptable to translation ⟨a word that doesn't ~ easily⟩ **2 :** to undergo a translation **3 :** LEAD, RESULT — usu. used with *into* ⟨tax cuts ~ into bigger savings⟩ — **trans·lat·abil·i·ty** \(ˌ)tran(t)s-ˌlāt-ə-ˈbil-ət-ē, (ˌ)tranz-\ *n* — **trans·lat·able** \tran(t)s-ˈlāt-ə-bəl, tranz-\ *adj* — **trans·la·tor** \-ˈlāt-ər\ *n*

trans·la·tion \tran(t)s-ˈlā-shən, tranz-\ *n* [ME *translacioun,* fr. MF or L; MF *tranlation,* fr. L *translation-, translatio,* fr. *translatus,* pp.] (14c) **1 :** an act, process, or instance of translating: as **a :** a rendering from one language into another; *also* : the product of such a rendering **b :** a change to a different substance, form, or appearance : CONVERSION **c (1) :** a transformation of coordinates in which the new axes are parallel to the old ones **(2) :** uniform motion of a body in a straight line **2 :** the process of forming a protein molecule at a ribosomal site of protein synthesis from information contained in messenger RNA — compare TRANSCRIPTION 3 — **trans·la·tion·al** \-shnəl, -shən-ᵊl\ *adj*

trans·la·tive \-ˈlāt-iv\ *adj* (1682) **1 :** of, relating to, or involving removal or transference from one person or place to another **2 :** of, relating to, or serving to translate from one language or system into another

trans·la·to·ry \ˈtran(t)s-lə-ˌtōr-ē, ˈtranz-, -ˌtȯr-; tran(t)s-ˈlāt-ə-rē, tranz-\ *adj* (1849) : of, relating to, or involving uniform motion in one direction

trans·lit·er·ate \tran(t)s-ˈlit-ə-ˌrāt, tranz-\ *vt* **-at·ed; -at·ing** [*trans-* + L *littera* letter] (1861) : to represent or spell in the characters of another alphabet — **trans·lit·er·a·tion** \(ˌ)tran(t)s-ˌlit-ə-ˈrā-shən, (ˌ)tranz-\ *n*

trans·lo·ca·tion \ˌtrans(t)s-lō-ˈkā-shən, ˌtranz-\ *n* (1624) : a change of location : DISPLACEMENT: as **a :** the conduction of soluble material (as metabolic products) from one part of a plant to another **b :** the exchange of parts between nonhomologous chromosomes — **trans·lo·cate** \ˈtrans(t)s-lō-ˌkāt, ˈtranz-, (ˈ)tran(t)s-ˈ, (ˈ)tranz-ˈ\ *vb*

trans·lu·cence \tran(t)s-ˈlüs-ᵊn(t)s, tranz-\ *n* (1755) : the quality or state of being translucent

trans·lu·cen·cy \-ᵊn-sē\ *n, pl* **-cies** (1611) **1 :** TRANSLUCENCE **2 :** something that is translucent

trans·lu·cent \-ᵊnt\ *adj* [L *translucent-, translucens,* prp. of *translucēre* to shine through, fr. *trans-* + *lucēre* to shine — more at LIGHT] (1607) **1 :** permitting the passage of light: **a :** CLEAR, TRANSPARENT ⟨~ water⟩ **b :** transmitting and diffusing light so that objects beyond cannot be seen clearly **2 :** free from disguise or falseness ⟨his ~ patriotism —*Newsweek*⟩ ***syn*** see CLEAR — **trans·lu·cent·ly** *adv*

trans·ma·rine \ˌtran(t)s-mə-ˈrēn, ˌtranz-\ *adj* [L *transmarinus,* fr. *trans-* + *mare* sea — more at MARINE] (1583) **1 :** being or coming from beyond or across the sea ⟨a ~ people⟩ **2 :** passing over or extending across the sea

trans·mem·brane \(ˈ)tran(t)s-ˈmem-ˌbrān, (ˈ)tranz-\ *adj* (1944) : taking place or existing across a membrane ⟨a ~ potential⟩

trans·mi·grate \(ˈ)tran(t)s-ˈmī-ˌgrāt, (ˈ)tranz-, ˈtran(t)s-ˌ, ˈtranz-ˌ\ *vb* [L *transmigratus,* pp. of *transmigrare* to migrate to another place, fr. *trans-* + *migrare* to migrate] *vt* (1559) : to cause to go from one state of existence or place to another ~ *vi* **1** *of the soul* : to pass at death from one body or being to another **2 :** MIGRATE — **trans·mi·gra·tion** \ˌtran(t)s-mī-ˈgrā-shen, ˌtranz-\ *n* — **trans·mi·gra·tor** \(ˈ)tran(t)s-ˈmī-ˌgrāt-ər, (ˈ)tranz-, ˈtran(t)s-ˌ, ˈtranz-ˌ\ *n* — **trans·mi·gra·to·ry** \tran(t)s-ˈmī-grə-ˌtōr-ē, tranz-, -ˌtȯr-\ *adj*

trans·mis·si·ble \tran(t)s-ˈmis-ə-bəl, tranz-\ *adj* (1644) : capable of being transmitted ⟨~ diseases⟩ — **trans·mis·si·bil·i·ty** \(ˌ)tran(t)s-ˌmis-ə-ˈbil-ət-ē, (ˌ)tranz-\ *n*

trans·mis·sion \tran(t)s-ˈmish-ən, tranz-\ *n* [L *transmission-, transmissio,* fr. *transmissus,* pp. of *transmittere* to transmit] (1611) **1 :** an act, process, or instance of transmitting ⟨~ of a nerve impulse across a synapse⟩ **2 :** the passage of radio waves in the space between transmitting and receiving stations; *also* : the act or process of transmitting by radio or television **3 :** an assembly of parts including the speed-changing gears and the propeller shaft by which the power is transmitted from an automobile engine to a live axle; *also* : the speed-changing gears in such an assembly **4 :** something that is transmitted : MESSAGE — **trans·mis·sive** \-ˈmis-iv\ *adj* — **trans·mis·siv·i·ty** \ˌtran(t)s-(ˌ)mis-ˈiv-ət-ē, ˌtranz-\ *n*

trans·mis·som·e·ter \ˌtran(t)s-(ˌ)mis-ˈäm-ət-ər, ˌtranz-\ *n* (ca. 1931) : an instrument for measuring the transmission of light through a fluid (as the atmosphere)

trans·mit \tran(t)s-ˈmit, tranz-\ *vb* **trans·mit·ted; trans·mit·ting** [ME *transmitten,* fr. L *transmittere,* fr. *trans-* + *mittere* to send] *vt* (15c) **1 a :** to send or convey from one person or place to another : FORWARD **b :** to cause or allow to spread: as **(1) :** to convey by or as if by inheritance or heredity : HAND DOWN **(2) :** to convey (infection) abroad or to another **2 a (1) :** to cause (as light or force) to pass or be conveyed through space or a medium **(2) :** to admit the passage of : CONDUCT ⟨glass ~s light⟩ **b :** to send out (a signal) either by radio waves or over a wire ~ *vi* : to send out a signal either by radio waves or over a wire — **trans·mit·ta·ble** \-ˈmit-ə-bəl\ *adj* — **trans·mit·tal** \-ˈmit-ᵊl\ *n*

trans·mit·tance \-ˈmit-ᵊn(t)s\ *n* (ca. 1864) **1 :** TRANSMISSION **2 :** the fraction of radiant energy that having entered a layer of absorbing matter reaches its farther boundary

trans·mit·ter \-ˈmit-ər\ *n* (1727) : one that transmits: as **a (1) :** a part on a telephone into which one speaks and which contains a mechanism for converting sound waves into equivalent electric waves **(2) :** the portion of a telegraph instrument by which the message is sent **b :** a radio or television transmitting set **c :** NEUROTRANSMITTER

trans·mog·ri·fy \tran(t)s-ˈmäg-rə-ˌfī, tranz-\ *vt* **-fied; -fy·ing** [origin unknown] (1656) : to change or alter greatly and often with grotesque or humorous effect ***syn*** see TRANSFORM — **trans·mog·ri·fi·ca·tion** \(ˌ)tran(t)s-ˌmäg-rə-fə-ˈkā-shən, (ˌ)tranz-\ *n*

trans·mon·tane \(ˈ)tran(t)s-ˈmän-ˌtān, (ˈ)tranz-; ˌtran(t)s-(ˌ)män-ˈ, ˌtranz-\ *adj* [L *transmontanus*] (1727) : TRAMONTANE

trans·moun·tain \(ˈ)tran(t)s-ˈmau̇nt-ᵊn, (ˈ)tranz-\ *adj* (1929) : crossing or extending over or through a mountain ⟨a ~ road⟩ ⟨a ~ tunnel⟩

trans·mu·ta·tion \ˌtran(t)s-myü-ˈtā-shən, ˌtranz-\ *n* [ME *transmutacioun,* fr. MF or L; MF *transmutation,* fr. L *transmutation-, transmutatio,* fr. *transmutatus,* pp. of *transmutare*] (14c) : an act or instance of transmuting or being transmuted: as **a :** the conversion of base metals into gold or silver **b :** the conversion of one element or nuclide into another either naturally or artificially — **trans·mut·ative** \tran(t)s-ˈmyüt-ət-iv, tranz-\ *adj*

trans·mute \tran(t)s-ˈmyüt, tranz-\ *vb* **trans·muted; trans·mut·ing** [ME *transmuten,* fr. L *transmutare,* fr. *trans-* + *mutare* to change — more at MISS] *vt* (15c) **1 :** to change or alter in form, appearance, or nature and esp. to a higher form **2 :** to subject (as an element) to transmutation ~ *vi* : to undergo transmutation ***syn*** see TRANSFORM — **trans·mut·able** \-ˈmyüt-ə-bəl\ *adj*

trans·na·tion·al \(ˈ)tran(t)s-ˈnash-nəl, (ˈ)tranz-, -ən-ᵊl\ *adj* (1921) : extending or going beyond national boundaries

trans·nat·u·ral \-ˈnach-(ə-)rəl\ *adj* (1569) : being above or beyond nature

trans·oce·an·ic \ˌtran(t)s-ˌō-shē-ˈan-ik, ˌtranz-\ *adj* (1827) **1 :** lying or dwelling beyond the ocean **2 :** crossing or extending across the ocean ⟨a ~ telephone cable⟩

tran·som \ˈtran(t)-səm\ *n* [ME *traunsom,* prob. fr. L *transtrum,* fr. *trans* across — more at THROUGH] (15c) **1 :** a transverse piece in a structure : CROSSPIECE: as **a :** LINTEL **b :** a horizontal crossbar in a window, over a door, or between a door and a window or fanlight above it **c :** the horizontal bar or member of a cross or gallows **d :** any of several transverse timbers or beams secured to the sternpost of a boat; *also* : the planking forming the stern of a square-ended boat **2 :** a window above a door or other window built on and commonly hinged to a transom — **over the transom** : without solicitation or prior arrangement ⟨the manuscript arrived *over the transom*⟩

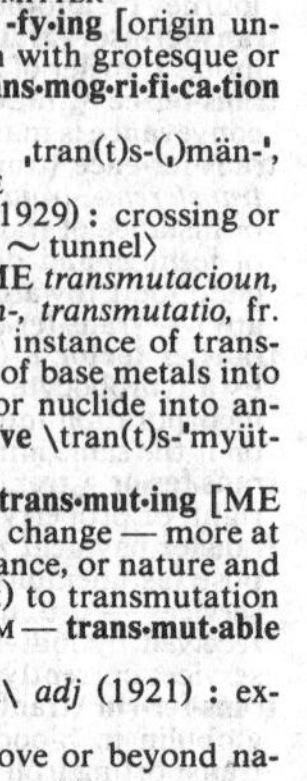

transom 1b

tran·son·ic *also* **trans–son·ic** \tran(t)s-ˈsän-ik, tran-ˈsän-\ *adj* [*trans-* + *-sonic* (as in *supersonic*)] (1945) **1 :** being or relating to a speed approximating the speed of sound in air which is a speed of about 1087 feet per second or about 741 miles per hour at sea level — often used of aeronautical speeds between 600 and 900 miles per hour **2 :** moving, capable of moving, or utilizing air currents moving at a transonic speed

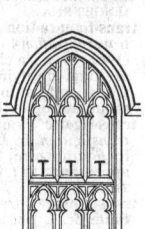

trans·pa·cif·ic \ˌtran(t)s-pə-ˈsif-ik\ *adj* (1891) **1 a :** crossing or extending across the Pacific ocean ⟨~ airlines⟩ **b :** relating to or involving crossing the Pacific ocean ⟨~ air fares⟩ **2 :** situated or occurring beyond the Pacific ocean

trans·par·ence \tran(t)s-ˈpar-ən(t)s, -ˈper-\ *n* (1594) : TRANSPARENCY 1

trans·par·en·cy \-ən-sē\ *n, pl* **-cies** (1615) **1 :** the quality or state of being transparent **2 :** something transparent; *esp* : a picture or design on glass, thin cloth, paper, or film designed to be viewed by light shining through it or by projection

trans·par·ent \-ənt\ *adj* [ME, fr. ML *transparent-, transparens,* prp. of *transparēre* to show through, fr. L *trans-* + *parēre* to show oneself — more at APPEAR] (15c) **1 a (1) :** having the property of transmitting light without appreciable scattering so that bodies lying beyond are entirely visible : PELLUCID **(2) :** pervious to a specified form of radiation (as X rays or ultraviolet light) **b :** fine or sheer enough to be seen through : DIAPHANOUS **2 a :** free from pretense or deceit : FRANK **b :** easily detected or seen through : OBVIOUS **c :** readily understood ***syn*** see CLEAR — **trans·par·ent·ly** *adv* — **trans·par·ent·ness** *n*

trans·par·ent·ize \-ən-ˌtīz\ *vt* **-ized; -iz·ing** (1925) : to make transparent or more nearly transparent ⟨~ tracing paper⟩

trans·per·son·al \(ˈ)tran(t)s-ˈpərs-nəl, -ən-ᵊl\ *adj* (1929) : extending or going beyond the personal or individual

tran·spic·u·ous \tran(t)s-ˈpik-yə-wəs\ *adj* [NL *transpicuus,* fr. L *transpicere* to look through, fr. *trans-* + *specere* to look, see — more at SPY] (1638) : clearly seen through or understood

trans·pierce \tran(t)s-ˈpi(ə)rs\ *vt* [MF *transpercer,* fr. OF, fr. *trans-* (fr. L) + *percer* to pierce] (1592) : to pierce through : PENETRATE

tran·spi·ra·tion \tran(t)s-pə-ˈrā-shən\ *n* (1551) : the act or process or an instance of transpiring; *esp* : the passage of watery vapor from a living

body through a membrane or pores — **tran·spi·ra·tion·al** \-shnəl, -shən-ᵊl\ *adj*

tran·spire \tran(t)s-ˈpī(ə)r\ *vb* **tran·spired; tran·spir·ing** [MF *transpirer,* fr. L *trans-* + *spirare* to breathe — more at SPIRIT] *vt* (1597) **:** to pass off or give passage to (a fluid) through pores or interstices; *esp* **:** to excrete (as water) in the form of a vapor through a living membrane (as the skin) ~ *vi* **1 :** to give off vaporous material; *specif* **:** to give off or exude watery vapor esp. from the surfaces of leaves **2 :** to pass in the form of a vapor from a living body **3 a :** to become known or apparent **:** DEVELOP **b :** to be revealed **:** come to light **4 :** to come to pass **:** OCCUR

usage Sense 4 of *transpire* is the frequent whipping boy of those who suppose sense 3 to be the only meaning of the word. Sense 4 appears to have developed in the late 18th century; it was well enough known to have been used by Abigail Adams in a letter to her husband in 1775 ⟨there is nothing new *transpired* since I wrote you last —Abigail Adams⟩ Noah Webster recognized the new sense in his dictionary of 1828. *Transpire* was evidently a popular word with 19th century journalists; sense 4 turns up in such pretentiously worded statements as "The police drill will transpire under shelter to-day in consequence of the moist atmosphere prevailing." Around 1870 the sense began to be attacked as a misuse on the grounds of etymology, and modern critics echo the damnation of 1870. Sense 4 has been in existence for about two centuries; it is firmly established as standard; it occurs now primarily in serious prose, not the ostentatiously flamboyant prose typical of 19th century journalism.

trans·pla·cen·tal \ˌtran(t)s-plə-ˈsent-ᵊl\ *adj* [ISV] (1929) **:** passing through or occurring by way of the placenta ⟨~ immunization⟩ — **trans·pla·cen·tal·ly** \-ᵊl-ē\ *adv*

¹**trans·plant** \tran(t)s-ˈplant\ *vb* [ME *transplaunten,* fr. LL *transplantare,* fr. L *trans-* + *plantare* to plant] *vt* (15c) **1 :** to lift and reset (a plant) in another soil or situation **2 :** to remove from one place or context and settle or introduce elsewhere **:** TRANSPORT **3 :** to transfer (an organ or tissue) from one part or individual to another ~ *vi* **:** to admit of being transplanted — **trans·plant·abil·i·ty** \ˌtran(t)s-ˌplant-ə-ˈbil-ət-ē\ *n* — **trans·plant·able** \tran(t)s-ˈplant-ə-bəl\ *adj* — **trans·plan·ta·tion** \ˌtran(t)s-ˌplan-ˈtā-shən\ *n* — **trans·plant·er** \tran(t)s-ˈplant-ər\ *n*

²**trans·plant** \ˈtran(t)s-ˌplant\ *n* (1756) **1 :** something transplanted **2 :** the act or process of transplanting

trans·po·lar \(ˈ)tran(t)s-ˈpō-lər\ *adj* (1850) **:** crossing or extending across either of the polar regions

tran·spon·der \tran(t)s-ˈpän-dər\ *n* [*trans*mitter + res*ponder*] (ca. 1944) **:** a radio or radar set that upon receiving a designated signal emits a radio signal of its own and that is used for the detection, identification, and location of objects

trans·pon·tine \tran(t)s-ˈpän-ˌtīn\ *adj* [*trans-* + L *pont-, pons* bridge — more at FIND] (1844) **1 :** situated on the farther side of a bridge **2 :** resembling or characteristic of melodramas once popular in the theaters of London south of the Thames

¹**trans·port** \tran(t)s-ˈpō(ə)rt, -ˈpȯ(ə)rt, ˈtran(t)s-ˌ\ *vt* [ME *transporten,* fr. MF or L; MF *transporter,* fr. L *transportare,* fr. *trans-* + *portare* to carry — more at FARE] (14c) **1 :** to transfer or convey from one place to another ⟨mechanisms of ~*ing* ions across a living membrane⟩ **2 :** to carry away with strong and often intensely pleasant emotion **3 :** to send to a penal colony overseas ***syn*** see BANISH — **trans·port·abil·i·ty** \(ˌ)tran(t)s-ˌpōrt-ə-ˈbil-ət-ē, -ˌpȯrt-\ *n* — **trans·port·able** \tran(t)s-ˈpōrt-ə-bəl, -ˈpȯrt-\ *adj*

²**trans·port** \ˈtran(t)s-ˌpō(ə)rt, -ˌpȯ(ə)rt\ *n* (1611) **1 :** an act or process of transporting **:** TRANSPORTATION **2 :** strong and often intensely pleasurable emotion ⟨~*s* of joy⟩ **3 a :** a ship for carrying soldiers or military equipment **b :** a vehicle (as a truck) used to transport persons or goods **c :** a system or means of usu. public conveyance **4 :** a transported convict **5 :** a mechanism for moving tape and esp. magnetic tape past a sensing or recording head ***syn*** see ECSTASY

trans·por·ta·tion \ˌtran(t)s-pər-ˈtā-shən\ *n* (1540) **1 :** an act, process, or instance of transporting or being transported **2 :** banishment to a penal colony **3 a :** means of conveyance or travel from one place to another **b :** public conveyance of passengers or goods esp. as a commercial enterprise — **trans·por·ta·tion·al** \-shnəl, -shən-ᵊl\ *adj*

trans·port·er \tran(t)s-ˈpōrt-ər, -ˈpȯrt-, ˈtran(t)s-ˌ\ *n* (1535) **:** one that transports; *esp* **:** a vehicle for transporting large or heavy loads

¹**trans·pose** \tran(t)s-ˈpōz\ *vt* **trans·posed; trans·pos·ing** [ME *transposen,* fr. MF *transposer,* fr. L *transponere* (perf. indic. *transposui*) to change the position of, fr. *trans-* + *ponere* to put, place — more at POSITION] (14c) **1 :** to change in form or nature **:** TRANSFORM **2 :** to render into another language, style, or manner of expression **:** TRANSLATE **3 :** to transfer from one place or period to another **:** SHIFT **4 :** to change the relative place or normal order of **:** alter the sequence of ⟨~ letters to change the spelling⟩ **5 :** to write or perform (a musical composition) in a different key **6 :** to bring (a term) from one side of an algebraic equation to the other with change of sign ***syn*** see REVERSE — **trans·pos·able** \-ˈpō-zə-bəl\ *adj*

²**trans·pose** \ˈtran(t)s-ˌpōz\ *n* (1947) **:** a matrix formed by interchanging the rows and columns of a given matrix

trans·po·si·tion \ˌtran(t)s-pə-ˈzish-ən\ *n* [ML *transposition-, transpositio,* fr. L *transpositus,* pp. of *transponere* to transpose] (1538) **1 :** an act, process, or instance of transposing or being transposed **2 a :** the transfer of any term of an equation from one side over to the other side with a corresponding change of the sign **b :** a mathematical permutation or interchange of two letters or symbols — **trans·po·si·tion·al** \-ˈzish-nəl, -ən-ᵊl\ *adj*

transposition cipher *n* (1939) **:** a cipher in which the letters of the plaintext are systematically rearranged into another sequence — compare SUBSTITUTION CIPHER

trans·sex·u·al \(ˈ)tran(t)s-ˈseksh-(ə-)wəl, -ˈsek-shəl\ *n* (ca. 1966) **:** a person with a psychological urge to belong to the opposite sex that may be carried to the point of undergoing surgery to modify the sex organs to mimic the opposite sex — **trans·sex·u·al·ism** \-wə-ˌliz-əm, -shə-ˌliz-\ *n* — **trans·sex·u·al·i·ty** \-ˌsek-shə-ˈwal-ət-ē\ *n*

trans·shape \tran(ch)-ˈshāp, tran(t)s-\ *vt, archaic* (1575) **:** to change into another shape **:** TRANSFORM

trans·ship \tran(ch)-ˈship, tran(t)s-\ *vt* (1792) **:** to transfer for further transportation from one ship or conveyance to another ~ *vi* **:** to change from one ship or conveyance to another — **trans·ship·ment** \-mənt\ *n*

trans·tho·rac·ic \ˌtran(t)s-thə-ˈras-ik\ *adj* (ca. 1923) **:** done or made by way of the thoracic cavity — **trans·tho·rac·i·cal·ly** \-i-k(ə-)lē\ *adv*

tran·sub·stan·tial \ˌtran(t)s-əb-ˈstan-chəl\ *adj* (1567) **:** changed or capable of being changed from one substance to another

tran·sub·stan·ti·ate \ˌtran(t)s-əb-ˈstan-chē-ˌāt\ *vb* **-at·ed; -at·ing** [ML *transubstantiatus,* pp. of *transubstantiare,* fr. L *trans-* + *substantia* substance] *vt* (1533) **1 :** to change into another substance **:** TRANSMUTE **2 :** to effect transubstantiation in (sacramental bread and wine) ~ *vi* **:** to undergo transubstantiation

tran·sub·stan·ti·a·tion \-ˌstan-chē-ˈā-shən\ *n* [ME *transubstacioun,* fr. ML *transubstantiation-, transubstantio,* fr. *transubstantus,* pp.] (14c) **1 :** an act or instance of transubstantiating or being transubstantiated **2 :** the miraculous change by which according to Roman Catholic and Eastern Orthodox dogma the eucharistic elements at their consecration become the body and blood of Christ while keeping only the appearances of bread and wine

tran·su·date \tran(t)s-ˈ(y)üd-ət, tranz-, -ˌāt; ˈtran(t)s-(y)u̇-ˌdāt, ˈtranz-\ *n* (1876) **:** a transuded substance

tran·su·da·tion \ˌtran(t)s-(y)ü-ˈdā-shən, ˌtranz-\ *n* (ca. 1612) **1 :** the act or process of transuding or being transuded **2 :** TRANSUDATE

tran·sude \tran(t)s-ˈ(y)üd, tranz-\ *vb* **tran·sud·ed; tran·sud·ing** [NL *transudare,* fr. L *trans-* + *sudare* to sweat — more at SWEAT] *vi* (1664) **:** to pass through a membrane or permeable substance **:** EXUDE ~ *vt* **:** to permit passage of

¹**trans·ura·nic** \ˌtran-shə-ˈran-ik, -ˈrā-nik, ˌtran-zhə-, ˌtran(t)s-yu̇-, ˌtranz-yu̇-\ *or* **trans·ura·ni·um** \-ˈrā-nē-əm\ *adj* (1937) **:** of, relating to, or being an element with an atomic number greater than that of uranium

²**transuranic** *n* (1950) **:** a transuranic element

trans·val·u·ate \(ˈ)tran(t)s-ˈval-yə-ˌwāt, (ˈ)tranz-\ *vt* **-at·ed; -at·ing** [back-formation fr. *transvaluation*] (1912) **:** TRANSVALUE

trans·val·u·a·tion \ˌtran(t)s-ˌval-yə-ˈwā-shən, ˌtranz-\ *n* (1898) **:** the act or process of transvaluing

trans·val·ue \(ˈ)tran(t)s-ˈval-(ˌ)yü, (ˈ)tranz-, -ˈval-yə(-w)\ *vt* **-val·ued; -valu·ing** (1911) **:** to reevaluate esp. on a basis that repudiates accepted standards

¹**trans·ver·sal** \tran(t)s-ˈvər-səl, tranz-\ *adj* [ME, fr. ML *transversalis,* fr. L *transversus*] (15c) **:** TRANSVERSE ⟨~ line⟩

²**transversal** *n* (ca. 1847) **:** a line that intersects a system of lines

¹**trans·verse** \tran(t)s-ˈvərs, tranz-, ˈtran(t)s-ˌ, ˈtranz-\ *adj* [L *transversus,* fr. pp. of *transvertere* to turn across, fr. *trans-* + *vertere* to turn — more at WORTH] (1621) **1 :** acting, lying, or being across **:** set crosswise **2 :** made at right angles to the anterior-posterior axis of the body ⟨a ~ section⟩ — **trans·verse·ly** *adv*

²**trans·verse** \ˈtran(t)s-ˌvərs, ˈtranz-\ *n* (1633) **:** something (as a piece, section, or part) that is transverse

transverse colon *n* (ca. 1860) **:** the middle portion of the colon that extends across the abdominal cavity

transverse process *n* (1696) **:** a lateral process of a vertebra — see VERTEBRA illustration

transverse wave *n* (1922) **:** a wave in which the vibrating element moves in a direction perpendicular to the direction of advance of the wave

trans·ves·tite \tran(t)s-ˈves-ˌtīt, tranz-\ *n* (ca. 1922) **:** a person and esp. a male who adopts the dress and often the behavior typical of the opposite sex esp. for purposes of emotional or sexual gratification — **trans·ves·tism** \-ˌtiz-əm\ *n* — **transvestite** *adj*

¹**trap** \ˈtrap\ *n* [ME, fr. OE *treppe* & OF *trape* (of Gmc origin); akin to MD *trappe* trap, stair, OE *treppan* to tread, Skt *dravati* he runs] (bef. 12c) **1 :** a device for taking game or other animals; *esp* **:** one that holds by springing shut suddenly **2 a :** something by which one is caught or stopped unawares **b :** a football play in which a defensive player is allowed to cross the line of scrimmage and then is blocked from the side while the ballcarrier advances through the spot vacated by the defensive player **3 a :** a device for hurling clay pigeons into the air **b :** SAND TRAP **c :** a piece of leather or section of interwoven leather straps between the thumb and forefinger of a baseball glove that forms an extension of the pocket **4** *slang* **:** MOUTH **5 :** a light usu. one-horse carriage with springs **6 :** any of various devices for preventing passage of something often while allowing other matter to proceed; *esp* **:** a device for drains or sewers consisting of a bend or partitioned chamber in which the liquid forms a seal to prevent the passage of sewer gas **7** *pl* **:** a group of percussion instruments (as a bass drum, snare drums, and cymbals) used esp. in a dance or jazz band **8** *pl* [*speed trap*] **:** a measured stretch of a course over which electronic timing devices measure the speed of a vehicle (as a racing car or dragster)

²**trap** *vb* **trapped; trap·ping** *vt* (14c) **1 a :** to catch or take in or as if in a trap **:** ENTRAP **b :** to place in a restricted position **:** CONFINE ⟨*trapped* in the burning wreck⟩ **2 :** to provide or set (a place) with traps **3 a :** STOP, HOLD ⟨these mountains ~ rains and fogs generated over the ocean —*Amer. Guide Series: Calif.*⟩ **b :** to separate out (as water from steam) **4 a :** to catch (as a baseball) immediately after a bounce **b :** to block out (a defensive football player) by means of a trap ~ *vi* **:** to engage in trapping animals (as for furs) ***syn*** see CATCH — **trap·per** *n*

³**trap** *vt* **trapped; trap·ping** [ME *trappen,* fr. *trappe* cloth, modif. of MF *drap* — more at DRAB] (14c) **:** to adorn with or as if with trappings

⁴**trap** *n* [Sw *trapp,* fr. *trappa* stair, fr. MLG *trappe;* akin to MD *trappe* stair] (ca. 1794) **:** any of various dark-colored fine-grained igneous rocks (as basalt or amygdaloid) used esp. in road making

trap·door \ˈtrap-ˈdō(ə)r, -ˈdȯ(ə)r\ *n* (14c) **:** a lifting or sliding door covering an opening (as in a roof, ceiling, or floor)

trap–door spider *n* (1826) **:** any of various often large burrowing spiders (esp. family Ctenizidae) that construct a tubular subterranean silk-lined nest topped with a hinged lid

\ə\ **abut** \ᵊ\ **kitten,** F **table** \ər\ **further** \a\ **ash** \ā\ **ace** \ä\ **cot, cart** \au̇\ **out** \ch\ **chin** \e\ **bet** \ē\ **easy** \g\ **go** \i\ **hit** \ī\ **ice** \j\ **job** \ŋ\ **sing** \ō\ **go** \ȯ\ **law** \ȯi\ **boy** \th\ **thin** \t͟h\ **the** \ü\ **loot** \u̇\ **foot** \y\ **yet** \zh\ **vision** \à, k̲, ⁿ, œ, œ̄, ue, ue̅, ʸ\ *see* Guide to Pronunciation

tra·peze \tra-'pēz *also* trə-\ *n* [F *trapèze*, fr. NL *trapezium*] (1861) : a gymnastic or acrobatic apparatus consisting of a short horizontal bar suspended by two parallel ropes
tra·pez·ist \-'pē-zəst\ *n* (1888) : a performer on the trapeze — called also *trapeze artist*
tra·pe·zi·um \trə-'pē-zē-əm, tra-\ *n, pl* **-zi·ums** *or* **-zia** \-zē-ə\ [NL, fr. Gk *trapezion*, lit., small table, dim. of *trapeza* table, fr. *tra-* four (akin to *tettares* four) + *peza* foot; akin to Gk *pod-*, *pous* foot — more at FOUR, FOOT] (ca. 1551) **1 a :** a quadrilateral having no two sides parallel **b** *Brit* **:** TRAPEZOID 1b **2 :** a bone in the wrist at the base of the thumb
tra·pe·zi·us \-zē-əs\ *n* [NL, fr. *trapezium*; fr. the pair on the back forming together the figure of a trapezium] (ca. 1704) : a large flat triangular superficial muscle of each side of the back
tra·pe·zo·he·dron \trə-ˌpē-zō-'hē-drən, ˌtrap-ə-\ *n, pl* **-drons** *or* **-dra** \-drə\ [NL, fr. *trapezium* + *-o-* + *-hedron*] (1816) : a crystalline form whose faces are trapeziums
trap·e·zoid \'trap-ə-ˌzȯid\ *n* [NL *trapezoïdes*, fr. Gk *trapezoeidēs* trapezium-shaped, fr. *trapeza* table] (1706) **1 a** *Brit* **:** TRAPEZIUM 1a **b :** a quadrilateral having only two sides parallel **2 :** a bone in the wrist at the base of the forefinger — **trap·e·zoi·dal** \ˌtrap-ə-'zȯid-ᵊl\ *adj*

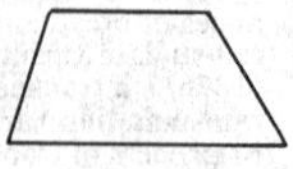
trapezoid

trap·nest \'trap-ˌnest\ *n* (1903) : a nest equipped with a hinged door designed to trap and confine a hen so that individual egg production may be determined — **trapnest** *vt*
trap·ping \'trap-iŋ\ *n* [ME, fr. gerund of *trappen* to adorn] (14c) **1 :** CAPARISON 1 — usu. used in pl. **2** *pl* **:** outward decoration or dress **:** ornamental equipment; *also* **:** outward signs ⟨conventional men with all the ~*s* . . . of banality —Robert Plank⟩
Trap·pist \'trap-əst\ *n* [F *trappiste*, fr. La Trappe, France] (1814) : a member of a reformed branch of the Roman Catholic Cistercian Order established by the Abbot de Rancé in 1664 at the monastery of La Trappe in Normandy — **Trappist** *adj*
trap·rock \'trap-'räk\ *n* (ca. 1813) : [4]TRAP
traps \'traps\ *n pl* [ME *trappe* cloth — more at TRAP] (1813) : personal belongings : LUGGAGE
trap·shoot·er \'trap-ˌshüt-ər\ *n* (1875) : one who engages in trapshooting
trap·shoot·ing \-ˌshüt-iŋ\ *n* (1875) : shooting at clay pigeons sprung from a trap into the air away from the shooter
tra·pun·to \trə-'pün-(ˌ)tō, -'pün-\ *n, pl* **-tos** [It, fr. pp. of *trapungere* to embroider, fr. *tra-* across (fr. L *trans-*) + *pungere* to prick, fr. L — more at TRANS-, PUNGENT] (ca. 1924) : a decorative quilted design in high relief worked through at least two layers of cloth by outlining the design in running stitch and padding it from the underside
[1]**trash** \'trash\ *n* [of Scand origin; akin to Norw *trask* trash; akin to OE *teran* to tear] (1518) **1 :** something worth little or nothing: as **a :** JUNK, RUBBISH **b** (1) **:** empty talk **:** NONSENSE (2) **:** inferior or worthless writing or artistic matter **2 :** something in a crumbled or broken condition or mass; *esp* **:** debris from pruning or processing plant material **3 :** a worthless person; *also* **:** such persons as a group **:** RIFFRAFF
[2]**trash** *vt* (ca. 1859) **1 :** VANDALIZE, DESTROY **2 :** ATTACK, ASSAULT **3 :** to subject to criticism or invective ~ *vi* **:** to trash something or someone
trash fish *n* (1945) **1 :** ROUGH FISH **2 :** any of various sea fishes that have no market value as human food but are sometimes processed for oil or meal for domestic animals
trash·man \'trash-ˌman, -mən\ *n* (1951) : one who collects and hauls away trash
trashy \'trash-ē\ *adj* **trash·i·er; -est** (1620) : resembling or containing trash : of inferior quality — **trash·i·ness** *n*
trass \'tras\ *n* [D] (1796) : a light-colored volcanic tuff that resembles pozzolana in composition and is sometimes ground and used together with lime or portland cement in a hydraulic cement mixture
trat·to·ria \ˌträt-ə-'rē-ə\ *n, pl* **-ri·as** *or* **-rie** \-'rē-ˌā\ [It, fr. *trattore* innkeeper, restaurant owner, fr. F *traiteur*, fr. *traiter* to treat, entertain (fr. OF *traitier*) + *-eur* -or — more at TREAT] (1832) : RESTAURANT
trau·ma \'trau̇-mə, 'trȯ-\ *n, pl* **trau·ma·ta** \-mət-ə\ *or* **traumas** [Gk *traumat-*, *trauma* wound — more at THROE] (1693) **1 a :** an injury (as a wound) to living tissue caused by an extrinsic agent ⟨surgical ~⟩ **b :** a disordered psychic or behavioral state resulting from mental or emotional stress or physical injury **2 :** an agent, force, or mechanism that causes trauma — **trau·mat·ic** \trə-'mat-ik, trȯ-, trau̇-\ *adj* — **trau·mat·i·cal·ly** \-i-k(ə-)lē\ *adv*
trau·ma·tism \'trau̇-mə-ˌtiz-əm, 'trȯ-\ *n* (1857) : the development or occurrence of trauma; *also* **:** TRAUMA
trau·ma·tize \-ˌtīz\ *vt* **-tized; -tiz·ing** (1903) : to inflict a trauma upon — **trau·ma·ti·za·tion** \ˌtrau̇-mət-ə-'zā-shən, ˌtrȯ-\ *n*
[1]**tra·vail** \trə-'vā(ə)l, 'trav-ˌāl\ *n* [ME, fr. OF, fr. *travaillier* to torture, travail, fr. (assumed) VL *tripaliare* to torture, fr. *tripalium* instrument of torture, fr. L *tripalis* having three stakes, fr. *tri-* + *palus* stake — more at POLE] (13c) **1 a :** work esp. of a painful or laborious nature **:** TOIL **b :** a physical or mental exertion or piece of work **:** TASK, EFFORT **c :** AGONY, TORMENT **2 :** LABOR, PARTURITION ***syn*** see WORK
[2]**travail** *like* [1]; *in prayer-book communion service usu* 'trav-ˌāl\ *vi* [ME *travailen*, fr. OF *travaillier*] (13c) **1 :** to labor hard **:** TOIL **2 :** LABOR 3
trave \'trāv\ *n* [ME, fr. MF, beam, fr. L *trabs* — more at THORP] (14c) **1 :** a traverse beam **2 :** a division or bay (as in a ceiling) made by or as if by traverse beams
[1]**trav·el** \'trav-əl\ *vb* **-eled** *or* **-elled; -el·ing** *or* **-el·ling** \-(ə-)liŋ\ [ME *travailen* to travail, journey, fr. OF *travaillier* to travail] *vi* (13c) **1 a :** to go on or as if on a trip or tour **:** JOURNEY **b** (1) **:** to go as if by traveling **:** PASS ⟨the news ~*ed* fast⟩ (2) **:** ASSOCIATE ⟨~*s* with a sophisticated crowd⟩ **c :** to go from place to place as a salesman or business agent **2 a :** to move or undergo transmission from one place to another ⟨goods ~*ing* by plane⟩ **b :** to move in a given direction or path or through a given distance ⟨the stylus ~*s* in a groove⟩ **c :** to move rapidly ⟨a car that can really ~⟩ **3 :** to walk or run with a basketball in violation of the rules ~ *vt* **1 a :** to journey through or over **b :** to follow (a course or path) as if by traveling **2 :** to traverse (a specified distance) **3 :** to cover (a place or region) as a commercial traveler — **travel light :** to travel with a minimum of equipment or baggage
[2]**travel** *n* (14c) **1 a :** the act of traveling **:** PASSAGE **b :** a journey esp. to a distant or unfamiliar place **:** TOUR, TRIP — often used in pl. **2** *pl* **:** an account of one's travels **3 :** the number traveling **:** TRAFFIC **4 a :** MOVEMENT, PROGRESSION ⟨the ~ of satellites around the earth⟩ **b :** the motion of a piece of machinery; *esp* **:** reciprocating motion
travel agency *n* (1947) : an agency engaged in selling and arranging personal transportation and accommodations for travelers — called also *travel bureau*
travel agent *n* (1927) : a person engaged in selling and arranging transportation, tours, or trips for travelers
trav·eled *or* **trav·elled** \'trav-əld\ *adj* (15c) **1 :** experienced in travel ⟨a widely ~ journalist⟩ **2 :** used by travelers ⟨a well-*traveled* highway⟩
trav·el·er *or* **trav·el·ler** \'trav-(ə-)lər\ *n* (14c) **1 :** one that travels: as **a :** one that goes on a trip or journey **b :** TRAVELING SALESMAN **2 a :** an iron ring sliding along a rope, bar, or rod of a ship **b :** a rod on the deck on which such a ring slides **3 :** any of various devices for handling something that is being transported laterally
traveler's check *n* (ca. 1909) : a draft purchased from a bank or express company and signed by the purchaser at the time of purchase and again at the time of cashing as a precaution against forgery
trav·el·ing *or* **trav·el·ling** \'trav-(ə-)liŋ\ *adj* (14c) **1 :** that travels ⟨a ~ opera company⟩ ⟨a ~ executive⟩ **2 :** carried, used by, or accompanying a traveler ⟨a ~ alarm clock⟩ ⟨a ~ companion⟩
traveling bag *n* (1836) : a bag carried by hand and designed to hold a traveler's clothing and personal articles
traveling case *n* (1835) : a usu. rigid and box-shaped traveling bag
traveling fellowship *n* (1789) : a fellowship whose terms permit or direct the holder to travel or go abroad for study or research
traveling salesman *n* (1885) : a traveling representative of a business concern who solicits orders usu. in an assigned territory
trav·el·ogue *or* **trav·el·og** \'trav-ə-ˌlȯg, -ˌläg\ *n* [*travel* + *-logue*] (1903) **1 :** a talk or lecture on travel usu. accompanied by a film or slides **2 :** a narrated motion picture about travel
travel trailer *n* (1961) : a trailer drawn esp. by a passenger automobile and equipped for use (as while traveling) as a dwelling
tra·vers·al \trə-'vər-səl *also* tra-' *or* 'tra-ˌ\ *n* (1897) : the act or an instance of traversing
[1]**tra·verse** \'tra-vərs *also* -ˌvərs, *esp for 6 & 8 also* trə-' *or* tra-'\ *n* [ME *travers*, fr. MF *traverse*, fr. *traverser* to cross, fr. LL *transversare*, fr. L *transversus*, pp., transverse — more at TRANSVERSE] (14c) **1 :** something that crosses or lies across **2 :** OBSTACLE, ADVERSITY **3 :** a formal denial of a matter of fact alleged by the opposite party in a legal pleading **4 a :** a compartment or recess formed by a partition, curtain, or screen **b :** a gallery or loft of communication from side to side in a large building **5 :** a route or way across or over: as **a :** a zigzag course of a sailing ship with contrary winds **b :** a curving or zigzag way up a steep grade **c :** the course followed in traversing **6 :** the act or an instance of traversing **:** CROSSING **7 :** a protective projecting wall or bank of earth in a trench **8 a :** a lateral movement (as of the saddle of a lathe carriage); *also* **:** a device for imparting such movement **b :** the lateral movement of a gun about a pivot or on a carriage to change direction of fire **9 :** a line surveyed across a plot of ground
[2]**tra·verse** \trə-'vərs *also* tra-' *or* 'tra-(ˌ)\ *vb* **tra·versed; tra·vers·ing** *vt* (14c) **1 a :** to go against or act in opposition to **:** OPPOSE, THWART **b :** to deny (as an allegation of fact or an indictment) formally at law **2 :** to pass through **:** PENETRATE ⟨light rays *traversing* a crystal⟩ **3 a :** to go or travel across or over **b :** to move along or through **4 :** to make a study of **:** EXAMINE **5 :** to lie or extend across **:** CROSS ⟨the bridge ~*s* a brook⟩ **6 a :** to move to and fro over or along **b :** to ascend, descend, or cross (a slope or gap) at an angle **c :** to move (a gun) to right or left on a pivot **7 :** to make or carry out a survey of by using traverses ~ *vi* **1 :** to move back and forth or from side to side **2 :** to move or turn laterally **:** SWIVEL **3 a :** to climb at an angle or in a zigzag course **b :** to ski across rather than straight down a hill **4 :** to make a survey by using traverses — **tra·vers·able** \-'vər-sə-bəl, -(ˌ)vər-\ *adj* — **tra·vers·er** *n*
[3]**tra·verse** \'tra-(ˌ)vərs, trə-', tra-'\ *adj* (15c) : lying across : TRANSVERSE
trav·erse jury \'trav-ərs-\ *n* (1823) : PETIT JURY
traverse rod *n* (1948) : a metal rod or track with a pulley mechanism for drawing curtains
trav·er·tine \'trav-ər-ˌtēn, -tən\ *n* [F *travertin*] (1797) : a mineral consisting of a massive usu. layered calcium carbonate (as aragonite or calcite) formed by deposition from spring waters or esp. from hot springs
[1]**trav·es·ty** \'trav-ə-stē\ *vt* **-tied; -ty·ing** (1673) : to make a travesty of : PARODY
[2]**travesty** *n, pl* **-ties** [obs. E *travesty*, disguised, parodied, fr. F *travesti*, pp. of *travestir* to disguise, fr. It *travestire*, fr. *tra-* across (fr. L *trans-*) + *vestire* to dress, fr. L — more at VEST] (1674) **1 :** a burlesque translation or literary or artistic imitation usu. grotesquely incongruous in style, treatment, or subject matter **2 :** a debased, distorted, or grossly inferior imitation ⟨a ~ of justice⟩ ***syn*** see CARICATURE
tra·vois \trə-'vȯi, 'trav-ˌȯi\ *n, pl* **tra·vois** *also* **tra·voises** \-'vȯiz, -ˌȯiz\ [CanF *travois*, alter. of F *travail* travel] (1847) : a primitive vehicle used by Plains Indians consisting of two trailing poles serving as shafts and bearing a platform or net for the load
[1]**trawl** \'trȯl\ *vb* [prob. fr. obs. D *tragelen*] *vi* (1561) **1 :** to fish with a trawl **2 :** TROLL 2 ~ *vt* **:** to catch (fish) with a trawl
[2]**trawl** *n* (1636) **1 :** a large conical net dragged along the sea bottom in gathering fish or other marine life **2 :** SETLINE
trawl·er \'trȯ-lər\ *n* (1630) **1 :** a person who fishes by trawling **2 :** a boat used in trawling
trawl·er·man \-mən\ *n* (1633) : a fisherman who trawls or one who mans a trawler
tray \'trā\ *n* [ME, fr. OE *trīg*, *trēg*; akin to OE *trēow* tree — more at TREE] (bef. 12c) : an open receptacle with a flat bottom and a low rim for holding, carrying, or exhibiting articles — **tray·ful** \-ˌfu̇l\ *n*
treach·er·ous \'trech-(ə-)rəs\ *adj* (14c) **1 :** characterized by or manifesting treachery **:** PERFIDIOUS **2 a :** likely to betray trust **:** UNRELIABLE ⟨a ~ memory⟩ **b :** providing insecure footing or support ⟨~ quicksand⟩ **c :** marked by hidden dangers, hazards, or perils ***syn*** see FAITHLESS — **treach·er·ous·ly** *adv* — **treach·er·ous·ness** *n*

treach·ery \'trech-(ə-)rē\ *n, pl* **-er·ies** [ME *trecherie,* fr. OF, fr. *trechier* to deceive] (13c) **1 :** violation of allegiance or of faith and confidence : TREASON **2 :** an act of perfidy or treason
trea·cle \'trē-kəl\ *n* [ME *triacle,* fr. MF, fr. L *theriaca,* fr. Gk *thēriakē* antidote against a poisonous bite, fr. fem. of *thēriakos* of a wild animal, fr. *thērion* wild animal, dim. of *thēr* wild animal — more at FIERCE] (14c) **1 :** a medicinal compound formerly in wide use as a remedy against poison **2** *chiefly Brit* **:** MOLASSES **3 :** something (as a tone of voice) heavily sweet and cloying
trea·cly \-k(ə-)lē\ *adj* (1733) **:** resembling treacle (as in quality or appearance) ⟨~ sentimentality⟩
1tread \'tred\ *vb* **trod** \'träd\ *also* **tread·ed; trod·den** \'träd-ᵊn\ *or* **trod; tread·ing** [ME *treden,* fr. OE *tredan;* akin to OHG *tretan* to tread] *vt* (bef. 12c) **1 a :** to step or walk on or over **b :** to walk along **:** FOLLOW **2 a :** to beat or press with the feet **:** TRAMPLE **b :** to subdue or repress as if by trampling **:** CRUSH **3 :** to copulate with — used of a male bird **4 a :** to form by treading **:** BEAT ⟨~ a path⟩ **b :** to execute by stepping or dancing ⟨~ a measure⟩ ~ *vi* **1 :** to move on foot **:** WALK **2 a :** to set foot **b :** to put one's foot **:** STEP **3 :** COPULATE 1 — **tread·er** *n* — **tread on one's toes :** to give offense (as by encroaching on one's rights or feelings) — **tread water :** to keep the body nearly upright in the water and the head above water by a treading motion of the feet usu. aided by the hands
2tread *n* (13c) **1 :** a mark (as a footprint or the imprint of a tire) made by or as if by treading **2 a (1) :** the action of treading **(2) :** an act or instance of treading **:** STEP **b :** manner of stepping **c :** the sound of treading **3 a :** the part of a sole that touches the ground; *also* **:** the pattern on the bottom of a sole **b (1) :** the part of a wheel or tire that makes contact with a road or rail **(2) :** the pattern of ridges or grooves made or cut in the face of a tire **4 :** the distance between the points of contact with the ground of the two front wheels or the two rear wheels of a vehicle **5 a :** the upper horizontal part of a step **b :** the width of such a tread — **tread·less** \-ləs\ *adj*
1trea·dle \'tred-ᵊl\ *n* [ME *tredel* step of a stair, fr. OE, fr. *tredan*] (15c) **:** a swiveling or lever device pressed by the foot to drive a machine
2treadle *vb* **trea·dled; trea·dling** \'tred-liŋ, -ᵊl-iŋ\ *vi* (1891) **:** to operate a treadle ~ *vt* **:** to operate (as a machine) by a treadle
tread·mill \'tred-,mil\ *n* (1822) **1 a :** a mill worked by persons treading on steps on the periphery of a wide wheel having a horizontal axis and used formerly in prison punishment **b :** a mill worked by an animal treading an endless belt **2 :** a wearisome or monotonous routine resembling continued activity on a treadmill
trea·son \'trēz-ᵊn\ *n* [ME *tresoun,* fr. OF *traison,* fr. ML *tradition-, traditio,* fr. L, act of handing over, fr. *traditus,* pp., betrayed — more at TRAITOR] (13c) **1 :** the betrayal of a trust **:** TREACHERY **2 :** the offense of attempting by overt acts to overthrow the government of the state to which the offender owes allegiance or to kill or personally injure the sovereign or his family
trea·son·able \'trēz-nə-bəl, -ᵊn-ə-bəl\ *adj* (14c) **:** relating to, consisting of, or involving treason — **trea·son·ably** \-blē\ *adv*
trea·son·ous \'trēz-nəs, -ᵊn-əs\ *adj* (15c) **:** TREASONABLE
trea·sur·able \'trezh-(ə-)rə-bəl, 'trāzh-\ *adj* (1607) **:** worthy of being treasured **:** PRECIOUS
1trea·sure \'trezh-ər, 'trāzh-\ *n* [ME *tresor,* fr. OF, fr. L *thesaurus* — more at THESAURUS] (12c) **1 a (1) :** wealth (as money, jewels, or precious metals) stored up or hoarded ⟨buried ~⟩ **(2) :** wealth of any kind or in any form **:** RICHES **b :** a store of money in reserve **2 :** something of great worth or value; *also* **:** a person esteemed as rare or precious **3 :** a collection of precious things
2treasure *vt* **trea·sured; trea·sur·ing** \-(ə-)riŋ\ (14c) **1 :** to collect and store up (something of value) for future use **:** HOARD **2 :** to hold or keep as precious **:** CHERISH, PRIZE ⟨she *treasured* those memories⟩ ***syn*** see APPRECIATE
trea·sur·er \'trezh-rər, 'trezh-ər-ər, 'trāzh-\ *n* (13c) **1 :** a guardian of a collection of treasures **:** CURATOR **2 :** an officer entrusted with the receipt, care, and disbursement of funds: as **a :** a governmental officer charged with receiving, keeping, and disbursing public revenues **b :** the executive financial officer of a club, society, or business corporation — **trea·sur·er·ship** \-,ship\ *n*
treasure trove \-,trōv\ *n* [AF *tresor trové,* lit., found treasure] (1550) **1 :** treasure that anyone finds; *specif* **:** gold or silver in the form of money, plate, or bullion which is found hidden and whose ownership is not known **2 :** a valuable or productive discovery
trea·sury \'trezh-(ə-)rē, 'trāzh-\ *n, pl* **-sur·ies** [ME *tresorie,* fr. OF, fr. *tresor* treasure] (13c) **1 a :** a place in which stores of wealth are kept **b :** the place of deposit and disbursement of collected funds; *esp* **:** one where public revenues are deposited, kept, and disbursed **c :** funds kept in such a depository **2** *obs* **:** TREASURE **3** *cap* **a :** a governmental department in charge of finances and esp. the collection, management, and expenditure of public revenues **b :** the building in which the business of such a governmental department is transacted **4** *cap* **:** a government security (as a note or bill) issued by the Treasury **5 :** a repository for treasures ⟨a ~ of poems⟩
treasury note *n* (1890) **1 :** a currency note issued by the U.S. Treasury in payment for silver bullion purchased under the Sherman Silver Purchase Act of 1890 **2 :** a U.S. government bond usu. with a maturity of not less than one year or more than seven years
treasury of merits (ca. 1921) **:** the superabundant satisfaction of Christ for men's sins and the excess of merit of the saints which according to Roman Catholic theology is effective for salvation of others and is available for dispensation through indulgences
treasury stock *n* (1903) **:** issued stock reacquired by a corporation and held as an asset
1treat \'trēt\ *vb* [ME *treten,* fr. OF *traitier,* fr. L *tractare* to handle, deal with, fr. *tractus,* pp. of *trahere* to draw — more at DRAW] *vi* (13c) **1 :** to discuss terms of accommodation or settlement **:** NEGOTIATE **2 :** to deal with a matter esp. in writing **:** DISCOURSE — usu. used with *of* ⟨a book ~*ing* of conservation⟩ **3 :** to pay another's expenses (as for a meal or drink) esp. as a compliment or as an expression of regard or friendship ~ *vt* **1 a :** to deal with in speech or writing **:** EXPOUND **b :** to present or represent artistically **c :** to deal with **:** HANDLE ⟨food is plentiful and ~*ed* with imagination —Cecil Beaton⟩ **2 a :** to bear oneself toward **:** USE ⟨~ a horse cruelly⟩ **b :** to regard and deal with in a specified manner — usu. used with *as* **3 a :** to provide with free food, drink, or entertainment **b :** to provide with enjoyment or gratification **4 :** to care for or deal with medically or surgically ⟨~ a disease⟩ **5 :** to act upon with some agent esp. to improve or alter ⟨~ a metal with acid⟩ — **treat·er** *n*
2treat *n* (1651) **1 :** an entertainment given without expense to those invited **2 :** an esp. unexpected source of joy, delight, or amusement
treat·able \'trēt-ə-bəl\ *adj* (14c) **:** capable of being treated **:** yielding or responsive to treatment ⟨a ~ disease⟩ — **treat·abil·i·ty** \,trēt-ə-'bil-ət-ē\ *n*
trea·tise \'trēt-əs *also* -əz\ *n* [ME *tretis,* fr. AF *tretiz,* fr. OF *traitier* to treat] (14c) **1 :** a systematic exposition or argument in writing including a methodical discussion of the facts and principles involved and conclusions reached ⟨a ~ on higher education⟩ **2** *obs* **:** ACCOUNT, TALE
treat·ment \'trēt-mənt\ *n* (1560) **1 a :** the act or manner or an instance of treating someone or something **:** HANDLING, USAGE **b :** the techniques or actions customarily applied in a specified situation **2 a :** a substance or technique used in treating **b :** an experimental condition
trea·ty \'trēt-ē\ *n, pl* **treaties** [ME *tretee,* fr. MF *traité,* fr. ML *tractatus,* fr. L, handling, treatment, fr. *tractatus,* pp. of *tractare* to treat] (14c) **1 :** the action of treating and esp. of negotiating **2 a :** an agreement or arrangement made by negotiation: **(1) :** PRIVATE TREATY **(2) :** a contract in writing between two or more political authorities (as states or sovereigns) formally signed by representatives duly authorized and usu. ratified by the lawmaking authority of the state **b :** a document in which such a contract is set down
treaty port *n* (1881) **:** any of numerous ports and inland cities in China, Japan, and Korea formerly open by treaty to foreign commerce
1tre·ble \'treb-əl\ *n* [ME, perh. fr. MF, trio, fr. *treble,* adj.] (14c) **1 a :** the highest voice part in harmonic music **:** SOPRANO **b :** one that performs a treble part; *also* **:** a member of a family of instruments having the highest range **c :** a high-pitched or shrill voice, tone, or sound **d :** the upper half of the whole vocal or instrumental tonal range — compare BASS **e :** the higher portion of the audio frequency range in sound recording and broadcasting **2 :** something treble in construction, uses, amount, number, or value
2treble *adj* [ME, fr. MF, fr. L *triplus* — more at TRIPLE] (14c) **1 a :** having three parts or uses **:** THREEFOLD **b :** triple in number or amount **2 a :** relating to or having the range or part of a treble **b :** HIGH-PITCHED, SHRILL **c :** of, relating to, or having the range of treble in sound recording and broadcasting ⟨~ frequencies⟩ — **tre·bly** \'treb-(ə-)lē\ *adv*
3treble *vb* **tre·bled; tre·bling** \'treb-(ə-)liŋ\ *vt* (14c) **:** to increase threefold ~ *vi* **1 :** to sing treble **2 :** to grow to three times the size, amount, or number
treble clef *n* [1*treble;* fr. its use for the notation of treble parts] (ca. 1903) **1 :** a clef that places G above middle C on the second line of the staff **2 :** TREBLE STAFF
treble staff *n* (ca. 1903) **:** the musical staff carrying the treble clef
treb·u·chet \,treb-(y)ə-'shet, -'chet\ *or* **treb·uc·ket** \,treb-ə-'ket\ *n* [ME *trebochet,* fr. MF *trebuchet*] (14c) **:** a medieval military engine for hurling missiles with great force
tre·cen·to \trā-'chen-(,)tō\ *n, pl* **-tos** [It, lit., three hundred, fr. L *tres* three + *centum* hundred — more at THREE, HUNDRED] (1841) **:** the 14th century; *specif* **:** the 14th century in Italian literature and art
tre·de·cil·lion \,trēd-i-'sil-yən\ *n, often attrib* [L *tredecim* thirteen (fr. *tres* three + *decem* ten) + E *-illion* (as in *million*) — more at THREE, TEN] (ca. 1934) — see NUMBER table
1tree \'trē\ *n* [ME, fr. OE *trēow;* akin to ON *trē* tree, Gk *drys,* Skt *dāru* wood] (bef. 12c) **1 a :** a woody perennial plant having a single usu. elongate main stem generally with few or no branches on its lower part **b :** a shrub or herb of arborescent form ⟨rose ~*s*⟩ ⟨a banana ~⟩ **2 a (1) :** a piece of wood (as a post or pole) usu. adapted to a particular use or forming part of a structure or implement **(2)** *archaic* **:** the cross on which Jesus was crucified **b** *archaic* **:** GALLOWS **3 :** something in the form of or resembling a tree: as **a :** a diagram or graph that branches usu. from a simple stem without forming loops or polygons ⟨genealogical ~⟩ **b :** an arborescent aggregation of crystals **c :** a much-branched system of channels esp. in an animal body ⟨the vascular ~⟩ — **tree·less** \-ləs\ *adj* — **tree·like** \-,līk\ *adj*
2tree *vt* **treed; tree·ing** (1700) **1 a :** to drive to or up a tree ⟨*treed* by a bull⟩ ⟨dogs ~*ing* game⟩ **b :** to put into a position of extreme disadvantage **:** CORNER; *esp* **:** to bring to bay **2 :** to furnish or fit (as a shoe) with a tree
treed \'trēd\ *adj* (1860) **:** planted or grown with trees **:** WOODED
tree farm *n* (1942) **:** an area of forest land managed to ensure continuous commercial production
tree fern *n* (1846) **:** a fern (chiefly of families Cyatheaceae and Marattiaceae) of arborescent habit with a woody caudex
tree frog *n* (1738) **:** any of numerous tailless amphibians (esp. family Hylidae) of arboreal habits
tree·hop·per \'trē-,häp-ər\ *n* (1836) **:** any of numerous small leaping homopterous insects (family Membracidae) living on a sap from branches and twigs
tree house *n* (ca. 1899) **:** a structure (as a playhouse) built among the branches of a tree
tree line *n* (1893) **:** TIMBERLINE
tree·nail *also* **tre·nail** \'trē-,nāl, 'tren-ᵊl, 'trən-ᵊl\ *n* (13c) **:** a wooden peg made usu. of dry compressed timber so as to swell in its hole when moistened
tree of heaven (1845) **:** an Asian ailanthus (*Ailanthus glandulosa*) that has foliage similar to that of the sumacs, has ill-scented staminate flowers, and is widely grown as a shade and ornamental tree
tree peony *n* (ca. 1891) **:** a shrubby Chinese peony (*Paeonia suffruticosa*) that has large showy flowers and is the source of many horticultural varieties

\ə\ abut \ᵊ\ kitten, F table \ər\ further \a\ ash \ā\ ace \ä\ cot, cart \au̇\ out \ch\ chin \e\ bet \ē\ easy \g\ go \i\ hit \ī\ ice \j\ job \ŋ\ sing \ō\ go \ȯ\ law \ȯi\ boy \th\ thin \t͟h\ the \ü\ loot \u̇\ foot \y\ yet \zh\ vision \ȧ, k̲, ⁿ, œ, œ̄, ue, ue̅, ʸ\ *see* Guide to Pronunciation

tree shrew *n* (ca. 1893) **:** any of a family (Tupaiidae) of arboreal insectivorous mammals sometimes classified as true insectivores and sometimes as primitive primates

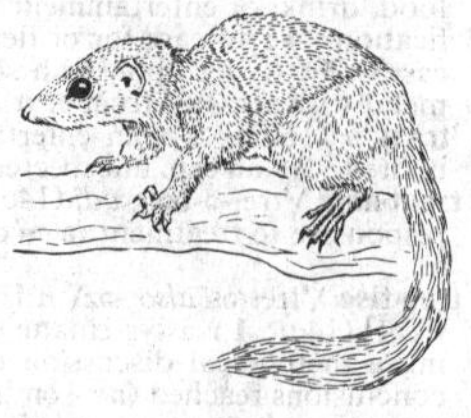

tree shrew

tree sparrow *n* (ca. 1770) **1 :** a European sparrow (*Passer montanus*) that has a black spot on the ear coverts **2 :** an American sparrow (*Spizella arborea*) that has a single dark spot on the breast and breeds in northern No. America and winters in the U.S.
tree surgeon *n* (1926) **:** a specialist in tree surgery
tree surgery *n* (1916) **:** operative treatment of diseased trees esp. for control of decay; *broadly* **:** practices forming part of the professional care of specimen or shade trees
tree toad *n* (1778) **:** TREE FROG
tree·top \ˈtrē-ˌtäp\ *n* (1530) **1 :** the topmost part of a tree **2** *pl* **:** the height or line marked by the tops of a group of trees
tre·foil \ˈtrē-ˌfȯil, ˈtref-ˌȯil\ *n* [ME, fr. MF *trefeuil,* fr. L *trifolium,* fr. *tri-* + *folium* leaf — more at BLADE] (15c) **1 a :** CLOVER; *broadly* **:** any of several trifoliolate leguminous herbs **b :** a trifoliolate leaf **2 :** an ornament or symbol in the form of a stylized trifoliolate leaf
tre·ha·lose \tri-ˈhäl-ˌōs, -ˌōz\ *n* [ISV *trehala* (a sweet substance constituting the pupal covering of a beetle) + *-ose*] (1862) **:** a crystalline disaccharide $C_{12}H_{22}O_{11}$ stored instead of starch by many fungi and found in the blood of many insects
treil·lage \tre-ˈyäzh\ *n* [F, fr. MF, fr. *treille* vine arbor, fr. L *trichila*] (1698) **:** latticework for vines **:** TRELLIS
[1]trek \ˈtrek\ *vi* **trekked; trek·king** [Afrik, fr. MD *trecken* to pull, haul, migrate; akin to OHG *trechan* to pull] (1821) **1** *chiefly So Afr* **a :** to travel by ox wagon **b :** to migrate by ox wagon or in a train of such **2 :** to make one's way arduously; *broadly* **:** to go on a journey — **trek·ker** *n*
[2]trek *n* [Afrik, fr. MD *treck* pull, haul, fr. *trecken*] (1835) **1** *chiefly So Afr* **:** a journey by ox wagon; *esp* **:** an organized migration by a group of settlers **2 :** a trip or movement esp. when involving difficulties or complex organization
[1]trel·lis \ˈtrel-əs\ *n* [ME *trelis,* fr. MF *treliz* fabric of coarse weave, trellis, fr. (assumed) VL *trilicius* woven with triple thread, fr. L *tri-* + *licium* thread] (15c) **1 :** a frame of latticework used as a screen or as a support for climbing plants **2 :** a construction (as a summerhouse) chiefly of latticework **3 :** an arrangement that forms or gives the effect of a lattice ⟨a ~ of interlacing streams⟩
[2]trellis *vt* (15c) **1 :** to provide with a trellis; *esp* **:** to train (as a vine) on a trellis **2 :** to cross or interlace on or through **:** INTERWEAVE
trel·lised \ˈtrel-əst\ *adj* (15c) **:** having or furnished with a trellis
trel·lis·work \ˈtrel-ə-ˌswərk\ *n* (1712) **:** LATTICEWORK
trem·a·tode \ˈtrem-ə-ˌtōd\ *n* [deriv. of Gk *trēmatōdēs* pierced with holes, fr. *trēmat-, trēma* hole, fr. *tetrainein* to bore — more at THROW] (ca. 1864) **:** any of a class (Trematoda) of parasitic flatworms including the flukes — **trematode** *adj*
[1]trem·ble \ˈtrem-bəl\ *vi* **trem·bled; trem·bling** \-b(ə-)liŋ\ [ME *tremblen,* fr. MF *trembler,* fr. ML *tremulare,* fr. L *tremulus* tremulous, fr. *tremere* to tremble; akin to Gk *tremein* to tremble] (14c) **1 :** to shake involuntarily (as with fear or cold) **:** SHIVER **2 :** to move, sound, pass, or come to pass as if shaken or tremulous ⟨the building *trembled* from the blast⟩ **3 :** to be affected with fear or doubt ⟨~ for the safety of another⟩ — **trem·bler** \-b(ə-)lər\ *n*
[2]tremble *n* (1609) **1 :** an act or instance of trembling; *esp* **:** a fit or spell of involuntary shaking or quivering **2** *pl but sing in constr* **:** severe poisoning of livestock and esp. cattle by a toxic alcohol present in a snakeroot (*Eupatorium rugosum*) and several rayless goldenrods (esp. *Haplopappus heterophyllus*) that is characterized by muscular tremors, weakness, and constipation
trem·bly \ˈtrem-b(ə-)lē\ *adj* (1849) **:** marked by trembling **:** TREMULOUS
tre·men·dous \tri-ˈmen-dəs\ *adj* [L *tremendus,* fr. gerundive of *tremere*] (1632) **1 :** being such as may excite trembling or arouse dread, awe, or terror **2 a :** astonishing by reason of extreme size, power, greatness, or excellence **b :** unusually large **:** HUGE ***syn*** see MONSTROUS — **tre·men·dous·ly** *adv* — **tre·men·dous·ness** *n*
trem·o·lite \ˈtrem-ə-ˌlīt\ *n* [F *trémolite,* fr. *Tremola,* valley in Switzerland] (1799) **:** a white or gray mineral $Ca_2Mg_5Si_8O_{22}(OH)_2$ of the amphibole group that is a calcium magnesium silicate — **trem·o·lit·ic** \ˌtrem-ə-ˈlit-ik\ *adj*
trem·o·lo \ˈtrem-ə-ˌlō\ *n, pl* **-los** [It, fr. *tremolo* tremulous, fr. L *tremulus*] (ca. 1801) **1 a :** the rapid reiteration of a musical tone or of alternating tones to produce a tremulous effect **b :** vocal vibrato esp. when prominent or excessive **2 :** a mechanical device in an organ for causing a tremulous effect
trem·or \ˈtrem-ər\ *n* [ME *tremour,* fr. MF, L *tremor,* fr. *tremere*] (1615) **1 :** a trembling or shaking usu. from physical weakness, emotional stress, or disease **2 :** a quivering or vibratory motion; *esp* **:** a discrete small movement following or preceding a major seismic event **3 a :** a feeling of uncertainty or insecurity **b :** a cause of such a feeling
trem·u·lant \ˈtrem-yə-lənt\ *adj* [ML *tremulant-, tremulans,* prp. of *tremulare* — more at TREMBLE] (1837) **:** TREMULOUS, TREMBLING
trem·u·lous \-ləs\ *adj* [L *tremulus* — more at TREMBLE] (1611) **1 :** characterized by or affected with trembling or tremors **2 :** affected with timidity **:** TIMOROUS **3 :** such as is caused by a tremulous state ⟨~ handwriting⟩ **4 :** exceedingly sensitive **:** easily shaken or disordered — **trem·u·lous·ly** *adv* — **trem·u·lous·ness** *n*
[1]trench \ˈtrench\ *n* [ME *trenche* track cut through a wood, fr. MF, act of cutting, fr. *trenchier* to cut] (15c) **1 :** a long cut in the ground **:** DITCH; *esp* **:** one used for military defense often with the excavated dirt thrown up in front **2 :** a long, narrow, and usu. steep-sided depression in the ocean floor — compare TROUGH
[2]trench *vt* (15c) **1 :** to make a cut in **:** CARVE **2 a :** to protect with or as if with a trench **b :** to cut a trench in **:** DITCH ~ *vi* **1 a :** ENTRENCH, ENCROACH ⟨~*ing* on other domains which were more vital — Sir Winston Churchill⟩ **b :** to come close **:** VERGE **2 :** to dig a trench
tren·chan·cy \ˈtren-chən-sē\ *n* (1866) **:** the quality or state of being trenchant
tren·chant \-chənt\ *adj* [ME, fr. MF, prp. of *trenchier*] (14c) **1 :** KEEN, SHARP **2 :** vigorously effective and articulate ⟨a ~ analysis⟩; *also* **:** CAUSTIC ⟨~ remarks⟩ **3 a :** sharply perceptive **:** PENETRATING **b :** CLEAR-CUT, DISTINCT ⟨the ~ divisions between right and wrong — Edith Wharton⟩ — **tren·chant·ly** *adv*
trench coat *n* (1917) **1 :** a waterproof overcoat with a removable lining designed for wear in trenches **2 :** a double-breasted raincoat with deep pockets, wide belt, and straps on the shoulders
trenched \ˈtrencht\ *adj* (1541) **1 :** furrowed or drained by trenches **2 :** provided with protective trenches
[1]tren·cher \ˈtren-chər\ *n* [ME, fr. MF *trencheoir,* fr. *trenchier* to cut] (14c) **:** a wooden platter for serving food
[2]trencher *adj* (15c) **1 :** of or relating to a trencher or to meals **2** *archaic* **:** having the nature of a parasite **:** SYCOPHANTIC
tren·cher·man \ˈtren-chər-mən\ *n* (1590) **1 :** a hearty eater **2** *archaic* **:** HANGER-ON, SPONGER
trench fever *n* (1915) **:** a rickettsial disease marked by fever and pain in muscles, bones, and joints and transmitted by the body louse
trench foot *n* (1915) **:** a painful foot disorder resembling frostbite and resulting from exposure to cold and wet
trench knife *n* (1918) **:** a knife with a strong double-edged blade about eight inches long suited for use in hand-to-hand fighting
trench mouth *n* (ca. 1923) **1 :** VINCENT'S ANGINA **2 :** VINCENT'S INFECTION
trench warfare *n* (1917) **:** warfare in which the opposing forces attack and counterattack from a relatively permanent system of trenches protected by barbed-wire entanglements
[1]trend \ˈtrend\ *vi* [ME *trenden* to turn, revolve, fr. OE *trendan;* akin to MHG *trendel* disk, spinning top, OE *teran* to tear — more at TEAR] (1598) **1 a :** to extend in a general direction **:** follow a general course ⟨mountain ranges ~*ing* north and south⟩ **b :** to veer in a new direction **:** BEND ⟨coastline that ~*s* westward⟩ **2 a :** to show a tendency **:** INCLINE ⟨prices ~*ing* upward⟩ **b :** to become deflected **:** SHIFT ⟨opinions ~*ing* toward conservatism⟩
[2]trend *n* (1777) **1 :** a line of general direction or movement ⟨the ~ of the coast turned toward the west⟩ **2 a :** a prevailing tendency or inclination **:** DRIFT **b :** a general movement **:** SWING ⟨the ~ toward suburban living⟩ **c :** a current style or preference **:** VOGUE ⟨new fashion ~*s*⟩ **d :** a line of development **:** APPROACH **3 :** the general movement in the course of time of a statistically detectable change; *also* **:** a statistical curve reflecting such a change ***syn*** see TENDENCY
trend·set·ter \ˈtren(d)-ˌset-ər\ *n* (1964) **:** one that sets a trend
trendy \ˈtren-dē\ *adj* **trend·i·er; -est** (1965) **1 :** very fashionable **:** UP-TO-DATE ⟨he's a ~ dresser —*Sunday Mirror*⟩ **2 :** marked by ephemeral, superficial, or faddish appeal or taste — **trend·i·ly** \-də-lē\ *adv* — **trend·i·ness** \-dē-nəs\ *n*
[1]tre·pan \tri-ˈpan\ *vt* **tre·panned; tre·pan·ning** (15c) **1 :** to use a trephine on (the skull) **2 :** to remove a disk or cylindrical core (as from metal for testing) — **trep·a·na·tion** \ˌtrep-ə-ˈnā-shən\ *n*
[2]tre·pan \ˈtrē-ˌpan, tri-ˈpan\ *n* [ME *trepane* trephine, fr. ML *trepanum,* fr. Gk *trypanon* auger, fr. *trypan* to bore, fr. *trypa* hole; akin to Gk *tetrainein* to pierce — more at THROW] (1877) **:** a heavy tool used in boring mine shafts
[3]tre·pan \tri-ˈpan\ *n* [origin unknown] (1641) **1** *archaic* **:** TRICKSTER **2** *archaic* **:** a deceptive device **:** SNARE
[4]tre·pan \tri-ˈpan\ *vt* **tre·panned; tre·pan·ning** *archaic* (ca. 1656) **:** ENTRAP, LURE
tre·pang \tri-ˈpaŋ, ˈtrē-ˌ\ *n* [Malay *tĕripang*] (1783) **:** any of several large sea cucumbers (esp. genera *Actinopyga* and *Holothuria*) that are taken mostly in northern Australia and the East Indies, boiled, dried, and used esp. by the Chinese for making soup — called also *bêche-de-mer*
treph·i·na·tion \ˌtref-ə-ˈnā-shən\ *n* (1874) **:** an act or instance of perforating the skull with a surgical instrument
tre·phine \ˈtrē-ˌfīn\ *n* [F *tréphine,* fr. obs. E *trefine, trafine,* fr. L *tres fines* three ends, fr. *tres* three + *fines,* pl. of *finis* end — more at THREE] (1628) **:** a surgical instrument for cutting out circular sections (as of bone or corneal tissue) — **trephine** *vt*
trep·id \ˈtrep-əd\ *adj* [L *trepidus*] (1650) **:** TIMOROUS
trep·i·dant \ˈtrep-əd-ənt\ *adj* [L *trepidant-, trepidans,* prp. of *trepidare*] (1892) **:** TIMID, TREMBLING
trep·i·da·tion \ˌtrep-ə-ˈdā-shən\ *n* [L *trepidation-, trepidatio,* fr. *trepidatus,* pp. of *trepidare* to tremble, fr. *trepidus* agitated; akin to OE *thrafian* to urge, push, Gk *trapein* to press grapes] (1605) **1** *archaic* **:** a tremulous motion **:** TREMOR **2 :** timorous uncertain agitation **:** APPREHENSION ***syn*** see FEAR
trepo·ne·ma \ˌtrep-ə-ˈnē-mə\ *n, pl* **-ma·ta** \-mət-ə\ *or* **-mas** [NL *Treponemat-, Treponema,* deriv. of Gk *trepein* to turn + *nēma* thread, fr. *nēn* to spin — more at TROPE, NEEDLE] (ca. 1908) **:** any of a genus (*Treponema*) of spirochetes that parasitize man and other warm-blooded animals and include organisms causing syphilis and yaws — **trepo·ne·mal** \-məl\ *adj*
trepo·ne·ma·to·sis \-ˌnē-mə-ˈtō-səs, -ˌnem-ə-\ *n, pl* **-to·ses** \-ˌsēz\ [NL] (ca. 1941) **:** infection with or disease caused by treponemata
trepo·neme \ˈtrep-ə-ˌnēm\ *n* (1919) **:** TREPONEMA
[1]tres·pass \ˈtres-pəs, -ˌpas\ *n* [ME *trespas,* fr. OF, crossing, trespass, fr. *trespasser* to go across] (13c) **1 a :** a violation of moral or social ethics **:** TRANSGRESSION; *esp* **:** SIN **b :** an unwarranted infringement **2 a (1) :** an unlawful act committed on the person, property, or rights of another **(2) :** the action for injuries done by such an act **b :** the tort of wrongful entry on real property
[2]trespass *same;* -ˌpas *more often than for* [1]\ *vb* [ME *trespassen,* fr. MF *trespasser,* fr. OF, lit., to go across, fr. *tres* across (fr. L *trans*) + *passer* to pass — more at THROUGH, PASS] *vi* (14c) **1 a :** ERR, SIN **b :** to make an unwarranted or uninvited incursion **2 :** to commit a trespass; *esp* **:** to enter unlawfully upon the land of another ~ *vt* **:** VIOLATE ⟨~ the bounds of good taste⟩ — **tres·pass·er** *n*
syn TRESPASS, ENCROACH, ENTRENCH, INFRINGE, INVADE mean to make inroads upon the property, territory, or rights of another. TRESPASS implies an unwarranted, unlawful, or offensive intrusion; ENCROACH suggests gradual or stealthy entrance upon another's territory or usurpation of his rights or possessions; ENTRENCH suggests establishing and maintaining oneself in a position of advantage or profit at the

expense of others; INFRINGE implies an encroachment clearly violating a right or prerogative; INVADE implies a hostile and injurious entry into the territory or sphere of another.

tress \ˈtres\ *n* [ME *tresse,* fr. OF *trece*] (13c) **1 :** a long lock of hair; *esp* **:** the long unbound hair of a woman — usu. used in pl. **2** *archaic* **:** a plait of hair **:** BRAID

tressed \ˈtrest\ *adj* (14c) **1** *obs* **:** being braided **:** PLAITED **2 :** having tresses — usu. used in combination ⟨golden-*tressed*⟩

tres·tle *also* **tres·sel** \ˈtres-əl *also* ˈtrəs-\ *n* [ME *trestel,* fr. MF, modif. of (assumed) VL *transtellum,* fr. L *transtillum,* dim. of *transtrum* traverse beam, transom — more at TRANSOM] (14c) **1 :** HORSE 2b **2 :** a braced frame serving as a support **3 :** a braced framework of timbers, piles, or steelwork for carrying a road or railroad over a depression

tres·tle·tree \-(ˌ)trē\ *n* (ca. 1625) **:** either of a pair of timber crosspieces fixed fore and aft on the masthead to support the crosstrees, top, and fid of the mast — usu. used in pl.

tres·tle·work \-ˌwərk\ *n* (1848) **:** a system of connected trestles supporting a structure (as a bridge)

trews \ˈtrüz\ *n pl* [ScGael *triubhas*] (1568) **1 :** tight-fitting trousers usu. of tartan **2 :** close-cut tartan shorts worn under the kilt in Highland dress

trey \ˈtrā\ *n, pl* **treys** [ME *treye, treis,* fr. MF *treie, treis,* fr. L *tres* three] (14c) **1 :** the side of a die or domino that has three spots **2 :** a card numbered three or having three main pips

tri- *comb form* [ME, fr. L (fr. *tri-, tres*) & Gk, fr. *tri-, treis* — more at THREE] **1 :** three ⟨*tri*costate⟩ **:** having three elements or parts ⟨*tri*graph⟩ **2 :** into three ⟨*tri*sect⟩ **3 :** thrice ⟨*tri*weekly⟩ **:** every third ⟨*tri*monthly⟩

tri·able \ˈtrī-ə-bəl\ *adj* (15c) **:** liable or subject to judicial or quasi-judicial examination or trial — **tri·able·ness** *n*

tri·ac·e·tate \(ˈ)trī-ˈas-ə-ˌtāt\ *n* [ISV] (1860) **1 :** an acetate containing three CH_3COO groups **2 :** a textile fiber or fabric consisting of cellulose that is completely or almost completely acetylated

1**tri·ac·id** \-ˈas-əd\ *adj* [ISV] (ca. 1890) **1 :** able to react with three molecules of a monobasic acid or one of a triacid to form a salt or ester — used esp. of bases **2 :** containing three hydrogen atoms replaceable by basic atoms or groups — used esp. of acid salts

2**triacid** *n* (ca. 1930) **:** an acid having three acid hydrogen atoms

tri·ad \ˈtrī-ˌad *also* -əd\ *n* [L *triad-, trias,* fr. Gk, fr. *treis* three] (1546) **1 :** a union or group of three **:** TRINITY **2 :** a chord of three tones consisting of a root with its third and fifth and constituting the harmonic basis of tonal music — called also *common chord* — **tri·ad·ic** \trī-ˈad-ik\ *adj* — **tri·ad·i·cal·ly** \-i-k(ə-)lē\ *adv*

tri·age \trē-ˈäzh, ˈtrē-ˌ\ *n* [F, sorting, sifting, fr. *trier* to sort, fr. OF — more at TRY] (1918) **:** the sorting of and allocation of treatment to patients and esp. battle and disaster victims according to a system of priorities designed to maximize the number of survivors

1**tri·al** \ˈtrī(-ə)l\ *n* [AF, fr. *trier* to try] (1526) **1 a :** the action or process of trying or putting to the proof **:** TEST **b :** a preliminary contest (as in a sport) **2 :** the formal examination before a competent tribunal of the matter in issue in a civil or criminal cause in order to determine such issue **3 :** a test of faith, patience, or stamina by suffering or temptation; *broadly* **:** a source of vexation or annoyance **4 a :** a tryout or experiment to test quality, value, or usefulness **b :** one of a number of repetitions of an experiment **5 :** ATTEMPT

2**trial** *adj* (1555) **1 :** of, relating to, or used in a trial **2 :** made or done as a test or experiment **3 :** used or tried out in a test or experiment

trial and error *n* (1806) **:** a finding out of the best way to reach a desired result or a correct solution by trying out one or more ways or means and by noting and eliminating errors or causes of failure; *also* **:** the trying of this and that until something succeeds

trial balance *n* (1838) **:** a list of the debit and credit balances of accounts in a double-entry ledger at a given date prepared primarily to test their equality

trial balloon *n* (ca. 1934) **1 :** a balloon sent up to test air currents and wind velocity **2 :** a project or scheme tentatively announced in order to test public opinion

trial court *n* (1904) **:** the court before which issues of fact and law are first determined as distinguished from an appellate court

trial examiner *n* (1949) **:** a person appointed to hold hearings and to investigate and report facts sometimes with recommendations to an administrative or quasi-judicial agency or tribunal

trial horse *n* (1901) **:** one set up as an opponent for a champion in trial competitions or workouts

trial jury *n* (ca. 1889) **:** a jury impaneled to try a cause **:** PETIT JURY

trial lawyer *n* (ca. 1914) **:** a lawyer who engages chiefly in the trial of cases before courts of original jurisdiction

tri·alogue \ˈtrī-ə-ˌlȯg, -ˌläg\ *n* [*tri-* + *-alogue* (as in *dialogue*)] (1532) **:** a scene, discourse, or colloquy in which three persons share

trial run *n* (1933) **:** a testing exercise **:** EXPERIMENT

tri·am·cin·o·lone \ˌtrī-ˌam-ˈsin-ᵊl-ˌōn\ *n* [*tri-* + *am*yl + *cin*ene (a terpene) + predniso*lone*] (1958) **:** a corticoid drug $C_{21}H_{27}FO_6$ used esp. in treating psoriasis and allergic skin and respiratory disorders

tri·an·gle \ˈtrī-ˌaŋ-gəl\ *n* [ME, fr. L *triangulum,* fr. neut. of *triangulus* triangular, fr. *tri-* + *angulus* angle] (14c) **1 :** a polygon having three sides — compare SPHERICAL TRIANGLE **2 a :** a percussion instrument consisting of a rod of steel bent into the form of a triangle open at one angle and sounded by striking with a small metal rod **b :** a drafting instrument consisting of a thin flat right-angled triangle of wood or plastic with acute angles of 45 degrees or of 30 degrees and 60 degrees **3 :** a situation involving the love of two persons of one sex for one of the opposite sex with the resulting complications ⟨the eternal ∼⟩

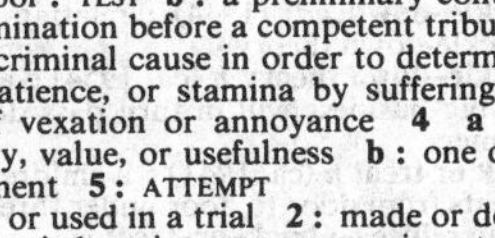

triangle 1: *1* equilateral, *2* isosceles, *3* scalene, *4* right-angled, *5* obtuse

triangle inequality *n* [fr. its application to the distances between three points in a coordinate system] (1965) **:** an inequality stating that the absolute value of a sum is less than or equal to the sum of the absolute value of the terms

tri·an·gu·lar \trī-ˈaŋ-gyə-lər\ *adj* [LL *triangularis,* fr. L *triangulum*] (1541) **1 a :** of, relating to, or having the form of a triangle ⟨a ∼ plot of land⟩ **b :** having a triangular base or principal surface ⟨a ∼ table⟩ ⟨a ∼ pyramid⟩ **2 a** (1) **:** of, relating to, or involving three elements ⟨the ∼ mother-father-child relationship⟩ (2) *of a military group* **:** based primarily on three units ⟨∼ division⟩ **b :** of or relating to a love triangle ⟨a ∼ love affair⟩ — **tri·an·gu·lar·i·ty** \(ˌ)trī-ˌaŋ-gyə-ˈlar-ət-ē\ *n* — **tri·an·gu·lar·ly** \trī-ˈaŋ-gyə-lər-lē\ *adv*

1**tri·an·gu·late** \trī-ˈaŋ-gyə-lət\ *adj* [ML *triangulatus,* pp. of *triangulare* to make triangles, fr. L *triangulum*] (1766) **:** consisting of or marked with triangles

2**tri·an·gu·late** \-ˌlāt\ *vt* **-lat·ed; -lat·ing** (1833) **1 :** to survey, map, or determine by triangulation **2 a :** to divide into triangles **b :** to give triangular form to

tri·an·gu·la·tion \(ˌ)trī-ˌaŋ-gyə-ˈlā-shən\ *n* (1818) **:** the measurement of the elements necessary to determine the network of triangles into which any part of the earth's surface is divided in surveying; *broadly* **:** any similar trigonometric operation for finding a position or location by means of bearings from two fixed points a known distance apart

tri·ar·chy \ˈtrī-ˌär-kē\ *n, pl* **-chies** [Gk *triarchia,* fr. *tri-* + *-archia* -archy] (ca. 1656) **1 :** government by three persons **:** TRIUMVIRATE **2 :** a country under three rulers

Tri·as·sic \trī-ˈas-ik\ *adj* [ISV, fr. L *trias* triad; fr. the three subdivisions of the European Triassic — more at TRIAD] (1841) **:** of, relating to, or being the earliest period of the Mesozoic era or the corresponding system of rocks — **Triassic** *n*

tri·ath·lete \trī-ˈath-ˌlēt\ *n* (1982) **:** an athlete who competes in a triathlon

tri·ath·lon \trī-ˈath-lən, -ˌlän\ *n* [*tri-* + *-athlon* (as in *decathlon*)] (1978) **:** an athletic contest that is a long-distance race consisting of three phases (as swimming, bicycling, and running)

tri·at·ic stay \(ˌ)trī-ˌat-ik-\ *n* [origin unknown] (ca. 1841) **:** a stay running horizontally between the heads of the foremast and mainmast

tri·atom·ic \ˌtrī-ə-ˈtäm-ik\ *adj* [ISV] (1862) **:** having three atoms in the molecule ⟨ozone is ∼ oxygen⟩

tri·ax·i·al \(ˈ)trī-ˈak-sē-əl\ *adj* [ISV] (1886) **:** having or involving three axes — **tri·ax·i·al·i·ty** \(ˌ)trī-ˌak-sē-ˈal-ət-ē\ *n*

tri·azine \ˈtrī-ə-ˌzēn, trī-ˈaz-ˌēn\ *n* [ISV] (1894) **:** any of three compounds $C_3H_3N_3$ containing a ring composed of three carbon and three nitrogen atoms; *also* **:** any of various derivatives of these including several used as herbicides

trib·al \ˈtrī-bəl\ *adj* (1632) **:** of, relating to, or characteristic of a tribe ⟨∼ customs⟩ — **trib·al·ly** \-bə-lē\ *adv*

trib·al·ism \-bə-ˌliz-əm\ *n* (1886) **1 :** tribal consciousness and loyalty; *esp* **:** exaltation of the tribe above other groups **2 :** strong in-group loyalty

tri·ba·sic \(ˈ)trī-ˈbā-sik\ *adj* (1837) **1 :** having three hydrogen atoms capable of replacement by basic atoms or groups — used of acids **2 :** containing three atoms of a univalent metal or their equivalent **3 :** having three basic hydroxyl groups and able to react with three molecules of a monobasic acid — used of bases and basic salts

tribe \ˈtrīb\ *n* [ME, fr. L *tribus,* a division of the Roman people, tribe] (13c) **1 a :** a social group comprising numerous families, clans, or generations together with slaves, dependents, or adopted strangers **b :** a political division of the Roman people orig. representing one of the three primitive tribes of ancient Rome **c :** PHYLE **2 :** a group of persons having a common character, occupation, or interest **3 :** a category of taxonomic classification sometimes equivalent to or ranking just below a suborder or ranking below a subfamily; *also* **:** a natural group irrespective of taxonomic rank ⟨the cat ∼⟩ ⟨rose ∼⟩

tribes·man \ˈtrībz-mən\ *n* (1798) **:** a member of a tribe

tribo- *comb form* [F, fr. Gk *tribein* to rub; akin to L *terere* to rub — more at THROW] **:** friction ⟨*tribo*luminescence⟩

tri·bo·elec·tric·i·ty \ˌtrī-bō-i-ˌlek-ˈtris-ət-ē, ˌtrib-ō-, -ˈtris-tē\ *n* (ca. 1917) **:** a charge of electricity generated by friction (as by rubbing glass with silk) — **tri·bo·elec·tric** \-ˈlek-trik\ *adj*

tri·bol·o·gy \trī-ˈbäl-ə-jē, trib-ˈäl-\ *n* [*tribo-*] (1966) **:** a study that deals with the design, friction, wear, and lubrication of interacting surfaces in relative motion (as in bearings or gears) — **tri·bo·log·i·cal** \ˌtrī-bə-ˈläj-i-kəl, ˌtrib-ə-\ *adj* — **tri·bol·o·gist** \trī-ˈbäl-ə-jəst, trib-ˈäl-\ *n*

tri·bo·lu·mi·nes·cence \ˈtrī-bō-ˌlü-mə-ˈnes-ᵊn(t)s, ˈtrib-ō-\ *n* [ISV] (1889) **:** luminescence due to friction — **tri·bo·lu·mi·nes·cent** \-ᵊnt\ *adj*

tri·bo·phys·ics \ˈtrī-bō-ˌfiz-iks, ˈtrib-ō-\ *n pl but sing or pl in constr* (1946) **:** the physics of friction

tri·brach \ˈtrī-ˌbrak\ *n* [L *tribrachys,* fr. Gk, having three short syllables, fr. *tri-* + *brachys* short — more at BRIEF] (1589) **:** a metrical foot of three short syllables of which two belong to the thesis and one to the arsis — **tri·brach·ic** \trī-ˈbrak-ik\ *adj*

trib·u·late \ˈtrib-yə-ˌlāt\ *vt* **-lat·ed; -lat·ing** [LL *tribulatus,* pp. of *tribulare*] (1637) **:** to cause to endure tribulation

trib·u·la·tion \ˌtrib-yə-ˈlā-shən\ *n* [ME *tribulacion,* fr. OF, fr. L *tribulation-, tribulatio,* fr. *tribulatus,* pp. of *tribulare* to press, oppress, perh. fr. *tribulum* drag used in threshing; akin to *terere* to rub — more at THROW] (13c) **:** distress or suffering resulting from oppression or persecution; *also* **:** a trying experience

tri·bu·nal \trī-ˈbyün-ᵊl, trib-ˈyün-\ *n* [L, platform for magistrates, fr. *tribunus* tribune] (1526) **1 :** 2TRIBUNE **2 :** a court or forum of justice **3 :** something that decides or determines ⟨the ∼ of public opinion⟩

tri·bu·nate \ˈtrib-yə-ˌnāt, trib-ˈyü-nət\ *n* (1546) **:** the office, function, or term of office of a tribune

1**tri·bune** \ˈtrib-ˌyün, trib-ˈ\ *n* [ME, fr. L *tribunus,* fr. *tribus* tribe] (14c) **1 :** a Roman official under the monarchy and the republic with the function of protecting the plebeian citizen from arbitrary action by the patrician magistrates **2 :** an unofficial defender of the rights of the individual — **tri·bune·ship** \-ˌship\ *n*

2**tribune** *n* [F, fr. It *tribuna,* fr. L *tribunal*] (1762) **:** a dais or platform from which an assembly is addressed

\ə\ abut \ᵊ\ kitten, F table \ər\ further \a\ ash \ā\ ace \ä\ cot, cart \au̇\ out \ch\ chin \e\ bet \ē\ easy \g\ go \i\ hit \ī\ ice \j\ job \ŋ\ sing \ō\ go \ȯ\ law \ȯi\ boy \th\ thin \t͟h\ the \ü\ loot \u̇\ foot \y\ yet \zh\ vision \à, k̲, ⁿ, œ, œ̄, ue, ue̅, ʸ\ *see* Guide to Pronunciation

1trib·u·tary \ˈtrib-yə-ˌter-ē\ *adj* [ME *tributarie,* fr. L *tributarius,* fr. *tributum* tribute] (14c) **1 :** paying tribute to another to acknowledge submission, to obtain protection, or to purchase peace : SUBJECT **2 :** paid or owed as tribute **3 :** channeling material or supplies into something more inclusive : CONTRIBUTORY

2tributary *n, pl* **-tar·ies** (15c) **1 :** a ruler or state that pays tribute to a conqueror **2 :** a stream feeding a larger stream or a lake

trib·ute \ˈtrib-(ˌ)yüt, -yət\ *n* [ME *tribut,* fr. L *tributum,* fr. neut. of *tributus,* pp. of *tribuere* to allot, bestow, grant, pay, fr. *tribus* tribe] (14c) **1 a :** a payment by one ruler or nation to another in acknowledgment of submission or as the price of protection; *also* **:** the tax levied for such a payment **b (1) :** an excessive tax, rental, or tariff imposed by a government, sovereign, lord, or landlord **(2) :** an exorbitant charge levied by a person or group having the power of coercion **c :** the liability to pay tribute **2 a :** something given or contributed voluntarily as due or deserved; *esp* **:** a gift or service showing respect, gratitude, or affection ⟨floral ~⟩ **b :** something (as material evidence or a formal attestation) that indicates the worth, virtue, or effectiveness of the one in question ⟨the vote was a ~ to their good sense⟩ ***syn*** see ENCOMIUM

tri·car·box·yl·ic \ˌtrī-ˌkär-ˌbäk-ˈsil-ik\ *adj* (1920) **:** containing three carboxyl groups in the molecule

tricarboxylic acid cycle *n* (1945) **:** KREBS CYCLE

1trice \ˈtrīs\ *vt* **triced; tric·ing** [ME *trisen, tricen* to pull, trice, fr. MD *trisen* to hoist] (15c) **:** to haul up or in and lash or secure (as a sail) with a small rope

2trice *n* [ME *trise,* lit., pull, fr. *trisen*] (15c) **:** a brief space of time **:** INSTANT — used chiefly in the phrase *in a trice*

tri·ceps \ˈtrī-ˌseps\ *n, pl* **tri·ceps·es** *also* **triceps** [NL *tricipit-, triceps,* fr. L, three-headed, fr. *tri-* + *capit-, caput* head — more at HEAD] (ca. 1704) **:** a muscle that arises from three heads; *esp* **:** the great extensor muscle along the back of the upper arm

tri·cer·a·tops \(ˈ)trī-ˈser-ə-ˌtäps\ *n* [NL, fr. *tri-* + *cerat-* + Gk *ōps* face — more at EYE] (1892) **:** any of a genus (*Triceratops*) of large herbivorous Cretaceous dinosaurs with three horns, a bony hood or crest on the neck, and hoofed toes

-trices *pl of* -TRIX

trich- *or* **tricho-** *comb form* [NL, fr. Gk, fr. *trich-, thrix* hair; akin to MIr gairb*driuch* bristle] **:** hair **:** filament ⟨*tricho*gyne⟩

tri·chi·a·sis \trik-ˈī-ə-səs\ *n* [LL, fr. Gk, fr. *trich* + *-iasis*] (ca. 1661) **:** a turning inward of the eyelashes often causing irritation of the eyeball

tri·chi·na \trik-ˈī-nə\ *n, pl* **-nae** \-(ˌ)nē\ *also* **-nas** [NL, fr. Gk *trichinos* made of hair, fr. *trich-, thrix* hair] (1857) **:** a small slender nematode worm (*Trichinella spiralis*) that in the larval state is parasitic in the voluntary muscles of flesh-eating mammals (as man and swine) — **tri·chi·nal** \-ˈīn-ᵊl\ *adj*

trich·i·nize \ˈtrik-ə-ˌnīz\ *vt* **-nized; -niz·ing** (1864) **:** to infest with trichinae ⟨*trichinized* pork⟩

trich·i·no·sis \ˌtrik-ə-ˈnō-səs\ *n* [NL] (1866) **:** infestation with or disease caused by trichinae and marked esp. by muscular pain, dyspnea, fever, and edema

tri·chi·nous \ˈtrik-ə-nəs, trik-ˈī-\ *adj* [ISV] (1857) **1 :** infested with trichinae ⟨~ meat⟩ **2 :** of, relating to, or involving trichinae or trichinosis ⟨~ infection⟩

trich·ite \ˈtrik-ˌīt\ *n* [G *trichit,* fr. Gk *trich-, thrix* hair] (ca. 1868) **:** a minute acicular body

tri·chlor·fon *also* **tri·chlor·phon** \(ˈ)trī-ˈklō(ə)r-ˌfän, -ˈklȯ(ə)r-\ *n* [*tri-* + *chlor-* + *-fon* (irreg. fr. *phosphonate* — a salt derived from phosphine)] (ca. 1960) **:** a crystalline compound $C_4H_8Cl_3O_4P$ used esp. as an insecticide

tri·chlo·ro·ace·tic acid \ˌtrī-ˌklōr-ō-ə-ˌsēt-ik-, -ˌklȯr-\ *n* [ISV] (ca. 1885) **:** a strong vesicant pungent acid $C_2Cl_3HO_2$ used in weed control and in medicine as a caustic and astringent

tri·chlo·ro·eth·y·lene \-ˈeth-ə-ˌlēn\ *n* [*tri-* + *chlor-* + *ethylene*] (ca. 1919) **:** a nonflammable liquid C_2HCl_3 used esp. as a solvent and in dry cleaning and removal of grease from metal

tricho·cyst \ˈtrik-ə-ˌsist\ *n* (ca. 1855) **:** any of the minute lassoing or stinging organs on the body of protozoans and esp. of many ciliates

tricho·gyne \-ˌjīn, -ˌgīn\ *n* [ISV] (ca. 1875) **:** a slender terminal prolongation of the ascogonium of a fungus or lichen that may serve as a fertilization tube; *also* **:** a similar reproductive structure in a red alga

tri·chol·o·gist \tri-ˈkäl-ə-jəst\ *n* (1887) **:** a person who cares for and dresses hair **:** HAIRDRESSER — **tri·chol·o·gy** \-jē\ *n*

tri·chome \ˈtrik-ˌōm, ˈtrī-ˌkōm\ *n* [G *trichom,* fr. Gk *trichōma* growth of hair, fr. *trichoun* to cover with hair, fr. *trich-, thrix* hair — more at TRICH-] (1875) **:** a filamentous outgrowth; *esp* **:** an epidermal hair structure on a plant

tricho·mo·na·cide \ˌtrik-ə-ˈmō-nə-ˌsīd\ *n* [*trichomonad* + *-cide*] (1949) **:** an agent used to destroy trichomonads — **tricho·mo·na·cid·al** \-ˌmō-nə-ˈsīd-ᵊl\ *adj*

tricho·mo·nad \ˌtrik-ə-ˈmō-ˌnad, -nəd\ *n* [NL *Trichomonad-, Trichomonas,* fr. *trich-* + LL *monad-, monas* monad] (1861) **:** any of a genus (*Trichomonas*) of flagellated protozoans parasitic in many animals including man — **trichomonad** *or* **tricho·mo·nal** \-ˈmōn-ᵊl\ *adj*

tricho·mo·ni·a·sis \ˌtrik-ə-mə-ˈnī-ə-səs\ *n, pl* **-a·ses** \-ˌsēz\ [NL, fr. *Trichomonas* + *-iasis*] (1917) **:** infection with or disease caused by trichomonads: as **a :** a human vaginitis characterized by a persistent discharge and caused by a trichomonad (*Trichomonas vaginalis*) that sometimes also invades the male urethra and bladder **b :** a venereal disease of domestic cattle marked by abortion and sterility **c :** one or more diseases of various birds resembling blackhead

tri·chop·ter·an \trik-ˈäp-tə-rən\ *n* [deriv. of Gk *trich-, thrix* hair + *pteron* wing — more at FEATHER] (ca. 1842) **:** any of an order (Trichoptera) of insects consisting of the caddis flies — **trichopteran** *adj*

tri·chot·o·mous \trī-ˈkät-ə-məs\ *adj* [LGk *trichotomein* to trisect, fr. Gk *tricha* in three (fr. *treis* three) + *-tomein* (akin to *temnein* to cut) — more at THREE, TOME] (1800) **:** divided or dividing into three parts or into threes ⟨~ branching⟩ — **tri·chot·o·mous·ly** *adv*

tri·chot·o·my \-mē\ *n, pl* **-mies** (1610) **:** division into three parts, elements, or classes

-tri·chous \tri-kəs\ *adj comb form* [Gk *-trichos,* fr. *trich-, thrix* hair — more at TRICH-] **:** having (such) hair ⟨peri*trichous*⟩

tri·chro·mat \ˈtrī-krō-ˌmat, (ˈ)trī-ˈ\ *n* [back-formation fr. *trichromatic*] (1931) **:** a person with normal color vision requiring that three primary colors be mixed in order to match the spectrum as he sees it

tri·chro·mat·ic \ˌtrī-krō-ˈmat-ik\ *adj* (ca. 1890) **1 :** of, relating to, or consisting of three colors ⟨~ light⟩ **2 a :** relating to or being the theory that human color vision involves three types of retinal sensory receptors **b :** characterized by trichromatism ⟨~ vision⟩

tri·chro·ma·tism \(ˈ)trī-ˈkrō-mə-ˌtiz-əm\ *n* (ca. 1890) **1 :** the quality or state of being trichromatic **:** the use of three colors (as in photography) **2 :** vision in which all of the fundamental colors are perceived though not necessarily with equal facility

1trick \ˈtrik\ *n* [ME *trik,* fr. ONF *trique,* fr. *trikier* to deceive, cheat] (15c) **1 a :** a crafty procedure or practice meant to deceive or defraud **b :** a mischievous act **:** PRANK **c :** an indiscreet or childish action **d :** a deceptive, dexterous, or ingenious feat designed to puzzle or amuse ⟨a juggler's ~*s*⟩ **2 a :** a habitual peculiarity of behavior or manner ⟨a horse with the ~ of shying⟩ **b :** a characteristic and identifying feature ⟨a ~ of speech⟩ **c :** a delusive appearance esp. when caused by art or legerdemain **:** an optical illusion ⟨a mere ~ of the light⟩ **3 a :** a quick or artful way of getting a result **:** KNACK **b :** a technical device (as of an art or craft) ⟨the ~*s* of stage technique⟩ **4 :** the cards played in one round of a card game often used as a scoring unit **5 a :** a turn of duty at the helm usu. lasting for two hours **b :** SHIFT 4b(1) **c :** a trip taken as part of one's employment **d :** a sexual act performed by a prostitute; *also* **:** JOHN 2 **6 :** an attractive child or pretty young woman ⟨a cute little ~⟩

syn TRICK, RUSE, STRATAGEM, MANEUVER, ARTIFICE, WILE, FEINT mean an indirect means to gain an end. TRICK may imply deception, roguishness, illusion, and either an evil or harmless end; RUSE stresses an attempt to mislead by a false impression; STRATAGEM implies a ruse used to entrap, outwit, circumvent, or surprise an opponent or enemy; MANEUVER suggests adroit and skillful avoidance of difficulty; ARTIFICE implies ingenious contrivance or invention; WILE suggests an attempt to entrap or deceive with false allurements; FEINT implies a diversion or distraction of attention away from one's real intent.

2trick *vt* (1500) **1 :** to dress or adorn fancifully or ornately **:** ORNAMENT ⟨~*ed* out in a gaudy uniform⟩ **2 :** to deceive by cunning or artifice **:** CHEAT ***syn*** see DUPE

3trick *adj* (1861) **1 a :** of or relating to or involving tricks or trickery ⟨~ photography⟩ ⟨~ dice⟩ **b :** skilled in or used for tricks ⟨a ~ horse⟩ **2 :** TRIG **3 a :** somewhat defective and unreliable ⟨a ~ lock⟩ **b :** inclined to give way unexpectedly ⟨a ~ knee⟩

trick·er \ˈtrik-ər\ *n* (1553) **:** one that tricks **:** TRICKSTER

trick·ery \ˈtrik-(ə-)rē\ *n* (1800) **:** the practice of crafty underhanded ingenuity to deceive or cheat ***syn*** see DECEPTION

trick·ish \ˈtrik-ish\ *adj* (1705) **:** given to or characterized by tricks or trickery **:** TRICKY — **trick·ish·ly** *adv* — **trick·ish·ness** *n*

1trick·le \ˈtrik-əl\ *vi* **trick·led; trick·ling** \-(ə-)liŋ\ [ME *triklen*] (14c) **1 a :** to issue or fall in drops **b :** to flow in a thin gentle stream **2 a :** to move or go one by one or little by little **b :** to dissipate slowly ⟨his enthusiasm *trickled* away⟩

2trickle *n* (ca. 1580) **:** a thin, slow, or intermittent stream or movement

trickle–down *adj* (1944) **:** relating to or working on the principle of trickle-down theory

trickle–down theory *n* (ca. 1954) **:** a theory that financial benefits given to big business will in turn pass down to smaller businesses and consumers

trick or treat *n* (ca. 1941) **:** a children's Halloween practice of asking for treats from door to door under threat of playing tricks on householders who refuse — **trick–or–treat** *vi*

trick·ster \ˈtrik-stər\ *n* (1711) **:** one who tricks: as **a :** a dishonest person who defrauds others by trickery **b :** a person (as a stage magician) skilled in the use of tricks and illusion

tricksy \ˈtrik-sē\ *adj* **tricks·i·er; -est** [*tricks,* pl. of *trick*] (1552) **1** *archaic* **:** smartly attired **:** SPRUCE **2 :** full of tricks **:** PRANKISH **3 a** *archaic* **:** having the craftiness of a trickster **b :** difficult to cope with or handle **:** TRYING ⟨a ~ job⟩ — **tricks·i·ness** *n*

tricky \ˈtrik-ē\ *adj* **trick·i·er; -est** (1786) **1 :** inclined to or marked by trickery **2 a :** giving a deceptive impression of easiness, simplicity, or order **:** TICKLISH ⟨a ~ path through the swamp⟩ **b :** TRICK 3 **3 :** requiring skill, knack, or caution (as in doing or handling); *also* **:** INGENIOUS ⟨a ~ rhythm⟩ ***syn*** see SLY — **trick·i·ly** \ˈtrik-ə-lē\ *adv* — **trick·i·ness** \ˈtrik-ē-nəs\ *n*

tri·clad \ˈtrī-ˌklad\ *n* [NL *Tricladida,* fr. *tri-* + Gk *klados* branch — more at GLADIATOR] (1888) **:** any of an order (Tricladida) of turbellarian flatworms (as a planarian) that have the intestine composed of a median anterior division and two lateral posterior divisions with side branches — **triclad** *adj*

tri·clin·ic \(ˈ)trī-ˈklin-ik\ *adj* [ISV] (1854) **:** having three unequal axes intersecting at oblique angles — used esp. of a crystal

tri·clin·i·um \trī-ˈklin-ē-əm\ *n, pl* **-ia** \-ē-ə\ [L, fr. Gk *triklinion,* fr. *tri-* + *klinein* to lean, recline — more at LEAN] (1646) **1 :** a couch used by ancient Romans for reclining at meals, extending round three sides of a table, and usu. divided into three parts **2 :** a dining room furnished with a triclinium

tric·o·lette \ˌtrik-ə-ˈlet\ *n* [*tricot* + *-lette* (as in *flannelette*)] (1919) **:** a usu. silk or rayon knitted fabric used esp. for women's clothing

1tri·col·or \ˈtrī-ˌkəl-ər *also* ˈtrē-, *esp Brit* ˈtrik-ə-lər\ *n* [F *tricolore,* fr. *tricolore* three-colored, fr. LL *tricolor,* fr. L *tri-* + *color* color] (1798) **:** a flag of three colors ⟨the French ~⟩

2tricolor *adj* [F *tricolore*] (1798) **1 a** *or* **tri·col·ored** \ˈtrī-ˈkəl-ərd\ **:** having or using three colors **b** *of a dog* **:** having a coat of black, tan, and white **2 :** of, relating to, or characteristic of a tricolor or a nation whose flag is a tricolor; *esp* **:** FRENCH

tri·corn \ˈtrī-ˌkȯ(ə)rn\ *adj* [L *tricornis*] (ca. 1844) **:** having three horns or corners

tri·corne *or* **tri·corn** \ˈtrī-ˌkȯ(ə)rn\ *n* [F *tricorne,* fr. *tricorne* three-cornered, fr. L *tricornis,* fr. *tri-* + *cornu* horn — more at HORN] (1876) **:** COCKED HAT 1

tri·cor·nered \ˈtrī-ˈkȯ(r)-nərd\ *adj* (1819) **:** having three corners

tri·cot \ˈtrē-(ˌ)kō, ˈtrī-kət\ *n* [F, fr. *tricoter* to knit, fr. MF, to agitate, hop, fr. OF *estriquier* to move actively, of Gmc origin; akin to OE *strican* to move, strike — more at STRIKE] (1872) **1 :** a plain warp-knitted fabric of nylon, wool, rayon, silk, or cotton with a close inelastic knit and used esp. in clothing (as underwear) **2 :** a twilled clothing fabric of wool with fine warp ribs or of wool and cotton with fine weft ribs

tri·co·tine \ˌtrik-ə-ˈtēn, ˌtrē-kə-\ *n* [F, fr. *tricot*] (ca. 1899) **:** a sturdy suiting woven of tightly twisted yarns in a double twill

tric·trac \ˈtrik-ˌtrak\ *n* [F] (1687) **:** an old form of backgammon played with pegs

1**tri·cus·pid** \(ˈ)trī-ˈkəs-pəd\ *adj* [L *tricuspid-, tricuspis,* fr. *tri-* + *cuspid-, cuspis* point] (1670) **:** having three cusps ⟨a ~ molar⟩

2**tricuspid** *n* (ca. 1860) **:** a tricuspid anatomical structure; *esp* **:** a tooth having three cusps

tricuspid valve *n* (1670) **:** a valve of three flaps that prevents reflux of blood from the right ventricle to the right atrium

tri·cy·cle \ˈtrī-ˌsik-əl\ *n* [F, fr. *tri-* + Gk *kyklos* wheel — more at WHEEL] (1868) **:** a 3-wheeled vehicle propelled by pedals, hand levers, or a motor

tri·cy·clic \(ˈ)trī-ˈsī-klik, -ˈsik-lik\ *adj* [*tri-* + *cyclic*] (1891) **:** being a chemical with three usu. fused rings in the molecular structure and esp. a tricyclic antidepressant

tricyclic antidepressant *n* (1966) **:** any of a group of antidepressant drugs (as imipramine, amitriptyline, desipramine, and nortriptyline) that potentiate the action of catecholamines and do not inhibit the action of monoamine oxidase — called also TRICYCLIC

1**tri·dent** \ˈtrīd-ᵊnt\ *adj* [L *trident-, tridens*] (1589) **:** having three teeth, processes, or points

2**trident** *n* [L *trident-, tridens,* fr. *trident-, tridens* having three teeth, fr. *tri-* + *dent-, dens* tooth — more at TOOTH] (1599) **1 :** a 3-pronged spear serving in classical mythology as the attribute of a sea god **2 :** a 3-pronged spear (as for fishing)

Tri·den·tine \trī-ˈden-ˌtīn, -ˌtēn; ˈtrīd-ᵊn-, ˈtrid-\ *adj* [NL *Tridentinus,* fr. L *Tridentum* Trent, Italy] (1561) **:** of or relating to a Roman Catholic Church council held at Trent from 1545 to 1563

tri·di·men·sion·al \ˌtrīd-ə-ˈmench-nəl, ˌtrīd-ī-, -ən-ᵊl\ *adj* [ISV] (1875) **:** of, relating to, or concerned with three dimensions ⟨~ space⟩ — **tri·di·men·sion·al·i·ty** \-ˌmen-chə-ˈnal-ət-ē\ *n*

trid·u·um \ˈtrij-ə-wəm, ˈtrid-yə-\ *n* [L, space of three days, fr. *tri-* + *-duum* (akin to *dies* day) — more at DEITY] (1883) **:** a period of three days of prayer usu. preceding a Roman Catholic feast

tried \ˈtrīd\ *adj* [ME, fr. pp. of *trien* to try, test] (15c) **1 :** found good, faithful, or trustworthy through experience or testing ⟨a ~ recipe⟩ **2 :** subjected to trials or distress ⟨a kind but much-*tried* father⟩

tried–and–true *adj* (1935) **:** proved good, desirable, or feasible **:** shown or known to be worthy ⟨a ~ sales technique⟩

tri·ene \ˈtrī-ˌēn\ *n* (ca. 1929) **:** a chemical compound containing three double bonds

tri·en·ni·al \(ˈ)trī-ˈen-ē-əl\ *adj* (1562) **1 :** consisting of or lasting for three years ⟨a ~ contract⟩ **2 :** occurring or being done every three years ⟨the ~ convention⟩ — **triennial** *n* — **tri·en·ni·al·ly** \-ē-ə-lē\ *adv*

tri·en·ni·um \trī-ˈen-ē-əm\ *n, pl* **-ni·ums** *or* **-nia** \-ē-ə\ [L, fr. *tri-* + *annus* year — more at ANNUAL] (1847) **:** a period of three years

tri·er \ˈtrī(-ə)r\ *n* (14c) **1 :** someone or something that tries **2 :** an implement (as a tapered hollow tube) used in obtaining samples of bulk material for examination and testing

tri·er·arch \ˈtrī(-ə)-ˌrärk\ *n* [L *trierarchus,* fr. Gk *triērarchos,* fr. *triērēs* trireme (fr. *tri-* + *-ērēs* — akin to L *remus* oar) + *-archos* -arch — more at ROW] (ca. 1656) **1 :** the commander of a trireme **2 :** an Athenian citizen who had to fit out a trireme for the public service

tri·er·ar·chy \-ˌrär-kē\ *n* (1837) **:** the ancient Athenian plan whereby individual citizens furnished and maintained triremes as a civic duty

tri·eth·yl \(ˈ)trī-ˈeth-əl\ *adj* [ISV] (ca. 1885) **:** containing three ethyl groups in the molecule

tri·fec·ta \trī-ˈfek-tə, ˈtrī-ˌ\ *n* [*tri-* + *perfecta*] (ca. 1974) **:** a variation of the perfecta in which a bettor wins by selecting the first three finishers of a race in the correct order of finish

tri·fid \ˈtrī-ˌfid, -fəd\ *adj* [L *trifidus* split into three, fr. *tri-* + *findere* to split — more at BITE] (ca. 1753) **:** being deeply and narrowly cleft into three teeth, processes, or points ⟨a spoon with a ~ top⟩

1**tri·fle** \ˈtrī-fəl\ *n* [ME *trufle, trifle,* fr. OF *trufe, trufle* mockery] (13c) **1 :** something of little value, substance, or importance **2 :** a dessert of many varieties typically including plain or sponge cake, sherry, rum, or brandy, jam or jelly, custard, and whipped cream — **a trifle :** to some small degree **:** SLIGHTLY ⟨*a trifle* annoyed⟩

2**trifle** *vb* **tri·fled; tri·fling** \-f(ə-)liŋ\ [ME *truflen, triflen,* fr. OF *trufer, trufler* to mock, trick] *vi* (14c) **1 a :** to talk in a jesting or mocking manner or with intent to delude or mislead **b :** to treat someone or something as unimportant **2 :** to handle something idly ~ *vt* **:** to spend or waste in trifling or on trifles — **tri·fler** \-f(ə-)lər\ *n*

syn TRIFLE, TOY, DALLY, FLIRT, COQUET mean to deal with or act toward without serious purpose. TRIFLE may imply playfulness, unconcern, indulgent contempt; TOY implies acting without full attention or serious exertion of one's powers; DALLY suggests indulging in thoughts or plans merely as an amusement; FLIRT implies an interest or attention that soon passes to another object; COQUET implies attracting interest or admiration without serious intention.

tri·fling \ˈtrī-fliŋ\ *adj* (1535) **:** lacking in significance or solid worth: as **a :** FRIVOLOUS ⟨~ talk⟩ **b :** TRIVIAL ⟨a ~ gift⟩ **c** *chiefly dial* **:** LAZY, SHIFTLESS ⟨a ~ fellow⟩

tri·fluo·per·a·zine \ˌtrī-ˌflü-ō-ˈper-ə-ˌzēn, -zən\ *n* [*tri-* + *fluor-* + *piperazine*] (ca. 1957) **:** a phenothiazine tranquilizer $C_{21}H_{24}F_3N_3S$ used esp. in the treatment of psychotic conditions (as schizophrenia) — compare STELAZINE

tri·flu·ra·lin \trī-ˈflu̇r-ə-lən\ *n* [*tri-* + *fluor-* + *aniline*] (ca. 1961) **:** an herbicide $C_{13}H_{16}F_3N_3O_4$ used in the control of weeds (as pigweed and annual grasses)

1**tri·fo·cal** \(ˈ)trī-ˈfō-kəl\ *adj* (1947) **:** having three focal lengths

2**trifocal** *n* (ca. 1948) **1 :** a trifocal glass or lens **2** *pl* **:** eyeglasses with trifocal lenses

tri·fo·li·ate \(ˈ)trī-ˈfō-lē-ət\ *adj* (ca. 1798) **1 :** having three leaves ⟨a ~ plant⟩ **2 :** TRIFOLIOLATE

trifoliate orange *n* (ca. 1900) **:** a hardy deciduous Chinese orange (*Poncirus trifoliata*) with trifoliolate leaves that is widely grown for ornament and esp. as a stock for budding other oranges

tri·fo·li·o·late \(ˈ)trī-ˈfō-lē-ə-ˌlāt\ *adj* [ISV] (ca. 1828) **:** having three leaflets ⟨a ~ leaf⟩

tri·fo·li·um \trī-ˈfō-lē-əm\ *n* [NL, fr. L, trefoil — more at TREFOIL] (1541) **:** any of a genus (*Trifolium*) of leguminous herbs comprising the typical clovers

tri·fo·ri·um \trī-ˈfōr-ē-əm, -ˈfȯr-\ *n, pl* **-ria** \-ē-ə\ [ML] (1703) **:** a gallery forming an upper story to the aisle of a church and typically an arcaded story between the nave arches and clerestory

tri·form \ˈtrī-ˌfȯrm\ *adj* [L *triformis,* fr. *tri-* + *forma* form] (15c) **:** having a triple form or nature

tri·fur·cate \(ˈ)trī-ˈfər-kət, -ˌkāt; ˈtrī-(ˌ)fər-ˌkāt\ *adj* [L *trifurcus,* fr. *tri-* + *furca* fork] (ca. 1811) **:** having three branches or forks **:** TRICHOTOMOUS — **tri·fur·cate** \ˈtrī-(ˌ)fər-ˌkāt, trī-ˈfər-\ *vi* — **tri·fur·ca·tion** \ˌtrī-(ˌ)fər-ˈkā-shən\ *n*

1**trig** \ˈtrig\ *adj* [ME, trusty, nimble, of Scand origin; akin to ON *tryggr* faithful; akin to OE *trēowe* faithful — more at TRUE] (1513) **1 :** stylishly or jauntily trim **2 :** extremely precise **:** PRIM **3** *dial chiefly Brit* **:** FIRM, VIGOROUS

2**trig** *n* [by shortening] (1899) **:** TRIGONOMETRY

tri·gem·i·nal \trī-ˈjem-ən-ᵊl\ *adj* [NL *trigeminus* trigeminal nerve, fr. L, threefold, fr. *tri-* + *geminus* twin] (1830) **:** of or relating to the trigeminal nerve

trigeminal nerve *n* (1830) **:** either of a pair of large mixed nerves that are the 5th cranial nerves and supply motor and sensory fibers mostly to the face — called also *trigeminal*

trigeminal neuralgia *n* (1874) **:** an intense paroxysmal neuralgia involving one or more branches of the trigeminal nerve

1**trig·ger** \ˈtrig-ər\ *n* [alter. of earlier *tricker,* fr. D *trekker,* fr. MD *trecker* one that pulls, fr. *trecken* to pull — more at TREK] (1621) **1 a :** a piece (as a lever) connected with a catch or detent as a means of releasing it; *esp* **:** the part of the action moved by the finger to fire a gun **b :** a similar movable part by which a mechanism is actuated ⟨~ of a spray gun⟩ **2 :** something that acts like a mechanical trigger in initiating a process or reaction — **trigger** *adj* — **trig·gered** \-ərd\ *adj*

2**trigger** *vb* **trig·gered; trig·ger·ing** \ˈtrig-(ə-)riŋ\ *vt* (1916) **1 a :** to release or activate by means of a trigger; *esp* **:** to fire by pulling a mechanical trigger ⟨~ a rifle⟩ **b :** to cause the explosion of ⟨~ a missile with a proximity fuze⟩ **2 :** to initiate, actuate, or set off by a trigger ⟨an indiscreet remark that ~*ed* a fight⟩ ⟨a stimulus that ~*ed* a reflex⟩ ~ *vi* **:** to release a mechanical trigger

trig·ger·fish \ˈtrig-ər-ˌfish\ *n* (ca. 1882) **:** any of numerous deep-bodied fishes (family Balistidae, esp. genus *Balistes*) of warm seas having an anterior dorsal fin with two or three stout erectile spines

trig·ger–hap·py \-ˌhap-ē\ *adj* (1943) **1 :** irresponsible in the use of firearms; *esp* **:** inclined to shoot before clearly identifying the target **2 a :** inclined to be irresponsible in matters that might precipitate war **b :** aggressively belligerent in attitude

trig·ger·man \-mən, -ˌman\ *n* (ca. 1925) **:** a gunman who shoots the victim (as in a gangland murder)

tri·glyc·er·ide \(ˈ)trī-ˈglis-ə-ˌrīd\ *n* [ISV] (ca. 1860) **:** an ester of glycerol that contains three ester groups and involves one, two, or three acids

tri·glyph \ˈtrī-ˌglif\ *n* [L *triglyphus,* fr. Gk *triglyphos,* fr. *tri-* + *glyphein* to carve — more at CLEAVE] (1563) **:** a slightly projecting rectangular tablet in a Doric frieze with two vertical channels of V section and two corresponding chamfers or half channels on the vertical sides — **tri·glyph·ic** \trī-ˈglif-ik\ *or* **tri·glyph·i·cal** \-i-kəl\ *adj*

tri·gon \ˈtrī-ˌgän\ *n* [L *trigonum,* fr. Gk *trigōnon,* fr. neut. of *trigōnos* triangular, fr. *tri-* + *gōnia* angle — more at -GON] (1563) **:** TRIPLICITY 1

tri·go·nal \trī-ˈgōn-ᵊl\ *adj* (1878) **:** of, relating to, or being the division of the hexagonal crystal system or the forms belonging to it characterized by a vertical axis of threefold symmetry — **tri·go·nal·ly** \-ᵊl-ē\ *adv*

trig·o·no·met·ric \ˌtrig-ə-nə-ˈme-trik\ *also* **trig·o·no·met·ri·cal** \-tri-kəl\ *adj* (1690) **:** of, relating to, or being in accordance with trigonometry — **trig·o·no·met·ri·cal·ly** \-tri-k(ə-)lē\ *adv*

trigonometric function *n* (1909) **1 :** a function (as the sine, cosine, tangent, cotangent, secant, or cosecant) of an arc or angle most simply expressed in terms of the ratios of pairs of sides of a right-angled triangle — called also *circular function* **2 :** the inverse (as the arcsine, arccosine, arctangent, arccotangent, arcsecant, or arccosecant) of a trigonometric function

trig·o·nom·e·try \ˌtrig-ə-ˈnäm-ə-trē\ *n* [NL *trigonometria,* fr. Gk *trigōnon* + *-metria* -metry] (ca. 1614) **:** the study of the properties of triangles and trigonometric functions and of their applications

tri·gram \ˈtrī-ˌgram\ *n* (1606) **1 :** TRIGRAPH 2 **2 :** any of the eight possible combinations of three whole or broken lines used esp. in Chinese divination

tri·graph \ˈtrī-ˌgraf\ *n* (ca. 1836) **1 :** three letters spelling a single consonant, vowel, or diphthong ⟨*eau* of *beau* is a ~⟩ **2 :** a cluster of three successive letters ⟨the letters *the* are a high frequency ~⟩ — **tri·graph·ic** \(ˈ)trī-ˈgraf-ik\ *adj*

tri·he·dral \(ˈ)trī-ˈhē-drəl\ *adj* (1789) **1 :** having three faces ⟨~ angle⟩ **2 :** of or relating to a trihedral angle — **trihedral** *n*

tri·hy·brid \-ˈhī-brəd\ *n* (1903) **:** an individual or strain that is heterozygous for three pairs of genes — **trihybrid** *adj*

tri·hy·droxy \ˌtrī-hī-ˌdräk-sē, -hə-\ *adj* [ISV] (ca. 1903) **:** containing three hydroxyl groups in the molecule

tri·io·do·thy·ro·nine \ˌtrī-ˌī-əd-ō-ˈthī-rə-ˌnēn\ *n* [*tri-* + *iod-* + *thyronine* (an amino acid of which thyroxine is a derivative)] (1954) **:** an iodine-containing amino acid $C_{15}H_{12}I_3NO_4$ that is made synthetically, may be formed naturally from thyroxine by loss of one iodine atom per molecule, and is used esp. in the treatment of hypothyroidism

tri·jet \ˈtrī-ˌjet\ *n* (1967) **:** an aircraft powered with three jet engines — **trijet** *adj*

tri·lat·er·al \(ˈ)trī-ˈlat-ə-rəl, -ˈla-trəl\ *adj* [L *trilaterus,* fr. *tri-* + *later-, latus* side] (1660) **:** having three sides or parties ⟨~ business ventures⟩

tril·by \ˈtril-bē\ *n, pl* **trilbies** [fr. the fact that such a hat was worn in the London stage version of *Trilby,* novel by George du Maurier] *chiefly Brit* (1897) **:** a soft felt hat with indented crown

tri·lin·ear \(ˈ)trī-ˈlin-ē-ər\ *adj* (1715) **:** of, relating to, or involving three lines ⟨~ coordinates⟩

tri·lin·gual \(ˈ)trī-ˈliŋ-g(yə-)wəl\ *adj* (1834) **:** consisting of, having, or expressed in three languages; *also* **:** familiar with or able to use three languages — **tri·lin·gual·ly** \-ē\ *adv*

¹tri·lit·er·al \-ˈlit-ə-rəl, -ˈli-trəl\ *adj* [*tri-* + L *littera* letter] (1751) **:** consisting of three letters and esp. of three consonants ⟨~ roots in Semitic languages⟩ — **tri·lit·er·al·ism** \-ˌiz-əm\ *n*

²triliteral *n* (ca. 1828) **:** a root or word that is triliteral

¹trill \ˈtril\ *vb* [ME *trillen*, prob. of Scand origin; akin to Sw *trilla* to roll; akin to MD *trillen* to vibrate] *vi* (14c) **1 :** to flow in a small stream or in drops **:** TRICKLE **2 :** TWIRL, REVOLVE **~** *vt* **:** to cause to flow in a small stream

²trill *n* [It *trillo*, fr. *trillare* to trill, prob. fr. D *trillen* to vibrate; akin to MD *trappe* step, trap] (1649) **1 a :** the alternation of two musical tones a diatonic second apart — called also *shake* **b :** VIBRATO **c :** a rapid reiteration of the same tone esp. on a percussion instrument **2 :** a sound resembling a musical trill **:** WARBLE **3 a :** the rapid vibration of one speech organ against another (as of the tip of the tongue against the teethridge) **b :** a speech sound made by a trill

³trill *vi* (1666) **:** to play or sing with a trill **:** QUAVER **~** *vt* **:** to utter as or with or as if with a trill ⟨~ the *r*⟩ — **trill·er** *n*

tril·lion \ˈtril-yən\ *n* [F, fr. *tri-* + *-illion* (as in *million*)] (ca. 1690) **1** — see NUMBER table **2 :** a very large number — **trillion** *adj* — **tril·lionth** \-yən(t)th\ *adj or n*

tril·li·um \ˈtril-ē-əm\ *n* [NL, fr. Sw *trilling* triplet; fr. its three leaves] (ca. 1760) **:** any of a genus (*Trillium*) of herbs of the lily family with short rootstocks and an erect stem bearing a whorl of three leaves and a large solitary flower

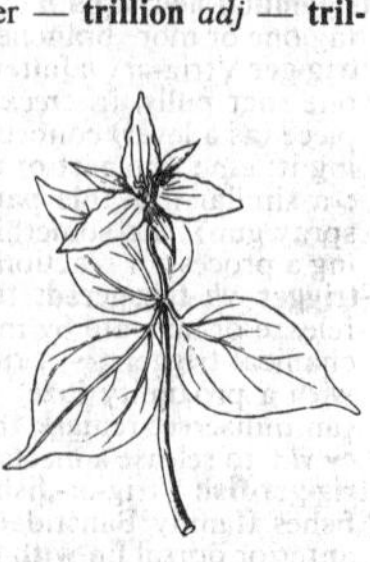

trillium

tri·lo·bate \(ˈ)trī-ˈlō-ˌbāt\ *adj* (1785) **:** TRILOBED

tri·lobed \ˈtrī-ˈlōbd\ *adj* (1826) **:** having three lobes ⟨a ~ leaf⟩

tri·lo·bite \ˈtrī-lə-ˌbīt\ *n* [deriv. of Gk *trilobos* three-lobed, fr. *tri-* + *lobos* lobe] (1832) **:** any of numerous extinct Paleozoic marine arthropods (group Trilobita) having the segments of the body divided by furrows on the dorsal surface into three lobes

tril·o·gy \ˈtril-ə-jē\ *n, pl* **-gies** [Gk *trilogia*, fr. *tri-* + *-logia* -logy] (ca. 1661) **:** a series of three dramas or literary works or sometimes three musical compositions that are closely related and develop a single theme

¹trim \ˈtrim\ *vb* **trimmed; trim·ming** [(assumed) ME *trimmen* to prepare, put in order, fr. OE *trymian, trymman* to strengthen, arrange, fr. *trum* strong, firm; akin to Skt *dāru* wood — more at TREE] *vt* (1516) **1 :** to embellish with or as if with ribbons, lace, or ornaments ⟨~ the Christmas tree⟩ ⟨the coat was *trimmed* with fur⟩ **2 a :** to administer a beating to **:** THRASH **b :** DEFEAT ⟨*trimmed* him at chess⟩ **3 a :** to make trim and neat esp. by cutting or clipping ⟨~ the hedges⟩ **b :** to free of excess or extraneous matter by or as if by cutting ⟨~ a budget⟩ ⟨~ down the inventory⟩ **c :** to remove by or as if by cutting ⟨*trimmed* thousands from federal payrolls —*Grit*⟩ **4 a (1) :** to cause (as a ship) to assume a desirable position in the water by arrangement of ballast, cargo, or passengers **(2) :** to adjust (as an airplane or submarine) for horizontal movement or for motion upward or downward **b :** to adjust (as cargo or a sail) to a desired position **5 :** to adjust (as one's opinions) for reasons of expediency — often used in the phrase *trim one's sails* **~** *vi* **1 a :** to maintain neutrality between opposing parties or to favor each equally **b :** to change one's views for reasons of expediency **2 :** to assume or cause a boat to assume a desired position in the water ⟨a boat that ~s badly⟩

²trim *adj* **trim·mer; trim·mest** (1521) **1 :** ready for service or use; *also* **:** in good physical condition ⟨keeps ~ by jogging⟩ **2** *obs* **:** EXCELLENT, FINE **3 :** exhibiting neatness, good order, or compactness of line or structure ⟨~ houses⟩ — **trim·ly** *adv* — **trim·ness** *n*

³trim *adv* (1529) **:** in a trim manner **:** TRIMLY — used chiefly in combination ⟨the *trim*-cut forest vistas —W. M. Thackeray⟩

⁴trim *n* (1590) **1 :** suitable or excellent condition ⟨tries to keep in ~⟩ **2 a :** one's clothing or appearance **b :** material used for ornament or trimming **c :** the lighter woodwork in the finish of a building esp. around openings **d :** the interior furnishings of an automobile **3 a :** the position of a ship or boat esp. with reference to the horizontal; *also* **:** the difference between the draft of a ship forward and that aft **b :** the relation between the plane of a sail and the direction of the ship **c :** the buoyancy status of a submarine **d :** the attitude of a lighter-than-air craft relative to a fore-and-aft horizontal plane **e :** the attitude with respect to wind axes at which an airplane will continue in level flight with free controls **4 :** something that is trimmed off or cut out

tri·ma·ran \ˈtrī-mə-ˌran, ˌtrī-mə-ˈ\ *n* [*tri-* + *-maran* (as in *catamaran*)] (1952) **:** a fast pleasure sailboat with three hulls side by side

tri·mer \ˈtrī-mər\ *n* [ISV] (ca. 1930) **:** a polymer formed from three molecules of a monomer — **tri·mer·ic** \trī-ˈmer-ik\ *adj*

trim·er·ous \ˈtrim-ə-rəs\ *adj* [NL *trimerus*, fr. Gk *tri-* + *meros* part — more at MERIT] (1826) **:** having the parts in threes — used of a flower and often written *3-merous*

tri·mes·ter \(ˈ)trī-ˈmes-tər, ˈtrī-ˌ\ *n* [F *trimestre*, fr. L *trimestris* of three months, fr. *tri-* + *mensis* month — more at MOON] (1821) **1 :** a period of three or about three months; *esp* **:** any of three periods of approximately three months each into which a human pregnancy is divided **2 :** one of three terms into which the academic year is sometimes divided

trim·e·ter \ˈtrim-ət-ər\ *n* [L *trimetrus*, fr. Gk *trimetros* having three measures, fr. *tri-* + *metron* measure — more at MEASURE] (ca. 1567) **:** a line of verse consisting of three dipodies or three metrical feet

tri·meth·o·prim \trī-ˈmeth-ə-ˌprim\ *n* [*tri-* + *meth-* + *-prim* (by shortening & alter. fr. *pyrimidine*)] (ca. 1964) **:** a synthetic antibacterial and antimalarial drug $C_{14}H_{18}N_4O_3$

tri·met·ro·gon \trī-ˈme-trə-ˌgän\ *n* [*tri-* + Gk *metron* measure + E *-gon*] (1943) **:** a system of aerial mapping involving the use of sets of one vertical and two oblique aerial photographs taken simultaneously over the area being mapped

trim·mer \ˈtrim-ər\ *n* (1555) **1 a (1) :** one that trims articles **(2) :** one that stows coal or freight on a ship so as to distribute the weight properly **b :** an instrument or machine with which trimming is done **c :** a circuit element (as a condenser) used to tune a circuit to a desired frequency **2 :** a beam that receives the end of a header in floor framing **3 :** a person who modifies his policy, position, or opinions out of expediency

trim·ming *n* (1519) **1 :** DEFEAT, BEATING **2 :** the act of one who trims **3 a :** a decorative accessory or additional item ⟨~s for a hat⟩ **b :** an additional garnishing ⟨turkey and all the ~s⟩

tri·month·ly \(ˈ)trī-ˈmən(t)th-lē\ *adj* (1856) **:** occurring every three months

tri·mor·phic \(ˈ)trī-ˈmȯr-fik\ *adj* [Gk *trimorphos* having three forms, fr. *tri-* + *-morphos* -morphous] (1866) **:** occurring in or having three distinct forms

tri·mo·tor \ˈtrī-ˌmōt-ər, -ˈmōt-\ *n* (1923) **:** an airplane powered by three engines

trim size *n* (ca. 1929) **:** the actual size (as of a book page) after excess material required in production has been cut off

Tri·mur·ti \tri-ˈmu̇(ə)rt-ē\ *n* [Skt *-trimūrti*, fr. *trimūrti* having three forms, fr. *tri-* tri- + *mūrti* body, form] (1810) **:** the great triad of Hindu gods comprising Brahma, Vishnu, and Siva

tri·nal \ˈtrīn-ᵊl\ *adj* [LL *trinalis*, fr. L *trini* three each — more at TRINE] (1590) **:** THREEFOLD

tri·na·ry \ˈtrī-nə-rē\ *adj* [LL *trinarius*, fr. L *trini*] (15c) **:** TERNARY

¹trine \ˈtrīn\ *adj* [ME, fr. MF *trin*, fr. L *trinus*, back-formation fr. *trini* three each; akin to L *tres* three — more at THREE] (14c) **1 :** THREEFOLD, TRIPLE **2 :** of, relating to, or being the favorable astrological aspect of two celestial bodies 120 degrees apart

²trine *n* (1552) **1 :** a group of three **:** TRIAD **2 :** the trine astrological aspect of two celestial bodies

trine immersion *n* (1637) **:** the practice of immersing a candidate for baptism three times in the names of the members of the Trinity

trin·i·tar·i·an \ˌtrin-ə-ˈter-ē-ən\ *adj* (1628) **1** *cap* **:** of or relating to the Trinity, the doctrine of the Trinity, or adherents to that doctrine **2 :** having three parts or aspects **:** THREEFOLD

Trinitarian *n* (ca. 1628) **1 :** a member of a religious teaching and nursing order for men founded in France in 1198 by John of Matha and Philip of Valois **2 :** one who subscribes to the doctrine of the Trinity — **Trin·i·tar·i·an·ism** \-ē-ə-ˌniz-əm\ *n*

tri·ni·tro·tol·u·ene \ˌtrī-ˌnī-trō-ˈtäl-yə-ˌwēn\ *n* [ISV] (ca. 1900) **:** a flammable toxic compound $C_7H_5N_3O_6$ obtained by nitrating toluene and used as a high explosive and in chemical synthesis — called also *TNT*

Trin·i·ty \ˈtrin-ət-ē\ *n* [ME *trinite*, fr. OF *trinité*, fr. LL *trinitat-, trinitas* state of being threefold, fr. L *trinus* trine] (13c) **1 :** the unity of Father, Son, and Holy Spirit as three persons in one Godhead according to Christian dogma **2** *not cap* **:** a group of three closely related persons or things **3 :** the Sunday after Whitsunday observed as a feast in honor of the Trinity

Trin·i·ty·tide \-ˌtīd\ *n* (1511) **:** the season of the church year between Trinity Sunday and Advent

¹trin·ket \ˈtriŋ-kət\ *n* [perh. fr. ME *trenket* small knife, fr. ONF *trenquet*] (1533) **1 :** a small ornament (as a jewel or ring) **2 :** a small article of equipment **3 :** a thing of little value **:** TRIFLE

²trinket *vi* [perh. fr. ¹*trinket*] (1646) **:** to deal clandestinely **:** INTRIGUE — **trin·ket·er** *n*

trin·ket·ry \-kə-trē\ *n* (1810) **:** small items of personal ornament

trin·oc·u·lar \(ˈ)trī-ˈnäk-yə-lər\ *adj* [alter. (influenced by *binocular*) of earlier *triocular*] (1960) **:** relating to or being a binocular microscope equipped with a lens for photographic recording during direct visual observation

¹tri·no·mi·al \trī-ˈnō-mē-əl\ *n* [*tri-* + *-nomial* (as in *binomial*)] (ca. 1674) **1 :** a polynomial of three terms **2 :** a trinomial name

²trinomial *adj* (ca. 1704) **1 :** consisting of three mathematical terms **2 :** of, relating to, or being biological taxa of three terms of which the first designates the genus, the second the species, and the third the subspecies or variety

tri·nu·cle·o·tide \(ˈ)trī-ˈn(y)ü-klē-ə-ˌtīd\ *n* (ca. 1923) **:** a nucleotide consisting of three mononucleotides in combination **:** CODON

trio \ˈtrē-(ˌ)ō\ *n, pl* **tri·os** [F, fr. It, fr. *tri-* (fr. L)] (ca. 1724) **1 a :** a musical composition for three voice parts or three instruments **b :** the secondary or episodic division of a minuet or scherzo, a march, or of various dance forms **2 :** the performers of a musical or dance trio **3 :** a group or set of three

tri·ode \ˈtrī-ˌōd\ *n* (1922) **:** an electron tube with an anode, a cathode, and a controlling grid

tri·ol \ˈtrī-ˌȯl, -ˌōl\ *n* (1936) **:** a chemical compound containing three hydroxyl groups

tri·o·let \ˈtrē-ə-lət, ˈtrī-\ *n* [F, prob. dim. of It *trio*] (1651) **:** a poem or stanza of eight lines in which the first line is repeated as the fourth and seventh and the second line as the eighth with a rhyme scheme of *ABaAabAB*

tri·ose \ˈtrī-ˌōs, -ˌōz\ *n* [ISV] (1894) **:** either of two simple sugars $C_3H_6O_3$ containing three carbon atoms

tri·ox·ide \(ˈ)trī-ˈäk-ˌsīd\ *n* [ISV] (ca. 1868) **:** an oxide containing three atoms of oxygen

¹trip \ˈtrip\ *vb* **tripped; trip·ping** [ME *trippen*, fr. MF *triper*, of Gmc origin; akin to OE *treppan* to tread — more at TRAP] *vi* (14c) **1 a :** to dance, skip, or caper with light quick steps **b :** to walk with light quick steps **2 :** to catch the foot against something so as to stumble **3 :** to make a mistake or false step (as in morality or accuracy) **4 :** to stumble in articulation when speaking **5 :** to make a journey **6 :** to run past the pallet of an escapement without previously locking — used of a tooth of the escapement wheel of a watch **7 a :** to actuate a mechanism **b :** to become operative **8 :** to get high on a psychedelic drug (as LSD) **:** TURN ON — often used with *out* **~** *vt* **1 a :** to cause to stumble **b :** to cause to fail **:** OBSTRUCT **2 :** to detect in a misstep, fault, or blunder; *also* **:** EXPOSE **3** *archaic* **:** to perform (as a dance) lightly or nimbly **4 :** to raise (an anchor) from the bottom so as to hang free **5 a :** to pull (a yard) into a perpendicular position for lowering **b :** to hoist (a topmast) far enough to enable the fid to be withdrawn preparatory to housing or lowering **6 :** to release or operate (a mechanism) esp. by releasing a catch or detent

²trip *n* (15c) **1 :** a stroke or catch by which a wrestler is made to lose footing **2 a :** VOYAGE, JOURNEY **b :** a single round or tour on a business errand **3 :** ERROR, MISSTEP **4 :** a quick light step **5 :** a faltering step caused by stumbling **6 a :** the action of tripping mechanically **b** (1) **:** a device for tripping a mechanism (as a catch or detent) (2) **:** TUP 2 **7 :** an intense visionary experience undergone by a person who has taken a psychedelic drug (as LSD) **8 :** pursuit of an absorbing or obsessive interest ⟨on a nostalgia ~⟩ **9 :** SCENE, LIFE-STYLE

tri·pack \ˈtrī-ˌpak\ *n* (1911) **:** a combination of three superposed films or emulsions each sensitive to a different primary color for simultaneous exposure in one camera

tri·par·tite \(ˈ)trī-ˈpär-ˌtīt\ *adj* [ME, fr. L *tripartitus,* fr. *tri-* + *partitus* partite] (15c) **1 :** divided into or composed of three parts **2 :** having three corresponding parts or copies **3 :** made between or involving three parties ⟨a ~ treaty⟩

tripe \ˈtrīp\ *n* [ME, fr. MF] (14c) **1 :** stomach tissue of a ruminant and esp. of the ox for use as a food: **a :** that of the rumen wall **b :** that of the reticulum wall **2 :** something poor, worthless, or offensive

1trip–ham·mer \ˈtrip-ˌham-ər\ *n* (1781) **:** a massive power hammer having a head that is tripped and allowed to fall by cam or lever action

2trip–hammer *adj* (1864) **:** suggesting a trip-hammer in loud pounding or persistent action

tri·phe·nyl·meth·ane \ˌtrī-ˌfen-ᵊl-ˈmeth-ˌān, -ˌfēn-\ *n* [ISV] (ca. 1885) **:** a crystalline hydrocarbon $CH(C_6H_5)_3$ that is the parent compound of many dyes

1tri·phib·i·an \(ˈ)trī-ˈfib-ē-ən\ *adj* [*tri-* + *-phibian* (as in *amphibian*)] (1943) **1 :** designed for or equipped to operate from a solid surface (as of land or ice) or water as well as in the air ⟨a ~ airplane⟩ **2 :** TRIPHIBIOUS 1 ⟨a ~ military operation⟩

2triphibian *n* (ca. 1951) **:** a triphibian airplane

tri·phib·i·ous \-ē-əs\ *adj* [fr. *triphibian;* after such pairs as *amphibious: amphibian*] (1941) **1 :** employing, involving, or constituted by land, naval, and air forces and often including airborne troops in coordinated attack ⟨~ operations⟩ **2 :** TRIPHIBIAN 1 ⟨~ marines⟩

tri·phos·phate \(ˈ)trī-ˈfäs-ˌfāt\ *n* (ca. 1826) **:** a salt or acid that contains three phosphate groups — see ATP, GTP

tri·phos·pho·pyr·i·dine nucleotide \ˈtrī-ˈfäs-fō-ˌpir-ə-ˌdēn-\ *n* (1937) **:** NADP

triph·thong \ˈtrif-ˌthȯŋ, ˈtrip-\ *n* [*tri-* + *-phthong* (as in *diphthong*)] (ca. 1599) **1 :** a speech item consisting of three successive sounds that serves or is capable of serving as a monosyllable **2 :** TRIGRAPH — **triph·thon·gal** \trif-ˈthȯŋ-(g)əl, trip-\ *adj*

tri·pin·nate \(ˈ)trī-ˈpin-ˌāt\ *adj* (ca. 1760) **:** bipinnate with each division pinnate — **tri·pin·nate·ly** *adv*

tri·plane \ˈtrī-ˌplān\ *n* (1909) **:** an airplane with three main supporting surfaces superposed

1tri·ple \ˈtrip-əl\ *vb* **tri·pled; tri·pling** \-(ə-)liŋ\ [ME *triplen,* fr. LL *triplare,* fr. L *triplus,* adj.] *vt* (14c) **1 :** to make three times as great or as many **2 a :** to score (a base runner) by a triple **b :** to bring about the scoring of (a run) by a triple ~ *vi* **1 :** to become three times as great or as numerous **2 :** to make a triple in baseball

2triple *n* [ME, fr. L *triplus,* adj.] (15c) **1 a :** a triple sum, quantity, or number **b :** a combination, group, or series of three **2 :** a base hit that allows the batter to reach third base safely **3 :** TRIFECTA

3triple *adj* [MF or L; MF, fr. L *triplus,* fr. *tri-* + *-plus* multiplied by — more at -FOLD] (1550) **1 :** being three times as great or as many **2 :** having three units or members **3 :** having a threefold relation or character ⟨worked as a double or even ~ agent —*Time*⟩ **4 :** three times repeated **:** TREBLE **5 :** marked by three beats per musical measure ⟨~ meter⟩ **6 a :** having units of three components ⟨~ feet⟩ **b** *of rhyme* **:** involving correspondence of three syllables (as in *unfortunate-importunate*)

triple bond *n* (1889) **:** a chemical bond in which three pairs of electrons are shared by two atoms in a molecule

triple counterpoint *n* (ca. 1869) **:** three-part musical counterpoint so written that any part may be transposed above or below any other

Triple Crown *n* (1897) **1 :** an unofficial title in horse racing representing the championship achieved by a horse that wins the three classic races for a designated category **2 :** the unofficial title representing the championship attained by a baseball player who at the end of a single season leads his league in batting average, home runs, and runs batted in

tri·ple–head·er \ˌtrip-əl-ˈhed-ər\ *n* (ca. 1949) **:** three games, contests, or events held consecutively on the same program

triple jump *n* (1964) **:** a jump for distance in track-and-field athletics usu. from a running start and combining a hop, a stride, and a jump in succession

triple play *n* (1869) **:** a play in baseball by which three players are put out

triple point *n* (1872) **:** the condition of temperature and pressure under which the gaseous, liquid, and solid phases of a substance can exist in equilibrium

tri·ple–space \ˌtrip-əl-ˈspās\ *vt* (ca. 1939) **:** to type (text) leaving two blank lines between lines of copy ~ *vi* **:** to type on every third line

trip·let \ˈtrip-lət\ *n* [2*triple*] (1656) **1 :** a unit of three lines of verse **2 a :** a combination, set, or group of three **b :** a group of three elementary particles (as positive, negative, and neutral pions) with different charge states but otherwise similar properties **c :** an atom or molecule with an even number of electrons that have a net magnetic moment **d :** CODON **3 :** one of three children or offspring born at one birth **4 :** a group of three musical notes or tones performed in the time of two of the same value

tri·ple·tail \ˈtrip-əl-ˌtāl\ *n* (ca. 1803) **:** a large edible marine percoid fish (*Lobotes surinamensis*) of the warm western Atlantic in which the long dorsal and anal fins extend backward and with the caudal fin appear like a 3-lobed tail

triple threat *n* (1924) **:** a football player adept at running, kicking, and passing; *broadly* **:** a person adept in three different fields of activity — **triple–threat** *adj*

tri·ple–tongue \ˌtrip-əl-ˈtəŋ\ *vi* (1879) **:** to articulate the notes of triplets in fast tempo on a wind instrument by using the tongue positions esp. for *t, k, t* for the notes of each successive triplet

1tri·plex \ˈtrip-ˌleks, ˈtrī-ˌpleks\ *n* (1601) **:** something (as an apartment) that is triplex

2triplex *adj* [L, fr. *tri-* + *-plex* -fold — more at -FOLD] (ca. 1654) **1 :** THREEFOLD, TRIPLE ⟨~ windows⟩ **2 :** having three apartments, floors, or sections ⟨~ buildings⟩ ⟨~ apartments⟩ ⟨a ~ theater⟩

1trip·li·cate \ˈtrip-li-kət\ *adj* [ME, fr. L *triplicatus,* pp. of *triplicare* to triple, fr. *triplic-, triplex* threefold] (15c) **:** consisting of or existing in three corresponding or identical parts or examples ⟨~ invoices⟩

2trip·li·cate \-lə-ˌkāt\ *vt* **-cat·ed; -cat·ing** (ca. 1623) **1 :** to make triple or threefold **2 :** to prepare in triplicate — **trip·li·ca·tion** \ˌtrip-lə-ˈkā-shən\ *n*

3trip·li·cate \-li-kət\ *n* (1810) **:** three copies all alike — used with *in* ⟨typed in ~⟩

tri·plic·i·ty \trip-ˈlis-ət-ē, trī-ˈplis-\ *n, pl* **-ties** [ME *triplicite,* fr. LL *triplicitas* condition of being threefold, fr. L *triplic-, triplex*] (14c) **1 :** one of the groups of three signs each distant 120 degrees from the other two into which the signs of the zodiac are divided — called also *trigon* **2 :** the quality or state of being triple or threefold

trip·lite \ˈtrip-ˌlīt\ *n* [G *triplit,* fr. L *triplus* triple; fr. its threefold cleavage] (ca. 1847) **:** a dark brown monoclinic mineral that consists of a basic phosphate of manganese, iron, magnesium, and calcium

trip·lo·blas·tic \ˌtrip-lō-ˈblas-tik\ *adj* [L *triplus* + E *-o-* + *-blastic*] (ca. 1888) **:** having three primary germ layers

trip·loid \ˈtrip-ˌlȯid\ *adj* [ISV, fr. L *triplus* triple] (1911) **:** having or being a chromosome number three times the monoploid number — **trip·loid** *n* — **trip·loi·dy** \-ˌlȯid-ē\ *n*

tri·ply \ˈtrip-(ə-)lē\ *adv* (1660) **:** in a triple degree, amount, or manner

tri·pod \ˈtrī-ˌpäd\ *n* [L *tripod-, tripus,* fr. Gk *tripod-, tripous,* fr. *tripod-, tripous,* adj., three-footed, fr. *tri-* + *pod-, pous* foot — more at FOOT] (1603) **1 :** a vessel (as a caldron) resting on three legs **2 :** a stool, table, or altar with three legs **3 :** a three-legged stand (as for a camera) — **tripod** *or* **tri·po·dal** \ˈtrip-əd-ᵊl, ˈtrī-ˌpäd-\ *adj*

trip·o·li \ˈtrip-ə-lē\ *n* [F, fr. *Tripoli,* region of Africa] (ca. 1601) **1 :** an earth consisting of very friable soft schistose deposits of silica and including diatomite and kieselguhr **2 :** an earth consisting of friable dustlike silica not of diatomaceous origin

tri·pos \ˈtrī-ˌpäs\ *n* [modif. of L *tripus*] (1589) **1** *archaic* **:** TRIPOD **2** [fr. the three-legged stool occupied by a participant in a disputation at the degree ceremonies] **:** a final honors examination at Cambridge university orig. in mathematics

trip·per \ˈtrip-ər\ *n* (1813) **1 :** one that takes a trip **:** TOURIST **2 :** a tripping device (as for operating a railroad signal)

trip·pet \ˈtrip-ət\ *n* [ME *tripet* tipcat peg, fr. *trippen* to trip] (ca. 1877) **:** a cam, wiper, or projecting piece that strikes another piece at definite times

trip·ping·ly \ˈtrip-iŋ-lē\ *adv* (1590) **:** in a nimble or lively manner ⟨speak the speech . . . ~ on the tongue —Shak.⟩

trip·tane \ˈtrip-ˌtān\ *n* [irreg. fr. *tri-* + *butane*] (ca. 1943) **:** a liquid hydrocarbon C_7H_{16} of high antiknock properties used esp. in aviation gasolines to increase their power

trip·tych \ˈtrip-(ˌ)tik\ *n* [Gk *triptychos* having three folds, fr. *tri-* + *ptychē* fold; akin to Gk *epi-* besides — more at EPI-] (1731) **1 :** an ancient Roman writing tablet with three waxed leaves hinged together **2 :** a picture or carving in three panels side by side; *esp* **:** an altarpiece with a central panel and two flanking panels half its size that fold over it

tri·que·trous \trī-ˈkwē-trəs, -ˈkwe-\ *adj* [L *triquetrus* three-cornered, fr. *tri-*] (ca. 1879) **:** having three acute angles ⟨~ stems⟩

tri·ra·di·ate \(ˈ)trī-ˈrād-ē-ət, -ē-ˌāt\ *adj* (1846) **:** having three rays or radiating branches ⟨a ~ sponge spicule⟩

tri·reme \ˈtrī-ˌrēm\ *n* [L *triremis,* fr. *tri-* + *remus* oar — more at ROW] (1601) **:** an ancient galley having three banks of oars

tris- \(ˌ)tris\ *prefix* [Gk *tris* — more at TER-] **:** thrice **:** tripled — esp. in complex chemical expressions

tri·sac·cha·ride \(ˈ)trī-ˈsak-ə-ˌrīd\ *n* [ISV] (ca. 1899) **:** a sugar that yields on complete hydrolysis three monosaccharide molecules

tri·sect \ˈtrī-ˌsekt, trī-ˈ\ *vt* (1695) **:** to divide into three usu. equal parts — **tri·sec·tion** \ˈtrī-ˌsek-shən, trī-ˈ\ *n* — **tri·sec·tor** \ˈtrī-ˌsek-tər, trī-ˈ\ *n*

tris·kai·deka·pho·bia \ˌtris-ˌkī-ˌdek-ə-ˈfō-bē-ə, ˌtris-kə-\ *n* [NL, fr. Gk *triskadeka, treiskaideka* thirteen (fr. *treis* three + *kai* and + *deka* ten) + NL *phobia* — more at THREE, TEN] (ca. 1911) **:** fear of the number 13

tri·skel·i·on \trī-ˈskel-ē-ən, tris-ˈkel-\ *or* **tri·skele** \ˈtrī-ˌskēl, ˈtris-ˌkēl\ *n* [*triskelion* fr. NL, fr. Gk *triskelēs* three-legged, fr. *tri-* + *skelos* leg; *triskele* fr. Gk *triskelēs* — more at CYLINDER] (1857) **:** a figure composed of three usu. curved or bent branches radiating from a center

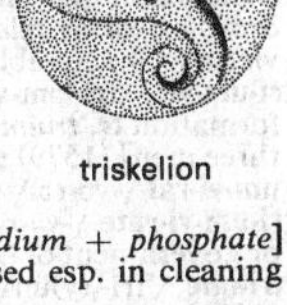

triskelion

tris·mus \ˈtriz-məs\ *n* [NL, fr. Gk *trismos* gnashing (of teeth), fr. *trizein* to squeak, gnash; akin to L *stridēre* to creak — more at STRIDENT] (ca. 1693) **:** spasm of the muscles of mastication **:** LOCKJAW

tris·oc·ta·he·dron \ˌtris-ˌäk-tə-ˈhē-drən\ *n* (ca. 1847) **:** a solid (as a crystal) having 24 congruent faces meeting on the edges of a regular octahedron

tri·so·di·um phosphate \ˌtrī-ˌsōd-ē-əm-\ *n* [*tri-* + *sodium* + *phosphate*] (1923) **:** a crystalline compound Na_3PO_4 that is used esp. in cleaning compositions

tri·so·my \ˈtrī-ˌsō-mē\ *n, pl* **-mies** [*tri-* + 3*-some* + *-y*] (1930) **:** the condition (as in Down's syndrome) of having one or a few chromosomes triploid in an otherwise diploid set — **tri·so·mic** \(ˈ)trī-ˈsō-mik\ *adj or n*

Tris·tan \ˈtris-tən, -ˌtän, -ˌtan\ *n* **:** TRISTRAM

triste \ˈtrēst\ *adj* [F, fr. L *tristis*] (15c) **:** SAD, MOURNFUL; *also* **:** WISTFUL

tri·stea·rin \(ˈ)trī-ˈstē-ə-rən, -ˈsti(-ə)r-ən\ *n* [ISV] (ca. 1856) **:** the crystallizable triglyceride $C_{57}H_{110}O_6$ of stearic acid that is found esp. in hard fats

tris·te·za \tris-ˈtā-zə\ *n* [Pg, lit., sadness, fr. L *tristitia,* fr. *tristis* sad] (ca. 1901) **:** a highly infectious virus disease of citrus trees grafted on sour orange rootstocks that is characterized by rotting of the rootlets and eventually causes the death of the trees

trist·ful \ˈtrist-fəl\ *adj* [ME *trist* sad, fr. MF *triste*] (15c) **:** SAD, MELANCHOLY — **trist·ful·ly** \-fə-lē\ *adv* — **trist·ful·ness** *n*

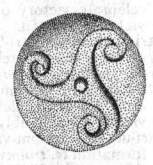

\ə\ abut \ᵊ\ kitten, F table \ər\ further \a\ ash \ā\ ace \ä\ cot, cart \au̇\ out \ch\ chin \e\ bet \ē\ easy \g\ go \i\ hit \ī\ ice \j\ job \ŋ\ sing \ō\ go \ȯ\ law \ȯi\ boy \th\ thin \t͟h\ the \ü\ loot \u̇\ foot \y\ yet \zh\ vision \à, k̲, ⁿ, œ, œ̄, ue, u̇e, ʸ\ *see* Guide to Pronunciation

tri·stim·u·lus \(ˈ)trī-ˈstim-yə-ləs\ *adj* (1933) **:** of or relating to values giving the amounts of the three colored lights red, green, and blue that when combined additively produce a match for the color being considered

Tris·tram \ˈtris-t(r)əm\ *n* [ME *Tristrem,* fr. AF *Tristan,* fr. OW *Trystan*] **:** the lover of Isolde of Ireland and husband of Isolde of Brittany in medieval legend

tri·sub·sti·tut·ed \ˈtrī-ˈsəb-stə-ˌt(y)üt-əd\ *adj* (ca. 1899) **:** having three substituent atoms or groups in the molecule

tri·syl·lab·ic \ˌtrī-sə-ˈlab-ik\ *adj* [L *trisyllabus,* fr. Gk *trisyllabos,* fr. *tri-* + *syllabē* syllable] (1637) **:** having three syllables ⟨a ~ word⟩ — **tri·syl·lab·i·cal·ly** \-i-k(ə-)lē\ *adv*

tri·syl·la·ble \ˈtrī-ˌsil-ə-bəl, (ˈ)trī-ˈ\ *n* (1589) **:** a word of three syllables

trite \ˈtrīt\ *adj* **trit·er; trit·est** [L *tritus,* fr. pp. of *terere* to rub, wear away — more at THROW] (1548) **:** hackneyed or boring from much use **:** not fresh or original — **trite·ly** *adv* — **trite·ness** *n*

syn TRITE, HACKNEYED, STEREOTYPED, THREADBARE mean lacking the freshness that evokes attention or interest. TRITE applies to a once effective phrase or idea spoiled from long familiarity ⟨"you win some, you lose some" is a *trite* expression⟩ HACKNEYED stresses being worn out by overuse so as to become dull and meaningless ⟨all of the metaphors and images in the poem are *hackneyed*⟩ STEREOTYPED implies falling invariably into the same pattern or form ⟨views of American Indians that are *stereotyped* and out-of-date⟩ THREADBARE applies to what has been used until its possibilities of interest have been totally exhausted ⟨a mystery novel with a *threadbare* plot⟩

tri·the·ism \ˈtrī-thē-ˌiz-əm\ *n* (1678) **:** the doctrine that the Father, Son, and Holy Spirit are three distinct Gods — **tri·the·ist** \-(ˌ)thē-əst\ *n or adj* — **tri·the·is·tic** \ˌtrī-thē-ˈis-tik\ *or* **tri·the·is·ti·cal** \-ˈis-ti-kəl\ *adj*

tri·thing \ˈtrī-thiŋ\ *n* [ME, alter. of (assumed) OE *thrithing, thriding*] *archaic* (13c) **:** [3]RIDING 1

tri·ti·at·ed \ˈtrit-ē-ˌāt-əd, ˈtrish-ē-\ *adj* (1953) **:** containing and esp. labeled with tritium

trit·i·ca·le \ˌtrit-ə-ˈkā-lē\ *n* [NL, blend of *Triticum,* genus of wheat, and *Secale,* genus of rye] (1952) **:** an amphidiploid hybrid between wheat and rye that has a high yield and rich protein content

tri·ti·um \ˈtrit-ē-əm, ˈtrish-ē-\ *n* [NL, fr. Gk *tritos* third — more at THIRD] (ca. 1933) **:** a radioactive isotope of hydrogen with atoms of three times the mass of ordinary light hydrogen atoms

trit·o·ma \ˈtrit-ə-mə\ *n* [NL, genus name, fr. Gk *tritomos* thrice cut, fr. *tri-* + *temnein* to cut; fr. their trimerous flowers — more at TOME] (1804) **:** any of a genus (*Kniphofia*) of African herbs of the lily family that are often grown for their spikes of showy red or yellow flowers

[1]**tri·ton** \ˈtrīt-ᵊn\ *n* [L, fr. Gk *Tritōn*] **1** *cap* **:** a son of Poseidon described as a demigod of the sea with the lower part of his body like that of a fish **2** [NL, genus name, fr. L *Triton*] **:** any of various large marine gastropod mollusks (esp. family Cymatiidae) with a heavy elongated conical shell; *also* **:** this shell

[2]**tri·ton** \ˈtrī-ˌtän\ *n* [*tritium* + *-on*] (ca. 1934) **:** the nucleus of tritium

tri·tone \ˈtrī-ˌtōn\ *n* [Gk *tritonon,* fr. *tri-* + *tonos* tone] (1609) **:** a musical interval of three whole steps

[1]**trit·u·rate** \ˈtrich-ə-ˌrāt\ *vt* **-rat·ed; -rat·ing** [LL *trituratus,* pp. of *triturare* to thresh, fr. L *tritura* act of rubbing, threshing, fr. *tritus,* pp. — more at TRITE] (ca. 1755) **1 :** CRUSH, GRIND **2 :** to pulverize and comminute thoroughly by rubbing or grinding — **trit·u·ra·ble** \ˈtrich-ə-rə-bəl\ *adj* — **trit·u·ra·tor** \-ˌrāt-ər\ *n*

[2]**trit·u·rate** \-rət\ *n* (ca. 1891) **:** a triturated substance **:** TRITURATION 2

trit·u·ra·tion \ˌtrich-ə-ˈrā-shən\ *n* (1646) **1 :** the act or process of triturating **:** the state of being triturated **:** COMMINUTION **2 :** a triturated medicinal powder made by triturating a substance with a diluent

[1]**tri·umph** \ˈtrī-əm(p)f\ *n, pl* **tri·umphs** \-əm(p)fs, -əm(p)s\ [ME *triumphe,* fr. MF, fr. L *triumphus*] (14c) **1 :** a ceremony attending the entering of Rome by a general who had won a decisive victory over a foreign enemy — compare OVATION 1 **2 :** the joy or exultation of victory or success **3 a :** a victory or conquest by or as if by military force **b :** a notable success — **tri·um·phal** \trī-ˈəm(p)-fəl\ *adj*

[2]**triumph** *vi* (1508) **1 a :** to receive the honor of a triumph **b :** to celebrate victory or success boastfully or exultingly **2 :** to obtain victory **:** PREVAIL

tri·um·phal·ism \trī-ˈəm(p)-fə-ˌliz-əm\ *n* (1964) **:** the doctrine, attitude, or belief that one religious creed is superior to all others — **tri·um·phal·ist** \-fə-ləst\ *n or adj*

tri·um·phant \trī-ˈəm(p)-fənt\ *adj* (15c) **1 :** VICTORIOUS, CONQUERING **2** *archaic* **:** of or relating to a triumph **3 :** rejoicing for or celebrating victory **4 :** notably successful — **tri·um·phant·ly** *adv*

tri·um·vir \trī-ˈəm-vər\ *n, pl* **-virs** *also* **-vi·ri** \-və-ˌrī, -ˌrē\ [L, back-formation fr. *triumviri,* pl., commission of three men, fr. *trium virum* of three men] (1579) **:** one of a commission or ruling body of three — **tri·um·vi·ral** \-və-rəl\ *adj*

tri·um·vi·rate \-və-rət\ *n* (1584) **1 :** a body of triumvirs **2 :** the office or government of triumvirs **3 :** a group or association of three

[1]**tri·une** \ˈtrī-ˌ(y)ün\ *n* [L *tri-* + *unus* one — more at ONE] *often cap* (1605) **:** TRINITY 1

[2]**triune** *adj* (1635) **:** three in one: **a** *often cap* **:** of or relating to the Trinity ⟨the ~ God⟩ **b :** consisting of three parts, members, or aspects

[1]**tri·va·lent** \(ˈ)trī-ˈvā-lənt\ *adj* [ISV] (1868) **:** having a valence of three

[2]**trivalent** *n* (1922) **:** a group of three synapsed homologous chromosomes in meiosis

triv·et \ˈtriv-ət\ *n* [ME *trevet,* fr. OE *trefet,* prob. modif. of LL *triped-, tripes,* fr. L, three-footed, fr. *tri-* + *ped-, pes* foot — more at FOOT] (15c) **1 :** a three-legged stand **:** TRIPOD **2 :** a usu. metal stand with short feet for use under a hot dish at table

triv·ia \ˈtriv-ē-ə\ *n pl but sing or pl in constr* [L, crossroads, pl. of *trivium,* influenced in meaning by E *trivial*] (1920) **:** unimportant matters **:** trivial facts or details; *also, sing in constr* **:** a quizzing game involving obscure facts

triv·i·al \ˈtriv-ē-əl\ *adj* [L *trivialis* found everywhere, commonplace, trivial, fr. *trivium* crossroads, fr. *tri-* + *via* way — more at VIA] (1589) **1 :** COMMONPLACE, ORDINARY **2 a :** of little worth or importance **b :** relating to or being the mathematically simplest case; *specif* **:** characterized by having all variables equal to zero ⟨a ~ solution to an equation⟩ **3 :** SPECIFIC 4 — **triv·i·al·ist** \-ə-ləst\ *n* — **triv·i·al·ly** \-ə-lē\ *adv*

trivialise *Brit var of* TRIVIALIZE

triv·i·al·i·ty \ˌtriv-ē-ˈal-ət-ē\ *n, pl* **-ties** (ca. 1598) **1 :** the quality or state of being trivial **2 :** something trivial **:** TRIFLE

triv·i·al·ize \ˈtriv-ē-ə-ˌlīz\ *vt* **-ized; -iz·ing** (1846) **:** to make trivial **:** reduce to triviality — **triv·i·al·iza·tion** \ˌtriv-ē-ə-lə-ˈzā-shən\ *n*

trivial name *n* (1759) **1 :** SPECIFIC EPITHET **2 :** a common or vernacular name of an organism or chemical

triv·i·um \ˈtriv-ē-əm\ *n, pl* **triv·ia** \-ē-ə\ [ML, fr. L, meeting of three ways, crossroads] (ca. 1804) **:** a group of studies consisting of grammar, rhetoric, and logic and forming the lower division of the seven liberal arts in medieval universities — compare QUADRIVIUM

[1]**tri·week·ly** \(ˈ)trī-ˈwē-klē\ *adj* (1832) **1 :** occurring or appearing three times a week **2 :** occurring or appearing every three weeks — **triweekly** *adv*

[2]**triweekly** *n, pl* **-lies** (1851) **:** a triweekly publication

-trix \(ˌ)triks\ *n suffix, pl* **-tri·ces** \trə-ˌsēz, ˈtrī-(ˌ)sēz\ *or* **-trix·es** \(ˌ)trik-səz\ [ME, fr. L, fem. of *-tor,* suffix denoting an agent, fr. *-tus* (pp. ending) + *-or* [1]-or — more at -ED] **1 :** female that does or is associated with a (specified) thing ⟨avia*trix*⟩ **2 :** geometric line, point, or surface ⟨genera*trix*⟩

tRNA \ˌtē-ˌär-ˌen-ˈā, ˈtē-ˌär-ˌen-ˌā\ *n* (ca. 1964) **:** TRANSFER RNA

tro·car *also* **tro·char** \ˈtrō-ˌkär\ *n* [F *trocart,* fr. *trois* three (fr. L *tres*) + *carre* side of a sword blade, fr. *carrer* to make square, fr. L *quadrare* — more at THREE, QUADRATE] (ca. 1706) **:** a sharp-pointed instrument fitted with a cannula and used esp. to insert the cannula into a body cavity as a drainage outlet

tro·cha·ic \trō-ˈkā-ik\ *adj* [MF *trochaïque,* fr. L *trochaicus,* fr. Gk *trochaikos,* fr. *trochaios* trochee] (1589) **:** of, relating to, or consisting of trochees — **trochaic** *n*

tro·chan·ter \trō-ˈkant-ər\ *n* [Gk *trochantēr;* akin to Gk *trechein* to run] (ca. 1615) **1 :** a rough prominence at the upper part of the femur of many vertebrates **2 :** the second segment counting from the base of the leg of an insect — **tro·chan·ter·al** \-ə-rəl\ *adj* — **tro·chan·ter·ic** \ˌtrō-kən-ˈter-ik, -ˌkan-\ *adj*

tro·che \ˈtrō-kē, *Brit usu* ˈtrōsh\ *n* [alter. of earlier *trochisk,* fr. LL *trochiscus,* fr. Gk *trochiskos,* fr. dim. of *trochos* wheel] (ca. 1597) **:** a usu. circular medicinal tablet or lozenge for slow dissolution in the mouth; *esp* **:** one used as a demulcent

tro·chee \ˈtrō-(ˌ)kē\ *n* [prob. fr. MF *trochée,* fr. L *trochaeus,* fr. Gk *trochaios,* fr. *trochaios* running, fr. *trochē* run, course, fr. *trechein* to run; akin to Gk *trochos* wheel, OIr *droch*] (1589) **:** a metrical foot consisting of one long syllable followed by one short syllable or of one stressed syllable followed by one unstressed syllable (as in *apple*)

troch·lea \ˈträk-lē-ə\ *n* [NL, fr. L, block of pulleys, fr. Gk *trochileia;* akin to Gk *trechein* to run] (ca. 1693) **:** an anatomical structure that is held to resemble a pulley; *esp* **:** the articular surface on the medial condyle of the humerus that articulates with the ulna

troch·le·ar \-ər\ *adj* (ca. 1681) **1 :** of, relating to, or being a trochlea **2 :** of, relating to, or being a trochlear nerve

trochlear nerve *n* (ca. 1890) **:** either of the 4th pair of cranial nerves that supply some of the eye muscles with motor fibers — called also *trochlear*

tro·choid \ˈtrō-ˌkȯid, ˈträk-ˌȯid\ *n* [Gk *trochoeidēs* like a wheel, fr. *trochos* wheel] (ca. 1704) **:** the curve generated by a point on the radius of a circle or the radius extended as the circle rolls on a fixed straight line — **tro·choi·dal** \trō-ˈkȯid-ᵊl, trä-\ *adj*

trocho·phore \ˈträk-ə-ˌfō(ə)r, -ˌfȯ(ə)r\ *n* [deriv. of Gk *trochos* wheel + *pherein* to carry — more at TROCHEE, BEAR] (ca. 1892) **:** a free-swimming ciliate larva typical of marine annelid worms but occurring in several invertebrate groups

trod *past and past part of* TREAD

trodden *past part of* TREAD

trof·fer \ˈträf-ər, ˈtrȯf-\ *n* [blend of *trough* and *coffer*] (1942) **:** an inverted trough serving as a support and reflector usu. for a fluorescent lighting unit

trog·lo·dyte \ˈträg-lə-ˌdīt\ *n* [L *troglodytae,* pl., fr. Gk *trōglodytai,* fr. *trōglē* hole, cave (akin to Gk *trōgein* to gnaw) + *dyein* to enter — more at ADYTUM] (1558) **1 :** a member of a primitive people dwelling in caves **2 :** a person resembling a troglodyte (as in reclusive habits or outmoded or reactionary attitudes) **3 :** APE 1b — **trog·lo·dyt·ic** \ˌträg-lə-ˈdit-ik\ *adj*

tro·gon \ˈtrō-ˌgän\ *n* [NL, genus name, fr. Gk *trōgōn,* prp. of *trōgein* to gnaw] (1792) **:** any of numerous nonpasserine tropical birds (family Trogonidae) with brilliant lustrous plumage

troi·ka \ˈtrȯi-kə\ *n* [Russ *troĭka,* fr. *troe* three; akin to OE *thrie* three] (1842) **1 :** a Russian vehicle drawn by three horses abreast; *also* **:** a team for such a vehicle **2 :** a group of three closely related persons or things: as **a :** an administrative or ruling body of three **b :** a group of three

troi·lite \ˈtrō-ə-ˌlīt, ˈtrȯi-ˌlīt\ *n* [G *troilit,* fr. Domenico *Troili,* 18th cent. Ital. scientist + G *-it* -ite] (ca. 1868) **:** a mineral FeS that is a variety of pyrrhotite and that is widely but sparsely distributed (as on earth, in meteorites, and in lunar soil samples)

Troi·lus \ˈtrȯi-ləs, ˈtrō-ə-ləs\ *n* [ME, fr. L, fr. Gk *Trōilos*] **:** a son of Priam who in medieval legend loved Cressida and lost her to Diomedes

[1]**Tro·jan** \ˈtrō-jən\ *n* [ME, fr. L *trojanus* of Troy, fr. *Troia, Troja* Troy, fr. Gk *Trōia*] (14c) **1 :** a native or inhabitant of Troy **2 :** one who shows qualities (as pluck, endurance, or determined energy) attributed to the defenders of ancient Troy **3 :** a gay, irresponsible, or disreputable companion

[2]**Trojan** *adj* (14c) **1 :** of, relating to, or resembling ancient Troy or its inhabitants **2 :** of, relating to, or constituting a Trojan horse

Trojan horse *n* [fr. the large hollow wooden horse filled with Greek soldiers and introduced within the walls of Troy by a stratagem] (ca. 1574) **:** someone or something intended to defeat or subvert from within

Trojan War *n* (1835) **:** a 10-year war between the Greeks and Trojans brought on by the abduction of Helen by Paris and ended with the destruction of Troy

[1]**troll** \ˈtrōl\ *vb* [ME *trollen*] *vt* (15c) **1 :** to cause to move round and round **:** ROLL **2 a :** to sing the parts of (as a round or catch) in succession **b :** to sing loudly **c :** to celebrate in song **3 a :** to angle for with a hook and line drawn through the water **b :** to angle in ⟨~ lakes⟩ **c :** to pull through the water in angling ⟨~ a lure⟩ ~ *vi* **1 :** to

move around : RAMBLE **2 :** to fish esp. by trolling a hook **3 :** to sing or play in a jovial manner **4 :** to speak rapidly — **troll·er** *n*

[2]troll *n* (1820) **:** a lure or a line with its lure and hook used in trolling

[3]troll *n* [Norw *troll* & Dan *trold,* fr. ON *troll* giant, demon; akin to MHG *trolle* monster] (1616) **:** a dwarf or giant in Teutonic folklore inhabiting caves or hills

[1]trol·ley *also* **trol·ly** \'träl-ē\ *n, pl* **trolleys** *also* **trollies** [prob. fr. [1]*troll*] (1823) **1** *dial Eng* **:** a cart of any of various kinds **2 a :** a device that carries electric current from an overhead wire to a trolley car **b :** TROLLEY CAR **3 :** a wheeled carriage running on an overhead rail or track **4** *chiefly Brit* **:** a cart or wheeled stand used for conveying something (as food or books)

[2]trolley *also* **trolly** *vb* **trol·leyed** *also* **trol·lied; trol·ley·ing** *also* **trol·ly·ing** *vt* (1882) **:** to convey by a trolley ~ *vi* **:** to ride on a trolley

trol·ley·bus \'träl-ē-,bəs\ *n* (ca. 1931) **:** a bus electrically propelled by power from two overhead wires and similar in appearance to a motor bus

trolley car *n* (1894) **:** a public conveyance for passengers that runs on tracks with motive power derived through a trolley

trol·lop \'träl-əp\ *n* [prob. irreg. fr. G dial. *trolle,* fr. MHG *trulle* prostitute — more at TRULL] (1615) **1 :** a slovenly woman **:** SLATTERN **2 :** a loose woman **:** WANTON

Trombe wall \'trōmb-, 'trämb-, 'trōⁿb-\ *n* [Felix *Trombe* 20th cent. Fr. designer] (1978) **:** a masonry wall that is usu. glazed on the exterior and is designed to absorb solar heat and release it into the interior of a building

trom·bi·di·a·sis \,träm-bə-'dī-ə-səs\ *n* [NL, fr. *Trombidium,* genus of mites] (1914) **:** infestation with chiggers

trom·bone \träm-'bōn, (,)trəm-', 'träm-,\ *n* [It, aug. of *tromba* trumpet, of Gmc origin; akin to OHG *trumba, trumpa* trumpet] (ca. 1724) **:** a brass instrument consisting of a long cylindrical metal tube with two turns and having a movable slide for varying the tone and a usual range one octave lower than that of the trumpet — **trom·bon·ist** \-'bō-nəst, -,bō-\ *n*

trom·mel \'träm-əl\ *n* [G, drum, fr. MHG *trummel,* dim. of *trumme* drum — more at DRUM] (ca. 1877) **:** a usu. cylindrical or conical revolving screen used esp. for screening or sizing rock, ore, or coal

tromp \'trämp, 'trömp\ *vb* [by alter.] *vi* (1883) **1 :** TRAMP 1 ⟨a lot of knocking on doors, ~*ing* from room to room —Sara Davidson⟩ **2 :** to step hard **:** STAMP ⟨~*ed* on the brake⟩ ~ *vt* **1 :** TRAMP **2 :** STAMP ⟨~*s* the accelerator to the floor —Jim Becker⟩ **3 a :** to give a physical beating to **b :** to defeat decisively

trompe l'oeil \(')trōmp-'ləi, trōⁿp-lœi\ *n, often attrib* [F *trompe-l'œil,* lit., deceive the eye] (1889) **1 :** a style of painting in which objects are depicted with photographically realistic detail; *also* **:** the use of similar technique in interior decorating **2 :** a trompe l'oeil painting or effect

-tron \,trän\ *n suffix* [Gk, suffix denoting an instrument; akin to OE *-thor,* suffix denoting an instrument, L *-trum*] **1 :** vacuum tube ⟨magne*tron*⟩ **2 :** device for the manipulation of subatomic particles ⟨cyclo*tron*⟩

tro·na \'trō-nə\ *n* [Sw, prob. fr. Ar *natrūn* natron— more at NATRON] (1799) **:** a gray-white or yellowish white monoclinic mineral $Na_3H(CO_3)_2 \cdot 2H_2O$ consisting of a hydrous acid sodium carbonate

trone \'trōn\ *n* [AF, fr. OF, fr. L *trutina* balance, scales, fr. Gk *trytanē;* akin to Gk *tryma* hole, *tetrainein* to pierce — more at THROW] *chiefly Scot* (15c) **:** a weighing machine for heavy wares

[1]troop \'trüp\ *n* [MF *trope, troupe* company, herd, of Gmc origin; akin to OE *thorp, throp* village — more at THORP] (1545) **1 a :** a group of soldiers **b :** a cavalry unit corresponding to an infantry company **c** *pl* **:** ARMED FORCES, SOLDIERS **2 :** a collection of people or things **:** COMPANY **3 :** a flock of mammals or birds **4 :** the basic organizational unit of Boy Scouts or Girl Scouts under an adult leader

[2]troop *vi* (1565) **1 :** to move or gather in crowds **2 :** to go one's way **:** WALK **3 :** to consort in company **:** ASSOCIATE **4 :** to move in large numbers

troop carrier *n* (1923) **:** a transport airplane used to carry troops

troop·er \'trü-pər\ *n* (1640) **1 a** (1) **:** an enlisted cavalryman (2) **:** the horse of a cavalryman **b :** PARATROOPER **c :** SOLDIER **2 a :** a mounted policeman **b :** a state policeman

troop·ship \'trüp-,ship\ *n* (1862) **:** a ship for carrying troops **:** TRANSPORT

troost·ite \'trü-,stīt, 'trō-\ *n* [Gerard *Troost* †1850 Am. geologist] (1835) **:** a variety of willemite occurring in large reddish crystals in which the zinc is partly replaced by manganese

trop- *or* **tropo-** *comb form* [ISV, fr. Gk *tropos*] **1 :** turn **:** turning **:** change ⟨*tropo*sphere⟩ **2 :** tropism ⟨*trop*ic⟩

trope \'trōp\ *n* [L *tropus,* fr. Gk *tropos* turn, way, manner, style, trope, fr. *trepein* to turn; akin to L *trepit* he turns] (1533) **1 :** the use of a word or expression in a figurative sense **:** FIGURE OF SPEECH **2 :** a phrase or verse added as an embellishment or interpolation to the sung parts of the Mass in the medieval period

troph- *or* **tropho-** *comb form* [F, fr. Gk, fr. *trophē* nourishment] **:** nutritive ⟨*tropho*plasm⟩

troph·al·lax·is \,trō-fə-'lak-səs\ *n* [NL, fr. *troph-* + Gk *allaxis* exchange, fr. *allassein* to change, exchange, fr. *allos* other — more at ELSE] (1918) **:** exchange of food (as from special glands) between organisms; *also* **:** the association of different organisms and esp. social insects on the basis of such a unilateral or mutual exchange

tro·phic \'trō-fik\ *adj* [F *trophique,* fr. Gk *trophikos,* fr. *trophē* nourishment, fr. *trephein* to nourish — more at ATROPHY] (1873) **1 :** of or relating to nutrition **:** NUTRITIONAL ⟨~ disorders⟩ **2 :** [3]TROPIC — **tro·phi·cal·ly** \-fi-k(ə-)lē\ *adv*

-tro·phic \'trō-fik\ *adj comb form* [NL *-trophia* -trophy] **1 a :** of, relating to, or characterized by (such) nutrition ⟨ecto*trophic*⟩ **b :** requiring or utilizing (such) a kind of nutrition ⟨poly*trophic*⟩ **2 :** -TROPIC ⟨lipo*trophic*⟩

trophic level *n* (1942) **:** one of the hierarchical strata of a food web characterized by organisms which are the same number of steps removed from the primary producers

tro·pho·blast \'trō-fə-,blast\ *n* [ISV] (1889) **:** a thin layer of ectoderm that forms the wall of many mammalian blastulas and functions in the nutrition and implantation of the embryo — **tro·pho·blas·tic** \,trō-fə-'blas-tik\ *adj*

tro·pho·zo·ite \,trō-fə-'zō-,īt\ *n* (ca. 1900) **:** a vegetative protozoan as distinguished from a reproductive or resting form

tro·phy \'trō-fē\ *n, pl* **trophies** [MF *trophee,* fr. L *tropaeum, trophaeum,* fr. Gk *tropaion,* fr. neut. of *tropaios* of a turning, of a rout, fr. *tropē* turn, rout, fr. *trepein* to turn — more at TROPE] (1513) **1 a :** a memorial of an ancient Greek or Roman victory raised on the field of battle or in case of a naval victory on the nearest land **b :** a representation of such a memorial (as on a medal); *also* **:** an architectural ornament representing a group of military weapons **2 :** something gained or given in victory or conquest esp. when preserved or mounted as a memorial — **trophy** *vt*

-tro·phy \trə-fē\ *n comb form* [NL *-trophia,* fr. Gk, fr. *-trophos* nourishing, fr. *trephein*] **:** nutrition **:** nurture **:** growth ⟨hypo*trophy*⟩

[1]trop·ic \'träp-ik\ *n* [ME *tropik,* fr. L *tropicus* of the solstice, fr. Gk *tropikos,* fr. *tropē* turn] (1503) **1 :** either of the two small circles of the celestial sphere on each side of and parallel to the equator at a distance of $23^{1}/_{2}$ degrees which the sun reaches at its greatest declination north or south **2 a :** either of the two parallels of terrestrial latitude corresponding to the celestial tropics — compare TROPIC OF CANCER, TROPIC OF CAPRICORN **b** *pl, often cap* **:** the region lying between these parallels of latitude

[2]tropic *adj* (1551) **:** of, relating to, or occurring in the tropics **:** TROPICAL

[3]tro·pic \'trō-pik\ *adj* [*trop-*] (1903) **1 :** of, relating to, or characteristic of tropism or of a tropism **2** *of a hormone* **:** influencing the activity of a specified gland

-tro·pic \'trō-pik, 'träp-ik\ *adj comb form* [F *-tropique,* fr. Gk *-tropos* -tropous] **1 :** turning, changing, or tending to turn or change in a (specified) manner or in response to a (specified) stimulus ⟨geo*tropic*⟩ **2 :** attracted to or acting upon (something specified) ⟨neuro*tropic*⟩

trop·i·cal *for 1* 'träp-i-kəl, *for 2* 'trōp- *also* 'träp-\ *adj* (1527) **1 a :** of, relating to, occurring in, or suitable for use in the tropics **b** *of a sign of the zodiac* **:** beginning at one of the tropics **2** [L *tropicus,* fr. Gk *tropikos,* fr. *tropos* trope] **:** FIGURATIVE 2 — **trop·i·cal·ly** \-i-k(ə-)lē\ *adv*

tropical aquarium *n* (ca. 1948) **:** an aquarium kept at a uniform warmth and used esp. for tropical fish

tropical cyclone *n* (1920) **:** a cyclone in the tropics characterized by winds rotating at the rate of 74 miles an hour or more

tropical fish *n* (1931) **:** any of various small usu. showy fishes of exotic origin often kept in the tropical aquarium

trop·i·cal·ize \'träp-i-kə-,līz\ *vt* **-ized; -iz·ing** (1885) **1 :** to make tropical (as in character, conditions, or appearance) **2 :** to fit or adapt for use in a tropical climate esp. by measures designed to combat the effects of fungi and moisture

tropical rain forest *n* (1926) **:** RAIN FOREST

tropical storm *n* (ca. 1945) **:** a tropical cyclone with strong winds of less than hurricane intensity

tropic bird *n* (ca. 1681) **:** any of several web-footed birds (genus *Phaethon* of the family Phaethontidae) that are related to the gannets, are found chiefly in tropical seas often far from land, and are marked by mostly white satiny plumage with a little black, a greatly elongated central pair of tail feathers, and a bright-colored bill

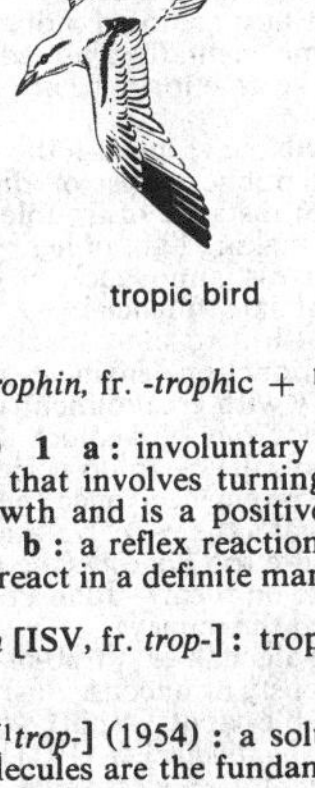

tropic bird

tropic of Cancer [fr. the sign of the zodiac which its celestial projection intersects] (1555) **:** the parallel of latitude that is approximately $23^{1}/_{2}$ degrees north of the equator and that is the northernmost latitude reached by the overhead sun

tropic of Capricorn [fr. the sign of the zodiac which its celestial projection intersects] (1555) **:** the parallel of latitude that is approximately $23^{1}/_{2}$ degrees south of the equator and that is the southernmost latitude reached by the overhead sun

-tro·pin \'trō-pən\ *or* **-tro·phin** \-fən\ *n comb form* [*-tropin,* alter. (influenced by *-trop*) of *-trophin,* fr. *-trophic* + [1]*-in*] **:** hormone ⟨gonado*tropin*⟩ ⟨somato*tropin*⟩

tro·pism \'trō-,piz-əm\ *n* [ISV *-tropism*] (1899) **1 a :** involuntary orientation by an organism or one of its parts that involves turning or curving by movement or by differential growth and is a positive or negative response to a source of stimulation **b :** a reflex reaction involving a tropism **2 :** an innate tendency to react in a definite manner to stimuli — **tro·pis·tic** \trō-'pis-tik\ *adj*

-tro·pism \trə-,piz-əm, 'trō-, ,trō-\ *n comb form* [ISV, fr. *trop-*] **:** tropism ⟨helio*tropism*⟩

tropo- — see TROP-

tro·po·col·la·gen \,träp-ə-'käl-ə-jən, ,trōp-\ *n* [[1]*trop-*] (1954) **:** a soluble substance whose elongated asymmetrical molecules are the fundamental building units of collagen fibers

tro·po·log·i·cal \,trōp-ə-'läj-i-kəl, ,träp-\ *also* **tro·po·log·ic** \-ik\ *adj* (14c) **1 :** characterized or varied by tropes **:** FIGURATIVE **2 :** of, relating to, or involving biblical interpretation stressing moral metaphor; *also* **:** MORAL — **tro·po·log·i·cal·ly** \-i-k(ə-)lē\ *adv*

tropo·my·o·sin \,träp-ə-'mī-ə-sən, ,trōp-\ *n* (1946) **:** a protein of muscle that forms a complex with troponin regulating the interaction of actin and myosin in muscular contraction

tro·po·nin \'trōp-ə-nən, 'träp-, -,nin\ *n* [*trop-* + *-n-* (arbitrary infix) + *-in*] (1966) **:** a protein of muscle that forms part of a regulatory protein complex with tropomyosin controlling the interaction of actin and myosin and that tends to inhibit muscular contraction unless combined with calcium ions

tro·po·pause \'trōp-ə-,pȯz, 'träp-\ *n* [ISV *tropo*sphere + *pause*] (ca. 1918) **:** the region at the top of the troposphere; *also* **:** a comparable layer of a celestial body

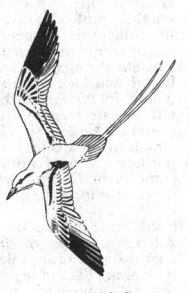

tro·po·sphere \'trōp-ə-,sfi(ə)r, 'träp-\ *n* [ISV] (ca. 1909) : the portion of the atmosphere which is below the stratosphere, which extends outward about 7 to 10 miles (11 to 16 kilometers) from the earth's surface, and in which generally temperature decreases rapidly with altitude, clouds form, and convection is active — **tro·po·spher·ic** \,trōp-ə-'sfi(ə)r-ik, ,träp-, -'sfer-\ *adj*

tro·po·tax·is \,trōp-ə-'tak-səs, ,träp-\ *n* [NL] (ca. 1939) : a taxis in which an organism orients itself through a process of simultaneous comparison of stimuli of different intensity acting on separate end organs

-tro·pous \trə-pəs\ *adj comb form* [Gk *-tropos,* fr. *trepein* to turn — more at TROPE] : turning or curving in (such) a way : exhibiting (such) a tropism ⟨ana*tropous*⟩

-tro·py \trə-pē\ *n comb form* [F *-tropie,* fr. Gk *-tropia,* fr. *-tropos*] : condition of turning or curving in (such) a way or of exhibiting (such) a tropism ⟨photo*tropy*⟩

1trot \'trät\ *n* [ME, fr. MF, fr. *troter* to trot, of Gmc origin; akin to OHG *trottōn* to tread, OE *tredan*] (14c) **1 a** (1) : a moderately fast gait of a quadruped (as a horse) in which the legs move in diagonal pairs (2) : a jogging gait of man that falls between a walk and a run **b** : a ride on horseback **2** : an old woman **3** : a literal translation of a foreign text **4** *pl* : DIARRHEA

2trot *vb* **trot·ted; trot·ting** *vi* (14c) **1** : to ride, drive, or proceed at a trot ⟨the fox *trotted* over the knoll⟩ **2** : to proceed briskly : HURRY ~ *vt* **1** : to cause to go at a trot **2** : to traverse at a trot

3trot *n* (1883) : TROTLINE; *also* : one of the short lines with hooks that are attached to it at intervals

1troth \'träth, 'trȯth, 'trōth, *or with* th\ *n* [ME *trouth,* fr. OE *trēowth* — more at TRUTH] (bef. 12c) **1** : loyal or pledged faithfulness : FIDELITY **2** : one's pledged word; *also* : BETROTHAL

2troth *vt* (15c) : PLEDGE, BETROTH

1troth·plight \'träth-,plīt, 'trȯth-, 'trōth-\ *n* (14c) : BETROTHAL

2trothplight *vt* (14c) : BETROTH

trot·line \'trät-,līn\ *n* [prob. fr. 2*trot*] (ca. 1835) : SETLINE; *esp* : a comparatively short setline used near shore or along streams

trot out *vt* (1838) **1** : to lead out and show the paces of (as a horse) **2** : to bring forward for display

Trots·ky·ism \'trät-skē-,iz-əm, 'trȯt-\ *n* (1925) : the political, economic, and social principles advocated by Trotsky; *esp* : the theory and practice of communism developed by or associated with Trotsky and usu. including adherence to the concept of worldwide revolution as opposed to socialism in one country — **Trots·ky·ist** \-skē-əst\ *n or adj* — **Trots·ky·ite** \-skē-,īt\ *n or adj*

trot·ter \'trät-ər\ *n* (14c) **1** : one that trots; *specif* : a standardbred horse trained for harness racing **2** : a pig's foot used as food

trou·ba·dour \'trü-bə-,dō(ə)r, -,dȯ(ə)r, -,dü(ə)r\ *n* [F, fr. OProv *trobador,* fr. *trobar* to compose, prob. fr. (assumed) VL *tropare,* fr. L *tropus* trope] (1727) : one of a class of lyric poets and poet-musicians often of knightly rank who flourished from the 11th to the end of the 13th century chiefly in the south of France and the north of Italy and whose major theme was courtly love — compare TROUVÈRE

1trou·ble \'trəb-əl\ *vb* **trou·bled; trou·bling** \'trəb-(ə-)liŋ\ [ME *troublen,* fr. OF *tourbler, troubler,* fr. (assumed) VL *turbulare,* alter. of L *turbidare,* fr. *turbidus* turbid, troubled — more at TURBID] *vt* (13c) **1 a** : to agitate mentally or spiritually : WORRY, DISTURB **b** (1) *archaic* : MISTREAT, OPPRESS (2) : to produce physical disorder in : AFFLICT ⟨*troubled* by a cold⟩ **c** : to put to exertion or inconvenience **2** : to put into confused motion ⟨the wind *troubled* the sea⟩ ~ *vi* **1** : to become mentally agitated : WORRY ⟨refused to ~ over trifles⟩ **2** : to make an effort : be at pains ⟨do not ~ to come⟩ — **trou·bler** \-(ə-)lər\ *n*

2trouble *n* (13c) **1** : the quality or state of being troubled esp. mentally **2** : public unrest or disturbance ⟨there's ~ brewing downtown⟩ **3** : an instance of trouble ⟨used to disguise her frustrations and despair by making light of her ~s —*Current Biog.*⟩ **4** : a state or condition of distress, annoyance, or difficulty ⟨in ~ with the law⟩ ⟨heading for ~⟩ ⟨got into financial ~⟩: as **a** : a condition of physical distress or ill health : AILMENT ⟨back ~⟩ ⟨heart ~⟩ **b** : a condition of mechanical malfunction ⟨engine ~⟩ **c** : a condition of doing something badly or only with great difficulty ⟨has ~ reading⟩ ⟨has ~ breathing⟩ **d** : pregnancy out of wedlock ⟨got a girl in ~⟩ **5** : an effort made : PAINS ⟨took the ~ to do it right⟩ **6 a** : a cause of distress, annoyance, or inconvenience ⟨once they get to six feet, they're ~ —Peter Benchley⟩ ⟨what's the ~?⟩ **b** : a negative feature : DRAWBACK ⟨the ~ with you is you're too honest⟩ ⟨the main ~ with electronic systems is the overreliance on them —John Perham⟩ **c** : the unhappy or sad fact ⟨the ~ is, I need the money⟩

trou·ble·mak·er \'trəb-əl-,mā-kər\ *n* (ca. 1914) : a person who consciously or unconsciously causes trouble

trou·ble·shoot \-,shüt\ *vb* **-shot** \-,shät\; **-shoot·ing** [back-formation fr. *troubleshooter*] *vi* (1931) : to operate or serve as a troubleshooter ⟨is ~*ing* for an electronics firm⟩ ~ *vt* : to investigate or deal with in the role of troubleshooter ⟨~*s* TV receivers⟩

trou·ble·shoot·er \-,shüt-ər\ *n* (1905) **1** : a skilled workman employed to locate trouble and make repairs in machinery and technical equipment **2** : one who is expert in resolving diplomatic or political disputes : a mediator of disputes that are at an impasse

trou·ble·some \-səm\ *adj* (1542) **1** : DIFFICULT, BURDENSOME **2** : giving trouble or anxiety : VEXATIOUS — **trou·ble·some·ly** *adv* — **trou·ble·some·ness** *n*

trou·blous \'trəb-(ə-)ləs\ *adj* (15c) **1** : full of trouble : STORMY ⟨these ~ times⟩ **2** : causing trouble : TROUBLESOME ⟨inflation is a ~ matter⟩ — **trou·blous·ly** *adv* — **trou·blous·ness** *n*

trou–de–loup \,trüd-ᵊl-'ü\ *n, pl* **trous–de–loup** \,trüd-ᵊl-'ü(z)\ [F, lit., wolf's hole] (ca. 1789) : a sloping pit with a pointed stake in the middle to form one of a group constructed as obstacles to the movements of an enemy — usu. used in pl.

trough \'trȯf, 'trȯth, *by bakers often* 'trō\ *n, pl* **troughs** \'trȯfs, 'trȯvz; 'trȯths, 'trȯ(th)z; 'trōz\ [ME, fr. OE *trog;* akin to OE *trēow* tree, wood — more at TREE] (bef. 12c) **1 a** : a long shallow often V-shaped receptacle for the drinking water or feed of domestic animals **b** : any of various domestic or industrial containers **2 a** : a conduit, drain, or channel for water; *esp* : a gutter along the eaves of a building **b** : a long and narrow or shallow channel or depression (as between waves or hills); *esp* : a long but shallow depression in the bed of the sea — compare TRENCH **3** : the minimum point of a complete cycle of a periodic function: as **a** : an elongated area of low barometric pressure **b** : the low point in a business cycle

trounce \'trau̇n(t)s\ *vt* **trounced; trounc·ing** [origin unknown] (1868) : to thrash or punish severely; *esp* : to defeat decisively

1troupe \'trüp\ *n* [F, fr. MF — more at TROOP] (1825) : COMPANY, TROOP; *esp* : a group of theatrical performers

2troupe *vi* **trouped; troup·ing** (1900) : to travel in a troupe; *also* : to perform as a member of a theatrical troupe — **troup·er** *n*

trou·pi·al \'trü-pē-əl\ *n* [F *troupiale,* fr. *troupe;* fr. its living in flocks] (1825) : any of a family (Icteridae) of birds including the American blackbirds, grackles, and orioles; *specif* : one of the large showy orioles (as *Icterus icterus*) of Central and So. America

1trou·ser \'trau̇-zər\ *n* [alter. of earlier *trouse,* fr. ScGael *triubhas*] (1613) : PANT — usu. used in pl.

2trouser *adj* (1762) **1** : of, relating to, or designed for trousers ⟨~ pockets⟩ **2** : of or relating to a male dramatic role played by a woman

trouser suit *n, chiefly Brit* (1967) : PANTSUIT

trous·seau \'trü-(,)sō, trü-'\ *n, pl* **trous·seaux** \-(,)sōz, -'sōz\ *or* **trous·seaus** [F, fr. OF, dim. of *trousse* bundle, fr. *trousser* to truss] (1817) : the personal possessions of a bride usu. including clothes, accessories, and household linens and wares

trout \'trau̇t\ *n, pl* **trout** *also* **trouts** [ME, fr. OE *trūht,* fr. LL *tructa,* a fish with sharp teeth, fr. Gk *trōktēs,* lit., gnawer, fr. *trōgein* to gnaw — more at TERSE] (bef. 12c) **1** : any of various food and sport fishes (family Salmonidae) mostly smaller than the typical salmons and restricted to cool clear fresh waters: **a** : any of various Old or New World fishes (genus *Salmo*) some of which are anadromous — compare RAINBOW TROUT **b** : any of various No. American fishes (genera *Salvelinus* or *Cristivomer*) : CHAR **2** : any of various fishes (as the largemouth bass) held to resemble the true trouts

trout lily *n* [prob. fr. its speckled leaves] (ca. 1898) : DOGTOOTH VIOLET

trout–perch \'trau̇t-,pərch\ *n* (1883) : a small freshwater fish (*Percopsis omiscomaycus*) of the central and eastern U.S.

trouty \'trau̇t-ē\ *adj* **trout·i·er; -est** (1676) : containing or likely to contain abundant trout

trou·vère \trü-'ve(ə)r\ *n* [F, fr. OF *troveor, troverre,* fr. *trover* to compose, find, fr. (assumed) VL *tropare* — more at TROUBADOUR] (1795) : one of a school of poets who flourished from the 11th to the 14th centuries and who composed mostly narrative works (as chansons de geste and fabliaux) — compare TROUBADOUR

trove \'trōv\ *n* [short for *treasure trove*] (1591) **1** : DISCOVERY, FIND **2** : a valuable collection : TREASURE; *also* : HAUL

tro·ver \'trō-vər\ *n* [MF *trover* to find, fr. OF] (1594) : a common law action to recover the value of goods wrongfully converted by another to his own use

trow \'trō\ *vb* [ME *trowen,* fr. OE *trēowan;* akin to OE *trēowe* faithful, true — more at TRUE] (bef. 12c) **1** *obs* : BELIEVE **2** *archaic* : THINK

1trow·el \'trau̇(-ə)l\ *n* [ME *truel,* fr. MF *truelle,* fr. LL *truella,* fr. L *trulla,* dim. of *trua* ladle; akin to L *turbare* to disturb — more at TURBID] (14c) : any of various hand tools used to apply, spread, shape, or smooth loose or plastic material; *also* : a scoop-shaped or flat-bladed garden tool for taking up and setting small plants

2trowel *vt* **-eled** *or* **-elled; -el·ing** *or* **-el·ling** (1670) : to smooth, mix, or apply with or as if with a trowel — **trow·el·er** *n*

troy \'trȯi\ *adj* [ME *troye,* fr. *Troyes,* France] (15c) : expressed in troy weight

troy weight *n* (15c) : a series of units of weight based on a pound of 12 ounces and the ounce of 20 pennyweights or 480 grains — see WEIGHT table

tru·an·cy \'trü-ən-sē\ *n, pl* **-cies** (1784) : an act or instance of playing truant : the state of being truant

1tru·ant \'trü-ənt\ *n* [ME, vagabond, idler, fr. OF, vagrant, of Celt origin; akin to ScGael *truaghan* wretch] (15c) : one who shirks duty; *esp* : one who stays out of school without permission

2truant *adj* (1561) **1** : shirking responsibility **2** : being, resembling or characteristic of a truant

3truant *vi* (1580) : to idle away time esp. while playing truant

truant officer *n* (1872) : ATTENDANCE OFFICER

tru·ant·ry \'trü-ən-trē\ *n, pl* **-ries** (15c) : TRUANCY

1truce \'trüs\ *n* [ME *trewes,* pl. of *trewe* agreement, fr. OE *trēow* fidelity; akin to OE *trēowe* faithful — more at TRUE] (13c) **1** : a suspension of fighting esp. of considerable duration by agreement of opposing forces : ARMISTICE, CEASE-FIRE **2** : a respite esp. from a disagreeable or painful state or action

2truce *vb* **truced; truc·ing** *vi* (1569) : to make a truce ~ *vt* : to end with a truce

1truck \'trək\ *vb* [ME *trukken,* fr. OF *troquer*] *vt* (13c) **1** : to give in exchange : SWAP **2** : to barter or dispose of by barter ~ *vi* **1** : to exchange commodities : BARTER **2** : to negotiate or traffic esp. in an underhanded way : have dealings

2truck *n* (1553) **1** : BARTER **2** : commodities appropriate for barter or for small trade **3** : close association : DEALINGS **4** : payment of wages in goods instead of cash **5** : vegetables grown for market **6** : heterogeneous small articles often of little value; *also* : RUBBISH

3truck *n* [prob. fr. L *trochus* iron hoop, fr. Gk *trochos* wheel — more at TROCHEE] (ca. 1611) **1** : a small wheel; *specif* : a small strong wheel for a gun carriage **2** : a small wooden cap at the top of a flagstaff or masthead usu. having holes for reeving flag or signal halyards **3** : a wheeled vehicle for moving heavy articles: as **a** : a strong horse-drawn or automotive vehicle for hauling **b** : a small barrow consisting of a rectangular frame having at one end a pair of handles and at the other end a pair of small heavy wheels and a projecting edge to slide under a load — called also *hand truck* **c** : a small heavy rectangular frame supported on four wheels for moving heavy objects **d** : a small flat-topped car pushed or pulled by hand **e** : a shelved stand mounted on casters **f** : an automotive vehicle equipped with a swivel for hauling a trailer; *also* : a truck with attached trailer **4 a** *Brit* : an open railroad freight car **b** : a swiveling carriage consisting of a frame with one or more pairs of wheels and springs to carry and guide one end (as of a railroad car) in turning sharp curves

[4]**truck** *vt* (1748) **:** to load or transport on a truck ~ *vi* **1 :** to transport goods by truck **2 :** to be employed in driving a truck **3 :** to roll along esp. in an easy untroubled way

truck·age \ˈtrək-ij\ *n* (1830) **1 :** money paid for conveyance on a truck **2 :** conveyance by truck

[1]**truck·er** \ˈtrək-ər\ *n* [[1]*truck*] (1598) **1 :** one that barters **2** *Scot* **:** PEDDLER

[2]**trucker** *n* [[4]*truck*] (ca. 1880) **1 :** one whose business is transporting goods by truck **2 :** a truck driver

truck farm *n* [[2]*truck*] (1866) **:** a farm devoted to the production of vegetables for the market — **truck farmer** *n*

truck·ing *n* (ca. 1809) **:** the process or business of transporting goods on trucks

truck·le \ˈtrək-əl\ *vi* **truck·led; truck·ling** \-(ə-)liŋ\ [fr. the lower position of the truckle bed] (1667) **:** to act in a subservient manner **:** SUBMIT *syn* see FAWN — **truck·ler** \-(ə-)lər\ *n*

truckle bed *n* [*truckle* (small wheel, pulley), fr. ME *trocle,* fr. L *trochlea* block of pulleys — more at TROCHLEA] (15c) **:** TRUNDLE BED

truck·line \ˈtrək-ˌlīn\ *n* (ca. 1924) **:** a transportation line using trucks

truck·load \-ˈlōd, -ˌlōd\ *n* (1862) **1 :** a load that fills a truck **2 :** the minimum weight required for shipping at truckload rates

truck·man \-mən\ *n* (1787) **1 :** [2]TRUCKER **2 :** a member of a fire department unit that operates a hook and ladder truck

truck·mas·ter \-ˌmas-tər\ *n, archaic* (1694) **:** an officer in charge of trade with Indians esp. among the early settlers

truck system *n* (1830) **:** the system of paying wages in goods instead of cash

tru·cu·lence \ˈtrək-yə-lən(t)s *also* ˈtrü-k-\ *n* (ca. 1727) **:** the quality or state of being truculent

tru·cu·len·cy \-lən-sē\ *n* (1569) **:** TRUCULENCE

tru·cu·lent \-lənt\ *adj* [L *truculentus,* fr. *truc-, trux* fierce] (1540) **1 :** feeling or displaying ferocity **:** CRUEL, SAVAGE **2 :** DEADLY, DESTRUCTIVE **3 :** scathingly harsh **:** VITRIOLIC **4 :** aggressively self-assertive **:** BELLIGERENT — **tru·cu·lent·ly** *adv*

[1]**trudge** \ˈtrəj\ *vb* **trudged; trudg·ing** [origin unknown] *vi* (1547) **:** to walk or march steadily and usu. laboriously ⟨*trudged* through deep snow⟩ ~ *vt* **:** to trudge along or over — **trudg·er** *n*

[2]**trudge** *n* (1835) **:** a long tiring walk **:** TRAMP

trud·gen stroke \ˈtrəj-ən-\ *n* [John *Trudgen,* 19th cent. Eng. swimmer] (1893) **:** a swimming stroke consisting of alternating overarm strokes and a scissors kick

[1]**true** \ˈtrü\ *adj* **tru·er; tru·est** [ME *trewe,* fr. OE *trēowe* faithful; akin to OHG *gitriuwi* faithful] (bef. 12c) **1 a :** STEADFAST, LOYAL **b :** HONEST, JUST **c** *archaic* **:** TRUTHFUL **2 a (1) :** being in accordance with the actual state of affairs ⟨~ description⟩ **(2) :** conformable to an essential reality **b :** IDEAL, ESSENTIAL **c :** being that which is the case rather than what is manifest or assumed ⟨the ~ dimension of the problem⟩ **d :** CONSISTENT ⟨~ to character⟩ **3 a :** properly so called ⟨~ love⟩ ⟨the ~ faith⟩ ⟨the ~ stomach⟩ **b (1) :** possessing the basic characters of and belonging to the same natural group as ⟨a whale is a ~ but not a typical mammal⟩ **(2) :** TYPICAL ⟨the ~ cats⟩ **4 :** LEGITIMATE, RIGHTFUL ⟨our ~ and lawful king⟩ **5 a :** that is fitted or formed or that functions accurately **b :** conformable to a standard or pattern **:** ACCURATE **6 :** determined with reference to the earth's axis rather than the magnetic poles ⟨~ north⟩ **7 :** logically necessary **8 :** NARROW, STRICT ⟨in the *truest* sense⟩ **9 :** corrected for error — **true·ness** *n*

[2]**true** *adv* (14c) **1 :** in accordance with fact or reality **2 a :** without deviation ⟨the bullet flew straight and ~⟩ **b :** without variation from type ⟨breed ~⟩

[3]**true** *n* (1812) **1 :** TRUTH, REALITY — usu. used with *the* **2 :** the quality or state of being accurate (as in alignment or adjustment) — used in the phrases *in true* and *out of true*

[4]**true** *vt* **trued; true·ing** *also* **tru·ing** (1841) **:** to make level, square, balanced, or concentric **:** bring or restore to a desired mechanical accuracy or form ⟨~ up a board⟩ ⟨~ up an engine cylinder⟩

true believer *n* (ca. 1820) **1 :** one who professes absolute belief in something **2 :** a zealous supporter of a particular cause

true bill *n* (1769) **:** a bill of indictment endorsed by a grand jury as warranting prosecution of the accused

true–blue *adj* (1674) **:** marked by unswerving loyalty (as to a party)

true blue *n* [fr. the old association of blue with constancy] (1672) **:** one who is true-blue

true·born \ˈtrü-ˈbȯ(ə)rn\ *adj* (1591) **:** genuinely such by birth ⟨a ~ Englishman —Shak.⟩

true bug *n* (1895) **:** BUG 1c

true–false test \ˈtrü-ˈfȯls-\ *n* (1924) **:** a test consisting of a series of statements to be marked as true or false

true·heart·ed \-ˈhärt-əd\ *adj* (15c) **:** FAITHFUL, LOYAL — **true·heart·ed·ness** *n*

true–life \ˌtrü-ˌlīf\ *adj* (1926) **:** true to life ⟨a ~ story⟩

true·love \ˈtrü-ˌləv\ *n* (14c) **:** one truly beloved or loving **:** SWEETHEART

true lover's knot *n* (1615) **:** a complicated ornamental knot not readily untied and symbolic of mutual love — called also *truelove knot;* see KNOT illustration

true·pen·ny \ˈtrü-ˌpen-ē\ *n* (1595) **:** an honest or trusty person

true rib *n* (1741) **:** any of the ribs having costal cartilages connected directly with the sternum and in man constituting the first seven pairs

truf·fle \ˈtrəf-əl, ˈtrüf-\ *n* [modif. of MF *truffe,* fr. OProv *trufa,* fr. VL *tufera,* akin to L *tuber* — more at TUBER] (1591) **1 :** the usu. dark and rugose edible subterranean fruiting body of several European ascomycetous fungi (genus *Tuber*); *also* **:** one of these fungi **2 :** a candy made of chocolate, butter, and sugar shaped into balls and coated with cocoa

truf·fled \-əld\ *adj* (1837) **:** cooked, stuffed, or garnished with truffles

tru·ism \ˈtrü-ˌiz-əm\ *n* (1708) **:** an undoubted or self-evident truth; *esp* **:** one too obvious for mention — **tru·is·tic** \trü-ˈis-tik\ *adj*

trull \ˈtrəl\ *n* [obs. G *trulle,* fr. MHG; akin to ON *troll* giant, demon — more at TROLL] (1519) **:** PROSTITUTE, STRUMPET

tru·ly \ˈtrü-lē\ *adv* (bef. 12c) **1 :** in all sincerity **:** SINCERELY — often used with *yours* as a complimentary close **2 :** in agreement with fact **:** TRUTHFULLY **3 :** with exactness of construction or operation **4 a :** INDEED — often used as an intensive ⟨~, she is fair⟩ or interjectionally to express astonishment or doubt **b :** without feigning, falsity, or inaccuracy in truth or fact **5 :** in a proper or suitable manner

[1]**trump** \ˈtrəmp\ *n* [ME *trompe,* fr. OF] (13c) **1 a :** TRUMPET **b** *chiefly Scot* **:** JEW'S HARP **2 :** a sound of or as if of trumpeting

[2]**trump** *n* [alter. of [1]*triumph*] (1529) **1 a :** a card of a suit any of whose cards will win over a card that is not of this suit **b :** the suit whose cards are trumps for a particular hand — often used in pl. **2 :** a decisive overriding factor or final resource **3 :** a dependable and exemplary person

[3]**trump** *vt* (1898) **1 :** to play a trump on (a card or trick) when another suit was led **2 :** to get the better of **:** OUTDO ~ *vi* **:** to play a trump when another suit was led

trump card *n* (1822) **:** [2]TRUMP 1a, 2

trumped–up \ˈtrəm(p)-ˈtəp\ *adj* (1728) **:** fraudulently concocted **:** SPURIOUS ⟨~ charges⟩

trum·pery \ˈtrəm-p(ə-)rē\ *n* [ME *tromperie* deceit, fr. MF, fr. *tromper* to deceive] (15c) **1 a :** worthless nonsense **b :** trivial or useless articles **:** JUNK ⟨a wagon loaded with household ~ —Washington Irving⟩ **2** *archaic* **:** tawdry finery — **trumpery** *adj*

[1]**trum·pet** \ˈtrəm-pət\ *n* [ME *trompette,* fr. MF, fr. OF *trompe* trump] (14c) **1 a :** a wind instrument consisting of a conical or cylindrical usu. metal tube, a cup-shaped mouthpiece, and a flared bell; *specif* **:** a valved brass instrument having a cylindrical tube with two turns and a usual range from F sharp below middle C upward for 2 1/2 octaves **b :** a musical instrument (as a cornet) resembling a trumpet **2 :** a trumpet player **3 :** something that resembles a trumpet or its tonal quality: as **a :** a funnel-shaped instrument (as a megaphone) for collecting, directing, or intensifying sound **b (1) :** a stentorian voice **(2) :** a penetrating cry (as of an elephant) — **trum·pet·like** *adj*

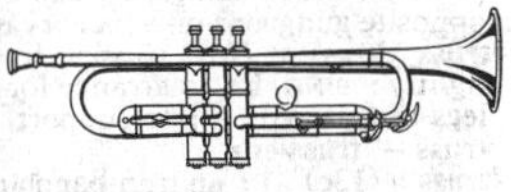
trumpet 1a

[2]**trumpet** *vi* (1530) **1 :** to blow a trumpet **2 :** to make a sound suggestive of that of a trumpet ~ *vt* **:** to sound or proclaim on or as if on a trumpet

trumpet creeper *n* (1818) **:** a No. American woody vine (*Campsis radicans* of the family Bignoniaceae, the trumpet-creeper family) having pinnate leaves and large red trumpet-shaped flowers

trum·pet·er \ˈtrəm-pət-ər\ *n* (15c) **1 a :** a trumpet player; *specif* **:** one that gives signals with a trumpet **b :** one that praises or advocates **:** EULOGIST, SPOKESMAN **2 a :** any of a genus (*Psophia*) of several large gregarious long-legged long-necked So. American birds related to the cranes **b :** any of an Asian breed of pigeons with a rounded crest and heavily feathered feet

trumpeter swan *n* (1709) **:** a rare pure white No. American wild swan (*Cygnus buccinator*) noted for its sonorous voice

trumpet flower *n* (ca. 1731) **1 :** any of various plants (as a trumpet creeper or a datura) with trumpet-shaped flowers **2 :** the flower of a trumpet flower

trumpet honeysuckle *n* (1731) **:** a No. American honeysuckle (*Lonicera sempervirens*) with coral-red or orange flowers and a trumpet-shaped corolla

trumpet vine *n* (ca. 1709) **:** TRUMPET CREEPER

trump up *vt* (1695) **1 :** to concoct esp. with intent to deceive **:** FABRICATE, INVENT **2** *archaic* **:** to cite as support for an action or claim

[1]**trun·cate** \ˈtrəŋ-ˌkāt, ˈtrən-\ *adj* [L *truncatus,* pp. of *truncare* to shorten, fr. *truncus* trunk — more at THRONG] (1716) **:** having the end square or even ⟨the ~ leaves of the tulip tree⟩

[2]**truncate** *vt* **trun·cat·ed; trun·cat·ing** (ca. 1727) **1 :** to shorten by or as if by cutting off **2 :** to replace (an edge or corner of a crystal) by a plane — **trun·ca·tion** \trəŋ-ˈkā-shən, trən-\ *n*

trun·cat·ed \-ˌkāt-əd\ *adj* (ca. 1704) **1 :** having the apex replaced by a plane section and esp. by one parallel to the base ⟨~ cone⟩ **2 a :** cut short **:** CURTAILED **b :** lacking an expected or normal element (as a syllable) at the beginning or end **:** CATALECTIC

[1]**trun·cheon** \ˈtrən-chən\ *n* [ME *tronchoun,* fr. MF *tronchon,* fr. (assumed) VL *truncion-, truncio,* fr. L *truncus* trunk] (14c) **1 :** a shattered spear or lance **2 a** *obs* **:** CLUB, BLUDGEON **b :** BATON 2 **c :** a police officer's billy club

[2]**truncheon** *vt, archaic* (1597) **:** to beat with a truncheon

[1]**trun·dle** \ˈtrən-dᵊl\ *n* [alter. of earlier *trendle,* fr. ME, circle, ring, wheel, fr. OE *trendel;* akin to OE *trendan* to revolve — more at TREND] (1542) **1 :** a small wheel or roller **2 :** a round or oval wooden tub **3 a :** a low-wheeled cart or truck **b :** TRUNDLE BED **4 :** the motion or sound of something rolling

[2]**trundle** *vb* **trun·dled; trun·dling** \-(d)liŋ, -dᵊl-iŋ\ *vt* (ca. 1598) **1 a :** to propel by causing to rotate **:** ROLL **b** *archaic* **:** to cause to revolve **:** SPIN **2 :** to transport in or as if in a wheeled vehicle **:** HAUL, WHEEL ~ *vi* **1 :** to progress by revolving **2 :** to move on or as if on wheels **:** ROLL — **trun·dler** \-(d)lər, -dᵊl-ər\ *n*

trundle bed *n* (1542) **:** a low bed usu. on casters that can be rolled or slid under a higher bed when not in use — called also *truckle bed*

trun·dle–tail \ˈtrən-dᵊl-ˌtāl\ *n, archaic* (15c) **:** a curly-tailed dog

trunk \ˈtrəŋk\ *n* [ME *tronke* box, trunk, fr. MF *tronc,* fr. L *truncus* trunk, torso — more at THRONG] (15c) **1 a :** the main stem of a tree apart from limbs and roots — called also *bole* **b (1) :** the human or animal body apart from the head and appendages **:** TORSO **(2) :** the thorax of an insect **c :** the central part of anything; *specif* **:** the shaft of a column or pilaster **2 a (1) :** a large rigid piece of luggage used usu. for transporting clothing and personal effects **(2) :** the luggage compartment of an automobile **b (1) :** a superstructure over a ship's hatches usu. level with the poop deck **(2) :** the part of the cabin of a boat projecting above the deck **(3) :** the housing for a centerboard or rudder **3 :** PROBOSCIS; *esp* **:** the long muscular proboscis of the elephant **4** *pl* **:** men's shorts worn chiefly for sports **5 a :** a usu. major channel or passage (as a chute or shaft) **b :** a circuit between two telephone exchanges for making connections between subscribers;

\ə\ abut \ᵊ\ kitten, F table \ər\ further \a\ ash \ā\ ace \ä\ cot, cart \au̇\ out \ch\ chin \e\ bet \ē\ easy \g\ go \i\ hit \ī\ ice \j\ job \ŋ\ sing \ō\ go \ȯ\ law \ȯi\ boy \th\ thin \th\ the \ü\ loot \u̇\ foot \y\ yet \zh\ vision \à, k, ⁿ, œ, œ̄, ue, ue̅, ʸ\ *see* Guide to Pronunciation

broadly : a usu. electronic path over which information is transmitted (as between computer memories) **6 a** : the principal channel of a tributary system ⟨an arterial ~⟩ ⟨~ of a river⟩ **b** : TRUNK LINE — **trunk·ful** \'trəŋk-ˌfu̇l\ *n*

trunked \'trəŋ(k)t\ *adj* (1640) : having a trunk esp. of a specified kind — usu. used in combination ⟨a gray-*trunked* tree⟩

trunk·fish \'trəŋk-ˌfish\ *n* (ca. 1804) : any of numerous small bright-colored fishes (family Ostraciidae) of tropical seas with the body and head enclosed in a bony carapace

trunk hose \'trəŋk-\ *n pl* [prob. fr. obs. E *trunk* (to truncate)] (1637) : short full breeches reaching about halfway down the thigh that were worn chiefly in the late 16th and early 17th centuries

trunk line *n* (1843) **1** : a transportation system (as an airline, railroad, or highway) handling long-distance through traffic **2 a** : a main supply channel (as for gas or oil) **b** : TRUNK 5b

trun·nel \'trən-ᵊl\ *var of* TREENAIL

trun·nion \'trən-yən\ *n* [F *trognon* core, stump] (ca. 1625) : a pin or pivot on which something can be rotated or tilted; *esp* : either of two opposite gudgeons on which a cannon is swiveled

[1]**truss** \'trəs\ *vt* [ME *trussen*, fr. OF *trousser*] (13c) **1 a** : to secure tightly : BIND **b** : to arrange for cooking by binding close the wings or legs of (a fowl) **2** : to support, strengthen, or stiffen by or as if by a truss — **truss·er** *n*

[2]**truss** *n* (13c) **1** : an iron band around a lower mast **2 a** : BRACKET 1 **b** : an assemblage of members (as beams) forming a rigid framework **3** : a device worn to reduce a hernia by pressure **4** : a compact flower or fruit cluster

truss bridge *n* (1840) : a bridge supported mainly by trusses — see BRIDGE illustration

truss·ing \'trəs-iŋ\ *n* (1840) **1** : the members forming a truss **2** : the trusses and framework of a structure

[1]**trust** \'trəst\ *n* [ME, prob. of Scand origin; akin to ON *traust* trust; akin to OE *trēowe* faithful — more at TRUE] (13c) **1 a** : assured reliance on the character, ability, strength, or truth of someone or something **b** : one in which confidence is placed **2 a** : dependence on something future or contingent : HOPE **b** : reliance on future payment for property (as merchandise) delivered : CREDIT **3 a** : a property interest held by one person for the benefit of another **b** : a combination of firms or corporations formed by a legal agreement; *esp* : one that reduces or threatens to reduce competition **4** *archaic* : TRUSTWORTHINESS **5 a (1)** : a charge or duty imposed in faith or confidence or as a condition of some relationship **(2)** : something committed or entrusted to one to be used or cared for in the interest of another **b** : responsible charge or office **c** : CARE, CUSTODY ⟨child committed to his ~⟩ — **in trust** : in the care or possession of a trustee

[2]**trust** *vi* (13c) **1 a** : to place confidence : DEPEND ⟨~ in God⟩ ⟨~ to luck⟩ **b** : to be confident : HOPE **2** : to sell or deliver on credit ~ *vt* **1 a** : to commit or place in one's care or keeping : ENTRUST **b** : to permit to stay or go or to do something without fear or misgiving **2 a** : to rely on the truthfulness or accuracy of : BELIEVE **b** : to place confidence in : rely on **c** : to hope or expect confidently **3** : to extend credit to — **trust·abil·i·ty** \ˌtrəs-tə-'bil-ət-ē\ *n* — **trust·able** \'trəs-tə-bəl\ *adj* — **trust·er** *n* — **trust·ing·ly** \'trəs-tiŋ-lē\ *adv* — **trust·ing·ness** *n*

trust·bust·er \'trəs(t)-ˌbəs-tər\ *n* (1903) : one who seeks to break up business trusts; *specif* : a federal official who prosecutes trusts under the antitrust laws — **trust–bust·ing** \-tiŋ\ *n*

trust company *n* (1834) : an incorporated trustee; *broadly* : a corporation that functions as a corporate and personal trustee and usu. also engages in the normal activities of a commercial bank

[1]**trust·ee** \ˌtrəs-'tē\ *n* (1647) **1 a** : one to whom something is entrusted **b** : a country charged with the supervision of a trust territory **2 a** : a natural or legal person to whom property is legally committed to be administered for the benefit of a beneficiary (as a person or a charitable organization) **b** : one (as a corporate director) occupying a position of trust and performing functions comparable to those of a trustee

[2]**trustee** *vb* **trust·eed; trust·ee·ing** *vt* (1818) : to commit to the care of a trustee ~ *vi* : to serve as trustee

trust·ee·ship \ˌtrəs-'tē-ˌship\ *n* (ca. 1730) **1** : the office or function of a trustee **2** : supervisory control by one or more countries over a trust territory

trust·ful \'trəst-fəl\ *adj* (1834) : full of trust : CONFIDING — **trust·ful·ly** \-fə-lē\ *adv* — **trust·ful·ness** *n*

trust fund *n* (1780) : property (as money or securities) settled or held in trust

trust·less \'trəst-ləs\ *adj* (1530) **1** : not deserving of trust : FAITHLESS **2** : DISTRUSTFUL

trust territory *n* (1945) : a non-self-governing territory placed under an administrative authority by the Trusteeship Council of the United Nations

trust·wor·thy \'trəst-ˌwər-t͟hē\ *adj* (1829) : worthy of confidence : DEPENDABLE — **trust·wor·thi·ly** \-t͟hə-lē\ *adv* — **trust·wor·thi·ness** *n*

[1]**trusty** \'trəs-tē\ *adj* **trust·i·er; -est** (14c) : TRUSTWORTHY, DEPENDABLE — **trust·i·ness** *n*

[2]**trusty** \'trəs-tē *also* ˌtrəs-'tē\ *n, pl* **trust·ies** (1573) : a trusty or trusted person; *specif* : a convict considered trustworthy and allowed special privileges

truth \'trüth\ *n, pl* **truths** \'trü͟thz, 'trüths\ [ME *trouthe*, fr. OE *trēowth* fidelity; akin to OE *trēowe* faithful — more at TRUE] (bef. 12c) **1 a** *archaic* : FIDELITY, CONSTANCY **b** : sincerity in action, character, and utterance **2 a (1)** : the state of being the case : FACT **(2)** : the body of real things, events, and facts : ACTUALITY **(3)** *often cap* : a transcendent fundamental or spiritual reality **b** : a judgment, proposition, or idea that is true or accepted as true ⟨~s of thermodynamics⟩ **c** : the body of true statements and propositions **3 a** : the property (as of a statement) of being in accord with fact or reality **b** *chiefly Brit* : TRUE 2 **c** : fidelity to an original or to a standard **4** *cap, Christian Science* : GOD — **in truth** : in accordance with fact : ACTUALLY

truth·ful \'trüth-fəl\ *adj* (1596) : telling or disposed to tell the truth — **truth·ful·ly** \-fə-lē\ *adv* — **truth·ful·ness** *n*

truth serum *n* (1925) : a hypnotic or anesthetic held to induce a subject under questioning to talk freely

truth set *n* (1940) : a mathematical or logical set containing all the elements that make a given statement of relationships true when substituted in it ⟨the equation $x + 7 = 10$ has as its *truth set* the single number 3⟩

truth table *n* (1921) : a table that shows the truth-value of a compound statement for every truth-value of its component statements; *also* : a similar table (as for a computer logic circuit) showing the value of the output for each value of each input

TRUTH TABLE

p a statement	q a statement	$\sim p$ not p denial	$p \cdot q$ p and q conjunction	$p \vee q$ p or q (inclusive) inclusive disjunction	p or q (exclusive) exclusive disjunction	$p \supset q$ if p then q conditional	$p \equiv q$ p if and only if q biconditional
T	T	F	T	T	F	T	T
T	F		F	T	T	F	F
F	T	T	F	T	T	T	F
F	F		F	F	F	T	T

T = true F = false

truth–value *n* (1903) : the truth or falsity of a proposition or statement

[1]**try** \'trī\ *vb* **tried; try·ing** [ME *trien*, fr. AF *trier*, fr. OF, to pick out, sift, prob. fr. LL *tritare* to rub to pieces, fr. *tritus*, pp. — more at TRITE] *vt* (14c) **1 a** : to examine or investigate judicially **b (1)** : to conduct the trial of **(2)** : to participate as counsel in the judicial examination of **2 a** : to put to test or trial ⟨~ one's luck⟩ — often used with *out* **b** : to subject to something (as undue strain or excessive hardship or provocation) that tests the powers of endurance **c** : DEMONSTRATE, PROVE **3 a** *obs* : PURIFY, REFINE **b** : to melt down and procure in a pure state : RENDER ⟨~ out whale oil from blubber⟩ **4** : to fit or finish with accuracy **5** : to make an attempt at — often used with an infinitive ~ *vi* : to make an attempt ***syn*** see AFFLICT, ATTEMPT — **try one's hand** : to attempt something for the first time

[2]**try** *n, pl* **tries** (1607) **1** : an experimental trial : ATTEMPT **2** : a play in rugby that is similar to a touchdown in football, scores usu. four points, and entitles the scoring side to attempt a placekick at the goal for additional points; *also* : the score made on a try

try for point (1924) : an attempt made after scoring a touchdown in football to score one or two additional points by kicking the ball over the crossbar or again carrying it into the opponents' end zone

try·ing \'trī-iŋ\ *adj* (1718) : severely straining the powers of endurance — **try·ing·ly** \-iŋ-lē\ *adv*

try on \(ˈ)trī-'ȯn, -'än\ *vt* (1693) **1** : to put on (a garment) in order to test the fit **2** : to use or test experimentally — **try–on** \'trī-ˌȯn, -ˌän\ *n*

try·out \'trī-ˌau̇t\ *n* (1903) : an experimental performance or demonstration: as **a** : a test of the ability (as of an athlete or actor) to fill a part or meet standards **b** : a performance of a play prior to its official opening to determine response and discover weaknesses

try out \(ˈ)trī-'au̇t\ *vi* (1898) : to compete for a position esp. on an athletic team or for a part in a play

try·pano·some \trip-'an-ə-ˌsōm\ *n* [NL *Trypanosoma*, fr. Gk *trypanon* auger + NL *-soma* -some — more at TREPAN] (1903) : any of a genus (*Trypanosoma*) of parasitic flagellate protozoans that infest the blood of various vertebrates including man, are usu. transmitted by the bite of an insect, and include some that cause serious disease (as sleeping sickness)

try·pano·so·mi·a·sis \trip-ˌan-ə-sə-'mī-ə-səs\ *n, pl* **-a·ses** \-ˌsēz\ (1902) : infection with or disease caused by trypanosomes

try–pot \'trī-ˌpät\ *n* (1795) : a metallic pot used on a whaler or on shore to render whale oil from blubber

tryp·sin \'trip-sən\ *n* [Gk *tryein* to wear down + ISV *-psin* (as in *pepsin*); akin to L *terere* to rub — more at THROW] (ca. 1876) : a proteolytic enzyme from pancreatic juice active in an alkaline medium; *also* : any of several similar enzymes

tryp·sin·o·gen \trip-'sin-ə-jən\ *n* [ISV] (ca. 1890) : the inactive substance released by the pancreas into the duodenum to form trypsin

trypt·amine \'trip-tə-ˌmēn\ *n* [*tryptophan* + *amine*] (1929) : a crystalline amine $C_{10}H_{12}N_2$ derived from tryptophan; *also* : any of various substituted derivatives of this amine of which some are significantly hallucinogenic or neurotoxic

tryp·tic \'trip-tik\ *adj* [ISV, fr. *trypsin*, after such pairs as ISV *pepsin: peptic*] (1888) : of, relating to, or produced by trypsin or its action

tryp·to·phan \'trip-tə-ˌfan\ *also* **tryp·to·phane** \-ˌfān\ *n* [ISV *tryptic* + *-o-* + *-phane*] (1890) : a crystalline amino acid $C_{11}H_{12}N_2O_2$ that is widely distributed in proteins and is essential to animal life

try·sail \'trī-ˌsāl, -səl\ *n* [obs. *at try* (lying to)] (1794) : a fore-and-aft sail bent to a gaff and hoisted on a lower mast or a small mast close abaft

try square *n* (ca. 1877) : an instrument used for laying off right angles and testing whether work is square

[1]**tryst** \'trist, *esp Brit* 'trīst\ *n* [ME, fr. MF *triste* watch post, prob. of Scand origin; akin to ON *traust* trust] (14c) **1** : an agreement (as between lovers) to meet **2** : an appointed meeting or meeting place

[2]**tryst** *vi* (14c) : to make or keep a tryst

try·works \'trī-ˌwərks\ *n pl* (1792) : a brick furnace in which try-pots are placed; *also* : the furnace with the pots

tsa·de \'(t)säd-ə, -ē\ *var of* SADHE

tsar \'zär, '(t)sär\ *var of* CZAR

tset·se fly \'(t)set-sē-, 'tet-, '(t)sēt-, 'tēt-\ *n* [Afrik, fr. Tswana (a Bantu language of southern Africa) *tsêtsê*] (1849) : any of several two-winged flies (genus *Glossina*) that occur in Africa south of the Sahara desert and include vectors of human and animal trypanosomes — called also *tsetse;* compare SLEEPING SICKNESS

Tshi \'chwē, chə-'wē, 'twē, 'chē\ *var of* TWI

Tshi·lu·ba \chi-'lü-bə\ *n* (ca. 1961) **:** one of the major trade languages of the Congo region esp. in the southern part

T–shirt \'tē-,shərt\ *n* (1944) **:** a collarless short-sleeved or sleeveless usu. cotton undershirt; *also* **:** an outer shirt of similar design — **T–shirt·ed** *adj*

T square *n* (1785) **:** a ruler with a crosspiece or head at one end used in making parallel lines

tsu·na·mi \(t)sü-'näm-ē\ *n* [Jp] (ca. 1907) **:** a great sea wave produced by submarine earth movement or volcanic eruption **:** TIDAL WAVE — **tsu·na·mic** \-ik\ *adj*

tsu·tsu·ga·mu·shi disease \,(t)süt-sə-gə-'mü-shē-, ,tüt-, -'gäm-ů-shē-\ *n* [Jp *tsutsugamushi* scrub typhus mite, fr. *tsutsuga* sickness + *mushi* insect] (ca. 1917) **:** an acute febrile disease that is caused by a rickettsia (*Rickettsia tsutsugamushi*) transmitted by mite larvae, resembles louse-borne typhus, and is widespread in the western Pacific area — called also *scrub typhus, tsutsugamushi*

t–test \'tē-'test\ *n* (ca. 1936) **:** a statistical test involving confidence limits for the random variable *t* of a t distribution and used esp. in testing hypotheses about means of normal distributions when the standard deviations are unknown

Tu·a·mo·tu \,tü-ə-'mō-(,)tü\ *n* (ca. 1925) **:** the Polynesian language of the Tuamotu archipelago

Tua·reg \'twä-,reg\ *n, pl* **Tuareg** *or* **Tuaregs** [Ar *Tawāriq*] (1826) **:** a member of the dominant nomadic people of the central and western Sahara and along the middle Niger from Tombouctou to Nigeria who have preserved their Hamitic speech but have adopted the Muslim religion

tu·a·ta·ra \,tü-ə-'tär-ə\ *n* [Maori *tuatàra*] (1890) **:** a large spiny quadrupedal reptile (*Sphenodon punctatum*) of islands off the coast of New Zealand that is the only surviving rhynchocephalian

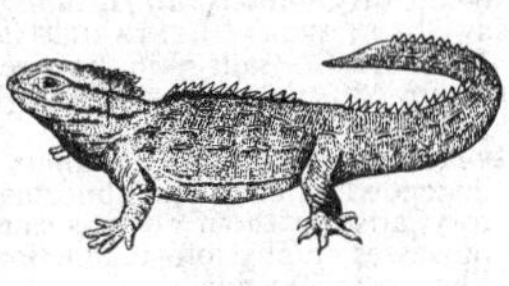

tuatara

[1]tub \'təb\ *n* [ME *tubbe,* fr. MD; akin to MLG *tubbe* tub] (14c) **1 :** a wide low vessel orig. formed with wooden staves, round bottom, and hoops **2 :** an old or slow boat **3 :** BATHTUB; *also* **:** BATH **4 :** the amount that a tub will hold — **tub·ful** \-,fůl\ *n* — **tub·like** \-,līk\ *adj*

[2]tub *vb* **tubbed; tub·bing** *vt* (1610) **1 :** to wash or bathe in a tub **2 :** to put or store in a tub ~ *vi* **1 :** BATHE **2 :** to undergo washing — **tub·ba·ble** \'təb-ə-bəl\ *adj* — **tub·ber** *n*

tu·ba \'t(y)ü-bə\ *n* [It, fr. L, trumpet] (ca. 1864) **:** a large low-pitched brass instrument usu. oval in shape and having a conical tube, a cup-shaped mouthpiece, and a usual range an octave lower than that of the euphonium — **tu·ba·ist** \-bə-(i)st\ *or* **tub·ist** \-bəst\ *n*

tub·al \'t(y)ü-bəl\ *adj* (1735) **:** of, relating to, or involving a tube and esp. a fallopian tube

tub·by \'təb-ē\ *adj* **tub·bi·er; -est** (1806) **1 :** sounding dull and without proper resonance or freedom of sound ⟨a ~ violin⟩ **2 :** PUDGY, FAT

tube \'t(y)üb\ *n* [F, fr. L *tubus;* akin to L *tuba* trumpet] (ca. 1611) **1 a** (1) **:** a slender channel within a plant or animal body **:** DUCT (2) **:** the narrow basal portion of a gamopetalous corolla or a gamosepalous calyx **b :** a hollow elongated cylinder; *esp* **:** one to convey fluids **2 :** any of various usu. cylindrical structures or devices: as **a :** a soft tubular container whose contents (as toothpaste) can be removed by squeezing **b** (1) **:** TUNNEL (2) *Brit* **:** SUBWAY b **c :** the basically cylindrical section between the mouthpiece and bell that is the fundamental part of a wind instrument **3 :** an airtight tube of rubber inside the casing of a pneumatic tire to hold air under pressure **4 :** ELECTRON TUBE **5 :** VACUUM TUBE **6 :** TELEVISION TUBE; *broadly* **:** TELEVISION **7 :** an article of clothing shaped like a tube ⟨~ top⟩ ⟨~ socks⟩ — **tubed** \'t(y)übd\ *adj* — **tube·like** \'t(y)ü-,blīk\ *adj* — **down the tube** *or* **down the tubes :** into a state of collapse, deterioration, or ruin

tube foot *n* (1888) **:** one of the small flexible tubular processes of most echinoderms that are extensions of the water-vascular system and are used esp. in locomotion and grasping

tube·less \'t(y)üb-ləs\ *adj* (1855) **:** lacking a tube; *specif* **:** being a pneumatic tire that does not depend on an inner tube for airtightness

tube nucleus *n* (1939) **:** the one of the two nuclei formed by mitotic division of a microspore during the formation of a pollen grain that is held to control subsequent growth of the pollen tube and that does not divide again — compare GENERATIVE NUCLEUS

tu·ber \'t(y)ü-bər\ *n* [L, lump, tuber, truffle — more at THUMB] (1668) **1 a :** a short fleshy usu. underground stem bearing minute scale leaves each of which bears a bud in its axil and is potentially able to produce a new plant — compare BULB, CORM **b :** a fleshy root or rhizome resembling a tuber **2 :** an anatomical prominence **:** TUBEROSITY

tu·ber·cle \'t(y)ü-bər-kəl\ *n* [L *tuberculum,* dim. of *tuber*] (1578) **1 :** a small knobby prominence or excrescence esp. on a plant or animal **:** NODULE: as **a :** a protuberance near the head of a rib that articulates with the transverse process of a vertebra **b :** any of several prominences in the central nervous system **c :** NODULE b **2 :** a small abnormal discrete lump in the substance of an organ or in the skin; *esp* **:** the specific lesion of tuberculosis

tubercle bacillus *n* (ca. 1890) **:** a bacterium (*Mycobacterium tuberculosis*) that is the cause of tuberculosis

tubercul- *or* **tuberculo-** *comb form* [NL, fr. L *tuberculum*] **1 :** tubercle ⟨*tubercular*⟩ **2 :** tubercle bacillus ⟨*tuberculin*⟩ **3 :** tuberculosis ⟨*tuberculoid*⟩

[1]tu·ber·cu·lar \t(y)ů-'bər-kyə-lər\ *adj* (1799) **1 :** characterized by tubercular lesions ⟨~ leprosy⟩ **2 :** relating to, resembling, or constituting a tubercle **:** TUBERCULATED **3 a :** of, relating to, or affected with tuberculosis **:** TUBERCULOUS **b :** caused by the tubercle bacillus ⟨~ meningitis⟩

[2]tubercular *n* (1925) **:** a person with tuberculosis

tu·ber·cu·lat·ed \t(y)ů-'bər-kyə-,lāt-əd\ *also* **tu·ber·cu·late** \-lət\ *adj* (1771) **:** having tubercles **:** characterized by or beset with tubercles

tu·ber·cu·lin \t(y)ů-'bər-kyə-lən\ *n* [ISV] (1890) **:** a sterile liquid containing the growth products of or specific substances extracted from the tubercle bacillus and used in the diagnosis of tuberculosis esp. in children and cattle

tuberculin test *n* (ca. 1901) **:** a test for hypersensitivity to tuberculin as an indication of past or present tubercular infection

tu·ber·cu·loid \t(y)ů-'bər-kyə-,lȯid\ *adj* [ISV] (ca. 1923) **:** resembling tuberculosis esp. in the presence of tubercles ⟨~ leprosy⟩

tu·ber·cu·lo·sis \t(y)ů-,bər-kyə-'lō-səs\ *n, pl* **-lo·ses** \-,sēz\ [NL] (1860) **:** a highly variable communicable disease of man and some other vertebrates caused by the tubercle bacillus and characterized by toxic symptoms or allergic manifestations which in man primarily affect the lungs

tu·ber·cu·lous \t(y)ů-'bər-kyə-ləs\ *adj* (1891) **1 :** constituting or affected with tuberculosis ⟨a ~ process⟩ **2 :** caused by or resulting from the presence or products of the tubercle bacillus ⟨~ peritonitis⟩

tube·rose \'t(y)ü-,brōz (*by folk etymology*), *also* -bə-,rōz, -bə-,rōs\ *n* [NL *tuberosa,* fr. L, fem. of *tuberosus* tuberous, fr. *tuber* tuber] (1664) **:** a Mexican bulbous herb (*Polianthes tuberosa*) of the amaryllis family cultivated for its spike of fragrant white single or double flowers

tu·ber·os·i·ty \,t(y)ü-bə-'räs-ət-ē\ *n, pl* **-ties** (ca. 1611) **:** a rounded prominence; *esp* **:** a large prominence on a bone usu. serving for the attachment of muscles or ligaments

tu·ber·ous \'t(y)ü-b(ə-)rəs\ *adj* (1650) **1 :** consisting of, bearing, or resembling a tuber **2 :** of, relating to, or being a plant tuber or tuberous root of a plant

tuberous root *n* (ca. 1668) **:** a thick fleshy storage root like a tuber but lacking buds or scale leaves — **tu·ber·ous–root·ed** \,t(y)ü-b(ə-)rəs-'rüt-əd, -'růt-\ *adj*

tu·bi·fex \'t(y)ü-bə-,feks\ *n, pl* **tubifex** *or* **tu·bi·fex·es** [NL *Tubific-, Tubifex,* fr. L *tubus* tube + *facere* to make — more at DO] (ca. 1948) **:** any of a genus (*Tubifex*) of slender reddish oligochaete worms that live in tubes in fresh or brackish water and are widely used as food for aquarium fish

tu·bi·fi·cid \t(y)ü-'bif-ə-səd, ,t(y)ü-bə-'fis-əd\ *n* [NL *Tubificidae,* fr. *Tubific-, Tubifex*] (1953) **:** any of a family (Tubificidae) of aquatic oligochaete worms that do not reproduce asexually — **tubificid** *adj*

tub·ing \'t(y)ü-biŋ\ *n* (1845) **1 :** material in the form of a tube; *also* **:** a length or piece of tube **2 :** a series or system of tubes

tu·bo·cu·ra·rine \,t(y)ü-bō-kyů-'rär-ən, -,ēn\ *n* [ISV *tubo-* (fr. L *tubus* tube) + *curare* + *-ine;* fr. its being shipped in sections of hollow bamboo] (1907) **:** a toxic alkaloid or its crystalline quaternary ammonium chloride $C_{38}H_{44}Cl_2N_2O_6{\cdot}5H_2O$ that is obtained chiefly from the bark and stems of a So. American vine (*Chondrodendron tomentosum* of the family Menispermaceae) and in its dextrorotatory form constitutes the chief active constituent of curare and is used esp. as a skeletal muscle relaxant

tub–thump·er \'təb-,thəm-pər\ *n* (ca. 1662) **:** a vociferous supporter (as of a cause) — **tub–thump** \-,thəmp\ *vb*

tu·bu·lar \'t(y)ü-byə-lər\ *adj* (1673) **1 a :** having the form of or consisting of a tube ⟨a ~ calyx⟩ **b :** made or provided with tubes **2 :** of, relating to, or sounding as if produced through tubes

tu·bule \'t(y)ü-(,)byü(ə)l\ *n* [L *tubulus,* dim. of *tubus*] (1677) **:** a small tube; *esp* **:** a slender elongated anatomical channel

tu·bu·lin \'t(y)ü-byə-lən\ *n* [*tubule* + *-in*] (ca. 1968) **:** a globular protein that polymerizes to form microtubules

tu·chun \'dü-'jün, -'jūen\ *n* [Chin (Pek) *tu[1] chun[1]*] (1920) **1 :** a Chinese military governor (as of a province) **2 :** a Chinese warlord

[1]tuck \'tək\ *n* (14c) **1 :** a fold stitched into cloth to shorten, decorate, or control fullness **2 :** the part of a vessel where the ends of the lower planks meet under the stern **3 a :** an act or instance of tucking **b :** something tucked or to be tucked in **4 a :** a body position (as in diving) in which the knees are bent, the thighs drawn tightly to the chest, and the hands clasped around the shins **b :** a skiing position in which the skier squats forward and holds his ski poles under his arms and parallel to the ground

[2]tuck *vb* [ME *tuken* to pull up sharply, scold, fr. OE *tūcian* to ill-treat; akin to OE *togian* to pull — more at TOW] *vt* (15c) **1 a :** to pull up into a fold **b :** to make a tuck in **2 :** to put into a snug often concealing or isolating place ⟨cottage ~*ed* away in the hill⟩ **3 a :** to push in the loose end of so as to hold tightly ⟨~ in your shirt⟩ **b :** to cover by tucking in bedclothes **4 :** EAT —usu. used with *away* or *in* **5 :** to put into a tuck position ~ *vi* **1 :** to draw together into tucks or folds **2 :** to eat heartily — usu. used with *into* ⟨~*ed* into a steamed lobster⟩ **3 :** to fit snugly

[3]tuck *n* [obs. E *tuk* (to beat the drum)] (1500) **:** a sound of or as if of a drumbeat

[4]tuck *n* [MF *estoc,* fr. OF, tree trunk, sword point, of Gmc origin; akin to OE *stocc* stump of a tree — more at STOCK] *archaic* (1508) **:** RAPIER

[5]tuck *n* [prob. fr. [1]*tuck*] (1878) **:** VIGOR, ENERGY ⟨seemed to kind of take the ~ all out of me —Mark Twain⟩

tuck·a·hoe \'tək-ə-,hō\ *n* [*tockawhoughe* (in some Algonquian language of Virginia)] (1612) **1 :** either of two American arums (*Peltandra virginica* and *Orantium aquaticum*) with rootstocks used as food by the Indians **2 :** the large edible sclerotium of a subterranean fungus (*Poria cocos*)

[1]tuck·er \'tək-ər\ *n* (ca. 1688) **1 :** a piece of lace or cloth in the neckline of a dress **2 :** one that tucks **3** *chiefly Austral* **:** FOOD

[2]tucker *vt* **tuck·ered; tuck·er·ing** \'tək-(ə-)riŋ\ [obs. E *tuck* (to reproach) + *-er* (as in [1]*batter*)] (1833) **:** EXHAUST — often used with *out*

tuck·er–bag \'tək-ər-,bag\ *n* [Austral *tucker* (food, rations)] *chiefly Austral* (1902) **:** a bag used esp. by travelers in the bush to hold food

tuck·et \'tək-ət\ *n* [prob. fr. obs. E *tuk* (to beat the drum, sound the trumpet)] (ca. 1593) **:** a fanfare on a trumpet

tuck–point \-,pȯint\ *vt* (ca. 1881) **:** to finish (the mortar joints between bricks or stones) with a narrow ridge of putty or fine lime mortar

tuck–shop \-,shäp\ *n* [Brit slang *tuck* (food, confectionery)] *Brit* (1857) **:** confectioner's shop **:** CONFECTIONERY

Tu·dor \'t(y)üd-ər\ *adj* [Henry *Tudor* (Henry VII of England)] (1779) **1 :** of or relating to the English royal house that ruled from 1485

to1603 **2 :** of, relating to, or characteristic of the Tudor period — **Tudor** *n*

Tudor arch *n* (ca. 1815) **:** a low elliptical 3-, 4-, or 5-centered arch; *esp* **:** a 4-centered pointed arch — see ARCH illustration

Tues·day \'t(y)üz-dē, -(,)dā\ *n* [ME *tiwesday*, fr. OE *tīwesdæg* (akin to OHG *ziostag* Tuesday), fr. OE *Tīw* Tiu + *dæg* day — more at DEITY] (bef. 12c) **:** the third day of the week — **Tues·days** \-dēz, -(,)dāz\ *adv*

tu·fa \'t(y)ü-fə\ *n* [It *tufo*, fr. L *tophus*] (1770) **1 :** TUFF **2 :** a porous rock formed as a deposit from springs or streams — **tu·fa·ceous** \t(y)ü-'fā-shəs\ *adj*

tuff \'təf\ *n* [MF *tuf*, fr. OIt *tufo* tufa] (ca. 1815) **:** a rock composed of the finer kinds of volcanic detritus usu. fused together by heat — **tuff·a·ceous** \,tə-'fā-shəs\ *adj*

tuf·fet \'təf-ət\ *n* [alter. of [1]*tuft*] (1553) **1 :** TUFT 1a **2 :** a low seat

[1]**tuft** \'təft\ *n* [ME, modif. of MF *tufe*] (14c) **1 a :** a small cluster of elongated flexible outgrowths attached or close together at the base and free at the opposite ends; *esp* **:** a growing bunch of grasses or close-set plants **b :** a bunch of soft fluffy threads cut off short and used as ornament **2 :** CLUMP, CLUSTER **3 :** MOUND — **tuft·ed** \'təf-təd\ *adj* — **tufty** \'təf-tē\ *adj*

[2]**tuft** *vt* (1535) **1 :** to provide or adorn with a tuft **2 :** to make (as a mattress) firm by stitching at intervals and sewing on tufts ~ *vi* **:** to form into or grow in tufts — **tuft·er** *n*

[1]**tug** \'təg\ *vb* **tugged; tug·ging** [ME *tuggen*; akin to OE *togian* to pull — more at TOW] *vi* (14c) **1 :** to pull hard **2 :** to struggle in opposition **:** CONTEND **3 :** to exert oneself laboriously **:** LABOR ~ *vt* **1 :** to pull or strain hard at **2 a :** to move by pulling hard **:** HAUL **b :** to carry with difficulty **:** LUG **3 :** to tow with a tugboat ***syn*** see PULL — **tug·ger** *n*

[2]**tug** *n* (15c) **1 a :** [3]TRACE 1 **b :** a short leather strap or loop **c :** a rope or chain used for pulling **2 a :** an act or instance of tugging **:** PULL **b :** a strong pulling force **3 a :** a straining effort **b :** a struggle between two people or opposite forces **4 :** TUGBOAT

tug·boat \'təg-,bōt\ *n* (1830) **:** a strongly built powerful boat used for towing and pushing — called also *towboat*

tug–of–war \,təg-ə(v)-'wȯ(ə)r\ *n, pl* **tugs–of–war** (1677) **1 :** a struggle for supremacy involving two antagonists **2 :** a contest in which two teams pull against each other at opposite ends of a rope with the object of pulling the middle of the rope over a mark on the ground

tu·grik *or* **tu·ghrik** \'tü-grik\ *n* [Mongolian *dughurik*, lit., round thing, wheel] (1927) — see MONEY table

tuille \'twē(ə)l\ *n* [ME *toile*, fr. MF *tuille* tile, fr. *tegula* — more at TILE] (15c) **:** one of the hinged plates before the thigh in plate armor — see ARMOR illustration

tu·ition \t(y)u̇-'ish-ən\ *n* [ME *tuicioun* protection, fr. OF *tuicion*, fr. L *tuition-, tuitio*, fr. *tuitus*, pp. of *tueri* to look at, look after] (15c) **1** *archaic* **:** CUSTODY, GUARDIANSHIP **2 :** the act or profession of teaching **:** INSTRUCTION ⟨pursued his studies under private ~⟩ **3 :** the price of or payment for instruction — **tu·ition·al** \-'ish-nəl, -ən-ᵊl\ *adj*

tu·la·re·mia \,t(y)ü-lə-'rē-mē-ə\ *n* [NL, fr. *Tulare* county, Calif.] (1921) **:** an infectious disease esp. of wild rabbits, rodents, man, and some domestic animals that is caused by a bacterium (*Pasteurella tularensis*), is transmitted esp. by the bites of insects, and in man is marked by symptoms (as fever) of toxemia — **tu·la·re·mic** \-mik\ *adj*

tu·le \'tü-lē\ *n* [Sp, fr. Nahuatl *tullin*] (1838) **:** either of two large New World bulrushes (*Scirpus californicus* and *S. acutus*) growing on overflowed land

tu·lip \'t(y)ü-ləp\ *n* [NL *tulipa*, fr. Turk *tülbent* turban] (1578) **:** any of a genus (*Tulipa*) of Eurasian bulbous herbs of the lily family that have linear or broadly lanceolate leaves and are widely grown for their showy flowers; *also* **:** the flower or bulb of a tulip

tulip tree *n* (1705) **1 :** a tall No. American timber tree (*Liriodendron tulipifera*) of the magnolia family having large greenish yellow tulip-shaped flowers and soft white wood used esp. for cabinetwork and woodenware **2 :** any of various trees other than the tulip tree with tulip-shaped flowers

tu·lip·wood \'t(y)ü-ləp-,wu̇d\ *n* (1843) **1 :** wood of the No. American tulip tree **:** WHITEWOOD **2 a :** any of several showily striped or variegated woods; *esp* **:** the rose-colored wood of a Brazilian tree (*Physocalymma scabberimum* of the family Lythraceae) that is much used by cabinetmakers for inlaying **b :** a tree that yields tulipwood

tulle \'tül\ *n* [F, fr. *Tulle*, France] (ca. 1818) **:** a sheer often stiffened silk, rayon, or nylon net used chiefly for veils or ballet costumes

[1]**tum·ble** \'təm-bəl\ *vb* **tum·bled; tum·bling** \-b(ə-)liŋ\ [ME *tumblen*, freq. of *tumben* to dance, fr. OE *tumbian*; akin to OHG *tūmōn* to reel] *vi* (14c) **1 a :** to perform gymnastic feats in tumbling **b :** to turn end over end in falling or flight **2 a :** to fall suddenly and helplessly **b :** to suffer a sudden downfall, overthrow, or defeat **c :** to decline suddenly and sharply (as in price) **:** DROP ⟨the stock market *tumbled*⟩ **d :** to fall into ruin **:** COLLAPSE **3 :** to roll over and over, to and fro, or end over end **:** TOSS **4 :** to issue forth hurriedly and confusedly **5 :** to come by chance **:** STUMBLE **6 :** to come to understand **:** CATCH ON ⟨didn't ~ to the seriousness of the problem⟩ ~ *vt* **1 :** to cause to tumble (as by pushing or toppling) **2 a :** to throw together in a confused mass **b :** RUMPLE, DISORDER **3 :** to whirl in a tumbling barrel

[2]**tumble** *n* (1634) **1 a :** a disordered mass of objects or material **b :** a disorderly state **2 :** an act or instance of tumbling

tum·ble·bug \'təm-bəl-,bəg\ *n* (ca. 1805) **:** any of various scarabaeid beetles (esp. genera *Scarabaeus, Canthon, Copris*, or *Phanaeus*) that roll dung into small balls, bury them in the ground, and lay eggs in them

tum·ble·down \,təm-bəl-,dau̇n\ *adj* (1818) **:** DILAPIDATED, RAMSHACKLE ⟨a ~ house at the edge of town —Sherwood Anderson⟩

tumble dry *vt* (1966) **:** to dry (as clothes) by tumbling in a dryer — **tumble dryer** *n* — **tumble drying** *n*

tum·bler \'təm-blər\ *n* (14c) **1 :** one that tumbles: as **a :** one that performs tumbling feats **:** ACROBAT **b :** any of various domestic pigeons that tumble or somersault backward in flight or on the ground **2 :** a drinking glass without foot or stem and orig. with pointed or convex base **3 a :** a movable obstruction in a lock (as a lever, latch, wheel, slide, or pin) that must be adjusted to a particular position (as by a key) before the bolt can be thrown **b :** a piece on which the mainspring acts in a gunlock **c (1) :** a projecting piece on a revolving shaft or rockshaft for actuating another piece **(2) :** the movable part of a reversing or speed-changing gear **4 :** a device or mechanism for tumbling (as a revolving cage in which clothes are dried) **5 :** a worker that operates a tumbler — **tum·bler·ful** \-,fu̇l\ *n*

tum·ble·weed \'təm-bəl-,wēd\ *n* (1887) **:** a plant (as Russian thistle or any of several amaranths or pigweeds) that breaks away from its roots in the autumn and is driven about by the wind as a light rolling mass

[1]**tum·bling** \'təm-b(ə-)liŋ\ *n* (14c) **:** the skill, practice, or sport of executing gymnastic feats (as somersaults and handsprings) without the use of apparatus

[2]**tumbling** *adj* (ca. 1716) **:** tipped or slanted out of the vertical — used esp. of a cattle brand

tumbling barrel *n* (ca. 1890) **:** a revolving cask in which objects or materials undergo a process (as drying or polishing) by being whirled about

tumbling verse *n* (ca. 1585) **:** an early modern English type of verse having four stresses but no prevailing type of foot and no regular number of syllables

tum·bril *also* **tum·brel** \'təm-brəl\ *n* [ME *tombrel*, fr. OF *tumberel* tipcart, fr. *tomber* to tumble, of Gmc origin; akin to OHG *tūmōn* to reel — more at TUMBLE] (15c) **1 :** a farm tipcart **2 :** a vehicle carrying condemned persons (as political prisoners during the French Revolution) to a place of execution

tu·me·fac·tion \,t(y)ü-mə-'fak-shən\ *n* [MF, fr. L *tumefactus*, pp. of *tumefacere* to cause to swell, fr. *tumēre* to swell + *facere* to make, do — more at THUMB, DO] (1597) **1 :** an action or process of swelling or becoming tumorous **2 :** SWELLING

tu·mes·cence \t(y)ü-'mes-ᵊn(t)s\ *n* (1859) **:** the quality or state of being tumescent; *esp* **:** readiness for sexual activity marked esp. by vascular congestion of the sex organs

tu·mes·cent \-ᵊnt\ *adj* [L *tumescent-, tumescens*, prp. of *tumescere* to swell up, incho. of *tumēre* to swell] (1882) **:** somewhat swollen ⟨~ tissue⟩

tu·mid \'t(y)ü-məd\ *adj* [L *tumidus*, fr. *tumēre*] (1541) **1 :** marked by swelling **:** SWOLLEN, ENLARGED ⟨a badly infected ~ leg⟩ **2 :** PROTUBERANT, BULGING ⟨sails ~ in the breeze⟩ **3 :** BOMBASTIC, TURGID

tum·my \'təm-ē\ *n, pl* **tummies** [baby-talk for *stomach*] (1867) **:** STOMACH 1c

tu·mor \'t(y)ü-mər\ *n* [L *tumor*, fr. *tumēre*] (1597) **1 :** a swollen or distended part **2 :** an abnormal mass of tissue that is not inflammatory, arises without obvious cause from cells of preexistent tissue, and possesses no physiologic function — **tu·mor·al** \-mə-rəl\ *adj* — **tu·mor·like** \-mər-,līk\ *adj*

tu·mor·i·gen·ic \,t(y)ü-mə-rə-'jen-ik\ *adj* (1941) **:** producing or tending to produce tumors; *also* **:** CARCINOGENIC — **tu·mor·i·gen·e·sis** \-'jen-ə-səs\ *n* — **tu·mor·i·ge·nic·i·ty** \-jə-'nis-ət-ē\ *n*

tu·mor·ous \'t(y)üm-(ə-)rəs\ *adj* (1547) **:** of, relating to, or resembling a tumor

tu·mour \'tyü-mər\ *chiefly Brit var of* TUMOR

tump \'təmp\ *n* [origin unknown] (1589) **1** *chiefly dial Eng* **:** MOUND, HUMMOCK **2 :** a clump of vegetation

tump·line \'təm-,plīn\ *n* [*tump*, of Algonquian origin; akin to Abnaki *mădûmbí* pack strap] (1796) **:** a sling formed by a strap slung over the forehead or chest and used for carrying or helping to support a pack on the back or in hauling loads

tu·mult \'t(y)ü-,məlt\ *n* [ME *tumulte*, fr. MF, fr. L *tumultus*; akin to Skt *tumula* noisy, L *tumēre* to swell — more at THUMB] (15c) **1 a :** disorderly agitation or milling about of a crowd usu. with uproar and confusion of voices **:** COMMOTION **b :** a turbulent uprising **:** RIOT **2 :** HUBBUB, DIN **3 a :** violent agitation of mind or feelings **b :** a violent outburst

tu·mul·tu·ary \t(y)u̇-'məl-chə-,wer-ē\ *adj* (1590) **:** attended or marked by tumult, riot, lawlessness, confusion, or impetuosity

tu·mul·tu·ous \t(y)u̇-'məlch-(ə-)wəs, -'məl-chəs\ *adj* (1548) **1 :** marked by tumult **2 :** tending or disposed to cause or incite a tumult **3 :** marked by violent or overwhelming turbulence or upheaval — **tu·mul·tu·ous·ly** *adv* — **tu·mul·tu·ous·ness** *n*

tu·mu·lus \'t(y)ü-myə-ləs, 'təm-yə-\ *n, pl* **-li** \-,lī, -,lē\ [L; akin to L *tumēre* to swell — more at THUMB] (1686) **:** an artificial hillock or mound (as over a grave); *esp* **:** an ancient grave **:** BARROW

tun \'tən\ *n* [ME *tunne*, fr. OE] (bef. 12c) **1 :** a large cask esp. for wine **2 :** any of various units of liquid capacity; *esp* **:** one equal to 252 gallons

[1]**tu·na** \'tü-nə\ *n* [Sp, fr. Taino] (ca. 1555) **1 :** any of various flat-jointed prickly pears (genus *Opuntia*); *esp* **:** one (*O. tuna*) common in tropical America **2 :** the edible fruit of a tuna

[2]**tu·na** \'t(y)ü-nə\ *n, pl* **tuna** *or* **tunas** [AmerSp, alter. of Sp *atún*, modif. of Ar *tūn*, fr. L *thunnus*, fr. Gk *thynnos*] (ca. 1884) **1 :** any of numerous large vigorous scombroid food and sport fishes (as an albacore or a bonito) **2 :** the flesh of a tuna esp. when canned for use as food — called also *tuna fish*

tun·able \'t(y)ü-nə-bəl\ *adj* (1500) **1** *archaic* **a :** TUNEFUL **b :** sounding in tune **:** CONCORDANT **2 :** capable of being tuned — **tun·abil·i·ty** \,t(y)ü-nə-'bil-ət-ē\ *n* — **tun·able·ness** \'t(y)ü-nə-bəl-nəs\ *n* — **tun·ably** \-blē\ *adv*

tun·dish \'tən-,dish\ *n* [ME, funnel for filling a tun] (ca. 1944) **:** a reservoir in the top part of a mold into which molten metal is poured

tun·dra \'tən-drə *also* 'tu̇n-\ *n* [Russ, of Finno-Ugric origin; akin to Lapp *tundar* hill] (ca. 1841) **:** a level or undulating treeless plain that is characteristic of arctic and subarctic regions, consists of black mucky soil with a permanently frozen subsoil, and supports a dense growth of often conspicuously flowering dwarf herbs

[1]**tune** \'t(y)ün\ *n* [ME, alter. of *tone*] (14c) **1 a** *archaic* **:** quality of sound **:** TONE **b :** manner of utterance **:** INTONATION; *specif* **:** phonetic modulation **2 a :** a succession of pleasing musical tones **:** MELODY **b :** a dominant theme **3 :** correct musical pitch or consonance — used chiefly in the phrases *in tune* and *out of tune* **4 a** *archaic* **:** a frame of mind **:** MOOD **b :** AGREEMENT, HARMONY ⟨in ~ with the times⟩ **c :** general attitude **:** APPROACH ⟨changed his ~ when the going got rough⟩ **5 :** AMOUNT, EXTENT ⟨custom-made to the ~ of $40 to $50 apiece —*Amer. Fabrics*⟩

[2]**tune** *vb* **tuned; tun·ing** *vt* (1505) **1 :** to adjust in musical pitch or cause to be in tune ⟨*tuned* his guitar⟩ **2 a :** to bring into harmony **:** ATTUNE **b :** to adjust for precise functioning — often used with *up* ⟨~ up an engine⟩ **3 :** to adjust with respect to resonance at a particular frequency: as **a :** to adjust (a radio or television receiver) to respond to waves of a particular frequency — often used with *in* **b :** to establish

radio contact with ⟨~ in a directional beacon⟩ **4 :** to adjust the frequency of the output of (a device) to a chosen frequency or range of frequencies; *also* **:** to alter the frequency of (radiation) ~ *vi* **1 :** to become attuned **2 :** to adjust a radio or television receiver to respond to waves of a particular frequency

tuned–in \ˈt(y)ün-ˈdin\ *adj* (ca. 1967) **:** TURNED-ON

tune·ful \ˈt(y)ün-fəl\ *adj* (1591) **:** MELODIOUS, MUSICAL — **tune·ful·ly** \-fə-lē\ *adv* — **tune·ful·ness** *n*

tune·less \ˈt(y)ün-ləs\ *adj* (1591) **1 :** not tuneful **2 :** not producing music — **tune·less·ly** *adv*

tune out *vt* (1910) **:** to become unresponsive to **:** IGNORE ~ *vi* **:** to dissociate oneself from what is happening

tun·er \ˈt(y)ü-nər\ *n* (ca. 1801) **1 :** one that tunes ⟨a piano ~⟩ **2 :** something used for tuning; *specif* **:** the part of a receiving set that converts radio signals into audio or video signals

tune·smith \ˈt(y)ün-ˌsmith\ *n* (1926) **:** a composer esp. of popular songs

tune–up \ˈt(y)ü-ˌnəp\ *n* (ca. 1947) **1 :** a preliminary trial **:** WARM-UP **2 :** a general adjustment to insure operation at peak efficiency

tung \ˈtəŋ\ *n* (ca. 1930) **:** TUNG TREE

tung oil *n* [part trans. of Chin (Pek) *yu2 t'ung2*] (1881) **:** a pale yellow pungent drying oil obtained from the seeds of tung trees and used chiefly in quick-drying varnishes and paints and as a waterproofing agent

tungst- *or* **tungsto-** *comb form* [ISV, fr. *tungsten*] **:** tungsten ⟨*tung*state⟩

tung·state \ˈtəŋ-ˌstāt\ *n* (1800) **:** a salt or ester of a tungstic acid and esp. of H_2WO_4

tung·sten \ˈtəŋ-stən\ *n* [Sw, fr. *tung* heavy + *sten* stone] (1796) **:** a gray-white heavy high-melting ductile hard polyvalent metallic element that resembles chromium and molybdenum in many of its properties and is used esp. for electrical purposes and in hardening alloys (as steel) — called also *wolfram;* see ELEMENT table

tung·stic \-stik\ *adj* [ISV] (1796) **:** of, relating to, or containing tungsten esp. with a valence of six

tungstic acid *n* (1796) **:** a yellow crystalline powder WO_3 that is the trioxide of tungsten; *also* **:** an acid (as H_2WO_4) derived from this

tung·stite \ˈtəŋ-ˌstīt\ *n* (1868) **:** a mineral $WO_3 \cdot H_2O(?)$ consisting of a hydrous tungsten trioxide and occurring in yellow or yellowish green pulverulent masses

tung tree *n* [Chin (Pek) *t'ung2*] (1895) **:** any of several trees (genus *Aleurites*) of the spurge family whose seeds yield a poisonous fixed drying oil; *esp* **:** a Chinese tree (*A. fordii*) widely grown in warm regions

Tun·gus \tu̇ŋ-ˈgüz, tən-\ *n, pl* **Tungus** *or* **Tun·gus·es** [Russ] (1674) **1 :** a member of a Mongoloid people widely spread over eastern Siberia **2 :** the Tungusic languages of the Tungus peoples

Tun·gu·sic \-ˈgü-zik\ *n* (ca. 1867) **:** a subfamily of Altaic languages spoken in Manchuria and northward — **Tungusic** *adj*

tu·nic \ˈt(y)ü-nik\ *n* [L *tunica,* of Sem origin; akin to Heb *kuttōneth* coat] (ca. 1609) **1 a :** a simple slip-on garment made with or without sleeves and usu. knee-length or longer, belted at the waist, and worn as an under or outer garment by men and women of ancient Greece and Rome **b :** SURCOAT **2 :** an enclosing or covering membrane or tissue ⟨the ~ of a seed⟩ **3 :** a long usu. plain close-fitting jacket with high collar worn esp. as part of a uniform **4 :** TUNICLE **5 a :** a short overskirt **b :** a hip-length or longer blouse or jacket

tu·ni·ca \ˈt(y)ü-ni-kə\ *n, pl* **tu·ni·cae** \-nə-ˌkē, -ˌkī, -ˌsē\ [L, tunic, membrane] (ca. 1828) **:** an enveloping membrane or layer of body tissue

1**tu·ni·cate** \ˈt(y)ü-ni-kət, -nə-ˌkāt\ *also* **tu·ni·cat·ed** \-nə-ˌkāt-əd\ *adj* [L *tunicatus,* fr. *tunica*] (ca. 1623) **1 a :** having or covered with a tunic or tunica **b :** having, arranged in, or made up of concentric layers ⟨a ~ bulb⟩ **2 :** of or relating to the tunicates

2**tu·ni·cate** \-ni-kət, -nə-ˌkāt\ *n* [NL *Tunicata,* fr. neut. pl. of L *tunicatus* tunicate] (1889) **:** any of a subphylum (Urochorda syn. Tunicata) of specialized or degenerate marine chordate animals that have clefts in the vascular walls of the pharyngeal gills, a thick secreted covering layer, a greatly reduced nervous system, and a heart able to reverse the direction of blood flow by changes of its contractions

tu·ni·cle \ˈt(y)ü-ni-kəl\ *n* [ME, fr. L *tunicula,* dim. of *tunica*] (15c) **:** a short vestment worn by a subdeacon over the alb during mass and by a bishop under the dalmatic at pontifical ceremonies — see VESTMENT illustration

tuning fork *n* (1799) **:** a 2-pronged metal implement that gives a fixed tone when struck and is useful for tuning musical instruments and ascertaining standard pitch

tuning pipe *n* (ca. 1926) **:** PITCH PIPE; *specif* **:** one of a set of pitch pipes used esp. for tuning stringed musical instruments

1**tun·nel** \ˈtən-ᵊl\ *n* [ME *tonel* tube-shaped net, fr. MF, tun, fr. OF, fr. *tonne* tun, fr. ML *tunna,* of Celt origin; akin to MIr *tonn* skin, hide; akin to L *tondēre* to shear — more at TOME] (1548) **1 :** a hollow conduit or recess **:** TUBE, WELL **2 a :** a covered passageway; *specif* **:** a horizontal passageway through or under an obstruction **b :** a subterranean gallery (as in a mine) **c :** BURROW — **tun·nel·like** \-ᵊl-ˌ(l)īk\ *adj*

2**tunnel** *vb* **-neled** *or* **-nelled; -nel·ing** *or* **-nel·ling** \ˈtən-liŋ, -ᵊl-iŋ\ *vi* (1795) **1 :** to make or use a tunnel **2** *physics* **:** to pass through a potential barrier ⟨electrons ~*ing* through an insulator between semiconductors⟩ ~ *vt* **:** to make a tunnel or similar opening through or under; *also* **:** to make (one's way) by or as if by making a tunnel — **tun·nel·er** \ˈtən-lər, -ᵊl-ər\ *n*

tunnel vision *n* (ca. 1942) **1 :** a field of vision of 70 percent or less from the straight-ahead position that results in elimination of the peripheral field **2 :** extreme narrowness of viewpoint **:** NARROWMINDEDNESS — **tun·nel–vi·sioned** \-ˈvizh-ənd\ *adj*

tun·ny \ˈtən-ē\ *n, pl* **tunnies** *also* **tunny** [modif. of MF *thon* or OIt *tonno;* both fr. OProv *ton,* fr. L *thunnus* — more at TUNA] (ca. 1530) **:** TUNA; *esp* **:** BLUEFIN TUNA

1**tup** \ˈtəp\ *n* [ME *tupe*] (14c) **1** *chiefly Brit* **:** RAM 1a **2 :** a heavy metal body (as the weight of a pendulum)

2**tup** *vt* **tupped; tup·ping** *chiefly Brit* (1604) **:** to copulate with (a ewe)

tu·pe·lo \ˈt(y)ü-pə-ˌlō\ *n, pl* **-los** [Creek *ito opilwa* swamp tree] (ca. 1730) **1 :** any of a genus (*Nyssa*) of mostly No. American trees that have simple alternate leaves, small greenish dioecious stalked flowers, and a rounded drupe; *esp* **:** BLACK GUM **2 :** the pale soft easily worked wood of a tupelo

Tu·pi \tü-ˈpē, ˈtü-(ˌ)\ *n, pl* **Tupi** *or* **Tupis** (ca. 1891) **1 :** a member of a group of Tupi-Guaranian peoples of Brazil living esp. in the Amazon valley **2 :** the language of the Tupi people

Tu·pi·an \tü-ˈpē-ən, ˈtü-(ˌ)\ *adj* (ca. 1904) **:** of, relating to, or constituting the Tupi or other Tupi-Guaranian peoples or their languages

Tu·pi–Gua·ra·ni \tü-ˌpē-ˌgwär-ə-ˈnē, ˈtü-(ˌ)pē-\ *n* (ca. 1901) **1 :** a member of a So. American people spread over an area from eastern Brazil to the Peruvian Andes and from the Guianas to Uruguay **2 :** TUPI-GUARANIAN

Tupi–Gua·ra·ni·an \-ˈnē-ən\ *n* (ca. 1902) **:** a language stock widely distributed in tropical So. America

-tu·ple \ˌtəp-əl, ˌtüp-\ *n comb form* [quin*tuple,* sex*tuple*] **:** set of (so many) elements — usu. used of sets with ordered elements ⟨the ordered 2-*tuple* (*a, b*)⟩

tup·pence *var of* TWOPENCE

tuque \ˈt(y)ük\ *n* [CanF, fr. F *toque* — more at TOQUE] (1871) **:** a warm knitted usu. pointed stocking cap

tu quo·que \ˈt(y)ü-ˈk(w)ō-kwē\ *n* [L, you too] (1614) **:** a retort charging an adversary with being or doing what he criticizes in others

Tu·ra·ni·an \t(y)u̇-ˈrā-nē-ən, -ˈrän-ē-\ *n* [Per *Tūrān* Turkestan, the region north of the Amu Darya] (ca. 1777) **1 :** a member of any of various peoples speaking Ural-Altaic languages **2 :** URAL-ALTAIC 1 — **Turanian** *adj*

tur·ban \ˈtər-bən\ *n* [MF *turbant,* fr. It *turbante,* fr. Turk *tülbent,* fr. Per *dulband*] (1588) **1 :** a headdress worn chiefly in countries of the eastern Mediterranean and southern Asia esp. by Muslims and made of a cap around which is wound a long cloth **2 :** a headdress resembling a Muslim turban; *specif* **:** a woman's close-fitting hat without a brim — **tur·baned** *or* **tur·banned** \-bənd\ *adj*

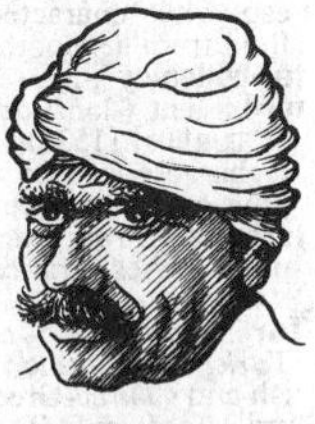

turban 1

tur·bel·lar·i·an \ˌtər-bə-ˈler-ē-ən, -ˈlar-\ *n* [deriv. of L *turbellae* (pl.) bustle, stir, dim. of *turba* confusion, crowd; fr. the tiny eddies created in water by the cilia] (1883) **:** any of a class (Turbellaria) of mostly aquatic and free-living flatworms; *esp* **:** PLANARIAN — **turbellarian** *adj*

tur·bid \ˈtər-bəd\ *adj* [L *turbidus* confused, turbid, fr. *turba* confusion, crowd; akin to OHG *dweran* to stir, L *turbare* to throw into disorder, disturb, Gk *tyrbē* confusion] (1626) **1 a :** thick or opaque with or as if with roiled sediment ⟨a ~ stream⟩ **b :** heavy with smoke or mist **2 a :** deficient in clarity or purity **:** FOUL, MUDDY ⟨~ depths of degradation and misery —C. I. Glicksberg⟩ **b :** characterized by or producing obscurity (as of mind or emotions) ⟨an emotionally ~ response⟩ — **tur·bid·i·ty** \ˌtər-ˈbid-ət-ē\ *n* — **tur·bid·ly** \ˈtər-bəd-lē\ *adv* — **tur·bid·ness** *n*

tur·bi·dim·e·ter \ˌtər-bə-ˈdim-ət-ər\ *n* [ISV *turbidi*ty + *-meter*] (ca. 1914) **1 :** an instrument for measuring and comparing the turbidity of liquids by viewing light through them and determining how much light is cut off **2 :** NEPHELOMETER — **tur·bi·di·met·ric** \ˌtər-bəd-ə-ˈme-trik, ˌtər-ˌbid-ə-\ *adj* — **tur·bi·di·met·ri·cal·ly** \-tri-k(ə-)lē\ *adv* — **tur·bi·dim·e·try** \ˌtər-bə-ˈdim-ə-trē\ *n*

tur·bi·dite \ˈtər-bə-ˌdīt\ *n* [*turbidi*ty current (a current flowing down a slope and spreading out on the ocean floor) + *-ite*] (ca. 1962) **:** a sedimentary deposit consisting of material that has moved down the steep slope at the edge of a continental shelf; *also* **:** a rock formed from this deposit

1**tur·bi·nate** \ˈtər-bə-nət, -ˌnāt\ *also* **tur·bi·nat·ed** \-ˌnāt-əd\ *adj* [L *turbinatus,* fr. *turbin-, turbo*] (1661) **1 :** shaped like a top or an inverted cone ⟨~ seed capsule⟩ **2 :** relating to or being a turbinate

2**turbinate** *n* (1802) **:** one of usu. several thin plicated membrane-covered bony or cartilaginous plates on the walls of the nasal chambers

tur·bine \ˈtər-bən, -ˌbīn\ *n* [F, fr. L *turbin-, turbo* top, whirlwind, whirl; akin to L *turbare* to disturb — more at TURBID] (1842) **:** a rotary engine actuated by the reaction or impulse or both of a current of fluid (as water, steam, or air) subject to pressure and usu. made with a series of curved vanes on a central rotating spindle

tur·bit \ˈtər-bət\ *n* [origin unknown] (ca. 1688) **:** a pigeon of a fancy breed having a short crested head, short beak, frilled breast, and mostly white plumage

tur·bo \ˈtər-(ˌ)bō\ *n, pl* **turbos** [*turbo-*] (1904) **1 :** TURBINE **2** [by shortening] **:** TURBOSUPERCHARGER

turbo- *comb form* [*turbine*] **1 :** coupled directly to a driving turbine ⟨*turbo*fan⟩ ⟨*turbo*generator⟩ **2 :** consisting of or incorporating a turbine ⟨*turbo*jet engine⟩ ⟨*turbo*machine⟩

tur·bo·car \ˈtər-bō-ˌkär\ *n* (1950) **:** an automotive vehicle propelled by a gas turbine

tur·bo·charged \-ˌchärjd\ *adj* (1945) **:** equipped with a turbocharger

tur·bo·charg·er \-ˌchär-jər\ *n* (1945) **:** a centrifugal blower driven by exhaust gas turbines and used to supercharge an engine

tur·bo·elec·tric \ˈtər-bō-i-ˈlek-trik\ *adj* (1904) **:** involving or depending as a power source on electricity produced by turbine generators

tur·bo·fan \-ˌfan\ *n* (1945) **1 :** a fan that is directly connected to and driven by a turbine and is used to supply air for cooling, ventilation, or combustion **2 :** a jet engine having a turbofan

tur·bo·jet \-ˌjet\ *n* (1945) **1 :** an airplane powered by turbojet engines **2 :** TURBOJET ENGINE

turbojet engine *n* (1944) **:** an airplane propulsion system in which the power developed by a turbine is used to drive a compressor that supplies air to a burner and hot gases from the burner pass through the turbine and thence to a rearward-directed thrust-producing exhaust nozzle

tur·bo·prop \ˈtər-bō-ˌpräp\ *n* (1945) **1 :** TURBO-PROPELLER ENGINE **2 :** an airplane powered by turbo-propeller engines

tur·bo–pro·pel·ler engine \ˌtər-bō-prə-ˈpel-ər-\ *n* (ca. 1947) **:** a jet engine having a turbine-driven propeller and designed to produce thrust principally by means of a propeller although additional thrust is usu. obtained from the hot exhaust gases which issue in a jet

tur·bo·prop–jet engine \-ˈpräp-ˌjet-\ *n* (1947) : TURBO-PROPELLER ENGINE

tur·bo·ram·jet engine \-ˈram-ˌjet-\ *n* (1947) : a jet engine consisting essentially of a turbojet engine with provisions for burning additional fuel in the tail pipe or the portion of the engine to the rear of the turbine

tur·bo·shaft \ˈtər-bō-ˌshaft\ *n* (1960) : a gas turbine engine that is similar in operation to a turboprop engine but instead of being used to power a propeller is used through a transmission system for powering other devices (as helicopter rotors and pumps)

tur·bo·su·per·charged \ˌtər-bō-ˈsü-pər-ˌchärjd\ *adj* (1942) : equipped with a turbosupercharger

tur·bo·su·per·charg·er \-ˌchär-jər\ *n* (1934) : a turbine compressor driven by hot exhaust gases of an airplane engine for feeding rarefied air at high altitudes into the carburetor of the engine at sea-level pressure so as to increase engine power

tur·bot \ˈtər-bət\ *n, pl* **turbot** *also* **turbots** [ME, fr. OF *tourbot*] (14c) **1** : a large European flatfish (*Psetta maxima*) that is a popular food fish and has a brownish upper surface marked with scattered tubercles and a white undersurface **2** : any of various flatfishes resembling the turbot

tur·bu·lence \ˈtər-byə-lən(t)s\ *n* (ca. 1598) : the quality or state of being turbulent: as **a** : wild commotion **b** : irregular atmospheric motion esp. when characterized by up-and-down currents **c** : departure in a fluid from a smooth flow

tur·bu·len·cy \-lən-sē\ *n, pl* **-cies** *archaic* (1607) : TURBULENCE

tur·bu·lent \-lənt\ *adj* [L *turbulentus,* fr. *turba* confusion, crowd — more at TURBID] (1538) **1** : causing unrest, violence, or disturbance **2 a** : characterized by agitation or tumult : TEMPESTUOUS **b** : exhibiting physical turbulence — **tur·bu·lent·ly** *adv*

turbulent flow *n* (ca. 1922) : a fluid flow in which the velocity at a given point varies erratically in magnitude and direction — compare LAMINAR FLOW

Tur·co- *or* **Tur·ko-** *comb form* [*Turco-* fr. ML *Turcus* Turk; *Turko-* fr. *Turk*] **1** : Turkic : Turkish : Turk ⟨*Turcophil*⟩ **2** \ˈtər-(ˌ)kō\ : Turkish and ⟨*Turco*-Greek⟩

turd \ˈtərd\ *n* [ME *tord, turd,* fr. OE *tord;* akin to MD *tort* dung, OE *teran* to tear — more at TEAR] (bef. 12c) **1** : a piece of excrement — sometimes considered vulgar **2** : a contemptible person — usu. considered vulgar

tu·reen \tə-ˈrēn, tyu̇-\ *n* [F *terrine,* fr. MF, fr. fem. of *terrin* of earth, fr. (assumed) VL *terrinus,* fr. L *terra* earth — more at TERRACE] (ca. 1706) **1** : a deep and usu. covered bowl from which foods (as soup) are served **2** : CASSEROLE 2

1turf \ˈtərf\ *n, pl* **turfs** \ˈtərfs\ *also* **turves** \ˈtərvz\ [ME, fr. OE; akin to OHG *zurba* turf, Skt *darbha* tuft of grass] (bef. 12c) **1 a** : the upper stratum of soil bound by grass and plant roots into a thick mat; *also* : a piece of this **b** : an artificial substitute for this (as on a playing field) **2 a** : PEAT **b** : a piece of peat dried for fuel **3 a** : a track or course for horse racing **b** : the sport or business of horse racing **4 a** : territory considered by a teenage gang to be under its control **b** : TERRITORY 2a ⟨looking for cheap thrills on strange ~ —*Playboy*⟩ — **turfy** \ˈtər-fē\ *adj*

2turf *vt* (15c) **1** : to cover with turf **2** *chiefly Brit* : to eject forcibly : KICK — usu. used with *out*

turf accountant *n, Brit* (1915) : BOOKMAKER 2

turf·man \ˈtərf-mən\ *n* (ca. 1818) : a devotee of horse racing; *esp* : one who owns and races horses

turf·ski \-ˌskē\ *n* (1967) : a short ski with rollers on the bottom that can be used to ski down a grassy slope — **turf·ski·ing** *n*

tur·ges·cent \ˌtər-ˈjes-ᵊnt\ *adj* [L *turgescent-, turgescens,* prp. of *turgescere* to swell, incho. of *turgēre* to be swollen] (ca. 1727) : becoming turgid, distended, or inflated : SWELLING — **tur·ges·cence** \-ᵊn(t)s\ *n*

tur·gid \ˈtər-jəd\ *adj* [L *turgidus,* fr. *turgēre* to be swollen; prob. akin to L *tumēre* to swell — more at THUMB] (1620) **1** : being in a state of distension : SWOLLEN, TUMID ⟨~ limbs⟩; *esp* : exhibiting turgor **2** : excessively embellished in style or language : BOMBASTIC, POMPOUS — **tur·gid·i·ty** \ˌtər-ˈjid-ət-ē\ *n* — **tur·gid·ly** \ˈtər-jəd-lē\ *adv* — **tur·gid·ness** *n*

tur·gor \ˈtər-gər, -ˌgȯ(ə)r\ *n* [LL, turgidity, swelling, fr. L *turgēre*] (1876) : the normal state of turgidity and tension in living cells; *esp* : the distension of the protoplasmic layer and wall of a plant cell by the fluid contents

Tu·ring machine \ˈt(y)u̇(ə)r-iŋ-\ *n* [A. M. *Turing* †1954 Eng. mathematician] (1937) : a hypothetical computing machine that has an unlimited amount of information storage

tu·ris·ta \tu̇-ˈrē-stə\ *n* [Sp, lit., tourist] (1962) : intestinal sickness and diarrhea commonly affecting a tourist in a foreign country; *esp* : MONTEZUMA'S REVENGE

Turk \ˈtərk\ *n* [ME, fr. MF or Turk; MF *Turc,* fr. ML or Turk; ML *Turcus,* fr. Turk *Türk*] (14c) **1** : a member of any of numerous Asian peoples speaking Turkic languages who live in the region ranging from the Adriatic to the Okhotsk **2** : a native or inhabitant of Turkey **3** *archaic* : one who is cruel or tyrannical **4** : MUSLIM; *specif* : a Muslim subject of the Turkish sultan **5** : a Turkish horse; *specif* : a Turkish strain of Arab and crossbred horses

tur·key \ˈtər-kē\ *n, pl* **turkeys** [*Turkey,* country in western Asia and southeastern Europe; fr. confusion with the guinea fowl, supposed to be imported from Turkish territory] (1555) **1** *also pl* **turkey** : a large American gallinaceous bird (*Meleagris gallopavo*) that is of wide range in No. America and is domesticated in most parts of the world **2** : FAILURE, FLOP; *esp* : a theatrical production that has failed **3** : three successive strikes in bowling **4** : a stupid, foolish, or inept person

tur·key–cock \ˈtər-kē-ˌkäk\ *n* (1578) **1** : GOBBLER **2** : a strutting pompous person

Tur·key red \ˌtər-kē-\ *n* [*Turkey*] (1789) **1 a** : a brilliant durable red produced on cotton by means of alizarin in connection with an aluminum mordant and fatty matter **b** : ALIZARIN 1 **2** : red iron oxide used as a pigment

tur·key shoot \ˈtər-kē-\ *n* (1845) : a marksmanship contest using a moving target with a turkey offered as a prize

turkey trot *n* (1908) : a ragtime dance danced with the feet well apart and with a characteristic rise on the ball of the foot followed by a drop upon the heel

turkey vulture *n* (1823) : an American vulture (*Cathartes aura*) common in So. and Central America and in the southern U.S. — called also *turkey buzzard*

Tur·ki \ˈtər-(ˌ)kē, ˈtu̇(ə)r-\ *adj* [Per *turkī,* fr. *Turk* Turk, fr. Turk *Türk*] (1800) **1** : of or relating to the peoples speaking Turkic **2** : of or relating to any central Asian Turkic language particularly of the eastern group — **Turki** *n*

Turk·ic \ˈtər-kik\ *adj* (ca. 1859) **1 a** : of, relating to, or constituting a subfamily of Altaic languages including Turkish **b** : of or relating to the peoples speaking Turkic **2** : TURKISH 1 — **Turkic** *n*

1Turk·ish \ˈtər-kish\ *adj* (1545) **1** : of, relating to, or characteristic of Turkey, the Turks, or Turkish **2** : TURKIC 1a

2Turkish *n* (1718) : the Turkic language of the Republic of Turkey

Turkish bath *n* (1644) : a bath in which the bather passes through a series of steam rooms of increasing temperature and then receives a rubdown, massage, and cold shower

Turkish coffee *n* (ca. 1919) : a sweetened decoction of pulverized coffee

Turkish delight *n* (ca. 1870) : a jellylike or gummy confection usu. cut in cubes and dusted with sugar — called also *Turkish paste*

Turkish towel *n* (1862) : a towel made of cotton terry cloth

Turk·ism \ˈtər-ˌkiz-əm\ *n* (1595) : the customs, beliefs, institutions, and principles of the Turks

Tur·ko·man *or* **Tur·co·man** \ˈtər-kə-mən\ *n, pl* **Turkomans** *or* **Turcomans** [ML *Turcomannus,* fr. Per *Turkmān,* fr. *turkmān* resembling a Turk, fr. *Turk*] (1600) : a member of a group of peoples of East Turkic stock living chiefly in the Turkmen, Uzbek, and Kazakh republics of the U.S.S.R.

Turk's head *n* (1833) : a turban-shaped knot worked on a rope with a piece of small line — see KNOT illustration

tur·mer·ic \ˈtər-mə-rik *also* ˈt(y)ü-mə-\ *n* [modif. of MF *terre merite* saffron, fr. ML *terra merita,* lit., deserving or deserved earth] (1545) **1** : an East Indian perennial herb (*Curcuma longa*) of the ginger family with a large aromatic deep yellow rhizome **2** : the cleaned, boiled, dried, and usu. pulverized rhizome of the turmeric plant used as a coloring agent, a condiment, or a stimulant **3** : a yellow to reddish brown dyestuff obtained from turmeric

tur·moil \ˈtər-ˌmȯil\ *n* [origin unknown] (1526) : a state or condition of extreme confusion, agitation, or commotion

1turn \ˈtərn\ *vb* [ME *turnen;* partly fr. OE *tyrnan* & *turnian* to turn, fr. ML *tornare,* fr. L, to turn on a lathe, fr. *tornus* lathe, fr. Gk *tornos;* partly fr. OF *torner, tourner* to turn, fr. ML *tornare;* akin to L *terere* to rub — more at THROW] *vt* (bef. 12c) **1 a** : to cause to move around an axis or a center : make rotate or revolve ⟨~ a wheel⟩ ⟨~ a crank⟩ **b** (1) : to cause to move around so as to effect a desired end (as of locking, opening, or shutting) ⟨~ a key⟩ (2) : to affect or alter the functioning of (as a mechanical device) by such movement ⟨~*ed* the oven to a higher temperature⟩ **c** : to execute or perform by rotating or revolving ⟨~ handsprings⟩ **d** : to twist out of line or shape : WRENCH ⟨had ~*ed* his ankle⟩ **2 a** (1) : to cause to change position by moving through an arc of a circle ⟨~*ed* his chair to the fire⟩ (2) : to cause to move around a center so as to show another side of ⟨~ the page⟩ (3) : to cause (as a scale) to move so as to register weight **b** : to revolve mentally : think over : PONDER **3 a** : to reverse the sides or surfaces of : INVERT ⟨~ pancakes⟩: (1) : to dig or plow so as to bring the lower soil to the surface (2) : to make (as a garment) over by reversing the material and resewing ⟨~ a collar⟩ (3) : to invert feet up and face down (as a character, rule, or slug) in setting type **b** : to reverse or upset the order or disposition of ⟨everything was ~*ed* topsy-turvy⟩ **c** : to disturb or upset the mental balance of : DERANGE, UNSETTLE ⟨a mind ~*ed* by grief⟩ **d** : to set in another esp. contrary direction **4 a** : to bend or change the course of : DIVERT **b** : to cause to retreat ⟨used fire hoses to ~ the mob⟩ **c** : to alter the drift, tendency, or expected result of **d** : to bend a course around or about : ROUND ⟨~*ed* the corner at full speed⟩ **5 a** (1) : to direct or point (as the face) in a specified way or direction (2) : to present by a change in direction or position ⟨~*ing* his back to his guests⟩ **b** : to bring to bear (as by aiming, pointing, or focusing) : TRAIN ⟨~*ed* his light into the dark doorway⟩ **c** : to direct (as the attention or mind) toward or away from something **d** : to direct the employment of : APPLY, DEVOTE ⟨~*ed* his skills to the service of mankind⟩ **e** (1) : to cause to rebound or recoil ⟨~*s* their argument against them⟩ (2) : to make antagonistic : PREJUDICE ⟨~ a child against its mother⟩ **f** (1) : to cause to go in a particular direction ⟨~*ed* his steps homeward⟩ (2) : DRIVE, SEND ⟨~ cows to pasture⟩ ⟨officers were ~*ed* adrift by the mutineers⟩ ⟨~*ing* hunters off his land⟩ (3) : to convey or direct into or out of a receptacle by inverting **6 a** (1) : to make acid or sour : CURDLE, FERMENT (2) : to change the color of (as foliage) **b** (1) : CONVERT, TRANSFORM ⟨~ defeat into victory⟩ (2) : TRANSLATE, PARAPHRASE **c** : to cause to become of a specified nature or appearance ⟨~*ed* him into a fiend⟩ ⟨illness ~*ed* her hair white⟩ **d** : to exchange for something else ⟨~ coins into paper money⟩ **7 a** : to shape esp. in a rounded form by applying a cutting tool while revolving in a lathe **b** : to give a rounded form to by any means ⟨~ the heel of a sock⟩ **c** : to shape or mold artistically, gracefully, or neatly ⟨well ~*ed* ankles⟩ ⟨a knack for ~*ing* a phrase⟩ **8** : to make a fold, bend, or curve in: **a** : to form by bending ⟨~ a lead pipe⟩ **b** : to cause (the edge of a blade) to bend back or over : BLUNT, DULL **9 a** : to keep (as money or goods) moving; *specif* : to dispose of (a stock) to make room for another **b** : to gain in the course of business ⟨~*ing* a quick profit⟩ **10** : to engage in (an act of prostitution) ⟨~ tricks⟩ ~ *vi* **1 a** : to move around on an axis or through an arc of a circle : ROTATE **b** : to become giddy or dizzy : REEL ⟨heights always made his head ~⟩ **c** (1) : HINGE ⟨argument ~*s* upon a point not of ethics but logic —Gail Kennedy⟩ (2) : to have a center (as of interest) in something specified **2 a** : to direct one's course **b** (1) : to reverse a course or direction (2) : to have a reactive usu. adverse effect : RECOIL **c** : to take a different course or direction ⟨~*ed* toward home⟩ ⟨the main road ~*s* sharply to the right⟩ **3 a** : to change position so as to face another way **b** : to face toward or away from someone or something **c** : to change one's attitude or reverse one's course of action to one of opposition or hostility ⟨felt the world had ~*ed* against him⟩ **d** : to make a sudden violent assault esp. without evident cause ⟨dogs ~*ing* on their owners⟩ **4 a** : to direct one's attention or thoughts to or away from someone or something **b** (1) : to change one's religion (2) : to go over to another side or party : DEFECT **c** : to have recourse : REFER, RESORT ⟨~*ed* to a friend for help⟩ ⟨~*ed* to his notes for the exact figures⟩ **d** : to direct one's efforts or interests : devote or apply oneself ⟨~*ed* to the study of the law⟩ **5 a** : to become changed, altered, or transformed: as (1) *archaic* : to become different (2) : to change color ⟨the leaves have ~*ed*⟩ (3) : to become sour, rancid, or tainted ⟨the milk had ~*ed*⟩ (4) : to be variable or inconstant (5) : to become mentally unbalanced : become deranged **b** (1) : to pass from one state to another : CHANGE ⟨water had ~*ed* to ice⟩ (2) : BECOME, GROW ⟨his hair had ~*ed* gray⟩ ⟨the weather ~*ed* bad⟩ ⟨just ~*ed* twenty⟩ (3) : to become someone or something specified by change from another state : change into ⟨~ traitor⟩ ⟨doctors ~*ed* authors⟩ **6** : to become curved or bent (as from pressure); *esp* : to become blunted by bending ⟨edge of the knife had ~*ed*⟩ **7** : to operate a lathe **8** *of merchandise* : to be stocked and disposed of : change hands — **turn·able** \ˈtər-nə-bəl\ *adj* — **turn a blind eye** : to refuse to see : be oblivious ⟨might *turn a blind eye* to the use of violence —Arthur Krock⟩ — **turn a deaf ear** : to refuse to listen — **turn a hair** : to give a sign of distress or disturbance ⟨did not *turn a hair* when told of the savage murder —*Times Lit. Supp.*⟩ — **turn color 1** : to become of a different color **2 a** : BLUSH, FLUSH **b** : to grow pale — **turn loose 1 a** : to set free ⟨*turned loose* the captured animal⟩ **b** : to free from all restraints ⟨*turned* them *loose* with a pile of theme paper to write whatever they liked —Elizabeth P. Schafer⟩ **2** : to fire off : DISCHARGE **3** : to open fire — **turn one's back on 1** : REJECT, DENY ⟨would be *turning one's back on* history —Pius Walsh⟩ **2** : FORSAKE ⟨*turned his back on* his obligations⟩ — **turn one's hand** *or* **turn a hand** : to set to work : apply oneself — **turn one's head** : to cause to become infatuated or conceited ⟨success had not *turned his head*⟩ — **turn one's stomach** : to disgust completely : SICKEN, NAUSEATE ⟨the foul smell *turned his stomach*⟩ — **turn tail** : to turn away so as to flee ⟨*turned tail* and ran⟩ — **turn the other cheek** : to respond to injury or unkindness with patience : forgo retaliation — **turn the scale** : to tip the scales — **turn the tables** : to bring about a reversal of the relative conditions or fortunes of two contending parties — **turn the trick** : to bring about the desired result or effect — **turn turtle** : CAPSIZE, OVERTURN

[2]**turn** *n* [ME; partly fr. OF *tourn, tour* lathe, circuit, turn (partly fr. L *tornus* lathe; partly fr. OF *torner, tourner* to turn); partly fr. ME *turnen* to turn] (13c) **1 a** : the action or an act of turning about a center or axis : REVOLUTION, ROTATION **b** : any of various rotating or pivoting movements in dancing **2 a** : the action or an act of giving or taking a different direction : change of course or posture ⟨illegal left ~⟩: as (1) : a drill maneuver in which troops in mass formation change direction without preserving alignment (2) : any of various shifts of direction in skiing (3) : an interruption of a curve in figure skating **b** : DEFLECTION, DEVIATION **c** : the action or an act of turning so as to face in the opposite direction : reversal of posture or course ⟨an about ~⟩ ⟨~ of the tide⟩ **d** : a change effected by turning over to another side ⟨~ of the cards⟩ **e** : a place at which something turns, turns off, or turns back : BEND, CURVE **3** : a short trip out and back or round about ⟨took a ~ through the park⟩ **4** : an act or deed affecting another esp. when incidental or unexpected ⟨one good ~ deserves another⟩ **5 a** : a period of action or activity : GO, SPELL; *specif* : a bout of wrestling **b** : a place, time, or opportunity accorded an individual or unit of a series in simple succession or in a scheduled order ⟨waiting her ~ in a doctor's office⟩ **c** : a period or tour of duty : SHIFT **d** : a short act (as for a variety show) **e** (1) : an event in any gambling game after which bets are settled (2) : the order of the last three cards in faro — used in the phrase *call the turn* **6** : something that revolves around a center: as **a** (1) : LATHE (2) : a catch or latch for a cupboard or cabinet door operated by turning a handle **b** : a musical ornament consisting of a group of four or more notes that wind about the principal note by including the notes next above and next below **7** : a special purpose or requirement — used chiefly in the phrase *serve one's turn* **8 a** : an act of changing : ALTERATION, MODIFICATION ⟨a nasty ~ in the weather⟩ **b** : a change in tendency, trend, or drift ⟨hoped for a ~ in his luck⟩ ⟨a ~ for the better⟩ **c** : the beginning of a new period of time ⟨the ~ of the century⟩ **9 a** : distinctive quality or character **b** (1) : a skillful fashioning of language or arrangement of words (2) : a particular form of expression or peculiarity of phrasing **c** : the shape or mold in which something is fashioned : CAST **10 a** : the state or manner of being coiled or twisted **b** : a single round (as of rope passed about an object or of wire wound on a core) **11** : natural or special ability or aptitude : BENT, INCLINATION ⟨a ~ for logic⟩ ⟨an optimistic ~ of mind⟩ **12** : a special twist, construction, or interpretation ⟨gave the old yarn a new ~⟩ **13 a** : a disordering spell or attack (as of illness, faintness, or dizziness) **b** : a nervous start or shock **14 a** : a complete transaction involving a purchase and sale of securities; *also* : a profit from such a transaction **b** : TURNOVER 7b **15** : something turned or to be turned: as **a** : a character or slug inverted in setting type **b** : a piece of type placed bottom up — **at every turn** : on every occasion : CONSTANTLY, CONTINUALLY ⟨they opposed her *at every turn*⟩ — **by turns** : one after another in regular succession : ALTERNATELY, SUCCESSIVELY — **in turn** : in due order of succession : SUCCESSIVELY, ALTERNATELY — **on the turn** : at the point of turning ⟨tide is *on the turn*⟩ — **out of turn 1** : not in due order of succession ⟨play *out of turn*⟩ **2** : at a wrong time or place : IMPRUDENTLY, UNWISELY ⟨talking *out of turn*⟩ — **to a turn** : to perfection

turn·about \ˈtər-nə-ˌbau̇t\ *n* (1789) **1** : MERRY-GO-ROUND **2 a** : a change or reversal of direction, trend, policy, role, or character **b** : a changing from one allegiance to another **c** : TURNCOAT, RENEGADE **d** : an act or instance of retaliating ⟨~ is fair play⟩

turn·around \-ˌrau̇nd\ *n* (1926) **1** : a space permitting the turning around of a vehicle **2** : TURNABOUT 2a, 2b **3** : the process of readying a vehicle for departure after its arrival esp. without any intervening delays; *also* : the time spent in this process

turn around \ˌtər-nə-ˈrau̇nd, ˈtər-\ *vi* (1822) : to act in an abrupt, different, or surprising manner — used with *and* ⟨after three years he just *turned around* and left school⟩

turn away *vt* (12c) **1** : DEFLECT, AVERT **2 a** : to send away : REJECT, DISMISS **b** : REPEL **c** : to refuse admittance or acceptance to ~ *vi* : to start to go away : DEPART

turn back *vi* (1535) **1 a** : to stop going forward **b** : to go in the reverse direction **2** : to refer to an earlier time or place ~ *vt* **1** : to drive back or away **2** : to stop the advance of **3** : to fold back **4** : GIVE BACK, RETURN — **turn back the clock** : to revert to a condition existing in the past

turn·buck·le \ˈtərn-ˌbək-əl\ *n* (ca. 1877) : a device that consists of a link with screw threads at both ends or a screw thread at one end and a swivel at the other, that is turned to bring the ends closer together, and that is used for tightening a rod or stay

turn·coat \-ˌkōt\ *n* (1557) : one who switches to an opposing side or party; *specif* : TRAITOR

[1]**turn·down** \ˌtərn-ˌdau̇n\ *adj* (1840) : capable of being turned down; *esp* : worn turned down ⟨~ collar⟩

[2]**turn·down** \ˈtərn-ˌdau̇n\ *n* (1849) **1** : something turned down **2** : REJECTION **3** : DOWNTURN

turn down \ˌtərn-ˈdau̇n, ˈtərn-\ *vi* (1601) : to be capable of being folded or doubled down ⟨collar *turns down*⟩ ~ *vt* **1** : to fold or double down **2** : to turn (a card) face downward **3** : to reduce the height or intensity of by turning a control ⟨*turn down* the radio⟩ **4** : to decline to accept : REJECT ⟨*turned down* the offer⟩

turned–on \ˈtərn-ˈdȯn, -ˈdän\ *adj* (1966) : keenly aware of and responsive to what is new and fashionable : HIP

[1]**turn·er** \ˈtər-nər\ *n* (15c) : one that turns or is used for turning ⟨a pancake ~⟩; *esp* : one who forms articles with a lathe

[2]**tur·ner** \ˈtər-nər, ˈtu̇(ə)r-\ *n* [G, fr. *turnen* to perform gymnastic exercises, fr. OHG *turnēn* to turn, fr. ML *tornare* — more at TURN] (1854) : a member of a turnverein : GYMNAST

Tur·ner's syndrome \ˈtər-nərz-\ *n* [Henry Hubert *Turner* †1970 Am. physician] (1942) : a genetically determined condition that is associated with the presence of one X chromosome and no Y chromosome and that is characterized by an outwardly female phenotype with incomplete and infertile gonads

turn·ery \ˈtər-nə-rē\ *n, pl* **-er·ies** (1644) : the work, products, or shop of a turner

turn–in \ˈtər-ˌnin\ *n* (1902) : something that turns in or is turned in

turn in \ˌtər-ˈnin, ˈtər-\ *vi* (1535) **1** : to make an entrance by turning from a road or path **2** : to go to bed ⟨*turned in* early⟩ ~ *vt* **1** : to deliver up : HAND OVER ⟨*turned in* his badge and quit⟩ **2 a** : to inform on : BETRAY **b** : to deliver to an authority ⟨urged the wanted man to *turn* himself *in*⟩ **3** : to acquit oneself of : PUT ON, PRODUCE ⟨*turned in* a good performance⟩

turn·ing *n* (14c) **1** : the act or course of one that turns **2** : a place of a change in direction **3 a** : a forming by use of a lathe; *broadly* : TURNERY **b** *pl* : waste produced in turning

turning chisel *n* (ca. 1877) : a chisel used for shaping or finishing work in a lathe

turning point *n* (1851) : a point at which a significant change occurs

tur·nip \ˈtər-nəp\ *n* [prob. fr. [1]*turn* + E dial. *neep* (turnip); fr. the well-rounded root] (1533) **1** : either of two biennial herbs of the mustard family with thick roots eaten as a vegetable or fed to stock: **a** : one (*Brassica rapa*) with hairy leaves and usu. flattened roots **b** : RUTABAGA **2** : a large pocket watch

[1]**turn·key** \ˈtərn-ˌkē\ *n, pl* **turnkeys** (1654) : one who has charge of a prison's keys

[2]**turnkey** *adj* (1927) : built, supplied, or installed complete and ready to operate ⟨a ~ nuclear plant⟩ ⟨a ~ computer system⟩; *also* : of or relating to a turnkey building or installation ⟨a ~ contract⟩ ⟨~ vendors⟩

turn·off \ˈtər-ˌnȯf\ *n* (ca. 1852) **1** : a turning off **2** : a place where one turns off; *esp* : an exit ramp on a turnpike **3** : one that causes loss of interest or enthusiasm ⟨the music was a ~⟩

turn off \ˌtər-ˈnȯf, ˈtər-\ *vt* (1564) **1 a** : DISMISS, DISCHARGE **b** : to dispose of : SELL **2** : DEFLECT, EVADE **3** : PRODUCE, ACCOMPLISH **4** : to stop the flow of or shut off by or as if by turning a control ⟨*turn* the water *off*⟩ **5** : HANG *vt* 1b **6 a** : to remove (material) by the process of turning **b** : to shape or produce by turning **7** : to cause to lose interest : BORE ⟨economics *turns* me *off*⟩; *also* : to evoke a negative feeling in ~ *vi* **1** : to deviate from a straight course or from a main road ⟨*turn off* into a side road⟩ **2 a** *Brit* : to turn bad : SPOIL **b** : to change to a specified state : BECOME **3** : to lose interest : WITHDRAW

turn on \(ˈ)tər-ˈnȯn, -ˈnän\ *vt* (1833) **1** : to cause to flow or operate by or as if by turning a control ⟨*turn* the water *on* full⟩ **2 a** : to cause to undergo an intense often visionary experience by taking a drug; *broadly* : to cause to get high **b** : to move pleasurably ⟨rock music *turns* her *on*⟩; *also* : to excite sexually **c** : to cause to gain knowledge or appreciation of something specified ⟨*turned* her *on* to ballet⟩ ~ *vi* : to become turned on — **turn–on** \ˈtər-ˌ\ *n*

turn·out \ˈtər-ˌnau̇t\ *n* (1688) **1** : an act of turning out **2** *chiefly Brit* **a** : STRIKE 3a **b** : STRIKER 1d **3** : a gathering of people for a special purpose ⟨a heavy voter ~⟩ **4 a** : a place where something (as a road) turns out or branches off **b** : a space adjacent to a highway in which vehicles may park or pull into to enable others to pass **c** : a railroad siding **5** : a clearing out and cleaning **6 a** : a coach or carriage together with the horses, harness, and attendants **b** : EQUIPMENT, RIG **c** : manner of dress : GETUP **7** : net quantity of produce yielded

turn out \ˌtər-ˈnau̇t, ˈtər-\ *vt* (1546) **1 a** : EXPEL, EVICT **b** : to put (as a horse) to pasture **2 a** : to turn inside out ⟨*turning out* his pockets⟩ **b** : to empty the contents of esp. for cleaning or rearranging; *also* : CLEAN **3** : to produce often rapidly or regularly by or as if by machine ⟨a writer *turning out* stories⟩ **4** : to equip, dress, or finish in a careful or elaborate way **5** : to put out by turning a switch ⟨*turn out* the lights⟩ **6** : to call (as the guard or a company) out from rest or shelter and into formation ~ *vi* **1 a** : to come or go out from home in answer to a summons ⟨voters *turned out* in droves⟩ **b** : to get out of bed **2 a** : to prove to be in the result or end ⟨the play *turned out* to be a flop⟩ **b** : to become in maturity ⟨nobody thought he'd *turn out* like this⟩ **c** : END ⟨stories that *turn out* happily⟩

[1]**turn·over** \ˈtər-ˌnō-vər\ *n* (14c) **1** : an act or result of turning over : UPSET **2** : a turning from one side, place, or direction to its opposite : SHIFT, REVERSAL **3** : a reorganization with a view to a shift in person-

nel : SHAKE-UP **4 :** something that is turned over **5 :** a filled pastry made by folding half of the crust over the other half **6 :** the amount of business done; *esp* **:** the volume of shares traded on a stock exchange **7 a :** movement (as of goods or people) into, through, and out of a place **b :** a cycle of purchase, sale, and replacement of a stock of goods; *also* **:** the ratio of sales for a stated period to average inventory **c :** the number of persons hired within a period to replace those leaving or dropped from a work force; *also* **:** the ratio of this number to the number in the average force maintained **8 :** the act or an instance of a team's losing possession of a ball through error or a minor violation of the rules (as in basketball or football)

2turn·over \ˌtər-ˌnō-vər\ *adj* (ca. 1849) **:** capable of being turned over

turn over \ˌtər-ˈnō-vər, ˈtər-\ *vt* (14c) **1 a :** to turn from an upright position **:** OVERTURN **b :** ROTATE ⟨*turn over* a stiff valve with a wrench⟩; *also* **:** to cause (an internal-combustion engine) to kick over **2 :** to search (as clothes or papers) by lifting or moving one by one **3 :** to think over **:** meditate on **4 :** to read or examine (as a book) slowly or idly **5 :** DELIVER, SURRENDER **6 a :** to receive and dispose of (a stock of merchandise) **b :** to do business to the amount of ⟨*turning over* $1000 a week⟩ ~ *vi* **1 :** UPSET, CAPSIZE **2 :** ROTATE **3 a** *of one's stomach* **:** to heave with nausea **b** *of one's heart* **:** to seem to leap or lurch convulsively with sudden fright — **turn over a new leaf :** to make a change for the better esp. in one's way of living

turn·pike \ˈtərn-ˌpīk\ *n* [ME *turnepike* revolving frame bearing spikes and serving as a barrier, fr. *turnen* to turn + *pike*] (1678) **1 :** TOLLGATE **2 a :** a toll road or one formerly maintained as such; *esp* **:** a toll expressway **b :** a main road; *esp* **:** a paved highway with crowned surface

turn·sole \ˈtərn-ˌsōl\ *n* [ME *turnesole*, fr. MF *tournesol*, fr. OIt *tornasole*, fr. *tornare* to turn (fr. ML) + *sole* sun, fr. L *sol* — more at TURN, SOLAR] (14c) **1 :** a European herb (*Chrozophora tinctoria*) of the spurge family with juice that is turned blue by ammonia; *also* **:** a purple dye obtained from it **2 :** HELIOTROPE 1

turn·spit \-ˌspit\ *n* (ca. 1576) **1 a :** one that turns a spit; *specif* **:** a small dog formerly used in a treadmill to turn a spit **b :** a roasting jack **2 :** a rotatable spit

turn·stile \-ˌstīl\ *n* (1643) **:** a post with arms pivoted on the top set in a passageway so that persons can pass through only on foot one by one

turn·stone \-ˌstōn\ *n* [fr. a habit of turning over stones to find food] (ca. 1674) **:** any of a genus (*Arenaria*) of various widely distributed migratory shorebirds resembling the related plovers and sandpipers; *esp* **:** a widely distributed bird (*A. interpres*) having the upper surfaces variegated with black and chestnut and a black breast

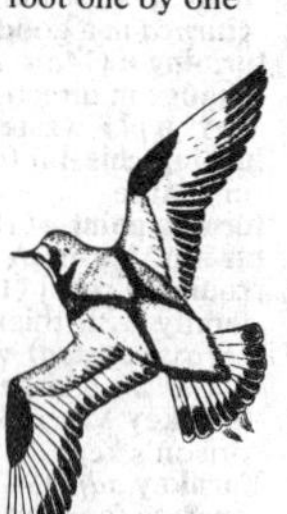

turnstone

turn·ta·ble \-ˌtā-bəl\ *n* (1835) **:** a revolvable platform: as **a :** a platform with a track for turning wheeled vehicles **b :** LAZY SUSAN **c :** a rotating platform that carries a phonograph record

turn to \ˈtərn-ˈtü\ *vi* (1813) **:** to apply oneself to work **:** act vigorously

1turn·up \ˌtər-ˌnəp\ *adj* (1685) **1 :** turned up ⟨a ~ nose⟩ **2 :** made or fitted to be turned up ⟨a ~ collar⟩

2turn·up \ˈtər-ˌnəp\ *n* (1688) **:** something that is turned up

turn up \ˌtər-ˈnəp, ˈtər-\ *vt* (1563) **1 :** FIND, DISCOVER **2 :** to raise or increase by or as if by turning a control **3** *Brit* **a :** to look up (as a word or fact) in a book **b :** to refer to or consult (a book) **4 :** to turn (a card) face upward **5 :** to reach a rotational speed of **:** develop power to the extent of ⟨engine *turns up* 101 horsepower⟩ ~ *vi* **1 :** to appear or come to light unexpectedly or after being lost ⟨new evidence has *turned up*⟩ **2 a (1) :** to turn out to be ⟨he *turned up* missing at roll call⟩ **(2) :** to become evident ⟨her name is always *turning up* in the newspapers⟩ **b :** to arrive or show up at an appointed or expected time or place ⟨*turned up* half an hour late⟩ **3 :** to happen or occur unexpectedly ⟨something always *turned up* to prevent their meeting⟩ **4** *of a ship* **:** TACK 1b — **turn up one's nose :** to show scorn or disdain

turn·ver·ein \ˈtərn-və-ˌrīn, ˈtu̇(ə)rn-\ *n* [G, fr. *turnen* to perform gymnastic exercises + *verein* club] (1852) **:** an athletic club

tu·ro·phile \ˈt(y)u̇r-ə-ˌfīl\ *n* [irreg. fr. Gk *tyros* cheese + E *-phile* — more at BUTTER] (1938) **:** a connoisseur of cheese **:** a cheese fancier

1tur·pen·tine \ˈtər-pən-ˌtīn, ˈtərp-ᵊm-\ *n* [ME *terbentyne, turpentyne*, fr. MF & ML; MF *terbentine, tourbentine*, fr. ML *terbentina*, fr. L *terebinthina*, fem. of *terebinthinus* of terebinth, fr. *terebinthus* terebinth, fr. Gk *terebinthos*] (14c) **1 a :** a yellow to brown semifluid oleoresin obtained as an exudate from the terebinth — called also *Chian turpentine* **b :** an oleoresin obtained from various conifers (as some pines and firs) **2 a :** an essential oil obtained from turpentines by distillation and used esp. as a solvent and thinner — called also *gum turpentine, oil of turpentine* **b :** a similar oil obtained by distillation or carbonization of pinewood — called also *wood turpentine*

2turpentine *vt* **-tined; -tin·ing** (1759) **1 :** to apply turpentine to **2 :** to extract turpentine from; *esp* **:** to tap (pine trees) in order to obtain turpentine

tur·pi·tude \ˈtər-pə-ˌt(y)üd\ *n* [MF, fr. L *turpitudo*, fr. *turpis* vile, base] (15c) **:** inherent baseness **:** DEPRAVITY ⟨moral ~⟩; *also* **:** a base act

turps \ˈtərps\ *n pl but sing in constr* [by shortening & alter.] (ca. 1823) **:** TURPENTINE

tur·quoise *also* **tur·quois** \ˈtər-ˌk(w)ȯiz\ *n* [ME *turkeis, turcas*, fr. MF *turquoyse*, fr. fem. of *turquoys* Turkish, fr. OF, fr. *Turc* Turk] (14c) **1 :** a mineral $CuAl_6(PO_4)_4(OH)_8{\cdot}5H_2O$ that is a blue, bluish green, or greenish gray hydrous basic copper aluminum phosphate, takes a high polish, changes sometimes to a green tint, but when sky blue is valued as a gem **2 :** a variable color averaging a light greenish blue

turquoise blue *n* (1799) **:** a variable color averaging a light greenish blue that is paler and slightly bluer than average turquoise

turquoise green *n* (1886) **:** a variable color averaging a light bluish green

tur·ret \ˈtər-ət, ˈtə-rət, ˈtür-ət\ *n* [ME *touret*, fr. MF *torete, tourete*, fr. OF, dim. of *tor, tur* tower — more at TOWER] (14c) **1 :** a little tower; *specif* **:** an ornamental structure at an angle of a larger structure **2 a :** a pivoted and revolvable holder in a machine tool **b :** a device (as on a microscope or a television camera) holding several lenses **3 a :** a tall building usu. moved on wheels and formerly used for carrying soldiers and equipment for breaching or scaling a wall **b (1) :** a gunner's fixed or movable enclosure in an airplane **(2) :** a revolving armored structure on a warship that protects one or more guns mounted within it **(3) :** a similar upper structure usu. for one gun on a tank

tur·ret·ed \-əd\ *adj* (1550) **:** furnished with or as if with turrets

1tur·tle \ˈtərt-ᵊl\ *n* [ME, fr. OE *turtla*, fr. L *turtur*] *archaic* (bef. 12c) **:** TURTLEDOVE

2turtle *n, pl* **turtles** *also* **turtle** *often attrib* [prob. by folk etymology fr. F *tortue*, prob. fr. (assumed) VL *tartaruca*, fr. LL *tartarucha*, fem of *tartaruchus* of Tartarus, fr. Gk *tartarouchos*, fr. *Tartaros* Tartarus] (1657) **:** any of an order (Testudinata) of land, freshwater, and marine reptiles that have a toothless horny beak and a shell of bony dermal plates usu. covered with horny shields enclosing the trunk and into which the head, limbs, and tail usu. may be withdrawn

3turtle *n* (1952) **:** TURTLENECK

tur·tle·back \ˈtərt-ᵊl-ˌbak\ *n* (1881) **:** a raised convex surface — **turtle-back** *or* **tur·tle–backed** \ˌtərt-ᵊl-ˈbakt\ *adj*

tur·tle·dove \ˈtərt-ᵊl-ˌdəv\ *n* (14c) **:** any of several small wild pigeons esp. of an Old World genus (*Streptopelia*) noted for plaintive cooing

tur·tle·head \-ˌhed\ *n* (1857) **:** any of a genus (*Chelone*) of perennial herbs of the figwort family with spikes of showy white or purple flowers

tur·tle·neck \-ˌnek\ *n* (ca. 1908) **1 :** a high close-fitting turnover collar used esp. for sweaters **2 :** a sweater with a turtleneck — **tur·tle-necked** \-ˌnekt\ *adj*

tur·tling \ˈtərt-liŋ, -ᵊl-iŋ\ *n* (1726) **:** the action or process of catching turtles

turves *pl of* TURF

1Tus·can \ˈtəs-kən\ *adj* [ME, fr. L *tuscanus* Etruscan, fr. *Tusci* Etruscans] (1563) **1 :** of or relating to one of the five classical orders of architecture that is of Roman origin and plain in style **2 :** of, relating to, or characteristic of Tuscany, the Tuscans, or Tuscan

2Tuscan *n* (1568) **1 a :** the Italian language spoken in Tuscany **b :** the standard literary dialect of Italian **2 :** a native or inhabitant of Tuscany

Tus·ca·ro·ra \ˌtəs-kə-ˈrōr-ə, -ˈrȯr-\ *n, pl* **Tuscarora** *or* **Tuscaroras** [Tuscarora *Skă-rū-rēⁿ*, lit., Indian hemp gatherers] (1713) **1 :** a member of an American Indian people orig. of No. Carolina and later of New York and Ontario **2 :** the language of the Tuscarora people

tu·sche \ˈtu̇sh-ə\ *n* [G, back-formation fr. *tuschen* to lay on color, fr. F *toucher*, lit., to touch, fr. OF *tuchier* — more at TOUCH] (ca. 1907) **:** a black liquid used in lithography for drawing and painting and in etching and the silk-screen process as a resist

1tush \ˈtəsh\ *n* [ME *tusch*, fr. OE *tūsc;* akin to OFris *tusk* tooth, OE *tōth* tooth] (bef. 12c) **:** a long pointed tooth; *esp* **:** a horse's canine

2tush *interj* [ME *tussch*] (15c) — used to express disdain or reproach

3tush \ˈtu̇sh\ *n* [Yiddish *toches*] *slang* (1970) **:** BUTTOCKS

1tusk \ˈtəsk\ *n* [ME, alter. of *tux*, fr. OE *tūx;* akin to OE *tūsc* tush] (bef. 12c) **1 :** an elongated greatly enlarged tooth that projects when the mouth is closed and serves for digging food or as a weapon; *broadly* **:** a long protruding tooth **2 :** one of the small projections on a tusk tenon — **tusked** \ˈtəskt\ *adj* — **tusk·like** \ˈtəs-ˌklīk\ *adj*

2tusk *vt* (1629) **:** to dig up with a tusk; *also* **:** to gash with a tusk

tusk·er \ˈtəs-kər\ *n* (1859) **:** an animal with tusks; *esp* **:** a male elephant with two normally developed tusks

tusk tenon *n* (ca. 1825) **:** a tenon strengthened by one or more smaller tenons underneath forming a steplike outline

tus·sah \ˈtəs-ə, -ˌȯ\ *or* **tus·sore** \-ˌō(ə)r, -ˌȯ(ə)r\ *n* [Hindi *tasar*] (1590) **:** silk or silk fabric from the brownish fiber produced by larvae of some saturniid moths (esp. *Antheraea paphia*)

tus·sive \ˈtəs-iv\ *adj* [L *tussis* cough] (ca. 1857) **:** of, relating to, or involved in coughing

1tus·sle \ˈtəs-əl\ *n* (1629) **1 :** a physical contest or struggle **:** SCUFFLE **2 :** an intense argument, controversy, or struggle

2tussle *vi* **tus·sled; tus·sling** \-(ə-)liŋ\ [ME *tussillen*, freq. of ME *-tusen, -tousen* to tousle — more at TOUSE] (1638) **:** to struggle roughly **:** SCUFFLE

tus·sock \ˈtəs-ək\ *n* [origin unknown] (1580) **:** a compact tuft esp. of grass or sedge; *also* **:** a hummock in marsh bound together by plant roots — **tus·socky** \-ə-kē\ *adj*

tussock grass *n* (1842) **:** a grass or sedge that typically grows in tussocks

tussock moth *n* (1826) **:** any of numerous dull-colored moths (esp. family Lymantriidae) that usu. have wingless females and larvae with long tufts or brushes of hair

tut *a t-sound made by suction rather than explosion; often read as* ˈtət\ *interj* (1529) — used to express disapproval or disbelief

tu·tee \t(y)ü-ˈtē\ *n* [*tutor* + *-ee*] (1927) **:** one who is being tutored

tu·te·lage \ˈt(y)üt-ᵊl-ij\ *n* [L *tutela* protection, guardian (fr. *tutus*, pp. of *tueri* to look at, guard) + E *-age*] (1605) **1 a :** an act or process of serving as guardian or protector **:** GUARDIANSHIP **b :** hegemony over a foreign territory **:** TRUSTEESHIP 2 **2 :** the state of being under a guardian or tutor **3 a :** instruction esp. of an individual **b :** a guiding influence

tu·te·lar \ˈt(y)üt-ᵊl-ər, -ᵊl-ˌär\ *adj or n* (1600) **:** TUTELARY

1tu·te·lary \ˈt(y)üt-ᵊl-ˌer-ē\ *adj* (1611) **1 :** having the guardianship of a person or a thing ⟨a ~ goddess⟩ **2 :** of or relating to a guardian

2tutelary *n, pl* **-lar·ies** (1652) **:** a tutelary power (as a deity)

1tu·tor \ˈt(y)üt-ər\ *n* [ME, fr. MF & L; MF *tuteur*, fr. L *tutor*, fr. *tutus*, pp. of *tueri*] (14c) **:** a person charged with the instruction and guidance of another: as **a :** a private teacher **b :** a teacher in a British university who gives individual instruction to undergraduates

2tutor *vt* (1592) **1 :** to have the guardianship, tutelage, or care of **2 :** to teach or guide usu. individually in a special subject or for a particular purpose **:** COACH ~ *vi* **1 :** to do the work of a tutor **2 :** to receive instruction esp. privately

tu·tor·age \ˈt(y)üt-ə-rij\ *n* (1617) **:** the function or work of a tutor

tu·tor·ess \ˈt(y)üt-ə-rəs\ *n* (1614) **:** a female tutor

1tu·to·ri·al \t(y)ü-ˈtōr-ē-əl, -ˈtȯr-\ *adj* (1822) **:** of, relating to, or involving a tutor

[2]tutorial *n* (1923) **1 :** a class conducted by a tutor for one student or a small number of students **2 :** a paper and esp. a technical paper written to give practical information about a specific subject

tu·tor·ship \ˈt(y)üt-ər-ˌship\ *n* (1581) **1 :** the office, function, or work of a tutor **2 :** TUTELAGE 3

tu·toy·er \tᵫ-twá-yā\ *vt* [F, to address with the familiar pronoun *tu* thou, fr. MF, fr. *tu* thou (fr. L) + *toi* thee, fr. L *te* (acc. of *tu*) — more at THOU] (1697) **:** to address familiarly

[1]tut·ti \ˈtüt-ē, ˈtu̇t-; ˈtü-ˌtē, ˈtu̇-\ *adj or adv* [It, masc. pl. of *tutto* all] (ca. 1724) **:** ALL — used as a direction in music for voices or instruments to perform together

[2]tutti *n* (1839) **:** a passage or section performed by all the performers

tut·ti-frut·ti \ˌtüt-i-ˈfrüt-ē, ˌtu̇t-\ *n* [It *tutti frutti,* lit., all fruits] (ca. 1876) **:** a confection or ice cream containing chopped usu. candied fruits

tut–tut *two t-sounds made by suction rather than explosion; often read as* ˈtət-ˈtət\ *interj* (1591) **:** TUT

tu·tu \ˈtü-(ˌ)tü\ *n* [F, fr. (baby talk) *cucu, tutu* backside, alter. of *cul* — more at CULET] (ca. 1927) **:** a very short projecting skirt worn by a ballerina

tu–whit tu–whoo \tə-ˌ(h)wit-tə-ˈ(h)wü\ *n* [imit.] (1588) **:** the cry of an owl

tux \ˈtəks\ *n* (1922) **:** TUXEDO

tux·e·do \ˌtək-ˈsēd-(ˌ)ō\ *n, pl* **-dos** *or* **-does** [*Tuxedo* Park, N.Y.] (1899) **1 :** a single-breasted or double-breasted usu. black or blackish blue jacket **2 :** semiformal evening clothes for men — **tux·e·doed** \-(ˌ)ōd\ *adj*

tu·yere \twē-ˈe(ə)r\ *n* [F *tuyère,* fr. MF, fr. *tuyau* pipe] (1781) **:** a nozzle through which an air blast is delivered to a forge or blast furnace

TV \ˈtē-ˈvē\ *n* [*television*] (1947) **:** TELEVISION

TV dinner \ˌtē-ˌvē-\ *n* [fr. its saving the television viewer from having to interrupt his viewing to prepare and serve a meal] (1954) **:** a quick-frozen packaged dinner (as of meat, potatoes, and a vegetable) that requires only heating before it is served

twa \ˈtwá\ *or* **twae** \ˈtwá, ˈtwē\ *Scot var of* TWO

[1]twad·dle \ˈtwäd-ᵊl\ *n* [prob. alter. of E dial. *twattle* (idle talk)] (1782) **1 :** silly idle talk **:** DRIVEL **2 :** one that twaddles **:** TWADDLER

[2]twaddle *vb* **twad·dled; twad·dling** \ˈtwäd-liŋ, -ᵊl-iŋ\ (1826) **:** PRATE, BABBLE — **twad·dler** \-lər, -ᵊl-ər\ *n*

[1]twain \ˈtwān\ *adj* [ME, fr. OE *twēgen* — more at TWO] *archaic* (bef. 12c) **:** TWO

[2]twain *pron* (bef. 12c) **:** TWO; *esp* **:** two fathoms ⟨mark ~⟩

[3]twain *n* (14c) **1 :** TWO **2 :** COUPLE, PAIR

[1]twang \ˈtwaŋ\ *n* [imit.] (1562) **1 :** a harsh quick ringing sound like that of a plucked bowstring **2 a :** nasal speech or resonance **b :** the characteristic speech of a region, locality, or group of people **3 a :** an act of plucking **b :** PANG, TWINGE — **twangy** \ˈtwaŋ-ē\ *adj*

[2]twang *vb* **twanged; twang·ing** \ˈtwaŋ-iŋ\ *vi* (1567) **1 :** to sound with a twang ⟨the gate ~*ed* and squealed⟩ **2 :** to speak or sound with a nasal intonation **3 :** to throb or twitch with pain or tension **~** *vt* **1 :** to cause to sound with a twang **2 :** to utter or pronounce with a nasal twang **3 :** to pluck the string of — **twang·er** *n*

[3]twang *n* [alter. of *tang*] (1611) **1 :** a persisting flavor, taste, or odor **:** TANG **2 :** SUGGESTION, TRACE

'twas \(ˈ)twəz, ˈtwäz\ [by contr.] **:** it was

twat \ˈtwät\ *n* [origin unknown] (ca. 1656) **:** VULVA — usu. considered vulgar

tway·blade \ˈtwā-ˌblād\ *n* [E dial. *tway* (two)] (1578) **:** any of several orchids (esp. genera *Listera* or *Liparis*) having a pair of opposite leaves

[1]tweak \ˈtwēk\ *vb* [prob. alter. of ME *twikken* to pull sharply, fr. OE *twiccian* to pluck — more at TWITCH] *vt* (1601) **1 :** to pinch and pull with a sudden jerk and twist **:** TWITCH ⟨~*ed* a bud from the stem⟩ **2 :** to pinch (a person or a body part) lightly or playfully ⟨~*ed* the baby's ear affectionately⟩ **~** *vi* **:** TWITCH 1

[2]tweak *n* (1609) **:** an act of tweaking **:** PINCH

twee \ˈtwē\ *adj* [baby-talk for *sweet*] *chiefly Brit* (1905) **:** affectedly or excessively dainty, delicate, cute, or quaint ⟨such a theme might sound ~ or corny —*Times Lit. Supp.*⟩

tweed \ˈtwēd\ *n* [alter. of Sc *tweel* twill, fr. ME *twyll*] (1841) **1 :** a rough woolen fabric made usu. in twill weaves and used esp. for suits and coats **2** *pl* **:** tweed clothing; *specif* **:** a tweed suit

Twee·dle·dum and Twee·dle·dee \ˌtwēd-ᵊl-ˈdəm-ən-ˌtwēd-ᵊl-ˈdē\ *n* [E *tweedle* (to chirp) + *dum* (imit. of a low musical note) & *dee* (imit. of a high musical note)] (1725) **:** two individuals or groups that are practically indistinguishable

tweedy \ˈtwēd-ē\ *adj* **tweed·i·er; -est** (1912) **1 :** of or resembling tweed **2 a :** given to wearing tweeds **b :** informal or suggestive of the outdoors in taste or habits — **tweed·i·ness** *n*

tween \(ˈ)twēn\ *prep* [ME *twene,* short for *betwene*] (14c) **:** BETWEEN

tweet \ˈtwēt\ *n* [imit.] (1845) **:** a chirping note — **tweet** *vi*

tweet·er \ˈtwēt-ər\ *n* (1939) **:** a small loudspeaker responsive only to the higher acoustic frequencies and reproducing sounds of high pitch

tweeze \ˈtwēz\ *vt* **tweezed; tweez·ing** [back-formation fr. *tweezers*] (1941) **:** to pluck, remove, or handle with tweezers

twee·zer \ˈtwē-zər\ *n* (1904) **:** TWEEZERS

twee·zers \-zərz\ *n pl but sing or pl in constr* [obs. E *tweeze,* n., short for obs. E *etweese,* fr. pl. of obs. E *etwee,* fr. F *étui* box of instruments, fr. OF *estui* container, fr. *estuier* to keep, preserve, perh. fr. (assumed) VL *studiare* to take care of, fr. L *studium* zeal, study — more at STUDY] (1654) **:** any of various small metal instruments that are usu. held between the thumb and forefinger, are used for plucking, holding, or manipulating, and consist of two legs joined at one end

Twelfth Day *n* [fr. its being the 12th day after Christmas] (bef. 12c) **:** EPIPHANY 1

Twelfth Night *n* (bef. 12c) **:** the evening or sometimes the eve of Epiphany

twelve \ˈtwelv\ *n* [ME, fr. *twelve,* adj., fr. OE *twelf;* akin to OHG *zwelif* twelve, OE *twā* two, *-leofan* (as in *endleofan* eleven) — more at TWO, ELEVEN] (bef. 12c) **1 —** see NUMBER table **2** *cap* **a :** the twelve original disciples of Jesus **b :** the books of the Minor Prophets in the Jewish Scriptures **3 :** the 12th in a set or series **4 :** something having 12 units or members **5** *pl* **:** TWELVEMO — **twelfth** \ˈtwelf(t)th\ *adj or n* — **twelve** *adj or pron*

twelve·mo \ˈtwelv-(ˌ)mō\ *n, pl* **-mos** (1819) **:** the size of a piece of paper cut 12 from a sheet; *also* **:** a book, a page, or paper of this size

twelve·month \-ˌmən(t)th\ *n* (13c) **:** YEAR

twelve–tone \-ˈtōn\ *adj* (1940) **:** of, relating to, or being serial music utilizing the 12 chromatic tones

twelve–tone row *n* (1941) **:** the 12 chromatic tones of the octave placed in a chosen fixed order and constituting with some permitted permutations and derivations the melodic and harmonic material of a musical piece

twen·ty \ˈtwent-ē\ *n, pl* **twenties** [ME, fr. *twenty,* adj., fr. OE *twēntig,* n., group of 20, fr. *twēn-* (akin to OE *twā* two) + *-tig* group of 10 — more at TWO, TEN] (bef. 12c) **1 —** see NUMBER table **2** *pl* **:** the numbers 20 to 29; *specif* **:** the years 20 to 29 in a lifetime or century **3 :** a 20-dollar bill — **twen·ti·eth** \-ē-əth\ *adj or n* — **twenty** *adj or pron*

twen·ty–four·mo \ˌtwent-ē-ˈfō(ə)r-(ˌ)mō, -ˈfȯ(ə)r-\ *n, pl* **-mos** (ca. 1841) **:** the size of a piece of paper cut 24 from a sheet; *also* **:** a book, a page, or paper of this size

twen·ty–one \ˌtwent-ē-ˈwən\ *n* (bef. 12c) **1 —** see NUMBER table **2** [trans. of F *vingt-et-un*] **:** BLACKJACK — **twenty–one** *adj or pron*

twenty–twenty *or* **20/20** \ˌtwent-ē-ˈtwent-ē\ *adj* [fr. the testing of vision by reading letters at a distance of 20 feet] *of the human eye* (1939) **:** meeting a standard of normal visual acuity ⟨~ vision⟩

twen·ty–two \ˌtwent-ē-ˈtü\ *n* (bef. 12c) **1 —** see NUMBER table **2 :** a .22-caliber firearm; *esp* **:** one firing rimfire cartridges — usu. written .22 — **twenty–two** *adj or pron*

'twere \(ˈ)twər\ [by contr.] **:** it were

twerp \ˈtwərp\ *n* [origin unknown] (ca. 1923) **:** a silly, insignificant, or contemptible person

Twi \ˈchwē, chə-ˈwē, ˈtwē, ˈchē\ *n* (ca. 1874) **1 :** a dialect of Akan **2 :** a literary language based on the Twi dialect and used by the Akan-speaking peoples (as the Ashanti)

twi- \ˈtwī\ *prefix* [ME, fr. OE; akin to OHG *zwi-* twi-, L *bi-,* Gk *di-,* OE *twā* two] **:** two **:** double **:** doubly **:** twice ⟨*twi*-headed⟩

twice \ˈtwīs\ *adv* [ME *twiges, twies,* fr. OE *twiga;* akin to OE *twi-*] (12c) **1 :** on two occasions ⟨~ absent⟩ **2 :** two times **:** in doubled quantity or degree ⟨~ two is four⟩ ⟨~ as much⟩

twice–born \-ˈbȯ(ə)rn\ *adj* (15c) **1 :** born a second time **2 :** having undergone a definite experience of fundamental moral and spiritual renewal **:** REGENERATE **3 :** of or forming one of the three upper Hindu caste groups in which boys undergo an initiation symbolizing spiritual birth

twice–laid \-ˈlād\ *adj* (1592) **:** made from the ends of rope and strands of used rope ⟨~ rope⟩

twice–told \-ˈtōld\ *adj* (1595) **:** well known from repeated telling — used chiefly in the phrase *a twice-told tale*

[1]twid·dle \ˈtwid-ᵊl\ *vb* **twid·dled; twid·dling** \ˈtwid-liŋ, -ᵊl-iŋ\ [origin unknown] *vi* (1540) **1 :** to play negligently with something **:** FIDDLE **2 :** to turn or jounce lightly ⟨~*s* round and round in the water —J. B. S. Haldane⟩ **~** *vt* **:** to rotate lightly or idly ⟨*twiddled* his cigar —James Lord⟩ — **twiddle one's thumbs :** to spend time idly **:** do nothing

[2]twiddle *n* (1774) **:** TURN, TWIST

[1]twig \ˈtwig\ *n* [ME *twigge,* fr. OE; akin to OHG *zwīg* twig, OE *twā* two] (bef. 12c) **1 :** a small shoot or branch usu. without its leaves **2 :** a minute branch of a nerve or artery — **twigged** \ˈtwigd\ *adj* — **twig·gy** \ˈtwig-ē\ *adj*

[2]twig *vb* **twigged; twig·ging** [perh. fr. ScGael *tuig* I understand] *vt* (1764) **1 :** NOTICE, OBSERVE **2 :** to understand the meaning of **:** COMPREHEND **~** *vi* **:** to gain a grasp **:** UNDERSTAND ⟨*twigged* instinctively about things —H. E. Bates⟩

[3]twig *n* [origin unknown] (ca. 1811) *Brit* **:** FASHION, STYLE

twi·light \ˈtwī-ˌlīt\ *n, often attrib* (15c) **1 :** the light from the sky between full night and sunrise or between sunset and full night produced by diffusion of sunlight through the atmosphere and its dust **2 a :** an intermediate state that is not clearly defined ⟨lived in the ~ of neutrality —*Newsweek*⟩ **b :** a period of decline ⟨the ~ of a great career⟩

twilight glow *n* (ca. 1960) **:** airglow seen at twilight

Twilight of the Gods [trans.] (1768) **:** RAGNAROK

twi·lit \ˈtwī-ˌlit\ *adj* [*twi*light + *lit*] (1869) **:** lighted by or as if by twilight

twill \ˈtwil\ *n* [ME *twyll,* fr. OE *twilic* having a double thread, modif. of L *bilic-, bilix,* fr. *bi-* + *licium* thread] (14c) **1 :** a fabric with a twill weave **2 :** a textile weave in which the filling threads pass over one and under two or more warp threads to give an appearance of diagonal lines

twilled \ˈtwild\ *adj* (15c) **:** made with a twill weave

twill·ing \ˈtwil-iŋ\ *n* (1894) **:** twilled fabric; *also* **:** the process of making it

[1]twin \ˈtwin\ *adj* [ME, fr. OE *twinn* twofold, two by two; akin to ON *tvinnr* two by two, OE *twā* two] (bef. 12c) **1 :** born with one other or as a pair at one birth ⟨~ brother⟩ ⟨~ girls⟩ **2 a :** made up of two similar, related, or connected members or parts **:** DOUBLE **b :** paired in a close or necessary relationship **:** MATCHING **c :** having or consisting of two identical units **d :** being one of a pair

[2]twin *vb* **twinned; twin·ning** *vt* (14c) **1 :** to bring together in close association **:** COUPLE **2 :** DUPLICATE, MATCH **~** *vi* **1 :** to bring forth twins **2 :** to grow as a twin crystal

[3]twin *n* (15c) **1 a :** either of two offspring produced at a birth **b** *pl, cap* **:** GEMINI **2 :** one of two persons or things closely related to or resembling each other **3 :** a compound crystal composed of two or more crystals or parts of crystals of the same kind that are grown together in a specific manner — **twin·ship** \-ˌship\ *n*

twin bed *n* (1920) **:** one of a pair of matching single beds

twin·ber·ry \ˈtwin-ˌber-ē\ *n* [fr. the occurrence of the berries in pairs] (1821) **1 :** a shrubby No. American honeysuckle (*Lonicera involucrata*) with purple involucrate flowers **2 :** PARTRIDGEBERRY

twin bill *n* (ca. 1949) **:** DOUBLEHEADER

twin·born \ˈtwin-ˈbȯ(ə)rn\ *adj* (1598) **:** born at the same birth

twin double *n* (1963) **:** a system of betting (as on horse races) in which the bettor must pick the winners of four stipulated races in order to win — compare DAILY DOUBLE

[1]**twine** \'twīn\ *n* [ME *twin,* fr. OE *twīn;* akin to MD *twijn* twine, OE *twā* two] (bef. 12c) **1 :** a strong string of two or more strands twisted together **2 :** a twined or interlaced part or object **3 :** an act of twining, interlacing, or embracing — **twiny** \'twī-nē\ *adj*

[2]**twine** *vb* **twined; twin·ing** *vt* (13c) **1 a :** to twist together **b :** to form by twisting **:** WEAVE **2 a :** INTERLACE ⟨the girl *twined* her hands —John Buchan⟩ **b :** to cause to encircle or enfold something **c :** to cause to be encircled ~ *vi* **1 :** to coil about a support **2 :** to stretch or move in a sinuous manner **:** MEANDER ⟨the river ~*s* through the valley⟩ — **twin·er** *n*

[3]**twine** *vb* **twined; twin·ing** [alter. of Sc *twin,* fr. ME *twinnen,* fr. *twin* double] *vt, chiefly Scot* (1722) **:** to cause (one) to lose possession **:** DEPRIVE ⟨*twined* him of his nose —J. C. Ransom⟩ ~ *vi, chiefly Scot* **:** PART ⟨you and me must ~ —R. L. Stevenson⟩

twin·flow·er \'twin-,flau̇(-ə)r\ *n* (ca. 1817) **:** a low prostrate subshrub (*Linnaea borealis*) of the honeysuckle family that is found in the northern parts of Europe, Asia and No. America and has opposite leaves and fragrant usu. pink flowers in pairs

[1]**twinge** \'twinj\ *vb* **twinged; twing·ing** \'twin-jiŋ\ *or* **twinge·ing** [ME *twengen,* fr. OE *twengan*] *vt* (bef. 12c) **1** *dial* **:** PLUCK, TWEAK **2 :** to affect with a sharp pain or pang ~ *vi* **:** to feel a sudden sharp local pain

[2]**twinge** *n* (1608) **1 :** a sudden sharp stab of pain **2 :** a moral or emotional pang ⟨a ~ of conscience⟩

twi–night \'twī-,nīt\ *adj* [*twi*light + *night*] (1946) **:** of, relating to, or being a baseball doubleheader in which the first game is played in the late afternoon and the second continues into the evening

[1]**twin·kle** \'twiŋ-kəl\ *vb* **twin·kled; twin·kling** \-k(ə-)liŋ\ [ME *twinklen,* fr. OE *twinclian;* akin to MHG *zwinken* to blink] *vi* (bef. 12c) **1 :** to shine with a flickering or sparkling light **:** SCINTILLATE **2 a :** to flutter the eyelids **b :** to appear bright esp. with merriment ⟨his eyes *twinkled*⟩ **3 :** to flutter or flit rapidly ~ *vt* **1 :** to cause to shine with fluctuating light **2 :** to flicker or flirt rapidly ⟨*twinkled* the straight, red-lacquered toes —Glenway Wescott⟩ — **twin·kler** \-k(ə-)lər\ *n*

[2]**twinkle** *n* (1548) **1 :** a wink of the eyelids **2 :** the instant's duration of a wink **:** TWINKLING **3 :** an intermittent radiance **:** FLICKER **4 :** a rapid flashing motion **:** FLIRT — **twin·kly** \-k(ə-)lē\ *adj*

twin·kling \'twiŋ-kliŋ\ *n* (14c) **:** the time required for a wink **:** INSTANT ⟨the kettle will boil in a ~ —*Punch*⟩

twin–size \'twin-'sīz\ *adj* [*twin bed*] (1926) **:** having the dimensions 39 inches by 75 inches — used of a bed; compare FULL-SIZE, KING-SIZE, QUEEN-SIZE

[1]**twirl** \'twər-(-ə)l\ *vb* [perh. of Scand origin; akin to Norw dial. *tvirla* to twirl; akin to OHG *dweran* to stir — more at TURBID] *vi* (1598) **1 :** to revolve rapidly **2 :** to pitch in a baseball game ~ *vt* **1 :** to cause to rotate rapidly **2 :** PITCH 2a — **twirl·er** \'twər-lər\ *n*

[2]**twirl** *n* (1598) **1 :** an act of twirling **2 :** COIL, WHORL — **twirly** \'twər-lē\ *adj*

twirp *var of* TWERP

[1]**twist** \'twist\ *vb* [ME *twisten,* fr. OE *-twist* rope; akin to MD *twist* quarrel, twine, OE *twā* two] *vt* (15c) **1 a :** to unite by winding ⟨~*ing* strands together⟩ **b :** to make by twisting strands together ⟨~ thread from yarn⟩ **c :** to mingle by interlacing **2 :** TWINE, COIL **3 a :** to wring or wrench so as to dislocate or distort; *esp* **:** SPRAIN ⟨~*ed* my ankle⟩ **b :** to alter the meaning of **:** DISTORT, PERVERT ⟨~*ed* the facts⟩ **c :** CONTORT ⟨~*ed* his face into a grin⟩ **d :** to pull off, turn, or break by torsion **e :** to cause to move with a turning motion **f :** to form into a spiral shape **g :** to cause to take on moral, mental, or emotional deformity **h :** to make (one's way) in a winding or devious manner to a destination or objective ~ *vi* **1 :** to follow a winding course **:** SNAKE **2 a :** to turn or change shape under torsion **b :** to assume a spiral shape **c :** SQUIRM, WRITHE **d :** to dance the twist **3** *of a ball* **:** to rotate while taking a curving path or direction **4 :** TURN 3a ⟨~*ed* around to see behind him⟩ — **twist one's arm :** to bring strong pressure to bear on one

[2]**twist** *n* (1555) **1 :** something formed by twisting or winding: as **a :** a thread, yarn, or cord formed by twisting two or more strands together **b :** a strong tightly twisted sewing silk **c :** a baked piece of twisted dough **d :** tobacco leaves twisted into a thick roll **e :** a strip of citrus peel used to flavor a drink **2 :** the fleshing between the hind legs esp. of cattle or sheep **3 a :** an act of twisting **:** the state of being twisted **b :** a dance performed with strenuous gyrations esp. of the hips **c :** the spin given the ball in any of various games **d :** a spiral turn or curve **e** (1) **:** torque or torsional stress applied to a body (as a rod or shaft) (2) **:** torsional strain (3) **:** the angle through which a thing is twisted **4 a :** a turning off a straight course **b :** ECCENTRICITY, IDIOSYNCRASY **c :** a distortion of meaning or sense **5 a :** an unexpected turn or development ⟨weird ~*s* of fate —W. L. Shirer⟩ **b :** a clever device **:** TRICK ⟨questions demanding special ~*s* of thinking —*New Yorker*⟩ **c :** a variant approach or method **:** GIMMICK ⟨a kind of ~ on the old triangle theme —Dave Fedo⟩ **6 :** a front or back dive in which the diver twists his body sideways a half or full turn before entering the water — **twisty** \'twis-tē\ *adj*

twist drill *n* (ca. 1875) **:** a drill having deep helical grooves extending from the point to the smooth portion of the shank

twist·er \'twis-tər\ *n* (1579) **1 :** one that twists; *esp* **:** a ball with a forward and spinning motion **2 :** a tornado, waterspout, or dust devil in which the rotatory ascending movement of a column of air is esp. apparent

twist·ing \'twis-tiŋ\ *n* (ca. 1905) **:** the use of misrepresentation or trickery to get someone to lapse a life insurance policy and buy another usu. in another company

[1]**twit** \'twit\ *n* (1528) **1 :** an act of twitting **:** TAUNT **2 :** a silly annoying person **:** FOOL

[2]**twit** *vt* **twit·ted; twit·ting** [ME *atwiten* to reproach, fr. OE *ætwītan,* fr. *æt* at + *wītan* to reproach; akin to OHG *wīzan* to punish, OE *witan* to know] (1530) **1 :** to subject to light ridicule or reproach **:** RALLY **2 :** to make fun of as a fault ***syn*** see RIDICULE

[1]**twitch** \'twich\ *vb* [ME *twicchen;* akin to OE *twiccian* to pluck, OHG *gizwickan* to pinch] *vt* (bef. 12c) **:** to move or pull with a sudden motion **:** JERK ~ *vi* **1 :** PULL 1a, PLUCK ⟨~*ed* at my sleeve⟩ **2 :** to move jerkily **:** QUIVER — **twitch·er** *n*

[2]**twitch** *n* (1523) **1 :** an act of twitching; *esp* **:** a short sudden pull or jerk **2 :** a physical or mental pang **3 :** a loop of rope or strap that is tightened over a horse's lip as a restraining device **4 a :** a short spastic contraction of the muscle fibers **b :** a slight jerk of a body part — **twitch·i·ly** \'twich-ə-lē\ *adv* — **twitchy** \'twich-ē\ *adj*

[3]**twitch** *n* [alter. of *quitch*] (1598) **:** QUACK GRASS

[1]**twit·ter** \'twit-ər\ *vb* [ME *twiteren;* akin to OHG *zwizzirōn* to twitter] *vi* (14c) **1 :** to utter successive chirping noises **2 a :** to talk in a chattering fashion **b :** GIGGLE, TITTER **3 :** to tremble with agitation **:** FLUTTER ~ *vt* **1 :** to utter in chirps or twitters ⟨the robin ~*ed* his morning song⟩ **2 :** to shake rapidly back and forth **:** FLUTTER — **twit·ter·er** \-ər-ər\ *n*

[2]**twitter** *n* (1678) **1 :** a trembling agitation **:** QUIVER **2 :** a small tremulous intermittent sound (as of birds) **3 a :** a light chattering **b :** a light silly laugh **:** GIGGLE — **twit·tery** \'twit-ə-rē\ *adj*

twixt \(')twikst\ *or* **'twixt** *prep* [ME *twix,* short for *betwix, betwixt*] (14c) **:** BETWEEN

[1]**two** \'tü\ *adj* [ME *twa, two,* fr. OE *twā* (fem. & neut.); akin to OE *twēgen* two (masc.), *tū* (neut.), OHG *zwēne,* L *duo,* Gk *dyo*] (bef. 12c) **1 :** being one more than one in number **2 :** being the second — used postpositively ⟨section ~ of the instructions⟩

[2]**two** *pron, pl in constr* (bef. 12c) **1 :** two countable individuals not specified ⟨only ~ were found⟩ **2 :** a small approximate number of indicated things ⟨only a shot or ~ were fired⟩

[3]**two** *n, pl* **twos** (bef. 12c) **1** — see NUMBER table **2 :** the second in a set or series ⟨the ~ of spades⟩ **3 :** a 2-dollar bill **4 :** something having two units or members

two–bag·ger \-'bag-ər\ *n* (1880) **:** DOUBLE

two–bit \,tü-,bit\ *adj* (1802) **1 :** of the value of two bits **2 :** cheap or trivial of its kind **:** PETTY, SMALL-TIME

two bits *n pl but sing or pl in constr* (1730) **1 :** the value of a quarter of a dollar **2 :** something of small worth or importance

[1]**two–by–four** \,tü-bə-'fō(ə)r, -'fȯ(ə)r\ *n* (1884) **:** a piece of lumber approximately 2 by 4 inches as sawed and usu. $1^5/_8$ by $3^5/_8$ inches if dressed

[2]**two–by–four** *adj* (1897) **1 :** measuring two units (as inches) by four **2 :** small or petty of its kind ⟨this house and its ~ garden —Philip Barry⟩

two cents *n* (1947) **1 :** a sum or object of very small value **:** practically nothing ⟨said angrily that for *two cents* he'd punch your nose⟩ **2** *or* **two cents worth :** an opinion offered on a topic under discussion ⟨each speaker . . . is getting in his *two cents worth* —Dwight Macdonald⟩

two–cycle *adj, of an internal-combustion engine* (1902) **:** having a 2-stroke cycle

two–dimensional *adj* (1898) **1 :** having two dimensions **2 :** lacking depth of characterization ⟨~ fiction⟩ — **two-dimensionality** *n*

two–faced \'tü-'fāst\ *adj* (1619) **1 :** DOUBLE-DEALING, FALSE **2 :** having two faces — **two–faced·ness** \-'fāst-nəs, -'fā-səd-nəs\ *n*

two·fer \'tü-fər\ *n* [alter. of *two for (one)*] (1890) **1 :** a cheap item of merchandise; *esp* **:** a cigar selling at two for a nickel **2 :** a free coupon entitling the bearer to purchase two tickets to a specified theatrical production for the price of one **3 :** two articles available for the price of one or about the price of one

two–fist·ed \-'fis-təd\ *adj* (1774) **:** marked by vigorous often virile energy **:** HARD-HITTING

two·fold \'tü-,fōld, -'fōld\ *adj* (1559) **1 :** having two units or members **2 :** being twice as great or as many — **twofold** \-'fōld\ *adv*

2,4–D \,tü-,fōr-'dē, -,fȯr-\ *n* (ca. 1945) **:** a white crystalline compound $C_8H_6Cl_2O_3$ used as a weed killer

2,4,5–T \-,fīv-'tē\ *n* (1946) **:** an irritant compound $C_8H_5Cl_3O_3$ used in brush and weed control

two–hand·ed \'tü-'han-dəd\ *adj* (15c) **1 :** used with both hands ⟨a ~ sword⟩ **2 :** requiring two persons ⟨a ~ saw⟩ **3** *archaic* **:** STOUT, STRONG **4 a :** having two hands **b :** efficient with either hand

two–line octave *n* (ca. 1931) **:** the musical octave that begins on the first C above middle C — see PITCH illustration

two–party *adj* (1925) **:** characterized by two major political parties of comparable strength

two·pence \'təp-ən(t)s, *US also* 'tü-,pen(t)s\ *n* (15c) **1 :** the sum of two British pennies **2** *pl* **twopence** *or* **two·pen·ces :** a coin worth twopence

two·pen·ny \'təp-(ə-)nē, *US also* 'tü-,pen-ē\ *adj* (1532) **:** costing or worth twopence

two–phase *adj* (ca. 1896) **:** DIPHASIC

[1]**two–piece** \,tü-,pēs\ *adj* (1910) **:** forming a clothing ensemble with matching top and bottom parts

[2]**two–piece** \'tü-,pēs\ *n* (1930) **:** a garment (as a bathing suit) that is two-piece

two–piec·er \'tü-'pē-sər\ *n* (1943) **:** TWO-PIECE

two–ply \-'plī\ *adj* (ca. 1847) **1 :** consisting of two thicknesses **2 a :** woven with two sets of warp thread and two of filling ⟨a ~ carpet⟩ **b :** consisting of two strands ⟨~ yarn⟩

two–sid·ed \-'sīd-əd\ *adj* (1884) **:** having two sides **:** BILATERAL

two·some \'tü-səm\ *n* (14c) **1 :** a group of two persons or things **:** COUPLE **2 :** a golf singles match

two–spot·ted spider mite \,tü-,spät-əd-\ *n* (1947) **:** a widely distributed plant-feeding mite (*Tetranychus urticae*) that feeds on various usu. herbaceous plants and is a serious pest in greenhouses

two–step \'tü-,step\ *n* (1895) **1 :** a ballroom dance in $^2/_4$ or $^4/_4$ time having a basic pattern of step-close-step **2 :** a piece of music for the two-step — **two–step** *vi*

two–suit·er \-'süt-ər\ *n* (1948) **:** a man's traveling bag designed to hold two suits and accessories

two–tailed \,tü-,tāl(d)\ *also* **two–tail** \-,tā(ə)l\ *adj* (ca. 1962) **:** being a statistical test for which the critical region consists of all values of the test statistic greater than a given value plus the values less than another given value — compare ONE-TAILED

two–time \'tü-,tīm\ *vt* (1928) **1 :** DOUBLE-CROSS **2 :** to betray (a spouse or lover) by secret lovemaking with another — **two–tim·er** *n*

two–tone \,tü-,tōn\ *adj* (ca. 1927) **:** colored in two colors or in two shades of one color ⟨~ shoes⟩

two–toned \'tü-'tōnd\ *adj* (ca. 1939) **:** TWO-TONE

two–way *adj* (1571) **1 :** being a cock or valve that will connect a pipe or channel with either of two others **2 :** moving or allowing movement in either direction ⟨a ~ bridge⟩ **3 a :** involving or allowing an exchange between two individuals or groups ⟨there must be good ~ communication —Jerrold Orne⟩; *esp* **:** designed for both sending and receiving messages ⟨~ radio⟩ **b :** involving mutual responsibility or reciprocal relationships ⟨political alliance is a ~ thing —T. H. White *b*1915⟩ **4 :** involving two participants ⟨a ~ race⟩ **5 :** usable in either of two manners ⟨a ~ lamp⟩

two–way street *n* (1948) **:** a situation or relationship requiring give-and-take ⟨marriage is a *two-way street*⟩

two–wheel·er \-ˈhwē-lər, -ˈwē-\ *n* (1861) **:** a 2-wheeled vehicle (as a bicycle)

two–winged fly \ˌtü-ˌwiŋ(d)-\ *n* (ca. 1753) **:** any of a large order (Diptera) of winged or rarely wingless insects (as the housefly, mosquito, or gnat) that have segmented often headless, eyeless, and legless larvae, the anterior wings functional, and the posterior wings reduced to balancers

-ty *n suffix* [ME *-te,* fr. OF *-té,* fr. L *-tat-, -tas* — more at -ITY] **:** quality **:** condition **:** degree ⟨aprior*ity*⟩

ty·coon \tī-ˈkün\ *n* [Jp *taikun,* fr. Chin (Pek) *ta*^{4} great + *chun*^{1} ruler] (1858) **1 :** SHOGUN **2 a :** a top leader (as in politics) **b :** a businessman of exceptional wealth and power **:** MAGNATE

tying *pres part of* TIE

tyke \ˈtīk\ *n* [ME *tyke,* fr. ON *tīk* bitch] (15c) **1 :** DOG; *esp* **:** an inferior or mongrel dog **2 a** *chiefly Brit* **:** a clumsy, churlish, or eccentric person **b :** a small child

tym·bal *n* [alter. of *timbal*] (1854) **:** the vibrating membrane in the shrilling organ of a cicada

tym·pan \ˈtim-pən\ *n* [in sense 1, fr. ME, fr. OE *timpana,* fr. L *tympanum;* in other senses, fr. ML & L *tympanum*] (bef. 12c) **1 :** DRUM **2 :** a sheet (as of paper or cloth) placed between the impression surface of a press and the paper to be printed **3 :** TYMPANUM 2

tympani, tympanist *var of* TIMPANI, TIMPANIST

tym·pan·ic \tim-ˈpan-ik\ *adj* [L & NL *tympanum*] (1808) **:** of, relating to, or being a tympanum

tympanic membrane *n* (ca. 1860) **:** a thin membrane that closes externally the cavity of the middle ear and functions in the mechanical reception of sound waves and in their transmission to the site of sensory reception — called also *eardrum;* see EAR illustration

tym·pa·ni·tes \ˌtim-pə-ˈnīt-ēz\ *n* [ME, fr. LL, fr. Gk *tympanitēs,* fr. *tympanon*] (14c) **:** a distension of the abdomen caused by accumulation of gas in the intestinal tract or peritoneal cavity — **tym·pa·nit·ic** \-ˈnit-ik\ *adj*

tym·pa·num \ˈtim-pə-nəm\ *n, pl* **-na** \-nə\ *also* **-nums** [ML & L; ML, eardrum, fr. L, drum, architectural panel, fr. Gk *tympanon* drum, kettledrum; akin to Gk *typtein* to beat] (1619) **1 a** (1) **:** TYMPANIC MEMBRANE (2) **:** MIDDLE EAR **b :** a thin tense membrane covering an organ of hearing of an insect — see INSECT illustration **c :** a membranous resonator in a sound-producing organ **2 a :** the recessed usu. triangular face of a pediment within the frame made by the upper and lower cornices **b :** the space within an arch and above a lintel or a subordinate arch **3 :** the diaphragm of a telephone

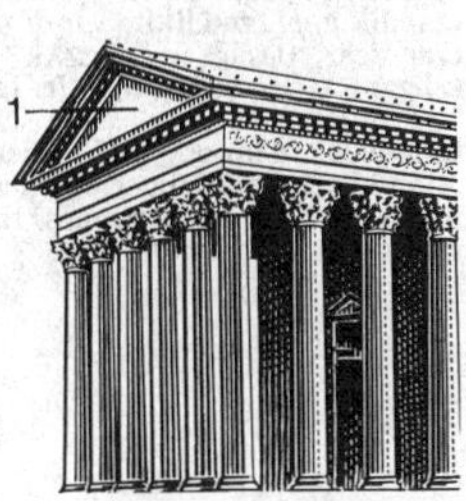

1 tympanum 2a

tym·pa·ny \-nē\ *n, pl* **-nies** [ML *tympanias,* fr. Gk, fr. *tympanon*] (1528) **1 :** TYMPANITES **2 :** BOMBAST, TURGIDITY

Tyn·dar·e·us \tin-ˈdar-ē-əs\ *n* [L, fr. Gk] **:** a king of Sparta and husband of Leda in Greek mythology

tyne *var of* TINE

typ·al \ˈtī-pəl\ *adj* (1853) **1 :** serving as a type **:** TYPICAL **2 :** of or relating to a type

[1]**type** \ˈtīp\ *n, often attrib* [ME, fr. LL *typus,* fr. L & Gk; L *typus* image, fr. Gk *typos* blow, impression, model, fr. *typtein* to strike, beat; akin to L *stupēre* to be benumbed, *tundere* to beat — more at STINT] (15c) **1 a :** a person or thing (as in the Old Testament) believed to foreshadow another (as in the New Testament) **b :** one having qualities of a higher category **:** MODEL **c :** a lower taxonomic category selected as a standard of reference for a higher category; *also* **:** a specimen or series of specimens on which a taxonomic species or subspecies is actually based **2 :** a distinctive mark or sign **3 a** (1) **:** a rectangular block usu. of metal bearing a relief character from which an inked print can be made (2) **:** a collection of such blocks ⟨a font of ~⟩ (3) **:** alphanumeric characters for printing ⟨the ~ for this book has been photoset⟩ **b :** TYPEFACE ⟨italic ~⟩ **c :** printed letters **d :** matter set in type **4 a :** qualities common to a number of individuals that distinguish them as an identifiable class: as (1) **:** the morphological, physiological, or ecological characters by which relationship between organisms may be recognized (2) **:** the form common to all instances of a linguistic element **b :** a typical and often superior specimen **c :** a member of an indicated class or variety of people ⟨the guests were mostly urban ~s —Lucy Cook⟩ **d :** a particular kind, class, or group **e :** something distinguishable as a variety **:** SORT ⟨what ~ of films to make —*Current Biog.*⟩

syn TYPE, KIND, SORT, NATURE, DESCRIPTION, CHARACTER mean a number of individuals thought of as a group because of a common quality or qualities. TYPE may suggest strong and clearly marked similarity throughout the items included so that each is typical of the group; KIND and SORT imply a group with less explicit resemblances; KIND may suggest natural grouping; SORT often suggests some disparagement; NATURE may imply inherent, essential resemblance rather than obvious or superficial likenesses; DESCRIPTION implies a group marked by agreement in all details belonging to a type as described or defined; CHARACTER implies a group marked by distinctive likenesses peculiar to the type.

usage The use of sense 4e as an attributive noun in place of *type of* ⟨I see the same *type* pitchers, the same *type* hitters —Ted Williams⟩ is criticized by several commentators. This sense of *type* is frequently used to form hyphenated modifiers by joining it to another noun or phrase ⟨neutralize the activities of . . . hate-*type* organizations —J.E. Hoover⟩ ⟨ad-agency-*type* news releases⟩ and esp. to a technical term ⟨a conveyor-*type* dishwasher⟩ or a proper name ⟨a Laurel-and-Hardy-*type* comedy⟩ ⟨an adult Western with an Othello-*type* plot —*Current Biog.*⟩ These constructions are not found in formal edited prose.

[2]**type** *vb* **typed; typ·ing** *vt* (1596) **1 :** to represent beforehand as a type **:** PREFIGURE **2 a :** to produce a copy of **b :** to represent in terms of typical characteristics **:** TYPIFY **3 :** TYPEWRITE; *also* **:** KEYBOARD **4 :** to identify as belonging to a type: as **a :** to determine the natural type of (as a blood sample) **b :** TYPECAST **~** *vi* **:** TYPEWRITE — **type·able** \ˈtī-pə-bəl\ *adj*

-type \ˌtīp\ *adj comb form* **:** of a specified type ⟨cheddar-*type*⟩ ***usage*** see TYPE

type·cast \-ˌkast\ *vt* **-cast; -cast·ing** (ca. 1935) **1 :** to cast (an actor or actress) in a part calling for the same characteristics as those possessed by the actor himself **2 :** to cast (an actor or actress) repeatedly in the same type of role **3 :** STEREOTYPE ⟨administrators . . . fearful of being ~ in the role of autocrats —F.M. Hechinger⟩

type·face \-ˌfās\ *n* (1904) **1 :** the face of printing type **2 :** all type of a single design

type·found·er \-ˌfau̇n-dər\ *n* (1797) **:** one engaged in the design and production of metal printing type for hand composition — **type·found·ing** \-diŋ\ *n*

type genus *n* (1840) **:** the genus of a taxonomic family or subfamily from which the name of the family or subfamily is formed

type I error \ˌtīp-ˌwən-\ *n* (1962) **:** rejection of the null hypothesis in statistical testing when it is true

type·script \ˈtīp-ˌskript\ *n* [*type* + manu*script*] (1893) **:** a typewritten manuscript; *esp* **:** one intended for use as printer's copy

type·set \-ˌset\ *vt* **-set; -set·ting** (1867) **:** to set in type **:** COMPOSE

type·set·ter \-ˌset-ər\ *n* (1883) **:** one that sets type

type species *n* (1840) **:** the species of a genus with which the generic name is permanently associated

type specimen *n* (ca. 1891) **:** a specimen or individual designated as type of a species or lesser group and serving as the final criterion of the characteristics of that group

type II error \ˌtīp-ˌtü-\ *n* (1962) **:** acceptance of the null hypothesis in statistical testing when it is false

type·write \ˈtī-ˌprīt\ *vb* **-wrote** \-ˌprōt\; **-writ·ten** \-ˌprit-ᵊn\ [back-formation fr. *typewriter*] *vt* (1887) **:** to write (as a letter) on a typewriter **~** *vi* **:** to use a typewriter

type·writ·er \ˈtī-ˌprīt-ər\ *n* (1868) **1 :** a machine for writing in characters similar to those produced by printer's type by means of keyboard-operated types striking through an inked ribbon **2 :** TYPIST

type·writ·ing \-ˌprīt-iŋ\ *n* (1868) **1 :** the act or study of or skill in using a typewriter **2 :** the printing done with a typewriter

typ·ey *also* **typy** \ˈtī-pē\ *adj* **typ·i·er; -est** [[1]*type*] (ca. 1923) **:** characterized by strict conformance to type; *also* **:** exhibiting superior bodily conformation ⟨a sound ~ heifer⟩

typh·lo·sole \ˈtif-lə-ˌsōl\ *n* [Gk *typhlos* blind + *sōlēn* pipe, channel — more at DEAF, SYRINGE] (1859) **:** a longitudinal fold of the intestinal wall that projects into the cavity esp. in bivalve mollusks, annelids, and starfishes

Ty·pho·eus \tī-ˈfō-ˌyüs, -yəs\ *n* [L, fr. Gk *Typhōeus*] **:** TYPHON — **Ty·phoe·an** \-ˈfē-ən\ *adj*

[1]**ty·phoid** \ˈtī-ˌfȯid, (ˌ)tī-ˈ\ *adj* [NL *typhus*] (1800) **1 :** of, relating to, or suggestive of typhus **2** [[2]*typhoid*] **:** of, relating to, or constituting typhoid

[2]**typhoid** *n* (ca. 1861) **1 :** TYPHOID FEVER **2 :** a disease of domestic animals resembling human typhus or typhoid

typhoid fever *n* (1845) **:** a communicable disease marked esp. by fever, diarrhea, prostration, headache, and intestinal inflammation and caused by a bacterium (*Salmonella typhosa*)

Typhoid Mary *n, pl* **Typhoid Marys** [*Typhoid Mary,* nickname of Mary Mallon †1938 Irish cook in U.S. who was found to be a typhoid carrier] (ca. 1931) **:** one that is by force of circumstances a center from which something undesirable spreads

Ty·phon \ˈtī-ˌfän\ *n* [L, fr. Gk *Typhōn*] **:** a monster with a tremendous voice who according to classical mythology was father of Cerberus, the Chimera, and the Sphinx

ty·phoon \tī-ˈfün\ *n* [alter. (influenced by Chin — Cant — *taaî fung* typhoon, fr. *taaî* great + *fung* wind) of earlier *touffon,* fr. Ar *ṭūfān* hurricane, fr. Gk *typhōn* whirlwind; akin to Gk *typhein* to smoke] (1588) **1 :** a tropical cyclone occurring in the region of the Philippines or the China sea **2 :** WHIRLWIND 2a ⟨a veritable ~ of interest and corporate investment —Norman Sklarewitz⟩

ty·phus \ˈtī-fəs\ *n* [NL, fr. Gk *typhos* fever; akin to Gk *typhein* to smoke — more at DEAF] (1785) **1 :** a severe human febrile disease marked by high fever, stupor alternating with delirium, intense headache, and a dark red rash, caused by a rickettsia (*Rickettsia prowazekii*), and transmitted esp. by body lice **2 :** MURINE TYPHUS **3 :** TSUTSUGAMUSHI DISEASE

typ·ic \ˈtip-ik\ *adj* (1601) **:** TYPICAL 1

typ·i·cal \ˈtip-i-kəl\ *adj* [LL *typicalis,* fr. *typicus,* fr. Gk *typikos,* fr. *typos* model — more at TYPE] (1612) **1 :** constituting or having the nature of a type **:** SYMBOLIC **2 a :** combining or exhibiting the essential characteristics of a group ⟨~ suburban houses⟩ **b :** conforming to a type ⟨a specimen ~ of the species⟩ ***syn*** see REGULAR — **typ·i·cal·i·ty** \ˌtip-ə-ˈkal-ət-ē\ *n* — **typ·i·cal·ness** \ˈtip-i-kəl-nəs\ *n*

typ·i·cal·ly \ˈtip-i-k(ə-)lē\ *adv* (1605) **1 :** in a typical manner ⟨~ American⟩ **2 :** on a typical occasion **:** in typical circumstances

typ·i·fy \ˈtip-ə-ˌfī\ *vt* **-fied; -fy·ing** (1634) **1 a :** to represent in typical fashion (as by an image, form, model, or resemblance) ⟨the anthropologist has tried to ~ the various strata of society —*Times Lit. Supp.*⟩ **b :** to constitute a typical mark or instance of ⟨realism . . . that *typified* his earlier work —*Current Biog.*⟩ **2 :** to embody the essential or sa-

\ə\ **abut** \ᵊ\ **kitten,** F **table** \ər\ **further** \a\ **ash** \ā\ **ace** \ä\ **cot, cart**
\au̇\ **out** \ch\ **chin** \e\ **bet** \ē\ **easy** \g\ **go** \i\ **hit** \ī\ **ice** \j\ **job**
\ŋ\ **sing** \ō\ **go** \ȯ\ **law** \ȯi\ **boy** \th\ **thin** \t͟h\ **the** \ü\ **loot** \u̇\ **foot**
\y\ **yet** \zh\ **vision** \à, k̟, ⁿ, œ, œ̄, ue, ue̅, ʸ\ *see* Guide to Pronunciation

lient characteristics of : be the type of — **typ·i·fi·ca·tion** \ˌtip-ə-fə-'kā-shən\ *n*

typ·ist \'tī-pəst\ *n* (1885) : one who typewrites

ty·po \'tī-(ˌ)pō\ *n, pl* **typos** [short for *typographical (error)*] (1922) : a typographical error

ty·po·graph \'tī-pə-ˌgraf\ *vt* (ca. 1933) : to produce (stamps) by letterpress

ty·pog·ra·pher \tī-'päg-rə-fər\ *n* (1643) : a person (as a compositor, printer, or designer) who specializes in the design, choice, and arrangement of type matter

ty·po·graph·ic \ˌtī-pə-'graf-ik\ *adj* (1778) : of, relating to, or occurring or used in typography or typeset matter ⟨a ~ character⟩

ty·po·graph·i·cal \-i-kəl\ *adj* (1593) : TYPOGRAPHIC ⟨a ~ error⟩ — **ty·po·graph·i·cal·ly** \-i-k(ə-)lē\ *adv*

ty·pog·ra·phy \tī-'päg-rə-fē\ *n* [ML *typographia*, fr. Gk *typos* impression, cast + *-graphia* -graphy — more at TYPE] (1697) : the style, arrangement, or appearance of typeset matter

ty·po·log·i·cal \ˌtī-pə-'läj-i-kəl\ *adj* (1845) : of or relating to typology or types — **ty·po·log·i·cal·ly** \-i-k(ə-)lē\ *adv*

ty·pol·o·gy \tī-'päl-ə-jē\ *n, pl* **-gies** (1845) **1** : a doctrine of theological types **2** : study of or analysis or classification based on types — **ty·pol·o·gist** \-jəst\ *n*

Tyr \'ti(ə)r\ *n* [ON *Tyr*; akin to OE *Tīw* Tiu — more at DEITY] : a god of war in Norse mythology

ty·ra·mine \'tī-rə-ˌmēn\ *n* [ISV *tyrosine* + *amine*] (ca. 1909) : a phenolic amine C₈H₁₁NO that has a sympathomimetic action and is derived from tyrosine

ty·ran·ni·cal \tə-'ran-i-kəl, tī-\ *also* **ty·ran·nic** \-ik\ *adj* [L *tyrannicus*, fr. Gk *tyrannikos*, fr. *tyrannos* tyrant] (15c) **1** : characteristic of a tyrant or tyranny ⟨~ rule⟩ **2** : characterized by oppressive, unjust, or arbitrary behavior or control : DESPOTIC ⟨a ~ ruler⟩ — **ty·ran·ni·cal·ly** \-i-k(ə-)lē\ *adv* — **ty·ran·ni·cal·ness** \-kəl-nəs\ *n*

ty·ran·ni·cide \tə-'ran-ə-ˌsīd, tī-\ *n* [in sense 1, fr. F, fr. L *tyrannicidium*, fr. *tyrannus* + *-i-* + *-cidium* -cide (killing); in sense 2, fr. F, fr. L *tyrannicida*, fr. *tyrannus* + *-i-* + *-cida*-cide (killer)] (1650) **1** : the act of killing a tyrant **2** : the killer of a tyrant

tyr·an·nize \'tir-ə-ˌnīz\ *vb* **-nized; -niz·ing** *vi* (15c) : to exercise arbitrary oppressive power or severity ⟨some ways the living ~ over the dying —Thomas Powers⟩ ~ *vt* : to treat tyrannically : OPPRESS — **tyr·an·niz·er** *n*

ty·ran·no·saur \tə-'ran-ə-ˌsȯ(ə)r, tī-\ *n* [NL *Tyrannosaurus*, genus name, deriv. of Gk *tyrannos* tyrant + *sauros* lizard — more at SAURIAN] (1924) : a very large bipedal carnivorous dinosaur (*Tyrannosaurus rex*) with small forelegs that occurs in the Upper Cretaceous of No. America

ty·ran·no·sau·rus \tə-ˌran-ə-'sȯr-əs, (ˌ)tī-\ *n* [NL] (ca. 1905) : TYRANNOSAUR

tyr·an·nous \'tir-ə-nəs\ *adj* (15c) : marked by tyranny; *esp* : unjustly severe — **tyr·an·nous·ly** *adv*

tyr·an·ny \'tir-ə-nē\ *n, pl* **-nies** [ME *tyrannie*, fr. MF, fr. ML *tyrannia*, fr. L *tyrannus* tyrant] (14c) **1** : oppressive power ⟨every form of ~ over

the mind of man —Thomas Jefferson⟩; *esp* : oppressive power exerted by government ⟨the ~ of a police state⟩ **2 a** : a government in which absolute power is vested in a single ruler; *esp* : one characteristic of an ancient Greek city-state **b** : the office, authority, and administration of a tyrant **3** : a rigorous condition imposed by some outside agency or force ⟨living under the ~ of the clock —Dixon Wecter⟩ **4** : a tyrannical act

ty·rant \'tī-rənt\ *n* [ME *tirant*, fr. OF *tyran, tyrant*, fr. L *tyrannus*, fr. Gk *tyrannos*] (13c) **1 a** : an absolute ruler unrestrained by law or constitution **b** : a usurper of sovereignty **2 a** : a ruler who exercises absolute power oppressively or brutally **b** : one resembling an oppressive ruler in the harsh use of authority or power

tyrant flycatcher *n* (ca. 1783) : any of various large American flycatchers (family Tyrannidae) that are usu. strictly insectivorous, take their prey on the wing, and have a flattened bill often hooked at the tip and usu. bristly at the gape

tyre *chiefly Brit var of* TIRE

Tyr·i·an purple \ˌtir-ē-ən-\ *n* [*Tyre*, maritime city of ancient Phoenicia] (1583) : a crimson or purple dye that is related to indigo, obtained by the ancient Greeks and Romans from gastropod mollusks, and now made synthetically

ty·ro \'tī-(ˌ)rō\ *n, pl* **tyros** [ML, fr. L *tiro* young soldier, tyro] (1611) : a beginner in learning : NOVICE **syn** see AMATEUR

ty·ro·ci·dine *also* **ty·ro·ci·din** \ˌtī-rə-'sīd-ʰn\ *n* [*tyro-* (as in *tyrothricin*) + *-cid-* (as in *gramicidin*) + *-ine*] (1942) : a basic polypeptide antibiotic produced by a soil bacillus (*Bacillus brevis*)

Ty·ro·le·an \tə-'rō-lē-ən, tī-; ˌtir-ə-'lē-\ *also* **Ty·ro·li·an** \tə-'rō-lē-ən, tī-\ *adj* (1859) **1** : of or relating to the Tirol **2** *of a hat* : of a style originating in the Tirol and marked by soft often green felt, a narrow brim and pointed crown, and an ornamental feather

ty·ros·i·nase \tə-'räs-ə-ˌnās, tī-, -ˌnāz\ *n* (1896) : an enzyme that promotes the oxidation of phenols (as tyrosine) and is widespread in plants and animals

ty·ro·sine \'tī-rə-ˌsēn\ *n* [ISV, irreg. fr. Gk *tyros* cheese — more at BUTTER] (1857) : a metabolically important phenolic amino acid C₉H₁₁NO₃ that is a precursor of various alkaloids

ty·ro·thri·cin \ˌtī-rə-'thrīs-ʰn\ *n* [NL *Tyrothoric-, Tyrothrix*, generic name formerly applied to various bacteria including *Bacillus brevis*] (1940) : an antibiotic mixture that consists chiefly of tyrocidine and gramicidin, is usu. extracted from a soil bacillus (*Bacillus brevis*) as a gray to brown powder, and is used for local applications esp. for infection caused by gram-positive bacteria

tzad·dik *n, pl* **tzad·dik·im** *var of* ZADDIK

tzar \'zär, '(t)sär\ *var of* CZAR

tzi·gane \(t)sē-'gän\ *n* [F, fr. Hung *cigány*] (1763) **1** : GYPSY 1 **2** : ROMANY 2

tzim·mes \'tsim-əs\ *n* [Yiddish *tsimes*] (1892) : a sweetened combination of vegetables (as carrots and potatoes) or of meat and carrots often with dried fruits (as prunes) that is stewed or baked in a casserole

tzi·tzis, tzi·tzit *var of* ZIZITH

U

u \'yü\ *n, pl* **u's** *or* **us** \'yüz\ *often cap, often attrib* **1 a** : the 21st letter of the English alphabet **b** : a graphic representation of this letter **c** : a speech counterpart of orthographic *u* **2 a** : a graphic device for reproducing the letter *u* **3** : one designated *u* esp. as the 21st in order or class **4** (abbr. for *unsatisfactory*) **a** : a grade rating a student's work as unsatisfactory **b** : one graded or rated with a U **5** : something shaped like the letter U

U \'yü\ *adj* [*upper class*] (1954) : characteristic of the upper classes

Uban·gi \(y)ü-'baŋ-(g)ē\ *n* [*Ubangi-Shari*, Africa] (1942) : a woman of the district of Kyabé village in Africa with lips pierced and distended to unusual dimensions with wooden disks

ubi·qui·none \yü-'bik-wə-ˌnōn, ˌyü-bə-kwin-'ōn\ *n* [blend of L *ubique* everywhere and E *quinone*; fr. its widespread occurrence in nature] (1958) : a quinone that contains a long isoprenoid side chain and that functions in the part of cellular respiration comprising oxidative phosphorylation as an electron-carrying coenzyme in the transport of electrons from organic substrates to oxygen esp. along the chain of reactions leading from the Krebs cycle — called also *coenzyme Q*

ubiq·ui·tous \yü-'bik-wət-əs\ *adj* (1837) : existing or being everywhere at the same time : constantly encountered : WIDESPREAD — **ubiq·ui·tous·ly** *adv* — **ubiq·ui·tous·ness** *n*

ubiq·ui·ty \-wət-ē\ *n* [L *ubique* everywhere, fr. *ubi* where + *-que*, enclitic generalizing particle; akin to L *quis* who and to L *-que* and — more at WHO, SESQUI-] (1585) : presence everywhere or in many places esp. simultaneously : OMNIPRESENCE

U-boat \'yü-ˌbōt, -ˌbōt\ *n* [trans. of G *u-boot*, short for *unterseeboot*, lit., undersea boat] (1916) : a German submarine

ud·der \'əd-ər\ *n* [ME, fr. OE *ūder*; akin to OHG *ūtar* udder, L *uber*, Gk *outhar*, Skt *ūdhar*] (bef. 12c) **1** : a large pendulous organ consisting of two or more mammary glands enclosed in a common envelope and each provided with a single nipple — see COW illustration **2** : MAMMARY GLAND

UFO \ˌyü-(ˌ)ef-'ō\ *n, pl* **UFO's** *or* **UFOs** \-'ōz\ [*unidentified flying object*] (1953) : an unidentified flying object; *esp* : FLYING SAUCER

ufol·o·gy \yü-'fäl-ə-jē\ *n, often cap* UFO [*UFO* + *-logy*] (1959) : the study of unidentified flying objects — **ufo·log·i·cal** \ˌyü-fə-'läj-i-kəl\ *adj, often cap* UFO — **ufol·o·gist** \yü-'fäl-ə-jəst\ *n, often cap* UFO

¹Uga·rit·ic \ˌ(y)ü-gə-'rit-ik\ *n* (1936) : the Semitic language of ancient Ugarit closely related to Phoenician and Hebrew

²Ugaritic *adj* (1938) : of, relating to, or characteristic of the ancient city of Ugarit, its inhabitants, or Ugaritic

ugh *often read as* 'əg *or* 'ək *or* 'ə\ *interj* (1837) — used to indicate the sound of a cough or grunt or to express disgust or horror

ug·li·fy \'əg-li-ˌfī\ *vt* **-fied; -fy·ing** (1576) : to make ugly — **ug·li·fi·ca·tion** \ˌəg-li-fə-'kā-shən\ *n*

ug·li·ness \'əg-lē-nəs\ *n* (14c) **1** : the quality or state of being ugly **2** : something that is ugly

ug·ly \'əg-lē\ *adj* **ug·li·er; -est** [ME, fr. ON *uggligr*, fr. *uggr* fear; akin to ON *ugga* to fear and perh. to OE *ecg* edge — more at EDGE] (13c) **1** : FRIGHTFUL, DIRE **2 a** : offensive to the sight : HIDEOUS **b** : offensive or unpleasing to any sense **3** : morally offensive or objectionable : REPULSIVE **4 a** : likely to cause inconvenience or discomfort ⟨the ~ truth⟩ **b** : SURLY, QUARRELSOME ⟨an ~ drunk⟩ — **ug·li·ly** \-lə-lē\ *adv*

Ugly American *n* [*The Ugly American* (1958), collection of stories by Eugene Burdick †1965 and William J. Lederer b1912 Am. authors] (1965) : an American in a foreign country whose behavior is offensive to the people of that country

ugly duckling *n* [*The Ugly Duckling*, story by Hans Christian Andersen] (1883) : something that appears very unpromising but often has great potential

Ugri·an \'(y)ü-grē-ən\ *n* [ORuss *Ugre* Hungarians] (1841) : a member of the eastern division of the Finno-Ugric peoples — **Ugrian** *adj*

Ugric \-grik\ *adj* (1854) : of, relating to, or characteristic of the languages of the Ugrians

ug·some \'əg-səm\ *adj* [ME, fr. *uggen* to fear, inspire fear, fr. ON *ugga* to fear] *archaic* (15c) : FRIGHTFUL, LOATHSOME

uh-huh *two m's separated by the voiceless sound* h; 'ən-(ˌ)hən, (ˌ)ən-'\ *interj* (1899) — used to indicate affirmation, agreement, or gratification

uh·lan \'ü-ˌlän, ü-'; '(y)ü-lən\ *n* [G, fr. Pol *ulan,* fr. Turk *oğlan* boy, servant] (1753) **:** any of a body of Prussian light cavalry orig. modeled on Tatar lancers

Ui·ghur *or* **Ui·gur** \'wē-ˌgu̇(ə)r\ *n* [Uighur *Uighur*] (1747) **1 :** a member of a Turkic people powerful in Mongolia and eastern Turkestan between the 8th and 12th centuries A.D. who constitute a majority of the population of Chinese Turkestan **2 :** the Turkic language of the Uighurs — **Uighur** *or* **Uigur** *adj*

uin·ta·ite *also* **uin·tah·ite** \yü-'int-ə-ˌīt\ *n* [*Uinta, Uintah,* mountains in Utah] (1888) **:** a black lustrous asphalt occurring esp. in Utah

Uit·land·er \'āt-ˌlan-dər\ *n* [Afrik, fr. MD *utelander* foreigner, fr. *utelant* foreign territory, fr. *ute* out + *lant* land] (1892) **:** FOREIGNER; *esp* **:** a British resident in the former republics of the Transvaal and Orange Free State

ukase \yü-'kās, -'kāz, 'yü-ˌ; ü-'käz\ *n* [F & Russ; F, fr. Russ *ukaz,* fr. *ukazat'* to show, order; akin to OSlav *u-* away, L *au-,* Skt *ava-* and to OSlav *kazati* to show] (1729) **1 :** a proclamation by a Russian emperor or government having the force of law **2 :** EDICT

uke \'yük\ *n* (1921) **:** UKULELE

uki·yo–e *also* **uki·yo–ye** \ü-ˌkē-ō-'yā, -ˌkē-yō-'ā\ *n* [Jp *ukiyo-e* genre picture, fr. *ukiyo* world, life + *e* picture] (1879) **:** a Japanese art movement that flourished from the 17th to the 19th century and produced paintings and prints depicting the everyday life and interests of the common people; *also* **:** the paintings and prints themselves

Ukrai·ni·an \yü-'krā-nē-ən *also* -'krī-\ *n* (1823) **1 :** a native or inhabitant of the Ukraine **2 :** the Slavic language of the Ukrainian people — **Ukrainian** *adj*

uku·le·le *also* **uke·le·le** \ˌyü-kə-'lā-lē, ˌü-\ *n* [Hawaiian *'ukulele,* fr. *'uku* flea + *lele* jumping] (1896) **:** a small guitar of Portuguese origin popularized in Hawaii in the 1880s and strung typically with four strings

-u·lar \(y)ə-lər\ *adj suffix* [L *-ularis,* fr. *-ulus, -ula, -ulum* -ule + *-aris* -ar] **:** of, relating to, or resembling ⟨valv*ular*⟩

ul·cer \'əl-sər\ *n* [ME, fr. L *ulcer-, ulcus;* akin to Gk *helkos* wound] (15c) **1 :** a break in skin or mucous membrane with loss of surface tissue, disintegration and necrosis of epithelial tissue, and often pus **2 :** something that festers and corrupts like an open sore — **ulcer** *vb*

ul·cer·ate \'əl-sə-ˌrāt\ *vb* **-at·ed; -at·ing** *vt* (15c) **:** to affect with or as if with an ulcer ~ *vi* **:** to undergo ulceration

ul·cer·ation \ˌəl-sə-'rā-shən\ *n* (15c) **1 :** the process of becoming ulcerated **:** the state of being ulcerated **2 :** ULCER — **ul·cer·ative** \'əl-sə-ˌrāt-iv, 'əls-(ə-)rət-\ *adj*

ul·cero·gen·ic \ˌəl-sə-rō-'jen-ik\ *adj* (1950) **:** tending to produce or develop into ulcers or ulceration

ul·cer·ous \'əls-(ə-)rəs\ *adj* (1577) **1 :** being or marked by an ulceration ⟨~ lesions⟩ **2 :** affected with or as if with an ulcer **:** ULCERATED

-ule \(ˌ)(y)ü(ə)l\ *n suffix* [F & L; F, fr. L *-ulus,* masc. dim. suffix, *-ula,* fem. dim. suffix, *-ulum,* neut. dim. suffix] **:** little one ⟨duct*ule*⟩

ule·ma *or* **ula·ma** \ˌü-lə-'mä\ *n* [Ar, Turk, & Per; Turk & Per *'ulemā,* fr. Ar *'ulamā*] (1768) **1** *pl* **:** the body of mullahs **2 :** MULLAH

-u·lent \(y)ə-lənt\ *adj suffix* [L *-ulentus*] **:** that abounds in (a specified thing) ⟨floc*culent*⟩

ulex·ite \'yü-lək-ˌsīt\ *n* [George L. *Ulex* †1883 Ger. chemist] (1867) **:** a mineral $NaCaB_5O_9 \cdot 8H_2O$ consisting of a hydrous sodium calcium borate and usu. occurring in loosely packed white fibers that transmit light lengthwise with nearly undiminished intensity

ul·lage \'əl-ij\ *n* [ME *ulage,* fr. MF *eullage* act of filling a cask, fr. *eullier* to fill a cask, fr. OF *ouil* eye, bunghole, fr. L *oculus* eye] (14c) **:** the amount that a container (as a tank or cask) lacks of being full

ul·na \'əl-nə\ *n* [NL, fr. L, elbow — more at ELL] (1541) **:** the bone on the little-finger side of the human forearm; *also* **:** a corresponding part of the forelimb of vertebrates above fishes — **ul·nar** \-nər, -ˌnär\ *adj*

-u·lose \(y)ə-ˌlōs, -ˌlōz\ *n suffix* [levulose] **:** ketose sugar ⟨hept*ulose*⟩

-u·lous \(y)ə-ləs\ *adj suffix* [L *-ulus,* dim. suffix] **:** being slightly or minutely (such) ⟨hirsut*ulous*⟩

ul·ster \'əl-stər\ *n* [*Ulster,* Ireland] (1876) **:** a long loose overcoat of Irish origin made of heavy material (as frieze)

ul·te·ri·or \ˌəl-'tir-ē-ər\ *adj* [L, farther, further, compar. of (assumed) L *ulter* situated beyond, fr. *uls* beyond; akin to L *ollus, ille,* that one, OIr *indoll* beyond] (1646) **1 a :** FURTHER, FUTURE **b :** more distant **:** REMOTER **c :** situated on the farther side **:** THITHER **2 :** going beyond what is openly said or shown and esp. what is proper ⟨~ motives⟩ — **ul·te·ri·or·ly** *adv*

ul·ti·ma \'əl-tə-mə\ *n* [L, fem. of *ultimus* last] (ca. 1864) **:** the last syllable of a word

ul·ti·ma·cy \'əl-tə-mə-sē\ *n, pl* **-cies** (1842) **1 :** the quality or state of being ultimate **2 :** ULTIMATE 1

ul·ti·ma ra·tio \ˌu̇l-tə-mə-'rät-ē-ˌō\ *n* [NL] (1780) **:** the final argument; *also* **:** the last resort (as force)

¹ul·ti·mate \'əl-tə-mət\ *adj* [ML *ultimatus* last, final, fr. LL, pp. of *ultimare* to come to an end, be last, fr. L *ultimus* farthest, last, final, superl. of (assumed) L *ulter* situated beyond — more at ULTERIOR] (1654) **1 a :** most remote in space or time **:** FARTHEST **b :** last in a progression or series ⟨their ~ destination was Paris⟩ **c :** EVENTUAL ⟨they hoped for ~ success⟩ **d :** EXTREME, UTMOST **2 :** finally reckoned **3 a :** BASIC, FUNDAMENTAL **b :** incapable of further analysis, division, or separation **4 :** MAXIMUM ***syn*** see LAST — **ul·ti·mate·ness** *n*

²ultimate *n* (1681) **1 :** something ultimate; *esp* **:** FUNDAMENTAL **2 :** ACME

³ul·ti·mate \-mət, -ˌmāt\ *vb* **-mat·ed; -mat·ing** (ca. 1834) **:** END

ul·ti·mate·ly \-mət-lē\ *adv* (1652) **1 :** in the end **:** FINALLY, FUNDAMENTALLY **2 :** EVENTUALLY

ul·ti·ma Thu·le \ˌəl-tə-mə-'th(y)ü-lē\ *n* [L, farthest Thule] (1665) **:** THULE

ul·ti·ma·tum \ˌəl-tə-'māt-əm, -'mät-\ *n, pl* **-tums** *or* **-ta** \-ə\ [NL, fr. ML, neut. of *ultimatus* final] (1731) **:** a final proposition, condition, or demand; *esp* **:** one whose rejection will end negotiations and cause a resort to force or other direct action

ul·ti·mo \'əl-tə-ˌmō\ *adj* [L *ultimo mense* in the last month] (1616) **:** of or occurring in the month preceding the present

ul·ti·mo·gen·i·ture \ˌəl-tə-mō-'jen-ə-ˌchu̇(ə)r, -i-chər, -ə-ˌt(y)u̇(ə)r\ *n* [L *ultimus* last + E *-o-* + *-geniture* (as in *primogeniture*)] (1882) **:** a system of inheritance by which the youngest son succeeds to the estate

¹ul·tra \'əl-trə\ *adj* [*ultra-*] (1818) **:** going beyond others or beyond due limit **:** EXTREME

²ultra *n* [*ultra-*] (1820) **:** one that is ultra **:** EXTREMIST

ultra- *prefix* [L, fr. *ultra* beyond, adv. & prep., fr. (assumed) L *ulter* situated beyond — more at ULTERIOR] **1 :** beyond in space **:** on the other side **:** TRANS- ⟨*ultra*violet⟩ **2 :** beyond the range or limits of **:** transcending **:** SUPER- ⟨*ultra*microscopic⟩ **3 :** beyond what is ordinary, proper, or moderate **:** excessively **:** extremely ⟨*ultra*modern⟩

ul·tra·abys·sal	**ul·tra·hype**	**ul·tra·re·al·ism**
ul·tra·care·ful	**ul·tra·left**	**ul·tra·re·al·ist**
ul·tra·ca·su·al	**ul·tra·left·ism**	**ul·tra·re·al·is·tic**
ul·tra·cau·tious	**ul·tra·left·ist**	**ul·tra·re·fined**
ul·tra·chic	**ul·tra·lib·er·al**	**ul·tra·rel·a·tiv·is·tic**
ul·tra·civ·i·lized	**ul·tra·lib·er·al·ism**	**ul·tra·re·li·able**
ul·tra·clean	**ul·tra·light·weight**	**ul·tra·re·spect·able**
ul·tra·com·mer·cial	**ul·tra·low**	**ul·tra·rev·o·lu·tion·ary**
ul·tra·com·pact	**ul·tra·mar·a·thon**	**ul·tra·rich**
ul·tra·com·pe·tent	**ul·tra·mas·cu·line**	**ul·tra·right**
ul·tra·con·ser·va·tism	**ul·tra·mil·i·tant**	**ul·tra·right·ist**
ul·tra·con·ser·va·tive	**ul·tra·mod·ern**	**ul·tra·ro·man·tic**
ul·tra·con·tem·po·rary	**ul·tra·mod·ern·ist**	**ul·tra·roy·al·ist**
ul·tra·con·ve·nient	**ul·tra·na·tion·al**	**ul·tra·safe**
ul·tra·cool	**ul·tra·na·tion·al·ism**	**ul·tra·se·cret**
ul·tra·crit·i·cal	**ul·tra·na·tion·al·ist**	**ul·tra·seg·re·ga·tion·ist**
ul·tra·dem·o·crat·ic	**ul·tra·na·tion·al·is·tic**	**ul·tra·sen·si·tive**
ul·tra·dense	**ul·tra·or·tho·dox**	**ul·tra·se·ri·ous**
ul·tra·dis·tance	**ul·tra·par·a·dox·i·cal**	**ul·tra·sharp**
ul·tra·dis·tant	**ul·tra·pas·teur·ized**	**ul·tra·sim·ple**
ul·tra·dry	**ul·tra·pa·tri·ot·ic**	**ul·tra·slick**
ul·tra·en·er·get·ic	**ul·tra·phys·i·cal**	**ul·tra·slow**
ul·tra·ex·clu·sive	**ul·tra·pow·er·ful**	**ul·tra·small**
ul·tra·fa·mil·iar	**ul·tra·prac·ti·cal**	**ul·tra·smart**
ul·tra·fash·ion·able	**ul·tra·pre·cise**	**ul·tra·soft**
ul·tra·fast	**ul·tra·pre·ci·sion**	**ul·tra·so·phis·ti·cat·ed**
ul·tra·fas·tid·i·ous	**ul·tra·pre·mi·um**	**ul·tra·speed**
ul·tra·fem·i·nine	**ul·tra·pro·gres·sive**	**ul·tra·thin**
ul·tra·fine	**ul·tra·pure**	**ul·tra·vac·u·um**
ul·tra·glam·or·ous	**ul·tra·pure·ly**	**ul·tra·vi·o·lence**
ul·tra·haz·ard·ous	**ul·tra·rad·i·cal**	**ul·tra·vi·o·lent**
ul·tra·heat	**ul·tra·rap·id**	**ul·tra·vir·ile**
ul·tra·heavy	**ul·tra·rare**	**ul·tra·vi·ril·i·ty**
ul·tra·hot	**ul·tra·rar·efied**	**ul·tra·wide**
ul·tra·hu·man	**ul·tra·ra·tio·nal**	

ul·tra·ba·sic \ˌəl-trə-'bā-sik\ *adj* [ISV] (1881) **:** extremely basic; *specif* **:** very low in silica and rich in iron and magnesium minerals — **ultrabasic** *n*

ul·tra·cen·trif·u·gal \-ˌsen-'trif-yə-gəl, -'trif-i-gəl\ *adj* (1930) **:** of, relating to, or obtained by means of an ultracentrifuge — **ul·tra·cen·trif·u·gal·ly** \-gə-lē\ *adv*

¹ul·tra·cen·tri·fuge \-'sen-trə-ˌfyüj\ *n* (1924) **:** a high-speed centrifuge able to sediment colloidal and other small particles and used esp. in determining sizes of such particles and molecular weights of large molecules

²ultracentrifuge *vt* (1930) **:** to subject to an ultracentrifuge — **ul·tra·cen·tri·fu·ga·tion** \-ˌsen-trə-fyü-'gā-shən\ *n*

ul·tra·fiche \'əl-trə-ˌfēsh\ *n* (1969) **:** a microfiche whose microimages are of printed matter reduced 90 or more times

ul·tra·fil·tra·tion \ˌəl-trə-fil-'trā-shən\ *n* (1908) **:** filtration through a medium (as a semipermeable capillary wall) which allows small molecules (as of water) to pass but holds back larger ones (as of protein)

ul·tra·high \-'hī\ *adj* (1947) **:** very high **:** exceedingly high ⟨~ vacuum⟩ ⟨at ~ temperatures⟩

ultrahigh frequency *n* (1932) **:** a radio frequency between superhigh frequency and very high frequency — see RADIO FREQUENCY table

ul·tra·ism \'əl-trə-ˌiz-əm\ *n* (1821) **1 :** the principles of those who advocate extreme measures (as radicalism) **2 :** an instance or example of radicalism — **ul·tra·ist** \-trə-əst\ *adj or n* — **ul·tra·is·tic** \ˌəl-trə-'is-tik\ *adj*

ul·tra·light \'əl-trə-ˌlīt\ *n* (1974) **:** a very light recreational aircraft powered by a small gasoline engine

ul·tra·maf·ic \ˌəl-trə-'maf-ik\ *adj* (1933) **:** ULTRABASIC

¹ul·tra·ma·rine \ˌəl-trə-mə-'rēn\ *n* [ML *ultramarinus* coming from beyond the sea, fr. L *ultra-* + *mare* sea — more at MARINE] (1598) **1 a** (1) **:** a blue pigment prepared by powdering lapis lazuli (2) **:** a similar pigment prepared from kaolin, soda ash, sulfur, and charcoal **b :** any of several related pigments **2 :** a vivid blue

²ultramarine *adj* (ca. 1656) **:** situated beyond the sea

ul·tra·mi·cro \ˌəl-trə-'mī-(ˌ)krō\ *adj* (1937) **:** being or dealing with something smaller than micro

ul·tra·mi·cro·scope \ˌəl-trə-'mī-krə-ˌskōp\ *n* [back-formation fr. *ultramicroscopic*] (1906) **:** an apparatus for making visible by scattered light particles too small to be perceived by the ordinary microscope

ul·tra·mi·cro·scop·ic \-ˌmī-krə-'skäp-ik\ *also* **ul·tra·mi·cro·scop·i·cal** \-i-kəl\ *adj* [ISV] (1870) **1 :** too small to be seen with an ordinary microscope **2 :** of or relating to an ultramicroscope — **ul·tra·mi·cro·scop·i·cal·ly** \-i-k(ə-)lē\ *adv*

ul·tra·mi·cro·tome \-'mī-krə-ˌtōm\ *n* (1946) **:** a microtome for cutting extremely thin sections for electron microscopy — **ul·tra·mi·crot·o·my** \-mī-'krät-ə-mē\ *n*

ul·tra·min·ia·ture \-'min-ē-ə-ˌchu̇(ə)r, -'min-i-ˌchu̇(ə)r, -'min-yə-, -chər, -ˌt(y)u̇(ə)r\ *adj* (1942) **:** SUBMINIATURE — **ul·tra·min·ia·tur·iza·tion** \-ˌmin-ē-ə-ˌchu̇r-ə-'zā-shən, ˌmin-i-ˌchu̇r-, ˌmin-yə-ˌchu̇r-, -chər-, -ˌt(y)u̇r-\ *n*

ul·tra·mon·tane \-'män-ˌtān, -ˌmän-'\ *adj* [ML *ultramontanus,* fr. L *ultra-* + *mont-, mons* mountain — more at MOUNT] (1618) **1 :** of or relating to countries or peoples beyond the mountains (as the Alps) **2 :** favoring greater or absolute supremacy of papal over national or diocesan

authority in the Roman Catholic Church — **ultramontane** *n, often cap* — **ul·tra·mon·tan·ism** \-'mänt-ən-,iz-əm\ *n*
ul·tra·short \-'shȯ(ə)rt\ *adj* (1926) **1 :** having a wavelength below 10 meters ⟨~ radiation⟩ **2 :** very short in duration ⟨an ~ pulse of light⟩
ul·tra·son·ic \-'sän-ik\ *adj* (1923) **1 :** having a frequency above the human ear's audibility limit of about 20,000 cycles per second — used of waves and vibrations **2 :** utilizing, produced by, or relating to ultrasonic waves or vibrations ⟨~ testing of metal⟩ — **ul·tra·son·i·cal·ly** \-i-k(ə-)lē\ *adv*
ul·tra·son·ics \,əl-trə-'sän-iks\ *n pl* (1924) **1 :** ultrasonic vibrations or compressional waves **2** *sing in constr* **:** the study of ultrasonic vibrations and their associated phenomena **3 :** ultrasonic devices
ul·tra·so·nog·ra·phy \-sə-'näg-rə-fē, -sō-\ *n* [[2]*ultrasonic* + *-o-* + *graphy*] (1951) **:** a diagnostic technique for the examination of internal body structures that involves the formation of a two-dimensional image by ultrasonic waves — **ul·tra·so·no·graph·ic** \-,sō-nə-'graf-ik, -,sän-ə-\ *adj*
ul·tra·sound \'əl-trə-,sau̇nd\ *n* (1923) **:** vibrations of the same physical nature as sound but with frequencies above the range of human hearing
ul·tra·struc·ture \'əl-trə-,strək-chər\ *n* (1939) **:** the invisible ultimate physiochemical organization of protoplasm — **ul·tra·struc·tur·al** \,əl-trə-'strək-chə-rəl, -'strək-shrəl\ *adj* — **ul·tra·struc·tur·al·ly** \-ē\ *adv*
ul·tra·vi·o·let \,əl-trə-'vī-ə-lət\ *adj* (1840) **1 :** situated beyond the visible spectrum at its violet end — used of radiation having a wavelength shorter than wavelengths of visible light and longer than those of X rays **2 :** relating to, producing, or employing ultraviolet radiation — **ultraviolet** *n*
ultraviolet light *n* (1904) **:** ultraviolet radiation
ul·tra vi·res \,əl-trə-'vī-(,)rēz\ *adv or adj* [NL, lit., beyond power] (1793) **:** beyond the scope or in excess of legal power or authority
ul·u·lant \'əl-yə-lənt\ *adj* (1868) **:** having a howling sound **:** WAILING ⟨dark wasteland . . . ~ with bitter wind —Rudi Blesh⟩
ul·u·late \-,lāt\ *vi* **-lat·ed; -lat·ing** [L *ululatus,* pp. of *ululare,* of imit. origin] (1623) **:** HOWL, WAIL — **ul·u·la·tion** \,əl-yə-'lā-shən\ *n*
ul·va \'əl-və\ *n* [NL, genus name, fr. L, sedge] (1706) **:** SEA LETTUCE
Ulys·ses \yu̇-'lis-(,)ēz\ *n* [L, modif. of Gk *Odysseus*] **:** ODYSSEUS
um·bel \'əm-bəl\ *n* [NL *umbella,* fr. L, umbrella — more at UMBRELLA] (1597) **:** a racemose inflorescence typical of the carrot family in which the axis is very much contracted so that the pedicels appear to spring from the same point to form a flat or rounded flower cluster — see INFLORESCENCE illustration
um·bel·late \'əm-bə-,lāt, ,əm-'bel-ət\ *adj* (1760) **1 :** bearing, consisting of, or arranged in umbels **2 :** resembling an umbel in form
um·bel·li·fer \,əm-'bel-ə-fər\ *n* [NL *Umbelliferae,* group name, fem. pl. of *umbellifer* bearing umbels] (1718) **:** a plant of the carrot family
um·bel·lif·er·ous \,əm-bə-'lif-(ə-)rəs\ *adj* (1662) **:** of or relating to the carrot family
[1]**um·ber** \'əm-bər\ *n* [prob. fr. obs. E, shade, color, fr. ME *umbre* shade, shadow, fr. MF, fr. L *umbra* — more at UMBRAGE] (1568) **1 :** a brown earth that is darker in color than ocher and sienna because of its content of manganese and iron oxides and is highly valued as a permanent pigment either in the raw or burnt state **2 a :** a moderate to dark yellowish brown **b :** a moderate brown
[2]**umber** *vt* **um·bered; um·ber·ing** \-b(ə-)riŋ\ (1610) **:** to darken with or as if with umber
[3]**umber** *adj* (1802) **:** of, relating to, or having the characteristics of umber; *specif* **:** of the color of umber
[1]**um·bil·i·cal** \,əm-'bil-i-kəl, *Brit also* ,əm-bə-'lī-kəl\ *adj* (1541) **1 :** of, relating to, or used at the navel **2 :** of or relating to the central region of the abdomen
[2]**umbilical** *n* (1774) **:** UMBILICAL CORD 2
umbilical cord *n* (1753) **1 :** a cord arising from the navel that connects the fetus with the placenta; *also* **:** YOLK STALK **2 :** a cable conveying power to a rocket or spacecraft before takeoff; *also* **:** a tethering or supply line (as for an astronaut outside a spacecraft or an aquanaut underwater)
um·bil·i·cate \,əm-'bil-i-kət\ *or* **um·bil·i·cat·ed** \-ə-,kāt-əd\ *adj* (1698) **1 :** depressed like a navel **2 :** having an umbilicus — **um·bil·i·ca·tion** \,əm-,bil-ə-'kā-shən\ *n*
um·bi·li·cus \,əm-bə-'lī-kəs, ,əm-'bil-i-\ *n, pl* **um·bi·li·ci** \,əm-bə-'lī-,kī, -,sī; ,əm-'bil-ə-,kī, -,kē\ *or* **um·bi·li·cus·es** [L — more at NAVEL] (ca. 1615) **1 a :** a small depression in the abdominal wall at the point of attachment of the umbilical cord to the embryo **b :** any of several morphological depressions; *esp* **:** HILUM 1a **2 :** a central point **:** CORE, HEART
um·bles \'əm-bəlz\ *n pl* [ME, alter. of *nombles,* fr. MF, pl. of *nomble* fillet of beef, pork loin, modif. of L *lumbulus,* dim. of *lumbus* loin — more at LOIN] (14c) **:** the edible viscera of an animal and esp. of a deer or hog
um·bo \'əm-(,)bō\ *n, pl* **um·bo·nes** \,əm-'bō-(,)nēz\ *or* **um·bos** [L; akin to L *umbilicus* — more at NAVEL] (1721) **1 :** the boss of a shield **2 :** a rounded elevation: as **a :** an inward projection of the tympanic membrane of the ear **b :** one of the lateral prominences just above the hinge of a bivalve shell — **um·bo·nal** \'əm-bən-əl, ,əm-'bōn-\ *adj* — **um·bo·nate** \'əm-bə-,nāt, ,əm-'bō-nət\ *adj*
um·bra \'əm-brə\ *n, pl* **umbras** *or* **um·brae** \-(,)brē, -,brī\ [L] (1638) **1 :** a shaded area **2 a :** a conical shadow excluding all light from a given source; *specif* **:** the conical part of the shadow of a celestial body excluding all light from the primary source **b :** the central dark part of a sunspot — **um·bral** \-brəl\ *adj*
um·brage \'əm-brij\ *n* [ME, fr. MF, fr. L *umbraticum,* neut. of *umbraticus* of shade, fr. *umbratus,* pp. of *umbrare* to shade, fr. *umbra* shade, shadow; akin to Lith *unksna* shadow] (15c) **1 :** SHADE, SHADOW **2 :** shady branches **:** FOLIAGE **3 a :** an indistinct indication **:** vague suggestion **:** HINT **b :** a reason for doubt **:** SUSPICION **4 :** a feeling of pique or resentment often at some fancied slight or insult ⟨took ~ at the speakers's remarks⟩
um·bra·geous \,əm-'brā-jəs\ *adj* (1587) **1 a :** SHADY **b :** filled with shadows **2 :** inclined to take offense easily — **um·bra·geous·ly** *adv* — **um·bra·geous·ness** *n*
[1]**um·brel·la** \,əm-'brel-ə, *esp Southern* 'əm-,\ *n* [It *ombrella,* modif. of L *umbella,* dim. of *umbra*] (1611) **1 :** a collapsible shade for protection against weather consisting of fabric stretched over hinged ribs radiating from a central pole; *esp* **:** a small one for carrying in the hand **2 :** the bell-shaped or saucer-shaped largely gelatinous structure that forms the chief part of the body of most jellyfishes **3 :** something which provides protection: as **a :** a defensive formation of aircraft maintained over surface operations or a landmass **b :** a heavy barrage **4 :** something which covers or embraces a broad range of elements or factors ⟨decided to expand . . . by building new colleges under a federation ~ —Diane Ravitch⟩
[2]**umbrella** *vt* **-laed; -la·ing** (1922) **:** to protect, cover, or provide with an umbrella
umbrella plant *n* (1874) **:** an African sedge (*Cyperus alternifolius*) that has large terminal whorls of slender leaves and is often grown as an ornamental
umbrella tree *n* (1738) **1 :** an American magnolia (*Magnolia tripetala*) having large leaves clustered at the ends of the branches **2 :** any of various trees or shrubs resembling an umbrella esp. in the arrangement of leaves or the shape of the crown
Um·bri·an \'əm-brē-ən\ *n* (1601) **1 :** a native or inhabitant of Umbria **2 :** the Italic language of ancient Umbria — see INDO-EUROPEAN LANGUAGES table — **Umbrian** *adj*
Um·bun·du \,əm-'bün-(,)dü\ *n* (ca. 1895) **:** a Congo language of central Angola
umi·ak \'ü-mē-,ak\ *n* [Esk] (1769) **:** an open Eskimo boat made of a wooden frame covered with hide and usu. propelled with broad paddles
[1]**um·laut** \'u̇m-,lau̇t, 'üm-\ *n* [G, fr. *um-* around, transformation + *laut* sound] (1844) **1 a :** the change of a vowel caused by partial assimilation to a succeeding sound; *esp* **:** the fronting or raising of a back or low vowel (as *a, o,* or *u*) caused by an *i* or *j* orig. standing in the following syllable but usu. lost or altered **b :** a vowel resulting from such partial assimilation **2 :** a diacritical mark ¨ placed esp. over a German vowel to indicate umlaut
[2]**umlaut** *vt* (1852) **1 :** to produce by umlaut **2 :** to write or print an umlaut over
[1]**ump** \'əmp\ *n* (ca. 1910) **:** UMPIRE 2
[2]**ump** *vi* (1928) **:** to act as umpire
[1]**um·pire** \'əm-,pī(ə)r\ *n* [ME *oumpere,* alter. (resulting fr. incorrect division of *a noumpere*) of *noumpere,* fr. MF *nomper* not equal, not paired, fr. *non-* + *per* equal, fr. L *par*] (15c) **1 :** one having authority to decide finally a controversy or question between parties: as **a :** one appointed to decide between arbitrators who have disagreed **b :** an impartial third party chosen to arbitrate disputes arising under the terms of a labor agreement **2 :** an official in a sport who rules on plays **3 :** a military officer who evaluates maneuvers
[2]**umpire** *vb* **um·pired; um·pir·ing** *vt* (1592) **:** to supervise or decide as umpire ~ *vi* **:** to act as umpire
ump·teen \'əm(p)-'tēn, ,əm(p)-\ *adj* [blend of *umpty* (such and such) and *-teen* (as in *thirteen*)] (ca. 1914) **:** very many **:** indefinitely numerous — **ump·teenth** \-'tēn(t)th\ *adj*
[1]**un-** \,ən, 'ən *before* '-stressed syllable, ,ən *before* ,-stressed or unstressed syllable\ *prefix* [ME, fr. OE; akin to OHG *un-* un-, L *in-,* Gk *a-, an-,* OE *ne* not — more at NO] **1 :** not **:** IN-, NON- — in adjectives formed from adjectives ⟨*unstrenuous*⟩ ⟨*unskilled*⟩ or participles ⟨*undressed*⟩, in nouns formed from nouns ⟨*unostentation*⟩, and rarely in verbs formed from verbs ⟨*unbe*⟩; sometimes in words that have a meaning that merely negates that of the base word and are thereby distinguished from words that prefix *in-* or a variant of it (as *im-*) to the same base word and have a meaning positively opposite to that of the base word ⟨*unartistic*⟩ ⟨*unmoral*⟩ **2 :** opposite of **:** contrary to — in adjectives formed from adjectives ⟨*unconstitutional*⟩ ⟨*ungraceful*⟩ ⟨*unmannered*⟩ or participles ⟨*unbelieving*⟩ and in nouns formed from nouns ⟨*unrest*⟩
[2]**un-** *prefix* [ME, fr. OE *un-, on-,* alter. of *and-* against — more at ANTE-] **1 :** do the opposite of **:** reverse (a specified action) **:** DE- 1a, DIS- 1a — in verbs formed from verbs ⟨*unbend*⟩ ⟨*undress*⟩ ⟨*unfold*⟩ **2 a :** deprive of **:** remove (a specified thing) from **:** remove — in verbs formed from nouns ⟨*unfrock*⟩ ⟨*unsex*⟩ **b :** release from **:** free from — in verbs formed from nouns ⟨*unhand*⟩ **c :** remove from **:** extract from **:** bring out of — in verbs formed from nouns ⟨*unbosom*⟩ **d :** cause to cease to be — in verbs formed from nouns ⟨*unman*⟩ **3 :** completely ⟨*unloose*⟩

un·abrad·ed
un·ab·sorbed
un·ab·sor·bent
un·ac·a·dem·ic
un·ac·a·dem·i·cal·ly
un·ac·cent·ed
un·ac·cept·ed
un·ac·cli·mat·ed
un·ac·cli·ma·tized
un·ac·com·mo·dat·ed
un·ac·com·mo·dat·ing
un·ac·cred·it·ed
un·ac·cul·tur·at·ed
un·achieved
un·ac·knowl·edged
un·ac·quaint·ed
un·act·able
un·act·ed
un·ac·tor·ish
un·adapt·able
un·adapt·ed
un·ad·dressed
un·ad·ju·di·cat·ed
un·ad·just·ed
un·ad·mired
un·ad·mit·ted
un·adopt·able
un·adult
un·ad·ven·tur·ous
un·ad·ver·tised
un·aes·thet·ic
un·af·fect·ing
un·af·fec·tion·ate
un·af·fec·tion·ate·ly
un·af·fil·i·at·ed
un·af·flu·ent
un·af·ford·able
un·afraid
un·ag·gres·sive
un·aid·ed
un·air–con·di·tioned
un·akin
un·alien·at·ed
un·alike
un·al·le·vi·at·ed
un·al·lo·cat·ed
un·al·tered
un·am·bi·tious
un·ame·na·ble
un·amend·ed
un·ami·a·ble
un·am·or·tized
un·am·pli·fied
un·amus·ing
un·an·a·lyz·able
un·an·a·lyzed
un·an·no·tat·ed
un·an·nounced
un·an·swered
un·apol·o·giz·ing
un·ap·par·ent
un·ap·peased
un·ap·pre·ci·at·ed
un·ap·pre·cia·tive
un·ap·pro·pri·at·ed
un·ap·proved
un·ar·gu·able
un·ar·gu·ably
un·ar·mored
un·ar·ro·gant
un·ar·tis·tic
un·as·pi·rat·ed
un·as·sailed
un·as·sem·bled
un·as·signed
un·as·sim·i·la·ble
un·as·sim·i·lat·ed
un·as·so·ci·at·ed
un·as·suaged
un·ath·let·ic
un·at·tain·able
un·at·tend·ed
un·at·ten·u·at·ed
un·at·test·ed
un·at·trib·ut·able
un·at·trib·ut·ed
un·at·tuned
un·au·dit·ed
un·au·then·tic
un·au·tho·rized
un·au·to·mat·ed
un·avail·abil·i·ty
un·avail·able
un·avowed
un·awak·ened
un·award·ed
un·awe·some
un·banned
un·bap·tized
un·barbed
un·bar·ri·cad·ed
un·bel·lig·er·ent
un·be·loved
un·be·mused
un·billed
un·bit·ten
un·bit·ter
un·bleached

un·blem·ished
un·blend·ed
un·blood·ed
un·book·ish
un·bought
un·bouncy
un·bowd·ler·ized
un·brack·et·ed
un·brake
un·breach·able
un·break·able
un·bridge·able
un·bridged
un·briefed
un·bright
un·bril·liant
un·bruised
un·brushed
un·bud·get·ed
un·buf·fered
un·build·able
un·bulky
un·bu·reau·crat·ic
un·bur·ied
un·burn·able
un·burned
un·burnt
un·busi·ness·like
un·bust·ed
un·busy
un·but·tered
un·cal·ci·fied
un·cal·cined
un·cal·i·brat·ed
un·called
un·cal·loused
un·can·celed
un·can·did
un·can·did·ly
un·ca·non·i·cal
un·cap
un·cap·i·tal·ized
un·cap·tioned
un·cap·tur·able
un·cared–for
un·car·ing
un·car·pet·ed
un·case
un·cas·trat·ed
un·cat·a·loged
un·catch·able
un·catchy
un·caught
un·cen·sored
un·cen·so·ri·ous
un·cen·sured
un·cer·ti·fied
un·chal·lenge·able
un·chal·lenged
un·chal·leng·ing
un·changed
un·chan·neled
un·chap·er·oned
un·char·is·mat·ic
un·charm·ing
un·char·tered
un·chau·vin·is·tic
un·check·able
un·checked
un·chew·able
un·chewed
un·chic
un·chic·ly
un·child·like
un·chlo·ri·nat·ed
un·cho·reo·graphed
un·church·ly
un·cil·i·at·ed
un·cin·e·mat·ic
un·clad
un·claimed
un·clar·i·fied
un·clas·si·fi·able
un·cleaned
un·clear
un·cleared
un·cli·ched
un·clip
un·cloy·ing
un·co·alesce
un·coat·ed
un·coat·ing
un·cod·ed
un·co·erced
un·co·er·cive
un·co·er·cive·ly
un·col·lect·ed
un·col·lect·ible
un·co·lored
un·com·bat·ive
un·combed

un·com·bined
un·come·ly
un·com·ic
un·com·mer·cial·ized
un·com·pas·sion·ate
un·com·pel·ling
un·com·pen·sat·ed
un·com·pla·cent
un·com·plet·ed
un·com·pound·ed
un·com·pre·hend·ed
un·com·pu·ter·ized
un·con·cealed
un·con·fined
un·con·firmed
un·con·found·ed
un·con·fused
un·con·ju·gat·ed
un·con·nect·ed
un·con·quered
un·con·se·crat·ed
un·con·strained
un·con·strict·ed
un·con·sumed
un·con·sum·mat·ed
un·con·tain·able
un·con·tain·er·ized
un·con·tam·i·nat·ed
un·con·tem·plat·ed
un·con·tem·po·rary
un·con·test·ed
un·con·tract·ed
un·con·tra·dict·ed
un·con·trolled
un·con·tro·ver·sial
un·con·tro·ver·sial·ly
un·con·vert·ed
un·con·vinced
un·con·voyed
un·cooked
un·cooled
un·co·op·er·a·tive
un·co·or·di·nat·ed
un·cor·rect·able
un·cor·rect·ed
un·cor·re·lat·ed
un·cor·rob·o·rat·ed
un·cor·rupt
un·cor·rupt·ed
un·count·able
un·cou·ra·geous
un·cov·e·nant·ed
un·coy
un·cracked
un·crate
un·cra·zy
un·cre·ative
un·cred·it·ed
un·crip·pled
un·cropped
un·cross·able
un·crowd·ed
un·crush·able
un·cuffed
un·cul·ti·va·ble
un·cul·ti·vat·ed
un·cul·tured
un·cured
un·cu·ri·ous
un·cur·rent
un·cur·tained
un·cus·tom·ari·ly
un·cus·tom·ary
un·cute
un·cyn·i·cal
un·cyn·i·cal·ly
un·dam·aged
un·damped
un·dance·able
un·dat·ed
un·de·ca·dent
un·de·cid·able
un·de·cid·ed
un·de·ci·pher·able
un·de·ci·phered
un·de·clared
un·de·com·posed
un·dec·o·rat·ed
un·ded·i·cat·ed
un·de·feat·ed
un·de·fend·ed
un·de·filed
un·de·fin·able
un·de·fined
un·de·fo·li·at·ed
un·de·formed
un·del·e·gat·ed
un·de·liv·er·able
un·de·liv·ered
un·de·lud·ed
un·de·mand·ing
un·de·nom·i·na·tion·al

un·de·pend·able
un·de·scrib·able
un·de·served
un·de·serv·ing
un·des·ig·nat·ed
un·de·sired
un·de·tect·able
un·de·tect·ed
un·de·ter·min·able
un·de·ter·mined
un·de·terred
un·de·vel·oped
un·di·ag·nosed
un·di·a·lec·ti·cal
un·di·dac·tic
un·dif·fer·en·ti·at·ed
un·di·gest·ed
un·di·gest·ible
un·dig·ni·fied
un·di·lut·ed
un·di·min·ished
un·dimmed
un·dis·charged
un·dis·ci·plined
un·dis·closed
un·dis·cour·aged
un·dis·cov·er·able
un·dis·cov·ered
un·dis·crim·i·nat·ing
un·dis·cussed
un·dis·mayed
un·dis·pu·ta·ble
un·dis·put·ed
un·dis·solved
un·dis·tin·guished
un·dis·tort·ed
un·dis·tract·ed
un·dis·trib·ut·ed
un·dis·turbed
un·di·vid·ed
un·do·able
un·doc·ile
un·doc·tored
un·doc·tri·naire
un·doc·u·ment·ed
un·do·mes·tic
un·do·mes·ti·cat·ed
un·dot·ted
un·doubt·able
un·doubt·ing
un·drained
un·dra·ma·tized
un·drilled
un·drink·able
un·dulled
un·du·pli·cat·ed
un·dyed
un·dy·nam·ic
un·ea·ger
un·ear·marked
un·eat·able
un·eat·en
un·ec·cen·tric
un·eco·log·i·cal
un·ed·i·fy·ing
un·ed·u·ca·ble
un·ed·u·cat·ed
un·elab·o·rat·ed
un·elect·able
un·elect·ed
un·elec·tri·fied
un·em·bar·rassed
un·em·bel·lished
un·em·bit·tered
un·em·phat·ic
un·em·phat·i·cal·ly
un·em·pir·i·cal
un·en·chant·ed
un·en·closed
un·en·cour·ag·ing
un·en·dear·ing
un·en·dur·able
un·en·dur·able·ness
un·en·dur·ably
un·en·dur·ing
un·en·force·able
un·en·forced
un·en·larged
un·en·light·ened
un·en·light·en·ing
un·en·riched
un·en·ter·pris·ing
un·en·thu·si·as·tic
un·en·thu·si·as·ti·cal·ly
un·en·vi·able
un·en·vi·ous
un·erot·ic
un·es·cap·able
un·eth·i·cal
un·eval·u·at·ed
un·ex·am·ined
un·ex·celled
un·ex·cit·able

un·ex·cit·ed
un·ex·cit·ing
un·ex·ot·ic
un·ex·pend·ed
un·ex·pired
un·ex·plain·able
un·ex·plained
un·ex·plod·ed
un·ex·plored
un·ex·posed
un·ex·pressed
un·ex·pur·gat·ed
un·ex·traor·di·nary
un·faked
un·fa·mous
un·fan·cy
un·fas·tid·i·ous
un·fazed
un·fea·si·ble
un·felt
un·fem·i·nine
un·fenced
un·fer·ment·ed
un·fer·tile
un·fer·til·ized
un·filled
un·fil·tered
un·fired
un·flam·boy·ant
un·flashy
un·fleshed
un·fly·able
un·fond
un·forced
un·fore·see·able
un·fore·seen
un·for·giv·able
un·forked
un·for·mu·lat·ed
un·forth·com·ing
un·for·ti·fied
un·fos·sil·if·er·ous
un·framed
un·free
un·free·dom
un·ful·filled
un·fun·ny
un·fur·nished
un·fused
un·gal·lant
un·gal·lant·ly
un·gar·nished
un·ge·nial
un·gen·teel
un·gen·tle
un·gen·tle·man·ly
un·ger·mi·nat·ed
un·gift·ed
un·gim·micky
un·glam·or·ized
un·glam·or·ous
un·glazed
un·grace·ful
un·grace·ful·ly
un·grace·ful·ness
un·grad·ed
un·grasp·able
un·ground·ed
un·grouped
un·guid·ed
un·hack·neyed
un·ham·pered
un·harmed
un·har·ness
un·har·vest·ed
un·hatched
un·healed
un·health·ful
un·heat·ed
un·hedged
un·heed·ed
un·heed·ing
un·help·ful
un·help·ful·ly
un·her·ald·ed
un·he·ro·ic
un·hin·dered
un·hip
un·his·tor·i·cal
un·ho·mog·e·nized
un·hon·ored
un·hope·ful
un·housed
un·hu·mor·ous
un·hurt
un·hy·drat·ed
un·hy·dro·lyzed

un·hy·gien·ic
un·hy·phen·at·ed
un·hys·ter·i·cal
un·hys·ter·i·cal·ly
un·iden·ti·fi·able
un·iden·ti·fied
un·ideo·log·i·cal
un·id·i·om·at·ic
un·ig·nor·able
un·imag·i·na·tive
un·imag·i·na·tive·ly
un·im·paired
un·im·pas·sioned
un·im·ped·ed
un·im·por·tant
un·im·pos·ing
un·im·pressed
un·im·pres·sive
un·in·cor·po·rat·ed
un·in·dexed
un·in·dict·ed
un·in·dus·tri·al·ized
un·in·fect·ed
un·in·flat·ed
un·in·flect·ed
un·in·flu·enced
un·in·for·ma·tive
un·in·for·ma·tive·ly
un·in·formed
un·in·hab·it·able
un·in·hab·it·ed
un·ini·ti·at·ed
un·in·jured
un·in·oc·u·lat·ed
un·in·spect·ed
un·in·spired
un·in·spir·ing
un·in·struct·ed
un·in·struc·tive
un·in·sur·able
un·in·sured
un·in·te·grat·ed
un·in·tel·lec·tu·al
un·in·tel·li·gence
un·in·tel·li·gent
un·in·tel·li·gent·ly
un·in·tel·li·gi·bil·i·ty
un·in·tel·li·gi·ble
un·in·tel·li·gi·ble·ness
un·in·tel·li·gi·bly
un·in·tend·ed
un·in·ten·tion·al
un·in·ten·tion·al·ly
un·in·ter·est·ing
un·in·ter·rupt·ed
un·in·ter·rupt·ed·ly
un·in·ter·rupt·ed·ness
un·in·tim·i·dat·ed
un·in·ven·tive
un·in·vit·ed
un·in·vit·ing
un·in·volved
un·iron·i·cal·ly
un·ir·ra·di·at·ed
un·ir·ri·gat·ed
un·is·sued
un·jad·ed
un·joint·ed
un·jus·ti·fi·able
un·jus·ti·fi·ably
un·jus·ti·fied
un·kept
un·knot
un·knowl·edge·able
un·ko·sher
un·la·beled
un·la·dy·like
un·la·ment·ed
un·laun·dered
un·leav·ened
un·lib·er·at·ed
un·li·censed
un·lik·able
un·lis·ten·able
un·lit
un·lit·er·ary
un·liv·able
un·lo·cal·ized
un·lov·able
un·loved
un·lov·ing
un·lyr·i·cal
un·ma·cho
un·mag·ni·fied
un·ma·li·cious
un·ma·li·cious·ly
un·man·age·able

un·man·age·ably
un·ma·nip·u·lat·ed
un·mapped
un·marked
un·mar·ket·able
un·marred
un·mas·cu·line
un·match·able
un·matched
un·meant
un·mea·sur·able
un·mea·sured
un·mech·a·nized
un·me·di·at·ed
un·med·i·cat·ed
un·me·lo·di·ous
un·me·lo·di·ous·ly
un·me·lo·di·ous·ness
un·mem·o·ra·ble
un·mem·o·ra·bly
un·mer·it·ed
un·mer·ry
un·met
un·me·tab·o·lized
un·mil·i·tary
un·milled
un·mixed
un·mod·ern·ized
un·mod·i·fied
un·mod·ish
un·mo·lest·ed
un·mon·i·tored
un·mo·ti·vat·ed
un·mount·ed
un·mov·able
un·moved
un·mu·si·cal
un·name·able
un·named
un·need·ed
un·ne·go·tia·ble
un·neu·rot·ic
un·news·wor·thy
un·no·tice·able
un·no·ticed
un·nour·ish·ing
un·ob·jec·tion·able
un·ob·serv·able
un·ob·served
un·ob·struct·ed
un·ob·tain·able
un·of·fi·cial
un·of·fi·cial·ly
un·open·able
un·opened
un·op·posed
un·or·dered
un·orig·i·nal
un·os·ten·ta·tious
un·os·ten·ta·tious·ly
un·owned
un·ox·y·gen·at·ed
un·paint·ed
un·par·a·sit·ized
un·par·don·able
un·pass·able
un·pas·teur·ized
un·pas·to·ral
un·pat·ent·able
un·paved
un·pe·dan·tic
un·per·ceived
un·per·ceiv·ing
un·per·cep·tive
un·per·form·able
un·per·formed
un·per·suad·ed
un·per·sua·sive
un·per·turbed
un·pic·tur·esque
un·placed
un·planned
un·plau·si·ble
un·play·able
un·pleased
un·pleas·ing
un·plowed
un·po·et·ic
un·po·liced
un·pol·ished
un·pol·lut·ed
un·posed
un·prac·ti·cal
un·pre·dict·abil·i·ty
un·pre·dict·able
un·prej·u·diced

un·pre·med·i·tat·ed
un·pre·pared
un·pre·pared·ness
un·pre·pos·sess·ing
un·pressed
un·pres·sured
un·pret·ty
un·pro·cessed
un·pro·duced
un·pro·duc·tive
un·pro·fes·sion·al
un·pro·gram·ma·ble
un·pro·grammed
un·pro·gres·sive
un·prompt·ed
un·pro·nounce·able
un·pro·pi·tious
un·pros·per·ous
un·pro·tect·ed
un·prov·able
un·proved
un·prov·en
un·pro·vid·ed
un·pro·voked
un·pruned
un·pub·li·cized
un·pub·lished
un·punc·tu·al
un·punc·tu·al·i·ty
un·pun·ished
un·quan·ti·fi·able
un·quench·able
un·ques·tioned
un·raised
un·ranked
un·rav·ished
un·reach·able
un·reached
un·read·able
un·readi·ness
un·ready
un·re·al·ism
un·re·al·iz·able
un·re·al·ized
un·re·cep·tive
un·re·claim·able
un·rec·og·niz·able
un·rec·og·niz·ably
un·rec·og·nized
un·rec·on·cil·able
un·rec·on·ciled
un·re·cord·ed
un·re·cov·er·able
un·re·cov·ered
un·re·deem·able
un·re·deemed
un·re·dressed
un·re·fined
un·re·flec·tive
un·re·formed
un·re·frig·er·at·ed
un·reg·u·lat·ed
un·re·hearsed
un·re·in·forced
un·re·lat·ed
un·re·laxed
un·re·li·abil·i·ty
un·re·li·able
un·re·lieved
un·re·lieved·ly
un·re·luc·tant
un·re·mark·able
un·re·mark·ably
un·re·mem·bered
un·rem·i·nis·cent
un·re·mov·able
un·re·peat·able
un·re·pen·tant
un·re·pen·tant·ly
un·re·port·ed
un·rep·re·sen·ta·tive
un·rep·re·sen·ta·tive·ness
un·rep·re·sent·ed
un·re·pressed
un·re·quit·ed
un·re·sis·tant
un·re·solv·able
un·re·solved
un·re·spect·able
un·re·spon·sive
un·re·spon·sive·ly
un·re·spon·sive·ness
un·rest·ful
un·re·stored
un·re·strict·ed
un·re·turn·able
un·re·vealed
un·re·viewed
un·re·vised
un·rev·o·lu·tion·ary
un·re·ward·ed
un·re·ward·ing

un·rhe·tor·i·cal
un·rhymed
un·rhyth·mic
un·rhyth·mi·cal
un·rid·able
un·ri·fled
un·rip·ened
un·ro·man·tic
un·ro·man·ti·cal·ly
un·ro·man·ti·cized
un·roofed
un·rushed
un·safe
un·sal·able
un·sal·a·ried
un·salt·ed
un·sal·vage·able
un·sanc·tioned
un·san·i·tary
un·sat·is·fied
un·scal·able
un·scarred
un·sched·uled
un·schol·ar·ly
un·screened
un·scrip·tur·al
un·sea·soned
un·sea·wor·thy
un·se·cured
un·seed·ed
un·seg·ment·ed
un·self-con·scious
un·self-con·scious·ly
un·self-con·scious·ness
un·sen·sa·tion·al
un·sen·si·tized
un·sen·ti·men·tal
un·sep·a·rat·ed
un·se·ri·ous
un·served
un·ser·vice·able
un·sex·u·al
un·sexy
un·shad·ed
un·shak·able
un·shak·ably
un·shak·en
un·shape·ly
un·shared
un·sharp
un·shav·en
un·shelled
un·shock·able
un·shorn
un·showy
un·signed
un·sink·able
un·sized
un·slaked
un·smart
un·smil·ing
un·smoothed
un·soiled
un·so·lic·it·ed
un·solv·able
un·solved
un·sort·ed
un·sound·ed
un·sown
un·spe·cial·ized
un·spec·i·fi·able
un·spec·if·ic
un·spec·i·fied
un·spec·tac·u·lar
un·spent
un·spir·i·tu·al
un·split
un·spoiled
un·spoilt
un·spo·ken
un·sprayed
un·stained
un·stan·dard·ized
un·star·tling
un·stat·ed
un·ster·ile
un·ster·il·ized
un·stint·ed
un·stitch
un·stoned
un·stop·per
un·strained
un·strat·i·fied
un·stuffy
un·styl·ish
un·sub·dued
un·sub·si·dized
un·sub·stan·ti·at·ed
un·sub·tle
un·sub·tly
un·suit·abil·i·ty

un·suit·able
un·suit·ably
un·suit·ed
un·sul·lied
un·su·per·vised
un·sup·port·able
un·sup·port·ed
un·sure
un·sur·pass·able
un·sur·passed
un·sur·prised
un·sur·pris·ing
un·sur·pris·ing·ly
un·sus·cep·ti·ble
un·sus·pect·ed
un·sus·pect·ing
un·sus·pi·cious
un·sus·tain·able
un·sweet·ened
un·sym·pa·thet·ic
un·sym·pa·thet·i·cal·ly
un·syn·chro·nized
un·sys·tem·at·ic
un·sys·tem·at·i·cal·ly
un·sys·tem·atized
un·tact·ful
un·tagged
un·taint·ed
un·tal·ent·ed
un·tam·able
un·tamed
un·tanned
un·tar·nished
un·teach·able
un·tech·ni·cal
un·tem·pered
un·ten·ant·ed
un·tend·ed
un·ten·ured
un·test·able
un·test·ed
un·threat·en·ing
un·thrifty
un·tilled
un·to·geth·er
un·trace·able
un·tracked
un·tra·di·tion·al
un·tra·di·tion·al·ly
un·trained
un·tram·meled
un·trans·formed
un·trans·lat·abil·i·ty
un·trans·lat·able
un·trans·lat·ed
un·trav·eled
un·tra·versed
un·treat·ed
un·trimmed
un·trust·ing
un·trust·wor·thy
un·tuck
un·tuft·ed
un·typ·i·cal
un·typ·i·cal·ly
un·un·der·stand·able
un·us·able
un·uti·lized
un·vac·ci·nat·ed
un·var·ied
un·vary·ing
un·ven·ti·lat·ed
un·ver·bal·ized
un·ver·i·fi·able
un·versed
un·vi·a·ble
un·vis·it·ed
un·want·ed
un·war·like
un·war·rant·ed
un·wa·ver·ing
un·wa·ver·ing·ly
un·waxed
un·weaned
un·weath·ered
un·wed
un·weed·ed
un·wel·come
un·white
un·willed
un·win·na·ble
un·wom·an·ly
un·won
un·work·abil·i·ty
un·work·able
un·worked
un·wor·ried
un·wound·ed
un·wo·ven
un·young

un·abashed \ˌən-ə-ˈbasht\ *adj* (1571) : not abashed : UNDISGUISED — **un·abash·ed·ly** \-ˈbash-əd-lē\ *adv*

un·abat·ed \ˌən-ə-ˈbāt-əd\ *adj* (ca. 1611) : not abated : being at full strength or force — **un·abat·ed·ly** *adv*

un·able \ˌən-ˈā-bəl, ˈən-\ *adj* (14c) : not able : INCAPABLE: as **a** : UNQUALIFIED, INCOMPETENT **b** : IMPOTENT, HELPLESS

un·abridged \ˌən-ə-ˈbrijd\ *adj* (1599) **1** : not abridged : COMPLETE ⟨an ∼ reprint of a novel⟩ **2** : being the most complete of its class : not based on one larger ⟨an ∼ dictionary⟩

un·ac·cept·able \ˌən-ik-ˈsep-tə-bəl, -ak-\ *adj* (15c) : not acceptable : not pleasing or welcome — **un·ac·cept·abil·i·ty** \-ˌsep-tə-ˈbil-ət-ē\ *n* — **un·ac·cept·ably** \-ˈsep-tə-blē\ *adv*

un·ac·com·pa·nied \ˌən-ə-ˈkəmp-(ə-)nēd\ *adj* (1545) : not accompanied; *esp* : being without instrumental accompaniment

un·ac·count·able \ˌən-ə-ˈkaůnt-ə-bəl\ *adj* (1643) **1** : not to be accounted for : INEXPLICABLE, STRANGE **2** : not to be called to account : not responsible — **un·ac·count·abil·i·ty** \-ˌkaůnt-ə-ˈbil-ət-ē\ *n* — **un·ac·count·ably** \-ˈkaůnt-ə-blē\ *adv*

un·ac·count·ed \-ˈkaůnt-əd\ *adj* (1799) : not accounted : UNEXPLAINED — often used with *for*

un·ac·cus·tomed \ˌən-ə-ˈkəs-təmd\ *adj* (1526) **1** : not customary : not usual or common **2** : not habituated — usu. used with *to* — **un·ac·cus·tomed·ly** \-təm-dlē\ *adv*

una cor·da \ˌü-nə-ˈkȯrd-ə, -ˈkȯr-(ˌ)dä\ *adv or adj* [It, lit., one string] (ca. 1854) : with soft pedal depressed — used as a direction in piano music

un·adorned \ˌən-ə-ˈdȯ(ə)rnd\ *adj* (1634) : not adorned : lacking embellishment or decoration : PLAIN, SIMPLE — **un·adorn·ment** \-ˈdȯ(ə)rn-mənt\ *n*

un·adul·ter·at·ed \ˌən-ə-ˈdəl-tə-ˌrāt-əd\ *adj* (1719) : PURE, UNMIXED — **un·adul·ter·at·ed·ly** *adv*

un·ad·vised \ˌən-əd-ˈvīzd\ *adj* (14c) **1** : done without due consideration : RASH ⟨a cruel and ∼ act⟩ **2** : not prudent : INDISCREET ⟨an ∼ love of gossip⟩ — **un·ad·vis·ed·ly** \-ˈvī-zəd-lē\ *adv*

un·af·fect·ed \ˌən-ə-ˈfek-təd\ *adj* (1586) **1** : not influenced or changed mentally, physically, or chemically **2** : free from affectation : GENUINE — **un·af·fect·ed·ly** *adv* — **un·af·fect·ed·ness** *n*

un·ag·ing *or* **un·age·ing** \ˌən-ˈā-jiŋ, ˈən-\ *adj* (1860) : AGELESS

unak·ite \ˈyü-nə-ˌkīt\ *n* (ca. 1874) : an altered igneous rock that is usu. opaque with green, black, pink, and white flecks and is usu. used as a gemstone

un·alien·able \ˌən-ˈāl-yə-nə-bəl, -ˈā-lē-ə-\ *adj* (1611) : INALIENABLE

un·aligned \ˌən-ə-ˈlīnd\ *adj* (ca. 1934) : NONALIGNED

un·al·loyed \ˌən-ə-ˈlȯid\ *adj* (1667) : not alloyed : UNMIXED, UNQUALIFIED, PURE ⟨∼ metals⟩ ⟨∼ happiness⟩

un·al·ter·able \ˌən-ˈȯl-t(ə-)rə-bəl, ˈən-\ *adj* (1611) : not capable of being altered or changed ⟨an ∼ resolve⟩ ⟨∼ hatred⟩ — **un·al·ter·abil·i·ty** \ˌən-ˌȯl-t(ə-)rə-ˈbil-ət-ē\ *n* — **un·al·ter·able·ness** \ˌən-ˈȯl-t(ə-)rə-bəl-nəs, ˈən-\ *n* — **un·al·ter·ably** \-blē\ *adv*

un·am·big·u·ous \ˌən-am-ˈbig-yə-wəs\ *adj* (1751) : not ambiguous : CLEAR, PRECISE — **un·am·big·u·ous·ly** *adv*

un·am·biv·a·lent \-ˈbiv-ə-lənt\ *adj* (1945) : not ambivalent : CLEAR-CUT, DEFINITE — **un·am·biv·a·lent·ly** *adv*

un-Amer·i·can \ˌən-ə-ˈmer-ə-kən\ *adj* (1818) : not American : not characteristic of or consistent with American customs, principles, or traditions

un·an·chor \ˌən-ˈaŋ-kər, ˈən-\ *vt* (1648) : to loosen from an anchor

un·aneled \ˌən-ə-ˈnē(ə)ld\ *adj* [*un-* + *aneled*, pp. of *anele* to anoint, fr. ME *anelen*, fr. *an* on + *elen* to anoint, fr. *ele* oil, fr. OE, fr. L *oleum* — more at OIL] *archaic* (1602) : not having received extreme unction

un·anes·the·tized \ˌən-ə-ˈnes-thə-ˌtīzd\ *adj* (1963) : not having been subjected to an anesthetic

una·nim·i·ty \ˌyü-nə-ˈnim-ət-ē\ *n* (15c) : the quality or state of being unanimous

unan·i·mous \yů-ˈnan-ə-məs\ *adj* [L *unanimus*, fr. *unus* one + *animus* mind — more at ONE, ANIMATE] (1624) **1** : being of one mind : AGREEING **2** : formed with or indicating unanimity : having the agreement and consent of all — **unan·i·mous·ly** *adv*

un·an·swer·able \ˌən-ˈan(t)s-(ə-)rə-bəl, ˈən-\ *adj* (1613) : not answerable; *esp* : IRREFUTABLE — **un·an·swer·abil·i·ty** \ˌən-ˌan(t)s-(ə-)rə-ˈbil-ət-ē\ *n* — **un·an·swer·ably** \ˌən-ˈan(t)s-(ə-)rə-blē\ *adv*

un·an·tic·i·pat·ed \ˌən-an-ˈtis-ə-ˌpāt-əd\ *adj* (ca. 1755) : not anticipated : UNEXPECTED, UNFORESEEN — **un·an·tic·i·pat·ed·ly** *adv*

un·apol·o·get·ic \ˌən-ə-ˌpäl-ə-ˈjet-ik\ *adj* (1834) : not apologetic : offered or put forward without apology — **un·apol·o·get·i·cal·ly** \-i-k(ə-)lē\ *adv*

un·ap·peal·able \ˌən-ə-ˈpē-lə-bəl\ *adj* (1635) : not appealable : not subject to appeal

un·ap·peal·ing \-ˈpē-liŋ\ *adj* (1846) : not appealing : UNATTRACTIVE — **un·ap·peal·ing·ly** \-liŋ-lē\ *adv*

un·ap·peas·able \-ˈpē-zə-bəl\ *adj* (1561) : not to be appeased : IMPLACABLE — **un·ap·peas·ably** \-blē\ *adv*

un·ap·pe·tiz·ing \ˌən-ˈap-ə-ˌtī-ziŋ, ˈən-\ *adj* (1891) : not appetizing : INSIPID, UNATTRACTIVE — **un·ap·pe·tiz·ing·ly** \-ˌtī-ziŋ-lē\ *adv*

un·ap·pre·ci·a·tion \ˌən-ə-ˌprē-shē-ˈā-shən\ *n* (1886) : failure to appreciate something

un·ap·proach·able \ˌən-ə-ˈprō-chə-bəl\ *adj* (1581) **1** : not approachable : physically inaccessible **2** : discouraging intimacies : RESERVED — **un·ap·proach·abil·i·ty** \-ˌprō-chə-ˈbil-ət-ē\ *n* — **un·ap·proach·ably** \-ˈprō-chə-blē\ *adv*

un·apt \ˌən-ˈapt, ˈən-\ *adj* (14c) **1** : INAPPROPRIATE, UNSUITABLE ⟨an ∼ quote⟩ **2** : not accustomed and not likely ⟨a teacher ∼ to tolerate carelessness⟩ **3** : DULL, BACKWARD ⟨∼ scholars⟩ — **un·apt·ly** \-ˈap-(t)lē\ *adv* — **un·apt·ness** \-ˈap(t)-nəs\ *n*

un·arm \ˌən-ˈärm, ˈən-\ *vt* (1560) : DISARM

un·armed \-ˈärmd\ *adj* (13c) **1** : not armed or armored **2** : having no hard and sharp projections (as spines, spurs, or claws)

un·ar·tic·u·lat·ed \ˌən-är-ˈtik-yə-ˌlāt-əd\ *adj* (1700) : not articulated; *esp* : not carefully reasoned or analyzed

una·ry \ˈyü-nə-rē\ *adj* [L *unus* one + E *-ary*] (1576) : having, consisting of, or acting on a single element, item, or component : MONADIC

un·ashamed \ˌən-ə-ˈshāmd\ *adj* (1600) : not ashamed : being without guilt, self-consciousness, or doubt — **un·asham·ed·ly** \-ˈshā-məd-lē\ *adv*

un·asked \ˌən-ˈas(k)t, ˈən-\ *adj* (13c) **1** : not asked ⟨∼ questions⟩ **2** : not being asked : UNINVITED **3** : not asked for ⟨∼ advice⟩

un·as·sail·able \ˌən-ə-ˈsā-lə-bəl\ *adj* (1596) **:** not assailable **:** not liable to doubt, attack, or question — **un·as·sail·abil·i·ty** \-ˌsā-lə-ˈbil-ət-ē\ *n* — **un·as·sail·able·ness** \-ˈsā-lə-bəl-nəs\ *n* — **un·as·sail·ably** \-blē\ *adv*
un·as·ser·tive \ˌən-ə-ˈsərt-iv\ *adj* (1861) **:** not assertive **:** MODEST, SHY — **un·as·ser·tive·ly** *adv*
un·as·sist·ed \ˌən-ə-ˈsis-təd\ *adj* (1614) **1 :** not assisted **:** lacking help **2 :** made or performed without an assist ⟨an ~ double play⟩
un·as·suage·able \ˌən-ə-ˈswā-jə-bəl\ *adj* (ca. 1611) **:** not capable of being assuaged
un·as·sum·ing \ˌən-ə-ˈsü-miŋ\ *adj* (1726) **:** not assuming **:** not arrogant or presuming **:** MODEST, RETIRING — **un·as·sum·ing·ness** *n*
un·at·tached \ˌən-ə-ˈtacht\ *adj* (ca. 1755) **1 a :** not assigned or committed (as to a particular task, organization, or person); *esp* **:** not married or engaged **b :** not seized as security for a legal judgment **2 :** not joined or united ⟨~ polyps⟩ ⟨~ buildings⟩
un·at·trac·tive \-ˈtrak-tiv\ *adj* (1775) **:** not attractive **:** PLAIN, DULL — **un·at·trac·tive·ly** *adv* — **un·at·trac·tive·ness** *n*
un·avail·ing \-ˈvā-liŋ\ *adj* (1670) **:** not availing **:** FUTILE, USELESS — **un·avail·ing·ly** \-liŋ-lē\ *adv* — **un·avail·ing·ness** *n*
un·av·er·age \ˌən-ˈav-(ə-)rij, ˈən-\ *adj* (1962) **:** not average **:** UNUSUAL, OUTSTANDING
un·avoid·able \ˌən-ə-ˈvȯid-ə-bəl\ *adj* (1577) **:** not avoidable **:** INEVITABLE — **un·avoid·ably** \-blē\ *adv*
[1]**un·aware** \-ə-ˈwa(ə)r, -ˈwe(ə)r\ *adv* (1592) **:** UNAWARES
[2]**unaware** *adj* (1704) **:** not aware **:** IGNORANT — **un·aware·ly** *adv* — **un·aware·ness** *n*
un·awares \-ˈwa(ə)rz, -ˈwe(ə)rz\ *adv* [*un-* + *aware* + *-s,* adv. suffix, fr. ME, fr. *-s,* gen. sing. ending of nouns — more at -s] (1535) **1 :** without design, attention, preparation, or premeditation **2 :** without warning **:** SUDDENLY, UNEXPECTEDLY
un·backed \ˌən-ˈbakt, ˈən-\ *adj* (1609) **:** lacking support or aid
[1]**un·bal·ance** \-ˈbal-ən(t)s\ *vt* (1856) **:** to put out of balance; *esp* **:** to derange mentally
[2]**unbalance** *n* (1887) **:** lack of balance **:** IMBALANCE
un·bal·anced \-ən(t)st\ *adj* (1650) **:** not balanced: as **a :** not in equilibrium **b :** mentally disordered or deranged **c :** not adjusted so as to make credits equal to debits ⟨an ~ account⟩
un·bal·last·ed \-ˈbal-ə-stəd\ *adj* (1657) **:** not furnished with or steadied by ballast **:** UNSTEADY
un·ban·dage \-ˈban-dij\ *vt* (1840) **:** to remove a bandage from
un·bar \ˌən-ˈbär, ˈən-\ *vt* (14c) **:** to remove a bar from **:** UNBOLT, OPEN
un·bar·bered \-ˈbär-bərd\ *adj* (1845) **:** having long and esp. unkempt hair
un·barred \-ˈbärd\ *adj* (1603) **1 :** not secured by a bar **:** UNLOCKED **2 :** not marked with bars
un·bat·ed \-ˈbāt-əd\ *adj* (1596) **1 :** UNABATED **2** *archaic* **:** not blunted
un·be \-ˈbē\ *vi, archaic* (15c) **:** to lack or cease to have being
un·bear·able \ˌən-ˈbar-ə-bəl, ˈən-, -ˈber-\ *adj* (15c) **:** not bearable **:** UNENDURABLE — **un·bear·ably** \-blē\ *adv*
un·beat·able \-ˈbēt-ə-bəl\ *adj* (1897) **1 :** not capable of being defeated **2 :** possessing unsurpassable qualities — **un·beat·ably** \-blē\ *adv*
un·beat·en \-ˈbēt-ᵊn\ *adj* (13c) **1 :** not pounded or beaten **:** not whipped **2 :** not traversed **:** UNTROD **3 :** not defeated
un·beau·ti·ful \-ˈbyüt-i-fəl\ *adj* (15c) **:** not beautiful **:** UNATTRACTIVE — **un·beau·ti·ful·ly** \-f(ə-)lē\ *adv*
un·be·com·ing \ˌən-bi-ˈkəm-iŋ\ *adj* (1598) **:** not becoming ⟨an ~ dress⟩; *esp* **:** not according with the standards appropriate to one's position or condition of life ⟨~ conduct⟩ ***syn*** see INDECOROUS — **un·be·com·ing·ly** \-iŋ-lē\ *adv* — **un·be·com·ing·ness** *n*
un·be·knownst \ˌən-bi-ˈnōn(t)st\ *also* **un·be·known** \-ˈnōn\ *adj* [[1]*un-* + obs. E *beknown* (known); *unbeknownst,* irreg. fr. *unbeknown*] (1636) **:** happening without one's knowledge **:** UNKNOWN — usu. used with *to*
un·be·lief \ˌən-bə-ˈlēf\ *n* (12c) **:** incredulity or skepticism esp. in matters of religious faith
un·be·liev·able \-ˈlē-və-bəl\ *adj* (1548) **:** too improbable for belief ⟨the plot is unreal and ~⟩; *also* **:** of such a superlative degree as to be hard to believe ⟨the destruction was ~⟩ ⟨made an ~ catch in center field⟩ — **un·be·liev·ably** \-blē\ *adv*
un·be·liev·er \-ˈlē-vər\ *n* (1526) **1 :** one that does not believe **:** an incredulous person **:** DOUBTER, SKEPTIC **2 :** one that does not believe in a particular religious faith
un·be·liev·ing \-ˈlē-viŋ\ *adj* (15c) **:** marked by unbelief **:** INCREDULOUS, SKEPTICAL — **un·be·liev·ing·ly** \-viŋ-lē\ *adv*
un·belt·ed \ˌən-ˈbel-təd, ˈən-\ *adj* (1814) **:** not furnished with a belt
un·bend \-ˈbend\ *vb* **-bent** \-ˈbent\; **-bend·ing** *vt* (13c) **1 :** to free from flexure **:** make or allow to become straight ⟨~ a bow⟩ **2 :** to cause (as the mind) to relax **3 a :** to unfasten (as a sail) from a spar or stay **b :** to cast loose or untie (as a rope) ~ *vi* **1 :** to relax one's severity, stiffness, or austerity **2 :** to cease to be bent **:** become straight
un·bend·able \-ˈben-də-bəl\ *adj* (1775) **:** SINGLE-MINDED, FIRM
un·bend·ing \-ˈben-diŋ\ *adj* [[1]*un-*] (ca. 1688) **1 :** not bending **:** UNYIELDING, INFLEXIBLE ⟨an ~ will⟩ **2 :** aloof or unsocial in manner **:** RESERVED
un·be·seem·ing \ˌən-bi-ˈsē-miŋ\ *adj* (1583) **:** not befitting **:** UNBECOMING
un·bi·ased \ˌən-ˈbī-əst, ˈən-\ *adj* (1647) **1 :** free from bias; *esp* **:** free from all prejudice and favoritism **:** eminently fair **2 :** having an expected value equal to a population parameter being estimated ⟨an ~ estimate of the population mean⟩ — **un·bi·ased·ness** \-əs(t)-nəs\ *n* ***syn*** see FAIR
un·bib·li·cal \ˌən-ˈbib-li-kəl, ˈən-\ *adj* (1828) **:** contrary to or unsanctioned by the Bible
un·bid·den \-ˈbid-ᵊn\ *also* **un·bid** \-ˈbid\ *adj* [ME *unbiden, unbeden,* fr. OE *unbeden,* fr. *un-* + *beden,* pp. of *biddan* to entreat — more at BID] (bef. 12c) **:** not bidden **:** UNASKED, UNINVITED
un·bind \-ˈbīnd\ *vt* **-bound** \-ˈbau̇nd\; **-bind·ing** (bef. 12c) **1 :** to remove a band from **:** free from fastenings **:** UNTIE, UNFASTEN **2 :** to set free **:** RELEASE
un·bit·ted \-ˈbit-əd\ *adj* [[2]*bit*] (ca. 1586) **:** UNBRIDLED, UNCONTROLLED
un·blenched \-ˈblencht\ *adj* (1634) **:** not disconcerted **:** UNDAUNTED
un·blessed *also* **un·blest** \ˌən-ˈblest, ˈən-\ *adj* (14c) **1 :** not blessed **2 :** EVIL, ACCURSED
un·blind·ed \-ˈblīn-dəd\ *adj* (ca. 1611) **:** not blinded; *esp* **:** free from illusion
un·blink·ing \-ˈbliŋ-kiŋ\ *adj* (ca. 1909) **1 :** not blinking **2 :** not showing signs of emotion, doubt, or confusion — **un·blink·ing·ly** \-kiŋ-lē\ *adv*
un·block \-ˈbläk\ *vt* (ca. 1611) **:** to free from being blocked
un·blush·ing \-ˈbləsh-iŋ\ *adj* (1595) **1 :** not blushing **2 :** SHAMELESS, UNABASHED — **un·blush·ing·ly** \-iŋ-lē\ *adv*
un·bod·ied \-ˈbäd-ēd\ *adj* (1532) **1 :** having no body **:** INCORPOREAL; *also* **:** freed from the body ⟨~ souls⟩ **2 :** FORMLESS
un·bolt \ˌən-ˈbōlt, ˈən-\ *vt* (ca. 1598) **:** to open or unfasten by withdrawing a bolt
[1]**un·bolt·ed** \-ˈbōl-təd\ *adj* [[2]*bolt*] (1580) **:** not fastened by bolts
[2]**unbolted** *adj* [[5]*bolt*] (1598) **:** not sifted ⟨~ flour⟩
un·bon·net·ed \ˌən-ˈbän-ət-əd, ˈən-\ *adj* (1604) **:** BAREHEADED
un·born \-ˈbȯ(ə)rn\ *adj* (bef. 12c) **1 :** not born **:** not brought into life **2 :** still to appear **:** FUTURE **3 :** existing without birth
un·bo·som \-ˈbu̇z-əm *also* -ˈbüz-\ *vt* (1588) **1 :** to give expression to **:** DISCLOSE, REVEAL **2 :** to disclose the thoughts or feelings of (oneself) ~ *vi* **:** to unbosom oneself
un·bound \-ˈbau̇nd\ *adj* (bef. 12c) **:** not bound: as **a** (1) **:** not fastened (2) **:** not confined **b :** not having the leaves fastened together ⟨an ~ book⟩ **c :** not bound together with other issues ⟨~ periodicals⟩ **d :** not held in chemical or physical combination
un·bound·ed \-ˈbau̇n-dəd\ *adj* (ca. 1598) **1 :** having no limit **2 :** UNRESTRAINED, UNCONTROLLED — **un·bound·ed·ness** *n*
un·bowed \ˌən-ˈbau̇d, ˈən-\ *adj* (14c) **1 :** not bowed down **2 :** not subdued
un·box \-ˈbäks\ *vt* (ca. 1611) **:** to remove from a box
un·brace \-ˈbrās\ *vt* (1593) **1 :** to free or detach by or as if by untying or removing a brace or bond **2 :** ENFEEBLE, WEAKEN
un·braid \-ˈbrād\ *vt* (ca. 1828) **:** to separate the strands of **:** UNRAVEL
un·branched \-ˈbrancht\ *adj* (1665) **1 :** having no branches ⟨a straight ~ trunk⟩ **2 :** not divided into branches ⟨a leaf with ~ veins⟩
un·brand·ed \-ˈbran-dəd\ *adj* (1886) **1 :** not marked with the owner's name or mark ⟨~ cattle⟩ **2 :** not sold under a brand name
un·breath·able \ˌən-ˈbrē-t͟hə-bəl\ *adj* (1846) **:** not fit for being breathed
un·bred \-ˈbred\ *adj* (1662) **1** *obs* **:** ILL-BRED **2 :** not taught **:** UNTRAINED **3 :** not bred **:** never having been bred ⟨an ~ heifer⟩
un·bri·dle \ˌən-ˈbrīd-ᵊl, ˈən-\ *vt* (15c) **:** to free or loose from a bridle; *broadly* **:** to set loose **:** free from restraint
un·bri·dled \-ˈbrīd-ᵊld\ *adj* (14c) **1 :** UNRESTRAINED ⟨~ enthusiasm⟩ **2 :** not confined by a bridle
un·broke \-ˈbrōk\ *adj* (14c) **:** UNBROKEN
un·bro·ken \-ˈbrō-kən\ *adj* (14c) **:** not broken: as **a :** not violated **b :** WHOLE, INTACT **c :** not subdued **:** UNTAMED; *esp* **:** not trained for service or use ⟨~ colts⟩ **d :** CONTINUOUS ⟨miles of ~ forest⟩ **e :** not plowed **f :** not disorganized ⟨advanced in ~ ranks⟩
un·buck·le \-ˈbək-əl\ *vt* (14c) **:** to loose the buckle of **:** UNFASTEN ~ *vi* **1 :** to loosen buckles **2 :** RELAX
un·budge·able \-ˈbəj-ə-bəl\ *adj* (1929) **:** not able to be budged or changed **:** INFLEXIBLE — **un·budge·ably** \-blē\ *adv*
un·budg·ing \-ˈbəj-iŋ\ *adj* (ca. 1934) **:** not budging **:** resisting movement or change — **un·budg·ing·ly** \-iŋ-lē\ *adv*
un·build \ˌən-ˈbild, ˈən-\ *vb* **-built** \-ˈbilt\; **-build·ing** *vt* (1607) **:** to pull down **:** DEMOLISH, RAZE ~ *vi* **:** to destroy something
un·built \-ˈbilt\ *adj* (15c) **1 :** not built **:** not yet constructed **2 :** not built on ⟨an ~ plot⟩ ⟨a forest which was ~ on⟩
un·bun·dle \-ˈbən-dᵊl\ *vi* (1969) **:** to give separate prices for equipment and supporting services ~ *vt* **:** to price separately
un·bur·den \-ˈbərd-ᵊn\ *vt* (ca. 1538) **1 :** to free or relieve from a burden **2 :** to relieve oneself of (as cares, fears, or worries) **:** cast off
un·bur·dened \-ˈbərd-ᵊnd\ *adj* (1548) **:** not burdened **:** having no weight or load
un·but·ton \-ˈbət-ᵊn\ *vt* (14c) **1 :** to loose the buttons of **2 :** to open by or as if by loosing buttons ~ *vi* **:** to undo buttons
un·but·toned \-ᵊnd\ *adj* (1583) **1 a :** not buttoned **b :** not provided with buttons **2 :** not under constraint **:** free and unrestricted in action and expression
un·cage \ˌən-ˈkāj, ˈən-\ *vt* (1620) **:** to release from or as if from a cage **:** free from restraint
un·cal·cu·lat·ed \-ˈkal-kyə-ˌlāt-əd\ *adj* (ca. 1828) **:** not planned or thought out beforehand **:** SPONTANEOUS
un·cal·cu·lat·ing \-ˌlāt-iŋ\ *adj* (ca. 1828) **:** not based on or marked by calculation
un·called–for \ˌən-ˈkȯl(d)-ˌfȯ(ə)r, ˈən-\ *adj* (ca. 1635) **1 :** not called for or needed **:** UNNECESSARY **2 :** being or offered without provocation or justification ⟨an ~ display of temper⟩ ⟨~ insults⟩
un·can·ny \-ˈkan-ē\ *adj* (1843) **1 a :** seeming to have a supernatural character or origin **:** EERIE, MYSTERIOUS **b :** being beyond what is normal or expected **:** suggesting superhuman or supernatural powers ⟨an ~ sense of direction⟩ **2** *chiefly Scot* **:** SEVERE, PUNISHING ***syn*** see WEIRD — **un·can·ni·ly** \-ˈkan-ᵊl-ē\ *adv* — **un·can·ni·ness** \-ˈkan-ē-nəs\ *n*
un·caused \-ˈkȯzd\ *adj* (1628) **:** having no antecedent cause
un·ceas·ing \-ˈsē-siŋ\ *adj* (14c) **:** never ceasing **:** CONTINUOUS, INCESSANT — **un·ceas·ing·ly** \-siŋ-lē\ *adv*
un·cel·e·brat·ed \-ˈsel-ə-ˌbrāt-əd\ *adj* (1660) **1 :** not formally honored or commemorated **2 :** not famous **:** OBSCURE
un·cer·e·mo·ni·ous \ˌən-ˌser-ə-ˈmō-nē-əs\ *adj* (1598) **1 :** not ceremonious **:** INFORMAL **2 :** ABRUPT, RUDE ⟨an ~ dismissal⟩ — **un·cer·e·mo·ni·ous·ly** *adv* — **un·cer·e·mo·ni·ous·ness** *n*
un·cer·tain \ˌən-ˈsərt-ᵊn, ˈən-\ *adj* (14c) **1 :** INDEFINITE, INDETERMINATE ⟨the time of departure is ~⟩ **2 :** not certain to occur **:** PROBLEMATICAL **3 :** not reliable **:** UNTRUSTWORTHY **4 a :** not known beyond doubt **:** DUBIOUS **b :** not having certain knowledge **:** DOUBTFUL **c :** not clearly identified or defined **5 :** not constant **:** VARIABLE, FITFUL — **un·cer·tain·ly** *adv* — **un·cer·tain·ness** \-ᵊn-(n)əs\ *n*
un·cer·tain·ty \-ᵊn-tē\ *n* (14c) **1 :** the quality or state of being uncertain **:** DOUBT **2 :** something that is uncertain

syn UNCERTAINTY, DOUBT, DUBIETY, SKEPTICISM, SUSPICION, MISTRUST mean lack of sureness about someone or something. UNCERTAINTY may range from a falling short of certainty to an almost complete lack of definite knowledge esp. about an outcome or result; DOUBT suggests both uncertainty and inability to make a decision; DUBIETY stresses a wavering between conclusions; SKEPTICISM implies unwillingness to believe without conclusive evidence; SUSPICION stresses lack of faith in the truth, reality, fairness, or reliability of something or someone; MISTRUST implies a genuine doubt based upon suspicion.

uncertainty principle *n* (ca. 1934) : a principle in quantum mechanics: it is impossible to assert in terms of the ordinary conventions of geometrical position and of motion that a particle (as an electron) is at the same time at a specified point and moving with a specified velocity

un·chain \ˌən-ˈchān, ˈən-\ *vt* (1582) : to free by or as if by removing a chain : set loose

un·chancy \-ˈchan(t)-sē\ *adj* (1533) **1** *chiefly Scot* : ILL-FATED **2** *chiefly Scot* : DANGEROUS

un·change·able \-ˈchān-jə-bəl\ *adj* (14c) : not changing or to be changed : IMMUTABLE — **un·change·abil·i·ty** \ˌən-ˌchān-jə-ˈbil-ət-ē\ *n* — **un·change·able·ness** \ˌən-ˈchān-jə-bəl-nəs, ˈən-\ *n* — **un·change·ably** \-blē\ *adv*

un·chang·ing \-ˈchān-jiŋ\ *adj* (1593) : CONSTANT, INVARIABLE — **un·chang·ing·ly** \-jiŋ-lē\ *adv* — **un·chang·ing·ness** *n*

un·char·ac·ter·is·tic \ˌən-ˌkar-ik-tə-ˈris-tik\ *adj* (1753) : not characteristic : not typical or distinctive — **un·char·ac·ter·is·ti·cal·ly** \-ti-k(ə-)lē\ *adv*

un·charge \ˌən-ˈchärj, ˈən-\ *vt, obs* (1602) : ACQUIT

un·charged \-ˈchärjd\ *adj* (1815) : not charged; *specif* : having no electric charge

un·char·i·ta·ble \-ˈchar-ət-ə-bəl\ *adj* (15c) : lacking in charity : severe in judging : HARSH — **un·char·i·ta·ble·ness** *n* — **un·char·i·ta·bly** \-blē\ *adv*

un·chart·ed \-ˈchärt-əd\ *adj* (ca. 1847) : not recorded or plotted on a map, chart, or plan; *broadly* : UNKNOWN

un·chaste \-ˈchāst\ *adj* (14c) : not chaste : lacking in chastity — **un·chaste·ly** *adv* — **un·chaste·ness** \-ˈchās(t)-nəs\ *n*

un·chas·ti·ty \-ˈchas-tət-ē\ *n* (14c) : the quality or state of being unchaste

un·chiv·al·rous \-ˈshiv-əl-rəs\ *adj* (1846) : not chivalrous : lacking in chivalry — **un·chiv·al·rous·ly** *adv*

un·choke \-ˈchōk\ *vt* (1588) : to clear of obstruction

un·chris·tian \-ˈkris(h)-chən\ *adj* (1555) **1** : not of the Christian faith **2 a** : contrary to the Christian spirit or character **b** : UNCIVILIZED, BARBAROUS

un·church \-ˈchərch\ *vt* (1620) **1** : to expel from a church : EXCOMMUNICATE **2** : to deprive of a church or of status as a church

un·churched \-ˈchərcht\ *adj* (1681) : not belonging to or connected with a church

unci *pl of* UNCUS

¹un·cial \ˈən-shəl, -chəl; ˈən(t)-sē-əl\ *adj* [L *uncialis* inch-high, fr. *uncia* twelfth part, ounce, inch] (1712) : written in the style or size of uncials — **un·cial·ly** \-ē\ *adv*

²uncial *n* (1775) **1** : a handwriting used esp. in Greek and Latin manuscripts of the 4th to the 8th centuries A.D. and made with somewhat rounded separated majuscules but having cursive forms for some letters **2** : an uncial letter **3** : a manuscript written in uncial

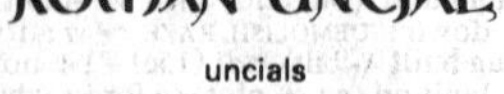

uncials

un·ci·form \ˈən(t)-sə-ˌfȯrm\ *adj* [NL *unciformis*, fr. L *uncus* hook + *-formis* -form — more at ANGLE] (1733) : hook-shaped : UNCINATE

un·ci·na·ri·a·sis \ˌən-ˌsin-ə-ˈrī-ə-səs\ *n* [NL] (1903) : ANCYLOSTOMIASIS

un·ci·nate \ˈən(t)-sə-ˌnāt\ *adj* (ca. 1760) : bent at the tip like a hook : HOOKED ⟨an ~ achene⟩

un·cir·cu·lat·ed \ˌən-ˈsər-kyə-ˌlāt-əd, ˈən-\ *adj* (1917) : issued for use as money but kept out of circulation (as for preservation in a collection)

un·cir·cum·cised \ˌən-ˈsər-kəm-ˌsīzd, ˈən-\ *adj* (14c) **1** : not circumcised **2** : spiritually impure : HEATHEN — **un·cir·cum·ci·sion** \ˌən-ˌsər-kəm-ˈsizh-ən\ *n*

un·civ·il \ˌən-ˈsiv-əl, ˈən-\ *adj* (1553) **1** : not civilized : BARBAROUS **2** : lacking in courtesy : ILL-MANNERED, IMPOLITE **3** : not conducive to civic harmony and welfare — **un·civ·il·ly** \-ə-lē\ *adv*

un·civ·i·lized \-ˈsiv-ə-ˌlīzd\ *adj* (1607) **1** : not civilized : BARBAROUS **2** : remote from settled areas : WILD

un·clamp \-ˈklamp\ *vt* (1809) : to loosen the clamp of : to free from a clamp

un·clar·i·ty \-ˈklar-ət-ē\ *n, pl* **-ties** (1923) : lack of clarity : AMBIGUITY, OBSCURITY

un·clasp \-ˈklasp\ *vt* (1530) **1** : to open the clasp of **2** : to open or cause to be opened (as a clenched hand) ~ *vi* : to loosen a hold

un·clas·si·cal \-ˈklas-i-kəl\ *adj* (1725) : not classical; *esp* : unconcerned with the classics

un·clas·si·fied \-ˈklas-ə-ˌfīd\ *adj* (1865) **1** : not placed or belonging in a class **2** : not subject to a security classification

un·cle \ˈəŋ-kəl\ *n* [ME, fr. OF, fr. L *avunculus* mother's brother; akin to OE *ēam* uncle, OIr *aue* grandson, L *avus* grandfather] (13c) **1 a** : the brother of one's father or mother **b** : the husband of one's aunt **2** : one who helps, advises, or encourages **3** — used as a cry of surrender ⟨was forced to cry ~⟩ **4** *cap* : UNCLE SAM

un·clean \ˌən-ˈklēn, ˈən-\ *adj* (bef. 12c) **1** : morally or spiritually impure **2** : infected with a harmful supernatural contagion; *also* : prohibited by ritual law for use or contact **3** : DIRTY, FILTHY **4** : lacking in clarity and precision of conception or execution — **un·clean·ness** \-ˈklēn-nəs\ *n*

¹un·clean·ly \-ˈklen-lē\ *adj* (bef. 12c) : morally or physically unclean — **un·clean·li·ness** *n*

²un·clean·ly \-ˈklēn-lē\ *adv* (bef. 12c) : in an unclean manner

un·clench \-ˈklench\ *vt* (1755) **1** : to open from a clenched position **2** : to release from a grip ~ *vi* : to become unclasped or relaxed

Un·cle Sam \ˌəŋ-kəl-ˈsam\ *n* [expansion of *U.S.*, abbr. of *United States*] (1813) **1** : the U.S. government **2** : the American nation or people

¹Uncle Tom \-ˈtäm\ *n* [*Uncle Tom*, pious and faithful Negro slave in *Uncle Tom's Cabin* (1851–52) by Harriet Beecher Stowe] (1927) **1** : a black who is overeager to win the approval of whites (as by obsequious behavior or uncritical acceptance of white values and goals) **2** : a member of a low-status group who is overly subservient to or cooperative with authority ⟨the worst floor managers and supervisors by far are women . . . Some of them are regular *Uncle Toms* —Jane Fonda⟩ — **Uncle Tom·ism** \-ˈtäm-ˌiz-əm\ *n*

²Uncle Tom *vi* **Uncle Tommed; Uncle Tom·ming** (1962) : to behave like an Uncle Tom

un·climb·able \ˌən-ˈklī-mə-bəl, ˈən-\ *adj* (1553) : not able to be climbed — **un·climb·able·ness** *n*

un·clinch \ˌən-ˈklinch, ˈən-\ *vt* (ca. 1598) : UNCLENCH

un·cloak \-ˈklōk\ *vt* (ca. 1598) **1** : to remove a cloak or cover from **2** : REVEAL, UNMASK ~ *vi* : to take off a cloak

un·clog \-ˈkläg\ *vt* (1607) : to free from a difficulty or obstruction

un·close \-ˈklōz\ *vt* (14c) **1** : OPEN **2** : DISCLOSE, REVEAL ~ *vi* : to become opened

un·closed \-ˈklōzd\ *adj* (15c) : not closed or settled : not concluded

un·clothe \-ˈklōth\ *vt* (14c) **1** : to strip of clothes **2** : DIVEST, UNCOVER

un·clothed \-ˈklōthd\ *adj* (15c) : not clothed

un·cloud·ed \-ˈklau̇d-əd\ *adj* (1595) : not covered by clouds : not darkened : CLEAR — **un·cloud·ed·ly** *adv*

un·clut·ter \-ˈklət-ər\ *vt* (ca. 1934) : to remove clutter from : make neat and orderly

un·clut·tered \-ərd\ *adj* (ca. 1934) : not cluttered

¹un·co \ˈəŋ-(ˌ)kō, -kə\ *adj* [ME (Sc) *unkow*, alter. of ME *uncouth*] (15c) **1** *chiefly Scot* **a** : STRANGE, UNKNOWN **b** : UNCANNY, WEIRD **2** *chiefly Scot* : EXTRAORDINARY

²unco *adv* (1724) : EXTREMELY, REMARKABLY, UNCOMMONLY

³unco *n, pl* **uncos** (1785) **1** *pl, chiefly Scot* : NEWS, TIDINGS **2** *chiefly Scot* : STRANGER

un·cock \ˌən-ˈkäk, ˈən-\ *vt* (1598) : to remove the hammer of (a firearm) from a cocked position

un·cof·fin \-ˈkȯ-fən\ *vt* (1923) : to remove from or as if from a coffin

un·cof·fined \-fənd\ *adj* (1648) : not placed in a coffin

un·coil \ˌən-ˈkȯi(ə)l, ˈən-\ *vt* (1713) : to release from a coiled state : UNWIND ~ *vi* : to become uncoiled

un·coiled \-ˈkȯi(ə)ld\ *adj* (ca. 1755) : not coiled

un·coined \-ˈkȯind\ *adj* (15c) **1** : not minted ⟨~ metal⟩ **2** : not fabricated : NATURAL

un·com·fort·able \ˌən-ˈkəm(p)(f)-tə(r)-bəl, ˈən-, -ˈkəm(p)-fə(r)t-ə-bəl, -ˈkəm-fə(r)-bəl\ *adj* (1592) **1** : causing discomfort or annoyance ⟨an ~ chair⟩ ⟨an ~ performance⟩ **2** : feeling discomfort : UNEASY ⟨was ~ with them⟩ — **un·com·fort·ably** \-blē\ *adv*

un·com·mer·cial \ˌən-kə-ˈmər-shəl\ *adj* (1768) **1** : not engaged in or related to commerce **2** : not based on commercial principles

un·com·mit·ted \-ˈmit-əd\ *adj* (1814) : not committed; *specif* : not pledged to a particular belief, allegiance, or program

un·com·mon \ˌən-ˈkäm-ən, ˈən-\ *adj* (ca. 1611) **1** : not ordinarily encountered : UNUSUAL **2** : REMARKABLE, EXCEPTIONAL *syn* see INFREQUENT — **un·com·mon·ly** *adv* — **un·com·mon·ness** \-ən-nəs\ *n*

un·com·mu·ni·ca·ble \ˌən-kə-ˈmyü-ni-kə-bəl\ *adj* (14c) : INCOMMUNICABLE

un·com·mu·ni·ca·tive \-ˈmyü-nə-ˌkāt-iv, -ni-kət-\ *adj* (1691) : not disposed to talk or impart information : RESERVED

un·com·pet·i·tive \-ˈpet-ət-iv\ *adj* (1885) : not competitive : unable to compete — **un·com·pet·i·tive·ness** *n*

un·com·plain·ing \-ˈplā-niŋ\ *adj* (1744) : not complaining : PATIENT — **un·com·plain·ing·ly** \-niŋ-lē\ *adv*

un·com·pli·cat·ed \ˌən-ˈkäm-plə-ˌkāt-əd, ˈən-\ *adj* (1775) **1** : not complicated by something outside itself; *specif* : not involving medical complications ⟨~ peptic ulcer⟩ **2** : not complex : SIMPLE ⟨~ machinery⟩

un·com·pli·men·ta·ry \ˌən-ˌkäm-plə-ˈment-ə-rē, -ˈmen-trē\ *adj* (1842) : not complimentary : DEROGATORY

un·com·pre·hend·ing \-pri-ˈhen-diŋ\ *adj* (1838) : not comprehending : lacking understanding — **un·com·pre·hend·ing·ly** \-diŋ-lē\ *adv*

un·com·pro·mis·able \ˌən-ˈkäm-prə-ˌmī-zə-bəl, ˈən-\ *adj* (1958) : not able to be compromised

un·com·pro·mis·ing \-ˌmī-ziŋ\ *adj* (ca. 1828) : not making or accepting a compromise : making no concessions : INFLEXIBLE, UNYIELDING — **un·com·pro·mis·ing·ly** \-ziŋ-lē\ *adv*

un·con·ceiv·able \ˌən-kən-ˈsē-və-bəl\ *adj* (ca. 1611) : INCONCEIVABLE

un·con·cern \ˌən-kən-ˈsərn\ *n* (1711) **1** : lack of care or interest : INDIFFERENCE **2** : freedom from excessive concern or anxiety

un·con·cerned \-ˈsərnd\ *adj* (1635) **1** : not involved : not having any part or interest **2** : not anxious or upset : free of worry *syn* see INDIFFERENT — **un·con·cerned·ly** \-ˈsər-nəd-lē, -ˈsərn-dlē\ *adv* — **un·con·cerned·ness** \-ˈsər-nəd-nəs, -ˈsərn(d)-nəs\ *n*

un·con·di·tion·al \ˌən-kən-ˈdish-nəl, -ˈdish-ən-ᵊl\ *adj* (1666) **1** : not conditional or limited : ABSOLUTE, UNQUALIFIED **2** : UNCONDITIONED 2 — **un·con·di·tion·al·ly** \-ē\ *adv*

un·con·di·tioned \-ˈdish-ənd\ *adj* (1631) **1** : not subject to conditions or limitations **2 a** : not dependent on or subjected to conditioning or learning : NATURAL ⟨~ responses⟩ **b** : producing an unconditioned response ⟨~ stimuli⟩

un·con·form·able \-ˈfȯr-mə-bəl\ *adj* (1594) **1** : not conforming **2** : exhibiting geological unconformity — **un·con·form·ably** \-blē\ *adv*

un·con·for·mi·ty \-ˈfȯr-mət-ē\ *n* (1600) **1** *archaic* : lack of conformity **2 a** : lack of continuity in deposition between rock strata in contact corresponding to a period of nondeposition, weathering, or erosion **b** : the surface of contact between unconformable strata

un·con·ge·nial \-ˈjē-nyəl, -nē-əl\ *adj* (1775) **1** : not sympathetic or compatible ⟨~ roommates⟩ **2 a** : not fitted : UNSUITABLE ⟨a soil ~ to most crops⟩ **b** : not to one's taste : DISAGREEABLE ⟨an ~ task⟩ — **un·con·ge·nial·i·ty** \-ˌjē-nē-ˈal-ət-ē, -ˌjēn-ˈyal-\ *n*

un·con·quer·able \ˌən-ˈkäŋ-k(ə-)rə-bəl, ˈən-\ *adj* (ca. 1598) **1** : incapable of being conquered : INDOMITABLE ⟨an ~ will⟩ **2** : incapable of being surmounted ⟨~ difficulties⟩ — **un·con·quer·ably** \-blē\ *adv*

un·con·scio·na·ble \-ˈkänch-(ə-)nə-bəl\ *adj* (1570) **1** : not guided or controlled by conscience : UNSCRUPULOUS ⟨an ~ villain⟩ **2 a** : EXCESSIVE, UNREASONABLE ⟨found an ~ number of defects in the car⟩ **b** : shockingly unfair or unjust ⟨~ sales practices⟩ — **un·con·scio·na·bil·i·ty** \ˌən-ˌkänch-(ə-)nə-ˈbil-ət-ē\ *n* — **un·con·scio·na·ble·ness** \ˌən-ˈkänch-(ə-)nə-bəl-nəs, ˈən-\ *n* — **un·con·scio·na·bly** \-blē\ *adv*

¹un·con·scious \ˌən-ˈkän-chəs, ˈən-\ *adj* (1712) **1 a** : not knowing or perceiving : not aware **b** : free from self-awareness **2 a** : not possessing mind or consciousness ⟨~ matter⟩ **b** (1) **:** not marked by conscious thought, sensation, or feeling ⟨~ motivation⟩ (2) **:** of or relating to the unconscious **c :** having lost consciousness ⟨was ~ for three days⟩ **3 :** not consciously held or deliberately planned or carried out ⟨~ bias⟩ — **un·con·scious·ly** *adv* — **un·con·scious·ness** *n*

[2]**unconscious** *n* (ca. 1919) **:** the part of the psychic apparatus that does not ordinarily enter the individual's awareness and that is manifested esp. by slips of the tongue or dissociated acts or in dreams

un·con·sid·ered \ˌən-kən-ˈsid-ərd\ *adj* (1587) **1 :** not considered or worth consideration **2 :** not resulting from consideration

un·con·sol·i·dat·ed \-ˈsäl-ə-ˌdāt-əd\ *adj* (1775) **:** loosely arranged ⟨~ subsidiaries⟩; *esp* **:** not stratified ⟨~ soil⟩

un·con·sti·tu·tion·al \ˌən-ˌkän(t)-stə-ˈt(y)üsh-nəl, -ən-ᵊl\ *adj* (1765) **:** not according or consistent with the constitution of a body politic (as a nation) — **un·con·sti·tu·tion·al·i·ty** \-ˌt(y)ü-shə-ˈnal-ət-ē\ *n* — **un·con·sti·tu·tion·al·ly** \-ˈt(y)üsh-nə-lē, -ən-ᵊl-ē\ *adv*

un·con·straint \ˌən-kən-ˈstrānt\ *n* (1711) **:** freedom from constraint **:** EASE

un·con·struct·ed \-ˈstrək-təd\ *adj, of clothing* (1970) **:** manufactured without added material for padding, stiffening, or shape retention

un·con·trol·la·ble \-ˈtrō-lə-bəl\ *adj* (1593) **1** *archaic* **:** free from control by a superior power **:** ABSOLUTE **2 :** incapable of being controlled **:** UNGOVERNABLE — **un·con·trol·la·bly** \-blē\ *adv*

un·con·ven·tion·al \-ˈvench-nəl, -ən-ᵊl\ *adj* (1839) **:** not conventional **:** not bound by or in accordance with convention **:** being out of the ordinary — **un·con·ven·tion·al·i·ty** \-ˌven-chə-ˈnal-ət-ē\ *n* — **un·con·ven·tion·al·ly** \-ˈvench-nə-lē, -ən-ᵊl-ē\ *adv*

un·con·vinc·ing \-ˈvin(t)-siŋ\ *adj* (1633) **:** not convincing **:** IMPLAUSIBLE — **un·con·vinc·ing·ly** \-siŋ-lē\ *adv* — **un·con·vinc·ing·ness** *n*

un·cool \ˌən-ˈkül, ˈən-\ *adj* (1958) **1 :** lacking in assurance **2 :** failing to accord with the mores of a particular group

un·cork \ˌən-ˈkȯ(ə)rk, ˈən-\ *vt* (1727) **1 :** to draw a cork from **2 a :** to release from a sealed or pent-up state ⟨~ a surprise⟩ **b :** to let go **:** RELEASE ⟨~ a wild pitch⟩

un·corked \-ˈkȯ(ə)rkt\ *adj* (1791) **:** not provided with a cork

un·cor·set·ed \-ˈkȯr-sət-əd\ *adj* (1856) **1 :** not wearing a corset **2 :** not controlled or inhibited

un·count·ed \-ˈkau̇nt-əd\ *adj* (1500) **1 :** not counted **2 :** INNUMERABLE

un·cou·ple \-ˈkəp-əl\ *vt* (14c) **1 :** to release (dogs) from a couple **2 :** DETACH, DISCONNECT ⟨~ railroad cars⟩ — **un·cou·pler** \-(ə-)lər\ *n*

un·couth \-ˈküth\ *adj* [ME, fr. OE *uncūth,* fr. *un-* + *cūth* familiar, known; akin to OHG *kund* known, OE *can* know — more at CAN] (bef. 12c) **1 a** *archaic* **:** not known or not familiar to one **:** seldom experienced **:** UNCOMMON, RARE **b** *obs* **:** MYSTERIOUS, UNCANNY **2 a :** strange or clumsy in shape or appearance **:** OUTLANDISH **b :** lacking in polish and grace **:** RUGGED ⟨~ verse⟩ **c :** awkward and uncultivated in appearance, manner, or behavior — **un·couth·ly** *adv* — **un·couth·ness** *n*

un·cov·er \-ˈkəv-ər\ *vt* (14c) **1 :** to make known **:** bring to light **:** DISCLOSE, REVEAL **2 :** to expose to view by removing some covering **3 a :** to take the cover from **b :** to remove the hat from **4 :** to deprive of protection **~** *vi* **1 :** to remove a cover or covering **2 :** to take off the hat as a token of respect

un·cov·ered \-ərd\ *adj* (ca. 1530) **:** not covered: as **a :** not supplied with a covering **b :** not covered by insurance or included in a social insurance or welfare program **c :** not covered by collateral ⟨an ~ note⟩

un·cre·at·ed \ˌən-krē-ˈāt-əd\ *adj* (1548) **1 :** not existing by creation **:** ETERNAL, SELF-EXISTENT **2 :** not yet created

un·crit·i·cal \ˌən-ˈkrit-i-kəl, ˈən-\ *adj* (1659) **1 :** not critical **:** lacking in discrimination **2 :** showing lack or improper use of critical standards or procedures — **un·crit·i·cal·ly** \-k(ə-)lē\ *adv*

un·cross \-ˈkrȯs\ *vt* (1599) **:** to change from a crossed position

un·crown \-ˈkrau̇n\ *vt* (14c) **:** to take the crown from **:** DEPOSE, DETHRONE

un·crum·ple \-ˈkrəm-pəl\ *vt* (ca. 1611) **:** to restore to an original smooth condition

un·crys·tal·lized \-ˈkris-tə-ˌlīzd\ *adj* (1759) **:** not crystallized; *also* **:** not finally or definitely formed

unc·tion \ˈəŋ(k)-shən\ *n* [ME *unctioun,* fr. L *unction-, unctio,* fr. *unctus,* pp. of *unguere* to anoint — more at OINTMENT] (14c) **1 :** the act of anointing as a rite of consecration or healing **2 :** something used for anointing **:** OINTMENT, UNGUENT **3 a :** religious or spiritual fervor or the expression of such fervor **b :** exaggerated, assumed, or superficial earnestness of language or manner **:** UNCTUOUSNESS

unc·tu·ous \ˈəŋ(k)-chə(-wə)s, ˈəŋ(k)sh-wəs\ *adj* [ME, fr. MF or ML; MF *unctueux,* fr. ML *unctuosus,* irreg. fr. L *unctum* ointment, fr. neut. of *unctus,* pp.] (14c) **1 a :** FATTY, OILY **b :** smooth and greasy in texture or appearance **2 a :** rich in organic matter and easily workable ⟨~ soil⟩ **b :** PLASTIC ⟨fine ~ clay⟩ **3 :** full of unction; *esp* **:** revealing or marked by a smug, ingratiating, and false earnestness or spirituality — **unc·tu·ous·ly** *adv* — **unc·tu·ous·ness** *n*

un·curl \ˌən-ˈkər(-ə)l, ˈən-\ *vi* (1588) **:** to become straightened out from a curled or coiled position **~** *vt* **:** to straighten the curls of **:** UNROLL

un·cus \ˈəŋ-kəs\ *n, pl* **un·ci** \ˈəŋ-ˌkī, -ˌkē; ˈən-ˌsī\ [NL, fr. L, hook — more at ANGLE] (1826) **:** a hooked anatomical part or process

un·cut \ˌən-ˈkət, ˈən-\ *adj* (1548) **1 :** not cut down or cut into **2 :** not shaped by cutting ⟨an ~ diamond⟩ **3** *of a book* **:** not having the folds of the leaves slit **4 :** not abridged or curtailed

un·daunt·able \ˌən-ˈdȯnt-ə-bəl, -ˈdänt-\ *adj* (1587) **:** incapable of being daunted **:** FEARLESS

un·daunt·ed \-əd\ *adj* (1587) **:** courageously resolute esp. in the face of danger or difficulty — **un·daunt·ed·ly** *adv*

un·de·bat·able \ˌən-di-ˈbāt-ə-bəl\ *adj* (1869) **:** not subject to debate **:** INDISPUTABLE — **un·de·bat·ably** \-blē\ *adv*

undec- *comb form* [L *undecim,* fr. *unus* one + *decem* ten — more at ONE, TEN] **:** eleven ⟨*undec*illion⟩

un·de·ceive \ˌən-di-ˈsēv\ *vt* (ca. 1598) **:** to free from deception, illusion, or error

un·de·cil·lion \ˌən-di-ˈsil-yən\ *n, often attrib* [*undec-* + *-illion* (as in *million*)] (1931) — see NUMBER table

un·dec·y·le·nic acid \ˌən-ˌdes-ə-ˌlen-ik-, -ˌlēn-\ *n* [*undecylene* ($C_{11}H_{22}$)] (1879) **:** an acid $C_{11}H_{20}O_2$ found in perspiration, obtained commercially from castor oil, and used in the treatment of fungous infections (as ringworm) of the skin

un·dem·o·crat·ic \ˌən-ˌdem-ə-ˈkrat-ik\ *adj* (1839) **:** not democratic **:** not agreeing with democratic practice or ideals — **un·dem·o·crat·i·cal·ly** \-i-k(ə-)lē\ *adv*

un·de·mon·stra·tive \ˌən-di-ˈmän(t)-strət-iv\ *adj* (1846) **:** restrained in expression of feeling **:** RESERVED — **un·de·mon·stra·tive·ly** *adv* — **un·de·mon·stra·tive·ness** *n*

un·de·ni·able \ˌən-di-ˈnī-ə-bəl\ *adj* (1547) **1 :** plainly true **:** INCONTESTABLE **2 :** unquestionably excellent or genuine ⟨an applicant with ~ references⟩ — **un·de·ni·able·ness** *n* — **un·de·ni·ably** \-blē\ *adv*

[1]**un·der** \ˈən-dər\ *adv* [ME, adv. & prep., fr. OE; akin to OHG *untar* under, L *inferus* situated beneath, lower, *infra* below, Skt *adha*] (bef. 12c) **1 :** in or into a position below or beneath something **2 :** below or short of some quantity or limit ⟨$10 or ~⟩ — often used in combination ⟨*under*-staffed⟩ **3 :** in or into a condition of subjection, subordination, or unconsciousness **4 :** so as to be covered

[2]**un·der** \ˌən-dər, ˈən-\ *prep* (bef. 12c) **1 :** below or beneath so as to be overhung, surmounted, covered, protected, or concealed by ⟨~ sunny skies⟩ ⟨a soft heart ~ a stern exterior⟩ ⟨~ cover of darkness⟩ **2 a :** subject to the authority, control, guidance, or instruction of ⟨served ~ the general⟩ ⟨~ the terms of the contract⟩ **b :** receiving or undergoing the action or effect of ⟨~ pressure⟩ ⟨courage ~ fire⟩ ⟨~ ether⟩ ⟨the image of a point ~ a mapping⟩ **3 :** within the group or designation of ⟨~ this heading⟩ **4 :** less or lower than (as in size, amount, or rank); *esp* **:** falling short of a standard or required degree ⟨~ the legal age⟩ ⟨~ par⟩

[3]**under** \ˈən-dər\ *adj* (14c) **1 a :** lying or placed below, beneath, or on the ventral side — often used in combination ⟨*under*lip⟩ **b :** facing or protruding downward **2 :** lower in rank or authority **:** SUBORDINATE **3 :** lower than usual, proper, or desired in amount, quality, or degree ⟨an ~ dose of medicine⟩

un·der·achieve \ˌən-də-rə-ˈchēv\ *vi* (1965) **:** to perform below an expected level of proficiency — **un·der·achieve·ment** *n* — **un·der·achiev·er** \-ˈchē-vər\ *n*

un·der·act \ˌən-də-ˈrakt\ *vt* (1623) **:** to perform (a dramatic part) with restraint for effect **:** UNDERPLAY **~** *vi* **:** to perform feebly or with restraint

un·der·ac·tive \-ˈrak-tiv\ *adj* (1959) **:** characterized by an abnormally low level of activity ⟨an ~ thyroid gland⟩ — **un·der·ac·tiv·i·ty** \-ˈtiv-ət-ē\ *n*

un·der·age \ˌən-də-ˈrāj\ *adj* (1594) **:** of less than mature or legal age

un·der·ap·pre·ci·at·ed \ˌən-də-rə-ˈprē-shē-ˌāt-əd\ *adj* (1968) **:** not duly appreciated

[1]**un·der·arm** \ˌən-də-ˌrärm\ *adj* (1816) **1 :** UNDERHAND 4 **2 :** placed under or on the underside of the arm ⟨~ seams⟩

[2]**un·der·arm** \ˌən-də-ˈrärm\ *adv* (ca. 1909) **:** UNDERHAND

[3]**un·der·arm** \ˈən-də-ˌrärm\ *n* (1923) **1 :** ARMPIT **2 :** the part of a garment that covers the underside of the arm

un·der·bel·ly \ˈən-dər-ˌbel-ē\ *n* (1607) **1 :** the underside of a body or mass **2 :** a vulnerable area

un·der·bid \ˌən-dər-ˈbid\ *vb* **-bid; -bid·ding** *vt* (ca. 1677) **1 :** to bid less than (a competing bidder) **2 :** to bid (a hand of cards) at less than the strength of the hand warrants **~** *vi* **:** to bid too low — **un·der·bid·der** *n*

un·der·body \ˈən-dər-ˌbäd-ē\ *n* (1879) **:** the lower part of something: as **a :** the lower part of an animal's body **:** UNDERPARTS **b :** the lower parts of the body of a vehicle

un·der·bred \ˌən-dər-ˈbred\ *adj* (1650) **:** marked by lack of good breeding **:** ILL-BRED

un·der·brim \ˈən-dər-ˌbrim\ *n* (1886) **:** a facing on the underside of a hat brim

un·der·brush \ˈən-dər-ˌbrəsh\ *n* (1775) **1 :** shrubs, bushes, or small trees growing beneath large trees in a wood or forest **:** BRUSH **2 :** a tangled, obstructing, or impeding mass

un·der·bud·get·ed \ˌən-dər-ˈbəj-ət-əd\ *adj* (1965) **:** provided with an inadequate budget

un·der·cap·i·tal·ized \-ˈkap-ət-ᵊl-ˌīzd, -ˈkap-tᵊl-\ *adj* (1967) **:** having too little capital for efficient operation

un·der·car·riage \ˈən-dər-ˌkar-ij\ *n* (1794) **1 :** a supporting framework (as of an automobile) **2 :** the landing gear of an airplane

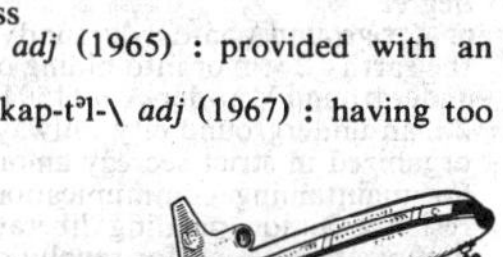

1 undercarriage 2

un·der·charge \ˌən-dər-ˈchärj\ *vt* (1633) **:** to charge (as a person) too little — **undercharge** \ˈən-dər-ˌ\ *n*

un·der·class \ˈən-dər-ˌklas\ *n* (1965) **:** LOWER CLASS

un·der·class·man \ˌən-dər-ˈklas-mən\ *n* (1871) **:** a member of the freshman or sophomore class in a school or college

un·der·clothes \ˈən-dər-ˌklō(th)z\ *n pl* (ca. 1859) **:** UNDERWEAR

un·der·cloth·ing \-ˌklō-thiŋ\ *n* (1835) **:** UNDERWEAR

un·der·coat \-ˌkōt\ *n* (1648) **1 :** a coat or jacket worn under another **2 :** a growth of short hair or fur partly concealed by a longer growth ⟨a dog's ~⟩ **3 a :** a coat (as of paint) applied as a base for another coat **b :** UNDERCOATING **4** *dial* **:** PETTICOAT

un·der·coat·ing \-ˌkōt-iŋ\ *n* (1924) **:** a usu. asphalt-based waterproof coating applied to the underside of a vehicle

un·der·cool \-ˈkül\ *vt* (1902) **:** SUPERCOOL

un·der·count \-ˈkau̇nt\ *vt* (1951) **:** to count fewer than the actual number of — **undercount** *n*

un·der·cov·er \-ˌkəv-ər\ *adj* (1925) **:** acting or executed in secret; *specif* **:** employed or engaged in spying or secret investigation ⟨an ~ agent⟩

un·der·croft \ˈən-dər-ˌkrȯft\ *n* [ME, fr. *under* + *crofte* crypt, fr. MD, fr. ML *crupta,* fr. L *crypta* — more at CRYPT] (14c) **:** a subterranean room; *esp* **:** a vaulted chamber under a church

\ə\ abut \ᵊ\ kitten, F table \ər\ further \a\ ash \ā\ ace \ä\ cot, cart \au̇\ out \ch\ chin \e\ bet \ē\ easy \g\ go \i\ hit \ī\ ice \j\ job \ŋ\ sing \ō\ go \ȯ\ law \ȯi\ boy \th\ thin \th\ the \ü\ loot \u̇\ foot \y\ yet \zh\ vision \à, k, ⁿ, œ, œ̄, ue, ue̅, ʸ\ *see* Guide to Pronunciation

un·der·cur·rent \\-ˌkər-ənt, -ˌkə-rənt\\ *n* (1683) **1 :** a current below the upper currents or surface **2 :** a hidden opinion or feeling often contrary to the one publicly shown — **undercurrent** *adj*

[1]**un·der·cut** \\ˌən-dər-ˈkət\\ *vb* **-cut; -cut·ting** *vt* (ca. 1598) **1 :** to cut away the underpart of ⟨~ a vein of ore⟩ **2 :** to cut away material from the underside of (an object) so as to leave an overhanging portion in relief **3 :** to offer to sell at lower prices than or to work for lower wages than (a competitor) **4 :** to cut obliquely into (a tree) below the main cut and on the side toward which the tree will fall **5 :** to strike (a ball) with a downward glancing blow so as to give a backspin or elevation to the shot **6 :** to undermine or destroy the force, value, or effectiveness of ⟨inflation ~s consumer buying power⟩ ~ *vi* **:** to perform the action of cutting away beneath

[2]**un·der·cut** \\ˈən-dər-ˌkət\\ *n* (1859) **1** *Brit* **:** TENDERLOIN 1 **2 :** the action or result of cutting away from the underside or lower part of something **3 :** a notch cut in the base of a tree before felling to determine the direction of falling and to prevent splitting

un·der·de·vel·oped \\ˌən-dər-di-ˈvel-əpt\\ *adj* (1892) **1 :** not normally or adequately developed ⟨~ muscles⟩ ⟨an ~ film⟩ **2 :** having a relatively low economic level of industrial production and standard of living (as from lack of capital) — **un·der·de·vel·op·ment** \\-əp-mənt\\ *n*

un·der·dog \\ˈən-dər-ˌdȯg\\ *n* (1887) **1 :** a loser or predicted loser in a struggle or contest **2 :** a victim of injustice or persecution

un·der·done \\ˌən-dər-ˈdən\\ *adj* (1683) **:** not thoroughly cooked **:** RARE

un·der·draw·ers \\ˈən-dər-ˌdrȯ(-ə)rz\\ *n pl* (1894) **:** an article of underwear for the lower body

un·der·ed·u·cat·ed \\ˌən-də-ˈrej-ə-ˌkāt-əd\\ *adj* (1856) **:** poorly educated

un·der·em·pha·sis \\ˌən-də-ˈrem(p)-fə-səs\\ *n* (1964) **:** less emphasis than is possible or desirable

un·der·em·pha·size \\-ˌsīz\\ *vt* (1967) **:** to fail to emphasize adequately

un·der·em·ployed \\ˌən-də-rim-ˈplȯid\\ *adj* (1937) **:** having less than full-time, regular, or adequate employment

un·der·em·ploy·ment \\-ˈplȯi-mənt\\ *n* (1910) **1 :** the condition in which people in a labor force are employed at less than full-time or regular jobs or at jobs inadequate with respect to their training or economic needs **2 :** the condition of being underemployed

un·der·es·ti·mate \\ˌən-də-ˈres-tə-ˌmāt\\ *vt* (1812) **1 :** to estimate as being less than the actual size, quantity, or number **2 :** to place too low a value on **:** UNDERRATE — **un·der·es·ti·mate** \\-mət\\ *n* — **un·der·es·ti·ma·tion** \\-ˌres-tə-ˈmā-shən\\ *n*

un·der·ex·pose \\ˌən-də-rik-ˈspōz\\ *vt* (1861) **:** to expose insufficiently; *esp* **:** to expose (as film) to insufficient radiation (as light) — **un·der·ex·po·sure** \\-ˈspō-zhər\\ *n*

un·der·feed \\ˌən-dər-ˈfēd\\ *vt* **-fed** \\-ˈfed\\; **-feed·ing** (1659) **1 :** to feed with too little food **2 :** to feed with fuel from the underside

un·der·fi·nanced \\-fə-ˈnan(t)st, -ˈfī-ˌ, -fī-ˈ\\ *adj* (1922) **:** inadequately financed

un·der·foot \\-ˈfu̇t\\ *adv* (13c) **1 :** under the foot esp. against the ground ⟨trampled the flowers ~⟩ **2 :** below, at, or before one's feet ⟨warm sand ~⟩ **3 :** in the way ⟨children always getting ~⟩

un·der·fund \\-ˈfənd\\ *vt* (1968) **:** to provide insufficient funds for

un·der·fur \\ˈən-dər-ˌfər\\ *n* (1877) **:** the thick soft undercoat of fur lying beneath the longer and coarser hair of a mammal

un·der·gar·ment \\-ˌgär-mənt\\ *n* (1530) **:** a garment to be worn under another

un·der·gird \\ˌən-dər-ˈgərd\\ *vt* (1526) **1 :** to make secure underneath ⟨~ a ship⟩ **2 :** to form the basis or foundation of **:** STRENGTHEN, SUPPORT ⟨faith ~s morals⟩

un·der·glaze \\ˈən-dər-ˌglāz\\ *adj* (1883) **:** applied or suitable for applying before the glaze is put on ⟨~ decorations⟩ ⟨~ colors⟩ — **underglaze** *n*

un·der·go \\ˌən-dər-ˈgō\\ *vt* **-went** \\-ˈwent\\; **-gone** \\-ˈgȯn *also* -ˈgän\\; **-going** \\-ˈgō-iŋ, -ˈgȯ(-)iŋ\\ (13c) **1 :** to submit to **:** ENDURE **2 :** to go through **:** EXPERIENCE **3** *obs* **:** UNDERTAKE **4** *obs* **:** to partake of

un·der·grad·u·ate \\ˌən-dər-ˈgraj-(ə-)wət, -ə-ˌwāt\\ *n* (1630) **:** a student at a college or university who has not taken a first and esp. a bachelor's degree

[1]**un·der·ground** \\ˌən-dər-ˈgrau̇nd\\ *adv* (1571) **1 :** beneath the surface of the earth **2 :** in or into hiding or secret operation

[2]**underground** \\ˈən-dər-ˌ\\ *n* (1594) **1 :** a subterranean space or channel **2 :** an underground city railway system **3 a :** a movement or group organized in strict secrecy among citizens esp. in an occupied country for maintaining communications, popular solidarity, and concerted resistive action pending liberation **b :** a clandestine conspiratorial organization set up for revolutionary or other disruptive purposes esp. against a civil order **c :** an unofficial, unsanctioned, or illegal but informal movement or group; *esp* **:** a usu. avant-garde group or movement that functions outside the establishment

[3]**un·der·ground** \\ˈən-dər-ˌgrau̇nd\\ *adj* (1610) **1 :** being, growing, operating, or situated below the surface of the ground **2 a :** conducted by secret means **b (1) :** existing outside the establishment ⟨an ~ literary reputation⟩ **(2) :** produced or published outside the establishment esp. by the avant-garde ⟨~ movies⟩ ⟨~ newspapers⟩; *also* **:** of or relating to the avant-garde underground ⟨an ~ moviemaker⟩ ⟨an ~ theater⟩

un·der·ground·er \\ˈən-dər-ˌgrau̇n-dər\\ *n* (1882) **:** a member of the underground

Underground Railroad *n* (1834) **:** a system of cooperation among active antislavery people in the U.S. before 1863 by which fugitive slaves were secretly helped to reach the North or Canada — called also *Underground Railway*

un·der·growth \\ˈən-dər-ˌgrōth\\ *n* (1600) **:** low growth on the floor of a forest including seedlings and saplings, shrubs, and herbs

[1]**un·der·hand** \\ˈən-dər-ˌhand\\ *adv* (1538) **1 a :** in a clandestine manner **b** *archaic* **:** in a quiet or unobtrusive manner **2 :** with the target seen below the hand holding the bow **3 :** with an underhand motion ⟨bowl ~⟩ ⟨pitch ~⟩

[2]**underhand** *adj* (1545) **1 :** aimed so that the target is seen below the hand holding the bow ⟨~ shooting at long range⟩ **2 :** UNDERHANDED **3 :** done so as to evade notice **4 :** made with the hand brought forward and up from below the shoulder level

[1]**un·der·hand·ed** \\ˌən-dər-ˈhan-dəd\\ *adv* (1825) **:** UNDERHAND

[2]**underhanded** *adj* (1834) **:** marked by secrecy, chicanery, and deception **:** not honest and aboveboard **:** SLY ***syn*** see SECRET — **un·der·hand·ed·ly** *adv* — **un·der·hand·ed·ness** *n*

un·der·in·flat·ed \\ˌən-də-rin-ˈflāt-əd\\ *adj* (1928) **:** not sufficiently inflated ⟨~ tires⟩ — **un·der·in·fla·tion** \\-ˈflā-shən\\ *n*

un·der·in·sured \\-ˈshu̇(ə)rd\\ *adj* (1967) **:** not sufficiently insured

un·der·laid \\ˌən-dər-ˈlād\\ *adj* (12c) **1 :** laid or placed underneath **2 :** having something laid or lying underneath

[1]**un·der·lay** \\-ˈlā\\ *vt* **-laid** \\-ˈlād\\; **-lay·ing** (bef. 12c) **1 :** to cover, line, or traverse the bottom of **:** give support to on the underside or below **2 :** to raise or support by something laid under

[2]**un·der·lay** \\ˈən-dər-ˌlā\\ *n* (1683) **:** something that is or is designed to be laid under

un·der·lay·ment \\ˌən-dər-ˈlā-mənt\\ *n* (1949) **:** UNDERLAY

un·der·let \\ˌən-dər-ˈlet\\ *vt* **-let; -let·ting** (1677) **1 :** to let below the real value **2 :** SUBLET

un·der·lie \\-ˈlī\\ *vt* **-lay** \\-ˈlā\\; **-lain** \\-ˈlān\\; **-ly·ing** \\-ˈlī-iŋ\\ (bef. 12c) **1** *archaic* **:** to be subject or amenable to **2 :** to lie or be situated under **3 :** to be at the basis of **:** form the foundation of **:** SUPPORT ⟨ideas *underlying* the revolution⟩ **4 :** to exist as a claim or security superior and prior to (another)

[1]**un·der·line** \\ˈən-dər-ˌlīn, ˌən-dər-ˈ\\ *vt* (1721) **1 :** to mark (as a word) with a line underneath **2 :** to put emphasis on **:** STRESS

[2]**un·der·line** \\ˈən-dər-ˌlīn\\ *n* (1886) **1 :** the outline of an animal's underbody **2 :** a horizontal line placed underneath something

un·der·ling \\ˈən-dər-liŋ\\ *n* (12c) **:** one who is under the orders of another **:** SUBORDINATE, INFERIOR

un·der·lip \\ˌən-dər-ˈlip\\ *n* (1669) **:** the lower lip

un·der·ly·ing \\ˌən-dər-ˌlī-iŋ\\ *adj* (ca. 1611) **1 a :** lying beneath or below ⟨the ~ rock is shale⟩ **b :** BASIC, FUNDAMENTAL ⟨an investigation of the ~ issues⟩ **2 :** evident only on close inspection **:** IMPLICIT **3 :** anterior and prior in claim ⟨~ mortgage⟩

un·der·manned \\ˌən-dər-ˈmand\\ *adj* (ca. 1867) **:** inadequately staffed

un·der·mine \\-ˈmīn\\ *vt* (14c) **1 :** to excavate the earth beneath **:** form a mine under **:** SAP **2 :** to wash away supporting material from under **3 :** to subvert or weaken insidiously or secretly **4 :** to weaken or ruin by degrees ***syn*** see WEAKEN

un·der·most \\ˈən-dər-ˌmōst\\ *adj* (1555) **:** lowest in relative position — **undermost** *adv*

[1]**un·der·neath** \\ˌən-dər-ˈnēth\\ *prep* [ME *underneþe*, prep. & adv., fr. OE *underneothan*, fr. *under* + *neothan* below — more at BENEATH] (bef. 12c) **1 a :** directly beneath ⟨write the date ~ the address⟩ **b :** close under esp. so as to be hidden ⟨treachery lying ~ a mask of friendliness⟩ ⟨wore a swimsuit ~ his slacks⟩ **2 :** under subjection to

[2]**underneath** *adv* (bef. 12c) **1 :** under or below an object or a surface **:** BENEATH **2 :** on the lower side — **underneath** *adj*

un·der·nour·ished \\ˌən-dər-ˈnər-isht, -ˈnə-risht\\ *adj* (1928) **1 :** supplied with less than the minimum amount of the foods essential for sound health and growth **2 :** poorly supplied with vital elements or qualities ⟨~ independent libraries⟩ — **un·der·nour·ish·ment** \\-ˈnər-ish-mənt, -ˈnə-rish-\\ *n*

un·der·nu·tri·tion \\-n(y)u̇-ˈtrish-ən\\ *n* (1899) **:** deficient bodily nutrition due to inadequate food intake or faulty assimilation

un·der·pants \\ˈən-dər-ˌpan(t)s\\ *n pl* (1925) **:** short or long pants worn under an outer garment **:** DRAWERS

un·der·part \\-ˌpärt\\ *n* (1783) **1 :** a part lying on the lower side esp. of a bird or mammal **2 :** a subordinate or auxiliary part or role

un·der·pass \\-ˌpas\\ *n* (1903) **:** a crossing of two highways or of a highway and pedestrian path or railroad at different levels where clearance to traffic on the upper level is obtained by depressing the lower level; *also* **:** the lower level of such a crossing

un·der·pay \\ˌən-dər-ˈpā\\ *vt* **-paid** \\-ˈpād\\; **-pay·ing** (1846) **:** to pay less than what is normal or required ⟨~ taxes⟩ — **un·der·pay·ment** *n*

un·der·pin \\-ˈpin\\ *vt* (1533) **1 :** to form part of, strengthen, or replace the foundation of ⟨~ a structure⟩ ⟨~ a sagging building⟩ **2 :** SUPPORT, SUBSTANTIATE ⟨~ a thesis with evidence⟩

un·der·pin·ning \\ˈən-dər-ˌpin-iŋ\\ *n* (1538) **1 :** the material and construction (as a foundation) used for support of a structure **2 :** something that serves as a foundation **:** BASIS, SUPPORT — often used in pl. ⟨the philosophical ~s of educational methods⟩ **3 :** UNDERWEAR — usu. used in pl. **4 :** a person's legs — usu. used in pl.

un·der·play \\ˌən-dər-ˈplā\\ *vt* (ca. 1909) **1 :** to play a card lower than (a held high card) **2 :** to act or present (as a role or a scene) with restraint **:** play down ~ *vi* **:** to play a role with subdued force

un·der·plot \\ˈən-dər-ˌplät\\ *n* (ca. 1668) **:** SUBPLOT 1

un·der·pop·u·lat·ed \\ˌən-dər-ˈpäp-yə-ˌlāt-əd\\ *adj* (1884) **:** having a lower density of population than is normal or desirable

un·der·powered \\-ˈpau̇(-ə)rd\\ *adj* (1907) **1 :** driven by an engine of insufficient power **2 :** having or supplied with insufficient power

un·der·pre·pared \\-prə-ˈpa(ə)rd, -ˈpe(ə)rd\\ *adj* (1964) **:** inadequately prepared

un·der·price \\-ˈprīs\\ *vt* (1756) **1 :** to price below what is normal or below the real value **2 :** to undercut (a competitor) in prices

un·der·priv·i·leged \\-ˈpriv-(ə-)lijd\\ *adj* (1925) **1 :** deprived through social or economic condition of some of the fundamental rights of all members of a civilized society **2 :** of or relating to underprivileged people ⟨~ areas of the city⟩

un·der·pro·duc·tion \\-prə-ˈdək-shən\\ *n* (1887) **:** the production of less than enough to satisfy the demand or of less than the usual amount

un·der·proof \\ˌən-dər-ˈprüf\\ *adj* (ca. 1890) **:** containing less alcohol than proof spirit

un·der·pub·li·cized \\-ˈpəb-lə-ˌsīzd\\ *adj* (1966) **:** not sufficiently publicized

un·der·rate \\ˌən-də(r)-ˈrāt\\ *vt* (1650) **:** to rate too low **:** UNDERVALUE

un·der·re·act \\-rē-ˈakt\\ *vi* (1968) **:** to react with less than appropriate force or intensity

un·der·re·port \\-ri-ˈpō(ə)rt, -ˈpȯ(ə)rt\\ *vt* (1949) **:** to report (as income) to be less than is actually the case **:** UNDERSTATE

un·der·rep·re·sent·ed \\-ˌrep-ri-ˈzent-əd\\ *adj* (1884) **:** inadequately represented — **un·der·rep·re·sen·ta·tion** \\-ˌzen-ˈtā-shən, -zən-\\ *n*

[1]**un·der·run** \\-ˈrən\\ *vt* **-ran** \\-ˈran\\; **-run; -run·ning** (1594) **1 :** to pass or extend under **2 :** to pass along under in order to examine (a cable)

[2]**un·der·run** \\ˈən-də(r)-ˌrən\\ *n* (1928) **:** the amount by which something produced (as a cut of lumber) falls below an estimate

un·der·sat·u·rat·ed \\ˌən-dər-ˈsach-ə-ˌrāt-əd\\ *adj* (ca. 1828) **:** less than normally or adequately saturated

1un·der·score \ˈən-dər-ˌskō(ə)r, -ˌskȯ(ə)r\ *vt* (1771) **1** : to draw a line under : UNDERLINE **2** : EMPHASIZE, STRESS **3** : to provide (action on film) with accompanying music

2underscore *n* (1901) **1** : a line drawn under a word or line esp. for emphasis or to indicate intent to italicize **2** : music accompanying the action and dialogue of a film

1un·der·sea \ˌən-dər-ˌsē\ *adj* (1613) **1** : being or carried on under the sea or under the surface of the sea ⟨~ oil deposits⟩ ⟨~ fighting⟩ **2** : designed for use under the surface of the sea ⟨an ~ fleet⟩

2un·der·sea \ˌən-dər-ˈsē\ *or* **un·der·seas** \-ˈsēz\ *adv* (1684) : under the sea : beneath the surface of the sea ⟨photographs taken ~⟩

un·der·sec·re·tar·i·at \-ˌsek-rə-ˈter-ē-ət\ *n* (1949) : the office and staff of an under secretary : a subdivision of a ministry

under secretary *n* (ca. 1687) : a secretary immediately subordinate to a principal secretary ⟨*under secretary* of state⟩

un·der·sell \ˌən-dər-ˈsel\ *vt* **-sold** \-ˈsōld\; **-sell·ing** (1622) **1** : to sell articles cheaper than ⟨~ a competitor⟩ **2** : to sell cheaper than ⟨imported cars that ~ domestic ones⟩

un·der·served \-ˈsərvd\ *adj* (1710) : provided with inadequate service

un·der·sexed \-ˈsekst\ *adj* (1949) : deficient in sexual desire

un·der·shirt \ˈən-dər-ˌshərt\ *n* (ca. 1648) : a collarless undergarment with or without sleeves — **un·der·shirt·ed** *adj*

un·der·shoot \ˌən-dər-ˈshüt\ *vt* **-shot** \-ˈshät\; **-shoot·ing** (1661) **1** : to shoot short of or below (a target) **2** : to fall short of (a runway) in landing an airplane

un·der·shorts \ˈən-dər-ˌshȯ(ə)rts\ *n pl* (1949) : 3SHORT 4b

un·der·shot \ˌən-dər-ˌshät\ *adj* (1881) **1** : having the lower incisor teeth or lower jaw projecting beyond the upper when the mouth is closed **2** : moved by water passing beneath ⟨an ~ wheel⟩

un·der·shrub \ˈən-dər-ˌshrəb, *esp Southern* -ˌsrəb\ *n* (ca. 1598) : SUBSHRUB

un·der·side \ˈən-dər-ˌsīd, ˌən-dər-ˈ\ *n* (1680) **1** : the side or surface lying underneath **2** : the side usu. hidden from sight; *specif* : the worse side

un·der·signed \ˈən-dər-ˌsīnd\ *n, pl* **undersigned** (1643) : one who signs his name at the end of a document ⟨the ~ all agree⟩

un·der·sized \ˌən-dər-ˈsīzd\ *also* **un·der·size** \-ˈsīz\ *adj* (1706) : of a size less than is common, proper, normal, or average ⟨~ trout⟩

un·der·skirt \ˈən-dər-ˌskərt\ *n* (1861) : a skirt worn under an outer skirt; *esp* : PETTICOAT

un·der·slung \ˌən-dər-ˈsləŋ\ *adj* (1903) **1** *of a vehicle frame* : suspended below the axles **2** : having a low center of gravity

un·der·spin \-ˌspin\ *n* (1901) : BACKSPIN

un·der·staffed \-ˈstaft\ *adj* (1891) : UNDERMANNED

un·der·stand \ˌən-dər-ˈstand\ *vb* **-stood** \-ˈstu̇d\; **-stand·ing** [ME *understanden*, fr. OE *understandan*, fr. *under* + *standan* to stand] *vt* (bef. 12c) **1** **a** : to grasp the meaning of ⟨~ Russian⟩ **b** : to grasp the reasonableness of ⟨his behavior is hard to ~⟩ **c** : to have thorough or technical acquaintance with or expertness in the practice of ⟨~ finance⟩ **d** : to be thoroughly familiar with the character and propensities of ⟨~s children⟩ **2** : to accept as a fact or truth or regard as plausible without utter certainty ⟨we ~ that he is returning from abroad⟩ **3** : to interpret in one of a number of possible ways **4** : to supply in thought as though expressed ⟨"to be married" is commonly *understood* after the word *engaged*⟩ ~ *vi* **1** : to have understanding : have the power of comprehension **2** : to achieve a grasp of the nature, significance, or explanation of something **3** : to believe or infer something to be the case **4** : to show a sympathetic or tolerant attitude toward something — **un·der·stand·abil·i·ty** \-ˌstan-də-ˈbil-ət-ē\ *n* — **un·der·stand·able** \-ˈstan-də-bəl\ *adj* — **un·der·stand·ably** \-blē\ *adv*

syn UNDERSTAND, COMPREHEND, APPRECIATE mean to have a clear or complete idea of. UNDERSTAND may differ from COMPREHEND in implying a result whereas COMPREHEND stresses the mental process of arriving at a result ⟨*understood* the instructions without *comprehending* their purpose⟩ APPRECIATE implies a just estimation of a thing's value ⟨failed to *appreciate* the risks involved⟩

1un·der·stand·ing \ˌən-dər-ˈstan-diŋ\ *n* (bef. 12c) **1** : a mental grasp : COMPREHENSION **2** **a** : the power of comprehending; *esp* : the capacity to apprehend general relations of particulars **b** : the power to make experience intelligible by applying concepts and categories **3** **a** : friendly or harmonious relationship **b** : an agreement of opinion or feeling : adjustment of differences **c** : a mutual agreement not formally entered into but in some degree binding on each side **4** : EXPLANATION, INTERPRETATION **5** : SYMPATHY 3a

2understanding *adj* (13c) **1** *archaic* : KNOWING, INTELLIGENT **2** : endowed with understanding : TOLERANT, SYMPATHETIC — **un·der·stand·ing·ly** \-ˈstan-diŋ-lē\ *adv*

un·der·state \ˌən-dər-ˈstāt\ *vt* (1824) **1** : to represent as less than is the case **2** : to state or present with restraint esp. for greater effect — **un·der·state·ment** \-mənt\ *n*

un·der·stat·ed \-ˈstāt-əd\ *adj* (ca. 1909) : avoiding obvious emphasis or embellishment — **un·der·stat·ed·ly** *adv*

un·der·steer \ˈən-dər-ˌsti(ə)r\ *n* (1951) : the tendency of an automobile to turn less sharply than the driver intends — **un·der·steer** \ˌən-dər-ˈ\ *vi*

un·der·stood \ˌən-dər-ˈstu̇d\ *adj* (1605) **1** : fully apprehended **2** : agreed upon **3** : IMPLICIT

un·der·sto·ry \ˈən-dər-ˌstōr-ē, -ˌstȯr-\ *n* (1902) : the plants of a forest undergrowth; *broadly* : an underlying layer of low vegetation

un·der·strap·per \-ˌstrap-ər\ *n* [3*under* + *strapper* (one who harnesses horses)] (1704) : a petty agent or subordinate : UNDERLING

un·der·strength \ˌən-dər-ˈstreŋ(k)th\ *adj* (1925) : deficient in strength; *esp* : lacking sufficient or prescribed personnel

1un·der·study \ˈən-dər-ˌstəd-ē, ˌən-dər-ˈ\ *vi* (1874) : to study another actor's part in order to be his substitute in an emergency ~ *vt* : to prepare (as a part) as understudy; *also* : to prepare as understudy to (as an actor)

2un·der·study \ˈən-dər-ˌstəd-ē\ *n* (1882) : one who is prepared to act another's part or take over another's duties

un·der·sup·ply \ˌən-dər-sə-ˈplī\ *n* (1848) : an inadequate supply or amount

1un·der·sur·face \ˈən-dər-ˌsər-fəs\ *n* (1733) : UNDERSIDE

2un·der·sur·face \ˌən-dər-ˌsər-fəs\ *adj* (ca. 1934) : existing or moving below the surface

un·der·take \ˌən-dər-ˈtāk\ *vb* **-took** \-ˈtu̇k\; **-tak·en** \-ˈtā-kən\; **-tak·ing** *vt* (14c) **1** : to take in hand : enter upon : set about : ATTEMPT ⟨~ a task⟩ **2** : to put oneself under obligation to perform : CONTRACT, COVENANT **3** : GUARANTEE, PROMISE **4** : to accept as a charge ⟨the lawyer who *undertook* the case⟩ ~ *vi, archaic* : to give surety or assume responsibility

un·der·tak·er \ˌən-dər-ˈtā-kər, *2 is* ˈən-dər-ˌ\ *n* (1615) **1** : one that undertakes : one that takes the risk and management of business : ENTREPRENEUR **2** : one whose business is to prepare the dead for burial and to arrange and manage funerals **3** : an Englishman taking over forfeited lands in Ireland in the 16th and 17th centuries

un·der·tak·ing \ˈən-dər-ˌtā-kiŋ, ˌən-dər-ˈ; *1b is* ˈən-dər-ˌ *only*\ *n* (15c) **1** **a** : the act of one who undertakes or engages in a project or business **b** : the business of an undertaker **2** : something undertaken : ENTERPRISE **3** : PLEDGE, GUARANTEE

un·der·ten·ant \ˈən-dər-ˌten-ənt\ *n* (1546) : one who holds lands or tenements by a sublease

under–the–counter *adj* [fr. the hiding of illicit wares under the counter of stores where they are sold] (1949) : surreptitious and usu. irregular or illicit ⟨~ liquor sales⟩

under–the–table *adj* (1948) : covert and usu. unlawful ⟨~ payoffs⟩

un·der·thrust \ˌən-dər-ˈthrəst\ *vt* **-thrust; -thrust·ing** (1893) : to insert (a faulted rock mass) into position under a passive rock mass

un·der·tone \ˈən-dər-ˌtōn\ *n* (1806) **1** : a low or subdued utterance or accompanying sound **2** : a quality (as of emotion) underlying the surface of an utterance or action **3** : a subdued color; *specif* : a color seen through and modifying another color

un·der·tow \-ˌtō\ *n* (ca. 1817) **1** : the current beneath the surface that sets seaward or along the beach when waves are breaking upon the shore **2** : an underlying current, force, or tendency that is in opposition to what is apparent

un·der·trick \-ˌtrik\ *n* (1903) : one of the tricks by which a declarer in bridge falls short of making his contract

un·der·used \ˌən-dər-ˈyüzd\ *adj* (1906) : not fully used

un·der·uti·lize \ˌən-dər-ˈyüt-ᵊl-ˌīz\ *vt* (1951) : to utilize less than fully or below the potential use — **un·der·uti·li·za·tion** \ˈən-dər-ˌyüt-ᵊl-ə-ˈzā-shən\ *n*

un·der·val·u·a·tion \ˌən-dər-ˌval-yə-ˈwā-shən\ *n* (1653) **1** : the act of undervaluing **2** : a value below the real worth

un·der·val·ue \-ˈval-(ˌ)yü, -yə(-w)\ *vt* (1599) **1** : to value, rate, or estimate below the real worth ⟨~ stock⟩ **2** : to treat as of little value : DEPRECIATE 2 ⟨was *undervalued* as a poet⟩

un·der·wa·ter \ˌən-dər-ˌwȯt-ər, -ˌwät-\ *adj* (1627) **1** : lying, growing, worn, or operating below the surface of the water **2** : being below the waterline of a ship — **un·der·wa·ter** \-ˈwȯt-, -ˈwät-\ *adv*

un·der·way \ˌən-dər-ˌwā\ *adj* (1743) : occurring, performed, or used while traveling or in motion ⟨~ refueling⟩

under way \-ˈwā\ *adv* [prob. fr. D *onderweg*, fr. MD *onderwegen*, lit., under or among the ways] (1751) **1** : in motion : not at anchor or aground **2** : into motion from a standstill **3** : in progress : AFOOT ⟨preparations were *under way*⟩

un·der·wear \ˈən-dər-ˌwa(ə)r, -ˌwe(ə)r\ *n* (ca. 1879) : clothing or an article of clothing worn next to the skin and under other clothing

under weigh *adv* [by folk etymology] (1777) : UNDER WAY

1un·der·weight \ˌən-dər-ˈwāt\ *n* (1596) : weight below normal, average, or requisite weight

2underweight *adj* (1890) : weighing less than the normal or requisite amount

un·der·whelm \-ˈhwelm, -ˈwelm\ *vt* [*under* + *-whelm* (as in *overwhelm*)] (1949) : to fail to impress or stimulate

1un·der·wing \ˈən-dər-ˌwiŋ\ *n* (1535) **1** : one of the posterior wings of an insect **2** : any of various noctuid moths (esp. genus *Catocala*) that have the hind wings banded with contrasting colors (as red and black) — called also *underwing moth*

2underwing *adj* (1896) : placed or growing underneath the wing ⟨~ rockets⟩

un·der·wood \ˈən-dər-ˌwu̇d\ *n* (14c) : UNDERGROWTH, UNDERBRUSH

un·der·wool \-ˌwu̇l\ *n* (1947) : short woolly underfur

un·der·world \-ˌwərld\ *n* (1608) **1** : the place of departed souls : HADES **2** *archaic* : EARTH **3** : the side of the earth opposite to one **4** : a social sphere below the level of ordinary life; *esp* : the world of organized crime

un·der·write \ˈən-də(r)-ˌrīt, ˌən-də(r)-ˈ\ *vb* **-wrote** \-ˌrōt, -ˈrōt\; **-writ·ten** \-ˌrit-ᵊn, -ˈrit-ᵊn\; **-writ·ing** \-ˌrīt-iŋ, -ˈrīt-\ *vt* (15c) **1** : to write under or at the end of something else **2** : to set one's name to (an insurance policy) for the purpose of thereby becoming answerable for a designated loss or damage on consideration of receiving a premium percent : insure on life or property; *also* : to assume liability for (a sum or risk) as an insurer **3** : to subscribe to : agree to **4** **a** : to agree to purchase (a security issue) usu. on a fixed date at a fixed price with a view to public distribution **b** : to guarantee financial support of ~ *vi* : to work as an underwriter

un·der·writ·er \ˈən-də(r)-ˌrīt-ər\ *n* (1622) **1** : one that underwrites : GUARANTOR **2** **a** : one that underwrites a policy of insurance : INSURER **b** : one who selects risks to be solicited or rates the acceptability of risks solicited **3** : one that underwrites a security issue

un·de·scend·ed \ˌən-di-ˈsen-dəd\ *adj* (1701) : retained within the inguinal region rather than descending into the scrotum ⟨an ~ testis⟩

un·de·sign·ing \ˌən-di-ˈzī-niŋ\ *adj* (1697) : having no ulterior or fraudulent purpose : SINCERE

1un·de·sir·able \-ˈzī-rə-bəl\ *adj* (1667) : not desirable : UNWANTED — **un·de·sir·abil·i·ty** \-ˌzī-rə-ˈbil-ət-ē\ *n* — **un·de·sir·able·ness** \-ˈzī-rə-bəl-nəs\ *n* — **un·de·sir·ably** \-blē\ *adv*

2undesirable *n* (1883) : one that is undesirable

un·de·vi·at·ing \ˌən-ˈdē-vē-ˌāt-iŋ, ˈən-\ *adj* (1732) : keeping a true course : UNSWERVING ⟨served their country with ~ loyalty and devotion⟩ — **un·de·vi·at·ing·ly** \-iŋ-lē\ *adv*

un·dies \'ən-dēz\ *n pl* [by shortening & alter.] (1900) : UNDERWEAR; *esp* : women's underwear
un·dine \,ən-'dēn, 'ən-,\ *n* [NL *undina*, fr. L *unda* wave — more at WATER] (1657) : an elemental being in the theory of Paracelsus inhabiting water : WATER NYMPH
un·dip·lo·mat·ic \,ən-,dip-lə-'mat-ik, 'ən-\ *adj* (ca. 1828) : not diplomatic : TACTLESS — **un·dip·lo·mat·i·cal·ly** \-i-k(ə-)lē\ *adv*
un·di·rect·ed \,ən-də-'rek-təd, -dī-\ *adj* (1596) : not directed : not planned or guided ⟨~ efforts⟩
un·dis·guised \,ən-dis-'gīzd\ *adj* (1500) : not disguised or concealed : FRANK, OPEN — **un·dis·guis·ed·ly** \-'gī-zəd-lē\ *adv*
un·dis·so·ci·at·ed \,ən-dis-'ō-s(h)ē-,āt-əd\ *adj* (ca. 1909) : not electrolytically dissociated
un·do \,ən-'dü, 'ən-\ *vb* **-did** \-'did\; **-done** \-'dən\; **-do·ing** \-'dü-iŋ\ *vt* (bef. 12c) **1** : to open or loose by releasing a fastening **2** : to make of no effect or as if not done : make null : REVERSE **3** **a** : to ruin the worldly means, reputation, or hopes of **b** : to disturb the composure of : UPSET **c** : SEDUCE 3 ~ *vi* : to come open or apart — **un·do·er** \-'dü-ər\ *n*
un·dock \-'däk\ *vi* (1924) : to move away from a dock (as at sailing time) ~ *vt* : UNCOUPLE ⟨~ the lunar module from the command module⟩
un·dog·mat·ic \,ən-dȯg-'mat-ik, -däg-\ *adj* (1857) : not dogmatic : not committed to dogma — **un·dog·mat·i·cal·ly** \-i-k(ə-)lē\ *adv*
un·do·ing \-'dü-iŋ\ *n* (14c) **1** : an act of loosening : UNFASTENING **2** : RUIN; *also* : a cause of ruin ⟨greed was to prove his ~⟩ **3** : ANNULMENT, REVERSAL
un·done \-'dən\ *adj* (14c) : not done : not performed or finished
un·dou·ble \,ən-'dəb-əl, 'ən-\ *vb* (ca. 1611) : UNFOLD, UNCLENCH
un·dou·bled \-'dəb-əld\ *adj* (1598) : not doubled
un·doubt·ed \-'dau̇t-əd\ *adj* (15c) : not doubted : GENUINE, UNDISPUTED — **un·doubt·ed·ly** *adv*
un·dra·mat·ic \,ən-drə-'mat-ik\ *adj* (1754) : lacking dramatic force or quality : UNSPECTACULAR — **un·dra·mat·i·cal·ly** \-i-k(ə-)lē\ *adv*
un·drape \,ən-'drāp, 'ən-\ *vt* (1869) : to strip of drapery : UNVEIL
un·draw \-'drȯ\ *vt* **-drew** \-'drü\; **-drawn** \-'drȯn\; **-draw·ing** (1677) : to draw aside (as a curtain) : OPEN
un·dreamed \-'drem(p)t, -'drēmd\ *also* **undreamt** \-'drem(p)t\ *adj* (1611) : not dreamed : not thought of : UNIMAGINED ⟨technical advances ~ of a few years ago⟩
[1]**un·dress** \-'dres\ *vt* (1615) **1** : to remove the clothes or covering of : DIVEST, STRIP **2** : EXPOSE, REVEAL ~ *vi* : to take off one's clothes : DISROBE
[2]**undress** *n* (1685) **1** : informal dress: as **a** : a loose robe or dressing gown **b** : ordinary dress — compare FULL DRESS **2** : the state of being undressed
un·dressed \,ən-'drest, 'ən-\ *adj* (1605) : not dressed: as **a** : partially, improperly, or informally clothed **b** : not fully processed or finished ⟨~ hides⟩ **c** : not cared for or tended ⟨an ~ wound⟩ ⟨~ fields⟩
un·drunk \-'drəŋk\ *adj* (1637) : not swallowed
un·due \-'d(y)ü\ *adj* (14c) **1** : not due : not yet payable **2** : exceeding or violating propriety or fitness
un·du·lant \'ən-jə-lənt, 'ən-d(y)ə-\ *adj* (ca. 1830) : rising and falling in waves : ROLLING
undulant fever *n* (1897) : a persistent human brucellosis marked by remittent fever, pain and swelling in the joints, and great weakness and contracted by contact with infected domestic animals or consumption of their products
[1]**un·du·late** \'ən-jə-lət, 'ən-d(y)ə-, -,lāt\ *or* **un·du·lat·ed** \-,lāt-əd\ *adj* [L *undulatus*, fr. (assumed) L *undula*, dim. of L *unda* wave — more at WATER] (1658) : having a wavy surface, edge, or markings ⟨the ~ margin of a leaf⟩
[2]**un·du·late** \-,lāt\ *vb* **-lat·ed; -lat·ing** [LL *undula* small wave, fr. (assumed) L] *vi* (1664) **1** : to form or move in waves : FLUCTUATE **2** : to rise and fall in volume, pitch, or cadence **3** : to present a wavy appearance ~ *vt* : to cause to move in a wavy, sinuous, or flowing manner ***syn*** see SWING
un·du·la·tion \,ən-jə-'lā-shən, ,ən-d(y)ə-\ *n* (1646) **1** **a** : a rising and falling in waves **b** : a wavelike motion to and fro in a fluid or elastic medium propagated continuously among its particles but with little or no permanent translation of the particles in the direction of the propagation : VIBRATION **2** : the pulsation caused by the vibrating together of two tones not quite in unison **3** : a wavy appearance, outline, or form : WAVINESS
un·du·la·to·ry \'ən-jə-lə-,tōr-ē, 'ən-d(y)ə-, -,tȯr-\ *adj* (1728) : of or relating to undulation : moving in or resembling waves : UNDULATING
undulatory theory *n* (1802) : a theory in physics: light is transmitted from luminous bodies to the eye and other objects by an undulatory movement — called also *wave theory*
un·du·ly \,ən-'d(y)ü-lē, 'ən-\ *adv* (1779) : in an undue manner : EXCESSIVELY
un·du·ti·ful \-'d(y)üt-i-fəl\ *adj* (1593) : not dutiful — **un·du·ti·ful·ly** \-fə-lē\ *adv* — **un·du·ti·ful·ness** *n*
un·dy·ing \-'dī-iŋ\ *adj* (14c) : not dying : IMMORTAL, PERPETUAL
un·earned \-'ərnd\ *adj* (1667) **1** : not gained by labor, service, or skill ⟨~ income⟩ **2** : scored as a result of an error by the opposing team ⟨~ run⟩
unearned increment *n* (1871) : an increase in the value of property (as land) that is due to no labor or expenditure of the owner but to natural causes (as the increase of population) that create an increased demand for it
un·earth \,ən-'ərth, 'ən-\ *vt* (15c) **1** : to dig up out of the earth : EXHUME, DISINTER ⟨~ a hidden treasure⟩ **2** : to make known or public : bring to light ⟨~ a plot⟩ ***syn*** see DISCOVER
un·earth·ly \-lē\ *adj* (1802) : not earthly: as **a** : not terrestrial ⟨~ radio sources⟩ **b** : PRETERNATURAL, SUPERNATURAL ⟨an ~ light⟩ **c** : WEIRD, EERIE ⟨~ howls⟩ **d** : not mundane : IDEAL ⟨~ love⟩ **e** : ABSURD 1 ⟨getting up at an ~ hour⟩ — **un·earth·li·ness** *n*
un·ease \,ən-'ēz, 'ən-\ *n* (14c) : mental or spiritual discomfort: as **a** : vague dissatisfaction : MISGIVING **b** : ANXIETY, DISQUIET **c** : lack of ease (as in social relations) : EMBARRASSMENT
un·eas·i·ly \-'ēz-ə-lē\ *adv* (14c) : in an uneasy manner
[1]**un·easy** \-'ē-zē\ *adj* (13c) **1** : causing physical or mental discomfort ⟨~ news of captures and killings —Marjory S. Douglas⟩ **2** : not easy : DIFFICULT **3** : marked by lack of ease : AWKWARD, EMBARRASSED ⟨gave an ~ laugh⟩ **4** : APPREHENSIVE, WORRIED **5** : RESTLESS, UNQUIET **6** : PRECARIOUS, UNSTABLE ⟨an ~ truce⟩ — **un·eas·i·ness** *n*
[2]**uneasy** *adv* (1596) : UNEASILY
un·eco·nom·ic \,ən-,ek-ə-'näm-ik, -,ē-kə-\ *also* **un·eco·nom·i·cal** \-i-kəl\ *adj* (1894) : not economically practicable : COSTLY, WASTEFUL
un·ed·it·ed \,ən-'ed-ət-əd, 'ən-\ *adj* (1829) : not edited: as **a** : left unrevised **b** : not yet edited ⟨~ books⟩ ⟨~ films⟩
un·emo·tion·al \,ən-i-'mō-shnəl, -shən-ᵊl\ *adj* (1876) : not emotional: as **a** : not easily aroused or excited : COLD **b** : involving a minimum of emotion : INTELLECTUAL — **un·emo·tion·al·ly** \-ē\ *adv*
un·em·ploy·able \,ən-im-'plȯi-ə-bəl\ *adj* (1887) : not acceptable for employment — **un·em·ploy·abil·i·ty** \-,plȯi-ə-'bil-ət-ē\ *n* — **unemployable** *n*
un·em·ployed \-'plȯid\ *adj* (1600) : not employed: **a** : not being used **b** : not engaged in a gainful occupation **c** : not invested — **unemployed** *n*
un·em·ploy·ment \-'plȯi-mənt\ *n* (1888) **1** : the state of being unemployed : involuntary idleness of workers; *also* : the rate of such unemployment **2** : UNEMPLOYMENT BENEFIT
unemployment benefit *n* (1928) : a sum of money paid at regular intervals (as by a government agency) to an unemployed worker esp. who has been laid off — called also *unemployment compensation*
unemployment insurance *n* (1923) : social insurance against involuntary unemployment that provides unemployment benefits for a limited period to unemployed workers
un·en·cum·bered \,ən-in-'kəm-bərd\ *adj* (1722) : free of encumbrance
un·end·ing \,ən-'en-diŋ, 'ən-\ *adj* (1661) : never ending : ENDLESS — **un·end·ing·ly** \-diŋ-lē\ *adv*
un–En·glish \,ən-'iŋ-glish, 'ən- *also* -'iŋ-lish\ *adj* (1633) **1** : not characteristically English **2** : not agreeing with standard or generally accepted usage of the English language
[1]**un·equal** \,ən-'ē-kwəl, 'ən-\ *adj* (1565) **1** **a** : not of the same measurement, quantity, or number as another **b** : not like or not the same as another in degree, worth, or status **2** : not uniform : VARIABLE, UNEVEN **3** **a** : badly balanced or matched ⟨an ~ contest⟩ **b** : contracted between unequals ⟨~ marriages⟩ **c** *archaic* : not equable **4** *archaic* : not equitable : UNJUST **5** : INADEQUATE, INSUFFICIENT ⟨~ to the task⟩ — **un·equal·ly** \-kwə-lē\ *adv*
[2]**unequal** *n* (1600) : one that is not equal to another
[3]**unequal** *adv, archaic* (1602) : in an unequal manner ⟨~ match'd —Shak.⟩
un·equaled *or* **un·equalled** \-kwəld\ *adj* (1600) : not equaled : UNPARALLELED
un·equiv·o·ca·bly \,ən-i-'kwiv-ə-kə-blē\ *adv* [by alter.] *nonstand* (1794) : UNEQUIVOCALLY
un·equiv·o·cal \,ən-i-'kwiv-ə-kəl\ *adj* (ca. 1755) : leaving no doubt : CLEAR, UNAMBIGUOUS
un·equiv·o·cal·ly \-kə-lē, -klē\ *adv* (1794) : in an unequivocal manner
un·err·ing \,ən-'e(ə)r-iŋ, ,ən-'ər-, 'ən-\ *adj* (1621) : committing no error : FAULTLESS, UNFAILING — **un·err·ing·ly** \-iŋ-lē\ *adv*
un·es·sen·tial \,ən-ə-'sen-chəl\ *adj* (1656) **1** : not essential : DISPENSABLE, UNIMPORTANT **2** *archaic* : void of essence : INSUBSTANTIAL
un–Eu·ro·pe·an \,ən-,yu̇r-ə-'pē-ən\ *adj* (1849) : not characteristically European
un·even \,ən-'ē-vən, 'ən-\ *adj* (bef. 12c) **1** **a** *archaic* : UNEQUAL 1a **b** : ODD 3a **2** **a** : not even : not level or smooth : RUGGED, RAGGED ⟨large ~ teeth⟩ ⟨~ handwriting⟩ **b** : varying from the straight or parallel **c** : not uniform : IRREGULAR ⟨~ combustion⟩ **d** : varying in quality ⟨an ~ performance⟩ **3** : UNEQUAL 3a ⟨an ~ confrontation⟩ ***syn*** see ROUGH — **un·even·ly** *adv*
un·even·ness \,ən-'ē-vən-nəs, 'ən-\ *n* (14c) : the quality or state of being uneven
un·event·ful \,ən-i-'vent-fəl\ *adj* (1800) : marked by no noteworthy or untoward incidents : PLACID — **un·event·ful·ly** \-fə-lē\ *adv*
un·ex·am·pled \,ən-ig-'zam-pəld\ *adj* (1610) : having no example or parallel : UNPRECEDENTED
un·ex·cep·tion·able \,ən-ik-'sep-sh(ə-)nə-bəl\ *adj* [*un-* + obs. *exception* (to take exception, object)] (1664) : not open to objection or criticism : beyond reproach : UNIMPEACHABLE — **un·ex·cep·tion·able·ness** *n* — **un·ex·cep·tion·ably** \-blē\ *adv*
un·ex·cep·tion·al \-shnəl, -shən-ᵊl\ *adj* (ca. 1891) : not out of the ordinary : COMMONPLACE
un·ex·pect·ed \,ən-ik-'spek-təd\ *adj* (1586) : not expected : UNFORESEEN — **un·ex·pect·ed·ly** *adv* — **un·ex·pect·ed·ness** *n*
un·ex·ploit·ed \,ən-ik-'splȯit-əd\ *adj* (1888) : not exploited or developed : not taken advantage of
un·ex·pres·sive \,ən-ik-'spres-iv\ *adj* (1755) **1** : not expressive : failing to convey the feeling or meaning intended **2** *obs* : INEFFABLE
un·fad·ing \,ən-'fād-iŋ, 'ən-\ *adj* (1652) **1** : not losing color or freshness **2** : not losing value or effectiveness — **un·fad·ing·ly** \-iŋ-lē\ *adv*
un·fail·ing \,ən-'fā-liŋ, 'ən-\ *adj* (15c) : not failing or liable to fail: **a** : CONSTANT, UNFLAGGING ⟨~ courtesy⟩ **b** : EVERLASTING, INEXHAUSTIBLE ⟨a subject of ~ interest⟩ **c** : INFALLIBLE, SURE ⟨an ~ test⟩ — **un·fail·ing·ly** \-liŋ-lē\ *adv*
un·fair \,ən-'fa(ə)r, 'ən-, -'fe(ə)r\ *adj* (1700) **1** : marked by injustice, partiality, or deception : UNJUST **2** : not equitable in business dealings — **un·fair·ness** *n*
un·fair·ly *adv* (1713) : in an unfair manner
un·faith \,ən-'fāth, 'ən-', 'ən-,\ *n* (15c) : absence of faith : DISBELIEF
un·faith·ful \,ən-'fāth-fəl, 'ən-\ *adj* (15c) : not faithful: **a** : not adhering to vows, allegiance, or duty : DISLOYAL **b** : not faithful to marriage vows **c** : INACCURATE, UNTRUSTWORTHY — **un·faith·ful·ly** \-fə-lē\ *adv* — **un·faith·ful·ness** *n*
un·fal·si·fi·able \,ən-,fȯl-sə-'fī-ə-bəl\ *adj* (ca. 1934) : not capable of being proved false ⟨~ hypotheses⟩
un·fal·ter·ing \,ən-'fȯl-t(ə-)riŋ\ *adj* (1727) : not wavering or weakening : FIRM — **un·fal·ter·ing·ly** \-t(ə-)riŋ-lē\ *adv*
un·fa·mil·iar \,ən-fə-'mil-yər\ *adj* (1594) : not familiar: **a** : not well-known : STRANGE ⟨an ~ place⟩ **b** : not well acquainted ⟨~ with the subject⟩ — **un·fa·mil·iar·i·ty** \-,mil-'yar-ət-ē, -,mil-ē-'(y)ar-\ *n* — **un·fa·mil·iar·ly** \-'mil-yər-lē\ *adv*

un·fash·ion·able \-'fash-(ə-)nə-bəl\ *adj* (1648) **1 :** not in keeping with the current fashion ⟨~ clothes⟩ **2 :** not favored socially ⟨~ neighborhoods⟩ — **un·fash·ion·ably** \-blē\ *adv*

un·fas·ten \-'fas-ᵊn\ *vt* (15c) **:** to make loose: as **a :** UNPIN, UNBUCKLE **b :** UNDO ⟨~ a button⟩ **c :** DETACH ⟨~ a boat from its moorings⟩

un·fa·thered \-'fäth-ərd\ *adj* (1597) **1 :** having no father **:** ILLEGITIMATE, BASTARD **2 :** having no known origin ⟨~ slanders⟩

un·fath·om·able \-'fath-ə-mə-bəl\ *adj* (1676) **:** not capable of being fathomed: **a :** impossible to comprehend **b :** IMMEASURABLE

un·fa·vor·able \,ən-'fāv-(ə-)rə-bəl, 'ən-, -'fā-vər-bəl\ *adj* (1548) **1 a :** OPPOSED, CONTRARY **b :** expressing disapproval **:** NEGATIVE ⟨~ reviews⟩ **2 :** not propitious **:** DISADVANTAGEOUS **3 :** not pleasing — **un·fa·vor·able·ness** *n* — **un·fa·vor·ably** \-blē\ *adv*

un·fa·vor·ite \-'fāv-(ə-)rət\ *adj* (1953) **:** not being a favorite; *esp* **:** being regarded with special disfavor or dislike

un·feel·ing \-'fē-liŋ\ *adj* (bef. 12c) **1 :** devoid of feeling **:** INSENSATE ⟨an ~ corpse⟩ **2 :** devoid of kindness or sympathy **:** HARDHEARTED, CRUEL ⟨an ~ wretch⟩ — **un·feel·ing·ly** \-liŋ-lē\ *adv* — **un·feel·ing·ness** *n*

un·feigned \-'fānd\ *adj* (14c) **:** not feigned or hypocritical **:** GENUINE *syn* see SINCERE — **un·feigned·ly** \-'fā-nəd-lē, -'fān-dlē\ *adv*

un·fet·ter \-'fet-ər\ *vt* (14c) **1 :** to free from fetters ⟨~ a prisoner⟩ **2 :** EMANCIPATE, LIBERATE ⟨~ the mind from prejudice⟩

un·fet·tered \-ərd\ *adj* (1601) **:** FREE, UNRESTRAINED

un·fil·ial \,ən-'fil-ē-əl, 'ən-, -'fil-yəl\ *adj* (1611) **:** not observing the obligations of a child to a parent **:** UNDUTIFUL — **un·fil·ial·ly** \-ē\ *adv*

un·find·able \,ən-'fīn-də-bəl, 'ən-\ *adj* (1791) **:** not capable of being found

un·fin·ished \-'fin-isht\ *adj* (1539) **:** not finished: **a :** not brought to an end or to the desired final state **b :** being in a rough state **:** UNPOLISHED **c :** subjected to no other processes (as bleaching or dyeing) after coming from the loom

¹un·fit \-'fit\ *adj* (1545) **:** not fit: **a :** not adapted to a purpose **:** UNSUITABLE **b :** not qualified **:** INCAPABLE, INCOMPETENT **c :** physically or mentally unsound — **un·fit·ly** *adv* — **un·fit·ness** *n*

²unfit *vt* (ca. 1611) **:** to make unfit **:** DISABLE, DISQUALIFY

un·fit·ted \,ən-'fit-əd, 'ən-\ *adj* (1592) **:** not adapted **:** UNQUALIFIED

un·fit·ting \-'fit-iŋ\ *adj* (1590) **:** not fitting **:** UNSUITABLE

un·fix \-'fiks\ *vt* (1597) **1 :** to loosen from a fastening **:** DETACH, DISENGAGE **2 :** to make unstable **:** UNSETTLE

un·flag·ging \-'flag-iŋ\ *adj* (1715) **:** not flagging **:** TIRELESS — **un·flag·ging·ly** \-iŋ-lē\ *adv*

un·flap·pa·ble \-'flap-ə-bəl\ *adj* [¹*un-* + *flap* (state of excitement) + *-able*] (1954) **:** marked by assurance and self-control — **un·flap·pa·bil·i·ty** \-,flap-ə-'bil-ət-ē\ *n* — **un·flap·pa·bly** \-'flap-ə-blē\ *adv*

un·flat·ter·ing \-'flat-ə-riŋ\ *adj* (1581) **:** not flattering; *esp* **:** UNFAVORABLE — **un·flat·ter·ing·ly** \-riŋ-lē\ *adv*

un·fledged \,ən-'flejd, 'ən-\ *adj* (1611) **1 :** not feathered **:** not ready for flight **2 :** not fully developed **:** IMMATURE ⟨an ~ writer⟩

un·flinch·ing \-'flin-chiŋ\ *adj* (1728) **:** not flinching or shrinking **:** STEADFAST, UNCOMPROMISING — **un·flinch·ing·ly** \-chiŋ-lē\ *adv*

un·fo·cused *also* **un·fo·cussed** \-'fō-kəst\ *adj* (ca. 1890) **1 :** not adjusted to a focus **2 :** not concentrated on one point or objective ⟨~ rage⟩

un·fold \-'fōld\ *vt* (bef. 12c) **1 a :** to open the folds of **:** spread or straighten out **:** EXPAND ⟨~*ed* the map⟩ **b :** to remove (as a package) from the folds **:** UNWRAP **2 :** to open to the view **:** REVEAL; *esp* **:** to make clear by gradual disclosure and often by recital ~ *vi* **1 a :** to open from a folded state **:** open out **:** EXPAND **b :** BLOSSOM **2 :** DEVELOP, EVOLVE ⟨as the story ~*s*⟩ **3 :** to open out gradually to the view or understanding **:** become known ⟨a panorama ~*s* before their eyes⟩ — **un·fold·ment** \-'fōl(d)-mənt\ *n*

un·fold·ed *adj* (1683) **:** not folded

un·for·get·ta·ble \,ən-fər-'get-ə-bəl\ *adj* (1806) **:** incapable of being forgotten **:** MEMORABLE — **un·for·get·ta·bly** \-'get-ə-blē\ *adv*

un·for·giv·ing \,ən-fər-'giv-iŋ\ *adj* (1713) **:** unwilling or unable to forgive — **un·for·giv·ing·ness** *n*

un·formed \-'fō(ə)rmd\ *adj* (14c) **:** not arranged in regular shape, order, or relations; *esp* **:** IMMATURE, UNDEVELOPED

¹un·for·tu·nate \-'fórch-(ə-)nət\ *adj* (1530) **1 a :** not favored by fortune **:** UNSUCCESSFUL, UNLUCKY ⟨an ~ young man⟩ **b :** marked or accompanied by or resulting in misfortune ⟨an ~ decision⟩ **2 a :** INFELICITOUS, UNSUITABLE ⟨an ~ choice of words⟩ **b :** DEPLORABLE, REGRETTABLE ⟨an ~ lack of taste⟩ — **un·for·tu·nate·ly** *adv*

²unfortunate *n* (1683) **:** an unfortunate person; *specif* **:** a social outcast

un·found·ed \,ən-'faun-dəd, 'ən-\ *adj* (ca. 1648) **:** lacking a sound basis **:** GROUNDLESS, UNWARRANTED

un·freeze \-'frēz\ *vt* **-froze** \-'frōz\; **-fro·zen** \-'frōz-ᵊn\; **-freez·ing** (1584) **1 :** to cause to thaw **2 :** to remove from a freeze

un·fre·quent·ed \,ən-frē-'kwent-əd; ,ən-'frē-kwənt-, 'ən-\ *adj* (1588) **:** not often visited or traveled over

un·friend·ed \,ən-'fren-dəd, 'ən-\ *adj* (1513) **:** having no friends **:** not befriended

un·friend·li·ness \-'fren-(d)lē-nəs\ *n* (1684) **:** the quality or state of being unfriendly **:** HOSTILITY

un·friend·ly \-'fren-(d)lē\ *adj* (15c) **:** not friendly: as **a :** HOSTILE, UNSYMPATHETIC **b :** INHOSPITABLE, UNFAVORABLE

un·frock \-'fräk\ *vt* (1644) **1 :** to deprive (as a priest) of the right to exercise the functions of office **2 :** to remove from a position of honor or privilege

un·froz·en \-'frōz-ᵊn\ *adj* (1596) **:** not frozen

un·fruit·ful \-'früt-fəl\ *adj* (14c) **:** not fruitful: as **a :** not producing offspring **:** BARREN **b :** yielding no valuable result ⟨an ~ conference⟩ — **un·fruit·ful·ly** \-fə-lē\ *adv* — **un·fruit·ful·ness** *n*

un·fund·ed \-'fən-dəd\ *adj* (1775) **1 :** not funded **:** FLOATING ⟨an ~ debt⟩ **2 :** not provided with funds ⟨~ schools⟩

un·furl \-'fər(-ə)l\ *vt* (1641) **:** to release from a furled state ~ *vi* **:** to open out from or as if from a furled state **:** UNFOLD

un·fussy \-'fəs-ē\ *adj* (1825) **:** not fussy: as **a :** not particular **:** UNCONCERNED **b :** not cluttered with pretentious or nonessential matters **:** UNCOMPLICATED — **un·fuss·i·ly** \-'fəs-ə-lē\ *adv*

un·gain·ly \-'gān-lē\ *adj* (1611) **1 a :** lacking in smoothness or dexterity **:** CLUMSY **b :** hard to handle **:** UNWIELDY **2 :** having an awkward appearance **:** UGLY — **un·gain·li·ness** *n*

un·gen·er·os·i·ty \,ən-,jen-ə-'räs-ət-ē, -'räs-tē\ *n* (1757) **:** lack of generosity

un·gen·er·ous \,ən-'jen-(ə-)rəs, 'ən-\ *adj* (1641) **:** not generous: **a :** PETTY, MEAN **b :** deficient in liberality **:** STINGY — **un·gen·er·ous·ly** *adv*

un·gird \-'gərd\ *vt* (bef. 12c) **:** to divest of a restraining band or girdle **:** UNBIND

un·girt \-'gərt\ *adj* (13c) **1 :** having the belt or girdle off or loose **2 :** lacking in discipline or compactness **:** LOOSE, SLACK

un·glue \-'glü\ *vt* (ca. 1548) **:** to separate by or as if by dissolving an adhesive

un·glued \-'glüd\ *adj* (1962) **:** UPSET, DISORDERED

un·god·li·ness \,ən-'gäd-lē-nəs, 'ən- *also* -'gȯd-\ *n* (1526) **:** the quality or state of being ungodly

un·god·ly \-lē\ *adj* (1526) **1 a :** denying God or disobedient to him **:** IMPIOUS, IRRELIGIOUS **b :** contrary to moral law **:** SINFUL, WICKED **2 :** OUTRAGEOUS ⟨gets up at an ~ hour⟩

un·got·ten \-'gät-ᵊn\ *or* **un·got** \-'gät\ *adj* (15c) **1** *obs* **:** not begotten **2 :** not obtained

un·gov·ern·able \-'gəv-ər-nə-bəl\ *adj* (1673) **:** not capable of being governed, guided, or restrained *syn* see UNRULY

un·gra·cious \-'grā-shəs\ *adj* (13c) **1** *archaic* **:** WICKED **2 :** not courteous **:** RUDE **3 :** not pleasing **:** DISAGREEABLE — **un·gra·cious·ly** *adv* — **un·gra·cious·ness** *n*

un·gram·mat·i·cal \,ən-grə-'mat-i-kəl\ *adj* (1654) **:** not following rules of grammar — **un·gram·mat·i·cal·i·ty** \-,mat-ə-'kal-ət-ē\ *n*

un·grate·ful \,ən-'grāt-fəl, 'ən-\ *adj* (1533) **1 :** showing no gratitude **:** making a poor return **2 :** DISAGREEABLE; *also* **:** THANKLESS — **un·grate·ful·ly** \-fə-lē\ *adv* — **un·grate·ful·ness** *n*

un·grudg·ing \-'grəj-iŋ\ *adj* (1768) **:** being without envy or reluctance

un·gual \'əŋ-gwəl, 'ən-\ *adj* [L *unguis* nail, claw, hoof — more at NAIL] (1834) **:** of, relating to, or resembling a nail, claw, or hoof

un·guard \,ən-'gärd, 'ən-\ *vt* [back-formation fr. *unguarded*] (1745) **:** to leave unprotected

un·guard·ed \-'gärd-əd\ *adj* (1593) **1 :** vulnerable to attack **:** UNPROTECTED **2 :** free from guile or wariness **:** DIRECT, INCAUTIOUS — **un·guard·ed·ly** *adv* — **un·guard·ed·ness** *n*

un·guent \'əŋ-gwənt, 'ən-; 'ən-jənt\ *n* [L *unguentum* — more at OINTMENT] (15c) **:** a soothing or healing salve **:** OINTMENT

un·guis \'əŋ-gwəs, 'ən-\ *n, pl* **un·gues** \-,gwēz\ [L — more at NAIL] (ca. 1790) **:** a nail, claw, or hoof esp. on a digit of a vertebrate

¹un·gu·late \'əŋ-gyə-lət, 'ən-, -,lāt\ *adj* [LL *ungulatus,* fr. L *ungula* hoof, fr. *unguis* nail, hoof] (1839) **1 :** having hoofs **2 :** of or relating to the ungulates

²ungulate *n* [deriv. of L *ungula*] (1842) **:** any of the group (Ungulata) consisting of the hoofed mammals (as a ruminant, swine, horse, tapir, rhinoceros, elephant, or hyrax) of which most are herbivorous and many are horned

un·hair \,ən-'ha(ə)r, 'ən-, -'he(ə)r\ *vt, archaic* (14c) **:** to deprive of hair

un·hal·low \-'hal-(,)ō, -'hal-ə(-w)\ *vt, archaic* (1535) **:** to make profane

un·hal·lowed \-(,)ōd, -əd\ *adj* [ME *unhalewed,* fr. OE *unhālgod,* fr. *un-* + *halgod,* pp. of *hālgian* to hallow — more at HALLOW] (bef. 12c) **1 :** not blessed **:** UNCONSECRATED, UNHOLY **2 a :** unsanctioned by or showing lack of reverence for religion **:** IMPIOUS, PROFANE **b :** contrary to accepted standards **:** IMMORAL

un·hand \,ən-'hand, 'ən-\ *vt* (1602) **:** to remove the hand from **:** let go

un·hand·some \-'han(t)-səm\ *adj* (ca. 1530) **:** not handsome: as **a :** not beautiful **:** HOMELY **b :** UNBECOMING, UNSEEMLY **c :** lacking in courtesy or taste **:** RUDE — **un·hand·some·ly** *adv*

un·handy \-'han-dē\ *adj* (1664) **1 :** hard to handle **:** INCONVENIENT **2 :** lacking in skill or dexterity **:** AWKWARD — **un·handi·ly** \-də-lē\ *adv* — **un·handi·ness** \-dē-nəs\ *n*

un·hap·py \-'hap-ē\ *adj* (14c) **1 :** not fortunate **:** UNLUCKY **2 :** not cheerful or glad **:** SAD, WRETCHED **3 a :** causing or subject to misfortune **:** INAUSPICIOUS **b :** INFELICITOUS, INAPPROPRIATE — **un·hap·pi·ly** \-'hap-ə-lē\ *adv* — **un·hap·pi·ness** *n*

un·healthy \-'hel-thē\ *adj* (1595) **1 :** not conducive to health ⟨an ~ climate⟩ **2 :** not in good health **:** SICKLY, DISEASED **3 a :** DANGEROUS, RISKY **b :** BAD, INJURIOUS **c :** morally contaminated **:** CORRUPT, UNWHOLESOME — **un·health·i·ly** \-thə-lē\ *adv* — **un·health·i·ness** \-thē-nəs\ *n*

un·heard \-'hərd\ *adj* (14c) **1 a :** not perceived by the ear **b :** not given a hearing **2** *archaic* **:** UNHEARD-OF

un·heard–of \-,əv, -,äv\ *adj* (1592) **:** previously unknown; *esp* **:** UNPRECEDENTED

un·hes·i·tat·ing \-'hez-ə-,tāt-iŋ\ *adj* (1753) **:** not hesitating **:** not checked or qualified — **un·hes·i·tat·ing·ly** \-iŋ-lē\ *adv*

un·hinge \-'hinj\ *vt* (1616) **1 :** to remove (as a door) from the hinges **2 :** to make unstable **:** UNSETTLE, DISRUPT ⟨~ the balance of world peace⟩ ⟨experiences that would ~ a lesser man⟩

un·hitch \-'hich\ *vt* (ca. 1706) **:** to free from or as if from being hitched

un·ho·ly \,ən-'hō-lē, 'ən-\ *adj* (bef. 12c) **1 :** showing disregard for what is holy **:** WICKED **2 :** SHOCKING, OUTRAGEOUS — **un·ho·li·ness** *n*

un·hood \-'hu̇d\ *vt* (1575) **:** to remove a hood or covering from

un·hook \-'hu̇k\ *vt* (ca. 1611) **1 :** to remove from a hook **2 :** to unfasten by disengaging a hook **3 :** to free from a habit or dependency

un·hoped \-'hōpt\ *adj, archaic* (14c) **:** not hoped for or expected

un·horse \-'hȯ(ə)rs\ *vt* (14c) **:** to dislodge from or as if from a horse

un·hou·seled \-'hau̇-zəld\ *adj, archaic* (1532) **:** not having received the Eucharist esp. shortly before death

un·hur·ried \-'hər-ēd, -'hə-rēd\ *adj* (1768) **:** not hurried **:** LEISURELY — **un·hur·ried·ly** *adv*

uni- *prefix* [ME, fr. MF, fr. L, fr. *unus* — more at ONE] **:** one **:** single ⟨*unicellular*⟩

uni·al·gal \,yü-nē-'al-gəl\ *adj* (1946) **:** of, relating to, or derived from a single algal individual or cell ⟨a ~ culture⟩

Uni·ate *or* **Uni·at** \'(y)ü-nē-,at\ *n* [Russ *uniyat,* fr. Pol *uniat,* fr. *unja* union (of the Greek and Roman Catholic churches), fr. LL *unio* —

more at UNION] (1833) : a Christian of a church adhering to an Eastern rite and discipline but submitting to papal authority — **Uniate** *adj*

uni·ax·i·al \ˌyü-nē-ˈak-sē-əl\ *adj* (ca. 1855) **1** : having only one axis **2** : of or relating to only one axis

uni·cam·er·al \ˌyü-ni-ˈkam-(ə-)rəl\ *adj* [*uni-* + LL *camera* room, chamber + E *-al* — more at CHAMBER] (1853) : having or consisting of a single legislative chamber — **uni·cam·er·al·ly** \-ē\ *adv*

uni·cel·lu·lar \ˌyü-ni-ˈsel-yə-lər\ *adj* (1858) : having or consisting of a single cell

uni·corn \ˈyü-nə-ˌkȯ(ə)rn\ *n* [ME *unicorne,* fr. OF, fr. LL *unicornis,* fr. L, having one horn, fr. *uni-* + *cornu* horn — more at HORN] (13c) : a mythical animal generally depicted with the body and head of a horse, the hind legs of a stag, the tail of a lion, and a single horn in the middle of the forehead

uni·cy·cle \ˈyü-ni-ˌsī-kəl\ *n* [*uni* + *-cycle* (as in *tricycle*)] (1869) : any of various vehicles that have a single wheel and are propelled usu. by pedals or applied draft — **uni·cy·clist** \-ˌsī-k(ə-)ləst\ *n*

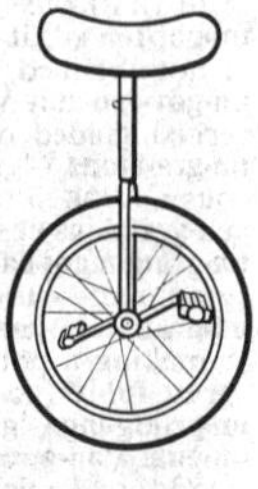
unicycle

uni·di·men·sion·al \ˌyü-ni-də-ˈmen-chən-ᵊl, -ˈmench-nəl *also* -ˈdī-\ *adj* (1883) : ONE-DIMENSIONAL — **uni·di·men·sion·al·i·ty** \-ˌmen-chə-ˈnal-ət-ē\ *n*

uni·di·rec·tion·al \ˌyü-ni-də-ˈrek-shnəl, -dī-, -shən-ᵊl\ *adj* (1883) **1** : involving, functioning, moving, or responsive in a single direction **2** : not subject to change or reversal of direction — **uni·di·rec·tion·al·ly** \-ē\ *adv*

unidirectional current *n* (1883) : DIRECT CURRENT

uni·fac·to·ri·al \ˌyü-ni-fak-ˈtōr-ē-əl, -ˈtȯr-\ *adj* (1933) : relating to or controlled by a single gene ⟨~ disorders⟩

uni·fi·ca·tion \ˌyü-nə-fə-ˈkā-shən\ *n* (1851) : the act, process, or result of unifying : the state of being unified

uni·fi·lar \ˌyü-ni-ˈfī-lər\ *adj* (1856) : having or involving use of only one thread, wire, or fiber

uni·fo·li·ate \-ˈfō-lē-ət\ *adj* (1849) **1** : having only one leaf **2** : UNIFOLIOLATE

uni·fo·li·o·late \-ˈfō-lē-ə-ˌlāt\ *adj, of a leaf* (ca. 1864) : compound but having only a single leaflet and distinguishable from a simple leaf by the basal joint

[1]**uni·form** \ˈyü-nə-ˌfȯrm\ *adj* [MF *uniforme,* fr. L *uniformis,* fr. *uni-* + *-formis* -form] (1540) **1** : having always the same form, manner, or degree : not varying or variable **2** : of the same form with others : conforming to one rule or mode : CONSONANT **3** : presenting an unvaried appearance of surface, pattern, or color ⟨~ red brick houses⟩ **4** : consistent in conduct or opinion ⟨~ interpretation of laws⟩ **5** : relating to or being convergence of a series whose terms are functions in such manner that the absolute value of the difference between the sum of the first *n* terms of the series and the sum of all terms can be made arbitrarily small for all values of the domain of the functions by choosing the *n*th term sufficiently far along in the series — **uni·form·ly** \ˈyü-nə-ˌfȯrm-lē, ˌyü-nə-ˈ\ *adv* — **uni·form·ness** \ˈyü-nə-ˌfȯrm-nəs\ *n*

[2]**uniform** *vt* (1681) **1** : to bring into uniformity **2** : to clothe with a uniform

[3]**uniform** *n* (1748) : dress of a distinctive design or fashion worn by members of a particular group and serving as a means of identification; *broadly* : distinctive or characteristic clothing

Uniform (ca. 1956) — a communications code word for the letter *u*

uni·for·mi·tar·i·an \ˌyü-nə-ˌfȯr-mə-ˈter-ē-ən\ *n* (1840) **1** : an adherent of the doctrine of uniformitarianism **2** : an advocate of uniformity — **uniformitarian** *adj*

uni·for·mi·tar·i·an·ism \-ē-ə-ˌniz-əm\ *n* (1865) : a geological doctrine that existing processes acting in the same manner as at present are sufficient to account for all geological changes

uni·for·mi·ty \ˌyü-nə-ˈfȯr-mət-ē\ *n, pl* **-ties** (15c) **1** : the quality or state of being uniform **2** : an instance of uniformity

uni·fy \ˈyü-nə-ˌfī\ *vt* **-fied; -fy·ing** [LL *unificare,* fr. L *uni-* + *-ficare* -fy] (1502) : to make into a unit or a coherent whole : UNITE — **uni·fi·able** \-ˌfī-ə-bəl\ *adj* — **uni·fi·er** \-ˌfī(-ə)r\ *n*

uni·lat·er·al \ˌyü-ni-ˈlat-ə-rəl, -ˈla-trəl\ *adj* (1802) **1 a** : done or undertaken by one person or party **b** : of, relating to, or affecting one side of a subject : ONE-SIDED **c** : constituting or relating to a contract or engagement by which an express obligation to do or forbear is imposed on only one party **2 a** : having parts arranged on one side ⟨a ~ raceme⟩ **b** : occurring on, performed on, or affecting one side of the body or one of its parts ⟨~ exophthalmos⟩ **3** : UNILINEAL **4** : having only one side — **uni·lat·er·al·ly** \-ē\ *adv*

uni·lin·eal \-ˈlin-ē-əl\ *adj* (1952) : tracing descent through either the maternal or paternal line only

uni·lin·ear \ˌyü-ni-ˈlin-ē-ər\ *adj* (1926) : developing in or involving a series of stages usu. from the primitive to the more advanced ⟨a ~ cultural sequence⟩

uni·lin·gual \ˌyü-ni-ˈliŋ-g(yə-)wəl\ *adj* [*uni-* + L *lingua* tongue, language — more at TONGUE] (1866) : composed in or using one language only

un·il·lu·sioned \ˌən-il-ˈü-zhənd, ˌən-ᵊl-\ *adj* (1926) : free from illusion

uni·loc·u·lar \ˌyü-ni-ˈläk-yə-lər\ *adj* (1753) : containing a single cavity

un·imag·in·able \ˌən-ə-ˈmaj-(ə-)nə-bəl\ *adj* (ca. 1611) : not imaginable or comprehensible — **un·imag·in·ably** \-blē\ *adv*

un·im·peach·able \ˌən-im-ˈpē-chə-bəl\ *adj* (1784) : not impeachable : not to be called in question : not liable to accusation : IRREPROACHABLE, BLAMELESS — **un·im·peach·ably** \-blē\ *adv*

[1]**un·im·proved** \-ˈprüvd\ *adj, obs* (1602) : not reproved or admonished

[2]**unimproved** *adj* (1665) : not improved: as **a** : not tilled, built on, or otherwise improved for use ⟨~ land⟩ **b** : not used or employed advantageously ⟨wasted time and ~ opportunities⟩ **c** : not selectively bred for better quality or productiveness

un·in·hib·it·ed \ˌən-in-ˈhib-ət-əd\ *adj* (ca. 1909) : free from inhibition; *also* : boisterously informal — **un·in·hib·it·ed·ly** *adv* — **un·in·hib·it·ed·ness** *n*

un·ini·tiate \ˌən-ə-ˈnish-(ē-)ət\ *adj* (1801) : not initiated : INEXPERIENCED

un·in·ter·est \(ˈ)ən-ˈin-trəst; -ˈint-ə-rəst, -ə-ˌrest, -ərst; -ˈin-ˌtrest\ *n* (1952) : lack of interest

un·in·ter·est·ed *adj* (1661) : not interested : not having the mind or feelings engaged ***usage*** see DISINTERESTED

uni·nu·cle·ate \ˌyü-ni-ˈn(y)ü-klē-ət\ *adj* (1885) : having a single nucleus ⟨a ~ yeast cell⟩

[1]**union** \ˈyün-yən\ *n* [ME, fr. MF, fr. LL *union-, unio* oneness, union, fr. L *unus* one — more at ONE] (15c) **1 a** : an act or instance of uniting or joining two or more things into one: as (1) : the formation of a single political unit from two or more separate and independent units (2) : a uniting in marriage; *also* : SEXUAL INTERCOURSE (3) : the growing together of severed parts **b** : a unified condition : COMBINATION, JUNCTION ⟨a gracious ~ of excellence and strength⟩ **2** : something that is made one : something formed by a combining or coalition of parts or members: as **a** : a confederation of independent individuals (as nations or persons) for some common purpose **b** : a political unit constituting an organic whole formed usu. from previously independent units (as England and Scotland in 1707) which have surrendered their principal powers to the government of the whole or to a newly created government (as the U.S. in 1789) **c** *cap* : an organization on a college or university campus providing recreational, social, cultural, and sometimes dining facilities; *also* : the building housing such an organization **d** : the set of all elements belonging to one or more of a given collection of two or more sets — called also *join, sum* **e** : LABOR UNION **3 a** : a device emblematic of the union of two or more sovereignties borne on a national flag typically in the upper inner corner or constituting the whole design of the flag **b** : the upper inner corner of a flag **4** : any of various devices for connecting parts (as of a machine); *esp* : a coupling for pipes or pipes and fittings

[2]**union** *adj* (1707) : of, relating to, dealing with, or constituting a union

union card *n* (1874) **1** : a card certifying personal membership in good standing in a labor union **2** : something that resembles a union card esp. in being necessary for employment or in providing evidence of in-group status

union church *n* (1847) : a local church uniting members of diverse denominational backgrounds in an interdenominational congregation

union·ism \ˈyün-yə-ˌniz-əm\ *n* (1845) : the principle or policy of forming or adhering to a union: as **a** *cap* : adherence to the policy of a firm federal union between the states of the United States esp. during the Civil War period **b** : the principles, theory, advocacy, or system of trade unions

union·ist \-nəst\ *n* (1799) : an advocate or supporter of union or unionism

union·iza·tion \ˌyün-yə-nə-ˈzā-shən\ *n* (1896) **1** : the quality or state of being unionized **2** : the action of unionizing

union·ize \ˈyün-yə-ˌnīz\ *vb* **-ized; -iz·ing** *vt* (1890) : to organize into a labor union ~ *vi* : to form or join a labor union

union·ized *adj* (1900) : characterized by the presence of labor unions ⟨~ states⟩

union jack *n, often cap U&J* (1674) : a jack consisting of the union of a national ensign

union shop *n* (ca. 1909) : an establishment in which the employer by agreement is free to hire nonmembers as well as members of the union but retains nonmembers on the payroll only on condition of their becoming members of the union within a specified time

union suit *n* (1901) : an undergarment with shirt and drawers in one piece

uni·pa·ren·tal \ˌyü-ni-pə-ˈrent-ᵊl\ *adj* (ca. 1909) : having or involving a single parent; *esp* : PARTHENOGENETIC — **uni·pa·ren·tal·ly** \-ᵊl-ē\ *adv*

uni·po·lar \ˌyü-ni-ˈpō-lər\ *adj* (1812) : having, produced by, or acting by a single magnetic or electrical pole — **uni·po·lar·i·ty** \-pō-ˈlar-ət-ē, -pə-\ *n*

unique \yu̇-ˈnēk\ *adj* [F, fr. L *unicus,* fr. *unus* one — more at ONE] (1602) **1** : being the only one : SOLE ⟨his ~ concern was his own comfort⟩ ⟨I can't walk away with a ~ copy. Suppose I lost it? —Kingsley Amis⟩ ⟨the ~ factorization of a number into prime factors⟩ **2 a** : being without a like or equal : UNEQUALED ⟨could stare at the flames, each one new, violent, ~ —Robert Coover⟩ **b** : distinctively characteristic : PECULIAR 1 ⟨this is not a condition ~ to California —Ronald Reagan⟩ **3** : UNUSUAL ⟨a very ~ ball-point pen⟩ ⟨we were fairly ~, the sixty of us, in that there wasn't one good mixer in the bunch —J.D. Salinger⟩ ***syn*** see STRANGE — **unique·ly** *adv* — **unique·ness** *n*

usage Many commentators have objected to the comparison or modification (as by *somewhat, almost,* or *very*) of *unique;* the statement that a thing is either unique or it is not has often been repeated by them. Objections are based chiefly on the assumption that *unique* has but a single absolute sense, an assumption contradicted by information readily available in a dictionary. *Unique* dates back to the 17th century but was little used until the end of the 18th when, according to the Oxford English Dictionary, it was reacquired from French. H.J. Todd entered it as a foreign word in his edition (1818) of Johnson's Dictionary, characterizing it as "affected and useless." Around the middle of the 19th century it ceased to be considered foreign and came into considerable popular use. With popular use came a broadening of application beyond the original two meanings (here numbered 1 and 2a). In modern use both comparison and modification are widespread and standard but are confined to the extended senses 2b and 3. When sense 1 or sense 2a is intended, *unique* is used without qualifying modifiers.

[1]**uni·sex** \ˈyü-nə-ˌseks\ *n* (1966) : the state or condition of not being distinguishable (as by hair or clothing) as to sex

[2]**unisex** *adj* (1968) **1** : not distinguishable as male or female ⟨a ~ face⟩ **2** : suitable or designed for both males and females ⟨~ clothes⟩

uni·sex·u·al \ˌyü-nə-ˈseksh-(ə-)wəl, -ˈsek-shəl\ *adj* (ca. 1802) **1** : of, relating to, or restricted to one sex: **a** : male or female but not hermaphroditic **b** : DICLINOUS ⟨a ~ flower⟩ **2** : UNISEX — **uni·sex·u·al·i·ty** \-ˌsek-shə-ˈwal-ət-ē\ *n*

uni·son \ˈyü-nə-sən, -nə-zən\ *n* [MF, fr. ML *unisonus* having the same sound, fr. L *uni-* + *sonus* sound — more at SOUND] (1575) **1 a** : identity in musical pitch; *specif* : the interval of a perfect prime **b** : the state of being so tuned or sounded **c** : the writing, playing, or singing of parts in a musical passage at the same pitch or in octaves **2** : a harmonious agreement or union : CONCORD — **unison** *adj* — **in unison** **1** : in perfect agreement : so as to harmonize exactly **2** : at the same time : SIMULTANEOUSLY

[1]**unit** \ˈyü-nət\ *n* [back-formation fr. *unity*] (1570) **1 a :** the first and least natural number : ONE **b :** a single quantity regarded as a whole in calculation **2 :** a determinate quantity (as of length, time, heat, or value) adopted as a standard of measurement: as **a :** an amount of work used in education in calculating student credits **b :** an amount of a biologically active agent (as a drug or antigen) required to produce a specific result under strictly controlled conditions **3 a :** a single thing, person, or group that is a constituent of a whole **b :** a part of a military establishment that has a prescribed organization (as of personnel and materiel) **c :** a piece or complex of apparatus serving to perform one particular function **d :** a part of a school course focusing on a central theme **e :** a local congregation of Jehovah's Witnesses

[2]**unit** *adj* (1844) **:** being, relating to, or measuring one unit

unit·age \ˈyü-nət-ij\ *n* (1935) **1 :** specifications of the amount constituting a unit **2 :** amount in units

uni·tar·i·an \ˌyü-nə-ˈter-ē-ən\ *n* [NL *unitarius,* fr. L *unitas* unity] (1687) **1 a** *often cap* **:** one who believes that the deity exists only in one person **b** *cap* **:** a member of a denomination that stresses individual freedom of belief, the free use of reason in religion, a united world community, and liberal social action **2 :** an advocate of unity or a unitary system — **unitarian** *adj, often cap* — **uni·tar·i·an·ism** \-ē-ə-ˌniz-əm\ *n, often cap*

uni·tary \ˈyü-nə-ˌter-ē\ *adj* (1861) **1 a :** of or relating to a unit **b :** based on or characterized by unity or units **2 :** having the character of a unit : UNDIVIDED, WHOLE — **uni·tar·i·ly** \ˌyü-nə-ˈter-ə-lē\ *adv*

unit cell *n* (ca. 1936) **:** the simplest polyhedron that embodies all the structural characteristics of and by indefinite repetition makes up the lattice of a crystal

unit character *n* (ca. 1909) **:** a natural character inherited on an all or none basis; *esp* **:** one dependent on the presence or absence of a single gene

unit circle *n* (1955) **:** a circle whose radius is one unit of length long

[1]**unite** \yu̇-ˈnīt\ *vb* **unit·ed; unit·ing** [ME *uniten,* fr. LL *unitus,* pp. of *unire* to make one, fr. L, fr. *unus* one — more at ONE] *vt* (15c) **1 a :** to put together to form a single unit **b :** to cause to adhere **c :** to link by a legal or moral bond **2 :** to possess (as qualities) in combination ~ *vi* **1 a :** to become one or as if one **b :** to become combined by or as if by adhesion or mixture **2 :** to act in concert ***syn*** see JOIN — **unit·er** *n*

[2]**unite** \ˈyü-ˌnīt\ *n* [obs. *unite* (united), fr. ME *unit,* fr. LL *unitus,* pp.] (1604) **:** an old British gold 20-shilling piece issued first by James I in 1604 for the newly united England and Scotland — called also *Jacobus*

unit·ed \yu̇-ˈnīt-əd\ *adj* (1552) **1 :** made one : COMBINED **2 :** relating to or produced by joint action **3 :** being in agreement : HARMONIOUS — **unit·ed·ly** *adv*

United Nations Day *n* (1947) **:** October 24 observed in commemoration of the founding of the United Nations

Unit·ed States \yu̇-ˌnīt-əd-, *esp Southern* ˈyü-\ *n pl but sing or pl in constr* (1617) **:** a federation of states esp. when forming a nation in a usu. specified territory ⟨advocating a *United States* of Europe⟩

uni·tive \ˈyü-nət-iv, yu̇-ˈnīt-\ *adj* (1526) **:** characterized by or tending to produce union

unit·ize \ˈyü-nət-ˌīz\ *vt* **-ized; -iz·ing** (1860) **1 :** to form or convert into a unit **2 :** to divide into units ⟨the added cost of *unitizing* bulk products⟩ — **unit·iza·tion** \ˌyü-nət-ə-ˈzā-shən\ *n*

unit magnetic pole *n* (ca. 1890) **:** a magnetic pole that will repel an equal and like pole at a distance of one centimeter in a vacuum with a force of one dyne

unit membrane *n* [fr. its being the basic structural unit of the cell] (1966) **:** a 3-layered membrane that consists of an inner lipid layer surrounded by a protein layer on each side

unit rule *n* (1884) **:** a rule under which a delegation to a national political convention casts its entire vote as a unit as determined by a majority vote

uni·trust \ˈyü-ni-ˌtrəst\ *n* (1970) **:** a trust from which the beneficiary receives annually a fixed percentage of the fair market value of its assets

units digit *n* (1955) **:** the numeral (as 6 in 456) occupying the units place in a number expressed in the Arabic system of writing numbers

units place *n* (1937) **:** the place immediately to the left of the decimal point in a number expressed in the Arabic system of writing numbers

unit train *n* (1964) **:** a railway train that transports a single commodity directly from producer to consumer

unit trust *n* (1940) **1** *Brit* **:** MUTUAL FUND **2 :** an investment company whose portfolio consists of long-term bonds that are held to maturity

uni·ty \ˈyü-nət-ē\ *n, pl* **-ties** [ME *unite,* fr. MF *unité,* fr. L *unitat-, unitas,* fr. *unus* one — more at ONE] (14c) **1 a :** the quality or state of not being multiple : ONENESS **b** (1) **:** a definite amount taken as one or for which 1 is made to stand in calculation ⟨in a table of natural sines the radius of the circle is regarded as ~⟩ (2) **:** IDENTITY ELEMENT **2 a :** a condition of harmony : ACCORD **b :** continuity without deviation or change (as in purpose or action) **3 a :** the quality or state of being made one : UNIFICATION **b :** a combination or ordering of parts in a literary or artistic production that constitutes a whole or promotes an undivided total effect; *also* **:** the resulting singleness of effect or symmetry and consistency of style and character **4 :** a totality of related parts : an entity that is a complex or systematic whole **5 :** any of three principles of dramatic structure derived by French classicists from Aristotle's *Poetics* and requiring a play to have a single action represented as occurring in one place and within one day **6** *cap* **:** a 20th century American religious movement for health and prosperity formerly affiliated with New Thought but closer to orthodox Christianity

[1]**uni·va·lent** \ˌyü-ni-ˈvā-lənt\ *n* (1928) **:** a chromosome that lacks a synaptic mate

[2]**univalent** *adj* (1933) **1 :** having a valence of one **2 :** being a chromosomal univalent

uni·valve \ˈyü-ni-ˌvalv\ *n* (1668) **1 :** a mollusk with a shell consisting of one valve; *esp* **:** GASTROPOD **2 :** a mollusk shell consisting of one piece — **univalve** *adj*

[1]**uni·ver·sal** \ˌyü-nə-ˈvər-səl\ *adj* [ME, fr. MF, fr. L *universalis,* fr. *universum* universe] (14c) **1 :** including or covering all or a whole collectively or distributively without limit or exception **2 a :** present or occurring everywhere **b :** existent or operative everywhere or under all conditions ⟨~ cultural patterns⟩ **3 a :** embracing a major part or the greatest portion (as of mankind) ⟨a ~ state⟩ ⟨~ practices⟩ **b :** comprehensively broad and versatile ⟨a ~ genius⟩ **4 a :** affirming or denying something of all members of a class or of all values of a variable **b :** denoting every member of a class ⟨a ~ term⟩ **5 :** adapted or adjustable to meet varied requirements (as of use, shape, or size) ⟨a ~ gear cutter⟩ — **uni·ver·sal·ly** \-s(ə-)lē\ *adv* — **uni·ver·sal·ness** \-səl-nəs\ *n*

syn UNIVERSAL, GENERAL, GENERIC mean of or relating to all or the whole. UNIVERSAL implies reference to every one without exception in the class, category, or genus considered; GENERAL implies reference to all or nearly all ⟨the theory has met *general* but not *universal* acceptance⟩ GENERIC implies reference to every member of a genus ⟨*generic* likenesses among all dogs⟩

[2]**universal** *n* (1553) **1 :** one that is universal: as **a :** a universal proposition in logic **b :** a predicable of traditional logic **c :** a general concept or term or something in reality to which it corresponds : ESSENCE **2 a :** a behavior pattern or institution (as the family) existing in all cultures **b :** a culture trait characteristic of all normal adult members of a particular society

uni·ver·sal·ism \ˌyü-nə-ˈvər-sə-ˌliz-əm\ *n* (1805) **1** *often cap* **a :** a theological doctrine that all men will eventually be saved **b :** the principles and practices of a liberal Christian denomination founded in the 18th century orig. to uphold belief in universal salvation and now united with Unitarianism **2 :** something that is universal in scope **3 :** the state of being universal : UNIVERSALITY — **uni·ver·sal·ist** \-s(ə-)ləst\ *n or adj, often cap*

uni·ver·sal·is·tic \-ˌvər-sə-ˈlis-tik\ *adj* (1872) **:** of or relating to the whole **:** universal in scope or nature

uni·ver·sal·i·ty \-(ˌ)vər-ˈsal-ət-ē\ *n* [ME *universalite,* fr. LL *universalitas,* fr. L *universalis*] (14c) **1 :** the quality or state of being universal **2 :** universal comprehensiveness in range

uni·ver·sal·ize \-ˈvər-sə-ˌlīz\ *vt* **-ized; -iz·ing** (1642) **:** to make universal : GENERALIZE — **uni·ver·sal·iza·tion** \-ˌvər-sə-lə-ˈzā-shən\ *n*

universal joint *n* (ca. 1882) **:** a shaft coupling capable of transmitting rotation from one shaft to another not collinear with it — called also *universal coupling*

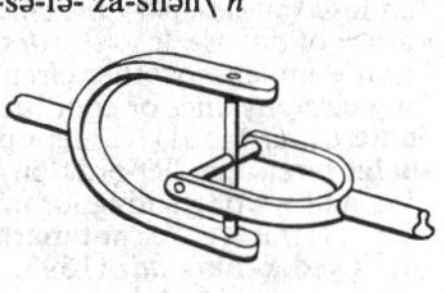

universal joint

universal motor *n* (1925) **:** an electric motor that can be used on either an alternating or a direct current supply

Universal Product Code *n* (1975) **:** a bar code that identifies a product's type and price

Universal time *n* (ca. 1890) **:** GREENWICH TIME

uni·verse \ˈyü-nə-ˌvərs\ *n* [L *universum,* fr. neut. of *universus* entire, whole, fr. *uni-* + *versus* turned toward, fr. pp. of *vertere* to turn — more at WORTH] (1589) **1 :** the whole body of things and phenomena observed or postulated : COSMOS **2 a :** a systematic whole held to arise by and persist through the direct intervention of divine power **b :** the world of human experience **c** (1) **:** the entire celestial cosmos (2) **:** MILKY WAY GALAXY (3) **:** an aggregate of stars comparable to the Milky Way galaxy **3 :** a distinct field or province of thought or reality that forms a closed system or self-inclusive and independent organization **4 :** POPULATION 4 **5 :** a set that contains all elements relevant to a particular discussion or problem **6 :** a great number or quantity ⟨a large enough ~ of stocks . . . to choose from —G. B. Clairmont⟩

universe of discourse (1881) **:** an inclusive class of entities that is tacitly implied or explicitly delineated as the subject of a statement, discourse, or theory

uni·ver·si·ty \ˌyü-nə-ˈvər-sət-ē, -ˈvər-stē\ *n, pl* **-ties** [ME *universite,* fr. MF *université,* fr. ML *universitat-, universitas,* fr. L *universus*] (14c) **1 :** an institution of higher learning providing facilities for teaching and research and authorized to grant academic degrees; *specif* **:** one made up of an undergraduate division which confers bachelor's degrees and a graduate division which comprises a graduate school and professional schools each of which may confer master's degrees and doctorates **2 :** the physical plant of a university

uni·vo·cal \yü-ˈniv-ə-kəl\ *adj* [LL *univocus,* fr. L *uni-* + *voc-, vox* voice — more at VOICE] (1656) **:** having one meaning only — **uni·vo·cal·ly** \-k(ə-)lē\ *adv*

un·joined \ˌən-ˈjoind\ *adj* (1538) **:** not joined

un·just \ˌən-ˈjəst, ˈən-\ *adj* (14c) **1 :** characterized by injustice : UNFAIR **2** *archaic* **:** DISHONEST, FAITHLESS — **un·just·ly** *adv* — **un·just·ness** \-ˈjəs(t)-nəs\ *n*

un·kempt \-ˈkem(p)t\ *adj* [*un-* + *kempt* (combed, neat)] (1599) **1 :** deficient in order or neatness ⟨~ individuals⟩ ⟨~ hotel rooms⟩; *also* **:** ROUGH, UNPOLISHED ⟨~ prose⟩ **2 :** not combed ⟨~ hair⟩

un·kenned \-ˈkend\ *adj, chiefly dial* (14c) **:** UNKNOWN, STRANGE

un·ken·nel \-ˈken-ᵊl\ *vt* (1576) **1 :** to drive (as a fox) from a hiding place or den **2 :** to bring out into the open : UNCOVER

un·kind \-ˈkīnd\ *adj* (14c) **1 :** not pleasing or mild : INCLEMENT ⟨an ~ climate⟩ **2 :** lacking in kindness or sympathy : HARSH, CRUEL — **un·kind·ness** \-ˈkīn(d)-nəs\ *n*

[1]**un·kind·ly** \-ˈkīn-(d)lē\ *adj* (13c) **:** not kindly — **un·kind·li·ness** *n*

[2]**unkindly** *adv* (14c) **:** in an unkind manner ⟨dwells ~ long on his final decline —A. H. Johnston⟩

un·kink \ˌən-ˈkiŋk, ˈən-\ *vt* (ca. 1899) **:** to free from kinks : STRAIGHTEN ~ *vi* **:** to become lax or loose : RELAX

un·knit \-ˈnit\ *vb* **-knit** *or* **-knit·ted; -knit·ting** (bef. 12c) **:** UNDO, UNRAVEL

un·know·able \ˌən-ˈnō-ə-bəl, ˈən-\ *adj* (14c) **:** not knowable; *esp* **:** lying beyond the limits of human experience or understanding

un·know·ing \-ˈnō-iŋ\ *adj* (14c) **:** not knowing — **un·know·ing·ly** \-iŋ-lē\ *adv*

[1]**un·known** \-ˈnōn\ *adj* (14c) **:** not known or not well-known; *also* **:** having an unknown value ⟨an ~ quantity⟩

²**unknown** *n* (1597) **1 :** one that is not known or not well-known; *esp* **:** a person who is little known (as to the public) **2 :** something that requires to be discovered, identified, or clarified: as **a :** a symbol in a mathematical equation representing an unknown quantity and often being one of the last letters of the alphabet **b :** a specimen (as of bacteria or mixed chemicals) required to be identified as an exercise in appropriate laboratory techniques

Unknown Soldier *n* (1923) **:** an unidentified soldier whose body is selected to receive national honors as a representative of all of the same nation who died in a war and esp. in one of the world wars

un·lace \ˌən-ˈlās, ˈən-\ *vt* (14c) **1 :** to loose by undoing a lacing **2** *obs* **:** UNDO, DISGRACE

un·lade \-ˈlād\ *vb* **-lad·ed; -laded** *or* **-lad·en** \-ˈlād-ᵊn\; **-lad·ing** *vt* (14c) **1 :** to take the load or cargo from **2 :** DISCHARGE, UNLOAD ~ *vi* **:** to discharge cargo

un·lash \-ˈlash\ *vt* (1748) **:** to untie the lashing of

un·latch \-ˈlach\ *vt* (1642) **:** to open or loose by lifting the latch ~ *vi* **:** to become loosed or opened

un·law·ful \ˌən-ˈlȯ-fəl, ˈən-\ *adj* (14c) **1 :** not lawful **:** ILLEGAL **2 :** not morally right or conventional — **un·law·ful·ly** \-f(ə-)lē\ *adv* — **un·law·ful·ness** \-fəl-nəs\ *n*

un·lay \-ˈlā\ *vb* **-laid** \-ˈlād\; **-lay·ing** *vt* (1726) **:** to untwist the strands of (as a rope) ~ *vi* **:** UNTWIST

un·lead·ed \-ˈled-əd\ *adj* (1611) **1 a :** stripped of lead **b :** not treated or mixed with lead or lead compounds ⟨~ fuels⟩ **2 :** not having leads between the lines in printing

un·learn \-ˈlərn\ *vt* (15c) **1 :** to put out of one's knowledge or memory **2 :** to undo the effect of **:** discard the habit of

un·learned \-ˈlər-nəd *for 1, 2,* -ˈlərnd *for 3*\ *adj* (15c) **1 :** possessing inadequate learning or education; *esp* **:** deficient in scholarly attainments **2 :** characterized by or revealing ignorance **3 :** not gained by study or training ***syn*** see IGNORANT

un·leash \-ˈlēsh\ *vt* (1671) **:** to free from or as if from a leash **:** let loose

¹**un·less** \ən-ˌles, ˌən-, *in some contexts* ᵊn-, ᵊm-, *or* ᵊŋ-\ *conj* [ME *unlesse,* alter. of *onlesse,* fr. *on* + *lesse* less] (1509) **1 :** except on the condition that **:** under any other circumstance than **2 :** without the accompanying circumstance or condition that **:** but that **:** BUT

²**unless** *prep* (1531) **:** except possibly **:** EXCEPT

un·let·tered \ˌən-ˈlet-ərd, ˈən-\ *adj* (14c) **1 a :** lacking facility in reading and writing and ignorant of the knowledge to be gained from books **b :** ILLITERATE **2 :** not marked with letters ***syn*** see IGNORANT

un·licked \-ˈlikt\ *adj* (1593) **1 :** lacking proper form or shape **2** *archaic* **:** not licked dry

¹**un·like** \-ˈlīk\ *adj* (13c) **:** not like: as **a :** marked by lack of resemblance **:** DIFFERENT ⟨the two books are quite ~⟩ **b :** marked by inequality **:** UNEQUAL ⟨contributed ~ amounts⟩ — **un·like·ness** *n*

²**unlike** *prep* (14c) **:** not like: as **a :** different from **b :** not characteristic of **c :** in a different manner from

un·like·li·hood \ˌən-ˈlī-klē-ˌhu̇d, ˈən-\ *n* (1550) **1 :** IMPROBABILITY **2 :** something unlikely

un·like·li·ness \-nəs\ *n* (1614) **:** IMPROBABILITY

un·like·ly \-ˈlī-klē\ *adj* (14c) **1 :** not likely **:** IMPROBABLE **2 :** likely to fail **:** UNPROMISING

un·lim·ber \ˌən-ˈlim-bər, ˈən-\ *vt* (ca. 1802) **1 :** to detach the limber from and so make ready ⟨~ a gun for action⟩ **2 :** to prepare for operation or performance ⟨~*ed* his banjo and began to sing⟩ ~ *vi* **:** to perform the task of preparing something for action

un·lim·it·ed \-ˈlim-ət-əd\ *adj* (15c) **1 :** lacking any controls **:** UNRESTRICTED **2 :** BOUNDLESS, INFINITE **3 :** not bounded by exceptions **:** UNDEFINED — **un·lim·it·ed·ly** *adv*

un·link \-ˈliŋk\ *vt* (1600) **:** to unfasten the links of **:** SEPARATE, DISCONNECT ~ *vi* **:** to become detached

un·linked \-ˈliŋ(k)t\ *adj* (1966) **:** not belonging to the same genetic linkage group ⟨~ genes⟩

un·list·ed \-ˈlis-təd\ *adj* (1644) **1 :** not appearing on a list; *esp* **:** not appearing in a telephone book ⟨~ numbers⟩ **2 :** being or involving a security not listed formally on an organized exchange **:** OVER-THE-COUNTER

un·live \-ˈliv\ *vt* (1614) **:** ANNUL, REVERSE

un·load \ˌən-ˈlōd, ˈən-\ *vt* (1523) **1 a** (1) **:** to take off **:** DELIVER (2) **:** to take the cargo from **b :** to give outlet to **:** pour forth ⟨~*ed* her bitter feelings⟩ **2 :** to relieve of something burdensome, unwanted, or oppressive ⟨~*ed* the pack animals⟩ ⟨~*ed* himself to his friend⟩ **3 :** to draw the charge from ⟨~*ed* the gun⟩ **4 :** to sell or dispose of esp. in large quantities **:** DUMP **5 :** to hit or propel with a great release of power ⟨~*ed* his ninth homer⟩ ~ *vi* **:** to perform the act of unloading — **un·load·er** *n*

un·lock \-ˈläk\ *vt* (15c) **1 :** to unfasten the lock of **2 :** OPEN, UNDO **3 :** to free from restraints or restrictions ⟨the shock ~*ed* a flood of tears⟩ **4 :** to furnish a key to **:** DISCLOSE ~ *vi* **:** to become unfastened or freed from restraints

un·looked–for \-ˈlu̇k-ˌtfȯ(ə)r\ *adj* (1535) **:** not foreseen **:** UNEXPECTED

un·loose \ˌən-ˈlüs, ˈən-\ *vt* (14c) **1 :** to relax the strain of ⟨~ a grip⟩ **2 :** to release from or as if from restraints **:** set free **3 :** to loosen the ties of ⟨~ traditional social bonds⟩

un·loos·en \-ˈlüs-ᵊn\ *vt* (15c) **:** UNLOOSE

un·love·ly \-ˈləv-lē\ *adj* (14c) **:** not likable **:** DISAGREEABLE, UNPLEASANT — **un·love·li·ness** \-lē-nəs\ *n*

un·lucky \-ˈlək-ē\ *adj* (1530) **1 :** marked by adversity or failure ⟨an ~ year⟩ **2 :** likely to bring misfortune **:** INAUSPICIOUS **3 :** having or meeting with bad luck ⟨~ people⟩ **4 :** producing dissatisfaction **:** REGRETTABLE — **un·luck·i·ly** \-ˈlək-ə-lē\ *adv* — **un·luck·i·ness** \-ˈlək-ē-nəs\ *n*

un·made \ˌən-ˈmād, ˈən-\ *adj* (13c) **:** not made ⟨an ~ bed⟩

un·make \-ˈmāk\ *vt* **-made** \-ˈmād\; **-mak·ing** (1605) **1 :** to cause to disappear **:** DESTROY **2 :** to deprive of rank or office **:** DEPOSE **3 :** to deprive of essential characteristics **:** change the nature of

un·man \ˌən-ˈman, ˈən-\ *vt* (1600) **1 :** to deprive of manly vigor, fortitude, or spirit **2 :** CASTRATE, EMASCULATE ***syn*** see UNNERVE

un·man·ly \-ˈman-lē\ *adj* (1547) **:** not manly: as **a :** being of weak character **:** COWARDLY **b :** EFFEMINATE — **un·man·li·ness** \-lē-nəs\ *n*

un·manned \-ˈmand\ *adj* (1544) **1 :** not manned ⟨an ~ spaceflight⟩ **2** *obs, of a hawk* **:** not trained

un·man·nered \-ˈman-ərd\ *adj* (1594) **1 :** marked by a lack of good manners **:** RUDE **2 :** characterized by an absence of artificiality **:** UNAFFECTED — **un·man·nered·ly** *adv*

¹**un·man·ner·ly** \-ˈman-ər-lē\ *adv* (14c) **:** in an unmannerly fashion

²**unmannerly** *adj* (14c) **:** not mannerly **:** DISCOURTEOUS — **un·man·ner·li·ness** \-lē-nəs\ *n*

un·mar·ried \-ˈmar-ēd\ *adj* (13c) **:** not married: **a :** not now or previously married **b :** being divorced **c :** being widowed — **unmarried** *n*

un·mask \ˌən-ˈmask, ˈən-\ *vt* (1602) **1 :** to remove a mask from **2 :** to reveal the true nature of **:** EXPOSE ~ *vi* **:** to remove one's mask

un·mean·ing \-ˈmē-niŋ\ *adj* (1704) **1 :** lacking intelligence **:** VAPID **2 :** having no meaning **:** SENSELESS

un·meet \-ˈmēt\ *adj* (1529) **:** not meet **:** UNSUITABLE, IMPROPER

¹**un·men·tion·able** \-ˈmench-(ə-)nə-bəl\ *adj* (1837) **:** not mentionable **:** UNSPEAKABLE

²**unmentionable** *n* (1928) **:** one that is not to be mentioned or discussed: as **a** *pl* **:** ³PANT 1 **b** *pl* **:** UNDERWEAR

un·mer·ci·ful \ˌən-ˈmər-si-fəl, ˈən-\ *adj* (15c) **1 :** not merciful **:** MERCILESS **2 :** EXCESSIVE, EXTREME ⟨chatted for an ~ length of time⟩ — **un·mer·ci·ful·ly** \-f(ə-)lē\ *adv*

un·mind·ful \-ˈmīn(d)-fəl\ *adj* (14c) **:** not carefully attentive or heedful **:** INATTENTIVE, CARELESS

un·mis·tak·able \ˌən-mə-ˈstā-kə-bəl\ *adj* (1666) **:** not capable of being mistaken or misunderstood **:** CLEAR — **un·mis·tak·ably** \-blē\ *adv*

un·mit·i·gat·ed \ˌən-ˈmit-ə-ˌgāt-əd, ˈən-\ *adj* (1599) **1 :** not lessened **:** UNRELIEVED ⟨sufferings ~ by any hope of early relief⟩ **2 :** being so definitely what is stated as to offer little chance of change or relief ⟨an ~ evil⟩ — **un·mit·i·gat·ed·ly** *adv* — **un·mit·i·gat·ed·ness** *n*

un·moor \-ˈmu̇(ə)r\ *vt* (15c) **:** to loose from or as if from moorings ~ *vi* **:** to cast off moorings

un·mor·al \-ˈmȯr-əl, -ˈmär-\ *adj* (1841) **1 :** having no moral perception or quality; *also* **:** not influenced or guided by moral considerations **2 :** lying outside the bounds of morals or ethics — **un·mo·ral·i·ty** \ˌən-mə-ˈral-ət-ē, -mȯ-\ *n*

un·muf·fle \ˌən-ˈməf-əl, ˈən-\ *vt* (1611) **:** to free from something that muffles

un·muz·zle \-ˈməz-əl\ *vt* (1601) **:** to free from or as if from a muzzle

un·my·elin·at·ed \-ˈmī-ə-lə-ˌnāt-əd\ *adj* (1919) **:** lacking a myelin sheath

un·nail \ˌən-ˈnā(ə)l, ˈən-\ *vt* (15c) **:** to unfasten by removing nails

un·nat·u·ral \ˌən-ˈnach-(ə-)rəl, ˈən-\ *adj* (15c) **1 :** not being in accordance with nature or consistent with a normal course of events **2 a :** not being in accordance with normal human feelings or behavior **:** PERVERSE **b :** lacking ease and naturalness **:** CONTRIVED ⟨her manner was forced and ~⟩ **c :** inconsistent with what is reasonable or expected ⟨an ~ alliance⟩ ***syn*** see IRREGULAR — **un·nat·u·ral·ly** \-ˈnach-(ə-)rə-lē, -ˈnach-ər-lē\ *adv* — **un·nat·u·ral·ness** \-ˈnach-(ə-)rəl-nəs\ *n*

un·nec·es·sar·i·ly \ˌən-ˌnes-ə-ˈser-ə-lē\ *adv* (1594) **:** not by necessity **:** to an unnecessary degree

un·nec·es·sary \ˌən-ˈnes-ə-ˌser-ē, ˈən-\ *adj* (1548) **:** not necessary

un·nerve \-ˈnərv\ *vt* (1601) **1 :** to deprive of courage, strength, or steadiness **2 :** to cause to become nervous **:** UPSET — **un·nerv·ing·ly** \-ˈnər-viŋ-lē\ *adv*

syn UNNERVE, ENERVATE, UNMAN, EMASCULATE mean to deprive of strength or vigor and the capacity for effective action. UNNERVE implies marked often temporary loss of courage, self-control, or power to act; ENERVATE suggests a gradual physical or moral weakening (as through luxury or indolence) until one is too feeble to make an effort; UNMAN implies a loss of manly vigor, fortitude, or spirit; EMASCULATE stresses a depriving of characteristic force by removing something essential.

un·nil·hex·i·um \ˌyün-ᵊl-ˈhek-sē-əm\ *n* [NL *unnil-* (fr. L *unus* one + *nil* nothing, zero) + Gk *hex* six + NL *-ium* — more at ONE, NIL, SIX] (ca. 1977) **:** the chemical element of atomic number 106 — see ELEMENT table

un·nil·pen·ti·um \-ˈpent-ē-əm\ *n* [NL *unnil-* + Gk *pente* five + NL *-ium* — more at FIVE] (ca. 1977) **:** the chemical element of atomic number 105 — see ELEMENT table

un·nil·qua·di·um \-ˈkwäd-ē-əm\ *n* [NL *unnil-* + *quadri-* + *-ium*] (ca. 1977) **:** the chemical element of atomic number 104 — see ELEMENT table

un·num·bered \ˌən-ˈnəm-bərd, ˈən-\ *adj* (14c) **1 :** INNUMERABLE **2 :** not having an identifying number ⟨~ pages⟩

un·ob·tru·sive \ˌən-əb-ˈtrü-siv, -ziv\ *adj* (1743) **:** not obtrusive **:** not blatant or aggressive **:** INCONSPICUOUS — **un·ob·tru·sive·ly** *adv* — **un·ob·tru·sive·ness** *n*

un·oc·cu·pied \ˌən-ˈäk-yə-ˌpīd, ˈən-\ *adj* (14c) **:** not occupied: as **a :** not busy **:** UNEMPLOYED **b :** not lived in **:** EMPTY

un·or·ga·nized \-ˈȯr-gə-ˌnīzd\ *adj* (ca. 1828) **1 a :** not brought into a coherent or well-ordered whole **b :** not belonging to a labor union **2 :** not having the characteristics of a living organism

un·or·tho·dox \-ˈȯr-thə-ˌdäks\ *adj* (1657) **:** not orthodox — **un·or·tho·dox·ly** *adv*

un·or·tho·doxy \-ˌdäk-sē\ *n* (1704) **1 :** the quality or state of being unorthodox **2 :** something (as an opinion or doctrine) that is unorthodox

un·pack \ˌən-ˈpak, ˈən-\ *vt* (15c) **1 a :** to remove the contents of ⟨~ a trunk⟩ **b :** UNBURDEN, REVEAL ⟨must . . . ~ my heart with words — Shak.⟩ **2 :** to remove or undo from packing or a container ⟨~*ed* his gear⟩ ~ *vi* **:** to engage in unpacking a container — **un·pack·er** *n*

un·paged \-ˈpājd\ *adj* (1874) **:** having no page numbers

un·paid \-ˈpād\ *adj* (14c) **1 :** not paid ⟨an ~ volunteer⟩ **2 :** not paying a salary ⟨an ~ position⟩

un·paired \-ˈpa(ə)rd, -ˈpe(ə)rd\ *adj* (1648) **1 a :** not paired; *esp* **:** not matched or mated **b :** characterized by the absence of pairing ⟨electrons in the ~ state⟩ **2 :** situated in the median plane of the body ⟨an ~ fin⟩

un·pal·at·able \-ˈpal-ət-ə-bəl\ *adj* (1682) **1 :** not palatable **:** DISTASTEFUL **2 :** UNPLEASANT, DISAGREEABLE — **un·pal·at·abil·i·ty** \ˌən-ˌpal-ət-ə-ˈbil-ət-ē\ *n*

un·par·al·leled \ˌən-ˈpar-ə-ˌleld, ˈən-, -ləld\ *adj* (1594) **:** having no parallel; *esp* **:** having no equal or match **:** unique in kind or quality

un·par·lia·men·ta·ry \ˌən-ˌpär-lə-ˈment-ə-rē, -ˌpärl-yə-, -ˈmen-trē\ *adj* (1626) **:** contrary to the practice of parliamentary bodies

un·peg \ˌən-ˈpeg, ˈən-\ *vt* (1602) **:** to remove a peg from **:** UNFASTEN

un·peo·ple \-ˈpē-pəl\ *vt* (1533) : DEPOPULATE
un·per·fect \-ˈpər-fikt\ *adj* (14c) : IMPERFECT
un·per·son \ˈən-ˈpərs-ᵊn, -ˌpərs-\ *n* (1962) : an individual who usu. for political or ideological reasons is removed completely from recognition or consideration
un·pick \ˌən-ˈpik, ˈən-\ *vt* (1775) : to undo (as sewing) by taking out stitches
un·pile \-ˈpī(ə)l\ *vt* (ca. 1611) : to take or disentangle from a pile
un·pin \-ˈpin\ *vt* (14c) **1** : to remove a pin from **2** : to loosen, free, or unfasten by or as if by removing a pin
un·pleas·ant \-ˈplez-ᵊnt\ *adj* (1538) : not pleasant : not amiable or agreeable : DISPLEASING ⟨~ odors⟩ — **un·pleas·ant·ly** *adv*
un·pleas·ant·ness *n* (ca. 1548) **1** : the quality or state of being unpleasant **2** : an unpleasant situation, experience, or event
un·plug \ˌən-ˈpləg, ˈən-\ *vt* (1775) **1 a** : to take a plug out of **b** : to remove an obstruction from **2 a** : to remove (as an electric plug) from a socket or receptacle **b** : to disconnect from an electric circuit by removing a plug ⟨~ the refrigerator⟩
un·plumbed \-ˈpləmd\ *adj* (1623) **1** : not tested with a plumb line **2 a** : not measured with a plumb **b** : not thoroughly explored
un·po·lar·ized \-ˈpō-lə-ˌrīzd\ *adj* (1827) : not polarized; *specif* : having a random pattern of vibrations
un·po·lit·i·cal \ˌən-pə-ˈlit-i-kəl\ *adj* (1643) : not political; *esp* : not interested or engaged in politics ⟨an ~ person⟩
un·pop·u·lar \ˌən-ˈpäp-yə-lər, ˈən-\ *adj* (1647) : not popular : viewed or received unfavorably by the public — **un·pop·u·lar·i·ty** \ˌən-ˌpäp-yə-ˈlar-ət-ē\ *n*
un·prec·e·dent·ed \ˌən-ˈpres-ə-ˌdent-əd, ˈən-\ *adj* (1623) : having no precedent : NOVEL, UNEXAMPLED — **un·prec·e·dent·ed·ly** *adv*
un·preg·nant \ˌən-ˈpreg-nənt\ *adj, obs* (1602) : INEPT 1
un·pre·tend·ing \ˌən-pri-ˈten-diŋ\ *adj* (1697) : UNPRETENTIOUS
un·pre·ten·tious \-ˈten-chəs\ *adj* (1859) : free from ostentation, elegance, or affectation : MODEST ⟨~ homes⟩ — **un·pre·ten·tious·ly** *adv* — **un·pre·ten·tious·ness** *n*
un·prin·ci·pled \ˌən-ˈprin(t)-s(ə-)pəld, ˈən-, -sə-bəld\ *adj* (1644) : lacking moral principles : UNSCRUPULOUS — **un·prin·ci·pled·ness** *n*
un·print·able \-ˈprint-ə-bəl\ *adj* (1871) : unfit to be printed
un·pro·fessed \ˌən-prə-ˈfest\ *adj* (15c) : not professed ⟨an ~ aim⟩
un·prof·it·able \ˌən-ˈpräf-ət-ə-bəl, ˈən-, -ˈpräf-tə-bəl\ *adj* (14c) : not profitable : USELESS, VAIN — **un·prof·it·able·ness** *n* — **un·prof·it·ably** \-blē\ *adv*
un·prom·is·ing \-ˈpräm-ə-siŋ\ *adj* (1663) : appearing unlikely to prove worthwhile or result favorably — **un·prom·is·ing·ly** \-siŋ-lē\ *adv*
un·pro·nounced \ˌən-prə-ˈnau̇n(t)st\ *adj* (1586) : not pronounced; *esp* : MUTE
un·pub·lish·able \-ˈpəb-lish-ə-bəl\ *adj* (1815) : UNPRINTABLE
un·qual·i·fied \ˌən-ˈkwäl-ə-ˌfīd, ˈən-\ *adj* (1556) **1** : not fit : not having requisite qualifications **2** : not modified or restricted by reservations : COMPLETE ⟨an ~ denial⟩ — **un·qual·i·fied·ly** \-ˌfī(-ə)d-lē\ *adv*
un·ques·tion·able \-ˈkwes(h)-chə-nə-bəl, *in rapid speech* -ˈkwesh-nə-\ *adj* (1631) : not questionable : INDISPUTABLE ⟨~ evidence⟩ — **un·ques·tion·ably** \-blē\ *adv*
un·ques·tion·ing \-ˈkwes(h)-chə-niŋ\ *adj* (ca. 1828) : not questioning : not expressing or marked by doubt or hesitation ⟨~ obedience⟩ — **un·ques·tion·ing·ly** \-niŋ-lē\ *adv*
un·qui·et \-ˈkwī-ət\ *adj* (1526) **1** : not quiet : AGITATED, TURBULENT **2** : physically, emotionally, or mentally restless : UNEASY — **un·qui·et·ly** *adv* — **un·qui·et·ness** *n*
un·quote \ˈən-ˌkwōt *also* -ˌkōt\ *n* (1915) — used orally to indicate the end of a direct quotation
un·rav·el \ˌən-ˈrav-əl, ˈən-\ *vt* (1603) **1 a** : to disengage or separate the threads of : DISENTANGLE **b** : to cause to come apart by or as if by separating the threads of **2** : to resolve the intricacy, complexity, or obscurity of : clear up ~ *vi* : to become unraveled
un·read \-ˈred\ *adj* (15c) **1** : not read : left unexamined **2** : lacking the experience or the benefits of reading ⟨~ in political science⟩
un·re·al \-ˈrē-(ə)l, -ˈri(-ə)l\ *adj* (1605) : lacking in reality, substance, or genuineness : ARTIFICIAL, ILLUSORY; *also* : INCREDIBLE, FANTASTIC
un·re·al·is·tic \ˌən-ˌrē-ə-ˈlis-tik, -ˌri-ə-\ *adj* (1865) : not realistic : inappropriate to reality or fact — **un·re·al·is·ti·cal·ly** \-ti-k(ə-)lē\ *adv*
un·re·al·i·ty \ˌən-rē-ˈal-ət-ē\ *n* (1751) **1 a** : the quality or state of being unreal : lack of substance or validity **b** : something unreal, insubstantial, or visionary : FIGMENT **2** : ineptitude in dealing with reality
un·rea·son \ˌən-ˈrēz-ᵊn, ˈən-ˈrēz-\ *n* (1827) : the absence of reason or sanity : IRRATIONALITY, MADNESS
un·rea·son·able \-ˈrēz-nə-bəl, -ᵊn-ə-\ *adj* (14c) **1 a** : not governed by or acting according to reason ⟨~ people⟩ **b** : not conformable to reason : ABSURD ⟨~ beliefs⟩ **2** : exceeding the bounds of reason or moderation ⟨working under ~ pressure⟩ — **un·rea·son·ably** \-blē\ *adv*
un·rea·son·able·ness \-bəl-nəs\ *n* (1532) : the quality or state of being unreasonable
un·rea·soned \-ˈrēz-ᵊnd\ *adj* (1790) : not founded on reason or reasoning
un·rea·son·ing \-ˈrēz-niŋ, -ᵊn-iŋ\ *adj* (1751) : not reasoning; *esp* : not moderated or controlled by reason ⟨~ fear⟩ — **un·rea·son·ing·ly** \-ˈrēz-niŋ-lē, -ᵊn-iŋ-\ *adv*
un·re·con·struct·ed \ˌən-ˌrē-kən-ˈstrək-təd\ *adj* (1869) : not reconciled to some political, economic, or social change; *esp* : holding stubbornly to principles, beliefs, or views that are outmoded
un·reel \ˌən-ˈrē(ə)l, ˈən-\ *vt* (1567) **1** : to unwind from a reel **2** : to perform successfully ⟨~*ed* a 66-yard pass play⟩ **3** : REEL OFF 1 ~ *vi* **1** : to become unwound **2** : to be presented ⟨the dress rehearsal ~*ed* flawlessly⟩
un·reeve \-ˈrēv\ *vt* **-rove** \-ˈrōv\ *or* **-reeved; -reev·ing** (1600) : to withdraw (a rope) from an opening (as a ship's block or thimble)
un·re·gen·er·ate \ˌən-ri-ˈjen-(ə-)rət\ *adj* (1612) **1** : not regenerated : UNREPENTANT **2 a** : not reformed : UNRECONSTRUCTED ⟨~ revolutionaries⟩ **b** : OBSTINATE, STUBBORN ⟨struggling against ~ impulses⟩ — **un·re·gen·er·ate·ly** *adv*
un·re·lent·ing \-ˈlent-iŋ\ *adj* (1588) **1** : not softening or yielding in determination : HARD, STERN ⟨an ~ leader⟩ **2** : not letting up or weakening in vigor or pace : CONSTANT ⟨~ struggles⟩ — **un·re·lent·ing·ly** \-iŋ-lē\ *adv*
un·re·marked \-ˈmärkt\ *adj* (1775) : not remarked : UNNOTICED
un·re·mit·ting \-ˈmit-iŋ\ *adj* (1728) : not remitting : CONSTANT, INCESSANT — **un·re·mit·ting·ly** \-iŋ-lē\ *adv*
un·re·serve \-ˈzərv\ *n* (1751) : absence of reserve : FRANKNESS
un·re·served \-ˈzərvd\ *adj* (1539) **1** : not limited or partial : ENTIRE, UNQUALIFIED ⟨~ enthusiasm⟩ **2** : not cautious or reticent : FRANK, OPEN **3** : not set aside for special use — **un·re·serv·ed·ly** \-ˈzər-vəd-lē\ *adv* — **un·re·served·ness** \-ˈzər-vəd-nəs, -ˈzərv(d)-nəs\ *n*
un·rest \ˌən-ˈrest, ˈən-\ *n* (14c) : a disturbed or uneasy state : TURMOIL
un·re·strained \ˌən-ri-ˈstrānd\ *adj* (1600) **1** : not restrained : IMMODERATE, UNCONTROLLED ⟨~ proliferation of technology⟩ **2** : free of constraint : SPONTANEOUS ⟨felt happy and ~⟩ — **un·re·strain·ed·ly** \-ˈstrā-nəd-lē\ *adv* — **un·re·strained·ness** \-ˈstrā-nəd-nəs, -ˈstrān(d)-nəs\ *n*
un·re·straint \-ˈstrānt\ *n* (1804) : freedom from or lack of restraint
un·rid·dle \ˌən-ˈrid-ᵊl, ˈən-\ *vt* (1586) : to find the explanation of : SOLVE
un·rig \-ˈrig\ *vt* (1579) : to strip of rigging ⟨~ a ship⟩
un·righ·teous \-ˈrī-chəs\ *adj* (bef. 12c) **1** : not righteous : SINFUL, WICKED **2** : UNJUST, UNMERITED ⟨intolerable and ~ interference in their lives —W. W. Wagar⟩ — **un·righ·teous·ly** *adv* — **un·righ·teous·ness** *n*
un·ripe \-ˈrīp\ *adj* (14c) **1** : not ripe : IMMATURE **2** : not ready : UNPREPARED — **un·ripe·ness** *n*
un·ri·valed *or* **un·ri·valled** \ˌən-ˈrī-vəld, ˈən-\ *adj* (1591) : having no rival : INCOMPARABLE, SUPREME
un·roll \-ˈrōl\ *vt* (15c) **1** : to unwind a roll of : open out : UNCOIL **2** : to spread out like a scroll for reading or inspection : UNFOLD, REVEAL ~ *vi* : to be unrolled : UNWIND
un·roof \-ˈrüf, -ˈru̇f\ *vt* (ca. 1598) : to strip off the roof or covering of
[1]**un·round** \ˌən-ˈrau̇nd, ˈən-\ *vt* (ca. 1909) **1** : to spread (the lips) laterally ⟨necessary to ~ the lips in pronouncing \ē\⟩ **2** : to pronounce (a sound) without lip rounding or with decreased lip rounding
[2]**unround** *adj* (1958) : pronounced with the lips not rounded : UNROUNDED
un·ruf·fled \ˌən-ˈrəf-əld, ˈən-\ *adj* (1659) **1** : poised and serene esp. in the face of setbacks or confusion **2** : not ruffled : SMOOTH ⟨~ water⟩ **syn** see COOL
un·ruly \-ˈrü-lē\ *adj* [ME *unreuly*, fr. *un-* + *reuly* disciplined, fr. *reule* rule] (15c) : not readily ruled, disciplined, or managed : TURBULENT — **un·rul·i·ness** *n*

syn UNRULY, UNGOVERNABLE, INTRACTABLE, REFRACTORY, RECALCITRANT, WILLFUL, HEADSTRONG mean not submissive to government or control. UNRULY implies lack of discipline or incapacity for discipline and often connotes waywardness or turbulence of behavior ⟨*unruly* children⟩ UNGOVERNABLE implies either an escape from control or guidance or a state of being unsubdued and incapable of controlling oneself or being controlled by others ⟨*ungovernable* rage⟩ INTRACTABLE suggests stubborn resistance to guidance or control ⟨the farmers were *intractable* in their opposition to the hazardous-waste dump⟩ REFRACTORY stresses resistance to attempts to manage or to mold ⟨special schools for *refractory* children⟩ RECALCITRANT suggests determined resistance to or defiance of authority ⟨acts of sabotage by a *recalcitrant* populace⟩ WILLFUL implies an obstinate determination to have one's own way ⟨a *willful* disregard for the rights of others⟩ HEADSTRONG suggests self-will impatient of restraint, advice, or suggestion ⟨a *headstrong* young cavalry officer⟩

un·sad·dle \ˌən-ˈsad-ᵊl, ˈən-\ *vt* (14c) **1** : to take the saddle from **2** : to throw from the saddle ~ *vi* : to remove the saddle from a horse
un·said \-ˈsed\ *adj* (bef. 12c) : not said; *esp* : not spoken aloud
un·sat·is·fac·to·ry \-ˌsat-əs-ˈfak-t(ə-)rē\ *adj* (1637) : not satisfactory — **un·sat·is·fac·to·ri·ly** \-t(ə-)rə-lē\ *adv* — **un·sat·is·fac·to·ri·ness** \-t(ə-)rē-nəs\ *n*
un·sat·u·rate \-ˈsach-(ə-)rət\ *n* (1936) : an unsaturated chemical compound
un·sat·u·rat·ed \-ˈsach-ə-ˌrāt-əd\ *adj* (1758) : not saturated: as **a** : capable of absorbing or dissolving more of something ⟨an ~ solution⟩ **b** : able to form products by chemical addition; *esp* : containing double or triple bonds between carbon atoms
un·saved \ˌən-ˈsāvd, ˈən-\ *adj* (1648) : not saved; *esp* : not absolved from eternal punishment : not regenerate
un·sa·vory \-ˈsāv-(ə-)rē\ *adj* (13c) **1** : INSIPID, TASTELESS **2 a** : unpleasant to taste or smell **b** : DISAGREEABLE, DISTASTEFUL ⟨an ~ assignment⟩; *esp* : morally offensive
un·say \-ˈsā, *Southern also* -ˈse\ *vt* **-said** \-ˈsed\; **-say·ing** \-ˈsā-iŋ\ (15c) : to make as if not said : RECANT, RETRACT
un·say·able \-ˈsā-ə-bəl\ *adj* (1905) : not sayable : not easily expressed or related
un·scathed \-ˈskāthd\ *adj* (14c) : wholly unharmed : not injured
un·schooled \-ˈsküld\ *adj* (1594) **1** : not schooled : UNTAUGHT, UNTRAINED ⟨an ~ woodsman⟩ **2** : not artificial : NATURAL ⟨~ talent⟩
un·sci·en·tif·ic \ˌən-ˌsī-ən-ˈtif-ik\ *adj* (1775) : not scientific: as **a** : not used in scientific work **b** : not being in accord with the principles and methods of science ⟨~ management of woodlands⟩ **c** : not showing scientific knowledge or familiarity with scientific methods — **un·sci·en·tif·i·cal·ly** \-i-k(ə-)lē\ *adv*
un·scram·ble \ˌən-ˈskram-bəl, ˈən-\ *vt* (1919) **1** : to separate (as a conglomeration or tangle) into original components : RESOLVE, CLARIFY **2** : to restore (scrambled communication) to intelligible form — **un·scram·bler** \-b(ə-)lər\ *n*
un·screw \-ˈskrü\ *vt* (1651) **1** : to draw the screws from **2** : to loosen or withdraw by turning ~ *vi* : to become or admit of being unscrewed
un·script·ed \-ˈskrip-təd\ *adj* (1944) : not following a prepared script
un·scru·pu·lous \-ˈskrü-pyə-ləs\ *adj* (1803) : not scrupulous : UNPRINCIPLED — **un·scru·pu·lous·ly** *adv* — **un·scru·pu·lous·ness** *n*
un·seal \-ˈsē(ə)l\ *vt* (15c) : to break or remove the seal of : OPEN
un·sealed \-ˈsē(ə)ld\ *adj* (15c) : not sealed
un·seam \ˌən-ˈsēm, ˈən-\ *vt* (1592) : to open the seams of
un·search·able \-ˈsər-chə-bəl\ *adj* (14c) : not capable of being searched or explored : INSCRUTABLE — **un·search·ably** \-blē\ *adv*

\ə\ abut \ᵊ\ kitten, F table \ər\ further \a\ ash \ā\ ace \ä\ cot, cart \au̇\ out \ch\ chin \e\ bet \ē\ easy \g\ go \i\ hit \ī\ ice \j\ job \ŋ\ sing \ō\ go \ȯ\ law \ȯi\ boy \th\ thin \th\ the \ü\ loot \u̇\ foot \y\ yet \zh\ vision \à, k, ⁿ, œ, œ̄, ue, ue̅, ʸ\ *see* Guide to Pronunciation

un·sea·son·able \-'sēz-nə-bəl, -'sēz-ᵊn-ə-\ *adj* (15c) **1 :** occurring at other than the proper time : UNTIMELY **2 :** not being in season **3 a :** not normal for the season of the year ⟨~ weather⟩ **b :** marked by unseasonable weather ⟨an ~ summer⟩ — **un·sea·son·able·ness** *n* — **un·sea·son·ably** \-blē\ *adv*

un·seat \-'sēt\ *vt* (1596) **1 :** to dislodge from one's seat esp. on horseback **2 :** to remove from a place or position; *esp* **:** to remove from political office

[1]**un·seem·ly** \-'sēm-lē\ *adj* (14c) **:** not seemly: as **a :** not according with established standards of good form or taste ⟨~ bickering⟩ **b :** not suitable for time or place : INAPPROPRIATE, UNSEASONABLE ***syn*** see INDECOROUS — **un·seem·li·ness** \-lē-nəs\ *n*

[2]**unseemly** *adv* (14c) **:** in an unseemly manner

un·seen \,ən-'sēn, 'ən-\ *adj* (13c) **1 :** not seen or perceived : INVISIBLE **2 :** SIGHT 1 ⟨an ~ translation⟩

un·seg·re·gat·ed \-'seg-ri-,gāt-əd\ *adj* (ca. 1909) **:** not segregated; *esp* **:** free from racial segregation

un·se·lect·ed \,ən(t)-sə-'lek-təd\ *adj* (ca. 1890) **:** not selected : chosen at random

un·se·lec·tive \-'lek-tiv\ *adj* (ca. 1925) **:** not marked by selection : RANDOM, INDISCRIMINATE

un·self·ish \,ən-'sel-fish, 'ən-\ *adj* (1698) **:** not selfish : GENEROUS — **un·self·ish·ly** *adv* — **un·self·ish·ness** *n*

un·sell \-'sel\ *vt* **-sold** \-'sōld\; **-sel·ling** (ca. 1929) **1 :** to dissuade from a belief in the truth, value, or desirability of something ⟨ads that ~ the public on energy consumption⟩ **2 :** to dissuade one from a belief in the truth, value, or desirability of ⟨I *unsold* the coat he wanted and sold him another⟩

un·set \-'set\ *adj* (1561) **:** not set: as **a :** not fixed in a setting : UNMOUNTED ⟨~ diamonds⟩ **b :** not firmed or solidified ⟨~ concrete⟩

un·set·tle \,ən-'set-ᵊl, 'ən-\ *vt* (1651) **1 :** to loosen or move from a settled state or condition : make unstable : DISORDER **2 :** to perturb or agitate mentally or emotionally : DISCOMPOSE ~ *vi* **:** to become unsettled — **un·set·tling·ly** \-'set-liŋ-lē, -ᵊl-iŋ-\ *adv*

un·set·tled \-'set-ᵊld\ *adj* (1591) **:** not settled: as **a** (1) **:** not calm or tranquil : DISTURBED ⟨~ political conditions⟩ (2) **:** likely to vary widely esp. in the near future : VARIABLE ⟨~ weather⟩ (3) **:** not settled down ⟨~ dust⟩ **b** (1) **:** not decided or determined : DOUBTFUL ⟨an ~ state of mind⟩ (2) **:** not resolved or worked out : UNDECIDED ⟨an ~ question⟩ **c :** characterized by irregularity ⟨an ~ life⟩ **d :** not inhabited or populated ⟨~ land⟩ **e :** mentally unbalanced **f** (1) **:** not disposed of according to law ⟨an ~ estate⟩ (2) **:** not paid or discharged ⟨~ debts⟩ — **un·set·tled·ness** \-ᵊl(d)-nəs\ *n*

un·set·tle·ment \-ᵊl-mənt\ *n* (1648) **1 :** an act, process, or instance of unsettling **2 :** the quality or state of being unsettled

un·sew \,ən-'sō, 'ən-\ *vt* **-sewed; -sewn** \-'sōn\ *or* **-sewed; -sew·ing** (14c) **:** to undo the sewing of

un·sex \-'seks\ *vt* (1605) **1 :** to deprive of sex or sexual power **2 :** to deprive of the qualities typical of one's sex

un·shack·le \-'shak-əl\ *vt* (ca. 1611) **:** to free from shackles

un·shaped \-'shāpt\ *adj* (1572) **:** not shaped: as **a :** not dressed or finished to final form ⟨an ~ timber⟩ **b :** imperfect in form or formulation ⟨~ ideas⟩

un·shap·en \-'shā-pən\ *adj* [ME, fr. [1]*un-* + *shapen,* pp. of *shapen* to shape] (14c) **:** UNSHAPED

un·sheathe \,ən-'shēth, 'ən-\ *vt* (1542) **:** to draw from or as if from a sheath or scabbard

un·shift \-'shift\ *vi* (1966) **:** to release the shift key (as on a typewriter)

un·ship \-'ship\ *vt* (15c) **1 :** to take out of a ship : DISCHARGE, UNLOAD **2 :** to remove (as an oar or tiller) from position : DETACH ~ *vi* **:** to become or admit of being detached or removed

un·shod \,ən-'shäd, 'ən-\ *adj* (bef. 12c) **:** not wearing or provided with shoes

[1]**un·sight** \-'sīt\ *vt* (1615) **:** to prevent from seeing

[2]**unsight** *adj* (1622) **:** not sighted or examined

un·sight·ly \,ən-'sīt-lē, 'ən-\ *adj* (15c) **:** not pleasing to the sight : not comely — **un·sight·li·ness** \-lē-nəs\ *n*

un·skilled \-'skild\ *adj* (1581) **1 :** not skilled in a branch of work : lacking technical training ⟨an ~ worker⟩ **2 :** not requiring skill ⟨~ jobs⟩ **3 :** marked by lack of skill ⟨produced ~ poems⟩

un·skill·ful \-'skil-fəl\ *adj* (1565) **:** not skillful : lacking in skill or proficiency — **un·skill·ful·ly** \-fə-lē\ *adv* — **un·skill·ful·ness** *n*

un·sling \-'sliŋ\ *vt* **-slung** \-'sləŋ\; **-sling·ing** \-'sliŋ-iŋ\ (1630) **1 :** to remove from being slung ⟨*unslung* his carbine⟩ **2 :** to take off the slings of esp. aboard ship : release from slings

un·snap \-'snap\ *vt* (1862) **:** to loosen or free by or as if by undoing a snap

un·snarl \-'snär(-ə)l\ *vt* (1555) **:** to disentangle a snarl in

un·so·cia·ble \,ən-'sō-shə-bəl, 'ən-\ *adj* (1600) **1 :** having or showing a disinclination for social activity : SOLITARY, RESERVED **2 :** not conducive to sociability — **un·so·cia·bil·i·ty** \,ən-,sō-shə-'bil-ət-ē\ *n* — **un·so·cia·ble·ness** \,ən-'sō-shə-bəl-nəs, 'ən-\ *n* — **un·so·cia·bly** \-blē\ *adv*

un·so·cial \-'sō-shəl\ *adj* (1731) **:** lacking a taste or desire for society or close association; *also* **:** marked by or arising from such a lack ⟨an ~ disposition⟩ — **un·so·cial·ly** \-'sōsh-(ə-)lē\ *adv*

un·sold \-'sōld\ *adj* (14c) **:** not sold

un·so·phis·ti·cat·ed \,ən(t)-sə-'fis-tə-,kāt-əd\ *adj* (1664) **:** not sophisticated: as **a :** not changed or corrupted : GENUINE **b** (1) **:** not worldly-wise : lacking social or economic sophistication (2) **:** lacking complexity of structure : SIMPLE, STRAIGHTFORWARD ⟨an ~ approach to a problem⟩ ***syn*** see NATURAL

un·so·phis·ti·ca·tion \-,fis-tə-'kā-shən\ *n* (1825) **:** lack of or freedom from sophistication

un·sought \,ən-'sȯt, 'ən-\ *adj* (13c) **:** not searched for or sought out ⟨~ compliments⟩

un·sound \-'saund\ *adj* (14c) **:** not sound: as **a :** not healthy or whole **b :** not mentally normal : not wholly sane **c :** not firmly made, placed, or fixed **d :** not valid or true : INVALID, SPECIOUS — **un·sound·ly** \-'saun-(d)lē\ *adv*

un·sound·ness \-'saun(d)-nəs\ *n* (1599) **1 :** the quality or state of being unsound **2 :** something (as a disease) that causes one to be unsound

un·spar·ing \-'spa(ə)r-iŋ, -'spe(ə)r-\ *adj* (1586) **1 :** not merciful or forbearing : HARD, RUTHLESS **2 :** not frugal : LIBERAL, PROFUSE — **un·spar·ing·ly** \-iŋ-lē\ *adv*

un·speak \-'spēk\ *vt, obs* (1605) **:** UNSAY

un·speak·able \-'spē-kə-bəl\ *adj* (15c) **1 a :** incapable of being expressed in words : UNUTTERABLE **b :** inexpressibly bad : HORRENDOUS **2 :** that may not or cannot be spoken ⟨the bawdy thoughts that come into one's head — the ~ words —L. P. Smith⟩ ⟨~ collections of consonants —Rosemary Jellis⟩ — **un·speak·ably** \-blē\ *adv*

un·sports·man·like \-'spōrt-smən-,līk, -'spȯrt-\ *adj* (1754) **:** not characteristic of or exhibiting good sportsmanship : not sportsmanlike

un·spot·ted \-'spät-əd\ *adj* (14c) **:** not spotted : free from spot or stain; *esp* **:** free from moral stain

un·sprung \-'sprəŋ\ *adj* (1600) **:** not sprung; *esp* **:** not equipped with springs

un·sta·ble \-'stā-bəl\ *adj* (13c) **:** not stable : not firm or fixed : not constant: as **a :** not steady in action or movement : IRREGULAR ⟨an ~ pulse⟩ **b :** wavering in purpose or intent : VACILLATING **c :** lacking steadiness : apt to move, sway, or fall ⟨an ~ tower⟩ **d :** readily changing (as by decomposing) in chemical composition or biological activity **e :** characterized by inability to control the emotions ***syn*** see INCONSTANT — **un·sta·ble·ness** *n* — **un·sta·bly** \-b(ə-)lē\ *adv*

[1]**un·steady** \,ən-'sted-ē, 'ən-\ *vt* (1532) **:** to make unsteady

[2]**unsteady** *adj* (ca. 1598) **:** not steady: as **a :** not firm or solid : not fixed in position : UNSTABLE **b :** marked by change or fluctuation : CHANGEABLE **c :** not uniform or even : IRREGULAR — **un·steadi·ly** \-'sted-ᵊl-ē\ *adv* — **un·steadi·ness** \-'sted-ē-nəs\ *n*

un·step \,ən-'step, 'ən-\ *vt* (1853) **:** to remove (a mast) from a step

un·stick \-'stik\ *vt* **-stuck** \-'stək\; **-stick·ing** (ca. 1706) **:** to release from a state of adhesion

un·stint·ing \-'stint-iŋ\ *adj* (1845) **:** giving or being given freely or generously ⟨an ~ volunteer⟩ ⟨~ praise⟩ — **un·stint·ing·ly** *adv*

un·stop \-'stäp\ *vt* (14c) **1 :** to free from an obstruction : OPEN **2 :** to remove a stopper from

un·stop·pa·ble \-'stäp-ə-bəl\ *adj* (1836) **:** incapable of being stopped — **un·stop·pa·bly** \-blē\ *adv*

un·strap \-'strap\ *vt* (1828) **:** to remove or loose a strap from

un·stressed \,ən-'strest, 'ən-\ *adj* (1883) **1 :** not bearing a stress or accent ⟨~ syllables⟩ **2 :** not subjected to stress ⟨~ wires⟩

un·string \-'striŋ\ *vt* **-strung** \-'strəŋ\; **-string·ing** \-'striŋ-iŋ\ (ca. 1611) **1 :** to loosen or remove the strings of **2 :** to remove from a string **3 :** to make weak, disordered, or unstable ⟨was *unstrung* by the news⟩

un·struc·tured \-'strək-chərd\ *adj* (1941) **:** not structured: as **a :** having few formal requirements ⟨an ~ college course⟩ **b :** not having a patterned social organization ⟨in a neighborhood gang . . . with a relatively ~ system —*Jour. of Social Issues*⟩

un·stud·ied \-'stəd-ēd\ *adj* (14c) **:** not studied: as **a :** not acquired by study **b :** not forced : not done or planned for effect

un·sub·stan·tial \,ən(t)-səb-'stan-chəl\ *adj* (15c) **:** not substantial : lacking substance, firmness, or strength — **un·sub·stan·ti·al·i·ty** \-,stan-chē-'al-ət-ē\ *n* — **un·sub·stan·tial·ly** \,ən(t)-səb-'stanch-(ə-)lē\ *adv*

un·suc·cess \,ən(t)-sək-'ses\ *n* (1586) **:** lack of success : FAILURE

un·suc·cess·ful \-fəl\ *adj* (1617) **:** not successful : not meeting with or producing success — **un·suc·cess·ful·ly** \-fə-lē\ *adv*

un·sung \,ən-'səŋ, 'ən-\ *adj* (15c) **1 :** not sung **2 :** not celebrated or praised (as in song or verse) ⟨an ~ hero⟩

un·swathe \-'swäth, -'swȯth, -'swāth\ *vt* (15c) **:** to free from something that swathes

un·swear \-'swa(ə)r, -'swe(ə)r\ *vb* **-swore** \-'swō(ə)r, -'swȯ(ə)r\; **-sworn** \-'swō(ə)rn, -'swȯ(ə)rn\; **swear·ing** *vi, archaic* (1596) **:** to unsay or retract something sworn ~ *vt, archaic* **:** to recant or recall (as an oath) esp. by a second oath

un·swerv·ing \-'swər-viŋ\ *adj* (1694) **1 :** not swerving or turning aside **2 :** STEADY ⟨~ loyalty⟩

un·sym·met·ri·cal \,ən(t)-sə-'me-tri-kəl\ *adj* (ca. 1755) **:** ASYMMETRIC — **un·sym·met·ri·cal·ly** \-k(ə-)lē\ *adv*

un·tan·gle \,ən-'taŋ-gəl, 'ən-\ *vt* (1550) **:** to loose from tangles or entanglement : straighten out ***syn*** see EXTRICATE

un·tapped \-'tapt\ *adj* (1775) **1 :** not subjected to tapping ⟨an ~ keg⟩ **2 :** not drawn upon or utilized ⟨as yet ~ markets⟩

un·taught \-'tȯt\ *adj* (14c) **1 :** not instructed or trained : IGNORANT **2 :** NATURAL, SPONTANEOUS ⟨~ kindness⟩

un·teach \-'tēch\ *vt* **-taught** \-'tȯt\; **-teach·ing** (1532) **1 :** to cause to unlearn something **2 :** to teach the contrary of

un·ten·a·ble \-'ten-ə-bəl\ *adj* (1647) **1 :** not able to be defended **2 :** not able to be occupied — **un·ten·a·bil·i·ty** \,ən-,ten-ə-'bil-ət-ē\ *n*

un·tent·ed \-'tent-əd\ *adj* [[1]*un-* + obs. E *tented,* pp. of *tent* (to probe)] (1605) **:** not probed or dressed ⟨the ~ woundings of a father's curse —Shak.⟩

un·teth·er \-'teth-ər\ *vt* (1775) **:** to free from a tether

un·think \-'thiŋk\ *vt* **-thought** \-'thȯt\; **-think·ing** (1600) **:** to put out of mind

un·think·able \-'thiŋ-kə-bəl\ *adj* (15c) **1 :** not capable of being grasped by the mind **2 :** being contrary to what is reasonable, desirable, or probable : being out of the question — **un·think·abil·i·ty** \,ən-,thiŋ-kə-'bil-ət-ē\ *n* — **un·think·ably** \,ən-'thiŋ-kə-blē, 'ən-\ *adv*

un·think·ing \,ən-'thiŋ-kiŋ, 'ən-\ *adj* (1676) **1 :** not taking thought : HEEDLESS, UNMINDFUL **2 :** not indicating thought or reflection **3 :** not having the power of thought — **un·think·ing·ly** \-kiŋ-lē\ *adv*

un·thought \-'thȯt\ *adj* (1548) **:** not anticipated : UNEXPECTED — often used with *of* ⟨an *unthought*-of development⟩

un·thread \,ən-'thred, 'ən-\ *vt* (1595) **1 :** to draw or take out a thread from **2 :** to loosen the threads or connections of **3 :** to make one's way through ⟨~ a maze⟩

un·throne \-'thrōn\ *vt* (ca. 1611) **:** to remove from or as if from a throne

un·ti·dy \-'tīd-ē\ *adj* (14c) **1 :** not neat : CARELESS, SLOVENLY **2 a :** not neatly organized or carried out ⟨an ~ manuscript⟩ **b :** conducive to a lack of neatness ⟨~ tasks like bathing the baby —*New Yorker*⟩ — **un·ti·di·ly** \-'tīd-ᵊl-ē\ *adv* — **un·ti·di·ness** \-'tīd-ē-nəs\ *n*

un·tie \-'tī\ *vb* **-tied; -ty·ing** *or* **-tie·ing** *vt* (bef. 12c) **1 :** to free from something that ties, fastens, or restrains : UNBIND **2 a :** to disengage the knotted parts of **b :** DISENTANGLE, RESOLVE ⟨~ a traffic jam⟩ ~ *vi* **:** to become loosened or unbound

[1]**un·til** \ən-,til, -tᵊl, -,tel, ,ən-, *in some contexts* ᵊn-, ᵊm-, *or* ᵊŋ-\ *prep* [ME, fr. *un-* unto, until (akin to OE *oth* to, until, OHG *unt* unto, until, OE *ende* end) + *til, till* till] (13c) **1** *chiefly Scot* **:** TO **2** — used as a func-

tion word to indicate continuance (as of an action or condition) to a specified time ⟨stayed ~ morning⟩ **3 :** BEFORE ⟨not available ~ tomorrow⟩

[2]**until** *conj* (14c) **:** up to the time that **:** till such time as ⟨play continued ~ it got dark⟩ ⟨never able to relax ~ he took up fishing⟩ ⟨ran ~ he was breathless⟩

[1]**un·time·ly** \ˌən-ˈtīm-lē, ˈən-\ *adv* (13c) **1 :** at an inopportune time **:** UNSEASONABLY **2 :** before the due, natural, or proper time **:** PREMATURELY

[2]**untimely** *adj* (1535) **1 :** occurring or done before the due, natural, or proper time **:** too early **:** PREMATURE ⟨~ death⟩ **2 :** INOPPORTUNE, UNSEASONABLE ⟨an ~ joke⟩ ⟨~ frost⟩ — **un·time·li·ness** *n*

un·time·ous \-ˈtī-məs\ *adj, chiefly Scot* (1500) **:** UNTIMELY

un·tir·ing \-ˈtī-riŋ\ *adj* (1822) **:** not becoming tired **:** INDEFATIGABLE ⟨an ~ worker⟩ — **un·tir·ing·ly** *adv*

un·ti·tled \-ˈtīt-ᵊld\ *adj* (1590) **1** *obs* **:** having no title or right to rule **2 :** not named ⟨an ~ novel⟩ **3 :** not called by a title ⟨~ nobility⟩

un·to \ˌən-tə(-w), ˈən-(ˌ)tü\ *prep* [ME, fr. *un-* unto, until + *to*] (14c) **1 :** TO **2** — used as a function word to indicate reference or concern ⟨they became a world ~ themselves —Anne T. Fleming⟩

un·told \ˈən-ˈtōld, ˈən-\ *adj* (15c) **1 :** too great or numerous to count **:** INCALCULABLE, VAST **2 a :** not told or related **b :** kept secret

un·touch·abil·i·ty \ˌən-ˌtəch-ə-ˈbil-ət-ē\ *n* (1922) **:** the quality or state of being untouchable; *esp* **:** the state of being an untouchable

[1]**un·touch·able** \ˌən-ˈtəch-ə-bəl, ˈən-\ *adj* (1567) **1 a :** forbidden to the touch **:** not to be handled **b :** exempt from criticism or control **2 :** lying beyond reach ⟨~ mineral resources buried deep within the earth⟩ **3 :** disagreeable or defiling to the touch

[2]**untouchable** *n* (1913) **:** one that is untouchable; *specif, often cap* **:** a member of a large formerly segregated hereditary group in India having in traditional Hindu belief the quality of defiling by contact a member of a higher caste

un·touched \ˌən-ˈtəcht, ˈən-\ *adj* (14c) **1 :** not subjected to touching **:** not handled **2 :** not described or dealt with **3 a :** not tasted **b :** being in the first or a primeval state or condition **4 :** not influenced **:** UNAFFECTED

un·to·ward \ˌən-ˈtō(-ə)rd, ˈən-, -ˈtō(-ə)rd; ˌən-tə-ˈwȯ(ə)rd\ *adj* (1526) **1 :** difficult to guide, manage, or work with **:** UNRULY, INTRACTABLE **2 a :** marked by trouble or unhappiness **:** UNLUCKY **b :** not favorable **:** ADVERSE, UNPROPITIOUS **3 :** IMPROPER, INDECOROUS — **un·to·ward·ly** *adv* — **un·to·ward·ness** *n*

un·tread \ˌən-ˈtred, ˈən-\ *vt, archaic* (1592) **:** to tread back **:** RETRACE

un·tried \-ˈtrīd\ *adj* (1526) **1 :** not tested or proved by experience or trial **2 :** not tried in court

un·trod \-ˈträd\ *or* **un·trod·den** \-ˈträd-ᵊn\ *adj* (1593) **:** not trod **:** UNTRAVERSED

un·trou·bled \-ˈtrəb-əld\ *adj* (15c) **1 :** not given trouble **:** not made uneasy **2 :** CALM, TRANQUIL

un·true \-ˈtrü\ *adj* (bef. 12c) **1 :** not faithful **:** DISLOYAL **2 :** not according with a standard of correctness **:** not level or exact **3 :** not according with the facts **:** FALSE — **un·tru·ly** \-ˈtrü-lē\ *adv*

un·truss \-ˈtrəs\ *vt* (1577) **1** *archaic* **:** UNTIE, UNFASTEN — used in the phrase *untruss one's points* **2** *archaic* **:** UNDRESS ~ *vi, archaic* **:** to unfasten or take off one's clothes and esp. one's breeches

un·truth \ˌən-ˈtrüth, ˈən-\ *n* (bef. 12c) **1** *archaic* **:** DISLOYALTY **2 :** lack of truthfulness **:** FALSITY **3 :** something that is untrue **:** FALSEHOOD

un·truth·ful \-ˈtrüth-fəl\ *adj* (ca. 1847) **:** not containing or telling the truth **:** FALSE, INACCURATE ⟨~ report⟩ ***syn*** see DISHONEST — **un·truth·ful·ly** \-fə-lē\ *adv* — **un·truth·ful·ness** *n*

un·tune \-ˈt(y)ün\ *vt* (ca. 1598) **1 :** to put out of tune **2 :** DISARRANGE, DISCOMPOSE

un·tu·tored \-ˈt(y)üt-ərd\ *adj* (1593) **1 a :** having no formal learning or training **b :** NAIVE, UNSOPHISTICATED **2 :** not produced or developed by instruction **:** NATIVE ⟨~ shrewdness⟩ ***syn*** see IGNORANT

un·twine \-ˈtwīn\ *vt* (15c) **1 :** to unwind the twisted or tangled parts of **:** DISENTANGLE **2 :** to remove by unwinding ~ *vi* **:** to become disentangled or unwound

un·twist \ˌən-ˈtwist, ˈən-\ *vt* (ca. 1538) **:** to separate the twisted parts of **:** UNTWINE ~ *vi* **:** to become untwined

un·twist·ed \-ˈtwis-təd\ *adj* (1575) **:** not twisted

un·used \-ˈyüzd, *in the phrase "unused to" usu* -ˈyüs(t)\ *adj* (13c) **1 :** not habituated **:** UNACCUSTOMED ⟨~ to crowds⟩ **2 :** not used: as **a :** FRESH, NEW ⟨set an ~ canvas on the easel⟩ **b :** not put to use **:** IDLE ⟨~ land⟩ **c :** not consumed **:** ACCRUED ⟨~ sick leave⟩

un·usu·al \-ˈyüzh-(ə-)wəl, -ˈyü-zhəl\ *adj* (1582) **:** not usual **:** UNCOMMON, RARE — **un·usu·al·ly** \-ē\ *adv* — **un·usu·al·ness** *n*

un·ut·ter·able \ˌən-ˈət-ə-rə-bəl, ˈən-\ *adj* (1586) **:** being beyond the powers of description **:** INEXPRESSIBLE — **un·ut·ter·ably** \-blē\ *adv*

un·val·ued \-ˈval-(ˌ)yüd, -yəd\ *adj* (1586) **1** *obs* **:** INVALUABLE **2 a :** not important or prized **:** DISREGARDED **b :** not appraised

un·var·nished \-ˈvär-nisht\ *adj* (1604) **1 a :** not adorned or glossed **:** PLAIN, STRAIGHTFORWARD ⟨told the ~ truth⟩ **b :** ARTLESS, FRANK ⟨the ~ candor of old people and children —Janet Flanner⟩ **2 :** not coated with or as if with varnish **:** CRUDE, UNFINISHED

un·veil \ˌən-ˈvā(ə)l, ˈən-\ *vt* (1599) **1 :** to remove a veil or covering from **2 :** to make public **:** DIVULGE, REVEAL ~ *vi* **:** to throw off a veil or protective cloak

un·veiled \-ˈvā(ə)ld\ *adj* (1606) **:** not veiled **:** OPEN, REVEALED

un·vo·cal \ˌən-ˈvō-kəl, ˈən-\ *adj* (1773) **1 :** not eloquent or outspoken **:** INARTICULATE **2 :** not musical **:** DISCORDANT

un·voice \-ˈvȯis\ *vt* (1637) **:** DEVOICE

un·voiced \-ˈvȯist\ *adj* (1859) **1 :** not verbally expressed **2 :** VOICELESS 2

un·war·rant·able \-ˈwȯr-ənt-ə-bəl, -ˈwär-\ *adj* (1612) **:** not justifiable **:** INEXCUSABLE — **un·war·rant·ably** \-blē\ *adv*

un·wary \ˌən-ˈwa(ə)r-ē, ˈən-, -ˈwe(ə)r-\ *adj* (1579) **:** not alert **:** easily fooled or surprised **:** HEEDLESS, GULLIBLE — **un·wari·ly** \-ˈwar-ə-lē, -ˈwer-\ *adv* — **un·wari·ness** \-ˈwar-ē-nəs, -ˈwer-\ *n*

[1]**un·washed** \-ˈwȯsht, -ˈwäsht\ *adj* (14c) **1 :** not cleaned with or as if with soap and water **2 :** IGNORANT, PLEBEIAN — **un·washed·ness** *n*

[2]**unwashed** *n* (1833) **:** an ignorant or underprivileged group **:** RABBLE

un·wea·ried \-ˈwi(ə)r-ēd\ *adj* (13c) **:** not tired or jaded **:** FRESH — **un·wea·ried·ly** *adv*

un·weave \-ˈwēv\ *vt* **-wove** \-ˈwōv\; **-wo·ven;** \-ˈwō-vən\; **-weav·ing** (1542) **:** DISENTANGLE, RAVEL

un·weet·ing \-ˈwēt-iŋ\ *adj, archaic* (14c) **:** UNWITTING — **un·weet·ing·ly** \-iŋ-lē\ *adv, archaic*

un·weight \-ˈwāt\ *vt* (ca. 1939) **:** to reduce momentarily the force exerted by (as a ski) upon a surface by shifting the weight or position of one's body ~ *vi* **:** to unweight something by shifting the weight or position of one's body

un·well \ˌən-ˈwel, ˈən-\ *adj* (15c) **1 :** being in poor health **:** AILING, SICK **2 :** undergoing menstruation

un·whole·some \-ˈhōl-səm\ *adj* (13c) **1 :** detrimental to physical, mental, or moral well-being **:** UNHEALTHY ⟨~ food⟩ ⟨~ pastimes⟩ **2 a :** CORRUPT, UNSOUND **b :** offensive to the senses **:** LOATHSOME — **un·whole·some·ly** *adv*

un·wieldy \-ˈwēl-dē\ *adj* (1530) **:** not easily managed or handled esp. because of bulk or weight **:** CUMBERSOME — **un·wield·i·ly** \-ˈwēl-də-lē\ *adv* — **un·wield·i·ness** \-dē-nəs\ *n*

un·will·ing \-ˈwil-iŋ\ *adj* (bef. 12c) **:** not willing: **a :** LOATH, RELUCTANT ⟨was ~ to learn⟩ **b :** done or given reluctantly ⟨~ approval⟩ **c :** offering opposition **:** OBSTINATE — **un·will·ing·ly** \-iŋ-lē\ *adv* — **un·will·ing·ness** *n*

un·wind \-ˈwīnd\ *vb* **-wound** \-ˈwau̇nd\; **-wind·ing** *vt* (14c) **1 a :** to cause to uncoil **:** wind off **:** UNROLL **b :** to free from or as if from a binding or wrapping **c :** to release from tension **:** RELAX **2** *archaic* **:** RETRACE ~ *vi* **1 :** to become uncoiled or disentangled **:** UNFOLD **2 :** to become released from tension

un·wis·dom \ˌən-ˈwiz-dəm, ˈən-\ *n* (bef. 12c) **:** lack of wisdom **:** FOOLISHNESS, FOLLY

un·wise \-ˈwīz\ *adj* (bef. 12c) **:** lacking wisdom or good sense **:** FOOLISH, IMPRUDENT — **un·wise·ly** *adv*

un·wish \-ˈwish\ *vt, obs* (1594) **:** to wish away

un·wit·ting \-ˈwit-iŋ\ *adj* (bef. 12c) **1 :** not intended **:** INADVERTENT ⟨an ~ mistake⟩ **2 :** not knowing **:** UNAWARE ⟨kept the truth from their ~ friends⟩ — **un·wit·ting·ly** \-iŋ-lē\ *adv*

un·wont·ed \-ˈwȯnt-əd, -ˈwōnt- *also* -ˈwənt- *or* -ˈwänt-\ *adj* (1553) **1 :** being out of the ordinary **:** RARE, UNUSUAL **2 :** not accustomed by experience — **un·wont·ed·ly** *adv* — **un·wont·ed·ness** *n*

un·world·ly \-ˈwər(-ə)l-dlē, -ˈwərl-lē\ *adj* (1707) **1 :** not of this world **:** UNEARTHLY; *specif* **:** SPIRITUAL **2 a :** not wise in the ways of the world **:** NAIVE **b :** not swayed by mundane considerations — **un·world·li·ness** \-ˈwərl-(d)lē-nəs\ *n*

un·worn \-ˈwō(ə)rn, -ˈwȯ(ə)rn\ *adj* (1586) **1 a :** not impaired by use **:** not worn away **b :** not worn **:** NEW **2 :** not jaded **:** FRESH, ORIGINAL

un·wor·thy \ˌən-ˈwər-t͟hē, ˈən-\ *adj* (13c) **1 a :** lacking in excellence or value **:** POOR, WORTHLESS **b :** BASE, DISHONORABLE **2 :** not meritorious **:** UNDESERVING ⟨~ of attention⟩ **3 :** not deserved **:** UNMERITED ⟨~ treatment⟩ **4 :** inappropriate to one' s condition or station ⟨actions ~ of a gentleman⟩ — **un·wor·thi·ly** \-t͟hə-lē\ *adv* — **un·wor·thi·ness** \-t͟hē-nəs\ *n*

un·wrap \-ˈrap\ *vt* (14c) **:** to remove the wrapping from **:** DISCLOSE ⟨~ a package⟩ ⟨~ evidence in a criminal case⟩

un·wreathe \-ˈrēt͟h\ *vt* (1591) **:** UNCOIL, UNTWIST

un·writ·ten \-ˈrit-ᵊn\ *adj* (14c) **1 :** not expressed in writing **:** ORAL, TRADITIONAL **2 :** containing no writing **:** BLANK

unwritten constitution *n* (1890) **:** a constitution not embodied in a single document but based chiefly on custom and precedent as expressed in statutes and judicial decisions

unwritten law *n* (1641) **:** law based chiefly on custom rather than legislative enactments

un·yield·ing \ˌən-ˈyē(ə)l-diŋ, ˈən-\ *adj* (1658) **1 :** characterized by lack of softness or flexibility **2 :** characterized by firmness or obduracy — **un·yield·ing·ly** \-diŋ-lē\ *adv*

un·yoke \-ˈyōk\ *vt* (bef. 12c) **1 :** to free from a yoke or harness **2 :** to take apart **:** DISJOIN ~ *vi* **1** *archaic* **:** to unharness a draft animal **2** *archaic* **:** to cease from work

un·zip \-ˈzip\ *vt* (1939) **:** to zip open ~ *vi* **:** to open by or as if by means of a zipper

[1]**up** \ˈəp\ *adv* [partly fr. ME *up* upward, fr. OE *ūp;* partly fr. ME *uppe* on high, fr. OE; both akin to OHG *ūf* up, L *sub* under, Gk *hypo* under, *hyper* over — more at OVER] (bef. 12c) **1 a (1) :** in or into a higher position or level; *esp* **:** away from the center of the earth **(2) :** from beneath the ground or water to the surface **(3) :** from below the horizon **(4) :** UPSTREAM **(5) :** in or into an upright position ⟨sit ~⟩; *esp* **:** out of bed **b :** upward from the ground or surface ⟨pull ~ a daisy⟩ **c :** so as to expose a particular surface **2 :** with greater intensity ⟨speak ~⟩ **3 a :** in or into a better or more advanced state **b :** at an end ⟨your time is ~⟩ **c :** in or into a state of greater intensity or excitement **d :** in a continual sequence ⟨from third grade ~⟩ **4 a (1) :** into existence, evidence, prominence, or prevalence ⟨put ~ several new buildings⟩ **(2) :** into operation or practical form **b :** into consideration or attention ⟨bring ~ for discussion⟩ **5 :** into possession or custody **6 a :** ENTIRELY, COMPLETELY ⟨button ~ your coat⟩ **b** — used as an intensifier ⟨clean ~ the house⟩ **7 :** in or into storage **:** BY ⟨lay ~ supplies⟩ **8 a :** so as to arrive or approach **b :** in a direction conventionally the opposite of down: **(1) :** to windward **(2) :** NORTHWARD **(3) :** to or at the top **(4) :** to or at the rear of a theatrical stage **9 :** in or into parts **10 :** to a stop — usu. used with *draw, bring, fetch,* or *pull* **11 :** for each side ⟨the score is 15 ~⟩

[2]**up** *adj* (bef. 12c) **1 a :** risen above the horizon ⟨the sun is ~⟩ **b :** STANDING **c :** being out of bed **d :** relatively high ⟨the river is ~⟩ ⟨was well ~ in her class⟩ **e :** being in a raised position **:** LIFTED ⟨windows are ~⟩ **f :** being in a state of completion **:** CONSTRUCTED, BUILT **g :** having the face upward **h :** mounted on a horse ⟨a new jockey ~⟩ **i :** grown above a surface ⟨the corn is ~⟩ **j (1) :** moving, inclining, or directed upward ⟨the ~ escalator⟩ **(2) :** bound in a direction regarded as up **2 a :** marked by agitation, excitement, or activity **b :** being above a former or normal level (as of quantity or intensity)

⟨attendance is ~⟩ ⟨the wind is ~⟩ **c :** exerting enough power (as for operation) ⟨sail when steam is ~⟩ **d :** READY; *specif* **:** highly prepared **e :** going on **:** taking place ⟨find out what is ~⟩ **3 a :** risen from a lower position ⟨men ~ from the ranks⟩ **b :** being at the same level or point ⟨did not feel ~ to par⟩ **c** (1) **:** well informed **:** ABREAST ⟨~ on the news⟩ (2) **:** being on schedule ⟨~ on his homework⟩ **d :** being ahead of one's opponent **4 a :** presented for or undergoing consideration ⟨contract ~ for negotiation⟩; *specif* **:** charged before a court ⟨~ for robbery⟩ **b :** placed at stake **:** WAGERED — **up to 1 :** capable of performing or dealing with ⟨feels *up to* her role⟩ **2 :** engaged in ⟨what is he *up to*⟩ **3 :** being the responsibility of ⟨it's *up to* me⟩

[3]**up** \(,)əp, 'əp\ *prep* (1509) **1 a** — used as a function word to indicate motion to or toward or situation at a higher point of **b :** up into or in the ⟨went ~ attic⟩ **2 a :** in a direction regarded as being toward or near the upper end or part of ⟨lives a few miles ~ the coast⟩ **b :** toward or near a point closer to the source or beginning of ⟨sail ~ the river⟩ **3 :** in the direction opposite to ⟨sailed ~ the wind⟩

[4]**up** \'əp\ *n* (1536) **1 :** one in a high or advantageous position **2 :** an upward slope **3 :** a period or state of prosperity or success **4 :** [3]UPPER

[5]**up** *vb* **upped** *or in vi 2* **up; upped; up·ping; ups** *or in vi 2* **up** *vi* (1643) **1 a :** to rise from a lying or sitting position **b :** to move upward **:** ASCEND **2** — used with *and* and another verb to indicate that the action of the following verb was either surprisingly or abruptly initiated ⟨he ~ and married a showgirl⟩ **~** *vt* **1 :** RAISE, LIFT **2 a :** to advance to a higher level: (1) **:** INCREASE (2) **:** PROMOTE 1a **b :** RAISE 8d, 8e

up–and–com·ing \,əp-ən-'kəm-iŋ, ,əp-ᵊm-\ *adj* (1889) **:** alertly active and likely to advance or succeed — **up–and–com·er** \-'kəm-ər\ *n*

up–and–down *adj* (ca. 1755) **1 :** marked by alternate upward and downward movement, action, or surface **2 :** PERPENDICULAR

up and down \,əp-ᵊm-'daůn, ,əp-ən-\ *adv* (13c) **1 :** to and fro **2 :** here and there esp. throughout an area **3 :** with regard to every particular **:** THOROUGHLY ⟨knew the territory *up and down*⟩

up–and–up \'əp-ən-,əp\ *n* (1863) **:** an honest or respectable course — used chiefly in the phrase *on the up-and-up*

Upa·ni·shad \ü-'pän-i-,shäd, yü-'pan-ə-,shad\ *n* [Skt *upaniṣad*] (1805) **:** one of a class of Vedic treatises dealing with broad philosophic problems — **Upa·ni·shad·ic** \(,)ü-,pän-i-'shäd-ik, (,)yü-,pan-ə-'shad-ik\ *adj*

upas \'yü-pəs\ *n* [Malay *pohon upas* poison tree] (1783) **1 a :** a tall Asian and East Indian tree (*Antiaris toxicaria*) of the mulberry family with a latex that contains poisonous glucosides used as an arrow poison **b :** a shrub or tree (*Strychnos tieuté* of the family Loganiaceae) of the same region also yielding an arrow poison **2 :** a poisonous concentrate of the juice or latex of a upas **3 :** a poisonous or harmful influence or institution

[1]**up·beat** \'əp-,bēt\ *n* (1869) **1 :** an unaccented beat in a musical measure; *specif* **:** the last beat of the measure **2 :** an increase in activity or prosperity ⟨business that is on the ~⟩

[2]**upbeat** *adj* (1947) **:** CHEERFUL, OPTIMISTIC

up–bow \'əp-,bō\ *n* (ca. 1890) **:** a stroke in playing a bowed instrument in which the bow is moved across the strings from the tip to the heel

up·braid \,əp-'brād\ *vt* [ME *upbreyden,* fr. OE *ūpbregdan*] (14c) **1 :** to criticize severely **:** find fault with **2 :** to reproach severely **:** scold vehemently ***syn*** see SCOLD — **up·braid·er** *n*

up·bring·ing \'əp-,briŋ-iŋ\ *n* (1520) **:** early training; *esp* **:** a particular way of bringing up a child ⟨had a strict Protestant ~⟩

up·build \,əp-'bild\ *vt* **-built** \-'bilt\; **-build·ing** (1513) **:** BUILD UP — **up·build·er** *n*

up·cast \'əp-,kast\ *n* (1890) **:** something cast up

up·chuck \'əp-,chək\ *vb* (1936) **:** VOMIT

up·com·ing \,əp-,kəm-iŋ\ *adj* (1944) **:** FORTHCOMING, APPROACHING

up–coun·try \,əp-,kən-trē\ *adj* (1835) **:** of, relating to, or characteristic of an inland, upland, or outlying region — **up–country** \'əp-,\ *n* — **up–country** \'əp-'\ *adv*

[1]**up·date** \,əp-'dāt\ *vt* (1910) **:** to bring up to date

[2]**up·date** \'əp-,dāt\ *n* (1965) **1 :** an act or instance of updating **2 :** current information for updating something **3 :** an up-to-date version, account, or report

up·do \'əp-(,)dü\ *n, pl* **updos** [*up*swept hair*do*] (1938) **:** an upswept hairdo

up·draft \'əp-,draft, -,dråft\ *n* (ca. 1887) **:** an upward movement of gas (as air)

up·end \,ə-'pend\ *vt* (1823) **1 :** to set or stand on end **2 a :** to affect to the point of being upset or flurried ⟨a . . . literary shocker, designed to ~ the credulous matrons —Wolcott Gibbs⟩ **b :** DEFEAT, BEAT **~** *vi* **:** to rise on an end

up·field \'əp-'fē(ə)ld\ *adv or adj* (ca. 1934) **:** in or into the part of the field toward which the offensive team is headed

up–front \,əp-'frənt, ,əp-,\ *adj* (1945) **:** being or coming in or at the front: as **a** (1) **:** being in a conspicuous or leading position (2) **:** FRANK, FORTHRIGHT **b :** playing in a front line (as in football) **c :** paid or payable in advance

up front *adv* (1937) **1 :** in or at the front **2 :** in advance

[1]**up·grade** \'əp-,grād\ *n* (1873) **1 :** an upward grade or slope **2 :** INCREASE, RISE

[2]**up·grade** \'əp-,grād, ,əp-'\ *vt* (1901) **:** to raise or improve the grade of: as **a :** to improve (livestock) by use of purebred sires **b :** to advance to a job requiring a higher level of skill esp. as part of a training program **c :** to raise the quality of (as a manufactured product) **d :** to raise the classification and usu. the price of (a product) without improving the quality **e :** to extend the usefulness of (as a device)

up·growth \'əp-,grōth\ *n* (1844) **:** the process of growing upward **:** DEVELOPMENT; *also* **:** a product or result of this

up·heav·al \,əp-'hē-vəl, (,)ə-'pē-\ *n* (1838) **1 :** the action or an instance of upheaving esp. of part of the earth's crust **2 :** extreme agitation or disorder **:** radical change; *also* **:** an instance of this

up·heave \,əp-'hēv, (,)ə-'pēv\ *vt* (14c) **:** to heave up **:** LIFT **~** *vi* **:** to move upward esp. with power — **up·heav·er** *n*

[1]**up·hill** \'əp-,hil\ *n* (1548) **:** rising ground **:** ASCENT

[2]**up·hill** \-'hil\ *adv* (1607) **1 :** upward on a hill or incline **2 :** against difficulties ⟨seemed to be talking ~ —Willa Cather⟩

[3]**up·hill** \-,hil\ *adj* (1613) **1 :** situated on elevated ground **2 a :** going up **:** ASCENDING **b :** being the higher one or part esp. of a set; *specif* **:** being nearer the top of an incline **3 :** DIFFICULT, LABORIOUS

up·hold \(,)əp-'hōld\ *vt* **-held** \-'held\; **-hold·ing** (13c) **1 a :** to give support to **b :** to support against an opponent **2 a :** to keep elevated **b :** to lift up ***syn*** see SUPPORT — **up·hold·er** *n*

up·hol·ster \(,)əp-'hōl-stər, (,)ə-'pōl-\ *vt* **-stered; -ster·ing** \-st(ə-)riŋ\ [back-formation fr. *upholstery*] (1853) **:** to furnish with or as if with upholstery — **up·hol·ster·er** \-stər-ər\ *n*

up·hol·stery \-st(ə-)rē\ *n, pl* **-ster·ies** [ME *upholdester* upholsterer, fr. *upholden* to uphold, fr. *up* + *holden* to hold] (1649) **:** materials (as fabric, padding, and springs) used to make a soft covering esp. for a seat

up·keep \'əp-,kēp\ *n* (1884) **1 :** the act of maintaining in good condition **:** the state of being maintained in good condition **2 :** the cost of maintaining in good condition

up·land \'əp-lənd, -,land\ *n* (1566) **1 :** high land esp. at some distance from the sea **:** PLATEAU **2 :** ground elevated above the lowlands along rivers or between hills — **upland** *adj* — **up·land·er** \-lən-dər, -,lan-\ *n*

upland cotton *n* (1819) **:** any of various usu. short-staple cottons cultivated esp. in the U.S.

upland plover *n* (1832) **:** a large sandpiper (*Bartramia longicauda*) of eastern No. America that frequents fields and uplands — called also *upland sandpiper*

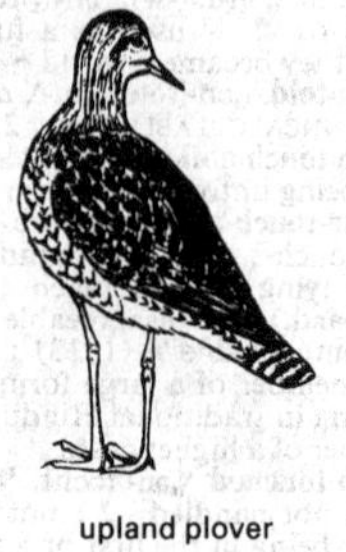

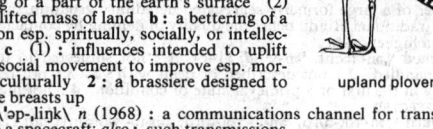

upland plover

[1]**up·lift** \(,)əp-'lift\ *vt* (14c) **1 :** to lift up **:** ELEVATE; *esp* **:** to cause (a portion of the earth's surface) to rise above adjacent areas **2 :** to improve the spiritual, social, or intellectual condition of **~** *vi* **:** RISE — **up·lift·er** *n*

[2]**up·lift** \'əp-,lift\ *n* (1853) **1 :** an act, process, result, or cause of uplifting: as **a** (1) **:** the uplifting of a part of the earth's surface (2) **:** an uplifted mass of land **b :** a bettering of a condition esp. spiritually, socially, or intellectually **c** (1) **:** influences intended to uplift (2) **:** a social movement to improve esp. morally or culturally **2 :** a brassiere designed to hold the breasts up

up·link \'əp-,liŋk\ *n* (1968) **:** a communications channel for transmissions to a spacecraft; *also* **:** such transmissions

up·man·ship \'əp-mən-,ship\ *n* (1959) **:** ONE-UPMANSHIP

up·mar·ket \,əp-,mär-kət\ *adj* (1972) **:** UPSCALE ⟨~ store⟩

up·most \'əp-,mōst\ *adj* (1560) **:** UPPERMOST

[1]**up·on** \ə-'pȯn, -'pän, -(,)pən\ *prep* (13c) **:** ON

[2]**up·on** \ə-'pȯn, -'pän\ *adv* (14c) **1** *obs* **:** on the surface **:** on it **2** *obs* **:** THEREAFTER, THEREON

[1]**up·per** \'əp-ər\ *adj* [compar. of [2]*up*] (14c) **1 a :** higher in physical position, rank, or order **b :** farther inland ⟨the ~ Mississippi⟩ **2 :** constituting the branch of a bicameral legislature that is usu. smaller and more restricted in membership and possesses greater traditional prestige than the lower house **3 a :** constituting a stratum relatively near the earth's surface **b** *cap* **:** being a later epoch or series of the period or series named ⟨*Upper* Cretaceous⟩ **4 :** NORTHERN ⟨~ Manhattan⟩

[2]**upper** *n* (1845) **:** one that is upper: as **a :** the parts of a shoe or boot above the sole **b :** an upper tooth or denture **c :** an upper berth — **on one's uppers :** in straitened circumstances **:** DESTITUTE

[3]**upper** *n* [*up* + [2]*-er*] (ca. 1968) **:** a stimulant drug; *esp* **:** AMPHETAMINE

upper atmosphere *n* (1933) **:** the part of the atmosphere that lies exterior to the troposphere and usu. includes the stratosphere, mesosphere, and thermosphere

[1]**up·per·case** \,əp-ər-'kās\ *adj* [fr. the compositor's practice of keeping capital letters in the upper of a pair of type cases] (ca. 1738) **:** CAPITAL 1

[2]**uppercase** *n* (1916) **:** capital letters

[3]**uppercase** *vt* **-cased; -cas·ing** (1949) **:** to print or set in capital letters

upper case *n* (1683) **:** a type case containing capitals and usu. small capitals, fractions, symbols, and accents

upper–class *adj* (1837) **:** of, relating to, or characteristic of the upper class

upper class *n* (1839) **:** a social class occupying a position above the middle class and having the highest status in a society

up·per·class·man \,əp-ər-'klas-mən\ *n* (1871) **:** a member of the junior or senior class in a school or college

upper crust *n* (ca. 1835) **:** the highest social class or group; *esp* **:** the highest circle of the upper class

up·per·cut \'əp-ər-,kət\ *n* (1856) **:** a swinging blow (as in boxing) directed upward with a bent arm — **uppercut** *vb*

upper hand *n* (15c) **:** MASTERY, ADVANTAGE, CONTROL ⟨was determined not to let the opposition get the *upper hand*⟩

up·per·most \'əp-ər-,mōst\ *adv* (15c) **:** in or into the highest or most prominent position — **uppermost** *adj*

up·per·part \-,pärt\ *n* (1805) **:** a part lying on the upper side (as of a bird)

upper partial *n* (1880) **:** OVERTONE 1a

up·pish \'əp-ish\ *adj* (ca. 1755) **:** UPPITY — **up·pish·ly** *adv* — **up·pish·ness** *n*

up·pi·ty \'əp-ət-ē\ *adj* [prob. fr. *up* + *-ity* (as in *persnickity,* var. of *persnickety*)] (1880) **:** putting on or marked by airs of superiority **:** ARROGANT, PRESUMPTUOUS ⟨was offended by the ~ attitude of the waiter⟩ — **up·pi·ty·ness** *n*

up quark *n* (1976) **:** a quark having an electric charge of + ⅔, zero charm, and zero strangeness

up·raise \(,)ə-'prāz\ *vt* (14c) **:** to raise or lift up **:** ELEVATE

up·rear \(,)ə-'pri(ə)r\ *vt* (14c) **1 :** to lift up **2 :** ERECT **~** *vi* **:** RISE

[1]**up·right** \'əp-,rīt\ *adj* [ME, fr. OE *ūpriht,* fr. *ūp* up + *riht* right; akin to OHG *ūfreht* upright] (bef. 12c) **1 a :** PERPENDICULAR, VERTICAL **b :** erect in carriage or posture **c :** having the main axis or a main part perpendicular ⟨~ freezer⟩ **2 :** marked by strong moral rectitude — **up·right·ly** *adv* — **up·right·ness** *n*

syn UPRIGHT, HONEST, JUST, CONSCIENTIOUS, SCRUPULOUS, HONORABLE mean having or showing a strict regard for what is morally right. UPRIGHT implies a strict adherence to moral principles; HONEST stresses adherence to such virtues as truthfulness, candor, fairness; JUST stresses conscious choice and regular practice of what is right or equitable; CONSCIENTIOUS and SCRUPULOUS imply an active moral sense governing all one's actions and painstaking efforts to follow one's conscience; HONORABLE suggests a firm holding to codes of right behavior and the guidance of a high sense of honor and duty.

[2]**upright** *adv* (1590) **:** vertically upward **:** in an upright position

[3]**upright** *n* (1683) **1 :** the state of being upright **:** PERPENDICULAR ⟨a pillar out of ~⟩ **2 :** something that stands upright **3 :** UPRIGHT PIANO

upright piano *n* (1896) **:** a piano with vertical frame and strings — compare GRAND PIANO

[1]**up·rise** \ˌə-ˈprīz\ *vi* **up·rose** \-ˈprōz\; **up·ris·en** \-ˈpriz-ᵊn\; **up·ris·ing** \-ˈprī-ziŋ\ (14c) **1 a :** to rise to a higher position **b** (1) **:** STAND UP (2) **:** to get out of bed **c :** to come into view esp. from below the horizon **2 :** to rise up in sound — **up·ris·er** \ˌə-ˈprī-zər, ˈəp-ˌrī-\ *n*

[2]**up·rise** \ˈəp-ˌrīz\ *n* (1588) **1 :** an act or instance of uprising **2 :** an upward slope

up·ris·ing \ˈəp-ˌrī-ziŋ\ *n* (1587) **:** an act or instance of rising up; *esp* **:** a usu. localized act of popular violence in defiance of an established government ***syn*** see REBELLION

up·riv·er \ˈəp-ˈriv-ər\ *adv or adj* (1836) **:** toward or at a point nearer the source of a river

up·roar \ˈəp-ˌrō(ə)r, -ˌrȯ(ə)r\ *n* [by folk etymology fr. D *oproer,* fr. MD, fr. *op* up (akin to OE *ūp*) + *roer* motion; akin to OE *hrēran* to stir] (1526) **:** a state of commotion, excitement, or violent disturbance

up·roar·i·ous \ˌə-ˈprōr-ē-əs, -ˈprȯr-\ *adj* (1819) **1 :** marked by uproar **2 :** very noisy and full **3 :** extremely funny ⟨an ~ comedy⟩ — **up·roar·i·ous·ly** *adv* — **up·roar·i·ous·ness** *n*

up·root \(ˌ)ə-ˈprüt, -ˈpru̇t\ *vt* (1695) **1 :** to pull up by the roots **2 :** to remove as if by pulling up **3 :** to displace from a country or traditional habitat ***syn*** see EXTERMINATE — **up·root·ed·ness** *n* — **up·root·er** *n*

up·rush \ˈəp-ˌrəsh\ *n* (1873) **1 :** an upward rush (as of gas or liquid) **2 :** a sudden increase

ups and downs *n pl* (1659) **:** alternating rise and fall esp. in fortune

up·scale \ˌəp-ˌskāl\ *adj* (1972) **:** relating to, being, or appealing to wealthy consumers

[1]**up·set** \(ˌ)əp-ˈset\ *vb* **-set; -set·ting** *vt* (1677) **1 :** to thicken and shorten (as a heated bar of iron) by hammering on the end **:** SWAGE **2 :** to force out of the usual upright, level, or proper position **:** OVERTURN **3 a :** to trouble mentally or emotionally **:** disturb the poise of **b :** to throw into disorder **c :** INVALIDATE **d :** to defeat unexpectedly **4 :** to cause a physical disorder in; *specif* **:** to make somewhat ill ~ *vi* **:** to become overturned ***syn*** see DISCOMPOSE — **up·set·ter** *n*

[2]**up·set** \ˈəp-ˌset\ *n* (1804) **1 :** an act of overturning **:** OVERTURN **2 a** (1) **:** an act of throwing into disorder **:** DERANGEMENT (2) **:** a state of disorder **:** CONFUSION **b :** an unexpected defeat **3 a :** a minor physical disorder ⟨a stomach ~⟩ **b :** an emotional disturbance ⟨went through a big ~ after his father's death⟩ **4 a :** a part of a rod (as the head on a bolt) that is upset **b :** the expansion of a bullet on striking **5 :** a swage used in upsetting

up·set price \ˌəp-ˌset-\ *n* (1814) **:** the minimum price set for property offered at auction or public sale

up·shift \ˈəp-ˌshift\ *vi* (1952) **:** to shift an automotive vehicle into a higher gear — **upshift** *n*

up·shot \ˈəp-ˌshät\ *n* (1604) **:** the final result **:** OUTCOME

up·side down \ˌəp-ˌsīd-ˈdau̇n\ *adv* [alter. of ME *up so doun,* fr. *up* + *so* + *doun* down] (14c) **1 :** in such a way that the upper and the lower parts are reversed in position **2 :** in or into great disorder — **upside–down** *adj*

upside–down cake *n* (1930) **:** a cake baked with its batter covering an arrangement of fruit (as pineapple) and served fruit side up

up·si·lon \ˈyüp-sə-ˌlän, ˈəp-, -lən, *Brit usu* yüp-ˈsī-lən\ *n* [MGk *y psilon,* lit., simple *y;* fr. the desire to distinguish it from *oi,* which was pronounced the same in later Greek] (1621) **:** the 20th letter of the Greek alphabet — see ALPHABET table

upsilon particle *n* (1976) **:** any of a group of unstable electrically neutral elementary particles of the meson family that have a mass about 10 times that of a proton

up·spring \ˌəp-ˈspriŋ\ *vi* **-sprang** \-ˈspraŋ\ *or* **-sprung** \-ˈsprəŋ\; **-sprung; -spring·ing** \-ˈspriŋ-iŋ\ (bef. 12c) **1 :** to spring up **2 :** to come into being

[1]**up·stage** \ˈəp-ˈstāj\ *adj* (1919) **1 :** of or relating to the rear of a stage **2** [[4]*upstage*]**:** HAUGHTY

[2]**upstage** *adv* (1925) **1 :** toward or at the rear of a theatrical stage **2 :** away from a motion-picture or television camera

[3]**up·stage** \ˈəp-ˌstāj\ *n* (1926) **:** the part of a stage that is farthest from the audience or camera

[4]**up·stage** \ˌəp-ˈstāj\ *vt* (1926) **1 :** to force (an actor) to face away from the audience by staying upstage **2 :** to steal the show from **3 :** to treat snobbishly

[1]**up·stairs** \ˈəp-ˈsta(ə)rz, -ˈste(ə)rz\ *adv* (1596) **1 :** up the stairs **:** on or to a higher floor **2 :** to or at a high altitude or higher position ⟨quietly moved him ~ to board chairman —*Newsweek*⟩ **3 :** in the head ⟨she's all vacant ~ —J. T. Farrell⟩

[2]**up·stairs** \ˌəp-ˌsta(ə)rz, -ˌste(ə)rz\ *adj* (1782) **:** situated above the stairs esp. on an upper floor ⟨an ~ bedroom⟩

[3]**up·stairs** \ˈəp-ˈ, ˈəp-ˌ\ *n pl but sing or pl in constr* (1842) **:** the part of a building above the ground floor

up·stand·ing \ˌəp-ˈstan-diŋ, ˈəp-ˌ\ *adj* (bef. 12c) **1 :** ERECT, UPRIGHT **2 :** marked by integrity — **up·stand·ing·ness** *n*

[1]**up·start** \ˌəp-ˈstärt\ *vi* (14c) **:** to jump up (as to one's feet) suddenly

[2]**up·start** \ˈəp-ˌstärt\ *n* (1555) **1 :** one that has risen suddenly (as from a low position to wealth or power) **:** PARVENU; *esp* **:** one that claims more personal importance than he warrants **2 :** a start-up enterprise — **upstart** \ˌəp-ˌ\ *adj*

up·state \ˈəp-ˌstāt\ *n* (1901) **:** the chiefly northerly sections of a state; *also* **:** the chiefly rural part of a state when the major metropolitan area is in the south — **up·state** \-ˈstāt\ *adv or adj* — **up·stat·er** \-ˈstāt-ər\ *n*

up·stream \ˈəp-ˈstrēm\ *adv or adj* (1681) **1 :** in the direction opposite to the flow of a stream **2 :** toward a portion of the production stream closer to basic extractive or manufacturing processes ⟨make most of its money ~, selling cheap crude . . . to refineries —John Quirt⟩

up·stroke \ˈəp-ˌstrōk\ *n* (1828) **:** a stroke made in an upward direction

up·surge \ˈəp-ˌsərj\ *n* (1917) **:** a rapid or sudden rise

[1]**up·sweep** \ˈəp-ˌswēp\ *vi* **-swept** \-ˌswept\; **-sweep·ing** (1791) **:** to sweep upward

[2]**upsweep** *n* (ca. 1890) **:** an upward sweep

up·swept \ˈəp-ˌswept\ *adj* (1938) **:** swept upward; *specif* **:** brushed up to the top of the head ⟨~ hairdo⟩

up·swing \ˈəp-ˌswiŋ\ *n* (1924) **1 :** an upward swing **2 :** a marked increase (as in activity)

up·take \ˈəp-ˌtāk\ *n* [Sc *uptake* to understand] (1726) **1 :** UNDERSTANDING, COMPREHENSION ⟨quick on the ~⟩ **2 :** a flue leading upward **3 :** an act or instance of absorbing and incorporating esp. into a living organism

up–tem·po \ˈəp-ˌtem-(ˌ)pō\ *n, often attrib* (1952) **:** a fast-moving tempo (as in jazz)

[1]**up·throw** \ˈəp-ˌthrō\ *vt* **-threw** \-ˌthrü\; **-thrown** \-ˌthrōn\; **-throw·ing** (1614) **:** to throw or thrust upward

[2]**upthrow** *n* (1807) **:** an upward displacement (as of a rock stratum) **:** UPHEAVAL, UPTHRUST

[1]**up·thrust** \ˈəp-ˌthrəst\ *vt* (1845) **:** to thrust up; *esp* **:** to elevate (a part of the earth's surface) in an upthrust ~ *vi* **:** to rise with an upward thrust

[2]**upthrust** *n* (1846) **:** an upward thrust; *specif* **:** an uplift of part of the earth's crust

up·tick \ˈəp-ˌtik\ *n* [*up* + [3]*tick*] (1955) **:** INCREASE, RISE

up·tight \ˈəp-ˈtīt, (ˌ)əp-ˈ, ˌəp-ˌ\ *adj* (1964) **1 a :** being tense, nervous, or uneasy **b :** ANGRY, INDIGNANT **c :** rigidly conventional **2 :** being in financial difficulties — **up·tight·ness** \(ˌ)əp-ˈtīt-nəs\ *n*

up·tilt \ˌəp-ˈtilt\ *vt* (ca. 1901) **:** to tilt upward

up·time \ˈəp-ˌtīm\ *n* (ca. 1960) **:** time during which a piece of equipment (as a computer) is functioning or able to function

up to *prep* (1809) **1 —** used as a function word to indicate extension as far as a specified place ⟨sank *up to* his knees in the mud⟩ **2 —** used as a function word to indicate a limit or boundary ⟨*up to* 50,000 copies a month⟩ ⟨worked *up to* the last minute⟩

up–to–date *adj* (1888) **1 :** extending up to the present time **:** including the latest information ⟨~ maps⟩ **2 :** abreast of the times **:** MODERN ⟨~ methods⟩ — **up–to–date·ly** *adv* — **up–to–date·ness** *n*

up–to–the–minute *adj* (1912) **1 :** extending up to the immediate present **:** including the very latest information **2 :** marked by complete up-to-dateness

up·town \ˈəp-ˌtau̇n\ *n* (1838) **:** the upper part of a town or city; *esp* **:** the residential district — **up·town** \ˈəp-ˈtau̇n\ *adj or adv*

up·trend \ˈəp-ˌtrend\ *n* (1943) **:** an upturn esp. in business or economic activity

[1]**up·turn** \ˈəp-ˌtərn, ˌəp-ˈ\ *vt* (1567) **1 :** to turn up or over **2 :** to direct upward ~ *vi* **:** to turn upward

[2]**up·turn** \ˈəp-ˌtərn\ *n* (1864) **:** an upward turn esp. toward better conditions or higher prices

[1]**up·ward** \ˈəp-wərd\ *or* **up·wards** \-wərdz\ *adv* (bef. 12c) **1 a :** in a direction from lower to higher ⟨the kite rose ~⟩ **b** (1) **:** toward the source (as of a river) (2) **:** toward the interior (as of a region) **c :** in a higher position ⟨held out his hand, palm ~⟩ **d :** in the upper parts **:** toward the head **:** ABOVE ⟨from the waist ~⟩ **2 :** toward a higher or better condition or level ⟨young lawyers moving ~⟩ **3 a :** to an indefinitely greater amount, figure, or rank ⟨from $5 ~⟩ **b :** toward a greater amount or higher number, degree, or rate ⟨attendance figures have risen ~⟩ **4 :** toward or into later years ⟨from his youth ~⟩

[2]**upward** *adj* (1607) **1 :** directed toward or situated in a higher place or level **:** ASCENDING **2 :** rising to a higher pitch — **up·ward·ly** *adv* — **up·ward·ness** *n*

upward mobility *n* (1949) **:** the capacity or facility for rising to a higher social or economic position — **upwardly mobile** *adj*

upwards of *also* **upward of** *adv* (1721) **:** more than **:** in excess of ⟨they cost *upwards of* $25⟩

up·well \ˌəp-ˈwel\ *vi* (1885) **:** to well up; *specif* **:** to move or flow upward

up·well·ing \-ˈwel-iŋ\ *n* (1896) **:** the process or an instance of rising or appearing to rise to the surface and flowing outward; *esp* **:** the process of upward movement to the surface of marine often nutrient-rich lower waters esp. along some shores due to the offshore drift of surface water (as from the action of winds and the Coriolis force)

up·wind \ˈəp-ˈwind\ *adv or adj* (1838) **:** in the direction from which the wind is blowing

[1]**ur-** *or* **uro-** *comb form* [NL, fr. Gk *our-, ouro-,* fr. *ouron* urine — more at URINE] **1 :** urine ⟨*uric*⟩ **2 :** urinary tract ⟨*urology*⟩ **3 :** urinary and ⟨*urogenital*⟩ **4 :** urea ⟨*uracil*⟩

[2]**ur-** *or* **uro-** *comb form* [NL, fr. Gk *our-, ouro-,* fr. *oura* tail — more at ASS] **:** tail ⟨*uropod*⟩

Ur- \ˈu̇(ə)r\ *prefix* [G, fr. OHG *ir-, ur-* thoroughly (perfective prefix) — more at ABIDE] **1 :** original **:** primitive ⟨*Ur*-form⟩ **2 :** original version of ⟨*Ur*-Hamlet⟩

ura·cil \ˈyu̇r-ə-ˌsil, -səl\ *n* [ISV [1]*ur-* + acetic + *-il* (substance relating to)] (ca. 1909) **:** a pyrimidine base $C_4H_4N_2O_2$ that is one of the four bases coding genetic information in the polynucleotide chain of RNA — compare ADENINE, CYTOSINE, GUANINE, THYMINE

urae·us \yu̇-ˈrē-əs\ *n, pl* **uraei** \-ˈrē-ˌī\ [NL, fr. LGk *ouraios,* a snake] (1832) **:** a representation of the sacred asp (*Naja haje*) on the headdress of ancient Egyptian rulers serving as a symbol of sovereignty

Ural–Al·ta·ic \ˌyu̇r-ə-lal-ˈtā-ik\ *n* (1855) **1 :** a postulated language group comprising the Uralic and Altaic languages **2 :** a language type showing agglutination and vowel harmony and occurring esp. in languages of Eurasia — **Ural–Altaic** *adj*

Ura·li·an \yu̇-ˈrā-lē-ən, -ˈral-ē-\ *adj* (ca. 1797) **1 :** of or relating to the Ural mountains **2 :** URALIC

[1]**Ural·ic** \yu̇-ˈral-ik\ *adj* (1861) **:** of, relating to, or constituting the Finno-Ugric and Samoyed languages

[2]**Uralic** *n* (ca. 1911) **:** a language family comprising the Finno-Ugric and Samoyed languages

ural·ite \ˈyu̇r-ə-ˌlīt\ *n* [G *uralit,* fr. *Ural* mountains] (1835) **:** a usu. fibrous and dark green amphibole resulting from alteration of pyroxene — **ural·it·ic** \ˌyu̇r-ə-ˈlit-ik\ *adj*

[1]**uran-** *or* **urano-** *comb form* [L, fr. Gk *ouran-, ourano-,* fr. *ouranos*] **:** sky **:** heaven ⟨*uranometry*⟩

\ə\ abut \ᵊ\ kitten, F table \ər\ further \a\ ash \ā\ ace \ä\ cot, cart \au̇\ out \ch\ chin \e\ bet \ē\ easy \g\ go \i\ hit \ī\ ice \j\ job \ŋ\ sing \ō\ go \ȯ\ law \ȯi\ boy \th\ thin \t͟h\ the \ü\ loot \u̇\ foot \y\ yet \zh\ vision \à, k̲, ⁿ, œ, œ̄, ue, ue̅, ʸ\ see Guide to Pronunciation

²uran- or **urano-** *comb form* [F, fr. NL *uranium*] : uranium ⟨*uranyl*⟩

Ura·nia \yu̇-ˈrā-nē-ə, -nyə\ *n* [L, fr. Gk *Ourania*] : the Greek Muse of astronomy

Ura·ni·an \yu̇-ˈrā-nē-ən, -nyən\ *adj* (1844) : of or relating to the planet Uranus

ura·nic \yu̇-ˈran-ik, -ˈrā-nik\ *adj* [ISV] (1837) : of, relating to, or containing uranium esp. with a valence higher than in uranous compounds

ura·ni·nite \yu̇-ˈrā-nə-ˌnīt\ *n* [G *uranin* uraninite (fr. NL *uranium*) + E *-ite*] (1879) : a mineral that is basically a black octahedral or cubic oxide UO_2 of uranium containing thorium, the cerium and yttrium metals, and lead, that often when heated yields a gas consisting chiefly of helium, and that is the chief ore of uranium

ura·ni·um \yu̇-ˈrā-nē-əm\ *n, often attrib* [NL, fr. *Uranus*] (ca. 1797) : a silvery heavy radioactive polyvalent metallic element that is found esp. in pitchblende and uraninite and exists naturally as a mixture of three isotopes of mass number 234, 235, and 238 in the proportions of 0.006 percent, 0.71 percent, and 99.28 percent respectively — see ELEMENT table

uranium hexa·flu·o·ride \-ˌhek-sə-ˈflu̇(-ə)r-ˌīd\ *n* [*uranium* + *hexa-* + *fluoride*] (1941) : a volatile compound UF_6 of uranium and fluorine that is used in one major process of isolating uranium 235

uranium trioxide *n* (ca. 1929) : a brilliant orange compound UO_3 that is formed in the course of refining uranium and that has been used as a coloring agent for ceramic wares

uranium 238 *n* (1942) : an isotope of uranium of mass number 238 that absorbs neutrons to form a uranium isotope of mass number 239 which then decays through neptunium to form plutonium of mass number 239

uranium 235 *n* (1940) : a light isotope of uranium of mass number 235 that is physically separable from natural uranium, that when bombarded with slow neutrons undergoes rapid fission into smaller atoms with the release of neutrons and atomic energy, and that is used in power plants and atom bombs

ura·nog·ra·phy \ˌyu̇r-ə-ˈnäg-rə-fē\ *n* [Gk *ouranographia* description of the heavens, fr. *ouran-* uran- + *-graphia* -graphy] (1675) : the construction of celestial representations (as maps)

ura·nous \yu̇-ˈrā-nəs, ˈyu̇r-ə-\ *adj* (1842) : of, relating to, or containing uranium esp. with a lower valence than in uranic compounds

Ura·nus \ˈyu̇r-ə-nəs, yu̇-ˈrā-\ *n* [LL, fr. Gk *Ouranos*] **1** : the sky personified as a god and father of the Titans in Greek mythology **2** : the planet seventh in order from the sun — see PLANET table

ura·nyl \ˈyu̇r-ə-ˌnil, yu̇-ˈrān-ᵊl\ *n* [ISV] (1850) : a bivalent radical UO_2 formed by uranium trioxide in acid solution

urate \ˈyu̇(ə)r-ˌāt\ *n* [F, fr. *urique* uric, fr. E *uric*] (1800) : a salt of uric acid — **urat·ic** \yu̇-ˈrat-ik\ *adj*

ur·ban \ˈər-bən\ *adj* [L *urbanus*, fr. *urbs* city] (1619) : of, relating to, characteristic of, or constituting a city

ur·bane \ˌər-ˈbān\ *adj* [L *urbanus* urban, urbane] (ca. 1623) : notably polite or finished in manner : POLISHED ***syn*** see SUAVE — **ur·bane·ly** *adv*

ur·ban·ism \ˈər-bə-ˌniz-əm\ *n* (1889) **1** : the characteristic way of life of city dwellers **2** : the study of the physical needs of urban societies **3** : URBANIZATION

ur·ban·ist \ˈər-bə-nəst\ *n* (1930) : a specialist in city planning — **ur·ban·is·tic** \ˌər-bə-ˈnis-tik\ *adj* — **ur·ban·is·ti·cal·ly** \-ti-k(ə-)lē\ *adv*

ur·ban·ite \ˈər-bə-ˌnīt\ *n* (1897) : one living in a city

ur·ban·i·ty \ˌər-ˈban-ət-ē\ *n, pl* **-ties** (1535) **1** : the quality or state of being urbane **2** *pl* : urbane acts or conduct

ur·ban·iza·tion \ˌər-bə-nə-ˈzā-shən\ *n* (1888) : the quality or state of being or becoming urbanized

ur·ban·ize \ˈər-bə-ˌnīz\ *vt* **-ized; -iz·ing** (1884) **1** : to cause to take on urban characteristics ⟨*urbanized* areas⟩ **2** : to impart an urban way of life to ⟨~ migrants from rural areas⟩

ur·ban·ol·o·gy \ˌər-bə-ˈnäl-ə-jē\ *n* (1961) : a study dealing with specialized problems of cities (as planning, education, sociology, and politics) — **ur·ban·ol·o·gist** \-jəst\ *n*

urban renewal *n* (1954) : a construction program to replace or restore substandard buildings in an urban area

urban sprawl *n* (1961) : the spreading of urban developments (as houses and shopping centers) on undeveloped land near a city

ur·bi·cul·ture \ˈər-bə-ˌkəl-chər\ *n* [L *urb-*, *urbs* city + E *-i-* + *culture*] (1954) : practices and problems peculiar to cities or to urban life

ur·ce·o·late \ˌər-ˈsē-ə-lət, ˈər-sē-ə-ˌlāt\ *adj* [NL *urceolatus*, fr. L *urceolus*, dim. of *urceus* pitcher] (1760) : shaped like an urn ⟨the ~ corolla of a blueberry⟩

ur·chin \ˈər-chən\ *n* [ME, fr. MF *herichon*, fr. L *ericius*, fr. *er*; akin to Gk *chēr* hedgehog, L *horrēre* to bristle, tremble — more at HORROR] (14c) **1** : HEDGEHOG **2** : a mischievous youngster : SCAMP **3** : SEA URCHIN

urd \ˈu̇(ə)rd, ˈərd\ *n* [Hindi] (ca. 1934) : an annual bean (*Phaseolus mungo*) widely grown in warm regions for its edible blackish seed, for green manure, or for forage

Ur·du \ˈu̇(ə)r-(ˌ)dü, ˈər-\ *n* [Hindi *urdū-zabān*, lit., camp language] (1796) : an Indic language that is an official literary language of Pakistan and is widely used in India

-ure *n suffix* [ME, fr. OF, fr. L *-ura*] **1** : act : process ⟨*exposure*⟩ **2** : office : function; *also* : body performing (such) a function ⟨*legislature*⟩

urea \yu̇-ˈrē-ə\ *n* [NL, fr. F *urée*, fr. *urine*] (1806) : a soluble weakly basic nitrogenous compound $CO(NH_2)_2$ that is the chief solid component of mammalian urine and an end product of protein decomposition, is synthesized from carbon dioxide and ammonia, and is used esp. in synthesis (as of resins and plastics) and in fertilizers and animal rations

urea–formaldehyde resin *n* (1943) : a thermosetting synthetic resin made by condensing urea with formaldehyde

ure·ase \ˈyu̇r-ē-ˌās, -ˌāz\ *n* (1900) : an enzyme that promotes the hydrolysis of urea

ure·din·i·um \ˌyu̇r-ə-ˈdin-ē-əm\ *n, pl* **-ia** \-ē-ə\ [NL, fr. L *uredin-*, *uredo* burning, blight, fr. *urere* to burn — more at EMBER] (ca. 1909) : a crowded usu. brownish mass of hyphae and spores of a rust fungus forming pustules that rupture the host's cuticle — **ure·din·i·al** \-ē-əl\ *adj*

ure·do·spore \yu̇-ˈrēd-ə-ˌspō(ə)r, -ˌspȯ(ə)r\ *also* **ure·dio·spore** \-ˈrēd-ē-ə-\ *n* [NL *uredium* + E *-o-* + *spore*] (1875) : one of the thin-walled spores that are produced in repeated crops by the uredinial hyphae of rust fungi, spread the fungus vegetatively, and follow the aecial spores

ure·ide \ˈyu̇r-ē-ˌīd\ *n* (1857) : a cyclic or acyclic acyl derivative of urea

ure·mia \yu̇-ˈrē-mē-ə\ *n* [NL] (ca. 1857) **1** : accumulation in the blood usu. in severe kidney disease of constituents normally eliminated in the urine producing a severe toxic condition **2** : the toxic bodily condition associated with uremia ⟨the patient was in ~⟩ — **ure·mic** \-mik\ *adj*

ureo·tel·ic \yu̇-ˌrē-ə-ˈtel-ik, ˌyu̇r-ē-ō-\ *adj* [*urea* + *-o-* + *tel-* + *-ic*; fr. the fact that urea is the end product] (1950) : excreting nitrogen mostly in the form of urea ⟨~ mammals⟩ — **ureo·te·lism** \-ˈtel-ˌiz-əm, ˌyu̇r-ē-ˈät-ᵊl-ˌiz-əm\ *n*

ure·ter \ˈyu̇r-ət-ər\ *n* [NL, fr. Gk *ourētēr*, fr. *ourein* to urinate — more at URINE] (1578) : a duct that carries away the urine from a kidney to the bladder or cloaca — **ure·ter·al** \yu̇-ˈrēt-ə-rəl\ *or* **ure·ter·ic** \ˌyu̇r-ə-ˈter-ik\ *adj*

ure·thane \ˈyu̇r-ə-ˌthān\ *or* **ure·than** \-ˌthan\ *n* [F *uréthane*, fr. *ur-* + *éth-* eth- + *-ane*] (1838) **1** **a** : a crystalline compound $C_3H_7NO_2$ that is the ethyl ester of carbamic acid and is used esp. as a solvent and medicinally as an antineoplastic agent **b** : an ester of carbamic acid other than the ethyl ester **2** : POLYURETHANE

urethr- *or* **urethro-** *comb form* [NL, fr. LL *urethra*] : urethra ⟨*urethritis*⟩ ⟨*urethroscope*⟩

ure·thra \yu̇-ˈrē-thrə\ *n, pl* **-thras** *or* **-thrae** \-(ˌ)thrē\ [LL, fr. Gk *ourēthra*, fr. *ourein* to urinate] (1634) : the canal that in most mammals carries off the urine from the bladder and in the male serves also as a genital duct — **ure·thral** \-thrəl\ *adj*

ure·thri·tis \ˌyu̇r-i-ˈthrīt-əs\ *n* [NL] (1823) : inflammation of the urethra

ure·thro·scope \yu̇-ˈrē-thrə-ˌskōp\ *n* [ISV] (1868) : an instrument for viewing the interior of the urethra

¹urge \ˈərj\ *vb* **urged; urg·ing** [L *urgēre* — more at WREAK] *vt* (1560) **1** : to present, advocate, or demand earnestly or pressingly ⟨his conviction was upheld on a theory never *urged* at his . . . trial —Leon Friedman⟩ **2** : to undertake the accomplishment of with energy, swiftness, or enthusiasm ⟨~ the attack⟩ **3** **a** : SOLICIT, ENTREAT **b** : to serve as a motive or reason for **4** : to force or impel in an indicated direction or into motion or greater speed ⟨the dog *urged* the sheep toward the gate⟩ **5** : STIMULATE, PROVOKE ~ *vi* : to declare, advance, or press earnestly a statement, argument, charge, or claim — **urg·er** *n*

²urge *n* (1618) **1** : the act or process of urging **2** : a force or impulse that urges; *esp* : a continuing impulse toward an activity or goal

ur·gen·cy \ˈər-jən-sē\ *n, pl* **-cies** (1540) **1** : the quality or state of being urgent : INSISTENCE **2** : a force or impulse that impels or constrains : URGE

ur·gent \ˈər-jənt\ *adj* [ME, fr. MF, fr. L *urgent-*, *urgens*, prp. of *urgēre*] (15c) **1** **a** : calling for immediate attention : PRESSING ⟨~ appeals⟩ **b** : conveying a sense of urgency **2** : urging insistently : IMPORTUNATE — **ur·gent·ly** *adv*

-ur·gy \(ˌ)ər-jē\ *n comb form* [NL *-urgia*, fr. Gk *-ourgia*, fr. *-ourgos* working, fr. *-o-* + *ergon* work — more at WORK] : technique or art of dealing or working with (such) a product, matter, or tool ⟨*chemurgy*⟩

-uria \ˈ(y)u̇r-ē-ə\ *n comb form* [NL, fr. Gk *-ouria*, fr. *ouron* urine — more at URINE] **1** : presence of (a specified substance) in urine ⟨*albuminuria*⟩ **2** : condition of having (such) urine ⟨*polyuria*⟩; *esp* : abnormal or diseased condition marked by the presence of (a specified substance) ⟨*pyuria*⟩

uri·al \ˈu̇r-ē-əl, -ˌäl\ *n* [Panjabi *hureāl*] (1887) : an upland wild sheep (*Ovis vignei*) of southern and central Asia that is reddish brown with a white neck and a beard

uric \ˈyu̇(ə)r-ik\ *adj* (1797) : of, relating to, or found in urine

uric acid *n* (1800) : a white odorless and tasteless nearly insoluble diacid $C_5H_4N_4O_3$ that is present in small quantity in mammalian urine, is present abundantly in the form of urates in the excreta of most lower vertebrates and in vertebrates as the chief nitrogenous waste, and occurs pathologically in renal calculi and the tophi of gout

uri·co·su·ric \ˌyu̇r-i-kə-ˈs(h)u̇r-ik\ *adj* [irreg. fr. *uric*] (ca. 1947) : relating to or promoting the excretion of uric acid in the urine

uri·co·tel·ic \ˌyu̇r-i-kō-ˈtel-ik\ *adj* [*uric* + *-o-* + *tel-* + *-ic*; fr. the fact that uric acid is the end product] (1947) : excreting nitrogen mostly in the form of uric acid ⟨birds are typical ~ animals⟩ — **uri·co·tel·ism** \-ˈtel-ˌiz-əm, -ˈkät-ᵊl-ˌiz-əm\ *n*

uri·dine \ˈyu̇r-ə-ˌdēn\ *n* [ISV ¹*ur-* + *-idine*] (1927) : a crystalline nucleoside $C_9H_{12}N_2O_6$ that is composed of uracil attached to ribose, is derived by hydrolysis from nucleic acids, and in the form of phosphate derivatives plays an important role in carbohydrate metabolism

Uri·el \ˈyu̇r-ē-əl\ *n* [Heb *Ūrī'ēl*] : one of the four archangels named in Hebrew tradition

Urim and Thum·mim \ˌ(y)u̇r-ə-mən-ˈthəm-əm, ˌu̇(ə)r-ˌē-mən-ˈtu̇m-ˌēm\ *n pl* [part trans. of Heb *ūrīm wĕthummīm*] (1537) : sacred lots used in early times by the Hebrews

urin- *or* **urino-** *comb form* [ME, fr. OF, fr. L, fr. *urina* urine] : ¹UR- ⟨*urinogenital*⟩ ⟨*urinary*⟩

uri·nal \ˈyu̇r-ən-ᵊl, *Brit also* yu̇-ˈrīn-ᵊl\ *n* [ME, fr. MF, fr. LL, fr. L *urina*] (15c) **1** : a vessel for receiving urine **2** : a building or enclosure with facilities for urinating; *also* : a fixture used for urinating

uri·nal·y·sis \ˌyu̇r-ə-ˈnal-ə-səs\ *n, pl* **-y·ses** [NL, irreg. fr. *urin-* + *analysis*] (1889) : chemical analysis of urine

uri·nary \ˈyu̇r-ə-ˌner-ē\ *adj* (1578) **1** : relating to, occurring in, affecting, or constituting the organs concerned with the formation and discharge of urine ⟨~ system⟩ ⟨~ caculi⟩ **2** : of, relating to, or for urine **3** : excreted as or in urine

urinary bladder *n* (1728) : a membranous sac in many vertebrates that serves for the temporary retention of urine and discharges by the urethra

uri·nate \ˈyu̇r-ə-ˌnāt\ *vi* **-nat·ed; -nat·ing** (1599) : to discharge urine : MICTURATE — **uri·na·tion** \ˌyu̇r-ə-ˈnā-shən\ *n*

urine \ˈyu̇r-ən\ *n* [ME, fr. MF, fr. L *urina*; akin to Gk *ouron* urine, *ourein* to urinate, OE *wæter* water] (14c) : waste material that is secreted by the kidney in vertebrates, is rich in end products of protein metabolism together with salts and pigments, and forms a clear amber and usu. slightly acid fluid in mammals but is semisolid in birds and reptiles — **urin·ous** \ˈyu̇r-ə-nəs\ *adj*

uri·no·gen·i·tal \ˌyu̇r-ə-nō-ˈjen-ə-tᵊl\ *adj* (1836) : UROGENITAL

uri·nom·e·ter \ˌyu̇r-ə-ˈnäm-ət-ər\ *n* [ISV] (1843) **:** a small hydrometer for determining the specific gravity of urine

urn \ˈərn\ *n* [ME *urne,* fr. L *urna*] (14c) **1 :** a vessel that is typically an ornamental vase on a pedestal and that is used for various purposes (as preserving the ashes of the dead after cremation) **2 :** a closed vessel usu. with a spigot for serving a hot beverage ⟨a coffee ~⟩

uro- — see UR-

uro·ca·nic acid \ˌyu̇r-ə-ˌkā-nik-, -ˌkan-ik-\ *n* [1*ur-* + *canine* + *-ic;* fr. its being first obtained from the urine of a dog] (ca. 1903) **:** a crystalline acid $C_6H_6N_2O_2$ that is normally present in human skin and is held to act as a screening agent for ultraviolet radiation

uro·chor·date \ˌyu̇r-ə-ˈkȯrd-ət, -ˌāt\ *n* [NL *Urochordata,* former group name, fr. 2*ur-* + *chordatus* having a notochord, fr. *chorda* notochord] (1948) **:** TUNICATE — **urochordate** *adj*

uro·chrome \ˈyu̇r-ə-ˌkrōm\ *n* (1864) **:** a yellow pigment to which the color of normal urine is principally due

uro·dele \ˈyu̇r-ə-ˌdēl\ *n* [F *urodèle,* deriv. of Gk *oura* tail + *dēlos* evident, showing — more at SQUIRREL] (ca. 1890) **:** any of an order (Caudata) of amphibians (as newts) that have a tail throughout life — **urodele** *adj*

uro·gen·i·tal \ˌyu̇r-ō-ˈjen-ə-tᵊl\ *adj* [ISV] (1848) **:** of, relating to, or being the organs or functions of excretion and reproduction

uro·ki·nase \ˌyu̇r-ō-ˈkī-ˌnās, -ˌnāz\ *n* (1952) **:** an enzyme that is similar to streptokinase, is found in human urine, and is used to dissolve blood clots (as in the heart)

uro·lith \ˈyu̇r-ə-ˌlith\ *n* [ISV] (ca. 1900) **:** a calculus in the urinary tract

uro·lith·i·a·sis \ˌyu̇r-ə-lith-ˈī-ə-səs\ *n* [NL, fr. ISV *urolith*] (ca. 1860) **:** a condition that is characterized by the formation or presence of calculi in the urinary tract

uro·log·ic \ˌyu̇r-ə-ˈläj-ik\ *also* **uro·log·i·cal** \-i-kəl\ *adj* (1855) **:** of or relating to the urinary tract or to urology

urol·o·gist \yu̇-ˈräl-ə-jəst\ *n* (1889) **:** a physician who specializes in the urinary or urogenital tract — **urol·o·gy** \-jē\ *n*

-u·ron·ic \(y)u̇-ˈrän-ik\ *adj suffix* [Gk *ouron* urine] **:** connected with urine — in names of certain aldehyde-acids derived from sugars or compounds of such acids ⟨hyal*uronic*⟩

uron·ic acid \yu̇-ˌrän-ik-\ *n* (1925) **:** any of a class of acidic compounds of the general formula $HOOC(CHOH)_nCHO$ that contain both carboxylic and aldehydic groups, are oxidation products of sugars, and occur combined in many polysaccharides and in urine

uro·pod \ˈyu̇r-ə-ˌpäd\ *n* [ISV 2*ur-* + Gk *pod-, pous* foot — more at FOOT] (ca. 1890) **:** either of the flattened lateral appendages of the last abdominal segment of a crustacean; *broadly* **:** an abdominal appendage of a crustacean

uro·py·gi·al gland \ˌyu̇r-ə-ˌpī-jē-əl-\ *n* (1870) **:** a large gland that occurs in most birds, opens dorsally at the base of the tail feathers, and usu. secretes an oily fluid which the bird uses in preening its feathers — called also *oil gland*

uro·py·gi·um \ˌyu̇r-ə-ˈpī-jē-əm\ *n* [NL, fr. Gk *ouropygion,* fr. *ouro-* 2ur- + *pygē* rump — more at STEATOPYGIA] (1771) **:** the fleshy and bony prominence at the posterior extremity of a bird's body that supports the tail feathers

uro·style \ˈyu̇r-ə-ˌstīl\ *n* [ISV 2*ur-* + Gk *stylos* pillar — more at STEER] (1875) **:** a long unsegmented bone that represents a number of fused vertebrae and forms the posterior part of the vertebral column of frogs and toads

-urous \ˈ(y)u̇r-əs\ *adj comb form* [NL *-urus,* fr. Gk *-ouros,* fr. *oura* tail — more at SQUIRREL] **:** -tailed ⟨macr*urous*⟩

Ur·sa Ma·jor \ˌər-sə-ˈmā-jər\ *n* [L (gen. *Ursae Majoris*), lit., greater bear] **:** a constellation that is the most conspicuous of the northern constellations, is situated near the north pole of the heavens, and contains the stars forming the Big Dipper two of which are in a line indicating the direction of the North Star — called also *Great Bear*

Ursa Mi·nor \-ˈmī-nər\ *n* [L (gen. *Ursae Minoris*), lit., lesser bear] **:** a constellation that includes the north pole of the heavens and the stars which form the Little Dipper with the North Star at the tip of the handle — called also *Little Bear*

ur·sine \ˈər-ˌsīn\ *adj* [L *ursinus,* fr. *ursus* bear — more at ARCTIC] (ca. 1550) **:** of, relating to, or resembling a bear or the bear family (Ursidae)

Ur·su·line \ˈər-sə-lən, -ˌlīn, -ˌlēn\ *n* [NL *Ursulina,* fr. *Ursula* St. Ursula, legendary Christian martyr] (1693) **:** a member of any of several Roman Catholic teaching orders of nuns; *esp* **:** a member of a teaching order founded by St. Angela Merici in Brescia, Italy, in 1535

ur·text \ˈu̇(ə)r-ˌtekst\ *n* [G, fr. *ur-* Ur- + *text* text, fr. ML *textus*] (ca. 1932) **:** the original text (as of a musical score)

ur·ti·car·ia \ˌərt-ə-ˈkar-ē-ə, -ˈker-\ *n* [NL, fr. L *urtica* nettle] (ca. 1771) **:** an allergic disorder marked by raised edematous patches of skin or mucous membrane and usu. intense itching and caused by contact with a specific precipitating factor either externally or internally (as by a food, drug, or inhalant) — **ur·ti·car·i·al** \-ē-əl\ *adj*

ur·ti·cate \ˈərt-ə-ˌkāt\ *vi* **-cat·ed; -cat·ing** [ML *urticatus,* pp. of *urticare* to sting, fr. L *urtica*] (1843) **:** to produce wheals or itching; *esp* **:** to induce urticaria — **ur·ti·ca·tion** \ˌərt-ə-ˈkā-shən\ *n*

urus \ˈyu̇r-əs\ *n* [L, of Gmc origin; akin to OHG *ūro* urus, *ohso* ox — more at OX] (1601) **:** an extinct large long-horned wild ox (*Bos primigenius*) of the German forests held to be a wild ancestor of domestic cattle

uru·shi·ol \(y)u̇-ˈrü-shē-ˌȯl, -ˌōl\ *n* [ISV, fr. Jp *urushi* lacquer] (1908) **:** a mixture of pyrocatechol derivatives with saturated or unsaturated side chains of 15 or 17 carbon atoms that is an oily toxic irritant principle present in poison ivy and some related plants (genus *Rhus*) and in oriental lacquers derived from such plants

us \(ˈ)əs\ *pron* [ME, fr. OE *ūs;* akin to OHG *uns* us, L *nos*] *objective case of* WE

us·able *also* **use·able** \ˈyü-zə-bəl\ *adj* (14c) **1 :** capable of being used **2 :** convenient and practicable for use — **us·abil·i·ty** \ˌyü-zə-ˈbil-ət-ē\ *n* — **us·able·ness** \ˈyü-zə-bəl-nəs\ *n* — **us·ably** \-blē\ *adv*

us·age \ˈyü-sij, -zij\ *n* [ME, fr. MF, fr. *us* use] (14c) **1 a :** firmly established and generally accepted practice or procedure **b :** a uniform certain reasonable lawful practice existing in a particular locality or occupation and binding persons entering into transactions chiefly on the basis of presumed familiarity **c :** the way in which words and phrases are actually used (as in a particular form or sense) in a language community **2 a :** the action, amount, or mode of using ⟨a decrease in the ~ of electricity⟩ **b :** manner of treating ⟨suffered ill ~ at the hands of his captors⟩ ***syn*** see HABIT

us·ance \ˈyüz-ᵊn(t)s\ *n* (14c) **1 :** USAGE 1a **2 :** USE, EMPLOYMENT **3 a** *obs* **:** USURY **b :** INTEREST **4 :** the time allowed by custom for payment of a bill of exchange in foreign commerce

1use \ˈyüs\ *n* [ME *us,* fr. OF, fr. L *usus,* fr. *usus,* pp. of *uti* to use] (13c) **1 a :** the act or practice of employing something **:** EMPLOYMENT, APPLICATION ⟨he made good ~ of his spare time⟩ **b :** the fact or state of being used ⟨a dish in daily ~⟩ **c :** a method or manner of employing or applying something ⟨gained practice in the ~ of the camera⟩ **2 a** (1) **:** habitual or customary usage (2) **:** an individual habit or group custom **b :** a liturgical form or observance; *esp* **:** a liturgy having modifications peculiar to a local church or religious order **3 a :** the privilege or benefit of using something ⟨gave him the ~ of her car⟩ **b :** the ability or power to use something (as a limb or faculty) **c :** the legal enjoyment of property that consists in its employment, occupation, exercise, or practice ⟨she had the ~ of the estate for life⟩ **4 a :** a particular service or end ⟨put learning to practical ~⟩ **b :** the quality of being suitable for employment ⟨saving things that might be of ~⟩ **c :** the occasion or need to employ ⟨took only what they had ~ for⟩ **5 a :** the benefit in law of one or more persons; *specif* **:** the benefit or profit of property established in one other than the legal possessor **b :** a legal arrangement by which such benefits and profits are so established **6 :** a favorable attitude **:** LIKING ⟨had no ~ for modern art⟩

2use \ˈyüz\ *vb* **used** \ˈyüzd, *in the phrase "used to" usu* ˈyüs(t)\; **us·ing** \ˈyü-ziŋ\ *vt* (13c) **1** *archaic* **:** ACCUSTOM, HABITUATE **2 :** to put into action or service **:** avail oneself of **:** EMPLOY **3 :** to consume or take (as liquor or drugs) regularly **4 :** to carry out a purpose or action by means of **:** UTILIZE; *also* **:** MANIPULATE 2b ⟨*used* him only as a means up the corporate ladder⟩ **5 :** to expend or consume by putting to use **6 :** to behave toward **:** act with regard to **:** TREAT ⟨*used* the prisoners cruelly⟩ **7 :** STAND 1d ⟨the house could ~ a coat of paint⟩ ~ *vi* — used in the past with *to* to indicate a former fact or state ⟨claims winters *used* to be harder⟩

syn USE, EMPLOY, UTILIZE mean to put into service esp. to attain an end. USE implies availing oneself of something as a means or instrument to an end; EMPLOY suggests the use of a person or thing that is available but idle, inactive, or disengaged; UTILIZE may suggest the discovery of a new, profitable, or practical use for something.

used \ˈyüzd, *in the phrase "used to" usu* ˈyüs(t)\ *adj* (14c) **1 :** employed in accomplishing something **2 :** that has endured use; *specif* **:** SECONDHAND ⟨a ~ car⟩ **3 :** ACCUSTOMED, HABITUATED

use·ful \ˈyüs-fəl\ *adj* (1595) **:** capable of being put to use **:** SERVICEABLE; *esp* **:** having utility — **use·ful·ly** \-fə-lē\ *adv*

use·ful·ness *n* (1617) **:** the quality of having utility and esp. practical worth or applicability

use·less \ˈyü-sləs\ *adj* (1593) **:** having or being of no use: **a :** INEFFECTUAL **b :** not able to give service or aid **:** INEPT — **use·less·ly** *adv* — **use·less·ness** *n*

us·er \ˈyü-zər\ *n* (15c) **:** one that uses

us·er–friend·ly \ˌyü-zər-ˈfren-(d)lē\ *adj* (1977) **:** easy to learn, use, understand, or deal with — **user–friendliness** *n*

use up *vt* (ca. 1785) **1 :** to consume completely ⟨*used up* all the sugar⟩ **2 :** to leave no capacity of force or use in ⟨land that has been *used up*⟩

1ush·er \ˈəsh-ər\ *n* [ME *ussher,* fr. MF *ussier,* fr. (assumed) VL *ustiarius* doorkeeper, fr. L *ostium, ustium* door, mouth of a river — more at OSTIUM] (14c) **1 a :** an officer or servant who has the care of the door of a court, hall, or chamber **b :** an officer who walks before a person of rank **c :** one who escorts persons to their seats (as in a theater) **2** *archaic* **:** an assistant teacher

2usher *vb* **ush·ered; ush·er·ing** \ˈəsh-(ə-)riŋ\ *vt* (1596) **1 :** to conduct to a place **2 :** to precede as an usher, forerunner, or harbinger **3 :** INAUGURATE, INTRODUCE — often used with *in* ⟨~ in a new era⟩ ~ *vi* **:** to serve as an usher ⟨~ at a wedding⟩

ush·er·ette \ˌəsh-ə-ˈret\ *n* (1925) **:** a female usher (as in a theater)

us·nea \ˈəs-nē-ə, ˈəz-\ *n* [NL, fr. Ar *ushnah* moss] (ca. 1597) **:** any of a genus (*Usnea*) of widely distributed lichens (as old-man's beard) that have a grayish or yellow pendulous freely branched thallus

us·que·baugh \ˈəs-kwi-ˌbȯ, -ˌbä\ *n* [IrGael *uisce beathadh*] (1581) *Irish & Scot* **:** WHISKEY

1usu·al \ˈyüzh-(ə-)wəl, ˈyüzh-əl\ *adj* [LL *usualis,* fr. L *usus* use] (14c) **1 :** accordant with usage, custom, or habit **:** NORMAL **2 :** commonly or ordinarily used ⟨followed his ~ route⟩ **3 :** found in ordinary practice or in the ordinary course of events **:** ORDINARY — **usu·al·ly** \ˈyüzh-(ə-)wə-lē, ˈyüzh-(ə-)lē *in rapid speech* ˈyüz-lē\ *adv* — **usu·al·ness** \ˈyüzh-(ə-)wəl-nəs, -əl-nəs\ *n*

syn USUAL, CUSTOMARY, HABITUAL, WONTED, ACCUSTOMED mean familiar through frequent or regular repetition. USUAL stresses the absence of strangeness or unexpectedness; CUSTOMARY applies to what accords with the practices, conventions, or usages of an individual or community; HABITUAL suggests a practice settled or established by much repetition; WONTED stresses habituation but usu. applies to what is favored, sought, or purposefully cultivated; ACCUSTOMED is less emphatic than WONTED or HABITUAL in suggesting fixed habit or invariable custom.

— **as usual :** in the accustomed or habitual way ⟨*as usual* they were late⟩

2usual *n* (1589) **:** something usual

usu·fruct \ˈyü-zə-ˌfrəkt, -sə-\ *n* [L *ususfructus,* fr. *usus et fructus* use and enjoyment] (1630) **1 :** the legal right of using and enjoying the fruits or profits of something belonging to another **2 :** the right to use or enjoy something

1usu·fruc·tu·ary \ˌyü-zə-ˈfrək-chə-ˌwer-ē, -sə-\ *n* (1618) **1 :** one having the usufruct of property **2 :** one having the use or enjoyment of something

2usufructuary *adj* (1710) **:** of, relating to, or having the character of a usufruct

usu·rer \'yü-zhər-ər, 'yüzh-rər\ *n* (13c) : one that lends money esp. at an exorbitant rate

usu·ri·ous \yü-'z(h)ùr-ē-əs\ *adj* (1610) **1** : practicing usury **2** : involving usury : of the character of usury — **usu·ri·ous·ly** *adv* — **usu·ri·ous·ness** *n*

usurp \yù-'sərp *also* -'zərp\ *vb* [ME *usurpen*, fr. MF *usurper*, fr. L *usurpare*, lit., to take possession of by use, fr. *usu* (abl. of *usus* use) + *rapere* to seize — more at RAPID] *vt* (14c) **1** : to seize and hold (as office, place, or powers) in possession by force or without right ⟨~ a throne⟩ **2** : to take the place of by or as if by force : SUPPLANT ~ *vi* : to seize or exercise authority or possession wrongfully — **usur·pa·tion** \,yü-sər-'pā-shən *also* ,yü-zər-\ *n* — **usurp·er** \yù-'sər-pər *also* -'zər-\ *n*

usu·ry \'yüzh-(ə-)rē\ *n*, *pl* **-ries** [ME, fr. ML *usuria*, alter. of L *usura*, fr. *usus*, pp. of *uti* to use] (14c) **1** *archaic* : INTEREST **2** : the lending of money with an interest charge for its use **3** : an unconscionable or exorbitant rate or amount of interest; *specif* : interest in excess of a legal rate charged to a borrower for the use of money

ut \'ət, 'üt, 'ùt\ *n* [ME, first note in the diatonic scale, fr. ML, fr. the syllable sung to this note in a medieval hymn to St. John the Baptist] (14c) : a syllable used for the first note in the diatonic scale in an early solmization system and later replaced by *do*

Ute \'yüt\ *n*, *pl* **Ute** *or* **Utes** [Ute *Yuta*] (1776) : a member of an American Indian people orig. ranging through Utah, Colorado, Arizona, and New Mexico

uten·sil \yù-'ten(t)-səl, 'yü-,\ *n* [ME, vessels for domestic use, fr. MF *utensile*, fr. L *utensilia*, fr. neut. pl. of *utensilis* useful, fr. *uti* to use] (14c) **1** : an implement, instrument, or vessel used in a household esp. a kitchen **2** : a useful tool or implement *syn* see IMPLEMENT

uter- *or* **utero-** \for 2, ,yüt-ə-rō\ *comb form* [L *uterus*] **1** : uterus ⟨*uterectomy*⟩ **2** : uterine and ⟨*uteroplacental*⟩

uter·ine \'yüt-ə-,rīn, -rən\ *adj* [ME, fr. LL *uterinus*, fr. L *uterus*] (15c) **1** : born of the same mother but by a different father **2** : of, relating to, or affecting the uterus ⟨~ cancer⟩

uter·us \'yüt-ə-rəs, 'yü-trəs\ *n*, *pl* **uteri** \'yüt-ə-,rī\ *also* **uter·us·es** [L] (1615) **1** : an organ of the female mammal for containing and usu. for nourishing the young during development previous to birth — called also *womb* **2** : a structure in some lower animals analogous to the uterus in which eggs or young develop

Uther \'ü-thər, 'yü-\ *n* : a legendary British king and father of Arthur

utile \'yüt-ᵊl, 'yü-,til\ *adj* [MF, fr. L *utilis*] (15c) : USEFUL

¹util·i·tar·i·an \(,)yù-,til-ə-'ter-ē-ən\ *n* (ca. 1780) : an advocate or adherent of utilitarianism

²utilitarian *adj* (1802) **1** : of or relating to or advocating utilitarianism **2** : marked by utilitarian views or practices **3 a** : of, relating to, or aiming at utility **b** : exhibiting or preferring mere utility ⟨spare ~ furnishings⟩

util·i·tar·i·an·ism \-ē-ə-,niz-əm\ *n* (1827) **1** : a doctrine that the useful is the good and that the determining consideration of right conduct should be the usefulness of its consequences; *specif* : a theory that the aim of action should be the largest possible balance of pleasure over pain or the greatest happiness of the greatest number **2** : utilitarian character, spirit, or quality

¹util·i·ty \yù-'til-ət-ē\ *n*, *pl* **-ties** [ME *utilite*, fr. MF *utilité*, fr. L *utilitat-, utilitas*, fr. *utilis* useful, fr. *uti* to use] (14c) **1** : fitness for some purpose or worth to some end **2** : something useful or designed for use **3 a** : PUBLIC UTILITY **b** (1) : a service (as light, power, or water) provided by a public utility (2) : equipment or a piece of equipment to provide such service or a comparable service

²utility *adj* (1851) **1** : capable of serving as a substitute in various roles or positions ⟨a ~ infielder⟩ **2 a** : kept for the production of a useful product rather than for show or as pets ⟨~ livestock⟩ **b** : being of a usable but inferior grade ⟨~ beef⟩ **3** : serving primarily for utility rather than beauty : UTILITARIAN **4** : designed or adapted for general use ⟨a ~ knife⟩ **5** : of or relating to a utility ⟨a ~ company⟩

uti·lize \'yüt-ᵊl-,īz\ *vt* **-lized; -liz·ing** [F *utiliser*, fr. *utile*] (1807) : to make use of : turn to practical use or account ⟨~ wasted skills⟩ *syn* see USE — **uti·liz·able** \-ᵊ-,ī-zə-bəl\ *adj* — **uti·li·za·tion** \,yüt-ᵊl-ə-'zā-shən\ *n* — **uti·liz·er** \'yüt-ᵊl-,ī-zər\ *n*

¹ut·most \'ət-,mōst, *esp Southern* -məst\ *adj* [ME, alter. of *utmest*, fr. OE *ūtmest*, superl. adj., fr. *ūt* out, adv. — more at OUT] (bef. 12c) **1** : situated at the farthest or most distant point : EXTREME ⟨the ~ point of the earth —John Hunt⟩ **2** : of the greatest or highest degree, quantity, number, or amount ⟨a matter of ~ concern⟩

²utmost *n* (bef. 12c) **1** : the most possible : the extreme limit : the highest attainable point or degree ⟨the ~ in reliability⟩ **2** : the highest, greatest, or best of one's abilities, powers, and resources ⟨will do our ~ to help⟩

Uto-Az·tec·an \,yüt-ō-'az-,tek-ən\ *n* [*Ute* + *-o-* + *Aztec*] (ca. 1909) : a language phylum comprising the Nahuatlan, Taracahitian, Piman, and Shoshonean families — **Uto-Aztecan** *adj*

uto·pia \yù-'tō-pē-ə\ *n* [*Utopia*, imaginary and ideal country in *Utopia* (1516) by Sir Thomas More, fr. Gk *ou* not, no + *topos* place — more at

TOPIC] (1610) **1** : an imaginary and indefinitely remote place **2** *often cap* : a place of ideal perfection esp. in laws, government, and social conditions **3** : an impractical scheme for social improvement

¹uto·pi·an \-pē-ən\ *adj, often cap* (1551) **1** : of, relating to, or having the characteristics of a utopia; *esp* : having impossibly ideal conditions esp. of social organization **2** : proposing or advocating impractically ideal social and political schemes ⟨~ idealists⟩ **3** : impossibly ideal : VISIONARY ⟨recognised the ~ nature of his hopes —C. S. Kilby⟩ **4** : believing in, advocating, or having the characteristics of utopian socialism ⟨~ doctrines⟩ ⟨~ novels⟩

²utopian *n* (1873) **1** : one that believes in the perfectibility of human society **2** : one that proposes or advocates utopian schemes

uto·pi·an·ism \-pē-ə-,niz-əm\ *n* (1661) **1** : a utopian idea or theory **2** *often cap* : the body of ideas, views, or aims of a utopian

utopian socialism *n* (ca. 1923) : socialism based on a belief that social ownership of the means of production can be achieved by voluntary and peaceful surrender of their holdings by propertied groups — **utopian socialist** *n*

uto·pism \'yüt-ə-,piz-əm, yù-'tō-\ *n* (ca. 1888) : UTOPIANISM **2** — **uto·pist** \yù-'tō-pəst\ *n* — **uto·pis·tic** \,yüt-ə-'pis-tik, yù-,tō-\ *adj*

utri·cle \'yü-tri-kəl\ *n* [L *utriculus*, dim. of *uter* leather bag] (1731) : any of various small pouches or saccate parts of an animal or plant body: as **a** : the part of the membranous labyrinth of the ear into which the semicircular canals open **b** : a small one-celled usu. indehiscent one-seeded or few-seeded achene with thin membranous pericarp — **utric·u·lar** \yù-'trik-yə-lər\ *adj*

utric·u·lar·ia \yù-,trik-yə-'lar-ē-ə, -'ler-\ *n* [NL, genus name, fr. L *utriculus*] (ca. 1753) : BLADDERWORT

utric·u·lus \yù-'trik-yə-ləs\ *n* [L, small bag] (1847) : UTRICLE a

¹ut·ter \'ət-ər\ *adj* [ME, remote, fr. OE *ūtera* outer, compar. adj. fr. *ūt* out, adv. — more at OUT] (15c) : carried to the utmost point or highest degree : ABSOLUTE, TOTAL ⟨~ darkness⟩ ⟨~ strangers⟩ — **ut·ter·ly** *adv*

²utter *vb* [ME *uttren*, fr. *utter* outside, adv., fr. OE *ūtor*, compar. of *ūt* out] *vt* (15c) **1** *obs* : to offer for sale **2 a** : to send forth as a sound **b** : to give utterance to : PRONOUNCE, SPEAK **c** : to give public expression to : express in words **3** : to put (as currency) into circulation; *specif* : to circulate (as a counterfeit note) as if legal or genuine ⟨~ false tokens⟩ **4** : to put forth or out : DISCHARGE ~ *vi* : to make a statement or sound *syn* see EXPRESS — **ut·ter·able** \'ət-ə-rə-bəl\ *adj* — **ut·ter·er** \'ət-ər-ər\ *n*

¹ut·ter·ance \'ət-ə-rən(t)s, 'ə-trən(t)s\ *n* [ME *uttraunce*, modif. of MF *outrance*] *archaic* (15c) : the last extremity : BITTER END

²ut·ter·ance \'ət-ə-rən(t)s *also* 'ə-trən(t)s\ *n* (15c) **1** : something uttered; *esp* : an oral or written statement : a stated or published expression **2** : vocal expression : SPEECH **3** : power, style, or manner of speaking

¹ut·ter·most \'ət-ər-,mōst\ *adj* [ME, alter. of *uttermest*, fr. ¹*utter* + *-mest* (as in *utmost* utmost)] (14c) **1** : OUTERMOST **2** : EXTREME, UTMOST

²uttermost *n* (14c) : UTMOST ⟨to the ~ of our capacity —H. S. Truman⟩

U-turn \(')yü-'tərn\ *n* (1930) **1** : a turn resembling the letter U; *esp* : a 180-degree turn made by a vehicle in a road **2** : something (as a reversal of policy) resembling a U-turn

U-val·ue \'val-(,)yü, -yə(-w)\ *n* [unit] (1949) : a measure of the heat transmission through a building part (as a wall or window) or a given thickness of insulating material expressed as the number of British thermal units transmitted through one square foot per hour per degree Fahrenheit temperature difference between the two sides so that the lower the number the higher the insulating effectiveness

uva·rov·ite \(y)ü-'vär-ə-,vīt\ *n* [G *uwarowit*, fr. Count Sergei S. *Uvarov* †1855 Russ. statesman] (1837) : an emerald green calcium-chromium garnet $Ca_3Cr_2(SiO_4)_3$

uvea \'yü-vē-ə\ *n* [ML, fr. L *uva* grape] (1525) : the posterior pigmented layer of the iris; *also* : the iris and ciliary body together with the choroid coat — **uve·al** \-vē-əl\ *adj*

uve·itis \,yü-vē-'īt-əs\ *n* [NL] (ca. 1848) : inflammation of the uvea of the eye

uvu·la \'yü-vyə-lə\ *n*, *pl* **-las** *or* **-lae** \-,lē, -,lī\ [ME, fr. ML, dim. of L *uva* grape, uvula; akin to OE *iw* yew] (15c) : the pendent fleshy lobe in the middle of the posterior border of the soft palate

uvu·lar \-lər\ *adj* (1843) **1** : of or relating to the uvula ⟨~ glands⟩ **2** : produced with the aid of the uvula

ux·o·ri·al \,ək-'sōr-ē-əl, -'sòr-; ,əg-'zōr-, -'zòr-\ *adj* [L *uxorius*] (1800) : of, relating to, or characteristic of a wife

ux·ori·cide \,ək-'sōr-ə-,sīd, -'sär-; ,əg-'zōr-, -'zär-\ *n* (1860) **1** [ML *uxoricidium*, fr. L *uxor* wife + *-i-* + *-cidium* -cide] : murder of a wife by her husband **2** [L *uxor* + E *-i-* + *-cide*] : a wife murderer

ux·o·ri·ous \,ək-'sōr-ē-əs, -'sòr-; ,əg-'zōr-, -'zòr-\ *adj* [L *uxorius* uxorious, uxorial, fr. *uxor* wife] (1598) : excessively fond of or submissive to a wife — **ux·o·ri·ous·ly** *adv* — **ux·o·ri·ous·ness** *n*

Uz·bek \'uz-,bek, 'əz-, ùz-\ *or* **Uz·beg** \-,beg, -'beg\ *n* (ca. 1890) **1** : a member of a Turkic people of Turkestan and esp. in the Uzbek Republic of the U.S.S.R. **2** : the Turkic language of the Uzbek people

V

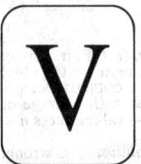

v \'vē\ *n, pl* **v's** *or* **vs** \'vēz\ *often cap, often attrib* **1 a :** the 22d letter of the English alphabet **b :** a graphic representation of this letter **c :** a speech counterpart of orthographic *v* **2 :** FIVE — see NUMBER table **3 :** a graphic device for reproducing the letter *v* **4 :** one designated *v* esp. as the 22d in order or class **5 :** something shaped like the letter V

va·can·cy \'vā-kən-sē\ *n, pl* **-cies** (1599) **1** *archaic* **:** an interval of leisure **2 :** physical or mental inactivity or relaxation **:** IDLENESS **3 a :** a vacating of an office, post, or piece of property **b :** the time such office or property is vacant **4 :** a vacant office, post, or tenancy **5 :** empty space **:** VOID; *specif* **:** unoccupied site for an atom or ion in a crystal **6 :** the state of being vacant **:** VACUITY

va·cant \'vā-kənt\ *adj* [ME, fr. OF, fr. L *vacant-, vacans,* prp. of *vacare* to be empty, be free — more at VACUUM] (13c) **1 :** not occupied by an incumbent, possessor, or officer ⟨a ~ office⟩ ⟨~ thrones⟩ **2 :** being without content or occupant ⟨a ~ seat in a bus⟩ ⟨a ~ room⟩ **3 :** free from activity or work **:** DISENGAGED ⟨~ hours⟩ **4 :** devoid of thought, reflection, or expression ⟨a ~ smile⟩ **5 :** not lived in ⟨~ houses⟩ **6 a :** not put to use ⟨~ land⟩ **b :** having no heir or claimant **:** ABANDONED ⟨a ~ estate⟩ ***syn*** see EMPTY — **va·cant·ly** *adv* — **va·cant·ness** *n*

va·cate \'vā-,kāt, vā-'\ *vb* **va·cat·ed; va·cat·ing** [L *vacatus,* pp. of *vacare*] *vt* (1649) **1 :** to make legally void **:** ANNUL **2 a :** to deprive of an incumbent or occupant **b :** to give up the incumbency or occupancy of ~ *vi* **:** to vacate an office, post, or tenancy

[1]**va·ca·tion** \vā-'kā-shən, və-\ *n, often attrib* [ME *vacacioun,* fr. MF *vacation,* fr. L *vacation-, vacatio* freedom, exemption, fr. *vacatus,* pp.] (14c) **1 :** a respite or a time of respite from something **:** INTERMISSION **2 a :** a scheduled period during which activity (as of a court or school) is suspended **b :** a period of exemption from work granted to an employee for rest and relaxation **3 :** a period spent away from home or business in travel or recreation ⟨had a restful ~ at the beach⟩ **4 :** an act or an instance of vacating

[2]**vacation** *vi* **-tioned; -tion·ing** \-sh(ə-)niŋ\ (1896) **:** to take or spend a vacation — **va·ca·tion·er** \-sh(ə-)nər\ *n*

va·ca·tion·ist \-sh(ə-)nəst\ *n* (1885) **:** a person taking a vacation

va·ca·tion·land \-shən-,land\ *n* (1927) **:** an area with recreational attractions and facilities for vacationists

vac·ci·nal \'vak-sən-ᵊl, vak-'sēn-\ *adj* (ca. 1860) **:** of or relating to vaccine or vaccination

vac·ci·nate \'vak-sə-,nāt\ *vb* **-nat·ed; -nat·ing** *vt* (1803) **1 :** to inoculate (a person) with cowpox virus in order to produce immunity to smallpox **2 :** to administer a vaccine to usu. by injection ~ *vi* **:** to perform or practice vaccination — **vac·ci·na·tor** \-,nāt-ər\ *n*

vac·ci·na·tion \,vak-sə-'nā-shən\ *n* (1800) **1 :** the act of vaccinating **2 :** the scar left by vaccinating

vac·cine \vak-'sēn, 'vak-,\ *n* [L *vaccinus,* adj., of or from cows, fr. *vacca* cow; akin to Skt *vaśa* cow] (1799) **1 :** matter or a preparation containing the virus of cowpox in a form used for vaccination **2 :** a preparation of killed microorganisms, living attenuated organisms, or living fully virulent organisms that is administered to produce or artificially increase immunity to a particular disease — **vaccine** *adj*

vac·ci·nee \,vak-sə-'nē\ *n* (1889) **:** a vaccinated individual

vac·cin·ia \vak-'sin-ē-ə\ *n* [NL, fr. *vaccinus*] (1803) **:** COWPOX — **vac·cin·i·al** \-ē-əl\ *adj*

vac·il·late \'vas-ə-,lāt\ *vi* **-lat·ed; -lat·ing** [L *vacillatus,* pp. of *vacillare* to sway, waver] (1597) **1 a :** to sway through lack of equilibrium **b :** FLUCTUATE, OSCILLATE **2 :** to waver in mind, will, or feeling **:** hesitate in choice of opinions or courses ***syn*** see HESITATE — **vac·il·lat·ing·ly** \-,lāt-iŋ-lē\ *adv* — **vac·il·la·tor** \-,lāt-ər\ *n*

vac·il·la·tion \,vas-ə-'lā-shən\ *n* [ME, fr. MF, fr. L *vacillation-, vacillatio* action of swaying, fr. *vacillare*] (15c) **1 :** an act or instance of vacillating **2 :** inability to take a stand **:** IRRESOLUTION, INDECISION

va·cu·ity \va-'kyü-ət-ē, və-\ *n, pl* **-ities** [L *vacuitas,* fr. *vacuus* empty] (1541) **1 :** an empty space **2 :** the state, fact, or quality of being vacuous **3 :** something (as an idea) that is vacuous or inane

vac·u·o·late \'vak-yə-(,)wō-,lāt\ *or* **vac·u·o·lat·ed** \-,lāt-əd\ *adj* (1859) **:** containing one or more vacuoles ⟨highly *vacuolated* cells⟩

vac·u·o·la·tion \,vak-yə-(,)wō-'lā-shən\ *n* (1858) **:** the development or formation of vacuoles

vac·u·ole \'vak-yə-,wōl\ *n* [F, lit., small vacuum, fr. L *vacuum*] (1853) **1 :** a small cavity or space in the tissues of an organism containing air or fluid **2 :** a cavity or vesicle in the protoplasm of a cell containing fluid — see CELL illustration — **vac·u·o·lar** \,vak-yə-'wō-lər, -,lär\ *adj*

vac·u·ous \'vak-yə-wəs\ *adj* [L *vacuus*] (1655) **1 :** emptied of or lacking content **2 :** marked by lack of ideas or intelligence **:** STUPID, INANE ⟨a ~ mind⟩ ⟨a ~ expression⟩ **3 :** devoid of serious occupation **:** IDLE ***syn*** see EMPTY — **vac·u·ous·ly** *adv* — **vac·u·ous·ness** *n*

[1]**vac·u·um** \'vak-yü-əm, -(,)yüm, -yəm\ *n, pl* **vac·u·ums** *or* **vac·ua** \-yə-wə\ [L, fr. neut. of *vacuus* empty; akin to L *vacare* to be empty] (1550) **1 :** emptiness of space **2 a :** a space absolutely devoid of matter **b :** a space partially exhausted (as to the highest degree possible) by artificial means (as an air pump) **c :** a degree of rarefaction below atmospheric pressure **3 a :** a state or condition resembling a vacuum **:** VOID ⟨the power ~ in Indochina after the departure of the French — Norman Cousins⟩ **b :** a state of isolation from outside influences ⟨people who live in a ~ . . . so that the world outside them is of no moment —W. S. Maugham⟩ **4 :** a device creating or utilizing a partial vacuum

[2]**vacuum** *adj* (1825) **1 :** of, containing, producing, or utilizing a partial vacuum ⟨separated by means of ~ distillation⟩ **2 :** of or relating to a vacuum device or system

[3]**vacuum** *vt* (1922) **:** to use a vacuum device (as a vacuum cleaner) on ~ *vi* **:** to operate a vacuum device

vacuum bottle *n* (1910) **:** a cylindrical container with a vacuum between an inner and an outer wall used to keep material and esp. liquids either hot or cold for considerable periods — called also *vacuum flask*

vacuum cleaner *n* (1903) **:** an electrical appliance for cleaning (as floors, carpets, tapestry, or upholstered work) by suction — called also *vacuum sweeper*

vacuum gauge *n* (ca. 1864) **:** a gauge indicating degree of rarefaction below atmospheric pressure

vac·u·um·ize \'vak-yü-(ə-),mīz\ *vt* **-ized; -iz·ing** (1909) **1 :** to produce a vacuum in **2 a :** to clean or dry by a vacuum mechanism **b :** to pack in a vacuum container

vac·u·um–packed \,vak-yü-əm-'pakt, -(,)yüm-, -yəm-\ *adj* (ca. 1926) **:** having much of the air removed before being hermetically sealed

vacuum pan *n* (1833) **:** a tank with a vacuum pump for rapid evaporation and condensation (as of sugar syrup) by boiling at a low temperature

vacuum pump *n* (ca. 1858) **:** a pump for exhausting gas from an enclosed space

vacuum tube *n* (1859) **:** an electron tube evacuated to a high degree of vacuum

va·de me·cum \,väd-ē-'mē-kəm, ,väd-ē-'mā-\ *n, pl* **vade mecums** [L, go with me] (1629) **1 :** a book for ready reference **:** MANUAL **2 :** something regularly carried about by a person

va·dose \'vā-,dōs\ *adj* [L *vadosus* shallow, fr. *vadum,* n., shallow, ford; akin to L *vadere* to go — more at WADE] (1894) **:** of, relating to, or being water or solutions in the earth's crust above the permanent groundwater level

vag- *or* **vago-** *comb form* [ISV, fr. NL *vagus*] **:** vagus nerve ⟨*vagal*⟩ ⟨*vagotomy*⟩

[1]**vag·a·bond** \'vag-ə-,bänd\ *adj* [ME, fr. MF, fr. L *vagabundus,* fr. *vagari* to wander] (15c) **1 :** moving from place to place without a fixed home **:** WANDERING **2 a :** of, relating to, or characteristic of a wanderer **b :** leading an unsettled, irresponsible, or disreputable life — **vag·a·bond·ish** \-,bän-dish\ *adj*

[2]**vagabond** *n* (15c) **:** one leading a vagabond life; *esp* **:** TRAMP — **vag·a·bond·age** \-,bän-dij\ *n* — **vag·a·bond·ism** \-,bän-,diz-əm\ *n*

[3]**vagabond** *vi* (1586) **:** to wander in the manner of a vagabond **:** roam about

va·gal \'vā-gəl\ *adj* [ISV] (1854) **:** of, relating to, mediated by, or being the vagus nerve — **va·gal·ly** \-gə-lē\ *adv*

va·gar·i·ous \vā-'ger-ē-əs, və-, -'gar-\ *adj* (1798) **:** marked by vagaries **:** CAPRICIOUS, WHIMSICAL — **va·gar·i·ous·ly** *adv*

va·ga·ry \'vā-gə-rē; və-'ge(ə)r-ē, -'ga(ə)r-, vā-; *also* 'vag-ə-rē\ *n, pl* **-ries** [prob. fr. L *vagari* to wander; akin to L *vagus* wandering] (1573) **:** an erratic, unpredictable, or extravagant manifestation, action, or notion ***syn*** see CAPRICE

vag·ile \'vaj-əl, -,īl\ *adj* [ISV, fr. L *vagus* wandering] (ca. 1890) **:** free to move about ⟨~ organisms⟩ — **va·gil·i·ty** \və-'jil-ət-ē, va-\ *n*

va·gi·na \və-'jī-nə\ *n, pl* **-nae** \-(,)nē\ *or* **-nas** [L, lit., sheath] (1682) **1 :** a canal in a female mammal that leads from the uterus to the external orifice of the genital canal **2 :** a canal that is similar in function or location to the vagina and occurs in various animals other than mammals

vag·i·nal \'vaj-ən-ᵊl\ *adj* (1726) **1 :** of or relating to a theca **2 :** of, relating to, or affecting the genital vagina — **vag·i·nal·ly** \-ᵊl-ē\ *adv*

vag·i·nis·mus \,vaj-ə-'niz-məs\ *n* [NL, fr. L *vagina*] (1866) **:** a painful spasmodic contraction of the vagina

vag·i·ni·tis \,vaj-ə-'nīt-əs\ *n* [NL] (1846) **:** inflammation of the vagina or of a sheath (as a tendon sheath)

va·got·o·my \vā-'gät-ə-mē\ *n, pl* **-mies** [ISV] (ca. 1903) **:** surgical division of the vagus nerve

va·go·to·nia \,vā-gə-'tō-nē-ə\ *n* [NL] (ca. 1915) **:** excessive excitability of the vagus nerve resulting typically in vasomotor instability, constipation, and sweating — **va·go·ton·ic** \-'tän-ik\ *adj*

va·gran·cy \'vā-grən(t)-sē\ *n, pl* **-cies** (1641) **1 :** VAGARY **2 :** the state or action of being vagrant **3 :** the offense of being a vagrant

[1]**va·grant** \'vā-grənt\ *n* [ME *vagraunt,* prob. modif. of MF *waucrant, wacrant* wandering, fr. OF, fr. prp. of *waucrer, wacrer* to roll, wander, of Gmc origin; akin to OE *wealcan* to roll — more at WALK] (15c) **1 a :** one who has no established residence and wanders idly from place to place without lawful or visible means of support **b :** one (as a prostitute or drunkard) whose conduct constitutes statutory vagrancy **2 :** WANDERER, ROVER

[2]**vagrant** *adj* (15c) **1 :** wandering about from place to place usu. with no means of support **2 a :** having a fleeting, wayward, or inconstant quality **b :** having no fixed course **:** RANDOM — **va·grant·ly** *adv*

va·grom \'vā-grəm\ *adj* (1599) **:** VAGRANT

vague \'vāg\ *adj* **vagu·er; vagu·est** [MF, fr. L *vagus,* lit., wandering] (1548) **1 a :** not clearly expressed **:** stated in indefinite terms ⟨~ accusation⟩ **b :** not having a precise meaning ⟨~ term of abuse⟩ **2 a :** not clearly defined, grasped, or understood **:** INDISTINCT ⟨only a ~ notion of what's needed⟩; *also* **:** SLIGHT ⟨a ~ hint of a thickening waistline⟩ ⟨hasn't the *vaguest* idea⟩ **b :** not clearly felt or sensed **:** somewhat subconscious ⟨a ~ longing⟩ **3 :** not thinking or expressing one's thoughts clearly or precisely ⟨~ about dates and places⟩ **4 :** lacking expression **:** VACANT **5 :** not sharply outlined **:** HAZY ***syn*** see OBSCURE — **vague·ly** *adv* — **vague·ness** *n*

va·gus nerve \'vā-gəs-\ *n* [NL *vagus nervus,* lit., wandering nerve] (1840) **:** either of the 10th pair of cranial nerves that arise from the medulla and supply chiefly the viscera esp. with autonomic sensory and motor fibers — called also *vagus*

vail \'vā(ə)l\ *vt* [ME *valen,* partly fr. MF *valer* (short for *avaler* to let fall) & partly short for ME *avalen* to let fall, fr. MF *avaler,* fr. OF, fr. *aval* downward, fr. *a* to (fr. L *ad*) + *val* valley — more at AT, VALE] (14c) **:** to lower often as a sign of respect or submission

vain \'vān\ *adj* [ME, fr. MF, fr. L *vanus* empty, vain — more at WANE] (14c) **1 :** having no real value **:** IDLE, WORTHLESS **2 :** marked by futility or ineffectualness **:** UNSUCCESSFUL, USELESS ⟨~ efforts to escape⟩ **3** *archaic* **:** FOOLISH, SILLY **4 :** having or showing undue or excessive pride in one's appearance or achievements **:** CONCEITED ***syn*** see FUTILE — **vain·ly** *adv* — **vain·ness** \'vān-nəs\ *n*

syn VAIN, NUGATORY, OTIOSE, IDLE, EMPTY, HOLLOW mean being without worth or significance. VAIN implies either absolute or relative absence of value; NUGATORY suggests triviality or insignificance; OTIOSE suggests that something serves no purpose and is either an encumbrance

\ə\ abut \ᵊ\ kitten, F table \ər\ further \a\ ash \ā\ ace \ä\ cot, cart \au̇\ out \ch\ chin \e\ bet \ē\ easy \g\ go \i\ hit \ī\ ice \j\ job \ŋ\ sing \ō\ go \ȯ\ law \ȯi\ boy \th\ thin \t͟h\ the \ü\ loot \u̇\ foot \y\ yet \zh\ vision \à, k̟, ⁿ, œ, œ̄, ue, ue̅, ʸ\ see Guide to Pronunciation

or a superfluity; IDLE suggests being incapable of worthwhile use or effect; EMPTY and HOLLOW suggest a deceiving lack of real substance or soundness or genuineness.

— **in vain** **1 :** to no end **:** without success or result **2 :** in an irreverent or blasphemous manner ⟨you shall not take the name of the Lord your God *in vain* — Deut 5:11 (RSV)⟩

vain·glo·ri·ous \(ˈ)vān-ˈglōr-ē-əs, -ˈglȯr-\ *adj* [ME *vanegloreous,* fr. MF, fr. ML *vainglorius,* fr. L *vanus* vain + *gloria* glory, vainglory] (15c) **:** marked by vainglory **:** BOASTFUL — **vain·glo·ri·ous·ly** *adv* — **vain·glo·ri·ous·ness** *n*

vain·glo·ry \ˈvān-ˌglōr-ē, -ˌglȯr-, (ˈ)vān-ˈ\ *n* [ME, fr. *vaine gloire,* fr. *vaine* (fem. of *vain* vain) + *gloire* glory, fr. L *gloria*] (14c) **1 :** excessive or ostentatious pride esp. in one's achievements **2 :** vain display or show **:** VANITY

vair \ˈva(ə)r, ˈve(ə)r\ *n* [ME *veir,* fr. OF *vair,* fr. *vair,* adj., variegated, fr. L *varius* variegated, various] (14c) **:** the bluish gray and white fur of a squirrel prized for ornamental use in medieval times

Vaish·na·va \ˈvīsh-nə-və\ *n* [Skt *vaiṣṇava* of Vishnu, fr. *Viṣṇu* Vishnu] (1815) **:** a member of a major Hindu sect devoted to the cult of Vishnu — **Vaishnava** *adj* — **Vaish·na·vism** \-ˌviz-əm\ *n*

Vais·ya \ˈvīsh-(y)ə\ *n* [Skt *vaiśya,* fr. *viś* settlement; akin to Gk *oikos* house — more at VICINITY] (1794) **:** a Hindu of an upper caste traditionally assigned to commercial and agricultural occupations

va·lance \ˈval-ən(t)s, ˈvāl-\ *n* [ME *vallance,* perh. fr. *Valence,* France] (15c) **1 :** a drapery hung along the edge of a bed, table, altar, canopy, or shelf **2 :** a short drapery or wood or metal frame used as a decorative heading to conceal the top of curtains and fixtures — **va·lanced** \-ən(t)st\ *adj*

vale \ˈvā(ə)l\ *n* [ME, fr. MF, fr. OF *val,* fr. L *valles, vallis;* akin to L *volvere* to roll — more at VOLUBLE] (14c) **1 :** VALLEY, DALE **2 :** WORLD ⟨this ~ of tears⟩

vale·dic·tion \ˌval-ə-ˈdik-shən\ *n* [L *valedictus,* pp. of *valedicere* to say farewell, fr. *vale* farewell + *dicere* to say — more at DICTION] (1614) **1 :** an act of bidding farewell **2 :** VALEDICTORY

vale·dic·to·ri·an \-ˌdik-ˈtōr-ē-ən, -ˈtȯr-\ *n* (1759) **:** the student usu. having the highest rank in a graduating class who delivers the valedictory address at the commencement exercises

1vale·dic·to·ry \-ˈdik-t(ə-)rē\ *adj* [L *valedictus*] (1651) **:** of or relating to a valediction **:** expressing or containing a farewell

2valedictory *n, pl* **-ries** (1779) **:** an address or statement of farewell or leave-taking

va·lence \ˈvā-lən(t)s\ *n* [LL *valentia* power, capacity, fr. L *valent-, valens,* prp. of *valēre* to be strong — more at WIELD] (1884) **1 a :** the degree of combining power of an element or chemical group as shown by the number of atomic weights of a univalent element (as hydrogen) with which the atomic weight of the element or the partial molecular weight of the group will combine or for which it can be substituted or with which it can be compared **b :** a unit of valence ⟨the four ~*s* of carbon⟩ **2 a :** relative capacity to unite, react, or interact (as with antigens or a biological substrate) **b :** the degree of attractiveness an individual, activity, or object possesses as a behavioral goal

valence electron *n* (1926) **:** a single electron or one of two or more electrons in the outer shell of an atom that is responsible for the chemical properties of the atom

Va·len·ci·ennes \və-ˌlen(t)-sē-ˈen(z), ˌval-ən-sē-\ *n* [*Valenciennes,* France] (1717) **:** a fine bobbin lace

-va·lent \ˈvā-lənt\ *adj comb form* [ISV, fr. L *valent-, valens*] **1 :** having a (specified) valence or valences ⟨bi*valent*⟩ ⟨multi*valent*⟩ **2 :** having (so many) chromosomal strands or homologous chromosomes ⟨uni*valent*⟩

val·en·tine \ˈval-ən-ˌtīn\ *n* (15c) **1 :** a sweetheart chosen or complimented on St. Valentine's Day **2 :** a gift or greeting sent or given esp. to a sweetheart on St. Valentine's Day; *esp* **:** a greeting card sent on this day

Valentine Day *or* **Valentine's Day** *n* (14c) **:** SAINT VALENTINE'S DAY

val·er·ate \ˈval-ə-ˌrāt\ *n* (1852) **:** a salt or ester of valeric acid

va·le·ri·an \və-ˈlir-ē-ən\ *n* [ME, fr. MF or ML; MF *valeriane,* fr. ML *valeriana,* prob. fr. fem. of *valerianus* of Valeria, fr. *Valeria,* Roman province formerly part of Pannonia] (14c) **1 :** any of a genus (*Valeriana* of the family Valerianaceae, the valerian family) of perennial herbs many of which possess medicinal properties **2 :** a drug consisting of the dried rootstock and roots of the garden heliotrope (*Valeriana officinalis*) formerly used as a carminative and sedative

va·le·ric acid \və-ˌlir-ik-, -ˌler-\ *n* [*valerian;* fr. its occurrence in the root of valerian] (1857) **:** any of four isomeric fatty acids $C_5H_{10}O_2$ or a mixture of these; *esp* **:** a liquid acid of disagreeable odor obtained from valerian or made synthetically and used esp. in organic synthesis

1va·let \ˈval-ət, ˈval-(ˌ)ā, va-ˈlā\ *n* [MF *vaslet, varlet, valet* young nobleman, page, domestic servant, fr. (assumed) ML *vassellittus,* dim. of ML *vassus* servant — more at VASSAL] (1567) **1 a :** a man's male servant who performs personal services (as taking care of clothing) **b :** an employee (as of a hotel or a public facility) who performs personal services for customers **2 :** a device (as a rack or tray) for holding clothing or personal effects

2valet *vt* (1840) **:** to serve as a valet

va·let de cham·bre \(ˌ)va-ˌlād-ə-ˈshäⁿbrᵊ\ *n, pl* **va·lets de chambre** *same*\ [F, lit., chamber valet] (1646) **:** VALET 1a

1val·e·tu·di·nar·i·an \ˌval-ə-ˌt(y)üd-ᵊn-ˈer-ē-ən\ *n* [L *valetudinarius* sickly, infirm, fr. *valetudin-, valetudo* state of health, sickness, fr. *valēre* to be strong, be well — more at WIELD] (1703) **:** a person of a weak or sickly constitution; *esp* **:** one whose chief concern is his invalidism

2valetudinarian *adj* (1713) **:** of, relating to, or characteristic of a valetudinarian **:** SICKLY, WEAK

val·e·tu·di·nar·i·an·ism \-ē-ə-ˌniz-əm\ *n* (1839) **:** the condition or state of mind of a valetudinarian

1val·e·tu·di·nary \-ˈt(y)üd-ᵊn-ˌer-ē\ *adj* [L *valetudinarius*] (1581) **:** VALETUDINARIAN

2valetudinary *n, pl* **-nar·ies** (1665) **:** VALETUDINARIAN

val·gus \ˈval-gəs\ *adj* [NL, fr. L, bowlegged — more at WALK] (1884) **:** of, relating to, or being a deformity in which an anatomical part is turned outward away from the midline of the body to an abnormal degree ⟨~ deformity of the ankle⟩ — **valgus** *n*

Val·hal·la \val-ˈhal-ə *also* väl-ˈhäl-\ *n* [G & ON; G *Walhalla,* fr. ON *Valhǫll,* lit., hall of the slain, fr. *valr* the slain (akin to OE *wæl* slaughter, the slain, OIr *fuil* blood) + *hǫll* hall; akin to OE *heall* hall] **:** the great hall in Norse mythology where the souls of heroes slain in battle are received

val·iance \ˈval-yən(t)s\ *n* (15c) **:** VALOR

val·ian·cy \-yən-sē\ *n* (1574) **:** VALOR

1val·iant \ˈval-yənt\ *adj* [ME *valiaunt,* fr. MF *vaillant,* fr. OF, fr. prp. of *valoir* to be of worth, fr. L *valēre* to be strong — more at WIELD] (14c) **1 :** possessing or acting with bravery or boldness **:** COURAGEOUS ⟨~ soldiers⟩ **2 :** marked by, exhibiting, or carried out with courage or determination **:** HEROIC ⟨~ feats⟩ — **val·iant·ly** *adv* — **val·iant·ness** *n*

2valiant *n* (1609) **:** a valiant person

val·id \ˈval-əd\ *adj* [MF or ML; MF *valide,* fr. ML *validus,* fr. L strong, fr. *valēre*] (1571) **1 :** having legal efficacy or force; *esp* **:** executed with the proper legal authority and formalities ⟨a ~ contract⟩ **2 a :** well-grounded or justifiable **:** being at once relevant and meaningful ⟨a ~ theory⟩ **b :** logically correct ⟨a ~ argument⟩ ⟨~ inference⟩ **3 :** appropriate to the end in view **:** EFFECTIVE ⟨every craft has its own ~ methods⟩ **4** *of a taxon* **:** conforming to accepted principles of sound biological classification — **va·lid·i·ty** \və-ˈlid-ət-ē, va-\ *n* — **val·id·ly** \ˈval-əd-lē\ *adv*

syn VALID, SOUND, COGENT, CONVINCING, TELLING mean having such force as to compel serious attention and usu. acceptance. VALID implies being supported by objective truth or generally accepted authority ⟨a contract which satisfies all the requirements for enforceability by a court is termed a *valid* contract —L. B. Howard⟩ SOUND implies a basis of flawless reasoning or of solid grounds ⟨a separate foundation designed to sponsor and support innovation in higher education is not a *sound* policy proposal —H. D. Gideonse⟩ COGENT may stress either weight of sound argument and evidence or lucidity of presentation ⟨a soul-searching melancholia through which he was to create a *cogent* universality of form and meaning —J. A. Dennis⟩ CONVINCING suggests a power to overcome doubt, opposition, or reluctance to accept ⟨the very lack of planning . . . is *convincing* proof that there was no conspiracy —Sylvan Fox⟩ TELLING stresses an immediate and crucial effect striking at the heart of a matter ⟨a *telling* attack, made with skill and shrewd insight —V. L. Parrington⟩

val·i·date \ˈval-ə-ˌdāt\ *vt* **-dat·ed; -dat·ing** [ML *validatus,* pp. of *validare* to validate, fr. *validus*] (1648) **1 a :** to make legally valid **b :** to grant official sanction to by marking **c :** to confirm the validity of (an election); *also* **:** to declare (a person) elected **2 :** to support or corroborate on a sound or authoritative basis ⟨experiments designed to ~ his hypothesis⟩ ***syn*** see CONFIRM

val·i·da·tion \ˌval-ə-ˈdā-shən\ *n* (ca. 1656) **:** an act, process, or instance of validating; *esp* **:** the determination of the degree of validity of a measuring device

va·line \ˈval-ˌēn, ˈvā-ˌlēn\ *n* [ISV, fr. *valeric* (*acid*)] (1915) **:** a crystalline essential amino acid $C_5H_{11}NO_2$ that occurs esp. in fibrous proteins

va·lise \və-ˈlēs\ *n* [F, fr. It *valigia*] (1615) **:** TRAVELING BAG

Val·ium \ˈval-ē-əm, ˈval-yəm\ *trademark* — used for a preparation of diazepam

Val·ky·rie \val-ˈkir-ē *also* val-ˈkī-rē, ˈval-kə-rē\ *n* [G & ON; G *walküre,* fr. ON *valkyrja,* lit., chooser of the slain; akin to OE *wælcyrige* witch, ON *valr* the slain, OHG *kiosan* to choose — more at CHOOSE] (1768) **:** any of the maidens of Odin who choose the heroes to be slain in battle and conduct them to Valhalla

val·late \ˈval-ˌāt\ *adj* [L *vallatus,* pp. of *vallare* to surround with a wall, fr. *vallum* wall, rampart — more at WALL] (1878) **:** having a raised edge surrounding a depression ⟨~ papillae of the tongue⟩

val·lec·u·la \va-ˈlek-yə-lə, və-\ *n, pl* **-u·lae** \-yə-ˌlē, -ˌlī\ [NL, fr. LL, little valley, dim. of L *valles* valley — more at VALE] (1859) **:** an anatomical groove, channel, or depression; *esp* **:** one between the base of the tongue and the epiglottis — **val·lec·u·lar** \-lər\ *adj*

val·ley \ˈval-ē\ *n, pl* **valleys** [ME *valey,* fr. OF *valee,* fr. *val* valley — more at VALE] (13c) **1 a :** an elongate depression of the earth's surface usu. between ranges of hills or mountains **b :** an area drained by a river and its tributaries **2 :** a low point or condition **3 a :** HOLLOW, DEPRESSION **b :** the place of meeting of two slopes of a roof that form on the plan a reentrant angle

valley fever *n* [fr. its prevalence in the San Joaquin valley of California] (ca. 1940) **:** COCCIDIOIDOMYCOSIS

Va·lois \ˈval-ˌwä, val-ˈ\ *adj* [Philippe de *Valois* (Philip VI of France)] (ca. 1888) **:** of or relating to the French royal house that ruled from 1328 to 1589

va·lo·nia \və-ˈlō-nē-ə, -nyə\ *n* [It *vallonia,* fr. MGk *balanidia,* pl. of *balanidion,* dim. of Gk *balanos* acorn — more at GLAND] (1722) **:** dried acorn cups esp. from a Eurasian evergreen oak (*Quercus aegilops*) used in tanning or dressing leather

val·or \ˈval-ər\ *n* [ME, fr. MF *valour,* fr. ML *valor* value, valor, fr. L *valēre* to be strong — more at WIELD] (14c) **:** strength of mind or spirit that enables a person to encounter danger with firmness **:** personal bravery

val·o·rize \ˈval-ə-ˌrīz\ *vt* **-rized; -riz·ing** [Pg *valorizare,* fr. *valor* value, price, fr. ML] (ca. 1906) **:** to enhance or try to enhance the price, value, or status of by organized and usu. governmental action ⟨using subsidies to ~ coffee⟩ — **val·o·ri·za·tion** \ˌval-ə-rə-ˈzā-shən\ *n*

val·or·ous \ˈval-ə-rəs\ *adj* (15c) **:** VALIANT — **val·or·ous·ly** *adv*

val·our \ˈval-ər\ *chiefly Brit var of* VALOR

val·po·li·cel·la \ˌväl-ˌpō-lə-ˈchel-ə, ˌval-\ *n, often cap* [*Valpolicella,* valley in northern Italy] (1941) **:** a dry red Italian table wine

Val·sal·va maneuver \val-ˌsal-və-\ *n* [Antonio Maria *Valsalva* †1723 Ital. anatomist] (1942) **:** the process of making a forceful attempt at expiration while holding the nostrils closed and keeping the mouth shut for the purpose of testing the patency of the eustachian tubes or of adjusting middle ear pressure — called also *Valsalva*

valse \ˈvȯls\ *n* [F, fr. G *walzer* — more at WALTZ] (1796) **:** WALTZ; *specif* **:** a concert waltz

1valu·able \ˈval-yə(-wə)-bəl\ *adj* (1589) **1 a :** having monetary value **b :** worth a good price **2 a :** having desirable or esteemed characteristics or qualities ⟨~ friendships⟩ **b :** of great use or service ⟨~ advice⟩ — **valu·able·ness** *n* — **valu·ably** \-blē\ *adv*

2valuable *n* (ca. 1775) **:** a usu. personal possession (as jewelry) of relatively great monetary value — usu. used in pl.

valuable consideration *n* (1638) **:** an equivalent or compensation having value that is given for something acquired or promised (as money or marriage) and that may consist either in a benefit accruing to one party or a loss falling upon the other

val·u·ate \'val-yə-,wāt\ *vt* **-at·ed; -at·ing** (1873) : to place a value on : APPRAISE

val·u·a·tion \,val-yə-'wā-shən\ *n* [MF, fr. *valuer* to value, fr. *value*] (1529) **1 :** the act or process of valuing; *specif* : appraisal of property **2 :** the estimated or determined market value of a thing **3 :** judgment or appreciation of worth or character — **val·u·a·tion·al** \-shnəl, -shən-ᵊl\ *adj* — **val·u·a·tion·al·ly** \-ē\ *adv*

val·u·a·tor \'val-yə-,wāt-ər\ *n* (1731) : one that valuates; *specif* : one that appraises

¹val·ue \'val-(,)yü, -yə(-w)\ *n* [ME, fr. MF, fr. (assumed) VL *valuta*, fr. fem. of *valutus*, pp. of L *valēre* to be worth, be strong — more at WIELD] (14c) **1 :** a fair return or equivalent in goods, services, or money for something exchanged **2 :** the monetary worth of something : marketable price **3 :** relative worth, utility, or importance : degree of excellence ⟨had nothing of ~ to say⟩ **4 a :** a numerical quantity that is assigned or is determined by calculation or measurement ⟨let *x* take on positive ~*s*⟩ ⟨a ~ for the age of the earth⟩ **b :** precise signification ⟨~ of a word⟩ **5 :** the relative duration of a musical note **6 a :** relative lightness or darkness of a color : LUMINOSITY **b :** the relation of one part in a picture to another with respect to lightness and darkness **7 :** something (as a principle or quality) intrinsically valuable or desirable ⟨sought material ~*s* instead of human ~*s* —W. H. Jones⟩ **8 :** DENOMINATION 2 — **val·ue·less** \-(,)yü-ləs, -yə-\ *adj* — **val·ue·less·ness** *n*

²value *vt* **val·ued; val·u·ing** (15c) **1 a :** to estimate or assign the monetary worth of : APPRAISE ⟨~ a necklace⟩ **b :** to rate or scale in usefulness, importance, or general worth : EVALUATE **2 :** to consider or rate highly : PRIZE, ESTEEM ⟨~*s* your friendship⟩ *syn* see ESTIMATE, APPRECIATE — **val·u·er** \-yə-wər\ *n*

val·ue–add·ed tax \,val-yə-,wad-əd-\ *n* (1967) : an incremental excise that is levied on the value added at each stage of the processing of a raw material or the production and distribution of a commodity and that typically has the impact of a sales tax on the ultimate consumer

val·ued \'val-(,)yüd, -yəd\ *adj* (1605) : having a value or values esp. of a specified kind or number — often used in combination ⟨real-*valued*⟩

value judgment *n* (1899) : a judgment assigning a value (as good or bad) to something

va·lu·ta \və-'lüt-ə, -'lü-(,)tä\ *n* [It, value, fr. (assumed) VL *valuta*] (1920) **1 :** the agreed upon or exchange value of a currency **2 :** FOREIGN EXCHANGE 2

val·vate \'val-,vāt\ *adj* (1829) : having valves or parts resembling a valve: as **a :** meeting at the edges without overlapping in the bud ⟨~ leaves⟩ **b :** opening as if by doors or valves ⟨~ capsules⟩ ⟨~ anthers⟩

valve \'valv\ *n* [L *valva*; akin to L *volvere* to roll — more at VOLUBLE] (14c) **1** *archaic* : a leaf of a folding or double door **2** [NL *valva*, fr. L] : a structure esp. in a vein or lymphatic that closes temporarily a passage or orifice or permits movement of fluid in one direction only **3 a :** any of numerous mechanical devices by which the flow of liquid, gas, or loose material in bulk may be started, stopped, or regulated by a movable part that opens, shuts, or partially obstructs one or more ports or passageways; *also* : the movable part of such a device **b :** a device in a brass instrument for quickly channeling air flow through an added length of tube in order to change the fundamental tone by some definite interval **c** *chiefly Brit* : ELECTRON TUBE **4** [NL *valva*, fr. L] : one of the distinct and usu. movably articulated pieces of which the shell of some shell-bearing animals (as lamellibranch mollusks, brachiopods, and barnacles) consists **5** [NL *valva*, fr. L] **a :** one of the segments or pieces into which a dehiscing capsule or legume separates **b :** the portion of various anthers (as of the barberry) resembling a lid **c :** one of the two encasing membranes of a diatom — **valved** \'valvd\ *adj* — **valve·less** \'valv-ləs\ *adj*

valve–in–head engine *n* (ca. 1931) : an internal-combustion engine in which both inlet and exhaust valves are located in the cylinder head

val·vu·la \'val-vyə-lə\ *n, pl* **-lae** \-,lē, -,lī\ [NL, dim. of L *valva*] (1615) : a small valve or fold

val·vu·lar \'val-vyə-lər\ *adj* (1797) **1 :** resembling or functioning as a valve; *also* : opening by valves **2 :** of or relating to a valve esp. of the heart ⟨~ disorders⟩

val·vu·li·tis \,val-vyə-'līt-əs\ *n* [NL] (ca. 1891) : inflammation of a valve esp. of the heart

va·moose \və-'müs, va-\ *vi* **va·moosed; va·moos·ing** [Sp *vamos* let us go, suppletive 1st pl. imper. (fr. L *vadere* to go) of *ir* to go, fr. L *ire* — more at WADE, ISSUE] (1840) : to depart quickly

¹vamp \'vamp\ *vt* (1599) **1 a :** to provide (a shoe) with a new vamp **b :** to piece (something old) with a new part : PATCH ⟨~ up old sermons⟩ **2 :** INVENT, FABRICATE ⟨~ up an excuse⟩ ~ *vi* : to play a musical vamp — **vamp·er** *n*

²vamp *n* [ME *vampe* sock, fr. OF *avantpié*, fr. *avant-* fore- + *pié* foot, fr. L *ped-, pes* — more at VANGUARD, FOOT] (1654) **1 :** the part of a shoe upper or boot upper covering esp. the forepart of the foot and sometimes also extending forward over the toe or backward to the back seam of the upper **2** [¹*vamp*] : an introductory musical passage of two or four measures often repeated several times (as in vaudeville) before a solo or between verses

³vamp *n* [short for *vampire*] (ca. 1911) : a woman who uses her charm or wiles to seduce and exploit men — **vamp·ish** \'vam-pish\ *adj*

⁴vamp *vt* (ca. 1915) : to practice seductive wiles on

vam·pire \'vam-,pī(ə)r\ *n* [F, fr. G *vampir*, of Slav origin; akin to Serb *vampir* vampire] (1734) **1 :** the reanimated body of a dead person believed to come from the grave at night and suck the blood of persons asleep **2 a :** one who lives by preying on others **b :** a woman who exploits and ruins her lover **3 :** any of various So. American bats (genera *Desmodus* and *Diphylla* of the family Desmodontidae) structurally adapted for subsisting on blood and dangerous to humans and domestic animals esp. as vectors of equine trypanosomiasis and of rabies; *also* : any of several other bats that do not feed on blood but are sometimes reputed to do so

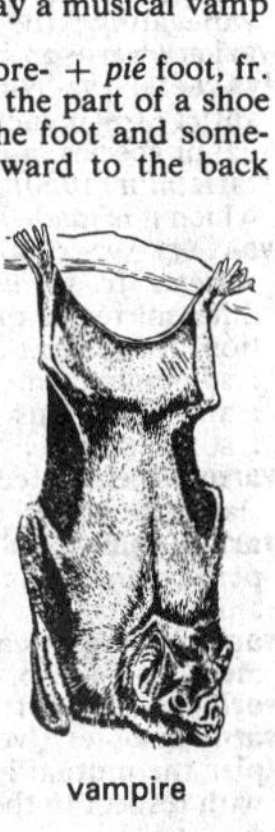
vampire

vam·pir·ism \-,pī(ə)r-,iz-əm\ *n* (1794) **1 :** belief in vampires **2 :** the actions of a vampire

¹van \'van\ *n* [ME, fr. MF, fr. L *vannus* — more at WINNOW] (14c) **1** *dial Eng* : a winnowing device (as a fan) **2 :** WING 1a

²van *n* [by shortening] (1610) : VANGUARD

³van *n* [short for *caravan*] (1829) **1 a :** a usu. enclosed wagon or motortruck used for transportation of goods or animals; *also* : CARAVAN 2a **b :** a multipurpose enclosed motor vehicle having a boxlike shape, rear or side doors, and side panels often with windows **c :** a detachable passenger cabin transportable by aircraft or truck **2** *chiefly Brit* : an enclosed railroad freight or baggage car

⁴van *vt* **vanned; van·ning** (1840) : to transport by van

van·a·date \'van-ə-,dāt\ *n* (1835) : a salt derived from vanadium pentoxide and containing pentavalent vanadium

va·na·dic \və-'nād-ik, -'nad-\ *adj* [NL *vanad*ium + E *-ic*] (1833) : of, relating to, or containing vanadium esp. with a higher valence than in vanadous compounds

vanadic acid *n* (1833) **1 :** any of various acids that are hydrates of vanadium pentoxide or are known esp. in the form of salts and esters **2 :** VANADIUM PENTOXIDE

va·na·di·nite \və-'nād-ᵊn-,īt, ,van-ə-'dēn-\ *n* [G *vanadinit*, fr. *vanadin* vanadium, fr. NL *vanadium*] (1855) : a mineral consisting of a lead vanadate and chloride and occurring in yellowish, brownish, or ruby-red hexagonal crystals

va·na·di·um \və-'nād-ē-əm\ *n* [NL, fr. ON *Vanadīs* Freya] (1835) : a grayish malleable ductile metallic element found combined in minerals and used esp. to form alloys (as vanadium steel) — see ELEMENT table

vanadium pentoxide *n* (ca. 1885) : a yellowish red crystalline compound V_2O_5 used esp. in glass manufacture and as a catalyst

va·na·dous \və-'nād-əs, 'van-əd-\ *adj* (1858) : of, relating to, or containing vanadium esp. with a lower valence than in vanadic compounds

Van Al·len belt \van-'al-ən-\ *n* [James A. *Van Allen*] (1958) : a belt of intense ionizing radiation that surrounds the earth in the outer atmosphere

va·nas·pa·ti \və-'nəs-pət-ē, -'näs-\ *n* [Skt, forest tree, soma plant, lit., lord of the forest, fr. *vana* forest + *pati* lord; akin to L *potis* able — more at POTENT] (ca. 1941) : a hydrogenated vegetable fat used as a butter substitute in India

van·dal \'van-dᵊl\ *n* [L *Vandalii* (pl.), of Gmc origin] (1555) **1** *cap* : a member of a Germanic people who lived in the area south of the Baltic between the Vistula and the Oder, overran Gaul, Spain, and northern Africa in the 4th and 5th centuries A.D., and in 455 sacked Rome **2 :** one who willfully or ignorantly destroys, damages, or defaces property belonging to another or to the public — **vandal** *adj, often cap* — **Van·dal·ic** \van-'dal-ik\ *adj*

van·dal·ism \'van-dᵊl-,iz-əm\ *n* (1798) : willful or malicious destruction or defacement of public or private property

van·dal·is·tic \,van-dᵊl-'is-tik\ *adj* (1854) : of or relating to vandalism

van·dal·ize \'van-dᵊl-,īz\ *vt* **-ized; -iz·ing** (1800) : to subject to vandalism : DAMAGE — **van·dal·iza·tion** \,van-dᵊl-ə-'zā-shən\ *n*

van·da orchid \'van-də-\ *n* [NL, fr. Hindi *vandā* mistletoe, fr. Skt, a parasitic plant] (1801) : any of a large genus (*Vanda*) of Indo-Malayan epiphytic orchids often grown for their loose racemes of showy flowers — called also *vanda*

Van de Graaff generator \,van-də-,graf-\ *n* [Robert J. *Van de Graaff* †1967 Am. physicist] (ca. 1937) : ELECTROSTATIC GENERATOR

van der Waals forces \,van-dər-,wólz-, -,välz-\ *n pl* [Johannes D. *van der Waals* †1923 Du. physicist] (ca. 1926) : the relatively weak attractive forces that act on neutral atoms and molecules and that arise because of the electric polarization induced in each of the particles by the presence of other particles

Van·dyke \van-'dīk, vən-\ *n* [Sir Anthony *Vandyke*] (1755) **1 a :** a wide collar with a deeply indented edge **b :** one of several V-shaped points forming a decorative edging **c :** a border of such points **2 :** a trim pointed beard — **van·dyked** \-'dīkt\ *adj*

Vandyke brown *n* [fr. its use by the painter Vandyke] (ca. 1850) : a natural brown-black pigment of organic matter obtained from bog earth or peat or lignite deposits; *also* : any of various synthetic brown pigments

vane \'vān\ *n* [ME (southern dial.), fr. OE *fana* banner; akin to OHG *fano* cloth, L *pannus* cloth, rag] (bef. 12c) **1 a :** a movable device attached to an elevated object (as a spire) for showing the direction of the wind **b :** one that is changeable or inconstant **2 :** a thin flat or curved object that is rotated about an axis by a flow of fluid or that rotates to cause a fluid to flow or that redirects a flow of fluid ⟨the ~*s* of a windmill⟩ **3 :** the web or flat expanded part of a feather **4 :** a feather fastened to the shaft near the nock of an arrow **5 a :** the target of a leveling rod **b :** one of the sights of a compass or quadrant — **vaned** \'vānd\ *adj*

van·guard \'van-,gärd *also* 'vaŋ-\ *n* [ME *vantgard*, fr. MF *avant-garde*, fr. OF, fr. *avant-* fore- (fr. *avant* before, fr. L *abante*) + *garde* guard — more at ADVANCE] (15c) **1 :** the troops moving at the head of an army **2 :** the forefront of an action or movement — **van·guard·ism** \-,iz-əm\ *n* — **van·guard·ist** \-əst\ *n*

¹va·nil·la \və-'nil-ə, -'nel-\ *n* [NL, fr. Sp *vainilla* vanilla (plant and fruit), dim. of *vaina* sheath, fr. L *vagina* sheath, vagina] (1662) **1 a :** VANILLA BEAN **b :** a commercially important extract of the vanilla bean that is used esp. as a flavoring **2 :** any of a genus (*Vanilla*) of tropical American climbing orchids

²vanilla *adj* (1846) **1 :** flavored with vanilla **2 :** lacking pizzazz : PLAIN, ORDINARY

vanilla bean *n* (1874) : the long capsular fruit of a vanilla (esp. *Vanilla planifolia*) that is an important article of commerce

van·il·lin \'van-ᵊl-ən\ *n* (ca. 1868) : a crystalline phenolic aldehyde $C_8H_8O_3$ that is the chief fragrant component of vanilla and is used esp. in flavoring and in perfumery

\ə\ abut \ᵊ\ kitten, F table \ər\ further \a\ ash \ā\ ace \ä\ cot, cart \aù\ out \ch\ chin \e\ bet \ē\ easy \g\ go \i\ hit \ī\ ice \j\ job \ŋ\ sing \ō\ go \ó\ law \ói\ boy \th\ thin \t͟h\ the \ü\ loot \ù\ foot \y\ yet \zh\ vision \á, k̲, ⁿ, œ, œ̄, ue, ue̅, ʸ\ *see* Guide to Pronunciation

Va·nir \ˈvän-ˌi(ə)r\ *n pl* [ON] **:** a race of Norse gods who become united with the Aesir

van·ish \ˈvan-ish\ *vb* [ME *vanisshen*, fr. MF *evaniss-*, stem of *evanir*, fr. (assumed) VL *exvanire*, alter. of L *evanescere* to dissipate like vapor, vanish, fr. *e-* + *vanescere* to vanish, fr. *vanus* empty] *vi* (14c) **1 a :** to pass quickly from sight **:** DISAPPEAR **b :** to pass completely from existence **2 :** to assume the value zero ∼ *vt* **:** to cause to disappear — **van·ish·er** *n*

vanishing cream *n* (1922) **:** a cosmetic preparation that is less oily than cold cream and is used chiefly as a foundation for face powder

van·ish·ing·ly \-iŋ-lē\ *adv* (1870) **:** so as to be almost nonexistent or invisible ⟨the difference is ∼ small⟩

vanishing point *n* (ca. 1797) **1 :** a point at which receding parallel lines seem to meet when represented in linear perspective **2 :** a point at which something disappears or ceases to exist

van·i·ty \ˈvan-ət-ē\ *n, pl* **-ties** [ME *vanite*, fr. OF *vanité*, fr. L *vanitat-, vanitas* quality of being empty or vain, fr. *vanus* empty, vain — more at WANE] (13c) **1 :** something that is vain, empty, or valueless **2 :** the quality or fact of being vain **3 :** inflated pride in oneself or one's appearance **:** CONCEIT **4 :** a fashionable trifle or knicknack **5 a :** [3]COMPACT a **b :** a small case or handbag for toilet articles used by women **6 :** DRESSING TABLE

vanity fair *n, often cap V&F* [*Vanity-Fair*, a fair held in the frivolous town of Vanity in *Pilgrim's Progress* (1678) by John Bunyan] (1816) **:** a scene or place characterized by frivolity and ostentation

vanity plate *n* (1966) **:** a license plate bearing letters or numbers designated by the owner of the vehicle

vanity press *n* (1950) **:** a publishing house that publishes books at the author's expense — called also *vanity publisher*

van·ner \ˈvan-ər\ *n* (1927) **:** a person who owns a usu. customized van

van·pool \ˈvan-ˌpül\ *n* [[3]*van* + car *pool*] (ca. 1974) **:** an arrangement by which a group of people commute to work in a van — **van·pool·ing** *n*

van·quish \ˈvaŋ-kwish, ˈvan-\ *vt* [ME *venquissen* fr. MF *venquis*, preterit of *veintre* to conquer, fr. L *vincere* — more at VICTOR] (14c) **1 :** to overcome in battle **:** subdue completely **2 :** to defeat in a conflict or contest **3 :** to gain mastery over (an emotion, passion, or temptation) ***syn*** see CONQUER — **van·quish·able** \-kwish-ə-bəl\ *adj* — **van·quish·er** *n*

van·tage \ˈvant-ij\ *n* [ME, fr. AF, fr. MF *avantage* — more at ADVANTAGE] (14c) **1** *archaic* **:** BENEFIT, GAIN **2 :** superiority in a contest **3 :** a position giving a strategic advantage, commanding perspective, or comprehensive view **4 :** ADVANTAGE 4 — **to the vantage** *obs* **:** in addition

vantage point *n* (1865) **:** a position or standpoint from which something is viewed or considered; *esp* **:** POINT OF VIEW

[1]**van·ward** \ˈvan-wərd\ *adj* (1820) **:** located in the vanguard **:** ADVANCED

[2]**vanward** *adv* (1827) **:** to or toward the vanguard **:** FORWARD

va·pid \ˈvap-əd, ˈvā-pəd\ *adj* [L *vapidus* flat tasting; akin to L *vappa* vapid wine and prob. to L *vapor* steam] (ca. 1656) **:** lacking liveliness, tang, briskness, or force **:** FLAT, UNINTERESTING ***syn*** see INSIPID — **va·pid·ly** *adv* — **va·pid·ness** *n*

va·pid·i·ty \va-ˈpid-ət-ē, vā-, və-\ *n, pl* **-ties** (ca. 1721) **1 :** the quality or state of being vapid **2 :** something vapid

[1]**va·por** \ˈvā-pər\ *n* [ME *vapour*, fr. MF *vapeur*, fr. L *vapor* steam, vapor] (14c) **1 :** diffused matter (as smoke or fog) suspended floating in the air and impairing its transparency **2 a :** a substance in the gaseous state as distinguished from the liquid or solid state **b :** a substance (as gasoline, alcohol, mercury, or benzoin) vaporized for industrial, therapeutic, or military uses; *also* **:** a mixture (as the explosive mixture in an internal-combustion engine) of such a vapor with air **3 a :** something unsubstantial or transitory **:** PHANTASM **b :** a foolish or fanciful idea **4** *pl* **a** *archaic* **:** exhalations of bodily organs (as the stomach) held to affect the physical or mental condition **b :** a depressed or hysterical nervous condition

[2]**vapor** *vi* **va·pored; va·por·ing** \-p(ə-)riŋ\ (15c) **1 a :** to rise or pass off in vapor **b :** to emit vapor **2 :** to indulge in bragging, blustering, or idle talk — **va·por·er** \-pər-ər\ *n*

vapor barrier *n* (ca. 1941) **:** a layer of material (as roofing paper or polyethylene film) used to retard or prevent the absorption of moisture into a construction (as a wall or floor)

va·po·ret·to \ˌvä-pə-ˈret-(ˌ)ō\ *n, pl* **-ret·ti** \-ˈret-ē\ *also* **-ret·tos** [It, dim. of *vapore* steamboat, fr. F *vapeur*, fr. *bateau à vapeur* steamboat] (1949) **:** a motorboat serving as a canal bus in Venice, Italy

va·por·ing \ˈvā-p(ə-)riŋ\ *n* (1630) **:** the act or speech of one that vapors; *specif* **:** an idle, extravagant, or high-flown expression or speech — usu. used in pl.

va·por·ise \ˈvā-pə-ˌrīz\ *Brit var of* VAPORIZE

va·por·ish \ˈvā-p(ə-)rish\ *adj* (ca. 1644) **1 :** resembling or suggestive of vapor **2 :** given to fits of the vapors — **va·por·ish·ness** *n*

va·por·ize \ˈvā-pə-ˌrīz\ *vb* **-ized; -iz·ing** *vt* (1634) **1 :** to convert (as by the application of heat or by spraying) into vapor **2 :** to cause to become dissipated ∼ *vi* **1 :** to become vaporized **2 :** VAPOR 2 — **va·por·iz·able** \-ˌrī-zə-bəl\ *adj* — **va·por·iza·tion** \ˌvā-pər-ə-ˈzā-shən\ *n*

va·por·iz·er \ˈvā-pə-ˌrī-zər\ *n* (ca. 1846) **:** one that vaporizes **:** as **a :** ATOMIZER **b :** an apparatus for vaporizing a heavy oil (as petroleum) for the explosive charge of an internal-combustion engine; *also* **:** a simple form of carburetor **c :** a device for converting water or a medicated liquid into a vapor for inhalation

vapor lock *n* (ca. 1926) **:** partial or complete interruption of flow of a fluid (as fuel in an internal-combustion engine) caused by the formation of bubbles of vapor in the feeding system

va·por·ous \ˈvā-p(ə-)rəs\ *adj* (1527) **1 :** consisting or characteristic of vapor **2 :** producing vapors **:** VOLATILE **3 :** containing or obscured by vapors **:** MISTY **4 a :** ETHEREAL, UNSUBSTANTIAL **b :** consisting of or indulging in vaporings — **va·por·ous·ly** *adv* — **va·por·ous·ness** *n*

vapor pressure *n* (ca. 1900) **:** the pressure exerted by a vapor that is in equilibrium with its solid or liquid form — called also *vapor tension*

vapor trail *n* (1943) **:** CONTRAIL

va·pory \ˈvā-p(ə-)rē\ *adj* (1598) **:** VAPOROUS, MISTY

va·pour \ˈvā-pər\ *chiefly Brit var of* VAPOR

va·que·ro \vä-ˈke(ə)r-(ˌ)ō\ *n, pl* **-ros** [Sp — more at BUCKAROO] (1831) **:** HERDSMAN, COWBOY

va·ra \ˈvär-ə\ *n* [Sp & Pg, lit., pole, fr. L, forked pole, fr. fem. of *varus* bent, crooked — more at PREVARICATE] (1604) **1 :** any of various Spanish, Portuguese, and Latin American units of length equal to between 31 and 34 inches (79 and 86 centimeters) **2 :** a Texas unit of length equal to 33.33 inches (84.66 centimeters)

vari- *or* **vario-** *comb form* [L *varius* — more at VARIOUS] **:** varied **:** diverse ⟨*vari*form⟩ ⟨*vario*coupler⟩

var·ia \ˈver-ē-ə, ˈvar-\ *n pl* [NL, fr. L, neut. pl. of *varius* various] (1926) **:** MISCELLANY; *esp* **:** a literary miscellany

[1]**vari·able** \ˈver-ē-ə-bəl, ˈvar-\ *adj* [ME, fr. MF, fr. L *variabilis*, fr. *variare* to vary] (14c) **1 a :** able or apt to vary **:** subject to variation or changes ⟨∼ winds⟩ ⟨∼ costs⟩ **b :** FICKLE, INCONSTANT **2 :** characterized by variations **3 :** having the characteristics of a variable **4 :** not true to type **:** ABERRANT — used of a biological group or character — **vari·abil·i·ty** \ˌver-ē-ə-ˈbil-ət-ē, ˌvar-\ *n* — **vari·able·ness** \ˈver-ē-ə-bəl-nəs, ˈvar-\ *n* — **vari·ably** \-blē\ *adv*

[2]**variable** *n* (1816) **1 a :** a quantity that may assume any one of a set of values **b :** a symbol representing a variable **2 :** something that is variable **3 :** VARIABLE STAR

variable rate mortgage *n* (1975) **:** a periodically renegotiable mortgage that has an interest rate indexed to the cost of funds to the lender

variable star *n* (1788) **:** a star whose brightness changes usu. in more or less regular periods

vari·ance \ˈver-ē-ən(t)s, ˈvar-\ *n* [ME *variaunce*, fr. MF, fr. L *variantia*, fr. *variant-, varians*, prp. of *variare* to vary] (14c) **1 :** the fact, quality, or state of being variable or variant **:** DIFFERENCE, VARIATION ⟨yearly ∼ in crops⟩ **2 :** the fact or state of being in disagreement **:** DISSENSION, DISPUTE **3 :** a disagreement between two parts of the same legal proceeding that must be consonant **4 :** a license to do some act contrary to the usual rule ⟨a zoning ∼⟩ **5 :** the square of the standard deviation ***syn*** see DISCORD — **at variance :** not in harmony or agreement

[1]**vari·ant** \ˈver-ē-ənt, ˈvar-\ *adj* (14c) **1** *obs* **:** VARIABLE **2 :** manifesting variety, deviation, or disagreement **3 :** varying usu. slightly from the standard form ⟨∼ readings⟩

[2]**variant** *n* (1848) **:** one of two or more persons or things exhibiting usu. slight differences: as **a :** one that exhibits variation from a type or norm **b :** one of two or more different spellings (as *labor* and *labour*) or pronunciations (as of *economics* \ek-, ēk-\) of the same word **c :** one of two or more words (as *geographic* and *geographical*) or word elements (as *mon-* and *mono-*) of essentially the same meaning differing only in the presence or absence of an affix

vari·ate \ˈver-ē-ˌāt, ˈvar-, -ət\ *n* (1899) **:** RANDOM VARIABLE

vari·a·tion \ˌver-ē-ˈā-shən, ˌvar-\ *n* [ME *varicioun*, fr. MF or L; MF *variation*, fr. L *variation-, variatio*, fr. *variatus*, pp. of *variare* to vary] (14c) **1 a :** the act or process of varying **:** the state or fact of being varied **b :** an instance of varying **c :** the extent to which or the range in which a thing varies **2 :** DECLINATION 6 **3 :** a change in the mean motion or mean orbit of a celestial body **4 a :** a change of algebraic sign between successive terms of a sequence **b :** a measure of the change in data, a variable, or a function **5 :** the repetition of a musical theme with modifications in rhythm, tune, harmony, or key **6 a :** divergence in qualities of an organism or biotype from those typical or usual to its group **b :** something (as an individual or group) that exhibits variation **7 a :** a solo dance in classic ballet **b :** a repetition in modern ballet of a movement sequence with changes — **vari·a·tion·al** \-shnəl, -shən-ᵊl\ *adj* — **vari·a·tion·al·ly** \-ē\ *adv*

var·i·cel·la \ˌvar-ə-ˈsel-ə\ *n* [NL, irreg. dim. of *variola*] (ca. 1771) **:** CHICKEN POX

var·i·co·cele \ˈvar-ə-kō-ˌsēl\ *n* [NL, fr. L *varic-, varix* + *-o-* + *-cele*] (1736) **:** a varicose enlargement of the veins of the spermatic cord

vari·col·ored \ˈver-i-ˌkəl-ərd, ˈvar-\ *adj* (1665) **:** having various colors **:** VARIEGATED ⟨∼ nuptial plumage of a bird⟩; *also* **:** of various colors

var·i·cose \ˈvar-ə-ˌkōs\ *adj* [L *varicosus* full of dilated veins, fr. *varic-, varix* dilated vein; akin to L *varus* stretched, bent, awry] (1730) **1 :** of, relating to, or exhibiting varices ⟨∼ mollusks⟩ **2** *also* **var·i·cosed** \-ˌkōst, -ˌkōzd\ **:** abnormally swollen or dilated ⟨∼ veins⟩

var·i·cos·i·ty \ˌvar-ə-ˈkäs-ət-ē\ *n, pl* **-ties** (1842) **1 :** the quality or state of being abnormally or markedly swollen or dilated **2 :** VARIX

var·ied \ˈve(ə)r-ēd, ˈva(ə)r-\ *adj* (1588) **1 :** VARIOUS, DIVERSE **2 :** VARIEGATED 1 — **var·ied·ly** *adv*

var·ie·gate \ˈver-ē-ə-ˌgāt, ˈver-i-ˌgāt, ˈvar-\ *vt* **-gat·ed; -gat·ing** [L *variegatus*, pp. of *variegare*, fr. *varius* various + *-egare* (akin to L *agere* to drive) — more at AGENT] (1653) **1 :** to diversify in external appearance esp. with different colors **:** DAPPLE **2 :** to enliven or give interest to by means of variety — **var·ie·ga·tor** \-ˌgāt-ər\ *n*

var·ie·gat·ed \-ˌgāt-əd\ *adj* (1661) **1 :** having discrete markings of different colors ⟨∼ leaves⟩ **2 :** VARIED 1

variegated cutworm *n* (1922) **:** a widespread noctuid moth (*Peridroma saucia*) whose larva is destructive to crops

var·ie·ga·tion \ˌver-ē-ə-ˈgā-shən, ˌver-i-ˈgā-, ˌvar-\ *n* (1646) **:** the act of variegating **:** the state of being variegated; *esp* **:** diversity of colors

vari·er \ˈver-ē-ər, ˈvar-\ *n* (1860) **:** one that varies

[1]**va·ri·etal** \və-ˈrī-ət-ᵊl\ *adj* (1866) **:** of, relating to, or characterizing a variety ⟨∼ name⟩; *also* **:** being a variety in distinction from an individual or species

[2]**varietal** *n* (1950) **:** a wine bearing the name of the principal grape from which it is made

va·ri·ety \və-ˈrī-ət-ē\ *n, pl* **-et·ies** [MF or L; MF *varieté*, fr. L *varietat-, varietas*, fr. *varius* various] (1548) **1 :** the quality or state of having different forms or types **:** MULTIFARIOUSNESS **2 :** a number or collection of different things esp. of a particular class **:** ASSORTMENT **3 a :** something differing from others of the same general kind **:** SORT **b :** any of various groups of plants or animals ranking below a species **:** SUBSPECIES **4 :** VARIETY SHOW

variety meat *n* (ca. 1946) **:** an edible part (as the liver or tongue) of a slaughter animal other than skeletal muscle

variety show *n* (1882) **:** a theatrical entertainment of successive separate performances (as of songs, dances, skits, acrobatic feats, and trained animal acts)

variety store *n* (ca. 1768) **:** a retail store that carries a large variety of merchandise esp. of low unit value

vario- — see VARI-

var·io·cou·pler \ˈver-ē-ō-ˌkəp-lər, ˈvar-\ *n* (ca. 1922) **:** an inductive coupler the mutual inductance of which is adjustable by moving one coil with respect to the other

va·ri·o·la \ˌver-ē-ˈō-lə, ˌvar-; və-ˈrī-ə-lə\ *n* [NL, fr. ML, pustule, pox, fr. LL, pustule] (ca. 1771) : any of several virus diseases (as smallpox or cowpox) marked by a pustular eruption

var·i·om·e·ter \ˌver-ē-ˈäm-ət-ər, ˌvar-\ *n* (ca. 1900) **1** : an instrument for measuring magnetic declination **2** : VARIOCOUPLER **3** : an aeronautical instrument for indicating rate of climb

[1]**var·i·o·rum** \ˌver-ē-ˈōr-əm, ˌvar-, -ˈȯr-\ *n* [L *variorum* of various persons (gen. pl. masc. of *varius*), in the phrase *cum notis variorum* with the notes of various persons] (1728) **1** : an edition or text with notes by different persons **2** : an edition containing variant readings of the text

[2]**variorum** *adj* (1763) : relating to or being a variorum; *also* : VARIANT ⟨~ readings⟩

var·i·ous \ˈver-ē-əs, ˈvar-\ *adj* [L *varius;* prob. akin to L *varus* bent, crooked] (1552) **1** *archaic* : VARIABLE, INCONSTANT **2** : VARICOLORED ⟨birds of ~ plumage⟩ **3 a** : of differing kinds : MULTIFARIOUS **b** : dissimilar in nature or form : UNLIKE ⟨animals as ~ as the jaguar and the sloth⟩ **4** : having a number of different aspects or characteristics ⟨a ~ place⟩ ⟨a ~ talent⟩ **5** : of an indefinite number greater than one ⟨stop at ~ towns⟩ **6** : INDIVIDUAL, SEPARATE ⟨rate increases granted in the ~ states⟩ ***syn*** see DIFFERENT — **var·i·ous·ness** *n*

var·i·ous·ly *adv* (1627) **1** : in various ways : at various times ⟨was ~ occupied teaching, farming, and clerking⟩ **2** : by various designations ⟨known ~ as principal, headmaster, and rector⟩

vari·sized \ˈver-i-ˌsīzd, ˈvar-\ *adj* (1941) : of various sizes

va·ris·tor \va-ˈris-tər, ve-\ *n* [*vari-* + *resistor*] (1943) : an electrical resistor whose resistance depends on the applied voltage

var·ix \ˈvar-iks\ *n, pl* **var·i·ces** \ˈvar-ə-ˌsēz\ [L *varic-, varix* — more at VARICOSE] (15c) **1** : an abnormally dilated and lengthened vein, artery, or lymph vessel; *esp* : a varicose vein **2** : one of the prominent ridges across each whorl of a gastropod shell

var·let \ˈvär-lət\ *n* [ME, fr. MF *vaslet, varlet* young nobleman, page — more at VALET] (15c) **1 a** : ATTENDANT, MENIAL **b** : a knight's page **2** : a base unprincipled person : KNAVE

var·let·ry \-lə-trē\ *n, archaic* (1606) : RABBLE

var·mint \ˈvär-mənt\ *n* [alter. of *vermin*] (1539) **1** : an animal or bird considered a pest; *specif* : an animal classed as vermin and unprotected by game law **2** : a contemptible person : RASCAL; *broadly* : PERSON, FELLOW

[1]**var·nish** \ˈvär-nish\ *n* [ME *vernisch,* fr. MF *vernis,* fr. OIt or ML; OIt *vernice,* fr. ML *veronic-, veronix* sandarac (resin)] (14c) **1 a** : a liquid preparation that when spread and allowed to dry on a surface forms a hard lustrous typically transparent coating **b** : the covering or glaze given by the application of varnish **c** (1) : something that suggests varnish by its gloss (2) : a coating (as of deposits in an internal-combustion engine) comparable to varnish **2** : outside show : GLOSS **3** *chiefly Brit* : a liquid nail polish — **var·nishy** \-ē\ *adj*

[2]**varnish** *vt* (14c) **1** : to apply varnish to **2** : to cover or conceal (as something unpleasant) with something that gives a fair appearance : [2]GLOSS **3** : ADORN, EMBELLISH — **var·nish·er** \-ər\ *n*

varnish tree *n* (1758) : any of various trees yielding a milky juice from which in some cases varnish or lacquer is prepared; *esp* : a Japanese sumac (*Rhus verniciflua*)

var·si·ty \ˈvär-sət-ē, -stē\ *n, pl* **-ties** [by shortening & alter. fr. *university*] (1646) **1** *Brit* : UNIVERSITY **2 a** : the principal squad representing a university, college, school, or club esp. in a sport **b** : [2]REGULAR 1d

Var·u·na \ˈvar-ə-nə\ *n* [Skt *Varuṇa*] : a chief Vedic god responsible for natural and moral order in the cosmos

var·us \ˈvar-əs, ˈver-\ *n* [NL, fr. L, bent, knock-kneed — more at VARICOSE] (1800) : a deformed position of a bodily part characterized by bending or turning inward toward the midline of the body to an abnormal degree ⟨a moderate right metatarsus ~ —*Jour. Amer. Med. Assoc.*⟩ — **varus** *adj*

varve \ˈvärv\ *n* [Sw *varv* turn, layer; akin to OE *hweorfan* to turn — more at WHARF] (ca. 1922) : a pair of layers of alternately finer and coarser silt or clay believed to comprise an annual cycle of deposition in a body of still water — **varved** \ˈvärvd\ *adj*

vary \ˈve(ə)r-ē, ˈva(ə)r-\ *vb* **var·ied; vary·ing** [ME *varien,* fr. MF or L; MF *varier,* fr. L *variare,* fr. *varius* various] *vt* (14c) **1 a** : to make a partial change in : make different in some attribute or characteristic **b** : to make differences between items in : DIVERSIFY **2** : to present under new aspects ⟨~ the rhythm and harmonic treatment⟩ ~ *vi* **1** : to exhibit or undergo change ⟨the sky was constantly ~*ing*⟩ **2** : DEVIATE, DEPART **3** : to take on successive values ⟨*y varies* inversely with *x*⟩ **4** : to exhibit divergence in structural or physiological characters from the typical form ***syn*** see CHANGE — **vary·ing·ly** \-iŋ-lē\ *adv*

varying hare *n* (1781) : any of several hares having white fur in winter; *esp* : SNOWSHOE RABBIT

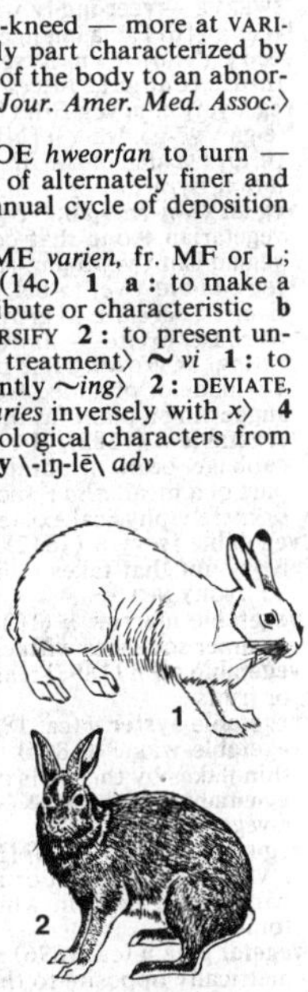

varying hare: *1* winter coat; *2* summer coat

vas \ˈvas\ *n, pl* **va·sa** \ˈvā-zə\ [NL, fr. L, vessel] (1651) : an anatomical vessel : DUCT — **va·sal** \-zəl\ *adj*

vas- *or* **vaso-** *comb form* [NL, fr. L *vas*] **1** : vessel: as **a** : blood vessel ⟨*vaso*motor⟩ **b** : vas deferens ⟨*vas*ectomy⟩ **2** : vascular and ⟨*vaso*vagal⟩ **3** : vasomotor ⟨*vaso*inhibitor⟩

va·sa ef·fer·en·tia \ˈvā-zə-ˌef-ə-ˈren-ch(ē-)ə\ *n pl* [NL, lit., efferent vessels] (ca. 1860) : the 12 to 20 tubes that lead from the rete of the testis to the vas deferens and except near their commencement are greatly convoluted and form the compact head of the epididymis

vas·cu·lar \ˈvas-kyə-lər\ *adj* [NL *vascularis,* fr. L *vasculum* small vessel, dim. of *vas*] (1672) **1** : of or relating to a channel for the conveyance of a body fluid (as blood of an animal or sap of a plant) or to a system of such channels; *also* : supplied with or made up of such channels and esp. blood vessels ⟨a ~ tumor⟩ ⟨a ~ system⟩ **2** : marked by vigor and ardor : SPIRITED, PASSIONATE — **vas·cu·lar·i·ty** \ˌvas-kyə-ˈlar-ət-ē\ *n*

vascular bundle *n* (ca. 1884) : a unit of the vascular system of a higher plant consisting usu. of vessels and sieve tubes together with parenchyma cells and fibers

vascular cylinder *n* (ca. 1889) : STELE

vas·cu·lar·iza·tion \ˌvas-kyə-lə-rə-ˈzā-shən\ *n* (1818) : the process of becoming vascular; *also* : abnormal or excessive formation of blood vessels (as in the retina or on the cornea)

vascular plant *n* (1861) : a plant having a specialized conducting system that includes xylem and phloem : TRACHEOPHYTE

vascular ray *n* (1672) : a band of usu. parenchymatous cells partly in the xylem and partly in the phloem of a plant root or stem that conducts fluids radially and appears in a cross section like a spoke of a wheel

vascular tissue *n* (1815) : plant tissue concerned mainly with conduction; *esp* : the specialized tissue of higher plants consisting essentially of phloem and xylem and forming a continuous system throughout the body

vas·cu·la·ture \ˈvas-kyə-lə-ˌchu̇(ə)r, -ˌt(y)u̇(ə)r\ *n* [L *vasculum* vessel + E *-ature* (as in *musculature*)] (ca. 1927) : the disposition or arrangement of blood vessels in an organ or part

vas·cu·li·tis \ˌvas-kyə-ˈlīt-əs\ *n, pl* **-lit·i·des** \-ˈlit-ə-ˌdēz\ [NL, fr. L *vasculum* vessel] (ca. 1903) : inflammation of a blood or lymph vessel

vas·cu·lum \ˈvas-kyə-ləm\ *n, pl* **-la** \-lə\ [NL, fr. L, small vessel] (1844) : a usu. metal and commonly cylindrical or flattened covered box used in collecting plants

vas def·er·ens \ˈvas-ˈdef-ə-rənz, -ˌrenz\ *n, pl* **va·sa def·er·en·tia** \ˈvā-zə-ˌdef-ə-ˈren-ch(ē-)ə\ [NL, lit., deferent vessel] (ca. 1885) : a spermatic duct esp. of a higher vertebrate forming in man a small thick-walled tube about two feet long greatly convoluted in its proximal portion

vase *US oftenest* ˈvās; *Canad usu & US also* ˈvāz; *Brit usu, Canad also, & US sometimes* ˈväz\ *n* [F, fr. L *vas* vessel; akin to Umbrian *vasor* vessels] (1563) : a usu. round vessel of greater depth than width used chiefly as an ornament or for holding flowers — **vase·like** \-ˌlīk\ *adj*

va·sec·to·mize \və-ˈsek-tə-ˌmīz, vā-ˈzek-\ *vt* **-mized; -miz·ing** (1900) : to perform a vasectomy on

va·sec·to·my \-tə-mē\ *n, pl* **-mies** [ISV] (1899) : surgical division or resection of all or part of the vas deferens usu. to induce permanent sterility

Vas·e·line \ˈvas-ə-ˌlēn, ˌvas-ə-ˈ\ *trademark* — used for petrolatum

va·so·ac·tive \ˌvā-zō-ˈak-tiv\ *adj* (ca. 1921) : affecting the blood vessels esp. in respect to the degree of their relaxation or contraction — **va·so·ac·tiv·i·ty** \-ak-ˈtiv-ət-ē\ *n*

va·so·con·stric·tion \-kən-ˈstrik-shən\ *n* [ISV] (1899) : narrowing of the lumen of blood vessels esp. as a result of vasomotor action

va·so·con·stric·tive \-ˈstrik-tiv\ *adj* (1890) : inducing vasoconstriction

va·so·con·stric·tor \-tər\ *n* (1877) : an agent (as a sympathetic nerve fiber or a drug) that induces or initiates vasoconstriction

va·so·di·la·tion \-dī-ˈlā-shən, -də-\ *or* **va·so·di·la·ta·tion** \-ˌdil-ə-ˈtā-shən, -ˌdī-lə-\ *n* [ISV] (1896) : widening of the lumen of blood vessels

va·so·di·la·tor \-ˌlāt-ər\ *n* (1881) : an agent (as a parasympathetic nerve fiber or a drug) that induces or initiates vasodilation

va·so·mo·tor \ˌvā-zə-ˈmōt-ər\ *adj* [ISV] (1865) : of, relating to, or being nerves or centers controlling the size of blood vessels

va·so·pres·sin \ˌvā-zō-ˈpres-ᵊn\ *n* [fr. *Vasopressin,* a trademark] (1927) : a polypeptide hormone secreted by the posterior lobe of the pituitary gland that increases blood pressure and decreases urine flow — called also *antidiuretic hormone*

va·so·pres·sor \-ˈpres-ər\ *adj* (1928) : causing a rise in blood pressure by exerting a vasoconstrictor effect — **vasopressor** *n*

va·so·spasm \ˈvā-zō-ˌspaz-əm\ *n* [ISV] (ca. 1909) : sharp and often persistent contraction of a blood vessel reducing its caliber and blood flow — **va·so·spas·tic** \ˌvā-zō-ˈspas-tik\ *adj*

va·so·to·cin \ˌvā-zə-ˈtōs-ᵊn\ *n* [*vaso-* + oxy*tocin*] (ca. 1963) : a polypeptide pituitary hormone of most lower vertebrates that is held to have an antidiuretic function

va·so·va·gal \ˌvā-zō-ˈvā-gəl\ *adj* (ca. 1923) : of, relating to, or involving both vascular and vagal factors

vas·sal \ˈvas-əl\ *n* [ME, fr. MF, fr. ML *vassallus,* fr. *vassus* servant, vassal, of Celt origin; akin to W *gwas* boy, servant] (14c) **1** : a person under the protection of a feudal lord to whom he has vowed homage and fealty : a feudal tenant **2** : one in a subservient or subordinate position — **vassal** *adj*

vas·sal·age \-ə-lij\ *n* (1594) **1** : the state of being a vassal **2** : the homage, fealty, or services due from a vassal **3** : a position of subordination or submission (as to a political power)

[1]**vast** \ˈvast\ *adj* [L *vastus;* akin to OIr *fot* length] (1575) : very great in size, amount, degree, intensity, or esp. in extent or range ***syn*** see ENORMOUS — **vast·ly** *adv* — **vast·ness** \ˈvas(t)-nəs\ *n*

[2]**vast** *n* (1604) : a boundless space ⟨the ~ of heaven —John Milton⟩

vas·ti·tude \ˈvas-tə-ˌt(y)üd\ *n* [L *vastitudo,* fr. *vastus*] (1623) : IMMENSITY, VASTNESS

vasty \ˈvas-tē\ *adj* (1596) : VAST ⟨call spirits from the ~ deep —Shak.⟩

[1]**vat** \ˈvat\ *n* [ME *fat, vat,* fr. OE *fæt;* akin to OHG *vaz* vessel, Lith *puodas* pot] (bef. 12c) **1** : a large vessel (as a cistern, tub, or barrel) esp. for holding liquors in an immature state or preparations for dyeing or tanning **2** : a liquor containing a dye converted into a soluble reduced colorless or weakly colored form that on textile material steeped in the liquor and exposed to the air is converted by oxidation to the original insoluble dye and precipitated in the fiber

[2]**vat** *vt* **vat·ted; vat·ting** (1784) : to put into or treat in a vat

vat dye *n* (ca. 1903) : a water-insoluble generally fast dye used in the form of a vat liquor — called also *vat color*

vat–dyed \ˈvat-ˈdīd\ *adj* (ca. 1947) : dyed with one or more vat dyes

vat·ic \ˈvat-ik\ *adj* [L *vates* seer, prophet; akin to OE *wōth* poetry, OHG *wuot* madness, OIr *fāith* seer, poet] (1603) : PROPHETIC, ORACULAR

Vat·i·can \'vat-i-kən\ *n* [L *Vaticanus* Vatican Hill (in Rome)] (1555) **1** : the papal headquarters in Rome **2** : the papal government — **Vatican** *adj*

va·tic·i·nal \və-'tis-ᵊn-əl, va-\ *adj* [L *vaticinus*, fr. *vaticinari* to foretell, prophesy] (1586) : PROPHETIC

va·tic·i·nate \-ᵊn-,āt\ *vb* **-nat·ed; -nat·ing** [L *vaticinatus*, pp. of *vaticinari*, fr. *vates* + *-cinari* (akin to L *canere* to sing) — more at CHANT] (ca. 1623) : PROPHESY, PREDICT — **va·tic·i·na·tor** \-,āt-ər\ *n*

va·tic·i·na·tion \-,tis-ᵊn-'ā-shən\ *n* [L *vaticination-*, *vaticinatio*, fr. *vaticinatus*, pp.] (1603) **1** : PREDICTION **2** : the act of prophesying

va·tu \'vä-,tü\ *n, pl* **vatu** [native name in Vanuatu] (1981) — see MONEY table

vaude·ville \'vȯd-(ə-)vəl, 'väd-, 'vōd-, -(ə-),vil\ *n* [F, fr. MF, popular satirical song, alter. of *vaudevire*, fr. *vau-de-Vire* valley of Vire, fr. *vau*, *val* valley + *de* from, of (fr. L) + *Vire*, town in northwest France where such songs were composed — more at VALE, DE-] (1739) **1** : a light often comic theatrical piece frequently combining pantomime, dialogue, dancing, and song **2** : stage entertainment consisting of various acts (as performing animals, acrobats, comedians, dancers, or singers) — **vaude·vil·lian** \,vȯd-(ə-)'vil-yən, ,väd-, ,vōd-\ *n or adj*

Vau·dois \vō-'dwä, 'vō-,\ *n pl* [MF, fr. ML *Valdenses*] (1560) : WALDENSES

1**vault** \'vȯlt\ *n* [ME *voute*, fr. MF, fr. (assumed) VL *volvita* turn, vault, prob. fr. *volvitare*] (14c) **1 a** : an arched structure of masonry usu. forming a ceiling or roof **b** : something (as the sky) resembling a vault **c** : an arched or dome-shaped anatomical structure **2 a** : a space covered by an arched structure; *esp* : an underground passage or room **b** : an underground storage compartment **c** : a room or compartment for the safekeeping of valuables **3 a** : a burial chamber **b** : a prefabricated container usu. of metal or concrete into which a casket is placed at burial — **vaulty** \'vȯl-tē\ *adj*

2**vault** *vt* (14c) : to form or cover with or as if with a vault : ARCH

3**vault** *vb* [MF *volter*, fr. OIt *voltare*, fr. (assumed) VL *volvitare* to turn, leap, freq. of L *volvere* to roll — more at VOLUBLE] *vi* (1538) **1** : to bound vigorously; *esp* : to execute a leap using the hands or a pole **2** : to do or achieve something as if by a leap ~ *vt* : to leap over; *esp* : to leap over by or as if by aid of the hands or a pole

4**vault** *n* (1576) : an act of vaulting : LEAP

vault·ed \'vȯl-təd\ *adj* (1533) **1** : built in the form of a vault : ARCHED **2** : covered with a vault

vault·er \-tər\ *n* (ca. 1552) : one that vaults; *esp* : an athlete who competes in the pole vault

1**vault·ing** \-tiŋ\ *n* (1512) : vaulted construction

2**vaulting** *adj* (1605) **1** : reaching or stretching for the heights ⟨~ ambition⟩ ⟨a ~ imagination⟩ **2** : designed for use in vaulting or in gymnastic exercises ⟨a ~ block⟩ — **vault·ing·ly** \-tiŋ-lē\ *adv*

vaulting horse *n* (ca. 1875) **1** : a gymnastics apparatus used in vaulting that consists of a padded rectangular or cylindrical form supported in a horizontal position above the floor **2** : an event in which vaults are made over a vaulting horse

1**vaunt** \'vȯnt, 'vänt\ *vb* [ME *vaunten*, fr. MF *vanter*, fr. LL *vanitare*, fr. L *vanitas* vanity] *vi* (15c) : to make a vain display of one's own worth or attainments : BRAG ~ *vt* : to call attention to pridefully and often boastfully ⟨people who ~ their ingenuity⟩ ***syn*** see BOAST — **vaunt·er** *n* — **vaunt·ing·ly** \-iŋ-lē\ *adv*

2**vaunt** *n* (15c) **1** : a vainglorious display of what one is or has or has done **2** : a bragging assertive statement

vaunt–cou·ri·er \vȯnt-'ku̇r-ē-ər, vänt-, -'kər-ē-, -'kə-rē-\ *n* [MF *avant-courrier*, lit., advance courier] *archaic* (1560) : FORERUNNER

vaunt·ful \'vȯnt-fəl, 'vänt-\ *adj* (1590) : VAINGLORIOUS, BOASTFUL

vaunty \'vȯnt-ē, 'vänt-\ *adj, Scot* (1724) : PROUD, BOASTFUL, VAIN

vav *var of* WAW

vav·a·sor *or* **vav·a·sour** \'vav-ə-,sȯ(ə)r, -,sō(ə)r, -,su̇(ə)r\ *n* [ME *vavasour*, fr. MF *vavassor*, prob. fr. ML *vassus vassorum* vassal of vassals] (14c) : a feudal tenant ranking directly below a baron

va·ward \'vau̇-,(w)ȯ(ə)rd\ *n* [ME *vauntwarde*, *vaward*, fr. ONF *avantwarde*, fr. *avant* before (fr. L *abante*) + *warde* guard, fr. *warder* to guard — more at ADVANCE, REWARD] *archaic* (14c) : the foremost part : FOREFRONT ⟨the ~ of our youth —Shak.⟩

VCR \,vē-(,)sē-'är\ *n* [videocassette recorder] (ca. 1971) : a video tape recorder that uses videocassettes

V–day \'vē-,dā\ *n* [victory *day*] (1942) : a day of victory

've \v, əv\ *vb* [by contr.] : HAVE ⟨we've been there⟩

Ve·adar \'vā-,ä-,där, 'vā-ə-\ *n* [Heb *wĕ-Adhār*, lit., and Adar (i.e., the second Adar)] (ca. 1864) : the intercalary month of the Jewish calendar following Adar in leap years

1**veal** \'vē(ə)l\ *n* [ME *veel*, fr. MF *veel*, fr. L *vitellus* small calf, dim. of *vitulus* calf — more at WETHER] (14c) **1** : the flesh of a young calf **2** : CALF; *esp* : VEALER

2**veal** *vt* (1664) : to kill and dress (a calf) for veal

veal·er \'vē-lər\ *n* (1895) : a calf grown for or suitable for veal

vealy \'vē-lē\ *adj* (1769) **1** : resembling or suggesting veal or a calf **2** : IMMATURE

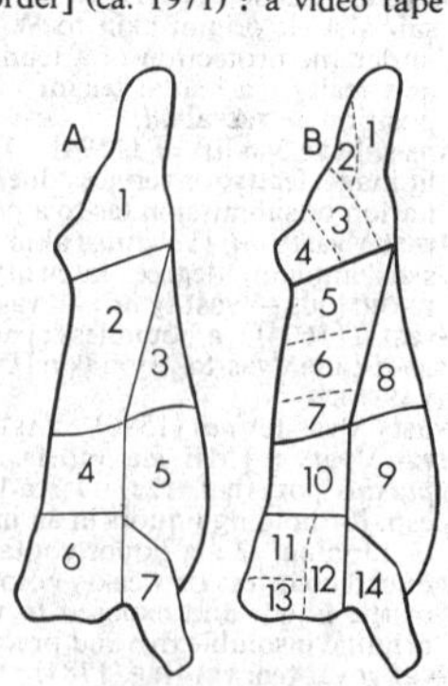

veal 1: *A* wholesale cuts: *1* leg, *2* loin, *3* flank, *4* rib, *5* breast, *6* shoulder, *7* shank; *B* retail cuts: *1* hind shank, *2* heel of round, *3* round, *4* rump roast, *5* sirloin steak, *6* loin chops, *7* kidney chops, *8* flank, *9* breast, *10* rib roast, *11* blade steak, *12* arm steak, *13* shoulder roast, *14* fore shank

1**vec·tor** \'vek-tər\ *n* [NL, fr. L, carrier, fr. *vectus*, pp. of *vehere* to carry — more at WAY] (1865) **1 a** : a quantity that has magnitude and direction and that is commonly represented by a directed line segment whose length represents the magnitude and whose orientation in space represents the direction; *broadly* : an element of a vector space **b** : a course or compass direction esp. of an airplane **2 a** : an organism (as an insect) that transmits a pathogen **b** : POLLINATOR a — **vector** *adj* — **vec·to·ri·al** \vek-'tōr-ē-əl, -'tȯr-\ *adj*

2**vector** *vt* **vec·tored; vec·tor·ing** \-t(ə-)riŋ\ (1941) **1** : to guide (as an airplane, its pilot, or a missile) in flight by means of a radioed vector **2** : to change the direction of (the thrust of a jet engine) for steering

vector product *n* (1878) : a vector *c* whose length is the product of the lengths of two vectors *a* and *b* and the sine of their included angle, whose direction is perpendicular to their plane, and whose direction is that in which a right-handed screw with axis *c* will move along *c* when *a* is rotated into *b* — called also *cross product*

vector space *n* (ca. 1943) : a set representing a generalization of a system of vectors and consisting of elements which comprise a commutative group under addition, each of which is left unchanged under multiplication by the multiplicative identity of a field, and for which multiplication by the multiplicative operation of the field is commutative, closed, distributive such that both $c(A + B) = cA + cB$ and $(c + d)A = cA + dA$, and associative such that $(cd)A = c(dA)$ where *A*, *B* are vectors and *c*, *d* are elements of the field

vector sum *n* (ca. 1901) : the sum of a number of vectors that for the sum of two vectors is geometrically represented by the diagonal of a parallelogram whose sides represent the two vectors being added

Ve·da \'vād-ə\ *n* [Skt, lit., knowledge; akin to Gk *eidenai* to know — more at WIT] (1734) : any of four canonical collections of hymns, prayers, and liturgical formulas that comprise the earliest Hindu sacred writings

ve·da·lia \vi-'dāl-yə\ *n* [NL] (ca. 1898) : an Australian ladybug (*Rodolia cardinalis*) introduced to many countries to control scale insects

Ve·dan·ta \vā-'dänt-ə, və-, -'dant-\ *n* [Skt *Vedānta*, lit., end of the Veda, fr. *Veda* + *anta* end; akin to OE *ende* end] (1788) : an orthodox system of Hindu philosophy developing esp. in a qualified monism the speculations of the Upanishads on ultimate reality and the liberation of the soul — **Ve·dan·tism** \-'dän-,tiz-əm, -'dan-\ *n* — **Ve·dan·tist** \-'dänt-əst, -'dant-\ *n*

Ve·dan·tic \-'dänt-ik, -'dant-\ *adj* (1882) **1** : of or relating to the Vedanta philosophy **2** : VEDIC

Ved·da *or* **Ved·dah** \'ved-ə\ *n* [Sinhalese *vedda* hunter] (1681) : a member of an aboriginal people of Ceylon (Sri Lanka)

Ved·doid \'ved-,ȯid\ *n* (ca. 1928) : a member of an ancient race of southern Asia characterized by wavy to curly hair, chocolate-brown skin color, slender body build, and fine features — **Veddoid** *adj*

ve·dette \vi-'det\ *n* [F, fr. It *vedetta*, alter. of *veletta*, prob. fr. Sp *vela* watch, fr. *velar* to keep watch, fr. L *vigilare* to wake, watch, fr. *vigil* awake — more at VIGIL] (1690) : a mounted sentinel stationed in advance of pickets

Ve·dic \'vād-ik\ *adj* (1859) : of or relating to the Vedas, the language in which they are written, or Hindu history and culture between 1500 B.C. and 500 B.C.

vee \'vē\ *n* (1883) **1** : something shaped like the letter V **2** : the letter *v*

vee·na *var of* VINA

veep \'vēp\ *n* [fr. *v. p.* (abbr. for *vice president*)] (1949) : VICE PRESIDENT

1**veer** \'vi(ə)r\ *vt* [ME *veren*, of LG or D origin; akin to MD *vieren* to slacken, MLG *viren*] (15c) : to let out (as a rope)

2**veer** *vb* [MF *virer*, prob. of Celt origin; akin to OIr *fiar* oblique; akin to OE *wīr* wire] *vi* (1582) **1** *of the wind* : to shift in a clockwise direction — compare BACK *vi* 2 **2** : to change direction or course **3** : to wear ship ~ *vt* : to direct to a different course; *specif* : WEAR 7 ***syn*** see SWERVE — **veer·ing·ly** \-iŋ-lē\ *adv*

3**veer** *n* (1611) : a change in course or direction ⟨a ~ to the right⟩

vee·ry \'vi(ə)r-ē\ *n, pl* **veeries** [perh. imit. of one of its notes] (1845) : a thrush (*Catharus fuscescens*) common in the eastern U.S.

veg \'vej\ *n, pl* **veg** *Brit* (1943) : VEGETABLE

Ve·ga \'vē-gə, 'vā-\ *n* [NL, fr. Ar (*al-Nasr*) *al-Wāqi'*, lit., the falling (vulture)] : a star of the first magnitude that is the brightest in the constellation Lyra

veg·an \'vej-ən, -,an; 'vē-gən\ *n* [by contr. fr. *vegetarian*] (1944) : a strict vegetarian : one that consumes no animal food or dairy products — **veg·an·ism** \'vej-ə-,niz-əm, 'vē-gə-\ *n*

1**veg·e·ta·ble** \'vej-tə-bəl, 'vej-ət-ə-\ *adj* [ME, fr. ML *vegetabilis* vegetative, fr. *vegetare* to grow, fr. L, to animate, fr. *vegetus* lively, fr. *vegēre* to rouse, excite — more at WAKE] (15c) **1 a** : of, relating to, constituting, or growing like plants **b** : consisting of plants : VEGETATIONAL **2** : made or obtained from plants or plant products **3** : resembling or suggesting a plant (as in monotony or passivity)

2**vegetable** *n* (1582) **1** : PLANT 1b **2** : a usu. herbaceous plant (as the cabbage, bean, or potato) grown for an edible part that is usu. eaten as part of a meal; *also* : such edible part **3** : a human being having a dull or merely physical existence

vegetable ivory *n* (1842) **1** : the hard white opaque endosperm of the ivory nut that takes a high polish and is used as a substitute for ivory **2** : IVORY NUT

vegetable marrow *n* (1816) : any of various smooth-skinned elongated summer squashes with creamy white to deep green skins

vegetable oil *n* (1897) : an oil of plant origin; *esp* : a fatty oil from seeds or fruits

vegetable oyster *n* (ca. 1817) : SALSIFY

vegetable wax *n* (1815) : a wax of plant origin secreted commonly in thin flakes by the walls of epidermal cells

veg·e·ta·bly \'vej-tə-blē, 'vej-ət-ə-\ *adv* (1651) : in the manner of or like a vegetable

veg·e·tal \'vej-ət-ᵊl\ *adj* [ML *vegetare* to grow] (15c) **1** : VEGETABLE **2** : VEGETATIVE **3** : of or relating to the vegetal pole of an egg or to that part of an egg from which the endoderm normally develops ⟨~ blastomeres⟩

vegetal pole *n* (ca. 1896) : the point on the surface of an egg that is diametrically opposite to the animal pole and usu. marks the center of the protoplasm containing more yolk, dividing more slowly and into larger blastomeres than that about the animal pole, and giving rise to the hypoblast of the embryo

1**veg·e·tar·i·an** \,vej-ə-'ter-ē-ən\ *n* [2*vegetable* + *-arian*] (1842) **1** : one who believes in or practices vegetarianism **2** : HERBIVORE

2**vegetarian** *adj* (1849) **1** : of or relating to vegetarians **2** : consisting wholly of vegetables ⟨a ~ diet⟩

veg·e·tar·i·an·ism \-ē-ə-ˌniz-əm\ *n* (ca. 1853) **:** the theory or practice of living on a diet made up of vegetables, fruits, grains, nuts, and sometimes animal products (as milk and cheese)

veg·e·tate \ˈvej-ə-ˌtāt\ *vb* **-tat·ed; -tat·ing** [ML *vegetatus,* pp. of *vegetare* to grow] *vi* (1605) **1 a :** to grow in the manner of a plant; *also* **:** to grow exuberantly or with proliferation of fleshy or warty outgrowths **b :** to produce vegetation **2 :** to lead a passive existence without exertion of body or mind ~ *vt* **:** to establish vegetation in or on

veg·e·ta·tion \ˌvej-ə-ˈtā-shən\ *n* [ML *vegetation-, vegetatio,* fr. *vegetatus,* pp.] (1564) **1 :** the act or process of vegetating **2 :** inert existence **3 :** plant life or total plant cover (as of an area) **4 :** an abnormal outgrowth upon a body part — **veg·e·ta·tion·al** \-shnəl, -shən-ᵊl\ *adj*

veg·e·ta·tive \ˈvej-ə-ˌtāt-iv\ *adj* [ME *vegetatif,* fr. ML *vegetativus,* fr. *vegetatus,* pp.] (14c) **1 a** (1) **:** growing or having the power of growing (2) **:** of, relating to, or engaged in nutritive and growth functions as contrasted with reproductive functions ⟨a ~ nucleus⟩ **b :** promoting plant growth ⟨the ~ properties of soil⟩ **c :** of, relating to, or involving propagation by nonsexual processes or methods **2 :** relating to, composed of, or suggesting vegetation ⟨~ cover⟩ **3 :** of or relating to the division of nature comprising the plant kingdom **4 :** affecting, arising from, or relating to involuntary bodily functions **5 :** VEGETABLE 3 — **veg·e·ta·tive·ly** *adv* — **veg·e·ta·tive·ness** *n*

ve·gete \və-ˈjēt\ *adj* [L *vegetus* — more at VEGETABLE] *archaic* (1639) **:** LIVELY, HEALTHY

veg·gie *also* **veg·ie** \ˈvej-ē\ *n* [*veg* + *-ie*] (1966) **1 :** VEGETABLE **2** *slang* **:** VEGETARIAN

ve·he·mence \ˈvē-ə-mən(t)s\ *n* (1529) **:** the quality or state of being vehement **:** INTENSITY

ve·he·ment \-mənt\ *adj* [ME, fr. MF, fr. L *vehement-, vehemens;* akin to L *vehere* to carry] (15c) **:** marked by forceful energy **:** POWERFUL ⟨a ~ wind⟩: as **a :** intensely emotional **:** IMPASSIONED, FERVID ⟨~ patriotism⟩ **b** (1) **:** deeply felt ⟨a ~ suspicion⟩ (2) **:** forcibly expressed ⟨~ denunciations⟩ **c :** bitterly antagonistic ⟨a ~ debate⟩ — **ve·he·ment·ly** *adv*

ve·hi·cle \ˈvē-ˌ(h)ik-əl, ˈvē-ə-kəl\ *n* [F *véhicule,* fr. L *vehiculum* carriage, conveyance, fr. *vehere* to carry — more at WAY] (1612) **1 a :** an inert medium (as a syrup) in which a medicinally active agent is administered **b :** any of various media acting usu. as solvents, carriers, or binders for active ingredients or pigments **2 :** an agent of transmission **:** CARRIER **3 :** a medium through which something is expressed, achieved, or displayed **4 :** a means of carrying or transporting something **:** CONVEYANCE: as **a :** MOTOR VEHICLE **b :** a piece of mechanized equipment

ve·hic·u·lar \vē-ˈhik-yə-lər\ *adj* (1616) **1 a :** of, relating to, or designed for vehicles and esp. motor vehicles **b :** transported by vehicle **2 :** serving as a vehicle

V–8 \ˈvē-ˈāt\ *n* (ca. 1948) **:** an internal-combustion engine having two banks of four cylinders each with the banks at an angle to each other; *also* **:** an automobile having such an engine

1**veil** \ˈvā(ə)l\ *n* [ME *veile,* fr. ONF, fr. L *vela,* pl. of *velum* veil] (13c) **1 a :** a length of cloth worn by women as a covering for the head and shoulders and often esp. in Eastern countries for the face; *specif* **:** the outer covering of a nun's headdress **b :** a length of veiling or netting worn over the head or face or attached for protection or ornament to a hat or headdress **c :** any of various liturgical cloths; *esp* **:** a cloth used to cover the chalice **2 :** the cloistered life of a nun **3 :** a concealing curtain or cover of cloth **4 :** something that hides or obscures like a veil **5 :** a covering body part or membrane: as **a :** VELUM **b :** CAUL

2**veil** *vt* (14c) **:** to cover, provide, obscure, or conceal with or as if with a veil ~ *vi* **:** to put on or wear a veil

veiled \ˈvā(ə)ld\ *adj* (1593) **1 a :** having or wearing a veil or a concealing cover ⟨a ~ hat⟩ **b :** characterized by a softening tonal distortion **2 :** obscured as if by a veil **:** DISGUISED ⟨~ threats⟩

veil·ing \ˈvā-liŋ\ *n* (14c) **1 :** VEIL **2 :** any of various light sheer fabrics

1**vein** \ˈvān\ *n* [ME *veine,* fr. OF, fr. L *vena*] (13c) **1 a :** a narrow water channel in rock or earth or in ice **b** (1) **:** LODE 2, 3 (2) **:** a bed of useful mineral matter **2 :** BLOOD VESSEL; *esp* **:** any of the tubular branching vessels that carry blood from the capillaries toward the heart **3 a :** any of the vascular bundles forming the framework of a leaf **b :** any of the thickened cuticular ribs that serve to stiffen the wings of an insect **4 :** something suggesting veins (as in reticulation); *specif* **:** a wavy variegation (as in marble) **5 a :** a distinctive mode of expression **:** STYLE **b :** a pervasive element or quality **:** STRAIN **c :** a line of thought or action **6 a :** a special aptitude **:** TALENT **b :** a usu. transitory and casually attained mood **c :** top form **:** FETTLE — **vein·al** \-ᵊl\ *adj*

2**vein** *vt* (1502) **:** to pattern with or as if with veins

veined \ˈvānd\ *adj* (1529) **:** patterned with or as if with veins **:** having venation **:** STREAKED ⟨a ~ leaf⟩ ⟨~ marble⟩

vein·er \ˈvā-nər\ *n* (1895) **:** a small V gouge used in wood carving

vein·ing \ˈvā-niŋ\ *n* (1826) **:** a pattern of veins **:** VENATION

vein·let \ˈvān-lət\ *n* (1831) **:** a small vein

veiny \ˈvā-nē\ *adj* (ca. 1611) **:** full of veins **:** VEINED

ve·la·men \və-ˈlā-mən\ *n, pl* **ve·lam·i·na** \-ˈlam-ə-nə\ [NL, fr. L, covering, fr. *velare* to cover, fr. *velum* veil] (1882) **:** the thick corky epidermis of aerial roots of an epiphytic orchid that absorbs water from the atmosphere

ve·lar \ˈvē-lər\ *adj* [NL *velaris,* fr. *velum*] (1876) **1 :** formed with the back of the tongue touching or near the soft palate ⟨the ~ \k\ of \ˈkül\ *cool*⟩ **2 :** of, forming, or relating to a velum and esp. the soft palate — **velar** *n*

ve·lar·i·um \vi-ˈlar-ē-əm, -ˈler-\ *n, pl* **-ia** \-ē-ə\ [L, fr. *velum* veil] (1834) **:** an awning over an ancient Roman theater or amphitheater

ve·lar·iza·tion \ˌvē-lə-rə-ˈzā-shən\ *n* (ca. 1937) **1 :** the quality or state of being velarized **2 :** an act or instance of velarizing

ve·lar·ize \ˈvē-lə-ˌrīz\ *vt* **-ized; -iz·ing** (ca. 1931) **:** to modify (as the \l\ of \ˈpül\ *pool*) by a simultaneous velar articulation

Vel·cro \ˈvel-(ˌ)krō\ *trademark* — used for a nylon fabric that can be fastened to itself

veld *or* **veldt** \ˈvelt, ˈfelt\ *n* [Afrik *veld,* fr. MD, field; akin to OE *feld* field] (1852) **:** a grassland esp. of southern Africa usu. with scattered shrubs or trees

ve·li·ger \ˈvē-lə-jər, ˈvel-ə-\ *n* [NL, fr. *velum* + *-ger* -gerous] (1877) **:** a larval mollusk in the stage when it has developed the velum

vel·le·ity \ve-ˈlē-ət-ē, və-\ *n, pl* **-ities** [NL *velleitas,* fr. L *velle* to wish, will — more at WILL] (1618) **1 :** the lowest degree of volition **2 :** a slight wish or tendency **:** INCLINATION

1**vel·lum** \ˈvel-əm\ *n* [ME *velim,* fr. MF *veelin,* fr. *veelin,* adj., of a calf, fr. *veel* calf — more at VEAL] (15c) **1 :** a fine-grained unsplit lambskin, kidskin, or calfskin prepared esp. for writing on or for binding books **2 :** a strong cream-colored paper

2**vellum** *adj* (1565) **1 :** of, resembling, or bound in vellum **2 :** slightly rough ⟨paper with a ~ finish⟩

ve·lo·ce \vā-ˈlō-(ˌ)chā\ *adv or adj* [It, fr. L *veloc-, velox*] (ca. 1823) **:** in a rapid manner — used as a direction in music

ve·lo·cim·e·ter \ˌvē-lō-ˈsim-ət-ər, ˌvel-ō-\ *n* [*velocity* + *-meter*] (1842) **:** a device for measuring speed (as of fluid flow or sound)

ve·loc·i·pede \və-ˈläs-ə-ˌpēd\ *n* [F *vélocipède,* fr. L *veloc-, velox* + *ped-, pes* foot — more at FOOT] (1819) **:** a lightweight wheeled vehicle propelled by the rider: as **a** *archaic* **:** BICYCLE **b :** TRICYCLE **c :** a 3-wheeled railroad handcar

ve·loc·i·ty \və-ˈläs-ət-ē, -ˈläs-tē\ *n, pl* **-ties** [MF *velocité,* fr. L *velocitat-, velocitas,* fr. *veloc-, velox* quick; akin to L *vehere* to carry — more at WAY] (1550) **1 :** quickness of motion **:** SPEED ⟨the ~ of sound⟩ **2 :** time rate of linear motion in a given direction **3 a :** rate of occurrence or action **:** RAPIDITY ⟨the ~ of historical change —R. J. Lifton⟩ **b :** rate of turnover ⟨the ~ of money⟩

ve·lo·drome \ˈvēl-ə-ˌdrōm, ˈvel-, ˈväl-\ *n* [F *vélodrome,* fr. *vélo* cycle (short for *vélocipède*) + *-drome*] (1895) **:** a track designed for cycling

ve·lour *or* **ve·lours** \və-ˈlu̇(ə)r\ *n, pl* **velours** \-ˈlu̇(ə)rz\ [F *velours* velvet, velour, fr. MF *velours, velour,* fr. OF *velous,* fr. L *villosus* shaggy, fr. *villus* shaggy hair — more at VELVET] (1706) **1 :** any of various fabrics with a pile or napped surface resembling velvet used in heavy weights for upholstery and curtains and in lighter weights for clothing; *also* **:** the article of clothing itself **2 :** a fur felt (as of rabbit or nutria) finished with a long velvety nap and used esp. for hats

ve·lum \ˈvē-ləm\ *n, pl* **ve·la** \-lə\ [NL, fr. L, curtain, veil] (1771) **1 :** a membrane or membranous part resembling a veil or curtain: as **a :** SOFT PALATE **b :** an annular membrane projecting inward from the margin of the umbrella in some jellyfishes (as the hydromedusans) **2 :** a swimming organ that is esp. well developed in the later larval stages of many marine gastropods

ve·lure \vel-ˈ(y)u̇(ə)r, ˈvel-yər\ *n* [modif. of MF *velour*] *obs* (1587) **:** VELVET; *also* **:** a fabric resembling velvet

1**vel·vet** \ˈvel-vət\ *n* [ME *veluet, velvet,* fr. MF *velu* shaggy, fr. (assumed) VL *villutus,* fr. L *villus* shaggy hair; akin to L *vellus* fleece — more at WOOL] (14c) **1 :** a clothing and upholstery fabric (as of silk, rayon, or wool) characterized by a short soft dense warp pile **2 a :** something suggesting velvet **b :** a characteristic (as softness or smoothness) of velvet **3 :** the soft vascular skin that envelops and nourishes the developing antlers of deer **4 a :** the winnings of a player in a gambling game **b :** a profit or gain beyond ordinary expectation

2**velvet** *adj* (14c) **1 :** made of or covered with velvet; *also* **:** clad in velvet **2 :** resembling or suggesting velvet **:** VELVETY ⟨a ~ voice⟩

velvet ant *n* (1748) **:** any of various solitary usu. brightly colored and hairy fossorial wasps (family Mutillidae) with the female wingless

velvet bean *n* (1898) **:** an annual legume (*Stizolobium deeringianum*) grown esp. in the southern U.S. for green manure and grazing; *also* **:** its seed often used as stock feed

vel·ve·teen \ˌvel-və-ˈtēn\ *n* (1776) **1 :** a clothing fabric usu. of cotton in twill or plain weaves made with a short close weft pile in imitation of velvet **2** *pl* **:** clothes made of velveteen

vel·vety \ˈvel-vət-ē\ *adj* (1752) **1 :** soft and smooth like velvet ⟨~ hair⟩ **2 :** smooth to the taste **:** MILD ⟨a ~ wine⟩

ven- *or* **veni-** *or* **veno-** *comb form* [L *vena*] **:** vein ⟨venation⟩ ⟨*veni*puncture⟩ ⟨*veno*stasis⟩

ve·na \ˈvē-nə\ *n, pl* **ve·nae** \-(ˌ)nē\ [ME, fr. L] (15c) **:** VEIN

ve·na ca·va \ˌvē-nə-ˈkā-və\ *n, pl* **ve·nae ca·vae** \-ni-ˈkā-(ˌ)vē\ [NL, lit., hollow vein] (1598) **:** any of the large veins by which in air-breathing vertebrates the blood is returned to the right atrium of the heart — **vena ca·val** \-vəl\ *adj*

ve·nal \ˈvēn-ᵊl\ *adj* [L *venalis,* fr. *venum* (acc.) sale; akin to Gk *ōneisthai* to buy, Skt *vasna* price] (1652) **1 :** capable of being bought or obtained for money or other valuable consideration **:** PURCHASABLE; *esp* **:** open to corrupt influence and esp. bribery **:** MERCENARY ⟨a ~ legislator⟩ **2 :** originating in, characterized by, or associated with corrupt bribery ⟨a ~ arrangement with the police⟩ — **ve·nal·i·ty** \vi-ˈnal-ət-ē\ *n* — **ve·nal·ly** \ˈvēn-ᵊl-ē\ *adv*

ve·na·tion \ve-ˈnā-shən, vē-\ *n* [L *vena* vein] (1646) **:** an arrangement or system of veins: as **a :** that in the tissue of a leaf blade **b :** that in the wing of an insect — **ve·na·tion·al** \-shnəl, -shən-ᵊl\ *adj*

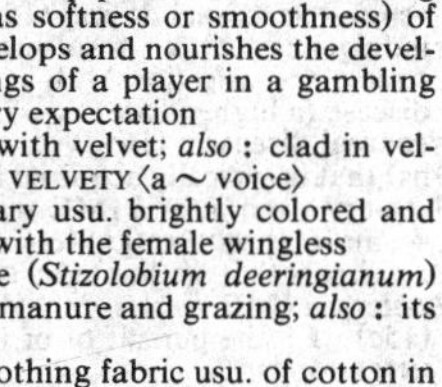

venation **a:** *1* pinnately veined, *2* palmately veined, *3* base to tip, *4* base to midrib, *5* midrib to margin

vend \ˈvend\ *vb* [L *vendere* to sell, v.t., contr. for *venum dare* to give for sale] *vi* (1622) **:** to dispose of something by sale **:** SELL; *also* **:** to engage in selling ~ *vt* **1 a :** to sell esp. as a hawker or peddler **b :** to sell by means of vending machines **2 :** to utter publicly

Ven·da \ˈven-də\ *n* (ca. 1939) **:** a Bantu language of the northern Transvaal

vend·ee \ven-ˈdē\ *n* (1547) **:** one to whom a thing is sold **:** BUYER

vend·er \ˈven-dər\ *n* (1596) **:** VENDOR

ven·det·ta \ven-ˈdet-ə\ *n* [It, lit., revenge, fr. L *vindicta* — more at VINDICTIVE] (1855) **1 :** BLOOD FEUD **2 :** a prolonged feud marked by bitter hostility

ven·deuse \vä^{n}-ˈdə(r)z, vän-ˈdüz\ *n* [F, fem. of *vendeur* salesman, fr. MF] (1926) : SALESWOMAN

vend·ible *or* **vend·able** \ˈven-də-bəl\ *adj* (14c) : capable of being vended : SALABLE — **vend·ibil·i·ty** \ˌven-də-ˈbil-ət-ē\ *n* — **vend·ibly** \ˈven-də-blē\ *adv*

vending machine *n* (ca. 1909) : a coin-operated machine for vending merchandise

ven·dor \ˈven-dər, *for 1 also* ven-ˈdȯ(ə)r\ *n* [MF *vendeur,* fr. *vendre* to sell, fr. L *vendere*] (1594) **1** : one that vends : SELLER **2** : VENDING MACHINE

ven·due \ˈven-ˌd(y)ü, ˈvän-, ˈfen-; ven-ˈ, vän-ˈ\ *n* [obs. F, fr. MF, fr. *vendre*] (1668) : a public sale at auction

[1]ve·neer \və-ˈni(ə)r\ *n* [G *furnier,* fr. *furnieren* to veneer, fr. F *fournir* to furnish — more at FURNISH] (1702) **1** : a thin sheet of a material: as **a** : a layer of wood of superior value or excellent grain to be glued to an inferior wood **b** : any of the thin layers bonded together to form plywood **2** : a protective or ornamental facing (as of brick or stone) **3** : a superficial or deceptively attractive appearance or display : GLOSS

[2]veneer *vt* (1728) **1** : to overlay or plate (as a common wood) with a thin layer of finer wood for outer finish or decoration; *broadly* : to face with a material giving a superior surface **2** : to cover over with a veneer; *esp* : to conceal (as a defect of character) under a superficial and deceptive attractiveness — **ve·neer·er** *n*

ve·neer·ing *n* (ca. 1706) **1** : a veneered surface **2** : material used as veneer

ven·er·a·ble \ˈven-ər(-ə)-bəl, ˈven-rə-bəl\ *adj* [ME, fr. L *venerabilis,* fr. *venerari* to venerate] (15c) **1** : deserving to be venerated — used as a title for an Anglican archdeacon or for a Roman Catholic who has been accorded the lowest of three degrees of recognition for sanctity **2** : made sacred esp. by religious or historical association **3** **a** : calling forth respect through age, character, and attainments; *broadly* : conveying an impression of aged goodness and benevolence **b** : impressive by reason of age ⟨under ~ pines⟩ ***syn*** see OLD — **ven·er·a·bil·i·ty** \ˌven-(ə-)rə-ˈbil-ət-ē\ *n* — **ven·er·a·ble·ness** \ˈven-ər(-ə)-bəl-nəs, ˈven-rə-\ *n* — **ven·er·a·bly** \-blē\ *adv*

ven·er·ate \ˈven-ə-ˌrāt\ *vt* **-at·ed; -at·ing** [L *veneratus,* pp. of *venerari,* fr. *vener-, venus* love, charm — more at WIN] (ca. 1623) : to regard with reverential respect or with admiring deference ***syn*** see REVERE — **ven·er·a·tor** \-ˌrāt-ər\ *n*

ven·er·a·tion \ˌven-ə-ˈrā-shən\ *n* [ME *veneracioun,* fr. *veneration-, veneratio,* fr. *veneratus,* pp.] (15c) **1** : respect or awe inspired by the dignity, wisdom, dedication, or talent of a person **2** : the act of venerating **3** : the condition of one that is venerated

ve·ne·re·al \və-ˈnir-ē-əl\ *adj* [ME *venerealle,* fr. L *venereus,* fr. *vener-, venus* love, sexual desire] (15c) **1** : of or relating to sexual pleasure or indulgence **2** **a** : resulting from or contracted during sexual intercourse ⟨~ infections⟩ **b** : of, relating to, or affected with venereal disease ⟨a high ~ rate⟩ **c** : involving the genital organs ⟨~ sarcoma⟩

venereal disease *n* (1658) : a contagious disease (as gonorrhea or syphilis) that is typically acquired in sexual intercourse

[1]ven·ery \ˈven-ə-rē\ *n* [ME *venerie,* fr. MF, fr. *vener* to hunt, fr. L *venari* — more at VENISON] (14c) **1** : the art, act, or practice of hunting **2** : animals that are hunted : GAME

[2]venery *n* [ME *venerie,* fr. ML *veneria,* fr. L *vener-, venus* sexual desire] (15c) **1** : the pursuit of or indulgence in sexual pleasure **2** : SEXUAL INTERCOURSE

ve·ne·sec·tion \ˈven-ə-ˌsek-shən, ˈvēn-\ *n* [NL *venae section-, venae sectio,* lit., cutting of a vein] (1661) : the operation of opening a vein for letting blood : PHLEBOTOMY

Ven·e·ti \ˈven-ə-ˌtī\ *n pl* [L *Veneti*] (1881) **1** : an ancient people in Gaul conquered by Caesar in 56 B.C. **2** : an ancient people in northeastern Italy allied politically to the Romans

ve·ne·tian blind \və-ˌnē-shən-\ *n* [*Venetian* of Venice, Italy] (1770) : a blind (as for a window) having numerous horizontal slats that may be set simultaneously at any of several angles so as to vary the amount of light admitted

venetian glass *n, often cap V* (ca. 1845) : often colored glassware made at Murano near Venice of a soda-lime metal and typically elaborately decorated (as with gilt, enamel, or engraving)

Venetian red *n* (ca. 1753) : an earthy hematite used as a pigment; *also* : a synthetic iron oxide pigment

Ve·net·ic \və-ˈnet-ik\ *n* [L *veneticus* of the Veneti, fr. *Veneti*] (1902) : the Italian language of the ancient Veneti of Italy — see INDO-EUROPEAN LANGUAGES table — **Venetic** *adj*

venge \ˈvenj\ *vt* **venged; veng·ing** [ME *vengen,* fr. MF *vengier,* fr. OF] *archaic* (14c) : AVENGE

ven·geance \ˈven-jən(t)s\ *n* [ME, fr. OF, fr. *vengier* to avenge, fr. L *vindicare* to lay claim to, avenge — more at VINDICATE] (13c) : punishment inflicted in retaliation for an injury or offense : RETRIBUTION — **with a vengeance** **1** : with great force or vehemence **2** : to an extreme or excessive degree

venge·ful \ˈvenj-fəl\ *adj* [obs. E *venge* (revenge)] (1586) : REVENGEFUL: as **a** : seeking to avenge **b** : serving to gain vengeance — **venge·ful·ly** \-fə-lē\ *adv* — **venge·ful·ness** *n*

V–en·gine \ˈvē-\ *n* (ca. 1922) : an internal-combustion engine whose cylinders are arranged in two banks forming an acute angle or a 90° degree angle

veni- *or* **veno-** — see VEN-

ve·nial \ˈvē-nē-əl, -nyəl\ *adj* [ME, fr. MF, fr. LL *venialis,* fr. L *venia* favor, indulgence, pardon; akin to L *venus* love, charm — more at WIN] (14c) : of a kind that can be remitted : FORGIVABLE, PARDONABLE; *also* : meriting no particular censure or notice : EXCUSABLE ⟨~ faults⟩ — **ve·nial·ly** \-ē\ *adv* — **ve·nial·ness** *n*

venial sin *n* (14c) : a sin that is relatively slight or that is committed without full reflection or consent and so according to Thomist theology does not deprive the soul of sanctifying grace — compare MORTAL SIN

ve·ni·punc·ture \ˈvēn-ə-ˌpəŋ(k)-chər, ˈven-ə-\ *n* (ca. 1903) : surgical puncture of a vein esp. for the withdrawal of blood or for intravenous medication

ve·ni·re \və-ˈnī-rē\ *n* [*venire facias*] (ca. 1665) : an entire panel from which a jury is drawn

ve·ni·re fa·ci·as \-ˌnī-rē-ˈfā-shē-əs\ *n* [ME, fr. ML, you should cause to come] (15c) : a judicial writ directing the sheriff to summon a specified number of qualified persons to serve as jurors

ve·ni·re·man \və-ˈnī-rē-mən, -ˈnir-ē-\ *n* (1776) : a member of a venire

ven·i·son \ˈven-ə-sən *also* -ə-zən, *Brit usu* ˈven-zən\ *n, pl* **venisons** *also* **venison** [ME, fr. OF *veneison* hunting, game, fr. L *venation-, venatio,* fr. *venatus,* pp. of *venari* to hunt, pursue; akin to OE *winnan* to struggle — more at WIN] (13c) **1** : the edible flesh of a wild animal taken by hunting **2** : the flesh of a deer

Ve·ni·te \və-ˈnīt-ē, -ˈnē-ˌtā\ *n* [L, O come, fr. *venire* to come; fr. the opening word of Ps 95:1 — more at COME] (13c) : a liturgical chant composed of parts of Psalms 95 and 96

Venn diagram \ˈven-\ *n* [John *Venn* †1923 Eng. logician] (ca. 1942) : a graph that employs circles to represent logical relations between and operations on sets and the terms of propositions by the inclusion, exclusion, or intersection of the circles

ve·nog·ra·phy \vi-ˈnäg-rə-fē, vā-\ *n* [ISV] (ca. 1927) : roentgenography of a vein after injection of an opaque substance

[1]ven·om \ˈven-əm\ *n* [ME *venim, venom,* fr. OF *venim,* fr. (assumed) VL *venimen,* alter. of L *venenum* magic charm, drug, poison; akin to L *venus* love, charm — more at WIN] (13c) **1** : poisonous matter normally secreted by some animals (as snakes, scorpions, or bees) and transmitted to prey or an enemy chiefly by biting or stinging; *broadly* : material that is poisonous **2** : ILL WILL, MALEVOLENCE

[2]venom *vt* (14c) : ENVENOM

ven·om·ous \ˈven-ə-məs\ *adj* (13c) **1** : full of venom: as **a** : POISONOUS, ENVENOMED **b** : NOXIOUS, PERNICIOUS ⟨expose a ~ dope ring —Don Porter⟩ **c** : SPITEFUL, MALEVOLENT ⟨~ criticism⟩ **2** : having a venom-producing gland and able to inflict a poisoned wound ⟨~ snakes⟩ — **ven·om·ous·ly** *adv* — **ven·om·ous·ness** *n*

ve·nous \ˈvē-nəs\ *adj* [L *venosus,* fr. *vena* vein] (1626) **1** : of, relating to, or full of veins ⟨a ~ rock⟩ ⟨a ~ system⟩ **2** *of blood* : having passed through the capillaries and given up oxygen for the tissues and become charged with carbon dioxide — **ve·nous·ly** *adv*

[1]vent \ˈvent\ *vt* [ME *venten,* prob. fr. MF *esventer* to expose to the air, fr. *es-* ex- (fr. L *ex-*) + *vent* wind, fr. L *ventus* — more at WIND] (14c) **1** : to provide with a vent **2** **a** : to serve as a vent for ⟨chimneys ~ smoke⟩ **b** : DISCHARGE, EXPEL **c** : to give often vigorous or emotional expression to **3** : to relieve by means of a vent ***syn*** see EXPRESS

[2]vent *n* (1508) **1** : an opportunity or means of escape, passage, or release : OUTLET ⟨finally gave ~ to his pent-up hostility⟩ **2** : an opening for the escape of a gas or liquid or for the relief of pressure: as **a** : the external opening of the rectum or cloaca : ANUS **b** : PIPE 3c, FUMAROLE **c** : an opening at the breech of a muzzle-loading gun through which fire is touched to the powder **d** *chiefly Scot* : CHIMNEY, FLUE — **vent·less** \-ləs\ *adj*

[3]vent *n* [ME *vente,* alter. of *fente,* fr. MF, slit, fissure, fr. *fendre* to split, fr. L *findere* — more at BITE] (15c) : a slit in a garment; *specif* : an opening in the lower part of a seam (as of a jacket or skirt) — **vent·less** *adj*

vent·age \ˈvent-ij\ *n* (1602) : a small hole (as a flute stop)

ven·tail \ˈven-ˌtāl\ *n* [ME, fr. MF *ventaille,* fr. *vent* wind] (15c) : the lower movable front of a medieval helmet

ven·ter \ˈvent-ər\ *n* [AF, fr. L, belly, womb; akin to OHG *wanast* paunch, L *vesica* bladder] (1544) **1** : a wife or mother that is a source of offspring **2** : a protuberant and often hollow anatomical structure: as **a** : the undersurface of the abdomen of an arthropod **b** : the swollen basal portion of an archegonium in which the egg of a vascular cryptogam is developed

ven·ti·fact \ˈvent-ə-ˌfakt\ *n* [L *ventus* + E *-ifact* (as in *artifact*)] (ca. 1931) : a stone worn, polished, or faceted by windblown sand

ven·ti·late \ˈvent-ᵊl-ˌāt\ *vt* **-lat·ed; -lat·ing** [LL *ventilatus,* pp. of *ventilare,* fr. L, to fan, winnow, fr. *ventulus,* dim. of *ventus* wind — more at WIND] (1527) **1** **a** : to examine, discuss, or investigate freely and openly : EXPOSE ⟨*ventilating* family quarrels in public⟩ **b** : to make public : UTTER ⟨*ventilated* their objections at length⟩ **2** *archaic* : to free from chaff by winnowing **3** **a** : to expose to air and esp. to a current of fresh air for purifying, curing, or refreshing ⟨~ stored grain⟩; *also* : OXYGENATE, AERATE ⟨~ blood in the lungs⟩ **b** : to subject the lungs to ventilation ⟨artificially ~ a patient in respiratory distress⟩ **4** **a** *of a current of air* : to pass or circulate through so as to freshen **b** : to cause fresh air to circulate through (as a room or mine) **5** : to provide an opening in (a burning structure) to permit escape of smoke and heat

ven·ti·la·tion \ˌvent-ᵊl-ˈā-shən\ *n* [ME, current of air, fr. L *ventilation-, ventilatio,* fr. *ventilatus,* pp.] (1519) **1** : the act or process of ventilating **2** **a** : circulation of air ⟨a room with good ~⟩ **b** : the circulation and exchange of gases in the lungs or gills that is basic to respiration **3** : a system or means of providing fresh air

ven·ti·la·tor \ˈvent-ᵊl-ˌāt-ər\ *n* (1743) : one that ventilates: as **a** : a contrivance for introducing fresh air or expelling foul or stagnant air **b** : RESPIRATOR 2

ven·ti·la·to·ry \ˈvent-ᵊl-ə-ˌtōr-ē, -ˌtȯr-\ *adj* (1850) : of, relating to, or provided with ventilation ⟨~ capacity of the lung⟩

ventr- *or* **ventro-** *comb form* [L *ventr-, venter* belly] : ventral and ⟨*ventro*lateral⟩

[1]ven·tral \ˈven-trəl\ *adj* [F, fr. L *ventralis,* fr. *ventr-, venter*] (1739) **1** **a** : of or relating to the belly : ABDOMINAL **b** : being or located near or on the anterior or lower surface of an animal opposite the back **2** : being or located on the lower surface of a dorsiventral plant structure — **ven·tral·ly** \-trə-lē\ *adv*

[2]ventral *n* (1834) : a ventral part (as a scale or fin)

ventral root *n* (ca. 1923) : the one of the two roots of a spinal nerve that passes ventrally from the spinal cord and consists of motor fibers — compare DORSAL ROOT

ven·tri·cle \ˈven-tri-kəl\ *n* [ME, fr. L *ventriculus,* fr. dim. of *ventr-, venter* belly] (15c) : a cavity of a bodily part or organ: as **a** : a chamber of the heart which receives blood from a corresponding atrium and from which blood is forced into the arteries — see HEART illustration **b** : any of the system of communicating cavities in the brain that are continuous with the central canal of the spinal cord — see BRAIN illustration

ven·tri·cose \-ˌkōs\ *adj* [NL *ventricosus,* fr. L *ventr-, venter* + *-icosus* (as in *varicosus* varicose)] (1756) : markedly swollen, distended, or inflated esp. on one side ⟨~ corollas⟩

ven·tric·u·lar \ven-ˈtrik-yə-lər, vən-\ *adj* (1822) **:** of, relating to, or being a ventricle or ventriculus

ven·tric·u·lus \ven-ˈtrik-yə-ləs, vən-\ *n, pl* **-li** \-ˌlī, -ˌlē\ [NL, fr. L, dim. of *venter*] (1693) **:** a digestive cavity: as **a :** STOMACH **b :** GIZZARD 1a **c :** the digestive part of an insect's stomach

ven·tril·o·quism \ven-ˈtril-ə-ˌkwiz-əm\ *n* [LL *ventriloquus* ventriloquist, fr. L *ventr-, venter* + *loqui* to speak; fr. the belief that the voice is produced from the ventriloquist's stomach] (ca. 1797) **:** the production of the voice in such a way that the sound seems to come from a source other than the vocal organs of the speaker — **ven·tri·lo·qui·al** \ˌven-trə-ˈlō-kwē-əl\ *adj* — **ven·tri·lo·qui·al·ly** \-ə-lē\ *adv*

ven·tril·o·quist \ven-ˈtril-ə-kwəst\ *n* (ca. 1656) **:** one who uses or is skilled in ventriloquism; *esp* **:** one who provides entertainment by using ventriloquism to carry on an apparent conversation with a hand-manipulated dummy — **ven·tril·o·quis·tic** \(ˌ)ven-ˌtril-ə-ˈkwis-tik\ *adj*

ven·tril·o·quize \ven-ˈtril-ə-ˌkwīz\ *vb* **-quized; -quiz·ing** *vi* (1844) **:** to use ventriloquism ~ *vt* **:** to utter in the manner of a ventriloquist

ven·tril·o·quy \-kwē\ *n* (1584) **:** VENTRILOQUISM

ven·tro·lat·er·al \ˌven-ˌtrō-ˈlat-ə-rəl, -ˈla-trəl\ *adj* (1835) **:** ventral and lateral

ven·tro·me·di·al \-ˈmēd-ē-əl\ *adj* (1928) **:** ventral and medial

[1]**ven·ture** \ˈven-chər\ *vb* **ven·tured; ven·tur·ing** \ˈvench-(ə-)riŋ\ [ME *venteren*, by shortening & alter. fr. *aventuren*, fr. *aventure* adventure] *vt* (15c) **1 :** to expose to hazard **:** RISK, GAMBLE **2 :** to undertake the risks and dangers of **:** BRAVE ⟨*ventured* the stormy sea⟩ **3 :** to offer at the risk of rebuff, rejection, or censure ⟨~ an opinion⟩ ~ *vi* **:** to proceed esp. in the face of danger — **ven·tur·er** \ˈvench-(ə-)rər\ *n*

[2]**venture** *n* (15c) **1** *obs* **:** DESTINY, FORTUNE, CHANCE **2 a :** an undertaking involving chance, risk, or danger; *esp* **:** a speculative business enterprise **b :** a venturesome act **3 :** something (as money or property) at hazard in a speculative venture — **at a venture :** at random ⟨a certain man drew a bow *at a venture*, and smote the king —1 Kings 22:34 (AV)⟩

venture capital *n* (1943) **:** capital (as retained corporate earnings or individual savings) invested or available for investment in the ownership element of new or fresh enterprise — called also *risk capital*

ven·ture·some \ˈven-chər-səm\ *adj* (1661) **1 :** involving risk **:** HAZARDOUS ⟨a ~ journey⟩ **2 :** inclined to court or incur risk or danger **:** DARING ⟨a ~ hunter⟩ *syn* see ADVENTUROUS — **ven·ture·some·ly** *adv* — **ven·ture·some·ness** *n*

ven·tu·ri \ven-ˈtu̇(ə)r-ē\ *n* [G. B. *Venturi* †1822 Ital. physicist] (1887) **:** a short tube with a tapering constriction in the middle that causes an increase in the velocity of flow of a fluid and a corresponding decrease in fluid pressure and that is used esp. in measuring fluid flow or for creating a suction (as for driving aircraft instruments or drawing fuel into the flow stream of a carburetor)

ven·tur·ous \ˈvench-(ə-)rəs\ *adj* (1565) **:** VENTURESOME — **ven·tur·ous·ly** *adv* — **ven·tur·ous·ness** *n*

ven·ue \ˈven-ˌyü\ *n* [ME *venyw* action of coming, fr. MF *venue*, fr. *venir* to come, fr. L *venire* — more at COME] (1531) **1 a :** the place or county in which take place the alleged events from which a legal action arises **b :** the place from which a jury is drawn and in which trial is held ⟨requested a change of ~⟩ **c :** a statement showing that a case is brought to the proper court or authority **2 :** LOCALE 1

ve·nule \ˈvēn-(ˌ)yü(ə)l, ˈven-\ *n* [L *venula*, dim. of *vena* vein] (ca. 1850) **:** a small vein; *esp* **:** any of the minute veins connecting the capillaries with the larger systemic veins

Ve·nus \ˈvē-nəs\ *n* [ME, fr. L *Vener-, Venus*] **1 :** the Roman goddess of love and beauty — compare APHRODITE **2 :** the planet second in order from the sun — see PLANET table

Ve·nus·berg \-ˌbərg\ *n* **:** a mountain in central Germany containing a cavern where in medieval legend Venus held court

Ve·nus·hair \-ˌha(ə)r, -ˌhe(ə)r\ *n* (1548) **:** a delicate maidenhair fern (*Adiantum capillus-veneris*) with a slender black stipe and branches

Ve·nu·sian \vi-ˈn(y)ü-zhən\ *adj* (ca. 1900) **:** of or relating to the planet Venus

Ve·nus's–fly·trap \ˌvē-nəs(-əz)-ˈflī-ˌtrap\ *n* (1770) **:** an insectivorous plant (*Dionaea muscipula*) of the sundew family of the Carolina coast with the leaf apex modified into an insect trap — called also *Venus flytrap*

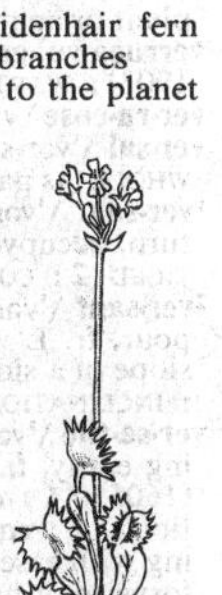
Venus's-flytrap

ve·ra·cious \və-ˈrā-shəs\ *adj* [L *verac-, verax* — more at VERY] (1677) **1 :** TRUTHFUL, HONEST **2 :** marked by truth **:** ACCURATE — **ve·ra·cious·ly** *adv* — **ve·ra·cious·ness** *n*

ve·rac·i·ty \və-ˈras-ət-ē\ *n, pl* **-ties** [NL *veracitas*, fr. L *verac-, verax*] (ca. 1623) **1 :** devotion to the truth **:** TRUTHFULNESS **2 :** power of conveying or perceiving truth **3 :** conformity with truth or fact **:** ACCURACY **4 :** something true ⟨makes his usual sound like *veracities*⟩

ve·ran·da *or* **ve·ran·dah** \və-ˈran-də\ *n* [Hindi *varandā*] (1711) **:** a usu. roofed open gallery or portico attached to the exterior of a building

ve·ran·daed *also* **ve·ran·dahed** \-dəd\ *adj* (1818) **:** having a veranda

ve·rap·a·mil \və-ˈrap-ə-ˌmil\ *n* [*vera-* (fr. NL *veratrum*) + *propyl* + *amino*] (ca. 1968) **:** a coronary vasodilator $C_{27}H_{38}N_2O_4$ used esp. in the form of its hydrochloride

ve·rat·ri·dine \və-ˈra-trə-ˌdēn\ *n* [*veratrine* + *-idine*] (ca. 1909) **:** a poisonous amorphous alkaloid $C_{36}H_{51}NO_{11}$ occurring esp. in sabadilla seed

ve·ra·trine \ˈver-ə-ˌtrēn, və-ˈra-trən\ *n* [NL *veratrina*, fr. *Veratrum*, genus of herbs] (1822) **:** a poisonous irritant mixture of alkaloids from sabadilla seed that has been used as a counterirritant, insecticide, and c-mitotic agent

ve·ra·trum \və-ˈrā-trəm\ *n* [NL, genus name, fr. L, hellebore] (14c) **:** HELLEBORE 2

verb \ˈvərb\ *n* [ME *verbe*, fr. MF, fr. L *verbum* word, verb — more at WORD] (14c) **:** a word that characteristically is the grammatical center of a predicate and expresses an act, occurrence, or mode of being, that in various languages is inflected for agreement with the subject, for tense, for voice, for mood, or for aspect, and that typically has rather full descriptive meaning and characterizing quality but is sometimes nearly devoid of these esp. when used as an auxiliary or linking verb — **verb·less** \ˈvər-bləs\ *adj*

[1]**ver·bal** \ˈvər-bəl\ *adj* [MF or LL; MF, fr. LL *verbalis*, fr. L *verbum* word] (15c) **1 a :** of, relating to, or consisting of words ⟨~ instructions⟩ **b :** of, relating to, or involving words rather than meaning or substance ⟨a consistency that is merely ~ and scholastic —B. N. Cardozo⟩ **c :** consisting of or using words only and not involving action ⟨a ~ protest⟩ **2 :** of, relating to, or formed from a verb ⟨a ~ adjective⟩ **3 :** spoken rather than written ⟨a ~ contract⟩ **4 :** VERBATIM, WORD-FOR-WORD ⟨a ~ translation⟩ **5 :** of or relating to facility in the use and comprehension of words ⟨~ aptitude⟩ — **ver·bal·ly** \-bə-lē\ *adv*

[2]**verbal** *n* (1530) **:** a word that combines characteristics of a verb with those of a noun or adjective — compare GERUND, INFINITIVE, PARTICIPLE

verbal auxiliary *n* (ca. 1958) **:** an auxiliary verb

ver·bal·ism \ˈvər-bə-ˌliz-əm\ *n* (1787) **1 a :** a verbal expression **:** TERM **b :** PHRASING, WORDING **2 :** words used as if they were more important than the realities they represent ⟨the emancipation of science from ~ —G. A. L. Sarton⟩ **3 a :** a wordy expression of little meaning **b :** VERBOSITY

ver·bal·ist \-ləst\ *n* (1609) **1 :** one who stresses words above substance or reality **2 :** a person who uses words skillfully — **ver·bal·is·tic** \ˌvər-bə-ˈlis-tik\ *adj*

ver·bal·ize \ˈvər-bə-ˌlīz\ *vb* **-ized; -iz·ing** *vi* (1609) **1 :** to speak or write verbosely **2 :** to express something in words ~ *vt* **1 :** to convert into a verb **2 :** to name or describe in words — **ver·bal·iza·tion** \ˌvər-bə-lə-ˈzā-shən\ *n* — **ver·bal·iz·er** \ˈvər-bə-ˌlī-zər\ *n*

verbal noun *n* (1706) **:** a noun derived directly from a verb or verb stem and in some uses having the sense and constructions of a verb

[1]**ver·ba·tim** \(ˌ)vər-ˈbāt-əm\ *adv* [ME, fr. ML, fr. L *verbum* word] (15c) **:** in the exact words **:** word for word

[2]**verbatim** *adj* (1737) **:** being in or following the exact words **:** WORD-FOR-WORD

ver·be·na \(ˌ)vər-ˈbē-nə\ *n* [NL, genus of herbs or subshrubs, fr. L, sing. of *verbenae* sacred boughs, certain medicinal plants — more at VERVAIN] (1562) **:** VERVAIN; *esp* **:** any of numerous garden plants of hybrid origin widely grown for their showy spikes of white, pink, red, or blue flowers which are borne in profusion over a long season

ver·biage \ˈvər-bē-ij *also* -bij\ *n* [F, fr. MF *verbier* to chatter, fr. *verbe* speech, fr. L *verbum* word] (1721) **1 :** superfluity of words in proportion to sense or content **:** WORDINESS **2 :** manner of expressing oneself in words **:** DICTION ⟨concise military ~⟩

ver·bi·cide \ˈvər-bə-ˌsīd\ *n* [L *verbum* word + E *-cide*] (1858) **1 :** deliberate distortion of the sense of a word (as in punning) **2 :** one who distorts the sense of a word

ver·bid \ˈvər-bəd\ *n* (1914) **:** VERBAL

ver·big·er·a·tion \(ˌ)vər-ˌbij-ə-ˈrā-shən\ *n* [ISV, fr. L *verbigeratus*, pp. of *verbigerare* to talk, chat, fr. *verbum* word + *gerere* to carry, wield — more at WORD, CAST] (1886) **:** continual repetition of stereotyped phrases (as in some forms of mental illness)

ver·bose \(ˌ)vər-ˈbōs\ *adj* [L *verbosus*, fr. *verbum* + *-osus* [1]-ose] (1672) **1 :** containing more words than necessary **:** WORDY ⟨a ~ reply⟩; *also* **:** impaired by wordiness ⟨a ~ style⟩ **2 :** given to wordiness ⟨a ~ orator⟩ *syn* see WORDY — **ver·bose·ly** *adv* — **ver·bose·ness** *n* — **ver·bos·i·ty** \-ˈbäs-ət-ē\ *n*

ver·bo·ten \vər-ˈbōt-ᵊn, fər-, ver-\ *adj* [G, fr. OHG *farboten*, pp. of *farbioten* to forbid (akin to OE *forbēodan* to forbid), fr. *far-, fur-* for- + *biotan* to offer — more at BID] (1912) **:** not allowed **:** FORBIDDEN; *esp* **:** prohibited by dictate

verb sap \ˈvərb-ˈsap\ (1841) **:** VERBUM SAP

ver·bum sap \ˌvər-bəm-ˈsap\ [short for NL *verbum sapienti* (*sat est*) a word to the wise (is sufficient)] (1818) **:** enough said — used to indicate that something left unsaid may or should be inferred

ver·dant \ˈvərd-ᵊnt\ *adj* [modif. of MF *verdoyant*, fr. prp. of *verdoyer* to be green, fr. OF *verdoier*, fr. *verd, vert* green, fr. L *viridis*, fr. *virēre* to be green; akin to OE *wise* sprout, ON *vīsir*] (1581) **1 a :** green in tint or color ⟨~ grass⟩ **b :** green with growing plants ⟨~ fields⟩ **2 :** unripe in experience or judgment **:** GREEN — **ver·dan·cy** \-ᵊn(t)-sē\ *n* — **ver·dant·ly** \-ᵊnt-lē\ *adv*

verd an·tique *or* **verde an·tique** \ˌvər-ˌdan-ˈtēk\ *n* [It *verde antico*, lit., ancient green] (1745) **:** a green mottled or veined serpentine marble or calcareous serpentine much used for indoor decoration esp. by the ancient Romans

ver·der·er *also* **ver·der·or** \ˈvərd-ər-ər\ *n* [AF, fr. OF *verdier*, fr. *verd* green] (1541) **:** a onetime English judicial officer in charge of the king's forest

ver·dict \ˈvər-(ˌ)dikt\ *n* [alter. of ME *verdit*, fr. AF, fr. OF *ver* true (fr. L *verus*) + *dit* saying, dictum, fr. L *dictum* — more at VERY] (13c) **1 :** the finding or decision of a jury on the matter submitted to it in trial **2 :** OPINION, JUDGMENT

ver·di·gris \ˈvərd-ə-ˌgrēs, -ˌgris, -grəs *also* -ˌgrē\ *n* [ME *vertegrez*, fr. OF *vert de Grice*, lit., green of Greece] (14c) **1 a :** a green or greenish blue poisonous pigment resulting from the action of acetic acid on copper and consisting of one or more basic copper acetates **b :** normal copper acetate $Cu(C_2H_3O_2)_2{\cdot}H_2O$ **2 :** a green or bluish deposit esp. of copper carbonates formed on copper, brass, or bronze surfaces

ver·din \ˈvərd-ᵊn\ *n* [prob. modif. of F *verdier* yellowhammer, fr. OF *verder*, deriv. of L *viridis* green — more at VERDANT] (1881) **:** a very small yellow-headed titmouse (*Auriparus flaviceps*) found from Texas to California and southward

ver·dure \ˈvər-jər\ *n* [ME, fr. MF, fr. *verd* green] (14c) **1 :** the greenness of growing vegetation; *also* **:** such vegetation itself **2 :** a condition of health and vigor — **ver·dur·ous** \ˈvərj-(ə-)rəs\ *adj*

ver·dured \ˈvər-jərd\ *adj* (1718) **:** covered with verdure

[1]**verge** \ˈvərj\ *n* [ME, fr. MF, fr. L *virga* rod, stripe — more at WHISK] (15c) **1 a** (1) **:** a rod or staff carried as an emblem of authority or symbol of office (2) *obs* **:** a stick or wand held by a person being admitted to tenancy while he swears fealty **b :** the spindle of a watch balance; *esp* **:** a spindle with pallets in an old vertical escapement **c**

: the male intromittent organ of any of various invertebrates **2 a** : something that borders, limits, or bounds: as (1) : an outer margin of an object or structural part (2) : the edge of roof covering (as tiling) projecting over the gable of a roof (3) *Brit* : the shoulder of a road **b** : BRINK, THRESHOLD ⟨a country on the ~ of destruction — Archibald MacLeish⟩

[2]**verge** *vi* **verged; verg·ing** (1787) **1** : to be contiguous **2** : to be on the verge or border

[3]**verge** *vi* **verged; verg·ing** [L *vergere* to bend, incline — more at WRENCH] (1610) **1 a** *of the sun* : to incline toward the horizon : SINK **b** : to move or extend in some direction or toward some condition **2** : to be in transition or change

verg·er \'vər-jər\ *n* (15c) **1** *chiefly Brit* : an attendant that carries a verge (as before a bishop or justice) **2** : a church official who keeps order during services or serves as an usher or a sacristan

ve·rid·i·cal \və-'rid-i-kəl\ *adj* [L *veridicus,* fr. *verus* true + *dicere* to say — more at VERY, DICTION] (1653) **1** : TRUTHFUL, VERACIOUS **2** : not illusory : GENUINE — **ve·rid·i·cal·i·ty** \-ˌrid-ə-'kal-ət-ē\ *n* — **ve·rid·i·cal·ly** \-k(ə-)lē\ *adv*

ver·i·fi·able \'ver-ə-ˌfī-ə-bəl\ *adj* (1593) : capable of being verified — **ver·i·fi·abil·i·ty** \ˌver-ə-ˌfī-ə-'bil-ət-ē\ *n* — **ver·i·fi·able·ness** *n*

ver·i·fi·ca·tion \ˌver-ə-fə-'kā-shən\ *n* (1523) : the act or process of verifying : the state of being verified

ver·i·fy \'ver-ə-ˌfī\ *vt* **-fied; -fy·ing** [ME *verifien,* fr. MF *verifier,* fr. ML *verificare,* fr. L *verus* true — more at VERY] (14c) **1** : to confirm or substantiate in law by oath **2** : to establish the truth, accuracy, or reality of ***syn*** see CONFIRM — **ver·i·fi·er** \-ˌfī(-ə)r\ *n*

ver·i·ly \'ver-ə-lē\ *adv* [ME *verraily,* fr. *verray* very] (14c) **1** : in truth : CERTAINLY **2** : TRULY, CONFIDENTLY

veri·sim·i·lar \ˌver-ə-'sim-(ə-)lər\ *adj* [L *verisimilis*] (1681) **1** : having the appearance of truth : PROBABLE **2** : depicting realism (as in art or literature) — **veri·sim·i·lar·ly** *adv*

veri·si·mil·i·tude \-sə-'mil-ə-ˌt(y)üd\ *n* [L *verisimilitudo,* fr. *verisimilis* verisimilar, fr. *veri similis* like the truth] (1603) **1** : the quality or state of being verisimilar **2** : something verisimilar — **veri·si·mil·i·tu·di·nous** \-ˌmil-ə-'t(y)üd-nəs, -ᵊn-əs\ *adj*

ve·rism \'vi(ə)r-ˌiz-əm, 've(ə)r-\ *n* [It *verismo,* fr. *vero* true, fr. L *verus*] (1892) : artistic use of contemporary everyday material in preference to the heroic or legendary esp. in grand opera — **ve·rist** \-əst\ *n or adj* — **ve·ris·tic** \vi(ə)r-'is-tik, ve(ə)r-\ *adj*

ve·ris·mo \vā-'rēz-(ˌ)mō\ *n* [It] (ca. 1915) : VERISM; *also* : REALISM 3

ver·i·ta·ble \'ver-ət-ə-bəl\ *adj* [ME, fr. MF, fr. *verité*] (15c) : being in fact the thing named and not false, unreal, or imaginary — often used to stress the aptness of a metaphor ⟨a ~ mountain of references⟩ ***syn*** see AUTHENTIC — **ver·i·ta·ble·ness** *n* — **ver·i·ta·bly** \-blē\ *adv*

vé·ri·té \ˌver-ə-'tā\ *n* [F, truth, fr. MF *verité*] (1966) : the art or technique of filming (as a motion picture) so as to convey candid realism

ver·i·ty \'ver-ət-ē\ *n, pl* **-ties** [ME *verite,* fr. MF *verité,* fr. L *veritat-, veritas,* fr. *verus* true] (14c) **1** : the quality or state of being true or real **2** : something (as a statement) that is true; *esp* : a fundamental and inevitably true value ⟨such eternal *verities* as honor, love, and patriotism⟩ **3** : the quality or state of being truthful or honest ⟨the king-becoming graces, as justice, ~ —Shak.⟩

ver·juice \'vər-ˌjüs\ *n* [ME *verjus,* fr. MF, fr. *vert jus,* lit., green juice] (14c) **1** : the sour juice of crab apples or of unripe fruit (as grapes or apples); *also* : an acid liquor made from verjuice **2** : acidity of disposition or manner

ver·meil *n* [MF, fr. *vermeil,* adj. — more at VERMILION] (15c) **1** \'vər-məl, -ˌmāl\ : VERMILION **2** \ve(ə)r-'mā\ : gilded silver — **vermeil** *adj*

vermi- *comb form* [NL, fr. LL, fr. L *vermis* — more at WORM] : worm ⟨*vermi*form⟩

ver·mi·cel·li \ˌvər-mə-'chel-ē, -'sel-\ *n* [It, fr. pl. of *vermicello,* dim. of *verme* worm, fr. L *vermis*] (1669) : pasta made in long solid strings smaller in diameter than spaghetti

ver·mi·cide \'vər-mə-ˌsīd\ *n* (1849) : an agent that destroys worms

ver·mic·u·lar \(ˌ)vər-'mik-yə-lər\ *adj* [NL *vermicularis,* fr. L *vermiculus,* dim. of *vermis*] (1672) **1 a** : resembling a worm in form or motion **b** : VERMICULATE **2** : of, relating to, or caused by worms

ver·mic·u·late \-lət\ *or* **ver·mic·u·lat·ed** \-ˌlāt-əd\ *adj* [L *vermiculatus,* fr. *vermiculus*] (1605) **1 a** : VERMIFORM **b** : marked with irregular fine lines or with wavy impressed lines ⟨a ~ nut⟩ **2** : TORTUOUS, INVOLUTE **3** : full of worms : WORM-EATEN — **ver·mic·u·la·tion** \-ˌmik-yə-'lā-shən\ *n*

ver·mic·u·lite \(ˌ)vər-'mik-yə-ˌlīt\ *n* [L *vermiculus* little worm] (1824) : any of various micaceous minerals that are hydrous silicates resulting usu. from expansion of the granules of mica at high temperatures to give a lightweight highly water-absorbent material

ver·mi·form \'vər-mə-ˌfȯrm\ *adj* [NL *vermiformis,* fr. *vermi-* + *-formis* form] (ca. 1730) : resembling a worm in shape

vermiform appendix *n* (ca. 1778) : a narrow blind tube usu. about three or four inches long that extends from the cecum in the lower right-hand part of the abdomen

ver·mi·fuge \'vər-mə-ˌfyüj\ *adj* [prob. fr. (assumed) NL *vermifugus,* fr. *vermi-* + L *fugare* to put to flight — more at -FUGE] (1697) : serving to destroy or expel parasitic worms : ANTHELMINTIC — **vermifuge** *n*

ver·mil·ion *also* **ver·mil·lion** \vər-'mil-yən\ *n* [ME *vermilioun,* fr. OF *vermeillon,* fr. *vermeil,* adj., bright red, vermilion, fr. LL *vermiculus* kermes, fr. L, little worm] (14c) **1** : a bright red pigment consisting of mercuric sulfide; *broadly* : any of various red pigments **2** : a variable color averaging a vivid reddish orange

ver·min \'vər-mən\ *n, pl* **vermin** [ME, fr. MF, fr. (assumed) L *vermin-, vermen* worm; akin to L *vermis* worm — more at WORM] (14c) **1 a** : small common harmful or objectionable animals (as lice or fleas) that are difficult to control **b** : birds and mammals that prey on game **2** : an offensive person

ver·min·ous \'vər-mə-nəs\ *adj* (1616) **1** : consisting of or being vermin : NOXIOUS **2** : forming a breeding place for or infested by vermin : FILTHY ⟨~ garbage⟩ **3** : caused by vermin ⟨~ disease⟩

ver·mouth \vər-'müth\ *n* [F *vermout,* fr. G *wermut* wormwood, fr. OHG *wermuota* — more at WORMWOOD] (1806) : a dry or sweet aperitif wine flavored with aromatic herbs and often used in mixed drinks

[1]**ver·nac·u·lar** \və(r)-'nak-yə-lər\ *adj* [L *vernaculus* native, fr. *verna* slave born in his master's house, native] (1601) **1 a** : using a language or dialect native to a region or country rather than a literary, cultured, or foreign language **b** : of, relating to, or being a nonstandard or substandard language or dialect of a place, region, or country **c** : of, relating to, or being the normal spoken form of a language **2** : applied to a plant or animal in the common native speech as distinguished from the Latin nomenclature of scientific classification **3** : of, relating to, or characteristic of a period, place, or group; *esp* : of, relating to, or being the common building style of a period or place — **ver·nac·u·lar·ly** *adv*

[2]**vernacular** *n* (1706) **1** : a vernacular language, expression, or mode of expression **2** : the mode of expression of a group or class **3** : a vernacular name of a plant or animal

ver·nac·u·lar·ism \və(r)-'nak-yə-lə-ˌriz-əm\ *n* (ca. 1846) : a vernacular word or idiom

ver·nal \'vərn-ᵊl\ *adj* [L *vernalis,* alter. of *vernus,* fr. *ver* spring; akin to Gk *ear* spring] (1534) **1** : of, relating to, or occurring in the spring ⟨~ equinox⟩ ⟨~ sunshine⟩ **2** : fresh or new like the spring; *also* : YOUTHFUL — **ver·nal·ly** \-ᵊl-ē\ *adv*

ver·nal·iza·tion \ˌvərn-ᵊl-ə-'zā-shən\ *n* (ca. 1932) : the act or process of hastening the flowering and fruiting of plants by treating seeds, bulbs, or seedlings so as to induce a shortening of the vegetative period — **ver·nal·ize** \'vərn-ᵊl-ˌīz\ *vt*

ver·na·tion \(ˌ)vər-'nā-shən\ *n* [NL *vernation-, vernatio,* fr. L *vernatus,* pp. of *vernare* to behave as in spring, fr. *vernus* vernal] (1793) : the arrangement of foliage leaves within the bud

Ver·ner's law \ˌve(ə)r-nərz-\ *n* [Karl A. *Verner*] (ca. 1892) : a statement in historical linguistics: in medial or final position in voiced environments and when the immediately preceding vowel did not bear the principal accent in Proto-Indo-European, the Proto-Germanic voiceless fricatives *f, þ,* and *χ* derived from the Proto-Indo-European voiceless stops *p, t,* and *k* and the Proto-Germanic voiceless fricative *s* derived from Proto-Indo-European *s* became the voiced fricatives *ƀ, ð, g,* and *z* represented in various recorded Germanic languages by *b, d, g,* and *r*

ver·ni·cle *or* **ver·na·cle** \'vər-ni-kəl\ *n* [ME *vernicle,* fr. MF *veronique, vernicle,* fr. ML *veronica*] (14c) : [2]VERONICA

[1]**ver·ni·er** \'vər-nē-ər\ *n* [Pierre *Vernier*] (ca. 1766) **1** : a short scale made to slide along the divisions of a graduated instrument for indicating parts of divisions **2 a** : a small auxiliary device used with a main device to obtain fine adjustment **b** : any of two or more small supplementary rocket engines or gas nozzles on a missile or a rocket vehicle for making fine adjustments in the speed or course or controlling the attitude — called also *vernier engine*

[2]**vernier** *adj* (1788) : having or comprising a vernier

vernier caliper *n* (ca. 1876) : a measuring device that consists of a main scale with a fixed jaw and a sliding jaw with an attached vernier

ver·nis·sage \ˌver-ni-'säzh\ *n* [F, day before an exhibition opens reserved for artists to varnish and put finishing touches to their paintings, lit., varnishing, fr. *vernis* varnish — more at VARNISH] (1926) : a private showing or preview of an art exhibition

[1]**ve·ron·i·ca** \və-'rän-i-kə\ *n* [NL, genus of herbs] (1527) : SPEEDWELL

[2]**veronica** *n* [ML, fr. *Veronica* St. Veronica] (1700) : an image of Christ's face said to have been impressed on the cloth that St. Veronica gave him to wipe his face with on the way to his crucifixion; *also* : a cloth resembling the legendary one of St. Veronica

[3]**veronica** *n* [Sp *verónica,* fr. St. *Veronica*] (1926) : a pase in bullfighting in which the cape is swung slowly away from the charging bull while the matador keeps his feet in the same position

Vé·ro·nique *also* **Ve·ro·nique** \ˌvā-rȯ-'nēk\ *adj* [F *Véronique* Veronica] (1927) : prepared or garnished with usu. white seedless grapes ⟨sole ~⟩

ver·ru·ca \və-'rü-kə\ *n, pl* **-cae** \-(ˌ)kē, -ˌkī, -ˌsī\ [L — more at WART] (1565) **1** : a wart or warty skin lesion **2** : a warty elevation on a plant or animal surface

verruca vul·ga·ris \-ˌvəl-'gar-əs, -'ger-\ *n* [NL, lit., common verruca] (ca. 1903) : WART 1a

ver·ru·cose \və-'rü-ˌkōs\ *adj* (1686) : covered with warty elevations

ver·sal \'vər-səl, 'vär-\ *adj* [short for *universal*] *archaic* (1592) : ENTIRE, WHOLE ⟨as pale as any clout in the ~ world —Shak.⟩

[1]**ver·sant** \'vərs-ᵊnt\ *adj* [L *versant-, versans,* prp. of *versare, versari* to turn, occupy oneself, meditate] (1645) **1** *archaic* : EXPERIENCED, PRACTICED **2** : CONVERSANT

[2]**ver·sant** \'vərs-ᵊnt, ve(ə)r-'sä^{n}\ *n* [F, fr. MF, fr. prp. of *verser* to turn, pour, fr. L *versare* to turn; fr. its shedding of water] (1851) **1** : the slope of a side of a mountain chain **2** : the general slope of a country : INCLINATION

ver·sa·tile \'vər-sət-ᵊl, *esp Brit* -sə-ˌtīl\ *adj* [F or L; F, fr. L *versatilis* turning easily, fr. *versatus,* pp. of *versare* to turn, fr. *versus,* pp. of *vertere*] (1605) **1** : changing or fluctuating readily : VARIABLE ⟨a ~ disposition⟩ **2** : embracing a variety of subjects, fields, or skills; *also* : turning with ease from one thing to another **3 a** (1) : capable of turning forward or backward : REVERSIBLE ⟨a ~ toe of a bird⟩ (2) : capable of moving laterally and up and down ⟨~ antennae⟩ **b** *of an anther* : having the filaments attached at or near the middle so as to swing freely **4** : having many uses or applications ⟨~ building material⟩ — **ver·sa·tile·ly** \-ᵊl-(l)ē, -ˌtīl-lē\ *adv* — **ver·sa·tile·ness** \-ᵊl-nəs, -ˌtīl-nəs\ *n*

ver·sa·til·i·ty \ˌvər-sə-'til-ət-ē\ *n* (ca. 1755) : the quality or state of being versatile ⟨a writer of great ~⟩

vers de so·ci·é·té \ˌve(ə)r-də-ˌsō-sē-ə-'tā\ *n* [F, society verse] (1803) : witty and typically ironic light verse

[1]**verse** \'vərs\ *n* [ME *vers,* fr. OF & OE; both fr. L *versus,* lit., turning, fr. *versus,* pp. of *vertere* to turn — more at WORTH] (bef. 12c) **1** : a line of metrical writing **2 a** (1) : metrical language (2) : metrical writing distinguished from poetry esp. by its lower level of intensity (3) : POETRY 2 **b** : POEM **c** : a body of metrical writing (as of a period or country) **3** : STANZA **4** : one of the short divisions into which a chapter of the Bible is traditionally divided

[2]**verse** *vb* **versed; vers·ing** *vi* (bef. 12c) : to make verse : VERSIFY ~ *vt* **1** : to tell or celebrate in verse **2** : to turn into verse

[3]**verse** *vt* **versed; vers·ing** [back-formation fr. *versed,* fr. L *versatus,* pp. of *versari* to be active, be occupied (in), pass. of *versare* to turn, fr. *versus,* pp.] (1673) : to familiarize by close association, study, or experience ⟨*versed* himself in the theater⟩

vers·et \'vərs-ət, ˌvər-'set\ *n* [ME, fr. OF, dim. of *vers* verse] (13c) : a short verse esp. from a sacred book (as the Koran)

ver·si·cle \ˈvər-si-kəl\ *n* [ME, fr. L *versiculus,* dim. of *versus* verse] (14c) **1 :** a short verse or sentence (as from a psalm) said or sung by a leader in public worship and followed by a response from the people **2 :** a little verse

ver·sic·u·lar \ˌvər-ˈsik-yə-lər\ *adj* [L *versiculus* little verse] (1812) **:** of or relating to verses or versicles

ver·si·fi·ca·tion \ˌvər-sə-fə-ˈkā-shən\ *n* [L *versification-, versificatio,* fr. *versificatus,* pp. of *versificare* to versify] (1603) **1 :** the making of verses **2 a :** metrical structure **:** PROSODY **b :** a particular metrical structure or style **3 :** a version in verse of something orig. in prose

ver·si·fi·er \ˈvər-sə-ˌfī(-ə)r\ *n* (14c) **:** one that versifies; *esp* **:** a writer of light or inferior verse

ver·si·fy \-ˌfī\ *vb* **-fied; -fy·ing** *vi* [ME *versifien,* fr. MF *versifier,* fr. L *versificare,* fr. *versus* verse, line] (14c) **:** to compose verses ~ *vt* **1 :** to relate or describe in verse **2 :** to turn into verse

ver·sion \ˈvər-zhən, -shən\ *n* [MF, fr. ML *version-, versio* act of turning, fr. L *versus,* pp. of *vertere* — more at WORTH] (1582) **1 :** a translation from another language; *esp* **:** a translation of the Bible or a part of it **2 a :** an account or description from a particular point of view esp. as contrasted with another account **b :** an adaptation of a literary work ⟨the movie ~ of the novel⟩ **c :** an arrangement of a musical composition **3 :** a form or variant of a type or original ⟨an experimental ~ of the plane⟩ **4 a :** a condition in which an organ and esp. the uterus is turned from its normal position **b :** manual turning of a fetus in the uterus to aid delivery — **ver·sion·al** \ˈvərzh-nəl, ˈvərsh-, -ən-ᵊl\ *adj*

vers li·bre \ve(ə)r-ˈlēbrᵊ\ *n, pl* **vers li·bres** *same*\ [F] (ca. 1916) **:** FREE VERSE

vers–li·brist \-ˈlē-brəst\ *n* [F *vers-libriste*] (1916) **:** a writer of free verse

ver·so \ˈvər-(ˌ)sō\ *n, pl* **versos** [NL *verso (folio)* the page being turned] (1839) **1 :** the side of a leaf (as of a manuscript) that is to be read second **2 :** a left-hand page — compare RECTO

verst \ˈvərst\ *n* [F *verste* & G *werst;* both fr. Russ *versta;* akin to L *vertere* to turn] (1555) **:** a Russian unit of distance equal to 0.6629 mile (1.067 kilometers)

ver·sus \ˈvər-səs, -səz\ *prep* [ML, towards, against, fr. L, adv., so as to face, fr. pp. of *vertere* to turn] (15c) **1 :** AGAINST **2 :** in contrast to or as the alternative of ⟨free trade ~ protection⟩

vert \ˈvərt\ *n* [ME *verte,* fr. MF *vert,* fr. *vert* green — more at VERDANT] (15c) **1 a :** green forest vegetation esp. when forming cover or providing food for deer **b :** the right or privilege (as in England) of cutting living wood or sometimes of pasturing animals in a forest **2 :** the heraldic color green

ver·te·bra \ˈvərt-ə-brə, -ˌbrā\ *n, pl* **-brae** \-ˌbrā, -(ˌ)brē, -brə\ *or* **-bras** [L, joint, vertebra, fr. *vertere* to turn — more at WORTH] (1578) **:** one of the bony or cartilaginous segments composing the spinal column, consisting in some lower vertebrates of several distinct elements which never become united, and in higher vertebrates having a short more or less cylindrical body whose ends articulate by pads of elastic or cartilaginous tissue with those of adjacent vertebrae and a bony arch that encloses the spinal cord

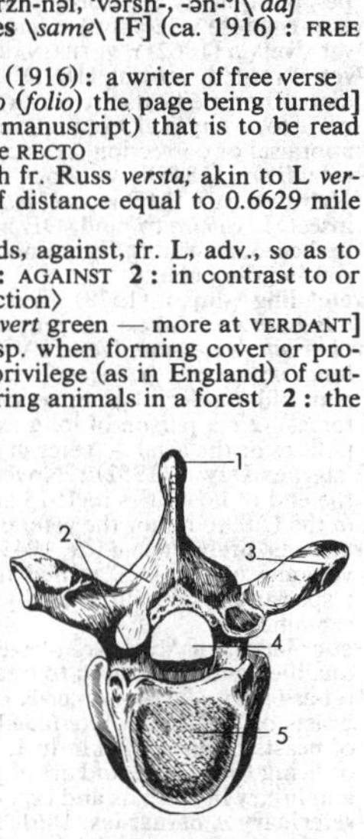

sixth thoracic vertebra, seen from above: *1* neural spine, *2* neural arch, *3* transverse process, *4* spinal foramen, *5* centrum

ver·te·bral \(ˌ)vər-ˈtē-brəl, ˈvərt-ə-\ *adj* (ca. 1681) **1 :** of, relating to, or being vertebrae or the vertebral column **:** SPINAL **2 :** composed of or having vertebrae

vertebral column *n* (1822) **:** SPINAL COLUMN

¹ver·te·brate \ˈvərt-ə-brət, -ˌbrāt\ *adj* [NL *vertebratus,* fr. L, jointed, fr. *vertebra*] (1826) **1 a :** having a spinal column **b :** of or relating to the vertebrates **2 :** organized or constructed in orderly or developed form

²vertebrate *n* [deriv. of NL *vertebratus*] (1826) **:** any of a comprehensive division (Vertebrata) usu. held to be a subphylum of chordates comprising animals (as mammals, birds, reptiles, amphibians, and fishes) with a segmented spinal column together with a few primitive forms in which the backbone is represented by a notochord

ver·tex \ˈvər-ˌteks\ *n, pl* **ver·ti·ces** \ˈvərt-ə-ˌsēz\ *also* **ver·tex·es** [L *vertic-, vertex, vortic-, vortex* whirl, whirlpool, top of the head, summit, fr. *vertere* to turn] (1570) **1 a** (1) **:** the point opposite to and farthest from the base in a figure (2) **:** a point (as of an angle, polygon, polyhedron, graph, or network) that terminates a line or curve or comprises the intersection of two or more lines or curves (3) **:** a point where an axis of an ellipse, parabola, or hyperbola intersects the curve itself **b :** ZENITH 1 **2 :** the top of the head **3 :** a principal or highest point **:** SUMMIT ⟨the ~ of the hill⟩

ver·ti·cal \ˈvərt-i-kəl\ *adj* [MF or LL; MF, fr. LL *verticalis,* fr. L *vertic-, vertex*] (1559) **1 a :** situated at the highest point **:** directly overhead or in the zenith **b :** being an aerial photograph taken with the camera pointing straight down or nearly so **2 a :** perpendicular to the plane of the horizon or to a primary axis **:** UPRIGHT **b** (1) **:** located at right angles to the plane of a supporting surface (2) **:** lying in the direction of an axis **:** LENGTHWISE **3 a :** relating to, involving, or integrating economic activity from basic production to point of sale ⟨~ monopoly⟩ **b :** of, relating to, or comprising persons of different status ⟨the ~ arrangement of society⟩ — **vertical** *n* — **ver·ti·cal·i·ty** \ˌvərt-ə-ˈkal-ət-ē\ *n* — **ver·ti·cal·ly** \ˈvərt-i-k(ə-)lē\ *adv* — **ver·ti·cal·ness** \-kəl-nəs\ *n*

syn VERTICAL, PERPENDICULAR, PLUMB mean being at right angles to a base line. VERTICAL suggests a line or direction rising straight upward toward a zenith; PERPENDICULAR may stress the straightness of a line making a right angle with any other line, not necessarily a horizontal one; PLUMB stresses an exact verticality determined (as with a plumb line) by earth's gravity.

vertical angle *n* (1571) **:** either of two angles lying on opposite sides of two intersecting lines

vertical circle *n* (1559) **:** a great circle of the celestial sphere whose plane is perpendicular to that of the horizon

vertical file *n* (ca. 1916) **:** a collection of articles (as pamphlets and clippings) that is maintained (as in a library) to answer brief questions or to provide points of information not easily located

vertical union *n* (1934) **:** INDUSTRIAL UNION

ver·ti·cil \ˈvərt-ə-ˌsil\ *n* [NL *verticillus,* dim. of L *vertex* whirl] (1793) **:** a circle of similar parts (as flowers around a stem or sensory hairs around an antennal joint) about the same point on the axis **:** WHORL

ver·ti·cil·late \ˌvərt-ə-ˈsil-ət\ *adj* (ca. 1793) **:** arranged in verticils

ver·ti·cil·li·um wilt \ˌvərt-ə-ˌsil-ē-əm-\ *n* [NL *Verticillium,* fr. *verticillus*] (ca. 1943) **:** a wilt disease of various plants that is caused by soil-borne imperfect fungi (genus *Verticillium*) having conidia borne singly at the apex of whorled branchlets

ver·tig·i·nous \(ˌ)vər-ˈtij-ə-nəs\ *adj* [L *vertiginosus,* fr. *vertigin-, vertigo*] (1608) **1 a :** characterized by or suffering from vertigo or dizziness **:** GIDDY **b :** inclined to frequent and often pointless change **:** INCONSTANT **2 :** causing or tending to cause dizziness ⟨the ~ heights⟩ **3 :** marked by turning **:** ROTARY ⟨the ~ motion of the earth⟩ — **ver·tig·i·nous·ly** *adv*

ver·ti·go \ˈvərt-i-ˌgō\ *n, pl* **-goes** *or* **-gos** [L *vertigin-, vertigo,* fr. *vertere* to turn] (1528) **1 a :** a disordered state in which the individual or his surroundings seem to whirl dizzily **:** GIDDINESS **b :** a dizzy confused state of mind **2 :** disordered vertiginous movement as a symptom of disease in lower animals; *also* **:** a disease (as gid) causing this

ver·tu \ˌvər-ˈtü, ve(ə)r-\ *var of* VIRTU

ver·vain \ˈvər-ˌvān\ *n* [ME *verveine,* fr. MF, fr. L *verbena,* sing. of *verbenae* sacred boughs, certain medicinal plants; akin to L *verber* rod, Gk *rhabdos*] (14c) **:** any of a genus (*Verbena* of the family Verbenaceae, the vervain family) of plants that have bracted flowers in heads or spikes, a regular corolla with a 5-lobed limb, and four 1-seeded nutlets; *esp* **:** one with small spicate flowers

verve \ˈvərv\ *n* [F, fantasy, caprice, animation, fr. L *verba,* pl. of *verbum* word — more at WORD] (1697) **1** *archaic* **:** special ability or talent **2 a :** the spirit and enthusiasm animating artistic composition or performance **:** VIVACITY **b :** ENERGY, VITALITY

ver·vet monkey \ˌvər-vət-\ *n* [F *vervet*] (ca. 1884) **:** a monkey of any of several southern and eastern African races of a guenon (*Cercopithecus aethiops*) having the face, chin, hands, and feet black — called also *vervet*

¹very \ˈver-ē\ *adj* **veri·er; -est** [ME *verray, verry,* fr. OF *verai,* fr. (assumed) VL *veracus,* alter. of L *verac-, verax* truthful, fr. *verus* true; akin to OE *wǣr* true, OHG *wāra* trust, care, Gk *ēra* (acc.) favor] (13c) **1 a :** properly entitled to the name or designation **:** TRUE ⟨the fierce hatred of a ~ woman —J. M. Barrie⟩ **b :** ACTUAL, REAL ⟨the ~ blood and bone of our grammar —H. L. Smith †1972⟩ **c :** SIMPLE, PLAIN ⟨in ~ truth⟩ **2 a :** being exactly as stated ⟨the ~ heart of the city⟩ **b :** exactly suitable or necessary ⟨the ~ thing for the purpose⟩ **3 a :** ABSOLUTE, UTTER ⟨the *veriest* fool alive⟩ **b :** UNQUALIFIED, SHEER ⟨the ~ shame of it⟩ **4 —** used as an intensive esp. to emphasize identity **5 :** MERE, BARE ⟨the ~ thought terrified him⟩ **6 :** being the same one **:** SELFSAME ⟨the ~ man I saw⟩ **7 :** SPECIAL, PARTICULAR ⟨the ~ essence of truth is plainness and brightness —John Milton⟩ ***syn*** see SAME

²very *adv* (14c) **1 :** in actual fact **:** TRULY ⟨the ~ best store in town⟩ ⟨told the ~ same story⟩ **2 :** to a high degree **:** EXCEEDINGLY ⟨~ hot⟩

very hard *adj, of cheese* (ca. 1943) **:** suitable chiefly for grating

very high frequency *n* (1928) **:** a radio frequency between ultrahigh frequency and high frequency — see RADIO FREQUENCY table

Ve·ry light \ˌver-ē-, ˌvi(ə)r-ē-\ *n* [Edward W. *Very* †1910 Am naval officer] (1915) **:** a pyrotechnic signal in a system of signaling using white or colored balls of fire projected from a special pistol

very low frequency *n* (ca. 1945) **:** a radio frequency between low frequency and voice frequency — see RADIO FREQUENCY table

Ve·ry pistol \ˌver-ē-, ˌvi(ə)r-ē-\ *n* (1915) **:** a pistol for firing Very lights

Very Reverend \ˌver-ē-\ (ca. 1847) — used as a title for various ecclesiastical officials (as cathedral deans and canons, rectors of Roman Catholic colleges and seminaries, and superiors of some religious houses)

ves·i·cal \ˈves-i-kəl\ *adj* [L *vesica* bladder — more at VENTER] (1797) **:** of or relating to a bladder and esp. to the urinary bladder ⟨~ burning⟩

ves·i·cant \-kənt\ *n* [L *vesica* bladder, blister] (1661) **:** an agent (as a drug or a war gas) that induces blistering — **vesicant** *adj*

ves·i·ca·tion \ˌves-ə-ˈkā-shən\ *n* (1543) **1 :** BLISTER **2 :** an instance or the process of blistering

ves·i·cle \ˈves-i-kəl\ *n* [MF *vesicule,* fr. L *vesicula* small bladder, blister, fr. dim. of *vesica*] (1578) **1 a :** a membranous and usu. fluid-filled pouch (as a cyst, vacuole, or cell) in a plant or animal **b :** a small abnormal elevation of the outer layer of skin enclosing a watery liquid **:** BLISTER **c :** a pocket of embryonic tissue that is the beginning of an organ **2 :** a small cavity in a mineral or rock

ve·sic·u·lar \və-ˈsik-yə-lər, ve-\ *adj* [NL *vesicula* vesicle, fr. L, small bladder] (1715) **1 :** containing, composed of, or characterized by vesicles ⟨~ lava⟩ **2 :** having the form or structure of a vesicle **3 :** of or relating to vesicles and esp. to the alveoli of the lungs — **ve·sic·u·lar·i·ty** \-ˌsik-yə-ˈlar-ət-ē\ *n*

vesicular stomatitis *n* (ca. 1903) **:** an acute virus disease esp. of horses and mules that is marked by erosive blisters in and about the mouth and that much resembles foot-and-mouth disease

ve·sic·u·late \və-ˈsik-yə-ˌlāt, ve-\ *vb* **-lat·ed; -lat·ing** *vt* (1865) **:** to make vesicular ~ *vi* **:** to become vesicular — **ve·sic·u·la·tion** \-ˌsik-yə-ˈlā-shən\ *n*

¹ves·per \ˈves-pər\ *n* [ME, fr. L, evening, evening star — more at WEST] (14c) **1** *cap* **:** EVENING STAR **2 :** a vesper bell **3** *archaic* **:** EVENING, EVENTIDE

²vesper *adj* (1791) **:** of or relating to vespers or the evening

ves·per·al \ˈves-p(ə-)rəl\ *adj* (ca. 1623) **:** VESPER ⟨a ~ breeze⟩

ves·pers \ˈves-pərz\ *n pl but sing or pl in constr, often cap* [F *vespres,* fr. ML *vesperae,* fr. L, pl. of *vespera* evening; akin to L *vesper* evening star]

\ə\ abut \ᵊ\ kitten, F table \ər\ further \a\ ash \ā\ ace \ä\ cot, cart \au̇\ out \ch\ chin \e\ bet \ē\ easy \g\ go \i\ hit \ī\ ice \j\ job \ŋ\ sing \ō\ go \ȯ\ law \ȯi\ boy \th\ thin \t͟h\ the \ü\ loot \u̇\ foot \y\ yet \zh\ vision \à, k̲, ⁿ, œ, œ̄, ue, ue̅, ʸ\ see Guide to Pronunciation

(1611) **1 :** the sixth of the canonical hours that is said or sung in the late afternoon **2 :** a service of evening worship
ves·per·til·ian \ˌves-pər-ˈtil-ē-ən, -ˈtil-yən\ *adj* [L *vespertilio* bat, fr. *vesper*] (1874) **:** of or relating to bats
ves·per·tine \ˈves-pər-ˌtīn\ *adj* [L *vespertinus,* fr. *vesper*] (1502) **1 :** of, relating to, or occurring in the evening ⟨~ shadows⟩ **2 :** active, flowering, or flourishing in the evening **:** CREPUSCULAR
ves·pid \ˈves-pəd\ *n* [deriv. of L *vespa* wasp — more at WASP] (ca. 1900) **:** any of a cosmopolitan family (Vespidae) of hymenopterous insects comprising the social wasps that live in colonies like bees — **vespid** *adj*
ves·pine \ˈves-ˌpīn\ *adj* [L *vespa* wasp] (1843) **:** of, relating to, or resembling wasps and esp. vespid wasps
ves·sel \ˈves-əl\ *n* [ME, fr. MF *vaissel,* fr. LL *vascellum,* dim. of L *vas* vase, vessel — more at VASE] (14c) **1 a :** a hollow or concave utensil (as a hogshead, bottle, kettle, cup, or bowl) for holding something **b :** a person into whom some quality (as grace) is infused ⟨a child of light, a true ~ of the Lord —H. J. Laski⟩ **2 a :** a hollow structure designed for navigation in or on the water; *esp* **:** one bigger than a rowboat **b :** any of various aircraft **3 a :** a tube or canal (as an artery) in which a body fluid is contained and conveyed or circulated **b :** a conducting tube in a vascular plant formed by the fusion and loss of end walls of a series of cells
¹**vest** \ˈvest\ *vb* [ME *vesten,* fr. MF *vestir* to clothe, invest, fr. L *vestire* to clothe, fr. *vestis* clothing, garment — more at WEAR] *vt* (15c) **1 a :** to place or give into the possession or discretion of some person or authority; *esp* **:** to give to a person a legally fixed immediate right of present or future enjoyment of (as an estate) **b :** to grant or endow with a particular authority, right, or property ⟨the retirement plan ~*s* the workers absolutely with the company's contribution after 10 years of continuous employment⟩ **2 :** to clothe with or as if with a garment; *esp* **:** to robe in ecclesiastical vestments ~ *vi* **1 :** to become legally vested **2 :** to put on garments; *esp* **:** to put on ecclesiastical vestments
²**vest** *n* [F *veste,* fr. It, fr. L *vestis* garment] (1613) **1** *archaic* **a :** a loose outer garment **:** ROBE **b :** CLOTHING, GARB **2 a :** a man's sleeveless garment for the upper body usu. worn under a suit coat; *also* **:** a similar garment for women **b :** a protective usu. sleeveless garment (as a life preserver) that extends to the waist **3 a** *chiefly Brit* **:** a man's sleeveless undershirt **b :** a knitted undershirt for women **4 :** a plain or decorative piece used to fill in the front neckline of a woman's outer garment (as a waist, coat, or gown) — **vest·like** \-ˌlīk\ *adj*
ves·ta \ˈves-tə\ *n* [L *Vesta*] **1** *cap* **:** the Roman goddess of the hearth — compare HESTIA **2 :** a short match with a shank of wax-coated threads; *also* **:** a short wooden match
¹**ves·tal** \ˈves-tᵊl\ *adj* (15c) **1 :** of or relating to the Roman goddess Vesta **2 a :** of or relating to a vestal virgin **b :** CHASTE
²**vestal** *n* (1549) **:** VESTAL VIRGIN
vestal virgin *n* (15c) **1 :** a virgin consecrated to the Roman goddess Vesta and to the service of watching the sacred fire perpetually kept burning on her altar **2 :** a chaste woman
vest·ed \ˈves-təd\ *adj* (ca. 1766) **:** fully and unconditionally guaranteed as a legal right, benefit, or privilege ⟨the ~ benefits of the pension plan⟩
vested interest *n* (1818) **1 a :** an interest (as a title to an estate) carrying a legal right of present or future enjoyment **b :** a right vested in an employee under a pension plan **2 :** a special concern or stake in maintaining or influencing a condition, arrangement, or action esp. for selfish ends **3 :** one having a vested interest in something; *specif* **:** a group enjoying benefits from an existing economic or political privilege
vest·ee \ve-ˈstē\ *n* (1904) **1 :** DICKEY; *esp* **:** one made to resemble a vest and worn under a coat **2 :** VEST 4
ves·ti·ary \ˈves-tē-ˌer-ē, ˈves(h)-chē-\ *n* [ME *vestiarie,* fr. MF, vestry — more at VESTRY] (15c) **1 :** a room where clothing is kept **2 :** CLOTHING, RAIMENT
ves·tib·u·lar \ve-ˈstib-yə-lər\ *adj* (1836) **:** of, relating to, or functioning as a vestibule
ves·ti·bule \ˈves-tə-ˌbyü(ə)l\ *n* [L *vestibulum*] (ca. 1728) **1 :** any of various bodily cavities esp. when serving as or resembling an entrance to some other cavity or space: as **a :** the central cavity of the bony labyrinth of the ear or the parts of the membranous labyrinth that it contains **b :** the part of the left ventricle below the aortic orifice **c :** the space between the labia minora containing the orifice of the urethra **d :** the part of the mouth cavity outside the teeth and gums **2 a :** a passage, hall, or room between the outer door and the interior of a building **:** LOBBY **b :** an enclosed entrance at the end of a railway passenger car **3 :** a course that offers access (as to something new) — **ves·ti·buled** \-ˌbyü(ə)ld\ *adj*
vestibule school *n* (1918) **:** a school organized in an industrial plant to train new workers in specific skills
ves·tib·u·lo·co·chle·ar nerve \ve-ˌstib-yə-lō-ˌkō-klē-ər-, -ˌkäk-lē-\ *n* (1962) **:** AUDITORY NERVE
ves·tige \ˈves-tij\ *n* [F, fr. L *vestigium* footstep, footprint, track, vestige] (1545) **1 a** (1) **:** a trace, mark, or visible sign left by something (as an ancient city or a condition or practice) vanished or lost (2) **:** the smallest quantity or trace **b :** FOOTPRINT 1 **2 :** a bodily part or organ that is small and degenerate or imperfectly developed in comparison to one more fully developed in an earlier stage of the individual, in a past generation, or in closely related forms ***syn*** see TRACE — **ves·ti·gial** \ve-ˈstij-(ē-)əl\ *adj* — **ves·ti·gial·ly** \-ē\ *adv*
vest·ing \ˈves-tiŋ\ *n* (1944) **:** the conveying to an employee of the inalienable right to share in a pension fund esp. in the event of termination of employment prior to the normal retirement age; *also* **:** the right so conveyed
vest·ment \ˈves(t)-mənt\ *n* [ME *vestement,* fr. MF, fr. L *vestimentum,* fr. *vestire* to clothe] (14c) **1 a :** an outer garment; *esp* **:** a robe of ceremony or office **b** *pl* **:** CLOTHING, GARB **2 :** a covering resembling a garment **3 :** one of the articles of the ceremonial attire and insignia worn by ecclesiastical officiants and assistants as indicative of their rank and appropriate to the rite being celebrated — **vest·men·tal** \ves(t)-ˈment-ᵊl\ *adj*

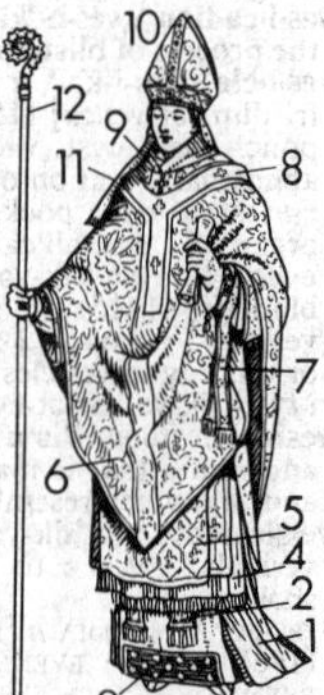

vestment 3 (of a 16th century archbishop): *1* alb, *2* stole, *3* apparel on alb, *4* tunicle, *5* dalmatic, *6* chasuble, *7* maniple, *8* pallium, *9* amice, *10* miter, *11* lappet, *12* crosier

vest–pocket *adj* (1848) **1 :** adapted to fit into the vest pocket ⟨a ~ edition of a book⟩ **2 :** of very small size or scope
vest–pocket park *n* (1966) **:** a very small urban park
ves·try \ˈves-trē\ *n, pl* **vestries** [ME *vestrie,* prob. modif. of MF *vestiarie,* fr. ML *vestiarium,* fr. L *vestire;* fr. its use as a robing room for the clergy] (14c) **1 a :** SACRISTY **b :** a room used for church meetings and classes **2 a :** the business meeting of an English parish **b :** an elective body in an Episcopal parish composed of the rector and a group of elected parishioners administering the temporal affairs of the parish
ves·try·man \-trē-mən\ *n* (1614) **:** a member of a vestry
¹**ves·ture** \ˈves(h)-chər\ *n* [ME, fr. MF, fr. *vestir* to clothe — more at VEST] (14c) **1 a :** a covering garment (as a robe or vestment) **b :** CLOTHING, APPAREL **2 :** something that covers like a garment
²**vesture** *vt* **ves·tured; ves·tur·ing** (1555) **:** to cover with vesture **:** CLOTHE
ve·su·vi·an \və-ˈsü-vē-ən\ *n* (1673) **1** [G, fr. *Vesuv* Vesuvius, volcano in Italy] **:** IDOCRASE **2** [*Vesuvian*] **:** a match used esp. formerly for lighting cigars
Ve·su·vi·an \və-ˈsü-vē-ən\ *adj* (1796) **1 :** of, relating to, or resembling the volcano Vesuvius **2 :** marked by sudden outbursts ⟨has a ~ temper, but quickly controls himself —Sidney Shalett⟩
ve·su·vi·an·ite \-vē-ə-ˌnīt\ *n* (ca. 1888) **:** IDOCRASE
¹**vet** \ˈvet\ *n* (1862) **:** VETERINARIAN, VETERINARY
²**vet** *vt* **vet·ted; vet·ting** (1891) **1 a :** to provide veterinary care for (an animal) or medical care for (a person) **b :** to subject (a person or animal) to a physical examination or checkup **2 :** to subject to expert appraisal or correction **:** EVALUATE
³**vet** *adj or n* (1848) **:** VETERAN
vetch \ˈvech\ *n* [ME *vecche,* fr. ONF *veche,* fr. L *vicia;* akin to OE *wicga* insect, L *vincire* to bind, OE *wīr* wire] (14c) **:** any of a genus (*Vicia*) of herbaceous twining leguminous plants including valuable fodder and soil-building plants
vetch·ling \-liŋ\ *n* (1578) **:** any of various small leguminous plants (genus *Lathyrus* and esp. *L. pratensis*)
vet·er·an \ˈvet-ə-rən, ˈve-trən\ *n* [L *veteranus,* fr. *veteranus,* adj., old, of long experience, fr. *veter-, vetus* old — more at WETHER] (1502) **1 a :** an old soldier of long service **b :** a former member of the armed forces **2 :** a person of long experience in some occupation or skill (as politics or the arts) — **veteran** *adj*
Veterans Day *n* (1952) **:** November 11 set aside in commemoration of the end of hostilities in 1918 and 1945 and observed as a legal holiday in the U.S. to honor the veterans of the armed forces
veterans' preference *n* (ca. 1941) **:** preferential treatment given qualified veterans of the U.S. armed forces under federal or state law; *specif* **:** special consideration (as by allowance of points) on a civil service examination
vet·er·i·nar·i·an \ˌvet-ə-rən-ˈer-ē-ən, ˌve-trən-, ˌvet-ᵊn-\ *n* (1646) **:** one qualified and authorized to treat diseases and injuries of animals
¹**vet·er·i·nary** \ˈvet-ə-rən-ˌer-ē, ˈve-trən-, ˈvet-ᵊn-\ *adj* [L *veterinarius* of beasts of burden, fr. *veterinae* beasts of burden, fr. fem. pl. of *veterinus* of beasts of burden; akin to L *veter-, vetus* old] (1790) **:** of, relating to, or being the science and art of prevention, cure, or alleviation of disease and injury in animals and esp. domestic animals
²**veterinary** *n, pl* **-nar·ies** (1861) **:** VETERINARIAN
veterinary surgeon *n, Brit* (ca. 1802) **:** VETERINARIAN
vet·i·ver \ˈvet-ə-vər\ *n* [F *vétiver,* fr. Tamil *veṭṭivēr*] (1846) **:** an East Indian grass (*Vetiveria zizanioides*) cultivated in warm regions esp. for its fragrant roots which are used for making mats and screens and in perfumes; *also* **:** its root
¹**ve·to** \ˈvēt-(ˌ)ō\ *n, pl* **vetoes** [L, I forbid, fr. *vetare* to forbid] (1629) **1 :** an authoritative prohibition **:** INTERDICTION **2 a :** a power of one department or branch of a government to forbid or prohibit finally or provisionally the carrying out of projects attempted by another department; *esp* **:** a power vested in a chief executive to prevent permanently or temporarily the enactment of measures passed by a legislature **b** (1) **:** the exercise of such authority (2) **:** a message communicating the reasons of an executive and esp. the president of the U.S. for vetoing a proposed law
²**veto** *vt* (1706) **:** to refuse to admit or approve **:** PROHIBIT; *also* **:** to refuse assent to (a legislative bill) so as to prevent enactment or cause reconsideration — **ve·to·er** \-ˌō(-ə)r\ *n*
ve·to–proof \-ˌprüf\ *adj* (1972) **:** having enough potential votes to be enacted over a veto or to override vetoes consistently ⟨a ~ bill⟩
vex \ˈveks\ *vt* **vexed** *also* **vext; vex·ing** [ME *vexen,* fr. MF *vexer,* fr. L *vexare* to agitate, trouble, vex] (15c) **1 a :** to bring trouble, distress, or agitation to ⟨~*ed* by a restless desire for change⟩ **b :** to bring physical distress to ⟨a headache ~*ed* him all morning⟩ **c :** to irritate or annoy by petty provocations **:** HARASS ⟨~*ed* by the children⟩ **d :** PUZZLE, BAFFLE ⟨a problem to ~ the keenest wit⟩ **2 :** to shake or toss about ***syn*** see ANNOY
vex·a·tion \vek-ˈsā-shən\ *n* (15c) **1 :** the act of harassing or vexing **:** TROUBLING **2 :** the quality or state of being vexed **:** IRRITATION **3 :** a cause of trouble **:** AFFLICTION
vex·a·tious \-shəs\ *adj* (1534) **1 a :** causing vexation **:** DISTRESSING **b :** intended to harass **2 :** full of disorder or stress **:** TROUBLED — **vex·a·tious·ly** *adv* — **vex·a·tious·ness** *n*
vexed \ˈvekst\ *adj* (1657) **:** debated or discussed at length ⟨a ~ question⟩
vexed·ly \ˈvek-səd-lē, ˈveks-tlē\ *adv* (1748) **:** in a vexed manner
vex·il·lol·o·gy \ˌvek-sə-ˈläl-ə-jē\ *n* [L *vexillum;* perh. akin to L *velum* curtain, veil] (1959) **:** the study of flags — **vex·il·lo·log·ic** \(ˌ)vek-ˌsil-ə-ˈläj-ik\ *or* **vex·il·lo·log·i·cal** \-ˈläj-i-kəl\ *adj* — **vex·il·lol·o·gist** \ˌvek-sə-ˈläl-ə-jəst\ *n*
vex·il·lum \vek-ˈsil-əm\ *n, pl* **-la** \-ə\ [L] (1726) **1 :** a square flag of the ancient Roman cavalry **2 :** the web or vane of a feather
via \ˌvī-ə, ˌvē-ə\ *prep* [L, abl. of *via* way; akin to Gk *hiesthai* to hurry — more at VIM] (1779) **1 :** by way of **2 :** through the medium or agency of; *also* **:** by means of

vi·a·ble \'vī-ə-bəl\ *adj* [F, fr. MF, fr. *vie* life, fr. L *vita* — more at VITAL] (ca. 1828) **1 :** capable of living; *esp* **:** capable of surviving outside the mother's womb without artificial support ⟨the human fetus usually becomes ~ by the end of the seventh month⟩ **2 :** capable of growing or developing ⟨~ seeds⟩ ⟨~ eggs⟩ **3 a :** capable of working, functioning, or developing adequately ⟨~ alternatives⟩ **b :** capable of existence and development as an independent unit ⟨the colony is now a ~ state⟩ **c :** having a reasonable chance of succeeding ⟨a ~ candidate⟩ — **vi·a·bil·i·ty** \,vī-ə-'bil-ət-ē\ *n* — **vi·a·bly** \'vī-ə-blē\ *adv*

via·duct \'vī-ə-,dəkt\ *n* [L *via* way, road + E *-duct* (as in *aqueduct*)] (1816) **1 :** a bridge esp. when resting on a series of narrow reinforced concrete or masonry arches, having high supporting towers or piers, and carrying a road or railroad over an obstruction (as a valley or highway) **2 :** a steel bridge made up of short spans carried on high steel towers

vi·al \'vī(-ə)l\ *n* [ME *fiole, viole,* fr. MF *fiole,* fr. OProv *fiola,* fr. L *phiala* — more at PHIAL] (14c) **:** a small closed or closable vessel esp. for liquids

via me·dia \,vī-ə-'mēd-ē-ə; ,vē-ə-'mäd-ē-ə, -'med-\ *n* [L] (1834) **:** a middle way

vi·and \'vī-ənd\ *n* [ME, fr. MF *viande,* fr. ML *vivanda* food, alter. of L *vivenda,* neut. pl. of *vivendus,* gerundive of *vivere* to live — more at QUICK] (15c) **1 :** an item of food; *esp* **:** a choice or tasty dish **2** *pl* **:** PROVISIONS, FOOD

vi·at·i·cum \vī-'at-i-kəm, vē-\ *n, pl* **-cums** *or* **-ca** \-kə\ [L — more at VOYAGE] (1562) **1 :** the Christian Eucharist given to a person in danger of death **2 a :** an allowance (as of transportation or supplies and money) for traveling expenses **b :** provisions for a journey

vibe \'vīb\ *n* (ca. 1967) **:** VIBRATION 4 ⟨seems to be in on every conversation, every deal, every ~ that is winging through the room —Albert Goldman⟩ — usu. used in pl. ⟨the good guy is someone who radiates good ~*s* . . . to others —Franklin Chu⟩

vibes \'vībz\ *n pl* (1940) **:** VIBRAPHONE — **vib·ist** \'vī-bəst\ *n*

vi·bra·harp \'vī-brə-,härp\ *n* [fr. *Vibra-Harp,* a trademark] (1927) **:** VIBRAPHONE — **vi·bra·harp·ist** \-,här-pəst\ *n*

vi·brance \'vī-brən(t)s\ *n* (1921) **:** VIBRANCY

vi·bran·cy \'vī-brən-sē\ *n* (ca. 1895) **:** the quality or state of being vibrant

vi·brant \-brənt\ *adj* (1550) **1 a** (1) **:** oscillating or pulsating rapidly (2) **:** pulsating with life, vigor, or activity ⟨a ~ personality⟩ **b** (1) **:** readily set in vibration (2) **:** RESPONSIVE, SENSITIVE **2 :** sounding as a result of vibration **:** RESONANT ⟨a ~ voice⟩ **3 :** BRIGHT 4 ⟨a ~ orange⟩ — **vi·brant·ly** *adv*

vi·bra·phone \'vī-brə-,fōn\ *n* [L *vibrare* + ISV *-phone*] (ca. 1926) **:** a percussion instrument resembling the xylophone but having metal bars and motor-driven resonators for sustaining the tone and producing a vibrato — **vi·bra·phon·ist** \-,fō-nəst\ *n*

vi·brate \'vī-,brāt, *esp Brit* vī-'\ *vb* **vi·brat·ed; vi·brat·ing** [L *vibratus,* pp. of *vibrare* to shake, vibrate — more at WIPE] *vt* (1616) **1 :** to swing or move to and fro **2 :** to emit with or as if with a vibratory motion **3 :** to mark or measure by oscillation ⟨a pendulum *vibrating* seconds⟩ **4 :** to set in vibration ~ *vi* **1 a :** to move to and fro or from side to side **:** OSCILLATE **b :** FLUCTUATE, VACILLATE ⟨~ between two choices⟩ **2 :** to have an effect as or as if of vibration ⟨music, when soft voices die, ~*s* in the memory —P. B. Shelley⟩ **3 :** to be in a state of vibration **:** QUIVER **4 :** to respond sympathetically **:** THRILL ⟨~ to the opportunity⟩ ***syn*** see SWING

vi·bra·tile \'vī-brət-ᵊl, -brə-,tīl\ *adj* (ca. 1826) **1 :** characterized by vibration **2 :** adapted to or used in vibratory motion ⟨the ~ organs of insects⟩

vi·bra·tion \vī-'brā-shən\ *n* [L *vibration-, vibratio,* fr. *vibratus,* pp.] (1655) **1 a :** a periodic motion of the particles of an elastic body or medium in alternately opposite directions from the position of equilibrium when that equilibrium has been disturbed (as when a stretched cord produces musical tones or particles of air transmit sounds to the ear) **b :** the action of vibrating **:** the state of being vibrated or in vibratory motion: as (1) **:** OSCILLATION (2) **:** a quivering or trembling motion **:** QUIVER **2 :** an instance of vibration **3 :** vacillation in opinion or action **:** WAVERING **4 a :** a characteristic emanation, aura, or spirit that infuses or vitalizes someone or something and that can be instinctively sensed or experienced — often used in pl. **b :** a distinctive usu. emotional atmosphere capable of being sensed — usu. used in pl. — **vi·bra·tion·al** \-shnəl, -shən-ᵊl\ *adj* — **vi·bra·tion·less** \-shən-ləs\ *adj*

vi·bra·to \vi-'brät-(,)ō, vī-\ *n, pl* **-tos** [It, fr. pp. of *vibrare* to vibrate, fr. L] (ca. 1876) **:** a slightly tremulous effect imparted to vocal or instrumental tone for added warmth and expressiveness by slight and rapid variations in pitch

vi·bra·tor \'vī-,brāt-ər\ *n* (1862) **1 :** one that vibrates or causes vibration: as **a :** a vibrating electrical apparatus used in massage or for sexual stimulation **b :** a vibrating device (as in an electric bell or buzzer) **2 :** an electromagnetic device that converts low direct current to pulsating direct current or alternating current

vi·bra·to·ry \'vī-brə-,tōr-ē, -,tȯr-\ *adj* (1728) **1 :** consisting in, capable of, or causing vibration or oscillation **2 :** characterized by vibration

vib·rio \'vib-rē-,ō\ *n, pl* **-rios** [NL, *Vibrion-, Vibrio,* fr. L *vibrare* to vibrate] (ca. 1864) **:** any of a genus (*Vibrio*) of short rigid motile bacteria typically shaped like a comma or an S — **vib·ri·on·ic** \,vib-rē-'än-ik\ *adj*

vib·ri·on \'vib-rē-,än\ *n* [NL *Vibrion-, Vibrio*] (1882) **:** VIBRIO; *also* **:** a motile bacterium

vib·ri·o·sis \,vib-rē-'ō-səs\ *n, pl* **-o·ses** \-,sēz\ [NL, fr. *Vibrio*] (1950) **:** abortion in sheep and cattle caused by a bacterium (*Campylobacter fetus* syn. *Vibrio fetus*) that invades the uterine and placental capillaries, interferes with fetal nutrition, and causes the death of the developing fetus

vi·bris·sa \vī-'bris-ə, və-\ *n, pl* **vi·bris·sae** \vī-'bris-(,)ē; və-'bris-(,)ē, -,ī\ [L; akin to L *vibrare*] (ca. 1693) **1 :** one of the stiff hairs that are located esp. about the nostrils or on other parts of the face in many mammals and that often serve as tactile organs **2 :** one of the bristly feathers near the mouth of many and esp. insectivorous birds that may help to prevent the escape of insects

vi·bur·num \vī-'bər-nəm\ *n* [NL, fr. L, a viburnum] (ca. 1731) **:** any of a genus (*Viburnum*) of widely distributed shrubs or trees of the honeysuckle family with simple leaves and white or rarely pink cymose flowers

vic·ar \'vik-ər\ *n* [ME, fr. L *vicarius,* fr. *vicarius* vicarious] (14c) **1 :** one serving as a substitute or agent; *specif* **:** an administrative deputy **2 :** an ecclesiastical agent: as **a :** a Church of England incumbent receiving a stipend but not the tithes of a parish **b :** a member of the Episcopal clergy or laity who has charge of a mission or chapel **c :** a member of the clergy who exercises a broad pastoral responsibility as the representative of a prelate — **vic·ar·ship** \-,ship\ *n*

vic·ar·age \'vik-(ə-)rij\ *n* (15c) **1 :** the benefice of a vicar **2 :** the house of a vicar **3 :** VICARIATE 1

vicar apostolic *n, pl* **vicars apostolic** (1766) **:** a Roman Catholic titular bishop who administers a territory not organized as a diocese

vic·ar·ate \'vik-ə-rət, -,rāt\ *n* (1883) **:** VICARIATE

vicar–general *n, pl* **vicars–general** (14c) **:** an administrative deputy of a Roman Catholic or Anglican bishop or of the head of a religious order

vi·car·i·al \vī-'ker-ē-əl, və-, -'kar-\ *adj* [L *vicarius*] (1617) **1 :** VICARIOUS 1 **2 :** of or relating to a vicar

vi·car·i·ate \-ē-ət\ *n* [ML *vicariatus,* fr. L *vicarius* vicar] (1610) **1 :** the office, jurisdiction, or tenure of a vicar **2 :** the office or district of a governmental administrative deputy

vi·car·i·ous \vī-'ker-ē-əs, və-, -'kar-\ *adj* [L *vicarius,* fr. *vicis* change, alternation, stead — more at WEEK] (1637) **1 a :** serving instead of someone or something else ⟨~ elements in a mineral⟩ **b :** that has been delegated ⟨~ authority⟩ **2 :** performed or suffered by one person as a substitute for another or to the benefit or advantage of another **:** SUBSTITUTIONARY ⟨a ~ sacrifice⟩ **3 :** experienced or realized through imaginative or sympathetic participation in the experience of another **4 :** occurring in an unexpected or abnormal part of the body instead of the usual one ⟨bleeding from the gums sometimes occurs in the absence of the normal discharge from the uterus in ~ menstruation⟩ — **vi·car·i·ous·ly** *adv* — **vi·car·i·ous·ness** *n*

Vicar of Christ (1570) **:** the Roman Catholic pope

¹vice \'vīs\ *n* [ME, fr. OF, fr. L *vitium* fault, vice] (13c) **1 a :** moral depravity or corruption **:** WICKEDNESS **b :** a moral fault or failing **c :** a habitual and usu. trivial defect or shortcoming **:** FOIBLE ⟨suffered from the ~ of curiosity⟩ **2 :** BLEMISH, DEFECT **3 :** a physical imperfection, deformity, or taint **4 a** *often cap* **:** a character representing one of the vices in an English morality play **b :** BUFFOON, JESTER **5 :** an abnormal behavior pattern in a domestic animal detrimental to its health or usefulness **6 :** sexual immorality; *esp* **:** PROSTITUTION ***syn*** see FAULT, OFFENSE

²vice *chiefly Brit var of* VISE

³vi·ce \'vī-sē\ *prep* [L, abl. of *vicis* change, alternation, stead — more at WEEK] (1770) **:** in the place of **:** SUCCEEDING

vice- \(')vīs, ,vīs\ *prefix* [ME *vis-, vice-,* fr. MF, fr. LL *vice-,* fr. L *vice,* abl. of *vicis*] **:** one that takes the place of ⟨*vice*-chancellor⟩

vice admiral *n* [MF *visamiral,* fr. *vis-* vice- + *amiral* admiral] (1520) **:** a commissioned officer in the navy or coast guard who ranks above a rear admiral and whose insignia is three stars

vice–chan·cel·lor \(')vīs-'chan(t)-s(ə-)lər\ *n* [ME *vichauncellor,* fr. MF *vischancelier,* fr. *vis-* + *chancelier* chancellor] (15c) **1 :** an officer ranking next below a chancellor and serving as deputy to the chancellor **2 :** chief administrative officer in a British university **3 :** a judge appointed to act for or to assist a chancellor

vice–con·sul \-'kän(t)-səl\ *n* (1559) **:** a consular officer subordinate to a consul general or to a consul

vice·ge·ren·cy \-'jir-ən-sē\ *n, pl* **-cies** (1596) **:** the office or jurisdiction of a vicegerent

vice·ge·rent \-'jir-ənt\ *n* [ML *vicegerent-, vicegerens,* fr. LL *vice-* + L *gerent-, gerens,* prp. of *gerere* to carry, carry on — more at CAST] (1536) **:** an administrative deputy of a king or magistrate

vi·cen·ni·al \vī-'sen-ē-əl\ *adj* [LL *vicennium* period of 20 years, fr. L *vicies* 20 times + *annus* year; akin to L *viginti* twenty — more at VIGESIMAL, ANNUAL] (ca. 1890) **:** occurring once every 20 years

vice presidency *n* (1804) **:** the office of vice president

vice president *n* (1574) **1 :** an officer next in rank to a president and usu. empowered to serve as president in that officer's absence or disability **2 :** any of several officers serving as a president's deputies in charge of particular locations or functions — **vice presidential** *adj*

vice·re·gal \(')vīs-'rē-gəl\ *adj* (1839) **:** of or relating to a viceroy or viceroyalty — **vice·re·gal·ly** \-gə-lē\ *adv*

vice–re·gent \-'rē-jənt\ *n* (1556) **:** a regent's deputy

vice·reine \'vīs-,rān\ *n* [F, fr. *vice-* + *reine* queen, fr. L *regina,* fem. of *reg-, rex* king — more at ROYAL] (1823) **1 :** the wife of a viceroy **2 :** a woman viceroy

vice·roy \'vīs-,rȯi\ *n* [MF *vice-roi,* fr. *vice-* + *roi* king, fr. L *reg-, rex* — more at ROYAL] (1524) **1 :** the governor of a country or province who rules as the representative of his king or sovereign **2 :** a showy American nymphalid butterfly (*Limenitis archippus*) closely mimicking the monarch in coloration but smaller

vice·roy·al·ty \'vīs-,rȯi(-ə)l-tē, vīs-'\ *n* (1703) **:** the office, jurisdiction, or term of service of a viceroy

vice·roy·ship \'vīs-,rȯi-,ship\ *n* (1609) **:** VICEROYALTY

vice squad *n* (1947) **:** a police squad charged with enforcement of laws concerning gambling, pornography, prostitution, and the illegal use of liquor and narcotics

vice ver·sa \,vī-si-'vər-sə, (')vīs-'vər-\ *adv* [L] (1601) **:** with the order changed **:** with the relations reversed **:** CONVERSELY

vi·chys·soise \,vish-ē-'swäz, ,vē-shē-\ *n* [F, fr. fem. of *vichyssois* of Vichy, fr. *Vichy,* France] (1917) **:** a soup made of pureed leeks or onions and potatoes, cream, and chicken stock and usu. served cold

Vi·chy water \'vish-ē-\ *n* (ca. 1858) **:** a natural sparkling mineral water from Vichy, France; *also* **:** an imitation of or substitute for this

vic·i·nage \'vis-ᵊn-ij, 'vis-nij\ *n* [ME *vesinage,* fr. MF, fr. *vesin* neighboring, fr. L *vicinus*] (14c) **:** a neighboring or surrounding district **:** VICINITY

vic·i·nal \'vis-ᵊn-əl, 'vis-nəl\ *adj* [L *vicinalis,* fr. *vicinus* neighbor, fr. *vicinus,* adj., neighboring] (ca. 1623) **1 :** of or relating to a limited district

\ə\ abut \ᵊ\ kitten, F table \ər\ further \a\ ash \ā\ ace \ä\ cot, cart \au̇\ out \ch\ chin \e\ bet \ē\ easy \g\ go \i\ hit \ī\ ice \j\ job \ŋ\ sing \ō\ go \ȯ\ law \ȯi\ boy \th\ thin \th\ the \ü\ loot \u̇\ foot \y\ yet \zh\ vision \à, k, ⁿ, œ, œ̄, ue, ue̅, ʸ\ *see* Guide to Pronunciation

: LOCAL **2** : of, relating to, or being subordinate forms or faces on a crystal which sometimes take the place of fundamental ones **3** : of, relating to, or substituted in adjacent sites in a molecule ⟨a ~ disulfide group⟩

vi·cin·i·ty \və-ˈsin-ət-ē\ *n, pl* **-ties** [MF *vicinité,* fr. L *vicinitat-, vicinitas,* fr. *vicinus* neighboring, fr. *vicus* row of houses, village; akin to Goth *weihs* village, Gk *oikos, oikia* house] (1560) **1** : the quality or state of being near : PROXIMITY **2** : a surrounding area or district : NEIGHBORHOOD **3** : NEIGHBORHOOD 3b

vi·cious \ˈvish-əs\ *adj* [ME, fr. MF *vicieus,* fr. L *vitiosus* full of faults, corrupt, fr. *vitium* vice] (14c) **1** : having the nature or quality of vice or immorality : DEPRAVED **2** : DEFECTIVE, FAULTY; *also* : INVALID **3** : IMPURE, NOXIOUS **4 a** : dangerously aggressive : SAVAGE ⟨a ~ dog⟩ **b** : marked by violence or ferocity : FIERCE ⟨a ~ fight⟩ **5** : MALICIOUS, SPITEFUL ⟨~ gossip⟩ **6** : worsened by internal causes that reciprocally augment each other ⟨a ~ wage-price spiral⟩ — **vi·cious·ly** *adv* — **vi·cious·ness** *n*

syn VICIOUS, VILLAINOUS, INIQUITOUS, NEFARIOUS, CORRUPT, DEGENERATE mean highly reprehensible or offensive in character, nature, or conduct. VICIOUS may directly oppose *virtuous* in implying moral depravity, or may connote malignancy, cruelty, or destructive violence; VILLAINOUS applies to any evil, depraved, or vile conduct or characteristic; INIQUITOUS implies absence of all signs of justice or fairness; NEFARIOUS suggests flagrant breaching of time-honored laws and traditions of conduct; CORRUPT stresses a loss of moral integrity or probity causing betrayal of principle or sworn obligations; DEGENERATE suggests having sunk to an esp. vicious or enervated condition.

vicious circle *n* (ca. 1792) **1** : a chain of events in which the response to one difficulty creates a new problem that aggravates the original difficulty **2** : an argument or definition that assumes something that is to be proved or defined

vi·cis·si·tude \və-ˈsis-ə-ˌt(y)üd, vī-\ *n* [MF, fr. L *vicissitudo,* fr. *vicissim* in turn, fr. *vicis* change, alternation — more at WEEK] (1570) **1 a** : the quality or state of being changeable : MUTABILITY **b** : natural change or mutation visible in nature or in human affairs **2 a** : a favorable or unfavorable event or situation that occurs by chance : a fluctuation of state or condition ⟨the ~*s* of daily life⟩ **b** : a difficulty or hardship attendant on a way of life, a career, or a course of action and usu. beyond one's control **c** : alternating change : SUCCESSION

vi·cis·si·tu·di·nous \və-ˌsis-ə-ˈt(y)üd-nəs, (ˌ)vī-, -ᵊn-əs\ *adj* [L *vicissitudin-, vicissitudo*] (ca. 1846) : marked by or filled with vicissitudes

vic·tim \ˈvik-təm\ *n* [L *victima;* akin to OHG *wīh* holy, Skt *vinakti* he sets apart] (15c) **1** : a living being sacrificed to a deity or in the performance of a religious rite **2** : one that is acted on and usu. adversely affected by a force or agent ⟨the schools are ~*s* of the social system⟩: as **a** (1) : one that is injured, destroyed, or sacrificed under any of various conditions ⟨a ~ of cancer⟩ ⟨a ~ of the auto crash⟩ (2) : one that is subjected to oppression, hardship, or mistreatment ⟨a frequent ~ of severe political attacks⟩ **b** : one that is tricked or duped ⟨a con man's ~⟩

vic·tim·ize \ˈvik-tə-ˌmīz\ *vt* **-ized; -iz·ing** (1830) **1** : to make a victim of **2** : to subject to deception or fraud : CHEAT — **vic·tim·iza·tion** \ˌvik-tə-mə-ˈzā-shən\ *n* — **vic·tim·iz·er** \ˈvik-tə-ˌmī-zər\ *n*

vic·tim·less \ˈvik-təm-ləs\ *adj* (1971) : having no victim ⟨~ crimes⟩

vic·tor \ˈvik-tər\ *n* [ME, fr. L, fr. *victus,* pp. of *vincere* to conquer, win; akin to OE *wīgan* to fight, OSlav *věkŭ* strength] (14c) : one that defeats an enemy or opponent : WINNER — **victor** *adj*

Victor (ca. 1942) — a communications code word for the letter *v*

vic·to·ria \vik-ˈtōr-ē-ə, -ˈtȯr-\ *n* [Queen *Victoria*] (ca. 1844) : a low four-wheeled pleasure carriage for two with a calash top and a raised seat in front for the driver

Victoria Cross *n* (1856) : a bronze Maltese cross awarded to members of the British armed services for acts of remarkable valor

Victoria Day *n* [Queen *Victoria*] (1901) **1** : formerly May 24 and now the Monday preceding May 25 observed in Canada as a legal holiday **2** : COMMONWEALTH DAY

[1]**Vic·to·ri·an** \vik-ˈtōr-ē-ən, -ˈtȯr-\ *adj* (1875) **1** : of, relating to, or characteristic of the reign of Queen Victoria of England or the art, letters, or tastes of her time **2** : typical of the moral standards, attitudes, or conduct of the age of Victoria esp. when considered stuffy or hypocritical

[2]**Victorian** *n* (1876) : a person living during Queen Victoria's reign; *esp* : a representative figure of that time

Vic·to·ri·ana \(ˌ)vik-ˌtōr-ē-ˈan-ə, -ˌtȯr-, -ˈän-, -ˈān-\ *n* [Queen *Victoria* + E *-ana*] (1940) : materials concerning or characteristic of the Victorian age; *also* : a collection of such materials

Vic·to·ri·an·ism \vik-ˈtōr-ē-ə-ˌniz-əm, -ˈtȯr-\ *n* (1905) **1** : a typical instance or product of Victorian expression, taste, or conduct **2** : the quality or state of being Victorian esp. in taste or conduct

vic·to·ri·ous \vik-ˈtōr-ē-əs, -ˈtȯr-\ *adj* (14c) **1 a** : having won a victory **b** : of, relating to, or characteristic of victory **2** : evincing moral harmony or a sense of fulfillment : FULFILLED — **vic·to·ri·ous·ly** *adv* — **vic·to·ri·ous·ness** *n*

vic·to·ry \ˈvik-t(ə-)rē\ *n, pl* **-ries** [ME, fr. MF *victorie,* fr. L *victoria,* fr. fem. of (assumed) L *victorius* of winning or conquest, fr. L *victus,* pp. of *vincere*] (14c) **1** : the overcoming of an enemy or antagonist **2** : achievement of mastery or success in a struggle or endeavor against odds or difficulties

[1]**vict·ual** \ˈvit-ᵊl\ *n* [alter. of ME *vitaille,* fr. MF, fr. LL *victualia,* pl., provisions, victuals, fr. neut. pl. of *victualis* of nourishment, fr. L *victus* nourishment, fr. *victus,* pp. of *vivere* to live — more at QUICK] (14c) **1** : food usable by man **2** *pl* : supplies of food : PROVISIONS

[2]**victual** *vb* **-ualed** *or* **-ualled; -ual·ing** *or* **-ual·ling** *vt* (14c) : to supply with food ~ *vi* **1** : EAT **2** : to lay in provisions

vict·ual·ler *or* **vict·ual·er** \ˈvit-ᵊl-ər\ *n* (14c) **1** : the keeper of a restaurant or tavern **2** : one that provisions an army, a navy, or a ship with food **3** : an army or navy provision ship

vi·cu·ña *or* **vi·cu·na** \vī-ˈkün-yə, vi-; vī-ˈk(y)ü-nə, və-\ *n* [Sp *vicuña,* fr. Quechua *wikúña*] (1593) **1** : a wild ruminant (*Lama vicugna*) of the Andes from Ecuador to Bolivia that is related to the domesticated llama and alpaca **2 a** : the wool from the vicuña's fine lustrous undercoat **b** : a fabric made of vicuña wool; *also* : a sheep's wool imitation of this

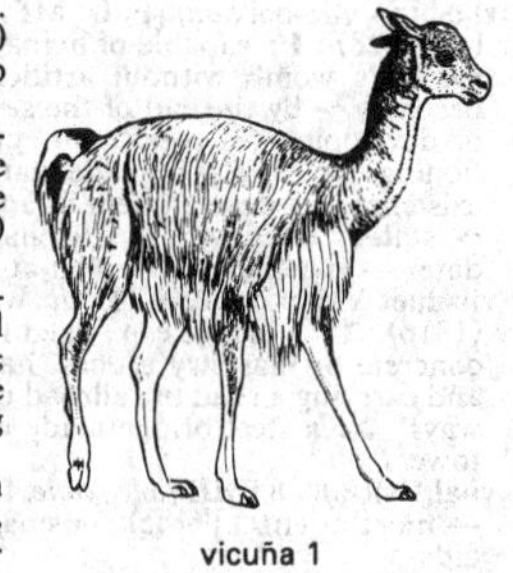

vicuña 1

vi·de \ˈvīd-ē, ˈvē-ˌdā\ *vb imper* [L, fr. *vidēre* to see — more at WIT] (1565) : SEE — used to direct a reader to another item

vi·de·li·cet \və-ˈdel-ə-ˌset, vī-; vi-ˈdā-li-ˌket\ *adv* [ME, fr. L, fr. *vidēre* to see + *licet* it is permitted, fr. *licēre* to be permitted — more at LICENSE] (15c) : that is to say : NAMELY

[1]**vid·eo** \ˈvid-ē-ˌō\ *n* (1937) **1** : TELEVISION ⟨~ drama⟩; *also* : the visual portion of television **2** : VIDEOTAPE; *esp* : a recording of a motion picture or television program for playing through a television set

[2]**video** *adj* [L *vidēre* to see + E *-o* (as in *audio*)] (1938) **1** : being, relating to, or used in the transmission or reception of the television image ⟨~ channel⟩ — compare AUDIO **2** : being, relating to, or involving images on a television screen or computer display ⟨~ terminal⟩

vid·eo·cas·sette \ˌvid-ē-ō-kə-ˈset, -ka-\ *n* (1970) **1** : a case containing videotape for use with a VCR **2** : a recording (as of a movie) on a videocassette

videocassette recorder *n* (ca. 1971) : VCR

vid·eo·con·fer·ence \-ˌkän-f(ə-)rən(t)s, -fərn(t)s\ *n* (1977) : a teleconference conducted by television — **vid·eo·con·fer·enc·ing** *n*

vid·eo·disc *or* **vid·eo·disk** \-ˌdisk\ *n* [*video* + *disc* or *disk*] (1967) : a disc similar in appearance and use to a phonograph record on which programs have been recorded for playback on a television set; *also* : OPTICAL DISC **2** : a recording (as of a movie) on a videodisc

video game *n* (1973) : an electronic game played by means of images on a video screen

vid·eo·land \-ˌland\ *n* (1967) : television as a medium or industry

vid·eo·phone \ˈvid-ē-ə-ˌfōn\ *n* (ca. 1950) : a telephone equipped for transmission of video as well as audio signals so that users can see each other

[1]**vid·eo·tape** \ˈvid-ē-ō-ˌtāp\ *n* (1953) : a recording of visual images and sound (as of a television production) made on magnetic tape; *also* : the magnetic tape used for such a recording

[2]**videotape** *vt* (1958) : to make a videotape of ⟨~ a show⟩ ⟨~ the president's speech⟩

videotape recorder *n* (1953) : a device for recording and playing back videotapes — called also *video recorder*

vid·eo·tex \-ˌteks\ *also* **vid·eo·text** \-ˌtekst\ *n* [*video* + *text*] (1978) : an interactive electronic system in which data is transmitted from a computer network over telephone or cable-television lines and is displayed on a subscriber's television or computer terminal screen

video vé·ri·té \-ˌver-ə-ˈtā\ *n* (1969) : the filming or videotaping of a television program (as a documentary) so as to convey candid realism

vi·dette *var of* VEDETTE

vid·icon \ˈvid-i-ˌkän\ *n, often cap* [*video* + *iconoscope*] (1950) : a camera tube using the principle of photoconductivity

vi·du·ity \vid-ˈ(y)ü-ət-ē\ *n* [ME (Sc) *viduite,* fr. MF *viduite,* fr. L *viduitat-, viduitas,* fr. *vidua* widow — more at WIDOW] (15c) : WIDOWHOOD

vie \ˈvī\ *vb* **vied; vy·ing** \ˈvī-iŋ\ [modif. of MF *envier* to invite, challenge, wager, fr. L *invitare* to invite] *vi* (1577) : to strive for superiority : CONTEND, COMPETE ~ *vt, archaic* : WAGER, HAZARD; *also* : to exchange in rivalry : MATCH ***syn*** see RIVAL — **vi·er** \ˈvī(-ə)r\ *n*

Vi·en·na sausage \vē-ˌen-ə-\ *n* [*Vienna,* Austria] (ca. 1902) : a short slender frankfurter

Viet·cong \vē-ˈet-ˈkäŋ, vyet-, ˌvē-ət-, vēt-, -ˈkȯŋ\ *n, pl* **Vietcong** [Vietnamese *Việt Nam cộng-sản* Vietnam communists] (1957) : a guerrilla member of the Vietnamese communist movement

Viet·minh \-ˈmin\ *n, pl* **Vietminh** [Vietnamese *Việt Nam Độc-Lập Đồng-Minh* League for the Independence of Vietnam] (1945) : an adherent of the Vietnamese communist movement from 1941 to 1951

Viet·nam·ese \vē-ˌet-nə-ˈmēz, ˌvyet-, ˌvē-ət-, ˌvēt-, -na-, -nä-, -ˈmēs\ *n, pl* **Vietnamese** (1947) **1** : a native or inhabitant of Vietnam **2** : the language of the largest group in Vietnam and the official language of the country — **Vietnamese** *adj*

[1]**view** \ˈvyü\ *n* [ME *vewe,* fr. MF *veue, vue,* fr. OF, fr. *veeir, voir* to see, fr. L *vidēre* — more at WIT] (15c) **1** : the act of seeing or examining : INSPECTION; *also* : SURVEY ⟨a ~ of English literature⟩ **2 a** : a mode or manner of looking at or regarding something **b** : an opinion or judgment colored by the feeling or bias of its holder ⟨in my ~ the conference has no chance of success⟩ **3** : SCENE, PROSPECT ⟨the lovely ~ from the balcony⟩ **4** : extent or range of vision : SIGHT ⟨tried to keep the ship in ~⟩ ⟨sat high in the bleachers to get a good ~⟩ **5** : something that is looked toward or kept in sight : OBJECT ⟨studied hard with a ~ to getting an A⟩ **6** : the foreseeable future ⟨no hope in ~⟩ **7** : a pictorial representation ***syn*** see OPINION — **in view of** : in regard to : in consideration of — **on view** : open to public inspection : on exhibition

[2]**view** *vt* (1523) **1** : to look at attentively : SCRUTINIZE, OBSERVE ⟨~ an exhibit⟩ ⟨~ the landscape⟩ **2 a** : SEE, WATCH ⟨~ a film⟩ **b** : to look on in a particular light : REGARD ⟨doesn't ~ himself as a rebel⟩ **3** : to survey or examine mentally : CONSIDER ⟨~ all sides of a question⟩ — **view·able** \-ə-bəl\ *adj*

view·data \ˈvyü-ˌdāt-ə *also* -ˌdat-\ *n* (1975) : VIDEOTEX

view·er \ˈvyü-ər\ *n* (15c) : one that views: as **a** : a person legally appointed to inspect and report on property **b** : an optical device used in viewing **c** : a person who watches television

view·er·ship \-ˌship\ *n* (1954) : a television audience esp. with respect to size or makeup

view·find·er \ˈvyü-ˌfīn-dər\ *n* (1889) : FINDER 3

view hal·loo \ˌvyü-hə-ˈlü\ *interj* (1761) — used in fox hunting on seeing a fox break cover

view·ing *n* (ca. 1548) : an act of seeing, watching, or taking a look; *esp* : an act of watching television

view·less \ˈvyü-ləs\ *adj* (1603) **1** : not perceivable : INVISIBLE **2** : affording no view **3** : expressing no views or opinions — **view·less·ly** *adv*

view·point \-ˌpȯint\ *n* (1855) : POINT OF VIEW, STANDPOINT

viewy \ˈvyü-ē\ *adj* (1848) **1 :** possessing visionary, impractical, or fantastic views **2 :** spectacular or arresting in appearance : SHOWY
vig \ˈvig\ *n* [by shortening] (1968) : VIGORISH
vi·ga \ˈvē-gə\ *n* [Sp, beam, rafter] (1844) : one of the heavy rafters and esp. a log supporting the roof in native Indian and Spanish architecture of the Southwest
vi·ges·i·mal \vī-ˈjes-ə-məl\ *adj* [L *vicesimus, vigesimus* twentieth; akin to L *viginti* twenty, Gk *eikosi*] (ca. 1656) : based on the number 20
vig·il \ˈvij-əl\ *n* [ME *vigile,* fr. OF, fr. LL & L; LL *vigilia* watch on the eve of a feast, fr. L, wakefulness, watch, fr. *vigil* awake, watchful; akin to L *vigēre* to be vigorous, *vegēre* to be active, rouse — more at WAKE] (13c) **1 a :** a watch formerly kept on the night before a religious feast with prayer or other devotions **b :** the day before a religious feast observed as a day of spiritual preparation **c :** evening or nocturnal devotions or prayers — usu. used in pl. **2 :** the act of keeping awake at times when sleep is customary; *also* **:** a period of wakefulness **3 :** an act or period of watching or surveillance : WATCH
vig·i·lance \ˈvij-ə-lən(t)s\ *n* (1570) : the quality or state of being vigilant
vigilance committee *n* (1835) : a committee of vigilantes
vig·i·lant \ˈvij-ə-lənt\ *adj* [ME, fr. MF, fr. L *vigilant-, vigilans,* fr. prp. of *vigilare* to keep watch, stay awake, fr. *vigil* awake] (15c) : alertly watchful esp. to avoid danger ***syn*** see WATCHFUL — **vig·i·lant·ly** *adv*
vig·i·lan·te \ˌvij-ə-ˈlant-ē\ *n* [Sp, watchman, guard, fr. *vigilante* vigilant, fr. L *vigilant-, vigilans*] (1865) : a member of a volunteer committee organized to suppress and punish crime summarily (as when the processes of law appear inadequate) — **vig·i·lan·tism** \-ˈlan-ˌtiz-əm\ *n*
vigil light *n* (ca. 1931) : a candle lighted devotionally (as in a Roman Catholic church) before a shrine or image — called also *vigil candle*
vi·gin·til·lion \ˌvī-jin-ˈtil-yən\ *n, often attrib* [L *viginti* twenty + E *-illion* (as in *million*) — more at VIGESIMAL] (ca. 1903) — see NUMBER table
vi·gne·ron \ˌvēn-yə-ˈrōn\ *n* [ME, fr. MF, fr. OF *vineron,* fr. *vine, vigne* vine, vineyard] (15c) : WINEGROWER
[1]**vi·gnette** \vin-ˈyet\ *n* [F, fr. MF *vignete,* fr. dim. of *vigne* vine — more at VINE] (15c) **1 :** a running ornament (as of vine leaves, tendrils, and grapes) put on or just before a title page or at the beginning or end of a chapter; *also* **:** a small decorative design or picture so placed **2 a :** a picture (as an engraving or photograph) that shades off gradually into the surrounding paper **b :** the pictorial part of a postage stamp design as distinguished from the frame and lettering **3 a :** a short descriptive literary sketch **b :** a brief incident or scene (as in a play or movie) — **vi·gnett·ist** \-ˈyet-əst\ *n*
[2]**vignette** *vt* **vi·gnett·ed; vi·gnett·ing** (ca. 1611) **1 :** to finish (as a photograph) in the manner of a vignette **2 :** to describe briefly — **vi·gnett·er** *n*
vig·or \ˈvig-ər\ *n* [ME, fr. MF *vigor,* fr. L, fr. *vigēre* to be vigorous] (14c) **1 :** active bodily or mental strength or force **2 :** active healthy well-balanced growth esp. of plants **3 :** intensity of action or effect : FORCE **4 :** effective legal status
vig·o·rish \ˈvig-ə-rish\ *n* [prob. fr. Yiddish, fr. Russ *vyigrysh* winnings, profit] (ca. 1943) **1 :** a charge taken (as by a bookie or a gambling house) on bets; *also* **:** the degree of such a charge ⟨a ~ of five percent⟩ **2 :** interest paid to a moneylender
vi·go·ro·so \ˌvig-ə-ˈrō-(ˌ)sō, ˌvē-gə-, -(ˌ)zō\ *adj or adv* [It, lit., vigorous, fr. MF *vigorous*] (ca. 1724) : energetic in style — used as a direction in music
vig·or·ous \ˈvig-(ə-)rəs\ *adj* [ME, fr. MF, fr. OF, fr. *vigor*] (14c) **1 :** possessing vigor : full of physical or mental strength or active force : STRONG ⟨a ~ youth⟩ ⟨a ~ plant⟩ **2 :** done with vigor : carried out forcefully and energetically ⟨~ exercises⟩ — **vig·or·ous·ly** *adv* — **vig·or·ous·ness** *n*
syn VIGOROUS, ENERGETIC, STRENUOUS, LUSTY, NERVOUS mean having great vitality and force. VIGOROUS further implies showing no signs of depletion or diminishing of freshness or robustness; ENERGETIC suggests a capacity for intense activity; STRENUOUS suggests a preference for coping with the arduous or the challenging; LUSTY implies exuberant energy and capacity for enjoyment; NERVOUS suggests esp. the forcibleness and sustained effectiveness resulting from mental vigor.
vig·our \ˈvig-ər\ *chiefly Brit var of* VIGOR
Vi·king \ˈvī-kiŋ\ *n* [ON *vīkingr*] (1807) **1 a :** one of the pirate Norsemen plundering the coasts of Europe in the 8th to 10th centuries **b** *not cap* **:** SEA ROVER **2 :** SCANDINAVIAN
vile \ˈvī(ə)l\ *adj* **vil·er** \ˈvī-lər\; **vil·est** \-ləst\ [ME, fr. OF *vil,* fr. L *vilis*] (13c) **1 a :** morally despicable or abhorrent ⟨nothing is so ~ as intellectual dishonesty⟩ **b :** physically repulsive : FOUL ⟨a ~ slum⟩ **2 :** of little worth or account : COMMON; *also* **:** MEAN **3 :** tending to degrade ⟨~ employments⟩ **4 :** disgustingly or utterly bad : OBNOXIOUS, CONTEMPTIBLE ⟨~ weather⟩ ⟨had a ~ temper⟩ ***syn*** see BASE — **vile·ly** \ˈvī(ə)l-lē\ *adv* — **vile·ness** *n*
vil·i·fi·ca·tion \ˌvil-ə-fə-ˈkā-shən\ *n* [ML *vilification-, vilificatio,* fr. LL *vilificatus,* pp. of *vilificare*] (1630) **1 :** the act of vilifying : ABUSE **2 :** an instance of vilifying : a defamatory utterance
vil·i·fy \ˈvil-ə-ˌfī\ *vt* **-fied; -fy·ing** [ME *vilifien,* fr. LL *vilificare,* fr. L *vilis* cheap, vile] (15c) **1 :** to lower in estimation or importance **2 :** to utter slanderous and abusive statements against : DEFAME ***syn*** see MALIGN — **vil·i·fi·er** \-ˌfī(-ə)r\ *n*
vil·i·pend \ˈvil-ə-ˌpend\ *vt* [ME *vilipenden,* fr. MF *vilipender,* fr. ML *vilipendere,* fr. L *vilis* + *pendere* to weigh, estimate — more at PENDANT] (15c) **1 :** to hold or treat as of little worth or account : CONTEMN **2 :** to express a low opinion of : DISPARAGE
vill \ˈvil\ *n* [AF, fr. OF *ville* village] (1596) **1 :** a division of a hundred : TOWNSHIP **2 :** VILLAGE
vil·la \ˈvil-ə\ *n* [It, fr. L; akin to L *vicus* row of houses — more at VICINITY] (1611) **1 :** a country estate **2 :** the rural or suburban residence of a wealthy person **3** *Brit* **:** a detached or semidetached urban residence with yard and garden space
vil·la·dom \ˈvil-əd-əm\ *n, Brit* (1880) : the world constituted by villas and their occupants
vil·lage \ˈvil-ij\ *n, often attrib* [ME, fr. MF, fr. OF, fr. *ville* farm, village, fr. L *villa*] (14c) **1 a :** a settlement usu. larger than a hamlet and smaller than a town **b :** an incorporated minor municipality **2 :** the residents of a village **3 :** something (as an aggregation of burrows or nests) suggesting a village **4 :** a territorial area having the status of a village esp. as a unit of local government
vil·lag·er \ˈvil-ij-ər\ *n* (ca. 1570) : an inhabitant of a village
vil·lage·ry \ˈvil-ij-(ə-)rē\ *n* (1590) : VILLAGES
vil·lain \ˈvil-ən\ *n* [ME *vilain, vilein,* fr. MF, fr. ML *villanus,* fr. L *villa*] (14c) **1 :** an uncouth person : BOOR **2 :** VILLEIN **3 :** a deliberate scoundrel or criminal **4 :** a scoundrel in a story or play **5 :** a person or thing blamed for a particular evil or difficulty ⟨automation as the ~ in job . . . displacement —M. H. Goldberg⟩
vil·lain·ess \-ə-nəs\ *n* (1586) : a woman who is a villain
vil·lain·ous \-ə-nəs\ *adj* (14c) **1 a :** befitting a villain (as in evil, depraved, or vile character) ⟨a ~ attack⟩ **b :** being or having the character of a villain : DEPRAVED ⟨the ~ foe⟩ **2 :** highly objectionable : WRETCHED ***syn*** see VICIOUS — **vil·lain·ous·ly** *adv* — **vil·lain·ous·ness** *n*
vil·lainy \-ə-nē\ *n, pl* **-lain·ies** (13c) **1 :** villainous conduct; *also* **:** a villainous act **2 :** the quality or state of being villainous : DEPRAVITY
vil·la·nel·la \ˌvil-ə-ˈnel-ə\ *n, pl* **-nel·le** \-ˈnel-ē\ [It, fr. *villano* villein, peasant, fr. ML *villanus*] (1597) **1 :** a 16th century Italian rustic part-song unaccompanied and in free form **2 :** an instrumental piece in the style of a rustic dance
vil·la·nelle \ˌvil-ə-ˈnel\ *n* [F, fr. It *villanella*] (1877) : a chiefly French verse form running on two rhymes and consisting typically of five tercets and a quatrain in which the first and third lines of the opening tercet recur alternately at the end of the other tercets and together as the last two lines of the quatrain
vil·lat·ic \vil-ˈat-ik\ *adj* [L *villaticus,* fr. *villa*] (1671) : RURAL
-ville \ˌvil, *esp Southern* -vəl\ *n suffix* [*-ville,* suffix occurring in names of towns, fr. F, fr. OF, fr. *ville* village] : place or category of a specified nature ⟨dulls*ville*⟩
vil·lein \ˈvil-ən, ˈvil-ˌān, vil-ˈān\ *n* [ME *vilain, vilein* — more at VILLAIN] (14c) **1 :** a free common villager or village peasant of any of the feudal classes lower in rank than the thane **2 :** a free peasant of a feudal class lower than a sokeman and higher than a cotter **3 :** an unfree peasant standing as the slave of his feudal lord but free in his legal relations with respect to all others
vil·len·age \ˈvil-ə-nij\ *n* [ME *vilenage,* fr. MF, fr. OF, fr. *vilein, vilain*] (14c) **1 :** tenure at the will of a feudal lord by villein services **2 :** the status of a villein
vil·li·form \ˈvil-ə-ˌfȯrm\ *adj* [ISV] (1849) : having the form or appearance of villi; *also* **:** resembling bristles or the pile of velvet ⟨a fish with ~ teeth⟩
vil·los·i·ty \vil-ˈäs-ət-ē\ *n, pl* **-ties** (1777) **1 :** the state of being villous **2 :** a villous patch or area
vil·lous \ˈvil-əs\ *adj* [ME, fr. L *villosus* hairy, shaggy, fr. *villus*] (15c) **1 :** covered or furnished with villi **2 :** having soft long hairs ⟨leaves ~ underneath⟩ — compare PUBESCENT
vil·lus \ˈvil-əs\ *n, pl* **vil·li** \ˈvil-ˌī, -(ˌ)ē\ [NL, fr. L, tuft of shaggy hair — more at VELVET] (ca. 1704) : a small slender often vascular process: as **a :** one of the minute finger-shaped processes of the mucous membrane of the small intestine that serve in the absorption of nutriment **b :** one of the branching processes of the surface of the chorion of the developing egg of most mammals that help to form the placenta
vim \ˈvim\ *n* [L, accus. of *vis* strength; akin to Gk *is* strength, *hiesthai* to hurry, OE *wāth* pursuit] (1843) : robust energy and enthusiasm
vi·na \ˈvē-nə\ *n* [Skt *vīṇā*] (1788) : a stringed instrument of India having usu. four strings on a long bamboo fingerboard with movable frets and a gourd resonator at each end
vi·na·ceous \vī-ˈnā-shəs, vin-ˈā-\ *adj* [L *vinaceus* of wine, fr. *vinum* wine — more at WINE] (1688) : of the color wine
vin·ai·grette \ˌvin-i-ˈgret\ *n* [F, fr. *vinaigre* vinegar] (1699) **1 :** a sauce made typically of oil and vinegar, onions, parsley, and herbs and used esp. on cold meats or fish — called also *vinaigrette dressing, vinaigrette sauce* **2 :** a small ornamental box or bottle with perforated top used for holding an aromatic preparation (as smelling salts)
vi·nal \ˈvī-ˌnal\ *n* [poly*vinyl al*cohol] (ca. 1939) : a synthetic textile fiber that is a long-chain polymer consisting largely of vinyl alcohol units
vin·blas·tine \(ˈ)vin-ˈblas-ˌtēn\ *n* [contr. of *vincaleukoblastine,* fr. *vinca* + *leukoblast* (developing leukocyte), fr. *leuk-* + *-blast*] (ca. 1962) : an alkaloid $C_{46}H_{58}N_4O_9$ from Madagascar periwinkle used esp. in the form of its sulfate to treat human neoplastic diseases
vin·ca \ˈviŋ-kə\ *n* [NL, short for L *pervinca* periwinkle] (ca. 1900) : [1]PERIWINKLE
Vin·cen·tian \vin-ˈsen-chən\ *n* (1854) : a member of the Roman Catholic Congregation of the Mission founded by St. Vincent de Paul in Paris, France, in 1625 and devoted to missions and seminaries — **Vincentian** *adj*
Vin·cent's angina \ˌvin(t)-sən(t)s-, (ˌ)vaⁿ-ˌsäⁿz-\ *n* [Jean Hyacinthe *Vincent* †1950 Fr. bacteriologist] (ca. 1903) : a contagious disease marked by ulceration of the mucous membrane of the mouth and adjacent parts and caused by a bacterium (*Fusobacterium fusiforme*) often in association with a spirochete (*Borrelia vincentii*) — called also *trench mouth*
Vincent's infection *n* (ca. 1922) : a bacterial infection of the respiratory tract and mouth marked by destructive ulceration esp. of the mucous membranes
vin·ci·ble \ˈvin(t)-sə-bəl\ *adj* [L *vincibilis,* fr. *vincere* to conquer — more at VICTOR] (1548) : capable of being overcome or subdued
vin·cris·tine \(ˈ)vin-ˈkris-ˌtēn\ *n* [*vinca* + L *crista* crest + E *-ine* — more at CREST] (ca. 1962) : an alkaloid $C_{46}H_{56}N_4O_{10}$ from Madagascar periwinkle used esp. in the form of its sulfate to treat some human neoplastic diseases (as leukemias)
vin·cu·lum \ˈviŋ-kyə-ləm\ *n, pl* **-lums** *or* **-la** \-lə\ [L, fr. *vincire* to bind — more at VETCH] (1661) **1 :** a unifying bond : LINK, TIE **2 :** a straight horizontal mark placed over two or more members of a compound mathematical expression and equivalent to parentheses or brackets about them (as in $a-\overline{b-c}=a-[b-c]$)
vin·di·ca·ble \ˈvin-di-kə-bəl\ *adj* (1647) : capable of being vindicated
vin·di·cate \ˈvin-də-ˌkāt\ *vt* **-cat·ed; -cat·ing** [L *vindicatus,* pp. of *vindicare* to lay claim to, avenge, fr. *vindic-, vindex* claimant, avenger] (1568) **1** *obs* **:** to set free : DELIVER **2 :** AVENGE **3 a :** EXONERATE,

\ə\ abut \ᵊ\ kitten, F table \ər\ further \a\ ash \ā\ ace \ä\ cot, cart \au̇\ out \ch\ chin \e\ bet \ē\ easy \g\ go \i\ hit \ī\ ice \j\ job \ŋ\ sing \ō\ go \ȯ\ law \ȯi\ boy \th\ thin \th\ the \ü\ loot \u̇\ foot \y\ yet \zh\ vision \à, k̲, ⁿ, œ, ᵫ, ue, ue̅, ʸ\ *see* Guide to Pronunciation

ABSOLVE **b** (1) : CONFIRM, SUBSTANTIATE (2) : to provide justification or defense for : JUSTIFY **c** : to protect from attack or encroachment : DEFEND **4** : to maintain a right to ***syn*** see EXCULPATE, MAINTAIN — **vin·di·ca·tor** \-ˌkāt-ər\ *n*
vin·di·ca·tion \ˌvin-də-ˈkā-shən\ *n* [ME, fr. L *vindication-, vindicatio*, fr. *vindicatus*, pp.] (15c) : an act of vindicating : the state of being vindicated; *specif* : justification against denial or censure : DEFENSE
vin·dic·a·tive \vin-ˈdik-ət-iv\ *adj* [ML *vindicatus*, fr. L *vindicatus*, pp.] (1521) **1** *obs* : VINDICTIVE, VENGEFUL **2** *archaic* : PUNITIVE
vin·di·ca·to·ry *adj* (1647) **1** \ˈvin-di-kə-ˌtōr-ē, -ˌtȯr-\ : providing vindication : JUSTIFICATORY **2** \vin-ˈdik-ə-\ : PUNITIVE, RETRIBUTIVE
vin·dic·tive \vin-ˈdik-tiv\ *adj* [L *vindicta* revenge, vindication, fr. *vindicare*] (1616) **1 a** : disposed to seek revenge : VENGEFUL **b** : intended for or involving revenge **2** : intended to cause anguish or hurt : SPITEFUL — **vin·dic·tive·ly** *adv* — **vin·dic·tive·ness** *n*
[1]**vine** \ˈvīn\ *n* [ME, fr. MF, fr. OF *vigne*, fr. L *vinea* vine, vineyard, fr. fem. of *vineus* of wine, fr. *vinum* wine — more at WINE] (14c) **1** : GRAPE 2 **2 a** : a plant whose stem requires support and which climbs by tendrils or twining or creeps along the ground; *also* : the stem of such a plant **b** : any of various sprawling herbaceous plants (as a tomato or potato) that lack specialized adaptations for climbing
[2]**vine** *vi* **vined; vin·ing** (1796) : to form or grow in the manner of a vine
vine·dress·er \ˈvīn-ˌdres-ər\ *n* (1560) : one that cultivates and prunes grapevines
vin·e·gar \ˈvin-i-gər\ *n* [ME *vinegre*, fr. MF *vinaigre*, fr. *vin* wine (fr. L *vinum*) + *aigre* keen, sour — more at EAGER] (14c) **1** : a sour liquid obtained by acetic fermentation of dilute alcoholic liquids and used as a condiment or preservative **2** : ill humor : SOURNESS **3** : VIM
vinegar eel *n* (1836) : a minute nematode worm (*Turbatrix aceti*) often found in great numbers in vinegar or acid fermenting vegetable matter
vinegar fly *n* [fr. its breeding in pickles] (ca. 1901) : DROSOPHILA
vin·e·gar·ish \ˈvin-i-g(ə-)rish\ *adj* (1844) : VINEGARY 2
vin·e·gary \ˈvin-i-g(ə-)rē\ *adj* (ca. 1730) **1** : resembling vinegar : SOUR **2** : disagreeable, bitter, or irascible in character or manner
vin·ery \ˈvīn-(ə-)rē\ *n, pl* **-er·ies** (15c) : an area or building in which vines are grown
vine·yard \ˈvin-yərd\ *n* (14c) **1** : a planting of grapevines **2** : an area or category of physical or mental occupation
vine·yard·ist \-əst\ *n* (1847) : one who owns or cultivates a vineyard
vingt–et–un \ˌvan-ˌtā-ˈən\ *n* [F, lit., twenty-one] (1781) : BLACKJACK 5
vi·ni·cul·ture \ˈvin-ə-ˌkəl-chər, ˈvī-nə-\ *n* [L *vinum* + ISV *-i-* + *culture*] (1871) : VITICULTURE
vi·nif·era \vī-ˈnif-(ə-)rə\ *adj* [NL, fr. L *vinifer* wine-producing, fr. *vinum* wine] (1900) : of, relating to, being, or derived from a common European grape (*Vitis vinifera*) that is the chief source of Old World wine grapes and table grapes — **vinifera** *n*
vi·ni·fi·ca·tion \ˌvin-ə-fə-ˈkā-shən, ˌvīn-\ *n* [F, fr. *vin* wine + *-i-* + *-fication*] (1880) : the conversion of fruit juices (as grape juice) into wine by fermentation
vin·i·fy \ˈvin-ə-ˌfī, ˈvīn-\ *vt* **-fied; -fy·ing** [prob. back-formation fr. *vinification*] (ca. 1969) : to convert into wine by fermentation
vi·no \ˈvē-(ˌ)nō\ *n* [It & Sp, fr. L *vinum*] (1898) : WINE
vin or·di·naire \ˌvan-ˌȯrd-i-ˈne(ə)r, -ˌȯrd-ᵊn-ˈe(ə)r\ *n* [F, ordinary wine] (1820) : inexpensive nonvintage table wine
vi·nos·i·ty \vī-ˈnäs-ət-ē\ *n, pl* **-ties** (1658) : the characteristic body, flavor, and color of a wine
vi·nous \ˈvī-nəs\ *adj* [L *vinosus*, fr. *vinum* wine] (1664) **1** : of, relating to, or made with wine ⟨~ medications⟩ **2** : showing the effects of the use of wine **3** : VINACEOUS — **vi·nous·ly** *adv*
[1]**vin·tage** \ˈvint-ij\ *n* [ME, alter. of *vendage*, fr. MF *vendenge*, fr. L *vindemia* grape-gathering, vintage, fr. *vinum* wine, grapes + *demere* to take off, fr. *de-* + *emere* to take — more at WINE, REDEEM] (15c) **1 a** (1) : a season's yield of grapes or wine from a vineyard (2) : WINE; *esp* : a usu. superior wine all or most of which comes from a single year **b** : a collection of contemporaneous and similar persons or things : CROP **2** : the act or time of harvesting grapes or making wine **3 a** : a period of origin or manufacture ⟨a piano of 1845 ~⟩ **b** : length of existence : AGE
[2]**vintage** *adj* (1601) **1** *of wine* : of, relating to, or produced in a particular vintage **2** : of old, recognized, and enduring interest, importance, or quality : CLASSIC **3** : OUTMODED, OLD-FASHIONED **4** : of the best and most characteristic — used with a proper noun ⟨~ Shaw: a wise and winning comedy —*Time*⟩
vin·tag·er \-ij-ər\ *n* (1589) : one concerned with the production of grapes and wine
vintage year *n* (ca. 1934) **1** : a year in which a vintage wine is produced **2** : a year of outstanding distinction or success
vint·ner \ˈvint-nər\ *n* [ME *vineter*, fr. MF *vinetier*, fr. ML *vinetarius*, fr. L *vinetum* vineyard, fr. *vinum* wine] (15c) **1** : a wine merchant **2** : a person who makes wine
viny \ˈvī-nē\ *adj* **vin·i·er; -est** (1570) **1** : of, relating to, or resembling vines ⟨~ plants⟩ **2** : covered with or abounding in vines
vi·nyl \ˈvī-ᵊl\ *n* [ISV, fr. L *vinum* wine] (1863) **1** : a univalent group $CH_2{=}CH$ derived from ethylene by removal of one hydrogen atom **2** : a polymer of a vinyl compound or a product (as a resin or a textile fiber) made from one — **vi·nyl·ic** \vī-ˈnil-ik\ *adj*
vinyl alcohol *n* (1873) : an unstable compound $CH_2{=}CHOH$ isolated only in the form of its polymers or derivatives
vinyl chloride *n* (1937) : a flammable gaseous carcinogenic compound C_2H_3Cl that is used esp. to make vinyl resins
vi·nyl·i·dene \vī-ˈnil-ə-ˌdēn\ *n* [ISV *vinyl* + *-ide* + *-ene*] (ca. 1930) : a bivalent group $CH_2{=}C$ derived from ethylene by removal of two hydrogen atoms from one carbon atom
vinylidene resin *n* (ca. 1948) : any of a group of tough thermoplastic resins that are formed by polymerization of a vinylidene compound and used esp. for filaments, films, and molded articles
vinyl resin *n* (ca. 1937) : any of various thermoplastic resinous materials that are essentially polymers of vinyl compounds
vi·ol \ˈvī(-ə)l, ˈvī-(ˌ)ōl\ *n* [ME, fr. MF *viole* viol, viola, fr. OProv *viola* viol] (15c) : a bowed stringed instrument chiefly of the 16th and 17th centuries having a deep body, flat back, sloping shoulders, usu. six strings, fretted fingerboard, and low-arched bridge and made in treble, alto, tenor, and bass sizes
[1]**vi·o·la** \vī-ˈō-lə, vē-; ˈvī-ə-\ *n* [L] (15c) : VIOLET 1a; *esp* : any of various garden hybrids with solitary white, yellow, or purple often variegated flowers resembling but smaller than typical pansies
[2]**vi·o·la** \vē-ˈō-lə\ *n* [It & Sp, viol, viola, fr. OProv, viol] (ca. 1724) : a musical instrument of the violin family that is intermediate in size and compass between the violin and cello and is tuned a fifth below the violin — **vi·o·list** \-ləst\ *n*
vi·o·la·ble \ˈvī-ə-lə-bəl\ *adj* [L *violabilis*, fr. *violare* to violate] (1552) : capable of being or likely to be violated — **vi·o·la·bil·i·ty** \ˌvī-ə-lə-ˈbil-ət-ē\ *n* — **vi·o·la·ble·ness** \ˈvī-ə-lə-bəl-nəs\ *n* — **vi·o·la·bly** \-blē\ *adv*
vi·o·la·ceous \ˌvī-ə-ˈlā-shəs\ *adj* [L *violaceus*, fr. *viola* violet] (1657) : of the color violet
vi·o·la da gam·ba \vē-ˌō-ləd-ə-ˈgäm-bə, -ˈgam-\ *n, pl* **vi·o·las da gamba** \-ləz-də-\ *or* **vi·o·le da gamba** \-(ˌ)lād-ə-\ [It, leg viol] (1597) : a bass member of the viol family having a range approximating the cello — **vi·o·list da gamba** \-ləs(t)-də-\ *n*
viola d'a·mo·re \-ləd-ə-ˈmōr-ē, -ˈmȯr-, -(ˌ)ā\ *n, pl* **violas d'amore** or **viole d'amore** [It, viol of love] (1697) : a tenor viol having usu. seven gut and seven wire strings
[1]**vi·o·late** \ˈvī-ə-ˌlāt\ *vt* **-lat·ed; -lat·ing** [ME *violaten*, fr. L *violatus*, pp. of *violare*; akin to L *violentus* violent, *vis* strength — more at VIM] (15c) **1** : BREAK, DISREGARD ⟨~ the law⟩ **2** : to do harm to the person or esp. the chastity of; *specif* : RAPE **3** : PROFANE, DESECRATE ⟨~ a shrine⟩ **4** : INTERRUPT, DISTURB ⟨~ the peace of a spring evening —Nancy Larter⟩ — **vi·o·la·tive** \-ˌlāt-iv\ *adj* — **vi·o·la·tor** \-ˌlāt-ər\ *n*
[2]**vi·o·late** \ˈvī-ə-lət\ *adj, archaic* (1503) : subjected to violation
vi·o·la·tion \ˌvī-ə-ˈlā-shən\ *n* [ME *violacioun*, fr. L *violation-, violatio*, fr. *violatus*, pp.] (15c) : the act of violating : the state of being violated: as **a** : INFRINGEMENT, TRANSGRESSION; *specif* : an infringement of the rules in sports that is less serious than a foul and usu. involves technicalities of play **b** : an act of irreverence or desecration : PROFANATION **c** : DISTURBANCE, INTERRUPTION **d** : RAPE, RAVISHMENT
vi·o·lence \ˈvī-ə-lən(t)s\ *n* [ME, fr. OF, fr. L *violentia*, fr. *violentus*] (13c) **1 a** : exertion of physical force so as to injure or abuse (as in effecting illegal entry into a house) **b** : an instance of violent treatment or procedure **2** : injury by or as if by distortion, infringement, or profanation : OUTRAGE **3 a** : intense, turbulent, or furious and often destructive action or force ⟨the ~ of the storm⟩ **b** : vehement feeling or expression : FERVOR; *also* : an instance of such action or feeling **c** : a clashing or jarring quality : DISCORDANCE **4** : undue alteration (as of wording or sense in editing a text)
vi·o·lent \-lənt\ *adj* [ME, fr. MF, fr. L *violentus*] (14c) **1** : marked by extreme force or sudden intense activity ⟨a ~ attack⟩ **2 a** : notably furious or vehement ⟨a ~ denunciation⟩; *also* : excited or mentally disordered to the point of loss of self-control ⟨the patient became ~ and had to be restrained⟩ **b** : EXTREME, INTENSE ⟨~ pain⟩ **3** : caused by force : not natural ⟨a ~ death⟩ — **vi·o·lent·ly** *adv*
violent storm *n* (ca. 1805) : STORM 1c(1) — see BEAUFORT SCALE table
vi·o·let \ˈvī-ə-lət\ *n* [ME, fr. MF *violete*, dim. of *viole* violet, fr. L *viola*] (14c) **1 a** : any of a genus (*Viola* of the family Violaceae, the violet family) of herbs or subshrubs with alternate stipulate leaves and both aerial and cleistogamous flowers; *esp* : one with smaller usu. solid-colored flowers as distinguished from the usu. larger-flowered violas and pansies **b** : any of several plants of genera other than that of the violet — compare DOGTOOTH VIOLET **2** : any of a group of colors of reddish blue hue, low lightness, and medium saturation
vi·o·lin \ˌvī-ə-ˈlin\ *n* [It *violino*, dim. of *viola*] (1579) : a bowed stringed instrument having four strings tuned at intervals of a fifth and a usual range from G below middle C upwards for more than 4½ octaves and distinguished from the viol in having a shallower body, shoulders at right angles to the neck, a fingerboard without frets, and a more curved bridge — **vi·o·lin·ist** \-əst\ *n* — **vi·o·lin·ist·ic** \-ə-lə-ˈnist-ik\ *adj*

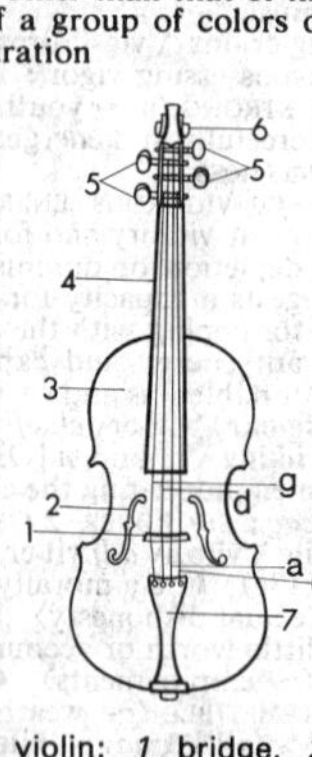

violin: *1* bridge, *2* sound hole, *3* soundboard, *4* fingerboard, *5* pegs, *6* scroll, *7* tailpiece, *g* G-string, *d* D-string, *a* A-string, *e* E-string

vi·o·lon·cel·lo \ˌvī-ə-lən-ˈchel-(ˌ)ō, ˌvē-\ *n* [It, dim. of *violone*, aug. of *viola*] (ca. 1724) : CELLO — **vi·o·lon·cel·list** \-ˈchel-əst\ *n*
vio·my·cin \ˌvī-ə-ˈmīs-ᵊn\ *n* [*violet* + *-mycin*, fr. the color of the soil organism] (ca. 1950) : a polypeptide antibiotic $C_{25}H_{43}N_{13}O_{10}$ that is produced by a soil actinomycete (*Streptomyces puniceus*) and is administered in the form of its sulfate in the treatment of tuberculosis
VIP \ˌvē-ˌī-ˈpē\ *n, pl* **VIPs** \-ˈpēz\ [very important person] (ca. 1944) : a person of great influence or prestige; *esp* : a high official with special privileges
vi·per \ˈvī-pər\ *n* [MF *vipere*, fr. L *vipera*] (1526) **1 a** : a common European venomous snake (*Vipera berus*) that attains a length of two feet, varies in color from red, brown, or gray with dark markings to black, occurs across Eurasia from England to Sakhalin, and is rarely fatal to man; *broadly* : any of various Old World venomous snakes (family Viperidae) **b** : PIT VIPER **c** : a venomous or reputedly venomous snake **2** : a vicious or treacherous person
vi·per·ine \-pə-ˌrīn\ *adj* (1550) : of, relating to, or resembling a viper : VENOMOUS
vi·per·ish \-p(ə-)rish\ *adj* (1755) : spitefully vituperative : VENOMOUS
vi·per·ous \-p(ə-)rəs\ *adj* (1535) **1** : VIPERINE **2** : having the qualities attributed to a viper : MALIGNANT, VENOMOUS — **vi·per·ous·ly** *adv*
viper's bugloss *n* (1597) : a coarse bristly Old World weed (*Echium vulgare*) of the borage family that is naturalized in No. America and has showy blue tubular flowers with exserted stamens
vi·ra·go \və-ˈräg-(ˌ)ō, -ˈrāg-; ˈvir-ə-ˌgō\ *n, pl* **-goes** *or* **-gos** [L *viragin-, virago*, fr. *vir* man — more at VIRILE] (14c) **1** : a woman of great stature, strength, and courage **2** : a loud overbearing woman : TERMAGANT — **vi·rag·i·nous** \və-ˈraj-ə-nəs\ *adj*
vi·ral \ˈvī-rəl\ *adj* (1937) : of, relating to, or caused by a virus — **vi·ral·ly** \-rə-lē\ *adv*
vir·e·lay \ˈvir-ə-ˌlā\ *n* [ME, fr. MF *virelai*] (14c) : a chiefly French verse form consisting of stanzas of indeterminate length and number with

alternating long and short lines and interlaced rhyme (as *abab bcbc cdcd dada*)
vi·re·mia \vī-ˈrē-mē-ə\ *n* [NL, fr. *virus* + *-emia*] (1946) : the presence of virus in the blood of a host — **vi·re·mic** \-mik\ *adj*
vir·eo \ˈvir-ē-ˌō\ *n, pl* **-e·os** [L, a small bird, fr. *virēre* to be green — more at VERDANT] (1834) : any of various small insectivorous American passerine birds (family Vireonidae) that are chiefly olivaceous and grayish in color
vires *pl of* VIS
vi·res·cence \və-ˈres-ᵊn(t)s, vī-\ *n* (ca. 1888) : the state or condition of becoming green; *esp* : such a condition due to the development of chloroplasts in plant organs (as petals) normally white or colored
vi·res·cent \-ᵊnt\ *adj* [L *virescent-, virescens,* prp. of *virescere* to become green, incho. of *virēre* to be green] (1826) **1** : beginning to be green : GREENISH **2** : developing or displaying virescence
vir·ga \ˈvər-gə\ *n* [NL, fr. L, branch, rod, streak in the sky suggesting rain — more at WHISK] (ca. 1938) : wisps of precipitation evaporating before reaching the ground
¹**vir·gate** \ˈvər-ˌgāt\ *n* [ML *virgata,* fr. *virga,* a land measure, fr. L, rod] (1655) : an old English unit of land area equal to one quarter of a hide or one quarter of an acre
²**virgate** *adj* [NL *virgatus,* fr. L, made of twigs, fr. *virga*] (1821) : shaped like a rod or wand ⟨a ~ one-flowered branch⟩
¹**vir·gin** \ˈvər-jən\ *n* [ME, fr. OF *virgine,* fr. L *virgin-, virgo* young woman, virgin] (13c) **1 a** : an unmarried woman devoted to religion **b** *cap* : VIRGO **2 a** : an absolutely chaste young woman **b** : an unmarried girl or woman **3** *cap* : VIRGIN MARY **4** : a person who has not had sexual intercourse **5** : a female animal that has never copulated
²**virgin** *adj* (14c) **1** : free of impurity or stain : UNSULLIED **2** : CHASTE **3** : characteristic of or befitting a virgin : MODEST **4** : FRESH, UNSPOILED; *specif* : not altered by human activity ⟨a ~ forest⟩ **5 a** : being used or worked for the first time **b** : INITIAL, FIRST **6 a** : NATIVE 8b ⟨~ sulfur⟩ **b** *of a vegetable oil* : obtained from the first light pressing and without heating **7** : produced directly from ore or by primary smelting — used of metal
¹**vir·gin·al** \ˈvər-jən-ᵊl, ˈvərj-nəl\ *adj* (15c) **1** : of, relating to, or characteristic of a virgin or virginity; *esp* : PURE, CHASTE **2** : PRISTINE, UNSULLIED — **vir·gin·al·ly** \-ē\ *adv*
²**virginal** *n* [prob. fr. L *virginalis* of a virgin, fr. *virgin-, virgo*] (1530) : a small rectangular spinet having no legs and only one wire to a note and popular in the 16th and 17th centuries — often used in pl.; called also *pair of virginals* — **vir·gin·al·ist** \-əst\ *n*
virgin birth *n* (1652) **1** : birth from a virgin **2** *often cap V&B* : the theological doctrine that Jesus was miraculously begotten of God and born of a virgin mother
Vir·gin·ia bluebells \vər-ˌjin-yə-, -ˌjin-ē-ə-\ *n pl* [*Virginia,* state of the U.S.] (ca. 1922) : BLUEBELL 2b
Virginia creeper *n* (1704) : a common No. American tendril-climbing vine (*Parthenocissus quinquefolia*) of the grape family with palmately compound leaves and bluish black berries — called also *woodbine*
Virginia fence *n* (1671) : WORM FENCE — called also *Virginia rail fence*
Virginia ham *n* (1824) : a flat lean hickory-smoked ham with dark red meat esp. from a peanut-fed razorback hog
Virginia pine *n* (1775) : a common often straggling pine (*Pinus virginiana*) of the eastern U.S. that has short needles occurring in pairs — called also *Jersey pine*
Virginia rail *n* (1785) : an American long-billed rail (*Rallus limicola*) that has gray cheeks
Virginia reel *n* (1817) : an American dance in which two lines of couples face each other and all couples in turn participate in a series of figures
Virginia snakeroot *n* (1694) : a birthwort (*Aristolochia serpentaria*) of the eastern U.S. with oblong leaves cordate at the base and a solitary basal very irregular flower
vir·gin·i·ty \(ˌ)vər-ˈjin-ət-ē\ *n, pl* **-ties** [ME, fr. MF *virginite,* fr. L *virginitat-, virginitas,* fr. *virgin-, virgo* virgin] (14c) **1** : the quality or state of being virgin; *esp* : MAIDENHOOD **2** : the unmarried life : CELIBACY, SPINSTERHOOD
vir·gin·ium \vər-ˈjin-ē-əm, -ˈjin-yəm\ *n* [NL, fr. *Virginia*] (ca. 1930) : FRANCIUM
Virgin Mary *n* : the mother of Jesus
virgin's bower *n* (1597) : any of several usu. small-flowered and climbing clematises
virgin wool *n* (ca. 1915) : wool not used before in manufacture
Vir·go \ˈvər-(ˌ)gō, ˈvi(ə)r-\ *n* [L (gen. *Virginis*), lit., virgin] **1** : a zodiacal constellation on the celestial equator that lies due south of the handle of the Big Dipper and is pictured as a woman holding a spike of grain **2 a** : the 6th sign of the zodiac in astrology — see ZODIAC table **b** : one born under this sign — **Vir·go·an** *n*
vir·gule \ˈvər-(ˌ)gyü(ə)l\ *n* [F, fr. L *virgula* small stripe, obelus, fr. dim. of *virga* rod — more at WHISK] (1837) : DIAGONAL 3
vi·ri·ci·dal \ˌvī-rə-ˈsīd-ᵊl\ *adj* [NL *virus* + E *-i-* + *-cide*] (1926) : VIRUCIDAL — **vi·ri·cide** \ˈvī-rə-ˌsīd\ *n*
vir·id \ˈvir-əd\ *adj* [L *viridis* green — more at VERDANT] (1600) : vividly green : VERDANT
vir·i·des·cent \ˌvir-ə-ˈdes-ᵊnt\ *adj* [L *viridis* green] (ca. 1847) : slightly green : GREENISH
vi·rid·i·an \və-ˈrid-ē-ən\ *n* [L *viridis*] (1882) : a chrome green that is probably a hydrated oxide of chrome $Cr_2O_3{\cdot}2H_2O$
vi·rid·i·ty \və-ˈrid-ət-ē\ *n* [ME *viridite,* fr. MF *viridité,* fr. L *viriditat-, viriditas,* fr. *viridis*] (15c) **1 a** : the quality or state of being green **b** : the color of grass or foliage **2** : naive innocence
vir·ile \ˈvir-əl, ˈvi(ə)r-ˌīl, *Brit also* ˈvi(ə)r-ˌīl\ *adj* [MF or L; MF *viril,* fr. L *virilis,* fr. *vir* man, male; akin to OE & OHG *wer* man, Skt *vīra*] (15c) **1** : having the nature, properties, or qualities of an adult male; *specif* : capable of functioning as a male in copulation **2** : ENERGETIC, VIGOROUS **3** : characteristic of or associated with men : MASCULINE **4** : MASTERFUL, FORCEFUL — **vir·ile·ly** \-ē\ *adv*
vir·il·ism \ˈvir-ə-ˌliz-əm\ *n* (1896) : the appearance of secondary male characteristics in the female
vi·ril·i·ty \və-ˈril-ət-ē, *Brit also* vī-\ *n* [L *virilitat-, virilitas,* fr. *virilis*] (1586) : the quality or state of being virile: **a** : MANHOOD **b** : manly vigor : MASCULINITY
vi·ri·on \ˈvī-rē-ˌän, ˈvir-ē-\ *n* [ISV *viri-* (fr. *virus*) + ²*-on*] (1964) : a complete virus particle that consists of RNA or DNA core with a protein coat sometimes with external envelopes and that is the extracellular infective form of a virus
virl \ˈvər(-ə)l\ *n* [ME *virole* — more at FERRULE] *Scot* (15c) : FERRULE 1
vi·roid \ˈvī-ˌrȯid\ *n* [NL *virus* + E *-oid*] (1971) : any of several causative agents of plant disease that consist solely of a single-stranded RNA of low molecular weight arranged in a closed loop or a linear chain
vi·rol·o·gy \vī-ˈräl-ə-jē\ *n* [NL *virus* + ISV *-logy*] (ca. 1935) : a branch of science that deals with viruses — **vi·ro·log·i·cal** \ˌvī-rə-ˈläj-i-kəl\ *or* **vi·ro·log·ic** \-ik\ *adj* — **vi·ro·log·i·cal·ly** \-i-k(ə-)lē\ *adv* — **vi·rol·o·gist** \vī-ˈräl-ə-jəst\ *n*
vir·tu \ˌvər-ˈtü, vi(ə)r-\ *n* [It *virtù,* lit., virtue, fr. L *virtut-, virtus*] (1722) **1** : a love of or taste for curios or objets d'art **2** : productions of art esp. of a curious or antique nature : OBJETS D'ART
vir·tu·al \ˈvərch-(ə-)wəl, ˈvər-chəl\ *adj* [ME, possessed of certain physical virtues, fr. ML *virtualis,* fr. L *virtus* strength, virtue] (1654) **1** : being such in essence or effect though not formally recognized or admitted ⟨a ~ dictator⟩ ⟨a ~ promise⟩ **2** : of, relating to, or using virtual memory
virtual focus *n* (1704) : a point from which divergent rays (as of light) seem to emanate but do not actually do so (as in the image of a point source seen in a plane mirror)
virtual image *n* (1859) : an image (as seen in a plane mirror) formed of virtual foci
vir·tu·al·i·ty \ˌvər-chə-ˈwal-ət-ē\ *n, pl* **-ties** (1646) **1** : ESSENCE **2** : potential existence : POTENTIALITY
vir·tu·al·ly \ˈvərch-(ə-)wə-lē, ˈvərch-(ə-)lē\ *adv* (15c) **1** : almost entirely : NEARLY **2** : for all practical purposes ⟨unnoticed and ~ unknown — Philip Brady⟩
virtual memory *n* (ca. 1966) : external memory (as magnetic disks) for a computer that can be used as if it were an extension of the computer's internal memory — called also *virtual storage*
vir·tue \ˈvər-(ˌ)chü, -chə(-w)\ *n* [ME *virtu,* fr. OF, fr. L *virtut-, virtus* strength, manliness, virtue, fr. *vir* man — more at VIRILE] (13c) **1 a** : conformity to a standard of right : MORALITY **b** : a particular moral excellence **2** *pl* : an order of angels — see CELESTIAL HIERARCHY **3** : a beneficial quality or power of a thing **4** : manly strength or courage : VALOR **5** : a commendable quality or trait : MERIT **6** : a capacity to act : POTENCY **7** : chastity esp. in a woman — **vir·tue·less** \-(ˌ)chü-ləs, -chə-\ *adj* — **by virtue of** *or* **in virtue of** : through the force of : by authority of
vir·tu·o·sa \ˌvər-chə-ˈwō-sə, -zə\ *n* [It, fem. of *virtuoso*] (1668) : a female virtuoso
vir·tu·os·i·ty \-ˈwäs-ət-ē\ *n, pl* **-ties** (1673) **1** : a taste for or interest in virtu **2** : great technical skill (as in the practice of a fine art)
vir·tu·o·so \-ˈwō-(ˌ)sō, -(ˌ)zō\ *n, pl* **-sos** *or* **-si** \-(ˌ)sē, -(ˌ)zē\ [It, fr. *virtuoso,* adj., virtuous, skilled, fr. LL *virtuosus* virtuous, fr. L *virtus*] (1620) **1** : an experimenter or investigator esp. in the arts and sciences : SAVANT **2** : one skilled in or having a taste for the fine arts **3** : one who excels in the technique of an art; *esp* : a highly skilled musical performer (as on the violin) — **vir·tu·o·sic** \-wō-sik, -zik\ *adj* — **virtuoso** *adj*
vir·tu·ous \ˈvərch-(ə-)wəs\ *adj* (14c) **1** : POTENT, EFFICACIOUS **2 a** : having or exhibiting virtue **b** : morally excellent : RIGHTEOUS **3** : CHASTE ***syn*** see MORAL — **vir·tu·ous·ly** *adv* — **vir·tu·ous·ness** *n*
vi·ru·cid·al \ˌvī-rə-ˈsīd-ᵊl\ *adj* [NL, *virus* + E *-cide*] (ca. 1927) : having the capacity to destroy or inactivate viruses — **vi·ru·cide** \ˈvī-rə-ˌsīd\ *n*
vir·u·lence \ˈvir-(y)ə-lən(t)s\ *n* (1663) : the quality or state of being virulent: as **a** : extreme bitterness or malignity of temper : RANCOR **b** : MALIGNANCY, VENOMOUSNESS ⟨ameliorate the ~ of a disease⟩ **c** : the relative capacity of a pathogen to overcome body defenses
vir·u·len·cy \-lən-sē\ *n* (1617) : VIRULENCE
vir·u·lent \-lənt\ *adj* [ME, fr. L *virulentus,* fr. *virus* poison] (15c) **1 a** : marked by a rapid, severe, and malignant course ⟨a ~ infection⟩ **b** : able to overcome bodily defensive mechanisms ⟨a ~ pathogen⟩ **2** : extremely poisonous or venomous : NOXIOUS **3** : full of malice : MALIGNANT ⟨~ racists⟩ **4** : objectionably harsh or strong — **vir·u·lent·ly** *adv*
vir·u·lif·er·ous \ˌvir-(y)ə-ˈlif-(ə-)rəs\ *adj* [*virulence* + *-iferous*] (ca. 1899) : containing, producing, or conveying an agent of infection ⟨offspring of ~ females⟩
vi·rus \ˈvī-rəs\ *n* [L, slimy liquid, poison, stench; akin to OE *wāse* marsh, Gk *ios* poison, Skt *visa;* in senses 2 & 4, fr. NL, fr. L] (1599) **1** *archaic* : VENOM 1 **2 a** : the causative agent of an infectious disease **b** : any of a large group of submicroscopic infective agents that are regarded either as extremely simple microorganisms or as extremely complex molecules, that typically contain a protein coat surrounding an RNA or DNA core of genetic material but no semipermeable membrane, that are capable of growth and multiplication only in living cells, and that cause various important diseases in man, lower animals, or plants; *also* : FILTERABLE VIRUS **c** : a disease caused by a virus **3** : something that poisons the mind or soul ⟨the force of this ~ of prejudice —V. S. Waters⟩ **4** : an antigenic but not infective material (as vaccine lymph) obtainable from a case of an infectious disease
vis \ˈvis\ *n, pl* **vi·res** \ˈvī-ˌrēz\ [L — more at VIM] (1601) : FORCE, POWER
¹**vi·sa** \ˈvē-zə *also* -sə\ *n* [F, fr. L, neut. pl. of *visus,* pp.] (1831) **1** : an endorsement made on a passport by the proper authorities denoting that it has been examined and that the bearer may proceed **2** : a signature of formal approval by a superior upon a document
²**visa** *vt* **vi·saed** \-zəd, -səd\; **vi·sa·ing** \-zə-iŋ, -sə-\ (ca. 1847) : to give a visa to (a passport)
vis·age \ˈviz-ij\ *n* [ME, fr. OF, fr. *vis* face, fr. L *visus* sight, fr. *visus,* pp. of *vidēre* to see — more at WIT] (14c) **1** : the face, countenance, or appearance of a person or sometimes an animal **2** : ASPECT, APPEARANCE ⟨grimy ~ of a mining town⟩ — **vis·aged** \-ijd\ *adj*

1vis–à–vis \ˈvēz-ə-ˈvē, ˌvēs- *also* -ä-ˈvē\ *prep* [F, lit., face-to-face] (1755) **1** : face-to-face with : OPPOSITE **2** : in relation to **3** : as compared with

2vis–à–vis *n, pl* **vis–à–vis** \-ə-ˈvē(z), -ä-\ (1757) **1** : one that is face-to-face with another **2 a** : ESCORT, DATE **b** : COUNTERPART **3** : TÊTE-À-TÊTE 1

3vis–à–vis *adv* (1946) : in company : TOGETHER

Vi·sa·yan \və-ˈsī-ən\ *var of* BISAYAN

vis·ca·cha \vis-ˈkäch-ə\ *n* [Sp *vizcacha,* fr. Quechua *wiskácha*] (1604) : any of several So. American burrowing rodents (genera *Lagostomus* and *Lagidium*) closely related to the chinchilla

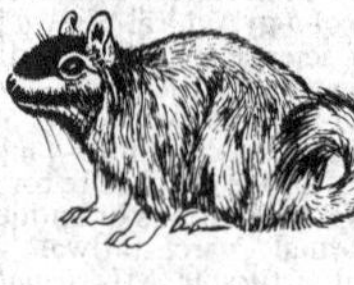
viscacha

viscera *pl of* VISCUS

vis·cer·al \ˈvis-ə-rəl\ *adj* (1575) **1** : felt in or as if in the viscera : DEEP ⟨~ conviction⟩ **2** : not intellectual : INSTINCTIVE, UNREASONING ⟨~ drives⟩ **3** : dealing with crude or elemental emotions : EARTHY ⟨a ~ novel⟩ **4** : of, relating to, or located on or among the viscera : SPLANCHNIC — **vis·cer·al·ly** \-rə-lē\ *adv*

vis·cero·mo·tor \ˌvis-ə-rə-ˈmōt-ər\ *adj* (1888) : causing or concerned in the functional activity of the viscera ⟨~ nerves⟩

vis·cid \ˈvis-əd\ *adj* [LL *viscidus,* fr. L *viscum* birdlime — more at VISCOUS] (1635) **1 a** : having an adhesive quality : STICKY **b** : having a glutinous consistency : VISCOUS **2** : covered with a sticky layer — **vis·cid·i·ty** \vis-ˈid-ət-ē\ *n* — **vis·cid·ly** \ˈvis-əd-lē\ *adv*

vis·co·elas·tic \ˌvis-kō-ə-ˈlas-tik\ *adj* [*viscous* + *elastic*] (1935) : having appreciable and conjoint viscous and elastic properties ⟨such ~ materials as asphalt⟩; *also* : constituting or relating to the state of viscoelastic materials ⟨~ data⟩ ⟨~ properties⟩ — **vis·co·elas·tic·i·ty** \-ˌlas-ˈtis-ət-ē, -ˈtis-tē\ *n*

vis·com·e·ter \vis-ˈkäm-ət-ər\ *n* [*viscosity* + *-meter*] (ca. 1883) : an instrument with which to measure viscosity — **vis·co·met·ric** \ˌvis-kə-ˈme-trik\ *adj* — **vis·com·e·try** \-ə-trē\ *n*

1vis·cose \ˈvis-ˌkōs, -ˌkōz\ *n* [obs. *viscose,* adj. (viscous)] (1896) **1** : a viscous golden-brown solution made by treating cellulose with caustic alkali solution and carbon disulfide and used in making rayon and films of regenerated cellulose **2** : viscose rayon

2viscose *adj* (1900) : of, relating to, or made from viscose

vis·co·sim·e·ter \ˌvis-kə-ˈsim-ət-ər\ *n* [ISV *viscosity* + *-meter*] (ca. 1868) : VISCOMETER — **vis·cosi·met·ric** \(ˌ)vis-ˌkäs-ə-ˈme-trik\ *adj*

vis·cos·i·ty \vis-ˈkäs-ət-ē\ *n, pl* **-ties** [ME *viscosite,* fr. MF *viscosité,* fr. ML *viscositat-, viscositas,* fr. LL *viscosus* viscous] (15c) **1** : the quality or state of being viscous **2** : the property of a fluid or semifluid that enables it to develop and maintain an amount of shearing stress dependent upon the velocity of flow and then to offer continued resistance to flow **3** : the ratio of the tangential frictional force per unit area to the velocity gradient perpendicular to the direction of flow of a liquid — called also *coefficient of viscosity*

viscosity index *n* (ca. 1937) : an arbitrary number assigned as a measure of the constancy of the viscosity of a lubricating oil with change of temperature with higher numbers indicating viscosities that change little with temperature

vis·count \ˈvī-ˌkau̇nt\ *n* [ME *viscounte,* fr. MF *viscomte,* fr. ML *vicecomit-, vicecomes,* fr. LL *vice-* vice- + *comit-, comes* count — more at COUNT] (15c) : a member of the peerage in Great Britain ranking below an earl and above a baron — **vis·count·cy** \-ˌkau̇n(t)-sē\ *n* — **vis·county** \-ˌkau̇nt-ē\ *n*

vis·count·ess \-ˌkau̇nt-əs\ *n* (15c) **1** : the wife or widow of a viscount **2** : a woman who holds the rank of viscount in her own right

vis·cous \ˈvis-kəs\ *adj* [ME *viscouse,* fr. LL *viscosus* full of birdlime, viscous, fr. L *viscum* mistletoe, birdlime; akin to OHG *wīhsila* cherry, Gk *ixos* mistletoe] (15c) **1** : VISCID **2** : having or characterized by viscosity ⟨~ flow⟩ — **vis·cous·ly** *adv* — **vis·cous·ness** *n*

vis·cus \ˈvis-kəs\ *n, pl* **vis·cera** \ˈvis-ə-rə\ [L (pl. *viscera*)] (1728) **1** : an internal organ of the body; *esp* : one (as the heart, liver, or intestine) located in the great cavity of the trunk proper **2** *pl* : HEART 4

1vise \ˈvīs\ *n* [MF *vis* something winding, fr. L *vitis* vine — more at WITHY] (1584) **1** : any of various tools with two jaws for holding work that close usu. by a screw, lever, or cam **2** : something likened to a vise ⟨economic ~ of slow growth and rampant price increases —David Milne⟩ — **vise·like** \ˈvī-ˌslīk\ *adj*

2vise *vt* **vised; vis·ing** (1602) : to hold, force, or squeeze with or as if with a vise

1vi·sé \ˈvē-ˌzā, vē-ˈ\ *vt* **vi·séd** *or* **vi·séed; vi·sé·ing** [F, pp. of *viser* to visa, fr. *visa*] (1810) : VISA

2visé *n* (ca. 1847) : VISA

Vish·nu \ˈvish-(ˌ)nü\ *n* [Skt *Viṣṇu*] : the preserver god of the Hindu sacred triad — compare BRAHMA, SIVA

vis·i·bil·i·ty \ˌviz-ə-ˈbil-ət-ē\ *n, pl* **-ties** (1581) **1** : the quality or state of being visible **2 a** : the degree of clearness of the atmosphere; *specif* : the greatest distance toward the horizon that prominent objects can be identified with the naked eye **b** : capability of being readily noticed **c** : capability of affording an unobstructed view **3** : a measure of the ability of radiant energy to evoke visual sensation

vis·i·ble \ˈviz-ə-bəl\ *adj* [ME, fr. MF or L; MF, fr. L *visibilis,* fr. *visus,* pp.] (14c) **1** : capable of being seen : perceptible to vision ⟨stars ~ to the naked eye⟩ ⟨~ light⟩ **2 a** : exposed to view ⟨the ~ horizon⟩ **b** : CONSPICUOUS **3** : capable of being discovered or perceived : RECOGNIZABLE ⟨no ~ means of support⟩ **4** : ACCESSIBLE 4 **5** : devised to keep a particular part or item always in full view or readily seen or referred to ⟨a ~ index⟩ — **vis·i·ble·ness** *n* — **vis·i·bly** \-blē\ *adv*

visible speech *n* (1865) **1** : a set of phonetic symbols based on symbols for articulatory position **2** : speech reproduced spectrographically

Visi·goth \ˈviz-ə-ˌgäth\ *n* [LL *Visigothi,* pl.] (1611) : a member of the western division of the Goths — **Visi·goth·ic** \ˌviz-ə-ˈgäth-ik\ *adj*

1vi·sion \ˈvizh-ən\ *n* [ME, fr. OF, fr. L *vision-, visio,* fr. *visus,* pp. of *vidēre* to see — more at WIT] (13c) **1 a** : something seen in a dream, trance, or ecstasy; *specif* : a supernatural appearance that conveys a revelation **b** : an object of imagination **c** : a manifestation to the senses of something immaterial ⟨look, not at ~*s,* but at realities —Edith Wharton⟩ **2 a** : the act or power of imagination **b** (1) : mode of seeing or conceiving (2) : unusual discernment or foresight ⟨a man of ~⟩ **c** : direct mystical awareness of the supernatural usu. in visible form **3 a** : the act or power of seeing : SIGHT **b** : the special sense by which the qualities of an object (as color, luminosity, shape and size) constituting its appearance are perceived and which is mediated by the eye **4 a** : something seen **b** : a lovely or charming sight — **vi·sion·al** \ˈvizh-nəl, -ən-ᵊl\ *adj* — **vi·sion·al·ly** \-ē\ *adv*

2vision *vt* **vi·sioned; vi·sion·ing** \ˈvizh-(ə-)niŋ\ (1795) : ENVISION

1vi·sion·ary \ˈvizh-ə-ˌner-ē\ *adj* (1648) **1 a** : of the nature of a vision : ILLUSORY **b** : IMPRACTICABLE, UTOPIAN ⟨a ~ scheme⟩ **c** : existing only in imagination : UNREAL **2 a** : able or likely to see visions **b** : disposed to reverie or imagining : DREAMY **3** : of, relating to, or characterized by visions or the power of vision ***syn*** see IMAGINARY — **vi·sion·ari·ness** \-ē-nəs\ *n*

2visionary *n, pl* **-ar·ies** (1702) **1** : one whose ideas or projects are impractical : DREAMER **2** : one who sees visions : SEER

vi·sioned \ˈvizh-ənd\ *adj* (1510) **1** : seen in a vision ⟨a ~ face⟩ **2** : produced by or experienced in a vision ⟨~ agony⟩ **3** : endowed with vision : INSPIRED

vi·sion·less \ˈvizh-ən-ləs\ *adj* (1820) **1** : SIGHTLESS, BLIND ⟨~ eyes⟩ **2** : lacking vision or inspiration ⟨a ~ leader⟩

1vis·it \ˈviz-ət\ *vb* **vis·it·ed** \ˈviz-ət-əd, ˈviz-təd\; **vis·it·ing** \ˈviz-ət-iŋ, ˈviz-tiŋ\ [ME *visiten,* fr. OF *visiter,* fr. L *visitare,* freq. of *visere* to go to see, fr. *vidēre* to see] *vt* (13c) **1 a** *archaic* : COMFORT — used of the Deity ⟨~ us with Thy salvation —Charles Wesley⟩ **b** (1) : AFFLICT ⟨~*ed* his people with distempers —Tobias Smollett⟩ (2) : INFLICT, IMPOSE ⟨~*ed* his wrath upon them⟩ **c** : AVENGE ⟨~*ed* the sins of the fathers upon the children⟩ **d** : to present itself to or come over momentarily ⟨was ~*ed* by a strange notion⟩ **2** : to go to see in order to comfort or help **3 a** : to pay a call on as an act of friendship or courtesy **b** : to reside with temporarily as a guest **c** : to go to see or stay at (a place) for a particular purpose (as business or sightseeing) **d** : to go or come officially to inspect or oversee ⟨a bishop ~*ing* his parish⟩ ~ *vi* **1** : to make a visit; *also* : to make frequent or regular visits **2** : CHAT, CONVERSE

2visit *n* (1621) **1 a** : a short stay : CALL **b** : a brief residence as a guest **c** : an extended stay : SOJOURN **2** : a journey to and stay or short sojourn at a place **3** : an official or professional call or tour : VISITATION **4** : the act of a naval officer in boarding a merchant ship on the high seas in exercise of the right of search

vis·it·able \ˈviz-ət-ə-bəl, ˈviz-tə-\ *adj* (1605) **1** : subject to or allowing visitation or inspection **2** : socially eligible to receive visits

vis·i·tant \ˈviz-ət-ənt, ˈviz-tənt\ *n* (1599) **1** : VISITOR; *esp* : one thought to come from a spirit world **2** : a migratory bird that appears at intervals for a limited period — **visitant** *adj*

vis·i·ta·tion \ˌviz-ə-ˈtā-shən\ *n* [ME *visitacioun,* fr. MF *visitation,* fr. L *visitation-, visitatio,* fr. *visitatus,* pp. of *visitare* to visit] (14c) **1** : an instance of visiting; *esp* : an official visit (as for inspection) **2 a** : a special dispensation of divine favor or wrath **b** : a severe trial : AFFLICTION **3** *cap* : the visit of the Virgin Mary to Elizabeth recounted in Luke and celebrated July 2 by a Christian feast — **vis·i·ta·tion·al** \-shnəl, -shən-ᵊl\ *adj*

vis·i·ta·to·ri·al \ˌviz-ət-ə-ˈtōr-ē-əl, ˌviz-tə-, -ˈtȯr-\ *adj* (1688) : of or relating to visitation or to a judicial visitor or superintendent

visiting card *n* (1782) : a small card bearing the name and sometimes the address of a person or married couple that is presented when calling

visiting fireman *n* (1939) : a usu. important or influential visitor whom it is desirable or expedient to show about or entertain impressively

visiting nurse *n* (ca. 1924) : a nurse employed by a hospital or social-service agency to perform public health services and esp. to visit sick persons in a community

visiting professor *n* (1949) : a professor invited to join a college or university faculty for a limited time (as an academic year)

visiting teacher *n* (ca. 1925) : an educational officer employed by a public school system to visit the homes of pupils in order to bring about cooperation between school and family and to enforce attendance regulations or to instruct sick or handicapped pupils unable to attend school

vis·i·tor \ˈviz-ət-ər, ˈviz-tər\ *n* (14c) : one that visits; *esp* : one that makes formal visits of inspection

vi·sive \ˈviz-iv, ˈvī-siv\ *adj* [ML *visivus,* fr. L *visus,* pp. of *vidēre* to see — more at WIT] *archaic* (1543) : of, relating to, or serving for vision

vi·sor \ˈvī-zər\ *n* [ME *viser,* fr. AF, fr. OF *visiere,* fr. *vis* face — more at VISAGE] (14c) **1** : the front piece of a helmet; *esp* : a movable upper piece **2 a** : a face mask **b** : DISGUISE **3 a** : a projecting front on a cap for shading the eyes **b** : a usu. movable flat sunshade attached at the top of an automobile windshield — **vi·sored** \-zərd\ *adj* — **vi·sor·less** \-zər-ləs\ *adj*

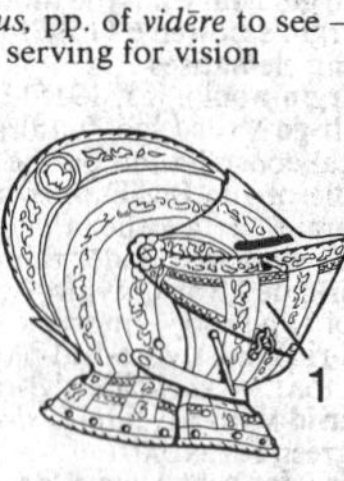
1 visor 1

vis·ta \ˈvis-tə\ *n* [It, sight, fr. *visto,* pp. of *vedere* to see, fr. L *vidēre* — more at WIT] (1644) **1** : a distant view through or along an avenue or opening : PROSPECT **2** : an extensive mental view (as over a stretch of time or a series of events)

vis·taed \ˈvis-təd\ *adj* (1835) **1** : affording or made to form a vista **2** : seen in or as if in a vista

1vi·su·al \ˈvizh-(ə-)wəl, ˈvizh-əl\ *adj* [ME, fr. LL *visualis,* fr. L *visus* sight, fr. *visus,* pp.] (15c) **1** : of, relating to, or used in vision ⟨~ organs⟩ **2** : attained or maintained by sight ⟨~ impressions⟩ **3** : VISIBLE **4** : producing mental images : VIVID **5** : done or executed by sight only ⟨~ navigation⟩ **6** : of, relating to, or employing visual aids — **vi·su·al·ly** \ˈvizh-(ə-)wə-lē, ˈvizh-(ə-)lē\ *adv*

2visual *n* (1938) : something (as a picture, chart, or film) that appeals to the sight and is used for illustration, demonstration, or promotion — usu. used in pl.

visual acuity *n* (1889) : the relative ability of the visual organ to resolve detail that is usu. expressed as the reciprocal of the minimum angular separation in minutes of two lines just resolvable as separate and that forms in the average human eye an angle of one minute

visual aid *n* (1911) **:** an instructional device (as a chart, map, or model) that appeals chiefly to vision; *esp* **:** an educational motion picture or filmstrip
visual field *n* (1880) **:** the entire expanse of space visible at a given instant without moving the eyes — called also *field of vision*
vi·su·al·iza·tion \ˌvizh-(ə-)wə-lə-ˈzā-shən, ˌvizh-ə-lə-\ *n* (1883) **1 :** formation of mental visual images **2 :** the act or process of interpreting in visual terms or of putting into visible form **3 :** the process of making a viscus visible by the introduction (as by swallowing, by an injection, or by an enema) of a radiopaque substance followed by roentgenography
vi·su·al·ize \ˈvizh-(ə-)wə-ˌlīz, ˈvizh-ə-ˌlīz\ *vb* **-ized; -iz·ing** *vt* (1817) **:** to make visible: as **a :** to see or form a mental image of **:** ENVISAGE **b :** to make (an organ) visible by roentgenographic visualization ~ *vi* **:** to form a mental visual image
vi·su·al·iz·er \-ˌlī-zər\ *n* (1886) **:** one that visualizes; *esp* **:** one whose mental imagery is prevailingly visual
visual literacy *n* (1971) **:** the ability to recognize and understand ideas conveyed through visible actions or images (as pictures)
visual purple *n* (1878) **:** a photosensitive red or purple pigment in the retinal rods of various vertebrates; *esp* **:** RHODOPSIN
vi·ta \ˈvēt-ə, ˈvīt-ə\ *n, pl* **vi·tae** \ˈvē-ˌtī, ˈvīt-ē\ [L, lit., life] (1939) **1 :** a brief biographical sketch **2 :** CURRICULUM VITAE
vi·tal \ˈvīt-ᵊl\ *adj* [ME, fr. MF, fr. L *vitalis* of life, fr. *vita* life; akin to L *vivere* to live — more at QUICK] (14c) **1 a :** existing as a manifestation of life **b :** concerned with or necessary to the maintenance of life ⟨~ organs⟩ ⟨blood and other ~ fluids⟩ **2 :** full of life and vigor **:** ANIMATED **3 :** characteristic of life or living beings **4 a :** fundamentally concerned with or affecting life or living beings: as **(1) :** tending to renew or refresh the living **:** INVIGORATING **(2) :** destructive to life **:** MORTAL **b :** of the utmost importance **5 :** recording data relating to lives **6 :** of, relating to, or constituting the staining of living tissues ***syn*** see ESSENTIAL — **vi·tal·ly** \-ᵊl-ē\ *adv*
vital capacity *n* (1852) **:** the breathing capacity of the lungs expressed as the number of cubic inches or cubic centimeters of air that can be forcibly exhaled after a full inspiration
vi·tal·ism \ˈvīt-ᵊl-ˌiz-əm\ *n* (1822) **1 :** a doctrine that the functions of a living organism are due to a vital principle distinct from physicochemical forces **2 :** a doctrine that the processes of life are not explicable by the laws of physics and chemistry alone and that life is in some part self-determining — **vi·tal·ist** \-ᵊl-əst\ *n or adj* — **vi·tal·is·tic** \ˌvīt-ᵊl-ˈis-tik\ *adj*
vi·tal·i·ty \vī-ˈtal-ət-ē\ *n, pl* **-ties** (1592) **1 a :** the peculiarity distinguishing the living from the nonliving **b :** capacity to live and develop; *also* **:** physical or mental vigor esp. when highly developed **2 a :** power of enduring **b :** lively and animated character
vi·tal·ize \ˈvīt-ᵊl-ˌīz\ *vt* **-ized; -iz·ing** (1678) **:** to endow with vitality **:** ANIMATE — **vi·tal·iza·tion** \ˌvīt-ᵊl-ə-ˈzā-shən\ *n*
vi·tals \ˈvīt-ᵊlz\ *n pl* (1610) **1 :** vital organs (as the heart, liver, lungs, and brain) **2 :** essential parts
vital signs *n pl* (ca. 1919) **:** signs of life; *specif* **:** the pulse rate, respiratory rate, body temperature, and sometimes blood pressure of a person
vital statistics *n pl* (1837) **1 :** statistics relating to births, deaths, marriages, health, and disease **2 :** facts (as physical dimensions or quantities) considered to be interesting or important; *esp* **:** a woman's bust, waist, and hip measurements
vi·ta·min \ˈvīt-ə-mən, *Brit usu* ˈvit-\ *n* [L *vita* life + ISV *amine*] (1912) **:** any of various organic substances that are essential in minute quantities to the nutrition of most animals and some plants, act esp. as coenzymes and precursors of coenzymes in the regulation of metabolic processes but do not provide energy or serve as building units, and are present in natural foodstuffs or sometimes produced within the body
vitamin A *n* (1920) **:** any of several fat-soluble vitamins (as retinol) found esp. in animal products (as egg yolk, milk, or fish-liver oils) or a mixture of them whose lack in the animal body causes epithelial tissues to become keratinous (as in the eye with resulting visual defects)
vitamin B *n* (1920) **1 :** VITAMIN B COMPLEX **2** *or* **vitamin B_1** \-ˈbē-ˈwən\ **:** THIAMINE
vitamin B complex *n* (ca. 1928) **:** a group of water-soluble vitamins found esp. in yeast, seed germs, eggs, liver and flesh, and vegetables that have varied metabolic functions and include coenzymes and growth factors — called also *B complex;* compare BIOTIN, CHOLINE, NICOTINIC ACID, PANTOTHENIC ACID
vitamin B_6 \-ˈbē-ˈsiks\ *n* (1934) **:** pyridoxine or a closely related compound found widely in combined form and considered essential to vertebrate nutrition
vitamin B_{12} \-ˈbē-ˈtwelv\ *n* (1948) **:** a complex cobalt-containing compound $C_{63}H_{88}CoN_{14}O_{14}P$ that occurs esp. in liver, is essential to normal blood formation, neural function, and growth, and is used esp. in treating pernicious and related anemias and in animal feed as a growth factor; *also* **:** any of several compounds of similar action but different chemistry
vitamin B_2 \-ˈbē-ˈtü\ *n* (1928) **:** RIBOFLAVIN
vitamin C *n* (1920) **:** a water-soluble vitamin $C_6H_8O_6$ found in plants and esp. in fruits and leafy vegetables or made synthetically and used in the prevention and treatment of scurvy and as an antioxidant for foods — called also *ascorbic acid*
vitamin D *n* (1921) **:** any or all of several fat-soluble vitamins chemically related to steroids, essential for normal bone and tooth structure, and found esp. in fish-liver oils, egg yolk, and milk or produced by activation (as by ultraviolet irradiation) of sterols: as **a** *or* **vitamin D_2** \-ˈdē-ˈtü\ **:** CALCIFEROL **b** *or* **vitamin D_3** \-ˈdē-ˈthrē\ **:** CHOLECALCIFEROL
vitamin E *n* (1925) **:** any of several fat-soluble vitamins that are chemically tocopherols, are essential in the nutrition of various vertebrates in which their absence is associated with infertility, degenerative changes in muscle, or vascular abnormalities, are found esp. in leaves and in seed germ oils, and are used chiefly in animal feeds and as antioxidants
vitamin G *n* (1929) **:** RIBOFLAVIN
vitamin H *n* (ca. 1935) **:** BIOTIN
vitamin K *n* [Dan *koagulation* coagulation] (1935) **1 :** either of two naturally occurring fat-soluble vitamins $C_{31}H_{46}O_2$ and $C_{41}H_{56}O_2$ essential for the clotting of blood because of their role in the production of prothrombin — called also respectively *vitamin K_1, vitamin K_2* **2 :** any of several synthetic compounds closely related chemically to natural vitamins K_1 and K_2 and of similar biological activity
vi·tel·line \vī-ˈtel-ən, -ˌēn, -ˌīn\ *adj* [L *vitellus* + E *-ine*] (15c) **1 :** resembling the yolk of an egg esp. in yellow color **2 :** of, relating to, or producing yolk
vitelline membrane *n* (1845) **:** a membrane enclosing the egg proper and corresponding to the plasmalemma of an ordinary cell; *esp* **:** a membrane separating from the surface of the egg in many invertebrates immediately after the egg is fertilized and thereby preventing other spermatozoa from entering
vi·tel·lo·gen·e·sis \vī-ˌtel-ō-ˈjen-ə-səs, və-\ *n* [NL, fr. L *vitellus* + NL *-o-* + *genesis*] (1947) **:** yolk formation
vi·tel·lus \-ˈtel-əs\ *n* [L, lit., small calf — more at VEAL] (1728) **:** the egg cell proper including the yolk but excluding any albuminous or membranous envelopes; *also* **:** YOLK 1c
vi·ti·ate \ˈvish-ē-ˌāt\ *vt* **-at·ed; -at·ing** [L *vitiatus,* pp. of *vitiare,* fr. *vitium* fault, vice] (1534) **1 :** to make faulty or defective often by the addition of something that impairs **2 :** to debase in moral or aesthetic status ⟨a spirit *vitiated* by luxury⟩ **3 :** to make ineffective or weak ***syn*** see DEBASE — **vi·ti·a·tion** \ˌvish-ē-ˈā-shən\ *n* — **vi·ti·a·tor** \ˈvish-ē-ˌāt-ər\ *n*
vi·ti·cul·ture \ˈvit-ə-ˌkəl-chər, ˈvīt-\ *n* [L *vitis* vine + E *culture* — more at WITHY] (1872) **:** the cultivation or culture of grapes — **vi·ti·cul·tur·al** \ˌvit-ə-ˈkəlch(-ə)-rəl, ˌvīt-\ *adj* — **vi·ti·cul·tur·al·ly** \-ē\ *adv* — **vi·ti·cul·tur·ist** \-rəst\ *n*
vit·i·li·go \ˌvit-ᵊl-ˈī-(ˌ)gō, -ˈē-\ *n* [NL, fr. L, tetter] (1842) **:** a skin disorder manifested by smooth white spots on various parts of the body
vit·rec·to·my \və-ˈtrek-tə-mē\ *n, pl* **-mies** [NL, fr. *vit*reous humor + *-ectomy*] (1968) **:** surgical removal of all or part of the vitreous humor
vit·re·ous \ˈvi-trē-əs\ *adj* [L *vitreus,* fr. *vitrum* glass — more at WOAD] (1646) **1 :** of, relating to, derived from, or consisting of glass **2 a :** resembling glass (as in color, composition, brittleness, or luster) **:** GLASSY ⟨~ rocks⟩ **b :** characterized by low porosity and usu. translucence due to the presence of a glassy phase ⟨~ china⟩ **3 :** of, relating to, or constituting the vitreous humor
vitreous enamel *n* (1916) **:** a fired-on opaque glassy coating on metal (as steel)
vitreous humor *n* (1663) **:** the clear colorless transparent jelly that fills the eyeball posterior to the lens — see EYE illustration
vitreous silica *n* (1925) **:** a chemically stable and refractory glass made from silica alone — compare QUARTZ GLASS
vit·ri·fy \ˈvi-trə-ˌfī\ *vb* **-fied; -fy·ing** [MF *vitrifier,* fr. L *vitrum* glass] *vt* (1594) **:** to convert into glass or a glassy substance by heat and fusion ~ *vi* **:** to become vitrified — **vit·ri·fi·able** \-ˌfī-ə-bəl\ *adj* — **vit·ri·fi·ca·tion** \ˌvi-trə-fə-ˈkā-shən\ *n*
vi·trine \və-ˈtrēn\ *n* [F, fr. *vitre* pane of glass, fr. OF, fr. L *vitrum*] (1880) **:** a glass showcase or cabinet esp. for displaying fine wares or specimens
vit·ri·ol \ˈvi-trē-əl\ *n* [ME, fr. MF, fr. ML *vitriolum,* alter. of LL *vitreolum,* neut. of *vitreolus* glassy, fr. L *vitreus* vitreous] (14c) **1 a :** a sulfate of any of various metals (as copper, iron, or zinc); *esp* **:** a glassy hydrate of such a sulfate **b :** OIL OF VITRIOL **2 :** something felt to resemble vitriol esp. in caustic quality; *esp* **:** virulence of feeling or of speech — **vit·ri·ol·ic** \ˌvi-trē-ˈäl-ik\ *adj*
vit·ta \ˈvit-ə\ *n, pl* **vit·tae** \ˈvit-ē, ˈvi-ˌtē, ˈvi-ˌtī\ [NL, fr. L, fillet; akin to L *viēre* to plait — more at WIRE] (1830) **1 :** one of the oil tubes in the fruits of plants of the carrot family **2 :** STRIPE, STREAK
vit·tles \ˈvit-ᵊlz\ *n pl* (14c) **:** VICTUALS
vi·tu·per·ate \vī-ˈt(y)ü-pə-ˌrāt, və-\ *vb* **-at·ed; -at·ing** [L *vituperatus,* pp. of *vituperare,* fr. *vitium* fault + *parare* to make — more at PARE] *vt* (1542) **:** to abuse or censure severely or abusively **:** BERATE ~ *vi* **:** to use harsh condemnatory language ***syn*** see SCOLD — **vi·tu·per·a·tor** \-ˌrāt-ər\ *n*
vi·tu·per·a·tion \(ˌ)vī-ˌt(y)ü-pə-ˈrā-shən, və-\ *n* [ME, fr. MF, fr. L *vituperation-, vituperatio,* fr. *vituperatus,* pp.] (15c) **1 :** sustained and bitter railing and condemnation **:** vituperative utterance **2 :** an act or instance of vituperating ***syn*** see ABUSE
vi·tu·per·a·tive \vī-ˈt(y)ü-p(ə-)rət-iv, -pə-ˌrāt-\ *adj* [LL *vituperativus,* fr L *vituperatus,* pp.] (1727) **:** uttering or given to censure **:** containing or characterized by verbal abuse — **vi·tu·per·a·tive·ly** *adv*
vi·tu·per·a·to·ry \-p(ə-)rə-ˌtōr-ē, -ˌtȯr-\ *adj* (ca. 1586) **:** VITUPERATIVE
vi·va \ˈvē-və, -ˌvä\ *interj* [It, long live, fr. 3d pers. sing. pres. subj. of *vivere* to live, fr. L — more at QUICK] (1674) — used to express goodwill or approval
[1]**vi·va·ce** \vē-ˈväch-(ˌ)ā, -ē\ *adv or adj* [It, vivacious, fr. L *vivac-, vivax*] (ca. 1683) **:** in a brisk spirited manner — used as a direction in music
[2]**vivace** *n* (ca. 1683) **:** a musical composition or movement in vivace tempo
vi·va·cious \və-ˈvā-shəs *also* vī-\ *adj* [L *vivac-, vivax,* lit., long-lived, fr. *vivere* to live — more at QUICK] (1645) **:** lively in temper or conduct **:** SPRIGHTLY ***syn*** see LIVELY — **vi·va·cious·ly** *adv* — **vi·va·cious·ness** *n*
vi·vac·i·ty \-ˈvas-ət-ē\ *n* [ME, fr. MF, fr. L *vivacitat-, vivacitas,* fr. *vivac-, vivax*] (15c) **:** the quality or state of being vivacious
vi·van·dière \ˌvē-ˌväⁿ-ˈdye(ə)r\ *n* [F, fem. of MF *vivandier,* fr. ML *vivanda* food — more at VIAND] (1848) **:** a female sutler
vi·var·i·um \vī-ˈvar-ē-əm, -ˈver-\ *n, pl* **-ia** \-ē-ə\ *or* **-i·ums** [L, park, preserve, fr. *vivus* alive — more at QUICK] (1853) **:** an enclosure for keeping or raising and observing animals or plants indoors; *esp* **:** one for terrestrial animals — compare TERRARIUM
[1]**vi·va vo·ce** \ˌvī-və-ˈvō-(ˌ)sē *or (as if fr It)* ˌvē-və-ˈvō-(ˌ)chā\ *adv* [ML, with the living voice] (1563) **:** by word of mouth **:** ORALLY
[2]**viva voce** *adj* (1654) **:** expressed or conducted by word of mouth **:** ORAL
[3]**viva voce** *n* (1842) **:** an examination conducted viva voce
vi·vax malaria \ˈvī-ˌvaks-\ *n* [NL *vivax,* specific epithet of *Plasmodium vivax,* parasite causing tertian] (ca. 1941) **:** malaria caused by a plas-

modium (*Plasmodium vivax*) that induces paroxysms at 48-hour intervals
vi·ver·rid \vī-'ver-əd\ *n* [NL *Viverridae*, fr. *Viverra*, type genus, fr. L *viverra* ferret] (1902) : any of a family (*Viverridae*) of carnivorous mammals (as a civet, a genet, or a mongoose) that are rarely larger than a domestic cat but are long, slender, and like a weasel in build with short more or less retractile claws and rounded feet — **viverrid** *adj*
vi·vers \'vē-vərz, 'vī-\ *n pl* [MF *vivres*, pl. of *vivre* food, fr. *vivre* to live, fr. L *vivere*] *chiefly Scot* (1536) : VICTUALS, FOOD
Viv·i·an *or* **Viv·i·en** \'viv-ē-ən\ *n* : the mistress of Merlin in Arthurian legend — called also *Lady of the Lake*
viv·id \'viv-əd\ *adj* [L *vividus*, fr. *vivere* to live — more at QUICK] (1638) **1** : having the appearance of vigorous life or freshness : LIVELY ⟨~ sketch⟩ **2** *of a color* : very strong : very high in chroma **3** : producing a strong or clear impression on the senses : SHARP, INTENSE; *specif* : producing distinct mental images ⟨a ~ description⟩ **4** : acting clearly and vigorously ⟨a ~ imagination⟩ ***syn*** see GRAPHIC — **viv·id·ly** *adv* — **viv·id·ness** *n*
vi·vif·ic \vī-'vif-ik\ *adj* [L *vivificus*] (1551) : imparting spirit or vivacity
viv·i·fy \'viv-ə-,fī\ *vt* **-fied; -fy·ing** [MF *vivifier*, fr. LL *vivificare*, fr. L *vivificus* enlivening, fr. *vivus* alive — more at QUICK] (1545) **1** : to endue with life or renewed life : ANIMATE ⟨rains that ~ the barren hills⟩ **2** : to impart vitality or vividness to ⟨concentrating this union of quality and meaning in a way which *vivifies* both — John Dewey⟩ ***syn*** see QUICKEN — **viv·i·fi·ca·tion** \,viv-ə-fə-'kā-shən\ *n* — **viv·i·fi·er** \'viv-ə-,fī(-ə)r\ *n*
vi·vi·par·i·ty \,vī-və-'par-ət-ē, ,viv-ə-\ *n* (1864) : the quality or state of being viviparous
vi·vip·a·rous \vī-'vip-(ə-)rəs, və-\ *adj* [L *viviparus*, fr. *vivus* alive + *-parus* -parous] (1646) **1** : producing living young instead of eggs from within the body in the manner of nearly all mammals, many reptiles, and a few fishes **2** : germinating while still attached to the parent plant ⟨the ~ seed of the mangrove⟩ — **vi·vip·a·rous·ly** *adv*
vivi·sect \'viv-ə-,sekt\ *vb* [back-formation fr. *vivisection*] *vt* (1864) : to perform vivisection on ~ *vi* : to practice vivisection — **vivi·sec·tor** \-,sek-tər\ *n*
vivi·sec·tion \,viv-ə-'sek-shən, 'viv-ə-,\ *n* [L *vivus* + E *section*] (1707) : the cutting of or operation on a living animal usu. for physiological or pathological investigation; *broadly* : animal experimentation esp. if considered to cause distress to the subject — **vivi·sec·tion·al** \,viv-ə-'sek-shnəl, -shən-ᵊl\ *adj* — **vivi·sec·tion·ist** \-'sek-sh(ə-)nəst\ *n*
vix·en \'vik-sən\ *n* [(assumed) ME (southern dial.) *vixen*, alter. of ME *fixen*, fr. OE *fyxe*, fem. of *fox*] (bef. 12c) **1** : a female fox **2** : a shrewish ill-tempered woman — **vix·en·ish** \-s(ə-)nish\ *adj*
viz·ard \'viz-ərd, -,ärd\ *n* [alter. of ME *viser* mask, visor] (1555) **1** : a mask for disguise or protection **2** : DISGUISE, GUISE
viz·ca·cha *var of* VISCACHA
vi·zier \və-'zi(ə)r\ *n* [Turk *vezir*, fr. Ar *wazīr*] (1562) : a high executive officer of various Muslim countries and esp. of the former Turkish Empire — **vi·zier·ate** \-'zir-ət, -'zi(ə)r-,āt\ *n* — **vi·zier·ial** \-'zir-ē-əl\ *adj* — **vi·zier·ship** \-'zi(ə)r-,ship\ *n*
vi·zor *var of* VISOR
vizs·la \'vizh-,lō\ *n* [*Vizsla*, Hungary] (ca. 1948) : any of a Hungarian breed of hunting dog resembling the weimaraner but having a rich deep red coat and brown eyes
V neck *n* (1905) : a V-shaped neck of a garment — **V–necked** *adj*
vo·ca·ble \'vō-kə-bəl\ *n* [MF, fr. L *vocabulum*, fr. *vocare* to call — more at VOICE] (1530) : TERM; *specif* : a word composed of various sounds or letters without regard to its meaning
vo·cab·u·lar \vō-'kab-yə-lər, və-\ *adj* [back-formation fr. *vocabulary*] (1608) : of or relating to words or phraseology : VERBAL
vo·cab·u·lary \vō-'kab-yə-,ler-ē, və-\ *n, pl* **-lar·ies** [MF *vocabulaire*, prob. fr. ML *vocabularium*, fr. neut. of *vocabularius* verbal, fr. L *vocabulum*] (1532) **1** : a list or collection of words or of words and phrases usu. alphabetically arranged and explained or defined : LEXICON **2 a** : a sum or stock of words employed by a language, group, individual, or work or in a field of knowledge **b** : a list or collection of terms or codes available for use (as in an indexing system) **3** : a supply of expressive techniques or devices (as of an art form)
vocabulary entry *n* (ca. 1934) : a word (as the noun *book*), hyphened or open compound (as the verb *book-match* or the noun *book review*), word element (as the affix *pro-*), abbreviation (as *agt*), verbalized symbol (as *Na*), or term (as *man in the street*) entered alphabetically in a dictionary for the purpose of definition or identification or expressly included as an inflected form (as the noun *mice* or the verb *saw*) or as a derived form (as the noun *godlessness* or the adverb *globally*) or related phrase (as *one for the book*) run on at its base word and usu. set in a type (as boldface) readily distinguishable from that of the lightface running text which defines, explains, or identifies the entry
¹vo·cal \'vō-kəl\ *adj* [ME, fr. L *vocalis*, fr. *voc-*, *vox* voice — more at VOICE] (14c) **1 a** : uttered by the voice : ORAL **b** : produced in the larynx : uttered with voice **2** : relating to, composed or arranged for, or sung by the human voice ⟨~ music⟩ **3** : VOCALIC **4 a** : having or exercising the power of producing voice, speech, or sound **b** : EXPRESSIVE **c** : full of voices : RESOUNDING **d** : given to expressing oneself freely or insistently : OUTSPOKEN **e** : expressed in words **5** : of, relating to, or resembling the voice ⟨~ impairment⟩ — **vo·cal·i·ty** \vō-'kal-ət-ē\ *n* — **vo·cal·ly** \'vō-kə-lē\ *adv*
²vocal *n* (1582) **1** : a vocal sound **2** : a usu. accompanied musical composition for the human voice : SONG; *also* : a performance of such a composition
vocal cords *n pl* (ca. 1852) : either of two pairs of folds of mucous membranes that project into the cavity of the larynx and have free edges extending dorsoventrally toward the middle line
¹vo·cal·ic \vō-'kal-ik, və-\ *adj* [L *vocalis* vowel, fr. *vocalis* vocal] (1814) **1** : marked by or consisting of vowels **2 a** : being or functioning as a vowel **b** : of, relating to, or associated with a vowel — **vo·cal·i·cal·ly** \-i-k(ə-)lē\ *adv*
²vocalic *n* (1924) : a vowel sound or sequence in its function as the most sonorous part of a syllable
vo·cal·ism \'vō-kə-,liz-əm\ *n* (ca. 1864) **1** : VOCALIZATION **2** : vocal art or technique : SINGING **3** : the vowel system of a language or dialect
vo·cal·ist \-kə-ləst\ *n* (1834) : ¹SINGER
vo·cal·ize \'vō-kə-,līz\ *vb* **-ized; -iz·ing** *vt* (1669) **1** : to give voice to : UTTER; *specif* : SING **2 a** : to make voiced rather than voiceless : VOICE **b** : to convert to a vowel **3** : to furnish (as a consonantal Hebrew or Arabic text) with vowels or vowel points ~ *vi* **1** : to utter vocal sounds **2** : SING; *specif* : to sing without words — **vo·cal·iza·tion** \,vō-kə-lə-'zā-shən\ *n* — **vo·cal·iz·er** \'vō-kə-,lī-zər\ *n*
vo·ca·tion \vō-'kā-shən\ *n* [ME *vocacioun*, fr. L *vocation-*, *vocatio* summons, fr. *vocatus*, pp. of *vocare* to call — more at VOICE] (15c) **1 a** : a summons or strong inclination to a particular state or course of action; *esp* : a divine call to the religious life **b** : an entry into the priesthood or a religious order **2 a** : the work in which a person is regularly employed : OCCUPATION **b** : the persons engaged in a particular occupation **3** : the special function of an individual or group
vo·ca·tion·al \-shnəl, -shən-ᵊl\ *adj* (1652) **1** : of, relating to, or concerned with a vocation **2** : of, relating to, or being in training in a skill or trade to be pursued as a career — **vo·ca·tion·al·ly** \-ē\ *adv*
vo·ca·tion·al·ism \-,iz-əm\ *n* (1924) : emphasis on vocational training in education — **vo·ca·tion·al·ist** \-əst\ *n*
¹voc·a·tive \'väk-ət-iv\ *adj* [ME *vocatif*, fr. MF, fr. L *vocativus*, fr. *vocatus*, pp.] (15c) **1** : of, relating to, or being a grammatical case marking the one addressed ⟨Latin *Domine* in *miserere, Domine* "have mercy, O Lord" is in the ~ case⟩ **2** *of a word or word group* : marking the one addressed ⟨*mother* in "mother, come here" is a ~ expression⟩ — **voc·a·tive·ly** *adv*
²vocative *n* (1522) **1** : the vocative case of a language **2** : a form in the vocative case
vo·cif·er·ant \vō-'sif-ə-rənt\ *adj* (1609) : CLAMOROUS, VOCIFEROUS
vo·cif·er·ate \-,rāt\ *vb* **-at·ed; -at·ing** [L *vociferatus*, pp. of *vociferari*, fr. *voc-*, *vox* voice + *ferre* to bear — more at VOICE, BEAR] *vt* (1599) : to utter loudly : SHOUT ~ *vi* : to cry out loudly : CLAMOR — **vo·cif·er·a·tion** \-,sif-ə-'rā-shən\ *n* — **vo·cif·er·a·tor** \-'sif-ə-,rāt-ər\ *n*
vo·cif·er·ous \vō-'sif-(ə-)rəs\ *adj* (1611) : marked by or given to vehement insistent outcry — **vo·cif·er·ous·ly** *adv* — **vo·cif·er·ous·ness** *n*
syn VOCIFEROUS, CLAMOROUS, BLATANT, STRIDENT, BOISTEROUS, OBSTREPEROUS mean so loud or insistent as to compel attention. VOCIFEROUS implies a vehement deafening shouting or calling out ⟨*vociferous* cries of protest and outrage⟩ CLAMOROUS may imply insistency as well as vociferousness in demanding or protesting ⟨*clamorous* demands for prison reforms⟩ BLATANT implies an offensive bellowing or insensitive loudness ⟨a *blatant* and abusive drunkard⟩ STRIDENT suggests harsh and discordant noise ⟨heard the *strident* cry of the crow⟩ BOISTEROUS suggests a noisiness and turbulence due to high spirits ⟨a *boisterous* crowd of party goers⟩ OBSTREPEROUS suggests unruly and aggressive noisiness and resistance to restraint ⟨the *obstreperous* demonstrators were removed from the hall⟩
vo·cod·er \'vō-'kōd-ər\ *n* [*voice coder*] (ca. 1939) : an electronic mechanism that reduces speech signals to slowly varying signals which can be transmitted over communication systems of limited frequency bandwidth
vod·ka \'väd-kə\ *n* [Russ, fr. *voda* water; akin to OE *wæter* water] (1802) : a colorless liquor of neutral spirits distilled from a mash (as of rye or wheat)
vodka martini *n* (1948) : a martini made with vodka instead of gin
vo·dun *also* **vo·doun** \vō-'düⁿ\ *n* [Haitian Creole] (ca. 1937) : VOODOO 1
vo·gie \'vō-gē\ *adj* [origin unknown] *Scot* (1712) : PROUD, VAIN
vogue \'vōg\ *n* [MF, action of rowing, course, fashion, fr. OIt *voga*, fr. *vogare* to row; akin to OSp *bogar* to row] (1571) **1** *archaic* : the leading place in popularity or acceptance **2 a** : popular acceptation or favor : POPULARITY **b** : a period of popularity **3** : one that is in fashion at a particular time ***syn*** see FASHION — **vogue** *adj*
vogu·ish \'vō-gish\ *adj* (1926) **1** : FASHIONABLE, SMART **2** : suddenly or temporarily popular — **vogu·ish·ness** *n*
¹voice \'vȯis\ *n* [ME, fr. OF *vois*, fr. L *voc-*, *vox*; akin to OHG *giwahanen* to mention, L *vocare* to call, Gk *epos* word, speech] (13c) **1 a** : sound produced by vertebrates by means of lungs, larynx, or syrinx; *esp* : sound so produced by human beings **b** (1) : musical sound produced by the vocal cords and resonated by the cavities of head and throat (2) : the power or ability to produce musical tones (3) : SINGER (4) : one of the melodic parts in a vocal or instrumental composition (5) : condition of the vocal organs with respect to production of musical tones (6) : the use of the voice (as in singing or acting) ⟨studying ~⟩ **c** : expiration of air with the vocal cords drawn close so as to vibrate audibly (as in uttering vowels and consonant sounds as \v\ or \z\) **d** : the faculty of utterance : SPEECH **2** : a sound resembling or suggesting vocal utterance **3** : an instrument or medium of expression ⟨the party became the ~ of the workers⟩ **4 a** : wish, choice, or opinion openly or formally expressed ⟨claimed to follow the ~ of the people⟩ **b** : right of expression; *also* : influential power **5** : distinction of form or a system of inflections of a verb to indicate the relation of the subject of the verb to the action which the verb expresses ⟨active and passive ~*s*⟩ — **with one voice** : without dissent : UNANIMOUSLY
²voice *vt* **voiced; voic·ing** (15c) **1** : to express in words : UTTER ⟨~ a complaint⟩ **2** : to adjust for producing the proper musical sounds **3** : to pronounce (as a consonant) with voice ***syn*** see EXPRESS
voice box *n* (1912) : LARYNX
voiced \'vȯist\ *adj* (1600) **1** : furnished with a voice — often used in combination ⟨soft-*voiced*⟩ **2** : uttered with vocal cord vibration ⟨a ~ consonant⟩ — **voiced·ness** \'vȯis(t)-nəs, 'vȯi-səd-nəs\ *n*
voice·ful \'vȯis-fəl\ *adj* (1611) : having a voice or vocal quality; *also* : having a loud voice or many voices — **voice·ful·ness** *n*
voice·less \'vȯi-sləs\ *adj* (1535) **1** : having no voice : MUTE **2** : not voiced : SURD ⟨a ~ consonant⟩ — **voice·less·ly** *adv* — **voice·less·ness** *n*
voice–over \'vȯi-,sō-vər\ *n* (ca. 1949) : the voice of an unseen narrator heard in a motion picture or a television program; *also* : the voice of a visible character indicating his thoughts but without motion of his lips
voice part *n* (1869) : VOICE 1b(4)
voice·print \'vȯi-,sprint\ *n* [*voice* + *-print* (as in *fingerprint*)] (ca. 1962) : an individually distinctive pattern of certain voice characteristics that is spectrographically produced
voic·er \'vȯi-sər\ *n* (1879) : one that voices; *specif* : one that voices organ pipes
voice vote *n* (ca. 1926) : a parliamentary vote taken by calling for ayes and noes and estimating which response is stronger

[1]**void** \'vȯid\ *adj* [ME *voide,* fr. OF, fr. (assumed) VL *vocitus,* deriv. of L *vacuus* — more at VACUUM] (13c) **1 :** containing nothing ⟨~ space⟩ **2 :** IDLE, LEISURE **3 a :** not occupied : VACANT ⟨a ~ bishopric⟩ **b :** not inhabited : DESERTED **4 a :** being without : DEVOID ⟨a nature ~ of all malice⟩ **b :** having no members or examples; *specif, of a suit* **:** having no cards represented in a particular hand ⟨bid a ~ suit as a slam signal⟩ **5 :** VAIN, USELESS **6 a :** of no legal force or effect : NULL ⟨a ~ contract⟩ **b :** VOIDABLE ***syn*** see EMPTY — **void·ness** *n*

[2]**void** *n* (1616) **1 a :** empty space : EMPTINESS, VACUUM **b :** OPENING, GAP **2 :** the quality or state of being without something : LACK, ABSENCE **3 :** a feeling of want or hollowness **4 :** absence of cards of a particular suit in a hand as dealt

[3]**void** *vb* [ME *voiden,* fr. MF *vuidier,* fr. (assumed) VL *vocitare,* fr. *vocitus*] *vt* (14c) **1 a :** to make empty or vacant : CLEAR **b** *archaic* **:** VACATE, LEAVE **2 :** DISCHARGE, EMIT ⟨~ excrement⟩ **3 :** NULLIFY, ANNUL ⟨~ a contract⟩ ~ *vi* **:** to eliminate solid or liquid waste from the body — **void·er** *n*

void·able \'vȯid-ə-bəl\ *adj* (15c) **:** capable of being voided; *specif* **:** capable of being adjudged void — **void·able·ness** *n*

void·ance \'vȯid-ᵊn(t)s\ *n* (14c) **1 :** the act of voiding **2** *of a benefice* **:** the state of being without an incumbent

void·ed \'vȯid-əd\ *adj* (1539) **:** having the inner part cut away or left vacant with a narrow border left at the sides — used of a heraldic charge

voi·là *also* **voi·la** \vwä-'lä\ *interj* [F, prep., there is] (ca. 1832) — used to call attention or to express satisfaction or approval

voile \'vȯi(ə)l\ *n* [F, veil, fr. L *vela,* neut. pl. of *velum*] (1889) **:** a fine soft sheer fabric used esp. for women's summer clothing or curtains

voir dire \(')(v)wär(r)-'di(ə)r\ *n* [AF, fr. OF, to speak the truth] (1676) **:** a preliminary examination to determine the competency of a witness or juror

vo·lant \'vō-lənt\ *adj* [MF, fr. L *volant-, volans,* prp. of *volare* to fly] (1572) **1 :** having the wings extended as if in flight — used of a heraldic bird **2 :** flying or capable of flying **3 :** QUICK, NIMBLE

vo·lan·te \vō-'län-(,)tā\ *adj* [It, lit., flying, fr. L *volant-, volans,* prp.] (ca. 1854) **:** moving with light rapidity — used as a direction in music

Vo·la·pük \'vō-lə-,pük, 'väl-ə-\ *n* [Volapük, lit., world's speech, fr. *vola* of the world (gen. of *vol* world, modif. of E *world*) + *pük* speech, modif. of E *speak*] (1885) **:** an artificial international language based largely on English but with some root words from German, French, and Latin

vo·lar \'vō-lər, -,lär\ *adj* [L *vola* palm of the hand, sole of the foot] (1814) **:** relating to the palm of the hand or the sole of the foot; *specif* **:** located on the same side as the palm of the hand ⟨the ~ part of the forearm⟩

[1]**vol·a·tile** \'väl-ət-ᵊl, *esp Brit* -ə-,tīl\ *n* [ME *volatil,* fr. MF, fr. *volatilie* group of birds, fr. ML *volatilia,* fr. L, neut. pl. of *volatilis* winged, volatile] (14c) **:** a volatile substance

[2]**volatile** *adj* [F, fr. L *volatilis,* fr. *volatus,* pp. of *volare* to fly] (1605) **1 :** readily vaporizable at a relatively low temperature **2 :** flying or having the power to fly **3 a :** LIGHTHEARTED, LIVELY **b :** easily aroused ⟨~ suspicions⟩ **c :** tending to erupt into violence : EXPLOSIVE **4 a :** unable to hold the attention fixed because of an inherent lightness or fickleness of disposition : CHANGEABLE **b :** characterized by rapid change **5 :** difficult to capture or hold permanently : EVANESCENT, TRANSITORY — **vol·a·tile·ness** *n* — **vol·a·til·i·ty** \,väl-ə-'til-ət-ē\ *n*

volatile oil *n* (1800) **:** an oil that vaporizes readily; *esp* **:** ESSENTIAL OIL

vol·a·til·ize \'väl-ət-ᵊl-,īz, *Brit also* və-'lat-\ *vb* **-ized; -iz·ing** *vt* (1657) **:** to make volatile; *esp* **:** to cause to pass off in vapor ~ *vi* **:** to pass off in vapor — **vol·a·til·iz·able** \-,ī-zə-bəl\ *adj* — **vol·a·til·iza·tion** \,väl-ət-ᵊl-ə-'zā-shən, *Brit also* və-,lat-\ *n*

vol–au–vent \,vȯ-lō-'vänⁿ\ *n* [F, lit., flight in the wind] (1828) **:** a large baked patty shell filled with a ragout of meat, fowl, game, or fish

[1]**vol·ca·nic** \väl-'kan-ik, vȯl- *also* -'kān-\ *adj* (1774) **1 a :** of, relating to, or produced by a volcano **b :** characterized by volcanoes **c :** made of materials from volcanoes **2 :** explosively violent : VOLATILE ⟨~ emotions⟩ — **vol·ca·ni·cal·ly** \-i-k(ə-)lē\ *adv*

[2]**volcanic** *n* (1894) **:** a volcanic rock

volcanic glass *n* (1840) **:** natural glass produced by the cooling of molten lava too rapidly to permit crystallization

vol·ca·nic·i·ty \,väl-kə-'nis-ət-ē, ,vȯl-\ *n* (1836) **:** VOLCANISM

vol·ca·nism \'väl-kə-,niz-əm, 'vȯl-\ *n* (ca. 1864) **:** volcanic power or action

vol·ca·no \väl-'kā-(,)nō, vȯl-\ *n, pl* **-noes** *or* **-nos** [It *vulcano,* fr. L *Volcanus, Vulcanus* Vulcan] (15c) **:** a vent in the crust of the earth or another planet from which usu. molten or hot rock and steam issue; *also* **:** a hill or mountain composed wholly or in part of the ejected material

vol·ca·no·log·i·cal \,väl-kən-ᵊl-'äj-i-kəl, ,vȯl-\ *also* **vol·ca·no·log·ic** \-ik\ *adj* (1949) **:** of, relating to, or involving volcanology or volcanic phenomena ⟨~ processes that shape the planets⟩

vol·ca·nol·o·gy \,väl-kə-'näl-ə-jē, ,vȯl-\ *n* (1886) **:** a branch of science that deals with volcanic phenomena — **vol·ca·nol·o·gist** \-jəst\ *n*

[1]**vole** \'vōl\ *n* [F, prob. fr. *voler* to fly — more at VOLLEY] (1675) **:** GRAND SLAM 1

[2]**vole** *n* [earlier *vole-mouse,* fr. *vole-* (of Scand origin; akin to ON *vǫllr* field) + *mouse;* akin to OE *weald* forest — more at WOLD] (1805) **:** any of various small rodents (family Cricetidae and esp. genus *Microtus*) that typically have a stout body, rather blunt nose, and short ears, that inhabit both moist meadows and dry uplands and do much damage to crops, and that are closely related to muskrats and lemmings but in general resemble stocky mice or rats

vo·li·tion \vō-'lish-ən, və-\ *n* [F, fr. ML *volition-, volitio,* fr. L *vol-* (stem of *velle* to will, wish) + *-ition-, -itio* (as in L *position-, positio* position) — more at WILL] (1615) **1 :** an act of making a choice or decision; *also* **:** a choice or decision made **2 :** the power of choosing or determining : WILL — **vo·li·tion·al** \-'lish-nəl, -ən-ᵊl\ *adj*

vol·i·tive \'väl-ət-iv\ *adj* (1660) **1 :** of or relating to the will **2 :** expressing a wish or permission

volks·lied \'fōk-,slēt, 'fȯlk-\ *n, pl* **volks·lie·der** \-,slēd-ər\ [G, fr. *volk* people (fr. OHG *folc*) + *lied* song — more at FOLK, LIED] (ca. 1854) **:** a folk song

[1]**vol·ley** \'väl-ē\ *n, pl* **volleys** [MF *volee* flight, fr. *voler* to fly, fr. L *volare*] (1573) **1 a :** a flight of missiles (as arrows) **b :** simultaneous discharge of a number of missile weapons **c :** one round per gun in a battery fired as soon as a gun is ready without regard to order **d** (1) **:** the flight of the ball (as in volleyball or tennis) or its course before striking the ground; *also* **:** a return of the ball before it touches the ground (2) **:** a kick of the ball in soccer before it rebounds (3) **:** the exchange of the shuttlecock in badminton following the serve **2 a :** a burst or emission of many things at once **b :** a burst of simultaneous or immediately sequential nerve impulses passing to an end organ, synapse, or center

[2]**volley** *vb* **vol·leyed; vol·ley·ing** *vt* (1591) **1 :** to discharge in or as if in a volley **2 :** to propel (an object) while in the air and before touching the ground; *esp* **:** to hit (a tennis ball) on the volley ~ *vi* **1 :** to become discharged in or as if in a volley **2 :** to make a volley; *specif* **:** to volley an object of play (as in tennis) — **vol·ley·er** *n*

vol·ley·ball \'väl-ē-,bȯl\ *n* (1896) **:** a game played by volleying a large inflated ball over a net; *also* **:** the ball used in this game

vol·plane \'väl-,plān, 'vȯl-\ *vi* **vol·planed; vol·plan·ing** [F *vol plané* gliding flight] (1909) **1 :** to glide in or as if in an airplane **2 :** GLIDE 3

Vol·sci \'vȯl-,skē, 'väl-,sī\ *n pl* [L] (14c) **:** a people of ancient Italy dwelling between the Latins and Samnites

Vol·scian \'väl-shən, 'vȯl-skē-ən\ *n, pl* **Volscians** (1513) **1 :** a member of the Volsci **2 :** the Italic language of the Volsci — **Volscian** *adj*

[1]**volt** \'vōlt, 'vȯlt\ *n* [F *volte,* fr. It *volta* turn, fr. *voltare* to turn, fr. (assumed) VL *volvitare,* freq. of L *volvere* to roll — more at VOLUBLE] (1688) **1 :** a leaping movement in fencing to avoid a thrust **2 a :** a tread or gait in which a horse going sideways makes a turn around a center **b :** a circle traced by a horse in this movement

[2]**volt** \'vōlt\ *n* [Alessandro *Volta*] (1873) **1 :** the practical meter-kilogram-second unit of electrical potential difference and electromotive force equal to the difference of potential between two points in a conducting wire carrying a constant current of one ampere when the power dissipated between these two points is equal to one watt and equivalent to the potential difference across a resistance of one ohm when one ampere is flowing through it **2 :** a unit of electrical potential difference and electromotive force equal to 1.00034 volts and formerly taken as the standard in the U. S. — called also *international volt*

volt·age \'vōl-tij\ *n* (1890) **1 :** electric potential or potential difference expressed in volts **2 :** intensity of feeling

voltage divider *n* (ca. 1922) **:** a resistor or series of resistors provided with taps at certain points and used to provide various potential differences from a single power source

vol·ta·ic \väl-'tā-ik, vōl-, vȯl-\ *adj* [Alessandro *Volta*] (1812) **:** of, relating to, or producing direct electric current by chemical action (as in a battery) : GALVANIC ⟨~ cell⟩

voltaic pile *n* (1815) **:** [3]PILE 4a

vol·ta·me·ter \vōl-'tam-ət-ər, 'vōl-tə-,mēt-\ *n* [ISV *voltaic* + *-meter*] (1836) **:** an apparatus for measuring the quantity of electricity passed through a conductor by the amount of electrolysis produced — **vol·ta·met·ric** \,vōl-tə-'me-trik\ *adj*

volt·am·me·ter \'vōl-'tam-,ēt-ər\ *n* [*volt* + *ampere* + *-meter*] (ca. 1889) **:** an instrument for indicating one or more ranges of volts and amperes by changing terminal connections

volt–am·pere \-'tam-,pi(ə)r *also* -,pe(ə)r\ *n* (ca. 1896) **:** a unit of electric measurement equal to the product of a volt and an ampere that for direct current constitutes a measure of power equivalent to a watt

volte–face \,vȯlt-(ə-)'fäs\ *n* [F, fr. It *voltafaccia,* fr. *voltare* to turn + *faccia* face, fr. (assumed) VL *facia* — more at VOLT] (1819) **:** a reversal in policy : ABOUT-FACE

-vol·tine \'vōl-,tēn, 'vȯl-\ *adj comb form* [F, fr. It *volta* time, occasion, lit., turn — more at VOLT] **:** having (so many) generations or broods in a season or year ⟨multi*voltine*⟩

volt·me·ter \'vōlt-,mēt-ər\ *n* [ISV] (1882) **:** an instrument (as a galvanometer) for measuring in volts the differences in potential between different points of an electrical circuit

vol·u·ble \'väl-yə-bəl\ *adj* [MF or L; MF, fr. L *volubilis,* fr. *volvere* to roll; akin to OE *wealwian* to roll, Gk *eilyein* to roll, wrap] (1588) **1 :** characterized by ready or rapid speech : GLIB, FLUENT **2 :** easily rolling or turning : ROTATING ***syn*** see TALKATIVE — **vol·u·bil·i·ty** \,väl-yə-'bil-ət-ē\ *n* — **vol·u·ble·ness** \'väl-yə-bəl-nəs\ *n* — **vol·u·bly** \-blē\ *adv*

[1]**vol·ume** \'väl-yəm, -(,)yüm\ *n* [ME, fr. MF, fr. L *volumen* roll, scroll, fr. *volvere* to roll] (14c) **1 a :** a series of printed sheets bound typically in book form : BOOK **b :** a series of issues of a periodical **c :** ALBUM 1c **2 :** SCROLL 1a **3 :** the amount of space occupied by a three-dimensional figure as measured in cubic units (as inches, quarts, or pecks) : cubic capacity — see METRIC SYSTEM table, WEIGHT table **4 a** (1) **:** AMOUNT; *also* **:** BULK, MASS (2) **:** a considerable quantity **b :** the amount of a substance occupying a particular volume **c :** mass or the

VOLUME FORMULAS

FIGURE	FORMULA	MEANING OF LETTERS
cube	$V = a^3$	a = length of one edge
rectangular prism	$V = abc$	a = length; b = width; c = depth
pyramid	$V = \frac{Ah}{3}$	A = area of base; h = height
cylinder	$V = \pi r^2 h$	π = 3.1416; r = radius of the base; h = height
cone	$V = \frac{\pi r^2 h}{3}$	π = 3.1416; r = radius of the base; h = height
sphere	$V = \frac{4\pi r^3}{3}$	π = 3.1416; r = radius

representation of mass in art or architecture **5 :** the degree of loudness or the intensity of a sound; *also* **:** LOUDNESS ***syn*** see BULK — **vol·umed** \-yəmd, -(ˌ)yümd\ *adj*

[2]**volume** *adj* (1661) **:** involving large quantities ⟨did a ~ business in staples⟩

[3]**volume** *vb* **vol·umed; vol·um·ing** *vi* (1815) **:** to roll or rise in volume ~ *vt* **:** to send or give out in volume

vol·u·meter \ˈväl-yü-ˌmēt-ər\ *n* [ISV, blend of *volume* and *-meter*] (1829) **:** an instrument for measuring volumes (as of gases or liquids) directly or (as of solids) by displacement of a liquid

vol·u·met·ric \ˌväl-yü-ˈme-trik\ *adj* (1826) **:** of, relating to, or involving the measurement of volume — **vol·u·met·ri·cal·ly** \-tri-k(ə-)lē\ *adv*

volumetric analysis *n* (1862) **1 :** quantitative analysis by the use of definite volumes of standard solutions of reagents **2 :** analysis of gases by volume

volume unit *n* (ca. 1940) **:** a unit equal to a decibel for specifying the power level in audio equipment of a signal above a value of 1 milliwatt in a 600-ohm circuit

vo·lu·mi·nos·i·ty \və-ˌlü-mə-ˈnäs-ət-ē\ *n* (1782) **:** the quality or state of being voluminous

vo·lu·mi·nous \və-ˈlü-mə-nəs\ *adj* [LL *voluminosus,* fr. L *volumin-, volumen*] (1611) **1 :** consisting of many folds, coils, or convolutions **:** WINDING **2 a :** having or marked by great volume or bulk **:** LARGE ⟨a ~ voice⟩; *also* **:** FULL ⟨a ~ skirt⟩ **b :** NUMEROUS ⟨trying to keep track of ~ white slips⟩ **3 a :** filling or capable of filling a large volume or several volumes ⟨a ~ literature on the subject⟩ **b :** writing or speaking much or at great length — **vo·lu·mi·nous·ly** *adv* — **vo·lu·mi·nous·ness** *n*

vol·un·ta·rism \ˈväl-ən-tə-ˌriz-əm\ *n* (1838) **1 :** the principle or system of doing something by or relying on voluntary action or volunteers **2 :** a theory that conceives will to be the dominant factor in experience or in the world — **vol·un·ta·rist** \-rəst\ *n* — **vol·un·ta·ris·tic** \ˌväl-ən-tə-ˈris-tik\ *adj*

[1]**vol·un·tary** \ˈväl-ən-ˌter-ē\ *adj* [ME, fr. L *voluntarius,* fr. *voluntas* will, fr. *velle* to will, wish — more at WILL] (14c) **1 :** proceeding from the will or from one's own choice or consent **2 :** unconstrained by interference **:** SELF-DETERMINING **3 :** done by design or intention **:** INTENTIONAL ⟨~ manslaughter⟩ **4 :** of, relating to, subject to, or regulated by the will ⟨~ behavior⟩ **5 :** having power of free choice ⟨man is a ~ agent⟩ **6 :** provided or supported by voluntary action ⟨a ~ hospital⟩ **7 :** acting or done of one's own free will without valuable consideration or legal obligation — **vol·un·tari·ly** *adv* — **vol·un·tari·ness** *n*

syn VOLUNTARY, INTENTIONAL, DELIBERATE, WILLING mean done or brought about of one's own will. VOLUNTARY implies freedom and spontaneity of choice or action without external compulsion; INTENTIONAL stresses an awareness of an end to be achieved; DELIBERATE implies full consciousness of the nature of one's act and its consequences; WILLING implies a readiness and eagerness to accede to or anticipate the wishes of another.

[2]**voluntary** *n, pl* **-tar·ies** (1565) **1 a :** a prefatory often extemporized musical piece **b :** an improvisatory organ piece played before, during, or after a religious service **2 :** one who participates voluntarily **:** VOLUNTEER

vol·un·tary·ism \ˈväl-ən-ˌter-ē-ˌiz-əm\ *n* (1835) **:** VOLUNTARISM — **vol·un·tary·ist** \-ē-əst\ *n*

voluntary muscle *n* (1788) **:** muscle (as most striated muscle) under voluntary control

[1]**vol·un·teer** \ˌväl-ən-ˈti(ə)r\ *n* [obs. F *voluntaire* (now *volontaire*), fr. *voluntaire,* adj., voluntary, fr. L *voluntarius*] (1618) **1 :** one who enters into or offers himself for a service of his own free will: as **a :** one who enters into military service voluntarily **b** (1) **:** one who renders a service or takes part in a transaction while having no legal concern or interest (2) **:** one who receives a conveyance or transfer of property without giving valuable consideration **2 :** a volunteer plant **3** *cap* [*Volunteers of America*] **:** a member of a quasi-military religious and philanthropic organization founded in 1896 by Commander and Mrs. Ballington Booth

[2]**volunteer** *adj* (1649) **1 :** being, consisting of, or engaged in by volunteers ⟨a ~ army⟩ ⟨~ activities to help the mentally handicapped⟩ **2 :** growing spontaneously without direct human control or supervision esp. from seeds lost from a previous crop

[3]**volunteer** *vi* (ca. 1755) **:** to offer oneself as a volunteer ~ *vt* **:** to offer or bestow voluntarily ⟨~ one's services⟩

vol·un·teer·ism \ˌväl-ən-ˈti(ə)r-ˌiz-əm\ *n* (1844) **:** VOLUNTARISM 1

vo·lup·tu·ary \və-ˈləp-chə-ˌwer-ē\ *n, pl* **-ar·ies** (1610) **:** one whose chief interest is luxury and the gratification of sensual appetites — **voluptuary** *adj*

vo·lup·tuous \-chə(-wə)s\ *adj* [ME, fr. L *voluptuosus,* fr. *voluptas* pleasure; akin to Gk *elpis* hope, L *velle* to wish — more at WILL] (14c) **1 :** full of delight or pleasure to the senses **:** conducive to or arising from sensuous or sensual gratification **:** LUXURIOUS ⟨a ~ dance⟩ ⟨~ ornamentation⟩ **2 :** given to or spent in enjoyments of luxury, pleasure, or sensual gratifications ⟨a long and ~ holiday —Edmund Wilson⟩ ***syn*** see SENSUOUS — **vo·lup·tuous·ly** *adv* — **vo·lup·tuous·ness** *n*

vo·lute \və-ˈlüt\ *n* [L *voluta,* fr. fem. of *volutus,* pp. of *volvere* to roll] (ca. 1696) **1 :** a spiral or scroll-shaped form **2 :** a spiral scroll-shaped ornament forming the chief feature of the Ionic capital **3 a :** any of numerous marine gastropod mollusks (family Volutidae) with a thick short-spired shell **b :** the shell of a volute — **volute** *or* **vo·lut·ed** \-ˈlüt-əd\ *adj*

vo·lu·tin \ˈväl-yə-ˌtin, və-ˈlüt-ᵊn\ *n* [G, fr. NL *volutans,* specific epithet of the bacterium *Spirillum volutans* in which it was first found] (1909) **:** a granular basophilic substance that is thought to be a nucleic acid compound and that is common in microorganisms

vol·va \ˈväl-və, ˈvȯl-\ *n* [NL, fr. L *volva, vulva* integument — more at VULVA] (ca. 1753) **:** a membranous sac or cup about the base of the stipe in many gill fungi

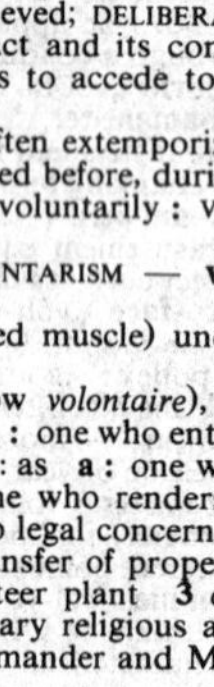

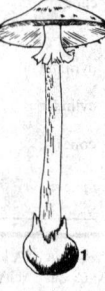

1 volva

vol·vox \-ˌväks\ *n* [NL, fr. L *volvere* to roll — more at VOLUBLE] (1864) **:** any of a genus (*Volvox*) of green flagellates that form spherical colonies

vol·vu·lus \ˈväl-vyə-ləs, ˈvȯl-\ *n* [NL, fr. L *volvere*] (1679) **:** a twisting of the intestine upon itself that causes obstruction

vo·mer \ˈvō-mər\ *n* [NL, fr. L, plowshare] (ca. 1704) **:** a bone of the skull of most vertebrates that is situated below the ethmoid region and in man forms part of the nasal septum — **vo·mer·ine** \ˈvō-mə-ˌrīn\ *adj*

[1]**vom·it** \ˈväm-ət\ *n* [ME, fr. MF, fr. L *vomitus,* fr. *vomitus,* pp. of *vomere* to vomit; akin to ON *vāma* nausea, Gk *emein* to vomit] (14c) **1 :** an act or instance of disgorging the contents of the stomach through the mouth; *also* **:** the disgorged matter **2 :** EMETIC

[2]**vomit** *vi* (15c) **1 :** to disgorge the stomach contents **2 :** to spew forth **:** BELCH, GUSH ~ *vt* **1 :** to disgorge (the contents of the stomach) through the mouth **2 :** to eject violently or abundantly **:** SPEW **3 :** to cause to vomit — **vom·it·er** *n*

vom·i·to·ry \ˈväm-ə-ˌtōr-ē, -ˌtȯr-\ *n, pl* **-ries** [LL *vomitorium,* fr. L *vomitus,* pp.; fr. its disgorging the spectators] (1730) **:** an entrance piercing the banks of seats of a theater, amphitheater, or stadium

vom·i·tus \ˈväm-ət-əs\ *n* [L] (ca. 1885) **:** material discharged by vomiting

V–1 \ˈvē-ˈwən\ *n* [G, abbr. for *vergeltungswaffe 1,* lit., reprisal weapon 1] (ca. 1944) **:** ROBOT BOMB

[1]**voo·doo** \ˈvüd-(ˌ)ü\ *n, pl* **voodoos** [LaF *voudou,* of African origin; akin to Ewe *voˡdu³* tutelary deity, demon] (1850) **1 :** a religion derived from African ancestor worship, practiced chiefly by Negroes of Haiti, and characterized by propitiatory rites and communication by trance with animistic deities **2 a :** one who deals in spells and necromancy **b** (1) **:** a sorcerer's spell **:** HEX (2) **:** a hexed object **:** CHARM — **voodoo** *adj*

[2]**voodoo** *vt* (1880) **:** to bewitch by or as if by means of voodoo **:** HEX

voo·doo·ism \ˈvüd-(ˌ)ü-ˌiz-əm\ *n* (1865) **1 :** VOODOO 1 **2 :** the practice of witchcraft — **voo·doo·ist** \-ˌü-əst\ *n* — **voo·doo·is·tic** \ˌvüd-(ˌ)ü-ˈis-tik\ *adj*

vo·ra·cious \vȯ-ˈrā-shəs, və-\ *adj* [L *vorac-, vorax,* fr. *vorare* to devour; akin to OHG *querdar* bait, L *gurges* whirlpool, Gk *bibrōskein* to devour] (1635) **1 :** having a huge appetite **:** RAVENOUS **2 :** excessively eager **:** INSATIABLE ⟨a ~ reader⟩ — **vo·ra·cious·ly** *adv* — **vo·ra·cious·ness** *n*

syn VORACIOUS, GLUTTONOUS, RAVENOUS, RAPACIOUS mean excessively greedy. VORACIOUS applies esp. to habitual gorging with food or drink ⟨teenagers are often *voracious* eaters⟩ GLUTTONOUS applies to one who delights in eating or acquiring things esp. beyond the point of necessity or satiety ⟨an admiral who was *gluttonous* for glory⟩ RAVENOUS implies excessive hunger and suggests violent or grasping methods of dealing with food or with whatever satisfies an appetite ⟨football practice usu. gives them *ravenous* appetites⟩ RAPACIOUS often suggests excessive and utterly selfish acquisitiveness or avarice ⟨*rapacious* land developers indifferent to the ruination of the environment⟩

vo·rac·i·ty \vȯ-ˈras-ət-ē, və-\ *n* (1526) **:** the quality or state of being voracious

vor·la·ge \ˈfōr-ˌläg-ə, ˈfȯr-\ *n* [G, lit., forward position, fr. *vor* fore + *lage* position, fr. OHG *lāga;* akin to OHG *ligen* to lie — more at LIE] (ca. 1936) **:** the position of a skier leaning forward from the ankles usu. without lifting the heels from the skis

-v·o·rous \v-(ə-)rəs\ *adj comb form* [L *-vorus,* fr. *vorare* to devour] **:** eating **:** feeding on ⟨frugi*vorous*⟩

vor·tex \ˈvȯ(ə)r-ˌteks\ *n, pl* **vor·ti·ces** \ˈvȯrt-ə-ˌsēz\ *also* **vor·tex·es** \ˈvȯr-ˌtek-səz\ [NL *vortic-, vortex,* fr. L *vertex, vortex* whirlpool — more at VERTEX] (1652) **1 a :** a mass of fluid and esp. of a liquid with a whirling or circular motion that tends to form a cavity or vacuum in the center of the circle and to draw toward this cavity or vacuum bodies subject to its action; *esp* **:** WHIRLPOOL, EDDY **b :** a region within a body of fluid in which the fluid elements have an angular velocity **2 :** something that resembles a whirlpool ⟨the hellish ~ of battle —*Time*⟩

vor·ti·cal \ˈvȯrt-i-kəl\ *adj* (1653) **:** of, relating to, or resembling a vortex **:** SWIRLING — **vor·ti·cal·ly** \-k(ə-)lē\ *adv*

vor·ti·cel·la \ˌvȯrt-ə-ˈsel-ə\ *n, pl* **-cel·lae** \-ˈsel-(ˌ)ē\ *or* **-cellas** [NL, fr. L *vortic-, vortex*] (ca. 1806) **:** any of a genus (*Vorticella*) of stalked bell-shaped ciliates

vor·ti·cism \ˈvȯrt-ə-ˌsiz-əm\ *n* [L *vortic-, vortex*] (1914) **:** an English abstract art movement from about 1912-15 embracing cubist and futurist concepts — **vor·ti·cist** \-səst\ *n*

vor·tic·i·ty \vȯr-ˈtis-ət-ē\ *n* (1895) **1 :** the state of a fluid in vortical motion; *broadly* **:** vortical motion **2 :** a measure of vortical motion; *esp* **:** a vector measure of local rotation in a fluid flow

vor·ti·cose \ˈvȯrt-i-ˌkōs\ *adj* (1783) **:** VORTICAL

vor·tig·i·nous \vȯr-ˈtij-ə-nəs\ *adj* [L *vortigin-, vortigo, vertigin-, vertigo* action of whirling, vertigo] *archaic* (1671) **:** VORTICAL

vo·ta·ress \ˈvōt-ə-rəs\ *n* (1589) **:** a female votary

vo·ta·rist \-rəst\ *n* (1603) **:** VOTARY

vo·ta·ry \ˈvōt-ə-rē\ *n, pl* **-ries** [L *votum* vow] (1546) **1** *archaic* **:** a sworn adherent **2 a :** ENTHUSIAST, DEVOTEE **b :** a devoted admirer **3 a :** a devout or zealous worshiper **b :** a staunch believer or advocate

[1]**vote** \ˈvōt\ *n* [ME (Sc), fr. L *votum* vow, wish — more at VOW] (15c) **1 a :** a usu. formal expression of opinion or will in response to a proposed decision; *esp* **:** one given as an indication of approval or disapproval of a proposal, motion, or candidate for office **b :** the total number of such expressions of opinion made known at a single time (as at an election) **c :** an expression of opinion or preference that resembles a vote **d :** BALLOT 1 **2 :** the collective opinion or verdict of a body of persons expressed by voting **3 :** the right to cast a vote; *specif* **:** the right of suffrage **:** FRANCHISE **4 a :** the act or process of voting ⟨brought the question to a ~⟩ **b :** a method of voting ⟨a voice ~⟩ **5 :** a formal expression of a wish, will, or choice voted by a meeting **6 a :** VOTER **b :** a group of voters with some common and identifying characteristics ⟨the labor ~⟩ **7** *chiefly Brit* **a :** a proposition to be voted on; *esp* **:** a legislative money item **b :** APPROPRIATION

[2]**vote** *vb* **vot·ed; vot·ing** *vi* (1552) **1 :** to express one's views in response to a poll; *esp* **:** to exercise a political franchise **2 :** to express an opinion ⟨consumers . . . ~ with their dollars —Lucia Mouat⟩ ~ *vt* **1 :** to choose, endorse, decide the disposition of, defeat, or authorize by vote **2 a :** to adjudge by general agreement **:** DECLARE **b :** to offer as a

suggestion : PROPOSE ⟨I ~ we all go home⟩ **3 a :** to cause to vote in a given way **b :** to cause to be cast for or against a proposal
vote·less \'vōt-ləs\ *adj* (1672) : having no vote; *esp* : denied the political franchise
vot·er \'vōt-ər\ *n* (1578) : one that votes or has the legal right to vote
voting machine *n* (1900) : a mechanical device for recording and counting votes cast in an election
vo·tive \'vōt-iv\ *adj* [L *votivus*, fr. *votum* vow] (1597) **1 :** consisting of or expressing a vow, wish, or desire ⟨a ~ prayer⟩ **2 :** offered or performed in fulfillment of a vow or in gratitude or devotion — **vo·tive·ly** *adv* — **vo·tive·ness** *n*
votive mass *n* (1738) : a mass celebrated for a special intention (as for a wedding or funeral) in place of the mass of the day
vo·tress \'vō-trəs\ *n* [by alter.] *archaic* (1590) : VOTARESS
¹**vouch** \'vaüch\ *vb* [ME *vochen, vouchen*, fr. MF *vocher*, fr. L *vocare* to call, summon — more at VOICE] *vt* (14c) **1 :** to summon into court to warrant or defend a title **2** *archaic* **a :** ASSERT, AFFIRM **b :** ATTEST **3** *archaic* : to cite or refer to as authority or supporting evidence **4 a** : PROVE, SUBSTANTIATE **b :** to verify (a business transaction) by examining documentary evidence ~ *vi* **1 :** to give a guarantee : become surety **2 a :** to supply supporting evidence or testimony **b :** to give personal assurance *syn* see CERTIFY
²**vouch** *n, obs* (1603) : ALLEGATION, DECLARATION
vouch·ee \vaü-'chē\ *n* (15c) : one for whom another vouches
¹**vouch·er** \'vaü-chər\ *n* [MF *vocher, voucher* to vouch] (1531) **1 :** an act of vouching **2 a :** a piece of supporting evidence : PROOF **b :** a documentary record of a business transaction **c :** a written affidavit or authorization : CERTIFICATE **d :** a form or check indicating a credit against future purchases or expenditures
²**voucher** *vt* (1609) **1 :** to establish the authenticity of **2 :** to prepare a voucher for
³**voucher** *n* [¹vouch + -er] *archaic* (1612) : one that guarantees : SURETY
vouch·safe \vaüch-'sāf, 'vaüch-,\ *vt* **vouch·safed; vouch·saf·ing** (14c) **1 a :** to grant or furnish often in a gracious or condescending manner **b :** to give by way of reply ⟨refused to ~ an explanation⟩ **2 :** to grant as a privilege or special favor *syn* see GRANT — **vouch·safe·ment** \vaüch-'sāf-mənt\ *n*
vous·soir \vü-'swär, 'vü-,\ *n* [F, fr. (assumed) VL *volsorium*, fr. *volsus*, pp. of L *volvere* to roll — more at VOLUBLE] (1728) : one of the wedge-shaped pieces forming an arch or vault — see ARCH illustration
¹**vow** \'vaü\ *n* [ME *vowe*, fr. OF *vou*, fr. L *votum*, fr. neut. of *votus*, pp. of *vovēre* to vow; akin to Gk *euchesthai* to pray, vow] (13c) : a solemn promise or assertion; *specif* : one by which a person binds himself to an act, service, or condition
²**vow** *vt* (14c) **1 :** to promise solemnly : SWEAR **2 :** to bind or consecrate by a vow ~ *vi* : to make a vow — **vow·er** \'vaü-(ə)r\ *n*
³**vow** *vt* [ME *vowen*, short for *avowen*] (14c) : AVOW, DECLARE
vow·el \'vaü-(ə)l\ *n* [ME, fr. MF *vouel*, fr. L *vocalis* — more at VOCALIC] (14c) **1 :** one of a class of speech sounds in the articulation of which the oral part of the breath channel is not blocked or is not constricted enough to cause audible friction; *broadly* : the one most prominent sound in a syllable **2 :** a letter or other symbol representing a vowel — usu. used in English of *a, e, i, o, u,* and sometimes *y*
vow·el·ize \'vaü-(ə-),līz\ *vt* **-ized; -iz·ing** (1883) : to furnish with vowel signs or points
vowel point *n* (1764) : a mark placed below or otherwise near a consonant in some languages (as Hebrew) and representing the vowel sound that precedes or follows the consonant sound
vowel rhyme *n* (1838) : ASSONANCE 2b
vox po·pu·li \'väk-'späp-yə-,lī, -'späp-(y)ə-,)lē\ *n* [L, voice of the people] (1550) : popular sentiment
¹**voy·age** \'voi-ij, 'vó(-)ij\ *n* [ME, fr. OF *voiage*, fr. LL *viaticum*, fr. L, traveling money, fr. neut. of *viaticus* of a journey, fr. *via* way — more at VIA] (13c) **1 :** an act or instance of traveling : JOURNEY **2 :** a course or period of traveling by other than land routes **3 :** an account of a journey esp. by sea
²**voyage** *vb* **voy·aged; voy·ag·ing** *vi* (15c) : to take a trip : TRAVEL ~ *vt* : SAIL, TRAVERSE — **voy·ag·er** *n*
voya·geur \,vói-ə-'zhər, ,vwä-yä-\ *n* [CanF, fr. F, traveler, fr. *voyager* to travel, fr. *voyage* voyage, fr. OF *voiage*] (1809) : a man employed by a fur company to transport goods and men to and from remote stations esp. in the Canadian Northwest
voy·eur \voi-'yər, vói-'ər\ *n* [F, lit., one who sees, fr. MF, fr. *voir* to see, fr. L *vidēre* — more at WIT] (ca. 1919) **1 :** one obtaining sexual gratification from seeing sex organs and sexual acts; *broadly* : one who habitually seeks sexual stimulation by visual means **2 :** a prying observer who is usu. seeking the sordid or the scandalous — **voy·eur·ism** \-,iz-əm\ *n* — **voy·eur·is·tic** \,vwä-(,)yər-'is-tik, ,vói-ər-\ *adj* — **voy·eur·is·ti·cal·ly** \-ti-k(ə-)lē\ *adv*
V–par·ti·cle \'vē-\ *n* [fr. the shape of its track in a cloud chamber] (ca. 1951) : a charged or uncharged short-lived elementary particle produced by collisions of very high-energy protons or neutrons with nuclei
vroom \'vrüm, və-'rüm\ *vi* [imit. of the noise of an engine] (1965) : to operate a motor vehicle at high speed or so as to create a great deal of engine noise
V sign *n* (1943) : a sign made by raising the index and middle fingers in a V and used as a victory salute or a gesture of approval

V–2 \'vē-'tü\ *n* [G, abbr. for *vergeltungswaffe 2*, lit., reprisal weapon 2] (ca. 1944) : a rocket-propelled bomb of German invention
vug \'vəg\ *n* [Corn dial. *vooga* underground chamber, fr. L *fovea* small pit] (1818) : a small unfilled cavity in a lode or in rock — **vug·gy** \'vəg-ē\ *adj*
Vul·can \'vəl-kən\ *n* [L *Volcanus, Vulcanus*] : the Roman god of fire and metalworking — compare HEPHAESTUS
vul·ca·ni·an \,vəl-'kā-nē-ən\ *adj* (1602) **1** *cap* : of or relating to Vulcan or to working in metals (as iron) **2 :** of or relating to a volcanic eruption in which highly viscous or solid lava is blown into fragments and dust
vul·ca·nic·i·ty \,vəl-kə-'nis-ət-ē\ *n* (1873) : VOLCANISM
vul·ca·nism \'vəl-kə-,niz-əm\ *n* (1877) : VOLCANISM
vul·ca·ni·zate \'vəl-kə-nə-,zāt, ,vəl-kə-'nī-\ *n* [back-formation fr. *vulcanization*] (ca. 1926) : a vulcanized product
vul·ca·ni·za·tion \,vəl-kə-nə-'zā-shən\ *n* (1846) : the process of treating crude or synthetic rubber or similar plastic material chemically to give it useful properties (as elasticity, strength, and stability)
vul·ca·nize \'vəl-kə-,nīz\ *vb* **nized; -niz·ing** [ISV, fr. L *Vulcanus* Vulcan, fire] *vt* (1846) : to subject to vulcanization ~ *vi* : to undergo vulcanization — **vul·ca·niz·er** *n*
vulcanized fiber *n* [fr. *Vulcanized Fibre*, a trademark] (ca. 1873) : a tough substance made by treatment of cellulose and used for luggage and electrical insulation and in packaging
vul·ca·nol·o·gy \,vəl-kə-'näl-ə-jē\ *n* [ISV] (1858) : VOLCANOLOGY — **vul·ca·nol·o·gist** \-jəst\ *n*
vul·gar \'vəl-gər\ *adj* [ME, fr. L *vulgaris* of the mob, vulgar, fr. *volgus, vulgus* mob, common people; akin to Skt *varga* group] (14c) **1 a :** generally used, applied, or accepted **b :** understood in or having the ordinary sense ⟨they reject the ~ conception of miracle —W. R. Inge⟩ **2 :** VERNACULAR ⟨the ~ name of a plant⟩ **3 a :** of or relating to the common people : PLEBEIAN **b :** generally current : PUBLIC ⟨the ~ opinion of that time⟩ **c :** of the usual, typical, or ordinary kind **4 a :** lacking in cultivation, perception, or taste : COARSE **b :** morally crude, undeveloped, or unregenerate : GROSS **c :** ostentatious or excessive in expenditure or display : PRETENTIOUS **5 a :** offensive in language : EARTHY **b :** lewdly or profanely indecent : OBSCENE *syn* see COMMON, COARSE — **vul·gar·ly** *adv*
vulgar era (1716) : CHRISTIAN ERA
vul·gar·i·an \,vəl-'gar-ē-ən, -'ger-\ *n* (1804) : a vulgar person
vul·gar·ism \'vəl-gə-,riz-əm\ *n* (1644) **1 a :** a word or expression originated or used chiefly by illiterate persons : a substandard use **b :** a coarse word or phrase : OBSCENITY **2 :** VULGARITY
vul·gar·i·ty \,vəl-'gar-ət-ē\ *n, pl* **-ties** (1579) **1 :** something vulgar **2 :** the quality or state of being vulgar
vul·gar·ize \'vəl-gə-,rīz\ *vt* **-ized; -iz·ing** (1709) **1 :** to diffuse generally : POPULARIZE **2 :** to make vulgar : COARSEN — **vul·gar·iza·tion** \,vəl-gə-rə-'zā-shən\ *n* — **vul·gar·iz·er** \'vəl-gə-,rī-zər\ *n*
Vulgar Latin *n* (1818) : the nonclassical Latin of ancient Rome including the speech of plebeians and the informal speech of the educated established by comparative evidence as the chief source of the Romance languages
vul·gate \'vəl-,gāt, -gət\ *n* [ML *vulgata*, fr. LL *vulgata editio* edition in general circulation] (1728) **1** *cap* : a Latin version of the Bible authorized and used by the Roman Catholic Church **2 :** a commonly accepted text or reading
vul·gus \'vəl-gəs\ *n* [prob. alter. of *vulgars* (English sentences to be translated into Latin)] (1856) : a short composition in Latin verse formerly common as an exercise in some English public schools
vul·ner·a·ble \'vəln-(ə-)rə-bəl, 'vəl-nər-bəl\ *adj* [LL *vulnerabilis*, fr. L *vulnerare* to wound, fr. *vulner-, vulnus* wound; akin to Goth *wilwan* to rob, L *vellere* to pluck, Gk *oulē* wound] (1605) **1 :** capable of being physically wounded **2 :** open to attack or damage : ASSAILABLE **3 :** liable to increased penalties but entitled to increased bonuses after winning a game in contract bridge — **vul·ner·a·bil·i·ty** \,vəln-(ə-)rə-'bil-ət-ē\ *n* — **vul·ner·a·ble·ness** \'vəln-(ə-)rə-bəl-nəs, 'vəl-nər-bəl-\ *n* — **vul·ner·a·bly** \-blē\ *adv*
¹**vul·ner·ary** \'vəl-nə-,rer-ē\ *adj* [L *vulnerarius*, fr. *vulner-, vulnus*] (1599) : used for or useful in healing wounds ⟨~ plants⟩
²**vulnerary** *n, pl* **-ar·ies** (1601) : a vulnerary remedy
vul·pine \'vəl-,pīn\ *adj* [L *vulpinus*, fr. *vulpes* fox; akin to Gk *alōpēx* fox] (1628) **1 :** of, relating to, or resembling a fox **2 :** FOXY, CRAFTY
vul·ture \'vəl-chər\ *n* [ME, fr. L *vultur*] (14c) **1 :** any of various large raptorial birds (families Aegypiidae and Cathartidae) that are related to the hawks, eagles, and falcons but have weaker claws and the head usu. naked and that subsist chiefly or entirely on carrion **2 :** a rapacious or predatory person — **vul·tur·ish** \-chə-rish\ *adj*
vul·tur·ine \-chə-,rīn\ *adj* (1647) **1 :** of, relating to, or characteristic of vultures **2 :** RAPACIOUS, PREDATORY ⟨~ legislators⟩
vul·tur·ous \'vəlch-(ə-)rəs\ *adj* (1623) : resembling a vulture esp. in rapacity or scavenging habits
vul·va \'vəl-və\ *n, pl* **vul·vae** \-,vē, -,vī\ [NL, fr. L *volva, vulva* integument, womb; akin to Skt *ulva* womb, L *volvere* to roll — more at VOLUBLE] (1548) : the external parts of the female genital organs — **vul·val** \'vəl-vəl\ *or* **vul·var** \-vər, -,vär\ *adj*
vul·vo·vag·i·ni·tis \,vəl-(,)vō-,vaj-ə-'nīt-əs\ *n, pl* **-ni·ti·des** \-'nīt-ə-,dēz\ [NL] (1897) : coincident inflammation of the vulva and vagina
vying *pres part of* VIE

W

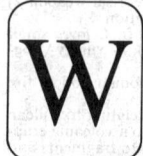

w \'dəb-əl-(ˌ)yü, -yə(-w), 'dəb(-ə)-yə(-w), 'dəb-yē\ *n, pl* **w's** *or* **ws** \-(ˌ)yüz, -yəz, -yēz\ *often cap, often attrib* **1 a :** the 23d letter of the English alphabet **b :** a graphic representation of this letter **c :** a speech counterpart of orthographic *w* **2 :** a graphic device for reproducing the letter *w* **3 :** one designated *w* esp. as the 23d in order or class **4 :** something shaped like the letter W

W *n* (1960) **:** W PARTICLE

wab·ble \'wäb-əl\ *var of* WOBBLE

Wac \'wak\ *n* [*Women's Army Corps*] (1943) **:** a member of the Women's Army Corps

wacko \'wak-(ˌ)ō\ *adj* [by alter.] *slang* (1975) **:** WACKY — **wacko** *n, slang*

wacky \'wak-ē\ *adj* **wack·i·er; -est** [perh. fr. E dial. *whacky* (fool)] (ca. 1935) **:** absurdly or amusingly eccentric or irrational **:** CRAZY — **wack·i·ly** \'wak-ə-lē\ *adv* — **wack·i·ness** \'wak-ē-nəs\ *n*

[1]wad \'wäd\ *n* [origin unknown] (1573) **1 :** a small mass, bundle, or tuft: as **a :** a soft mass esp. of a loose fibrous material variously used (as to stop an aperture, pad a garment, or hold grease around an axle) **b** (1) **:** a soft plug used to retain a powder charge or to avoid windage esp. in a muzzle-loading gun (2) **:** a felt or paper disk used to separate the components of a shotgun cartridge **c :** a small mass of a chewing substance ⟨a ~ of gum⟩ **2 :** a considerable amount (as of money) **3 a :** a roll of paper money **b :** MONEY

[2]wad *vt* **wad·ded; wad·ding** (1579) **1 a :** to insert a wad into ⟨~ a gun⟩ **b :** to hold in by a wad ⟨~ a bullet in a gun⟩ **2 :** to form into a wad or wadding; *esp* **:** to roll or crush into a tight wad **3 :** to stuff or line with some soft substance — **wad·der** *n*

wad·ding \'wäd-iŋ\ *n* (1627) **1 :** wads or material for making wads **2 :** a soft mass or sheet of short loose fibers used for stuffing or padding

[1]wad·dle \'wäd-ᵊl\ *vi* **wad·dled; wad·dling** \'wäd-liŋ, -ᵊl-iŋ\ [freq. of *wade*] (1592) **1 :** to walk with short steps swinging the forepart of the body from side to side **2 :** to move clumsily in a manner suggesting a waddle — **wad·dler** \-lər, -ᵊl-ər\ *n*

[2]waddle *n* (1691) **:** an awkward clumsy swaying gait

[1]wad·dy \'wäd-ē\ *n, pl* **waddies** [native name in Australia] *Austral* (1800) **:** CLUB 1a

[2]waddy *vt* **wad·died; wad·dy·ing** (1855) *Austral* **:** to attack or beat with a waddy

[3]wad·dy *or* **wad·die** \'wäd-ē\ *n, pl* **waddies** [origin unknown] *West* (1927) **:** COWBOY

[1]wade \'wād\ *vb* **wad·ed; wad·ing** [ME *waden*, fr. OE *wadan*; akin to OHG *watan* to go, wade, L *vadere* to go] *vi* (bef. 12c) **1 :** to step in or through a medium (as water) offering more resistance than air **2 :** to move or proceed with difficulty or labor **3 :** to set to work or attack with determination or vigor — used with *in* or *into* ⟨~ into a task⟩ ~ *vt* **:** to pass or cross by wading — **wad·able** *or* **wade·able** \-ə-bəl\ *adj*

[2]wade *n* (1665) **:** an act of wading ⟨a ~ in the brook⟩

wad·er \'wād-ər\ *n* (1673) **1 :** one that wades **2 :** SHOREBIRD; *also* **:** WADING BIRD **3** *pl* **:** high waterproof boots or trousers used for wading

wa·di \'wäd-ē\ *n* [Ar *wādiy*] (1839) **1 :** the bed or valley of a stream in regions of southwestern Asia and northern Africa that is usu. dry except during the rainy season and that often forms an oasis **:** GULLY, WASH **2 :** a shallow usu. sharply defined depression in a desert region

wading bird *n* (ca. 1847) **:** any of an order (Ciconiiformes) of long-legged birds (as herons, bitterns, storks, and flamingos) that wade in water in search of food

wading pool *n* (1923) **:** a shallow pool of portable or permanent construction used by children for wading

wad·mal *or* **wad·mol** *or* **wad·mel** \'wäd-məl\ *n* [ME *wadmale*, fr. ON *vathmāl*, lit., standard cloth, fr. *vāth* cloth, clothing + *māl* measure; akin to L *metiri* to measure — more at WEED, MEASURE] (14c) **:** a coarse rough woolen fabric formerly used in the British Isles and Scandinavia for protective coverings and warm clothing

wae·sucks \'wā-ˌsəks\ *interj* [Sc *wae* woe (fr. ME *wa*) + *sucks*, alter. of E *sakes* — more at WOE] *Scot* (1772) — used to express pity

Waf \'waf\ *n* [*Women in the Air Force*] (1948) **:** a member of the women's component of the air force formed after World War II

[1]wa·fer \'wā-fər\ *n* [ME, fr. ONF *waufre*, of Gmc origin; akin to MD *wafel, wafer* waffle] (14c) **1 a :** a thin crisp cake, candy, or cracker **b :** a round thin piece of unleavened bread used in the celebration of the Eucharist **2 :** an adhesive disk of dried paste with added coloring matter used as a seal **3 a :** a thin disk or ring resembling a wafer and variously used (as for a valve or diaphragm) **b :** a thin slice of semiconductor (as silicon) used as a base for an electronic component or circuit

[2]wafer *vt* **wa·fered; wa·fer·ing** \-f(ə-)riŋ\ (1748) **1 :** to seal, close, or fasten with a wafer **2 :** to divide (as a silicon rod) into wafers

waff \'waf\ *n* [E dial. *waff* (to wave)] (1600) **1** *chiefly Scot* **:** a waving motion **2** *chiefly Scot* **:** PUFF, GUST

[1]waf·fle \'wäf-əl, 'wȯf-\ *vi* **waf·fled; waf·fling** \-(ə-)liŋ\ [freq. of obs. *woff* to yelp, of imit. origin] (ca. 1701) **1 :** to talk or write foolishly **:** BLATHER ⟨can ~ . . . tiresomely off the point —*Times Lit. Supp.*⟩ **2 :** EQUIVOCATE

[2]waffle *n* [D *wafel*, fr. MD *wafel, wafer*; akin to OE *wefan* to weave] (1744) **:** a crisp cake of batter baked in a waffle iron

[3]waffle *n* (ca. 1888) **:** empty or pretentious words **:** TRIPE

waffle iron *n* (ca. 1794) **:** a cooking utensil having two hinged metal parts that shut upon each other and impress surface projections on waffles that are being cooked

waf·fle·stomp·er \'wäf-əl-ˌstäm-pər, 'wȯf-, -ˌstȯm-\ *n* [[2]*waffle* + *stomp* + *-er*; fr. the pattern left by the soles] (1972) **:** a hiking boot with a lug sole

[1]waft \'wäft, 'waft\ *vb* [(assumed) ME *waughten* to guard, convoy, fr. MD or MLG *wachten* to watch, guard; akin to OE *wæccan* to watch — more at WAKE] *vi* (1562) **:** to move or go lightly on or as if on a buoyant medium ~ *vt* **:** to cause to move or go lightly by or as if by the impulse of wind or waves — **waft·er** *n*

[2]waft *n* (1607) **1 :** a slight breeze **:** PUFF **2 :** something (as an odor) that is wafted **:** WHIFF **3 :** the act of waving **4 :** a pennant or flag used to signal or to show wind direction

waft·age \'wäf-tij, 'waf-\ *n* (1558) **:** the act of wafting or state of being wafted; *broadly* **:** CONVEYANCE

waf·ture \'wäf-chər, 'waf-\ *n* (1601) **:** the act of waving or a wavelike motion

[1]wag \'wag\ *vb* **wagged; wag·ging** [ME *waggen*; akin to MHG *wacken* to totter, OE *wegan* to move — more at WAY] *vi* (13c) **1 :** to be in motion **:** STIR **2 :** to move to and fro or up and down esp. with quick jerky motions **3 :** to move in chatter or gossip ⟨scandal caused tongues to ~⟩ **4** *archaic* **:** DEPART **5 :** WADDLE ~ *vt* **1 :** to swing to and fro or up and down esp. with quick jerky motions **:** SWITCH; *specif* **:** to nod (the head) or shake (a finger) at (as in assent or mild reproof) **2 :** to move (as the tongue) animatedly in conversation — **wag·ger** *n*

[2]wag *n* (1589) **:** an act of wagging **:** SHAKE

[3]wag *n* [prob. short for obs. E *waghalter* (gallows bird), fr. E [1]*wag* + *halter*] (ca. 1550) **1 :** WIT, JOKER **2** *obs* **:** a young man **:** CHAP

[1]wage \'wāj\ *vb* **waged; wag·ing** [ME *wagen* to pledge, give as security, fr. ONF *wagier*, fr. *wage*] *vt* (15c) **:** to engage in or carry on ⟨~ war⟩ ⟨~ a campaign⟩ ~ *vi* **:** to be in process of occurring ⟨the riot *waged* for several hours —*Amer. Guide Series: Md.*⟩

[2]wage *n* [ME, pledge, wage, fr. ONF, of Gmc origin; akin to Goth *wadi* pledge — more at WED] (14c) **1 a :** a payment usu. of money for labor or services usu. according to contract and on an hourly, daily, or piecework basis — often used in pl. **b** *pl* **:** the share of the national product attributable to labor as a factor in production **2 :** RECOMPENSE, REWARD — usu. used in pl. but sing. or pl. in constr. ⟨the ~s of sin is death — Rom 6:23 (RSV)⟩ — **wage·less** \'wāj-ləs\ *adj*

wage earner *n* (1885) **:** one who works for wages or salary

[1]wa·ger \'wā-jər\ *n* [ME, pledge, bet, fr. AF *wageure*, fr. ONF *wagier* to pledge] (14c) **1 a :** something (as a sum of money) risked on an uncertain event **:** STAKE **b :** something on which bets are laid **:** GAMBLE ⟨do a stunt as a ~⟩ **2** *archaic* **:** an act of giving a pledge to take and abide by the result of some action

[2]wager *vb* **wa·gered; wa·ger·ing** \'wāj-(ə-)riŋ\ *vi* (1602) **:** to make a bet ~ *vt* **:** to risk or venture on a final outcome; *specif* **:** to lay as a gamble ⟨~ $5 on a horse⟩ — **wa·ger·er** \'wā-jər-ər\ *n*

wage scale *n* (1902) **:** a schedule of wage rates for related tasks; *broadly* **:** the general level of wages in an industry or region

wage slave *n* (1886) **:** a person dependent on wages or a salary for a livelihood

wage·work·er \'wāj-ˌwər-kər\ *n* (1876) **:** WAGE EARNER

wag·gery \'wag-ə-rē\ *n, pl* **-ger·ies** (1594) **1 :** mischievous merriment **:** PLEASANTRY **2 :** JEST; *esp* **:** PRACTICAL JOKE

wag·gish \'wag-ish\ *adj* (1589) **1 :** done or made in waggery or for sport **:** HUMOROUS **2 :** resembling or characteristic of a wag ⟨a ~ disposition⟩ — **wag·gish·ly** *adv* — **wag·gish·ness** *n*

[1]wag·gle \'wag-əl\ *vb* **wag·gled; wag·gling** \-(ə-)liŋ\ [freq. of [1]*wag*] *vi* (1594) **:** to reel, sway, or move from side to side **:** WAG ~ *vt* **:** to move frequently one way and the other **:** WAG — **wag·gly** \-(ə-)lē\ *adj*

[2]waggle *n* (ca. 1866) **1 :** an instance of waggling **:** a jerky motion back and forth or up and down **2 :** a preliminary swinging of a golf club head back and forth over the ball before the swing

wag·gon *chiefly Brit var of* WAGON

[1]Wag·ne·ri·an \väg-'nir-ē-ən, -'ner-\ *adj* [Richard *Wagner*] (1873) **:** of, relating to, characteristic, or suggestive of Wagner or his music or theories

[2]Wagnerian *n* (1882) **:** an admirer of the musical theories and style of Wagner

Wag·ner·ite \'väg-nə-ˌrīt\ *n* (1855) **:** WAGNERIAN

[1]wag·on \'wag-ən\ *n* [D *wagen*, fr. MD — more at WAIN] (1523) **1 a :** a usu. four-wheel vehicle for transporting bulky commodities and drawn orig. by animals **b :** a lighter typically horse-drawn vehicle for transporting goods or passengers **c :** PATROL WAGON **2** *Brit* **:** a railway freight car **3 :** a low four-wheel vehicle with an open rectangular body and a retroflex tongue made for the play or use (as for carrying newspapers) of a child **4 :** a small wheeled table used for the service of a dining room **5 :** a delivery truck ⟨milk ~⟩ **6 :** STATION WAGON — **off the wagon :** no longer abstaining from alcoholic beverages — **on the wagon :** abstaining from alcoholic beverages

[2]wagon *vi* (1606) **:** to travel or transport goods by wagon ~ *vt* **:** to transport (goods) by wagon

wag·on·er \'wag-ə-nər\ *n* (1544) **1 :** one who drives a wagon **2** *cap* **:** AURIGA **3** *cap* **:** DIPPER 3a

wag·on·ette \ˌwag-ə-'net\ *n* (ca. 1858) **:** a light wagon with two facing seats along the sides back of a transverse front seat

wa·gon–lit \vå-gōⁿ-lē\ *n, pl* **wagons–lits** *or* **wagon–lits** \-gōⁿ-lē(z)\ [F, fr. *wagon* railroad car + *lit* bed] (1884) **:** a railroad sleeping car

wagon master *n* (1645) **:** a person in charge of one or more wagons

wagon train *n* (1810) **:** a column of wagons (as of supplies for a group of settlers) traveling overland

wag·tail \'wag-ˌtāl\ *n* (ca. 1510) **:** any of numerous chiefly Old World birds (family Motacillidae) related to the pipits and having a trim slender body and a very long tail that they habitually jerk up and down

Wah·ha·bi *or* **Wa·ha·bi** \wə-'häb-ē, wä-\ *n* [Ar *wahhābīy*, fr. Muḥammad b. 'Abd al-*Wahhāb* (Abdul-Wahhab) †1787 Arab. religious reformer] (1807) **:** a member of a puritanical Muslim sect founded in Arabia in the 18th century by Muhammad ibn-Abdul Wahhab and revived by ibn-Saud in the 20th century — **Wah·hab·ism** \-'häb-ˌiz-əm\ *n* — **Wah·hab·ite** \-ˌīt\ *adj or n*

wa·hi·ne \wä-'hē-nē, -(ˌ)nā\ *n* [Maori & Hawaiian, woman] (ca. 1773) **1 :** a Polynesian woman **2 :** a female surfer

[1]wa·hoo \'wä-ˌhü, 'wȯ-\ *n, pl* **wahoos** [Creek *ûhawhu*] (1770) **:** WINGED ELM

[2]wahoo *n, pl* **wahoos** [Dakota *wāhu*, lit., arrowwood] (ca. 1810) **:** a shrubby No. American spindle tree (*Euonymus atropurpureus*) having purple capsules which in dehiscence expose the scarlet-ariled seeds — called also *burning bush*

[3]wahoo *n, pl* **wahoos** [origin unknown] (ca. 1900) **:** a large vigorous mackerel (*Acanthocybium solandri*) that is common in warm seas and esteemed as a food and sport fish

[4]wa·hoo \'wä-'hü\ *interj, chiefly West* (ca. 1924) — used to express exuberance or enthusiasm or to attract attention

wah-wah pedal *var of* WA-WA PEDAL

[1]waif \'wāf\ *n* [ME, fr. ONF, adj., lost, unclaimed] (14c) **1 a :** a piece of property found (as washed up by the sea) but unclaimed **b** *pl* **:** sto-

len goods thrown away by a thief in flight **2 a :** something found without an owner and esp. by chance **b :** a stray person or animal; *esp* **:** a homeless child

²**waif** *n* (1530) **:** WAFT 4

¹**wail** \ˈwā(ə)l\ *vb* [ME *wailen,* of Scand origin; akin to ON *væla, vāla* to wail; akin to ON *vei* woe — more at WOE] *vi* (14c) **1 :** to express sorrow audibly **:** LAMENT **2 :** to make a sound suggestive of a mournful cry **3 :** to express dissatisfaction plaintively **:** COMPLAIN ~ *vt, archaic* **:** BEWAIL — **wail·er** \ˈwā-lər\ *n*

²**wail** *n* (15c) **1 :** the act or practice of wailing **:** loud lamentation **2 a :** a usu. prolonged cry or sound expressing grief or pain **b :** a sound suggestive of wailing ⟨the ~ of an air-raid siren⟩ **c :** a querulous expression of grievance **:** COMPLAINT

wail·ful \ˈwā(ə)l-fəl\ *adj* (1544) **1 :** uttering a sound suggestive of wailing **2 :** expressing grief or pain **:** SORROWFUL, MOURNFUL — **wail·ful·ly** \-fə-lē\ *adv*

wailing wall *n* (1919) **1** *cap* **:** a surviving section of the wall which in ancient times formed a part of the enclosure of Herod's temple near the Holy of Holies and at which Jews traditionally gather for prayer and religious lament **2 :** a source of comfort and consolation in misfortune ⟨a soldier making the chaplain's office his *wailing wall*⟩

wain \ˈwān\ *n* [ME, wagon, chariot, fr. OE *wægn;* akin to MD *wagen* wagon, OE *wegan* to move — more at WAY] (bef. 12c) **1 :** a usu. large and heavy vehicle for farm use **2** *cap* [short for *Charles's Wain*] **:** DIPPER 3a

¹**wain·scot** \ˈwān-skət, -ˌskōt, -ˌskät\ *n* [ME, fr. MD *wagenschot*] (14c) **1** *Brit* **:** a fine grade of oak imported for woodwork **2 a (1) :** a usu. paneled wooden lining of an interior wall **(2) :** a lining of an interior wall irrespective of material **b :** the lower three or four feet of an interior wall when finished differently from the remainder of the wall

²**wainscot** *vt* **-scot·ed** *or* **-scot·ted; -scot·ing** *or* **-scot·ting** (ca. 1570) **:** to line with or as if with boards or paneling

wain·scot·ing *or* **wain·scot·ting** \-ˌskōt-iŋ, -ˌskät-, -skət-\ *n* (1580) **1 :** WAINSCOT 2 **2 :** material used to wainscot a surface

wain·wright \ˈwān-ˌrīt\ *n* [OE *wægnwyrhta,* fr. *wægn* wagon + *wyrhta* worker, maker — more at WRIGHT] (bef. 12c) **:** a maker and repairer of wagons

waist \ˈwāst\ *n* [ME *wast;* akin to OE *weaxan* to grow — more at WAX] (14c) **1 a :** the narrowed part of the body between the thorax and hips **b :** the greatly constricted basal part of the abdomen of some insects (as wasps and flies) **2 :** the part of something corresponding to or resembling the human waist: as **a (1) :** the part of a ship's deck between the poop and forecastle **(2) :** the middle part of a sailing ship between foremast and mainmast **b :** the middle section of the fuselage of an airplane **3 :** a garment or the part of a garment covering the body from the neck to the waistline or just below: **a :** BODICE 1 **b :** BLOUSE — **waist·ed** \ˈwā-stəd\ *adj*

waist·band \ˈwās(t)-ˌband\ *n* (1584) **:** a band (as of trousers or a skirt) fitting around the waist

waist·coat \ˈwes-kət, ˈwās(t)-ˌkōt\ *n* (1519) **1 :** an ornamental garment worn under a doublet **2** *chiefly Brit* **:** VEST 2a — **waist·coat·ed** \-əd\ *adj*

waist·line \ˈwāst-ˌlīn\ *n* (1897) **1 :** an arbitrary line encircling the narrowest part of the waist; *also* **:** the part of a garment that covers this line or may be above or below it as fashion dictates **2 :** body circumference at the waist

¹**wait** \ˈwāt\ *vb* [ME *waiten,* fr. ONF *waitier* to watch, of Gmc origin; akin to OHG *wahta* watch, OE *wæccan* to watch — more at WAKE] *vt* (13c) **1 :** to stay in place in expectation of **:** AWAIT **2 :** to delay serving (a meal) **3 :** to serve as waiter for ⟨~ table⟩ ~ *vi* **1 a :** to remain stationary in readiness or expectation ⟨~ for a train⟩ **b :** to pause for another to catch up **2 a :** to look forward expectantly ⟨just ~*ing* to see his rival lose⟩ **b :** to hold back expectantly ⟨~*ing* for a chance to strike⟩ **3 :** to serve at meals — usu. used in the phrases *wait at table* or *wait on table* **4 a :** to be ready and available ⟨slippers ~*ing* by the bed⟩ **b :** to remain temporarily neglected or unrealized ***syn*** see STAY

usage Linguistic investigators have found *wait on* in place of *wait for* to be widespread in the U.S. but concentrated primarily in Southern and Midland speech areas. A British commentator has noted its occurrence in the British press in the mid-20th century and has ascribed it to American influence. Commentators on usage consider *wait on* regional or informal or incorrect. Our written evidence does not quite agree with any of these judgments ⟨no groups of idle or of busy reapers could here stand *waiting on* the guidance of a master —Thomas Carlyle⟩ ⟨actual initiation had to *wait on* new endowment —*Report: Pres. of Harvard Univ. to Board of Overseers, 1939-40*⟩ ⟨settlement of the big problems still *waited on* Russia —*Time*⟩ Our written evidence, while sparse, does not show any discernible regional pattern and is not limited in formality. While considerably less common than *wait for, wait on* appears to be gaining slightly in frequency in edited prose. We also have evidence of a variant *wait upon* ⟨we do not propose to *wait upon* the economy to produce the earnings improvement that sound financing . . . clearly requires —J. D. de Butts⟩

— **wait on** *or* **wait upon 1 a :** to attend as a servant **b :** to supply the wants of **:** SERVE **2 :** to make a formal call on **3 :** to wait for — **wait up :** to delay going to bed

²**wait** *n* [ME *waite* watchman, public musician, wait, fr. ONF, watchman, watch, of Gmc origin; akin to OHG *wahta* watch] (13c) **1 a :** one of a band of public musicians in England employed to play for processions or public entertainments **b (1) :** one of a group who serenade for gratuities esp. at the Christmas season **(2) :** a piece of music by such a group **2 a :** a hidden or concealed position — used chiefly in the expression *lie in wait* **b :** a state or attitude of watchfulness and expectancy ⟨anchored in ~ for early morning fishing —Fred Zimmer⟩ **3 :** an act or period of waiting ⟨a long ~ in line⟩

wait·er \ˈwāt-ər\ *n* (15c) **1 :** one that waits on another; *esp* **:** a man who waits on table (as in a restaurant) **2 :** a tray on which something (as a tea service) is carried **:** SALVER

waiting game *n* (1890) **:** a strategy in which one or more participants withhold action temporarily in the hope of having a favorable opportunity for more effective action later

waiting list *n* (1897) **:** a list or roster of those waiting (as for election to a club or admission to an educational institution)

waiting room *n* (1683) **:** a room (as in a doctor's office) for the use of persons (as patients) who are waiting

wait out *vt* (1941) **:** to await an end to ⟨*wait* the storm *out*⟩

wait·ress \ˈwā-trəs\ *n* (1834) **:** a girl or woman who waits on table (as in a restaurant) — **waitress** *vi*

waive \ˈwāv\ *vt* **waived; waiv·ing** [ME *weiven,* fr. ONF *weyver,* fr. *waif* lost, unclaimed] (14c) **1** *archaic* **:** GIVE UP, FORSAKE **2 :** to throw away (stolen goods) **3** *archaic* **:** to shunt aside (as a danger or duty) **:** EVADE **4 a :** to relinquish voluntarily (as a legal right) ⟨~ a jury trial⟩ **b :** to refrain from pressing or enforcing (as a claim or rule) **:** FORGO **5 :** to put off from immediate consideration **:** POSTPONE **6 :** to dismiss with or as if with a wave of the hand ⟨*waived* the problem aside⟩ ***syn*** see RELINQUISH

waiv·er \ˈwā-vər\ *n* [AF *weyver,* fr. ONF *weyver* to abandon, waive] (1628) **1 :** the act of intentionally relinquishing or abandoning a known right, claim, or privilege; *also* **:** the legal instrument evidencing such an act **2 :** the act of a club's waiving the right to claim a professional ball player who is being removed from another club's roster

Wa·kash·an \wō-ˈkash-ən, ˈwō-ˌ\ *n* (ca. 1895) **:** a language family of the Mosan phylum

¹**wake** \ˈwāk\ *vb* **woke** \ˈwōk\ *also* **waked** \wākt\; **wo·ken** \ˈwō-kən\ *also* **waked** *or* **woke; wak·ing** [partly fr. ME *waken* (past *wook,* pp. *waken*), fr. OE *wacan* to awake (past *wōc,* pp. *wacen*); partly fr. ME *wakien, waken* (past & pp. *waked*), fr. OE *wacian* to be awake (past *wacode,* pp. *wacod*); akin to OE *wæccan* to watch, L *vegēre* to rouse, excite] *vi* (bef. 12c) **1 a :** to be or remain awake **b** *archaic* **:** to remain awake on watch esp. over a corpse **c** *obs* **:** to stay up late in revelry **2 :** AWAKE — often used with *up* ~ *vt* **1 :** to stand watch over (as a dead body); *esp* **:** to hold a wake over **2 a :** to rouse from or as if from sleep **:** AWAKE — often used with *up* **b :** STIR, EXCITE ⟨*woke* up latent possibilities —Norman Douglas⟩ **c :** to arouse conscious interest in **:** ALERT — usu. used with *to* ⟨*woke* the publishers to the fact that there was an enormous . . . audience —Harrison Smith⟩ — **wak·er** *n*

²**wake** *n* (13c) **1 :** the state of being awake **2 a (1) :** an annual English parish festival formerly held in commemoration of the church's patron saint **(2) :** VIGIL 1a **b :** the festivities orig. connected with the wake of an English parish church — usu. used in pl. but sing. or pl. in constr. **c** *Brit* **:** an annual holiday or vacation — usu. used in pl. but sing. or pl. in constr. **3 :** a watch held over the body of a dead person prior to burial and sometimes accompanied by festivity

³**wake** *n* [of Scand origin; akin to ON *vǫk* hole in ice; akin to ON *vǫkr* damp — more at HUMOR] (1547) **1 :** the track left by a moving body (as a ship) in a fluid (as water); *broadly* **:** a track or path left **2 :** AFTERMATH 3 — **in the wake of 1 :** close behind and in the same path of travel ⟨*in the wake of* trappers and . . . riflemen came . . . settlers —*Amer. Guide Series: Ind.*⟩ **2 :** as a result of **:** as a consequence of ⟨power vacuums left *in the wake of* the second world war —A. M. Schlesinger b1917⟩

wake·ful \ˈwāk-fəl\ *adj* (1549) **:** not sleeping or able to sleep **:** SLEEPLESS — **wake·ful·ly** \-fə-lē\ *adv* — **wake·ful·ness** *n*

wake·less \ˈwā-kləs\ *adj* (1824) **:** SOUND, UNBROKEN ⟨~ sleep⟩

wak·en \ˈwā-kən\ *vb* **wak·ened; wak·en·ing** \ˈwāk-(ə-)niŋ\ [ME *waknen,* fr. OE *wæcnian;* akin to ON *vakna* to awaken, OE *wæccan* to watch] *vi* (bef. 12c) **:** AWAKE — often used with *up* ~ *vt* **:** to rouse esp. out of sleep **:** WAKE

wak·en·er \ˈwāk-(ə-)nər\ *n, archaic* (1573) **:** one that causes to waken

wake·rife \ˈwā-ˌkrif\ *adj* [ME (Sc) *walkryfe,* fr. *walk* awake (fr. *waken, walken* to wake) + *ryfe* rife] *Scot* (15c) **:** WAKEFUL, ALERT

wake–rob·in \ˈwā-ˌkräb-ən\ *n* (ca. 1530) **1 :** TRILLIUM **2 :** JACK-IN-THE-PULPIT

wak·ing \ˈwā-kiŋ\ *adj* (1567) **:** passed in a conscious or alert state ⟨every ~ hour⟩

Wal·den·ses \wȯl-ˈden(t)-(ˌ)sēz, wäl-\ *n pl* [ME *Waldensis,* fr. ML *Waldenses, Valdenses,* fr. Peter *Waldo* (or *Valdo*)] (15c) **:** a Christian sect arising in southern France in the 12th century, adopting Calvinist doctrines in the 16th century, and later living chiefly in Piedmont — **Wal·den·sian** \-ˈden-chən, -ˈden(t)-sē-ən\ *adj or n*

Wal·dorf salad \ˌwȯl-ˌdȯrf-\ *n* [*Waldorf*-Astoria Hotel, New York City] (ca. 1902) **:** a salad made typically of diced apples, celery, nuts, and mayonnaise

¹**wale** \ˈwā(ə)l\ *n* [ME, fr. OE *walu;* akin to ON *valr* round, L *volvere* to roll — more at VOLUBLE] (bef. 12c) **1 a :** a streak or ridge made on the skin esp. by the stroke of a whip **:** WEAL **b :** a narrow raised surface **:** RIDGE **2 :** one of a number of strakes usu. of extra thick and strong planks in the sides of a wooden ship — usu. used in pl. **3 a :** one of a series of even ribs in a fabric **b :** the texture esp. of a fabric **4 :** a horizontal constructional member (as of timber or steel) used for bracing vertical members

²**wale** *vt* **waled; wal·ing** (15c) **:** to mark (as the skin) with welts

³**wale** *n* [ME (Sc & northern dial.) *wal,* fr. ON *val;* akin to OHG *wala* choice, OE *wyllan* to wish — more at WILL] (14c) **1** *dial Brit* **:** CHOICE **2** *dial Brit* **:** the best part **:** PICK

⁴**wale** *vb, dial Brit* (14c) **:** CHOOSE

wal·er \ˈwā-lər\ *n, often cap* [New So. *Wales,* Australia] (1849) **:** a horse from New So. Wales; *esp* **:** a rather large rugged saddle horse of mixed ancestry formerly exported in quantity from Australia to British India for military use

Wal·hal·la \väl-ˈhäl-ə\ *n* [G] **:** VALHALLA

¹**walk** \ˈwȯk\ *vb* [partly fr. ME *walken* (past *welk,* pp. *walken*), fr. OE *wealcan* to roll, toss, journey about (past *weolc,* pp. *wealcen*) and partly fr. ME *walkien* (past *walked,* pp. *walked*), fr. OE *wealcian* to roll up, muffle up; akin to MD *walken* to knead, press, full, L *valgus* bowlegged] *vi* (bef. 12c) **1 a** *obs* **:** ROAM, WANDER **b** *of a spirit* **:** to move about in visible form **:** APPEAR **c** *of a ship* **:** to make headway **2 a :** to move along on foot **:** advance by steps **b :** to come or go easily or readily **c :** to go on foot for exercise or pleasure **d :** to go at a walk **3 a :** to pursue a course of action or way of life **:** conduct oneself

: BEHAVE ⟨~ warily⟩ **b :** to be or act in association : continue in union ⟨the British and American peoples will . . . ~ together side by side . . . in peace —Sir Winston Churchill⟩ **4 :** to go to first base as a result of a base on balls **5** *of an inanimate object* **a :** to move in a manner that is suggestive of walking **b :** to stand with an appearance suggestive of strides ⟨pylons ~*ing* across the valley⟩ **6** *of an astronaut* **:** to move about in space outside a spacecraft ~ *vt* **1 a :** to pass on foot or as if on foot through, along, over, or upon : TRAVERSE, PERAMBULATE ⟨~ the streets⟩ ⟨~ a tightrope⟩ **b :** to perform or accomplish by going on foot ⟨~ guard⟩ **2 a :** to cause (an animal) to go at a walk ⟨~*ing* a dog⟩ **b :** to cause to move by walking ⟨~*ed* his bicycle up the hill⟩; *specif* : to haul (as an anchor) by walking round the capstan **3 :** to follow on foot for the purpose of measuring, surveying, or inspecting ⟨~ a boundary⟩ **4 a :** to accompany on foot : walk with ⟨~*ed* her home⟩ **b :** to compel to walk (as by a command) **c :** to bring to a specified condition by walking ⟨~*ed* us off our feet⟩ **5 :** to move (an object) in a manner suggestive of walking **6 :** to perform (a dance) at a walking pace ⟨~ a quadrille⟩ **7 :** to give a base on balls to — **walk away from 1 :** to outrun or get the better of without difficulty **2 :** to survive (an accident) with little or no injury — **walk off with 1 a :** to steal and take away **b :** to take over unexpectedly from someone else : STEAL 1d ⟨*walked off with* the show⟩ **2 :** to win or gain esp. by outdoing one's competitors without difficulty — **walk on :** to take advantage of : ABUSE — **walk over :** to treat contemptuously — **walk the plank 1 :** to walk under compulsion over the side of a ship into the sea **2 :** to resign an office or position under compulsion — **walk through 1 :** to go through (as a theatrical role or familiar activity) perfunctorily (as in an early stage of rehearsal) **2 :** to deal with or carry out perfunctorily

²walk *n* (14c) **1 a :** an act or instance of going on foot esp. for exercise or pleasure ⟨go for a ~⟩ **b :** SPACE WALK **2 :** an accustomed place of walking : HAUNT **3 :** a place designed for walking: **a :** a railed platform above the roof of a dwelling house **b** (1) **:** a path specially arranged or paved for walking (2) **:** SIDEWALK **c :** a public avenue for promenading : PROMENADE **d :** ROPEWALK **4 :** a place or area of land in which animals feed and exercise with minimal restraint **5 :** distance to be walked ⟨a quarter mile ~ from here⟩ **6** *Brit* **:** a ceremonial procession **7 :** manner of living : CONDUCT, BEHAVIOR **8 a :** the gait of a biped in which the feet are lifted alternately with one foot not clear of the ground before the other touches **b :** the gait of a quadruped in which there are always at least two feet on the ground; *specif* : a four-beat gait of a horse in which the feet strike the ground in the sequence near hind, near fore, off hind, off fore **c :** a low rate of speed ⟨the shortage of raw materials slowed production to a ~⟩ **9 :** a route regularly traversed by a person in the performance of a particular activity (as patrolling, begging, or vending) **10 :** characteristic manner of walking ⟨his ~ is just like his father's⟩ **11 a :** social or economic status ⟨all ~*s* of life⟩ **b** (1) **:** range or sphere of action : FIELD, PROVINCE (2) **:** VOCATION **12 :** BASE ON BALLS

walk·about \ˈwȯ-kə-ˌbau̇t\ *n* (1907) **1 :** a short period of wandering bush life engaged in by an Australian aborigine as an occasional interruption of regular work **2 :** a walking tour : walking trip

walk·a·thon \ˈwȯ-kə-ˌthän\ *n* [*walk* + *-athon* (as in *marathon*)] (1932) **:** a walk covering a considerable distance organized esp. to raise money for a cause

walk·away \ˈwȯ-kə-ˌwā\ *n* (1888) **:** an easily won contest

walk·er \ˈwȯ-kər\ *n* (14c) **1 :** one that walks: as **a :** one who conducts himself in a specified way **b :** a competitor in a walking race **c :** a peddler going on foot **2 :** something used in walking: as **a :** a framework designed to support a baby learning to walk or a crippled or handicapped person **b :** a walking shoe

walk·ie–look·ie \ˌwȯ-kē-ˈlu̇k-ē\ *n* (ca. 1946) **:** a portable one-man television camera

walk·ie–talk·ie \-ˈtȯ-kē, ˈwȯ-kē-ˌ\ *n* (ca. 1939) **:** a compact easily transportable battery-operated radio transmitting and receiving set

¹walk–in \ˌwȯ-ˌkin\ *adj* (1926) **1 :** large enough to be walked into ⟨a ~ closet⟩ **2 :** arranged so as to be entered directly rather than through a lobby ⟨a ~ apartment⟩ **3 a :** being a person who walks in without an appointment ⟨a ~ blood donor⟩ **b :** of or relating to such persons ⟨~ clinic⟩

²walk–in \ˈwȯ-ˌkin\ *n* (1944) **1 :** a walk-in refrigerator or cold storage room **2 :** an easy election victory **3 :** one who walks in without an appointment

¹walk·ing \ˈwȯ-kiŋ\ *n* (15c) **1 :** the action of one that walks ⟨~ is good exercise⟩ **2 :** the condition of a surface for one going on foot ⟨the ~ is slippery⟩

²walking *adj* (15c) **1 a :** able to walk : AMBULATORY ⟨the ~ wounded⟩ **b :** being the personification of a nonhuman quality or thing ⟨a ~ encyclopedia⟩ **2 a :** used for or in walking ⟨~ shoes⟩ **b :** characterized by or consisting of the action of walking ⟨a ~ tour⟩ **3 :** that moves or appears to move in a manner suggestive of walking; *esp* **:** that swings or rocks back and forth ⟨~ beam⟩ **4 :** guided or operated by a person on foot ⟨a ~ plow⟩

walking catfish *n* (1968) **:** an Asian catfish (*Clarias batrachus*) that is able to move about on land and has been inadvertently introduced into Florida waters

walking delegate *n* (ca. 1890) **:** a labor union representative appointed to visit members and their places of employment, to secure enforcement of union rules and agreements, and at times to represent the union in dealing with employers

walking leaf *n* (ca. 1817) **:** any of a family (Phasmatidae) of insects with wings and legs resembling leaves

walking papers *n pl* (1825) **:** DISMISSAL, DISCHARGE — called also *walking ticket*

walking stick *n* (1580) **1 :** a stick used in walking **2** *usu* **walk·ing·stick :** STICK INSECT; *esp* **:** a phasmid (*Diapheromera femorata*) common in parts of the U.S.

walk–on \ˈwȯ-ˌkȯn, -ˌkän\ *n* (1902) **:** a small part or brief appearance esp. in a dramatic production

walk·out \ˈwȯ-ˌkau̇t\ *n* (1888) **1 :** STRIKE 3a **2 :** the action of leaving a meeting or organization as an expression of disapproval

walk out \(ˈ)wȯ-ˈkau̇t\ *vi* (ca. 1840) **1 :** to leave suddenly often as an expression of disapproval **2 :** to go on strike — **walk out on :** to leave in the lurch : ABANDON, DESERT

walk·over \ˈwȯ-ˌkō-vər\ *n* (1838) **1 :** a one-sided contest : an easy or uncontested victory **2 :** a horse race with only one starter

walk–through \ˈwȯk-ˌthrü\ *n* (1940) **1 :** a perfunctory performance of a play or acting part (as in an early stage of rehearsal) **2 :** a television rehearsal without cameras

¹walk–up \ˌwȯ-ˌkəp\ *adj* (1919) **1 :** located above the ground floor in a building with no elevator ⟨a ~ apartment⟩ **2 :** consisting of several stories and having no elevator ⟨a ~ tenement⟩ **3 :** designed to allow pedestrians to be served without entering a building ⟨the ~ window of a bank⟩

²walk–up \ˈwȯ-ˌkəp\ *n* (1924) **:** a building or apartment house of several stories that has no elevator; *also* **:** an apartment or office in such a building

walk·way \ˈwȯ-ˌkwā\ *n* (1792) **:** a passage for walking : WALK

Wal·ky·rie \väl-ˈkir-ē *also* väl-ˈkī-rē & ˈväl-kə-rē\ *n* [G *walküre* & ON *valkyrja*] **:** VALKYRIE

¹wall \ˈwȯl\ *n* [ME, fr. OE *weall;* akin to MHG *wall;* both fr. L *vallum* rampart, fr. *vallus* stake, palisade; akin to ON *vǫlr* round stick, L *volvere* to roll — more at VOLUBLE] (bef. 12c) **1 a :** a high thick masonry structure forming a long rampart or an enclosure chiefly for defense — often used in pl. **b :** a masonry fence around a garden, park, or estate **c :** a structure that serves to hold back pressure (as of water or sliding earth) **2 :** one of the sides of a room or building connecting floor and ceiling or foundation and roof **3 :** the side of a footpath next to buildings **4 :** an extreme or desperate position or a state of defeat, failure, or ruin — usu. used in the phrase *to the wall* **5 :** a material layer enclosing space ⟨the ~ of a container⟩ ⟨heart ~*s*⟩ **6 :** something resembling a wall (as in appearance, function, or effect); *esp* **:** something that acts as a barrier or defense ⟨a ~ of reserve⟩ ⟨tariff ~⟩ — **walled** \ˈwȯld\ *adj* — **wall–like** \ˈwȯl-ˌlīk\ *adj* — **up the wall** *slang* **:** into a state of intense agitation, annoyance, or frustration ⟨the noise drove me *up the wall*⟩

²wall *vt* (bef. 12c) **1 a :** to provide, cover with, or surround with or as if with a wall ⟨~ in the garden⟩ **b :** to separate by or as if by a wall ⟨~*ed* off half the house⟩ **2 a :** IMMURE **b :** to close (an opening) with or as if with a wall

³wall *vb* [ME (Sc) *wawlen,* prob. fr. ME *wawil-* (in *wawil-eghed* walleyed)] *vt* (15c) **:** to roll (one's eyes) in a dramatic manner ~ *vi, of the eyes* **:** to roll in a dramatic manner

wal·la·by \ˈwäl-ə-bē\ *n, pl* **wallabies** *also* **wallaby** [*wolabā,* native name in New So. Wales, Australia] (ca. 1798) **:** any of various small or medium-sized usu. brightly colored kangaroos (esp. genus *Macropus*)

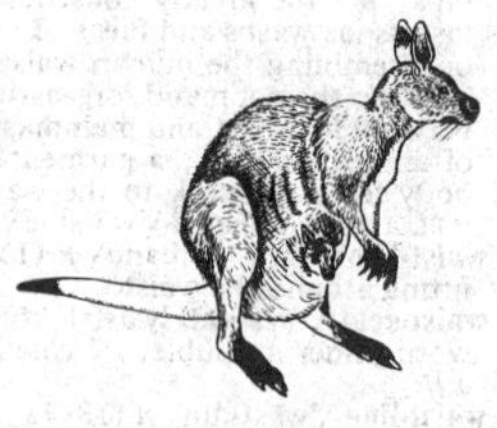

wallaby

Wal·lace's line \ˌwäl-ə-səz-\ *n* [Alfred Russel *Wallace*] (ca. 1868) **:** a hypothetical boundary separating the characteristic Asian flora and fauna from those of Australasia and forming the common boundary of the Australian and Oriental biogeographic regions

wal·lah \ˈwäl-ə, *in combination usu* ˌwäl-ə\ *n* [Hindi *-wālā* man, one in charge, fr. Skt *pāla* protector; akin to Skt *pāti* he protects — more at FUR] (1782) **:** a person who is associated with a particular work or who performs a specific duty or service — usu. used in combination ⟨the book ~ was an itinerant peddler —George Orwell⟩

wal·la·roo \ˌwäl-ə-ˈrü\ *n, pl* **-roos** [*wolarū,* native name in New So. Wales, Australia] (1827) **:** a large reddish gray kangaroo (*Macrobus robustus*) — called also *euro*

wall·board \ˈwȯl-ˌbō(ə)rd, -ˌbȯ(ə)rd\ *n* (1906) **:** a structural boarding of any of various materials (as wood pulp, gypsum, or plastic) made in large rigid sheets and used esp. for sheathing interior walls and ceilings

wal·let \ˈwäl-ət\ *n* [ME *walet*] (14c) **1 :** a bag for carrying miscellaneous articles while traveling **2 a :** a folding pocketbook with compartments for personal papers and usu. unfolded paper money; *also* **:** BILLFOLD **b :** a container that resembles a money wallet: as (1) **:** a usu. flexible folding case fitted for carrying specific items (as tools or fishing flies) (2) **:** FOLDER 3

wall·eye \ˈwȯ-ˌlī\ *n* [back-formation fr. *walleyed*] (1523) **1 a :** an eye with a whitish iris **b :** an eye with an opaque white cornea **2 a :** strabismus in which the eye turns outward away from the nose **b** *pl* **:** eyes affected with divergent strabismus **3 :** a large vigorous American freshwater food and sport fish (*Stizostedion vitreum*) that has prominent eyes and is related to the perches but resembles the true pike — called also *walleyed pike*

wall·eyed \-ˈlīd\ *adj* [by folk etymology fr. ME *wawil-eghed,* part trans. of ON *vagl-eygr* walleyed, fr. *vagl* beam, roost (akin to OE *wegan* to move, carry) + *eygr* eyed — more at WAY] (15c) **1 :** having walleyes or affected with walleye **2 :** marked by a wild irrational staring of the eyes

wall·flow·er \ˈwȯl-ˌflau̇(-ə)r\ *n* (1578) **1 a :** any of several Old World herbaceous or somewhat woody perennial plants (genus *Cheiranthus*) of the mustard family; *esp* **:** a hardy erect herb (*C. cheiri*) widely cultivated for its showy fragrant flowers **b :** any of a related genus (*Erysimum*) with alternate leaves and yellow flowers **2 :** a person who from shyness or unpopularity remains on the sidelines of a social activity (as a dance)

Wal·loon \wä-ˈlün\ *n* [MF *Wallon,* adj. & n., of Gmc origin; prob. akin to OHG *Walah* Celt, Roman, OE *Wealh* Celt, Welshman — more at WELSH] (1530) **1 :** a French dialect of the Walloons **2 :** a member of a chiefly Celtic people of southern and southeastern Belgium and adjacent parts of France — **Walloon** *adj*

¹wal·lop \ˈwäl-əp\ *vb* [ME *walopen* to gallop, fr. ONF *waloper*] *vi* (14c) **1 a :** to move with reckless or disorganized haste : advance in a headlong rush **b :** WALLOW, FLOUNDER **2 :** to boil noisily ~ *vt* **1 a :** to thrash soundly : LAMBASTE **b :** to beat by a wide margin : TROUNCE **2 :** to hit with force : SOCK — **wal·lop·er** *n*

²wallop *n* [ME, gallop, fr. ONF *walop,* fr. *waloper* to gallop] (ca. 1823) **1 a :** a powerful blow : ²PUNCH 2 **b :** something resembling a wallop esp. in suddenness of force **c :** the ability (as of a boxer) to hit hard **2**

a : emotional or psychological force or influence : IMPACT **b :** an exciting emotional response : THRILL **3** *Brit* **:** BEER
wal·lop·ing *adj* (ca. 1847) **1 :** LARGE, WHOPPING **2 :** exceptionally fine or impressive : SMASHING
[1]**wal·low** \'wäl-(,)ō, -ə(-w)\ *vi* [ME *walwen,* fr. OE *wealwian* to roll — more at VOLUBLE] (bef. 12c) **1 :** to roll oneself about in an indolent or ungainly manner **2 :** to billow forth : SURGE **3 :** to devote oneself entirely; *esp* **:** to take unrestrained pleasure : DELIGHT **4 a :** to become abundantly supplied : LUXURIATE ⟨a family that ~*s* in money⟩ **b :** to indulge oneself immoderately ⟨~*ing* in self-pity⟩ **5 :** to become or remain helpless ⟨allowed them to ~ in their ignorance⟩ — **wal·low·er** \'wäl-ə-wər\ *n*
[2]**wallow** *n* (15c) **1 :** an act or instance of wallowing **2 a :** a muddy area or one filled with dust used by animals for wallowing **b :** a depression formed by or as if by the wallowing of animals **3 :** a state of degradation or degeneracy
wall painting *n* (ca. 1854) **:** FRESCO
[1]**wall·pa·per** \'wȯl-,pā-pər\ *n* (1827) **:** decorative paper for the walls of a room
[2]**wallpaper** *vt* (1924) **:** to provide the walls of (a room) with wallpaper ~ *vi* **:** to put wallpaper on a wall
wall plate *n* (14c) **:** PLATE 5
wall plug *n* (1888) **:** an electric receptacle in a wall
wall rock *n* (1876) **:** a rock through which a fault or vein runs
wall rocket *n* (ca. 1611) **:** any of several plants (genus *Diplotaxis*) of the mustard family; *esp* **:** a yellow-flowered European weed (*D. tenuifolia*) adventive in No. America
Wall Street \'wȯl-\ *n* [*Wall Street,* New York City, site of the New York Stock Exchange] (1836) **:** the influential financial interests of the U.S. economy
Wall Street·er \-,strēt-ər\ *n* (1885) **:** one who is involved in Wall Street
wall system *n* (1968) **:** a set of shelves often with cabinets or bureaus that can be variously arranged along a wall
wall–to–wall *adj* (1946) **1 :** covering the entire floor ⟨~ carpeting⟩ **2 a :** covering or filling one entire space or time ⟨a disco crammed with ~ bodies —*Women's Wear Daily*⟩ **b :** occurring or found everywhere : UBIQUITOUS
wal·ly \'wā-lē\ *adj* [prob. fr. [3]*wale*] *Scot* (1500) **:** FINE, STURDY
wal·ly·drai·gle \'wā-lē-,drā-gəl, 'wal-ē-\ *n* [origin unknown] *chiefly Scot* (1500) **:** a feeble, imperfectly developed, or slovenly creature
wal·nut \'wȯl-(,)nət\ *n* [ME *walnot,* fr. OE *wealhhnutu,* lit., foreign nut, fr. *Wealh* Welshman, foreigner + *hnutu* nut — more at WELSH, NUT] (bef. 12c) **1 a :** an edible nut of any of a genus (*Juglans* of the family Juglandaceae, the walnut family) of trees; *esp* **:** the large edible nut of a Eurasian tree (*J. regia*) with a hard richly figured wood **b :** a tree that bears walnuts **c :** the wood of a walnut that is often valued for cabinetmaking and veneers **2 :** a moderate reddish brown
Wal·pur·gis·nacht \väl-'pu̇r-gə-,snäkt\ *n* [G] (1822) **:** WALPURGIS NIGHT
Wal·pur·gis Night \väl-'pu̇r-gəs-\ *n* [part trans. of G *walpurgisnacht,* fr. *Walpurgis* St. Walburga †A.D. 779 Eng. saint whose feast day falls on May Day + G *nacht* night] (1823) **1 :** the eve of May Day on which witches are held to ride to an appointed rendezvous **2 :** something (as an event or situation) having a nightmarish quality
wal·rus \'wȯl-rəs, 'wäl-\ *n, pl* **walrus** *or* **wal·rus·es** [D, of Scand origin; akin to Dan & Norw *hvalros* walrus, ON *rosmhvalr*] (1728) **:** a large marine mammal (*Odobenus rosmarus* of the family Odobenidae) with two ivory tusks that is related to the seals, is found in Arctic seas, feeds mostly on bivalve mollusks, and has long been a source of food and other materials for maritime Eskimo peoples
Wal·ter Mit·ty \,wȯl-tər-'mit-ē\ *n* [*Walter Mitty,* daydreaming hero of a story by James Thurber] (1949) **:** a commonplace unadventurous person who seeks escape from reality through daydreaming — **Walter Mit·ty·ish** \-ē-ish\ *adj*
[1]**waltz** \'wȯl(t)s\ *vi* (1712) **1 :** to dance a waltz **2 :** to move or advance in a lively or conspicuous manner : FLOUNCE **3 a :** to advance easily and successfully : BREEZE — usu. used with *through* **b :** to approach boldly — used with *up* ⟨can't just ~ up and introduce ourselves⟩ ~ *vt* **1 :** to dance a waltz with **2 :** to grab and lead (as a person) unceremoniously : MARCH — **waltz·er** *n*
[2]**waltz** *n* [G *walzer,* fr. *walzen* to roll, dance, fr. OHG *walzan* to turn, roll — more at WELTER] (1781) **1 :** a ballroom dance in 3/4 time with strong accent on the first beat and a basic pattern of step-step-close **2 :** music for a waltz or a concert composition in 3/4 time
[1]**wam·ble** \'wäm-bəl\ *vi* **wam·bled; wam·bling** \-b(ə-)liŋ\ [ME *wamlen;* akin to Dan *vamle* to become nauseated, L *vomere* to vomit — more at VOMIT] (14c) **1 a :** to feel nausea **b** *of a stomach* **:** RUMBLE 1 **2 :** to move unsteadily or with a weaving or rolling motion
[2]**wamble** *n* (1552) **1 :** a wambling esp. of the stomach **2 :** a reeling or staggering gait or movement
wame \'wām\ *n* [ME, alter. of *wamb* — more at WOMB] *chiefly Scot* (15c) **:** BELLY
wam·pum \'wäm-pəm\ *n* [short for *wampumpeag*] (1636) **1 :** beads of polished shells strung in strands, belts, or sashes and used by No. American Indians as money, ceremonial pledges, and ornaments **2** *slang* **:** MONEY
wam·pum·peag \-,pēg\ *n* [Narraganset *wampompeag,* fr. *wampan* white + *api* string + *-ag,* pl. suffix] (1627) **:** WAMPUM; *esp* **:** that made of the less valuable white shell beads
[1]**wan** \'wän\ *adj* **wan·ner; wan·nest** [ME, fr. OE *wann* dark, livid] (bef. 12c) **1 a :** suggestive of poor health : SICKLY, PALLID **b :** lacking vitality : FEEBLE **2 :** DIM, FAINT **3 :** LANGUID ⟨a ~ smile⟩ — **wan·ly** *adv* — **wan·ness** \'wän-nəs\ *n*
[2]**wan** *vi* **wanned; wan·ning** (1582) **:** to grow or become pale or sickly
wand \'wänd\ *n* [ME, slender stick, fr. ON *vǫndr;* akin to OE *windan* to wind, twist — more at WIND] (15c) **1 :** a slender staff carried in a procession : VERGE **2 :** a slender rod used by conjurers and magicians **3 :** a slat 6 feet by 2 inches used as a target in archery; *also* **:** a narrow strip of paper pasted vertically on a target face **4 :** any of various pipelike devices; *esp* **:** the rigid tube between the hose and the nozzle of a vacuum cleaner
wan·der \'wän-dər\ *vb* **wan·dered; wan·der·ing** \-d(ə-)riŋ\ [ME *wandren,* fr. OE *wandrian;* akin to MHG *wandern* to wander, OE *windan* to wind, twist] *vi* (bef. 12c) **1 a :** to move about without a fixed course, aim, or goal **b :** to go idly about : RAMBLE **2 :** to follow a winding course : MEANDER **3 a :** to deviate (as from a course) : STRAY **b :** to go astray morally : ERR **c :** to lose normal mental contact : stray in thought ~ *vt* **:** to roam over — **wander** *n* — **wan·der·er** \-dər-ər\ *n*
syn WANDER, ROAM, RAMBLE, ROVE, TRAIPSE, MEANDER mean to move about more or less aimlessly. WANDER implies an absence of or an indifference to a fixed course ⟨found her *wandering* about the square⟩ ROAM suggests wandering about freely and often far afield ⟨liked to *roam* through the woods⟩ RAMBLE stresses carelessness and indifference to one's course or objective ⟨the speaker *rambled* on without ever coming to the point⟩ ROVE suggests vigorous and sometimes purposeful roaming ⟨armed brigands *roved* over the countryside⟩ TRAIPSE implies an erratic if purposeful course ⟨*traipsed* all over town looking for the right dress⟩ MEANDER implies a winding or intricate course suggestive of aimless or listless wandering ⟨the river *meanders* for miles through rich farmland⟩
[1]**wan·der·ing** *adj* (bef. 12c) **:** characterized by aimless, slow, or pointless movement: as **a :** that winds or meanders ⟨a ~ course⟩ **b :** not keeping a rational or sensible course : VAGRANT **c :** NOMADIC ⟨~ tribes⟩ **d** *of a plant* **:** having long runners or tendrils
[2]**wandering** *n* (14c) **1 :** a going about from place to place — often used in pl. **2 :** movement away from the proper, normal, or usual course or place — often used in pl.
Wandering Jew *n* **1 :** a Jew of medieval legend condemned by Christ to wander the earth till Christ's second coming **2** *not cap W* **:** any of several plants (genera *Zebrina* and *Tradescantia*) of the spiderwort family; *esp* **:** either of two trailing or creeping plants (*Z. pendula* and *T. fluminensis*) cultivated for their showy and often white-striped foliage
wan·der·lust \'wän-dər-,ləst\ *n* [G, fr. *wandern* to wander + *lust* desire, pleasure] (1902) **:** strong longing for or impulse toward wandering
[1]**wane** \'wān\ *vi* **waned; wan·ing** [ME *wanen,* fr. OE *wanian;* akin to OHG *wanōn* to wane, OE *wan* wanting, deficient, L *vanus* empty, vain] (bef. 12c) **1 :** to decrease in size, extent, or degree : DWINDLE: as **a :** to diminish in phase or intensity — used chiefly of the moon **b :** to become less brilliant or powerful : DIM **c :** to flow out : EBB **2 :** to fall gradually from power, prosperity, or influence ***syn*** see ABATE
[2]**wane** *n* (14c) **1 a :** the act or process of waning ⟨strength on the ~⟩ **b :** a period or time of waning; *specif* **:** the period from full phase of the moon to the new moon **2** [ME, defect, fr. OE *wana;* akin to OE *wan* deficient] **:** a defect in lumber characterized by bark or a lack of wood at a corner or edge
wan·gle \'waŋ-gəl\ *vb* **wan·gled; wan·gling** \-g(ə-)liŋ\ [perh. alter. of *waggle*] *vi* (ca. 1820) **1 :** to extricate oneself (as from difficulty) : WIGGLE **2 :** to resort to trickery or devious methods ~ *vt* **1 :** SHAKE, WIGGLE **2 :** to adjust or manipulate for personal or fraudulent ends **3 :** to make or get by devious means : FINAGLE ⟨~ an invitation⟩ — **wan·gler** \-g(ə-)lər\ *n*
wan·i·gan *or* **wan·ni·gan** \'wän-i-gən\ *n* [of Algonquian origin; akin to Abnaki *waniigan* trap, lit., that into which something strays] (ca. 1848) **:** a shelter (as for sleeping, eating, or storage) often mounted on wheels or tracks and towed by tractor or mounted on a raft or boat
wan·ion \'wän-yən\ *n* [fr. the obs. phrase *in the waniand* unluckily, lit., in the waning (moon), fr. ME, fr. *waniand,* northern prp. of *wanien, wanen* to wane] *archaic* (1549) **:** PLAGUE, VENGEANCE — used in the phrase *with a wanion*
Wan·kel engine \,väŋ-kəl-, ,waŋ-\ *n* [Felix *Wankel* b1902 Ger. engineer] (1961) **:** an internal-combustion rotary engine that has a rounded triangular rotor functioning as a piston and rotating in a space in the engine and that has only two major moving parts
wan·na–be \'wä-nə-,bē\ *n* [fr. the phrase *want to be*] (1986) **:** a person who wants to be someone or something else
[1]**want** \'wȯnt *also* 'wänt & 'wənt\ *vb* [ME *wanten,* fr. ON *vanta;* akin to OE *wan* deficient] *vi* (13c) **1 :** to be needy or destitute **2 :** to have or feel need ⟨never ~*s* for friends⟩ **3 :** to be necessary or needed **4 :** to desire to come, go, or be ⟨the cat ~*s* in⟩ ⟨~*s* out of the deal⟩ ~ *vt* **1 :** to fail to possess esp. in customary or required amount : LACK ⟨his answer ~*s* courtesy⟩ **2 a :** to have a strong desire for ⟨~*ed* a chance to rest⟩ **b :** to have an inclination to : LIKE ⟨say what you ~, he is efficient⟩ **3 a :** to have need of : REQUIRE ⟨the motor ~*s* a tune-up⟩ **b :** to suffer from the lack of ⟨thousands still ~ food and shelter⟩ **4 :** to wish or demand the presence of **5 :** to hunt or seek in order to apprehend ⟨he is ~*ed* for murder⟩ ***syn*** see DESIRE
[2]**want** *n* (14c) **1 a :** DEFICIENCY, LACK ⟨he suffers from a ~ of good sense⟩ **b :** grave and extreme poverty that deprives one of the necessities of life **2 :** something wanted : NEED, DESIRE **3 :** personal defect : FAULT ***syn*** see POVERTY
want ad *n* (1897) **:** a newspaper advertisement stating that something (as an employee, employment, or a specified item) is wanted
[1]**want·ing** *adj* (14c) **1 :** not present or in evidence : ABSENT **2 a :** not being up to standards or expectations **b :** lacking in ability or capacity : DEFICIENT
[2]**wanting** *prep* (1693) **1 :** WITHOUT ⟨a book ~ a cover⟩ **2 :** LESS, MINUS ⟨a month ~ two days⟩
[1]**wan·ton** \'wȯnt-ᵊn, 'wänt-\ *adj* [ME, fr. *wan-* deficient, wrong, mis- (fr. OE, fr. *wan* deficient) + *towen,* pp. of *teen* to draw, train, discipline, fr. OE *tēon* — more at TOW] (14c) **1 a** *archaic* **:** hard to control : UNDISCIPLINED, UNRULY **b :** playfully mean or cruel : MISCHIEVOUS **2 a :** LEWD, BAWDY **b :** causing sexual excitement : LUSTFUL, SENSUAL **3 a :** MERCILESS, INHUMANE ⟨~ cruelty⟩ **b :** having no just foundation or provocation : MALICIOUS ⟨a ~ attack⟩ **4 :** being without check or limitation: as **a :** luxuriantly rank ⟨~ vegetation⟩ **b :** unduly lavish : EXTRAVAGANT ***syn*** see SUPEREROGATORY — **wan·ton·ly** *adv* — **wan·ton·ness** \-ᵊn-nəs\ *n*
[2]**wanton** *n* (1526) **1 :** a pampered person or animal : PET; *esp* **:** a spoiled child **2 :** a frolicsome child or animal **3 a :** one given to self-indulgent flirtation or trifling — used esp. in the phrase *play the wanton* **b :** a lewd or lascivious person

\ə\ abut \ᵊ\ kitten, F table \ər\ further \a\ ash \ā\ ace \ä\ cot, cart \au̇\ out \ch\ chin \e\ bet \ē\ easy \g\ go \i\ hit \ī\ ice \j\ job \ŋ\ sing \ō\ go \ȯ\ law \ȯi\ boy \th\ thin \th\ the \ü\ loot \u̇\ foot \y\ yet \zh\ vision \à, k, ⁿ, œ, œ̄, ue, ue̅, ʸ\ *see* Guide to Pronunciation

[3]**wanton** *vi* (1582) : to be wanton or act wantonly ~ *vt* : to pass or waste wantonly or in wantonness — **wan·ton·er** *n*

wa·pen·take \ˈwap-ən-ˌtāk, ˈwäp-\ *n* [ME, fr. OE *wǣpentæc*, fr. ON *vāpnatak* act of grasping weapons, fr. *vāpn* weapon + *tak* act of grasping, fr. *taka* to take; prob. fr. the brandishing of weapons as an expression of approval when the chief of the wapentake entered upon his office — more at WEAPON, TAKE] (bef. 12c) : a subdivision of some English shires corresponding to a hundred

wa·pi·ti \ˈwäp-ət-ē\ *n, pl* **wapiti** *or* **wapitis** [of Algonquian origin; akin to Cree *wapitew* white, whitish; fr. its white rump and tail] (1806) : ELK 1b

wap·pen·schaw·ing \ˈwap-ən-ˌshȯ(-)iŋ, ˈwäp-\ *n* [ME (northern dial.) *wapynschawing*, fr. *wapen* weapon (fr. ON *vāpn*) + *schawing*, gerund of *schawen* to show, fr. OE *scēawian* to look, look at — more at WEAPON, SHOW] (15c) : an inspection or muster of soldiers formerly held at various times in each district of Scotland

[1]**war** \ˈwȯ(ə)r\ *n, often attrib* [ME *werre*, fr. ONF, of Gmc origin; akin to OHG *werra* strife; akin to OHG *werran* to confuse] (12c) **1 a** (1) : a state of usu. open and declared armed hostile conflict between states or nations (2) : a period of such armed conflict (3) : STATE OF WAR **b** : the art or science of warfare **c** (1) *obs* : weapons and equipment for war (2) *archaic* : soldiers armed and equipped for war **2 a** : a state of hostility, conflict, or antagonism **b** : a struggle or competition between opposing forces or for a particular end ⟨a class ~⟩ ⟨a ~ against disease⟩ **c** : VARIANCE, ODDS 3 — **war·less** \-ləs\ *adj*

[2]**war** *vi* **warred; war·ring** (13c) **1** : to be in active or vigorous conflict **2** : to engage in warfare

[3]**war** \ˈwär\ *adv or adj* [ME *werre*, fr. ON *verri*, adj., *verr*, adv. — more at WORSE] *chiefly Scot* (13c) : WORSE

[4]**war** \ˈwär\ *vt* **warred; war·ring** *Scot* (15c) : WORST, OVERCOME

war baby *n* (1901) : a child born or conceived during a war

[1]**war·ble** \ˈwȯr-bəl\ *n* [ME *werble* tune, fr. ONF, of Gmc origin; akin to MHG *wirbel* whirl, tuning peg, OHG *wirbil* whirlwind — more at WHIRL] (14c) **1** : a melodious succession of low pleasing sounds **2** : a musical trill **3** : the action of warbling

[2]**warble** *vb* **war·bled; war·bling** \-b(ə-)liŋ\ *vi* (1536) **1** : to sing in a trilling manner or with many turns and variations **2** : to become sounded with trills, quavers, and rapid modulations in pitch **3** : SING ~ *vt* : to render with turns, runs, or rapid modulations : TRILL

[3]**warble** *n* [perh. of Scand origin; akin to obs. Sw *varbulde* boil, fr. *var* pus + *bulde* swelling] (1585) **1** : a swelling under the hide esp. of the back of cattle, horses, and wild mammals caused by the maggot of a botfly or warble fly **2** : the maggot of a warble fly — **war·bled** \-bəld\ *adj*

warble fly *n* (1877) : any of various two-winged flies (family Oestridae) whose larvae live under the skin of various mammals and cause warbles

war·bler \ˈwȯr-blər\ *n* (ca. 1611) **1** : one that warbles : SINGER, SONGSTER **2 a** : any of numerous small Old World singing birds (family Sylviidae) many of which are noted songsters and are closely related to the thrushes **b** : any of numerous small brightly colored American songbirds (family Parulidae) with a usu. weak and unmusical song — called also *wood warbler*

war·bon·net \ˈwȯr-ˌbän-ət\ *n* (1845) : an American Indian ceremonial headdress with a feathered extension down the back

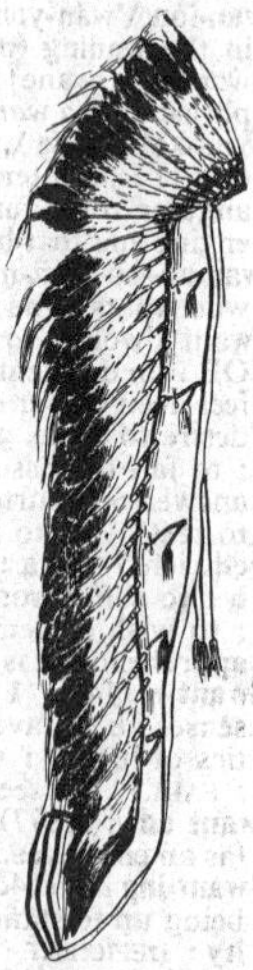

warbonnet

war bride *n* (1916) **1** : a woman who marries a serviceman ordered into active service in time of war **2** : a woman who marries a serviceman esp. of a foreign nation met during a time of war

war chest *n* (1901) : a fund accumulated to finance a war; *broadly* : a fund earmarked for a specific purpose, action, or campaign

war club *n* (1776) : a club-shaped implement used as a weapon esp. by American Indians

war cry *n* (1748) **1** : a cry used by a body of fighters in war **2** : a slogan used esp. to rally people to a cause

[1]**ward** \ˈwȯ(ə)rd\ *n* [ME, fr. OE *weard*; akin to OHG *warta* act of watching, OE *warian* to beware of, guard, *wær* careful — more at WARY] (bef. 12c) **1 a** : the action or process of guarding **b** : a body of guards **2** : the state of being under guard; *esp* : CUSTODY **3 a** : the inner court of a castle or fortress **b** : a division (as a cell or block) of a prison **c** : a division in a hospital; *esp* : a large room in a hospital where a number of patients often requiring similar treatment are accommodated **4 a** : a division of a city for representative, electoral, or administrative purposes **b** : a division of some English and Scottish counties corresponding to a hundred **c** : the Mormon local congregation having auxiliary organizations (as Sunday schools and relief societies) and one or more quorums of each office of the Aaronic priesthood **5** : a projecting ridge of metal in a lock casing or keyhole permitting only the insertion of a key with a corresponding notch; *also* : a corresponding notch in a bit of a key **6** : a person or thing under guard, protection, or surveillance: as **a** : a minor subject to wardship **b** : a person who by reason of incapacity (as minority or lunacy) is under the protection of a court either directly or through a guardian appointed by the court — called also *ward of court* **c** : a person or body of persons under the protection or tutelage of a government **7** : a means of defense : PROTECTION — **ward·ed** \ˈwȯrd-əd\ *adj*

[2]**ward** *vt* [ME *warden*, fr. OE *weardian*; akin to OHG *wartēn* to watch, ON *vartha* to guard, OE *weard* ward] (bef. 12c) **1** : to keep watch over : GUARD **2** : to turn aside (something threatening) : DEFLECT — usu. used with *off*

[1]**-ward** \wərd\ *also* **-wards** \wərdz\ *adj suffix* [*-ward* fr. ME, fr. OE *-weard*; akin to OHG *-wart*, *-wert* -ward, L *vertere* to turn; *-wards* fr. *-wards*, adv. suffix — more at WORTH] **1** : that moves, tends, faces, or is directed toward ⟨river*ward*⟩ **2** : that occurs or is situated in the direction of ⟨left*ward*⟩

[2]**-ward** *or* **-wards** *adv suffix* [*-ward* fr. ME, fr. OE *-weard*, fr. *-weard*, adj. suffix; *-wards* fr. ME, fr. OE *-weardes*, gen. sing. neut. of *-weard*, adj. suffix] **1** : in a (specified) spatial or temporal direction ⟨up*ward*⟩ ⟨after*ward*⟩ **2** : toward a (specified) point, position, or area ⟨earth*ward*⟩

war dance *n* (1711) : a dance performed by primitive peoples as preparation for battle or in celebration of victory

ward·ed \ˈwȯr-dəd\ *adj* (1572) : provided with a ward ⟨a ~ lock⟩

war·den \ˈwȯrd-ᵊn\ *n* [ME *wardein*, fr. ONF, fr. *warder* to guard, of Gmc origin; akin to OHG *wartēn* to watch] (13c) **1** : one having care or charge of something : GUARDIAN, KEEPER **2 a** : REGENT 2 **b** : the governor of a town, district, or fortress **c** : a member of the governing body of a guild **3 a** : an official charged with special supervisory duties or with the enforcement of specified laws or regulations ⟨game ~⟩ ⟨air raid ~⟩ **b** : an official in charge of the operation of a prison **c** : any of various British officials having designated administrative functions ⟨~ of the mint⟩ **4 a** : one of two ranking lay officers of an Episcopal parish **b** : any of various British college officials whose duties range from the administration of academic matters to the supervision of student discipline

war·den·ship \-ˌship\ *n* (14c) : the office, jurisdiction, or powers of a warden

[1]**ward·er** \ˈwȯrd-ər\ *n* [ME, fr. AF *wardere*, fr. *warde* act of guarding, of Gmc origin; akin to OHG *warta* act of watching] (15c) **1** : WATCHMAN, PORTER **2** *Brit* **a** : WARDEN **b** : a prison guard

[2]**war·der** *n* [ME, perh. fr. *warden* to ward] (1548) : a truncheon used by a king or commander in chief to signal orders

ward heeler *n* (1888) : a worker for a political boss in a ward or other local area

ward·ress \ˈwȯr-drəs\ *n* (1878) : a woman supervising female prisoners (as in a jail)

ward·robe \ˈwȯr-ˌdrōb\ *n* [ME *warderobe*, fr. ONF, fr. *warder* to guard + *robe* robe] (14c) **1 a** : a room or closet where clothes are kept **b** : CLOTHESPRESS **c** : a large trunk in which clothes may be hung upright **2 a** : a collection of wearing apparel (as of one person or for one activity) ⟨a summer ~⟩ **b** : a collection of stage costumes and accessories **3** : the department of a royal or noble household entrusted with the care of wearing apparel, jewels, and personal articles

ward·room \ˈwȯr-ˌdrüm, -ˌdrům\ *n* (1801) : the space in a warship allotted for living quarters to the commissioned officers excepting the captain; *specif* : the mess assigned to these officers

ward·ship \ˈwȯrd-ˌship\ *n* (15c) **1 a** : care and protection of a ward **b** : the right to the custody of an infant heir of a feudal tenant and of his property **2** : the state of being under a guardian

[1]**ware** \ˈwa(ə)r, ˈwe(ə)r\ *adj* [ME *war*, *ware* careful, aware, fr. OE *wær* — more at WARY] (bef. 12c) **1** : AWARE, CONSCIOUS ⟨was ~ of black looks cast at me —Mary Webb⟩ **2** *archaic* : WARY, VIGILANT

[2]**ware** *vt* **wared; war·ing** [ME *waren*, fr. OE *warian*; akin to OHG *biwarōn* to protect, OE *wær* aware] (bef. 12c) : to beware of : AVOID — used chiefly as a command to hunting animals

[3]**ware** *n* [ME, fr. OE *waru*; akin to MHG *ware* ware and prob. to OE *wær* aware — more at WARY] (bef. 12c) **1 a** : manufactured articles, products of art or craft, or farm produce : GOODS — often used in combination ⟨tin*ware*⟩ **b** : an article of merchandise **2** : articles (as pottery or dishes) of fired clay ⟨earthen*ware*⟩ **3** : an intangible item (as a service) that is a marketable commodity

[4]**ware** *vt* **wared; war·ing** [ME *waren*, fr. ON *verja* to clothe, invest, spend — more at WEAR] *Scot* (14c) : SPEND, EXPEND

[1]**ware·house** \ˈwa(ə)r-ˌhau̇s, ˈwe(ə)r-\ *n* (14c) : a structure or room for the storage of merchandise or commodities

[2]**ware·house** \-ˌhau̇z, -ˌhau̇s\ *vt* (1799) : to deposit, store, or stock in or as if in a warehouse

ware·house·man \-ˌhau̇-smən\ *n* (1653) : one who manages or works in a warehouse

ware·hous·er \-ˌhau̇-zər, -sər\ *n* (ca. 1927) : WAREHOUSEMAN

ware·room \ˈwa(ə)r-ˌrüm, ˈwe(ə)r-, -ˌru̇m\ *n* (1811) : a room in which goods are exhibited for sale

war·fare \ˈwȯr-ˌfa(ə)r, -ˌfe(ə)r\ *n* [ME, fr. *werre*, *warre* war + *fare* journey, passage — more at FARE] (15c) **1** : military operations between enemies : HOSTILITIES, WAR; *also* : an activity undertaken by a political unit (as a nation) to weaken or destroy another ⟨economic ~⟩ **2** : struggle between competing entities : CONFLICT

war·fa·rin \ˈwȯr-fə-rən\ *n* [*W*isconsin *A*lumni *R*esearch *F*oundation (its patentee) + coum*arin*] (ca. 1950) : a crystalline anticoagulant compound $C_{19}H_{16}O_4$ used as a rodent poison and in medicine

war footing *n* (1894) : the condition of being prepared to undertake or maintain war

war–game *vt* (1828) : to plan or conduct in the manner of a war game ⟨*war-gamed* an invasion —*Newsweek*⟩ ~ *vi* : to conduct a war game

war game *n* (1942) **1** : a simulated battle or campaign to test military concepts and usu. conducted in conferences by officers acting as the opposing staffs **2** : a two-sided umpired training maneuver with actual elements of the armed forces participating

war gas *n* (1918) : a gas for use in warfare

war hawk *n* (1798) : one who clamors for war; *esp* : an American jingo favoring war with Britain around 1812

war·head \ˈwȯ(ə)r-ˌhed\ *n* (1898) : the section of a missile containing the explosive, chemical, or incendiary charge

war–horse \-ˌhȯ(ə)rs\ *n* (1653) **1** : a horse used in war : CHARGER **2** : a veteran soldier or public person (as a politician) **3** : a work of art (as a musical composition) that has become hackneyed due to much repetition in the standard repertoire

war·i·son \ˈwar-ə-sən\ *n* [prob. a misunderstanding by Sir Walter Scott in the *Lay of the Last Minstrel* (1805) of ME *waryson* reward, fr. ONF *warison* defense, possessions, fr. *warir* to protect, provide, of Gmc origin; akin to OHG *werien* to defend — more at WEIR] (1805) : a bugle call to attack

war·like \ˈwȯ(ə)r-ˌlīk\ *adj* (15c) **1** *obs* : ready for war : equipped to fight **2** : fit for, disposed to, or fond of war : BELLICOSE **3** : of, relating to, or useful in war **4** : befitting or characteristic of war or a soldier

war·lock \-ˌläk\ *n* [ME *warloghe*, fr. OE *wǣrloga* one that breaks faith, the Devil, fr. *wǣr* faith, troth + *-loga* (fr. *lēogan* to lie); akin to OE *wǣr* true — more at VERY, LIE] (14c) **1** : a man practicing the black arts : SORCERER — compare WITCH **2** : CONJURER

war·lord \-ˌlȯ(ə)rd\ *n* (1856) **1 :** a supreme military leader **2 :** a military commander exercising civil power by force usu. in a limited area — **war·lord·ism** \-ˌiz-əm\ *n*

[1]**warm** \ˈwȯ(ə)rm\ *adj* [ME, fr. OE *wearm;* akin to OHG *warm* warm, L *formus,* Gk *thermos* warm, hot] (bef. 12c) **1 a :** having or giving out heat to a moderate or adequate degree **b :** serving to maintain or preserve heat esp. to a satisfactory degree ⟨a ~ sweater⟩ **c :** feeling or causing sensations of heat brought about by strenuous exertion **2 :** comfortably established : SECURE ⟨a ~ existence in his old age⟩ **3 a :** marked by strong feeling : ARDENT **b :** marked by excitement, disagreement, or anger ⟨a ~ debate⟩ **4 :** marked by or readily showing affection, gratitude, cordiality, or sympathy ⟨a ~ welcome⟩ ⟨~ regards⟩ **5 :** emphasizing or exploiting sexual imagery or incidents **6 :** accompanied or marked by extreme danger or duress **7 :** newly made : FRESH ⟨a ~ scent⟩ **8 :** having the color or tone of something that imparts heat; *specif* **:** of a hue in the range yellow through orange to red **9 :** near to a goal, object, or solution sought — **warm·ish** \ˈwȯr-mish\ *adj* — **warm·ness** \ˈwȯrm-nəs\ *n*

[2]**warm** *vt* (bef. 12c) **1 :** to make warm **2 a :** to infuse with a feeling of love, friendship, well-being, or pleasure **b :** to fill with anger, zeal, or passion **3 :** to reheat (cooked food) for eating — often used with *over* **4 :** to make ready for operation or performance by preliminary exercise or operation — often used with *up* ~ *vi* **1 :** to become warm **2 a :** to become ardent or interested **b :** to become filled with affection or love — used with *to* or *toward* **3 :** to experience feelings of pleasure : BASK **4 :** to become ready for operation or performance by preliminary activity — often used with *up*

[3]**warm** *adv* (bef. 12c) **:** WARMLY — usu. used in combination ⟨*warm*=clad⟩

warm–blood·ed \ˈwȯrm-ˈbləd-əd\ *adj* (1793) **1 :** having warm blood; *specif* **:** having a relatively high and constant body temperature relatively independent of the surroundings **2 :** fervent or ardent in spirit — **warm–blood·ed·ness** *n*

warmed–over \ˈwȯrm-ˈdō-vər\ *adj* (1887) **1 :** not fresh or new : STALE ⟨~ ideas⟩ **2 :** heated again ⟨~ beans⟩

warm·er \ˈwȯr-mər\ *n* (1595) **:** one that warms; *esp* **:** a device for keeping something warm ⟨a hand ~⟩

warm front *n* (ca. 1921) **:** an advancing edge of a warm air mass

warm·heart·ed \ˈwȯ(-ə)rm-ˈhärt-əd\ *adj* (1500) **:** marked by ready affection, cordiality, generosity, or sympathy — **warm·heart·ed·ness** *n*

warming pan *n* (15c) **:** a long-handled covered pan filled with live coals that is used to warm a bed

warm·ly \ˈwȯ(ə)rm-lē\ *adv* (1529) **1 :** in a manner characterized or accompanied by warmth of emotion **2 :** in a manner that causes or maintains warmth

war·mon·ger \ˈwȯ(ə)r-ˌməŋ-gər, -ˌmäŋ-\ *n* (1590) **:** one who urges or attempts to stir up war : JINGO — **war·mon·ger·ing** \-g(ə-)riŋ\ *n*

war·mouth \ˈwȯ(ə)r-ˌmau̇th\ *n* [origin unknown] (ca. 1883) **:** a freshwater sunfish (*Lepomis gulosus*) of the eastern U.S. — called also *warmouth bass*

warm spot *n* (ca. 1927) **:** a lasting affection for a particular person or object

warmth \ˈwȯ(ə)rm(p)th\ *n* (12c) **1 :** the quality or state of being warm in temperature **2 :** the quality or state of being warm in feeling ⟨a child needing human ~ and family life⟩ **3 :** a glowing effect that is often produced by the use of warm colors

warm–up \ˈwȯr-ˌməp\ *n* (1846) **1 :** the act or an instance of warming up; *also* **:** a preparatory activity or procedure **2 :** SWEAT SUIT — often used in pl.

warm up \(ˈ)wȯr-ˈməp\ *vi* (1940) **1 :** to engage in exercise or practice esp. before entering a game or contest; *broadly* **:** to get ready **2 :** to approach a state of violence, conflict, or danger

warn \ˈwȯ(ə)rn\ *vb* [ME *warnen,* fr. OE *warnian;* akin to OHG *warnōn* to take heed, OE *wær* careful, aware — more at WARY] *vt* (bef. 12c) **1 a :** to give notice to beforehand esp. of danger or evil **b :** to give admonishing advice to : COUNSEL **c :** to call to one's attention : INFORM **2 :** to order to go or stay away — often used with *off* ~ *vi* **:** to give a warning — **warn·er** *n*

[1]**warn·ing** \ˈwȯr-niŋ\ *n* (bef. 12c) **1 :** the act of warning : the state of being warned ⟨he had ~ of his illness⟩ **2 :** something that warns or serves to warn

[2]**warning** *adj* (ca. 1552) **:** serving as an alarm, signal, summons, or admonition ⟨~ bell⟩ ⟨~ shot⟩ — **warn·ing·ly** \ˈwȯr-niŋ-lē\ *adv*

warning coloration *n* (ca. 1928) **:** conspicuous coloration possessed by an animal otherwise effectively but not obviously defended that serves to warn off potential enemies

warning track *n* (1966) **:** a usu. dirt or cinder strip around the outside edge of a baseball outfield to warn a fielder when running to make a catch that he is approaching the fence — called also *warning path*

war of nerves (1939) **:** a conflict characterized by psychological tactics (as bluff, threats, and intimidation) designed primarily to create confusion, indecision, or breakdown of morale

[1]**warp** \ˈwȯ(ə)rp\ *n* [ME, fr. OE *wearp;* akin to OHG *warf* warp, OE *weorpan* to throw, ON *verpa,* Gk *rhembein* to whirl] (bef. 12c) **1 a (1) :** a series of yarns extended lengthwise in a loom and crossed by the woof **(2) :** the cords forming the carcass of a pneumatic tire **b :** FOUNDATION, BASE ⟨the ~ of the economic structure is agriculture — *Amer. Guide Series: N.C.*⟩ **2 :** a rope for warping a ship or boat **3** [[2]*warp*] **a :** a twist or curve that has developed in something orig. flat or straight ⟨a ~ in a door panel⟩ **b :** a mental twist or aberration — **war·page** \ˈwȯr-pij\ *n*

[2]**warp** *vt* (13c) **1 :** to arrange (yarns) so as to form a warp **2 a :** to turn or twist out of or as if out of shape *esp* **:** to twist or bend out of a plane **b :** to cause to judge, choose, or act wrongly : PERVERT **c :** FALSIFY, DISTORT ⟨intellect and learning . . . ~*ed* by prejudices — Irving Wallace⟩ **d :** to deflect from a course **3 :** to move (as a ship) by hauling on a line attached to a fixed object ~ *vi* **1 :** to become warped **2 :** to move a ship by warping ***syn*** see DEFORM — **warp·er** *n*

war paint *n* (1826) **1 :** paint put on parts of the body (as the face) by American Indians as a sign of going to war **2 :** ceremonial dress : REGALIA **3 :** MAKEUP 3a

warp and woof *n* (1842) **:** FOUNDATION, BASE ⟨the vigorous Anglo-Saxon base had become the *warp and woof* of English speech —H. R. Warfel⟩

war party *n* (1755) **1 :** a group of American Indians on the warpath **2 :** a usu. jingoistic political party advocating or upholding a war

war·path \ˈwȯ(ə)r-ˌpath, -ˌpȧth\ *n* (1755) **1 :** the route taken by a party of American Indians going on a warlike expedition or to a war **2 :** a hostile course of action or frame of mind

warp beam *n* (ca. 1831) **:** a roll on which warp is wound for a loom

warp–knit·ted \-ˈnit-əd\ *adj* (ca. 1920) **:** produced in machine knitting with the yarns running in a lengthwise direction — **warp knit** *n* — **warp knitting** *n*

war·plane \ˈwȯ(ə)r-ˌplān\ *n* (ca. 1911) **:** a military airplane; *esp* **:** one armed for combat

war power *n* (1766) **:** the power to make war; *specif* **:** an extraordinary power exercised usu. by the executive branch of a government in the prosecution of a war

[1]**war·rant** \ˈwȯr-ənt, ˈwär-\ *n* [ME, protector, warrant, fr. ONF *warant,* OHG *werēnto* guarantor, *werēn* to warrant, OE *wǣr* true — more at VERY] (13c) **1 a (1) :** SANCTION, AUTHORIZATION; *also* **:** evidence for or token of authorization **(2) :** GUARANTEE, SECURITY **b (1) :** GROUND, JUSTIFICATION **(2) :** CONFIRMATION, PROOF **2 a :** a commission or document giving authority to do something; *specif* **:** a writing that authorizes a person to pay or deliver to another and the other to receive money or other consideration **b :** a precept or writ issued by a competent magistrate authorizing an officer to make an arrest, a seizure, or a search or to do other acts incident to the administration of justice **c :** an official certificate of appointment issued to an officer of lower rank than a commissioned officer **d (1) :** a short-term obligation of a governmental body (as a municipality) issued in anticipation of revenue **(2) :** an instrument issued by a corporation giving to the holder the right to purchase the capital stock of the corporation at a stated price either prior to a stipulated date or at any future time — **war·rant·less** \-ləs\ *adj*

[2]**warrant** *vt* [ME *warranten,* fr. ONF *warantir,* fr. *warant*] (13c) **1 :** to guarantee security or immunity to : SECURE ⟨I'll ~ him from drowning —Shak.⟩ **2 a :** to declare or maintain with certainty : be sure that ⟨I'll ~ he'll be here by noon⟩ **b :** to assure (a person) of the truth of what is said **3 a :** to guarantee to a person good title to and undisturbed possession of (as an estate) **b :** to provide a guarantee of the security of (as title to property sold) usu. by an express covenant in the deed of conveyance **c :** to guarantee to be as represented **d :** to guarantee (as goods sold) esp. in respect of the quality or quantity specified **4 :** to give warrant or sanction to : AUTHORIZE ⟨the law ~s this procedure⟩ **5 a :** to give proof of the authenticity or truth of **b :** to give assurance of the nature of or for the undertaking of : GUARANTEE **6 :** to serve as or give adequate ground or reason for ⟨promising enough to ~ further consideration⟩

war·rant·able \ˈwȯr-ənt-ə-bəl, ˈwär-\ *adj* (1581) **:** capable of being warranted : JUSTIFIABLE — **war·rant·able·ness** *n* — **war·rant·ably** \-blē\ *adv*

war·ran·tee \ˌwȯr-ən-ˈtē, ˌwär-\ *n* (1706) **:** the person to whom a warranty is made

warrant officer *n* (1693) **1 :** an officer in the armed forces holding rank by virtue of a warrant and ranking above a noncommissioned officer and below a commissioned officer **2 :** a commissioned officer ranking below an ensign in the navy or coast guard and below a second lieutenant in the marine corps

war·ran·tor \ˌwȯr-ən-ˈtȯ(ə)r, ˌwär-; ˈwȯr-ənt-ər, ˈwär-\ *also* **war·rant·er** \ˈwȯr-ənt-ər, ˈwär-\ *n* (1583) **:** one that warrants or gives a warranty

war·ran·ty \ˈwȯr-ənt-ē, ˈwär-\ *n, pl* **-ties** [ME *warantie,* fr. ONF, fr. *warantir* to warrant] (14c) **1 a :** a real covenant binding the grantor of an estate and his heirs to warrant and defend the title **b :** a collateral undertaking that a fact regarding the subject of a contract is or will be as it is expressly or by implication declared or promised to be **2 :** something that authorizes, sanctions, supports, or justifies : WARRANT **3 :** a usu. written guarantee of the integrity of a product and of the maker's responsibility for the repair or replacement of defective parts

warranty deed *n* (1779) **:** a deed warranting that the grantor has a good title free and clear of all liens and encumbrances and will defend the grantee against all claims

war·ren \ˈwȯr-ən, ˈwär-\ *n* [ME *warenne,* fr. ONF] (14c) **1** *chiefly Brit* **a :** a place legally authorized for keeping small game (as hare or pheasant) **b :** the privilege of hunting game in such a warren **2 a (1) :** an area (as of uncultivated ground) where rabbits breed **(2) :** a structure where rabbits are kept or bred **b :** the rabbits of a warren **3 a :** a crowded tenement or district **b :** a maze of passageways or cubbies

war·ren·er \-ə-nər\ *n* (13c) **1 :** GAMEKEEPER **2 :** one that maintains a rabbit warren

war·rior \ˈwȯr-yər, ˈwȯr-ē-ər, ˈwär-ē- *also* ˈwär-yər\ *n, often attrib* [ME *werriour,* fr. ONF *werreieur,* fr. *werreier* to make war, fr. *werre* war — more at WAR] (13c) **:** a man engaged or experienced in warfare; *broadly* **:** a person engaged in some struggle or conflict ⟨poverty ~*s*⟩

war·saw \ˈwȯr-(ˌ)sȯ\ *n* [modif. of AmerSp *guasa*] (ca. 1884) **:** a large grouper (esp. *Epinephelus nigritus*) — called also *warsaw grouper*

war·ship \ˈwȯ(ə)r-ˌship\ *n* (1533) **:** a military ship; *esp* **:** one armed for combat

war·sle *or* **wars·tle** \ˈwä(r)s-əl\ *vb* [ME *werstelen, warstelen,* alter. of *wrestlen, wrastlen*] *Scot* (14c) **:** WRESTLE, STRUGGLE — **warsle** *n, Scot*

wart \ˈwȯ(ə)rt\ *n* [ME, fr. OE *wearte;* akin to OHG *warza* wart, L *verruca*] (bef. 12c) **1 a :** a horny projection on the skin usu. of the extremities that is caused by a virus — called also *verruca vulgaris* **b :** any of numerous similar skin lesions **2 :** an excrescence or protuberance resembling a true wart; *esp* **:** a glandular excrescence or hardened protuberance on a plant **3 a :** one that suggests a wart esp. in smallness, unpleasantness, or unattractiveness **b :** DEFECT, IMPERFECTION — often used in the phrase *warts and all* — **wart·ed** \ˈwȯrt-əd\ *adj* — **wart·less** \ˈwȯrt-ləs\ *adj* — **warty** \ˈwȯrt-ē\ *adj*

wart·hog \'wȯ(ə)rt-,hȯg, -,häg\ *n* (ca. 1840) **:** any of a genus (*Phacochoerus*) of African wild hogs with two pairs of rough warty excrescences on the face and large protruding tusks

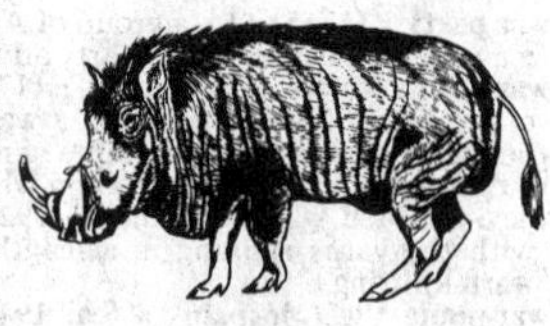

warthog

war·time \'wȯ(ə)r-,tīm\ *n, often attrib* (14c) **:** a period during which a war is in progress

war whoop *n* (1739) **:** a war cry esp. of American Indians

wary \'wa(ə)r-ē, 'we(ə)r-\ *adj* **wari·er; -est** [[1]*ware,* fr. ME *war, ware,* fr. OE *wær* careful, aware, wary; akin to OHG *giwar* aware, attentive, L *vereri* to fear, Gk *horan* to see] (ca. 1552) **:** marked by keen caution, cunning, and watchful prudence in detecting and escaping danger ***syn*** see CAUTIOUS — **wari·ly** \'war-ə-lē, 'wer-\ *adv* — **wari·ness** \'war-ē-nəs, 'wer-\ *n*

war zone *n* (1917) **1 :** a zone in which belligerents are waging war **2 :** a designated area esp. on the high seas within which rights of neutrals are not respected by a belligerent nation in time of war

was [ME, fr. OE, 1st & 3d sing. past indic. of *wesan* to be; akin to ON *vera* to be, *var* was, Skt *vasati* he lives, dwells] *past 1st & 3d sing of* BE

[1]**wash** \'wȯsh, 'wäsh, *chiefly Midland also* 'wȯ(ə)rsh *or* 'wärsh\ *vb* [ME *washen,* fr. OE *wascan;* akin to OHG *waskan* to wash and perh. to OE *wæter* water] *vt* (bef. 12c) **1 a :** to cleanse by or as if by the action of liquid (as water) **b :** to remove (as dirt) by rubbing or drenching with liquid **2 :** to cleanse (fur) by licking or by rubbing with a paw moistened with saliva **3 a :** to flush or moisten (a bodily part or injury) with a liquid **b** (1) **:** to wet thoroughly **:** DRENCH (2) **:** to overspread with light **:** SUFFUSE **c :** to pass water over or through esp. so as to carry off material from the surface or interior **4 :** to flow along or dash or overflow against **:** LAVE ⟨waves *~ing* the shore⟩ **5 :** to move, carry, or deposit by or as if by the force of water in motion ⟨houses *~ed* away by the flood⟩ **6 a :** to subject (as crushed ore) to the action of water to separate valuable material **b :** to separate (particles) from a substance (as ore) by agitation with or in water **c** (1) **:** to pass through a bath to carry off impurities or soluble components (2) **:** to pass (a gas or gaseous mixture) through or over a liquid to purify it esp. by removing soluble components **7 a :** to cover or daub lightly with or as if with an application of a thin liquid (as whitewash or varnish) **b :** to depict or paint by a broad sweep of thin color with a brush **8 :** to cause to swirl ⟨*~ing* coffee around in his cup⟩ **9 :** LAUNDER 3 ⟨how the mob *~es* its money through corrupt bankers —Vincent Teresa⟩ **~** *vi* **1 :** to wash oneself or a part of one's body **2 :** to become worn away by the action of water **3 :** to clean something by rubbing or dipping in water **4 a :** to become carried along on water **:** DRIFT ⟨cakes of ice *~ing* along⟩ **b :** to pour, sweep, or flow in a stream or current ⟨waves of pioneers *~ing* westward —Green Peyton⟩ **5 :** to serve as a cleansing agent ⟨this soap *~es* thoroughly⟩ **6 a :** to undergo laundering ⟨this dress doesn't ~ well⟩ **b** (1) **:** to undergo testing successfully ⟨an interesting theory, but it just won't ~⟩ (2) **:** to gain acceptance **:** inspire belief ⟨his story didn't ~ with me⟩ — **wash one's hands of :** to disclaim interest in, responsibility for, or further connection with

[2]**wash** *n* (bef. 12c) **1 a :** the act or process or an instance of washing or being washed **b :** articles to be washed or being washed **2 :** the surging action of waves **3 a :** a piece of ground washed by the sea or river **b :** BOG, MARSH **c** (1) **:** a shallow body of water (2) **:** a shallow creek **d** *West* **:** the dry bed of a stream — called also *dry wash* **4 a :** worthless esp. liquid waste **:** REFUSE **b :** an insipid beverage **c :** vapid writing or speech **5 a :** a sweep or splash esp. of color made by or as if by a long stroke of a brush **b :** a thin coat of paint (as watercolor) **c :** a thin liquid used for coating a surface (as a wall) **6 :** LOTION **7 :** loose or eroded surface material of the earth (as rock debris) transported and deposited by running water **8 a :** BACKWASH 1 **b :** a disturbance in the air produced by the passage of an airfoil or propeller **9 :** WASHOUT 2

[3]**wash** *adj* (1634) **1 :** WASHABLE ⟨~ fabric⟩ **2 :** involving essentially simultaneous purchase and sale of the same security ⟨spurious market activity resulting from ~ trading⟩

wash·able \'wȯsh-ə-bəl, 'wäsh-\ *adj* (1821) **:** capable of being washed without damage — **wash·abil·i·ty** \,wȯsh-ə-'bil-ət-ē, ,wäsh-\ *n*

wash–and–wear *adj* (ca. 1956) **:** of, relating to, or constituting a fabric or garment that needs little or no ironing after washing

wash·a·te·ria *also* **wash·e·te·ria** \,wäsh-ə-'tir-ē-ə, ,wȯsh-\ *n* [[2]*wash* + *-ateria* or *-eteria* (as in *cafeteria*)] *chiefly Southern* (1937) **:** a self-service laundry

wash·ba·sin \'wȯsh-,bās-ᵊn, 'wäsh-\ *n* (1812) **:** WASHBOWL

wash·board \'wȯsh-,bō(ə)rd, 'wäsh-, -,bȯ(ə)rd\ *n* (1742) **1 :** a broad thin plank along a gunwale or on the sill of a lower deck port to keep out the sea **2 :** BASEBOARD **3 a :** a corrugated rectangular surface that is used for scrubbing clothes **b :** a road or pavement so worn by traffic as to be corrugated transversely

wash·bowl \-,bōl\ *n* (1816) **:** a large bowl for water that is used to wash one's hands and face

wash·cloth \-,klȯth\ *n* (ca. 1900) **:** a cloth that is used for washing one's face and body — called also *facecloth, washrag*

wash down *vt* (1600) **1 :** to move or carry downward by action of a liquid; *esp* **:** to facilitate the passage of (food) down the gullet with accompanying swallows of liquid **2 :** to wash the whole length or extent of ⟨*washed down* and scrubbed the front porch⟩

wash drawing *n* (1889) **:** watercolor painting in or chiefly in washes esp. in black, white, and gray tones only

washed–out \'wȯsh-'taůt, 'wäsh-\ *adj* (1837) **1 :** faded in color **2 :** depleted in vigor or animation **:** EXHAUSTED

washed–up \'wȯsh-'təp, 'wäsh-\ *adj* (1923) **:** no longer successful, popular, or needed **:** THROUGH

wash·er \'wȯsh-ər, 'wäsh-\ *n* (13c) **1 :** a flat thin ring or a perforated plate used in joints or assemblies to ensure tightness, prevent leakage, or relieve friction **2 :** one that washes; *esp* **:** WASHING MACHINE

wash·er·man \-mən\ *n* (1715) **:** LAUNDRYMAN; *also* **:** a man operating any of various industrial washing machines

wash·er·wom·an \-,wům-ən\ *n* (ca. 1632) **:** LAUNDRYWOMAN; *esp* **:** one who takes in washing

wash·house \'wȯsh-,haůs, 'wäsh-\ *n* (bef. 12c) **:** a building used or equipped for washing; *esp* **:** one for washing clothes

wash·ing \'wȯsh-iŋ, 'wäsh-\ *n* (13c) **1 :** the act or action of one that cleanses with water **2 :** material obtained by washing **3 :** a thin covering or coat ⟨a ~ of silver⟩ **4 :** articles washed or to be washed **:** WASH

washing machine *n* (1799) **:** a machine for washing; *esp* **:** one for washing clothes and household linen

washing soda *n* (1865) **:** SAL SODA

Wash·ing·ton pie \,wȯsh-iŋ-tən-, ,wäsh-, *chiefly Midland also* ,wȯr-shiŋ- *or* ,wär-shiŋ-\ *n* [George *Washington*] (1905) **:** cake layers put together with a jam or jelly filling

Washington's Birthday *n* [George *Washington*] (1829) **1 :** February 22 formerly observed as a legal holiday in most of the states of the U.S. **2 :** the third Monday in February observed as a legal holiday in most of the states of the U.S. — called also *Presidents' Day*

wash·out \'wȯsh-,aůt, 'wäsh-\ *n* (1873) **1 a :** the washing out or away of something and esp. of earth in a roadbed by a freshet **b :** a place where earth is washed away **2 :** one that fails to measure up **:** FAILURE; as **a :** one who fails in a course of training or study **b :** an unsuccessful enterprise or undertaking

wash out \(ˈ)wȯsh-'aůt, (ˈ)wäsh-\ *vt* (1555) **1 :** to wash free of an extraneous substance (as dirt) **2 a :** to cause to fade by or as if by laundering **b :** to deplete the strength or vitality of **c :** to eliminate as useless or unsatisfactory **:** REJECT **3 a :** to destroy or make useless by the force or action of water ⟨the storm *washed out* the bridge⟩ **b :** RAIN OUT ⟨the game was *washed out*⟩ **~** *vi* **1 :** to become depleted of color or vitality **:** FADE **2 :** to fail to meet requirements or measure up to a standard

wash·rag \'wȯsh-,rag, 'wäsh-\ *n* (1890) **:** WASHCLOTH

wash·room \-,rüm, -,rům\ *n* (1806) **:** a room that is equipped with washing and toilet facilities **:** LAVATORY

wash·stand \-,(s)tand\ *n* (1839) **1 :** a stand holding articles needed for washing one's face and hands **2 :** a washbowl permanently set in place and attached to water and drainpipes

wash·tub \-,təb\ *n* (1602) **:** a tub in which clothes are washed or soaked

wash–up \-,əp\ *n* (1884) **:** the act or process of washing clean

wash up \(ˈ)wȯsh-'əp, (ˈ)wäsh-\ *vt* (1751) **1 :** to get rid of by washing ⟨*wash up* the spilled milk⟩ **2 :** EXHAUST, FINISH **~** *vi* **1 :** to wash one's face and hands **2** *Brit* **:** to wash the dishes after a meal

wash·wom·an \'wȯsh-,wům-ən, 'wäsh-\ *n* (1590) **:** WASHERWOMAN

washy \'wȯsh-ē, 'wäsh-\ *adj* **wash·i·er; -est** (1566) **1 a :** WEAK, WATERY ⟨~ tea⟩ **b :** deficient in color **:** PALLID **c :** lacking in vigor, individuality, or definiteness **2 :** lacking in condition and in firmness of flesh

wasn't \'wəz-ᵊnt, 'wäz-, *dial also* 'wət-ᵊn(t)\ **:** was not

wasp \'wäsp, 'wȯsp\ *n* [ME *waspe,* fr. OE *wæps, wæsp;* akin to OHG *wafsa* wasp, L *vespa* wasp, OE *wefan* to weave — more at WEAVE] (bef. 12c) **1 :** any of numerous social or solitary winged hymenopterous insects (esp. families Sphecidae and Vespidae) that usu. have a slender smooth body with the abdomen attached by a narrow stalk, well-developed wings, biting mouthparts, and in the females and workers an often formidable sting, and that are largely carnivorous and often provision their nests with caterpillars, insects, or spiders killed or paralyzed by stinging for their larvae to feed on — compare BEE **2 :** any of various hymenopterous insects (as a chalcid or ichneumon fly) other than wasps with larvae that are parasitic on other arthropods — **wasp·like** \-,līk\ *adj*

WASP *or* **Wasp** \'wäsp, 'wȯsp\ *n* [white *A*nglo-*S*axon *P*rotestant] (1960) **:** an American of Northern European and esp. British stock and of Protestant background; *esp* **:** a member of the dominant and the most privileged class of people in the U.S. — sometimes used disparagingly — **Wasp·dom** \-dəm\ *n* — **Wasp·ish** \'wäs-pish, 'wȯs-\ *adj* — **Wasp·ish·ness** *n* — **Waspy** \-pē\ *adj*

wasp·ish \'wäs-pish, 'wȯs-\ *adj* (1566) **1 :** resembling a wasp in behavior; *esp* **:** SNAPPISH, PETULANT **2 :** resembling a wasp in form; *esp* **:** slightly built — **wasp·ish·ly** *adv* — **wasp·ish·ness** *n*

wasp waist *n* (1870) **:** a very slender waist — **wasp–waist·ed** \'wäsp-'wā-stəd, 'wȯsp-\ *adj*

[1]**was·sail** \'wäs-əl *also* wä-'sā(ə)l\ *n* [ME *wæs hæil,* fr. ON *ves heill* be well, fr. *ves* (imper. sing. of *vera* to be) + *heill* healthy — more at WAS, WHOLE] (13c) **1 :** an early English toast to someone's health **2 :** a hot drink made with wine, beer, or cider, spices, sugar, and usu. baked apples and that is traditionally served in a large bowl esp. at Christmastime **3 :** riotous drinking **:** REVELRY

[2]**wassail** *vi* (14c) **1 :** to indulge in wassail **:** CAROUSE **2** *dial Eng* **:** to sing carols from house to house at Christmas **~** *vt* **:** to drink to the health or thriving of

was·sail bowl \'wäs-əl-\ *n* (1606) **1 :** a bowl that is used for the serving of wassail **2 :** WASSAIL 2

was·sail·er \'wäs-ə-lər *also* wä-'sā-lər\ *n* (1634) **1 :** one that carouses **:** REVELER **2** *archaic* **:** one who goes about singing carols

Was·ser·mann reaction \'wäs-ər-mən-, 'väs-\ *n* [August von *Wassermann*] (1911) **:** the complement-fixing reaction that occurs in a positive complement-fixation test for syphilis using the serum of an infected individual

Wassermann test *n* (1914) **:** a test for the detection of syphilitic infection using the Wassermann reaction — called also *Wasserman*

wast \wəst, (ˈ)wäst\ *archaic past 2d sing of* BE

wast·age \'wā-stij\ *n* (1756) **:** loss, decrease, or destruction of something (as by use, decay, erosion, or leakage); *esp* **:** wasteful or avoidable loss of something valuable

[1]**waste** \'wāst\ *n* [ME *waste, wast;* in sense 1, fr. ONF *wast,* fr. *wast,* adj., desolate, waste, fr. L *vastus;* akin to OHG *wuosti* desolate, waste, L *vanus* empty; in other senses, fr. ME *wasten* to waste — more at WANE] (13c) **1 a :** a sparsely settled or barren region **:** DESERT **b :** uncultivated land **c :** a broad and empty expanse (as of water) **2 :** the act or an instance of wasting **:** the state of being wasted **3 a :** loss through breaking down of bodily tissue **b :** gradual loss or decrease by use, wear, or decay **4 a :** damaged, defective, or superfluous material produced by a manufacturing process: as (1) **:** material rejected during a textile manufacturing process and used usu. for wiping away dirt and oil ⟨cotton ~⟩ (2) **:** SCRAP (3) **:** an unwanted by-product of

a manufacturing process, chemical laboratory, or nuclear reactor ⟨toxic ~⟩ ⟨hazardous ~⟩ ⟨nuclear ~⟩ **b :** refuse from places of human or animal habitation: as (1) **:** GARBAGE, RUBBISH (2) *pl* **:** EXCREMENT (3) **:** SEWAGE **c :** material derived by mechanical and chemical weathering of the land and moved down sloping surfaces or carried by streams to the sea

²waste *vb* **wast·ed; wast·ing** [ME *wasten,* fr. ONF *waster,* fr. L *vastare,* fr. *vastus* desolate, waste] *vt* (13c) **1 :** to lay waste; *esp* **:** to damage or destroy gradually and progressively ⟨reclaiming land *wasted* by strip-mining⟩ **2 :** to cause to shrink in physical bulk or strength **:** EMACIATE, ENFEEBLE **3 :** to wear away or diminish gradually **:** CONSUME **4 a :** to spend or use carelessly **:** SQUANDER **b :** to allow to be used inefficiently or become dissipated **5 :** KILL; *also* **:** to injure severely ~ *vi* **1 :** to lose weight, strength, or vitality — often used with *away* **2 a :** to become diminished in bulk or substance **b :** to become consumed **3 :** to spend money or consume property extravagantly or improvidently *syn* see RAVAGE — **waste one's breath :** to accomplish nothing by speaking

³waste *adj* [ME *waste, wast,* fr. ONF *wast*] (13c) **1 a** (1) **:** being wild and uninhabited **:** DESOLATE (2) **:** ARID, EMPTY **b :** not cultivated **:** not productive **2 :** being in a ruined or devastated condition **3** [¹*waste*] **a :** discarded as worthless, defective, or of no use **:** REFUSE ⟨~ material⟩ **b :** excreted from or stored in inert form in a living body as a byproduct of vital activity ⟨~ disposal in birds⟩ **4** [¹*waste*] **:** serving to conduct or hold refuse material; *specif* **:** carrying off superfluous water **5 :** WASTED 4

waste·bas·ket \'wās(t)-,bas-kət\ *n* (1850) **:** a receptacle for refuse and esp. for wastepaper — called also *wastepaper basket*

wast·ed *adj* (15c) **1 :** laid waste **:** RAVAGED **2 :** impaired in strength or health **:** EMACIATED **3** *archaic* **:** gone by **:** ELAPSED ⟨the chronicle of ~ time —Shak.⟩ **4 :** unprofitably used, made, or expended ⟨~ effort⟩ **5** *slang* **:** intoxicated from drugs or alcohol

waste·ful \'wāst-fəl\ *adj* (14c) **:** given to or marked by waste **:** LAVISH, PRODIGAL — **waste·ful·ly** \-fə-lē\ *adv* — **waste·ful·ness** *n*

waste·land \'wāst-,land *also* -lənd\ *n* (13c) **1 :** barren or uncultivated land ⟨a desert ~⟩ **2 :** an ugly often devastated or barely inhabitable place or area **3 :** something (as a way of life) that is spiritually and emotionally arid and unsatisfying

waste·pa·per \'wās(t)-'pā-pər\ *n* (ca. 1585) **:** paper discarded as used, superfluous, or not fit for use

waste pipe *n* (1512) **:** a pipe for carrying off waste fluid

wast·er \'wā-stər\ *n* (14c) **1 a** (1) **:** one that spends or consumes extravagantly and without thought for the future (2) **:** a dissolute person **b :** one that uses wastefully or causes or permits waste ⟨a procedure that is a ~ of time⟩ **c :** one that lays waste **:** DESTROYER **2 :** an imperfect or inferior manufactured article or object

waste·wa·ter \'wāst-,wȯt-ər, -,wät-\ *n* (15c) **:** water that has been used (as in a manufacturing process) **:** SEWAGE

wast·ing \'wā-stiŋ\ *adj* (13c) **1 :** laying waste **:** DEVASTATING **2 :** undergoing or causing decay or loss of strength ⟨~ diseases such as tuberculosis⟩

wast·rel \'wā-strəl *also* 'wäs-trəl\ *n* [irreg. fr. ²*waste*] (ca. 1841) **1 :** VAGABOND, WAIF **2 :** one who dissipates his resources foolishly and self-indulgently **:** PROFLIGATE

¹watch \'wäch, 'wȯch\ *vb* [ME *wacchen,* fr. OE *wæccan* — more at WAKE] *vi* (bef. 12c) **1 a :** to keep vigil as a devotional exercise **b :** to be awake during the night **2 a :** to be attentive or vigilant **b :** to keep guard **3 a :** to keep someone or something under close observation **b :** to observe as a spectator ⟨the country ~*ed* as stocks fell sharply⟩ **4 :** to be expectant **:** WAIT ⟨~ for the signal⟩ ~ *vt* **1 :** to keep under guard **2 a :** to observe closely in order to check on action or change ⟨he's being ~*ed* by the police⟩ **b :** to look at **:** OBSERVE ⟨sat and ~*ed* the crowd⟩ **c :** to look on at ⟨~ television⟩ ⟨~ a ball game⟩ **3 a :** to take care of **:** TEND **b :** to be careful of ⟨~*es* his diet⟩ **4 :** to be on the alert for **:** BIDE ⟨~*ed* his opportunity⟩ — **watch it :** look out **:** be careful ⟨*watch it* when you handle the glassware⟩ — **watch one's step :** to proceed with extreme care **:** act or talk warily — **watch over :** to have charge of **:** SUPERINTEND

²watch *n* (bef. 12c) **1 a :** the act of keeping awake to guard, protect, or attend **b** *obs* **:** the state of being wakeful **c :** a wake over a dead body **d :** a state of alert and continuous attention **e :** close observation **:** SURVEILLANCE **2 a :** any of the definite divisions of the night made by ancient peoples **b :** one of the indeterminate wakeful intervals marking the passage of night — usu. used in pl. ⟨the silent ~*es* of the night⟩ **3 a :** one that watches **:** LOOKOUT, WATCHMAN **b** *archaic* **:** the office or function of a sentinel or guard **4 a :** a body of soldiers or sentinels making up a guard **b :** a watchman or body of watchmen formerly assigned to patrol the streets of a town at night, announce the hours, and act as police **5 a** (1) **:** a portion of time during which a part of a ship's company is on duty (2) **:** the part of a ship's company required to be on duty during a particular watch (3) **:** a sailor's assigned duty period **b :** a period of duty **:** SHIFT **6 a :** a portable timepiece that has a movement driven in any of several ways (as by a spring or a battery) and is designed to be worn (as on the wrist) or carried in the pocket — compare CLOCK **b :** a ship's chronometer

watch·able \'wäch-ə-bəl, 'wȯch-\ *adj* (1954) **:** worth watching — **watch·able** *n*

watch and ward *n* (14c) **1 :** continuous unbroken vigilance and guard **2 :** service as a watchman or sentinel required from a feudal tenant

watch·band \'wäch-,band, 'wȯch-\ *n* (1948) **:** the bracelet or strap of a wristwatch

watch cap *n* (ca. 1886) **:** a knitted close-fitting navy-blue cap worn esp. by enlisted men in the U.S. navy in cold or stormy weather

watch·case \'wäch-,kās, 'wȯch-\ *n* (1671) **:** the outside metal covering of a watch

¹watch·dog \-,dȯg\ *n* (1610) **1 :** a dog kept to guard property **2 :** one that guards against loss, waste, theft, or undesirable practices

²watchdog *vt* (1902) **:** to act as a watchdog for

watch·er \'wäch-ər, 'wȯch-\ *n* (1509) **:** one that watches: as **a :** one that sits up or continues awake at night **b :** WATCHMAN **c** (1) **:** one that keeps watch beside a dead person (2) **:** one that attends a sick person at night **d :** OBSERVER, VIEWER **e :** a representative of a party or candidate who is stationed at the polls on an election day to watch the conduct of officials and voters

watch·eye \-,ī\ *n* (ca. 1938) **:** WALLEYE 1; *esp* **:** a walleye of a dog

watch fire *n* (1801) **:** a fire lighted as a signal or for the use of a guard

watch·ful \'wäch-fəl, 'wȯch-\ *adj* (1548) **1** *archaic* **a :** not able or accustomed to sleep or rest **:** WAKEFUL **b :** causing sleeplessness **c :** spent in wakefulness **:** SLEEPLESS **2 :** carefully observant or attentive **:** being on the watch — **watch·ful·ly** \-fə-lē\ *adv* — **watch·ful·ness** *n*

syn WATCHFUL, VIGILANT, WIDE-AWAKE, ALERT mean being on the lookout esp. for danger or opportunity. WATCHFUL is the least explicit term; VIGILANT suggests intense, unremitting, wary watchfulness; WIDE-AWAKE applies to watchfulness for opportunities and developments more often than dangers; ALERT stresses readiness or promptness in meeting danger or in seizing opportunity.

watch·mak·er \-,mā-kər\ *n* (1630) **:** one that makes or repairs watches or clocks — **watch·mak·ing** \-,mā-kiŋ\ *n*

watch·man \-mən\ *n* (15c) **:** one who keeps watch **:** GUARD

watch night *n* (1742) **:** a devotional service lasting until after midnight esp. on New Year's Eve

watch out *vi* (1845) **:** to be vigilant or alert **:** be on the lookout — usu. used with *for*

watch pocket *n* (1837) **:** a small pocket just below the front waistband of men's trousers

watch·tow·er \'wäch-,tau̇(-ə)r, 'wȯch-\ *n* (1544) **:** a tower for a lookout

watch·word \-,wərd\ *n* (15c) **1 :** a word or phrase used as a sign of recognition among members of the same society, class, or group **2 :** a motto that embodies a principle or guide to action of an individual or group **:** SLOGAN

¹wa·ter \'wȯt-ər, 'wät-\ *n, often attrib* [ME, fr. OE *wæter;* akin to OHG *wazzar* water, Gk *hydōr,* L *unda* wave] (bef. 12c) **1 a :** the liquid that descends from the clouds as rain, forms streams, lakes, and seas, and is a major constituent of all living matter and that is an odorless, tasteless, very slightly compressible liquid oxide of hydrogen H_2O which appears bluish in thick layers, freezes at 0° C and boils at 100° C, has a maximum density at 4° C and a high specific heat, is feebly ionized to hydrogen and hydroxyl ions, and is a poor conductor of electricity and a good solvent **b :** a natural mineral water — usu. used in pl. **2 a** (1) *pl* **:** the water occupying or flowing in a particular bed (2) *chiefly Brit* **:** LAKE, POND **b :** a quantity or depth of water adequate for some purpose (as navigation) **c** *pl* (1) **:** a band of seawater abutting on the land of a particular sovereignty and under the control of that sovereignty (2) **:** the sea of a particular part of the earth **d :** WATER SUPPLY ⟨threatened to turn off the ~⟩ **3 :** travel or transportation on water ⟨we went by ~⟩ **4 :** the level of water at a particular state of the tide **:** TIDE **5 :** liquid containing or resembling water: as **a** (1) **:** a pharmaceutical or cosmetic preparation made with water (2) **:** a watery solution of a gaseous or readily volatile substance — compare AMMONIA WATER **b** *archaic* **:** a distilled fluid (as an essence); *esp* **:** a distilled alcoholic liquor **c :** a watery fluid (as tears, urine, or sap) formed or circulating in a living body **6 a :** the limpidity and luster of a precious stone and esp. a diamond **b :** degree of excellence ⟨a scholar of the first ~⟩ **c :** a wavy lustrous pattern (as of a textile) **7 :** WATERCOLOR **8 a :** capital stock not representing assets of the issuing company and not backed by earning power **b :** fictitious or exaggerated asset entries that give a stock an unrealistic book value — **above water :** out of difficulty

²water *vt* (bef. 12c) **1 :** to moisten, sprinkle, or soak with water **2 :** to supply with water for drink **3 :** to supply water to **4 :** to treat with or as if with water; *specif* **:** to impart a lustrous appearance and wavy pattern to (cloth) by calendering **5 a :** to dilute by the addition of water — often used with *down* ⟨~ down the punch⟩ **b :** to add to the aggregate par value of (securities) without a corresponding addition to the assets represented by the securities ~ *vi* **1 :** to form or secrete water or watery matter (as tears or saliva) **2 :** to get or take water: as **a :** to take on a supply of water **b :** to drink water

water back *n* (1864) **:** a water heater set in the firebox of a stove

water bag *n* (1638) **1 :** a bag for holding water; *esp* **:** one designed to keep water cool for drinking by evaporation through a slightly porous surface **2 :** the fetal membranes enclosing the amniotic fluid — used esp. of domestic animals

water balance *n* (1911) **:** the ratio between the water assimilated into the body and that lost from the body; *also* **:** the condition of the body when this ratio approximates unity

water ballet *n* (ca. 1926) **:** a synchronized sequence of movements performed by a group of swimmers

water bear *n* (1852) **:** TARDIGRADE

Water Bearer *n* **:** AQUARIUS 1, 2a

water bed *n* (1853) **:** a bed whose mattress is a plastic bag filled with water

water beetle *n* (ca. 1668) **:** any of numerous oval flattened aquatic beetles (esp. family Dytiscidae) that swim by means of their fringed hind legs which act together as oars

water bird *n* (15c) **:** a swimming or wading bird — compare WATERFOWL

water biscuit *n* (1790) **:** a cracker of flour and water and sometimes fat

water blister *n* (1895) **:** a blister with a clear watery content that is not purulent or sanguineous

water bloom *n* (1906) **:** an accumulation of algae and esp. of blue-green algae at or near the surface of a body of water

water boatman *n* (1815) **1 :** BACK SWIMMER **2 :** any of various aquatic bugs (family Corixidae) with one pair of legs modified into paddles

wa·ter·borne \'wȯt-ər-,bō(ə)rn, 'wät-, -,bȯ(ə)rn\ *adj* (1558) **:** supported or carried by water ⟨~ commerce⟩ ⟨~ infection⟩

water boy *n* (1859) **:** one who keeps a group (as of football players) supplied with drinking water

wa·ter·buck \'wȯt-ər-,bək, 'wät-\ *n, pl* **waterbuck** *or* **waterbucks** (1850) **:** any of several African antelopes (genus *Kobus,* esp. *K. ellipsiprymnus* and *K. defassa*) that commonly frequent streams or wet areas

\ə\ abut \ᵊ\ kitten, F table \ər\ further \a\ ash \ā\ ace \ä\ cot, cart \au̇\ out \ch\ chin \e\ bet \ē\ easy \g\ go \i\ hit \ī\ ice \j\ job \ŋ\ sing \ō\ go \ȯ\ law \ȯi\ boy \th\ thin \t͟h\ the \ü\ loot \u̇\ foot \y\ yet \zh\ vision \ȧ, k̲, ⁿ, œ, œ̄, ue, u̅e, ʸ\ see Guide to Pronunciation

water buffalo *n* (ca. 1890) **:** an often domesticated Asian buffalo (*Bubalus bubalis*)

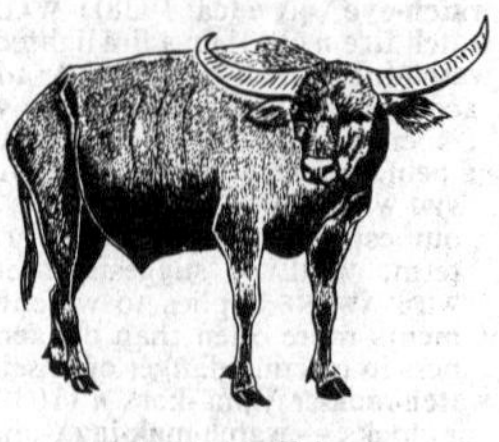

water buffalo

water bug *n* (1750) **:** any of various small arthropods (as insects) that frequent damp or wet places: as **a :** GERMAN COCKROACH **b :** WATER BOATMAN

water cannon *n* (1968) **:** a large truck-mounted nozzle for directing a high-pressure stream of water (as at a crowd of rioters or demonstrators)

water chestnut *n* (1854) **1 :** any of a genus (*Trapa* and esp. *T. natans* and *T. bicornis*) of aquatic herbs of the evening-primrose family; *also* **:** its edible nutlike spiny-angled fruit — called also *water caltrop* **2 :** a Chinese sedge (*Eleocharis tuberosa*); *also* **:** its edible tuber

water clock *n* (1601) **:** an instrument designed to measure time by the fall or flow of a quantity of water — called also *clepsydra*

water closet *n* (1755) **1 :** a compartment or room for defecation and excretion into a toilet bowl **2 :** a toilet bowl and its accessories

wa·ter·col·or \'wȯt-ər-ˌkəl-ər, 'wät-\ *n* (1596) **1 :** a paint of which the liquid is a water dispersion of the binding material (as glue, casein, or gum) **2 :** the art or method of painting with watercolors **3 :** a picture or design executed in watercolors — **watercolor** *adj* — **wa·ter·col·or·ist** \-ˌkəl-ə-rəst\ *n*

wa·ter–cool \ˌwȯt-ər-'kül, ˌwät-\ *vt* (ca. 1898) **:** to cool by means of water and esp. circulating water (as in a water jacket)

wa·ter·cool·er \'wȯt-ər-ˌkü-lər, 'wät-\ *n* (1846) **:** a device for dispensing refrigerated drinking water

wa·ter·course \'wȯt-ər-ˌkō(ə)rs, -ˌkȯ(ə)rs\ *n* (1510) **1 :** a natural or man-made channel through which water flows **2 :** a stream of water (as a river, brook, or underground stream)

wa·ter·craft \-ˌkraft\ *n* (1566) **1 :** skill in aquatic activities (as managing boats) **2 a :** SHIP, BOAT **b :** craft for water transport

wa·ter·cress \-ˌkres\ *n* (14c) **:** any of several water-loving cresses; *esp* **:** a perennial cress (*Nasturtium officinale*) found chiefly in springs or running water and used esp. in salads or as a potherb

water dog *n* (14c) **1 :** any of several large American salamanders; *esp* **:** any of a genus (*Necturus* of the family Proteidae) with external gills **2 :** a person (as a skilled sailor) who is quite at ease in or on water

water down *vt* (1850) **:** to reduce or temper the force or effectiveness of — **wa·tered–down** *adj*

wa·ter·er \'wȯt-ər-ər, 'wät-\ *n* (1549) **:** one that waters: as **a :** a person who obtains or supplies drinking water **b :** a device used for supplying water to livestock and poultry — called also *drinker*

wa·ter·fall \-ˌfȯl\ *n* (bef. 12c) **1 a :** a perpendicular or very steep descent of the water of a stream **b :** an artificial waterfall (as in a hotel lobby or a nightclub) **2 :** something resembling a waterfall

water flea *n* (1585) **:** any of various small active dark or brightly colored aquatic entomostracan crustaceans (as of the genera *Cyclops* and *Daphnia*)

[1]**wa·ter·flood** \-ˌfləd\ *n* (ca. 1936) **:** the process of waterflooding an oil well

[2]**waterflood** *vi* (1964) **:** to pump water into the ground around an oil well nearing depletion in order to loosen and force out additional oil

wa·ter·fowl \'wȯt-ər-ˌfau̇l, 'wät-\ *n* (14c) **1 :** a bird that frequents water; *esp* **:** a swimming bird **2 waterfowl** *pl* **:** swimming game birds as distinguished from upland game birds and shorebirds

wa·ter·fowl·er \-ˌfau̇-lər\ *n* (1968) **:** a hunter of waterfowl — **wa·ter·fowl·ing** \-liŋ\ *n*

wa·ter·front \-ˌfrənt\ *n* (1766) **:** land, land with buildings, or a section of a town fronting or abutting on a body of water

water gap *n* (1756) **:** a pass in a mountain ridge through which a stream runs

water gas *n* (1851) **:** a poisonous flammable gaseous mixture that consists chiefly of carbon monoxide and hydrogen with small amounts of methane, carbon dioxide, and nitrogen, is usu. made by blowing air and then steam over red-hot coke or coal, and is used as a fuel or after carbureting as an illuminant

Wa·ter·gate \-ˌgāt\ *n* [*Watergate*, apartment and office complex in Washington, D.C.] (1973) **:** a scandal usu. involving abuses of office, skulduggery, and a cover-up

water gate *n* (14c) **1 :** a gate (as of a building) giving access to a body of water **2 :** FLOODGATE

water gauge *n* (ca. 1706) **:** an instrument to measure or find the depth or quantity of water or to indicate the height of its surface esp. in a steam boiler

water glass *n* (1612) **1 :** a glass vessel (as a drinking glass) for holding water **2 :** WATER CLOCK **3 :** an instrument consisting of an open box or tube with a glass bottom used for examining objects in or under water **4 :** a substance that consists usu. of the silicate of sodium, is found in commerce as a glassy mass, a stony powder, or dissolved in water as a viscous syrupy liquid, and is used esp. as a cement, a protective coating, and as a fireproofing agent **5 :** WATER GAUGE

water gun *n* (1951) **:** WATER PISTOL

water hammer *n* (ca. 1890) **:** a concussion or sound of concussion of moving water against the sides of a containing pipe or vessel (as a steam pipe)

water haul *n* [fr. the figure of a fishing net that catches nothing but water] (1823) **:** a fruitless effort

water heater *n* (ca. 1876) **:** an apparatus for heating and usu. storing hot water (as for domestic use)

water hemlock *n* (1764) **:** a tall poisonous Eurasian perennial herb (*Cicuta virosa*) of the carrot family; *also* **:** any of several poisonous No. American plants (esp. *Cicuta maculata* and *C. douglasii*) of the same genus

water hen *n* (1529) **:** any of various birds (as a coot or gallinule) related to the rails

water hole *n* (ca. 1653) **1 :** a natural hole or hollow containing water **2 :** a hole in a surface of ice

water hyacinth *n* (1897) **:** a showy So. American floating aquatic plant (*Eichhornia crassipes* of the family Pontederiaceae) that often clogs waterways in warm regions (as of the southern U.S.)

water ice *n* (1818) **:** a frozen dessert of water, sugar, and flavoring

wa·ter–inch \ˌwȯt-ə-'rinch, ˌwät-\ *n* (ca. 1855) **:** a unit of hydraulic measure that equals the discharge from a circular orifice one inch in diameter which is commonly estimated at 14 pints per minute

watering can *n* (1692) **:** a vessel usu. with a spout used to sprinkle or pour water esp. on plants — called also *watering pot*

watering hole *n* (1955) **:** a place where people gather socially; *esp* **:** WATERING PLACE 3

watering place *n* (15c) **1 :** a place where water may be obtained; *esp* **:** one where animals and esp. livestock come to drink **2 :** a health or recreational resort featuring mineral springs or bathing **3 :** a place (as a nightclub, bar, or lounge) where drink is available

wa·ter·ish \'wȯt-ə-rish, 'wät-\ *adj* (1530) **:** somewhat watery — **wa·ter·ish·ness** *n*

water jacket *n* (1869) **:** an outer casing which holds water or through which water circulates to cool the interior; *specif* **:** the enclosed space surrounding the cylinder block of an internal-combustion engine and containing the cooling liquid

water jump *n* (1875) **:** an obstacle (as in a steeplechase) consisting of a pool, stream, or ditch of water

wa·ter·leaf \'wȯt-ər-ˌlēf, 'wät-\ *n, pl* **-leafs** \-ˌlēfs\ (1760) **:** any of a genus (*Hydrophyllum* of the family Hydrophyllaceae, the waterleaf family) of perennial woodland herbs with lobed or pinnate toothed leaves and cymes of bell-shaped flowers

wa·ter·less \-ləs\ *adj* (bef. 12c) **1 :** lacking or destitute of water **:** DRY **2 :** not requiring water (as for cooling or cooking) — **wa·ter·less·ly** *adv* — **wa·ter·less·ness** *n*

water level *n* (1563) **1 :** an instrument to show the level by means of the surface of water in a trough or in a U-shaped tube **2 :** the surface of still water: as **a :** the level assumed by the surface of a particular body or column of water **b :** the waterline of a vessel **c :** WATER TABLE 2

water lily *n* (15c) **:** any of a family (Nymphaeaceae, the water-lily family) of aquatic plants with floating leaves and usu. showy flowers; *broadly* **:** an aquatic plant (as a water hyacinth) with showy flowers

wa·ter·line \'wȯt-ər-ˌlīn, 'wät-\ *n* (ca. 1625) **:** any of several lines that are marked upon the outside of a ship and correspond with the surface of the water when it is afloat on an even keel

wa·ter·log \-ˌlȯg, -ˌläg\ *vt* [back-formation fr. *waterlogged*] (1779) **1 :** to make (as a boat) unmanageable by flooding **2 :** to saturate with water to the point of sogginess or loss of buoyancy

wa·ter·logged \-ˌlȯgd, -ˌlägd\ *adj* [[1]*water* + *log* (to accumulate in the hold)] (ca. 1769) **:** so filled or soaked with water as to be heavy or hard to manage ⟨~ boats⟩

wa·ter·loo \ˌwȯt-ər-'lü, ˌwät-\ *n, pl* **-loos** [*Waterloo*, Belgium, scene of Napoleon's defeat in 1815] (1816) **:** a decisive defeat

water main *n* (1803) **:** a pipe or conduit for conveying water

wa·ter·man \'wȯt-ər-mən, 'wät-\ *n* (15c) **:** one who works or lives on the water: as **a :** a man who makes his living from the water (as by fishing) **b :** a boatman who plies for hire usu. on inland waters or harbors

wa·ter·man·ship \-ˌship\ *n* (1882) **:** the business, skill, or art of a waterman: as **a :** technique or expertness in rowing **b :** technique or expertness in swimming

[1]**wa·ter·mark** \'wȯt-ər-ˌmärk, 'wät-\ *n* (1678) **1 :** a mark indicating the height to which water has risen **2 :** a marking in paper resulting from differences in thickness usu. produced by pressure of a projecting design in the mold or on a processing roll and visible when the paper is held up to the light; *also* **:** the design of or the metal pattern producing the marking

[2]**watermark** *vt* (1866) **1 :** to mark (paper) with a watermark **2 :** to impress (a given design) as a watermark

wa·ter·mel·on \-ˌmel-ən\ *n* (1615) **1 :** a large oblong or roundish fruit with a hard green or white rind often striped or variegated, a sweet watery pink, yellowish, or red pulp, and many seeds **2 :** a widely grown African vine (*Citrullus vulgaris*) of the gourd family that bears watermelons

water meter *n* (ca. 1858) **:** an instrument for recording the quantity of water passing through a particular outlet

water milfoil *n* (1578) **:** any of a genus (*Myriophyllum* of the family Haloragaceae) of aquatic plants with finely pinnate submersed leaves

water mill *n* (15c) **:** a mill whose machinery is moved by water

water moccasin *n* (1821) **1 :** a venomous semiaquatic pit viper (*Agkistrodon piscivorus*) of the southern U.S. closely related to the copperhead — called also *cotton mouth, cottonmouth moccasin* **2 :** an American water snake (genus *Natrix*)

water mold *n* (ca. 1899) **:** an aquatic fungus (as of the genus *Saprolegnia*)

water nymph *n* (14c) **:** a nymph (as a naiad, Nereid, or Oceanid) associated with a body of water

water oak *n* (1687) **:** any of several American oaks (esp. *Quercus nigra*) that thrive in wet soils

water of constitution (ca. 1889) **:** water so combined into a molecule that it cannot be removed without disrupting the entire molecule — compare WATER OF HYDRATION

water of crystallization (1791) **:** water of hydration present in many crystallized substances that is usu. essential for maintenance of a particular crystal structure

water of hydration (ca. 1889) **:** water that is chemically combined with a substance to form a hydrate and can be expelled (as by heating) without essentially altering the composition of the substance — compare WATER OF CONSTITUTION

water ouzel *n* (1622) **:** DIPPER 1

water parting *n* (1859) **:** a summit or boundary line separating the drainage districts of two streams or coasts

water pepper *n* (ca. 1538) **:** an annual smartweed (*Polygonum hydropiper*) of moist soils with extremely acrid peppery juice

water pimpernel *n* (ca. 1760) **:** either of two small white-flowered herbs (*Samolus valerandi* of Europe and *S. floribundus* of the U.S.) of the primrose family that grow in wet places

water pipe *n* (15c) **1 :** a pipe for conveying water **2 :** a tobacco smoking device that consists of a bowl mounted on a vessel of water which is provided with a long tube and so arranged that the smoke is drawn through the water where it is cooled and up the tube to the mouth

water pistol *n* (1905) **:** a toy pistol designed to squirt a jet of liquid — called also *water gun, squirt gun*

water plantain *n* (ca. 1538) **:** any of a genus (*Alisma* of the family Alismaceae, the water-plantain family) of marsh or aquatic herbs with acrid sap and scapose 3-petaled flowers

water polo *n* (1888) **:** a goal game similar to soccer that is played in water by teams of swimmers using a ball resembling a soccer ball

wa·ter·pow·er \ˈwȯt-ər-ˌpau̇(-ə)r, ˈwät-\ *n* (1827) **1 a :** the power of water employed to move machinery **b :** a fall of water suitable for such use **2 :** a water privilege for a mill

water privilege *n* (1749) **:** the right to use water esp. as a source of mechanical power

[1]**wa·ter·proof** \ˈwȯt-ər-ˌprüf, ˈwät-\ *adj* (1736) **:** impervious to water; *esp* **:** covered or treated with a material (as a solution of rubber) to prevent permeation by water — **wa·ter·proof·ness** *n*

[2]**waterproof** *n* (1799) **1 :** a waterproof fabric **2** *chiefly Brit* **:** RAINCOAT

[3]**waterproof** *vt* (1841) **:** to make waterproof — **wa·ter·proof·er** *n*

wa·ter·proof·ing \-ˈprü-fiŋ\ *n* (1845) **1 a :** the act or process of making something waterproof **b :** the condition of being made waterproof **2 :** something (as a coating) capable of imparting waterproofness

water race *n* (1771) **:** [1]RACE 2c

water rat *n* (ca. 1552) **1 :** a rodent that frequents water **2 :** a waterfront loafer or petty thief

wa·ter–re·pel·lent \ˌwȯt-ə(r)-ri-ˈpel-ənt, ˌwät-\ *adj* (ca. 1896) **:** treated with a finish that is resistant but not impervious to penetration by water

wa·ter–re·sis·tant \-ri-ˈzis-tənt\ *adj* (1921) **:** WATER-REPELLENT

water right *n* (1793) **:** a right to the use of water (as for irrigation); *esp* **:** RIPARIAN RIGHT

water sapphire *n* (1698) **:** a deep blue cordierite sometimes used as a gem

wa·ter·scape \ˈwȯt-ər-ˌskāp, ˈwät-\ *n* (1854) **:** a water or sea view **:** SEASCAPE 1

water scorpion *n* (1681) **:** any of numerous aquatic bugs (family Nepidae) with the end of the abdomen prolonged by a long breathing tube

wa·ter·shed \ˈwȯt-ər-ˌshed, ˈwät-\ *n* (1803) **1 :** WATER PARTING **2 :** a region or area bounded peripherally by a water parting and draining ultimately to a particular watercourse or body of water **3 :** a crucial dividing point, line, or factor **:** TURNING POINT — **watershed** *adj*

water shield *n* (ca. 1817) **:** an aquatic plant (*Brasenia schreberi*) of the water-lily family having floating oval leaves with a gelatinous coating and small dull purple flowers; *also* **:** any of a related genus (*Cabomba*)

[1]**wa·ter·side** \ˈwȯt-ər-ˌsīd, ˈwät-\ *n* (14c) **:** the margin of a body of water **:** WATERFRONT

[2]**waterside** *adj* (1663) **1 :** employed along the waterside ⟨~ workers⟩; *also* **:** of or relating to the workers along the waterside ⟨a ~ strike⟩ **2 :** of, relating to, or located on the waterside ⟨a ~ café⟩

water ski *n* (1931) **:** a ski used in planing over water while being towed by a speedboat — **wa·ter–ski** *vi*

wa·ter–ski·er \ˈwȯt-ər-ˌskē-ər, ˈwät-\ *n* (1954) **:** one that water-skis

wa·ter·ski·ing \-ˌskē-iŋ\ *n* (1946) **:** the sport of planing and jumping on water skis

water snake *n* (1601) **:** any of numerous snakes (esp. genus *Natrix*) that frequent or inhabit fresh waters and feed largely on aquatic animals

wa·ter–soak \ˈwȯt-ər-ˌsōk, ˈwät-\ *vt* (1791) **:** to soak in water

water spaniel *n* (1566) **:** a spaniel of either of two breeds: **a :** AMERICAN WATER SPANIEL **b :** IRISH WATER SPANIEL

water spot *n* (ca. 1939) **:** a physiological disorder of citrus fruits in the rainy season in which the epidermal air spaces of the rind become filled with liquid

wa·ter·spout \ˈwȯt-ər-ˌspau̇t, ˈwät-\ *n* (14c) **1 :** a pipe, duct, or orifice from which water is spouted or through which it is carried **2 :** a funnel-shaped or tubular column of rotating cloud-filled wind usu. extending from the underside of a cumulus or cumulonimbus cloud down to a cloud of spray torn up by the whirling winds from the surface of an ocean or lake

water sprite *n* (1798) **:** a sprite believed to inhabit or haunt water **:** WATER NYMPH

water sprout *n* (ca. 1892) **:** an extremely vigorous but usu. unproductive shoot from an adventitious or latent bud on a tree

water strider *n* (1888) **:** any of various long-legged bugs (family Gerridae) that move about on the surface of the water

water supply *n* (ca. 1882) **:** source, means, or process of supplying water (as for a community) usu. including reservoirs, tunnels, and pipelines

water system *n* (1833) **1 :** a river with its tributaries **2 :** WATER SUPPLY

water table *n* (15c) **1 :** a stringcourse or similar member when projecting so as to throw off water **2 :** the upper limit of the portion of the ground wholly saturated with water

water·thrush \ˈwȯt-ər-ˌthrəsh, ˈwät-\ *n* (ca. 1808) **:** either of two No. American warblers (*Seiurus noveboracensis* and *S. motacilla*) usu. living in the vicinity of streams

wa·ter·tight \ˌwȯt-ər-ˈtīt, ˌwät-\ *adj* (14c) **1 :** of such tight construction or fit as to be impermeable to water except when under sufficient pressure to produce structural discontinuity **2 :** leaving no possibility of misconstruction or evasion ⟨a ~ lease⟩ — **wa·ter·tight·ness** *n*

water tower *n* (ca. 1882) **:** a tower or standpipe serving as a reservoir to deliver water at a required head

water turkey *n* (1836) **:** a New World anhinga (*Anhinga anhinga*)

water vapor *n* (ca. 1880) **:** water in a vaporous form esp. when below boiling temperature and diffused (as in the atmosphere)

water–vascular system *n* (1870) **:** a system of vessels in echinoderms containing a circulating watery fluid that is used for the movement of tentacles and tube feet and may also function in excretion and respiration

water wagon *n* (1904) **:** a wagon or motortruck equipped with a tank or barrels for hauling water or for sprinkling — **on the water wagon :** abstaining from alcoholic beverages

water wave *n* (1882) **:** a method or style of setting hair by dampening with water and forming into waves — **wa·ter–waved** \ˈwȯt-ər-ˌwāvd, ˈwät-\ *adj*

wa·ter·way \ˈwȯt-ər-ˌwā, ˈwät-\ *n* (bef. 12c) **1 :** a way or channel for water **2 :** a groove at the edge of a ship's deck for draining the deck **3 :** a navigable body of water

wa·ter·weed \-ˌwēd\ *n* (1842) **:** any of various aquatic plants (as a pondweed) with inconspicuous flowers — compare WATER LILY

wa·ter·wheel \-ˌhwēl, -ˌwēl\ *n* (15c) **1 :** a wheel made to rotate by direct action of water **2 :** a wheel for raising water

water wings *n pl* (ca. 1908) **:** a pneumatic device to give support to the body of a person swimming or learning to swim

water witch *n* (1817) **:** one that dowses for water — **water witch·ing** \-ˌwich-iŋ\ *n*

water witch·er \-ˌwich-ər\ *n* (1917) **:** WATER WITCH

wa·ter·works \ˈwȯt-ər-ˌwərks, ˈwät-\ *n pl* (1586) **1 :** an ornamental fountain or cascade **2 :** the system of reservoirs, channels, mains, and pumping and purifying equipment by which a water supply is obtained and distributed (as to a city) **3 :** the shedding of tears **:** TEARS

wa·ter·worn \-ˌwō(ə)rn, -ˌwȯ(ə)rn\ *adj* (1815) **:** worn, smoothed, or polished by the action of water

wa·tery \ˈwȯt-ə-rē, ˈwät-\ *adj* (bef. 12c) **1 a :** consisting of or filled with water **b :** containing, sodden with, or yielding water or a thin liquid ⟨a ~ solution⟩ ⟨~ vesicles⟩ **2 a :** felt to resemble water or watery matter esp. in thin fluidity, soggy texture, paleness, or lack of savor ⟨~ blood⟩ ⟨~ sunlight⟩ ⟨a ~ soup⟩ **b :** exhibiting weakness and vapidity **:** WISHY-WASHY ⟨a ~ writing style⟩ — **wa·ter·i·ly** \-ə-rə-lē\ *adv* — **wa·ter·i·ness** \-ə-rē-nəs\ *n*

wa·ter·zooi \ˈwȯt-ər-ˌzü-ē, ˈwät-\ *n* [Flem, prob. modif. of D *waterzootje*] (1949) **:** a stew of fish or chicken and vegetables in a well-seasoned stock thickened with cream and egg yolks

Wat·son–Crick \ˌwät-sən-ˈkrik\ *adj* (1958) **:** of or relating to the Watson-Crick model ⟨*Watson-Crick* helix⟩ ⟨*Watson-Crick* structure⟩

Watson–Crick model *n* [J. D. *Watson* b1928 Am. biologist and F. H. C. *Crick* b1916 Eng. biologist] (1958) **:** a model of DNA structure in which the molecule is a cross-linked double-stranded helix, each strand is composed of alternating links of phosphate and deoxyribose, and the strands are cross-linked by pairs of purine and pyrimidine bases projecting inward from the deoxyribose sugars and joined by hydrogen bonds with adenine paired with thymine and with cytosine paired with guanine — compare DOUBLE HELIX

watt \ˈwät\ *n* [James *Watt* †1819] (1882) **:** the absolute meter-kilogram-second unit of power equal to the work done at the rate of one absolute joule per second or to the rate of work represented by a current of one ampere under a pressure of one volt and taken as the standard in the U.S. **:** $^{1}/_{746}$ horsepower

watt·age \ˈwät-ij\ *n* (1903) **:** amount of power expressed in watts

Wat·teau \(ˌ)wä-ˈtō\ *adj* [Antoine *Watteau*] (1887) **1** *of women's dress* **:** having back pleats falling loosely from neckline to hem **2** *of a hat* **:** shallow-crowned with wide brim turned up at the back to hold flower trimmings

-watt·er \ˈwät-ər\ *n comb form* **:** one having a specified wattage

watt–hour \ˈwät-ˈau̇(ə)r\ *n* (1888) **:** a unit of work or energy equivalent to the power of one watt operating for one hour

[1]**wat·tle** \ˈwät-ᵊl\ *n* [ME *wattel,* fr. OE *watel;* akin to OHG *wadal* bandage] (bef. 12c) **1 a :** a fabrication of poles interwoven with slender branches, withes, or reeds and used esp. formerly in building **b :** material for such construction **c** *pl* **:** poles laid on a roof to support thatch **2 :** a fleshy dependent process usu. about the head or neck (as of a bird) — see COCK illustration **3** *Austral* **:** ACACIA 2 — **wat·tled** \-ᵊld\ *adj*

[2]**wattle** *vt* **wat·tled; wat·tling** \ˈwät-liŋ, -ᵊl-iŋ\ (14c) **1 :** to form or build of or with wattle **2 a :** to form into wattle **:** interlace to form wattle **b :** to unite or make solid by interweaving light flexible material

wattle and daub *n* (1808) **:** a framework of woven rods and twigs covered and plastered with clay and used in building construction

wat·tle·bird \ˈwät-ᵊl-ˌbərd\ *n* (1820) **:** any of several Australasian honey eaters (genus *Anthochaera*) having fleshy pendulous ear wattles

watt·me·ter \ˈwät-ˌmēt-ər\ *n* [ISV] (1887) **:** an instrument for measuring electric power in watts

[1]**wave** \ˈwāv\ *vb* **waved; wav·ing** [ME *waven,* fr. OE *wafian* to wave with the hands; akin to OE *wǣfre* restless — more at WAVER] *vi* (bef. 12c) **1 :** to motion with the hands or with something held in them in signal or salute **2 :** to float, play, or shake in an air current **:** move loosely to and fro **:** FLUTTER **3** *of water* **:** to move in waves **:** HEAVE **4 :** to become moved or brandished to and fro ⟨his sword *waved* and flashed⟩ **5 :** to move before the wind with a wavelike motion ⟨field of *waving* grain⟩ **6 :** to follow a curving line or take a wavy form **:** UNDULATE ~ *vt* **1 :** to swing (something) back and forth or up and down **2 :** to impart a curving or undulating shape to ⟨*waved* her hair⟩ **3 a :** to motion to (someone) to go in an indicated direction or to stop **:** FLAG, SIGNAL ⟨looked at his papers, then *waved* him on⟩ **b :** to gesture with (the hand or an object) in greeting or farewell or in homage **c :** to dismiss or put out of mind **:** DISREGARD — usu. used with *aside* **d :** to convey by waving ⟨*waved* farewell⟩ **4 :** BRANDISH, FLOURISH ⟨*waved* a pistol menacingly⟩ ***syn*** see SWING

[2]**wave** *n* (14c) **1 a :** a moving ridge or swell on the surface of a liquid (as of the sea) **b :** open water **2 a :** a shape or outline having successive curves **b :** a waviness of the hair **c :** an undulating line or streak or a pattern formed by such lines **3 :** something that swells and dies away: as **a :** a surge of sensation or emotion ⟨a ~ of anger swept over her⟩ **b :** a movement sweeping large numbers in a common direction ⟨~s of protest⟩ **c :** a peak or climax of activity ⟨a ~ of buying⟩ **4 :** a sweep of hand or arm or of some object held in the hand used as a signal or greeting **5 :** a rolling or undulatory movement or one of a series of such movements passing along a surface or through the air **6 :** a movement like that of an ocean wave: as **a :** a surging movement of a group ⟨a big new ~ of incoming freshmen⟩ **b :** one of a succession of influxes of people migrating into a region **c (1) :** a moving group of animals of one kind **(2) :** a sudden rapid increase in a popu-

lation **d** : a line of attacking or advancing troops or airplanes **7 a** : a disturbance or variation that transfers energy progressively from point to point in a medium and that may take the form of an elastic deformation or of a variation of pressure, electric or magnetic intensity, electric potential, or temperature **b** : one complete cycle of such a disturbance **8** : a marked change in temperature : a period of hot or cold weather **9** : an undulating or jagged line constituting a graphic representation of an action — **wave·less** \'wāv-ləs\ *adj* — **wave·less·ly** *adv* — **wave·like** \-,līk\ *adj*

Wave \'wāv\ *n* [*W*omen *A*ccepted for *V*olunteer *E*mergency Service] (ca. 1942) : a woman serving in the navy

wave band *n* (1923) : a band of radio-wave frequencies

waved \'wāvd\ *adj* (1547) : having a wavelike form or outline: as **a** : having wavy lines of color : WATERED ⟨~ cloth⟩ **b** : marked by undulations : CURVING ⟨the ~ cutting edge of a bread knife⟩

wave equation *n* (ca. 1929) : a partial differential equation of the second order whose solutions describe wave phenomena

wave·form \'wāv-,fȯrm\ *n* (1846) : a usu. graphic representation of the shape of a wave that indicates its characteristics (as frequency and amplitude) — called also *waveshape*

wave front *n* (ca. 1864) : a surface composed at any instant of all the points just reached by a vibrational disturbance in its propagation through a medium

wave·guide \'wāv-,gīd\ *n* (ca. 1932) : a device (as a duct, coaxial cable, or glass fiber) designed to confine and direct the propagation of electromagnetic waves including light waves; *esp* : a metal tube for channeling ultrahigh-frequency waves

wave·length \-,leŋ(k)th\ *n* (ca. 1860) **1** : the distance in the line of advance of a wave from any one point to the next point of corresponding phase **2** : a particular course or line of thought esp. as related to mutual understanding ⟨got on with people only when they were on his private ~ —Robert Wernick⟩

wave·let \-lət\ *n* (1810) : a little wave : RIPPLE

wave mechanics *n pl but sing or pl in constr* (1927) : a theory of matter that is based on the concept of the possession of wave properties by elementary particles (as electrons, protons, or neutrons) and that affords a mathematical interpretation of the structure of matter on the basis of these properties

wave number *n* (ca. 1902) : the number of waves per unit distance of radiant energy of a given wavelength : the reciprocal of the wavelength

wave of the future (1940) : a movement that is viewed as representing forces or a trend that will inevitably prevail

wave packet *n* (ca. 1928) : a pulse of radiant energy that is the resultant of a number of wave trains of differing wavelengths

[1]**wa·ver** \'wā-vər\ *vi* **wa·vered; wa·ver·ing** \'wāv-(ə-)riŋ\ [ME *waveren;* akin to OE *wǣfre* restless, *wefan* to weave — more at WEAVE] (14c) **1** : to vacillate irresolutely between choices : fluctuate in opinion, allegiance, or direction **2 a** : to weave or sway unsteadily to and fro : REEL, TOTTER **b** : QUIVER, FLICKER ⟨~*ing* flames⟩ **c** : to hesitate as if about to give way : FALTER **3** : to give an unsteady sound : QUAVER *syn* see SWING, HESITATE — **wa·ver·er** \'wā-vər-ər\ *n* — **wa·ver·ing·ly** \'wāv-(ə-)riŋ-lē\ *adv*

[2]**waver** *n* (1519) : an act of wavering, quivering, or fluttering

[3]**wav·er** \'wā-vər\ *n* (1835) : one that waves

wa·very \'wāv-(ə-)rē\ *adj* (1820) : that waves : WAVERING

wave·shape \'wāv-,shāp\ *n* (1907) : WAVEFORM

wave theory *n* (1833) : UNDULATORY THEORY

wave train *n* (1897) : a succession of similar waves at equal intervals

wavy \'wā-vē\ *adj* **wav·i·er; -est** (1562) **1** : rising or swelling in waves; *also* : abounding in waves ⟨~ hair⟩ **2** : moving with an undulating motion : FLUCTUATING; *also* : marked by wavering **3** : marked by undulation : ROLLING — **wav·i·ly** \'wā-və-lē\ *adv* — **wav·i·ness** \-vē-nəs\ *n*

waw \'väv, 'vȯv\ *n* [Heb *wāw*] (14c) : the 6th letter of the Hebrew alphabet — see ALPHABET table

wa–wa pedal \'wä-,wä-\ *n* [imit.] (1968) : an electronic device that is connected to an amplifier and operated by a foot pedal and that is used (as with an electric guitar) to produce a fluctuating muted effect

[1]**wax** \'waks\ *n* [ME, fr. OE *weax;* akin to OHG *wahs* wax, Lith *vaškas*] (bef. 12c) **1** : a substance that is secreted by bees and is used by them for constructing the honeycomb, that is a dull yellow solid plastic when warm, and that is composed of a mixture of esters, cerotic acid, and hydrocarbons — called also *beeswax* **2** : any of various substances resembling beeswax: as **a** : any of numerous substances of plant or animal origin that differ from fats in being less greasy, harder, and more brittle and in containing principally esters of higher fatty acids and higher alcohols, free higher acids and alcohols, and saturated hydrocarbons **b** : a solid substance (as ozokerite or paraffin wax) of mineral origin consisting usu. of higher hydrocarbons **c** : a pliable or liquid composition used esp. in uniting surfaces, excluding air, making patterns or impressions, or producing a polished surface **d** : a resinous preparation used by shoemakers for rubbing thread **3** : something likened to wax as soft, impressionable, or readily molded **4** : a waxy secretion; *esp* : CERUMEN **5** : a phonograph recording — **wax-like** \'wak-,slīk\ *adj*

[2]**wax** *vt* (14c) **1** : to treat or rub with wax usu. for polishing or stiffening **2** : to record on phonograph records

[3]**wax** *vi* [ME *waxen,* fr. OE *weaxan;* akin to OHG *wahsan* to increase, Gk *auxanein,* L *augēre* — more at EKE] (bef. 12c) **1 a** : to increase in size, numbers, strength, prosperity, or intensity **b** : to grow in volume or duration **c** : to grow toward full development **2** : to increase in phase or intensity — used chiefly of the moon, other satellites, and inferior planets **3** : to assume a (specified) characteristic, quality, or state : BECOME ⟨~ indignant⟩

[4]**wax** *n* (14c) : INCREASE, GROWTH — usu. used in the phrase *on the wax*

[5]**wax** *n* [perh. fr. [3]*wax*] (1854) : a fit of temper : RAGE

wax bean *n* (ca. 1905) : a kidney bean with pods that turn creamy yellow to bright yellow when mature enough for use as snap beans

wax·bill \-,bil\ *n* (1757) : any of numerous Old World birds (family Ploceidae and esp. genera *Estrilda* and *Lagonosticta*) having white, pink, or reddish bills of a waxy appearance

waxed paper *n* (1853) : paper coated or otherwise treated with wax to make it resistant to water and grease and used esp. as a wrapping

wax·en \'wak-sən\ *adj* (bef. 12c) **1** : made of or covered with wax **2** : resembling wax: as **a** : easily molded : PLIABLE **b** : seeming to lack vitality or animation : PALLID **c** : lustrously smooth

wax·er \-sər\ *n* (1875) **1** : one whose work is applying or polishing with wax **2** : a device for applying wax

wax·ing *n* (15c) **1** : the act of applying wax (as in polishing) **2** : the process of removing body hair with a depilatory wax

wax light *n* (1648) : a wax candle : TAPER

wax moth *n* (1766) : a dull brownish or ashen pyralid moth (*Galleria mellonella*) with a larva that feeds on the wax of the combs of the honeybee

wax museum *n* (1953) : a place where wax effigies (as of famous historical persons) are exhibited

wax myrtle *n* (1806) : any of a genus (*Myrica* of the family Myricaceae, the wax-myrtle family) of trees or shrubs with aromatic foliage; *esp* : an American shrub (*M. cerifera*) having small hard berries with a thick coating of white wax used for candles

wax palm *n* (ca. 1828) : any of several palms that yield wax: as **a** : an Andean pinnate-leaved palm (*Ceroxylon andicolum*) whose stem yields a resinous wax used in candles **b** : CARNAUBA

wax paper *n* (ca. 1844) : WAXED PAPER

wax·wing \'wak-,swiŋ\ *n* (1817) : any of a genus (*Bombycilla*) of American and Eurasian passerine birds (as a cedar waxwing) that are chiefly brown with a showy crest and velvety plumage

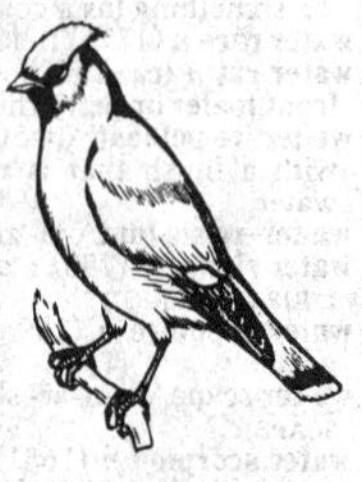
waxwing

wax·work \'wak-,swərk\ *n* (1697) **1** : an effigy in wax usu. of a person **2** *pl but sing or pl in constr* : WAX MUSEUM

waxy \'wak-sē\ *adj* **wax·i·er; -est** (ca. 1552) **1** : made of, abounding in, or covered with wax : WAXEN ⟨a ~ surface⟩ ⟨~ berries⟩ **2** : resembling wax: as **a** : readily shaped or molded **b** : marked by smooth or lustrous whiteness ⟨a ~ complexion⟩ — **wax·i·ness** *n*

[1]**way** \'wā\ *n* [ME, fr. OE *weg;* akin to OHG *weg* way, OE *wegan* to move, L *vehere* to carry] (bef. 12c) **1 a** : a thoroughfare for travel or transportation from place to place **b** : an opening for passage ⟨this door is the only ~ out of the room⟩ **2** : the course traveled from one place to another : ROUTE **3 a** : a course (as a series of actions or sequence of events) leading in a direction or toward an objective ⟨led the ~ to eventual open heart operations —*Current Biog.*⟩ **b** (1) : a course of action ⟨took the easy ~ out⟩ (2) : opportunity, capability, or fact of doing as one pleases ⟨always manages to get her own ~⟩ **c** : a possible decision, action, or outcome : POSSIBILITY ⟨they were rude — no two ~s about it⟩ **4 a** : manner or method of doing or happening; *also* : method of accomplishing : MEANS **b** : FEATURE, RESPECT ⟨in no ~ resembles her mother⟩ **c** : a usu. specified degree of participation in an activity or enterprise ⟨active in real estate in a small ~⟩ **5** : characteristic, regular, or habitual manner or mode of being, behaving, or happening ⟨knows nothing of the ~s of women⟩ **6** : the length of a course : DISTANCE ⟨has come a long ~ in her studies⟩ **7** : movement or progress along a course ⟨working his ~ through college⟩ **8 a** : DIRECTION ⟨is coming this ~⟩ **b** : PARTICIPANT — usu. used in combination ⟨three-*way* discussion⟩ **9** : state of affairs : CONDITION, STATE ⟨that's the ~ things are⟩ **10 a** *pl but sometimes sing in constr* : an inclined structure upon which a ship is built or supported in launching **b** *pl* : the guiding surfaces on the bed of a machine along which a table or carriage moves **11** : CATEGORY, KIND — usu. used in the phrase *in the way of* ⟨doesn't require much in the ~ of expensive equipment —*Forbes*⟩ **12** : motion or speed of a ship or boat through the water *syn* see METHOD — **by way of 1** : for the purpose of **2** : by the route through : VIA — **in a way 1** : within limits : with reservations **2** : from one point of view — **in one's way** *also* **in the way 1** : in a position to be encountered by one : in or along one's course ⟨an opportunity had been put *in my way* —Ellen Glasgow⟩ **2** : in a position to hinder or obstruct — **on the way** *or* **on one's way** : moving along in one's course : in progress — **out of the way 1** : WRONG, IMPROPER ⟨didn't know he'd said anything *out of the way*⟩ **2 a** : in or to a secluded place **b** : UNUSUAL, REMARKABLE ⟨the house wasn't anything *out of the way*⟩ **3** : DONE, COMPLETED ⟨got his homework *out of the way*⟩

[2]**way** *adj* (1799) : of, connected with, or constituting an intermediate point on a route ⟨visited five major countries plus ~ points⟩

[3]**way** *adv* (1849) **1** : AWAY 7 ⟨is ~ ahead of the class⟩ **2** : all the way ⟨pull the switch ~ back⟩ — **from way back** : of long standing ⟨friends *from way back*⟩

way·bill \'wā-,bil\ *n* (1791) : a document prepared by the carrier of a shipment of goods that contains details of the shipment, route, and charges

way car *n* (1879) **1** : CABOOSE 2 **2** : a freight car for less-than-carload shipments to way stations

way·far·er \'wā-,far-ər, -,fer-\ *n* [ME *weyfarere,* fr. *wey, way* way + *-farere* traveler, fr. *faren* to go — more at FARE] (15c) : a traveler esp. on foot — **way·far·ing** \-,far-iŋ, -,fer-\ *adj*

way·go·ing \'wā-,gō-ən, -iŋ\ *n, chiefly Scot* (1633) : the act of leaving : DEPARTURE

Way·land \'wā-lən(d)\ *n* [OE *Wēland*] : an heroic smith of Germanic legend

way·lay \'wā-,lā\ *vt* **-laid** \-,lād\; **-lay·ing** (1513) : to lie in wait for or attack from ambush *syn* see SURPRISE

way·less \-ləs\ *adj* (12c) : having no road or path

Way of the Cross (1868) : STATIONS OF THE CROSS

way–out \'wā-'au̇t\ *adj* [*way out* (adverbial phrase), fr. [3]*way* + *out*] (ca. 1954) : FAR-OUT

ways \'wāz\ *n pl but sing in constr* [ME *wayes,* fr. gen. of [1]*way*] (1588) : WAY 6 ⟨a long ~ from home⟩

-ways \,wāz\ *adv suffix* [ME, fr. *ways,* gen. of *way*] : in (such) a way, course, direction, or manner ⟨side*ways*⟩ ⟨flat*ways*⟩

ways and means *n pl* (15c) **1** : methods and resources for accomplishing something and esp. for defraying expenses **2** *often cap W&M* **a** : methods and resources for raising the necessary revenues for the

expenses of a nation or state **b :** a legislative committee concerned with this function
way·side \'wā-,sīd\ *n* (15c) **:** the side of or land adjacent to a road or path — **wayside** *adj*
way station *n* (1849) **1 :** an intermediate station between principal stations on a line of travel (as a railroad) **2 :** an intermediate stopping place
way·ward \'wā-wərd\ *adj* [ME, short for *awayward* turned away, fr. *away,* adv. + *-ward*] (14c) **1 :** following one's own capricious, wanton, or depraved inclinations **:** UNGOVERNABLE **2 :** following no clear principle or law **:** UNPREDICTABLE **3 :** opposite to what is desired or expected **:** UNTOWARD ⟨~ fate⟩ *syn* see CONTRARY — **way·ward·ly** *adv* — **way·ward·ness** *n*
way·worn \-,wō(ə)rn, -,wȯ(ə)rn\ *adj* (1788) **:** wearied by traveling
we \(')wē\ *pron, pl in constr* [ME, fr. OE *wē;* akin to OHG *wir* we, Skt *vayam*] (bef. 12c) **1 :** I and the rest of a group that includes me **:** you and I **:** you and I and another or others **:** I and another or others not including you — used as pronoun of the first person plural; compare I, OUR, OURS, US **2 :** [1]I — used by sovereigns; used by writers to keep an impersonal character
weak \'wēk\ *adj* [ME *weike,* fr. ON *veikr;* akin to OE *wīcan* to yield, L *vicis* change — more at WEEK] (14c) **1 :** lacking strength: as **a :** deficient in physical vigor **:** FEEBLE, DEBILITATED **b :** not able to sustain or exert much weight, pressure, or strain **c :** not able to resist external force or withstand attack **2 a :** mentally or intellectually deficient **b :** not firmly decided **:** VACILLATING **c :** resulting from or indicating lack of judgment or discernment **d :** not able to withstand temptation or persuasion **3 :** not factually grounded or logically presented ⟨a ~ argument⟩ **4 a :** not able to function properly **b** (1) **:** lacking skill or proficiency ⟨tutoring for ~*er* students⟩ (2) **:** indicative of a lack of skill or aptitude ⟨math was my ~*est* subject⟩ **c :** wanting in vigor of expression or effect **5 a :** deficient in the usual or required ingredients **:** DILUTE ⟨~ coffee⟩ **b :** lacking normal intensity or potency ⟨~ strain of virus⟩ **6 a :** not having or exerting authority or political power ⟨~ government⟩ **b :** INEFFECTIVE, IMPOTENT **7 :** of, relating to, or constituting a verb or verb conjugation that in English forms the past tense and past participle by adding the suffix *-ed* or *-d* or *-t* **8 a :** bearing the minimal degree of stress occurring in the language ⟨~ syllable⟩ **b :** having little or no stress and obscured vowel sound ⟨*'d* is the ~ form of *would*⟩ **9 :** tending toward a lower price ⟨a ~ market⟩ **10 :** ionizing only slightly in solution ⟨~ acids and bases⟩ — **weak·ly** *adv*

syn WEAK, FEEBLE, FRAIL, FRAGILE, INFIRM, DECREPIT mean not strong enough to endure strain, pressure, or strenuous effort. WEAK applies to deficiency or inferiority in strength or power of any sort; FEEBLE suggests extreme weakness inviting pity or contempt; FRAIL implies delicacy and slightness of constitution or structure; FRAGILE suggests frailty and brittleness unable to resist rough usage; INFIRM suggests instability, unsoundness, and insecurity due to old age or crippling illness; DECREPIT implies being worn-out or broken-down from long use or old age.

weak·en \'wē-kən\ *vb* **weak·ened; weak·en·ing** \'wēk-(ə-)niŋ\ *vt* (1530) **1 :** to make weak **:** lessen the strength of **2 :** to reduce in intensity or effectiveness ~ *vi* **:** to become weak — **weak·en·er** \-(ə-)nər\ *n*

syn WEAKEN, ENFEEBLE, DEBILITATE, UNDERMINE, SAP, CRIPPLE, DISABLE mean to lose or cause to lose strength or vigor. WEAKEN may imply loss of physical strength, health, soundness, or stability or of quality, intensity, or effective power; ENFEEBLE implies an obvious and pitiable condition of weakness and helplessness; DEBILITATE suggests a less marked or more temporary impairment of strength or vitality; UNDERMINE and SAP suggest a weakening by something working surreptitiously and insidiously; CRIPPLE implies causing a serious loss of functioning power through damaging or removing an essential part or element; DISABLE suggests a usu. sudden crippling or enfeebling.

weak·fish \'wēk-,fish\ *n* [obs. D *weekvis,* fr. D *week* soft + *vis* fish; fr. its tender flesh] (1796) **1 :** a common marine percoid sport and market fish (*Cynoscion regalis*) of the eastern coast of the U.S. — called also *sea trout* **2 :** any of several food fishes congeneric with the weakfish
weak·heart·ed \-'härt-əd\ *adj* (1549) **:** lacking courage **:** FAINTHEARTED
weak interaction *n* (1963) **:** a fundamental interaction experienced by elementary particles that is responsible for some particle decay processes, for nuclear beta decay, and for emission and absorption of neutrinos — called also *weak force*
weak·ish \'wē-kish\ *adj* (1594) **:** somewhat weak ⟨~ tea⟩
weak–kneed \'wēk-'nēd\ *adj* (1863) **:** lacking willpower or resolution
weak·ling \'wē-kliŋ\ *n* (1548) **:** one that is weak in body, character, or mind — **weakling** *adj*
weak·ly \'wē-klē\ *adj* (1577) **:** FEEBLE, WEAK — **weak·li·ness** *n*
weak–mind·ed \'wēk-'mīn-dəd\ *adj* (ca. 1878) **:** having or indicating a weak mind: **a :** lacking in judgment or good sense **:** FOOLISH **b :** FEEBLEMINDED — **weak–mind·ed·ness** *n*
weak·ness \-nəs\ *n* (14c) **1 :** the quality or state of being weak; *also* **:** an instance or period of being weak ⟨agreed in a moment of ~ to go along⟩ **2 :** FAULT, DEFECT **3 :** an object of special desire or fondness ⟨has a ~ for chocolates⟩
weak side *n* (1940) **:** the side of a football formation having the smaller number of players; *specif* **:** the side of a formation away from the tight end
weak sister *n* (1857) **:** a member of a group who needs aid; *also* **:** something that is weak and ineffective as compared with others in the group
[1]weal \'wē(ə)l\ *n* [ME *wele,* fr. OE *wela;* akin to OE *wel* well] (bef. 12c) **1 :** a sound, healthy, or prosperous state **:** WELL-BEING **2** *obs* **:** BODY POLITIC, COMMONWEAL
[2]weal *n* [alter. of *wale*] (ca. 1798) **:** WELT
weald \'wē(ə)ld\ *n* [the *Weald,* England, fr. ME *weeld,* fr. OE *weald* forest — more at WOLD] (bef. 12c) **1 :** a heavily wooded area **:** FOREST ⟨*Weald* of Kent⟩ **2 :** a wild or uncultivated usu. upland region
wealth \'welth *also* 'weltth\ *n* [ME *welthe,* fr. *wele* weal] (13c) **1** *obs* **:** WEAL, WELFARE **2 :** abundance of valuable material possessions or resources **3 :** abundant supply **:** PROFUSION **4 a :** all property that has a money value or an exchangeable value **b :** all material objects that have economic utility; *esp* **:** the stock of useful goods having economic value in existence at any one time ⟨national ~⟩
wealthy \'wel-thē *also* 'welt-\ *adj* **wealth·i·er; -est** (14c) **1 :** having wealth **:** extremely affluent **2 :** characterized by abundance **:** AMPLE *syn* see RICH — **wealth·i·ly** \-thə-lē\ *adv* — **wealth·i·ness** \-thē-nəs\ *n*
wean \'wēn\ *vt* [ME *wenen,* fr. OE *wenian* to accustom, wean; akin to OE *wunian* to be used to — more at WONT] (bef. 12c) **1 :** to accustom (as a child) to take food otherwise than by nursing **2 :** to detach from a cause of dependence or preoccupation **:** free from a usu. unwholesome interest *syn* see ESTRANGE
wean·er \'wē-nər\ *n* (1579) **1 :** one that weans **2 :** a young animal recently weaned from its mother
wean·ling \'wēn-liŋ\ *n* (1532) **:** a child or animal newly weaned — **weanling** *adj*
[1]weap·on \'wep-ən\ *n* [ME *wepen,* fr. OE *wǣpen;* akin to ON *vāpn* weapon] (bef. 12c) **1 :** an instrument of offensive or defensive combat **:** something to fight with **2 :** a means of contending against another
[2]weapon *vt* (bef. 12c) **:** ARM
weap·on·less \'wep-ən-ləs\ *adj* (bef. 12c) **:** lacking weapons **:** UNARMED
weap·on·ry \-rē\ *n* (1844) **1 :** WEAPONS **2 :** the science of designing and making weapons
[1]wear \'wa(ə)r, 'we(ə)r\ *vb* **wore** \'wō(ə)r, 'wȯ(ə)r\; **worn** \'wō(ə)rn, 'wȯ(ə)rn\; **wear·ing** [ME *weren,* fr. OE *werian;* akin to ON *verja* to clothe, invest, spend, L *vestis* clothing, garment, Gk *hennynai* to clothe] *vt* (bef. 12c) **1 :** to bear or have on the person ⟨*wore* a coat⟩ **2 a :** to use habitually for clothing, adornment, or assistance ⟨~*s* a toupee⟩ ⟨~ glasses⟩ **b :** to carry on the person ⟨~ a sword⟩ **3 a :** to hold the rank or dignity or position signified by (an ornament) ⟨~ the royal crown⟩ **b :** to have or show an appearance of ⟨*wore* a happy smile⟩ **c :** to show or fly (a flag or colors) on a ship **4 a :** to cause to deteriorate by use **b :** to impair or diminish by use or attrition **:** consume or waste gradually ⟨letters on the stone *worn* away by weathering⟩ **5 :** to produce gradually by friction or attrition ⟨~ a hole in the rug⟩ **6 :** to exhaust or lessen the strength of **:** WEARY, FATIGUE **7 :** to cause (a ship) to go about with the stern presented to the wind ~ *vi* **1 a :** to endure use **:** last under use or the passage of time ⟨material that will ~ for years⟩ **b :** to retain quality or vitality **2 a :** to diminish or decay through use ⟨the heels of his shoes began to ~⟩ **b :** to diminish or fail with the passage of time ⟨the effect of the drug *wore* off⟩ ⟨the day *wore* on⟩ **c :** to grow or become by attrition or use **3** *of a ship* **:** to change to an opposite tack by turning the stern to the wind — compare TACK — **wear·er** *n* — **wear on :** IRRITATE, FRAY — **wear the trousers** or **wear the pants :** to have the controlling authority in a household — **wear thin 1 :** to become weak or ready to give way ⟨my patience was *wearing thin*⟩ **2 :** to become trite, unconvincing, or out-of-date ⟨an argument that quickly *wore thin*⟩
[2]wear *n* (15c) **1 :** the act of wearing **:** the state of being worn **:** USE ⟨clothes for everyday ~⟩ **2 a :** clothing or an article of clothing usu. of a particular kind; *esp* **:** clothing worn for a special occasion or popular during a specific period **b :** FASHION, VOGUE **3 :** wearing quality **:** durability under use **4 :** the result of wearing or use **:** diminution or impairment due to use ⟨*wear*-resistant surface⟩
[1]wear·able \'war-ə-bəl, 'wer-\ *adj* (1590) **:** capable of being worn **:** suitable to be worn — **wear·abil·i·ty** \,war-ə-'bil-ət-ē, ,wer-\ *n*
[2]wearable *n* (1711) **:** GARMENT — usu. used in pl.
wear and tear *n* (1666) **:** the loss or injury to which something is subjected by or in the course of use; *esp* **:** normal depreciation
wear down *vt* (1803) **:** to weary and overcome by persistent resistance or pressure
wea·ri·ful \'wir-ē-fəl\ *adj* (15c) **1 :** causing weariness; *esp* **:** TEDIOUS **2 :** full of weariness **:** WEARIED — **wea·ri·ful·ly** \-fə-lē\ *adv* — **wea·ri·ful·ness** *n*
wea·ri·less \'wir-ē-ləs\ *adj* (15c) **:** TIRELESS — **wea·ri·less·ly** *adv*
[1]wear·ing \'wa(ə)r-iŋ, 'we(ə)r-\ *adj* (15c) **:** intended for wear ⟨~ apparel⟩
[2]wearing *adj* (1811) **:** subjecting to or inflicting wear; *esp* **:** causing fatigue ⟨a ~ journey⟩ — **wear·ing·ly** \-iŋ-lē\ *adv*
wea·ri·some \'wir-ē-səm\ *adj* (15c) **:** causing weariness **:** TIRESOME — **wea·ri·some·ly** *adv* — **wea·ri·some·ness** *n*
wear out *vt* (14c) **1 :** TIRE, EXHAUST **2 :** to make useless esp. by long or hard usage **3 :** ERASE, EFFACE **4 :** to endure through **:** OUTLAST ⟨*wear out* a storm⟩ **5 :** to consume (as time) tediously ⟨*wear out* idle days⟩ ~ *vi* **:** to become useless from long or excessive wear or use
[1]wea·ry \'wi(ə)r-ē\ *adj* **wea·ri·er; -est** [ME *wery,* fr. OE *wērig;* akin to OHG *wuorag* intoxicated, Gk *hōrakian* to faint] (bef. 12c) **1 :** exhausted in strength, endurance, vigor, or freshness **2 :** expressing or characteristic of weariness **3 :** having one's patience, tolerance, or pleasure exhausted — used with *of* **4 :** WEARISOME — **wea·ri·ly** \'wir-ə-lē\ *adv* — **wea·ri·ness** \'wir-ē-nəs\ *n*
[2]weary *vb* **wea·ried; wea·ry·ing** *vi* (bef. 12c) **:** to become weary ~ *vt* **:** to make weary *syn* see TIRE
wea·sand \'wēz-ᵊnd, 'wiz-ᵊn(d)\ *n* [ME *wesand,* fr. (assumed) OE *wǣsend* gullet; akin to OE *wāsend* gullet, OHG *weisunt* windpipe] (bef. 12c) **:** THROAT, GULLET; *also* **:** WINDPIPE
[1]wea·sel \'wē-zəl\ *n, pl* **weasels** [ME *wesele,* fr. OE *weosule;* akin to OHG *wisula* weasel, and prob. to L *virus* slimy liquid, stench — more at VIRUS] (bef. 12c) **1** *or pl* **weasel :** any of various small slender active carnivorous mammals (genus *Mustela* of the family Mustelidae, the weasel family) that consume small birds and mammals and esp. great numbers of vermin (as mice or rats) and are mostly reddish brown with white or yellowish underparts and in northern forms turn white in winter **2 :** a light self-propelled tracked vehicle built either for traveling over snow, ice, or sand or as an amphibious vehicle

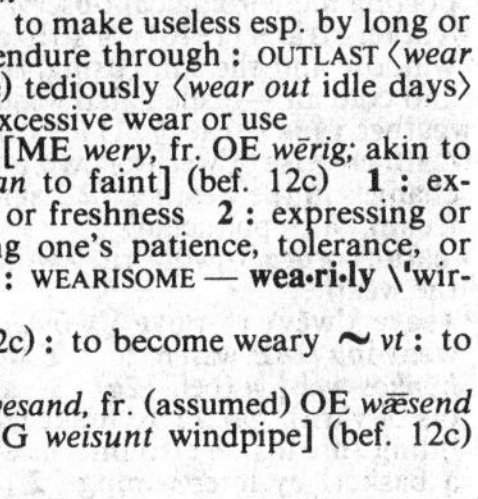
weasel 1

2weasel *vi* **wea·seled; wea·sel·ing** \'wēz-(ə-)liŋ\ [*weasel word*] (1900) **1** : to use weasel words : EQUIVOCATE **2** : to escape from or evade a situation or obligation — often used with *out*

weasel word *n* [fr. the weasel's reputed habit of sucking the contents out of an egg while leaving the shell superficially intact] (1900) : a word used in order to evade or retreat from a direct or forthright statement or position

1weath·er \'weth-ər\ *n* [ME *weder*, fr. OE; akin to OHG *wetar* weather, OSlav *vetrŭ* wind] (bef. 12c) **1** : state of the atmosphere with respect to heat or cold, wetness or dryness, calm or storm, clearness or cloudiness **2** : state of life or fortune **3** : disagreeable atmospheric conditions: as **a** : RAIN, STORM **b** : cold air with dampness **4** : WEATHERING — **under the weather 1** : ILL **2** : DRUNK

2weather *vb* **weath·ered; weath·er·ing** \'weth-(ə-)riŋ\ *vt* (15c) **1** : to expose to the open air : subject to the action of the elements **2** : to sail or pass to the windward of **3** : to bear up against and come safely through ⟨~ a storm⟩ ~ *vi* : to undergo or endure the action of the elements

3weather *adj* (1625) : WINDWARD — compare LEE

weath·er·abil·i·ty \,weth-(ə-)rə-'bil-ət-ē\ *n* (1947) : capability of withstanding the weathering process ⟨~ of a plastic⟩

weath·er–beat·en \'weth-ər-,bēt-ᵊn\ *adj* (1530) **1** : toughened, tanned, or bronzed by the weather ⟨~ face⟩ **2** : worn or damaged by exposure to weather

weath·er·board \-,bō(ə)rd, -,bȯ(ə)rd\ *n* (1539) **1** : CLAPBOARD, SIDING **2** : the weather side of a ship

weath·er·board·ing \-,bōrd-iŋ, -,bȯrd-\ *n* (1632) : CLAPBOARDS, SIDING

weath·er–bound \-,baủnd\ *adj* (1590) : kept in port or at anchor or from travel or sport by bad weather

weather bureau *n* (ca. 1870) : a bureau engaged in the collection of weather reports as a basis for weather predictions, storm warnings, and the compiling of statistical records

weath·er–burned \'weth-ər-,bərnd\ *adj* (1906) : browned by sun and wind

weath·er·cock \-,käk\ *n* (14c) **1** : a vane often in the figure of a cock mounted so as to turn freely with the wind and show its direction **2** : a person or thing that changes readily or often

weather deck *n* (1850) : a deck having no overhead protection from the weather

weath·ered \'weth-ərd\ *adj* (1789) **1 a** : seasoned by exposure to the weather **b** : altered in color, texture, composition, or form by such exposure or by artificial means producing a similar effect ⟨~ oak⟩ **2** : made sloping so as to throw off water ⟨~ windowsill⟩

weather eye *n* (1839) **1** : an eye quick to observe coming changes in the weather **2** : constant and shrewd watchfulness and alertness

weath·er·glass \'weth-ər-,glas\ *n* (1626) : a simple instrument for showing changes in atmospheric pressure by the changing level of liquid in a spout connected with a closed reservoir; *broadly* : BAROMETER

weath·er·ing *n* (1548) : the action of the elements in altering the color, texture, composition, or form of exposed objects; *specif* : the physical disintegration and chemical decomposition of earth materials at or near the earth's surface

weath·er·ize \'weth-ə-,rīz\ *vt* (1943) : to make (as a house) better protected against winter weather esp. by adding insulation and by caulking joints — **weath·er·iza·tion** \,weth-(ə-)rə-'zā-shən\ *n*

weath·er·ly \'weth-ər-lē\ *adj* (1729) : able to sail close to the wind with little leeway

weath·er·man \-,man\ *n* (1859) : one who reports and forecasts the weather : METEOROLOGIST

weather map *n* (1871) : a map or chart showing the principal meteorological elements at a given hour and over an extended region

weath·er·proof \,weth-ər-'prüf\ *adj* (1620) : able to withstand exposure to weather without damage or loss of function — **weatherproof** *vt* — **weath·er·proof·ness** *n*

weather ship *n* (1946) : a ship that makes observations for use by meteorologists

weather station *n* (ca. 1909) : a station for taking, recording, and reporting meteorological observations

weather strip *n* (1846) : a strip of material to cover the joint of a door or window and the sill, casing, or threshold so as to exclude rain, snow, and cold air — called also *weather stripping* — **weath·er–strip** *vt*

weather vane *n* (ca. 1721) : VANE 1a

weath·er–wise \'weth-ər-,wīz\ *adj* (14c) **1** : skillful in forecasting changes in the weather **2** : skillful in forecasting changes in opinion or feeling ⟨a ~ politician⟩

weath·er·worn \-,wō(ə)rn, -,wȯ(ə)rn\ *adj* (1609) : worn by exposure to the weather

1weave \'wēv\ *vb* **wove** \'wōv\ *or* **weaved; wo·ven** \'wō-vən\ *or* **weaved; weav·ing** [ME *weven*, fr. OE *wefan*; akin to OHG *weban* to weave, Gk *hyphos* web] *vt* (bef. 12c) **1 a** : to form (cloth) by interlacing strands (as of yarn); *specif* : to make (cloth) on a loom by interlacing warp and filling threads **b** : to interlace (as threads) into cloth **c** : to make (as a basket) by intertwining **2** : SPIN — used of spiders and insects **3** : to interlace esp. to form a texture, fabric, or design **4 a** : to produce by elaborately combining elements : CONTRIVE **b** : to unite in a coherent whole **c** : to introduce as an appropriate element : work in — usu. used with *in* or *into* **5** : to direct (as the body) in a winding or zigzag course esp. to avoid obstacles ~ *vi* **1** : to work at weaving : make cloth **2** : to move in a devious, winding, or zigzag course esp. to avoid obstacles

2weave *n* (1581) **1** : something woven; *esp* : woven cloth **2** : any of the patterns or methods for interlacing the threads of woven fabrics

3weave *vi* **weaved; weav·ing** [ME *weven* to move to and fro, wave; akin to ON *veifa* to wave, Skt *vepate* he trembles] (1596) : to move waveringly from side to side : SWAY

weav·er \'wē-vər\ *n* (14c) **1** : one that weaves esp. as an occupation **2** : WEAVERBIRD

weav·er·bird \-,bərd\ *n* (ca. 1826) : any of numerous Old World passerine birds (family Ploceidae) that resemble finches and mostly construct elaborate nests of interlaced vegetation — called also *weaver*

weaver's knot *n* (1532) : SHEET BEND — called also *weaver's hitch*

1web \'web\ *n* [ME, fr. OE; akin to ON *vefr* web, OE *wefan* to weave] (bef. 12c) **1** : a fabric on a loom or in process of being removed from a loom **2 a** : COBWEB 1, 2 **b** : SNARE, ENTANGLEMENT **3** : a tissue or membrane of an animal or plant; *esp* : that uniting fingers or toes either at their bases (as in man) or for a greater part of their length (as in many water birds) **4 a** : a thin metal sheet, plate, or strip **b** : the plate connecting the upper and lower flanges of a girder or rail **c** : the arm of a crank **5** : an intricate structure suggestive of something woven : NETWORK **6** : the series of barbs implanted on each side of the shaft of a feather : VANE **7 a** : a continuous sheet of paper manufactured or undergoing manufacture on a paper machine **b** : a roll of paper for use in a rotary printing press **8** : the part of a ribbed vault between the ribs — **webbed** \'webd\ *adj* — **web·like** \'web-,līk\ *adj*

2web *vb* **webbed; web·bing** *vi* (1604) : to construct or form a web ~ *vt* **1** : to cover with a web or network **2** : ENSNARE, ENTANGLE **3** : to provide with a web

web·bing \'web-iŋ\ *n* (1794) **1** : a strong narrow closely woven tape designed for bearing weight and used esp. for straps, harness, or upholstery **2** : TRAP 3c

web·by \'web-ē\ *adj* (1661) : of, relating to, or consisting of a web

we·ber \'web-ər, 'vā-bər\ *n* [Wilhelm E. *Weber* †1891 Ger. physicist] (ca. 1891) : the practical meter-kilogram-second unit of magnetic flux equal to that flux which in linking a circuit of one turn produces in it an electromotive force of one volt as the flux is reduced to zero at a uniform rate of one ampere per second : 10^8 maxwells

web·fed \'web-,fed\ *adj* (1947) : of, relating to, or printed by a web press

web·foot *n* (1765) **1** \'web-'fủt\ : a foot having webbed toes **2** \-,fủt\ : an animal having web feet — **web–foot·ed** \-'fủt-əd\ *adj*

web member *n* (ca. 1890) : one of the several members joining the top and bottom chords of a truss or lattice girder

web offset *n* (1967) : offset printing by web press

web press *n* (1875) : a press that prints a continuous roll of paper

web spinner *n* (ca. 1907) : an insect that spins a web; *esp* : any of an order (Embiodea) of small slender insects with biting mouthparts that live in silken tunnels which they spin

web·ster \'web-stər\ *n* [ME, fr. OE *webbestre* female weaver, fr. *webbian* to weave; akin to OE *wefan* to weave] *archaic* (bef. 12c) : WEAVER

web·worm \'web-,wərm\ *n* (1797) : any of various caterpillars that are more or less gregarious and spin large webs

wed \'wed\ *vb* **wed·ded** *also* **wed; wed·ding** [ME *wedden*, fr. OE *weddian*; akin to MHG *wetten* to pledge, OE *wedd* pledge, OHG *wetti*, Goth *wadi*, L *vad-*, *vas* bail, security] *vt* (bef. 12c) **1** : to take for wife or husband by a formal ceremony : MARRY **2** : to join in marriage **3** : to unite as if by the bond of marriage ~ *vi* : to enter into matrimony — **wed·der** *n*

we'd \(,)wēd\ : we had : we would : we should

wed·ding \'wed-iŋ\ *n, often attrib* (bef. 12c) **1** : a marriage ceremony usu. with its accompanying festivities : NUPTIALS **2** : an act, process, or instance of joining in close association **3** : a wedding anniversary or its celebration — usu. used in combination

wedding march *n* (1850) : a march of slow tempo and stately character composed or played to accompany the bridal procession

wedding ring *n* (14c) : a ring often of plain gold or platinum given by the groom to the bride during the wedding service; *also* : a similar ring given by the bride to the groom in a double-ring service

we·del \'vād-ᵊl\ *vi* [back-formation fr. *wedeln*] (ca. 1966) : to ski downhill by means of wedeln

we·deln \'vād-ᵊln\ *n* [G, fr. *wedeln* to fan, wag the tail, fr. *wedel* fan, tail, fr. OHG *wadal*; akin to ON *vēli* bird's tail] (ca. 1957) : a style of skiing in which a skier moves the rear of the skis quickly from side to side while following the fall line

1wedge \'wej\ *n* [ME *wegge*, fr. OE *wecg*; akin to OHG *wecki* wedge, Lith *vagis*] (bef. 12c) **1** : a piece of a substance (as wood or iron) that tapers to a thin edge and is used for splitting wood and rocks, raising heavy bodies, or for tightening by being driven into something **2 a** : something (as a policy) causing a breach or separation **b** : something used to initiate an action or development **3** : something wedge-shaped: as **a** : an array of troops or tanks in the form of a wedge **b** : the wedge-shaped stroke in cuneiform characters **c** : a shoe having a heel extending from the back of the shoe to the front of the shank and a tread formed by an extension of the sole **d** : an iron golf club with a broad low-angled face for maximum loft

2wedge *vb* **wedged; wedg·ing** *vt* (15c) **1** : to fasten or tighten by driving in a wedge **2 a** : to force or press (something) into a narrow space : CRAM **b** : to force (one's way) into or through ⟨*wedged* his way into the crowd⟩ **3** : to separate or force apart with or as if with a wedge ~ *vi* : to become wedged

wedged \'wejd, 'wej-əd\ *adj* (ca. 1552) : shaped like a wedge

wedg·ie \'wej-ē\ *n* [*wedge* + *-ie*] (ca. 1938) : a shoe having a wedge-shaped piece serving as the heel and joining the half sole to form a continuous flat undersurface

Wedg·wood \'wej-,wủd\ *trademark* — used for ceramic wares (as bone china or jasper)

wedgy \'wej-ē\ *adj* (1799) : resembling a wedge in shape

wed·lock \'wed-,läk\ *n* [ME *wedlok*, fr. OE *wedlāc* marriage bond, fr. *wedd* pledge + *-lāc*, suffix denoting activity] (13c) : the state of being married : MARRIAGE, MATRIMONY — **out of wedlock** : with the natural parents not legally married to each other

Wednes·day \'wenz-dē, -(,)dā; *Brit also* 'wed-ᵊnz-\ *n* [ME, fr. OE *wōdnesdæg*; (akin to ON *ōthinsdagr* Wednesday); akin to OE *Wōden* Odin and *dæg* day] (bef. 12c) : the fourth day of the week — **Wednes·days** \-dēz, -(,)dāz\ *adv*

wee \'wē\ *adj* [ME *we*, fr. *we*, n., little bit, fr. OE *wǣge* weight; akin to OE *wegan* to move, weigh — more at WAY] (15c) **1** : very small : DIMINUTIVE **2** : very early ⟨~ hours of the morning⟩

1weed \'wēd\ *n* [ME, fr. OE *wēod* weed, herb; akin to OS *wiod* weed] (bef. 12c) **1 a** (1) : a plant that is not valued where it is growing and is usu. of rank growth; *esp* : one that tends to overgrow or choke out more desirable plants (2) : a weedy growth of plants **b** : an aquatic plant; *esp* : SEAWEED **c** (1) : TOBACCO (2) : MARIJUANA **2 a** : an obnoxious growth, thing, or person **b** : something like a weed in detrimental quality; *esp* : an animal unfit to breed from

2weed *vi* (12c) : to remove weeds or something harmful ~ *vt* **1 a** : to clear of weeds ⟨~ a garden⟩ **b** (1) : to free from something hurtful or offensive (2) : to remove the less desirable portions of **2** : to get rid of (something harmful or superfluous) — often used with *out*

[3]**weed** *n* [ME *wede,* fr. OE *wǣd, gewǣde;* akin to ON *vāth* cloth, clothing, Lith *austi* to weave] (bef. 12c) **1 :** GARMENT — often used in pl. **2 a :** dress worn as a sign of mourning (as by a widow) — usu. used in pl. **b :** a band of crape worn on a man's hat as a sign of mourning — usu. used in pl.
weed·er \ˈwēd-ər\ *n* (15c) **:** one that weeds; *specif* **:** any of various devices for removing weeds from an area
weedy \ˈwēd-ē\ *adj* (15c) **1 :** abounding with or consisting of weeds **2 :** resembling a weed esp. in rank growth or ready propagation **3 :** noticeably lean and scrawny **:** LANKY — **weed·i·ness** *n*
week \ˈwēk\ *n* [ME *weke,* fr. OE *wicu, wucu;* akin to OHG *wehha* week, L *vicis* change, alternation] (bef. 12c) **1 a :** one of a series of 7-day cycles used in various calendars **b** (1) **:** a week beginning with a specified day or containing a specified holiday ⟨the ~ of the 18th⟩ ⟨Easter ~⟩ (2) **:** a week appointed for public recognition of some cause ⟨Fire Prevention *Week*⟩ **2 a :** any seven consecutive days **b :** a series of regular working, business, or school days during each 7-day period **3 :** a time seven days before or after a specified day
week·day \ˈwēk-ˌdā\ *n* (15c) **:** a day of the week except Sunday or sometimes except Saturday and Sunday
week·days \-ˌdāz\ *adv* (1777) **:** on weekdays repeatedly **:** on any weekday ⟨takes a bus ~⟩
[1]**week·end** \ˈwē-ˌkend\ *n* (1878) **:** the end of the week; *specif* **:** the period between the close of one working or business or school week and the beginning of the next
[2]**weekend** *vi* (1901) **:** to spend the weekend
weekend bag *n* (1921) **:** a traveling bag of a size to carry clothing and personal articles for a weekend trip — called also *weekend case*
week·end·er \ˈwē-ˈken-dər\ *n* (ca. 1880) **1 :** one that vacations or visits for a weekend **2 :** WEEKEND BAG
week·ends \ˈwē-ˌken(d)z\ *adv* (1946) **:** on weekends repeatedly **:** on any weekend ⟨travels ~⟩
[1]**week·ly** \ˈwē-klē\ *adv* (15c) **:** every week **:** once a week **:** by the week
[2]**weekly** *adj* (15c) **1 :** occurring, appearing, or done weekly **2 :** reckoned by the week
[3]**weekly** *n, pl* **weeklies** (1833) **:** a weekly newspaper or periodical
week·night \ˈwēk-ˌnīt\ *n* (1859) **:** a weekday night
week·nights \-ˌnīts\ *adv* (1965) **:** on weeknights repeatedly **:** on any weeknight
ween \ˈwēn\ *vt* [ME *wenen,* fr. OE *wēnan;* akin to ON *væna* to hope, L *venus* love, charm — more at WIN] *archaic* (bef. 12c) **:** IMAGINE
wee·nie *var of* WIENIE
wee·ny \ˈwē-nē\ *also* **ween·sy** \ˈwēn(t)-sē\ *adj* [alter. of *wee*] (ca. 1781) **:** exceptionally small **:** TINY
weep \ˈwēp\ *vb* **wept** \ˈwept\; **weep·ing** [ME *wepen,* fr. OE *wēpan;* akin to OHG *wuoffan* to weep, OSlav *vabiti* to call to] *vt* (bef. 12c) **1 :** to express deep sorrow for usu. by shedding tears **:** BEWAIL **2 :** to pour forth (tears) from the eyes **3 :** to exude (a fluid) slowly **:** OOZE ~ *vi* **1 :** to express passion (as grief) by shedding tears **2 a :** to give off or leak fluid slowly **:** OOZE **b** *of a fluid* **:** to flow sluggishly or in drops **3 :** to droop over **:** BEND
weep·er \ˈwē-pər\ *n* (14c) **1 a :** one that weeps **b :** a professional mourner **2 :** a small statue of a figure in mourning on a funeral monument **3 :** a badge of mourning worn esp. in the 18th and 19th centuries **4** *pl* **:** long and flowing side-whiskers **5 :** TEARJERKER
weep hole *n* (1851) **:** a hole (as in a wall or foundation) that is designed to drain off accumulated water
weep·ing \ˈwē-piŋ\ *adj* (bef. 12c) **1 :** TEARFUL **2** *archaic* **:** RAINY **3 :** having slender pendent branches
weeping willow *n* (ca. 1731) **:** an Asian willow (*Salix babylonica*) with weeping branches
weepy \ˈwē-pē\ *adj* (1602) **:** inclined to weep **:** TEARFUL
weet \ˈwēt\ *vb* [ME *weten,* alter. of *witen* — more at WIT] *archaic* (1547) **:** KNOW
wee·vil \ˈwē-vəl\ *n* [ME *wevel,* fr. OE *wifel;* akin to OHG *wibil* beetle, OE *wefan* to weave] (bef. 12c) **:** any of a taxon (suborder Rhynchophora) of beetles which have the head prolonged into a more or less distinct snout and which include many that are injurious esp. as larvae to nuts, fruit, and grain or to living plants; *esp* **:** any of a family (Curculionidae) having a well-developed snout curved downward with the jaws at the tip and clubbed usu. elbowed antennae — **wee·vily** *or* **wee·vil·ly** \ˈwēv-(ə-)lē\ *adj*
weft \ˈweft\ *n* [ME, fr. OE; akin to ON *veptr* weft, OE *wefan* to weave — more at WEAVE] (bef. 12c) **1 a :** [1]WOOF 1a **b :** yarn used for the woof **2 :** WEB, FABRIC; *also* **:** an article of woven fabric
weft–knit·ted \-ˌnit-əd\ *adj* (1943) **:** produced in machine knitting with the yarns running crosswise or in a circle
wei·ge·la \wī-ˈjē-lə\ *n* [NL, fr. Christian E. *Weigel* †1831 Ger. physician] (ca. 1879) **:** any of a genus (*Weigela*) of showy shrubs of the honeysuckle family; *esp* **:** one (*W. florida*) of China widely grown for its pink or red flowers
[1]**weigh** \ˈwā\ *vb* [ME *weyen,* fr. OE *wegan* to move, carry, weigh — more at WAY] *vt* (bef. 12c) **1 :** to ascertain the heaviness of by or as if by a balance **2 a :** OUTWEIGH **b :** COUNTERBALANCE **c :** to make heavy **:** WEIGHT **3 :** to consider carefully esp. by balancing opposing factors or aspects in order to reach a choice or conclusion **:** EVALUATE **4 :** to heave up (an anchor) preparatory to sailing **5 :** to measure or apportion (a definite quantity) on or as if on a scales ~ *vi* **1 a :** to have a certain heaviness **:** experience a specific force of attraction due to gravity **b :** to register a weight (as on a scales) — used with *in* or *out;* compare WEIGH IN **2 :** to merit consideration as important **:** COUNT ⟨evidence will ~ heavily against him⟩ **3 a :** to press down with or as if with a heavy weight **b :** to have a saddening or disheartening effect **4 :** to weigh anchor ***syn*** see CONSIDER — **weigh·able** \ˈwā-ə-bəl\ *adj* — **weigh·er** *n*
[2]**weigh** *n* [alter. of *way*] (1785) **:** WAY — used in the phrase *under weigh*
weigh down *vt* (14c) **1 :** to cause to bend down **:** OVERBURDEN **2 :** OPPRESS, DEPRESS
weigh–in \ˈwā-ˌin\ *n* (1939) **:** an act or instance of weighing in as a contestant esp. in sport
weigh in \(ˈ)wā-ˈin\ *vi* (1879) **1 :** to have oneself or one's possessions (as baggage) weighed; *esp* **:** to have oneself weighed in connection with an athletic contest **2 :** to enter as a participant
[1]**weight** \ˈwāt\ *n* [ME *wight, weght,* fr. OE *wiht;* akin to ON *vætt* weight, OE *wegan* to weigh] (bef. 12c) **1 a :** the amount that a thing weighs **b** (1) **:** the standard or established amount that a thing should weigh (2) **:** one of the classes into which contestants in a sports event are divided according to body weight (3) **:** poundage required to be carried by a horse in a handicap race **2 a :** a quantity or thing weighing a fixed and usu. specified amount **b :** a heavy object (as a metal ball) thrown, put, or lifted as an athletic exercise or contest **3 a :** a unit of weight or mass — see METRIC SYSTEM table **b :** a piece of material (as metal) of known specified weight for use in weighing articles **c :** a system of related units of weight **4 a :** something heavy **:** LOAD **b :** a heavy object to hold or press something down or to counterbalance **5 a :** BURDEN, PRESSURE **b :** the quality or state of being ponderous **c :** CORPULENCE **6 a :** relative heaviness **:** MASS **b :** the force with which a body is attracted toward the earth or a celestial body by gravitation and which is equal to the product of the mass and the local gravitational acceleration **7 a :** the relative importance or authority accorded something **b :** measurable influence esp. on others **8 :** overpowering force **9 :** the quality (as lightness) that makes a fabric or garment suitable for a particular use or season — often used in combination ⟨summer-*weight*⟩ **10 :** a numerical coefficient assigned to an item to express its relative importance in a frequency distribution ***syn*** see IMPORTANCE, INFLUENCE
[2]**weight** *vt* (1647) **1 :** to oppress with a burden ⟨~*ed* down with cares⟩ **2 a :** to load or make heavy with or as if with a weight **b :** to increase in heaviness by adding an ingredient **3 a :** WEIGH 1 **b :** to feel the weight of **:** HEFT **4 :** to assign a statistical weight to **5 :** to cause to incline in a particular direction by manipulation ⟨the tax structure . . . which was ~*ed* so heavily in favor of the upper classes —A. S. Link⟩ **6 :** to shift the burden of weight upon ⟨~ the inside ski⟩
weight·ed *adj* (1732) **1 :** made heavy **:** LOADED ⟨~ silk⟩ **2 a :** having a statistical weight attached ⟨a ~ test score⟩ **b :** compiled or calculated from weighted data ⟨a ~ mean⟩
weight·less \ˈwāt-ləs\ *adj* (1547) **:** having little weight **:** lacking apparent gravitational pull — **weight·less·ly** *adv* — **weight·less·ness** *n*
weight lifter *n* (1897) **:** one that lifts barbells in competition or as an exercise — **weight lifting** *n*
weight man *n* (ca. 1949) **:** an athlete who competes in any of the field events in which a weight is thrown or put
weighty \ˈwāt-ē\ *adj* **weight·i·er; -est** (15c) **1 a :** of much importance or consequence **:** MOMENTOUS **b :** SOLEMN **2 a :** weighing a considerable amount **b :** heavy in proportion to its bulk ⟨~ metal⟩ **3 :** POWERFUL, TELLING ⟨~ arguments⟩ ***syn*** see HEAVY — **weight·i·ly** \ˈwāt-ᵊl-ē\ *adv* — **weight·i·ness** \ˈwāt-ē-nəs\ *n*
wei·ma·ra·ner \ˌvī-mə-ˈrän-ər, ˌwī-; ˈvī-mə-ˌ, ˈwī-\ *n* [G, fr. *Weimar,* Germany] (ca. 1943) **:** any of a German breed of large gray short-haired sporting dogs
wei·ner \ˈwē-nər, ˈwē-nē, ˈwin-ē\ *var of* WIENER
weir \ˈwa(ə)r, ˈwe(ə)r, ˈwi(ə)r\ *n* [ME *were,* fr. OE *wer;* akin to ON *ver* fishing place, OHG *werien, werren* to defend] (bef. 12c) **1 :** a fence or enclosure set in a waterway for taking fish **2 :** a dam in a stream to raise the water level or divert its flow
[1]**weird** \ˈwi(ə)rd\ *n* [ME *wird, werd,* fr. OE *wyrd;* akin to ON *urthr* fate, OE *weorthan* to become — more at WORTH] (bef. 12c) **1 :** FATE, DESTINY; *esp* **:** ill fortune **2 :** SOOTHSAYER
[2]**weird** *adj* (15c) **1 :** of, relating to, or caused by witchcraft or the supernatural **:** MAGICAL **2 :** of strange or extraordinary character **:** ODD, FANTASTIC — **weird·ly** *adv* — **weird·ness** *n*
syn WEIRD, EERIE, UNCANNY mean mysteriously strange or fantastic. WEIRD may imply an unearthly or supernatural strangeness or it may stress queerness or oddness; EERIE suggests an uneasy or fearful consciousness that mysterious and malign powers are at work; UNCANNY implies disquieting strangeness or mysteriousness.
weird·ie \ˈwi(ə)rd-ē\ *or* **weirdy** *n, pl* **weird·ies** (ca. 1894) **:** one that is extraordinarily strange, eccentric, or queer
weirdo \ˈwi(ə)rd-(ˌ)ō\ *n, pl* **weird·os** (ca. 1955) **:** WEIRDIE
Weird Sisters *n pl* **:** FATES
wei·sen·hei·mer *var of* WISENHEIMER
Weis·mann·ism \ˈwī-smə-ˌniz-əm, ˈvī-\ *n* (1894) **:** the theories of heredity proposed by August Weismann stressing particularly the continuity of the germ plasm and the separateness of the germ cells and soma
weka \ˈwek-ə\ *n* [Maori] (1845) **:** a flightless New Zealand rail (*Gallirallus australis*)
welch \ˈwelch\, **welcher** *var of* WELSH, WELSHER
Welch \ˈwelch\ *var of* WELSH
[1]**wel·come** \ˈwel-kəm\ *interj* [ME, alter. of *wilcume,* fr. OE, fr. *wilcuma* desirable guest; akin to OHG *willicomo* desirable guest, OE *willa, will* desire, *cuman* to come — more at WILL, COME] (bef. 12c) — used to express a greeting to a guest or newcomer upon his arrival
[2]**welcome** *vt* **wel·comed; wel·com·ing** (bef. 12c) **1 :** to greet hospitably and with courtesy or cordiality **2 :** to accept with pleasure the occurrence of ⟨~*s* danger⟩ — **wel·com·er** *n*
[3]**welcome** *adj* (bef. 12c) **1 :** received gladly into one's presence or companionship ⟨was always ~ in their home⟩ **2 :** giving pleasure **:** received with gladness or delight esp. in response to a need ⟨a ~ relief⟩ **3 :** willingly permitted or admitted ⟨he was ~ to come and go —W. M. Thackeray⟩ **4** — used in the phrase "You're welcome" as a reply to an expression of thanks — **wel·come·ly** *adv* — **wel·come·ness** *n*
[4]**welcome** *n* (1525) **:** a greeting or reception upon arrival
[1]**weld** \ˈweld\ *vb* [alter. of obs. E *well* to weld, fr. ME *wellen* to boil, well, weld] *vi* (1599) **:** to become or be capable of being welded ~ *vt* **1 a :** to unite (metallic parts) by heating and allowing the metals to flow together or by hammering or compressing with or without previous heating **b :** to unite (plastics) in a similar manner by heating **c :** to repair (as an article) by this method **d :** to produce or create as if by such a process **2 :** to unite or reunite closely or intimately — **weld-**

able \'wel-də-bəl\ *adj*
²**weld** *n* (1831)   **1** : a welded joint   **2** : union by welding : the state or condition of being welded
weld·er \'wel-dər\ *n* (ca. 1828) : one that welds: as   **a** *or* **weldor** : one whose work is welding   **b** : a machine used in welding
weld·ment \'wel(d)-mənt\ *n* (1941) : a unit formed by welding together an assembly of pieces
¹**wel·fare** \'wel-,fa(ə)r, -,fe(ə)r\ *n* [ME, fr. the phrase *wel faren* to fare well] (14c)   **1** : the state of doing well esp. in respect to good fortune, happiness, well-being, or prosperity   **2** : WELFARE WORK   **3** : RELIEF 2b
²**welfare** *adj* (1904)   **1** : of, relating to, or concerned with welfare and esp. with improvement of the welfare of disadvantaged social groups ⟨~ legislation⟩   **2** : receiving public welfare benefits ⟨~ mothers⟩
welfare state *n* (1945)   **1** : a social system based on the assumption by a political state of primary responsibility for the individual and social welfare of its citizens   **2** : a nation or state characterized by the operation of the welfare state system
welfare work *n* (ca. 1908) : organized efforts by a community or organization for the social betterment of a group in society — **welfare worker** *n*
wel·far·ism \'wel-,fa(ə)r-,iz-əm, -,fe(ə)r-\ *n* (1949) : the complex of policies, attitudes, and beliefs associated with the welfare state — **wel·far·ist** \-əst\ *n or adj*
wel·kin \'wel-kən\ *n* [ME, lit., cloud, fr. OE *wolcen*; akin to OHG *wol-*

kan cloud, OSlav *vlaga* moisture] (12c)   **1   a** : the vault of the sky : FIRMAMENT   **b** : the celestial abode of God or the gods : HEAVEN   **2** : the upper atmosphere
¹**well** \'wel\ *n* [ME *welle*, fr. OE *welle*; akin to OHG *wella* wave, OE *weallan* to bubble, boil, L *volvere* to roll — more at VOLUBLE] (bef. 12c)   **1   a** : an issue of water from the earth : a pool fed by a spring   **b** : FOUNTAIN, WELLSPRING   **2** : a pit or hole sunk into the earth to reach a supply of water   **3   a** : an enclosure in the middle of a ship's hold to protect from damage and facilitate the inspection of the pumps   **b** : a compartment in the hold of a fishing boat in which fish are kept alive   **4** : a shaft or hole sunk to obtain oil, brine, or gas   **5** : an open space extending vertically through floors of a structure   **6** : a space having a construction or shape suggesting a well for water   **7   a** : something resembling a well in being damp, cool, deep, or dark   **b** : a deep vertical hole   **c** : a source from which something may be drawn as needed   **8** : a pronounced minimum of a variable in physics ⟨a potential ~⟩
²**well** *vi* (bef. 12c)   **1** : to rise to the surface and usu. flow forth ⟨tears ~ed from her eyes⟩   **2** : to rise to the surface like a flood of liquid ⟨longing ~ed up in his breast⟩ **~** *vt* : to emit in a copious free flow
³**well** *adv* **bet·ter** \'bet-ər\; **best** \'best\ [ME *wel*, fr. OE; akin to OHG *wela* well, OE *wyllan* to wish — more at WILL] (bef. 12c)   **1   a** : in a good or proper manner : JUSTLY, RIGHTLY   **b** : satisfactorily with respect to conduct or action ⟨did ~ in math⟩   **2** : in a kindly or friendly

WEIGHTS AND MEASURES[1]

UNIT	ABBR. OR SYMBOL	EQUIVALENTS IN OTHER UNITS OF SAME SYSTEM	METRIC EQUIVALENT
WEIGHT *avoirdupois*			
ton			
short ton		20 short hundredweight, 2000 pounds	0.907 metric ton
long ton		20 long hundredweight, 2240 pounds	1.016 metric tons
hundredweight	cwt		
short hundredweight		100 pounds, 0.05 short ton	45.359 kilograms
long hundredweight		112 pounds, 0.05 long ton	50.802 kilograms
pound	lb *or* lb avdp *also* #	16 ounces, 7000 grains	0.454 kilogram
ounce	oz *or* oz avdp	16 drams, 437.5 grains	28.350 grams
dram	dr *or* dr avdp	27.344 grains, 0.0625 ounce	1.772 grams
grain	gr	0.037 dram, 0.002286 ounce	0.0648 gram
troy			
pound	lb t	12 ounces, 240 pennyweight, 5760 grains	0.373 kilogram
ounce	oz t	20 pennyweight, 480 grains	31.103 grams
pennyweight	dwt *also* pwt	24 grains, 0.05 ounce	1.555 grams
grain	gr	0.042 pennyweight, 0.002083 ounce	0.0648 gram
apothecaries'			
pound	lb ap	12 ounces, 5760 grains	0.373 kilogram
ounce	oz ap *or* ℥	8 drams, 480 grains	31.103 grams
dram	dr ap *or* ℨ	3 scruples, 60 grains	3.888 grams
scruple	s ap *or* ℈	20 grains, 0.333 dram	1.296 grams
grain	gr	0.05 scruple, 0.002083 ounce, 0.0166 dram	0.0648 grams
CAPACITY *U.S. liquid measure*			
gallon	gal	4 quarts (231 cubic inches)	3.785 liters
quart	qt	2 pints (57.75 cubic inches)	0.946 liter
pint	pt	4 gills (28.875 cubic inches)	0.473 liter
gill	gi	4 fluidounces (7.219 cubic inches)	118.294 milliliters
fluidounce	fl oz *or* f ℥	8 fluidrams (1.805 cubic inches)	29.573 milliliters
fluidram	fl dr *or* f ℨ	60 minims (0.226 cubic inch)	3.697 milliliters
minim	min *or* ♏	¹⁄₆₀ fluidram (0.003760 cubic inch)	0.061610 milliliter
U.S. dry measure			
bushel	bu	4 pecks (2150.42 cubic inches)	35.239 liters
peck	pk	8 quarts (537.605 cubic inches)	8.810 liters
quart	qt	2 pints (67.201 cubic inches)	1.101 liters
pint	pt	½ quart (33.600 cubic inches)	0.551 liter
British imperial liquid and dry measure			
bushel	bu	4 pecks (2219.36 cubic inches)	0.036 cubic meter
peck	pk	2 gallons (554.84 cubic inches)	0.0091 cubic meter
gallon	gal	4 quarts (277.420 cubic inches)	4.546 liters
quart	qt	2 pints (69.355 cubic inches)	1.136 liters
pint	pt	4 gills (34.678 cubic inches)	568.26 cubic centimeters
gill	gi	5 fluidounces (8.669 cubic inches)	142.066 cubic centimeters
fluidounce	fl oz *or* f ℥	8 fluidrams (1.7339 cubic inches)	28.412 cubic centimeters
fluidram	fl dr *or* f ℨ	60 minims (0.216734 cubic inch)	3.5516 cubic centimeters
minim	min *or* ♏	¹⁄₆₀ fluidram (0.003612 cubic inch)	0.059194 cubic centimeters
LENGTH			
mile	mi	5280 feet, 320 rods, 1760 yards	1.609 kilometers
rod	rd	5.50 yards, 16.5 feet	5.029 meters
yard	yd	3 feet, 36 inches	0.9144 meter
foot	ft *or* '	12 inches, 0.333 yard	30.48 centimeters
inch	in *or* "	0.083 foot, 0.028 yard	2.54 centimeters
AREA			
square mile	sq mi *or* mi²	640 acres, 102,400 square rods	2.590 square kilometers
acre		4840 square yards, 43,560 square feet	0.405 hectare, 4047 square meters
square rod	sq rd *or* rd²	30.25 square yards, 0.00625 acre	25.293 square meters
square yard	sq yd *or* yd²	1296 square inches, 9 square feet	0.836 square meter
square foot	sq ft *or* ft²	144 square inches, 0.111 square yard	0.093 square meter
square inch	sq in *or* in²	0.0069 square foot, 0.00077 square yard	6.452 square centimeters
VOLUME			
cubic yard	cu yd *or* yd³	27 cubic feet, 46,656 cubic inches	0.765 cubic meter
cubic foot	cu ft *or* ft³	1728 cubic inches, 0.0370 cubic yard	0.028 cubic meter
cubic inch	cu in *or* in³	0.00058 cubic foot, 0.000021 cubic yard	16.387 cubic centimeters

[1]For U.S. equivalents of metric units see Metric System table

manner ⟨spoke ~ of your idea⟩ 3 a : with skill or aptitude : EXPERTLY ⟨paints ~⟩ b : SATISFACTORILY c : with good appearance or effect : ELEGANTLY ⟨carried himself ~⟩ 4 : with careful or close attention : ATTENTIVELY 5 : to a high degree ⟨~ deserved the honor⟩ ⟨*well*-equipped kitchen⟩ 6 : FULLY, QUITE ⟨~ worth the price⟩ 7 a : in a way appropriate to the facts or circumstances : FITTINGLY, RIGHTLY b : in a prudent manner : SENSIBLY — used with *do* 8 : in accordance with the occasion or circumstances : with propriety or good reason ⟨cannot ~ refuse⟩ 9 a : as one could wish : FAVORABLY b : with material success : ADVANTAGEOUSLY ⟨married ~⟩ 10 a : EASILY, READILY ⟨could ~ afford a new car⟩ b : in all likelihood : INDEED ⟨it may ~ be true⟩ 11 : in a prosperous or affluent manner ⟨he lives ~⟩ 12 : to an extent approaching completeness : THOROUGHLY ⟨after being ~ dried with a sponge⟩ 13 : without doubt or question : CLEARLY ⟨~ knew the penalty⟩ 14 : in a familiar manner ⟨knew her ~⟩ 15 : to a large extent or degree : CONSIDERABLY, FAR ⟨~ over a million⟩ ***usage*** see GOOD — **as well** 1 : in addition : ALSO ⟨there were other features *as well*⟩ 2 : to the same extent or degree : as much ⟨open *as well* to the poor as to the rich⟩ 3 : with equivalent or comparable effect ⟨might just *as well* have stayed home⟩

4**well** *interj* (bef. 12c) 1 — used to indicate resumption of discourse or to introduce a remark 2 — used to express surprise or expostulation

5**well** *adj* (bef. 12c) 1 a : PROSPEROUS, WELL-OFF b : being in satisfactory condition or circumstances 2 : being in good standing or favor 3 : SATISFACTORY, PLEASING ⟨all's ~ that ends well⟩ 4 : ADVISABLE, DESIRABLE ⟨it might be ~ for you to leave⟩ 5 a : free or recovered from infirmity or disease : HEALTHY ⟨a ~ man⟩ b : completely cured or healed ⟨the wound is nearly ~⟩ 6 : pleasing or satisfactory in appearance 7 : being a cause for thankfulness : FORTUNATE ⟨it is ~ that this has happened⟩ ***syn*** see HEALTHY — **well•ness** *n*

we'll \(ˌ)wē(ə)l, wil\ : we will : we shall

well–ad•vised \ˌwel-əd-ˈvīzd\ *adj* (14c) 1 : acting with wisdom, wise counsel, or proper deliberation : PRUDENT 2 : resulting from, based on, or showing careful deliberation or wise counsel ⟨~ plans⟩

well–ap•point•ed \ˌwel-ə-ˈpȯint-əd\ *adj* (ca. 1530) : having good and complete equipment : properly fitted out ⟨a ~ house⟩

wel•la•way \ˌwel-ə-ˈwā, ˈwel-ə-ˌ\ *interj* [ME *welaway*, fr. OE *weilāwei*, lit., woe! lo! woe!, alter. of *wālāwā*, fr. *wā* woe + *lā* lo + *wā* woe — more at WOE] *archaic* (bef. 12c) — used to express sorrow or lamentation

well–be•ing \ˈwel-ˈbē-iŋ\ *n* (1613) : the state of being happy, healthy, or prosperous : WELFARE

well–be•loved \ˌwel-bi-ˈləvd\ *adj* (14c) 1 : sincerely and deeply loved ⟨my ~ wife⟩ 2 : sincerely respected — used in various ceremonial forms of address

well•born \ˈwel-ˈbȯ(ə)rn\ *adj* (bef. 12c) : born of good stock either socially or genetically

well–bred \-ˈbred\ *adj* (1597) 1 : having or displaying good breeding : REFINED 2 : having a good pedigree ⟨~ swine⟩

well–con•di•tioned \ˌwel-kən-ˈdish-ənd\ *adj* (15c) 1 : characterized by proper disposition, morals, or behavior 2 : having a good physical condition : SOUND

well–de•fined \ˌwel-di-ˈfīnd\ *adj* (1704) 1 : having clearly distinguishable limits, boundaries, or features ⟨a ~ scar⟩ 2 : clearly stated or described ⟨~ policies⟩

well–dis•posed \-dis-ˈpōzd\ *adj* (14c) : having a good disposition; *esp* : disposed to be friendly, favorable, or sympathetic

well–done \ˈwel-ˈdən\ *adj* (15c) 1 : rightly or properly performed 2 : cooked thoroughly

Wel•ler•ism \ˈwel-ə-ˌriz-əm\ *n* [Sam *Weller*, witty servant of Mr. Pickwick in the story *Pickwick Papers* (1836-37) by Charles Dickens] (1854) : an expression of comparison comprising a usu. well-known quotation followed by a facetious sequel (as " 'every one to his own taste,' said the old woman as she kissed the cow")

well–fa•vored \ˈwel-ˈfā-vərd\ *adj* (15c) : GOOD-LOOKING, HANDSOME — **well–fa•vored•ness** *n*

well–fixed \-ˈfikst\ *adj* (1822) : having plenty of money or property

well–found \-ˈfau̇nd\ *adj* (1793) : fully furnished : properly equipped ⟨a ~ ship⟩

well–found•ed \-ˈfau̇n-dəd\ *adj* (14c) : based on excellent reasoning, information, judgment, or grounds

well–groomed \-ˈgrümd, -ˈgru̇md\ *adj* (1886) 1 : well-dressed and scrupulously neat ⟨~ men⟩ 2 : made neat, tidy, and attractive down to the smallest details ⟨a ~ lawn⟩

well–ground•ed \-ˈgrau̇n-dəd\ *adj* (14c) : having a firm foundation ⟨~ in Latin and Greek⟩

well–han•dled \-ˈhan-dᵊld\ *adj* (15c) 1 : managed or administered efficiently 2 : having been handled a great deal ⟨~ goods for sale⟩

well•head \ˈwel-ˌhed\ *n* (14c) 1 : the source of a spring or a stream 2 : principal source : FOUNTAINHEAD 3 : the top of or a structure built over a well

wellhead price *n* (1953) : the price less transportation costs charged by the producer for petroleum or natural gas

well–heeled \-ˈhē(ə)ld\ *adj* (1897) : having plenty of money : WELL-FIXED

well–in•formed \-in-ˈfȯ(ə)rmd\ *adj* (15c) 1 : having extensive knowledge esp. of current topics and events 2 : thoroughly knowledgeable in a particular subject

Wel•ling•ton \ˈwel-iŋ-tən\ *n* [Arthur Wellesley, 1st Duke of *Wellington*] (1817) : a leather boot having a loose top with the front usu. coming above the knee

well–in•ten•tioned \ˌwel-in-ˈten-chənd\ *adj* (1598) : WELL-MEANING

well–knit \ˈwel-ˈnit\ *adj* (15c) : firmly knit ⟨a ~ group⟩; *esp* : firmly and strongly constructed, compacted, or framed ⟨a ~ drama⟩

well–known \-ˈnōn\ *adj* (15c) : fully or widely known

well–mean•ing \-ˈmē-niŋ\ *adj* (14c) : having or based on good intentions ⟨~ but misguided idealists⟩

well–nigh \-ˈnī\ *adv* (12c) : ALMOST, NEARLY ⟨~ impossible⟩

well–off \-ˈȯf\ *adj* (1733) 1 : being in good condition or favorable circumstances ⟨doesn't know when he's ~⟩ 2 : having no lack — usu. used with *for* 3 a : being in easy or affluent circumstances : WELL-TO-DO b : suggesting prosperity ⟨the house had a sleek ~ look⟩

well–or•dered \-ˈȯrd-ərd\ *adj* (1606) 1 : having an orderly procedure or arrangement ⟨a ~ household⟩ 2 : partially ordered with every subset containing a first element and exactly one of the relationships "greater than", "less than", or "equal to" holding for any given pair of elements — **well–or•der•ing** \-ˈȯrd-(ə-)riŋ\ *n*

well–read \-ˈred\ *adj* (1596) : well informed or deeply versed through reading ⟨~ in history⟩

well–round•ed \-ˈrau̇n-dəd\ *adj* (ca. 1875) : fully or broadly developed: as a : having a broad educational background ⟨schools that turn out ~ graduates⟩ b : COMPREHENSIVE ⟨a ~ program of activities⟩

well–set \-ˈset\ *adj* (14c) 1 : well or firmly established ⟨~ in his own values —William Johnson⟩ 2 : strongly built ⟨a ~ athlete⟩

well–spo•ken \ˈwel-ˈspō-kən\ *adj* (15c) 1 : speaking well, fitly, or courteously 2 : spoken with propriety ⟨~ words⟩

well•spring \-ˌspriŋ\ *n* (bef. 12c) 1 : a source of continual supply ⟨a ~ of information⟩ 2 : FOUNTAINHEAD 1

well–tak•en \-ˈtā-kən\ *adj* (1761) : WELL-GROUNDED, JUSTIFIABLE ⟨your point is ~⟩

well–thought–of \wel-ˈthȯt-ˌəv, -ˌäv\ *adj* (1579) : being of good repute

well–timed \ˈwel-ˈtīmd\ *adj* (1635) : happening at an opportune moment : TIMELY ⟨a ~ announcement⟩

well–to–do \ˌwel-tə-ˈdü\ *adj* (1825) : having more than adequate financial resources : PROSPEROUS ⟨a ~ family⟩

well–turned \ˈwel-ˈtərnd\ *adj* (1616) 1 : symmetrically shaped or rounded : SHAPELY 2 : concisely and appropriately expressed ⟨a ~ phrase⟩ 3 : expertly rounded or turned ⟨a ~ column⟩

well–wish•er \ˈwel-ˌwish-ər, -ˈwish-\ *n* (1590) : one that wishes well to another — **well–wish•ing** \-iŋ\ *adj or n*

well–worn \-ˈwō(ə)rn, -ˈwȯ(ə)rn\ *adj* (1621) 1 a : having been much used or worn ⟨~ shoes⟩ b : made trite by overuse : HACKNEYED ⟨a ~ quotation⟩ 2 *archaic* : worn well or properly

Wels•bach \ˈwelz-ˌbak, -ˌbäk\ *trademark* — used for a burner for producing gaslight by the combustion of a mixture of air and gas or vapor to heat to incandescence a gas mantle or for the mantle used with such a burner

welsh \ˈwelsh, ˈwelch\ *vi* [prob. fr. *Welsh*, adj.] (1857) 1 : to avoid payment — used with *on* ⟨~*ed* on his debts⟩ 2 : to break one's word : RENEGE ⟨~*ed* on his promises⟩ — **welsh•er** *n*

Welsh \ˈwelsh *also* ˈwelch\ *n* [ME *Walsche*, *Welsse*, fr. *walisch*, *welisch*, adj., Welsh, fr. OE *wælisc*, *welisc* Celtic, Welsh, foreign, fr. OE *Wealh* Celt, Welshman, foreigner, of Celt origin; akin to the source of L *Volcae*, a Celtic people of southeastern Gaul] (bef. 12c) 1 : the Celtic language of the Welsh people 2 *pl in constr* : the natives or inhabitants of Wales 3 : a breed of cattle or of swine developed in Wales — **Welsh** *adj*

Welsh corgi *n* (1926) : a short-legged long-backed dog with foxy head of either of two breeds of Welsh origin: a : CARDIGAN WELSH CORGI b : PEMBROKE WELSH CORGI

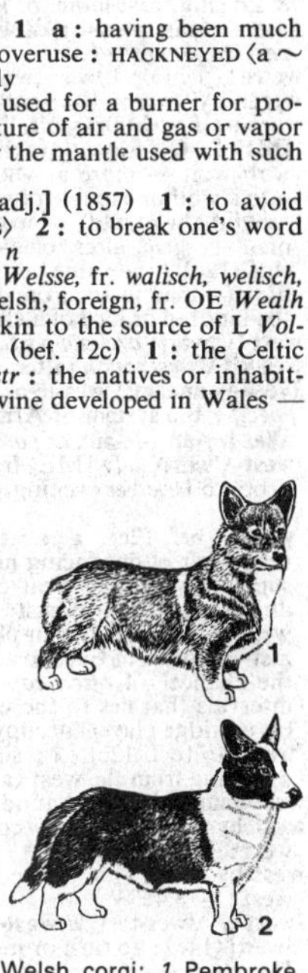

Welsh corgi: *1* Pembroke, *2* Cardigan

Welsh•man \-mən\ *n* (bef. 12c) : a native or inhabitant of Wales

Welsh rabbit *n* (1725) : melted often seasoned cheese poured over toast or crackers

Welsh rare•bit \-ˈra(ə)r-bət, -ˈre(ə)r-\ *n* [by alter.] (ca. 1785) : WELSH RABBIT

Welsh springer spaniel *n* (ca. 1929) : any of a Welsh breed of red and white or orange and white small-eared springer spaniels

Welsh terrier *n* (ca. 1886) : any of a breed of wiry-coated terriers resembling Airedales but smaller and developed in Wales for hunting

Welsh•wom•an \ˈwelsh-ˌwu̇m-ən *also* ˈwelch-\ *n* (15c) : a woman who is a native or inhabitant of Wales

1**welt** \ˈwelt\ *n* [ME *welte*] (15c) 1 : a strip between a shoe sole and upper through which they are stitched or stapled together 2 : a doubled edge, strip, insert, or seam (as on a garment) for ornament or reinforcement 3 a : a ridge or lump raised on the body usu. by a blow b : a heavy blow

2**welt** *vt* (15c) 1 : to furnish with a welt 2 a : to raise a welt on the body of b : to hit hard

welt•an•schau•ung \ˈvel-ˌtän-ˌshau̇-əŋ, -tən-\ *n, pl* **weltanschauungs** \-əŋz\ *or* **welt•an•schau•ung•en** \-əŋ-ən\ *often cap* [G, fr. *welt* world + *anschauung* view] (ca. 1868) : a comprehensive conception or apprehension of the world esp. from a specific standpoint

1**wel•ter** \ˈwel-tər\ *vi* **wel•tered; wel•ter•ing** \-t(ə-)riŋ\ [ME *welteren*; akin to MD *welteren* to roll, OHG *walzan*, L *volvere* — more at VOLUBLE] (14c) 1 a : WRITHE, TOSS; *also* : WALLOW b : to rise and fall or toss about in or with waves 2 : to become deeply sunk, soaked, or involved 3 : to be in turmoil

2**welter** *n* (1596) 1 : a state of wild disorder : TURMOIL 2 : a chaotic mass or jumble ⟨a bewildering ~ of data⟩

3**welter** *n* (1900) : WELTERWEIGHT

wel•ter•weight \ˈwel-tər-ˌwāt\ *n* [*welter* (prob. fr. 1*welt*) + *weight*] (ca. 1892) : a boxer in a weight division having a maximum limit of 147 pounds — compare LIGHTWEIGHT, MIDDLEWEIGHT

welt•schmerz \ˈvelt-ˌshme(ə)rts\ *n, often cap* [G, fr. *welt* world + *schmerz* pain, fr. OHG *smerzo*; akin to OHG *smerzan* to pain — more at SMART] (1875) 1 : mental depression or apathy caused by comparison of the actual state of the world with an ideal state 2 : a mood of sentimental sadness

1**wen** \ˈwen\ *n* [ME *wenn*, fr. OE; akin to MLG *wene* wen] (bef. 12c) : a cyst formed by obstruction of a sebaceous gland and filled with sebaceous material

²**wen** *n* [OE *wen, wynn,* lit., joy — more at WINSOME] (bef. 12c) : a runic letter used in Old English and Middle English to represent the consonant \w\
¹**wench** \'wench\ *n* [ME *wenche,* short for *wenchel* child, fr. OE *wencel;* akin to OHG *winchan* to stagger — more at WINK] (13c) **1 a :** a young woman : GIRL **b :** a female servant **2 :** a lewd woman : PROSTITUTE
²**wench** *vi* (1599) : to consort with lewd women; *esp* : to practice fornication — **wench·er** *n*
wend \'wend\ *vb* [ME *wenden,* fr. OE *wendan;* akin to OHG *wenten* to turn, OE *windan* to twist — more at WIND] *vi* (bef. 12c) : to direct one's course : TRAVEL ~ *vt* : to proceed on (one's way) : DIRECT
Wend \'wend\ *n* [G *Wende,* fr. OHG *Winida;* akin to OE *Winedas,* pl., Wends] (1786) : a member of a Slavic people of eastern Germany
¹**Wend·ish** \'wen-dish\ *adj* (1614) : of or relating to the Wends or their language
²**Wendish** *n* (1617) : the West Slavic language of the Wends
went [ME, past & pp. of *wenden*] *past of* GO
wen·tle·trap \'went-ᵊl-ˌtrap\ *n* [D *wenteltrap* winding stair, fr. MD *wendeltrappe,* fr. *wendel* turning (fr. *wenden* to turn; akin to OHG *wenten*) + *trappe* stairs — more at TRAP] (1758) : any of a family (Epitoniidae) of marine snails with usu. white shells; *also* : one of the shells
wept *past and past part of* WEEP
were [ME *were* (suppletive sing. past subj. & 2d sing. past indic. of *been* to be), *weren* (suppletive past pl. of *been*), fr. OE *wǣre* (sing. past subj. & 2d sing. past indic. of *wesan* to be), *wǣron* (past pl. indic. of *wesan*), *wǣren* (past pl. subj. of *wesan*) — more at WAS] *past 2d sing, past pl, or past subjunctive of* BE
we're \(ˌ)wi(ə)r, (ˌ)wər, ˌwē-ər\ : we are
weren't \(ˈ)wərnt, 'wər-ənt\ : were not
were·wolf \'wi(ə)r-ˌwu̇lf, 'we(ə)r-, 'wər-\ *n, pl* **were·wolves** \-ˌwu̇lvz\ [ME, fr. OE *werwulf* (akin to OHG *werwolf* werewolf), fr. *wer* man + *wulf* wolf — more at VIRILE, WOLF] (bef. 12c) : a person transformed into a wolf or capable of assuming a wolf's form
wer·gild \'wər-ˌgild\ *or* **wer·geld** \-ˌgeld\ *n* [ME *wergeld,* fr. OE, fr. *wer* man + *-geld,* alter. of *gield, geld* payment, tribute — more at GELD] (bef. 12c) : the value set in Anglo-Saxon and Germanic law upon the life of a man in accordance with his rank and paid as compensation to the kindred or lord of a slain person
wert \(ˈ)wərt\ *archaic past 2d sing of* BE
wes·kit \'wes-kət\ *n* [alter. of *waistcoat*] (ca. 1856) : VEST 2a
Wes·ley·an·ism \'wes-lē-ə-ˌniz-əm *also* 'wez-\ *n* (1774) : METHODISM 1; *specif* : the system of Arminian Methodism taught by John Wesley — **Wes·ley·an** \-lē-ən\ *adj or n*
¹**west** \'west\ *adv* [ME, fr. OE; akin to OHG *westar* to the west and prob. to L *vesper* evening, Gk *hesperos*] (bef. 12c) : to, toward, or in the west
²**west** *n* (bef. 12c) **1 a :** the general direction of sunset : the direction to the left of one facing north **b :** the place on the horizon where the sun sets when it is near one of the equinoxes **c :** the compass point directly opposite to east **2** *cap* **a :** regions or countries lying to the west of a specified or implied point of orientation **b :** the noncommunist countries of Europe and America **3 :** the end of a church opposite the chancel **4** *often cap* **a :** the one of four positions at 90-degree intervals that lies to the west or at the left of a diagram **b :** a person (as a bridge player) occupying this position during a specified activity
³**west** *adj* (bef. 12c) **1 :** situated toward or at the west ⟨the ~ exit⟩ **2 :** coming from the west ⟨a ~ wind⟩
west·bound \'wes(t)-ˌbau̇nd\ *adj* (1881) : traveling or heading west
west by north (15c) : a compass point that is one point north of due west : N78°45′W
west by south (15c) : a compass point that is one point south of due west : S78°45′W
¹**west·er** \'wes-tər\ *vi* **west·ered; west·er·ing** \-t(ə-)riŋ\ [ME *westren,* fr. ¹*west*] (14c) : to turn or move westward ⟨the half moon ~s low —A. E. Housman⟩
²**wester** *n* [³*west*] (1922) : a westerly wind; *esp* : a storm with west winds
¹**west·er·ly** \'wes-tər-lē\ *adj or adv* [obs. *wester* (western)] (1577) **1 :** situated toward or belonging to the west ⟨the ~ end of the farm⟩ **2 :** coming from the west ⟨a ~ breeze⟩
²**westerly** *n, pl* **-lies** (1876) : a wind from the west
¹**west·ern** \'wes-tərn\ *adj* [ME *westerne,* fr. OE; akin to OHG *westrōni* western, OE *west*] (bef. 12c) **1 a :** lying toward the west **b :** coming from the west ⟨a ~ storm⟩ **2** *cap* : of, relating to, or characteristic of a region conventionally designated West: as **a :** steeped in or stemming from the Greco-Roman traditions **b :** of or relating to the noncommunist countries of Europe and America **c :** of or relating to the American West **3** *cap* : of or relating to the Roman Catholic or Protestant segment of Christianity ⟨*Western* liturgies⟩ — **west·ern·most** \-ˌmōst\ *adj*
²**western** *n* (1612) **1 :** one that is produced in or characteristic of a western region and esp. the western U.S. **2** *often cap* : a novel, story, motion picture, or broadcast dealing with life in the western U.S. esp. during the latter half of the 19th century
West·ern·er \'wes-tə(r)-nər\ *n* (1837) **1 :** a native or inhabitant of the West; *esp* : a native or resident of the western part of the U.S. **2 :** one advocating the adoption of western European culture esp. in 19th century Russia
western hemisphere *n, often cap W&H* (1624) : the half of the earth comprising No. and So. America and surrounding waters
west·ern·iza·tion \ˌwes-tər-nə-'zā-shən\ *n, often cap* (1904) : conversion to or adoption of western traditions or techniques
west·ern·ize \'wes-tər-ˌnīz\ *vb, often cap* **-ized; -iz·ing** *vt* (1837) : to imbue with qualities native to or associated with a western region and esp. the noncommunist countries of Europe and America ~ *vi* : to become westernized
western omelet *n* (1951) : an omelet made usu. with diced ham, green pepper, and onion
western saddle *n, often cap W* (1911) : STOCK SADDLE
West Germanic *n* (1894) : a subdivision of the Germanic languages including English, Frisian, Dutch, and German — see INDO-EUROPEAN LANGUAGES table
West Highland white terrier *n* (ca. 1904) : a small white long-coated dog of a breed developed in Scotland
west·ing \'wes-tiŋ\ *n* (1628) : westerly progress : a going westward
west–northwest *n* (14c) : a compass point that is two points north of due west : N67°30′W
West·pha·lian ham \wes(t)-ˌfāl-yən-, -ˌfā-lē-ən-\ *n* [*Westphalia,* Germany] (1664) : a ham of distinctive flavor produced by smoking with juniper brush
West Saxon *n* (14c) **1 :** a native or inhabitant of the West Saxon kingdom **2 :** a dialect of Old English used as the chief literary dialect in England before the Norman Conquest
west–southwest *n* (14c) : a compass point that is two points south of due west : S67°30′W
¹**west·ward** \'wes-twərd\ *adv or adj* (bef. 12c) : toward the west — **westwards** \-twərdz\ *adv*
²**westward** *n* (1652) : westward direction or part ⟨sail to the ~⟩
¹**wet** \'wet\ *adj* **wet·ter; wet·test** [ME, partly fr. pp. of *weten* to wet & partly fr. OE *wǣt* wet; akin to ON *vātr* wet, OE *wæter* water] (bef. 12c) **1 a :** consisting of, containing, covered with, or soaked with liquid (as water) **b** *of natural gas* : containing appreciable quantities of readily condensable hydrocarbons **2 :** RAINY **3 :** still moist enough to smudge or smear ⟨~ paint⟩ **4 a :** DRUNK ⟨a ~ driver⟩ **b (1) :** permitting the manufacture and sale of alcoholic liquor ⟨a ~ county⟩ **(2) :** advocating a policy of permitting such traffic ⟨a ~ candidate⟩ **5 :** preserved in liquid **6 :** employing or done by means of or in the presence of water or other liquid ⟨~ extraction of copper⟩ **7** *Brit* : lacking strength of character : WEAK, SPINELESS ⟨thought him ~ and violence petrified him —William Golding⟩ — **wet·ly** *adv* — **wet·ness** *n*
syn WET, DAMP, DANK, MOIST, HUMID mean covered or more or less soaked with liquid. WET usu. implies saturation but may suggest a covering of a surface with water or something (as paint) not yet dry; DAMP implies a slight or moderate absorption and often connotes an unpleasant degree of moisture; DANK implies a more distinctly disagreeable or unwholesome dampness; MOIST applies to what is slightly damp or not felt as dry; HUMID applies to the presence of much water vapor in the air.
— **all wet :** completely wrong : in error — **wet behind the ears :** IMMATURE, INEXPERIENCED
²**wet** *n* (bef. 12c) **1 :** WATER; *also* : MOISTURE, WETNESS **2 :** rainy weather : RAIN **3 :** an advocate of a policy of permitting the sale of intoxicating liquors
³**wet** *vb* **wet** *or* **wet·ted; wet·ting** [ME *weten,* fr. OE *wǣtan,* fr. *wǣt,* adj.] *vt* (bef. 12c) **1 :** to make wet **2 :** to urinate in or on ~ *vi* **1 :** to become wet **2 :** URINATE — **wet one's whistle :** to take a drink esp. of liquor
wet·back \'wet-ˌbak\ *n* (ca. 1942) : a Mexican who enters the U.S. illegally — sometimes taken to be offensive
wet bar *n* (1967) : a bar for mixing drinks (as in a home) that contains a sink with running water
wet blanket *n* (1857) : one who quenches or dampens enthusiasm or pleasure
wet down *vt* (1840) : to dampen by sprinkling with water
wet dream *n* (ca. 1926) : an erotic dream culminating in orgasm and in the male accompanied by seminal emission
weth·er \'weth-ər\ *n* [ME, ram, fr. OE; akin to OHG *widar* ram, L *vitulus* calf, *vetus* old, Gk *etos* year] (bef. 12c) : a male sheep castrated before sexual maturity
wet·land \'wet-ˌland, -lənd\ *n* (1778) : land or areas (as tidal flats or swamps) containing much soil moisture — usu. used in pl.
wet–nurse *vt* (1784) **1 :** to act as wet nurse to **2 :** to give constant and often excessive care to
wet nurse *n* (1620) : one that cares for and suckles young not her own
wet suit *n* (1960) : a close-fitting suit made of material (as sponge rubber) that traps a thin layer of water against the body to retain body heat and that is worn (as by a skin diver) esp. in cold water
wet·ta·bil·i·ty \ˌwet-ə-'bil-ət-ē\ *n* (ca. 1927) : the quality or state of being wettable : the degree to which something can be wet
wet·ta·ble \'wet-ə-bəl\ *adj* (1885) : capable of being wetted
wet·ter \'wet-ər\ *n* (1737) : one that wets; *also* : WETTING AGENT
wetting agent *n* (ca. 1936) : a substance that by becoming adsorbed prevents a surface from being repellent to a wetting liquid and is used esp. in mixing solids with liquids or spreading liquids on surfaces
wet·tish \'wet-ish\ *adj* (1648) : somewhat wet : MOIST
wet wash *n* (1916) : laundry returned damp and not ironed
we've \(ˌ)wēv\ : we have
¹**whack** \'hwak, 'wak\ *vb* [prob. imit. of the sound of a blow] *vt* (1719) **1 a :** to strike with a smart or resounding blow **b :** to cut with or as if with a whack : CHOP **2** *chiefly Brit* : to get the better of : DEFEAT ~ *vi* : to strike a smart or resounding blow — **whack·er** *n*
²**whack** *n* (1736) **1 :** a smart or resounding blow; *also* : the sound of or as if of such a blow **2 :** PORTION, SHARE **3 :** CONDITION, STATE **4 a :** an opportunity or attempt to do something ⟨take a ~ at it⟩ **b :** a single action or occasion ⟨borrowed $50 all at one ~⟩ — **out of whack 1 :** out of proper order or shape ⟨threw his knee *out of whack*⟩ **2 :** not in accord ⟨feeling *out of whack* with her contemporaries —S.E. Rubin⟩
whacked–out \'(h)wak-ˌdau̇t, ˌ(h)wak-'\ *adj* (1967) **1 :** WORN-OUT, EXHAUSTED **2 :** WACKY **3 :** STONED ⟨~ on drugs⟩
whack·ing \'hwak-iŋ, 'wak-\ *adj* (1806) : very large : WHOPPING
whack off *vb* (1969) : MASTURBATE — usu. considered vulgar
whack up *vt* (1891) : to divide into shares
whacky \'hwak-ē, 'wak-\ *var of* WACKY
¹**whale** \'hwā(ə)l, 'wā(ə)l\ *n, pl* **whales** *often attrib* [ME, fr. OE *hwæl;* akin to OHG *hwal* whale, L *squalus* sea fish, *squama* scale] (bef. 12c) **1** *or pl* **whale :** any of an order (Cetacea) of marine mammals that lack hind limbs and have the front limbs modified into flippers, have the tail flattened and extended laterally into horizontal flukes, and usu. have the nares opening externally at the top of the head; *esp* : one of the larger members of this group **2 :** one that is impressive esp. in size ⟨a ~ of a difference⟩ — **whale·like** \-ˌlīk\ *adj*
²**whale** *vi* **whaled; whal·ing** (1700) : to engage in whale fishing
³**whale** *vt* **whaled; whal·ing** [origin unknown] (ca. 1790) **1 :** LASH, THRASH **2 :** to strike or hit vigorously **3 :** to defeat soundly
whale·back \'hwā(ə)l-ˌbak, 'wā(ə)l-\ *n* (1886) : something shaped like the back of a whale; *specif* : a freight steamer with a convex upper deck

whale·boat \-ˌbōt\ *n* (1682) **1 :** a long narrow rowboat made with both ends sharp and raking, often steered with an oar, and formerly used by whalers for hunting whales **2 :** a long narrow rowboat or motorboat that is sharp and rounded at both ends in the manner of the original whaleboats and is often carried by warships and merchant ships

whale·bone \-ˌbōn\ *n* (1601) **1 :** a horny substance found in two rows of plates from 2 to 12 feet long attached along the upper jaw of whalebone whales **2 :** an article made of whalebone

whalebone whale *n* (1725) **:** any of various usu. large whales (suborder Mysticeti) having whalebone instead of teeth — called also *baleen whale;* compare TOOTHED WHALE

whal·er \'hwā-lǝr, 'wā-\ *n* (1684) **1 :** a person or ship engaged in whale fishing **2 :** WHALEBOAT 2

whal·ing \-liŋ\ *n* (1688) **:** the occupation of catching and extracting commercial products from whales

¹wham \'hwam, 'wam\ *n* [imit.] (1739) **1 :** a solid blow **2 :** the loud sound of a hard impact

²wham *vb* **whammed; wham·ming** *vt* (1925) **:** to propel, strike, or beat so as to produce a loud impact ~ *vi* **:** to hit or explode with a loud impact

wham·my \'hwam-ē, 'wam-\ *n, pl* **whammies** [prob. fr. ¹*wham*] (1943) **1 a :** a supernatural power bringing bad luck **b :** a magic curse or spell **2 :** a potent force or attack; *specif* **:** a paralyzing or lethal blow

¹whang \'hwaŋ, 'waŋ\ *n* [alter. of ME *thong, thwang*] (1536) **1** *dial* **a :** THONG **b :** RAWHIDE **2** *Brit* **:** a large piece **:** CHUNK **3 :** PENIS — often considered vulgar

²whang *vt* (1684) **1** *dial* **:** BEAT, THRASH **2 :** to propel or strike with force ~ *vi* **:** to beat or work with force or violence

³whang *n* [imit.] (ca. 1824) **:** a loud sharp vibrant or resonant sound

⁴whang *vi* (1875) **:** to make a whang ~ *vt* **:** to strike with a whang

whan·gee \hwaŋ-'(g)ē, waŋ-\ *n* [prob. fr. Chin (Pek) *huang² li²*, fr. *huang²* yellow + *li²* bamboo cane] (1790) **1 :** any of several Chinese bamboos (genus *Phyllostachys*) **2 :** a walking stick or riding crop of whangee

whap \'hwäp, 'wäp\ *var of* WHOP

wharf \'hwȯrf, 'wȯrf\ *n, pl* **wharves** \'hwȯrvz, 'wȯrvz\ *also* **wharfs** [ME, fr. OE *hwearf* embankment, wharf; akin to OE *hweorfan* to turn, OHG *hwerban*, Gk *karpos* wrist] (bef. 12c) **1 :** a structure built along or at an angle from the shore of navigable waters so that ships may lie alongside to receive and discharge cargo and passengers **2** *obs* **:** the bank of a river or the shore of the sea

wharf·age \'hwȯr-fij, 'wȯr-\ *n* (15c) **1 a :** the provision or the use of a wharf **b :** the handling or stowing of goods on a wharf **2 :** the charge for the use of a wharf **3 :** the wharf accommodations of a place **:** WHARVES

wharf·in·ger \-fǝn-jǝr\ *n* [irreg. fr. *wharfage*] (1552) **:** the operator or manager of a commercial wharf

wharf·mas·ter \'hwȯrf-ˌmas-tǝr, 'wȯrf-\ *n* (1618) **:** the manager of a wharf **:** WHARFINGER

¹what \(')hwät, (')hwȯt, (')wät, 'wǝt\ *pron* [ME, fr. OE *hwæt*, neut. of *hwā* who — more at WHO] (bef. 12c) **1 a** (1) — used as an interrogative expressing inquiry about the identity, nature, or value of an object or matter ⟨~ is this⟩ ⟨~ is wealth without friends⟩ ⟨~ does he earn⟩ ⟨~ hath God wrought⟩ (2) — often used to ask for repetition of an utterance or part of an utterance not properly heard or understood ⟨you said ~⟩ **b** (1) *archaic* **:** WHO 1 — used as an interrogative expressing inquiry about the identity of a person (2) — used as an interrogative expressing inquiry about the character, nature, occupation, position, or role of a person ⟨~ do you think I am, a fool⟩ ⟨~ is she, that all our swains commend her —Shak.⟩ **c** — used as an exclamation expressing surprise or excitement and frequently introducing a question ⟨~, no breakfast⟩ **d** — used in expressions directing attention to a statement that the speaker is about to make ⟨you know ~⟩ **e** — used at the end of a question to express inquiry about additional possibilities ⟨is it raining, or snowing, or ~⟩ **f** *chiefly Brit* — used at the end of an utterance as a form of tag question ⟨a clever play, ~⟩ **2** *chiefly substand* **:** ⁴THAT 1, WHICH 3, WHO 3 **3 :** that which **:** the one or ones that ⟨no income but ~ he gets from his writings⟩ — sometimes used in reference to a clause or phrase that is yet to come or is not yet complete ⟨gave also, ~ is more valuable, understanding⟩ **4 a :** WHATEVER 1a ⟨say ~ you will⟩ **b** *obs* **:** WHOEVER — **what for 1 :** for what purpose or reason **:** WHY — usu. used with the other words of a question between *what* and *for* ⟨*what* did you do that *for*⟩ except when used alone **2 :** punishment esp. by blows or by a sharp reprimand ⟨gave him *what for*⟩ in violent Spanish —*New Yorker*⟩ — **what have you :** ¹WHATNOT ⟨novels, plays, short stories, travelogues, and *what have you* —Haldeen Braddy⟩ — **what if 1 :** what will or would be the result if **2 :** what does it matter if — **what it takes :** the qualities or resources needed for success or for attainment of a goal — **what of 1 :** what is the situation with respect to **2 :** what importance can be assigned to — **what's what :** the true state of things ⟨knows *what's what* when it comes to fashion⟩ — **what though :** what does it matter if ⟨*what though* the rose have prickles, yet 'tis plucked —Shak.⟩

²what *adv* (bef. 12c) **1** *obs* **:** WHY **2 :** in what respect **:** HOW ⟨~ does he care⟩ **3** — used to introduce prepositional phrases in parallel construction or a prepositional phrase that expresses cause and usu. has more than one object; used principally before phrases beginning with *with* ⟨~ with unemployment and high prices⟩ ⟨~ with the war, the sweat, ~ with the gallows, and ~ with poverty, I am customa shrunk —Shak.⟩

³what *adj* (bef. 12c) **1 a** — used as an interrogative expressing inquiry about the identity, nature, or value of a person, object, or matter ⟨~ minerals do we export⟩ **b :** how remarkable or striking for good or bad qualities — used esp. in exclamatory utterances and dependent clauses ⟨~ mountains⟩ ⟨remember ~ fun we had⟩ ⟨~ a suggestion⟩ ⟨~ a charming girl⟩ **2 a** (1) **:** WHATEVER 1a (2) **:** ANY ⟨ornament of ~ description soever⟩ **b :** the . . . that **:** as much or as many . . . as ⟨rescued ~ survivors they found⟩

¹what·ev·er \hwät-'ev-ǝr, wät-, ˌ(h)wǝt-\ *pron* (14c) **1 a :** anything or everything that ⟨take ~ you want⟩ **b :** no matter what ⟨he says, they won't believe him⟩ **c :** WHATNOT ⟨buffalo or rhinoceros or ~ —Alan Moorehead⟩ **2 :** WHAT 1a(1) — used to express astonishment or perplexity ⟨~ do you mean by that⟩

²whatever *adj* (14c) **1 a :** any . . . that **:** all . . . that ⟨buy peace . . . on ~ terms could be obtained —C. S. Forester⟩ **b :** no matter what ⟨money, in ~ hands, will confer power —Samuel Johnson⟩ **2 :** of any kind at all — used after the substantive it modifies with *any* or with an expressed or implied negative ⟨in any order ~ —W. G. Moulton⟩ ⟨no food ~⟩

³whatever *adv* (1951) **:** in any case

¹what·not \'hwät-ˌnät, 'hwȯt-, 'wät-, 'wǝt-\ *pron* [*what not?*] (1540) **:** any of various other things that might also be mentioned ⟨paper clips, pins, and ~⟩

²whatnot *n* (1602) **1 :** a nondescript person or thing **2 :** a light open set of shelves for bric-a-brac

what·so·ev·er \ˌhwät-sǝ-'wev-ǝr, ˌhwǝt-, ˌwät-, ˌwǝt-\ *pron or adj* (13c) **:** WHATEVER

whaup \'hwȯp, 'wȯp\ *n, pl* **whaup** *also* **whaups** [imit.] *chiefly Scot* (ca. 1512) **:** a European curlew (*Numenius arquata*)

wheal \'hwē(ǝ)l, 'wē(ǝ)l\ *n* [alter. of *wale*] (1808) **:** a suddenly formed elevation of the skin surface: as **a :** WELT **b :** a flat burning or itching eminence on the skin

wheat \'hwēt, 'wēt\ *n, often attrib* [ME *whete*, fr. OE *hwǣte*; akin to OHG *weizzi* wheat, *hwiz, wiz* white — more at WHITE] (bef. 12c) **1 :** a cereal grain that yields a fine white flour, is the chief breadstuff of temperate climates, is used also in pastas (as macaroni or spaghetti), and is important in animal feeds **2 :** any of various grasses (genus *Triticum*) of wide climatic adaptability that are cultivated in most temperate areas for the wheat they yield; *esp* **:** an annual cereal grass (*T. aestivum*) known only as a cultigen

wheat bread *n* (14c) **:** a bread made of a combination of white and whole wheat flours as distinguished from bread made entirely of white or whole wheat flour

wheat cake *n* (1772) **:** a pancake made of wheat flour

wheat·ear \'hwēt-ˌi(ǝ)r, 'wēt-\ *n* [back-formation fr. earlier *wheatears wheatear*, prob. by folk etymology or euphemism fr. *white + arse*] (1591) **:** a small white-rumped northern bird (*Oenanthe oenanthe*) related to the stonechat and whinchat

¹wheat·en \'hwēt-ⁿn, 'wēt-\ *adj* (bef. 12c) **:** of, relating to, or made of wheat

²wheaten *n* (ca. 1931) **:** a pale yellowish to ruddy fawn color characteristic of the coat of some dogs

wheat germ *n* (ca. 1902) **:** the embryo of the wheat kernel separated in milling and used esp. as a source of vitamins

wheat rust *n* (ca. 1884) **:** a destructive disease of wheat caused by rust fungi; *also* **:** a fungus (as *Puccinia graminis*) causing a wheat rust

Wheat·stone bridge \'hwēt-ˌstōn-, ˌwēt-, *chiefly Brit* -stǝn-\ *n* [Sir Charles *Wheatstone*] (1872) **:** a bridge for measuring electrical resistances that consists of a conductor joining two branches of a circuit

whee \'hwē, 'wē\ *interj* (1898) — used to express delight or exuberance

whee·dle \'hwēd-ⁿl, 'wēd-\ *vb* **whee·dled; whee·dling** \'(h)wēd-liŋ, -ⁿl-iŋ\ [origin unknown] (ca. 1661) **1 :** to influence or entice by soft words or flattery **2 :** to gain or get by wheedling ⟨~ his way into favor⟩ ~ *vi* **:** to use soft words or flattery

¹wheel \'hwē(ǝ)l, 'wē(ǝ)l\ *n, often attrib* [ME, fr. OE *hweogol, hwēol;* akin to ON *hvēl* wheel, Gk *kyklos* circle, wheel, Skt *cakra*, L *colere* to cultivate, inhabit, Gk *telos* end] (bef. 12c) **1 :** a circular frame of hard material that may be solid, partly solid, or spoked and that is capable of turning on an axle **2 :** a contrivance or apparatus having as its principal part a wheel: as **a :** a chiefly medieval instrument of torture designed for mutilating a victim (as by stretching or disjointing) **b :** BICYCLE **c :** any of many revolving disks or drums used as gambling paraphernalia **3 a :** an imaginary turning wheel symbolizing the inconstancy of fortune **b :** a recurring course, development, or action **:** CYCLE **4 :** something resembling a wheel in shape or motion: as **a :** a round flat cheese **b :** a firework that rotates while burning **c :** a propeller on a boat **5 a :** a curving or circular movement **b :** a rotation or turn usu. about an axis or center; *specif* **:** a turning movement of troops or ships in line in which the units preserve alignment and relative positions as they change direction **6 a :** a moving or essential part of something compared to a machine ⟨the ~s of government⟩ **b :** a directing or controlling force **c :** a person of importance esp. in an organization ⟨a big ~⟩ **7 :** the refrain or burden of a song **8 a :** a circuit of theaters or places of entertainment **b :** a sports league **9** *pl, slang* **:** a wheeled vehicle; *esp* **:** AUTOMOBILE — **wheel·less** \'hwē(ǝ)l-lǝs, 'wē(ǝ)l-\ *adj*

²wheel *vi* (13c) **1 :** to turn on or as if on an axis **:** REVOLVE **2 :** to change direction as if revolving on a pivot ⟨the battalion would have ~ed to the flank —Walter Bernstein⟩ ⟨her mind will ~ around to the other extreme —Liam O'Flaherty⟩ **3 :** to move or extend in a circle or curve ⟨birds in ~ing flight⟩ ⟨valleys where young cotton ~ed slowly in fanlike rows —William Faulkner⟩ **4 :** to drive or go on or as if on wheels or in a wheeled vehicle ~ *vt* **1 :** to cause to turn on or as if on an axis **:** ROTATE **2 :** to convey or move on or as if on wheels or in a wheeled vehicle; *esp* **:** to drive (a vehicle) at high speed **3 :** to cause to change direction as if revolving on a pivot **4 :** to make or perform in a circle or curve — **wheel and deal :** to pursue one's interest esp. in a shrewd or unscrupulous manner

wheel and axle *n* (1773) **:** a mechanical device consisting of a grooved wheel turned by a cord or chain with a rigidly attached axle (as for winding up a weight) together with the supporting standards

wheel animal *n* (1788) **:** ROTIFER

wheel animalcule *n* (1834) **:** ROTIFER

¹wheel·bar·row \'hwē(ǝ)l-ˌbar-(ˌ)ō, -bar-ǝ\, -ˌbar-ǝ-(w)\ *n* (14c) **:** a small usu. single-wheeled vehicle that is used for carrying small loads and is fitted with handles at the rear by which it can be pushed and guided

²wheelbarrow *vt* (1721) **:** to convey in a wheelbarrow

wheel·base \'hwē(ǝ)l-ˌbās, 'wē(ǝ)l-\ *n* (1886) **:** the distance in inches between the front and rear axles of an automotive vehicle

---

\ǝ\ abut \ᵊ\ kitten, F table \ǝr\ further \a\ ash \ā\ ace \ä\ cot, cart
\au̇\ out \ch\ chin \e\ bet \ē\ easy \g\ go \i\ hit \ī\ ice \j\ job
\ŋ\ sing \ō\ go \ȯ\ law \ȯi\ boy \th\ thin \t̲h̲\ the \ü\ loot \u̇\ foot
\y\ yet \zh\ vision \a, k, ⁿ, œ, œ̄, ᵫ, ᵫ̄, �\ *see* Guide to Pronunciation

wheel bug *n* (1815) : a large No. American bug (*Arilus cristatus*) that has a high serrated crest on its prothorax and that sucks the blood of other insects

wheel·chair \'hwē(ə)l-ˌche(ə)r, 'wē(ə)l-, -ˌcha(ə)r\ *n* (1700) : a chair mounted on wheels esp. for the use of invalids

wheeled \'hwē(ə)ld, 'wē(ə)ld\ *adj* (1606) **1 :** equipped with wheels ⟨~ vehicles⟩ **2 :** moving or functioning by means of wheels ⟨~ traffic⟩

wheel·er \'hwē-lər, 'wē-\ *n* (1683) **1 :** one that wheels **2 :** a draft animal (as a horse) pulling in the position nearest the front wheels of a wagon **3 :** something (as a vehicle or ship) that has wheels — used esp. in combination ⟨side-*wheeler*⟩

wheeler and dealer *n* (1965) : WHEELER-DEALER

wheel·er–deal·er \ˌhwē-lər-'dē-lər, ˌwē-\ *n* [fr. the vb. phrase *wheel and deal*] (1954) : a shrewd operator esp. in business or politics

wheel·horse \'hwē(ə)l-ˌhȯ(ə)rs, 'wē(ə)l-\ *n* (1708) **1 :** a horse (as in a tandem) in a position nearest the wheels **2 :** a steady and effective worker esp. in a political body

wheel·house \-ˌhau̇s\ *n* (ca. 1813) : PILOTHOUSE

wheel·ie \'hwē-lē, 'wē-\ *n* (ca. 1965) : a maneuver in which a wheeled vehicle (as a bicycle) is momentarily balanced on its rear wheel or wheels

wheel·ing \'hwē-liŋ, 'wē-\ *n* (15c) **1 :** the act or process of one that wheels **2 :** the condition of a road relative to passage on wheels

wheel lock *n* (1670) : a gunlock for a muzzle-loading firearm in which sparks are struck from a flint or a piece of iron pyrites by a revolving wheel

wheel·man \'hwē(ə)l-mən, 'wē(ə)l-\ *n* (1865) **1 a :** HELMSMAN **b :** the driver of an automobile **2 :** CYCLIST

wheels·man \'hwē(ə)lz-mən, 'wē(ə)lz-\ *n* (1885) : one who steers with a wheel; *esp* : HELMSMAN

wheel·work \'hwē(ə)l-ˌwərk, 'wē(ə)l-\ *n* (1670) : wheels in gear and their connections in a machine or mechanism

wheel·wright \-ˌrīt\ *n* (13c) : a maker and repairer of wheels and wheeled vehicles

[1]**ween** \'hwēn, 'wēn\ *adj* [ME (Sc) *quheyne*, fr. OE *hwǣne, hwēne*, adv., somewhat, fr. instr. of *hwōn* little, few] *dial Brit* (14c) : FEW 2

[2]**ween** *n, dial Brit* (1757) : a considerable number or amount

[1]**wheeze** \'hwēz, 'wēz\ *vi* **wheezed; wheez·ing** [ME *whesen*, prob. of Scand origin; akin to ON *hvæsa* to hiss; akin to OE *hwǣst* action of blowing, L *queri* to complain] (15c) **1 :** to breathe with difficulty usu. with a whistling sound **2 :** to make a sound resembling that of wheezing

[2]**wheeze** *n* (1834) **1 :** a sound of wheezing **2 a :** an often repeated and widely known joke used esp. by entertainers **b :** a trite saying or proverb

wheezy \'hwē-zē, 'wē-\ *adj* **wheez·i·er; -est** (1818) **1 :** inclined to wheeze **2 :** having a wheezing sound — **wheez·i·ly** \-zə-lē\ *adv* — **wheez·i·ness** \-zē-nəs\ *n*

[1]**whelk** \'hwelk, 'welk, 'wilk\ *n* [ME *welke*, fr. OE *weoloc;* akin to L *volvere* to turn — more at VOLUBLE] (bef. 12c) : any of numerous large marine snails (as of the genus *Buccinum*); *esp* : one (*B. undatum*) much used as food in Europe

[2]**whelk** \'hwelk, 'welk\ *n* [ME *whelke*, fr. OE *hwylca*, fr. *hwelian* to suppurate] (bef. 12c) : PAPULE, PUSTULE

whelm \'hwelm, 'welm\ *vb* [ME *whelmen*] *vt* (14c) **1 :** to turn (as a dish or vessel) upside down usu. to cover something : cover or engulf completely with usu. disastrous effect **2 :** to overcome in thought or feeling : OVERWHELM ~ *vi* : to pass or go over something so as to bury or submerge it

[1]**whelp** \'hwelp, 'welp\ *n* [ME, fr. OE *hwelp;* akin to OHG *hwelf* whelp] (bef. 12c) **1 a :** one of the young of various carnivorous mammals and esp. of the dog **b :** a young boy or girl **2 :** an ill-considered or despised person or his offspring

[2]**whelp** *vt* (13c) : to give birth to — used of various carnivores and esp. the dog ~ *vi* : to bring forth young

[1]**when** \(ˈ)hwen, (ˈ)wen, (h)wən\ *adv* [ME, fr. OE *hwanne, hwenne;* akin to OHG *hwanne* when, OE *hwā* who — more at WHO] (bef. 12c) **1 :** at what time ⟨~ will he return⟩ **2 a :** at or during which time **b :** and then **3 :** at a former and usu. less prosperous time ⟨brag fondly of having known him ~ —Vance Packard⟩

[2]**when** *conj* [ME, fr. OE *hwanne, hwenne*, fr. *hwanne, hwenne*, adv.] (bef. 12c) **1 a :** at or during the time that : WHILE ⟨went fishing ~ he was a boy⟩ **b :** just at the moment that ⟨stop writing ~ the bell rings⟩ **c :** at any or every time that ⟨~ he listens to music, he falls asleep⟩ **2 :** in the event that : IF ⟨a contestant is disqualified ~ he disobeys the rules⟩ **3 a :** considering that ⟨why use water at all ~ you can drown in it —Stuart Chase⟩ **b :** in spite of the fact that : ALTHOUGH ⟨quit politics ~ he might have had a great career in it⟩

[3]**when** \ˌhwen, ˌwen\ *pron* (14c) : what or which time ⟨in 1934, since ~ he has been working at landscapes and portraits —*Horizon*⟩

[4]**when** \'hwen, 'wen\ *n* (1616) : the time in which something is done or comes about ⟨troubled his head very little about the hows and ~*s* of life —Laurence Sterne⟩

when·as \hwe-'naz, we-, (h)wə-\ *conj* [ME (Sc) *when as*, fr. ME *when* + *as*] *archaic* (15c) : WHEN

[1]**whence** \(ˈ)hwen(t)s, (ˈ)wen(t)s\ *adv* [ME *whennes*, fr. *whenne* whence (fr. OE *hwanon*) + *-s*, adv. suffix, fr. *-s*, gen. sing. ending; akin to OHG *hwanān* whence, OE *hwā* who] (14c) : from what place, source, or cause ⟨then ~ comes this paradox —*Changing Times*⟩

[2]**whence** *conj* (14c) **1 :** from what place, source, or cause ⟨inquired ~ the water came —Maria Edgeworth⟩ **2 a :** from or out of which place, source, or cause ⟨the lawless society ~ the ballads sprang —DeLancey Ferguson⟩ **b :** by reason of which fact : WHEREFORE ⟨nothing broke — ~ I infer that my bones are not yet chalky —O. W. Holmes †1935⟩

whence·so·ev·er \'hwen(t)(s)-sə-ˌwev-ər, 'wen(t)(s)-\ *conj* (1511) : from whatever place or source

[1]**when·ev·er** \hwe-'nev-ər, we-, (h)wə-\ *conj* (14c) : at any or every time that

[2]**whenever** *adv* (1667) : at whatever time

[1]**when·so·ev·er** \'hwen(t)-sə-ˌwev-ər, 'wen(t)-\ *conj* (14c) : WHENEVER

[2]**whensoever** *adv, obs* (1604) : at any time whatever

[1]**where** \(ˈ)hwe(ə)r, (ˈ)hwa(ə)r, (ˈ)we(ə)r, (ˈ)wa(ə)r, (ˌ)(h)wər\ *adv* [ME, fr. OE *hwǣr;* akin to OHG *hwār* where, OE *hwā* who — more at WHO] (bef. 12c) **1 a :** at, in, or to what place ⟨~ is the house⟩ ⟨~ are we going⟩ **b :** at, in, or to what situation, position, direction, circumstances, or respect ⟨~ does this plan lead⟩ ⟨~ am I wrong⟩ **2** *archaic* : HERE, THERE ⟨lo, ~ it comes again —Shak.⟩

[2]**where** *conj* (bef. 12c) **1 a :** at, in, or to what place ⟨knows ~ the house is⟩ **b :** at, in, or to what situation, position, direction, circumstances, or respect ⟨shows ~ the plan leads⟩ **c :** the place or point at, in, or to which ⟨couldn't see from ~ he was sitting⟩ **2 :** WHEREVER ⟨goes ~ he likes⟩ **3 a :** at, in, or to which place ⟨the town ~ she lives⟩ **b :** at or in which ⟨has reached the size ~ traffic is a problem⟩ **4 a :** at, in, or to the place at, in, or to which ⟨stay ~ you are⟩ ⟨send him away ~ he'll forget⟩ **b :** in a case, situation, or respect in which ⟨outstanding ~ endurance is called for⟩

[3]**where** \'hwe(ə)r, 'hwa(ə)r, 'we(ə)r, 'wa(ə)r\ *n* (15c) **1 :** PLACE, LOCATION ⟨the ~ and the how of the accident⟩ **2 :** what place, source, or cause ⟨~ is he from⟩ — **where it's at 1 a :** a place of central interest or activity **b :** something (as a topic or field of interest) of primary concern or importance ⟨education is *where it's at*⟩ **2 :** the true nature of things — **where one is at :** one's true position, state, or nature

[1]**where·abouts** \-ə-ˌbau̇ts\ *also* **where·about** \-ˌbau̇t\ *adv* [ME *wherabоutes* (fr. *wher aboute* + *-s*, adv. suffix) & *wher aboute*, fr. *where, wher* where + *about, aboute* about — more at WHENCE] (14c) : about where : near what place ⟨~ is the house⟩

[2]**whereabouts** *also* **whereabout** *conj* (14c) **1** *obs* : on what business or errand **2 :** near what place : WHERE ⟨know ~ he lives⟩

[3]**whereabouts** *n pl but sing or pl in constr, also* **whereabout** (1605) : the place or general locality where a person or thing is ⟨his present ~ are a secret⟩

[1]**where·as** \hwer-'az, hwar-, wer-, war-, (ˌ)(h)wər-\ *conj* [ME *where as*, fr. *where* + *as*] (14c) **1 a :** while on the contrary **b :** ALTHOUGH **2 :** in view of the fact that : SINCE — used esp. to introduce a preamble

[2]**whereas** *n* (1795) **1 :** an introductory statement of a formal document : PREAMBLE **2 :** a conditional or qualifying statement

where·at \-'at\ *conj* (15c) **1 :** at or toward which **2 :** in consequence of which : WHEREUPON

[1]**where·by** \hwe(ə)r-'bī, hwa(ə)r-, we(ə)r-, wa(ə)r-, (ˌ)(h)wər-\ *conj* (13c) : by, through, or in accordance with which

[2]**whereby** *adv, obs* (14c) : by what : HOW

[1]**where·fore** \'hwe(ə)r-ˌfō(ə)r, 'hwa(ə)r-, 'we(ə)r-, 'wa(ə)r-, -ˌfȯ(ə)r\ *adv* [ME *wherfor, wherfore*, fr. *where, wher* + *for, fore* for] (13c) **1 :** for what reason or purpose : WHY **2 :** THEREFORE

[2]**wherefore** *n* (1590) : an answer or statement giving an explanation : REASON ⟨wants to know the whys and ~*s*⟩

where·from \-ˌfrəm, -ˌfräm\ *conj* (15c) : from which

[1]**where·in** \hwer-'in, hwar-, wer-, war-, (ˌ)(h)wər-\ *adv* (13c) : in what : in what particular or respect ⟨~ was I wrong⟩

[2]**wherein** *conj* (14c) **1 a :** in which : WHERE ⟨the city ~ he lives⟩ **b :** during which **2 :** in what way : HOW ⟨showed me ~ I was wrong⟩

where·in·to \-'in-(ˌ)tü, -tə(-w)\ *conj* (1539) : into which

[1]**where·of** \-'əv, -'äv\ *conj* (14c) **1 :** of what ⟨knows ~ she speaks⟩ **2 a :** of which ⟨books ~ the best are lost⟩ **b :** of whom **3** *archaic* : with or by which

[2]**whereof** *adv, archaic* (15c) : of what ⟨~ are you made —Shak.⟩

[1]**where·on** \-'ȯn, -'än\ *conj* (13c) **1** *archaic* : on what ⟨tell me ~ the likelihood depends —Shak.⟩ **2 :** on which ⟨the base ~ it rests⟩

[2]**whereon** *adv, archaic* (15c) : on what ⟨~ do you look —Shak.⟩

where·so·ev·er \'hwer-sə-ˌwev-ər, 'hwar-, 'wer-, 'war-\ *conj* (13c) : WHEREVER

where·through \'hwe(ə)r-ˌthrü, 'hwa(ə)r-, 'we(ə)r-, 'wa(ə)r-\ *conj* (13c) : through which

[1]**where·to** \-ˌtü\ *adv* (13c) : to what place, purpose, or end ⟨~ tends all this —Shak.⟩

[2]**whereto** *conj* (14c) : to which

where·un·to \hwer-'ən-(ˌ)tü, hwar-, wer-, war-, (ˌ)(h)wər-, -'ən-tə(-w)\ *adv or conj* (15c) : WHERETO

where·up·on \'hwer-ə-ˌpȯn, 'hwar-, 'wer-, 'war-, -ˌpän\ *conj* (14c) **1 :** on which **2 :** closely following and in consequence of which

[1]**wher·ev·er** \hwer-'ev-ər, hwar-, wer-, war-, (ˌ)(h)wər-\ *adv* (13c) **1 :** where in the world ⟨~ did she get that hat⟩ **2 :** anywhere at all ⟨explore northward or ~ —Bernard De Voto⟩

[2]**wherever** *conj* (14c) **1 :** at, in, or to any or all places that ⟨thrives ~ he goes⟩ **2 :** in any circumstance in which ⟨~ it is possible, he tries to help⟩

[1]**where·with** \'hwe(ə)r-ˌwith, 'hwa(ə)r-, 'we(ə)r-, 'wa(ə)r-, -ˌwith\ *conj* (13c) : with or by means of which ⟨metal tools ~ to break ground —Russell Lord⟩

[2]**wherewith** *pron, archaic* (13c) : that with or by which — used with an infinitve ⟨so shall I have ~ to answer him — Ps 119:42 (AV)⟩

[3]**wherewith** *adv, obs* (13c) : with what ⟨~ shall it be salted —Mt 5:13 (AV)⟩

[1]**where·with·al** \'hwe(ə)r-with-ˌȯl, 'hwa(ə)r-, 'we(ə)r-, 'wa(ə)r-, -with-\ *conj* [*where* + *withal*] (1578) : WHEREWITH

[2]**wherewithal** *pron* (1583) : that with or by which

[3]**wherewithal** *n* (1659) : MEANS, RESOURCES; *specif* : MONEY ⟨didn't have the ~ for an expensive dinner⟩

wher·ry \'hwer-ē, 'wer-\ *n, pl* **wherries** [ME *whery*] (15c) **1 :** any of various light boats: as **a :** a long light rowboat made sharp at both ends and used to transport passengers on rivers and about harbors **b :** a racing scull for one person **2 :** a large light barge, lighter, or fishing boat varying in type in different parts of Great Britain

[1]**whet** \'hwet, 'wet\ *vt* **whet·ted; whet·ting** [ME *whetten*, fr. OE *hwettan;* akin to OHG *wezzen* to whet, *waz* sharp] (bef. 12c) **1 :** to sharpen by rubbing on or with something (as a stone) ⟨~ a knife⟩ **2 :** to make keen or more acute : EXCITE, STIMULATE ⟨~ the appetite⟩ — **whet·ter** *n*

[2]**whet** *n* (1641) **1** *dial* **a :** a spell of work done with a scythe between the time it is sharpened and the time it needs to be sharpened again **b :** TIME, WHILE **2 :** something that sharpens or makes keen: **a :** GOAD, INCITEMENT **b :** APPETIZER; *also* : a drink of liquor

[1]**wheth·er** \'hweth-ər, 'weth-, (ˌ)(h)wəth-\ *n* [ME, fr. OE *hwæther, hwether;* akin to OHG *hwedar* which of two, L *uter*, Gk *poteros*, OE *hwā* who — more at WHO] (bef. 12c) **1** *archaic* : which one of the two **2** *archaic* : whichever one of the two

[2]**whether** *conj* (bef. 12c) — used as a function word usu. with correlative *or* or with *or whether* to indicate (1) until the early 19th century a direct

question involving alternatives; (2) an indirect question involving alternatives ⟨decide ~ he should agree or raise objections⟩; (3) alternative conditions or possibilities ⟨see me no more, ~ he be dead or no —Shak.⟩ ⟨seated him next to her ~ by accident or design⟩ — **whether or no** *or* **whether or not** : in any case

whet·stone \ˈhwet-ˌstōn, ˈwet-\ *n* (bef. 12c) : a stone for whetting edge tools

whew *often read as* ˈhwü, ˈwü, ˈhyü; *the interj is a whistle concluded with a voiceless* ü\ *n* [imit.] (1513) **1** : a whistling sound **2** : a sound like a half-formed whistle uttered as an exclamation ⟨gave a long ~ when he realized the size of the job⟩ — used interjectionally chiefly to express amazement, discomfort, or relief

whey \ˈhwā, ˈwā\ *n* [ME, fr. OE *hwæg;* akin to MD *wey* whey] (bef. 12c) : the serum or watery part of milk that is separated from the coagulable part or curd esp. in the process of making cheese and that is rich in lactose, minerals, and vitamins and contains lactalbumin and traces of fat

whey–face \ˈhwā-ˌfās, ˈwā-\ *n* (1605) : a person having a pale face (as from fear) — **whey–faced** \-ˌfāst\ *adj*

1**which** \(ˈ)hwich, (ˈ)wich\ *adj* [ME, of what kind, which, fr. OE *hwilc;* akin to OHG *wilīh* of what kind, which, OE *hwā* who & *-līc* -ly — more at WHO, -LY] (bef. 12c) **1** : being what one or ones out of a group — used as an interrogative ⟨~ tie should I wear⟩ ⟨kept a record of ~ employees took their vacations in July⟩ **2** : 1WHICHEVER ⟨it will not fit, turn it ~ way you like⟩ **3** — used as a function word to introduce a nonrestrictive relative clause and to modify a noun in that clause and to refer together with that noun to a word or word group in a preceding clause or to an entire preceding clause or sentence or longer unit of discourse ⟨in German, ~ language might . . . have been the medium of transmission —Thomas Pyles⟩ ⟨that this city is a rebellious city . . . : for ~ cause was this city destroyed —Ezra 4:15 (AV)⟩

2**which** *pron* (bef. 12c) **1** : what one or ones out of a group — used as an interrogative ⟨~ of those houses do you live in⟩ ⟨~ of you want tea and ~ want lemonade⟩ ⟨he is swimming or canoeing, I don't know ~⟩ **2** : WHICHEVER ⟨take ~ you like⟩ **3** — used as a function word to introduce a relative clause; used in any grammatical relation except that of a possessive; used esp. in reference to animals, inanimate objects, groups, or ideas ⟨the bonds ~ represent the debt —G. B. Robinson⟩ ⟨the Samnite tribes, ~ settled south and southeast of Rome —Ernst Pulgram⟩; used freely in reference to persons recently as the 17th century ⟨our Father ~ art in heaven —Mt 6:9 (AV)⟩, and still occas. so used but usu. with some implication of emphasis on the function or role of the person rather than on the person himself ⟨chiefly they wanted husbands, ~ they got easily —Lynn White⟩; used by speakers on all educational levels and by many reputable writers, though disapproved by some grammarians, in reference to an idea expressed by a word or group of words that is not necessarily a noun or noun phrase ⟨he resigned that post, after ~ he engaged in ranching —*Current Biog.*⟩

1**which·ev·er** \hwich-ˈev-ər, wich-\ *adj* (14c) : being whatever one or ones out of a group : no matter which ⟨its soothing . . . effect will be the same ~ way you take it —*Punch*⟩

2**whichever** *pron* (15c) : whatever one or ones out of a group ⟨take two of the four elective subjects, ~ you prefer⟩

which·so·ev·er \ˌhwich-sə-ˈwev-ər, ˌwich-\ *pron or adj* (15c) : WHICHEVER

whick·er \ˈhwik-ər, ˈwik-\ *vi* **whick·ered; whick·er·ing** \-(ə-)riŋ\ [imit.] (ca. 1808) : NEIGH, WHINNY — **whicker** *n*

whid \ˈhwid, ˈwid\ *vi* **whid·ded; whid·ding** [Sc *whid* silent rapid motion] *Scot* (1728) : to move nimbly and silently

whidah *var of* WHYDAH

1**whiff** \ˈhwif, ˈwif\ *n* [origin unknown] (1591) **1** **a** : a quick puff or slight gust esp. of air, odor, gas, smoke, or spray **b** : an inhalation of odor, gas, or smoke **c** : a slight puffing or whistling sound **2** : a slight trace **3** : STRIKEOUT

2**whiff** *vi* (1591) **1** : to move with or as if with a puff of air **2** : to emit whiffs : PUFF **3** : to inhale an odor **4** : STRIKE OUT 3 ~ *vt* **1** **a** : to carry or convey by or as if by a whiff : BLOW **b** : to expel or puff out in a whiff : EXHALE **c** : SMOKE 3 **2** : FAN 8

whif·fet \ˈhwif-ət, ˈwif-\ *n* [prob. alter. of *whippet*] (1839) : a small, young, or unimportant person

whif·fle \ˈhwif-əl, ˈwif-\ *vb* **whif·fled; whif·fling** \-(ə-)liŋ\ [prob. freq. of *whiff*] *vi* (1568) **1** **a** *of the wind* : to blow unsteadily or in gusts **b** : VACILLATE **2** : to emit or produce a light whistling or puffing sound ~ *vt* : to blow, disperse, emit, or expel with or as if with a whiff

1**whif·fler** \ˈhwif-lər, ˈwif-\ *n* [alter. of earlier *wifler,* fr. obs. *wifle* (battle-ax)] *Brit* (1539) : one that clears the way for a procession

2**whif·fler** \ˈhwif-(ə-)lər, ˈwif-\ *n* [*whiffle*] (1607) **1** : one that frequently changes his opinion or course **2** : one that uses shifts and evasions in argument

whif·fle·tree \ˈhwif-əl-(ˌ)trē, ˈwif-\ *n* [alter. of *whippletree*] (ca. 1828) : the pivoted swinging bar to which the traces of a harness are fastened and by which a vehicle or implement is drawn

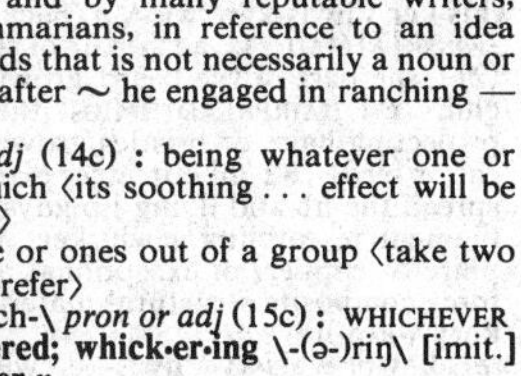

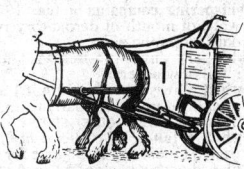

1 whiffletree

Whig \ˈhwig, ˈwig\ *n* [short for *Whiggamore* (member of a Scottish group that marched to Edinburgh in 1648 to oppose the court party)] (ca. 1680) **1** : a member or supporter of a major British political group of the 18th and early 19th centuries seeking to limit the royal authority and increase parliamentary power — compare TORY **2** : an American favoring independence from Great Britain during the American Revolution **3** : a member or supporter of an American political party formed about 1834 in opposition to the Jacksonian Democrats, associated chiefly with manufacturing, commercial, and financial interests, and succeeded about 1854 by the Republican party — **Whig** *adj* — **Whig·gish** \ˈhwig-ish, ˈwig-\ *adj* — **Whig·gism** \-ˌiz-əm\ *n*

Whig·gery \ˈhwig-ə-rē, ˈwig-\ *n* (1682) : the principles or practices of Whigs

whig·ma·lee·rie \ˌhwig-mə-ˈli(ə)r-ē, ˌwig-\ *n* [origin unknown] (1730) **1** : WHIM **2** : an odd or fanciful contrivance : GIMCRACK

1**while** \ˈhwī(ə)l, ˈwī(ə)l\ *n* [ME, fr. OE *hwīl;* akin to OHG *hwīla* time, L *quies* rest, quiet] (bef. 12c) **1** : a period of time esp. when short and marked by the occurrence of an action or a condition : TIME ⟨stay here for a ~⟩ **2** : the time and effort used (as in the performance of an action) : TROUBLE ⟨worth your ~⟩

2**while** *conj* (12c) **1** **a** : during the time that ⟨take a nap ~ I'm out⟩ **b** : as long as ⟨~ there's life there's hope⟩ **2** **a** : when on the other hand : WHEREAS ⟨easy for an expert, ~ it is dangerous for a novice⟩ **b** : in spite of the fact that : ALTHOUGH ⟨~ respected, he is not liked⟩ **3** : similarly and at the same time that ⟨~ the book will be welcomed by scholars, it will make an immediate appeal to the general reader —*Brit. Book News*⟩

3**while** *prep, archaic* (14c) : UNTIL

4**while** *vt* **whiled; whil·ing** (1635) : to cause to pass esp. without boredom or in a pleasant manner — usu. used with *away* ⟨~ away the time⟩

1**whiles** \ˈhwī(ə)lz, ˈwī(ə)lz\ *conj* [ME, fr. *while* + *-s,* adv. suffix — more at WHENCE] *archaic* (13c) : WHILE

2**whiles** *adv, chiefly Scot* (15c) : SOMETIMES

1**whi·lom** \ˈhwī-ləm, ˈwī-\ *adv* [ME, lit., at times, fr. OE *hwīlum,* dat. pl. of *hwīl* time, while] *archaic* (13c) : FORMERLY

2**whilom** *adj* (15c) : FORMER

whilst \ˈhwī(ə)lst, ˈwī(ə)lst\ *conj* [ME *whilest,* alter. of *whiles*] *chiefly Brit* (14c) : WHILE

whim \ˈhwim, ˈwim\ *n* [short for *whim-wham*] (1678) **1** : a capricious or eccentric and often sudden idea or turn of the mind : FANCY **2** : a large capstan that is made with one or more radiating arms to which a horse may be yoked and that is used in mines for raising ore or water **syn** see CAPRICE

whim·brel \ˈhwim-brəl, ˈwim-\ *n* [origin unknown] (1530) : a small European curlew (*Numenius phaeopus*); *broadly* : any small curlew

1**whim·per** \ˈhwim-pər, ˈwim-\ *vi* **whim·pered; whim·per·ing** \-p(ə-)riŋ\ [imit.] (1513) **1** : to make a low whining plaintive or broken sound **2** : to complain or protest with or as if with a whimper

2**whimper** *n* (ca. 1700) **1** : a whimpering cry or sound **2** : a petulant complaint or protest

whim·si·cal \ˈhwim-zi-kəl, ˈwim-\ *adj* [*whimsy*] (1653) **1** : full of, actuated by, or exhibiting whims **2** **a** : resulting from or characterized by whim or caprice **b** : subject to erratic behavior or unpredictable change — **whim·si·cal·i·ty** \ˌhwim-zə-ˈkal-ət-ē, ˌwim-\ *n* — **whim·si·cal·ly** \ˈhwim-zi-k(ə-)lē, ˈwim-\ *adv* — **whim·si·cal·ness** \-kəl-nəs\ *n*

whim·sied \ˈhwim-zēd, ˈwim-\ *adj* (1624) : WHIMSICAL

whim·sy *or* **whim·sey** \ˈhwim-zē, ˈwim-\ *n, pl* **whimsies** *or* **whimseys** [irreg. fr. *whim-wham*] (1605) **1** : WHIM, CAPRICE **2** : a fanciful or fantastic device, object, or creation esp. in writing or art

whim–wham \ˈhwim-ˌhwam, ˈwim-ˌwam\ *n* [origin unknown] (1500) **1** : a whimsical object or device esp. of ornament or dress **2** : FANCY, WHIM **3** *pl* : JITTERS

whin \ˈhwin, ˈwin\ *n* [ME *whynne,* of Scand origin; akin to Norw *kvein* bent grass] (15c) : FURZE

whin·chat \ˈhwin-ˌchat, ˈwin-\ *n* [*whin*] (1678) : a small brown and buff European singing bird (*Saxicola rubetra*) of grassy meadows

1**whine** \ˈhwīn, ˈwīn\ *vb* **whined; whin·ing** [ME *whinen,* fr. OE *hwīnan* to whiz; akin to ON *hvīna* to whiz] *vi* (13c) **1** **a** : to utter a high-pitched plaintive or distressed cry **b** : to make a sound similar to such a cry ⟨the wind *whined* in the chimney⟩ **2** : to utter a complaint with or as if with a whine **3** : to move or proceed with the sound of a whine ⟨the bullet *whined* . . . across the ice —Berton Roueché⟩ ~ *vt* : to utter or express with or as if with a whine — **whin·er** *n* — **whin·ing·ly** \ˈhwī-niŋ-lē, ˈwī-\ *adv*

2**whine** *n* (1633) **1** **a** : a prolonged high-pitched cry usu. expressive of distress or pain **b** : a sound resembling such a cry **2** : a complaint uttered with or as if with a whine — **whiny** *or* **whin·ey** \ˈhwī-nē, ˈwī-\ *adj*

whing–ding \ˈwiŋ-ˌdiŋ, ˈhwiŋ-\ *n* [by alter.] (ca. 1945) : WINGDING

1**whin·ny** \ˈhwin-ē, ˈwin-\ *vb* **whin·nied; whin·ny·ing** [prob. imit.] *vi* (1530) : to neigh esp. in a low or gentle way ~ *vt* : to utter with or as if with a whinny

2**whinny** *n, pl* **whinnies** (ca. 1823) **1** : the loud prolonged cry of a horse : NEIGH **2** : a sound resembling a neigh

whin·stone \ˈhwin-ˌstōn, ˈwin-\ *n* (ca. 1513) : basaltic rock : TRAP; *also* : any of various other dark resistant rocks (as chert)

1**whip** \ˈhwip, ˈwip\ *vb* **whipped; whip·ping** [ME *wippen, whippen;* akin to MD *wippen* to move up and down, sway, OE *wīpian* to wipe] *vt* (14c) **1** : to take, pull, snatch, jerk, or otherwise move very quickly and forcefully ⟨*whipped* out his gun —Green Peyton⟩ **2** **a** (1) : to strike with a slender lithe implement (as a lash or rod) esp. as a punishment (2) : SPANK **b** : to drive or urge on by or as if by using a whip **c** : to strike as a lash does ⟨rain *whipped* the pavement⟩ **3** **a** : to bind or wrap (as a rope or fishing rod) with cord for protection and strength **b** : to wind or wrap around something **4** : to belabor with stinging words : ABUSE **5** : to seam or hem with shallow overcasting stitches **6** : to overcome decisively : DEFEAT **7** : to stir up : INCITE — usu. used with *up* ⟨trying to ~ up a new emotion —Ellen Glasgow⟩ **8** : to produce in a hurry — usu. used with *up* ⟨a sketch . . . an artist might ~ up —*N.Y. Times*⟩ **9** : to fish (water) with rod, line, and artificial lure **10** : to beat (as eggs or cream) into a froth with a utensil (as a whisk or fork) **11** : to gather together or hold together for united action in the manner of a party whip ~ *vi* **1** : to proceed nimbly or quickly : WHISK ⟨*whipping* through the supper dishes —C. B. Davis⟩ **2** : to thrash about flexibly in the manner of a whiplash ⟨a flag . . . *whipping* out from its staff —H. A. Calahan⟩ — **whip·per** *n* — **whip into shape** : to bring forcefully to a desired state or condition

2**whip** *n* (14c) **1** : an instrument consisting usu. of a handle and lash forming a flexible rod that is used for whipping **2** : a stroke or cut with or as if with a whip **3** **a** : a dessert made by whipping a portion of the ingredients ⟨prune ~⟩ **b** : a kitchen utensil made of braided or coiled wire or perforated metal with a handle and used in whipping **4**

: one of the arms of a windmill **5** : a hoisting apparatus; *esp* : a purchase consisting of a single block and a small rope for lifting light articles **6** : one that handles a whip: as **a** : a driver of horses : COACHMAN **b** : WHIPPER-IN 1 **7** **a** : a member of a legislative body appointed by his political party to enforce party discipline and to secure the attendance of party members at important sessions **b** *often cap* : a notice of forthcoming business sent weekly to each member of a political party in the British House of Commons **8** : a whipping or thrashing motion **9** : the quality of resembling a whip esp. in being flexible **10** : any of various pieces of machinery that operate with a quick vibratory motion (as a spring in an electrical device for making a circuit) **11** : a flexible vertical rod radio antenna — called also *whip antenna* — **whip·like** \'hwip-,līk, 'wip-\ *adj*

whip·cord \'hwip-,kȯ(ə)rd, 'wip-\ *n* [fr. its use in making whips] (14c) **1** : a thin tough cord made of braided or twisted hemp or catgut **2** : a cloth that is made of hard-twisted yarns and has fine diagonal cords or ribs

whip hand *n* (1680) **1** : positive control : ADVANTAGE **2** : the hand holding the whip in driving

whip in *vt* (1769) **1** : to collect or keep together (members of a political party) for legislative action **2** : to keep (hounds in a pack) from scattering by use of a whip

whip·lash \'hwip-,lash, 'wip-\ *n* (14c) **1** : the lash of a whip **2** : something resembling a blow from a whip ⟨the ~ of fear —R. S. Banay⟩ **3** : WHIPLASH INJURY

whiplash injury *n* (ca. 1953) : injury resulting from a sudden sharp whipping movement of the neck and head (as of a person in a vehicle that is struck head-on or from the rear by another vehicle)

whip·per–in \,hwip-ə-'rin, ,wip-\ *n, pl* **whip·pers–in** \-ər-'zin\ (1739) **1** : a huntsman's assistant who whips in the hounds **2** : WHIP 7a

whip·per·snap·per \'hwip-ər-,snap-ər, 'wip-\ *n* [alter. of *snippersnapper*] (1700) : a diminutive, insignificant, or presumptuous person

whip·pet \'hwip-ət, 'wip-\ *n* [prob. fr. [1]*whip*] (1610) **1** : any of a breed of small swift slender dogs that are widely used for racing **2** : a small tank used in World War I by the Allied armies

whip·ping *n* (1540) **1** : the act of one that whips: as **a** : a severe beating or chastisement **b** : a stitching with small overcasting stitches **2** : material used to whip or bind

whipping boy *n* (1647) **1** : a boy formerly educated with a prince and punished in his stead **2** : SCAPEGOAT

whipping post *n* (1600) : a post to which offenders are tied to be legally whipped

whip·ple·tree \'hwip-əl-(,)trē, 'wip-\ *n* [perh. irreg. fr. *whip* + *tree*] (1733) : WHIFFLETREE

whip·poor·will \'hwip-ər-,wil, ,hwip-ər-', 'wip-, ,wip-\ *n* [imit.] (1709) : a nocturnal goatsucker (*Caprimulgus vociferus*) of the eastern U.S. and Canada related to the European nightjar

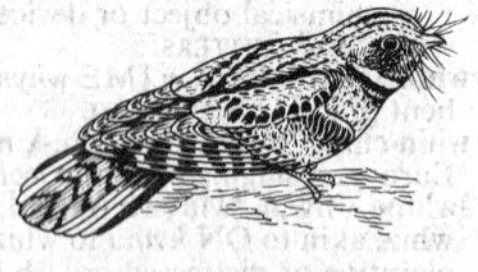
whippoorwill

whip·py \'hwip-ē, 'wip-\ *adj* **whip·pi·er; -est** (1867) **1** : unusually resilient : SPRINGY ⟨a ~ fishing rod⟩ **2** : of, relating to, or resembling a whip

whip–round \'hwip-,raund, 'wip-\ *n, chiefly Brit* (1887) : a collection of money made usu. for a benevolent purpose ⟨had a ~ to help the couple pay for a Paris honeymoon —*The People*⟩

[1]**whip·saw** \'hwip-,sȯ, 'wip-\ *n* [[2]*whip*] (1538) **1** : a narrow pit saw tapering from butt to point, having hook teeth, and averaging from 5 to 7½ feet (1.5 to 2.3 meters) in length **2** : a two-man crosscut saw

[2]**whipsaw** *vt* (1842) **1** : to saw with a whipsaw **2** : to worst or victimize in two opposite ways at once, by a two-phase operation, or by the collusive action of two opponents

whip·sawed \-,sȯd\ *adj* (1892) : subjected to a double market loss through trying inopportunely to recoup a loss by a subsequent short sale of the same security

whip scorpion *n* (ca. 1890) : any of an order (Pedipalpida) of arachnids somewhat resembling true scorpions but having a long slender caudal process and no sting

whip stall *n* (1924) : a stall during a vertical climb in which the nose of the airplane whips violently forward and then downward

[1]**whip·stitch** \'hwip-,stich, 'wip-\ *vt* (1592) : WHIP 5

[2]**whipstitch** *n* (1640) : a shallow overcasting stitch

whip·stock \-,stäk\ *n* (ca. 1530) : the handle of a whip

whip·worm \-,wərm\ *n* (1875) : a parasitic nematode worm (family Trichuridae) with a body that is thickened posteriorly and that is very long and slender anteriorly; *esp* : one (*Trichuris trichiura*) of the human intestine

[1]**whir** *also* **whirr** \'hwər, 'wər\ *vb* **whirred; whir·ring** [ME (Sc) *quirren*, prob. of Scand origin; akin to Dan *hvirre* to whirl, whir; akin to OE *hweorfan* to turn — more at WHARF] *vi* (15c) : to fly, revolve, or move rapidly with a whir ~ *vt* : to move or carry rapidly with a whir

[2]**whir** *also* **whirr** *n* (ca. 1677) : a continuous fluttering or vibratory sound made by something in rapid motion

[1]**whirl** \'hwər(-ə)l, 'wər(-ə)l\ *vb* [ME *whirlen*, prob. of Scand origin; akin to ON *hvirfla* to whirl; akin to OHG *wirbil* whirlwind, OE *hweorfan* to turn — more at WHARF] *vi* (13c) **1** : to move in a circle or similar curve esp. with force or speed **2** **a** : to turn on or around an axis like a wheel : ROTATE **b** : to turn abruptly around or aside : WHEEL **3** : to pass, move, or go quickly ⟨she ~*ed* down the hallway⟩ **4** : to become giddy or dizzy : REEL ⟨my head is ~*ing*⟩ ~ *vt* **1** : to drive, impel, or convey with or as if with a rotary motion **2** **a** : to cause to turn usu. rapidly on or around an axis : ROTATE **b** : to cause to turn abruptly around or aside **3** *obs* : to throw or hurl violently with a revolving motion — **whirl·er** \'hwər-lər, 'wər-\ *n*

[2]**whirl** *n* (15c) **1** **a** : a rapid rotating or circling movement **b** : something undergoing such a movement **2** **a** : a confused tumult : BUSTLE ⟨the social ~⟩ **b** : a confused or disturbed mental state : TURMOIL ⟨a ~ of febrile excitement —Emily Skeel⟩ **3** : an experimental or brief attempt : TRY ⟨gave it a ~⟩

whirl·i·gig \'hwər-li-,gig, 'wər-\ *n* [ME *whirlegigg*, fr. *whirlen* to whirl + *gigg* top — more at GIG] (15c) **1** : a child's toy having a whirling motion **2** : MERRY-GO-ROUND **3** **a** : one that continuously whirls, moves, or changes **b** : a whirling or circling course (as of events)

whirligig beetle *n* (ca. 1855) : any of numerous beetles (family Gyrinidae) that live mostly on the surface of water where they move swiftly about in curves

whirl·pool \'hwər(-ə)l-,pül, 'wər(-ə)l-\ *n* (1529) **1** **a** : a confused tumult and bustle : WHIRL **b** : a magnetic or impelling force by which something may be engulfed ⟨refusing to be drawn into this ~ of intrigue —A. D. White⟩ **2** **a** : water moving rapidly in a circle so as to produce a depression in the center into which floating objects may be drawn : EDDY, VORTEX **b** : WHIRLPOOL BATH

whirlpool bath *n* (ca. 1916) : a therapeutic bath in which all or part of the body is exposed to forceful whirling currents of hot water

[1]**whirl·wind** \-,wind\ *n* (14c) **1** : a small rotating windstorm of limited extent marked by an inward and upward spiral motion of the lower air that is followed by an outward and upward spiral motion and usu. a progressive motion at all levels **2** **a** : a confused rush : WHIRL **b** : a destructive force or agency

[2]**whirlwind** *adj* (1614) : resembling a whirlwind esp. in speed or force ⟨a ~ campaign⟩ ⟨a ~ romance⟩

[1]**whirly** \'hwər-lē, 'wər-\ *adj* (15c) : marked by or exhibiting a whirling motion

[2]**whirly** *n, pl* **whirl·ies** (ca. 1914) : a small whirlwind

whirly·bird \-,bərd\ *n* (1951) : HELICOPTER

whir·ry \'hwər-ē, 'wər-, '(h)wə-rē\ *vb* **whir·ried; whir·ry·ing** [perh. blend of *whir* and *hurry*] *vt, Scot* (1582) : to convey quickly ~ *vi, Scot* : HURRY

[1]**whish** \'hwish, 'wish\ *vb* [imit.] *vt* (1518) : to urge on or cause to move with a whish ~ *vi* **1** : to make a sibilant sound **2** : to move with a whish esp. at high speed ⟨an elevator . . . ~*es* down to the lower level —Natalie Cooper⟩

[2]**whish** *n* (ca. 1802) : a rushing sound : SWISH

whisht \'hwisht, 'wisht\ *vi* [imit.] *chiefly Irish* (15c) : HUSH — often used interjectionally to enjoin silence

[1]**whisk** \'hwisk, 'wisk\ *n* [ME *wisk*, prob. of Scand origin; akin to ON *visk* wisp; akin to OE *wiscian* to plait, L *virga* branch, rod] (14c) **1** : a quick light brushing or whipping motion **2** **a** : a small usu. wire kitchen utensil used for beating food by hand **b** : a flexible bunch (as of twigs, feathers, or straw) attached to a handle for use as a brush

[2]**whisk** *vi* (15c) : to move nimbly and quickly ~ *vt* **1** : to move or convey briskly ⟨~*ed* the children off to bed⟩ **2** : to mix or fluff up by or as if by beating with a whisk ⟨~ egg whites⟩ **3** : to brush or wipe off lightly

whisk broom *n* (1857) : a small broom with a short handle used esp. as a clothes brush

whis·ker \'hwis-kər, 'wis-\ *n* [back-formation fr. *whiskers* (mustache), fr. [2]*whisk*] (1600) **1** **a** : a hair of the beard **b** *pl* (1) *archaic* : MUSTACHE (2) : the part of the beard growing on the sides of the face or on the chin **c** : HAIRBREADTH ⟨lost the race by a ~⟩ **2** : one of the long projecting hairs or bristles growing near the mouth of an animal (as a cat or bird) **3** : an outrigger extending on each side of the bowsprit to spread the jib and flying jib guys — usu. used in pl. **4** **a** : a shred or filament resembling a whisker **b** : a thin hairlike crystal (as of sapphire or copper) of exceptional mechanical strength used esp. to reinforce composite structural material — **whis·kered** \-kərd\ *adj* — **whis·kery** \-k(ə-)rē\ *adj*

whis·key *or* **whis·ky** \'hwis-kē, 'wis-\ *n, pl* **whiskeys** *or* **whiskies** [IrGael *uisce beathadh* & ScGael *uisge beatha*, lit., water of life] (1715) **1** : a liquor distilled from the fermented mash of grain (as rye, corn, or barley) **2** : a drink of whiskey

Whiskey (ca. 1952) — a communications code word for the letter *w*

whiskey sour *n* (ca. 1891) : a cocktail usu. consisting of whiskey, sugar, and lemon juice shaken with ice

[1]**whis·per** \'hwis-pər, 'wis-\ *vb* **whis·pered; whis·per·ing** \-p(ə-)riŋ\ [ME *whisperen*, fr. OE *hwisperian*; akin to OHG *hwispalōn* to whisper, ON *hvīsla* — more at WHISTLE] *vi* (bef. 12c) **1** : to speak softly with little or no vibration of the vocal cords esp. to avoid being overheard **2** : to make a sibilant sound that resembles whispering ~ *vt* **1** : to address in a whisper **2** : to utter or communicate in or as if in a whisper

[2]**whisper** *n* (1596) **1** : something communicated by or as if by whispering; *esp* : RUMOR ⟨~*s* of scandal⟩ **2** **a** : an act or instance of whispering; *esp* : speech without vibration of the vocal cords **b** : a sibilant sound that resembles whispered speech **3** : HINT, TRACE

whis·per·er \-pər-ər\ *n* (1547) : one that whispers; *specif* : RUMORMONGER

[1]**whis·per·ing** *n* (bef. 12c) **1** **a** : whispered speech **b** : GOSSIP, RUMOR **2** : a sibilant sound : WHISPER

[2]**whispering** *adj* (1547) **1** : making a sibilant sound **2** : spreading confidential and esp. derogatory reports ⟨~ tongues can poison truth —S. T. Coleridge⟩ — **whis·per·ing·ly** \-p(ə-)riŋ-lē\ *adv*

whispering campaign *n* (ca. 1920) : the systematic dissemination by word of mouth of derogatory rumors or charges esp. against a candidate for public office

whis·pery \'hwis-p(ə-)rē, 'wis-\ *adj* (1834) **1** : resembling a whisper **2** : full of whispers

[1]**whist** \'hwist, 'wist\ *vi* [imit.] *dial Brit* (14c) : to be silent : HUSH — often used interjectionally to enjoin silence

[2]**whist** *adj* (15c) : QUIET, SILENT

[3]**whist** *n* [alter. of earlier *whisk*, prob. fr. [2]*whisk*; fr. whisking up the tricks] (1663) : a card game for four players in two partnerships that is played with a pack of 52 cards and that scores one point for each trick in excess of six

[1]**whis·tle** \'hwis-əl, 'wis-\ *n, often attrib* [ME, fr. OE *hwistle*; akin to ON *hvīsla* to whisper, *hvīna* to whiz — more at WHINE] (bef. 12c) **1** **a** : a small wind instrument in which sound is produced by the forcible passage of breath through a slit in a short tube ⟨police ~⟩ **b** : a device through which air or steam is forced into a cavity or against a thin edge to produce a loud sound ⟨a factory ~⟩ **2** **a** : a shrill clear sound produced by forcing breath out or air in through the puckered lips **b** : the sound produced by a whistle **c** : a signal given by or as if by whistling **3** : a sound that resembles a whistle; *esp* : a shrill clear note of or as if of a bird

[2]**whistle** *vb* **whis·tled; whis·tling** \-(ə-)liŋ\ *vi* (bef. 12c) **1** **a** : to utter a shrill clear sound by blowing or drawing air through the puckered lips

b : to utter a shrill note or call resembling a whistle **c :** to make a shrill clear sound esp. by rapid movement ⟨the wind *whistled*⟩ **d :** to blow or sound a whistle **2 a :** to give a signal or issue an order or summons by or as if by whistling **b :** to make a demand without result ⟨did a sloppy job so he can ~ for his money⟩ **~** *vt* **1 :** to send, bring, signal, or call by or as if by whistling **2 :** to produce, utter, or express by whistling ⟨~ a tune⟩ — **whis·tle·able** \-ə-lə-bəl\ *adj* — **whistle in the dark :** to keep up one's courage by or as if by whistling

whis·tle–blow·er \-ˌblō(-ə)r\ *n* (1970) **:** one who reveals something covert or who informs against another ⟨pledges to protect ~*s* who fear reprisals —*Wall Street Jour.*⟩ — **whis·tle–blow·ing** \-ˌblō-iŋ\ *n*

whis·tler \ˈhwis-(ə-)lər, ˈwis-\ *n* (bef. 12c) **:** one that whistles: as **a :** any of various birds; *esp* **:** any of a genus (*Pachycephala*) of Australian and Polynesian birds that are related to the shrikes and have a whistling call **b :** a large mountain marmot (*Marmota caligata*) of northwestern No. America **c :** a broken-winded horse **d :** an electromagnetic signal of audio or radio frequency that is generated by lightning discharge and that travels along the earth's magnetic lines of force

¹whis·tle–stop \ˈhwis-əl-ˌstäp, ˈwis-\ *n* (ca. 1925) **1 a :** a small station at which trains stop only on signal **:** FLAG STOP **b :** a small community **2 :** a brief personal appearance esp. by a political candidate usu. on the rear platform of a train during the course of a tour

²whistle–stop *vi* (1952) **:** to make a tour esp. in a political campaign with many brief personal appearances in small communities

whis·tling *n* (14c) **:** the act or sound of one that whistles **:** WHISTLE

whistling swan *n* (1785) **:** a native No. American swan (*Olor columbianus*) with a soft musical note that breeds in the Arctic tundra and winters in shallow fresh or salt water esp. along the eastern and western coasts of the U.S.

whit \ˈhwit, ˈwit\ *n* [prob. alter. of ME *wiht, wight* creature, thing — more at WIGHT] (15c) **:** the smallest part or particle imaginable **:** BIT ⟨have not contributed one ~ to our knowledge of man —Nehemiah Jordan⟩

¹white \ˈhwīt, ˈwīt\ *adj* **whit·er; whit·est** [ME, fr. OE *hwīt;* akin to OHG *hwīz* white, Skt *śveta*] (bef. 12c) **1 a :** free from color **b :** of the color of new snow or milk; *specif* **:** of the color white **c :** light or pallid in color ⟨~ hair⟩ ⟨lips ~ with fear⟩ **d :** lustrous pale gray **:** SILVERY; *also* **:** made of silver **2 a :** being a member of a group or race characterized by reduced pigmentation and usu. specif. distinguished from persons belonging to groups marked by black, brown, yellow, or red skin coloration **b :** of, relating to, characteristic of, or consisting of white people **c :** marked by upright fairness **3 :** free from spot or blemish: as **a (1) :** free from moral impurity **:** INNOCENT **(2) :** marked by the wearing of white by the woman as a symbol of purity ⟨a ~ wedding⟩ **b :** unmarked by writing or printing **c :** not intended to cause harm ⟨a ~ lie⟩ ⟨~ magic⟩ **d :** FAVORABLE, FORTUNATE ⟨one of the ~ days of his life —Sir Walter Scott⟩ **4 a :** wearing or habited in white **b :** marked by the presence of snow **:** SNOWY ⟨a ~ Christmas⟩ **5 a :** heated to the point of whiteness **b :** notably ardent **:** PASSIONATE ⟨~ fury⟩ **6 a :** ultraconservative or reactionary in political outlook and action **b :** instigated or carried out by reactionary forces as a counterrevolutionary measure ⟨a ~ terror⟩ **7 :** of, relating to, or constituting a musical tone quality characterized by a controlled pure sound, a lack of warmth and color, and a lack of resonance **8 :** consisting of a wide range of frequencies — used of light, sound, and electromagnetic radiation — **whit·ish** \ˈhwīt-ish, ˈwīt-\ *adj*

²white *n* (bef. 12c) **1 :** the achromatic object color of greatest lightness characteristically perceived to belong to objects that reflect diffusely nearly all incident energy throughout the visible spectrum **2 a :** a white or light-colored part of something: as **(1) :** a mass of albuminous material surrounding the yolk of an egg **(2) :** the white part of the ball of the eye **(3) :** the light-colored pieces in a two-handed board game; *also* **:** the player by whom these are played **b (1)** *archaic* **:** a white target **(2) :** the fifth or outermost circle of an archery target; *also* **:** a shot that hits it **3 :** one that is or approaches the color white: as **a :** white clothing — often used in pl. **b :** WHITE WINE **c :** a white mammal (as a horse or a hog) **d :** a white-colored product (as flour, pins, or sugar) — usu. used in pl. **4** *pl* **:** LEUKORRHEA **5 :** a person belonging to a light-skinned race **6 :** a member of an ultraconservative or reactionary political group

³white *vt* **whit·ed; whit·ing** [ME *whiten,* fr. *white,* adj.] *archaic* (bef. 12c) **:** WHITEN

white amur \-ä-ˈmu̇(ə)r\ *n* [*amur,* fr. *Amur* river] (1968) **:** GRASS CARP

white ant *n* (1684) **:** TERMITE

white·bait \ˈhwīt-ˌbāt, ˈwīt-\ *n* (1758) **1 :** the young of any of several European herrings and esp. of the common herring (*Clupea harengus*) or of the sprat (*C. sprattus*) **2 :** any of various small fishes likened to the European whitebait and used as food

white bass *n* (1813) **:** a No. American freshwater food fish (*Morone chrysops*)

white·beard \ˈhwīt-ˌbi(ə)rd, ˈwīt-\ *n* (15c) **:** an old man **:** GRAYBEARD

white blood cell *n* (1885) **:** a blood cell that does not contain hemoglobin **:** LEUKOCYTE — called also *white blood corpuscle*

white book *n* (15c) **:** an official report of government affairs bound in white

white·cap \ˈhwīt-ˌkap, ˈwīt-\ *n* (1773) **:** a wave crest breaking into white foam

white cedar *n* (1674) **:** any of several No. American timber trees or their wood: as **a :** a strong-scented evergreen swamp tree (*Chamaecyparis thyoides*) of the eastern coast of the U.S. that has smaller leaves than an arborvitae and globose cones with peltate scales **b :** NORTHERN WHITE CEDAR

white cell *n* (1861) **:** WHITE BLOOD CELL

white chip *n* (1897) **1 :** a white-colored poker chip usu. of minimum value **2 :** a thing or quantity of little worth — compare BLUE CHIP

white clover *n* (bef. 12c) **:** a Eurasian clover (*Trifolium repens*) with round heads of white flowers that is widely used in lawn and pasture grass-seed mixtures and is an important source of nectar for bees — called also *white Dutch clover*

white–col·lar \ˈhwīt-ˈkäl-ər, ˈwīt-\ *adj* (1920) **:** of, relating to, or constituting the class of salaried employees whose duties do not call for the wearing of work clothes or protective clothing — compare BLUE-COLLAR

white corpuscle *n* (ca. 1860) **:** WHITE BLOOD CELL

white crappie *n* (ca. 1926) **:** a silvery No. American sunfish (*Pomoxis annularis*) with 5 or 6 protruding spines on the dorsal fins that is used as a panfish and often for stocking small ponds

whit·ed \ˈhwīt-əd, ˈwīt-\ *adj* (14c) **1 :** covered with white or whiting and esp. with whitewash **2 :** made white **:** WHITENED

whited sepulcher *n* [fr. the simile in Mt 23:27 (AV)] (1582) **:** a person inwardly corrupt or wicked but outwardly or professedly virtuous or holy **:** HYPOCRITE

white dwarf *n, pl* **white dwarfs** (1924) **:** a whitish star of low intrinsic brightness usu. with a mass approximately equal to that of the sun but with a density many times larger

white elephant *n* (15c) **1 :** an Indian elephant of a pale color that is sometimes venerated in India, Sri Lanka, Thailand, and Burma **2 a :** a property requiring much care and expense and yielding little profit **b :** an object no longer of value to its owner but of value to others **c :** something of little or no value

white·face \ˈhwīt-ˌfās, ˈwīt-\ *n* (1709) **1 :** a white-faced animal; *specif* **:** HEREFORD **2 :** dead-white facial makeup ⟨a clown in ~⟩

white–faced \-ˈfāst\ *adj* (1595) **1 :** having a wan pale face **2 :** having the face white in whole or in part — used esp. of an animal otherwise dark in color

white feather *n* [fr. the superstition that a white feather in the plumage of a gamecock is a mark of a poor fighter] (ca. 1785) **:** a mark or symbol of cowardice — used chiefly in the phrase *show the white feather*

white·fish \ˈhwīt-ˌfish, ˈwīt-\ *n* (15c) **1 a :** any of various freshwater food fishes (esp. of genera *Coregonus* and *Prosopium*) related to the salmons and trouts **b :** any of various fishes resembling the true whitefishes **c** *Brit* **:** any of various market fishes with white flesh that is not oily **2 :** the flesh of a whitefish esp. as an article of food

white flag *n* (1600) **1 :** a flag of plain white used as a flag of truce or as a token of surrender **2 :** a token of weakness or yielding

white flight *n* (1967) **:** the departure of white families usu. from urban neighborhoods undergoing racial integration or from cities implementing school desegregation

white·fly \ˈhwīt-ˌflī, ˈwīt-\ *n* (ca. 1890) **:** any of numerous small homopterous insects (family Aleyrodidae) that are injurious plant pests related to the scale insects

white–foot·ed mouse \ˌhwīt-ˌfu̇t-əd-, ˌwīt-\ *n* (1869) **:** a common woodland mouse (*Peromyscus leucopus*) of the eastern U.S.; *also* **:** any of several related mice

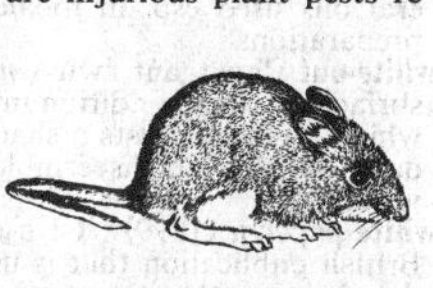

white-footed mouse

white friar *n, often cap W&F* [fr. his white habit] (15c) **:** CARMELITE

white–fringed beetle \ˌhwīt-ˌfrinj(d)-, ˌwīt-\ *n* (1939) **:** any of a genus (*Graphognathus*) of So. American flightless beetles of which one (*G. leucoloma*) has been accidentally introduced into the southeastern U.S. where it is a pest on cultivated plants

white gasoline *n* (1926) **:** gasoline containing no tetraethyllead — called also *white gas*

white gold *n* (ca. 1666) **:** a pale alloy of gold esp. with nickel or palladium that resembles platinum in appearance

white goods *n pl* (ca. 1871) **1 a :** white fabrics esp. of cotton or linen **b :** articles (as sheets, towels, or curtains) orig. or typically made of white cloth **2 :** major household appliances (as stoves and refrigerators) that are typically finished in white enamel

white grub *n* (1817) **:** a grub that is the larva of a june beetle and a destructive pest of grass roots

White·hall \ˈhwīt-ˌhȯl, ˈwīt-\ *n* [*Whitehall,* thoroughfare of London in which are located the chief offices of British government] (1850) **:** the British government

white·head \-ˌhed\ *n* (ca. 1931) **:** MILIUM

white–head·ed \-ˈhed-əd\ *adj* (1525) **1 :** having the hair, fur, or plumage of the head white or very light **2 :** specially favored **:** FORTUNATE — used esp. in the phrase *white-headed boy*

white heat *n* (ca. 1710) **1 :** a temperature (as for copper and iron from 1500° to 1600° C) which is higher than red heat and at which a body becomes brightly incandescent **2 :** a state of intense mental or physical strain, emotion, or activity

white hole *n* (1971) **:** a hypothetical extremely dense celestial object that radiates enormous amounts of energy and matter—compare BLACK HOLE

white hope *n* (ca. 1910) **1** *slang* **:** a white contender for a boxing championship held by a black; *also* **:** one who is felt to represent whites **2 :** one from whom much is expected; *esp* **:** a person undertaking a difficult task

White Horde *n* (ca. 1911) **:** a Mongolian people powerful in Russia in the 14th century

white–hot \ˈhwīt-ˈhät, ˈwīt-\ *adj* (1820) **1 :** being at or radiating white heat **2 :** ardently zealous **:** FERVID

White House \-ˌhau̇s\ *n* [the *White House,* mansion in Washington, D.C. assigned to the use of the president of the U.S.] (1811) **1 :** the executive department of the U.S. government **2 :** a residence of the president of the U.S.

white hunter *n* (1945) **:** a white man serving as guide and professional hunter to an African safari

white knight *n* (1951) **1 :** one that comes to the rescue; *esp* **:** a corporation invited to buy out a second corporation in order to prevent an undesired takeover by a third **2 :** one that champions a cause

white–knuck·le \ˈhwīt-ˈnək-əl, ˈwīt-\ *adj* (1974) **:** showing or causing tense nervousness ⟨a ~ ride on a roller coaster⟩

white lead *n* (15c) **:** any of several white lead-containing pigments; *esp* **:** a heavy poisonous basic carbonate of lead of variable composition that is marketed as a powder or as a paste in linseed oil, has good hiding power, and is used chiefly in exterior paints

white lightning *n* (1915) **:** MOONSHINE 3

\ə\ abut \ᵊ\ kitten, F table \ər\ further \a\ ash \ā\ ace \ä\ cot, cart
\au̇\ out \ch\ chin \e\ bet \ē\ easy \g\ go \i\ hit \ī\ ice \j\ job
\ŋ\ sing \ō\ go \ȯ\ law \ȯi\ boy \th\ thin \t͟h\ the \ü\ loot \u̇\ foot
\y\ yet \zh\ vision \à, k̟, ⁿ, œ, œ̄, ue, ue̅, ʸ\ *see* Guide to Pronunciation

white line *n* (15c) : a band or edge of something white; *esp* : a stripe painted on a road and used to guide traffic
white list \-ˌlist\ *n* (ca. 1909) : a list of approved or favored items — compare BLACKLIST — **white–list·ed** \-ˌlis-təd\ *adj*
white–liv·ered \-ˈliv-ərd\ *adj* [fr. the former belief that the choleric temperament depends on the body's producing large quantities of yellow bile] (ca. 1548) : PUSILLANIMOUS, LILY-LIVERED
white·ly \ˈhwīt-lē, ˈwīt-\ *adv* (14c) : with an effect of whiteness : so as to show or appear white
white man's burden *n* ["The White Man's Burden" (1899), poem by Rudyard Kipling] (1899) : the alleged duty of the white peoples to manage the affairs of the less developed nonwhite peoples
white matter *n* (1839) : neural tissue that consists largely of myelinated nerve fibers, has a whitish color, and underlies the gray matter of the brain and spinal cord or is gathered into nerves
white metal *n* (1613) **1** : any of several light-colored alloys used esp. as a base for plated silverware and ornaments and novelties **2** : any of several lead-base or tin-base alloys (as babbitt metal) used esp. for bearings, fusible plugs, and type metal
white mustard *n* (1731) : a Eurasian mustard (*Brassica hirta*) grown for its seeds which yield mustard and mustard oil
whit·en \ˈhwīt-ᵊn, ˈwīt-\ *vb* **whit·ened; whit·en·ing** \ˈhwīt-niŋ, ˈwīt-, -ᵊn-iŋ\ *vt* (14c) : to make white or whiter ⟨snow ~*ed* the hills⟩ ~ *vi* : to become white or whiter
whit·en·er \ˈhwīt-nər, -ᵊn-ər, ˈwīt-\ *n* (1611) : one that whitens; *specif* : an agent (as a bleach) used to impart whiteness to something
white·ness \ˈhwīt-nəs, ˈwīt-\ *n* (bef. 12c) **1** : the quality or state of being white: as **a** : white color **b** : PALLOR, PALENESS **c** : freedom from stain : CLEANNESS **2** : white substance
whit·en·ing *n* (1601) **1** : the act or process of making or becoming white **2** : something that is used to make white : WHITING
white oak *n* (1635) : any of various oaks (esp. *Quercus alba* of No. America) with acorns that mature in one year and leaf veins that never extend beyond the margin of the leaf; *also* : its hard strong durable wood
white of egg *n, pl* **whites of egg** *or* **whites of eggs** (15c) : WHITE 2a(1)
white oil *n* (ca. 1900) : any of various colorless odorless tasteless mineral oils used esp. in medicine and in pharmaceutical and cosmetic preparations
white·out \ˈhwīt-ˌau̇t, ˈwīt-\ *n* [*white* + *-out* (as in *blackout*)] (1942) : a surface weather condition in a snow-covered area (as a polar region) in which no object casts a shadow, the horizon cannot be seen, and only dark objects are discernible; *also* : a blizzard that severely reduces visibility
white paper *n* (1899) **1** : a government report on any subject; *esp* : a British publication that is usu. less extensive than a blue book **2** : a detailed or authoritative report
white pepper *n* (14c) : a pungent condiment that consists of the fruit of an East Indian plant (*Piper nigrum*) ground after the black husk has been removed
white perch *n* (1775) **1** : a small silvery anadromous sea bass (*Morone americana*) of the coast and coastal streams of the eastern U.S. **2** : FRESHWATER DRUM **3** : WHITE CRAPPIE
white pine *n* (1682) **1 a** : a tall-growing pine (*Pinus strobus*) of eastern No. America with leaves in clusters of five — called also *eastern white pine* **b** : any of several trees that resemble the white pine esp. in having leaves in bundles of five **2** : the wood of a white pine and esp. of the eastern white pine
white–pine blister rust *n* (1916) : a destructive disease of white pine caused by a rust fungus (*Cronartium ribicola*) that passes part of its complex life cycle on currant or gooseberry bushes; *also* : this fungus
white potato *n* (ca. 1890) : POTATO 2b
white room *n* (1962) : CLEAN ROOM
White Russian *n* (1866) : BELORUSSIAN
white rust *n* (ca. 1884) : any of various plant diseases caused by phycomycetous fungi (genus *Albugo* of the order Peronosporales) and characterized by the presence of masses of white spores that escape through ruptures of the host tissue; *also* : a fungus causing a white rust
white sale *n* (1923) : a sale of white goods
white sauce *n* (1723) : a sauce consisting essentially of a roux with milk, cream, or stock and seasoning
white sea bass *n* (1884) : a large croaker (*Cynoscion nobilis*) of the Pacific coast that is an important sport and food fish
white shark *n* (ca. 1674) : a large mackerel shark (*Carcharodon carcharias*) of warm seas that is bluish when young but becomes whitish with age and is a man-eater — called also *great white shark* — see SHARK illustration
white slave *n* (1857) : a woman or girl held unwillingly for purposes of commercial prostitution
white slav·er \-ˈslā-vər\ *n* (1912) : one engaged in white-slave traffic
white slavery *n* (1857) : enforced prostitution
white·smith \ˈhwīt-ˌsmith, ˈwīt-\ *n* (14c) **1** : TINSMITH **2** : a worker in iron who finishes or polishes the work
white space *n* (1849) : the areas of a page (as in a book) not covered by print or pictures
white spruce *n* (ca. 1803) **1** : any of several spruces; *esp* : a widely distributed spruce (*Picea glauca*) of cooler parts of No. America that has short blue-green leaves and slender cones **2** : the wood of a white spruce; *esp* : the light pale tough straight-grained wood of the common white spruce (*Picea glauca*) used esp. for construction and as a source of paper pulp
white sucker *n* (ca. 1902) : a common and widespread edible sucker (*Catostomus commersoni*) of the U.S. and Canada
white supremacist *n* (1945) : an advocate of or believer in white supremacy
white supremacy *n* (1867) : a doctrine based on a belief in the inherent superiority of the white race over the black race and the correlative necessity for the subordination of blacks to whites in all relationships
white·tail \ˈhwīt-ˌtāl, ˈwīt-\ *n* (1872) : WHITE-TAILED DEER
white–tailed deer \ˌhwīt-ˌtāl-ˈdi(ə)r, ˌwīt-\ *n* (1849) : a No. American deer (*Odocoileus virginianus*) with a rather long tail white on the undersurface and forward-arching antlers
white·throat \ˈhwīt-ˌthrōt, ˈwīt-\ *n* (1676) : any of several birds with white on the throat: as **a** : an Old World warbler (*Sylvia communis*) with rusty upper surfaces and largely pale buff underparts **b** : WHITE-THROATED SPARROW
white–throated sparrow \ˌhwīt-ˌthrōt-əd-, ˌwīt-\ *n* (1811) : a common brown sparrow (*Zonotrichia albicollis*) of eastern No. America with a striped crown and a large white patch on the throat
white–tie *adj* (1953) : characterized by or requiring the wearing of formal evening dress by men ⟨a ~ dinner⟩ — compare BLACK-TIE
white trash *n sing but pl in constr* (1855) : POOR WHITE — usu. used disparagingly
white·wall \ˈhwīt-ˌwȯl, ˈwīt-\ *n* (1951) : an automobile tire having a white band on the sidewall
white walnut *n* (ca. 1743) **1** : BUTTERNUT 1b **2** : the light-colored wood of a butternut
[1]**white·wash** \ˈhwīt-ˌwȯsh, ˈwīt-, -ˌwäsh\ *vt* (ca. 1591) **1** : to whiten with whitewash **2 a** : to gloss over or cover up (as vices or crimes) **b** : to exonerate by means of a perfunctory investigation or through biased presentation of data **3** : to hold (an opponent) scoreless in a game or contest — **white·wash·er** *n*
[2]**whitewash** *n* (1689) **1** : a liquid composition for whitening a surface: as **a** : a preparation for whitening the skin **b** : a composition (as of lime and water or whiting, size, and water) for whitening structural surfaces **2** : an act or instance of glossing over or of exonerating **3** : a defeat in a contest in which the loser fails to score
white·wash·ing \-iŋ\ *n* (1663) : an act or instance of applying whitewash; *also* : WHITEWASH 3
white water *n* (1586) : frothy water (as in breakers, rapids, or falls)
white way *n* [the *Great White Way*, nickname for the theatrical section of Broadway, New York City] (1909) : a brilliantly lighted street or avenue esp. in a city's business or theater district
white whale *n* (ca. 1834) : a cetacean (*Delphinapterus leucas*) that is about 10 feet (3.0 meters) long and white when adult — called also *beluga*
white wine *n* (14c) : a wine ranging in color from faintly yellow to amber that is produced from the juice alone of dark- or light-colored grapes
white·wing \ˈhwīt-ˌwiŋ, ˈwīt-\ *n* (1898) : a person and esp. a street sweeper wearing a white uniform
white·wood \-ˌwu̇d\ *n* (1663) **1** : any of various trees with pale or white wood: as **a** : TULIP TREE 1 **b** : an Australian tree (*Atalaya hemiglauca* of the family Sapindaceae) **2** : the wood of a whitewood; *esp* : the pale soft wood of the tulip tree
whit·ey \ˈhwīt-ē, ˈwīt-\ *n, often cap* (1828) : the white man : white society — usu. used disparagingly
[1]**whith·er** \ˈhwith-ər, ˈwith-\ *adv* [ME, fr. OE *hwider;* akin to L *quis* who and to OE *hider* hither — more at WHO, HITHER] (bef. 12c) **1** : to what place ⟨~ will they go⟩ **2** : to what situation, position, degree, or end ⟨~ will this abuse drive him⟩
[2]**whither** *conj* (bef. 12c) **1 a** : to what place ⟨knew ~ to go —Daniel Defoe⟩ **b** : to what situation, position, degree, or end **2 a** : to the place at, in, or to which **b** : to which place **3** : to whatever place
whith·er·so·ev·er \ˌhwith-ər-sə-ˈwev-ər, ˌwith-\ *conj* (14c) : to whatever place ⟨will go ~ you lead⟩
whith·er·ward \ˈhwith-ər-wərd, ˈwith-\ *adv, archaic* (13c) : toward what or which place
[1]**whit·ing** \ˈhwīt-iŋ, ˈwīt-\ *n* [ME, fr. MD *witinc,* fr. *wit* white; akin to OE *hwīt* white] (15c) : any of various marine food fishes: as **a** : a common European fish (*Merlangus merlangus*) related to the cod **b** : SILVER HAKE
[2]**whiting** *n* [ME, fr. gerund of *whiten* to white] (15c) : calcium carbonate prepared as fine powder by grinding and washing and used esp. as a pigment and extender, in putty, and in rubber compounding and paper coating
whit·low \ˈhwit-(ˌ)lō, ˈwit-\ *n* [ME *whitflawe, whitflowe, whitlowe*] (15c) : a deep usu. suppurative inflammation of the finger or toe esp. near the end or around the nail — called also *felon*
Whit·mon·day \ˈhwit-ˈmən-dē, ˈwit-, -ˈmən-\ *n* [*Whit-* (as in *Whitsunday*) + *Monday*] (1557) : the day after Whitsunday observed as a legal holiday in England, Wales, and Ireland
Whit·sun \ˈhwit-sən, ˈwit-\ *adj* [ME *Whitson,* fr. *Whitsonday*] (13c) : of, relating to, or observed on Whitsunday or at Whitsuntide
Whit·sun·day \-ˈsən-dē, -sən-ˌdā\ *n* [ME *Whitsonday,* fr. OE *hwīta sunnandæg,* lit., white Sunday; prob. fr. the custom of wearing white robes by those newly baptized at this season] (12c) : PENTECOST 2
Whit·sun·tide \-sən-ˌtīd\ *n* (13c) : the week beginning with Whitsunday and esp. the first three days of this week
[1]**whit·tle** \ˈhwit-ᵊl, ˈwit-\ *n* [ME *whittel,* alter. of *thwitel,* fr. *thwiten* to whittle, fr. OE *thwītan;* akin to ON *thveita* to hew] *archaic* (15c) : a large knife
[2]**whittle** *vb* **whit·tled; whit·tling** \ˈhwit-liŋ, -ᵊl-iŋ, ˈwit-\ *vt* (1552) **1 a** : to pare or cut off chips from the surface of (wood) with a knife **b** : to shape or form by so paring or cutting **2** : to reduce, remove, or destroy gradually as if by cutting off bits with a knife : PARE ⟨~ down expenses⟩ ~ *vi* **1** : to cut or shape something (as wood) by or as if by paring it with a knife **2** : to wear oneself or another out with fretting — **whit·tler** \-lər, -ᵊl-ər\ *n*
whit·tling *n* (1854) **1** : the act or art of whittling **2** : a piece cut away in whittling
whit·tret \ˈhwi-trət, ˈwi-\ *n* [ME *whitrat,* fr. *white, whit* white + *rat* rat] *chiefly Scot* (15c) : WEASEL
whity *or* **whit·ey** \ˈhwīt-ē, ˈwīt-\ *adj* (1593) : somewhat white : WHITISH — usu. used in combination
[1]**whiz** *or* **whizz** \ˈhwiz, ˈwiz\ *vb* **whizzed; whiz·zing** [imit.] *vi* (1547) **1** : to hum, whir, or hiss like a speeding object (as an arrow or ball) passing through air **2** : to fly or move swiftly esp. with a whiz ~ *vt* : to cause to whiz; *esp* : to rotate very rapidly
[2]**whiz** *or* **whizz** *n, pl* **whiz·zes** (1620) **1** : a hissing, buzzing, or whirring sound **2** : a movement or passage of something accompanied by a whizzing sound
[3]**whiz** *n, pl* **whiz·zes** [prob. by shortening & alter.] (1917) : WIZARD 3 ⟨a ~ at math⟩
whiz–bang *also* **whizz–bang** \ˈhwiz-ˌbaŋ, ˈwiz-, -ˈbaŋ\ *n* (ca. 1914) : one that is conspicuous for noise, speed, excellence, or startling effect — **whiz–bang** *adj*

whiz kid *also* **whizz kid** *n* [[3]*whiz*] (ca. 1942) **:** a person who is unusually intelligent, clever, or successful esp. at an early age

whiz·zer \ˈhwiz-ər, ˈwiz-\ *n* (1881) **:** one that whizzes; *esp* **:** a centrifugal machine for drying something (as grain, sugar, or nitrated cotton)

who \(ˈ)hü, ü\ *pron* [ME, fr. OE *hwā;* akin to OHG *hwer,* interrog. pron., who, L *quis,* Gk *tis,* L *qui,* rel. pron., who] (bef. 12c) **1 :** what or which person or persons — used as an interrogative ⟨~ was elected president⟩ ⟨find out ~ they are⟩; used by speakers on all educational levels and by many reputable writers, though disapproved by some grammarians, as the object of a verb or a following preposition ⟨~ did I see but a Spanish lady —Padraic Colum⟩ ⟨do not know ~ the message is from —G. K. Chesterton⟩ **2 :** the person or persons that **:** WHOEVER **3** — used as a function word to introduce a relative clause; used esp. in reference to persons ⟨my father, ~ was a lawyer⟩ but also in reference to groups ⟨a generation ~ had known nothing but war —R. B. West⟩ or to animals ⟨dogs ~ . . . fawn all over tramps —Nigel Balchin⟩ or to inanimate objects esp. with the implication that the reference is really to a person ⟨earlier sources ~ maintain a Davidic ancestry —F. M. Cross⟩; used by speakers on all educational levels and by many reputable writers, though disapproved by some grammarians, as the object of a verb or a following preposition ⟨a character ~ we are meant to pity —*Times Lit. Supp.*⟩ ***usage*** see WHOM — **as who** *archaic* **:** as one that **:** as if someone — **as who should say** *archaic* **:** so to speak — **who is who** *or* **who's who** *or* **who was who :** the identity of or the noteworthy facts about each of a number of persons

whoa \ˈwō, ˈhō, ˈhwō\ *vb imper* [ME *whoo, who*] (15c) — a command (as to a draft animal) to stand still

who·dun·it *also* **who·dun·nit** \hü-ˈdən-ət\ *n* [substandard *who done it?*] (1930) **:** a detective story or mystery story presented as a novel, play, or motion picture

who·ev·er \hü-ˈev-ər\ *pron* (12c) **:** whatever person **:** no matter who — used in any grammatical relation except that of a possessive ⟨sells to ~ has the money to buy⟩

[1]**whole** \ˈhōl\ *adj* [ME *hool* healthy, unhurt, entire, fr. OE *hāl;* akin to OHG *heil* healthy, unhurt, ON *heill,* OSlav *cělŭ*] (bef. 12c) **1 a** (1) **:** free of wound or injury **:** UNHURT (2) **:** recovered from a wound or injury **:** RESTORED (3) **:** being healed ⟨~ of an ancient evil, I sleep sound —A. E. Housman⟩ **b :** free of defect or impairment **:** INTACT **c :** physically sound and healthy **:** free of disease or deformity **d :** mentally or emotionally sound **2 :** having all its proper parts or components **:** COMPLETE, UNMODIFIED ⟨~ milk⟩ ⟨a ~ egg⟩ **3 a :** constituting the total sum or undiminished entirety **:** ENTIRE ⟨owns the ~ island⟩ **b :** each or all of the ⟨took part in the ~ series of athletic events⟩ **4 a :** constituting an undivided unit **:** UNBROKEN, UNCUT ⟨a ~ roast suckling pig⟩ **b :** directed to one end **:** CONCENTRATED ⟨promised to give it his ~ attention⟩ **5 a :** seemingly complete or total ⟨the ~ idea is to help, not hinder⟩ **b :** very great ⟨feels a ~ lot better now⟩ **6 :** constituting a person in his full nature or development ⟨the university is supposed to educate the ~ man —J. W. Scott⟩ **7 :** having the same father and mother ⟨~ brother⟩ ***syn*** see PERFECT — **whole·ness** *n*

syn WHOLE, ENTIRE, TOTAL, ALL mean including everything or everyone without exception. WHOLE implies that nothing has been omitted, ignored, abated, or taken away; ENTIRE may suggest a state of completeness or perfection to which nothing can be added; TOTAL implies that everything has been counted, weighed, measured, or considered; ALL may equal WHOLE, ENTIRE, or TOTAL.

[2]**whole** *n* (14c) **1 :** a complete amount or sum **:** a number, aggregate, or totality lacking no part, member, or element **2 :** something constituting a complex unity **:** a coherent system or organization of parts fitting or working together as one — **in whole :** to the full or entire extent **:** WHOLLY — usu. used in the phrase *in whole or in part* — **on the whole 1 :** in view of all the circumstances or conditions **:** all things considered **2 :** in general **:** in most instances **:** TYPICALLY

[3]**whole** *adv* (14c) **1 :** WHOLLY, ENTIRELY ⟨a ~ new age group —Henry Chauncey⟩ **2 :** as a complete entity

whole cloth *n* (1840) **:** pure fabrication — usu. used in the phrase *out of whole cloth*

whole gale *n* (ca. 1805) **:** wind having a speed of 55 to 63 miles per hour — see BEAUFORT SCALE table

whole·heart·ed \ˈhōl-ˈhärt-əd\ *adj* (1840) **1 :** completely and sincerely devoted, determined, or enthusiastic ⟨a ~ student of social problems⟩ **2 :** marked by complete earnest commitment **:** free from all reserve or hesitation ⟨gave the movement his ~ support⟩ ***syn*** see SINCERE — **whole·heart·ed·ly** *adv*

whole–hog *adj* (1829) **:** committed without reservation **:** THOROUGHGOING ⟨a ~ patriot⟩

[1]**whole hog** *n* (1829) **:** the whole way or farthest limit — usu. used adverbially in the phrase *go the whole hog*

[2]**whole hog** *adv* (1844) **:** to the fullest extent **:** without reservation **:** COMPLETELY ⟨accepting *whole hog* the standards . . . of the majority —R. B. Kaplan⟩

whole note *n* (1597) **:** a musical note equal in time value to four quarter notes or two half notes

whole number *n* (1557) **:** INTEGER

whole rest *n* (ca. 1890) **:** a musical rest corresponding in time value to a whole note

[1]**whole·sale** \ˈhōl-ˌsāl\ *n* (15c) **:** the sale of commodities in quantity usu. for resale (as by a retail merchant)

[2]**wholesale** *adj* (1642) **1 :** performed or existing on a large scale esp. without discrimination ⟨~ slaughter⟩ **2 :** of, relating to, or engaged in the sale of commodities in quantity for resale ⟨a ~ grocer⟩

[3]**wholesale** *adv* (1759) **:** in a wholesale manner

[4]**wholesale** *vb* **whole·saled; whole·sal·ing** *vt* (1800) **:** to sell (something) in quantity usu. for resale ~ *vi* **:** to sell in quantity usu. for resale

whole·sal·er \ˈhōl-ˌsā-lər\ *n* (1857) **:** a merchant middleman who sells chiefly to retailers, other merchants, or industrial, institutional, and commercial users mainly for resale or business use

whole·some \ˈhōl-səm\ *adj* (13c) **1 :** promoting health or well-being of mind or spirit **2 :** promoting health of body **3 a :** sound in body, mind, or morals **b :** having the simple health or vigor of normal domesticity **4 a :** based on well-grounded fear **:** PRUDENT ⟨a ~ respect for the law⟩ **b :** SAFE ⟨it wouldn't be ~ for you to go down there —Mark Twain⟩ ***syn*** see HEALTHFUL, HEALTHY — **whole·some·ly** *adv* — **whole·some·ness** *n*

whole–souled \ˈhōl-ˈsōld\ *adj* (1834) **:** moved by ardent enthusiasm or single-minded devotion **:** WHOLEHEARTED

whole step *n* (ca. 1899) **:** a musical interval (as C–D or G–A) comprising two half steps — called also *whole tone*

whole wheat *adj* (1880) **:** made of ground entire wheat kernels

who·lis·tic \hō-ˈlis-tik\ *var of* HOLISTIC

whol·ly \ˈhōl-(l)ē\ *adv* [ME *hoolly,* fr. *hool* whole] (14c) **1 :** to the full or entire extent **:** COMPLETELY ⟨a ~ owned subsidiary⟩ **2 :** to the exclusion of other things **:** SOLELY ⟨a book dealing ~ with herbs⟩

whom \(ˈ)hüm, üm\ *pron, objective case of* WHO [ME, fr. OE *hwām,* dat. of *hwā* who] (bef. 12c) — used as an interrogative or relative; used as object of a verb or a preceding preposition ⟨to know for ~ the bell tolls —John Donne⟩ or less frequently as the object of a following preposition ⟨the man ~ you wrote to⟩ though now often considered stilted esp. as an interrogative and esp. in oral use; occas. used as predicate nominative with a copulative verb or as subject of a verb esp. in the vicinity of a preposition or a verb of which it might mistakenly be considered the object ⟨~ say ye that I am — Mt 16:15 (AV)⟩ ⟨people . . . ~ you never thought would sympathize —Shea Murphy⟩

usage Observers of the language have been predicting the demise of *whom* from about 1870 down to the present day ⟨one of the pronoun cases is visibly disappearing — the objective case *whom* —R.G. White (1870)⟩ ⟨*whom* is dying out in England, where "Whom did you see?" sounds affected —Anthony Burgess (1980)⟩ Our evidence shows that no one — English or not — should expect *whom* to disappear momentarily; it shows every indication of persisting quite a while yet. Actual usage of *who* and *whom* — accurately described at the entries in this dictionary — does not appear to be markedly different from the usage of Shakespeare's time. But the 18th century grammarians, propounding rules and analogies, rejecting other rules and analogies, and usu. justifying both with appeals to Latin or Greek, have intervened between us and Shakespeare. It seems clear that the grammarians' rules have had little effect on the traditional uses. One thing they have accomplished is to encourage hypercorrect uses of *whom* ⟨*whom* shall I say is calling?⟩ Another is that they have made some people unsure of themselves ⟨said he was asked to step down, although it is not known exactly *who* or *whom* asked him —*Redding (Conn.) Pilot*⟩

whom·ev·er \hü-ˈmev-ər\ *pron, objective case of* WHOEVER

[1]**whomp** \ˈhwämp, ˈhwȯmp, ˈwämp, ˈwȯmp\ *n* [imit.] (1926) **:** a loud slap, crash, or crunch

[2]**whomp** *vi* (1942) **:** to strike with a sharp noise or thump ~ *vt* **1 :** to hit or slap sharply **2 :** to defeat decisively **:** TROUNCE **3 :** to create or put together esp. hastily — usu. used with *up*

whomp up *vt* (1949) **:** to stir up **:** AROUSE

whom·so \ˈhüm-(ˌ)sō\ *pron, objective case of* WHOSO

whom·so·ev·er \ˌhüm-sə-ˈwev-ər\ *pron, objective case of* WHOSOEVER

[1]**whoop** \ˈhüp, ˈhu̇p, *least frequently for vi 3* ˈhwüp *or* ˈhwu̇p\ *vb* [ME *whopen,* fr. MF *houpper,* of imit. origin] *vi* (15c) **1 :** to utter a whoop in expression of eagerness, enthusiasm, or enjoyment **:** SHOUT **2 :** to utter the cry of an owl **:** HOOT **3 :** to make the characteristic whoop of whooping cough **4 a :** to go or pass with a loud noise **b :** to be rushed through by acclamation or with noisy support ⟨the bill ~*ed* through both houses⟩ ~ *vt* **1 a :** to utter or express with a whoop **b :** to urge, drive, or cheer on with a whoop **2 :** to agitate in behalf of **3 :** RAISE, BOOST ⟨~ up the price⟩ — **whoop it up 1 :** to celebrate riotously **:** CAROUSE **2 :** to stir up enthusiasm

[2]**whoop** *n* (1600) **1 a :** a loud yell expressive of eagerness, exuberance, or jubilation — often used interjectionally **b :** a shout of hunters or of men in battle or pursuit **2 :** the cry of an owl **:** HOOT **3 :** the crowing intake of breath following a paroxysm in whooping cough **4 :** a minimum amount or degree (as of care or consideration) **:** the least bit ⟨not worth a ~⟩

whoop–de–do *or* **whoop–de–doo** \ˌh(w)üp-dē-ˈdü, ˌh(w)u̇p-, -tē-\ *n* [prob. irreg. fr. [2]*whoop*] (1936) **1 :** noisy and exuberant or attention-getting activity (as at a social affair or in a political campaign) **2 :** a lively social affair **3 :** agitated public discussion or debate

[1]**whoop·ee** \ˈ(h)wu̇p-(ˌ)ē, ˈ(h)wu̇-(ˌ)pē; (h)wu̇-ˈpē, (h)wü-\ *interj* [irreg. fr. [2]*whoop*] (15c) — used to express exuberance

[2]**whoop·ee** \ˈ(h)wu̇p-(ˌ)ē, ˈ(h)wü-(ˌ)pē\ *n* (1924) **:** boisterous convivial fun

whoop·er \ˈh(w)ü-pər, ˈh(w)u̇p-ər\ *n* (1660) **:** one that whoops; *specif* **:** WHOOPING CRANE

whooping cough *n* (1739) **:** an infectious disease esp. of children caused by a bacterium (*Bordetella pertussis*) and marked by a convulsive spasmodic cough sometimes followed by a crowing intake of breath — called also *pertussis*

whooping crane *n* (1730) **:** a large white nearly extinct No. American crane (*Grus americana*) noted for its loud whooping note

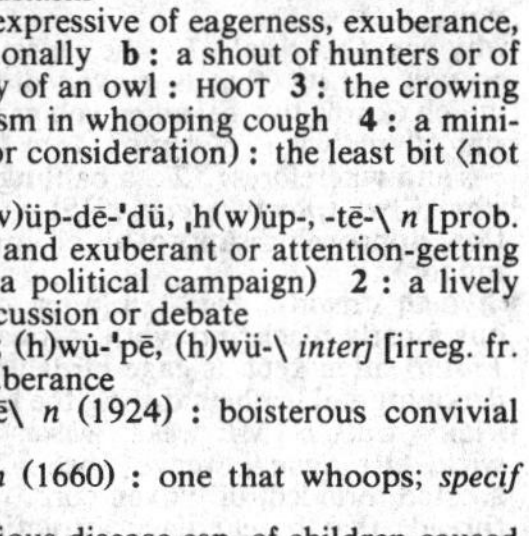
whooping crane

whoop·la \ˈh(w)üp-ˌlä, ˈh(w)u̇p-\ *n* [alter. of *hoopla*] (1931) **1 :** a noisy commotion **2 :** boisterous merrymaking

whoops \ˈ(w)u̇(ə)ps\ *var of* OOPS

[1]**whoosh** \ˈhwüsh, ˈwüsh, ˈ(h)wu̇sh\ *n* [imit.] (1906) **:** a swift or explosive rush

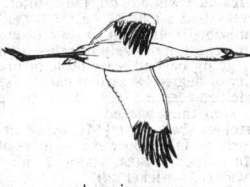

[2]**whoosh** *vi* (1917) **:** to rush past or move explosively ⟨cars ~*ing* along the expressway⟩ ~ *vt* **:** to move (a person or thing) with an explosive or sibilant rush

[1]**whop** \ˈhwäp, ˈwäp\ *vt* **whopped; whop·ping** [ME *whappen,* alter. of *wappen* to throw violently] (15c) **1 :** to pull or whip out **2 a :** BEAT, STRIKE **b :** to defeat totally

[2]**whop** *n* (15c) **:** a heavy blow **:** THUMP

whop·per \'hwäp-ər, 'wäp-\ *n* [[1]*whop*] (ca. 1785) **1 :** something unusually large or otherwise extreme of its kind **2 :** an extravagant or monstrous lie

whop·ping \'hwäp-iŋ, 'wäp-\ *adj* (1625) **:** extremely large; *also* **:** EXTRAORDINARY, INCREDIBLE

[1]**whore** \'hō(ə)r, 'hȯ(ə)r, 'hu̇(ə)r\ *n* [ME *hore,* fr. OE *hōre;* akin to ON *hōrr* adulterer — more at CHARITY] (bef. 12c) **:** a woman who practices promiscuous sexual intercourse esp. for hire **:** PROSTITUTE

[2]**whore** *vb* **whored; whor·ing** *vi* (15c) **1 :** to have unlawful sexual intercourse as or with a whore **2 :** to pursue a faithless, unworthy, or idolatrous desire ~ *vt, obs* **:** to corrupt by lewd intercourse **:** DEBAUCH

whore·dom \'hōrd-əm, 'hȯrd-, 'hu̇rd-\ *n* [ME *hordom* sexual immorality, idolatrous practices, fr. ON *hōrdōmr* adultery, fr. *hōrr* + *-dom* -dom] (12c) **1 :** the practice of whoring **:** PROSTITUTION **2 :** faithless, unworthy, or idolatrous practices or pursuits

whore·house \'hō(ə)r-,hau̇s, 'hȯ(ə)r-, 'hu̇(ə)r-\ *n* (14c) **:** a building in which prostitutes are available

whore·mas·ter \-,mas-tər\ *n* (14c) **:** a man consorting with whores or given to lechery

whore·mon·ger \-,məŋ-gər, -,mäŋ-\ *n* (14c) **:** WHOREMASTER

whore·son \'hōrs-ᵊn, 'hȯrs-, 'hu̇rs-\ *n, often attrib* (14c) **1 :** BASTARD **2 :** a coarse fellow — used as a generalized term of abuse

whor·ish \'hōr-ish, 'hȯr-, 'hu̇r-\ *adj* (1535) **:** of or befitting a whore

whorl \'hwȯr(-ə)l, 'wȯr(-ə)l, '(h)wər(-ə)l\ *n* [ME *wharle, whorle,* prob. alter. of *whirle,* fr. *whirlen* to whirl] (15c) **1 :** a drum-shaped section on the lower part of a spindle in spinning or weaving machinery serving as a pulley for the tape drive that rotates the spindle **2 :** an arrangement of similar anatomical parts (as leaves) in a circle around a point on an axis **3 :** something that whirls, coils, or spirals or whose form suggests such movement **:** SWIRL ⟨~s of snow⟩ **4 :** one of the turns of a univalve shell **5 :** a fingerprint in which the central papillary ridges turn through at least one complete circle

whorled \'hwȯr(-ə)ld, 'wȯr(-ə)ld, '(h)wər(-ə)ld\ *adj* (ca. 1776) **:** having or arranged in whorls

whor·tle·ber·ry \'hwərt-ᵊl-,ber-ē, 'wərt-\ *n* [alter. of earlier *hurtleberry,* fr. ME *hurtilberye,* irreg. fr. OE *horte* whortleberry + ME *berye* berry] (1578) **1 :** a European blueberry (*Vaccinium myrtillus*); *also* **:** its glaucous blackish edible berry **2 :** BLUEBERRY

[1]**whose** \(')hüz, üz\ *adj* [ME *whos,* gen. of *who, what*] (bef. 12c) **:** of or relating to whom or which esp. as possessor or possessors ⟨~ gorgeous vesture heaps the ground —Robert Browning⟩, agent or agents ⟨the law courts, ~ decisions were important —F. L. Mott⟩, or object or objects of an action ⟨the first poem ~ publication he ever sanctioned —J. W. Krutch⟩

[2]**whose** *pron, sing or pl in constr* (13c) **:** that which belongs to whom — used without a following noun as a pronoun equivalent in meaning to the adjective *whose* ⟨tell me ~ it was —Shak.⟩

whose·so·ev·er \,hüz-sə-'wev-ər\ *adj* (1611) **:** of or relating to whomsoever ⟨~ sins ye remit —Jn 20:23 (AV)⟩

who·so \'hü-(,)sō\ *pron* (12c) **:** WHOEVER

who·so·ev·er \,hü-sə-'wev-ər\ *pron* (13c) **:** WHOEVER

who's who \,hüz-'hü\ *n, often cap both Ws* (ca. 1849) **1 :** a compilation of brief biographical sketches of prominent persons in a particular field ⟨a *who's who* of sports figures⟩ **2 :** the leaders of a group **:** ELITE

whump \'hwəmp, 'wəmp\ *vi* [imit.] (1897) **:** BANG, THUMP — **whump** *n*

[1]**why** \(')hwī, (')wī\ *adv* [ME, fr. OE *hwȳ,* instr. case of *hwæt* what — more at WHAT] (bef. 12c) **:** for what cause, reason, or purpose ⟨~ did you do it⟩

[2]**why** *conj* (bef. 12c) **1 :** the cause, reason, or purpose for which ⟨know ~ you did it⟩ ⟨that is ~ you did it⟩ **2 :** for which **:** on account of which ⟨know the reason ~ you did it⟩

[3]**why** \'hwī, 'wī\ *n, pl* **whys** (14c) **1 :** REASON, CAUSE ⟨wants to know the ~s and wherefores⟩ **2 :** a baffling problem **:** ENIGMA

[4]**why** \(,)wī, (,)hwī\ *interj* (1519) — used to express mild surprise, hesitation, approval, disapproval, or impatience ⟨~, here's what I was looking for⟩

whyd·ah \'hwid-ə, 'wid-\ *n* [alter. of *widow (bird)*] (1783) **:** any of various mostly black and white African weaverbirds (genera *Euplectes* and *Vidua*) often kept as cage birds and distinguished in the male by long drooping tail feathers during the breeding season

[1]**wick** \'wik\ *n* [ME *weke, wicke,* fr. OE *wēoce;* akin to OHG *wiohha* wick, OIr *figim* I weave] (bef. 12c) **:** a bundle of fibers or a loosely twisted, braided, or woven cord, tape, or tube usu. of soft spun cotton threads that by capillary attraction draws up to be burned a steady supply of the oil in lamps or the melted tallow or wax in candles

[2]**wick** *vt* (1949) **:** to carry (as moisture) by capillary action — often used with *away* ⟨a fabric that ~s away perspiration⟩

wick·ed \'wik-əd\ *adj* [ME, alter. of *wicke* wicked] (13c) **1 :** morally very bad **:** EVIL **2 a :** FIERCE, VICIOUS ⟨a ~ dog⟩ **b :** disposed to mischief **:** ROGUISH **3 a :** disgustingly unpleasant **:** VILE ⟨a ~ odor⟩ **b :** causing or likely to cause harm, distress, or trouble ⟨a ~ storm⟩ **4 :** going beyond reasonable or predictable limits **:** of exceptional quality or degree ⟨~ skill at cards⟩ ***syn*** see BAD — **wick·ed·ly** *adv*

wick·ed·ness *n* (14c) **1 :** the quality or state of being wicked **2 :** something wicked

wick·er \'wik-ər\ *n* [ME *wiker,* of Scand origin; akin to Sw dial. *vikker* willow, ON *veikr* weak — more at WEAK] (14c) **1 :** a small pliant twig or branch **:** OSIER, WITHE **2 a :** WICKERWORK **b :** something made of wicker — **wicker** *adj*

wick·er·work \-,wərk\ *n* (1719) **:** work consisting of interlaced osiers, twigs, or rods ⟨a cage of ~⟩

wick·et \'wik-ət\ *n* [ME *wiket,* fr. ONF, of Gmc origin; akin to MD *wiket* wicket, OE *wīcan* to yield — more at WEAK] (13c) **1 :** a small gate or door; *esp* **:** one forming part of or placed near a larger gate or door **2 :** an opening like a window; *esp* **:** a grilled or grated window through which business is transacted **3 :** a small gate for emptying the chamber of a canal lock or regulating the amount of water passing through a channel **4 a :** either of the two sets of three stumps topped by two crosspieces and set 22 yards (20 meters) apart at which the ball is bowled in cricket **b :** an area 10 feet (3.0 meters) wide bounded by these wickets **c :** one innings of a batsman; *specif* **:** one that is not completed or never begun ⟨win by three ~s⟩ **5 :** an arch or hoop in croquet

wick·ing \'wik-iŋ\ *n* (1846) **:** material for wicks

wick·i·up \'wik-ē-,əp\ *n* [Fox *wikiyap* dwelling] (1852) **:** a hut used by the nomadic Indians of the arid regions of the western and southwestern U.S. with a usu. oval base and a rough frame covered with reed mats, grass, or brushwood; *also* **:** a rude temporary shelter or hut

wic·o·py \'wik-ə-pē\ *n* [Cree *wikupiy* inner bark of basswood] (1704) **1 :** LEATHERWOOD **2 :** a basswood (*Tilia americana*)

wid·der·shins \'wid-ər-shənz\ *adv* [MLG *weddersinnes,* fr. MHG *widersinnes,* fr. *widersinnen* to go back, go against, fr. *wider* back against (fr. OHG *widar*) + *sinnen* to travel, go; akin to OHG *sendan* to send — more at WITH, SEND] (1513) **:** in a left-handed, wrong, or contrary direction **:** COUNTERCLOCKWISE — compare DEASIL

wid·dy \'wid-ē\ *n, pl* **widdies** [ME (Sc), fr. ME *withy*] (15c) **1** *Scot & dial Eng* **:** a rope of osiers **:** WITHY **2** *Scot & dial Eng* **:** a hangman's noose

[1]**wide** \'wīd\ *adj* **wid·er; wid·est** [ME, fr. OE *wīd;* akin to OHG *wīt* wide] (bef. 12c) **1 a :** having great extent **:** VAST ⟨a ~ area⟩ **b :** extending over a vast area **:** EXTENSIVE ⟨a ~ reputation⟩ **c :** extending throughout a specified area or scope — usu. used in combination ⟨nation*wide*⟩ **d :** COMPREHENSIVE 1, INCLUSIVE 1 ⟨a ~ assortment⟩ **2 a :** having a specified extension from side to side ⟨3 feet ~⟩ **b :** having much extent between the sides **:** BROAD ⟨a ~ doorway⟩ **c :** fully opened ⟨*wide*-eyed⟩ **d :** LAX 4 **3 a :** extending or fluctuating considerably between limits ⟨a ~ variation⟩ **b :** straying or deviating from something specified — used with *of* ⟨his remark was ~ of the truth⟩ **4** *of an animal ration* **:** relatively rich in carbohydrate as compared with protein ***syn*** see BROAD — **wide·ness** *n*

[2]**wide** *adv* **wid·er; wid·est** (bef. 12c) **1 a :** over a great distance or extent **:** WIDELY ⟨searched far and ~⟩ **b :** over a specified distance, area, or extent — usu. in combination ⟨expanded the business country-*wide*⟩ **2 a :** so as to leave much space or distance between **b :** so as to pass at or clear by a considerable distance ⟨ran ~ around left end⟩ **3 :** to the fullest extent **:** COMPLETELY, FULLY ⟨~ open⟩

wide-an·gle \'wī-'daŋ-gəl\ *adj* (1878) **1 :** having or covering an angle of view wider than the ordinary — used esp. of lenses of shorter than normal focal length **2 :** having, involving the use of, or relating to a wide-angle lens ⟨a ~ camera⟩

wide-awake \,wīd-ə-'wāk\ *n* (1837) **1 :** a soft felt hat with a low crown and a wide brim **2 :** SOOTY TERN

wide-awake *adj* (1818) **1 :** fully awake **2 :** alertly watchful esp. for advantages or opportunities ***syn*** see WATCHFUL

wide·band \'wīd-,band\ *adj* (1937) **:** BROADBAND

wide-eyed \'wīd-'īd\ *adj* (1853) **1 :** having the eyes wide open esp. with wonder or astonishment **2 :** marked by unsophisticated or uncritical acceptance or admiration **:** NAIVE ⟨~ innocence⟩

wide·ly *adv* (1663) **1 :** to a great extent ⟨departed ~ from the previous edition⟩ **2 :** over or through a wide area ⟨has traveled ~⟩ **3 :** by or among a large well-dispersed group of people ⟨a ~ known political figure⟩ **4 :** over a broad range ⟨persons with ~ fluctuating incomes —*Current Biog.*⟩

wide·mouthed \'wīd-'mau̇thd, -'mau̇tht\ *adj* (1593) **1 :** having one's mouth opened wide (as in awe) **2 :** having a wide mouth ⟨~ jars⟩

wid·en \'wīd-ᵊn\ *vb* **wid·ened; wid·en·ing** \'wīd-niŋ, -ᵊn-iŋ\ *vt* (1650) **:** to increase the width, scope, or extent of ~ *vi* **:** to become wide or wider — **wid·en·er** \-nər, -ᵊn-ər\ *n*

wide-rang·ing \'wī-,drān-jiŋ\ *adj* (1816) **:** extensive in scope **:** COMPREHENSIVE ⟨~ interests⟩

wide receiver *n* (ca. 1968) **:** a football receiver who normally lines up several yards to the side of the offensive formation

wide-screen *adj* (1953) **:** of or relating to a projected picture whose aspect ratio is substantially greater than 1.33:1

wide·spread \'wīd-'spred\ *adj* (1705) **1 :** widely diffused or prevalent ⟨~ public interest⟩ **2 :** widely extended or spread out ⟨low, ~ hood and fenders —*Time*⟩ ⟨a ~ erosion surface —C. B. Hitchcock⟩

wide-spread·ing \-iŋ\ *adj* (1591) **1 :** stretching or extending over a wide space or area ⟨~ thatch roofs —*Nat'l Geographic*⟩ **2** *archaic* **:** spreading over or affecting a wide area

wid·get \'wij-ət\ *n* [alter. of *gadget*] (1926) **1 :** GADGET **2 :** an unnamed article considered for purposes of hypothetical example

wid·ish \'wīd-ish\ *adj* (1845) **:** somewhat wide

[1]**wid·ow** \'wid-(,)ō, 'wid-ə(-w)\ *n* [ME *widewe,* fr. OE *wuduwe;* akin to OHG *wituwa* widow, L *vidua* widow, *-videre* to separate, Gk *ēitheos* unmarried youth] (bef. 12c) **1 a :** a woman who has lost her husband by death and usu. has not remarried **b :** GRASS WIDOW 2 **2 :** an extra hand or part of a hand of cards dealt face down and usu. placed at the disposal of the highest bidder **3 :** a single usu. short last line (as of a paragraph) separated from its related text and appearing at the top of a printed page or column

[2]**widow** *vt* (14c) **1 :** to bereave of a spouse; *esp* **:** to cause to become a widow **2** *obs* **:** to survive as the widow of **3 :** to deprive of something greatly valued or needed

wid·ow·er \'wid-ə-wər\ *n* [ME *widewer,* alter. of *wedow* widow, widower, fr. OE *wuduwa* widower; akin to OE *wuduwe* widow] (bef. 12c) **:** a man who has lost his wife by death and usu. has not remarried

wid·ow·er·hood \-,hu̇d\ *n* (1796) **1 :** the quality or state of being a widower **2 :** the period during which a man remains a widower

wid·ow·hood \'wid-ō-,hu̇d, 'wid-ə-,hu̇d\ *n* (bef. 12c) **1 :** the quality or state of being a widow **2 :** the period during which a woman remains a widow

widow's peak *n* (ca. 1849) **:** PEAK 7

widow's walk *n* (1937) **:** a railed observation platform atop a usu. coastal house

width \'width, 'witth\ *n* [[1]*wide*] (1627) **1 :** the measurement taken at right angles to the length **:** BREADTH **2 :** largeness of extent or scope **3 :** a measured and cut piece of material ⟨a ~ of calico⟩ ⟨a ~ of lumber⟩

wield \'wē(ə)ld\ *vt* [ME *welden* to control, fr. OE *wieldan;* akin to OHG *waltan* to rule, L *valēre* to be strong, be worth] (bef. 12c) **1** *chiefly dial* **:** to deal successfully with **:** MANAGE **2 :** to handle (as a tool) esp. effectively ⟨~ a broom⟩ **3 a :** to exert one's authority by means of ⟨~ influence⟩ **b :** have at one's command or disposal ⟨did not ~ appropriate credentials —G. W. Bonham⟩ ***syn*** see HANDLE — **wield·er** *n*

wieldy \'wē(ə)l-dē\ *adj* (14c) **:** capable of wielding or of being wielded easily

wie·ner \'wē-nər, 'wē-nē, 'win-ē\ *n* [short for *wienerwurst*] (1900) : FRANKFURTER

Wie·ner schnit·zel \'vē-nər-ˌs(h)nit-səl, 'wē-nər-ˌsnit-\ *n* [G, lit., Vienna cutlet] (1862) : a thin breaded veal cutlet

wie·ner·wurst \'wē-nə(r)-ˌwərst, -ˌwu̇(ə)rst; 'wē-nər-ˌwu̇s(h)t\ *n* [G, fr. *Wiener* of Vienna + *wurst* sausage] (1889) **1** : VIENNA SAUSAGE **2** : FRANKFURTER

wie·nie \'wē-nē, 'win-ē\ *n* (1867) : FRANKFURTER

wife \'wīf\ *n, pl* **wives** \'wīvz\ [ME *wif,* fr. OE *wīf;* akin to OHG *wīb* wife] (bef. 12c) **1 a** *dial* : WOMAN **b** : a woman acting in a specified capacity — used in combination ⟨fish*wife*⟩ **2** : a married woman — **wife·hood** \'wīf-ˌhu̇d, 'wī-ˌfu̇d\ *n* — **wife·less** \'wī-fləs\ *adj*

1**wife·like** \'wī-ˌflīk\ *adv* (1598) : in a wifely manner

2**wifelike** *adj* (1613) : WIFELY

wife·ly \'wī-flē\ *adj* (bef. 12c) : of, relating to, or befitting a wife — **wife·li·ness** \-flē-nəs\ *n*

1**wig** \'wig\ *n* [short for *periwig*] (1675) **1 a** : a manufactured covering of natural or synthetic hair for the head **b** : TOUPEE 2 **2** : an act of wigging : REBUKE

2**wig** *vt* **wigged; wig·ging** (1829) : to scold severely : REBUKE

wig·an \'wig-ən\ *n* [*Wigan,* England] (ca. 1875) : a stiff plain-weave cotton fabric used for interlining

wi·geon *or* **wid·geon** \'wij-ən\ *n, pl* **wigeon** *or* **wigeons** *or* **widgeon** *or* **widgeons** [origin unknown] (1513) : any of several freshwater ducks (genus *Anas*): as **a** : an Old World duck (*Anas penelope*) with a large white patch on each wing and in the male with a red brown head and a buff crown **b** : BALDPATE 2

wigged \'wigd\ *adj* (1777) : wearing a wig ⟨the mute, blond-*wigged* . . . member of the team —*Current Biog.*⟩

1**wig·gle** \'wig-əl\ *vb* **wig·gled; wig·gling** \-(ə-)liŋ\ [ME *wiglen,* fr. or akin to MD or MLG *wiggelen* to totter; akin to OE *wegan* to move — more at WAY] *vi* (13c) **1** : to move to and fro with quick jerky or shaking motions : JIGGLE **2** : to proceed with or as if with twisting and turning movements : WRIGGLE ~ *vt* : to cause to wiggle

2**wiggle** *n* (1816) **1** : the act of wiggling **2** : shellfish or fish in cream sauce with peas — **wig·gly** \'wig-(ə-)lē\ *adj*

wig·gler \'wig-(ə-)lər\ *n* (1859) **1** : a larva or pupa of the mosquito — called also *wriggler* **2** : one that wiggles

1**wight** \'wīt\ *n* [ME, creature, thing, fr. OE *wiht;* akin to OHG *wiht* creature, thing, OSlav *veštĭ* thing] (bef. 12c) : a living being : CREATURE; *esp* : a human being

2**wight** *adj* [ME, of Scand origin; akin to ON *vīgr* skilled in fighting (neut. *vīgt*); akin to OE *wīgan* to fight — more at VICTOR] *archaic* (13c) : VALIANT, STALWART

wig·let \'wig-lət\ *n* (1831) : a small wig used esp. to enhance a hairstyle

1**wig·wag** \'wig-ˌwag\ *vb* [E dial. *wig* to move + E *wag*] *vt* (1892) **1** : to signal by wigwagging **2** : to cause to wigwag ~ *vi* **1** : to send a signal by or as if by a flag or light waved according to a code **2** : to make a signal (as with the hand or arm)

2**wigwag** *n* (1886) **1** : the art or practice of wigwagging **2** : the act of wigwagging

wig·wam \'wig-ˌwäm\ *n* [Abnaki & Massachuset *wīkwām*] (1628) : a hut of the Indians of the Great Lakes region and eastward having typically an arched framework of poles overlaid with bark, rush mats, or hides; *also* : a rough hut

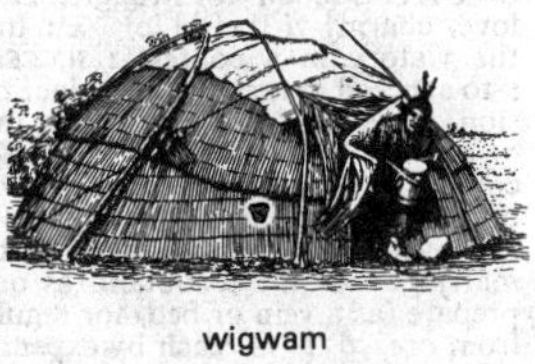

wigwam

wil·co \'wil-(ˌ)kō\ *interj* [*will* comply] (ca. 1938) — used esp. in radio and signaling to indicate that a message received will be complied with

1**wild** \'wī(ə)ld\ *adj* [ME *wilde,* fr. OE; akin to OHG *wildi* wild, W *gwyllt*] (bef. 12c) **1 a** : living in a state of nature and not ordinarily tame or domesticated ⟨~ duck⟩ **b** (1) : growing or produced without the aid and care of man ⟨~ honey⟩ (2) : related to or resembling a corresponding cultivated or domesticated organism **c** : of or relating to wild organisms ⟨the ~ state⟩ **2 a** : not inhabited or cultivated ⟨~ land⟩ **b** : not amenable to human habitation or cultivation; *also* : DESOLATE **3 a** (1) : loose from restraint or regulation : UNCONTROLLED ⟨~ mobs⟩ (2) : emotionally overcome ⟨~ with grief⟩; *also* : passionately eager or enthusiastic ⟨was ~ to own a toy train —J. C. Furnas⟩ (3) : not amenable to control or restraint : UNRULY ⟨the zebra is too ~ to be used as a draft animal⟩ **b** : marked by turbulent agitation : STORMY ⟨a ~ night⟩ **c** : going beyond normal or conventional bounds : FANTASTIC **d** : indicative of strong passion, desire, or emotion ⟨a ~ gleam of delight in his eyes —*Irish Digest*⟩ **4** : UNCIVILIZED, BARBARIC **5** : characteristic of, appropriate to, or expressive of wilderness, wildlife, or a simple or uncivilized society **6 a** : deviating from the intended or expected course ⟨~ spelling —C. W. Cunnington⟩ ⟨the throw was ~⟩ **b** : having no basis in known or surmised fact ⟨a ~ guess⟩ **7** *of a playing card* : able to represent any card designated by the holder — **wild·ish** \'wīl-dish\ *adj* — **wild·ly** \'wī(ə)l-(d)lē\ *adv* — **wild·ness** \'wī(ə)l(d)-nəs\ *n*

2**wild** *adv* (1549) : in a wild manner: as **a** : without regulation or control **b** : off an intended or expected course

3**wild** *n* (1596) **1** : a sparsely inhabited or uncultivated region or tract : WILDERNESS **2** : a wild, free, or natural state or existence

wild bergamot *n* (ca. 1843) : a fragrant No. American herb (*Monarda fistulosa*) having a terminal capitate cluster of rather large pink or purple flowers

wild boar *n* (13c) : an Old World wild hog (*Sus scrofa*) from which most domestic swine have been derived

wild card *n* [*wild card,* playing card with arbitrarily determined value] (1972) **1** : one picked to fill a leftover tournament berth after regularly qualifying competitors have all been seeded **2** : an unknown or unpredictable factor

wild carrot *n* (ca. 1538) : a widely naturalized Eurasian weed (*Daucus carota*) that is prob. the original of the cultivated carrot and has an acrid ill-flavored root — called also *Queen Anne's lace*

1**wild·cat** \'wī(ə)l(d)-ˌkat\ *n, pl* **wildcats** (14c) **1 a** : either of two cats (*Felis sylvestris* of Europe and *F. ocreata* of Africa) that resemble but are heavier in build than the domestic tabby cat and are usu. held to be among the ancestors of the domestic cat **b** *or pl* **wildcat** : any of various small or medium-sized cats (as the lynx or ocelot) **c** : a feral domestic cat **2** : a savage quick-tempered person **3 a** : wildcat money **b** : a wildcat oil or gas well **c** : a wildcat strike

2**wildcat** *adj* (1838) **1 a** (1) : financially irresponsible or unreliable ⟨~ banks⟩ (2) : issued by a financially irresponsible banking establishment ⟨~ currency⟩ **b** : operating, produced, or carried on outside the bounds of standard or legitimate business practices ⟨~ insurance schemes —H. H. Reichard⟩ **c** : of, relating to, or being an oil or gas well drilled in territory not known to be productive **d** : initiated by a group of workers without formal union approval or in violation of a contract ⟨a ~ strike⟩ ⟨~ work stoppages⟩ **2 a** *of a cartridge* : having a bullet of standard caliber but using an expanded case or a case designed for a bullet of greater caliber necked down for the smaller bullet **b** *of a firearm* : using wildcat cartridges

3**wildcat** *vi* **wild·cat·ted; wild·cat·ting** (ca. 1903) : to prospect and drill an experimental oil or gas well or sink a mine shaft in territory not known to be productive

wild·cat·ter \-ˌkat-ər\ *n* (1883) **1** : one that drills wells in the hope of finding oil in territory not known to be an oil field **2** : one that promotes unsafe and unreliable enterprises; *esp* : one that sells stocks in enterprises of this kind **3** : one that designs, builds, or fires wildcat cartridges and firearms **4** : a worker who goes out on an unauthorized strike

wild celery *n* (1874) : TAPE GRASS

wil·de·beest \'wil-də-ˌbēst\ *n, pl* **wildebeests** *also* **wildebeest** [D or Afrik; D, fr. *wilde* wild + *beest* beast (fr. L *bestia*); Afrik *wildebees,* fr. *wilde* wild + *bees* ox] (ca. 1838) : GNU

wil·der \'wil-dər\ *vb* [prob. irreg. fr. *wilderness*] *vt* (1613) **1** *archaic* : to lead astray **2** *archaic* : BEWILDER, PERPLEX ~ *vi, archaic* : to move at random : WANDER — **wil·der·ment** \-dər-mənt\ *n, archaic*

wil·der·ness \'wil-dər-nəs\ *n* [ME, fr. *wildern* wild, fr. OE *wilddēoren* of wild beasts] (13c) **1 a** (1) : a tract or region uncultivated and uninhabited by human beings (2) : an area essentially undisturbed by human activity together with its naturally developed life community **b** : an empty or pathless area or region ⟨in remote ~*es* of space groups of nebulae are found —G. W. Gray †1960⟩ **c** : a part of a garden devoted to wild growth **2** *obs* : wild or uncultivated state **3 a** : a confusing multitude or mass : an indefinitely great number or quantity ⟨I would not have given it for a ~ of monkeys —Shak.⟩ **b** : a bewildering situation ⟨those moral ~*es* of civilized life —Norman Mailer⟩

wilderness area *n, often cap W&A* (1928) : an often large tract of public land maintained essentially in its natural state and protected against introduction of intrusive artifacts (as roads and buildings)

wild–eyed \'wī(ə)l-'dīd\ *adj* (1817) **1** : having a wild expression in the eyes **2** : consisting of or favoring extreme political or social measures ⟨~ schemes⟩

wild·fire \'wī(ə)l(d)-ˌfī(ə)r\ *n* (12c) **1** : a sweeping and destructive conflagration **2** : GREEK FIRE **3** : a phosphorescent glow (as ignis fatuus or fox fire) **4** : a destructive bacterial disease of tobacco — **like wildfire** : very rapidly

wild·flow·er \-ˌflau̇(-ə)r\ *n* (1797) : the flower of a wild or uncultivated plant or the plant bearing it

wild·fowl \'wī(ə)l(d)-ˌfau̇l\ *n* (bef. 12c) : a game bird; *esp* : a game waterfowl (as a wild duck or goose) — **wild·fowl·er** \-ˌfau̇-lər\ *n* — **wild·fowl·ing** \-liŋ\ *n*

wild geranium *n* (1882) **1** : any of several geraniums related to the wild geranium **2** : a common geranium (*Geranium maculatum*) of eastern No. America with deeply parted leaves and flowers of rosy purple

wild ginger *n* (1804) : a No. American perennial herb (*Asarum canadense*) of the birthwort family with a pungent creeping rhizome

wild–goose chase *n* (1592) : a fruitless pursuit or search

wild hyacinth *n* (1847) : any of several plants with flowers suggestive of hyacinths: as **a** : a camas (*Camassia scilloides*) with white racemose flowers **b** : BLUEBELL 2a **c** : any of several western No. American plants (genus *Brodiaea*) of the lily family with grasslike basal leaves and variously colored flowers

wild indigo *n* (1744) : any of a genus (*Baptisia*) of American leguminous plants; *esp* : a tumbleweed (*B. tinctoria*) with bright yellow flowers and trifoliolate leaves

1**wild·ing** \'wīl-diŋ\ *n* [1*wild* + 2*-ing*] (ca. 1525) **1 a** : a plant growing uncultivated in the wild either as a native or an escape; *esp* : a wild apple or crab apple **b** : the fruit of a wilding **2** : a wild animal

2**wilding** *adj* (1697) : not domesticated or cultivated : WILD

wild·land \'wī(ə)l-ˌ(d)land\ *n* (1813) : land that is uncultivated or unfit for cultivation

wild·life \'wī(ə)l-ˌ(d)līf\ *n, often attrib* (1933) : living things that are neither human nor domesticated; *esp* : mammals, birds, and fishes hunted by man

wild·ling \'wī(ə)l-(d)liŋ\ *n* (1840) : WILDING

wild marjoram *n* (1550) : OREGANO 1

wild mustard *n* (ca. 1597) : CHARLOCK

wild oat *n* (15c) **1** : any of several wild grasses (genus *Avena*); *esp* : a European annual weed (*A. fatua*) common in meadows and pastures **2** *pl* : offenses and indiscretions ascribed to youthful exuberance — usu. used in the phrase *sow one's wild oats*

wild olive *n* (14c) : any of various trees that resemble the olive or have fruits resembling its fruit

wild pansy *n* (ca. 1900) : JOHNNY-JUMP-UP

wild pink *n* (1814) : an American catchfly (*Silene caroliniana*) of the eastern U.S. with pink or whitish flowers

wild pitch *n* (1867) : a pitched baseball not hit by the batter that cannot be caught or controlled by the catcher with ordinary effort and that enables a base runner to advance — compare PASSED BALL

wild rice *n* (1778) : a tall aquatic No. American perennial grass (*Zizania aquatica*) that yields an edible grain

wild rye *n* (15c) : any of several grasses (genus *Elymus*)
wild sarsaparilla *n* (ca. 1814) : a common No. American perennial herb (*Aralia nudicaulis*) with long-stalked basal compound leaves, umbels of greenish flowers, and an aromatic root used as a substitute of true sarsaparilla
wild type *n* (1914) : the typical form of an organism as ordinarily encountered in nature in contrast to natural or laboratory mutant individuals — **wild–type** *adj*
wild West *n* (1849) : the western U.S. in its frontier period
wild·wood \'wī(ə)l-,(d)wu̇d\ *n* (12c) : a wood unaltered or unfrequented by man
[1]**wile** \'wī(ə)l\ *n* [ME *wil,* fr. (assumed) ONF, prob. of Gmc origin; akin to OE *wigle* divination — more at WITCH] (12c) **1 :** a trick or stratagem intended to ensnare or deceive; *also* **:** a beguiling or playful trick **2 :** skill in outwitting : TRICKERY, GUILE ***syn*** see TRICK
[2]**wile** *vt* **wiled; wil·ing** (15c) **1 :** to lure by or as if by a magic spell : ENTICE **2** [perh. alter. of *while*] **:** to pass or spend pleasurably
[1]**will** \wəl, (ə)l, ᵊl, (')wil\ *vb, past* **would** \wəd, (ə)d, (')wu̇d\; *pres sing & pl* **will** [ME (1st & 3d sing. pres. indic.), fr. OE *wille* (infin. *wyllan*); akin to OHG *wili* (3d sing. pres. indic.) wills, L *velle* to wish, will] *vt* (bef. 12c) : DESIRE, WISH ⟨call it what you ~⟩ ~ *verbal auxiliary* **1** — used to express desire, choice, willingness, consent, or in negative constructions refusal ⟨could find no one who *would* take the job⟩ ⟨if we ~ all do our best⟩ ⟨~ you please stop that racket⟩ **2** — used to express frequent, customary, or habitual action or natural tendency or disposition ⟨~ get angry over nothing⟩ ⟨~ work one day and loaf the next⟩ **3** — used to express futurity ⟨tomorrow morning I ~ wake up in this first-class hotel suite —Tennessee Williams⟩ **4** — used to express capability or sufficiency ⟨back seat ~ hold three passengers⟩ **5** — used to express probability and often equivalent to the simple verb ⟨that ~ be the milkman⟩ **6 a** — used to express determination, insistence, persistence, or willfulness ⟨I have made up my mind to go and go I ~⟩ **b** — used to express inevitability ⟨accidents ~ happen⟩ **7** — used to express a command, exhortation, or injunction ⟨you ~ do as I say, at once⟩ ~ *vi* **:** to have a wish or desire ⟨whether we ~ or no⟩ ***usage*** see SHALL
[2]**will** \'wil\ *n* [ME, fr. OE *willa* will, desire; akin to OE *wille*] (bef. 12c) **1 :** DESIRE, WISH: as **a :** DISPOSITION, INCLINATION ⟨where there's a ~ there's a way⟩ **b :** APPETITE, PASSION **c :** CHOICE, DETERMINATION **2 a :** something desired; *esp* **:** a choice or determination of one having authority or power **b** (1) *archaic* **:** REQUEST, COMMAND (2) [fr. the phrase *our will is* which introduces it] **:** the part of a summons expressing a royal command **3 :** the act, process, or experience of willing **:** VOLITION **4 a :** mental powers manifested as wishing, choosing, desiring, or intending **b :** a disposition to act according to principles or ends **c :** the collective desire of a group ⟨the ~ of the people⟩ **5 :** the power of control over one's own actions or emotions ⟨a man of iron~⟩ **6 :** a legal declaration of a person's mind as to the manner in which he would have his property or estate disposed of after his death; *esp* **:** a written instrument legally executed by which a person makes disposition of his estate to take effect after his death — **at will :** as one wishes **:** as or when it pleases or suits oneself
[3]**will** \'wil\ *vt* (bef. 12c) **1 a :** to order or direct by a will **b :** to dispose of by or as if by a will **:** BEQUEATH **2 a :** to determine by an act of choice **b :** DECREE, ORDAIN ⟨Providence ~s it⟩ **c :** INTEND, PURPOSE **d :** to cause or change by an act of will; *also* **:** to try to do so ~ *vi* **1 :** to exercise the will **2 :** CHOOSE
willed \'wild\ *adj* (14c) **1 :** having a will esp. of a specified kind — usu. used in combination ⟨strong-*willed*⟩ **2 :** DELIBERATE
wil·lem·ite \'wil-ə-,mīt\ *n* [G *willemit,* fr. *Willem* (William) I †1843 king of the Netherlands] (ca. 1841) **:** a mineral Zn_2SiO_4 consisting of zinc silicate, occurring in hexagonal prisms and in massive or granular forms, and varying in color
wil·let \'wil-ət\ *n, pl* **willet** [imit.] (1709) **:** a large shorebird (*Catoptrophorus semipalmatus*) of central and southern Canada to the Gulf of Mexico and the West Indies that winters in the southern U.S. and as far south as Brazil
will·ful *or* **wil·ful** \'wil-fəl\ *adj* (13c) **1 :** obstinately and often perversely self-willed **2 :** done deliberately **:** INTENTIONAL ***syn*** see UNRULY — **will·ful·ly** \-fə-lē\ *adv* — **will·ful·ness** *n*
Wil·liam Tell \,wil-yəm-'tel\ *n* **:** an heroic archer in Swiss legend who complies with an order to shoot an apple off his son's head
wil·lies \'wil-ēz\ *n pl* [origin unknown] (ca. 1895) **:** a fit of nervousness **:** JITTERS — used with *the*
will·ing \'wil-iŋ\ *adj* (14c) **1 :** inclined or favorably disposed in mind **:** READY **2 :** prompt to act or respond **3 :** done, borne, or accepted by choice or without reluctance **4 :** of or relating to the will or power of choosing **:** VOLITIONAL ***syn*** see VOLUNTARY — **will·ing·ly** \-iŋ-lē\ *adv* — **will·ing·ness** *n*
wil·li·waw \'wil-i-,wȯ\ *n* [origin unknown] (1842) **1 a :** a sudden violent gust of cold land air common along mountainous coasts of high latitudes **b :** a sudden violent wind **2 :** a violent commotion
will–less \'wil-ləs\ *adj* (1747) **1 :** involving no exercise of the will **:** INVOLUNTARY ⟨~ fealty⟩ **2 :** not exercising the will ⟨~ slaves⟩
will–o'–the–wisp \,wil-ə-t͟hə-'wisp\ *n* [*Will* (nickname for *William*) + *of* + *the* + *wisp*] (1608) **1 :** IGNIS FATUUS **2 :** a delusive or elusive goal — **will–o'–the–wisp** *adj*
wil·low \'wil-(,)ō, 'wil-ə(-w)\ *n* [ME *wilghe, wilowe,* fr. OE *welig;* akin to MHG *wilge* willow, Gk *helikē*] (bef. 12c) **1 :** any of a genus (*Salix* of the family Salicaceae, the willow family) of trees and shrubs bearing aments of apetalous flowers and including forms of value for wood, osiers, or tanbark and a few ornamentals **2 :** an object made of willow wood; *esp* **:** a cricket bat — **wil·low·like** \-ō-,līk, -ə-,līk\ *adj*
willow herb *n* (1578) **1 :** any of a genus (*Epilobium*) of herbs of the evening-primrose family; *esp* **:** FIREWEED b **2 :** LOOSESTRIFE; *esp* **:** PURPLE LOOSESTRIFE
wil·low·ware \'wil-ə-,wa(ə)r, 'wil-ō-, -,we(ə)r\ *n* (1885) **:** dinnerware that is usu. blue-and-white and that is decorated with a story-telling design featuring a large willow tree by a little bridge
wil·lowy \'wil-ə-wē\ *adj* (1766) **1 :** abounding with willows **2 :** resembling a willow: **a :** PLIANT **b :** gracefully tall and slender
will·pow·er \'wil-,pau̇(-ə)r\ *n* (1874) **:** energetic determination
will to power (1896) **1 :** the drive of the superman in the philosophy of Nietzsche to perfect and transcend the self through the possession and exercise of creative power **2 :** a conscious or unconscious desire to exercise authority over others
wil·ly–nil·ly \,wil-ē-'nil-ē\ *adv or adj* [alter. of *will I nill I* or *will ye nill ye* or *will he nill he*] (1608) **1 :** by compulsion **:** without choice **2 :** in a haphazard or spontaneous manner
Wilms' tumor \'vilmz-(əz-)\ *n* [Max *Wilms* †1918 Ger. surgeon] (ca. 1910) **:** a rapidly developing cancer of the kidney that affects esp. children and is made up of embryonic elements
Wil·son's disease \'wil-sənz-\ *n* [Samuel A. K. *Wilson* †1937 Eng. neurologist] (ca. 1915) **:** a hereditary disease that is determined by an autosomal recessive gene and is marked esp. by cirrhotic changes in the liver and severe mental disorder due to a ceruloplasmin deficiency and resulting inability to metabolize copper
[1]**wilt** \wəlt, (')wilt\ *archaic pres 2d sing of* WILL
[2]**wilt** \'wilt\ *vb* [alter. of earlier *welk,* fr. ME *welken,* prob. fr. MD; akin to OHG *erwelkēn* to wilt] *vi* (ca. 1691) **1 :** to lose freshness and become flaccid (as a plant on a dry day) **:** DROOP **2 :** to grow weak or faint **:** LANGUISH ~ *vt* **:** to cause to wilt
[3]**wilt** \'wilt\ *n* (1855) **1 :** an act or instance of wilting **:** the state of being wilted **2 a :** a disorder (as a fungus disease) of plants marked by loss of turgidity in soft tissues with subsequent drooping and often shriveling — called also *wilt disease* **b :** a destructive virus disease of various caterpillars marked by visceral liquefaction and shriveling of the body
Wil·ton \'wilt-ᵊn\ *n* [*Wilton,* borough in England] (1774) **:** a carpet woven with loops like the Brussels carpet but having a velvet cut pile and being generally of better materials
wily \'wī-lē\ *adj* **wil·i·er; -est** (14c) **:** full of wiles **:** CRAFTY — **wil·i·ly** \-lə-lē\ *adv* — **wil·i·ness** \-lē-nəs\ *n*
[1]**wim·ble** \'wim-bəl\ *n* [ME, fr. AF, fr. MD *wimmel* auger; akin to MLG *wimmel* auger] (13c) **:** any of various instruments for boring holes
[2]**wimble** *vt* **wim·bled; wim·bling** \-b(ə-)liŋ\ *archaic* (15c) **:** to bore with or as if with a wimble
wimp \'wimp\ *n* [perh. fr. Brit. slang *wimp* girl, woman, of unknown origin] (ca. 1963) **:** a weak or ineffectual person — **wimp·ish** \'wim-pish\ *adj* — **wimpy** \'wim-pē\ *adj*
[1]**wim·ple** \'wim-pəl\ *n* [ME *wimpel,* fr. OE; akin to OE *wīpian* to wipe] (bef. 12c) **1 :** a cloth covering worn over the head and around the neck and chin esp. by women in the late medieval period and by some nuns **2** *Scot* **a :** a crafty turn **:** TWIST **b :** CURVE, BEND

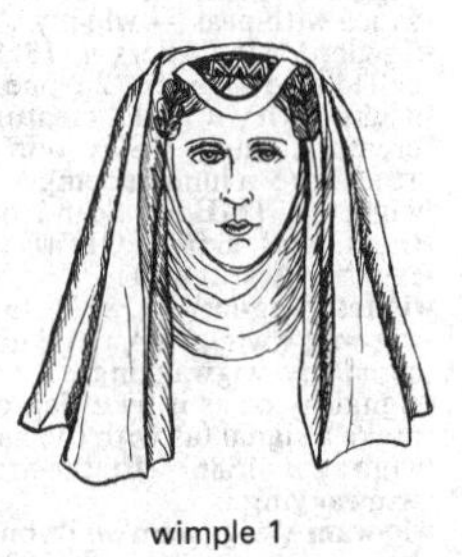
wimple 1

[2]**wimple** *vb* **wim·pled; wim·pling** \-p(ə-)liŋ\ *vt* (13c) **1 :** to cover with or as if with a wimple **:** VEIL **2 :** to cause to ripple ~ *vi* **1** *archaic* **:** to fall or lie in folds **2** *chiefly Scot* **:** to follow a winding course **:** MEANDER **3 :** RIPPLE
[1]**win** \'win\ *vb* **won** \'wən\; **win·ning** [ME *winnen,* fr. OE *winnan* to struggle; akin to OHG *winnan* to struggle, L *venus* love, charm] *vi* (bef. 12c) **1 :** to gain the victory in a contest **:** SUCCEED **2 :** to succeed in arriving at a place or a state ~ *vt* **1 a :** to get possession of by effort or fortune **b :** to obtain by work **:** EARN ⟨striving to ~ a living from the sterile soil⟩ **2 a :** to gain in or as if in battle or contest **b :** to be the victor in ⟨*won* the war⟩ **3 a :** to make friendly or favorable to oneself or to one's cause — often used with *over* ⟨*won* him over with persuasive arguments⟩ **b :** to induce to accept oneself in marriage **4 a :** to obtain (as ore, coal, or clay) by mining **b :** to prepare (as a vein or bed) for regular mining **c :** to recover (as metal) from ore **5 :** to reach by expenditure of effort — **win·less** \'win-ləs\ *adj* — **win·na·ble** \'win-ə-bəl\ *adj*
[2]**win** *n* (1862) **:** VICTORY; *esp* **:** first place at the finish (as of a horse race)
wince \'win(t)s\ *vi* **winced; winc·ing** [ME *wenchen* to be impatient, dart about, fr. (assumed) ONF *wenchier,* of Gmc origin; akin to OHG *wankōn* to totter, OE *wincian* to wink] (13c) **:** to shrink back involuntarily (as from pain) **:** FLINCH ***syn*** see RECOIL — **wince** *n*
[1]**winch** \'winch\ *n* [ME *winche* roller, reel, fr. OE *wince;* akin to OE *wincian* to wink] (bef. 12c) **1 :** any of various machines or instruments for hauling or pulling; *esp* **:** a powerful machine with one or more drums on which to coil a rope, cable, or chain for hauling or hoisting **:** WINDLASS **2 :** a crank with a handle for giving motion to a machine (as a grindstone)
[2]**winch** *vt* (1529) **:** to hoist or haul with or as if with a winch — **winch·er** *n*
Win·ches·ter \'win-,ches-tər\ *adj* [fr. the code name used by the original developer] (1973) **:** relating to or being computer disk technology that permits high-density storage by sealing the rigid metal disks against dust
[1]**wind** \'wind, *archaic or poetic* 'wīnd\ *n, often attrib* [ME, fr. OE; akin to OHG *wint* wind, L *ventus,* Gk *aēnai* to blow, Skt *vāti* it blows] (bef. 12c) **1 a :** a natural movement of air of any velocity; *esp* **:** the earth's air or the gas surrounding a planet in natural motion horizontally **b :** an artificially produced movement of air **c :** SOLAR WIND, STELLAR WIND **2 a :** a destructive force or influence **b :** a force or agency that carries along or influences **:** TENDENCY, TREND ⟨withstood the ~s of popular opinion —Felix Frankfurter⟩ **3 a :** BREATH 4a **b :** BREATH 2a **c :** the pit of the stomach **:** SOLAR PLEXUS **4 :** gas generated in the stomach or the intestines **5 a :** compressed air or gas **b** *archaic* **:** AIR **6 :** something that is insubstantial: as **a :** mere talk **:** idle words **b :** NOTHING, NOTHINGNESS **c :** vain self-satisfaction **7 a :** air carrying a scent (as of a hunter or game) **b :** slight information esp. about something secret **:** INTIMATION ⟨got ~ of the rumors about him⟩ **8 a :** musical wind instruments esp. as distinguished from strings and percussion **b** *pl* **:** players of wind instruments **9 a :** a direction from which the wind may blow **:** a point of the compass; *esp* **:** one of the cardinal points **b :** the direction from which the wind is blowing — **wind·less** \-ləs\ *adj* — **wind·less·ly** *adv* — **before the wind :** in the same direction as the main force of the wind — **close to the wind :** as nearly as possible against the main force of the wind — **have the wind of 1 :** to be to windward of **2 :** to be on the scent of **3 :** to have a superior position to — **in the wind :** about to happen **:** ASTIR, AFOOT ⟨other

projects than a new building were *in the wind* —Ben Riker⟩ — **near the wind 1 :** close to the wind **2 :** close to a point of danger : near the permissible limit — **off the wind :** away from the direction from which the wind is blowing — **on the wind :** toward the direction from which the wind is blowing — **under the wind 1 :** to leeward **2 :** in a place protected from the wind : under the lee

[2]**wind** \'wind\ *vt* (15c) **1 :** to detect or follow by scent **2 :** to expose to the air or wind : dry by exposing to air **3 :** to make short of breath **4 :** to regulate the wind supply of (an organ pipe) **5 :** to rest (as a horse) in order to allow the breath to be recovered ~ *vi* **1 :** to scent game **2** *dial* **:** to pause for breath

[3]**wind** \'wīnd, 'wind\ *vb* **wind·ed** \'wīn-dəd, 'win-\ *or* **wound** \'waùnd\; **wind·ing** [[1]*wind*] *vt* (1586) **1 :** to cause (as a horn) to sound by blowing : BLOW **2 :** to sound (as a call or note) on a horn ⟨*wound* a rousing call —R. L. Stevenson⟩ ~ *vi* **:** to produce a sound on a horn

[4]**wind** \'wīnd\ *vb* **wound** \'waùnd\ *also* **wind·ed; wind·ing** [ME *winden,* fr. OE *windan* to twist, move with speed or force, brandish; akin to OHG *wintan* to wind, Umbrian ohav*endu* let him turn aside] *vi* (bef. 12c) **1 :** BEND, WARP **2 a :** to have a curving course or shape : extend in curves **b :** to proceed as if by winding **3 :** to move so as to encircle something **4 :** to turn when lying at anchor ~ *vt* **1 a** *obs* **:** WEAVE **b :** ENTANGLE, INVOLVE **c :** to introduce sinuously or stealthily : INSINUATE **2 a :** to encircle or cover with something pliable : bind with loops or layers **b :** to turn completely or repeatedly about an object : COIL, TWINE **c (1) :** to hoist or haul by means of a rope or chain and a windlass **(2) :** to move (a ship) by hauling on a capstan **d (1) :** to tighten the spring of ⟨~ a clock⟩ **(2)** *obs* **:** to make tighter : TIGHTEN, TUNE **(3) :** CRANK **e :** to raise to a high level (as of excitement or tension) — usu. used with *up* **3 a :** to cause to move in a curving line or path **b** *archaic* **:** to turn the course of; *esp* **:** to lead (a person) as one wishes **c (1) :** to cause (as a ship) to change direction : TURN **(2) :** to turn (a ship) end for end **d :** to traverse on a curving course ⟨the river ~*s* the valley⟩ **e :** to effect by or as if by curving

[5]**wind** \'wīnd\ *n* (14c) **1 :** a mechanism (as a winch) for winding **2 :** an act of winding : the state of being wound **3 :** COIL, TURN **4 :** a particular method of winding

wind·age \'win-dij\ *n* [[1]*wind*] (ca. 1710) **1 a :** the space between the projectile of a smoothbore gun and the surface of the bore **b :** the difference between the diameter of the bore of a muzzle-loading rifled cannon and that of the projectile cylinder **2 a :** the amount of sight deflection necessary to compensate for wind displacement in aiming a gun **b (1) :** the influence of the wind in deflecting the course of a projectile **(2) :** the amount of deflection due to the wind **3 :** the disturbance of the air caused by a passing object (as a projectile) **4 :** the surface exposed (as by a ship) to the wind

wind·bag \'win(d)-ˌbag\ *n* (1827) **:** an exhaustively talkative person

wind–bell \-ˌbel\ *n* (1901) **1 :** a cluster of small pieces of glass or metal tied loosely together in such a way that they tinkle when blown by the wind — usu. used in pl. **2 :** a bell that is light enough to be moved and sounded by the wind

wind·blast \-ˌblast\ *n* (1942) **:** the destructive effect of air friction on a pilot ejected from a high-speed airplane

wind·blown \-ˌblōn\ *adj* (1600) **1 :** blown by the wind; *esp* **:** having a permanent set or character of growth determined by the prevailing winds ⟨~ trees⟩ **2** *of hair* **:** cut so that the ends turn outward and to the front as if blown by a wind from behind

wind–borne \-ˌbō(ə)rn, -ˌbȯ(ə)rn\ *adj* (1842) **:** carried by the wind ⟨~ pollen⟩ ⟨~ soil deposits⟩

wind·break \-ˌbrāk\ *n* (1861) **:** a growth of trees or shrubs serving to break the force of wind; *broadly* **:** a shelter (as a fence) from the wind

wind·break·er \-ˌbrā-kər\ *n* [fr. a trademark] (ca. 1918) **:** an outer jacket made of wind-resistant material

wind–bro·ken \-ˌbrō-kən\ *adj, of a horse* (1603) **:** affected with pulmonary emphysema or with heaves

wind·burn \-ˌbərn\ *n* (1925) **:** irritation of the skin caused by wind — **wind·burned** \-ˌbərnd\ *adj*

wind·cheat·er \'-win(d)-ˌchēt-ər\ *n, chiefly Brit* (1940) **:** WINDBREAKER

wind·chill \'win(d)-ˌchil\ *n* (1939) **:** a still-air temperature that would have the same cooling effect on exposed human flesh as a given combination of temperature and wind speed — called also *chill factor, windchill factor, windchill index*

wind chime *n* (ca. 1927) **:** WIND-BELL 1 — usu. used in pl.

wind cone *n* (ca. 1917) **:** WIND SOCK

wind down *vi* (1952) **1 :** to draw gradually toward an end **2 :** RELAX, UNWIND ~ *vt* **:** to cause a gradual lessening of usu. with the intention of bringing to an end

wind·er \'wīn-dər\ *n* [[4]*wind*] (1553) **:** one that winds: as **a :** a worker who winds yarn or thread **b :** any of various textile machines for winding thread and yarn **c :** a key for winding a mechanism (as a clock) **d :** a step that is wider at one end than at the other (as in a spiral staircase)

wind·fall \'win(d)-ˌfȯl\ *n* (15c) **1 :** something (as a tree or fruit) blown down by the wind **2 :** an unexpected or sudden gain or advantage

wind farm *n* (1980) **:** an area of land with a cluster of wind turbines for driving electrical generators

wind·flaw \'win(d)-ˌflȯ\ *n* (1913) **:** a gust of wind : FLAW

wind·flow·er \-ˌflaù(-ə)r\ *n* (1551) **:** ANEMONE 1

wind·gall \-ˌgȯl\ *n* (1523) **:** a soft tumor or synovial swelling on a horse's leg in the region of the fetlock joint

wind gap *n* (1769) **:** a notch in the crest of a mountain ridge : a pass not occupied by a stream

wind·hov·er \'wind-ˌhəv-ər, -ˌhäv-\ *n, Brit* (1674) **:** KESTREL

[1]**wind·ing** \'wīn-diŋ\ *n* (bef. 12c) **1 :** material (as wire) wound or coiled about an object (as an armature); *also* **:** a single turn of the wound material **2 a :** the act of one that winds **b :** the manner of winding something **3 :** a curved or sinuous course, line, or progress

[2]**winding** *adj* (1530) **:** marked by winding: as **a :** having a pronounced curve; *esp* **:** SPIRAL ⟨a ~ stairway⟩ **b :** having a course that winds ⟨a ~ road⟩

wind·ing–sheet \'wīn-diŋ-ˌshēt\ *n* (15c) **:** a sheet in which a corpse is wrapped

wind instrument *n* (1582) **:** a musical instrument (as a trumpet, clarinet, or organ) sounded by wind; *esp* **:** one sounded by the player's breath

wind·jam·mer \'win(d)-ˌjam-ər\ *n* (1899) **:** a sailing ship; *also* **:** one of its crew — **wind·jam·ming** \-iŋ\ *n*

[1]**wind·lass** \'win-(d)ləs\ *n* [ME *wyndlas,* alter. of *wyndas,* fr. ON *vindāss,* fr. *vinda* to wind (akin to OHG *wintan* to wind) + *āss* pole; akin to Goth *ans* pole] (15c) **:** any of various machines for hoisting or hauling: as **a :** a horizontal barrel supported on vertical posts and turned by a crank so that the hoisting rope is wound around the barrel **b :** a steam or electric winch with horizontal or vertical shaft and two drums used to raise a ship's anchor

[2]**windlass** *vt* (1870) **:** to hoist or haul with a windlass

win·dle·straw \'win-(d)ᵊl-ˌstrȯ\ *n* [(assumed) ME, fr. OE *windel-strēaw,* fr. *windel* basket (fr. *windan* to wind) + *strēaw* straw] *Brit* (bef. 12c) **:** a dry thin stalk of grass

[1]**wind·mill** \'win(d)-ˌmil\ *n* (13c) **1 a :** a mill operated by the wind usu. acting on oblique vanes or sails that radiate from a horizontal shaft; *esp* **:** a wind-driven water pump **b :** the wind-driven wheel of a windmill **2 :** something that resembles or suggests a windmill: as **a :** PINWHEEL 2 **b :** HELICOPTER **3** [fr. the episode in *Don Quixote* by Cervantes in which the hero attacks windmills under the illusion that they are giants] **:** an imaginary wrong, evil, or opponent — usu. used in the phrase *to tilt at windmills*

[2]**windmill** *vi* (1694) **:** to move like a windmill ~ *vt* **:** to cause to move like a windmill

win·dow \'win-(ˌ)dō, -də(-w)\ *n, often attrib* [ME *windowe,* fr. ON *vindauga,* fr. *vindr* wind (akin to OE *wind*) + *auga* eye; akin to OE *ēage* eye — more at EYE] (13c) **1 a :** an opening esp. in the wall of a building for admission of light and air that is usu. closed by casements or sashes containing transparent material (as glass) and capable of being opened and shut **b :** WINDOWPANE **2 :** a means of entrance or access; *esp* **:** a means of obtaining information **3 :** an opening (as a shutter, slot, or valve) that resembles or suggests a window **4 :** the transparent panel of a window envelope **5 :** the framework (as a shutter or sash with its fittings) that closes a window opening **6 :** CHAFF 4 **7 :** a range of wavelengths in the electromagnetic spectrum to which a planet's atmosphere is transparent **8 a :** an interval of time within which a rocket or spacecraft must be launched to accomplish a particular mission **b :** an interval of time during which conditions are favorable or an opportunity exists **9 :** an area at the limits of the earth's sensible atmosphere through which a spacecraft must pass for successful reentry **10 :** any of the areas into which a computer display may be divided and on which distinctly different types of information are displayed — **win·dow·less** \-dō-ləs, -də-\ *adj*

window box *n* (ca. 1885) **1 :** a box designed to hold soil for growing plants on a windowsill **2 :** one of the hollows in the sides of a window frame for the weights that counterbalance a lifting sash

window dressing *n* (1895) **1 :** the display of merchandise in a retail store window **2 a :** the act or an instance of making something appear deceptively attractive or favorable **b :** something used to create a deceptively favorable or attractive impression — **win·dow–dress** \'win-dō-ˌdres\ *vt* — **window dresser** *n*

win·dowed \'win-(ˌ)dōd, -dəd\ *adj* (15c) **:** having windows esp. of a specified kind — often used in combination

window envelope *n* (1914) **:** an envelope having an opening through which the address on the enclosure is visible

win·dow·pane \'win-dō-ˌpān, -də-\ *n* (1819) **1 :** a pane in a window **2 :** TATTERSALL

window seat *n* (ca. 1755) **1 :** a seat built into a window recess **2 :** a seat at a window (as in a bus or airplane)

window shade *n* (1810) **:** a shade or curtain for a window

win·dow–shop \'win-dō-ˌshäp, -də-\ *vi* (1926) **:** to look at the displays in retail store windows without going inside the stores to make purchases — **win·dow–shop·per** *n*

win·dow·sill \-ˌsil\ *n* (1703) **:** the horizontal member at the bottom of a window opening

wind·pipe \'win(d)-ˌpīp\ *n* (ca. 1530) **:** the passage for the breath from the larynx to the lungs : TRACHEA

wind–pol·li·nat·ed \-'päl-ə-ˌnāt-əd\ *adj* (ca. 1884) **:** pollinated by wind-borne pollen

wind·proof \-'prüf\ *adj* (1616) **:** impervious to wind ⟨a ~ jacket⟩

wind rose \'win-ˌdrōz\ *n* [G *windrose* compass card] (1846) **:** a diagram showing for a given place the relative frequency or frequency and strength of winds from different directions

[1]**wind·row** \'win-ˌ(d)rō\ *n* (1523) **1 a :** a row of hay raked up to dry before being baled or stored **b :** a similar row of cut vegetation (as grain) for drying **2 :** a row heaped up by or as if by the wind **3 a :** a long low ridge of road-making material scraped to the side of a road **b :** BANK, RIDGE, HEAP

[2]**windrow** *vt* (1729) **:** to form (as hay) into a windrow

wind scale *n* (ca. 1909) **:** a series of numbers or words corresponding to various ranges of wind speeds for indicating the force of the wind

wind·screen \'win(d)-ˌskrēn\ *n* (1858) **1 :** a screen that protects against the wind **2** *Brit* **:** an automobile windshield

wind shake *n* (1545) **:** shake in timber attributed to high winds

wind shear *n* (1941) **:** a radical shift in wind speed and direction between slightly different altitudes

wind·shield \'win(d)-ˌshēld\ *n* (1902) **:** a transparent screen (as of glass) in front of the occupants of a vehicle

wind sock *n* (1928) **:** a truncated cloth cone open at both ends and mounted in an elevated position to indicate the direction of the wind — called also *wind sleeve*

Wind·sor chair \ˌwin-zər-\ *n* [*Windsor,* England] (1724) **:** a wooden chair with spindle back, raking legs, and usu. a saddle seat

Windsor knot *n* [prob. after Edward, Duke of *Windsor*] (1947) **:** a necktie knot that is wider than the usual four-in-hand knot

Windsor tie *n* (ca. 1897) **:** a broad necktie usu. tied in a loose bow

wind sprint *n* (1948) : a sprint performed as a training exercise to develop breathing capacity esp. during exertion
wind·storm \'win(d)-,stȯ(ə)rm\ *n* (14c) : a storm marked by high wind with little or no precipitation
Wind·surf·er \-,sər-fər\ *trademark* — used for a sailboard
wind·swept \'win(d)-,swept\ *adj* (1812) : swept by or as if by wind
wind tee *n* (1932) : a large weather vane shaped like a horizontal letter T on or near a landing field
wind tunnel *n* (1911) : a tunnellike passage through which air is blown at a known velocity to determine the effects of wind pressure on an object (as an airplane part or model or a guided missile) placed in the passage
wind turbine *n* (1909) : a turbine driven by the wind
[1]**wind-up** \'wīn-,dəp\ *n* (1573) **1 a** : the act of bringing to an end **b** : a concluding act or part : FINISH **2** : a series of regular and distinctive motions (as swinging the arms) made by a pitcher preparatory to releasing a pitch
[2]**windup** *adj* (1784) : having a spring wound up by hand for operation
wind up \(')wīn-'dəp\ *vt* (1583) **1** : to bring to a conclusion : END **2** : to put in order : SETTLE ~ *vi* **1 a** : to come to a conclusion **b** : to arrive in a place, situation, or condition at the end or as a result of a course of action ⟨*wound up* as millionaires⟩ **2** : to make a pitching windup
[1]**wind·ward** \'wind-(d)wərd\ *n* (1549) : the side or direction from which the wind is blowing — **to windward** : into or in an advantageous position
[2]**windward** *adj* (1627) : being in or facing the direction from which the wind is blowing — compare LEEWARD
wind·way \'win-,(d)wā\ *n* (ca. 1875) : a passage for air (as in an organ pipe)
wind–wing \-,(d)wiŋ\ *n* (1952) : a small panel in an automobile window that can be turned outward for ventilation
windy \'win-dē\ *adj* **wind·i·er; -est** (bef. 12c) **1 a** (1) : WINDSWEPT (2) : marked by strong wind or by more wind than usual **b** : VIOLENT, STORMY **2** : FLATULENT 1 ⟨a ~ bellyache⟩ **3 a** : VERBOSE, BOMBASTIC **b** : lacking substance : EMPTY — **wind·i·ly** \-də-lē\ *adv* — **wind·i·ness** \-dē-nəs\ *n*
[1]**wine** \'wīn\ *n, often attrib* [ME *win,* fr. OE *wīn;* akin to OHG *wīn* wine; both fr. L *vinum* wine, of non-IE origin; akin to the source of Gk *oinos* wine] (bef. 12c) **1 a** : the fermented juice of fresh grapes used as a beverage **b** : wine or a substitute used in Christian communion services **2** : the usu. fermented juice of a plant product (as a fruit) used as a beverage **3** : something that invigorates or intoxicates **4** : a variable color averaging a dark red
[2]**wine** *vb* **wined; win·ing** *vi* (1829) : to drink wine ~ *vt* : to give wine to ⟨*wined* and dined his friends⟩
wine cellar *n* (14c) : a room for storing wines; *also* : a stock of wines
wine cooler *n* (1815) : a vessel or container in which wine is cooled
wine·glass \'wīn-,glas\ *n* (1709) **1** : a stemware drinking glass for wine **2** : a 4-ounce unit of measure used in mixing drinks
wine·grow·er \-,grō(-ə)r\ *n* (1844) : one that cultivates a vineyard and makes wine
wine·press \'wīn-,pres\ *n* (1526) : a vat in which juice is expressed from grapes by treading or by means of a plunger
win·ery \'wīn-(ə-)rē\ *n, pl* **-er·ies** (1882) : a wine-making establishment
wine·shop \'wīn-,shäp\ *n* (1848) : a tavern that specializes in serving wine
wine·skin \-,skin\ *n* (1821) : a bag that is made from the skin of an animal (as a goat) and that is used for holding wine
wine taster *n* (1632) **1** : one who tastes and evaluates wine esp. professionally **2** : a small shallow vessel used to sample wine
win·ey *var of* WINY
[1]**wing** \'wiŋ\ *n, often attrib* [ME *winge,* of Scand origin; akin to Dan & Sw *vinge* wing; akin to Skt *vāti* it blows — more at WIND] (12c) **1 a** : one of the movable feathered or membranous paired appendages by means of which a bird, bat, or insect is able to fly; *also* : such an appendage even though rudimentary if possessed by an animal belonging to a group characterized by the power of flight **b** : any of various organic structures esp. of a flying fish or flying lemur providing means of limited flight **2** : an appendage or part resembling a wing in appearance, position, or function: as **a** : a device worn under the arms to aid a person in swimming or staying afloat **b** : ALA **c** : a turned-back or extended edge on an article of clothing **d** : a sidepiece at the top of an armchair **e** (1) : a foliaceous, membranous, or woody expansion of a plant esp. along a stem or on a samara or capsule (2) : either of the two lateral petals of a papilionaceous flower **f** : a vane of a windmill or arrow **g** : SAIL **h** : one of the airfoils that develop a major part of the lift which supports a heavier-than-air aircraft **3** : a means of flight or rapid progress **4** : the act or manner of flying : FLIGHT **5** : a side or outlying region or district **6** : a part or feature usu. projecting from and subordinate to the main or central part **7 a** : one of the pieces of scenery at the side of a stage **b** *pl* : the area at the side of the stage out of sight **8 a** : a left or right section of an army or fleet : FLANK **b** : one of the offensive positions or players on either side of a center position in certain team sports; *also* : FLANKER **9 a** : either of two opposing groups within an organization or society : FACTION **b** : a section of an organized body (as a legislative chamber) representing a group or faction holding distinct opinions or policies — compare LEFT WING, RIGHT WING **10 a** : a unit of the U.S. Air Force higher than a group and lower than a division **b** : two or more squadrons of naval airplanes **11** : a dance step marked by a quick outward and inward rolling glide of one foot **12** *pl* : insignia consisting of an outspread pair of stylized bird's wings which are awarded on completion of prescribed training to a qualified pilot, aircrew member, or military balloon pilot — **wingy** \-ē\ *adj* — **in the wings 1** : out of sight in the stage wings **2** : close at hand in the background : readily available ⟨had an alternative plan waiting *in the wings*⟩ — **on the wing 1** : in flight : FLYING **2** : in motion — **under one's wing** : under one's protection : in one's care

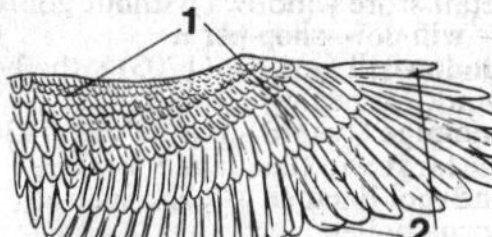

wing 1a: *1* covert feathers, *2* primary feathers, *3* secondary feathers

[2]**wing** *vt* (1591) **1 a** : to fit with wings **b** : to enable to fly or move swiftly **2 a** : to traverse with or as if with wings **b** : to effect or achieve by flying **3** : to let fly : DISPATCH ⟨would start to ~ punches —A.J. Liebling⟩ **4 a** : to wound in the wing : disable the wing of ⟨~*ed* the duck⟩ **b** : to wound (as with a bullet) without killing ⟨~*ed* by a sniper⟩ ~ *vi* : to go with or as if with wings : FLY — **wing it** : to act or perform without preparation or guidelines : IMPROVISE
wing and wing *adv* (1781) : with sails extended on both sides
wing·back \'wiŋ-,bak\ *n* (1933) : an offensive back in football who lines up outside the tight end; *also* : the position of a player so stationed
wing bar *n* (1855) : a line of contrasting color across the middle of a bird's wing made by markings on the wing coverts — see COCK illustration
wing bow *n* (1867) : the lesser coverts of the upper part of a bird's wing when distinctively colored — see COCK illustration
wing case *n* (1661) : ELYTRON
wing chair *n* (1904) : an upholstered armchair with high solid back and sides that provide a rest for the head and protection from drafts
wing commander *n* (1914) : a commissioned officer in the British air force who ranks with a lieutenant colonel in the army
wing covert *n* (1815) : one of the feathers covering the bases of the wing quills
wing·ding \'wiŋ-,diŋ\ *n* [origin unknown] (1944) : a wild, lively, or lavish party
winged \'wiŋd *also except for 1a(2)* 'wiŋ-əd\ *adj* (14c) **1 a** (1) : having wings ⟨~ seeds⟩ (2) : having wings of a specified kind — used in combination ⟨strong-*winged*⟩ **b** : using wings in flight **2 a** : soaring with or as if with wings : ELEVATED **b** : SWIFT, RAPID
winged elm *n* (1820) : a No. American elm (*Ulmus alata*) having twigs and young branches with prominent corky projections
wing·er \'wiŋ-ər\ *n, chiefly Brit* (1896) : a player (as in soccer) in a wing position
wing–foot·ed \'wiŋ-'fu̇t-əd\ *adj* (1591) **1** : having winged feet **2** : SWIFT
wing·less \'wiŋ-ləs\ *adj* (1591) : having no wings or very rudimentary wings — **wing·less·ness** *n*
wing·let \'wiŋ-lət\ *n* (1816) : a very small or rudimentary wing
wing·like \-,līk\ *adj* (ca. 1804) : resembling a wing in form or lateral position
wing·man \-mən\ *n* (1942) : a pilot who flies behind and outside the leader of a flying formation
wing nut *n* (ca. 1900) : a nut with wings that provide a grip for the thumb and finger
wing·over \'wiŋ-,ō-vər\ *n* (1927) : a flight maneuver in which a plane is put into a climbing turn until nearly stalled after which the nose is allowed to fall while the turn is continued until normal flight is attained in a direction opposite to that in which the maneuver was entered
wing shooting *n* (1881) : the act or practice of shooting at game birds in flight or at flying targets
wing·span \'wiŋ-,span\ *n* (ca. 1917) : the distance from the tip of one of a pair of wings to that of the other; *also* : SPAN 2c
wing·spread \-,spred\ *n* (1897) : the spread of the wings : WINGSPAN; *specif* : the extreme measurement between the tips or outer margins of the wings (as of a bird or insect)
wing tip *n* (ca. 1908) **1** : a toe cap having a point that extends back toward the throat of the shoe and curving sides that extend toward the shank **2** : a shoe having a wing tip **3** *usu* **wingtip** : the outer end of an airplane wing
[1]**wink** \'wiŋk\ *vb* [ME *winken,* fr. OE *wincian;* akin to OHG *winchan* to stagger, wink, L *vacillare* to sway] *vi* (bef. 12c) **1** : to shut one eye briefly as a signal or in teasing **2** : to close and open the eyelids quickly **3** : to avoid seeing or noting something — usu. used with *at* **4** : to gleam or flash intermittently : TWINKLE **5 a** : to come to an end — usu. used with *out* **b** : to stop shining — usu. used with *out* **6** : to signal a message with a light ~ *vt* **1** : to cause to open and shut **2** : to affect or influence by or as if by blinking the eyes
[2]**wink** *n* (14c) **1** : a brief period of sleep : NAP **2 a** : a hint or sign given by winking **b** : an act of winking **3** : the time of a wink : INSTANT ⟨quick as a ~⟩ **4** : a flicker of the eyelids : BLINK
wink·er \'wiŋ-kər\ *n* (1549) **1** : one that winks **2** : a horse's blinder : BLINKER
[1]**win·kle** \'wiŋ-kəl\ *n* [by shortening] (ca. 1585) : [2]PERIWINKLE
[2]**winkle** *vi* **win·kled; win·kling** \-k(ə-)liŋ\ [freq. of *wink*] (1791) : TWINKLE
[3]**winkle** *vt* **win·kled; win·kling** \-k(ə-)liŋ\ ['*winkle;* fr. the process of extracting a winkle from its shell] *chiefly Brit* (1918) : to displace, extract, or evict from a position — usu. used with *out*
win·ner \'win-ər\ *n* (14c) : one that wins: as **a** : one that is successful esp. through praiseworthy ability and hard work **b** : a victor esp. in games and sports **c** : one that wins admiration
winner's circle *n* (1951) : an enclosure near a racetrack where the winning horse and jockey are brought for photographs and awards
Win·nie \'win-ē\ *n* [*winner* + *-ie*] (ca. 1942) : an award presented annually by a professional organization for notable achievement in fashion design
[1]**win·ning** \'win-iŋ\ *n* (14c) **1** : the act of one that wins : VICTORY **2** : something won: as **a** : a captured territory : CONQUEST **b** : money won by success in a game or competition — usu. used in pl. **3 a** : a shaft or pit opening made to win coal **b** : a more or less isolated section of a mine
[2]**winning** *adj* (15c) **1 a** : of, relating to, or used for or in the act of winning ⟨the ~ ticket⟩ **b** : successful esp. in competition ⟨a ~ team⟩ **2** : tending to please or delight ⟨a ~ smile⟩ — **win·ning·ly** \-iŋ-lē\ *adv*
win·nock \'win-ək\ *n* [ME (Sc) *windok, windowe*] *Scot* (15c) : WINDOW
[1]**win·now** \'win-(,)ō, 'win-ə(-w)\ *vb* [ME *winewen,* fr. OE *windwian* to fan, winnow; akin to OHG *wintōn* to fan, L *vannus* winnowing fan, *ventus* wind — more at WIND] *vt* (bef. 12c) **1 a** (1) : to remove (as chaff) by a current of air (2) : to get rid of (something undesirable or unwanted) : REMOVE — often used with *out* ⟨~ out certain inaccuracies —Stanley Walker⟩ **b** (1) : SEPARATE, SIFT ⟨an old hand at ~*ing* what

is true and significant —Oscar Lewis⟩ (2) : SELECT **2 a :** to treat (as grain) by exposure to a current of air so that waste matter is eliminated **b :** to free of unwanted or inferior elements : PARE **3 :** to blow on : FAN ⟨the wind ~*ing* his thin white hair —*Time*⟩ ~ *vi* **1 :** to separate chaff from grain by fanning **2 :** to separate desirable and undesirable elements — **win·now·er** \'win-ə-wər\ *n*

²**winnow** *n* (1580) **1 :** a device for winnowing **2 a :** the action of winnowing **b :** a motion resembling that of winnowing

wino \'wī-(,)nō\ *n, pl* **win·os** (ca. 1915) : one who is chronically addicted to drinking wine

win·some \'win(t)-səm\ *adj* [ME *winsum*, fr. OE *wynsum*, fr. *wynn* joy; akin to OHG *wunna* joy, L *venus* love — more at WIN] (bef. 12c) **1 :** generally pleasing and engaging often because of a childlike charm and innocence **2 :** CHEERFUL, GAY — **win·some·ly** *adv* — **win·some·ness** *n*

¹**win·ter** \'wint-ər\ *n* [ME, fr. OE; akin to OHG *wintar* winter] (bef. 12c) **1 :** the season between autumn and spring comprising in the northern hemisphere usu. the months of December, January, and February or as reckoned astronomically extending from the December solstice to the March equinox **2 :** the colder half of the year **3 :** YEAR ⟨happened many ~*s* ago⟩ **4 :** a period of inactivity or decay

²**winter** *adj* (bef. 12c) **1 :** of, relating to, or suitable for winter ⟨a ~ vacation⟩ ⟨~ clothes⟩ **2 :** sown in the autumn and harvested in the following spring or summer ⟨~ wheat⟩ ⟨~ rye⟩ — compare SUMMER

³**winter** *vb* **win·tered; win·ter·ing** \'wint-ə-riŋ, 'win-triŋ\ *vi* (14c) **1 :** to pass the winter **2 :** to feed or find food during the winter — used with *on* ~ *vt* **:** to keep, feed, or manage during the winter

winter aconite *n* (1794) : a small Old World perennial herb (*Eranthis hyemalis*) of the buttercup family grown for its bright yellow flowers which often bloom through the snow

win·ter·ber·ry \'wint-ər-,ber-ē\ *n* (1759) **1 :** an eastern No. American shrub (*Ilex verticillata*) of the holly family with clusters of axillary flowers, usu. bright red berries, and deciduous leaves that turn black in the fall — called also *black alder* **2 :** a shrub (*Ilex laevigata*) similar to the winterberry but of more restricted range

win·ter·bourne \-,bō(ə)rn, -,bȯ(ə)rn, -,bu̇(ə)rn\ *n* (bef. 12c) : a stream that flows only or chiefly in winter

winter crookneck *n* (ca. 1909) : any of several crooknecks that are winter squashes of the pumpkin group noted for their keeping qualities

win·ter·er \'wint-ər-ər\ *n* (1783) : one that winters; *specif* : a winter resident or visitor

winter flounder *n* (1814) : a rusty brown flounder (*Pseudopleuronectes americanus*) of the northwestern Atlantic important as a market fish esp. in winter

win·ter·green \'wint-ər-,grēn\ *n* (1548) **1 :** any of a genus (*Pyrola* of the family Pyrolaceae, the wintergreen family) of evergreen perennial herbs related to the heaths; *esp* : one (*P. minor*) with small round basal leaves **2 a :** any of a genus (*Gaultheria*) of the heath family; *esp* : a low evergreen plant (*G. procumbens*) with white flowers and spicy red berries — compare CHECKERBERRY **b (1) :** an essential oil from this plant **(2) :** the flavor of this oil ⟨~ lozenges⟩

win·ter·ize \'wint-ə-,rīz\ *vt* **-ized; -iz·ing** (1934) : to make ready for winter or winter use and esp. resistant or proof against winter weather ⟨~ a car⟩ — **win·ter·iza·tion** \,wint-ə-rə-'zā-shən\ *n*

win·ter–kill \'wint-ər-,kil\ *vt* (1817) : to kill (as a plant) by exposure to winter conditions ~ *vi* **:** to die as a result of exposure to winter conditions — **winterkill** *n*

win·ter·ly \'wint-ər-lē\ *adj* (bef. 12c) : of, relating to, or occurring in winter : WINTRY

winter melon *n* (ca. 1900) : a muskmelon (*Cucumis melo inodorus*) with smooth rind and sweet white or greenish flesh that keeps well — compare CASABA

winter quarters *n pl but sing or pl in constr* (1641) : a winter residence or station (as of a military unit or a circus)

winter savory *n* (1597) : a perennial European herb (*Satureia montana*) used for seasoning — compare SUMMER SAVORY

winter squash *n* (1775) : any of various squashes derived from a natural species (*Cucurbita maxima*) or pumpkins from a species (*C. moschata*) that can be stored for several months

win·ter·tide \'wint-ər-,tīd\ *n* (bef. 12c) : WINTERTIME

win·ter·time \-,tīm\ *n* (14c) : the season of winter

win through *vi* (1644) : to survive difficulties and reach a desired or satisfactory end

win·tle \'win(t)-ᵊl\ *vi* **win·tled; win·tling** \'win(t)-liŋ, -ᵊl-iŋ\ [perh. fr. Flem *windtelen* to reel] (1786) **1** *Scot* : STAGGER, REEL **2** *Scot* : WRIGGLE

win·try \'win-trē\ *also* **win·tery** \'wint-ə-rē, 'win-trē\ *adj* **win·tri·er; -est** [OE *wintrig*, fr. *winter*] (bef. 12c) **1 :** of, relating to, or characteristic of winter **2 a :** weathered by or as if by winter : AGED, HOARY **b :** CHEERLESS, CHILLING ⟨a bitter ~ smile⟩ — **win·tri·ness** \'win-trē-nəs\ *n*

winy \'wī-nē\ *adj* **win·i·er; -est** (14c) **1 :** having the taste or qualities of wine : VINOUS **2** *of the air* : crisply fresh : EXHILARATING

¹**winze** \'winz\ *n* [alter. of earlier *winds*, prob. fr. pl. of ⁵*wind*] (1757) : a steeply inclined passageway connecting a mine working place with a lower one

²**winze** *n* [Flem or D *wensch* wish] *Scot* (1785) : CURSE

¹**wipe** \'wīp\ *vb* **wiped; wip·ing** [ME *wipen*, fr. OE *wīpian*; akin to OHG *wīfan* to wind around, L *vibrare* to vibrate] *vt* (bef. 12c) **1 a :** to rub with or as if with something soft for cleaning **b :** to clean or dry by rubbing **c :** to draw, pass, or move for or as if for rubbing or cleaning **2 a :** to remove by or as if by rubbing **b :** to expunge completely ⟨~ from memory the gruesome scenes —*Amer. Guide Series: Del.*⟩ **3 a :** to spread by or as if by wiping **b :** to form (a joint between lead pipes) by applying solder in repeated increments individually spread and shaped with greased cloth pads ~ *vi* **:** to make a motion of or as if of wiping something — **wipe one's boots on :** to treat with indignity — **wipe the floor with** *or* **wipe the ground with :** to defeat decisively

²**wipe** *n* (1550) **1 a :** BLOW, STRIKE **b :** JEER, GIBE **2 a :** an act or instance of wiping **b :** a transition from one scene or picture to another (as in movies or television) made by a line moving across the screen **3 :** something (as a towel) used for wiping

wiped out *adj, slang* (1965) : INTOXICATED, HIGH

wipe·out \'wī-,pau̇t\ *n* (1921) **1 :** the act or an instance of wiping out : complete or utter destruction **2 :** a fall from a surfboard caused usu. by losing control or being knocked off by a wave

wipe out \(')wī-'pau̇t\ *vt* (1535) : to destroy completely : ANNIHILATE ~ *vi* **1 :** to fall from a surfboard **2 :** to fall while skiing

wip·er \'wī-pər\ *n* (1552) **1 :** one that wipes **2 a :** something (as a towel or sponge) used for wiping **b :** a projecting tooth, tumbler, eccentric, tappet, or cam on a rotating or oscillating piece used esp. for raising a stamper, the helve of a power hammer, or other part intended to fall by its own weight **c :** a moving contact for making connections with the terminals of an electrical device (as a rheostat) **d :** a usu. motor-driven arm with a flexible blade for wiping a window (as the windshield of an automobile or airplane)

¹**wire** \'wī(ə)r\ *n, often attrib* [ME, fr. OE *wīr*; akin to OHG *wiara* fine gold, L *viēre* to plait, Gk *iris* rainbow] (bef. 12c) **1 a :** metal in the form of a usu. very flexible thread or slender rod **b :** a thread or rod of such material **2 a :** WIREWORK **b :** the meshwork of parallel or woven wire on which the wet web of paper forms **3 :** something (as a thin plant stem) that is wirelike **4** *pl* **a :** a system of wires used to operate the puppets in a puppet show **b :** hidden influences controlling the action of a person or organization **5 a :** a line of wire for conducting electrical current — compare CORD 3b **b :** a telephone or telegraph wire or system; *esp* : WIRE SERVICE **c :** TELEGRAM, CABLEGRAM **6 :** fencing or a fence of usu. barbed wire **7 :** the finish line of a race — **wire·like** \-,līk\ *adj* — **under the wire 1 :** at the finish line **2 :** at the last moment

²**wire** *vb* **wired; wir·ing** *vt* (14c) **1 :** to provide with wire : use wire on for a specific purpose **2 :** to send or send word to by telegraph **3 :** to connect by a wire ~ *vi* **:** to send a telegraphic message — **wir·able** \'wī-rə-bəl\ *adj* — **wir·er** \'wīr-ər\ *n*

wire cloth *n* (1798) : a fabric of woven metallic wire (as for strainers)

wired \'wī(ə)rd\ *adj* (15c) **1 :** reinforced by wire (as for strength) **2 :** furnished with wires (as for electric connections) **3 :** bound with wire ⟨a ~ container⟩ **4 :** having a wirework netting or fence **5 :** feverishly excited

wire·draw \'wī(ə)r-,drȯ\ *vt* (1598) **1 :** to draw or stretch forcibly : ELONGATE **2 :** to draw or spin out to great length, tenuity, or overrefinement : ATTENUATE — **wire·draw·er** \-drȯ(-ə)r\ *n*

wire·drawn \-,drȯn\ *adj* (1603) : excessively minute and subtle ⟨curious speculations, ~ comparisons, obsolete erudition —Virginia Woolf⟩

wire gauge *n* (1833) **1 :** a gauge esp. for measuring the diameter of wire or the thickness of sheet metal **2 :** any of various systems consisting of a series of standard sizes used in describing the diameter of wire or the thickness of sheet metal

wire gauze *n* (1816) : a gauzelike texture of fine wires

wire glass *n* (ca. 1896) : a glass with wire netting embedded in it

wire grass *n* (1751) : any of various grasses or rushes having wiry culms or leaves; *esp* : a European slender-stemmed meadow grass (*Poa compressa*) widely naturalized in the U.S. and Canada

wire·hair \'wī(ə)r-,ha(ə)r, -,he(ə)r\ *n* (1884) : a wirehaired fox terrier

wire·haired \-'ha(ə)rd, -'he(ə)rd\ *adj* (1801) : having a stiff wiry outer coat of hair — used esp. of a dog

wirehaired pointing griffon *n* (ca. 1929) : any of a breed of sporting dogs that originated in Holland and have a long head and a harsh wiry gray or grayish outer coat often with chestnut markings

wirehaired terrier *n* (ca. 1885) : a wirehaired fox terrier

¹**wire·less** \'wī(ə)r-ləs\ *adj* (1894) **1 :** having no wire or wires **2** *chiefly Brit* : of or relating to radiotelegraphy, radiotelephony, or radio

²**wireless** *vi* (1899) : to send a message by wireless ~ *vt* **:** to send by wireless : RADIO ⟨the lightship ~*ed* a warning to vessels in the vicinity —*Amer. Guide Series: N.C.*⟩

³**wireless** *n* (1903) **1 :** WIRELESS TELEGRAPHY **2 :** two-way wireless transmission of sound using radio waves **3** *chiefly Brit* : RADIO

wireless telegraphy *n* (1898) : telegraphy carried on by radio waves and without connecting wires — called also *wireless telegraph*

wireless telephone *n* (1894) : RADIOTELEPHONE

wire·man \'wī(ə)r-mən\ *n* (1547) **1 :** a maker of or worker with wire; *esp* : LINEMAN 1 **2 :** WIRETAPPER

wire netting *n* (1801) : a texture of woven wire coarser than wire gauze

Wire·pho·to \'wī(ə)r-'fōt-(,)ō\ *trademark* — used for a photograph transmitted by electrical signals over telephone wires

wire–pull·er \-,pu̇l-ər\ *n* (1832) : one who uses secret or underhanded means to influence the acts of a person or organization — **wire–pull·ing** \-,pu̇l-iŋ\ *n*

wire recorder *n* (1943) : a magnetic recorder using magnetic wire — **wire–re·cord·ing** *n*

wire rope *n* (1841) : a rope formed wholly or chiefly of wires

wire service *n* (1944) : a news agency that sends out syndicated news copy by wire to subscribers

¹**wire·tap** \'wī(ə)r-,tap\ *vi* (1904) : to tap a telephone or telegraph wire in order to get information ~ *vt* **:** to tap the telephone of

²**wiretap** *n* (1948) **1 :** the act or an instance of wiretapping **2 :** an electrical connection for wiretapping

wire·tap·per \-,tap-ər\ *n* (1893) : one that taps telephone or telegraph wires

wire·way \'wī(ə)r-,wā\ *n* (1906) : a conduit for wires

wire·work \-,wərk\ *n* (1587) **1 :** a work of wires; *esp* : meshwork, netting, or grillwork of wire ⟨plan the ~ for new circuitry⟩ **2 :** walking on wires esp. by acrobats

wire·worm \-,wərm\ *n* (1790) : a worm that is the slender hard-coated larva of various click beetles and is esp. destructive to plant roots

wir·ing \'wī(ə)r-iŋ\ *n* (1809) **1 :** the act of providing or using wire **2 :** a system of wires; *esp* : an arrangement of wires used for electric distribution

wir·ra \'wir-ə\ *interj* [*oh wirra*, fr. IrGael *a Muire*, lit., O Mary] *Irish* (1829) — usu. used to express lament, grief, or concern

wiry \'wī(ə)r-ē\ *adj* **wir·i·er** \'wī-rē-ər\; **-est** (1588) **1 a :** made of wire **b :** resembling wire esp. in form and flexibility **c** *of sound* **:** produced by or suggestive of the vibration of wire ⟨the violinist . . . often let his tone go nasal and ~ —D. J. Henahan⟩ **2 :** being lean, supple, and vigorous **:** SINEWY — **wir·i·ly** \'wī-rə-lē\ *adv* — **wir·i·ness** \-rē-nəs\ *n*

wis \'wis\ *vb* [by incorrect division fr. *iwis* (understood as *I wis,* with *wis* taken to be an archaic pres. indic. of [1]*wit*)] *archaic* (1508) **:** KNOW

wis·dom \'wiz-dəm\ *n* [ME, fr. OE *wīsdōm,* fr. *wīs* wise] (bef. 12c) **1 a :** accumulated philosophic or scientific learning **:** KNOWLEDGE **b :** ability to discern inner qualities and relationships **:** INSIGHT **c :** good sense **:** JUDGMENT **2 :** a wise attitude or course of action **3 :** the teachings of the ancient wise men ***syn*** see SENSE

Wisdom *n* **:** a didactic book included in the Roman Catholic canon of the Old Testament and corresponding to the Wisdom of Solomon in the Protestant Apocrypha — see BIBLE table

Wisdom of Sol·o·mon \-'säl-ə-mən\ **:** a didactic book included in the Protestant Apocrypha — see BIBLE table

wisdom tooth *n* [fr. being cut usu. in the late teens] (1848) **:** the third molar that is the last tooth to erupt on each side of the upper and lower jaws in man

[1]**wise** \'wīz\ *n* [ME, fr. OE *wīse;* akin to OHG *wīsa* manner, Gk *eidos* form, *idein* to see — more at WIT] (bef. 12c) **:** MANNER, WAY ⟨in any ~⟩

[2]**wise** *adj* **wis·er; wis·est** [ME *wis,* fr. OE *wīs;* akin to OHG *wīs* wise, OE *witan* to know — more at WIT] (bef. 12c) **1 a :** characterized by wisdom **:** marked by deep understanding, keen discernment, and a capacity for sound judgment **b :** exercising sound judgment **:** PRUDENT **2 a :** evidencing or hinting at the possession of inside information **:** KNOWING **b :** possessing inside information **c :** CRAFTY, SHREWD **3** *archaic* **:** skilled in magic or divination **4 :** INSOLENT, SMART-ALECKY, FRESH— **wise·ly** *adv* — **wise·ness** *n*

syn WISE, SAGE, SAPIENT, JUDICIOUS, PRUDENT, SENSIBLE, SANE mean having or showing sound judgment. WISE suggests great understanding of people and of situations and unusual discernment and judgment in dealing with them; SAGE suggests wide experience, great learning, and wisdom; SAPIENT suggests great sagacity and discernment; JUDICIOUS stresses a capacity for reaching wise decisions or just conclusions; PRUDENT suggests exercise of the restraint of sound practical wisdom and discretion; SENSIBLE applies to action guided and restrained by good sense and rationality; SANE stresses mental soundness, rationality, and levelheadedness.

[3]**wise** *vb* **wised; wis·ing** *vt* (1905) **:** to give instruction or information to **:** TEACH — usu. used with *up* ~ *vi* **:** to become informed or knowledgeable **:** LEARN — used with *up*

[4]**wise** *vt* **wised; wis·ing** [ME *wisen,* fr. OE *wīsian;* akin to ON *vīsa* to show the way, OE *wīs* wise] (bef. 12c) **1** *chiefly Scot* **a :** DIRECT, GUIDE **b :** ADVISE, PERSUADE **2** *chiefly Scot* **:** to divert or impel in a given direction **:** SEND

-wise \,wīz\ *adv comb form* [ME, fr. OE *-wīsan,* fr. *wīse* manner] **1 a :** in the manner of ⟨crab*wise*⟩ ⟨fan*wise*⟩ **b :** in the position or direction of ⟨slant*wise*⟩ ⟨clock*wise*⟩ **2 :** with regard to **:** in respect of ⟨dollar*wise*⟩

wise·acre \'wī-,zā-kər\ *n* [MD *wijssegger* soothsayer, modif. of OHG *wīzzago;* akin to OE *witega* soothsayer, *witan* to know] (1595) **:** one who pretends to knowledge or cleverness **:** SMART ALECK

wise·ass \-,zas\ *n* (1971) **:** SMART ALECK

[1]**wise·crack** \'wīz-,krak\ *n* (ca. 1920) **:** a sophisticated or knowing witticism ***syn*** see JEST

[2]**wisecrack** *vi* (1924) **:** to make a wisecrack — **wise·crack·er** *n*

wise guy \'wīz-,gī\ *n* (1896) **:** SMART ALECK

wise man *n* (bef. 12c) **1 :** a man of unusual learning, judgment, or insight **:** SAGE **2 :** a man versed in esoteric lore (as of magic or astrology); *specif* **:** MAGUS 2

wi·sen·hei·mer \'wīz-ᵊn-,hī-mər\ *n* [[2]*wise* + G *-enheimer* (as in G family names such as *Guggenheimer, Oppenheimer*)] (1904) **:** SMART ALECK

wi·sent \'vē-,zent\ *n* [G, fr. OHG *wisunt* — more at BISON] (1866) **:** a European bison (*Bison bonasus*) — called also *aurochs*

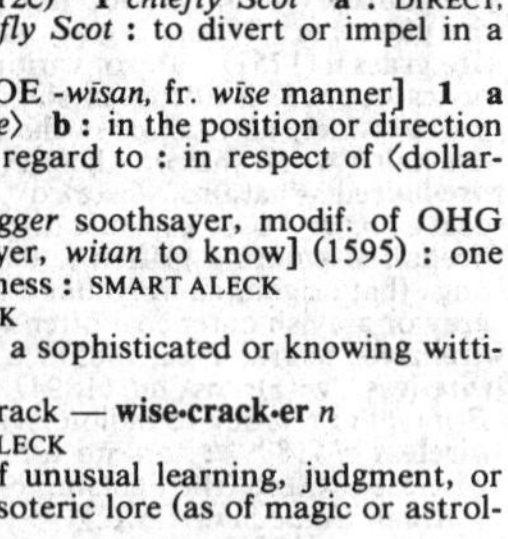
wisent

wise·wom·an \'wīz-,wu̇m-ən\ *n* (14c) **:** a woman versed in charms, conjuring, or fortune-telling

[1]**wish** \'wish\ *vb* [ME *wisshen,* fr. OE *wȳscan;* akin to OHG *wunsken* to wish, L *venus* love, charm — more at WIN] *vt* (bef. 12c) **1 :** to have a desire for (as something unattainable) ⟨~*ed* he could live his life over⟩ **2 :** to give expression to as a wish **:** BID ⟨~ him good night⟩ **3 a :** to give form to (a wish) **b :** to express a wish for **c :** to request in the form of a wish **:** ORDER **d :** to desire (a person or thing) to be as specified ⟨cannot ~ our problems away⟩ **4 :** to confer (something unwanted) on someone **:** FOIST ~ *vi* **1 :** to have a desire **:** WANT **2 :** to make a wish ***syn*** see DESIRE — **wish·er** *n*

[2]**wish** *n* (14c) **1 a :** an act or instance of wishing or desire **:** WANT **b :** an object of desire **:** GOAL **2 a :** an expressed will or desire **:** MANDATE **b :** a request or command couched as a wish **3 :** an invocation of good or evil fortune on someone

wisha \'wish-ə\ *interj* [IrGael *ō* oh + *muise* indeed] *chiefly Irish* (1842) — used as an intensive or to express surprise

wish·bone \'wish-,bōn\ *n* [fr. the superstition that when two persons pull it apart the one getting the longer fragment will have his wish granted] (1853) **1 :** a furcula in front of the breastbone in a bird consisting chiefly of the two clavicles fused at their median or lower end **2 :** a variation of the T formation in which the halfbacks line up farther from the line of scrimmage than the fullback does

wish·ful \'wish-fəl\ *adj* (1593) **1 a :** expressive of a wish **:** HOPEFUL **b :** having a wish **:** DESIROUS **2 :** according with wishes rather than reality — **wish·ful·ly** \-fə-lē\ *adv* — **wish·ful·ness** *n*

wish fulfillment *n* (1908) **:** the gratification of a desire esp. symbolically (as in dreams, daydreams, or neurotic symptoms)

wishful thinking *n* (1932) **:** the attribution of reality to what one wishes to be true and the tenuous justification of what one wants to believe

wish·ing *adj* (ca. 1530) **1** *archaic* **:** WISHFUL **2 :** regarded as having the power to grant wishes ⟨threw a coin in the ~ well⟩

wish list *n* (1972) **:** a list of desired but often realistically unobtainable items

wish–wash \'wish-,wȯsh, -,wäsh\ *n* [redupl. of [2]*wash*] (1786) **1 :** a weak drink **2 :** insipid talk or writing

wishy–washy \'wish-ē-,wȯsh-ē, -,wäsh-\ *adj* [redupl. of *washy*] (1693) **1 :** lacking in character or determination **:** INEFFECTUAL **2 :** lacking in strength or flavor **:** WEAK — **wishy–wash·i·ness** *n*

[1]**wisp** \'wisp\ *n* [ME] (14c) **1 :** a small handful (as of hay or straw) **2 a :** a thin strip or fragment **b :** a thready streak ⟨a ~ of smoke⟩ **c :** something frail, slight, or fleeting ⟨a ~ of a girl⟩ ⟨a ~ of a smile⟩ **3 :** WILL-O'-THE-WISP — **wisp·i·ly** \'wis-pə-lē\ *adv* — **wisp·i·ness** \'wis-pē-nəs\ *n* — **wispy** \'wis-pē\ *adj*

[2]**wisp** *vt* (1753) **1 :** to roll into a wisp **2 a :** to make wisps of ⟨a cigarette ~*ing* smoke at the corner of his mouth —Raymond Chandler⟩ **b :** to cover with wisps ⟨the sky all ~*ed* with mist —W. F. Wray⟩ ~ *vi* **:** to emerge or drift in wisps ⟨her hair began to ~ into her eyes —Mary Manning⟩

wisp·ish \'wis-pish\ *adj* (1896) **:** resembling a wisp **:** INSUBSTANTIAL

wist \'wist\ *vt* [alter. of *wis*] *archaic* (1508) **:** KNOW

wis·te·ria \wis-'tir-ē-ə\ *or* **wis·tar·ia** \-'tir-ē-ə *also* -'ter-\ *n* [NL *Wisteria,* fr. Caspar *Wistar* †1818 Am. physician] (1876) **:** any of a genus (*Wisteria*) of chiefly Asian mostly woody leguminous vines having pinnately compound leaves and showy blue, white, purple, or rose pealike flowers in long racemes and including several grown as ornamentals

wist·ful \'wist-fəl\ *adj* [blend of *wishful* and obs. E *wistly* (intently)] (1714) **1 :** full of unfulfilled longing or desire **:** YEARNING **2 :** musingly sad **:** PENSIVE — **wist·ful·ly** \-fə-lē\ *adv* — **wist·ful·ness** *n*

[1]**wit** \'wit\ *vb* **wist** \'wist\; **wit·ting;** *pres 1st & 3d sing* **wot** \'wät\ [ME *witen* (1st & 3d sing. pres. *wot,* past *wiste*), fr. OE *witan* (1st & 3d sing. pres. *wāt,* past *wisse, wiste*); akin to OHG *wizzan* to know, L *vidēre* to see, Gk *eidenai* to know, *idein* to see] (bef. 12c) **1** *archaic* **:** KNOW **2** *archaic* **:** to come to know **:** LEARN

[2]**wit** *n* [ME, fr. OE; akin to OHG *wizzi* knowledge, OE *witan* to know] (bef. 12c) **1 a :** MIND, MEMORY **b :** reasoning power **:** INTELLIGENCE **2 a :** SENSE 2a — usu. used in pl. ⟨alone and warming his five ~*s,* the white owl in the belfry sits —Alfred Tennyson⟩ **b (1) :** mental soundness **:** SANITY — usu. used in pl. **(2) :** mental capability and resourcefulness **:** INGENUITY **3 a :** astuteness of perception or judgment **:** ACUMEN **b :** the ability to relate seemingly disparate things so as to illuminate or amuse **c (1) :** a talent for banter or persiflage **(2) :** a witty utterance or exchange **4 a :** a person of superior intellect **:** THINKER **b :** an imaginatively perceptive and articulate individual esp. skilled in banter or persiflage

syn WIT, HUMOR, IRONY, SARCASM, SATIRE, REPARTEE mean a mode of expression intended to arouse amusement. WIT suggests the power to evoke laughter by remarks showing verbal felicity or ingenuity and swift perception esp. of the incongruous; HUMOR implies an ability to perceive the ludicrous, the comical, and the absurd in human life and to express these usu. without bitterness; IRONY applies to a manner of expression in which the intended meaning is the opposite of what is seemingly expressed; SARCASM applies to expression frequently in the form of irony that is intended to cut or wound; SATIRE applies to writing that exposes or ridicules conduct, doctrines, or institutions either by direct criticism or more often through irony, parody, or caricature; REPARTEE implies the power of answering quickly, pointedly, or wittily.

— **at one's wit's end** *or* **at one's wits' end :** at a loss for a means of solving a problem

wi·tan \'wi-,tän\ *n pl* [OE, pl. of *wita* sage, adviser; akin to OHG *wizzo* sage, OE *witan* to know] (bef. 12c) **:** members of the witenagemot

[1]**witch** \'wich\ *n* [ME *wicche,* fr. OE *wicca,* masc., wizard & *wicce,* fem., witch; akin to MHG *wicken* to bewitch, OE *wigle* divination, OHG *wīh* holy — more at VICTIM] (bef. 12c) **1 :** one that is credited with usu. malignant supernatural powers; *esp* **:** a woman practicing usu. black witchcraft often with the aid of a devil or familiar **:** SORCERESS — compare WARLOCK **2 :** an ugly old woman **:** HAG **3 :** a charming or alluring girl or woman — **witch·like** \'wich-,līk\ *adj* — **witchy** \'wich-ē\ *adj*

[2]**witch** *vt* (14c) **1 :** to affect injuriously with witchcraft **2** *archaic* **:** to influence or beguile with allure or charm ~ *vi* **:** DOWSE

witch·craft \'wich-,kraft\ *n* [ME *wicchecraft,* fr. OE *wiccecræft* witchcraft, sorcery, fr. *wicce* + *cræft* skill, power — more at CRAFT] (bef. 12c) **1 a :** the use of sorcery or magic **b :** communication with the devil or with a familiar **2 :** an irresistible influence or fascination

witch doctor *n* (1718) **:** a professional worker of magic usu. in a primitive society who often works to cure sickness

witch·ery \'wich-(ə-)rē\ *n, pl* **-er·ies** (1546) **1 a :** the practice of witchcraft **:** SORCERY **b :** an act of witchcraft **2 :** an irresistible fascination

witches' brew *n* (1929) **:** a potent or fearsome mixture ⟨a *witches' brew* of untamed sex and brutality —Harrison Smith⟩

witch·es'–broom \'wich-əz-,brüm, -,bru̇m\ *n* (1881) **:** an abnormal tufted growth of small branches on a tree or shrub caused esp. by fungi or viruses

witches' Sabbath *n* (1676) **:** a midnight assembly of witches, devils, and sorcerers for the celebration of rites and orgies

witch·grass \'wich-,gras\ *n* [prob. alter. of *quitch* (*grass*)] (1790) **1 :** QUACK GRASS **2** [[1]*witch*] **:** a No. American grass (*Panicum capillare*) with slender brushy panicles that is often a weed on cultivated land

witch ha·zel \'wich-,hā-zəl\ *n* [*witch* (a tree with pliant branches)] (1541) **1 :** any of a genus (*Hamamelis* of the family Hamamelidaceae, the witch-hazel family) of shrubs with slender-petaled yellow flowers borne in late fall or early spring; *esp* **:** one (*H. virginiana*) of eastern No. America that blooms in the fall **2 :** an alcoholic solution of a distillate of the bark of a witch hazel (*H. virginiana*) used as a soothing and mildly astringent lotion

witch–hunt \'wich-,hənt\ *n* (1885) **1 :** a searching out for persecution of persons accused of witchcraft **2 :** the searching out and deliberate harassment of those (as political opponents) with unpopular views — **witch–hunt·er** *n* — **witch–hunt·ing** *n or adj*

[1]**witch·ing** \'wich-iŋ\ *n* (bef. 12c) **:** the practice of witchcraft **:** SORCERY

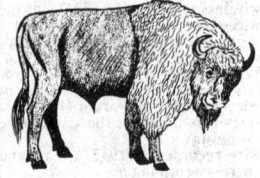

[2]**witching** *adj* (14c) **:** of, relating to, or suitable for sorcery or supernatural occurrences ⟨the very ~ time of night —Shak.⟩

witch of Agne·si \-än-ˈyā-zē\ *n* [*witch* (trans. of It *avversiera,* by confusion with It *versiera,* lit., turning — Agnesi's name for the curve) + *of* + Maria Gaetana *Agnesi* †1799 Ital. mathematician] (1875) **:** a plane cubic curve that is symmetric about the y-axis and approaches the x-axis as an asymptote, that is constructed by drawing lines from the origin intersecting an upright circle tangent to the x-axis at the origin and taking the locus of points of intersection of pairs of lines parallel to the x-axis and y-axis each pair of which consists of a line parallel to the x-axis through the point where a line through the origin intersects the circle and a line parallel to the y-axis through the point where the same line through the origin intersects the line parallel to the x-axis through the point of intersection of the circle and the y-axis, and that has the equation $x^2y = 4a^2(2a - y)$ — called also *witch*

witch·weed \ˈwich-ˌwēd\ *n* (1904) **:** any of a genus (*Striga* of the figwort family) of yellow-flowered Old World plants that are damaging root parasites of grasses (as sorghum and maize) and that include one (*S. lutea*) which is an introduced pest in parts of the southeastern U.S.

[1]**wite** \ˈwīt\ *vt* **wit·ed; wit·ing** *chiefly Scot* (bef. 12c) **:** BLAME

[2]**wite** *n* [ME, fr. OE *wīte* punishment; akin to OHG *wīzi* punishment, OE *witan* to know] *chiefly Scot* (13c) **:** BLAME, RESPONSIBILITY

wi·te·na·ge·mot *or* **wi·te·na·ge·mote** \ˈwit-ᵊn-ə-gə-ˌmōt, -yə-ˌmōt\ *n* [OE *witena gemōt,* fr. *witena* (gen. pl. of *wita* sage, adviser) + *gemōt* gemot] (bef. 12c) **:** an Anglo-Saxon council made up of a varying number of nobles, prelates, and influential officials and convened from time to time to advise the king on administrative and judicial matters

with \(ˈ)wit͟h, (ˈ)with, wət͟h, wəth\ *prep* [ME, against, from, with, fr. OE; akin to OE *wither* against, OHG *widar* against, back, Skt *vi* apart] (bef. 12c) **1 a :** in opposition to **:** AGAINST ⟨had a fight ~ his brother⟩ **b :** so as to be separated or detached from ⟨broke ~ her family⟩ **2 a** — used as a function word to indicate a participant in an action, transaction, or arrangement ⟨works ~ his father⟩ ⟨a talk ~ a friend⟩ ⟨got into an accident ~ the car⟩ **b** — used as a function word to indicate the object of attention, behavior, or feeling ⟨get tough ~ him⟩ ⟨angry ~ her⟩ **c :** in respect to **:** so far as concerns ⟨on friendly terms ~ all nations⟩ **d** — used to indicate the object of an adverbial expression of imperative force ⟨off ~ his head⟩ **e :** OVER, ON ⟨no longer has any influence ~ him⟩ **f :** in the performance, operation, or use of ⟨the trouble ~ this machine⟩ **3 a** — used as a function word to indicate the object of a statement of comparison or equality ⟨a dress identical ~ her hostess's⟩ **b** — used as a function word to express agreement or sympathy ⟨must conclude, ~ you, that the painting is a forgery⟩ **c :** on the side of **:** FOR ⟨if he's for lower taxes, I'm ~ him⟩ **d :** as well as ⟨can pitch ~ the best of them⟩ **4 a** — used as a function word to indicate combination, accompaniment, presence, or addition ⟨heat milk ~ honey⟩ ⟨went there ~ her⟩ ⟨his money, ~ his wife's, comes to a million⟩ **b :** inclusive of ⟨costs $5 ~ the tax⟩ **5 a :** in the judgment or estimation of ⟨stood well ~ his classmates⟩ **b :** in or according to the experience or practice of ⟨~ many of us, our ideas seem to fall by the wayside —W. J. Reilly⟩ **6 a** — used as a function word to indicate the means, cause, agent, or instrumentality ⟨hit him ~ a rock⟩ ⟨pale ~ anger⟩ ⟨threatened ~ tuberculosis⟩ ⟨he amused the crowd ~ his antics⟩ **b** *archaic* **:** by the direct act of **7 a** — used as a function word to indicate manner of action ⟨ran ~ effort⟩ ⟨acknowledge your contribution ~ thanks⟩ **b** — used as a function word to indicate an attendant fact or circumstance ⟨stood there ~ his hat on⟩ **c** — used as a function word to indicate a result attendant on a specified action ⟨got off ~ a light sentence⟩ **8 a** (1) **:** in possession of **:** HAVING ⟨came ~ good news⟩ (2) **:** in the possession or care of ⟨left the money ~ his mother⟩ **b :** characterized or distinguished by ⟨a person ~ a sharp nose⟩ **9 a** — used as a function word to indicate a close association in time ⟨~ the outbreak of war they went home⟩ ⟨mellows ~ time⟩ **b :** in proportion to ⟨the pressure varies ~ the depth⟩ **10 a :** in spite of **:** NOTWITHSTANDING ⟨a really tip-top man, ~ all his wrongheadedness —H. J. Laski⟩ **b :** except for ⟨finds that, ~ one group of omissions and one important addition, they reflect that curriculum —Gilbert Highet⟩ **11 :** in the direction of ⟨~ the wind⟩ ⟨~ the grain⟩

[1]**with·al** \wit͟h-ˈȯl, with-\ *adv* [ME, fr. *with* + *all, al* all] (13c) **1 :** together with this **:** BESIDES ⟨a supporter of all constructive work and ~ an excellent businessman —A. W. Long⟩ **2** *archaic* **:** THEREWITH 1 **3 :** on the other hand **:** NEVERTHELESS

[2]**withal** *prep, archaic* (14c) **:** WITH — used postpositively with a relative or interrogative pronoun as object

with·draw \wit͟h-ˈdrȯ, with-\ *vb* **-drew** \-ˈdrü\; **-drawn** \-ˈdrȯn\; **-draw·ing** \-ˈdrȯ(-)iŋ\ [ME *withdrawen,* fr. *with* from + *drawen* to draw] *vt* (13c) **1 a :** to take back or away **:** REMOVE ⟨pressure upon educational administrators to ~ academic credit —J. W. Scott⟩ **b :** to remove from use or cultivation **c :** to remove (money) from a place of deposit **d :** to turn away (as the eyes) from an object of attention ⟨*withdrew* his gaze⟩ **e :** to draw (as a curtain) back or aside **2 a :** to remove from consideration or set outside a group ⟨*withdrew* his name from the list of nominees⟩ ⟨*withdrew* her son from the school⟩ **b** (1) **:** TAKE BACK, RETRACT (2) **:** to recall or remove (a motion) under parliamentary procedure ~ *vi* **1 a :** to move back or away **:** RETIRE **b :** to draw back from a battlefield **:** RETREAT **2 a :** to remove oneself from participation **b :** to become socially or emotionally detached ⟨had *withdrawn* farther and farther into herself —Ethel Wilson⟩ **3 :** to recall a motion under parliamentary procedure — **with·draw·able** \-ˈdrȯ-ə-bəl\ *adj*

with·draw·al \-ˈdrȯ(-ə)l\ *n* (1749) **1 a :** the act of taking back or away something that has been granted or possessed **b :** removal from a place of deposit or investment **c :** the discontinuance of administration or use of a drug **2 a :** retreat or retirement esp. into a more secluded or less exposed place or position **b :** an operation by which a military force disengages from the enemy **c** (1) **:** social or emotional detachment (2) **:** a pathological retreat from objective reality (as in some schizophrenic states) **3 :** RETRACTION, REVOCATION ⟨threatened us with ~ of his consent⟩ **4 :** the act of drawing someone or something back from or out of a place or position

withdrawing room *n* (1591) **:** a room to retire to (as from a dining room); *esp* **:** DRAWING ROOM

with·drawn \wit͟h-ˈdrȯn\ *adj* (1615) **1 :** removed from immediate contact or easy approach **:** ISOLATED **2 :** socially detached and unresponsive **:** exhibiting withdrawal **:** INTROVERTED — **with·drawn·ness** \-ˈdrȯn-nəs\ *n*

withe \ˈwith, ˈwit͟h, ˈwīt͟h\ *n* [ME, fr. OE *withthe;* akin to OE *wīthig* withy] (bef. 12c) **:** a slender flexible branch or twig; *esp* **:** one used as a band or line

with·er \ˈwit͟h-ər\ *vb* **with·ered; with·er·ing** \-(ə-)riŋ\ [ME *widren;* prob. akin to ME *weder* weather] *vi* (14c) **1 :** to become dry and sapless; *esp* **:** to shrivel from or as if from loss of bodily moisture **2 :** to lose vitality, force, or freshness ~ *vt* **1 :** to cause to wither **2 :** to make speechless or incapable of action **:** STUN ⟨~*ed* him with a look —Dorothy Sayers⟩

with·ered *adj* (15c) **:** shriveled and shrunken from drying

with·er·ing *adj* (1579) **:** acting or serving to cut down or destroy **:** DEVASTATING ⟨a ~ fire from the enemy⟩ — **with·er·ing·ly** \-(ə-)riŋ-lē\ *adv*

with·er·ite \ˈwit͟h-ə-ˌrīt\ *n* [G *witherit,* irreg. fr. William *Withering* †1799 Eng. physician] (1794) **:** a mineral $BaCO_3$ consisting of a carbonate of barium in the form of white or gray twin crystals or columnar or granular masses

withe rod *n* (1847) **:** a No. American viburnum (*Viburnum cassinoides*) with tough slender shoots

with·ers \ˈwit͟h-ərz\ *n pl* [prob. fr. obs. E *wither-* (against), fr. ME, fr. OE, fr. *wither* against; fr. the withers being the parts which resist the pull in drawing a load — more at WITH] (1580) **1 :** the ridge between the shoulder bones of a horse — see HORSE illustration **2 :** a part corresponding to the withers in a quadruped other than a horse

with·er·shins \ˈwit͟h-ər-shənz\ *var of* WIDDERSHINS

with·hold \with-ˈhōld, wit͟h-\ *vb* **-held** \-ˈheld\; **-hold·ing** [ME *withholden,* fr. *with* from + *holden* to hold — more at WITH] *vt* (13c) **1 :** to hold back from action **:** CHECK **2** *archaic* **:** to keep in custody **3 :** to refrain from granting, giving, or allowing ⟨~ permission⟩ **4 :** to deduct (withholding tax) from income ~ *vi* **:** FORBEAR, REFRAIN **syn** see KEEP — **with·hold·er** *n*

withholding tax *n* (1941) **:** a deduction (as from wages, fees, or dividends) levied at a source of income as advance payment on income tax

[1]**with·in** \wit͟h-ˈin, with-\ *adv* [ME *withinne,* fr. OE *withinnan,* fr. *with* + *innan* inwardly, within, fr. *in*] (bef. 12c) **1 :** in or into the interior **:** INSIDE **2 :** in one's inner thought, disposition, or character **:** INWARDLY ⟨search ~ for a creative impulse —Kingman Brewster, Jr.⟩

[2]**within** *prep* (12c) **1** — used as a function word to indicate enclosure or containment **2** — used as a function word to indicate situation or circumstance in the limits or compass of: as **a :** before the end of ⟨gone ~ a week⟩ **b** (1) **:** not beyond the quantity, degree, or limitations of ⟨lives ~ his income⟩ (2) **:** in or into the scope or sphere of ⟨~ the jurisdiction of the state⟩ (3) **:** in or into the range of ⟨~ reach⟩ ⟨~ sight⟩ (4) — used as a function word to indicate a specified difference or margin ⟨came ~ two points of a perfect mark⟩ ⟨~ a mile of the town⟩ **3 :** to the inside of **:** INTO

[3]**within** *n* (15c) **:** an inner place or area ⟨revolt from ~⟩

[4]**within** *adj* (1748) **:** being inside **:** ENCLOSED ⟨the ~ indictment⟩

with·in·doors \wit͟h-ˌin-ˈdō(ə)rz, with-, -ˈdȯ(ə)rz\ *adv* (1579) **:** INDOORS

with–it \ˈwit͟h-ət\ *adj* (ca. 1950) **:** attuned to a social or cultural vanguard **:** socially or culturally up-to-date ⟨the intelligent, disaffected, ~ young —Eliot Fremont-Smith⟩

[1]**with·out** \wit͟h-ˈau̇t, with-\ *prep* [ME *withoute,* fr. OE *withūtan,* fr. *with* + *ūtan* outside, fr. *ūt* out — more at OUT] (bef. 12c) **1 :** OUTSIDE **2** — used as a function word to indicate the absence or lack of something or someone ⟨fight ~ fear⟩ ⟨left ~ him⟩ ⟨looks ~ seeing⟩

[2]**without** *adv* (bef. 12c) **1 :** on the outside **:** EXTERNALLY **2 :** with something lacking or absent ⟨has learned to do ~⟩

[3]**without** *conj, chiefly dial* (13c) **:** UNLESS ⟨you don't know about me ~ you have read a book —Mark Twain⟩

[4]**without** *n* (15c) **:** an outer place or area ⟨came from ~⟩

with·out·doors \wit͟h-ˌau̇t-ˈdō(ə)rz, with-\ *adv* (13c) **:** OUTDOORS

with·stand \with-ˈstand, wit͟h-\ *vt* **-stood** \-ˈstu̇d\; **-stand·ing** [ME *withstanden,* fr. OE *withstandan,* fr. *with* against + *standan* to stand] (bef. 12c) **1 a :** to stand up against **:** oppose with firm determination; *esp* **:** to resist successfully **b :** to be proof against **:** resist the effect of ⟨~ the impact of a landing —*Current Biog.*⟩ **2** *archaic* **:** to stop or obstruct the course of **syn** see OPPOSE

[1]**withy** \ˈwit͟h-ē\ *n, pl* **with·ies** [ME, fr. OE *wīthig;* akin to OHG *wīda* willow, L *vitis* vine, *viēre* to plait, Gk *in-, is* tendon, sinew — more at WIRE] (bef. 12c) **1 :** WILLOW; *esp* **:** OSIER 1 **2 :** a flexible slender twig or branch (as of osier) **:** WITHE

[2]**withy** \ˈwith-ē, ˈwit͟h-ē, ˈwī-t͟hē\ *adj* [*withe*] (1598) **:** flexibly tough

wit·less \ˈwit-ləs\ *adj* (bef. 12c) **1 :** destitute of wit or understanding **:** FOOLISH **2 :** mentally deranged **:** CRAZY ⟨drive one ~ with anxiety —William Styron⟩ — **wit·less·ly** *adv* — **wit·less·ness** *n*

wit·ling \-liŋ\ *n* (1693) **1 :** a would-be wit **2 :** a person of little wit

wit·loof \ˈwit-ˌlōf, -ˌlüf\ *n* [D dial. *witloof* chicory, fr. D *wit* white (akin to OE *hwīt* white) + *loof* foliage, fr. MD; akin to OE *lēaf* leaf — more at WHITE, LEAF] (1885) **:** CHICORY 1; *also* **:** ENDIVE 2

[1]**wit·ness** \ˈwit-nəs\ *n* [ME *witnesse,* fr. OE *witnes* knowledge, testimony, witness, fr. *wit* intelligence] (bef. 12c) **1 :** attestation of a fact or event **:** TESTIMONY **2 :** one that gives evidence; *specif* **:** one who testifies in a cause or before a judicial tribunal **3 :** one asked to be present at a transaction so as to be able to testify to its having taken place **4 :** one who has personal knowledge of something **5 a :** something serving as evidence or proof **:** SIGN **b :** public affirmation by word or example of usu. religious faith or conviction ⟨the heroic ~ to divine life —*Pilot*⟩ **6** *cap* **:** a member of the Jehovah's Witnesses

[2]**witness** *vt* (14c) **1 :** to testify to **:** ATTEST **2 :** to act as legal witness of **3 :** to furnish proof of **:** BETOKEN **4 a :** to have personal or direct cognizance of **:** see for oneself ⟨~*ed* the historic event⟩ **b :** to take note of ⟨our grammar — ~ our verb system — is a marvel of flexibility, variety, and exactitude —Charlton Laird⟩ **5 :** to constitute the

scene or time of ⟨structures . . . which this striking Dorset hilltop once ~ed —*Times Lit. Supp.*⟩ ~ *vi* **1 :** to bear witness **:** TESTIFY **2 :** to bear witness to one's religious convictions ⟨opportunity to ~ for Christ —Billy Graham⟩ ***syn*** see CERTIFY

wit·ness–box \-ˌbäks\ *n, chiefly Brit* (1806) **:** an enclosure in which a witness sits or stands while testifying in court

witness stand *n* (1885) **:** a stand or an enclosure from which a witness gives evidence in a court

wit·ted \ˈwit-əd\ *adj* (14c) **:** having wit or understanding — usu. used in combination ⟨dull-*witted*⟩ ⟨quick-*witted*⟩

wit·ti·cism \ˈwit-ə-ˌsiz-əm\ *n* [*witty* + *-cism* (as in *criticism*)] (1651) **:** a cleverly witty and often biting or ironic remark ***syn*** see JEST

[1]**wit·ting** \ˈwit-ᵊn, -iŋ\ *n* (14c) **1** *chiefly dial* **:** knowledge or awareness of something **:** COGNIZANCE **2** *chiefly dial* **:** information obtained or communicated **:** NEWS

[2]**witting** \-iŋ\ *adj* (14c) **1 :** cognizant or aware of something **:** CONSCIOUS **2 :** done deliberately **:** INTENTIONAL — **wit·ting·ly** \-iŋ-lē\ *adv*

wit·tol \ˈwit-ᵊl\ *n* [ME *wetewold,* fr. *weten, witen* to know + *-wold* (as in *cokewold* cuckold)] (15c) **1** *archaic* **:** a man who knows of his wife's infidelity and puts up with it **2** *archaic* **:** a witless person

wit·ty \ˈwit-ē\ *adj* **wit·ti·er; -est** (bef. 12c) **1** *archaic* **:** having good intellectual capacity **:** INTELLIGENT **2 :** amusingly or ingeniously clever in conception or execution ⟨the costumes are sumptuous and ~ —Virgil Thomson⟩ ⟨the musical background is . . . often ~ —Wolcott Gibbs⟩ **3 :** marked by or full of wit **:** smartly facetious or jocular **4 :** quick or ready to see or express illuminating or amusing relationships or insights — **wit·ti·ly** \ˈwit-ᵊl-ē\ *adv* — **wit·ti·ness** \ˈwit-ē-nəs\ *n*

syn WITTY, HUMOROUS, FACETIOUS, JOCULAR, JOCOSE mean provoking or intended to provoke laughter. WITTY suggests cleverness and quickness of mind and often a caustic tongue; HUMOROUS applies broadly to anything that evokes usu. genial laughter and may contrast with WITTY in suggesting whimsicality or eccentricity; FACETIOUS stresses a desire to produce laughter and may be derogatory in implying dubious or ill-timed attempts at wit or humor; JOCULAR implies a usu. habitual fondness for jesting and joking; JOCOSE is somewhat less derogatory than FACETIOUS in suggesting habitual waggishness or playfulness.

wive \ˈwīv\ *vb* **wived; wiv·ing** [ME *wiven,* fr. OE *wīfian,* fr. *wīf* woman, wife] *vi* (bef. 12c) **:** to marry a woman ~ *vt* **1 :** to marry to a wife **2 :** to take for a wife

wives *pl of* WIFE

wiz \ˈwiz\ *n* (ca. 1902) **:** WIZARD 3

[1]**wiz·ard** \ˈwiz-ərd\ *n* [ME *wysard,* fr. *wis, wys* wise] (15c) **1** *archaic* **:** a wise man **:** SAGE **2 :** one skilled in magic **:** SORCERER **3 :** a very clever or skillful person

[2]**wizard** *adj* (1579) **1** *archaic* **:** having magical influence or power **2** *archaic* **:** of or relating to wizardry **:** ENCHANTED **3** *chiefly Brit* **:** worthy of the highest praise **:** EXCELLENT

wiz·ard·ly \ˈwiz-ərd-lē\ *adj* (1588) **1 :** having characteristics of a wizard **2 :** marvelous in construction or operation ⟨uses ~ circuitry to distort images —*Time*⟩

wiz·ard·ry \ˈwiz-ə(r)-drē\ *n, pl* **-ries** (1583) **1 :** the art or practices of a wizard **:** SORCERY **2 a :** a seemingly magical transforming power or influence ⟨electronic ~⟩ **b :** great skill or cleverness in an activity

[1]**wiz·en** \ˈwiz-ᵊn\ *vb* [ME *wisenen,* fr. OE *wisnian;* akin to OHG *wesanēn* to wither, L *viēre* to twist together, plait — more at WIRE] *vi* (bef. 12c) **:** to become dry, shrunken, and wrinkled often as a result of aging or of failing vitality ~ *vt* **:** to cause to wizen

[2]**wizen** *adj* [alter. of *wizened*] (1786) **:** that is wizened

woad \ˈwōd\ *n* [ME *wod,* fr. OE *wād;* akin to OHG *weit* woad, L *vitrum* woad, glass] (bef. 12c) **:** a European herb (*Isatis tinctoria*) of the mustard family formerly grown for the blue dyestuff yielded by its leaves; *also* **:** this dyestuff

[1]**wob·ble** \ˈwäb-əl\ *vb* **wob·bled; wob·bling** \-(ə-)liŋ\ [prob. fr. LG *wabbeln;* akin to OE *wǣfre* restless — more at WAVER] *vi* (1657) **1 a :** to move or proceed with an irregular rocking or staggering motion or unsteadily and clumsily from side to side **b :** TREMBLE, QUAVER **2 :** WAVER, VACILLATE ~ *vt* **:** to cause to wobble — **wob·bler** \-(ə-)lər\ *n* — **wob·bli·ness** \ˈwäb-lē-nəs\ *n* — **wob·bly** \ˈwäb-(ə-)lē\ *adj*

[2]**wobble** *n* (1699) **1 a :** a hobbling or rocking unequal motion (as of a wheel unevenly mounted) **b :** an uncertainly directed movement **2 :** an intermittent variation (as in volume of sound)

wobble pump *n* (ca. 1930) **:** an auxiliary hand pump used on an airplane to supply fuel to the carburetor of an engine when the power-driven pump fails or to force fuel from an extra tank

Wob·bly \ˈwäb-lē\ *n, pl* **Wobblies** [origin unknown] (ca. 1910) **:** a member of the Industrial Workers of the World

Wo·den \ˈwōd-ᵊn\ *n* [OE *Wōden*] **:** ODIN

[1]**woe** \ˈwō\ *interj* [ME *wa, wo,* fr. OE *wā;* akin to ON *vei,* interj., woe, L *vae*] (bef. 12c) — used to express grief, regret, or distress

[2]**woe** *n* (13c) **1 :** a condition of deep suffering from misfortune, affliction, or grief **2 :** ruinous trouble **:** CALAMITY, AFFLICTION ⟨economic ~s⟩ ***syn*** see SORROW

woe·be·gone \ˈwō-bi-ˌgȯn *also* -ˌgän\ *adj* [ME *wo begon,* fr. *wo* [2]woe + *begon,* pp. of *begon* to go about, beset, fr. OE *begān,* fr. *be-* + *gān* to go — more at GO] (14c) **1 :** strongly affected with woe **:** WOEFUL **2 a :** exhibiting great woe, sorrow, or misery ⟨a ~ expression⟩ **b :** being in a sorry state ⟨~ tattered clothes⟩ — **woe·be·gone·ness** *n*

woe·ful *also* **wo·ful** \ˈwō-fəl\ *adj* (14c) **1 :** full of woe **:** GRIEVOUS ⟨~ prophecies⟩ **2 :** involving or bringing woe **3 :** lamentably bad or serious **:** DEPLORABLE ⟨~ ignorance⟩ — **woe·ful·ly** \-f(ə-)lē\ *adv* — **woe·ful·ness** \-fəl-nəs\ *n*

wog \ˈwäg, ˈwȯg\ *n* [prob. short for *golliwog*] *chiefly Brit* (ca. 1934) **:** a dark-skinned foreigner; *esp* **:** one from the Middle East or Far East — usu. used disparagingly

wok \ˈwäk\ *n* [Chin (Cant) *wôk*] (ca. 1960) **:** a bowl-shaped cooking utensil used esp. in the preparation of Chinese food

woke *past and past part of* WAKE

woken *past part of* WAKE

wold \ˈwōld\ *n* [ME *wald, wold,* fr. OE *weald, wald* forest; akin to OHG *wald* forest] (bef. 12c) **1 :** a usu. upland area of open country **2** *cap* **:** a hilly or rolling region — used in names of various English geographical areas ⟨Yorkshire ~s⟩

[1]**wolf** \ˈwu̇lf\ *n, pl* **wolves** \ˈwu̇lvz\ *often attrib* [ME, fr. OE *wulf;* akin to OHG *wolf,* L *lupus,* Gk *lykos*] (bef. 12c) **1** *pl also* **wolf a :** any of various large predatory mammals (genus *Canis* and esp. *C. lupus*) that resemble the related dogs, are destructive to game and livestock, and may rarely attack man esp. when in a pack — compare COYOTE, JACKAL **b :** the fur of a wolf **2 a** (1) **:** a fierce, rapacious, or destructive person (2) **:** a man forward, direct, and zealous in amatory attentions to women **b :** dire poverty **:** STARVATION ⟨keep the ~ from the door⟩ **c :** the maggot of a warble fly **3** [G; fr. the howling sound] **a** (1) **:** dissonance in some chords on organs, pianos, or other instruments with fixed tones tuned by unequal temperament (2) **:** an instance of such dissonance **b :** a harshness due to faulty vibration in various tones in a bowed instrument — **wolf·like** \ˈwu̇l-ˌflīk\ *adj* — **wolf in sheep's clothing :** one who cloaks a hostile intention with a friendly manner

[2]**wolf** *vt* (1862) **:** to eat greedily **:** DEVOUR

wolf·ber·ry \ˈwu̇lf-ˌber-ē\ *n* (1834) **:** a white-berried western American shrub (*Symphoricarpos occidentalis*) of the honeysuckle family

wolf dog *n* (1652) **1 :** any of various large dogs formerly kept for hunting wolves **2 :** the offspring of a wolf and a domestic dog

wolf·er \ˈwu̇l-fər\ *n* (1871) **:** a hunter of wolves

wolff·ian body \ˌwu̇l-fē-ən-\ *n, often cap W* [Kaspar Friedrich *Wolff*] (ca. 1844) **:** MESONEPHROS

Wolffian duct *n* (ca. 1879) **:** the duct of the mesonephros persisting in the female as the ureter and in the male as the common urogenital duct

wolf·fish \ˈwu̇lf-ˌfish\ *n* (1569) **:** any of several large marine blennies (genus *Anarhichas* of the family Anarhicadidae) notable for their strong teeth and ferocity

wolf·hound \ˈwu̇lf-ˌhau̇nd\ *n* (1786) **:** any of several large dogs used esp. formerly in hunting large animals (as wolves)

wolf·ish \ˈwu̇l-fish\ *adj* (ca. 1570) **1 :** of or relating to wolves **2 a :** suggestive of a wolf ⟨~ mongrel dogs —Hoffman Birney⟩ ⟨a ~ and withdrawn youth —Marshall Frady⟩ **b :** befitting or characteristic of a wolf (as in fierceness or rapacity) ⟨a ~ appetite⟩ — **wolf·ish·ly** *adv* — **wolf·ish·ness** *n*

wolf pack *n* (1942) **:** a group of submarines that make a coordinated attack on shipping; *also* **:** a group of two or more fighter planes making a coordinated attack

wol·fram \ˈwu̇l-frəm\ *n* [G] (1757) **1 :** WOLFRAMITE **2 :** TUNGSTEN

wol·fram·ic \wu̇l-ˈfram-ik\ *adj* (1860) **:** TUNGSTIC

wol·fram·ite \ˈwu̇l-frə-ˌmīt\ *n* [G *wolframit,* fr. *wolfram*] (ca. 1868) **:** a mineral $(Fe,Mn)WO_4$ that consists of a tungstate of iron and manganese usu. of a brownish or grayish black color and slightly metallic luster, occurs in monoclinic crystals and in granular or columnar masses, and is used as a source of tungsten

wolfs·bane \ˈwu̇lfs-ˌbān\ *n* (1548) **:** MONKSHOOD; *esp* **:** a highly variable yellow-flowered Eurasian herb (*Aconitum vulparia*)

wolf spider *n* (1608) **:** any of various active wandering ground spiders (family Lycosidae)

wolf whistle *n* (1946) **:** a distinctive whistle sounded by a male to express sexual admiration for a girl or woman in his vicinity

wol·las·ton·ite \ˈwu̇l-ə-stə-ˌnīt, ˈwäl-\ *n* [William H. *Wollaston* †1828 Eng. chemist] (1823) **:** a triclinic mineral $CaSiO_3$ of a white to gray, red, yellow, or brown color consisting of a native calcium silicate occurring usu. in cleavable masses

Wo·lof \ˈwō-ˌlȯf\ *n* (ca. 1895) **:** a Niger-Congo language of Senegambia

wol·ver·ine \ˌwu̇l-və-ˈrēn\ *n, pl* **wolverines** [prob. irreg. fr. *wolv-* (as in *wolves*)] (1574) **1** *pl also* **wolverine a :** a carnivorous usu. solitary mammal (*Gulo gulo*) of the weasel family of northern forests and associated tundra that is blackish with a light brown band on each side of the body and is noted esp. for its strength **b :** the fur of the wolverine **2** *cap* **:** a native or resident of Michigan — used as a nickname

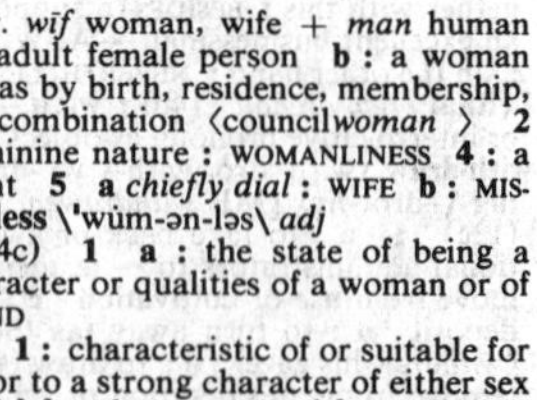

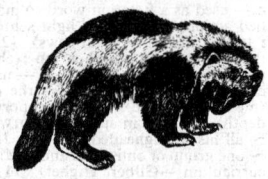

wolverine 1a

wom·an \ˈwu̇m-ən\ *n, pl* **wom·en** \ˈwim-ən\ [ME, fr. OE *wīfman,* fr. *wīf* woman, wife + *man* human being, man] (bef. 12c) **1 a :** an adult female person **b :** a woman belonging to a particular category (as by birth, residence, membership, or occupation) — usu. used in combination ⟨council*woman*⟩ **2 :** WOMENKIND **3 :** distinctively feminine nature **:** WOMANLINESS **4 :** a female servant or personal attendant **5 a** *chiefly dial* **:** WIFE **b :** MISTRESS **c :** GIRLFRIEND 2 — **wom·an·less** \ˈwu̇m-ən-ləs\ *adj*

wom·an·hood \ˈwu̇m-ən-ˌhu̇d\ *n* (14c) **1 a :** the state of being a woman **b :** the distinguishing character or qualities of a woman or of womankind **2 :** WOMEN, WOMENKIND

wom·an·ish \ˈwu̇m-ə-nish\ *adj* (14c) **1 :** characteristic of or suitable for a woman **2 :** unsuitable to a man or to a strong character of either sex **:** EFFEMINATE ⟨~ fears⟩ — **wom·an·ish·ly** *adv* — **wom·an·ish·ness** *n*

wom·an·ize \ˈwu̇m-ə-ˌnīz\ *vb* **-ized; -iz·ing** *vt* (1590) **:** to make effeminate ~ *vi* **:** to pursue freewheeling relationships with women — **wom·an·iz·er** *n*

wom·an·kind \ˈwu̇m-ən-ˌkīnd\ *n sing but sing or pl in constr* (14c) **:** WOMENKIND

[1]**wom·an·like** \-ˌlīk\ *adj* (15c) **:** WOMANLY

[2]**womanlike** *adv* (15c) **:** in the manner of a woman

wom·an·ly \-lē\ *adj* (13c) **1 :** having qualities generally associated with a woman **2 :** appropriate in character to a woman — **wom·an·li·ness** *n*

woman of the street (1928) **:** PROSTITUTE

wom·an·pow·er \ˈwu̇m-ən-ˌpau̇(-ə)r\ *n* (1942) **:** women available and prepared for work (as in industry or a particular line of endeavor)

woman's rights *n pl* (1840) **1 :** legal, political, and social rights for women equal to those of men **2 :** FEMINISM 2

woman suffrage *n* (1867) **:** possession and exercise of suffrage by women

womb \ˈwüm\ *n* [ME *wamb, womb,* fr. OE; akin to OHG *wamba* belly] (bef. 12c) **1 :** UTERUS **2 a :** a cavity or space that resembles a womb in containing and enveloping **b :** a place where something is generated — **wombed** \ˈwümd\ *adj*

wom·bat \ˈwäm-ˌbat\ *n* [native name in New So. Wales] (1798) **:** any of several stocky Australian marsupials (family Vombatidae) resembling small bears

wom·en·folk \ˈwim-ən-ˌfōk\ *also* **wom·en·folks** \-ˌfōks\ *n pl* (1833) **:** WOMEN

wom·en·kind \-ˌkīnd\ *n* (14c) **:** female human beings **:** women esp. as distinguished from men

women's room *n* (1853) **:** LADIES' ROOM

wom·mera \ˈwäm-ə-rə\ *var of* WOOMERA

1won \ˈwən, ˈwōn\ *vi* **wonned; won·ning** [ME *wonen,* fr. OE *wunian* — more at WONT] *archaic* (bef. 12c) **:** DWELL 2a, ABIDE 2

2won \ˈwən\ *past and past part of* WIN

3won \ˈwón\ *n, pl* **won** [Korean *wǒn*] (ca. 1917) — see MONEY table

1won·der \ˈwən-dər\ *n* [ME, fr. OE *wundor;* akin to OHG *wuntar* wonder] (bef. 12c) **1 a :** a cause of astonishment or admiration **:** MARVEL ⟨it's a ~, considering the chances he took, that he wasn't killed⟩ **b :** MIRACLE **2 :** the quality of exciting amazed admiration **3 a :** rapt attention or astonishment at something awesomely mysterious or new to one's experience **b :** a feeling of doubt or uncertainty

2wonder *vb* **won·dered; won·der·ing** \-d(ə-)riŋ\ *vi* (bef. 12c) **1 a :** to be in a state of wonder **b :** to feel surprise **2 :** to feel curiosity or doubt ~ *vt* **:** to be curious or in doubt about — **won·der·er** \-dər-ər\ *n*

3wonder *adj* (12c) **:** WONDROUS, WONDERFUL: as **a :** exciting amazement or admiration **b :** effective or efficient far beyond anything previously known or anticipated

wonder drug *n* (1939) **:** MIRACLE DRUG

won·der·ful \ˈwən-dər-fəl\ *adj* (12c) **1 :** exciting wonder **:** MARVELOUS, ASTONISHING ⟨a sight ~ to behold⟩ **2 :** unusually good **:** ADMIRABLE — **won·der·ful·ly** \-f(ə-)lē\ *adv* — **won·der·ful·ness** \-fəl-nəs\ *n*

won·der·land \ˈwən-dər-ˌland, -lənd\ *n* (1790) **1 :** an imaginary place of delicate beauty or magical charm **2 :** a place that excites admiration or wonder

won·der·ment \-mənt\ *n* (1535) **1 :** ASTONISHMENT, SURPRISE **2 :** a cause of or occasion for wonder **3 :** curiosity about something

won·der·work \-də(r)-ˌwərk\ *n* (bef. 12c) **:** a marvelous act, work, or accomplishment

won·der–work·er \-ˌwər-kər\ *n* (1599) **:** one that performs wonders

won·der–work·ing \-kiŋ\ *adj* (1594) **:** producing wonders

won·drous \ˈwən-drəs\ *adj* [alter. of ME *wonders,* fr. gen. of 1*wonder*] (15c) **:** that is to be marveled at **:** EXTRAORDINARY — **wondrous** *adv, archaic* — **won·drous·ly** *adv* — **won·drous·ness** *n*

won·ky \ˈwäŋ-kē\ *adj* [alter. of E dial. *wankle,* fr. ME *wankel,* fr. OE *wancol*] (1919) **1** *Brit* **:** UNSTEADY, SHAKY **2** *Brit* **:** AWRY, WRONG

1wont \ˈwónt, ˈwōnt *also* ˈwənt, ˈwänt\ *adj* [ME *woned, wont,* fr. pp. of *wonen* to dwell, be used to, fr. OE *wunian;* akin to OHG *wonēn* to dwell, be used to, L *venus* love, charm — more at WIN] (bef. 12c) **1 :** ACCUSTOMED, USED ⟨got up early as he is ~ to do⟩ **2 :** INCLINED, APT ⟨revealing as letters are ~ to be —Gladys M. Wrigley⟩

2wont *n* (14c) **:** habitual way of doing **:** USE ***syn*** see HABIT

3wont *vb* **wont; wont** *or* **wont·ed; wont·ing** *vt* (15c) **:** ACCUSTOM, HABITUATE ~ *vi* **:** to have the habit of doing something

won't \(ˈ)wōnt; *NewEng, upstate NY, nPa* ˌwənt, ˈwənt; *greater NYC* (ˈ)wünt; *eSC* (ˈ)wünt, (ˈ)wůnt\ **:** will not

wont·ed \ˈwónt-əd, ˈwōnt- *also* ˈwənt- *or* ˈwänt-\ *adj* (15c) **:** usual or ordinary esp. by reason of established habit ⟨spoke with his ~ slowness⟩ ***syn*** see USUAL — **wont·ed·ly** *adv* — **wont·ed·ness** *n*

won·ton \ˈwän-ˌtän\ *n* [Chin (Cant) *wan t'an*] (1934) **:** filled pockets of noodle dough boiled in and eaten with soup

woo \ˈwü\ *vb* [ME *wowen,* fr. OE *wōgian*] *vt* (bef. 12c) **1 :** to sue for the affection of and usu. marriage with **:** COURT **2 :** to solicit or entreat esp. with importunity **3 :** to seek to gain or bring about ~ *vi* **:** to court a woman — **woo·er** *n*

1wood \ˈwüd, ˈwōd, ˈwůd\ *adj* [ME, fr. OE *wōd* insane; akin to OHG *wuot* madness — more at VATIC] *archaic* (bef. 12c) **:** violently mad

2wood \ˈwůd\ *n* [ME *wode,* fr. OE *widu, wudu;* akin to OHG *witu* wood, OIr *fid* tree] (bef. 12c) **1 a :** a dense growth of trees usu. greater in extent than a grove and smaller than a forest — often used in pl. but sing. or pl. in constr. **b :** WOODLAND **2 a :** the hard fibrous substance basically xylem that makes up the greater part of the stems and branches of trees or shrubs beneath the bark and is found to a limited extent in herbaceous plants **b :** wood suitable or prepared for some use (as burning or building) **3 a :** something made of wood **b :** a golf club having a thick wooden head; *also* **:** a golf club having a similar head made of metal

3wood \ˈwůd\ *adj* (bef. 12c) **1 :** WOODEN **2 :** suitable for cutting or working with wood ⟨a ~ saw⟩ **3** *or* **woods** \ˈwůdz\ **:** living, growing, or existing in woods ⟨*woods* trails⟩

4wood \ˈwůd\ *vt* (1538) **:** to cover with a growth of trees or plant with trees ~ *vi* **:** to gather or take on wood

wood alcohol *n* (1861) **:** METHANOL

wood anemone *n* (1657) **:** any of several anemones; *esp* **:** a common anemone (*Anemone quinquefolia*) of the eastern U.S. with solitary often pink-tinged flowers

wood bet·o·ny \-ˈbet-ᵊn-ē\ *n* [ME *betone,* fr. OF *betoine,* fr. L *vettonica, betonica,* fr. *Vettones,* an ancient people inhabiting the Iberian peninsula] (1657) **:** a lousewort (*Pedicularis canadensis*) of eastern No. America with pinnately parted leaves and red or yellowish flowers in bracted spikes

wood·bine \ˈwůd-ˌbīn\ *n* [ME *wodebinde,* fr. OE *wudubinde,* fr. *wudu* wood + *bindan* to tie, bind; fr. its winding around trees] (bef. 12c) **1 :** any of several honeysuckles; *esp* **:** a European twining shrub (*Lonicera periclymenum*) **2 :** VIRGINIA CREEPER

wood·block \-ˌbläk\ *n* (1837) **:** WOODCUT — **wood–block** *adj*

wood–bor·ing \-ˌbōr-iŋ, -ˌbór-\ *adj* (1815) **:** excavating galleries in wood in feeding or in constructing a nest — used chiefly of an insect

wood carving *n* (1847) **:** the art of fashioning or ornamenting objects of wood by cutting with a sharp hand-held implement; *also* **:** an object of wood so fashioned or ornamented — **wood–carv·er** \-ˌkär-vər\ *n*

wood·chat shrike \ˌwůd-ˌchat-\ *n* (1705) **:** a European shrike (*Lanius senator*) — called also *woodchat*

wood·chop·per \-ˌchäp-ər\ *n* (1779) **:** one engaged esp. in chopping down trees

wood·chuck \-ˌchək\ *n* [by folk etymology fr. Ojibwa *otchig* fisher, marten, or Cree *otcheck*] (1674) **1 :** a grizzled thickset marmot (*Marmota monax*) of the northeastern U.S. and Canada — called also *groundhog* **2 :** any of several marmots of mountainous western No. America

wood·cock \ˈwůd-ˌkäk\ *n, pl* **woodcocks** (bef. 12c) **1** *or pl* **woodcock :** a widespread Old World woodland bird (*Scolopax rusticola* of the family Scolopacidae); *also* **:** a smaller related American game bird (*Scolopax minor* syn. *Philohela minor*) **2** [fr. the ease with which the woodcock is snared] *archaic* **:** SIMPLETON

wood·craft \-ˌkraft\ *n* (14c) **1 :** skill and practice in anything relating to the woods and esp. in maintaining oneself and making one's way in the woods **2 :** skill in shaping or constructing articles from wood

wood·cut \-ˌkət\ *n* (1662) **1 :** a relief printing surface consisting of a wooden block with a usu. pictorial design cut with the grain **2 :** a print from a woodcut

wood·cut·ter \-ˌkət-ər\ *n* (1761) **:** one that cuts wood

wood·cut·ting \-ˌkət-iŋ\ *n* (1683) **1 :** the action or occupation of cutting wood or timber **2 :** the producing of woodcuts

wood duck *n* (1777) **:** a showy American duck (*Aix sponsa*) that nests in trees and in the male has a large crest and plumage varied with green, purple, black, white, and chestnut

wood·ed \ˈwůd-əd\ *adj* (1605) **:** covered with growing trees

wood·en \ˈwůd-ᵊn\ *adj* (ca. 1538) **1 :** made or consisting of wood **2 :** lacking ease or flexibility **:** awkwardly stiff — **wood·en·ly** *adv* — **wood·en·ness** \-ᵊn-(n)əs\ *n*

wood engraving *n* (1816) **1 :** a relief printing surface consisting of a wooden block with a usu. pictorial design cut in the end grain **2 :** a print from a wood engraving

wood·en·head \ˈwůd-ᵊn-ˌhed\ *n* (1831) **:** BLOCKHEAD

wood·en·head·ed \ˌwůd-ᵊn-ˈhed-əd\ *adj* (ca. 1854) **:** DENSE, STUPID

wooden Indian *n* (1879) **:** a wooden image of a standing American Indian brave used esp. formerly as a sign for a cigar store

wood·en·ware \ˈwůd-ᵊn-ˌwa(ə)r, -ˌwe(ə)r\ *n* (1647) **:** articles made of wood for domestic use

wood fiber *n* (1875) **:** any of various fibers in or associated with xylem

wood ibis *n* (1785) **:** a large wading bird (*Mycteria americana* of the family Ciconiidae) that frequents wooded swamps of So. and Central America and the southern U.S. — called also *wood stork*

1wood·land \ˈwůd-lənd, -ˌland\ *n* (bef. 12c) **:** land covered with woody vegetation **:** TIMBERLAND, FOREST — **wood·land·er** \-ər\ *n*

2woodland *adj* (14c) **1 :** growing, living, or existing in woodland **2 :** of, relating to, or being woodland

wood·lore \-ˌlōr, -ˌlór\ *n* (1918) **:** knowledge of the woods

wood·lot \ˈwůd-ˌlät\ *n* (1643) **:** a restricted area of woodland usu. privately maintained as a source of fuel, posts, and lumber

wood louse *n* (1611) **:** a terrestrial isopod crustacean (suborder Oniscoidea) with a flattened elliptical body often capable of being rolled into a ball — called also *pill bug, sow bug*

wood·man \ˈwůd-mən\ *n* (15c) **1 :** WOODSMAN **2** *cap* [Modern *Woodmen* of America & *Woodmen* of the World] **:** a member of either of two independent benevolent and fraternal societies

wood·note \-ˌnōt\ *n* [fr. its likeness to the call of a bird in the woods] (1632) **:** verbal expression that is natural and artless

wood nymph *n* (1577) **:** a nymph living in woods — called also *dryad*

wood·peck·er \ˈwůd-ˌpek-ər\ *n* (ca. 1530) **:** any of numerous birds (family Picidae) with zygodactyl feet, stiff spiny tail feathers used in climbing or resting on tree trunks, a usu. extensile tongue, a very hard bill used to drill the bark or wood of trees for insect food or to excavate nesting cavities, and generally showy parti-colored plumage

wood·pile \-ˌpīl\ *n* (ca. 1552) **:** a pile of wood (as firewood) — **in the woodpile :** doing or responsible for covert mischief

wood pulp *n* (1866) **:** pulp from wood used in making cellulose derivatives (as paper or rayon)

wood pussy *n* (ca. 1899) **:** SKUNK

wood rat *n* (1763) **:** any of numerous cricetid rodents (esp. genus *Neotoma*) of the southern U.S. and western No. America with soft fur, well-furred tails, and large ears

wood ray *n* (1925) **:** XYLEM RAY

wood·ruff \ˈwůd-(ˌ)rəf\ *n* [ME *woderove,* fr. OE *wudurofe,* fr. *wudu* wood + *-rofe* (perh. akin to OHG *rāba* turnip) — more at RAPE] (bef. 12c) **:** any of a genus (*Asperula*) of herbs of the madder family; *esp* **:** a small European sweet-scented herb (*A. odorata*) used in perfumery and for flavoring wine

1wood·shed \-ˌshed\ *n* (1844) **1 :** a shed for storing wood and esp. firewood **2 :** a place, means, or session for administering discipline

2woodshed *vi* **-shed·ded; -shed·ding** [prob. fr. the former use of woodsheds for private practicing] (ca. 1936) **:** PRACTICE; *esp* **:** to practice on a musical instrument

wood shot *n* (1938) **1 :** a golf shot played with a wood **2 :** a stroke in a racket game in which the ball or shuttlecock is hit with the frame of the racket rather than the strings

woods·man \ˈwůdz-mən\ *n* (1688) **:** one who frequents or works in the woods; *esp* **:** one skilled in woodcraft

wood sorrel *n* (1525) **:** any of a genus (*Oxalis* of the family Oxalidaceae, the wood-sorrel family) of herbs with acid sap, compound leaves, and regular flowers; *esp* **:** a stemless herb (*O. montana* or *O. acetosella*) with trifoliolate leaves sometimes held to be the original shamrock

wood spirit *n* (ca. 1842) **:** METHANOL

wood sugar *n* (ca. 1900) **:** XYLOSE

woodsy \ˈwůd-zē\ *adj* (1860) **:** characteristic or suggestive of woods

wood tar *n* (1857) **:** tar obtained by the destructive distillation of wood either as a deposit from pyroligneous acid or as a residue from the distillation of the acid or of wood turpentine

wood tick *n* (1668) **:** any of various ixodid ticks whose young cling to bushes whence they readily drop on and attach themselves to passing animals where they may produce troublesome sores or serve as vectors for disease-producing microorganisms — compare ROCKY MOUNTAIN SPOTTED FEVER

\ə\ abut \ᵊ\ kitten, F table \ər\ further \a\ ash \ā\ ace \ä\ cot, cart \aů\ out \ch\ chin \e\ bet \ē\ easy \g\ go \i\ hit \ī\ ice \j\ job \ŋ\ sing \ō\ go \ó\ law \ói\ boy \th\ thin \t͟h\ the \ü\ loot \ů\ foot \y\ yet \zh\ vision \à, k̲, ⁿ, œ, œ̄, ue, ue̅, ʸ\ see Guide to Pronunciation

wood turning *n* (ca. 1876) : the art or process of fashioning wooden pieces or blocks into various forms and shapes by means of a lathe
wood turpentine *n* (ca. 1909) : TURPENTINE 2b
wood warbler *n* (1817) : WARBLER 2b
wood·wind \-ˌwind\ *n* (1876) **1** : one of a group of wind instruments (as a clarinet, flute, oboe, or saxophone) that is characterized by a cylindrical or conical tube of wood or metal usu. ending in a slightly flared bell, that produces tones by the vibration of one or two reeds in the mouthpiece or by the passing of air over a mouth hole, and that usu. has finger holes or keys by which the player may produce all the tones within the instrument's range **2** *pl* : the woodwind section of a band or orchestra
wood·work \-ˌwərk\ *n* (1650) **1** : work made of wood; *esp* : interior fittings (as moldings or stairways) of wood **2** : a place of retirement, seclusion, or hiding ⟨witnesses came out of the ~ when a reward was offered⟩
[1]**wood·work·ing** \-ˌwər-kiŋ\ *adj* (1872) : used for woodworking ⟨~ tools⟩
[2]**woodworking** *n* (1875) : the act, process, or occupation of working with wood — **wood·work·er** \-kər\ *n*
[1]**woody** \'wu̇d-ē\ *adj* **wood·i·er; -est** (14c) **1** : abounding or overgrown with woods **2 a** : of or containing wood or wood fibers : LIGNEOUS ⟨~ tissues⟩ **b** : having woody parts : rich in xylem and associated structures ⟨~ plants⟩ **3** : characteristic of or suggestive of wood ⟨wine with a ~ flavor⟩ — **wood·i·ness** *n*
[2]**woody** *or* **wood·ie** \'wu̇d-ē\ *n, pl* **woodies** [alter. of [3]*wood*] (1961) : a wood-paneled station wagon
[1]**woof** \'wu̇f, 'wüf\ *n* [alter. of ME *oof,* fr. OE *ōwef,* fr. *ō-* (fr. *on*) + *wefan* to weave — more at WEAVE] (bef. 12c) **1 a** : a filling thread or yarn in weaving **b** : woven fabric; *also* : the texture of such a fabric **2** : a basic or essential element or material
[2]**woof** \'wu̇f\ *vi* [imit.] (1804) **1** : to make the sound of a woof **2** : to express oneself in a usu. stylized boastful, aggressive, or exaggeratedly deceitful manner
[3]**woof** *n* (1839) **1** : a low gruff sound typically produced by a dog **2** : a low note emitted by sound reproducing equipment
woof·er \'wu̇f-ər\ *n* (ca. 1939) : a loudspeaker usu. larger than a tweeter, responsive only to the lower acoustic frequencies, and used for reproducing sounds of low pitch
wool \'wu̇l\ *n, often attrib* [ME *wolle,* fr. OE *wull;* akin to OHG *wolla* wool, L *vellus* fleece, *lana* wool, *lanugo* down] (bef. 12c) **1** : the soft wavy or curly hypertrophied undercoat of various hairy mammals and esp. the sheep made up of fibers of keratin molecules within a matrix and covered with minute scales **2** : a product of wool; *esp* : a woven fabric or garment of such fabric **3 a** : a dense felted pubescence esp. on a plant : TOMENTUM **b** : a filamentous mass — usu. used in combination; compare MINERAL WOOL, STEEL WOOL
-wooled \'wu̇ld\ *adj comb form* : having wool of (such) quality ⟨coarse-*wooled*⟩
[1]**wool·en** *or* **wool·len** \'wu̇l-ən\ *adj* (bef. 12c) **1** : made of wool — compare WORSTED **2** : of or relating to the manufacture or sale of woolen products ⟨~ mills⟩ ⟨the ~ industry⟩
[2]**woolen** *or* **woollen** *n* (14c) **1** : a fabric made of wool **2** : garments of woolen fabric — usu. used in pl.
wool fat *n* (1875) : wool grease esp. after refining : LANOLIN
wool–gath·er \'wu̇l-ˌgath-ər, -ˌgeth-\ *vi* (1850) : to indulge in woolgathering — **wool·gath·er·er** \-ər-ər\ *n*
wool·gath·er·ing \-ˌgath-(ə-)riŋ, -ˌgeth-\ *n* (1553) : the act of indulging in idle daydreaming
wool grease *n* (1875) : a fatty slightly sticky wax coating the surface of the fibers of sheep's wool — compare WOOL FAT
[1]**wool·ly** *also* **wooly** \'wu̇l-ē\ *adj* **wool·li·er; -est** (1578) **1 a** : of, relating to, or bearing wool **b** : resembling wool **2 a** : lacking in clearness or sharpness of outline ⟨a ~ TV picture⟩ **b** : marked by mental confusion ⟨~ thinking⟩ **3** : marked by boisterous roughness or lack of order or restraint ⟨where the West is still ~ —Paul Schubert⟩ — **wool·li·ness** *n*
[2]**wool·ly** *also* **wool·ie** *or* **wooly** \'wu̇l-ē\ *n, pl* **wool·lies** (ca. 1865) **1** : a garment made from wool; *esp* : underclothing of knitted wool — usu. used in pl. **2** *West & Austral* : SHEEP
woolly aphid *n* (1842) : a plant louse (genus *Eriosoma*) covered with a dense coat of white filaments — called also *woolly aphis*
woolly bear *n* (ca. 1841) : any of various rather large very hairy caterpillars; *esp* : one that is the larva of a tiger moth
wool·ly–head·ed \ˌwu̇l-ē-'hed-əd\ *adj* (1650) **1** : having hair suggesting wool **2** : marked by vague or confused perception or thinking
wool·pack \'wu̇l-ˌpak\ *n* (13c) **1 a** : a wrapper of strong fabric into which fleeces are packed for shipment **b** : the complete package of wool and wrapper **2** : a rounded cumulus cloud springing from a horizontal base
wool·sack \-ˌsak\ *n* (14c) **1** *archaic* : WOOLPACK 1b **2** : the official seat of the Lord Chancellor or his deputy in the House of Lords
wool·shed \-ˌshed\ *n* (1850) : a building or range of buildings (as on an Australian sheep station) in which sheep are sheared and wool is prepared for market
wool·skin \-ˌskin\ *n* (15c) : a sheepskin having the wool still on it
wool·sort·er's disease \'wu̇l-ˌsȯrt-ərz-\ *n* (1880) : pulmonary anthrax resulting esp. from inhalation of bacterial spores (*Bacillus anthracis*) from contaminated wool or hair
wool stapler *n* (15c) : a dealer in wool
woom·era \'wu̇m-ə-rə\ *n* [native name in Australia] (1793) : a wooden rod with a hooked end used by Australian aborigines for throwing a spear
woops \'(w)u̇(ə)ps\ *var of* OOPS
woo·zy \'wü-zē, 'wu̇z-ē\ *adj* **woo·zi·er; -est** [prob. alter. of *oozy*] (1897) **1** : mentally unclear or hazy ⟨seems a little ~, not quite knowing what to say —J. A. Lukacs⟩ **2** : affected with dizziness, mild nausea, or weakness : SICK — **woo·zi·ly** *adv* — **woo·zi·ness** *n*
wop \'wäp\ *n, often cap* [It dial. *guappo* blusterer, swaggerer, bully, tough] (1908) : ITALIAN — usu. used disparagingly
Worces·ter \'wu̇s-tər\ *n* (1802) : low-fired porcelain containing a frit and steatite produced at Worcester, England from about 1751 — called also *Worcester china, Worcester porcelain*
Worces·ter·shire sauce \'wu̇s-tə(r)-ˌshi(ə)r-, -shər- *also* -ˌshī(ə)r-\ *n* [*Worcestershire,* England, where it was orig. made] (1843) : a pungent sauce whose ingredients include soy, vinegar, and garlic
[1]**word** \'wərd\ *n* [ME, fr. OE; akin to OHG *wort* word, L *verbum,* Gk *eirein* to say, speak] (bef. 12c) **1 a** : something that is said **b** *pl* (1) : TALK, DISCOURSE ⟨putting one's feelings into ~*s*⟩ (2) : the text of a vocal musical composition **c** : a brief remark or conversation ⟨would like to have a ~ with you⟩ **2 a** (1) : a speech sound or series of speech sounds that symbolizes and communicates a meaning without being divisible into smaller units capable of independent use (2) : the entire set of linguistic forms produced by combining a single base with various inflectional elements without change in the part of speech elements **b** (1) : a written or printed character or combination of characters representing a spoken word ⟨the number of ~*s* to a line⟩ (2) : any segment of written or printed discourse ordinarily appearing between spaces or between a space and a punctuation mark **c** : a combination of electrical or magnetic impulses conveying a quantum of information in communication and computer work **3** : ORDER, COMMAND ⟨don't move till I give the ~⟩ **4** *often cap* **a** : LOGOS **b** : GOSPEL 1a **c** : the expressed or manifested mind and will of God **5 a** : NEWS, INFORMATION ⟨sent ~ that he would be late⟩ **b** : RUMOR **6** : the act of speaking or of making verbal communication **7** : SAYING, PROVERB **8** : PROMISE, DECLARATION ⟨kept her ~⟩ **9** : a quarrelsome utterance or conversation — usu. used in pl. **10** : a verbal signal : PASSWORD — **good word 1** : a favorable statement ⟨put in a *good word* for me⟩ **2** : good news ⟨what's the *good word*⟩ — **in a word** : in short — **in so many words 1** : in exactly those terms ⟨implied that such actions were criminal but did not say so *in so many words*⟩ **2** : in plain forthright language ⟨*in so many words,* she wasn't fit to be seen —Jean Stafford⟩ — **of few words** : not inclined to say more than is necessary : LACONIC ⟨a man *of few words*⟩ — **of one's word** : that can be relied on to keep a promise — used only after *man* or *woman* ⟨a man *of his word*⟩ — **upon my word** : with my assurance : INDEED, ASSUREDLY ⟨*upon my word,* I've never heard of such a thing⟩
[2]**word** *vi, archaic* (13c) : SPEAK ~ *vt* : to express in words : PHRASE
word·age \'wərd-ij\ *n* (1829) **1 a** : WORDS **b** : VERBIAGE 1 **2** : the number or quantity of words **3** : WORDING
word–association test *n* (1946) : a test of personality and mental function in which the subject is required to respond to each of a series of words with the first one that comes to mind or with one of a specified class of words
word·book \'wərd-ˌbu̇k\ *n* (1598) : VOCABULARY, DICTIONARY
word class *n* (1914) : a linguistic form class whose members are words; *esp* : PART OF SPEECH
word–for–word *adj* (1611) : being in the exact words : VERBATIM
word for word *adv* (14c) : in the exact words : VERBATIM
word–hoard \'wərd-ˌhō(ə)rd, -ˌhȯ(ə)rd\ *n* [trans. of OE *wordhord*] (ca. 1869) : a supply of words : VOCABULARY
word·ing \'wərd-iŋ\ *n* (1649) : the act or manner of expressing in words
word·less \'wərd-ləs\ *adj* (13c) **1** : not expressed in or accompanied by words **2** : SILENT, SPEECHLESS — **word·less·ly** *adv* — **word·less·ness** *n*
word·mon·ger \-ˌməŋ-gər, -ˌmäŋ-\ *n* (1590) : a writer who uses words for show or without particular regard for meaning
word–mon·ger·ing \-g(ə-)riŋ\ *n* (1879) : the use of empty or bombastic words
word–of–mouth \ˌwərd-ə(v)-'mau̇th\ *adj* (1802) : orally communicated
word of mouth (1553) : oral communication
word order *n* (1892) : the order or arrangement of words in a phrase, clause, or sentence
word·play \'wərd-ˌplā\ *n* (1855) : verbal wit
word processing *n* (1970) : the production of typewritten documents (as business letters) with automated and usu. computerized typing and text-editing equipment
word processor *n* (1970) : a keyboard-operated terminal usu. with a video display and a magnetic storage device for use in word processing; *also* : software (as for a computer system) to perform word processing
word·smith \'wərd-ˌsmith\ *n* (1896) : a person who works with words; *esp* : a skillful writer
word square *n* (ca. 1879) : a series of words of equal length arranged in a square pattern to read the same horizontally and vertically
word stress *n* (ca. 1914) : the manner in which stresses are distributed on the syllables of a word — called also *word accent*
wordy \'wərd-ē\ *adj* **word·i·er; -est** (12c) **1** : using or containing many and usu. too many words **2** : of or relating to words : VERBAL — **word·i·ly** \'wərd-ᵊl-ē\ *adv* — **word·i·ness** \'wərd-ē-nəs\ *n*
syn WORDY, VERBOSE, PROLIX, DIFFUSE mean using more words than necessary to express thought. WORDY may also imply loquaciousness or garrulity; VERBOSE suggests a resulting dullness, obscurity, or lack of incisiveness or precision; PROLIX suggests unreasonable and tedious dwelling on details; DIFFUSE stresses lack of compactness and pointedness of style.
wore *past of* WEAR
[1]**work** \'wərk\ *n* [ME *werk, work,* fr. OE *werc, weorc;* akin to OHG *werc,* Gk *ergon*] (bef. 12c) **1** : activity in which one exerts strength or faculties to do or perform something: **a** : sustained physical or mental effort to overcome obstacles and achieve an objective or result **b** : the labor, task, or duty that is one's accustomed means of livelihood **c** : a specific task, duty, function, or assignment often being a part or phase of some larger activity **2 a** : energy expended by natural phenomena **b** : the result of such energy ⟨sand dunes are the ~ of sea and wind⟩ **c** : the transference of energy that is produced by the motion of the point of application of a force and is measured by multiplying the force and the displacement of its point of application in the line of action **3 a** : something that results from a particular manner or method of working, operating, or devising ⟨careful police ~⟩ ⟨clever camera ~⟩ **b** : something that results from the use or fashioning of a particular material ⟨porcelain ~⟩ **4 a** : a fortified structure (as a fort, earthen barricade, or trench) **b** *pl* : structures in engineering (as docks, bridges, or embankments) or mining (as shafts or tunnels) **5** *pl but sing or pl in constr* : a place where industrial labor is carried on : PLANT, FACTORY **6** *pl* : the working or moving parts of a mechanism ⟨~*s* of a clock⟩ **7 a** : something produced or accomplished by effort, exertion, or exercise of skill ⟨this book is the ~ of many hands⟩ **b** : something produced by the exercise of creative talent or expenditure

of creative effort : artistic production **8** *pl* : performance of moral or religious acts ⟨salvation by ~*s*⟩ **9 a** : effective operation : EFFECT, RESULT ⟨wait for time to do its healing ~⟩ **b** : manner of working : WORKMANSHIP, EXECUTION **10** : the material or piece of material that is operated upon at any stage in the process of manufacture **11** *pl* **a** : everything possessed, available, or belonging ⟨the whole ~*s*, rod, reel, tackle box, went overboard⟩ **b** : subjection to drastic treatment : all possible abuse — usu. used with *get* ⟨get the ~*s*⟩ or *give* ⟨gave them the ~*s*⟩

syn WORK, LABOR, TRAVAIL, TOIL, DRUDGERY, GRIND mean activity involving effort or exertion. WORK may imply activity of body, of mind, of a machine, or of a natural force; LABOR applies to physical or intellectual work involving great and often strenuous exertion; TRAVAIL is bookish for labor involving pain or suffering; TOIL implies prolonged and fatiguing labor; DRUDGERY suggests dull and irksome labor; GRIND implies labor exhausting to mind or body.

syn WORK, EMPLOYMENT, OCCUPATION, CALLING, PURSUIT, MÉTIER, BUSINESS mean a specific sustained activity engaged in esp. in earning one's living; WORK may apply to any purposeful activity whether remunerative or not; EMPLOYMENT implies work for which one has been engaged and is being paid by an employer; OCCUPATION implies work in which one engages regularly esp. as a result of training; CALLING applies to an occupation viewed as a vocation or profession; PURSUIT suggests a trade, profession, or avocation followed with zeal or steady interest; MÉTIER implies a calling or pursuit for which one believes oneself to be esp. fitted; BUSINESS suggests activity in commerce or the management of money and affairs.

— **at work** **1** : engaged in working : BUSY; *esp* : engaged in one's regular occupation **2** : having effect : OPERATING, FUNCTIONING — **in the works** : in process of preparation, development, or completion — **in work** **1** : in process of being done **2** *of a horse* : in training — **out of work** : without regular employment : JOBLESS

[2]**work** *adj* (14c) **1** : used for work ⟨~ elephant⟩ **2** : suitable or styled for wear while working ⟨~ clothes⟩ **3** : involving or engaged in work ⟨~ gang⟩

[3]**work** *vb* **worked** \ˈwərkt\ *or* **wrought** \ˈrȯt\; **work·ing** [ME *werken, worken*, fr. OE *wyrcan;* akin to OE *weorc*] *vt* (bef. 12c) **1** : to bring to pass : EFFECT ⟨~ miracles⟩ **2 a** : to fashion or create a useful or desired product by expending labor or exertion on : FORGE, SHAPE ⟨~ flint into tools⟩ **b** : to make or decorate with needlework; *esp* : EMBROIDER **3 a** : to prepare for use by stirring or kneading **b** : to bring into a desired form by a gradual process of cutting, hammering, scraping, pressing, or stretching ⟨~ cold steel⟩ **4** : to set or keep in motion, operation, or activity : cause to operate or produce ⟨a pump ~*ed* by hand⟩ ⟨~ farmland⟩ **5** : to solve (a problem) by reasoning or calculation — often used with *out* **6 a** : to cause to toil or labor ⟨~*ed* their horses nearly to death⟩ **b** : to make use of : EXPLOIT **c** : to control or guide the operation of ⟨switches are ~*ed* from a central tower⟩ **7** : to carry on an operation through or in or along ⟨the salespeople ~*ed* both sides of the street⟩ **8** : to pay for with labor or service ⟨~*ed* my way through college⟩ **9 a** : to get (oneself or an object) into or out of a condition or position by gradual stages **b** : CONTRIVE, ARRANGE ⟨we can ~ it so that you can take your vacation⟩ **10 a** : to practice trickery or cajolery on for some end ⟨~*ed* the management for a free ticket⟩ **b** : EXCITE, PROVOKE ⟨~*ed* myself into a rage⟩ ~ *vi* **1 a** : to exert oneself physically or mentally esp. in sustained effort for a purpose or under compulsion or necessity **b** : to perform or carry through a task requiring sustained effort or continuous repeated operations ⟨~*ed* all day over a hot stove⟩ **c** : to perform work or fulfill duties regularly for wages or salary **2** : to function or operate according to plan or design ⟨hinges ~ better with oil⟩ **3** : to exert an influence or tendency **4** : to produce a desired effect or result : SUCCEED **5 a** : to make way slowly and with difficulty : move or progress laboriously ⟨~*ed* up to the presidency⟩ **b** : to sail to windward **6** : to permit of being worked : react in a specified way to being worked ⟨this wood ~*s* easily⟩ **7 a** : to be in agitation or restless motion **b** : FERMENT 1 **c** : to move slightly in relation to another part **d** : to get into a specified condition by slow or imperceptible movements ⟨the knot ~*ed* loose⟩ — **work on** **1** : AFFECT ⟨*worked on* my sympathies⟩ **2** : to strive to influence or persuade — **work upon** : to have effect upon : operate on : INFLUENCE

work·able \ˈwər-kə-bəl\ *adj* (1545) **1** : capable of being worked **2** : PRACTICABLE, FEASIBLE ⟨a ~ system⟩ — **work·abil·i·ty** \ˌwər-kə-ˈbil-ət-ē\ *n* — **work·able·ness** \ˈwər-kə-bəl-nəs\ *n*

work·a·day \ˈwər-kə-ˌdā\ *adj* [alter. of earlier *workyday*, fr. obs. *workyday*, n. (workday)] (1554) **1** : of, relating to, or suited for working days **2** : ORDINARY, PROSAIC

work·a·hol·ic \ˌwər-kə-ˈhȯl-ik, -ˈhäl-\ *n* [*work* + connective *-a-* + *-holic* (as in *alcoholic*)] (1971) : a compulsive worker — **work·a·hol·ism** \ˈwər-kə-ˌhȯl-ˌiz-əm, -ˌhäl-\ *n*

work·bag \ˈwərk-ˌbag\ *n* (1775) : a bag for implements or materials for work; *esp* : a bag for needlework

work·bas·ket \-ˌbas-kət\ *n* (1743) : a basket for needlework

work·bench \-ˌbench\ *n* (1781) : a bench on which work esp. of mechanics, machinists, and carpenters is performed

work·boat \-ˌbōt\ *n* (1937) : a boat used for work purposes (as commercial fishing and ferrying supplies) rather than for sport or for passenger or naval service

work·book \-ˌbu̇k\ *n* (1910) **1** : a booklet outlining a course of study **2** : a worker's manual **3** : a record of work done **4** : a student's book of problems to be solved directly on the pages

work·box \-ˌbäks\ *n* (1811) : a box for work instruments and materials

work camp *n* (1941) : a camp for workers: as **a** : PRISON CAMP 1 **b** : a short-term group project in which individuals from one or more religious organizations volunteer their labor

work·day \ˈwərk-ˌdā\ *n* (15c) **1** : a day on which work is performed as distinguished from a day off **2** : the period of time in a day during which work is performed — **workday** *adj*

worked \ˈwərkt\ *adj* (1740) : that has been subjected to some process of development, treatment, or manufacture ⟨a newly ~ field⟩

worked up *adj* (1903) : emotionally aroused : EXCITED

work·er \ˈwər-kər\ *n* (14c) **1 a** : one that works esp. at manual or industrial labor or with a particular material — often used in combination **b** : a member of the working class **2** : one of the sexually underdeveloped and usu. sterile members of a colony of social ants, bees, wasps, or termites that perform most of the labor and protective duties of the colony — see HONEYBEE illustration **3** : a usu. electrotype plate from which printing is done

worker–priest *n* (1953) : a French Roman Catholic priest who for missionary purposes spends part of each weekday as a worker in a secular job

work ethic *n* (1951) : a belief in work as a moral good

work·fare \ˌwərk-ˌfa(ə)r, -ˌfe(ə)r\ *n* [*work* + *-fare* (as in *welfare*)] (1968) : a welfare program in which recipients are required to perform usu. public-service work

work farm *n* (1953) : a farm on which persons guilty of minor law violations are confined

work·folk \ˈwərk-ˌfōk\ *or* **work·folks** \-ˌfōks\ *n pl* (15c) : working people; *esp* : farm workers

work force *n* (ca. 1943) **1** : the workers engaged in a specific activity ⟨the factory's *work force*⟩ **2** : the number of workers potentially assignable for any purpose ⟨the nation's *work force*⟩

work·horse \ˈwərk-ˌhȯ(ə)rs\ *n* (1543) **1** : a horse used chiefly for labor as distinguished from driving, riding, or racing **2 a** : a person who performs most of the work of a group task **b** : a markedly useful or durable vehicle, craft, or machine

work·house \-ˌhau̇s\ *n* (1652) **1** *Brit* : POORHOUSE **2** : a house of correction for persons guilty of minor law violations

work in *vt* (1576) **1** : to insert or cause to penetrate by repeated or continued effort **2** : to interpose or insinuate gradually or unobtrusively ⟨*worked in* a few topical jokes⟩

[1]**work·ing** *adj* (14c) **1** : adequate to permit work to be done ⟨a ~ majority⟩ **2** : assumed or adopted to permit or facilitate further work or activity ⟨~ draft⟩ **3** : engaged in work ⟨a ~ journalist⟩ **4** : spent at work ⟨~ life⟩

[2]**working** *n* (14c) **1** : the manner of functioning or operating : OPERATION — usu. used in pl. **2** : an excavation or group of excavations made in mining, quarrying, or tunneling — usu. used in pl.

working asset *n* (ca. 1914) : an asset other than a capital asset

working capital *n* (ca. 1901) : capital actively turned over in or available for use in the course of business activity: **a** : the excess of current assets over current liabilities **b** : all capital of a business except that invested in capital assets

work·ing–class *adj* (1839) : of, relating to, deriving from, or suitable to the class of wage earners ⟨~ virtues⟩ ⟨~ family⟩

working class *n* (1813) : the class of people who work for wages usu. at manual labor

working day *n* (15c) : WORKDAY

working dog *n* (1891) : a dog fitted by size, breeding, or training for useful work (as draft or herding) esp. as distinguished from one fitted primarily for pet, show, or sporting use

working fluid *n* (ca. 1903) : a fluid working substance

work·ing·man \ˈwər-kiŋ-ˌman\ *n* (1638) : one who works for wages usu. at manual labor

working order *n* (1845) : a condition of a machine in which it functions properly

working papers *n pl* (1928) : official documents legalizing the employment of a minor

working substance *n* (ca. 1897) : a usu. fluid substance that through changes of temperature, volume, and pressure is the means of carrying out thermodynamic processes or cycles (as in a heat engine)

work·less \ˈwər-kləs\ *adj* (15c) : being without work : UNEMPLOYED — **work·less·ness** *n*

work load *n* (1943) **1** : the amount of work or of working time expected from or assigned to an employee **2** : the amount of work performed or capable of being performed (as by a mechanical device) usu. within a specific period

work·man \ˈwərk-mən\ *n* (bef. 12c) **1** : WORKINGMAN **2** : ARTISAN

work·man·like \-ˌlīk\ *adj* (1739) : worthy of a good workman : SKILLFUL

work·man·ly \-lē\ *adj* (1545) : WORKMANLIKE

work·man·ship \-ˌship\ *n* (1523) **1** : something effected, made, or produced : WORK **2** : the art or skill of a workman : CRAFTSMANSHIP; *also* : the quality imparted to a thing in the process of making ⟨a vase of exquisite ~⟩

work·mate \ˈwərk-ˌmāt\ *n, chiefly Brit* (1851) : a fellow worker

workmen's compensation insurance *n* (ca. 1917) : insurance that reimburses an employer for damages that must be paid to an employee for injury occurring in the course of his or her employment

work of art (1834) **1** : a product of one of the fine arts; *esp* : a painting or sculpture of high artistic quality **2** : something giving high aesthetic satisfaction to the beholder or auditor

work off *vt* (1678) : to dispose of or get rid of by work or activity

work·out \ˈwər-ˌkau̇t\ *n* (ca. 1894) **1** : a practice or exercise to test or improve one's fitness for athletic competition, ability, or performance **2** : a test of one's ability, capacity, stamina, or suitability

work out \ˌwər-ˈkau̇t, ˈwər-\ *vt* (1534) **1 a** : to bring about by labor and exertion ⟨*work out* your own salvation —Phil 2:12 (AV)⟩ **b** : to devise, arrange, or achieve by resolving difficulties ⟨after many years of wrangling, *worked out* a definite agreement —A.A. Butkus⟩ **c** : DEVELOP ⟨the final situation is not *worked out* with psychological profundity —Leslie Rees⟩ **2** : to discharge (as a debt) by labor **3** : to exhaust (as a mine) by working ~ *vi* **1 a** : to prove effective, practicable, or suitable ⟨how this will actually *work out* I don't know —Milton Kotler⟩ **b** : to amount to a total or calculated figure — used with *at* or *to* **2** : to engage in a workout ⟨*works out* in gymnasiums . . . to keep in shape —*Current Biog.*⟩

work over *vt* (1883) **1** : to do over : REWORK ⟨saved the play by *working* the first act *over*⟩ **2** : to subject to thorough examination, study, or treatment ⟨shelf stock would get thoroughly *worked over* by shop-

\ə\ **abut** \ᵊ\ **kitten,** F **table** \ər\ **further** \a\ **ash** \ā\ **ace** \ä\ **cot, cart**
\au̇\ **out** \ch\ **chin** \e\ **bet** \ē\ **easy** \g\ **go** \i\ **hit** \ī\ **ice** \j\ **job**
\ŋ\ **sing** \ō\ **go** \ȯ\ **law** \ȯi\ **boy** \th\ **thin** \t͟h\ **the** \ü\ **loot** \u̇\ **foot**
\y\ **yet** \zh\ **vision** \à, k̟, ⁿ, œ, œ̄, ue, ue̅, ʸ\ *see* Guide to Pronunciation

pers⟩ 3 : to beat up or manhandle with thoroughness ⟨the gang *worked* me *over*⟩

work·peo·ple \ˈwərk-ˌpē-pəl\ *n pl, chiefly Brit* (1708) : WORKERS, EMPLOYEES

work·piece \-ˌpēs\ *n* (1926) : a piece of work in process of manufacture

work·place \-ˌplās\ *n* (1828) : a place (as a shop or factory) where work is done

work print *n* (1937) : a completely edited motion-picture print used as a guide in cutting the original negative from which the final production prints will be made

work·room \ˈwər-ˌkrüm, -ˌkru̇m\ *n* (1828) : a room used esp. for manual work

work·shop \ˈwərk-ˌshäp\ *n* (1562) **1** : a small establishment where manufacturing or handicrafts are carried on **2** : WORKROOM **3** : a usu. brief intensive educational program for a relatively small group of people that emphasizes participation in problem-solving

work song *n* (1925) : a song sung in rhythm with work

work·sta·tion \-ˌstā-shən\ *n* (1931) : an area with equipment for a single worker; *also* : a usu. intelligent terminal connected to a data-processing or word-processing network

work stoppage *n* (1945) : concerted cessation of work by a group of employees usu. more spontaneous and less serious than a strike

work–study program *n* (1946) : a program planned to give high school or college students work experience

work·ta·ble \ˈwərk-ˌtā-bəl\ *n* (1800) : a table for holding working materials and implements; *esp* : a small table with drawers and other conveniences for needlework

work·up \ˈwər-ˌkəp\ *n* (1939) : an intensive diagnostic study

work–up \ˈwər-ˌkəp\ *n* (1903) : an unintended mark on a printed sheet caused by the rising of spacing material

work up \ˌwər-ˈkəp, ˈwər-\ *vi* (1681) : to rise gradually in intensity or emotional tone ~ *vt* **1** : to stir up : ROUSE **2** : to produce by mental or physical work ⟨*worked up* a comedy act⟩ ⟨*worked up* a sweat in the gymnasium⟩

work·week \ˈwər-ˌkwēk\ *n* (1921) : the hours or days of work in a calendar week ⟨40-hour ~⟩ ⟨a 5-day ~⟩ ⟨a shortened ~⟩

work·wom·an \ˈwər-ˌkwu̇m-ən\ *n* (ca. 1530) : a woman who works

[1]**world** \ˈwər(-ə)ld\ *n* [ME, fr. OE *woruld* human existence, this world, age; akin to OHG *weralt* age, world] (bef. 12c) **1 a** : the earthly state of human existence **b** : life after death — used with a qualifier ⟨the next ~⟩ **2** : the earth with its inhabitants and all things upon it **3** : individual course of life : CAREER **4** : the inhabitants of the earth : the human race **5 a** : the concerns of the earth and its affairs as distinguished from heaven and the life to come **b** : secular affairs **6** : the system of created things : UNIVERSE **7 a** : a division or generation of the inhabitants of the earth distinguished by living together at the same place or at the same time ⟨the medieval ~⟩ **b** : a distinctive class of persons or their sphere of interest ⟨the academic ~⟩ ⟨the sports ~⟩ **8** : human society ⟨withdraw from the ~⟩ **9** : a part or section of the earth that is a separate independent unit **10** : the sphere or scene of one's life and action ⟨living in your own little ~⟩ **11** : an indefinite multitude or a great quantity or distance ⟨makes a ~ of difference⟩ ⟨a ~ away⟩ **12** : the whole body of living persons : PUBLIC ⟨announced their discovery to the ~⟩ **13** : KINGDOM 5 ⟨the animal ~⟩ **14** : a celestial body (as a planet); *esp* : one that is inhabited — **for all the world** : in every way : EXACTLY ⟨copies which look *for all the world* like the original⟩ — **in the world** : among innumerable possibilities : EVER — used as an intensive ⟨what *in the world* is it⟩ — **out of this world** : of extraordinary excellence : SUPERB

[2]**world** *adj* (12c) **1** : of or relating to the world ⟨a ~ championship⟩ **2 a** : extending or found throughout the world : WORLDWIDE ⟨brought about ~ peace⟩ **b** : involving or applying to part of or the whole world ⟨a ~ tour⟩ ⟨a ~ state⟩

world–beat·er \ˈwərl(d)-ˌbēt-ər\ *n* (ca. 1888) : one that excels all others of its kind : CHAMPION

world–class *adj* (1968) : being of the highest caliber in the world ⟨a ~ polo player⟩

world federalism *n* (1950) **1** : federalism on a worldwide basis **2** *cap W&F* **a** : the principles and policies of the World Federalists **b** : the body or movement composed of World Federalists

world federalist *n* (1951) **1** : an adherent or advocate of world federalism **2** *cap W&F* : a member of a movement arising after World War II advocating the formation of a federal union of the nations of the world with limited but positive governmental powers

World Island *n* (ca. 1942) : the landmass consisting of Europe, Asia, and Africa held by geopoliticians to have strategic advantages for mastery of the world

world·ling \ˈwər(-ə)l-dliŋ, ˈwərl-liŋ\ *n* (1549) : a person engrossed in the concerns of this present world

world·ly \ˈwər(-ə)l-dlē, ˈwərl-lē\ *adj* (bef. 12c) **1** : of, relating to, or devoted to this world and its pursuits rather than to religion or spiritual affairs **2** : WORLDLY-WISE ***syn*** see EARTHLY — **world·li·ness** *n*

world·ly–mind·ed \ˌwərl-(d)lē-ˈmīn-dəd\ *adj* (1601) : devoted to or engrossed in worldly interests — **world·ly–mind·ed·ness** *n*

world·ly–wise \ˈwərl-(d)lē-ˌwīz\ *adj* (15c) : possessing a practical and often shrewd and materialistic understanding of human affairs ***syn*** see SOPHISTICATED

world power *n* (1900) : a political unit (as a nation or state) powerful enough to affect the entire world by its influence or actions

world premiere *n* (1925) : the first regular performance (as of a theatrical production) anywhere in the world

World Series *n* (1889) : a series of baseball games played each fall between the pennant winners of the major leagues to decide the professional championship of the U.S.

world's fair *n* (1850) : an international exposition featuring exhibits and participants from all over the world

world–shak·ing \ˈwərl(d)-ˌshā-kiŋ\ *adj* (1598) : EARTHSHAKING

world soul *n* (1848) : an animating spirit or creative principle related to the world as the soul is to the individual being

world·view \-ˌvyü\ *n* (1858) : WELTANSCHAUUNG

world war *n* (1909) : a war engaged in by all or most of the principal nations of the world; *esp, cap both Ws* : either of two such wars of the first half of the 20th century

world–wea·ry \ˈwərl-ˌdwi(ə)r-ē\ *adj* (1768) : feeling or showing fatigue from or boredom with the life of the world and esp. material pleasures — **world–wea·ri·ness** *n*

[1]**world·wide** \ˈwər(-ə)l-ˈdwīd\ *adj* (1632) : extended throughout or involving the entire world

[2]**worldwide** *adv* (1892) : throughout the world

[1]**worm** \ˈwərm\ *n, often attrib* [ME, fr. OE *wyrm* serpent, worm; akin to OHG *wurm* serpent, worm, L *vermis* worm] (bef. 12c) **1 a** : EARTHWORM; *broadly* : an annelid worm **b** : any of numerous relatively small elongated usu. naked and soft-bodied animals: as (1) : an insect larva; *esp* : one that is a destructive grub, caterpillar, or maggot (2) : SHIPWORM (3) : BLINDWORM **2 a** : a human being who is an object of contempt, loathing, or pity : WRETCH **b** : something that torments or devours from within **3** *archaic* : SNAKE, SERPENT **4** : HELMINTHIASIS — usu. used in pl. **5** : something (as a mechanical device) spiral or vermiculate in form or appearance: as **a** : the thread of a screw **b** : a short revolving screw whose threads gear with the teeth of a worm wheel or a rack **c** : a spiral condensing tube used in distilling **d** : ARCHIMEDES' SCREW; *also* : a conveyor working on the principle of such a screw — **worm·like** \-ˌlīk\ *adj*

[2]**worm** *vt* (1564) **1** : to free (as a dog) from worms **2** : to obtain or extract by artful or insidious questioning or by pleading, asking, or persuading — usu. used with *out of* **3** : to wind rope or yarn spirally round and between the strands of (a cable or rope) before serving **4 a** : to cause to move or proceed in or as if in the manner of a worm **b** : to insinuate or introduce (oneself) by devious or subtle means **c** : to proceed or make (one's way) insidiously or deviously ⟨tried to ~ her way out of the situation⟩ ~ *vi* : to move or proceed sinuously or insidiously — **worm·er** *n*

worm–eat·en \ˈwər-ˌmēt-ᵊn\ *adj* (14c) **1 a** : eaten or burrowed by worms ⟨~ timber⟩ **b** : PITTED **2** : WORN-OUT, ANTIQUATED

worm fence *n* (1652) : a zigzag fence consisting of interlocking rails supported by crossed poles — called also *snake fence, Virginia fence*

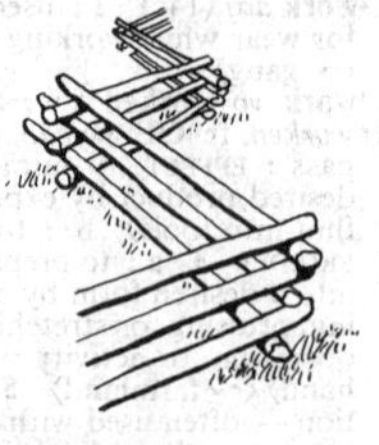
worm fence

worm gear *n* (ca. 1876) **1** : WORM WHEEL **2** : a gear of a worm and a worm wheel working together

worm·hole \ˈwərm-ˌhōl\ *n* (1593) : a hole or passage burrowed by a worm

worm·seed \-ˌsēd\ *n* (15c) : any of various plants whose seeds possess anthelmintic properties: as **a** : any of several artemisias **b** : a goosefoot (*Chenopodium ambrosioides*)

worm's–eye \ˌwərm-ˌzī\ *adj* (1911) : seen from ground level or from the lowest levels of a hierarchy ⟨the bird's-eye view of the executive and the ~ view of the employee — *Current Biog.*⟩

worm snake *n* (1885) : any of various small harmless burrowing snakes (esp. family Typhlopidae) suggesting earthworms

worm wheel *n* (1677) : a toothed wheel gearing with the thread of a worm

worm·wood \ˈwərm-ˌwu̇d\ *n* [ME *wormwode*, alter. of *wermode*, fr. OE *wermōd;* akin to OHG *wermuota* wormwood] (15c) **1** : ARTEMISIA; *esp* : a European plant (*Artemisia absinthium*) yielding a bitter slightly aromatic dark green oil used in absinthe **2** : something bitter or grievous : BITTERNESS

wormy \ˈwər-mē\ *adj* **worm·i·er; -est** (15c) **1** : containing, abounding in, or infested with or as if with worms ⟨~ flour⟩ ⟨a ~ dog⟩; *also* : damaged by worms : WORM-EATEN ⟨~ timbers⟩ **2** : resembling or suggestive of a worm

worn *past part of* WEAR

worn–out \ˈwō(ə)r-ˈnau̇t, ˈwȯ(ə)r-\ *adj* (1593) : exhausted or used up by or as if by wear

wor·ri·ment \ˈwər-ē-mənt, ˈwə-rē-\ *n* (1832) : an act or instance of worrying; *also* : TROUBLE, WORRY

wor·ri·some \-səm\ *adj* (1845) **1** : causing distress or worry **2** : inclined to worry or fret — **wor·ri·some·ly** *adv* — **wor·ri·some·ness** *n*

[1]**wor·ry** \ˈwər-ē, ˈwə-rē\ *vb* **wor·ried; wor·ry·ing** [ME *worien*, fr. OE *wyrgan;* akin to OHG *wurgen* to strangle, Lith *veržti* to constrict] *vt* (bef. 12c) **1** *dial Brit* : CHOKE, STRANGLE **2 a** : to harass by tearing, biting, or snapping esp. at the throat **b** : to shake or pull at with the teeth ⟨a terrier ~*ing* a rat⟩ **c** : to touch or disturb something repeatedly **d** : to change the position of or adjust by repeated pushing or hauling **3 a** : to assail with rough or aggressive attack or treatment : TORMENT **b** : to subject to persistent or nagging attention or effort **4** : to afflict with mental distress or agitation : make anxious ~ *vi* **1** *dial Brit* : STRANGLE, CHOKE **2** : to move, proceed, or progress by unceasing or difficult effort : STRUGGLE **3** : to feel or experience concern or anxiety : FRET — **wor·ried·ly** \-(r)ēd-lē, -(r)əd-\ *adv* — **wor·ri·er** \-(r)ē-ər\ *n*

syn WORRY, ANNOY, HARASS, HARRY, PLAGUE, PESTER, TEASE mean to disturb or irritate by persistent acts. WORRY implies an incessant goading or attacking that drives one to desperation ⟨pursued a policy of *worrying* the enemy⟩ ANNOY implies disturbing one's composure or peace of mind by intrusion, interference, or petty attacks ⟨you're doing that just to *annoy* me⟩ HARASS implies petty persecutions or burdensome demands that exhaust one's nervous or mental power ⟨*harassed* on all sides by creditors⟩ HARRY may imply heavy oppression or maltreatment ⟨*harried* mothers trying to cope with small children⟩ PLAGUE implies a painful and persistent affliction ⟨*plagued* all her life by poverty⟩ PESTER stresses the repetition of petty attacks ⟨the bureau was constantly *pestered* with trivial complaints⟩ TEASE suggests an attempt to break down one's resistance or rouse to wrath ⟨malicious children *teased* the dog⟩

— **not to worry** : nothing to be concerned about : don't worry

[2]**worry** *n, pl* **worries** (1804) **1 a** : mental distress or agitation resulting from concern usu. for something impending or anticipated : ANXIETY **b** : an instance or occurrence of such distress or agitation **2** : a cause of worry : TROUBLE, DIFFICULTY ***syn*** see CARE

worry beads *n pl* (1956) : a string of beads fingered so as to keep one's hands occupied

wor·ry·wart \ˈwər-ē-ˌwȯ(ə)rt, ˈwə-rē-\ *n* (1936) : one who is inclined to worry unduly

[1]**worse** \'wərs\ *adj, comparative of* BAD *or of* ILL [ME *werse, worse,* fr. OE *wiersa, wyrsa;* akin to OHG *wirsiro* worse] (bef. 12c) **1 :** of more inferior quality, value, or condition **2 a :** more unfavorable, difficult, unpleasant, or painful **b :** more faulty, unsuitable, or incorrect **c :** less skillful or efficient **3 :** bad, evil, or corrupt in a greater degree **:** more reprehensible **4 :** being in poorer health **:** SICKER

[2]**worse** *n* (bef. 12c) **:** one that is worse ⟨thought he was an atheist and ~ —Van Wyck Brooks⟩

[3]**worse** *adv, comparative of* BAD *or of* ILL (bef. 12c) **:** in a worse manner **:** to a worse extent or degree

wors·en \'wərs-ᵊn\ *vb* **wors·ened; wors·en·ing** \'wərs-niŋ, -ᵊn-iŋ\ *vt* (13c) **:** to make worse ~ *vi* **:** to become worse

wors·er \'wər-sər\ *adj or adv* [*worse* + *-er*] *archaic* (15c) **:** WORSE ⟨I cannot hate thee ~ than I do —Shak.⟩

[1]**wor·ship** \'wər-shəp\ *n* [ME *worshipe* worthiness, repute, respect, reverence paid to a divine being, fr. OE *weorthscipe* worthiness, repute, respect, fr. *weorth* worthy, worth + *-scipe* -ship] (bef. 12c) **1** *chiefly Brit* **:** a person of importance — used as a title for various officials (as magistrates and some mayors) ⟨sent a petition to his *Worship*⟩ **2 :** reverence offered a divine being or supernatural power; *also* **:** an act of expressing such reverence **3 :** a form of religious practice with its creed and ritual **4 :** extravagant respect or admiration for or devotion to an object of esteem ⟨~ of the dollar⟩

[2]**worship** *vb* **-shiped** *or* **-shipped; -ship·ing** *or* **-ship·ping** *vt* (13c) **1 :** to honor or reverence as a divine being or supernatural power **2 :** to regard with great, even extravagant respect, honor, or devotion ~ *vi* **:** to perform or take part in worship or an act of worship ***syn*** see REVERE — **wor·ship·er** *or* **wor·ship·per** *n*

wor·ship·ful \'wər-shəp-fəl\ *adj* (14c) **1 a** *archaic* **:** NOTABLE, DISTINGUISHED **b** *chiefly Brit* — used as a title for various persons or groups of rank or distinction **2 :** giving worship or veneration — **wor·ship·ful·ly** \-fə-lē\ *adv* — **wor·ship·ful·ness** *n*

wor·ship·less \-shə-pləs\ *adj* (1765) **:** lacking worship or worshipers

[1]**worst** \'wərst\ *adj, superlative of* BAD *or of* ILL [ME *werste, worste,* fr. OE *wierresta, wyrsta,* superl. of the root of OE *wiersa* worse] (bef. 12c) **1 :** most corrupt, bad, evil, or ill **2 a :** most unfavorable, difficult, unpleasant, or painful **b :** most unsuitable, faulty, unattractive, or ill-conceived **c :** least skillful or efficient **3 :** most wanting in quality, value, or condition — **the worst way :** very much ⟨such men . . . need indoctrination *the worst way* —J. G. Cozzens⟩ — often used with *in* ⟨wanted a new bicycle in *the worst way*⟩

[2]**worst** *adv, superlative of* ILL *or* ILLY *or of* BAD *or* BADLY (bef. 12c) **1 :** to the extreme degree of badness or inferiority **2 :** to the greatest or highest degree ⟨groups who need the subsidies ~ lose out —T. W. Arnold⟩

[3]**worst** *n, pl* **worst** (14c) **:** one that is worst — **at worst :** under the worst circumstances

[4]**worst** *vt* (1636) **:** to get the better of **:** DEFEAT

worst–case *adj* (1964) **:** involving, projecting, or providing for the worst possible circumstances or outcome of a given situation

wor·sted \'wu̇s-təd, 'wər-stəd\ *n* [ME, fr. *Worsted* (now *Worstead*), England] (13c) **1 :** a fabric made from worsted yarns **2 :** a smooth compact yarn from long wool fibers used esp. for firm napless fabrics, carpeting, or knitting — **worsted** *adj*

[1]**wort** \'wərt, 'wȯ(ə)rt\ *n* [ME, fr. OE *wyrt* root, herb, plant — more at ROOT] (bef. 12c) **:** PLANT; *esp* **:** an herbaceous plant — usu. used in combination ⟨louse*wort*⟩

[2]**wort** *n* [ME, fr. OE *wyrt;* akin to MHG *würze* brewer's wort, OE *wyrt* root, herb] (bef. 12c) **:** a liquid formed by soaking mash in hot water and then fermented to make beer

[1]**worth** \'wərth\ *vi* [ME *worthen,* fr. OE *weorthan;* akin to OHG *werdan* to become, L *vertere* to turn] *archaic* (bef. 12c) **:** BECOME — usu. used in the phrase *woe worth*

[2]**worth** *adj* [ME, fr. OE *weorth* worthy, of (a specified) value; akin to OHG *werd* worthy, worth] (bef. 12c) **1** *archaic* **:** having monetary or material value **2** *archaic* **:** ESTIMABLE

[3]**worth** *prep* (bef. 12c) **1 a :** equal in value to **b :** having possessions or income equal to **2 :** deserving of ⟨well ~ the effort⟩ — **worth one's salt :** of substantial or significant value or merit

[4]**worth** *n* (bef. 12c) **1 a :** monetary value ⟨farmhouse and lands of little ~⟩ **b :** the equivalent of a specified amount or figure ⟨a dollar's ~ of gas⟩ **2 :** the value of something measured by its qualities or by the esteem in which it is held ⟨a literary heritage of great ~⟩ **3 a :** moral or personal value ⟨trying to teach human ~⟩ **b :** MERIT, EXCELLENCE ⟨a field in which we have proved our ~⟩ **4 :** WEALTH, RICHES

worth·ful \'wərth-fəl\ *adj* (bef. 12c) **1 :** full of merit ⟨a good and ~ person⟩ **2 :** having value ⟨the ~ aspects of their culture⟩

worth·less \'wərth-ləs\ *adj* (1588) **1 a :** lacking worth **:** VALUELESS ⟨~ currency⟩ **b :** USELESS ⟨~ to continue searching⟩ **2 :** CONTEMPTIBLE, DESPICABLE — **worth·less·ly** *adv* — **worth·less·ness** *n*

worth·while \-'hwī(ə)l, -'wī(ə)l\ *adj* (1900) **1 :** being worth the time or effort spent **2 :** WORTHY 1 — **worth·while·ness** *n*

[1]**wor·thy** \'wər-t͟hē\ *adj* **wor·thi·er; -est** (13c) **1 a :** having worth or value **:** ESTIMABLE ⟨a ~ cause⟩ **b :** HONORABLE, MERITORIOUS ⟨~ candidates⟩ **2 :** having sufficient worth or importance ⟨~ to be remembered⟩ — **wor·thi·ly** \'wər-t͟hə-lē\ *adv* — **wor·thi·ness** \-t͟hē-nəs\ *n*

[2]**worthy** *n, pl* **worthies** (14c) **:** a worthy or prominent person

-wor·thy \ˌwər-t͟hē\ *adj comb form* **1 :** fit or safe for ⟨a sea*worthy* vessel⟩ **2 :** of sufficient worth for ⟨a news*worthy* event⟩

[1]**wot** *pres 1st & 3d sing of* WIT

[2]**wot** \'wät\ *vb* **wot·ted; wot·ting** [ME *woten,* alter. of *witen* — more at WIT] *chiefly Brit* (14c) **:** KNOW — often used with *of*

would \wəd, əd, d, (ˈ)wu̇d\ *past of* WILL [ME *wolde,* fr. OE; akin to OHG *wolta* wished, desired] (bef. 12c) **1 a** *archaic* **:** WISHED, DESIRED **b** *archaic* **:** wish for **:** WANT **c (1) :** strongly desire **:** WISH ⟨I ~ I were young again⟩ **(2)** — used in auxiliary function with *rather* or *sooner* to express preference ⟨he ~ sooner die than face them⟩ **2 a** — used in auxiliary function to express wish, desire, or intent ⟨those who ~ forbid gambling⟩ **b** — used in auxiliary function to express willingness or preference ⟨as ye ~ that men should do to you —Lk 6:31 (AV)⟩ **c** — used in auxiliary function to express plan or intention ⟨said we ~ come⟩ **3** — used in auxiliary function to express custom or habitual action ⟨we ~ meet often for lunch⟩ **4** — used in auxiliary function to express consent or choice ⟨~ put it off if he could⟩ **5 a** — used in auxiliary function in the conclusion of a conditional sentence to express a contingency or possibility ⟨if he were coming, he ~ be here now⟩ **b** — used in auxiliary function in a noun clause (as one completing a statement of desire, request, or advice) ⟨we wish that he ~ go⟩ **6** — used in auxiliary function to express probability or presumption in past or present time ⟨~ have won if I had not tripped⟩ **7 :** COULD ⟨the barrel ~ hold 20 gallons⟩ **8** — used in auxiliary function to express a request with which voluntary compliance is expected ⟨~ you please help us⟩ **9** — used in auxiliary function to express doubt or uncertainty ⟨the explanation . . . ~ seem satisfactory⟩ **10 :** SHOULD ⟨knew I ~ enjoy the trip⟩ ⟨~ be glad to know the answer⟩

would–be \ˌwu̇d-ˌbē\ *adj* (14c) **:** desiring, professing, or having the potential to be

would·est \'wu̇d-əst\ *archaic past 2d sing of* WILL

wouldn't \'wu̇d-ᵊnt, -ᵊn, *dial also* 'wu̇t-ᵊn(t) *or* (ˌ)wu̇nt\ **:** would not

wouldst \wədst, (ˈ)wu̇dst, wətst\ *archaic past 2d sing of* WILL

[1]**wound** \'wünd, *archaic or dial* 'wau̇nd\ *n* [ME, fr. OE *wund;* akin to OHG *wunta* wound] (bef. 12c) **1 a :** an injury to the body (as from violence, accident, or surgery) that involves laceration or breaking of a membrane (as the skin) and usu. damage to underlying tissues **b :** a cut or breach in a plant due to external violence **2 :** a mental or emotional hurt or blow **3 :** something resembling a wound in appearance or effect; *esp* **:** a rift in or blow to a political body or social group

[2]**wound** *vt* (bef. 12c) **:** to cause a wound to or in ~ *vi* **:** to inflict a wound

[3]**wound** \'wau̇nd\ *past and past part of* WIND

[1]**wound·ed** \'wün-dəd\ *n pl* (bef. 12c) **:** wounded persons

[2]**wounded** *adj* (14c) **:** injured, hurt by, or suffering from a wound

wound·less \'wün-(d)ləs\ *adj* (1579) **1 :** free from wounds **:** UNWOUNDED **2** *obs* **:** INVULNERABLE ⟨the ~ air —Shak.⟩

wove *past of* WEAVE

[1]**woven** *past part of* WEAVE

[2]**wo·ven** \'wō-vən\ *n* (1930) **:** a woven fabric

wove paper \'wōv-\ *n* [*wove* (archaic pp. of *weave*)] (1815) **:** paper made with a revolving roller covered with wires so woven as to produce no fine lines running across the grain — compare LAID PAPER

[1]**wow** \'wau̇\ *interj* (1513) — used to express strong feeling (as pleasure or surprise)

[2]**wow** *n* (1920) **:** a striking success **:** HIT

[3]**wow** *vt* (1924) **:** to excite to enthusiastic admiration or approval

[4]**wow** *n* [imit.] (1932) **:** a distortion in reproduced sound consisting of a slow rise and fall of pitch caused by speed variation in the reproducing system

wow·ser \'wau̇-zər\ *n* [origin unknown] *chiefly Austral* (ca. 1890) **:** an obtrusively puritanical person

W particle *n* [weak] (1963) **:** an elementary particle about 80 times heavier than a proton that along with the Z particle is a transmitter of the weak interaction and that can have a positive or negative charge

[1]**wrack** \'rak\ *n* [ME *wrak,* fr. MD or MLG; akin to OE *wrecan* to drive, punish; something driven by the sea] (14c) **1 a :** a wrecked ship **b :** WRECKAGE **c :** WRECK **d** *dial* **:** the violent destruction of a structure, machine, or vehicle **2 a :** marine vegetation; *esp* **:** KELP **b :** dried seaweeds

[2]**wrack** *n* [ME, fr. OE *wræc* misery, punishment, something driven by the sea; akin to OE *wrecan* to drive, punish — more at WREAK] (15c) **1 :** RUIN, DESTRUCTION **2 :** a remnant of something destroyed

[3]**wrack** *vt* (1562) **:** to utterly ruin **:** WRECK

[4]**wrack** *vb* [by alter.] (1553) **:** [4]RACK

[5]**wrack** *n* (1591) **:** [3]RACK 2

[6]**wrack** *n* (1796) **:** [1]RACK

wrack·ful \'rak-fəl\ *adj* (1558) **:** DESTRUCTIVE

wraith \'rāth\ *n, pl* **wraiths** \'rāths *also* 'rāt͟hz\ [origin unknown] (1513) **1 a :** an apparition of a living person in his exact likeness seen usu. just before his death **b :** GHOST, SPECTER **2 :** an insubstantial appearance **:** SHADOW **3 :** a barely visible gaseous or vaporous column — **wraith·like** \-ˌlīk\ *adj*

[1]**wran·gle** \'raŋ-gəl\ *vb* **wran·gled; wran·gling** \-g(ə-)liŋ\ [ME *wranglen;* akin to OHG *ringan* to struggle — more at WRING] *vi* (14c) **1 :** to dispute angrily or peevishly **:** BICKER **2 :** to engage in argument or controversy ~ *vt* **1 :** to obtain by persistent arguing **:** WANGLE **2 :** to herd and care for (livestock and esp. horses) on the range

[2]**wrangle** *n* (1547) **1 :** an angry, noisy, or prolonged dispute or quarrel **2 :** the action or process of wrangling

wran·gler \-g(ə-)lər\ *n* (1515) **1 :** a bickering disputant **2 :** a ranch hand who takes care of the saddle horses; *broadly* **:** COWBOY

[1]**wrap** \'rap\ *vb* **wrapped; wrap·ping** [ME *wrappen*] *vt* (14c) **1 a :** to cover esp. by winding or folding **b :** to envelop and secure for transportation or storage **:** BUNDLE **c :** ENFOLD, EMBRACE **d :** to coil, fold, draw, or twine about something **2 a :** SURROUND, ENVELOP **b :** to suffuse or surround with an aura or state ⟨the affair was *wrapped* in scandal⟩ **c :** to involve completely **:** ENGROSS **3 :** to conceal or obscure as if by enveloping **4 :** to enclose as if with a protective covering ~ *vi* **1 :** to wind, coil, or twine so as to encircle or cover something **2 :** to put on clothing **:** DRESS — usu. used with *up* **3 :** to be subject to covering, enclosing, or packaging — usu. used with *up*

[2]**wrap** *n* (15c) **1 a (1) :** WRAPPER, WRAPPING **(2) :** material used for wrapping ⟨plastic ~⟩ **b :** an article of clothing that may be wrapped round a person; *esp* **:** an outer garment (as a coat or shawl) **c :** BLANKET **2 :** a single turn or convolution of something wound round an object **3** *pl* **a :** RESTRAINT **b :** a shroud of secrecy ⟨a plan kept under ~s⟩

[1]**wrap·around** \ˌrap-ə-ˌrau̇nd\ *adj* (1926) **1 :** made to be wrapped around something and esp. the body ⟨a ~ skirt⟩ **2 :** shaped to follow a contour; *esp* **:** made to curve from the front around to the side ⟨~ sunglasses⟩ ⟨~ windows⟩ ⟨~ terraces⟩

[2]**wrap·around** \'rap-\ *n* (1926) **1 :** a garment (as a dress) made with a full-length opening and adjusted to the figure by wrapping around **2 :** an object that encircles or esp. curves and laps over another

\ə\ abut \ᵊ\ kitten, F table \ər\ further \a\ ash \ā\ ace \ä\ cot, cart \au̇\ out \ch\ chin \e\ bet \ē\ easy \g\ go \i\ hit \ī\ ice \j\ job \ŋ\ sing \ō\ go \ȯ\ law \ȯi\ boy \th\ thin \t͟h\ the \ü\ loot \u̇\ foot \y\ yet \zh\ vision \à, k̲, ⁿ, œ, œ̄, ue, u̅e, ʸ\ *see* Guide to Pronunciation

wrap·per \'rap-ər\ *n* (15c) **1 :** that in which something is wrapped: as **a :** a tobacco leaf used for the outside covering esp. of cigars **b** (1) **:** JACKET 3c(1) (2) **:** the paper cover of a book not bound in boards **c :** a paper wrapped around a newspaper or magazine in the mail **2 :** one that wraps **3 :** an article of clothing worn wrapped around the body

wrap·ping \'rap-iŋ\ *n* (14c) **:** something used to wrap an object **:** WRAPPER

wrap–up \'rap-,əp\ *n* (1951) **:** a summarizing report

wrap up \(')rap-'əp\ *vt* (1568) **1 :** SUMMARIZE, SUM UP **2 :** to bring to a usu. successful conclusion

wrasse \'ras\ *n* [Corn *gwragh, wragh* hag, wrasse] (ca. 1672) **:** any of numerous elongate compressed usu. brilliantly colored marine spiny-finned fishes (family Labridae) that include important food fishes esp. of warm seas as well as some believed to be poisonous

¹wrath \'rath, *chiefly Brit* 'rȯth\ *n* [ME, fr. OE *wrǣththo*, fr. *wrāth* wroth — more at WROTH] (bef. 12c) **1 :** strong vengeful anger or indignation **2 :** retributory punishment for an offense or a crime **:** divine chastisement *syn* see ANGER

²wrath *adj* [alter. of *wroth*] *archaic* (1535) **:** WRATHFUL

wrath·ful \-fəl\ *adj* (14c) **1 :** filled with wrath **:** IRATE **2 :** arising from, marked by, or indicative of wrath — **wrath·ful·ly** \-fə-lē\ *adv* — **wrath·ful·ness** *n*

wrathy \-ē\ *adj* (1828) **:** WRATHFUL

wreak \'rēk *also* 'rek\ *vt* [ME *wreken*, fr. OE *wrecan* to drive, punish, avenge; akin to OHG *rehhan* to avenge, L *urgēre* to drive on, urge] (bef. 12c) **1 a** *archaic* **:** AVENGE **b :** to cause the infliction of (vengeance or punishment) **2 :** to give free play or course to (malevolent feeling) **3 :** BRING ABOUT, CAUSE ⟨~ havoc⟩

wreath \'rēth\ *n, pl* **wreaths** \'rēthz, 'rēths\ [ME *wrethe*, fr. OE *writha;* akin to OE *wrīthan* to twist — more at WRITHE] (bef. 12c) **:** something intertwined into a circular shape; *esp* **:** GARLAND, CHAPLET

wreathe \'rēth\ *vb* **wreathed; wreath·ing** [*wreath*] *vt* (1530) **1 a :** to shape into a wreath **b :** INTERWEAVE **c :** to cause to coil about something **2 :** to twist or contort so as to show folds or creases **3 :** to encircle or adorn with or as if with a wreath ~ *vi* **1 :** to twist in coils **:** WRITHE **2 a :** to take on the shape of a wreath **b :** to move or extend in circles or spirals

wreathy \'rē-thē, -thē\ *adj* (1644) **1 :** having the form of a wreath **2 :** constituting a wreath

¹wreck \'rek\ *n* [ME *wrek*, fr. AF, of Scand origin; akin to ON *rek* wreck; akin to OE *wrecan* to drive] (13c) **1 :** something cast up on the land by the sea esp. after a shipwreck **2 a :** SHIPWRECK **b :** the action of wrecking or fact or state of being wrecked **:** DESTRUCTION **3 a :** a hulk or the ruins of a wrecked ship **b :** the broken remains of something wrecked or otherwise ruined **c :** something disabled or in a state of ruin or dilapidation; *also* **:** a person or animal of broken constitution, health, or spirits

²wreck *vt* (15c) **1 :** to cast ashore **2 a :** to reduce to a ruinous state by or as if by violence **b :** SHIPWRECCK **c :** to ruin, damage, or imperil by a wreck **d :** to involve in disaster or ruin **3 :** WREAK 3 ~ *vi* **1 :** to become wrecked **2 :** to rob, salvage, or repair wreckage or a wreck

wreck·age \'rek-ij\ *n* (1837) **1 :** the act of wrecking **:** the state of being wrecked **2 a :** something that has been wrecked **b :** broken and disordered parts or material from something wrecked

wreck·er \'rek-ər\ *n* (1802) **1 a :** one that searches for or works on the wrecks of ships (as for rescue or for plunder) **b :** an automotive vehicle with hoisting apparatus and equipment for towing wrecked or disabled automobiles or freeing automobiles stalled in snow or mud **c :** one that salvages junked automobile parts and material **2 :** one that wrecks; *esp* **:** one whose work is the demolition of buildings

wrecker's ball *n* (1967) **:** a heavy iron or steel ball swung or dropped by a derrick to demolish old buildings — called also *wrecking ball*

wrecking bar *n* (ca. 1943) **:** a small crowbar with a claw for pulling nails at one end and a slight bend for prying at the other end

wren \'ren\ *n* [ME *wrenne*, fr. OE *wrenna;* akin to OHG *rentilo* wren] (bef. 12c) **1 :** any of a family (Troglodytidae) of numerous small more or less brown singing birds; *esp* **:** a very small European bird (*Troglodytes troglodytes*) that has a short erect tail and is noted for its song **2 :** any of numerous small singing birds resembling the true wrens in size and habits

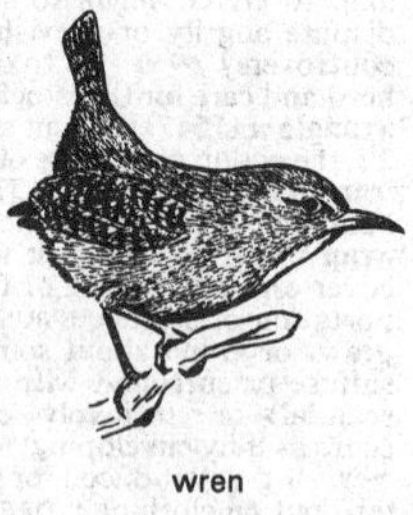
wren

¹wrench \'rench\ *vb* [ME *wrenchen*, fr. OE *wrencan;* akin to OHG *renken*, L *vergere* to bend, incline] *vi* (bef. 12c) **1 :** to move with a violent twist; *also* **:** to undergo twisting **2 :** to pull or strain at something with violent twisting ~ *vt* **1 :** to twist violently **2 :** to injure or disable by a violent twisting or straining **3 :** CHANGE; *esp* **:** DISTORT, PERVERT **4 a :** to pull or tighten by violent twisting or with violence **b :** to snatch forcibly **:** WREST **5 :** to cause to suffer mental anguish **:** RACK — **wrench·ing·ly** \'ren-chiŋ-lē\ *adv*

²wrench *n* (1530) **1 a :** a violent twisting or a pull with or as if with twisting **b :** a sharp twist or sudden jerk straining muscles or ligaments; *also* **:** the resultant injury (as of a joint) **c :** a distorting or perverting alteration **d :** acute emotional distress **:** sudden violent mental change **2 :** a hand or power tool for holding, twisting, or turning an object (as a bolt or nut) **3 :** MONKEY WRENCH 2

¹wrest \'rest\ *vt* [ME *wrasten, wresten*, fr. OE *wrǣstan;* akin to OE *wrīthan* to twist — more at WRITHE] (bef. 12c) **1 :** to pull, force, or move by violent wringing or twisting movements **2 :** to gain with difficulty by or as if by force, violence, or determined labor

²wrest *n* (14c) **1 :** the action of wresting **:** WRENCH **2** *archaic* **:** a key or wrench used for turning pins in a stringed instrument (as a harp or piano)

¹wres·tle \'res-əl, 'ras-\ *vb* **wres·tled; wres·tling** \-(ə-)liŋ\ [ME *wrastlen, wrestlen*, fr. OE *wrǣstlian*, freq. of *wrǣstan*] *vi* (13c) **1 :** to contend by grappling with and striving to trip or throw an opponent down or off balance **2 :** to combat an opposing tendency or force ⟨*wrestling* with his conscience⟩ **3 :** to engage in deep thought, consideration, or debate **4 :** to engage in or as if in a violent or determined struggle ⟨*wrestling* with cumbersome luggage⟩ ~ *vt* **1 a :** to engage in (a match, bout, or fall) in wrestling **b :** to wrestle with ⟨~ an alligator⟩ **2 :** to move by or as if by force — **wres·tler** \'res-lər, 'ras-\ *n*

²wrestle *n* (1593) **:** the action or an instance of wrestling **:** STRUGGLE; *esp* **:** a wrestling bout

wres·tling \'res-liŋ\ *n* (bef. 12c) **:** a sport or contest in which two unarmed individuals struggle hand to hand with each attempting to subdue or unbalance the other

wretch \'rech\ *n* [ME *wrecche*, fr. OE *wrecca* outcast, exile; akin to OE *wrecan* to drive, drive out — more at WREAK] (bef. 12c) **1 :** a miserable person **:** one who is profoundly unhappy or in great misfortune **2 :** a base, despicable, or vile person

wretch·ed \'rech-əd\ *adj* [irreg. fr. *wretch*] (13c) **1 :** deeply afflicted, dejected, or distressed in body or mind **2 :** extremely or deplorably bad or distressing ⟨was in ~ health⟩ ⟨a ~ accident⟩ **3 a :** being or appearing mean, miserable, or contemptible ⟨dressed in ~ old clothes⟩ **b :** very poor in quality or ability **:** INFERIOR ⟨~ workmanship⟩ — **wretch·ed·ly** *adv* — **wretch·ed·ness** *n*

¹wrig·gle \'rig-əl\ *vb* **wrig·gled; wrig·gling** \-(ə-)liŋ\ [ME *wrigglen*, fr. or akin to MLG *wriggeln* to wriggle; akin to OE *wrigian* to turn — more at WRY] *vi* (15c) **1 :** to move the body or a bodily part to and fro with short writhing motions like a worm **:** SQUIRM **2 :** to move or advance by twisting and turning **3 :** to extricate or insinuate oneself or reach a goal as if by wriggling ~ *vt* **1 :** to cause to move in short quick contortions **2 :** to introduce, insinuate, or bring into a state or place by or as if by wriggling — **wrig·gly** \-(ə-)lē\ *adj*

²wriggle *n* (1709) **1 :** a short or quick writhing motion or contortion **2 :** a formation or marking of sinuous design

wrig·gler \'rig-(ə-)lər\ *n* (1631) **:** one that wriggles; *esp* **:** WIGGLER 1

wright \'rīt\ *n* [ME, fr. OE *wyrhta, wryhta* worker, maker; akin to OE *weorc* work — more at WORK] (bef. 12c) **:** a worker esp. in wood — usu. used in combination ⟨ship*wright*⟩ ⟨wheel*wright*⟩

wring \'riŋ\ *vb* **wrung** \'rəŋ\; **wring·ing** \'riŋ-iŋ\ [ME *wringen*, fr. OE *wringan;* akin to OHG *ringan* to struggle, OE *wyrgan* to strangle — more at WORRY] *vt* (bef. 12c) **1 :** to squeeze or twist esp. so as to make dry or to extract moisture or liquid ⟨~ a towel dry⟩ **2 :** to extract or obtain by or as if by twisting and compressing ⟨~ water from a towel⟩ ⟨~ a confession from the suspect⟩ **3 a :** to twist so as to strain or sprain into a distorted shape ⟨I could ~ your neck⟩ **b :** to twist together (clasped hands) as a sign of anguish **4 :** to affect painfully as if by wringing **:** TORMENT ⟨a tragedy that ~s the heart⟩ ~ *vi* **:** SQUIRM, WRITHE — **wring** *n*

wring·er \'riŋ-ər\ *n* (14c) **:** one that wrings: as **a :** a machine or device for pressing out liquid or moisture ⟨a clothes ~⟩ **b :** something that causes pain, hardship, or exertion

¹wrin·kle \'riŋ-kəl\ *n* [ME, back-formation fr. *wrinkled* twisted, winding, prob. fr. OE *gewrinclod*, pp. of *gewrinclian* to wind, fr. *ge-*, perfective prefix + *-wrinclian* (akin to *wrencan* to wrench) — more at CO-, WRENCH] (15c) **1 :** a small ridge or furrow esp. when formed on a surface by the shrinking or contraction of a smooth substance **:** CREASE; *specif* **:** one in the skin esp. when due to age, care, or fatigue **2 a :** METHOD, TECHNIQUE ⟨the latest ~ in selling⟩ **b :** a change in a customary procedure or method **c :** something new or different **:** INNOVATION **3 :** IMPERFECTION, IRREGULARITY — **wrin·kly** \-k(ə-)lē\ *adj*

²wrinkle *vb* **wrin·kled; wrin·kling** \-k(ə-)liŋ\ *vi* (1528) **:** to become marked with or contracted into wrinkles ~ *vt* **:** to contract into wrinkles **:** PUCKER

wrist \'rist\ *n* [ME, fr. OE; akin to OE *wrǣstan* to twist, wrest — more at WREST] (bef. 12c) **1 :** the joint or the region of the joint between the human hand and the arm or a corresponding part on a lower animal **2 :** the part of a garment or glove covering the wrist

wrist·band \'ris(t)-,band\ *n* (1571) **1 :** the part of a sleeve covering the wrist **2 :** a band encircling the wrist

wrist·let \'ris(t)-lət\ *n* (1847) **:** a band encircling the wrist; *esp* **:** a close-fitting knitted band attached to the top of a glove or the end of a sleeve

wrist·lock \'rist-,läk\ *n* (1921) **:** a wrestling hold in which one contestant is thrown or made helpless by a twisting grip on the wrist

wrist pin *n* (ca. 1875) **:** a stud or pin that forms a journal (as in a crosshead) for a connecting rod

wrist·watch \'ris-,twäch\ *n* (1896) **:** a small watch that is attached to a bracelet or strap and is worn around the wrist

wrist wrestling *n* (1968) **:** a form of arm wrestling in which opponents interlock thumbs instead of gripping hands

wristy \'ris-tē\ *adj* (1888) **:** involving or using a lot of wrist movement (as in stroking a ball)

writ \'rit\ *n* [ME, fr. OE; akin to OE *wrītan* to write] (bef. 12c) **1 :** something written **:** WRITING ⟨Sacred *Writ*⟩ **2 a :** a formal written document; *specif* **:** a legal instrument in epistolary form issued under seal in the name of the English monarch **b :** an order or mandatory process in writing issued under seal in the name of the sovereign or of a court or judicial officer commanding the person to whom it is directed to perform or refrain from performing an act specified therein ⟨~ of detinue⟩ ⟨~ of entry⟩ ⟨~ of execution⟩ **c :** such a written order constituting a symbol of the power and authority of the issuer — usu. used with *run* ⟨outside the United States where . . . our ~ does not run — Dean Acheson⟩

writ·able \'rīt-ə-bəl\ *adj* (1782) **:** capable of being put in writing

write \'rīt\ *vb* **wrote** \'rōt\; **writ·ten** \'rit-ᵊn\ *also* **writ** \'rit\; **writ·ing** \'rīt-iŋ\ [ME *writen*, fr. OE *wrītan* to scratch, draw, inscribe; akin to OHG *rizan* to tear, Gk *rhinē* file, rasp] *vt* (bef. 12c) **1 a :** to form (as characters or symbols) on a surface with an instrument (as a pen) **b :** to form (as words) by inscribing the characters or symbols of on a surface **c :** to spell in writing ⟨words *written* alike but pronounced differently⟩ **d :** to cover, fill, or fill in by writing ⟨*wrote* ten pages⟩ ⟨~ a check⟩ **2 :** to set down in writing: as **a :** DRAW UP, DRAFT ⟨~ a will⟩ **b** (1) **:** to be the author of **:** COMPOSE ⟨~s poems and essays⟩ (2) **:** to compose in musical form ⟨~ a string quartet⟩ **c :** to express in literary form ⟨if I could ~ the beauty of your eyes —Shak.⟩ **d :** to communicate by letter ⟨~s that he is coming⟩ **e :** to use or exhibit (a specific script, language, or literary form or style) in writing ⟨~ Braille⟩ ⟨~s French with ease⟩ **f :** to write contracts or orders for; *esp* **:** UNDERWRITE ⟨~ life insurance⟩ **3 :** to make a permanent impression of

4 : to communicate with in writing ⟨we'll ~ you when we get there⟩ 5 : ORDAIN, FATE ⟨so be it, it is *written* —D. C. Peattie⟩ 6 : to make evident or obvious ⟨guilt *written* on his face⟩ 7 : to force, effect, introduce, or remove by writing ⟨~ oneself into fame and fortune —Charles Lee⟩ 8 : to take part in or bring about (something worth recording) 9 a : to introduce (information) into the storage device or medium of a computer b : to transfer (information) from the memory store of a computer to its output storage device or medium 10 : SELL ⟨~ a stock option⟩ ~ *vi* 1 a : to make significant characters or inscriptions; *also* : to permit or be adapted to writing b : to form or produce written letters, words, or sentences 2 : to compose, communicate by, or send a letter 3 a : to produce a written work b : to compose music — **write one's own ticket** : to select a course of action or position entirely according to one's wishes — **writ large** : on a larger scale or in a more prominent manner ⟨the problems of modern totalitarianism are only our own problems *writ large* —*Times Lit. Supp.*⟩ — **writ small** : on a smaller scale

write–down \'rīt-ˌdau̇n\ *n* (1932) : a deliberate reduction in the book value of an asset (as to reflect the effect of obsolescence)

write down \(ˈ)rīt-'dau̇n\ *vt* (1588) 1 : to record in written form 2 a : to depreciate, disparage, or injure by writing b : to reduce in status, rank, or value; *esp* : to reduce the book value of ~ *vi* : to write so as to appeal to a lower level of taste, comprehension, or intelligence

write–in \'rīt-ˌin\ *n* (1932) 1 : a vote cast by writing in the name of a candidate 2 : a candidate whose name is written in

write in \(ˈ)rīt-'in\ *vt* (14c) 1 : to insert in a document or text 2 a : to insert (a name not listed on a ballot or voting machine) in an appropriate space b : to cast (a vote) in this manner

write–off \'rīt-ˌȯf\ *n* (1905) 1 : an elimination of an item from the books of account 2 : a reduction in book value of an item (as by way of depreciation)

write off \(ˈ)rīt-'ȯf\ *vt* (1682) 1 a : to reduce the estimated or book value of : DEPRECIATE b : to take off the books : CANCEL ⟨*write off* a bad debt⟩ 2 : to regard or concede to be lost ⟨most were content to *write off* 1979 and look optimistically ahead —*Money*⟩; *also* : DISMISS ⟨was *written off* as an expatriate highbrow —Brendan Gill⟩

write out *vt* (1548) : to write esp. in a full and complete form

writ·er \'rīt-ər\ *n* (bef. 12c) : one who writes: as a : AUTHOR b : one who writes stock options

writ·er·ly \'rīt-ər-lē\ *adj* (1957) : of, relating to, or typical of a writer

writer's block *n* (1950) : a psychological inhibition preventing a writer from proceeding with a piece

writer's cramp *n* (1853) : a painful spasmodic cramp of muscles of the hand or fingers brought on by excessive writing

write–up \'rīt-ˌəp\ *n* (1885) 1 : a written account; *esp* : a flattering article 2 : a deliberate increase in the book value of an asset (as to reflect the effect of inflation)

write up \(ˈ)rīt-'əp\ *vt* (15c) 1 : to make a write-up 2 : to report (a person) esp. for some violation of law or rules

writhe \'rīth\ *vb* **writhed; writh·ing** [ME *writhen*, fr. OE *wrīthan;* akin to ON *ritha* to twist, OE *wrigian* to turn — more at WRY] *vt* (bef. 12c) 1 a : to twist into coils or folds b : to twist so as to distort : WRENCH c : to twist (the body or a bodily part) in pain 2 : INTERTWINE ~ *vi* 1 : to move or proceed with twists and turns 2 : to twist from or as if from pain or struggling 3 : to suffer keenly — **writhe** *n*

writh·en \'rith-ən\ *adj* [ME, fr. OE, fr. pp. of *wrīthan*] (bef. 12c) : being twisted or contorted ⟨~ trees⟩ ⟨a ~ smile⟩

writ·ing \'rīt-iŋ\ *n* (13c) 1 : the act or process of one who writes: as a : the act or art of forming visible letters or characters; *specif* : HANDWRITING 1 b : the act or practice of literary or musical composition 2 : something written: as a : letters or characters that serve as visible signs of ideas, words, or symbols b : a letter, note, or notice used to communicate or record c : a written composition d : INSCRIPTION 3 : a style or form of composition 4 : the occupation of a writer; *esp* : the profession of authorship — **writing on the wall** : HANDWRITING ON THE WALL

writing desk *n* (ca. 1611) : a desk that often has a sloping top for writing on; *also* : a portable case that contains writing materials and has a surface for writing

writing paper *n* (ca. 1548) : paper that is usu. finished with a smooth surface and sized and that can be written on with ink

Writ·ings \'rīt-iŋz\ *n pl* [trans. of LHeb *kĕthūbhīm*] (14c) : HAGIOGRAPHA

writ of assistance (1706) 1 : a writ issued to a law officer (as a sheriff or marshal) for the enforcement of a court order or decree 2 : a writ issued to a law officer to aid in the search for smuggled or illegal goods

writ of certiorari (ca. 1823) : CERTIORARI

writ of election (1936) : a writ used to order the holding of an election; *specif* : one used to call a special election for filling a vacancy in an elective office

writ of error (15c) : a writ used to direct a court usu. to remit the record of a legal action to an appellate court in order that some alleged error in the proceedings or in the judgment may be corrected if it exists

writ of extent (ca. 1861) : a writ formerly used to recover debts of record to the British crown and under which the lands, goods, and person of the debtor might all be seized to secure payment

writ of privilege (15c) : a writ used to deliver a privileged person from custody when arrested in a civil suit

writ of prohibition (ca. 1876) : a writ issued by a superior tribunal to direct an inferior court to cease from the prosecution of a suit depending before it

writ of protection (ca. 1811) : a judicial writ issued to a person required to attend court as party or juror and intended to secure him from arrest in coming, staying, and returning

writ of summons (1660) : a writ issued on behalf of the British monarch summoning a lord spiritual or a lord temporal to attend parliament

[1]**wrong** \'rȯŋ\ *n* [ME, fr. OE *wrang*, fr. (assumed) *wrang*, adj., wrong] (bef. 12c) 1 a : an injurious, unfair, or unjust act : action or conduct inflicting harm without due provocation or just cause b : a violation or invasion of the legal rights of another; *esp* : TORT 2 : something wrong, immoral, or unethical; *esp* : principles, practices, or conduct contrary to justice, goodness, equity, or law 3 : the state, position, or fact of being or doing wrong: as a : the state of being mistaken or incorrect b : the state of being guilty ***syn*** see INJUSTICE

[2]**wrong** *adj* **wrong·er** \'rȯŋ-ər\; **wrong·est** \'rȯŋ-əst\ [ME, fr. (assumed) OE *wrang*, of Scand origin; akin to ON *rangr* awry, wrong; akin to OE *wringan* to wring] (13c) 1 : not according to the moral standard : SINFUL, IMMORAL ⟨thought that war was ~⟩ 2 : not right or proper according to a code, standard, or convention : IMPROPER ⟨it was ~ not to thank your host⟩ 3 : not according to truth or facts : INCORRECT ⟨gave a ~ date⟩ 4 : not satisfactory (as in condition, results, health, or temper) 5 : not in accordance with one's needs, intent, or expectations ⟨took the ~ bus⟩ 6 : of, relating to, or constituting the side of something that is usu. held to be opposite to the principal one, that is the one naturally or by design turned down, inward, or away, or that is the least finished or polished — **wrong·ly** \'rȯŋ-lē\ *adv* — **wrong·ness** *n* — **wrong side of the tracks** : a run-down or unfashionable neighborhood

[3]**wrong** *adv* (13c) 1 : without accuracy : INCORRECTLY ⟨guessed ~⟩ 2 : without regard for what is proper or just 3 : in a wrong direction 4 a : in an unsuccessful or unfortunate way b : out of working order or condition 5 : in a false light ⟨don't get me ~⟩

[4]**wrong** *vt* **wronged; wrong·ing** \'rȯŋ-iŋ\ (14c) 1 a : to do wrong to : INJURE, HARM b : to treat disrespectfully or dishonorably : VIOLATE 2 : DEFRAUD — usu. used with *of* 3 : DISCREDIT, MALIGN — **wrong·er** \'rȯŋ-ər\ *n*

syn WRONG, OPPRESS, PERSECUTE, AGGRIEVE mean to injure unjustly or outrageously. WRONG implies inflicting injury either unmerited or out of proportion to what one deserves; OPPRESS suggests inhumane imposing of burdens one cannot endure or exacting more than one can perform; PERSECUTE implies a relentless and unremitting subjection to annoyance or suffering; AGGRIEVE implies suffering caused by an infringement or denial of rights.

wrong·do·er \'rȯŋ-'dü-ər\ *n* (14c) : one that does wrong; *esp* : one who transgresses moral laws

wrong·do·ing \-'dü-iŋ\ *n* (15c) 1 : evil behavior or action 2 : an instance of doing wrong

wronged *adj* (1547) : being injured unjustly : suffering a wrong

wrong·ful \'rȯŋ-fəl\ *adj* (14c) 1 : WRONG, UNJUST 2 a : having no legal sanction : UNLAWFUL b : ILLEGITIMATE — **wrong·ful·ly** \-fə-lē\ *adv* — **wrong·ful·ness** *n*

wrong·head·ed \'rȯŋ-'hed-əd\ *adj* (1732) : stubborn in adherence to wrong opinion or principles : PERVERSE — **wrong·head·ed·ly** *adv* — **wrong·head·ed·ness** *n*

wrote *past of* WRITE

wroth \'rȯth *also* 'rōth\ *adj* [ME, fr. OE *wrāth;* akin to OHG *reid* twisted, OE *wrīthan* to writhe] (bef. 12c) : intensely angry : highly incensed : WRATHFUL

wrought \'rȯt\ *adj* [ME, fr. pp. of *worken* to work] (13c) 1 : worked into shape by artistry or effort : FASHIONED, FORMED ⟨carefully ~ essays⟩ 2 : elaborately embellished : ORNAMENTED 3 : processed for use : MANUFACTURED ⟨~ silk⟩ 4 : beaten into shape by tools : HAMMERED — used of metals 5 : deeply stirred : EXCITED — often used with *up* ⟨gets easily ~ up over nothing⟩

wrought iron *n* (1678) : a commercial form of iron that is tough, malleable, and relatively soft, contains less than 0.3 percent and usu. less than 0.1 percent carbon, and carries 1 or 2 percent of slag mechanically mixed with it

wrung *past and past part of* WRING

[1]**wry** \'rī\ *vb* **wried; wry·ing** [ME *wrien*, fr. OE *wrigian* to turn; akin to MHG *rigel* kerchief wound around the head, Gk *rhoikos* crooked] *vi* (14c) : TWIST, WRITHE ~ *vt* : to pull out of or as if out of proper shape : make awry

[2]**wry** *adj* **wry·er** \'rī(-ə)r\; **wry·est** \'rī-əst\ (1523) 1 : having a bent or twisted shape or condition ⟨a ~ smile⟩; *esp* : turned abnormally to one side ⟨a ~ neck⟩ 2 : marked by perversity : WRONGHEADED 3 : cleverly and often ironically or grimly humorous — **wry·ly** \'rī-lē\ *adv* — **wry·ness** *n*

wry·neck \'rī-ˌnek\ *n* (ca. 1585) 1 : either of two woodpeckers (*Jynx torquilla* or *J. ruficollis*) that differ from the typical woodpeckers in having soft tail feathers and a peculiar manner of writhing the neck 2 : TORTICOLLIS

Wu \'wü\ *n* [Chin (Pek) *wu*[2]] (1908) : a group of Chinese dialects spoken in the lower Yangtze valley

wud \'wüd\ *adj* [alter. of [1]*wood*] *chiefly Scot* (1772) : INSANE, MAD

wul·fen·ite \'wu̇l-fə-ˌnīt\ *n* [G *wulfenit*, fr. F. X. von *Wulfen* †1805 Austrian mineralogist] (1849) : a tetragonal mineral $PbMoO_4$ that is a complex oxide of lead and molybdenum and that occurs usu. in bright orange-yellow to red, gray, green, or brown tabular crystals

wun·der·kind \'vu̇n-dər-ˌkint\ *n, pl* **wun·der·kin·der** \-ˌkin-dər\ [G, fr. *wunder* wonder (fr. OHG *wuntar*) + *kind* child — more at WONDER] (1891) : a child prodigy; *also* : one who succeeds in a competitive or highly difficult field or profession at an early age

wurst \'wərst, 'wu̇(ə)rst, 'wu̇s(h)t\ *n* [G, fr. OHG; akin to OHG *werran* to confuse — more at WAR] (1855) : SAUSAGE

wurzel *n* (1888) : MANGEL-WURZEL

Wy·an·dot \'wī-ən-ˌdät *also* 'wīn-\ *n* (1749) : a member of a subgroup of the Hurons

wy·an·dotte \-ˌdät\ *n* [prob. fr. *Wyandotte* (Wyandot)] (1884) : any of an American breed of medium-sized domestic fowls raised for meat and eggs

Wyc·liff·ite \'wik-lə-ˌfīt\ *n* [John *Wycliffe*] (1580) : LOLLARD — **Wycliffite** *adj*

wye \'wī\ *n* (1857) 1 : a Y-shaped part or object 2 : the letter *y*

wy·lie·coat \'wī-lē-ˌkōt, 'wil-ē-\ *n* [ME (Sc) *wyle cot*] (15c) 1 *chiefly Scot* : a warm undergarment 2 *chiefly Scot* : PETTICOAT

wyn *or* **wynn** \'win\ *var of* [2]WEN

\ə\ abut \ᵊ\ kitten, F table \ər\ further \a\ ash \ā\ ace \ä\ cot, cart \au̇\ out \ch\ chin \e\ bet \ē\ easy \g\ go \i\ hit \ī\ ice \j\ job \ŋ\ sing \ō\ go \ȯ\ law \ȯi\ boy \th\ thin \t͟h\ the \ü\ loot \u̇\ foot \y\ yet \zh\ vision \á, k̟, ⁿ, œ, œ̄, ue, ue̅, ʸ\ *see* Guide to Pronunciation

wynd \'wind\ *n* [ME (Sc) *wynde*, prob. fr. *wynden* to wind, proceed, go, fr. OE *windan* to twist — more at WIND] *chiefly Scot* (15c) : a very narrow street

wy·vern \'wī-vərn\ *n* [alter. of ME *wyvere* viper, fr. ONF *wivre*, modif. of L *vipera*] (1610) : a mythical animal usu. represented as a 2-legged winged creature resembling a dragon

¹x \'eks\ *n, pl* **x's** *or* **xs** \'ek-saz\ *often cap, often attrib* **1 a** : the 24th letter of the English alphabet **b** : a graphic representation of this letter **c** : a speech counterpart of orthographic *x* **2** : TEN — see NUMBER table **3** : a graphic device for reproducing the letter *x* **4** : one designated *x* esp. as the 24th in order or class, or the first in an order or class that includes x, y, and sometimes z **5** : an unknown quantity **6** : something shaped like or marked with the letter X
²x *vt* **x-ed** *also* **x'd** *or* **xed** \'ekst\; **x-ing** *or* **x'ing** \'ek-sin\ (1849) **1** : to mark with an *x* **2** : to cancel or obliterate with a series of *x*'s — usu. used with *out*
X \'eks\ *adj, of a motion picture* (1950) : of such a nature that admission is denied to persons under a specified age (as 17) — compare G, PG, PG-13, R
Xan·a·du \'zan-ə-,d(y)ü\ *n* [*Xanadu*, locality in *Kubla Khan* (1798), poem by Samuel T. Coleridge] (1919) : a place (as a town or village) of idyllic beauty
xanth- *or* **xantho-** *comb form* [NL, fr. Gk, fr. *xanthos*; akin to L *canus* gray, white — more at HARE] : yellow ⟨*xanthene*⟩
xan·thate \'zan-,thāt\ *n* (1831) : a salt or ester of any of various thio acids and esp. $C_3H_6OS_2$
xan·thene \-,thēn\ *n* (1898) **1** : a white crystalline heterocyclic compound $C_{13}H_{10}O$; *also* : an isomer of this that is the parent of the colored forms of the xanthene dyes **2** : any of various derivatives of xanthene
xanthene dye *n* (1930) : any of various brilliant fluorescent yellow to pink to bluish red dyes that are characterized by the presence of the xanthene nucleus
xan·thine \'zan-,thēn\ *n* [ISV] (1857) : a feebly basic compound $C_5H_4N_4O_2$ that occurs esp. in animal or plant tissue, is derived from guanine, and yields uric acid on oxidation; *also* : any of various derivatives of this
Xan·thip·pe \zan-'t(h)ip-ē\ *or* **Xan·tip·pe** \-'tip-ē\ *n* [Gk *Xanthippē*, shrewish wife of Socrates] (1691) : an ill-tempered woman
xan·thoch·roi \zan-'thäk-rə-,wī, -'thäk-,rȯi\ *n pl* [NL, fr. *xanth-* + Gk *ōchroi*, nom. pl. masc. of *ōchros* pale] (1866) : white persons having light hair and fair skin — **xan·tho·chro·ic** \,zan(t)-thə-'krō-ik\ *adj* — **xan·tho·chroid** \'zan(t)-thə-,krȯid, zan-'thäk-,rȯid\ *adj or n*
xan·thone \'zan-,thōn\ *n* [ISV] (1894) : a ketone $C_{13}H_8O_2$ that is the parent of several natural yellow pigments
xan·tho·phyll \'zan(t)-thə-,fil\ *n* [F *xanthophylle*, fr. *xanth-* + *-phylle* -phyll] (1838) : any of several neutral yellow to orange carotenoid pigments that are oxygen derivatives of carotenes; *esp* : LUTEIN
Xa·ve·ri·an Brother \zā-,vir-ē-ən-, za-\ *n* [*Xaverian* (of St. Francis Xavier)] (1882) : a member of a Roman Catholic congregation of lay brothers founded by Theodore J. Ryken in Bruges, Belgium, in 1839 and dedicated to education
x-ax·is \'ek-,sak-səs\ *n* (1886) **1** : the axis in a plane Cartesian coordinate system parallel to which abscissas are measured **2** : one of the three axes in a three-dimensional rectangular coordinate system
X chromosome *n* (1911) : a sex chromosome that usu. occurs paired in each female cell and single in each male cell in species in which the male typically has two unlike sex chromosomes — compare Y CHROMOSOME
x-co·or·di·nate \,ek-skō-'ȯrd-nət, -ʼn-ət, -ʼn-,āt\ *n* (1927) : a coordinate whose value is determined by measuring parallel to an x-axis; *specif* : ABSCISSA
xe·bec \'zē-,bek, zi-\ *n* [prob. modif. of F *chebec*, fr. Ar *shabbāk*] (1756) : a usu. 3-masted Mediterranean sailing ship with long overhanging bow and stern
xen- *or* **xeno-** *comb form* [LL, fr. Gk, fr. *xenos* stranger, guest, host] **1** : guest : foreigner ⟨*xenophobia*⟩ **2** : strange : foreign ⟨*xenolith*⟩
xe·nia \'zē-nē-ə, -nyə\ *n* [NL, fr. Gk, hospitality, fr. *xenos* host] (1899) : the effect of genes introduced by a male nucleus on structures (as endosperm or the fruit of a seed plant) other than the embryo

xebec

xe·no·bi·ot·ic \,zen-ō-bī-'ät-ik, ,zēn-, -bē-\ *n* (ca. 1919) : a chemical compound (as a drug, pesticide, or carcinogen) that is foreign to a living organism — **xenobiotic** *adj*
xe·no·di·ag·no·sis \-,dī-ig-'nō-səs, ,zēn-\ *n* [NL] (ca. 1929) : the detection of a parasite (as of man) by feeding a suitable intermediate host (as an insect) on supposedly infected material (as blood) and later examining it for the parasite — **xe·no·di·ag·nos·tic** \-'näs-tik\ *adj*
xe·no·ge·ne·ic \-jə-'nē-ik\ *adj* [*xen-* + *-geneic* (alter. of *-genic*] (1961) : derived from, originating in, or being a member of another species
xe·no·graft \'zen-ə-,graft, 'zēn-\ *n* (ca. 1961) : a tissue graft carried out between members of different species

xe·no·lith \'zen-ʼl-,ith, 'zēn-\ *n* (1903) : a fragment of a rock included in another rock — **xe·no·lith·ic** \,zen-ʼl-'ith-ik, ,zēn-\ *adj*
xe·non \'zē-,nän, 'zen-,än\ *n* [Gk, neut. of *xenos* strange] (ca. 1898) : a heavy, colorless, and relatively inert gaseous element that occurs in air as about one part in 20 million by volume and is used in thyratrons and specialized flashtubes — see ELEMENT table
xe·no·phile \'zen-ə-,fil, 'zēn-\ *n* [ISV] (1948) : one attracted to foreign things (as styles or people) — **xe·noph·i·lous** \ze-'näf-ə-ləs, zi-\ *adj*
xe·no·phobe \'zen-ə-,fōb, 'zēn-\ *n* [ISV] (1915) : one unduly fearful of what is foreign and esp. of people of foreign origin — **xe·no·pho·bic** \,zen-ə-'fō-bik, ,zēn-\ *adj*
xe·no·pho·bia \,zen-ə-'fō-bē-ə, ,zēn-\ *n* [NL] (1903) : fear and hatred of strangers or foreigners or of anything that is strange or foreign
xe·no·tro·pic \-'träp-ik, -trōp-\ *adj* (1973) : replicating or reproducing only in cells other than those of the host species ⟨~ viruses⟩
xer- *or* **xero-** *comb form* [Gk, fr. Gk *xēr-*, *xēro-*, fr. *xēros* — more at SERENE] : dry ⟨*xeric*⟩ ⟨*xerophyte*⟩
xe·ric \'zir-ik, 'zer-\ *adj* (1926) : characterized by, relating to, or requiring only a small amount of moisture ⟨a ~ habitat⟩ ⟨a ~ plant⟩ — compare HYDRIC, MESIC
xe·ro·der·ma pig·men·to·sum \,zir-ə-'dər-mə-,pig-mən-'tō-səm, -,men-\ *n* [NL *xer-* + *-derma* + *pigmentosum*, fr. L *pigmentum* pigment + L *-osum*, neut. of *-osus -ose*] (1884) : a genetic condition inherited as a recessive autosomal trait that is caused by a defect in mechanisms that repair DNA mutations (as those caused by ultraviolet light) and is characterized by the development of pigment abnormalities and multiple skin cancers in body areas exposed to the sun
xe·rog·ra·phy \zə-'räg-rə-fē, zir-'äg-\ *n* [ISV] (1948) : a process for copying graphic matter by the action of light on an electrically charged photoconductive insulating surface in which the latent image is developed with a resinous powder — **xe·ro·graph·ic** \,zir-ə-'graf-ik\ *adj* — **xe·ro·graph·i·cal·ly** \-i-k(ə-)lē\ *adv*
xe·roph·i·lous \zə-'räf-ə-ləs, zir-'äf-\ *or* **xe·ro·phile** \'zir-ə-,fil\ *adj* (1863) : thriving in or tolerant or characteristic of a xeric environment — **xe·roph·i·ly** \zə-'räf-ə-lē, zir-'äf-\ *n*
xe·roph·thal·mia \,zir-,äf-'thal-mē-ə, -,äp-'thal-\ *n* [LL, fr. Gk *xēroph-thalmia*, fr. *xēr- xer-* + *ophthalmia* ophthalmia] (1656) : a dry thickened lusterless condition of the eyeball resulting from a severe systemic deficiency of vitamin A — **xe·roph·thal·mic** \-mik\ *adj*
xe·ro·phyte \'zir-ə-,fit\ *n* (1897) : a plant structurally adapted for life and growth with a limited water supply esp. by means of mechanisms that limit transpiration or that provide for the storage of water — **xe·ro·phyt·ic** \,zir-ə-'fit-ik\ *adj* — **xe·ro·phyt·ism** \'zir-ə-,fit-,iz-əm\ *n*
xe·ro·ra·di·og·ra·phy \,zir-ō-,rād-ē-'äg-rə-fē\ *n* (1949) : radiography used esp. in screening for breast cancer that produces an image on paper using X rays in a manner similar to the way an image is produced by light in xerography
xe·ro·ther·mic \,zir-ō-'thər-mik\ *adj* (1904) **1** : characterized by heat and dryness **2** : adapted to or thriving in a hot dry environment
Xe·rox \'zi(ə)r-,äks, 'zē-,räks\ *trademark* — used for a xerographic copier
x height *n* (ca. 1949) : the height of a lowercase x used to represent the height of the main body of a lowercase letter
xi \'zī, 'ksī\ *n, pl* **xis** [Gk *xei*] (1823) : the 14th letter of the Greek alphabet — see ALPHABET table
x-in·ter·cept \'ek-'sint-ər-,sept\ *n* (ca. 1939) : the x-coordinate of a point where a line, curve, or surface intersects the x-axis
xi·phi·ster·num \,zī-fə-'stər-nəm, ,zif-ə-\ *n, pl* **-na** \-nə\ [NL, fr. Gk *xiphos* sword + NL *sternum*] (ca. 1860) : XIPHOID PROCESS
xi·phoid \'zī-,fȯid, 'zif-,ȯid\ *n* [NL *xiphoides*, fr. Gk *xiphoeidēs*, fr. *xiphos*] (1860) : XIPHOID PROCESS — **xiphoid** *adj*
xiphoid process *n* (1873) : the segment of the human sternum that is the third and lowest to the feet
x-ir·ra·di·a·tion \,ek-sir-,ād-ē-'ā-shən\ *n, often cap* (ca. 1899) : X-RADIATION 1
Xmas \'kris-məs *also* 'ek-sməs\ *n* [*X* (symbol for *Christ*, fr. the Gk letter chi (X), initial of *Christos* Christ) + *-mas* (in *Christmas*)] (1551) : CHRISTMAS
x-ra·di·a·tion \,eks-,rād-ē-'ā-shən\ *n, often cap* (1896) **1** : exposure to X rays **2** : radiation composed of X rays
Xray \'eks-,rā\ (1943) : a communications code word for the letter x
x-ray \'eks-,rā\ *vt, often cap* (1899) : to examine, treat, or photograph with X rays
X ray \'eks-,rā\ *n* (1896) **1** : any of the electromagnetic radiations of the same nature as visible radiation but of an extremely short wavelength less than 100 angstroms that is produced by bombarding a metallic target with fast electrons in vacuum or by transition of atoms to lower energy states and that has the properties of ionizing gases upon passage through it, of penetrating various thicknesses of all solids, of producing secondary radiations by impinging on material bodies, of acting on photographic films and plates as light does, and of causing fluorescent screens to emit light **2** : a photograph obtained by use of X rays — **X-ray** \'eks-,rā\ *adj*

X-ray astronomy *n* (1963) : astronomy dealing with investigations of celestial bodies by means of the X rays they emit

X-ray diffraction *n* (1942) : a scattering of X rays by the atoms of a crystal that produces an interference effect so that the diffraction pattern gives information on the structure of the crystal or the identity of a crystalline substance

X-ray photograph *n* (ca. 1934) : a shadow picture made with X rays

X-ray star *n* (1964) : a luminous celestial object emitting a major portion of its radiation in the form of X rays — called also *X-ray source*

X-ray therapy *n* (1926) : medical treatment (as of cancer) by controlled application of X rays

X-ray tube *n* (ca. 1909) : a vacuum tube in which a concentrated stream of electrons strikes a metal target and produces X rays

x-sec·tion \'krös-'sek-shən, -,sek-\ *n* [*x*, rebus for *cross*] (1962) : CROSS SECTION — **x-sec·tion·al** \-shnəl, -shən-²l\ *adj*

xu \'sü\ *n, pl* **xu** [Vietnamese, fr. F *sou* sou] (1948) **1** : a former coin of South Vietnam equivalent to the cent **2** — see *dong* at MONEY table

xyl- *or* **xylo-** *comb form* [L, fr. Gk, fr. *xylon*] **1** : wood ⟨*xylophone*⟩ **2** : xylene ⟨*xylic*⟩

xy·lan \'zī-,lan\ *n* [ISV] (ca. 1894) : a yellow gummy pentosan that yields xylose on hydrolysis and is abundantly present in plant cell walls and woody tissue

xy·lem \'zī-ləm, -,lem\ *n* [G, fr. Gk *xylon*] (1873) : a complex tissue in the vascular system of higher plants that consists of vessels, tracheids, or both usu. together with wood fibers and parenchyma cells, functions chiefly in conduction but also in support and storage, and typically constitutes the woody element (as of a plant stem) — compare PHLOEM

xylem ray *n* (1875) : a vascular ray or portion of a vascular ray located in xylem — called also *wood ray*; compare PHLOEM RAY

xy·lene \'zī-,lēn\ *n* [ISV] (1851) : any of three toxic flammable oily isomeric aromatic hydrocarbons C_8H_{10} that are di-methyl homologues of benzene and are usu. obtained from petroleum or natural gas distillates; *also* : a mixture of xylenes and ethyl-benzene used chiefly as a solvent

xy·li·dine \'zī-lə-,dēn\ *n* [ISV] (1850) : any or a mixture of six toxic liquid or low-melting crystalline isomeric amino derivatives $C_8H_{11}N$ of the xylenes used chiefly as intermediates for azo dyes and in organic synthesis

xy·li·tol \'zī-lə-,tȯl, -,tōl\ *n* [*xyl-* + *-itol*] (ca. 1919) : a crystalline alcohol $C_5H_{12}O_5$ that is a derivative of xylose, is obtained esp. from birch bark, and is used as a sweetener

xy·log·ra·phy \zī-'läg-rə-fē\ *n* [F *xylographie*, fr. *xyl-* + *-graphie* -graphy] (1816) : the art of making engravings on wood — **xy·lo·graph** \'zī-lə-,graf\ *n* — **xy·log·ra·pher** \zī-'läg-rə-fər\ *n* — **xy·lo·graph·ic** \,zī-lə-'graf-ik\ *also* **xy·lo·graph·i·cal** \-i-kəl\ *adj*

xy·lol \'zī-,lȯl, -,lōl\ *n* [ISV] (1851) : XYLENE

xy·loph·a·gous \zī-'läf-ə-gəs\ *adj* [Gk *xylophagos*, fr. *xyl-* + *-phagos* -phagous] (1842) : feeding on or in wood

xy·lo·phone \'zī-lə-,fōn *also* 'zil-ə-\ *n* (1866) : a percussion instrument consisting of a series of wooden bars graduated in length to produce the musical scale, supported on belts of straw or felt, and sounded by striking with two small wooden hammers — **xy·lo·phon·ist** \-,fō-nəst\ *n*

xy·lose \'zī-,lōs, -,lōz\ *n* [ISV] (ca. 1894) : a crystalline aldose sugar $C_5H_{10}O_5$ that is not fermentable with ordinary yeasts and occurs esp. as a constituent of xylans from which it is obtained by hydrolysis

---

Y

y \'wī\ *n, pl* **y's** *or* **ys** \'wīz\ *often cap, often attrib* **1 a** : the 25th letter of the English alphabet **b** : a graphic representation of this letter **c** : a speech counterpart of orthographic *y* **2 a** : a graphic device for reproducing the letter *y* **3** : one designated *y* esp. as the 25th in order or class or the second in order or class when x is made the first **4** : something shaped like the letter Y

Y \'wī\ *n* (ca. 1915) : YMCA

¹-y *also* **-ey** \ē\ *in some dialects, esp Brit, Southern, NewEng, often* i *but not shown as individual entries\ adj suffix* [ME, fr. OE *-ig*; akin to OHG *-ig* -y, L *-icus*, Gk *-ikos*, Skt *-ika*] **1 a** : characterized by : full of ⟨*blossomy*⟩ ⟨*dirty*⟩ ⟨*muddy*⟩ ⟨*clayey*⟩ **b** : having the character of : composed of ⟨*waxy*⟩ **c** : like : like that of ⟨*homey*⟩ ⟨*wintry*⟩ — often with a disparaging connotation ⟨*stagy*⟩ **d** : devoted to : addicted to : enthusiastic over ⟨*horsy*⟩ **2 a** : tending or inclined to ⟨*sleepy*⟩ ⟨*chatty*⟩ **b** : giving occasion for (specified) action ⟨*teary*⟩ **c** : performing (specified) action ⟨*curly*⟩ **3 a** : somewhat : rather ⟨*chilly*⟩ **b** : having (such) characteristics to a marked degree or in an affected or superficial way ⟨*Frenchy*⟩

²-y \same\ *n suffix, pl* **-ies** [ME *-ie*, fr. OF, fr. L *-ia*, fr. Gk *-ia*, *-eia*] **1** : state : condition : quality ⟨*beggary*⟩ **2** : activity, place of business, or goods dealt with ⟨*chandlery*⟩ ⟨*laundry*⟩ **3** : whole body or group ⟨*soldiery*⟩

³-y *n suffix, pl* **-ies** [ME *-ie*, fr. AF, fr. L *-ium*] : instance of a (specified) action ⟨*entreaty*⟩ ⟨*inquiry*⟩

⁴-y — see -IE

yab·ber \'yab-ər\ *n* [prob. modif. (influenced by E *jabber*) of *yabba*, native name in Australia] *Austral* (1874) : TALK, JABBER ⟨all ∼ and chatter ceased around the campfires —Francis Birtles⟩ — **yabber** *vi*

¹yacht \'yät\ *n* [obs. D *jaght*, fr. MLG *jacht*, short for *jachtschiff*, lit., hunting ship] (1557) : any of various relatively small sailing or mechanically driven ships that characteristically have a sharp prow and graceful lines and are ordinarily used for pleasure cruising or racing

²yacht *vi* (1836) : to race or cruise in a yacht

yacht club *n* (1837) : a club organized to promote and regulate yachting and boating

yacht·ing *n* (1836) : the action, fact, or pastime of racing or cruising in a yacht

yachts·man \'yät-smən\ *n* (1862) : a person who owns or sails a yacht

YAG \'yag\ *n* [*y*ttrium *a*luminum *g*arnet] (1965) : a synthetic yttrium aluminum garnet of marked hardness and high refractive index that is used esp. as a gemstone and in laser technology

ya·gi \'yäg-ē, 'yag-\ *n* [Hidetsugu *Yagi* b1886 Jp. engineer] (1945) : a highly directional and selective shortwave antenna consisting of a horizontal conductor of one or two dipoles connected with the receiver or transmitter and of a set of nearly equal insulated dipoles parallel to and on a level with the horizontal conductor

ya·hoo \'yä-(,)hü, 'yä-\ *n, pl* **yahoos** (1726) **1** *cap* : a member of a race of brutes in Swift's *Gulliver's Travels* who have the form and all the vices of man **2** : a boorish, crass, or stupid person — **ya·hoo·ism** \-,iz-əm\ *n*

Yah·weh \'yä-(,)wä, -(,)vä *also* **Yah·veh** \-(,)vä\ *n* [Heb *Yahweh*] : the God of the Hebrews — compare TETRAGRAMMATON

Yah·wism \-,wiz-əm, -,viz-\ *n* (1867) : the worship of Yahweh among the ancient Hebrews

Yah·wis·tic \yä-'wis-tik, -'vis-\ *adj* (ca. 1890) **1** : characterized by the use of *Yahweh* as the name of God **2** : of or relating to Yahwism

¹yak \'yak\ *n, pl* **yaks** *also* **yak** [Tibetan *gyak*] (1795) : a large long-haired wild or domesticated ox (*Bos grunniens*) of Tibet and adjacent elevated parts of central Asia

²yak \'yäk, 'yak\ *n* [imit.] (1946) **1** *slang* : LAUGH **2** *slang* : JOKE, GAG

³yak *also* **yack** *vi* **yakked** *also* **yacked; yak·king** *also* **yack·ing** [origin unknown] (1949) : to talk persistently : CHATTER

⁴yak *also* **yack** \'yak\ *n* (ca. 1950) : persistent or voluble talk

Yak·i·ma \'yak-ə-,mȯ\ *n, pl* **Yakima** *or* **Yakimas** (1838) **1** : a member of a group of Shahaptian peoples of the lower Yakima river valley, south central Washington **2** : the language of the Yakima people

ya·ki·to·ri \,yä-ki-'tȯr-ē\ *n* [Jp, lit., grilled chicken, fr. *yaki* roasting + *tori* bird, chicken] (1964) : bite-sized marinated chicken pieces on skewers

y'all \'yȯl\ *var of* YOU-ALL

yam \'yam\ *n* [earlier *iname*, fr. Pg *inhame* & Sp *ñame*] (1657) **1** : the edible starchy tuberous root of various plants (genus *Dioscorea* of the family Dioscoreaceae) used as a staple food in tropical areas; *also* : a plant producing yams **2** : a moist-fleshed and usu. orange-fleshed sweet potato

ya·men \'yäm-ən\ *n* [Chin (Pek) *ya²-men²*] (1858) : the headquarters or residence of a Chinese government official or department

yam·mer \'yam-ər\ *vi* **yam·mered; yam·mer·ing** \-(ə-)riŋ\ [alter. of ME *yomeren* to murmur, be sad, fr. OE *gēomrian*; akin to OHG *jāmaron* to be sad] (15c) **1 a** : to utter repeated cries of distress or sorrow **b** : WHIMPER **2** : to utter persistent complaints : WHINE **3** : to talk persistently or volubly and often loudly ⟨caused the purists to ∼ for censorship —D. W. Maurer⟩ — **yammer** *n*

yang \'yäŋ, 'yaŋ\ *n* [Chin (Pek) *yang²*] (1893) : the masculine active principle in nature that in Chinese cosmology is exhibited in light, heat, or dryness and that combines with yin to produce all that comes to be

¹yank \'yaŋk\ *n* [origin unknown] (1818) : a strong sudden pull : JERK

²yank *vi* (1848) **1** : to pull or extract with a quick vigorous movement **2** : to remove in or as if in an abrupt manner ⟨∼ed the story from the evening edition⟩ ∼ *vi* : to pull on something with a quick vigorous movement

Yank \'yaŋk\ *n* (1778) : YANKEE

¹Yan·kee \'yaŋ-kē\ *n* [origin unknown] (1758) **1 a** : a native or inhabitant of New England **b** : a native or inhabitant of the northern U.S. **2** : a native or inhabitant of the U.S. — **Yan·kee·dom** \-kēd-əm\ *n* — **Yan·kee·ism** \-kē-,iz-əm\ *n*

²Yankee (ca. 1952) — a communications code word for the letter *y*

Yan·kee–Doo·dle \,yaŋ-kē-'düd-²l\ *n* [*Yankee Doodle*, popular song during the American Revolution] (1770) : YANKEE

yan·qui \'yäŋ-kē\ *n, often cap* [Sp, fr. E *Yankee*] (1928) : a citizen of the U.S. as distinguished from a Latin American

yan·tra \'yən-trə, 'yan-, 'yän-\ *n* [Skt] (ca. 1921) : a geometrical diagram used like an icon usu. in meditation

yap \'yap\ *vi* **yapped; yap·ping** [imit.] (1668) **1** : to bark snappishly : YELP **2** : to talk in a shrill insistent way : CHATTER, SCOLD — **yap·per** *n*

---

[2]**yap** *n* (1826) **1 a :** a quick sharp bark : YELP **b :** shrill insistent talk : CHATTER **2 :** an unsophisticated, ignorant, or uncouth person : BUMPKIN **3** *slang* **:** MOUTH

Ya·qui \'yäk-ē\ *n* (1899) **1 a :** a Taracahitian-speaking people of Sonora, Mexico **b :** a member of such people **2 :** the language of the Yaqui people

Yar·bor·ough \'yär-ˌbər-ə, -ˌbə-rə, -b(ə-)rə\ *n* [Charles Anderson Worsley, 2d Earl of *Yarborough* †1897 Eng. nobleman said to have bet a thousand to one against the dealing of such a hand] (1900) **:** a hand in bridge or whist containing no ace and no card higher than a nine

[1]**yard** \'yärd\ *n* [ME, fr. OE *geard* enclosure, yard; akin to OHG *gart* enclosure, L *hortus* garden] (bef. 12c) **1 a :** a small usu. walled and often paved area open to the sky and adjacent to a building : COURT **b :** the grounds of a building or group of buildings **2 a :** an enclosure for livestock (as poultry) **b** (1) **:** an area with its buildings and facilities set aside for a particular business or activity (2) **:** an assembly or storage area **c :** a system of tracks for storage and maintenance of cars and making up trains **3 :** a locality in a forest where deer herd in winter

[2]**yard** *adj* (1580) **1 :** of, relating to, or employed in the yard surrounding a building ⟨~ light⟩ **2 :** of, relating to, or employed in a railroad yard ⟨~ engine⟩

[3]**yard** *vt* (1758) **1 :** to drive into or confine in a restricted area : HERD, PEN **2 :** to deliver to or store in a yard ~ *vi* **:** to congregate in or as if in a yard

[4]**yard** *n* [ME *yarde*, fr. OE *gierd* twig, measure, yard; akin to OHG *gart* stick, L *hasta* spear] (14c) **1 :** any of various units of measure: as **a :** a unit of length equal in the U.S. to 0.9144 meter — see WEIGHT table **b :** a unit of volume equal to a cubic yard **2 a :** a great length or quantity ⟨remembered ~*s* of facts and figures⟩ **b** *slang* **:** one hundred dollars **3 :** a long spar tapered toward the ends to support and spread the head of a square sail, lateen, or lugsail

[1]**yard·age** \'yärd-ij\ *n* [[1]*yard*] (ca. 1865) **1 :** the use of a livestock enclosure for animals in transit provided by a railroad at a station **2 :** a charge made by a railroad for the use of a livestock enclosure

[2]**yardage** *n* [[4]*yard*] (1900) **1 a :** an aggregate number of yards **b :** the length, extent, or volume of something as measured in yards **2 :** YARD GOODS

yard·arm \'yärd-ˌärm\ *n* (1553) **:** either end of the yard of a square-rigged ship

yard·bird \-ˌbərd\ *n* [[1]*yard*] (ca. 1941) **1 :** a soldier assigned to a menial task or restricted to a limited area as a disciplinary measure **2 :** an untrained or inept enlisted man

yard goods *n pl* (1905) **:** fabrics sold by the yard : PIECE GOODS

yard grass *n* [[1]*yard*] (1822) **:** a coarse annual grass (*Eleusine indica*) with digitate spikes that is widely distributed as a weed — called also *goose grass*

yard line *n* (1949) **:** any of a series of marked or imaginary lines one yard apart on a football field that are parallel to the goal lines and that indicate the distance to the nearest goal line

yard·man \'yärd-mən, -ˌman\ *n* (ca. 1825) **1 :** a man employed to do outdoor work (as mowing lawns) **2 :** one who works in the yard of a commercial establishment; *esp* **:** one who supervises the handling of building materials in a lumberyard **3 :** a railroad man employed in yard service

yard·mas·ter \-ˌmas-tər\ *n* (1872) **:** the man in charge of operations in a railroad yard

yard of ale (ca. 1890) **1 :** a slender horn-shaped glass about three feet tall that holds two or three pints **2 :** the amount contained in a yard of ale

yard sale *n* (1972) **:** GARAGE SALE

yard·stick \'yärd-ˌstik\ *n* (1816) **1 a :** a graduated measuring stick three feet (0.9144 meter) long **b :** a standard basis of calculation **2 :** a standard for making a critical judgment : CRITERION ***syn*** see STANDARD

yare \'ya(ə)r, 'ye(ə)r, 'yär\ *adj* [ME, fr. OE *gearu;* akin to OHG *garo* ready] (bef. 12c) **1** *archaic* **:** set for action : READY **2** *or* **yar** \'yär\ **a :** characterized by speed and agility : NIMBLE, LIVELY **b** *of a ship* **:** easily handled : MANEUVERABLE — **yare** *adv, archaic* — **yare·ly** *adv, archaic*

yar·mul·ke *also* **yar·mel·ke** \'yäm-ə-kə, 'yär-mə(l)-kə\ *n* [Yiddish, fr. Ukrainian & Pol *jarmułka* skullcap] (1944) **:** a skullcap worn esp. by Orthodox and Conservative Jewish males in the synagogue and the home

[1]**yarn** \'yärn\ *n* [ME, fr. OE *gearn;* akin to OHG *garn* yarn, Gk *chordē* string, L *hernia* rupture] (bef. 12c) **1 a :** a continuous often plied strand composed of either natural or man-made fibers or filaments and used in weaving and knitting to form cloth **b :** a similar strand of metal, glass, asbestos, paper, or plastic **2 :** a narrative of adventures; *esp* **:** a tall tale

[2]**yarn** *vi* (1812) **:** to tell a yarn — **yarn·er** *n*

yarn–dye \'yärn-ˌdī\ *vt* (ca. 1939) **:** to dye before weaving or knitting

yar·row \'yar-(ˌ)ō, -ə(-w)\ *n* [ME *yarowe*, fr. OE *gearwe;* akin to OHG *garwa* yarrow] (bef. 12c) **:** a widely naturalized strong-scented Eurasian composite herb (*Achillea millefolium*) with finely dissected leaves and small usu. white corymbose flowers; *also* **:** any of several congeneric plants

yash·mak *also* **yas·mak** \'yas(h)-ˌmak\ *n* [Turk *yaşmak*] (1844) **:** a veil worn by Muslim women that is wrapped around the upper and lower parts of the face so that only the eyes remain exposed to public view

yat·a·ghan \'yat-ə-ˌgan, 'yat-i-gən\ *n* [Turk *yatağan*] (1819) **:** a long knife or short saber common among Muslims that is made without a cross guard and usu. with a double curve to the edge and a nearly straight back

yauld \'yȯl(d)\ *adj* [origin unknown] *chiefly Scot* (1786) **:** VIGOROUS, ENERGETIC

yau·pon \'yü-ˌpän *also* 'yō-, 'yō-\ *n* [Catawba *yopún*, dim. of *yop* tree] (1709) **:** a holly (*Ilex vomitoria*) of the southern U.S. with smooth elliptical leaves and emetic and purgative properties

yau·tia \yau̇t-ē-ə\ *n* [AmerSp *yautía*, fr. Taino] (1901) **:** any of several aroid plants (genus *Xanthosoma*, esp. *X. sagittifolium*) chiefly of tropical America with starchy edible tubers that are cooked and eaten like yams or potatoes; *esp* **:** one of these tubers

[1]**yaw** \'yȯ\ *n* [origin unknown] (1546) **1 :** the action of yawing; *esp* **:** a side to side movement **2 :** the extent of the movement in yawing

[2]**yaw** *vi* (1586) **1 a** *of a ship* **:** to deviate erratically from a course (as when struck by a heavy sea) **b** *of an airplane, spacecraft, or projectile* **:** to turn by angular motion about the vertical axis **2 :** ALTERNATE ⟨restlessly ~*ing* between apparent extremes —Martin Kasindorf⟩

yawl \'yȯl\ *n* [LG *jolle*] (1670) **1 :** a ship's small boat : JOLLY BOAT **2 :** a fore-and-aft rigged sailboat carrying a mainsail and one or more jibs with a mizzenmast far aft

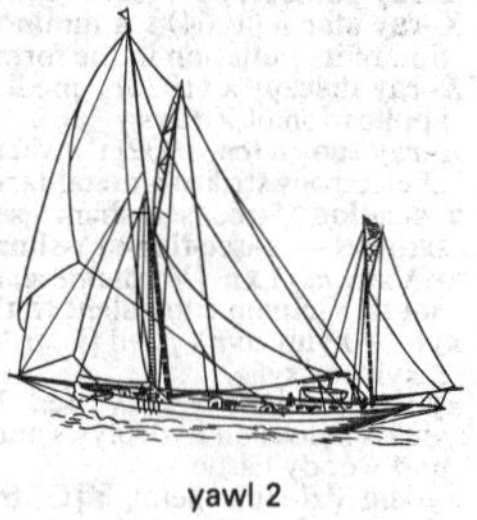

yawl 2

[1]**yawn** \'yȯn, 'yän\ *vb* [ME *yenen, yanen*, fr. OE *ginian;* akin to OHG *ginēn* to yawn, L *hiare*, Gk *chainein*] *vi* (bef. 12c) **1 :** to open wide : GAPE **2 :** to open the mouth wide usu. as an involuntary reaction to fatigue or boredom ~ *vt* **1 :** to utter with a yawn **2 :** to accomplish with or impel by yawns ⟨his grandchildren ~*ed* him to bed —L.L. King⟩

[2]**yawn** *n* (1602) **1 :** GAP, CAVITY **2 :** a deep usu. involuntary intake of breath through the wide open mouth often as an involuntary reaction to fatigue or boredom; *also* **:** a reaction resembling a yawn ⟨a . . . success at the box office but drew only ~*s* from critics —*Current Biog.*⟩ **3 :** [5]BORE

yawn·er *n* (1687) **1 :** one that yawns **2 :** one that causes boredom ⟨the show was a real ~⟩

yawn·ing *adj* (bef. 12c) **1 :** wide open : CAVERNOUS ⟨a ~ hole⟩ **2 :** showing fatigue or boredom by yawns ⟨a ~ audience⟩ — **yawn·ing·ly** \'yō-niŋ-lē\ *adv*

[1]**yawp** *or* **yaup** \'yȯp\ *vi* [ME *yolpen*] (14c) **1 :** to make a raucous noise : SQUAWK **2 :** CLAMOR, COMPLAIN — **yawp·er** *n*

[2]**yawp** *also* **yaup** *n* (1824) **1 :** a raucous noise : SQUAWK **2 :** something suggestive of a raucous noise; *specif* **:** rough vigorous language

yawp·ing *n* (1876) **:** a strident utterance

yaws \'yȯz\ *n pl but sing or pl in constr* [of Cariban origin; akin to Calinago *yáya* yaws] (1679) **:** an infectious contagious tropical disease caused by a spirochete (*Treponema pertenue*) closely resembling the causative agent of syphilis and marked by ulcerating lesions with later bone involvement — called also *frambesia*

y–ax·is \'wī-ˌak-səs\ *n* (1927) **1 :** the axis of a plane Cartesian coordinate system parallel to which ordinates are measured **2 :** one of the three axes in a three-dimensional rectangular coordinate system

Y chromosome *n* (1923) **:** a sex chromosome that is characteristic of male cells in species in which the male typically has two unlike sex chromosomes — compare X CHROMOSOME

yclept *or* **ycleped** [ME, fr. OE *geclipod*, pp. of *clipian* to cry out, name] *past part of* CLEPE

y–co·or·di·nate \ˌwī-kō-'ȯrd-nət, -ᵊn-ət, -ᵊn-ˌāt\ *n* (1927) **:** a coordinate whose value is determined by measuring parallel to a y-axis; *specif* **:** ORDINATE

[1]**ye** \(ˈ)yē\ *pron* [ME, fr. OE *gē;* akin to OHG *ir* you — more at YOU] (bef. 12c) **:** YOU 1 — used orig. only as a plural pronoun of the second person in the subjective case and now used esp. in ecclesiastical or literary language and in various English dialects

[2]**ye** \yē, yə, *or like* [1]THE\ *definite article* [alter. of OE *þē* the; fr. the use by early printers of the letter *y* to represent þ (*th*) of manuscripts] *archaic* (1551) **:** THE ⟨*Ye* Olde Gifte Shoppe⟩

[1]**yea** \'yā\ *adv* [ME *ye, ya*, fr. OE *gēa;* akin to OHG *jā* yes] (bef. 12c) **1 :** YES — used in oral voting **2 :** more than this : not only so but — used as a function word to introduce a more explicit or emphatic phrase ⟨yet the impression, ~ the evidence, is inescapable —J.G. Harrison⟩

[2]**yea** *n* (13c) **1 :** AFFIRMATION, ASSENT **2 a :** an affirmative vote **b :** a person casting a yea vote

yeah \'ye-ə, 'yeu̇, 'ya-ə\ *adv* [by alter.] (1902) **:** YES

yean \'(y)ēn\ *vi* [ME *yenen*, fr. (assumed) OE *geēanian*, fr. OE *ge-*, perfective prefix + *ēanian* to yean; akin to L *agnus* lamb, Gk *amnos*] (ca. 1548) **:** to bring forth young — used of a sheep or goat

yean·ling \-liŋ, -lən\ *n* (1637) **:** LAMB, KID 1a

year \'yi(ə)r\ *n* [ME *yere*, fr. OE *gēar;* akin to OHG *jār* year, Gk *hōros* year, *hōra* season, hour, L *ire* to go — more at ISSUE] (bef. 12c) **1 a :** the period of about 365¼ solar days required for one revolution of the earth around the sun **b :** the time required for the apparent sun to return to an arbitrary fixed or moving reference point in the sky **2 a :** a cycle in the Gregorian calendar of 365 or 366 days divided into 12 months beginning with January and ending with December **b :** a period of time equal to one year of the Gregorian calendar but beginning at a different time **3 :** a calendar year specified usu. by a number ⟨died in the ~ 1900⟩ **4** *pl* **:** a time or era having a special significance **5 a :** 12 months that constitute a measure of age or duration ⟨her 21st ~⟩ — often used in combination ⟨a *year*-old child⟩ **b** *pl* **:** AGE ⟨a man in ~*s* but a child in understanding⟩; *also* **:** the final stage of the normal life span **6 :** a period of time (as the usu. nine-month period in which a school is in session) other than a calendar year

year·book \-ˌbu̇k\ *n* (1710) **1 :** a book published yearly as a report or summary of statistics or facts : ANNUAL **2 :** a school publication that is compiled usu. by a graduating class and that serves as a record of the year's activities

year·ling \'yi(ə)r-liŋ, 'yər-lən\ *n* (15c) **:** one that is a year old: as **a :** an animal one year old or in the second year of its age **b :** a racehorse between January 1st of the year after the year in which it was foaled and the next January 1st — **yearling** *adj*

year·long \'yi(ə)r-'lȯŋ\ *adj* (1813) **:** lasting through a year

[1]**year·ly** \'yi(ə)r-lē\ *adj* (bef. 12c) **1 :** reckoned by the year **2 :** occurring, appearing, made, done, or acted upon every year or once a year : ANNUAL

[2]**yearly** *adv* (bef. 12c) **:** every year : ANNUALLY

Yearly Meeting *n* (1927) **:** an organization uniting several Quarterly Meetings of the Society of Friends

yearn \'yərn\ *vi* [ME *yernen*, fr. OE *giernan;* akin to OHG *gerōn* to desire, L *hortari* to urge, encourage, Gk *chairein* to rejoice] (bef. 12c) **1**

: to long persistently, wistfully, or sadly 2 : to feel tenderness or compassion *syn* see LONG — **yearn·er** *n* — **yearn·ing·ly** \'yər-niŋ-lē\ *adv*

yearn·ing *n* (bef. 12c) : a tender or urgent longing

year of grace (13c) : a year of the Christian era ⟨the *year of grace* 1962⟩

year–round \'yi(ə)r-'raund, 'yiə-'raund\ *adj* (1924) : effective, employed, staying, or operating for the full year : not seasonal ⟨a ~ resort⟩ — **year–round** *adv*

yea–say·er \'yā-,sā-ər, -,se(-ə)r\ *n* (1920) 1 : one whose attitude is that of confident affirmation 2 : YES-MAN

[1]**yeast** \'yēst, *esp Southern & Midland* 'ēst\ *n* [ME *yest,* fr. OE *gist;* akin to MHG *jest* foam, Gk *zein* to boil] (bef. 12c) 1 a : a yellowish surface froth or sediment that occurs esp. in saccharine liquids (as fruit juices) in which it promotes alcoholic fermentation, consists largely of cells of a fungus (family Saccharomycetaceae), and is used esp. in the making of alcoholic liquors and as a leaven in baking b : a commercial product containing yeast plants in a moist or dry medium c (1) : a minute fungus (esp. *Saccharomyces cerevisiae*) that is present and functionally active in yeast, usu. has little or no mycelium, and reproduces by budding (2) : any of various similar fungi (esp. orders Endomycetales and Moniliales) 2 : the foam or spume of waves 3 : something that causes ferment or activity ⟨were all seething with the ~ of revolt —J. F. Dobie⟩

[2]**yeast** *vi* (1819) : FERMENT, FROTH

yeasty \'yē-stē, 'ē-stē\ *adj* **yeast·i·er; -est** (1598) 1 : of, relating to, or resembling yeast 2 a : IMMATURE, UNSETTLED b : marked by change c : full of vitality d : FRIVOLOUS — **yeast·i·ness** \-stē-nəs\ *n*

yech *or* **yecch** \'yək, 'yək, 'yek, 'yek\ *interj* [imit.] (1972) — used to express rejection or disgust

yegg \'yeg, 'yāg\ *n* [origin unknown] (1903) : SAFECRACKER; *also* : ROBBER

[1]**yell** \'yel\ *vb* [ME *yellen,* fr. OE *giellan;* akin to OHG *gellan* to yell, OE *galan* to sing] *vi* (13c) 1 : to utter a loud cry, scream, or shout 2 : to give a cheer usu. in unison ~ *vt* : to utter or declare with or as if with a yell : SHOUT — **yell·er** *n*

[2]**yell** *n* (14c) 1 : SCREAM, SHOUT 2 : a usu. rhythmic cheer used esp. in schools or colleges to encourage athletic teams

[1]**yel·low** \'yel-(,)ō, -ə(-w)\ *adj* [ME *yelwe, yelow,* fr. OE *geolu;* akin to OHG *gelo* yellow, L *helvus* light bay, Gk *chlōros* greenish yellow, Skt *hari* yellowish] (bef. 12c) 1 a : of the color yellow b : become yellowish through age, disease, or discoloration : SALLOW c : having a yellow or light brown complexion or skin 2 a : featuring sensational or scandalous items or ordinary news sensationally distorted ⟨~ journalism⟩ b : MEAN, COWARDLY — **yel·low·ish** \'yel-ə-wish\ *adj*

[2]**yellow** *n* (bef. 12c) 1 : something yellow or marked by a yellow color: as a : a person having yellow or light brown skin b : the yolk of an egg 2 a : a color whose hue resembles that of ripe lemons or sunflowers or is that of the portion of the spectrum lying between green and orange b : a pigment or dye that colors yellow 3 *pl* : JAUNDICE 4 *pl but sing in constr* : any of several plant diseases caused esp. by viruses and marked by yellowing of the foliage and stunting

[3]**yellow** *vt* (1598) : to make yellow : give a yellow tinge or color to ⟨~*ed* by time⟩ ~ *vi* : to become or turn yellow

yellow bile *n* (1881) : a humor believed in medieval physiology to be secreted by the liver and to cause irascibility

yellow birch *n* (1787) : a No. American birch (*Betula lutea*) with thin lustrous gray or yellow bark; *also* : its strong hard pale wood

yel·low–dog \,yel-ō-'dȯg, -ə-'dȯg\ *adj* (1880) 1 : MEAN, CONTEMPTIBLE 2 : of or relating to opposition to trade unionism or a labor union

yellow–dog contract *n* (1920) : an employment contract in which a worker disavows membership in and agrees not to join a labor union during the period of his employment

yellow dwarf *n* (1928) : any of several virus diseases of plants and esp. cereal grasses characterized by yellowing and stunting

yellow enzyme *n* (1938) : a yellow flavoprotein respiratory enzyme

yellow fever *n* (1739) : an acute destructive infectious disease of warm regions marked by sudden onset, prostration, fever, albuminuria, jaundice, and often hemorrhage and caused by a virus transmitted by a mosquito — called also *yellow jack*

yellow–fever mosquito *n* (1905) : a small dark-colored mosquito (*Aëdes aegypti*) that is the usual vector of yellow fever

yel·low·fin tuna \,yel-ō-,fin-, ,yel-ə-\ *n* (1939) : a rather small and nearly cosmopolitan tuna (*Thunnus albacares*) with yellow-tipped fins and delicate light flesh — called also *yellowfin*

yellow–green alga *n* (1930) : any of a division (Chrysophyta) of algae with the chlorophyll masked by brown or yellow pigment

yel·low·ham·mer \'yel-ō-,ham-ər, 'yel-ə-\ *n* [alter. of earlier *yelambre,* fr. (assumed) ME *yelwambre,* fr. ME *yelwe* yellow + (assumed) ME *ambre* yellowhammer, fr. OE *amore;* akin to OHG *amaro* yellowhammer, *amari* emmer] (1556) 1 : a common European finch (*Emberiza citrinella*) having the male largely bright yellow — called also *yellow bunting* 2 : YELLOW-SHAFTED FLICKER

yellow jack *n* (1836) 1 : YELLOW FEVER 2 : a silvery and golden food fish (*Caranx bartholomaei*) of Florida and the West Indies

yellow jacket *n* (1796) 1 : any of various small yellow-marked social wasps (family Vespidae) that commonly nest in the ground 2 *slang* : pentobarbital esp. in a yellow capsule

yellow jessamine *n* (1709) : a twining evergreen shrub (*Gelsemium sempervirens*) of the family Loganiaceae with fragrant yellow flowers — called also *yellow jasmine*

yel·low·legs \'yel-ō-,legz, 'yel-ə-, -,lāgz\ *n pl but sing or pl in constr* (1772) : either of two American shorebirds: a : GREATER YELLOWLEGS b : LESSER YELLOWLEGS

yellow ocher *n* (15c) 1 : a mixture of limonite usu. with clay and silica used as a pigment 2 : a moderate orange yellow

yellow pages *n pl* (1954) : the section of a telephone directory that lists business and professional firms alphabetically by category and that includes classified advertising; *also* : a listing of products or services that is independently published

yellow perch *n* (1805) : a common No. American perch (*Perca flavescens*) that is yellowish with dark green bands and is an excellent food and sport fish

yellow peril *n, often cap Y&P* (1898) 1 : a danger to Western civilization held to arise from expansion of the power and influence of Oriental peoples 2 : a threat to Western living standards from the influx of Oriental laborers willing to work for very low wages

yellow pine *n* (1709) 1 : any of several No. American pines (as a Ponderosa pine) with yellowish wood 2 : the wood of a yellow pine

yellow poplar *n* (1774) 1 : the American tulip tree 2 : TULIPWOOD 1

yel·low–shaft·ed flicker \,yel-ō-,shaf-təd-, ,yel-ə-\ *n* (ca. 1890) : a common large woodpecker (*Colaptes auratus*) of eastern No. America with bright symmetrical markings among which are a black crescent on the breast, red nape, white rump, and yellow shafts to the tail and wing feathers — called also *yellowhammer*

yellow spot *n* (1869) : MACULA LUTEA

yel·low·tail \'yel-ō-,tāl, 'yel-ə-\ *n, pl* **yellowtail** *or* **yellowtails** (1709) : any of various fishes having a yellow or yellowish tail: as a : any of several carangid fishes (genus *Seriola*); *esp* : a sport fish (*S. lalandei*) of the California coast and southward that reaches a length of three feet (0.9144 meter) b : SILVER PERCH a c : a common snapper (*Ocyurus chrysurus*) of the tropical western Atlantic and West Indies that is olive above and broadly striped with yellow along the sides and on the tail and highly esteemed for sport and food — called also *yellowtail snapper*

yel·low·throat \-,thrōt\ *n* (1702) : any of several largely olive American warblers (genus *Geothlypis*); *esp* : one (*G. trichas*) with yellow breast and throat and a whitish belly

yel·low·wood \-,wu̇d\ *n* (1666) 1 : any of various trees having yellowish wood or yielding a yellow extract; *esp* : a leguminous tree (*Cladrastis lutea*) of the southern U.S. having showy white fragrant flowers and yielding a yellow dye 2 : the wood of a yellowwood tree

[1]**yelp** \'yelp\ *n* (ca. 1500) : a sharp shrill bark or cry (as of a dog); *also* : SQUEAL

[2]**yelp** *vb* [ME *yelpen* to boast, cry out, fr. OE *gielpan* to boast, exult; akin to OHG *gelph* outcry, Lith *gulbinti* to praise] *vi* (1553) : to utter a sharp quick shrill cry ⟨dogs ~⟩ ~ *vt* : to utter with a yelp

yelp·er \'yel-pər\ *n* (1673) 1 : one that yelps; *esp* : a yelping dog 2 : an instrument used by hunters to produce a call or whistle imitating the yelp of the wild turkey hen

[1]**yen** \'yen\ *n, pl* **yen** [Jp *en*] (1875) — see MONEY table

[2]**yen** *n* [obs. E slang *yen-yen* craving for opium, fr. Chin (Cant) *in-yăn,* fr. *in* opium + *yăn* craving] (1908) : a strong desire or propensity : LONGING; *also* : URGE

[3]**yen** *vi* **yenned; yen·ning** (1921) : to have an intense desire : LONG, YEARN

yen–shee \'yen-'shē\ *n* [Chin (Cant) *in shí,* fr. *in* opium + *shí* excrement, filth] (1912) : the residue formed in the bowl of an opium pipe by smoking

yen·ta \'yent-ə\ *n* [Yiddish *yente* vulgar woman, prob. fr. the name *Yente*] (1939) : one that meddles; *also* : BLABBERMOUTH, GOSSIP

yeo·man \'yō-mən\ *n* [ME *yoman*] (14c) 1 a : an attendant or officer in a royal or noble household b : a person attending or assisting another : RETAINER c : YEOMAN OF THE GUARD d : a naval petty officer who performs clerical duties 2 a : a small farmer who cultivates his own land; *specif* : one belonging to a class of English freeholders below the gentry b : a person of the social rank of yeoman 3 : one that performs great and loyal service ⟨did a ~'s job in seeing the program through⟩

[1]**yeo·man·ly** \-lē\ *adv* (14c) : in a manner befitting a yeoman : BRAVELY

[2]**yeomanly** *adj* (1576) 1 : of, relating to, or having the rank of a yeoman 2 : becoming or suitable to a yeoman : STURDY, LOYAL

yeoman of the guard (15c) : a member of a military corps attached to the British royal household that serves as ceremonial attendants of the sovereign and as warders of the Tower of London

yeo·man·ry \'yō-mən-rē\ *n* (14c) 1 : the body of yeomen; *specif* : the body of small landed proprietors of the middle class 2 : a British volunteer cavalry force created from yeomen in 1761 as a home defense force and reorganized in 1907 as part of the territorial force

yep \'yep, *or with glottal stop instead of* p\ *adv* [by alter.] (1891) : YES

-yer — see -ER

yer·ba ma·té \,yer-bə-'mä-,tā, ,yər-\ *n* [AmerSp *yerba mate,* fr. *yerba* herb (fr. L *herba*) + *mate* maté] (1843) : MATÉ

[1]**yerk** \'yərk\ *vt* [ME *yerken* to bind tightly] (ca. 1520) 1 *dial* : to beat vigorously : THRASH 2 *dial* : to attack or excite vigorously : GOAD

[2]**yerk** *n* (1581) 1 *Scot* : a lashing out : KICK 2 *dial* : JERK 1

[1]**yes** \'yes, 'yeu̇, 'e-(y)ə *are three of many variants*\ *adv* [ME, fr. OE *gēse*] (bef. 12c) 1 — used as a function word to express assent or agreement ⟨are you ready? *Yes,* I am⟩ 2 — used as a function word usu. to introduce correction or contradiction of a negative assertion or direction ⟨don't say that! *Yes,* I will⟩ 3 — used as a function word to introduce a more emphatic or explicit phrase 4 — used as a function word to indicate uncertainty or polite interest or attentiveness

[2]**yes** \'yes\ *n* (bef. 12c) : an affirmative reply : YEA

ye·shi·va *or* **ye·shi·vah** \yə-'shē-və\ *n, pl* **yeshivas** *or* **ye·shi·voth** \-,shē-'vōt(h)\ [LHeb *yĕshībhāh*] (1926) 1 : a school for talmudic study 2 : an Orthodox Jewish rabbinical seminary 3 : a Jewish day school providing secular and religious instruction

yes–man \'yes-,man\ *n* (1913) : a person who agrees with everything that is said to him; *esp* : one who endorses or supports without criticism every opinion or proposal of an associate or superior

yes·ter \'yes-tər\ *adj, archaic* (1577) : of or relating to yesterday

[1]**yes·ter·day** \'yes-tərd-ē, -(,)ā\ *adv* [ME *yisterday,* fr. OE *giestran dæg,* fr. *giestran* yesterday + *dæg* day; akin to OHG *gestaron* yesterday, L *heri,* Gk *chthes*] (bef. 12c) 1 : on the day last past : on the day preceding today 2 : at a time not long past : only a short time ago ⟨I wasn't born ~⟩ — **yesterday** *adj*

[2]**yesterday** *n* (bef. 12c) 1 : the day last past : the day next before the present 2 : recent time : time not long past 3 : past time — usu. used in pl.

yes·ter·year \'yes-tər-,yi(ə)r\ *n* [*yesterday* + *year*] (1870) 1 : last year 2 : the recent past — **yesteryear** *adv*

yes·treen \ye-ˈstrēn\ *n* [ME (Sc) *yistrevin,* fr. *yisterday* + *evin* evening, alter. of *even* [1]even] *chiefly Scot* (14c) : last evening or night — **yes·treen** *adv*

[1]**yet** \(ˈ)yet\ *adv* [ME, fr. OE *giet;* akin to OFris *ieta* yet] (bef. 12c) **1 a** : in addition : BESIDES ⟨gives ~ another reason⟩ **b** : EVEN 2c ⟨a ~ higher speed⟩ **c** : on top of everything else : no less ⟨had wells going dry. Between two large lakes, ~ —J.H. Buzard⟩ **2 a** (1) : up to now : so far ⟨hasn't done much ~⟩ (2) : at this or that time : so soon as now ⟨not time to go ~⟩ **b** : continuously up to the present or a specified time : STILL ⟨is ~ a new country⟩ **c** : at a future time : EVENTUALLY ⟨may ~ see the light⟩ **3** : NEVERTHELESS, HOWEVER — **as yet** : up to the present time

[2]**yet** *conj* (bef. 12c) : but nevertheless : BUT

ye·ti \ˈyet-ē, ˈyāt-\ *n* [Tibetan] (1951) : ABOMINABLE SNOWMAN

yeuk \ˈyük\ *vi* [ME (northern) *yukyn,* fr. OE *giccan*] *chiefly Scot* (1551) : ITCH

yew \ˈyü\ *n* [ME *ew,* fr. OE *īw;* akin to OHG *īwa* yew, OIr *éo*] (bef. 12c) **1 a** : any of a genus (*Taxus* of the family Taxaceae, the yew family) of evergreen trees and shrubs with stiff linear leaves and fruits with a fleshy aril: as (1) : a long-lived Eurasian tree or shrub (*T. baccata*) — called also *English yew* (2) : a low straggling bush (*T. canadensis*) of the eastern U.S. and Canada **b** : the wood of a yew; *esp* : the heavy fine-grained wood of English yew **2** *archaic* : an archery bow made of yew

Ygerne \ē-ˈge(ə)rn\ *n* : IGRAINE

Ygg·dra·sil \ˈig-drə-ˌsil\ *n* [ON] : a huge ash tree in Norse mythology that overspreads the world and binds earth, hell, and heaven together

YHWH \ˈyä-(ˌ)wā, -(ˌ)vā\ *n* : YAHWEH — compare TETRAGRAMMATON

Yid·dish \ˈyid-ish\ *n* [Yiddish *yidish,* short for *yidish daytsh,* lit., Jewish German, fr. MHG *jüdisch diutsch,* fr. *jüdisch* Jewish (fr. *Jude* Jew) + *diutsch* German] (1886) : a High German language usu. written in Hebrew characters that is spoken by Jews chiefly in eastern Europe and areas to which eastern European Jews have migrated — **Yiddish** *adj*

Yid·dish·ism \ˈyid-i-ˌshiz-əm\ *n* (1904) **1** : a usage, word, phrase, or idiom peculiar to Yiddish **2** : a movement characterized by advocacy of the Yiddish language and culture — **Yid·dish·ist** \-i-shəst\ *n or adj*

[1]**yield** \ˈyē(ə)ld\ *vb* [ME *yielden,* fr. OE *gieldan;* akin to OHG *geltan* to pay] *vt* (bef. 12c) **1** *archaic* : RECOMPENSE, REWARD **2** : to give or render as fitting, rightfully owed, or required **3** : to give up possession of on claim or demand: as **a** : to give up (as one's breath) and so die **b** : to surrender or relinquish to the physical control of another : hand over possession of **c** : to surrender or submit (oneself) to another **d** : to give (oneself) up to an inclination, temptation, or habit **e** : to relinquish one's possession of (as a position of advantage or point of superiority) ⟨~ precedence⟩ **4 a** : to bear or bring forth as a natural product esp. as a result of cultivation ⟨the tree always ~*s* good fruit⟩ **b** : to furnish as return or produce as a result of expended effort ⟨properly handled this soil should ~ good crops⟩ **c** (1) : to produce as return from an expenditure or investment : furnish as profit or interest ⟨a bond that ~*s* 12 percent⟩ (2) : to produce as revenue : BRING IN ⟨the tax is expected to ~ millions⟩ **5** : to give up (as a hit or run) in baseball ⟨~*ed* two runs in the third inning⟩ ~ *vi* **1** : to be fruitful or productive : BEAR, PRODUCE **2** : to give up and cease resistance or contention : SUBMIT, SUCCUMB **3** : to give way to pressure or influence : submit to urging, persuasion, or entreaty **4** : to give way under physical force (as bending, stretching, or breaking) **5 a** : to give place or precedence : acknowledge the superiority of someone else **b** : to be inferior ⟨our beer ~*s* to none⟩ **c** : to give way to or become succeeded by someone or something else **6** : to relinquish the floor of a legislative assembly

syn YIELD, SUBMIT, CAPITULATE, SUCCUMB, RELENT, DEFER mean to give way to someone or something that one can no longer resist. YIELD may apply to any sort or degree of giving way before force, argument, persuasion, or entreaty ⟨after some further argument I *yielded* the point —W.H. Hudson †1922⟩ SUBMIT suggests full surrendering after resistance or conflict to the will or control of another ⟨not only has faith in divine Providence but *submits* to it humbly —Herbert Agar⟩ CAPITULATE stresses the fact of ending all resistance and may imply either a coming to terms (as with an adversary) or hopelessness in the face of an irresistible opposing force ⟨the universities would *capitulate* to a young, vigorous and revolutionary creed —Walter Moberly⟩ SUCCUMB implies weakness and helplessness to the one that gives way or an overwhelming power to the opposing force ⟨the best of constitutions will not prevent ambitious politicians from *succumbing* . . . to the temptations of power —Aldous Huxley⟩ RELENT implies a yielding through pity or mercy by one who holds the upper hand ⟨when a second appeal, couched in more urgent terms, was dispatched to him, he *relented* —Bennet Cerf⟩ DEFER implies a voluntary yielding or submitting out of respect or reverence for or deference and affection toward another ⟨she *deferred* in all things to her uncle —Upton Sinclair⟩ ***syn*** see in addition RELINQUISH

[2]**yield** *n* (15c) **1** : something yielded : PRODUCT; *esp* : the amount or quantity produced or returned ⟨~ of wheat per acre⟩ **2** : the capacity of yielding produce

yield·er \ˈyēl-dər\ *n* (1733) : one that yields: as **a** : a person who surrenders, concedes, or gives in **b** : something that yields produce or products

yield·ing \-diŋ\ *adj* (1533) **1** : PRODUCTIVE ⟨a high-*yielding* wheat⟩ **2** : lacking rigidity or stiffness : FLEXIBLE **3** : disposed to submit or comply

yin \ˈyin\ *n* [Chin (Pek) *yin*[1]] (1893) : the feminine passive principle in nature that in Chinese cosmology is exhibited in darkness, cold, or wetness and that combines with yang to produce all that comes to be

y–in·ter·cept \ˈwī-ˈint-ər-ˌsept\ *n* (ca. 1939) : the y-coordinate of a point where a line, curve, or surface intersects the y-axis

yip \ˈyip\ *vi* **yipped; yip·ping** [imit.] (1907) **1** : to bark sharply, quickly, and often continuously **2** : to utter a short sharp cry — **yip** *n*

yip·pee \ˈyip-ē\ *interj* (1914) — used to express exuberant delight or triumph

-yl \əl, ᵊl, (ˌ)il, ˌēl, *chiefly Brit* ˌīl\ *n comb form* [Gk *hylē* matter, material, lit., wood] : chemical and usu. univalent group ⟨eth*yl*⟩

ylang–ylang \ˌē-ˌläŋ-ˈē-ˌläŋ\ *n* [Tag] (1876) **1** : a tree (*Canangium odoratum*) of the custard-apple family of the Malay archipelago, the Philippines, and adjacent areas that has very fragrant greenish yellow flowers **2** : a perfume distilled from the flowers of the ylang-ylang tree

YMCA \ˌwī-ˌem-(ˌ)sē-ˈā\ *n* [*Y*oung *M*en's *C*hristian *A*ssociation] (1881) : an international organization that promotes the spiritual, intellectual, social, and physical welfare orig. of young men

YMHA \ˌwī-ˌem-ˌā-ˈchā\ *n* [*Y*oung *M*en's *H*ebrew *A*ssociation] (1918) : an organization that promotes the religious, intellectual, social, and physical welfare of Jewish young men

Ymir \ˈē-ˌmi(ə)r\ *n* [ON] : a giant from whose body the gods create the world in Norse mythology

yob \ˈyäb\ *n* [backward spelling for *boy*] *Brit* (1908) : YOBBO

yob·bo \ˈyä-bō\ *n, pl* **yobbos** *or* **yobboes** [*yob* + *-o*] (1938) **1** *Brit* : LOUT, YOKEL **2** *Brit* : HOODLUM

yock \ˈyäk\ *var of* [2]YAK

yod \ˈyȯd, ˈyu̇d\ *n* [Heb *yōdh*] (1735) : the 10th letter of the Hebrew alphabet — see ALPHABET table

[1]**yo·del** \ˈyōd-ᵊl\ *vb* **-deled** *or* **-delled; -del·ing** *or* **-del·ling** \ˈyōd-liŋ, -ᵊl-iŋ\ [G *jodeln*] *vi* (1838) : to sing by suddenly changing from a natural voice to a falsetto and back; *also* : to shout or call in a similar manner ~ *vt* : to sing (a tune) by yodeling — **yo·del·er** \ˈyōd-lər, -ᵊl-ər\ *n*

[2]**yodel** *n* (1849) : a song or refrain sung by yodeling; *also* : a yodeled shout or cry

yo·ga \ˈyō-gə\ *n* [Skt, lit., yoking, fr. *yunakti* he yokes; akin to L *jungere* to join — more at YOKE] (1820) **1** *cap* : a Hindu theistic philosophy teaching the suppression of all activity of body, mind, and will in order that the self may realize its distinction from them and attain liberation **2** : a system of exercises for attaining bodily or mental control and well-being — **yo·gic** \-gik\ *adj, often cap*

yogh \ˈyōk, ˈyōg, ˈyōk\ *n* [ME *yogh*] (14c) : the letter ȝ used in Old English to represent voiced velar and palatal stops and fricatives (as \g\ and \y\) and in Middle English chiefly to represent voiced and voiceless velar and palatal fricatives (as \k̲\ and \y\)

yo·gi \ˈyō-gē\ *also* **yo·gin** \-gən, -ˌgin\ *n* [Skt *yogin,* fr. *yoga*] (1619) **1** : a person who practices yoga **2** *cap* : an adherent of Yoga philosophy **3** : a markedly reflective or mystical person

yo·gurt *also* **yo·ghurt** \ˈyō-gərt\ *n* [Turk *yoğurt*] (1625) : a fermented slightly acid often flavored semisolid food made of whole or skimmed cow's milk and milk solids to which cultures of two bacteria (*Lactobacillus bulgaricus* and *Streptococcus thermophilus*) have been added

yo·him·bine \yō-ˈhim-ˌbēn, -bən\ *n* [ISV, fr. *yohimbe* (an African tree)] (1898) : an alkaloid $C_{21}H_{26}N_2O_3$ that is a weak blocker of alpha-adrenergic receptors and has been used as an aphrodisiac

yoicks \ˈyȯiks\ *interj* (1774) — used as a cry of encouragement to foxhounds

[1]**yoke** \ˈyōk\ *n, pl* **yokes** [ME *yok,* fr. OE *geoc;* akin to OHG *joh* yoke, L *jugum,* Gk *zygon,* Skt *yuga,* L *jungere* to join] (bef. 12c) **1 a** : a wooden bar or frame by which two draft animals (as oxen) are joined at the heads or necks for working together **b** : an arched device formerly laid on the neck of a defeated person **c** : a frame fitted to a person's shoulders to carry a load in two equal portions **d** : a bar by which the end of the tongue of a wagon or carriage is suspended from the collars of the harness **e** (1) : a crosspiece on the head of a boat's rudder (2) : an airplane lever operating the elevators and the ailerons **f** : a frame from which a bell is hung **g** : a clamp or similar piece that embraces two parts to hold or unite them in position **2** *pl usu* **yoke** : two animals yoked or worked together **3 a** (1) : an oppressive agency (2) : SERVITUDE, BONDAGE **b** : TIE, LINK; *esp* : MARRIAGE **4** : a fitted or shaped piece at the top of a skirt or at the shoulder of various garments

[2]**yoke** *vb* **yoked; yok·ing** *vt* (bef. 12c) **1 a** (1) : to put a yoke on (2) : to join in or with a yoke **b** : to attach a draft animal to; *also* : to attach (a draft animal) to something **2** : to join as if by a yoke **3** : to put to work ~ *vi* : to become joined or linked

yoke·fel·low \ˈyōk-ˌfel-(ˌ)ō, -ə(-w)\ *n* (1526) : a close companion : MATE

yo·kel \ˈyō-kəl\ *n* [perh. fr. E dial. *yokel* green woodpecker, of imit. origin] (ca. 1812) : a naive or gullible inhabitant of a rural area or small town

yolk \ˈyōk, ˈyelk (*in cultivated speech, esp Southern*), *also* ˈyōlk, ˈyȯlk, ˈyälk, ˈyəlk\ *also* **yoke** \ˈyōk\ *n* [ME *yolke,* fr. OE *geoloca,* fr. *geolu* yellow — more at YELLOW] (bef. 12c) **1 a** : the yellow spheroidal mass of stored food that forms the inner portion of the egg of a bird or reptile and is surrounded by the white — see EGG illustration **b** *archaic* : the whole contents of an ovum consisting of a protoplasmic formative portion and an inert nutritive portion **c** : material stored in an ovum that supplies food to the developing embryo and consists chiefly of proteins, lecithin, and cholesterol **2** [akin to MD *ieke* yolk (of wool), OE *ēowu* ewe] : oily material in unprocessed sheep wool consisting of wool fat, suint, and debris — **yolked** *adj* — **yolky** *adj*

yolk sac *n* (1861) : a membranous sac that is attached to an embryo and encloses food yolk, that is continuous in most forms through the vitelline duct with the intestinal cavity of the embryo, that being abundantly supplied with blood vessels is throughout embryonic life and in some forms later the chief organ of nutrition, and that in placental mammals is nearly vestigial and functions chiefly prior to the elaboration of the placenta

yolk stalk *n* (1900) : the narrow tubular stalk connecting the yolk sac with the embryo

Yom Kip·pur \ˌyōm-ki-ˈpu̇(ə)r, ˌyȯm-, ˌyäm-; -ˈkip-ər, -(ˌ)u̇(ə)r\ *n* [Heb *yōm kippūr,* fr. *yōm* day + *kippūr* atonement] (1903) : a Jewish holiday observed with fasting and prayer on the 10th day of Tishri in accordance with the rites described in Leviticus 16 — called also *Day of Atonement*

[1]**yon** \ˈyän\ *adj* [ME, fr. OE *geon;* akin to OHG *ienēr,* adj., that, Gk *enē* day after tomorrow] (bef. 12c) : YONDER

[2]**yon** *pron, dial* (14c) : that or those yonder

[3]**yon** *adv* (15c) **1** : YONDER **2** : THITHER ⟨ran hither and ~⟩

[1]**yond** \ˈyänd\ *adv* [ME, fr. OE *geond;* akin to OE *geon*] *archaic* (14c) : YONDER

[2]**yond** *adj, dial* (14c) : YONDER

[1]**yon·der** \ˈyän-dər\ *adv* [ME, fr. *yond* + *-er* (as in *hither*)] (14c) : at or in that indicated more or less distant place usu. within sight

[2]**yonder** *adj* (14c) **1** : farther removed : more distant **2** : being at a distance within view or at a place or in a direction known or indicated

[3]**yonder** *pron* (14c) **:** something that is or is in an indicated more or less distant place

yo·ni \ˈyō-nē\ *n* [Skt, vulva] (1799) **:** a stylized representation of the female genitalia symbolizing the feminine principle in Hindu cosmology — compare LINGAM — **yo·nic** \ˈyō-nik\ *adj*

yoo–hoo \ˈyü-(ˌ)hü\ *interj* (1924) — used to attract attention or as a call to persons

yore \ˈyō(ə)r, ˈyȯ(ə)r\ *n* [ME, fr. *yore,* adv., long ago, fr. OE *gēara,* fr. *gēar* year — more at YEAR] (bef. 12c) **:** time past and esp. long past — usu. used in the phrase *of yore*

York·ist \ˈyȯr-kəst\ *adj* [Edward, Duke of *York* (Edward IV of England)] (1823) **:** of or relating to the English royal house that ruled from 1461 to 1485 — **Yorkist** *n*

York rite \ˈyȯ(ə)rk-\ *n* [*York,* England] (ca. 1909) **1 :** a ceremonial observed by one of the Masonic systems **2 :** a system or organization that observes the York rite and confers in the U.S. 13 degrees of which the last three are in commanderies of Knights Templar — compare SCOTTISH RITE

York·shire \ˈyȯ(ə)rk-ˌshi(ə)r, -shər\ *n* (1906) **:** a white swine of any of several breeds or strains originated in Yorkshire, England

Yorkshire pudding *n* (1747) **:** batter consisting of eggs, flour, and milk that is baked in meat drippings

Yorkshire terrier *n* (1885) **:** any of a breed of compact toy terriers with long straight silky hair mostly bluish gray but tan on the head and chest

Yor·u·ba \ˈyȯr-ə-bə\ *n, pl* **Yoruba** *or* **Yorubas** (1894) **1 :** a member of a Negro people of the eastern Guinea coast mainly between Benin and the lower Niger **2 :** the language of the Yorubas — **Yo·ru·ban** \ˈyȯr-ə-bən\ *n or adj*

you \(ˈ)yü, yə, yē\ *pron* [ME, fr. OE *ēow,* dat. & accus. of *gē* you; akin to OHG *iu,* dat. of *ir* you, Skt *yūyam* you] (bef. 12c) **1 :** the one or ones being addressed — used as the pronoun of the second person singular or plural in any grammatical relation except that of a possessive ⟨~ may sit in that chair⟩ ⟨~ are my friends⟩ ⟨can I pour ~ a cup of tea⟩; used formerly only as a plural pronoun of the second person in the dative or accusative case as direct or indirect object of a verb or as object of a preposition; compare THEE, THOU, YE, YOUR, YOURS **2 :** [3]ONE 2a

you–all \(ˈ)yü-ˈȯl, ˈyü-, ; ˈyȯl\ *pron, chiefly Southern* (1824) **:** YOU — usu. used in addressing two or more persons or sometimes one person as representing also another or others

you'd \(ˌ)yüd, (ˌ)yu̇d, yəd\ **:** you had **:** you would

you'll \(ˌ)yü(ə)l, (ˌ)yu̇l, yəl\ **:** you will **:** you shall

[1]**young** \ˈyəŋ\ *adj* **young·er** \ˈyəŋ-gər\; **young·est** \ˈyəŋ-gəst\ [ME *yong,* fr. OE *geong;* akin to OHG *jung* young, L *juvenis*] (bef. 12c) **1 a :** being in the first or an early stage of life, growth, or development **b :** JUNIOR 1a **c :** of an early, tender, or desirable age for use as food or drink ⟨fresh ~ lamb⟩ ⟨a ~ wine⟩ **2 :** having little experience **3 a :** recently come into being **:** NEW **b :** YOUTHFUL 5 **4 :** of, relating to, or having the characteristics of youth or a young person **5** *cap* **:** representing a new or rejuvenated esp. political group or movement — **young·ish** \ˈyəŋ-ish\ *adj* — **young·ness** \ˈyəŋ-nəs\ *n*

[2]**young** *n, pl* **young** (bef. 12c) **1** *pl* **a :** young persons **:** YOUTH **b :** immature offspring esp. of lower animals **2 :** a single recently born or hatched animal — **with young :** PREGNANT — used of a female animal

young·ber·ry \ˈyəŋ-ˌber-ē\ *n* [B. M. *Young fl* 1900 Am. fruit grower] (1931) **:** the large sweet reddish black fruit of a hybrid between a trailing blackberry and a southern dewberry grown in western and southern U.S.; *also* **:** the trailing hybrid bramble

youn·ger \ˈyəŋ-gər\ *n* (bef. 12c) **:** an inferior in age **:** JUNIOR — usu. used with a possessive pronoun ⟨is several years his ~⟩

youn·gest \ˈyəŋ-gəst\ *n, pl* **youngest** (bef. 12c) **:** one that is the least old; *esp* **:** the youngest child or member of a family

young·ling \ˈyəŋ-liŋ\ *n* (bef. 12c) **:** one that is young; *esp* **:** a young person or animal — **youngling** *adj*

young·ster \ˈyəŋ(k)-stər\ *n* (1589) **1 a :** a young person **:** YOUTH **b :** CHILD **2 :** a young mammal, bird, or plant esp. of a domesticated or cultivated breed or type

Young Turk *n* [*Young Turks,* a 20th cent. revolutionary party in Turkey] (1901) **:** an insurgent or a member of an insurgent group esp. in a political party **:** RADICAL; *broadly* **:** one advocating changes within a usu. established group

youn·ker \ˈyəŋ-kər\ *n* [D *jonker* young nobleman] (1513) **1 :** a young man **2 :** CHILD, YOUNGSTER

your \yər, (ˈ)yu̇(ə)r, (ˈ)yō(ə)r, (ˈ)yȯ(ə)r\ *adj* [ME, fr. OE *ēower;* akin to OE *ēow* you — more at YOU] (bef. 12c) **1 :** of or relating to you or yourself or yourselves esp. as possessor or possessors ⟨~ bodies⟩, agent or agents ⟨~ contributions⟩, or object or objects of an action ⟨~ discharge⟩ **2 :** of or relating to one or oneself ⟨when you face the north, east is at ~ right⟩ **3** — used with little or no meaning almost as an equivalent to the definite article *the* ⟨a trait . . . that sets him apart from ~ average professor —James Breckenridge⟩

you're \yər, (ˌ)yu̇(ə)r, (ˌ)yō(ə)r, (ˌ)yȯ(ə)r, ˌyü-ər\ **:** you are

yours \ˈyu̇(ə)rz, ˈyō(ə)rz, ˈyȯ(ə)rz\ *pron, sing or pl in constr* [ME fr. *your* + *-s* -'s] (1526) **:** that which belongs to you — used without a following noun as a pronoun equivalent in meaning to the adjective *your;* often used esp. with an adverbial modifier in the complimentary close of a letter ⟨~ truly⟩ — **yours truly :** I, ME, MYSELF ⟨I can take care of *yours truly*⟩

your·self \yər-ˈself, *Southern also* -ˈsef\ *pron* (14c) **1 a :** that identical one that is you — used reflexively ⟨you might hurt ~⟩, for emphasis ⟨carry them ~⟩, or in absolute constructions **b :** your normal, healthy, or sane condition **2 :** ONESELF

your·selves \-ˈselvz, *Southern also* -ˈsevz\ *pron pl* (1523) **1 :** those identical ones that are you — used reflexively ⟨get ~ a treat⟩, for emphasis, or in absolute constructions **2 :** your normal, healthy, or sane condition

youth \ˈyüth\ *n, pl* **youths** \ˈyüt͟hz, ˈyüths\ *often attrib* [ME *youthe,* fr. OE *geoguth;* akin to OE *geong* young — more at YOUNG] (bef. 12c) **1 a :** the time of life when one is young; *esp* **:** the period between childhood and maturity **b :** the early period of existence, growth, or development **2 a :** a young person; *esp* **:** a young male between adolescence and maturity **b :** young persons or creatures — usu. pl. in constr. **3 :** the quality or state of being youthful **:** YOUTHFULNESS

youth·ful \ˈyüth-fəl\ *adj* (1590) **1 :** of, relating to, or characteristic of youth **2 :** being young and not yet mature **3 :** marked by or possessing youth **4 :** having the vitality or freshness of youth **:** VIGOROUS **5 :** having accomplished or undergone little erosion — **youth·ful·ly** \-fə-lē\ *adv* — **youth·ful·ness** *n*

youth hostel *n* (1939) **:** HOSTEL 2

youth·quake \-ˌkwāk\ *n* [*youth* + *-quake* (as in *earthquake*)] (1966) **:** the impact of the values, tastes, and mores of youth on the established norms of society

you've \(ˌ)yüv, yəv\ **:** you have

[1]**yowl** \ˈyau̇(ə)l\ *vb* [ME *yowlen*] *vi* (13c) **1 :** to utter a loud long cry of grief, pain, or distress **:** WAIL **2 :** to complain or protest with or as if with yowls ~ *vt* **:** to express with yowling

[2]**yowl** *n* (15c) **:** a loud long mournful wail or howl (as of a cat)

[1]**yo–yo** \ˈyō-(ˌ)yō\ *n, pl* **yo–yos** [native name in Philippines] (1916) **1 :** a thick grooved double disk with a string attached to its center which is made to fall and rise to the hand by unwinding and rewinding on the string **2 :** one that resembles a yo-yo esp. in moving up and down unexpectedly or repeatedly **3 :** a stupid or foolish person

[2]**yo–yo** *adj* (1947) **:** shifting back and forth or up and down uncertainly or unexpectedly

[3]**yo–yo** *vi* **yo–yoed; yo–yo·ing** (1967) **:** to move from one position to another repeatedly **:** FLUCTUATE

yt·ter·bi·um \i-ˈtər-bē-əm\ *n* [NL, fr. *Ytterby,* town in southern Sweden] (1879) **:** a metallic element of the rare-earth group that resembles yttrium and occurs with it and related elements in several minerals — see ELEMENT table

yt·tri·um \ˈi-trē-əm\ *n* [NL, fr. *yttria* yttrium oxide (Y_2O_3), irreg. fr. *Ytterby,* town in southern Sweden] (1822) **:** a metallic element usu. included among the rare-earth metals which it resembles chemically and with which it usu. occurs in minerals — see ELEMENT table

yu·an \ˈyü-ən, yu̇-ˈän\ *n, pl* **yuan** [Chin (Pek) *yüan*[2]] (1917) **1** — see MONEY table **2 :** the dollar of the Republic of China (Taiwan)

Yu·ca·tec \ˈyü-kə-ˌtek\ *n* [Sp *yucateco,* fr. *Yucatán* peninsula, Mexico] (1920) **1 :** a member of an Indian people of the Yucatán peninsula, Mexico **2 :** a Mayan language of the Yucatecs — **Yu·ca·tec·an** \ˌyü-kə-ˈtek-ən\ *adj or n*

yuc·ca \ˈyək-ə\ *n* [NL, fr. Sp *yuca,* of unknown origin] (1664) **:** any of a genus (*Yucca*) of sometimes arborescent plants of the lily family having long often rigid fibrous-margined leaves on a woody base and bearing a large panicle of white blossoms

[1]**yuck** \ˈyək\ *var of* [2]YAK

[2]**yuck** *also* **yuk** *interj* [imit.] (1975) — used to express rejection or disgust ⟨spending hours over some dish and getting, "~, I hate that" —Anne Dowie⟩

yucky \ˈyək-ē\ *adj, slang* (1970) **:** OFFENSIVE, DISTASTEFUL

yu·ga \ˈyu̇g-ə, ˈyüg-\ *n* [Skt, yoke, age — more at YOKE] (1784) **:** one of the four ages of a Hindu world cycle

yuk \ˈyək\ *var of* [2]YAK

Yu·kon time \ˈyü-ˌkän-\ *n* (1950) **:** the time of the 9th time zone west of Greenwich that includes the Yukon Territory and formerly part of southern Alaska — called also *Yukon standard time*

yule \ˈyü(ə)l\ *n, often cap* [ME *yol,* fr. OE *geōl;* akin to ON *jōl* yule] (bef. 12c) **:** the feast of the nativity of Jesus Christ **:** CHRISTMAS

Yule log *n* (1725) **:** a large log formerly put on the hearth on Christmas Eve as the foundation of the fire

yule·tide \ˈyü(ə)l-ˌtīd\ *n, often cap* (15c) **:** CHRISTMASTIDE

Yu·man \ˈyü-mən\ *n* (ca. 1895) **:** an American Indian language family of southwestern U.S. and northern Mexico — **Yuman** *adj*

yum·my \ˈyəm-ē\ *adj* **yum·mi·er; -est** [*yum-yum*] (1926) **:** highly attractive or pleasing; *esp* **:** DELICIOUS, DELECTABLE

yum–yum \ˈyəm-ˈyəm\ *interj* [imit. of the sound of smacking the lips] (ca. 1883) — used to express pleasurable satisfaction esp. in the taste of food

yup \ˈyəp\ *var of* YEP

yup·pie \ˈyə-pē\ *n, often cap* [prob. fr. young urban professional + *-ie*] (1983) **:** a young college-educated adult who is employed in a well-paying profession and who lives and works in or near a large city

Yu·rak \yu̇-ˈrak, ˈyu̇(ə)r-ˌak\ *n* (1931) **:** a Uralic language of northern Russia and Siberia

yurt \ˈyu̇(ə)rt\ *n* [Russ *yurta,* of Turkic origin; akin to Turk *yurt* dwelling] (ca. 1890) **:** a circular domed tent of skins or felt stretched over a collapsible lattice framework and used by the Kirghiz and other Mongol nomads of Siberia; *also* **:** a structure that resembles a yurt usu. in size and design

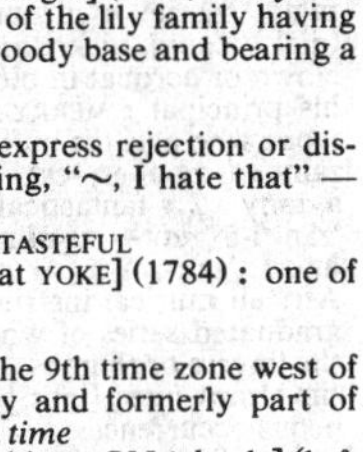

yurt

YWCA \ˌwī-ˌdəb-əl-yü-(ˌ)sē-ˈā, -ˌdəb-ə-yü-\ *n* [*Young Women's Christian Association*] (1887) **:** an international organization that promotes the spiritual, intellectual, social, and physical welfare orig. of young women

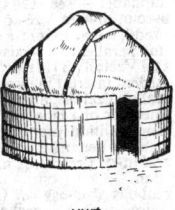

YWHA \-ˌā-ˈchā\ *n* [*Young Women's Hebrew Association*] (1918) **:** an organization that promotes the religious, intellectual, social, and physical welfare of Jewish young women

\ə\ **abut** \ᵊ\ **kitten, F table** \ər\ **further** \a\ **ash** \ā\ **ace** \ä\ **cot, cart** \au̇\ **out** \ch\ **chin** \e\ **bet** \ē\ **easy** \g\ **go** \i\ **hit** \ī\ **ice** \j\ **job** \ŋ\ **sing** \ō\ **go** \ȯ\ **law** \ȯi\ **boy** \th\ **thin** \t͟h\ **the** \ü\ **loot** \u̇\ **foot** \y\ **yet** \zh\ **vision** \à, k̲, ⁿ, œ, œ̄, ue, ue̅, ʸ\ *see* **Guide to Pronunciation**

z \'zē, *Canad, Brit, & Austral* 'zed, *chiefly dial* 'iz-ərd\ *n, pl* **z's** *or* **zs** *often cap, often attrib* **1 a :** the 26th and last letter of the English alphabet **b :** a graphic representation of this letter **c :** a speech counterpart of orthographic *z* **2 :** a graphic device for reproducing the letter *z* **3 :** one designated *z* esp. as the 26th in order or class or the third in order or class when x is made the first **4 :** something shaped like the letter Z

Z *n* (1967) **:** Z PARTICLE

za·ba·glio·ne \ˌzäb-əl-'yō-nē\ *n* [It] (1924) **:** a frothy sauce of whipped egg yolks, sugar, and usu. Marsala wine that is often served on fruit

Zach·a·ri·as \ˌzak-ə-'rī-əs\ *n* [LL, fr. Gk, fr. Heb *Zĕkharyāh*] **:** ZECHARIAH

zad·dik \'tsäd-ik\ *n, pl* **zad·dik·im** \tsä-'dik-əm\ [Heb *ṣaddīq* just, righteous] (ca. 1902) **1 :** a righteous and saintly person by Jewish religious standards **2 :** the spiritual leader of a modern Hasidic community

zaf·fer *or* **zaf·fre** \'zaf-ər\ *n* [It *zaffera,* prob. fr. L *sapphirus* sapphire — more at SAPPHIRE] (1662) **:** an impure oxide of cobalt used in the manufacture of smalt and as a blue ceramic coloring

zaf·tig *also* **zof·tig** \'zäf-tig, 'zȯf-\ *adj* [Yiddish *zaftik* juicy, succulent, fr. G *saftig,* fr. *saft* juice, fr. OHG *saf* — more at SAP] *of a woman* (ca. 1936) **:** having a full rounded figure **:** pleasingly plump

[1]**zag** \'zag\ *n* [zigzag] (1793) **1 a :** one of the sharp turns, angles, or alterations in a zigzag course **b :** one of the short straight lines or sections of a zigzag course at an angle to a zig **2 :** ZIG 2

[2]**zag** *vi* **zagged; zag·ging** (1900) **:** to execute a zag

zaire \zä-'i(ə)r *also* 'zī(ə)r\ *n, pl* **zaires** *or* **zaire** [F *zaïre,* fr. *Zaïre,* former name of Congo river] (1967) — see MONEY table

za·mia \'zā-mē-ə\ *n* [NL, fr. L *zamiae nuces* false MS reading for *azaniae nuces* pine nuts] (1819) **:** any of a genus (*Zamia*) of American cycads with a short thick woody base, a crown of palmlike leaves, and oblong cones

za·min·dar *or* **ze·min·dar** \'zam-ən-ˌdär, 'zem-; zə-ˌmēn-'där\ *n* [Hindi *zamīndār,* fr. Per, fr. *zamīn* land + *-dār* holder] (1683) **1 :** a collector of the land revenue of a district for the government during the period of Muslim rule in India **2 :** a feudal landlord in British India paying the government a fixed revenue

za·min·dari *or* **ze·min·dary** \ˌzam-ən-'där-ē, ˌzem-; zə-ˌmēn-\ *n, pl* **-dar·is** *or* **-dar·ies** [Hindi *zamīndārī,* fr. Per, fr. *zamīndār*] (1757) **1 :** the system of landholding and revenue collection by zamindars **2 :** the land held or administered by a zamindar

zan·der \'zan-dər, 'tsän-\ *n, pl* **zander** *or* **zanders** [G] (1854) **:** a pike perch (*Stizostedion lucioperca*) of central Europe related to the walleyed pike

[1]**za·ny** \'zā-nē\ *n, pl* **zanies** [It *zanni,* a traditional masked clown, fr. It (dial.) *Zanni,* nickname for *Giovanni* John] (1588) **1 :** a subordinate clown or acrobat in old comedies who mimics ludicrously the tricks of his principal **:** MERRY-ANDREW **2 :** a slavish follower **:** TOADY **3 a :** one who acts the buffoon to amuse others **b :** NUT, KOOK

[2]**zany** *adj* **za·ni·er; -est** (1616) **1 :** being or having the characteristics of a zany **2 :** fantastically or absurdly ludicrous — **za·ni·ly** \'zā-nə-lē, 'zān-ᵊl-ē\ *adv* — **za·ni·ness** \'zā-nē-nəs\ *n*

zan·za \'zan-zə\ *n* [Ar *ṣanj* castanets, cymbals, fr. Per *sanj*] (1864) **:** an African musical instrument that consists of a wooden box set with a graduated series of wooden or metal tongues which are plucked with the fingers or thumbs

[1]**zap** \'zap\ *interj* [imit.] (1962) — used to indicate a sudden or instantaneous occurrence

[2]**zap** *n* (1963) **:** ZIP 2

[3]**zap** *vb* **zapped; zap·ping** *vt* (ca. 1942) **1 a :** to destroy or kill by or as if by shooting **b :** to strike with or as if with an electrical charge **2 :** to propel suddenly or speedily ~ *vi* **:** to move with speed or force

za·pa·te·ado \ˌzäp-ə-tā-'äd-(ˌ)ō, ˌsäp-ə-tā-'äu̇\ *n* [Sp, fr. *zapatear* to strike or tap with the shoe, fr. *zapato* shoe] (ca. 1890) **:** a Latin-American dance marked by rhythmic stamping or tapping of the feet

za·pa·teo \ˌzäp-ə-'tā-(ˌ)ō, ˌsäp-\ *n* [Sp, fr. *zapatear*] (1922) **:** ZAPATEADO

Za·po·tec \ˌzäp-ə-'tek, ˌsäp-\ *n* (1904) **:** a member of an Indian people of Mexico

zap·py \'zap-ē\ *adj* (1969) **:** ZIPPY

za·re·ba *or* **za·ri·ba** \zə-'rē-bə\ *n* [Ar *zarībah* enclosure] (1849) **:** an improvised stockade constructed esp. of thorny bushes in parts of Africa

zar·zue·la \ˌzärz-(ə-)'wā-lə\ *n* [Sp, prob. fr. *La Zarzuela,* royal residence near Madrid where it was first performed] (ca. 1890) **:** a usu. comic Spanish operetta

z–ax·is \'zē-ˌak-səs; *Canad, Brit, & Austral* 'zed-\ *n* (ca. 1949) **:** one of the axes in a three-dimensional rectangular coordinate system

za·yin \'zä-yən, 'zī-(ə)n\ *n* [Heb] (1823) **:** the 7th letter of the Hebrew alphabet — see ALPHABET table

z–co·or·di·nate \ˌzē-kō-'ȯrd-nət, -ᵊn-ət, -ᵊn-ˌāt; *Canad, Brit, & Austral* ˌzed-\ *n* (ca. 1956) **:** a coordinate whose value is determined by measuring parallel to a z-axis

zeal \'zē(ə)l\ *n* [ME *zele,* fr. LL *zelus,* fr. Gk *zēlos*] (15c) **:** eagerness and ardent interest in pursuit of something **:** FERVOR ***syn*** see PASSION

zeal·ot \'zel-ət\ *n* [LL *zelotes,* fr. Gk *zēlōtēs,* fr. *zēlos*] (14c) **1** *cap* **:** a member of a fanatical sect arising in Judea during the first century A.D. and militantly opposing the Roman domination of Palestine **2 :** a zealous person; *esp* **:** a fanatical partisan — **zealot** *adj*

zeal·ot·ry \'zel-ə-trē\ *n, pl* **-ries** (1656) **:** excess of zeal **:** fanatical devotion

zeal·ous \'zel-əs\ *adj* (1535) **:** filled with or characterized by zeal ⟨~ missionaries⟩ — **zeal·ous·ly** *adv* — **zeal·ous·ness** *n*

ze·atin \'zē-ə-tən\ *n* [NL *Zea,* genus of grasses including Indian corn + *-tin* (as in *kinetin*) — more at ZEIN] (1964) **:** a cytokinin first isolated from the endosperm of Indian corn

ze·bra \'zēb-rə, *Canad & Brit also* 'zeb-\ *n, pl* **zebras** *also* **zebra** [It, fr. Sp *cebra,* fr. OSp *zebra, enzebro* wild ass, perh. deriv. of L *equifer, equiferus,* lit., wild horse, fr. L *equus* horse + *ferus* wild, trans. of Gk *hippagros* — more at EQUINE, FIERCE] (1600) **:** any of several fleet African mammals (genus *Equus*) related to the horse but distinctively and conspicuously patterned in stripes of black or dark brown and white or buff — **ze·brine** \-ˌrīn\ *adj or n*

ze·bra crossing \'zeb-rə-, 'zēb-\ *n, Brit* (1951) **:** a crosswalk marked by a series of broad white stripes to indicate a crossing-point at which pedestrians have the right-of-way

zebra finch *n* (1889) **:** a small largely gray-and-white Australian weaverbird (*Poephila guttata*) that has black bars on the tail coverts and is often kept as a cage bird

zebra fish *n* (1771) **:** any of various barred fishes; *esp* **:** a very small blue-and-silver-striped Indian danio (*Brachydanio rerio*) often kept in the tropical aquarium

ze·bra·wood \'zēb-rə-ˌwu̇d, 'zeb-\ *n* (1783) **1 :** any of several trees or shrubs having mottled or striped wood; *esp* **:** any of various leguminous African timber trees (genus *Brachystegia*) with pale golden heartwood uniformly striped with dark brown or black **2 :** the wood of a zebrawood

ze·bu \'zē-(ˌ)b(y)ü\ *n* [F *zébu*] (1774) **:** an Asian ox (*Bos indicus*) domesticated and differentiated into many breeds, used chiefly for draft or for milk or flesh, and distinguished from European cattle with which it crosses freely by the presence of a large fleshy hump over the shoulders, a loose skin prolonged into dewlap and folds under the belly, large pendulous ears, and marked resistance to the injurious effects of heat and insect attack

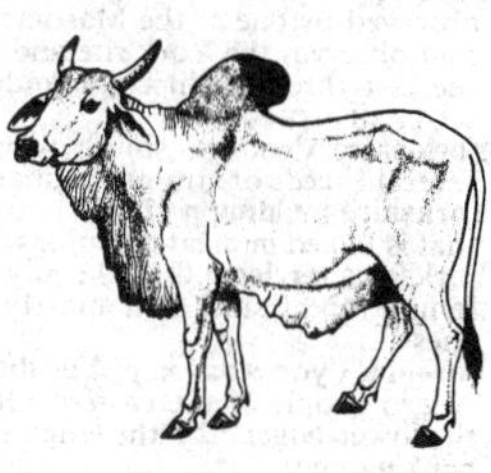

zebu

Zeb·u·lun \'zeb-yə-lən\ *n* [Heb *Zĕbhūlūn*] **:** a son of Jacob and the traditional eponymous ancestor of one of the tribes of Israel

zec·chi·no \ze-'kē-(ˌ)nō, tse-\ *n, pl* **-ni** \-(ˌ)nē\ *or* **-nos** [It — more at SEQUIN] (1617) **:** SEQUIN 1

Zech·a·ri·ah \ˌzek-ə-'rī-ə\ *n* [Heb *Zĕkharyāh*] **1 :** a Hebrew prophet of the 6th century B.C. **2 :** a prophetic book of canonical Jewish and Christian Scripture — see BIBLE table

ze·chin \'zek-ən, ze-'kēn\ *n* [It *zecchino*] (1575) **:** SEQUIN 1

zed \'zed\ *n* [ME, fr. MF *zede,* fr. LL *zeta* zeta, fr. Gk *zēta*] *chiefly Brit* (15c) **:** the letter *z*

zee \'zē\ *n* (1677) **:** the letter *z*

ze·in \'zē-ən\ *n* [NL *Zea,* genus of grasses including Indian corn, fr. Gk, wheat; akin to Skt *yava* barley] (1822) **:** a protein from Indian corn that lacks lysine and tryptophan and is used esp. in making textile fibers, plastics, printing inks, coatings (as varnish), and adhesives and sizes

zeit·ge·ber \'tsīt-ˌgā-bər, 'zīt-\ *n* [G, fr. *zeit* time (fr. OGH *zīt*) + *geber,* lit., giver, donor, fr. *geben* to give, fr. OHG *geban;* akin to OE *giefan* to give — more at TIDE, GIVE] (1968) **:** an environmental agent or event (as the occurrence of light or dark) that provides the stimulus setting or resetting a biological clock of an organism

zeit·geist \'tsīt-ˌgīst, 'zīt-\ *n, often cap* [G, fr. *zeit* + *geist* spirit, fr. OHG — more at GHOST] (1884) **:** the general intellectual, moral, and cultural climate of an era

zel·ko·va tree \'zel-kə-və-, zel-'kō-və-\ *n* [NL, fr. Georgian *tselkva*] (ca. 1890) **:** a tall widely spreading Japanese tree (*Zelkova serrata*) resembling the American elm and often replacing the latter as an ornamental and shade tree because of its resistance to Dutch elm disease — called also *zelkova*

zemst·vo \'zem(p)st-(ˌ)vō, -və\ *n, pl* **zemstvos** [Russ; akin to Russ *zemlya* earth, land, L *humus* — more at HUMBLE] (1865) **:** one of the district and provincial assemblies established in Russia in 1864

Zen \'zen\ *n* [Jp, religious meditation, fr. Chin (Pek) *ch'an²,* fr. Pali *jhāna,* fr. Skt *dhyāna,* fr. *dhyāti* he thinks — more at SEMANTIC] (1902) **:** a Japanese sect of Mahayana Buddhism that aims at enlightenment by direct intuition through meditation

ze·na·na \zə-'nän-ə\ *n* [Hindi *zanāna*] (1760) **:** HAREM, SERAGLIO

Zend–Aves·ta \ˌzen-də-'ves-tə\ *n* [F, fr. MPer *Avastāk va Zand* Avesta and commentary] (1630) **:** AVESTA

ze·ner diode \ˌzē-nər-, ˌzen-ər-\ *n, often cap Z* [Clarence M. *Zener* b1905 Am. physicist] (1960) **:** a silicon semiconductor device used esp. as a voltage regulator

ze·nith \'zē-nəth, *Canad also & Brit usu* 'zen-əth, -ith\ *n* [ME *senith,* fr. MF *cenith,* fr. ML, fr. OSp *zenit,* modif. of Ar *samt (ar-ra's)* way (of the head)] (14c) **1 :** the point of the celestial sphere that is directly opposite the nadir and vertically above the observer **2 :** the highest point reached in the heavens by a celestial body **3 :** culminating point **:** ACME ⟨at the ~ of his powers —John Buchan⟩

ze·nith·al \-əl\ *adj* (1860) **1 :** of, relating to, or located at or near the zenith **2 :** showing correct directions from the center ⟨a ~ map⟩

ze·o·lite \'zē-ə-ˌlīt\ *n* [Sw *zeolit,* fr. Gk *zein* to boil + *-o-* + Sw *-lit* -lite, fr. F *-lite* — more at YEAST] (ca. 1777) **:** any of various hydrous silicates that are analogous in composition to the feldspars, occur as secondary minerals in cavities of lavas, and can act as ion-exchangers; *also* **:** any of various natural or synthesized silicates of similar structure used esp. in water softening and as adsorbents and catalysts — **ze·o·lit·ic** \ˌzē-ə-'lit-ik\ *adj*

Zeph·a·ni·ah \ˌzef-ə-'nī-ə\ *n* [Heb *Ṣĕphanyāh*] **1 :** a Hebrew prophet of the 7th century B.C. **2 :** an apocalyptic book of canonical Jewish and Christian Scripture — see BIBLE table

zeph·yr \'zef-ər\ *n* [ME *Zephirus,* west wind (personified), fr. L *Zephyrus,* god of the west wind (fr. Gk *Zephyros,* fr. *zephyros*), & *zephyrus* west wind, zephyr, fr. Gk *zephyros* west wind, zephyr] (bef. 12c) **1 a :** a breeze from the west **b :** a gentle breeze **2 :** any of various lightweight fabrics and articles of clothing

Zeph·y·rus \'zef-ə-rəs\ *n* [L] **:** the Greek god of the west wind

zep·pe·lin \'zep-(ə-)lən\ *n* [Count Ferdinand von *Zeppelin*] (1900) **:** a rigid airship consisting of a cylindrical trussed and covered frame supported by internal gas cells; *broadly* **:** AIRSHIP

[1]**ze·ro** \'zē-(ˌ)rō, 'zi(ə)r-(ˌ)ō\ *n, pl* **zeros** *also* **zeroes** [F or It; F *zéro,* fr. It *zero,* fr. ML *zephirum,* fr. Ar *ṣifr*] (1604) **1 a :** the arithmetical symbol 0 or Ø denoting the absence of all magnitude or quantity **b :** ADDITIVE IDENTITY; *specif* **:** the number between the set of all negative numbers and the set of all positive numbers **c :** a value of an independent variable that makes a function equal to zero ⟨+2 and −2 are ~s of *f*(*x*)

$= x^2 - 4$〉 2 — see NUMBER table 3 a (1) : the point of departure in reckoning; *specif* : the point from which the graduation of a scale (as of a thermometer) begins (2) : the temperature represented by the zero mark on a thermometer b : the setting or adjustment of the sights of a firearm that causes it to shoot to point of aim at a desired range 4 : an insignificant person or thing : NONENTITY 5 a : a state of total absence or neutrality b : the lowest point : NADIR 6 : something arbitrarily or conveniently designated zero

[2]**zero** *adj* (1879) 1 a : of, relating to, or being a zero b : having no magnitude or quantity : not any 〈~ growth〉 c (1) : ABSENT, LACKING 〈the ~ modification in the past tense of *cut*〉 (2) : having no modified inflectional form 〈a ~ plural〉 2 a *of a cloud ceiling* : limiting vision to 50 feet (15 meters) or less b *of horizontal visibility* : limited to 165 feet (50.3 meters) or less

[3]**zero** *vt* (1913) 1 : to determine or adjust the zero of (as a rifle) 2 a : to concentrate firepower on the exact range of — usu. used with *in* b : to bring to bear on the exact range of a target — usu. used with *in* ~ *vi* 1 : to adjust fire (as of artillery) on a specific target — usu. used with *in* 2 : to move near to or focus attention as if on a target : CLOSE — usu. used with *in*

zero–based *or* **zero–base** *adj* (ca. 1970) : having each item justified on the basis of cost or need 〈~ budgeting〉

zero hour *n* [fr. its being marked by the count of zero in a countdown] (1917) 1 a : the hour at which a planned military operation is scheduled to start b : the time at which a usu. significant or notable event is scheduled to take place 2 : a time when a vital decision or decisive change must be made

zero–sum *adj* (1949) : of, relating to, or being a situation (as a game or relationship) in which a gain for one side entails a corresponding loss for the other side

ze•roth \ˈzē-(ˌ)rōth, ˈzi(ə)r-(ˌ)ōth\ *adj* (1896) : being numbered zero in a series; *also* : ZERO 1 〈the ~ power of a number〉

zero tillage *n* (1963) : NO-TILLAGE

zero vector *n* (ca. 1901) : a vector which is of zero length and all of whose components are zero

zero–zero *adj* (ca. 1939) 1 : characterized by or being atmospheric conditions that reduce ceiling and visibility to zero 2 : limited to zero by atmospheric conditions

zest \ˈzest\ *n* [obs. F (now *zeste*), orange or lemon peel (used as flavoring)] (1709) 1 : a piece of the peel or of the thin outer skin of an orange or lemon used as flavoring 2 : an enjoyably exciting quality : PIQUANCY 3 : keen enjoyment : RELISH, GUSTO — **zest•ful** \-fəl\ *adj* — **zest•ful•ly** \-fə-lē\ *adv* — **zest•ful•ness** *n*

zesty \ˈzes-tē\ *adj* **zest•i•er; -est** (1930) : having or characterized by zest

ze•ta \ˈzāt-ə, ˈzēt-\ *n* [Gk *zēta*] (1823) : the 6th letter of the Greek alphabet — see ALPHABET table

zeug•ma \ˈzüg-mə\ *n* [L, fr. Gk, lit., joining, fr. *zeugnynai* to join; akin to L *jungere* to join — more at YOKE] (ca. 1523) : the use of a word to modify or govern two or more words usu. in such a manner that it applies to each in a different sense or makes sense with only one 〈"opened the door and her heart to the homeless boy" is an example of ~〉

Zeus \ˈzüs\ *n* [Gk] : the king of the gods and husband of Hera in Greek mythology — compare JUPITER

zib•e•line *or* **zib•el•line** \ˈzib-ə-ˌlēn, -ˌlīn\ *n* [MF, sable, fr. OIt *zibellino*, of Slav origin; akin to Russ *sobol'* sable] (1892) : a soft lustrous wool fabric with mohair, alpaca, or camel's hair

zi•do•vu•dine \zi-ˈdō-vyü-ˌdēn\ *n* [*azido*thymidine + connective *-v-* + *-udine* (n. comb. form) nonhalogenated thymidine derivative] (1987) : AZIDOTHYMIDINE

[1]**zig** \ˈzig\ *n* [zigzag] (1840) 1 a : one of the sharp turns, angles, or alterations in a zigzag course b : one of the short straight lines or sections of a zigzag course at an angle to a zag 2 : a sharp alteration or change of direction (as in a process or policy) 〈the quick ~s and zags of his international maneuverings —*N.Y. Times*〉

[2]**zig** *vi* **zigged; zig•ging** (1940) : to execute a zig

zig•gu•rat \ˈzig-ə-ˌrat\ *n* [Akkadian *ziqqurratu* pinnacle] (1877) : an ancient Mesopotamian temple tower consisting of a lofty pyramidal structure built in successive stages with outside staircases and a shrine at the top

[1]**zig•zag** \ˈzig-ˌzag\ *n* [F] (1712) : one of a series of short sharp turns, angles, or alterations in a course; *also* : something having the form or character of such a series 〈a blouse with green ~*s*〉

[2]**zigzag** *adv* (ca. 1730) : in or by a zigzag path or course

[3]**zigzag** *adj* (1750) : having short sharp turns or angles 〈a ~ trail〉

[4]**zigzag** *vb* **zig•zagged; zig•zag•ging** *vt* (1777) : to form into a zigzag ~ *vi* : to lie in, proceed along, or consist of a zigzag course

zilch \ˈzilch\ *adj or n* [origin unknown] (ca. 1966) : ZERO, NOTHING

zil•lion \ˈzil-yən\ *n* [*z* + *-illion* (as in *million*)] (1934) : an indeterminately large number 〈~*s* of mosquitoes〉

[1]**zinc** \ˈziŋk\ *n, often attrib* [G *zink*] (1641) : a bluish white crystalline metallic element of low to intermediate hardness that is ductile when pure but in the commercial form is brittle at ordinary temperatures and becomes ductile on slight heating, occurs abundantly in minerals, is an essential micronutrient for both plants and animals, and is used esp. as a protective coating for iron and steel — see ELEMENT table

[2]**zinc** *vt* **zinced** *or* **zincked** \ˈziŋ(k)t\; **zinc•ing** *or* **zinck•ing** \ˈziŋ-kiŋ\ (1841) : to treat or coat with zinc : GALVANIZE

zinc•ate \ˈziŋ-ˌkāt\ *n* (1872) : a compound formed by reaction of zinc oxide or zinc with solutions of alkalies

zinc blende *n* (1842) : SPHALERITE

zinc chloride *n* (1851) : a poisonous caustic deliquescent salt $ZnCl_2$ used esp. as a wood preservative, drying agent, and catalyst

zinc•ite \ˈziŋ-ˌkīt\ *n* [G *zinkit*, fr. *zink*] (1854) : a brittle deep-red to orange-yellow hexagonal mineral that consists essentially of zinc oxide and occurs in massive or granular form

zincky *or* **zinky** *or* **zincy** \ˈziŋ-kē\ *adj* (1757) : containing or having the appearance of zinc

zinc oxide *n* (1849) : an infusible white solid ZnO used esp. as a pigment, in compounding rubber, and in pharmaceutical and cosmetic preparations

zinc oxide ointment *n* (1936) : an ointment that contains about 20 percent of zinc oxide and is used in treating skin disorders — called also *zinc ointment*

zinc sulfate *n* (1851) : a crystalline salt $ZnSO_4$ used esp. in making a white paint pigment, in printing and dyeing, in sprays and fertilizers, and in medicine as an astringent and emetic

zinc sulfide *n* (1851) : a fluorescent white to yellowish compound ZnS used esp. as a white pigment and a phosphor

zinc white *n* (1847) : a white pigment that consists of zinc oxide

zin•fan•del \ˈzin-fən-ˌdel\ *n* [origin unknown] (1896) : a red table wine of the claret type made from a small black grape that is grown chiefly in California

[1]**zing** \ˈziŋ\ *n* [imit.] (1911) 1 : a shrill humming noise 2 : ENERGY, VIM

[2]**zing** *vi* (1920) 1 : to make or move with a humming sound 2 : ZIP, SPEED ~ *vt* 1 : ZAP 1a 2 : to attack with words : CRITICIZE, SATIRIZE

zing•er \ˈziŋ-ər\ *n* (1955) 1 : something causing or meant to cause interest, surprise, or shock 2 : a pointed witty remark or retort

zingy \ˈziŋ-ē\ *adj* **zing•i•er; -est** [[1]zing] (1945) 1 : enjoyably exciting 〈a ~ musical〉 2 : strikingly attractive or appealing 〈wore a ~ new outfit〉

zinj•an•thro•pus \zin-ˈjan(t)-thrə-pəs, ˌzin-ˌjan-ˈthrō-\ *n, pl* **-pi** \-ˌpī, -ˌpē\ *or* **-pus•es** [NL, fr. Ar *Zīnj* eastern Africa + Gk *anthrōpos* human being] (1959) : a fossil hominid (*Australopithecus boisei*, syn. *Zinjanthropus boisei*) based on skeletal remains from the Late Pliocene or Early Pleistocene of eastern Africa and characterized by very low brow and large molars — **zin•jan•thro•pine** \zin-ˈjan(t)-thrə-ˌpīn\ *adj or n*

zin•nia \ˈzin-ē-ə, ˈzin-yə, ˈzēn-\ *n* [NL, fr. Johann G. Zinn †1759 Ger. botanist] (1767) : any of a small genus (*Zinnia*) of tropical American composite herbs and low shrubs with showy flower heads and long-lasting ray flowers

Zi•on \ˈzī-ən\ *n* [*Zion*, citadel in Palestine which was the nucleus of Jerusalem, fr. ME *Sion*, fr. OE, fr. LL, fr. Heb *Ṣiyōn*] (14c) 1 a : the Jewish people : ISRAEL b : the Jewish homeland that is symbolic of Judaism or of Jewish national aspiration c : the ideal nation or society envisaged by Judaism 2 : HEAVEN 3 : UTOPIA

Zi•on•ism \ˈzī-ə-ˌniz-əm\ *n* (1896) : an international movement orig. for the establishment of a Jewish national or religious community in Palestine and later for the support of modern Israel — **Zi•on•ist** \-nəst\ *adj or n* — **Zi•on•is•tic** \ˌzī-ə-ˈnis-tik\ *adj*

[1]**zip** \ˈzip\ *vb* **zipped; zip•ping** [imit. of the sound of a speeding object] *vi* (1852) 1 : to move or act with speed and vigor 2 : to travel with a sharp hissing or humming sound ~ *vt* 1 : to impart speed or force to 2 : to add zest, interest, or life to — often used with *up* 3 : to transport with speed

[2]**zip** *n* (1875) 1 : a sudden sharp hissing or sibilant sound 2 : ENERGY, VIM — **zip•less** \-ləs\ *adj*

[3]**zip** *n* [origin unknown] (ca. 1900) : NOTHING, ZERO 〈the final score was 27 to ~〉

[4]**zip** *n, chiefly Brit* (1920) : ZIPPER

[5]**zip** *vb* **zipped; zip•ping** [back-formation fr. *zipper*] *vt* (1932) 1 a : to close or open with or as if with a zipper b : to enclose or wrap by fastening a zipper 2 : to cause (a zipper) to open or shut ~ *vi* : to become open, closed, or attached by means of a zipper

[6]**zip** *n, often cap Z&I&P* (1965) : ZIP CODE

zip–code *vt* (1964) : to furnish with a zip code

zip code *n, often cap Z&I&P* [zone improvement plan] (1963) : a number that identifies each postal delivery area in the U.S.

zip fastener *n, chiefly Brit* (1927) : ZIPPER

zip gun *n* (1950) : a crudely homemade single-shot pistol

[1]**zip•per** \ˈzip-ər\ *n* [fr. *Zipper*, a trademark] (1926) : a fastener consisting of two rows of metal or plastic teeth on strips of tape and a sliding piece that closes an opening by drawing the teeth together

[2]**zipper** *vt* (1930) : [5]ZIP

zip•pered \-ərd\ *adj* (1939) : equipped with a zipper

zip•py \ˈzip-ē\ *adj* **zip•pi•er; -est** (1904) : full of zip : BRISK, SNAPPY

zi•ram \ˈzī-ˌram\ *n* [*zinc* + *-ram* (as in *thiram*)] (1949) : an organic zinc salt $C_6H_{12}N_2S_4Zn$ used as a rubber accelerator and agricultural fungicide

zir•con \ˈzər-ˌkän, -kən\ *n* [G, modif. of F *jargon* jargoon, zircon, fr. It *giargone*] (1794) : a tetragonal mineral $ZrSiO_4$ consisting of a zirconium silicate and occurring usu. in brown or grayish square prisms of adamantine luster or sometimes in transparent forms which are used as gems

zir•co•nia \ˌzər-ˈkō-nē-ə\ *n* [NL, fr. ISV *zircon*] (1797) : ZIRCONIUM OXIDE

zir•con•ic \ˌzər-ˈkän-ik\ *adj* (1804) : of, relating to, or containing zirconium

zir•co•ni•um \ˌzər-ˈkō-nē-əm\ *n* [NL, fr. ISV *zircon*] (1808) : a steel-gray strong ductile metallic element with a high melting point that occurs widely in combined form (as in zircon), is highly resistant to corrosion, and is used esp. in alloys and in refractories and ceramics — see ELEMENT table

zirconium oxide *n* (1868) : a white crystalline compound ZrO_2 used esp. in refractories, in thermal and electric insulation, in abrasives, and in enamels and glazes — called also *zirconia*

zit \ˈzit\ *n* [origin unknown] *slang* (ca. 1966) : PIMPLE 1

zith•er \ˈzit͟h-ər, ˈzith-\ *n* [G, fr. L *cithara* cithara] (1850) : a stringed instrument having usu. 30 to 40 strings over a shallow horizontal soundboard and played with pick and fingers — **zith•er•ist** \-ə-rəst\ *n*

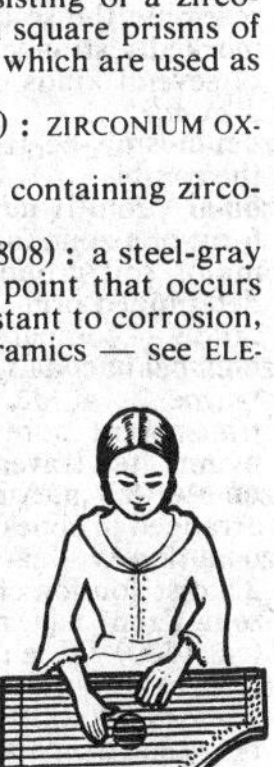

zither

zi•ti \ˈzēt-ē\ *n, pl* **ziti** [It, lit., boys, pl. of *zito* boy, modif. of *citto* boy, youth] (ca. 1845) : medium-sized tubular pasta

zi•zith \ˈtsit-səs, tsēt-ˈsēt\ *n pl* [Heb *ṣīṣith*] (1675) : the fringes or tassels worn on traditional

\ə\ abut \ᵊ\ kitten, F table \ər\ further \a\ ash \ā\ ace \ä\ cot, cart \au̇\ out \ch\ chin \e\ bet \ē\ easy \g\ go \i\ hit \ī\ ice \j\ job \ŋ\ sing \ō\ go \ȯ\ law \ȯi\ boy \th\ thin \t͟h\ the \ü\ loot \u̇\ foot \y\ yet \zh\ vision \á, k̲, ⁿ, œ, œ̄, ue, ue̅, ʸ\ *see* Guide to Pronunciation

or ceremonial garments by Jewish males as reminders of the commandments of Deut 22:12 and Num 15:37–41

Z line *n* (1916) **:** any of the dark thin lines across a striated muscle fiber that mark the boundaries between adjacent sarcomeres

zlo·ty \ˈzlȯt-ē, zə-ˈlȯt-\ *n, pl* **zlo·tys** \-ēz\ *or* **zloty** *also* **zlo·tych** \-ik, -ik\ *or* **zlo·te** \-ē\ *or* **zlo·ties** \-ēz\ [Pol *złoty*] (1915) — see MONEY table

zo- *or* **zoo-** *comb form* [Gk *zōi-, zōio-,* fr. *zōion;* akin to Gk *zōē* life — more at QUICK] **1 :** animal **:** animal kingdom or kind ⟨zooid⟩ ⟨zoology⟩ **2** [Gk *zō-* alive, fr. *zōos;* akin to Gk *zōē*] **:** motile ⟨zoospore⟩

-zoa \ˈzō-ə\ *n pl comb form* [NL, fr. Gk *zōia,* pl. of *zōion*] **:** animals — in taxa ⟨Meta*zoa*⟩

zo·an·thar·i·an \ˌzō-ən-ˈther-ē-ən, -ˈthar-\ *n* [deriv. of *zo-* + Gk *anthos* flower — more at ANTHOLOGY] (1887) **:** any of a subclass (Zoantharia) of anthozoans having a hexamerous arrangement of tentacles or septa or both and including most of the recent corals and sea anemones — **zoantharian** *adj*

zo·ar·i·um \zō-ˈar-ē-əm, -ˈer-\ *n, pl* **-ia** \-ē-ə\ [NL] (1880) **:** a colony of colonial bryozoans — **zo·ar·i·al** \-ē-əl\ *adj*

zo·di·ac \ˈzōd-ē-ˌak\ *n* [ME, fr. MF *zodiaque,* fr. L *zodiacus,* fr. Gk *zōidiakos,* fr. *zōidiakos,* adj., of carved figures, of the zodiac, fr. *zōidion* carved figure, sign of the zodiac, fr. dim. of *zōion* living being, figure; akin to Gk *zōē* life — more at QUICK] (14c) **1 a :** an imaginary belt in the heavens usu. 18 degrees wide that encompasses the apparent paths of all the principal planets except Pluto, has the ecliptic as its central line, and is divided into 12 constellations or signs each taken for astrological purposes to extend 30 degrees of longitude **b :** a figure representing the signs of the zodiac and their symbols **2 :** a cyclic course ⟨a ~ of feasts and fasts —R. W. Emerson⟩ — **zo·di·a·cal** \zō-ˈdī-ə-kəl, zə-\ *adj*

SIGNS OF THE ZODIAC

NUMBER	NAME	SYMBOL	SUN ENTERS
1	Aries the Ram	♈	March 21
2	Taurus the Bull	♉	April 20
3	Gemini the Twins	♊	May 21
4	Cancer the Crab	♋	June 22
5	Leo the Lion	♌	July 23
6	Virgo the Virgin	♍	August 23
7	Libra the Balance	♎	September 23
8	Scorpio the Scorpion	♏	October 24
9	Sagittarius the Archer	♐	November 22
10	Capricorn the Goat	♑	December 22
11	Aquarius the Water Bearer	♒	January 20
12	Pisces the Fishes	♓	February 19

zodiacal light *n* (1734) **:** a diffuse glow seen in the west after twilight and in the east before dawn

zo·ea \zō-ˈē-ə\ *n, pl* **zo·eae** \-ˈē-ˌē\ *or* **zo·eas** \-ˈē-əz\ [NL, fr. Gk *zōē* life] (ca. 1890) **:** an early larval form of many decapod crustaceans and esp. crabs with a relatively large cephalothorax, conspicuous eyes, and large fringed antennae and mouthparts used for swimming

[1]**-zo·ic** \ˈzō-ik\ *adj comb form* [Gk *zōikos* of animals, fr. *zōion* animal — more at ZO-] **:** having a (specified) animal mode of existence ⟨holozoic⟩ ⟨endozoic⟩ ⟨saprozoic⟩

[2]**-zoic** *adj comb form* [Gk *zōē* life] **:** of, relating to, or being a (specified) geological era ⟨Archeozoic⟩ ⟨Mesozoic⟩

zois·ite \ˈzȯi-ˌsīt\ *n* [G *zoisit,* fr. Baron Sigismund *Zois* von Edelstein †1819 Slovenian nobleman] (1805) **:** an orthorhombic mineral $Ca_2Al_3Si_3O_{12}OH$ that consists of a basic calcium aluminum silicate and is related to epidote

zom·bie *also* **zom·bi** \ˈzäm-bē\ *n* [of Niger-Congo origin; akin to Kongo *nzambi* god] (ca. 1871) **1** *usu zombi* **a :** the voodoo snake deity **b :** the supernatural power that according to voodoo belief may enter into and reanimate a dead body **c :** a will-less and speechless human in the West Indies capable only of automatic movement who is held to have died and been reanimated but often believed to have been drugged into a catalepsy for the hours of interment **2 a :** a person held to resemble the so-called walking dead; *esp* **:** AUTOMATON **b :** a person markedly strange in appearance or behavior **3 :** a mixed drink made of several kinds of rum, liqueur, and fruit juice — **zom·bie·like** \-bē-ˌlīk\ *adj*

zom·bi·ism \-bē-ˌiz-əm\ *n* (1932) **:** the beliefs and practices of the cult of the zombi

zon·al \ˈzōn-ᵊl\ *adj* (1873) **1 :** of, relating to, affecting, or having the form of a zone ⟨a ~ boundary⟩ **2 :** of, relating to, or being a soil or a major soil group marked by well-developed characteristics that are determined primarily by the action of climate and organisms esp. vegetation — compare AZONAL, INTRAZONAL — **zon·al·ly** \-ᵊl-ē\ *adv*

zo·na pel·lu·ci·da \ˌzō-nə-pə-ˈlü-sə-də, -pel-ˈyü-\ *n, pl* **zo·nae pel·lu·ci·dae** \-(ˌ)nē . . . -(ˌ)dē, -ˌnī . . . -ˌdī\ [NL, transparent zone] (1841) **:** the transparent more or less elastic outer layer or envelope of a mammalian ovum often traversed by numerous radiating striae

zon·ate \ˈzō-ˌnāt\ *also* **zon·at·ed** \-ˌnāt-əd\ *adj* (1803) **:** marked with or arranged in zones

zo·na·tion \zō-ˈnā-shən\ *n* (1902) **1 :** zonate structure or arrangement **2 :** distribution of kinds of organisms in biogeographic zones

[1]**zone** \ˈzōn\ *n* [L *zona* belt, zone, fr. Gk *zōnē;* akin to Lith *juosti* to gird] (ca. 1500) **1 a :** any of five great divisions of the earth's surface with respect to latitude and temperature — compare FRIGID ZONE, TEMPERATE ZONE, TORRID ZONE **b :** a portion of the surface of a sphere included between two parallel planes **2** *archaic* **:** GIRDLE, BELT **3 a :** an encircling anatomical structure **b (1) :** a subdivision of a biogeographic region that supports a similar fauna and flora throughout its extent **(2) :** such a zone dominated by a particular life form **c :** a distinctive belt, layer, or series of layers of earth materials (as rock) **4 :** a region or area set off as distinct from surrounding or adjoining parts **5 :** one of the sections of an area or territory created for a particular purpose: as **a :** a zoned section of a city **b :** any of the eight concentric bands of territory centered on a given postal shipment point designated as a distance bracket for U.S. parcel post to which mail is charged at a single rate — called also *parcel post zone* **c :** a distance within which the same fare is charged by a common carrier **d :** an area on a field of play **e :** a stretch of roadway or a space in which certain traffic regulations are in force

[2]**zone** *vt* **zoned; zon·ing** (1795) **1 :** to surround with a zone **:** ENCIRCLE **2 :** to arrange in or mark off into zones; *specif* **:** to partition (a city, borough, or township) by ordinance into sections reserved for different purposes (as residence, business, or manufacturing) — **zon·er** *n*

[3]**zone** *adj* (1795) **1 :** ZONAL 1 **2 :** of, relating to, or being a system of defense (as in basketball or football) in which each player guards an assigned area rather than a specified opponent

zone refining *n* (1952) **:** a technique for the purification of a crystalline material and esp. a metal in which a molten region travels through the material to be refined, picks up impurities at its advancing edge, and then allows the purified part to recrystallize at its opposite edge — called also *zone melting* — **zone–refined** *adj*

Zon·ian \ˈzō-nē-ən, -nyən\ *n* (1910) **:** a U.S. citizen who lives in the Panama Canal Zone

zonk \ˈzäŋk, ˈzȯŋk\ *vb* [back-formation fr. *zonked*] *vt* (ca. 1961) **:** STUN, STUPEFY; *also* **:** STRIKE, ZAP — often used with *out* ~ *vi* **:** to pass out from or as if from alcohol or a drug — often used with *out*

zonked \ˈzäŋkt, ˈzȯŋ(k)t\ *adj* [origin unknown] (1959) **:** being or acting as if under the influence of alcohol or a drug (as LSD) **:** HIGH

Zon·ti·an \ˈzänt-ē-ən\ *n* [*Zonta International*] (1934) **:** a member of a service club made up of executive women each of whom is a sole representative of one business or profession in a community

zoo \ˈzü\ *n, pl* **zoos** [short for *zoological garden*] (ca. 1847) **1 a :** ZOOLOGICAL GARDEN **b :** a collection of living animals usu. for public display **2 :** a place, situation, or group marked by crowding, confusion, or unrestrained behavior ⟨the convention was a ~⟩

zoo- — see ZO-

zoo·gen·ic \ˌzō-ə-ˈjen-ik\ *adj* [ISV] (ca. 1864) **:** caused by or associated with animals or their activities ⟨~ humus⟩

zoo·ge·og·ra·phy \ˌzō-ə-jē-ˈäg-rə-fē\ *n* [ISV] (1868) **:** a branch of biogeography concerned with the geographical distribution of animals and esp. with the determination of the areas characterized by special groups of animals and the study of the causes and significance of such groups — **zoo·ge·og·ra·pher** \-fər\ *n* — **zoo·geo·graph·ic** \-ˌjē-ə-ˈgraf-ik\ *or* **zoo·geo·graph·i·cal** \-i-kəl\ *adj* — **zoo·geo·graph·i·cal·ly** \-i-k(ə-)lē\ *adv*

zo·oid \ˈzō-ˌȯid\ *n* (1851) **:** one of the asexually produced individuals of a compound organism (as a bryozoan, hydroid, or coral colony)

zoo·keep·er \ˈzü-ˌkē-pər\ *n* (1924) **:** one who maintains or cares for animals in a zoo

zooks \ˈzu̇ks\ *interj* [short for *gadzooks*] *archaic* (1634) — used as a mild oath

zo·ol·a·try \zō-ˈäl-ə-trē, zə-ˈwäl-\ *n* [NL *zoolatria,* fr. *zo-* + LL *-latria* -latry] (1817) **:** animal worship

zoo·log·i·cal \ˌzō-ə-ˈläj-i-kəl\ *also* **zoo·log·ic** \-ik\ *adj* (1807) **1 :** of, relating to, or occupied with zoology **2 :** of, relating to, or affecting lower animals often as distinguished from man — **zoo·log·i·cal·ly** \-i-k(ə-)lē\ *adv*

zoological garden *n* (1829) **:** a garden or park where wild animals are kept for exhibition

zo·ol·o·gy \zō-ˈäl-ə-jē, zə-ˈwäl-\ *n* [NL *zoologia,* fr. *zo-* + *-logia* -logy] (1669) **1 :** a science that deals with animals and is the branch of biology concerned with the animal kingdom and its members as individuals and classes and with animal life **2 :** a treatise on zoology **3 a :** animal life (as of a region) **:** FAUNA **b :** the properties and vital phenomena exhibited by an animal, animal type, or group — **zo·ol·o·gist** \-jəst\ *n*

[1]**zoom** \ˈzüm\ *vb* [imit.] *vi* (1886) **1 a :** to move with a loud low hum or buzz **b :** to go speedily **:** ZIP **2** *of an airplane* **:** to climb for a short time at an angle greater than that which can be maintained in steady flight so that the machine is carried upward at the expense of stored kinetic energy **3 :** to focus a camera or microscope on an object using a special lens that permits the apparent distance of the object to be varied or that gives the effect of motion toward or away from the object — often used with *in* or *out* **4 :** to increase sharply ⟨retail sales ~*ed*⟩ ~ *vt* **:** to cause to zoom

[2]**zoom** *n* (1917) **1 :** an act or process of zooming; *specif* **:** a sharp upward movement **2 :** a zooming sound **3 :** ZOOM LENS

zoom lens *n* (1936) **:** a camera or projector lens in which the image size can be varied continuously so that the image remains in focus at all times

zoo·mor·phic \ˌzō-ə-ˈmȯr-fik\ *adj* [ISV] (1872) **1 :** having the form of an animal ⟨a ~ orchid⟩ **2 :** of, relating to, or being a deity conceived of in animal form or with the attributes of an animal

-zo·on \ˈzō-ˌän *also* -ən\ *n comb form, pl* **-zoa** \ˈzō-ə\ [NL, fr. Gk *zōion*] **:** animal **:** zooid ⟨hemato*zoon*⟩ ⟨spermato*zoon*⟩

zoo·no·sis \zō-ˈän-ə-səs, ˌzō-ə-ˈnō-səs\ *n, pl* **-no·ses** \-ˌsēz\ [NL, fr. *zo-* + Gk *nosos* disease] (1876) **:** a disease communicable from lower animals to man under natural conditions — **zoo·not·ic** \ˌzō-ə-ˈnät-ik\ *adj*

zo·oph·a·gous \zō-ˈäf-ə-gəs, zə-ˈwäf-\ *adj* [ISV] (1842) **:** feeding on animals **:** CARNIVOROUS

zoo·phil·ic \ˌzō-ə-ˈfil-ik\ *or* **zo·oph·i·lous** \zō-ˈäf-ə-ləs, zə-ˈwäf-\ *adj* (1886) **:** having an attraction to or preference for animals; *esp, of an insect* **:** preferring lower animals to man as a source of food

zoo·phyte \ˈzō-ə-ˌfīt\ *n* [Gk *zōophyton,* fr. *zōi-, zō-* zo- + *phyton* plant — more at PHYT-] (1644) **:** an invertebrate animal (as a coral or sponge) more or less resembling a plant in appearance or mode of growth

zoo·plank·ter \ˈzō-ə-ˌplaŋ(k)-tər\ *n* (1943) **:** a planktonic animal

zoo·plank·ton \ˌzō-ə-ˈplaŋ(k)-tən, -ˌtän\ *n* (1901) **:** animal life of the plankton — **zoo·plank·ton·ic** \-ˌplaŋ(k)-ˈtän-ik\ *adj*

zoo·spo·ran·gi·um \ˌzō-ə-spə-ˈran-jē-əm\ *n* [NL] (1874) **:** a spore case or sporangium bearing zoospores

zoo·spore \ˈzō-ə-ˌspō(ə)r, -ˌspȯ(ə)r\ *n* [ISV] (1846) **:** an independently motile spore; *esp* **:** a motile usu. naked and flagellated asexual spore esp. of an alga or lower fungus — **zoo·spor·ic** \ˌzō-ə-ˈspōr-ik, -ˈspȯr-\ *adj*

zo·os·ter·ol \zō-ˈäs-tə-ˌrȯl, -ˌrōl\ *n* (1926) **:** a sterol (as cholesterol) of animal origin — compare PHYTOSTEROL

zoo·tech·ni·cal \ˌzō-ə-ˈtek-ni-kəl\ *adj* (1926) **:** of or relating to the technology of animal husbandry — **zoo·tech·nics** \-ˈtek-niks\ *n pl but sing or pl in constr*

zoot suit \ˈzüt-\ *n* [coined by Harold C. Fox *b*1910 Am. clothier and bandleader] (1942) **:** a flashy suit of extreme cut typically consisting of a thigh-length jacket with wide padded shoulders and peg pants with narrow cuffs — **zoot–suit·er** \-ˌsüt-ər\ *n*

zo·o·xan·thel·la \ˌzō-ə-zan-ˈthel-ə\ *n, pl* **-lae** \-(ˌ)ē\ [NL, fr. *zo-* + *xanth-* + *-ella* (dim. suffix)] (ca. 1891) : any of various symbiotic dinoflagellates that live within the cells of other organisms (as reef-building coral polyps)

zo·ri \ˈzōr-ē, ˈzór-\ *n, pl* **zori** [Jp *zōri*] (1823) : a flat thonged sandal usu. made of straw, leather, or rubber

Zorn's lemma \ˈzó(ə)rnz-\ *n* [Max August Zorn *b*1906 Ger. mathematician] (1950) : a lemma in set theory: if a set S is partially ordered and if each subset for which every pair of elements is related by exactly one of the relationships "less than," "equal to," or "greater than" has an upper bound in S, then S contains at least one element for which there is no greater element in S

Zo·ro·as·tri·an·ism \ˌzór-ə-ˈwas-trē-ə-ˌniz-əm\ *n* (1854) : a Persian religion founded in the 6th century B.C. by the prophet Zoroaster, promulgated in the Avesta, and characterized by worship of a supreme god Ahura Mazda who requires men's good deeds for help in his cosmic struggle against the evil spirit Ahriman — **Zo·ro·as·tri·an** \-trē-ən\ *adj or n*

zoster *n* [L, fr. Gk *zōstēr* girdle; akin to Gk *zōnē* zone] (1706) : HERPES ZOSTER

Zou·ave \zü-ˈäv\ *n* [F, fr. Berber *Zwāwa*, Algerian tribe] (1830) **1** : a member of a French infantry unit orig. composed of Algerians wearing a brilliant uniform and conducting a quick spirited drill **2** : a member of a military unit adopting the dress and drill of the Zouaves

zounds \ˈz(w)aůn(d)z, ˈz(w)ün(d)z\ *interj* [euphemism for *God's wounds*] (ca. 1600) — used as a mild oath

zoy·sia \ˈzói-shə, -zhə, -sē-ə, -zē-ə\ *n* [NL, alter. of *Zoisia*, fr. Karl von *Zois* †1800 Ger. botanist] (1924) : any of a genus (*Zoisia*) of creeping perennial grasses having fine wiry leaves and including some suitable for lawn grasses esp. in warm regions

Z particle *n* (1979) : a neutral elementary particle about 90 times heavier than a proton that along with the W particle is a transmitter of the weak interaction — called also *Z⁰* or *Zᵒ particle*

zuc·chet·to \zü-ˈket-(ˌ)ō, tsü-\ *n, pl* **-tos** [It, dim. of *zucca* gourd, head, fr. LL *cucutia* gourd] (1854) : a small round skullcap worn by Roman Catholic ecclesiastics in colors that vary according to the rank of the wearer

zuc·chi·ni \zü-ˈkē-nē\ *n, pl* **-ni** *or* **-nis** [It, pl. of *zucchino*, dim. of *zucca* gourd] (1929) : a summer squash of bushy growth with smooth cylindrical dark green fruits; *also* : its fruit

¹Zu·lu \ˈzü-(ˌ)lü\ *n* (1824) **1** : a member of a Bantu-speaking people of Natal **2** : a Bantu language of the Zulus — **Zulu** *adj*

²Zulu (1952) — a communications code word for the letter *z*

Zu·ni \ˈzü-nē\ *or* **Zu·ñi** \ˈzün-yē\ *n, pl* **Zuni** *or* **Zunis** *or* **Zuñi** *or* **Zuñis** [AmerSp *Zuñi*] (1834) **1 a** : an American Indian people of western New Mexico **b** : a member of this people **2** : the language of the Zuni people — **Zu·ni·an** \ˈzü-nē-ən\ *or* **Zu·ñi·an** \ˈzün-yē-ən\ *adj*

Zunian *or* **Zuñian** (ca. 1895) : a language family consisting of Zuni only

zup·pa in·gle·se \ˌtsü-pə-iṇ-ˈglā-(ˌ)zā, ˌzü-, -in-, -(ˌ)sā\ *n, often cap I* [It, lit., English soup] (1941) : a dessert consisting of sponge cake and custard or pudding that is flavored with rum, covered with cream, and garnished with fruit

zwie·back \ˈswē-ˌbak, ˈswī-, ˈzwē-, ˈzwī-, -ˌbäk\ *n* [G, lit., twice baked, fr. *zwie-* twice (fr. OHG *zwi-*) + *backen* to bake, fr. OHG *bahhan* — more at TWI-, BAKE] (1894) : a usu. sweetened bread enriched with eggs that is baked and then sliced and toasted until dry and crisp

Zwing·li·an \ˈzwiṇ-(g)lē-ən, ˈswiṇ-; ˈtsfiṇ-lē-\ *adj* (1532) : of or relating to Ulrich Zwingli or his teachings and esp. his doctrine that Christ's

presence in the Eucharist is not corporeal but symbolic — **Zwinglian** *n* — **Zwing·li·an·ism** \-ə-ˌniz-əm\ *n*

zwit·ter·ion \ˈtsvit-ər-ˌī-ˌän *also* ˈzwit-\ *n* [G, fr. *zwitter* hybrid (fr. OHG *zwitaran*, fr. *zwi-*) + *ion* ion — more at TWI-] (1906) : a dipolar ion — **zwit·ter·ion·ic** \ˌzwit-ə-rī-ˈän-ik, ˌswit-\ *adj*

zyg- *or* **zygo-** *comb form* [NL, fr. Gk, fr. *zygon* — more at YOKE] **1** : yoke ⟨*zygo*morphic⟩ **2** : pair ⟨*zygo*dactyl⟩ **3** : union ⟨*zygo*spore⟩

zyg·apoph·y·sis \ˌzī-gə-ˈpäf-ə-səs\ *n, pl* **-y·ses** \-ˌsēz\ (1854) : any of the articular processes of the neural arch of a vertebra of which there are usu. two anterior and two posterior

zy·go·dac·tyl \ˌzī-gə-ˈdak-t²l\ *adj* [ISV *zyg-* + Gk *daktylos* toe] (1831) : having the toes arranged two in front and two behind — used of a bird

zy·go·dac·ty·lous \-tə-ləs\ *adj* (ca. 1828) : ZYGODACTYL

zy·go·ma \zī-ˈgō-mə\ *n, pl* **-ma·ta** \-mət-ə\ *also* **-mas** [NL *zygomat-*, *zygoma*, fr. Gk *zygōma*, fr. *zygoun* to join, fr. *zygon* yoke] (ca. 1684) **1 a** : ZYGOMATIC ARCH **b** : a slender bony process of the zygomatic arch **2** : ZYGOMATIC BONE

zy·go·mat·ic \ˌzī-gə-ˈmat-ik\ *adj* (1709) : of, relating to, constituting, or situated in the region of the zygoma and esp. the zygomatic arch

zygomatic arch *n* (1825) : the arch of bone that extends along the front or side of the skull beneath the orbit

zygomatic bone *n* (1709) : a bone of the side of the face below the eye that in mammals forms part of the zygomatic arch and part of the orbit — called also *cheekbone*

zygomatic process *n* (1741) : any of several bony processes that enter into or strengthen the zygomatic arch

zy·go·mor·phic \ˌzī-gə-ˈmór-fik\ *adj* (1875) : having one or more similar parts unequal in size or form so that the whole structure is capable of division into essentially symmetrical halves by only one longitudinal plane passing through the axis ⟨the flower of the pea is ∿⟩ — **zy·go·mor·phy** \ˈzī-gə-ˌmór-fē\ *n*

zy·gos·i·ty \zī-ˈgäs-ət-ē\ *n* (1946) : the makeup or characteristics of a particular zygote

zy·go·spore \ˈzī-gə-ˌspō(ə)r, -ˌspó(ə)r\ *n* [ISV] (1864) : a plant spore that is formed by union of two similar sexual cells, usu. serves as a resting spore, and produces the sporophytic phase of the plant — compare OOSPORE

zy·gote \ˈzī-ˌgōt\ *n* [Gk *zygōtos* yoked, fr. *zygoun* to join together — more at ZYGOMA] (1887) : a cell formed by the union of two gametes; *broadly* : the developing individual produced from such a cell — **zy·got·ic** \zī-ˈgät-ik\ *adj*

zy·go·tene \ˈzī-gə-ˌtēn\ *n* [ISV] (1911) : the stage of meiotic prophase which immediately follows the leptotene and during which synapsis of homologous chromosomes occurs — **zygotene** *adj*

-zy·gous \ˈzī-gəs\ *adj comb form* [Gk *-zygos* yoked, fr. *zygon* yoke — more at YOKE] : having (such) a zygotic constitution ⟨hetero*zygous*⟩

zym- *or* **zymo-** *comb form* [NL, fr. Gk, leaven, fr. *zymē*] **1** : fermentation ⟨*zym*urgy⟩ **2** : enzyme ⟨*zymo*gen⟩

zy·mase \ˈzī-ˌmās, -ˌmāz\ *n* [ISV] (1875) : an enzyme or enzyme complex that promotes glycolysis

-zyme \ˌzīm\ *n comb form* [Gk *zymē* leaven] : enzyme ⟨lyso*zyme*⟩

zy·mo·gen \ˈzī-mə-jən\ *n* [ISV] (1877) : an inactive protein precursor of an enzyme secreted by living cells and activated by catalysis (as by a kinase or an acid) — called also *proenzyme*

zy·mo·gram \ˈzī-mə-ˌgram\ *n* (ca. 1959) : an electrophoretic strip (as of starch gel) or a representation of it exhibiting the pattern of separated proteins or protein components after electrophoresis

zy·mo·san \ˈzī-mə-ˌsan\ *n* [NL *zymosis* fermentation (fr. Gk *zymōsis*, fr. *zymoun* to ferment, fr. *zymē*) + *-an*] (1943) : an insoluble largely polysaccharide fraction of yeast cell walls

---

Abbreviations

AND SYMBOLS FOR CHEMICAL ELEMENTS

The following list of abbreviations is not intended to be all-inclusive; it does, however, contain many of those most commonly used. Symbols for chemical elements are also included. Most of these abbreviations have been normalized to one form. In practice, however, there is considerable variation in the use of periods and in capitalization (as *mph, m.p.h., Mph,* and *MPH*), and stylings other than those given in this dictionary are often acceptable.

For a list of abbreviations regularly used in this dictionary, see the section Abbreviations in This Work in the front matter.

For a list of special signs and symbols not readily alphabetizable, see the section Signs and Symbols in the back matter.

a absent, acceleration, acre, adult, alto, anode, answer, ante, anterior, are, area, atto-, author

A ace, ampere, argon

A angstrom unit

aa ana

AA Alcoholics Anonymous, antiaircraft, associate in arts, author's alterations

AAA Agricultural Adjustment Administration, American Automobile Association

AAAL American Academy of Arts and Letters

AAAS American Association for the Advancement of Science

A and M agricultural and mechanical, ancient and modern

A and R artists and repertory

AAR against all risks

AAS associate in applied science

AAU Amateur Athletic Union

AAUP American Association of University Professors

AAUW American Association of University Women

ab about

AB able-bodied seaman, airborne, airman basic, Alberta, [NL *artium baccalaureus*] bachelor of arts

ABA American Bankers Association, American Bar Association, American Basketball Association, American Booksellers Association

abbr abbreviation

ABC American Bowling Congress, American Broadcasting Company, Australian Broadcasting Corporation

ABCD accelerated business collection and delivery

abd *or* **abdom** abdomen, abdominal

abl ablative

abn airborne

abp archbishop

abr abridged, abridgment

abs absolute, abstract

ABS American Bible Society

abstr abstract

ac account, acre

Ac actinium, altocumulus

AC air-conditioning, alternating current, [L *ante Christum*] before Christ; [L *ante cibum*] before meals; area code, athletic club

acad academic, academy

AC and U Association of Colleges and Universities

acc accusative

accel accelerando

acct account, accountant

accus accusative

ACE American Council on Education

ack acknowledge, acknowledgment

ACLU American Civil Liberties Union

ACP American College of Physicians

acpt acceptance

ACS American Chemical Society, American College of Surgeons

act active, actor, actual

ACT American College Test, Association of Classroom Teachers, Australian Capital Territory

actg acting

ACV actual cash value, air-cushion vehicle

AD active duty, after date, air-dried, anno Domini — often printed in small capitals; assembly district, assistant director, athletic director

ADA American Dental Association, Americans for Democratic Action, average daily attendance

ADC aide-de-camp, Aid to Dependent Children, Air Defense Command, assistant division commander

ADD American Dialect Dictionary

addn addition

addnl additional

ADF automatic direction finder

ADH antidiuretic hormone

ad int ad interim

ADIZ air defense identification zone

adj adjective, adjunct, adjustment, adjutant

ad loc [L *ad locum*] to or at the place

adm administration, administrative

ADM admiral

admin administration

admrx administratrix

ADP automatic data processing

adv adverb, [L *adversus*] against; advertisement, advertising, advisory

ad val ad valorem

advt advertisement

AEC Atomic Energy Commission

AEF American Expeditionary Force

aeq [L *aequalis*] equal

aero aeronautical, aeronautics

aet *or* **aetat** [L *aetatis*] of age, aged

af affix

AF air force, audio frequency

AFAM Ancient Free and Accepted Masons

AFB air force base

AFC American Football Conference, automatic frequency control

A/1C airman first class

AFDC Aid to Families with Dependent Children

aff affirmative

afft affidavit

AFL American Football League

AFL–CIO American Federation of Labor and Congress of Industrial Organizations

Afr Africa, African

aft afternoon

AFT American Federation of Teachers, automatic fine tuning

AFTRA American Federation of Television and Radio Artists

Ag [L *argentum*] silver

AG adjutant general, attorney general

AGC advanced graduate certificate

agcy agency

agr *or* **agric** agricultural, agriculture

agt agent

AH ampere-hour, anno hegirae, arts and humanities

AHL American Hockey League

AI ad interim, airborne intercept, air interception, artificial insemination, artificial intelligence

AID Agency for International Development

AIM American Indian Movement

AK Alaska

aka also known as

AKC American Kennel Club

Al aluminum

AL Alabama, American League, American Legion

Ala Alabama

ALA American Library Association, Automobile Legal Association

Alb Albania, Albanian

alc alcohol

ALCS American League Championship Series

ald alderman

alg algebra

alk alkaline

alky alkalinity

allo allegro

ALS autographed letter signed

alt alternate, altitude, alto

Alta Alberta

alw allowance

Am America, American, americium

AM airmail, Air Medal, [L *anno mundi*] in the year of the world — often printed in small capitals; ante meridiem — often not cap.; [NL *artium magister*] master of arts

AMA American Medical Association

amb ambassador

amdt amendment

Amer America, American

AmerInd American Indian

AMG allied military government

Amn airman

amp ampere

amp hr ampere-hour

AMS Agricultural Marketing Service

amt amount

AMU atomic mass unit

AMVETS American Veterans (of World War II)

an annum

AN airman (Navy)

ANA American Newspaper Association, American Nurses Association

anal analogy, analysis, analytic

anat anatomical, anatomy

anc ancient

Angl Anglican

anhyd anhydrous

ann annals, annual

anon anonymous, anonymously

ANOVA analysis of variance

ans answer

ant antenna, antonym

Ant Antarctica, Antrim

anthrop anthropological, anthropology

antiq antiquarian, antiquary

AO account of, and others

aor aorist

ap apostle, apothecaries'

AP additional premium, airplane, American plan, antipersonnel, arithmetic progression, armor-piercing, Associated Press, author's proof

APB all points bulletin

APC armored personnel carrier

API air position indicator

APO army post office

Apoc Apocalypse, Apocrypha, apocryphal

app apparatus, appendix

appl applied

approx approximate, approximately

appt appoint, appointed, appointment

apptd appointed

Apr April

APR annual percentage rate

apt apartment, aptitude

aq aqua, aqueous

ar arrival, arrive

Ar Arabic, argon

AR accounts receivable, acknowledgment of receipt, all rail, all risks, annual return, Arkansas,

army regulation, autonomous republic
Arab Arabian, Arabic
ARC AIDS-related complex, American Red Cross
arccos arccosine
arccot arccotangent
arccsc arccosecant
arch archaic, archery, architect, architectural, architecture
Arch Archbishop
archeol archeology
arcsec arcsecant
arcsin arcsine
arctan arctangent
arg argent, argument
Arg Argentina, Argyll
arith arithmetic, arithmetical
Ariz Arizona
Ark Arkansas
Arm Armagh, Armenian
ARP air-raid precautions
arr arranged, arrival, arrive
ARRT American Registered Respiratory Therapist
art article, artificial, artillery
arty artillery
ARV American Revised Version
ARVN Army of the Republic of Vietnam (South Vietnam)
As altostratus, arsenic
AS after sight, airspeed, American Samoa, Anglo-Saxon, antisubmarine, associate in science
ASA American Standards Association
ASAP as soon as possible
asb asbestos
ASCAP American Society of Composers, Authors and Publishers
ASCU Association of State Colleges and Universities
ASE American Stock Exchange
ASEAN Association of Southeast Asian Nations
asgd assigned
asgmt assignment
ASI airspeed indicator
ASL American Sign Language
ASR airport surveillance radar, air-sea rescue
assn association
assoc associate, associated, association
ASSR Autonomous Soviet Socialist Republic
asst assistant
asstd assented, assorted
assy assembly
Assyr Assyrian
ASTM American Society for Testing and Materials
ASTP army specialized training program
astrol astrologer, astrology
astron astronomer, astronomy
ASV American Standard Version
at airtight, atomic
At astatine
AT air temperature, ampere-turn, automatic transmission
Atl Atlantic
atm atmosphere, atmospheric
ATM automated teller machine, automatic teller machine
at no atomic number
att attached, attention, attorney
attn attention
attrib attributive, attributively
atty attorney
atty gen attorney general
ATV all-terrain vehicle
at wt atomic weight
Au [L *aurum*] gold
AU angstrom unit, astronomical unit
AUC [L *ab urbe condita*] from the year of the founding of the city (of Rome)
aud audit, auditor
aug augmentative
Aug August
Aus Austria, Austrian
AUS Army of the United States
Austral Australia
auth authentic, author, authorized
auto automatic
aux or **auxil** auxiliary
av avenue, average, avoirdupois
AV ad valorem, audiovisual, Authorized Version
AVC automatic volume control
avdp avoirdupois

ave avenue
avg average
avn aviation
AW actual weight, aircraft warning, all water, articles of war, automatic weapon
ax axiom, axis
AYC American Youth Congress
AYD American Youth for Democracy
AYH American Youth Hostels
Ayr Ayrshire
az azimuth, azure
AZ Arizona
b bachelor, bacillus, back, bag, bale, bass, basso, bat, Baumé, before, Bible, billion, bishop, black, blue, bolivar, book, born, brick, brightness, British, bulb, butut
B boron
Ba barium
BA bachelor of arts, batting average, Buenos Aires
BAA bachelor of applied arts
BAAE bachelor of aeronautical and astronautical engineering
bac [ML *baccalaureus*] bachelor
bact bacterial, bacteriology, bacterium
BAE bachelor of aeronautical engineering, bachelor of agricultural engineering, bachelor of architectural engineering, bachelor of art education, bachelor of arts in education
BAEd bachelor of arts in education
BAeE bachelor of aeronautical engineering
BAEE bachelor of arts in elementary education
BAg bachelor of agriculture
bal balance
BAM bachelor of applied mathematics, bachelor of arts in music
B and B bed-and-breakfast
B and E breaking and entering
b and w black and white
Bap or **Bapt** Baptist
bar barometer, barometric, barrel
Bar Baruch
BAr bachelor of architecture
BAR Browning automatic rifle
Bart baronet
BAS bachelor of applied science, bachelor of arts and sciences
BAT bachelor of arts in teaching
Bav Bavaria, Bavarian
BB bachelor of business, ball bearing, base on balls, blue book, B'nai B'rith
BBA bachelor of business administration
BBB Better Business Bureau
BBC British Broadcasting Corporation
BBE bachelor of business education
bbl barrel, barrels
BC bachelor of commerce, before Christ — often printed in small capitals; British Columbia
BCE bachelor of chemical engineering, bachelor of civil engineering
bcf billion cubic feet
BCh bachelor of chemistry
BChE bachelor of chemical engineering
BCL bachelor of canon law, bachelor of civil law
bcn beacon
BCS bachelor of chemical science, bachelor of commercial science
BCSE Board of Civil Service Examiners
bd barrels per day, board, bound, boundary, bundle
BD bachelor of divinity, bank draft, bills discounted, bomb disposal, brought down
BDA bachelor of domestic arts, bachelor of dramatic art
bd ft board foot
bdl or **bdle** bundle
bdrm bedroom
Be beryllium
BE bachelor of education, bachelor of engineering, bill of exchange
Bé Baumé
BEC Bureau of Employees' Compensation

BEd bachelor of education
Beds Bedfordshire
BEE bachelor of electrical engineering
bef before
BEF British Expeditionary Force
beg begin, beginning
Belg Belgian, Belgium
BEM bachelor of engineering of mines, British Empire Medal
BEngr bachelor of engineering
BEngS bachelor of engineering science
Berks Berkshire
Berw Berwick
bet between
BeV billion electron volts
bf boldface
BF bachelor of forestry, board foot, brought forward
BFA bachelor of fine arts
bg background, bag, beige, being
BG or **B Gen** brigadier general
BH bill of health, Brinell hardness
bhd bulkhead
BHE Bureau of Higher Education
BHL bachelor of Hebrew letters, bachelor of Hebrew literature
BHN Brinell hardness number
bhp bishop
Bi bismuth
BIA bachelor of industrial arts, Braille Institute of America, Bureau of Indian Affairs
bib Bible, biblical
BID bachelor of industrial design, [L *bis in die*] twice a day
BIE bachelor of industrial engineering
biog biographer, biographical, biography
biol biologic, biological, biologist, biology
BJ bachelor of journalism
bk bank, book, break, brook
Bk berkelium
bkg banking, bookkeeping, breakage
bkgd background
bks barracks
bkt basket, bracket
bl bale, barrel, black, block, blue
BL bachelor of law, bachelor of letters, baseline, bats left, bill of lading, breadth-length
bld blond, blood
bldg building
Bldg E building engineer
bldr builder
BLitt or **BLit** [ML *baccalaureus litterarum*] bachelor of letters, bachelor of literature
blk black, block, bulk
BLS bachelor of liberal studies, bachelor of library science, Bureau of Labor Statistics
blvd boulevard
bm beam
BM bachelor of medicine, bachelor of music, basal metabolism, bill of material, board measure, bowel movement, bronze medal
BME bachelor of mechanical engineering, bachelor of mining engineering, bachelor of music education
BMOC big man on campus
BMR basal metabolic rate
BMS bachelor of marine science
BMT bachelor of medical technology
bn baron, battalion, beacon, been
BN bachelor of nursing, bank note, Bureau of Narcotics
BNDD Bureau of Narcotics and Dangerous Drugs
BNS bachelor of naval sciences
BO back order, body odor, box office, branch office, buyer's option
BOD biochemical oxygen demand, biological oxygen demand
BOQ bachelor officers' quarters
bor borough
bot botanical, botanist, botany, bottle, bottom, bought
botan botanical
bp baptized, birthplace, bishop
BP beautiful people, before the present, bills payable, blood pressure, blueprint, boiling point
bpd barrels per day

BPE bachelor of petroleum engineering, bachelor of physical education
BPh bachelor of philosophy
bpi bits per inch, bytes per inch
bpl birthplace
BPOE Benevolent and Protective Order of Elks
BPW Board of Public Works, Business and Professional Women's Clubs
br branch, brass, brown
Br Britain, British, bromine
BR bats right, bedroom, bills receivable
Braz Brazil, Brazilian
BRE bachelor of religious education
Breck Brecknockshire
brig brigade, brigadier
Brig Gen brigadier general
Brit Britain, British
brl barrel
bro brother, brothers
bros brothers
BS bachelor of science, balance sheet, bill of sale, British standard
BSA bachelor of science in agriculture, Boy Scouts of America
BSAA bachelor of science in applied arts
BSAE bachelor of science in aeronautical engineering, bachelor of science in agricultural engineering, bachelor of science in architectural engineering
BSAg bachelor of science in agriculture
BSArch bachelor of science in architecture
BSB bachelor of science in business
BSc bachelor of science
BSCh bachelor of science in chemistry
BSEc or **BSEcon** bachelor of science in economics
BSEd or **BSE** bachelor of science in education
BSEE bachelor of science in electrical engineering, bachelor of science in elementary education
BSFor bachelor of science in forestry
BSFS bachelor of science in foreign service
BSI British Standards Institution
bskt basket
BSL bachelor of sacred literature, bachelor of science in languages, bachelor of science in law, bachelor of science in linguistics
BSME bachelor of science in mechanical engineering
BSN bachelor of science in nursing
Bt baronet
btry battery
Btu British thermal unit
bu bureau, bushel
Bucks Buckinghamshire
Bulg Bulgaria, Bulgarian
bull bulletin
bur bureau
bus business
BV Blessed Virgin
bvt brevet
BW bacteriological warfare, biological warfare, black and white
BWI British West Indies
bx box
BX base exchange
by billion years
BYO bring your own
BYOB bring your own booze, bring your own bottle
byp bypass
c calm, calorie, Canadian, canceled, candle, carat, case, castle, catcher, Catholic, cedi, cent, centavo, center, centi-, centime, centimeter, centum, century, chairman, chapter, circa, circuit, circumference, clockwise, cloudy, cocaine, codex, coefficient, college, colon, color, colt, [L *congius*] gallon; congress, conservative, contralto, copyright, cost, cubic, cup, curie
C capacitance, carbon, Celsius, centigrade, Coulomb
ca circa
Ca calcium
CA California, chartered accountant, chief accountant, chronolog-

ical age, commercial agent, controller of accounts, current account
CAB Civil Aeronautics Board
CAD computer-aided design
CAF cost and freight
CAGS Certificate of Advanced Graduate Study
CAI computer-aided instruction, computer-assisted instruction
cal calendar, caliber, calorie, small calorie
Cal California, large calorie
calc calculate, calculated
Calif California
CAM computer-aided manufacturing
Cambs Cambridgeshire
can canceled, cancellation, cannon, canto
Can or **Canad** Canada, Canadian
canc canceled
C and F cost and freight
C and W country and western
Cant Canticle of Canticles, Cantonese
cap capacity, capital, capitalize, capitalized
CAP Civil Air Patrol
caps capitals, capsule
Capt captain
Car Carlow
CAR civil air regulations
card cardinal
CARE Cooperative for American Relief to Everywhere
CAS certificate of advanced study
cat catalog, catalyst
CAT clear-air turbulence, college ability test, computerized axial tomography
cath cathedral, cathode
CATV community antenna television
caus causative
cav cavalry, cavity
CAVU ceiling and visibility unlimited
Cb columbium, cumulonimbus
CBC Canadian Broadcasting Corporation
CBD cash before delivery, central business district
CBI computer-based instruction, Cumulative Book Index
CBS Columbia Broadcasting System
CBW chemical and biological warfare
cc cubic centimeter
Cc cirrocumulus
CC carbon copy, chief clerk, common carrier, community college, country club
CCAT Cooperative College Ability Test
CCC Civilian Conservation Corps
CCD Confraternity of Christian Doctrine
CCF Chinese communist forces, Cooperative Commonwealth Federation (of Canada)
cckw counterclockwise
CCTV closed-circuit television
CCU cardiac care unit, coronary care unit, critical care unit
ccw counterclockwise
cd candela, candle, cord
Cd cadmium
CD carried down, certificate of deposit, civil defense, [F *corps diplomatique*] diplomatic corps
CDD certificate of disability for discharge
cdg commanding
CDP certificate in data processing
CDR commander
CDT central daylight time
Ce cerium
CE chemical engineer, civil engineer, (International Society of) Christian Endeavor, Corps of Engineers
CEA College English Association, Council of Economic Advisors
CED Committee for Economic Development
cem cement
CEMF counter electromotive force
cent centigrade, central, centum, century
Cent Central
CENTO Central Treaty Organization

CEO chief executive officer
CER conditioned emotional response
cert certificate, certification, certified, certify
CETA Comprehensive Employment and Training Act
cf calf, [L *confer*, imper. of *conferre* to compare — more at CONFER] compare
Cf californium
CF carried forward, centrifugal force, cost and freight, cystic fibrosis
CFI certified flight instructor, chief flying instructor; cost, freight, and insurance
cfm cubic feet per minute
CFO chief financial officer
cfs cubic feet per second
cg or **cgm** centigram
CG center of gravity, coast guard, commanding general
cgs centimeter-gram-second
CGT [F *Confédération Générale du Travail*] General Confederation of Labor
ch chain, champion, chaplain, chapter, chief, child, children, church
CH clearinghouse, courthouse, customhouse
chan channel
chap chapter
chem chemical, chemist, chemistry
Ches Cheshire
chg change, charge
Chin Chinese
chm chairman, checkmate
Chmn chairman
chron chronicle, chronological, chronology
Chron Chronicles
Ci cirrus, curie
CI cast iron, certificate of insurance, cost and insurance
CIA Central Intelligence Agency, certified internal auditor
cia [Sp *compañia*] company
CIAA Central Intercollegiate Athletic Association
CIC counterintelligence corps
CID Criminal Investigation Department, cubic inch displacement
cie [F *compagnie*] company
CIF central information file; cost, insurance, and freight
C in C commander in chief
CIP Cataloging in Publication
cir circle, circuit, circular, circumference
circ circular
cit citation, cited, citizen
civ civil, civilian
CJ chief justice
ck cask, check
cl centiliter, class, clause, close, closet, cloth
Cl chlorine
CL carload, center line, civil law, common law
cld called, cleared
CLEP College Level Examination Program
Clev Cleveland
clin clinical
clk clerk
clo clothing
clr clear, clearance
CLU chartered life underwriter
cm centimeter, cumulative
Cm curium
CM center matched, circular mil, common meter, [Commonwealth of the Northern Mariana Islands] Northern Mariana Islands, Congregation of the Mission
CMA certified medical assistant
cmd command
cmdg commanding
cmdr commander
CMG Companion of the Order of St. Michael and St. George
cml commercial
CMSgt chief master sergeant
CN credit note
CNO chief of naval operations
CNS central nervous system
co company, county
Co cobalt
CO cash order, Colorado, commanding officer, conscientious objector

c/o care of
cod codex
COD cash on delivery, collect on delivery
coeff or **coef** coefficient
C of C Chamber of Commerce
C of S chief of staff
cog cognate
col colonial, colony, color, colored, column, counsel
col or **coll** collateral, collect, collected, collection, college, collegiate
Col colonel, Colorado, Colossians
COL colonel, cost of living
COLA cost-of-living allowance
collat collateral
Colo Colorado
colloq colloquial
colog cologarithm
com comedy, comic, comma
COM computer output microfilm, computer output microfilmer
comb combination, combined, combining, combustion
comd command
comdg commanding
comdr commander
comdt commandant
COMECON Council for Mutual Economic Assistance
coml commercial
comm command, commandant, commander, commanding, commentary, commerce, commercial, commission, commissioned, commissioner, committee, common, commoner, commonwealth, commune, communication, communist, community
commo commodore
comp comparative, compare, compensation, compiled, compiler, composition, compound, comprehensive, comptroller
compd compound
comr commissioner
con [L *conjunx*] consort; consolidated, consul, continued
conc concentrate, concentrated, concentration, concrete
conch or **conchol** conchology
concn concentration
cond condition, conductivity
conf conference, confidential
Confed Confederate
cong congress, congressional
conj conjunction, conjunctive
Conn Connecticut
cons consecrated, conservative, consigned, consignment, consol, consolidated, consonant, constable, constitution, construction, consul, consulting
consol consolidated
const constant, constitution, constitutional, construction
constr construction
cont containing, contents, continent, continental, continued, control
contd continued
contg containing
contr contract, contraction, contralto, contrary, control, controller
contrib contribution, contributor
conv convention, conventional, convertible, convocation
COO chief operating officer
cop copper, copulative, copy, copyright
Cop or **Copt** Coptic
cor corner, coroner, corpus, corresponding
Cor Corinthians
CORE Congress of Racial Equality
Corn Cornish, Cornwall
corp corporal, corporation
corr correct, corrected, correction, correspondence, correspondent, corresponding, corrupt, corruption
cos companies, consul, consulship, cosine, counties
COS cash on shipment, chief of staff
cosec cosecant
cot cotangent
cp compare, coupon
CP candlepower, Cape Province, center of pressure, charter party, chemically pure, command post,

communist party, Congregation of the Passion, custom of port
CPA certified public accountant
CPB Corporation for Public Broadcasting
CPCU chartered property casualty underwriter
cpd compound
CPFF cost plus fixed fee
CPI consumer price index
cpl complete, compline
Cpl corporal
CPM cost per thousand, cycles per minute
CPO chief petty officer
CPOM master chief petty officer
CPOS senior chief petty officer
CPR cardiopulmonary resuscitation
CPS cards per second, certified professional secretary, characters per second, Civilian Public Service, cycles per second
CPT captain
cpu central processing unit
CQ call to quarters, charge of quarters, commercial quality
CQT College Qualification Test
cr center, circular, commander, cream, creased, credit, creditor, creek, crescendo, cruzeiro
Cr chromium
CR carrier's risk, cathode ray, class rate, conditioned reflex, conditioned response, consciousness-raising, Costa Rica, current rate
CRC Civil Rights Commission
cresc crescendo
crim criminal
crim con criminal conversation
criminol criminologist, criminology
crit critical, criticism, criticized
CRNA certified registered nurse anesthetist
CRT cathode-ray tube
cryst crystalline, crystallized
cs case, cases, census, consciousness, consul
Cs cesium, cirrostratus
CS capital stock, chief of staff, Christian Science practitioner, civil service, conditioned stimulus, county seat
C/S cycles per second
CSA Confederate States of America
csc cosecant
CSC Civil Service Commission
CSF cerebrospinal fluid
CSM command sergeant major
CST central standard time, convulsive shock therapy
ct carat, cent, count, county, court
CT central time, certificated teacher, certified teacher, code telegram, Connecticut
CTC centralized traffic control
ctf certificate
ctg or **ctge** cartage
ctn carton, cotangent
cto concerto
c to c center to center
ctr center, counter
cu cubic, cumulative
Cu cumulus, [L *cuprum*] copper
CU close-up
cum cumulative
Cumb Cumbria
cur currency, current
cv or **cvt** convertible
CV cardiovascular, chief value, curriculum vitae
CVA Columbia Valley Authority
cw clockwise
CW chemical warfare, chief warrant officer, continuous wave
CWO cash with order, chief warrant officer
cwt hundredweight
CY calendar year
cyc or **cycl** cyclopedia
cyl cylinder
CYO Catholic Youth Organization
cytol cytological, cytology
CZ Canal Zone
d date, daughter, day, dead, deceased, deci-, degree, [L *denarius*, *denarii*] penny, pence; depart, departure, diameter, differential, dimensional, distance, dorsal, drive, driving

D Democrat, derivative, deuterium, Dutch
da deka-
DA days after acceptance, delayed action, deposit account, Dictionary of Americanisms, district attorney, doctor of arts, documents against acceptance, documents for acceptance, don't answer
DAB Dictionary of American Biography
DAE Dictionary of American English
dag dekagram
DAH Dictionary of American History
dal dekaliter
dam dekameter
Dan Daniel, Danish
D & C dilation and curettage
DAR Daughters of the American Revolution
dat dative
DAT differential aptitude test, digital audiotape
dau daughter
DAV Disabled American Veterans
db debenture
dB *or* **db** decibel
DB daybook
d/b/a doing business as
DBA doctor of business administration
DBE Dame Commander of the Order of the British Empire
DBH diameter at breast height
dbl double
DBMS data base management system
DC [It *da capo*] from the beginning; decimal classification, direct current, District of Columbia, doctor of chiropractic, double crochet
DChE doctor of chemical engineering
DCL doctor of canon law, doctor of civil law
dd dated, delivered
DD days after date, demand draft, dishonorable discharge, doctor of divinity, due date
DDC Dewey Decimal Classification
DDD direct distance dialing
DDS doctor of dental science, doctor of dental surgery
DE defensive end, Delaware, doctor of engineering
deb debenture
dec deceased, declaration, declared, declination, decorated, decorative, decrease, decrescendo
Dec December
decd deceased
def defendant, defense, deferred, defined, definite, definition
deg degree
del delegate, delegation, delete
Del Delaware
dely delivery
dem demonstrative, demurrage
Dem Democrat, Democratic
Den Denmark
dent dental, dentist, dentistry
dep depart, department, departure, deponent, deposed, deposit, depot, deputy
depr depreciation, depression
dept department
der *or* **deriv** derivation, derivative
Derbys Derbyshire
derm dermatologist, dermatology
det detached, detachment, detail, determine
detd determined
detn detention, determination
Deut Deuteronomy
dev deviation
Devon Devonshire
DEW distant early warning
DF damage free, direction finder, direction finding
DFA doctor of fine arts
DFC Distinguished Flying Cross
DFM Distinguished Flying Medal
dft defendant, draft
dg decigram
DG [LL *Dei gratia*] by the grace of God; director general
DH designated hitter, doctor of humanities

DHL doctor of Hebrew letters, doctor of Hebrew literature
DI drill instructor
dia diameter
diag diagonal, diagram
dial dialect, dialectical
diam diameter
dict dictionary
dif *or* **diff** difference
dig digest
dil dilute
dim dimension, diminished, diminuendo, diminutive
dimin diminuendo
din dinar
dip diploma
dir director
dis discharge, discount, distance
disc discount
disp dispensary
diss dissertation
dist distance, district
distn distillation
distr distribute, distribution
div divided, dividend, division, divorced
DJ disc jockey, district judge, doctor of jurisprudence, dust jacket
DJIA Dow-Jones Industrial Average
dk dark, deck, dock
dkg dekagram
dkl dekaliter
dkm dekameter
dl deciliter
DLitt *or* **DLit** [L *doctor litterarum*] doctor of letters, doctor of literature
DLO dead letter office, dispatch loading only
DLS doctor of library science
dm decimeter
DM deutsche mark
DMA doctor of musical arts
DMD [NL *dentariae medicinae doctor*] doctor of dental medicine
DML doctor of modern languages
DMin doctor of ministry
DMZ demilitarized zone
dn down
DNB Dictionary of National Biography
do ditto
DO defense order, doctor of osteopathy
DOA dead on arrival
DOB date of birth
doc document
DOD Department of Defense
DOE Department of Energy
dol dollar
dom domestic, dominant, dominion
DOM [ML *Deo optimo maximo*] to God, the best and greatest
Don Donegal
Dors Dorset
DOS disk operating system
DOT Department of Transportation
doz dozen
DP data processing, degree of polymerization, dew point, doctor of podiatry, double play
DPE doctor of physical education
DPh doctor of philosophy
DPH department of public health, doctor of public health
DPM doctor of podiatric medicine
dpt department, deponent
DPT diphtheria, pertussis, tetanus
dr debtor, drachma, dram, drive, drum
Dr doctor
DR dead reckoning, dining room
dram dramatic, dramatist
DS [It *dal segno*] from the sign; days after sight, detached service, document signed
DSc doctor of science
DSC Distinguished Service Cross, doctor of surgical chiropody
DSM Distinguished Service Medal
DSO Distinguished Service Order
DSP [L *decessit sine prole*] died without issue
DST daylight saving time, doctor of sacred theology
DSW doctor of social welfare
DT daylight time, doctor of theology, double time
DTh doctor of theology

DTP desktop publishing; diphtheria, tetanus, pertussis
Du Dutch
Dub Dublin
DUI driving under the influence
Dumf Gal Dumfries and Galloway
dup duplex, duplicate
Dur Durham
DV [L *Deo volente*] God willing; Douay Version
DVM doctor of veterinary medicine
DW deadweight, delayed weather, distilled water, dust wrapper
DWI driving while intoxicated, Dutch West Indies
dwt deadweight ton, pennyweight
DX distance
dy delivery, deputy, duty
Dy dysprosium
dynam dynamics
dz dozen
e earth, east, easterly, eastern, edge, eldest, ell, empty, end, energy, erg, error, excellent
E electromotive force, energy, English
ea each
EA enemy aircraft
E and OE errors and omissions excepted
EB eastbound
eccl ecclesiastic, ecclesiastical
Eccles Ecclesiastes
Ecclus Ecclesiasticus
ECG electrocardiogram
ECM European Common Market
ecol ecological, ecology
econ economics, economist, economy
ECT electroconvulsive therapy
Ecua Ecuador
ed edited, edition, editor, education
ED extra duty
EdD doctor of education
EDD English Dialect Dictionary
EDP electronic data processing
EdS specialist in education
EDT eastern daylight time
educ education, educational
EE electrical engineer
EEC European Economic Community
EEG electroencephalogram, electroencephalograph
EENT eye, ear, nose, and throat
EEO equal employment opportunity
eff efficiency
EFT *or* **EFTS** electronic funds transfer (system)
e.g. [L *exempli gratia*] for example
Eg Egypt, Egyptian
Egypt Egyptian
EHF extremely high frequency
EHP effective horsepower, electric horsepower
EHV extra high voltage
EKG [G *elektrokardiogramm*] electrocardiogram, electrocardiograph
el elevation
elec electric, electrical, electricity
elem elementary
elev elevation
ELF extremely low frequency
Eliz Elizabethan
ELSS extravehicular life support system
EM electromagnetic, electron microscope, end matched, engineer of mines, enlisted man
embryol embryology
emer emeritus
emf electromotive force
EMG electromyograph
emp emperor, empress
EMP electromagnetic pulse
emu electromagnetic unit
enc *or* **encl** enclosure
ency *or* **encyc** encyclopedia
ENE east-northeast
eng engine, engineer, engineering
Eng England, English
engr engineer, engraved, engraver, engraving
enl enlarged, enlisted
ENS ensign
entom *or* **entomol** entomological, entomology
env envelope
EO executive order
EOM end of month

EP estimated position, European plan, extended play
EPA Environmental Protection Agency
Eph *or* **Ephes** Ephesians
epil epilepsy, epileptic
Episc Episcopal
eq equal, equation
equip equipment
equiv equivalency, equivalent
Er erbium
ER earned run, emergency room
ERA earned run average, Equal Rights Amendment
Es einsteinium
ESB electrical stimulation of the brain
Esd Esdras
ESE east-southeast
Esk Eskimo
ESL English as a second language
ESOP employee stock ownership plan
esp especially
Esq *or* **Esqr** esquire
est established, estimate, estimated
EST eastern standard time
Esth Esther
esu electrostatic unit
ESV earth satellite vehicle
Et ethyl
ET eastern time
ETA estimated time of arrival
et al [L *et alii* (masc.), *et aliae* (fem.), or *et alia* (neut.)] and others
etc et cetera
ETD estimated time of departure
ethnol ethnologist, ethnology
ETO European theater of operations
et seq [L *et sequens*] and the following one; [L *et sequentes* (masc. & fem. pl.), or *et sequentia* (neut. pl.)] and the following ones
et ux [L *et uxor*] and wife
ETV educational television
Eu europium
Eur Europe, European
eV electron volt
EVA extravehicular activity
evap evaporate
evg evening
EW enlisted woman
ex example, exchange, executive, express, extra
Ex Exodus
exc excellent, except
exch exchange, exchanged
exec executive
exhbn exhibition
Exod Exodus
exor executor
exp expense, experiment, experimental, exponent, export, express
expt experiment
exptl experimental
expy expressway
exrx executrix
ext extension, exterior, external, externally, extra, extract
extg extracting
Ez *or* **Ezr** Ezra
Ezech Ezechiel
Ezek Ezekiel
f failure, false, family, farad, faraday, feast, female, feminine, femto-, fermi, fine, finish, fluid, fluidness, focal length, [following] and the following one; force, forte, fragile, French, frequency, from, full
F Fahrenheit, fluorine
FA field artillery, fielding average, football association
FAA Federal Aviation Administration, free of all average
fac facsimile, faculty
FADM fleet admiral
Fah *or* **Fahr** Fahrenheit
fam familiar, family
F and A fore and aft
FAO Food and Agriculture Organization of the United Nations
FAQ fair average quality
far farthing
FAS firsts and seconds, Foreign Agricultural Service, free alongside (ship)
fasc fascicle
fath fathom
FB foreign body, freight bill
FBI Federal Bureau of Investigation

FC fire control, fire controlman, follow copy, food control, footcandle
FCA Farm Credit Administration
FCC Federal Communications Commission
fcp foolscap
fcy fancy
FD fire department, free dock
FDA Food and Drug Administration
FDIC Federal Deposit Insurance Corporation
Fe [L *ferrum*] iron
Feb February
fec [L *fecit*] he made it
fed federal, federation
fedn federation
fem female, feminine
FEPA Fair Employment Practices Act
FEPC Fair Employment Practices Commission
FERA Federal Emergency Relief Administration
Ferm Fermanagh
ff folios, [*following*] and the following ones; fortissimo
FG fine grain
FHA Federal Housing Administration
FICA Federal Insurance Contributions Act
fict fiction, fictitious
fi fa fieri facias
FIFO first in, first out
fig figurative, figuratively, figure
fin finance, financial, finish
Finn Finnish
fin sec financial secretary
FIO free in and out
fir firkin
fl flanker, floor, florin, [L *floruit*] flourished; fluid
FL Florida, focal length, foreign language
Fla Florida
fl dr fluidram
Flem Flemish
Flint *or* **Flints** Flintshire
fl oz fluidounce
FLSA Fair Labor Standards Act
fm fathom
Fm fermium
FM field manual
FMB Federal Maritime Board
FMCS Federal Mediation and Conciliation Service
fn footnote
fo *or* **fol** folio
FO field officer, field order, finance officer, flight officer, foreign office, forward observer
FOB free on board
FOC free of charge
FOE Fraternal Order of Eagles
FOIA Freedom of Information Act
for foreign, forestry
FOR free on rail
forz forzando
FOS free on steamer
FOT free on truck
4WD four-wheel drive
fow first open water
fp freezing point
FPA Foreign Press Association, free of particular average
FPC Federal Power Commission, fish protein concentrate
fpm feet per minute
FPO fleet post office
fps feet per second, foot-pound-second, frames per second
fr father, franc, friar, from
Fr France, francium, French
FRB Federal Reserve Board
freq frequency, frequent, frequentative, frequently
FRG Federal Republic of Germany
Fri Friday
front frontispiece
FRS Federal Reserve System
frt freight
frwy freeway
FS filmstrip, Foreign Service
FSH follicle-stimulating hormone
FSLIC Federal Savings and Loan Insurance Corporation
FSO Foreign Service Officer
FSP Food Stamp Program
ft feet, foot, fort
FT free throw, full time

FTC Federal Trade Commission
fth fathom
ft lb foot-pound
fund fundamental
fur furlong
fut future
FV [L *folio verso* the page being turned] on the back of the page
fwd foreword, forward
FWD front-wheel drive
FX foreign exchange
FY fiscal year
FYI for your information
fz [It *forzando, forzato*] accented
g acceleration of gravity, game, gauge, gender, good, gram, grand, gravity
G German, giga-, Gulf
ga gauge
Ga gallium, Georgia
GA Gamblers Anonymous, general agent, general assembly, general average, general of the army, Georgia
gal gallery, gallon
Gal Galatians
galv galvanized
GAO General Accounting Office
GAPA ground-to-air pilotless aircraft
gar garage
GAR Grand Army of the Republic
GATT General Agreement on Tariffs and Trade
GAW guaranteed annual wage
gaz gazette
GB Great Britain
GBF Great Books Foundation
GC gigacycle
GCA ground-controlled approach
GCB Knight Grand Cross of the Bath
GCD greatest common divisor
GCF greatest common factor
GCT Greenwich civil time
gd good
Gd gadolinium
GDR German Democratic Republic
Ge germanium
GE gilt edges
GED General Educational Development (tests), general equivalency diploma
GEM ground-effect machine
gen general, genitive, genus
Gen Genesis
Gen AF general of the air force
genl general
geog geographic, geographical, geography
geol geologic, geological, geology
geom geometric, geometrical, geometry
ger gerund
Ger German, Germany
GeV giga-electron-volt
GFE government-furnished equipment
GHQ general headquarters
GHz gigahertz
gi gill
GI galvanized iron, gastrointestinal, general issue, government issue
Gib *or* **Gibr** Gibraltar
GIGO garbage in, garbage out
GIT Group Inclusive Tour
Gk Greek
Glos Gloucestershire
gm gram
GM general manager, grand master, guided missile
GMT Greenwich mean time
GMW gram-molecular weight
gn guinea
GNI gross national income
GNP gross national product
GO general order
GOP Grand Old Party (Republican)
Goth Gothic
gov government, governor
govt government
gp group
GP general practice, general practitioner, geometric progression
GPA grade point average
GPD gallons per day
GPH gallons per hour
GPM gallons per minute
GPO general post office, Government Printing Office
GPS gallons per second

GQ general quarters
gr grade, grain, gram, gravity, gross
Gr Greece, Greek
grad graduate, graduated
gram grammar, grammatical
Gramp Grampian
GRAS generally recognized as safe
GRE graduate record examination
gro gross
gr wt gross weight
GS general staff, ground speed
GSA General Services Administration, Girl Scouts of America
GSC general staff corps
GSO general staff officer
GSR galvanic skin response
GST Greenwich sidereal time
GSUSA Girl Scouts of the United States of America
GSV guided space vehicle
gt gilt top, great,
GT gross ton
Gt Brit Great Britain
gtd guaranteed
Gtr Man Greater Manchester
gtt [L *gutta*, pl. *guttae*] drop
GU genitourinary, Guam
Gwyn Gwynedd
gyn *or* **gynecol** gynecology
Gy Sgt gunnery sergeant
h half, harbor, hard, hardness, hecto-, height, heroin, high, hit, hour, humidity, hundred, Hungary, husband
H Hamiltonian, henry, hydrogen
ha hectare
HA hour angle
Hab Habakkuk
hab corp habeas corpus
Hag Haggai
Hants Hampshire
Hb hemoglobin
HBM Her Britannic Majesty, His Britannic Majesty
h.c. [L *honoris causa*] for the sake of honor
HC Holy Communion, House of Commons
HCF highest common factor
HCG human chorionic gonadotropin
HCL high cost of living
hd head
HD heavy-duty
hdbk handbook
hdkf handkerchief
HDTV high-definition television
hdwe hardware
He helium
HE Her Excellency, high explosive, His Eminence, His Excellency
Heb Hebrew, Hebrews
her heraldry
Heref/Worcs Hereford and Worcester
Herts Hertfordshire
HEW Department of Health, Education, and Welfare
hex hexagon, hexagonal
hf half
Hf hafnium
HF height finding, high frequency, home forces
hg hectogram, heliogram, hemoglobin
Hg [NL *hydrargyrum*, lit., water silver] mercury
HGH human growth hormone
hgt height
hgwy highway
HH Her Highness, His Highness, His Holiness
HHD [NL *humanitatum doctor*] doctor of humanities
HHFA Housing and Home Finance Agency
HHS Department of Health and Human Services
HI Hawaii, high intensity, humidity index
Hind Hindi, Hindustani
hist historian, historical, history
Hitt Hittite
HIV human immunodeficiency virus
HJ [L *hic jacet*] here lies
HJR House joint resolution
hl hectoliter
HL House of Lords
hld hold
HLF Heart and Lung Foundation
hlqn harlequin

HLS [L *hoc loco situs*] laid in this place; holograph letter signed
hlt halt
hm hectometer
HM Her Majesty, Her Majesty's, His Majesty, His Majesty's
HMAS Her Majesty's Australian ship, His Majesty's Australian ship
HMBS Her Majesty's British ship, His Majesty's British ship
HMC Her Majesty's Customs, His Majesty's Customs
HMCS Her Majesty's Canadian ship, His Majesty's Canadian ship
HMF Her Majesty's Forces, His Majesty's Forces
HMS Her Majesty's ship, His Majesty's ship
HN head nurse
HNS Holy Name Society
hny honey
Ho holmium
hom homiletics, homily
hon honor, honorable, honorary
Hon *or* **Hond** Honduras
HOP high oxygen pressure
HOPE Health Opportunity for People Everywhere
hor horizontal
horol horology
hort horticultural, horticulture
Hos Hosea
hosp hospital
HP half pay, high pressure, hire purchase, horsepower
HPA high-power amplifier
HPF highest possible frequency, high power field
HPGC heading per gyrocompass
HQ headquarters
hr here, hour
HR House of Representatives
hrdwre hardware
H Res House resolution
HRH Her Royal Highness, His Royal Highness
HRI height-range indicator
hrzn horizon
HS high school
HSGT high-speed ground transport
HSL high-speed launch
HST Hawaiian standard time, hypersonic transport
ht height
HT halftime, halftone, hardtop, Hawaii time, high-tension, high tide, [L *hoc tempore*] at this time; [L *hoc titulo*] under this title
HUAC House Un-American Activities Committee
HUD Department of Housing and Urban Development
Humber Humberside
Hung Hungarian, Hungary
hv have
HV high velocity, high voltage
hvy heavy
hw how
HW high water, highway, hot water
HWM high-water mark
hwy highway
hy henry
hyd hydraulics, hydrostatics
hyp hypothesis, hypothetical
Hz hertz
i Indian, industrial, initial, intelligence, intensity, interstate, intransitive, island, isle, Israeli
I electric current, iodine
Ia *or* **IA** Iowa
IAA indoleacetic acid
IAAF International Amateur Athletic Federation
IABA International Amateur Boxing Association
IAEA International Atomic Energy Agency
IALC instrument approach and landing chart
IAM International Association of Machinists and Aerospace Workers
IAP international airport
IAS indicated airspeed
IATA International Air Transport Association
IAU International Association of Universities, International Astronomical Union
ib *or* **ibid** ibidem

IB in bond, incendiary bomb
IBRD International Bank for Reconstruction and Development
IBY International Biological Year
ICA International Cooperation Administration, International Cooperative Alliance
ICAO International Civil Aviation Organization
ICC Indian Claims Commission, International Chamber of Commerce, Interstate Commerce Commission
Ice Iceland
ICE internal-combustion engine, International Cultural Exchange
Icel Icelandic
ICFTU International Confederation of Free Trade Unions
ichth ichthyology
ICJ International Court of Justice
ICRC International Committee of the Red Cross
ICU intensive care unit
id idem
ID Idaho, identification, industrial design, inner diameter, inside dimensions, intelligence department, internal diameter
IDP international driving permit
i.e. [L *id est*] that is
IE industrial engineer
IEEE The Institute of Electrical and Electronics Engineers
IF intermediate frequency
IFC International Finance Corporation
iff if and only if
IFO identified flying object
IFR instrument flight rules
Ig immunoglobulin
IG inspector general
IGY International Geophysical Year
IHP indicated horsepower
IL Illinois
ILA International Longshoremen's Association
ILGWU International Ladies' Garment Workers' Union
ill illustrated, illustration, illustrator
Ill Illinois
illust *or* **illus** illustrated, illustration
ILO International Labor Organization
ILS instrument landing system
IM individual medley, intramural
IMCO Inter-Governmental Maritime Consultative Organization
imdtly immediately
IMF International Monetary Fund
imit imitative
immun immunity, immunization
immunol immunology
imp imperative, imperfect, imperial, import, imported
imperf imperfect, imperforate
in inch, inlet
In indium
IN Indiana
inc incomplete, incorporated, increase
incl including, inclusive
incog incognito
incr increase, increased
ind independent, index, industrial, industry
Ind Indian, Indiana
IND investigational new drug
IndE industrial engineer
indef indefinite
indic indicative
indiv individual
indn indication
Indon Indonesia, Indonesian
indus industrial, industry
inf infantry, infinitive
infl influenced
INH [*iso-ni*cotinic acid *hydrazide*] isoniazid
inorg inorganic
INP International News Photo
inq inquire
INRI [L *Iesus Nazarenus Rex Iudaeorum*] Jesus of Nazareth, King of the Jews
ins inches, insurance
INS Immigration and Naturalization Service
insol insoluble
insp inspector

inst instant, institute, institution, institutional
instr instructor, instrument, instrumental
insur insurance
int intelligence, intercept, interest, interim, interior, interjection, interleaved, intermediate, internal, international, interpreter, intersection, interval, interview, intransitive
interj interjection
interrog interrogative
intl *or* **intnl** international
intrans intransitive
in trans [L *in transitu*] in transit
introd introduction
intsv intensive
inv inventor, invoice
I/O input/output
IOC International Olympic Committee
Ion Ionic
IOOF Independent Order of Odd Fellows
IORM Improved Order of Red Men
IP initial point, innings pitched, intermediate pressure
ipm inches per minute
IPPF International Planned Parenthood Federation
ips inches per second
IPTS International Practical Temperature Scale
iq [L *idem quod*] the same as
Ir iridium, Irish
IR information retrieval, infrared, inland revenue, intelligence ratio, internal revenue
IRA individual retirement account, Irish Republican Army
IRBM intermediate range ballistic missile
Ire Ireland
irid iridescent
irred irredeemable
irreg irregular
IRS Internal Revenue Service
is island, isle
Isa *or* **Is** Isaiah
ISBN International Standard Book Number
ISC interstate commerce
isl island
isoln isolation
Isr Israel, Israeli
ISSN International Standard Serial Number
IST insulin shock therapy
isth isthmus
ISV International Scientific Vocabulary
It Italian, Italy
ital italic, italicized
Ital Italian
ITO International Trade Organization
ITU International Telecommunication Union, International Typographical Union
ITV instructional television
IU international unit
IV intravenous, intravenously
IW inside width, Isle of Wight, isotopic weight
IWW Industrial Workers of the World
j jack, journal, judge, justice
J joule
JA joint account, judge advocate
JAG judge advocate general
Jam Jamaica
Jan January
Jas James
Jav Javanese
JBS John Birch Society
JC junior college
JCB junior college of business, [NL *juris canonici baccalaureus*] bachelor of canon law
JCD [NL *juris canonici doctor*] doctor of canon law
JCL [NL *juris canonici licentiatus*] licentiate in canon law
JCS joint chiefs of staff
jct junction
JD [L *juris doctor*] doctor of jurisprudence, doctor of law; [L *jurum doctor*] doctor of laws; justice department; juvenile delinquent
Jer Jeremiah, Jeremias
jg junior grade
JIT job instruction training

Jn *or* **Jno** John
JND just noticeable difference
jnr *Brit* junior
Jo Joel
Jon Jonah, Jonas
Josh Joshua
jour journal, journeyman
JP jet propulsion, justice of the peace
Jpn Japan, Japanese
Jr junior
JRC Junior Red Cross
JSD [NL *juris scientiae doctor*] doctor of science of law
jt *or* **jnt** joint
Jud Judith
Judg Judges
Jul July
jun junior
Jun June
junc junction
juv juvenile
JV junior varsity
k karat, kindergarten, king, kitchen, knit, knot, koruna, kosher, kyat
K [NL *kalium*] potassium; Kelvin, strikeout
ka [G *kathode*] cathode
Kan *or* **Kans** Kansas
kb *or* **kbar** kilobar
KB kilobyte
kc kilocycle
KC Kansas City, King's Counsel, Knights of Columbus
kcal kilocalorie, kilogram calorie
KCB knight commander of the Order of the Bath
kc/s kilocycles per second
KD kiln-dried, knocked down
Ker Kerry
keV kilo-electron volt
kg keg, kilogram, king
kG kilogauss
KG knight of the Order of the Garter
KGB [Russ *Komitet Gosudarstvennoi Bezopasnosti*] (Soviet) State Security Committee
KGPS kilograms per second
kHz kilohertz
KIA killed in action
Kild Kildare
Kilk Kilkenny
Kin Kinross-shire
KJV King James Version
KKK Ku Klux Klan
kl kiloliter
km kilometer
KMPS kilometers per second
kn knot
K of C Knights of Columbus
K of P Knights of Pythias
Kor Korea, Korean
kpc kiloparsec
kph kilometers per hour
Kr krypton
KS Kansas
kt karat, knight, knot
kv kilovolt
kw kilowatt
kwhr *or* **kwh** kilowatt-hour
Ky *or* **KY** Kentucky
l lady, lake, lambert, land, large, late, left, [L *libra*] pound; line, liquid, lira, lire, liter, little, low
L Lagrangian, Latin, long
La lanthanum, Louisiana
LA law agent, Los Angeles, Louisiana
Lab Labrador
lam laminated
Lam Lamentations
Lancs Lancashire
lang language
lat latitude
Lat Latin, Latvia
LAT local apparent time
lav lavatory
lb [L *libra*] pound
LB Labrador
LBO leveraged buyout
lc lowercase
LC landing craft, left center, letter of credit, Library of Congress
LCD least common denominator, lowest common denominator
LCDR lieutenant commander
LCL less-than-carload lot
LCM least common multiple, lowest common multiple, [NL *legis comparativae magister*] master of comparative law
LCpl lance corporal

LCS League Championship Series
LCT local civil time
ld load, lord
LD learning disabled, learning disability; lethal dose — often used with a numerical subscript to indicate the percent of a test group of organisms the dose is expected to kill ⟨LD_{50}⟩; line of departure
LDC less developed country
ldg landing, loading
LDH lactate dehydrogenase, lactic dehydrogenase
ldr leader
LDS Latter-day Saints
LE leading edge
lea leather
Leb Lebanese, Lebanon
lect lecture, lecturer
leg legal, legato, legislative, legislature
legis legislation, legislative, legislature
Leics Leicestershire
Leit Leitrim
Lev *or* **Levit** Leviticus
lf lightface
LF ledger folio, low frequency
lg large, long
LH left hand, lower half, luteinizing hormone
LHD [L *litterarum humaniorum doctor*] doctor of humane letters, doctor of humanities
li link
Li lithium
LI Long Island
lib liberal, librarian, library
lieut lieutenant
LIFO last in, first out
Lim Limerick
lin lineal, linear
Lincs Lincolnshire
ling linguistics
liq liquid, liquor
lit liter, literal, literally, literary, literature
lith lithographic, lithography
Litt B *or* **Lit B** [ML *litterarum baccalaureus*] bachelor of letters, bachelor of literature
Litt D *or* **Lit D** [ML *litterarum doctor*] doctor of letters, doctor of literature
Lk Luke
ll lines
LL lending library, limited liability, lower left
LLB [NL *legum baccalaureus*] bachelor of laws
LLD [NL *legum doctor*] doctor of laws
LLM [NL *legum magister*] master of laws
LM Legion of Merit, long meter, lunar module
LMG light machine gun
LMT local mean time
ln lane, natural logarithm
lndg landing
LNG liquefied natural gas
loc cit [L *loco citato*] in the place cited
log logic
Lond London, Londonderry
long longitude
Long Longford
LOOM Loyal Order of Moose
loq [L *loquitur*] he speaks, she speaks
LOS line of scrimmage, line of sight
Loth Lothian
Lou Louth
LP low pressure
LPG liquefied petroleum gas
LPGA Ladies Professional Golf Association
Lr lawrencium
LR living room, log run, lower right
LRT light-rail transit
LRV light-rail vehicle
LS left side, letter signed, library science, [L *locus sigilli*] place of the seal; long shot
LSAT Law School Admission Test
LSI large-scale integrated, large-scale integration
LSM letter-sorting machine
LSS lifesaving service, lifesaving station, life-support system

LST landing ship, tank; local sidereal time
lt light
Lt lieutenant
LT long ton, low-tension
LTC or **Lt Col** lieutenant colonel
Lt Comdr lieutenant commander
ltd limited
LTG or **Lt Gen** lieutenant general
lt gov lieutenant governor
LTh licentiate in theology
LTJG lieutenant, junior grade
LTL less than truckload
ltr letter, lighter
LTS launch telemetry station, launch tracking system
Lu lutetium
lub lubricant, lubricating
Luth Lutheran
lv leave
LVT landing vehicle, tracked
LW low water
LWM low-water mark
LWV League of Women Voters
LZ landing zone
m male, manual, married, martyr, masculine, mass, mega-, meridian, [L *meridies*] noon; meter, middle, mile, [L *mille*] thousand; milli-, minute, molal, molality, molar, molarity, mole, month, moon, morning, muscle
m- meta-
M Mach, March, May, medium, million, monsieur
ma or **mA** milliampere
MA [ML *magister artium*] master of arts; Massachusetts, mental age, Middle Ages
MAA master of applied arts
Mac Machabees
Mac or **Macc** Maccabees
MAC military airlift command
mach machine, machining, machinist
MAD mutual assured destruction
MAE or **MA Ed** master of arts in education
mag magnesium, magnetism, magneto, magnitude
Maj major
Maj Gen major general
Mal Malachi
MALS master of arts in library science
man manual
Man Manitoba
manuf manufacture, manufacturing
MAO monoamine oxidase
MAP modified American plan
mar maritime
Mar March
masc masculine
MASH mobile army surgical hospital
Mass Massachusetts
MAT master of arts in teaching, Miller analogy test
math mathematical, mathematician
matric matriculated, matriculation
Matt Matthew
max maximum
mb millibar
MB bachelor of medicine, Manitoba, megabyte, municipal borough
MBA master of business administration
mbd million barrels per day
MBE member of the Order of the British Empire
MBS Mutual Broadcasting System
mc megacycle, millicurie
MC member of Congress
MCAT Medical College Admission Test
mcf thousand cubic feet
mcg microgram
MCL Marine Corps League, master of civil law, master of comparative law
MCP male chauvinist pig
MCPO master chief petty officer
Md Maryland, mendelevium
MD [NL *medicinae doctor*] doctor of medicine; [It *mano destra*] right hand; Maryland, medical department, months after date, muscular dystrophy
MDiv master of divinity
mdnt midnight

mdse merchandise
MDT mountain daylight time
Me Maine, methyl
ME Maine, mechanical engineer, medical examiner
Mea Meath
meas measure
mech mechanical, mechanics
med medicine, medieval, medium
Med Mediterranean
MEd master of education
meg megohm
mem member, memoir, memorial
mer meridian
Mersey Merseyside
met meteorological, meteorology, metropolitan
metal or **metall** metallurgical, metallurgy
metaph metaphysics
METO Middle East Treaty Organization
MeV million electron volts
Mex Mexican, Mexico
mf or **mF** millifarad
MF medium frequency, mezzo forte, microfiche
MFA master of fine arts
mfd manufactured
mfg manufacturing
MFH master of foxhounds
MFN most favored nation
mfr manufacture, manufacturer
mg milligram
Mg magnesium
MG machine gun, major general, military government
mgal milligal
MGB [Russ *Ministerstvo Gosudarstvennoi Bezopasnosti*] Ministry of State Security
mgd million gallons per day
mgr manager, monseigneur, monsignor
mgt or **mgmt** management
MGy Sgt master gunnery sergeant
mh millihenry
MH medal of honor, mobile home
MHA master of hospital administration
MHD magnetohydrodynamic, magnetohydrodynamics
mhg mahogany
MHW mean high water
MHz megahertz
mi mile, mileage, mill
MI Michigan, military intelligence
Mic Micah
Mich Michigan
MICR magnetic ink character recognition
mid middle
Middx Middlesex
Mid Glam Mid Glamorgan
midn midshipman
mil military, million
min minim, minimum, mining, minister, minor, minute
Minn Minnesota
MIO minimum identifiable odor
MIPS million instructions per second
misc miscellaneous
Miss Mississippi
mixt mixture
mk mark, markka
Mk Mark
mks meter-kilogram-second
mktg marketing
ml milliliter
mL millilambert
MLA Member of the Legislative Assembly
MLD median lethal dose, minimum lethal dose
MLF multilateral force
Mlle [F] mademoiselle
Mlles [F] mesdemoiselles
MLS master of library science
MLW mean low water
mm millimeter
MM [F] messieurs; mutatis mutandis
Mme [F] madame
mmf magnetomotive force
MMPI Minnesota Multiphasic Personality Inventory
Mn manganese
MN magnetic north, Minnesota
mo month
Mo Missouri, molybdenum
MO mail order, medical officer, Missouri, modus operandi, money order

mod moderate, modern, modification, modified, modulo, modulus
modif modification
mol molecular, molecule
MOL manned orbiting laboratory
mol wt molecular weight
MOM middle of month
mon monastery, monetary
Mon Monaghan, Monday
Mont Montana
mor morocco
MOR middle of the road
morph morphology
mos months
MOS metal-oxide semiconductor
MOSFET metal-oxide-semiconductor field effect transistor
MP melting point, member of parliament, metropolitan police, military police, military policeman
mpg miles per gallon
mph miles per hour
MPM meters per minute
MPS meters per second
MPX multiplex
mr milliroentgen
MR map reference, mentally retarded, mill run
mRNA messenger RNA
ms millisecond
MS [It *mano sinistra*] left hand; manuscript, master of science, military science, Mississippi, motor ship, multiple sclerosis
MSAT Minnesota Scholastic Aptitude Test
MSc master of science
msec millisecond
msg message
MSG master sergeant, monosodium glutamate
msgr monseigneur, monsignor
MSgt master sergeant
MSH melanocyte-stimulating hormone
MSL mean sea level
MSN master of science in nursing
MSS manuscripts
MST mountain standard time
MSTS Military Sea Transportation Service
MSW master of social welfare, master of social work
mt mount, mountain
Mt Matthew
MT machine translation, metric ton, Montana, mountain time
mtg meeting, mortgage
mtge mortgage
mtn mountain
MTO Mediterranean theater of operations
mun or **munic** municipal
mus museum, music, musical, musician
mv or **mV** millivolt
MV main verb, mean variation, motor vessel
MVA Missouri Valley Authority
MVD [Russ *Ministerstvo Vnutrennikh Del*] Ministry of Internal Affairs
MVP most valuable player
MW megawatt
MWe megawatts electric
mxd mixed
my million years
myc or **mycol** mycology
Myr million years
n name, navy, net, neuter, *usu ital* neutron, noon, normal, north, northern, note, noun, number
N newton, nitrogen
Na [NL *natrium*] sodium
NA national association, no account, North America, not applicable, not available
NAACP National Association for the Advancement of Colored People
NAB New American Bible
NACU National Association of Colleges and Universities
NAD no appreciable disease
Nah Nahum
NAIA National Association of Intercollegiate Athletes
NAMH National Association for Mental Health
NAS National Academy of Sciences, naval air station

NASA National Aeronautics and Space Administration
NASCAR National Association of Stock Car Auto Racing
NASL North American Soccer League
nat national, native, natural
natl national
NATO North Atlantic Treaty Organization
naut nautical
nav naval, navigable, navigation
Nb niobium
NB New Brunswick, northbound; nota bene
NBA National Basketball Association, National Boxing Association
NBC National Broadcasting Company
NBS National Bureau of Standards
NC no charge, no credit, North Carolina, nurse corps
NCAA National Collegiate Athletic Association
NCE New Catholic Edition
NCV no commercial value
Nd neodymium
ND no date, North Dakota
N Dak North Dakota
Ne neon
NE Nebraska, New England, no effects, northeast
NEA National Education Association
Neb or **Nebr** Nebraska
NEB New English Bible
NED New English Dictionary
neg negative
Neh Nehemiah
NEI not elsewhere included
nem con [NL *nemine contradicente*] no one contradicting
nem diss [NL *nemine dissentiente*] no one dissenting
NEP New Economic Policy
NES not elsewhere specified
NET National Educational Television
NETFS National Educational Television Film Service
Neth Netherlands
neurol neurological, neurology
neut neuter
Nev Nevada
New Eng New England
NF Newfoundland, no funds
NFC National Football Conference
NFL National Football League
Nfld Newfoundland
NFS not for sale
ng nanogram
NG national guard, no good
NGF nerve growth factor
NGk New Greek
NGU nongonococcal urethritis
NH never hinged, New Hampshire
NHL National Hockey League
NHP nominal horsepower
Ni nickel
NIC newly industrialized country, newly industrializing country
NIH National Institutes of Health
NIT National Invitational Tournament
NJ New Jersey
NKVD [Russ *Narodnyi Komissariat Vnutrennikh Del*] People's Commissariat of Internal Affairs
NL National League, new line, night letter, [L *non licet*] it is not permitted; north latitude
NLCS National League Championship Series
NLF National Liberation Front
NLRB National Labor Relations Board
NLT night letter
nm nanometer
NM nautical mile, New Mexico, no mark, not marked
N Mex New Mexico
NMI no middle initial
NMR nuclear magnetic resonance
NNE north-northeast
NNW north-northwest
no north, northern, [L *numero*, abl. of *numerus*] number
No nobelium
NOIBN not otherwise indexed by name
nom nominative

non obst *or* **non obs** non obstante
non seq non sequitur
NOP not otherwise provided for
Nor Norway, Norwegian
NORAD North American Air Defense Command
Norf Norfolk
norm normal
Northants Northamptonshire
Norw Norway, Norwegian
nos numbers
NOS not otherwise specified
Notts Nottinghamshire
nov novelist
Nov November
NOW National Organization for Women, negotiable order of withdrawal
NO$_x$ nitrogen oxide
np no pagination, no place (of publication)
Np neptunium
NP neuropsychiatric, neuropsychiatry, no protest, notary public, noun phrase
NPF not provided for
NPN nonprotein nitrogen
NPR National Public Radio
nr near
NR not rated
NRA National Recovery Administration, National Rifle Association
NRC National Research Council, Nuclear Regulatory Commission
Ns nimbostratus
NS national special, new series, new style, not specified, not sufficient, Nova Scotia, nuclear ship
NSA National Security Agency
NSC National Security Council
nsec *also* **ns** nanosecond
NSF National Science Foundation, not sufficient funds
NSW New South Wales
NT New Testament, Northern Territory, Northwest Territories
Nthmb Northumberland
NTP normal temperature and pressure
nt wt *or* **n wt** net weight
NU name unknown
num numeral
Num *or* **Numb** Numbers
numis numismatic, numismatical, numismatics
NV Nevada, nonvoting
NW northwest
NWT Northwest Territories
NY New York
NYA National Youth Administration
NYC New York City
NYSE New York Stock Exchange
NZ New Zealand
o ocean, ohm, old, order, oriental, over
O Ohio, oxygen, [NL *octarius*] pint
o- ortho-
o/a on or about
OAS Organization of American States
OAU Organization of African Unity
ob [L *obiit*] he died, she died; observation, obstetrical, obstetrician
Ob *or* **Obad** Obadiah
OBE Officer of the Order of the British Empire
ob-gyn obstetrician gynecologist, obstetrics gynecology
obj object, objective
obl oblique, oblong
obstet obstetrical, obstetrics
obv obverse
oc ocean
OC off center, officer candidate, on center, on course
occas occasionally
OCDM Office of Civil and Defense Mobilization
oceanog oceanography
OCR optical character reader, optical character recognition
OCS officer candidate school
oct octavo
Oct October
OCTV open-circuit television
OD doctor of optometry, [L *oculus dexter*] right eye; officer of the day, olive drab, on demand, outside diameter, outside dimension, overdraft, overdrawn
Oe oersted

OE Old English
OECD Organization for Economic Cooperation and Development
OED Oxford English Dictionary
OEO Office of Economic Opportunity
OES Order of the Eastern Star
OF outfield
off office, officer, official
offic official
OG officer of the guard, original gum
OH Ohio
OHMS on Her Majesty's service, on His Majesty's service
OIT Office of International Trade
OJ orange juice
OJT on-the-job training
OK Oklahoma, outer keel
Okla Oklahoma
OM order of merit
OMB Office of Management and Budget
ON *or* **Ont** Ontario
OOB off-off Broadway
op opus
OP observation post, out of print
op cit [L *opere citato*] in the work cited
OPEC Organization of Petroleum Exporting Countries
opp opposite
opt optical, optician, optics, optional
OR operating room, operations research, Oregon, owner's risk
orch orchestra
ord order, ordnance
Oreg *or* **Ore** Oregon
org organic, organization, organized
orig original, originally, originator
Ork Orkney
ornith ornithology
Os osmium
OS [L *oculus sinister*] left eye; old series, old style, ordinary seaman, out of stock
OSHA Occupational Safety and Health Administration
OSS Office of Strategic Services
OT occupational therapy, Old Testament, overtime
OTB offtrack betting
OTC over-the-counter
OTS officers' training school
OW one-way
Oxon [L *Oxonia*] Oxford; Oxfordshire, [L *Oxoniensis*] of Oxford
oz [obs. It *onza* (now *oncia*)] ounce; ounces
p page, parental generation, part, participle, past, pater, pawn, pence, penny, per, peseta, peso, petite, piano, pico-, pint, pipe, pitch, pole, port, power, pressure, pro, proton, purl
P phosphorus, [F *poids*] weight
p- para-
Pa pascal, Pennsylvania, protactinium
PA particular average, passenger agent, Pennsylvania, per annum, personal appearance, physician's assistant, power amplifier, power of attorney, press agent, private account, professional association, public address, purchasing agent
Pac Pacific
PAC Political Action Committee
paleon paleontology
pam pamphlet
Pan Panama
p and h postage and handling
P and L profit and loss
par paragraph, parallel, parish
part participial, participle, particular
PAS para-aminosalicylic acid
pass passenger, passive
pat patent
path *or* **pathol** pathological, pathology
PAU Pan American Union
PAYE pay as you earn, pay as you enter
payt payment
Pb [L *plumbum*] lead
PB power brakes
PBS Public Broadcasting Service
PBX private branch exchange
pc parsec
PC Peace Corps, percent, percentage, personal computer, postcard,

[L *post cibum*] after meals; professional corporation
pct percent, percentage
pd paid
Pd palladium
PD per diem, police department, postal district, potential difference, public domain
PDA predicted drift angle
PDD past due date
PDT Pacific daylight time
PE physical education, printer's error, probable error
P/E price/earnings
PEI Prince Edward Island
pen peninsula
PEN International Association of Poets, Playwrights, Editors, Essayists and Novelists
Penn *or* **Penna** Pennsylvania
per period, person
perf perfect, perforated, performance
perh perhaps
perm permanent
perp perpendicular
pers person, personal, personnel
Pers Persia, Persian
pert pertaining
pet petroleum
Pet Peter
pf personal foul, pfennig, picofarad, preferred
PF power factor, pianoforte, [It *più forte*] louder
PFC private first class
pfd preferred
pg page, picogram
Pg Portugal, Portuguese
PG paying guest, postgraduate, prostaglandin
PGA Professional Golfers' Association
ph phase
PH pinch hit, public health, Purple Heart
phar pharmacopoeia, pharmacy
pharm pharmaceutical, pharmacist, pharmacy
PhB [L *philosophiae baccalaureus*] bachelor of philosophy
PhD [L *philosophiae doctor*] doctor of philosophy
phil *or* **philol** philological, philology
philos philosopher, philosophy
phon phonetics
photog photographic, photography
phr phrase
phys physical, physics
physiol physiologist, physiology
pi *or* **pias** piaster
PI Philippine Islands, programmed instruction
PIN personal identification number
PINS persons in need of supervision
pinx [L *pinxit*] he painted it, she painted it
pizz pizzicato
pk park, peak, peck, pike
pkg package
pkt packet, pocket
PKU phenylketonuria
pkwy parkway
pl place, plate, plural
PL partial loss, private line
plat plateau, platoon
plf plaintiff
PLO Palestine Liberation Organization
PLSS portable life-support system
pm phase modulation, premium
Pm promethium
PM paymaster, permanent magnet, police magistrate, postmaster, post meridiem — often not cap.; postmortem, prime minister, provost marshal
pmk postmark
pmt payment
PN promissory note
pnxt [L *pinxit*] he painted it, she painted it
Po polonium
PO [L *per os*] by mouth, orally; petty officer, postal order, post office, purchase order
POC port of call
POD pay on delivery, post office department
POE port of embarkation, port of entry

Pol Poland, Polish
polit political, politician
poly polytechnic
pon pontoon
POO post office order
pop population
por portrait
POR pay on return
Port Portugal, Portuguese
pos position, positive
poss possessive
pot potential, potentiometer
pp pages, [L *per procurationem*] by proxy; pianissimo
PP parcel post, past participle, postpaid, prepaid
ppa per power of attorney
ppb parts per billion
ppd postpaid, prepaid
ppm parts per million
PPS [L *post postscriptum*] an additional postscript
ppt parts per thousand, parts per trillion, precipitate
pptn precipitation
PQ previous question, Province of Quebec
pr pair, price, printed
Pr praseodymium, propyl
PR payroll, proportional representation, public relations, Puerto Rico
PRC People's Republic of China
prec preceding
pred predicate
pref preface, preferred, prefix
prem premium
prep preparatory, preposition
prepd prepared
prepg preparing
prepn preparation
pres present, president
Presb Presbyterian
prev previous, previously
prf proof
prim primary, primitive
prin principal, principle
priv private, privately, privative
PRN [L *pro re nata*] for the emergency; as needed
PRO public relations officer
prob probable, probably, probate, problem
proc proceedings
prod product, production
prof professional, professor
prom promontory
pron pronoun, pronounced, pronunciation
prop property, proposition, proprietor
pros prosody
Prot Protestant
prov province, provincial, provisional
Prov Proverbs
prox proximo
ps picosecond
Ps *or* **Psa** Psalms
PS [L *postscriptum*] postscript; power steering, power supply, public school
psec picosecond
pseud pseudonym, pseudonymous
psf pounds per square foot
PSG platoon sergeant
psi pounds per square inch
psig pounds per square inch gauge
PST Pacific standard time
psych psychology
psychol psychologist, psychology
pt part, payment, pint, point, port
Pt platinum
PT Pacific time, part-time, physical therapy, physical training
pta peseta
PTA Parent-Teacher Association
pte *Brit* private
ptg printing
PTO Parent-Teacher Organization, please turn over
PTV public television
pty *Brit* proprietary
Pu plutonium
PU pickup
pub public, publication, published, publisher, publishing
publ publication, published, publisher
PUD pickup and delivery
pulv [L *pulvis*] powder
PV polyvinyl
PVA polyvinyl acetate
PVC polyvinyl chloride

pvt private
PVT pressure, volume, temperature
PW prisoner of war
pwr power
pwt pennyweight
PX please exchange, post exchange
q quart, quartile, quarto, queen, query, question, quetzal, quire
QB queen's bench
QC quality control, queen's counsel
QD [L *quaque die*] daily
QED quantum electrodynamics, [L *quod erat demonstrandum*] which was to be demonstrated
QEF [L *quod erat faciendum*] which was to be done
QEI [L *quod erat inveniendum*] which was to be found out
QF quick-firing
QID [L *quater in die*] four times a day
Qld Queensland
QM [L *quoque matutino*] every morning; quartermaster
QMC quartermaster corps
QMG quartermaster general
qp *or* **q pl** [L *quantum placet*] as much as you please
qq questions
qq v [L *quae vide*] which (*pl*) see
qr quarter, quire
QS [L *quantum sufficit*] as much as suffices
qt quantity, quart
qtd quartered
qto quarto
qty quantity
qu *or* **ques** question
quad quadrant
qual qualitative, quality
quant quantitative
quar quarterly
Que Quebec
quot quotation
qv [L *quod vide*] which see
qy query
r rabbi, radius, rain, range, Rankine, rare, real, Reaumur, recto, red, repeat, Republican, rerun, resistance, right, river, roentgen, rook, rough, ruble, run, rupee
R radical — used esp. of a univalent hydrocarbon radical; recipe; registered trademark — often enclosed in a circle; regular
ra range
Ra radium
RA regular army, right ascension, Royal Academician, Royal Academy
RAAF Royal Australian Air Force
rad radical, radian, radiator, radio, radius, radix
RADM rear admiral
RAF Royal Air Force
RAM random-access memory
R & B rhythm and blues
R and R rest and recreation, rest and recuperation
rap rapid
Rb rubidium
RBC red blood cells, red blood count
RBE relative biological effectiveness
RC Red Cross, resistance-capacitance, Roman Catholic
RCAF Royal Canadian Air Force
RCMP Royal Canadian Mounted Police
RCN Royal Canadian Navy
rct recruit
rd road, rod, round
RD refer to drawer, rural delivery
RDA recommended daily allowance, recommended dietary allowance
RDF radio direction finder, radio direction finding
Re rhenium
REA Railway Express Agency, Rural Electrification Administration
rec receipt, record, recording, recreation
recd received
recip reciprocal, reciprocity
rec sec recording secretary
rect receipt, rectangle, rectangular, rectified
rec ve recreational vehicle
red reduce, reduction

ref reference, referred, refining, reformed, refunding
refl reflex, reflexive
refr refraction
refrig refrigerating, refrigeration
reg region, register, registered, registration, regular
regd registered
regt regiment
REIT real estate investment trust
rel relating, relative, released, religion, religious
relig religion
rep repair, report, reporter, representative, republic
Rep Republican
repl replace, replacement
rept report
req request, require, required, requisition
reqd required
res research, reservation, reserve, residence, resolution
RES reticuloendothelial system
resp respective, respectively
ret retain, retired, return
retd retained, retired, returned
rev revenue, reverse, review, reviewed, revised, revision, revolution
Rev Revelation, reverend
rf refunding
RF radio frequency
RFD rural free delivery
Rh rhodium
RH relative humidity, right hand
rhet rhetoric
RI refractive index, Rhode Island
RIA radioimmunoassay
RIF reduction in force
RIP [L *requiescat in pace*] may he rest in peace, may she rest in peace; [L *requiescant in pace*] may they rest in peace
rit ritardando
riv river
RJ road junction
rm ream, room
rms root-mean-square
RMS Royal Mail Service, Royal Mail Steamer, Royal Mail Steamship
Rn radon
RN registered nurse, Royal Navy
rnd round
RNZAF Royal New Zealand Air Force
ROC Republic of China (Taiwan)
ROG receipt of goods
ROI return on investment
ROK Republic of Korea (South Korea)
Rom Roman, Romance, Romania, Romanian
ROM read-only memory
ROP record of production, run-of-paper
Ros *or* **Rosc** Roscommon
rot rotating, rotation
ROTC Reserve Officers' Training Corps
RP Received Pronunciation, relief pitcher, reply paid, reprint, reprinting
RPM revolutions per minute
RPS revolutions per second
rpt repeat, report
RQ respiratory quotient
RR railroad, rural route
RS recording secretary, revised statutes, right side, Royal Society
RSFSR [Russ *Rossiĭskaya Sovetskaya Federativnaya Sotsialisticheskaya Respublika*] Russian Soviet Federated Socialist Republic
RSV Revised Standard Version
RSVP [F *répondez s'il vous plaît*] please reply
RSWC right side up with care
rt right
RT radiotelephone, room temperature
rte route
rtw ready-to-wear
Ru ruthenium
Rum Rumania, Rumanian
Russ Russia, Russian
RV recreational vehicle
RW radiological warfare, right worshipful, right worthy
rwy *or* **ry** railway
s sabbath, saint, schilling, scruple, second, secondary, section, sen-

ate, series, shilling, [L *signa*] label; siemens, signor, sine, singular, small, smooth, snow, society, son, sou, south, southern, subject, symmetrical
S satisfactory, short, standard deviation of a sample, sulfur, svedberg
SA Salvation Army, seaman apprentice, sex appeal, [L *sine anno* without year] without date; South Africa, South America, South Australia, subject to approval
SAC Strategic Air Command
SAE self-addressed envelope, stamped addressed envelope
SALT Strategic Arms Limitation Talks
Sam *or* **Saml** Samuel
S and M sadism and masochism, sadist and masochist
sanit sanitary, sanitation
SASE self-addressed stamped envelope
Sask Saskatchewan
sat saturate, saturated, saturation
Sat Saturday
satd saturated
S Aust South Australia
sb substantive
Sb [L *stibium*] antimony
SB [NL *scientiae baccalaureus*] bachelor of science; simultaneous broadcast, southbound
SBA Small Business Administration
SBN Standard Book Number
sc scale, scene, science, scilicet, screw, [L *sculpsit*] he carved it, she carved it; he engraved it, she engraved it
Sc scandium, Scots, stratocumulus
SC small capitals, South Carolina, supercalendered, supreme court
Scand Scandinavia, Scandinavian
SCAT School and College Ability Test, supersonic commercial air transport
ScD doctor of science
sch school
sci science, scientific
scil scilicet
Scot Scotland, Scottish
SCP single-cell protein
SCPO senior chief petty officer
script scripture
sct scout
sctd scattered
sd said, sewed
SD sea-damaged, sine die, South Dakota, special delivery, stage direction, standard deviation
SDA specific dynamic action
S Dak South Dakota
SDI Strategic Defense Initiative
SDR special drawing rights
SDS Students for a Democratic Society
Se selenium
SE southeast, Standard English, stock exchange, straight edge
SEATO Southeast Asia Treaty Organization
sec secant, second, secondary, secretary, section, [L *secundum*] according to
SEC Securities and Exchange Commission
sect section, sectional
secy secretary
sed sediment, sedimentation
sel select, selected, selection
sem semicolon, seminar, seminary
Sem Semitic
sen senate, senator, senior
sep separate, separated
Sep September
sepd separated
sepg separating
sepn separation
Sept September
seq [L *sequens, sequentes, sequentia*] the following
seqq [L *sequentia*] the following ones
ser serial, series, service
Serb Serbian
serg *or* **sergt** sergeant
serv service
SES socioeconomic status
sf *or* **sfz** sforzando
SF sacrifice fly, science fiction, sinking fund
SFC sergeant first class

SG senior grade, sergeant, solicitor general, *often not cap* specific gravity; surgeon general
sgd signed
Sgt sergeant
Sgt Maj sergeant major
Shak Shakespeare
Shet Shetland
SHF superhigh frequency
shipt shipment
SHP shaft horsepower
shpt shipment
sht sheet
shtg shortage
Si silicon
SI [F *Système International d'Unités*] International System of Units
SIDS sudden infant death syndrome
sig signal, signature, signor
Sig [L *signa*] label
SIG special interest group
sigill [L *sigillum*] seal
sin sine
sing singular
SJ Society of Jesus
SK Saskatchewan
Skt Sanskrit
sl slightly, slow
SL salvage loss, sea level, south latitude
SLAN [L *sine loco, anno*, (*vel*) *nomine*] without place, year, or name
Slav Slavic
SLBM submarine-launched ballistic missile
sld sailed, sealed, sold
SLE systemic lupus erythematosus
Slo Sligo
SLR single-lens reflex
sm small
Sm samarium
SM [NL *scientiae magister*] master of science; sergeant major, service mark, soldier's medal, stage manager, station master
S–M *or* **S/M** sadomasochism, sadomasochist
SMA sergeant major of the army
SMaj sergeant major
SMSA Standard Metropolitan Statistical Area
SMSgt senior master sergeant
SMV slow-moving vehicle
Sn [LL *stannum*] tin
SNCC Student Nonviolent Coordinating Committee
SNG substitute natural gas, synthetic natural gas
so south, southern
SO seller's option, strikeout
soc social, society
sociol sociologist, sociology
sol solicitor, soluble, solution
soln solution
Som Somersetshire
SOP standard operating procedure, standing operating procedure
soph sophomore
SO$_x$ sulfur oxide
sp special, species, specific, specimen, spelling, spirit
Sp Spain, Spanish
SP self-propelled, shore patrol, shore patrolman, shore police, [L *sine prole*] without issue; single pole, specialist
Span Spanish
SPCA Society for the Prevention of Cruelty to Animals
SPCC Society for the Prevention of Cruelty to Children
spec special, specifically
specif special, specifically
sp gr specific gravity
sp ht specific heat
SPOT satellite positioning and tracking
spp *pl* species
SPQR [L *senatus populusque Romanus*] the senate and the people of Rome; small profits, quick returns
sps [L *sine prole superstite*] without surviving issue
sq squadron, square
Sr senior, senor, señor, sister, strontium
SR seaman recruit, sedimentation rate, shipping receipt

Sra senora, señora
SRO single-room occupancy, standing room only
Srta senorita, señorita
ss [L *semis*] one half
SS saints, same size, Social Security, steamship, sworn statement
SSA Social Security Administration
SSE south-southeast
SSG *or* **SSgt** staff sergeant
SSM staff sergeant major
ssp subspecies
SSPE subacute sclerosing panencephalitis
SSR Soviet Socialist Republic
SSS Selective Service System
SSW south-southwest
st stanza, state, stitch, stone, street
St saint, stratus
ST short ton, single throw, standard time
sta station, stationary
Staffs Staffordshire
stat [L *statim*] immediately; statute
STB [L *sacrae theologiae baccalaureus*] bachelor of sacred theology; [L *scientiae theologicae baccalaureus*] bachelor of theology
stbd starboard
std standard
STD [L *sacrae theologiae doctor*] doctor of sacred theology
Ste [F *sainte*] saint (female)
ster *or* **stg** sterling
stge storage
stk stock
STL [NL *sacrae theologiae licentiatus*] licentiate of sacred theology
STOL short takeoff and landing
stor storage
STP standard temperature and pressure
str steamer, strophe
stud student
STV subscription television
sub subaltern, subtract, suburb
subg subgenus
subj subject, subjunctive
suff sufficient, suffix
Suff Suffolk
Sun Sunday
sup superior, supplement, supplementary, supply, supra
supp *or* **suppl** supplement, supplementary
supr supreme
supt superintendent
supvr supervisor
sur surface
surg surgeon, surgery, surgical
surv survey, surveying, surveyor
Suss Sussex
sv sailing vessel, saves, [L *sub verbo* or *sub voce*] under the word
svc *or* **svce** service
svgs savings
sw switch
Sw Sweden, Swedish
SW seawater, shipper's weight, shortwave, southwest
SWA South-West Africa
SWAT Special Weapons and Tactics
Swed Sweden, Swedish
SWG standard wire gauge
Switz Switzerland
syl *or* **syll** syllable
sym symbol, symmetrical
syn synonym, synonymous, synonymy
syst system
t tablespoon, target, teaspoon, technical, temperature, [L *tempore*] in the time of; tense, tension, tera-, tertiary, time, ton, township, transitive, troy, true
T tesla, tritium
Ta tantalum
TA teaching assistant
TAC Tactical Air Command
TAG the adjutant general
tan tangent
TAT thematic apperception test
taxon taxonomic, taxonomy
Tay Tayside
tb tablespoon, tablespoonful
Tb terbium
TB trial balance, tubercle bacillus
TBA *often not cap* to be announced
tbs *or* **tbsp** tablespoon, tablespoonful

TBS talk between ships
tc tierce
Tc technetium
TC teachers college, terra-cotta, till countermanded
TD tank destroyer, touchdown, Treasury Department
TDD telecommunications device for the deaf
TDN total digestible nutrients
TDY temporary duty
Te tellurium
tec technical, technician
tech technical, technically, technician, technological, technology
technol technological, technology
TEFL teaching English as a foreign language
tel telegram, telegraph, telephone
teleg telegraphy
temp temperance, temperature, template, temporal, temporary, [L *tempore*] in the time of
Tenn Tennessee
ter terrace, territory
terr territory
TESL teaching English as a second language
TESOL Teachers of English to Speakers of Other Languages
Test Testament
Tex Texas
TF task force, territorial force
tfr transfer
TG transformational grammar, type genus
TGIF thank God it's Friday
tgt target
Th thorium, Thursday
TH true heading
Thai Thailand
theat theater, theatrical
theol theological, theology
therm thermometer
Thess Thessalonians
ThM [NL *theologiae magister*] master of theology
Thurs *or* **Thu** Thursday
Ti titanium
TID [L *ter in die*] three times a day
Tim Timothy
tinc tincture
Tip Tipperary
tit title
Tit Titus
tk tank, truck
tkt ticket
Tl thallium
TL total loss, truckload
TLC tender loving care, thin-layer chromatography
TLO total loss only
tlr tailor, trailer
Tm thulium
TM trademark, transcendental meditation
TMO telegraph money order
tn ton, town, train
TN Tennessee, true north
tng training
tnpk turnpike
TO table of organization, telegraph office, traditional orthography, turn over
TOEFL Test of English as a Foreign Language
tonn tonnage
topo topographic, topographical
topog topography
tot total
TOT time on target
tp title page, township
tpk *or* **tpke** turnpike
tps townships, troops
tr translated, translation, translator, transpose, troop, trustee
trag tragedy, tragic
trans transaction, transitive, translated, translation, translator, transportation, transverse
transf transfer, transferred
transl translation, translated
transp transportation
trav travel, traveler, travels
treas treasurer, treasury
trib tributary
trit triturate
trop tropic, tropical
ts tensile strength
TSgt technical sergeant
TSH thyroid-stimulating hormone
tsp teaspoon, teaspoonful

TT telegraphic transfer, teletypewriter, Trust Territories
TTY teletypewriter
Tu Tuesday
TU trade union, transmission unit
TUC Trades Union Congress
Tues *or* **Tue** Tuesday
Turk Turkey, Turkish
TV terminal velocity, transvestite
TVA Tennessee Valley Authority
Tvl Transvaal
twp township
TWX teletypewriter exchange
TX Texas
Tyr Tyrone
u uncle, unit, unsymmetrical, upper
U [*Union of Orthodox Hebrew Congregations*] kosher certification — often enclosed in a circle; university, unsatisfactory, uranium
UAE United Arab Emirates
UAR United Arab Republic
UAW United Automobile Workers
UC undercharge, uppercase
UFT United Federation of Teachers
ugt urgent
UHF ultrahigh frequency
UK United Kingdom
ult ultimate, ultimo
UMW United Mine Workers
UN United Nations
unan unanimous
UNESCO United Nations Educational, Scientific, and Cultural Organization
Unh unnilhexium
UNICEF [*United Nations International Children's Emergency Fund*, its former name] United Nations Children's Fund
univ universal, university
unp unpaged
Unp unnilpentium
Unq unnilquadium
UNRWA United Nations Relief and Works Agency
uns unsymmetrical
UP underproof
UPC Universal Product Code
UPI United Press International
urol urological, urology
US [L *ubi supra*] where above mentioned; United States, [L *ut supra*] as above
USA United States Army, United States of America
USAF United States Air Force
USCG United States Coast Guard
USDA United States Department of Agriculture
USES United States Employment Service
USIA United States Information Agency
USM United States Mail
USMC United States Marine Corps
USN United States Navy
USO United Service Organizations
USP United States Pharmacopeia
USPS United States Postal Service
USS United States ship
USSR Union of Soviet Socialist Republics
usu usual, usually
UT Universal time, Utah
UTC Coordinated Universal Time
ut dict [L *ut dictum*] as directed
util utility
UV ultraviolet
UW underwriter
ux [L *uxor*] wife
UXB unexploded bomb
v vector, velocity, verb, verse, verso, versus, very, vice, victory, vide, voice, voltage, volume, vowel
V vanadium, volt
Va Virginia
VA Veterans Administration, vicar apostolic, vice admiral, Virginia, visual aid, volt-ampere
vac vacuum
VADM vice admiral
val value, valued
var variable, variant, variation, variety, various
VAR visual-aural range, volt-ampere reactive
VAT value-added tax

vb verb, verbal
VC veterinary corps, vice-chancellor, vice-consul, Victoria Cross, Vietcong
VD vapor density, various dates, venereal disease
VDRL venereal disease research laboratory
VDT video display terminal
VDU visual display unit
veg vegetable
vel vellum, velocity
Ven venerable
ver verse
vers versed sine
vert vertebrate, vertical
VF very fair, very fine, video frequency, visual field, voice frequency
VFD volunteer fire department
VFR visual flight rules
VFW Veterans of Foreign Wars
VG very good, vicar-general
VHF very high frequency
vi verb intransitive, [L *vide infra*] see below
VI Virgin Islands, viscosity index, volume indicator
vic vicinity
Vic Victoria
vil village
VIN vehicle identification number
vis visibility, visual
VISTA Volunteers in Service to America
viz videlicet
VLF very low frequency
VOA Voice of America
voc vocational, vocative
vocab vocabulary
vol volcano, volume, volunteer
VOM volt-ohmmeter
VOR very-high-frequency omnidirectional radio range
vou voucher
VP variable pitch, various places, verb phrase, vice president
VRM variable rate mortgage
vs verse, versus
VS veterinary surgeon, [L *vide supra*] see above
vss verses, versions
V/STOL vertical short takeoff and landing
vt verb transitive
Vt Vermont
VT vacuum tube, variable time, Vermont, voice type
VTOL vertical takeoff and landing
VTR videotape recorder
VU volume unit
Vulg Vulgate
vv verses, vice versa
w warden, water, week, weight, Welsh, west, western, white, wicket, wide, width, wife, with, withdrawal, work
W energy, [G *Wolfram*] tungsten; watt
WA Washington, Western Australia
war warrant
Warks Warwickshire
Wash Washington
Wat Waterford
WATS Wide-Area Telecommunications Service
W Aust Western Australia
WB water ballast, waybill, weather bureau, westbound
WBC white blood cells
WC water closet, without charge
WCTU Women's Christian Temperance Union
wd wood, word, would
WD War Department
Wed Wednesday
Westm Westmeath, Westmorland
Wex Wexford
WFTU World Federation of Trade Unions
wh which, white
WH watt-hour
WHA World Hockey Association
whf wharf
WHO World Health Organization
whr watt-hour
whs *or* **whse** warehouse
whsle wholesale
wi when issued
WI West Indies, Wisconsin, wrought iron
WIA wounded in action
Wick Wicklow

wid widow, widower
Wilts Wiltshire
Wis *or* **Wisc** Wisconsin
Wisd Wisdom
wk week, work
wkly weekly
WL waterline, wavelength
wm wattmeter
wmk watermark
WNW west-northwest
WO warrant officer
w/o without
W/O water-in-oil
WOC without compensation
WP weather permitting, wettable powder, white phosphorus, without prejudice, word processing, word processor
WPA Works Progress Administration

WPC watts per candle
WPM words per minute
wpn weapon
WR warehouse receipt
WRAC Women's Royal Army Corps
WRAF Women's Royal Air Force
WRNS Women's Royal Naval Service
wrnt warrant
WSW west-southwest
wt weight
WT watertight, wireless telegraphy
WV *or* **W Va** West Virginia
WVS Women's Voluntary Services
WW warehouse warrant, with warrants, world war
w/w wall-to-wall

WY *or* **Wyo** Wyoming
x cross, ex, experimental, extra
XC *or* **xcp** ex coupon
XD *or* **x div** ex dividend
Xe xenon
XI *or* **x in** *or* **x int** ex interest
XL extra large, extra long
Xn Christian
Xnty Christianity
XR ex rights
XS extra small
XW ex warrants
y yard, year, yen, yeoman
Y yttrium
YA young adult
Yb ytterbium
YB yearbook
yd yard
yeo *or* **yeom** yeomanry

YO year old
YOB year of birth
Yorks Yorkshire
yr year, younger, your
yrbk yearbook
YT Yukon Territory
Yug Yugoslavia
z zero, zone
Z *or* **ZD** zenith distance
Zach Zacharias
Zech Zechariah
Zeph Zephaniah
ZI zone of interior
Zl zloty
Zn [azimuth + *north*] azimuth; zinc
zool zoological, zoology
ZPG zero population growth
Zr zirconium

Foreign Words and Phrases

ab·eunt stu·dia in mo·res \'äb-e-,ünt-'stüd-ē-,ä-,in-'mō-,rās\ [L] : practices zealously pursued pass into habits

à bien·tôt \à-byaⁿ-tō\ [F] : so long

ab in·cu·na·bu·lis \,äb-,iⁿ-kə-'näb-ə-,lēs\ [L] : from the cradle : from infancy

à bon chat, bon rat \à-bōⁿ-'shà bōⁿ-'rà\ [F] : to a good cat, a good rat : retaliation in kind

à bouche ou·verte \à-bü-shü-vert\ [F] : with open mouth : eagerly : uncritically

ab ovo us·que ad ma·la \äb-'ō-vō-,ùs-kwe-,äd-'mäl-ä\ [L] : from egg to apples : from soup to nuts : from beginning to end

à bras ou·verts \à-brà-zü-ver\ [F] : with open arms : cordially

ab·sit in·vi·dia \'äb-,sit-in-'wid-ē-,ä\ [L] : let there be no envy or ill will

ab uno dis·ce om·nes \äb-'ü-nō-,dis-ke-'ōm-,näs\ [L] : from one learn to know all

ab ur·be con·di·ta \äb-'ùr-be-'kōn-də-,tä\ [L] : from the founding of the city (Rome, founded 753 B.C.) — used by the Romans in reckoning dates

ab·usus non tol·lit usum \'äb-,ü-səs-,nōn-,tó-lət-'ü-səm\ [L] : abuse does not take away use, i.e., is not an argument against proper use

à compte \à-'kōⁿt\ [F] : on account

à coup sûr \à-kü-sūr\ [F] : with sure stroke : surely

acte gra·tuit \àk-tə-grà-twē\ [F] : gratuitous impulsive act

ad ar·bi·tri·um \,ad-är-'bit-rē-əm\ [L] : at will : arbitrarily

ad as·tra per as·pe·ra \ad-'as-trə-,pər-'as-pə-rə\ [L] : to the stars by hard ways — motto of Kansas

ad ex·tre·mum \,ad-ik-'strē-məm\ [L] : to the extreme : at last

ad ka·len·das Grae·cas \,äd-kə-'len-dəs-'grī-,käs\ [L] : at the Greek calends : never (since the Greeks had no calends)

ad ma·jo·rem Dei glo·ri·am \ad-,mä-'yōr-,em-'de-,ē-'glōr-ē-,äm, -'yòr-, -'glòr-\ [L] : to the greater glory of God — motto of the Society of Jesus

ad pa·tres \äd-'pä-,trās\ [L] : (gathered) to his fathers : deceased

ad re·fe·ren·dum \,äd-,ref-ə-'ren-dəm\ [L] : for reference : for further consideration by one having the authority to make a final decision

à droite \à-drwàt\ [F] : to or on the right hand

ad un·guem \äd-'ùŋ-,gwem\ [L] : to the fingernail : to a nicety : exactly (from the use of the fingernail to test the smoothness of marble)

ad utrum·que pa·ra·tus \,äd-ü-'trùm-kwe-pə-'rät-əs\ [L] : prepared for either (event)

ad vi·vum \äd-'wē-,wùm\ [L] : to the life

ae·gri som·nia \,ī-grē-'sóm-nē-,ä\ [L] : a sick man's dreams

ae·quam ser·va·re men·tem \'ī-,kwäm-sər-,wä-rē-'men-,tem\ [L] : to preserve a calm mind

ae·quo an·i·mo \,ī-kwō-'än-ə-,mō\ [L] : with even mind : calmly

ae·re per·en·ni·us \'ī-rā-pə-'ren-ē-,ùs\ [L] : more lasting than bronze

à gauche \à-gōsh\ [F] : to or on the left hand

age quod agis \'äg-e-,kwód-'äg-,is\ [L] : do what you are doing : to the business at hand

à grands frais \à-gräⁿ-fre\ [F] : at great expense

à huis clos \à-wʸē-klō\ [F] : with closed doors

aide-toi, le ciel t'ai·de·ra \ed-twà lə-'syel-te-drà\ [F] : help yourself (and) heaven will help you

aî·né \e-nā\ [F] : elder : senior (masc.)

aî·née \e-nā\ [F] : elder : senior (fem.)

à l'aban·don \à-là-bäⁿ-dōⁿ\ [F] : carelessly : in disorder

à la belle étoile \à-là-bel-ā-twàl\ [F] : under the beautiful star : in the open air at night

à la bonne heure \à-là-bò-nœr\ [F] : at a good time : well and good : all right

à la fran·çaise \à-là-fräⁿ-sez\ [F] : in the French style

à l'an·glaise \à-läⁿ-glez\ [F] : in the English style

alea jac·ta est \'äl-ē-,ä-,yäk-tə-'est\ [L] : the die is cast

à l'im·pro·viste \à-laⁿ-prō-vēst\ [F] : unexpectedly

ali·quan·do bo·nus dor·mi·tat Ho·me·rus \,äl-ə-,kwän-dō-'bō-nəs-dór-'mē-,tät-hō-'mer-əs\ [L] : sometimes (even) good Homer nods

alis vo·lat pro·pri·is \'äl-,ēs-'wò-,lät-'prō-prē-,ēs\ [L] : she flies with her own wings — motto of Oregon

al·ki \'al-,kī, -kē\ [Chinook Jargon] : by and by — motto of Washington

alo·ha oe \ä-,lō-hä-'ói, -'ō-ē\ [Hawaiian] : love to you : greetings : farewell

al·ter idem \,ól-tər-'ī-,dem, äl-tər-'ē-\ [L] : second self

a max·i·mis ad mi·ni·ma \ä-'mäk-sə-,mēs-,äd-'min-ə-,mä\ [L] : from the greatest to the least

à mer·veille \à-mer-vey\ [F] : marvelously

ami·cus hu·ma·ni ge·ne·ris \à-'mē-kəs-hü-,män-ē-'gen-ə-rəs\ [L] : friend of the human race

ami·cus us·que ad aras \-,ùs-kwe-,äd-'är-,äs\ [L] : a friend as far as to the altars, i.e., except in what is contrary to one's religion; also : a friend to the last extremity

ami de cour \à-,mēd-ə-'kür\ [F] : court friend : insincere friend

amor pa·tri·ae \,äm-,ór-'pä-trē-,ī\ [L] : love of one's country

amor vin·cit om·nia \'ä-,mór,wiŋ-kət-'óm-nē-ə\ [L] : love conquers all things

an·cienne no·blesse \äⁿ-syen-nó-bles\ [F] : old-time nobility : the French nobility before the Revolution of 1789

an·guis in her·ba \,äŋ-gwəs-in-'her,bä\ [L] : snake in the grass

an·i·mal bi·pes im·plu·me \'än-i-,mäl-,bip-,äs-im-'plü-me\ [L] : two-legged animal without feathers (i.e., man)

an·i·mis opi·bus·que pa·ra·ti \'än-ə-,mēs-,ó-pə-'bùs-kwe-pə-'rät-ē\ [L] : prepared in mind and resources — one of the mottoes of South Carolina

an·no ae·ta·tis su·ae \'än-ō-ī-,tät-əs-'sü-,ī\ [L] : in the (specified) year of his (or her) age

an·no mun·di \,än-ō-'mùn-dē\ [L] : in the year of the world — used in reckoning dates from the supposed period of the creation of the world, esp. as fixed by James Ussher at 4004 B.C. or by the Jews at 3761 B.C.

an·no ur·bis con·di·tae \,än-ō-,ùr-bəs-'kōn-də-,tī\ [L] : in the year of the founded city (Rome, founded 753 B.C.)

an·nu·it coep·tis \,än-ə-,wit-'kóip-,tēs\ [L] : He (God) has smiled on our undertakings — motto on the reverse of the Great Seal of the United States

à peu près \à-pœ-pre\ [F] : nearly : approximately

à pied \à-pyā\ [F] : on foot

après moi le dé·luge \à-pre-mwà-lə-dā-lūezh\ [F] : after me the deluge (attributed to Louis XV)

à pro·pos de bottes \à-prə-pōd-ə-bòt\ [F] : apropos of boots — used to change the subject

à pro·pos de rien \-,ryaⁿ\ [F] : apropos of nothing

aqua et ig·ni in·ter·dic·tus \,äk-wä-et-'ig-nē-,int-ər-'dik-təs\ [L] : forbidden to be furnished with water and fire : outlawed

Ar·ca·des am·bo \,är-kə-,des-'äm-bō\ [L] : both Arcadians : two persons of like occupations or tastes; also : two rascals

ar·rec·tis au·ri·bus \à-'rek-,tēs-'aù-ri-,bùs\ [L] : with ears pricked up : attentively

ar·ri·ve·der·ci \,är-e-vä-'der-chē\ [It] : till we meet again : farewell

ars est ce·la·re ar·tem \,ärs-,est-kä-,lär-ē-'är-,tem\ [L] : it is (true) art to conceal art

ars lon·ga, vi·ta bre·vis \ärs-'lóŋ-,gä ,wē-,tä-'bre-wəs\ [L] : art is long, life is short

a ter·go \ä-'ter-(,)gō\ [L] : from behind

à tort et à tra·vers \à-tór-tā-à-trà-ver\ [F] : wrong and crosswise : at random : without rhyme or reason

au bout de son la·tin \ō-büd-ə-sōⁿ-là-taⁿ\ [F] : at the end of one's Latin : at the end of one's mental resources

au con·traire \ō-kōⁿ-trer\ [F] : on the contrary

au·de·mus ju·ra nos·tra de·fen·de·re \aù-'dā-məs-,yùr-ə-'nó-strə-dā-'fen-də-rē\ [L] : we dare defend our rights — motto of Alabama

au·den·tes for·tu·na ju·vat \aù-'den-,täs-fór-,tü-nə-'yù-,wät\ [L] : fortune favors the bold

au·di al·te·ram par·tem \'aù-,dē-,äl-tə-,räm-'pär-,tem\ [L] : hear the other side

au fait \ō-fet, -fe\ [F] : to the point : fully competent : fully informed : socially correct

au fond \ō-fōⁿ\ [F] : at bottom : fundamentally

au grand sé·rieux \ō-gräⁿ-sā-ryœ\ [F] : in all seriousness

au mieux \ō-myœ\ [F] : on the best terms : on intimate terms

au pays des aveugles les borgnes sont rois \ō-pā-ē-dā-zà-vœgl²-lā-bórn²-ə-sōⁿ-rwà, -rwä\ [F] : in the country of the blind the one-eyed men are kings

au·rea me·di·o·cri·tas \'aù-rē-ə-,med-ē-'ó-krə-,täs\ [L] : the golden mean

au reste \ō-rest\ [F] : for the rest : besides

au sé·rieux \ō-sā-ryœ\ [F] : seriously

au·spi·ci·um me·li·o·ris ae·vi \aù-'spik-ē-,üm,mel-ē-,ōr-əs-'ī-,wē\ [L] : an omen of a better age — motto of the Order of St. Michael and St. George

aus·si·tôt dit, aus·si·tôt fait \ō-sē-tō-dē ō-sē-tō-fe\ [F] : no sooner said than done

---

\ə\ abut \ᵊ\ kitten, F table \ər\ further \a\ ash \ā\ ace \ä\ cot, cart \aù\ out \ch\ chin \e\ bet \ē\ easy \g\ go \i\ hit \ī\ ice \j\ job \ŋ\ sing \ō\ go \ò\ law \òi\ boy \th\ thin \t̲h̲\ the \ü\ loot \ù\ foot \y\ yet \zh\ vision \à, k̲, ⁿ, œ, œ̄, ʉ, ̄ʉ, ʸ\ see Guide to Pronunciation

aut Cae·sar aut ni·hil \aut-'kī-sär-,aut-'ni-,hil\ [L] : either a Caesar or nothing

aut Caesar aut nul·lus \-'nul-əs\ [L] : either a Caesar or a nobody

au·tres temps, au·tres mœurs \ō-trə-tän̄ ō-trə-mœrs\ [F] : other times, other customs

aut vin·ce·re aut mo·ri \aut-'wiŋ-kə-rē-,aut-'mó-,rē\ [L] : either to conquer or to die

aux armes \ō-zärm\ [F] : to arms

avant–pro·pos \av-än̄-prō-pō\ [F] : preface

ave at·que va·le \'ä-,wät-kwe-'wä-,lā\ [L] : hail and farewell

à vo·tre san·té \à-vót-sän-,tā, -vó-trə\ [F] : to your health — used as a toast

beaux yeux \bō-zyœ\ [F] : beautiful eyes : beauty of face

bien en·ten·du \byan̄-nän̄-tän-dw̄e\ [F] : well understood : of course

bien–pen·sant \byan̄-pä-sän̄\ [F] : right-minded : one who holds orthodox views

bien·sé·ance \byan̄-sā-än̄s\ [F] : propriety

bis dat qui ci·to dat \,bis-,dät-kwē-'ki-tō-,dät\ [L] : he gives twice who gives promptly

bon ap·pé·tit \bó-nà-pā-tē\ [F] : good appetite : enjoy your meal

bon gré, mal gré \'bōn̄-,grä-'mál-,grä\ [F] : whether with good grace or bad : willy-nilly

bo·nis avi·bus \,bó-,nēs-'ä-wi-,bùs\ [L] : under good auspices

bon·jour \bōn̄-zhür\ [F] : good day : good morning

bonne foi \bón-fwä\ [F] : good faith

bon·soir \bōn̄-swár\ [F] : good evening

bru·tum ful·men \,brüt-əm-'fùl-mən\ [L] : insensible thunderbolt : a futile threat or display of force

ca·dit quae·stio \,käd-ət-'kwī-stē-,ō\ [L] : the question drops : the argument collapses

carte d'iden·ti·té \kàrt-dē-dän̄-tē-tā\ [F] : identity card

cau·sa si·ne qua non \'kaù-sä-,sin-ē-kwä-'nōn\ [L] : an indispensable cause or condition

ca·ve·at lec·tor \'käv-ē-,ät-'lek-,tór, 'kav-\ [L] : let the reader beware

ca·ve ca·nem \,kä-wā-'kän-,em\ [L] : beware the dog

ce·dant ar·ma to·gae \'kā-,dänt-,är-mə-'tō-,gī\ [L] : let arms yield to the toga : let military power give way to civil power — motto of Wyoming

ce n'est que le pre·mier pas qui coûte \snek-lə-prə-myä-pä-kē-küt\ [F] : it is only the first step that costs

c'est–à–dire \se-tà-dēr\ [F] : that is to say : namely

c'est au·tre chose \se-tōt-shōz, -tō-trə-\ [F] : that's a different thing

c'est la guerre \se-là-ger\ [F] : that's war : it cannot be helped

c'est la vie \se-là-vē\ [F] : that's life : that's how things happen

c'est plus qu'un crime, c'est une faute \se-plœ-kœn̄-krēm se-tw̄en-fōt\ [F] : it is worse than a crime, it is a blunder

ce·te·ra de·sunt \,kāt-ə-,rä-'dā-,sùnt\ [L] : the rest is missing

cha·cun à son goût \shä-kœn̄-nà-sōn̄-gü\ [F] : everyone to his taste

châ·teau en Es·pagne \shä-tō-än̄-nes-pàn̄\ [F] : castle in Spain : a visionary project

cher·chez la femme \sher-shā-là-fàm\ [F] : look for the woman

che sa·rà, sa·rà \kā-sä-,rä-sä-'rä\ [It] : what will be, will be

che·val de ba·taille \shə-vál-də-bà-tä\ [F] : war-horse : argument constantly relied on : favorite subject

ci–gît \sē-zhē\ [F] : here lies — used preceding a name on a tombstone

co·gi·to, er·go sum \'kō-gə-,tō-,er-gō-'sùm\ [L] : I think, therefore I exist

co·mé·die hu·maine \kò-mā-dē-ū̄e-men\ [F] : human comedy : the whole variety of human life

comédie lar·moy·ante \-làr-mwä-yän̄t\ [F] : tearful comedy : sentimental comedy

comme ci, comme ça \kóm-sē-kòm-sä\ [F] : so-so

com·pa·gnon de voy·age \kōn̄-pà-nyōn̄-də-vwä-yàzh\ [F] : traveling companion

compte ren·du \kōn̄t-rän̄-dw̄e\ [F] : report (as of proceedings in an investigation)

con·cor·dia dis·cors \kän-'kórd-ē-ä-'dis-,kórs\ [L] : discordant harmony

con·fes·sio fi·dei \kən-'fes-ē-ō-'fid-ē-,ē\ [L] : confession of faith

con·temp·tus mun·di \kən-'tem(p)-tə-'smùnd-ē\ [L] : contempt for the world

cor·rup·tio op·ti·mi pes·si·ma \kə-'rúp-tē-,ō-'äp-tə-,mē-'pes-ə-,mä\ [L] : the corruption of the best is the worst of all

coup de maî·tre \küd-(ə-)metr\ [F] : masterstroke

coup d'es·sai \kü-dä-se\ [F] : experiment : trial

coûte que coûte \küt-kə-küt\ [F] : cost what it may

cre·do quia ab·sur·dum est \,krä-dō-'kwē-ä-äp-,sùrd-əm-'est\ [L] : I believe it because it is absurd

cre·do ut in·tel·li·gam \,krä-dō-,ùt-in-'tel-ə-,gäm\ [L] : I believe so that I may understand

cres·cit eun·do \,kres-kət-'eùn-dō\ [L] : it grows as it goes — motto of New Mexico

crise de conscience \krēz-də-kōn̄-syän̄s\ [F] : crisis of conscience : agonizing period of moral uncertainty

crise de nerfs or **crise des nerfs** \krēz-də-ner\ [F] : crisis of nerves : nervous collapse : hysterical fit

crux cri·ti·co·rum \'krùks-,krit-ə-'kōr-əm\ [L] : crux of critics

cum gra·no sa·lis \kùm-,grän-ō-'säl-əs\ [L] : with a grain of salt

cus·tos mo·rum \,kùs-tōs-'mōr-əm\ [L] : guardian of manners or morals : censor

d'ac·cord \dá-kór\ [F] : in accord : agreed

dame d'hon·neur \dàm-dó-nœr\ [F] : lady-in-waiting

dam·nant quod non in·tel·li·gunt \'däm-,nänt-,kwód-,nōn-in-'tel-ə-,gùnt\ [L] : they condemn what they do not understand

de bonne grâce \də-bòn-gräs\ [F] : with good grace : willingly

de gus·ti·bus non est dis·pu·tan·dum \dē-'gùs-tə-,bùs-,nōn-,est-,dis-pù-'tän-,dùm\ [L] : there is no disputing about tastes

Dei gra·tia \dē-,ē-'grät-ē-,ä\ [L] : by the grace of God

de in·te·gro \dā-'int-ə-,grō\ [L] : anew : afresh

de l'au·dace, en·core de l'au·dace, et tou·jours de l'au·dace \də-lō-'däs än̄-,kór-də-lō-däs ä-tü-'zhür-də-lō-däs\ [F] : audacity, more audacity, and ever more audacity

de·len·da est Car·tha·go \dā-'len-dä-,est-kär-'täg-ō\ [L] : Carthage must be destroyed

de·li·ne·a·vit \dā-,lē-nä-'ä-wit\ [L] : he (or she) drew it

de mal en pis \də-má-län̄-pē\ [F] : from bad to worse

de mi·ni·mis non cu·rat lex \dā-'min-ə-,mēs-,nōn-,kü-,rät-'leks\ [L] : the law takes no account of trifles

de mor·tu·is nil ni·si bo·num \dā-'mórt-ə-,wēs-,nēl-,nis-ē-'bó-,nùm\ [L] : of the dead (say) nothing but good

de nos jours \də-nō-zhür\ [F] : of our time : contemporary — used postpositively esp. after a proper name

Deo fa·ven·te \,dā-ō-fə-'vent-ē\ [L] : with God's favor

Deo gra·ti·as \,dā-ō-'grät-ē-,äs\ [L] : thanks (be) to God

de pro·fun·dis \dā-prō-'fùn-dēs, -'fən-\ [L] : out of the depths

der Geist der stets ver·neint \dər-'gist-dər-,shtäts-fer-'nint\ [G] : the spirit that ever denies — applied originally to Mephistopheles

de·si·pe·re in lo·co \dā-'sip-ə-rē-in-'lō-kō\ [L] : to indulge in trifling at the proper time

De·us vult \,dā-əs-'wùlt\ [L] : God wills it — rallying cry of the First Crusade

di·es fau·stus \,dē-,äs-'faù-stəs\ [L] : lucky day

dies in·fau·stus \-'in-,faù-stəs\ [L] : unlucky day

dies irae \-'ē-,rī, -,rä\ [L] : day of wrath — used of the Judgment Day

Dieu et mon droit \dyœ-ā-mōn̄-drwä\ [F] : God and my right — motto on the British royal arms

Dieu vous garde \dyœ-vü-gárd\ [F] : God keep you

di·ri·go \'dē-ri-,gō\ [L] : I direct — motto of Maine

dis ali·ter vi·sum \,dēs-,äl-ə-,ter-'wē-,sùm\ [L] : the Gods decreed otherwise

di·tat De·us \dē-,tät-'dā-,ùs\ [L] : God enriches — motto of Arizona

di·vi·de et im·pe·ra \'dē-wi-,de-,et-'im-pə-,rä\ [L] : divide and rule

do·cen·do dis·ci·mus \dō-,ken-dō-'dis-ki-,mùs\ [L] : we learn by teaching

dol·ce stil nuo·vo \'dòl-chā-stēl-'nwó-vō\ [It] : sweet new style

Do·mi·ne, di·ri·ge nos \'dò-mi-,ne,-dē-ri-,ge-'nōs\ [L] : Lord, direct us — motto of the City of London

Do·mi·nus vo·bis·cum \,dó-mi-,nùs-wō-'bēs-,kúm\ [L] : the Lord be with you

dul·ce et de·co·rum est pro pa·tria mo·ri \,dùl-,ket-de-'kór-,est-prō-,pä-trē-,ä-'mó-,rē\ [L] : it is sweet and seemly to die for one's country

dum spi·ro, spe·ro \dùm-'spē-rō-'spä-rō\ [L] : while I breathe I hope — one of the mottoes of South Carolina

dum vi·vi·mus vi·va·mus \,dùm-'wē-wē-,mùs-wē-'wäm-ùs\ [L] : while we live, let us live

dux fe·mi·na fac·ti \,dùks-,fā-mi-nä-'fäk-,tē\ [L] : a woman was leader of the exploit

ec·ce sig·num \,ek-e-'sig-,nùm\ [L] : behold the sign : look at the proof

e con·tra·rio \,ā-kōn-'trär-ē-,ō\ [L] : on the contrary

écra·sez l'in·fâme \ā-krä-zä-lan̄-fàm\ [L] : crush the infamous thing

eheu fu·ga·ces la·bun·tur an·ni \,ā-,heù-fú-'gä-,käs-lä-,bùn-,túr-'än-,ē\ [L] : alas! the fleeting years glide on

ein' fes·te Burg ist un·ser Gott \in-,fes-tə-'bùrk-ist-,ùn-zər-'gót\ [G] : a mighty fortress is our God

em·bar·ras de ri·chesses \än̄-bá-,räd-(ə-)rē-shes\ [F] : embarrassing surplus of riches : confusing abundance

em·bar·ras du choix \än̄-bà-rä-dw̄e-shwä\ [F] : embarrassing variety of choice

en ami \än̄-nà-mē\ [F] : as a friend

en ef·fet \än̄-nä-fe\ [F] : in fact : indeed

en fa·mille \än̄-fà-mēy\ [F] : in or with one's family : at home : informally

en·fant ché·ri \än̄-fän̄-shä-rē\ [F] : loved or pampered child : one that is highly favored

en·fant gâ·té \än̄-fän̄-gä-tä\ [F] : spoiled child

en·fants per·dus \än̄-fän̄-per-dw̄e\ [F] : lost children : soldiers sent to a dangerous post

en·fin \än̄-fan̄\ [F] : in conclusion : in a word

en gar·çon \än̄-gàr-sōn̄\ [F] : as or like a bachelor

en garde \än̄-gàrd\ [F] : on guard

en pan·tou·fles \än̄-pän̄-tüfl\ [F] : in slippers : at ease : informally

en plein air \än̄-plen-er\ [F] : in the open air

en plein jour \än̄-plan̄-zhür\ [F] : in broad day

en poste \än̄-póst\ [F] : in a diplomatic post

en règle \än̄-regl\ [F] : in order : in due form

en re·tard \än̄r-(ə-)tär\ [F] : behind time : late

en re·traite \än̄r-rə-trät\ [F] : in retreat : in retirement

en re·vanche \än̄r-(ə-)vän̄sh\ [F] : in return : in compensation

en se·condes noces \än̄s-(ə-)gōn̄d-nós\ [F] : in a second marriage

en·se pe·tit pla·ci·dam sub li·ber·ta·te qui·e·tem \,en-se-,pet-ət-'pläk-i-,däm-sùb-,lē-ber-,tä-te-kwē-'ä-,tem\ [L] : with the sword she seeks calm repose under liberty — motto of Massachusetts

eo ip·so \ä-ō-'ip-(,)sō\ [L] : by that itself : by that fact

épa·ter les bour·geois \ā-pä-tä-lä-bür-zhwä\ [F] : to shock the middle classes

e plu·ri·bus unum \,ā-,plùr-ə-bəs-'(y)ü-nəm, ,ä-,plùr-\ [L] : one out of many — used on the Great Seal of the U.S. and on several U.S. coins

ep·pur si muo·ve \,āp-,pür-sē-'mwó-vä\ [It] : and yet it does move — attributed to Galileo after recanting his assertion of the earth's motion

Erin go bragh \,er-ən-gə-'brò, -gō-'brä\ [IrGael *go bráth*, lit., till doomsday] : Ireland forever

er·ra·re hu·ma·num est \e-'rär-e-hü-,män-əm-'est\ [L] : to err is human

es·prit de l'es·ca·lier \es-prēd-les-kä-lyä\ or **es·prit d'es·ca·lier** \-prē-des-\ [F] : spirit of the staircase : repartee thought of only too late, on the way home

es·se quam vi·de·ri \'es-ē-,kwäm-wi-'dā-rē\ [L] : to be rather than to seem — motto of North Carolina

est mo·dus in re·bus \,est-'mó-,dùs-in-'rä-,bùs\ [L] : there is a proper measure in things, i.e., the golden mean should always be observed

es·to per·pe·tua \,es-,tō-pər-'pet-ə-,wä\ [L] : may she endure forever — motto of Idaho

et hoc ge·nus om·ne \et-,hōk-,gen-əs-'óm-ne\ or **et id genus omne** \et-,id-\ [L] : and everything of this kind

et in Ar·ca·dia ego \et-in-är-,käd-ē-ə-'eg-ō\ [L] : I too (lived) in Arcadia

et sic de si·mi·li·bus \et-,sēk-dā-sə-'mil-ə-,bùs\ [L] : and so of like things

et tu Bru·te \et-'tü-'brü-te\ [L] : thou too, Brutus — exclamation attributed to Julius Caesar on seeing his friend Brutus among his assassins

eu·re·ka \yù-'rē-kə\ [Gk] : I have found it — motto of California

Ewig–Weib·li·che \,ā-vik-'vīp-li-kə\ [G] : eternal feminine ex an·i·mo \ek-'sän-ə-ˌmō\ [L] : from the heart : sincerely

ex·cel·si·or \ik-'sel-sē-ər, eks-'kel-sē-ˌór\ [L] : still higher — motto of New York

ex·cep·tio pro·bat re·gu·lam de re·bus non ex·cep·tis \eks-'kep-tē-ˌō-ˌprō-bät-'rä-gə-ˌläm-dā-'rä-ˌbús-ˌnōn-eks-'kep-tēs\ [L] : an exception establishes the rule as to things not excepted

ex·cep·tis ex·ci·pi·en·dis \eks-'kep-ˌtēs-eks-ˌkip-ē-'en-ˌdēs\ [L] : with the proper or necessary exceptions

ex·i·tus ac·ta pro·bat \'ek-sə-ˌtüs-ˌäk-tə-'prò-ˌbät\ [L] : the event justifies the deed

ex li·bris \eks-'lē-brəs\ [L] : from the books of — used on bookplates

ex me·ro mo·tu \eks-ˌmer-ō-'mō-tü\ [L] : out of mere impulse : of one's own accord

ex ne·ces·si·ta·te rei \eks-nə-ˌkes-ə-'tä-te-'rā(-ˌē)\ [L] : from the necessity of the case

ex ni·hi·lo ni·hil fit \eks-'ni-hi-ˌlō-ˌni-ˌhil-'fit\ [L] : from nothing nothing is produced

ex pe·de Her·cu·lem \eks-ˌped-e-'her-kə-ˌlem\ [L] : from the foot (we may judge of the size of) Hercules : from a part we may judge of the whole

ex·per·to cre·de \eks-ˌpert-ō-'kräd-e\ or experto cre·di·te \-'kräd-ə-ˌte\ [L] : believe one who has had experience

ex un·gue le·o·nem \eks-ˌún-gwe-lē-'ō-ˌnem\ [L] : from the claw (we may judge of) the lion : from a part we may judge of the whole

ex vi ter·mi·ni \eks-ˌwē-'ter-mə-ˌnē\ [L] : from the force of the term

fa·ci·le prin·ceps \ˌfäk-i-le-'prin-ˌkeps\ [L] : easily first

fa·ci·lis de·scen·sus Aver·no \'fäk-i-ˌlis-dā-ˌskän-ˌsùs-ä-'wer-nō\ or facilis descensus Aver·ni \-(ˌ)nē\ [L] : the descent to Avernus is easy : the road to evil is easy

fa·çon de par·ler \fä-sōⁿ-də-pár-lā\ [F] : manner of speaking : figurative or conventional expression

faire suivre \fer-swēvr\ [F] : have forwarded : please forward

fas est et ab ho·ste do·ce·ri \fäs-'est-et-äb-'hò-ste-dò-'kā-(ˌ)rē\ [L] : it is right to learn even from an enemy

Fa·ta vi·am in·ve·ni·ent \ˌfä-tä-'wē-ˌäm-in-'wen-ē-ˌent\ [L] : the Fates will find a way

fat·ti mas·chii, pa·ro·le fe·mi·ne \ˌfät-tē-'mäs-ˌkē pä-ˌrò-lā-'fā-mē-ˌnä\ [It] : deeds are males, words are females : deeds are more effective than words — motto of Maryland, where it is generally interpreted as meaning "manly deeds, womanly words"

faux bon·homme \fō-bò-nòm\ [F] : pretended good fellow

faux–naïf \fō-nä-ēf\ [F] : pretending to be childlike

femme de cham·bre \ˌfäm-də-shäⁿbr\ [F] : chambermaid : lady's maid

fes·ti·na len·te \fe-ˌstē-nä-'len-ˌtä\ [L] : make haste slowly

feux d'ar·ti·fice \fœ-dár-tē-fēs\ [F] : fireworks : display of wit

fi·at ex·per·i·men·tum in cor·po·re vi·li \'fē-ˌät-ek-ˌsper-ē-'men-tùm-in-ˌkór-pə-re-'wē-lē\ [L] : let experiment be made on a worthless body

fi·at ju·sti·tia, ru·at cae·lum \ˌfē-ˌät-yùs-'tit-ē-ä ˌrú-ˌät-'kī-ˌlúm\ [L] : let justice be done though the heavens fall

fi·at lux \fē-ˌät-'lúks\ [L] : let there be light

Fi·dei De·fen·sor \ˌfid-e-ˌī-'fän-ˌsór\ [L] : Defender of the Faith — a title of the sovereigns of England

fi·dus Acha·tes \ˌfēd-əs-ä-'kä-ˌtäs\ [L] : faithful Achates : trusty friend

fille de cham·bre \fēy-də-shäⁿbr\ [F] : lady's maid

fille d'hon·neur \fēy-dò-nœr\ [F] : maid of honor

fils \fēs\ [F] : son — used after French proper names to distinguish a son from his father

fi·nem re·spi·ce \'fē-ˌnem-'rä-spi-ˌke\ [L] : consider the end

fi·nis co·ro·nat opus \ˌfē-nəs-kə-ˌrō-ˌnät-'ō-ˌpús\ [L] : the end crowns the work

fluc·tu·at nec mer·gi·tur \'flúk-tə-ˌwät-ˌnek-'mer-gə-ˌtùr\ [L] : it is tossed by the waves but does not sink — motto of Paris

fo·lie de gran·deur or fo·lie des gran·deurs \fò-lē-də-grä°-dœr\ [F] : delusion of greatness : megalomania

fors an et haec olim me·mi·nis·se ju·va·bit \ˌfòr-ˌsän-ˌet-'hīk-ò-lim-ˌmem-ə-'nis-e-yù-'wä-bit\ [L] : perhaps this too will be a pleasure to look back on one day

for·tes for·tu·na ju·vat \'fòr-ˌtäs-fòr-ˌtü-nə-'yù-ˌwät\ [L] : fortune favors the brave

fron·ti nul·la fi·des \'fròn-ˌtē-ˌnúl-ə-'fid-ˌās\ [L] : no reliance can be placed on appearance

fu·it Ili·um \'fù-ət-'il-ē-əm\ [L] : Troy has been (i.e., is no more)

fu·ror lo·quen·di \ˌfúr-ˌór-lò-'kwen-(ˌ)dē\ [L] : rage for speaking

furor po·e·ti·cus \-ˌpò-'āt-i-kùs\ [L] : poetic frenzy

furor scri·ben·di \-ˌskrē-'ben-(ˌ)dē\ [L] : rage for writing

Gal·gen·hu·mor \'gäl-gən-hü-ˌmòr\ [G] : gallows humor

Gal·li·ce \'gäl-ə-ˌke\ [L] : in French : after the French manner

gar·çon d'hon·neur \gär-ˌsōⁿ-dò-nœr\ [F] : bridegroom's attendant

garde du corps \gärd-dü-kór\ [F] : bodyguard

gar·dez la foi \gär-dā-lä-fwä\ [F] : keep faith

gau·de·a·mus igi·tur \gaùd-ē-'äm-əs-'ig-ə-ˌtùr\ [L] : let us then be merry

gens d'é·glise \zhä°-dā-glēz\ [F] : church people : clergy

gens de guerre \zhä°-də-ger\ [F] : military people : soldiery

gens du monde \zhä°-dü°-mō°d\ [F] : people of the world : fashionable people

gno·thi se·au·ton \gə-'nō-thē-ˌse-aú-'tòn\ [Gk] : know thyself

goût de ter·roir \gü-də-te-rwär\ [F] : taste of the earth

grand monde \grä°-mō°d\ [F] : great world : high society

guerre à ou·trance \ger-ä-ü-trä°s\ [F] : war to the uttermost

gu·ten Tag \güt-°n-'täk\ [G] : good day

has·ta la vis·ta \ˌästä-lä-'vēs-tə\ [Sp] : good-bye

haute vul·ga·ri·sa·tion \ōt-ˌvūel-gä-rē-zä-syōⁿ\ [F] : high popularization : effective presentation of a difficult subject to a general audience

haut goût \ō-gü\ [F] : high flavor : slight taint of decay

hic et ubi·que \ˌhēk-et-ü-'bē-kwe\ [L] : here and everywhere

hic ja·cet \hik-'jä-sət, hēk-'yäk-ət\ [L] : here lies — used preceding a name on a tombstone

hinc il·lae la·cri·mae \ˌhiŋk-ˌil-ˌī-'läk-ri-ˌmī\ [L] : hence those tears

hoc age \hōk-'äg-e\ [L] : do this : apply yourself to what you are about

hoc opus, hic la·bor est \hōk-'ō-ˌpús-ˌhēk-lä-ˌbòr-'est\ [L] : this is the hard work, this is the toil

homme d'af·faires \òm-dä-fer\ [F] : man of business : business agent

homme d'es·prit \-des-prē\ [F] : man of wit

homme moyen sen·suel \òm-mwá-yaⁿ-sän-swᵚel\ [F] : the average nonintellectual man

ho·mo sum: hu·ma·ni nil a me ali·e·num pu·to \'hò-mō-ˌsùm hü-ˌmän-ē-'nēl-ä-ˌmä-ˌäl-ē-'ä-nəm-'pù-tō\ [L] : I am a man: I regard nothing that concerns man as foreign to my interests

ho·ni soit qui mal y pense \ò-nē-swä-kē-mäl-ē-päⁿs\ [F] : shamed be he who thinks evil of it — motto of the Order of the Garter

hon·nête homme \ò-net-òm\ [F] : honest man : respectable and honorable citizen of the middle class

hors com·merce \òr-kò-mers\ [F] : outside the trade : not offered through regular commercial channels

hu·ma·num est er·ra·re \hü-ˌmän-əm-ˌest-e-'rär-e\ [L] : to err is human

ich dien \ik-'dēn\ [G] : I serve — motto of the Prince of Wales

ici on parle fran·çais \ē-sē-ōⁿ-párl(-ə)-frä°-se\ [F] : French is spoken here

id est \id-'est\ [L] : that is

ig·no·ran·tia ju·ris ne·mi·nem ex·cu·sat \ig-nə-ˌränt-ē-ä-'yúr-əs-'nä-mə-ˌnem-eks-'kü-ˌsät\ [L] : ignorance of the law excuses no one

ig·no·tum per ig·no·ti·us \ig-ˌnòt-əm-ˌper-ig-'nòt-ē-ˌùs\ [L] : (explaining) the unknown by means of the more unknown

il faut cul·ti·ver no·tre jar·din \ē-ˌfō-kūel-tē-vä-nòt-zhär-daⁿ, -nó-trə-zhär-\ [F] : we must cultivate our garden : we must tend to our own affairs

ils ne pas·se·ront pas \ēl-nə-pás(-ə)-rōⁿ-pä\ [F] : they shall not get past

in ae·ter·num \in-i-'ter-ˌnúm\ [L] : forever

in du·bio \in-'dùb-ē-ˌō\ [L] : in doubt : undetermined

in fu·tu·ro \in-fə-'túr-ō\ [L] : in the future

in hoc sig·no vin·ces \in-hōk-'sig-nō-'wiŋ-ˌkās\ [L] : by this sign (the Cross) you will conquer

in li·mi·ne \in-'lē-mə-ˌne\ [L] : on the threshold : at the beginning

in om·nia pa·ra·tus \in-'òm-nē-ə-pə-'rä-ˌtùs\ [L] : ready for all things

in par·ti·bus in·fi·de·li·um \in-'pärt-ə-ˌbús-in-fə-'dä-lē-ˌùm\ [L] : in the regions of the infidels — used of a titular bishop having no diocesan jurisdiction, usu. in non-Christian countries

in prae·sen·ti \ˌin-pri-'sen-ˌtē\ [L] : at the present time

in sae·cu·la sae·cu·lo·rum \in-'sī-kú-ˌlä-ˌsī-kə-'lòr-əm, -'sä-kú-ˌlä-sä-\ [L] : for ages of ages : forever and ever

insh·al·lah \in-shä-'lä\ [Ar] : if Allah wills : God willing

in sta·tu quo an·te bel·lum \in-'stä-tü-kwō-ˌänt-ē-'bel-əm\ [L] : in the same state as before the war

in·te·ger vi·tae sce·le·ris·que pu·rus \in-tə-ˌger-'wē-ˌtī-skel-ə-'ris-kwe-'pü-rəs\ [L] : upright of life and free from wickedness

in·ter nos \ˌint-ər-'nòs\ [L] : between ourselves

in·tra mu·ros \in-ˌträ-'mü-ˌrōs\ [L] : within the walls

in usum Del·phi·ni \in-ˌü-səm-del-'fē-nē\ [L] : for the use of the Dauphin : expurgated

in utrum·que pa·ra·tus \in-ü-'trúm-kwe-pə-'rä-ˌtùs\ [L] : prepared for either (event)

in·ve·nit \in-'wä-nit\ [L] : he (or she) devised it

in vi·no ve·ri·tas \in-wē-nō-'wä-rə-ˌtäs\ [L] : there is truth in wine

in·vi·ta Mi·ner·va \in-ˌwē-tä-mi-'ner-ˌwä\ [L] : Minerva being unwilling : without natural talent or inspiration

ip·sis·si·ma ver·ba \ip-ˌsis-ə-mä-'wer-ˌbä\ [L] : the very words

ira fu·ror bre·vis est \ē-rä-'fúr-ˌór-'bre-wəs-ˌest\ [L] : anger is a brief madness

j'ac·cuse \zhá-küez\ [F] : I accuse : bitter denunciation

jac·ta alea est \'yäk-ˌtä-ˌä-lē-ˌä-'est\ [L] : the die is cast

j'adoube \zhá-dúb\ [F] : I adjust — used in chess when touching a piece without intending to move it

ja·nu·is clau·sis \ˌyän-ə-wēs-'klaú-ˌses\ [L] : behind closed doors

je main·tien·drai \zhə-maⁿ-tyaⁿ-drā\ [F] : I will maintain — motto of the Netherlands

jeu de mots \zhœd-(ə-)mō\ [F] : play on words : pun

Jo·an·nes est no·men eius \yō-'än-äs-est-ˌnō-men-'ä-yùs\ [L] : John is his name — motto of Puerto Rico

jo·lie laide \zhó-lē-led\ [F] : good-looking ugly woman : woman who is attractive though not conventionally pretty

jour·nal in·time \zhür-nál-aⁿ-tēm\ [F] : intimate journal : private diary

jus di·vi·num \yùs-di-'wē-nùm\ [L] : divine law

jus·ti·tia om·ni·bus \yùs-ˌtit-ē-ˌä-'òm-ni-ˌbùs\ [L] : justice for all — motto of the District of Columbia

j'y suis, j'y reste \zhē-swē-zhē-'rest\ [F] : here I am, here I remain

Kin·der, Kir·che, Küche \'kin-dər 'kir-kə 'kuek-ə\ [G] : children, church, kitchen

kte·ma es aei \(kə-)'tä-ˌmä-ˌes-ä-'ā\ [Gk] : a possession for ever — applied to a work of art or literature of enduring significance

la belle dame sans mer·ci \lá-bel-dàm-säⁿ-mer-sē\ [F] : the beautiful lady without mercy

la·bo·ra·re est ora·re \'läb-ō-ˌrär-e-ˌest-'ō-ˌrär-e\ [L] : to work is to pray

la·bor om·nia vin·cit \'lä-ˌbòr-ˌòm-nē-ä-'wiŋ-kit\ [L] : labor conquers all things — motto of Oklahoma

la·cri·mae re·rum \ˌläk-ri-ˌmī-'rä-ˌrúm\ [L] : tears for things : pity for misfortune; also : tears in things : tragedy of life

lais·sez–al·ler or lais·ser–al·ler \ˌle-sā-ä-lā\ [F] : letting go : lack of restraint

lap·sus ca·la·mi \ˌläp-sùs-'käl-ə-ˌmē, ˌlap-səs-'kal-ə-ˌmī\ [L] : slip of the pen

lap·sus lin·guae \ˌlap-səs-'liŋ-ˌgwī, ˌläp-ˌsùs-\ [L] : slip of the tongue

la reine le veut \lä-ren-lə-vœ\ [F] : the queen wills it

la·scia·te ogni spe·ran·za, voi ch'en·tra·te \ˌläsh-shä-tä-ˌō-nᵛē-spä-'rän-tsä-ˌvō-ē-kän-'trä-tä\ [It] : abandon all hope, ye who enter

lau·da·tor tem·po·ris ac·ti \laù-ˌdä-ˌtòr-ˌtem-pə-ris-'äk-ˌtē\ [L] : one who praises past times

laus Deo \laùs-'dā-ˌō\ [L] : praise (be) to God

le cœur a ses rai·sons que la rai·son ne con·naît point \lə-kœr-á-sä-re-zōⁿ-kə-lä-re-zōⁿ-(ˌ)kò-ne-pwaⁿ\ [F] : the heart has its reasons that reason knows nothing of

---

\ə\ abut \ᵊ\ kitten, F table \ər\ further \a\ ash \ā\ ace \ä\ cot, cart \aú\ out \ch\ chin \e\ bet \ē\ easy \g\ go \i\ hit \ī\ ice \j\ job \ŋ\ sing \ō\ go \ò\ law \òi\ boy \th\ thin \th̸\ the \ü\ loot \ú\ foot \y\ yet \zh\ vision \à, ᶄ, ⁿ, œ, œ̄, ue, ūe, ᵛ\ see Guide to Pronunciation

le roi est mort, vive le roi \lə-rwä-e-mòr vēv-lə-rwä\ [F] : the king is dead, long live the king

le roi le veut \lə-vœ\ [F] : the king wills it

le roi s'avi·se·ra \-sä-vēz-rá\ [F] : the king will consider

le style, c'est l'homme \lə-stēl-se-lóm\ [F] : the style is the man

l'état, c'est moi \lā-tä-se-mwä\ [F] : the state, it is I

l'étoile du nord \lā-twál-dūe-nòr\ [F] : the star of the north — motto of Minnesota

Lie·der·kranz \'lēd-ər-‚kräns\ [G] : wreath of songs : German singing society

lit·tera scrip·ta ma·net \lit-ə-‚rä-‚skrip-tə-'män-et\ [L] : the written letter abides

lo·cus in quo \‚ló-kəs-in-'kwō\ [L] : place in which

l'union fait la force \lūe-nyòⁿ-fe-lá-fórs\ [F] : union makes strength — motto of Belgium

lu·sus na·tu·rae \‚lü-səs-nə-'túr-ē, -'túr-‚ī\ [L] : freak of nature

ma foi \má-fwä\ [F] : my faith! : indeed

mag·na est ve·ri·tas et prae·va·le·bit \‚mäg-nä-‚est-'wā-ri-‚täs-et-‚prī-wä-'lä-bit\ [L] : truth is mighty and will prevail

mag·ni no·mi·nis um·bra \‚mäg-nē-‚nō-mə-nis-'úm-brä\ [L] : the shadow of a great name

mai·son de san·té \mā-zōⁿd-(ə)-‚säⁿ-tä\ [F] : private hospital : asylum

ma·lade ima·gi·naire \má-lád-ē-má-zhē-ner\ [F] : imaginary invalid : hypochondriac

ma·lis avi·bus \‚mäl-‚ēs-'ä-wi-‚bús\ [L] : under evil auspices

mal vu \mál-vūe\ [F] : badly regarded : disapproved of

ma·no a ma·no \‚män-ō-ä-'män-ō\ [Sp] : hand to hand : in direct competition or confrontation

man spricht Deutsch \man-shprikt-'dòich\ [G] : German spoken

ma·riage de con·ve·nance \má-ryàzh-də-kōⁿv-näⁿs\ [F] : marriage of convenience

ma·ri com·plai·sant \má-rē-kōⁿ-ple-zäⁿ\ [F] : complaisant husband : cuckold who accepts his wife's infidelity

mau·vaise honte \mō-vez-ōⁿt\ [F] : bad shame : bashfulness

mau·vais quart d'heure \mò-ve-kár-dœr\ [F] : bad quarter hour : an uncomfortable though brief experience

me·den agan \(‚)mā-‚den-'äg-‚än\ [Gk] : nothing in excess

me·dio tu·tis·si·mus ibis \‚med-ē-ō-‚tü-‚tis-ə-mús-'ē-bəs\ [L] : you will go most safely by the middle course

me ju·di·ce \mā-'yüd-ə-ke\ [L] : I being judge : in my judgment

mens sa·na in cor·po·re sa·no \‚mäns-'sän-ə-in-‚kòr-pə-re-'sän-ō\ [L] : a sound mind in a sound body

met·teur en scène \‚me-tœr-äⁿ-'sen\ [F] : one who puts on the stage : director of a play or film

me·um et tu·um \‚mē-əm-‚et-'tü-əm, ‚me-əm-\ [L] : mine and thine : distinction of private property

mi·ra·bi·le vi·su \mə-‚räb-ə-lē-'wē-sü\ [L] : wonderful to behold

mi·ra·bi·lia \‚mir-ə-'bil-ē-ə\ [L] : wonders : miracles

mœurs \mœr(s)\ [F] : mores : attitudes, customs, and manners of a society

mo·le ru·it sua \'mō-le-‚rú-it-‚sú-ä\ [L] : it collapses from its own bigness

monde \mōⁿd\ [F] : world : fashionable world : society

mon·ta·ni sem·per li·be·ri \mòn-'tän-ē-‚sem-pər-'lē-bə-‚rē\ [L] : mountaineers are always free men — motto of West Virginia

mo·nu·men·tum ae·re per·en·ni·us \‚mò-nə-'men-tùm-‚ī-re-pə-'ren-ē-ùs\ [L] : a monument more lasting than bronze — used of an immortal work of art or literature

mo·re suo \‚mòr-ā-'sü-ō\ [L] : in his (or her) own manner

mo·ri·tu·ri te sa·lu·ta·mus \‚mòr-ə-‚túr-ē-‚tä-‚säl-ə-'täm-ùs\ *or* **morituri te sa·lu·tant** \-'säl-ə-‚tänt\ [L] : we (or those) who are about to die salute thee

mul·tum in par·vo \‚múl-təm-in-'pär-vō, -'pär-wō\ [L] : much in little

mu·sée ima·gi·naire \mue-zä-ē-má-zhē-ner\ [F] : imaginary museum

mu·ta·to no·mi·ne de te fa·bu·la nar·ra·tur \mü-‚tät-ō-'nō-mə-ne-dä-'tä-‚fáb-ə-lä-nä-'rä-‚túr\ [L] : with the name changed the story applies to you

na·tu·ram ex·pel·las fur·ca, ta·men us·que re·cur·ret \nä-'tü-‚räm-ek-‚spel-äs-'fúr-‚kä ‚tä-mən-'üs-kwe-re-'kúr-et\ [L] : you may drive nature out with a pitchfork, but she will keep coming back

na·tu·ra non fa·cit sal·tum \nä-'tü-rä-‚nōn-‚fäk-ət-'säl-‚tùm\ [L] : nature makes no leap

ne ce·de ma·lis \nä-‚kä-de-'mäl-‚ēs\ [L] : yield not to misfortunes

ne·mo me im·pu·ne la·ces·sit \‚nä-mō-‚mä-im-‚pü-nä-lä-'kes-ət\ [L] : no one attacks me with impunity — motto of Scotland and of the Order of the Thistle

ne quid ni·mis \‚nä-‚kwid-'nim-əs\ [L] : not anything in excess

n'est-ce pas? \nes-'pä\ [F] : isn't it so?

nicht wahr? \nikt-'vär\ [G] : not true? : isn't it so?

nil ad·mi·ra·ri \'nēl-‚äd-mə-'rär-ē\ [L] : to be excited by nothing : equanimity

nil de·spe·ran·dum \‚nēl-‚de-spə-'rän-dùm\ [L] : never despair

nil si·ne nu·mi·ne \‚nēl-‚sin-e-'nü-mə-ne\ [L] : nothing without the divine will — motto of Colorado

n'im·porte \naⁿ-'pòrt\ [F] : it's no matter

no·lens vo·lens \‚nō-‚lenz-'vō-‚lenz\ [L] : unwilling (or) willing : willy-nilly

non om·nia pos·su·mus om·nes \‚nōn-‚óm-nē-ä-‚pò-sə-mùs-'òm-‚näs\ [L] : we can't all (do) all things

non om·nis mo·ri·ar \‚nōn-‚óm-nəs-'mòr-ē-‚är\ [L] : I shall not wholly die

non sans droict \nōⁿ-säⁿ-drwä\ [OF] : not without right — motto on Shakespeare's coat of arms

non sum qua·lis eram \‚nōn-‚sùm-‚kwäl-əs-'er-‚äm\ [L] : I am not what I used to be

nos·ce te ip·sum \‚nòs-ke-tā-'ip-‚sùm\ [L] : know thyself

nos·tal·gie de la boue \‚nòs-‚täl-zhēd-(ə)-lä-bü\ [F] : nostalgia for the mud : homesickness for the gutter

nous avons chan·gé tout ce·la \nü-zá-vōⁿ-shäⁿ-zhä-tü-s(l)á\ [F] : we have changed all that

nous ver·rons ce que nous ver·rons \nü-ve-rōⁿs-(ə)-kə-nü-ve-rōⁿ\ [F] : we shall see what we shall see

no·vus ho·mo \‚nó-wəs-'hó-mō\ [L] : new man : man newly ennobled : upstart

no·vus or·do se·clo·rum \-'òr-‚dō-sä-'klōr-əm\ [L] : a new cycle of the ages — motto on the reverse of the Great Seal of the United States

nu·gae \'nü-‚gī\ [L] : trifles

nuit blanche \nwē-bläⁿsh\ [F] : white night : a sleepless night

nyet \'nyet\ [Russ] : no

ob·iit \'ó-bē-‚it\ [L] : he (or she) died

ob·scu·rum per ob·scu·ri·us \əb-'skyúr-əm-‚per-əb-'skyúr-ē-əs\ [L] : (explaining) the obscure by means of the more obscure

ode·rint dum me·tu·ant \'òd-ə-‚rint-‚dùm-met-ə-‚wänt\ [L] : let them hate, so long as they fear

odi et amo \‚ò-‚dē-et-'äm-‚(‚)ō\ [L] : I hate and I love

omer·tà \‚ò-mer-tä\ [It] : submission : code chiefly among members of the criminal underworld that enjoins private vengeance and the refusal to give information to outsiders (as the police)

om·ne ig·no·tum pro mag·ni·fi·co \‚óm-ne-ig-‚nō-‚tùm-prō-mäg-'nif-i-‚kō\ [L] : everything unknown (is taken) as grand : the unknown tends to be exaggerated in importance or difficulty

om·nia mu·tan·tur, nos et mu·ta·mur in il·lis \‚óm-nē-ä-'mü-‚tän-‚túr ‚nōs-‚et-mü-‚täm-ər-in-'il-‚ēs\ [L] : all things are changing, and we are changing with them

om·nia vin·cit amor \'òm-nē-ä-‚wiⁿ-kət-'äm-‚ór\ [L] : love conquers all

onus pro·ban·di \‚ō-nəs-prō-'ban-‚dī, -dē\ [L] : burden of proof

ora pro no·bis \‚ō-rä-prō-'nō-‚bēs\ [L] : pray for us

ore ro·tun·do \‚ör-ē-rō-'tən-dō\ [L] : with round mouth : eloquently

oro y pla·ta \‚ór-ō-ē-'plät-ə\ [Sp] : gold and silver — motto of Montana

o tem·po·ra! o mo·res! \ō-'tem-pə-rä-ō-'mō-‚räs\ [L] : oh the times! oh the manners!

oti·um cum dig·ni·ta·te \‚ōt-ē-‚úm-‚kúm-‚dig-nə-'tä-te\ [L] : leisure with dignity

où sont les neiges d'an·tan? \ü-sōⁿ-lä-nezh-däⁿ-täⁿ\ [F] : where are the snows of yesteryear?

pal·li·da Mors \‚pal-əd-ə-'mórz\ [L] : pale Death

pa·nem et cir·cen·ses \'pän-‚em-et-kir-'kän-‚säs\ [L] : bread and circuses : provision of the means of life and recreation by government to appease discontent

pan·ta rhei \‚pän-‚tä-'(h)rä, ‚pant-ə-'rä\ [Gk] : all things are in flux

par avance \‚pär-á-väⁿs\ [F] : in advance : by anticipation

par avion \‚pär-á-vyōⁿ\ [F] : by airplane — used on airmail

par ex·em·ple \‚pär-äg-zäⁿpl\ [F] : for example

par·tu·ri·unt mon·tes, nas·ce·tur ri·di·cu·lus mus \‚pär-‚túr-ē-‚ùnt-'mòn-‚täs ‚näs-'kä-‚túr-ri-‚dik-ə-lús-'müs\ [L] : the mountains are in labor, and a ridiculous mouse will be brought forth

pa·ter pa·tri·ae \‚pä-‚ter-'pä-trē-‚ī\ [L] : father of his country

pau·cis ver·bis \‚paù-‚kēs-'wer-‚bès\ [L] : in a few words

pax vo·bis·cum \‚päks-vō-'bēs-‚kùm\ [L] : peace (be) with you

peine forte et dure \pen-fór-tä-düer\ [F] : strong and hard punishment : torture

per an·gus·ta ad au·gus·ta \‚per-'äⁿ-‚gùs-tə-äd-'aù-‚gùs-tə, per-'äⁿ-\ [L] : through difficulties to honors

père \per\ [F] : father — used after French proper names to distinguish a father from his son

per·eant qui an·te nos nos·tra dix·e·runt \'per-e-‚änt-kwē-‚än-te-'nōs-‚nós-trä-dēk-'sä-‚rùnt\ [L] : may they perish who have expressed our bright ideas before us

per·eunt et im·pu·tan·tur \'per-e-‚ùnt-et-‚im-pə-'tän-‚túr\ [L] : they (the hours) pass away and are reckoned on (our) account

per·fide Al·bion \per-‚fēd-ál-byōⁿ\ [F] : perfidious Albion (England)

peu à peu \‚pœ-á-pœ\ [F] : little by little

peu de chose \‚pœd-(ə)-shōz\ [F] : a trifle

pièce d'oc·ca·sion \pyes-dó-kä-zyōⁿ\ [F] : piece for a special occasion

pièce jus·ti·fi·ca·tive \pyes-zhūes-tē-fē-kä-tēv\ [F] : justificatory paper : document serving as evidence

pièce mon·tée \pyes-mōⁿ-tä\ [F] : set piece : food that has been decoratively shaped or arranged

pinx·it \'piŋk-sət\ [L] : he (or she) painted it

place aux dames \‚pläs-ō-dám\ [F] : (make) room for the ladies

ple·no ju·re \‚plä-nō-'yùr-e\ [L] : with full right

plus ça change, plus c'est la même chose \plue-sä-shäⁿzh plue-se-lá-mem-shōz\ [F] : the more that changes, the more it is the same thing

plus roy·a·liste que le roi \plue-rwá-yá-lēst-kəl-rwä\ [F] : more royalist than the king

po·cas pa·la·bras \‚pō-käs-pä-'läv-räs\ [Sp] : few words

po·eta nas·ci·tur, non fit \pó-‚ā-tä-'näs-kə-‚túr nōn-'fit\ [L] : a poet is born, not made

point de re·père \pwaⁿ-də-rä-per\ [F] : point of reference

pol·li·ce ver·so \‚pó-li-ke-'wer-sō\ [L] : with thumb turned : with a gesture or expression of condemnation

post hoc, er·go prop·ter hoc \‚pōst-‚hòk ‚er-gō-'próp-ter-‚hòk\ [L] : after this, therefore on account of it (a fallacy of argument)

post ob·itum \pōst-'ò-bə-‚tùm\ [L] : after death

pour ac·quit \‚pür-á-kē\ [F] : received payment

pour le mé·rite \‚pür-lə-mā-rēt\ [F] : for merit

pour rire \pür-rēr\ [F] : for laughing : not to be taken seriously

pro aris et fo·cis \‚prō-‚ä-‚rēs-et-'fó-‚kēs\ [L] : for altars and firesides

pro bo·no pu·bli·co \‚prō-‚bò-nō-'pü-bli-‚kō\ [L] : for the public good

pro hac vi·ce \‚prō-‚häk-'wik-e\ [L] : for this occasion

pro pa·tria \prō-'pä-trē-ä\ [L] : for one's country

pro re·ge, le·ge, et gre·ge \prō-'rä-‚ge-'lä-‚ge-et-'greg-‚e\ [L] : for the king, the law, and the people

pro re na·ta \‚prō-‚rä-'nät-ə\ [L] : for an occasion that has arisen : as needed — used in medical prescriptions

quand même \käⁿ-mem\ [F] : even though : whatever may happen

quan·tum mu·ta·tus ab il·lo \‚kwänt-əm-mü-'tät-əs-äb-'il-ō\ [L] : how changed from what he once was

quan·tum suf·fi·cit \‚kwänt-əm-'səf-ə-‚kit\ [L] : as much as suffices : a sufficient quantity — used in medical prescriptions

¿quién sa·be? \kyān-'sä\ [Sp] : who knows?

qui fa·cit per ali·um fa·cit per se \kwē-‚fäk-it-‚per-'äl-ē-‚úm-‚fäk-it-‚per-'sä\ [L] : he who does (anything) through another does it through himself

quis cus·to·di·et ip·sos cus·to·des? \‚kwis-kús-'tōd-ē-‚et-‚ip-‚sōs-kús-'tō-‚däs\ [L] : who will keep the keepers themselves?

qui s'ex·cuse s'ac·cuse \kē-'sek-‚skūez-'sá-‚kūez\ [F] : he who excuses himself accuses himself

quis se·pa·ra·bit? \‚kwis-‚sä-pə-'räb-it\ [L] : who shall separate (us)? — motto of the Order of St. Patrick

qui trans·tu·lit sus·ti·net \kwē-'träns-tə-‚lit-'sùs-tə-‚net\ [L] : He who transplanted sustains (us) — motto of Connecticut

qui va là? \kē-vá-lá\ [F] : who goes there?

quo·ad hoc \‚kwò-‚ad-'hòk\ [L] : as far as this : to this extent

quod erat de·mon·stran·dum \‚kwòd-'er-‚ät-‚dem-ən-'stran-dəm, -‚dā-‚mòn-'strän-‚dùm\ [L] : which was to be proved

quod erat fa·ci·en·dum \-‚fäk-ē-'en-‚dùm\ [L] : which was to be done

quod sem·per, quod ubi·que, quod ab om·ni·bus \kwòd-'sem-‚per kwòd-'ùb-i-‚kwā‚kwòd-äb-'òm-ni-‚bùs, -‚kwòd-ù-'bē-(‚)kwā-\ [L] : what (has been held) always, everywhere, by everybody

quod vi·de \kwòd-'wid-‚e\ [L] : which see

quo·rum pars mag·na fui \'kwòr-əm-‚pärs-‚mäg-nə-'fù-ē\ [L] : in which I played a great part

quos de·us vult per·de·re pri·us de·men·tat \kwòs-'de-ùs-‚wùlt-'perd-ə-‚re‚pri-ùs-dā-'men-‚tät\ [L] : those whom a god wishes to destroy he first drives mad

quot ho·mi·nes, tot sen·ten·ti·ae \kwòt-'hò-mə-‚näs-‚tòt-sen-'ten-tē-‚ī\ [L] : there are as many opinions as there are men

quo va·dis? \kwò-'wäd-əs, -'väd-\ [L] : whither are you going?

rai·son d'état \re-zōⁿ-dā-tá\ [F] : reason of state

re·cu·ler pour mieux sau·ter \rə-kūē-lā-pür-myōē-sō-tā\ [F] : to draw back in order to make a better jump

reg·nat po·pu·lus \‚reg-‚nät-'pò-pə-‚lùs\ [L] : the people rule — motto of Arkansas

re in·fec·ta \‚rā-in-'fek-‚tä\ [L] : the business being unfinished : without accomplishing one's purpose

re·li·gio lo·ci \re-‚lig-ē-‚ō-'lò-‚kē\ [L] : religious sanctity of a place

rem acu te·ti·gis·ti \rem-‚ä-kü-‚tet-ə-'gis-tē\ [L] : you have touched the point with a needle : you have hit the nail on the head

ré·pon·dez s'il vous plaît \rā-pōⁿ-dā-sēl-vü-ple\ [F] : reply, if you please

re·qui·es·cat in pa·ce \‚rek-wē-‚es-‚kät-in-'päk-‚e, ‚rā-kwē-‚es-‚kät-in-'päch-‚ā\ [L] : may he (or she) rest in peace — used on tombstones

re·spi·ce fi·nem \‚rā-spi-‚ke-'fē-‚nem\ [L] : look to the end : consider the outcome

re·sur·gam \re-'sùr-‚gäm\ [L] : I shall rise again

re·te·nue \rət-nǖ\ [F] : self-restraint : reserve

re·ve·nons à nos mou·tons \rəv-nōⁿ-á-nō-mü-tōⁿ\ [F] : let us return to our sheep : let us get back to the subject

ruse de guerre \rūēz-də-ger\ [F] : war stratagem

rus in ur·be \‚rüs-in-'ùr-‚be\ [L] : country in the city

sae·va in·dig·na·tio \‚si-wä-‚in-dig-'nät-ē-‚ō\ [L] : fierce indignation

sal At·ti·cum \‚sal-'at-i-kəm\ [L] : Attic salt : wit

salle à man·ger \sál-á-mä⁴-zhä\ [F] : dining room

sal·to mor·ta·le \‚säl-tō-mòr-'täl-‚ā\ [It] : deadly jump : full somersault : dangerous or crucial undertaking

sa·lus po·pu·li su·pre·ma lex es·to \‚säl-‚üs-‚pò-pə-‚lē-sü-‚prä-mə-‚leks-'es-‚tō\ [L] : let the welfare of the people be the supreme law — motto of Missouri

sans doute \sä⁴-'düt\ [F] : without doubt

sans gêne \sä⁴-zhen\ [F] : without embarrassment or constraint

sans peur et sans re·proche \sä⁴-‚pœr-ā-sä⁴-rə-'prȯsh\ [F] : without fear and without reproach

sans sou·ci \sä⁴-sü-sē\ [F] : without worry

sa·yo·na·ra \‚sä-yə-'när-ə, ‚sä-yə-\ [Jp] : good-bye

scène à faire \sen-á-fer\ [F] : obligatory scene

sculp·sit \'skəlp-‚sət, 'skülp-\ [L] : he (or she) carved it

scu·to bo·nae vo·lun·ta·tis tu·ae co·ro·nas·ti nos \'skü-‚tō-'bò-‚nī-‚vò-lùn-‚tät-əs-‚tü-‚ī-‚kòr-ə-‚näs-tē-'nōs\ [L] : Thou hast crowned us with the shield of Thy good will — a motto on the Great Seal of Maryland

se·cun·dum ar·tem \se-‚kùn-dəm-'är-‚tem\ [L] : according to the art : according to the accepted practice of a profession or trade

secundum na·tu·ram \-nä-'tü-‚räm\ [L] : according to nature : naturally

se de·fen·den·do \‚sā-‚fen-‚den-'dō\ [L] : in self-defense

se ha·bla es·pa·ñol \sā-‚äv-lä-‚äs-pä-'nyòl\ [Sp] : Spanish spoken

sem·per ea·dem \‚sem-‚per-'e-ä-‚dem\ [L] : always the same (fem.) — motto of Queen Elizabeth I

sem·per fi·de·lis \‚sem-pər-fə-'dā-ləs\ [L] : always faithful — motto of the U.S. Marine Corps

sem·per idem \‚sem-‚per-'ē-‚dém\ [L] : always the same (masc.)

sem·per pa·ra·tus \‚sem-pər-pə-'rät-əs\ [L] : always prepared — motto of the U.S. Coast Guard

se non è ve·ro, è ben tro·va·to \sä-‚nōn-e-'vä-rō-e-‚ben-trō-'vä-tō\ [It] : even if it is not true, it is well conceived

si jeu·nesse sa·vait, si vieil·lesse pou·vait! \sē-'zhœ-nes-'sá-ve sē-'vye-yes-'pü-ve\ [F] : if youth only knew, if age only could!

si·lent le·ges in·ter ar·ma \‚sil-‚ent-'lā-‚gäs-‚int-ər-'är-mä\ [L] : the laws are silent in the midst of arms

s'il vous plaît \sēl-vü-ple\ [F] : if you please

si·mi·lia si·mi·li·bus cu·ran·tur \sim-'il-ē-ä-sim-'il-ə-bùs-kü-'rän-‚tùr\ [L] : like is cured by like

si·mi·li si·mi·li gau·det \'sim-ə-ləs-'sim-ə-lē-'gaù-‚det\ [L] : like takes pleasure in like

si mo·nu·men·tum re·qui·ris, cir·cum·spi·ce \sē-‚mò-nə-‚ment-əm-re-'kwē-rəs kir-'kùm-spi-‚ke\ [L] : if you seek his monument, look around — epitaph of Sir Christopher Wren in St. Paul's, London, of which he was architect

si quae·ris pen·in·su·lam amoe·nam, cir·cum·spi·ce \sē-‚kwī-ris-pā-‚nin-sə-‚läm-ə-‚mē-‚näm kir-‚kùm-spi-ke\ [L] : if you seek a beautiful peninsula, look around — motto of Michigan

sis·te vi·a·tor \‚sis-te-wē-'ä-‚tòr\ [L] : stop, traveler — used on Roman roadside tombs

si vis pa·cem, pa·ra bel·lum \sē-‚wēs-'pä-‚kem ‚pä-rä-'bel-‚ùm\ [L] : if you wish peace, prepare for war

sol·vi·tur am·bu·lan·do \'sòl-wə-‚tùr-‚äm-bə-'län-dō\ [L] : it is solved by walking : the problem is solved by a practical experiment

splen·di·de men·dax \‚splen-də-‚dā-'men-‚däks\ [L] : nobly untruthful

spo·lia opi·ma \‚spō-lē-ə-ō-'pē-mə\ [L] : rich spoils : the arms taken by the victorious from the vanquished general

sta·tus in quo \‚stät-əs-in-'kwō\ [L] : state in which : the existing state

sta·tus quo an·te bel·lum \'stät-əs-kwō-‚änt-e-'bel-‚úm\ [L] : the state existing before the war

Stim·mung \shtim-‚ùŋ\ [G] : tone : mood : atmosphere

sua·vi·ter in mo·do, for·ti·ter in re \'swä-wə-‚ter-in-'mòd-ō 'fòrt-ə-‚ter-in-‚rä\ [L] : gently in manner, strongly in deed

sub ver·bo \‚sùb-'wer-bō, ‚səb-'vər-bō\ or **sub vo·ce** \‚sùb-'wō-ke, ‚səb-'vō-se\ [L] : under the word — introducing a cross-reference in a dictionary or index

sunt la·cri·mae re·rum \‚sùnt-‚läk-ri-‚mī-'rä-rúm\ [L] : there are tears for things : tears attend trials

suo ju·re \‚sù-ō-'yùr-e\ [L] : in his (or her) own right

suo lo·co \-'lō-kō\ [L] : in its proper place

suo Mar·te \-'mär-te\ [L] : by one's own exertions

sur place \sùer-plás\ [F] : in place : on the spot

su·um cui·que \‚sù-əm-'kwik-we\ [L] : to each his own

tant mieux \tä⁴-myōē\ [F] : so much the better

tant pis \-pē\ [F] : so much the worse

tem·po·ra mu·tan·tur, nos et mu·ta·mur in il·lis \‚tem-pə-rä-mü-'tän-‚tùr ‚nōs-‚et-mü-‚täm-ər-in-'il-‚ēs\ [L] : the times are changing, and we are changing with them

tem·pus edax re·rum \'tem-pùs-‚ed-‚äks-'rä-rúm\ [L] : time, that devours all things

tem·pus fu·git \‚tem-pəs-'fyü-jət, -'fü-git\ [L] : time flies

ti·meo Da·na·os et do·na fe·ren·tes \‚tim-ē-‚ō-‚dän-ä-‚ōs-‚et-‚dō-nä-fe-'ren-‚täs\ [L] : I fear the Greeks even when they bring gifts

to·ti·dem ver·bis \‚tòt-ə-‚dem-'wer-‚bēs\ [L] : in so many words

to·tis vi·ri·bus \‚tō-‚tēs-'wē-ri-‚bùs\ [L] : with all one's might

to·to cae·lo \‚tō-tō-'kī-lō\ or **toto coe·lo** \-'kȯi-lō\ [L] : by the whole extent of the heavens : diametrically

tou·jours per·drix \tü-zhür-per-drē\ [F] : always partridge : too much of a good thing

tour d'ho·ri·zon \tür-dȯ-rē-zōⁿ\ [F] : circuit of the horizon : general survey

tous frais faits \tü-fre-fe\ [F] : all expenses defrayed

tout à fait \tü-tá-fe\ [F] : altogether : quite

tout au con·traire \tü-tō-kō⁴-trer\ [F] : quite the contrary

tout à vous \tü-tá-vü\ [F] : wholly yours : at your service

tout bien ou rien \tü-'byaⁿ-nü-'ryaⁿ\ [F] : everything well (done) or nothing (attempted)

tout com·pren·dre c'est tout par·don·ner \'tü-kō⁴-prä⁴-drə se-'tü-pár-dȯ-nä\ [F] : to understand all is to forgive all

tout court \tü-kür\ [F] : quite short : simply; also : brusquely

tout de même \tüt-mem\ [F] : all the same : nevertheless

tout de suite \tüt-swēt\ [F] : immediately; also : all at once : consecutively

tout en·sem·ble \tü-tä⁴-sä⁴blⁿ\ [F] : all together : general effect

tout est per·du fors l'hon·neur \tü-te-per-dūē-fȯr-lȯ-nœr\ or **tout est perdu hors l'honneur** \-dūē-ȯr-\ [F] : all is lost save honor

tout le monde \tül-mō⁴d\ [F] : all the world : everybody

tranche de vie \trä⁴sh-də-vē\ [F] : slice of life

tria junc·ta in uno \‚trī-ä-'yùŋk-tä-in-'ü-nō\ [L] : three joined in one — motto of the Order of the Bath

trist·esse \trē-stes\ [F] : melancholy

tru·di·tur di·es die \‚trü-ə-‚tùr-‚dī-‚äs-'di-‚ä\ [L] : day is pushed forth by day : one day hurries on another

tu·e·bor \tü-'ä-‚bòr\ [L] : I will defend — a motto on the Great Seal of Michigan

ua mau ke ea o ka ai·na i ka po·no \‚ù-ä-'mä-ù-ke-'e-ä-ō-kä-'ä-ē-nä-‚ē-kä-'pō-nō\ [Hawaiian] : the life of the land is established in righteousness — motto of Hawaii

ue·ber·mensch \'üē-bər-‚mench\ [G] : superman

ul·ti·ma ra·tio re·gum \'ùl-ti-mä-‚rät-ē-ō-'rä-gùm\ [L] : the final argument of kings, i.e., war

und so wei·ter \ùnt-zō-'vī-tər\ [G] : and so on

uno an·i·mo \‚ü-nō-'än-ə-‚mō\ [L] : with one mind : unanimously

ur·bi et or·bi \‚ùr-bē-‚et-'òr-bē\ [L] : to the city (Rome) and the world

uti·le dul·ci \‚üt-ⁿl-e-'dùl-‚kē\ [L] : the useful with the agreeable

ut in·fra \‚üt-'in-frä\ [L] : as below

ut su·pra \‚üt-'sü-prä\ [L] : as above

va·de re·tro me, Sa·ta·na \‚wä-de-'rä-trō-‚mä-'sä-tə-‚nä\ [L] : get thee behind me, Satan

va et vient \vá-ā-vyä⁴\ [F] : coming and going : active movement : traffic

vae vic·tis \‚wī-'wik-‚tēs\ [L] : woe to the vanquished

va·ria lec·tio \‚wär-ē-‚äk-tē-‚ō\ pl **va·ri·ae lec·ti·o·nes** \'wär-ē-‚ī-‚lek-tē-'ō-‚näs\ [L] : variant reading

va·ri·um et mu·ta·bi·le sem·per fe·mi·na \‚wär-ē-‚et-‚mü-'tä-bə-le-‚sem-‚per-'fä-mə-nä\ [L] : woman is ever a fickle and changeable thing

ve·di Na·po·li e poi mo·ri \‚vä-dē-'nä-pō-lē-ä-‚pȯ-ē-'mȯ-rē\ [It] : see Naples, and then die

ve·ni, vi·di, vi·ci \‚wä-nē-‚wēd-ē-'wē-kē\ [L] : I came, I saw, I conquered

ven·tre à terre \vä⁴-trá-ter\ [F] : belly to the ground : at very great speed

ver·ba·tim ac lit·te·ra·tim \wer-‚bä-tim-‚äk-‚lit-ə-'rä-tim\ [L] : word for word and letter for letter

ver·bum sat sa·pi·en·ti est \‚wer-‚bùm-‚sät-‚säp-ē-'ent-ē-‚est\ [L] : a word to the wise is sufficient

vin·cit om·nia ve·ri·tas \‚wiŋ-kət-'ȯm-nē-ä-'wä-rə-‚täs\ [L] : truth conquers all things

vin·cu·lum ma·tri·mo·nii \‚wiŋ-kə-‚lùm-‚mä-trə-'mō-nē-‚ē\ [L] : bond of marriage

---

\ə\ abut \ⁿ\ kitten, F table \ər\ further \a\ ash \ā\ ace \ä\ cot, cart
\aú\ out \ch\ chin \e\ bet \ē\ easy \g\ go \i\ hit \ī\ ice \j\ job
\ŋ\ sing \ō\ go \ȯ\ law \ȯi\ boy \th\ thin \t̲h̲\ the \ü\ loot \ù\ foot
\y\ yet \zh\ vision \a̲, ḵ, ⁿ, œ, œ̄, ue, ūe, ᵊ\ see Guide to Pronunciation

vir·gi·ni·bus pu·e·ris·que \wir-'gin-ə-bús-,pú-ə-'rēs-kwe\ [L] : for girls and boys

vir·tu·te et ar·mis \wir-'tü-te-,et-'är-mēs\ [L] : by valor and arms — motto of Mississippi

vis me·di·ca·trix na·tu·rae \'wēs-,med-i-'kä-triks-nä-'tü-,rī\ [L] : the healing power of nature

vi·ta nuo·va \,vē-tä-'nwó-vä\ [It] : new life

vive la dif·fé·rence \vēv-(-ə)-lä-dē-fä-rä"s\ [F] : long live the difference (between the sexes)

vive la reine \vēv-lá-ren\ [F] : long live the queen

vive le roi \vēv-lə-rwä\ [F] : long live the king

vix·e·re for·tes an·te Aga·mem·no·na \wik-,sä-re-'fôr-,tās-,änt-,äg-ə-'mem-nə-,nä\ [L] : brave men lived before Agamemnon

vogue la ga·lère \vóg-lá-gá-ler\ [F] : let the galley be kept rowing : keep on, whatever may happen

voi·là tout \vwá-lá-tü\ [F] : that's all

vo·lup·té \vó-lūep-tā\ [F] : pleasure : sensuality

vou·lu \vü-lūē\ [F] : willed : contrived or forced

vox et prae·te·rea ni·hil \'wōks-et-prī-,ter-e-ä-'ni-,hil\ [L] : voice and nothing more

vox po·pu·li vox Dei \wōks-'pó-pə-,lē-,wōks-'de-ē\ [L] : the voice of the people is the voice of God

Wan·der·jahr \'vän-dər-,yär\ [G] : year of wandering

Welt·bild \'velt-,bilt\ [G] : conception of the world

Wert·frei·heit \'vert-,frī-,hit\ [G] : freedom from value judgments : ethical neutrality

wie geht's? \vē-'gäts\ [G] : how goes it?

Wis·sen·schaft \'vis-ən-,shäft\ [G] : learning : science

wun·der·bar \'vun-dər-,bär\ [G] : wonderful

Biographical Names

This section contains the names of persons both living and deceased. Persons are generally entered under the name or title by which they are most commonly known. Entries typically consist of last name, personal names, birth and death dates, nationality, and occupation or status. Also included, when appropriate, are pseudonyms, original names, epithets, alternate names, reign names, and titles. The pronunciation and syllabication of elements in boldface are usually shown. The pronunciation and syllabication of names or titles in italics or roman are given only occasionally. Transliterations of names from alphabets other than the roman have been made as exact and consistent as possible. For most Chinese names, the traditional Wade-Giles system has been used. The Pinyin system has been used only for Chinese still living or recently deceased.

A number of names contain connectives like *d'*, *de*, *di*, *van*, and *von*. With some exceptions, chiefly American or British, names are not alphabetized under these connectives but rather under the principal element of the surname. If the surname of a person is usually construed as containing this connective, the entry appears at the principal element and the connective appears immediately after, separated by a comma:

Gogh, van . . . Vincent

If the full name contains a connective which is not usually construed as an inseparable part of the surname, then the connective follows the personal name.

Bee·tho·ven . . . Ludwig van

Birth and death dates about which there is little or no doubt are entered without qualification. Doubtful dates are followed by a question mark, and approximate dates are preceded by *ca* (circa). In some instances only the years of principal activity are given, preceded by the abbreviation *fl* (flourished). The dates of a reign or other term of office are enclosed in parentheses.

At the end of many entries are derivative adjectives with such endings as *-ian*, *-ic*, or *-esque*. While it is possible to form these derivatives from any name, only the more common are shown:

Ru·bens . . . Peter Paul . . . . — **Ru·ben·esque** . . . *adj* — **Ru·ben·si·an** . . . *adj*

Of necessity many abbreviations have been used. For a key see the section Abbreviations in This Work in the front matter.

Ab·bey \'ab-ē\ Edwin Austin 1852–1911 Am. painter & illustrator

Ab·bott \'ab-ət\ Sir John Joseph Caldwell 1821–1893 Canad. polit.; prime min. (1891–92)

Abbott Lyman 1835–1922 Am. clergyman & author

Ab·del·ka·der \,ab-,del-'käd-ər\ *or* **Abd al-Qā·dir** \-,dal-\ 1808–1883 Arab leader in Algeria

'Ab·dor·rah·mān Khān \,ab-,dór-rə-'män-,kän\ *ca* 1844–1901 emir of Afghanistan (1880–1901)

Ab·dül·a·ziz \,ab-,dül-ə-'zēz\ 1830–1876 Ottoman sultan (1861–76)

Ab·dül·ha·mīd II \,ab-,dül-hä-'mēd\ 1842–1918 Ottoman sultan (1876–1909)

Abd·ul·lah \,ab-də-'lä\ 1882–1951 *'Abd Allāh ibn al-Husayn* emir of Transjordan (1921–46); king of Jordan (1946–51)

Ab·dül·me·cid I \,ab-,dül-mə-'jēd\ 1823–1861 Ottoman sultan (1839–61)

Abel \'ā-bəl\ Sir Frederick Augustus 1827–1902 Eng. chem.

Abe·lard \'ab-ə-,lärd\ Peter *F* Pierre **Abé·lard** *or* **Abai·lard** \-,ab-ā-'lär\ 1079–?1144 Fr. philos. & theol.

Ab·er·crom·bie *or* **Ab·er·crom·by** \'ab-ər-,kräm-bē, -,krəm-\ James 1706–1781 Brit. gen. in America

Abercromby Sir Ralph 1734–1801 Brit. gen.

Ab·er·nathy \'ab-ər-,nath-ē\ Ralph David 1926–1990 Am. clergyman & civil rights leader

Ab·ing·ton \'ab-iŋ-tən\ Fanny 1737–1815 née *Frances Barton* Eng. actress

Abruz·zi Duke of the — see LUIGI AMEDEO

Abū al-Qā·sim \ə-,búl-'käs-əm\ *or* **Abul Ka·sim** *L* **Al·bu·ca·sis** \,al-byü-'kā-səs\ *ca* 936–*ca* 1013 Span. Arab physician & medical writer

Abū Bakr \ə-,bü-'bak-ər\ *ca* 573–634 1st caliph of Mecca

Ach·e·son \'ach-ə-sən\ Dean Gooderham 1893–1971 Am. statesman

Ac·ton \'ak-tən\ 1st Baron 1834–1902 *John Emerich Edward Dal·berg-Acton* \,dal-,bərg-\ Eng. hist.

Ad·am \'ad-əm\ Robert 1728–1792 & his bro. James 1730–1794 Scot. architects & furniture designers

Ad·ams \'ad-əmz\ Ansel Easton 1902–1984 Am. photographer

Adams Charles Francis 1807–1886 *son of J.Q.* Am. author & diplomat

Adams Franklin Pierce 1881–1960 *known as F.P.A.* Am. journalist

Adams Henry Brooks 1838–1918 *son of C.F.* Am. hist.

Adams James Truslow 1878–1949 Am. hist.

Adams John 1735–1826 Am. diplomat & 2d pres. of the U.S. (1797–1801)

Adams John Quin·cy \'kwin-zē, 'kwin(t)-sē\ 1767–1848 *son of John* 6th pres. of the U.S. (1825–29)

Adams Maude 1872–1953 orig. *Maude Kiskadden* Am. actress

Adams Samuel 1722–1803 Am. Revolutionary patriot

Adams Samuel Hopkins 1871–1958 Am. author

Ad·dams \'ad-əmz\ Jane 1860–1935 Am. social worker

Ad·di·son \'ad-ə-sən\ Joseph 1672–1719 Eng. essayist & poet — **Ad·di·so·nian** \,ad-ə-'sō-nē-ən, -nyən\ *adj*

Ade \'ād\ George 1866–1944 Am. humorist & playwright

Ade·nau·er \'ad-ᵊn-,aú(-ə)r, 'äd-\ Konrad 1876–1967 chancellor of West Germany (1949–63)

Ad·ler \'äd-lər, 'ad-\ Alfred 1870–1937 Austrian psychiatrist

Adler \'ad-\ Cyrus 1863–1940 Am. educ. & scholar

Adler \'ad-\ Felix 1851–1933 Am. educ. & reformer

Adler \'ad-\ Mortimer Jerome 1902– Am. philos.

\ə\ abut \ᵊ\ kitten, F table \ər\ further \a\ ash \ā\ ace \ä\ cot, cart \aú\ out \ch\ chin \e\ bet \ē\ easy \g\ go \i\ hit \ī\ ice \j\ job \ŋ\ sing \ō\ go \ó\ law \ói\ boy \th\ thin \t̲h̲\ the \ü\ loot \ú\ foot \y\ yet \zh\ vision \å, k̲, ⁿ, œ, ᴔ, ᵫ, ᴇ, ʸ\ see Guide to Pronunciation

Adri·an \'ā-drē-ən\ name of 6 popes: esp. **IV** (*Nicholas Break·spear* \'bräk-ˌspi(ə)r\) 1100?–1159 the only Eng. pope (1154–59)
Adrian Rom. emp. — see HADRIAN
Adrian Edgar Douglas 1889–1977 1st Baron of *Cambridge* Eng. physiol.
Æ — see George William RUSSELL
Æl·fric \'al-frik\ *ca* 955–*ca* 1010 Eng. abbot & writer
Aeneas Silvius *or* Sylvius — see PIUS II
Aes·chi·nes \'es-kə-ˌnēz, 'ēs-\ 389–314 B.C. Athenian orator
Aes·chy·lus \'es-kə-ləs, 'ēs-\ 525–456 B.C. Greek dram. — Aes·chy·le·an \ˌes-kə-'lē-ən, ˌēs-\ *adj*
Ae·sop \'ē-ˌsäp, -səp\ Greek fabulist; prob. legendary
Aeth·el·bert \'ath-əl-ˌberkt\ *or* Eth·el·bert \'eth-əl-ˌbert, 'eth-, -ˌbərt\ *or* Aed·il·berct \'ad-ᵊl-ˌberkt\ *d* 616 king of Kent (560–616)
Aeth·el·red \'ath-əl-ˌred\ *or* Eth·el·red II \'eth-\ 968?–1016 *the Unready* king of England (978–1016)
Afon·so \ə-'fōn(n)-sü\ name of 6 kings of Portugal: esp **I** Hen·ri·ques \ān-'rē-kish\ 1109?–1185 (1st king of Portugal; 1139–85); **V** 1432–1481 (reigned 1438–81)
Aga Khan III \ˌäg-ə-'kän, ˌag-\ 1877–1957 *Aga Sultan Sir Mohammed Shah* head of Ismailian Muslims (1885–1957)
Aga Khan IV 1936– *grandson of prec.*, *Shah Karim* head of Ismailian Muslims (1957–)
Ag·as·siz \'ag-ə-(ˌ)sē\ Alexander 1835–1910 *son of J.L.R.* Am. zool.
Agassiz (Jean) Louis (Rodolphe) 1807–1873 Am. (Swiss-born) naturalist
Agath·o·cles \ə-'gath-ə-ˌklēz\ 361–289 B.C. tyrant of Syracuse
Agee \'ā-(ˌ)jē\ James 1909–1955 Am. author
Ages·i·la·us II \ə-ˌjes-ə-'lā-əs\ *ca* 444–360 B.C. king of Sparta (399–360)
Ag·nes \'ag-nəs\ Saint *d* A.D. 304 virgin martyr
Ag·new \'ag-ˌn(y)ü\ Spi·ro \'spi(ə)r-(ˌ)ō\ Theodore 1918– Am. polit.; vice pres. of the U.S. (1969–73)
Ag·non \'ag-ˌnän\ Shmuel Yosef 1888–1970 Israeli (Austrian-born) author
Agric·o·la \ə-'grik-ə-lə\ Gnaeus Julius A.D. 40–93 Rom. gen.
Agrip·pa \ə-'grip-ə\ Marcus Vipsanius 63?–12 B.C. Rom. statesman
Ag·rip·pi·na \ˌag-rə-'pī-nə, -'pē-\ the elder *ca* 14 B.C.–A.D. 33 *dau. of Agrippa, wife of Germanicus Caesar, mother of Caligula*
Agrippina the younger A.D. 15?–59 *dau. of prec. & mother of Emp. Nero*
Agt \'äkt\ Andries A.M. van 1931– prime min. of the Netherlands (1977–82)
Agui·nal·do \ˌäg-ē-'näl-(ˌ)dō\ Emilio 1869–1964 Filipino leader
Ah·med III \ä-'met, -'med\ 1673–1736 Ottoman sultan (1703–30)
Ai·ken \'ā-kən\ Conrad Potter 1889–1973 Am. writer
Ai·ley \'ā-lē\ Alvin 1931–1989 Am. dancer & choreographer
Ains·worth \'änz-(ˌ)wərth\ (William) Harrison 1805–1882 Eng. nov.
Ai·shah \'ä-ē-shə\ 611–678 *favorite wife of Muhammad*
Ak·bar \'ak-bər, -ˌbär\ 1542–1605 Mughal emp. of India (1556–1605)
à Kempis — see THOMAS À KEMPIS
Aken·side \'ā-kən-ˌsīd\ Mark 1721–1770 Eng. poet & physician
Akhe·na·ton \ˌäk-(ə-)'nät-ᵊn\ *also* Ikh·na·ton \ik-'nät-ᵊn\ king of Egypt (1379–1362 B.C.)
Aki·ba ben Jo·seph \ä-'kiv-ä-ben-'jō-zəf\ A.D. 40–135 Jewish sage & martyr in Palestine
Aki·hi·to \ˌäk-ē-'hē-(ˌ)tō\ 1933– emp. of Japan (1989–)
'Alam·gir \'äl-əm-gi(ə)r\ Muhī-ud-Din Muhammad 1618–1707 *Aurangzeb* Mughal emp. of India
Alanbrooke Viscount — see Sir Alan Francis BROOKE
Alar·cón, de \ˌäl-ˌär-'kōn, -'kón\ Pedro Antonio 1833–1891 Span. writer & statesman
Al·a·ric \'al-ə-rik\ *ca* 370–410 Visigoth king; conqueror of Rome
Alaric II *d* 507 Visigoth king; issued legal code
Al·bee \'ól-(ˌ)bē, 'al-\ Edward Franklin 1928– Am. dram.
Albemarle Duke of — see George MONCK
Al·bé·niz \äl-'bā-(ˌ)nēs, -(ˌ)nēth\ Isaac 1860–1909 Span. pianist & composer
Al·bers \'al-bərz, 'äl-bərs\ Josef 1888–1976 Am. (Ger.-born) painter
Al·bert I \'al-bərt\ 1875–1934 king of Belgium (1909–34)
Albert Carl Bert 1908– Am. polit.
Albert of Saxe-Co·burg-Go·tha \-ˌsaks-ˌkō-bərg-'gō-thə, -'gót-ə\ 1819–1861 *prince consort of Queen Victoria of Great Britain* (1840–61)
Al·ber·tus Mag·nus \al-'bərt-ə-'smag-nəs\ Saint *ca* 1200–1280 *Albert Count von Boll·städt* \-'ból-ˌshtet\ Ger. philos. & theol.
Al·boin \'al-ˌbóin, -bə-wən\ *d* 572 Lombard king (*ca* 565–572)
Albucasis — see ABŪ AL-QĀSIM
Al·bu·quer·que, de \'al-bə-ˌkər-kē, ˌal-bə-'\ Afonso 1453–1515 Port. viceroy & conqueror in India
Al·cae·us \al-'sē-əs\ *ca* 620–*ca* 580 B.C. Greek poet
Al·ci·bi·a·des \ˌal-sə-'bī-ə-ˌdēz\ *ca* 450–404 B.C. Athenian gen. & polit.
Al·cott \'ól-kət, 'al-, -ˌkät\ Amos Bronson 1799–1888 Am. teacher & philos.
Alcott Louisa May 1832–1888 *dau. of A.B.* Am. author
Al·cuin \'al-kwən\ *ca* 732–804 Anglo-Saxon theol. & scholar
Al·da \'ól-də, 'ól-, 'al-\ Frances 1883–1952 orig. *Frances Davis* N.Z.-born soprano
Al·den \'ól-dən\ John 1599?–1687 *Mayflower* pilgrim
Al·der \'äl-dər\ Kurt 1902–1958 Ger. chem.
Al·drich \'ól-drich\ Thomas Bailey 1836–1907 Am. author
Al·drin \'ól-drən\ Edwin Eugene Jr. 1930– Am. astronaut; 2d man on the moon
Alei·chem Sha·lom \ˌshó-ləm-ə-'lā-kəm\ 1859–1916 pseud. of Sholem Rabinowitz Am. (Russ.-born) humorist
Aleix·an·dre \ˌä-ˌlā-'sän-dre\ Vicente 1898–1984 Span. poet
Ale·mán \ˌäl-ā-'män\ Mateo 1547–*ca* 1614 Span. nov.
Ale·mán Val·dés \-väl-'dēs\ Miguel 1902–1983 Mex. lawyer; pres. of Mexico (1946–52)
Alem·bert, d' \ˌdal-əm-'ba(ə)r, -'be(ə)r\ Jean Le Rond 1717–1783 Fr. math. & philos.
Al·ex·an·der \ˌal-ig-'zan-dər, ˌel-\ name of 8 popes: esp. **VI** (*Rodrigo Borgia*) 1431–1503 (pope 1492–1503)
Alexander III of Macedon 356–323 B.C. *the Great* king (336–323)
Alexander Russ Alek·sandr name of 3 emps. of Russia: **I** 1777–1825 (reigned 1801–25); **II** 1818–1881 (reigned 1855–81); **III** 1845–1894 (reigned 1881–94)

Alexander Serb Aleksandar Obre·no·vić \-ō-'bren-ə-ˌvich\ 1876–1903 king of Serbia (1889–1903)
Alexander Harold Rupert Leofric George 1891–1969 1st Earl Alexander of Tunis Brit. field marshal; gov.-gen. of Canada (1946–52)
Alexander I 1888–1934 king of Yugoslavia (1929–34)
Alexander Nev·sky \-'nev-skē, -'nef-\ *ca* 1220–1263 Russ. saint & mil. hero
Alexander Severus — see SEVERUS ALEXANDER
Alex·is I Mi·khay·lo·vich \ə-ˌlek-səs-mi'ki-lə-ˌvich\ 1629–1676 *father of Peter the Great* czar of Russia (1645–76)
Alex·is Pe·tro·vich \-pe-'trō-vich\ 1690–1718 *son of Peter the Great* czarevitch of Russia
Alex·i·us I Com·ne·nus \ə-'lek-sē-əs-ˌkäm-'nē-nəs\ 1048–1118 Byzantine emp. (1081–1118)
Al·fie·ri \ˌal-fē-'er-ē\ Conte Vittorio 1749–1803 Ital. tragic poet
Al·fon·so XIII \al-'fän(t)-(ˌ)sō, -'fän-(ˌ)zō\ 1886–1941 king of Spain (1886–1931)
Al·fred *or* Æl·fred \'al-frəd, -fərd\ 849–899 *the Great* king of Wessex (871–899)
Alf·vén \ˌalf-'vän, -'ven\ Hannes Olof Gösta 1908– Swed. astrophysicist
Al·ger \'al-jər\ Horatio 1832–1899 Am. author
Al·gren \'ól-grən\ Nelson 1909–1981 Am. author
'Alī \ä-'lē, 'äl-ē\ *or* Ar 'Alī ibn Abī Tā·lib \-ˌib-ən-ˌäb-ē-'tä-lib\ *ca* 600–661 *cousin & son-in-law of Muhammad* 4th orthodox caliph (656–661)
Ali Pa·şa \-'päsh-ə, -'pash-; -pə-'shä\ 1741–1822 *the Lion of Janina* Turk. pasha
Ali Muhammad 1942– orig. *Cassius Marcellus Clay* Am. boxer
Al·lais \'al-ˌā\ Maurice 1911– Fr. econ.
Al·len \'al-ən\ Ethan 1738–1789 Am. Revolutionary soldier
Allen William 1532–1594 Eng. cardinal
Al·len·by \'al-ən-bē\ Edmund Henry Hynman 1st Viscount 1861–1936 Brit. field marshal
Allen·de Gos·sens \ä-ˌyen-dā-'gó-ˌsen(t)s\ Salvador 1908–1973 Chilean Marxist; pres. of Chile (1970–73)
Al·leyne \'al-ən, -ˌēn, -ˌān\ Edward 1566–1626 Eng. actor
All·ston \'ól-stən\ Washington 1779–1843 Am. painter
Al·ma–Tad·e·ma \ˌal-mə-'tad-ə-mə\ Sir Lawrence 1836–1912 Eng. (Du.-born) painter
Alt·man \'ólt-mən\ Sidney 1939– Am. (Canad.-born) biophysicist
Alva Duke of — see ÁLVAREZ DE TOLEDO
Al·va·ra·do, de \ˌäl-vä-'rä-thō\ Pedro *ca* 1485–1541 Span. soldier; companion of Cortes in Mexico
Al·va·rez \'al-və-ˌrez\ Luis Walter 1911–1988 Am. physicist
Al·va·rez de To·le·do \ˌäl-vä-ˌräth-thā-tō-'lā-thō\ Fernando 1507–1582 3d Duke of Al·ba \'al-bə\ *or* Al·va \'al-və\ Span. gen.
Alvarez Quin·te·ro \-ˌkēn-'tā-rō\ Serafín 1871–1938 & his bro. Joaquín 1873–1944 Span. dram.
A·ma·ti \ä-'mät-ē, ə-\ family of Ital. violin makers of Cremona: esp. Nicolò 1596–1684
Am·brose \'am-ˌbrōz\ Saint 339–397 bishop of Milan — Am·bro·sian \am-'brō-zhən, -zē-ən\ *adj*
Amen·ho·tep \ˌäm-ən-'hō-ˌtep, ˌam-\ *or* Am·e·no·phis \ˌam-ə-'nō-fəs\ name of 4 kings of Egypt: esp. **III** (1417–1379 B.C.); **IV** — see AKHENATON
Amerigo Vespucci — see VESPUCCI
Am·herst \'am-(ˌ)ərst\ Jeffrey 1717–1797 *Baron Amherst* Brit. gen.; gov.-gen. of Brit. No. America (1760–63)
Amis \'ā-məs\ Kingsley 1922– Eng. author
Am·père \ˌän-'pe(ə)r\ André-Marie 1775–1836 Fr. physicist
Amund·sen \'äm-ən-sən\ Roald 1872–1928 Norw. polar explorer; disc. south pole (1911)
Anac·re·on \ə-'nak-rē-ən\ *ca* 582–*ca* 485 B.C. Greek poet
An·ax·ag·o·ras \ˌan-ˌak-'sag-ə-rəs\ *ca* 500–*ca* 428 B.C. Greek philos. — An·ax·ag·o·re·an \-ˌsag-ə-'rē-ən\ *adj*
Anax·i·man·der \ə-'nak-sə-ˌman-dər\ 610–*ca* 547 B.C. Greek philos. & astron. — Anax·i·man·dri·an \-ˌnak-sə-'man-drē-ən\ *adj*
An·ders \'än-dərs, -dərz\ Władysław 1892–1970 Pol. gen.
An·der·sen \'an-dər-sən\ Hans Christian 1805–1875 Dan. writer of fairy tales
An·der·son \'an-dər-sən\ Carl David 1905– Am. physicist
Anderson John 1882–1958 1st Viscount Wa·ver·ley \'wā-vər-lē\ Brit. polit.
Anderson Dame Judith 1898– orig. *Frances Margaret Anderson* Austral. actress
Anderson Marian 1902– Am. contralto
Anderson Maxwell 1888–1959 Am. dram.
Anderson Philip Warren 1923– Am. physicist
Anderson Sherwood 1876–1941 Am. writer
An·drás·sy \'än-ˌdräsh-ē\ Gyula, count; father 1823–1890 & son 1860–1929 Hung. statesmen
An·dré \'än-ˌdrā, 'än-(ˌ)drā\ John 1750–1780 Brit. spy
An·drea del Sar·to \ˌän-ˌdrā-ə-ˌdel-'sär-(ˌ)tō\ 1486–1530 *Andrea d'Agnolo* Florentine painter
An·drews \'an-ˌdrüz\ Roy Chapman 1884–1960 Am. naturalist
An·dre·yev \än-'drā-(y)əf\ Leonid Nikolayevich 1871–1919 Russ. author
An·drić \'än-drich\ Ivo 1892–1975 Serbo-Croatian author
An·dro·pov \än-'drò-ˌpóv\ Yuri Vladimirovich 1914–1984 Russ. polit; pres. U.S.S.R. (1982–84); 1st secy. of communist party (1982–84)
An·dros \'an-drəs, -dräs\ Sir Edmund 1637–1714 Brit. colonial gov. in America
An·fin·sen \'an-fən-sən\ Christian Boehmer 1916– Am. chem.
An·ge·la Me·ri·ci \ˌan-jə-lə-mə-'rē-chē\ Saint 1474?–1540 Ital. religious; founder of Ursuline order (1535)
An·gel·i·co \an-'jel-i-ˌkō\ Fra *ca* 1400–1455 orig. *Guido di Pietro* Florentine painter
An·gell \'an-jəl\ Sir Norman 1872–1967 orig. *Ralph Norman Angell Lane* Eng. author & lecturer
Ang·ström \'aŋ-strəm, 'óŋ\ Anders Jonas 1814–1874 Swed. physicist
An·na Iva·nov·na \'an-ə-ē-'vän-əv-nə\ 1693–1740 empress of Russia (1730–40)
Anne \'an\ 1665–1714 *dau. of James II* queen of Great Britain (1702–14)

Anne of Austria 1601–1666 *consort of Louis XIII of France* regent (1643–51) for her son Louis XIV

Anne of Cleves \'klēvz\ 1515–1557 *4th wife of Henry VIII of England*

Annunzio, D' Gabriele — see D'ANNUNZIO

Anouilh \a-'nü-ē\ Jean 1910–1987 Fr. dram.

An·selm \'an-,selm\ Saint 1033/34–1109 archbishop of Canterbury (1093–1109)

An·tho·ny \'an(t)-thə-nē, *chiefly Brit* 'an-tə-\ Saint *ca* 250–355 Egypt. monk; regarded as founder of Christian monasticism

Anthony Mark — see Marcus ANTONIUS

Anthony Susan Brownell 1820–1906 Am. suffragist

Anthony *or* **An·to·ny** \'an-tə-nē\ of **Padua** Saint 1195–1231 Franciscan monk

An·tig·o·nus I \an-'tig-ə-nəs\ 382–301 B.C. *Antigonus Cyclops* gen. of Alexander the Great & king of Macedonia (306–301)

An·ti·o·chus \an-'tī-ə-kəs\ name of 13 Seleucid kings of Syria: esp. **III** *the Great* 242–187 B.C. (reigned 223–187); **IV** *Epiph·a·nes* \-i-'pif-ə-,nēz\ *ca* 215–164 B.C. (reigned 175–164)

An·tip·a·ter \an-'tip-ət-ər\ *ca* 397–*ca* 319 B.C. Macedonian gen.

An·tis·the·nes \an-'tis-thə-,nēz\ *ca* 445–*ca* 365 B.C. Athenian philos.

An·to·ne·scu \,an-tə-'nes-(,)kü\ Ion \'yon\ 1882–1946 Romanian gen.; dictator (1940–44)

An·to·ni·nus \,an-tə-'nī-nəs\ Marcus Au·re·lius \ȯ-'rēl-yəs, -'rē-lē-əs\ A.D. 121–180 *nephew, son-in-law, and adopted son of Antoninus Pius* Rom. emp. (161–180) & Stoic philos.

Antoninus Pi·us \-'pī-əs\ A.D. 86–161 Rom. emp. (138–161)

An·to·ni·us \an-'tō-nē-əs\ Marcus *E* Mark *or* Marc An·to·ny *or* An·tho·ny \'an(t)-thə-nē, *chiefly Brit* 'an-tə-\ *ca* 82–30 B.C. Rom. orator, triumvir, & gen.

Apel·les \ə-'pel-ēz\ 4th cent. B.C. Greek painter

Apol·li·naire \ə-,päl-ə-'na(ə)r, -'ne(ə)r\ Guillaume 1880–1918 orig. *Wilhelm Apollinaris de Kos·tro·wit·zki* \,kȯs-trə-'vēt-skē\ Fr. poet

Ap·ol·lo·ni·us \,ap-ə-'lō-nē-əs\ **of Rhodes** 3d cent. B.C. Greek poet — **Ap·ol·lo·nian** \-nē-ən, -nyən\ *adj*

Appius Claudius — see CLAUDIUS

Appleseed Johnny — see John CHAPMAN

Ap·ple·ton \'ap-əl-tən\ Sir Edward 1892–1965 Eng. physicist

Apra·ksin *or* **Aprax·in** \ə-'prak-sən\ Fyodor Matveyevich 1661–1728 Russ. admiral

Ap·u·le·ius \,ap-ə-'lā-əs\ Lucius *ca* A.D. 124–after 170? Rom. philos. & rhetorician

Aqui·nas Saint Thomas — see THOMAS AQUINAS

Aqui·no \ə-'kē-nō\ Corazon 1933– pres. of Philippines (1986–)

Ar·am \'ar-əm, 'er-\ Eugene 1704–1759 Eng. philologist & murderer

Ara·nha \ə-'ran-yə\ Oswaldo 1894–1960 Braz. lawyer & polit.

Ar·ber \'är-bər\ Werner 1929– Swiss microbiologist

Arblay, d' Madame — see Fanny BURNEY

Ar·buth·not \är-'bəth-nət, 'är-bəth-,nät\ John 1667–1735 Scot. physician & author

Ar·cher \'är-chər\ William 1856–1924 Scot. critic & dram.

Ar·chi·me·des \,är-kə-'mēd-ēz\ *ca* 287–212 B.C. Greek math. & inventor — **Ar·chi·me·de·an** \-'mēd-ē-ən, -mi-'dē-\ *adj*

Ar·chi·pen·ko \,är-kə-'peŋ-(,)kō\ Aleksandr Porfiryevich 1887–1964 Am. (Ukrainian-born) sculptor

Are·ti·no \,ar-ə-'tē-nō, ,är-\ Pietro 1492–1556 Ital. satirist

Ar·gall \'är-,gȯl, -gəl\ Sir Samuel *ca* 1572–*ca* 1626 Eng. mariner

Ar·gyll \är-'gi(ə)l, 'är-,gil\ 9th Duke of — see John D.S. CAMPBELL

Ar·i·as Sán·chez \är-ē-,äs-'sän-chez\ Oscar 1941– pres. of Costa Rica (1986–)

Ari·os·to \,är-ē-'ō-(,)stō\ Ludovico 1474–1533 Ital. poet

Ar·is·tar·chus \,ar-ə-'stär-kəs\ *ca* 217–145 B.C. Greek grammarian

Aristarchus of Samos *fl ca* 270 B.C. Greek astron.

Ar·is·ti·des *or* **Ar·is·tei·des** \,ar-ə-'stīd-ēz\ *ca* 530–*ca* 468 B.C. *the Just* Athenian statesman

Ar·is·tip·pus \,ar-ə-'stip-əs\ *ca* 435–366 B.C. Greek philos.

Ar·is·toph·a·nes \,ar-ə-'stäf-ə-,nēz\ *ca* 450–*ca* 388 B.C. Athenian dram. — **Ar·is·to·phan·ic** \,ar-ə-stə-'fan-ik\ *adj*

Aristophanes of Byzantium *ca* 257–180 B.C. Greek scholar

Ar·is·tot·le \'ar-ə-,rit\ Sir Richard 1732–1792 Eng. inventor

Ark·wright \'ärk-,rīt\ Sir Richard 1732–1792 Eng. inventor

Ar·len \'är-lən\ Michael 1895–1956 orig. *Di·kran* \dik-'rän\ *Kou·youm·djian* \kü-'yüm-jē-,än\ Brit. (Bulg.-born) nov.

Ar·min·i·us \är-'min-ē-əs\ *or* **Ar·min** \är-'mēn\ 18 B.C.?–A.D. 19 sometimes *Her·mann* \'he(ə)r-,män\ Ger. hero

Arminius Jacobus 1560–1609 *Jacob Har·men·sen* \'här-mən-sən\ *or* *Hermansz* \'he(ə)r-,män(t)s\ Du. theol.

Ar·mour \'är-mər\ Philip Danforth 1832–1901 Am. industrialist

Arm·strong \'ärm-,strȯŋ\ Hamilton Fish 1893–1973 Am. editor

Armstrong Louis 1901–1971 *Satch·mo* \'sach-,mō\ Am. jazz musician

Armstrong Neil Alden 1930– Am. astronaut; 1st man on the moon

Armstrong William George 1810–1900 Baron *Armstrong of Cragside* Eng. inventor & industrialist

Armstrong–Jones \-'jōnz\ Antony Charles Robert 1930– Earl of *Snowdon* Eng. photographer

Arne \'ärn\ Thomas Augustine 1710–1778 Eng. composer

Ar·nold \'ärn-ʰld\ Benedict 1741–1801 Am. gen. in Revolution & traitor

Arnold Henry Harley 1886–1950 Am. gen.

Arnold Matthew 1822–1888 *son of Thomas* Eng. poet & critic — **Ar·nold·ian** \är-'nōld-ē-ən\ *adj*

Arnold Thomas 1795–1842 Eng. educ.

Ar·nold·son \'ärn-ʰl-sən\ Klas Pontus 1844–1916 Swed. pacifist

Arou·et \är-we\ François-Marie — see VOLTAIRE

Arp \'ärp\ Jean (*or* Hans) 1887–1966 Fr. artist & poet

Ar·pád \'är-,päd\ *d* 907 Hung. national hero

Ar·rhe·ni·us \ə-'rē-nē-əs, -'rā-\ Svante August 1859–1927 Swed. physicist & chem.

Ar·row \'ar-(,)ō\ Kenneth Joseph 1921– Am. econ.

Ar·son·val, d' \'därs-ʰn-,väl\ Jacques Arsène 1851–1940 Fr. biophysicist

Ar·ta·xer·xes \,ärt-ə(g)-'zərk-,sēz\ name of 3 Pers. kings: **I** *d* 425 B.C. (reigned 465–25); **II** *d* 359/58 B.C. (reigned 404–359/58); **III** *d* 338 B.C. (reigned 359/58–338)

Ar·te·vel·de, van \'ärt-ə-,vel-də\ Jacob *ca* 1295–1345 & his son Philip 1340–1382 Flem. leaders

---

Ar·thur \'är-thər\ Chester Alan 1829–1886 21st pres. of the U.S. (1881–85)

As·bury \'az-,ber-ē, -b(ə-)rē\ Francis 1745–1816 Methodist bishop

Asch \'ash\ Sho·lem \'shō-ləm\ *or* Sha·lom \shə-'lōm\ *or* Sho·lom \'shō-ləm\ 1880–1957 Am. (Pol.-born) Yiddish writer

As·cham \'as-kəm\ Roger 1515–1568 Eng. scholar & author

Ashburton Baron — see Alexander BARING

Ashton Winifred — see Clemence DANE

Ashur·ba·ni·pal *also* **As·sur·ba·ni·pal** *or* **Asur·ba·ni·pal** \,äs(h)-ər-'bän-ə-,päl\ king of Assyria (668–627 B.C.)

Aso·ka *or* **Aço·ka** \ə-'s(h)ō-kə\ *d* 238 *or* 232 B.C. king of Magadha, India (*ca* 265–238 *or* *ca* 273–232 B.C.)

As·pa·sia \as-'pā-zh(ē-)ə\ 470?–410 B.C. *consort of Pericles*

As·quith \'as-,kwith, -kwəth\ Herbert Henry 1852–1928 *1st Earl of Oxford and Asquith* Brit. statesman

Assad, al- \al-'ä-,säd\ Hafiz 1928– pres. of Syria (1971–)

As·ser \'äs-ər\ Tobias Michael Carel 1838–1913 Du. jurist

Astaire \ə-'sta(ə)r, -'ste(ə)r\ Fred 1899–1987 Am. dancer & actor

As·ton \'as-tən\ Francis William 1877–1945 Eng. physicist

As·tor \'as-tər\ John Jacob 1763–1848 Am. (Ger.-born) fur trader & capitalist

Astor Nancy Witcher 1879–1964 *Viscountess Astor* 1st woman member of Brit. Parliament (1919–45)

As·tu·ri·as \ə-'st(y)ùr-ē-əs\ Miguel Angel 1899–1974 Guatemalan author

Ata·huall·pa *or* **Ata·hual·pa** \,ät-ə-'wäl-pə\ *ca* 1502–1533 last Inca king of Peru

Ath·a·na·si·us \,ath-ə-'nā-zh(ē-)əs, -'nā-sh(ē-)əs\ Saint *ca* 293–373 Greek church father

Ath·el·stan \'ath-əl-,stan\ *d* 939 Anglo-Saxon ruler

Ath·er·ton \'ath-ərt-ʰn\ Gertrude Franklin 1857–1948 née *Horn* Am. nov.

'At·tār \'at-ər, 'a-,tär\ Farīd od-Dīn Moḥammad ebn Ebrāhīm *ca* 1142–*ca* 1220 Pers. mystical poet

At·ti·la \'at-ʰl-ə, ə-'til-ə\ 406?–453 *the Scourge of God* king of the Huns

Att·lee \'at-lē\ Clement Richard 1883–1967 *1st Earl Attlee* Eng. polit.

At·tucks \'at-əks\ Crispus 1723?–1770 Am. patriot; one of 5 men killed in Boston Massacre

Au·ber \ō-'be(ə)r\ Daniel-François-Esprit 1782–1871 Fr. composer

Au·brey \'ō-brē\ John 1626–1697 Eng. antiquarian

Au·chin·closs \'ō-kən-,kläs\ Louis Stanton 1917– Am. writer

Au·den \'ȯd-ʰn\ Wystan Hugh 1907–1973 Am. (Eng.-born) poet — **Au·den·esque** \,ȯd-ʰn-'esk\ *adj*

Au·du·bon \'ȯd-ə-bən, -,bän\ John James 1785–1851 Am. (Haitian-born) artist & ornithologist

Au·er·bach \'aù(-ə)r-,bäk, -,bäk\ Berthold 1812–1882 Ger. nov.

Au·gier \ō-'zh(y)ā, ,ō-zhē-'ā\ Emile 1820–1889 Fr. poet & dram.

Au·gus·tine \'ȯ-gə-,stēn; ȯ-'gəs-tən, ə-\ Saint 354–430 church father; bishop of Hippo (396–430)

Augustine *also* **Austin** Saint *d* 604 *Apostle of the English* 1st archbishop of Canterbury (601–04)

Au·gus·tus \ȯ-'gəs-təs, ə-\ 63 B.C.–A.D. 14 orig. *Gaius Octavius* then *Gaius Julius Caesar* 1st Rom. emp. (27 B.C.–A.D. 14)

Aurangzeb — see 'ALAMGIR

Au·re·lian \ȯ-'rēl-yən\ *ca* A.D. 215–275 *Lucius Domitius Aurelianus* Rom. emp. (270-275)

Au·riol \,ȯr-ē-'ȯl, -'ōl\ Vincent 1884–1966 Fr. polit.; 1st pres. of 4th Republic (1947–54)

Au·ro·bin·do \,ȯr-ə-'bin-dō\ Sri 1872–1950 orig. *Sri Aurobindo Ghose* \'gōs\ Indian seer, poet, & nationalist

Aus·ten \'ȯs-tən, 'äs-\ Jane 1775–1817 Eng. nov.

Aus·tin \'ȯs-tən, 'äs-\ Alfred 1835–1913 Eng. poet; poet laureate (1896–1913)

Austin John 1790–1859 Eng. jurist

Austin Mary 1868–1934 née *Hunter* Am. nov.

Austin Stephen Fuller 1793–1836 Am. colonizer in Texas

Avebury 1st Baron — see LUBBOCK

Avenzoar — see IBN ZUHR

Aver·ro·ës *or* **Aver·rho·ës** \ə-'ver-ə-,wēz, ,av-ə-'rō-(,)ēz\ 1126–1198 *also Ibn-Rushd* Span.-Arab philos. & physician

Avery \'ā-v(ə-)rē\ Milton Clark 1885–1965 Am. artist

Av·i·cen·na \,av-ə-'sen-ə\ 980–1037 *also Ibn Sīnā* Islamic (Pers.-born) philos. & scientist

Avi·la Ca·ma·cho \'äv-ē-lə-kə-'mäch-(,)ō\ Manuel 1897–1955 Mex. soldier & polit.; pres. of Mexico (1940–46)

Avo·ga·dro \,av-ə-'gäd-(,)rō, ,äv-\ Amedeo 1776–1856 *Conte di Quaregna e Ceretto* Ital. chem. & physicist

Avon Earl of — see Anthony EDEN

Ax·el·rod \'ak-səl-,räd\ Julius 1912– Am. biochem.

Ay·de·lotte \'ād-ʰl-,ät\ Frank 1880–1956 Am. educ.

Ayl·win Azó·car \'āl-win-ä-'sō-kär\ Patricio 1918– pres. of Chile (1990–)

Aza·ña y Dí·az \ə-'zän-yə-ē-'thē-äth\ Manuel 1880–1940 Span. polit.; pres. of Spain (1936–39)

Azu·ma \ə-'zü-mə, 'äz-ə-,mä\ Tokuho 1909– Jp. dancer

Ba'al Shem Tov — see ISRAEL BEN ELIEZER

Bab·bitt \'bab-ət\ Irving 1865–1933 Am. scholar

Ba·beuf \bä-'bəf\ François-Noël 1760–1797 Fr. agitator

Bab·ing·ton \'bab-iŋ-tən\ Anthony 1561–1586 Eng. R.C. conspirator against Queen Elizabeth I

Bab·son \'bab-sən\ Roger Ward 1875–1967 Am. statistician

Bā·bur \'bäb-ər\ 1483–1530 *Zahīr-ud-Dīn Muhammad* founder of Mogul dynasty of India; emp. (1526–30)

Ba·bu·ren \bä-'bǖ-rən, -'bir-ən\ Dirck van *ca* 1590–1624 Du. painter

Bach \'bäk, 'bäk\ Carl Philipp Emanuel 1714–1788 *son of J.S.* Ger. composer

Bach Johann Christian 1735–1782 *son of J.S.* Ger. organist & composer

---

Bach Johann Sebastian 1685–1750 Ger. organist & composer
Bach Wilhelm Friedemann 1710–1784 *son of J.S.* Ger. organist & composer
Ba·con \'bā-kən\ Francis 1561–1626 1st Baron *Ver·u·lam* \'ver-(y)ə-ləm\ Viscount *St. Al·bans* \sănt-'ȯl-bənz, sənt-\ Eng. philos.
Bacon Francis 1909– Brit. painter
Bacon Nathaniel 1647–1676 Am. colonial leader
Bacon Roger *ca* 1220–1292 Eng. philos. and scientist
Ba·den–Pow·ell \,băd-ⁿ-'pō-əl\ Robert Stephenson Smyth 1857–1941 1st Baron of *Gilwell* founder of Boy Scout movement
Ba·do·glio \bə-'dȯl-(,)yō\ Pietro 1871–1956 Ital. soldier
Bae·yer, von \'bā-(y)ər\ Adolf 1835–1917 Ger. chem.
Baf·fin \'baf-ən\ William *ca* 1584–1622 Eng. navigator
Bage·hot \'baj-ət\ Walter 1826–1877 Eng. econ. & journalist
Ba·gra·tion \bə-,grät-ē-'ȯn, ,bäg-rə-'tyȯn\ Prince Pyotr Ivanovich 1765–1812 Russ. gen.
Ba·hā' Al·lāh or Ba·ha·ul·lah \,bä-,hä-ü-'lä\ Mírzá Ḥoseyn Alī Nūrī 1817–1892 Pers. founder of the Bahā'ī faith
Bai·ley \'bā-lē\ Liberty Hyde 1858–1954 Am. botanist
Bailey Nathan *or* Nathaniel *d* 1742 Eng. lexicographer
Bailey Pearl Mae 1918– Am. singer
Bail·lie \'bā-lē\ Joanna 1762–1851 Scot. dram. & poet
Bain \'bān\ Alexander 1818–1903 Scot. psychol.
Baird \'ba(ə)rd, 'be(ə)rd\ John Logie 1888–1946 *father of television* Scot. inventor
Bairns·fa·ther \'ba(ə)rnz-,făth-ər, 'be(ə)rnz-\ Bruce 1888–1959 Eng. cartoonist
Ba·jer \'bī(-ə)r\ Fredrik 1837–1922 Dan. statesman & writer
Ba·ker \'bā-kər\ James Addison 1930– U.S. secy. of treasury (1985–88); secy. of state (1989–   )
Baker Newton Diehl 1871–1937 Am. statesman
Baker Ray Stannard 1870–1946 pseud. *David Gray·son* \'grās-ⁿ\ Am. author
Baker Sir Samuel White 1821–1893 Eng. explorer in Africa
Bakst \'bäkst\ Léon 1866–1924 orig. *Lev Samoylovich Rosenberg* Russ. painter
Ba·ku·nin \bə-'kün-(y)ən, bä-\ Mikhail Aleksandrovich 1814–1876 Russ. anarchist
Bal·an·chine \,bal-ən-'shēn, 'bal-ən-,\ George 1904–1983 *Georgy Melitonovich Balanchivadze* Am. (Russ.-born) choreographer
Bal·bo \'bäl-(,)bō\ Italo 1896–1940 Ital. aviator & polit.
Bal·boa, de \,bal-'bō-ə\ Vasco Núñez 1475–1519 Span. explorer; disc. Pacific ocean
Balch \'bȯlch\ Emily Greene 1867–1961 Am. econ. & sociol.
Bald·win I \'bȯl-dwən\ 1058?–1118 *bro. of Godfrey of Bouillon* king of Jerusalem (1100–18)
Baldwin James 1924–1987 Am. writer
Baldwin James Mark 1861–1934 Am. psychol.
Baldwin Stanley 1867–1947 1st Earl *Baldwin of Bewd·ley* \'byüd-lē\ Eng. statesman
Balfe \'balf\ Michael William 1808–1870 Irish composer & singer
Bal·four \'bal-fər, -,fȯr, -,fȯr\ Arthur James 1848–1930 1st Earl of Balfour; Brit. philos. & statesman
Ba·liol *or* Bal·liol \'bāl-yəl\ John de 1249–1315 king of Scotland (1292–96)
Ball \'bȯl\ John *d* 1381 Eng. priest & social agitator
Bal·lan·tyne \'bal-ən-,tīn\ James 1772–1833 Scot. printer
Bal·ti·more \'bȯl-tə-,mō(ə)r, -,mȯ(ə)r, -mər\ David 1938– Am. microbiologist
Baltimore Baron — see George CALVERT
Bal·zac \'bȯl-,zak, 'bal-, *F* bȧl-zȧk\ Honoré de 1799–1850 Fr. nov. —
Bal·za·cian \bȯl-'zä-shən, bal-, -'zak-ē-ən\ *adj*
Ban·croft \'ban-,krȯft, 'baŋ-\ George 1800–1891 Am. hist.
Bancroft Richard 1544–1610 Eng. prelate; archbishop of Canterbury (1604–10)
Ban·del·lo \ban-'del-(,)ō, bän-\ Matteo 1485–1561 Ital. writer
Bangs \'baŋz\ John Kendrick 1862–1922 Am. humorist
Banks \'baŋ(k)s\ Sir Joseph 1743–1820 Eng. naturalist
Ban·ting \'bant-iŋ\ Sir Frederick Grant 1891–1941 Canad. physician
Ba·ra·nov \bə-'rän-əf\ Aleksandr Andreyevich 1747–1819 Russ. fur trader; 1st gov. of Russ. America
Bá·rány \'bär-,än-yə\ Robert 1876–1936 Austrian physician
Bar·ba·ros·sa \,bär-bə-'räs-ə, -'rȯs-\ — see FREDERICK I
Barbarossa *d* 1546 *Khayr ad-Dīn* Barbary pirate
Bar·ber \'bär-bər\ Samuel 1910–1981 Am. composer
Bar·bie \'bär-bē\ Klaus 1913– Ger. Nazi leader
Bar·busse \bär-büs, bär-'b(y)üs\ Henri 1873–1935 Fr. author
Bar·clay \'bär-klē\ Robert 1648–1690 Scot. Quaker author
Bar·clay de Tol·ly \,bär-,klī-də-'tȯ-lē, -,klä-\ Prince Mikhail 1761–1818 Russ. field marshal
Bar·deen \'bär-'dēn\ John 1908– Am. physicist
Ba·rents \'bar-ən(t)s, 'bär-\ Willem *ca* 1550–1597 Du. navigator
Bar·ing \'bar-iŋ\ Alexander 1774–1848 1st Baron *Ash·bur·ton* \'ash-,bərt-ⁿ\ Brit. financier & diplomat
Baring Evelyn 1841–1917 1st Earl of *Cro·mer* \'krō-mər\ Brit. diplomat
Bark·la \'bär-klə\ Charles Glover 1877–1944 Eng. physicist
Bark·ley \'bär-klē\ Al·ben \'al-bən\ William 1877–1956 Am. lawyer & polit.; vice pres. of U.S. (1949–53)
Bar·low \'bär-,lō\ Joel 1754–1812 Am. poet & diplomat
Bar·nard \'bär-nərd, -,närd\ Christiaan Neethling 1922– So. African surgeon
Bar·nard \'bär-nərd\ George Grey 1863–1938 Am. sculptor
Barnevelt Jan van Olden — see OLDENBARNEVELT
Bar·num \'bär-nəm\ Phineas Taylor 1810–1891 Am. showman
Ba·ro·ja \bä-'rō-(,)hä\ Pío 1872–1956 Span. writer
Barozzi Giacomo — see VIGNOLA
Bar·rès \bä-'res\ Auguste-Maurice 1862–1923 Fr. nov. & polit.
Bar·rie \'bar-ē\ Sir James Matthew 1860–1937 Scot. nov. & dram.
Bar·ros \'bär-üsh\ João de *ca* 1496–1570 Port. hist.
Bar·row \'bar-(,)ō, 'bär-ə(-w)\ Isaac 1630–1677 Eng. math. & theol.
Bar·ry \'ba-rē\ Jeanne Bécu 1743–1793 *Comtesse du Barry* mistress of Louis XV of France
Bar·ry \'bar-ē\ Philip 1896–1949 Am. dram.

Bar·ry·more \'bar-i-,mō(ə)r, -,mȯ(ə)r\ family of Am. actors: Maurice 1847–1905 real name *Herbert Blythe;* his wife Georgiana Emma 1854–1893 *dau. of John Drew;* their children Lionel 1878–1954, Ethel 1879–1959, & John Blythe 1882–1942
Bart \'bär\ *or* Barth \'bärt\ Jean 1650–1702 Fr. naval hero
Barth \'bärth\ John Simmons 1930– Am. author
Barth \'bärt, 'bärth\ Karl 1886–1968 Swiss theol. — Barth·ian \-ē-ən\ *adj*
Bar·thol·di \bär-'t(h)äl-dē, -'t(h)ȯl-\ Frédéric-Auguste 1834–1904 Fr. sculptor
Bart·lett \'bärt-lət\ John 1820–1905 Am. publisher & editor
Bartlett Vernon 1894– Eng. author
Bar·tók \'bär-,täk, -,tók\ Bé·la \'bā-lä\ 1881–1945 Hung. composer
Bar·to·lom·meo \,bär-,tȯl-ə-'mä-(,)ō\ Fra 1472–1517 *Baccio della Porta* Florentine painter
Bar·ton \'bärt-ⁿ\ Clara 1821–1912 in full *Clarissa Harlow Barton* founder of Am. Red Cross Society
Barton Sir Derek Harold Richard 1918– Brit. chem.
Bar·tram \'bär-trəm\ John 1699–1777 Am. botanist
Bartram William 1739–1823 *son of John* Am. naturalist
Ba·ruch \bə-'rük\ Bernard Man·nes \'man-əs\ 1870–1965 Am. businessman & statesman
Bashō — see MATSUO
Ba·sie \'bā-sē\ William 1904–1984 *Count* Am. bandleader & composer
Bas·il \'baz-əl, 'bäs-, 'bas-, 'bāz-\ *or* Ba·sil·i·us \bə-'sil-ē-əs, -'zil-\ Saint *ca* 329–379 *the Great* church father; bishop of Caesarea
Bas·ker·ville \'bas-kər-,vil\ John 1706–1775 Eng. typographer
Ba·sov \'bä-,sȯf, -,sȯv\ Nikolay Gennadiyevich 1922– Russ. physicist
Bates \'bāts\ Katharine Lee 1859–1929 Am. poet & educ.
Ba·tis·ta y Zal·di·var \bə-'tēs-tə-,zäl-'dē-,vär\ Fulgencio 1901–1973 Cuban soldier; pres. of Cuba (1940–44; 1952–59)
Bat·tā·nī, al- \,al-bə-'tän-ē\ *ca* 858–929 *Al·ba·te·gni* \,al-bə-'tän-yē\ *or* Al·ba·te·ni·us \-'tē-nē-əs\ Arab astron.
Bau·de·laire \bōd-'la(ə)r, -'le(ə)r\ Charles-Pierre 1821–1867 Fr. poet —
Bau·de·lair·ean *also* Bau·de·lair·ian \-ē-ən\ *adj*
Bau·douin \bō-'dwanⁿ\ 1930– king of Belgium (1951–   )
Baum \'bäm\ Lyman Frank 1856–1919 Am. journalist & writer
Baum \'baúm\ Vicki 1888–1960 Am. (Austrian-born) nov.
Bau·mé \bō-'mä\ Antoine 1728–1804 Fr. chem.
Bax·ter \'bak-stər\ Richard 1615–1691 Eng. Puritan scholar & writer
Ba·yard \'bī-ərd, 'bā-ərd, *F* bȧ-yȧr\ Pierre Terrail *ca* 1473–1524 *Seigneur de Bayard* Fr. mil. hero
Bayle \'bā(ə)l, 'bel\ Pierre 1647–1706 Fr. philos. & critic
Beaconsfield Earl of — see Benjamin DISRAELI
Bea·dle \'bēd-ⁿl\ George Wells 1903–1989 Am. biol.
Beard \'bi(ə)rd\ Charles Austin 1874–1948 & his wife Mary née *Ritter* 1876–1958 Am. historians
Beard Daniel Carter 1850–1941 Am. painter & illustrator; organizer of Boy Scouts in U.S. (1910)
Beards·ley \'bi(ə)rdz-lē\ Aubrey Vincent 1872–1898 Eng. illustrator
Be·a·trix \'bā-ə-,triks\ 1938– queen of the Netherlands (1980–   )
Beat·tie \'bēt-ē\ James 1735–1803 Scot. poet
Beau·fort \'bō-fərt\ Sir Francis 1774–1857 Brit. admiral
Beaufort Henry *ca* 1374–1447 Eng. cardinal & statesman
Beau·har·nais, de \,bō-,är-'nā\ Fr. family including: Vicomte Alexandre 1760–1794 gen.; his wife Joséphine 1763–1814 later the *1st wife of Napoleon I;* their son Eugène 1781–1824 prince of Eich·stätt \'īk-,shtet\; their daughter Hortense 1783–1837 *wife of Louis Bonaparte & mother of Napoleon III*
Beau·mar·chais, de \,bō-,mär-'shā\ Pierre-Augustin Caron 1732–1799 Fr. dram. & businessman
Beau·mont \'bō-,mänt, -mənt\ Francis 1584–1616 Eng. dram.
Beau·mont \-,mänt\ William 1785–1853 Am. surgeon
Beau·re·gard \'bōr-ə-,gärd, 'bȯr-\ Pierre Gustave Toutant 1818–1893 Am. Confed. gen.
Beau·voir, de \bōv-'wär\ Simone 1908–1986 Fr. author
Bea·ver·brook \'bē-vər-,brük\ 1st Baron 1879–1964 *William Maxwell Aitken* Brit. (Canad.-born) newspaper publisher
Be·bel \'bā-bəl\ August 1840–1913 Ger. Social Democrat leader & writer
Beck·et \'bek-ət\ Saint Thomas *ca* 1118–1170 *Thomas à Becket* \-ə-\ archbishop of Canterbury (1162–70)
Beck·ett \'bek-ət\ Samuel 1906–1989 Irish author in France
Beck·ford \'bek-fərd\ William 1760–1844 Eng. author
Bec·que·rel \,be-'krel, ,bek-ə-'rel\ family of Fr. physicists including: Antoine-César 1788–1878; his son Alexandre-Edmond 1820–1891; the latter's son Antoine-Henri 1852–1908
Bed·does \'bed-(,)ōz\ Thomas Lovell 1803–1849 Eng. writer
Bede \'bēd\ *or* Bae·da *or* Be·da \'bēd-ə\ Saint *ca* 672–735 *the Venerable Bede* Anglo-Saxon scholar, hist., & theol.
Bed·ford \'bed-fərd\ Duke of — see JOHN OF LANCASTER
Bed·norz \'bed-,nȯrts\ Johannes Georg 1950– Ger. physicist
Bee·be \'bē-bē\ Charles William 1877–1962 Am. naturalist & explorer
Bee·cham \'bē-chəm\ Sir Thomas 1879–1961 Eng. conductor
Bee·cher \'bē-chər\ Henry Ward 1813–1887 Am. clergyman
Beecher Lyman 1775–1863 *father of H.W. & of Harriet Beecher Stowe* Am. Presbyterian clergyman
Beer·bohm \'bi(ə)r-,bōm, -bəm\ Sir Max 1872–1956 Eng. critic & caricaturist
Beer·naert \'be(ə)r-,närt\ Auguste Marie François 1829–1912 Belg. statesman
Bee·tho·ven \'bā-,tō-vən\ Ludwig van 1770–1827 Ger. composer —
Bee·tho·ve·nian \,bā-,tō-'vē-nyən\ *adj*
Be·gin \'bā-gin, bē-gin\ Me·na·chem \mə-'näk-əm\ 1913– prime min. of Israel (1977–83)
Be·han \'bē-ən\ Brendan Francis 1923–1964 Irish dram.
Beh·ring \'be(ə)r-iŋ\ Emil von 1854–1917 Ger. bacteriol.
Behr·man \'be(ə)r-mən\ Samuel Nathaniel 1893–1973 Am. dram.
Bé·ké·sy \'bā-kə-shē\ Georg von 1899–1972 Am. (Hung.-born) physicist
Be·las·co \bə-'las-(,)kō\ David 1853–1931 Am. dram. & producer
Bel·i·sar·i·us \,bel-ə-'sar-ē-əs, -'ser-\ *ca* 505–565 Byzantine gen.

Bell \'bel\ Alexander Graham 1847–1922 Am. (Scot.-born) inventor of the telephone
Bel·la·my \'bel-ə-mē\ Edward 1850–1898 Am. author
Bel·lay, du \ˌd(y)ü-bə-'lā\ Joachim ca 1522–1560 Fr. poet
Bel·li·ni \bə-'lē-nē\ family of Venetian painters including: Jacopo ca 1400–ca 1470 and his sons Gentile ca 1429–1507 and Giovanni ca 1430–1516
Bellini Vincenzo 1801–1835 Ital. composer
Bel·loc \'bel-ˌäk, -ək\ (Joseph-Pierre) Hilaire 1870–1953 Eng. author
Bel·low \'bel-(ˌ)ō, -ə(-w)\ Saul 1915–   Am. (Canad.-born) writer
Bel·lows \'bel-(ˌ)ōz, -əz\ George Wesley 1882–1925 Am. painter & lithographer
Be·na·cer·raf \be-'nas-ə-ˌräf\ Baruj 1920–   Am. (Venezuelan-born) pathologist
Be·na·ven·te y Mar·tí·nez \ˌben-ə-ˌvent-ē-,ē-mär-'tē-nəs\ Jacinto 1866–1954 Span. dram.
Bench·ley \'bench-lē\ Robert Charles 1889–1945 Am. humorist
Ben·e·dict \'ben-ə-ˌdikt\ name of 15 popes: esp. XIV (Prospero Lambertini) 1675–1758 (pope 1740–58); XV (Giacomo della Chiesa) 1854–1922 (pope 1914–22)
Benedict of Nur·sia \'nər-sh(ē-)ə\ Saint ca 480–ca 547 Ital. founder of Benedictine order
Benedict Ruth 1887–1948 née Fulton Am. anthropol.
Be·neš \'ben-ˌesh\ Edvard 1884–1948 Czech statesman; pres. (1935–38; 1940–48)
Be·nét \bə-'nā\ Stephen Vincent 1898–1943 bro. of W.R. Am. poet
Benét William Rose 1886–1950 Am. poet, nov., & editor
Ben–Gu·rion \ˌben-gùr-'yòn, ben-'gùr-ē-ən\ David 1886–1973 Israeli (Pol.-born) statesman; prime min. of Israel (1949–53; 1955–63)
Ben·ja·min \'benj-(ə-)mən\ Judah Philip 1811–1884 Am. Confed. statesman & lawyer
Ben·nett \'ben-ət\ (Enoch) Arnold 1867–1931 Eng. nov.
Bennett James Gordon 1795–1872 Am. (Scot.-born) journalist
Bennett Richard Bedford 1870–1947 Viscount Bennett Canad. prime min. (1930–35)
Bennett William John 1943–   U.S. secy. of education (1985–88)
Be·noît de Sainte–Maure \ben-'wäd-ə-(ˌ)saⁿ(n)t-'mò(ə)r\ 12th cent. Fr. trouvère
Ben·son \'ben(t)-sən\ Edward White 1829–1896 Brit. prelate; archbishop of Canterbury (1882–96)
Ben·tham \'ben(t)-thəm\ Jeremy 1748–1832 Eng. jurist & philos.
Ben·tinck \'bent-i(ŋ)k\ Lord William Cavendish 1774–1839 son of W.H.C. 1st gov.-gen. of India (1833)
Bentinck William Henry Cavendish 1738–1809 3d Duke of Portland Brit. prime min. (1783; 1807–09)
Bent·ley \'bent-lē\ Richard 1662–1742 Eng. clergyman, scholar, & critic
Ben·ton \'bent-ᵊn\ Thomas Hart 1782–1858 Old Bullion Am. polit.
Benton Thomas Hart 1889–1975 Am. painter
Bé·ran·ger \bā-rän-zhā\ Pierre-Jean de 1780–1857 Fr. poet
Ber·dya·yev \bərd-'yä-yəf, bər-'jä-\ Nikolay Aleksandrovich 1874–1948 Russ. philos.
Ber·en·son \'ber-ən-sən\ Bernard 1865–1959 Am. (Lith.-born) art critic
Berg \'be(ə)rg\ Alban 1885–1935 Austrian composer
Berg \'bərg\ Paul 1926–   Am. chem.
Bergerac, de Cyrano — see CYRANO DE BERGERAC
Ber·gi·us \'ber-gē-əs\ Friedrich 1884–1949 Ger. chem.
Berg·man \'bərg-mən, Sw 'ber-mán\ Ingmar 1918–   Swed. film & theater director
Berg·son \'berg-sən, berk-sōⁿ\ Henri-Louis 1859–1941 Fr. philos. — Berg·son·ian \ˌberg-'sō-nē-ən, berk-\ adj
Berg·ström \'berg-strəm, 'bar-ē-strüm\ K. Sune D. 1916–   Swed. biochem.
Be·ria or Be·ri·ya \'ber-ē-ə\ Lavrenty Pavlovich 1899–1953 Russ. polit.
Be·ring \'bi(ə)r-iŋ, 'be(ə)r-\ Vitus Jonassen 1681–1741 Dan. navigator; disc. Bering strait and Bering sea
Berke·ley \'bär-klē, 'bər-\ George 1685–1753 Irish bishop & philos.
Berke·ley \'bər-klē\ Sir William 1606–1677 colonial gov. of Virginia
Ber·lich·in·gen \ber-'lik-,iŋ-ən\ Götz or Gottfried von 1480–1562 Ger. knight
Ber·lin \(ˌ)bər-'lin\ Irving 1888–1989 Am. (Russ.-born) composer
Ber·li·ner \'bər-lə-nər\ Emile 1851–1929 Am. (Ger.-born) inventor
Ber·li·oz \'ber-lē-ˌōz\ Hector 1803–1869 in full Louis-Hector Berlioz Fr. composer — Ber·li·oz·ian \ˌber-lē-'ō-zē-ən\ adj
Ber·na·dette of Lourdes \ˌbər-nə-'det\ Saint 1844–1879 Marie-Bernarde Sou·bi·rous \ˌsü-bē-'rü\ Fr. religious
Bernadotte Jean Baptiste Jules — see CHARLES XIV JOHN
Ber·nard \ber-'när\ Claude 1813–1878 Fr. physiol.
Ber·nard of Clair·vaux \bər-'närd-əv-ˌkla(ə)r-'vō, ber-'när-, -ˌklä(ə)r-\ Saint 1090–1153 Fr. ecclesiastic — Ber·nar·dine \'bər-nə(r)-ˌdēn\ adj
Ber·nar·din de Saint–Pierre \ˌber-nər-'daⁿ-də-ˌsänt-pē-'e(ə)r\ Jacques-Henri 1737–1814 Fr. author
Berners Baron — see TYRWHITT-WILSON
Bern·hardt \'bərn-ˌhärt, ber-'när\ Sarah 1844–1923 orig. Henriette-Rosine Ber·nard \ber-nár\ Fr. actress
Ber·ni·ni \bər-'nē-nē\ Gian or Giovanni Lorenzo 1598–1680 Ital. sculptor, architect, & painter
Bern·stein \'bərn-ˌstīn also -ˌstēn\ Leonard 1918–   Am. conductor & composer
Bern·storff \'be(ə)rn-ˌshtòrf\ Johann-Heinrich 1862–1939 Graf von Bernstorff Ger. diplomat
Ber·ry·man \'ber-ē-mən\ John 1914–1972 Am. poet
Ber·thier \ber-'tyā\ Louis-Alexandre 1753–1815 Prince de Neuchâtel; Prince de Wagram Fr. soldier; marshal of France
Ber·til·lon \ˌbert-ē-'(y)ōⁿ, 'bərt-ᵊl-ˌän\ Alphonse 1853–1914 Fr. anthropol. & criminol.
Ber·ze·li·us \(ˌ)bər-'zē-lē-əs, -'zä-\ Baron Jöns Jakob 1779–1848 Swed. chem.
Bes·ant \'bes-ᵊnt, 'bez-\ Annie 1847–1933 née Wood Eng. theosophist
Bes·se·mer \'bes-ə-mər\ Henry 1813–1898 Eng. engineer
Be·tan·court \ˌbe-ˌtän-'kù(ə)r(t), -ˌtäŋ-\ Rómulo 1908–1981 Venezuelan pres. (1959–64)
Be·the \'bāt-ə\ Hans Albrecht 1906–   Am. (Ger.-born) physicist

Beth·mann–Holl·weg \ˌbet-mən-'hòl-ˌväg, -ˌmän-\ Theobald Theodor Friedrich Alfred von 1856–1921 Ger. statesman; chancellor (1909–17)
Be·thune \bə-'th(y)ün\ Mary 1875–1955 née McLeod Am. educ.
Bet·je·man \'bech-ə-mən\ Sir John 1906–1984 Brit. author; poet laureate (1972–84)
Bet·tel·heim \'bet-əl-ˌhīm\ Bruno 1903–1990 Am. (Austrian-born) psychol.
Bet·ter·ton \'bet-ərt-ᵊn\ Thomas ca 1635–1710 Eng. actor
Bev·er·idge \'bev-(ə-)rij\ Albert Jeremiah 1862–1927 Am. polit. & hist.
Beveridge William Henry 1879–1963 1st Baron Beveridge of Tug·gal \'təg-əl\ Eng. econ.
Bev·in \'bev-ən\ Ernest 1881–1951 Brit. labor leader & polit.
Beyle Marie-Henri — see STENDHAL
Bhu·mi·bol Adul·ya·dej \'pü-mē-ˌpōn-ä-'dùn-lə-ˌdät —sic \ 1927–   king of Thailand (1946–)
Bhut·to \'bü-tō\ Benazir 1953–   prime min. of Pakistan (1988–)
Bi·dault \bē-'dō\ Georges 1899–1983 Fr. statesman
Bid·dle \'bid-ᵊl\ John 1615–1662 founder of Eng. Unitarianism
Biddle Nicholas 1786–1844 Am. financier
Bien·ville \'bē-'en-ˌvil, -vəl; byaⁿ-'vēl\ Jean-Baptiste Le Moyne, sieur de 1680–1768 Fr. colonial gov. of Louisiana
Bierce \'bi(ə)rs\ Ambrose Gwinnett 1842–?1914 Am. author
Bier·stadt \'bi(ə)r-ˌstat\ Albert 1830–1902 Am. (Ger.-born) painter
Bing·ham \'biŋ-əm\ George Caleb 1811–1879 Am. painter
Bin·nig \'bin-ik\ Gerd 1947–   Ger. physicist
Bi·on \'bī-ˌän, -ən\ fl 100 B.C. Greek bucolic poet
Birk·beck \'bər(k)-ˌbek\ George 1776–1841 Eng. physician
Bir·ken·head \'bər-kən-ˌhed\ 1st Earl of 1872–1930 Frederick Edwin Smith Eng. jurist & statesman
Bi·ron \'bē-ˌrón\ Ernst Johann 1690–1772 orig. Büh·ren \'büe-rən\ Duke of Kurland Ger. polit. in Russia
Bish·op \'bish-əp\ Elizabeth 1911–1979 Am. poet
Bishop John Michael 1936–   Am. microbiologist
Bis·marck \'biz-ˌmärk\ Prince Otto Eduard Leopold von 1815–1898 in full Bismarck-Schön·hau·sen \-ˌshōen-'haúz-ᵊn\ 1st chancellor of Ger. Empire (1871–90) — Bis·marck·ian \biz-'märk-ē-ən\ adj
Bi·zet \bē-'zā\ Alexandre-César-Léopold 1838–1875 called Georges Fr. composer
Bjørn·son \'byørn-sən\ Bjørnstjerne Martinius 1832–1910 Norw. poet, dram., & nov.
Black \'blak\ Hugo LaFayette 1886–1971 Am. jurist & polit.
Black Sir James Whyte 1924–   Brit. pharmacologist
Black·ett \'blak-ət\ Patrick Maynard Stuart 1897–1974 Brit. physicist
Black Hawk \'blak-ˌhòk\ 1767–1838 Ma-ka-ta-ī-me-she-kia-kiak Am. Indian chief
Black·more \'blak-ˌmō(ə)r, -ˌmó(ə)r\ Richard Doddridge 1825–1900 Eng. nov.
Black·mun \'blak-mən\ Harry Andrew 1908–   Am. jurist
Black·stone \'blak-ˌstōn, chiefly Brit -stən\ Sir William 1723–1780 Eng. jurist
Black·well \'blak-ˌwel, -wəl\ Elizabeth 1821–1910 Am. physician
Black·wood \'blak-ˌwùd\ William 1776–1834 Scot. publisher
Blaine \'blān\ James Gillespie 1830–1893 Am. statesman
Blake \'blāk\ Eugene Carson 1906–1985 Am. clergyman
Blake Robert 1599–1657 Eng. admiral
Blake William 1757–1827 Eng. artist, poet, & mystic — Blak·ean \'blā-kē-ən\ adj
Blanc \'blaŋk\ Melvin Jerome 1908–1989 Mel Am. actor
Blas·co Ibá·ñez \'bläs-(ˌ)kō-ē-'bän-(ˌ)yäs\ Vicente 1867–1928 Span. nov.
Bla·vat·sky \blə-'vat-skē, -'vät-\ Helena Petrovna 1831–1891 née Hahn Russ. traveler & theosophist
Blé·riot \'bler-ē-ˌō\ Louis 1872–1936 Fr. engineer & pioneer aviator
Bligh \'blī\ William 1754–1817 Eng. naval officer
Bloch \'bläk, 'blók, 'blōk\ Ernest 1880–1959 Am. (Swiss-born) composer
Bloch \'bläk\ Felix 1905–1983 Am. physicist
Bloch \'bläk, 'blók, 'blōk\ Konrad Emil 1912–   Am. (Ger.-born) biochem.
Block \'bläk\ Herbert Lawrence 1909–   Her·block \'hər-ˌbläk\ Am. editorial cartoonist
Bloem·ber·gen \'blüm-ˌbər-gən\ Nicolaas 1920–   Am. (Du.-born) physicist
Bloom·er \'blü-mər\ Amelia 1818–1894 née Jenks Am. reformer
Bloom·field \'blüm-ˌfēld\ Leonard 1887–1949 Am. linguist
Blü·cher \'blü-kər, 'blue-ər\ Gebhard Leberecht von 1742–1819 prince of Wahlstatt Pruss. field marshal
Blum \'blüm\ Léon 1872–1950 Fr. polit.; provisional pres. (1946–47)
Blum·berg \'bləm-ˌbərg, 'blüm-\ Baruch Samuel 1925–   Am. virologist
Bluntsch·li \'blúnch-lē\ Johann Kaspar 1808–1881 Swiss legal scholar
Boabdil — see MUHAMMAD XI
Boadicea — see BOUDICCA
Bo·as \'bō-ˌaz\ Franz 1858–1942 Am. (Ger.-born) anthropol. & ethnol.
Bo·ba·di·lla \ˌbō-bə-'dē-(y)ə\ Francisco de d 1502 Span. viceroy of Indies
Boc·cac·cio \bō-'käch-(ē-)ˌō\ Giovanni 1313–1375 Ital. author
Boc·che·ri·ni \ˌbäk-ə-'rē-nē\ Luigi 1743–1805 Ital. composer
Bod·ley \'bäd-lē\ Sir Thomas 1545–1613 Eng. diplomat & founder of Bodleian library
Bo·do·ni \bə-'dō-nē\ Giambattista 1740–1813 Ital. printer & type designer
Bo·ethi·us \bō-'ē-thē-əs\ Anicius Manlius Severinus ca 480–524 Rom. philos.
Boh·len \'bō-lən\ Charles Eustis 1904–1974 Am. diplomat
Böh·me \'bø(r)m-ə, 'boe-mə\ Ja·kob \'yä-ˌkòp\ 1575–1624 Ger. mystic
Bohr \'bō(ə)r, 'bò(ə)r\ Aage Niels 1922–   son of Niels Dan. physicist
Bohr Niels Henrik David 1885–1962 Dan. physicist

Bo·iar·do \bȯi-'ärd-(,)ō, bō-'yärd-\ Matteo Maria 1441?–1494 Ital. poet
Boi·leau–Des·pré·aux \'bwäl-ō-,dā-prē-'ō\ Nicolas 1636–1711 Fr. critic & poet
Boj·er \'bȯi-ər\ Johan \yō-'hän\ 1872–1959 Norw. writer
Bok \'bäk\ Edward William 1863–1930 Am. (Du.-born) editor
Bo·leyn \bu̇-'lin, 'bu̇l-ən\ Anne 1507?–1536 *2d wife of Henry VIII of England & mother of Queen Elizabeth I*
Bo·ling·broke \'bäl-iŋ-,bru̇k, 'bu̇l-* (*usu Brit pronuncs*), 'bō-liŋ-, -,brȯk\ 1st Viscount 1678–1751 *Henry St. John* \'sin-jən (*usu Brit pronunc*), (,)sänt-'jän, sənt-\ Eng. statesman
Bo·li·var Si·món \sē-,mōn-bə-'lē-,vär, ,sī-mən-'bäl-ə-vər\ 1783–1830 So. Am. liberator
Böll \'bəl, 'bœl\ Heinrich Theodor 1917–1985 Ger. writer
Bo·na·parte \'bō-nə-,pärt\ *It* **Buo·na·par·te** \,bwȯn-ə-'pärt-ē\ Corsican family including Na·po·leon I \nə-'pōl-yən, -'pō-lē-ən\ (*q.v.*) & his bros.: Joseph 1768–1844 king of Naples & Spain; Lucien 1775–1840 prince of Ca·ni·no \kə-'nē-(,)nō\; Louis 1778–1846 *father of Napoleon III* king of Holland; Jérôme 1784–1860 king of Westphalia
Bonar Law — see LAW
Bon·a·ven·tu·ra \,bän-ə-,ven-'t(y)u̇r-ə\ *or* **Bon·a·ven·ture** \,bän-ə-'ven-chər, 'bän-ə-,\ Saint *ca* 1217–1274 *the Seraphic Doctor* Ital. philos.
Bone \'bōn\ Sir Muirhead 1876–1953 Scot. etcher & painter
Bon·heur \bä-'nər\ Rosa 1822–1899 *Marie-Rosalie* Fr. painter
Bon·i·face \'bän-ə-fəs, -,fās\ Saint *ca* 675–754 *Wynfrid* or *Wynfrith* Eng. missionary in Germany
Boniface name of 9 popes: esp. **VIII** (*Benedict Caetani*) *ca* 1235(or 1240)–1303 (pope 1294–1303)
Bon·nard \bȯ-'när\ Pierre 1867–1947 Fr. painter
Bon·ner *or* **Bon·er** \'bän-ər\ Edmund *ca* 1500–1569 Eng. prelate
Bon·net \bȯ-'nā\ Georges-Etienne 1889–1973 Fr. polit. & diplomat
Bon·ney \'bän-ē\ William orig. *Henry* 1859–1881 *Billy the Kid* Am. outlaw
Bon·temps \bän-'täm\ Arna Wendell 1902–1973 Am. writer
Boone \'bün\ Daniel 1734–1820 Am. pioneer
Booth \'büth, *chiefly Brit* 'bü͟th\ family of Am. actors: Junius Brutus 1796–1852 *b* in England & his sons Edwin Thomas 1833–1893 & John Wilkes 1838–1865 assassin of Lincoln
Booth William 1829–1912 Eng. founder of Salvation Army *father of:* William Bramwell 1856–1929 Salvation Army gen.; Ballington 1857–1940 founder of Volunteers of America; Evangeline Cory 1865–1950 Salvation Army gen.
Boothe Clare — see Clare Boothe LUCE
Bo·rah \'bōr-ə, 'bȯr-\ William Edgar 1865–1940 Am. polit.
Bor·den \'bȯrd-ᵊn\ Sir Robert (Laird) 1854–1937 Canad. lawyer & statesman; prime min. (1911–20)
Bor·det \bȯr-'dā\ Jules 1870–1961 Belg. bacteriol.
Bor·ges \'bȯr-,hās\ Jorge Luis 1899–1986 Argentine author
Bor·gia \'bȯr-(,)jä, -jə, -zhə\ Cesare 1475(or 1476)–1507 *son of Rodrigo* Ital. cardinal & mil. leader
Borgia Lucrezia 1480–1519 *dau. of Rodrigo* duchess of Ferrara
Borgia Rodrigo see Pope ALEXANDER VI
Bor·glum \'bȯr-gləm\ (John) Gut·zon \'gət-sən\ (de la Mothe) 1867–1941 Am. sculptor
Bo·ris III \'bȯr-əs, 'bor-, 'bär-\ 1894–1943 czar of Bulgaria (1918–43)
Bor·laug \'bȯr-,lȯg\ Norman Ernest 1914–   Am. agronomist
Born \'bȯ(ə)rn\ Max 1882–1970 Ger. physicist
Bo·ro·din \,bȯr-ə-'dēn, ,bär-\ Aleksandr Porfiryevich 1833–1887 Russ. composer & chem.
Bor·row \'bär-(,)ō, -ə(-w)\ George Henry 1803–1881 Eng. author
Bosch \'bäsh, 'bȯsh\ Carl 1874–1940 Ger. industrial chem.
Bosch \'bäsh, 'bȯsh, *D* 'bäs, 'bȯs\ Hieronymus *ca* 1450–*ca* 1516 Du. painter
Bo·sco \'bäs-kō\ Saint Giovanni Melchior 1815–1888 *Don Bosco* Ital. religious; founder of Society of St. Francis de Sales
Bose \'bōs, 'bōs(h)\ Sir Ja·ga·dis \'jəg-ə-'dēs\ Chan·dra \'chən-drə\ 1858–1937 Indian physicist & plant physiol.
Bos·suet \bȯ-'swä\ Jacques-Bénigne 1627–1704 Fr. bishop
Bos·well \'bäz-,wel, -wəl\ James 1740–1795 Scot. lawyer & author; biographer of Samuel Johnson
Bo·tha \'b(w)ō-tə\ Louis 1862–1919 Boer gen.; 1st prime min. of Transvaal (1907) & of Union of So. Africa (1910–19)
Botha Pieter Willem 1916–   prime min. of Republic of So. Africa (1978–89)
Bo·the \'bōt-ə\ Walther Wilhelm Georg Franz 1891–1957 Ger. physicist
Bot·ti·cel·li \,bät-ə-'chel-ē\ Sandro 1445–1510 *Alessandro di Mariano Filipepi* Ital. painter
Bou·cher \bü-'shā\ François 1703–1770 Fr. painter
Bou·ci·cault \'bü-si-,kō\ *or* **Bour·ci·cault** \'bu̇r-\ Dion 1820(or 1822)–1890 *Dionysius Lardner Boursiquot* Am. (Irish-born) actor & dram.
Bou·dic·ca \bü-'dik-ə\ *also* **Bo·a·di·cea** \,bō-əd-ə-'sē-ə\ *d* A.D. 60 ancient Brit. queen
Bou·gain·ville \'bü-gən-,vil, bü-gaⁿ-vēl\ Louis-Antoine de 1729–1811 Fr. navigator
Bou·lan·ger \bü-läⁿ-zhā\ Georges-Ernest-Jean-Marie 1837–1891 Fr. gen.
Bou·lez \bü-'lez\ Pierre 1925–   Fr. composer & conductor
Bour·bon \bü(ə)r-bən, bu̇r-'bōⁿ\ Charles de 1490–1527 *Duc de Bourbon* Fr. gen.; constable of France
Bour·geois \bu̇rzh-'wä, 'bu̇(ə)rzh-,\ Léon-Victor-Auguste 1851–1925 Fr. statesman
Bour·get \bu̇r-'zhā\ Paul-Charles-Joseph 1852–1935 Fr. author
Bour·gui·ba \bu̇r-'gē-bə\ Habib ibn Ali 1902(or 1903)–   Tunisian pres. (1957–87)
Bo·vet \bō-'vā\ Daniel 1907–   Ital. (Swiss-born) pharmacologist
Bow·ditch \'bau̇d-ich\ Nathaniel 1773–1838 Am. math. & astron.
Bow·ell \'bō-əl\ Sir Mackenzie 1823–1917 Canad. polit.; prime min. of Canada (1894–96)
Bow·en \'bō-ən\ Elizabeth 1899–1973 Irish author
Bowen Otis Ray 1918–   U.S. secy. of health & human services (1985–89)
Bow·ie \'bü-ē, 'bō-\ James 1796–1836 hero of Texas revolution
Bowles \'bōlz\ Chester 1901–1986 Am. econ. & diplomat

Boy·den \'bȯid-ᵊn\ Seth 1788–1870 Am. inventor
Boyd Orr \'bȯid-'ȯ(ə)r, -'ō(ə)r\ John 1880–1971 *Baron Boyd-Orr of Brechin Mearns* Scot. agriculturist
Boyle \'bȯi(ə)l\ Kay 1903–   Am. author
Boyle Robert 1627–1691 Brit. physicist & chem.
Brad·bury \'brad-,ber-ē, -b(ə-)rē\ Ray Douglas 1920–   Am. writer
Brad·dock \'brad-ək\ Edward 1695–1755 Brit. gen. in America
Brad·ford \'brad-fərd\ Gamaliel 1863–1932 Am. biographer
Bradford William 1590–1657 Pilgrim father; 2d gov. of Plymouth colony
Bradford William 1663–1752 Am. printer
Brad·ley \'brad-lē\ Francis Herbert 1846–1924 Eng. philos. — **Brad·le·ian** *also* **Brad·ley·an** \'brad-lē-ən, brad-'\ *adj*
Bradley Henry 1845–1923 Eng. philologist & lexicographer
Bradley Omar Nelson 1893–1981 Am. gen.
Brad·street \'brad-,strēt\ Anne *ca* 1612–1672 née *Dudley*; wife of Simon Am. poet
Bradstreet Simon 1603–1697 colonial gov. of Massachusetts
Bra·dy \'brād-ē\ Mathew B. 1823?–1896 Am. photographer
Brady Nicholas Frederick 1930–   U.S. secy. of treasury (1989–)
Bragg \'brag\ Braxton 1817–1876 Am. Confed. gen.
Bragg Sir (William) Lawrence 1890–1971 *son of W.H.* Eng. physicist
Bragg Sir William Henry 1862–1942 Eng. physicist
Bra·he \'brä; 'brä-hē, -hä Ty·cho \'tē-(,)kō, 'tī-\ 1546–1601 Dan. astron.
Brahms \'brämz\ Johannes 1833–1897 Ger. composer & pianist — **Brahms·ian** \'bräm-zē-ən\ *adj*
Braille \'brā(ə)l, 'brī\ Louis 1809–1852 Fr. blind teacher of the blind
Bra·man·te \brə-'mänt-ē, -'män-(,)tä\ Donato 1444–1514 orig. *Donato d'Agnolo* or *d'Angelo* Ital. architect
Bran·cu·si \bran-'kü-sē\ Constantin 1876–1957 Fr. (Romanian-born) sculptor
Bran·deis \'bran-,dīs, -,dīz\ Louis Dembitz 1856–1941 Am. jurist
Bran·des \'brän-dəs\ Georg Morris 1842–1927 Dan. lit. critic
Brandt \'bränt, 'brant\ Wil·ly \'vil-ē, 'wil-ē\ 1913–   W. Ger. polit.; chancellor of West Germany (1969–74)
Bran·ting \'bränt-iŋ\ Karl Hjal·mar \'yäl-,mär\ 1860–1925 Swed. statesman & socialist leader
Braque \'bräk, 'bräk\ Georges 1882–1963 Fr. painter
Brat·tain \'brat-ᵊn\ Walter Houser 1902–1987 Am. physicist
Brau·chitsch \'brau̇k-ich, 'brau̇k-\ Heinrich Alfred Hermann Walther von 1881–1948 Ger. gen.
Braun \'brau̇n\ Karl Ferdinand 1850–1918 Ger. physicist
Braun Wernher von 1912–1977 Am. (Ger.-born) engineer
Breas·ted \'bres-təd\ James Henry 1865–1935 Am. orientalist
Brecht \'brekt, 'brekt\ Bertolt 1898–1956 Ger. dram. — **Brecht·ian** \-ē-ən\ *adj*
Breck·in·ridge \'brek-ən-(,)rij\ John Cabell 1821–1875 Am. polit.; vice pres. of the U.S. (1857–61)
Bren·nan \'bren-ən\ William Joseph, Jr. 1906–   Am. jurist
Bre·ton \brə-tōⁿ\ André 1896–1966 Fr. surrealist poet
Brew·ster \'brü-stər\ William 1567–1644 Pilgrim father
Brezh·nev \'brezh-,nef\ Leonid Ilyich 1906–1982 Russ. polit.; pres. of U.S.S.R. (1960–64; 1977–82); 1st secy. of Communist party (1964–82)
Bri·an \'brī-ən, 'brēn\ *also* **Brian Bo·ru** \bə-'rü\ 941–1014 king of Ireland (1002–14)
Bri·and \brē-äⁿ\ Aristide 1862–1932 Fr. statesman
Brid·ger \'brij-ər\ James 1804–1881 Am. pioneer & scout
Brid·ges \'brij-əz\ Robert Seymour 1844–1930 Eng. poet; poet laureate (1913–30)
Bridg·man \'brij-mən\ Percy Williams 1882–1961 Am. physicist
Bright \'brīt\ John 1811–1889 Eng. orator & statesman
Brig·it \'brij-ət, 'brē-ət\ *also* **Brid·get** \'brij-ət\ *or* **Brig·id** \'brij-əd, 'brē-əd\ *or* **Brighid** \'brēd\ *or* **Bride** \'brīd\ **of Kildare** *or* **of Ireland** Saint *d* *ca* 524–528 a patron saint of Ireland
Bril·lat–Sa·va·rin \brē-'(y)ä-,sav-ə-'raⁿ, -'sav-ə-rən\ Anthelme 1755–1826 Fr. gastronome
Brit·ten \'brit-ᵊn\ (Edward) Benjamin 1913–1976 Baron *Britten of Aldeburgh* Eng. composer
Brod·sky \'bräd-skē\ Joseph 1940–   Am. (Russ.-born) poet & essayist
Bro·gan \'brō-gən\ Sir Denis William 1900–1974 Brit. hist.
Broglie, de \brȯi\ Louis-Victor-Pierre-Raymond 1892–1987 Fr. physicist
Bron·të \'bränt-ē, 'brän-(,)tā\ a family of Eng. writers: Charlotte 1816–1855 & her sisters Emily 1818–1848 & Anne 1820–1849
Brooke \'bru̇k\ Sir Alan Francis 1883–1963 1st Viscount *Al·an·brooke* \'al-ən-,bru̇k\ Brit. field marshal
Brooke Edward William 1919–   Am. polit.
Brooke Rupert 1887–1915 Eng. poet
Brooks \'bru̇ks\ Gwendolyn Elizabeth 1917–   Am. poet
Brooks Phillips 1835–1893 Am. bishop
Brooks Van Wyck \van-'wik, vən-\ 1886–1963 Am. essayist & critic
Bro·sio \'brō-zē-,ō, 'brō-\ Manlio 1897–1980 Ital. diplomat; secy.-gen. of NATO (1964–71)
Brow·der \'brau̇d-ər\ Earl 1891–1973 Am. Communist polit.
Brown \'brau̇n\ Charles Brockden 1771–1810 Am. nov.
Brown Ford Mad·ox \'mad-əks\ 1821–1893 Eng. painter
Brown Herbert Charles 1912–   Am. (Eng.-born) chem.
Brown John 1800–1859 *Old Brown of Osa·wat·o·mie* \,ō-sə-'wät-ə-mē\ Am. abolitionist
Brown John Mason 1900–1969 Am. lit. critic
Brown Michael Stuart 1941–   Am. biochemist
Browne \'brau̇n\ Charles Farrar 1834–1867 pseud. *Ar·te·mus* \'ärt-ə-məs\ *Ward* Am. humorist
Browne Sir Thomas 1605–1682 Eng. physician & author
Brow·ning \'brau̇-niŋ\ Elizabeth Barrett 1806–1861 *wife of Robert* Eng. poet
Browning Robert 1812–1889 Eng. poet
Broz Josip — see TITO
Bruce \'brüs\ Sir David 1855–1931 Brit. physician & bacteriol.
Bruce David Kirkpatrick Este 1898–1977 Am. diplomat
Bruce Robert — see ROBERT I the Bruce
Bruce Stanley Melbourne 1883–1967 1st Viscount *Bruce of Melbourne* Austral. statesman; prime min. (1923–29)

Bruck·ner \'brúk-nər\ Anton 1824–1896 Austrian composer
Brue·ghel *or* Breu·ghel \'brü-gəl, 'brói-, *Dutch* 'brœ̄-kəl\ family of Flem. painters including: Pieter *ca* 1525(or 1530)–1569 & his sons Pieter 1564–1638 & Jan 1568–1625
Brum·mell \'brəm-əl\ George Bryan 1778–1840 *Beau Brummell* Eng. dandy
Bru·nel·le·schi \,brün-ºl-'es-kē\ *or* Bru·nel·le·sco \-(,)kō\ Filippo 1377–1446 Ital. architect
Bru·ne·tière \,brü-nə-'tye(ə)r, ,brüē-\ Vincent de Paul-Marie-Ferdinand 1849–1906 Fr. critic
Brü·ning \'brü-niŋ, 'brüē-\ Heinrich 1885–1970 chancellor of Germany (1930–32)
Bru·no \'brü-(,)nō\ Giordano 1548–1600 Ital. philos.
Bru·tus \'brüt-əs\ Marcus Junius 85–42 B.C. Rom. polit.; one of Caesar's assassins
Bry·an \'brī-ən\ William Jennings 1860–1925 Am. lawyer & polit.
Bry·ant \'brī-ənt\ William Cul·len \'kəl-ən\ 1794–1878 Am. poet & editor
Bu·ber \'bü-bər\ Martin 1878–1965 Israeli (Austrian-born) philos.
Buch·an \'bək-ən, 'bək-\ Sir John 1875–1940 1st Baron *Tweeds·muir* \'twēdz-,myü(ə)r\ Scot. author; gov.-gen. of Canada (1935–40)
Bu·chan·an \byü-'kan-ən, bə-\ James 1791–1868 Am. polit. & diplomat; 15th pres. of the U.S. (1857–61)
Buchanan James McGill 1919– Am. econ.
Buch·man \'búk-mən, 'bək-\ Frank Nathan Daniel 1878–1961 Am. evangelist
Buch·ner \'búk-nər, 'bük-\ Eduard 1860–1917 Ger. chem.
Buck \'bək\ Pearl 1892–1973 née *Sy·den·strick·er* \'sīd-ºn-,strik-ər\ Am. nov.
Buckingham 1st & 2d Dukes of — *see* VILLIERS
Buck·ley \'bək-lē\ William Frank 1925– Am. editor & writer
Buck·ner \'bək-nər\ Simon Bolivar 1823–1914 Am. Confed. gen. & polit.
Buckner Simon Bolivar 1886–1945 *son of prec.* Am. gen.
Buddha — *see* SIDDHĀRTHA GAUTAMA
Bu·den·ny \bü-'dyón-ē, bü-'den-\ Semyon Mikhaylovich 1883–1973 Russ. gen.
Buffalo Bill — *see* William Frederick CODY
Buf·fon \,bə-'fōⁿ, byü-, büē-\ Comte Georges-Louis Leclerc de 1707–1788 Fr. naturalist
Buis·son \bwē-'sōⁿ\ Ferdinand-Édouard 1841–1932 Fr. educ.
Bu·kha·rin \bü-'kär-ən\ Nikolay Ivanovich 1888–1938 Russ. Communist leader & editor
Bul·finch \'bül-,finch\ Charles 1763–1844 Am. architect
Bul·ga·nin \bül-'gan-ən\ Nikolay Aleksandrovich 1895–1975 Russ. polit. & marshal
Bull \'bül\ Ole \'ō-lə\ Bornemann 1810–1880 Norw. violinist
Bul·litt \'bül-ət\ William Christian 1891–1967 Am. diplomat
Bü·low \'byü-(,)lō, 'büē-\ Bernhard Heinrich Martin Karl 1849–1929 Prince *von Bülow* Ger. diplomat & statesman; chancellor of Germany (1900–09)
Bul·wer \'bül-wər\ William Henry Lytton Earle 1801–1872 *bro. of 1st Baron Lytton* Brit. diplomat
Bulwer–Lytton — *see* LYTTON
Bunche \'bench\ Ralph Johnson 1904–1971 Am. diplomat
Bu·nin \'bün-(y)ən, -,(y)ēn\ Ivan Alekseyevich 1870–1953 Russ. poet & nov.
Bun·ker \'bəŋ-kər\ Ellsworth 1894–1984 Am. diplomat
Bun·sen \'bün-zən, 'bən(t)-sən\ Robert Wilhelm 1811–1899 Ger. chem.
Bun·yan \'bən-yən\ John 1628–1688 Eng. preacher & author
Buonaparte Ital. spelling of BONAPARTE
Bur·bage \'bər-bij\ Richard *ca* 1567–1619 Eng. actor
Bur·bank \'bər-,baŋk\ Luther 1849–1926 Am. horticulturist
Burch·field \'bərch-,fēld\ Charles Ephraim 1893–1967 Am. painter
Bur·ger \'bər-gər\ Warren Earl 1907– Am. jurist; chief justice U.S. Supreme Court (1969–86)
Bür·ger \'bər-gər, 'bir-, 'büēr-\ Gottfried August 1747–1794 Ger. poet
Bur·gess \'bər-jəs\ Anthony 1917– Brit. writer
Burgess (Frank) Gelett 1866–1951 Am. humorist & illustrator
Burgess Thornton Waldo 1874–1965 Am. writer
Burghley *or* Burleigh 1st Baron — *see* William CECIL
Bur·goyne \(,)bər-'góin, 'bər-,\ John 1722–1792 Brit. gen. in America & dram.
Burk \'bərk\ Martha Jane 1852?–1903 née *Cannary* pseud. *Calamity Jane* Am. frontier figure
Burke \'bərk\ Edmund 1729–1797 Brit. statesman & orator — Burk·ean *or* Burk·ian \'bər-kē-ən\ *adj*
Bur·lin·game \'bər-lən-,gām\ An·son \'an(t)-sən\ 1820–1870 Am. diplomat
Burne–Jones \'bərn-'jōnz\ Sir Edward Co·ley \'kō-lē\ 1833–1898 orig. surname *Jones* Eng. painter & designer
Bur·net \(,)bər-'net, 'bər-nət\ Sir (Frank) Macfarlane 1899–1985 Austral. physician
Bur·nett \(,)bər-'net, 'bər-nət\ Frances Eliza 1849–1924 née *Hodg·son* \'häj-sən\ Am. (Eng.-born) writer
Bur·ney \'bər-nē\ Fanny 1752–1840 orig. *Frances;* *Madame d'Ar·blay* \'där-,blā\ Eng. nov. & diarist
Burns \'bərnz\ Robert 1759–1796 Scot. poet — Burns·ian \'bərn-zē-ən\ *adj*
Burn·side \'bərn-,sīd\ Ambrose Everett 1824–1881 Am. gen.
Burr \'bər\ Aaron 1756–1836 3d vice pres. of the U.S. (1801–05)
Bur·roughs \'bər-(,)ōz, 'bə-(,)rōz\ Edgar Rice 1875–1950 Am. writer
Burroughs John 1837–1921 Am. naturalist
Burroughs William Seward 1914– Am. writer
Bur·ton \'bərt-ºn\ Harold Hitz 1888–1964 Am. jurist
Burton Richard 1925–1984 Brit. actor
Burton Sir Richard Francis 1821–1890 Brit. explorer & orientalist
Burton Robert 1577–1640 Eng. clergyman & author
Bush \'büsh\ George Herbert Walker 1924– Am. polit.; 41st pres. of the U.S. (1989–)
Bush Van·ne·var \və-'nē-vər\ 1890–1974 Am. electrical engineer
Bu·so·ni \b(y)ü-'zō-nē\ Ferruccio Benvenuto 1866–1924 Ital. composer & pianist

Bu·sta·man·te y Sir·vén \bü-stə-'män-(,)tā-ē-sir-'ven\ Antonio Sánchez 1865–1951 Cuban jurist
Bu·te·nandt \'büt-ºn-,änt\ Adolph Friedrich Johann 1903– Ger. chem.
But·ler \'bət-lər\ Benjamin Franklin 1818–1893 Am. gen. & polit.
Butler Joseph 1692–1752 Eng. theol.
Butler Nicholas Murray 1862–1947 Am. educ.
Butler Samuel 1612–1680 Eng. satirical poet
Butler Samuel 1835–1902 Eng. nov. & satirist
Bux·te·hu·de \,búk-stə-'hüd-ə\ Dietrich 1637–1707 Dan. organist & composer
Byng \'biŋ\ George 1663–1733 1st Viscount *Torrington* Brit. admiral
Byng Julian Hedworth George 1862–1935 1st Viscount *Byng of Vimy* Brit. gen.; gov.-gen. of Canada (1921–26)
Byrd \'bərd\ Richard Evelyn 1888–1957 Am. admiral & polar explorer
Byrnes \'bərnz\ James Francis 1879–1972 Am. polit. & jurist
By·ron \'bī-rən\ Lord 1788–1824 *in full George Gordon Byron, 6th Baron Byron* Eng. poet — By·ron·ic \bī-'rän-ik\ *adj*
Ca·be·za de Va·ca \kə-,bā-zə-də-'väk-ə\ Alvar Núñez *ca* 1490–*ca* 1560 Span. explorer
Ca·ble \'kā-bəl\ George Washington 1844–1925 Am. nov.
Cab·ot \'kab-ət\ John *ca* 1450–*ca* 1499 It. *Giovanni Ca·bo·to* \kä-'bō-(,)tō\ Venetian navigator; disc. continent of No. America for England
Cabot Sebastian 1476?–1557 *son of John* Eng. navigator
Ca·bral \kə-'bräl\ Pedro Álvares 1467(or 1468)–1520 Port. navigator
Ca·bril·ho \kə-'brē-(,)(y)ō, -'bril-(,)ō\ João Rodrigues *d* 1543 Sp. *Juan Rodríguez Cabrillo* Span. (Port.-born) explorer in Mexico & California
Ca·bri·ni \kə-'brē-nē\ Saint Frances Xavier 1850–1917 *Mother Cabrini* 1st Am. citizen canonized (1946)
Cade \'kād\ John *d* 1450 *Jack* Eng. rebel
Cad·il·lac \'kad-ºl-,ak, F kȧ-dē-yȧk\ Antoine de la Mothe, sieur de 1658–1730 Fr. founder of Detroit
Caed·mon \'kad-mən\ *fl* 658–680 Anglo-Saxon poet
Cae·sar \'sē-zər\ Gaius Julius 100–44 B.C. Rom. gen., statesman, & writer
Cage \'kāj\ John Milton 1912– Am. composer
Ca·glio·stro \kal-'yō-(,)strō, käl-\ Count Alessandro di 1743–1795 orig. *Giuseppe Bal·sa·mo* \bäl-sə-,mō\ Ital. imposter
Caine \'kān\ Sir (Thomas Henry) Hall 1853–1931 Eng. nov.
Calamity Jane — *see* Martha Jane BURK
Cal·der \'kȯl-dər\ Alexander 1898–1976 Am. sculptor
Cal·de·rón de la Bar·ca \,käl-də-'rōn-dā-lə-'bär-kə\ Pedro 1600–1681 Span. dram. & poet
Cald·well \'kȯl-,dwel, -dwəl, 'käl-\ Erskine 1903–1987 Am. nov.
Caldwell (Janet) Taylor 1900–1985 Am. (Eng.-born) author
Cal·houn \kal-'hün\ John Caldwell 1782–1850 Am. polit.; vice pres. of the U.S. (1825–32)
Ca·lig·u·la \kə-'lig-yə-lə\ A.D. 12–41 *Gaius Caesar* Rom. emp. (37–41)
Cal·la·ghan \'kal-ə-hən, -,han\ (Leonard) James 1912– Brit. prime min. (1976–79)
Cal·las \'kal-əs, 'käl-\ Maria 1923–1977 orig. *Maria Anna Sofia Cecilia Kalogeropoulos* Am. soprano
Cal·les \'kä-,yäs\ Plutarco Elías 1877–1945 Mex. gen.; pres. of Mexico (1924–28)
Cal·lim·a·chus \kə-'lim-ə-kəs\ 5th cent. B.C. Greek sculptor
Callimachus *ca* 305–*ca* 240 B.C. Greek scholar & Alexandrian librarian
Cal·lis·the·nes \kə-'lis-thə-,nēz\ *ca* 360–328 B.C. Greek philos. & hist.
Cal·lis·tra·tus \kə-'lis-trət-əs\ *d* 355 B.C. Athenian orator & gen.
Cal·vert \'kal-vərt\ George 1580?–1632 1st Baron *Baltimore* Eng. proprietor in America
Calvert Leonard 1606–1647 *son of George* gov. of Maryland province (1634–47)
Cal·vin \'kal-vən\ John 1509–1564 orig. *Jean Chau·vin* \shō-vaⁿ\ *or* *Caul·vin* \kōl-vaⁿ\ Fr. theol. & reformer
Calvin Melvin 1911– Am. chem.
Cal·vo So·te·lo y Bus·te·lo \,käl-vō-sō-'tel-ō-ē-bü-'stel-ō\ Leopoldo 1926– premier of Spain (1981–82)
Camacho Manuel Ávila — *see* ÁVILA CAMACHO
Cam·ba·cé·rès \,käⁿ-,bȧs-ā-'res, -,bäs-\ Jean-Jacques-Régis de 1753–1824 Duc de *Parme* Fr. jurist; counselor of Napoleon I
Cambridge 1st Baron of — *see* Edgar Douglas ADRIAN
Cam·by·ses II \kam-'bī-(,)sēz\ *d* 522 B.C. *son of Cyrus II the Great* king of Persia (529–22)
Cam·den \'kam-dən\ William 1551–1623 Eng. antiquarian & hist.
Cam·er·on of Loch·iel \'kam-(ə-)rə-nəv-lä-'kē(ə)l, -'kē(ə)l\ 1629–1719 *Sir Ewen Cameron* Scot. chieftain
Cameron of Lochiel 1695?–1748 *Donald Cameron; the gentle Lochiel* Scot. chieftain
Ca·mões \kə-'móiⁿsh\ *E* Ca·mo·ëns \kə-'mō-ənz, 'kam-ə-wənz\ Luiz Vaz de 1524(or 1525)–1580 Port. poet
Camp \'kamp\ Walter Chauncey 1859–1925 Am. football coach
Camp·bell \'kam-(b)əl\ Alexander 1788–1866 Am. (Irish-born) founder of Disciples of Christ
Campbell Colin 1792–1863 orig. surname *Mac·li·ver* \mə-'klē-vər\; Baron *Clyde* Brit. field marshal
Campbell John 1705–1782 4th Earl of *Lou·doun* \'laúd-ºn\ Brit. gen. in America
Campbell John Douglas Sutherland 1845–1914 9th Duke of *Argyll* gov.= gen. of Canada (1878–83)
Campbell Joseph 1904–1987 Am. mythologist & folklorist
Campbell Thomas 1777–1844 Brit. poet
Campbell–Ban·ner·man \-'ban-ər-mən\ Sir Henry 1836–1908 Brit. statesman; prime min. (1905–08)
Cam·pi \'käm-(,)pē\ Ital. family of painters in Cremona including: Galeazzo 1477–1536 & his three sons Giulio 1502–1572, Antonio 1536–*ca* 1591, & Vincenzo 1536–1591
Cam·pi·on \'kam-pē-ən\ Thomas 1567–1620 Eng. poet & composer

Ca·mus \kȧ-mǖ\ Albert 1913–1960 Fr. nov., essayist, & dram.
Ca·na·let·to \ˌkän-ᵊl-'et-(ˌ)ō\ 1697–1768 orig. *Giovanni Antonio Canal* Ital. painter
Can·by \'kan-bē\ Henry Sei·del \'sīd-ᵊl\ 1878–1961 Am. editor & author
Can·dolle \kä-'dòl\ Augustin Pyrame de 1778–1841 Swiss botanist
Can·dra·gup·ta \ˌkən-drə-'gùp-tə\ *or* Chan·dra·gup·ta \ˌchən-\ *d ca* 297 B.C. Indian emp. (*ca* 321–*ca* 297 B.C.)
Can·dra Gup·ta II \'kən-drə-'gùp-tə\ *also* Chan·dra Gup·ta II \'chən-\ Indian ruler of Gupta dynasty (*ca* 380–*ca* 415)
Ca·net·ti \kə-'net-ē\ Elias 1905– Bulg.-born author writing in German
Canfield Dorothy — see Dorothy Canfield FISHER
Can·ning \'kan-iŋ\ Charles John 1812–1862 Earl *Canning* Brit. gov.-gen. of India (1856–58); 1st viceroy of India (1858–62)
Canning George 1770–1827 *father of C.J.* Brit. statesman; prime min. (1827)
Canning Stratford 1786–1880 1st Viscount *Stratford de Red·cliffe* \'red-ˌklif\ Brit. diplomat
Can·non \'kan-ən\ Joseph Gurney 1836–1926 *Uncle Joe* Am. polit.
Ca·no·va \kə-'nō-və, -'nò-\ Antonio 1757–1822 Ital. sculptor
Ca·nute \kə-'n(y)üt\ *d* 1035 *the Great* king of England (1016–35); of Denmark (1018–35); of Norway (1028–35)
Ca·pek \'chäp-ˌek\ Ka·rel \'kär-əl\ 1890–1938 Czech nov. & dram.
Capet Hugh — see HUGH CAPET
Ca·pone \kə-'pōn\ Alphonse 1899–1947 *Scarface* Am. gangster
Ca·pote \kə-'pō-tē\ Truman 1924–1984 Am. writer
Car·a·cal·la \ˌkar-ə-'kal-ə\ A.D. 188–217 *Marcus Aurelius Antoninus* orig. *Bas·si·a·nus* \ˌbas-ē-'än-əs\ Rom. emp. (211–217)
Ca·ra·vag·gio \ˌkar-ə-'väj-(ē-ˌ)ō, -'väzh-ō\ Michelangelo da 1573–1610 *Michelangelo Merisi* Ital. painter — Ca·ra·vag·gesque \ˌkär-ə-ˌvä-'jesk\ *adj*
Car·ber·ry \'kär-ˌber-ē, -bə-rē\ John Joseph 1904– Am. cardinal
Cár·de·nas \'kärd-ᵊn-ˌäs, 'kär-thə-ˌnäs\ Lázaro 1895–1970 Mex. gen. & polit.; pres. of Mexico (1934–40)
Car·do·zo \kär-'dō-(ˌ)zō\ Benjamin Nathan 1870–1938 Am. jurist
Car·duc·ci \kär-'dü-(ˌ)chē\ Giosuè 1835–1907 Ital. poet
Ca·rew \kə-'rü; 'ka(ə)r-ē, 'ke(ə)r-\ Thomas 1595?–?1640 Eng. poet
Carl XVI Gus·taf \'kärl-'gəs-ˌtäv, -'gùs-, -ˌtäf\ 1946– king of Sweden (1973–)
Carle·ton \'kär(-ə)l-tən, 'kärlt-ᵊn\ Sir Guy 1724–1808 1st Baron *Dorchester* Brit. gen. & administrator in America
Car·los \'kär-ləs, -ˌlōs\ Don 1788–1855 infante & pretender to Span. throne
Carlos de Aus·tria \-thä-'aù-strē-ə\ Don 1545–1568 *son of Philip II of Spain* prince of Asturias & heir to Span. throne
Car·lo·ta \kär-'lōt-ə, -'lät-\ 1840–1927 *Marie-Charlotte-Amélie-Augustine-Victoire-Clémentine-Léopoldine* empress of Mexico (1864–67)
Car·lyle \kär-'lī(ə)l, 'kär-ˌ\ Thomas 1795–1881 Scot. essayist & hist. — Car·lyl·ian \kär-'lī-lē-ən\ *adj*
Car·mo·na \kär-'mō-nə\ António Óscar de Fragoso 1869–1951 Port. gen.; pres. of Portugal (1928–51)
Car·ne·gie \'kär-nə-gē, kär-'neg-ē\ Andrew 1835–1919 Am. (Scot.-born) industrialist & philanthropist
Car·not \kär-'nō\ Lazare-Nicolas-Marguerite 1753–1823 Fr. statesman & gen.
Carnot Marie-François-Sadi 1837–1894 pres. of France (1887–94)
Car·ol II \'kar-əl\ 1893–1953 king of Romania (1930–40)
Car·pac·cio \kär-'päch-(ē-ˌ)ō\ Vittore *ca* 1460–1525(or 1526) Ital. painter
Car·ran·za \kə-'ran-zə, -'rän-\ Venustiano 1859–1920 pres. of Mexico (1915–20)
Car·rel \kä-'rel, 'kar-əl\ Alexis 1873–1944 Fr. surgeon & biol.
Car·rère \kə-'re(ə)r\ John Merven 1858–1911 Am. architect
Car·roll \'kar-əl\ Charles 1737–1832 *Carroll of Carrollton* Am. patriot
Carroll Lewis — see Charles Lutwidge DODGSON — Car·roll·ian \kə-'rō-lē-ən\ *adj*
Car·son \'kärs-ᵊn\ Christopher 1809–1868 *Kit* \'kit\ Am. trapper & frontiersman
Carson Rachel Louise 1907–1964 Am. scientist & writer
Car·stens \'kär-stən(t)s\ Karl 1914– pres. of West Germany (1979–84)
Carte, D'Oy·ly \ˌdòi-lē-'kärt\ Richard 1844–1901 Eng. opera impresario
Car·ter \'kärt-ər\ Howard 1873–1939 Eng. archaeol.
Carter Jimmy 1924– *James Earl, Jr.* Am. polit.; 39th pres. of the U.S. (1977–81)
Car·ter·et \ˌkärt-ə-'ret, 'kärt-ə-ˌ\ John 1690–1763 Earl *Gran·ville* \'gran-ˌvil\ Eng. statesman
Car·tier \kär-'tyā, 'kärt-ē-ˌā\ George Étienne 1814–1873 Canad. statesman
Cartier Jacques 1491–1557 Fr. navigator & explorer; disc. St. Lawrence river
Cart·wright \'kärt-ˌrīt\ Edmund 1743–1823 Eng. inventor
Ca·ru·so \kə-'rü-(ˌ)sō, -(ˌ)zō\ En·ri·co \en-'rē-(ˌ)kō\ 1873–1921 orig. *Errico* Ital. tenor
Car·ver \'kär-vər\ George Washington *ca* 1864–1943 Am. botanist
Carver John 1576–1621 Eng. *Mayflower* pilgrim; 1st gov. of Plymouth colony
Cary \'ka(ə)r-ē, 'ke(ə)r-ē\ (Arthur) Joyce (Lunel) 1888–1957 Brit. nov.
Cary Henry Francis 1772–1844 Eng. clergyman & translator
Ca·sals \kə-'sälz, -'zälz\ Pablo 1876–1973 Catalan *Pau* Span.-born cellist, conductor, & composer
Ca·sa·no·va \ˌkaz-ə-'nō-və, ˌkas-\ Giovanni Giacomo 1725–1798 *Chevalier de Seingalt* Ital. adventurer
Ca·sau·bon \kə-'sò-bən, ˌkaz-ō-'bōⁿ\ Isaac 1559–1614 Fr. theol. & scholar
Case·ment \'kā-smənt\ Sir Roger David 1864–1916 Irish rebel
Ca·si·mir-Pé·rier \ˌkaz-ə-ˌmi(ə)r-'per-ē-ˌā\ Jean-Paul-Pierre 1847–1907 Fr. statesman; pres. of France (1894–95)
Cas·lon \'kaz-lən\ William 1692–1766 Eng. typefounder
Cass \'kas\ Lewis 1782–1866 Am. statesman
Cas·satt \kə-'sat\ Mary Stevenson 1845–1926 Am. painter in France

Cas·sin \ka-'saⁿ, kä-\ René-Samuel 1887–1976 Fr. statesman
Cas·si·o·do·rus \ˌkas-ē-ə-'dòr-əs, -'dòr-\ Flavius Magnus Aurelius *ca* 490–*ca* 585 Rom. statesman & author
Cas·sius Lon·gi·nus \'kash-(ē)-ə,ˌslän-'ji-nəs, 'kas-ē-ə-\ Gaius *d* 42 B.C. Rom. gen. & conspirator
Cas·te·lar y Ri·poll \ˌkas-tə-'lär-ē-rē-'pòl\ Emilio 1832–1899 Span. statesman & writer
Ca·stel·ve·tro \kä-ˌstel-'ve-(ˌ)trō\ Lodovico *ca* 1505–1571 Ital. critic & philologist
Ca·sti·glio·ne \ˌkäs-tēl-'yō-(ˌ)nā\ Baldassare 1478–1529 Ital. statesman & author
Cas·ti·lho \käs(h)-'tēl-(ˌ)yü\ António Feliciano de 1800–1875 Port. poet
Castlereagh Viscount — see Robert STEWART
Cas·tro \'kas-(ˌ)trō, 'käs-\ Cipriano 1858–1924 Venezuelan gen.; pres. of Venezuela (1902–08)
Castro Inés de 1320?–1355 Span. noblewoman
Castro (Ruz) \'rüs\ Fi·del \fē-'del\ 1926– Cuban leader (1959–)
Cates·by \'kāts-bē\ Mark 1679?–1749 Eng. naturalist
Catesby Robert 1573–1605 Eng. rebel
Cath·er \'kath-ər\ Willa Sibert 1873–1947 Am. nov.
Cath·er·ine \'kath-(ə-)rən\ name of 1st, 5th, & 6th wives of Henry VIII of England: Catherine of Aragon 1485–1536; Catherine Howard 1520?–1542; Catherine Parr \'pär\ 1512–1548
Catherine I 1684–1727 *wife of Peter the Great* empress of Russia (1725–27)
Catherine II 1729–1796 *the Great* empress of Russia (1762–96)
Catherine of Braganza 1638–1705 *queen of Charles II of England*
Cath·er·ine de Mé·di·cis \'kath-(ə-)rən-də-'med-ə-(ˌ)chē, -ˌmäd-ə-'sē(s)\ *It* Caterina de' Me·di·ci \'med-ə-(ˌ)chē\ 1519–1589 *queen of Henry II of France*
Cat·i·line \'kat-ᵊl-ˌīn\ *ca* 108–62 B.C. *Lucius Sergius Cat·i·li·na* \ˌkat-ᵊl-'ī-nə, -'ē-nə\ Rom. polit. & conspirator
Cat·lin \'kat-lən\ George 1796–1872 Am. artist
Ca·to \'kāt-(ˌ)ō\ Marcus Porcius 234–149 B.C. *the Elder; the Censor* Rom. statesman
Cato Marcus Porcius 95–46 B.C. *the Younger; great-grandson of prec.* Rom. statesman
Catt \'kat\ Carrie Chapman 1859–1947 née *Lane* Am. suffragist
Cat·tell \kə-'tel\ James McKeen 1860–1944 Am. psychol. & editor
Cat·ton \'kat-ᵊn\ (Charles) Bruce 1899–1978 Am. journalist & hist.
Ca·tul·lus \kə-'təl-əs\ Gaius Valerius *ca* 84–*ca* 54 B.C. Rom. poet
Cau·lain·court \ˌkō-ˌlaⁿ-'kü(ə)r\ Marquis Armand-Augustin-Louis de 1773–1827 Fr. gen. & diplomat
Ca·va·zos \kə-'vä-zòs\ Lauro Fred 1927– U.S. secy. of education (1988–)
Ca·vell \'kav-əl, kə-'vel\ Edith Louisa 1865–1915 Eng. nurse
Cav·en·dish \'kav-ən-(ˌ)dish\ Henry 1731–1810 Eng. scientist
Cavendish Spencer Compton 1833–1908 8th Duke of *Devonshire* Eng. statesman
Cavendish Sir William 1505?–1557 Eng. statesman
Cavendish William 1640–1707 1st Duke of *Devonshire* Eng. statesman
Ca·vour \kä-'vü(ə)r, kä-\ Con·te \'kōn-(ˌ)tā-\ Camillo Benso di 1810–1861 Ital. statesman
Ca·xi·as \kə-'shē-əs\ Du·que \'dü-kə\ de 1803–1880 *Luiz Alves de Lima e Silva* Braz. gen. & statesman
Cax·ton \'kak-stən\ William *ca* 1422–1491 1st Eng. printer
Ceau·șes·cu \chaù-'shes-(ˌ)kü\ Nicolae 1918–1989 pres. of Romania (1974–1989)
Cech \'chek\ Thomas Robert 1947– Am. biochem.
Ce·cil \'ses-əl, 'sis-\ (Edgar Algernon) Robert 1864–1958 1st Viscount *Cecil of Chel·wood* \'chel-ˌwùd\ Eng. statesman
Cecil Lord (Edward Christian) David 1902–1986 Eng. biographer
Cecil Robert 1563–1612 1st Earl of *Salisbury* & 1st Viscount *Cran·borne* \'kran-ˌbó(ə)rn\ Eng. statesman
Cecil Robert Arthur Talbot Gas·coyne- \'gas-ˌkòin-\ 1830–1903 3d Marquis of *Salisbury* Eng. statesman
Cecil William 1520–1598 1st Baron *Burgh·ley* or *Bur·leigh* \'bər-lē\ Eng. statesman
Ce·la \'sā-lə\ Camilo José 1916– Span. writer
Cel·li·ni \chə-'lē-nē\ Ben·ve·nu·to \ˌben-və-'nü-(ˌ)tō\ 1500–1571 Ital. goldsmith & sculptor
Cel·sius \'sel-sē-əs, -shəs\ Anders 1701–1744 Swed. astron.
Cen·ci \'chen-(ˌ)chē\ Bea·tri·ce \ˌbä-ä-'trē-(ˌ)chä\ 1577–1599 Ital. woman executed for parricide
Cer·van·tes \sər-'van-ˌtēz, -'vän-ˌtäs\ Miguel de 1547–1616 full surname *Cervantes Saa·ve·dra* \ˌsä-(ə-)'vā-drə\ Span. writer
Cé·zanne \sā-'zan\ Paul 1839–1906 Fr. painter — Cé·zann·esque \(ˌ)sā-ˌzan-'esk\ *adj*
Cha·bri·er \ˌshäb-rē-'ā, shab-\ (Alexis) Emmanuel 1841–1894 Fr. composer
Chad·wick \'chad-(ˌ)wik\ Sir James 1891–1974 Eng. physicist
Cha·gall \shə-'gäl, -'gal\ Marc 1887–1985 Russ. painter in France
Chag·a·tai \ˌchag-ə-'tī\ *or* Jag·a·tai \ˌjag-\ *d* 1241 *2d son of Genghis Khan* Mongol ruler
Chain \'chān\ Ernst Boris 1906–1979 Brit. (Ger.-born) biochem.
Cha·lia·pin \shəl-'yäp-(ˌ)ēn, -ən\ Fyodor Ivanovich 1873–1938 Russ. basso
Chal·mers \'chal-mərz, 'chäm-ərz\ Alexander 1759–1834 Scot. biographer & editor
Cham·ber·lain \'chām-bər-lən\ Joseph 1836–1914 & his sons Sir (Joseph) Austen 1863–1937 & (Arthur) Neville 1869–1940 Brit. statesmen
Chamberlain Owen 1920– Am. physicist
Cham·ber·lin \'chām-bər-lən\ Thomas Chrow·der \'kraùd-ər\ 1843–1928 Am. geologist
Cham·bers \'chām-bərz\ Robert 1802–1871 Scot. publisher & editor
Cham·bord \shäⁿ-'bó(ə)r\ Comte de 1820–1883 *Henri-Charles-Ferdinand-Marie Dieudonné d'Artois Duc de Bordeaux* Bourbon claimant to Fr. throne
Cha·mor·ro \chä-'mòr-(ˌ)rō\ Violeta Barrios de 1929– pres. of Nicaragua (1990–)
Cham·plain \(ˌ)sham-'plān, shäⁿ-pla(ⁿ)\ Samuel de *ca* 1567–1635 Fr. explorer in America; founder of Quebec
Cham·pol·lion \shäⁿ-pòl-yōⁿ\ Jean-François 1790–1832 Fr. Egyptologist

Cham·pol·lion–Fi·geac \-fē-zhȧk\ Jacques-Joseph 1778–1867 *bro. of prec.* Fr. archaeol.

Chan·dra·gup·ta — see CANDRAGUPTA

Chandra Gupta II — see CANDRA GUPTA II

Chan·dra·se·khar \ˌchən-drə-'shä-kär\ Subrahmanyan 1910– Am. (Indian-born) physicist

Cha·nel \shə-'nel, sha-\ Gabrielle 1883–1971 *Co·co* \'kō-(ˌ)kō\ Fr. fashion designer & perfumer

Chang Hsüeh–liang \'jäŋ-shŭ-'ä-lē-'äŋ\ *son of Chang Tso-lin* 1898– Chin. gen.

Chang Tso–lin \-'(t)sō-'lin\ 1873–1928 Chin. gen.

Chan·ning \'chan-iŋ\ William Ellery 1780–1842 Am. clergyman

Chao K'uang–yin \'jaù-'kwäŋ-'yin\ 927–976 *T'ai Tsu* \'tīd-'zü\ Chin. emp. (960–976); founder of Sung dynasty

Chap·lin \'chap-lən\ Sir Charles Spencer 1889–1977 Brit. actor & producer — Chap·lin·esque \ˌchap-lə-'nesk\ *adj*

Chap·man \'chap-mən\ Frank Mich·ler \'mik-lər\ 1864–1945 Am. ornithologist

Chapman George 1559?–1634 Eng. dram. & translator

Chapman John 1774–1845 *Johnny Ap·ple·seed* \'ap-əl-ˌsēd\ Am. pioneer

Char·cot \shär-'kō, 'shär-\ Jean-Mar·tin \-mär-'taⁿ\ 1825–1893 Fr. neurologist

Char·din \shär-'daⁿ\ Jean-Baptiste-Siméon 1699–1779 Fr. painter

Char·le·magne \'shär-lə-ˌmän\ 742–814 *Charles the Great* or *Charles I* Frankish king (768–814) & emp. of the West (800–814)

Charles I \'chär(-ə)lz\ 1600–1649 *Charles Stuart* king of Great Britain (1625–49)

Charles II 1630–1685 *son of Charles I* king of Great Britain (1660–85)

Charles 1948– *son of Elizabeth II* prince of Wales

Charles I 1771–1847 archduke of Austria

Charles I 1887–1922 *Charles Francis Joseph; nephew of Francis Ferdinand* emp. of Austria & (as *Charles IV*) king of Hungary (1916–18)

Charles I or II 823–877 *the Bald* king of France as *Charles I* (840–877); Holy Rom. emp. as *Charles II* (875–877)

Charles IV 1294–1328 *the Fair* king of France (1322–28)

Charles V 1337–1380 *the Wise* king of France (1364–80)

Charles VI 1368–1422 *the Mad* or *the Beloved* king of France (1380–1422)

Charles VII 1403–1461 king of France (1422–61)

Charles IX 1550–1574 king of France (1560–74)

Charles X 1757–1836 king of France (1824–30)

Charles V 1500–1558 Holy Rom. emp. (1519–56); king of Spain as *Charles I* (1516–56)

Charles XII 1682–1718 king of Sweden (1697–1718)

Charles Prince 1903–1983 *bro. of King Leopold* regent of Belgium (1944–50)

Charles XIV John 1763–1844 orig. *Jean-Baptiste-Jules Bernadotte* king of Sweden & Norway (1818–44)

Charles Edward 1720–1788 *the Young Pretender; (Bonnie) Prince Charlie* Brit. prince

Charles Mar·tel \-mär-'tel\ *ca* 688–741 *grandfather of Charlemagne* Frankish ruler (719–741)

Charlotte Empress of Mexico — see CARLOTA

Chase \'chās\ Mary Ellen 1887–1973 Am. educ. & author

Chase Sal·mon \'sam-ən, 'sal-mən\ Portland 1808–1873 Am. statesman, chief justice U.S. Supreme Court (1864–73)

Cha·teau·bri·and \(ˌ)sha-ˌtō-brē-'äⁿ\ Vi·comte \vē-kōⁿt\ François⸗Auguste-René de 1768–1848 Fr. author

Chatham 1st Earl of — see William PITT

Chatrian Alexandre — see ERCKMANN-CHATRIAN

Chat·ter·jee \'chät-ər-jē\ Ban·kim \'bôⁿ-kim\ Chan·dra \'chŏn-(ˌ)drô\ 1838–1894 Indian nov.

Chat·ter·ton \'chat-ərt-ⁿn\ Thomas 1752–1770 Eng. poet

Chau·cer \'chȯ-sər\ Geoffrey *ca* 1342–1400 Eng. poet — Chau·ce·ri·an \chȯ-'sir-ē-ən\ *adj*

Chau·temps \shō-'täⁿ\ Camille 1885–1963 Fr. lawyer & polit.; premier (1930; 1933–34; 1937–38)

Chavannes, de — see PUVIS DE CHAVANNES

Chá·vez \'chäv-əs, -ˌez\ Carlos 1899–1978 Mex. conductor & composer

Chee·ver \'chē-vər\ John 1912–1982 Am. writer

Che·khov *also* Che·kov \'chek-ˌȯf, -ˌȯv\ Anton Pavlovich 1860–1904 Russ. dram. & writer — Che·kho·vi·an \che-'kō-vē-ən\ *adj*

Che·ney \'chē-nē\ Richard Bruce 1941– U.S. secy. of defense (1989–)

Ché·nier \shän-'yä\ André-Marie de 1762–1794 Fr. poet

Chen·nault \shə-'nȯlt\ Claire Lee 1890–1958 Am. gen.

Cheops — see KHUFU

Che·ren·kov \chə-'reŋ-kəf\ Pavel Alekseyevich 1904– Russ. physicist

Cher·nen·ko \cher-'ⁿyeŋ-kō\ Konstantin Ustinovich 1911–1985 Soviet polit.; pres. U.S.S.R. (1984–85); 1st secy. of Communist party (1984–85)

Cher·ny·shev·sky \ˌcher-ni-'shef-skē, -'shev-\ Nikolay Gavrilovich 1829–1889 Russ. revolutionary & author

Che·ru·bi·ni \ˌker-ə-'bē-nē, ˌkä-rü-\ (Maria) Lu·i·gi \lü-'ē-(ˌ)jē\ Carlo Zenobio Salvatore 1760–1842 Ital. composer

Ches·ter·field \'ches-tər-ˌfēld\ 4th Earl of 1694–1773 *Philip Dormer Stan·hope* \'stan-əp\ Eng. statesman & author

Ches·ter·ton \'ches-tərt-ⁿn\ Gilbert Keith 1874–1936 Eng. journalist & author — Ches·ter·to·nian \ˌches-tər-'tō-nē-ən, -nyən\ *adj*

Che·va·lier \shə-'val-(ˌ)yä\ Mau·rice \mȯ-'rēs\ 1888–1972 Fr. entertainer

Chiang Kai–shek \jē-'äŋ-'kī-'shek, 'chaŋ-\ 1887–1975 pinyin *Jiang Jie·shi* \jē-'äŋ-jē-'ä-'shē\ Chin. gen. & polit.; pres. of China (1948–49; Taiwan, 1950–75)

Ch'ien–lung \chē-'en-'lùŋ\ 1711–1799 Chin. emp. (1736–96)

Chif·ley \'chif-lē\ Joseph Benedict 1885–1951 prime min. of Australia (1945–49)

Chi·ka·ma·tsu \ˌchē-kə-'mät-(ˌ)sü\ Monzaemon 1653–1724 *the Shakespeare of Japan* Jp. dram.

Child \'chī(ə)ld\ Francis James 1825–1896 Am. philologist & ballad editor

Childe \'chī(ə)ld\ Vere Gordon 1892–1957 Brit. anthropol. & archaeol.

Chil·ders \'chil-dərz\ Erskine Hamilton 1905–1974 Irish (Eng.-born) polit.; pres. of Ireland (1973–74)

Ch'in Shih Huang Ti \'chin-'shi(ə)r-'hwän-'dē\ *ca* 259–210 B.C. prename *Cheng* \'jen\ Chin. emp. (221–210 B.C.)

Chip·pen·dale \'chip-ən-ˌdāl\ Thomas 1718–1779 Eng. cabinetmaker

Chi·rac \shē-räk\ Jacques-René 1932– prime min. of France (1974–76; 1986–88)

Chi·ri·co, De \'kir-i-ˌkō, 'kē-ri-\ Gior·gio \'jōr-(ˌ)jō\ 1888–1978 Ital. painter

Choate \'chōt\ Joseph Hod·ges \'häj-əz\ 1832–1917 Am. lawyer & diplomat

Choate Rufus 1799–1859 Am. jurist

Choi·seul \shwä-'zəl, -'zər(-ə)l, -'zœl\ Étienne-François de 1719–1785 *duc de Choiseul* Fr. statesman

Chom·sky \'chäm-skē\ (Avram) Noam 1928– Am. linguist

Cho·pin \'shō-ˌpan, -ˌpaⁿ\ Frédéric François 1810–1849 Pol. pianist & composer

Chou En–lai \'jō-'en-'lī\ 1898–1976 pinyin *Jou En-lai* Chin. Communist polit.

Chré·tien de Troyes \krā-tyaⁿ-də-trwä\ *fl* 1170 Fr. trouvère

Christ Jesus — see JESUS

Chris·tian X \'kris(h)-chən\ 1870–1947 king of Denmark (1912–47)

Chris·tie \'kris-tē\ Dame Agatha 1890–1976 née *Miller* Eng. writer

Chris·ti·na \kris-'tē-nə\ 1626–1689 *dau. of Gustav II Adolphus* queen of Sweden (1632–54)

Chris·tophe \krē-stóf\ Henri 1767–1820 king of Haiti (1811–20)

Chris·ty \'kris-tē\ Howard Chandler 1873–1952 Am. artist

Chry·sos·tom \'kris-əs-təm, kris-'äs-təm\ Saint John *ca* 347–407 church father & patriarch of Constantinople

Chu Hsi \'jü-'shē\ 1130–1200 Chin. philos.

Chun Doo–Hwan \'jün-'dō-'hwän\ 1931– pres. of So. Korea (1980–88)

Church \'chərch\ Frederic Edwin 1826–1900 Am. painter

Chur·chill \'chər-ˌchil, 'chərch-ˌhil\ John 1650–1722 1st Duke of Marl·bor·ough \'märl-ˌbər-ə, 'mȯl-, -ˌbə-rə, -b(ə-)rə\ Eng. gen.

Churchill Randolph Henry Spencer 1849–1895 Lord *Randolph Churchill* Brit. statesman

Churchill Sir Winston Leonard Spencer 1874–1965 *son of Lord Randolph* Brit. statesman; prime min. (1940–45; 1951–55) — Chur·chill·ian \ˌchər-'chil-ē-ən, 'chərch-'hil-\ *adj*

Chu Teh \'jü-'də\ 1886–1976 Chin. gen.

Cia·no \'chän-(ˌ)ō\ Galeazzo 1903–1944 *Conte di Cortellazzo* Ital. statesman

Ciar·di \'chärd-ē\ John 1916–1986 Am. poet

Cib·ber \'sib-ər\ Col·ley \'käl-ē\ 1671–1757 Eng. dram. & actor; poet laureate (1730–57)

Cic·e·ro \'sis-ə-ˌrō\ Marcus Tullius 106–43 B.C. Rom. statesman, orator, & author — Cic·e·ro·nian \ˌsis-ə-'rō-nyən, -nē-ən\ *adj*

Cid, El \'sid\ *ca* 1043–1099 *Rodrigo Díaz de Vi·var* \vē-'vär\ Span. soldier & hero

Ci·ma·bue \ˌchē-mə-'bü-(ˌ)ä\ Giovanni *ca* 1251–1302 orig. *Bencivieni di Pepo* Florentine painter

Ci·mon \'sī-mən, -ˌmän\ *ca* 570–*ca* 451 B.C. Athenian gen. & statesman

Cin·cin·na·tus \ˌsin(t)-sə-'nat-əs, -'nät-\ Lucius Quinctius *b ca* 519 B.C. Rom. gen. & statesman

Clare of Assisi \'kla(ə)r, 'kle(ə)r\ Saint 1194–1253 Ital. nun

Clarendon Earl of — see Edward HYDE

Clark \'klärk\ Champ \'champ\ 1850–1921 *James Beau·champ* \'bē-chəm\ *Clark* Am. polit.

Clark George Rogers 1752–1818 Am. soldier & frontiersman

Clark Joe 1939– *Charles Joseph* Canad. polit.; prime min. (1979)

Clark Kenneth Bancroft 1914– Am. psychol.

Clark Kenneth Mackenzie 1903–1983 Baron *Clark of Saltwood* Brit. art hist.

Clark Mark Wayne 1896–1984 Am. gen.

Clark Tom Campbell 1899–1977 Am. jurist

Clark William 1770–1838 *bro. of G.R.* Am. explorer (with Meriwether Lewis)

Clarke \'klärk\ Charles Cow·den \'kaùd-ⁿn\ 1787–1877 & his wife Mary Victoria Cowden-Clarke 1809–1898 Eng. Shakespearean scholars

Claude \'klȯd\ Albert 1898–1983 Belg. physiol. in U.S.

Claude Lor·rain \klōd-lȯ-raⁿ\ 1600–1682 pseud. of *Claude Gel·lée* \zhə-lä\ Fr. painter

Clau·di·us \'klȯd-ē-əs\ Rom. gens including: Ap·pi·us \'ap-ē-əs\ Clau·dius Cras·sus \'kras-əs\ consul (471 & 451 B.C.) & decemvir (451–450 B.C.); Appius Claudius Cae·cus \'sē-kəs\ censor (312–307 B.C.), consul (307 & 296 B.C.), & dictator who began building of the Appian Way (312 B.C.)

Claudius I 10 B.C.–A.D. 54 *Tiberius Claudius Drusus Ne·ro* \'nē-(ˌ)rō, 'ni(ə)r-(ˌ)ō\ *Germanicus* Rom. emp. (41–54)

Claudius II A.D. 214–270 *Marcus Aurelius Claudius Gothicus* Rom. emp. (268–270)

Clau·se·witz \'klaù-zə-ˌvits\ Carl von 1780–1831 Pruss. gen. & military strategist

Clay \'klā\ Henry 1777–1852 Am. statesman & orator

Clay Lucius Du Bi·gnon \dü-'bin-yən\ 1897–1978 Am. gen.

Cle·an·thes \klē-'an-ˌthēz\ 331(or 330)–232(or 231) B.C. Greek Stoic philos.

Cle·ar·chus \klē-'är-kəs\ 5th cent. B.C. Greek soldier; gov. of Byzantium

Cleis·the·nes \'klīs-thə-ˌnēz\ *or* Clis·the·nes \'klis-\ *ca* 570–after 508 B.C. Athenian statesman

Cle·men·ceau \ˌklem-ən-'sō, klā-män-'sō\ Georges 1841–1929 Fr. statesman

Clem·ens \'klem-ənz\ Samuel Langhorne 1835–1910 pseud. *Mark Twain* \'twän\ Am. writer

Clem·ent \'klem-ənt\ name of 14 popes: esp. *VII (Giulio de'Me·di·ci* \'med-ə-(ˌ)chē\ 1478–1534 (pope 1523–34)

Cle·men·ti \klə-'ment-ē\ Muzio 1752–1832 Ital. pianist & composer in England
Clement of Alexandria Saint *ca* 150–between 211 and 215 *Titus Flavius Cle·mens* \'klem-,enz\ Greek Christian theol. & church father
Cle·om·e·nes \klē-'äm-ə-,nēz\ name of 3 kings of Sparta: esp. **III** (reigned 235–222 B.C.)
Cle·o·pa·tra \,klē-ə-'pa-trə, -'pä-, -'pä-\ 69–30 B.C. queen of Egypt (51–30)
Cleve·land \'klēv-lənd\ (Stephen) Grover 1837–1908 22d & 24th pres. of the U.S. (1885–89; 1893–97)
Cli·burn \'klī-bərn\ Van \'van\ 1934–   *Harvey Lavan Cliburn* Am. pianist
Clin·ton \'klint-ᵊn\ De Witt \di-'wit\ 1769–1828 Am. statesman
Clinton George 1739–1812 vice pres. of the U.S. (1805–12)
Clinton Sir Henry 1738–1795 Eng. gen. in America
Clive \'klīv\ Robert 1725–1774 Baron *Clive of Plassey* Brit. gen.; founder of the empire of Brit. India
Cloots \'klōts\ Baron de 1755–1794 *Jean-Baptiste du Val-de-Grâce;* known as *An·a·char·sis* \,an-ə-'kär-səs\ *Cloots* Pruss.-Fr. revolutionary
Clough \'kləf\ Arthur Hugh 1819–1861 Eng. poet
Clo·vis I \'klō-vəs\ *G Chlod·wig* \'klōt-(,)vik\ *ca* 466–511 king of the Salian Franks (481–511)
Clyde Baron — see Colin CAMPBELL
Cnut \kə-'n(y)üt\ *var of* CANUTE
Coates \'kōts\ Joseph Gordon 1878–1943 N. Z. statesman
Cobb \'käb\ Tyrus Raymond 1886–1961 *Ty* Am. baseball player
Cob·bett \'käb-ət\ William 1763–1835 pseud. *Peter Porcupine* Eng. polit. writer
Cob·den \'käb-dən\ Richard 1804–1865 Eng. statesman & econ.
Cobham Lord — see Sir John OLDCASTLE
Co·chise \kō-'chēs\ 1812?–1874 Chiricahua Apache Indian chief
Cock·croft \'käk-,(k)ròft\ Sir John Douglas 1897–1967 Brit. physicist
Coc·teau \käk-'tō, kók-\ Jean 1889–1963 Fr. author & artist
Co·dy \'kōd-ē\ John Patrick 1907–1982 Am. cardinal
Cody William Frederick 1846–1917 *Buffalo Bill* Am. scout, Indian fighter, & showman
Coen \'kün\ Jan Pie·ters·zoon \'pēt-ər-sən\ 1587–1629 Du. colonial gov.; founder of Du. East Indian empire
Coeur de Lion — see RICHARD I of England
Cof·fin \'kóf-ən, 'käf-\ Robert Peter Tristram 1892–1955 Am. author
Cog·gan \'käg-ən\ Frederick Donald 1909–   archbishop of Canterbury (1974–80)
Co·han \'kō-,han\ George Michael 1878–1942 Am. actor, dram., & producer
Co·hen \'kō-ən\ Stanley 1922–   Am. biochem.
Cohn \'kōn\ Ferdinand Julius 1828–1898 Ger. botanist
Coke \'kúk, 'kōk\ Sir Edward 1552–1634 *Lord Coke* Eng. jurist
Col·bert \kól-'be(ə)r, 'kòl-,\ Jean-Baptiste 1619–1683 Fr. statesman & financier
Cole \'kōl\ Thomas 1801–1848 Am. (Eng.-born) painter
Cole·pep·er or **Cul·pep·er** \'kòl-,pep-ər\ Thomas 1635–1689 2d Baron *Colepeper* Eng. colonial administrator; gov. of Virginia
Cole·ridge \'kōl-rij, 'kō-lə-rij\ Samuel Taylor 1772–1834 Eng. poet — **Cole·ridg·ean** *also* **Cole·ridg·ian** \,kōl-(ə-)'rij-ē-ən\ *adj*
Col·et \'käl-ət\ John 1466(or 1467)–1519 Eng. theol. & scholar
Co·lette \kó-'let\ Sidonie-Gabrielle 1873–1954 Fr. author
Col·fax \'kōl-,faks\ Schuy·ler \'skī-lər\ 1823–1885 vice pres. of the U.S. (1869–73)
Co·li·gny \,kò-,lēn-'yē, kə-'lēn-yē\ Gaspard II de 1519–1572 *Seigneur de Châtillon* Fr. admiral & Huguenot leader
Col·lier \'käl-yər, 'käl-ē-ər\ Jeremy 1650–1726 Eng. clergyman
Collier John Payne 1789–1883 Eng. editor
Collier Peter Fen·e·lon \'fen-ᵊl-ən\ 1849–1909 Am. publisher
Col·lins \'käl-ənz\ Michael 1890–1922 Irish revolutionary
Collins Michael 1930–   Am. astronaut
Collins William 1721–1759 Eng. poet
Collins (William) Wilkie 1824–1889 Eng. nov.
Col·lor de Mel·lo \kō-'lòr-də-'me-lü\ Fernando Affonso 1949–   pres. of Brazil (1990–   )
Col·man \'kōl-mən\ George 1732–1794 Eng. dram.
Col·um \'käl-əm\ Pad·raic \'póth-rig\ 1881–1972 Am. (Irish-born) writer
Co·lum·ba \kə-'ləm-bə\ *Ir Col·um* \'kəl-əm\ *or* **Col·um·cille** \'kəl-əm-,kil\ Saint *ca* 521–597 Irish missionary in Scotland
Co·lum·bus \kə-'ləm-bəs\ Christopher *It* Christoforo **Co·lom·bo** \kə-'lòm-(,)bō\ *Sp* Cristóbal **Co·lón** \kə-'lòn\ 1451–1506 Ital. navigator; disc. America
Co·me·ni·us \kə-'mē-nē-əs\ John Amos *Czech* Jan Ámos **Ko·men·ský** \'kó-men-skē\ 1592–1670 Czech theol. & educ.
Com·ma·ger \'käm-i-jər\ Henry Steele 1902–   Am. hist.
Com·mo·dus \'käm-ə-dəs\ Lucius Aelius Aurelius A.D. 161–192 Rom. emp. (180–192)
Com·mo·ner \'käm-ə-nər\ Barry 1917–   Am. biol. & educ.
Com·mynes or **Co·mines** or **Com·mines** \kò-'mēn\ Philippe de *ca* 1447–1511 Fr. polit. & chronicler
Comp·ton \'käm(p)-tən\ Arthur Holly 1892–1962 Am. physicist
Compton Karl Taylor 1887–1954 *bro. of A.H.* Am. physicist
Com·stock \'käm-,stäk *also* 'kəm-\ Anthony 1844–1915 Am. reformer
Comte \'kōⁿ(n)t\ Auguste 1798–1857 in full *Isidore-Auguste-Marie-François-Xavier* Fr. math. & philos.
Conan Doyle — see DOYLE
Co·nant \'kō-nənt\ James Bryant 1893–1978 Am. chem. & educ.
Con·dé \kōⁿ-'dā\ Prince de 1621–1686 *Louis II de Bour·bon* \'bü(ə)r-bən, bür-'bōⁿ\; Duc *d'En·ghien* \däⁿ-gaⁿ\ Fr. gen.
Con·don \'kän-dən\ Edward Uhler 1902–1974 Am. physicist
Con·dor·cet \kōⁿ-dòr-sā\ Marquis de 1743–1794 *Marie-Jean-Antoine-Nicholas de Ca·ri·tat* \,kar-ə-'tä\ Fr. philos. & polit.
Con·fu·cius \kən-'fyü-shəs\ *Chin* **K'ung K'ung-Fu-tzu** \'kúŋ-'füd-'zü\ *or* **K'ung-tzu** \,kúŋd-'zü\ 551–479 B.C. Chin. philos.
Con·greve \'kän-,grēv, 'käŋ-\ William 1670–1729 Eng. dram.
Con·ing·ham \'kən-iŋ-,ham, *chiefly Brit* -iŋ-əm\ Sir Arthur 1895–1948 Brit. air marshal

Con·rad \'kän-,rad\ Joseph 1857–1924 orig. *Józef Teodor Konrad Kor·ze·niow·ski* \,kō-zhən-'yòf-skē, -'yòv-\ Brit. (Ukrainian-born of Pol. parents) nov.
Con·sta·ble \'kən(t)-stə-bəl, 'kän(t)-\ John 1776–1837 Eng. painter
Cons·tant de Re·becque \kōⁿ-'stän-də-rə-'bek\ Benjamin 1767–1830 Fr. writer & polit.
Con·stan·tine \'kän(t)-stən-,tēn, -,tīn\ name of 2 kings of Greece: **I** 1868–1923 (reigned 1913–17; 1920–22); **II** 1940–   (reigned 1964–73; deposed)
Constantine I *d* 337 *the Great* Rom. emp. (306–337) — **Con·stan·tin·ian** \,kän(t)s-tən-'tin-ē-ən\ *adj*
Con·ta·ri·ni \,känt-ə-'rē-nē\ Venetian family including esp. Gasparo 1483–1542 cardinal & diplomat
Con·ti \'kōnt-ē, 'känt-\ Niccolò de' *ca* 1395–1469 Venetian traveler
Cook \'kúk\ Capt. James 1728–1779 Eng. navigator & explorer
Cooke \'kúk\ (Alfred) Al·is·tair \'al-ə-stər\ 1908–   Am. (Brit.-born) essayist & journalist
Cooke Terence James 1921–1983 Am. cardinal
Coo·lidge \'kü-lij\ (John) Calvin 1872–1933 30th pres. of the U.S. (1923–29)
Coo·per \'kü-pər, 'kúp-ər\ Anthony Ashley — see SHAFTESBURY
Cooper James Fen·i·more \'fen-ə-,mó(ə)r, -,mó(ə)r\ 1789–1851 Am. nov.
Cooper Leon N. 1930–   Am. physicist
Cooper Peter 1791–1883 Am. manufacturer & philanthropist
Co·per·ni·cus \kō-'pər-ni-kəs\ Nicolaus *Pol* Mikołaj **Ko·per·nik** \kò-'per-nēk\ *or* Niklas **Kop·per·nigk** \'käp-ər-,nik\ 1473–1543 Pol. astron.; founder of modern astronomy
Cop·land \'kō-plənd\ Aaron 1900–   Am. composer
Cop·ley \'käp-lē\ John Sin·gle·ton \'siŋ-gəl-tən\ 1738–1815 Am. portrait painter
Co·que·lin \,kók-(ə-)'laⁿ\ Benoît-Constant 1841–1909 Fr. actor
Cor·bu·sier, Le \lə-kòr-büs-'yä\ 1887–1965 orig. *Charles-Édouard Jean·ne·ret* \zhän-'re\ Fr. (Swiss-born) architect, painter, & sculptor
Cor·co·ran \'kòr-k(ə-)rən\ Thomas Gardiner 1900–1981 Am. lawyer & polit.
Cor·day \kòr-'dā, 'kòr-\ Charlotte 1768–1793 *Marie-Anne-Charlotte Corday d'Ar·mont* \där-'mōⁿ\ Fr. patriot; assassinated Marat
Co·rel·li \kə-'rel-ē\ Arcangelo 1653–1713 Ital. violinist & composer
Co·ri \'kòr-ē, 'kór-\ Carl Ferdinand 1896–1984 & his wife Ger·ty \'gert-ē\ Theresa 1896–1957 née *Rad·nitz* \'räd-,nits\ Am. (Czech-born) biochemists
Cor·mack \'kòr-mək\ Allan MacLeod 1924–   Am. (So. African-born) physicist
Cor·neille \kòr-'nā\ Pierre 1606–1684 Fr. dram.
Cor·ne·lia \kòr-'nēl-yə, -'nē-lē-ə\ 2d cent. B.C. *Mother of the Gracchi* Rom. matron
Cornelia *d* 67? B.C. *wife of Julius Caesar*
Cor·ne·lius \kòr-'nāl-yəs, -'nä-lē-əs\ Pe·ter \'pāt-ər\ von 1783–1867 Ger. painter
Cor·nell \kòr-'nel\ Ezra 1807–1874 Am. financier & philanthropist
Cornell Katharine 1893–1974 Am. actress
Corn·forth \'kòrn-fərth, -,fō(ə)rth, -,fó(ə)rth\ John Warcup 1917–   Brit. (Austral.-born) chem.
Corn·wal·lis \kòrn-'wäl-əs\ 1st Marquis 1738–1805 *Charles Cornwallis* Brit. gen. & statesman
Co·ro·na·do \,kòr-ə-'näd-(,)ō, ,kär-\ Francisco Vásquez de *ca* 1510–1554 Span. explorer of southwestern U.S.
Co·rot \kə-'rō, kò-\ Jean-Baptiste-Camille 1796–1875 Fr. painter
Cor·reg·gio \kə-'rej-(ē-,)ō\ 1494–1534 *Antonio Allegri da Correggio* Ital. painter
Cor·ri·gan \'kòr-i-gən\ Mairead 1944–   Irish peace worker
Cor·tés \kòr-'tez, 'kòr-\ Hernán *or* Hernando 1485–1547 Span. conqueror of Mexico
Cos·grave \'käz-,grāv\ Liam 1920–   prime min. of Ireland (1973–77)
Cosgrave William Thomas 1880–1965 *father of Liam* Irish statesman
Cos·ta Ca·bral \,kós(h)-tə-kə-'bräl\ António Bernardo da 1803–1889 *Conde de Thomar* Port. statesman
Cos·tel·lo \'käs-tə-,lō\ John Aloysius 1891–1976 prime min. of Ireland (1948–51; 1954–57)
Cot·ton \'kät-ᵊn\ Charles 1630–1687 Eng. author & translator
Cotton John 1585–1652 Eng. Puritan clergyman in America
Co·ty \kò-'tē, kō-\ René-Jules-Gustave 1882–1962 Fr. lawyer; 2d pres. of 4th Republic (1954–59)
Cou·lomb \kü-lōⁿ; 'kü-,läm, -,lōm, kü-'\ Charles-Augustin de 1736–1806 Fr. physicist
Cou·pe·rin \,küp-(ə-)'raⁿ\ François 1668–1733 Fr. composer
Cou·pe·rus \kü-'pā-rəs, -'per-əs\ Louis Marie Anne 1863–1923 Du. nov.
Cour·bet \kúr-'bā\ Gustave 1819–1877 Fr. painter
Cour·nand \kúr-'näⁿ\ André Frédéric 1895–1988 Am. (Fr.-born) physiol.
Cou·sin \kü-zaⁿ\ Victor 1792–1867 Fr. philos.
Cous·ins \'kəz-ᵊnz\ Norman 1912–   Am. editor & essayist
Cous·teau \kü-'stō\ Jacques-Yves 1910–   Fr. marine explorer
Co·var·ru·bias \,kō-və-'rü-bē-əs\ Miguel 1904–1957 Mex. artist
Cov·er·dale \'kəv-ər-,dāl\ Miles 1488?–1569 Eng. Bible translator
Cow·ard \'kaú-(ə)rd\ Sir Noël Peirce 1899–1973 Eng. actor & dram.
Cow·ell \'kaú(-ə)l\ Henry Dixon 1887–1965 Am. composer
Cow·en \'kaú-ən, 'kō-\ Sir Zelman 1919–   gov.-gen. of Australia (1977–82)
Cowl \'kaú(ə)l\ Jane 1883–1950 orig. *Cowles* Am. actress
Cow·ley \'kaú-lē\ Abraham 1618–1667 Eng. poet
Cowley Malcolm 1898–1989 Am. lit. critic
Cow·per \'kü-pər, 'kúp-ər, 'kaú-pər\ William 1731–1800 Eng. poet
Cox·ey \'käk-sē\ Jacob Sechler 1854–1951 Am. polit. reformer
Coz·zens \'kəz-ᵊnz\ James Gould 1903–1978 Am. author
Crabbe \'krab\ George 1754–1832 Eng. poet
Craig·av·on \krā-'gav-ən\ 1st Viscount 1871–1940 *James Craig* Brit. statesman; 1st prime min. of Northern Ireland (1921–40)
Crai·gie \'krā-gē\ Sir William Alexander 1867–1957 Brit. philologist & lexicographer
Cram \'kram\ Donald James 1919–   Am. chem.
Cram Ralph Adams 1863–1942 Am. architect & author
Cra·nach \'krä-,äk\ Lucas 1472–1553 Ger. painter & engraver
Cranborne Viscount — see Robert CECIL

Crane \'krān\ (Harold) Hart 1899–1932 Am. poet
Crane Stephen 1871–1900 Am. writer
Crane Walter 1845–1915 Eng. artist
Cran·mer \'kran-mər\ Thomas 1489–1556 Eng. reformer; archbishop of Canterbury (1533–56)
Cras·sus \'kras-əs\ Marcus Licinius 115?–53 B.C. *Di·ves* \'dī-(ˌ)vēz\ Rom. polit.
Crazy Horse \'krā-zē-ˌhȯrs\ 1842–1877 *Ta-sunko-witko* or *Tashunca⸗ Uitco* Sioux Indian chief
Cré·bil·lon \ˌkrā-bē-'(y)ȯⁿ\ 1674–1762 pseud. of *Prosper Jolyot* Fr. dram.
Cre·mer \'krē-mər\ Sir William Randal 1838–1908 Eng. pacifist
Cres·ton \'kres-tən\ Paul 1906–1985 orig. *Giuseppe Guttoveggio* Am. composer
Crève·coeur \krev-'kər, krēv-, -'kü(ə)r\ Michel-Guillaume-Jean de 1735–1813 pseud. *J. Hector St. John* Am. (Fr.-born) essayist
Crich·ton \'krīt-ᵊn\ James 1560–1582 *the Admirable Crichton* Scot. man of letters
Crick \'krik\ Francis Harry Compton 1916–   Brit. biophysicist
Crile \'krī(ə)l\ George Washington 1864–1943 Am. surgeon
Cripps \'krips\ Sir (Richard) Stafford 1889–1952 Brit. statesman
Cri·spi \'kris-pē, 'krēs-\ Francesco 1819–1901 Ital. statesman; premier (1887–91; 1893–96)
Cris·ti·ani \ˌkris-tē-'än-ē\ Alfredo 1947–   pres. of El Salvador (1989–)
Cro·ce \'krō-(ˌ)chā\ Benedetto 1866–1952 Ital. philos. & statesman
Crock·ett \'kräk-ət\ David 1786–1836 *Davy* Am. frontiersman & polit.
Croe·sus \'krē-səs\ *d ca* 546 B.C. king of Lydia (*ca* 560–546)
Cro·ker \'krō-kər\ John Wilson 1780–1857 Brit. essayist & editor
Cromer Earl of — see Evelyn BARING
Cromp·ton \'kräm(p)-tən\ Samuel 1753–1827 Eng. inventor of the spinning mule
Crom·well \'kräm-ˌwel, 'krəm-, -wəl\ Oliver 1599–1658 Eng. gen. & statesman; lord protector of England (1653–58) — Crom·well·ian \ˌkräm-'wel-ē-ən, -wəl-\ *adj*
Cromwell Richard 1626–1712 *son of Oliver* lord protector (1658–59)
Cromwell Thomas 1485?–1540 Earl of *Essex* Eng. statesman
Cro·nin \'krō-nən\ Archibald Joseph 1896–1981 Eng. physician & nov.
Cronin James Watson 1931–   Am. physicist
Cron·je \'krȯn-'yä\ Piet Arnoldus *ca* 1835–1911 Boer leader & gen.
Crookes \'krúks\ Sir William 1832–1919 Eng. physicist & chem.
Cross \'krȯs\ Wilbur Lucius 1862–1948 Am. educ. & polit.
Crouse \'kraús\ Russel 1893–1966 Am. journalist & dram.
Cru·den \'krüd-ᵊn\ Alexander 1701–1770 Scot. compiler of a biblical concordance
Cruik·shank \'krúk-ˌshaŋk\ George 1792–1878 Eng. caricaturist & illustrator
Cud·worth \'kad-(ˌ)wərth\ Ralph 1617–1688 Eng. philos.
Cul·pep·er \'kəl-ˌpep-ər\ *var of* COLEPEPER
Cum·mings \'kəm-iŋz\ Edward Estlin 1894–1962 known as *e. e. cummings* Am. poet
Cu·nha Tris·tão da \ˌtris-tən-də-'kü-nə, trēs(h)-ˌtaúⁿ-də-'kün-yə\ 1460–1540 Port. navigator & explorer
Cun·ning·ham \'kən-iŋ-ˌham, *chiefly Brit* -iŋ-əm\ Allan 1784–1842 Scot. author
Cunningham Merce 1919?–   Am. choreographer
Cu·rie \kyü-'rē, 'kyü(ə)r-(ˌ)ē\ Eve 1904–   *dau. of Marie & Pierre* Am. (Fr.-born) author
Curie Marie 1867–1934 née *Maria Skło·dow·ska* \sklə-'dȯf-skə, -'dȯv-\ Fr. (Pol.-born) chem.
Curie Pierre 1859–1906 *husband of Marie* Fr. chem.
Curie Joliot — see JOLIOT-CURIE
Cur·ley \'kər-lē\ James Michael 1874–1958 Am. polit.
Cur·ri·er \'kər-ē-ər, 'kə-rē-\ Nathaniel 1813–1888 Am. lithographer
Cur·ry \'kər-ē, 'kə-rē\ John Steuart 1897–1946 Am. painter
Cur·tin \'kərt-ᵊn\ John 1885–1945 Austral. polit.; prime min. (1941–45)
Cur·tis \'kərt-əs\ Charles 1860–1936 vice pres. of the U.S. (1929–33)
Curtis Cyrus Hermann Kotzschmar 1850–1933 Am. publisher
Curtis George Ticknor 1812–1894 Am. lawyer & writer
Curtis George William 1824–1892 Am. author & editor
Cur·tiss \'kərt-əs\ Glenn Hammond 1878–1930 Am. aviator & inventor
Cur·ti·us \'kürt-sē-əs\ Ernst 1814–1896 Ger. hist. & archaeol.
Cur·wen \'kər-wən\ John 1816–1880 Eng. music teacher
Cur·zon \'kərz-ᵊn\ George Nathaniel 1859–1925 1st Baron & 1st Marquis *Curzon of Ked·le·ston* \'ked-ᵊl-stən\ Eng. statesman; viceroy of India (1899–1905)
Cush·ing \'kúsh-iŋ\ Caleb 1800–1879 Am. lawyer & diplomat
Cushing Harvey 1869–1939 Am. surgeon
Cushing Richard James 1895–1970 Am. cardinal
Cush·man \'kúsh-mən\ Charlotte Saunders 1816–1876 Am. actress
Cus·ter \'kəs-tər\ George Armstrong 1839–1876 Am. gen.
Cuth·bert \'kəth-bərt\ Saint 635?–687 Eng. monk
Cu·vier \k(y)ü-vē-ˌā, kūē-vyā\ Baron Georges 1769–1832 orig. *Jean⸗ Léopold-Nicolas-Frédéric Cuvier* Fr. naturalist
Cuyp *or* Cuijp \'kīp\ Aelbert Jacobsz 1620–1691 Du. painter
Cyn·e·wulf \'kin-ə-ˌwúlf\ *or* Cyn·wulf \'kin-ˌwúlf\ 9th cent. Anglo⸗ Saxon poet
Cyp·ri·an \'sip-rē-ən\ Saint *d* 258 *Thascius Caecilius Cyprianus* Christian martyr; bishop of Carthage (*ca* 248–258)
Cy·ran·kie·wicz \ˌ(t)sir-ən-'kyä-vich\ Józef 1911–1989 Pol. polit.; prime min. (1947–52; 1954–70)
Cy·ra·no de Ber·ge·rac \ˌsir-ə-ˌnō-də-'ber-zhə-ˌrak\ Savinien de 1619–1655 Fr. poet & soldier
Cyr·il \'sir-əl\ Saint *ca* 827–869 *Constantine* apostle to the Slavs
Cy·rus II \'sī-rəs\ *ca* 585–*ca* 529 B.C. *the Great* or *the Elder* king of Persia (*ca* 550–529)
Cyrus 424?–401 B.C. *the Younger* Persian prince & satrap
Czer·ny \'cher-nē, 'chɔr-\ Carl 1791–1857 Austrian pianist & composer
D', De, Du, etc. for many names beginning with these elements see the specific family names
Da·guerre \də-'ge(ə)r\ Louis-Jacques-Mandé 1789–1851 Fr. painter; inventor of the daguerreotype
Daim·ler \'dīm-lər\ Gottlieb Wilhelm 1834–1900 Ger. automotive manufacturer
Da·kin \'dā-kən\ Henry Drys·dale \'drīz-ˌdāl\ 1880–1952 Eng. chem.

Da·la·dier \də-'läd-ē-ˌā, ˌdal-əd-'yā\ Édouard 1884–1970 Fr. statesman
Da·lai La·ma \ˌdäl-ˌī-'läm-ə\ 1935–   *Tenzin Gyatso* Tibetan religious & political leader
D' Al·bert \'dal-bərt\ Eugen Francis Charles 1864–1932 Scot. pianist & composer
Dalcroze Émile Jaques — see Émile JAQUES-DALCROZE
Dale \'dā(ə)l\ Sir Henry Hallett 1875–1968 Eng. physiol.
Dale Sir Thomas *d* 1619 Eng. colonial administrator in Virginia (1611–16)
Da·lén \'dä-lən\ Nils Gustaf 1869–1937 Swed. inventor
Da·ley \'dā-lē\ Richard Joseph 1902–1976 Am. polit.
Dalhousie Earl & Marquis of — see RAMSAY
Da·lí \'däl-ē, *by himself* dä-'lē\ Salvador 1904–1989 Span. surrealistic painter — Da·li·esque \ˌdäl-ē-'esk\ *adj*
Dal·las \'dal-əs, -is\ George Mifflin 1792–1864 vice pres. of the U.S. (1845–49)
Dal·rym·ple \dal-'rim-pəl, 'dal-ˌ\ Sir James 1619–1695 1st Viscount *Stair* Scot. jurist
Dalrymple Sir John 1673–1747 2d Earl of *Stair* Brit. gen. & diplomat
Dal·ton \'dȯlt-ᵊn\ Baron 1887–1962 *Hugh Dalton* Brit. polit.
Dalton John 1766–1844 Eng. chem. & physicist
Da·ly \'dā-lē\ (John) Augustin 1838–1899 Am. dram. & theater manager
Dam \'dam, 'däm\ (Carl Peter) Henrik 1895–1976 Dan. biochem.
Da·mien \'dā-mē-ən, ˌdam-ē-'aⁿ\ Father 1840–1889 orig. *Joseph de Veuster* Belg. R.C. missionary to lepers on Molokai
Dam·pier \'dam-pē-ər\ William 1652–1715 Eng. buccaneer & navigator
Dam·rosch \'dam-ˌräsh\ Walter Johannes 1862–1950 Am. (Ger.-born) musician & conductor
Da·na \'dā-nə\ Charles Anderson 1819–1897 Am. newspaper editor
Dana James Dwight 1813–1895 Am. geologist
Dana Richard Henry 1815–1882 Am. lawyer & author
Dane \'dān\ Clemence 1888–1965 pseud. of *Winifred Ash·ton* \'ash-tən\ Eng. nov.
Dan·iel \'dan-yəl\ Samuel 1562?–1619 Eng. poet
Dan·iels \'dan-yəlz\ Josephus 1862–1948 Am. journalist & statesman
Da·ni·lo·va \də-'nē-lə-və\ Aleksandra 1904–   Russ. ballet dancer in U.S.
D'An·nun·zio \dä-'nün(t)-sē-ˌō\ Gabriele 1863–1938 Ital. author & soldier
Dan·te \'dän-(ˌ)tā, 'dan-, -(ˌ)tē; 'dant-ē, 'dänt-\ 1265–1321 *Dante* or *Durante Ali·ghie·ri* \ˌal-əg-'ye(ə)r-ē\ Ital. poet — Dan·te·an \'dant-ē-ən, 'dänt-\ *or* Dan·tes·can \dan-'tes-kən, dän-\ *or* Dan·tesque \-'tesk\ *adj*
Dan·ton \dä⁻-tōⁿ\ Georges-Jacques 1759–1794 Fr. revolutionary
Dare \'da(ə)r, 'de(ə)r\ Virginia 1587–? 1st child born in America of Eng. parents
Da·ri·us \də-'rī-əs\ name of 3 kings of Persia: esp. I 550–486 B.C. (reigned 522–486) *Darius Hys·tas·pes* \his-'tas-pəs\; *the Great*
Dar·lan \'där-ˌläⁿ\ Jean-Louis-Xavier-François 1881–1942 Fr. admiral
Darn·ley \'därn-lē\ Lord 1545–1567 *Henry Stewart* or *Stuart; husband of Mary, Queen of Scots*
Dar·row \'dar-(ˌ)ō\ Clarence Seward 1857–1938 Am. lawyer & author
Dar·win \'där-wən\ Charles Robert 1809–1882 Eng. naturalist
Darwin Erasmus 1731–1802 *grandfather of C. R.* Eng. physiol. & poet
Dau·bi·gny \ˌdō-bēn-'yē, ˌdō-bē-nyē\ Charles-François 1817–1878 Fr. painter
Dau·det \dō-'dā\ Alphonse 1840–1897 Fr. nov.
Daudet Léon 1867–1942 *son of Alphonse* Fr. journalist & writer
Dau·mier \dō-myā, 'dō-mē-ˌā\ Honoré 1808–1879 Fr. caricaturist & painter
Daus·set \dō-se, -sä\ Jean-Baptiste-Gabriel 1916–   Fr. physician
Dav·e·nant *or* D'Av·e·nant \'dav-(ə-)nənt\ Sir William 1606–1668 Eng. poet & dram.; poet laureate (1638–68)
Dav·en·port \'dav-ən-ˌpō(ə)rt, 'dav-ᵊm-, -ˌpó(ə)rt\ John 1597–1670 Eng. clergyman; founder of New Haven colony
Da·vid I \'dā-vəd\ *ca* 1082–1153 king of Scotland (1124–53)
Da·vid \'däv-ət\ Gerard *ca* 1460–1523 Du. painter
Da·vid \'dä-ˌvēd\ Jacques-Louis 1748–1825 Fr. painter
Da·vid d'An·gers \dä⁻-ˌzhä\ Pierre-Jean 1788–1856 Fr. sculptor
Da·vid·son \'dā-vəd-sən\ Jo 1883–1952 Am. sculptor
Davidson Randall Thomas 1848–1930 archbishop of Canterbury (1903–28)
Da·vies \'dā-vēz\ Arthur Bowen 1862–1928 Am. painter
Dá·vi·la Pa·di·lla \'däv-i-lə-pä-'dē-(y)ə\ Agustín 1562–1604 Mex. monk & hist.
Da·vis \'dā-vəs\ Bette 1908–1989 orig. *Ruth Elizabeth Davis* Am. actress
Davis Dwight Filley 1879–1945 Am. statesman
Davis Elmer Holmes 1890–1958 Am. radio broadcaster & news commentator
Davis Harold Le·noir \lə-'nō(ə)r, -'nȯ(ə)r\ 1896–1960 Am. writer
Davis Jefferson 1808–1889 Am. statesman; pres. of Confed. states (1861–65)
Da·vis·son \'dā-və-sən\ Clinton Joseph 1881–1958 Am. physicist
Da·vout \də-'vü\ Louis-Nicolas 1770–1823 Duc *d'Au·er·städt* \daú(ə)r-ˌstet\ & Prince *d'Eck·mühl* \'dek-ˌmyül\ marshal of France
Da·vy \'dā-vē\ Sir Humphry 1778–1829 Eng. chem.
Dawes \'dȯz\ Charles Gates 1865–1951 Am. lawyer & financier; vice pres. of U.S. (1925–29)
Daw·son \'dȯs-ᵊn\ Sir John William 1820–1899 Canad. geologist
Day \'dā\ Clarence Shepard, Jr. 1874–1935 Am. author
Day Thomas 1748–1789 Eng. author
Day William Rufus 1849–1923 Am. statesman & jurist
Da·yan \dä-'yän\ Moshe 1915–1981 Israeli soldier and statesman
Day–Lew·is \'dā-'lü-əs\ Cecil 1904–1972 pseud. *Nicholas Blake* Brit. writer; poet laureate (1968–72)
De·ák \'dā-ˌäk\ Fe·renc \'fer-ˌen(t)s\ 1803–1876 Hung. statesman

---

\ə\ abut \ᵊ\ kitten, F table \ər\ further \a\ ash \ā\ ace \ä\ cot, cart
\aú\ out \ch\ chin \e\ bet \ē\ easy \g\ go \i\ hit \ī\ ice \j\ job
\ŋ\ sing \ō\ go \ȯ\ law \ȯi\ boy \th\ thin \t͟h\ the \ü\ loot \ú\ foot
\y\ yet \zh\ vision \á, k̲, ⁿ, œ, œ̄, ᵫ, ᵬ, ᵺ\ *see* Guide to Pronunciation

Dean \'dēn\ Sir Patrick 1909–   Brit. diplomat
Deane \'dēn\ Silas 1737–1789 Am. lawyer & diplomat
Dear·den \'di(ə)rd-ᵊn\ John Francis 1907–1988 Am. cardinal
De·bierne \də-'bye(ə)rn\ André-Louis 1874–1949 Fr. chem.
De·breu \də-'brœ\ Gerard 1921–   Am. (Fr.-born) econ.
Debs \'debz\ Eugene Victor 1855–1926 Am. socialist
De·bus·sy \ˌdeb-yü-'sē, ˌdāb-; də-'byü-sē\ (Achille-) Claude 1862–1918 Fr. composer — De·bus·sy·an \ˌdeb-yü-'sē-ən, ˌdāb-; də-'byü-sē-ən\ adj
De·bye \də-'bī\ Peter Joseph William 1884–1966 Du.-born physicist in America
De·ca·tur \di-'kāt-ər\ Stephen 1779–1820 Am. naval officer
De·cazes \də-käz\ Duc Élie 1780–1860 Fr. statesman
De·cius \'dē-sh(ē-)əs\ Gaius Messius Quintus Trajanus ca 201–251 Rom. emp. (249–51)
Dee·ping \'dē-piŋ\ (George) Warwick 1877–1950 Eng. nov.
Deere \'di(ə)r\ John 1804–1886 Am. inventor
Def·fand, du \də-fäⁿ\ Marquise 1697–1780 née Marie de Vichy-Chamrond \-shäⁿ-rōⁿ\ Fr. woman of letters
De·foe \di-'fō\ Daniel 1660–1731 Eng. journalist & nov.
De For·est \di-'fȯr-əst, -'fär-\ Lee 1873–1961 Am. inventor
De·gas \də-gä\ (Hilaire-Germain-) Edgar 1834–1917 Fr. artist
de Gaulle Charles—see GAULLE
Deh·melt \'dā-məlt\ Hans Georg 1922–   Am. (Ger.-born) physicist
Dei·sen·hof·er \'diz-ən-ˌhōf-ər\ Johann 1943–   Ger. biochem.
Dek·ker \'dek-ər\ Thomas 1572?–?1632 Eng. dram.
de Klerk \də-'klərk\ Frederik Willem 1936–   pres. of Republic of So. Africa (1989–   )
de Koo·ning \də-'kō-niŋ\ Willem 1904–   Am. (Du.-born) painter
de Kruif \də-'krīf\ Paul Henry 1890–1971 Am. bacteriol. & author
De·la·croix \ˌdel-ə-'k(r)wä\ (Ferdinand-Victor-) Eugène 1798–1863 Fr. painter
de la Mare \ˌdel-ə-'ma(ə)r, -'me(ə)r\ Walter John 1873–1956 Eng. poet & nov.
De·land \də-'land\ Margaret 1857–1945 née Margaretta Wade Campbell Am. nov.
De La Rey \ˌdel-ə-'rī, -'rā\ Jacobus Hercules 1847–1914 Boer gen. & statesman
De·la·roche \ˌdel-ə-'rōsh, -'rȯsh\ (Hippolyte-) Paul 1797–1859 Fr. painter
De·la·vigne \ˌdel-ə-'vēn, -'vēn-yə\ Jean-François-Casimir 1793–1843 Fr. poet & dram.
De La Warr \'del-ə-ˌwa(ə)r, -ˌwe(ə)r\ Baron 1577–1618 Thomas West; Lord Delaware Eng. colonial administrator in America
Del·brück \'del-ˌbrʊk, -ˌbrük\ Max 1906–1981 Am. (Ger.-born) biol.
De·led·da \dā-'led-ə, də-\ Grazia 1875–1936 Ital. author
De·libes \də-'lēb\ (Clément-Philibert-) Léo 1836–1891 Fr. composer
De·lius \'dē-lē-əs, 'dēl-yəs\ Frederick 1862–1934 Eng. composer
Del·la Rob·bia \ˌdel-ə-'räb-ē-ə, -'rȯb-\ Luca 1399(or 1400)–1482 orig. Luca di Simone di Marco Florentine sculptor
De Long \də-'lȯŋ\ George Washington 1844–1881 Am. naval officer & explorer
De·lorme or de l'Orme \də-'lȯ(ə)rm\ Philibert 1515?–1570 Fr. architect
de Mille \də-'mil\ Agnes George 1909?–   Am. dancer & choreographer
de·Mille \də-'mil\ Cec·il \'ses-əl\ Blount \'blənt\ 1881–1959 Am. motion-picture producer
De·moc·ri·tus \di-'mäk-rət-əs\ ca 460–ca 370 B.C. the Laughing Philosopher Greek philos.
De Mor·gan \di-'mȯr-gən\ William Frend 1839–1917 Eng. artist & nov.
De·mos·the·nes \di-'mäs-thə-ˌnēz\ 384–322 B.C. Athenian orator & statesman — De·mos·then·ic \di-ˌmäs-'then-ik, ˌdē-\ adj
Demp·sey \'dem(p)-sē\ William Harrison 1895–1983 Jack Am. boxer
Deng Xiaoping—see TENG HSIAO-P'ING
De·ni·ker \ˌdä-nē-'ke(ə)r\ Joseph 1852–1918 Fr. anthropol.
De·nis or De·nys \'den-əs, də-nē\ Saint d 258? 1st bishop of Paris; patron saint of France
Dent \'dent\ Joseph Mal·a·by \'mal-ə-bē\ 1849–1926 Eng. publisher
De·pew \di-'pyü\ Chauncey Mitchell 1834–1928 Am. lawyer & polit.
De Quin·cey \di-'kwin(t)-sē, -'kwin-zē\ Thomas 1785–1859 Eng. author
De·rain \də-raⁿ\ André 1880–1954 Fr. painter
Der·win·ski \dər-'win-skē\ Edward Joseph 1926–   U.S. secy. of veterans affairs (1989–   )
Der·zha·vin \der-'zhäv-ən\ Gavrila Romanovich 1743–1816 Russ. poet
De·sai \de-'sī\ Morarji Ranchhodji 1896–   prime min. of India (1977–79)
De·saix de Vey·goux \də-ˌsäd-ə-(ˌ)vā-'gü\ Louis-Charles-Antoine 1768–1800 Fr. gen.
De·sargues \də-'zärg\ Gérard or Girard 1591–1661 Fr. math.
Des·cartes \dā-'kärt\ René 1596–1650 L. Renatus Cartesius Fr. math. & philos. — Car·te·sian \kär-'tē-zhən\ n
Des·cha·nel \ˌdā-shə-'nel\ Paul-Eugène-Louis 1855–1922 Fr. statesman; pres. of France (1920)
De Se·ver·sky \də-sə-'ver-skē\ Alexander Procofieff 1894–1974 Am. (Russ.-born) aeronautical engineer
Des·mou·lins \ˌdā-mü-laⁿ\ Camille 1760–1794 Lucie-Simplice-Camille-Benoît Desmoulins Fr. revolutionary
de So·to Hernando — see SOTO
Des Prez Josquin — see JOSQUIN DES PREZ
Des·saix \de-'sā\ Comte Joseph-Marie 1764–1834 Fr. gen.
Des·sa·lines \ˌdäs-ə-'lēn, ˌdes-\ Jean-Jacques 1758?–1806 emp. as Jacques I of Haiti (1804–06)
De·taille \də-'tī\ (Jean-Baptiste-) Édouard 1848–1912 Fr. painter
De·us Ra·mos \dā-əsh-'ram-(ˌ)üsh\ João \zhwaúⁿ\ de 1830–1896 Port. poet
De Va·le·ra \ˌdev-ə-'ler-ə, -'lir-ə\ Ea·mon \'ā-mən\ 1882–1975 Irish polit.; prime min. of Ireland (1937–48; 1951–54; 1957–59); pres. of Ireland (1959–73)
De Vere \də-'vi(ə)r\ Aubrey Thomas 1814–1902 Irish poet
Dev·er·eux \'dev-ə-ˌrü(ks)\ Robert 1566–1601 2d Earl of Essex Eng. soldier & courtier
Devonshire dukes of — see CAVENDISH
De Vo·to \di-'vōt-(ˌ)ō\ Bernard Augustine 1897–1955 Am. author
De Vries Hugo — see VRIES
Dew·ar \'d(y)ü-ər\ Sir James 1842–1923 Scot. chem. & physicist

De Wet Christiaan Rudolph — see WET
Dew·ey \'d(y)ü-ē\ George 1837–1917 Am. admiral
Dewey John 1859–1952 Am. philos. & educ. — Dew·ey·an \-ən\ adj
Dewey Melvil 1851–1931 Am. librarian
Dewey Thomas Edmund 1902–1971 Am. lawyer & polit.
De Witt Johan — see WITT
Dia·ghi·lev \dē-'äg-ə-ˌlef\ Sergey Pavlovich 1872–1929 Russ. ballet producer & art critic
Di·as \'dē-ˌäsh\ Bartholomeu ca 1450–1500 Port. navigator; disc. Cape of Good Hope
Dí·az \'dē-ˌäts\ Armando 1861–1928 Duca della Vittoria Ital. gen.; marshal of Italy
Dí·az \'dē-ˌäs, -ˌäz\ Porfirio 1830–1915 José de la Cruz Porfirio Mex. gen.; pres. of Mexico (1877–80; 1884–1911)
Díaz de Vivar — see CID
Dí·az Or·daz \ˌdē-ə-sȯr-'däz\ Gustavo 1911–1979 pres. of Mexico (1964–70)
Dick \'dik\ George Frederick 1881–1967 & Gladys Henry 1881–1963 Am. physicians
Dick·ens \'dik-ənz\ Charles John Huffam 1812–1870 pseud. Boz \'bäz, 'bōz\ Eng. nov. — Dick·en·si·an \dik-'en-zē-ən, -sē-\ adj
Dick·in·son \'dik-ən-sən\ Emily Elizabeth 1830–1886 Am. poet
Dickinson John 1732–1808 Am. statesman
Di·de·rot \'dē-drō, ˌdēd-ə-ˌrō\ Denis 1713–1784 Fr. encyclopedist
Die·fen·ba·ker \'dē-fən-ˌbä-kər\ John George 1895–1979 prime min. of Canada (1957–63)
Diels \'dē(ə)lz, 'dē(ə)ls\ Otto Paul Hermann 1876–1954 Ger. chem.
Die·sel \'dē-zəl, -səl\ Rudolf 1858–1913 Ger. mechanical engineer
Diez \'dēts\ Friedrich Christian 1794–1876 Ger. philologist
Dig·by \'dig-bē\ Sir Ken·elm \'ken-ˌelm\ 1603–1665 Eng. naval commander, diplomat, & author
Dill \'dil\ Sir John Greer 1881–1944 Brit. gen.
Dil·lon \'dil-ən\ John 1851–1927 Irish nationalist polit.
Di·Mag·gio \də-'mäzh-ē-(ˌ)ō, -'maj-(ē)-(ˌ)ō\ Joseph Paul 1914–   Am. baseball player
Di·ne·sen \'dē-nə-sən, 'din-ə-\ Isak \'ē-ˌsäk\ 1885–1962 pseud. of Karen Christence Dinesen, Baroness Blixen-Finecke Dan. author
Din·wid·die \din-'wid-ē\ Robert 1693–1770 Eng. colonial administrator in America
Di·o·cle·tian \ˌdī-ə-'klē-shən\ 245(or 248)–313(or 316) Gaius Aurelius Valerius Diocletianus Rom. emp. (284–305)
Di·o·ge·nes \dī-'äj-ə-ˌnēz\ d ca 320 B.C. Greek Cynic philos.
Di·o·ny·sius \ˌdī-ə-'nis(h)-ē-əs, -'nish-əs, -'nī-sē-əs\ ca 430–367 B.C. the Elder Greek tyrant of Syracuse (405–367)
Dionysius the Younger tyrant of Syracuse (367–356; 354–343 B.C.)
Dionysius Ex·ig·u·us \eg-'zig-yə-wəs\ ca 500–ca 560 Christian monk; introduced method of reckoning the Christian era
Dionysius of Alexandria Saint ca 200–ca 265 theol. & bishop of Alexandria (247)
Dionysius of Halicarnassus fl ca 20 B.C. Greek scholar
Di·rac \di-'rak\ Paul Adrien Maurice 1902–1984 Eng. physicist
Dirk·sen \dərk-sən\ Everett McKinley 1896–1969 Am. polit.
Dis·ney \'diz-nē\ Walter Elias 1901–1966 Am. film producer
Dis·rae·li \diz-'rā-lē\ Benjamin 1804–1881 1st Earl of Bea·cons·field \'bē-kənz-ˌfēld\ Brit. polit. & author; prime min. (1868; 1874–80)
Dit·mars \'dit-ˌmärz\ Raymond Lee 1876–1942 Am. naturalist
Dix \'diks\ Dorothea Lynde 1802–1887 Am. social reformer
Dix Dorothy — see Elizabeth Meriwether GILMER
Dix·on \'dik-sən\ Jeremiah d 1777 Eng. surveyor in America
Dmow·ski \də-'mȯf-skē, 'mȯv-\ Roman 1864–1939 Pol. statesman
Dö·be·rei·ner \'də(r)b-ə-ˌri-nər, 'dēb-\ Johann Wolfgang 1780–1849 Ger. chem.
Do·bie \'dō-bē\ James Frank 1888–1964 Am. folklorist
Do·brée \'dō-ˌbrā\ Bon·a·my \'bän-ə-mē\ 1891–1974 Eng. scholar
Dob·son \'däb-sən\ (Henry) Austin 1840–1921 Eng. poet & essayist
Dodge \'däj\ Mary Elizabeth 1831–1905 née Mapes \'māps\ Am. author
Dodg·son \'däj-sən, 'däd-\ Charles Lut·widge \'lət-wij\ 1832–1898 pseud. Lewis Car·roll \'kar-əl\ Eng. math. & writer
Dods·ley \'dädz-lē\ Robert 1703–1764 Eng. author & bookseller
Doi·sy \'dȯi-zē\ Edward Adelbert 1893–1986 Am. biochem.
Dole \'dōl\ Elizabeth Hanford 1936–   U.S. secy. of transportation (1983–87); secy. of labor (1989–   )
Dole Sanford Ballard 1844–1926 Am. jurist; pres. (1894–1900) & gov. (1900–03) of Hawaii
Doll·fuss \'dȯl-ˌfüs\ Engelbert 1892–1934 Austrian statesman
Do·magk \'dō-ˌmäk\ Gerhard 1895–1964 Ger. bacteriol.
Do·me·ni·chi·no \(ˌ)dō-ˌmā-nə-'kē-(ˌ)nō\ 1581–1641 Domenico Zam·pie·ri \ˌtsäm-pē-'e(ə)r-ē, ˌzäm-\ Ital. painter
Dom·i·nic \'däm-ə-(ˌ)nik\ Saint ca 1170–1221 Domingo de Guz·mán \güz-'män, güs-\ Span.-born founder of the Dominican order of friars
Do·mi·tian \də-'mish-ən\ A.D. 51–96 Titus Flavius Domitianus Rom. emp. (81–96)
Do·na·tel·lo \ˌdän-ə-'tel-(ˌ)ō\ 1386?–1466 Donato de Betto di Bardi Florentine sculptor
Don·gen \'dȯn-ən\ Kees van 1877–1968 orig. Cornelis Theodorus Maria Dongen Fr. (Du.-born) painter
Dö·nitz \'də(r)n-əts, 'dœn-\ Karl 1891–1980 Ger. admiral
Don·i·zet·ti \ˌdän-ə-'zet-ē, ˌdōn-\ Gaetano 1797–1848 Ital. composer
Donne \'dən also \'dän\ John 1572–1631 Eng. poet & clergyman — Donn·ean or Donn·ian \ˌdän-ē-ən, 'dän-\ adj
Don·o·van \'dän-ə-vən, 'dən-\ Raymond J. 1930–   U.S. secy. of labor (1981–85)
Donovan William Joseph 1883–1959 Wild Bill Am. lawyer & gen.
Doo·lit·tle \'dü-ˌlit-ᵊl\ James Harold 1896–   Am. aviator & gen.
Dopp·ler \'däp-lər\ Christian Johann 1803–1853 Austrian physicist
Do·ra·ti \də-'rät-ē\ An·tal \'än-ˌtäl\ 1906–1988 Am. (Hung.-born) conductor
Do·ré \dȯ-'rā, də-\ (Paul-) Gustave 1832–1883 Fr. illustrator & painter
Dor·ge·les \ˌdȯr-zhə-'les\ Roland 1886–1973 Fr. nov.
Dor·nier \'dȯrn-ˌyā\ Claudius 1884–1969 Ger. airplane builder
Dorr \'dȯ(ə)r\ Thomas Wilson 1805–1854 Am. lawyer & polit.
Dorset 1st Earl of — see Thomas SACKVILLE
Dos Pas·sos \däs-'pas-əs\ John Roderigo 1896–1970 Am. writer

Dos·to·yev·ski \ˌdäs-tə-'yef-skē, -'yev-\ Fyodor Mikhaylovich 1821–1881 Russ. nov. — Dos·to·yev·ski·an or Dos·to·ev·ski·an \-skē-ən\ adj
Dou or Douw \'daů\ Gerrit or Gerard 1613–1675 Du. painter
Dough·ty \'daůt-ē\ Charles Montagu 1843–1926 Eng. poet & traveler
Doug·las \'dəg-ləs\ John Shol·to \'shōl-(ˌ)tō\ 1844–1900 8th Marquis & Earl of Queens·ber·ry \'kwēnz-ˌber-ē, -b(ə-)rē\ Scot. boxing patron
Douglas Stephen Arnold 1813–1861 Am. polit.
Douglas William Orville 1898–1980 Am. jurist
Douglas–Home — see HOME
Douglas of Kir·tle·side \'kərt-ᵊl-ˌsīd\ 1st Baron 1893–1969 William Sholto Douglas Brit. air marshal
Doug·lass \'dəg-ləs\ Frederick 1817–1895 orig. Frederick Augustus Washington Bailey Am. abolitionist
Dou·mer \dü-'mer\ Paul 1857–1932 pres. of France (1931–32)
Dou·mergue \dü-'merg\ Gaston 1863–1937 Fr. statesman; pres. of France (1924–31)
Dow·den \'daůd-ᵊn\ Edward 1843–1913 Irish lit. critic
Dow·ie \'daů-ē\ John Alexander 1847–1907 Scot.-born religious leader in America
Downes \'daůnz\ (Edwin) Olin \'ō-lən\ 1886–1955 Am. music critic
Dow·son \'daůs-ᵊn\ Ernest Christopher 1867–1900 Eng. lyric poet
Dox·ia·dis \ˌdok-sē-'ä-ˌthēs\ Konstantinos Apostolos 1913–1975 Greek architect
Doyle \'dȯi(ə)l\ Sir Arthur Co·nan \'kō-nən\ 1859–1930 Brit. physician, nov., & detective-story writer
D'Oyly Carte — see CARTE
Drach·mann \'dräk-mən\ Holger Henrik Herholdt 1846–1908 Dan. author
Dra·co \'drā-(ˌ)kō\ late 7th cent. B.C. Athenian lawgiver
Drake \'drāk\ Sir Francis 1540(or 1543)–1596 Eng. navigator & admiral
Dra·per \'drā-pər\ Henry 1837–1882 Am. astron.
Dray·ton \'drāt-ᵊn\ Michael 1563–1631 Eng. poet
Drei·ser \'drī-sər, -zər\ Theodore 1871–1945 Am. editor & nov.
Drew \'drü\ John 1827–1862 Am. (Irish-born) actor
Drew John 1853–1927 son of prec. Am. actor
Drey·fus \'drī-fəs, 'drā-; dre-füs\ Alfred 1859–1935 Fr. army officer
Driesch \'drēsh\ Hans Adolf Eduard 1867–1941 Ger. biol. & philos.
Drink·wa·ter \'driŋk-ˌwȯt-ər, -ˌwät-\ John 1882–1937 Eng. poet & dram.
Drou·et \drü-'e, -'ā\ Jean-Baptiste 1765–1844 Comte d'Er·lon \der-'lōⁿ\ Fr. gen.; marshal of France
Drum·mond \'drəm-ənd\ Henry 1851–1897 Scot. clergyman & writer
Drummond William Henry 1854–1907 Canad. (Irish-born) poet
Drummond of Haw·thorn·den \'hȯ-ˌthȯrn-dən\ William 1585–1649 Scot. poet
Dru·sus \'drü-səs\ 38–9 B.C. Ne·ro \'nē-(ˌ)rō, 'ni(ə)r-(ˌ)ō\ Claudius Drusus Ger·man·i·cus \(ˌ)jer-'man-i-kəs\ Rom. gen.
Dry·den \'drīd-ᵊn\ John 1631–1700 Eng. poet & dram.; poet laureate (1668–88) — Dry·de·ni·an \(')drī-'dē-nē-ən, -'den-ē-\ adj
Du Barry Comtesse — see Jeanne BARRY
Du·bois \d(y)ü-'bwä, dᵫ-bwä\ Paul 1829–1905 Fr. sculptor
Dubois (François-Clément-) Théodore 1837–1924 Fr. composer
Du Bois \d(y)ü-'bȯis\ William Edward Burghardt 1868–1963 Am. educ. & writer
Du·buf·fet \d(y)ü-bə-'fā, dᵫ-bᵫ-fe\ Jean 1901–1985 Fr. artist
Du Cange \d(y)ü-'känzh\ Sieur Charles Du Fresne 1610–1688 Fr. scholar & glossarist
Du Chail·lu \d(y)ü-'shal-(ˌ)ü, -'shī-(ˌ)ü\ Paul Belloni 1831–1903 Am. (Fr.-born) explorer in Africa
Du·champ \d(y)ü-'shäⁿ\ Marcel 1887–1968 Fr. painter
Du·com·mun \d(y)ü-kə-'mœⁿ\ Élie 1833–1906 Swiss journalist
Dudevant Aurore — see George SAND
Dud·ley \'dəd-lē\ Robert 1532(or 1533)–1588 1st Earl of Leicester Eng. courtier
Dudley Thomas 1576–1653 colonial administrator in Massachusetts Bay Colony
Duf·fer·in and Ava \ˌdəf-(ə-)rə-nə-'näv-ə\ 1st Marquis of 1826–1902 Frederick Temple Hamilton-Temple-Blackwood Brit. diplomat
Duff–Gor·don \'dəf-'gȯrd-ᵊn\ Lady Lucie 1821–1869 Eng. author
Duf·fy \'dəf-ē\ Sir Charles Gavan 1816–1903 Irish nationalist & Austral. polit.
Du·fy \d(y)ü-'fē\ Raoul 1877–1953 Fr. painter
Du Gard Roger Martin — see MARTIN DU GARD
Du Gues·clin Bertrand — see GUESCLIN
Du·ha·mel \d(y)ü-ä-'mel, dᵫ-ä-mel\ Georges 1884–1966 Fr. writer
Du·ka·kis \d(y)ü-'käk-is\ Michael Stanley 1933– Am. polit.
Duke \d(y)ük\ Benjamin Newton 1855–1929 & his bro. James Buchanan 1856–1925 Am. tobacco industrialists
Dul·bec·co \(ˌ)dəl-'bek-(ˌ)ō\ Renato 1914– Am. (Ital.-born) virologist
Dul·les \'dəl-əs\ John Foster 1888–1959 Am. diplomat; secy. of state (1953–59)
Du·mas \d(y)ü-'mä, d(y)ü-,\ Alexandre 1802–1870 Dumas père \'pe(ə)r\ Fr. nov. & dram.
Dumas Alexandre 1824–1895 Dumas fils \'fēs\ Fr. nov. & dram.
du Mau·rier \d(y)ü-'mȯr-ē-ˌā\ Dame Daphne 1907–1989 Brit. writer
du Mau·rier George Louis Palmella Busson 1834–1896 grandfather of prec. Brit. artist & nov.
Du·mou·riez \d(y)ü-'műr-ē-ˌā\ Charles-François du Périer 1739–1823 Fr. gen.
Du·nant \d(y)ü-'näⁿ\ Jean-Henri 1828–1910 Swiss philanthropist; founder of the Red Cross
Dun·bar \'dən-ˌbär\ Paul Laurence 1872–1906 Am. poet
Dunbar \'dən-ˌbär, ˌdən-'\ William 1460?–?1530 Scot. poet
Dun·can \'dən-kən\ Isadora 1877–1927 Am. dancer
Dun·das \ˌdən-'das\ Henry 1742–1811 1st Viscount Melville & Baron Dun·ira \ˌdə-'nīr-ə\ Brit. statesman
Dun·lop \'dən-ˌläp, 'dən-,\ John Boyd 1840–1921 Scot. inventor
Dunne \'dən\ Finley Peter 1867–1936 Am. humorist
Du·nois \d(y)ün-'wä\ Comte de 1403–1468 Jean d'Orléans; the bastard of Orléans Fr. gen.

Dun·sa·ny \ˌdən-'sä-nē\ 18th Baron 1878–1957 Edward John Moreton Drax Plunkett Irish poet & dram.
Duns Sco·tus \ˌdən(z)-'skōt-əs\ John 1266?–1308 Scot. scholastic theol.
Dun·stan \'dən(t)-stən\ Saint 924–988 archbishop of Canterbury (959–988)
Du·pleix \d(y)ü-'pleks\ Marquis Joseph-François 1697–1763 Fr. colonial administrator in India
Duplessis–Mornay — see Philippe de MORNAY
Du Pont \d(y)ü-'pänt, 'd(y)ü-,\ Éleuthère Irénée 1771–1834 son of P.S. Du Pont de Nemours Am. (Fr.-born) industrialist
Du Pont de Ne·mours \-də-nə-'mü(ə)r\ Pierre-Samuel 1739–1817 Fr. econ. & statesman
Du·quesne \d(y)ü-'kän\ Marquis Abraham 1610–1688 Fr. naval officer
Du·rant \d(y)ü-'rant\ William James 1885–1981 Am. educ. & writer
Dü·rer \'d(y)ůr-ər\ Albrecht 1471–1528 Ger. painter & engraver — Dü·rer·esque \d(y)ůr-ər-'esk, ˌdůr-\ adj
D'Ur·fey \'dər-fē\ Thomas 1653–1723 Eng. songwriter & dram.
Dur·kheim \důr-'kem\ Émile 1858–1917 Fr. sociol. — Dur·kheim·ian \-'kem-ē-ən\ adj
Du·roc \d(y)ü-'räk\ Géraud-Christophe-Michel 1772–1813 Duc de Frioul Fr. gen. under Napoleon
Dur·rell \'dər-əl, ˌdü-rəl\ Lawrence 1912– Eng. nov. & poet
Dür·ren·matt \'dur-ən-ˌmät, 'dür-\ Friedrich 1921– Swiss author
Du·ruy \ˌdür-(ē-)'wē\ Victor 1811–1894 Fr. hist.
Du·se \'dü-(ˌ)zā\ Eleonora 1858–1924 Ital. actress
Du·tra \'dü-trə\ Eurico Gaspar 1885–1974 Braz. gen.; pres. of Brazil (1946–51)
Du·va·lier \d(y)ü-'val-(ˌ)yā\ François 1907–1971 Papa Doc pres. of Haiti (1957–71)
Du·ve \'dü-və\ Christian René Marie Joseph 1917– Belg. (Eng.-born) physiol.
Du Vi·gneaud \d(y)ü-'vēn-(ˌ)yō\ Vincent 1901–1978 Am. biochem.
Dvo·řák \(də-)'vȯr-ˌzhäk\ Antonín 1841–1904 Bohemian composer
Dwig·gins \'dwig-ənz\ William Addison 1880–1956 Am. type designer
Dwight \'dwīt\ Timothy 1752–1817 Am. clergyman; pres. Yale U. (1795–1817)
Dwight Timothy 1828–1916 grandson of prec. Am. clergyman; pres. Yale U. (1886–99)
Dwyfor Earl of — see LLOYD GEORGE
Dyce \'dīs\ Alexander 1798–1869 Scot. editor
Dy·er \'dī(-ə)r\ John 1699–1757 Brit. poet
Dyer Mary d 1660 Am. Quaker martyr
Eads \'ēdz\ James Buchanan 1820–1887 Am. engineer & inventor
Ea·kins \'ā-kənz\ Thomas 1844–1916 Am. artist
Ear·hart \'e(ə)r-ˌhärt, ½(ə)r-\ Amelia 1897–1937 Am. aviator
Ear·ly \'ər-lē\ Ju·bal \'jü-bəl\ Anderson 1816–1894 Am. Confed. gen.
Earp \'ərp\ Wyatt 1848–1929 Am. lawman
East·man \'ēst-mən\ George 1854–1932 Am. inventor & industrialist
Eastman Max Forrester 1883–1969 Am. editor & writer
Ea·ton \'ēt-ᵊn\ Theophilus 1590–1658 Eng. colonial administrator in America; gov. of New Haven colony (1638–58)
Ebert \'ā-bərt\ Friedrich 1871–1925 pres. of Germany (1919–25)
Ec·cles \'ek-əlz\ Sir John Carew 1903– Brit. physiol.
Eccles Marriner Stoddard 1890–1977 Am. banker & econ.
Eche·ga·ray y Ei·za·guir·re \ˌā-chə-gə-'rī-ˌē-ˌä-thə-'gwi(ə)r-(ˌ)ā, -ˌē-ˌä-sə-\ José 1832–1916 Span. dram.
Eche·ver·ría \ˌā-chə-və-'rē-ə-'al-və-ˌrez, ˌech-ə-\ Luis 1922– pres. of Mexico (1970–76)
Eck \'ek\ Johann 1486–1543 orig. Maier Ger. R.C. theol.
Ecke·hart \'ek-ə-ˌhärt\ or Eck·art or Eck·hart \'ek-,(h)ärt\ Johannes 1260?–?1327 Meister Eckehart Ger. Dominican theol.; founder of Ger. mysticism
Eck·er·mann \'ek-ər-ˌmän, -mən\ Johann Peter 1792–1854 Ger. writer
Ed·ding·ton \'ed-iŋ-tən\ Sir Arthur Stanley 1882–1944 Eng. astron.
Ed·dy \'ed-ē\ Mary Morse 1821–1910 née Baker Am. founder of the Christian Science Church
Ed·el·man \'ed-ᵊl-mən\ Gerald Maurice 1929– Am. biochem.
Eden \'ēd-ᵊn\ (Robert) Anthony 1897–1977 Earl of Avon \'ā-vən\ Eng. statesman; prime min. (1955–57)
Edge·worth \'ej-(ˌ)wərth\ Maria 1767–1849 Brit. nov.
Edinburgh Duke of — see PHILIP
Ed·i·son \'ed-ə-sən\ Thomas Alva 1847–1931 Am. inventor
Ed·mund or Ead·mund II \'ed-mənd\ ca 993–1016 Ironside king of the English (1016)
Ed·ward \'ed-wərd\ name of 8 post-Norman Eng. (Brit.) kings: I 1239–1307 (reigned 1272–1307); II 1284–1327 (reigned 1307–27); III 1312–1377 (reigned 1327–77); IV 1442–1483 (reigned 1461–70; 1471–83); V 1470–1483 (reigned 1483); VI 1537–1553 (reigned 1547–53) son of Henry VIII & Jane Seymour; VII 1841–1910 (reigned 1901–10) Albert Edward, son of Victoria; VIII 1894–1972 (reigned 1936; abdicated) Duke of Windsor, son of George V
Edward 1330–1376 the Black Prince; son of Edward III prince of Wales
Edward or Ead·ward \'ed-\ 1003?–1066 the Confessor king of the English (1042–66)
Ed·wards \'ed-wərdz\ Jonathan 1703–1758 Am. theol. — Ed·ward·ean \ˌed-'wärd-ē-ən, -'wȯrd-\ adj
Ed·win or Ead·wine \'ed-wən\ 585?–633 king of Northumbria (616–633)
Egas Mo·niz \'ā-gäs-mō-'nēz\ António Caetano de Abreu Freire 1874–1955 Port. neurologist & polit.
Eg·bert \'eg-bərt\ d 839 king of the West Saxons (802–839) & 1st king of the English (828–839)
Eg·gle·ston \'eg-əl-stən\ Edward 1837–1902 Am. writer
Eggleston George Cary 1839–1911 bro. of Edward Am. writer
Eg·mond \'eg-ˌmänt\ or Eg·mont Lamoraal 1522–1568 Graaf van Egmond Flem. gen. & statesman
Eh·ren·burg \'er-ən-ˌbů(ə)rg, -ˌbů(ə)rk\ Ilya Grigoryevich 1891–1967 Russ. writer

---

\ə\ abut \ᵊ\ kitten, F table \ər\ further \a\ ash \ā\ ace \ä\ cot, cart \aů\ out \ch\ chin \e\ bet \ē\ easy \g\ go \i\ hit \ī\ ice \j\ job \ŋ\ sing \ō\ go \ȯ\ law \ȯi\ boy \th\ thin \th\ the \ü\ loot \ů\ foot \y\ yet \zh\ vision \à, k̲, ⁿ, œ, œ̄, ᵫ, ᵫ̄, ᵊ\ see Guide to Pronunciation

Ehr·lich \'e(ə)r-lik\ Paul 1854–1915 Ger. bacteriol.
Ehr·lich \'ər-lik\ Paul Ralph 1932–   Am. biol.
Eif·fel \'ī-fəl, e-fel\ Alexandre-Gustave 1832–1923 Fr. engineer
Ei·gen \'ī-gən\ Manfred 1927–   Ger. chem.
Eijk·man \'īk-,män, 'āk-\ Christiaan 1858–1930 Du. pathologist
Ein·stein \'īn-,stīn\ Albert 1879–1955 Am. (Ger.-born) physicist — Ein·stein·ian \īn-'stī-nē-ən\ adj
Eint·ho·ven \'īnt-,hō-vən, 'änt-\ Willem 1860–1927 Du. physiol.
Ei·sen·how·er \'īz-ᵊn-,haú(-ə)r\ Dwight David 1890–1969 Am. gen.; 34th pres. of the U.S. (1953–61)
Ei·sen·stein \'īz-ᵊn-,stīn\ Sergey Mikhaylovich 1898–1948 Russ. film director
El·a·gab·a·lus \el-ə-'gab-ə-ləs\ Gk He·li·o·gab·a·lus \,hē-lē-ō-'gab-ə-ləs\ 204–222 Rom. emp. (218–222)
El·don \'el-dən\ 1st Earl of 1751–1838 John Scott Eng. jurist
El·ea·nor \'el-ə-nər, -,nó(ə)r\ of Aquitaine 1122?–1204 queen of Louis VII of France (divorced 1152) & of Henry II of England
Eleanor of Castile 1246–1290 queen of Edward I of England
Eleanor of Provence 1223–1291 queen of Henry III of England
El·gar \'el-,gär, -gər\ Sir Edward 1857–1934 Eng. composer
El·i·on \'el-ē-ən\ Gertrude Belle 1918–   Am. biochem.
El·iot \'el-ē-ət, 'el-yət\ Charles William 1834–1926 Am. educ.; pres. Harvard U. (1869–1909)
Eliot George 1819–1880 pseud. of Mary Ann (or Marian) Evans Eng. nov.
Eliot Sir John 1592–1632 Eng. statesman
Eliot John 1604–1690 apostle to the Indians Am. clergyman
Eliot Thomas Stearns 1888–1965 Brit. (Am.-born) poet & critic — El·i·ot·ic \,el-ē-'ät-ik\ adj
Eliz·a·beth \i-'liz-ə-bəth\ name of 2 Eng. (Brit.) queens: I 1533–1603 dau. of Henry VIII & Anne Boleyn (reigned 1558–1603); II 1926–   Elizabeth Alexandra Mary; dau. of George VI, wife of Prince Philip; mother of Prince Charles (reigned 1952–   )
Elizabeth also Elizabeth Stu·art \-'st(y)ü-ərt, 'st(y)ù(-ə)rt\ 1596–1662 queen of Frederick V of Bohemia
Elizabeth 1900–   Elizabeth Angela Marguerite Bowes-Ly·on \'bōz-'lī-ən\ queen of George VI of Great Britain
Elizabeth 1843–1916 pseud. Carmen Syl·va \,kär-mən-'sil-və\ queen of Romania & writer
Elizabeth Pe·trov·na \-pə-'tróv-nə\ 1709–1762 empress of Russia (1741–62)
Ellenborough 1st Baron — see LAW
El·ling·ton \'el-iŋ-tən\ Edward Kennedy 1899–1974 Duke Am. bandleader & composer
El·liott \'el-ē-ət, 'el-yət\ Maxine 1868–1940 pseud. of Jessie Dermot Am. actress
El·lis \'el-əs\ Alexander John 1814–1890 orig. surname Sharpe Eng. philologist
Ellis (Henry) Have·lock \'hav-,läk, -lək\ 1859–1939 Eng. psychol. & writer
El·li·son \'el-ə-sən\ Ralph Waldo 1914–   Am. writer
Ells·worth \'elz-(,)wərth\ Lincoln 1880–1951 Am. explorer
Ellsworth Oliver 1745–1807 Am. jurist; chief justice U.S. Supreme Court (1796–1800)
El·man \'el-mən\ Mi·scha \'mē-shə\ 1891–1967 Am. (Russ.-born) violinist
El·phin·stone \'el-fən-,stōn, chiefly Brit -stən\ Mount·stu·art \maúnt-'st(y)ü-ərt\ 1779–1859 Brit. statesman in India
Elphinstone William 1431–1514 Scot. bishop & statesman
El·yot \'el-ē-ət, 'el-yət\ Sir Thomas 1490?–1546 Eng. scholar & diplomat
El·y·tis \'el-ē-(,)tēs\ Odysseus 1911–   Greek poet
El·ze·vir or El·ze·vier \'el-zə-,vi(ə)r\ family of Du. printers including esp. Lodewijk or Louis 1546?–1617, his son Bonaventura 1583–1652, & his grandson Abraham 1592–1652
Em·er·son \'em-ər-sən\ Ralph Waldo 1803–1882 Am. essayist & poet — Em·er·so·nian \,em-ər-'sō-nē-ən, -nyən\ adj
Em·met \'em-ət\ Robert 1778–1803 Irish nationalist & rebel
Em·ped·o·cles \em-'ped-ə-,klēz\ ca 490–430 B.C. Greek philos. & statesman
En·de·cott or En·di·cott \'en-di-kət, -də-,kät\ John 1588–1665 colonial gov. of Massachusetts
En·ders \'en-dərz\ John Franklin 1897–1985 Am. bacteriol.
Enes·cu \ə-'nes-(,)kü\ Gheorghe or George Fr Enes·co \-(,)kō\ Georges 1881–1955 Romanian composer
Eng·els \'eŋ-(g)əlz, G 'eŋ-əls\ Friedrich 1820–1895 Ger. socialist; collaborator with Karl Marx
En·ver Pa·şa \en-,ve(ə)r-'päsh-ə, -'pash-ə, -pə-'shä\ 1881–1922 Turk. soldier & polit.
Epam·i·non·das \i-,pam-ə-'nän-dəs\ ca 410–362 B.C. Theban gen. & statesman
Ep·ic·te·tus \,ep-ik-'tēt-əs\ ca A.D. 55–ca135 Greek Stoic philos. in Rome — Ep·ic·te·tian \-'tē-shən\ adj
Ep·i·cu·rus \,ep-i-'kyür-əs\ 341–270 B.C. Greek philos.
Ep·stein \'ep-,stīn\ Sir Jacob 1880–1959 Brit. (Am.-born) sculptor
Eras·mus \i-'raz-məs\ Desiderius 1466?–1536 Du. scholar — Eras·mi·an \-mē-ən\ adj
Er·a·tos·the·nes \,er-ə-'täs-thə-,nēz\ ca 276–ca 194 B.C. Greek astron.
Erck·mann–Cha·tri·an \'erk-,män-,shä-trē-'äⁿ, -,sha-\ joint pseud. of Émile Erckmann 1822–1899 & Alexandre Chatrian 1826–1890 Fr. authors
Er·hard \'e(ə)r-härt\ Ludwig 1897–1977 chancellor of West Germany (1963–66)
Er·ics·son \'er-ik-sən\ John 1803–1889 Am. (Swed.-born) engineer & inventor
Erig·e·na \i-'rij-ə-nə\ John Scotus ca 810–ca 877 Scot. (Irish-born) philos. & theol.
Er·ik \'er-ik\ the Red 10th cent. Norw. navigator; explored Greenland coast
Eriksson Leif — see LEIF ERIKSSON
Er·lan·der \er-'län-dər\ Tage Frithiof 1901–1985 Swed. polit.
Er·lang·er \'ər-,laŋ-ər\ Joseph 1874–1965 Am. physiol.
Er·len·mey·er \'ər-lən-,mī(-ə)r, 'er-\ Richard August Carl Emil 1825–1909 Ger. chem.

Ernst \'e(ə)rn(t)st, 'ərn(t)st\ Max 1891–1976 Ger. painter
Er·skine \'ər-skən\ John 1879–1951 Am. educ. & writer
Erskine of Car·nock \'kär-nək\ John 1695–1768 Scot. jurist
Er·vine \'ər-vən\ St. John \sänt-'jän, sənt-; 'sin-jən\ Greer 1883–1971 Irish dram. & nov.
Erz·ber·ger \'erts-,ber-gər\ Matthias 1875–1921 Ger. statesman
Es·a·ki \ə-'säk-ē\ Leo 1925–   Jp. physicist
Esch·er \'esh-ər, 'es-kər\ Maurits Cornelis 1898–1972 Du. graphic artist
Esh·kol \esh-'kōl\ Levi 1895–1969 prime min. of Israel (1963–69)
Es·par·te·ro \,es-pər-'te(ə)r-(,)ō\ Baldomero 1793–1879 Conde de Luchana Span. gen. & statesman
Es·qui·vel \,ä-skē-'vel\ Adolfo Pérez 1932–   Argentine sculptor and dissident
Es·sen \'es-ᵊn\ Count Hans Henrik von 1755–1824 Swed. field marshal & statesman
Essex 2d Earl of — see DEVEREUX
Es·taing, d' \des-taⁿ\ Comte Jean-Baptiste-Charles-Henri-Hector 1729–1794 Fr. admiral
Este \'es-(,)tā\ Ital. princely family beginning with Alberto Az·zo II \'äd-(,)zō\ 996–1097 & ending with Er·co·le III \'er-kə-,lā\ Rinaldo 1727–1803
Es·ter·ha·zy \'es-tər-,häz-ē\ Marie-Charles-Ferdinand-Walsin 1847–1923 Fr. army officer
Es·tienne \ā-'tyen\ or Étienne Fr. family of printers & booksellers including esp.: Henri I ca1470–1520; his son Robert 1503–1559; & Robert's son Henri II 1528–1598
Es·tra·da Pal·ma \ā-'sträth-ə-'päl-mə\ Tomás 1835–1908 1st pres. of Cuba (1902–06)
Ethelbert — see AETHELBERHT
Ethelred — see AETHELRED
Eth·er·ege \'eth-(ə-)rij\ Sir George 1635?–1692 Eng. dram.
Euck·en \'òi-kən\ Rudolf Christoph 1846–1926 Ger. philos.
Eu·clid \'yü-kləd\ fl ca 300 B.C. Greek geometer
Eu·gene \yü-'jēn, 'yü-, F œ-zhen\ 1663–1736 François-Eugène de Savoie-Carignan prince of Savoy & Austrian gen.
Eu·gé·nie \yü-jə-,nē; yü-'jā-nē, -'je-; F œ-zhā-nē\ 1826–1920 Eugénia Maria de Montijo de Guzmán; wife of Napoleon III empress of the French (1853–71)
Eu·ler \'òi-lər\ Leonhard 1707–1783 Swiss math. & physicist
Eu·ler–Chel·pin \,òi-lər-'kel-pən\ Hans Karl August Simon von 1873–1964 Swed. (Ger.-born) chem.
Eu·rip·i·des \yü-'rip-ə-,dēz\ ca 484–406 B.C. Greek dram. — Eu·rip·i·de·an \-,rip-ə-'dē-ən\ adj
Eus·den \'yüz-dən\ Laurence 1688–1730 Eng. poet; poet laureate (1718–30)
Eu·se·bi·us of Caesarea \yü-'sē-bē-əs\ ca 260–ca 339 theol. & church hist.
Eu·sta·chio \eú-'stäk-ē-,ō\ Bartolommeo 1520–1574 L. Eu·sta·chius \yü-'stā-kē-əs, -'stä-kē(-)əs\ Ital. anatomist
Ev·ans \'ev-ənz\ Sir Arthur John 1851–1941 Eng. archaeol.
Evans Herbert McLean 1882–1971 Am. anatomist & embryologist
Evans Maurice 1901–1989 Am. (Eng.-born) actor
Evans Rudulph 1878–1960 Am. sculptor
Evans Walker 1903–1975 Am. photographer
Ev·arts \'ev-ərts\ William Maxwell 1818–1901 Am. lawyer & statesman
Ev·att \'ev-ət\ Herbert Vere 1894–1965 Austral. jurist & statesman
Eve·lyn \'ēv-lən, 'ev-\ John 1620–1706 Eng. diarist
Ev·er·ett \'ev-(ə-)rət\ Edward 1794–1865 Am. clergyman, orator, & statesman
Ewald \'iv-,äl\ Johannes 1743–1781 Dan. poet & dram.
Ewell \'yü-əl\ Richard Stoddert 1817–1872 Am. Confed. gen.
Eyck, van \van-'īk\ Hubert or Huybrecht ca1370–1426 & his bro. Jan before 1395–1441 Flem. painters
Eze·kiel \i-'zēk-yəl\ Moses Jacob 1844–1917 Am. sculptor
Fa·bi·o·la \,fab-ē-'ō-lə, fəb-'yō-\ 1928–   queen of King Baudouin I of Belgium
Fa·bi·us \'fā-bē-əs\ d 203 B.C. Quintus Fabius Maximus Verrucosus Cuncta·tor \,kəŋk-'tāt-ər\ Rom. gen. against Hannibal
Fa·bre \fäbrᵊ\ Jean-Henri 1823–1915 Fr. entomologist
Fad·den \'fad-ᵊn\ Sir Arthur William 1895–1973 Austral. statesman
Fad·i·man \'fad-ə-mən\ Clifton 1904–   Am. writer & editor
Fahd \'fäd\ 1922–   Fahd ibn Abd al-Aziz Al Saud king of Saudi Arabia (1982–   )
Fah·ren·heit \'far-ən-,hīt, 'fär-\ Daniel Gabriel 1686–1736 Ger. physicist
Fair·banks \'fa(ə)r-,baŋ(k)s, 'fe(ə)r-\ Charles Warren 1852–1918 Am. lawyer & polit.; vice pres. of U.S. (1905–09)
Fairbanks Douglas Elton 1883–1939 Am. actor
Fair·child \'fa(ə)r-,child, 'fe(ə)r-\ David Grandison 1869–1954 Am. botanist
Fair·fax \'fa(ə)r-,faks, 'fe(ə)r-\ Baron Thomas 1612–1671 Eng. gen.
Fairfax Baron Thomas 1692–1782 proprietor in Virginia
Fai·sal \'fī-səl, 'fā-\ ca 1906–1975 king of Saudi Arabia (1964–75)
Fai·sal I Ar Fay·sal \'fī-səl, 'fā-\ 1885–1933 king of Syria (1920), of Iraq (1921–1933)
Faisal II Ar Fay·sal 1935–1958 king of Iraq (1939–58)
Fa·lier \fəl-'ye(ə)r\ or Fa·lie·ro \-(,)ō\ Marino 1274–1355 doge of Venice (1354–55)
Fal·ken·hau·sen \'fäl-kən-,haúz-ᵊn, 'fal-\ Ludwig 1844–1936 Freiherr von Falkenhausen Ger. gen.
Fal·ken·hayn \'fäl-kən-,hīn, 'fal-\ Erich von 1861–1922 Ger. gen.
Falkner William — see FAULKNER
Fal·la \'fä(l)-yə, 'fī-ə\ Manuel de 1876–1946 Span. composer
Fal·lières \fal-'ye(ə)r\ Clément-Armand 1841–1931 Fr. statesman; pres. of France (1906–13)
Fan·euil \'fan-yəl, 'fan-ᵊl, 'fan-yə-wəl\ Peter 1700–1743 Am. merchant
Far·a·day \'far-ə-,dā, -əd-ē\ Michael 1791–1867 Eng. chem. & physicist
Far·ley \'fär-lē\ James Aloysius 1888–1976 Am. polit.
Far·man \'fär-,män, 'fär-mən\ Henri 1874–1958 & his bro. Maurice 1877–1964 Fr. pioneer aviators and airplane manufacturers
Far·mer \'fär-mər\ Fannie Merritt 1857–1915 Am. cookery expert
Farmer James Leonard 1920–   Am. civil rights leader
Far·ne·se \fär-'nā-zē, -sē\ Alessandro 1545–1592 Duke of Parma Ital. gen. in Span. service

Fa·rouk I \fə-'rük\ *Ar* Fā·rūq al–Aw·wal \fär-'ük-al-'a-wal\ 1920–1965 king of Egypt (1936–52; abdicated)

Far·quhar \'fär-k(w)ər\ George 1678–1707 Brit. dram.

Far·ra·gut \'far-ə-gət\ David Glasgow 1801–1870 Am. admiral

Far·rar \'far-ər\ Frederic William 1831–1903 Eng. clergyman & writer

Far·rar \fə-'rär\ Geraldine 1882–1967 Am. soprano

Far·rell \'far-əl\ James Thomas 1904–1979 Am. nov.

Fa·ruk *var of* FAROUK

Fāt·i·mah \'fat-ə-mə\ *ca* 606–633 *az-Zahrā'* ('Shining One') dau. of Muhammad

Faulk·ner \'fók-nər\ William Cuthbert 1897–1962 *orig. Falkner* Am. nov. — Faulk·ner·ian \fók-'nir-ē-ən, -'ner-\ *adj*

Faure \'fó(ə)r, 'fó(ə)r\ François-Félix 1841–1899 Fr. statesman; pres. of France (1895–99)

Fau·ré \fó-'rā\ Gabriel-Urbain 1845–1924 Fr. composer

Faus·ta \'fó-stə, 'faü-\ 289–326 *Flavia Maximiana Fausta; wife of Constantine the Great* Rom. empress

Fawkes \'fóks\ Guy 1570–1606 Eng. conspirator

Fech·ner \'fek-nər, 'fek-\ Gustav Theodor 1801–1887 Ger. physicist & psychol.

Feif·fer \'fi-fər\ Jules 1929– Am. cartoonist and writer

Fei·ning·er \'fi-niŋ-ər\ Lyonel Charles Adrian 1871–1956 Am. painter

Feke \'fēk\ Robert *ca* 1705–*ca* 1750 Am. painter

Fel·li·ni \fel-'lē-nē\ Federico 1920– Ital. film director — Fel·li·ni·esque \fə-‚lē-nē-'esk\ *adj*

Fell·tham \'fel-thəm\ Owen 1602?–1668 Eng. writer

Fé·ne·lon \‚fän-ᵊl-'ōⁿ, fen-'lōⁿ\ François de Salignac de La Mothe-1651–1715 Fr. prelate & writer

Feng Yü–hsiang \'fəŋ-'yü-shē-'äŋ\ 1882–1948 Chin. gen.

Fer·ber \'fər-bər\ Edna 1887–1968 Am. writer

Fer·di·nand I \'ferd-ᵊn-‚and\ 1503–1564 Holy Rom. emp. (1558–64)

Ferdinand II 1578–1637 king of Bohemia (1617–19; 1620–27) & of Hungary (1618–25); Holy Rom. emp. (1619–37)

Ferdinand III 1608–1657 king of Hungary (1625–47); Holy Rom. emp. (1637–57)

Ferdinand I 1861–1948 king of Bulgaria (1908–18)

Ferdinand I 1016(or 1018)–1065 *the Great* king of Castile (1035–65); of León (1037–65)

Ferdinand II of Aragon *or* V of Castile 1452–1516 *the Catholic* king of Castile (1474–1504); of Aragon (1479–1516); of Naples (1504–16); founder of the Span. monarchy

Ferdinand VII 1784–1833 king of Spain (1808; 1814–33)

Fer·mat \fer-'mä\ Pierre de 1601–1665 Fr. math.

Fer·mi \'fe(ə)r-(‚)mē\ Enrico 1901–1954 Am. (Ital.-born) physicist

Fer·nán·dez \fər-'nan-‚dez\ Juan *ca* 1536–*ca* 1604 Span. navigator

Fernández de Cór·do·ba \-thä-'kór-də-bə, -və\ Gonzalo 1453–1515 *El Gran Capitán* Span. soldier & statesman

Fer·re·ro \fə-'re(ə)r-(‚)ō\ Guglielmo 1871–1943 Ital. hist. & author

Fes·sen·den \'fes-ᵊn-dən\ William Pitt 1806–1869 Am. polit.; secy. of the treasury (1864–65)

Fes·tus \'fes-təs\ Porcius *d ca* A.D. 62 Rom. procurator of Judea (58 or 60–62)

Feucht·wang·er \'fóikt-‚väŋ-ər, 'fóikt-\ Li·on \'lē-‚ón\ 1884–1958 Ger. nov. & dram.

Feuil·let \‚fə-'yä\ Octave 1821–1890 Fr. nov. & dram.

Feyn·man \'fïn-mən\ Richard Phillips 1918–1988 Am. physicist

Fi·bi·ger \'fē-bē-gər\ Johannes Andreas Grib 1867–1928 Dan. pathologist

Fich·te \'fik-tə, 'fik-\ Johann Gottlieb 1762–1814 Ger. philos. — Fich·te·an \-tē-ən\ *adj*

Fied·ler \'fēd-lər\ Arthur 1894–1979 Am. conductor

Field \'fē(ə)ld\ Cyrus West 1819–1892 Am. financier

Field Eugene 1850–1895 Am. poet & journalist

Field Marshall 1834–1906 Am. merchant

Fiel·ding \'fē(ə)l-diŋ\ Henry 1707–1754 Eng. nov.

Fields \'fē(ə)ldz\ W.C. 1880–1946 *orig. William Claude Dukenfield* Am. actor

Figl \'fē-gəl\ Leopold 1902–1965 Austrian polit.

Fi·guei·re·do \‚fē-ger-'ā-(‚)dü\ João Baptista de Oliveira 1918– pres. of Brazil (1979–85)

Fi·gue·roa \‚fē-gə-'rō-ə\ Francisco de *ca* 1536–*ca* 1620 Span. poet

Fill·more \'fil-‚mō(ə)r, -‚mó(ə)r\ Millard 1800–1874 13th pres. of the U.S. (1850–53)

Fin·lay \fin-'lī\ Carlos Juan 1833–1915 Cuban physician & biol.

Finn·bo·ga·dot·tir \'fin-‚bō-gə-‚dót-ər\ Vigdis 1930– pres. of Iceland (1980–)

Fin·sen \'fin(t)-sən\ Niels Ryberg 1860–1904 Dan. physician

Fir·bank \'fir-‚baŋk\ (Arthur Annesley) Ronald 1886–1926 Eng. author

Fir·daw·sī *or* Fer·dow·sī \far-'daü-sē, -'dó-\ *or* Fir·du·si \-'dü-\ *or* Fir·dou·si \-'daü-, -'dó-\ *ca* 935–*ca* 1020 (or 1026) *orig. Abū ol-Qāsem Mansūr* Pers. poet

Fire·stone \'fi(ə)r-‚stōn\ Harvey Samuel 1868–1938 Am. industrialist

Fi·scher \'fish-ər\ Emil 1852–1919 Ger. chem.

Fischer Ernst Otto 1918– Ger. chem.

Fischer Hans 1881–1945 Ger. chem.

Fish \'fish\ Hamilton 1808–1893 Am. statesman

Fish·bein \'fish-‚bīn\ Morris 1889–1976 Am. physician & editor

Fish·er \'fish-ər\ Dorothy 1879–1958 *Dorothea Frances* née Can·field \'kan-‚fēld\ Am. nov.

Fisher Irving 1867–1947 Am. econ.

Fisher John Arbuthnot 1841–1920 1st Baron *Fisher of Kil·ver·stone* \'kil-vər-stən\ Brit. admiral

Fiske \'fisk\ John 1842–1901 *orig. Edmund Fisk Green* Am. philos. & hist.

Fitch \'fich\ (William) Clyde 1865–1909 Am. dram.

Fitch John 1743–1798 Am. inventor

Fitch Val Logsdon 1923– Am. physicist

Fitz·ger·ald \fits-'jer-əld\ Ella 1918– Am. singer

Fitzgerald Francis Scott Key 1896–1940 Am. writer

FitzGerald Edward 1809–1883 Eng. poet & translator

FitzGerald Garret 1926– prime min. of Ireland (1981–87)

Fitz·her·bert \fits-'hər-bərt\ Maria Anne 1756–1837 née *Smythe; wife of George IV of England*

Flagg \'flag\ James Montgomery 1877–1960 Am. painter, illustrator, & writer

Flag·stad \'fläg-‚stä, 'flag-‚stad\ Kir·sten \'kish-tən, 'ki(ə)r-stən\ 1895–1962 Norw. soprano

Fla·min·i·us \flə-'min-ē-əs\ Gaius *d* 217 B.C. Rom. gen. & statesman

Flam·ma·rion \flä-‚mar-ē-'ōⁿ\ (Nicolas-) Camille 1842–1925 Fr. astron. & writer

Flan·a·gan \'flan-i-gən\ Edward Joseph 1886–1948 Am. (Irish-born) R. C. priest & founder of Boys Town

Flan·din \fläⁿ-daⁿ\ Pierre-Étienne 1889–1958 Fr. polit.; premier (1934–35)

Flau·bert \flō-'be(ə)r\ Gustave 1821–1880 Fr. nov. — Flau·ber·tian \-'bər-shən, -'bert-ē-ən\ *adj*

Flax·man \'flak-smən\ John 1755–1826 Eng. sculptor

Fleet·wood \'flēt-‚wúd\ Charles *d* 1692 Eng. gen.

Flem·ing \'flem-iŋ\ Sir Alexander 1881–1955 Brit. bacteriol.

Fleming Ian Lancaster 1908–1964 Brit. writer

Fleming Sir John Ambrose 1849–1945 Eng. electrical engineer

Fletch·er \'flech-ər\ John 1579–1625 Eng. dram.

Fleu·ry \flər-'ē\ André-Hercule de 1653–1743 Fr. cardinal & statesman

Fleury Claude 1640–1723 Fr. ecclesiastical hist.

Flint \'flint\ Austin: father 1812–1886 & son 1836–1915 Am. physicians

Flo·res \'flōr-‚ās, 'flór-\ Juan José 1800–1864 Ecuadorian soldier; pres. of Ecuador (1830–35; 1839–45)

Flo·rey \'flōr-ē, 'flór-\ Sir Howard Walter 1898–1968 Brit. pathologist

Flo·rio \'flōr-ē-‚ō, 'flór-\ John *ca* 1553–*ca* 1625 Eng. lexicographer & translator

Flo·ry \'flōr-ē, 'flór-\ Paul John 1910–85 Am. chem.

Flo·tow \'flō-(‚)tō\ Friedrich 1812–1883 Freiherr *von Flotow* Ger. composer

Foch \'fosh, 'fäsh\ Ferdinand 1851–1929 Fr. gen.; marshal of France

Fo·kine \'fō-‚ken, fó-'\ Michel 1880–1942 Am. (Russ.-born) choreographer

Fok·ker \'fäk-ər, 'fók-\ Anthony Herman Gerard 1890–1939 Am. (Du.-born) aircraft designer & builder

Fol·ger \'fōl-gər\ Henry Clay 1857–1930 Am. bibliophile

Fon·tanne \fän-'tan, 'fän-‚\ Lynn 1887?–1983 *wife of Alfred Lunt* Am. (Eng.-born) actress

Fon·teyn \fän-'tän, 'fän-‚\ Dame Margot 1919– *orig. Margot Hookham* \'húk-əm\ Eng. ballerina

Foote \'füt\ Andrew Hull 1806–1863 Am. admiral

Foote Samuel 1720–1777 Eng. actor & playwright

Forbes–Rob·ert·son \‚fórbz-'räb-ərt-sən\ Sir Johnston 1853–1937 Eng. actor

Ford \'fō(ə)rd, 'fó(ə)rd\ Ford Mad·ox \'mad-əks\ 1873–1939 *orig. Huef·fer* \'(h)wef-ər\ Eng. author

Ford Gerald Rudolph 1913– Am. polit.; 38th pres. of the U.S. (1974–77)

Ford Henry 1863–1947 Am. automobile manuf.

Ford John 1586–?1639 Eng. dram.

For·es·ter \'fór-əs-tər, 'fär-\ Cecil Scott 1899–1966 Brit. writer

Forrest \'fór-əst, 'fär-\ Edwin 1806–1872 Am. actor

Forrest Nathan Bedford 1821–1877 Am. Confed. gen.

For·res·tal \'fór-əs-tᵊl, 'fär-, -‚tól\ James Vincent 1892–1949 Am. banker; 1st secy. of defense (1947–49)

Forss·mann \'fór-‚smän\ Werner Theodor Otto 1904–1979 Ger. surgeon

For·ster \'fór-stər\ Edward Morgan 1879–1970 Brit. nov. — For·ste·ri·an \'fór-'stir-ē-ən\ *adj*

For·syth \'fór-‚sīth, fər-\ John 1780–1841 Am. statesman

For·tas \'fórt-əs\ Abe 1910–1982 Am. jurist

Fos·dick \'fäz-(‚)dik\ Harry Emerson 1878–1969 Am. clergyman

Fos·ter \'fós-tər, 'fäs-\ Stephen Collins 1826–1864 Am. songwriter

Foster William Zebulon 1881–1961 Am. Communist

Fou·cault \fü-'kō\ Jean-Bernard-Léon 1819–1868 Fr. physicist

Fou·qué \fü-'kā\ Friedrich Heinrich Karl de la Motte 1777–1843 Freiherr *Fouqué* Ger. author

Fou·quet *or* Fouc·quet \fü-'kā\ Nicolas 1615–1680 Fr. superintendent of finance

Fou·quier–Tin·ville \fü-kyä-taⁿ-'vēl\ Antoine-Quentin 1746–1795 Fr. polit.

Four·dri·nier \‚fór-drə-'ni(ə)r, ‚fór-; ‚fúr-'drin-ē-ər, ‚fór-, ‚fór-\ Henry 1766–1854 & his bro. Sealy *d* 1847 Eng. papermakers & inventors

Fou·ri·er \'fúr-ē-‚ā\ (François-Marie-) Charles 1772–1837 Fr. sociol. & reformer

Fow·ler \'faú-lər\ Henry Watson 1858–1933 Eng. lexicographer

Fowler William Alfred 1911– Am. physicist

Fox \'fäks\ Charles James 1749–1806 Eng. statesman & orator

Fox George 1624–1691 Eng. preacher; founder of Society of Friends (Quakers)

Fox Henry 1705–1774 1st Baron *Hol·land* \'häl-ənd\ Brit. statesman

Foxe \'fäks\ John 1516–1587 Eng. martyrologist

Foxe *or* Fox Richard *ca* 1448–1528 Eng. prelate & statesman

Fra·go·nard \‚frag-ə-'när\ Jean-Honoré 1732–1806 Fr. painter & engraver

France \'fran(t)s, fräⁿs\ Anatole 1844–1924 *pseud. of Jacques-Anatole-François Thibault* Fr. nov. & satirist

Francesca Piero della — see PIERO DELLA FRANCESCA

Francesca da Rimini — see POLENTA

Fran·cis I \'fran(t)-səs\ 1494–1547 king of France (1515–47)

Francis II 1768–1835 last Holy Rom. emp. (1792–1806); emp. of Austria (as *Francis I*) 1804–35

Francis Ferdinand 1863–1914 archduke of Austria; assassinated

Francis Joseph I 1830–1916 emp. of Austria (1848–1916)

Francis of Assisi Saint 1181(or 1182)–1226 in full *Francesco di Pietro di Bernardone* Ital. friar; founder of Franciscan order

Francis of Sales \'sä(ə)lz\ Saint 1567–1622 Fr. R. C. bishop of Geneva

Franck \'fräŋk\ César Auguste 1822–1890 Belg.-Fr. organist & composer

Franck James 1882–1964 Am. (Ger.-born) physicist

Francke \'fräŋ-kə\ Kuno 1855–1930 Am. (Ger.-born) hist. & educ.

Fran·co \'fräŋ-(ˌ)kō, 'fraŋ-\ Francisco 1892–1975 *Francisco Paulino Hermenegildo Teódulo Franco Bahamonde* Span. gen. & head of Span. state (1936–75)

Frank \'fraŋk, 'fräŋk\ Ilya Mikhaylovich 1908–   Russ. physicist

Frank·furt·er \'fraŋk-fə(r)t-ər, -ˌfərt-\ Felix 1882–1965 Am. (Austrian-born) jurist

Frank·lin \'fraŋ-klən\ Benjamin 1706–1790 Am. statesman & philos.

Franklin Sir John 1786–1847 Eng. arctic explorer

Franks \'fraŋ(k)s\ Baron 1905–   *Oliver Shewell Franks* Eng. philos. & diplomat

Fra·ser \'frā-zər, -zhər\ James Earle 1876–1953 Am. sculptor

Fraser (John) Malcolm 1930–   prime min. of Australia (1975–83)

Fraser Peter 1884–1950 N.Z. statesman; prime min. (1940–49)

Fraun·ho·fer \'fraun-ˌhō-fər\ Joseph von 1787–1826 Bavarian optician & physicist

Fra·zer \'frā-zər, -zhər\ Sir James George 1854–1941 Scot. anthropol.

Fré·chette \frā-'shet\ Louis-Honoré 1839–1908 Canad. journalist & poet

Fred·er·ick I \'fred-(ə-)rik\ ca 1123–1190 *Frederick Bar·ba·ros·sa* \ˌbär-bə-'räs-ə, -'rös-\ Holy Rom. emp. (1152–90)

Frederick II 1194–1250 Holy Rom. emp. (1215–50); king of Sicily (1198–1250)

Frederick I 1657–1713 king of Prussia (1701–13)

Frederick II 1712–1786 *the Great* king of Prussia (1740–86)

Frederick IX 1899–1972 king of Denmark (1947–72)

Frederick William 1620–1688 *the Great Elector* elector of Brandenburg (1640–88)

Frederick William name of 4 kings of Prussia: I 1688–1740 (reigned 1713–40); II 1744–1797 (reigned 1786–97); III 1770–1840 (reigned 1797–1840); IV 1795–1861 (reigned 1840–61)

Free·man \'frē-mən\ Douglas Sou·thall \'sau-ˌthöl, -ˌthöl\ 1886–1953 Am. editor & hist.

Freeman Mary Eleanor 1852–1930 née *Wilkins* Am. writer

Fre·ling·huy·sen \'frē-liŋ-ˌhīz-ʰn\ Frederick Theodore 1817–1885 Am. statesman

Fré·mont \'frē-ˌmänt\ John Charles 1813–1890 Am. gen. & explorer

French \'french\ Daniel Chester 1850–1931 Am. sculptor

Fre·neau \fri-'nō\ Philip Morin 1752–1832 Am. poet

Fres·co·bal·di \ˌfres-kə-'bäl-dē, -'böl-\ Girolamo 1583–1643 Ital. composer

Fres·nel \frā-'nel\ Augustin-Jean 1788–1827 Fr. physicist

Freud \'fröid\ Sigmund 1856–1939 Austrian neurologist; founder of psychoanalysis

Frey·berg \'frī-ˌbərg\ 1st Baron 1889–1963 *Bernard Cyril Freyberg* N.Z. gen.

Frey·tag \'frī-ˌtäk, -ˌtäg\ Gustav 1816–1895 Ger. author

Frick \'frik\ Henry Clay 1849–1919 Am. industrialist

Fried \'frēt, 'frēd\ Alfred Hermann 1864–1921 Austrian pacifist

Fried·man \'frēd-mən\ Milton 1912–   Am. econ.

Frie·drich \'frē-drik\ Caspar David 1774–1840 Ger. painter

Frisch \'frish\ Karl von 1886–1982 Austrian zool.

Frisch Ragnar 1895–1973 Norw. econ.

Fro·bi·sher \'frō-bi-shər\ Sir Martin 1535?–1594 Eng. navigator

Froe·bel or Frö·bel \'frā-bəl, 'frē-, 'frœ-\ Friedrich Wilhelm August 1782–1852 Ger. educ.

Froh·man \'frō-mən\ Charles 1860–1915 Am. theater manager

Frois·sart \'fröi-ˌgärt, f(r)wä-'sär\ Jean 1333?–ca 1405 Fr. chronicler

Fromm \'fröm, 'främ\ Erich 1900–1980 Am. (Ger.-born) psychoanalyst

Fron·di·zi \frän-'dē-zē, -sē\ Arturo 1908–   Argentine pres. (1958–62)

Fron·te·nac et Pal·lu·au \ˌfröⁿ-tə-nä-kä-pä-lwʻö\ Comte de 1622–1698 *Louis de Buade* \'bwʻäd\ Fr. gen. & colonial administrator in America

Frost \'fröst\ Robert Lee 1874–1963 Am. poet — Frost·ian \-ē-ən\ adj

Froude \'früd\ James Anthony 1818–1894 Eng. hist.

Fry \'frī\ Christopher 1907–   Eng. dram.

Fu·ʻād I \fu-'äd\ 1868–1936 sultan (1917–22) & king (1922–36) of Egypt

Fu·en·tes \fü-'en-ˌtäs\ Carlos 1928–   Mex. author

Fuer·tes \'fyü(ə)rt-(ˌ)ēz\ Louis Agassiz 1874–1927 Am. illustrator

Fu·gard \'fü-ˌgärd\ Athol 1932–   So. African playwright

Fu·ji·mo·ri \ˌfüj-ē-'mö-rē\ Alberto 1938–   pres. of Peru (1990–   )

Fu·kui \'fük-ü-ē, fü-'kü-ē\ Kenichi 1918–   Jp. chem.

Ful·bright \'ful-ˌbrīt\ (James) William 1905–   Am. polit.

Ful·ler \'ful-ər\ Melville Weston 1833–1910 Am. jurist; chief justice U.S. Supreme Court (1888–1910)

Fuller (Richard) Buckminster 1895–1983 Am. engineer

Fuller (Sarah) Margaret 1810–1850 Marchioness Os·so·li \'ö-sə-(ˌ)lē\ Am. critic & reformer

Fuller Thomas 1608–1661 Eng. divine & author

Ful·ton \'fult-ʰn\ Robert 1765–1815 Am. engineer & inventor

Funk \'fuŋk, 'faŋk\ Casimir 1884–1967 Am. (Pol.-born) biochem.

Funk \'faŋk\ Isaac Kauffman 1839–1912 Am. editor & publisher

Fun·ston \'fən(t)-stən\ Frederick 1865–1917 Am. gen.

Fur·ness \'fər-nəs, -ˌnes\ Horace Howard: father 1833–1912 & son 1865–1930 Am. Shakespeare scholars

Fur·ni·vall \'fər-nə-vəl\ Frederick James 1825–1910 Eng. philologist

Furt·wäng·ler \'fürt-ˌveŋ-lər\ (Gustav Heinrich Ernst Martin) Wilhelm 1886–1954 Ger. conductor

Ga·ble \'gā-bəl\ (William) Clark 1901–1960 Am. actor

Ga·bo \'gäb-(ˌ)ō\ Naum 1890–1977 orig. *Naum Pevs·ner* \'pevz-nər\ Am. (Russ.-born) sculptor

Ga·bor \'gäb-(ˌ)ör, gə-'bö(ə)r\ Dennis 1900–1979 Brit. (Hung.-born) physicist

Ga·bo·riau \ˌgə-'bör-ē-,ō\ Émile 1832(or 1833 or 1835)–ca 1873 Fr. writer

Ga·bri·eli \ˌgäb-rē-'el-ē\ Giovanni ca 1556–1612 Ital. composer

Gads·den \'gadz-dən\ James 1788–1858 Am. army officer & diplomat

Ga·ga·rin \gə-'gär-yən\ Yu·ry \'yùr-ē\ Alekseyevich 1934–1968 Russ. astronaut; 1st man in space (1961)

Gage \'gāj\ Thomas 1721–1787 Brit. gen. & colonial gov. in America

Gail·lard \gil-'yärd\ David DuBose \-d(y)ü-'böz\ 1859–1913 Am. army officer & engineer

Gaines \'gänz\ Edmund Pendleton 1777–1849 Am. gen.

Gains·bor·ough \'gänz-,bər-ə, -,bə-rə, -b(ə-)rə\ Thomas 1727–1788 Eng. painter

Gait·skell \'gät-skəl\ Hugh Todd Naylor 1906–1963 Eng. polit.

Ga·ius \'gä-(y)əs, 'gī-əs\ *fl* A.D. 130–180 Rom. jurist

Gaj·du·sek \'gī-də-,shek\ D(aniel) Carleton 1923–   Am. virologist

Gal·ba \'gal-bə, 'göl-\ Servius Sulpicius 3 B.C.–A.D. 69 Rom. emp. (68–69)

Gal·braith \'gal-,brāth\ John Kenneth 1908–   Am. (Canad.-born) econ.

Gale \'gā(ə)l\ Zona 1874–1938 Am. nov.

Ga·len \'gā-lən\ A.D. 129–ca 199 Greek physician & writer — Ga·len·ic \gə-'len-ik\ *or* Ga·len·i·cal \-i-kəl\ adj

Ga·le·ri·us \gə-'lir-ē-əs\ d 311 *Gaius Galerius Valerius Maximianus* Rom. emp. (305–311)

Ga·li·lei \ˌgal-ə-'lā-,ē\ Ga·li·leo \ˌgal-ə-'lē-(ˌ)ō, -'lā-\ 1564–1642 usu. called *Galileo* Ital. astron. & physicist

Gal·land \ga-'läⁿ\ Antoine 1646–1715 Fr. orientalist & translator

Gal·la·tin \'gal-ət-ʰn\ (Abraham Alfonse) Albert 1761–1849 Am. (Swiss-born) financier & statesman

Gal·lau·det \ˌgal-ə-'det\ Thomas Hopkins 1787–1851 Am. teacher of the hearing- and speech-impaired

Ga·lle·gos Fre·ire \gä-'yä-(ˌ)gös-'frā-(ˌ)rä\ Rómulo 1884–1969 Venezuelan nov.; pres. of Venezuela (1948)

Gal·li-Cur·ci \ˌgal-i-'kür-chē, ˌgäl-, -'kər-\ Amelita 1889–1963 née *Galli* Am. (Ital.-born) soprano

Gal·lie·ni \ˌgal-yä-'nē, ˌgal-'yä-nē\ Joseph-Simon 1849–1916 Fr. gen. & colonial administrator

Gal·lie·nus \ˌgal-ē-'ē-nəs, -'ā-nəs\ Publius Licinius Valerianus Egnatius d 268 Rom. emp. (253–268)

Gal·lup \'gal-əp\ George Horace 1901–1984 Am. statistician

Ga·lois \gal-'wä\ Évariste 1811–1832 Fr. math.

Gals·wor·thy \'gölz-,wər-thē\ John 1867–1933 Eng. nov. & dram.

Galt \'gölt\ John 1779–1839 Scot. nov.

Gal·ton \'gölt-ʰn\ Sir Francis 1822–1911 Eng. scientist — Gal·to·nian \ˌgöl-'tō-nē-ən, -nyən\ adj

Gal·va·ni \gal-'vän-ē, gäl-\ Luigi 1737–1798 Ital. physician & physicist

Gál·vez \'gäl-,ves\ José 1729–1787 Marqués *de la Sonora* Span. jurist & colonial administrator

Ga·ma, da \'gam-ə, 'gäm-\ Vasco ca 1460–1524 Port. navigator

Ga·mar·ra \gə-'mär-ə\ Agustín 1785–1841 Peruvian gen.; pres. of Peru (1829–33; 1839–41)

Gam·bet·ta \gam-'bet-ə, ˌgäⁿ-bə-'tä\ Léon-Michel 1838–1882 Fr. lawyer & statesman

Ga·me·lin \ˌgam-ə-)'lan\ Maurice-Gustave 1872–1958 Fr. gen.

Gan·dhi \'gän-dē, 'gan-\ In·dira \in-'dir-ə, 'in-də-rə\ Nehru 1917–1984 *dau. of Jawaharlal Nehru* prime min. of India (1966–77; 1980–84)

Gandhi Mohandas Karamchand 1869–1948 *Ma·hat·ma* \mə-'hät-mə, -'hat-\ Indian nationalist leader — Gan·dhi·an \-ən\ adj

Gandhi Ra·jiv \rä-'jēv\ Ratna 1944–   *son of Indira* prime min. of India (1984–89)

Gar·a·mond \'gar-ə-,mänd, ,gar-ə-'möⁿ\ *or* Gar·a·mont \-,mänt, -'möⁿ\ Claude ca 1480–1561 Fr. typefounder

Ga·rand \gə-'rand, 'gar-ənd\ John Cantius 1888–1974 Am. (Canad.-born) inventor

Gar·bo \'gär-(ˌ)bō\ Greta 1905–1990 orig. *Greta Lovisa Gustafsson* Am. (Swed.-born) actress

Gar·cía Gu·tiér·rez \gär-'sē-ə-gü-'tyer-əs\ Antonio 1813–1884 Span. dram.

García Íñi·guez \-'ēn-yi-,gäs\ Calixto 1839–1898 Cuban revolutionary

García Lor·ca \-'lör-kə\ Federico 1898–1936 Span. poet & dram.

García Már·quez \-'mär-,käs\ Gabriel 1928–   Colombian author

García Mo·re·no \-mə-'rä-(ˌ)nö\ Gabriel 1821–1875 Ecuadorian journalist; pres. of Ecuador (1861–65; 1869–75)

Gar·ci·la·so de la Ve·ga \gär-si-'läs-ö-,dä-lə-'vä-gə\ 1539–1616 *El Inca* Peruvian hist.

Gar·den \'gärd-ʰn\ Mary 1874–1967 Am. (Scot.-born) soprano

Gar·di·ner \'gärd-nər, -ʰn-ər\ Samuel Rawson 1829–1902 Eng. hist.

Gardiner Stephen ca 1482–1555 Eng. prelate & statesman

Gard·ner \'gärd-nər\ Erle Stanley 1889–1970 Am. writer

Gar·field \'gär-,fēld\ James Abram 1831–1881 20th pres. of the U.S. (1881)

Gar·i·bal·di \ˌgar-ə-'böl-dē\ Giuseppe 1807–1882 Ital. patriot — Gar·i·bal·di·an \-dē-ən\ adj

Gar·land \'gär-lənd\ (Hannibal) Hamlin 1860–1940 Am. nov.

Gar·ner \'gär-nər\ John Nance 1868–1967 Am. polit.; vice pres. of the U.S. (1933–41)

Gar·nett \'gär-nət\ Constance 1862–1946 née *Black* Eng. translator

Gar·rick \'gar-ik\ David 1717–1779 Eng. actor

Gar·ri·son \'gar-ə-sən\ William Lloyd 1805–1879 Am. abolitionist

Gar·shin \'gär-shən\ Vsevolod Mikhaylovich 1855–1888 Russ. writer

Gar·vey \'gär-vē\ Marcus Moziah 1887–1940 Jamaican black leader

Gary \'gar-ē, 'ger-ē\ Elbert Henry 1846–1927 Am. industrialist

Gas·coigne \'gas-,köin\ George ca 1525–1577 Eng. poet

Gas·kell \'gas-kəl\ Elizabeth Cleghorn 1810–1865 née *Stevenson* Eng. nov.

Gas·ser \'gas-ər\ Herbert Spencer 1888–1963 Am. physiol.

Gates \'gāts\ Horatio ca 1728–1806 Am. gen. in Revolution

Gau·guin \gō-gaⁿ\ (Eugène-Henri-) Paul 1848–1903 Fr. painter — Gau·guin·esque \(ˌ)gō-gaⁿ-'esk\ adj

Gaulle, de \di-'göl, -'göl\ Charles-André-Marie-Joseph 1890–1970 Fr. gen. & polit.; pres. of Fifth Republic (1958–69)

Gauss \'gaus\ Carl Friedrich 1777–1855 Ger. math. & astron.

Gautama Buddha — see SIDDHĀRTHA GAUTAMA

Gau·tier \gö-tyä\ Théophile 1811–1872 Fr. author

Gay \'gā\ John 1685–1732 Eng. poet & dram.

Gay-Lus·sac \ˌgā-lə-'sak\ Joseph-Louis 1778–1850 Fr. chem. & physicist

Ge·ber — see JĀBIR IBN ḤAYYĀN

Ged·des \'ged-ēz\ Norman Bel \'bel\ 1893–1958 Am. designer

Gei·kie \'gē-kē\ Sir Archibald 1835–1924 Scot. geologist

Gei·sel \'gī-zəl\ Theodor Seuss 1904–   pseud. *Dr. Seuss* \'süs\ Am. writer & illustrator

Gellée Claude — see CLAUDE LORRAIN
Gell–Mann \'gel-ˌmän\ Murray 1929–   Am. physicist
Ge·net \zhə-'na\ Edmond-Charles-Édouard 1763–1834 Fr. diplomat in U.S.
Genet Jean 1910–1986 Fr. dram. & nov.
Gen·ghis Khan \ˌjeŋ-gə-'skän, ˌgeŋ-\ ca 1162–1227 Mongol conqueror
Gen·ser·ic \'gen(t)-sə-rik, 'jen(t)-\ or Gai·se·ric \'gī-zə-(ˌ)rik, -sə-\ d 477 king of the Vandals (428–477)
Gen·ti·le da Fa·bri·a·no \jen-'tē-lē-də-ˌfäb-rē-'än-(ˌ)ō\ ca 1370–1427 orig. Niccolò di Giovanni di Massio Ital. painter
Gen·ti·les·chi \ˌjent-ᵊl-'es-kē\ Orazio Lomi ca 1562–ca 1647 & his dau. Artemisia ca1597–after 1651 Ital. painters
Geof·frey of Monmouth \'jef-rē-\ ca 1100–1154 Brit. ecclesiastic & chronicler
George \'jȯ(ə)rj\ Saint 3d cent. Christian martyr & patron saint of England
George name of 6 kings of Great Britain: I 1660–1727 (reigned 1714–27); II 1683–1760 (reigned 1727–60); III 1738–1820 (reigned 1760–1820); IV 1762–1830 (reigned 1820–30); V 1865–1936 (reigned 1910–36); VI 1895–1952 (reigned 1936–52)
George name of 2 kings of Greece: I 1845–1913 (reigned 1863–1913); II 1890–1947 (reigned 1922–23; 1935–47)
George David Lloyd — see David LLOYD GEORGE
George Henry 1839–1897 Am. econ.
Ge·rard \jə-'rärd, 'jer-ˌärd\ Charles 1618?–1694 1st Baron Gerard of Bran·don \'bran-dən\; Viscount Brandon Eng. royalist commander
Gé·rard \zhā-'rär\ Comte Étienne-Maurice 1773–1852 Fr. Napoleonic gen.; marshal of France
Ger·hard·sen \'ge(ə)r-ˌhärs-ᵊn\ Einar Henry 1897–1987 Norw. polit.
Gé·ri·cault \ˌzhā-ri-'kō\ (Jean-Louis-André-) Théodore 1791–1824 Fr. painter
Ger·man·i·cus Cae·sar \jər-ˌman-i-kə(s)-'sē-zər\ 15 B.C.–A.D. 19 Rom. gen.
Gé·rôme \zhā-'rōm\ Jean-Léon 1824–1904 Fr. painter
Ge·ron·i·mo \jə-'rän-ə-ˌmō\ 1829–1909 Goyathlay Chiricahua Apache chieftain
Ger·ry \'ger-ē\ Elbridge 1744–1814 Am. statesman; vice pres. of the U.S. (1813–14)
Gersh·win \'gərsh-wən\ George 1898–1937 orig. Jacob Gershvin Am. composer
Ge·sell \gə-'zel\ Arnold Lucius 1880–1961 Am. psychol. & pediatrician
Ges·ner \'ges-nər\ Conrad 1516–1565 Swiss naturalist
Get·ty \'get-ē\ Jean Paul 1892–1976 Am. business executive
Gha·zā·li, al- \ˌal-gə-'zal-ē\ 1058–1111 Abu Hāmid Muḥammad ibn Muḥammad at-Ṭūsi al-Ghazālī Islamic jurist, theol., & mystic
Ghi·ber·ti \gē-'bert-ē\ Lorenzo ca 1378–1455 Florentine goldsmith, painter, & sculptor
Ghir·lan·da·jo or Ghir·lan·da·io \ˌgir-lən-'dä-(ˌ)yō, -'dī-(ˌ)ō\ Domenico 1449–1494 orig. Domenico di Tommaso Bigordi Florentine painter
Ghose Sri Aurobindo — see AUROBINDO
Gia·co·met·ti \ˌjäk-ə-'met-ē\ Alberto 1901–1966 Swiss artist
Giae·ver \'yā-vər\ Ivar 1929–   Norw. physicist in U.S.
Gi·auque \jē-'ōk\ William Francis 1895–1982 Am. chem.
Gib·bon \'gib-ən\ Edward 1737–1794 Eng. hist.
Gib·bons \'gib-ənz\ James 1834–1921 Am. cardinal
Gibbons Orlando 1538–1625 Eng. organist & composer
Gibbs \'gibz\ James 1682–1754 Brit. architect
Gibbs Josiah Willard 1839–1903 Am. math. & physicist
Gib·ran or Jib·ran \jə-'brän\ Kahlil 1883–1931 Jubrān Khalīl Jubrān Lebanese nov., poet, & artist in U.S.
Gib·son \'gib-sən\ Charles Dana 1867–1944 Am. illustrator
Gibson William 1914–   Am. dram.
Gide \'zhēd\ André 1869–1951 Fr. nov., critic, & essayist
Giel·gud \'gil-ˌgüd, 'gēl-\ Sir (Arthur) John 1904–   Eng. actor
Gie·rek \'gyer-ək\ Edward 1913–   1st secy. of Polish Communist party (1970–80)
Gie·se·king \'gē-zə-kiŋ\ Walter Wilhelm 1895–1956 Ger. (Fr.-born) pianist
Gil·bert \'gil-bərt\ Cass 1859–1934 Am. architect
Gilbert Sir Humphrey ca 1539–1583 Eng. navigator
Gilbert Walter 1932–   Am. biochem.
Gilbert William 1540–1603 Eng. physician & physicist
Gilbert Sir William Schwenck 1836–1911 Eng. librettist & poet; collaborator with Sir Arthur Sullivan — Gil·bert·ian \(')gil-'bərt-ē-ən\ adj
Gil·lette \jə-'let\ King Camp 1855–1932 Am. inventor & manuf.
Gillette William Hooker 1855–1937 Am. actor
Gil·man \'gil-mən\ Daniel Coit \'kȯit\ 1831–1908 Am. educ.; pres. Johns Hopkins U. (1875–1901)
Gil·mer \'gil-mər\ Elizabeth 1870–1951 née Mer·i·weth·er \'mer-ə-ˌweth-ər\ pseud. Dorothy Dix \'diks\ Am. journalist
Gil·pin \'gil-pən\ Charles Sidney 1878–1930 Am. actor
Gi·na·ste·ra \ˌhē-nə-'ster-ə\ Alberto Evaristo 1916–1983 Argentine composer
Gins·berg \'ginz-ˌbərg\ Allen 1926–   Am. poet
Gior·gio·ne \(ˌ)jȯr-'jō-nē\ ca 1477–1511 Giorgione da Castelfranco Venetian painter
Giot·to \'jȯ(t)-(ˌ)tō, jē-'ät-(ˌ)ō\ 1266/67(or 1276)–1337 Giotto di Bondone Florentine painter, architect, & sculptor
Gi·rard \jə-'rärd\ Jean-Baptiste 1765–1850 Swiss Franciscan & educ.
Gi·rard \jə-'rärd\ Stephen 1750–1831 Am. (Fr.-born) financier & philanthropist
Gi·raud \zhē-'rō\ Henri-Honoré 1879–1949 Fr. gen.
Gi·rau·doux \zhē-rō-'dü\ (Hyppolyte-) Jean 1882–1944 Fr. writer
Gir·tin \'gərt-ᵊn\ Thomas 1775–1802 Eng. founder of art of modern watercolor painting
Gis·card d'Es·taing \zhis-kär-des-taⁿ, -ˌkär-des-'taŋ\ Valéry 1926–   pres. of France (1974–81)
Gis·sing \'gis-iŋ\ George Robert 1857–1903 Eng. nov.
Giu·lio Ro·ma·no \ˌjül-yō-rə-'män-(ˌ)ō\ ca 1499–1546 Giulio di Pietro di Filippo de' Gianuzzi Ital. painter & architect
Gjel·le·rup \'gel-ə-ˌrüp\ Karl 1857–1919 Dan. writer
Glad·stone \'glad-ˌstōn, chiefly Brit -stən\ William Ewart 1809–1898 Brit. statesman; prime min. (1868–74; 1880–85; 1886; 1892–94)
Gla·ser \'glā-zər\ Donald Arthur 1926–   Am. physicist

Glas·gow \'glas-(ˌ)kō, -(ˌ)gō; 'glaz-(ˌ)gō\ Ellen Anderson Gholson 1873–1945 Am. nov.
Glash·ow \'glash-(ˌ)ō\ Sheldon Lee 1932–   Am. physicist
Glas·pell \'glas-ˌpel\ Susan 1882–1948 Am. nov. & dram.
Glass \'glas\ Carter 1858–1946 Am. statesman
Gla·zu·nov \'glaz-ə-ˌnȯf, -ˌnȯv, ˌglaz-ü-'\ Aleksandr Konstantinovich 1865–1936 Russ. composer
Glen·dow·er \'glen-ˌdaù(-ə)r\ Owen ca 1359–ca 1416 Welsh chieftain & rebel against Henry IV of England
Glenn \'glen\ John Herschel 1921–   Am. astronaut & polit.; 1st Am. to orbit the earth (1962)
Glin·ka \'gliŋ-kə\ Mikhail Ivanovich 1804–1857 Russ. composer
Gloucester Duke of — see HUMPHREY
Glov·er \'gləv-ər\ John 1732–1797 Am. gen. in Revolution
Glover Sarah Ann 1785–1867 Eng. music teacher; invented tonic sol-fa system of notation
Gluck \'glük\ Alma 1884–1938 née (Reba) Fiersohn Am. (Romanian-born) soprano
Gluck Christoph Willibald 1714–1787 Ger. composer
Go·bat \gō-'bä\ Charles Albert 1834–1914 Swiss statesman
God·dard \'gäd-ərd\ Robert Hutchings 1882–1945 Am. physicist
God·frey of Bouil·lon \ˌgäd-frē-əv-(ˌ)bü-'yōⁿ\ F Godefroy de Bouillon ca 1060–1100 Fr. crusader
Go·dol·phin \gə-'däl-fən\ Sidney 1645–1712 1st Earl of Godolphin Eng. statesman
Go·doy \gō-'dȯi\ Manuel de 1767–1851 Span. statesman
Go·du·nov \'gōd-ᵊn-ˌȯf, 'gȯd-, 'gäd-\ Boris Fyodorovich ca 1551–1605 czar of Russia (1598–1605)
God·win \'gäd-wən\ or God·wine \'gäd-(ˌ)win-ə\ d 1053 earl of Wessex
Godwin William 1756–1836 Eng. philos. & nov. — God·win·ian \gäd-'win-ē-ən\ adj
Godwin–Aus·ten \-'ȯs-tən, -'äs-\ Henry Haversham 1834–1923 Eng. explorer & geologist
Goeb·bels \'gə(r)b-əlz, 'gœb-əls\ (Paul) Joseph 1897–1945 Ger. Nazi propagandist
Goering var of GÖRING
Goes \'güs\ Hugo van der ca 1440–1482 Du. painter
Goe·thals \'gō-thəlz\ George Washington 1858–1928 Am. gen. & engineer
Goe·the \'gə(r)-tə, 'gœt-ə\ Johann Wolfgang von 1749–1832 Ger. poet & dram. — Goe·the·an \-tē-ən\ adj
Gogh, van \van-'gō, -'gäk, -'kȯk\ Vincent Willem 1853–1890 Du. painter
Go·gol \'gȯ-gəl, 'gō-ˌgȯl\ Nikolay Vasilyevich 1809–1852 Russ. writer — Go·gol·ian \gō-'gōl-yən, gə-'gōl-\ adj
Gold·berg \'gōl(d)-ˌbərg\ Arthur Joseph 1908–1990 Am. lawyer and jurist; U.S. ambassador to U.N. (1965–68)
Gol·den \'gōl-dən\ Harry Lewis 1902–1981 Am. journalist
Gol·den·wei·ser \'gōl-dən-ˌwī-zər\ Alexander Alexandrovich 1880–1940 Am. (Russ.-born) anthropol. & sociol.
Gol·ding \'gōl-diŋ\ William Gerald 1911–   Eng. author
Gol·do·ni \gäl-'dō-nē\ Carlo 1707–1793 Ital. dram.
Gold·smith \'gōl(d)-ˌsmith\ Oliver 1730–1774 Brit. author
Gold·stein \'gōl(d)-ˌstīn\ Joseph Leonard 1940–   Am. medical geneticist
Gold·wa·ter \'gōl-ˌdwȯt-ər, -ˌdwät-\ Barry Morris 1909–   Am. polit.
Gold·wyn \'gōl-dwən\ Samuel 1879?–1974 orig. Schmuel Gelbfisz Am. (Pol.-born) motion-picture producer
Gol·gi \'gȯl-(ˌ)jē\ Camillo \kä-'mēl-(ˌ)lō\ 1843(or 1844)–1926 Ital. physician
Gol·lancz \gə-'lan(t)s\ Sir Hermann 1852–1930 Eng. Semitic scholar
Gó·mez \'gō-ˌmez\ Juan Vicente 1864–1935 Venezuelan gen. & polit.; dictator (1908–35)
Gom·pers \'gäm-pərz\ Samuel 1850–1924 Am. (Brit.-born) labor leader
Go·muł·ka \gō-'mùl-kə, -'məl-\ Władysław 1905–1982 Pol. polit.
Gon·çal·ves Di·as \gōn-ˌsäl-vəs-'dē-əs\ Antônio 1823–1864 Braz. poet
Gon·cha·ro·va \gən-'chär-ə-və\ Nathalie 1883–1962 Russ. artist
Gon·court \gōⁿ-'kü(ə)r\ Edmond-Louis-Antoine Huot de 1822–1896 & his bro. Jules-Alfred Huot de 1830–1870 Fr. nov. & collaborators
Gon·do·mar \ˌgän-də-'mär\ Conde de 1567–1626 Diego Sarmiento de Acuña Span. diplomat
Gon·za·ga \gən-'zäg-ə, gän-, -'zag\ Saint Aloysius 1568–1591 Ital. Jesuit
Gon·zá·lez \gən-'zäl-əs\ Manuel 1833–1893 Mex. gen.; pres. of Mexico (1880–84)
Gonzalo de Córdoba — see FERNÁNDEZ DE CÓRDOBA
Good·hue \'gùd-(ˌ)(h)yü\ Bertram Grosvenor 1869–1924 Am. architect
Good·man \'gùd-mən\ Benjamin David 1909–1986 Benny Am. musician and bandleader
Good·rich \'gùd-(ˌ)rich\ Samuel Griswold 1793–1860 pseud. Peter Parley \'pär-lē\ Am. writer
Good·year \'gùd-ˌyi(ə)r, 'gùj-ˌi(ə)r\ Charles 1800–1860 Am. inventor
Gor·ba·chev \ˌgȯr-bə-'chȯf\ Mikhail Sergeyevich 1931–   Soviet polit.; 1st secy. of communist party (1985–   ); pres. of U.S.S.R. (1990–   )
Gor·cha·kov \ˌgȯr-chə-'kȯf, -'kȯv\ Prince Aleksandr Mikhaylovich 1798–1883 Russ. statesman & diplomat
Gor·din \'gȯrd-ᵊn\ Jacob 1853–1909 Am. (Russ.-born) Yiddish dram.
Gor·don \'gȯrd-ᵊn\ Charles George 1833–1885 Chinese Gordon, Gordon Pasha Brit. soldier
Gordon Charles William 1860–1937 pseud. Ralph Connor Canad. clergyman & nov.
Gordon Lord George 1751–1793 Eng. polit. agitator
Go·re·my·kin \gə-'rē-mə-kən\ Ivan Logginovich 1839–1917 Russ. statesman; prime min. (1906; 1914–16)
Gor·gas \'gȯr-gəs\ William Crawford 1854–1920 Am. army surgeon & sanitation expert

---

Gö·ring \\'gər-iŋ, 'ger-, 'gœr-\\ Hermann 1893–1946 Ger. Nazi polit.
Gor·ky \\'gȯr-kē\\ Maksim 1868–1936 pseud. of *Aleksey Maksimovich Pesh·kov* \\'pesh-ˌkȯf, -ˌkȯv\\ Russ. writer
Gor·ky \\'gȯr-kē\\ Arshile 1905–1948 Am. (Armenian-born) artist
Gort Viscount — see VEREKER
Gosse \\'gäs\\ Sir Edmund William 1849–1928 Eng. poet & critic
Gott·schalk \\'gäch-ˌȯk, 'gät-ˌshȯk\\ Louis Moreau 1829–1869 Am. composer
Gou·dy \\'gaȯd-ē\\ Frederic William 1865–1947 Am. type designer
Gough \\'gäf\\ Hugh 1779–1869 1st Viscount *Gough* Eng. field marshal
Gould \\'güld\\ Jay orig. *Jason* 1836–1892 Am. financier
Gou·nod \\'gü-ˌnō\\ Charles-François 1818–1893 Fr. composer
Gour·mont \\'gu̇r-'mōⁿ\\ Remy de 1858–1915 Fr. writer
Gow·er \\'gau̇(-ə)r, 'gō(-ə)r, 'gȯ(-ə)r\\ John 1330?–1408 Eng. poet
Go·ya y Lu·cien·tes \\'gȯi-(y)ə-ˌē-ˌlü-sē-'en-ˌtäs\\ Francisco José de 1746–1828 Span. painter — **Go·ya·esque** \\ˌgȯi-(y)ə-'esk\\ *or* **Go·yesque** \\gȯi-'(y)esk\\ *adj*
Goy·en *or* **Goij·en, van** \\'gȯi-(y)ən\\ Jan Josephszoon 1596–1656 Du. painter
Grac·chus \\'grak-əs\\ Gaius Sempronius 153–121 B.C. & his bro. Tiberius Sempronius 163–133 B.C. *the Grac·chi* \\'grak-ˌī\\ Rom. statesmen
Gra·ham \\'grā-əm, 'gra(-ə)m\\ John 1648–1689 *Graham of Cla·ver·house* \\'klā-vər-ˌhau̇s\\; *Bonny Dundee;* 1st Viscount of *Dundee* Scot. Jacobite
Graham Martha 1893–   Am. dancer
Graham Thomas 1805–1869 Scot. chem.
Graham William Franklin 1918–   *Billy* Am. evangelist
Gra·hame \\'grā-əm, 'gra(-ə)m\\ Kenneth 1859–1932 Brit. writer
Gramme \\'gram\\ Zénobe Théophile 1826–1901 Belg. engineer
Gra·na·dos \\grə-'näd-(ˌ)ōs\\ Enrique 1867–1916 Span. composer
Gran·di \\'grän-(ˌ)dē\\ Dino 1895–1988 Conte *di Mordano* Ital. Fascist polit.
Gra·nit \\grä-'nēt\\ Ragnar Arthur 1900–   Swed. (Finn.-born) physiol.
Grant \\'grant\\ Ulysses 1822–1885 orig. *Hiram Ulysses Grant* Am. gen.; 18th pres. of the U.S. (1869–77)
Gran·ville–Bar·ker \\ˌgran-ˌvil-'bär-kər\\ Harley Granville 1877–1946 Eng. actor, manager, & dram.
Grass \\'gräs\\ Günter Wilhelm 1927–   Ger. writer
Grasse \\'gras, 'gräs\\ François-Joseph-Paul 1722–1788 Comte *de Grasse* & Marquis de *Grasse-Tilly* \\-tē-'yē\\ Fr. naval officer
Gra·tian \\'grā-sh(ē-)ən\\ *L Flavius Gratianus* 359–383 Rom. emp. (367–383)
Grat·tan \\'grat-ᵊn\\ Henry 1746–1820 Irish orator & statesman
Grau San Mar·tín \\'grau̇-ˌsan-(ˌ)mär-'tēn, -ˌsän-\\ Ramón 1887–1969 Cuban physician & polit.; pres. of Cuba (1944–48)
Graves \\'grāvz\\ Robert Ranke 1895–1985 Brit. author
Gray \\'grā\\ Asa 1810–1888 Am. botanist
Gray Thomas 1716–1771 Eng. poet
Grayson David — see Ray Stannard BAKER
Gra·zia·ni \\ˌgrät-sē-'ä-nē\\ Rodolfo 1882–1955 Marchese *di Neghelli* Ital. marshal & colonial administrator
Gre·co, El \\el-'grek-(ˌ)ō *also* -'gräk-\\ 1541–1614 *Doménikos Theotokópoulos* Span. (Cretan-born) painter
Gree·ley \\'grē-lē\\ Horace 1811–1872 Am. journalist & polit.
Gree·ly \\'grē-lē\\ Adolphus Washington 1844–1935 Am. gen. & arctic explorer
Green \\'grēn\\ John Richard 1837–1883 Eng. hist.
Green Julien 1900–   Fr. nov.
Green William 1873–1952 Am. labor leader
Gree·na·way \\'grē-nə-ˌwā\\ Catherine 1846–1901 *Kate* Eng. painter & illustrator
Greene \\'grēn\\ Graham 1904–   Brit. nov.
Greene Nathanael 1742–1786 Am. gen. in Revolution
Greene Robert 1558?–1592 Eng. poet & dram.
Gree·nough \\'grē-(ˌ)nō\\ Horatio 1805–1852 Am. sculptor
Greg·o·ry \\'greg-(ə-)rē\\ name of 16 popes: esp. **I** Saint *ca* 540–604 *the Great* (pope 590–604); **VII** Saint orig. *Hil·de·brand* \\'hil-də-ˌbrand\\ *ca* 1020–1085 (pope 1073–85); **XIII** orig. *Ugo Buoncompagni* 1502–1585 (pope 1572–85)
Gregory Lady Isabella Augusta 1852–1932 née *Persse* Irish dram.
Gregory of Nys·sa \\-'nis-ə\\ Saint *ca* 335–*ca* 394 Eastern church father
Gregory of Tours Saint 538–594 Frankish ecclesiastic & hist.
Gren·fell \\'gren-ˌfel, -fəl\\ Sir Wilfred Thomason 1865–1940 Eng. medical missionary
Gren·ville \\'gren-ˌvil, -vəl\\ George 1712–1770 Eng. statesman
Grenville *or* **Greyn·ville** \\'grän-\\ Sir Richard 1542–1591 Brit. naval commander
Gresh·am \\'gresh-əm\\ Sir Thomas 1519–1579 Eng. financier
Greuze \\'grœz\\ Jean-Baptiste 1725–1805 Fr. painter
Gré·vy \\grā-'vē\\ (François-Paul-) Jules 1807–1891 Fr. lawyer; 3d pres. of the Republic (1879–87)
Grey \\'grā\\ 2d Earl 1764–1845 *Charles Grey* Eng. statesman; prime min. (1830–34)
Grey Edward 1862–1933 Viscount *Grey of Fal·lo·don* \\'fal-əd-ᵊn\\ Eng. statesman
Grey Lady Jane 1537–1554 titular queen of England for 9 days
Grey Zane 1875–1939 Am. nov.
Grieg \\'grēg, 'grig\\ Edvard Hagerup 1843–1907 Norw. composer
Grieve Christopher Murray — see Hugh MACDIARMID
Grif·fin \\'grif-ən\\ Walter Burley 1876–1937 Am. architect
Grif·fith \\'grif-əth\\ Arthur 1872–1922 Irish journalist & nationalist
Griffith David Lewelyn Wark 1875–1948 Am. motion-picture producer & director
Gri·gnard \\grēn-'yär\\ (François-Auguste-) Victor 1871–1935 Fr. chem.
Grill·par·zer \\'gril-ˌpärt-sər\\ Franz 1791–1872 Austrian dram. & poet
Grimm \\'grim\\ Jacob 1785–1863 & his bro. Wilhelm 1786–1859 Ger. philologists & folklorists
Gris \\'grēs\\ Juan 1887–1927 *José Victoriano González* Span. painter in France
Gro·fé \\grō-'fā\\ Ferd·e \\'fərd-ē\\ 1892–1972 Am. conductor & composer
Gro·lier de Ser·vières \\grōl-yā-də-ˌser-vē-'e(ə)r\\, 'grōl-yər-\\ Jean 1479–1565 Vicomte *d'Aguisy* Fr. bibliophile
Gro·my·ko \\grə-'mē-(ˌ)kō, grō-\\ Andrey Andreyevich 1909–1989 Russ. econ. & diplomat; pres. of U.S.S.R. (1985–88)

Groo·te \\'grōt-ə\\ Gerhard 1340–1384 *Ge·rar·dus Mag·nus* \\jə-ˌrärd-ə-'smag-nəs\\ Du. religious reformer
Gro·pi·us \\'grō-pē-əs\\ Walter 1883–1969 Ger.-born architect in America
Grop·per \\'gräp-ər\\ William 1897–1977 Am. artist
Gros·ve·nor \\'grōv-(ə-)nər\\ Gilbert Hovey 1875–1966 Am. geographer and editor
Grosz \\'grōs\\ George 1893–1959 Am. (Ger.-born) painter
Grosz Ka·roly \\kä-rói\\ 1930–   1st secy. of Hung. Communist party (1988–89)
Grote \\'grōt\\ George 1794–1871 Eng. hist.
Gro·tius \\'grō-sh(ē-)əs\\ Hugo 1583–1645 *Huigh de Groot* \\'grōt\\ Du. jurist & statesman
Grou·chy \\grü-'shē\\ Emmanuel 1766–1847 Marquis *de Grouchy* Fr. gen.
Grove \\'grōv\\ Sir George 1820–1900 Eng. writer on music
Groves \\'grōvz\\ Leslie Richard 1896–1970 Am. gen.
Grü·ne·wald \\'grü-nə-ˌwȯld, 'grᵫ-nə-ˌvält\\ Matthias *ca* 1455–1528 Ger. painter
Gryph·i·us \\'grif-ē-əs\\ Andreas 1616–1664 *G Greif* \\'grīf\\ Ger. poet & dram.
Guar·ne·ri \\gwär-'ne(ə)r-ē\\ *L* **Guar·ne·ri·us** \\gwär-'nir-ē-əs, -'ner-\\ family of Ital. violin makers: esp. Giuseppe Antonio 1687–1745
Gu·de·ri·an \\gü-'der-ē-ən\\ Heinz Wilhelm 1888–1954 Ger. gen.
Gue·dal·la \\gwi-'dal-ə\\ Philip 1889–1944 Eng. writer
Gue·rin \\ger-ən\\ Jules 1866–1946 Am. painter
Gues·clin \\ges-'klaⁿ\\ Bertrand du *ca* 1320–1380 Fr. soldier
Guesde \\ged\\ Jules 1845–1922 *Mathieu Basile* Fr. socialist
Guest \\'gest\\ Edgar Albert 1881–1959 Am. journalist & poet
Gue·va·ra \\ge-'vär-ə, gä-'vär-ə\\ Ernesto 1928–1967 *Che* Latin-Am. revolutionary leader
Gui·do of Arezzo \\'gwēd-(ˌ)ō\\ *or* **Guido Are·ti·nus** \\-ˌar-ə-'tē-nəs\\ *ca* 991–1050 Benedictine monk & music reformer
Guil·laume \\gē-'yōm\\ Charles Édouard 1861–1938 Fr. physicist
Guille·min \\gē(-yə)-'maⁿ\\ Roger Charles Louis 1924–   Am. (Fr.-born) physiol.
Guiscard Robert — see ROBERT GUISCARD
Guise, de \\'gēz *also* 'gwēz\\ 2d Duc 1519–1563 *François de Lorraine* Fr. soldier & polit.
Guise, de 3d Duc 1550–1588 *Henri I de Lorraine* Fr. soldier & polit.
Gui·te·ras \\gē-'ter-əs\\ Juan 1852–1925 Cuban physician
Gui·zot \\gē-'zō\\ François-Pierre-Guillaume 1787–1874 Fr. hist. & statesman
Gull·strand \\'gəl-ˌstran(d)\\ Allvar 1862–1930 Swed. ophthalmologist
Gun·nars·son \\'gən-ər-sən\\ Gunnar 1889–1975 Icelandic writer
Gun·ter \\'gənt-ər\\ Edmund 1581–1626 Eng. math.
Gus·tav \\'gu̇s-ˌtäv\\ *or* **Gus·ta·vus** \\(ˌ)gə-'stä-vəs, -'stäv-əs\\ name of 6 kings of Sweden, the first 4 of the Vasa dynasty: **I** (*Gustav Eriksson*) 1496?–1560 (reigned 1523–60); **II** (*Gustav Adolph*) 1594–1632 (reigned 1611–32); **III** 1746–1792 (reigned 1771–92); **IV** (*Gustav Adolph*) 1778–1837 (reigned 1792–1809); **V** 1858–1950 (reigned 1907–50); **VI** (*Gustav Adolph*) 1882–1973 (reigned 1950–73)
Gu·ten·berg \\'güt-ᵊn-ˌbərg\\ Johannes *ca* 1390–1468 Ger. inventor of printing from movable type
Guth·rie \\'gəth-rē\\ Woodrow Wilson 1912–1967 *Woody* Am. folksinger
Gutz·kow \\'gu̇ts-(ˌ)kō\\ Karl Ferdinand 1811–1878 Ger. journalist, nov., & dram.
Guz·mán Blan·co \\gü-ˌsmän-'blän-(ˌ)kō\\ Antonio 1829–1899 Venezuelan soldier & statesman; dictator of Venezuela (1870–89)
Gwin·nett \\gwin-'et\\ Button *ca* 1735–1777 Am. Revolutionary leader
Gwyn *or* **Gwynn** *or* **Gwynne** \\'gwin\\ Eleanor 1650–1687 *Nell* Eng. actress *mistress of Charles II*
Haa·kon VII \\'hȯ-kən, -ˌkän\\ 1872–1957 king of Norway (1905–57)
Haa·vel·mo \\'hȯ-vəl-ˌmō\\ Trygve 1911–   Norw. econ.
Ha·ber \\'häb-ər\\ Fritz 1868–1934 Ger. chem.
Há·cha \\'hä-(ˌ)kä\\ Emil 1872–1945 Czech jurist & statesman
Had·field \\'had-ˌfēld\\ Sir Robert Abbott 1858–1940 Eng. metallurgist
Had·ley \\'had-lē\\ Henry Kimball 1871–1937 Am. composer
Had·ow \\'had-(ˌ)ō\\ Sir (William) Henry 1859–1937 Eng. educ. & writer on music
Ha·dri·an \\'hā-drē-ən\\ *var of* ADRIAN
Hadrian A.D. 76–138 Rom. emp. (117–138)
Haeck·el \\'hek-əl\\ Ernst Heinrich 1834–1919 Ger. biol. & philos.
Hā·fez \\hä-'fez\\ 1325(or 1326)–1389(or 1390) *Mohammad Shams od-Din Hāfez* Pers. poet
Hag·gard \\'hag-ərd\\ Sir (Henry) Ri·der \\-'rīd-ər\\ 1856–1925 Eng. nov.
Hahn \\'hän\\ Otto 1879–1968 Ger. physical chem.
Hah·ne·mann \\'hän-ə-mən\\ (Christian Friedrich) Samuel 1755–1843 Ger. physician; founder of homeopathy
Haider Ali — see HYDER ALI
Haig \\'hāg\\ 1st Earl 1861–1928 *Douglas Haig* Brit. field marshal
Hai·le Se·las·sie \\ˌhī-lē-sə-'las-ē, -'läs-\\ 1892–1975 Ras *Tafari* emp. of Ethiopia (1930–36; 1941–74)
Hak·luyt \\'hak-ˌlüt\\ Richard *ca* 1552–1616 Eng. geographer & hist.
Hal·dane \\'hȯl-ˌdān, -dən\\ John Burdon Sanderson 1892–1964 *son of J.S.* Brit. scientist
Haldane John Scott 1860–1936 Brit. physiol.
Haldane Richard Burdon 1856–1928 Viscount *Haldane of Cloan* \\'klōn\\; *bro. of J.S.* Brit. lawyer, philos., & statesman
Hal·der \\'häl-dər\\ Franz 1884–1972 Ger. gen.
Hale \\'hā(ə)l\\ Edward Everett 1822–1909 Am. Unitarian clergyman & writer
Hale George Ellery 1868–1938 Am. astron.
Hale Sir Matthew 1609–1676 Eng. jurist
Hale Nathan 1755–1776 Am. Revolutionary hero
Ha·lé·vy \\ˌ(h)al-ā-'vē, ˌ(h)äl-\\ (Jacques-François-) Fromental (-Elíe) 1799–1862 pseud. of *Élie Lévy* \\lā-'vē\\ Fr. composer
Halévy Ludovic 1834–1908 *nephew of prec.* Fr. dram. & nov.
Hal·i·fax \\'hal-ə-ˌfaks\\ Earl of 1881–1959 *Edward Frederick Lindley Wood* Eng. statesman & diplomat
Hall \\'hȯl\\ Charles Francis 1821–1871 Am. arctic explorer
Hall Charles Martin 1863–1914 Am. chem. & manuf.
Hall Granville Stanley 1844–1924 Am. psychol. & educ.
Hall James Norman 1887–1951 Am. nov.
Hal·lam \\'hal-əm\\ Henry 1777–1859 Eng. hist.
Hal·leck \\'hal-ək, -ik\\ Fitz-Greene 1790–1867 Am. poet

Halleck Henry Wager 1815–1872 Am. gen.
Hal·ley \'hal-ē *also* 'hā-lē\ Edmond *or* Edmund 1656–1742 Eng. astron.
Hals \'hälz, 'häls\ Frans *ca* 1581–1666 Du. painter
Hal·sey \'hól-sē, -zē\ William Frederick 1882–1959 Am. admiral
Hal·sted \'hól-stəd, -,sted\ William Stewart 1852–1922 Am. surgeon
Ham·bro \'häm-,brō\ Carl Joachim 1885–1964 Norw. statesman
Ha·mil·car Bar·ca \hə-'mil-,kär-'bär-kə, 'ham-əl-\ *or* **Bar·cas** \-'bär-kəs\ 270?–229(or 228) B.C. *father of Hannibal* Carthaginian gen.
Ham·il·ton \'ham-əl-tən, -əlt-ᵊn\ Alexander 1755–1804 Am. statesman — **Ham·il·to·nian** \,ham-əl-'tō-nē-ən, -nyən\ *adj*
Hamilton Edith 1867–1963 Am. classicist
Hamilton Lady Emma 1765–1815 née *Amy Lyon* mistress of Lord Nelson
Ham·lin \'ham-lən\ Hannibal 1809–1891 Am. polit.; vice pres. of the U.S. (1861–65)
Ham·mar·skjöld \'ham-ər-,shəld, 'häm-, -,shúld, -,shēld\ Dag \'däg\ Hjalmar Agne Carl 1905–1961 Swed. U.N. official; secy.-gen. (1953–61)
Ham·mer·stein \'ham-ər-,stīn, -,stēn\ Oscar 1846–1919 Ger.-born theater manager in America
Hammerstein Oscar 1895–1960 *grandson of prec.* Am. dram.
Ham·mett \'ham-et\ (Samuel) Dashiell 1894–1961 Am. writer
Ham·mond \'ham-ənd\ John Hays 1855–1936 Am. mining engineer
Hammond John Hays 1888–1965 *son of prec.* Am. electrical engineer & inventor
Hammond Laurens 1895–1973 Am. inventor
Ham·mu·ra·bi \,ham-ə-'räb-ē\ *or* **Ham·mu·ra·pi** \-'räp-ē\ *d* 1750 B.C. king of Babylon (1792–50)
Hamp·den \'ham(p)-dən\ John 1594–1643 Eng. statesman
Hampden Walter 1879–1955 stage name of *W. H. Dougherty* Am. actor
Hamp·ton \'ham(p)-tən\ Wade 1751?–1835 Am. gen.
Hampton Wade 1818–1902 *grandson of prec.* Am. polit. & Confed. gen.
Ham·sun \'häm-sən\ Knut 1859–1952 pseud. of *Knut Pedersen* Norw. writer
Han·cock \'han-,käk\ John 1737–1793 Am. statesman in Revolution
Hancock Winfield Scott 1824–1886 Am. gen. & polit.
Hand \'hand\ (Billings) Learned 1872–1961 Am. jurist
Han·del \'han-dᵊl\ George Frideric 1685–1759 Brit. (Ger.-born) composer — **Han·de·li·an** \han-'dē-lē-ən\ *adj*
Han·dy \'han-dē\ William Christopher 1873–1958 Am. blues musician
Han·na \'han-ə\ Marcus Alonzo 1837–1904 *Mark* Am. businessman & polit.
Han·nay \'han-,ā, 'han-ē\ James Owen 1865–1950 Irish clergyman & nov.
Han·ni·bal \'han-ə-bəl\ 247–183 B.C. *son of Hamilcar Barca* Carthaginian gen.
Han·no \'han-(,)ō\ 3d cent. B.C. *the Great* Carthaginian statesman
Ha·no·taux \,an-ə-'tō, än-\ (Albert-Auguste-) Gabriel 1853–1944 Fr. hist. & statesman
Han·sard \'han-,särd, 'han(t)-sərd\ Luke 1752–1828 Eng. printer
Han·son \'han(t)-sən\ Howard 1896–1981 Am. composer
Hans·son \'han(t)-sən\ Per Albin 1885–1946 Swed. statesman
Han Wu Ti \'hän-'wü-'dē\ 156–87 B.C. orig. *Liu Ch'e* often called *Wu Ti* Chin. emp. (140–87)
Han Yü \'hän-'yü\ 768–824 *Han Wen-kung* Chin. poet, essayist, & philos.
Har·bach \'här-,bäk\ Otto Abels 1873–1963 Am. dram. & musical-comedy librettist
Har·de·ca·nute *or* **Har·di·ca·nute** \,härd-i-kə-'n(y)üt\ *ca* 1019–1042 king of Denmark (1028–42) and of England (1040–42)
Har·den \'härd-ᵊn\ Sir Arthur 1865–1940 Eng. chem.
Harden Maximilian 1861–1927 orig. *Felix Ernst Witkowski* Ger. writer
Har·den·berg \'härd-ᵊn-,bərg, -,berk\ Prince Karl August von 1750–1822 Pruss. statesman
Har·ding \'härd-iŋ\ Warren Gamaliel 1865–1923 29th pres. of the U.S. (1921–23)
Har·dy \'härd-ē\ Thomas 1840–1928 Eng. nov. & poet — **Har·dy·esque** \,härd-ē-'esk\ *adj*
Har·greaves \'här-,grēvz\ James *d* 1778 Eng. inventor
Har·ing·ton *or* **Har·ring·ton** \'har-iŋ-tən\ Sir John 1561–1612 Eng. writer & translator
Ha·rī·rī, al– \,al-hə-'ri(ə)r-ē\ 1054–1122 Arab scholar & poet
Har·lan \'här-lən\ John Marshall 1833–1911 & his grandson 1899–1971 Am. jurists
Har·ley \'här-lē\ Robert 1661–1724 1st Earl of *Oxford* Eng. statesman
Harms·worth \'härmz-(,)wərth\ Alfred Charles William 1865–1922 Viscount *North·cliffe* \'nórth-,klif\ Eng. publisher & polit.
Harmsworth Harold Sidney 1868–1940 1st Viscount *Roth·er·mere* \'räth-ər-mi(ə)r\ *bro. of A.C.W.* Eng. publisher & polit.
Har·old \'har-əld\ name of 2 kings of the English: I *d* 1040 *Harold Harefoot* \'ha(ə)r-,fút, 'he(ə)r-\ (reigned 1035–40); II *ca* 1022–1066 (reigned 1066)
Harold name of 3 kings of Norway: esp. III *Hard·raa·de* \'hór-,ród-ə\ 1015–1066 (reigned 1045–66)
Har·ri·man \'har-ə-mən\ William Aver·ell \'āv-(ə-)rəl\ 1891–1986 Am. businessman, diplomat, & polit.
Har·ring·ton \'har-iŋ-tən\ (Edward) Michael 1928–1989 Am. writer and polit.
Har·ris \'har-əs\ Barbara Clementine 1930– Am. bishop
Harris Frank 1856–1931 Am. (Irish-born) writer
Harris Joel Chandler 1848–1908 Am. writer
Harris Roy 1898–1979 Am. composer
Harris William Torrey 1835–1909 Am. philos. & educ.
Har·ri·son \'har-ə-sən\ Benjamin 1833–1901 *grandson of W. H. Harrison* 23d pres. of the U.S. (1889–93)
Harrison Frederic 1831–1923 Eng. writer & philos.
Harrison Sir Rex 1908–1990 orig. *Reginald Carey Harrison* Brit. actor
Harrison William Henry 1773–1841 9th pres. of the U.S. (1841)
Hart \'härt\ Albert Bushnell 1854–1943 Am. hist. & editor
Hart Basil Henry Liddell — see LIDDELL HART
Hart Lorenz 1895–1943 Am. lyricist
Hart Moss 1904–1961 Am. librettist & dram.
Hart Sir Robert 1835–1911 Brit. diplomat
Hart William Surrey 1872–1946 Am. actor

Harte \'härt\ Francis Brett 1836–1902 known as *Bret* Am. writer
Hart·line \'härt-,lin\ Haldan Keffer 1903–1983 Am. biophysicist
Har·tung \'här-,túŋ\ Hans 1904–1989 Fr. (Ger.-born) painter
Hā·rūn ar–Ra·shīd \hə-,rü-när-rə-'shēd\ 763(or 766)–809 *Hārūn ar-Rashīd ibn Muhammad al-Mahdī ibn al-Mansūr al-'Abbāsī* caliph of Baghdad (786–809)
Har·vard \'här-vərd\ John 1607–1638 Am. clergyman
Har·vey \'här-vē\ George Brinton McClellan 1864–1928 Am. journalist & diplomat
Harvey Sir John Martin 1863–1944 Eng. actor & producer
Harvey William 1578–1657 Eng. physician & anatomist
Has·dru·bal \'haz-,drü-bəl, haz-'\ *d* 207 B.C. *bro. of Hannibal* Carthaginian gen.
Has·sam \'has-əm\ (Frederick) Childe 1859–1935 Am. artist
Has·sel \'häs-əl\ Odd 1897–1981 Norw. chem.
Hass·ler \'häs-lər\ Hans Leo 1564–1612 Ger. composer
Has·tings \'hā-stiŋz\ 1st Marquess of 1754–1826 *Francis Raw·don-Hastings* \,ród-ᵊn-\ Brit. gen. & colonial administrator
Hastings Warren 1732–1818 Eng. statesman & administrator in India
Haugh·ey \'hók-ē\ Charles James 1925– prime min. of Ireland (1979–81; 1982; 1987–)
Haupt·man \'haúp(t)-mən\ Herbert Aaron 1917– Am. biophysicist
Haupt·mann \'haúp(t)-,män\ Gerhart 1862–1946 Ger. writer
Haus·ho·fer \'haús-,hō-fər\ Karl Ernst 1869–1946 Ger. gen. & geographer
Hauss·mann \ō-'smän, 'haús-mən\ Baron Georges-Eugène 1809–1891 Fr. administrator
Ha·vel \'hä-vel, 'häv-əl\ Vá·clav \'vät-,släf\ 1936– Czech writer & polit.; pres. of Czechoslovakia (1989–)
Have·lock \'hav-,läk, -lok\ Sir Henry 1795–1857 Brit. gen.
Hawke \'hók\ 1st Baron 1705–1781 *Edward Hawke* Eng. admiral
Hawke Robert James Lee 1929– prime min. of Australia (1983–)
Haw·kins \'hó-kənz\ Sir Anthony Hope 1863–1933 pseud. *Anthony Hope* Eng. nov. & dram.
Hawkins *or* **Haw·kyns** Sir John 1532–1595 Eng. admiral
Haw·orth \'haú-ərth\ Sir (Walter) Norman 1883–1950 Eng. chem.
Haw·thorne \'hó-,thó(ə)rn\ Nathaniel 1804–1864 Am. author
Hay \'hā\ John Milton 1838–1905 Am. statesman
Hay·den \'häd-ᵊn\ Carl Trumbull 1877–1972 Am. polit.
Haydn \'hīd-ᵊn\ (Franz) Joseph 1732–1809 Austrian composer
Hay·ek \'hī-(y)ək\ Friedrich August von 1899– Austrian econ.
Hayes \'häz\ Helen 1900– *Helen Hayes Brown, wife of Charles MacArthur* Am. actress
Hayes Isaac Israel 1832–1881 Am. arctic explorer
Hayes Roland 1887–1977 Am. tenor
Hayes Rutherford Birchard 1822–1893 19th pres. of the U.S. (1877–81)
Haynes \'hānz\ Elwood 1857–1925 Am. inventor
Hays \'hāz\ Will Harrison 1879–1954 Am. lawyer & polit.
Ha·zard \ä-'zär\ Paul-Gustave-Marie-Camille 1878–1944 Fr. lit. hist.
Haz·litt \'haz-lət, 'häz-\ William 1778–1830 Eng. essayist
Hea·ly \'hē-lē\ Timothy Michael 1855–1931 Irish statesman
Hearn \'hərn\ Laf·ca·dio \laf-'käd-ē-,ō\ 1850–1904 Jp. *Yakumo Koizumi* Am. (Greek-born) writer in Japan
Hearst \'hərst\ William Randolph 1863–1951 Am. newspaper publisher
Heath \'hēth\ Edward 1916– Brit. prime min. (1970–74)
Heav·i·side \'hev-ē-,sīd\ Oliver 1850–1925 Eng. physicist
Heb·bel \'heb-əl\ (Christian) Friedrich 1813–1863 Ger. dram.
He·ber \'hē-bər\ Reginald 1783–1826 Eng. prelate & hymn writer
Hé·bert \ā-'be(ə)r\ Jacques-René 1757–1794 Fr. radical journalist
He·din \hā-'dēn\ Sven Anders 1865–1952 Swed. explorer
Heem \'hām\ Jan Davidsz de 1606–1683(or 1684) Du. painter
He·gel \'hā-gəl\ Georg Wilhelm Friedrich 1770–1831 Ger. philos.
Hei·deg·ger \'hi-,deg-ər, 'hīd-i-gər\ Martin 1889–1976 Ger. philos.
Hei·den·stam \'häd-ᵊn-,stam, -,stäm\ (Carl Gustaf) Verner von 1859–1940 Swed. writer
Hei·fetz \'hī-fəts\ Ja·scha \'yäsh-ə\ 1901–1987 Am. (Russ.-born) violinist
Hei·ne \'hī-nə *also* -nē\ Heinrich 1797–1856 Ger. poet & critic
Hei·sen·berg \'hīz-ᵊn-bərg, -,berk\ Werner Karl 1901–1976 Ger. physicist
Heliogabalus — see ELAGABALUS
Hel·ler \'hel-ər\ Joseph 1923– Am. nov.
Hell·man \'hel-mən\ Lillian 1905–1984 Am. dram.
Helm·holtz \'helm-,hólts\ Hermann Ludwig Ferdinand von 1821–1894 Ger. physicist, anatomist, & physiol.
Hé·lo·ise \'ā-lə-,wēz, 'el-ə-\ *ca* 1098–1164 *wife of Abelard* Fr. abbess
Hel·vé·tius \hel-'vā-sh(ē-)əs, -'vē-; (h)el-,väs-'yüs, -'yēs\ Claude-Adrien 1715–1771 Fr. philos.
He·mans \'hem-ənz, 'hē-mənz\ Felicia Dorothea 1793–1835 née *Browne* Eng. poet
Hem·inge *or* **Hem·minge** \'hem-iŋ\ John *ca* 1556–1630 Eng. actor
Hem·ing·way \'hem-iŋ-,wā\ Ernest Miller 1899–1961 Am. writer & journalist — **Hem·ing·way·esque** \,hem-iŋ-,wā-'esk\ *adj*
Hench \'hench\ Philip Showalter 1896–1965 Am. physician
Hen·der·son \'hen-dər-sən\ Arthur 1863–1935 Brit. labor leader & statesman
Henderson Sir Nev·ile \'nev-əl\ Meyrick 1882–1942 Brit. diplomat
Hen·gist *or* **Hen·gest** \'heŋ-gəst, -,gist\ & *his bro.* **Hor·sa** \'hór-sə\ 5th cent. Jute invaders of Britain
Hen·ley \'hen-lē\ William Ernest 1849–1903 Eng. editor & author
Hen·ne·pin \'hen-ə-pən, ,en-ə-'pa[n]\ Louis 1626–after 1701 Belg. friar & explorer in America
Hen·ri \'hen-rē\ Robert 1865–1929 Am. painter

Hen·ry \'hen-rē\ name of 8 kings of England: **I** 1068–1135 (reigned 1100–35); **II** 1133–1189 (reigned 1154–89); **III** 1207–1272 (reigned 1216–72); **IV** 1366–1413 (reigned 1399–1413); **V** 1387–1422 (reigned 1413–22); **VI** 1421–1471 (reigned 1422–61 & 1470–71); **VII** 1457–1509 (reigned 1485–1509); **VIII** 1491–1547 (reigned 1509–47)
Henry name of 4 kings of France: **I** *ca* 1008–1060 (reigned 1031–60); **II** 1519–1559 (reigned 1547–59); **III** 1551–1589 (reigned 1574–89); **IV** (Henry III of Navarre) 1553–1610 (reigned 1589–1610)
Henry 1394–1460 *the Navigator* Port. prince
Henry Joseph 1797–1878 Am. physicist
Henry O. — see William Sydney PORTER
Henry Patrick 1736–1799 Am. statesman & orator
Hens·lowe \'henz-,(,)lō\ Philip *ca* 1550–1616 Eng. theater manager
Hep·burn \'hep-,(,)bərn\ Katharine 1909–   Am. actress
Hep·ple·white \'hep-əl-,(h)wīt\ George *d* 1786 Eng. cabinetmaker and designer
Hep·worth \'hep-,(,)wərth\ Dame Barbara 1903–1975 Brit. sculptor
Her·a·clei·tus *or* **Her·a·cli·tus** \,her-ə-'klīt-əs\ *ca* 540–*ca* 480 B.C. Greek philos. — **Her·a·cli·te·an** \-'klīt-ē-ən, -,klī-'tē-\ *adj*
He·ra·cli·us \,her-ə-'klī-əs, hi-'rak-lē-\ *ca* 575–641 Byzantine emp. (610–641)
Her·bart \'he(ə)r-,bärt\ Johann Friedrich 1776–1841 Ger. philos. & educ.
Her·bert \'hər-bərt\ George 1593–1633 Eng. divine & poet
Herbert Victor 1859–1924 Am. (Irish-born) composer & conductor
Herbert William 1580–1630 3d Earl of *Pembroke* Eng. statesman & poet
Herblock — see Herbert Lawrence BLOCK
Her·der \'herd-ər\ Johann Gottfried von 1744–1803 Ger. philos. & writer
He·re·dia \ā-rā-'dyä, (h)ā-'räd-ē-ə\ José María de 1842–1905 Fr. (Cuban-born) poet
Her·ford \'hər-fərd\ Oliver 1863–1935 Eng. writer & illustrator
He·ring \'her-iŋ, 'hā-riŋ\ Ewald 1834–1918 Ger. physiol. & psychol.
Her·ki·mer \'hər-kə-mər\ Nicholas 1728–1777 Am. gen. in Revolution
Her·man \'hər-mən\ Woodrow Charles 1913–1987 *Woody* Am. musician & bandleader
Hern·don \'hərn-dən\ William Henry 1818–1891 Am. lawyer
He·ro \'hē-(,)rō, 'hi(ə)r-(,)ō\ *or* **He·ron** \'hē-,rän\ 1st cent. A.D. Greek scientist
Her·od \'her-əd\ 73–4 B.C. *the Great* Rom. king of Judea (37–4)
Herod An·ti·pas \-'ant-ə-,pas, -pəs\ 21 B.C.–A.D. 39 *son of prec.* Rom. tetrarch of Galilee (4 B.C.–A.D. 39)
He·rod·o·tus \hi-'räd-ə-təs\ *ca* 484–between 430 and 420 B.C. Greek hist. — **He·rod·o·te·an** \-,räd-ə-'tē-ən\ *adj*
Her·re·ra \(h)ə-'rer-ə\ Francisco de 1576–*ca* 1656 *el Viejo* Span. painter
Her·rick \'her-ik\ Robert 1591–1674 Eng. poet
Her·ring·ton \'her-iŋ-tən\ John 1939–   U.S. secy. of energy (1985–89)
Her·riot \,er-ē-'ō\ Édouard 1872–1957 Fr. statesman
Hersch·bach \'hərsh-,bäk\ Dudley Robert 1932–   Am. chem.
Her·schel \'hər-shəl\ Sir John Frederick William 1792–1871 & his father Sir William 1738–1822 Eng. astronomers
Her·sey \'hər-sē\ John Richard 1914–   Am. nov.
Her·shey \'hər-shē\ Alfred Day 1908–   Am. geneticist
Her·ter \'hərt-ər\ Christian Archibald 1895–1966 Am. diplomat; secy. of state (1959–61)
Hertz \'he(ə)rts, 'hərts\ Gustav Ludwig 1887–1975 Ger. physicist
Hertz Heinrich Rudolf 1857–1894 Ger. physicist
Herz·zog \'hert-,sôk\ James Barry Munnik 1866–1942 So. African gen.
Herz·berg \'hərts-,bərg\ Gerhard 1904–   Canad. (Ger.-born) physicist
Herzl \'hert-s²l\ Theodor 1860–1904 Austrian (Hung.-born) Zionist
He·si·od \'hē-sē-əd, 'hes-ē-\ *fl ca* 800 B.C. Greek poet
Hess \'hes\ Dame Myra 1890–1965 Eng. pianist
Hess (Walther Richard) Rudolf 1894–1987 Ger. Nazi polit.
Hess Victor Franz 1883–1964 Austrian physicist
Hess Walter Rudolf 1881–1973 Swiss physiol.
Hes·se \'hes-ə\ Hermann 1877–1962 Ger. author
He·ve·sy \'hā-ə-shē, -,esh-ē\ Georg Karl 1885–1966 Hung. chem.
Hew·ish \'hyü-ish\ Antony 1924–   Brit. astron.
Hey·drich \'hī-drik, -drik\ Reinhard 1904–1942 *the Hangman* Ger. Nazi administrator
Hey·er·dahl \'hā-ər-,däl\ Thor 1914–   Norw. explorer & writer
Hey·mans \ā-'män(t)s, -'man(t)s\ Corneille-Jean-François 1892–1968 Belg. physiol.
Hey·rov·ský \'hā-,rôf-skē, -,rôv-\ Jaroslav 1890–1967 Czech chem.
Hey·se \'hī-zə\ Paul Johann Ludwig von 1830–1914 Ger. nov., dram., & poet
Hey·ward \'hā-wərd\ (Edwin) Du·Bose \d(y)ù-'bōz\ 1885–1940 Am. author
Hey·wood \'hā-,wud\ John 1497?–?1580 Eng. author
Heywood Thomas 1574?–1641 Eng. dram.
Hick·ok \'hik-,äk\ James Butler 1837–1876 *Wild Bill* Am. scout & U.S. marshal
Hicks \'hiks\ Edward 1780–1849 Am. painter
Hicks Sir John Richard 1904–1989 Brit. econ.
Hi·ero I \'hī-ə-,rō\ *or* **Hi·er·on** \-,rän\ *d* 467(or 466) B.C. tyrant of Syracuse (478–467 or 466)
Hieronymus Saint Eusebius — see JEROME
Hig·gin·son \'hig-ən-sən\ Thomas Wentworth Storrow 1823–1911 Am. clergyman & writer
Hil·bert \'hil-bərt\ David 1862–1943 Ger. math.
Hildebrand — see Pope GREGORY VII
Hill \'hil\ Ambrose Powell 1825–1865 Am. Confed. gen.
Hill Archibald Vivian 1886–1977 Eng. physiol.
Hill James Jerome 1838–1916 Am. financier
Hill Sir Rowland 1795–1879 Eng. postal reformer
Hil·la·ry \'hil-ə-rē\ Sir Edmund Percival 1919–   N.Z. mountaineer & explorer
Hil·lel \'hil-əl, -,el\ 1st cent. B.C.–1st cent. A.D. Jewish teacher
Hil·liard \'hil-yərd\ Nicholas 1547–1619 Eng. painter
Hill·man \'hil-mən\ Sidney 1887–1946 Am. labor leader
Hil·ton \'hilt-²n\ Conrad Nicholson 1887–1979 Am. hotelier

Hilton James 1900–1954 Eng. nov.
Himm·ler \'him-lər\ Heinrich 1900–1945 Ger. Nazi polit.
Hin·de·mith \'hin-də-,mit(h), -mət(h)\ Paul 1895–1963 Am. (Ger.-born) violist & composer
Hin·den·burg \'hin-dən-,bərg, -,bú(ə)rg\ Paul von 1847–1934 *Paul Ludwig Hans Anton von Beneckendorff und von Hindenburg* Ger. field marshal; pres. of Germany (1925–34)
Hin·shel·wood \'hin-chəl-,wùd\ Sir Cyril Norman 1897–1967 Brit. chem.
Hip·par·chus \hip-'är-kəs\ *d* 514 B.C. tyrant of Athens (527–514)
Hipparchus *or* **Hipparchos** *fl* 146–127 B.C. Greek astron.
Hip·pi·as \'hip-ē-əs\ *d* 490 B.C. *bro. of Hipparchus* ruled Athens with his brother
Hip·poc·ra·tes \hip-'äk-rə-,tēz\ *ca* 460–*ca* 377 B.C. *father of medicine* Greek physician
Hi·ro·hi·to \,hir-ō-'hē-(,)tō\ 1901–1989 emp. of Japan (1926–89)
Hi·ro·shi·ge \,hir-ə-'shē-gä\ Ando 1797–1858 Jp. painter
Hitch·cock \'hich-,käk\ Sir Alfred Joseph 1899–1980 Brit. film director — **Hitch·cock·ian** \hich-'käk-ē-ən\ *adj*
Hitchcock Edward 1793–1864 Am. geologist
Hitch·ings \'hich-iŋz\ George Herbert 1905–   Am. biochem.
Hit·ler \'hit-lər\ Adolf 1889–1945 Ger. chancellor & führer — **Hit·ler·ian** \hit-'lir-ē-ən, -'ler-\ *adj*
Hit·ti \'hit-ē\ Philip Khuri 1886–1978 Am. (Lebanese-born) orientalist
Hit·torf \'hi-,tórf\ Johann Wilhelm 1824–1914 Ger. physicist
Hoare \'hō(ə)r, 'hó(ə)r\ Sir Samuel John Gurney 1880–1959 Viscount *Templewood* Eng. statesman
Ho·bart \'hō-,bärt, -bərt\ Garret Augustus 1844–1899 Am. polit.; vice pres. of the U.S. (1897–99)
Hob·be·ma \'häb-ə-mə\ Meindert *or* Meyndert 1638–1709 Du. painter
Hobbes \'häbz\ Thomas 1588–1679 Eng. philos.
Hoc·cleve \'häk-,lēv\ *or* **Oc·cleve** \'äk-\ Thomas 1368(or 1369)–*ca* 1450 Eng. poet
Ho Chi Minh \,hō-,chē-'min, ,hō-,shē-\ 1890–1969 orig. *Nguyen That Thanh* pres. of No. Vietnam (1945–69)
Hock·ing \'häk-iŋ\ William Ernest 1873–1966 Am. philos.
Ho·del \hō-'del\ Donald Paul 1935–   U.S. secy. of energy (1982–85); secy. of the interior (1985–89)
Hodg·kin \'häj-kin\ Sir Alan Lloyd 1914–   Brit. physiol.
Hodgkin Dorothy Mary Crowfoot 1910–   Brit. physicist
Hoe \'hō\ Richard March 1812–1886 *son of Robert* Am. inventor
Hoe Robert 1784–1833 Am. (Eng.-born) printing-press manuf.
Ho·fer \'hō-fər\ Andreas 1767–1810 Tyrolese patriot
Hof·fa \'häf-ə\ James Riddle 1913–?1975 Am. labor leader
Hoff·man \'häf-mən, 'hóf-\ Mal·vi·na \mal-'vē-nə\ 1887–1966 Am. sculptor
Hoff·mann \'häf-mən, 'hóf-, -,män\ August Heinrich 1798–1874 Ger. poet, philologist, & hist.
Hoffmann Ernst Theodor Wilhelm 1776–1822 known as *Ernst Theodor Amadeus Hoffmann* Ger. composer, writer, & illustrator
Hoffmann Roald 1937–   Am. (Pol.-born) chem.
Hof·mann \'häf-mən, 'hóf-, -,män\ August Wilhelm von 1818–1892 Ger. chem.
Hofmann Hans 1880–1966 Am. (Ger.-born) painter
Hofmann Josef Casimir 1876–1957 Pol. pianist
Hof·manns·thal \'häf-mənz-,täl, 'hóf-\ Hugo von 1874–1929 Austrian poet & dram.
Hof·stadt·er \'hóf-,stat-ər\ Robert 1915–   Am. physicist
Ho·garth \'hō-,gärth\ William 1697–1764 Eng. painter & engraver — **Ho·garth·ian** \hō-'gär-thē-ən\ *adj*
Hog·ben \'hóg-bən, 'häg-\ Lancelot Thomas 1895–1975 Eng. scientist
Hogg \'hóg, 'häg\ James 1770–1835 *the Ettrick Shepherd* Scot. poet
Hohenzollern Michael — see MICHAEL
Ho·ku·sai \'hō-kü-,sī, ,hō-kú-'\ Katsushika 1760–1849 Jp. artist
Hol·bein \'hōl-,bīn, 'hól-\ Hans 1465?–1524 *the Elder* & Hans 1497?–1543 *the Younger* Ger. painters
Hol·berg \'hōl-,berg\ Baron 1684–1754 *Ludwig Holberg* Dan. (Norw.-born) author
Hol·in·shed \'häl-ən-,shed\ *or* **Hol·lings·head** \-iŋz-,hed\ Raphael *d ca* 1580 Eng. chronicler
Hol·land \'häl-ənd\ John Philip 1840–1914 Am. (Irish-born) inventor
Holland Sir Sidney George 1893–1961 prime min. of New Zealand (1949–57)
Hol·ley \'häl-ē\ Robert William 1922–   Am. biochem.
Holman–Hunt William — see Holman HUNT
Holmes \'hōmz, 'hōlmz\ Oliver Wendell 1809–1894 Am. physician & author
Holmes Oliver Wendell 1841–1935 *son of prec.* Am. jurist
Holst \'hōlst\ Gustav Theodore 1874–1934 Eng. composer
Holt \'hōlt\ Harold Edward 1908–1967 Austral. polit.; prime min. (1966–67)
Holt Luther Emmett 1855–1924 Am. pediatrician
Hol·yoake \'hōl-,yōk, 'hō-lē-,ōk\ Sir Keith Jacka 1904–1983 prime min. of New Zealand (1960–72)
Home \'hyüm\ Sir Alec Douglas- 1903–   Brit. prime min. (1963–64)
Home William Douglas- 1912–   Brit. dram.
Ho·mer \'hō-mər\ 9th–8th? cent. B.C. Greek epic poet
Homer Winslow 1836–1910 Am. artist
Ho·neck·er \'hō-nə-kər\ Erich 1912–   gen. secy. of East German Communist party (1971–89)
Ho·neg·ger \,ō-nä-'ge(ə)r, '(h)än-i-gər\ Arthur 1892–1955 Fr. composer
Ho·no·ri·us \hə-'nōr-ē-əs, -'nór-\ Flavius 384–423 Rom. emp. of the West (395–423)
Hont·horst \'hónt-,hórst\ Gerrit van 1590–1656 Du. painter
Hooch *or* **Hoogh** \'hōk\ Pieter de 1629–after 1684 Du. painter
Hood \'hud\ John Bell 1831–1879 Am. Confed. gen.
Hood Samuel 1724–1816 1st Viscount *Hood* Brit. admiral
Hood Thomas 1799–1845 Eng. poet
Hooke \'huk\ Robert 1635–1703 Eng. scientist
Hook·er \'huk-ər\ Joseph 1814–1879 Am. gen.
Hooker Sir Joseph Dalton 1817–1911 Eng. botanist
Hooker Richard 1554–1600 Eng. theol.
Hooker Thomas 1586?–1647 Eng. Puritan clergyman; a founder of Connecticut

Hoo·ton \'hüt-ᵊn\ Earnest Albert 1887–1954 Am. anthropol.

Hoo·ver \'hü-vər\ Herbert Clark 1874–1964 31st pres. of the U.S. (1929–33)

Hoover John Edgar 1895–1972 Am. criminologist; F.B.I. director (1924–72)

Hope \'hōp\ Anthony — see Sir Anthony Hope HAWKINS

Hope Victor Alexander John 1887–1951 8th Earl of *Hope·toun* \'hōp-tən\ & 2d Marquis of *Lin·lith·gow* \lin-'lith-(,)gō\ Brit. soldier; viceroy of India (1936–43)

Hop·kins \'häp-kənz\ Sir Frederick Gow·land \'gaú-lənd\ 1861–1947 Eng. biochem.

Hopkins Gerard Manley 1844–1889 Eng. poet

Hopkins Harry Lloyd 1890–1946 Am. polit. & administrator

Hopkins Johns \'jänz\ 1795–1873 Am. financier

Hopkins Mark 1802–1887 Am. educ.

Hop·kin·son \'häp-kən-sən\ Francis 1737–1791 Am. lawyer & satirist

Hop·pe \'häp-ē\ William Frederick 1887–1959 Am. billiard player

Hop·per \'häp-ər\ Edward 1882–1967 Am. artist

Hopper (William) DeWolf 1858–1935 Am. actor

Hop·wood \'häp-,wúd\ (James) Avery 1882–1928 Am. dram.

Hor·ace \'hór-əs, 'här-\ 65–8 B.C. *Quintus Horatius Flaccus* Rom. poet & satirist — Ho·ra·tian \hə-'rā-shən\ adj

Hore–Be·li·sha \,hō(ə)r-bə-'lē-shə, ,hó(ə)r-\ Leslie 1893–1957 Eng. polit.

Hor·na·day \'hòr-nə-,dā\ William Temple 1854–1937 Am. zool.

Hor·ney \'hòr-,nī\ Karen 1885–1952 née *Danielsen* Am. (Ger.-born) psychoanalyst & author

Ho·ro·witz \'hór-ə-,wits, 'här-\ Vladimir 1903–1989 Am. (Russ.-born) pianist

Horsa — see HENGIST

Hortense de Beauharnais — see BEAUHARNAIS

Hor·thy de Nagy·bán·ya \'hórt-ē-dä-'näj-,bán-yə\ Miklós 1868–1957 Hung. admiral; regent of Hungary (1920–44)

Hou·di·ni \hü-'dē-nē\ Harry 1874–1926 orig. *Erik Weisz* Am. (Hung.₌ born) magician

Hou·don \'hü-,dän, ü-dōⁿ\ Jean-Antoine 1741–1828 Fr. sculptor

Houns·field \'haúnz-,fē(ə)ld\ Godfrey Newbold 1919– Brit. engineer & inventor

House \'haús\ Edward Mandell 1858–1938 *Colonel House* Am. diplomat

Hous·man \'haú-smən\ Alfred Edward 1859–1936 Eng. classical scholar & poet

Housman Laurence 1865–1959 bro. of prec. Eng. writer & illustrator

Hous·say \ü-'sī\ Bernardo Alberto 1887–1971 Argentine physiol.

Hous·ton \'(h)yü-stən\ Samuel 1793–1863 Am. gen.; pres. of the Republic of Texas (1836–38; 1841–44)

How·ard \'haú(-ə)rd\ Catherine — see CATHERINE

Howard Henry 1517?–1547 Earl of *Surrey* Eng. soldier & poet

Howard Oliver Otis 1830–1909 Am. gen. & educ.

Howard Sidney Coe 1891–1939 Am. dram.

Howe \'haú\ Ed 1853–1937 *Edgar Watson* Am. journalist

Howe Elias 1819–1867 Am. inventor

Howe Julia 1819–1910 née *Ward* Am. suffragist & reformer

Howe Richard 1726–1799 *Earl Howe* Eng. admiral

Howe William 1729–1814 5th Viscount *Howe; bro. of prec.* Eng. gen. in America

How·ells \'haú-əlz\ William Dean 1837–1920 Am. author

Hr·dlič·ka \'hərd-lich-,kä\ Aleš \'äl-,esh\ 1869–1943 Am. (Bohemian₌ born) anthropol.

Hsüan–t'ung — see P'U-I

Hua Kuo–feng \'hwä-'gwó-'fəŋ\ 1920– pinyin *Hua Guo·feng* Chin. premier (1976–80)

Huás·car \'wäs-,kär\ d 1532 Inca prince

Hub·bard \'həb-ərd\ Elbert Green 1856–1915 Am. writer

Hub·ble \'həb-əl\ Edwin Powell 1889–1953 Am. astron.

Hu·bel \'(h)yü-bəl\ David Hunter 1926– Am. (Canad.-born) neurobiologist

Hu·ber \'hü-bər\ Robert 1937– Ger. biochem.

Hud·son \'həd-sən\ Henry d 1611 Eng. navigator & explorer

Hudson Manley Ottmer 1886–1960 Am. jurist

Hudson William Henry 1841–1922 Eng. naturalist & writer

Huer·ta \'wert-ə, ü-'ert-\ Victoriano 1854–1916 Mex. gen.; provisional pres. of Mexico (1913–14)

Hug·gins \'həg-ənz\ Charles Brenton 1901– Am. (Canad.-born) physician

Huggins Sir William 1824–1910 Eng. astron.

Hugh Ca·pet \'hyü-'kā-pət, -'kap-ət, -,ka-'pā\ ca 938–996 king of France (987–996)

Hughes \'hyüz also 'yüz\ Charles Evans 1862–1948 Am. jurist; chief justice U.S. Supreme Court (1930–41)

Hughes Howard Robard 1905–1976 Am. businessman

Hughes (James) Langston 1902–1967 Am. writer

Hughes Ted 1930– Brit. poet; poet laureate (1984–)

Hughes Thomas 1822–1896 Eng. jurist, reformer, & writer

Hughes William Morris 1864–1952 Austral. statesman

Hu·go \'(h)yü-(,)gō\ Victor-Marie 1802–1885 Fr. poet, nov., & dram. — Hu·go·esque \,(h)yü-(,)gō-'esk\ adj

Hui·zinga \'hī-ziŋ-ə\ Johan 1872–1945 Du. hist.

Hü·le·gü \'hü-'lä-(,)gü\ ca 1217–ca 1265 *grandson of Genghis Khan* Mongol ruler

Hull \'həl\ Cordell 1871–1955 Am. statesman; secy. of state (1933–44)

Hull Isaac 1773–1843 Am. naval officer

Hull William 1753–1825 Am. gen.

Hu·mā·yün \hü-'mä-,yün\ 1508–1556 Mogul emp. of India (1530–56)

Hum·boldt \'həm-,bōlt, haú-\ (Friedrich Wilhelm Karl Heinrich) Alexander von 1769–1859 Ger. naturalist, traveler, & statesman

Humboldt (Karl) Wilhelm von 1767–1835 bro. of prec. Ger. philologist & diplomat

Hume \'hyüm also 'yüm\ David 1711–1776 Scot. philos. & hist. — Hum·ean or Hum·ian \'hyü-mē-ən\ adj

Hum·per·dinck \'húm-pər-,diŋk, 'həm-\ Engelbert 1854–1921 Ger. composer

Hum·phrey \'həm(p)-frē\ 1391–1447 *son of Henry IV* Duke of *Gloucester (the Good Duke)* & Earl of *Pembroke* Eng. statesman & book collector

Humphrey Hubert Horatio 1911–1978 Am. polit.; vice pres. of the U.S. (1965–69)

Hun·e·ker \'hən-i-kər\ James Gibbons 1860–1921 Am. critic

Hung–wu \'hún-'wü\ 1328–1398 *Chu Yüan-chang* \'jü-yü-'än-'jäŋ\ Chin. emp. (1368–98); founder of Ming dynasty

Hunt \'hənt\ (James Henry) Leigh 1784–1859 Eng. writer

Hunt (William) Hol·man \'hōl-mən\ 1827–1910 Eng. painter

Hun·ter \'hənt-ər\ John 1728–1793 Brit. anatomist & surgeon

Hun·ting·ton \'hənt-iŋ-tən\ Collis Potter 1821–1900 Am. pioneer railroad builder

Huntington Ellsworth 1876–1947 Am. geographer & explorer

Huntington Henry Edwards 1850–1927 Am. bibliophile

Huntington Samuel 1731–1796 Am. Revolutionary patriot

Hun·tzi·ger \,(h)ənt-sē-'zhe(ə)r\ Charles-Léon-Clément 1880–1941 Fr. gen.

Hu·nya·di \'hún-,yäd-ē, -,yód-\ Já·nos \'yän-(,)ösh\ 1407?–1456 Hung. soldier & hero

Hur·ley \'hər-lē\ Patrick Jay 1883–1963 Am. lawyer & diplomat

Hurst \'hərst\ Sir Cecil James Barrington 1870–1963 Eng. jurist

Hurst Fannie 1889–1968 Am. writer

Hus \'həs, 'hús\ Jan 1372(or 1373)–1415 Bohemian religious reformer

Hu·sák \'h(y)ü-(,)säk\ Gustav 1913– pres. of Czechoslovakia (1975–87)

Hu·sayn ibn 'Alī \hü-'sä-,nib-ən-ä-'lē\ ca1854–1931 1st king of the Hejaz (1916–24)

Hu Shih \'hü-'shi(ə)r\ 1891–1962 Chin. philos.

Hus·sein I \hü-'sān\ 1935– king of Jordan (1952–)

Hussein Saddam al-Tikriti 1937– pres. of Iraq (1979–)

Hus·serl \'hús-ə-rəl\ Edmund 1859–1938 Ger. philos.

Hus·ton \'(h)yü-stən\ John 1906–1987 Am. motion-picture director, writer, & actor

Hu·szár \'hús-,är\ Károly 1882–1941 Hung. journalist & polit.

Hutch·ins \'həch-ənz\ Robert Maynard 1899–1977 Am. educ.

Hutch·in·son \'həch-ə(n)-sən\ Anne 1591–1643 née *Marbury* religious leader in America

Hutchinson Thomas 1711–1780 Am. colonial administrator

Hut·ten \'hút-ᵊn\ Ulrich von 1488–1523 Ger. humanist & supporter of Luther

Hux·ley \'hək-slē\ Al·dous \'öl-dəs\ Leonard 1894–1963 bro. of J.S. Eng. nov. & critic — Hux·lei·an \,hək-'slē-ən, 'hək-slē-\ or Hux·ley·an \'hək-slē-ən\ adj

Huxley Andrew Fielding 1917– Brit. physiol. & educ.

Huxley Sir Julian Sorell 1887–1975 *grandson of T.H.* Eng. biol.

Huxley Thomas Henry 1825–1895 Eng. biol.

Huy·gens \'hī-gənz, 'hói-\ Christian 1629–1695 Du. math., physicist, & astron.

Huys·mans \wē-'smäⁿs\ Camille 1871–1968 Belg. polit.

Huysmans Joris-Karl 1848–1907 orig. *Georges-Charles* Fr. nov.

Hy·att \'hī-ət\ Alpheus 1838–1902 Am. naturalist

Hyde \'hīd\ Douglas 1860–1949 pseud. *An Craoibhín Aoibhinn* Irish author; pres. of Republic of Ireland (1938–45)

Hyde Edward 1609–1674 1st Earl of *Clarendon* Eng. statesman & hist.

Hy·der Ali or Hai·dar Ali \,hīd-ə-rä-'lē\ 1722–1782 Indian ruler and soldier

Hy·mans \'hī-,män(t)s, ē-mäⁿs\ Paul 1865–1941 Belg. statesman

Hy·pse·lan·tes \,ēp-sə-'län-dēs\ var of YPSILANTIS

Ibáñez Vicente Blasco- — see BLASCO IBÁÑEZ

Iber·ville \'ē-bər-,vil, -,vēl; 'ē-bar,vil\ Sieur d' 1661–1706 *Pierre Le Moyne* Fr.-Canad. explorer; founder of Louisiana

Ibn–Khal·dūn \,ib-ən-,kal-'dün, -,kal-\ 1332–1406 Arab hist.

Ibn–Rushd — see AVERROËS

Ibn Sa·'ūd \,ib-ən-sä-'üd, -'saúd\ ca 1880–1953 king of Saudi Arabia (1932–53)

Ibn Zuhr \,ib-ən-'zü(ə)r\ L Av·en·zo·ar \,av-ən-'zō-ər, -zō-'är\ or Abu·me·ron \,ab-yü-'mer-,än\ ca 1090–1162 Muslim physician

Ibrā·hīm Pa·sha \,ib-,brä-'him-'päsh-ə, -'pash-ə, -pə-'shä\ 1789–1848 Egypt. gen. & viceroy

Ib·sen \'ib-sən, 'ip-\ Henrik 1828–1906 Norw. poet & dram. — Ib·se·ni·an \ib-'sē-nē-ən, ip-, -'sen-ē-\ adj

Ick·es \'ik-əs\ Harold LeClair 1874–1952 Am. polit.

Ic·ti·nus \ik-'tī-nəs\ 5th cent. B.C. Greek architect

Ig·na·tius \ig-'nā-sh(ē-)əs\ Saint d ca A.D. 110 *Theophorus* bishop of Antioch & church father

Ignatius of Loyola Saint 1491–1556 orig. *Iñigo de Oñaz y Loyola* Span. religious; founder of Society of Jesus — Ig·na·tian \-sh(ē-)ən\ adj

Ike·da \ē-'käd-ə, -'ked-\ Hayato 1899–1965 Jp. polit.; prime min. (1960–64)

Ikhnaton — see AKHENATON

Il·ies·cu \il-ē-'es-(,)kü, il-'yes-\ Ion 1930– pres. of Romania (1989–)

Im·mel·mann \'im-əl-,män, -mən\ Max 1890–1916 Ger. aviator

In·dy, d' \'dan-dē; dan-'dē, daⁿ-\ (Paul-Marie-Théodore-) Vincent 1851–1931 Fr. composer

Inés de Castro — see CASTRO

Inge \'inj\ William 1913–1973 Am. playwright

Inge \'iŋ\ William Ralph 1860–1954 Eng. prelate & author

In·ger·soll \'in-gər-,sól, -,säl\ Robert Green 1833–1899 Am. orator

In·gres \'aⁿ(')gr\ Jean-Auguste-Dominique 1780–1867 Fr. painter

In·ness \'in-əs\ George: father 1825–1894 & son 1854–1926 Am. painters

In·no·cent \'in-ə-sənt\ name of 13 popes: esp. II d 1143 (pope 1130–43); III 1160(or 1161)–1216 (pope 1198–1216); IV d 1254 (pope 1243–54); XI 1611–1689 (pope 1676–89)

Inö·nü \,in-ə-'n(y)ü\ **İs·met** \is-'met\ 1884–1973 Turk. statesman; pres. of Turkey (1938–50); premier (1961–65)
In·sull \'in(t)-səl\ Samuel 1859–1938 Am. (Eng.-born) utilities executive
Io·nes·co \ē-ə-'nes-(,)kō\ Eugène 1912–   Fr. (Rom.-born) dram.
Ipa·tieff \i-'pät-ē-,ef, -'päch-əf\ Vladimir Nikolayevich 1867–1952 Am. (Russ.-born) chem.
Ire·dell \'ī(ə)r-,del\ James 1751–1799 Am. jurist
Ire·ton \'ī(ə)rt-ᵊn\ Henry 1611–1651 Eng. soldier & polit.
Iri·go·yen \i-ri-'gō-,yen\ Hi·pó·li·to \ē-'pō-lē-,tō\ 1852–1933 pres. of Argentina (1916–22; 1928–30)
Iron·side \'ī-(,)rn-,sīd\ William Edmund 1880–1959 1st Baron *Ironside* Brit. field marshal
Ir·ving \'ər-viŋ\ Sir Henry 1838–1905 orig. *John Henry Brodribb* Eng. actor
Irving Washington 1783–1859 Am. essayist, nov., & hist.
Ir·win \'ər-wən\ William Henry 1873–1948 *Will* Am. journalist
Isaacs \'ī-ziks, -zəks\ Sir Isaac Alfred 1855–1948 Austral. jurist & statesman; gov.-gen. of Australia (1931–36)
Isaacs Rufus Daniel — see Marquis of READING
Is·a·bel·la I \,iz-ə-'bel-ə\ 1451–1504 *wife of Ferdinand V of Castile* queen of Castile (1474–1504) & of Aragon (1479–1504); aided Columbus
Ish·er·wood \'ish-ər-,wůd\ Christopher William Bradshaw 1904–1986 Am. (Brit.-born) writer
Ishii \'ē-shē-,ē, 'ish-ē-,ē\ Viscount Kikujiro 1866–1945 Jp. diplomat
Is·i·dore of Seville \'iz-ə-,dō(ə)r, -,dȯ(ə)r\ Saint *ca* 560–636 L. *Isidorus Hispalensis* Span. prelate & scholar
Iskender Bey — see SKANDERBEG
Is·mā·'īl Pa·sha \is-'mä-,ēl-'päsh-ə, -'pash-ə, -pə-'shä\ 1830–1895 viceroy of Egypt (1863–79)
Isoc·ra·tes \ī-'säk-rə-,tēz\ 436–338 B.C. Athenian orator
Is·ra·el ben Eli·ezer \'iz-rē-əl-,ben-,el-ē-'ä-zər\ *ca* 1700–1760 *Ba'al Shem Tov* Pol.-Jewish religious leader
Ito \'ē-(,)tō\ Prince Hirobumi 1841–1909 Jp. statesman
Itur·bi \i-'tůr-bē\ José 1895–1980 Span.-born pianist & conductor
Itur·bi·de \,ē-,tür-'bē-(,)thā\ Agustín de 1783–1824 Mex. soldier; emp. of Mexico (1822–23)
Ivan III \ē-'vän, 'ī-vən\ **Va·si·lye·vich** \və-'sil-yə-,vich\ 1440–1505 *the Great* grand prince of Russia (1462–1505)
Ivan IV Vasilyevich 1530–1584 *the Terrible* ruler of Russia (1533–84)
Ives \'īvz\ Charles Edward 1874–1954 Am. composer — **Ives·ian** \'īv-zē-ən\ *adj*
Ives James Merritt 1824–1895 Am. lithographer
Iyeyasu or **Ieyasu** — see TOKUGAWA
Jā·bir ibn Ḥay·yān \'jab-,ir-,ib-ən-hī-'(y)an\ Abū Mūsā *ca* 721–*ca* 815 L. *Geber* Arab alchemist & mystic
Jack·son \'jak-sən\ Andrew 1767–1845 Am. gen.; 7th pres. of the U.S. (1829–37)
Jackson Helen Maria Hunt 1830–1885 née *Fiske* Am. nov.
Jackson Jesse Louis 1941–   Am. clergyman & polit.
Jackson Robert Hough·wout \'haů-ət\ 1892–1954 Am. jurist
Jackson Thomas Jonathan 1824–1863 *Stone·wall* \'stōn-,wȯl\ *Jackson* Am. Confed. gen.
Ja·cob \zhä-kȯb\ François 1920–   Fr. geneticist
Ja·co·po del·la Quer·cia \yä-'kō-(,)pō-,dā-lä-'kwer-chä\ *ca* 1374–1438 Ital. sculptor
Jac·quard \zha-'kär, 'jak-,ärd\ Joseph-Marie 1752–1834 Fr. inventor
Jacques I — see Jean-Jacques DESSALINES
Jag·a·tai — see CHAGATAI
Ja·hän–gīr \jə-'hän-,gi(ə)r\ 1569–1627 emp. of India (1605–27)
Ja·lāl ad–Dīn ar–Rū·mī \jə-'läl-ə-,dēn-är-'rü-mē\ *ca* 1207–1273 Pers. poet
James \'jāmz\ name of 6 kings of Scotland & 2 kings of Great Britain: esp. **VI** 1566–1625 of Scotland (reigned 1567–1603) *or* **I** of Great Britain (reigned 1603–25); **II** 1633–1701 (reigned 1685–88)
James Henry 1811–1882 Am. philos.
James Henry 1843–1916 *son of prec.* Brit. (Am.-born) writer
James Jesse Woodson 1847–1882 Am. outlaw
James William 1842–1910 *bro. of Henry* Am. psychol. & philos.
James Edward 1688–1766 *James Francis Edward Stuart; the Old Pretender* Eng. prince
Jame·son \'jām-sən, 'jem-ə-sən\ Sir Leander Starr 1853–1917 *Doctor Jameson* Scot. physician & administrator in So. Africa
Jā·mī \'jäm-ē\ 1414–1492 Pers. poet & mystic
Ja·ná·ček \'yän-ə-,chek\ Leoš 1854–1928 Czech composer
Jan·sen \'jan(t)-sən, 'yän(t)-\ Cor·ne·lis \kȯr-'nā-ləs\ 1585–1638 L. *Cornelius Jansenius* Du. R.C. theol.
Jaques–Dal·croze \'zhäk-,dal-'krȯz, 'zhak-\ Émile 1865–1950 Swiss composer & creator of eurythmics
Ja·rīr \jə-'ri(ə)r\ *ca* 650–*ca* 729 Arab poet
Jar·rell \jə-'rel, ja-\ Randall 1914–1965 Am. writer
Ja·ru·zel·ski \,yär-ü-'zel-skē\ Woj·ciech \'vȯi-,chek\ Witold 1923–   gen.; 1st secy. of the communist party in Poland (1981–89)
Jas·pers \'yäs-pərs\ Karl Theodor 1883–1969 Ger. philos.
Jauregg Julius Wagner von — see WAGNER VON JAUREGG
Jau·rès \zhō-res\ Jean-Joseph-Marie-Auguste 1859–1914 Fr. socialist
Jay \'jā\ John 1745–1829 Am. jurist & statesman; 1st chief justice U.S. Supreme Court (1789–95)
Jeanne d'Arc — see JOAN OF ARC
Jeans \'jēnz\ Sir James Hopwood 1877–1946 Eng. physicist, astron., & author
Jebb \'jeb\ Sir Richard Claverhouse 1841–1905 Scot. scholar
Jef·fers \'jef-ərz\ (John) Robinson 1887–1962 Am. poet
Jef·fer·son \'jef-ər-sən\ Thomas 1743–1826 3d pres. of the U.S. (1801–09) — **Jef·fer·so·ni·an** \,jef-ər-'sō-nē-ən, -nyən\ *adj*
Jef·frey \'jef-rē\ Lord Francis 1773–1850 Scot. critic & jurist
Jef·freys \'jef-rēz\ George 1645–1689 1st Baron *Jeffreys of Wem* Eng. jurist
Jel·li·coe \'jel-i-,kō\ 1st Earl 1859–1935 *John Rushworth Jellicoe* Brit. admiral
Jen·ner \'jen-ər\ Edward 1749–1823 Eng. physician — **Jen·ne·ri·an** \je-'nir-ē-ən\ *adj*
Jenner Sir William 1815–1898 Eng. physician
Jen·sen \'yen-zən\ (Johannes) Hans Daniel 1907–1973 Ger. physicist

Jen·sen \'yen(t)-sən, 'jen(t)-\ Johannes Vilhelm 1873–1950 Dan. poet & nov.
Jen·son \'jen-sən, zhäⁿ-sōⁿ\ Nicolas *ca* 1420–1480 Fr. printer & engraver in Venice
Jerne \'yer-ne\ Niels Kai 1911–   Dan. (Eng.-born) immunologist
Je·rome \jə-'rōm\ Saint *ca* 347–419(or 420) L. *Eusebius Hieronymus* church father
Jer·vis \'jər-vəs, 'jär-\ John 1735–1823 Earl of *St. Vincent* Brit. admiral
Jes·per·sen \'yes-pər-sən\ (Jens) Otto Harry 1860–1943 Dan. philologist
Je·sus \'jē-zəs, -zəz\ *or* **Jesus Christ** \'krīst\ *or* **Christ Jesus** *ca* 6 B.C.–A.D. 30 *Jesus of Nazareth; the Son of Mary* source of the Christian religion & Savior in the Christian faith
Jev·ons \'jev-ənz\ William Stanley 1835–1882 Eng. econ.
Jew·ett \'jü-ət\ Sarah Orne 1849–1909 Am. writer
Ji·ang Ze·min \jē-'äŋ-zə-'min\ 1926–   gen. secy. of Chin. communist party (1989–   )
Ji·mé·nez \hē-'mā-nes\ Juan Ramón 1881–1958 Span. poet
Jiménez de Cis·ne·ros \-,dä-sis-'ner-əs\ Francisco 1436–1517 Span. prelate & statesman
Jin·nah \'jin-(,)ä, 'jin-ə\ Mohammed Ali 1876–1948 Indian polit.; 1st gov.-gen. of dominion of Pakistan (1947–48)
Jo·achim \yō-'äk-im, -'äk-; 'yō-ə-,kim, -,kim\ Joseph 1831–1907 Hung. violinist
Joan of Arc \jōn-əv-'ärk\ *F* **Jeanne d'Arc** \zhän-dȧrk\ Saint *ca* 1412–1431 *the Maid of Orleans* Fr. national heroine
Jodl \'yōd-ᵊl\ Alfred 1890–1946 Ger. gen.
Jof·fre \zhȯfrᵊ\ Joseph-Jacques-Césaire 1852–1931 Fr. field marshal; marshal of France
John \'jän\ name of 21 popes: esp. **XXIII** (*Angelo Giuseppe Roncalli*) 1881–1963 (pope 1958–63)
John 1167–1216 *John Lack·land* \'lak-,land\ king of England (1199–1216)
John I 1357–1433 *the Great* king of Portugal (1385–1433)
John Augustus Edwin 1878–1961 Brit. painter & etcher
John of Austria 1547–1578 Don *John* Span. gen.
John of Gaunt \'gȯnt, 'gänt\ 1340–1399 Duke of *Lancaster; son of Edward III of England*
John of Lancaster 1389–1435 Duke of *Bedford; son of Henry IV of England*
John of Leiden *ca* 1509–1536 Du. Anabaptist
John of Salisbury 1115(or 1120)–1180 Eng. ecclesiastic
John Paul \-'pȯl\ name of 2 popes: esp. **II** (*Karol Wojtyla*) 1920–   (pope 1978–   )
John III So·bies·ki \sō-'byes-kē, ,sō-bē-'es-\ 1629–1696 king of Poland (1674–96)
John·son \'jän(t)-sən\ Andrew 1808–1875 17th pres. of the U.S. (1865–69) — **John·so·nian** \jän-'sō-nē-ən, -nyən\ *adj*
Johnson (Jonathan) Eastman 1824–1906 Am. painter
Johnson \'yün-sȯn\ Eyvind 1900–1976 Swed. author
Johnson \'jän(t)-sən\ James Weldon 1871–1938 Am. author
Johnson Lyndon Baines 1908–1973 Am. polit.; 36th pres. of the U.S. (1963–69) — **John·so·nian** \jän-'sō-nē-ən, -nyən\ *adj*
Johnson Philip Cortelyou 1906–   Am. architect
Johnson Richard Mentor 1780–1850 vice pres. of the U.S. (1837–41)
Johnson Samuel 1709–1784 *Dr. Johnson* Eng. lexicographer & author — **John·so·nian** \jän-'sō-nē-ən, -nyən\ *adj*
Johnson Sir William 1715–1774 Brit. administrator in America
John·ston \'jän(t)-stən, -sən\ Albert Sidney 1803–1862 Am. Confed. gen.
Johnston Joseph Eggleston 1807–1891 Am. Confed. gen.
Join·ville \zhwaⁿ-'vēᵊl\ Jean de *ca* 1224–1317 Fr. chronicler
Jó·kai \'yō-,kȯi\ Mór 1825–1904 Hung. nov. & dram.
Jo·liot–Cu·rie \zhȯl-,yō-kyü-'rē, -'kyü(ə)r-(,)ē\ (Jean-) Frédéric 1900–1958 orig. *Joliot* Fr. physicist
Joliot–Curie Irène 1897–1956 formerly *Irène Curie-Joliot, dau. of Marie & Pierre Curie & wife of prec.* Fr. physicist
Jol·liet or **Jo·liet** \zhȯl-'yä\ Louis 1645–1700 Fr. explorer
Jo·mi·ni \,zhō-mə-'nē\ Henri de 1779–1869 Swiss-born soldier & mil. strategist
Jones \'jōnz\ Anson 1798–1858 pres. of the Republic of Texas (1844–46)
Jones Daniel 1881–1967 Eng. phonetician
Jones Howard Mumford 1892–1980 Am. educ. & critic
Jones In·i·go \'in-i-,gō\ 1573–1652 Eng. architect
Jones John Paul 1747–1792 orig. in full *John Paul* Am. (Scot.-born) naval officer
Jones Thomas Hudson 1892–1969 Am. sculptor
Jon·son \'jän(t)-sən\ Ben 1572–1637 orig. *Benjamin* Eng. dram. — **Jon·so·nian** \jän-'sō-nē-ən, -nyən\ *adj*
Jop·lin \'jäp-lən\ Scott 1868–1917 Am. pianist & composer
Jor·daens \'yȯr-dän(t)s\ Jacob 1593–1678 Flem. painter
Jor·dan \'jȯrd-ᵊn\ David Starr 1851–1931 Am. biol. & educ.
Jør·gen·sen \'yœr-gən-sən, 'yər-\ Anker 1922–   Dan. polit.; prime min. (1975–82)
Jo·seph \'jō-zəf *also* -səf\ *ca* 1840–1904 *In-mut-too-yah-lat-lat* Nez Percé Indian chief
Joseph II 1741–1790 Holy Rom. emp. (1765–90)
Jo·se·phine \'jō-zə-,fēn\ Empress — see BEAUHARNAIS
Jo·seph·son \jō-zəf-sən *also* -səf-\ Brian David 1940–   Brit. physicist
Jo·se·phus \jō-'sē-fəs\ Flavius *ca* A.D. 37–*ca* 100 Jewish hist.
Jos·quin des Prez \zhō-'skaⁿ-de-'prā\ *or* **Des·prez** \de-'prā\ *ca* 1440–1521 Fr. composer
Jou·bert \zhü-'be(ə)r\ Joseph 1754–1824 Fr. essayist & moralist
Joubert \zhü-'be(ə)r, yō-\ Petrus Jacobus 1834–1900 known as *Piet* Boer gen. & statesman
Jou·haux \zhü-ō\ Léon 1879–1954 Fr. trade-union leader
Joule \'jül\ James Prescott 1818–1889 Eng. physicist
Jour·dan \zhür-'dän\ Comte Jean-Baptiste 1762–1833 Fr. soldier; marshal of France
Jo·vi·an \'jō-vē-ən\ *ca* 331–364 *Flavius Jovianus* Rom. emp. (363–364)
Jow·ett \'jaů-ət, 'jō-\ Benjamin 1817–1893 Eng. Greek scholar
Joyce \'jȯis\ James Augustine 1882–1941 Irish writer — **Joyce·an** \'jȯi-sē-ən\ *adj*

Juan Car·los \'(h)wän-'kär-,lōs, -ləs\ 1938–   king of Spain (1975–)
Juan Manuel Don — see MANUEL
Juá·rez \'(h)wär-əs\ Benito Pablo 1806–1872 Mex. lawyer; pres. of Mexico (1861–65; 1867–72)
Judas Maccabaeus — see MACCABEES
Ju·gur·tha \jü-'gər-thə\ or Iu·gur·tha \yü-\ ca 160–104 B.C. king of Numidia (118–105 B.C.)
Ju·lian \'jül-yən\ ca 331–363 Flavius Claudius Julianus, the Apostate Rom. emp. (361–363)
Ju·li·ana \,jü-lē-'an-ə\ 1909–   dau. of Wilhelmina queen of the Netherlands (1948–80)
Jung \'yun\ Carl Gustav 1875–1961 Swiss psychol.
Ju·nius \'jü-nyəs, -nē-əs\ Franciscus 1589–1677 Eng. (Ger.-born) philologist
Jun·kers \'yun-kərz, -kərs\ Hugo 1859–1935 Ger. airplane designer & builder
Ju·not \zhü-'nō\ Andoche 1771–1813 Duc d'Abran·tès \,dab-,räⁿ-'tes\ Fr. gen. under Napoleon
Jus·se·rand \zhües-(ə-)räⁿ\ Jean-(Adrien-Antoine-) Jules 1855–1932 Fr. scholar & diplomat
Jus·tin \'jəs-tən\ Saint ca 100–ca 165 Justin (the) Martyr church father
Jus·tin·i·an I \,jə-'stin-ē-ən\ 483–565 the Great Byzantine emp. (527–565)
Ju·ve·nal \'jü-vən-°l\ A.D. 55 to 60–ca 127 Decimus Junius Juvenalis Rom. poet & satirist — Ju·ve·na·lian \,jü-və-'nāl-yən\ adj
Ká·dár \'kád-,är\ János 1912–1989 1st secy. of Hung. communist party (1956–88)
Kaf·ka \'käf-kə, 'kaf-\ Franz 1883–1924 Austrian writer — Kaf·ka·esque \,käf-kə-'esk, ,kaf-\ adj
Ka·ga·wa \kä-'gä-wə\ Toyohiko 1888–1960 Jp. social reformer
Kai·fu \'kī-(,)fü\ Toshiki 1931–   prime min. of Japan (1989–)
Kai·ser \'kī-zər\ Henry John 1882–1967 Am. industrialist
Kalb \'kälp, 'kalb\ Johann 1721–1780 Baron de Kalb \di-'kalb\ Ger. gen. in America
Ká·li·dā·sa \,käl-i-'däs-ə\ 5th cent. A.D. Indian dram. & poet
Ka·li·nin \kə-'lē-n(y)ən\ Mikhail Ivanovich 1875–1946 Russ. polit.; formal head of Soviet state (1919–46)
Ka·me·ha·me·ha I \kə-,mā-ə-'mā-(,)hä\ 1758?–1819 the Great king of Hawaii (1795–1819)
Ka·me·nev \'käm-(y)ə-,nef, 'kam-\ Lev Borisovich 1883–1936 Russ. Communist leader
Ka·mer·lingh On·nes \,käm-ər-lin-'ón-əs\ Heike 1853–1926 Du. physicist
Kan·din·sky \kan-'din(t)-skē\ Wassily 1866–1944 Russ. painter
Kane \'kān\ Elisha Kent 1820–1857 Am. arctic explorer
K'ang–hsi \'kän-'shē\ 1654–1722 Chin. emp. (1661–1722)
Kant \'kant, 'känt\ Immanuel 1724–1804 Ger. philos. — Kant·ian \-ē-ən\ adj
Kan·to·ro·vich \,kän-tə-'róv-ich\ Leonid Vitalyevich 1912–1986 Russ. econ.
Ka·pit·sa \'käp-yit-sə\ Pyotr Leonidovich 1894–1984 Russ. physicist
Kar·a·george \,kar-ə-jó(ə)rj\ 1762–1817 orig. George Petrović Karageorge Serbian nationalist; founder of Kar·a·geor·ge·vić \-'jór-jə-,vich\ dynasty
Ka·ra·jan \'kär-ə-,yän\ Herbert von 1908–1989 Austrian conductor
Ka·ra·man·lis \,kär-ə-,män-'lēs, -'man-\ Konstantinos 1907–   prime min. (1974–80) & pres. (1980–85) of Greece
Karle \'kärl\ Jerome 1918–   Am. physical chem.
Karl·feldt \'kärl(ə)l-,felt\ Erik Axel 1864–1931 Swed. poet
Ká·ro·lyi \'kar-əl-,yē, 'kär-\ Count Mihály 1875–1955 Hung. polit.
Kar·rer \'kär-ər\ Paul 1889–1971 Swiss chem.
Kar·sa·vi·na \kär-'säv-ə-nə, -'sav-\ Tamara 1885–1978 Russ. dancer
Kas·tler \'käst-lər\ Alfred 1902–1984 Fr. physicist
Kastriota George — see SKANDERBEG
Katz \'kats\ Sir Bernhard 1911–   Brit. (Ger.-born) biophysicist
Kauf·man \'kóf-mən\ George Simon 1889–1961 Am. dram.
Kau·nitz \'kaú-nəts\ Wenzel Anton von 1711–1794 Prince von Kaunitz–Rietberg Austrian statesman
Kaut·sky \'kaút-skē\ Karl Johann 1854–1938 Ger. socialist writer
Ka·wa·ba·ta \kä-wə-'bät-ə, kə-'wäb-ə-,tä\ Yasunari 1899–1972 Jp. writer
Kaye–Smith \'kā-'smith\ Sheila 1887–1956 Eng. nov.
Ka·zan·tza·kis \,käz-°n-'tsäk-ēs\ Nikos 1885–1957 Greek poet, nov., & translator
Kean \'kēn\ Edmund 1789–1833 Eng. actor
Kear·ny \'kär-nē\ Philip 1814–1862 Am. gen.
Keats \'kēts\ John 1795–1821 Eng. poet — Keats·ian \'kēt-sē-ən\ adj
Ke·ble \'kē-bəl\ John 1792–1866 Eng. clergyman & poet
Ke·fau·ver \'kē-,fó-vər\ (Carey) Estes 1903–1963 Am. polit.
Kei·tel \'kīt-°l\ Wilhelm 1882–1946 Ger. field marshal
Kek·ko·nen \'kek-ə-nən, -,nen\ Urho Kaleva 1900–1986 pres. of Finland (1956–81)
Kel·ler \'kel-ər\ Helen Adams 1880–1968 Am. deaf & blind lecturer
Kel·logg \'kel-,óg, -,äg\ Frank Billings 1856–1937 Am. statesman
Kel·vin \'kel-vən\ 1st Baron 1824–1907 William Thomson Brit. math. & physicist
Ke·mal Ata·türk \kə-,mal-'at-ə-,tərk, -'ät-\ 1881–1938 orig. Mustafa Kemal Turk. gen.; pres. of Turkey (1923–38)
Kem·ble \'kem-bəl\ Frances Anne 1809–1893 Fanny Eng. actress
Kemble John Philip 1757–1823 Eng. actor
Kemp \'kemp\ Jack French 1935–   U.S. secy. of housing & urban development (1989–)
Kempis Thomas à — see THOMAS A KEMPIS
Ken or Kenn \'ken\ Thomas 1637–1711 Eng. prelate & hymn writer
Ken·dall \'ken-d°l\ Edward Calvin 1886–1972 Am. biochem.
Ken·drew \'ken-(,)drü\ Sir John Cowdery 1917–   Brit. chem.
Ken·nan \'ken-ən\ George Frost 1904–   Am. hist. & diplomat
Ken·ne·dy \'ken-əd-ē\ Anthony M. 1936–   Am. jurist
Kennedy John Fitzgerald 1917–1963 Am. polit.; 35th pres. of the U.S. (1961–63)
Kennedy Joseph Patrick 1888–1969 father of J. F. & R. F. Am. businessman & diplomat
Kennedy Robert Francis 1925–1968 Am. polit.; atty. gen. (1961–64)
Ken·nel·ly \'ken-°l-ē\ Arthur Edwin 1861–1939 Am. engineer

Ken·ny \'ken-ē\ Elizabeth 1880–1952 Sister Kenny Austral. nurse & physiotherapist
Kent \'kent\ James 1763–1847 Am. jurist
Kent Rockwell 1882–1971 Am. painter and illustrator
Ken·yon \'ken-yən\ John Samuel 1874–1959 Am. phonetician
Kep·ler \'kep-lər\ Johannes 1571–1630 Ger. astron. — Kep·ler·ian \,kep-'lir-ē-ən, -'ler-\ adj
Kep·pel \'kep-əl\ 1st Viscount 1725–1786 Augustus Keppel Brit. admiral
Ker \'ke(ə)r, 'kər, 'kär\ William Paton 1855–1923 Brit. scholar
Ke·ren·sky \'ker-ən-skē, ker-'en-\ Aleksandr Fyodorovich 1881–1970 Russ. revolutionary
Kern \'kərn\ Jerome David 1885–1945 Am. composer
Ker·ou·ac \'ker-ə-,wak\ Jack 1922–1969 Jean-Louis Am. writer
Kes·sel·ring \'kes-əl-rin\ Albert 1885–1960 Ger. field marshal
Ket·ter·ing \'ket-ə-rin\ Charles Franklin 1876–1958 Am. electrical engineer & inventor
Key \'kē\ Francis Scott 1779–1843 Am. lawyer; author of "The Star-Spangled Banner"
Keynes \'kānz\ John Maynard 1883–1946 1st Baron Keynes of Tilton Eng. econ. — Keynes·ian \'kānz-ē-ən\ adj
Key·ser·ling \'kī-zər-lin\ Hermann Alexander 1880–1946 Graf Keyserling Ger. philos. & writer
Kha·cha·tu·ri·an \,käch-ə-'túr-ē-ən, ,kach-\ Aram Ilich 1903–1978 Russ.-Armenian composer
Khā·lid \'kä-lid, 'kä-\ in full Khālid ibn 'Abd al-'Azīz ibn 'Abd ar-Raḥmān al-Sa'ūd 1913–1982 king of Saudi Arabia (1975–82)
Kha·me·nei \'kä-'mä-nä\ Hojatolislam Sayyed Ali 1939–   religious leader of Iran (1989–)
Khayyám Omar — see OMAR KHAYYAM
Khe·ra·skov \kə-'räs-kəf\ Mikhail Matveyevich 1733–1807 Russ. poet
Kho·mei·ni \kō-'mā-nē, kō-, hō-\ Ayatollah Ruholla Mussaui 1900–1989 religious leader of Iran (1979–89)
Kho·ra·na \kō-'rän-ə\ Har Gobind 1922–   Am. (Indian-born) biochem.
Khru·shchev \krüsh-'(ch)óf, -'(ch)óv, -'(ch)ef, -'(ch)ev, 'krüsh-,\ Ni·ki·ta \nə-'kēt-ə\ Sergeyevich 1894–1971 Russ. polit.; premier of Soviet Union (1958–64) — Khru·shchev·ian \krüsh-'(ch)óv-ē-ən, -'(ch)óv-, -'(ch)ev-\ adj — Khru·shchev·ite \-'(ch)óv-,īt, -'(ch)ev-, 'krüsh-,\ adj
Khu·fu \'kü-(,)fü\ Gk Che·ops \'kē-,äps\ 26th cent. B.C. king of Egypt & pyramid builder
Khwa·riz·mi, al– \al-'kwär-əz-mē, -'kwár-\ ca 780–ca 850 Muḥammad ibn Mūsā al-Khwārizmi Arab math.
Kidd \'kid\ William ca1645–1701 Captain Kidd Scot. pirate
Kie·ran \'kir-ən\ John Francis 1892–1981 Am. journalist
Kier·ke·gaard \'kir-kə-,gär(d), -,gó(ə)r\ Søren Aabye 1813–1855 Dan. philos. & theol. — Kier·ke·gaard·ian \,kir-kə-'gärd-ē-ən, -'górd-\ adj
Kie·sing·er \'kē-zin-ər\ Kurt Georg 1904–1988 chancellor of West Germany (1966–69)
Kil·lian \'kil-ē-ən, 'kil-yən\ James Rhyne 1904–1988 Am. educ.
Kil·mer \'kil-mər\ (Alfred) Joyce 1886–1918 Am. poet
Kim Il Sung \'kim-'il-'sən, -'sún\ 1912–   No. Korean leader (1948–) and pres. (1972–)
Kim·mel \'kim-əl\ Husband Edward 1882–1968 Am. admiral
Kin·di, al– \al-'kin-dē\ d ca 870 Arab philos.
King \'kin\ Ernest Joseph 1878–1956 Am. admiral
King Martin Luther, Jr. 1929–1968 Am. clergyman & civil rights leader
King Rufus 1755–1827 Am. polit. & diplomat
King William Lyon Mackenzie 1874–1950 Canad. statesman; prime min. (1921–26; 1926–30; 1935–48)
King William Rufus de Vane 1786–1853 Am. polit.; vice pres. of the U.S. (1853)
Kings·ley \'kinz-lē\ Charles 1819–1875 Eng. clergyman & nov.
Kin·kaid \kin-'kād\ Thomas Cassin 1888–1972 Am. admiral
Kin·sey \'kin-zē\ Alfred Charles 1894–1956 Am. sexologist
Kip·ling \'kip-lin\ (Joseph) Rud·yard \'rəd-yərd, 'rəj-ərd\ 1865–1936 Eng. author — Kip·ling·esque \,kip-lin-'esk\ adj
Kir·by–Smith \,kər-bē-'smith\ Edmund 1824–1893 orig. surname Smith Am. Confed. gen.
Kirch·hoff \'ki(ə)r-,kóf\ Gustav Robert 1824–1887 Ger. physicist
Kirch·ner \'ki(ə)rk-nər, 'ki(ə)rk-\ Ernst Ludwig 1880–1938 Ger. painter
Kirch·schlae·ger \'ki(ə)rk-,shleg-ər\ Rudolf 1915–   pres. of Austria (1974–86)
Ki·rov \'kē-,róf, -,róv\ Sergey Mironovich 1886–1934 Soviet polit.
Kir·wan \'kər-wən\ Richard 1733–1812 Irish chem.
Kis·sin·ger \'kis-°n-jər\ Henry Alfred 1923–   Am. (Ger.-born) scholar & govt. official; secy. of state (1973–77)
Kitch·e·ner \'kich-(ə-)nər\ Horatio Herbert 1850–1916 1st Earl Kitchener of Khartoum and of Broome Brit. field marshal
Kit·tredge \'ki-trij\ George Lyman 1860–1941 Am. educ.
Klee \'klā\ Paul 1879–1940 Swiss painter
Klein \'klīn\ Lawrence Robert 1920–   Am. econ.
Kleist \'klīst\ (Bernd) Heinrich Wilhelm von 1777–1811 Ger. dram.
Kleist Ewald von 1881–1954 Ger. gen.
Klem·per·er \'klem-pər-ər\ Otto 1885–1973 Ger. conductor
Klitz·ing \'klits-in\ Klaus von 1943–   Ger. physicist
Klop·stock \'kläp-,stäk, 'klóp-,shtók\ Friedrich Gottlieb 1724–1803 Ger. poet
Klug \'klüg\ Aaron 1926–   So. African (Lith.-born) molecular biol.
Knel·ler \'nel-ər\ Sir Godfrey 1646(or 1649)–1723 orig. Gottfried Kniller Eng. (Ger.-born) painter
Knox \'näks\ Henry 1750–1806 Am. gen. in Revolution
Knox John ca 1514–1572 Scot. reformer & statesman
Knox Philander Chase 1853–1921 Am. statesman
Knud·sen \kə-'nüt\ William Signius 1879–1948 Am. (Dan.-born) industrialist & administrator
Knut \kə-'n(y)üt\ var of CANUTE
Koch \'kók, 'kók, or ō, ä\ Robert 1843–1910 Ger. bacteriol.

Ko·cher \'kŏk-ər, 'kŏk-\ Emil Theodor 1841–1917 Swiss surgeon
Kock \'kŏk\ Charles-Paul de 1793–1871 Fr. nov. & dram.
Ko·dály \'kō-,dī\ Zol·tán \'zōl-,tän\ 1882–1967 Hung. composer
Koest·ler \'kes(t)-lər\ Arthur 1905–1983 Brit. (Hung.-born) writer
Kohl \'kōl\ Helmut 1930– chancellor of West Germany (1982–)
Koh·ler \'kō-lər\ Foy David 1908– Am. diplomat
Köhler \'kœ-lər\ Georges J. F. 1946– Ger. immunologist
Koi·so \'kŏi-(,)sō, 'kō-ē-(,)sō\ Kuniaki 1880–1950 Jp. gen.
Kokh·ba \'kŏk-bä\ Bar *d* A.D. 135 orig. *Sim·e·on bar Ko·zi·ba* \'sim-ē-ən-bär-'kō-zē-,bä\ Jewish leader in Palestine
Ko·kosch·ka \kō-'kŏsh-kə\ Oskar 1886–1980 Brit. (Austrian-born) painter
Kol·chak \kŏl-'chäk\ Aleksandr Vasilyevich 1873–1920 Russ. admiral & counterrevolutionary
Kol·lon·tay \,käl-ən-'tī\ Aleksandra Mikhaylovna 1872–1952 Russ. diplomat
Koll·witz \'kōl-,wits, 'kŏl-,vits\ Käthe 1867–1945 Ger. artist
Kol·mo·go·rov \kəl-mə-'gŏ-rəf\ Andrey Nikolayevich 1903–1987 Soviet math.
Kol·tsov \kōlt-'sŏf, -'sŏv\ Aleksey Vasilyevich 1808–1842 Russ. poet
Ko·mu·ra \kō-'mùr-ä, kō-mə-,rä\ Marquis Jutarō 1855–1911 Jp. diplomat
Kon·dí·lis \kŏn-'dē-ləs, -lēs\ Geórgios 1879–1936 Greek gen. & polit.
Ko·nev \'kŏn-,yef, -,yev, -yəf\ Ivan Stepanovich 1897–1973 Russ. gen. & marshal of Soviet Union
Ko·noe \kə-'nŏ-(,)ā\ Prince Fumimaro 1891–1945 Jp. statesman
Koo \'kü\ Vi Kyuin Wel·ling·ton \'wel-iŋ-tən\ 1888–1985 orig. *Ku Wei≈ chün* Chin. statesman & diplomat
Koop·mans \'küp-mənz\ Tjalling Charles 1910–1985 Am. (Du.-born) econ.
Kopernik *or* **Koppernigk** — see COPERNICUS
Korn·berg \'kó(ə)rn-,bərg\ Arthur 1918– Am. biochem.
Korn·gold \'kó(ə)rn-,gōld, -,gŏlt\ Erich Wolfgang 1897–1957 Am. (Austrian-born) composer, conductor, & pianist
Kor·ni·lov \kŏr-'nē-ləf\ Lavr Georgiyevich 1870–1918 Russ. gen. & counterrevolutionary
Ko·ro·len·ko \,kŏr-ə-'leŋ-(,)kō, ,kär-\ Vladimir Galaktionovich 1853–1921 Russ. nov.
Kor·zyb·ski \kə-'zhip-skē, kŏr-'zib-\ Alfred Habdank Skarbek 1879–1950 Am. (Pol.-born) scientist & writer
Koś·ciusz·ko \,käs-ē-'əs-,kō, kŏsh-'chüsh-(,)kō\ Tadeusz Andrzej Bonawentura 1746–1817 Pol. patriot and Am. Revolutionary soldier
Kos·sel \'kŏs-əl\ Albrecht 1853–1927 Ger. biochem.
Kos·suth \'kä-,süth, kä-'; 'kŏ-,shüt\ La·jos \'lói-,ōsh\ 1802–1894 Hung. patriot & statesman
Ko·sy·gin \kə-'sē-gən\ Aleksey Nikolayevich 1904–1980 Russ. polit.; premier of Soviet Union (1964–80)
Kot·ze·bue \'kät-sə-,bü, 'kŏt-\ August Friedrich Ferdinand von 1761–1819 Ger. dram.
Kous·se·vitz·ky \,kü-sə-'vit-skē\ Serge \'sərj, 'se(ə)rzh\ 1874–1951 *Sergey Aleksandrovich Kusevitsky* Am. (Russ.-born) conductor
Krafft–Ebing \'kräf-'tä-biŋ, 'kraf-\ Richard 1840–1902 Freiherr *von Krafft-Ebing* Ger. neurologist
Krebs \'krebz\ Sir Hans Adolf 1900–1981 Brit. (Ger.-born) biochem.
Kreis·ky \'krī-skē\ Bruno 1911– chancellor of Austria (1970–83)
Kreis·ler \'krī-slər\ Fritz 1875–1962 Am. (Austrian-born) violinist
Krogh \'krŏg\ (Schack) August Steenberg 1874–1949 Dan. physiol.
Krol \'krŏl\ John Joseph 1910– Am. cardinal
Kro·pot·kin \krə-'pät-kən\ Pyotr Alekseyevich 1842–1921 Russ. geographer & revolutionary
Kru·ger \'krü-gər *Afrik* 'krüē-ər\ Paul 1825–1904 *Stephanus Johannes Paulus* So. African statesman
Krupp \'krúp, 'krəp\ family of Ger. munition makers: including Friedrich 1787–1826; his son Alfred 1812–1887; Alfred's son Friedrich Alfred 1854–1902; Friedrich Alfred's daughter Bertha 1886–1957; & Bertha's son Alfried 1907–1967
Krup·ska·ya \'krüp-skə-yə\ Nadezhda Konstantinovna 1869–1939 *wife of Lenin* Russ. social worker
Krutch \'krüch\ Joseph Wood 1893–1970 Am. author & critic
Ku·bi·tschek de Oli·vei·ra \'kü-bə-,chek-dä-ō-lē-'vā-rə\ Juscelino 1902–1976 pres. of Brazil (1956–61)
Ku·blai Khan \,kü-,blə-'kän, -,blī-\ 1215–1294 founder of Mongol dynasty in China
Ku·brick \'k(y)ü-brik\ Stanley 1928– Am. film director, writer, and producer
Kuhn \'kün\ Richard 1900–1967 Austrian chem.
Kui·by·shev \'kwē-bə-,shef, 'kü-ē-bə-, -,shev\ Valerian Vladimirovich 1888–1935 Russ. Bolshevik
Kun \'kün\ Béla \'bā-lə\ 1885–1937 Hung. Communist
Kung \'güŋ\ Prince 1833–1898 Manchu statesman
K'ung \'güŋ\ H. H. 1881–1967 orig. *K'ung Hsiang-hsi* Chin. statesman
Ku·ro·pat·kin \,kùr-ə-'pat-kən, -'pät-\ Aleksey Nikolayevich 1848–1921 Russ. gen.
Kusch \'kùsh\ Polykarp 1911– Am. (Ger.-born) physicist
Ku·tu·zov \kə-'tü-,zŏf, -,zŏv\ Mikhail Illarionovich 1745–1813 Prince of *Smolensk* Russ. field marshal
Kuz·nets \'kəz-(,)nets\ Simon 1901–1985 Am. (Ukrainian-born) econ.
Kyd *or* **Kid** \'kid\ Thomas 1558–1594 Eng. dram.
Kynewulf *var of* CYNEWULF
La Bru·yère \lä-brü-'ye(ə)r, -brē-'e(ə)r\ Jean de 1645–1696 Fr. moralist
La·chaise \lä-'shäz\ Gaston 1882–1935 Am. (Fr.-born) sculptor
La Farge \lə-'färzh, -'färj\ John 1835–1910 Am. artist
La Farge Oliver Hazard Perry 1901–1963 Am. writer & anthropol.
La·fa·yette \,läf-ē-'et, ,laf-\ Marquis de 1757–1834 *Marie-Joseph-Paul≈ Yves-Roch-Gilbert du Motier* Fr. gen. & statesman
Laf·fite *or* **La·fitte** \lə-'fēt, la-\ Jean *ca* 1780–*ca* 1826 Fr. pirate in America
La Fol·lette \lə-'fäl-ət\ Robert Marion 1855–1925 Am. polit.
La·fon·taine \,lä-,fōⁿ-'ten\ Henri 1854–1943 Belg. lawyer & statesman
La Fon·taine \,lä-,fōⁿ-'ten\ Jean 1621–1695 Fr. poet
La·ger·kvist \'läg-ər-,kfist, -,kwist\ Pär Fabian 1891–1974 Swed. dram., poet, & nov.

La·ger·löf \'läg-ər-,lə(r)v\ Selma Ottiliana Lovisa 1858–1940 Swed. nov. & poet
La·grange \lə-'gränj, -'gränzh\ Joseph-Louis 1736–1813 Comte *de Lagrange* Fr. math.
La Guar·dia \lə-'g(w)ärd-ē-ə\ Fi·o·rel·lo \,fē-ə-'rel-(,)ō\ Henry 1882–1947 Am. polit.
Laing \'laŋ\ Ronald David 1927–1989 Brit. psychiatrist — **Laing·ian** \-ē-ən\ *adj*
Lake \'lāk\ Simon 1866–1945 Am. naval architect
La·marck \lə-'märk\ Jean-Baptiste de Monet de 1744–1829 Chevalier *de Lamarck* Fr. naturalist
La·mar·tine \,läm-,är-'tēn, ,lam-ər-\ Alphonse-Marie-Louis de Prat de 1790–1869 Fr. poet
Lamas Carlos Saavedra — see Carlos SAAVEDRA LAMAS
Lamb \'lam\ Charles 1775–1834 Eng. essayist & critic
Lamb William 1779–1848 2d Viscount *Melbourne* Eng. statesman
Lamb Willis Eugene 1913– Am. physicist
Lam·bert \'lam-bərt\ John 1619–1683 Eng. gen.
Lam·masch \'läm-,äsh\ Heinrich 1853–1920 Austrian jurist
La Motte–Fouqué — see FOUQUÉ
L'Amour \lä-'mór, -'mü(ə)r\ Louis Dearborn 1908–1988 Am. writer
Land \'land\ Edwin Herbert 1909– Am. inventor & industrialist
Lan·dau \län-'daù\ Lev Davidovich 1908–1968 Russ. physicist
Lan·dis \'lan-dəs\ Ken·e·saw \'ken-ə-,só\ Mountain 1866–1944 Am. jurist & baseball commissioner
Lan·don \'lan-dən\ Alfred Mossman 1887–1987 Am. polit.
Lan·dor \'lan-,dó(ə)r, -dər\ Walter Savage 1775–1864 Eng. author
Lan·dow·ska \lan-'dóf-skə, -'dóv-\ Wanda Louise 1879–1959 Pol. pianist
Land·seer \'lan(d)-,si(ə)r\ Sir Edwin Henry 1802–1873 Eng. painter
Land·stei·ner \'lan(d)-,stī-nər, 'länt-,shtī-\ Karl 1868–1943 Austrian≈ born pathologist in America
Lane \'lān\ Edward William 1801–1876 Eng. orientalist
Lan·franc \'lan-,fraŋk\ 1005?–1089 Ital.-born prelate in England
Lang \'laŋ\ Andrew 1844–1912 Scot. scholar & author
Lang Cosmo Gordon 1864–1945 Brit. prelate; archbishop of Canterbury (1928–42)
Lange \'läŋ-ə\ Christian Louis 1869–1938 Norw. pacifist & hist.
Lange \'lóŋ-ē\ David Russell 1942– prime min. of New Zealand (1984–89)
Lang·er \'laŋ-ər\ Susanne Knauth 1895–1985 Am. philos. & educ.
Lang·land \'laŋ-lənd\ William *ca* 1330–*ca* 1400 Eng. poet
Lang·ley \'laŋ-lē\ Samuel Pierpont 1834–1906 Am. astron. & airplane pioneer
Lang·muir \'laŋ-,myü(ə)r\ Irving 1881–1957 Am. chem.
Lang·ton \'laŋ(k)-tən\ Stephen *d* 1228 Eng. prelate
Lang·try \'laŋ(k)-trē\ Lillie 1853–1929 née (*Emilie Charlotte*) *Le Breton;* the *Jersey Lily* Brit. actress
La·nier \lə-'ni(ə)r\ Sidney 1842–1881 Am. poet
Lan·kes·ter \'laŋ-kəs-tər; 'lan-,kes-, 'laŋ-\ Sir Edwin Ray 1847–1929 Eng. zool.
Lannes \'län, 'lan\ Jean 1769–1809 Duc *de Montebello* Fr. soldier
Lan·sing \'lan(t)-siŋ\ Robert 1864–1928 Am. lawyer & statesman
Lao–tzu \'laùd-'zə\ orig. *Li Erh* \'lē-'er\ 6th cent. B.C. Chin. philos.
La Pé·rouse \,lä-pā-'rüz, -pə-\ Comte de 1741–1788 *Jean-François de Galoup* Fr. navigator & explorer
La·place \lə-'pläs\ Pierre-Simon 1749–1827 Marquis *de Laplace* Fr. astron. & math.
Lard·ner \'lärd-nər\ Ring 1885–1933 in full *Ringgold Wilmer Lardner* Am. writer
La·re·do Brú \lə-,räd-ō-'brü\ Federico 1875–1946 Cuban soldier; pres. of Cuba (1936–40)
La Roche·fou·cauld \lä-,rŏsh-fü-'kō, -,rōsh-\ François 1613–1680 Duc *de La Rochefoucauld* Fr. writer & moralist
La·rousse \lä-'rüs\ Pierre-Athanase 1817–1875 Fr. grammarian & lexicographer
Lar·tet \lär-'tä\ Édouard-Armand-Isidore-Hippolyte 1801–1871 Fr. archaeol.
La Salle \lə-'sal\ Sieur de 1643–1687 *René-Robert Cavelier* Fr. explorer in America
Las Ca·sas \läs-'käs-əs\ Bartolomé de 1474–1566 Span. Dominican missionary & hist.
Las·ki \'las-kē\ Harold Joseph 1893–1950 Eng. polit. scientist
Las·salle \lə-'sal, -'säl\ Ferdinand 1825–1864 Ger. socialist
Lat·i·mer \'lat-ə-mər\ Hugh *ca* 1485–1555 Eng. religious reformer
La Tour \lə-'tù(ə)r\ Georges de 1593–1652 Fr. painter
La Tour Maurice-Quentin de 1704–1788 Fr. painter
La·trobe \lə-'trōb\ Benjamin Henry 1764–1820 Am. (Eng.-born) architect & engineer
Lat·ti·more \'lat-ə-,mō(ə)r, -,mó(ə)r\ Owen 1900–1989 Am. orientalist
Lattimore Richmond 1906–1984 Am. poet & translator
Lau·bach \'laù-,bäk\ Frank Charles 1884–1970 Am. educator & missionary
Laud \'lód\ William 1573–1645 Eng. prelate; archbishop of Canterbury (1633–45)
Lau·der \'lód-ər\ Sir Harry Maclennan 1870–1950 Scot. singer
Laue \'laù-ə\ Max von 1879–1960 Ger. physicist
Laugh·ton \'lót-ᵊn\ Charles 1899–1962 Am. (Eng.-born) actor
Lau·rence \'lór-ən(t)s, 'lär-\ (Jean) Margaret 1926–1987 née *Wemyss* Can. author
Lau·ren·cin \,lò-räⁿ-saⁿ\ Marie 1885–1956 Fr. painter
Lau·ri·er \'lòr-ē-,ā, 'lär-\ Sir Wilfrid 1841–1919 Canad. statesman
Lautrec — see TOULOUSE-LAUTREC
La·val \lə-'val, -'väl\ Pierre 1883–1945 Fr. polit.
La·val·lière \lä-,val-'ye(ə)r\ Duchesse de 1644–1710 *Françoise-Louise de La Baume Le Blanc* mistress of Louis XIV of France
La·ve·ran \,lav-ə-'räⁿ\ Charles-Louis-Alphonse 1845–1922 Fr. physiol. & bacteriol.
La Vé·ren·drye \lä-,ver-ən-'drē, -'ver-ən-,drī\ Sieur de 1685–1749 *Pierre Gaultier de Varennes* Canad. explorer in America
La·very \'läv-(ə-)rē, 'lav-\ Sir John 1856–1941 Brit. painter
La·voi·sier \lə-'vwäz-ē-,ā\ Antoine-Laurent 1743–1794 Fr. chem.
Law \'ló\ (Andrew) Bon·ar \'bän-ər\ 1858–1923 Brit. (Canad.-born) statesman

Law Edward 1750–1818 1st Baron *Ellenborough* Eng. jurist
Law John 1671–1729 Scot. financier & speculator
Law William 1686–1761 Eng. writer
Lawes \'lôz\ Henry 1596–1662 Eng. composer
Lawes Lewis Edward 1883–1947 Am. penologist
Law·rence \'lȯr-ən(t)s, 'lär-\ David 1888–1973 Am. journalist
Lawrence David Herbert 1885–1930 Eng. nov. — **Law·ren·tian** *or* **Lau·ren·tian** \lȯ-'ren-ch(ē-)ən\ *adj*
Lawrence Ernest Orlando 1901–1958 Am. physicist
Lawrence Gertrude 1898–1952 orig. *Gertrud Alexandra Dagmar Lawrence Klasen* Eng. actress
Lawrence James 1781–1813 Am. naval officer
Lawrence Sir Thomas 1769–1830 Eng. painter
Lawrence Thomas Edward 1888–1935 *Lawrence of Arabia* later surname *Shaw* Brit. archaeol., soldier, & writer
Lax·ness \'läk‚snes\ Halldór Kiljan 1902–   Icelandic writer
Lay·a·mon \'lī-ə-mən, 'lä-ə-\ *fl* 1200 Eng. poet
Lay·ard \'lā-‚ärd, -ərd\ Sir Austen Henry 1817–1894 Eng. archaeol. & diplomat
Lea·cock \'lē-‚käk\ Stephen Butler 1869–1944 Canad. econ. & humorist
Leadbelly — see Huddie LEDBETTER
Lea·hy \'lā-(‚)hē\ William Daniel 1875–1959 Am. admiral
Lea·key \'lē-kē\ Louis Seymour Bazett 1903–1972 Brit. paleontologist
Lean \'lēn\ Sir David 1908–   Brit. film director
Lear \'li(ə)r\ Edward 1812–1888 Eng. painter & nonsense poet
Le·brun \lə-'brəⁿn, -'brœⁿ\ Albert 1871–1950 Fr. statesman; pres. of France (1932–40)
Lebrun Mme. Vigée·— see VIGÉE-LEBRUN
Le Brun *or* Le·brun Charles 1619–1690 Fr. painter
Lecky \'lek-ē\ William Edward Hartpole 1838–1903 Irish hist.
Le·conte de Lisle \lə-‚kōⁿ(n)t-də-'lē(ə)l\ Charles-Marie 1818–1894 orig. *Leconte* Fr. poet
Le Corbusier — see CORBUSIER
Led·bet·ter \'led-‚bet-ər\ Huddie 1888–1949 *Lead·bel·ly* \'led-‚bel-ē\ Am. blues singer
Le·der·berg \'läd-ər-‚bərg\ Joshua 1925–   Am. geneticist
Le·der·man \'läd-ər-mən\ Leon Max 1922–   Am. physicist
Le Duc Tho \‚läd-‚ək-'tō\ 1911–   Vietnamese diplomat
Lee \'lē\ Ann 1736–1784 Eng. mystic; founder of Shaker society in U.S.
Lee Charles 1731–1782 Am. (Eng.-born) gen.
Lee Fitzhugh 1835–1905 *nephew of R. E. Lee* Am. gen.
Lee Francis Lightfoot 1734–1797 Am. statesman in Revolution
Lee Henry 1756–1818 *Light-Horse Harry* Am. gen.
Lee Richard Henry 1732–1794 Am. statesman in Revolution
Lee Robert Edward 1807–1870 Am. Confed. gen.
Lee Sir Sidney 1859–1926 Eng. editor & scholar
Lee Yuan Tseh 1936–   Am. (Taiwanese-born) chem.
Lee Tsung–Dao \'lē-'dzún-'daú\ 1926–   Chin. physicist
Leeu·wen·hoek \'lā-vən-‚húk\ Antonie van 1632–1723 Du. naturalist
Le·feb·vre \lə-'fevr⁾\ François-Joseph 1755–1820 Duc *de Dantzig* Fr. gen.; marshal of France
Le Gal·lienne \lə-'gal-yən\ Eva 1899–   Am. (Eng.-born) actress
Le Gallienne Richard 1866–1947 Eng. writer
Le·gen·dre \lə-'zhäⁿ(n)dr⁾\ Adrien-Marie 1752–1833 Fr. math.
Lé·ger \lā-'zhā\ Alexis Saint-Léger 1887–1975 pseud. *St. John Perse* \saⁿ-‚jön-'pe(ə)rs\ Fr. diplomat & poet
Léger Fernand 1881–1955 Fr. painter
Le·guía y Sal·ce·do \lā-'gē-ə-‚ē-säl-'säd-(‚)ō, -'sä-(‚)thō\ Augusto Bernardino 1863–1932 Peruvian banker; pres. of Peru (1908–12; 1919–30)
Le·hár \'lā-‚här\ Franz 1870–1948 Hung. composer
Leh·man \'lē-mən\ Herbert Henry 1878–1963 Am. banker & polit.
Leh·mann \'lā-‚män\ Lotte 1888–1976 Ger. soprano
Lehn \'lān\ Jean-Marie 1939–   Fr. chem.
Leib·niz \'līb-nəts, G 'līp-nits\ Gottfried Wilhelm 1646–1716 Ger. philos. & math. — **Leib·niz·ian** \līb-'nit-sē-ən, līp-\ *adj*
Leicester 1st Earl of — see Robert DUDLEY; see also de MONTFORT
Leif Er·iks·son \‚lā-'ver-ik-sən, ‚lē-'fer-\ *or* Er·ics·son *fl* 1000 *son of Erik the Red* Norw. explorer
Leigh·ton \'lāt-ᵊn\ Frederick 1830–1896 Baron *Leighton of Stretton* Eng. painter
Leins·dorf \'līnz-‚dȯrf, 'līn(t)s-\ Erich 1912–   Am. (Austrian-born) conductor
Le·jeune \lə-'jün\ John Archer 1867–1942 Am. marine-corps gen.
Le·land \'lē-lənd\ John 1506?–1552 Eng. antiquarian
Leloir \lə-'lwär\ Luis Federico 1906–1987 Argentine biochem.
Le·ly \'lē-lē\ Sir Peter 1618–1680 orig. *Pieter Van der Faes* Du. painter in England
Le·maî·tre \lə-'metr⁾\ (François-Élie) Jules 1853–1914 Fr. writer
Lemaître (Abbé) Georges Henri 1894–1966 Belg. astrophysicist
Lemoyne Pierre — see IBERVILLE
Le·nard \'lā-‚närt\ Philipp 1862–1947 Ger. physicist
Len·clos \lä⁴-klō\ Anne de 1620–1705 *Ninon de Lenclos* Fr. courtesan
L'En·fant \'läⁿ-‚fänt, lä⁴-fä⁴\ Pierre-Charles 1754–1825 Fr. engineer in America
Le·nin \'len-ən\ 1870–1924 orig. *Vladimir Ilyich Ul·ya·nov* \úl-'yän-əf, -‚ȯf, -‚ȯv\ Russ. Communist leader
Leo \'lē-(‚)ō\ name of 13 popes: esp. I Saint *d* 461 (pope 440–61); III Saint *d* 816 (pope 795–816); XIII 1810–1903 (pope 1878–1903)
Leon·ard \'len-ərd\ William Ellery 1876–1944 Am. educ. & poet
Le·o·nar·do da Vin·ci \‚lē-ə-'när-(‚)dō-də-'vin-chē, ‚lā-, -'vēn-\ 1452–1519 It. painter, sculptor, architect, & engineer — **Le·o·nar·desque** \‚lē-ə-‚närd-'esk, ‚lā-\ *adj*
Le·on·ca·val·lo \‚lā-‚ōn-kə-'väl-(‚)ō\ Ruggiero 1858–1919 Ital. composer & librettist
Le·on·i·das \lē-'än-əd-əs\ *d* 480 B.C. Greek hero; king of Sparta (490?–480)
Le·ont·ief \l(y)ē-'ȯnt-yəf\ Wassily 1906–   Am. (Russ.-born) econ.
Le·o·par·di \‚lā-ə-'pärd-ē\ Giacomo 1798–1837 Ital. poet
Le·o·pold I \'lē-ə-‚pōld\ 1640–1705 king of Hungary (1655–1705) & Holy Rom. emp. (1658–1705)
Leopold II 1747–1792 Holy Rom. emp. (1790–92)
Leopold I 1790–1865 king of Belgium (1831–65)
Leopold II 1835–1909 king of Belgium (1865–1909)
Leopold III 1901–1983 king of Belgium (1934–51)

Lep·i·dus \'lep-əd-əs\ Marcus Aemilius *d* 13(or 12) B.C. Rom. triumvir
Ler·mon·tov \'ler-mən-‚tȯf, -‚tȯv\ Mikhail Yuryevich 1814–1841 Russ. poet & nov.
Ler·ner \'lər-nər\ Alan Jay 1918–1986 Am. dram. & librettist
Le·sage \lə-'säzh\ Alain-René 1668–1747 Fr. nov. & dram.
Le·sche·tiz·ky \‚lesh-ə-'tit-skē\ Theodor 1830–1915 Pol. pianist & composer
Les·seps \lā-'seps, 'les-əps\ Ferdinand-Marie de 1805–1894 Vicomte *de Lesseps* Fr. diplomat; promoter of Suez Canal
Les·sing \'les-iŋ\ Gotthold Ephraim 1729–1781 Ger. critic & dram.
L'Es·trange \lə-'stränj\ Sir Roger 1616–1704 Eng. journalist & translator
Leu·tze \'lȯit-sə\ Emanuel 1816–1868 Am. (Ger.-born) painter
Le·ver \'lē-vər\ Charles James 1806–1872 Brit. nov.
Le·vi–Mon·tal·ci·ni \‚lā-vē-‚mȯn-täl-'chē-nē\ Rita 1909–   Am. (Ital.=born) neurologist
Lé·vi–Strauss \‚lā-vē-'straús, ‚lev-ē-\ Claude 1908–   Fr. (Belg.-born) social anthropol. — **Lé·vi–Straus·si·an** \-'straú-sē-ən\ *adj*
Lew·es \'lü-əs\ George Henry 1817–1878 Eng. philos. & critic
Lewis Cecil Day — see DAY-LEWIS
Lewis \'lü-əs\ Sir (William) Arthur 1915–   Brit. econ.
Lewis Clive Staples 1898–1963 Eng. nov. & essayist
Lewis Isaac Newton 1858–1931 Am. army officer & inventor
Lewis John Llewellyn 1880–1969 Am. labor leader
Lewis Matthew Gregory 1775–1818 *Monk Lewis* Eng. author
Lewis Meriwether 1774–1809 Am. explorer
Lewis (Harry) Sinclair 1885–1951 Am. nov.
Lewis (Percy) Wyndham 1882–1957 Brit. painter & author
Ley \'lī\ Robert 1890–1945 Ger. Nazi leader
Lib·by \'lib-ē\ Willard Frank 1908–1980 Am. chem.
Lich·ten·stein \'lik-tən-‚stīn, -‚shtīn\ Roy 1923–   Am. artist
Li·cin·i·us \lə-'sin-ē-əs\ *d* 325 *Valerius Licinianus Licinius* Rom. emp. (308–324)
Lid·dell Hart \‚lid-ᵊl-'härt\ Sir Basil Henry 1895–1970 Eng. mil. scientist
Lie \'lē\ Jonas 1833–1908 Norw. nov. & dram.
Lie Trygve Halvdan 1896–1968 Norw. lawyer; secy.-gen. of U.N. (1946–52)
Lie·big \'lē-big\ Justus von 1803–1873 Freiherr *von Liebig* Ger. chem.
Lieb·knecht \'lēp-(kə-)‚nekt\ Karl 1871–1919 Ger. socialist leader
Li·far \'lē-‚fär, lē-'\ Serge 1905–1986 Russ. dancer
Li Hung–chang \'lē-'huŋ-'jäŋ\ 1823–1901 Chin. statesman
Lil·ien·thal \'lil-yən-‚täl, -‚thȯl\ Otto 1848–1896 Ger. aeronautical engineer
Li·li·u·o·ka·la·ni \li-‚lē-ə-(‚)wō-kə-'län-ē\ 1838–1917 *Lydia Paki Liliuokalani; Liliu Kamakaeha* queen of the Hawaiian Islands (1891–93)
Lil·lo \'lil-(‚)ō\ George 1693–1739 Eng. dram.
Li·món \li-'mōn\ José Arcadio 1908–1972 Am. (Mex.-born) dancer & choreographer
Lin·a·cre \'lin-i-kər\ Thomas *ca* 1460–1524 Eng. humanist & physician
Lin·coln \'liŋ-kən\ Abraham 1809–1865 16th pres. of the U.S. (1861–65) — **Lin·coln·esque** \‚liŋ-kə-'nesk\ *or* **Lin·coln·ian** \liŋ-'kō-nē-ən\ *adj*
Lincoln Benjamin 1733–1810 Am. gen. in Revolution
Lind \'lind\ Jenny 1820–1887 orig. *Johanna Maria; the Swedish Nightingale* Swed. soprano
Lind·bergh \'lin(d)-‚bərg\ Anne Spencer 1906–   née *Morrow; wife of C. A.* Am. author
Lindbergh Charles Augustus 1902–1974 Am. aviator
Lind·ley \'lin-(d)lē\ John 1799–1865 Eng. botanist — **Lind·ley·an** \-ən\ *adj*
Lind·say \'lin-zē\ Howard 1889–1968 Am. dram. & actor
Lindsay (Nicholas) Va·chel \'vā-chəl\ 1879–1931 Am. poet
Link·la·ter \'liŋ-‚klät-ər, -klət-\ Eric 1899–1974 Brit. writer
Linlithgow Marquis of — see HOPE
Lin·nae·us \lə-'nē-əs, -'nā-\ Carolus 1707–1778 Sw. *Carl von Lin·né* \lə-'nā\ Swed. botanist
Lin Yü–t'ang \'lin-'yü-'täŋ\ 1895–1976 Chin. author & philologist
Li·o·tard \‚lē-ō-'tär\ Jean-Étienne 1702–1789 Swiss painter
Lip·chitz \'lip-shəts\ Jacques 1891–1973 Am. (Latvian-born) sculptor
Li Peng \'lē-'pəŋ\ 1928–   Chin. Communist leader (1987–   )
Lip·mann \'lip-mən\ Fritz Albert 1899–1986 Am. (Ger.-born) biochem.
Li Po \'lē-'bȯ, -'pȯ\ 701–762 Chin. poet
Lip·pi \'lip-ē\ Fra Filippo *ca* 1406–1469 Florentine painter
Lippi Filippo *or* Filippino *ca* 1457–1504 *son of prec.* Florentine painter
Lipp·mann \'lēp-‚män, -'man\ Gabriel 1845–1921 Fr. physicist
Lipp·mann \'lip-mən\ Walter 1889–1974 Am. journalist & author
Lips·comb \'lip-skəm\ William Nunn, Jr. 1919–   Am. chem.
Lip·ton \'lip-tən\ Sir Thomas Johnstone 1850–1931 Eng. merchant & yachtsman
Li Shih–min — see T'ANG T'AI TSUNG
Lisle, de — see LECONTE DE LISLE, ROUGET DE LISLE
Lis·ter \'lis-tər\ Joseph 1827–1912 1st Baron *Lister of Lyme Regis* Eng. surgeon
Liszt \'list\ Franz 1811–1886 Hung. pianist & composer — **Liszt·ian** \-ē-ən\ *adj*
Lit·tle·ton *or* Lyt·tel·ton \'lit-ᵊl-tən\ *or* Lut·tel·ton \'lət-\ Sir Thomas 1422–1481 Eng. jurist
Lit·tré \li-'trā\ Maximilien-Paul-Émile 1801–1881 Fr. lexicographer
Lit·vi·nov \'lit-‚vē-‚nȯf, -‚nȯv, -nəf\ Maksim Maksimovich 1876–1951 Soviet diplomat
Liu Shao–ch'i \'lē-‚ü-'shaú-'chē\ 1898–1974 Chin. Communist polit.
Liv·ing·ston \'liv-iŋ-stən\ Robert R. 1746–1813 Am. statesman
Liv·ing·stone \'liv-iŋ-stən\ David 1813–1873 Scot. missionary and explorer in Africa
Livy \'liv-ē\ 59 B.C.–A.D. 17 *Titus Livius* Rom. hist.

\ə\ abut \ᵊ\ kitten, F table \ər\ further \a\ ash \ā\ ace \ä\ cot, cart
\aú\ out \ch\ chin \e\ bet \ē\ easy \g\ go \i\ hit \ī\ ice \j\ job
\ŋ\ sing \ō\ go \ȯ\ law \ȯi\ boy \th\ thin \th\ the \ü\ loot \ú\ foot
\y\ yet \zh\ vision \á, k̲, ⁿ, œ, œ̄, uė, ūė, ᵜ\ *see* Guide to Pronunciation

Lloyd George \'lȯid-'jȯ(ə)rj\ David 1863–1945 1st Earl of *Dwy·for* \'dü-ē-,vȯ(ə)r\ Brit. statesman; prime min. (1916–22)

Llull \'lyül\ Ramon *ca* 1235–1316 *Raymond Lul·ly* \'lül-ē\ Catalan mystic & poet

Lo·ba·chev·sky \,lō-bə-'chef-skē, ,läb-ə-, -'chev-\ Nikolay Ivanovich 1792–1856 Russ. math.

Lo·ben·gu·la \,lō-bən-'g(y)ü-lə\ *ca* 1836–1894 Zulu king of the Matabele

Locke \'läk\ John 1632–1704 Eng. philos.

Lock·hart \'läk-ərt, 'läk-,(h)ärt\ John Gibson 1794–1854 Scot. nov. & biographer

Lock·yer \'läk-yər\ Sir Joseph Norman 1836–1920 Eng. astron.

Lodge \'läj\ Henry Cabot 1850–1924 Am. statesman & author

Lodge Henry Cabot 1902–1985 *grandson of prec.* Am. polit. & diplomat

Lodge Sir Oliver Joseph 1851–1940 Eng. physicist

Lodge Thomas 1558–1625 Eng. poet & dram.

Loeb \'lōb\ Jacques 1859–1924 Ger.-born physiol. in America

Loewe \'lō\ Frederick 1901–1988 Am. (Austrian-born) composer

Loewi \'lō-ē\ Otto 1873–1961 Am. (Ger.-born) pharmacologist

Löff·ler \'lef-lər\ Friedrich August Johannes 1852–1915 Ger. bacteriol.

Lo·max \'lō-,maks\ John Avery 1867–1948 and his son Alan 1915– Am. folklorists

Lombard Peter — see PETER LOMBARD

Lom·bro·so \lȯm-'brō-(,)sō\ Ce·sa·re \'chä-zä-,rā\ 1836–1909 Ital. physician & psychiatrist

Lon·don \'lən-dən\ John Griffith 1876–1916 *Jack* Am. writer

Long \'lȯŋ\ Crawford Williamson 1815–1878 Am. surgeon

Long Hu·ey \'hyü-ē\ Pierce 1893–1935 Am. polit.

Long Stephen Harriman 1784–1864 Am. army officer & explorer

Long·fel·low \'lȯŋ-,fel-(,)ō, -fel-ə-(w)\ Henry Wads·worth \'wädz-(,)wərth\ 1807–1882 Am. poet

Lon·gi·nus \län-'jī-nəs\ 1st cent. A.D. Greek critic

Long·street \'lȯŋ-,strēt\ James 1821–1904 Am. Confed. gen.

Lönn·rot \'lœn-,rüt\ Elias 1802–1884 Finn. folklorist

Lons·dale \'länz-,dāl\ Frederick 1881–1954 Brit. dram.

Ló·pez \'lō-,pez\ Carlos Antonio 1790–1862 pres. of Paraguay (1844–62)

López Francisco Solano 1827–1870 *son of prec.* pres. of Paraguay (1862–70)

López Ma·te·os \,-mə-'tā-əs, -(,)ōs\ Adolfo 1910–1969 pres. of Mexico (1958–64)

López Por·til·lo \-pȯr-'tē-(y)ō\ José 1920– pres. of Mexico (1976–82)

Lorca Federico García — see Federico GARCÍA LORCA

Lo·rentz \'lȯr-,en(t)s, 'lȯr-\ Hendrik Antoon 1853–1928 Du. physicist

Lo·renz \'lȯr-,en(t)s, 'lȯr-\ Konrad 1903–1989 Ger. (Austrian-born) ethologist

Lorrain Claude — see CLAUDE LORRAIN

Lo·thair I \lō-'t(h)a(ə)r, -'t(h)e(ə)r, 'lō-,\ 795–855 Holy Rom. emp. (840–855)

Lothair II (*or* **III**) 1075–1137 king of Germany & Holy Rom. emp. (1125–37)

Lo·ti \lō-'tē, lō-\ Pierre 1850–1923 pseud. of *Louis-Marie-Julien Viaud* Fr. naval officer & nov.

Lou·bet \lü-'bā\ Émile-François 1838–1929 Fr. statesman; pres. of France (1899–1906)

Loudoun 4th Earl of — see John CAMPBELL

Lou·is \'lü-ē, lü-'ē\ name of 18 kings of France: esp. **I** 778–840 (reigned 814–840); **V** (*le Fainéant*) 967–987 (reigned — last Carolingian — 986–987); **IX** (*Saint*) 1214–1270 (reigned 1226–70); **XI** 1423–1483 (reigned 1461–83); **XII** 1462–1515 (reigned 1498–1515); **XIII** 1601–1643 (reigned 1610–43); **XIV** 1638–1715 (reigned 1643–1715); **XV** 1710–1774 (reigned 1715–74); **XVI** 1754–1793 (reigned 1774–92; guillotined); **XVII** 1785–1795 (nominally reigned 1793–95); **XVIII** 1755–1824 (reigned 1814–15; 1815–24)

Louis IV 1283?–1347 *Duke of Bavaria* king of Germany & Holy Rom. emp. (1314–47)

Louis II de Bourbon — see CONDÉ

Louis–Napoléon — see NAPOLÉON III

Louis Phi·lippe \-fi-'lēp\ 1773–1850 *the Citizen King* king of the French (1830–48)

L'Ouverture — see Pierre Dominique TOUSSAINT LOUVERTURE

Lou·ÿs \lü-'ē\ Pierre 1870–1925 Fr. writer

Love·lace \'ləv-,lās\ Richard 1618–1657 Eng. Cavalier poet

Lov·ell \'ləv-əl\ Sir (Alfred Charles) Bernard 1913– Brit. astron.

Lov·er \'ləv-ər\ Samuel 1797–1868 Irish nov.

Low \'lō\ Sir David Alexander Cecil 1891–1963 Brit. cartoonist

Low·ell \'lō-əl\ Amy 1874–1925 Am. poet & critic

Lowell James Russell 1819–1891 Am. poet, essayist, & dram.

Lowell Percival 1855–1916 *bro. of Amy* Am. astron.

Lowell Robert Traill Spence 1917–1977 Am. poet

Lowes \'lōz\ John Livingston 1867–1945 Am. educ.

Lowndes \'laün(d)z\ William Thomas 1798–1843 Eng. bibliographer

Low·ry \'laü(ə)r-ē\ (Clarence) Malcolm 1909–1957 Brit. writer

Loyola Saint Ignatius — see IGNATIUS OF LOYOLA

Lub·bock \'ləb-ək\ Sir John 1834–1913 1st Baron *Avebury; son of Sir J. W.* Eng. financier & author

Lubbock Sir John William 1803–1865 Eng. astron. & math.

Luc·an \'lü-kən\ A.D. 39–65 *Marcus Annaeus Lucanus* Rom. poet

Luce \'lüs\ Clare 1903–1987 née *Boothe* \'büth\ *wife of H. R.* Am. dram., polit., & diplomat

Luce Henry Robinson 1898–1967 Am. editor & publisher

Lu·cre·tius \lü-'krē-sh(ē-)əs\ *ca* 96–*ca* 55 B.C. *Titus Lucretius Carus* Rom. poet & philos. — **Lu·cre·tian** \-shən\ *adj*

Lu·cul·lus \lü-'kəl-əs\ Lucius Licinius *ca* 117–58(or 56) B.C. Rom. gen. & epicure — **Lu·cul·lan** \-'kəl-ən\ *adj*

Lu·den·dorff \'lüd-ən-,dȯrf\ Erich Friedrich Wilhelm 1865–1937 Ger. gen.

Lu Hsün \'lü-'shün\ 1881–1936 pseud. of *Chou Shu-Jen* Chin. writer

Lu·i·gi Ame·deo \lə-'wē-jē-,äm-ə-'dā-(,)ō\ 1873–1933 Duca *D'Abruzzi* & Prince of *Savoy-Aosta* Ital. explorer & naval officer

Lu·jan \'lü-hən\ Manuel, Jr. 1928– U.S. secy. of interior (1989–)

Lul·ly \lü-'lē\ Jean-Baptiste 1632–1687 Fr. (Ital.-born) composer

Lully Raymond — see Ramon LLULL

Lunt \'lənt\ Alfred 1893–1977 Am. actor

Lu·ria \'lür-ē-ə\ Salvador Edward 1912– Am. (Ital.-born) microbiologist

Lu·ther \'lü-thər\ Martin 1483–1546 Ger. Reformation leader

Lu·thu·li \lü-'t(h)ü-lē\ Albert John 1898–1967 So. African reformer

Lux·em·burg \'lək-səm-,bərg, 'lük-səm-,bürk\ Rosa 1870–1919 Ger. socialist leader

Lwoff \'lwȯf, lə-'wȯf\ André-Michael 1902– Fr. microbiologist

Lyau·tey \lē-,ō-'tā\ Louis-Hubert-Gonzalve 1854–1934 Fr. soldier; marshal of France

Ly·cur·gus \lī-'kər-gəs\ 9th cent. B.C. Spartan lawgiver

Lyd·gate \'lid-,gāt, -gət\ John *ca* 1370–*ca* 1450 Eng. poet

Ly·ell \'lī-əl\ Sir Charles 1797–1875 Brit. geologist

Lyly \'lil-ē\ John 1554?–1606 Eng. author

Lynd \'lind\ Robert Staugh·ton \'stȯt-ʰn\ 1892–1970 & his wife Helen née *Merrell* 1896–1982 Am. sociologists

Ly·nen \'lǖ-nən\ Feodor Felix Konrad 1911–1979 Ger. biochem.

Lyng \'liŋ\ Richard Edmund 1918– U.S. secy. of agriculture (1986–89)

Ly·on \'lī-ən\ Mary 1797–1849 Am. educ.

Ly·ons \'lī-ənz\ Joseph Aloysius 1879–1939 Austral. statesman; prime min. (1931–39)

Ly·san·der \lī-'san-dər\ *d* 395 B.C. Spartan commander

Ly·sen·ko \lə-'sen-(,)kō\ Trofim Denisovich 1898–1976 Soviet biol.

Lys·i·as \'lis-ē-əs\ *ca* 445–after 380 B.C. Athenian orator

Ly·sim·a·chus \lī-'sim-ə-kəs\ *ca* 355–*ca* 281 B.C. Macedonian gen. under Alexander the Great; king of Thrace (306)

Ly·sip·pus \lī-'sip-əs\ 4th cent. B.C. Greek sculptor

Lyt·ton \'lit-ʰn\ 1st Baron 1803–1873 *Edward George Earle Bul·wer* *Lytton* \,bül-wər-\; *bro. of Sir Henry Bulwer* Eng. author

Lytton 1st Earl of 1831–1891 (*Edward*) Robert Bulwer-Lytton; pseud. *Owen Meredith; son of prec.* Brit. statesman & poet

Mac·Ar·thur \mə-'kär-thər\ Arthur 1845–1912 Am. gen.

MacArthur Charles 1895–1956 Am. dram.

MacArthur Douglas 1880–1964 *son of Arthur* Am. gen.

Ma·cau·lay \mə-'kȯ-lē\ Dame Rose 1881–1958 Eng. nov.

Macaulay Thomas Babington 1800–1859 1st Baron *Macaulay* Eng. hist., author, & statesman

Mac·beth \mək-'beth\ *d* 1057 king of Scotland (1040–57)

Mac·Bride \mək-'brīd\ Seán 1904–1988 Irish statesman

Mac·ca·bees \'mak-ə-,bēz\ Judas *or* Judah *d* 161 B.C. surname *Mac·ca·ba·eus* \,mak-ə-'bē-əs\ Jewish patriot

Mac·Diar·mid \mək-'dər-məd, -mət\ Hugh 1892–1978 pseud. of *Christopher Murray Grieve* Scot. poet

Mac·don·ald \mək-'dän-ʰld\ George 1824–1905 Scot. nov. & poet

Macdonald Sir John Alexander 1815–1891 Canad. statesman; 1st prime min. of Dominion of Canada (1867–73) and again (1878–91)

Mac·Don·ald \mək-'dän-ʰld\ (James) Ramsay 1866–1937 Brit. statesman

Mac·don·ough \mək-'dän-ə, -'dən-\ Thomas 1783–1825 Am. naval officer

Mac·Dow·ell \mək-'daù-(ə)l\ Edward Alexander 1860–1908 Am. composer

Mach \'mäk, 'mäk\ Ernst 1838–1916 Austrian physicist & philos.

Ma·cha·do y Mo·ra·les \mä-'chäd-ō-,ē-mə-'räl-əs\ Gerardo 1871–1939 pres. of Cuba (1925–33)

Ma·chi·a·vel·li \,mak-ē-ə-'vel-ē\ Niccolò 1469–1527 Ital. polit. philos.

Mac·Kaye \mə-'kī\ Percy 1875–1956 Am. poet & dram.

Mack·en·sen \'mäk-ən-zən\ August von 1849–1945 Ger. field marshal

Mack·en·zie \mə-'ken-zē\ Alexander 1822–1892 Canad. (Scot.-born) statesman; prime min. (1873–78)

Mackenzie Sir Alexander Campbell 1847–1935 Brit. composer & conductor

Mackenzie Sir Compton 1883–1972 Eng. nov.

Mackenzie William Lyon 1795–1861 Canad. (Scot.-born) insurgent leader

Mac·kin·der \mə-'kin-dər\ Sir Halford John 1861–1947 Eng. geographer

Maclaren Ian — see John WATSON

Mac·Leish \mə-'klēsh\ Archibald 1892–1982 Am. poet & administrator

Mac·Len·nan \mə-'klen-ən\ Hugh 1907– Canad. nov.

Mac·leod \mə-'klaüd\ John James Rickard 1876–1935 Scot. physiol.

Mac–Ma·hon \,mak-mä-'ōⁿ; mək-'ma(-)ən, -'man\ Marie-Edme-Patrice-Maurice 1808–1893 Comte *de Mac-Mahon*; duc *de Magenta* marshal (1859) & pres. (1873–79) of France

Mac·mil·lan \mək-'mil-ən\ (Maurice) Harold 1894–1986 Brit. prime min. (1957–63)

Mac·Mil·lan \mək-'mil-ən\ Donald Baxter 1874–1970 Am. explorer

Mac·Neice \mək-'nēs\ Louis 1907–1963 Irish poet

Mac·pher·son \mək-'fər-ʰn\ James 1736–1796 Scot. writer

Mac·rea·dy \mə-'krēd-ē\ William Charles 1793–1873 Eng. actor

Ma·da·ria·ga y Ro·jo \,mäd-ə-rē-'äg-ə-(,)'rō-(,)hō\ Salvador de 1886–1978 Span. writer & diplomat

Ma·de·ro \mə-'ðer-(,)ō\ Francisco Indalecio 1873–1913 pres. of Mexico (1911–13)

Mad·i·son \'mad-ə-sən\ Dolley 1768–1849 née (*Dorothea*) *Payne; wife of James* Am. hostess

Madison James 1751–1836 4th pres. of the U.S. (1809–17) — **Mad·i·so·nian** \,mad-ə-'sō-nē-ən, -nyən\ *adj*

Mae·ce·nas \mi-'sē-nəs\ Gaius *ca* 70–8 B.C. Rom. statesman & patron of literature

Maes \'mäs\ Nicolaes 1634–1693 also called *Nicolas Maas* Du. painter

Mae·ter·linck \'mät-ər-,liŋk *also* 'met-, 'mat-\ Maurice-Polydore-Marie-Bernard 1862–1949 Belg. poet, dram., & essayist — **Mae·ter·linck·ian** \,mät-ər-'liŋ-kē-ən, ,met-, ,mat-\ *adj*

Ma·gel·lan \mə-'jel-ən, *chiefly Brit* -'gel-\ Ferdinand *ca* 1480–1521 Pg. *Fernão de Magalhães* Port. navigator

Ma·gi·not \,mazh-ə-'nō, ,maj-\ André 1877–1932 Fr. polit.

Ma·gritte \mə-'grēt\ René-François-Ghislain 1898–1967 Belg. painter

Mag·say·say \mäg-'sī-,sī, -,sī-'sī\ Ramon 1907–1957 pres. of Philippines (1953-57)

Mah·fouz \mäk-füz\ Naguib 1911– Egypt. writer

Mah·ler \'mäl-ər\ Gustav 1860–1911 Austrian composer — **Mah·ler·ian** \mä-'lir-ē-ən, -'ler-\ *adj*

Mah·mud II \mä-'müd\ 1785–1839 Ottoman sultan (1808–39)

Mai·ler \'mā-lər\ Norman 1923–   Am. author

Mail·lol \mä-'yȯl, -'yōl\ Aristide 1861–1944 Fr. sculptor

Mai·mon·i·des \mī-'män-ə-,dēz\ Moses 1135–1204 Heb. *Moses ben Maimon* Jewish philos., jurist, & physician

Maine \'mān\ Sir Henry James Sumner 1822–1888 Eng. jurist

Main·te·non \maⁿ(n)t-^ən-'ōⁿ, maⁿ(n)t-^ənōⁿ\ Marquise de 1635–1719 *Françoise d'Aubigné; consort of Louis XIV*

Mait·land \'māt-lənd\ Frederic William 1850–1906 Eng. hist.

Mal·a·mud \'mal-ə-(,)məd\ Bernard 1914–1986 Am. writer

Ma·lan \mə-'lan, -'län\ Daniel François 1874–1959 So. African editor; prime min. (1948–54)

Mal·colm X \,mal-kə-'meks\ 1925–1965 orig. *Malcolm Little* Am. civil rights leader

Male·branche \,mal-(ə-)'brän̄sh, mäl-\ Nicolas de 1638–1715 Fr. philos.

Ma·len·kov \ma-'len-,kȯf, -,kȯv, -'len̄-kȯf; ,mal-ən-'kȯf, -'kȯv\ Georgy Maksimilianovich 1902–1988 Soviet polit.

Mal·herbe \ma-'le(ə)rb, mä-\ François de 1555–1628 Fr. poet

Ma·li·nov·sky \,mal-ə-'nȯf-skē, ,mäl-, -'nȯv-\ Rodion Yakovlevich 1898–1967 Soviet gen.

Ma·li·now·ski \,mal-ə-'nȯf-skē, ,mäl-, -'nȯv-\ Bronislaw Kasper 1884–1942 Am. (Pol.-born) anthropol.

Mal·kiel \mäl-'kyel\ Yakov 1914–   Am. (Russ.-born) Romance philologist & etymologist

Mal·lar·mé \,mal-,är-'mā\ Stéphane 1842–1898 Fr. poet

Ma·lone \mə-'lōn\ Edmond 1741–1812 Irish scholar

Mal·o·ry \'mal-(ə-)rē\ Sir Thomas *fl* 1470 Eng. author

Mal·pi·ghi \mal-'pē-gē, -'pig-ē\ Marcello 1628–1694 Ital. anatomist — **Mal·pi·ghi·an** \-ən\ *adj*

Mal·raux \mal-'rō\ André 1901–1976 Fr. writer & art historian

Mal·thus \'mal-thəs\ Thomas Robert 1766–1834 Eng. econ.

Mam·et \'mam-ət\ David Alan 1947–   Am. dram.

Man·del \mä(n)-'del\ Georges 1885–1944 orig. *Louis-Georges Rothschild* Fr. polit.

Man·de·la \man-'del-ə\ Nelson Rolihlahla 1918–   So. African black political leader

Man·de·ville \'man-də-,vil\ Bernard de 1670–1733 Brit. (Du.-born) satirist & philos.

Mandeville Sir John *fl* 1356 pseud. of an unidentified travel writer

Ma·net \ma-'nā, mä-\ Édouard 1832–1883 Fr. painter

Ma·nil·i·us \mə-'nil-ē-əs\ Gaius 1st cent. B.C. Rom. polit.

Mann \'man\ Horace 1796–1859 Am. educ.

Mann \'män, 'man\ Thomas 1875–1955 Am. (Ger.-born) author

Man·ner·heim \'män-ər-,hām, 'man-, -,hïm\ Baron Carl Gustaf Emil von 1867–1951 Finn. gen. & statesman

Man·ning \'man-in̄\ Henry Edward 1808–1892 Eng. cardinal

Mans·field \'mans-,fēld, 'manz-\ Katherine 1888–1923 pseud. of *Kathleen Mansfield Beau·champ* \'bē-chəm\ Brit. (N.Z.-born) writer

Man·son \'man(t)-sən\ Sir Patrick 1844–1922 Brit. parasitologist

Man·ṣūr, al- \,al-,man-'sú(ə)r\ 709(to 714)–775 in full *Abū Ja'far al= Manṣūr* or *al-Manṣūr al-'Abbāsī* Arab caliph (754–775); founder of Baghdad

Man·te·gna \män-'tän-yə\ Andrea 1431–1506 Ital. painter & engraver

Man·uel \män-'wel\ Don Juan 1282–1349 Span. nobleman & writer

Man·zo·ni \män(d)-'zō-nē\ Alessandro Francesco Tommaso Antonio 1785–1873 Ital. nov. & poet

Mao Tse-tung \maú(d)-zə-'dún̄, ,maút-sə-\ 1893–1976 pinyin *Mao Ze-dong* Chin. Communist; leader of People's Republic of China (1949–76)

Map \'map\ Walter *ca* 1140– *ca* 1209 Eng. writer

Ma·rat \mə-'rä\ Jean-Paul 1743–1793 Fr. (Swiss-born) revolutionary

Mar·cel·lus \mär-'sel-əs\ Marcus Claudius 268?–208 B.C. Rom. gen.

March 1st Earl of — see Roger de MORTIMER

Mar·co·ni \mär-'kō-nē\ Guglielmo 1874–1937 Ital. physicist & inventor

Marco Polo — see POLO

Mar·cos \'mär-(,)kōs\ Ferdinand Edralin 1917–1989 pres. of the Philippines (1965–86)

Marcus Aurelius — see Marcus Aurelius ANTONINUS

Mar·cu·se \mär-'kü-zə\ Herbert 1898–1979 Am. (Ger.-born) social & polit. philos.

Mar·ga·ret \'mär-g(ə-)rət\ **of Angoulême** 1492–1549 queen of *Henry of Navarre* & writer

Margaret of Anjou 1430–1482 queen of Henry VI of England

Margaret of Valois or **Margaret of France** 1553–1615 queen consort of *Henry of Navarre*

Margaret Rose 1930–   princess of Great Britain

Mar·gre·the II \mär-'grät-ə\ 1940–   queen of Denmark (1972–   )

Ma·ria The·re·sa \mə-,rē-ə-tə-'rā-sə, -'rā-zə\ 1717–1780 *wife of Holy Rom. Emp. Francis I* archduchess of Austria & queen of Hungary & Bohemia

Ma·rie \mə-'rē\ 1875–1938 queen of Romania (1914–27); queen dowager (1927–38)

Marie An·toi·nette \-,an-t(w)ə-'net\ 1755–1793 *dau. of Maria Theresa & wife of Louis XVI of France*

Marie-Louise 1791–1847 *dau. of Francis II of Austria & 2d wife of Napoléon I*

Marie de Mé·di·cis \-də-'med-ə-(,)chē, -,mād-ə-'sē(s)\ 1573–1642 *2d wife of Henry IV of France* regent for Louis XIII

Mar·in \'mar-ən\ John Cheri 1870–1953 Am. painter

Ma·ri·net·ti \,mar-ə-'net-ē, ,mär-\ (Emilio) Filippo Tommaso 1876–1944 Ital. poet

Ma·ri·ni \mə-'rē-nē\ or **Ma·ri·no** \-(,)nō\ Giambattista 1569–1625 Ital. poet

Mar·ion \'mer-ē-ən, 'mar-ē-\ Francis 1732?–1795 *the Swamp Fox* Am. commander in Revolution

Ma·ri·tain \,mar-ə-'taⁿ\ Jacques 1882–1973 Fr. philos. & diplomat

Ma·ri·us \'mer-ē-əs, 'mar-\ Gaius *ca* 157–86 B.C. Rom. gen.

Ma·ri·vaux \,mar-ə-'vō\ Pierre Carlet de Chamblain de 1688–1763 Fr. dram. & nov.

Mark Antony or **Anthony** — see Marcus ANTONIUS

Mark·ham \'mär-kəm\ Edwin 1852–1940 orig. *Charles Edward Anson Markham* Am. poet

Mar·ko·va \mär-'kō-və\ Dame Ali·cia \ə-'lē-sē-ə\ 1910–   orig. *Lilian Alicia Marks* Eng. dancer

Marlborough 1st Duke of — see John CHURCHILL

Mar·lowe \'mär-,lō\ Christopher 1564–1593 Eng. dram. — **Mar·lo·vi·an** \mär-'lō-vē-ən, -vyən\ *adj*

Marlowe Julia 1866–1950 orig. *Sarah Frances Frost* Am. (Eng.-born) actress

Mar·mont \mär-'mōⁿ\ Auguste-Frédéric-Louis Viesse de 1774–1852 *Duc de Raguse* Fr. gen.; marshal of France

Mar·mon·tel \,mär-(,)mōⁿ-'tel\ Jean-François 1723–1799 Fr. author

Ma·rot \ma-'rō\ Clément 1496?–1544 Fr. poet

Mar·quand \mär-'kwänd\ John Phillips 1893–1960 Am. nov.

Mar·quette \mär-'ket\ Jacques 1637–1675 *Père* \,pi(ə)r, ,pe(ə)r\ *Marquette* Fr.-born Jesuit missionary & explorer in America

Mar·quis \'mär-kwəs\ Donald Robert Perry 1878–1937 Am. humorist

Mar·ry·at \'mar-ē-ət\ Frederick 1792–1848 Eng. naval commander & nov.

Marsh \'märsh\ Dame (Edith) Ngaio \'nī-(,)ō\ 1899–1982 N.Z. writer

Mar·shall \'mär-shəl\ George Catlett 1880–1959 Am. gen. & statesman

Marshall John 1755–1835 Am. jurist; chief justice U.S. Supreme Court (1801–35)

Marshall John Ross 1912–   prime min. of New Zealand (1972)

Marshall Thomas Riley 1854–1925 vice pres. of the U.S. (1913–21)

Marshall Thurgood 1908–   Am. jurist

Mar·sil·i·us \mär-'sil-ē-əs\ **of Padua** *ca* 1280–*ca* 1343 Ital. scholar

Mar·ston \'mär-stən\ John 1576–1634 Eng. dram.

Martel Charles — see CHARLES MARTEL

Mar·tens \'märt-^ənz\ Fyodor Fyodorovich 1845–1909 Russ. jurist

Martens Wilfried 1936–   prime min. of Belgium (1979–   )

Mar·tial \'mär-shəl\ *ca* A.D. 40–*ca* 103 *Marcus Valerius Martialis* Rom. epigrammatist

Mar·tin \'märt-^ən, mär-taⁿ\ Saint *ca* 316–397 *Martin of Tours* \-'tú(ə)r\ patron saint of France

Mar·tin \'märt-^ən\ Archer John Porter 1910–   Brit. chem.

Martin Glenn Luther 1886–1955 Am. airplane manuf.

Martin Homer Dodge 1836–1897 Am. painter

Martin Joseph William 1884–1968 Am. publisher & polit.

Mar·tin du Gard \,mär-ta-dē-'gär\ Roger 1881–1958 Fr. author

Mar·ti·neau \'märt-^ən-,ō\ Harriet 1802–1876 Eng. nov. & econ.

Martineau James 1805–1900 *bro. of Harriet* Eng. theol. & philos.

Mar·ti·ni \mär-'tē-nē\ Simone *ca* 1284–1344 Ital. painter

Mar·tin·son \'mär-tēn-(,)sòn\ Harry Edmund 1904–1978 Swed. author

Mar·vell \'mär-vəl\ Andrew 1621–1678 Eng. poet & satirist

Marx \'märks\ Karl Heinrich 1818–1883 Ger. polit. philos. & socialist — **Marx·ian** \'märk-sē-ən\ *adj*

Mary I \'me(ə)r-ē, 'ma(ə)r-ē, 'mā-rē\ 1516–1558 *Mary Tudor; Bloody Mary* queen of England (1553–58)

Mary II 1662–1694 joint Brit. sovereign with William III

Mary Stuart 1542–1587 *Mary, Queen of Scots* queen of Scotland (1542–87)

Ma·sac·cio \mə-'zäch-(ē-,)ō\ 1401–1428 orig. *Tommaso di Giovanni di Simone Guidi* Ital. painter

Ma·sa·ryk \'mäs-ə-(,)rik, 'mas-\ Jan \'yän, 'yan\ Gar·rigue \gə-'rēg\ 1886–1948 *son of T. G.* Czech diplomat & polit.

Masaryk To·máš \'tò-,mäsh, 'täm-əs\ Garrigue 1850–1937 Czech philos. & statesman; 1st pres. of Czechoslovakia (1918–35)

Ma·sca·gni \mä-'skän-yē, ma-\ Pietro 1863–1945 Ital. composer

Mase·field \'mās-,fēld\ John 1878–1967 Eng. author; poet laureate (1930–67)

Mas·i·nis·sa or **Mas·si·nis·sa** \,mas-ə-'nis-ə\ *ca* 240–148 B.C. king of Numidia

Ma·son \'mās-^ən\ Charles 1728–1786 Eng. astron. & surveyor

Mason George 1725–1792 Am. statesman in Revolution

Mas·sa·soit \,mas-ə-'sòit\ *d* 1661 sachem of Wampanoag Indians in eastern Massachusetts

Mas·sé·na \,mas-ā-'nä, mə-'sā-nə\ André 1758–1817 *Duc de Rivoli; Prince d'Ess·ling* \des-len̄\ Fr. gen.

Mas·se·net \,mas-^ən-'ā, ma-'snä\ Jules-Émile-Frédéric 1842–1912 Fr. composer

Mas·sey \'mas-ē\ William Ferguson 1856–1925 N.Z. statesman

Mas·sine \ma-'sēn\ Léonide 1896–1979 orig. *Leonid Fedorovich Miassin* Am. (Russ.-born) dancer & choreographer

Mas·sin·ger \'mas-^ən-jər\ Philip 1583–1640 Eng. dram.

Mas·son \'mas-^ən\ David 1822–1907 Scot. editor & author

Mas·sys \'mäs-,is\ or **Mat·sys** \'mät-'sis\ or **Mes·sys** \'mes-'is\ or **Met·sys** \'met-,sis\ Quentin *ca* 1466–1530 Flem. painter

Mas·ters \'mas-tərz\ Edgar Lee 1869–1950 Am. author

Math·er \'math-ər, 'math-\ Cotton 1663–1728 Am. clergyman & author

Mather Increase 1639–1723 *father of Cotton* Am. clergyman & author; pres. Harvard College (1685–1701)

Ma·tisse \ma-'tēs, mə-\ Henri-Émile-Benoît 1869–1954 Fr. painter

Ma·tsuo \mät-'sü-ō, 'mät-sü-ō\ Bashō 1644–1694 pseud. of *Matsuo Munefusa* Jp. haiku poet

Ma·tsu·o·ka \,mat-sə-'wō-kə, ,mät-, -(,)kä\ Yōsuke 1880–1946 Jp. statesman

Mat·te·ot·ti \,mat-ē-'ōt-ē, ,mät-, -'òt-\ Giacomo 1885–1924 Ital. socialist

Mat·thews \'math-(,)yüz\ (James) Brander 1852–1929 Am. educ. & author

Maugham \'mòm\ (William) Somerset 1874–1965 Eng. nov. & dram.

Mau·nou·ry \,mō-nə-'rē\ Michel-Joseph 1847–1923 Fr. gen.

Mau·pas·sant \,mō-pə-'säⁿ\ (Henri-René-Albert-) Guy de 1850–1893 Fr. short-story writer

Mau·riac \mòr-'yäk, ,mòr-ē-'äk\ François 1885–1970 Fr. author

Mau·rice of Nassau 1567–1625 Prince of *Orange* Du. gen. & statesman

Mau·rice \'mòr-əs, 'mär-; mò-'rēs\ *G* **Mo·ritz** \'mōr-,äts, 'mòr-\ 1521–1553 elector of Saxony (1547–53) & gen.

Mau·rois \mòr-'wä\ André 1885–1967 pseud. of *Émile-Salomon= Wilhelm Her·zog* \-zòg\ Fr. writer

Mau·ry \'mòr-ē, 'mär-\ Matthew Fontaine 1806–1873 Am. naval officer & oceanographer

\ə\ abut \^ə\ kitten, F table \ər\ further \a\ ash \ā\ ace \ä\ cot, cart
\aú\ out \ch\ chin \e\ bet \ē\ easy \g\ go \i\ hit \ī\ ice \j\ job
\n̄\ sing \ō\ go \ò\ law \òi\ boy \th\ thin \t̲h̲\ the \ü\ loot \ú\ foot
\y\ yet \zh\ vision \a, k, ⁿ, œ, œ̄, ue, ᵫ, ^y\ see Guide to Pronunciation

Mau·ser \\'maů-zər\\ Peter Paul 1838–1914 & his bro. Wilhelm 1834–1882 Ger. inventors
Maw·son \\'mós-ᵊn\\ Sir Douglas 1882–1958 Austral. explorer & geologist
Max·im \\'mak-səm\\ Sir Hiram Stevens 1840–1916 Brit. (Am.-born) inventor
Maxim Hudson 1853–1927 *bro. of Sir Hiram* Am. inventor
Max·i·mil·ian \\,mak-sə-'mil-yən\\ 1832–1867 *bro. of Francis Joseph I of Austria* emp. of Mexico (1864–67)
Maximilian I 1459–1519 Holy Rom. emp. (1493–1519)
Maximilian II 1527–1576 Holy Rom. emp. (1564–76)
Max·well \\'mak-,swel, -swəl\\ James Clerk \\'klärk\\ 1831–1879 Scot. physicist — **Max·wel·li·an** \\mak-'swel-ē-ən\\ *adj*
May \\'mā\\ Sir Thomas Erskine 1815–1886 1st Baron *Farn·bor·ough* \\'färn-,bər-ə, -,bə-rə, -b(ə-)rə\\ Eng. jurist
Ma·ya·kov·ski \\,mä-yə-'kóf-skē, ,mī-ə-, -'kòv-\\ Vladimir Vladimirovich 1893–1930 Russ. poet
May·er \\'mī(-ə)r\\ Maria Goeppert 1906–1972 Am. (Ger.-born) physicist
Mayo \\'mā-(,)ō\\ Charles Horace 1865–1939 & his bro. William James 1861–1939 Am. surgeons
Ma·za·rin \\,maz-ə-'raⁿ\\ Jules 1602–1661 Fr. cardinal & statesman
Ma·zo·wie·cki \\,mä-zō-'vyet-skē\\ Tadeusz 1927–   prime min. of Poland (1989–   )
Maz·zi·ni \\mät-'sē-nē, mäd-'zē-\\ Giuseppe 1805–1872 Ital. patriot
Mc·Adoo \\'mak-ə-,dü\\ William Gibbs 1863–1941 Am. administrator
M'·Car·thy \\mə-'kär-thē *also* -'kärt-ē\\ Justin 1830–1912 Irish writer & polit.
Mc·Car·thy \\mə-'kär-thē *also* -'kärt-ē\\ Eugene Joseph 1916–   Am. polit.
McCarthy Joseph Raymond 1908–1957 Am. polit.
McCarthy Mary Therese 1912–1989 Am. writer
Mc·Clel·lan \\mə-'klel-ən\\ George Brinton 1826–1885 Am. gen. & polit.
Mc·Clin·tock \\mə-'klin-tək\\ Barbara 1902–   Am. botanist
Mc·Clos·key \\mə-'kläs-kē\\ John 1810–1885 1st Am. cardinal
Mc·Cloy \\mə-'klói\\ John Jay 1895–1989 Am. banker & govt. official
Mc·Clure \\mə-'klů(ə)r\\ Samuel Sidney 1857–1949 Am. (Irish-born) editor & publisher
Mc·Cor·mack \\mə-'kòr-mək, -mik\\ John 1884–1945 Am. (Irish-born) tenor
McCormack John William 1891–1980 Am. polit.
Mc·Cor·mick \\mə-'kòr-mik\\ Cyrus Hall 1809–1884 Am. inventor
McCormick Robert Rutherford 1880–1955 Am. newspaper publisher
Mc·Cul·lers \\mə-'kəl-ərz\\ Carson 1917–1967 née *Smith* Am. writer
Mc·Dow·ell \\mak-'daů(-ə)l\\ Ephraim 1771–1830 Am. surgeon
McDowell Irvin 1818–1885 Am. gen.
Mc·Gill \\mə-'gil\\ James 1744–1813 Canad. (Scot.-born) businessman & philanthropist
Mc·Gov·ern \\mə-'gəv-ərn\\ George Stanley 1922–   Am. polit.
Mc·Guf·fey \\mə-'gəf-ē\\ William Holmes 1800–1873 Am. educ.
Mc·Ken·na \\mə-'ken-ə\\ Sio·bhan \\shə-'vòn\\ 1923?–1986 Irish actress
Mc·Kim \\mə-'kim\\ Charles Follen 1847–1909 Am. architect
Mc·Kin·ley \\mə-'kin-lē\\ William 1843–1901 25th pres. of the U.S. (1897–1901)
Mc·Lu·han \\mə-'klü-ən\\ (Herbert) Marshall 1911–1980 Canad. educ.
Mc·Ma·hon \\mək-'mä(-ə)n\\ Sir William 1908–1988 prime min. of Australia (1971–72)
Mc·Mil·lan \\mək-'mil-ən\\ Edwin Mattison 1907–   Am. chem.
Mc·Na·mara \\,mak-nə-'mar-ə, ,mak-nə-,mar-ə\\ Robert Strange 1916–   U.S. secy. of defense (1961–68)
Mc·Naugh·ton \\mək-'nòt-ᵊn\\ Andrew George Latta 1887–1966 Canad. gen. & diplomat
Mead \\'mēd\\ Margaret 1901–1978 Am. anthropol.
Meade \\'mēd\\ George Gordon 1815–1872 Am. gen.
Meade James Edward 1907–   Brit. econ.
Mea·ny \\'mē-nē\\ George 1894–1980 Am. labor leader
Med·a·war \\'med-ə-wər\\ Peter Brian 1915–1987 Eng. anatomist
Me·dei·ros \\mə-'der-əs, -(,)ōs\\ Humberto 1915–1983 Am. (Port.-born) cardinal
Me·di·ci, de' \\'med-ə-(,)chē\\ Catherine — see CATHERINE DE MÉDICIS
Medici, de' Cosimo 1389–1464 *the Elder* Florentine financier & ruler
Medici, de' Cosimo I 1519–1574 *the Great;* Duke of *Florence;* Grand Duke of *Tuscany*
Medici, de' Giulio — see CLEMENT VII
Medici, de' Lorenzo 1449–1492 *the Magnificent* Florentine statesman, ruler, & patron
Me·di·na-Si·do·nia \\mə-'dē-nə-sə-'dōn-yə\\ Duque de *d* 1619 *Alonso Pérez de Guzmán* Span. admiral
Meer van Delft, van der — see Jan VERMEER
Meese \\'mēs\\ Edwin 1931–   U.S. atty. gen. (1985–88)
Meigh·en \\'mē-ən\\ Arthur 1874–1960 Canad. statesman; prime min. (1920–21; 1926)
Me·ir \\me-'i(ə)r\\ Golda 1898–1978 orig. *Goldie Mabovitch,* later *Goldie Myerson* prime min. of Israel (1969–74)
Meis·so·nier \\,mās-ᵊn-'yā, mā-'sòn-(,)yā\\ Jean-Louis-Ernest 1815–1891 Fr. painter
Meit·ner \\'mīt-nər\\ Li·se \\'lē-zə\\ 1878–1968 Ger. physicist
Me·lanch·thon \\mə-'laŋ(k)-t(h)ən\\ Philipp 1497–1560 orig. surname *Schwartzerd* Ger. scholar & religious reformer
Mel·ba \\'mel-bə\\ Dame Nellie 1861–1931 orig. *Helen Porter Mitchell* Austral. soprano
Mel·chers \\'mel-chərz\\ (Julius) Gari 1860–1932 Am. painter
Mel·chi·or \\'mel-kē-,ó(ə)r\\ Lau·ritz \\'laů-rəts\\ Lebrecht Hommel 1890–1973 Am. (Dan.-born) tenor
Mel·lon \\'mel-ən\\ Andrew William 1855–1937 Am. financier
Mel·ville \\'mel-,vil\\ Herman 1819–1891 Am. nov.
Mem·ling \\'mem-liŋ\\ *or* **Mem·linc** \\-,liŋk\\ Hans *ca* 1430–1494 Flem. painter
Me·nan·der \\mə-'nan-dər\\ 342–292 B.C. Greek dram.
Men·cius — see MENG-TZU
Menck·en \\'meŋ-kən, 'men-\\ Henry Louis 1880–1956 Am. editor — **Menck·e·nian** \\meŋ-'kē-nē-ən, men-\\ *adj*
Men·del \\'men-dᵊl\\ Gregor Johann 1822–1884 Austrian botanist — **Men·del·ian** \\men-'del-ē-ən, -'dē-lē-ən\\ *adj*

Men·de·le·yev \\,men-də-'lā-əf\\ Dmitry Ivanovich 1834–1907 Russ. chem.
Men·dels·sohn \\'men-dᵊl-sən\\ Moses 1729–1786 Ger. philos.
Mendelssohn–Bar·thol·dy \\-bär-'t(h)ól-dē\\ (Jakob Ludwig) Felix 1809–1847 *grandson of prec.* Ger. composer, pianist, & conductor — **Men·dels·sohn·ian** \\,men-dᵊl-'sō-nē-ən, -,nyən\\ *adj*
Mendès-France \\,maⁿ-des-fräⁿs\\ Pierre 1907–1982 Fr. statesman
Men·do·za \\men-'dō-zə\\ Antonio de *ca* 1490–1552 Span. colonial gov.
Men·e·lik II \\'men-ᵊl-(,)ik\\ 1844–1913 emp. of Ethiopia (1889–1913)
Men·em \\'men-,em, -əm\\ Carlos Saúl 1930–   pres. of Argentina (1989–   )
Me·nén·dez de Avi·lés \\mə-'nen-dəs-dā-,äv-ə-'läs\\ Pedro 1519–1574 Span. admiral; colonizer of Florida
Me·nes \\'mē-(,)nēz\\ *fl ca* 3100 B.C. king of Egypt
Mengs \\'men(k)s\\ Anton Raphael 1728–1779 Ger. painter
Meng–tzu \\'məŋd-'zü\\ *ca* 371–*ca* 289 B.C. orig. *Meng K'o* L. **Men·cius** \\'men-ch(ē-)əs\\ Chin. philos.
Men·ning·er \\'men-iŋ-ər\\ Karl Augustus 1893–   Am. psychiatrist
Men·no Si·mons \\'men-ō-'sim-ōns\\ 1469–1561 Dutch religious reformer
Me·not·ti \\mə-'nät-ē, -'nòt-\\ Gian Carlo 1911–   Am. (Ital.-born) composer
Me·nu·hin \\'men-yə-wən\\ Ye·hu·di \\yə-'hüd-ē\\ 1916–   Am. violinist
Men·zies \\'men-(,)zēz\\ Sir Robert Gordon 1894–1978 Austral. statesman; prime min. (1939–41; 1949–66)
Mer·ca·tor \\(,)mər-'kät-ər\\ Gerardus 1512–1594 *Gerhard Kremer* Flem. cartographer
Mer·cier \\mer-'syā, 'mer-sē-,ā\\ Désiré-Joseph 1851–1926 Belg. cardinal & philos.
Mer·e·dith \\'mer-əd-əth\\ George 1828–1909 Eng. nov. & poet
Meredith Owen — see E. R. Bulwer-LYTTON
Mer·gen·tha·ler \\'mər-gən-,thäl-ər, 'mer-gən-,täl-\\ Ottmar 1854–1899 Am. (Ger.-born) inventor
Mé·ri·mée \\'mer-ə-,mā, ,mā-rə-'\\ Prosper 1803–1870 Fr. writer
Mer·ri·field \\'mer-i-,fēld\\ Robert Bruce 1921–   Am. biochem.
Mer·ton \\'mərt-ᵊn\\ Thomas 1915–1968 Am. religious & author
Mes·mer \\'mez-mər, 'mes-\\ Franz *or* Friedrich Anton 1734–1815 Ger. physician
Mes·sa·la (*or* **Mes·sal·la**) **Cor·vi·nus** \\mə-'säl-ə-,kòr-'vī-nəs\\ Marcus Valerius *ca* 64 B.C.–A.D. 8 Rom. gen. & statesman
Mes·sa·li·na \\,mes-ə-'lī-nə, -'lē-\\ Valeria *ca* A.D. 22–48 *3d wife of Emp. Claudius*
Mes·ser·schmitt \\'mes-ər-,shmit\\ Willy 1898–1978 Ger. aircraft designer & manuf.
Mes·sier \\mäs-yā, 'mes-ē-,ā\\ Charles 1730–1817 Fr. astron.
Meš·tro·vić \\'mes(h)-trə-,vich\\ Ivan 1883–1962 Am. (Yugoslavian-born) sculptor
Me·tax·as \\me-,täk-'säs\\ Ioannis 1871–1941 Greek gen. & dictator
Metch·ni·koff \\'mech-nə-,kóf\\ Élie 1845–1916 orig. *Ilya Ilich Mech·ni·kov* \\'myäch-nyi-,kóf\\ Fr. (Russ.-born) zool. & bacteriol.
Met·ter·nich \\'met-ər-(,)nik, -(,)nik\\ Klemens Wenzel Nepomuk Lothar 1773–1859 Fürst *von Metternich* Austrian statesman — **Met·ter·nich·ian** \\,met-ər-'nik-ē-ən, -'nik-\\ *adj*
Mey·er \\'mī(-ə)r\\ Annie 1867–1951 née *Nathan* Am. educ. & writer
Mey·er·beer \\'mī-ər-,bi(ə)r, -,be(ə)r\\ Giacomo 1791–1864 orig. *Jakob Liebmann Beer* Ger. composer
Mey·er·hof \\'mī-ər-,hóf\\ Otto 1884–1951 Ger. biochem.
Mi·chael \\'mī-kəl\\ *Romanian* **Mi·hai** \\mē-'hi\\ 1921–   *Michael Hohenzollern* king of Romania (1927–30; 1940–47); abdicated
Mich·el \\'mik-əl\\ Hartmut 1948–   Ger. biochem.
Mi·chel·an·ge·lo \\,mī-kə-'lan-jə-(,)lō, ,mik-ə-'lan-, ,mē-kə-'län-\\ 1475–1564 *Michelangelo di Lodovico Buonarroti Simoni* Ital. sculptor, painter, architect, & poet — **Mi·chel·an·ge·lesque** \\-,lan-jə-'lesk\\ *adj*
Mi·che·let \\mēsh-(ə-)'lā\\ Jules 1798–1874 Fr. hist.
Mi·chel·son \\'mī-kəl-sən\\ Albert Abraham 1852–1931 Am. (Ger.-born) physicist
Mich·ener \\'mish-nər\\ (Daniel) Roland 1900–   Canad. polit.; gov. gen. (1967–74)
Michener James Albert 1907–   Am. author
Mic·kie·wicz \\mits-'kyä-vich\\ Adam 1798–1855 Pol. poet
Mid·dle·ton \\'mid-ᵊl-tən\\ Thomas 1570?–1627 Eng. dram.
Mies van der Ro·he \\,mēs-,van-də-'rō(-ə), ,mēz-\\ Ludwig 1886–1969 Am. (Ger.-born) architect — **Mies** \\'mēs\\ *van·der* \\'mē-sə-shən\\ *adj*
Miff·lin \\'mif-lən\\ Thomas 1744–1800 Am. gen. in Revolution
Mi·haj·lo·vić \\mi-'hī-lə-,vich\\ Dragoljub 1893–1946 *Draža* \\'dräzh-ə\\ Yugoslav gen.
Mi·ki \\'mē-kē\\ Tak·eo \\'täk-ā-ō\\ 1907–1988 Jp. premier (1974–76)
Mi·ko·yan \\,mē-kō-'yän\\ Ana·stas \\,än-ə-'stäs\\ Ivanovich 1895–1978 Soviet polit.; head of Presidium (1964–65)
Miles \\'mi(ə)lz\\ Nelson Appleton 1839–1925 Am. gen.
Mi·lhaud \\mē-'(y)ō\\ Darius 1892–1974 Fr. composer
Mill \\'mil\\ James 1773–1836 Scot. philos., hist., & econ.
Mill John Stuart 1806–1873 *son of James* Eng. philos. & econ.
Mil·lais \\'mil-,ā, mil-'ā\\ Sir John Everett 1829–1896 Eng. painter
Mil·lay \\mil-'ā\\ Edna St. Vincent 1892–1950 Am. poet
Mil·ler \\'mil-ər\\ Arthur 1915–   Am. dram. & nov.
Miller Henry 1891–1980 Am. writer
Miller Joa·quin \\wä-'kēn, wó-\\ 1837–1913 pseud. of *Cincinnatus Hiner Miller* Am. poet
Miller Perry Gilbert Eddy 1905–1963 Am. lit. critic & scholar
Miller William 1782–1849 Am. religious leader
Mil·le·rand \\mēl-(ə-)'räⁿ\\ Alexandre 1859–1943 Fr. statesman; pres. of France (1920–24)
Mil·les \\'mil-əs\\ Carl 1875–1955 Swed. sculptor
Mil·let \\mē-'yā, mi-'lā\\ Jean-François 1814–1875 Fr. painter
Mil·li·kan \\'mil-i-kən\\ Robert Andrews 1868–1953 Am. physicist
Mil·man \\'mil-mən\\ Henry Hart 1791–1868 Eng. poet & hist.
Milne \\'mil(n)\\ Alan Alexander 1882–1956 Eng. poet & dram.
Mi·losz \\'mē-lòsh\\ Czeslaw 1911–   Pol. writer
Mil·stein \\'mil-,stīn, -,stēn\\ César 1927–   Brit. (Argentine-born) immunologist
Mil·ti·a·des \\mil-'tī-ə-,dēz\\ *ca* 554–?489 B.C. *the Younger* Athenian gen.
Mil·ton \\'milt-ᵊn\\ John 1608–1674 Eng. poet — **Mil·to·nian** \\mil-'tō-nē-ən, -nyən\\ *or* **Mil·ton·ic** \\-'tän-ik\\ *adj*

Mil·yu·kov \\,mil-yə-'kóf, -'kòv\\ Pavel Nikolayevich 1859–1943 Russ. polit. & hist.

Mi·not \\'mī-nət\\ George Richards 1885–1950 Am. physician

Min·ton \\'mint-ᵊn\\ Sherman 1890–1965 Am. jurist

Min·u·it \\'min-yə-wət\\ or **Min·ne·wit** \\'min-ə-,wit\\ Peter 1580–1638 Du. colonial administrator in America

Mi·ra·beau \\'mir-ə-,bō\\ Comte de 1749–1791 Honoré-Gabriel Riqueti Fr. orator & revolutionary

Mi·ró \\mē-'rō\\ Joan \\zhù-'än\\ 1893–1983 Span. painter

Mi·shi·ma \\'mē-shi-,mä, mə-'shē-mə\\ Yukio 1925–1970 Jp. writer

Mis·tral \\mi-'sträl, -'sträl\\ Frédéric 1830–1914 Provençal poet

Mis·tral \\mi-'sträl, -'sträl\\ Gabriela 1889–1957 orig. Lucila Godoy Alcayaga Chilean poet & educ.

Mitch·ell \\'mich-əl\\ John 1870–1919 Am. labor leader

Mitchell Margaret Munnerlyn 1900–1949 Am. nov.

Mitchell Maria 1818–1889 Am. astron.

Mitchell Peter Dennis 1920–   Brit. chem.

Mitchell William 1879–1936 Billy Am. gen.

Mit·ford \\'mit-fərd\\ Mary Russell 1787–1855 Eng. nov. & dram.

Mitford William 1744–1827 Eng. hist.

Mith·ra·da·tes VI Eu·pa·tor \\,mith-rə-'dāt-ēz-'yü-,pāt-ər\\ d 63 B.C. the Great king of Pontus (120–63)

Mi·tro·pou·los \\mə-'träp-ə-ləs\\ Di·mi·tri \\də-'mē-trē\\ 1896–1960 Am. (Greek-born) conductor

Mit·ter·rand \\,mē-ter-'äⁿ\\ François-Maurice 1916–   pres. of France (1981–   )

Mo·bu·tu Se·se Se·ko \\mə-'bü-(,)tü-'sā-sā-'sā-(,)kō\\ 1930–   orig. Joseph-Désiré Mobutu pres. of Zaire (1965–   )

Mo·di·glia·ni \\,mō-dēl-'yän-ē, ,mōd-ᵊl-\\ Amedeo 1884–1920 Ital. painter

Modigliani Franco 1918–   Am. (Ital.-born) econ.

Mo·djes·ka \\mə-'jes-kə\\ Helena 1840–1909 Am. (Pol.-born) actress

Mo·ham·mad Re·za Pah·la·vi \\mō-'ham-əd-ri-'zä-'pal-ə-(,)vē, -'häm-\\ 1919–1980 shah of Iran (1941–79)

Mohammed var of MUHAMMAD

Mois·san \\mwä-'säⁿ\\ Henri 1852–1907 Fr. chem.

Mo·ley \\'mō-lē\\ Raymond Charles 1886–1975 Am. journalist

Mo·lière \\mōl-'ye(ə)r, 'mōl-,\\ 1622–1673 orig. Jean-Baptiste Poquelin Fr. actor & dram.

Molina Tirso de — see TIRSO DE MOLINA

Mol·nár \\'mōl-,när, 'mòl-\\ Fe·renc \\'fer-ən(t)s\\ 1878–1952 Hung. author

Mo·lo·tov \\'mäl-ə-,tóf, 'mòl-, 'mōl-, -,tòv\\ Vyacheslav Mikhaylovich 1890–1986 orig. surname Skryabin Soviet statesman

Molt·ke \\'mōlt-kə\\ Helmuth Karl Bernhard 1800–1891 Graf von Moltke Pruss. field marshal

Momm·sen \\'mȯm-zən\\ Theodor \\'tā-ō-,dōr\\ 1817–1903 Ger. classical scholar & hist.

Monck or **Monk** \\'məŋk\\ George 1608–1670 1st Duke of Albemarle Eng. gen.

Mon·dale \\'män-,dāl\\ Walter Frederick 1928–   Am. polit.; vice pres. of the U.S. (1977–81)

Mon·dri·an \\'mòn-drē-,än\\ Piet 1872–1944 Pieter Cornelis Mondriaan Du. painter

Mo·net \\mō-'nā\\ Claude 1840–1926 Fr. painter

Mo·ne·ta \\mō-'nät-ə\\ Ernesto Teodoro 1833–1918 Ital. journalist & pacifist

Mo·niz Antonio Egas — see EGAS MONIZ

Mon·mouth \\'mən-məth, 'män-\\ Duke of 1649–1685 James Scott, son of Charles II of England Eng. rebel & claimant to the throne

Mon·net \\mō-'ne\\ Jean-Omer-Marie-Gabriel 1888–1979 Fr. econ. & diplomat

Mo·nod \\mō-'nō\\ Jacques-Lucien 1910–1976 Fr. biochem.

Mon·roe \\mən-'rō\\ James 1758–1831 5th pres. of U.S. (1817–25)

Mon·ta·gna \\mən-'tän-yə\\ Bartolommeo ca 1450–1523 Ital. painter

Mon·ta·gu \\'mänt-ə-,gyü, 'mənt-\\ Lady Mary Wortley 1689–1762 Eng. letter writer & poet

Mon·taigne \\män-'tän, mōⁿ-ten³\\ Michel Eyquem de 1533–1592 Fr. essayist

Mon·ta·le \\mōn-'täl-(,)ā\\ Eugenio 1896–1981 Ital. poet

Mont·calm de Saint-Véran \\mänt-'kä(l)m-də-,saⁿ-vā-'räⁿ\\ Marquis de 1712–1759 Louis-Joseph de Montcalm-Grozon Fr. field marshal

Mon·tes·pan \\mōⁿ-tes-päⁿ, 'mänt-ə-,span\\ Marquise de 1641–1707 née (Françoise-Athénaïs) Rochechouart de Mortemart mistress of Louis XIV

Mon·tes·quieu \\,mänt-əs-'kyü, -'kyə(r), -'kyœ\\ Baron de La Brède et de 1689–1755 Charles-Louis de Secondat Fr. lawyer & polit. philos.

Mon·tes·so·ri \\,mänt-ə-'sōr-ē, -'sòr-\\ Maria 1870–1952 Ital. physician & educ.

Mon·teux \\mōⁿ-'tə(r), -'tœ\\ Pierre 1875–1964 Am. (Fr.-born) conductor

Mon·te·ver·di or **Mon·te·ver·de** \\,mänt-ə-'verd-ē, -'vərd-\\ Claudio 1567–1643 Ital. composer

Mon·te·zu·ma II \\,mänt-ə-'zü-mə\\ or **Moc·te·zu·ma** \\,mäk-tə-\\ 1466–1520 last Aztec emp. of Mexico (1502–20)

Mont·fort \\'mänt-fərt, mōⁿ-'fò(ə)r\\ Simon de 1165?–1218 Simon IV de Montfort l'Amaury Fr. soldier

Montfort \\'mänt-fərt\\ Simon de ca 1208–1265 Earl of Leicester Eng. soldier & statesman

Mont·gol·fier \\mänt-'gäl-fē-ər, -fē-,ā\\ Joseph-Michel 1740–1810 & his bro. Jacques-Étienne 1745–1799 Fr. inventors & balloonists

Mont·gom·ery \\(,)mən(t)-'gəm-(ə-)rē, män(t)-, -'gäm-\\ Bernard Law 1887–1976 1st Viscount Montgomery of Alamein Brit. field marshal

Mont·mo·ren·cy \\,mänt-mə-'ren(t)-sē\\ Anne 1493–1567 1st duc de Montmorency Fr. soldier; constable (1537)

Mon·trose \\män-'trōz\\ 1st Marquess of 1612–1650 James Graham Scot. Royalist

Moo·dy \\'müd-ē\\ Dwight Lyman 1837–1899 Am. evangelist

Moody William Vaughn 1869–1910 Am. poet & dram.

Moore \\'mō(ə)r, 'mò(ə)r, 'mù(ə)r\\ George 1852–1933 Irish author

Moore George Edward 1873–1958 Eng. philos.

Moore Henry 1898–1986 Brit. sculptor

Moore John Bassett 1860–1947 Am. jurist

Moore Marianne Craig 1887–1972 Am. poet

Moore Stanford 1913–1982 Am. biochem.

Moore Thomas 1779–1852 Irish poet

Mo·ra·via \\mō-'räv-ē-ə\\ Alberto 1907–   pseud. of Alberto Pincherle Ital. writer

More \\'mō(ə)r, 'mò(ə)r\\ Hannah 1745–1833 Eng. religious writer

More Henry 1614–1687 Eng. philos.

More Paul Elmer 1864–1937 Am. essayist & critic

More Sir Thomas 1478–1535 Saint Eng. statesman & author

Mo·reau \\mò-rō\\ (Jean-) Victor-Marie 1763–1813 Fr. gen.

Mor·gan \\'mòr-gən\\ Daniel 1736–1802 Am. gen. in Revolution

Morgan Sir Henry 1635–1688 Eng. buccaneer

Morgan John Hunt 1825–1864 Am. Confed. cavalry officer

Morgan John Pier·pont \\'pi(ə)r-,pänt\\ 1837–1913 Am. financier

Morgan John Pierpont 1867–1943 son of J. P. Am. financier

Morgan Thomas Hunt 1866–1945 Am. geneticist

Mor·gen·thau \\'mòr-gən-,thò\\ Henry 1891–1967 U.S. secy. of the treasury (1934–45)

Mor·i·son \\'mòr-ə-sən, 'mär-\\ Samuel Eliot 1887–1976 Am. hist.

Morison Stanley 1889–1968 Eng. type designer

Mo·ri·sot \\,mò-rē-zō\\ Berthe 1841–1895 Fr. painter

Mor·ley \\'mòr-lē\\ Christopher Darlington 1890–1957 Am. writer

Morley John 1838–1923 Viscount Morley Eng. statesman & writer

Mor·nay \\mòr-nā\\ Philippe de 1549–1623 Seigneur du Plessis-Marly; usu. called Duplessis-Mornay Fr. Huguenot

Mor·ris \\'mòr-əs, 'mär-\\ Gou·ver·neur \\,gəv-ə(r)-'ni(ə)r\\ 1752–1816 Am. statesman & diplomat

Morris Robert 1734–1806 Am. financier & statesman

Morris William 1834–1896 Eng. poet, artist, & socialist

Mor·ri·son \\'mòr-ə-sən, 'mär-\\ Herbert Stanley 1888–1965 Baron Morrison of Lambeth Eng. polit.

Morrison Robert 1782–1834 Scot. missionary

Morrison Toni 1931–   orig. Chloe Anthony Wofford Am. novelist

Morse \\'mò(ə)rs\\ Samuel Finley Breese 1791–1872 Am. artist & inventor

Mor·ti·mer \\'mòrt-ə-mər\\ Roger de 1287–1330 1st Earl of March & 8th Baron of Wigmore Welsh rebel & paramour of Isabella, Queen of Edward II of England

Mor·ton \\'mòrt-ᵊn\\ Levi Parsons 1824–1920 Am. banker & polit.; vice pres. of the U.S. (1889–93)

Morton William Thomas Green 1819–1868 Am. dentist

Mos·bach·er \\'mòz-,bäk-ər\\ Robert Adam 1927–   U.S. secy. of commerce (1989–   )

Mos·by \\'mòz-bē\\ John Singleton 1833–1916 Am. cavalry officer

Moś·cic·ki \\mòsh-'chēt-skē, -'chit-\\ Ignacy 1867–1946 Pol. chem.; pres. of Poland (1926–39)

Mo·ses \\'mō-zəz also -zəs\\ Anna Mary née Robertson 1860–1961 Grandma Moses Am. painter

Mos·ley \\'mòz-lē\\ Sir Oswald Er·nald \\'ərn-ᵊld\\ 1896–1980 Eng. polit.

Möss·bau·er \\'mœs-,baù(-ə)r, 'mes-\\ Rudolf Ludwig 1929–   Ger. physicist

Moth·er·well \\'məth-ər-,wel, -wəl\\ Robert 1915–   Am. artist

Mo Ti — see MO-TZU

Mot·ley \\'mät-lē\\ John Lothrop 1814–1877 Am. hist.

Mo·ton \\'mōt-ᵊn\\ Robert Russa 1867–1940 Am. educ.

Mott \\'mät\\ John Raleigh 1865–1955 Am. religious leader

Mott Lucretia 1793–1880 née Coffin Am. social reformer

Mott Sir Nevill Francis 1905–   Brit. physicist

Mot·tel·son \\'mòt-ᵊl-sən, -(,)sòn\\ Ben Roy 1926–   Dan. (Am.-born) physicist

Mot·teux \\mä-'tə(r), 'mä-,\\ Peter Anthony 1660–1718 Brit. (Fr.-born) dram. & translator

Mo·tzu \\'mȯd-'zə\\ 470?–?391 B.C. orig. Mo Ti \\'mō-'dē\\ L. Mi·cius \\'mē-sh(ē-)əs\\ Chin. philos.

Moul·ton \\'mōlt-ᵊn\\ Forest Ray 1872–1952 Am. astron.

Moul·trie \\'mül-trē, 'mòl-\\ William 1730–1805 Am. gen. in Revolution

Mount·bat·ten \\maùnt-'bat-ᵊn\\ Louis 1900–1979 1st Earl Mountbatten of Burma Brit. admiral; 1st gov.-gen. of India (1947–48); chief of defense staff (1959–65)

Mountbatten Philip, Duke of Edinburgh — see Prince PHILIP

Mo·zart \\'mōt-,särt\\ Wolfgang Amadeus 1756–1791 Austrian composer — **Mo·zart·ean** or **Mo·zart·ian** \\mōt-'särt-ē-ən\\ adj

Mu·bar·ak \\mù-'bär-ək\\ Muhammad Hosni 1929–   pres. of Egypt (1981–   )

Muench \\'minch\\ Aloisius Joseph 1889–1962 Am. cardinal

Mu·ga·be \\mù-'gäb-ē\\ Robert Gabriel 1924–   prime min. of Zimbabwe (1980–   )

Mu·ham·mad \\mō-'ham-əd, -'häm- also mü-\\ ca 570–632 Abū al-Qāsim Muhammad ibn 'Abd Allāh ibn 'Abd al-Muṭṭalib ibn Hāshim Arab prophet & founder of Islam

Mu·ham·mad \\mō-'ham-əd, mü-\\ Elijah 1897–1975 orig. E. Poole Am. religious leader

Muhammad XI \\mō-'ham-əd, -'häm- also mü-\\ d 1527 Abū 'Abd Allāh Muhammad Sp. Boabdil last sultan of Granada

Müh·len·berg \\'myü-lən-,bərg\\ Henry Melchior 1711–1787 Am. (Ger.-born) Lutheran clergyman

Muir \\'myu(ə)r\\ John 1838–1914 Am. (Scot.-born) naturalist

Mul·ler \\'məl-ər\\ Hermann Joseph 1890–1967 Am. geneticist

Mül·ler \\'myül-ər, 'mil-, 'məl-\\ (Friedrich) Max 1823–1900 Brit. (Ger.-born) philologist

Müller Johann 1436–1476 Regiomontanus Ger. astron.

Müller Karl Alexander 1927–   Swiss physicist

Müller Paul Hermann 1899–1965 Swiss chem.

Mul·li·ken \\'məl-ə-kən\\ Robert Sanderson 1896–1986 Am. chem. & physicist

Mul·ro·ney \\məl-'rü-nē\\ (Martin) Brian 1939–   Canad. polit.; prime min. (1984–   )

Mum·ford \\'məm(p)-fərd\\ Lewis 1895–1990 Am. writer

Munch \\'munch, 'müench\\ Charles 1891–1968 Fr.-born conductor

Munch \\'muŋk\\ Edvard 1863–1944 Norw. painter

Münch·hau·sen \\'mуenk-,haúz-ᵊn\\ Karl Friedrich Hieronymus von 1720–1797 Baron *Mun·chau·sen* \\'mən-,chaúz-ᵊn, 'mún-, -,chȯz-\\ Ger. hunter, soldier, & raconteur

Mu·ñoz Ma·rín \\(,)mün-,yōs-mə-'rēn, -,yōz-\\ Luis 1898–1980 Puerto Rican polit.

Mun·ro \\(,)mən-'rō\\ Hector Hugh 1870–1916 pseud. *Saki* Scot. writer

Mün·ster·berg \\'mùn(t)-stər-,bərg, 'myün(t)-, 'mən(t)-\\ Hugo 1863–1916 Am. (Ger.-born) psychol.

Mu·ra·sa·ki \\,m(y)ùr-ə-'säk-ē\\ Shikibu 978?–?1026 Jp. court lady & nov.

Mu·rat \\myü-'rä, mue-\\ Joachim 1767–1815 Fr. gen.; marshal of France; king of Naples (1808–15)

Mur·doch \\'mər-dək, -,däk\\ Dame (Jean) Iris 1919–   Brit. (Irish-born) writer

Mu·ril·lo \\myù-'ril-(,)ō, m(y)ù-'rē-(,)ō\\ Bartolomé Esteban 1617–1682 Span. painter

Mur·phy \\'mər-fē\\ Frank 1890–1949 Am. jurist

Murphy Robert Daniel 1894–1978 Am. diplomat

Murphy William Parry 1892–   Am. physician

Mur·ray \\'mər-ē, 'mə-rē\\ (George) Gilbert Aimé 1866–1957 Brit. classical scholar

Murray Sir James Augustus Henry 1837–1915 Brit. lexicographer

Murray Lindley 1745–1826 Am. grammarian

Murray Philip 1886–1952 Am. labor leader

Mur·row \\'mər-(,)ō, -ə-(,)rō\\ Edward Roscoe 1908–1965 Am. journalist

Mus·kie \\'məs-kē\\ Edmund Sixtus 1914–   Am. polit.

Mus·set \\myü-'sā\\ (Louis-Charles-) Alfred de 1810–1857 Fr. poet

Mus·so·li·ni \\,mü-sə-'lē-nē, ,müs-ə-\\ Be·ni·to \\bə-'nēt-(,)ō\\ 1883–1945 *Il Du·ce* \\'dü-(,)chā\\ Ital. Fascist premier (1922–43)

Mus·sorg·sky \\'mú-'sȯrg-skē, -'zȯrg-\\ Mo·dest \\mō-'dest\\ Petrovich 1839–1881 Russ. composer

Mustafa Kemal — see KEMAL ATATÜRK

Mu·tsu·hi·to \\,müt-sə-'hē-(,)tō\\ 1852–1912 *Mei·ji* \\'mā-(,)jē\\ emp. of Japan (1867–1912)

Mu·zo·re·wa \\,müz-ə-'rä-wə\\ Abel Tendekayi 1925–   prime min. of Zimbabwe Rhodesia (1979–80)

Muz·zey \\'məz-ē\\ David Saville 1870–1965 Am. hist.

Myr·dal \\'mуer-,däl, 'mər-, 'miər-\\ Alva 1902–1986 Swed. sociologist & diplomat

Myrdal (Karl) Gunnar 1898–1987 Swed. econ.

My·ron \\'mī-rən\\ *fl ca* 480–440 B.C. Greek sculptor

Na·bo·kov \\nə-'bȯ-kəf\\ Vladimir Vladimirovich 1899–1977 Am. (Russ.-born) nov. & poet — **Na·bo·ko·vi·an** \\,nab-ə-'kō-vē-ən\\ *adj*

Na·der \\'näd-ər\\ Ralph 1934–   Am. consumer advocate

Nai·du \\'nīd-(,)ü\\ Sarojini 1879–1949 Indian poet & reformer

Na·ka·so·ne \\,nä-kə-'sō-nē\\ Yasuhiro 1918–   prime min. of Japan (1982–87)

Na·mier \\'nā-,mi(ə)r\\ Sir Lewis Bernstein 1888–1960 Brit. hist.

Nā·nak \\'nän-ək\\ 1469–1539 founder of the Sikh faith in India

Nan·sen \\nän(t)-sən, 'nan(t)-\\ Frid·tjof \\'frich-,ȯf\\ 1861–1930 Norw. arctic explorer, zool., & statesman

Na·pier \\'nā-pē-ər, -,pi(ə)r; nə-'pi(ə)r\\ Sir Charles James 1782–1853 Brit. gen.

Napier *or* **Ne·per** \\'nā-pər\\ John 1550–1617 Laird of *Mer·chis·ton* \\'mər-kə-stən\\ Scot. math.

Napier Robert Cornelis 1810–1890 1st Baron *Napier of Mag·da·la* \\'mag-də-lə\\ Brit. field marshal

Na·po·léon I \\nə-'pōl-yən, -'pō-lē-ən\\ *or* **Napoléon Bo·na·parte** \\'bō-nə-,pärt\\ 1769–1821 emp. of the French (1804–15) — **Na·po·le·on·ic** \\nə-,pō-lē-'än-ik\\ *adj*

Napoléon II 1811–1832 Duc *de Reichstadt; son of Napoléon I & Marie Louise*

Napoléon III 1808–1873 *Louis-Napoléon; son of Louis Bonaparte & nephew of Napoléon I* emp. of the French (1852–71)

Nar·vá·ez \\när-'vä-,äs\\ Pánfilo de *ca* 1480–1528 Span. soldier

Nash \\'nash\\ Ogden 1902–1971 Am. poet

Nash *or* **Nashe** \\'nash\\ Thomas 1567–1601 Eng. satirist & dram.

Nash Walter 1882–1968 prime min. of New Zealand (1957–60)

Na·smyth \\'nā-,smith, 'nāz-məth\\ Alexander 1758–1840 Scot. painter

Nas·ser \\'näs-ər, 'nas-\\ Ga·mal \\gə-'mäl\\ Ab·del \\'äb-d'l\\ 1918–1970 Egypt. polit.; pres. of Egypt (1956–70)

Nast \\'nast\\ Thomas 1840–1902 Am. (Ger.-born) cartoonist

Na·than \\'nā-thən\\ George Jean 1882–1958 Am. editor & drama critic

Na·thans \\'nā-thənz\\ Daniel 1928–   Am. microbiologist

Na·tion \\'nā-shən\\ Car·ry \\'kar-ē\\ Amelia 1846–1911 née *Moore* Am. temperance agitator

Nat·ta \\'nät-(,)tä\\ Giulio 1903–1979 Ital. chem.

Neb·u·cha·drez·zar \\,neb-(y)ə-kə-'drez-ər\\ *also* **Neb·u·chad·nez·zar** \\-kəd-'nez-\\ *ca* 630–562 B.C. Chaldean king of Babylon (605–562)

Nec·ker \\nä-'ke(ə)r, 'nek-ər\\ Jacques 1732–1804 *father of Mme. de Staël* Fr. (Swiss-born) financier & statesman

Né·el \\nā-el\\ Louis-Eugène-Félix 1904–   Fr. physicist

Neh·ru \\'nā-(,)rü-(,)ü, 'ne(ə),rü\\ Ja·wa·har·lal \\jə-'wä-hər-,läl\\ 1889–1964 *son of Motilal* Indian nationalist; prime min. (1947–64)

Nehru Pan·dit \\'pən-dət\\ Mo·ti·lal \\'mōt-ᵊl-,äl\\ 1861–1931 Indian nationalist

Neil·son \\'nē(ə)l-sən\\ William Allan 1869–1946 Am. (Scot.-born) educ.; pres. Smith College (1917–39)

Nel·son \\'nel-sən\\ Horatio 1758–1805 Viscount *Nelson* Brit. admiral

Ne·pos \\'nē-,päs, 'nep-,äs\\ Cornelius *ca* 100–*ca* 25 B.C. Rom. hist.

Ne·ri \\'ne(ə)r-ē, 'nā-rē\\ Saint Philip 1515–1595 It. *Filippo Neri* Ital. founder (1564) of "Fathers of the Oratory"

Nernst \\'nern(t)st\\ Walther Hermann 1864–1941 Ger. physicist & chem.

Ne·ro \\'nē-(,)rō, 'ni(ə)r-(,)ō\\ A.D. 37–68 *Nero Claudius Caesar Drusus Germanicus* orig. *Lucius Domitius Ahenobarbus* Rom. emp. 54–68 — **Ne·ro·ni·an** \\ni-'rō-nē-ən\\ *or* **Ne·ron·ic** \\-'rän-ik\\ *adj*

Ne·ru·da \\nā-'rüd-ə, -'rü-(,)thä\\ Pablo 1904–1973 *Neftalí Ricardo Reyes Basoalto* Chilean poet & diplomat

Ner·va \\'nər-və\\ Marcus Cocceius *ca* A.D. 30–98 Rom. emp. (96–98)

Ner·vi \\'ne(ə)r-vē\\ Pier Luigi 1891–1979 Ital. engineer & architect

Nes·to·ri·us \\ne-'stōr-ē-əs, -'stȯr-\\ *d ca* 451 patriarch of Constantinople (428–431)

Neu·rath \\'nȯi-,rät\\ Konstantin 1873–1956 Freiherr *von Neurath* Ger. diplomat

Nev·el·son \\'nev-əl-sən\\ Louise 1900–1988 Am. (Russ.-born) sculptor

Neville Richard — see Earl of WARWICK

Nev·in \\'nev-ən\\ Ethelbert Woodbridge 1862–1901 Am. composer

Nev·ins \\'nev-ənz\\ Allan 1890–1971 Am. hist.

New·bolt \\'n(y)ü-,bōlt\\ Sir Henry John 1862–1938 Eng. author

New·comb \\'n(y)ü-kəm\\ Simon 1835–1909 Am. (Canad.-born) astron.

New·man \\'n(y)ü-mən\\ John Henry 1801–1890 Eng. cardinal & writer

New·ton \\'n(y)üt-ᵊn\\ Sir Isaac 1642–1727 Eng. math. & physicist — **New·to·ni·an** \\n(y)ü-'tō-nē-ən, -nyən\\ *adj*

Ney \\'nā\\ Michel 1769–1815 Duc *d'Elchingen; Prince de la Moskova* Fr. soldier; marshal of France

Nich·o·las \\'nik-(ə-)ləs\\ Saint 4th cent. Christian prelate

Nicholas name of 2 czars of Russia: **I** 1796–1855 (reigned 1825–55); **II** 1868–1918 (reigned 1894–1917)

Nicholas *Russ* **Ni·ko·lay** **Ni·ko·lay·e·vich** \\'nyē-kə-,lī-,nyē-kə-'lī-(-əv)-,yich\\ 1856–1929 Russ. grand duke & army officer

Nicholas of Cu·sa \\-'kyü-sə, -zə\\ 1401–1464 Ger. cardinal, math., & philos.

Nich·ol·son \\'nik-əl-sən\\ Ben 1894–1982 Brit. painter

Ni·ci·as \\'nis(h)-ē-əs\\ *d* 413 B.C. Athenian gen. & statesman

Nic·o·lay \\'nik-ə-,lā\\ John George 1832–1901 Am. biographer

Nic·o·let \\,nik-ə-'lā\\ Jean 1598–1642 Fr. explorer in No. America

Ni·colle \\nē-kȯl\\ Charles-Jean-Henri 1866–1936 Fr. physician & bacteriol.

Nic·ol·son \\'nik-əl-sən\\ Sir Harold George 1886–1968 Eng. biographer & diplomat

Nie·buhr \\'nē-,bú(ə)r, -bər\\ Barthold Georg 1776–1831 Ger. hist., statesman, & philologist

Niebuhr Rein·hold \\'rīn-,hōld\\ 1892–1971 Am. theol. — **Nie·buhr·ian** \\nē-'bùr-ē-ən\\ *adj*

Niel·sen \\'nēl-sən\\ Carl August 1865–1931 Dan. composer

Niem·ce·wicz \\(ne-),em-'sä-vich\\ Julian Ursyn 1758–1841 Pol. patriot & writer

Nie·mey·er \\'nē-,mi(-ə)r\\ Oscar 1907–   in full *Oscar Niemeyer Soares Filho* Braz. architect

Nie·möl·ler \\'nē-,mə(r)l-ər, -,mœl-\\ (Friedrich Gustav Emil) Martin 1892–1984 Ger. anti-Nazi Protestant theol.

Nietz·sche \\'nē-chə, -chē\\ Friedrich Wilhelm 1844–1900 Ger. philos. — **Nietz·sche·an** \\-chē-ən\\ *adj*

Night·in·gale \\'nīt-ᵊn-,gāl, -iŋ-\\ Florence 1820–1910 Eng. nurse & philanthropist

Ni·jin·ska \\nə-'zhin-skə, -'jin-\\ Bro·ni·sła·wa \\,brän-ə-'släv-ə\\ 1891–1972 *sister of following* Russ. (Pol.-born) dancer & choreographer

Ni·jin·sky \\nə-'zhin-skē, -'jin-\\ Vas·lav \\'vät-släf\\ Fomich 1890–1950 Russ. dancer

Nils·son \\'nil-sən\\ Birgit 1918–   Swed. soprano

Nim·itz \\'nim-əts\\ Chester William 1885–1966 Am. admiral

Nin \\'nēn\\ Anaïs 1903–1977 Am. (Fr.-born) author

Ni·ren·berg \\'nir-ən-,bərg\\ Marshall Warren 1927–   Am. geneticist

Nit·ti \\'nit-ē, 'nēt-\\ Francesco Saverio 1868–1953 Ital. econ. & statesman

Nix·on \\'nik-sən\\ Richard Milhous 1913–   Am. polit.; 37th pres. of the U.S. (1969–74) — **Nix·o·ni·an** \\nik-'sō-nē-ən, -nyən\\ *adj*

Nkru·mah \\en-'krü-mə, en-\\ Kwa·me \\'kwäm-ē\\ 1909–1972 prime min. (1952–60) & 1st pres. (1960–66) of Ghana

No·bel \\nō-'bel\\ Alfred Bernhard 1833–1896 Swed. manuf., inventor, & philanthropist

No·bi·le \\'nō-bə-,lā\\ Umberto 1885–1978 Ital. arctic explorer & aeronautical engineer

No·el-Ba·ker \\,nō-əl-'bā-kər\\ Philip John 1889–1982 Brit. polit.

No·gu·chi \\nō-'gü-chē\\ Hideyo 1876–1928 Am. (Jp.-born) bacteriol.

Noguchi Isamu 1904–1988 Am. sculptor

Nor·dau \\'nō(ə)r-,daú\\ Max Simon 1849–1923 orig. *Süd·feld* \\'zúet-,felt\\ Ger. (Hung.-born) physician, author, & Zionist

Nor·den·skiöld \\'nùrd-ᵊn-,shəld, -,shúld, -,shēld\\ Baron (Nils) Adolf Erik 1832–1901 Swed. arctic explorer

Nor·ris \\'nȯr-əs, 'när-\\ Benjamin Franklin 1870–1902 *Frank; bro. of C.G.* Am. nov.

Norris Charles Gilman 1881–1945 Am. nov.

Norris George William 1861–1944 Am. statesman

Nor·rish \\'nȯr-ish\\ Ronald George Wreyford 1897–1978 Brit. chem.

North \\'nō(ə)rth\\ Christopher — see John WILSON

North Frederick 1732–1792 *Lord North* Eng. statesman; prime min. (1770–82)

North Sir Thomas 1535–?1603 Eng. translator

Northcliffe Viscount — see Alfred C.W. HARMSWORTH

Nor·throp \\'nor-thrəp\\ John Howard 1891–1987 Am. biochem.

Nor·ton \\'nȯrt-ᵊn\\ Charles Eliot 1827–1908 Am. author & educ.

Norton Thomas 1532–1584 Eng. lawyer & poet

Nos·tra·da·mus \\,näs-trə-'dä-məs, ,nōs-trə-'däm-əs\\ 1503–1566 *Michel de Notredame* or *Nostredame* Fr. physician & astrologer

Noyes \\'nȯiz\\ Alfred 1880–1958 Eng. poet

Nu·re·yev \\nú-'rā-yəf\\ Rudolf Hametovich 1938–   Brit. (Russ.-born) ballet dancer

Nut·ting \\'nət-iŋ\\ Wallace 1861–1941 Am. antiquarian

Nye \\'nī\\ Edgar Wilson 1850–1896 *Bill* Am. humorist

Oates \\'ōts\\ Joyce Carol 1938–   Am. writer

Oates Titus 1649–1705 Brit. fabricator of the Popish Plot

O'Boyle \\ō-'bȯi(ə)l\\ Patrick Aloysius 1896–1987 Am. cardinal

Obrenović Alexander I — see ALEXANDER

O'Bri·en \\ō-'brī-ən\\ Lawrence Francis 1917–   U.S. postmaster general (1965–68)

O'Ca·sey \\ō-'kä-sē\\ Sean \\'shȯn\\ 1880–1964 orig. *John Casey* Irish dram.

Oc·cleve \\'äk-,lēv\\ — see Thomas HOCCLEVE

Ochoa \\ō-'chō-ə\\ Severo 1905–   Am. (Span.-born) biochem.

Ochs \\'äks\\ Adolph Simon 1858–1935 Am. newspaper publisher

Ock·ham *or* **Oc·cam** \\'äk-əm\\ William of *ca* 1285–?1349 Eng. philos. — **Ock·ham·is·tic** *or* **Oc·cam·is·tic** \\,äk-ə-'mis-tik\\ *adj*

O'Con·nell \\ō-'kän-ᵊl\\ Daniel 1775–1847 Irish nationalist

O'Connell William Henry 1859–1944 Am. cardinal

O'Con·nor \\ō-'kän-ər\\ (Mary) Flannery 1925–1964 Am. writer

O'Con·nor Frank 1903–1966 pseud. of *Michael John O'Donovan* Irish author
O'Con·nor Sandra Day 1930–   Am. jurist
O'Con·nor Thomas Power 1848–1929 *Tay Pay* \'tā-'pā\ Irish journalist
Oc·ta·vian *or* Oc·ta·vi·a·nus — see AUGUSTUS
Odets \ō-'dets\ Clifford 1906–1963 Am. dram.
Odo·a·cer \'ōd-ə-,wā-sər, 'äd-\ *also* Odo·va·car *or* Odo·va·kar \-vä-kər\ 433–493 1st barbarian ruler of Italy (476–493)
Oeh·len·schlä·ger \'ə(r)l-ən-,shlä-gər, 'œl-\ Adam Gottlob 1779–1850 Dan. poet & dram.
O'·Fao·láin \,ō-fə-'lón\ Seán \'shón\ 1900–   Irish author
Of·fen·bach \'óf-ən-,bäk, -,bäk\ Jacques 1819–1880 Fr. composer
O'·Fla·her·ty \ō-'fla-(h)ər-tē\ Li·am \'lē-əm\ 1896–1984 Irish nov.
Og·den \'ôg-dən, 'äg-\ Charles Kay 1889–1957 Brit. psychol.
Ogle·thorpe \'ō-gəl-,thórp\ James Edward 1696–1785 Eng. philanthropist & gen.; founder of Georgia
Ögö·dei \'ö-gə-,dā\ *also* Oga·dai \-,dī\ *or* Og·dai \'óg-,dī\ *or* Uge·dei \'ü-gə-,dā\ 1185–1241 Mongol Khan (1229–41)
O'·Hara \ō-'har-ə\ John Henry 1905–1970 Am. author
O'·Hig·gins \ō-'hig-ənz, ō-'ē-gən(t)s\ Bernardo 1778–1842 *Liberator of Chile* Chilean soldier & statesman
Ohira \ō-'hir-ə\ Masayoshi 1910–1980 prime min. of Japan (1978–80)
Oh·lin \'ō-lin\ Bertil Gotthard 1899–1979 Swed. econ.
Ohm \'ōm\ Georg Simon 1787–1854 Ger. physicist
Ois·trakh \'ois-trək\ David Fyodorovich 1908–1974 Russ. violinist
O'Keeffe \ō-'kēf\ Georgia 1887–1986 Am. painter
O'·Kel·ly \ō-'kel-ē\ Seán \'shón\ Thomas 1883–1966 Irish journalist; pres. of Republic of Ireland (1945–59)
O'Kelly Seu·mas \'shā-məs\ 1881–1918 Irish writer
Olaf name of 5 kings of Norway: esp. **Olaf I Tryg·va·son** \'trig-və-sən\ *ca* 964–1000 (reigned 995–1000); **Olaf II Har·alds·son** \'har-əl(d)-sən\ *Saint Olaf* 995?–1030 (reigned 1016–28); **Olaf V** 1903–   (reigned 1957–   )
Old·cas·tle \'ōl(d)-,kas-əl\ Sir John 1377?–1417 Baron *Cob·ham* \-'käb-əm\ Eng. Lollard leader
Ol·den·bar·ne·velt \,ōl-dən-'bär-nə-vəlt\ Johan van 1547–1619 Du. statesman
Oliv·i·er \ō-'liv-ē-,ā\ Laurence Kerr 1907–1989 Baron *Olivier of Brighton* Eng. actor
Olm·sted \'ōm-,sted, 'äm-, -stəd\ Frederick Law 1822–1903 Am. landscape architect
Omar Khay·yám \,ō-,mär-,kī-'(y)äm, ,ō-mər-, -'(y)am\ 1048?–1122 Pers. poet & astron.
O'·Neill \ō-'nē(ə)l\ Eugene Gladstone 1888–1953 Am. dram.
On·ions \'ən-yənz\ Charles Talbut 1873–1965 Eng. lexicographer
On·sa·ger \'ón-,säg-ər\ Lars 1903–1976 Am. (Norw.-born) chem.
Op·pen·heim \'äp-ən-,hīm\ Edward Phillips 1866–1946 Eng. nov.
Op·pen·hei·mer \'äp-ən-,hī-mər\ (Julius) Robert 1904–1967 Am. physicist
Or·ca·gna \ór-'kän-yə\ Andrea *ca* 1308–*ca* 1368 *Andrea di Cione* Florentine painter, sculptor, & architect
Or·czy \'órt-sē\ Baroness Em·mus·ka \'em-əsh-kə\ 1865–1947 Eng. (Hung.-born) nov. & dram.
Orff \'ó(ə)rf\ Carl 1895–1982 Ger. composer
Or·i·gen \'ór-ə-jən, 'är-\ 185?–?254 Greek writer, teacher, & church father
Or·lan·do \ór-'lan-(,)dō, -'län-\ Vittorio Emanuele 1860–1952 Ital. statesman
Or·man·dy \'ór-mən-dē\ Eugene 1899–1985 Am. (Hung.-born) conductor
Oroz·co \ō-'rō-(,)skō\ José Clemente 1883–1949 Mex. painter
Ør·sted \'ə(r)-stəd, 'œr-\ Hans Christian 1777–1851 Dan. physicist & chem.
Or·te·ga y Gas·set \ór-'tā-gə-,ē-gä-'set\ José 1883–1955 Span. philos., writer, & statesman
Or·tiz Ru·bio \ór-,tēz-'rü-bē-,ō\ Pascual 1877–1963 pres. of Mexico (1930–32)
Or·well \'ór-,wel, -wəl\ George 1903–1950 pseud. of *Eric Blair* Eng. author — **Or·well·ian** \ór-'wel-ē-ən\ *adj*
Os·born \'äz-bərn, -,bórn\ Henry Fairfield 1857–1935 Am. paleontologist
Os·borne \'äz-bərn, -,bó(ə)rn, -,bō(ə)rn\ John James 1929–   Brit. dram.
Osborne Thomas Mott 1859–1926 Am. penologist
Os·car II \'äs-kər\ 1829–1907 king of Sweden (1872–1907) & of Norway (1872–1905)
Osce·o·la \,äs-ē-'ō-lə, ,ō-sē-\ *ca* 1800–1838 Seminole Indian chief
Os·ler \'ō-slər, 'óz-lər\ Sir William 1849–1919 Canad. physician
Os·man I \ös-'män\ 1258–*ca* 1326 founder of the Ottoman Empire
Os·me·ña \óz-'män-yə, ōs-\ Sergio 1878–1961 pres. of Philippine Commonwealth (1944–46)
Os·si·etz·ky \,äs-ē-'et-skē\ Carl von 1889–1938 Ger. writer & pacifist
Ossoli Marchioness — see Margaret FULLER
Ost·wald \'ós-,twóld\ Friedrich Wilhelm 1853–1932 Ger. physical chem. & philos.
Otis \'ōt-əs\ Elwell Stephen 1838–1909 Am. gen.
Otis Harrison Gray 1837–1917 Am. gen. & journalist
Otis James 1725–1783 Am. statesman in Revolution
Ot·ter·bein \'ät-ər-,bīn\ Philip William 1726–1813 Am. (Ger.-born) clergyman
Ot·to I \'ät-(,)ō\ 912–973 *the Great* Holy Rom. emp. (936–973)
Ot·way \'ät-,wā\ Thomas 1652–1685 Eng. dram.
Ouida — see Marie Louise de la RAMÉE
Ov·id \'äv-əd\ 43 B.C.–?A.D. 17 *Publius Ovidius Naso* Rom. poet — **Ovid·ian** \ä-'vid-ē-ən\ *adj*
Ow·en \'ō-ən\ Robert 1771–1858 Welsh social reformer
Owen Wilfred 1893–1918 Brit. poet
Ox·en·stier·na \'úk-sen-,sher-nä\ Count Axel Gustafsson 1583–1654 Swed. statesman
Oxford Earl of — see Robert HARLEY
Paa·si·ki·vi \'pä-sə-,kē-vē\ Ju·ho \'yü-(,)hó\ Kusti 1870–1956 Finn. businessman; pres. of Finland (1946–56)
Pa·de·rew·ski \,pad-ə-'ref-skē, -'rev-\ Ignacy \ēn-'yäs\ Jan \'yän\ 1860–1941 Pol. pianist, composer, & statesman

Pa·ga·ni·ni \,pag-ə-'nē-nē, ,päg-\ Niccolò 1782–1840 Ital. violinist
Page \'pāj\ Thomas Nelson 1853–1922 Am. nov. & diplomat
Page Walter Hines 1855–1918 Am. journalist & diplomat
Pag·et \'paj-ət\ Sir James 1814–1899 Eng. surgeon & pathologist
Pahlavi — see REZA SHAH PAHLAVI & MOHAMMAD REZA PAHLAVI
Paine \'pān\ Albert Bigelow 1861–1937 Am. author
Paine Thomas 1737–1809 Am. (Eng.-born) polit. philos. & author
Pain·le·vé \pa⁼-lə-vä\ Paul 1863–1933 Fr. math. & statesman
Pa·la·de \pə-'läd-ē\ George Emil 1912–   Am. (Romanian-born) biol.
Pa·le·stri·na \,pal-ə-'strē-nə\ Giovanni Pierluigi da *ca* 1525–1594 Ital. composer
Pa·ley \'pā-lē\ William 1743–1805 Eng. theol. & philos.
Pal·grave \'pal-,grāv, 'pól-\ Francis Turner 1824–1897 Eng. poet & critic
Pal·la·dio \pə-'läd-ē-,ō\ Andrea 1508–1580 Ital. architect
Palma Tomás Estrada see ESTRADA PALMA
Palm·er \'päm-ər, 'päl-mər\ Alice Elvira 1855–1902 née *Freeman; wife of G. H.* Am. educ.
Palmer Daniel David 1845–1913 Am. chiropractor
Palmer Geoffrey 1942–   prime min. of New Zealand (1989–   )
Palmer George Herbert 1842–1933 Am. scholar & educ.
Palm·er·ston \'päm-ər-stən, 'päl-mər-\ 3d Viscount 1784–1865 *Henry John Temple* Eng. statesman; prime min. (1855–58; 1859–65) — **Palm·er·sto·nian** \,päm-ər-'stō-nē-ən, ,päl-mər-, -nyən\ *adj*
Palm·gren \'päm-grən, 'pälm-\ Selim 1878–1951 Finn. pianist & composer
Pā·ni·ni \'pän-(y)ə-(,)nē\ *fl ca* 400 B.C. Indian grammarian of Sanskrit
Pank·hurst \'paŋk-,hərst\ Emmeline 1858–1928 née *Goulden* Eng. suffragist
Pan·ni·ni *or* Pa·ni·ni \pä-'nē-(,)nē\ Giovanni Paolo 1691–1765 Ital. painter
Pa·o·li \'paú-lē, 'pä-ō-(,)lē\ Pasquale 1725–1807 Corsican patriot
Pa·pen \'päp-ən\ Franz von 1879–1969 Ger. diplomat
Pap·pen·heim \'päp-ən-,hīm, 'pap-\ Gottfried Heinrich 1594–1632 Graf *zu Pappenheim* Ger. gen.
Par·a·cel·sus \,par-ə-'sel-səs\ 1493–1541 pseud. of *Philippus Aureolus Theophrastus Bombast von Hohenheim* Swiss-born alchemist & physician
Pa·re·to \pə-'rāt-(,)ō\ Vilfredo 1848–1923 Ital. econ. & sociol.
Pa·ris \pä-'rēs, pə-\ (Bruno-Paulin-) Gaston 1839–1903 Fr. philologist
Par·is \'par-əs\ Matthew *d* 1259 Eng. monk & hist.
Park Chung Hee \'pärk-'chəŋ-'hē\ 1917–1979 So. Korean leader (1961–79) & pres. (1963–79)
Park \'pärk\ Mungo 1771–1806 Scot. explorer in Africa
Par·ker \'pär-kər\ Dorothy 1893–1967 née *Rothschild* Am. writer
Parker Sir Gilbert 1862–1932 Canad. author
Parker Matthew 1504–1575 Eng. theol.
Parker Theodore 1810–1860 Am. Unitarian clergyman
Parkes \'pärks\ Sir Henry 1815–1896 Austral. statesman
Park·man \'pärk-mən\ Francis 1823–1893 Am. hist.
Parks \'pärks\ Rosa Lee 1913–   Am. civil rights leader
Parley Peter — see Samuel Griswold GOODRICH
Par·men·i·des \pär-'men-ə-,dēz\ *b ca* 515 B.C. Greek philos.
Par·mi·gia·ni·no \,pär-mi-jä-'nē-(,)nō\ *or* Par·mi·gia·no \-mə-'jän-(,)ō\ 1503–1540 *Girolamo Francesco Maria Mazzuoli* or *Mazzola* Ital. painter
Par·nell \pär-'nel *also* 'pärn-ʔl\ Charles Stewart 1846–1891 Irish nationalist
Parr Catherine — see CATHERINE
Par·ring·ton \'par-iŋ-tən\ Vernon Louis 1871–1929 Am. lit. hist.
Par·rish \'par-ish\ Maxfield Frederick 1870–1966 Am. painter
Par·ry \'par-ē\ Sir William Edward 1790–1855 Eng. explorer
Par·sons \'pärs-ʔnz\ William 1800–1867 3d Earl of *Rosse* Irish astron.
Pas·cal \pas-'kal, päs-kál\ Blaise 1623–1662 Fr. math. & philos.
Pa·šić \'päsh-(,)ich\ Nicola \'nē-kō-lä\ 1845–1926 Serbian & Yugoslav statesman
Passfield 1st Baron — see WEBB
Pas·sy \pa-'sē, pä-\ Frédéric 1822–1912 Fr. econ. & statesman
Passy Paul-Edouard 1859–1940 *son of prec.* Fr. phonetician
Pas·ter·nak \'pas-tər-,nak\ Boris Leonidovich 1890–1960 Russ. poet, nov., & translator
Pas·teur \pas-'tər\ Louis 1822–1895 Fr. chem. — **Pas·teur·i·an** \-ē-ən\ *adj*
Pa·ter \'pāt-ər\ Walter Horatio 1839–1894 Eng. essayist & critic
Pat·more \'pat-,mō(ə)r, -,mó(ə)r\ Coventry Kersey Dighton 1823–1896 Eng. poet
Pa·ton \'pāt-ʔn\ Alan Stewart 1903–1988 So. African writer
Pat·rick \'pa-trik\ Saint 5th cent. A.D. apostle & patron saint of Ireland
Pat·ti \'pat-ē, 'pät-ē\ Adelina 1843–1919 Am. (Span.-born) soprano
Pat·ti·son \'pat-ə-sən\ Mark 1813–1884 Eng. scholar & author
Pat·ton \'pat-ʔn\ George Smith 1885–1945 Am. gen.
Paul \'pól\ name of 6 popes: esp. **III** 1468–1549 (pope 1534–49); **V** 1552–1621 (pope 1605–21); **VI** (*Giovanni Battista Montini*) 1897–1978 (pope 1963–78)
Paul I 1754–1801 emp. of Russia (1796–1801)
Paul I 1901–1964 king of Greece (1947–64)
Paul Jean — see RICHTER
Paul \'paúl\ Wolfgang 1913–   Ger. physicist
Paul–Bon·cour \'pól-(,)bō⁼-'kü(ə)r\ Joseph 1873–1972 Fr. lawyer & statesman
Pauld·ing \'pól-diŋ\ James Kirke 1778–1860 Am. author
Pau·li \'paú-lē\ Wolfgang 1900–1958 Am. (Austrian-born) physicist
Pau·ling \'pó-liŋ\ Li·nus \'lī-nəs\ Carl 1901–   Am. chem.
Pau·lus \'paú-ləs\ Friedrich 1890–1957 Ger. field marshal
Paulus \'pó-ləs\ Julius 2d–3d cent. A.D. Rom. jurist
Pau·sa·ni·as \pó-'sā-nē-əs\ *fl* A.D. 143–176 Greek traveler & geographer
Pav·lov \'päv-,lóf, 'pav-, -,lóv\ Ivan Petrovich 1849–1936 Russ. physiol. — **Pav·lov·ian** \pav-'lō-vē-ən, -'lō-; -'lō-fē-\ *adj*

Pa·vlo·va \'pav-lə-və, pav-'lō-\ Anna 1882–1931 Russ. ballerina
Paz \'päs, 'päz\ Octavio 1914–   Mex. author
Pea·body \'pē-,bäd-ē, -bəd-ē\ Endicott 1857–1944 Am. educ.
Peabody George 1795–1869 Am. merchant & philanthropist
Pea·cock \'pē-,käk\ Thomas Love 1785–1866 Eng. nov. & poet
Peale \'pē(ə)l\ Charles Willson 1741–1827 & his bro. James 1749–1831 & Charles's son Rembrandt 1778–1860 Am. painters
Pear·son \'pi(ə)rs-ᵊn\ Karl 1857–1936 Eng. math.
Pearson Lester Bowles 1897–1972 prime min. of Canada (1963–68)
Pea·ry \'pi(ə)r-ē\ Robert Edwin 1856–1920 Am. explorer
Pe·der·sen \'pēd-ər-sən\ Charles John 1904–1989 Am. (Korean-born) chem.
Pe·dro \'pä-drō, -drü\ Dom; name of 2 emps. of Brazil: I 1798–1834 (reigned as emp. 1822–31; as king of Portugal 1826); II 1825–1891 (reigned 1831–1889)
Peel \'pē(ə)l\ Sir Robert 1788–1850 Eng. statesman
Peele \'pē(ə)l\ George 1556–1596 Eng. dram. & poet
Pei \'pā\ Ieoh Ming 1917–   Am. (Chin.-born) architect
Peirce \'pərs, 'pi(ə)rs\ Charles Sanders 1839–1914 Am. physicist, math., & logician
Pei·sis·tra·tus or Pi·sis·tra·tus \pi-'sis-trət-əs, pə-\ d 527 B.C. Athenian tyrant
Pe·la·gius \pə-'lā-j(ē-)əs\ ca 354–after 418 Brit. monk & theol.
Pe·lop·i·das \pə-'läp-əd-əs\ d 364 B.C. Theban gen.
Pen·de·rec·ki \,pen-də-'ret-skē\ Krzysztof 1933–   Pol. composer
Penn \'pen\ Sir William 1621–1670 Eng. admiral
Penn William 1644–1718 son of prec. Eng. Quaker; founder of Pennsylvania
Pen·nell \'pen-ᵊl, pə-'nel\ Joseph 1857–1926 Am. etcher
Pen·zi·as \'pent-sē-əs\ Arno Allan 1933–   Am. (Ger.-born) physicist
Pép·in III \'pep-ən\ 714?–768 the Short king of the Franks (751–768)
Pepys \'pēps\ Samuel 1633–1703 Eng. diarist — Pepys·ian \-ē-ən\ adj
Per·cy \'pər-sē\ Sir Henry 1364–1403 Hotspur Eng. soldier
Percy Thomas 1729–1811 Eng. antiquarian & poet
Percy Walker 1916–1990 Am. writer
Per·el·man \'pər-əl-mən (his own pron.), 'pər(-ə)l-\ Sidney Joseph 1904–1979 Am. writer
Pé·rez Gal·dós \,per-əs-(,)gäl-'dōs\ Benito 1843–1920 Span. writer
Per·go·le·si \,pər-gə-'lā-zē, ,per-gə-'lā-sē\ Giovanni Battista 1710–1736 Ital. composer
Per·i·cles \'per-ə-,klēz\ ca 495–429 B.C. Athenian statesman — Per·i·cle·an \,per-ə-'klē-ən\ adj
Per·kins \'pər-kənz\ Frances 1882–1965 Am. public official
Pe·rón \pā-'rōn, pə-\ Juan Domingo 1895–1974 Argentine polit.; pres. of Argentina (1946–55; 1973–74)
Per·rault \pə-'rō, pe-\ Charles 1628–1703 Fr. fairy tale writer
Per·rin \pə-'ra(n)n, pe-\ Jean-Baptiste 1870–1942 Fr. physicist
Per·ry \'per-ē\ Bliss 1860–1954 Am. educ. & critic
Perry Matthew Calbraith 1794–1858 Am. commodore
Perry Oliver Hazard 1785–1819 bro. of prec. Am. naval officer
Perry Ralph Barton 1876–1957 Am. philos. & educ.
Perse St. John — see Aléxis Saint-Léger LÉGER
Per·shing \'pər-shiŋ, -zhiŋ\ John Joseph 1860–1948 Am. gen.
Per·sius \'pər-shəs, 'pər-sē-əs\ A.D. 34–62 Aulus Persius Flaccus Rom. satirist
Pe·ru·gi·no \,per-ə-'jē-(,)nō\ ca 1450–1523 Pietro di Cristoforo Vannucci Ital. painter
Per·utz \pə-'rüts\ Max Ferdinand 1914–   Brit. (Austrian-born) chem.
Pe·ruz·zi \pə-'rüt-sē, pā-\ Baldassare 1481–1536 Ital. architect & painter
Pes·ta·loz·zi \,pes-tə-'lät-sē\ Johann Heinrich 1746–1827 Swiss educ.
Pé·tain \pā-taⁿ\ Philippe 1856–1951 Fr. gen.; marshal of France; premier of Vichy France (1940–44)
Pe·ter I \'pēt-ər\ 1672–1725 the Great czar of Russia (1682–1725)
Peter I 1844–1921 king of Serbia (1903–21)
Peter II 1923–1970 king of Yugoslavia (1934–45)
Peter Lom·bard \-'läm-,bärd\ ca 1095–1160 L. Petrus Lombardus Ital. theol.
Peter the Hermit ca 1050–1115 Fr. preacher of the 1st Crusade
Pe·ters \'pāt-ərz, -ərs\ Carl 1856–1918 Ger. explorer
Pe·tő·fi \'pet-ə-fē\ Sán·dor \'shän-,dó(ə)r\ 1823–1849 Hung. poet
Pe·trarch \'pē-,trärk, 'pe-\ 1304–1374 It. Francesco Petrarca Ital. poet — Pe·trarch·an \pē-'trär-kən, pe-\ adj
Pe·trie \'pē-trē\ Sir (William Matthew) Flin·ders \'flin-dərz\ 1853–1942 Eng. Egyptologist
Pe·tro·ni·us \pi-'trō-nē-əs\ d A.D. 66 in full prob. Titus Petronius Niger Rom. satirist — Pe·tro·ni·an \-nē-ən\ adj
Pet·ty \'pet-ē\ Sir William 1623–1687 Eng. polit. econ.
Pevs·ner \'pevz-nər\ Antoine 1886–1962 bro. of Naum Gabo Fr. (Russ.²born) sculptor & painter
Pevsner Sir Nikolaus 1902–1983 Brit. (Ger.-born) art hist.
Phae·drus \'fē-drəs\ 5th cent. B.C. Greek philos.
Phaedrus ca 15 B.C.–ca A.D. 50 Rom. creator of fables
Phid·i·as \'fid-ē-əs\ fl ca 490–430 B.C. Greek sculptor
Phil·ip \'fil-əp\ 1639?–1676 Meta·com·et \,met-ə-'käm-ət\ sachem of the Wampanoag Indians
Philip name of 6 kings of France: esp. II or Philip Augustus 1165–1223 (reigned 1179–1223); IV (the Fair) 1268–1314 (reigned 1285–1314); VI 1293–1350 (reigned 1328–50)
Philip name of 5 kings of Spain: esp. II 1527–1598 (reigned 1556–98); V 1683–1746 (reigned 1700–24, 1724–46)
Philip II 382–336 B.C. king of Macedon (359–336)
Philip III 1396–1467 the Good Duke of Burgundy (1419–67)
Philip Prince 1921–   consort of Queen Elizabeth II of Great Britain 3d Duke of Edinburgh
Phil·ips \'fil-əps\ Ambrose 1674–1749 Nam·by-Pam·by \,nam-bē-'pam-bē\ Eng. poet & dram.
Phil·lips \'fil-əps\ Wendell 1811–1884 Am. orator & reformer
Phill·potts \'fil-,päts\ Eden 1862–1960 Eng. nov. & dram.
Phi·lo Ju·dae·us \'fī-(,)lō-jü-'dē-əs, -'dā-\ ca 13 B.C.–A.D. 45 to 50 Jewish philos. of Alexandria
Pho·ci·on \'fō-sē-,än\ ca 402–318 B.C. Athenian gen. & statesman
Phyfe \'fīf\ Duncan 1768–1854 Am. (Scot.-born) cabinetmaker

Pia·get \pyä-'zhā\ Jean 1896–1980 Swiss psychol. — Pia·get·ian \,pē-ə-'jet-ē-ən, pyä-'zhā-ən\ adj
Pi·card \pē-'kär, pik-'ärd\ Jean 1620–1682 Fr. astron.
Pi·cas·so \pi-'käs-(,)ō, -'kas-\ Pablo 1881–1973 Span. painter & sculptor in France
Pic·card \pi-'kär, pik-'ärd\ Auguste 1884–1962 Swiss physicist
Piccard Jacques-Ernst 1922–   son of Auguste Swiss (Belg.-born) oceanographer; developer of bathyscaphe
Pick·er·ing \'pik-(ə-)riŋ\ Edward Charles 1846–1919 & his bro. William Henry 1858–1938 Am. astron.
Pick·ett \'pik-ət\ George Edward 1825–1875 Am. Confed. gen.
Pi·co del·la Mi·ran·do·la \'pē-(,)kō-,del-ə-mə-'ran-də-lə, -'rän-\ Conte Giovanni 1463–1494 Ital. humanist
Pierce \'pi(ə)rs\ Franklin 1804–1869 14th pres. of the U.S. (1853–57)
Pierce Samuel Riley, Jr. 1922–   U.S. secy. of housing & urban development (1981–89)
Pie·ro del·la Fran·ces·ca \'pyer-ō-,del-ə-fran-'ches-kə, -frän-\ or de'Fran·ces·chi \-dä-fran-'ches-kē, -frän-\ ca 1420–1492 Ital. painter
Pike \'pīk\ Zebulon Montgomery 1779–1813 Am. gen. & explorer
Pi·late \'pī-lət\ Pon·tius \'pän-chəs, 'pən-chəs\ d after A.D. 36 Rom. procurator of Judea (26–ca 36)
Pił·sud·ski \pil-'süt-skē, -'züt-\ Józef Klemens 1867–1935 Pol. gen. & statesman
Pin·chot \'pin-,shō\ Gifford 1865–1946 Am. forester & polit.
Pinck·ney \'piŋk-nē\ Charles Cotesworth 1746–1825 Am. statesman
Pin·dar \'pin-dər, -,där\ ca 522–ca 438 B.C. Greek poet
Pi·ne·ro \pə-'ni(ə)r-(,)ō, -'ne(ə)r-\ Sir Arthur Wing 1855–1934 Eng. dram.
Pin·ker·ton \'piŋ-kərt-ᵊn\ Allan 1819–1884 Am. (Scot.-born) detective
Pi·no·chet Ugar·te \,pē-nō-'chet-ü-'gär-tä\ Augusto 1915–   Chilean gen.; pres. of Chile (1974–90)
Pin·ter \'pint-ər\ Harold 1930–   Eng. dram. — Pin·ter·esque \,pint-ə-'resk\ adj
Pin·tu·ric·chio \,pint-ə-'rē-kē-,ō\ ca 1454–1513 Bernardino di Betto di Biago Ital. painter
Pin·zón \pin-'zōn\ Martín Alonso ca 1441–1493 & his bro. Vicente Yáñez ca 1460–ca 1523 Span. navigators with Columbus
Piozzi \pē-'ót-sē\ Hester Lynch 1741–1821 Mrs. Thrale \'thrā(ə)l\ Eng. writer
Pi·ran·del·lo \,pir-ən-'del-(,)ō\ Luigi 1867–1936 Ital. author — Pi·ran·del·li·an \-'del-ē-ən\ adj
Pi·ra·ne·si \,pir-ə-'nä-zē\ Giambattista 1720–1778 Ital. architect, painter, & engraver
Pire \'pi(ə)r\ Dominique Georges 1910–1969 Belg. clergyman & humanitarian
Pi·sa·no \pi-'sän-(,)ō, -'zän-\ Giovanni ca 1250–after 1314 & his father Nicola ca 1220–1278(or 1284) Ital. sculptors
Pisistratus — see PEISISTRATUS
Pis·sar·ro \pə-'sär-(,)ō\ Camille 1830–1903 Fr. painter
Pis·ton \'pis-tən\ Walter Hamor 1894–1976 Am. composer
Pit·man \'pit-mən\ Sir Isaac 1813–1897 Eng. phonographer
Pitt \'pit\ William 1708–1778 Earl of Chatham; the Elder Pitt Eng. statesman
Pitt William 1759–1806 the Younger Pitt; son of prec. Eng. statesman
Pitt–Riv·ers \'pit-'riv-ərz\ Augustus Henry 1827–1900 Eng. archaeol.
Pi·us \'pī-əs\ name of 12 popes: esp. II (Enea Silvio Piccolomini or Aeneas Silvius or Sylvius) 1405–1464 (pope 1458–64); VII 1742–1823 (pope 1800–23); IX 1792–1878 (pope 1846–78); X 1835–1914 (pope 1903–14); XI (Ambrogio Damiano Achille Ratti) 1857–1939 (pope 1922–39); XII (Eugenio Pacelli) 1876–1958 (pope 1939–58)
Pi·zar·ro \pə-'zär-(,)ō\ Francisco ca 1475–1541 Span. conqueror of Peru
Planck \'pläŋk\ Max Karl Ernst Ludwig 1858–1947 Ger. physicist
Plan·tin \plän-taⁿ\ Christophe ca 1520–1589 Fr. printer
Plath \'plath\ Sylvia 1932–1963 Am. poet
Pla·to \'plāt-(,)ō\ ca 428–348(or 347) B.C. Greek philos.
Plau·tus \'plót-əs\ Titus Maccius ca 254–184 B.C. Rom. dram. — Plau·tine \'plò-,tīn\ adj
Ple·kha·nov \plə-'kän-,óf, pli-'kän-\ Georgy Valentinovich 1857–1918 Russ. Marxist philos.
Ple·ven \plā-'ven\ René 1901–   Fr. polit.
Pliny \'plin-ē\ A.D. 23–79 Gaius Plinius Secundus; the Elder Rom. scholar
Pliny A.D. 61(or 62)–ca 113 Gaius Plinius Caecilius Secundus; the Younger; nephew of prec. Rom. author
Plo·ti·nus \plō-'tī-nəs\ A.D. 205–270 Rom. (Egypt.-born) philos. — Plo·tin·i·an \-'tin-ē-ən\ adj
Plu·tarch \'plü-,tärk\ ca A.D. 46–after 119 Greek biographer & moralist — Plu·tarch·an \-kən\ or Plu·tarch·ian \-kē-ən\ adj
Po·ca·hon·tas \,pō-kə-'hänt-əs\ ca 1595–1617 dau. of Powhatan Am. Indian
Pod·gor·ny \päd-'gór-nē\ Nikolay Viktorovich 1903–1983 Soviet polit.; head of Presidium (1965–77)
Poe \'pō\ Edgar Allan 1809–1849 Am. poet & short-story writer
Poin·ca·ré \,pwaⁿ(n)-,kä-'rā\ Jules-Henri 1854–1912 Fr. math.
Poincaré Raymond 1860–1934 cousin of J. H. Fr. statesman; pres. of France (1913–20)
Po·lan·yi \pō-'län-yē\ John Charles 1929–   Canad. (Ger.-born) chem.
Pole \'pōl, 'pül\ Reginald 1500–1558 Eng. cardinal; archbishop of Canterbury (1556–58)
Po·len·ta \pō-'len-tə\ Francesca da d 1283(or 1284) Francesca da Rimini Ital. noblewoman famous for tragic adulterous love affair
Po·li·tian \pə-'lish-ən\ 1454–1494 Angelo Poliziano or Angelo Ambrogini Ital. classical scholar & poet
Polk \'pōk\ James Knox 1795–1849 11th pres. of the U.S. (1845–49)
Pol·lio \'päl-ē-,ō\ Gaius Asinius 76 B.C.–A.D. 4 Rom. soldier, orator, & polit.
Pol·lock \'päl-ək\ Sir Frederick 1845–1937 Eng. jurist
Pollock (Paul) Jackson 1912–1956 Am. painter
Po·lo \'pō-(,)lō\ Mar·co \'mär-(,)kō\ 1254–1324 Venetian traveler
Po·lyb·i·us \pə-'lib-ē-əs\ ca 200–ca 118 B.C. Greek hist.
Pol·y·carp \'päl-i-,kärp\ Saint 2d cent. Christian martyr & Apostolic Father; bishop of Smyrna

Pol·y·cli·tus *or* Pol·y·clei·tus \,päl-i-'klīt-əs\ 5th cent. B.C. Greek sculptor & architect
Po·lyc·ra·tes \pə-'lik-rə-,tēz\ *d ca* 522 B.C. tyrant of Samos
Pol·y·do·rus \,päl-i-'dōr-əs, -'dór-\ 1st cent. B.C. Rhodian sculptor
Pol·yg·no·tus \,päl-ig-'nōt-əs\ *ca* 500–*ca* 440 B.C. Greek painter
Pom·pa·dour \'päm-pə-,dō(ə)r, -,dȯ(ə)r, -,dü(ə)r\ Madame de 1721–1764 *Jeanne-Antoinette Poisson; mistress of Louis XV*
Pom·pey \'päm-pē\ 106–48 B.C. *Gnaeus Pompeius Magnus; the Great* Rom. gen. & statesman
Pom·pi·dou \'päm-pi-,dü\ Georges-Jean-Raymond 1911–1974 Fr. polit.; premier (1962–68) & pres. (1969–74) of France
Ponce de Le·ón \,pän(t)-sə-,dä-lē-'ōn, ,pänts-də-'lē-ən\ Juan 1460–1521 Span. explorer
Pon·chi·el·li \,pȯn-kē-'el-ē\ Amilcare 1834–1886 Ital. composer
Pons \'pȯns\ Lily 1904–1976 Am. (Fr.-born) soprano
Pon·selle \pän-'sel\ Rosa Melba 1897–1981 Am. soprano
Pon·ti·ac \'pänt-ē-,ak\ *ca* 1720–1769 Ottawa Indian chief
Pon·top·pi·dan \pän-'täp-ə-,dan\ Henrik 1857–1943 Dan. nov.
Pon·tor·mo \pōn-'tȯr-(,)mō\ Jacopo da 1494–1557 orig. *J. Carrucci* Ital. painter
Pope \'pōp\ Alexander 1688–1744 Eng. poet — Pop·ian *also* Pop·ean \'pō-pē-ən\ *adj*
Pope John 1822–1892 Am. gen.
Por·son \'pȯrs-ᵊn\ Richard 1759–1808 Eng. scholar
Por·tal \'pȯrt-ᵊl, 'pȯrt-\ Charles Frederick Algernon 1893–1971 1st Viscount *Portal of Hungerford* Brit. air marshal
Por·ter \'pȯrt-ər, 'pȯrt-\ Cole Albert 1892?–1964 Am. composer & lyricist
Porter David 1780–1843 & his son David Dixon 1813–1891 Am. naval officers
Porter Gene 1868–1924 née *Stratton* Am. nov.
Porter Sir George 1920–   Brit. chem.
Porter Katherine Anne 1890–1980 Am. writer
Porter Noah 1811–1892 Am. philos. & lexicographer
Porter Rodney Robert 1917–1985 Brit. biochem.
Porter William Sydney 1862–1910 pseud. *O. Hen·ry* \(ᵊ)ō-'hen-rē\ Am. short-story writer
Portland Duke of — see BENTINCK
Post \'pōst\ Emily 1872–1960 née *Price* Am. columnist & writer
Po·tem·kin \pə-'tyóm(p)-kən, pō-'tem(p)-\ Grigory Aleksandrovich 1739–1791 Russ. field marshal & statesman
Pot·ter \'pät-ər\ Beatrix 1866–1943 Brit. writer & illustrator
Potter Paul *or* Paulus 1625–1654 Du. painter
Pou·lenc \'pü-,laŋk\ Fran·cis \frä-'sēs\ 1899–1963 Fr. composer
Pound \'paúnd\ Ezra Loomis 1885–1972 Am. poet
Pound Roscoe 1870–1964 Am. jurist
Pous·sin \pü-saⁿ\ Nicolas 1594–1665 Fr. painter
Pow·ell \'paú(-ə)l\ Adam Clayton 1908–1972 Am. clergyman & polit.
Powell \'pō-əl, 'paú(-ə)l\ Anthony 1905–   Eng. writer
Powell Cecil Frank 1903–1969 Brit. physicist
Powell \'paú(-ə)l\ Colin Luther 1937–   Am. gen.
Powell John Wesley 1834–1902 Am. geologist & explorer
Powell Lewis Franklin 1907–   Am. jurist
Pow·ers \'paú(-ə)rz\ Hiram 1805–1873 Am. sculptor
Pow·ha·tan \,paú-ə-'tan, paú-'hat-ᵊn\ 1550?–1618 *Wa-hun-sen-a-cawh or Wahunsonacock; father of Pocahontas* Am. Indian chief
Pow·ys \'pō-əs\ John Cow·per \'kü-pər\ 1872–1963 & his bros. Theodore Francis 1875–1953 & Llewelyn 1884–1939 Eng. authors
Pra·do Ugar·te·che \'präd-(,)ō-,ü-gär-'tä-chē\ Manuel 1889–1967 Peruvian banker; pres. of Peru (1939–45; 1956–62)
Pra·ji·di·pok \prä-'chät-i-,päk\ 1893–1941 king of Siam (1925–35)
Pratt \'prat\ Edwin John 1883–1964 Canad. poet
Prax·it·e·les \prak-'sit-ᵊl-,ēz\ *fl* 370–330 B.C. Athenian sculptor — Prax·it·e·le·an \(,)prak-,sit-ᵊl-'ē-ən\ *adj*
Pre·ble \'preb-əl\ Edward 1761–1807 Am. naval officer
Pregl \'prā-gəl\ Fritz 1869–1930 Austrian chem.
Pre·log \'prel-,ōg\ Vladimir 1906–   Swiss (Yugoslavian-born) chem.
Pres·cott \'pres-kət *also* -,kät\ William Hickling 1796–1859 Am. hist.
Pre·to·ri·us \pri-'tōr-ē-əs, -'tór-\ Andries Wilhelmus Jacobus 1798–1853 & his son Marthinus Wessels 1819–1901 So. African Du. colonizers & soldiers
Pré·vost d'Ex·iles \prā-'vō-,deg-'zē(ə)l\ Antoine-François 1697–1763 Fr. abbé & writer
Price \'prīs\ (Mary) Le·on·tyne \lē-'än-,tēn; 'lē-ən-,, 'lä-\ 1927–   Am. soprano
Pride \'prīd\ Thomas *d* 1658 Eng. parliamentary commander
Priest·ley \'prēst-lē\ John Boynton 1894–1984 Eng. author
Priestley Joseph 1733–1804 Eng. clergyman & chem.
Pri·go·gine \prə-'gō-zhən, -(,)gō-'zhēn\ Ilya 1917–   Belg. (Russ.-born) chem.
Pri·mo de Ri·ve·ra y Or·ba·ne·ja \'prē-(,)mō-thä-ri-'ver-ə-,ē-,ȯr-bə-'nä-(,)hä\ Miguel 1870–1930 Marqués *de Estella* Span. gen. & polit.
Primrose Archibald Philip — see ROSEBERY
Prior \'prī(-ə)r\ Matthew 1664–1721 Eng. poet
Pris·cian \'prish-ən, 'prish-ē-ən\ *fl* A.D. 500 *Priscianus Caesariensis* Latin grammarian at Constantinople
Pro·clus \'prō-kləs, 'präk-ləs\ 410?–485 Greek philos.
Pro·co·pi·us \prə-'kō-pē-əs\ 6th cent. Byzantine hist.
Pro·kho·rov \,prō-kə-'rȯf\ Aleksandr Mikhaylovich 1916–   Russ. physicist
Pro·kof·iev \prə-'kȯf-yəf, -,yef, -,yev\ Sergey Sergeyevich 1891–1953 Russ. composer — Pro·kof·iev·ian \-,kȯf-'yev-ē-ən\ *adj*
Pro·per·tius \prō-'pər-sh(ē-)əs\ Sextus *ca* 50–*ca* 15 B.C. Rom. poet
Pro·tag·o·ras \prō-'tag-ə-rəs\ *ca* 485–410 B.C. Greek philos. — Pro·tag·o·re·an \-,tag-ə-'rē-ən\ *adj*
Prou·dhon \prü-'dōⁿ\ Pierre-Joseph 1809–1865 Fr. journalist
Proust \'prüst\ Marcel 1871–1922 Fr. nov. — Proust·ian \'prü-stē-ən\ *adj*
Prynne \'prin\ William 1600–1669 Eng. Puritan pamphleteer
Przhe·val·sky \,pər-zhə-'väl-skē, ,(p)shə-'väl-\ Nikolay Mikhaylovich 1839–1888 Russ. explorer
Ptol·e·my \'täl-ə-mē\ name of 15 kings of Egypt 323–30 B.C.
Ptolemy 2d cent. A.D. *Claudius Ptolemaeus* Alexandrian astron.
Puc·ci·ni \pü-'chē-nē\ Giacomo 1858–1924 Ital. composer

P'u–i \'pü-'ē\ Henry 1906–1967 *Hsüan-T'ung* Chin. emp. (1908–12); last of Manchu dynasty; puppet emp. of Manchukuo (1934–45)
Pu·las·ki \pə-'las-kē, pyü-\ Kazimierz 1747–1779 Pol. soldier in Am. Revolution
Pu·lit·zer \'púl-ət-sər (*family's pron.*), 'pyü-lət-\ Joseph 1847–1911 Am. (Hung.-born) journalist
Pull·man \'púl-mən\ George Mortimer 1831–1897 Am. inventor
Pu·pin \p(y)ü-'pēn\ Michael Idvorsky 1858–1935 Am. (Yugoslavian-born) physicist & inventor
Pur·cell \(,)pər-'sel\ Edward Mills 1912–   Am. physicist
Pur·cell \'pər-səl, (,)pər-'sel\ Henry *ca* 1659–1695 Eng. composer
Pur·chas \'pər-chəs\ Samuel *ca* 1577–1626 Eng. compiler of travel books
Pur·ky·ně *or* Pur·kin·je \'púr-kən-,yā, (,)pər-'kin-jē\ Jan Evangelista 1787–1869 Bohemian physiol.
Pu·sey \'pyü-zē\ Edward Bouverie 1800–1882 Eng. theol.
Push·kin \'púsh-kən\ Aleksandr Sergeyevich 1799–1837 Russ. poet — Push·kin·ian \,púsh-'kin-ē-ən\ *adj*
Put·nam \'pət-nəm\ Israel 1718–1790 Am. gen. in Revolution
Putnam Rufus 1738–1824 *cousin of prec.* Am. gen. in Revolution
Pu·vis de Cha·vannes \pǖ-,vē-də-shä-,vän, -,vēs-; pyü-,vē(s)-də-shä-'vän\ Pierre-Cécile 1824–1898 Fr. painter & muralist
Pye \'pī\ Henry James 1745–1813 Eng. poet laureate (1790–1813)
Pyle \'pi(ə)l\ Ernest Taylor 1900–1945 *Ernie* Am. journalist
Pym \'pim\ John 1584–1643 Eng. statesman
Pyr·rhus \'pir-əs\ 319–272 B.C. king of Epirus (306–302; 297–272 B.C.)
Py·thag·o·ras \pə-'thag-ə-rəs, pī-\ *ca* 580–*ca* 500 B.C. Greek philos. & math.
Qad·da·fi \kə-'däf-ē\ Mu'ammar Muḥammad al- 1942–   Libyan leader (1969–   )
Qua·dros \'kwäd-,rōs\ Jânio da Silva 1917–   pres. of Brazil (1960–61)
Quarles \'kwȯr(ə)lz, 'kwär(ə)lz\ Francis 1592–1644 Eng. poet
Qua·si·mo·do \kwä-'zē-mə-,dō\ Salvatore \,säl-vä-'tō-(,)rä\ 1901–1968 Ital. poet & critic
Quayle \'kwā(ə)l\ James Danforth 1947–   *Dan* Am. polit.; vice pres. of the U.S. (1989–   )
Queensberry Marquis of — see DOUGLAS
Quercia, della Jacopo — see JACOPO DELLA QUERCIA
Ques·nay \kā-'nä\ François 1694–1774 Fr. physician & econ.
Que·zon y Mo·li·na \'kā-,sò-,nē-mə-'lē-nə\ Manuel Luis 1878–1944 pres. of the Philippine Commonwealth (1935–44)
Quid·de \'kfid-ə, 'kwid-\ Ludwig 1858–1941 Ger. hist. & pacifist
Quil·ler–Couch \'kwil-ər-,küch\ Sir Arthur Thomas 1863–1944 pseud. *Q* Eng. author
Quin·cy \'kwin-zē, 'kwin(t)-sē\ Josiah 1744–1775 Am. lawyer
Quine \'kwīn\ Willard Van Orman 1908–   Am. philos.
Quintero Serafín & Joaquín — see ALVAREZ QUINTERO
Quin·til·ian \kwin-'til-yən\ *ca* A.D. 35–*ca* 100 *Marcus Fabius Quintilianus* Rom. rhetorician
Qui·ri·no \ki-'rē-(,)nō\ Elpidio 1890–1956 pres. of the Philippine Republic (1948–53)
Quoirez Françoise — see Françoise SAGAN
Ra·be·lais \'rab-ə-,lā, ,rab-ə-'lā\ François *ca* 1483–1553 Fr. humorist & satirist
Ra·bi \'räb-ē\ Isidor Isaac 1898–1988 Am. (Austrian-born) physicist
Ra·bin \'rä-'bēn\ Yitzhak 1922–   prime min. of Israel (1974–77)
Rabinowitz Solomon — see Shalom ALEICHEM
Rach·ma·ni·noff \räk-'män-ə-,nȯf\ Sergey Vasilyevich 1873–1943 Russ. composer, pianist, & conductor
Ra·cine \ra-'sēn, rə-\ Jean 1639–1699 Fr. dram.
Rack·ham \'rak-əm\ Arthur 1867–1939 Brit. illustrator
Rad·cliffe \'rad-,klif\ Ann 1764–1823 née *Ward* Eng. nov.
Ra·detz·ky \rə-'det-skē\ Joseph 1766–1858 Graf *Radetzky von Radetz* Austrian field marshal
Rae \'rā\ John 1813–1893 Scot. explorer
Rae·burn \'rä-(,)bərn\ Sir Henry 1756–1823 Scot. painter
Rae·der \'räd-ər\ Erich 1876–1960 Ger. admiral
Rae·mae·kers \'räm-,äk-ərz, -ərs\ Louis 1869–1956 Du. cartoonist
Raf·san·ja·ni \,räf-sän-jä-nē\ Ali Akbar Hashemi 1934–   pres. of Iran (1989–   )
Rag·lan \'rag-lən\ 1st Baron 1788–1855 *FitzRoy James Henry Somerset* Brit. field marshal
Rai·mon·di \rī-'män-dē, -'mōn-\ Marcantonio *ca* 1480–*ca* 1534 Ital. engraver
Rain·wa·ter \'rän-,wȯt-ər, -,wät-\ L(eo) James 1917–1986 Am. physicist
Ra·ja·go·pa·la·cha·ri \'räj-ə-(,)gō-,päl-ə-'chär-ē\ Chakravarti 1879–1972 Indian polit.; gov.-gen. of India (1948–50)
Ra·kow·ski \rä-'kȯf-skē\ Mieczysław Franciszek 1926–   1st secy. of the communist party in Poland (1989–   )
Ra·leigh *or* Ra·legh \'rȯl-ē, 'ral- *also* 'ral-\ Sir Walter 1554–1618 Eng. courtier, navigator, & hist.
Ral·lis \'räl-(,)ēs\ George 1918–   prime min. of Greece (1980–81)
Ra·ma·krish·na \,räm-ə-'krish-nə\ 1836–1886 Hindu religious
Ra·man \'räm-ən\ Sir Chan·dra·se·kha·ra \,chən-drə-'shä-kə-rə\ Venkata 1888–1970 Indian physicist
Ra·meau \ra-'mō\ Jean-Philippe 1683–1764 Fr. composer
Ra·mée \rə-'mā\ Marie Louise de la 1839–1908 pseud. *Oui·da* \'wēd-ə\ Eng. nov.
Ra·món y Ca·jal \rə-,mōn-(,)ē-kə-'häl\ Santiago 1852–1934 Span. histologist
Ram·say \'ram-zē\ Allan 1686–1758 Scot. poet
Ramsay James Andrew Broun 1812–1860 10th Earl & 1st Marquis of *Dal·hou·sie* \dal-'haú-zē\ Brit. colonial administrator
Ramsay Sir William 1852–1916 Brit. chem.
Ram·ses \'ram-,sēz\ *or* Ram·e·ses \'ram-ə-,sēz\ name of 11 kings of Egypt: esp. **II** (reigned 1304–1237 B.C.); **III** (reigned 1198–1166 B.C.)

\ə\ abut	\ᵊ\ kitten, F table	\ər\ further	\a\ ash	\ā\ ace	\ä\ cot, cart
\aú\ out	\ch\ chin	\e\ bet	\ē\ easy	\g\ go	\i\ hit	\ī\ ice	\j\ job
\ŋ\ sing	\ō\ go	\ȯ\ law	\ȯi\ boy	\th\ thin	\t̲h̲\ the	\ü\ loot	\ú\ foot
\y\ yet	\zh\ vision	\à, ᵏ, ⁿ, œ, œ̄, ū̆, ᵘ̈, ᵞ\ see Guide to Pronunciation			

Ram·sey \\'ram-zē\\ (Arthur) Michael 1904–1988 archbishop of Canterbury (1961–74)
Ramsey Norman Foster 1915–   Am. physicist
Rand \\'rand\\ Ayn \\'īn\\ 1905–1982 Am. (Russ.-born) writer
Ran·dolph \\'ran-,dälf\\ Asa Philip 1889–1979 Am. labor leader
Randolph Edmund Jennings 1753–1813 Am. statesman
Randolph John 1773–1833 *John Randolph of Roanoke* Am. statesman
Ra·nier III \\rə-'ni(ə)r, ra-\\ 1923–   prince of Monaco (1949–)
Ran·jit Singh \\,rən-jət-'siŋ\\ 1780–1839 *Lion of the Punjab* founder of Sikh kingdom
Ran·ke \\'räŋ-kə\\ Leopold von 1795–1886 Ger. hist.
Ran·som \\'ran(t)-səm\\ John Crowe 1888–1974 Am. educ. & poet
Ra·pha·el \\'raf-ē-əl, 'rä-fē-, 'räf-ē-\\ 1483–1520 It. *Raffaello Sanzio* Ital. painter — **Ra·pha·el·esque** \\,raf-ē-ə-'lesk, ,rä-fē-, ,räf-ē-\\ adj
Rask \\'rask, 'räsk\\ Rasmus Kristian 1787–1832 Dan. philologist & orientalist
Ras·mus·sen \\'ras-mə-sən, 'räs-,mùs-ᵊn\\ Knud Johan Victor 1879–1933 Dan. explorer & ethnologist
Ras·pu·tin \\ra-'sp(y)üt-ᵊn, -'spùt-\\ Grigory Yefimovich 1872–1916 Russ. mystic
Ra·the·nau \\'rät-ᵊn-,aù, 'rath-ən-\\ Emil 1838–1915 Ger. industrialist
Rausch·en·berg \\'raù-shən-,berg\\ Robert 1925–   Am. artist
Ra·vel \\rə-'vel, ra-\\ Mau·rice \\mò-'rēs\\ Joseph 1875–1937 Fr. composer
Raw·lin·son \\'rò-lən-sən\\ Sir Henry Cres·wicke \\'krez-ik\\ 1810–1895 Eng. orientalist
Ray \\'rā\\ John 1627–1705 Eng. naturalist
Ray·burn \\'rā-,bərn\\ Samuel Taliaferro 1882–1961 Am. polit.
Ray·leigh \\'rā-lē\\ Lord 1842–1919 *John William Strutt* Eng. math. & physicist
Read \\'rēd\\ George 1733–1798 Am. lawyer & revolutionary
Read Sir Herbert 1893–1968 Eng. writer
Reade \\'rēd\\ Charles 1814–1884 Eng. nov. & dram.
Read·ing \\'red-iŋ\\ 1st Marquis of 1860–1935 *Rufus Daniel Isaacs* Brit. statesman; viceroy of India (1921–26)
Rea·gan \\'rā-gən\\ Ronald Wilson 1911–   Am. actor & polit.; 40th pres. of the U.S. (1981–89)
Ré·au·mur \\,rā-ō-'myù(ə)r; rā-'ō-mər, -,myù(ə)r\\ René-Antoine Ferchault de 1683–1757 Fr. naturalist & physicist
Ré·ca·mi·er \\rā-'kam-ē-,ā, rā-kà-myä\\ Jeanne-Françoise-Julie-Adélaïde 1777–1849 Fr. society wit
Red Cloud \\'red-,klaùd\\ 1822–1909 Sioux Indian chief
Red·mond \\'red-mənd\\ John Edward 1856–1918 Irish polit.
Re·don \\rə-'dōⁿ\\ Odilon 1840–1916 Fr. artist
Reed \\'rēd\\ John 1887–1920 Am. journalist, poet, & Communist
Reed Stanley Forman 1884–1980 Am. jurist
Reed Thomas Brackett 1839–1902 Am. polit.
Reed Walter 1851–1902 Am. army surgeon
Re·gan \\'rē-gən\\ Donald Thomas 1918–   U.S. secy. of the treasury (1981–85)
Reg·u·lus \\'reg-yə-ləs\\ Marcus Atilius d ca 250 B.C. Rom. gen.
Rehn·quist \\'ren-,kwist\\ William Hubbs 1924–   Am. jurist; chief justice U.S. Supreme Court (1986–)
Reich·stein \\'rīk-,s(h)tīn\\ Tadeus 1897–   Swiss (Pol.-born) chem.
Reid \\'rēd\\ Thomas 1710–1796 Scot. philos.
Reid Whitelaw 1837–1912 Am. journalist & diplomat
Rei·ner \\'rī-nər\\ Fritz 1888–1963 Am. (Hung.-born) conductor
Rein·hardt \\'rīn-,härt\\ Max 1873–1943 orig. surname *Goldmann* Austrian theater director
Re·marque \\rə-'märk\\ Erich Maria 1898–1970 Am. (Ger.-born) nov.
Rem·brandt \\'rem-,brant also -,bränt\\ 1606–1669 in full *Rembrandt Harmensz (or Harmenszoon) van Rijn (or Ryn)* Du. painter — **Rem·brandt·esque** \\,rem-,brant-'esk, -,bränt-\\ adj
Rem·ing·ton \\'rem-iŋ-tən\\ Frederic 1861–1909 Am. artist
Rem·sen \\'rem(p)-sən, 'rem-zən\\ Ira 1846–1927 Am. chem.
Re·nan \\rə-'näⁿ(n)\\ Joseph Ernest 1823–1892 Fr. philologist & hist.
Re·nault \\rə-'nō\\ Louis 1843–1918 Fr. jurist & pacifist
Re·ni \\'rā-nē\\ Guido 1575–1642 Ital. painter
Ren·ner \\'ren-ər\\ Karl 1870–1950 pres. of Austria (1945–50)
Re·noir \\'ren-,wär, rən-'\\ Jean 1894–1979 *son of P.-A.* Fr. film director & writer
Renoir Pierre-Auguste 1841–1919 Fr. painter
Ren·wick \\'ren-(,)wik\\ James 1818–1895 Am. architect
Rep·plier \\'rep-,li(ə)r, -lē-ər\\ Agnes 1855–1950 Am. essayist
Re·spi·ghi \\rā-'spē-gē, re-\\ Ottorino 1879–1936 Ital. composer
Res·ton \\'res-tən\\ James Barrett 1909–   Am. journalist
Retz \\'rets, Fr re(s)\\ Cardinal de 1613–1679 *Jean-François-Paul de Gondi* Fr. ecclesiastic & polit.
Reuch·lin \\'ròik-lən; 'ròi-klēn, ròi-'\\ Johannes 1455–1522 *Cap·nio* \\'kap-nē-,ō\\ Ger. humanist
Reu·ter \\'ròit-ər\\ Baron Paul Julius von 1816–1899 orig. *Israel Beer Josaphat* Brit. (Ger.-born) journalist
Reu·ther \\'rü-thər\\ Walter Philip 1907–1970 Am. labor leader
Re·vere \\ri-'vi(ə)r\\ Paul 1735–1818 Am. patriot & silversmith
Rex·roth \\'reks-,ròth\\ Kenneth 1905–1982 Am. writer
Rey·mont \\'rā-,mänt\\ or **Rej·ment** \\'rā-,ment\\ Władysław \\vlä-'dis-,läf\\ Sta·ni·sław \\stä-nē-,släf\\ 1867–1925 Pol. nov.
Rey·naud \\rā-'nō\\ Paul 1878–1966 premier of France (1940)
Reyn·olds \\'ren-ᵊl(d)z\\ Sir Joshua 1723–1792 Eng. painter
Re·za Shah Pah·la·vi \\ri-'zä-'shä-'pal-ə-(,)vē, -'shò-\\ 1878–1944 *father of Mohammed Reza Pahlavi* shah of Iran (1925–41)
Rhee \\'rē\\ Syng·man \\'siŋ-mən, 'sig-\\ 1875–1965 So. Korean polit.; pres. of So. Korea (1948–60)
Rhodes \\'rōdz\\ Cecil John 1853–1902 Brit. administrator & financier in So. Africa
Rhond·da \\'rän-də, -thə\\ 1st Viscount 1856–1918 *David Alfred Thomas* Brit. industrialist & administrator
Rib·ben·trop \\'rib-ən-,träp, -,tròp\\ Joachim von 1893–1946 Ger. diplomat
Ri·be·ra \\ri-'ber-ə\\ José (or Jusepe) de 1588–1652 *Lo Spa·gno·let·to* \\,lō-,spän-yə-'let-(,)ō\\ Span. painter & etcher in Italy
Ri·car·do \\rik-'ärd-(,)ō\\ David 1772–1823 Eng. econ.
Rice \\'rīs\\ Elmer Leopold 1892–1967 orig. *Elmer Reizenstein* Am. dram.

Rich·ard \\'rich-ərd\\ name of 3 kings of England: **I** (*Coeur de Li·on* \\,kərd-ᵊl-'ī-ən, -'ē-ən, -ē-'ōⁿ\\) 1157–1199 (reigned 1189–99); **II** 1367–1400 (reigned 1377–99); **III** 1452–1485 (reigned 1483–85)
Rich·ards \\'rich-ərdz\\ Dickinson Woodruff 1895–1973 Am. physician
Richards Theodore William 1868–1928 Am. chem.
Rich·ard·son \\'rich-ərd-sən\\ Henry Handel 1870–1946 pseud. of *Ethel Florence Lindesay Richardson* Austral. nov.
Richardson Henry Hobson 1838–1886 Am. architect
Richardson Sir Owen Willans 1879–1959 Eng. physicist
Richardson Sir Ralph David 1902–1983 Brit. actor
Richardson Samuel 1689–1761 Eng. nov.
Ri·che·lieu \\'rish-əl-,(y)ü, rē-shə-lyœ̄\\ Duc de 1585–1642 *Armand-Jean du Plessis* Fr. cardinal & statesman
Ri·chet \\rē-'shā\\ Charles Robert 1850–1935 Fr. physiol.
Rich·ter \\'rik-tər\\ Burton 1931–   Am. physicist
Richter Charles Francis 1900–1985 Am. seismologist
Rich·ter \\'rik-tər, 'rik-\\ Jean Paul Friedrich 1763–1825 pseud. *Jean Paul* \\'zhäⁿ-'paù(ə)l, 'jēn-'pòl\\ Ger. writer
Ric·i·mer \\'ris-ə-mər\\ Flavius d 472 Rom. gen.
Rick·en·back·er \\'rik-ən-,bak-ər\\ Edward Vernon 1890–1973 Am. aviator
Rick·o·ver \\'rik-,ō-vər\\ Hyman George 1900–1986 Am. admiral
Rid·ley \\'rid-lē\\ Nicholas ca 1503–1555 Eng. reformer & martyr
Ri·el \\rē-'el\\ Louis 1844–1885 Canad. insurgent
Rie·mann \\'rē-,män\\ Georg Friedrich Bernhard 1826–1866 Ger. math. — **Rie·mann·ian** \\rē-'män-ē-ən\\ adj
Rien·zo \\'ryent-sō\\ Cola di 1313–1354 prename *Niccolò* Ital. leader
Ries·man \\'rēs-mən\\ David 1909–   Am. social scientist
Riis \\'rēs\\ Jacob August 1849–1914 Am. (Dan.-born) social reformer & writer
Ri·ley \\'rī-lē\\ James Whit·comb \\'hwit-kəm, 'wit-\\ 1849–1916 Am. poet
Ril·ke \\'ril-kə, -kē\\ Rai·ner \\'rī-nər\\ Maria 1875–1926 Ger. poet
Rim·baud \\raⁿ(m)-'bō, 'ram-,\\ (Jean-Nicholas-) Arthur 1854–1891 Fr. poet
Rimini Francesca da — see POLENTA
Rim·sky–Kor·sa·kov \\,rim(p)-skē-'kòr-sə-,kòf, -,kòv, -,kòr-sə-'\\ Nikolay Andreyevich 1844–1908 Russ. composer
Rine·hart \\'rīn-,härt\\ Mary 1876–1958 née *Roberts* Am. writer
Ri·os \\'rē-,ōs\\ Juan Antonio 1888–1946 pres. of Chile (1942–46)
Rip·ley \\'rip-lē\\ George 1802–1880 Am. lit. critic & socialist
Ri·ve·ra \\ri-'ver-ə\\ Diego 1886–1957 Mex. painter
Riv·ers \\'riv-ərz\\ Larry 1923–   Am. artist
Ri·zal \\ri-'zäl, -'säl\\ José Protasio 1861–1896 Filipino patriot
Riza Shah Pahlavi *var of* REZA SHAH PAHLAVI
Riz·zio \\'rit-sē-,ō\\ *or* **Ric·cio** \\'rich-ē-,ō\\ David ca 1533–1566 Ital. musician & favorite of Mary, Queen of Scots
Robbe–Gril·let \\,rò-bə-grē-'yā\\ Alain 1922–   Fr. writer
Robbia, della Luca — see DELLA ROBBIA
Rob·bins \\'räb-ənz\\ Frederick Chapman 1916–   Am. physician
Robbins Jerome 1918–   Am. dancer & choreographer
Robert I \\'räb-ərt\\ d 1035 *the Devil* Duke of Normandy (1027–35) *father of William the Conqueror*
Robert I 1274–1329 *the Bruce* \\'brüs\\ king of Scotland (1306–1329)
Robert Guis·card \\-gē-'skär\\ ca 1015–1085 *Robert de Hauteville* Norman mil. leader
Rob·erts \\'räb-ərts\\ Sir Charles George Douglas 1860–1943 Canad. poet
Roberts Frederick Sleigh 1832–1914 1st Earl *Roberts* Brit. field marshal
Roberts Kenneth 1885–1957 Am. nov.
Roberts Owen Josephus 1875–1955 Am. jurist
Rob·ert·son \\'räb-ərt-sən\\ William 1721–1793 Scot. hist.
Robe·son \\'rōb-sən\\ Paul Bustill 1898–1976 Am. actor & singer
Robes·pierre \\'rōbz-,pi(ə)r, -,pye(ə)r; ,rō-,bes-'pye(ə)r\\ Maximilien-François-Marie-Isidore de 1758–1794 Fr. revolutionary
Rob·in·son \\'räb-ən-sən\\ Edwin Arlington 1869–1935 Am. poet
Robinson George Frederick Samuel 1827–1909 1st Marquis & 2d Earl of *Ripon* Brit. statesman
Robinson James Harvey 1863–1936 Am. hist.
Robinson Sir Robert 1886–1975 Eng. chem.
Ro·card \\,rò-'cár\\ Michel-Louis-Léon 1930–   prime min. of France (1988–)
Ro·cham·beau \\,rō-,sham-'bō\\ Comte de 1725–1807 *Jean-Baptiste- Donatien de Vimeur* Fr. gen.
Rocke·fel·ler \\'räk-i-,fel-ər, 'räk-,fel-\\ John Davison father 1839–1937 & son 1874–1960 Am. oil magnates & philanthropists
Rockefeller Nelson Aldrich 1908–1979 *grandson & son of prec.* Am. polit.; vice pres. of the U.S. (1974–77)
Rock·ing·ham \\'räk-iŋ-əm, US also -iŋ-,ham\\ 2d Marquis of 1730–1782 *Charles Watson-Wentworth* Eng. statesman
Rock·ne \\'räk-nē\\ Knute \\'nüt\\ Kenneth 1888–1931 Am. (Norw.-born) football coach
Rock·well \\'räk-,wel, -wəl\\ Norman 1894–1978 Am. illustrator
Ro·de \\'rō-thə\\ Hel·ge \\'hel-gə\\ 1870–1937 Dan. poet
Rod·gers \\'räj-ərz\\ Richard 1902–1979 Am. composer
Ro·din \\rō-'daⁿ(n)\\ (François-)Auguste(-René) 1840–1917 Fr. sculptor
Rod·ney \\'räd-nē\\ George Bryd·ges \\'brij-əz\\ 1718–1792 1st Baron *Rodney* Eng. admiral
Ro·dri·guez Pe·dot·ti \\ròth-'rē-gäs-pā-'dòt-tē\\ Andrés 1923–   pres. of Paraguay (1989–)
Roeb·ling \\'rō-bliŋ\\ John Augustus 1806–1869 Am. (Ger.-born) civil engineer
Roentgen — see RÖNTGEN
Roe·rich \\'rər-ik, 're(ə)r-\\ Nikolay Konstantinovich 1874–1947 Russ. painter
Roeth·ke \\'ret(h)-kē\\ Theodore 1908–1963 Am. poet
Rog·ers \\'räj-ərz\\ Bruce 1870–1957 Am. printer & book designer
Rogers Carl Ranson 1902–1987 Am. psychol.
Rogers Henry Hut·tle·ston \\'hət-ᵊl-stən\\ 1840–1909 Am. financier
Rogers Robert 1731–1795 Am. frontiersman
Rogers William Penn Adair 1879–1935 *Will* Am. actor & humorist
Ro·get \\rō-'zhā, 'rō-,\\ Peter Mark 1779–1869 Eng. physician & scholar
Rohr·er \\'ròr-ər\\ Heinrich 1933–   Swiss physicist
Roh Tae Woo \\'rō-'tā-'ü\\ 1932–   pres. of So. Korea (1988–)

Ro·kos·sov·sky \,räk-ə-'sȯf-skē, -'sȯv-\ Konstantin Konstantinovich 1896–1968 marshal of Soviet Union
Rolfe \'rälf\ John 1585–1622 Eng. colonist
Rol·land \rȯ-'läⁿ, rȯ-\ Romain 1866–1944 Fr. author
Röl·vaag \'rȯl-,väg\ Ole \'ō-lə\ Ed·vart \'ed-,värt\ 1876–1931 Am. (Norw.-born) educ. & nov.
Ro·mains \rō-'maⁿ\ Jules 1885–1972 pseud. of *Louis-Henri-Jean Farigoule* Fr. author
Romano Giulio — see GIULIO ROMANO
Ro·ma·nov *or* **Ro·ma·noff** \rō-'män-əf, 'rō-mə-,näf\ Michael 1596–1645 1st czar (1613–45) of Russ. Romanov dynasty (1613–1917)
Rom·berg \'räm-,bərg\ Sigmund 1887–1951 Am. (Hung.-born) composer
Rom·mel \'räm-əl\ Erwin Johannes Eugen 1891–1944 Ger. field marshal
Rom·ney \'räm-nē, 'rəm-\ George 1734–1802 Eng. painter
Ron·sard \rōⁿ-'sär\ Pierre de 1524–1585 Fr. poet
Rönt·gen *or* **Roent·gen** \'rent-gən, 'rənt-, -jən; 'ren-chən, 'rən-\ Wilhelm Conrad 1845–1923 Ger. physicist
Roo·se·velt \'rō-zə-,velt (*Roosevelts' usual pron.*), -,velt *also* 'rü-\ (Anna) Eleanor 1884–1962 née *Roosevelt, wife of F.D.* Am. humanitarian & writer
Roosevelt Franklin Del·a·no \'del-ə-,nō\ 1882–1945 32d pres. of the U.S. (1933–45) — **Roo·se·velt·ian** \,rō-zə-'vel-tē-ən, -sh(ē-)ən\ *adj*
Roosevelt Theodore 1858–1919 26th pres. of the U.S. (1901–09)
Root \'rüt, 'rut\ Elihu 1845–1937 Am. lawyer & statesman
Ro·rem \'rōr-əm, 'rȯr-\ Ned 1923– Am. composer
Ro·sa \'rō-zə\ Salvator 1615–1673 Ital. painter & poet
Rose·bery \'rōz-,ber-ē, -b(ə-)rē\ 5th Earl of 1847–1929 *Archibald Philip Primrose* Eng. statesman
Rose·crans \'rō-zə-,kranz, 'rōz-,kran(t)s\ William Starke 1819–1898 Am. gen.
Ro·sen·berg \'rōz-əⁿ-,bərg, -,be(ə)rg\ Alfred 1893–1946 Ger. Nazi & writer
Ro·sen·wald \'rōz-əⁿ-,wȯld\ Julius 1862–1932 Am. merchant & philanthropist
Ross \'rȯs\ Betsy 1752–1836 née *Griscom* reputed maker of 1st Am. flag
Ross Sir James Clark 1800–1862 Scot. explorer
Ross Sir John 1777–1856 *uncle of prec.* Scot. explorer
Ross Sir Ronald 1857–1932 Brit. physician
Rosse Earl of — see William PARSONS
Ros·set·ti \rō-'zet-ē, -'set-\ Christina Georgina 1830–1894 *sister of D.G.* Eng. poet
Rossetti Dante Gabriel 1828–1882 Eng. painter & poet
Ros·si \'rȯs-ē\ Bruno 1905– Am. (Ital.-born) physicist
Ros·si·ni \rȯ-'sē-nē, rə-\ Gio·ac·chi·no \,jō-ə-'kē-(,)nō\ Antonio 1792–1868 Ital. composer
Ros·tand \rȯ-stäⁿ, 'räs-,tand\ Edmond 1868–1918 Fr. poet & dram.
Roth \'rȯth\ Philip 1933– Am. writer
Roth·ko \'räth-(,)kō\ Mark 1903–1970 Am. (Russ.-born) painter
Roth·schild \'rȯth(s)-,chīld, 'rȯs-, G 'rōt-,shilt\ Mayer Amschel 1744–1812 Ger. financier
Rothschild Nathan Mayer 1777–1836 *son of prec.* financier in London
Rou·ault \rü-'ō\ Georges 1871–1958 Fr. painter
Rou·get de Lisle \(,)rü-,zhä-də-'lē(ə)l\ Claude-Joseph 1760–1836 Fr. army officer & composer
Rous \'raus\ Francis Peyton 1879–1970 Am. pathologist
Rous·seau \rü-'sō, 'rü-,\ Henri-Julien-Félix 1844–1910 *le Douanier* Fr. painter
Rousseau Jean-Jacques 1712–1778 Fr. (Swiss-born) philos. & writer
Rousseau (Pierre-Étienne-) Théodore 1812–1867 Fr. painter
Rowe \'rō\ Nicholas 1674–1718 Eng. poet & dram.; poet laureate (1715–18)
Row·land·son \'rō-lən(d)-sən\ Thomas 1756–1827 Eng. caricaturist
Row·ley \'rō-lē, 'rau\ William 1585?–?1642 Eng. actor & dram.
Rox·as y Acu·ña \'rō-,häs-,ē-ə-'kün-yə\ Manuel 1892–1948 Philippine statesman; pres. of the Philippine Republic (1946–48)
Roy·all \'rȯi(-ə)l\ Kenneth Claiborne 1894–1971 Am. statesman
Royce \'rȯis\ Josiah 1855–1916 Am. philos.
Rub·bia \'rü-bē-ə\ Carlo 1934– Ital. physicist
Ru·bens \'rü-bənz\ Peter Paul 1577–1640 Flem. painter — **Ru·ben·esque** \,rü-bə-'nesk\ *adj* — **Ru·ben·si·an** \rü-'ben-zē-ən\ *adj*
Ru·bin·stein \'rü-bən-,stīn\ An·ton \än-'tȯn\ 1829–1894 Russ. pianist & composer
Rubinstein Arthur 1887–1982 Am. (Pol.-born) pianist
Rud·olf \'rü-,dälf\ 1858–1889 archduke & crown prince of Austria
Rudolf I 1218–1291 Holy Rom. emp. (1273–91); 1st of the Hapsburgs
Ruis·dael *or* **Ruys·dael** \'rīz-,däl, 'rīs-\ Jacob van 1628(or 1629)–1682 & his uncle Salomon van *ca* 1602–1670 Du. painters
Rumford Count — see Benjamin THOMPSON
Run·cie \'rən(t)-sē\ Robert Alexander Kennedy 1921– archbishop of Canterbury (1980–)
Rund·stedt \'run(t)-,s(h)tet\ Karl Rudolf Gerd von 1875–1953 Ger. field marshal
Ru·ne·berg \'rü-nə-,berg, -,ber-ē\ Johan Ludvig 1804–1877 Finn. poet
Run·yon \'rən-yən\ (Alfred) Da·mon \'dā-mən\ 1884–1946 Am. author — **Run·yon·esque** \,rən-yə-'nesk\ *adj*
Ru·pert \'rü-pərt\ Prince 1619–1682 Count *Palatine of Rhine* & Duke of *Bavaria* Ger.-Eng. gen. & admiral
Rush \'rəsh\ Benjamin 1745–1813 Am. physician & Revolutionary patriot
Rush Richard 1780–1859 *son of prec.* Am. diplomat & statesman
Rusk \'rəsk\ (David) Dean 1909– U.S. secy. of state (1961–69)
Rus·ka \'rus-kə\ Ernst August Friedrich 1906–1988 Ger. physicist
Rus·kin \'rəs-kən\ John 1819–1900 Eng. essayist, critic, & reformer — **Rus·kin·ian** \,rəs-'kin-ē-ən\ *adj*
Rus·sell \'rəs-əl\ Bertrand Arthur William 1872–1970 3d Earl *Russell* Eng. math. & philos.
Russell Charles Taze 1852–1916 Am. religious leader
Russell George William 1867–1935 pseud. Æ \'ā-,ē\ Irish author
Russell John 1792–1878 1st Earl *Russell of Kingston Russell* Brit. statesman
Russell Lillian 1861–1922 *Helen Louise Leonard* Am. singer & actress
Rus·tin \'rəs-tən\ Bayard 1910–1987 Am. civil rights leader

Ruth \'rüth\ George Herman 1895–1948 *Babe* Am. baseball player
Ruth·er·ford \'rəth-ə(r)-fərd, 'rəth-\ Ernest 1871–1937 1st Baron *Rutherford of Nelson* Brit. physicist
Rutherford Joseph Franklin 1869–1942 Am. leader of Jehovah's Witnesses
Rut·ledge \'rət-lij\ John 1739–1800 Am. statesman & jurist; chief justice U.S. Supreme Court (1795)
Rutledge Wiley Blount \'blənt\ 1894–1949 Am. jurist
Ru·žič·ka \'rü-,z(h)ich-kə, -,zhits-\ Leopold 1887–1976 Yugoslav chem.
Ry·der \'rīd-ər\ Albert Pinkham 1847–1917 Am. painter
Rydz-Śmig·ły \'rits-'shmēg-lē\ Edward 1886–1941 Pol. gen.
Ryle \'rī(ə)l\ Sir Martin 1918–1984 Brit. astron.

Saa·ri·nen \'sär-ə-nən\ Ee·ro \'e(ə)r-(,)ō\ 1910–1961 Am. architect
Saarinen (Gottlieb) Eliel 1873–1950 *father of prec.* Finn. architect
Saa·ve·dra La·mas \sä-,väd-rə-'läm-əs, -,vǟth-\ Carlos 1878–1959 Argentine lawyer & diplomat
Sa·ba·tier \,sab-ə-'tyā\ Paul 1854–1941 Fr. chem.
Sa·ba·ti·ni \,sab-ə-'tē-nē, ,säb-\ Rafael 1875–1950 Eng. (Ital.-born) author
Sa·bin \'sā-bin\ Albert Bruce 1906– Am. physician
Sac·a·ga·wea *also* **Sac·a·ja·wea** \,sak-ə-jə-'wē-ə\ 1786?–1812 Am. Indian guide
Sac·co \'sak-(,)ō\ Nicola 1891–1927 & **Van·zet·ti** \van-'zet-ē\ Bartolomeo 1888–1927 Am. (Ital.-born) anarchists
Sachs \'zäks, 'saks\ Hans 1494–1576 Ger. poet & Meistersinger
Sachs \'saks, 'zäks\ Nelly 1891–1970 Swed. (Ger.-born) dram. & poet
Sack·ville \'sak-,vil\ Thomas 1536–1608 1st Earl of *Dorset* Eng. poet & diplomat
Sackville–West \-'west\ Victoria Mary 1892–1962 Brit. writer
Sa·dat \sə-'dat, -'dät\ Anwar as- 1918–1981 pres. of Egypt (1970–81)
Sade, de \'säd\ Comte Donatien-Alphonse-François 1740–1814 Marquis *de Sade* Fr. soldier & pervert
Sa·gan \sä-'gäⁿ\ Françoise 1935– pseud. of *Françoise Quoirez* Fr.
Sage \'sāj\ Russell 1816–1906 Am. financier
St. Den·is \sänt-'den-əs, sənt-\ Ruth 1878–1968 Am. dancer
Sainte–Beuve \saⁿt-'bœv; säⁿt-'bə(r)v, sənt-\ Charles-Augustin 1804–1869 Fr. critic & author
Saint–Gau·dens \sänt-'gȯd-ᵊnz, sənt-\ Augustus 1848–1907 Am. (Irish-born) sculptor
St. John Henry — see BOLINGBROKE
Saint–Just \saⁿ-zhᵫst; sänt-'jəst, sənt-\ Louis-Antoine-Léon de 1767–1794 Fr. revolutionary
St. Lau·rent \saⁿ-lȯ-räⁿ\ Louis Stephen 1882–1973 Canad. polit.; prime min. (1948–57)
Saint–Pierre — see BERNARDIN DE SAINT-PIERRE
Saint–Saëns \saⁿ-säⁿs\ (Charles-) Camille 1835–1921 Fr. composer
Saints·bury \'sānts-,ber-ē, -b(ə-)rē\ George Edward Bateman 1845–1933 Eng. critic
Saint–Si·mon \saⁿ-sē-mōⁿ\ Claude-Henri de Rouvroy 1760–1825 Comte *de Saint-Simon* Fr. philos. & social scientist
Saint–Simon Louis de Rouvroy 1675–1755 Duc *de Saint-Simon* Fr. soldier, statesman, & writer
Sai·on·ji \sī-'än-jē, -'ȯn-\ Prince Kimmochi 1849–1940 Jp. statesman
Sa·kha·rov \'säk-ə-,rȯf, 'säk-, -,rȯv\ Andrey Dmitriyevich 1921–1989 Russ. physicist
Sa·ki \'säk-ē\ — see H. H. MUNRO
Sal·a·din \'sal-əd-ən\ 1137(or 1138)–1193 *Salāḥ Ad-dīn Yūsuf Ibn Ayyūb* Syrian commander & vizier in Egypt
Sa·lam \sä-'läm\ Abdus 1926– Pakistani physicist
Sa·la·zar \,sal-ə-'zär, ,säl-\ Antonio de Oliveira 1889–1970 Port. dictator (1932–68)
Sa·li·nas de Gor·ta·ri \sä-'lē-näs-thä-gȯr-'tä-rē\ Carlos 1948– pres. of Mexico (1988–)
Sal·in·ger \'sal-ən-jər\ Jerome David 1919– Am. nov.
Salisbury 1st Earl of & 3d Marquis of — see CECIL
Salk \'sȯ(l)k\ Jonas Edward 1914– Am. physician
Sal·lust \'sal-əst\ *ca* 86–35(or 34) B.C. *Gaius Sallustius Crispus* Rom. hist. & polit. — **Sal·lus·ti·an** \sə-'ləs-tē-ən, sa-\ *adj*
Sal·o·mon \'sal-ə-mən\ Haym 1740–1785 Am. (Pol.-born) merchant
Sam·u·el·son \'sam-yə(-wə)l-sən\ Paul Anthony 1915– Am. econ.
Sam·u·els·son \'sam-y(ə-w)əl-sən\ Bengt I. 1934– Swed. biochem.
Sánchez de Bustamante y Sirvén Antonio — see BUSTAMANTE Y SIRVÉN
Sand \'sand, 'säⁿ(n)d, säⁿ\ George 1804–1876 pseud. of *Amandine-Aurore-Lucie* (*or -Lucile*) *Dudevant* née *Dupin* Fr. writer
Sand·burg \'san(d)-,bərg\ Carl 1878–1967 Am. author
San·gal·lo \sän-'gäl-(,)ō, säŋ-\ Giuliano da 1445?–1516 Florentine architect & sculptor
Sang·er \'saŋ-ər\ Frederick 1918– Brit. chem.
Sanger Margaret 1883–1966 née *Higgins* Am. birth-control leader
San Mar·tín \,san-(,)mär-'tēn, ,sän-\ José de 1778–1850 So. Am. soldier & statesman
San·ta An·na \,sant-ə-'an-ə, ,sänt-ə-'än-ə\ Antonio López de 1794–1876 Mex. gen., revolutionary, & pres.
San·tan·der \,san-,tän-'de(ə)r, ,san-,tan-\ Francisco de Paula 1792–1840 Colombian gen. & polit.
San·ta·ya·na \,sant-ə-'yän-ə, ,sant-ē-'än-ə, ,sänt-\ George 1863–1952 Am. (Span.-born) philos. & poet
San·tos–Du·mont \,sant-əs-d(y)ü-'mänt, säⁿ-tōs-dᵫ-'mōⁿ\ Alberto 1873–1932 Fr. (Braz.-born) aviation pioneer
Sa·pir \sə-'pi(ə)r\ Edward 1884–1939 Am. (Pomeranian-born) anthropol. & linguist
Sap·pho *also* **Psap·pho** \'saf-(,)ō\ *fl ca* 610–*ca* 580 B.C. Greek poet
Sar·da·na·pa·lus *or* **Sar·da·na·pal·lus** \,särd-ᵊn-'ap-(ə-)ləs, -ᵊn-ə-'pā-ləs\ king of Assyria; sometimes identified with Ashurbanipal (reigned 668–627 B.C.)
Sar·dou \sär-'dü\ Victorien 1831–1908 Fr. dram.

Sar·gent \\'sär-jənt\\ John Sing·er \\'siŋ-ər\\ 1856–1925 Am. painter
Sar·gon II \\'sär-ˌgän, -gən\\ king of Assyria (722–705 B.C.)
Sa·roy·an \\sə-'roi-ən\\ William 1908–1981 Am. writer
Sar·tre \\'särtrᵊ\\ Jean-Paul 1905–1980 Fr. philos., dram., & nov. — **Sar·tre·an** or **Sar·tri·an** \\'sär-trē-ən\\ adj
Sas·soon \\sä-'sün, sə-\\ Siegfried Lorraine 1886–1967 Eng. writer
Sa·tie \\sa-'tē, sä-\\ Erik-Alfred-Leslie 1866–1925 Fr. composer
Sa·ud \\sä-'üd\\ 1902–1969 king of Saudi Arabia (1953–64)
Saus·sure \\sō-sᵿēr\\ Ferdinand de 1857–1913 Swiss linguist — **Saus·sur·ian** or **Saus·sur·ean** \\sō-'sᵿr-ē-ən, sō-\\ adj
Sav·age \\'sav-ij\\ Michael Joseph 1872–1940 prime min. of New Zealand (1935–40)
Savage Richard 1697?–1743 Eng. poet
Sa·vo·na·ro·la \\ˌsav-ə-nə-'rō-lə, sə-ˌvän-ə-'rō-\\ Gi·ro·la·mo \\ji-'rōl-ə-ˌmō\\ 1452–1498 Ital. reformer
Saxe \\'saks\\ Hermann-Maurice 1696–1750 Comte de Saxe Fr. soldier; marshal of France
Saxo Gram·mat·i·cus \\ˌsak-(ˌ)sō-grə-'mat-i-kəs\\ ca 1150–after 1216 Dan. hist.
Say·ers \\'sā-ərz, 'se(ə)rz\\ Dorothy Leigh 1893–1957 Eng. writer
Sca·lia \\skə-'lē-ə\\ Antonin 1936–   Am. jurist
Scal·i·ger \\'skal-ə-jər\\ Joseph Justus 1540–1609 Fr. scholar
Scaliger Julius Caesar 1484–1558 father of prec. Ital. physician
Scanderbeg — see SKANDERBEG
Scar·lat·ti \\skär-'lät-ē\\ (Pietro) Alessandro Gaspare 1660–1725 & his son (Giuseppe) Domenico 1685–1757 Ital. composers
Scar·ron \\ska-'rōⁿ\\ Paul 1610–1660 Fr. author
Schacht \\'shäkt, 'shäkt\\ (Horace Greeley) Hjal·mar \\'yäl-ˌmär\\ 1877–1970 Ger. financier
Schal·ly \\'shal-ē\\ Andrew Victor 1926–   Am. (Pol.-born) physiol.
Scharn·horst \\'shärn-ˌhȯrst\\ Gerhard Johann David von 1755–1813 Pruss. gen.
Schar·wen·ka \\shär-'veŋ-kə\\ Philipp 1847–1917 & his bro. Xaver 1850–1924 Ger. pianists & composers
Schaw·low \\'shȯ-(ˌ)lō\\ Arthur Leonard 1921–   Am. physicist
Schei·de·mann \\'shīd-ə-ˌmän\\ Philipp 1865–1939 Ger. polit.
Schel·ling \\'shel-iŋ\\ Friedrich Wilhelm Joseph von 1775–1854 Ger. philos. — **Schel·ling·ian** \\she-'liŋ-ē-ən\\ adj
Schia·pa·rel·li \\skē-ˌäp-ə-'rel-ē, ˌskap-\\ Giovanni Virginio 1835–1910 Ital. astron.
Schick \\'shik\\ Bé·la \\'bā-lə\\ 1877–1967 Am. (Hung.-born) pediatrician
Schil·ler \\'shil-ər\\ (Johann Christoph) Friedrich von 1759–1805 Ger. poet & dram.
Schi·rach \\'shē-ˌräk, -ˌräk\\ Baldur von 1907–1974 Ger. Nazi polit.
Schle·gel \\'shlā-gəl\\ August Wilhelm von 1767–1845 Ger. author
Schlegel Friedrich von 1772–1829 bro. of prec. Ger. philos. & writer
Schlei·cher \\'shlī-kər, -kər\\ Kurt von 1882–1934 Ger. soldier & polit.
Schlei·er·ma·cher \\'shlī-ər-ˌmäk-ər, -ˌmäk\\ Friedrich Ernst Daniel 1768–1834 Ger. theol. & philos.
Schle·sing·er \\'shlā-ziŋ-ər\\ Arthur Meier father 1888–1965 & son 1917–   Am. historians
Schley \\'sh(h)lī\\ Winfield Scott 1839–1909 Am. admiral
Schlie·mann \\'shlē-ˌmän\\ Heinrich 1822–1890 Ger. archaeol.
Schmidt \\'shmit\\ Helmut 1918–   chancellor West Germany (1974–82)
Schna·bel \\'shnäb-əl\\ Ar·tur \\'är-ˌtu̇(ə)r\\ 1882–1951 Austrian pianist & composer
Schnitz·ler \\'shnit-slər\\ Arthur 1862–1931 Austrian physician, dram., & nov.
Scho·field \\'skō-ˌfēld\\ John McAllister 1831–1906 Am. gen.
Schön·berg \\'sha(r)n-ˌbərg, 'shœn-ˌberk\\ Arnold 1874–1951 Am. (Austrian-born) composer — **Schön·berg·ian** \\-ē-ən\\ adj
Scho·pen·hau·er \\'shō-pən-ˌhau̇(-ə)r\\ Arthur 1788–1860 Ger. philos.
Schrey·er \\'shrī-ər\\ Edward Richard 1935–   Canad. polit.; gov.-gen. (1979–84)
Schrief·fer \\'shrē-fər\\ John Robert 1931–   Am. physicist
Schrö·ding·er \\'shrȫd-iŋ-ər, shräd-\\ Erwin 1887–1961 Austrian physicist
Schu·bert \\'shü-bərt, -ˌbert\\ Franz Peter 1797–1828 Austrian composer — **Schu·bert·ian** \\-ē-ən\\ adj
Schultz \\'shu̇lts\\ Theodore 1902–   Am. econ.
Schulz \\'shu̇lts\\ Charles Monroe 1922–   Am. cartoonist
Schu·man \\'shü-ˌmän, -mən\\ Robert 1886–1963 Fr. statesman
Schu·man \\'shü-mən\\ William Howard 1910–   Am. composer
Schu·mann \\'shü-ˌmän, -mən\\ Robert 1810–1856 Ger. composer
Schu·mann–Heink \\'shü-mən-'hiŋk\\ Ernestine 1861–1936 née Roessler Am. (Austrian-born) contralto
Schur·man \\'shu̇(ə)r-mən, 'shər-\\ Jacob Gould 1854–1942 Am. philos. & diplomat
Schurz \\'shu̇(ə)rts, 'shərts\\ Carl 1829–1906 Am. (Ger.-born) lawyer, gen., & polit.
Schusch·nigg \\'shu̇sh-(ˌ)nik, -(ˌ)nig\\ Kurt von 1897–1977 Austrian statesman
Schuy·ler \\'skī-lər\\ Philip John 1733–1804 Am. gen. & statesman
Schwartz \\'shwȯ(ə)rts\\ Melvin 1932–   Am. physicist
Schweit·zer \\'s(h)wīt-sər, 'shvīt-\\ Albert 1875–1965 Fr. theol., philos., missionary physician, & music scholar
Schwing·er \\'shwiŋ-ər\\ Julian Seymour 1918–   Am. physicist
Scip·io \\'sip-ē-ˌō, 'skip-\\ **Aemilianus Af·ri·ca·nus** \\-ˌaf-rə-'kä-nəs, -'kän-, -ˌkän-\\ **Numantinus** Publius Cornelius 185(or 184)–129 B.C. Scipio the Younger Rom. gen.
Scipio Africanus Publius Cornelius 236–184(or 183) B.C. Scipio the Elder Rom. gen.
Scopes \\'skōps\\ John Thomas 1900–1970 Am. teacher
Scott \\'skät\\ Dred \\'dred\\ 1795?–1858 Am. slave
Scott Sir George Gilbert 1811–1878 Eng. architect
Scott Robert Falcon 1868–1912 Eng. explorer
Scott Sir Walter 1771–1832 Scot. poet & nov.
Scott Winfield 1786–1866 Am. gen.
Scotus Duns — see DUNS SCOTUS
Scotus John — see ERIGENA
Scria·bin or **Skrya·bin** \\skrē-'äb-ən\\ Aleksandr Nikolayevich 1872–1915 Russ. composer
Scribe \\skrēb\\ Augustin-Eugène 1791–1861 Fr. dram.

Scu·dé·ry \\ˌskȕd-ə-'rē, skü̇-dä-rē\\ Madeleine de 1607–1701 Sa·pho \\sȧ-fō\\ Fr. poet, nov., & lady of fashion
Sea·borg \\'sē-ˌbȯ(ə)rg\\ Glenn Theodore 1912–   Am. chem.
Sears \\'si(ə)rz\\ Richard Warren 1863–1914 Am. merchant
See \\'sē\\ Thomas Jefferson Jackson 1866–1962 Am. astron. & math.
Seeckt \\zäkt\\ Hans von 1866–1936 Ger. army officer
See·ger \\'sē-gər\\ Peter 1919–   Pete Am. folksinger
Se·fe·ri·a·des \\ˌsef-ˌer-'yäth-ēs\\ Giorgos Stylianou 1900–1971 pseud. George Se·fe·ris \\se-'fer-ēs\\ Greek diplomat & poet
Se·go·via \\sā-'gō-vyə, -vē-ə\\ Andrés 1893?–1987 Span. guitarist & composer
Se·grè \\sə-'grā, sā-\\ Emilio Gino 1905–1989 Am. (Ital.-born) physicist
Sei·fert \\'zī-fərt\\ Jaroslav 1901–1986 Czech poet
Se·ja·nus \\si-'jā-nəs\\ Lucius Aelius d A.D. 31 Rom. conspirator
Sel·den \\'sel-dən\\ George Baldwin 1846–1922 Am. lawyer & inventor
Selden John 1584–1654 Eng. jurist & antiquarian
Se·leu·cus I Ni·ca·tor \\sə-ˌlü-kə-'snī-ˌkāt-ər\\ 358(to 354)–281 B.C. Macedonian gen; founder of Seleucid dynasty
Sel·kirk \\'sel-ˌkərk\\ Alexander 1676–1721 Scot. sailor; original of Defoe's Robinson Crusoe
Se·me·nov \\sə-'myȯn-əf\\ Nikolay Nikolayevich 1896–1986 Russ. chem.
Semmes \\'semz\\ Raphael 1809–1877 Am. Confed. admiral
Sen·e·ca \\'sen-i-kə\\ Lucius Annaeus 4 B.C.–A.D. 65 Rom. statesman, dram., & philos. — **Sen·e·can** \\-kən\\ adj
Sen·ghor \\sen-'gȯ(ə)r, sän-'gȯ(ə)r\\ Léopold Sédar 1906–   pres. of Senegal (1960–80)
Sen·nach·er·ib \\sə-'nak-ə-rəb\\ d 681 B.C. king of Assyria (704–681)
Se·quoya or **Se·quoy·ah** or **Se·quoia** \\si-'kwȯi-ə\\ ca1760–1843 George Guess Cherokee Indian scholar
Ser·kin \\'sər-kən\\ Rudolf 1903–   Am. (Bohemian-born) pianist
Ser·ra \\'ser-ə\\ Ju·ni·pe·ro \\hü̇-'nē-pə-ˌrō\\ 1713–1784 orig. Miguel José Span. missionary in Mexico & California
Ser·to·ri·us \\(ˌ)sər-'tōr-ē-əs, -'tȯr-\\ Quintus ca123–72 B.C. Rom. gen. & statesman
Ser·ve·tus \\(ˌ)sər-'vēt-əs\\ Michael 1511?–1553 Span. Miguel Serveto Span. theol. & physician
Ser·vice \\'sər-vəs\\ Robert William 1874–1958 Canad. writer
Ses·sions \\'sesh-ənz\\ Roger Huntington 1896–1985 Am. composer
Se·ton \\'set-ᵊn\\ Saint Elizabeth Ann née Bayley 1774–1821 Mother Seton Am. religious leader
Seton Ernest Thompson 1860–1946 orig. surname Thompson Am. (Eng.-born) writer & illustrator
Seu·rat \\sə-'rä\\ Georges 1859–1891 Fr. painter
Seuss — see Theodor Seuss GEISEL
Se·ve·rus \\sə-'vir-əs\\ Lucius Septimius A.D. 146–211 Rom. emp. (193–211)
Sé·vi·gné \\ˌsā-(ˌ)vēn-'yā, sā-'vēn-(ˌ)yā\\ Marquise de 1626–1696 née (Marie) de Rabutin-Chantal Fr. writer & lady of fashion
Sew·ard \\'sü-ərd, 'sǘ(-ə)rd\\ William Henry 1801–1872 Am. statesman; secy. of state (1861–69)
Sew·ell \\'sü-əl\\ Anna 1820–1878 Brit. writer
Sey·mour \\'sē-ˌmō(ə)r, -ˌmó(ə)r\\ Jane 1509?–1537 3d wife of Henry VIII of England & mother of Edward VI
Seyss–In·quart \\'zis-'iŋk-ˌvärt\\ Ar·tur \\'är-ˌtü(ə)r\\ 1892–1946 Austrian Nazi polit.
Shack·le·ton \\'shak-əl-tən, -ˌəlt-ᵊn\\ Sir Ernest Henry 1874–1922 Brit. explorer
Shad·well \\'shad-ˌwel, -wəl\\ Thomas 1642?–1692 Eng. dram.; poet laureate (1688–92)
Shaf·ter \\'shaf-tər\\ William Rufus 1835–1906 Am. gen.
Shaftes·bury \\'shaf(t)s-ˌber-ē, -b(ə-)rē\\ 1st Earl of 1621–1683 Anthony Ashley Cooper Eng. statesman
Shāh Jā·han \\ˌshäj-ə-'hän\\ 1592–1666 Mogul emp. of India (1628–57 or 58)
Shahn \\'shän\\ Ben 1898–1969 Am. (Lithuanian-born) painter
Shake·speare \\'shāk-ˌspi(ə)r\\ William 1564–1616 Eng. dram. & poet
Sha·mir \\shə-'mēr\\ Yitzhak 1914–   orig. surname Yizernitzky prime min. of Israel (1983–   )
Sha·pi·ro \\shə-'pi(ə)r-(ˌ)ō\\ Karl Jay 1913–   Am. poet & critic
Shas·tri \\'shäs-trē\\ Lal \\'läl\\ Bahadur 1904–1966 Indian polit.; prime min. (1964–66)
Shaw \\'shȯ\\ George Bernard 1856–1950 Brit. (Irish-born) author
Shaw Thomas Edward — see T. E. LAWRENCE
Shawn \\'shȯn\\ Ted 1891–1972 Am. dancer & choreographer
Shays \\'shāz\\ Daniel 1747?–1825 Am. soldier & insurrectionist
Shee·ler \\'shē-lər\\ Charles 1883–1965 Am. painter & photographer
Shel·ley \\'shel-ē\\ Mary Woll·stone·craft \\'wu̇l-stən-ˌkraft\\ 1797–1851 née Godwin; wife of P. B. Eng. nov.
Shelley Percy Bysshe \\'bish\\ 1792–1822 Eng. poet — **Shel·ley·an** \\'shel-ē-ən\\ or **Shel·ley·an** \\'shel-ē-'esk\\ adj
Shen·stone \\'shen-ˌstōn, 'shen(t)-stən\\ William 1714–1763 Eng. poet
Shep·ard \\'shep-ərd\\ Alan Bartlett 1923–   Am. astronaut; 1st Am. in space (1961)
Sher·a·ton \\'sher-ət-ᵊn\\ Thomas 1751–1806 Eng. furniture designer
Sher·i·dan \\'sher-əd-ᵊn\\ Philip Henry 1831–1888 Am. gen.
Sheridan Richard Brins·ley \\'brinz-lē\\ 1751–1816 Irish dram. & orator
Sher·man \\'shər-mən\\ James Schoolcraft 1855–1912 vice pres. of the U.S. (1909–12)
Sherman John 1823–1900 bro. of W. T. Am. statesman
Sherman Roger 1721–1793 Am. jurist & statesman
Sherman William Tecumseh 1820–1891 Am. gen.
Sher·riff \\'sher-əf\\ Robert Cedric 1896–1975 Eng. writer
Sher·ring·ton \\'sher-iŋ-tən\\ Sir Charles Scott 1857–1952 Eng. physiol.
Sher·wood \\'shər-ˌwu̇d\\ also 'she(ə)r-\\ Robert Emmet 1896–1955 Am. dram.
Shev·ard·nad·ze \\ˌshev-ər(d)-'näd-zə\\ Eduard Amvrosiyevich 1928–   Soviet foreign minister (1985–   )
Shev·chen·ko or **Sev·čen·ko** \\shef-'cheŋ-(ˌ)kō\\ Taras Hryhorovych 1814–1861 Ukrainian poet
Shi·de·ha·ra \\ˌshēd-ə-'här-ə\\ Kijūrō Baron 1872–1951 Jp. diplomat & statesman
Shi·ge·mit·su \\ˌshē-gə-'mit-(ˌ)sü, ˌshig-ə-\\ Mamoru 1887–1957 Jp. diplomat
Shih Huang–ti — see CH'IN SHIH HUANG TI

Shin·well \'shin-,wel, -wəl\ Emanuel 1884–1986 Brit. polit.
Shi·rer \'shir-ər\ William Lawrence 1904–   Am. author
Shir·ley \'shər-lē\ James 1596–1666 Eng. dram.
Shock·ley \'shäk-lē\ William Bradford 1910–1989 Am. physicist
Sho·lo·khov \'shól-ə,kóf, -,kóv\ Mikhail Aleksandrovich 1905–1984 Russ. nov.
Sho·sta·ko·vich \,shäs-tə-'kō-vich, ,shós-, -'kò-\ Dmi·try \də-'mē-trē\ Dmitriyevich 1906–1975 Russ. composer
Shultz \'shúlts\ George Pratt 1920–   U.S. secy. of labor (1969–70); secy. of the treasury (1972–73); secy. of state (1982–89)
Shute \'shüt\ Nev·il \'nev-əl\ 1899–1960 pseud. of Nevil Shute Norway Eng. aeronautical engineer & writer
Shver·nik \'shfer-nik\ Nikolay Mikhaylovich 1888–1970 Russ. polit.; chairman of the Presidium (1946–54)
Si·be·lius \sə-'bāl-yəs, -'bā-lē-əs\ Jean \'zhän, 'yän\ 1865–1957 Finn. composer
Sick·les \'sik-əlz\ Daniel Edgar 1825–1914 Am. gen. & polit.
Sid·dhār·tha Gau·ta·ma \'sid-är-tə-'gaút-ə-mə\ ca 563–ca 483 B.C. The Bud·dha \'búd-ə, 'bùd-\ Indian philos.; founder of Buddhism
Sid·dons \'sid-²nz\ Sarah 1755–1831 née Kemble Eng. actress
Sid·ney \'sid-nē\ Sir Philip 1554–1586 Eng. poet, statesman, & soldier
Sieg·bahn \'sēg-,bän\ Kai Manne 1918–   Swed. physicist
Siegbahn Karl Manne Georg 1886–1978 Swed. physicist
Sie·mens \'sē-mənz\ Sir William 1823–1883 Brit. (Ger.-born) inventor
Sien·kie·wicz \shen-'kyä-vich\ Henryk 1846–1916 pseud. Litwas Pol. nov.
Sie·yès \sē-,ā-'yes\ Emmanuel-Joseph 1748–1836 Fr. revolutionary
Sig·is·mund \'sig-ə-smənd\ 1368–1437 Holy Rom. emp. (1433–37)
Sigs·bee \'sigz-bē\ Charles Dwight 1845–1923 Am. admiral
Si·gurds·son \'sig-ərd-sən, -ərth-\ Jón \'yōn\ 1811–1879 Icelandic statesman & author
Si·kor·ski \sə-'kór-skē\ Władysław 1881–1943 Pol. gen. & statesman
Si·kor·sky \sə-'kór-skē\ Igor Ivan 1889–1972 Am. (Russ.-born) aeronautical engineer
Sil·lan·pää \'sil-ən-,pa\ Frans Eemil 1888–1964 Finn. nov.
Si·lo·ne \si-'lō-nē\ Ignazio 1900–1978 pseud. of Secondo Tranquilli Ital. author
Si·me·non \,sē-mə-'nōⁿ\ Georges-Joseph-Christian 1903–1989 Fr. (Belg.-born) writer
Sim·e·on Sty·li·tes \,sim-ē-ən-stə-'līt-ēz, -,stī-\ Saint ca 390–459 Syrian ascetic & pillar dweller
Si·mon \sē-mōⁿ\ Claude 1913–   Fr. writer
Si·mon \'sī-mən\ 1st Viscount 1873–1954 John Allsebrook Simon Brit. jurist & statesman
Simon Herbert Alexander 1916–   Am. econ.
Simon Neil 1927–   Am. dram.
Si·mon·i·des \sī-'män-ə-,dēz\ of Ceos ca 556–ca 468? B.C. Greek poet
Sims \'simz\ William Sow·den \'saúd-²n\ 1858–1936 Am. admiral
Sin·clair \sin-'kler, sin\ Upton Beall \'bel\ 1878–1968 Am. writer & polit.
Sing·er \'siŋ-ər\ Isaac Bashevis 1904–   Am. (Pol.-born) author
Singer Isaac Merrit 1811–1875 Am. inventor
Singh \'siⁿ-hə, 'siŋ\ Vishwanath Pratap 1931–   prime min. of India (1989–   )
Si·quei·ros \si-'kā-(,)rōs\ David Alfaro 1896–1974 Mex. painter
Si·raj-ud-Daw·lah \sə-,räj-ə-'daù-lə\ ca 1732–1757 nawab of Bengal (1756–57)
Sis·ley \'siz-lē, sēs-le\ Alfred 1839–1899 Fr. (Eng.-born) painter
Sis·mon·di \sis-'män-dē, sēs-mōⁿ-dē\ Jean-Charles-Léonard Simonde de 1773–1842 Swiss hist. & econ.
Sit·ter \'sit-ər\ Willem de 1872–1934 Du. astron.
Sit·ting Bull \,sit-iŋ-'búl\ ca 1831–1890 Sioux leader
Sit·well \'sit-,wel, -wəl\ Sir George Reres·by \'ri(ə)rz-bē\ 1860–1943 & his 3 children: Dame Edith 1887–1964; Sir Osbert 1892–1969; & Sa·chev·er·ell \sə-'shev-(ə-)rəl\ 1897–1988 Eng. authors
Skan·der·beg or Scan·der·beg \'skan-dər-,beg\ 1405–1468 orig. George Kastrioti; Turk. Iskender Bey Albanian hero
Skeat \'skēt\ Walter William 1835–1912 Eng. philologist
Skel·ton \'skelt-²n\ John ca 1460–1529 Eng. poet — Skel·ton·ic \skel-'tän-ik\ adj
Skin·ner \'skin-ər\ Burrhus Frederic 1904–1990 Am. psychol. — Skin·ner·ian \skin-'nir-ē-ən, -'ner-\ adj
Skinner Cornelia Otis 1901–1979 dau. of Otis Am. actress
Skinner Otis 1858–1942 Am. actor
Skinner Samuel K. 1938–   U.S. secy. of transportation (1989–   )
Sko·da \'skōd-ə, 'shkòd-(,)ä\ Emil von 1839–1900 Czech engineer & industrialist
Sla·ter \'slāt-ər\ Samuel 1768–1835 Am. (Eng.-born) industrialist
Sli·dell \sli-'del, by collateral descendants 'slīd-²l\ John 1793–1871 Am. Confed. diplomat
Sloan \'slōn\ John French 1871–1951 Am. painter
Slo·cum \'slō-kəm\ Henry Warner 1827–1894 Am. gen.
Slo·nim·sky \slō-'nim(p)-skē\ Nicolas 1894–   Russ.-born composer & musicologist in America
Sme·ta·na \'smet-²n-ə\ Be·dřich \'bed-ər-,zhik\ 1824–1884 Czech composer
Smig·ly–Rydz Edward — see RYDZ-ŚMIGŁY
Smith \'smith\ Adam 1723–1790 Scot. econ.
Smith Alfred Emanuel 1873–1944 Am. polit.
Smith Bessie 1894(or 1898)–1937 Am. blues singer
Smith David 1906–1965 Am. sculptor
Smith Edmund Kirby — see KIRBY-SMITH
Smith Hamilton Othanel 1931–   Am. microbiologist
Smith John ca 1580–1631 Eng. colonist in America
Smith Joseph 1805–1844 Am. founder of Mormon Church
Smith Sydney 1771–1845 Eng. essayist
Smith Walter Be·dell \bə-'del\ 1895–1961 Am. gen. & diplomat
Smith William 1769–1839 Eng. geologist
Smith–Dor·ri·en \'smith-'dór-ē-ən, -'där-\ Sir Horace Lockwood 1858–1930 Brit. gen.
Smith·son \'smith-sən\ James 1765–1829 Brit. chem. & mineralogist & benefactor of Smithsonian Inst.
Smol·lett \'smäl-ət\ Tobias George 1721–1771 Brit. author

Smuts \'smɔts, 'smœts\ Jan \'yän\ Christiaan 1870–1950 So. African field marshal; prime min. (1919–24; 1939–48)
Smyth \'smīth\ Henry DeWolf 1898–1986 Am. physicist
Snell \'snel\ George 1903–   Am. research geneticist
Snor·ri Stur·lu·son \,snór-ē-'stər-lə-sən, ,snär-\ 1179–1241 Icelandic statesman & hist.
Snow \'snō\ Baron 1905–1980 Charles Percy Snow Eng. nov. & physicist
Snow·den \'snōd-²n\ Philip 1864–1937 1st Viscount Snowden of Ick·orn·shaw \'ik-,òrn-,shò\ Eng. polit.
Snow·don \'snōd-²n\ Earl of — see ARMSTRONG-JONES
Sny·der \'snid-ər\ John Wesley 1895–1985 Am. banker & administrator
Sny·ders \'snīd-ərs\ Frans 1579–1657 Flem. painter
Soar·es \'swär-ish, -sh\ Má·rio 1924–   prime min. of Portugal (1976–78; 1983–85) & pres. (1986–   )
Sobieski John — see JOHN III SOBIESKI
So·ci·nus \sō-'sī-nəs\ Faustus 1539–1604 Fausto Soz·zi·ni or So·ci·ni or Soz·zi·ni \-sōt-'sē-nē\ Ital. theol.
Soc·ra·tes \'säk-rə-,tēz\ ca 470–399 B.C. Greek philos.
Sod·dy \'säd-ē\ Frederick 1877–1956 Eng. chem.
Sö·der·blom \'sə(r)d-ər-,blüm, 'sœd-\ Nathan 1866–1931 Swed. theol.
So·do·ma \'sòd-ə-mə\ 1477–1549 Giovanni Antonio Bazzi Ital. painter
So·lon \'sō-lən, -,län\ ca 630–ca 560 B.C. Athenian lawgiver
So·low \'sō-lō\ Robert Merton 1924–   Am. econ.
Sol·zhe·ni·tsyn \,sōl-zhə-'nēt-sən, ,sól-\ Aleksandr Isayevich 1918–   Russ. nov.
Som·er·ville \'səm-ər-,vil\ Sir James Fownes \'fònz\ 1882–1949 Brit. admiral
Soong Ai–ling \'sùn-'ī-'liŋ\ 1888–1973 wife of H. H. K'ung
Soong Ch'ing–ling \-'chiŋ-'liŋ\ 1892–1981 wife of Sun Yat-sen
Soong Mei–ling \-'mā-'liŋ\ 1897–   wife of Chiang Kai-shek
Soong Tzu–wen or Tse–ven or Tsü–wên \-'tsü-'wən\ 1894–1971 T. V. Soong; bro. of prec. Chin. financier & statesman
Soph·o·cles \'säf-ə-,klēz\ ca 496–406 B.C. Greek dram. — Soph·o·cle·an \,säf-ə-'klē-ən\ adj
Sor·del·lo \sòr-'del-(,)ō\ ca 1200–before 1269 Ital. troubadour
So·rol·la y Bas·ti·da \sə-'ról-yə-,ē-bä-'stē-də, -'rói-ə-, -'stē-thə\ Joaquín 1863–1923 Span. painter
So·to, de \thä-'sōt-(,)ō, di-\ Hernando 1496(or 1499 or 1500)–1542 Span. explorer
Soult \'sült\ Nicolas-Jean de Dieu 1769–1851 Duc de Dal·ma·tie \dál-má-sē\ Fr. soldier; marshal of France
Sou·sa \'sü-zə, 'sü-sə\ John Philip 1854–1932 the March King Am. bandmaster & composer
South \'saúth\ Robert 1634–1716 Eng. clergyman
Sou·they \'saú-thē, 'səth-ē\ Robert 1774–1843 Eng. author; poet laureate (1813–43)
Sou·tine \sü-'tēn\ Chaim 1893–1943 Fr. (Lith.-born) painter
So·yin·ka \shò-'yiŋ-ka\ Wo·le \'wò-lā\ 1934–   Nigerian dram. & poet
Spaak \'späk\ Paul-Henri Charles 1899–1972 Belg. lawyer & polit.; premier (1938–39; 1947–50); secy.-gen. of NATO (1957–61)
Spaatz \'späts\ Carl 1891–1974 Am. gen.
Spal·ding \'spòl-diŋ\ Albert 1888–1953 Am. violinist & composer
Spark \'spärk\ Muriel Sarah 1918–   née Camberg Brit. writer
Sparks \'spärks\ Jar·ed \'jar-əd, 'jer-\ 1789–1866 Am. hist.
Spar·ta·cus \'spärt-ə-kəs\ d 71 B.C. Rom. slave & insurrectionist
Spell·man \'spel-mən\ Francis Joseph 1889–1967 Am. cardinal
Spe·mann \'shpā-,män\ Hans 1869–1941 Ger. embryologist
Spen·cer \'spen(t)-sər\ Herbert 1820–1903 Eng. philos.
Spen·der \'spen(t)-sər\ Stephen Harold 1909–   Eng. poet & critic
Speng·ler \'s(h)peŋ-lər\ Oswald 1880–1936 Ger. philos.
Spen·ser \'spen(t)-sər\ Edmund 1552–1599 Eng. poet — Spen·se·ri·an \spen-'sir-ē-ən\ adj
Sper·ry \'sper-ē\ Elmer Ambrose 1860–1930 Am. inventor
Sperry Roger Wolcott 1913–   Am. psychobiologist
Spiel·berg \'spē(ə)l-,bərg\ Steven 1947–   Am. motion-picture director, writer, & producer
Spi·no·za \spin-'ō-zə\ Benedict de 1632–1677 Hebrew prename Baruch Du. philos. — Spi·no·zis·tic \spin-ə-,nō-'zis-tik, ,spin-ə-\ adj
Spit·te·ler \'s(h)pit-²l-ər, 's(h)pit-lər\ Carl 1845–1924 pseud. Felix Tandem \'tän-,dem\ Swiss writer
Spock \'späk\ Benjamin McLane 1903–   Am. physician
Spode \'spōd\ Josiah 1754–1827 Eng. potter
Spru·ance \'sprü-ən(t)s\ Raymond Ames 1886–1969 Am. admiral
Spy·ri \'s(h)pi(ə)r-ē\ Johanna 1827–1901 née Heusser Swiss author
Staël, de \'stäl\ Mme. Anne-Louise-Germaine 1766–1817 née Necker Baronne de Staël-Holstein Fr. writer
Ståhl·berg \'stòl-,bərg, -,ber-ē\ Kaarlo Ju·ho \'yü-(,)hò\ 1865–1952 Finn. statesman
Stair Viscount & Earl of — see DALRYMPLE
Sta·lin \'stäl-ən, 'stal-, -,ēn\ Joseph 1879–1953 Iosif Vissarionovich Dzhugash·vi·li \,jü-gəsh-'vē-lē\ Soviet leader
Stan·dish \'stan-dish\ Myles or Miles 1584?–1656 Am. colonist
Stan·is·lav·sky \,stan-i-'släf-skē\ Konstantin 1863–1938 pseud. of Konstantin Sergeyevich Alekseyev Russ. actor, director, & producer
Stan·is·ław I \'stan-ə-,slòv, -,släv\ Lesz·czyń·ski \lesh-'chin-skē\ 1677–1766 king of Poland (1704–09; 1733–35)
Stan·ley \'stan-lē\ Edward George Geoffrey Smith 1799–1869 Earl of Derby Brit. statesman
Stanley Sir Henry Morton 1841–1904 orig. John Rowlands Brit. explorer
Stanley Wendell Meredith 1904–1971 Am. biochem.
Stan·ton \'stant-²n\ Edwin McMasters 1814–1869 Am. lawyer & secy. of war (1862–68)
Stanton Elizabeth 1815–1902 née Cady Am. suffragist
Star·hem·berg \'stär-əm-,bərg, 'shtär-əm-,berk\ Ernst Rüdiger 1899–1956 Fürst von Starhemberg Austrian polit.

\ə\ abut \²\ kitten, F table \ər\ further \a\ ash \ā\ ace \ä\ cot, cart
\aú\ out \ch\ chin \e\ bet \ē\ easy \g\ go \i\ hit \ī\ ice \j\ job
\ŋ\ sing \ō\ go \ò\ law \òi\ boy \th\ thin \t̲h̲\ the \ü\ loot \ú\ foot
\y\ yet \zh\ vision \à, ᴋ, ⁿ, œ, œ̄, ᵫ, ᵫ̄, ᐟ\ see Guide to Pronunciation

Stark \\'stärk\\ Harold Raynsford 1880–1972 Am. admiral
Stark \\'s(h)tärk\\ Johannes 1874–1957 Ger. physicist
Stark \\'stärk\\ John 1728–1822 Am. Revolutionary gen.
Stas·sen \\'stas-ᵊn\\ Harold Edward 1907–   Am. polit.
Sta·tius \\'stā-sh(ē-)əs\\ Publius Papinius *ca* A.D. 45–96 Rom. poet
Stau·ding·er \\'s(h)taůd-iŋ-ər\\ Hermann 1881–1965 Ger. chem.
Steele \\'stē(ə)l\\ Sir Richard 1672–1729 Brit. essayist & dram.
Steen \\'stān\\ Jan 1626–1679 Du. painter
Ste·fans·son \\'stef-ən-sən\\ Vil·hjal·mur \\'vil-,yaůl-mər\\ 1879–1962 Am. (Canad.-born) explorer
Stef·fens \\'stef-ənz\\ (Joseph) Lincoln 1866–1936 Am. journalist
Stei·chen \\'stī-kən\\ Edward Jean 1879–1973 Am. photographer
Stein \\'stīn\\ Gertrude 1874–1946 Am. writer
Stein William Howard 1911–   Am. biochem.
Stein \\'s(h)tīn\\ (Heinrich Friedrich) Karl 1757–1831 Freiherr *vom und zum Stein* Pruss. statesman
Stein·beck \\'stīn-,bek\\ John Ernst 1902–1968 Am. nov.
Stein·berg·er \\'stīn-,bər-gər\\ Jack 1921–   Am. (Ger.-born) physicist
Stein·metz \\'s(h)tīn-,mets\\ Charles Proteus 1865–1923 Am. (Ger.-born) electrical engineer
Sten·dhal \\sten-'däl, stan-, *F* staⁿ-dál\\ 1783–1842 pseud. of *Marie-Henri Beyle* \\'bel\\ Fr. writer — **Sten·dhal·ian** \\-'däl-ē-ən\\ *adj*
Ste·phen \\'stē-vən\\ *ca* 1097–1154 king of England (1135–54)
Stephen Sir Leslie 1832–1904 Eng. philos., critic, & biographer
Ste·phens \\'stē-vənz\\ Alexander Hamilton 1812–1883 Am. polit.; vice pres. of the Confed. states
Stephens James 1882–1950 Irish poet & nov.
Ste·phen·son \\'stē-vən-sən\\ George 1781–1848 Eng. inventor & founder of railroads
Stephenson Robert 1803–1859 *son of George* Eng. engineer
Stern \\'stərn\\ Isaac 1920–   Am. (Russ.-born) violinist
Stern Otto 1888–1969 Am. (Ger.-born) physicist
Stern·berg \\'stərn-,bərg\\ George Miller 1838–1915 Am. physician & bacteriol.
Sterne \\'stərn\\ Laurence 1713–1768 Brit. nov.
Stet·tin·i·us \\stə-'tin-ē-əs, ste-\\ Edward Reilly 1900–1949 Am. financier & statesman
Steu·ben, von \\'st(y)ü-bən, 'shtȯi-; st(y)ü-'ben\\ Baron Friedrich Wilhelm Ludolf Gerhard Augustin 1730–1794 Pruss.-born gen. in Am. Revolution
Ste·vens \\'stē-vənz\\ John 1749–1838 Am. inventor
Stevens John Paul 1920–   Am. jurist
Stevens Thaddeus 1792–1868 Am. polit.
Stevens Wallace 1879–1955 Am. poet
Ste·ven·son \\'stē-vən-sən\\ Ad·lai \\'ad-lē, -(,)lā\\ Ewing 1835–1914 Am. polit.; vice pres. of U.S. (1893–97)
Stevenson Adlai Ewing 1900–1965 *grandson of prec.* Am. polit.
Stevenson Robert Louis Balfour 1850–1894 Scot. author
Stew·art \\'st(y)ü-ərt, 'st(y)ů(-ə)rt\\ Du·gald \\'dü-gəld\\ 1753–1828 Scot. philos.
Stewart Potter 1915–1985 Am. jurist
Stewart Robert 1769–1822 Viscount *Cas·tle·reagh* \\'kas-əl-,rā\\ Eng. statesman
Steyn \\'stīn\\ Marthinus Theunis 1857–1916 So. African statesman
Stieg·litz \\'stēg-ləts, -,lits\\ Alfred 1864–1946 Am. photographer & editor
Stig·ler \\'stig-lər\\ George J. 1911–   Am. econ.
Stil·i·cho \\'stil-i-,kō\\ Flavius *ca* 365–408 Rom. gen. & statesman
Still \\'stil\\ Andrew Taylor 1828–1917 Am. physician; founder of osteopathy
Stil·well \\'stil-,wel, -wəl\\ Joseph Warren 1883–1946 Am. gen.
Stim·son \\'stim(p)-sən\\ Henry Lewis 1867–1950 Am. statesman
Stin·nes \\'s(h)tin-əs\\ Hugo 1870–1924 Ger. industrialist
Stock·mar \\'stäk-,mär\\ Christian Friedrich 1787–1863 Baron *von Stockmar* Anglo-Belg. statesman
Stock·ton \\'stäk-tən\\ Francis Richard 1834–1902 *Frank R.* Am. writer
Stod·dard \\'städ-ərd\\ Richard Henry 1825–1903 Am. poet & critic
Sto·ker \\'stō-kər\\ Bram 1847–1912 Brit. writer
Stokes \\'stōks\\ Sir Frederick Wilfrid Scott 1860–1927 Eng. engineer & inventor
Sto·kow·ski \\stə-'kȯf-skē, -'kȯv- *also* -'kaů-\\ Leopold Antoni Stanislaw Boleslawowicz 1882–1977 Am. (Eng.-born) conductor
Stone \\'stōn\\ Edward Durell 1902–1978 Am. architect
Stone Harlan Fiske 1872–1946 Am. jurist; chief justice U.S. Supreme Court (1941–46)
Stone Irving 1903–1989 orig. *I. Tennenbaum* Am. writer
Stone Lucy 1818–1893 Am. suffragist
Stone Sir (John) Richard Nicholas 1913–   Eng. econ.
Stoph \\'stȯf\\ Willi 1914–   prime min. of East Germany (1976–   )
Sto·ry \\'stōr-ē, 'stȯr-ē\\ Joseph 1779–1845 Am. jurist
Story William Wetmore 1819–1895 *son of prec.* Am. sculptor
Stow \\'stō\\ John 1525–1605 Eng. hist. & antiquarian
Stowe \\'stō\\ Harriet Elizabeth 1811–1896 *née Beecher* Am. author
Stra·bo \\'strā-(,)bō\\ 64(or 63) B.C.–after A.D. 23 Greek geographer
Stra·chey \\'strā-chē\\ (Evelyn) John St. Loe 1901–1963 Eng. socialist
Strachey (Giles) Lytton 1880–1932 Eng. biographer
Stra·di·va·ri \\,strad-ə-'vär-ē, -'var-, -'ver-\\ Antonio 1644–1737 L. *Antonius Strad·i·var·i·us* \\,strad-ə-'var-ē-əs, -'ver-\\ Ital. violin maker
Straf·ford \\'straf-ərd\\ 1st Earl of 1593–1641 *Thomas Wentworth* Eng. statesman
Stratford de Redcliffe Viscount — see Stratford CANNING
Strath·co·na \\strath-'kō-nə\\ **and Mount Royal** 1st Baron 1820–1914 *Donald Alexander Smith* Canad. (Scot.-born) railroad builder & polit.
Straus \\'s(h)traůs\\ Oscar 1870–1954 Fr. (Austrian-born) composer
Strauss \\'s(h)traůs\\ David Friedrich 1808–1874 Ger. theol. & philos.
Strauss Johann father 1804–1849 & his sons Johann Baptist 1825–1899 & Josef 1827–1870 Austrian composers
Strauss Ri·chard \\'rik-,ärt, 'rik-\\ 1864–1949 Ger. composer
Stra·vin·sky \\strə-'vin(t)-skē\\ Igor \\'ē-,gȯ(ə)r\\ Fyodorovich 1882–1971 Am. (Russ.-born) composer — **Stra·vin·sky·an** or **Stra·vin·ski·an** \\-skē-ən\\ *adj*
Strei·cher \\'s(h)trī-kər, -,kər\\ Julius 1885–1946 Ger. Nazi administrator
Stre·se·mann \\'s(h)trā-zə-,män\\ Gustav 1878–1929 Ger. statesman

Strij·dom \\'strīd-əm, 'sträd-\\ Johannes Gerhardus 1893–1958 prime min. of So. Africa (1954–58)
Strind·berg \\'strin(d)-,bərg, *Sw* 'strin-,ber-ē\\ August 1849–1912 Swed. dram. & nov. — **Strind·berg·ian** \\strin(d)-'bər-gē-ən\\ *adj*
Stroess·ner \\'stres-nər\\ Alfredo 1912–   pres. of Paraguay (1954–89)
Stru·en·see \\'s(h)trü-ən-,zā\\ Johann Friedrich 1737–1772 Graf *Struensee* Ger.-Dan. physician & polit.
Stu·art \\'st(y)ü-ərt, 'st(y)ů(-ə)rt\\ — see CHARLES I & MARY STUART
Stuart Charles *the Young Pretender* — see CHARLES EDWARD
Stuart Gilbert Charles 1755–1828 Am. painter
Stuart James Ewell Brown 1833–1864 *Jeb* Am. Confed. gen.
Stuart James Francis Edward *the Old Pretender* — see JAMES EDWARD
Stubbs \\'stəbz\\ George 1724–1806 Eng. painter
Stubbs William 1825–1901 Eng. hist. & prelate
Stülp·na·gel \\'s(h)tůlp-,näg-əl, 'shtůelp-\\ Karl Heinrich von 1886–1944 Ger. gen.
Sturluson — see SNORRI STURLUSON
Stur·sa \\'shtů(ə)r-sə\\ Jan \\'yän\\ 1880–1925 Czech sculptor
Stuy·ve·sant \\'stī-və-sənt\\ Peter *ca* 1610–1672 Du. administrator in America
Sty·ron \\'stī-rən\\ William 1925–   Am. writer
Sua·rez Gon·zá·lez \\,swär-əz-gən-'zäl-əs\\ Adolfo 1932–   prime min. of Spain (1976–81)
Suck·ling \\'sək-liŋ\\ Sir John 1609–1642 Eng. Cavalier poet
Su·cre \\'sü-(,)krā\\ Antonio José de 1795–1830 So. Am. liberator
Sue \\'sü, süē\\ Eugène 1804–1857 orig. *Marie-Joseph Sue* Fr. nov.
Sue·to·ni·us \\swē-'tō-nē-əs, ,sü-ə-'tō-\\ *ca* A.D. 69–after 122 Gaius *Suetonius Tranquillus* Rom. biographer & hist.
Su·gi·ya·ma \\,sü-gē-'yäm-ə\\ Gen 1880–1945 Jp. field marshal
Su·har·to \\sə-'härt-(,)ō, sü-\\ 1921–   pres. of Indonesia (1967–   )
Su·kar·no \\sü-'kär-(,)nō\\ 1901–1970 pres. of Indonesian Republic (1945–1967)
Sü·ley·man *or* **So·li·man** *or* **Su·lei·man I** \\sü-lā-,män, -li-\\ 1494(or 1495)–1566 *the Magnificent* Ottoman sultan (1520–66)
Sul·la \\'səl-ə\\ 138–78 B.C. *Lucius Cornelius Sulla Felix* Rom. gen. & polit.
Sul·li·van \\'səl-ə-vən\\ Sir Arthur Seymour 1842–1900 Eng. composer
Sullivan John 1740–1795 Am. Revolutionary gen.
Sullivan John Lawrence 1858–1918 Am. boxer
Sullivan John Lawrence 1899–1982 Am. lawyer & administrator
Sullivan Louis Henri 1856–1924 Am. architect
Sullivan Louis Wade 1933–   U.S. secy. of health & human services (1989–   )
Sul·ly \\'səl-ē, (,)sə-'lē, süēl-lē\\ Duc de 1560–1641 *Maximilien de Béthune* Baron *de Ros·ny* \\-rō-'nē\\ Fr. statesman
Sul·ly \\'səl-ē\\ Thomas 1783–1872 Am. (Eng.-born) painter
Sully Pru·dhomme \\-prü-dom, prüē-, -'dȯm\\ 1839–1907 pseud. of *René-François-Armand Prudhomme* Fr. poet & critic
Sum·ner \\'səm-nər\\ Charles 1811–1874 Am. statesman & orator
Sumner James Batcheller 1887–1955 Am. biochem.
Sumner William Graham 1840–1910 Am. sociol. & educ.
Sun·day \\'sən-dē\\ William Ashley 1862–1935 *Billy* Am. evangelist
Sun Yat·sen \\'sůn-'yät-'sen\\ 1866–1925 orig. *Sun Wen* or *Sun Chung=shan* Chin. statesman
Surrey Earl of — see Henry HOWARD
Sur·tees \\'sərt-(,)ēz\\ Robert Smith 1803–1864 Eng. nov. & editor
Suth·er·land \\'səth-ər-lənd\\ Earl Wilbur, Jr. 1915–1974 Am. physiol.
Sutherland Dame Joan 1926–   Austral. soprano
Sut·ter \\'sət-ər, 'süt-\\ John Augustus 1803–1880 orig. *Johann August Suter* Am. (Ger.-born) pioneer
Sutt·ner \\'zůt-nər, 'süt-\\ Bertha 1843–1914 *née Kinsky* Baroness *von Suttner* Austrian writer & pacifist
Su·vo·rov \\sů-'vȯr-əf, -'vär-\\ Aleksandr Vasilyevich 1729–1800 Russ. field marshal
Sved·berg \\'sfed-,bərg, *Sw* -,ber-ē\\ The *or* Theodor 1884–1971 Swed. chem.
Sver·drup \\'sve(ə)r-drəp\\ Otto Neumann 1855–1930 Norw. explorer
Sver·rir \\'sver-ər\\ *ca* 1149–1202 *Sverrir Si·gurds·son* \\'sig-ərd-sən\\ king of Norway (1184–1202)
Swe·den·borg \\'swēd-ᵊn-,bȯrg\\ Emanuel 1688–1772 orig. *Svedberg* Swed. philos. & religious writer
Swee·linck \\'swā-liŋk\\ Jan Pieterszoon 1562–1621 Du. organist & composer
Sweet \\'swēt\\ Henry 1845–1912 Eng. phonetician
Swift \\'swift\\ Gustavus Franklin 1839–1903 Am. meat packer
Swift Jonathan 1667–1745 Eng. satirist — **Swift·ian** \\'swif-tē-ən\\ *adj*
Swin·burne \\'swin-(,)bərn\\ Algernon Charles 1837–1909 Eng. poet — **Swin·burn·ian** \\swin-'bər-nē-ən\\ *adj*
Swin·ner·ton \\'swin-ərt-ᵊn\\ Frank Arthur 1884–1982 Eng. nov. & critic
Sylva Carmen — see ELIZABETH Queen of Romania
Sy·ming·ton \\'sī-miŋ-tən\\ (William) Stuart 1901–1988 Am. industrialist & polit.
Sy·monds \\'sim-ən(d)z, 'sim-\\ John Addington 1840–1893 Eng. scholar
Sy·mons \\'sim-ənz, 'sim-\\ Arthur William 1865–1945 Brit. poet & critic
Synge \\'siŋ\\ John Millington 1871–1909 Irish poet & dram.
Synge Richard Laurence Millington 1914–   Brit. biochem.
Sy·se \\'süē-sə, 's(y)ü-\\ Jan Peder 1930–   prime min. of Norway (1989–   )
Szell \\'sel, 'zel\\ George 1897–1970 Am. (Hung.-born) conductor
Szent–Györ·gyi \\sänt-'jȯrj(-ē)\\ Albert von Nagyrapolt 1893–1986 Am. (Hung.-born) chem.
Szi·lard \\'zil-,ärd, zə-'lärd\\ Leo 1898–1964 Am. (Hung.-born) physicist
Szold \\'zōld\\ Henrietta 1860–1945 Am. Zionist; founder of Hadassah
Tac·i·tus \\'tas-ət-əs\\ Cornelius *ca* A.D. 56–*ca* 120 Rom. hist. — **Tac·i·te·an** \\,tas-ə-'tē-ən\\ *adj*
Taft \\'taft\\ Lo·ra·do \\lə-'räd-(,)ō\\ 1860–1936 Am. sculptor
Taft Robert Alphonso 1889–1953 *son of W.H.* Am. polit.
Taft William Howard 1857–1930 27th pres. of the U.S. (1909–13); chief justice U.S. Supreme Court (1921–30)
Ta·gore \\tə-'gȯ(ə)r, -'gȯ(ə)r\\ Ra·bin·dra·nath \\rə-'bin-drə-,nät\\ 1861–1941 Indian poet
Taine \\'tān, 'ten\\ Hippolyte-Adolphe 1828–1893 Fr. philos. & critic
Tait \\'tāt\\ Archibald Campbell 1811–1882 archbishop of Canterbury (1869–82)

T'ai–tsu — see CHAO K'UANG-YIN
Ta·ke·shi·ta \tä-'kä-shə-,tä\ Noboru 1924– Jp. prime min. (1987–89)
Tall·chief \'tȯl-,chēf\ Maria 1925– Am. dancer
Tal·ley·rand–Pé·ri·gord \'tal-ē-,ran(d)-,per-ə-'gȯ(ə)r, F tál-(e-)räⁿ-\ Charles-Maurice de 1754–1838 Prince de Bénévent Fr. statesman
Ta·ma·yo \tə-'mī-(,)ō\ Rufino 1899– Mex. painter
Tamerlane or Tamburlaine — see TIMUR
Tamm \'täm, 'tam\ Igor Yevgenyevich 1895–1971 Russ. physicist
Tan·cred \'taŋ-krəd\ 1078?–1112 Norman leader in 1st Crusade
Ta·ney \'tȯ-nē\ Roger Brooke 1777–1864 Am. jurist; chief justice U.S. Supreme Court (1836–64)
Tan·ge \'tän-gä\ Kenzo 1913– Jp. architect
T'ang T'ai Tsung \'tän-'tīd-'zùn\ 600–649 prename Li Shih-min Chin. emp.; real founder of T'ang dynasty
Tan·guy \tän-'gē\ Yves 1900–1955 Am. (Fr.-born) artist
Tar·bell \'tär-bəl\ Ida Minerva 1857–1944 Am. author
Tar·dieu \tär-'dyə(r), -'dyœ\ André-Pierre-Gabriel-Amédée 1876–1945 Fr. statesman
Tar·king·ton \'tär-kiŋ-tən\ (Newton) Booth 1869–1946 Am. nov.
Tas·man \'taz-mən\ Abel Janszoon 1603?–?1659 Du. mariner
Tas·so \'tas-(,)ō, 'täs-\ Tor·qua·to \tȯr-'kwät-(,)ō\ 1544–1595 Ital. poet
Tate \'tāt\ (John Orley) Allen 1899–1979 Am. poet & critic
Tate Nahum 1652–1715 Brit. dram.; poet laureate (1692–1715)
Ta·tum \'tāt-əm\ Edward Lawrie 1909–1975 Am. biochem.
Taube \'taùb\ Henry 1915– Am. (Canad.-born) chem.
Taw·ney \'tȯ-nē\ Richard Henry 1880–1962 Eng. economic hist.
Tay·lor \'tā-lər\ (James) Bay·ard \'bī-ərd, 'bā-\ 1825–1878 Am. writer
Taylor (Joseph) Deems 1885–1966 Am. composer & music critic
Taylor Edward 1645?–1729 Am. clergyman & poet
Taylor Jeremy 1613–1667 Eng. prelate & author
Taylor Maxwell Davenport 1901–1987 Am. gen.
Taylor Tom 1817–1880 Eng. dram.
Taylor Zachary 1784–1850 12th pres. of the U.S. (1849–50)
Tchai·kov·sky \chī-'kȯf-skē, chə-, -'kȯv-\ Pyotr Ilich 1840–1893 Russ. composer — Tchai·kov·sky·an or Tchai·kov·ski·an \-skē-ən\ adj
Teas·dale \'tēz-,dāl\ Sara 1884–1933 Am. poet
Te·cum·seh \tə-'kəm(p)-sə, -sē\ or Te·cum·tha \-'kəm(p)-thə\ or Ti·kam·the \-'kəm(p)-thə, -'käm(p)-\ 1768–1813 Shawnee Indian chief
Ted·der \'ted-ər\ 1st Baron 1890–1967 Arthur William Tedder Brit. air marshal
Teil·hard de Char·din \tā-yár-də-shár-daⁿ\ Pierre 1881–1955 Fr. philos. & paleontologist
Tek·a·kwitha \,tek-ə-'kwith-ə\ or Teg·a·kwitha \,teg-\ or Teg·a·kouita \,teg-ə-'kwit-ə\ Ka·teri \'kät-ə-rē\1656–1680 Lily of the Mohawks Am. Indian religious
Te·le·mann \'tā-lə-,män\ Georg Philipp 1681–1767 Ger. composer
Tel·ler \'tel-ər\ Edward 1908– Am. (Hung.-born) physicist
Téllez Gabriel — see TIRSO DE MOLINA
Tem·in \'tem-ən\ Howard Martin 1934– Am. oncologist
Tem·ple \'tem-pəl\ Frederick 1821–1902 archbishop of Canterbury (1896–1902)
Temple Shirley 1928– Am. actress & polit.
Temple Sir William 1628–1699 Brit. statesman
Temple William 1881–1944 son of Frederick archbishop of Canterbury (1942–44)
Templewood Viscount — see HOARE
Teng Hsiao–p'ing or Deng Xiao·ping \'dəŋ-'shaù-'piŋ\ 1904– Chin. Communist leader (1977–)
Te·niers \tə-'ni(ə)rs, ə-'tə·'nyä\ David the Elder 1582–1649 & the Younger 1610–1690 Flem. painters
Ten·niel \'ten-yəl\ Sir John 1820–1914 Eng. cartoonist & illustrator
Ten·ny·son \'ten-ə-sən\ Alfred 1809–1892 1st Baron Tennyson known as Alfred, Lord Tennyson Eng. poet; poet laureate (1850–92) — Ten·ny·so·nian \,ten-ə-'sō-nē-ən, -nyən\ adj
Ter·borch or Ter Borch \tər-'bȯrk, -'bȯrk\ Gerard 1617–1681 Du. painter
Ter·brug·ghen \tər-'brü-gən\ Hendrik 1588–1629 Du. painter
Ter·ence \'ter-ən(t)s\ 186(or 185)–?159 B.C. Publius Terentius Afer Rom. dram.
Te·re·sa \tə-'rä-zə, -'rē-sə\ Mother 1910– Agnes Gonxha Bojaxhiu Albanian religious in India
Teresa of Avila Saint 1515–1582 Span. Carmelite & mystic
Te·resh·ko·va \,ter-əsh-'kȯ-və, -'kō-\ Valentina Vladimirovna 1937– Russ. cosmonaut; 1st woman in space (1963)
Ter·hune \(,)tər-'hyün\ Albert Payson 1872–1942 Am. author
Ter·ry \'ter-ē\ (Alice) Ellen 1847–1928 Eng. actress
Ter·tul·lian \(,)tər-'təl-yən\ ca A.D. 155(or 160)–after 220 Quintus Septimius Florens Tertullianus church father
Tes·la \'tes-lə\ Nikola 1856–1943 Am. (Croatian-born) electrical engineer & inventor
Tet·zel or Te·zel \'tet-səl\ Johann ca1465–1519 Ger. Dominican monk
Thack·er·ay \'thak(-ə)-rē\ William Makepeace 1811–1863 Eng. author — Thack·er·ay·an \-rē-ən\ adj
Tha·les \'thā-(,)lēz\ of Miletus 625?–?547 B.C. Greek philos. — Tha·le·sian \thā-'lē-zhən\ adj
Thant \'thant, 'thänt\ U \'ü\ 1909–1974 Burmese U.N. official; secy.= gen. (1961–71)
Thatch·er \'thach-ər\ Margaret Hilda 1925– née Roberts Brit. prime min. (1979–)
Thayer \'tha(ə)r, 'the(ə)r, 'thā-ər\ Sylvanus 1785–1872 father of West Point Am. army officer & educ.
Thei·ler \'tī-lər\ Max 1899–1972 Am. (So. African-born) microbiologist
The·mis·to·cles \thə-'mis-tə-,klēz\ ca 524–ca 460 B.C. Athenian gen. & statesman
The·oc·ri·tus \thē-'äk-rət-əs\ ca 310–250 B.C. Greek poet
The·od·o·ric \thē-'äd-ə-rik\ 454?–526 the Great king of the Ostrogoths (493–526)
The·o·do·sius I \,thē-ə-'dō-sh(ē-)əs\ 347–395 the Great Rom. gen. & emp. (379–395)
The·o·phras·tus \,thē-ə-'fras-təs\ ca 372–ca 287 B.C. Greek philos. & naturalist
The·o·rell \,tā-ə-'rel\ Axel Hugo Theodor 1903–1982 Swed. biochem.
Theresa Saint — see TERESA OF AVILA

Thes·pis \'thes-pəs\ 6th cent. B.C. Greek poet
Thiers \tē-'e(ə)r\ Louis-Adolphe 1797–1877 Fr. statesman & hist.
Tho·mas \tȯ-'mä\ (Charles-Louis-)Ambroise 1811–1896 Fr. composer
Thom·as \'täm-əs\ Augustus 1857–1934 Am. dram.
Thomas Dyl·an \'dil-ən\ Marlais 1914–1953 Welsh poet
Thomas Norman Mat·toon \ma-'tün, mə-\ 1884–1968 Am. socialist polit.
Thomas Seth 1785–1859 Am. clock manuf.
Thomas (Christian Friedrich) Theodore 1835–1905 Am. (Ger.-born) conductor
Thomas à Becket — see BECKET
Thomas à Kem·pis \-ə-'kem-pəs, -(,)ä-'kem-\ 1379(or 1380)–1471 orig. Thomas Hemerken Du. ecclesiastic & writer
Thomas Aqui·nas \-ə-'kwī-nəs\ Saint 1224(or 1225)–1274 Ital. Tommaso d'Aquino Ital. religious & philos.
Thomas of Er·cel·doune \-ər-səl-,dün\ fl 1220–1297 Thomas the Rhymer and Thomas Learmont Scot. seer & poet
Thomp·son \'täm(p)-sən\ Benjamin 1753–1814 Count Rum·ford \'rəm(p)-fərd\ Brit. (Am.-born) physicist & statesman
Thompson Dorothy 1894–1961 Am. journalist
Thompson Francis 1859–1907 Eng. poet
Thompson Sir John Sparrow David 1844–1894 Canad. statesman; prime min. (1892–94)
Thom·son \'täm(p)-sən\ Sir George Pag·et \'paj-ət\ 1892–1975 son of Sir Joseph John Eng. physicist
Thomson James 1700–1748 Scot. poet
Thomson James 1834–1882 B. V. or Bysshe Vanolis Scot. poet
Thomson John Arthur 1861–1933 Scot. biol.
Thomson Sir Joseph John 1856–1940 Eng. physicist
Thomson Virgil Garnett 1896–1989 Am. composer & critic
Thomson William — see Baron KELVIN
Tho·reau \thə-'rō, thō-\ Henry David 1817–1862 orig. David Henry Thoreau Am. writer — Tho·reau·vi·an \thə-'rō-vē-ən, thō-\ adj
Tho·rez \tȯ-'rez\ Maurice 1900–1964 Fr. polit.
Thorn·burgh \'thȯrn-,bərg\ Richard L. 1932– U.S. atty. gen. (1988–)
Thorn·dike \'thȯrn-,dīk\ Ashley Horace 1871–1933 & his brother Lynn 1882–1965 Am. educators
Thorndike Dame (Agnes) Sybil 1882–1976 Brit. actress
Thorn·ton \'thȯrnt-ʰn\ William 1759–1828 Am. architect
Thorpe \'thȯ(ə)rp\ James Francis 1866–1953 Jim Am. athlete
Thor·vald·sen or Thor·wald·sen \'t(h)ȯr-,wȯl-sən, 'tùr-,väl-sən\ Ber·tel \'bert-ʰl\ 1768(or 1770)–1844 Dan. sculptor
Thras·y·bu·lus \,thras-ə-'byü-ləs\ d 388 B.C. Athenian gen.
Thu·cyd·i·des \th(y)ü-'sid-ə-,dēz\ d ca 401 B.C. Greek hist. — Thu·cyd·i·de·an \(,)th(y)ü-,sid-ə-'dē-ən\ adj
Thur·ber \'thər-bər\ James Grover 1894–1961 Am. writer
Thut·mo·se \'thüt-'mō-sə\ name of 4 kings of Egypt: esp. III d 1450 B.C. (reigned 1504–1450 B.C.)
Thys·sen \'tis-ʰn\ Fritz 1873–1951 Ger. industrialist
Tib·bett \'tib-ət\ Lawrence Mervil 1896–1960 Am. baritone
Ti·be·ri·us \tī-'bir-ē-əs\ 42 B.C.–A.D. 37 Tiberius Claudius Nero Caesar Augustus Rom. emp. (14–37)
Ti·bul·lus \tə-'bəl-əs\ Albius ca 55–ca 19 B.C. Rom. poet
Tieck \'tēk\ (Johann) Ludwig 1773–1853 Ger. author
Tie·po·lo \tē-'ā-pə-,lō, -'ep-ə-\ Giovanni Battista 1696–1770 Ital. painter
Tif·fa·ny \'tif-ə-nē\ Charles Lewis 1812–1902 Am. jeweler
Tiffany Louis Comfort 1848–1933 son of C.L. Am. artist & glass manuf.
Tig·lath–pi·le·ser III \'tig-,lath-(,)pī-'lē-zər-, -pə-\ d 727 B.C. king of Assyria (745–727)
Til·den \'til-dən\ Samuel Jones 1814–1886 Am. polit.
Til·dy \'til-dē\ Zol·tán \'zōl-,tän\ 1889–1961 Hung. polit.
Til·lich \'til-ik\ Paul Johannes 1886–1965 Am. (Ger.-born) theol.
Til·lot·son \'til-ət-sən\ John 1630–1694 Eng. divine
Til·ly \'til-ē\ Graf von 1559–1632 Johann Tser·claes \tsər-'kläs\ Bavarian gen.
Ti·mo·shen·ko \,tim-ə-'shen-(,)kō\ Semyon \səm-'yȯn\ Konstantinovich 1895–1970 Soviet marshal
Tim·ur \'tim-,(,)ù(ə)r\ or Timur Lenk \-'leŋk\ 1336–1405 E. Tam·er·lane \'tam-ər-,lān\ or Tam·bur·laine \'tam-bər-,lān\ Turkic conqueror
Tin·ber·gen \'tin-,ber-kə(n)\ Jan 1903– Du. econ.
Tinbergen Nikolaas 1907–1988 bro. of Jan Du. ethologist
Ting \'tiŋ\ Samuel Chao Chung 1936– Am. physicist
Ting·ley \'tiŋ-lē\ Katherine Augusta 1847–1929 née Westcott Am. theosophist
Tin·to·ret·to \,tin-tə-'ret-(,)ō\ ca 1518–1594 Jacopo Robusti Ital. painter
Ti·pu or Tip·pu Sul·tan \tip-(,)ü-'sùl-,tän\ 1749(or 1753)–1799 sultan of Mysore (1782–99)
Tir·pitz \'ti(ə)r-pəts, 'tər-\ Alfred von 1849–1930 Ger. admiral
Tir·so de Mo·li·na \'ti(ə)r-(,)sō-,dā-mə-'lē-nə\ ca 1584–1648 pseud. of Gabriel Téllez Span. dram.
Ti·se·li·us \tə-'sä-lē-əs, -'zä-\ Arne Wilhelm Kaurin 1902–1971 Swed. biochem.
Ti·so \'tē-(,)sō\ Josef or Joseph 1887–1947 Slovak priest & polit.
Titch·en·er \'tich-ə-nər\ Edward Bradford 1867–1927 Am. psychol.
Ti·tian \'tish-ən\ ca1488–1576 Tiziano Vecellio Ital. painter — Ti·tian·esque \,tish-ə-'nesk\ adj
Tito \'tēt-(,)ō\ 1892–1980 orig. Josip Broz; usu. called Marshal Tito leader of Yugoslavia (1943–80)
Ti·tus \'tīt-əs\ A.D. 39–81 Titus Flavius Vespasianus Rom. emp. (79–81)
To·bin \'tō-bən\ James 1918– Am. econ.
Tocque·ville \'tōk-,vil, 'tōk-; 'täk-, -,vil, -vəl\ Alexis-Charles-Henri Clérel de 1805–1859 Fr. statesman & author
Todd \'täd\ Sir Alexander Robertus 1907– Brit. chem.
Todt \'tōt\ Fritz 1891–1942 Ger. military engineer
To·gliat·ti \tōl-'yät-ē\ Pal·mi·ro \päl-'mē-(,)rō\ 1893–1964 Ital. Communist

Tō·gō \'tō-(ˌ)gō\ Marquis Heihachirō 1848–1934 Jp. admiral
Tō·jō \'tō-(ˌ)jō\ Hideki 1884–1948 Jp. gen. & polit.
To·ku·ga·wa \ˌtō-kü-'gä-wə\ Ieyasu 1543–1616 orig. *Matsudaira Take-chiyo* Jp. shogun (1603–05); founder of last Jp. shogunate (1603–1867)
Tol·kien \'tòl-ˌkēn\ John Ronald Reuel 1892–1973 Eng. author
Tol·ler \'tòl-ər, 'täl-\ Ernst 1893–1939 Ger. dram. & polit.
Tol·stoy \tòl-'stòi, tōl-', täl-', 'tòl-, , 'tōl-, , 'täl-,\ Count Lev Nikolaye-vich 1828–1910 Russ. nov., philos., & mystic — **Tol·stoy·an** *also* **Tol·stoi·an** \-ən\ *adj*
Tom·baugh \'täm-ˌbò\ Clyde William 1906– Am. astron.
Tom·ma·si·ni \ˌtäm-ə-'zē-nē\ Vincenzo 1878–1950 Ital. composer
To·mo·na·ga \ˌtō-mə-'näg-ə, -mō-\ Shin'ichirō 1906–1979 Jp. physicist
Tomp·kins \'täm(p)-kənz\ Daniel D. 1774–1825 Am. polit.; vice pres. of the U.S. (1817–25)
Tone \'tōn\ (Theobald) Wolfe 1763–1798 Irish revolutionary
To·ne·ga·wa \ˌtō-nə-'gä-wə\ Susumu 1939– Am. (Jp.-born) biol.
Tooke \'tuk\ (John) Horne 1736–1812 Eng. polit. radical & philologist
Toombs \'tümz\ Robert Augustus 1810–1885 Am. polit.
Tor·que·ma·da \ˌtòr-kə-'mäd-ə, -'mäth-ə\ Tomás de 1420–1498 Span. grand inquisitor
Tor·ri·cel·li \ˌtòr-ə-'chel-ē, ˌtär-\ Evangelista 1608–1647 Ital. math. & physicist
Tos·ca·ni·ni \ˌtäs-kə-'nē-nē, ˌtòs-\ Ar·tu·ro \är-'tü(ə)r-(ˌ)ō\ 1867–1957 Ital. conductor
Tou·louse–Lau·trec (**–Mon·fa**) \tü-ˌlüz-lō-'trek(-mōⁿ-'fä)\ Henri-Marie-Raymond de 1864–1901 Fr. painter
Tour·neur \'tər-nər\ Cyril *ca* 1575–1626 Eng. dram.
Tous·saint–Lou·ver·ture \'tü-ˌsan-'lü-vər-ˌt(y)ü(ə)r\ *ca* 1743–1803 orig. *François-Dominique Toussaint* Haitian gen. & liberator
Townes \'taunz\ Charles Hard 1915– Am. physicist
Toyn·bee \'tòin-bē\ Arnold Joseph 1889–1975 Eng. hist.
Tra·jan \'trā-jən\ A.D. 53–117 orig. *Marcus Ulpius Traiánus* usu. called *Germanicus* Rom. emp. (98–117)
Trau·bel \'trau-bəl\ Helen 1903–1972 Am. soprano
Tree \'trē\ Sir Herbert Draper Beerbohm 1853–1917 Eng. actor–manager
Treitsch·ke \'trīch-kə\ Heinrich von 1834–1896 Ger. hist.
Tre·vel·yan \tri-'vel-yən, -'vil-\ George Macaulay 1876–1962 Eng. hist.
Trevelyan Sir George Otto 1838–1928 *father of prec.* Eng. polit., biographer, & hist.
Trol·lope \'träl-əp\ Anthony 1815–1882 Eng. nov. — **Trol·lo·pi·an** \trä-'lō-pē-ən\ *adj*
Tromp \'trómp, 'trämp\ Maarten Harpertszoon 1598–1653 Du. admiral
Trots·ky \'trät-skē *also* 'tròt-\ Leon 1879–1940 orig. *Lev Davidovich Bronstein* Russ. Communist
Tru·deau \'trü-(ˌ)dō, trü-'\ Pierre Elliott 1919– Canad. polit.; prime min. (1968–79; 1980–84)
Tru·ji·llo Mo·li·na \trü-'hē-(ˌ)(y)ō-mə-'lē-nə\ Rafael Leónidas 1891–1961 Dominican gen. & polit.; pres. of Dominican Republic (1930–38; 1942–52)
Tru·man \'trü-mən\ Harry S 1884–1972 33d pres. of the U.S. (1945–53)
Trum·bull \'trəm-bəl\ John 1756–1843 Am. painter
Trumbull Jonathan 1710–1785 *father of prec.* Am. statesman
Ts'ao Chan \'tsau-'jän\ 1715?–1763 *Ts'ao Hsüeh-ch'in* Chin. nov.
Tschaikovsky *var of* TCHAIKOVSKY
Tu Fu \'tü-'fü\ 712–770 Chin. poet
Tub·man \'təb-mən\ Harriet *ca*1820–1913 Am. abolitionist
Tubman William Vacanarat Shadrach 1895–1971 Liberian lawyer; pres. of Liberia (1944–71)
Tuch·man \'tək-mən\ Barbara 1912–1989 Am. hist.
Tu·dor \'t(y)üd-ər\ Antony 1908 (or 1909)–1987 Am. (Brit.-born) ballet dancer & choreographer
Tul·si·dās \ˌtül-sē-'däs\ 1543?–1623 Hindu poet
Tup·per \'təp-ər\ Sir Charles 1821–1915 Canad. polit.; prime min. (1896)
Tu·renne \tü-'ren\ Vicomte de 1611–1675 *Henri de La Tour d'Auvergne* marshal of France
Tur·ge·nev \tur-'gän-yəf, -'gen-\ Ivan Sergeyevich 1818–1883 Russ. nov.
Tur·got \tur-'gō\ Anne-Robert-Jacques 1727–1781 Baron *de l'Aulne* \'lōn\ Fr. statesman & econ.
Tur·ner \'tər-nər\ Frederick Jackson 1861–1932 Am. hist.
Turner Joseph Mallord William 1775–1851 Eng. painter
Turner Nat 1800–1831 Am. slave insurrectionist
Tut·ankh·a·men \ˌtü-ˌtaŋ-'käm-ən, -ˌtän-\ *or* **Tut·ankh·a·ten** \-'kät-ⁿn\ *ca*1370–1352 B.C. king of Egypt (1361–1352 B.C.)
Tutu \'tü-ˌtü\ Desmond Mpilo 1931– So. African clergyman
Twacht·man \'twäk(t)-mən\ John Henry 1853–1902 Am. painter
Twain Mark — *see* CLEMENS
Tweed \'twēd\ William Marcy 1823–1878 *Boss Tweed* Am. polit.
Tweedsmuir — *see* BUCHAN
Ty·ler \'tī-lər\ John 1790–1862 10th pres. of the U.S. (1841–45)
Tyler Wat \'wät\ *or* Walter *d* 1381 Eng. leader of Peasants' Revolt (1381)
Tyn·dale *or* **Tin·dal** *or* **Tin·dale** \'tin-dᵊl\ William *ca*1494–1536 Eng. reformer & translator
Tyn·dall \'tin-dᵊl\ John 1820–1893 Brit. physicist
Tyr·whitt–Wil·son \ˌtir-ət-'wil-sən\ Gerald Hugh 1883–1950 14th Baron *Ber·ners* \'bər-nərz\ Eng. composer & painter
Tz'u–hsi \'tsü-'shē\ 1835–1908 Chin. empress dowager
Uc·cel·lo \ü-'chel-(ˌ)ō\ Paolo 1397–1475 orig. *Paolo di Dono* Florentine painter
Udall \'yü-ˌdòl, 'yüd-ᵊl\ Nicholas 1505–1556 Eng. schoolmaster & dram.
Ugar·te \ü-'gärt-ē\ Manuel 1874–1951 Argentine writer
Uh·land \'ü-ˌlänt\ Johann Ludwig 1787–1862 Ger. poet & hist.
Ul·bricht \'ul-ˌbrikt, -ˌ)brikt\ Walter 1893–1973 East German polit.
Ul·fi·las \'ul-fə-ˌläs, -əl-, -ˌləs, -ˌlas\ *or* Goth. **Wul·fi·la** \'wul-fə-lə\ *ca* 311–*ca* 382 Gothic missionary
Ul·pi·an \'əl-pē-ən\ *d* A.D. 228 *Domitius Ulpianus* Rom. jurist
Um·ber·to \(ˌ)əm-'ber-(ˌ)tō\ name of 2 kings of Italy: **I** 1844–1900 Duke of *Savoy* (reigned 1878–1900); **II** 1904–1983 Prince of *Piedmont;* Count of *Sarre* (reigned 1946)
Una·mu·no y Ju·go \ˌü-nə-'mü-(ˌ)nō-ē-'hü-(ˌ)gō\ Miguel de 1864–1936 Span. philos. & writer

Un·cas \'ən-kəs\ 1588?–?1683 Pequot Indian chief
Und·set \'ún-ˌset\ Si·grid \'sig-rē, -rəd\ 1882–1949 Norw. nov.
Uno \u-(ˌ)nō\ Sousuke 1922– prime min. of Japan (1989)
Un·ter·mey·er \'ənt-ər-ˌmī(-ə)r\ Louis 1885–1977 Am. poet
Up·dike \'əp-ˌdīk\ John Hoyer 1932– Am. writer
Up·john \'əp-ˌjän\ Richard 1802–1878 Am. (Eng.-born) architect
Up·ton \'əp-tən\ Emory 1839–1881 Am. gen. & author
Ur·ban \'ər-bən\ name of 8 popes: esp. **II** (*Odo* \'öd-(ˌ)ō\ *of Lagery*) *ca* 1035–1099 (pope 1088–99)
Urey \'yu(ə)r-ē\ Harold Clayton 1893–1981 Am. chem.
Ur·quhart \'ər-kərt, -ˌkärt\ *or* **Ur·chard** \ər-chərd\ Sir Thomas 1611–1660 Scot. author & translator
Ussher \'əsh-ər\ James 1581–1656 Irish prelate
Utril·lo \yü-'tril-(ˌ)ō; ˌyü-trē-'ō, ˌü-\ Maurice 1883–1955 Fr. painter
Val·de·mar \'väl-də-ˌmär, 'val-\ *or* **Wal·de·mar** \'wòl-\ name of 4 kings of Denmark: esp. **I** 1131–1182 (reigned 1157–82)
Valdes Peter — *see* WALDO
Val·di·via \val-'dē-vē-ə\ Pedro de *ca* 1498–1553 Span. conqueror of Chile
Va·lens \'vā-lənz, -ˌlenz\ 328?–378 Rom. emp. of the East (364–378)
Val·en·tin·ian \ˌval-ən-'tin-ē-ən, -'tin-yən\ *L* **Val·en·tin·i·a·nus** \'val-ən-ˌtin-ē-'ā-nəs\ name of 3 Rom. emperors: **I** 321–375 (reigned 364–375); **II** 371–392 (reigned 375–392); **III** 419–455 (reigned 425–455)
Valera Eamon de — *see* DE VALERA
Va·le·ra y Al·ca·lá Ga·lia·no \və-'ler-ə-ˌē-ˌäl-kə-'lä-ˌgal-ē-'än-(ˌ)ō, -ˌäl-kə-, -ˌgäl-\ Juan 1824–1905 Span. writer & statesman
Va·le·ri·an \və-'lir-ē-ən\ *d* A.D. 260 *Publius Licinius Valerianus* Rom. emp. (253–260)
Va·lé·ry \ˌval-ə-'rē, 'val-ə-rē\ (Ambroise-) Paul-Toussaint-Jules 1871–1945 Fr. poet & philos.
Val·le·jo \və-'lā-(ˌ)ō, -'yā-(ˌ)(h)ō\ Mariano Guadalupe 1808–1890 Am. soldier & pioneer
Van Al·len \van-'al-ən\ James Alfred 1914– Am. physicist
Van·brugh \'van-brə, van-'brü\ Sir John 1664–1726 Eng. dram. & architect
Van Bu·ren \van-'byür-ən, vən-\ Martin 1782–1862 8th pres. of the U.S. (1837–41)
Van·cou·ver \van-'kü-vər\ George 1757–1798 Eng. navigator & explorer
Van·de·grift \'van-də-ˌgrift\ Alexander Archer 1887–1973 Am. marine-corps gen.
Van·den·berg \'van-dən-ˌbərg\ Arthur Hendrick 1884–1951 Am. journalist & polit.
Van·der·bilt \'van-dər-ˌbilt\ Cornelius 1794–1877 Am. industrialist
van der Meer \ˌvän-dər-'me(ə)r\ Simon 1925– Du. physicist
Van Dine — *see* Willard Huntington WRIGHT
van Dongen Kees — *see* DONGEN
Van Do·ren \van-'dōr-ən, vən-, -'dòr-\ Carl Clinton 1885–1950 & his bro. Mark 1894–1972 Am. writers & editors
Van Dyck *or* **Van·dyke** \van-'dīk, vən-\ Sir Anthony 1599–1641 Flem. painter
Vane \'vān\ Sir Henry 1613–1662 *the Younger* Eng. statesman
Vane John R. 1927– Eng. pharmacologist
Van Eyck — *see* EYCK, VAN
Van Rens·se·laer \ˌvan-ˌren(t)-sə-'li(ə)r, -, ren-'sli(ə)r, vən-; -'ren(t)-s(ə-)lər\ Stephen 1764–1839 Am. gen. & polit.
van't Hoff \vänt-'hòf, vant-\ Jacobus Hen·dri·cus \hen-'drē-kəs\ 1852–1911 Du. physical chem.
Van Vleck \van-'vlek\ John Hasbrouck 1899–1980 Am. physicist
Vanzetti Bartolomeo — *see* Nicola SACCO
Va·rèse \və-'räz, -'rez\ Edgard 1883–1965 orig. *Edgar Victor Achille Charles Varèse* Am. (Fr.-born) composer
Var·gas \'vär-gəs\ Getúlio Dornelles 1883–1954 Braz. lawyer; pres. of Brazil (1930–45; 1951–54)
Var·mus \'vär-məs\ Harold Elliot 1939– Am. microbiologist
Var·ro \'var-(ˌ)ō\ Marcus Terentius 116–27 B.C. Rom. scholar
Va·sa·ri \və-'zär-ē\ Giorgio 1511–1574 Ital. artist & art hist.
Vasco da Gama — *see* GAMA
Va·tu·tin \və-'tü-tin\ Nikolay Fyodorovich 1900–1944 Russ. gen.
Vau·ban \vō-'bäⁿ\ Sébastien Le Prestre de 1633–1707 Fr. mil. engineer; marshal of France
Vaughan \'vòn, 'vän\ Henry 1621?–1695 Brit. poet
Vaughan Sarah Lois 1924–1990 Am. singer
Vaughan Wil·liams \-'wil-yəmz\ Ralph 1872–1958 Eng. composer
Ve·blen \'veb-lən\ Thor·stein \'thò(ə)r-ˌstīn\ Bunde 1857–1929 Am. sociol. & econ. — **Veb·le·ni·an** \veb-'lē-nē-ən\ *adj*
Ve·ga \'vā-gə\ Lo·pe \'lō-(ˌ)pä\ de 1562–1635 *Lope Félix de Vega Carpio* Span. dram.
Ve·láz·quez \və-'las-kəs\ Diego Rodríguez de Silva 1599–1660 Span. painter
Ven·dôme \väⁿ(n)-'dōm\ Duc de 1654–1712 *Louis-Joseph* Fr. soldier; marshal of France
Ve·ni·zé·los \ˌven-ə-'zā-ləs, -'zel-əs\ Eleuthérios 1864–1936 Greek statesman
Ver·di \'ve(ə)rd-ē\ Giuseppe Fortunio Francesco 1813–1901 Ital. composer — **Ver·di·an** \-ən\ *adj*
Ve·re·ker \'ver-ə-kər\ John Standish Surtees Prendergast 1886–1946 6th Viscount *Gort* Brit. soldier
Ve·re·shcha·gin \ˌver-əsh-'chäg-ən, ˌver-ə-'shäg-\ Vasily Vasilyevich 1842–1904 Russ. painter
Vergil — *see* VIRGIL
Ver·laine \ve(ə)r-'län, -'len\ Paul 1844–1896 Fr. poet
Ver·meer \vər-'me(ə)r, -'mi(ə)r\ Jan 1632–1675 also called *Jan van der Meer van Delft* Du. painter
Verne Jules \'jülz-'vərn, 'zhül-'ve(ə)rn\ 1828–1905 Fr. writer
Ver·ner \'ve(ə)r-nər\ Karl Adolph 1846–1896 Dan. philologist
Ver·nier \ver-ˌnyā\ *or* Pierre *ca*1580–1637 Fr. math.
Ver·non \'vər-nən\ Edward 1684–1757 Eng. admiral
Ve·ro·ne·se \ˌver-ə-'nā-sē, -'nā-zē\ Paolo 1528–1588 orig. *Paolo Caliari* Ital. painter
Ver·raz·za·no *or* **Ver·raz·za·no** \ˌver-ə-'zän-(ˌ)ō, -ət-'sän-\ Giovanni da 1485?–?1528 Florentine navigator
Ver·roc·chio \və-'rōk-ē-ˌō\ Andrea del 1435–1488 orig. *Andrea di Michele Cione* Florentine sculptor & painter
Verulam — *see* Francis BACON

Ve·rus \'vir-əs\ Lucius Aurelius A.D. 130–169 orig. *Lucius Ceionius Commodus* Rom. emp. (161–169)
Ver·woerd \fər-'vů(ə)rt, fer-\ Hendrik Frensch 1901–1966 So. African polit.; prime min. (1958–66)
Ve·sa·li·us \və-'sāl-ē-əs, -'zāl-\ Andreas 1514–1564 Belg. anatomist
Ve·sey \'vē-zē\ Denmark *ca* 1767–1822 Am. slave insurrectionist
Ves·pa·sian \ve-'spā-zh(ē-)ən\ A.D. 9–79 *Titus Flavius Sabinus Vespasianus* Rom. emp. (69–79)
Ves·puc·ci \ve-'sp(y)ü-chē\ Ame·ri·go \ə-'mer-i-,gō, It ,äm-ə-'rē-(,)gō\ 1454–1512 L. *Amer·i·cus Ves·pu·cius* \ə-'mer-ə-kəs,-ves-'pyü-sh(ē-)əs\ Ital. navigator; eponym of *America*
Vi·co \'vē-kō\ Giambattista 1668–1744 Ital. philos.
Vic·tor Em·man·u·el I \,vik-tər-i-'man-yə-wəl\ 1759–1824 king of Sardinia (1802–21)
Victor Emmanuel II 1820–1878 king of Sardinia-Piedmont (1849–61) & 1st king of Italy (1861–78)
Victor Emmanuel III 1869–1947 king of Italy (1900–46)
Vic·to·ria \vik-'tōr-ē-ə, -'tor-\ 1819–1901 *Alexandrina Victoria* queen of Great Britain (1837–1901)
Victoria Tomás Luis de *ca* 1548–1611 Span. composer
Vi·da \'vēd-ə\ Marco Girolamo *ca* 1490–1566 Ital. poet
Vi·gée–Le·brun \vē-'zhä-lə-'brəⁿ(n), -'brœⁿ\ Marie-Louise-Élisabeth 1755–1842 Fr. painter
Vi·gno·la \vēn-'yō-lə\ Giacomo da 1507–1573 Ital. architect
Vi·gny \vēn-'yē\ Alfred-Victor de 1797–1863 Fr. author
Vil·la \'vē-(y)ə\ Francisco usu. called Pan·cho \'pän-(,)chō, 'pan-\ 1878–1923 orig. *Doroteo Arango* Mex. bandit & revolutionary
Vil·la–Lo·bos \,vē-lə-'lō-(,)bōs, -bəs\ Heitor \'ā-,tòr\ 1887–1959 Braz. composer
Vil·lard \və-'lär(d)\ Oswald Garrison 1872–1949 Am. journalist
Vil·lars \vi-'lär\ Claude-Louis-Hector 1653–1734 Duc *de Villars* Fr. soldier; marshal of France
Ville·neuve \,vēl(-ə)-'nœ(r)v, -'nœv\ Pierre-Charles-Jean-Baptiste-Silvestre de 1763–1806 Fr. admiral
Vil·liers \'vil-(y)ərz\ George 1592–1628 1st Duke of *Buck·ing·ham* \'bək-iŋ-əm, *US also* -iŋ-,ham\ Eng. courtier & polit.
Villiers George 1628–1687 2d Duke of *Buckingham, son of prec.* Eng. courtier & dram.
Vil·lon \vē-'(y)ōⁿ *also* -'lōⁿ\ François 1431–after 1463 orig. *François de Montcorbier or Des Loges* Fr. poet
Vil·lon \vē-'lōⁿ, -'yōⁿ\ Jacques 1875–1963 orig. *Gaston Duchamp; bro. of Marcel Duchamp* Fr. painter
Vin·cent de Paul \,vin(t)-sənt-də-'pòl\ Saint 1581–1660 Fr. religious
Vinci, da Leonardo — see LEONARDO DA VINCI
Vi·no·gra·doff \,vin-ə-'grad-,òf\ Sir Paul Gavrilovitch 1854–1925 Brit. (Russ.-born) jurist & hist.
Vin·son \'vin(t)-sən\ Frederick Moore 1890–1953 Am. jurist; chief justice U.S. Supreme Court (1946–53)
Viol·let–le–Duc \,vē-ə-'lā-lə-'d(y)ük, vyò-le-lə-dūēk\ Eugène-Emmanuel 1814–1879 Fr. architect
Vir·chow \'fi(ə)r-(,)kō, 'vi(ə)r-\ Rudolf 1821–1902 Ger. pathologist
Vir·gil *also* Ver·gil \'vər-jəl\ *Publius Vergilius Maro* Rom. poet 70–19 B.C. poet — Vir·gil·ian *also* Ver·gil·ian \(,)vər-'jil-ē-ən\ *adj*
Vir·ta·nen \'vi(ə)r-tə-,nen\ Art·tu·ri \'ärt-ə-rē\ Ilmari 1895–1973 Finn. biochem.
Vi·tru·vi·us \və-'trü-vē-əs\ *fl* 1st cent. B.C. *Marcus Vitruvius Pollio* Rom. architect & engineer
Vi·val·di \vi-'väl-dē, -'vòl-\ Antonio Lucio 1678–1741 Ital. composer
Vla·di·mir I \'vlad-ə-,mi(ə)r, vlə-'dē-,mi(ə)r\ *ca* 956–1015 grand prince of Kiev (980–1015)
Vla·minck \vlə-'maŋk\ Maurice de 1876–1958 Fr. painter
Vo·gler \'fō-glər\ Georg Joseph 1749–1814 Abt \äpt, apt\ *or* Abbé *Vogler* Ger. composer & writer
Vol·stead \'väl-,sted, 'vòl-, 'vōl-, -stəd\ Andrew John 1860–1947 Am. legislator
Vol·ta \'vōl-tə, 'väl-, 'vòl-\ Conte Alessandro Giuseppe Antonio Anastasio 1745–1827 Ital. physicist
Vol·taire \vōl-'ta(ə)r, väl-, vòl-, -'te(ə)r\ 1694–1778 orig. *François-Marie Arouet* Fr. writer — Vol·tair·ean *or* Vol·tair·ian \-'tar-ē-ən, -'ter-\ *adj*
Von Braun Wernher — see BRAUN
Von Eu·ler \'fòn-'òi-lər\ Ulf Svante 1905–1983 Swed. physiol.
Von·ne·gut \'vän-i-gət\ Kurt 1922–   Am. writer
Vo·ro·shi·lov \,vòr-ə-'shē-,lòf, ,vär-, -,lòv\ Kliment Yefremovich 1881–1969 Soviet marshal; chairman of the Presidium (1953–60)
Vor·ster \'fòr-stər\ Balthazar Johannes 1915–1983 prime min. of Republic of So. Africa (1966–78)
Voz·ne·sen·sky \,väz-nə-'sen(t)-skē\ Andrey 1933–   Soviet poet
Vries \'vrēs\ Hugo Marie de 1848–1935 Du. botanist & geneticist
Vuil·lard \vwē-'yär\ (Jean-) Édouard 1868–1940 Fr. painter
Vy·shin·sky \vi-'shin(t)-skē\ Andrey Yanuaryevich 1883–1954 Soviet lawyer & statesman
Waals, van der \'van-dər-,wòlz\ Johannes Diderik 1837–1923 Du. physicist
Wace \'wās, 'wäs\ *ca* 1100–after 1174 Anglo-Norman poet
Wag·ner \'väg-nər\ (Wilhelm) Ri·chard \'rik-,ärt, 'rik-\ 1813–1883 Ger. composer — Wag·ner·ian \väg-'nir-ē-ən, -'ner-\ *adj*
Wagner von Jau·regg *or* Wagner–Jau·regg \-'yaù-,rek\ Julius 1857–1940 Austrian neurologist & psychiatrist
Wain·wright \'wān-,rīt\ Jonathan Mayhew 1883–1953 Am. gen.
Wainwright Richard father 1817–1862 & his son 1849–1926 Am. naval officers
Waite \'wāt\ Morrison Remick 1816–1888 Am. jurist; chief justice U.S. Supreme Court (1874–88)
Waks·man \'wäk-smən, 'wak-\ Sel·man \'sel-mən\ Abraham 1888–1973 Am. (Ukrainian-born) microbiologist
Wald \'wòld\ George 1906–   Am. biol.
Wald Lillian D. 1867–1940 Am. social worker
Waldemar — see VALDEMAR
Wal·der·see \'väl-dər-,zā, 'wòl-\ Alfred von 1832–1904 Ger. soldier
Wald·heim \'väld-,hīm\ Kurt 1918–   Austrian U.N. official; secy. gen. (1972–82); pres. of Austria (1986–   )
Wal·do \'wòl-(,)dō, 'wäl-\ *or* Val·des \'val-(,)däs, 'väl-\ Peter *d* before 1218 Fr. religious leader
Wa·le·sa \və-'len-sə, wä-\ Lech 1943–   Pol. labor leader

Walk·er \'wò-kər\ Francis Am·a·sa \'am-ə-sə\ 1840–1897 Am. econ.
Walker William 1824–1860 Am. filibuster
Wal·lace \'wäl-əs\ Alfred Russel 1823–1913 Eng. naturalist
Wallace George Corley 1919–   Am. polit.
Wallace Henry Agard \'ā-,gärd\ 1888–1965 Am. agriculturist, editor, & polit.; vice pres. of the U.S. (1941–45)
Wallace Lewis 1827–1905 *Lew* Am. lawyer, gen., & nov.
Wallace Sir William *ca* 1270–1305 Scot. patriot
Wal·lach \'wäl-ək, 'väl-\ Otto 1847–1931 Ger. chem.
Wal·len·berg \'wäl-ən-,berg, *Sw* -,ber-ē\ Raoul 1912–1947? Swed. diplomat & hero of the Holocaust
Wal·len·stein \'wäl-ən-,stīn\ Albrecht Eusebius Wenzel von 1583–1634 Duke of *Friedland and Mecklenburg;* Prince of *Sagan* Austrian gen.
Wal·ler \'wäl-ər\ Edmund 1606–1687 Eng. poet
Wal·pole \'wòl-,pōl, 'wäl-\ Horace 1717–1797 orig. *Horatio* 4th Earl of *Or·ford* \'òr-fərd\ Eng. author
Walpole Sir Hugh Seymour 1884–1941 Eng. nov.
Walpole Sir Robert 1676–1745 1st Earl of *Orford; father of Horace* Eng. statesman — Wal·pol·ian \wòl-'pō-lē-ən, wäl-\ *adj*
Wal·ter \'väl-tər, 'wòl-\ Bruno 1876–1962 orig. *Bruno Schle·sing·er* \'s(h)lā-ziŋ-ər\ Am. (Ger.-born) conductor
Wal·ther von der Vo·gel·wei·de \'väl-tər,-fòn-dər-'fō-gəl-,vīd-ə\ *ca* 1170–*ca* 1230 Ger. minnesinger & poet
Wal·ton \'wòlt-ᵊn\ Ernest Thomas Sinton 1903–   Irish physicist
Walton Izaak \'ī-zik, -zək\ 1593–1683 Eng. writer
Walton Sir William Turner 1902–1983 Eng. composer
Wan·a·ma·ker \'wän-ə-,mā-kər\ John 1838–1922 Am. merchant
Wang Ching–wei \'wäŋ-'jiŋ-'wä\ 1883–1944 Chin. polit.
War·beck \'wòr-,bek\ Perkin 1474–1499 Flem. imposter
War·burg \'wòr-,bərg, 'vär-,bů(ə)rk\ Otto Heinrich 1883–1970 Ger. biochem.
Ward \'wò(ə)rd\ Aaron Montgomery 1843–1913 Am. merchant
Ward Ar·te·mas \'ärt-ə-məs\ 1727–1800 Am. gen. in Revolution
Ward Artemus — see Charles Farrar BROWNE
Ward Barbara 1914–1981 Baroness *Jackson of Lodsworth* Eng. econ.
Ward Sir Joseph George 1856–1930 N.Z. statesman
Ward Mary Augusta 1851–1920 *Mrs. Humphry Ward* née *Arnold* Eng. nov.
War·hol \'wòr-,hòl, -,hōl\ Andy 1927?–1987 Am. artist & filmmaker
War·ner \'wòr-nər\ Charles Dudley 1829–1900 Am. editor & essayist
War·ren \'wòr-ən, 'wär-\ Earl 1891–1974 Am. jurist; chief justice U.S. Supreme Court (1953–69)
Warren Gou·ver·neur \,gəv-ə(r)-'ni(ə)r\ Kemble 1830–1882 Am. gen.
Warren Joseph 1741–1775 Am. physician & gen.
Warren Robert Penn 1905–1989 Am. author & educ.; poet laureate (1986–87)
War·ton \'wòrt-ᵊn\ Thomas 1728–1790 Eng. lit. hist. & critic; poet laureate (1785–90)
War·wick \'wär-ik, *US also* 'wòr-ik, 'wòr-(,)wik\ Earl of 1428–1471 *Richard Nev·ille* \'nev-əl\; *the Kingmaker* Eng. soldier & statesman
Wash·ing·ton \'wòsh-iŋ-tən, 'wäsh-, *chiefly Midland also* 'wòr-shiŋ- *or* 'wär-shiŋ-\ Book·er \'bůk-ər\ Tal·ia·ferro \'täl-ə-vər\ 1856–1915 Am. educ.
Washington George 1732–1799 Am. gen.; 1st pres. of the U.S. (1789–97) — Wash·ing·to·nian \,wòsh-iŋ-'tō-nē-ən, ,wäsh-, -nyən\ *adj*
Was·ser·mann \'wäs-ər-mən, 'väs-\ August von 1866–1925 Ger. bacteriol.
Wa·ters \'wòt-ərz, 'wät-\ Ethel 1896–1977 Am. actress & singer
Wat·kins \'wät-kənz\ James David 1927–   U.S. secy. of energy (1989–   )
Wat·son \'wät-sən\ James Dewey 1928–   Am. geneticist
Watson John 1850–1907 pseud. *Ian Mac·lar·en* \mə-'klar-ən\ Scot. clergyman & author
Watson John Broadus 1878–1958 Am. psychol.
Watson Sir (John) William 1858–1935 Eng. poet
Watson–Watt \-'wät\ Sir Robert Alexander 1892–1973 Scot. physicist
Watt \'wät\ James 1736–1819 Scot. inventor
Wat·teau \wä-'tō, vä-\ (Jean-) Antoine 1684–1721 Fr. painter
Wat·ter·son \'wät-ər-sən, 'wòt-\ Henry 1840–1921 Am. journalist & polit.
Watts \'wäts\ George Frederic 1817–1904 Eng. painter & sculptor
Watts Isaac 1674–1748 Eng. theol. & hymn writer
Watts–Dun·ton \-'dənt-ᵊn\ Walter Theodore 1832–1914 Eng. critic & poet
Waugh \'wò\ Evelyn Arthur St. John 1903–1966 Eng. writer
Wa·vell \'wā-vəl\ 1st Earl 1883–1950 *Archibald Percival Wavell* Brit. field marshal; viceroy of India (1943–47)
Wayne \'wān\ Anthony 1745–1796 *Mad Anthony* Am. gen. in Revolution
Webb \'web\ Beatrice 1858–1943 née *Potter; wife of S.J.* Eng. socialist
Webb Sidney James 1859–1947 1st Baron *Passfield* Eng. socialist
Weber Carl Maria von 1786–1826 Ger. composer & conductor
Weber Max 1864–1920 Ger. sociol. & econ. — We·be·ri·an \vā-'bir-ē-ən\ *adj*
Web·er \'web-ər\ Max 1881–1961 Am. (Russ.-born) painter
We·bern \'vā-bərn\ Anton von 1883–1945 Austrian composer
Web·ster \'web-stər\ Daniel 1782–1852 Am. statesman & orator
Webster John *ca* 1580–*ca* 1625 Eng. dram.
Webster Noah 1758–1843 Am. lexicographer & author
Wedg·wood \'wej-,wůd\ Josiah 1730–1795 Eng. potter
Weems \'wēmz\ Mason Locke 1759–1825 *Parson Weems* Am. clergyman & biographer
Weill \'wī(ə)l, 'vī(ə)l\ Kurt \'ků(ə)rt\ 1900–1950 Am. (Ger.-born) composer
Wein·berg \'wīn-,bərg\ Steven 1933–   Am. physicist

Wein·ber·ger \'wīn-,bər-gər\ Caspar Willard 1917– U.S. secy. of defense (1981–87)
Weir \'wi(ə)r\ Robert Walter 1803–1889 Am. painter
Weis·mann \'vī-,smän, 'wī-smən\ August Friedrich Leopold 1834–1914 Ger. biol.
Weiz·mann \'vīt-smən, 'wīt-\ Chaim \'kim, 'hīm\ Azriel 1874–1952 Israeli (Russ.-born) chem.; 1st pres. of Israel (1949–52)
Welch \'welch, 'welsh\ William Henry 1850–1934 Am. pathologist
Wel·ler \'wel-ər\ Thomas Huckle 1915– Am. virologist
Welles \'welz\ (George) Or·son \'ôrs-ᵊn\ 1915–1985 Am. film & theater director, writer, producer, & actor
Welles Gideon 1802–1878 Am. polit. & writer
Welles Sumner 1892–1961 Am. diplomat
Welles·ley \'welz-lē\ 1st Marquis of 1760–1842 *Richard Colley Welles-ley* Brit. statesman; gov.-gen. of India (1797–1805)
Wel·ling·ton \'wel-iŋ-tən\ 1st Duke of 1769–1852 *Arthur Wellesley; the Iron Duke* Brit. gen. & statesman
Wells \'welz\ Herbert George 1866–1946 Eng. nov. & hist. — **Wells·ian** \'wel-zē-ən\ *adj*
Wel·ty \'wel-tē\ Eudora 1909– Am. writer
Wen·ces·las \'wen(t)-sə-,slôs, -sləs\ *G* **Wen·zel** \'ven(t)-səl\ 1361–1419 king of Germany & Holy Rom. emp. (1378–1400) & (as Wenceslas IV) king of Bohemia (1378–1419)
Wen·dell \'wen-dᵊl\ Barrett 1855–1921 Am. scholar
Went·worth \'went-(,)wərth\ William Charles 1793–1872 Austral. statesman
Wer·fel \'ver-fəl\ Franz 1890–1945 Ger. author
Wer·ner \'ve(ə)r-nər\ Alfred 1866–1919 Swiss chem.
Wes·ley \'wes-lē, 'wez-\ Charles 1707–1788 *bro. of John* Eng. Methodist preacher & hymn writer
Wesley John 1703–1791 Eng. theol., evangelist, & founder of Methodism
West \'west\ Benjamin 1738–1820 Am. painter
West Nathanael 1903–1940 orig. *Nathan Wallenstein Weinstein* Am. nov.
West Dame Rebecca 1892–1983 pseud. of *Cicily Isabel Andrews* née *Fairfield* Eng. critic & nov.
West Thomas — see DE LA WARR
Wes·ter·marck \'wes-tər-,märk\ Edward Alexander 1862–1939 Finn. philos. & anthropol.
Wes·ting·house \'wes-tiŋ-,haùs\ George 1846–1914 Am. inventor
Wet \'vät\ Christiaan Rudolf de 1854–1922 Boer soldier & polit.
Wey·den \'vīd-ᵊn, 'vād-\ Rogier van der 1399?–1464 Flem. painter
Wey·gand \vā-gän\ Maxime 1867–1965 Fr. gen.
Whar·ton \'hwort-ᵊn, 'wort-\ Edith Newbold 1862–1937 née *Jones* Am. nov.
Whate·ly \'hwāt-lē, 'wāt-\ Richard 1787–1863 Eng. theol. & logician
Wheat·ley \'hwēt-lē, 'wēt-\ Phillis 1753?–1784 Am. (African-born) poet
Wheat·stone \'hwēt-,stōn, 'wēt-, *chiefly Brit* -stən\ Sir Charles 1802–1875 Eng. physicist & inventor
Whee·ler \'hwē-lər, 'wē-\ Joseph 1836–1906 Am. gen.
Wheeler William Almon 1819–1887 Am. polit.; vice pres. of the U.S. (1877–81)
Whee·lock \'hwē-,läk, 'wē-\ Eleazar 1711–1779 Am. clergyman & educ.
Whip·ple \'hwip-əl, 'wip-\ George Hoyt 1878–1976 Am. pathologist
Whis·tler \'hwis-lər, 'wis-\ James Abbott McNeill 1834–1903 Am. painter & etcher — **Whis·tler·ian** \(h)wis-'lir-ē-ən\ *adj*
White \'hwīt, 'wīt\ Andrew Dickson 1832–1918 Am. educ. & diplomat
White Byron Raymond 1917– Am. jurist & polit.
White Edward Douglass 1845–1921 Am. jurist; chief justice U.S. Supreme Court (1910–21)
White Elwyn Brooks 1899–1985 Am. journalist & writer
White Gilbert 1720–1793 Eng. clergyman & naturalist
White Patrick Victor Martindale 1912– Austral. writer
White Stanford 1853–1906 Am. architect
White Stewart Edward 1873–1946 Am. writer
White Theodore Harold 1915–1986 Am. writer
White William Allen 1868–1944 Am. journalist & writer
White·field \'hwīt-,fēld, 'hwit-, 'wīt-, 'wit-\ George 1714–1770 Eng. Methodist revivalist
White·head \'hwīt-,hed, 'wīt-\ Alfred North 1861–1947 Eng. math. & philos.
Whitehead William 1715–1785 Eng. dram.; poet laureate (1757–85)
Whit·man \'hwit-mən, 'wit-\ Marcus 1802–1847 & his wife Narcissa 1808–1847 née *Prentiss* Am. missionaries & pioneers in the Oregon region
Whitman Walt \'wôlt\ 1819–1892 orig. *Walter* Am. poet — **Whit·man·esque** \,(h)wit-mə-'nesk\ *or* **Whit·ma·ni·an** \(h)wit-'mā-nē-ən\ *adj*
Whit·ney \'hwit-nē, 'wit-\ Eli 1765–1825 Am. inventor
Whitney Josiah Dwight 1819–1896 Am. geologist
Whitney William Dwight 1827–1894 *bro. of J.D.* Am. philologist
Whit·ta·ker \'hwit-i-kər, 'wit-\ Charles Evans 1901–1973 Am. jurist
Whit·ti·er \'hwit-ē-ər, 'wit-\ John Greenleaf 1807–1892 Am. poet
Wic·lif *or* **Wick·liffe** *var of* WYCLIFFE
Wi·dor \vē-'dô(ə)r\ Charles-Marie 1844–1937 Fr. organist & composer
Wie·land \'vē-,länt\ Christoph Martin 1733–1813 Ger. author
Wieland Heinrich 1877–1957 Ger. chem.
Wien \'vēn\ Wilhelm 1864–1928 Ger. physicist
Wie·ner \'wē-nər\ Norbert 1894–1964 Am. math.
Wie·sel \vē-'zel, wē-\ El·ie \'el-ē\ 1928– Am. (Rom.-born) writer
Wie·sel \vē-səl\ Torsten N. 1924– Swed. neurobiologist
Wig·gin \'wig-ən\ Kate Douglas 1856–1923 Am. writer & educ.
Wig·ner \'wig-nər\ Eugene Paul 1902– Am. (Hung.-born) physicist
Wil·ber·force \'wil-bər-,fō(ə)rs, -,fó(ə)rs\ William 1759–1833 Eng. philanthropist & abolitionist
Wil·bur \'wil-bər\ Richard Purdy 1921– Am. poet & translator; poet laureate (1987–)
Wilde \'wī(ə)ld\ Oscar Fingal O'Flahertie Wills 1854–1900 Irish writer — **Wil·de·an** \'wil-dē-ən\ *adj*
Wil·der \'wīl-dər\ Thornton Niven 1897–1975 Am. author
Wi·ley \'wī-lē\ Harvey Washington 1844–1930 Am. chem. & reformer
Wil·hel·mi·na \,wil-(,)hel-'mē-nə, ,wil-ə-'mē-\ 1880–1962 queen of the Netherlands (1890–1948)
Wilkes \'wilks\ Charles 1798–1877 Am. naval officer & explorer

Wilkes John 1725–1797 Eng. polit.
Wil·kins \'wil-kənz\ Sir George Hubert 1888–1958 Austral. explorer
Wilkins Mary Eleanor — see Mary E. FREEMAN
Wilkins Maurice Hugh Frederick 1916– Brit. biophysicist
Wilkins Roy 1901–1981 Am. civil rights leader
Wil·kin·son \'wil-kən-sən\ Ellen Cicely 1891–1947 Eng. feminist & polit.
Wilkinson Sir Geoffrey 1921– Brit. chem.
Wilkinson James 1757–1825 Am. gen. & adventurer
Wil·lard \'wil-ərd\ Emma 1787–1870 née *Hart* Am. educ.
Willard Frances Elizabeth Caroline 1839–1898 Am. educ. & reformer
Will·cocks \'wil-,käks\ Sir William 1852–1932 Brit. engineer
Wil·liam \'wil-yəm\ name of 4 kings of England: **I** (*the Conqueror*) *ca*1028–1087 (reigned 1066–87); **II** (*Ru·fus* \'rü-fəs\ *ca*1056–1100 (reigned 1087–1100); **III** 1650–1702 (reigned 1689–1702 — see MARY); **IV** 1765–1837 (reigned 1830–37)
William I 1533–1584 *the Silent* prince of Orange & founder of the Du. Republic
William I 1797–1888 *Wilhelm Friedrich Ludwig* king of Prussia (1861–88) Ger. emp. (1871–88)
William II 1859–1941 *Friedrich Wilhelm Viktor Albert* Ger. emp. & king of Prussia (1888–1918)
William 1882–1951 *Friedrich Wilhelm Victor August Ernst* crown prince of Germany (1888–1918)
William of Malmes·bury \'mämz-,ber-ē, 'mälmz-, -b(ə)rē\ *ca* 1090–*ca* 1143 Eng. hist.
Wil·liams \'wil-yəmz\ Elizabeth 1943– *Betty* Irish peace worker
Williams Ralph Vaughan — see VAUGHAN WILLIAMS
Williams Roger 1603?–1683 Am. (Eng.-born) clergyman; founder of Rhode Island colony
Williams Tennessee 1911–1983 orig. *Thomas Lanier Williams* Am. dram.
Williams William Carlos 1883–1963 Am. writer
Wil·lis \'wil-əs\ Nathaniel Parker 1806–1867 Am. editor & writer
Will·kie \'wil-kē\ Wendell Lewis 1892–1944 Am. polit.
Wil·loch \'vil-ək\ Kå·re \'kôr-ə\ Isaachsen 1928– prime min. of Norway (1981–86)
Will·stät·ter \'vil-,shtet-ər, 'wil-,stet-\ Richard 1872–1942 Ger. chem.
Wil·son \'wil-sən\ Charles Thomson Rees 1869–1959 Scot. physicist
Wilson Edmund 1895–1972 Am. writer
Wilson Sir (James) Harold 1916– Brit. prime min. (1964–70; 1974–76)
Wilson Henry 1812–1875 orig. *Jeremiah Jones Colbath* Am. polit.; vice pres. of the U.S. (1873–75)
Wilson John 1785–1854 pseud. *Christopher North* Scot. author
Wilson Kenneth G. 1936– Am. physicist
Wilson Robert Woodrow 1936– Am. physicist
Wilson (Thomas) Wood·row \'wùd-,rō\ 1856–1924 28th pres. of the U.S. (1913–21) — **Wil·so·ni·an** \wil-'sō-nē-ən\ *adj*
Winck·el·mann \'viŋ-kəl-,män, 'wiŋ-kəl-mən\ Johann Joachim 1717–1768 Ger. archaeol. & art hist.
Win·daus \'vin-,daùs\ Adolf Otto Reinhold 1876–1959 Ger. chem.
Win·disch·grätz \,vin-dish-'grets\ Alfred Candidus Ferdinand 1787–1862 Fürst *zu Windischgrätz* Austrian field marshal
Windsor Duke of — see EDWARD VIII
Win·gate \'win-,gāt, -gət\ Orde \'ó(ə)rd\ Charles 1903–1944 Brit. gen.
Wingate Sir (Francis) Reginald 1861–1953 Brit. gen.
Wins·low \'winz-,lō\ Edward 1595–1655 gov. of Plymouth colony
Win·sor \'win-zər\ Justin 1831–1897 Am. librarian & hist.
Win·throp \'win(t)-thrəp\ John 1588–1649 1st gov. of Massachusetts Bay colony
Winthrop John 1606–1676 *son of prec.* gov. of Connecticut colony
Winthrop John 1638–1707 *son of prec.* gov. of Connecticut colony
Wise \'wīz\ Stephen Samuel 1874–1949 Am. (Hung.-born) rabbi
Wise Thomas James 1859–1937 Eng. bibliophile & forger
Wise·man \'wiz-mən\ Nicholas Patrick Stephen 1802–1865 Eng. cardinal & author
Wiss·ler \'wis-lər\ Clark 1870–1947 Am. anthropol.
Wis·ter \'wis-tər\ Owen 1860–1938 Am. nov.
With·er \'with-ər\ George 1588–1667 Eng. poet & pamphleteer
Witt \'vit\ Johan de 1625–1672 Du. statesman
Wit·te \'vit-ə\ Emanuel de 1617–1692 Du. painter
Witte Sergey Yulyevich 1849–1915 Russ. statesman
Wit·te·kind \'vit-ə-,kint\ *or* **Wi·du·kind** \'vēd-ə-\ *d ca* 807 Saxon warrior
Witt·gen·stein \'vit-gən-,s(h)tīn\ Ludwig Josef Johan 1889–1951 Brit. (Austrian-born) philos. — **Witt·gen·stein·ian** \,vit-gən-'s(h)tī-nē-ən\ *adj*
Wit·tig \'vit-ik\ Georg 1897–1987 Ger. chem.
Wode·house \'wùd-,haùs\ Sir Pel·ham \'pel-əm\ Grenville 1881–1975 Am. (Eng.-born) writer
Wof·fing·ton \'wäf-iŋ-tən\ Margaret *ca*1714–1760 *Peg* Irish actress
Wol·cott \'wùl-kət\ Oliver 1726–1797 *son of Roger* gov. of Connecticut (1796–97)
Wolcott Oliver 1760–1833 *son of prec.* gov. of Connecticut (1817–27)
Wolcott Roger 1679–1767 gov. of Connecticut (1751–54)
Wolf \'vólf\ Friedrich August 1759–1824 Ger. philologist
Wolf Hugo Philipp Jakob 1860–1903 Austrian composer
Wolfe \'wùlf\ Charles 1791–1823 Irish poet
Wolfe James 1727–1759 Brit. gen.
Wolfe Thomas Clayton 1900–1938 Am. nov.
Wolff \'vólf\ Caspar Friedrich 1734–1794 Ger. anatomist
Wolff *or* **Wolf** \'vólf\ Christian 1679–1754 Freiherr *von Wolff* Ger. philos. & math.
Wol·fram \'wùl-frəm, 'vól-,främ\ **von Esch·en·bach** \'esh-ən-,bäk, -,bäk\ *ca*1170–*ca*1220 Ger. poet
Wol·las·ton \'wùl-ə-stən\ William Hyde 1766–1828 Eng. chem. & physicist
Wolse·ley \'wùlz-lē\ 1st Viscount 1833–1913 *Garnet Joseph Wolseley* Brit. field marshal
Wol·sey \'wùl-zē\ Thomas *ca*1475–1530 Eng. cardinal & statesman
Wood \'wùd\ Grant 1892–1942 Am. painter
Wood Leonard 1860–1927 Am. physician & gen.
Wood·ward \'wùd-wərd\ Robert Burns 1917–1979 Am. chem.
Woolf \'wùlf\ (Adeline) Virginia 1882–1941 née *Stephen* Eng. author

Wooll·cott \'wůl-kət\ Alexander 1887–1943 Am. writer
Wool·ley \'wůl-ē\ Sir Charles Leonard 1880–1960 Eng. archaeol.
Wool·worth \'wůl-(ˌ)wərth\ Frank Winfield 1852–1919 Am. merchant
Worces·ter \'wůs-tər\ Joseph Emerson 1784–1865 Am. lexicographer
Worde \'wȯ(ə)rd\ Wynkyn de *d* 1534? Eng. (Alsatian-born) printer
Words·worth \'wərdz-(ˌ)wərth\ William 1770–1850 Eng. poet; poet laureate (1843–50) — **Words·worth·ian** \ˌwərdz-'wər-thē-ən, -thē-\ *adj*
Wot·ton \'wůt-ᵊn, 'wät-\ Sir Henry 1568–1639 Eng. diplomat & poet
Wran·gel \'raŋ-gəl\ Baron Pyotr Nikolayevich 1878–1928 Russ. gen.
Wren \'ren\ Sir Christopher 1632–1723 Eng. architect
Wright \'rīt\ Frank Lloyd 1867–1959 Am. architect
Wright Joseph 1734–1797 *Wright of Derby* Eng. painter
Wright Louis Booker 1899–1984 Am. educ. & librarian
Wright Or·ville \'ȯr-vəl\ 1871–1948 & his bro. Wilbur 1867–1912 Am. pioneers in aviation
Wright Richard 1908–1960 Am. author
Wright Willard Huntington 1888–1939 pseud. *S. S. Van Dine* \van-'dīn, vən-\ Am. writer
Wundt \'vůnt\ Wilhelm 1832–1920 Ger. physiol. & psychol.
Wu–ti — see HAN WU TI
Wy·att *or* **Wy·at** \'wī-ət\ Sir Thomas 1503–1543 Eng. poet & diplomat
Wych·er·ley \'wich-ər-lē\ William 1640–1716 Eng. dram.
Wyc·liffe \'wik-ˌlif, -ləf\ John *ca*1330–1384 Eng. religious reformer & theol. — **Wyc·liff·ian** \wik-'lif-ē-ən\ *adj*
Wy·eth \'wī-əth\ Andrew Newell 1917–   Am. painter
Wyeth Newell Convers 1882–1945 *father of A. N.* Am. painter
Wyld \'wī(ə)ld\ Henry Cecil Kennedy 1870–1945 Eng. lexicographer
Wy·lie \'wī-lē\ Elinor Morton 1885–1928 *Mrs. William Rose Benét, née Hoyt* Am. poet & nov.
Wylie Philip Gordon 1902–1971 Am. writer
Wynd·ham \'win-dəm\ George 1863–1913 Eng. polit. & writer
Xan·thip·pe \zan-'t(h)ip-ē\ 5th cent. B.C. *wife of Socrates*
Xa·vi·er \'zāv-yər, 'zä-vē-ər, ig-'zā-\ Saint Francis 1506–1552 Span. *Francisco Ja·vier* \hä-'vye(ə)r\ Span. Jesuit missionary
Xe·noc·ra·tes \zi-'näk-rə-ˌtēz\ 396–314 B.C. Greek philos.
Xe·noph·a·nes \zi-'näf-ə-ˌnēz\ *ca* 560–*ca* 478 B.C. Greek philos.
Xen·o·phon \'zen-ə-fən\ *ca* 431–*ca* 352 B.C. Greek hist.
Xer·xes I \'zərk-ˌsēz\ *ca* 519–465 B.C. *the Great* king of Persia (486–465)
Yale \'yā(ə)l\ Elihu 1649–1721 Eng. (Am.-born) colonial administrator
Yal·ow \'yal-(ˌ)ō\ Rosalyn Sussman 1921–   Am. med. physicist
Ya·ma·ga·ta \ˌyäm-ə-'gät-ə\ Prince Aritomo 1838–1922 Jp. gen. & statesman
Ya·ma·mo·to \ˌyäm-ə-'mōt-(ˌ)ō\ Isoroku 1884–1943 Jp. admiral
Ya·ma·shi·ta \yä-'mäsh-i-ˌtä\ Tomoyuki 1885–1946 Jp. gen.
Yang Chen Ning \'yäŋ-'jən-'niŋ\ 1922–   Chin. physicist
Yeats \'yāts\ William Butler 1865–1939 Irish poet & dram. — **Yeats·ian** \'yāt-sē-ən\ *adj*
Yen Hsi–shan \'yen-'shē-'shän\ 1883–1960 Chin. gen.
Yer·kes \'yər-kēz\ Charles Ty·son \'tīs-ᵊn\ 1837–1905 Am. financier
Yeut·ter \'yī-tər\ Clayton Keith 1930–   U.S. secy. of agriculture (1989–   )
Yev·tu·shen·ko \ˌyef-tə-'sheŋ-(ˌ)kō\ Yevgeny Aleksandrovich 1933–   Russ. writer
Yo·nai \'yō-ˌnī\ Mitsumasa 1880–1948 Jp. admiral & statesman
York \'yȯ(ə)rk\ Alvin Cullum 1887–1964 Am. soldier
Yo·shi·hi·to \ˌyō-shi-'hē-(ˌ)tō\ 1879–1926 emp. of Japan (1912–26)
You·mans \'yü-mənz\ Vincent 1898–1946 Am. composer
Young \'yəŋ\ Andrew Jackson, Jr. 1932–   U.S. ambassador to U.N. (1977–79)
Young Brig·ham \'brig-əm\ 1801–1877 Am. Mormon leader
Young Edward 1683–1765 Eng. poet
Young Francis Brett 1884–1954 Eng. nov.
Young Owen D. 1874–1962 Am. lawyer
Young Whitney Moore 1921–1971 Am. civil rights leader

Young·hus·band \'yəŋ-ˌhəz-bənd\ Sir Francis Edward 1863–1942 Brit. explorer & author
Your·ce·nar \ˌyür-sə-'när\ Marguerite 1903–1987 orig. surname *de Crayencour* Fr. author
Yp·si·lan·tis \ˌip-sə-'lant-ē\ Alexandros 1792–1828 & his bro. Demetrios 1793–1832 Greek revolutionaries
Yüan Shih–k'ai \yü-'än-'shi(ə)r-'kī, -'shē\ 1859–1916 Chin. soldier & statesman; pres. of China (1913–16)
Yu·ka·wa \yü-'kä-wə\ Hideki 1907–1981 Jp. physicist
Yung–lo \'yůŋ-'lȯ\ 1360–1424 orig. *Chu Ti; often called Ch'eng Tsu* Chin. emp. (1402–24)
Zagh·lūl \zag-'lůl\ Sa'd \'såd\ 1857–1927 *Sa'd Zaghlūl Pasha ibn Ibrāhīm* Egypt. statesman
Za·ha·roff \zə-'här-əf, -ˌȯf\ Sir Basil 1849–1936 orig. *Basileios Zacharias* Fr. (Russ.-born) banker & armament contractor
Za·i·mis \zä-'ē-məs, -mēs\ Alexandros 1855–1936 Greek statesman
Zan·gwill \'zaŋ-ˌ(g)wil\ Israel 1864–1926 Eng. dram. & nov.
Zee·man \'zā-ˌmän, -mən\ Pieter 1865–1943 Du. physicist
Zeng·er \'zeŋ-(g)ər\ John Peter 1697–1746 Am. (Ger.-born) journalist & printer
Ze·no of Citium \'zē-(ˌ)nō-əv-'sish(-ē)-əm\ *ca* 335–*ca* 263 B.C. Greek philos.; founder of Stoic school
Zeno of Elea \-'ē-lē-ə\ *ca* 495–*ca* 430 B.C. Greek philos.
Ze·no·bia \zə-'nō-bē-ə\ *d* after A.D. 274 queen of Palmyra (267 or 268–272)
Zep·pe·lin \ˌtsep-ə-'lēn, 'zep-(ə-)lən\ Ferdinand Adolf August Heinrich 1838–1917 Graf *von Zeppelin* Ger. gen. & aeronaut
Zer·ni·ke \'zer-ni-kə, 'zər-\ Frits 1888–1966 Du. physicist
Zeux·is \'zük-səs\ 5th cent. B.C. Greek painter
Zhao Zi·yang *or* **Chao Tzu–yang** \ˌjaü(d)-zə-'yäŋ\ 1919–   Chin. Communist leader (1987–89)
Zhda·nov \zhə-'dän-əf, 'shtän-\ Andrey Aleksandrovich 1896–1948 Soviet polit.
Zhu·kov \'zhü-ˌkȯf, -ˌkȯv\ Georgy Konstantinovich 1896–1974 Soviet marshal
Zieg·feld \'zig-ˌfeld, 'zēg- *also* -ˌfēld, -fəld\ Florenz 1869–1932 Am. theatrical producer
Zieg·ler \'tsē-glər\ Karl 1898–1973 Ger. chem.
Zim·mer·mann \'zim-ər-mən, 'tsim-ər-ˌmän\ Arthur 1864–1940 Ger. statesman
Zi·nov·yev *or* **Zi·nov·iev** \zyin-'ȯf-yəf\ Grigory Yevseyevich 1883–1936 orig. *Ovsel Gershon Aronov Radomyslsky* Soviet revolutionary
Zins·ser \'zin(t)-sər\ Hans 1878–1940 Am. bacteriol.
Zin·zen·dorf \'zin-zən-ˌdȯrf, 'tsin-sən-\ Nikolaus Ludwig 1700–1760 Graf *von Zinzendorf* religious reformer
Žiž·ka \'zhish-kə\ Count Jan *ca*1376–1424 Bohemian gen. & Hussite leader
Zog I \'zȯg\ 1895–1961 prename *Ahmed Bey Zogu* king of the Albanians (1928–39)
Zo·la \'zō-lə, 'zȯ-ˌlä, zō-'lä\ Émile 1840–1902 Fr. nov. — **Zo·la·esque** \ˌzō-lə-'esk, -lä-\ *adj*
Zorn \'sȯ(ə)rn, 'zȯ(ə)rn\ Anders Leonhard 1860–1920 Swed. painter, etcher, & sculptor
Zo·ro·as·ter \'zȯr-ə-ˌwas-tər, ˌzȯr-\ *Old Iranian* **Zar·a·thu·shtra** \ˌzar-ə-'thüs(h)-trə, -'thəs(h)-\ *ca* 628–*ca* 551 B.C. founder of Zoroastrianism
Zor·ri·lla y Mo·ral \zə-'rē-(y)ə-ē-mə-'räl\ José 1817–1893 Span. poet & dram.
Zsig·mon·dy \'zhig-ˌmȯn-dē\ Richard 1865–1929 Ger. chem.
Zu·lo·a·ga \ˌzü-lə-'wäg-ə\ Ignacio 1870–1945 Span. painter
Zur·ba·rán \ˌzür-bə-'rän\ Francisco de 1598–1664 Span. painter
Zweig \'zwīg, 'swīg, 'tsfīk\ Arnold 1887–1968 Ger. author
Zweig Stefan 1881–1942 Austrian writer
Zwing·li \'zwiŋ-(g)lē, 'swiŋ-; 'tsfiŋ-lē\ Huldrych 1484–1531 Swiss Reformation leader

Geographical Names

This section gives basic information about the countries of the world and their most important regions, cities, and physical features. The information includes spelling, syllabication, and pronunciation of the name, nature of the feature, its location, and for the more important entries statistical data. Cities in the United States having 16,500 or more inhabitants at the 1980 census and incorporated places in Canada having 16,500 or more inhabitants at the 1981 census have been included.

This section complements the A-Z vocabulary by entering many derivative forms:

Ab·ys·sin·ia . . . . — Ab·ys·sin·ian . . . *adj or n*

Cos·ta Ri·ca . . . . — Cos·ta Ri·can . . . *adj or n*

Mo·na·co . . . — Mo·na·can . . . *adj or n* — Mon·e·gasque . . . *adj or n*

The abbreviations used are listed in the section Abbreviations in This Work or in the back-matter section Abbreviations and Symbols for Chemical Elements. The letters N, E, S, and W when not followed by a period indicate direction and are not part of a place-name; thus N Vietnam indicates northern Vietnam and not North Vietnam. The symbol * denotes a capital. Areas, altitudes, and lengths are given first in conventional units with metric equivalents in parentheses.

The Wade-Giles transliteration of People's Republic of China place-names is the first spelling shown; the Pinyin transliteration is second. Where no variant is given, the two spellings are identical.

Aa·chen \'äk-ən\ *or F* **Aix–la–Cha·pelle** \,äk-,slä-shə-'pel, ,ek-\ city W W. Germany near Belgian & Dutch borders *pop* 243,947

Aai·ún, El \,el-ī-'ün\ *or* **Ai·un** \ī-'ün\ town NW Africa * of Western Sahara

Aaland — see AHVENANMAA

Aalborg — see ÅLBORG

Aalst \'älst\ *or* **Alost** \ä-'lóst\ commune *cen* Belgium WNW of Brussels *pop* 78,938

Aa·rau \'är-,aú\ commune N Switzerland * of Aargau canton *pop* 15,788

Aa·re \'är-ə\ *or* **Aar** \'är\ river 175 *mi* (280 *km*), *cen* & N Switzerland flowing E & NE into the Rhine

Aar·gau \'är-,gaú\ *or F* **Ar·go·vie** \,är-gə-'vē\ canton N Switzerland * Aarau *area* 542 *sq mi* (1409 *sq km*), *pop* 453,442

Aarhus — see ÅRHUS

Ab·a·co \'ab-ə-,kō\ two islands of the Bahamas (**Great Abaco & Little Abaco**) N of New Providence Is. *area* 776 *sq mi* (2018 *sq km*)

Aba·dan \,äb-ə-'dän, ,ab-ə-'dan\ **1** island W Iran in Shatt-al-Arab delta **2** city & port on Abadan Is. *pop* 272,962

Ab·bai \ä-'bī\ the upper course of the Blue Nile

Ab·be·ville \ab-'vēl, 'ab-i,vil\ commune N France on the Somme NW of Amiens *pop* 25,252

Ab·er·dare \,ab-ər-'da(ə)r, -'de(ə)r\ town S Wales in Mid Glamorgan *pop* 36,621

Ab·er·deen **1** \'ab-ər-,dēn\ city NE S.Dak. *pop* 25,956 **2** city & port W Wash. on Grays Harbor *pop* 18,739 **3** \,ab-ər-'dēn\ *or* **Ab·er·deen·shire** \-,shi(ə)r, -shər\ former county NE Scotland **4** city & port NE Scotland * of Grampian *pop* 190,200 — **Ab·er·do·ni·an** \,ab-ər-'dō-nē-ən\ *adj or n*

Ab·er·yst·wyth \,ab-ə-'ris-,twith, -'rəs-\ borough W Wales in Dyfed on Cardigan Bay *pop* 8666

Ab–i–Diz — see DEZ

Ab·i·djan \,ab-i-'jän\ city & port * of Ivory Coast *pop* 685,828

Abila — see MUSA (Jebel)

Ab·i·lene \'ab-ə-,lēn\ city NW *cen* Tex. *pop* 98,315

Ab·i·tibi \,ab-ə-'tib-ē\ **1** lake Canada on E boundary of Ont. *area* 356 *sq mi* (926 *sq km*) **2** river 230 *mi* (368 *km*) Canada flowing N into Moose river

Ab·khaz Republic \ab-'käz\ *or* **Ab·kha·zia** \ab-'kä-zh(ē-)ə, -'käz-ē-ə\ autonomous republic U.S.S.R. in NW Georgia on Black sea * Sukhumi *area* 3358 *sq mi* (8731 *sq km*), *pop* 499,000 — **Ab·khas** \-'käs\ *n* — **Ab·kha·sian** *or* **Ab·kha·zian** \-'kä-zhən, -'käz-ē-ən\ *adj or n*

Abo·mey \,ab-ə-'mā, ə-'bō-mē\ city S Benin *pop* 54,418

Abruz·zi \ä-'brüt-sē, ə-\ region *cen* Italy bordering on the Adriatic & including highest of the Apennines * L'Aquila; with Molise (to S), formerly comprised **Abruzzi e Mo·li·se** \-,ä-'mó-lə-,zā\ region

Ab·sa·ro·ka \ab-'sär-ə-kə, -'só(ə)r-kē, -'zó(ə)r-\ mountain range S Mont. & NW Wyo. E of Yellowstone National Park — see FRANCS PEAK

Ab·se·con \ab-'sē-kən\ inlet SE N.J. bet. barrier islands N of Atlantic City

Abu Dha·bi \,äb-ü-'thäb-ē, -'däb-\ **1** sheikhdom, member of United Arab Emirates **2** town, its * & * United Arab Emirates *pop* 347,000

Ab·u·kir \,ab-(,)ü-'ki(ə)r, ,äb-\ **1** bay N Egypt bet. Alexandria & Rosetta mouth of the Nile **2** village on this bay — see CANOPUS

Abu Sim·bel \,äb-ü-'sim-bəl\ *or* **Ip·sam·bul** \,ip-səm-'bül\ locality S Egypt on left bank of the Nile SW of Aswân; site of two rock temples which were moved 1964–66 to higher ground when area was flooded after completion of Aswan High Dam

Aby·dos \ə-'bīd-əs\ **1** ancient town Asia Minor on the Hellespont **2** ancient town S Egypt on left bank of the Nile S of Thebes

Abyla — see MUSA (Jebel)

Ab·ys·sin·ia \,ab-ə-'sin-ē-ə, -'sin-yə\ — see ETHIOPIA — **Ab·ys·sin·ian** \-ē-ən, -yən\ *adj or n*

Aca·dia \ə-'kād-ē-ə\ *or F* **Aca·die** \ä-kà-dē\ an early name for Nova Scotia

Acadia National Park section of coast of Maine including chiefly mountainous areas on Mount Desert Is. & Isle au Haut

Aca·pul·co \,äk-ə-'pül-(,)kō, ,ak-\ *or* **Acapulco de Juá·rez** \-də-'wär-əs\ city & port S Mexico in Guerrero on the Pacific *pop* 309,254

Ac·ar·na·nia \,ak-ər-'nä-nē-ə, -'nä-nyə\ *or NGk* **Akar·na·nia** \,äk-,är-nə-'nē-ə\ region W Greece on Ionian sea — **Ac·ar·na·nian** \,ak-ər-'nä-nē-ən, -'nä-nyən\ *adj or n*

Ac·cad \'ak-,ad, 'äk-,äd\ — see AKKAD — **Ac·ca·di·an** \ə-'käd-ē-ən, -'käd-\ *adj or n*

Ac·cra \ə-'krä\ city & port * of Ghana on Gulf of Guinea *pop* 1,045,381

Ac·cring·ton \'ak-riŋ-tən\ town NW England in SE Lancashire N of Manchester *pop* 35,891

Achaea \ə-'kē-ə\ *or* **Acha·ia** \ə-'kī-ə, -'kā-(y)ə\ region S Greece in N Peloponnisos bordering on gulfs of Corinth & Patras — **Achae·an** \ə-'kē-ən\ *or* **Acha·ian** \ə-'kī-ən, -'kā-(y)ən\ *adj or n*

Ach·e·lo·us *or NGk* **Akhe·ló·os** *or* **Ach·e·lo·os** \,ak-ə-'ló-əs\ river 100 *mi* (160 *km*) W Greece flowing S to Ionian sea

Ach·ill \'ak-əl\ island 15 *mi* (24 *km*) long NW Ireland in County Mayo

Achray, Loch \ə-'krä\ lake *cen* Scotland in SW Tayside

Acon·ca·gua \ak-ən-'käg-wə, äk-, -ən-\ mountain 22,834 *ft* (6960 *m*) W Argentina WNW of Mendoza near Chilean border; highest in Andes & western hemisphere

Açores — see AZORES

Acragas — see AGRIGENTO

Acre \'äk-rə, 'ā-(,)krä\ state W Brazil bordering on Peru & Bolivia ✳ Rio Branco *area* 57,153 *sq mi* (148,598 *sq km*), *pop* 306,893

Acre \'äk-ər, 'ā-kər, 'äk-rə\ *or Heb* **Ak·ko** *or* **Ac·cho** \ä-'kō\ *or anc* **Ptol·e·ma·is** \,täl-ə-'mā-əs\ city & port NW Israel N of Mt. Carmel *pop* 33,900

Ac·te *or* **Ak·te** \'ak-(,)tē\ peninsula NE Greece, the most easterly of the three peninsulas of Chalcidice — see ATHOS

Ac·ti·um \'ak-shē-əm, 'ak-tē-\ promontory & ancient town W Greece in NW Acarnania

Ac·ton \'ak-tən\ city NE Mass. SSE of Lowell *pop* 17,544

Adak \'ā-,dak\ island SW Alaska in Andreanof group

Adalia — see ANTALYA

Ad·ams, Mount \'ad-əmz\ **1** mountain 5798 *ft* (1767 *m*) N N.H. in White mountains N of Mt. Washington **2** mountain 12,307 *ft* (3751 *m*) SW Wash. in Cascade range SSE of Mt. Rainier

Ad·am's Bridge \,ad-əmz-\ chain of shoals 30 *mi* (48 *km*) long bet. Sri Lanka & SE India

Adam's Peak *or Sinhalese* **Sa·ma·na·la** \'səm-ə-nə-lə\ mountain 7360 *ft* (2243 *m*) S *cen* Sri Lanka

Ada·na \'äd-ə-nə, -,nä, ə-'dän-ə\ *or* **Sey·han** \sā-'hän\ city S Turkey on Seyhan river *pop* 568,513

Ada·pa·za·ri \,äd-ə-,päz-ə-'rē\ city NW Turkey E of Istanbul *pop* 152,171

Ad·dis Aba·ba \,ad-ə-'sab-ə-bə\ city cen Ethiopia, its ✳ *pop* 1,408,068

Ad·di·son \'ad-ə-sən\ village NE Ill. W of Chicago *pop* 29,759

Ad·e·laide \'ad-ᵊl-,ād\ city Australia ✳ of S. Australia *pop* (with suburbs) 882,520

Aden \'äd-ᵊn, 'ād-, 'ad-\ **1** former Brit. protectorate S Arabia comprising coastal area bet. Yemen N & Oman on E; became part of People's Democratic Republic of Yemen 1967 *area* 112,000 *sq mi* (291,200 *sq km*) **2** former Brit. colony on coast of & surrounded by Aden protectorate comprising Aden & Little Aden peninsulas, a small area of hinterland, & Perim Is.; became part of People's Democratic Republic of Yemen 1967 *area* 75 *sq mi* (195 *sq km*) **3** city & port S Yemen; formerly ✳ of People's Democratic Republic of Yemen & before that ✳ of Aden colony & protectorate *pop* 240,370

Aden, Gulf of arm of Indian ocean between Aden & Somalia

Adi·ge \'äd-ə-jā\ river 220 *mi* (354 *km*) N Italy flowing SE into the Adriatic

Ad·i·ron·dack \,ad-ə-'rän-,dak\ mountains NE N.Y.

Ad·mi·ral·ty \'ad-m(ə)-ral-tē\ **1** island 100 *mi* (161 *km*) long SE Alaska in N Alexander archipelago **2** islands W Pacific N of New Guinea in Bismarck archipelago *area* 800 *sq mi* (2080 *sq km*), *pop* 30,160

Adour \ə-'dü(ə)r\ river 200 *mi* (322 *km*) SW France flowing from the Pyrenees NW & W into Bay of Biscay

Adri·an \'ā-drē-ən\ city SE Mich. SW of Detroit *pop* 21,186

Adrianople — see EDIRNE

Adri·at·ic \,ā-drē-'at-ik, ,ad-rē-\ sea arm of the Mediterranean bet. Italy & Balkan peninsula

Adu·wa *or* **Ado·wa** \'äd-ə-wə, 'ad-\ *or* **Ad·wa** \'äd-(,)wä\ city N Ethiopia S of Asmara *pop* 26,782

Ad·vent Bay \,ad-,vent-, -,vənt\ inlet of Arctic ocean West Spitsbergen on W coast

Ady·gei *or* **Adi·gey** \,äd-ə-'gā\ autonomous region U.S.S.R. in S Soviet Russia, Europe ✳ Maikop *area* 1505 *sq mi* (3913 *sq km*), *pop* 400,000

Adzhar Republic \,aj-,är-\ autonomous republic U.S.S.R. in SW Georgia on Black sea ✳ Batum *area* 1080 *sq mi* (2808 *sq km*), *pop* 339,000 — **Adzhar** \'aj-,är\ *n* — **Adzhar·i·an** \ə-'jär-ē-ən\ *adj or n*

Aegates — see EGADI

Ae·ge·an \i-'jē-ən\ **1** sea arm of the Mediterranean between Asia Minor & Greece **2** islands Aegean sea including the Cyclades & the Northern & Southern Sporades

Ae·gi·na \i-'jī-nə\ *or NGk* **Ai·gi·na** \'ā-yē-,nä\ island & ancient state SE Greece in Saronic gulf — **Ae·gi·ne·tan** \,ē-jə-'nēt-ᵊn\ *adj or n*

Ae·gos·pot·a·mi \,ē-gə-'spät-ə-,mī\ *or* **Ae·gos·pot·a·mos** \-məs\ river & town of ancient Thrace in the Chersonese

Aemilia — see EMILIA-ROMAGNA

Ae·o·lis \'ē-ə-ləs\ *or* **Ae·o·lia** \ē-'ō-lē-ə, -'ōl-yə\ ancient country of NW Asia Minor

Ae·to·lia \ē-'tō-lē-ə, -'tōl-yə\ region W *cen* Greece N of Gulf of Patras & E of Acarnania — **Ae·to·lian** \-lē-ən, -yən\ *adj or n*

Afars and the Issas, French Territory of the — see DJIBOUTI

Af·ghan·i·stan \af-'gan-ə-,stan\ country W Asia E of Iran; a republic ✳ Kabul *area* 250,000 *sq mi* (650,000 *sq km*), *pop* 13,051,358

Afog·nak \ə-'fòg-,nak, -'fäg-\ island S Alaska N of Kodiak Is.

Af·ri·ca \'af-ri-kə\ continent of the eastern hemisphere S of the Mediterranean & adjoining Asia on NE *area* 11,596,000 *sq mi* (30,149,600 *sq km*)

Afyon·ka·ra·hi·sar \ä-'fyōn-,kär-ə-his-'är\ *or* **Afyon** \ä-'fyōn\ city W *cen* Turkey *pop* 73,832

Aga·dir \,äg-ə-'di(ə)r, ,ag-\ city & port SW Morocco *pop* 110,479

Aga·na \ə-'gän-yə\ town W of Guam on W coast *pop* 881

Agar·ta·la \,og-ər-tə-'lä\ city E India ✳ of Tripura *pop* 131,513

Ag·ate Fossil Beds National Monument \'ag-ət-\ reservation W Nebr.

Aga·wam \'ag-ə-,wäm\ town SW Mass. *pop* 26,271

Age·nais \,äzh-ə-'nā\ *or* **Age·nois** \,äzh-ən-'wä\ ancient region SW France S of Périgord ✳ Agen

Aghrim — see AUGHRIM

Agincourt — see AZINCOURT

Ag·no \'äg-(,)nō\ river 128 *mi* (206 *km*) Philippines in NW Luzon

Agra \'äg-rə\ **1** region N India roughly equivalent to present Uttar Pradesh excluding Oudh region **2** city N India in W Uttar Pradesh SSE of Delhi *pop* 770,352

Agri Dagi — see ARARAT

Agri·gen·to \,äg-ri-'jen-(,)tō, ,ag-\ *or formerly* **Gir·gen·ti** \jər-'jent-ē\ *or anc* **Ac·ra·gas** \'ag-rə-,gas\ *or* **Ac·ra·gas** \'ak-rə-gəs\ commune Italy in SW Sicily near coast *pop* 51,682

Agua·di·lla \,äg-wə-'thē-(y)ə\ city NW Puerto Rico *pop* 22,039

Aguas·ca·lien·tes \,äg-wəs-,käl-'yen-,täs\ **1** state cen Mexico *area* 2499 *sq mi* (6497 *sq km*), *pop* 503,410 **2** city, its ✳ *pop* 222,105

Agul·has, Cape \ə-'gəl-əs\ headland Republic of S. Africa in S Cape Province; southernmost point of Africa, at 34°50'S, 20°E

Ahag·gar \ə-'häg-ər, ,ä-hə-'gär\ *or* **Hog·gar** \'häg-ər, hə-'gär\ mountains S Algeria in W *cen* Sahara; highest Tahat 9573 *ft* (2918 *m*)

Ah·mad·abad *or* **Ah·med·abad** \'äm-əd-ə-,bäd\ city W India N of Bombay in Gujarat *pop* 1,550,779

Ah·ven·an·maa \'ä(k)-və-,nän-,mä\ *or Sw* **Åland** *or* **Aa·land** \'ō-,länd\ **1** archipelago SW Finland in Baltic sea ✳ Mariehamn **2** island, chief of this group

Ah·waz \ä-'wäz\ city SW Iran on the Karun *pop* 329,006

Ail·sa Craig \,āl-zə-,krāg\ small rocky island Scotland S of Arran at mouth of Firth of Clyde

Ain \aⁿ\ river 118 *mi* (190 *km*) E France rising in Jura mountains & flowing SSW into the Rhône

Aintab — see GAZIANTEP

Air·drie \'a(ə)r-drē, 'e(ə)r-\ burgh S *cen* Scotland in Strathclyde E of Glasgow *pop* 45,643

Aire \'a(ə)r, 'e(ə)r\ river 70 *mi* (113 *km*) N England in W Yorkshire flowing to the Ouse; its valley is **Aire·dale** \-,dāl\

Aisne \'ān\ river *ab* 175 *mi* (282 *km*) N France flowing NW & W from Argonne forest into the Oise near Compiègne

Aiun — see AAIÚN, EL

Aix–en–Pro·vence \,āk-,sän-prō-'väⁿs, ,ek-\ *or* **Aix** \'āks, 'eks\ city SE France N of Marseilles *pop* 91,665

Aix–la–Chapelle — see AACHEN

Aix–les–Bains \,äk-slā-'baⁿ, ,ek-\ commune E France N of Chambéry *pop* 21,884

Ajac·cio \ä-'yäch-(,)ō, ,ä-zhák-syō\ city & port France in Corsica *pop* 47,065

Ajan·ta \ə-'jənt-ə\ village W *cen* India in N *cen* Maharashtra in Ajanta range NNE of Aurangabad; caves

Ajax \'ā-,jaks\ town Canada in SE Ont. *pop* 25,475

Aj·man \äj-'man\ sheikhdom, member of United Arab Emirates

Aj·mer \,əj-'mi(ə)r, -'me(ə)r\ **1** *or* **Ajmer–Mer·wa·ra** \-,me(ə)r-'wär-ə\ former state NW India, now part of Rajasthan *area* 2425 *sq mi* (6305 *sq km*) **2** city, its ✳, SW of Delhi *pop* 374,350

Akaba — see 'AQABA

Akarnania — see ACARNANIA

Aka·shi \ä-'käsh-ē\ city Japan in SW Honshu on Akashi strait W of Kobe *pop* 258,640

Akheloos — see ACHELOUS

Ak·hi·sar \,äk-(h)is-'är\ *or anc* **Thy·a·ti·ra** \,thī-ə-'tī-rə\ city W Turkey in Asia NE of Izmir *pop* 46,167

Aki·ta \ä-'kēt-ə, 'äk-i-,tä\ city & port Japan in N Honshu on Sea of Japan *pop* 287,791

Ak·kad *or* **Ac·cad** \'ak-,ad, 'äk-,äd\ **1** the N division of ancient Babylonia **2** *or* **Aga·de** \ə-'gäd-ə\ ancient city, its ✳

Akkerman — see BELGOROD-DNESTROVSKIY

Akko — see ACRE

Ak·ron \'ak-rən\ city NE Ohio SE of Cleveland *pop* 237,177

Ak·sum *or* **Ax·um** \'äk-,süm\ town N Ethiopia ✳ of an ancient kingdom (the Axumite Empire)

Akte — see ACTE

Akyab — see SITTWE

Al·a·bama \,al-ə-'bam-ə\ **1** river 315 *mi* (507 *km*) S Ala. flowing SW into Tensaw & Mobile rivers — see TALLAPOOSA **2** state SE U.S. ✳ Montgomery *area* 51,609 *sq mi* (134,183 *sq km*), *pop* 3,893,888 — **Al·a·bam·i·an** \-'bam-ē-ən\ *or* **Al·a·bam·an** \-'bam-ən\ *adj or n*

Ala·go·as \,al-ə-'gō-əs\ state NE Brazil ✳ Maceió *area* 11,031 *sq mi* (28,681 *sq km*), *pop* 2,011,875

Alai \ä-'lī\ mountain range U.S.S.R. in Soviet Central Asia in SW Kirghiz Republic; highest peak 19,554 *ft* (5960 *m*)

Al·a·me·da \,al-ə-'mēd-ə\ city & port W Calif. on island in San Francisco Bay near Oakland *pop* 63,852

Ala·mein *or* **El Alamein** \,el-,al-ə-'mān\ village NW Egypt on the Mediterranean N of NE corner of Qattara Depression

Al·a·mo·gor·do \,al-ə-mə-'gòrd-(,)ō\ city S N.Mex. *pop* 24,024

Ala·se·hir \,al-ə-shə-'hi(ə)r, ,äl-\ *or anc* **Philadelphia** city W Turkey 75 *mi* (121 *km*) E of Izmir *pop* 23,243

Alas·ka \ə-'las-kə\ **1** state (territory 1912–59) of the U.S. NW N. America ✳ Juneau *area* 586,412 *sq mi* (1,524,671 *sq km*), *pop* 400,481 **2** peninsula SW Alaska SW of Cook inlet **3** mountain range S Alaska extending from Alaska peninsula to Yukon boundary — see MCKINLEY (Mount) — **Alas·kan** \-kən\ *adj or n*

Alaska, Gulf of inlet of the Pacific off S Alaska between Alaska peninsula on W & Alexander archipelago on E

Ala Tau \,al-ə-'taů, ,äl-\ several ranges of the Tien Shan mountain system Soviet Central Asia in E Kazakhstan & Kirghiz Republic around & NE of Issyk Kul

Ala·va \'äl-ə-və\ province N Spain S of Vizcaya; one of the Basque Provinces ✳ Vitoria *area* 1175 *sq mi* (3055 *sq km*), *pop* 286,499

Ail·a·va, Cape \'al-ə-və\ cape NW Wash. S of Cape Flattery; westernmost point of conterminous U.S., at 124°44'W

Al·ba·ce·te \,al-bə-'sät-ē\ **1** province SE Spain N of Murcia province *area* 5737 *sq mi* (14,916 *sq km*), *pop* 317,498 **2** commune, its ✳ *pop* 116,484

Al·ba Lon·ga \,al-bə-'lón-gə\ ancient city cen Italy SE of Rome

Al·ban hills \,ol-bən-, ,al-\ *or* **Al·ba·nus Mons** \äl-,bän-ə-'smón(t)s\ mountain group Italy SE of Rome

Al·ba·nia \al-'bā-nē-ə, -nyə *also* ȯl-\ **1** ancient country Europe in E Caucasus region on W side of Caspian sea **2** country S Europe in Balkan peninsula on the Adriatic; a republic ✳ Tiranë *area* 10,630 *sq mi* (27,638 *sq km*), *pop* 2,841,000

Al·ba·no, Lake \al-'bän-(,)ō, äl-\ *or anc* **La·cus Al·ba·nus** \,läk-ə-säl-'bän-əs\ lake Italy SE of Rome

Al·ba·ny \'òl-bə-nē\ **1** city SW Ga. *pop* 74,059 **2** city ✳ of N.Y., on Hudson river *pop* 101,727 **3** city NW Oreg. S of Salem *pop* 26,546 **4** river 610 *mi* (982 *km*) Canada in N Ont. flowing E into James Bay — **Al·ba·ni·an** \òl-'bā-nē-ən\ *adj or n*

Al·be·marle \'al-bə-,märl\ **1** sound inlet of Atlantic ocean NE N.C. **2** — see ISABELA

Al·bert, Lake \'al-bərt\ lake 100 *mi* (161 *km*) long E Africa bet. Uganda & Zaire in course of the Victoria Nile

Al·ber·ta \al-'bərt-ə\ province W Canada ✳ Edmonton *area* 248,800 *sq mi* (646,880 *sq km*), *pop* 2,237,724 — **Al·ber·tan** \-'bərt-ᵊn\ *adj or n*
Al·bert Lea \ˌal-bərt-'lē\ city S Minn. *pop* 19,200
Albert Nile — see NILE
Albertville — see KALEMIE
Al·bi \al-'bē\ commune S France NE of Toulouse *pop* 43,942
Al Biqa — see BEKAA
Al·borg *or* **Aal·borg** \'ȯl-ˌbȯ(ə)rg\ city & port Denmark in NE Jutland *pop* 154,385
Al·bu·quer·que \'al-b(y)ə-ˌkər-kē\ city *cen* N.Mex. *pop* 331,767 — **Al·bu·quer·que·an** \-kē-ən\ *n*
Al·ca·mo \'äl-kə-ˌmō\ commune Italy in NW Sicily *pop* 42,059
Al·ca·traz \'al-kə-ˌtraz\ island Calif. in San Francisco Bay
Al·coy \äl-'kȯi\ commune E Spain N of Alicante *pop* 61,371
Al·da·bra \al-'dä-brə\ island (atoll) NW Indian ocean N of Madagascar, chief of Aldabra group belonging to Seychelles
Al·dan \äl-'dän\ river 1500 *mi* (2414 *km*) U.S.S.R. in E Soviet Russia, Asia, in SE Yakut Republic flowing into the Lena
Al·der·ney \'ȯl-dər-nē\ island in English channel, northernmost of the Channel islands ✳ St. Anne *area* 3 *sq mi* (7.8 *sq km*), *pop* 2086
Al·der·shot \'ȯl-dər-ˌshät\ borough S England in NE Hampshire *pop* 32,654
Aleksandrovsk — see ZAPOROZH'YE
Aleksandrovsk Grushevski — see SHAKHTY
Alen·çon \ˌal-ˌän-'sōⁿ\ city NW France N of Le Mans *pop* 32,917
Alep·po \ə-'lep-(ˌ)ō\ *or anc* **Be·roea** *or* **Be·rea** \bə-'rē-ə\ city N Syria *pop* 639,000 — **Alep·pine** \ə-'lep-ˌən, -ˌin, -ˌēn\ *adj or n*
Ales·san·dria \ˌal-ə-'san-drē-ə\ commune NW Italy *pop* 100,518
Aleu·tian \ə-'lü-shən\ **1** islands SW Alaska extending in an arc 1200 *mi* (1931 *km*) SW & W from Alaska peninsula — see ANDREANOF, FOX, NEAR, RAT **2** mountain range SW Alaska, the SW extension of Alaska range, running along NW shore of Cook inlet to SW tip of Alaska peninsula with mountains of the Aleutian chain forming its SW extension — see SHISHALDIN
Al·ex·an·der \ˌal-ig-'zan-dər, ˌel-\ archipelago of *ab* 1100 islands SE Alaska — see ADMIRALTY, BARANOF, CHICHAGOF, KUPREANOF, PRINCE OF WALES, REVILLAGIGEDO
Alexander I island Antarctica W of base of Antarctic peninsula
Alexandretta — see ISKENDERUN
Al·ex·an·dria \ˌal-ig-'zan-drē-ə, ˌel-\ **1** city *cen* La. *pop* 51,565 **2** city N Va. on the Potomac S of Washington, D.C. *pop* 103,217 **3** city & port N Egypt between Lake Mareotis & the Mediterranean *pop* 2,317,705 — **Al·ex·an·dri·an** \-drē-ən\ *adj or n*
Al·föld \'ȯl-ˌfə(r)ld\ the central plain of Hungary
Al·gar·ve \äl-'gär-və, al-\ medieval Moorish kingdom now a province of Portugal on S coast
Al·ge·ci·ras \ˌal-jə-'sir-əs\ city & port SW Spain W of Gibraltar on Bay of Algeciras *pop* 81,662
Al·ge·ria \al-'jir-ē-ə\ country NW Africa bordering on the Mediterranean ✳ Algiers *area* 919,352 *sq mi* (2,390,315 *sq km*), *pop* 16,948,000 — **Al·ge·ri·an** \-ē-ən\ *adj or n*
Al·giers \al-'ji(ə)rz\ **1** former Barbary state N Africa now Algeria **2** city & port ✳ of Algeria on Bay of Algiers (inlet of Mediterranean) *pop* 1,365,400 — **Al·ge·rine** \ˌal-jə-'rēn\ *adj or n*
Al·goa Bay \al-ˌgō-ə\ inlet of Indian ocean S Republic of S. Africa on SE coast of Cape Province
Al Hamad — see HAMAD, AL
Al·ham·bra \al-'ham-brə\ **1** city SW Calif. E of Los Angeles *pop* 64,615 **2** hill in Granada, Spain; site of remains of the palace of the Moorish kings
Al Hijāz — see HEJAZ
Al·i·ba·tes Flint Quarries National Monument \ˌal-ə-'bät-ēz-\ archaeological site N Tex. NE of Amarillo
Ali·can·te \ˌal-ə-'kant-ē, ˌäl-ə-'känt-ē\ **1** province E Spain on the Mediterranean S of Valencia province *area* 2185 *sq mi* (5681 *sq km*), *pop* 1,217,729 **2** city & port, its ✳ *pop* 245,963
Ali·garh \ˌal-i-'gär\ city N India in W Uttar Pradesh N of Agra *pop* (including old town of **Ko·il** \'kō-əl\) 319,981
Al·i·quip·pa \ˌal-ə-'kwip-ə\ borough W Pa. *pop* 17,094
Al Ittihad — see MEDINA AS-SHAAB
Al Jazirah — see GEZIRA, EL
Alk·maar \'alk-ˌmär\ commune NW Netherlands *pop* 80,992
Al Ku·frah \al-'kü-frə\ *or* **Ku·fra** \'kü-frə\ group of five oases SE Libya
Al–Kut — see KUT
Al·lah·abad \'al-ə-hə-ˌbad, -ˌbäd\ city N India in S Uttar Pradesh on the Ganges W of Banaras *pop* 642,420
Al·le·ghe·ny \ˌal-ə-'gā-nē *also* -'gen-ē\ **1** river 325 *mi* (523 *km*) W Pa. & SW N.Y. uniting with the Monongahela at Pittsburgh to form the Ohio **2** mountains of Appalachian system E U.S. in Pa., Md., Va., & W.Va. — **Al·le·ghe·ni·an** \ˌ-gā-nē-ən, ˌ-gen-ē-ən\ *adj*
Al·len Park \ˌal-ən-\ city SE Mich. WSW of Detroit *pop* 34,196
Allenstein — see OLSZTYN
Al·len·town \'al-ən-ˌtaún\ city E Pa. on the Lehigh *pop* 103,758
Al·ep·pey \ə-'lep-ē\ city & port S India in Kerala *pop* 169,934
Al·li·ance \ə-'lī-ən(t)s\ city NE Ohio N of Canton *pop* 24,315
Al·lier \al-'yā\ river *ab* 250 *mi* (402 *km*) S *cen* France flowing to the Loire
Al·ma \'al-mə\ **1** river 50 *mi* (80 *km*) U.S.S.R. in S Soviet Russia, Europe, in SW Crimea **2** city Canada in E Que. on the Saguenay *pop* 25,638
Al·ma–Ata \ˌal-mə-ə-'tä\ *or formerly* **Ver·nyi** \'ve(ə)rn-yē\ city U.S.S.R. in Soviet Central Asia ✳ of Kazakhstan *pop* 730,000
Al·ma·dén \ˌal-mə-'dän, ˌäl-\ town S *cen* Spain in Sierra Morena
Al·me·lo \'äl-mə-ˌlō\ commune E Netherlands *pop* 63,079
Al·me·ría \ˌal-mə-'rē-ə\ **1** province S Spain SE of Granada province *area* 3360 *sq mi* (8736 *sq km*), *pop* 389,922 **2** city & port, its ✳ *pop* 140,745
Al Minyā — see MINYĀ, AL
Alor \'al-ˌó(ə)r, 'äl-\ island Indonesia in Lesser Sundas N of Timor; with **Pan·tar** \'pan-ˌtär\, forms **Alor islands** group
Alor Se·tar \sə-'tär\ city Malaysia in NW Peninsular Malaysia ✳ of Kedah *pop* 66,179
Alost — see AALST

Al·phe·us \al-'fē-əs\ *or* NGk **Al·fiós** \äl-'fyós\ river *ab* 75 *mi* (121 *km*) S Greece in W Peloponnisos flowing NW into Ionian sea
Alps \'alps\ mountain system S *cen* Europe extending from Mediterranean coast at border bet. France & Italy into NW & W Yugoslavia — see MONT BLANC
Al·sace \al-'sas, -'säs, 'al-ˌ\ *or* G **El·sass** \'el-ˌzäs\ *or anc* **Al·sa·tia** \al-'sā-sh(ē-)ə\ region & former province NE France bet. Rhine river & Vosges mountains — **Al·sa·tian** \al-'sā-shən\ *adj or n*
Alsace–Lor·raine \ˌ-lə-'rān, -lō-\ region NE France including Alsace & part of Lorraine
Al·sek \'al-ˌsek\ river 260 *mi* (418 *km*) NW Canada & SE Alaska flowing S into the Pacific
Al·sip \'ȯl-səp, 'äl-\ city NE Ill. SSW of Chicago *pop* 17,134
Al·ta California \'al-tə\ former Spanish & Mexican province (1772–1848) comprising the present state of Calif. — a name used to differentiate it from Baja California
Al·tai \'al-ˌtī\ **1** mountain system *cen* Asia bet. Mongolia (republic) & Sinkiang Uighur region of W China & bet. Kazakhstan & Soviet Russia, Asia — see TABUN BOGDO **2** territory U.S.S.R. in SW Soviet Russia, Asia ✳ Barnaul *area* 71,885 *sq mi* (186,901 *sq km*)
Al·ta·ma·ha \ˌȯl-tə-mə-ˌhȯ\ river 137 *mi* (220 *km*) SE Ga. formed by junction of the Ocmulgee & the Oconee & flowing SE into **Altamaha Sound** (estuary)
Al·ta·mi·ra \ˌal-tə-'mir-ə\ caverns N Spain WSW of Santander
Al·ta·monte Springs \ˌal-tə-ˌmänt-\ city *cen* Fla. *pop* 22,028
Alt·dorf \'alt-ˌdȯrf, 'ält-\ *or* **Al·torf** \'al-ˌtȯrf, 'äl-\ town *cen* Switzerland ✳ of Uri canton *pop* 8230
Al·ten·burg \'ält-ᵊn-ˌbú(ə)rg\ city S E. Germany E of Weimar *pop* 55,468
Al·to Adi·ge \ˌält-(ˌ)tō-'äd-i-ˌjä\ *or* **Upper Adige** *or* **South Tirol** district N Italy in S Tirol in N Trentino-Alto Adige region
Al·ton \'ȯlt-ᵊn\ city SW Ill. on the Mississippi *pop* 34,171
Al·too·na \al-'tü-nə\ city *cen* Pa. *pop* 57,078
Alto Paraná — see PARANÁ
Al·trin·cham \'ȯl-triŋ-əm\ borough NW England in Greater Manchester SSW of Manchester *pop* 39,641
Al·tus \'al-təs\ city SW Okla. *pop* 23,101
Al·tyn Tagh \ˌal-ˌtin-'täg\ *or* **Al·tun Shan** \ˌal-tən-'shän\ mountain range W China in S Sinkiang Uighur; highest peak 20,213 *ft* (6161 *m*)
Al·vin \'al-vən\ city SE Tex. S of Houston *pop*. 16,515
Ama·ga·sa·ki \ˌam-ə-gə-'säk-ē\ city Japan in W *cen* Honshu on Osaka Bay *pop* 519,141
Amal·fi \ə-'mäl-fē\ commune & port S Italy in Campania on Gulf of Salerno *pop* 6052 — **Amal·fi·an** \-fē-ən\ *adj or n*
Ama·mi \ə-'mäm-ē\ island group W Pacific in *cen* Ryukyus *area* 498 *sq mi* (1295 *sq km*)
Ama·pá \ˌam-ə-'pä\ territory N Brazil NW of Amazon delta ✳ Macapá *area* 55,489 *sq mi* (144,271 *sq km*), *pop* 180,078
'Ama·ra \ä-'mär-ə\ city SE Iraq on the Tigris
Am·a·ril·lo \ˌam-ə-'ril-(ˌ)ō, -'ril-ə\ city NW Tex. *pop* 149,230
Am·a·zon \'am-ə-ˌzän, -zən\ river *ab* 3900 *mi* (6276 *km*) N S. America flowing from Peruvian Andes into the Atlantic in N Brazil — see UCAYALI, SOLIMÕES
Ama·zo·nas \ˌam-ə-'zō-nəs\ state NW Brazil ✳ Manaus *area* 595,474 *sq mi* (1,548,232 *sq km*), *pop* 1,449,135
Ama·zo·nia \ˌam-ə-'zō-nē-ə\ region N S. America, the basin of the Amazon
Am·ba·to \äm-'bät-(ˌ)ō\ city *cen* Ecuador S of Quito *pop* 75,300
Am·bon \'am-ˌbän\ *or* **Am·boi·na** \am-'bȯi-nə\ **1** island E Indonesia in the Moluccas S of Ceram *area* 314 *sq mi* (816 *sq km*), *pop* 72,679 **2** city & port on Ambon Is. ✳ of Maluku — **Am·bo·nese** \ˌam-bə-'nēz, -'nēs\ *or* **Am·boi·nese** \ˌam-ˌbȯi-'nēz, am-'bȯi-\ *adj or n*
Am·bra·cian Gulf \am-ˌbrā-shən-\ *or* **Gulf of Ar·ta** \'ärt-ə\ *or* NGk **Am·vra·ki·kós Kól·pos** \ˌam-'vräk-i-ˌkȯ-'skȯl-ˌpȯs\ inlet of Ionian sea 25 *mi* (40 *km*) long W Greece in S Epirus
Am·brose \ˌam-ˌbrōz\ dredged channel SE N.Y. at entrance to N.Y. harbor N of Sandy Hook; 40 *ft* (12 *m*) deep, 2000 *ft* (606 *m*) wide
Am·chit·ka \am-'chit-kə\ island SW Alaska at E end of Rat group
Amer·i·ca \ə-'mer-ə-kə\ **1** either continent (N. America or S. America) of the western hemisphere **2** *or* **the Amer·i·cas** \-kəz\ the lands of the western hemisphere including N., Central, & S. America & the W. Indies **3** UNITED STATES OF AMERICA
American Samoa *or* **Eastern Samoa** island group of E Samoa SW *cen* Pacific ✳ Pago Pago (on Tutuila Is.) *area* 76 *sq mi* (198 *sq km*), *pop* 32,297
Amers·foort \'äm-ərz-ˌfō(ə)rt, -ərs-, -ˌfó(ə)rt\ commune *cen* Netherlands NE of Utrecht *pop* 87,451
Ames \'āmz\ city *cen* Iowa N of Des Moines *pop* 45,775
Am·ga \äm-'gä\ river 800 *mi* (1280 *km*) U.S.S.R. in E Soviet Russia, Asia, flowing NE to the Aldan
Am·hara \äm-'här-ə,-'här-ə\ former kingdom now province of NW Ethiopia ✳ Gondar
Am·herst \'am-(ˌ)ərst, *chiefly by outsiders* -ˌhərst\ town W *cen* Mass. N of Springfield *pop* 33,229
Amiens \am-'yäⁿ\ city N France on the Somme *pop* 129,453
Amin·di·vi \ˌam-ən-'dē-vē\ island group India in the N Laccadives
Am·i·rante \'am-ə-ˌrant\ islands W Indian ocean S of Seychelles; a dependency of Seychelles
Am·man \ä-'män, -'man\ *or anc* **Philadelphia** *or* bib **Rab·bah** \'rab-ə\ *or* **Rab·bath** \'rab-əth\ city ✳ of Jordan, NE of Dead sea *pop* 711,850
Am·mon \'am-ən\ ancient country NW Arabia E of Gilead ✳ Rabbah
Ammonium — see SIWA
Am·ne Ma·chin \ˌäm-ə-mə-'jin\ *or* **A'nyê·ma·qên** \ˌän-'yem-'ä -'chen\ *or* **A–ni–ma–ch'ing** \ˌän-ē-'mä-'chiŋ\ range of the Kunlun mountains W China in E *cen* Koko Nor; highest peak *ab* 25,000 *ft* (7620 *m*)
Amor·gos \ə-'mȯr-gəs\ *or* NGk **Amor·gós** \ˌäm-(,)ȯr-'gȯs\ island Greece in the Aegean in SE Cyclades SE of Naxos *area* 52 *sq mi* (135 *sq km*)
Amoy — see HSIA-MEN

Am·ra·va·ti \ˌəm-ˈräv-ət-ē, äm-\ *or* **Am·rao·ti** \-ˈrau̇t-ē\ city *cen* India in NE Maharashtra, chief city of Berar region *pop* 261,387
Am·rit·sar \ˌəm-ˈrit-sər\ city N India in NW Punjab *pop* 589,229
Am·ster·dam \ˈam(p)-stər-ˌdam\ **1** city E N.Y. on the Mohawk *pop* 21,872 **2** city & port, official * of Netherlands *pop* 688,100 — **Am·ster·dam·mer** \-ər\ *n*
Amu Dar·ya \ˌäm-ü-ˈdär-yə\ *or* **Ox·us** \ˈäk-səs\ river over 1400 *mi* (2253 *km*), *cen* & W Asia flowing from Pamir plateau into Aral sea
Amund·sen \ˈäm-ən-sən, ˈam-\ **1** sea, arm of the S Pacific W Antarctica off Marie Byrd Land **2** gulf, arm of Beaufort sea N Canada
Amur \ä-ˈmu̇(ə)r\ river 1780 *mi* (2865 *km*) E Asia formed by junction of the Shilka & the Argun, flowing into the Pacific at N end of Tatar strait, & forming part of boundary bet. China & Soviet Russia, Asia
Ana·dyr *or* **Ana·dir** \ˌän-ə-ˈdi(ə)r, ˌan-\ river 450 *mi* (724 *km*) U.S.S.R. in Soviet Russia, Asia, flowing S & E to Gulf of Anadyr
Anadyr, Gulf of inlet of N Bering sea U.S.S.R. in Soviet Russia, Asia, S of Chukotski peninsula
An·a·heim \ˈan-ə-ˌhīm\ city SW Calif. E of Long Beach *pop* 221,847
Aná·huac \ə-ˈnä-ˌwäk\ the central plateau of Mexico
An·a·to·lia \ˌan-ə-ˈtō-lē-ə, -ˈtōl-yə\ the part of Turkey comprising the peninsula of Asia Minor
An–ch'ing *or* **An·qing** \ˈän-ˈchiŋ\ *or* **An·king** \-ˈkiŋ\ *or formerly* **Hwai·ning** \ˈhwī-ˈniŋ\ city E China in Anhwei on the Yangtze *pop* 105,300
An·chor·age \ˈaŋ-k(ə-)rij\ city S *cen* Alaska at head of Cook inlet *pop* 174,431
An·co·hu·ma \ˌaŋ-kə-ˈh(y)ü-mə\ mountain peak 20,873 *ft* (6362 *m*) W Bolivia; highest in the Illampu massif
An·co·na \aŋ-ˈkō-nə, an-\ city & port *cen* Italy * of the Marches on the Adriatic *pop* 106,421
An·da·lu·sia \ˌan-də-ˈlü-zh(ē-)ə\ *or Sp* **An·da·lu·cía** \ˌän-də-(ˌ)lü-ˈsē-ə\ region S Spain including Sierra Nevada & valley of the Guadalquivir — **An·da·lu·sian** \ˌan-də-ˈlü-zhən\ *adj or n*
An·da·man \ˈan-də-mən, -ˌman\ **1** islands India in Bay of Bengal S of Myanmar & N of Nicobar islands *area* 2508 *sq mi* (6521 *sq km*) **2** sea SE Asia, the E section of Bay of Bengal — **An·da·man·ese** \ˌan-də-mə-ˈnēz, -ˈnēs\ *adj or n*
Andaman and Nic·o·bar \ˈnik-ə-ˌbär\ union territory India comprising Andaman & Nicobar groups * Port Blair *area* 3143 *sq mi* (8172 *sq km*), *pop* 188,254
An·der·lecht \ˈän-dər-ˌlekt\ commune *cen* Belgium, *pop* 94,764
An·der·matt \ˈän-dər-ˌmät\ commune *cen* Switzerland S of Altdorf
An·der·son \ˈan-dər-sən\ **1** city *cen* Ind. *pop* 64,695 **2** city NW S.C. *pop* 27,313 **3** river 430 *mi* (692 *km*) Canada in NW Mackenzie district flowing W & N into Beaufort sea
An·des \ˈan-(ˌ)dēz\ mountain system of S. America extending along W coast from Panama to Tierra del Fuego — see ACONCAGUA — **An·de·an** \ˈan-(ˌ)dē-ən, an-ˈ\ *adj* — **An·dine** \ˈan-ˌdēn, -ˌdīn\ *adj*
An·dhra Pra·desh \ˌän-drə-prə-ˈdāsh, -ˈdesh\ state SE India N of Tamil Nadu state bordering on Bay of Bengal * Hyderabad *area* 105,677 *sq mi* (274,760 *sq km*), *pop* 53,403,619
An·di·zhan \ˌan-di-ˈzhan, ˌän-di-ˈzhän\ city U.S.S.R. in Uzbek Republic ESE of Tashkent *pop* 188,000
An·dor·ra \an-ˈdȯr-ə, -ˈdär-ə\ country SW Europe in E Pyrenees bet. France & Spain; a republic * Andorra la Vella *area* 179 *sq mi* (465 *sq km*), *pop* 40,000 — **An·dor·ran** \-ən\ *adj or n*
An·do·ver \ˈan-ˌdō-vər, -də-\ town NE Mass. *pop* 26,370
An·dre·a·nof \ˌan-drē-ˈan-əf, -ˌȯf\ islands SW Alaska in *cen* Aleutian chain — see ADAK, ATKA
An·dria \ˈän-drē-ə\ commune SE Italy in Apulia *pop* 83,319
Andropov — see RYBINSK
An·dros **1** \ˈan-drəs\ island, largest of the Bahamas *area* 1600 *sq mi* (4160 *sq km*) **2** \ˈan-drəs, -ˌdräs\ island 25 *mi* (40 *km*) long Greece in N Cyclades
An·dros·cog·gin \ˌan-drə-ˈskäg-ən\ river 157 *mi* (253 *km*) NE N.H. & SW Maine flowing into the Kennebec
Ane·to, Pi·co de \ˈpē-(ˌ)kō-ˌdā-ə-ˈnāt-(ˌ)ō\ *or F* **Pic de Né·thou** \ˌpēk-də-(ˌ)nā-ˈtü\ mountain 11,168 *ft* (3404 *m*) NE Spain; highest in the Pyrenees
An·ga·ra \ˌäŋ-gə-ˈrä\ river 1100 *mi* (1770 *km*) U.S.S.R. in Soviet Russia, Asia, flowing from Lake Baikal into the Yenisei — see TUNGUSKA
An·garsk \an-ˈgärsk\ city U.S.S.R. in E *cen* Soviet Russia, Asia, on the Angara NW of Irkutsk *pop* 224,000
An·gel Falls \ˌān-jəl-\ waterfall 3212 *ft* (979 *m*) SE Venezuela on Auyán-tepuí mountain in a headstream of the Caroní
An·gers \äⁿ-zhā\ city W France ENE of Nantes *pop* 136,603
Ang·kor \ˈaŋ-ˌkȯ(ə)r\ ruins of ancient city NW Cambodia N of Tonle Sap; * of the Khmers
An·gle·sey *or* **An·gle·sea** \ˈaŋ-gəl-sē\ **1** *or anc* **Mo·na** \ˈmō-nə\ island NW Wales **2** former county comprising Anglesey Is. & Holyhead Is. * Llangefni
Anglia **1** — see ENGLAND **2** — see EAST ANGLIA — **An·gli·an** \ˈaŋ-glē-ən\ *adj or n*
Anglo–Egyptian Sudan — see SUDAN
An·go·la \aŋ-ˈgō-lə, an-\ *or formerly* **Portuguese West Africa** country SW Africa S of mouth of the Congo; until 1975 a dependency of Portugal * Luanda *area* 481,351 *sq mi* (1,251,513 *sq km*), *pop* 6,761,000 — **An·go·lan** \-lən\ *adj or n*
An·gou·lême \ˌäⁿ-gü-ˈlām, -ˈlem\ city W France *pop* 46,293
An·gou·mois \ˌäⁿ-güm-ˈwä\ region & former duchy & province W France S of Poitou * Angoulême
An·guil·la \aŋ-ˈgwil-ə, an-\ island Brit. W. Indies NW of St. Kitts *area* 34 *sq mi* (88 *sq km*) — **An·guil·lan** \-ˈgwil-ən\ *adj or n*
An·gus \ˈaŋ-gəs\ *or earlier* **For·far** \ˈfȯr-fər\ *or* **For·far·shire** \-ˌshi(ə)r-, -shər\ former county E Scotland * Forfar
An·halt \ˈän-ˌhält\ former state *cen* Germany * Dessau
An·hwei *or* **An·hui** \ˈän-ˈ(h)wā\ province E China W of Kiangsu * Hofei *area* 54,015 *sq mi* (140,439 *sq km*), *pop* 49,665,724
An·i·ak·chak Crater \ˌan-ē-ˈak-ˌchak\ active volcano 4420 *ft* (1347 *m*) SW Alaska on Alaska peninsula in **Aniakchak National Monument;** crater 6 *mi* (10 *km*) in diameter
A–ni–ma–ch'ing — see AMNE MACHIN
An·jou \ˈan-ˌjü, äⁿ-zhü\ **1** region & former province NW France in Loire valley * Angers **2** town Canada in S Que. *pop* 37,346
An·ka·ra \ˈaŋ-kə-rə, ˈäŋ-\ *or formerly* **An·go·ra** \aŋ-ˈgōr-ə, an-, -ˈgȯr-\ *or anc* **An·cy·ra** \an-ˈsī-rə\ city * of Turkey in N *cen* Anatolia *pop* 2,203,729
Ann, Cape \ˈan\ peninsula NE Mass.
An·na·ba \ə-ˈnäb-ə\ *or formerly* **Bône** \ˈbōn\ commune & port NE Algeria NE of Constantine *pop* 255,900
An Nafūd — see NAFŪD, AN
An Na·jaf \an-ˈnaj-ˌaf\ city S *cen* Iraq W of the Euphrates *pop* 134,027
An·nam \a-ˈnam, ə-; ˈan-ˌam\ region & former kingdom E Indochina in *cen* Vietnam * Hue *area* 57,000 *sq mi* (148,200 *sq km*)
An·nap·o·lis \ə-ˈnap-(ə-)ləs\ city & port * of Md. *pop* 31,740
Annapolis Basin inlet of Bay of Fundy Canada in W N.S.
An·na·pur·na *or* **An·a·pur·na** \ˌan-ə-ˈpu̇r-nə, -ˈpər-\ massif N Nepal in the Himalayas; highest peak Annapurna I 26,334 *ft* (8027 *m*)
Ann Ar·bor \a-ˈnär-bər\ city SE Mich. W of Detroit *pop* 107,966
An·ne·cy \ˌan-ə-ˈsē\ city E France ENE of Lyons *pop* 53,058
An Nhon \ˈän-ˈnōn\ *or formerly* **Binh Dinh** \ˈbin-ˈdin\ city *cen* Vietnam in S Annam
An·nis·ton \ˈan-ə-stən\ city NE Ala. *pop* 29,523
Anqing — see AN-CH'ING
An·shan \ˈän-ˈshän\ city NE China in E *cen* Liaoning SSW of Mukden *pop* 833,000
An·so·nia \an-ˈsō-nē-ə, -ˈsōn-yə\ city SW Conn. *pop* 19,039
An·ta·kya \ˌant-ə-ˈkyä\ *or* **An·ta·ki·yah** \-ˈkē-(y)ə\ *or anc* **An·ti·och** \ˈant-ē-ˌäk\ city S Turkey on the Orontes *pop* 91,551
An·tal·ya \ˌänt-ᵊl-ˈyä\ *or formerly* **Ada·lia** \ˌäd-ᵊl-ē-ˈ(y)ä\ city & port SW Turkey on Gulf of Antalya *pop* 176,446
An·ta·nan·a·ri·vo \ˌan-tə-ˌnan-ə-ˈrē-(ˌ)vō\ *or Malagasy* **Ta·nan·a·ri·vo** \tə-ˌnan-ə-ˈrē-(ˌ)vō\ *or formerly* **Ta·nan·a·rive** \tə-ˈnan-ə-ˌrēv\ city * of Madagascar *pop* 339,233
Ant·arc·tic \(ˈ)ant-ˈärk-tik, -ˈärt-ik\ **1** ocean surrounding Antarctica including the southern regions of the S. Atlantic, S. Pacific, & Indian oceans esp. S of *ab* 60° S **2** the Antarctic regions **3** *or formerly* **Palmer peninsula** \ˌpäm-ər, ˌpäl-mər\ *or* **Gra·ham Land** \ˈgrā-əm, ˈgra(-ə)m\ peninsula 1200 *mi* (1931 *km*) long W Antarctica S of S end of S. America **4** *or* **Palmer archipelago** islands W of N end of Antarctic peninsula in Falkland Islands Dependencies
Ant·arc·ti·ca \-ˈärk-ti-kə, -ˈärt-i-\ *or* **Antarctic continent** body of land around the S. Pole; a plateau covered by a great ice cap & mountain peaks *area ab* 5,500,000 *sq mi* (14,300,000 *sq km*), divided into **West Antarctica** (including Antarctic peninsula) & **East Antarctica** by Transantarctic mountains
An·tibes \äⁿ-tēb\ city & port SE France SW of Nice *pop* 44,226
Antibes, Cap d' — see CAP D'ANTIBES
An·ti·cos·ti \ˌant-ə-ˈkȯ-stē\ island E Canada in E Que. at mouth of the St. Lawrence *area* 3043 *sq mi* (7912 *sq km*)
An·tie·tam \an-ˈtēt-əm\ creek S Pa. & N Md. flowing S into the Potomac N of Harpers Ferry, W.Va.
An·ti·gua \an-ˈtē-g(w)ə\ **1** island Brit. W. Indies in the Leewards *area* 108 *sq mi* (281 *sq km*); with Barbuda an independent nation (**Antigua and Barbuda**) since 1981 (*pop* 77,000) — see WEST INDIES ASSOCIATED STATES **2** *or* **Antigua Guatemala** city S *cen* Guatemala; former * of Guatemala *pop* 27,014 — **An·ti·guan** \an-ˈtē-g(w)ən\ *adj or n*
An·ti–Leb·a·non \ˈant-i-ˈleb-ə-nən, -ˌnän\ mountains SW Asia E of Bekaa valley on Syria-Lebanon border — see HERMON (Mount)
Antilles the W. Indies excluding the Bahamas — see GREATER ANTILLES, LESSER ANTILLES — **An·til·le·an** \an-ˈtil-ē-ən\ *adj*
An·ti·och \ˈant-ē-ˌäk\ **1** city W Calif. NE of Oakland *pop* 43,559 **2** — see ANTAKYA **3** ancient city Asia Minor in Pisidia, at certain periods within boundaries of Phrygia; ruins in W *cen* Turkey — **An·ti·o·chene** \an-ˈtī-ə-ˌkēn, ˌant-ē-ˌä-ˈkēn\ *adj or n*
An·ti·sa·na \ˌant-i-ˈsän-ə\ volcano 18,714 *ft* (5704 *m*) N *cen* Ecuador
An·to·fa·gas·ta \ˌant-ə-fə-ˈgäs-tə\ city & port N Chile N of Santiago *pop* 125,081
An·trim \ˈan-trəm\ district E Northern Ireland, established 1974 *area* 217 *sq mi* (564 *sq km*), *pop* 44,384
Antung — see TAN-TUNG
Ant·werp \ˈant-ˌwərp, ˈan-ˌtwərp\ *or F* **An·vers** \äⁿ-ˈve(ə)r(s)\ *or Flem* **Ant·wer·pen** \ˈänt-ˌver-pə(n)\ **1** province N Belgium *area* 1104 *sq mi* (2870 *sq km*), *pop* 1,569,876 **2** city & port, its *, on the Scheldt *pop* 185,897
Anu·ra·dha·pu·ra \ˌən-ə-ˌräd-ə-ˈpu̇r-ə\ town N *cen* Sri Lanka; an ancient * of Ceylon *pop* 16,531
An·yang \ˈän-ˈyäŋ\ city E China in N Honan
A'nyêmaqên — see AMNE MACHIN
An·zio \ˈan-zē-ˌō, ˈän-\ city & port Italy SSE of Rome *pop* 27,094
Ao·mo·ri \ˈau̇-mə-(ˌ)rē\ city & port N Japan in NE Honshu on Mutsu Bay *pop* 289,329
Aorangi — see COOK (Mount)
Aos·ta \ä-ˈō-stə\ **1** commune NW Italy in Piedmont at junction of Great & Little St. Bernard passes *pop* 37,682 **2** — see VAL D'AOSTA
Ap·a·lach·i·co·la \ˌap-ə-ˌlach-i-ˈkō-lə\ river 90 *mi* (145 *km*) NW Fla. flowing from Lake Seminole S into **Apalachicola Bay** (inlet of Gulf of Mexico)
Apa·po·ris \ˌäp-ə-ˈpōr-(ˌ)ēs, -ˈpȯr-\ river *ab* 500 *mi* (805 *km*) S Colombia flowing SE into the Japurá on Colombia-Brazil boundary
Apel·doorn \ˈap-əl-ˌdō(ə)rn, -ˌdȯ(ə)rn\ commune E *cen* Netherlands N of Arnhem *pop* 143,276
Ap·en·nines \ˈap-ə-ˌnīnz\ mountain chain Italy extending the length of the peninsula — see CORNO (Monte) — **Ap·en·nine** \-ˌnīn\ *adj*
Apia \ə-ˈpē-ə\ town & port Samoa * of Western Samoa on Upolu Is.
Apo, Mount \ˈäp-(ˌ)ō\ volcano 9689 *ft* (2953 *m*) S Philippines in SE Mindanao; highest peak in the Philippines
Ap·pa·la·chia \ˌap-ə-ˈlā-chə, -ˈlach-ə, -ˈlā-shə\ region E U.S. comprising Appalachian mountains from S *cen* N.Y. to *cen* Ala.
Ap·pa·la·chian \ˌap-ə-ˈlā-ch(ē-)ən, -sh(ē-)ən; -ˈlach-(ē-)ən\ mountain system E N. America extending from SE Que., Nfld., & N.B. SW to N Ala.; highest peak Mt. Mitchell 6684 *ft* (2037 *m*)
Ap·pen·zell \ˈap-ən-ˌzel, ˈäp-ən(t)-ˌsel\ former canton NE Switzerland, now divided into two cantons (formerly half cantons): **Appenzell In·ner Rhodes** \-ˈin-ə(r)-ˌrōdz\ *or G* **Appenzell Inner Rho·den** \-ˌrōd-ᵊn\ (* Appenzell *area* 61 *sq mi or* 159 *sq km*, *pop* 13,700) & **Appenzell Out·er Rhodes** \-ˈau̇t-ə(r)-\ *or G* **Appenzell Aus·ser Rhoden** \-ˈau̇-sə(r)-\ (* Herisau *area* 101 *sq mi or* 263 *sq km*, *pop* 48,500)

Ap·pi·an Way \'ap-ē-ən-\ ancient paved highway extending from Rome to the Adriatic (in Apulia)

Ap·ple·ton \'ap-əl-tən\ city E Wis. *pop* 59,032

Apple Valley city SE Minn. *pop* 21,818

Apra Harbor \'äp-rə\ seaport Guam on W coast

Ap·she·ron \,äp-shə-'rȯn\ peninsula U.S.S.R. projecting into the Caspian sea on coast of E Azerbaijan

Apu·lia \ə-'pyül-yə, -'pyü-lē-ə\ *or It* **Pu·glia** \'pül-yä\ *or* **Le Pu·glie** \lä-'pül-yä\ region SE Italy on the Adriatic & Gulf of Taranto ✱ Bari — **Apu·lian** \ə-'pyül-yən, -'pyü-lē-ən\ *adj or n*

Apu·re \ə-'pü(ə)r-(,)ā\ river 420 *mi* (676 *km*) W Venezuela flowing E into the Orinoco

Apu·rí·mac \,äp-ə-'rē-,mäk\ river 550 *mi* (885 *km*) S & *cen* Peru flowing N to unite with the Urubamba forming the Ucayali

'Aqa·ba *or* **Aka·ba** \'äk-ə-bə\ *or anc* **Elath** \'ē-,lath\ town & port SW Jordan on border of Israel at head of NE arm (**Gulf of 'Aqaba**) of Red sea

Aquid·neck \ə-'kwid-,nek\ *or* **Rhode** island SE R.I. in Narragansett Bay; site of city of Newport

Aq·ui·taine \,ak-wə-,tān\ old region of SW France comprising area later known as Guienne ✱ Toulouse

Aq·ui·ta·nia \,ak-wə-'tā-nyə, -nē-ə\ a Roman division of SW Gaul under Caesar consisting of country between Pyrenees mountains & Garonne river & under Augustus expanded to Loire & Allier rivers — **Aq·ui·ta·nian** \-nyən, -nē-ən\ *adj or n*

Ara·ba, Wa·di el \,wäd-ē-,el-'ar-ə-bə\ *or* **Ar·a·bah** \'ar-ə-bə\ valley extending S from Dead sea to Gulf of 'Aqaba

Ara·bia \ə-'rā-bē-ə\ peninsula of SW Asia *ab* 1400 *mi* (2253 *km*) long & 1250 *mi* (2012 *km*) wide including Saudi Arabia, Yemen, & Persian Gulf States; in earlier times divided into **Arabia Pe·traea** \-pə-'trē-ə\, "Rocky Arabia", the NW part; **Arabia De·ser·ta** \-di-'zərt-ə\, "Desert Arabia", the N part; & **Arabia Fe·lix** \-'fē-liks\, "Fertile Arabia", the main part of the peninsula but by some geographers restricted to Yemen — **Ara·bi·an** \-bē-ən\ *adj or n*

Arabian **1** desert E Egypt between the Nile & the Red sea **2** sea, NW section of the Indian ocean between India & Arabia

Ar·a·by \'ar-ə-bē\ ARABIA

Ara·ca·ju \,ar-ə-kə-'zhü\ city & port NE Brazil ✱ of Sergipe *pop* 293,285

Arad \ä-'räd\ city W Romania on the Mures *pop* 178,248

Ara·fu·ra \,ar-ə-'für-ə\ sea bet. N Australia & W New Guinea

Ar·a·gon \'ar-ə-,gän, -gən\ region NE Spain bordering on France; once an independent kingdom ✱ Zaragoza — **Ar·a·go·nese** \,ar-ə-gə-'nēz, -'nēs\ *adj or n*

Ara·gua·ia *or* **Ara·gua·ya** \,är-ə-'gwī-ə\ river *ab* 1100 *mi* (1770 *km*), *cen* Brazil flowing N to the Tocantins

Arak \ä-'räk, ə-'rak\ city W Iran SW of Tehran *pop* 114,507

Ara·kan \,ar-ə-'kän, -'kan\ coast region SW Myanmar on Bay of Bengal; chief town Sittwe

Araks \ə-'räks\ *or* **Aras** \ə-'räs\ *or anc* **Arax·es** \ə-'rak-(,)sēz\ river 635 *mi* (1022 *km*) W Asia rising in mountains of Turkish Armenia & flowing E to join the Kura in E Azerbaijan, U.S.S.R.

Aral sea \'ar-əl\ *or formerly* **Lake Aral** brackish lake U.S.S.R. in SW Soviet Central Asia bet. Kazakhstan & Uzbek Republic *area* 26,000 *mi* (67,600 *sq km*)

Ar·am \'ar-əm, 'er-\ ancient Syria — its Hebrew name

Ar·an \'ar-ən\ islands W Ireland off coast of Galway; largest island Inishmore

Aran·sas Bay \ə-'ran(t)-səs\ inlet of Gulf of Mexico S Tex. NE of Corpus Christi Bay between mainland & St. Joseph Is.

Aransas Pass channel S Tex. bet. Mustang & St. Joseph islands leading to Corpus Christi & Aransas bays

Ar·a·rat \'ar-ə-,rat\ *or* **Ağ·rı Da·gi** \,ä(g)-rē-dä(g)-'ē\ mountain 16,946 *ft* (5165 *m*) E Turkey near border of Iran

Arau·ca·nia \ə-,raù-'kän-ē-ə, ,är-,aù-\ region *cen* Chile S of the Bío-Bío

Ara·val·li \ə-'räv-ə-(,)lē\ mountain range NW India E of Thar desert; highest peak Mt. Abu 5650 *ft* (1722 *m*)

Ar·bil *or* **Ir·bil** *or* **Er·bil** \ər-'bēl\ *or anc* **Ar·be·la** \är-'bē-lə\ city N Iraq E of Mosul *pop* 460,758

Ar·bon \är-'bȯn\ commune NE Switzerland *pop* 11,333

Ar·buck·le mountains \'är-,bək-əl\ hilly region S *cen* Okla.

Ar·ca·dia \är-'kād-ē-ə\ **1** city SW Calif. ENE of Los Angeles *pop* 45,994 **2** mountainous region S Greece in *cen* Peloponnisos

Archangel, Gulf of — see DVINA GULF

Arch·es National Park \'är-chəz\ reservation E Utah including wind-eroded natural arch formations

Ar·cos de la Fron·te·ra \'är-kōs-,del-ə-,frən-'ter-ə\ commune SW Spain NE of Cádiz *pop* 16,217

Ar·cot \är-'kät\ city SE India in Tamil Nadu WSW of Madras; once ✱ of the nawabs of Carnatic *pop* 30,230

Arc·tic \'ärk-tik, 'ärt-ik\ **1** ocean N of the Arctic circle **2** Arctic regions **3** archipelago N & E Northwest Territories, Canada in Arctic ocean

Arctic Red river 310 *mi* (499 *km*) Canada in W Northwest Territories, flowing N into the Mackenzie

Ar·cueil \är-'kœi\ commune N France S of Paris *pop* 20,303

Ar·da·bil *or* **Ar·de·bil** \,ärd-ə-'bē(ə)l\ city NW Iran in E Azerbaijan province *pop* 147,404

Ar·den \'ärd-ᵊn\ district *cen* England in SW Warwickshire W of Stratford-upon-Avon; site of former **Forest of Arden**

Ar·dennes \är-'den\ wooded plateau region in NE France, W Luxembourg, & SE Belgium E of the Meuse

Ard·more \'ärd-,mō(ə)r, -,mȯ(ə)r\ city S Okla. *pop* 23,689

Ards \'ärdz\ district E Northern Ireland, established 1974 *area* 143 *sq mi* (372 *sq km*), *pop* 57,626

Are·ci·bo \,ar-ə-'sē-(,)bō\ city & port N Puerto Rico *pop* 48,779

Are·na, Point \ə-'rē-nə\ promontory N Calif. in the Pacific *ab* midway bet. Cape Mendocino & San Francisco

Are·qui·pa \,ar-ə-'kē-pə\ city S Peru at foot of El Misti *pop* 108,023

Arez·zo \ə-'ret-(,)sō, ä-\ commune *cen* Italy in Tuscany *pop* 84,839

Ar·gen·tan \,är-zhən-'tän\ commune NW France in Normandy NNW of Alençon *pop* 16,063

Ar·gen·teuil \,är-zhən-'tœi\ commune N France on the Seine NNW of Paris *pop* 101,542

Ar·gen·ti·na \,är-jən-'tē-nə\ *or* **the Ar·gen·tine** \'är-jən-,tīn, -,tēn\ country S S. America bet. the Andes & the Atlantic S of the Pilcomayo; a federal republic ✱ Buenos Aires *area* 1,079,965 *sq mi* (2,807,909 *sq km*), *pop* 27,947,446 — **Argentine** *adj or n* — **Ar·gen·tin·ean** *or* **Ar·gen·tin·i·an** \,är-jən-'tin-ē-ən\ *adj or n*

Ar·gi·nu·sae \,är-jə-'n(y)ü-(,)sē\ group of small islands in the Aegean SE of Lésvos

Ar·go·lis \'är-gə-ləs\ district & ancient country S Greece in E Peloponnisos comprising a plain around Argos & area between Gulf of Argolis & Saronic gulf — **Ar·gol·ic** \är-'gäl-ik\ *adj*

Argolis, Gulf of *or* **Gulf of Nau·plia** \'nȯ-plē-ə\ inlet of the Aegean S Greece on E coast of Peloponnisos

Ar·gonne \är-'gän, 'är-,\ wooded plateau NE France S of the Ardennes near Belgian border bet. the Meuse & the Aisne

Ar·gos \'är-,gäs, -gəs\ town Greece in E Peloponnisos on Argive plain at head of Gulf of Argolis; once a Greek city-state

Argovie — see AARGAU

Ar·guel·lo, Point \är-'gwel-(,)ō\ cape SW Calif. WNW of Santa Barbara

Ar·gun \är-'gün\ river 450 *mi* (724 *km*) NE Asia forming boundary between Inner Mongolia (China) & U.S.S.R. & uniting with the Shilka to form the Amur

Ar·gyll \är-'gi(ə)l, 'är-,gil\ *or* **Ar·gyll·shire** \-,shi(ə)r, -shər\ former county W Scotland ✱ Lochgilphead

Ar·hus *or* **Aar·hus** \'ȯ(ə)r-,hùs\ city & port Denmark in E Jutland on the Kattegat *pop* 245,565

Aria \'ar-ē-ə, ə-'rī-ə\ **1** an E province of ancient Persian Empire; district now in NW Afghanistan & E Iran **2** — see HERAT

Ari·ca \ə-'rē-kə\ city & port N Chile *pop* 63,160 — see TACNA

Ar·i·ma·thea *or* **Ar·i·ma·thaea** \,ar-ə-mə-'thē-ə\ town in ancient Palestine; location not certainly identified

Ariminum — see RIMINI

Ari·pua·nã \,ar-əp-wə-'na⁴\ river 600 *mi* (966 *km*) W *cen* Brazil rising in Mato Grosso state & flowing N into the Madeira

Arius — see HARI RUD

Ar·i·zo·na \,ar-ə-'zō-nə\ state SW U.S. ✱ Phoenix *area* 113,909 *sq mi* (296,163 *sq km*), *pop* 2,718,215 — **Ar·i·zo·nan** \-nən\ *or* **Ar·i·zo·nian** \-nē-ən, -nyən\ *adj or n*

Ar·kan·sas \'är-kən-,sȯ; *1 is also* är-'kan-zəs\ **1** river 1450 *mi* (2334 *km*) SW *cen* U.S. rising in *cen* Colo. & flowing E & SE through S Kans., NE Okla., & Ark. into the Mississippi **2** state S *cen* U.S. ✱ Little Rock *area* 53,104 *sq mi* (138,070 *sq km*), *pop* 2,285,513 — **Ar·kan·san** \är-'kan-zən\ *adj or n*

Ar·khan·gel'sk \är-'kän-,gelsk\ *or* **Arch·an·gel** \'är-,kān-jəl\ city & port U.S.S.R. in N Soviet Russia, Europe, on the Northern Dvina *pop* 385,000

Arl·berg \'ärl(-ə)l-,bərg, -,berg\ Alpine valley, pass, & tunnel W Austria in the Tirol

Arles \'ärl\ **1** medieval kingdom E & SE France; also called Kingdom of Burgundy **2** *or anc* **Ar·e·las** \'ar-ə-,las\ *or* **Ar·e·la·te** \,ar-ə-'lāt-ē\ city SE France on the Rhône *pop* 37,337 — **Ar·le·sian** \är-'lē-zhən\ *n*

Ar·ling·ton \'är-liŋ-tən\ **1** town E Mass. NW of Boston *pop* 48,219 **2** city N Tex. E of Fort Worth *pop* 160,113

Arlington Heights village NE Ill. NW of Chicago *pop* 66,116

Ar·lon \är-'lōⁿ\ commune SE Belgium ✱ of Luxembourg province *pop* 22,279

Ar·magh \är-'mä, 'är-,\ **1** district Northern Ireland, established 1974 *area* 260 *sq mi* (676 *sq km*), *pop* 47,618 **2** town *cen* Armagh district, Northern Ireland *pop* 12,700

Ar·ma·gnac \,är-mən-'yak\ district SW France in old province of Gascony; chief town Auch

Ar·me·nia \är-'mē-nē-ə, -nyə\ **1** *or bib* **Min·ni** \'min-,ī\ former kingdom W Asia in mountainous region SE of Black sea & SW of Caspian sea; area now divided bet. U.S.S.R., Turkey, & Iran **2** *or* **Armenian Republic** constituent republic of U.S.S.R. in S Transcaucasia ✱ Yerevan *area* 11,580 *sq mi* (30,108 *sq km*), *pop* 3,031,000 — see LESSER ARMENIA

Ar·men·tières \,är-mən-'tye(ə)r, -'ti(ə)rz\ commune N France W of Lille *pop* 23,850

Ar·mor·i·ca \är-'mȯr-i-kə, -'mär-\ **1** *or* **Ar·e·mor·i·ca** \,ar-ə-\ ancient region NW France bet. the Seine & the Loire **2** BRITTANY

Arn·hem \'ärn-,hem, 'är-nəm\ commune E Netherlands ✱ of Gelderland *pop* 128,641

Arn·hem Land \'är-nəm\ region N Australia on N coast of Northern Territory

Ar·no \'är-(,)nō\ *or anc* **Ar·nus** \-nəs\ river 140 *mi* (225 *km*) *cen* Italy flowing W from the Apennines through Florence into Ligurian sea

Ar·nold \'ärn-ᵊld\ city E Mo. *pop* 19,141

Aroos·took \ə-'rüs-tək, -'rüs-\ river 140 *mi* (225 *km*) N Maine flowing NE across N.B. border & into St. John river

Ar·ran \'ar-ən\ island SW Scotland in Firth of Clyde *area* 165 *sq mi* (429 *sq km*)

Ar·ras \ə-'räs, 'ar-əs\ city N France SSW of Lille *pop* 45,804

Arsanias — see MURAT

Arta, Gulf of — see AMBRACIAN GULF

Ar·tois \är-'twä\ former province N France bet. Flanders & Picardy ✱ Arras

Aru *or* **Aroe** *or* **Ar·roe** \är-(,)ü\ islands E Indonesia S of W New Guinea *area* 3305 *sq mi* (8593 *sq km*), *pop* 29,604

Aru·ba \ä-'rü-bə\ internally self-governing Dutch island off NW Venezuela; chief town Oranjestad *area* 69 *sq mi* (179 *sq km*), *pop* 60,312

Arun·a·chal Pra·desh \,är-ə-,näch-əl-prə-'dāsh, -'desh\ *or formerly* **North East Frontier Agency** state NE India N of Assam ✱ Itanagar *area* 31,439 *sq mi* (81,741 *sq km*), *pop* 628,050

Aru·wi·mi \,är-ə-'wē-mē, ,ar-\ river 800 *mi* (1287 *km*) N Zaire flowing SW & W into Congo river

Ar·va·da \är-'vad-ə\ city *cen* Colo. NW of Denver *pop* 84,576

Arwad \är-ˈwad, -ˈwäd\ or **Ru·ad** \rü-ˈad\ or bib **Ar·vad** \ˈär-ˌvad\ island Syria off coast of S Latakia
Asa·hi·ka·wa \ˌäs-ə-hē-ˈkä-wə\ or **Asa·hi·ga·wa** \-ˈgä-wə\ city Japan in cen Hokkaido pop 353,255
Asa·ma \ə-ˈsäm-ə\ or **Asa·ma·ya·ma** \ə-ˌsäm-ə-ˈyäm-ə\ volcano 8340 ft (2542 m) Japan in cen Honshu
Asan·sol \ˈäs-ᵊn-ˌsōl\ city NE India in W. Bengal pop 365,371
As·bury Park \ˈaz-ˌber-ē, -b(ə-)rē\ city E N.J. on the Atlantic pop 17,015
As·cen·sion \ə-ˈsen-chən\ island in S Atlantic belonging to Brit. colony of St. Helena area 34 sq mi (88 sq km), pop 849
As·co·li Pi·ce·no \ˌäs-kə-(ˌ)lē-pi-ˈchā-(ˌ)nō\ or anc **As·cu·lum Pi·ce·num** \ˌas-kyə-ləm-(ˌ)pi-ˈsē-nəm\ commune cen Italy in the Marches NE of Rome pop 54,193
Ascoli Sa·tria·no \-ˌsä-trē-ˈän-(ˌ)ō\ or anc **As·cu·lum Ap·u·lum** \ˌas-kyə-lə-ˈmap-yə-ləm\ or **Aus·cu·lum Apulum** \ˌȯs-\ commune SE Italy in Apulia S of Foggia pop 7524
As·cot \ˈas-kət\ village S England in Berkshire SW of London
As·cut·ney, Mount \ə-ˈskət-nē\ mountain 3144 ft (958 m) SE Vt.
Ashan·ti \ə-ˈshant-ē, -ˈshänt-\ or **Asan·te** \ə-ˈsänt-ē\ region cen Ghana; formerly a native kingdom & later a Brit. colony * Kumasi area 24,379 sq mi (63,385 sq km), pop 1,996,821
Ash·bur·ton \ˈash-ˌbərt-ᵊn\ river 500 mi (805 km) Australia in NW Western Australia flowing NW into Indian ocean
Ash·dod \ˈash-ˌdäd\ city & port Israel W of Jerusalem pop 40,500
Ashe·ville \ˈash-ˌvil, -vəl\ city W N.C. pop 53,583
Ashi·ka·ga \ˌäsh-i-ˈkäg-ə\ city Japan in cen Honshu pop 166,132
Ash·ke·lon \ˈash-kə-ˌlän\ or **As·ca·lon** \ˈas-kə-\ ancient city & port SW Palestine, site in Israel WSW of Jerusalem
Ashkh·a·bad \ˈash-kə-ˌbad, -ˌbäd\ or formerly **Pol·to·ratsk** \ˌpäl-tə-ˈrätsk\ city U.S.S.R. in Soviet Central Asia * of Turkmen Republic pop 312,000
Ash·land \ˈash-lənd\ **1** city NE Ky. on the Ohio pop 27,064 **2** city N cen Ohio pop 20,326
Ash·ley \ˈash-lē\ river 40 mi (64 km) S S.C. flowing SE into Charleston harbor
Ash·ta·bu·la \ˌash-tə-ˈbyü-lə\ city NE Ohio on Lake Erie pop 23,449
Asia \ˈā-zhə, -shə\ continent of the eastern hemisphere N of equator forming a single landmass with Europe (the conventional dividing line bet. Asia & Europe being the Ural mountains & main range of the Caucasus mountains); has numerous large offshore islands including Cyprus, Sri Lanka, Malay archipelago, Taiwan, the Japanese chain, & Sakhalin area 16,988,000 sq mi (44,168,800 sq km)
Asia Mi·nor \-ˈmī-nər\ peninsula forming W extremity of Asia between Black sea on N, Mediterranean sea on S, & Aegean sea on W — see ANATOLIA
Asir \a-ˈsi(ə)r\ province S Saudi Arabia on Red sea SE of Hejaz * As Sabya area 13,857 sq mi (36,028 sq km)
As·ma·ra \az-ˈmär-ə, -ˈmar-ə\ city N Ethiopia * of Eritrea pop 474,241
As·nières \an-ˈye(ə)r, än-\ commune N France NW of Paris
Aso \ˈäs-(ˌ)ō\ or **Aso·san** \ˌäs-ō-ˈsän\ volcanic mountain Japan in cen Kyushu; has five volcanic cones grouped around crater 15 mi (24 km) long with walls 2000 ft (610 m) high
Aso·lo \ˈäz-ə-ˌlō\ commune NE Italy NW of Treviso pop 6387
Asphaltites, Lacus — see DEAD SEA
As·sam \ə-ˈsam, a-; ˈas-ˌam\ state NE India on edge of Himalayas * Dispur area 30,318 sq mi (78,827 sq km), pop 19,902,226
As·sen \ˈäs-ᵊn\ commune NE Netherlands * of Drenthe
As·sin·i·boine \ə-ˈsin-ə-ˌbȯin\ river 450 mi (724 km) Canada rising in SE Sask. & flowing S & E across S Man. into Red river
Assiniboine, Mount mountain 11,870 ft (3618 m) Canada in SW Alta. on B.C. border
As·si·si \ə-ˈsis-ē, -ˈsē-zē, -ˈsē-sē, -ˈsiz-ē\ commune cen Italy ESE of Perugia pop 24,440
As·syr·ia \ə-ˈsir-ē-ə\ or bib **As·sur** \ä-ˈsu̇(ə)r, ˈä-ˌ\ or **Ashur** \ˈäsh-ˌu̇(ə)r\, ancient empire W Asia extending along middle Tigris & over foothills to the E; early * Calah, later * Nineveh
Astacus — see IZMIT
Asterabad — see GORGAN
Asti \ˈäs-tē\ commune NW Italy W of Alessandria pop 76,950
As·tra·khan \ˈas-trə-ˌkan, -kən\ city U.S.S.R. in Soviet Russia, Europe, on the Volga at head of its delta pop 461,000
As·tu·ri·as \ə-ˈst(y)u̇r-ē-əs, a-\ **1** region & old kingdom NW Spain on Bay of Biscay **2** OVIEDO (province) — **As·tu·ri·an** \-ē-ən\ adj or n
Asun·ción \ə-ˌsün(t)-sē-ˈōn, (ˌ)ä-\ city * of Paraguay on Paraguay river at confluence with the Pilcomayo pop 455,517
As·wân \a-ˈswän, ä-\ or anc **Sy·e·ne** \sī-ˈē-nē\ city S Egypt on right bank of the Nile near site of dam built 1898–1902 & of **Aswân High Dam** (completed 1970 to form **Lake Nas·ser** \ˈnäs-ər, ˈnas-\) pop 144,654
As·yût or **As·siout** or **As·siut** \äs-ˈyüt\ city cen Egypt on left bank of the Nile pop 213,751
Ata·ca·ma \ˌat-ə-ˈkäm-ə\ **1** desert N Chile bet. Copiapó & Peru border **2** — see PUNA DE ATACAMA
At·ba·ra \ˈat-bə-rə\ river ab 500 mi (805 km) NE Africa rising in N Ethiopia & flowing through E Sudan into the Nile
Atchaf·a·laya \(ə-)ˌchaf-ə-ˈlī-ə\ river 225 mi (362 km) S La. flowing S into **Atchafalaya Bay** (inlet of Gulf of Mexico)
Ath·a·bas·ca or **Ath·a·bas·ka** \ˌath-ə-ˈbas-kə\ **1** river 765 mi (1231 km) Canada in Alta. flowing NE & N into Athabasca lake **2** lake Canada on Alta.-Sask. boundary area 3058 sq mi (7951 sq km)
Ath·ens \ˈath-ənz\ **1** city NE Ga. pop 42,549 **2** city SE Ohio pop 19,743 **3** or NGk **Athí·nai** \ä-ˈthē-(ˌ)nā\ or anc **Athe·nae** \ə-ˈthē-(ˌ)nē\ city * of Greece near Saronic Gulf pop 885,136 — **Athe·nian** \ə-ˈthē-nē-ən, -nyən\ adj or n
Athos \ˈath-ˌäs, ˈā-ˌthäs\ mountain NE Greece at E end of Acte peninsula; site of a number of monasteries comprising **Mount Athos** (autonomous area)
Ati·tlán \ˌät-ē-ˈtlän\ lake 24 mi (39 km) long SW Guatemala at 4700 ft (1432 m) altitude occupying a crater 1000 ft (305 m) deep N of **Atitlán Volcano**
At·ka \ˈat-kə, ˈät-\ island SW Alaska in Andreanof group
At·lan·ta \ət-ˈlant-ə, at-\ city NW cen Ga., its * pop 425,022 — **At·lan·tan** \-ˈlant-ᵊn\ adj or n
At·lan·tic \ət-ˈlant-ik, at-\ ocean separating N. & S. America from Europe & Africa area 41,105,000 sq mi (106,873,000 sq km)
Atlantic City city SE N.J. on Atlantic coast pop 40,199
Atlantic Provinces the Canadian provinces of Nfld., N.B., N.S., & P.E.I. — see MARITIME PROVINCES
At·las \ˈat-ləs\ mountains NW Africa extending from SW Morocco to NE Tunisia; its highest peaks are in the **Grand**, or **High, Atlas** in SW cen Morocco — see TOUBKAL (Jebel)
Atrek \ə-ˈtrek\ or **Atrak** \-ˈtrak\ river 300 mi (483 km) NE Iran flowing into the Caspian on U.S.S.R. border
Atropatene — see AZERBAIJAN
At·ta·wa·pis·kat \ˌat-ə-wə-ˈpis-kət\ river 465 mi (748 km) Canada in N Ont. flowing E into James Bay
At·ti·ca \ˈat-i-kə\ region E Greece, chief city Athens; a state of ancient Greece
At·tle·boro \ˈat-ᵊl-ˌbər-ə, -ˌbə-rə\ city SE Mass. pop 34,196
At·tu \ˈa-(ˌ)tü\ island SW Alaska, most westerly of the Aleutians, in Near group — see WRANGELL (Cape)
Aube \ˈōb\ river 125 mi (201 km) N cen France flowing into the Seine
Au·ber·vil·liers \ˌō-bər-ˌvēl-ˈyā\ commune N France pop 72,859
Au·burn \ˈȯ-bərn\ **1** city E Ala. pop 28,471 **2** city SW Maine pop 23,128 **3** city cen N.Y. pop 32,548 **4** city W Wash. pop 26,417
Auck·land \ˈȯ-klənd\ city & port N New Zealand on North Is. pop 144,963
Audenarde — see OUDENAARDE
Au·ghra·bies Falls \ȯ-ˈgräb-ēz\ or **King George's Falls** waterfall 480 ft (146 m) Republic of S. Africa in Orange river in NW Cape Province
Au·ghrim or **Aghrim** \ˈȯ-grəm, -krəm\ town W Ireland in E Galway
Augs·burg \ˈȯgz-ˌbərg, ˈau̇gz-ˌbu̇(ə)rg\ city S W. Germany in Bavaria on the Lech pop 248,346
Au·gus·ta \ȯ-ˈgəs-tə, ə-\ **1** city E Ga. on Savannah river pop 47,532 **2** city * of Maine on the Kennebec pop 21,819
Au·lis \ˈȯ-ləs\ harbor E Greece in Boeotia on Evripos strait
Au·nis \ō-ˈnēs\ former province W France on Gironde estuary & Bay of Biscay * La Rochelle
Au·rang·a·bad \au̇-ˈrəŋ-(g)ə-ˌbäd\ city W India in cen Maharashtra ENE of Bombay pop 316,244
Au·rès \ȯ-ˈres\ massif ab 7600 ft (2316 m) NE Algeria in Saharan Atlas
Au·ri·gnac \ˌō-rēn-ˈyak\ village SW France SW of Toulouse
Au·ril·lac \ˌō-rē-ˈ(y)ak\ city S cen France pop 29,458
Au·ro·ra \ə-ˈrōr-ə, ō-, -ˈrȯr-\ **1** city N cen Colo. E of Denver pop 158,588 **2** city NE Ill. pop 81,293
Au·sa·ble \ȯ-ˈsā-bəl\ river 20 mi (32 km) NE N.Y. flowing E into Lake Champlain through **Ausable Chasm** gorge
Auschwitz — see OŚWIĘCIM
Austerlitz — see SLAVKOV
Aus·tin \ˈȯs-tən, ˈäs-\ **1** city S Minn. pop 23,020 **2** city * of Tex. on the Colorado pop 345,496
Austral — see TUBUAI
Aus·tral·asia \ˌȯs-trə-ˈlā-zhə, ˌäs-, -ˈlā-shə\ Australia, Tasmania, New Zealand, & Melanesia — **Aus·tral·asian** \-zhən, -shən\ adj or n
Aus·tra·lia \ȯ-ˈstrāl-yə, ä-, ə-\ **1** continent of the E hemisphere SE of Asia & S of the equator area 2,948,366 sq mi (7,665,751 sq km) **2** or **Commonwealth of Australia** dominion of the Commonwealth including the continent of Australia & island of Tasmania * Canberra area 2,967,909 sq mi (7,716,563 sq km), pop 14,574,488
Australian Alps mountain range SE Australia in E Victoria & SE New S. Wales forming S end of Great Dividing range
Australian Capital Territory or formerly **Federal Capital Territory** district SE Australia including two areas, one around Canberra & the other on Jervis Bay, surrounded by New S. Wales area 939 sq mi (2441 sq km), pop 221,609
Aus·tra·sia or **Os·tra·sia** \ȯ-ˈstrā-zhə, ä-, -shə\ the E dominions of the Merovingian Franks extending from the Meuse to Böhmerwald — **Aus·tra·sian** \-zhən, -shən\ adj or n
Aus·tria \ˈȯs-trē-ə, ˈäs-\ or G **Ös·ter·reich** \ˈœ-stə(r)-ˌrīk\ country cen Europe in & N of E Alps with the Danube crossing it in N; a republic * Vienna area 32,375 sq mi (84,175 sq km), pop 7,555,338 — **Aus·tri·an** \-ən\ adj or n
Austria–Hun·ga·ry \-ˈhəŋ-gə-rē\ dual monarchy 1867–1918 cen Europe including Bohemia, Moravia, Bukovina, Transylvania, Galicia, and what is now Austria, Hungary, NW half of Yugoslavia, & NE Italy — **Aus·tro–Hun·gar·i·an** \ˈȯs-(ˌ)trō-ˌhəŋ-ˈgar-ē-ən, ˈäs-, -ˈger-\ adj or n
Aus·tro·ne·sia \ˌȯs-trə-ˈnē-zhə, ˌäs-, -ˈnē-shə\ **1** the islands of the S Pacific **2** area extending from Madagascar through the Malay peninsula & archipelago to Hawaii & Easter Is.
Au·teuil \ō-ˈtəi, -ˈtə(r)\ district in W Paris, France
Au·vergne \ō-ˈve(ə)rn(-yə), -ˈvərn\ **1** region & former province S cen France * Clermont (now Clermont-Ferrand) **2** mountains S cen France; highest in the Massif Central — see SANCY (Puy de)
Aux Cayes — see CAYES
Aux Sources, Mont \ˌmōⁿ-ˌtō-ˈsu̇(ə)rs\ mountain 10,822 ft (3298 m) N Lesotho in Drakensberg mountains on Natal border
Au·yán–te·puí \au̇-ˌyän-təp-ˈwē\ or **Devil Mountain** plateau ab 20 mi (32 km) long SE Venezuela E of the Caroní — see ANGEL FALLS
Au·yuit·tuq National Park \au̇-ˈyü-ət-ək-\ reservation NE Canada in E Baffin island
Av·a·lon \ˈav-ə-ˌlän\ peninsula Canada in SE Newfoundland
Avalon, Isle of — see ISLE OF AVALON
Ave·bury \ˈāv-b(ə-)rē, US also -ˌber-ē\ village S England in Wiltshire E of Bristol; has megalithic remains
Ave·lla·ne·da \ˌav-ə-zhə-ˈnā-də\ city E Argentina, E suburb of Buenos Aires, on Río de la Plata pop 330,654
Avenches \a-ˈväⁿsh\ or anc **Aven·ti·cum** \ə-ˈvent-i-kəm\ town W Switzerland in Vaud canton * of ancient Helvetia pop 2177
Av·en·tine \ˈav-ən-ˌtīn, -ˌtēn\ hill in Rome, Italy, one of seven (including also the Caelian, Capitoline, Esquiline, Palatine, Quirinal, & Viminal) on which the ancient city was built
Aver·nus \ə-ˈvər-nəs\ or It **Aver·no** \ä-ˈve(ə)r-(ˌ)nō\ lake S Italy in crater of extinct volcano W of Naples
Avi·gnon \ˌa-(ˌ)vēn-ˈyōⁿ\ city SE France pop 73,482
Avi·la \ˈäv-i-lə\ **1** province cen Spain area 3042 sq mi (7909 sq km), pop 165,427 **2** city, its *, WNW of Madrid pop 36,745
Avlona — see VLORË
Avon \ˈā-vən, ˈav-ən, US also ˈā-ˌvän\ **1** river 96 mi (154 km) cen England rising in Northamptonshire & flowing WSW past Stratford-

Upon-Avon into Severn river at Tewkesbury **2** river 65 *mi* (105 *km*) S England rising near Devizes in Wiltshire & flowing S into English channel **3** river 62 *mi* (100 *km*) SW England rising in Gloucestershire & flowing S & W through city of Bristol into Bristol channel at Avonmouth **4** \'av-ən\ — see SWAN **5** \'ā-vən, 'av-ən, *US also* 'ā-,vän\ county SW England ✱ Bristol *area* 520 *sq mi* (1352 *sq km*), *pop* 925,700
Avranches \av-'räⁿsh\ town NW France in SW Normandy
Awa·ji \ə-'wäj-ē\ island Japan S of Honshu & NE of Shikoku
Awash \'ä-,wäsh\ river 500 *mi* (805 *km*) E Ethiopia flowing NE
Ax·el Hei·berg \,ak-səl-'hī-,bərg\ island N Canada in the Sverdrup islands W of Ellesmere Is. *area* 15,779 *sq mi* (41,025 *sq km*)
Axum — see AKSUM — **Ax·um·ite** \'ak-sə-mīt\ *adj or n*
Aya·cu·cho \,ī-ə-'kü-(,)chō\ town S Peru SE of Lima
Ay·dın \ī-'din\ city SW Turkey SE of Izmir *pop* 71,576
Ayers Rock \'a(ə)rz-, 'e(ə)rz-\ outcrop *cen* Australia in SW Northern Territory; 1143 *ft* (348 *m*) high
Ayles·bury \'ā(ə)lz-b(ə-)rē, *US also* -,ber-ē\ borough SE *cen* England ✱ of Buckinghamshire *pop* 41,288
Ayl·mer \'ā(ə)l-mər\ town Canada in SW Que. *pop* 26,695
Ayr \'a(ə)r, 'e(ə)r\ **1** *or* **Ayr·shire** \-,shi(ə)r, -shər\ former county SW Scotland **2** burgh & port SW Scotland in Strathclyde *pop* 49,481
Ayut·tha·ya \ä-'yüt-ə-yə\ city S Thailand N of Bangkok
Azer·bai·jan *or* **Azer·bai·dzhan** *or* **Azerbaijan Republic** \,az-ər-,bī-'jän, ,äz-\ constituent republic of the U.S.S.R. in E Transcaucasia bordering on Caspian sea ✱ Baku *area* 33,200 *sq mi* (86,320 *sq km*), *pop* 6,028,000
Azerbaijan *or anc* **At·ro·pa·te·ne** \,a-trō-pə-'tē-nē\ *or* **Me·dia Atropatene** \'mēd-ē-ə-\ region NW Iran; chief city Tabriz
Azin·court \â-zaⁿ-kür\ *or earlier* **Agin·court** \'aj-ən-,kō(ə)rt, -,kó(ə)rt; 'azh-ən-,kù(ə)r\ village N France WNW of Arras
Azores \'ā-,zō(ə)rz, -,zó(ə)rz, ə-'\ *or Pg* **Aço·res** \ə-'sōr-ēsh\ islands N Atlantic belonging to Portugal & lying *ab* 800 *mi* (1287 *km*) off coast of Portugal; chief town Ponta Delgada *area* 888 *sq mi* (2309 *sq km*), *pop* 336,100 — **Azor·e·an** *or* **Azor·i·an** \ā-'zōr-ē-ən, -'zór-, ə-\ *adj or n*
Azov, Sea of \'az-,óf, 'āz-, -,äv\ gulf of the Black sea E of Crimea connected with the Black sea by the Kerch strait *area* 14,520 *sq mi* (37,752 *sq km*)
Az·tec Ruins National Monument \,az-,tek-\ reservation NW N.Mex. NE of Farmington; site of a prehistoric pueblo
Azu·sa \ə-'zü-sə\ city SW Calif. ENE of Los Angeles *pop* 29,380
Az Zaqāziq — see ZAGAZIG
Baal·bek \'bā-əl-,bek, 'bäl-,bek\ town E Lebanon N of Damascus on site of ancient city of **He·li·op·o·lis** \,hē-lē-'äp-(ə-)ləs\
Ba·bar \'bäb-,är\ islands Indonesia ENE of Timor
Bab el Man·deb \,bab-əl-'man-dəb\ strait between SW Arabia & Africa connecting Red sea & Gulf of Aden
Ba·bel·thu·ap \,bäb-əl-'tü-,äp\ island W Pacific, chief island in Belau *area* 143 *sq mi* (372 *sq km*)
Babian — see BLACK 4
Ba·bu·yan \,bäb-ü-'yän\ **1** islands N Philippines N of Luzon *area* 225 *sq mi* (585 *sq km*) **2** chief island of the group
Bab·y·lon \'bab-ə-lən, -,län\ ancient city ✱ of Babylonia; its site *ab* 50 *mi* (80 *km*) S of Baghdad near the Euphrates
Bab·y·lo·nia \,bab-ə-'lō-nyə, -nē-ə\ ancient country in valley of the lower Euphrates & the Tigris ✱ Babylon
Back \'bak\ river 605 *mi* (974 *km*) Canada in NE Mackenzie district & NW Keewatin district flowing ENE into Arctic ocean
Ba·co·lod \bä-'kō-,lód\ city Philippines on Negros Is. *pop* 262,415
Bactra — see BALKH
Bac·tria \'bak-trē-ə\ ancient country SW Asia between Hindu Kush & Oxus river ✱ Bactra — see BALKH — **Bac·tri·an** \'bak-trē-ən\ *adj or n*
Ba·da·joz \,bäth-ə-'hōs, ,bäd-ə-'hōz\ **1** province SW Spain in valley of the Guadiana *area* 8451 *sq mi* (21,973 *sq km*), *pop* 572,798 **2** city, its ✱ *pop* 111,456
Ba·da·lo·na \,bäth-ə-'lō-nə, ,bäd-ᵊl-'ō-nə\ city & port NE Spain on the Mediterranean NE of Barcelona *pop* 229,780
Bad Ems — see EMS
Ba·den \'bäd-ᵊn\ **1** region SW W. Germany bordering on Switzerland & France; formerly a grand duchy (1805–1918), a state of the Weimar Republic (1918–33), an administrative division of the Third Reich (1933–49), & a state of the Bonn Republic (1949–51) ✱ Karlsruhe — see BADEN-WÜRTTEMBERG **2** BADEN-BADEN
Ba·den–Ba·den \,bäd-ᵊn-'bäd-ᵊn\ city & spa SW W. Germany in Baden-Württemberg SSW of Karlsruhe *pop* 49,142
Ba·den–Würt·tem·berg \,bäd-ᵊn-'wərt-əm-,bərg, -'wùrt-; -'vuert-əm-,berk\ state SW W. Germany W of Bavaria; formed 1951 from former Baden, Württemberg-Baden, & Württemberg-Hohenzollern states ✱ Stuttgart *area* 13,800 *sq mi* (35,880 *sq km*), *pop* 9,258,947
Bad·ga·stein \,bät-gä-'stīn\ town W *cen* Austria S of Salzburg
Bad Godesberg — see GODESBERG
Bad Homburg — see HOMBURG
Badlands National Park reservation SW S.Dak. E of Black Hills comprising an area of badlands topography
Bad Mergentheim — see MERGENTHEIM
Baf·fin \'baf-ən\ island NE Canada N of Hudson strait; largest in Arctic archipelago *area* 183,810 *sq mi* (477,906 *sq km*)
Baffin Bay inlet of the Atlantic bet. W Greenland & E Baffin Is.
Ba·fing \bə-'faŋ\ river 350 *mi* (560 *km*) W Africa in W Mali & Guinea; the upper course of the Senegal
Bagh·dad *or* **Bag·dad** \'bag-,dad\ city ✱ of Iraq on the middle Tigris *pop* 1,490,759 — **Bagh·dadi** \bag-'dad-ē\ *n*
Ba·guio \,bäg-ē-'ō\ city, summer ✱ of the Philippines, in NW *cen* Luzon *pop* 119,009
Ba·ha·ma \bə-'häm-ə, *by outsiders also* -'hā-mə\ islands in the Atlantic SE of Fla.; an independent member of the Commonwealth since 1973 ✱ Nassau *area* 4404 *sq mi* (11,450 *sq km*), *pop* 223,455 — see TURKS AND CAICOS — **Ba·ha·mi·an** \bə-'hā-mē-ən, -'häm-ē-\ *or* **Ba·ha·man** \-'hā-mən, -'häm-ən\ *adj or n*
Ba·ha·wal·pur \bə-'hä-wəl-,pù(ə)r\ region Pakistan in SW Punjab in Thar desert; until 1947 a princely state of India
Ba·hia \bə-'hē-ə, bä-'ē-ə\ **1** *or formerly* **Ba·ía** \bä-'ē-ə\ state E Brazil ✱ Salvador *area* 215,329 *sq mi* (559,855 *sq km*), *pop* 9,597,393 **2** — see SALVADOR — **Ba·hi·an** \-ən\ *adj or n*
Ba·hía Blan·ca \bə-,hē-ə-'blaŋ-kə, bä-,ē-ə-'bläŋ-\ city & port E Argentina SW of Buenos Aires *pop* 182,158
Bahnasa, El — see OXYRHYNCHUS
Bah·rain *or* **Bah·rein** \bä-'rān\ **1** islands in Persian Gulf off coast of Arabia; an independent sultanate ✱ Manama (on Bahrain Is.) *area* 213 *sq mi* (554 *sq km*), *pop* 358,857 **2** island, largest of the group, 27 *mi* (43 *km*) long — **Bah·raini** *or* **Bah·reini** \-'rā-nē\ *adj or n*
Bahr el Gha·zal \'bär-ál-gə-'zal\ river *ab* 500 *mi* (800 *km*) SW Sudan flowing E to unite with the Bahr el Jebel forming the White Nile
Bai·kal, Lake *or* **Lake Bay·kal** \bī-'käl, -'kal\ lake U.S.S.R. in S Soviet Russia, Asia; 5712 *ft* (1731 *m*) deep, *ab* 375 *mi* (600 *km*) long
Baile Atha Cliath — see DUBLIN
Ba·ja California \'bä-(,)hä-\ peninsula 760 *mi* (1216 *km*) long NW Mexico bet. the Pacific & Gulf of California; divided into the states of **Baja California Nor·te** \'nór-tē\ (to the N ✱ Mexicali *area* 27,653 *sq mi or* 71,898 *sq km*, *pop* 1,225,436) & **Baja California Sur** \'sù(ə)r\ (to the S ✱ La Paz *area* 27,976 *sq mi or* 72,738 *sq km*, *pop* 221,389)
Bakan — see SHIMONOSEKI
Ba·ker \'bā-kər\ island (atoll) *cen* Pacific near the equator at 176°31′W; belongs to U.S.
Baker, Mount mountain 10,778 *ft* (3266 *m*) NW Wash. in Cascade range
Baker Lake — see DUBAWNT
Ba·kers·field \'bā-kərz-,fēld\ city S *cen* Calif. on the Kern *pop* 105,611
Bakh·ta·ran \,bäk-tə-'rän\ *or formerly* **Ker·man·shah** \,ker-,män-'shä\ city W Iran *pop* 290,861
Ba·ku \bä-'kü\ city U.S.S.R. ✱ of Azerbaijan *pop* 1,022,000
Bakwanga — see MBUJI-MAYI
Ba·la·kla·va *or* **Ba·la·cla·va** \,bal-ə-'klav-ə, ,bäl-ə-'kläv-ə\ village U.S.S.R. in S Soviet Russia, Europe, in Crimea SE of Sevastopol
Bal·a·ton \'bal-ə-,tän, 'ból-ə-,tōn\ *or G* **Plat·ten·see** \'plät-ᵊn-,zā\ lake W Hungary; largest in *cen* Europe *area* 266 *sq mi* (692 *sq km*)
Bal·boa Heights \(,)bal-,bō-ə-\ town Panama, at Pacific entrance to Panama canal adjacent to Panama (city); former administrative center of Canal Zone
Bal·dwin \'ból-dwən\ borough SW Pa. S of Pittsburgh *pop* 24,598
Baldwin Park city SW Calif. E of Los Angeles *pop* 50,554
Bâle — see BASEL
Bal·e·ar·es \,bal-ē-'ar-ēz\ **1** the Balearic islands **2** province E Spain comprising the Balearic islands ✱ Palma *area* 1936 *sq mi* (5034 *sq km*)
Bal·e·ar·ic \,bal-ē-'ar-ik\ islands E Spain in the W Mediterranean — see BALEARES, IBIZA, MAJORCA, MINORCA
Ba·li \'bäl-ē\ island Indonesia off E Java *area* 2147 *sq mi* (5582 *sq km*), *pop* 2,247,000 — **Ba·li·nese** \,bäl-i-'nēz, ,bal-, -'nēs\ *adj or n*
Ba·lı·ke·sir \,bäl-ē-ke-'si(ə)r\ city NW Turkey in Asia *pop* 124,122
Ba·lik·pa·pan \,bäl-ik-'päp-,än\ city & port Indonesia on SE Borneo on inlet of Makassar strait *pop* 280,675
Bal·kan \'ból-kən\ **1** mountain range *cen* Bulgaria extending from Yugoslavia border to Black sea; highest point Botev Peak 7746 *ft* (2324 *m*) **2** peninsula SE Europe bet. Adriatic & Ionian seas on W & Aegean & Black seas on E — **Balkan** *or* **Bal·kan·ic** \ból-'kan-ik\ *adj*
Bal·kans \'ból-kənz\ *or* **Balkan States** the countries occupying the Balkan peninsula: Yugoslavia, Romania, Bulgaria, Albania, Greece, & Turkey in Europe
Bal·kar·ia \ból-'kar-ē-ə, bal-, -'ker-\ mountain region U.S.S.R. in S Soviet Russia, Europe, in S Kabardin-Balkar Republic
Balkh \'bälk\ **1** district N Afghanistan corresponding closely to ancient Bactria **2** *or anc* **Bac·tra** \'bak-trə\ town N Afghanistan ✱ of ancient Bactria
Bal·khash \bal-'kash, bäl-'käsh\ lake 440 *mi* (704 *km*) long U.S.S.R. in Soviet Central Asia in SE Kazakhstan *area* 6700 *sq mi* (17,420 *sq km*)
Bal·la·rat \'bal-ə-,rat\ city SE Australia in *cen* Victoria *pop* 62,641
Bal·ly·me·na \,bal-ē-'mē-nə\ district NE Northern Ireland, established 1974 *area* 246 *sq mi* (640 *sq km*), *pop* 54,426
Bal·ly·mon·ey \,bal-ē-'mən-ē\ district N Northern Ireland, established 1974 *area* 162 *sq mi* (421 *sq km*), *pop* 22,873
Bal·sas \'ból-səs, 'bäl-\ river 426 *mi* (682 *km*) *cen* Mexico flowing from Tlaxcala to the Pacific on border bet. Michoacán & Guerrero
Bal·tic \'ból-tik\ sea arm of the Atlantic N Europe enclosed by Denmark & the Scandinavian peninsula *area ab* 160,000 *sq mi* (256,000 *sq km*)
Bal·ti·more \'ból-tə-,mō(ə)r, -,mó(ə)r, 'ból-(tə-)mər\ city & port N *cen* Md. on the Patapsco estuary near Chesapeake Bay *pop* 786,775 — **Bal·ti·mor·ean** \,ból-tə-'mōr-ē-ən, -'mór-\ *n*
Bal·ti·stan \,ból-tə-'stan\ region Ladakh district N Kashmir
Ba·lu·chi·stan \bə-,lü-chə-'stan\ **1** arid region S Asia bordering on Arabian sea in SW Pakistan & SE Iran S & SW of Afghanistan **2** province SW Pakistan ✱ Quetta *pop* 4,305,000
Ba·ma·ko \,bäm-ə-'kō\ city ✱ of Mali on Niger river *pop* 435,313
Bam·ba·ri \'bäm-bə-rē\ town S *cen* Central African Republic
Bam·berg \'bam-,bərg, 'bäm-,be(ə)rg\ city E W. Germany in N Bavaria NNW of Nuremberg *pop* 71,928
Ba·na·hao \bə-'nä-,haù\ extinct volcano 7141 *ft* (2142 *m*) Philippines on S Luzon SE of Manila
Ba·nana river \bə-,nan-ə-\ lagoon E Fla. between Canaveral peninsula & Merritt Is.
Ba·na·ras *or* **Be·na·res** \bə-'när-əs, -ēz\ *or* **Va·ra·na·si** \və-'rän-ə-(,)sē\ city N India in SE Uttar Pradesh *pop* 793,542
Ba·nat \bə-'nät, 'bän-,ät\ region SE *cen* Europe in Danube basin bet. the Tisza & the Mures & the Transylvanian Alps; once entirely in Hungary, divided 1919 bet. Yugoslavia & Romania
Ban·bridge \ban-'brij\ district SE Northern Ireland, established 1974 *area* 171 *sq mi* (445 *sq km*), *pop* 29,885
Ban·da \'ban-də, 'bän-\ **1** islands Indonesia in Moluccas S of Ceram *area* 16 *sq mi* (42 *sq km*) **2** sea E Malay archipelago SE of Celebes, S of the Moluccas, W of Aru islands, & NE of Timor
Ban·da Ori·en·tal \'bän-də-,ōr-ē-,en-'täl, -,ór-\ URUGUAY — a former name, used with reference to its position on E shore of Río de la Plata

Bandar — see MACHILIPATNAM
Ban·dar Kho·mei·ni \,bən-dər-,kō-mā-'nē\ town & port SW Iran at head of Persian Gulf ENE of Abadan
Bandar Se·ri Be·ga·wan \,bən-dər-,ser-ē-bə-'gä-wən\ *or formerly* **Brunei** town, ✻ of Brunei *pop* 49,902
Ban·de·lier National Monument \,ban-də-'li(ə)r\ reservation N *cen* N.Mex. W of Santa Fe containing cliff-dweller ruins
Ban·djar·ma·sin *or* **Ban·jer·ma·sin** \,ban-jər-'mäs-ᵊn, ,bän-\ city Indonesia in S Borneo *pop* 331,286
Ban·dung *or* D **Ban·doeng** \'bän-,dúŋ\ city Indonesia in W Java SE of Djakarta *pop* 1,462,637
Banff \'bam(p)f\ *or* **Banff·shire** \-,shi(ə)r, -,shər\ former county NE Scotland ✻ Banff
Banff National Park reservation W Canada in SW Alta. on E slope of Rocky mountains
Ban·ga·lore \'baŋ-gə-,lō(ə)r, -,ló(ə)r\ city S India W of Madras ✻ of Karnataka *pop* 2,913,537
Bang·ka *or* **Ban·ka** \'baŋ-kə\ island, Indonesia off SE Sumatra; chief town Pangkalpinang *area* 4609 *sq mi* (11,983 *sq km*), *pop* 251,639
Bang·kok \'baŋ-,käk, baŋ-'\ *or Thai* **Krung Thep** \'krüŋ-'tep\ city & port ✻ of Thailand on the Chao Phraya *ab* 20 *mi* (32 *km*) above its mouth *pop* 2,132,000
Ban·gla·desh \,bäŋ-glə-'desh, ,baŋ-, ,bəŋ-, -'däsh\ country S Asia E of India on Bay of Bengal; a republic in the Commonwealth since 1971 ✻ Dacca *area* 55,126 *sq mi* (143,328 *sq km*), *pop* 87,052,024 — see EAST PAKISTAN — **Ban·gla·deshi** \-ē\ *adj or n*
Ban·gor \'baŋ-,gó(ə)r & 'ban-,gó(ə)r (*these usual for* 1), 'baŋ-gər\ **1** city E *cen* Maine on the Penobscot *pop* 31,643 **2** municipal borough SE Northern Ireland in North Down district *pop* 46,585 **3** borough & city NW Wales in Gwynedd *pop* 12,174
Ban·gui \bäⁿ-gē\ city ✻ of Central African Republic, on the Ubangi *pop* 300,723
Bang·we·u·lu, Lake \-,baŋ-wē-'ü-(,)lü\ lake *ab* 50 *mi* (80 *km*) long N Zambia in swamp region; its area fluctuates seasonally; drains into the Luapula, a headstream of Congo river
Ban·jul \'bän-,jül\ *or formerly* **Bath·urst** \'bath-(,)ərst\ city & port ✻ of Gambia on estuary of St. Mary in Gambia river *pop* 39,476
Banks \'baŋ(k)s\ **1** island N Canada at W end of Canadian Arctic archipelago *area* 23,230 *sq mi* (60,398 *sq km*) **2** islands SW Pacific N of Vanuatu
Ban·nock·burn \'ban-ək-,bərn, ,ban-ək-'\ town *cen* Scotland in Central region SSE of Stirling
Ban·tam \'bant-əm\ village Indonesia in NW corner of Java; once ✻ of Sultanate of Bantam
Ban·try Bay \,ban-trē-\ bay SW Ireland in SW County Cork
Baoding — see PAOTING
Baoji — see PAO-CHI
Baotou — see PAO-T'OU
Ba·paume \ba-'pōm, ba-\ town N France S of Arras *pop* 3683
Ba·ra·cal·do \,bar-ə-'käl-(,)dō, ,bär-\ commune N Spain W of Bilbao *pop* 118,615
Ba·ra·coa \,bar-ə-'kō-ə, ,bär-\ city & port E Cuba on N coast near E tip of island *pop* 76,873
Ba·ra·na·gar \bə-'rän-ə-gər\ city E India in W. Bengal N of Calcutta *pop* 136,842
Ba·ra·nof \'bar-ə-,nóf, bə-'rän-əf\ island SE Alaska in Alexander archipelago S of Chichagof Is. *area ab* 1600 *sq mi* (4160 *sq km*)
Bar·a·tar·ia Bay \,bar-ə-'tar-ē-ə, -'ter-\ lagoon SE La. on coast NW of delta of Mississippi river
Bar·ba·dos \bär-'bād-əs, -(,)ōz, -(,)äs, -(,)ōs\ island Brit. W. Indies in Lesser Antilles E of the Windward group; a dominion of the Commonwealth since 1966 ✻ Bridgetown *area* 166 *sq mi* (432 *sq km*), *pop* 249,000 — **Bar·ba·di·an** \-'bād-ē-ən\ *adj or n*
Bar·ba·ry \'bär-b(ə-)rē\ region N Africa on **Barbary Coast** extending from Egyptian border to the Atlantic & including the former **Barbary States** (Morocco, Algiers, Tunis, & Tripoli) — a chiefly former name
Bar·bers Point \'bär-bərz-\ *or* **Ka·la·e·loa Point** \kə-,lä-(,)ā-,lō-ə-\ cape Hawaii at SW corner of Oahu W of Pearl Harbor
Bar·ber·ton \'bär-bərt-ᵊn\ city NE Ohio SW of Akron *pop* 29,751
Bar·bi·zon \'bär-bə-'zōⁿ\ village N France SSE of Paris
Bar·bu·da \bär-'büd-ə\ island Brit. W. Indies in the Leewards *area* 62 *sq mi* (161 *sq km*) — see ANTIGUA 1
Bar·ca *or* **Bar·ka** \'bär-kə\ town Libya in NW Cyrenaica
Bar·ce·lo·na \,bär-sə-'lō-nə\ **1** province NE Spain in Catalonia on the Mediterranean *area* 2968 *sq mi* (7717 *sq km*), *pop* 4,949,892 **2** city & port, its ✻ *pop* 1,752,627 **3** city NE Venezuela near coast *pop* 78,201 — **Bar·ce·lo·nan** \-'lō-nən\ *n* — **Bar·ce·lo·nese** \-lō-'nēz, -'nēs, -'lō-,\ *adj or n*
Bar·dia \'bärd-ē-ə\ town & port Libya in NE Cyrenaica
Ba·reil·ly *or* **Ba·re·li** \bə-'rā-lē\ **1** city N India in NW *cen* Uttar Pradesh ESE of Delhi *pop* 437,801 **2** — see ROHILKHAND
Ba·rents \'bär-ən(t)s, 'bär-\ sea comprising the part of the Arctic ocean between Spitsbergen & Novaya Zemlya
Ba·ri \'bär-ē\ *or anc* **Bar·i·um** \'bar-ē-əm, 'ber-\ commune & port SE Italy ✻ of Apulia on the Adriatic *pop* 370,781
Ba·ri·lo·che \,bar-ə-'lō-chē\ *or* **San Car·los de Bariloche** \san-'kär-ləs-də-\ city SW Argentina on Lake Nahuel Huapi *pop* 15,995
Bar·i·sal \'bar-ə-,sól\ city S Bangladesh in Ganges delta *pop* 98,127
Bar·king \'bär-kiŋ\ *or* **Barking Town** borough of E Greater London, England *pop* 150,900
Bar·let·ta \bär-'let-ə\ commune & port SE Italy in Apulia on the Adriatic *pop* 83,719
Bar·na·ul \,bär-nə-'ül\ city U.S.S.R. in Soviet Russia, Asia, on the Ob ✻ of Altai territory *pop* 533,000
Bar·ne·gat Bay \'bär-ni-,gat, -,gət\ inlet of the Atlantic E N.J.
Barnes \'bärnz\ former municipal borough SE England, now part of Richmond
Bar·net \'bär-nət\ borough of N Greater London, England *pop* 296,300
Barns·ley \'bärnz-lē\ borough N England in S. Yorkshire *pop* 73,646
Barn·sta·ble \'bärn-stə-bəl\ town SE Mass. *pop* 30,898
Ba·ro·da \bə-'rōd-ə\ **1** former state W India near head of Gulf of Cambay ✻ Baroda *area* 8176 *sq mi* (21,258 *sq km*) **2** city W India in SE Gujarat SE of Ahmadabad *pop* 744,043

Ba·rot·se·land \bə-'rät-sē-,land\ region W Zambia; formerly a protectorate
Bar·qui·si·me·to \,bär-kə-sə-'māt-(,)ō\ city NW Venezuela *pop* 504,000
Bar·ran·qui·lla \,bar-ən-'kē-(y)ə\ city & port N Colombia on the Magdalena *pop* 703,488
Barren Grounds treeless plains N Canada W of Hudson bay
Bar·rie \'bar-ē\ city Canada in SE Ont. *pop* 38,423
Bar·row, Point \-'bar-(,)ō\ most northerly point of Alaska & of the U.S., at *ab* 71°25′N, 156°30′W
Bar·row–in–Fur·ness \,bar-ə-wən-'fər-nəs\ borough NW England in S Cumbria *pop* 73,900
Bar·stow \'bär-,stō\ city S Calif. NNE of San Bernardino *pop* 17,690
Bar·tles·ville \'bärt-ᵊlz-,vil\ city NE Okla. *pop* 34,568
Bart·lett \'bärt-lət\ city SW Tenn. *pop* 17,170
Ba·rú \bär-'ü\ *or formerly* **Chi·ri·qui** \chir-i-'kē\ volcano 11,400 *ft* (3475 *m*) Panama near Costa Rican border
Ba·sel \'bäz-əl\ *or* F **Bâle** *or older* **Basle** \'bäl\ **1** former canton NW Switzerland, now divided into two half cantons: **Ba·sel–Land** \'bäz-əl-,länt\ (✻ Liestal *area* 165 *sq mi* or 429 *sq km*, *pop* 219,822) & **Ba·sel–Stadt** \-,shtät\ (✻ Basel *area* 14 *sq mi* or 36 *sq km*, *pop* 203,915) **2** city NW Switzerland ✻ of Basel-Stadt *pop* 182,143
Ba·shan \'bā-shən\ region in ancient Palestine E & NE of Sea of Galilee
Ba·shi channel \'bäsh-ē\ strait between Philippines & Taiwan
Bash·kir·ia \bash-'kir-ē-ə\ *or* **Bash·kir Republic** \,bash-,ki(ə)r-\ autonomous republic U.S.S.R. in E Soviet Russia, Europe, in S Ural mountains ✻ Ufa *area* 54,233 *sq mi* (141,006 *sq km*), *pop* 3,819,000
Ba·si·lan \bä-'sē-,län\ **1** island Philippines SW of Mindanao *area* 495 *sq mi* (1287 *sq km*) **2** city comprising Basilan Is. and several small nearby islands
Bas·il·don \'baz-əl-dən\ town SE England in Essex *pop* 152,301
Ba·si·li·ca·ta \bə-,zil-ə-'kät-ə, -,sil-\ *or formerly* **Lu·ca·nia** \lü-'kän-yə, 'kän-\ region S Italy on Gulf of Taranto ✻ Potenza
Basin ranges — see GREAT BASIN
Basque Provinces \'bask\ autonomous region N Spain on Bay of Biscay including provinces of Alava, Guipúzcoa, & Vizcaya
Bas·ra \'bäs-rə, 'bəs-, 'bas-, 'bäz-, 'bəz-, 'baz-\ *or* **Bus·ra** \'bäs-rə, 'bəs-\ city & port S Iraq on Shatt-al-Arab *pop* 310,950
Bass \'bas\ strait separating Tasmania & continent of Australia
Bas·sein \bə-'sān\ city S Myanmar W of Yangon *pop* 126,045
Basse·terre \bäs-'te(ə)r, bäs-\ city & town & port Brit. W. Indies ✻ of St. Kitts Is. & of St. Kitts-Nevis state *pop* 14,725
Basse–Terre \bäs-'te(ə)r, bäs-\ **1** island French W. Indies constituting the W part of Guadeloupe *area* 364 *sq mi* (946 *sq km*) **2** town & port ✻ of Guadeloupe *pop* 13,796
Bas·tia \'bas-tē-ə, 'bäs-\ city & port France on NE coast of Corsica *pop* 45,387
Bas·togne \ba-'stōn\ town SE Belgium in the Ardennes
Basutoland — see LESOTHO
Ba·ta \'bät-ə\ city ✻ of Mbini, Equatorial Guinea *pop* 30,474
Ba·taan \bə-'tan, -'tän\ peninsula Philippines in W Luzon on W side of Manila Bay
Ba·ta·via \bə-'tā-vē-ə\ **1** city NW N.Y. *pop* 16,703 **2** — see DJAKARTA — **Ba·ta·vi·an** \-vē-ən\ *adj or n*
Batavian Republic the Netherlands under the French (1795-1806)
Bath \'bath, 'bäth\ city SW England in Avon *pop* 79,965
Bath·urst \'bath-(,)ərst\ **1** — see BANJUL **2** island N Canada in Parry group *area* 6041 *sq mi* (15,707 *sq km*)
Bat·on Rouge \,bat-ᵊn-'rüzh\ city ✻ of La. on Mississippi river *pop* 219,419
Bat·ter·sea \'bat-ər-sē\ former metropolitan borough SW London, England, on S bank of the Thames, now part of Wandsworth
Bat·tle Creek \'bat-ᵊl-,krēk\ city S Mich. *pop* 35,724
Ba·tu·mi \bə-'tü-mē\ *or* **Ba·tum** \-'tüm\ city & port U.S.S.R. in SW Georgia on Black sea ✻ of Adzhar Republic *pop* 82,000
Baut·zen \'baut-sən\ city SE E. Germany on the Spree ENE of Dresden *pop* 48,866
Ba·var·ia \bə-'ver-ē-ə, -'var-\ *or* G **Bay·ern** \'bī-ərn\ state SE W. Germany bordering on Austria & Czechoslovakia ✻ Munich *area* 27,232 *sq mi* (70,803 *sq km*), *pop* 10,928,151
Ba·ya·món \,bä-yä-'mōn\ city NE *cen* Puerto Rico *pop* 185,087
Bay City **1** city E Mich. near head of Saginaw Bay *pop* 41,593 **2** city SE Tex. *pop* 17,837
Ba·yeux \bī-'(y)ü, bä-; bä-'yə(r); bá-yœ\ town NW France WNW of Caen
Baykal, Lake — see BAIKAL, LAKE
Ba·yonne \bā-'ōn, bä-'yón\ city SW France on the Adour near Bay of Biscay *pop* 41,281
Bay·reuth \bī-'ròit, 'bī-,\ city E W. Germany in Bavaria NE of Nuremberg *pop* 70,633
Bay·town \'bā-,taún\ city SE Tex. on Galveston Bay *pop* 56,923
Bay Village city NE Ohio W of Cleveland *pop* 17,846
Beachy Head \,bē-chē-\ headland SE England on coast of E. Sussex
Bea·cons·field \'bē-kənz-,fēld\ city Canada in S Que. on Montreal Is. SSW of Montreal *pop* 19,613
Bear \'ba(ə)r, 'be(ə)r\ **1** river 75 *mi* (121 *km*) N Calif. flowing SW to Feather river **2** river 350 *mi* (563 *km*) N Utah, SW Wyo., & SE Idaho flowing to Great Salt Lake
Beard·more \'bi(ə)rd-,mō(ə)r, -,mó(ə)r\ glacier Antarctica descending to Ross Ice Shelf at *ab* 170°E
Bear Mountain mountain 1314 *ft* (401 *m*) SE N.Y. on the Hudson
Bé·arn \bā-'ärn\ region & former province SW France in Pyrenees SW of Gascony ✻ Pau
Be·as *or* **Bi·as** \'bē-,äs\ river 300 *mi* (483 *km*) N India in the Punjab
Beau·fort \'bō-fərt\ sea comprising the part of the Arctic ocean NE of Alaska & NW of Canada
Beau·mar·is \bō-'mar-əs\ borough NW Wales in Gwynedd on E Anglesey Is. on Beaumaris Bay *pop* 2088
Beau·mont \'bō-,mänt, bō-'\ city & port SE Tex. on the Neches *pop* 118,102
Beaune \'bōn\ commune E France SSW of Dijon *pop* 16,386
Beau·port \'bō-pórt, -pó(r)t\ city Canada in S Que. *pop* 60,447
Beau·so·leil \,bō-sə-'lā\ commune SE France N of Monaco
Beau·vais \bō-'vā\ commune N France NNW of Paris *pop* 53,493

Bea·ver \ˈbē-vər\ **1** river 280 *mi* (451 *km*) NW Okla. forming upper course of the N. Canadian **2** river 305 *mi* (491 *km*) Canada in Alta. & Sask. flowing E into the Churchill
Bea·ver·head \ˈbē-vər-ˌhed\ mountains on Idaho-Mont. boundary; SE part of Bitterroot range of the Rockies — see GARFIELD
Bea·ver·ton \ˈbē-vərt-^{ə}n\ city NW Oreg. W of Portland *pop* 30,582
Bé·char \bā-ˈshär\ *or formerly* **Co·lomb-Bé·char** \kə-ˌlō^{n}(m)-\ commune NW Algeria SSE of Oran *pop* 72,800
Bech·u·a·na·land \ˌbech-(ə-)ˈwän-ə-ˌland\ **1** region S Africa N of Orange river & W of Transvaal & including Kalahari desert & Okovanggo Basin **2** — see BOTSWANA **3** *or* **British Bechuanaland** former Brit. colony in the region S of the Molopo; became part of Union of S. Africa 1895 — **Bech·u·a·na** \ˌbech-(ə-)ˈwän-ə\ *adj or n*
Beck·en·ham \ˈbek-(ə-)nəm\ former urban district SE England in Kent, now part of Bromley
Beck·ley \ˈbek-lē\ city S W.Va. *pop* 20,492
Bed·ford \ˈbed-fərd\ **1** city N Tex. *pop* 20,821 **2** borough SE *cen* England ✻ of Bedfordshire *pop* 74,245
Bed·ford·shire \ˈbed-fərd-ˌshi(ə)r, -shər\ *or* **Bed·ford** \ˈbed-fərd\ county SE *cen* England *area* 477 *sq mi* (1240 *sq km*), *pop* 509,200
Bed·loe's \ˈbed-ˌlōz\ — see LIBERTY
Będ·zin \ˈben-ˌjēn\ commune S Poland in Silesia *pop* 76,868
Beer·she·ba \bi(ə)r-ˈshē-bə, be(ə)r-, bər-\ city S Israel in N Negeb, in Bible times marking extreme S limit of Palestine *pop* 101,000
Behistun — see BISITUN
Bei·da \ˈbād-ə\ town NE Libya in Cyrenaica NE of Benghazi
Beijing — see PEKING
Bei·ra \ˈbā-rə\ town & port SE Mozambique; chief port for *cen* Mozambique & landlocked Zimbabwe & Malawi *pop* 130,398
Bei·rut \bā-ˈrüt\ *or anc* **Be·ry·tus** \bə-ˈrīt-əs\ city & port ✻ of Lebanon
Be·jaïa \bā-ˈzhī-ə\ *or formerly* **Bou·gie** \bü-ˈzhē\ city & port NE Algeria *pop* 89,500
Be·kaa \bi-ˈkä\ *or* **Al Bi·qa** \ˌal-bi-ˈkä\ *or anc* **Coe·le–Syr·ia** \ˌsē-lē-ˈsir-ē-ə\ valley Lebanon bet. Lebanon & anti-Lebanon mountain ranges
Bé·kés·csa·ba \ˈbā-ˌkāsh-ˌchò-ˌbò\ city SE Hungary *pop* 67,266
Be·lau \bə-ˈlau̇\ *or formerly* **Pa·lau** \pə-ˈlau̇\ *or* **Pe·lew** \pə-ˈlü\ district SW Trust Territory of the Pacific Islands; usu. considered part of the Carolines
Be·la·wan \bə-ˈlä-ˌwän\ town & port Indonesia in NE Sumatra
Be·la·ya \ˈbel-ə-yə\ river 700 *mi* (1126 *km*) U.S.S.R. in Soviet Russia, Europe, rising in the S Urals & flowing S, W, & NW to the Kama
Be·lém \bə-ˈlem\ *or* **Pa·rá** \pə-ˈrä\ city N Brazil ✻ of Pará state on Pará river *pop* 934,322
Bel·fast \ˈbel-ˌfast, bel-ˈ\ **1** district E Northern Ireland, established 1974 *area* 54 *sq mi* (140 *sq km*), *pop* 295,223 **2** city & port ✻ of Northern Ireland at head of **Belfast Lough** (inlet) *pop* 295,223
Bel·fort \bel-ˈfò(ə)r, bā-ˈfò(ə)r\ commune E France commanding **Belfort Gap** (wide pass bet. Vosges & Jura mountains) *pop* 54,469
Belgian Congo *or earlier* **Congo Free State** former Belgian colony W *cen* Africa — see ZAIRE
Belgian East Africa — see RUANDA-URUNDI
Bel·gium \ˈbel-jəm\ *or F* **Bel·gique** \bel-zhēk\ *or Flem* **Bel·gië** \ˈbel-gē-ə\ country W Europe bordering on North sea; a constitutional monarchy ✻ Brussels *area* 11,774 *sq mi* (30,612 *sq km*), *pop* 9,848,647
Bel·go·rod–Dnes·trov·skiy \ˈbel-gə-ˌräd-(ˌ)ne-ˈstròf-skē, -ˈstròv-, ˈbyel-gə-rət-\ *or formerly Turk & Russ* **Ak·ker·man** \ˌäk-ər-ˈmän\ city U.S.S.R. in SW Ukrainian Republic on the Dniester estuary *pop* 29,000
Bel·grade \ˈbel-ˌgrād, -ˌgräd, -ˌgrad, bel-ˈ\ *or* **Beo·grad** \ˈbeu̇-ˌgräd\ city ✻ of Yugoslavia & of Serbia *pop* 727,945
Bel·gra·via \bel-ˈgrā-vē-ə\ district of W *cen* London, England, in Kensington and Chelsea borough S of Hyde Park
Be·li·tung \bə-ˈlēt-əŋ\ *or* **Bil·li·ton** \-ˈlē-ˌtän\ island Indonesia bet. Sumatra & Borneo *area* 1866 *sq mi* (4852 *sq km*), *pop* 102,375
Be·lize \bə-ˈlēz\ *or formerly* **British Honduras** country Central America bordering on the Caribbean; an independent member of the Commonwealth ✻ Belmopan *area* 8866 *sq mi* (23,052 *sq km*), *pop* 144,857 — **Be·liz·ean** \-ˈlē-zē-ən\ *adj or n*
Bell \ˈbel\ city SW Calif. SE of Los Angeles *pop* 25,450
Bel·la Coo·la \ˌbel-ə-ˈkü-lə\ river *ab* 60 *mi* (96 *km*) Canada in B.C. flowing W to Burke channel E of Queen Charlotte Sound
Bel·leau \be-ˈlō, ˈbe-ˌ\ village N France NW of Château-Thierry & N of **Bel·leau Wood** (*F* **Bois de Bel·leau** \ˌbwäd-ə-be-ˈlō\)
Belle Fourche \(ˈ)bel-ˈfüsh\ river *ab* 290 *mi* (467 *km*) NE Wyo. & W S.Dak. flowing NE & E into Cheyenne river
Belle Glade \ˈbel-ˌglād, bel-ˈ\ city SE Fla. *pop* 16,535
Belle Isle, Strait of \be-ˈlī(ə)l\ channel between N tip of Newfoundland (island) & SE Labrador
Belle·ville \ˈbel-ˌvil\ **1** city SW Ill. *pop* 41,580 **2** town NE N.J. N of Newark *pop* 35,367 **3** city Canada in SE Ont. *pop* 34,881
Belle·vue \ˈbel-ˌvyü\ **1** city E Nebr. S of Omaha *pop* 21,813 **2** city W Wash. E of Seattle *pop* 73,903
Bell·flow·er \ˈbel-ˌflau̇(-ə)r\ city SW Calif. E of Los Angeles *pop* 53,441
Bell Gardens city SW Calif. E of Los Angeles *pop* 34,117
Bel·ling·ham \ˈbel-iŋ-ˌham\ city & port NW Wash. on **Bellingham Bay** (inlet at N end of Puget Sound) *pop* 45,794
Bel·lings·hau·sen \ˈbel-iŋz-ˌhau̇z-^{ə}n\ sea comprising a large bay of the S Pacific W of base of Antarctic peninsula
Bel·lin·zo·na \ˌbel-ən-ˈzō-nə\ commune S Switzerland E of Locarno ✻ of Ticino *pop* 16,743
Bell·wood \ˈbel-ˌwu̇d\ village NE Ill. W of Chicago *pop* 19,811
Bel·mont \ˈbel-ˌmänt\ **1** city W Calif. SE of San Francisco *pop* 24,505 **2** town E Mass. W of Boston *pop* 26,100
Bel·mo·pan \ˌbel-mō-ˈpan\ city ✻ of Belize *pop* 2932
Bel·oeil \bel-ˈī(ə)l\ town Canada in S Que. *pop* 17,540
Be·lo Ho·ri·zon·te \ˈbā-lō-ˌhòr-ə-ˈzänt-ē, ˈbel-ō-, -ˌhär-\ city E Brazil ✻ of Minas Gerais *pop* 1,781,924
Be·loit \bə-ˈlòit\ city S Wis. on Ill. border *pop* 35,207
Be·lo·rus·sia \ˌbel-ō-ˈrəsh-ə\ *or* **Bye·lo·rus·sia** \bē-ˌel-ō-\ *or* **White Russian Republic** *or* **Be·lo·rus·sian Republic** \-ˌrəsh-ən-\ constituent republic of the U.S.S.R. bordering on Poland, Lithuania, & Latvia ✻ Minsk *area* 88,044 *sq mi* (228,914 *sq km*), *pop* 9,560,000
Beloye More — see WHITE
Bel·sen \ˈbel-zən\ *or* **Ber·gen–Belsen** \ˌber-gən-, ˌbər-\ locality NE W. Germany on Lüneburg Heath NW of Celle
Be·lu·kha \bə-ˈlü-kə\ mountain 15,157 *ft* (4620 *m*) U.S.S.R. in S Soviet Russia, Asia; highest in Altai mountain region
Benares — see BANARAS
Bend \ˈbend\ city *cen* Oreg. on the Deschutes *pop* 17,263
Ben·di·go \ˈben-di-ˌgō\ city SE Australia in N Victoria NNW of Melbourne *pop* 31,841
Be·ne·lux \ˈben-^{ə}l-ˌəks\ economic union comprising Belgium, the Netherlands, & Luxembourg; formed 1947
Be·ne·ven·to \ˌben-ə-ˈven-(ˌ)tō\ commune S Italy in Campania NE of Naples *pop* 61,443
Ben·gal \ben-ˈgòl, beŋ-\ region E India (subcontinent) including delta of the Ganges & the Brahmaputra; formerly a presidency & (1937–47) a province of Brit. India; divided 1947 between Pakistan & India (republic) — see EAST BENGAL, EAST PAKISTAN, WEST BENGAL — **Ben·gal·ese** \ˌbeŋ-gə-ˈlēz, ˌben-, -ˈlēs\ *adj or n*
Bengal, Bay of arm of the Indian ocean between India & Sri Lanka on the W & Myanmar & Malay peninsula on the E
Ben·gha·zi \ben-ˈgäz-ē, beŋ-ˈgaz-\ *or anc* **Ber·e·ni·ce** \ˌber-ə-ˈnī-sē\ city & port NE Libya, a former ✻ of Libya *pop* 267,700
Ben·guela \ben-ˈg(w)el-ə\ city & port W Angola *pop* 40,996
Be·ni \ˈbā-nē\ river 1000 *mi* (1609 *km*) *cen* & N Bolivia flowing N to unite with Mamoré river forming Madeira river
Be·nin \bə-ˈnin, -ˈnēn; ˈben-ən\ **1** river *ab* 100 *mi* (161 *km*) S Nigeria W of the Niger flowing into Bight of Benin **2** former kingdom W Africa on lower Niger river; incorporated in Nigeria after 1897 **3** *or formerly* **Da·ho·mey** \də-ˈhō-mē\ country W Africa on Gulf of Guinea; a republic, formerly a territory of French W. Africa ✻ Porto-Novo *area* 44,749 *sq mi* (116,347 *sq km*), *pop* 3,338,240 **4** *or* **Benin City** city SW Nigeria in W delta of Niger river *pop* 161,700 — **Be·ni·nese** \bə-ˌnin-ˈēz, -ˌnēn-; ˌben-i-ˈnēz, -ˈnēs\ *adj or n*
Benin, Bight of the N section of Gulf of Guinea W Africa SW of Nigeria
Be·ni Su·ef \ˌben-ē-sü-ˈāf\ city N *cen* Egypt *pop* 117,910
Ben Lomond — see LOMOND (Ben)
Ben Nev·is \ben-ˈnev-əs\ mountain 4406 *ft* (1343 *m*) W Scotland in Grampian mountains; highest in Great Britain
Be·no·ni \bə-ˈnō-nē\ city NE Republic of S. Africa in S Transvaal on the Witwatersrand E of Johannesburg *pop* 151,294
Ben·ton \ˈbent-^{ə}n\ city *cen* Ark. SW of Little Rock *pop* 17,717
Be·nue \ˈbān-(ˌ)wā\ river 870 *mi* (1400 *km*) W Africa flowing W into Niger river
Benxi — see PEN-CH'I
Bep·pu \ˈbep-(ˌ)ü\ city Japan in NE Kyushu on **Beppu Bay** (arm of Inland sea) *pop* 136,449
Be·rar \bā-ˈrär, bə-\ region W *cen* India; in Central Provinces & Berar 1903–47, in Madhya Pradesh 1947–56, in Bombay 1956–60, in Maharashtra since 1960; chief city Amravati
Ber·be·ra \ˈbər-b(ə-)rə\ town & port N Somalia *pop* 12,219
Be·rea \bə-ˈrē-ə\ **1** city NE Ohio SW of Cleveland *pop* 19,567 **2** — see VÉROIA
Be·re·zi·na \bə-ˈrāz-^{ə}n-ə, -ˈrez-\ river 350 *mi* (563 *km*) U.S.S.R. in Belorussia flowing SE into the Dnieper
Bergama — see PERGAMUM
Ber·ga·mo \ˈbe(ə)r-gə-ˌmō, ˈbər-\ commune N Italy in Lombardy NE of Milan *pop* 121,846
Ber·gen **1** \ˈbər-gən, ˈbe(ə)r-\ city & port SW Norway *pop* 207,753 **2** — see MONS
Ber·gen·field \ˈbər-gən-ˌfēld\ borough NE N.J. *pop* 25,568
Be·ring \ˈbi(ə)r-iŋ, ˈbe(ə)r-\ **1** sea arm of the N Pacific bet. Alaska & NE Siberia & bet. the Aleutians & Bering strait *area* 878,000 *sq mi* (2,282,800 *sq km*) **2** strait *ab* 56 *mi* (90 *km*) wide separating Asia (U.S.S.R.) from N. America (Alaska)
Berke·ley \ˈbər-klē\ city W Calif. on San Francisco Bay N of Oakland *pop* 103,328
Berk·ley \ˈbər-klē\ city SE Mich. NW of Detroit *pop* 18,637
Berk·shire \ˈbərk-ˌshi(ə)r, -shər\ **1** hills W Mass. W of Connecticut river — see GREYLOCK (Mount) **2** *Brit usu* ˈbärk-\ county S England in Thames river basin ✻ Reading *area* 485 *sq mi* (1261 *sq km*), *pop* 688,100
Ber·lin \(ˌ)bər-ˈlin, *G* ber-ˈlēn\ city E *cen* E. Germany on Spree river, before 1945 ✻ of Germany & of Prussia, divided under postwar occupation bet. E. & W. Germany, E. Berlin being made ✻ of E. Germany (1949) & W. Berlin a state (not formally incorporated) of W. Germany — **Ber·lin·er** \(ˌ)bər-ˈlin-ər\ *n*
Ber·me·jo \bər-ˈmā-(ˌ)hō, ber-\ river 1000 *mi* (1609 *km*) N Argentina rising on Bolivian frontier & flowing SE into Paraguay river
Ber·mond·sey \ˈbər-mən(d)-zē\ former metropolitan borough E *cen* London, England, now part of Southwark
Ber·mu·da \(ˌ)bər-ˈmyüd-ə\ islands W Atlantic ESE of Cape Hatteras; a self-governing Brit. colony ✻ Hamilton *area* 21 *sq mi* (55 *sq km*), *pop* 67,761 — **Ber·mu·di·an** \-ˈmyüd-ē-ən\ *or* **Ber·mu·dan** \-ˈmyüd-^{ə}n\ *adj or n*
Bern \ˈbərn, ˈbe(ə)rn\ **1** canton NW & W *cen* Switzerland *area* 2658 *sq mi* (6911 *sq km*), *pop* 912,022 **2** city, its ✻ & ✻ of Switzerland on the Aare *pop* 145,254 — **Bern·ese** \(ˌ)bər-ˈnēz, -ˈnēs\ *adj or n*
Bern·burg \ˈbərn-ˌbərg, ˈbe(ə)rn-ˌbu̇(ə)rg\ city W *cen* E. Germany W of Dessau *pop* 44,428
Ber·ner Al·pen \ˌber-nər-ˈäl-pən\ *or* **Ber·nese Ober·land** \(ˌ)bər-ˌnē-ˈzō-bər-ˌlänt, -ˈsō-\ *or* **Bernese Alps** \(ˌ)bər-ˌnē-ˈzalps, -ˈsalps\ *or* **Ober·land** \ˈō-bər-ˌlänt\ section of the Alps S Switzerland in Bern & Valais cantons bet. Thuner See & Brienz on the N & the valley of the upper Rhône on the S
Ber·ni·cia \(ˌ)bər-ˈnish-(ē-)ə\ Anglian kingdom of 6th century A.D. located bet. Tyne & Forth rivers ✻ Bamborough
Ber·ni·na \(ˌ)bər-ˈnē-nə\ the S extension of Rhaetian Alps on border bet. Italy & Switzerland; highest peak **Piz Bernina** \ˌpēts-\ (highest in the Rhaetian Alps) 13,200 *ft* (4023 *m*)
Beroea **1** — see ALEPPO **2** — see VÉROIA

Ber·ry or **Ber·ri** \be-'rē\ former province cen France ✳ Bourges
Ber·thoud \'bər-thəd\ mountain pass 11,315 ft (3449 m) N Colo. in Front range WNW of Denver
Ber·wick \'ber-ik\ or **Ber·wick·shire** \-,shi(ə)r, -shər\ former county SE Scotland ✳ Duns
Ber·wyn \'bər-wən\ city NE Ill. W of Chicago pop 46,849
Berytus — see BEIRUT
Be·san·çon \bə-'zan(t)-sən, bə-zän-sōⁿ\ city E France E of Dijon pop 119,803
Bes·kids \'bes-,kidz, be-'skēdz\ mountain ranges cen Europe in W Carpathians; include **West Beskids** (in Poland & Czechoslovakia W of Tatry mountains) & **East Beskids** (in NE Czechoslovakia)
Bes·sa·ra·bia \,bes-ə-'rā-bē-ə\ region SE Europe bet. the Dniester & Prut rivers; now mostly in Moldavia, U.S.S.R. — **Bes·sa·ra·bi·an** \-bē-ən\ adj or n
Bes·se·mer \'bes-ə-mər\ city N cen Ala. pop 31,729
Beth·a·ny \'beth-ə-nē\ **1** city cen Okla. pop 22,130 **2** village Palestine E of Jerusalem on Mount of Olives pop 3560
Be·thel \'beth-əl, be-'thel\ ruined town Palestine in W Jordan N of Jerusalem
Beth·el Park \,beth-əl-\ borough SW Pa. pop 34,755
Beth·le·hem \'beth-li-,hem, -lē-(h)əm\ **1** city E Pa. on the Lehigh pop 70,419 **2** city Palestine in Judea SW of Jerusalem pop 16,313
Beth·nal Green \,beth-nəl-\ former metropolitan borough E London, England, now part of Tower Hamlets
Beth·sa·i·da \beth-'sā-əd-ə\ ruined town Palestine on NE side of Sea of Galilee E of the Jordan; its site in SE Syria
Be·tio \'bā-chē-,ō, -shē-; 'bät-sē-\ islet & village W Pacific in N Kiribati at S end of Tarawa
Bet·ten·dorf \'bet-ᵊn-,dȯrf\ city E Iowa E of Davenport pop 27,381
Beuthen — see BYTOM
Bev·er·ley \'bev-ər-lē\ town N England in Humberside pop 16,433
Bev·er·ly \'bev-ər-lē\ city NE Mass. pop 37,655
Beverly Hills city SW Calif. within city of Los Angeles pop 32,367
Bex·ley \'bek-slē\ borough of E Greater London, England pop 216,900
Bey·o·glu \,bā-ə-'(g)lü\ or formerly **Pera** \'per-ə\ section of Istanbul, Turkey, comprising N of the Golden Horn
Bé·ziers \bāz-'yā\ city S France SW of Montpellier pop 79,213
Bezwada — see VIJAYAWADA
Bha·gal·pur \'bäg-əl-,pu(ə)r\ city E India in E Bihar pop 221,276
Bhak·ra Dam \,bäk-rə-\ hydroelectric & irrigation dam 680 ft (207 m) high N India in Punjab NW of Bilaspur in gorge of the Sutlej
Bha·mo \bə-'mó, -'mō\ city N Burma on the upper Irrawaddy pop 13,767
Bhat·pa·ra \bät-'pär-ə\ city E India in W. Bengal pop 204,750
Bhav·na·gar or **Bhau·na·gar** \baú-'nəg-ər\ city & port W India in S Gujarat on Gulf of Cambay pop 308,194
Bho·pal \bō-'päl\ **1** former state N cen India in & N of Vindhya mountains ✳ Bhopal; now part of Madhya Pradesh **2** city N cen India NW of Nagpur of Madhya Pradesh pop 672,329
Bhu·ba·nes·war or **Bhu·va·nesh·war** \,búv-ə-'näsh-wər\ city E India S of Cuttack ✳ of Orissa pop 219,419
Bhu·tan \bü-'tan, -'tän\ country Asia in Himalayas on NE border of India; a protectorate of India ✳ Thimbu area 18,000 sq mi (46,800 sq km), pop 1,333,000 — **Bhu·ta·nese** \,büt-ᵊn-'ēz, -'ēs\ adj or n
Bi·a·fra, Bight of \bē-'af-rə, bī-, -'äf-\ or **Bight of Bon·ny** \-'bän-ē\ the E section of Gulf of Guinea, W Africa
Bi·ak \bē-'(y)äk\ island off W New Guinea; largest of the Schoutens
Bia·ly·stok \bē-'äl-i-,stók\ city NE Poland pop 229,651
Biar·ritz \,bē-ə-'rits, 'bē-ə-,\ commune SW France on Bay of Biscay pop 27,453
Bias — see BEAS
Bid·de·ford \'bid-ə-fərd\ city SW Maine SW of Portland pop 19,638
Biel \'bē(ə)l\ or F **Bienne** \bē-'en\ commune NW Switzerland in Bern canton NE of **Lake of Biel** (10 mi or 17 km long) pop 53,793
Bie·le·feld \'bē-lə-,felt\ city cen W. Germany E of Münster pop 312,708
Big Bend 1 area W Tex. in large bend of the Rio Grande; partly included in **Big Bend National Park 2** section of Columbia river E cen Wash.
Big Black river 330 mi (531 km) W cen Miss. flowing to Mississippi river
Big Diomede — see DIOMEDE
Big·horn \'big-,hȯ(ə)rn\ **1** river 336 mi (541 km) N Wyo. & SE Mont. flowing N into Yellowstone river — see WIND **2** mountains N Wyo. extending S from Mont. border E of Bighorn river — see CLOUD PEAK
Big Sandy river 22 mi (35 km) bet. W.Va. & Ky. flowing N into Ohio river
Big Sioux \'sü\ river 300 mi (483 km) S.Dak. & Iowa flowing S to Missouri river & forming Iowa-S.Dak. boundary
Big Spring city W Tex. SW of Odessa pop 24,804
Big Stone lake ab 30 mi (48 km) long bet. W Minn. & NE S.Dak. — see MINNESOTA (river)
Big Sur \'sər\ region W Calif. centering on Big Sur river & extending ab 80 mi (129 km) along coast SE of Point Sur
Big Thicket wilderness area E Tex. NE of Houston area ab 450 sq mi (1170 sq mi)
Bi·har \bi-'här\ **1** state NE India bordering on Nepal; winter ✳ Patna, summer ✳ Ranchi area 67,164 sq mi (174,626 sq km), pop 59,823,154 **2** city cen Bihar state SE of Patna pop 151,308
Bijanagar — see VIJAYANAGAR
Bi·ka·ner \,bik-ə-'ne(ə)r, ,bē-kə-, -'ni(ə)r\ city NW India in N Rajasthan in Thar desert pop 280,366
Bi·ki·ni \bə-'kē-nē\ island (atoll) W Pacific in Marshall islands — **Bi·ki·ni·an** \-ən\ adj or n
Bi·las·pur \bə-'läs,pú(ə)r\ city E cen India in SE Madhya Pradesh SE of Jabalpur pop 186,885
Bil·bao \bil-'bä-,ō, -'baú, -'bä-(,)ō\ city N Spain ✳ of Vizcaya pop 433,115
Bil·ler·i·ca \(')bil-'rik-ə, ,bel-ə-'rik-ə\ town NE Mass. pop 36,727
Bil·lings \'bil-iŋz\ city S cen Mont. pop 66,798
Billiton — see BELITUNG
Bi·lox·i \bə-'lək-sē, -'läk-\ city & port SE Miss. pop 49,311
Bim·i·ni \'bim-ə-nē\ two islands of the Bahamas NW of Andros
Bing·en \'biŋ-ən\ city W W. Germany pop 23,528

Bing·ham·ton \'biŋ-əm-tən\ city S cen N.Y. pop 55,860
Binh Dinh — see AN NHON
Bío–Bío \,bē-ō-'bē-(,)ō\ river 238 mi (383 km) S cen Chile flowing into the Pacific at Concepción
Bi·o·ko \bē-'ō-(,)kō\ or formerly **Fer·nan·do Po** \fər-,nan-(,)dō-'pō\ or 1973-79 **Ma·ci·as Ngue·ma Bi·yo·go** \'mä-thē-ə-sən-'(g)wä-mə-bi-'yō-(,)gō\ island Equatorial Guinea in Bight of Biafra area 778 sq mi (2023 sq km)
Bir·ken·head \'bər-kən-,hed, ,bər-kən-'\ borough NW England in Merseyside on the Mersey estuary opposite Liverpool pop 123,907
Bir·ming·ham \'bər-miŋ-,ham, Brit usu -miŋ-əm\ **1** city N cen Ala. pop 284,413 **2** city SE Mich. N of Detroit pop 21,689 **3** city & borough W cen England in West Midlands pop 920,389
Bi·ro·bi·dzhan \,bir-ō-bi-'jän, -'jan\ city U.S.S.R. ✳ of Jewish Autonomous Oblast pop 69,000
Bisayas — see VISAYAN
Biscay or **Biscaya** — see VIZCAYA — **Bis·cay·an** \bis-'kī-ən, -'kā-\ adj or n
Bis·cay, Bay of \'bis-,kā, -kē\ inlet of the Atlantic between W coast of France & N coast of Spain
Bis·cayne Bay \bis-'kān, 'bis-,\ inlet of the Atlantic SE Fla.; S part forms Biscayne National Park
Bi·sho \'bē-(,)shō\ town ✳ of Ciskei
Bi·si·tun \,bē-sə-'tün\ or **Be·his·tun** \,bā-his-\ or **Bi·so·tun** \bē-sə-\ ruined town W Iran E of Kermanshah
Bisk \'bisk, 'bēsk\ or **Biysk** or **Biisk** \'bē(-ə)sk\ city U.S.S.R. in Soviet Russia, Asia, in E Altai territory pop 212,000
Bis·kra \'bis-krə, -(,)krä\ city NE Algeria at an oasis on S edge of Atlas mountains pop 90,500
Bis·marck \'biz-,märk\ **1** sea comprising the part of the W Pacific enclosed by the islands of the Bismarck archipelago **2** archipelago W Pacific N of E end of New Guinea area 22,290 sq mi (57,954 sq km) **3** mountain range North-East New Guinea NW of Owen Stanley range; highest point Mt. Wilhelm 14,107 ft (4300 m) **4** city ✳ of N.Dak. on Missouri river pop 44,485
Bis·sau \bis-'aú\ city & port ✳ of Guinea-Bissau pop 105,273
Bi·thyn·ia \bə-'thin-ē-ə\ ancient country NW Asia Minor bordering on the Sea of Marmara & Black sea — **Bi·thyn·i·an** \-ē-ən\ adj or n
Bi·to·la \'bēt-ᵊl-,yä\ or **Bi·tolj** \'bē-,tōl(-y)ə\, -,tói\ or **Mon·a·stir** \,män-ə-'sti(ə)r\ city S Yugoslavia in S Macedonia pop 64,467
Bitter Lakes two lakes (Great Bitter Lake & Little Bitter Lake) in NE Egypt N of Suez; connected & traversed by the Suez canal
Bit·ter·root \'bit-ə(r)-,rüt, -,rút\ range of the Rocky mountains on Idaho-Mont. boundary — see BEAVERHEAD, GARFIELD
Bi·wa \'bē-(,)wä\ lake 40 mi (64 km) long Japan on W cen Honshu
Bi·zerte \bə-'zərt-ē, bi-'ze(ə)rt\ or **Bi·zer·ta** \bə-'zərt-ə\ city & port N Tunisia on **Lake Bizerte** (a deep lagoon) pop 62,856
Black 1 mountains W N.C.; a range of the Blue Ridge mountains — see MITCHELL (Mount) **2** canyon of Colorado river between Ariz. & Nev. S of Hoover Dam **3** canyon of the Gunnison river SW cen Colo. partly in **Black Canyon of the Gunnison National Monument 4** or **Babian** \'bä-bē-'än\ or **Pa-Pien Chiang** \'pä-bē-'en-chē-'äŋ\ river 500 mi (800 km) SE Asia rising in cen Yunnan, China, & flowing SE to Red river
Black·burn \'blak-(,)bərn\ borough NW England in Lancashire pop 88,236
Blackburn, Mount mountain 16,390 ft (4996 m) S Alaska; highest in the Wrangell mountains
Black Forest or G **Schwarz·wald** \'shfärts-,vält, 'shwȯrt-,swȯld\ forested mountain region SW W. Germany along the upper Rhine between the Neckar river & Swiss border
Black Hills mountains W S.Dak. & NE Wyo. — see HARNEY PEAK
Black·pool \'blak-,pül\ borough NW England in Lancashire on Irish sea pop 147,854
Blacks·burg \'blaks-,bərg\ city W Va. W of Roanoke pop 30,638
Black sea or anc **Pon·tus Eux·i·nus** \'pänt-əs-,yük-'si-nəs\ or **Pontus** sea bet. Europe & Asia connected with Aegean sea through the Bosporus, Sea of Marmara, & Dardanelles area 168,500 sq mi (438,100 sq km)
Black Volta — see VOLTA
Black Warrior river 178 mi (286 km) cen Ala. flowing into the Tombigbee
Bla·go·vesh·chensk \,bläg-ə-'vesh-(ch)ən(t)sk\ city U.S.S.R. in E Soviet Russia, Asia, on the Amur pop 172,000
Blaine \'blān\ city E Minn. N of St. Paul pop 28,558
Blanc, Cape \'blaŋk, 'blän\ **1** cape N Tunisia; northernmost point of Africa, at 37°14'N **2** promontory NW Africa on the Atlantic in Mauritania at SW tip of Rio de Oro
Blanc, Mont — see MONT BLANC
Blan·ca Peak \'blaŋ-kə\ mountain 14,317 ft (4364 m) S Colo.; highest in Sangre de Cristo mountains
Blan·co, Cape \'blaŋ-(,)kō\ cape SW Oreg.
Blan·tyre \'blan-,ti(ə)r\ city S Malawi pop 222,153
Blar·ney \'blär-nē\ town SW Ireland in cen County Cork
Blas·ket \'blas-kət\ islands SW Ireland N of Dingle Bay
Bled \'bled\ resort Yugoslavia in Slovenia NW of Ljubljana
Blen·heim \'blen-əm\ or G **Blind·heim** \'blint-,him\ village S W. Germany in Bavaria NNW of Augsburg pop 1619
Bli·da \'blēd-ə\ city N Algeria SW of Algiers pop 160,900
Block \'bläk\ island R.I. SW of Point Judith
Bloem·fon·tein \'blüm-fən-,tān, -,fän-\ city Republic of S. Africa ✳ of Orange Free State & judicial ✳ of the Republic pop 149,836
Blois \blə-'wä\ city N cen France SW of Orléans pop 49,134
Bloom·field \'blüm-,fēld\ **1** town cen Conn. NW of Hartford pop 18,608 **2** town NE N.J. pop 47,792
Bloo·ming·ton \'blü-miŋ-tən\ **1** city cen Ill. pop 44,189 **2** city SW cen Ind. pop 52,044 **3** village SE Minn. pop 81,831
Blooms·bury \'blümz-b(ə-)rē, US also -,ber-ē\ district of N cen London, England, in borough of Camden
Blue 1 mountains NE Oreg. & SE Wash. W of Wallowa mountains; highest Rock Creek Butte 9105 ft (2775 m) **2** mountains SE Australia in Great Dividing range in E New S. Wales; highest 4460 ft (1359 m) **3** mountains E Jamaica; highest Blue Mountain Peak 7402 ft (2256 m)
Blue·field \'blü-,fēld\ city S W.Va. on Va. border pop 16,060
Blue Grotto sea cave Italy on N shore of Capri

Blue Island city NE Ill. S of Chicago *pop* 21,853

Blue Nile river 850 *mi* (1368 *km*) Ethiopia & Sudan flowing from Lake Tana NNW into the Nile at Khartoum — see ABBAI

Blue Ridge the E range of the Appalachians E U.S. extending from South Mountain, S Pa. into N Ga. — see MITCHELL (Mount)

Blue Springs city N Mo. SE of Independence *pop* 25,927

Bluff \'bləf\ town S New Zealand; port for Invercargill *pop* 2720

Blythe·ville \'blī-vəl, 'blith-,vil\ city NE Ark. *pop* 23,844

Bo·bruisk \bȯ-'brü-isk\ city U.S.S.R. in Belorussia on the Berezina *pop* 138,000

Bo·ca Ra·ton \,bȯ-kə-rə-'tōn\ city SE Fla. N of Fort Lauderdale *pop* 49,505

Bo·chum \'bō-kəm\ city W W. Germany in Ruhr valley *pop* 400,757

Bodensee — see CONSTANCE (Lake)

Bod·min \'bäd-min\ borough SW England, a ✳ of Cornwall and Isles of Scilly *pop* 12,148

Boe·o·tia \bē-'ō-sh(ē-)ə\ or *NGk* **Voi·o·tía** \vyȯ-'tē-ə\ district E *cen* Greece NW of Attica — **Boe·o·tian** \bē-'ō-shən\ *adj or n*

Bo·ga·lu·sa \,bō-gə-'lü-sə\ city E La. NNE of New Orleans *pop* 16,976

Bo·gor \'bō-,gȯr\ or *formerly* **Bui·ten·zorg** \'bīt-ᵊn-,zȯrg\ city Indonesia in W Java S of Djakarta *pop* 247,409

Bo·go·tá \,bō-gə-'tȯ, -'tä\ city ✳ of Colombia on plateau in the Andes *pop* 2,293,919

Bohai — see PO HAI

Bo·he·mia \bō-'hē-mē-ə\ or **Če·chy** \'chek-ē\ region W Czechoslovakia; once a kingdom, later a province ✳ Prague

Böh·mer·wald \'ba(r)m-ər-,vält, 'bœm-\ or **Bohemian Forest** forested mountain region Czechoslovakia & W. Germany along boundary between E Bavaria & SW Bohemia

Bo·hol \bō-'hȯl\ island S *cen* Philippines, one of the Visayan islands, N of Mindanao *area* 1492 *sq mi* (3879 *sq km*)

Bois de Belleau — see BELLEAU

Bois de Bou·logne \,bwäd-ə-bü-'lȯn, -'lȯin\ park France W of Paris

Boi·se \'bȯi-sē, -zē\ city ✳ of Idaho on Boise river (60 *mi or* 96 *km* long) *pop* 102,451

Bo·ja·dor, Cape \'bäj-ə-,dȯ(ə)r\ headland NW Africa in the Atlantic on W coast of Western Sahara

Bokhara — see BUKHARA

Boks·burg \'bäks-,bərg\ city NE Republic of S. Africa in S Transvaal E of Johannesburg *pop* 108,850

Bo·lan \bō-'län\ mountain pass 5900 *ft* (1798 *m*) Pakistan in N Baluchistan

Bolbitine — see ROSETTA

Bo·ling·brook \'bō-liŋ-,brük\ city NE Ill. SW of Chicago *pop* 37,261

Bo·lí·var, Cer·ro \,ser-(,)ō-bə-'lē-,vär\ or *formerly* **La Pa·ri·da** \läp-ə-'rēd-ə\ iron mountain 2018 *ft* (615 *m*) E Venezuela S of Ciudad Bolívar

Bo·lí·var, Pi·co \,(,)kō-bə-'lē-,vär\ mountain 16,427 *ft* (5007 *m*) W Venezuela in Cordillera Mérida; highest in Venezuela

Bo·liv·ia \bə-'liv-ē-ə\ country W *cen* S. America; a republic; administrative ✳ La Paz, constitutional ✳ Sucre *area* 424,200 *sq mi* (1,102,920 *sq km*), *pop* 6,547,000 — **Bo·liv·i·an** \-ē-ən\ *adj or n*

Bo·lo·gna \bə-'lōn-(y)ə\ or *anc* **Bo·no·nia** \bə-'nō-nē-ə\ commune N Italy ✳ of Emilia-Romagna at foot of the Apennines *pop* 455,853 — **Bo·lo·gnan** \bə-'lōn-yən\ or **Bo·lo·gnese** \,bō-lən-'(y)ēz, -'(y)ēs\ *adj or n*

Bol·se·na, Lake \bȯl-'sā-nə\ lake *cen* Italy in N Latium

Bol·ton \'bōlt-ᵊn\ borough NW England in NW Greater Manchester *pop* 147,099

Bol·za·no \bȯlt-'sän-(,)ō, bȯl-'zän-\ **1** former province N Italy in S Tirol, now part of Trentino-Alto Adige region **2** commune in Trentino-Alto Adige region *pop* 104,606

Bo·ma \'bō-mə\ city & port W Congo on Congo river *pop* 79,230

Bom·bay \bäm-'bā\ **1** former state W India ✳ Bombay; divided 1960 into Gujarat & Maharashtra states; once a presidency & (1937–47) a province of Brit. India **2** island W India on which city of Bombay is situated *area* 24 *sq mi* (62 *sq km*) **3** city & port W India ✳ of Maharashtra & of former Bombay state *pop* 8,227,332

Bo·mu \'bō-(,)mü\ or **Mbo·mou** \əm-'bō-(,)mü\ river 500 *mi* (805 *km*) W *cen* Africa forming boundary bet. Zaire & Central African Republic & uniting with the Uele to form the Ubangi

Bon, Cape \'bōⁿ\ or **Ras el Tib** \,räs-,el-'tib\ headland NE Tunisia on **Cape Bon Peninsula**

Bo·na, Mount \'bō-nə\ mountain 16,420 *ft* (5005 *m*) S Alaska at W end of Wrangell mountains

Bon·aire \bə-'na(ə)r, -'ne(ə)r\ island Netherlands Antilles E of Curaçao *area* 95 *sq mi* (247 *sq km*), *pop* 8099

Bon·di \'bän-'dī\ town SE Australia, SE suburb of Sydney, S of entrance to Port Jackson on **Bondi Beach**

Bône — see ANNABA

Bo·nin \bō-'nən\ or **Oga·sa·wa·ra** \(,)ō-,gäs-ə-'wär-ə\ islands W Pacific *ab* 600 *mi* (966 *km*) SSE of Tokyo; belong to Japan; administered by U.S. 1945–68 *area* 40 *sq mi* (104 *sq km*), *pop* 1507

Bonn \'bän, 'bȯn\ city W W. Germany on the Rhine SSE of Cologne ✳ of Federal Republic of Germany (often called **Bonn Republic**) *pop* 288,148

Bon·ne·ville Salt Flats \'bän-ə-,vil\ or **Bonneville Flats** broad level area of Great Salt Lake desert E of Wendover, Utah

Bonny, Bight of — see BIAFRA, BIGHT OF

Booker T. Washington National Monument historic site W *cen* Va. SE of Roanoke

Boo·thia \'bü-thē-ə\ peninsula N Canada W of Baffin Is.; its N tip (at *ab* 72°N, 94°W) is the northernmost point on N. American mainland

Boothia, Gulf of gulf N Canada between Baffin Is. & Melville peninsula on E & Boothia peninsula on W

Boo·tle \'büt-ᵊl\ borough NW England in W Merseyside *pop* 62,463

Bo·phu·tha·tswa·na \,bō-(,)püt-ät-'swän-ə\ group of noncontiguous black enclaves in the Republic of S. Africa granted independence 1977 ✳ Mmabatho *pop* 1,039,000

Bo·ra Bo·ra \,bȯr-ə-'bȯr-ə, ,bȯr-ə-'bȯr-ə\ island S Pacific in Leeward group of the Society islands NW of Tahiti *area ab* 15 *sq mi* (38 *sq km*)

Bo·rah Peak \,bȯr-ə\ mountain 12,662 *ft* (3859 *m*) E *cen* Idaho in Lost River range; highest point in state

Bo·rås \bü-'rȯs\ city SW Sweden E of Göteborg *pop* 102,129

Bor·deaux \bȯr-'dō\ city & port SW France on the Garonne *pop* 220,830

Bor·ders \'bȯrd-ərz\ region S Scotland, established 1975 ✳ Newtown St. Boswells *area* 1804 *sq mi* (4690 *sq km*), *pop* 99,248

Bor·di·ghe·ra \,bȯrd-i-'ger-ə\ commune & port NW Italy in SW Liguria *pop* 11,896

Bor·ger·hout \'bȯr-gər-,haȯt\ commune N Belgium, E suburb of Antwerp *pop* 43,521

Borgne, Lake \'bȯ(ə)rn\ inlet of the Mississippi sound E of New Orleans, La.

Bor·neo \'bȯr-nē-,ō\ island Malay archipelago SW of Philippines *area* 290,012 *sq mi* (754,031 *sq km*) — see BRUNEI, KALIMANTAN, SABAH, SARAWAK — **Bor·ne·an** \-nē-ən\ *adj or n*

Born·holm \'bȯrn-,hō(l)m\ island Denmark in Baltic sea ✳ Rönne *area* 228 *sq mi* (593 *sq km*), *pop* 47,241

Bos·nia \'bäz-nē-ə\ region W *cen* Yugoslavia; formerly a kingdom, now part of **Bosnia and Her·ze·go·vi·na** \,hert-sə-gō-'vē-nə, ,hərt-\ federated republic (✳ Sarajevo *area* 19,904 *sq mi* or 51,750 *sq km, pop* 4,021,000) — **Bos·ni·an** \-nē-ən\ *adj or n*

Bos·po·rus \'bäs-p(ə-)rəs\ or **Bos·pho·rus** \-f(ə-)rəs\ strait *ab* 18 *mi* (29 *km*) long bet. Turkey in Europe & Turkey in Asia connecting Sea of Marmara & Black sea — **Bos·po·ran** \-pə-rən\ *adj*

Bos·sier City \,bō-zhər-\ city NW La. *pop* 50,817

Bos·ton \'bȯ-stən\ **1** mountains NW Ark. & E Okla. in Ozark plateau **2** city & port ✳ of Mass. on Massachusetts Bay *pop* 562,994 **3** borough & port E England in SE Lincolnshire in Parts of Holland *pop* 26,425 — **Bos·ton·ese** \,bȯ-stə-'nēz, -'nēs\ *adj* — **Bos·to·nian** \bȯ-'stō-nē-ən, -nyən\ *adj or n*

Bo·ta·fo·go Bay \,bät-ə-'fō-(,)gō\ inlet of Guanabara Bay in Rio de Janeiro, Brazil

Bot·a·ny Bay \'bät-ᵊn-ē, 'bät-nē\ inlet of the S Pacific SE Australia in New S. Wales on S border of city of Sydney

Both·nia, Gulf of \'bäth-nē-ə\ arm of Baltic sea bet. Sweden & Finland

Bo·tswa·na \bät-'swän-ə\ country S Africa N of the Molopo; an independent republic since 1966, formerly Brit. protectorate of Bechuanaland ✳ Gaborone *area ab* 222,000 *sq mi* (577,200 *sq km*), *pop* 936,600

Bot·trop \'bä-,träp\ city W W. Germany NNW of Essen *pop* 114,571

Bou·cher·ville \'bü-shər-,vil, ,bü-,shä-'\ town Canada in S Que. NE of Montreal *pop* 29,704

Bou·gain·ville \'büg-ən-,vil, 'bōg-, 'bȯg-\ island S Pacific, largest of the Solomons; chief town Kieta *area* 3880 *sq mi* (10,088 *sq km*)

Bougie — see BEJAIA

Bouil·lon \bü-'yōⁿ\ town SE Belgium in the Ardennes

Boul·der \'bōl-dər\ city N *cen* Colo. *pop* 76,685

Boulder Dam — see HOOVER DAM

Bou·logne \bü-'lōn, -'lȯin\ or **Bou·logne–sur–Mer** \-,sü(ə)r-'me(ə)r\ city & port N France on English channel *pop* 48,309

Boulogne–Bil·lan·court \-,bē-(y)äⁿ-'kü(ə)r\ commune N France SW of Paris on the Seine *pop* 103,527

Boundary Peak mountain 13,140 *ft* (4005 *m*) SW Nev. in White mountains; highest in state

Bountiful city N Utah N of Salt Lake City *pop* 32,877

Bour·bon·nais \,bür-bə-'nā\ former province *cen* France W of Burgundy

Bourges \'bü(ə)rzh\ commune *cen* France SSE of Orléans *pop* 75,200

Bourgogne — see BURGUNDY

Bourne·mouth \'bō(ə)rn-məth, 'bȯ(ə)rn-, 'bü(ə)rn-\ town S England in Dorset on English channel *pop* 144,803

Bou·vet \'bü-(,)vä\ island S Atlantic SSW of Cape of Good Hope at *ab* 54°S, 5°E; belongs to Norway

Bow \'bō\ river 315 *mi* (507 *km*) Canada in SW Alta. rising in Banff National Park

Bow·ie \'bü-ē\ town Md. NE of Washington, D.C. *pop* 33,695

Bowling Green 1 city S Ky. *pop* 40,450 **2** city NW Ohio S of Toledo *pop* 25,728

Boyne \'bȯin\ river 70 *mi* (113 *km*) E Ireland in Leinster flowing to Irish sea S of Drogheda

Boyn·ton Beach \,bȯint-ᵊn-\ city SE Fla. *pop* 35,624

Bo·yo·ma Falls \bȯi-,äm-ə-\ or *formerly* **Stanley Falls** series of seven cataracts NE Zaire in the Lualaba near head of Congo river with total fall of *ab* 200 *ft* (61 *m*) in 60 *mi* (96 *km*)

Boz·ca·a·da \,bȯz-jä-'dä\ or *anc* **Ten·e·dos** \'ten-ə-,däs\ island Turkey in NE Aegean sea S of the Dardanelles

Boze·man \'bōz-mən\ city SW Mont. *pop* 21,645

Bra·bant \brə-'bant, -'bänt\ **1** old duchy of W Europe including region now forming N. Brabant province of the Netherlands & Brabant & Antwerp provinces of Belgium **2** province *cen* Belgium ✳ Brussels *pop* 2,221,222

Bra·den·ton \'brād-ᵊn-tən\ city & port W Fla. N of Sarasota *pop* 30,170

Brad·ford \'brad-fərd\ city N England in W. Yorkshire *pop* 280,691

Bra·ga \'bräg-ə\ commune NW Portugal NNE of Porto *pop* 124,800

Bra·gan·ça \brə-'gan(t)-sə\ commune NE Portugal near Spanish border *pop* 34,803

Brah·ma·pu·tra \,bräm-ə-'p(y)ü-trə\ river 1680 *mi* (2704 *km*) S Asia flowing from the Himalayas in Tibet to the Ganges delta in E India (subcontinent) — see JAMUNA, TSANGPO

Bra·ila \brə-'ē-lə\ city E Romania on the Danube *pop* 214,940

Brain·tree \'brān-(,)trē\ town E Mass. S of Boston *pop* 36,337

Brak·pan \'brak-,pan\ city NE Republic of S. Africa in S Transvaal on the Witwatersrand S of Johannesburg *pop* 85,044

Bramp·ton \'bram(p)-tən\ town Canada in SE Ont. *pop* 149,030

Bran·co \'braŋ-(,)kō, -(,)kü\ river 350 *mi* (563 *km*) N Brazil flowing S into Negro river

Bran·den·burg \'bran-dən-,bərg, 'brän-dən-,bu(ə)rg\ **1** region & former province NE *cen* Germany **2** city *cen* E. Germany *pop* 94,071

Bran·don \'bran-dən\ city Canada in SW Man. *pop* 36,242

Bran·dy·wine \'bran-dē-,win\ creek *ab* 20 *mi* (32 *km*) SE Pa. & N Del. flowing SE to Wilmington, Del.

Bran·ford \'bran-fərd\ town S Conn. E of New Haven *pop* 23,363

Brant·ford \'brant-fərd\ city Canada in SE Ont. *pop* 74,315
Bras d'Or Lake \brad-'ȯ(ə)r\ tidal lake *ab* 50 *mi* (80 *km*) long Canada in N.S. on Cape Breton Is.
Bra·sí·lia \brə-'zil-yə\ city ✻ of Brazil in Federal District *pop* 246,580
Bra·sov \brä-'shȯv\ *or formerly* **Sta·lin** \'stäl-ən, 'stal-, -ēn\ *or* **Ora·sul Stalin** \ȯr-ə-,shül-, ,ȯr-\ city *cen* Romania in foothills of Transylvanian Alps *pop* 304,670
Bra·ti·sla·va \,brat-ə-'släv-ə, ,brät-\ *or G* **Press·burg** \'pres-,bərg, -,bu̇(ə)rg\ *or Hung* **Po·zsony** \'pō-,zhōn-yə\ city Czechoslovakia, chief city of Slovakia, on the Danube *pop* 380,259
Bratsk \'brätsk\ city U.S.S.R. in E *cen* Soviet Russia, Asia, NNE of Irkutsk near site of **Bratsk Dam** (in the Angara) *pop* 214,000
Braunschweig — *see* BRUNSWICK
Bravo, Río — *see* RIO GRANDE
Bra·zil *or Pg* **Bra·sil** \brə-'zil\ country E S. America; a federal republic ✻ Brasília *area* 3,286,169 *sq mi* (8,544,039 *sq km*), *pop* 118,674,604 — **Bra·zil·ian** \brə-'zil-yən\ *adj or n*
Braz·os \'braz-əs\ river *ab* 950 *mi* (1529 *km*), *cen* Tex. flowing SE into Gulf of Mexico
Braz·za·ville \'braz-ə-,vil, 'bräz-ə-,vēl\ city & port ✻ of Congo on W bank of Stanley Pool in Congo river *pop* 302,460
Brea \'brā-ə\ city SW Calif. SE of Los Angeles *pop* 27,913
Brec·on \'brek-ən\ *or* **Breck·nock** \'brek-,näk, -nək\ **1** *or* **Brec·on·shire** *or* **Breck·nock·shire** \-,shi(ə)r, -shər\ former county SE Wales ✻ Brecon **2** borough SE Wales in Powys *pop* 7422
Brecon Beacons two mountain peaks SE Wales in S Powys
Bre·da \brā-'dä\ commune S Netherlands in N. Brabant province *pop* 118,813
Bre·genz \'brā-,gen(t)s\ commune W Austria on Lake Constance ✻ of Vorarlberg *pop* 24,683
Bre·men \'brem-ən, 'brā-mən\ **1** former duchy N Germany bet. the lower Weser & the lower Elbe **2** state N W. Germany *area* 156 *sq mi* (406 *sq km*), *pop* 693,846 **3** city & port, its ✻, on the Weser *pop* 555,118
Bre·mer·ha·ven \'brem-ər-,häv-ən, ,brā-mər-'häf-ən\ city & port N W. Germany in Bremen state at mouth of the Weser; includes former city of Wesermünde *pop* 138,728
Brem·er·ton \'brem-ərt-ən, -ərt-ᵊn\ city & port W Wash. on Puget Sound *pop* 36,208
Bren·ner \'bren-ər\ mountain pass 4495 *ft* (1370 *m*) in the Alps between Austria & Italy
Brent \'brent\ *or formerly* **Brent·ford and Chis·wick** \,brent-fərd-ᵊn-'chiz-ik\ borough of W Greater London, England *pop* 254,400
Bren·ta \'brent-ə\ river 100 *mi* (161 *km*) N Italy flowing SE into the Adriatic S of Chioggia
Bre·scia \'bresh-ə, 'brā-shə\ *or anc* **Brix·ia** \'brik-sē-ə\ commune N Italy in E Lombardy ENE of Milan *pop* 206,460
Brest \'brest\ **1** commune & port NW France in Brittany *pop* 163,940 **2** *or formerly* **Brest Li·tovsk** \,brest-lə-'tȯfsk, -'tȯvsk\ city U.S.S.R. in SW Belorussia on Bug river *pop* 177,000
Bre·ton, Cape \kāp-'bret-ᵊn, kə-'bret-, -'brit-\ headland Canada, eastern-most point of Cape Breton Is. & of N.S., at 59°48' W
Bri·an·çon \brē-än-'sōⁿ\ town SE France SE of Grenoble
Briansk — *see* BRYANSK
Bridge·port \'brij-,pō(ə)rt, -,pȯ(ə)rt\ city SW Conn. on Long Is. Sound *pop* 142,546
Bridge·ton \'brij-tən\ **1** city E Mo. NW of St. Louis *pop* 18,445 **2** city SW N.J. *pop* 18,795
Bridge·town \'brij-,tau̇n\ city & port Brit. W. Indies ✻ of Barbados *pop* 8868
Bridge·wa·ter \'brij-,wȯt-ər, -,wät-\ city SE Mass. S of Brockton *pop* 17,202
Brie \brē\ district & medieval county NE France E of Paris; chief town Meaux
Bri·enne \brē-en\ **1** former county NE France in Champagne NNE of Troyes **2** town, its ✻
Bri·enz \brē-'en(t)s\ town Switzerland in SE Bern canton at NE end of **Lake of Brienz** (9 *mi* or 14 *km* long, in course of the Aare)
Brigh·ton \'brīt-ᵊn\ borough S England in E. Sussex on English channel *pop* 146,134
Brin·di·si \'brin-də-(,)zē, 'brēn-\ *or anc* **Brun·di·si·um** \,brən-'diz(h)-ē-əm\ city & port SE Italy in Apulia *pop* 88,947
Bris·bane \'briz-bən, -,bān\ city & port E Australia ✻ of Queensland on **Brisbane** river (215 *mi* or 344 *km*) near its mouth *pop* 942,836
Bris·tol \'bris-tᵊl\ **1** city W *cen* Conn. WSW of Hartford *pop* 57,370 **2** town E R.I. SE of Providence *pop* 20,128 **3** city NE Tenn. *pop* 23,986 **4** city SW Va. *pop* 19,042 **5** channel between S Wales & SW England **6** city & port SW England in Avon on Avon river near Severn estuary *pop* 387,977 — **Bris·to·li·an** \bris-'tō-lē-ən, -'tōl-yən\ *n*
Bristol Bay arm of Bering sea SW Alaska of Alaska peninsula
Brit·ain \'brit-ᵊn\ **1** *or L* **Bri·tan·nia** \brə-'tan-yə, -'tan-ē-ə\ the island of Great Britain **2** UNITED KINGDOM **3** COMMONWEALTH
British America 1 *or* **British North America** CANADA **2** all Brit. possessions in & adjacent to N. & S. America
British Bechuanaland — *see* BECHUANALAND
British Cameroons former Brit. trust territory W equatorial Africa comprising two areas in the Cameroons bet. Nigeria & Cameroon ✻ Buea; divided 1961 bet. Nigeria (N section) & Cameroon (S section)
British Columbia province W Canada on Pacific coast ✻ Victoria *area* 359,279 *sq mi* (934,125 *sq km*), *pop* 2,744,467
British East Africa 1 KENYA — a former name **2** the former Brit. dependencies in E Africa: Kenya, Uganda, Zanzibar, & Tanganyika
British Empire Great Britain & the Brit. dominions & dependencies — a former usage
British Guiana — *see* GUYANA
British Honduras — *see* BELIZE
British India the part of India formerly under direct Brit. administration — *see* INDIAN STATES
British Indian Ocean Territory Brit. colony in Indian ocean comprising Chagos archipelago & formerly Aldabra, Farquhar, & Desroches islands (returned to Seychelles 1976) *area* 30 *sq mi* (78 *sq km*)
British Isles island group W Europe comprising Great Britain, Ireland, & adjacent islands

British Malaya former dependencies of Great Britain on Malay peninsula & in Malay archipelago including Malaya (federation), Singapore, N. Borneo, Sarawak, & Brunei
British Solomon Islands former Brit. protectorate comprising the Solomons (except Bougainville, Buka, & adjacent small islands) & the Santa Cruz islands ✻ Honiara (on Guadalcanal)
British Somaliland former Brit. protectorate E Africa bordering on Gulf of Aden ✻ Hargeisa; since 1960 part of Somalia
British Virgin Islands the E islands of the Virgin islands group; a Brit. possession ✻ Road Town (on Tortola Is.) *area* 58 *sq mi* (151 *sq km*), *pop* 12,000
British West Indies islands of the W. Indies including Jamaica, the Bahamas, Caymans, Brit. Virgin islands, Brit. Leeward & Windward islands, Trinidad, & Tobago
Brit·ta·ny \'brit-ᵊn-ē\ *or F* **Bre·tagne** \brə-tányᵊ\ region & former province NW France SW of Normandy
Br·no \'bər-(,)nō\ *or G* **Brünn** \'bru̇en, 'bru̇n\ city *cen* Czechoslovakia, chief city of Moravia *pop* 371,463
Broad 1 river 220 *mi* (354 *km*) N.C. & S.C. — *see* SALUDA **2** river 70 *mi* (113 *km*) S S.C. flowing into the Atlantic
Broads \'brȯdz\ low-lying district E England in Norfolk (the **Norfolk Broads**) & Suffolk (the **Suffolk Broads**)
Brock·en \'bräk-ən\ mountain 3747 *ft* (1142 *m*) E. Germany near W. German border; highest in Harz mountains
Brock·ton \'bräk-tən\ city SE Mass. *pop* 95,172
Brock·ville \'bräk-,vil\ city Canada in SE Ont. *pop* 19,896
Bro·ken Hill \,brō-kən-\ **1** city SE Australia in W New S. Wales *pop* 26,913 **2** — *see* KABWE
Bromberg — *see* BYDGOSZCZ
Brom·ley \'bräm-lē\ borough of SE Greater London, England *pop* 299,500
Bronx \'brän(k)s\ *or* **The Bronx** borough of New York City on the mainland NE of Manhattan Is. *pop* 1,168,972
Brook·field \'bru̇k-,fēld\ **1** village NE Ill. W of Chicago *pop* 19,395 **2** city SE Wis. W of Milwaukee *pop* 34,035
Brook·line \'bru̇k-,līn\ town E Mass. W of Boston *pop* 55,062
Brook·lyn \'bru̇k-lən\ borough of New York City at SW end of Long Is. *pop* 2,601,852 — **Brook·lyn·ite** \-lə-,nīt\ *n*
Brooklyn Center village SE Minn. NW of Minneapolis *pop* 31,230
Brooklyn Park village E Minn. NW of Minneapolis *pop* 43,332
Brook Park \,bru̇k-\ city NE Ohio *pop* 26,195
Brooks \'bru̇ks\ mountain range N Alaska extending from Kotzebue Sound to Canadian border; highest peak Mt. Michelson 9239 *ft* (2816 *m*)
Broom·field \'brüm-,fēld, 'bru̇m-\ city N *cen* Colo. NNW of Denver *pop* 20,730
Bros·sard \brȯ-'sär(d)\ town Canada in S Que. *pop* 52,232
Browns·ville \'brau̇nz-,vil, -vəl\ city & port S Tex. *pop* 84,997
Brown·wood \'brau̇n-,wu̇d\ city *cen* Tex. *pop* 19,396
Bruges \'brüzh, brüezh\ *or Flem* **Brug·ge** \'brüeg-ə\ commune NW Belgium ✻ of W. Flanders *pop* 118,020
Bru·nei \bru̇-'nī, 'bru̇-,nī\ **1** independent sultanate & former Brit. protectorate NW Borneo ✻ Bandar Seri Begawan *area* 2226 *sq mi* (5788 *sq km*), *pop* 192,832 **2** — *see* BANDAR SERI BEGAWAN
Bruns·wick \'brənz-(,)wik\ **1** city & port SE Ga. on Atlantic coast *pop* 17,605 **2** town SW Maine *pop* 17,366 **3** city NE Ohio SSW of Cleveland *pop* 28,104 **4** *or G* **Braun·schweig** \'brau̇n-,shwig, -,shfīk\ former state *cen* Germany ✻ Brunswick **5** *or G* **Braunschweig** city E W. Germany W of Berlin *pop* 261,141
Brus·sels \'brəs-əlz\ *or F* **Bru·xelles** \brüe(k)-sel\ *or Flem* **Brus·sel** \'brües-əl\ city ✻ of Belgium & of Brabant *pop* 139,678 — **Bru·xel·lois** \brüe(k)-sel-wá\ *adj or n*
Bruttium — *see* CALABRIA
Bry·an \'brī-ən\ city E *cen* Tex. *pop* 44,337
Bryansk *or* **Briansk** \brē-'än(t)sk\ city U.S.S.R. in SW Soviet Russia, Europe, SW of Moscow *pop* 394,000
Bryce Canyon National Park \'brīs\ reservation S Utah NE of Zion National Park
Bu·bas·tis \byü-'bas-təs\ ancient city N Egypt near modern Zagazig
Bu·ca·ra·man·ga \,bü-kə-rə-'mäŋ-gə\ city N Colombia NNE of Bogotá *pop* 291,661
Bu·cha·rest \'b(y)ü-kə-,rest\ *or Romanian* **Bu·cu·res·ti** \,bü-kə-'resht(-ē)\ city ✻ of Romania *pop* 1,861,027
Bu·chen·wald \'bü-kən-,wȯld, -,vält\ village SW E. Germany NW of Weimar
Buck·ing·ham·shire \'bək-iŋ-əm-,shi(ə)r, -shər, *US also* -iŋ-,ham-\ *or* **Buckingham** *or* **Bucks** \'bəks\ county SE *cen* England ✻ Aylesbury *area* 727 *sq mi* (1890 *sq km*), *pop* 571,600
Buck Island Reef National Monument \,bək-\ reservation St. Croix, Virgin Islands; contains marine gardens
Bu·da·pest \'büd-ə-,pest *also* 'byüd-, 'bu̇d-, -,pesht\ city ✻ of Hungary on the Danube *pop* 2,060,170
Buddh Ga·ya \,bu̇d-gə-'yä\ village NE India in *cen* Bihar
Budweis — *see* CESKE BUDEJOVICE
Bue·na Park \,byü-nə-\ city Calif. W of Anaheim *pop* 64,165
Bue·na·ven·tu·ra \,bwen-ə-ven-'t(y)u̇r-ə, ,bwä-nə-\ city & port W Colombia on the Pacific *pop* 115,770
Bue·nos Ai·res \,bwā-nəs-'ar-ēz, *Sp* ,bwä-nōs-'ī-räs\ city & port ✻ of Argentina on Río de la Plata *pop* 2,908,001
Buenos Aires, Lake lake 80 *mi* (129 *km*) long S Argentina & S Chile
Buf·fa·lo \'bəf-ə-,lō\ city & port W N.Y. on Lake Erie & the Niagara *pop* 357,870 — **Buf·fa·lo·ni·an** \,bəf-ə-'lō-nē-ən\ *n*
Buffalo Grove city NE Ill. *pop* 22,230
Bug \'bü̇g\ **1** river 450 *mi* (724 *km*) *cen* Poland rising in W Ukrainian Republic, U.S.S.R., & flowing into the Vistula **2** river 500 *mi* (805 *km*) U.S.S.R. in SW Ukrainian Republic flowing SE to the Dnieper estuary
Bu·gan·da \b(y)ü-'gan-də\ region & former native kingdom E Africa in SE Uganda ✻ Kampala
Buitenzorg — *see* BOGOR
Bu·jum·bu·ra \,bü-jəm-'bu̇r-ə\ *or formerly* **Usum·bu·ra** \,ü-səm-\ city ✻ of Burundi on Lake Tanganyika *pop* 376,000
Bu·ka \'bü-kə\ island W Pacific in the Solomons N of Bougainville *pop* 33,770

Bu·ka·vu \bü-ˈkäv-(ˌ)ü\ *or formerly* **Cos·ter·mans·ville** \ˈkäs-tər-mənz-ˌvil\ city E Zaire at S end of Lake Kivu *pop* 152,193
Bu·kha·ra \bü-ˈkär-ə, -ˈkar-, -ˈhär-, -ˈhar-\ *or* **Bo·kha·ra** \bō-\ **1** former emirate W Asia around city of Bukhara **2** city U.S.S.R. in Soviet Central Asia in W Uzbek Republic E of the Amu Darya *pop* 139,000 — **Bu·kha·ran** *or* **Bo·kha·ran** \-ən\ *adj or n*
Bu·kit·ting·gi \ˌbü-kə-ˈtiŋ-gē\ *or formerly* **Fort de Kock** \-də-ˈkȯk, -ˈkäk\ city Indonesia in W *cen* Sumatra *pop* 70,771
Bu·ko·vi·na *or* **Bu·co·vi·na** \ˌbü-kə-ˈvē-nə\ region E *cen* Europe in foothills of E Carpathians; now in NE Romania & W Ukrainian Republic
Bu·la·wayo *or* **Bu·lu·wayo** \ˌbu̇l-ə-ˈwā-(ˌ)ō, -ˈwī-\ city SW Zimbabwe, chief town of Matabeleland *pop* 359,000
Bul·gar·ia \ˌbəl-ˈgar-ē-ə, bu̇l-, -ˈger-\ country SE Europe on Black sea; a republic ✱ Sofia *area* 42,858 *sq mi* (111,431 *sq km*), *pop* 8,942,976
Bull Run \ˈbu̇l-ˈrən\ stream 20 *mi* (32 *km*) N Va. W of Washington, D.C., flowing into Occoquan creek (small tributary of the Potomac)
Bun·del·khand \ˈbu̇n-dᵊl-ˌkənd\ region N *cen* India containing headwaters of the Jumna; now chiefly in N Madhya Pradesh
Bundesrepublik Deutschland — see GERMANY
Bun·ker Hill \ˌbəŋ-kər-\ height in Charlestown section of Boston, Mass.
Bur·bank \ˈbər-ˌbaŋk\ **1** city SW Calif. *pop* 84,625 **2** city NE Ill. *pop* 28,462
Bur·gas \bu̇r-ˈgäs\ city & port SE Bulgaria *pop* 144,449
Bur·gen·land \ˈbər-gən-ˌland, ˈbu̇r-gən-ˌlänt\ province E Austria SE of Vienna on Hungarian border ✱ Eisenstadt
Bur·gos \ˈbu̇(ə)r-ˌgōs\ **1** province N Spain *area* 5480 *sq mi* (14,248 *sq km*), *pop* 327,926 **2** city, its ✱ & once ✱ of Old Castile *pop* 152,545
Bur·gun·dy \ˈbər-gən-dē\ *or F* **Bour·gogne** \bür-gȯnʸ\ **1** region & former kingdom, duchy, & province E France S of Champagne **2** county France E of Burgundy province; later called **Franche–Com·té** \fräⁿsh-(ə-)kōⁿ-tā\ — **Bur·gun·di·an** \(ˌ)bər-ˈgən-dē-ən\ *adj or n*
Bur·ki·na Fa·so \bu̇r-ˈkē-nə-ˈfä-sō\ *or formerly* **Upper Vol·ta** \-ˈvōl-tə, -ˈvȯl-\ republic W Africa; until 1958 a French territory ✱ Ouagadougou *area* 121,892 *sq mi* (316,919 *sq km*), *pop* 7,967,019
Bur·lin·game \ˈbər-lən-ˌgām\ city W Calif. *pop* 26,173
Bur·ling·ton \ˈbər-liŋ-tən\ **1** city SE Iowa *pop* 29,529 **2** town NE Mass. *pop* 23,486 **3** city N *cen* N.C. *pop* 37,266 **4** city NW Vt. *pop* 37,712 **5** town Canada in SE Ont. N of Hamilton *pop* 114,853
Burma — see MYANMAR
Bur·na·by \ˈbər-nə-bē\ city Canada in SW B.C. *pop* 131,599
Burn·ley \ˈbərn-lē\ borough NW England in SE Lancashire *pop* 69,864
Burns·ville \ˈbərnz-ˌvil\ village SE Minn. S of Minneapolis *pop* 35,674
Bur·rard \bə-ˈrärd\ inlet of Strait of Georgia, W Canada, in B.C.; city of Vancouver is situated on it
Bur·sa \bu̇r-ˈsä, ˈbər-sə\ *or formerly* **Bru·sa** \brü-ˈsä, ˈbrü-sə\ city NW Turkey in Asia near Sea of Marmara *pop* 466,178
Bur·ton \ˈbərt-ᵊn\ city SE *cen* Mich. SE of Flint *pop* 29,976
Bu·run·di \bu̇-ˈrün-dē\ *or formerly* **Urun·di** \u̇-ˈrün-\ country E *cen* Africa; a republic ✱ Usumbura *area* 10,744 *sq mi* (27,934 *sq km*), *pop* 3,992,130 — see RUANDA-URUNDI — **Bu·run·di·an** \-dē-ən\ *adj or n*
Bury \ˈber-ē\ borough NW England in Greater Manchester NNW of Manchester *pop* 67,529
Bur·yat *or* **Bur·iat Republic** \bu̇r-ˌyät-, ˌbu̇r-ē-ˌät-\ autonomous republic U.S.S.R. in S Soviet Russia, Asia, adjacent to Mongolia & E of Lake Baikal ✱ Ulan-Ude *area* 127,020 *sq mi* (330,252 *sq km*), *pop* 812,000 — **Buryat** *or* **Buriat** *n*
Bury Saint Ed·munds \ˌber-ē-sānt-ˈed-mən(d)z, -sənt-\ borough SE England in Suffolk *pop* 28,914
Bu·shire \bü-ˈshi(ə)r\ city & port SW Iran *pop* 57,681
Busra — see BASRA
Butaritari — see MAKIN
Bute \ˈbyüt\ **1** island SW Scotland W of Firth of Clyde **2** *or* **Bute·shire** \-ˌshi(ə)r, -shər\ former county SW Scotland comprising several islands in the Firth of Clyde ✱ Rothesay (on Bute)
But·ler \ˈbət-lər\ city W Pa. N of Pittsburgh *pop* 17,026
Butte \ˈbyüt\ city SW Mont. in plateau of Rockies *pop* 36,817
Bu·tung \ˈbü-ˌtu̇ŋ\ island Indonesia off SE Celebes *area ab* 2000 *sq mi* (5200 *sq km*), *pop* 253,262
Bu·zau \bə-ˈzō, -ˈzau̇\ city E Romania *pop* 112,760
Buz·zards Bay \ˌbəz-ərdz-\ inlet of the Atlantic SE Mass. W of Cape Cod
Byd·goszcz \ˈbid-ˌgȯsh(ch)\ *or G* **Brom·berg** \ˈbräm-ˌbərg, ˈbrȯm-ˌberk\ city NW *cen* Poland NE of Poznan *pop* 352,424
Byelgorod–Dnestrovski — see BELGOROD-DNESTROVSKIY
Byelorussia — see BELORUSSIA — **Byelorussian** *adj or n*
By·tom \ˈbē-ˌtȯm, ˈbi-\ *or G* **Beu·then** \ˈbȯit-ᵊn\ city SW Poland in Silesia *pop* 237,828
Byzantium — see ISTANBUL
Ca·ba·na·tuan \ˌkäb-ə-nə-ˈtwän\ city Philippines in S *cen* Luzon *pop* 138,298
Ca·bin·da \kə-ˈbin-də\ territory W equatorial Africa on the Atlantic bet. Congo & Zaire; belongs to Angola ✱ Cabinda *area* 3000 *sq mi* (7800 *sq km*), *pop* 58,547
Cab·ot \ˈkab-ət\ strait *ab* 70 *mi* (113 *km*) wide E Canada bet. SW Newfoundland & Cape Breton Is. connecting Gulf of St. Lawrence with the Atlantic
Ca·bril·lo National Monument \kə-ˈbrē(l)-(ˌ)yō-\ historic site SW Calif. on San Diego Bay
Ca·ca·hua·mil·pa \ˌkäk-ə-wə-ˈmil-pə\ caverns S Mexico in Guerrero NNE of Taxco
Cá·ce·res \ˈkäs-ə-ˌrās\ **1** province W Spain in N Estremadura *area* 7667 *sq mi* (19,934 *sq km*), *pop* 380,020 **2** city, its ✱ *pop* 67,392
Cache la Pou·dre \ˌkash-lə-ˈpüd-ər\ river 125 *mi* (201 *km*) N Colo. flowing into the S. Platte
Cad·do \ˈkad-(ˌ)ō\ lake 20 *mi* (32 *km*) long NW La. & NE Tex. draining to Red river
Cá·diz \kə-ˈdiz; ˈkād-əz, ˈkäd-, ˈkad-; *Sp* ˈkä-(ˌ)t͟hēs\ **1** province SW Spain in Andalusia *area* 2834 *sq mi* (7368 *sq km*), *pop* 992,296 **2** *or anc* **Ga·dir** \ˈgād-ər\ *or* **Ga·des** \ˈgād-(ˌ)ēz\ city & port, its ✱, on Bay of Cádiz NW of Gibraltar *pop* 156,711
Cadiz, Gulf of arm of the Atlantic SW Spain
Cae·li·an \ˈsē-lē-ən\ hill in Rome, Italy, one of seven on which the ancient city was built — see AVENTINE
Caen \käⁿ\ city NW France in Normandy *pop* 116,987
Caerdydd — see CARDIFF
Caer·nar·von *or* **Caer·nar·fon** \kär-ˈnär-vən, kə(r)-\ **1** *or* **Caer·nar·von·shire** \-ˌshi(ə)r, -shər\ former county NW Wales **2** borough NW Wales ✱ of Gwynedd *pop* 9506
Cae·sa·rea \ˌsē-zə-ˈrē-ə; ˌses-ə-, ˌsez-\ **1** ancient seaport Palestine S of Haifa **2** *or* **Caesarea Mazaca** — see KAYSERI
Caesarea Phi·lip·pi \-ˈfil-ə-ˌpī, -fə-ˈlip-ˌī\ ancient city N Palestine SW of Mt. Hermon; site at modern village of Baniyas \ˌban-ē-ˈyas\ in SW Syria
Caesena — see CESENA
Ca·ga·yan \ˌkäg-ə-ˈyän\ *or* **Rio Gran·de de Cagayan** \ˌrē-ō-ˈgrän-dē-ˌdā-\ river 220 *mi* (354 *km*) Philippines in NE Luzon flowing N
Ca·glia·ri \ˈkäl-yə-(ˌ)rē\ commune & port Italy ✱ of Sardinia *pop* 221,427
Ca·guas \ˈkä(g)-ˌwäs\ city E *cen* Puerto Rico *pop* 87,214
Ca·ho·kia \kə-ˈhō-kē-ə\ village SW Ill. S of E. St. Louis *pop* 18,904
Cahokia Mounds group of prehistoric Indian mounds Ill. ENE of E. St. Louis
Ca·hors \kä-ˈ(h)ȯ(ə)r\ city SW France N of Toulouse *pop* 19,288
Caicos — see TURKS AND CAICOS
Cairn·gorm \ˈka(ə)rn-ˌgȯ(ə)rm, ˈke(ə)rn-\ **1** mountain range of the Grampians NE *cen* Scotland; highest point Ben Macdhui 4296 *ft* (1309 *m*) **2** mountain 4084 *ft* (1245 *m*) in Cairngorm mountains on boundary bet. Highlands and Grampian regions
Cai·ro \ˈkī-(ˌ)rō\ city N Egypt, its ✱ *pop* 5,074,016 — **Cai·rene** \kī-ˈrēn\ *adj or n*
Caith·ness \ˈkāth-nəs\ *or* **Caith·ness–shire** \-nəs(h)-ˌshi(ə)r, -shər\ former county N Scotland ✱ Wick
Ca·ja·mar·ca \ˌkä-hə-ˈmär-kə\ city NW Peru *pop* 77,182
Ca·jon \kə-ˈhōn\ pass 4301 *ft* (1303 *m*) S Calif. NW of San Bernardino bet. San Bernardino & San Gabriel mountains
Cal·a·bar \ˈkal-ə-ˌbär\ city & port SE Nigeria *pop* 122,800
Ca·la·bria \kə-ˈlā-brē-ə, -ˈläb-rē-\ **1** district of ancient Italy comprising area forming heel of the Italian peninsula; now the S part of Apulia **2** *or It* **Le Ca·la·brie** \ˌlā-kə-ˈläb-rē-ˌä\ *or anc* **Brut·ti·um** \ˈbrüt-ē-əm, ˈbrət-\ region S Italy occupying toe of the Italian peninsula ✱ Catanzaro *area* 5823 *sq mi* (15,140 *sq km*), *pop* 2,030,505 — **Ca·la·bri·an** \kə-ˈlā-brē-ən, -ˈläb-rē-\ *adj or n*
Ca·lah \ˈkā-lə\ *or* **Kal·hu** \ˈkal-(ˌ)hü\ ancient city ✱ of Assyria on the Tigris 20 *mi* (32 *km*) SE of modern Mosul, Iraq; site now called **Nim·rud** \nim-ˈrüd\
Ca·lais \ka-ˈlā, ˈkal-(ˌ)ā\ city & port N France on Strait of Dover *pop* 73,009
Calais, Pas de — see DOVER (Strait of)
Ca·la·mian \ˌkäl-ə-mē-ˈän\ islands W Philippines NE of Palawan Is.
Cal·ca·sieu \ˈkal-kə-ˌshü\ river 200 *mi* (322 *km*) SW La. flowing through **Calcasieu Lake** (*ab* 15 *mi or* 24 *km* long) & **Calcasieu Pass** (channel 5 *mi or* 8 *km* long) into Gulf of Mexico
Cal·cut·ta \kal-ˈkət-ə\ city & port E India on the Hooghly ✱ of West Bengal *pop* 9,165,650 — **Cal·cut·tan** \-ˈkət-ᵊn\ *n*
Cald·well \ˈkȯl-ˌdwel, -dwəl, ˈkäl-\ city SW Idaho W of Boise *pop* 17,699
Cal·e·don \ˈkal-ə-dən\ town Canada in SE Ont. *pop* 26,645
Cal·e·do·nia \ˌkal-ə-ˈdō-nyə, -nē-ə\ — see SCOTLAND — **Cal·e·do·nian** \-nyən, -nē-ən\ *adj or n*
Caledonian Canal ship canal N Scotland connecting Loch Linnhe & Moray firth & uniting lochs Ness, Oich, Lochy, & Eil
Cal·ga·ry \ˈkal-gə-rē\ city Canada in SW Alta. *pop* 592,743
Ca·li \ˈkäl-ē\ city W Colombia on the Cauca *pop* 820,809
Cal·i·cut \ˈkal-i-kət\ *or* **Ko·zhi·kode** \ˈkō-zhə-ˌkōd\ city & port SW India on Malabar coast in Kerala *pop* 546,060
Cal·i·for·nia \ˌkal-ə-ˈfȯr-nyə\ state SW U.S. ✱ Sacramento *area* 158,693 *sq mi* (412,602 *sq km*), *pop* 23,668,562 — **Cal·i·for·nian** \-nyən\ *adj or n* — **Cal·i·for·nio** \-nyō\ *n*
California, Gulf of arm of the Pacific NW Mexico bet. Baja California & states of Sonora & Sinaloa
Ca·llao \kə-ˈyä-(ˌ)ō, -ˈyau̇\ city & port W Peru on Callao Bay W of Lima *pop* 260,581
Ca·loo·sa·hatch·ee \kə-ˌlü-sə-ˈhach-ē\ river 75 *mi* (121 *km*) S Fla. flowing W into Gulf of Mexico
Calpe — see GIBRALTAR (Rock of)
Cal·ta·nis·set·ta \ˌkäl-tə-ni-ˈset-ə, ˌkal-\ commune Italy in *cen* Sicily *pop* 60,713
Cal·u·met \ˈkal-yə-ˌmet, -mət\ industrial region NW Ind. & NE Ill. SE of & adjacent to Chicago; includes chiefly cities of E. Chicago, Gary, & Hammond, Ind., & Calumet City & Lansing, Ill.
Calumet City city NE Ill. S of Chicago *pop* 39,697
Cal·va·dos Reef \ˌkal-və-ˈdōs\ *or F* **Ro·chers du Calvados** \rō-ˌshād-ə-\ long reef of rocks NW France in English channel at mouth of the Orne
Cal·va·ry \ˈkalv-(ə-)rē\ *or Heb* **Gol·go·tha** \ˈgäl-gə-thə, gäl-ˈgäth-ə\ place outside ancient Jerusalem where Christ was crucified
Cal·y·don \ˈkal-ə-ˌdän, -əd-ᵊn\ ancient city *cen* Greece in S Aetolia near Gulf of Patras — **Cal·y·do·nian** \ˌkal-ə-ˈdō-nyən, -nē-ən\ *adj*
Cam \ˈkam\ river 40 *mi* (64 *km*) E *cen* England in Cambridgeshire flowing into the Ouse
Ca·ma·güey \ˌkam-ə-ˈgwā\ city E *cen* Cuba *pop* 261,831
Ca·margue \kə-ˈmärg\ *or* **La Camargue** \ˌläk-ə-\ marshy island S France in delta of the Rhône
Cam·a·ril·lo \ˌkam-ə-ˈrē-(ˌ)ō\ city SW Calif. W of Los Angeles *pop* 37,732
Cam·bay \kam-ˈbā\ city W India in Gujarat W of Baroda *pop* 51,291
Cambay, Gulf of inlet of Arabian sea in India N of Bombay
Cam·ber·well \ˈkam-bər-ˌwel, -wəl\ **1** city SE Australia in S Victoria E of Melbourne *pop* 85,883 **2** former metropolitan borough S London, England, now part of Southwark
Cam·bo·dia \kam-ˈbōd-ē-ə\ *or* **Kam·pu·chea** \ˌkam-pə-ˈchē-ə\ *or 1970–75* **Khmer Republic** \kə-ˈme(ə)r-\ country SE Asia bordering on Gulf of Siam ✱ Phnom Penh *area* 69,866 *sq mi* (181,652 *sq km*), *pop* 7,492,000

Cam·brai *or formerly* **Cam·bray** \kam-'brā, kä^{n}-\ city N France on the Scheldt *pop* 38,706
Cam·bria \'kam-brē-ə\ — see WALES
Cam·bri·an \'kam-brē-ən\ mountains *cen* Wales
Cam·bridge \'kām-brij\ **1** city E Mass. W of Boston *pop* 95,322 **2** city Canada in SE Ont. *pop* 72,383; includes former cities of Galt & Preston **3** *or ML* **Can·ta·brig·ia** \,kant-ə-'brij-(ē-)ə\ city & borough E England ✱ of Cambridgeshire *pop* 90,440
Cam·bridge·shire \'kām-brij-,shi(ə)r, -shər\ *or* **Cambridge** *or formerly* **Cambridgeshire and Isle of Ely** \'ē-lē\ county E England ✱ Cambridge *area* 1316 *sq mi* (3422 *sq km*), *pop* 540,300
Cam·den \'kam-dən\ **1** city & port SW N.J. on Delaware river opposite Philadelphia, Pa. *pop* 84,910 **2** borough of N Greater London, England *pop* 183,800
Cam·er·oon \,kam-ə-'rün\ **1** *or* **Fa·ko** \'fäk-(,)ō\ massif 13,350 *ft* (4069 *m*) Cameroon (republic) NW of Buea **2** *or* **Cam·er·oun** \-'rün\ country W equatorial Africa in Cameroons region; a republic, formerly a trust territory under France ✱ Yaoundé *area* 183,080 *sq mi* (476,008 *sq km*), *pop* 10,446,000 — **Cam·er·oo·nian** \-'rü-nē-ən, -nyən\ *adj or n*
Cam·er·oons \,kam-ə-'rünz\ region W Africa bordering on NE Gulf of Guinea formerly comprising Brit. & French Cameroons but now divided bet. Nigeria & Cameroon — **Cam·er·oo·nian** \-'rü-nē-ən, -nyən\ *adj or n*
Ca·mi·guin \,kam-ə-'gēn\ **1** island N Philippines N of Luzon; site of Camiguin Volcano 2602 *ft* (793 *m*) **2** island S Philippines off N coast of Mindanao — see HIBOKHIBOK
Ca·mo·tes \kə-'mō-,tās\ sea S *cen* Philippines W of Leyte
Cam·pa·gna di Ro·ma \kam-,pän-yə-dē-'rō-mə, -'pan-\ *or* **Roman Campagna** region *cen* Italy around Rome
Cam·pa·nia \kam-'pā-nyə, -nē-ə\ region S Italy bordering on Tyrrhenian sea ✱ Naples *area* 5214 *sq mi* (13,556 *sq km*), *pop* 5,408,298 — **Cam·pa·nian** \-nyən, -nē-ən\ *adj or n*
Camp·bell \'kam-(b)əl\ city W Calif. SW of San José *pop* 27,067
Cam·pe·che \kam-'pē-chē, käm-'pā-chā\ **1** state SE Mexico in W Yucatán peninsula *area* 19,670 *sq mi* (51,142 *sq km*), *pop* 372,277 **2** city & port, its ✱, on Bay of Campeche *pop* 59,627
Campeche, Bay of the SW section of Gulf of Mexico
Cam·pi·na Gran·de \kam-,pē-nə-'gran-də, -dē\ city E Brazil in E Paraíba *pop* 247,964
Cam·pi·nas \kam-'pē-nəs\ city SE Brazil in E São Paulo state *pop* 664,356
Cam·po·bel·lo \,kam-pə-'bel-(,)ō\ island Canada in SW N.B.
Cam·po·for·mi·do \,kam-(,)pō-'fòr-mə-,dō\ *or formerly* **Cam·po For·mio** \-mē-,ō\ village NE Italy SW of Udine *pop* 6196
Cam·po Gran·de \,käm-(,)pō-'grän-dā\ city SW Brazil ✱ of Mato Grosso do Sul *pop* 291,807
Cam·pos \'kam-pəs\ city SE Brazil in Rio de Janeiro state on the Paraíba *pop* 349,036
Cam Ranh Bay \,kam-,ran-\ inlet of S. China sea SE Vietnam *ab* 180 *mi* (290 *km*) NE of Ho Chi Minh City
Ca·na \'kā-nə\ village in Galilee NE of Nazareth; now in Israel
Ca·naan \'kā-nən\ ancient region corresponding vaguely to later Palestine
Can·a·da \'kan-əd-ə\ country N N. America including Newfoundland & Arctic islands N of mainland; a dominion of the Commonwealth ✱ Ottawa *area* 3,851,809 *sq mi* (10,014,703 *sq km*), *pop* 24,098,473
Ca·na·di·an \kə-'nād-ē-ən\ *or, above its junction with the N. Canadian,* **South Canadian** river 906 *mi* (1458 *km*) S *cen* U.S. flowing E from NE N. Mex. to Arkansas river in E Okla.
Canadian Shield *or* **Lau·ren·tian Shield** \lò-,ren-chən-\ plateau region E Canada & NE U.S. extending from Mackenzie basin E to Davis strait & S to S Que., NE Minn., N Wis., NW Mich., & NE N.Y. including the Adirondacks
Canal Zone *or* **Panama Canal Zone** strip of territory Panama; ceased to exist as a formal political entity Oct. 1, 1979, but remains under U.S. control through 1999 for administration of the Panama canal
Can·an·dai·gua \,kan-ən-'dā-gwə\ lake 15 *mi* (24 *km*) long W *cen* N.Y.; one of the Finger Lakes
Ca·nary \kə-'ner-ē\ islands in the Atlantic off NW Africa belonging to Spain *area* 2807 *sq mi* (7298 *sq km*), *pop* 1,367,646 — see LAS PALMAS, SANTA CRUZ DE TENERIFE — **Ca·nar·i·an** \kə-'ner-ē-ən\ *adj or n*
Ca·nav·er·al \kə-'nav-(ə-)rəl\ **1** peninsula E Fla. enclosing Mosquito lagoon & Indian river (lagoon) **2** *or 1963–1973 officially* **Cape Ken·ne·dy** \-'ken-ə-dē\ cape on E shore of Canaveral peninsula; site of Air Force Missile Test Center & John F. Kennedy Space Center.
Can·ber·ra \'kan-b(ə-)rə, -,ber-ə\ city ✱ of Australia in Australian Capital Territory SW of Sydney *pop* 196,538
Can·cún \,kan-'kün\ resort SE Mexico on island off NE coast of Yucatán peninsula
Can·dia \'kan-dē-ə\ **1** CRETE **2** — see IRÁKLION
Candia, Sea of — see CRETE (Sea of)
Ca·nea \kə-'nē-ə\ *or NGk* **Kha·niá** \kän-'yä\ *or anc* **Cy·do·nia** \sī-'dō-nē-ə, -nyə\ city & port Greece ✱ of Crete *pop* 47,804
Can·nae \'kan-(,)ē\ ancient town SE Italy in Apulia WSW of modern Barletta
Can·na·nore \'kan-ə-,nō(ə)r, -,nò(ə)r\ **1** *or* **Ka·na·nur** \,kən-ə-'nù(ə)r\ city SW India in Kerala NNW of Calicut *pop* 157,777 **2** — see LACCADIVE
Cannes \'kan\ commune & port SE France SW of Nice *pop* 70,226
Ca·no·pus \kə-'nō-pəs\ ancient city N Egypt E of Alexandria at modern Abukir — **Ca·no·pic** \kə-'nō-pik, -'näp-ik\ *adj*
Can·so, Cape \'kan(t)-(,)sō\ cape Canada on NE N.S. mainland
Canso, Strait of narrow channel Canada separating Cape Breton Is. from N.S. mainland
Can·ta·bri·an \kan-'tā-brē-ən\ mountains N & NW Spain running E–W near coast of Bay of Biscay — see CERREDO
Cantabrigia — see CAMBRIDGE
Can·ter·bury \'kant-ə(r)-,ber-ē, -b(ə-)rē\ **1** city SE Australia in E New S. Wales, SW suburb of Sydney **2** city & county borough SE England in Kent *pop* 34,404 — **Can·ter·bu·ri·an** \,kant-ə(r)-'byùr-ē-ən\ *adj*
Can·ti·gny \kä^{n}-,tēn-'yē\ village N France S of Amiens
Can·ton \'kant-^{ə}n\ **1** town E Mass. S of Boston *pop* 18,182 **2** city NE Ohio SSE of Akron *pop* 94,730 **3** \'kan-,tän, kan-'\ *or* **Guang·zhou** *or* **Kuang–chou** \'gwäŋ-'jō\ city & port SE China ✱ of Kwangtung on Chu river *pop* 1,840,000
Canyon de Chel·ly National Monument \də-'shā\ reservation NE Ariz. containing cliff-dweller ruins
Can·yon·lands National Park \'kan-yən-,lan(d)z\ reservation SE Utah surrounding junction of Colorado & Green rivers
Cap d'An·tibes \,kap-dä^{n}-'tēb\ cape SE France SW of Antibes
Cap–de–la–Ma·de·leine \,kap-də-,lä-,mad-^{ə}l-'ān\ city Canada in S Que. on St. Lawrence river ENE of Trois-Rivières *pop* 32,626
Cape Bret·on \kāp-'bret-^{ə}n, kə-'bret-, -'brit-\ **1** island Canada in NE N.S. *area* 3970 *sq mi* (10,322 *sq km*) **2** — see BRETON (Cape)
Cape Breton Highlands National Park reservation Canada in NE N.S. near N end of Cape Breton Is.
Cape Cod Bay the S end of Massachusetts Bay W of Cape Cod
Cape Cor·al \'kòr-əl, 'kär-\ city SW Fla. *pop* 32,103
Cape Fear \'fi(ə)r\ **1** river 202 *mi* (325 *km*) *cen* & SE N.C. flowing SE into the Atlantic **2** — see FEAR (Cape)
Cape Gi·rar·deau \-jə-'rär-(,)dō, -jə-'räd-ə\ city SE Mo. on Mississippi river *pop* 34,361
Cape Kru·sen·stern National Monument \'krü-zən-,stərn\ reservation NW Alaska on Chukchi sea
Cape of Good Hope **1** — see GOOD HOPE (Cape of) **2** *or* **Cape Province** *or* **Kaap·land** \'käp-,länt\ *or formerly* **Cape Colony** province S Republic of S. Africa ✱ Cape Town *area* 278,465 *sq mi* (724,009 *sq km*), *pop* 6,199,634
Ca·per·na·um \kə-'pər-nē-əm\ city of ancient Palestine on NW shore of Sea of Galilee
Cape Sa·ble \'sā-bəl\ **1** island 7 *mi* (11 *km*) long Canada off S coast of N.S. **2** — see SABLE (Cape)
Cape Town \'kāp-,taùn\ city & port, legislative ✱ of Republic of S. Africa & ✱ of Cape of Good Hope, on Table Bay *pop* 790,880 — **Cape·to·ni·an** \kāp-'tō-nē-ən\ *n*
Cape Verde \-'vərd\ **1** islands in the Atlantic off W Africa: a republic; until 1975 belonged to Portugal ✱ Praia *area* 1557 *sq mi* (4048 *sq km*), *pop* 303,000 **2** — see VERDE (Cape) — **Cape Verd·ean** \-'vərd-ē-ən\ *n*
Cape York Peninsula \'yō(ə)rk\ peninsula NE Australia in N Queensland having at its N tip **Cape York** (on Torres strait)
Cap Hai·tien \kap-'hā-shən\ *or F* **Cap–Ha·ï·tien** \kà-pà-ē-syã^{n}, -ē-tyã^{n}\ city & port N Haiti *pop* 74,761
Cap·i·to·line \'kap-ət-^{ə}l-,īn, *Brit often* kə-'pit-^{ə}l-\ hill in Rome, Italy, one of seven on which the ancient city was built — see AVENTINE
Capitol Reef National Park reservation S *cen* Utah containing archaeological remains, petrified forests, & unusual erosion forms
Capodistria — see KOPER
Caporetto — see KOBARID
Cap·pa·do·cia \,kap-ə-'dō-sh(ē-)ə\ ancient district E Asia Minor chiefly in valley of the upper Kizil Irmak in modern Turkey ✱ Caesarea Mazaca — **Cap·pa·do·cian** \-sh(ē-)ən\ *adj or n*
Ca·pri \ka-'prē, kə-; 'käp-(,)rē, 'kap-\ *or anc* **Cap·re·ae** \'kap-rē-,ē\ island Italy S Bay of Naples *area* 5 *sq mi* (13 *sq km*) — **Ca·pri·ote** \'kap-rē-,ōt, 'käp-, -rē-ət\ *n*
Capsa — see GAFSA
Cap·ua \'kap-yə-wə\ commune S Italy on the Volturno N of Naples NW of site of ancient city of Capua *pop* 18,053
Cap·u·lin, Mount \'kap-(y)ə-lən\ cinder cone 8215 *ft* (2504 *m*) NE N. Mex.; main feature of **Capulin Mountain National Monument**
Ca·ra·cas \kə-'rak-əs, -'räk-\ city ✱ of Venezuela near Caribbean coast *metropolitan area pop* 2,299,700
Car·bon·dale \'kär-bən-,dāl\ city SW Ill. *pop* 26,287
Car·cas·sonne \,kär-kə-'sòn, -'sōn\ city S France *pop* 38,887
Car·che·mish \'kär-kə-,mish, kär-'kē-mish\ ruined city S Turkey on the Euphrates at Syrian border N of modern Jerablus, Syria
Cár·de·nas \'kärd-^{ə}n-,äs\ city & port N Cuba E of Matanzas *pop* 73,521
Car·diff \'kärd-əf\ *or W* **Caer·dydd** \kī(ə)r-'dēth\ borough & port ✱ of Wales & of S. Glamorgan *pop* 260,574
Car·di·gan \'kärd-i-gən\ *or* **Car·di·gan·shire** \-,shi(ə)r, -shər\ former county W Wales ✱ Aberystwyth
Cardigan Bay inlet of St. George's channel on W coast of Wales
Ca·ren·tan \,kar-ən-'tä^{n}\ town NW France at base of Cotentin peninsula
Car·ia \'kar-ē-ə, 'ker-\ ancient region SW Asia Minor bordering on Aegean sea ✱ Halicarnassus — **Car·i·an** \-ē-ən\ *adj or n*
Ca·rib·be·an \,kar-ə-'bē-ən, kə-'rib-ē-\ sea arm of the Atlantic bounded on N & E by W. Indies, on S by S. America, & on W by Cen. America
Car·ib·bees \'kar-ə-,bēz\ LESSER ANTILLES
Car·i·boo \'kar-ə-,bü\ mountains W Canada in E *cen* B.C. W of the Rocky mountains; highest point *ab* 11,750 *ft* (3581 *m*)
Ca·rin·thia \kə-'rin(t)-thē-ə\ region *cen* Europe in E Alps; once a duchy, Austrian crown land 1849–1918, divided between Austria & Yugoslavia 1918 — **Ca·rin·thi·an** \-thē-ən\ *adj or n*
Car·lisle \kär-'lī(ə)l, kər-, 'kär-,\ **1** borough S *cen* Pa. *pop* 18,314 **2** city & borough NW England ✱ of Cumbria *pop* 70,930
Car·low \'kär-,lō\ **1** county SE Ireland in Leinster *area* 346 *sq mi* (900 *sq km*), *pop* 39,820 **2** urban district, its ✱ *pop* 11,722
Carls·bad \'kär(-ə)lz-,bad\ **1** caverns SE N. Mex. in **Carlsbad Caverns National Park** **2** city SW Calif. NNW of San Diego *pop* 35,490 **3** city SE N. Mex. on the Pecos *pop* 25,496
Carmana, Carmania — see KERMAN
Car·mar·then \kär-'mär-thən, kə(r)-\ **1** *or* **Car·mar·then·shire** \-,shi(ə)r, -shər\ former county S Wales ✱ Carmarthen **2** borough & port S Wales ✱ of Dyfed *pop* 12,302
Car·mel \'kär-məl\ city *cen* Ind. N of Indianapolis *pop* 18,272
Car·mel, Mount \'kär-məl\ mountain ridge NW Israel; highest point 1791 *ft* (546 *m*)
Car·men de Pat·a·go·nes \'kär-mən-dā-,pat-ə-'gō-nəs\ town Argentina on the Negro river opposite Viedma *pop* 13,981
Car·nat·ic \kär-'nat-ik\ region SE India between Eastern Ghats & Coromandel coast now in Andhra Pradesh & Karnataka
Car·nic Alps \,kär-nik-\ mountain range E Alps between Austria & Italy
Car·nio·la \,kär-nē-'ō-lə, kärn-'yō-\ region NW Yugoslavia NE of Istrian peninsula — **Car·nio·lan** \-lən\ *adj*
Car·o·li·na \,kar-ə-'lī-nə\ English colony 1663–1729 on E coast of N. America divided 1729 into N.C. & S.C. (the **Car·o·li·nas** \-nəz\)

Ca·ro·li·na \,kär-ə-'lē-nə\ city NE cen Puerto Rico pop 147,835
Car·o·line \'kar-ə-,līn, -lən\ islands S Trust Territory of the Pacific Islands comprising Belau & the Federated States of Micronesia
Ca·ro·ní \,kär-ə-'nē\ river 373 mi (600 km) E Venezuela flowing N into the Orinoco
Car·pa·thi·an \kär-'pā-thē-ən\ mountain system E cen Europe along boundary between Czechoslovakia & Poland & in N & cen Romania — see GERLACHOVKA, TATRA, TRANSYLVANIAN ALPS
Carpathian Ruthenia — see RUTHENIA
Car·pen·tar·ia, Gulf of \,kär-pən-'ter-ē-ə, -'tar-\ inlet of Arafura sea on N coast of Australia
Car·pen·ters·ville \'kär-pən-tərz-,vil\ village NE Ill. NW of Chicago pop 23,272
Car·qui·nez \kär-'kē-nəs\ strait 8 mi (13 km) long Calif. joining San Pablo & Suisun bays
Car·ran·tuo·hill \,kar-ən-'tü-əl\ mountain 3414 ft (1041 m) SW Ireland in County Kerry; highest in Macgillicuddy's Reeks & in Ireland
Car·ra·ra \kə-'rär-ə\ commune N Italy ESE of La Spezia pop 68,460
Car·rhae \'kar-(,)ē\ ancient city N Mesopotamia SSE of modern Urfa
Car·rick·fer·gus \,kar-ik-'fər-gəs\ district E Northern Ireland, established 1974 area 34 sq mi (88 sq km), pop 28,458
Car·rick on Shan·non \,kar-i-,kòn-'shan-ən, -,kän-\ town N cen Ireland ✳ of County Leitrim
Car·roll·ton \'kar-əl-tən, -əlt-ᵊn\ city N Tex. pop 40,595
Car·shal·ton \kär-'shòlt-ᵊn, kər-\ former urban district S England in Surrey, now part of Sutton
Carso — see KRAS
Car·son \'kärs-ᵊn\ 1 river 125 mi (201 km) W Nev. flowing NE into Carson Lake 2 city SW Calif. SE of Los Angeles pop 81,221
Carson City city ✳ of Nev. E of Lake Tahoe pop 32,022
Carson Sink intermittent lake W Nev. S of Humboldt Lake
Car·stensz, Mount — see DJAJA (Mount)
Car·ta·ge·na \,kärt-ə-'gā-nə, -'hä-\ 1 city & port NW Colombia pop 292,512 2 city & port SE Spain on the Mediterranean pop 167,936
Car·ta·go \kär-'täg-(,)ō\ city cen Costa Rica pop 21,753
Car·ter·et \,kärt-ə-'ret\ borough NE N.J. S of Elizabeth pop 20,598
Car·thage \'kär-thij\ or anc Car·tha·go \kär-'täg-(,)ō\ ancient city & state N Africa on coast NE of modern Tunis — Car·tha·gin·ian \,kär-thə-'jin-yən, -'jin-ē-ən\ adj or n
Cary \'ka(ə)r-ē, 'ke(ə)r-ē\ city E cen N.C. pop 21,763
Ca·sa·blan·ca \,kas-ə-'blaŋ-kə, ,kaz-\ or Ar Dar el Bei·da \,där-,el-bā-'dä\ city & port W Morocco on the Atlantic pop 2,139,204
Casa Gran·de Ruins National Monument \,kas-ə-'gran-dē\ reservation S Ariz. SE of Phoenix; prehistoric ruins
Cas·cade \(')kas-'kād\ mountain range W U.S., N continuation of the Sierra Nevada extending N from Lassen Peak, N Calif., across Oreg. & Wash. — see RAINIER (Mount), COAST
Cas·co Bay \'kas-(,)kō\ inlet of the Atlantic S Maine
Ca·ser·ta \kə-'zert-ə, -'zərt-\ commune S Italy pop 66,754
Cash·el \'kash-əl\ urban district S Ireland in cen Tipperary at base of Rock of Cashel (hill with ruins of cathedral & castle)
Cashmere — see KASHMIR
Ca·si·qui·a·re \,käs-i-'kyär-ē\ river 125 mi (201 km) S Venezuela connecting the upper course of Negro river with Orinoco river
Cas·per \'kas-pər\ city cen Wyo. on N. Platte river pop 51,016
Cas·pi·an \'kas-pē-ən\ sea (salt lake) bet. Europe & Asia; ab 85 ft (30 m) below sea level area 169,381 sq mi (440,391 sq km)
Caspian Gates pass on W shore of Caspian sea near Derbent
Cas·si·no \kə-'sē-(,)nō\ commune cen Italy ESE of Frosinone; site of Monte Cassino monastery pop 31,139
Cas·tel Gan·dol·fo \(,)käs-,tel-gän-'dòl-(,)fō\ commune cen Italy on Lake Albano SE of Rome pop 6239
Cas·tel·lón or Castellón de la Pla·na \,kas-tə(l)-'yòn-,del-ə-'plän-ə\ 1 province E Spain area 2495 sq mi (6487 sq km), pop 430,171 2 city & port, its ✳, on the Mediterranean pop 124,487
Castellorizo or Castelrosso — see KASTELLORIZON
Cas·tile \kas-'tēl\ or Sp Cas·ti·lla \kä-'stē-l'yä, -'stē-yä\ region & ancient kingdom cen & N Spain divided by the Sierra de Guadarrama into regions & old provinces of Old Castile or Sp Castilla la Vieja \-'vyä-hä\ (to the N, ✳ Burgos) & New Castile or Sp Castilla la Nue·va \-län-'wä-vä\ (to the S, ✳ Toledo)
Cas·til·lo de San Mar·cos National Monument \kas-'tē-(y)ōd-ə-san-'mär-(,)kōs\ historic site NE Fla.; contains a Spanish fort
Cas·tle·bar \,kas-əl-'bär\ urban district NW Ireland ✳ of Mayo
Castle Clin·ton National Monument \'klint-ᵊn\ historic site Manhattan Is. SE N.Y.; contains a fort
Cast·le·reagh \'kas-əl-(,)rā\ district E Northern Ireland, established 1974 area 33 sq mi (86 sq km), pop 60,757
Castres \'kästrᵉ\ city S France E of Toulouse pop 41,037
Cas·tries \'kas-,trēz, -,trēs\ city & port ✳ of St. Lucia pop 4254
Ca·strop–Rauxel or Ka·strop–Rauxel \,käs-,tròp-'raúk-səl\ city W W. Germany SSW of Münster pop 78,877
Ca·tal·ca \chät-ᵊl-'jä\ city Turkey in Europe W of Istanbul
Cat·a·li·na \,kat-ᵊl-'ē-nə\ or San·ta Catalina \,sant-ə-\ island SW Calif. in Channel islands area 70 sq mi (182 sq km)
Cat·a·lo·nia \,kat-ᵊl-'ō-nyə, -nē-ə\ or Sp Ca·ta·lu·ña \,kät-ᵊl-'ü-nyə\ autonomous region NE Spain bordering on France & the Mediterranean; chief city Barcelona area 12,431 sq mi (32,321 sq km) — Cat·a·lo·nian \-'ō-nyən, -nē-ən\ adj or n
Ca·ta·marc·a \,kät-ə-'märk-ə\ city NW Argentina pop 64,410
Ca·ta·nia \kə-'tän-yə, -'tän-\ or anc Cat·a·na \'kat-ə-nə\ commune Italy in E Sicily on E coast on Gulf of Catania pop 378,521
Ca·ta·ño \kə-'tän-(,)yō\ town NE cen Puerto Rico pop 26,243
Ca·tan·za·ro \,kä,-tän-'(d)zär-(,)ō\ city S Italy ✳ of Calabria pop 100,637
Ca·taw·ba \kə-'tò-bə\ river 250 mi (402 km) flowing S from W N.C. into S.C. — see WATEREE
Ca·thay \ka-'thā\ CHINA — an old name
Catherine, Mount — see KATHERINA (Gebel)
Ca·toc·tin Mountain \kə-'täk-tən\ mountain ridge NW Md. & N Va. in Blue Ridge mountains
Cats·kill \'kat-,skil\ mountains SE N.Y. in the Appalachian system W of Hudson river — see SLIDE MOUNTAIN
Cattaro — see KOTOR

Cau·ca \'kaú-kə\ river 600 mi (966 km) W Colombia flowing N into the Magdalena
Cau·ca·sus \'kó-kə-səs\ 1 mountain system U.S.S.R. — see ELBRUS 2 or Cau·ca·sia \kó-'kā-zhə, -shə\ region U.S.S.R. bet. the Black & Caspian seas; divided by Caucasus mountains into Cis·cau·ca·sia \,sis-\ (to the N) & Trans·cau·ca·sia \,tran(t)s-\ (to the S)
Caucasus Indicus — see HINDU KUSH
Cau·dine Forks \'kó-,dēn-, -,dēn-\ two mountain passes S Italy in the Apennines bet. Benevento & Capua
Caul·field \'kòl-,fēld\ city SE Australia in S Victoria SE of Melbourne; part of Greater Melbourne pop 69,922
Causses \'kōs\ limestone region S cen France on S border of Massif Central
Cau·ve·ry \'kò-və-rē\ or Ka·ve·ri \'käv-ə-rē\ river 475 mi (764 km) S India flowing E & entering Bay of Bengal in a wide delta
Cauvery Falls waterfall 300 ft (91 m) India in the Cauvery on Karnataka-Tamil Nadu boundary
Cav·an \'kav-ən\ 1 county NE Ireland (republic) in Ulster area 730 sq mi (1898 sq km), pop 53,855 2 urban district, its ✳ pop 3240
Ca·vi·te \kə-'vēt-ē\ city Philippines in Luzon on Cavite peninsula in Manila Bay SW of Manila pop 87,666
Ca·xi·as \kə-'shē-əs\ 1 town NE Brazil in Maranhão WNW of Teresina pop 125,771 2 — see DUQUE DE CAXIAS 3 or Caxias do Sul \-də-'sül\ city S Brazil in Rio Grande do Sul pop 220,725
Cay·enne \kī-'en, kā-\ city & port ✳ of French Guiana on island in Cayenne river near the coast pop 38,135
Cayes or Aux Cayes \'kā\ city & port SW Haiti pop 105,383
Ca·yey \kä-'yä\ city SE cen Puerto Rico pop 23,305
Cay·man \'kā-,man, attributively 'kä-mən\ islands W. Indies NW of Jamaica; a Brit. colony ✳ George Town (on Grand Cayman, chief island) area 93 sq mi (242 sq km), pop 16,677 — Cay·man·i·an \kā-'man-ē-ən\ adj or n
Ca·yu·ga \kē-'ü-gə, 'kyü-, kā-'(y)ü-\ lake 40 mi (64 km) long W cen N.Y.; one of the Finger Lakes
Ce·a·rá \,sā-ə-'rä\ state NE Brazil bordering on the Atlantic ✳ Fortaleza area 57,371 sq mi (149,165 sq km), pop 5,380,432
Ce·bu \sā-'bü\ 1 island E cen Philippines, one of the Visayans area 1707 sq mi (4438 sq km) pop 2,091,602 2 city on E Cebu Is. pop 490,281
Cechy — see BOHEMIA
Ce·dar \'sēd-ər\ river 329 mi (529 km) SE Minn. & E Iowa flowing SE into the Iowa
Cedar Breaks National Monument reservation SW Utah NE of Zion National Park containing unusual erosion forms
Cedar Falls city NE Iowa NW of Waterloo pop 36,322
Cedar Rapids city E Iowa on the Cedar pop 110,243
Ce·le·bes \'sel-ə-,bēz, sə-'lē-bēz\ 1 or Su·la·we·si \,sü-lə-'wä-sē\ island Indonesia E of Borneo ✳ Makassar area 69,255 sq mi (180,063 sq km), pop 8,925,000 2 sea arm of W Pacific enclosed on N by Mindanao & Sulu archipelago, on S by Celebes, & on W by Borneo — Cel·e·be·sian \,sel-ə-'bē-zhən\ adj
Celestial Empire the former Chinese Empire
Cel·le \'(t)sel-ə\ city NE W. Germany NE of Hannover pop 72,820
Celt·ic \'kel-tik, 'sel-\ sea inlet of the Atlantic British Isles SE of Ireland, SW of Wales, & W of Cornwall
Ce·nis, Mont \,mōⁿ-sə-'nē\ 1 mountain pass 6831 ft (2082 m) bet. France & Italy over Mont Cenis massif (11,792 ft or 3573 m) in Graian Alps 2 or Fré·jus \frā-'zhüs, -'zhūs\ tunnel 8.5 mi (13.6 km) long piercing the Fréjus massif SW of Mont Cenis
Cen·ter·ville \'sent-ər-,vil, -vəl\ city SW Ohio pop 18,886
Central region cen Scotland, established 1975 ✳ Stirling area 972 sq mi (2527 sq km), pop 373,078
Central African Republic or 1976-79 Central African Empire or earlier Ubangi–Shari republic N cen Africa ✳ Bangui area 240,376 sq mi (624,978 sq km), pop 2,740,000
Central America 1 the narrow S portion of N. America connecting with S. America & extending from the Isthmus of Tehuantepec to the Isthmus of Panama 2 the republics of Guatemala, El Salvador, Honduras, Nicaragua, & Costa Rica & often also Panama & Belize
Central Falls city N R.I. N of Providence pop 16,995
Central India former group of 89 Indian states N cen India ✳ Indore; area now chiefly in W & N Madhya Pradesh
Central Karroo — see KARROO
Central Provinces and Be·rar \bā-'rär, bə-\ former province of India reorganized 1950 & renamed Madhya Pradesh
Central Valley valley cen Calif. comprising the valleys of the Sacramento & San Joaquin rivers
Ceos — see KEOS
Ceph·a·lo·nia \,sef-ə-'lō-nyə, -nē-ə\ or NGk Ke·fal·li·nía \,kef-ə-lə-'nē-ə\ island W Greece in the Ionians area 277 sq mi (720 sq km)
Ce·ram or Se·ram \'sā-,räm\ island E Indonesia in cen Moluccas area 6621 sq mi (17,215 sq km), pop 96,797
Cerigo — see KITHIRA
Cernauti — see CHERNOVTSY
Cer·re·do \sə-'räd-(,)ō\ or Tor·re de Cerredo \'tòr-ē-də-\ mountain 8787 ft (2678 m) N Spain SW of Santander; highest in the Cantabrians
Cer·ri·tos \sə-'rēt-əs\ city SW Calif. NE of Long Beach pop 53,020
Cerro Bolívar — see BOLÍVAR (Cerro)
Cer·ro de Pas·co \,ser-ō-də-'pas-(,)kō\ 1 mountain 15,100 ft (4602 m) cen Peru NE of Lima 2 city near the mountain pop 71,558
Cerro de Pun·ta \-'pünt-ə\ mountain 4390 ft (1338 m), cen Puerto Rico in Cordillera Central; highest on the island
Cer·ro Gor·do \,ser-ə-'górd-(,)ō\ mountain pass E Mexico bet. Veracruz & Jalapa
Cervin, Mont — see MATTERHORN
Ce·se·na \chə-'zā-nə\ or anc Cae·se·na \sə-'zē-nə\ commune N Italy in Emilia-Romagna SE of Forlì pop 89,640

\ə\ abut \ᵊ\ kitten, F table \ər\ further \a\ ash \ā\ ace \ä\ cot, cart
\aú\ out \ch\ chin \e\ bet \ē\ easy \g\ go \i\ hit \ī\ ice \j\ job
\ŋ\ sing \ō\ go \ò\ law \òi\ boy \th\ thin \ṯh\ the \ü\ loot \ú\ foot
\y\ yet \zh\ vision \à, ḵ, ⁿ, œ, œ̄, ᵫ, ᵾ, ᵊ\ see Guide to Pronunciation

Čes·ke Bu·de·jo·vi·ce \'ches-kə-'büd-ə-,yō-vət-sə\ *or G* **Bud·weis** \'büt-,vīs\ city W Czechoslovakia in S Bohemia *pop* 90,415
Ce·ti·nje \'(t)set-^{ə}n-,yä\ town S Yugoslavia SE of Kotor near coast; formerly ✱ of Montenegro *pop* 12,089
Cette — see SÈTE
Ceu·ta \'sä-,üt-ə, 'seü-(,)tä\ city & port N Morocco opposite Gibraltar; a Spanish presidio *pop* 67,187
Cé·vennes \sä-'ven\ mountain range S France W of the Rhône at E edge of Massif Central — see MÉZENC
Cey·lon \si-'län, sā-\ *or* **Lan·ka** \'laŋ-kə\ **1** *or Ar* **Ser·en·dib** \'ser-ən-,dib, -,dip\ *or L & Gk* **Ta·prob·a·ne** \tə-'präb-ə-(,)nē\ island 270 *mi* (434 *km*) long & 140 *mi* (225 *km*) wide in Indian ocean off S India **2** — see SRI LANKA — **Cey·lon·ese** \,sä-lə-'nēz, ,sē-lə-, ,sel-ə-, -'nēs\ *adj or n*
Cha·co \'chäk-(,)ō\ *or* **Gran Chaco** \(')grän-\ region S *cen* S. America drained by the Paraguay & its chief W tributaries the Pilcomayo & Bermejo; divided bet. Argentina, Bolivia, & Paraguay
Chad *or F* **Tchad** \'chad\ country N *cen* Africa ✱ N'Djamena; a republic; until 1959 a territory of French Equatorial Africa *area* 495,752 *sq mi* (1,288,955 *sq km*), *pop* 4,681,000 — **Chad·ian** \'chad-ē-ən\ *adj or n*
Chad, Lake shallow lake N *cen* Africa at junction of boundaries of Chad, Niger, & Nigeria
Chae·ro·nea \,ker-ə-'nē-ə, ,kir-\ *or* **Chae·ro·neia** \-'nī-ə\ ancient city E *cen* Greece in W Boeotia SE of Mt. Parnassus
Cha·gos \'chä-gəs\ archipelago *cen* Indian ocean S of Maldives; comprises Brit. Indian Ocean Territory — see DIEGO GARCIA
Cha·gres \'chäg-rəs, 'chag-\ river Panama flowing through Gatun Lake to the Caribbean
Cha·gua·ra·mas \,chäg-wə-'räm-əs\ district NW Trinidad W of Port of Spain on **Chaguaramas Bay** (inlet of Gulf of Paria)
Cha·har \'chä-'här\ former province NE China in E Inner Mongolia ✱ Kalgan
Chalcedon — see KADIKOY
Chal·cid·i·ce \kal-'sid-ə-(,)sē\ *or NGk* **Khal·ki·di·kí** \,käl-kə-thi-'kē\ peninsula NE Greece in E Macedonia projecting SE into N Aegean sea; terminates in three peninsulas: Kassandra (ancient Pallene), Sithonia, & Acte — see ACTE
Chalcis — see KHALKÍS — **Chal·cid·i·an** \kal-'sid-ē-ən\ *adj or n*
Chal·dea *or* **Chal·daea** \kal-'dē-ə\ ancient region SW Asia on Euphrates river & Persian gulf
Cha·leur Bay \shə-'lü(ə)r, -'lər\ inlet of Gulf of St. Lawrence SE Canada bet. N N.B. & Gaspé peninsula, Que.
Cha·lon \shä-'lōn\ *or* **Chalon–sur–Saône** \-,sü(ə)r-'sōn\ city E *cen* France N of Mâcon *pop* 55,495
Châ·lons \shä-'lōn\ *or* **Châlons–sur–Marne** \-,sü(ə)r-'märn\ commune NE France on the Marne *pop* 50,870
Cham·bal \'chəm-bəl\ river 650 *mi* (1046 *km*) *cen* India flowing from Vindhya mountains E into the Jumna
Cham·bé·ry \shä^{n}-bā-rē\ city E France E of Lyons *pop* 52,286
Cham·bord \shä^{n}-'bō(ə)r\ village N *cen* France NE of Blois *pop* 166
Cha·mi·zal \,sham-ə-'zäl, ,chäm-i-'säl\ tract of land 630 *acres* (252 *hectares*) on N bank of the Rio Grande formerly in El Paso, Tex.; ceded to Mexico 1963 — see CORDOVA ISLAND
Cha·mo·nix \,sham-ə-'nē\ **1** valley SE France NW of Mont Blanc **2** *or* **Chamonix–Mont–Blanc** \-'mōn-'blän\ town SE France in Chamonix valley *pop* 5907
Cham·pagne \sham-'pān\ region & former province NE France W of Lorraine & N of Burgundy ✱ Troyes
Cham·paign \sham-'pān\ city E *cen* Ill. *pop* 58,133
Cham·pi·gny–sur–Marne \,shä^{n}-(,)pēn-'yē-,sü(ə)r-'märn\ commune N France, SSE suburb of Paris *pop* 80,189
Cham·plain, Lake \sham-'plān\ lake 125 *mi* (201 *km*) long bet. N.Y. & Vt. extending N into Que. *area* 600 *sq mi* (1560 *sq km*)
Chan–chiang *or* **Zhan·jiang** \'jän-jē-'äŋ\ *or formerly* **Fort Bay·ard** \'bā-ərd, 'bī-\ city SE China in SW Kwangtung *pop* 170,000
Chan·der·na·gore \,chən-dər-nə-'gō(ə)r, -'gȯ(ə)r\ *or* **Chan·dan·na·gar** \,chən-də-'nəg-ər\ *or* **Chan·dar·na·gar** \-dər-'nəg-\ city E India in W. Bengal N of Calcutta; before 1950 part of French India *pop* 421,256
Chan·di·garh \'chən-dē-gər\ city N India N of Delhi; a union territory administered by the national government; ✱ of Punjabi Suba & of Haryana; founded 1953, *pop* 450,061
Chan·dler \'chan-(d)lər\ city SW *cen* Ariz. *pop* 29,673
Chan·dra·pur \,chən-drə-'pü(ə)r\ *or formerly* **Chan·da** \,chən-də\ town *cen* India in E Maharashtra *pop* 115,352; ✱ of anc. Gond dynasty
Changan — see SIAN
Ch'ang–chia–k'ou — see KALGAN
Chang–chou *or* **Zhang·zhou** \'jäŋ-'jō\ *or* **Chang·chow** *same or* 'chaŋ-'chaü\ *or formerly* **Lung·ki** \'lüŋ-kē\ city SE China in S Fukien
Ch'ang–chou *or* **Chang·zhou** \'chäŋ-'jō\ *or* **Chang·chow** *same or* 'chaŋ-'chaü\ *or formerly* **Wu·tsin** \'wüd-'zin\ city E China in S Kiangsu *pop* 300,000
Chang·chun \'chäŋ-'chün\ city NE China ✱ of Kirin *pop* 975,000
Chang·hua \'chäŋ-'(h)wä\ city China in W Taiwan *pop* 58,227
Chang·sha \'chäŋ-'shä\ city SE *cen* China ✱ of Hunan on the Hsiang *pop* 975,000
Chang·shu \'chäŋ-'shü\ city E China in S Kiangsu *pop* 101,000
Chang·teh *or* **Chang·de** \'chäŋ-'də\ city SE *cen* China in N Hunan on the Yuan *pop* 120,000
Chang·tu *or* **Zhang·du** \'jäŋ-'dü\ town SW China in E Tibet on the Mekong
Channel **1** *or* **Santa Barbara** islands Calif. in the Pacific off SW coast — see CATALINA, SAN CLEMENTE, SANTA CRUZ, SANTA ROSA **2** islands in English channel; a possession of Brit. Crown *area* 75 *sq mi* (195 *sq km*), *pop* 129,000 — see ALDERNEY, GUERNSEY, JERSEY, SARK
Channel Islands National Park reserve SW Calif. in Channel islands including areas on Anacapa islands (E of Santa Cruz Is.) & Santa Barbara Is. (W of Santa Catalina Is.)
Chan·til·ly \shä^{n}-tē-yē, shan-'til-ē\ town N France NNE of Paris
Ch'ao–an \'chaü-'än\ *or* **Zhao·'an** \'jaü-'än\ *or* **Chao·chow** \'chaü-'jō\ city E China in NE Kwangtung on Han river *pop* 101,000
Chao Phra·ya \chaü-'prī-ə\ *or* **Me Nam** \mā-'näm\ river 160 *mi* (257 *km*) W *cen* Thailand formed by confluence of Nan & Ping rivers & flowing S into Gulf of Siam
Cha·pa·la \chə-'päl-ə\ lake 50 *mi* (80 *km*) long W *cen* Mexico in Jalisco & Michoacán SE of Guadalajara
Chapel Hill town N N.C. SW of Durham *pop* 32,421
Cha·rente \shə-'ränt\ river 225 *mi* (362 *km*) W France flowing W into Bay of Biscay
Cha·ri *or* **Sha·ri** \'shär-ē\ river 1400 *mi* (2253 *km*) N *cen* Africa in Chad flowing NW into Lake Chad
Char·i·ton \'shar-ət-^{ə}n\ river 280 *mi* (451 *km*) S Iowa & N Mo. flowing S into the Missouri
Charle·roi \'shär-lə-,rȯi, -lər-,wä\ city SW Belgium in Hainaut *pop* 222,343
Charles \'chär(ə)lz\ river 47 *mi* (76 *km*) Mass. flowing into Boston harbor
Charles, Cape cape E Va. N of entrance to Chesapeake Bay
Charles·bourg \shärl-'bü(ə)r, 'chärlz-,bərg\ city Canada in SE Que. NE of Quebec city *pop* 68,326
Charles·ton \'chärl-stən\ **1** city E *cen* Ill. *pop* 19,355 **2** city & port SE S.C. *pop* 69,510 **3** city ✱ of W. Va. on the Kanawha *pop* 63,968 — **Charles·to·nian** \chärl-'stō-nē-ən, -nyən\ *n*
Charleston Peak mountain 11,919 *ft* (3633 *m*) SE Nev. WNW of Las Vegas
Charles·town \'chärl-,staün\ section of Boston, Mass., on Boston harbor between mouths of Charles & Mystic rivers
Char·lotte \'shär-lət\ city S N.C. near S.C. border *pop* 314,447
Charlotte Ama·lie \ə-'mäl-yə\ *or formerly* **Saint Thomas** city & port ✱ of Virgin Islands of the U.S., on St. Thomas Is. *pop* 11,671
Charlotte Harbor inlet of Gulf of Mexico SW Fla.
Char·lottes·ville \'shär-ləts-,vil, -vəl\ city *cen* Va. *pop* 39,916
Char·lotte·town \'shär-lət-,taün\ city & port Canada ✱ of P.E.I. on Northumberland Strait *pop* 15,282
Chartres \'shärt, 'shärtr^{ə}\ city N *cen* France SW of Paris *pop* 38,574
Châ·teau·guay \'shat-ə-,gā\ town Canada in S Que. SW of Montreal *pop* 36,928
Châ·teau·roux \shä-tō-rü\ commune *cen* France S of Orléans *pop* 53,166
Châ·teau–Thier·ry \,sha-,tō-,tye-'rē, ,shä-\ town N France on the Marne SW of Reims *pop* 13,379
Chat·ham \'chat-əm\ **1** — see SAN CRISTÓBAL **2** islands S Pacific belonging to New Zealand & comprising two islands (Chatham & Pitt) *area* 372 *sq mi* (967 *sq km*) **3** strait SE Alaska bet. Admiralty Is. & Kuiu Is. on E & Baranof Is. & Chichagof Is. on W **4** city Canada in SE Ont. E of Lake St. Clair *pop* 40,952 **5** borough SE England in Kent *pop* 61,909
Chat·ta·hoo·chee \,chat-ə-'hü-chē\ river 410 *mi* (660 *km*) SE U.S. rising in N Ga., flowing SW & S along Ala.-Ga. boundary into Lake Seminole
Chat·ta·noo·ga \,chat-ə-'nü-gə, ,chat-^{ə}n-'ü-\ city SE Tenn. on Tennessee river *pop* 169,565
Chau·tau·qua \shə-'tȯ-kwə\ lake 18 *mi* (29 *km*) long SW N.Y.
Che·bok·sa·ry \,cheb-,äk-'sär-ē\ city U.S.S.R. in Soviet Russia, Europe ✱ of Chuvash Republic WNW of Kazan *pop* 308,000
Che·cheno–In·gush Republic \chə-,chen-ō-in-'güsh\ autonomous republic of the U.S.S.R. in SE Soviet Russia, Europe, on N slopes of Caucasus mountains *area* 6064 *sq mi* (15,766 *sq km*), *pop* 1,065,000
Che·du·ba \chə-'dü-bə\ island W Burma *area* 220 *sq mi* (572 *sq km*), *pop* 2635
Che·foo \'jə-'fü\ *or* **Yan·tai** \'yän-'tī\ *or* **Yen–t'ai** \'yən-'tī\ city & port E China in NE Shantung on Shantung peninsula on Po Hai *pop* 140,000
Che·ju \'chē-jü\ *or* **Quel·part** \'kwel-,pärt\ **1** island S. Korea in N E. China sea *area* 710 *sq mi* (1846 *sq km*) **2** city & port on N coast of the island *pop* 167,546
Che·kiang *or* **Zhe·jiang** \'jəj-ē-'äŋ\ province E China bordering on E. China sea ✱ Hangchow *area* 39,305 *sq mi* (102,193 *sq km*), *pop* 38,884,603
Che·lan \shə-'lan\ lake *ab* 55 *mi* (88 *km*) long N *cen* Wash.
Chelms·ford **1** \'chem-sfərd *also* 'chelm-\ town NE Mass. S of Lowell *pop* 31,174 **2** \'chelm-, 'chem-\ borough SE England ✱ of Essex *pop* 58,159
Chel·sea \'chel-sē\ **1** city E Mass. NE of Boston *pop* 25,431 **2** former metropolitan borough SW London, England, on N bank of Thames river, now part of Kensington and Chelsea
Chel·ten·ham \'chelt-nəm, -^{ə}n-əm, *US also* -^{ə}n-,ham\ borough SW *cen* England in Gloucestershire *pop* 73,229
Che·lya·binsk \chel-'yä-bən(t)sk\ city U.S.S.R. in W Soviet Russia, Asia, S of Sverdlovsk *pop* 1,030,000
Che·lyu·skin, Cape \chel-'yü-skən\ headland U.S.S.R. in NW Soviet Russia, Asia, on Taimyr peninsula; northernmost point of Asian mainland, at 77°35'N, 105°E
Chemnitz — see KARL-MARX-STADT
Chemulpo — see INCHON
Che·nab \chə-'näb\ river 590 *mi* (950 *km*) NW India (subcontinent) in Kashmir & the Punjab flowing SW to unite with the Sutlej forming the Panjnad
Chen–chiang *or* **Zhen·jiang** \'jən-jē-'äŋ\ *or* **Chin·kiang** \'jin-jē-'äŋ\ city & port E China in NW *cen* Kiangsu *pop* 190,000
Cheng–chou *or* **Zheng·zhou** *or* **Cheng·chow** \'jəŋ-'jō\ city NE *cen* China ✱ of Honan on the Hwang *pop* 766,000
Cheng·teh *or* **Cheng·de** *or* **Ch'eng–te** \'chəŋ-'də\ city NE China in NE Hopeh NE of Peking *pop* 120,000
Ch'eng–tu *or* **Cheng·du** \'chəŋ-'dü\ city SW *cen* China ✱ of Szechwan on Min river *pop* 1,107,000
Chenstokhov — see CZESTOCHOWA
Cher \'she(ə)r\ river 220 *mi* (354 *km*), *cen* France flowing into the Loire
Cher·bourg \'she(ə)r-,bü(ə)r(g), sher-'bü(ə)r\ city & port NW France on Cotentin peninsula on English channel *pop* 31,333
Che·rem·kho·vo \chə-'rem-kə-və, ,cher-əm-'kō-və\ city U.S.S.R. in E *cen* Soviet Russia, Asia, NW of Irkutsk *pop* 77,000
Cheribon — see TJIREBON
Cher·kessk \chər-'kesk\ city U.S.S.R. in SE Soviet Russia, Europe, in N Caucasus region SE of Stavropol ✱ of Karachayevo-Cherkess Autonomous Region *pop* 91,000
Cher·ni·gov \cher-'nē-gəf\ city U.S.S.R. in Ukrainian Repubic *pop* 238,000
Cher·nov·tsy \cher-'nȯft-sē\ *or Romanian* **Cer·na·u·ti** \,cher-nə-'üts(-ē)\ city U.S.S.R. in W Ukrainian Republic on the Prut *pop* 187,000
Cher·o·kee Outlet *or* **Cherokee Strip** \,cher-ə-(,)kē-\ strip of land N Okla. along S border of Kans. E of 100°W opened to settlement 1893; 50 *mi* (80 *km*) wide, *ab* 220 *mi* (354 *km*) long

Cher·so·nese \'kər-sə-ˌnēz, -ˌnēs\ *or anc* **Cher·so·ne·sus** \ˌkər-sə-'nē-səs\ any of several peninsulas: as (1) Jutland (the **Cim·bri·an Chersonese** \'sim-brē-ən\ **Cim·bric Chersonese** \-brik\); (2) the Malay peninsula (the **Golden Chersonese**); (3) the Crimea (the **Tau·ric Chersonese** \'tȯr-ik\); (4) the Gallipoli peninsula (the **Thra·cian Chersonese** \'thrā-shən\)

Cher·well \'chär-wəl\ river 30 *mi* (48 *km*) *cen* England in Northamptonshire & Oxfordshire flowing S into the Thames at Oxford

Ches·a·peake \'ches-(ə-)ˌpēk\ city SE Va. S of Norfolk *pop* 114,486

Chesapeake Bay inlet of the Atlantic 200 *mi* (322 *km*) long in Va. & Md.

Chesh·ire \'chesh-ər, 'chesh-ˌi(ə)r\ **1** town S Conn. SW of Meriden *pop* 21,788 **2** *or* **Ches·ter** \'ches-tər\ county NW England ✻ Chester *area* 899 *sq mi* (2337 *sq km*), *pop* 928,300

Ches·ter \'ches-tər\ **1** city SE Pa. *pop* 45,794 **2** city NW England ✻ of Cheshire on Dee river *pop* 58,436

Ches·ter·field \'ches-tər-ˌfēld\ **1** inlet *ab* 250 *mi* (402 *km*) long N Canada on NW coast of Hudson bay **2** borough N *cen* England in Derbyshire S of Sheffield *pop* 70,546

Che·tu·mal \ˌchā-tü-'mäl\ city SE Mexico ✻ of Quintana Roo

Che·vi·ot \'chev-ē-ət, 'chē-vē-ət\ **1** hills extending NE to SW along English-Scottish border **2** peak 2676 *ft* (816 *m*) highest in the Cheviots

Chey·enne \shī-'an, -'en\ **1** river 290 *mi* (467 *km*) S. Dak. flowing NE into Missouri river **2** city ✻ of Wyo. *pop* 47,283

Chi·ai \jē-'ī\ city W *cen* Taiwan *pop* 200,000

Chia·mu·ssu \jē-'ä-'mü-'sü\ *or* **Jia·mu·si** \jē-'ä-'mü-'sē\ *or* **Kia·mu·sze** \jē-'ä-'mü-'sü\ city NE China in E Heilungkiang *pop* 300,000

Chiang Mai \jē-'äŋ-'mī\ *or* **Chieng·mai** \jē-'eŋ-'mī\ city NW Thailand on the Ping *pop* 89,272

Chia·pas \chē-'äp-əs\ state SE Mexico bordering on the Pacific ✻ Tuxtla Gutiérrez *area* 28,729 *sq mi* (74,695 *sq km*), *pop* 2,096,812

Chi·ba \'chē-bə\ city E Japan in Honshu on Tokyo Bay E of Tokyo *pop* 755,729

Chi·ca·go \shə-'käg-(ˌ)ō, -'kȯg-, -ə\ **1** river Chicago, Ill., having two branches (N. Branch & S. Branch) & *orig.* flowing E into Lake Michigan but now flowing S through S. Branch & Chicago Sanitary & Ship canal into Des Plaines river **2** city & port NE Ill. on Lake Michigan *pop* 3,005,072 — **Chi·ca·go·an** \-'käg-ə-wən, -'kȯg-\ *n*

Chicago Heights city NE Ill. S of Chicago *pop* 37,026

Chich·a·gof \'chich-ə-ˌgȯf, -ˌgäf\ island SE Alaska in Alexander archipelago N of Baranof Is. *area* 2060 *sq mi* (5460 *sq km*)

Chi·chén It·zá \chə-ˌchen-ət-'sä\ village SE Mexico in Yucatán ESE of Mérida at site of important Mayan city

Chich·es·ter \'chich-ə-stər\ city & borough S England ENE of Portsmouth ✻ of W. Sussex *pop* 24,189

Ch'i-ch'i-ha-erh — see TSITSIHAR

Chick·a·hom·i·ny \ˌchik-ə-'häm-ə-nē\ river 90 *mi* (145 *km*) E Va. flowing SE into James river

Chi·cla·yo \chə-'klī-(ˌ)ō\ city NW Peru near coast *pop* 207,269

Chi·co \'chē-(ˌ)kō\ city W Calif. N of Sacramento *pop* 26,601

Chi·co·pee \'chik-ə-(ˌ)pē\ city SW Mass. *pop* 55,112

Chi·cou·ti·mi \shə-'küt-ə-mē\ **1** river 100 *mi* (161 *km*) Canada in S Que. flowing N into the Saguenay **2** city Canada in S *cen* Que. on the Saguenay *pop* 60,064

Chihli — see HOPEH

Chihli, Gulf of — see PO HAI

Chi·hua·hua \chə-'wä-(ˌ)wä, shə-, -wə\ **1** state N Mexico bordering on the U.S. *area* 94,822 *sq mi* (246,537 *sq km*), *pop* 1,933,856 **2** city, its ✻ *pop* 363,850

Chi·le \'chil-ē, 'chē-(ˌ)lā\ country S S. America bet. the Andes & the Pacific; a republic ✻ Santiago *area* 286,396 *sq mi* (744,630 *sq km*), *pop* 11,275,440 — **Chil·ean** \'chil-ē-ən, chə-'lā-ən\ *adj or n*

Chil·koot \'chil-ˌküt\ pass 3502 *ft* (1067 *m*) bet. SE Alaska & SW Yukon Territory, Canada, in N Coast mountains

Chi·llán \chē-'(y)än\ city *cen* Chile NE of Concepción *pop* 128,515

Chil·li·cothe \ˌchil-ə-'käth-ē, -'kȯ-thē\ city S Ohio *pop* 23,420

Chil·li·wack \'chil-ē-ˌwak\ city Canada in S B.C. *pop* 8634

Chi·loé \ˌchil-ə-'wā\ island S *cen* Chile *area* 4700 *sq mi* (12,220 *sq km*), *pop* 65,161

Chil·pan·cin·go \ˌchil-pən-'siŋ-(ˌ)gō\ city S Mexico ✻ of Guerrero *pop* 36,193

Chil·tern \'chil-tərn\ hills S *cen* England in Oxfordshire, Buckinghamshire, Hertfordshire, & Bedfordshire

Chim·bo·ra·zo \ˌchim-bə-'räz-(ˌ)ō\ mountain 20,561 *ft* (6267 *m*) W *cen* Ecuador

Chim·kent \chim-'kent\ city U.S.S.R. in S Kazakhstan N of Tashkent *pop* 322,000

Chin \'chin\ hills W Burma; highest Mt. Victoria 10,016 *ft* (3053 *m*)

Chi·na, People's Republic of \-'chī-nə\ country E Asia; a republic, ✻ Peking; *area* 3,691,502 *sq mi* (9,597,905 *sq km*), *pop* 1,031,882,511

China, Republic of — see TAIWAN

China sea the E. & S. China seas

Chinan — see TSINAN

Chin–chou *or* **Jin·zhou** *or* **Chin·chow** \'jin-'jō\ city NE China in SW Liaoning *pop* 400,000

Chin·co·teague \ˌchiŋ-kə-'tēg\ bay Md. & Va. on Atlantic coast

Chin·dwin \'chin-'dwin\ river 550 *mi* (885 *km*) NW Myanmar flowing S into the Irrawaddy

Chinese Turkestan region W China in W & *cen* Sinkiang Uighur

Ch'ing Hai — see KOKO NOR

Ch'in–huang–tao *or* **Qin·huang·dao** *or* **Chin·wang·tao** \'chin-'(h)wäŋ-'daů\ city & port NE China in NE Hopeh *pop* 210,000

Chin·ju \'jin-'jü\ city S S. Korea W of Pusan *pop* 202,753

Chinkiang — see CHEN-CHIANG

Chinnampo — see NAMPO

Chinnereth, Sea of — see GALILEE (Sea of)

Chi·no \'chē-(ˌ)nō\ city SW Calif. E of Los Angeles *pop* 40,165

Chiog·gia \kē-'ò-jə\ commune & port NE Italy on island in Lagoon of Venice *pop* 53,566

Chi·os \'kī-ˌäs\ *or NGk* **Khí·os** \'kē-ˌȯs\ island E Greece in the Aegean off W coast of Turkey *area* 355 *sq mi* (923 *sq km*) — **Chi·an** \'kī-ən\ *adj or n*

Chip·pe·wa \'chip-ə-ˌwä, -wə\ river 183 *mi* (294 *km*) NW Wis. flowing S into Mississippi river

Chir·i·ca·hua National Monument \ˌchir-i-'kä-wə, *locally also* 'chir-i-ˌkaů\ reservation SE Ariz. containing curious natural rock formations

Chiriquí — see BARÚ

Chis·holm Trail \'chiz-əm-\ pioneer cattle trail bet. San Antonio (Tex.) & Abilene (in E *cen* Kans.), used esp. 1866–85

Chisinau — see KISHINEV

Chis·le·hurst and Sid·cup \'chiz-əl-ˌhər-stən-'sid-kəp\ former urban district SE England in Kent, now partly in Bexley, partly in Bromley

Chi·ta \chi-'tä\ city U.S.S.R. in SE Soviet Russia, Asia, E of Lake Baikal *pop* 303,000

Chi·tral \chi-'träl\ **1** river 300 *mi* (483 *km*) N Pakistan & Afghanistan flowing SW into Kabul river **2** district N North-West Frontier Province Pakistan ✻ Chitral

Chit·ta·gong \'chit-ə-ˌgäŋ, -ˌgȯŋ\ city & port SE Bangladesh on Bay of Bengal *pop* 889,760

Chiungchow — see HAINAN **2**

Chiu·si \kē-'ü-sē\ *or anc* **Clu·si·um** \'klü-z(h)ē-əm\ town *cen* Italy in Tuscany SE of Siena *pop* 9206

Chkalov — see ORENBURG

Choaspes — see KARKHEH

Choi·seul \shwä-'zə(r)l\ island W Pacific in the Solomons SE of Bougainville Is. *area* 1500 *sq mi* (3900 *sq km*); nearly surrounded by barrier reef

Choi·sy *or* **Choisy–le–Roi** \shwä-ˌzē-lər-'wä\ commune N France on the Seine SSE of Paris *pop* 38,629

Cho·lon \shə-'lȯn, chə-'lȯn\ former city S Vietnam, now part of Ho Chi Minh City

Cho·lu·la \chə-'lü-lə\ town SE *cen* Mexico in Puebla state

Cho·mo Lha·ri \ˌchō-mō-'lär-ē\ mountain 23,997 *ft* (7314 *m*) in the Himalayas bet. Tibet & NW Bhutan; sacred to Buddhists

Chomolungma — see EVEREST

Chong·jin \'chȯŋ-ˌjin\ city & port NE N. Korea on Sea of Japan *pop* 265,000

Chong·ju \'chȯŋ-ˌjü\ city W *cen* S. Korea N of Taejon *pop* 252,985

Chon·ju \'jən-ˌjü\ city SW S. Korea SW of Taejon *pop* 366,997

Cho Oyu \ˌchō-ō-'yü\ mountain 26,749 *ft* (8153 *m*) Nepal & Tibet in the Himalayas; 6th highest in the world

Cho·ras·mia \kə-'raz-mē-ə\ province of ancient Persia on Oxus river extending W to Caspian sea; equivalent to Khwarazm — see KHIVA

Cho·rzow \'kȯr-ˌzhüf, -ˌzhüv\ city SW Poland in Silesia *pop* 149,649

Chosen — see KOREA

Cho·ta Nag·pur \ˌchōt-ə-'näg-ˌpůr\ plateau region E India N of Mahanadi basin in N Orissa & S Bihar

Chou–shan *or* **Zhou·shan** \'jaů-'shän\ archipelago E China in East China sea at entrance to Hangchow Bay

Cho·wan \chə-'wän\ river 50 *mi* (80 *km*) NE N.C. flowing into Albemarle sound

Christ·church \'krīs(t)-ˌchərch\ city New Zealand on E coast of South Is. *pop* 164,680 — see LYTTELTON

Christiania — see OSLO

Chris·tians·haab \'kris(h)-chənz-ˌhȯb\ town W Greenland on Disko Bay SE of Godhavn

Chris·tian·sted \'kris(h)-chən-ˌsted\ town Virgin Islands of the U.S. on N coast of St. Croix Is. *pop* 2904

Christ·mas \'kris-məs\ **1** island E Indian ocean 225 *mi* (360 *km*) S of W end of Java; administered by Australia *area* 64 *sq mi* (166 *sq km*), *pop* 2871 **2** — see KIRITIMATI

Chu \'chü\ **1** *or* **Zhu** \'jü\ *or* **Pearl** \'pər(-ə)l\ river SE China SE of Canton at E side of the Hsi delta **2** river 600 *mi* (966 *km*) U.S.S.R. in Soviet Central Asia in SE Kazakhstan flowing E into Issyk Kul

Ch'iian–chou *or* **Quan·zhou** *or* **Chuan·chow** \chə-'wän-'jō\ city SE China in SE Fukien on Formosa strait *pop* 110,000

Chubb Crater — see NEW QUEBEC CRATER

Chu·but \chə-'büt, -'vüt\ river 500 *mi* (805 *km*) S Argentina flowing E across Patagonia into the Atlantic

Chudskoe — see PEIPUS (Lake)

Chu·gach \'chü-ˌgach *also* -ˌgash\ mountains S Alaska extending along coast from Cook inlet to St. Elias range; highest Mt. Marcus Baker 13,176 *ft* (4016 *m*)

Chuk·chi *or* **Chuck·chee** \'chək-chē, 'chůk-\ sea of the Arctic ocean N of Bering strait

Chu·kot·ski \chə-'kät-skē\ *or* **Chu·kot** \-'kät\ peninsula U.S.S.R. in NE Soviet Russia, Asia, bet. Bering & Chukchee seas

Chu·la Vis·ta \ˌchü-lə-'vis-tə\ city SW Calif. S of San Diego *pop* 83,927

Chu·lym *or* **Chu·lim** \chə-'lim\ river 700 *mi* (1126 *km*) U.S.S.R. in E *cen* Soviet Russia, Asia, flowing W into the Ob

Chun·chon \'chün-ˌchȯn\ city N *cen* S. Korea NE of Seoul *pop* 155,214

Chung·king \'chůŋ-'kiŋ\ *or* **Chong·qing** \'chůŋ-'chiŋ\ *or* **Ch'ung–ch'ing** city ✻ of China 1937–46 in SE Szechwan on the Yangtze *pop* 3,500,000

Chur \'kůr\ *or F* **Coire** \'kwär\ commune E Switzerland ✻ of Graubünden canton *pop* 32,037

Chur·chill \'chər-ˌchil\ **1** river *ab* 1000 *mi* (1609 *km*) Canada flowing E across N Sask. & N Man. into Hudson bay **2** *or formerly* **Hamilton** river 208 *mi* (335 *km*) Canada in Nfld. in S *cen* Labrador flowing E to Lake Melville

Churchill Falls *or formerly* **Grand Falls** waterfall 245 *ft* (75 *m*) high Canada in W Labrador in Churchill river

Chu·vash Republic \chü-ˌväsh-\ autonomous republic U.S.S.R. in E *cen* Soviet Russia, Europe, S of the Volga ✻ Cheboksary *area* 6909 *sq mi* (17,963 *sq km*), *pop* 1,224,000

Chu·zen·ji \chü-'zen-jē\ lake Japan in *cen* Honshu W of Nikko

---

Cí·bo·la \ˈsē-bə-lə, ˈsib-ə-\ historical region in present N N. Mex. including seven pueblos (the **Seven Cities of Cíbola**) believed by early Spanish explorers to contain vast treasures
Cic·ero \ˈsis-ə-ˌrō\ town NE Ill. W of Chicago *pop* 61,232
Cien·fue·gos \sē-ˌen-ˈfwā-(ˌ)gōs\ city & port W *cen* Cuba on S coast on **Cienfuegos Bay** *pop* 114,650
Cie·szyn \ˈchesh-ən\ *or G* **Te·schen** \ˈtesh-ən\ region *cen* Europe in Silesia; once an Austrian duchy; divided 1920 bet. Poland & Czechoslovakia
Ci·li·cia \sə-ˈlish-(ē-)ə\ ancient country SE Asia Minor extending along Mediterranean coast S of Taurus mountains — see LESSER ARMENIA — **Ci·li·cian** \-ˈlish-ən\ *adj or n*
Cilician Gates mountain pass S Turkey in Taurus mountains
Cim·ar·ron \ˈsim-ə-ˌrän, -ˌrōn, -rən\ river 600 *mi* (966 *km*) flowing E from NE N. Mex. through SW Kans. into Arkansas river in NE Okla.
Cimbrian Chersonese *or* **Cimbric Chersonese** — see CHERSONESE
Cim·me·ri·an Bosporus \sə-ˌmir-ē-ən-\ the Kerch strait
Cin·cin·nati \ˌsin(t)-sə-ˈnat-ē, -ˈnat-ə\ city SW Ohio on Ohio river *pop* 385,457 — **Cin·cin·nati·an** \-ˈnat-ē-ən\ *n*
Cinque Ports \ˈsiŋk\ group of seaport towns SE England on coast of Kent & Sussex, orig. five (Dover, Sandwich, Romney, Hastings, & Hythe) to which were later added Winchelsea, Rye, & other minor places, granted special privileges (abolished in 19th century) in return for services in coast defense
Cintra — see SINTRA
Circars — see NORTHERN CIRCARS
Cir·cas·sia \(ˌ)sər-ˈkash-(ē-)ə\ region U.S.S.R. in S Soviet Russia, Europe, on Black sea N of W end of Caucasus mountains
Cirenaica — see CYRENAICA
Cis·al·pine Gaul \sis-ˌal-ˌpīn-\ the part of Gaul lying S & E of the Alps
Ciscaucasia — see CAUCASUS 2
Cis·kei \ˈsis-ˌkī\ black enclave in the Republic of S. Africa; granted independence 1981; ✱ Bisho
Ci·thae·ron \sə-ˈthē-ˌrän\ *or NGk* **Ki·thai·rón** \ˌkē-the-ˈrōn\ *or formerly* **El·a·tea** \ˌel-ə-ˈtē-ə\ mountain 4623 *ft* (1409 *m*) Greece on NW border of ancient Attica
Ci·tlal·te·petl \sē-ˌtläl-ˈtā-ˌpet-ᵊl\ *or* **Ori·za·ba** \ˌōr-ə-ˈzäb-ə, ˌȯr-\ inactive volcano 18,700 *ft* (5700 *m*) SE Mexico on Puebla-Veracruz boundary; highest mountain in Mexico & 3d highest in N. America
Città del Vaticano — see VATICAN CITY
Ci·u·dad Bo·lí·var \ˌsē-ü-ˌthä-bə-ˈlē-ˌvär, -ü-ˌdad-\ city & port E *cen* Venezuela on the Orinoco *pop* 103,663
Ciudad Gua·ya·na \gwə-ˈyän-ə\ city E Venezuela near junction of the Caroní & the Orinoco *pop* 140,319
Ciudad Juá·rez *or* **Juárez** \ˈ(h)wär-əs\ city Mexico in Chihuahua on Rio Grande opposite El Paso, Tex. *pop* 424,135
Ciudad Re·al \-rā-ˈäl\ **1** province S *cen* Spain *area* 7620 *sq mi* (19,812 *sq km*), *pop* 438,621 **2** commune, its ✱, S of Toledo *pop* 48,115
Ciudad Trujillo — see SANTO DOMINGO
Ciudad Vic·to·ria \ˌvik-ˈtōr-ē-ə, -ˈtȯr-\ city E *cen* Mexico ✱ of Tamaulipas *pop* 94,304
Ci·vi·ta·vec·chia \ˌchē-vē-tä-ˈvek-(ˌ)yä\ commune & port *cen* Italy in Latium on Tyrrhenian sea WNW of Rome *pop* 45,836
Clack·man·nan \klak-ˈman-ən\ *or* **Clack·man·nan·shire** \-ˌshi(ə)r, -shər\ **1** former county *cen* Scotland bordering on the Forth **2** town, its ✱
Clac·ton \ˈklak-tən\ *or* **Clacton–on–Sea** town SE England in Essex on North sea *pop* 43,571
Clare \ˈkla(ə)r, ˈkle(ə)r\ county W Ireland in Munster ✱ Ennis *area* 1231 *sq mi* (3201 *sq km*), *pop* 87,567
Clare·mont \-ˌmänt\ city SW Calif. E of Los Angeles *pop* 30,950
Clark Fork \ˈklärk\ river 300 *mi* (483 *km*) W Mont. & N Idaho flowing NW into Pend Oreille Lake
Clarks·burg \ˈklärks-ˌbərg\ city N W. Va. *pop* 22,371
Clarks·dale \ˈklärks-ˌdāl\ city NW Miss. *pop* 21,137
Clarks·ville \ˈklärks-ˌvil, -vəl\ city N Tenn. NW of Nashville *pop* 54,777
Clear, Cape \ˈkli(ə)r\ cape SW Ireland at S end of Clear Is.
Clear·field \ˈkli(ə)r-ˌfēld\ city N Utah S of Ogden *pop* 17,982
Clear·wa·ter \ˈkli(ə)r-ˌwȯt-ər, -ˌwät-\ **1** mountains N *cen* Idaho; highest *ab* 8000 *ft* (2438 *m*) **2** city W Fla. NW of St. Petersburg on Gulf of Mexico *pop* 85,528
Cle·burne \ˈklē-bərn\ city NE *cen* Tex. *pop* 19,218
Clee \ˈklē\ hills W England in S Salop
Cler·mont–Fer·rand \ˌkler-ˌmō^{n}-fə-ˈrä^{n}\ city S *cen* France in Allier valley on edge of Auvergne mountains *pop* 153,379
Cleve·land \ˈklēv-lənd\ **1** city & port NE Ohio on Lake Erie *pop* 573,822 **2** city SE Tenn. ENE of Chattanooga *pop* 26,415 **3** county N England N of N. Yorkshire ✱ Middlesbrough *area* 226 *sq mi* (588 *sq km*), *pop* 568,400; includes the **Cleveland hills** — **Cleve·land·er** \-lən-dər\ *n*
Cleveland, Mount mountain 10,448 *ft* (3184 *m*) N Mont., highest in Glacier National Park
Cleveland Heights city NE Ohio E of Cleveland *pop* 56,438
Cli·chy \klē-ˈshē\ commune N France NW of Paris *pop* 47,731
Cliff·side Park \ˈklif-(ˌ)sīd-\ borough NE N.J. *pop* 21,464
Clif·ton \ˈklif-tən\ city NE N.J. N of Newark *pop* 74,388
Clinch \ˈklinch\ river 200 *mi* (322 *km*) SW Va. & E Tenn. flowing SW into Tennessee river
Cling·mans Dome \ˌkliŋ-mənz-\ mountain 6642 *ft* (2024 *m*) on N.C.-Tenn. boundary; highest in Great Smoky mountains
Clin·ton \ˈklint-ᵊn\ city E Iowa on Mississippi river *pop* 32,828
Clon·mel \klän-ˈmel\ municipal borough S Ireland ✱ of County Tipperary *pop* 12,407
Cloud Peak mountain 13,165 *ft* (4013 *m*) N Wyo.; highest in Bighorn mountains
Clo·vis \ˈklō-vəs\ **1** city *cen* Calif. NE of Fresno *pop* 33,021 **2** city E N. Mex. *pop* 31,194
Cluj–Na·po·ca \ˈklüzh-ˈnäp-ō-kə\ city NW *cen* Romania in Transylvania *pop* 283,647
Clu·ny \ˈklü-nē, klü-ˈ\ town E *cen* France NNW of Lyons *pop* 4335
Clusium — see CHIUSI
Clu·tha \ˈklü-thə\ river 210 *mi* (338 *km*) New Zealand in SE South Is. flowing SE into the Pacific
Clwyd \ˈklüid\ county NE Wales ✱ Mold *area* 937 *sq mi* (2436 *sq km*), *pop* 392,200
Clyde \ˈklīd\ river 106 *mi* (171 *km*) SW Scotland flowing NW into **Firth of Clyde** (estuary)
Clyde·bank \ˈklīd-ˌbaŋk\ burgh W *cen* Scotland in Strathclyde on Clyde river *pop* 51,656
Clydes·dale \ˈklīdz-ˌdāl\ valley of the upper Clyde river, Scotland
Cni·dus \ˈnīd-əs\ ancient town SW Asia Minor in Caria
Cnossus — see KNOSSOS
Coa·chel·la \kō-ə-ˈchel-ə\ valley SE Calif. bet. Salton sea & San Bernardino mountains
Coa·hui·la \ˌkō-ə-ˈwē-lə, kwä-ˈwē-\ state N Mexico bordering on the U.S. ✱ Saltillo *area* 58,062 *sq mi* (150,961 *sq km*), *pop* 1,558,401
Coast **1** mountains Canada in W B.C.; N continuation of Cascade range **2** mountain ranges W N. America extending along Pacific coast W of Sierra Nevada & Cascade range & N through Vancouver Is., B.C., to Kenai peninsula & Kodiak Is., Alaska — see LOGAN (Mount)
Coat·bridge \ˈkōt-(ˌ)brij\ burgh S *cen* Scotland in Strathclyde *pop* 50,866
Coats Land \ˈkōts\ section of Antarctica SE of Weddell sea
Cobh \ˈkōv\ *or formerly* **Queens·town** \ˈkwēn-ˌstau̇n\ urban district & port SW Ireland on island in Cork harbor *pop* 6587
Coblenz — see KOBLENZ
Co·burg **1** \ˈkō-ˌbərg\ city SE Australia in S Victoria, N suburb of Melbourne *pop* 55,035 **2** \-ˌbərg, -ˌbu̇(ə)rg\ city E W. Germany in N Bavaria NW of Bayreuth *pop* 45,633
Co·cha·bam·ba \ˌkō-chə-ˈbäm-bə\ city W *cen* Bolivia *pop* 204,684
Co·chin \ˈkō-chən\ region SW India in Kerala on Malabar coast — see TRAVANCORE
Co·chin China \ˌkō-chən-\ region S Vietnam bordering on S. China sea & Gulf of Siam *area* 29,974 *sq mi* (77,932 *sq km*)
Co·chi·nos, Ba·hía de \ˈbä-hyə-ˌthä-kō-ˈchē-nəs\ *or* **Bay of Pigs** bay W Cuba on S coast
Co·co \ˈkō-(ˌ)kō\ *or* **Se·go·via** \sā-ˈgō-vyə, -vē-ə\ river 450 *mi* (724 *km*) N Nicaragua flowing NE into the Caribbean & forming part of Honduras-Nicaragua boundary
Co·co·ni·no \ˌkō-kə-ˈnē-(ˌ)nō, -ˈnē-nə\ plateau NW Ariz. S of Grand Canyon
Co·cos \ˈkō-kəs\ *or* **Kee·ling** \ˈkē-liŋ\ islands E Indian ocean belonging to Australia *area* 1 *sq mi* (2.6 *sq km*), *pop* 555
Cod, Cape \ˈkäd\ peninsula 65 *mi* (105 *km*) long SE Mass. — **Cape Cod·der** \ˈkäd-ər\ *n*
Coele–Syria — see BEKAA
Coeur d'Alene \ˌkōrd-ᵊl-ˈān\ **1** lake *ab* 25 *mi* (40 *km*) long N Idaho E of Spokane, Wash.; drained by Spokane river **2** city N Idaho *pop* 20,054
Co·glians, Mon·te \ˌmōnt-ē-kōl-ˈyän(t)s\ mountain 9121 *ft* (2780 *m*) on Austria-Italy border; highest in the Carnic Alps
Co·hoes \kə-ˈhōz\ city E N.Y. NW of Troy *pop* 18,144
Coim·ba·tore \ˌkȯim-bə-ˈtō(ə)r, -ˈtȯ(ə)r\ city S India in W Tamil Nadu on S slope of Nilgiri hills *pop* 917,155
Co·im·bra \kō-ˈim-brə, ku̇-\ city W *cen* Portugal *pop* 147,143
Coire — see CHUR
Col·ches·ter \ˈkōl-ˌches-tər, -chəs-\ borough SE England in Essex *pop* 81,945
Col·chis \ˈkäl-kəs\ ancient country bordering on Black sea S of Caucasus mountains; area now constitutes W part of Georgia, U.S.S.R. — **Col·chi·an** \ˈkäl-kē-ən\ *adj or n*
Cole·raine \kōl-ˈrān, ˈkōl-ˌ\ district N Northern Ireland, established 1974 *area* 187 *sq mi* (486 *sq km*), *pop* 46,272
Co·li·ma \kə-ˈlē-mə\ **1** volcano SW Mexico in S Jalisco **2** state SW Mexico bordering on the Pacific *area* 2009 *sq mi* (5223 *sq km*), *pop* 339,202 **3** city, its ✱, SSW of Guadalajara *pop* 70,219
College Park **1** city NW Ga. S of Atlanta *pop* 24,632 **2** city SW Md. NE of Washington, D.C. *pop* 23,614
College Station city E *cen* Tex. SE of Bryan *pop* 37,272
Col·lins·ville \ˈkäl-ənz-ˌvil\ city SW Ill. NE of E. St. Louis *pop* 19,613
Col·mar *or* **Kol·mar** \ˈkōl-ˌmär, kōl-ˈ\ commune NE France at E edge of Vosges mountains *pop* 58,585
Co·logne \kə-ˈlōn\ *or G* **Köln** \ˈkœln\ city W W. Germany in N. Rhine-Westphalia on the Rhine *pop* 976,694
Colomb–Béchar — see BÉCHAR
Co·lombes \kə-ˈlō^{n}(m)b\ commune N France, NW suburb of Paris *pop* 83,241
Co·lom·bia \kə-ˈləm-bē-ə *also* -ˈlōm-\ country NW S. America bordering on Caribbean sea & Pacific ocean ✱ Bogotá *area* 439,825 *sq mi* (1,143,545 *sq km*), *pop* 27,867,326 — **Co·lom·bi·an** \-bē-ən\ *adj or n*
Co·lom·bo \kə-ˈləm-(ˌ)bō\ city & port ✱ of Sri Lanka *pop* 585,776
Co·lón \kə-ˈlōn\ city & port N Panama on the Caribbean at entrance to Panama canal *pop* 59,043
Colón, Archipiélago de — see GALÁPAGOS ISLANDS
Colonial Heights city SE Va. N of Petersburg *pop* 16,509
Col·o·phon \ˈkäl-ə-fən, -ˌfän\ ancient city W Asia Minor in Lydia
Col·o·ra·do \ˌkäl-ə-ˈrad-(ˌ)ō, -ˈräd-\ **1** river 1450 *mi* (2334 *km*) SW U.S. & NW Mexico rising in N Colo. & flowing SW into Gulf of California **2** river 840 *mi* (1352 *km*) S Tex. flowing SE into Gulf of Mexico **3** desert SE Calif. W of Colorado river **4** plateau SW U.S. W of Rocky mountains in Colorado river basin in N Ariz., S & E Utah, W Colo., & NW N. Mex. **5** state W U.S. ✱ Denver *area* 104,247 *sq mi* (271,042 *sq km*), *pop* 2,889,964 **6** river 530 *mi* (853 *km*) *cen* Argentina flowing SE to the Atlantic — **Col·o·ra·dan** \-ˈrad-ᵊn, -ˈräd-\ *adj or n* — **Col·o·ra·do·an** \-ˈrad-ə-wən, -ˈräd-\ *adj or n*
Colorado National Monument reservation W Colo. W of Grand Junction containing many unusual erosion formations
Colorado Springs city *cen* Colo. E of Pikes Peak *pop* 215,150
Co·los·sae \kə-ˈläs-(ˌ)ē\ ancient city SW *cen* Asia Minor in SW Phrygia — **Co·los·sian** \kə-ˈläsh-ən\ *adj or n*
Col·ton \ˈkōlt-ᵊn\ city SW Calif. S of San Bernardino *pop* 21,310
Co·lum·bia \kə-ˈləm-bē-ə\ **1** river 1270 *mi* (2044 *km*) SW Canada & NW U.S. rising in SE B.C. & flowing S & W into the Pacific **2** plateau E Wash., E Oreg., & SW Idaho in Columbia river basin **3** city *cen* Mo. *pop* 62,061 **4** city ✱ of S.C. *pop* 99,296 **5** city *cen* Tenn. *pop* 26,372 — **Co·lum·bi·an** \-bē-ən\ *adj or n*
Columbia, Cape cape N Canada on Ellesmere Is.; northernmost point of Canada, at 83°07′N
Columbia, District of — see DISTRICT OF COLUMBIA
Columbia Heights city SE Minn. N of Minneapolis *pop* 20,029

Co·lum·bus \kə-'ləm-bəs\ 1 city W Ga. on the Chattahoochee *pop* 169,441 2 city S *cen* Ind. *pop* 30,614 3 city E Miss. *pop* 27,383 4 city E Nebr. *pop* 17,328 5 city *cen* Ohio, its ✱ *pop* 564,871

Col·ville \'kōl-,vil, 'käl-\ river 320 *mi* (515 *km*) N Alaska flowing NE into Beaufort sea

Col·wyn Bay \,käl-wən-\ borough N Wales in Clwyd *pop* 26,278

Co·mil·la \kə-'mil-ə\ city E Bangladesh SE of Dacca *pop* 86,446

Commander — see KOMANDORSKIE

Common Market — see EUROPEAN ECONOMIC COMMUNITY

Com·mon·wealth \'käm-ən-,wel(t)th\ *or* Commonwealth of Nations United Kingdom of Great Britain and Merrihern Ireland & the Brit. dominions, republics, & dependencies

Communism Peak \'käm-yə-,niz-əm\ *or* Russ Pik Kom·mu·niz·ma \'pēk-kə-mü-'nēz-mə\ mountain 24,590 *ft* (7495 *m*) Soviet Central Asia in SE Tadzhik Republic in the Pamirs; highest in the U.S.S.R.

Co·mo \'kō-(,)mō\ commune N Italy in Lombardy at SW end of Lake Como (37 *mi or* 59 *km* long) *pop* 95,183

Co·mo·do·ro Ri·va·da·via \,käm-ə-'dōr-(,)ō,-rē-və-'däv-ē-ə, -'dōr-\ city & port S Argentina *pop* 96,865

Com·o·rin, Cape \'käm-ə-rən; kə-'mōr-ən, -'mòr-, -'mär-\ cape S India in Tamil Nadu; southernmost point of India, at 8°5'N

Com·o·ro Islands \'käm-ə-,rō\ country off SE Africa bet. Mozambique & Madagascar; formerly a French possession; a republic (except for Mayotte Is., which remains French) since 1975 ✱ Moroni *area* 790 *sq mi* (2054 *sq km*) *pop* 421,000

Com·piègne \kōmp-'yän\ town N France on the Oise *pop* 37,009

Compostela SANTIAGO DE COMPOSTELA

Comp·ton \'käm(p)-tən\ city SW Calif. SSE of Los Angeles *pop* 81,286

Com·stock lode \'käm-,stäk-\ gold & silver lode at Virginia City, Nev.

Con·a·kry *or* Kon·a·kry \'kän-ə-krē\ city & port ✱ of Guinea on the Atlantic *pop* 581,000

Co·nan·i·cut \kə-'nan-i-kət\ island R.I. in Narragansett Bay W of Aquidneck Is.

Con·cep·ción \,kän-,sep-sē-'ōn, -'sep-shən\ city S *cen* Chile *pop* 202,396

Con·chos \'kän-chəs\ river 300 *mi* (483 *km*) N Mexico flowing NE into Rio Grande

Con·cord 1 \'kän-,kó(ə)rd, 'kän-\ city W Calif. NE of Oakland *pop* 103,255 2 \'käŋ-kərd\ town E Mass. NW of Boston *pop* 16,293 3 \'kän-kərd\ city ✱ of N.H. on the Merrimack *pop* 30,400 4 \'kän-,kó(ə)rd, 'kän-\ city S *cen* N.C. *pop* 16,942

Co·ney Island \'kō-nē-\ resort section of New York City in S Brooklyn; formerly an island

Con·ga·ree \'käŋ-gə-(,)rē\ river 60 *mi* (96 *km*) *cen* S.C. flowing SE to unite with the Wateree forming the Santee

Congaree Swamp National Monument reservation *cen* S.C. S of Columbia

Con·go \'käŋ-(,)gō\ 1 *or* Zaire river *ab* 3000 *mi* (4828 *km*) *cen* Africa flowing N, W, & SW into the Atlantic — see LUALABA 2 — see ZAIRE 3 *or* Congo Republic *or formerly* Middle Congo country W *cen* Africa W of the lower Congo ✱ Brazzaville *area* 132,046 *sq mi* (343,320 *sq km*), *pop* 1,853,828 — see FRENCH EQUATORIAL AFRICA — Con·go·lese \,käŋ-gə-'lēz, -'lēs\ *adj or n*

Congo Free State — see BELGIAN CONGO

Con·nacht \'kän-,ót\ *or formerly* Con·naught province W Ireland *area* 6611 *sq mi* (17,189 *sq km*), *pop* 389,763

Con·nect·i·cut \kə-'net-i-kət\ 1 river 407 *mi* (655 *km*) NE U.S. rising in N N.H. & flowing S into Long Is. Sound 2 state NE U.S. ✱ Hartford *area* 5009 *sq mi* (13,023 *sq km*), *pop* 3,107,576

Con·ne·ma·ra \,kän-ə-'mär-ə\ district Ireland in W Galway

Con·ners·ville \'kän-ərz-,vil\ city E Ind. *pop* 17,023

Con·roe \'kän-(,)rō\ city E Tex. *pop* 18,034

Con·stance \'kän(t)-stən(t)s\ *or* G Kon·stanz \'kón-,stän(t)s\ commune SW W. Germany on Lake Constance *pop* 68,305

Constance, Lake *or* G Bo·den·see \'bód-ᵊn-,zā\ lake 46 *mi* (74 *km*) long W Europe on border bet. W. Germany, Austria, & Switzerland

Con·stan·tine \'kän(t)-stən-,tēn\ city NE Algeria *pop* 335,100

Constantinople — see ISTANBUL — Con·stan·ti·no·pol·i·tan \,kän-,stant-ᵊn-ō-'päl-ət-ᵊn \ *adj*

Con·stan·tsa \kän(t)-stän(t)-sə\ city & port SE Romania on Black sea

Con·ti·nen·tal Di·vide \,känt-ᵊn-,ent-ᵊl-di-'vīd\ *or* Great Divide the watershed of the N. American continent extending SSE from NW Canada to S. America where it joins the Andes

Con·way \'kän-,wā\ city *cen* Ark. N of Little Rock *pop* 20,375

Cooch Be·har \,küch-bə-'här\ former state NE India W of Assam; since 1947 attached to West Bengal

Cook \'kúk\ 1 islands S Pacific SW of Society islands; self-governing territory of New Zealand ✱ Avarua (on Rarotonga Is.) *area* 89 *sq mi* (231 *sq km*), *pop* 18,128 2 strait New Zealand bet. North Is. & South Is. 3 inlet of the Pacific S Alaska W of Kenai peninsula

Cook, Mount *or* Ao·rangi \aú-'räŋ-ē\ mountain 12,349 *ft* (3764 *m*) New Zealand in W *cen* South Is.; highest peak in Southern Alps & New Zealand

Cooke·ville \'kúk-,vil, -vəl\ city N *cen* Tenn. *pop* 20,535

Cooks·town \'kúk-,staún\ district *cen* Northern Ireland, established 1974 *area* 241 *sq mi* (627 *sq km*), *pop* 30,826

Coon Rapids \'kün\ city E Minn. N of St. Paul *pop* 35,826

Coorg *or* Kurg \'kú(ə)rg\ former state S India ✱ Mercara; merged with Mysore state (now Karnataka) 1956

Coo·sa \'kü-sə\ river 286 *mi* (460 *km*) NW Ga. & N Ala. flowing SW to join Tallapoosa river forming Alabama river

Coos Bay \'küs\ inlet of the Pacific SW Oreg.

Co·pán \kō-'pän\ ruined Mayan city W Honduras

Co·pen·ha·gen \,kō-pən-'hā-gən, -'häg-ən\ *or* Dan Kö·ben·havn \,kœ-bən-'haún\ city & port ✱ of Denmark on E Sjælland Is. & N Amager Is. *pop* 654,437 — Co·pen·ha·gen·er \,kō-pən-'hā-gə-nər, -'häg-ə-\ n

Co·pia·pó \,kō-pē-ə-'pō\ 1 volcano 19,948 *ft* (6080 *m*) N *cen* Chile 2 city W of the volcano *pop* 36,767

Cop·per·as Cove \'käp-(ə-)rəs-\ city *cen* Tex. *pop* 19,469

Cop·per·mine \'käp-ər-,mīn\ river 525 *mi* (845 *km*) N Canada in Northwest Territories flowing NW into Arctic ocean

Coquilhatville — see MBANDAKA

Co·quim·bo \kō-'kim-(,)bō, -'kēm-\ city & port N *cen* Chile *pop* 73,953

Coral sea arm of the SW Pacific bounded on W by Queensland, Australia, on N by the Solomons, & on E by Vanuatu & New Caledonia

Coral Gables city SE Fla. SW of Miami *pop* 43,241

Cor·al Springs \'kór-əl, 'kär-\ city SE Fla. *pop* 37,349

Cor·co·va·do \,kór-kə-'väd-(,)ō\ mountain 2310 *ft* (704 *m*) SE Brazil on S side of city of Rio de Janeiro

Cor·di·lle·ra Cen·tral \,kórd-ᵊl-'(y)er-ə-,sen-'träl, ,kórd-ē-'er-\ 1 range of the Andes in Colombia 2 range of the Andes in Peru E of the Marañón 3 chief range of the Dominican Republic 4 range Philippines in N Luzon — see PULOG 5 range S *cen* Puerto Rico — see CERRO DE PUNTA

Cordillera Mé·ri·da \-'mer-əd-ə\ *or* Sier·ra Ne·va·da de Mérida \sē-,er-ə-nə-'väd-ə-də-, -'vad-\ mountain range W Venezuela — see BOLÍVAR (Pico)

Cór·do·ba \'kórd-ə-bə, -ə-və\ 1 province S Spain *area* 5299 *sq mi* (13,777 *sq km*) *pop* 684,974 2 *or* Cor·do·va \'kórd-ə-və\ city, its ✱, on the Guadalquivir *pop* 279,386 3 city N *cen* Argentina *pop* 586,015 — Cor·do·ban \-bən\ *adj or n*

Cor·do·va Island \,kórd-ə-və\ tract on the Rio Grande 382 *acres* (153 *hectares*) adjoining Chamizal, formerly belonging to Mexico; 191 *acres* (76 *hectares*) ceded to U.S. in 1963

Cor·fu \'kór-'fü, 'kór-,)f(y)ü\ *or NGk* Kér·ky·ra *or* Kér·ki·ra \'ker-ki-rə\ *or anc* Cor·cy·ra \'kór-'si-rə\ 1 island NW Greece, one of the Ionian islands *area* 227 *sq mi* (590 *sq km*) 2 city & port on E Corfu *pop* 35,787 — Cor·fi·ote \'kór-fē-,ōt, -ət\ *n*

Cor·inth \'kór-ən(t)th, 'kär-\ *or NGk* Kó·rin·thos \'kór-ən-,thós\ 1 *or* Co·rin·thia \kə-'rin(t)-thē-ə\ region of ancient Greece occupying most of Isthmus of Corinth & part of NE Peloponnisos 2 city & port Greece on Isthmus of Corinth at head of Gulf of Corinth NE of site of ancient city of Corinth *pop* 22,495

Corinth, Gulf of *or* Gulf of Le·pan·to \'lep-ən-,tō, li-'pan-(,)tō\ inlet of Ionian sea *cen* Greece W of Isthmus of Corinth (neck of land 20 *mi or* 32 *km* long connecting Peloponnisos with rest of Greece)

Cork \'kó(ə)rk\ 1 county SW Ireland in Munster *area* 2881 *sq mi* (7491 *sq km*), *pop* 402,465 2 city & county borough & port, its ✱, at head of Cork harbor *pop* 136,344

Corn \'kó(ə)rn\ two small islands Nicaragua in the Caribbean

Cor·ner Brook \'kó(r)-nər-,brúk\ city Canada on W Nfld. on Gulf of St. Lawrence *pop* 24,339

Corneto — see TARQUINIA

Cor·no, Mon·te \,mänt-ē-'kór-(,)nō\ mountain 9560 *ft* (2897 *m*) *cen* Italy NE of Rome; highest in the Apennines

Corn·wall \'kórn-,wòl, -wəl\ 1 city Canada in SE Ont. *pop* 46,144 2 *or since 1974* Cornwall and Isles of Scil·ly \-'sil-ē\ county SW England ✱ Bodmin & ✱ Truro *area* 1375 *sq mi* (3575 *sq km*), *pop* 426,500

Co·ro \'kór-(,)ō, 'kór-\ city NW Venezuela near coast at base of Paraguaná peninsula *pop* 68,701

Cor·o·man·del \,kór-ə-'man-d°l, ,kär-\ coast region SE India on Bay of Bengal S of the Krishna

Co·ro·na \kə-'rō-nə\ city SW Calif. E of Los Angeles *pop* 37,791

Cor·o·na·do \,kór-ə-'näd-(,)ō, ,kär-\ city SW Calif. on San Diego Bay opposite San Diego *pop* 16,859

Cor·pus Chris·ti \,kór-pə-'skris-tē\ city & port S Tex. on Corpus Christi Bay (inlet of Gulf of Mexico) at mouth of the Nueces *pop* 231,999

Cor·reg·i·dor \kə-'reg-ə-,dó(ə)r\ island N Philippines at entrance to Manila Bay *area ab* 2 *sq mi* (5 *sq km*)

Cor·rien·tes \,kór-ē-'en-tas, ,kär-\ city NE Argentina *pop* 179,590

Cor·si·ca \'kór-si-kə\ *or F* Corse \'kórs\ island France in the Mediterranean N of Sardinia *area* 3367 *sq mi* (8754 *sq km*), *pop* 289,842 — Cor·si·can \'kór-si-kən\ *adj or n*

Cor·si·ca·na \,kór-sə-'kan-ə\ city NE *cen* Tex. *pop* 21,712

Cor·ti·na *or* Cortina d'Am·pez·zo \kór-'tē-nə-,däm-'pet-(,)sō\ resort village N Italy in the Dolomites N of Belluno

Cort·land \'kórt-lənd\ city S *cen* N.Y. *pop* 20,138

Cor·to·na \kór-'tō-nə\ commune *cen* Italy NW of Perugia *pop* 22,281

Coruña, La; Corunna — see LA CORUÑA

Cor·val·lis \kór-'val-əs\ city W Oreg. SW of Salem *pop* 40,960

Cos — see KOS

Co·sen·za \kō-'zen(t)-sə\ commune S Italy in Calabria *pop* 105,806

Cos·ta Bra·va \,käs-tə-'bräv-ə, ,kòs-, ,kōs-\ coast region NE Spain in Catalonia on the Mediterranean extending NE from Barcelona

Costa del Sol \-del-'sól, -'sōl\ coast region S Spain on the Mediterranean extending E from Gibraltar

Cos·ta Me·sa \,kōs-tə-'mā-sə\ city SW Calif. SE of Long Beach on Pacific coast *pop* 82,562

Cos·ta Ri·ca \,käs-tə-'rē-kə, ,kòs-, ,kōs-\ country Central America bet. Nicaragua & Panama; a republic ✱ San José *area* 19,238 *sq mi* (50,019 *sq km*), *pop* 2,435,000 — Cos·ta Ri·can \-kən\ *adj or n*

Costermansville — see BUKAVU

Côte d'A·zur \,kōt-də-'zü(ə)r\ coast region SE France on the Mediterranean; part of the Riviera

Côte d'Ivoire — see IVORY COAST

Côte d'Or \,kōt-'dó(ə)r\ range of hills E France SW of Dijon

Co·ten·tin \,kō-,tän-'tan\ peninsula NW France projecting into English channel W of mouth of the Seine

Côte-Saint-Luc \,kōt-sänt-'lük, -sənt-\ city Canada in S Que. W of Montreal *pop* 27,531

Co·to·nou \,kōt-ə-'nü\ city & port S Benin, former ✱ of Dahomey *pop* 449,000

Co·to·paxi \,kōt-ə-'pak-sē, -'päk-\ volcano 19,347 *ft* (5897 *m*) N *cen* Ecuador

Cots·wold \'kät-,swōld\ hills SW *cen* England in Gloucestershire; highest point Cleeve Cloud 1031 *ft* (314 *m*)

Cottage Grove city E Minn. *pop* 18,994

Cott·bus *or* Kott·bus \'kät-bəs, -,bús\ city SE E. Germany on Spree river SE of Berlin *pop* 114,840

Cot·ti·an Alps \,kät-ē-ən-\ range of W Alps France & Italy — see VISO

Couls·don and Pur·ley \'kōlz-də-nən-'pər-lē\ former urban district S England in Surrey, now part of Croydon

Coun·cil Bluffs \ˌkau̇n(t)-səl-ˈbləfs\ city SW Iowa on Missouri river *pop* 56,449
Cou·ran·tyne *or* **Co·ren·tyne** \ˈkōr-ən-ˌtīn, ˈkȯr-\ *or D* **Co·ran·tijn** \-ˌtīn\ river 300 *mi* (483 *km*) N S. America flowing N into the Atlantic & forming boundary bet. Guyana & Suriname
Cour·be·voie \ˌku̇r-bəv-ˈwä\ commune N France on the Seine NW of Paris *pop* 54,391
Courland — see KURLAND
Courland Lagoon — see KURISCHES HAFF
Cour·ma·yeur \ˌku̇r-mə-ˈyər\ resort village NW Italy in Valle d'Aosta SE of Mont Blanc *pop* 2741
Courtrai — see KORTRIJK
Cov·en·try **1** \ˈkəv-ən-trē\ town W R.I. *pop* 27,065 **2** \ˈkäv-, ˈkəv-\ city & borough *cen* England in W. Midlands *pop* 312,605
Co·vi·na \kō-ˈvē-nə\ city SW Calif. E of Los Angeles *pop* 33,751
Cov·ing·ton \ˈkəv-iŋ-tən\ city N Ky. *pop* 49,563
Cowes \ˈkau̇z\ town S England on Isle of Wight *pop* 19,663
Cow·litz \ˈkau̇-ləts\ river 150 *mi* (241 *km*) SW Wash. flowing into Columbia river
Co·zu·mel \ˌkō-zə-ˈmel\ island SE Mexico off Quintana Roo
Cracow — see KRAKOW
Craig·av·on \krā-ˈgav-ən\ district *cen* Northern Ireland, established 1974 *area* 147 *sq mi* (382 *sq km*), *pop* 71,202
Cra·io·va \krə-ˈyō-və\ city S Romania *pop* 227,444
Cran·ston \ˈkran(t)-stən\ city E R.I. S of Providence *pop* 71,992
Cra·ter \ˈkrāt-ər\ lake 1932 *ft* (589 *m*) deep SW Oreg. in Cascade range at altitude of 6164 *ft* (1879 *m*); main feature of **Crater Lake National Park**
Craters of the Moon National Monument reservation SE *cen* Idaho including lava flows & other volcanic formations
Cré·cy \krā-ˈsē, ˈkres-ē\ *or* **Cré·cy–en–Pon·thieu** \krā-ˈsē-ˌäⁿ-pōⁿ-ˈtyə(r), -ˈtyœ̄\ commune N France NW of Amiens
Cre·mo·na \kri-ˈmō-nə\ commune N Italy in Lombardy on the Po ESE of Milan *pop* 80,758 — **Crem·o·nese** \ˌkrem-ə-ˈnēz, -ˈnēs\ *adj*
Crete \ˈkrēt\ *or NGk* **Kríti** \ˈkrēt-ē\ island Greece in the E Mediterranean ✱ Canea *area* 3199 *sq mi* (8317 *sq km*), *pop* 483,075 — **Cre·tan** \ˈkrēt-ᵊn\ *adj or n*
Crete, Sea of *or* **Sea of Can·dia** \ˈkan-dē-ə\ the S section of Aegean sea between Crete & the Cyclades
Crewe \ˈkrü\ borough NW England in Cheshire *pop* 47,759
Cri·mea \krī-ˈmē-ə, krə-\ *or Russ* **Krim** \ˈkrim\ peninsula U.S.S.R. in S Soviet Russia, Europe, extending into Black sea SW of Sea of Azov — **Cri·me·an** \krī-ˈmē-ən, krə-\ *adj*
Cris·to·bal \kris-ˈtō-bəl\ *or Sp* **Cris·tó·bal** town N Panama adjoining Colón at Caribbean entrance to Panama canal
Cro·atan \ˌkrō-ə-ˈtan\ *or* **Cro·ato·an** \-ˈtō-ən\ island of uncertain identity, prob. Ocracoke Is., off coast of N.C. bet. Pamlico Sound & the Atlantic thought to be place to which Raleigh's Roanoke Is. colony moved 1587
Cro·atia \krō-ˈā-sh(ē-)ə\ **1** region SE Europe in NW Yugoslavia SE of Slovenia **2** constituent republic of Yugoslavia comprising Croatia, Slavonia, & most of Istria & the Dalmatian coast ✱ Zagreb *area* 21,726 *sq mi* (56,488 *sq km*), *pop* 4,396,397
Crocodile — see LIMPOPO
Cros·by \ˈkrȯz-bē\ *or* **Great Crosby** borough NW England in Merseyside on Irish Sea NNW of Liverpool *pop* 53,660
Cross \ˈkrȯs\ river 300 *mi* (483 *km*) W Africa in W Cameroon & SE Nigeria flowing W & S into Gulf of Guinea
Cro·to·ne \krə-ˈtō-nē\ *or anc* **Cro·to·na** \-nə\ *or* **Cro·ton** \ˈkrō-ˌtän, ˈkrōt-ᵊn\ commune S Italy in Calabria on Gulf of Taranto *pop* 58,281
Croy·don \ˈkrȯid-ᵊn\ borough of S Greater London, England *pop* 322,000
Cro·zet \krō-ˈzā\ islands S Indian ocean WNW of Kerguelen; a French dependency
Crys·tal \ˈkris-tᵊl\ city SE Minn. N of Minneapolis *pop* 25,543
Crystal Lake city N Ill. *pop* 18,590
Cte·si·phon \ˈtes-ə-ˌfän, ˈtē-sə-\ ancient city *cen* Iraq on the Tigris opposite Seleucia ✱ of Parthia & of later Sassanid empire
Cuan·za \ˈkwän-zə\ river 500 *mi* (805 *km*) SW Africa in *cen* Angola flowing NW into the Atlantic
Cu·ba \ˈkyü-bə\ **1** island in the W. Indies N of Caribbean sea *area* 41,634 *sq mi* (108,248 *sq km*) **2** country largely coextensive with island; a republic ✱ Havana *area* 46,736 *sq mi* (121,514 *sq km*), *pop* 9,706,369 — **Cu·ban** \-bən\ *adj or n*
Cu·ban·go \kü-ˈvän(ŋ)-(ˌ)gü\ *or* **Oka·van·go** \ˌō-kə-ˈvaŋ-(ˌ)gō\ river 1000 *mi* (1609 *km*) SW *cen* Africa rising in *cen* Angola & flowing S & E to empty into **Okavango Swamp** (great marsh N of Lake Ngami in NW Botswana)
Cú·cu·ta \ˈkü-kət-ə\ city N Colombia near Venezuela border *pop* 219,772
Cud·a·hy \ˈkəd-ə-(ˌ)hē\ **1** city SW Calif. NW of Downey *pop* 17,984 **2** city SE Wis. *pop* 19,547
Cuen·ca \ˈkweŋ-kə\ **1** city S Ecuador *pop* 104,470 **2** province E *cen* Spain *area* 6636 *sq mi* (17,254 *sq km*), *pop* 188,958 **3** commune, its ✱, ESE of Madrid *pop* 39,403
Cuer·na·va·ca \ˌkwer-nə-ˈväk-ə, -ˈvak-\ city S *cen* Mexico S of Mexico City ✱ of Morelos *pop* 239,814
Cu·lia·cán \ˌkül-yə-ˈkän\ **1** river 175 *mi* (282 *km*) NW Mexico flowing SW into the Pacific at mouth of Gulf of California **2** city NW Mexico on the Culiacán ✱ of Sinaloa *pop* 228,001
Cul·lo·den Moor \kə-ˌläd-ᵊn-, -ˌlōd-\ moorland N Scotland in N Highland region E of Inverness
Cul·ver City \ˌkəl-vər\ city SW Calif. *pop* 38,139
Cu·mae \ˈkyü-(ˌ)mē\ ancient town S Italy on Tyrrhenian coast W of modern Naples — **Cu·mae·an** \kyü-ˈmē-ən\ *adj*
Cu·ma·ná \ˌkü-mə-ˈnä\ city & port NE Venezuela on the Caribbean NE of Barcelona *pop* 119,751
Cum·ber·land \ˈkəm-bər-lənd\ **1** river 687 *mi* (1106 *km*) S Ky. & N Tenn. flowing W into Ohio river **2** falls SE Ky. in upper course of Cumberland river **3** caverns *cen* Tenn. SE of McMinnville **4** city NW Md. on the Potomac *pop* 25,933 **5** town NE R.I. *pop* 27,069 **6** former county NW England ✱ Carlisle — see CUMBRIA
Cumberland Gap mountain pass 1304 *ft* (397 *m*) NE Tenn. through a ridge of the Cumberlands SE of Middlesboro, Ky.
Cumberland plateau *or* **Cumberland mountains** mountain region E U.S., part of the S Appalachian mountains W of Tennessee river extending from S W.Va. to NE Ala.
Cumbre, La — see USPALLATA
Cum·bria \ˈkəm-brē-ə\ **1** — see STRATHCLYDE **2** county NW England including former counties of Cumberland & Westmorland ✱ Carlisle *area* 2659 *sq mi* (6913 *sq km*), *pop* 476,700 — **Cum·bri·an** \ˈkəm-brē-ən\ *adj or n*
Cumbrian mountains NW England chiefly in Cumbria & Lancashire — see SCAFELL PIKE
Cu·naxa \kyü-ˈnak-sə\ town in ancient Babylonia NW of Babylon
Cu·ne·ne *or* **Ku·ne·ne** \kü-ˈnā-nə\ river 700 *mi* (1126 *km*) SW Africa in SW Angola flowing S & W into the Atlantic
Cu·par \ˈkü-pər\ burgh E Scotland ✱ of Fife *pop* 6642
Cu·per·ti·no \ˌkü-pər-ˈtē-(ˌ)nō\ city W Calif. W of San José *pop* 34,015
Cu·ra·çao \ˈk(y)u̇r-ə-ˌsō, -ˌsau̇, ˌk(y)u̇r-ə-ˈ\ island Netherlands Antilles in the S Caribbean; chief town Willemstad *area* 210 *sq mi* (546 *sq km*), *pop* 143,778
Cu·ri·ti·ba \ˌku̇r-ə-ˈtē-bə\ city S Brazil ✱ of Paraná *pop* 1,025,979
Cush or **Kush** \ˈkəsh, ˈku̇sh\ ancient country NE Africa in Nile valley S of Egypt — **Cush·ite** \-ˌīt\ *adj or n* — **Cush·it·ic** \ˌkəsh-ˈit-ik, ku̇sh-\ *adj*
Cus·ter Battlefield National Monument \ˈkəs-tər\ site SE Mont. on the Little Bighorn of battle 1876
Cutch — see KUTCH
Cut·tack \ˈkət-ək\ city E India in Orissa *pop* 326,463
Cux·ha·ven \ku̇ks-ˈhäf-ən\ city & port N W. Germany on North sea at mouth of the Elbe *pop* 58,666
Cuy·a·hoga \ˌkī-(ə-)ˈhō-gə, kə-ˈhō-, -ˈhä-, -ˈhō-\ river 100 *mi* (161 *km*) NE Ohio flowing into Lake Erie at Cleveland
Cuyahoga Falls city NE Ohio N of Akron *pop* 43,890
Cu·yu·ni \kü-ˈyü-nē\ river 300 *mi* (483 *km*) N S. America rising in E Venezuela & flowing E into the Essequibo in N Guyana
Cuz·co *or* **Cus·co** \ˈkü-(ˌ)skō\ city S Peru *pop* 88,104
Cwm·bran \ku̇m-ˈbrän\ urban district SE Wales ✱ of Gwent
Cyc·la·des \ˈsik-lə-ˌdēz\ *or NGk* **Ki·klá·dhes** \kē-ˈklät͟h-əs\ islands Greece in the S Aegean *area* 996 *sq mi* (2590 *sq km*) — **Cy·clad·ic** \sik-ˈlad-ik, sī-ˈklad-\ *adj*
Cydonia — see CANEA — **Cy·do·nian** \sī-ˈdō-nē-ən, -ˈdō-nyən\ *adj or n*
Cymru — see WALES
Cy·press \ˈsī-prəs\ city SW Calif. SE of Los Angeles *pop* 40,391
Cy·prus \ˈsī-prəs\ **1** island E Mediterranean S of Turkey **2** country coextensive with the island; a republic of the Commonwealth ✱ Nicosia *area* 3572 *sq mi* (9287 *sq km*), *pop* 612,851 — **Cyp·ri·ot** \ˈsip-rē-ət, -rē-ˌät\ *or* **Cyp·ri·ote** \-ˌōt, -ət\ *adj or n*
Cy·re·na·ica \ˌsir-ə-ˈnā-ə-kə, ˌsī-rə-\ *or It* **Ci·re·na·ica** \ˌchē-rā-ˈnä-ē-kä\ **1** *or* **Cy·re·ne** \sī-ˈrē-(ˌ)nē\ ancient coastal region N Africa dominated by city of Cyrene **2** region E Libya, formerly a province — **Cy·re·na·ic** \ˌsir-ə-ˈnā-ik, ˌsīr-\ *adj or n* — **Cy·re·na·ican** \-ˈnā-ə-kən\ *adj or n*
Cy·re·ne \sī-ˈrē-(ˌ)nē\ ancient city N Africa on the Mediterranean in NE Libya — **Cy·re·ni·an** \-nē-ən\ *adj or n*
Cyz·i·cus \ˈsiz-i-kəs\ **1** — see KAPIDAGI **2** ancient city in Mysia on isthmus leading to Kapidagi peninsula
Czecho·slo·va·kia \ˌchek-ə-slō-ˈväk-ē-ə, -ˈvak-\ country *cen* Europe; a republic ✱ Prague *area* 49,373 *sq mi* (128,370 *sq km*), *pop* 15,283,095 — **Czecho·slo·vak** \-ˈslō-ˌväk, -ˌvak\ *adj or n* — **Czecho·slo·va·ki·an** \-slō-ˈväk-ē-ən, -ˈvak-\ *adj or n*
Cze·sto·cho·wa \ˌchen(t)-stə-ˈkō-və\ *or Russ* **Chen·sto·khov** \ˈchen(t)-stə-ˈkȯf, -ˈkȯv\ city S Poland on the Warta *pop* 237,713
Da — see GRAND 7
Dac·ca *or* **Dha·ka** \ˈdak-ə, ˈdäk-ə\ city ✱ of Bangladesh *pop* 1,679,572
Da·chau \ˈdäk-ˌau̇\ city SE W. Germany in S Bavaria *pop* 33,950
Da·cia \ˈdā-sh(ē-)ə\ ancient country & Roman province SE Europe roughly equivalent to Romania & Bessarabia — **Da·cian** \-shən\ *adj or n*
Da·dra and Na·gar Ha·ve·li \də-ˈdrä . . . ˌnəg-ər-ə-ˈvel-ē\ union territory India bordering on Gujarat and Maharashtra *area* 189 *sq mi* (491 *sq km*) *pop* 103,677
Dag·en·ham \ˈdag-(ə-)nəm\ former municipal borough SE England in Essex, now part of Barking
Da·ge·stan \ˌdag-ə-ˈstan, ˌdäg-ə-ˈstän\ autonomous republic U.S.S.R. in SE Soviet Russia, Europe, on W shore of the Caspian ✱ Makhachkala *area* 13,124 *sq mi* (34,122 *sq km*), *pop* 1,429,000
Dahomey — see BENIN — **Da·ho·man** \-mən\ *adj or n* — **Da·ho·me·an** \-mē-ən\ *adj or n* — **Da·ho·mey·an** \-mē-ən\ *adj or n*
Dai·ren \ˈdī-ˈren\ *or* **Lü–ta** \ˈlü-ˈdä\ *or* **Lü·da** \ˈlü-ˈdä\ city NE China in S Liaoning on Liaotung peninsula NE of Port Arthur
Da·kar \ˈdak-ˌär, də-ˈkär\ city & port ✱ of Senegal *pop* 798,792
Dakh·la \ˈdäk-lə\ *or formerly* **Vi·lla Cis·ne·ros** \ˌvē-(y)ə-sis-ˈner-əs\ town & port NW Africa in Western Sahara ✱ of Río de Oro
Da·ko·ta \də-ˈkōt-ə\ territory (1861–89) NW U.S. divided 1889 into states of N.D. & S.D. (the **Da·ko·tas** \-əz\) — **Da·ko·tan** \-ˈkōt-ᵊn\ *adj or n*
Dal·e·car·lia \ˌdal-ə-ˈkär-lē-ə\ region W *cen* Sweden — **Dal·e·car·li·an** \-lē-ən\ *adj*
Dal·las \ˈdal-əs, ˈda-lis\ city NE Tex. on Trinity river *pop* 904,078 — **Dal·las·ite** \ˈdal-ə-ˌsīt\ *n*
Dal·ma·tia \dal-ˈmā-sh(ē-)ə\ region W Yugoslavia on the Adriatic — **Dal·ma·tian** \-shən\ *adj or n*
Dal·ton \ˈdȯlt-ᵊn\ city NW Ga. *pop* 20,939
Da·ly City \ˌdā-lē-\ city W Calif. S of San Francisco *pop* 78,519
Da·man \də-ˈman\ *or* **Da·mão** \də-ˈmau̇ⁿ\ district W India on Gulf of Cambay; a constituent part of the union territory of **Daman and Diu** *area* 148 *sq mi* (385 *sq km*) — see GOA, PORTUGUESE INDIA
Da·man·hûr \ˌdam-ən-ˈhu̇(ə)r\ city N Egypt E of Alexandria *pop* 170,633
Da·mas·cus \də-ˈmas-kəs\ city SW Syria, its ✱ *pop* 1,251,028
Dam·a·vand \ˈdam-ə-ˌvand\ *or* **Dem·a·vend** \ˈdem-ə-ˌvend\ mountain 18,934 *ft* (5771 *m*) N Iran; highest in Elburz mountains
Dam·i·et·ta \ˌdam-ē-ˈet-ə\ city & port N Egypt *pop* 93,488
Dam·mam \də-ˈmam\ town & port Saudi Arabia on Persian gulf
Da·mo·dar \ˈdäm-ə-ˌdär\ river 350 *mi* (563 *km*) NE India in *cen* Bihar & W. Bengal flowing ESE into the Hooghly
Dan \ˈdan\ **1** river 180 *mi* (290 *km*) S Va. & N N.C. flowing E into Roanoke river **2** ancient village at N extremity of Palestine

Da Nang \(')dä-'nän\ *or formerly* Tou·rane \tü-'rän\ city & port *cen* Vietnam in Annam
Dan·bury \'dan-,ber-ē, -b(ə-)rē\ city SW Conn. *pop* 60,470
Dandong — see TAN-TUNG
Danger islands — see PUKAPUKA
Danish West Indies the W islands of the Virgin islands group that were until 1917 a Danish possession & now constitute the Virgin Islands of the U.S.
Danmark — see DENMARK
Dan·ube \'dan-,yüb\ *or G* Do·nau \'dō-,naù\ *or anc* Da·nu·bi·us \də-'n(y)ü-bē-əs, da-\ *or* Is·ter \'is-tər\ river 1725 *mi* (2776 *km*) *cen* & SE Europe flowing SE from S W. Germany into Black sea — Da·nu·bi·an \da-'nyü-bē-ən\ *adj*
Dan·vers \'dan-vərz\ town NE Mass. N of Lynn *pop* 24,100
Dan·ville 1 \'dan-,vil\ city E Ill. *pop* 38,985 2 \-,vil, -vəl\ city S Va. on Dan river *pop* 45,642
Dan·zig \'dan(t)-sig, 'dän(t)-\ 1 — see GDANSK 2 territory surrounding & including Gdansk that (1920–39) constituted a free city under the League of Nations
Danzig, Gulf of — see GDANSK, GULF OF
Dar·da·nelles \,därd-ə-n-'elz\ *or* Hel·les·pont \'hel-ə-,spänt\ *or anc* Hel·les·pon·tus \,hel-ə-'spänt-əs\ strait NW Turkey connecting Sea of Marmara with the Aegean
Dar el Beida — see CASABLANCA
Dar es Sa·laam \,där-,es-sə-'läm\ city & port ✻ of Tanzania & of Tanganyika on Indian ocean *pop* 757,346
Dar·fur \där-'fú(ə)r\ region W Sudan; chief city El Fasher
Dar·i·en \,där-ē-'en, ,der-\ 1 town SW Conn. on Long Is. Sound *pop* 18,892 2 Spanish colonial settlement Central America W of Gulf of Darien
Darien, Gulf of inlet of the Caribbean bet. E Panama & NW Colombia
Darien, Isthmus of — see PANAMA, ISTHMUS OF
Dar·jee·ling *or* Dar·ji·ling \där-'jē-liŋ\ city NE India in W. Bengal on Sikkim border *pop* 42,873
Dar·ling \'där-liŋ\ 1 river 1160 *mi* (1867 *km*) SE Australia in Queensland & New S. Wales flowing SW into Murray river 2 mountain range SW Western Australia extending *ab* 250 *mi* (400 *km*) N–S along coast; highest point Mt. Cooke 1910 *ft* (582 *m*)
Dar·ling·ton \'där-liŋ-tən\ borough N England in Durham *pop* 85,396
Darm·stadt \'därm-,stat, -,s(h)tät\ city *cen* W. Germany in Hesse SSW of Frankfurt am Main *pop* 138,201
Dart·moor \'därt-,mú(ə)r, -,mō(ə)r, -,mó(ə)r\ tableland SW England in S Devon *area* 215 *sq mi* (559 *sq km*)
Dart·mouth \'därt-məth\ 1 town SE Mass. W of New Bedford *pop* 23,966 2 city Canada in S N.S. on Halifax harbor opposite Halifax *pop* 62,277 3 borough & port SW England in S Devon on Dart river *pop* 6298
Dar·win \'där-wən\ city & port N Australia ✻ of Northern Territory on Port Darwin (inlet of Timor sea) *pop* 56,482
Dar·yal Gorge *or* Dar·ial Gorge \,där-'yal-\ mountain pass U.S.S.R. in S Soviet Russia, Europe, through Caucasus mountains
Datong — see TATUNG
Dau·gav·pils \'daú-gəf-,pilz\ *or Russ* Dvinsk \də-'vin(t)sk\ city U.S.S.R. in E Latvia on Dvina river *pop* 116,000
Dau·phi·né \,dō-fi-'nā\ region & former province SE France N of Provence ✻ Grenoble
Da·vao \'däv-,aú, dä-'vaú\ 1 gulf of the Pacific, Philippines in SE Mindanao 2 city Philippines on Davao gulf *pop* 610,375
Dav·en·port \'dav-ən-,pō(ə)rt, 'dav-²m-, -,pó(ə)rt\ city E Iowa on Mississippi river *pop* 103,264
Da·vie \'dā-vē\ city SE Fla. *pop* 20,877
Da·vis \'dā-vəs\ 1 mountains W Tex. N of the Big Bend of the Rio Grande 2 strait connecting Baffin Bay with the Atlantic 3 city W Calif. W of Sacramento *pop* 36,640
Daw·son \'dòs-²n\ city N Canada in Yukon
Dax \'daks\ commune SW France in the Landes on the Adour NE of Biarritz *pop* 18,019
Day·ton \'dāt-²n\ city SW Ohio on Miami river *pop* 203,371
Day·to·na Beach \dā-,tō-nə-, də-\ city NE Fla. *pop* 54,176
Dead sea \'ded\ *or bib* Salt sea \'sólt\ *or L* La·cus As·phal·ti·tes \'lā-kə-,sas-,fòl-'tīt-ēz\ salt lake *ab* 50 *mi* (80 *km*) long on boundary bet. Israel & Jordan *area* 370 *sq mi* (962 *sq km*), surface 1286 *ft* (392 *m*) below sea level
Dean, Forest of \'dēn\ forested district SW England in W Gloucester between Severn & Wye rivers; an ancient royal forest
Dear·born \'di(ə)r-,bó(ə)rn, -bərn\ city SE Mich. *pop* 90,660
Dearborn Heights city SE Mich. W of Detroit *pop* 67,706
Death Valley arid valley E Calif. & S Nev. containing lowest point in the U.S. at 280 *ft* (85 *m*) below sea level; most of area included in Death Valley National Monument
Deau·ville \'dō-,vil, dō-'vē(ə)l\ town NW France on Bay of the Seine SSW of Le Havre *pop* 5655
De·bre·cen \'deb-rət-,sen\ city E Hungary *pop* 192,484
De·cap·o·lis \di-'kap-ə-ləs\ confederation of 10 ancient cities N Palestine in region chiefly SE of Sea of Galilee
De·ca·tur \di-'kāt-ər\ 1 city N Ala. *pop* 42,002 2 city NW *cen* Ga. E of Atlanta *pop* 18,404 3 city *cen* Ill. *pop* 94,081
Dec·can \'dek-ən, -,an\ plateau region S *cen* India lying between Eastern Ghats & Western Ghats
Ded·ham \'ded-əm\ town E Mass. SW of Boston *pop* 25,298
Dee \'dē\ 1 river 90 *mi* (145 *km*) NE Scotland flowing E into North sea 2 river 50 *mi* (80 *km*) S Scotland flowing S into Solway firth 3 river 70 *mi* (113 *km*) N Wales & W England flowing E & N into Irish sea
Deer·field Beach city SE Fla. N of Fort Lauderdale *pop* 39,193
Deer Park city SE Tex. *pop* 22,648
De·fi·ance \di-'fī-ən(t)s\ city NW Ohio *pop* 16,810
Deh·ra Dun \,der-ə-'dün\ city N India in NW Uttar Pradesh *pop* 293,628
De Kalb \di-'kalb\ city N Ill. *pop* 33,099
Del·a·goa Bay \,del-ə-,gō-ə-\ inlet of Indian ocean S Mozambique
Del·a·ware \'del-ə-,wa(ə)r, -,we(ə)r, -,wər\ 1 river 296 *mi* (476 *km*) E U.S. flowing S from S N.Y. into Delaware Bay 2 state E U.S. ✻ Dover *area* 2057 *sq mi* (5348 *sq km*), *pop* 594,338 3 city *cen* Ohio NNW of Columbus *pop* 18,780 — Del·a·war·ean \,del-ə-'war-ē-ən, -'wer-\ *n*

Delaware Bay inlet of the Atlantic between SW N.J. & E Del.
Del City \'del\ city *cen* Okla. E of Oklahoma City *pop* 28,424
De·lé·mont \də-lā-'mōⁿ\ commune NW Switzerland ✻ of Jura canton
Delft \'delft\ commune SW Netherlands *pop* 86,287
Del·ga·do, Cape \del-'gäd-(,)ō\ cape NE Mozambique
Del·hi \'del-ē\ 1 union territory N India W of Uttar Pradesh ✻ Delhi *area* 578 *sq mi* (1503 *sq km*) 2 city, its ✻ *pop* 5,713,581 — see NEW DELHI
Dells of the Wisconsin *or* Wisconsin Dells \'delz\ gorge of Wisconsin river in S *cen* Wis. N of Baraboo
Del·mar·va \del-'mär-və\ peninsula E U.S. bet. Chesapeake & Delaware bays comprising Del. & parts of Md. & Va. — see EASTERN SHORE
Del·men·horst \'del-mən-,hòrst\ city N W. Germany in Lower Saxony WSW of Bremen *pop* 72,370
De·los \'dē-,läs\ *or NGk* Dhí·los \'thē-\ island Greece in *cen* Cyclades *area* 2 *sq mi* (5.2 *sq km*) — Del·i·an \'dēl-yən\ *adj or n*
Del·phi \'del-,fī\ ancient town *cen* Greece in Phocis on S slope of Mt. Parnassus near present village of Dhel·foi \thel-'fē\
Del·ray Beach \(,)del-'rā-\ city SE Fla. S of Palm Beach *pop* 34,325
Del Rio \del-'rē-(,)ō, -'rē-ə\ city S Tex. on Rio Grande *pop* 30,034
Del·ta \'del-tə\ municipality Canada in SW B.C. *pop* 74,692
Delta, The region NW Miss. bet. Mississippi & Yazoo rivers
Demavend — see DAMAVAND
Dem·e·ra·ra \,dem-ə-'rär-ə, -'rar-, -'rer-\ river 200 *mi* (322 *km*) Guyana flowing N into the Atlantic
Denali, Denali National Park — see MCKINLEY (Mount)
Den·bigh \'den-bē\ *or* Den·bigh·shire \-,shi(ə)r, -shər\ former county N Wales ✻ Ruthin
Den·der·mon·de \,den-dər-'män-də\ *or* Ter·monde \te(ə)r-'mōⁿ(n)d\ commune NW *cen* Belgium *pop* 22,119
Den Hel·der \də(n)-'hel-dər\ commune W Netherlands in N. Holland on an outlet from Wadden Zee to North sea *pop* 63,647
Den·i·son \'den-ə-sən\ city NE Tex. on Red river *pop* 23,884
De·niz·li \,den-əz-'lē\ city SW Turkey SE of Izmir *pop* 134,673
Den·mark \'den-,märk\ *or Dan* Dan·mark \'dän-,märk\ 1 country N Europe occupying most of Jutland peninsula & adjacent islands in Baltic & North seas; a kingdom ✻ Copenhagen *area* 16,576 *sq mi* (43,098 *sq km*), *pop* 5,119,000 2 strait 130 *mi* (209 *km*) wide bet. SE Greenland & Iceland connecting Arctic ocean with the Atlantic
Dent Blanche \däⁿ-bläⁿsh\ mountain 14,295 *ft* (4357 *m*) S Switzerland in Pennine Alps
Dent du Mi·di \,däⁿ-də-mi-'dē\ mountain 10,686 *ft* (3257 *m*) SW Switzerland in W Alps
Den·ton \'dent-²n\ city N Tex. NW of Dallas *pop* 48,063
D'En·tre·cas·teaux \,däⁿ-trə-'kas-(,)tō\ islands SW Pacific N of E tip of New Guinea belonging to Papua New Guinea *area* 1200 *sq mi* (3120 *sq km*), *pop* 38,894
Den·ver \'den-vər\ city NE *cen* Colo., its ✻ *pop* 492,365 — Den·ver·ite \-və-,rīt\ *n*
De·pew \di-'pyü\ village NW N.Y. E of Buffalo *pop* 19,819
Dept·ford \'det-fərd\ former metropolitan borough SE London, England, now part of Lewisham
Der·be \'dər-(,)bē\ ancient town S Asia Minor in S Lycaonia on border of Cilicia; exact site unknown
Der·bent *or* Der·bend \dər-'bent\ city U.S.S.R. in SE Soviet Russia, Europe, in Dagestan on Caspian sea *pop* 61,000
Der·by \'där-bē, *chiefly U.S.* 'dər-\ borough N *cen* England in Derbyshire *pop* 215,736
Der·by·shire \'där-bē-,shi(ə)r, -shər; *US also* 'dər-\ *or* Derby county N *cen* England ✻ Matlock *area* 1016 *sq mi* (2642 *sq km*), *pop* 910,200
Der·na \'de(ə)r-nə\ city N E Libya *pop* 36,900
Der·ry \'der-ē\ 1 city SE N.H. SE of Manchester *pop* 18,875 2 *or* Lon·don·der·ry \,lən-dən-'der-ē, 'lən-dən-,\ district NW Northern Ireland, established 1974 *area* 148 *sq mi* (385 *sq km*), *pop* 83,384 3 *or* Londonderry county borough & port, NW Derry district *pop* 62,697
Der·went \'dər-wənt\ river 130 *mi* (209 *km*) Australia in Tasmania flowing SE into Tasman sea
Derwent Water lake NW England in Lake District in Cumbria
Desaguadero — see SALADO
Des·chutes \dā-'shüt\ river 250 *mi* (402 *km*) *cen* & N Oreg. E of Cascade range flowing N into Columbia river
Des·er·et \,dez-ə-'ret\ provisional state of the U.S. S of 42d parallel & W of the Rockies organized 1849 by Mormons
Des Moines \di-'móin\ 1 river 327 *mi* (526 *km*) Iowa flowing SE into Mississippi river 2 city ✻ of Iowa on Des Moines river *pop* 191,003
Des·na \'dā-'snä\ river 550 *mi* (885 *km*) U.S.S.R. in SW Soviet Russia, Europe, & N Ukrainian Republic flowing S into the Dnieper
Des Plaines \di-'plänz\ 1 river 150 *mi* (241 *km*) NE Ill. flowing S to unite with Kankakee river forming Illinois river 2 city NE Ill. NW of Chicago *pop* 53,568
Des·roches \dā-'ròsh\ island NW Indian ocean NNE of Madagascar belonging to Seychelles
Des·sau \'des-,aú\ city *cen* E. Germany NE of Halle *pop* 102,957
De·troit \di-'tròit\ 1 river 31 *mi* (50 *km*) Ont. & SE Mich. connecting Lake Erie & Lake St. Clair 2 city SE Mich. on Detroit river *pop* 1,203,339 — De·troit·er \-ər\ *n*
Detskoe Selo — see PUSHKIN
Deur·ne \'dərn-(ə)\ commune N Belgium, E suburb of Antwerp *pop* 77,635
Deutsche Demokratische Republik — see GERMANY
Deutschland — see GERMANY
De·ven·ter \'dā-vən-tər\ commune E Netherlands *pop* 64,453
Devil Mountain — see AUYÁN-TEPUÍ
Devil's Island *or F* Ile du Dia·ble \,ēl-dū-dyäbl'\ island French Guiana in the Safety islands group; former penal colony

---

\ə\ abut \ᵊ\ kitten, F table \ər\ further \a\ ash \ā\ ace \ä\ cot, cart \aú\ out \ch\ chin \e\ bet \ē\ easy \g\ go \i\ hit \ī\ ice \j\ job \ŋ\ sing \ō\ go \ò\ law \ói\ boy \th\ thin \t̲h̲\ the \ü\ loot \ú\ foot \y\ yet \zh\ vision \à, ḵ, ⁿ, œ, œ̄, ᵫ, ᵿ, ᴴ\ *see* Guide to Pronunciation

Devils Post·pile \-'pōst-,pīl\ lava formation E cen Calif. SE of Yosemite National Park; feature of **Devils Postpile National Monument**

Devils Tower or **Ma·to Tepee** \,mät-(,)ō-\ columnar rock formation NE Wyo. rising 865 ft (264 m) in **Devils Tower National Monument**

Dev·on \'dev-ən\ 1 island Northwest Territories, Canada in E Parry islands N of Baffin Is. area 20,861 sq mi (54,239 sq km) 2 or **Dev·on·shire** \'dev-ən-,shi(ə)r, -shər\ county SW England ✱ Exeter area 2591 sq mi (6737 sq km) pop 959,700

Dews·bury \'d(y)üz-,ber-ē, -b(ə-)rē\ borough N England in W. Yorkshire S of Leeds pop 48,339

Dez \'dez\ or **Ab–i–Diz** \,äb-i-'dēz\ river 250 mi (402 km) W Iran flowing S to the Karun

Dezh·nev, Cape \,dezh-nē-'óf, ,desh-, -'óv\ or **East Cape** cape U.S.S.R. in NE Soviet Russia, Asia, at E end of Chukotski peninsula

Dhah·ran \dä-'rän, 'dä-,rän\ town SE Saudi Arabia on Persian Gulf near Bahrain islands pop 12,500

Dhaka — see DACCA

Dhau·la·gi·ri \,daù-lə-'gi(ə)r-ē\ mountain 26,810 ft (8172 m) W cen Nepal in the Himalayas

Di·a·blo, Mount \dē-'äb-(,)lō, dī-'ab-\ mountain 3849 ft (1173 m) cen Calif. at N end of **Diablo range**

Di·a·man·ti·na 1 \,dī-ə,man-'tē-nə\ river 470 mi (756 km) E cen Australia in SW Queensland flowing SW into The Warburton 2 \,dē-ə-\ city E Brazil in cen Minas Gerais pop 36,018

Di·a·mond \'dī-(ə-)mənd\ or **Kum·gang** \'kùm-,gäŋ\ mountains SE N. Korea; highest 5374 ft (1638 m)

Diamond Head promontory Hawaii on Oahu Is. in SE Honolulu

Die·go Gar·cia \dē-,ä-gō-,gär-'sē-ə\ island in Indian ocean, chief island of Chagos archipelago

Dié·go–Sua·rez \dē-,ä-gō-'swär-əs\ city & port Madagascar near N tip of island pop 40,443

Dien Bien Phu \,dyen-,byen-'fü\ village NW Vietnam

Di·eppe \dē-'ep\ city & port N France N of Rouen pop 25,607

Di·jon \dē-zhōⁿ\ city E France pop 149,899

Diks·mui·de or **Dix·mui·de** \dik-'smīd-ə\ or **Dix·mude** \dēk-smǖd\ town W Belgium in W. Flanders N of Ieper pop 15,347

Di·li \'dē-lē\ city & port N Timor, formerly ✱ of Portuguese Timor

Di·mi·trov·grad \də-'mē-trəf-,grad\ city S Bulgaria on the Maritsa ESE of Plovdiv pop 45,596

Di·mi·tro·vo — see PERNIK

Di·nar·ic Alps \də-,nar-ik-\ range of E Alps W Yugoslavia; highest point Djeravica (SW of Pec) 8714 ft (2656 m)

Din·gle Bay \'diŋ-gəl-\ inlet of the Atlantic SW Ireland

Ding·wall \'diŋ-,wòl\ burgh N Scotland NW of Inverness pop 4815

Dinosaur National Monument reservation NW Colo. & NE Utah at junction of Green & Yampa rivers; rich fossil deposits

Di·o·mede \'dī-ə-,mēd\ islands in Bering strait comprising **Big Diomede** (U.S.S.R.) & **Little Diomede** (U.S.)

Diospolis — see THEBES

Di·re·dawa \dir-ə-'daù-ə\ city E Ethiopia pop 91,629

Dis·ko \'dis-(,)kō\ island W Greenland in Davis strait

Dismal or **Great Dismal** swamp SE Va. & NE N.C. between Chesapeake Bay & Albemarle sound ab 40 mi (64 km) long, 10 mi (16 km) wide

District of Co·lum·bia \-kə-'ləm-bē-ə\ federal district E U.S. coextensive with city of Washington area 67 sq mi (174 sq km), pop 638,333

Dis·tri·to Fe·de·ral \di-'strē-tō-,feth-ə-'räl\ 1 district E Argentina largely comprising ✱ city of Buenos Aires area 74 sq mi (192 sq km) 2 — see FEDERAL DISTRICT 1 3 or **Federal District** district cen Mexico including ✱ city of Mexico City area 573 sq mi (1490 sq km) 4 or **Federal District** district N Venezuela including ✱ city of Caracas area 745 sq mi (1937 sq km)

Diu \'dē-(,)ü\ district W India at S end of Kathiawar peninsula; a constituent part of the union territory of Daman and Diu area 20 sq mi (52 sq km) — see GOA, PORTUGUESE INDIA

Dix·on Entrance \,dik-sən-\ strait between N Queen Charlotte islands, B.C., & Prince of Wales Is., Alaska

Di·yar·ba·kir \di-,yär-bä-'kə(ə)r\ or **Di·ar·bekr** \-'bek-ər\ city SE Turkey on the Tigris pop 233,289

Diz·ful \diz-'fül\ city SW Iran on the Karun pop 110,287

Dja·ja, Mount \'jä-yə\ or formerly **Mount Car·stensz** \'kär-stənz\ mountain 16,503 ft (5030 m) Indonesia in W. Irian in Sudirman range; highest in New Guinea

Dja·ja·pu·ra \,jä-yə-'pùr-ə\ or formerly **Hol·lan·dia** \hä-'lan-dē-ə\ or **Ko·ta·ba·ru** \,kōt-ə-'bär-(,)ü\ or **Su·kar·na·pu·ra** \sü-,kär-nə-'pùr-ə\ city & port Indonesia W of W. Irian

Dja·kar·ta or **Ja·kar·ta** \jə-'kärt-ə\ or formerly **Ba·ta·via** \bə-'tā-vē-ə\ city & port ✱ of Indonesia in NW Java pop 6,503,449

Djambi — see TELANAIPURA

Djawa — see JAVA

Djer·ba or **Jer·ba** \'jər-bə\ island SE Tunisia in the Mediterranean at entrance to Gulf of Gabes area 16 sq mi (42 sq km), pop 70,217

Dji·bou·ti \jə-'büt-ē\ 1 or formerly **French Territory of the Afars and the Is·sas** \'äf-,är(z) . . . -ē-'sä(z)\ or earlier **French Somaliland** country E Africa on Gulf of Aden; a republic area 8880 sq mi (23,088 sq km), pop 456,000 2 or **Ji·bu·ti** city, its ✱

Djokjakarta — see YOGYAKARTA

Dne·pro·dzer·zhinsk \'nep-(,)rō-dər-'zhin(t)sk\ city U.S.S.R. in E cen Ukrainian Republic on the Dnieper W of Dnepropetrovsk pop 227,000

Dne·pro·pe·trovsk \,pə-'trófsk\ or formerly **Eka·te·ri·no·slav** \i-,kat-ə-'rē-nə-,släf, -,släv\ city U.S.S.R. in E Ukrainian Republic pop 863,000

Dnie·per \'nē-pər\ river 1400 mi (2253 km) U.S.S.R. rising in S Valdai hills & flowing S through Ukrainian Republic into Black sea

Dnies·ter \'nēs-tər\ river 850 mi (1368 km) U.S.S.R. rising on N slope of Carpathian mountains & flowing SE into Black sea

Do·be·rai \'dō-bə-,rī\ or **Vo·gel·kop** \'vō-gəl-,käp\ peninsula Indonesia in NW W. Irian

Do·bru·ja or **Do·bru·dja** \'dō-brə-jä\ region S Europe in Romania & Bulgaria on Black sea S of the Danube

Do·de·ca·nese \dō-'dek-ə-,nēz, ,dō-di-kə-, -,nēs\ islands Greece in the SE Aegean comprising the Southern Sporades S of Icaria & Samos; belonged to Italy 1923–47 area 486 sq mi (1264 sq km) — see RHODES — **Do·de·ca·ne·sian** \(,)dō-,dek-ə-'nē-zhən, ,dō-di-kə-'nē-zhən, ,dō-dē-kə-, -shən\ adj or n

Dodge City \'däj-\ city S Kans. on Arkansas river pop 18,001

Dog·ger Bank \,dòg-ər-, ,däg-\ submerged sandbank ab 150 mi (241 km) long in North sea E of N England

Do·ha \'dō-(,)hä\ city & port ✱ of Qatar on Persian Gulf pop 150,000

Dol·gel·lau \dòl-'ge-,(h)lī\ or **Dol·gel·ley** or **Dol·gel·ly** \-'ge-(h)lē\ town W Wales in Gwynedd, formerly ✱ of Merionethshire

Dol·lard–des–Or·meaux \dò-'lär-,dā-,zòr-'mō\ town Canada in S Que. NW of Montreal pop 39,940

Do·lo·mites \'dō-lə-,mīts, 'däl-ə-\ or **Dolomite Alps** range of E Alps NE Italy between the Adige & the Piave — see MARMOLADA

Dol·ton \'dōlt-ᵊn\ village NE Ill. S of Chicago pop 24,766

Dôme, Puy de \-pwēd-ə-'dōm\ mountain 4806 ft (1465 m) S cen France in Auvergne mountains

Dom·i·ni·ca \,däm-ə-'nē-kə, də-'min-ə-kə\ island Brit. W. Indies in the Lesser Antilles; a republic of the Commonwealth since 1978 ✱ Roseau area 305 sq mi (793 sq km), pop 74,089

Do·min·i·can Republic \də-,min-i-kən-\ or formerly **San·to Do·min·go** \,sant-ə-'d·min-(,)gō\ or **San Domingo** \,san-\ country W. Indies on E Hispaniola; a republic ✱ Santo Domingo area 18,700 sq mi (48,620 sq km), pop 5,647,977 — **Do·min·i·can** \-'min-\ adj or n

Don \'dän\ river 1200 mi (1931 km) U.S.S.R. in SW Soviet Russia, Europe, flowing SE & then SW into Sea of Azov

Donau — see DANUBE

Don·cas·ter \'däŋ-kə-stər\ borough N England in S. Yorkshire pop 81,610

Don·e·gal \,dän-i-'gòl, ,dən-\ county NW Ireland (republic) in Ulster ✱ Lifford area 1865 sq mi (4849 sq km), pop 125,112

Donegal Bay inlet of the Atlantic NW Ireland

Do·nets \də-'nets\ river 670 mi (1078 km) U.S.S.R. in SE Ukrainian Republic & SW Soviet Russia, Europe, flowing SE into Don river

Donets Basin or **Don·bass** or **Don·bas** \,dən-'bas\ region U.S.S.R. in E Ukrainian Republic SW of the Donets

Do·netsk \də-'netsk\ or formerly **Sta·li·no** \'stäl-i-,nō, 'stal-\ or **Sta·lin** \'stäl-ən, 'stal-, -,ēn\ or **Yu·zov·ka** \'yü-zəf-kə\ city U.S.S.R. in E Ukrainian Republic in Donets basin pop 879,000

Don·ner \'dän-ər\ mountain pass 7135 ft (2175 m) E Calif. in Sierra Nevada

Don·ny·brook \'dän-ē-,brùk\ city E Ireland in Leinster, SE suburb of Dublin

Door \'dòr\ peninsula E Wis. between Green Bay & Lake Michigan

Doornik — see TOURNAI

Dor·ches·ter \'dòr-chə-stər, -,ches-tər\ borough S England ✱ of Dorset pop 14,049

Dor·dogne \dòr-'dōn(-yə)\ river 300 mi (483 km) SW France flowing SW & W to unite with the Garonne forming the Gironde estuary

Dor·drecht \'dòr-,drekt\ or **Dordt** or **Dort** \'dòr)t\ commune SW Netherlands in S. Holland on the Meuse pop 107,947

Dore, Monts \mōⁿ-'dō(ə)r, -'dòr\ mountain group S cen France in Auvergne mountains — see SANCY (Puy de)

Do·ris \'dōr-əs, 'dòr-, 'där-\ 1 ancient country cen Greece bet. Mounts Oeta & Parnassus 2 ancient district SW Asia Minor on coast of Caria

Dor·noch \'dòr-nək, -,näk\ royal burgh N Scotland in Highland region N of Inverness

Dorpat — see TARTU

Dor·set \'dòr-sət\ or **Dor·set·shire** \-,shi(ə)r, -shər\ county S England ✱ Dorchester area 973 sq mi (2530 sq km), pop 596,600

Dorset, Cape cape Canada in SW Baffin Is. on Foxe peninsula

Dort·mund \'dò(ə)rt-,mùnt, -mənd\ city W cen W. Germany in the Ruhr pop 608,297

Dor·val \dòr-'val, -'väl\ city Canada in S Que. pop 17,722

Do·than \'dō-thən\ city SE Ala. pop 48,750

Dou·ai \dü-'ā\ city N France S of Lille pop 43,954

Dou·a·la or **Du·a·la** \dü-'äl-ə\ city & port SW Cameroon on Bight of Biafra pop 458,426

Doug·las \'dəg-ləs\ borough ✱ of Isle of Man pop 20,385

Dou·ro \'dòr-,ü, 'dòr-\ or **Sp Due·ro** \'dwe(ə)r-(,)ō\ river 485 mi (781 km) N Spain & N Portugal flowing W into the Atlantic

Do·ver \'dō-vər\ 1 city cen Del., its ✱ pop 23,512 2 city SE N.H. pop 22,377 3 borough SE England in Kent on Strait of Dover pop 32,843

Dover, Strait of or **F Pas de Ca·lais** \päd-(ə)-kä-le\ channel between SE England & N France, easternmost section of English channel; 20 mi (32 km) wide at narrowest point

Down \'daùn\ district SE Northern Ireland, established 1974 area 250 sq mi (650 sq km), pop 52,869

Dow·ners Grove \,daù-nərz-\ village NE Ill. pop 42,572

Dow·ney \'daù-nē\ city SW Calif. SE of Los Angeles pop 82,602

Down·pat·rick \,daùn-'pa·trik\ town SE Northern Ireland in Down district pop 8245

Downs \'daùnz\ 1 two ranges of hills SE England — see NORTH DOWNS, SOUTH DOWNS 2 roadstead in English channel along E coast of Kent protected by the Goodwin Sands

Dra·chen·fels \'dräk-ən-,felz\ hill 1053 ft (321 m) W W. Germany in the Siebengebirge on the Rhine S of Bonn

Dra·cut \'drā-kət\ town NE Mass. N of Lowell pop 21,249

Dra·kens·berg \'dräk-ənz-,bərg\ or **Quath·lam·ba** \,kwät-'läm-bə\ mountains E Republic of S. Africa in & Lesotho; highest Thabana Ntlenyana 11,425 ft (3482 m)

Drake Passage \'dräk\ strait S of S. America bet. Cape Horn & S. Shetlands

Dram·men \'dräm-ən\ city & port SE Norway pop 49,533

Dran·cy \drän-'sē\ commune N France, NE of Paris pop 64,258

Dra·va or **Dra·ve** \'dräv-ə\ river 450 mi (724 km) S Austria & N Yugoslavia flowing SE into the Danube

Dren·the or **Dren·te** \'dren-tə\ province NE Netherlands ✱ Assen area 1030 sq mi (2678 sq km), pop 424,694

Dres·den \'drez-dən\ city SE E. Germany in Saxony pop 516,604

Dri·na \'drē-nə\ river 160 mi (257 km) cen Yugoslavia flowing N along the border bet. Bosnia & Serbia into the Sava

Dro·ghe·da \'dró(i)-əd-ə, 'dròid-ə\ municipal borough E Ireland in County Louth on the Boyne pop 23,247

Drug — see DURG

Drum·mond·ville \'drəm-ən-,(d)vil\ city Canada in S Que. NE of Montreal pop 27,347

Dry Tor·tu·gas \(,)tòr-'tü-gəz\ island group S Fla. W of Key West; site of **Fort Jef·fer·son National Monument** \'jef-ər-sən\

Duar·te \'dwärt-ē, dů-'ärt-\ city SW Calif. *pop* 16,766

Du·bai \(.)dü-'bī\ 1 sheikhdom, member of United Arab Emirates 2 city, its ✻ *pop.* 265,702

Du·bawnt \dů-'bônt\ 1 lake N Canada in SE Northwest Territories E of Great Slave Lake *area* 1654 *sq mi* (4300 *sq km*) 2 river 580 *mi* (933 *km*) N Canada flowing NE through Dubawnt lake to **Ba·ker Lake** \,bā-kər-\ (W expansion of Chesterfield inlet)

Dub·lin \'dəb-lən\ *or IrGael* **Bai·le Atha Cli·ath** \blä-'klē-ə\ 1 county E Ireland in Leinster *area* 356 *sq mi* (926 *sq km*), *pop* 1,003,164 2 city & county borough & port ✻ of Ireland (republic) & of County Dublin at mouth of the Liffey on Dublin Bay (inlet of Irish sea) *pop* 422,786 — **Dub·lin·er** \'dəb-lə-nər\ *n*

Du·brov·nik \'dü-,brôv-nik\ city & port SW Yugoslavia in Croatia *pop* 31,213

Du·buque \də-'byük\ city E Iowa on Mississippi river *pop* 62,321

Dud·ley \'dəd-lē\ borough W *cen* England in W. Midlands WNW of Birmingham *pop* 187,228

Duis·burg \'dü-əs-,bərg, 'd(y)üz-, *G* 'düēs-,bůrk\ *or formerly* **Duisburg–Ham·born** \-häm-'bô(ə)rn\ city W W. Germany at junction of Rhine & Ruhr rivers *pop* 558,089

Du·luth \də-'lüth\ city & port NE Minn. at W end of Lake Superior *pop* 92,811 — **Du·luth·ian** \-'lü-thē-ən\ *adj or n*

Dul·wich \'dəl-ij, -ich\ a SE district of London, England

Dum·bar·ton \'dəm-'bärt-'n\ 1 burgh W *cen* Scotland in Strathclyde *pop* 23,204 2 *or* **Dum·bar·ton·shire** \-,shi(ə)r, -shər\ DUNBARTON

Dum·fries \,dəm-'frēs\ 1 *or* **Dum·fries·shire** \-'frēs(h)-,shi(ə)r, -shər\ former county S Scotland ✻ Dumfries 2 burgh S Scotland ✻ of Dumfries and Galloway *pop* 32,084

Dumfries and Gal·lo·way \-'gal-ə-,wā\ region S Scotland, established 1975 ✻ Dumfries *area* 2460 *sq mi* (6396 *sq km*), *pop* 145,078

Du·mont \'d(y)ü-,mänt\ borough NE N.J. E of Paterson *pop* 18,334

Dun·bar·ton \,dən-'bärt-'n\ *or* **Dun·bar·ton·shire** \-,shi(ə)r, -shər\ former county W *cen* Scotland ✻ Dumbarton

Dun·can \'dən-kən\ city S Okla. *pop* 22,517

Dun·can·ville \'dən-kən-,vil, -vəl\ city NE Tex. *pop* 27,781

Dun·dalk \,dən-'dô(l)k\ urban district & port NE Ireland (republic) on Dundalk Bay ✻ of County Louth *pop* 25,663

Dun·das \'dən-dəs\ town Canada in SE Ont. *pop* 19,586

Dun·dee \,dən-'dē\ city & port E Scotland ✻ of Tayside on Firth of Tay *pop* 174,746

Dun·edin \,dən-'nēd-²n\ 1 city W Fla. N of Clearwater *pop* 30,203 2 — see EDINBURGH 3 city New Zealand on SE coast of South Is. at head of Otago Harbor *pop* 77,176

Dun·ferm·line \,dən-'fərm-lən\ royal burgh E Scotland in Fife *pop* 52,057

Dun·gan·non \dən-'gan-ən\ district S Northern Ireland, established 1974 *area* 301 *sq mi* (783 *sq km*), *pop* 41,073

Dun·kerque *or* **Dun·kirk** \'dən-,kərk, ,dən-'\ city & port N France on Strait of Dover *pop* 78,171

Dun Laoghai·re \,dən-'lē(ə)r-ə\ *or formerly* **Kings·town** \'kiṅ-,staůn\ borough & port E Ireland in Leinster on Dublin Bay *pop* 53,171

Dun·more \'dən-,mō(ə)r, -,mô(ə)r\ borough NE Pa. *pop* 16,781

Dun·net Head \,dən-ət-\ headland N Scotland on N coast W of John o' Groat's; northernmost point of mainland, at 58°50'N

Duns \'dənz\ burgh SE Scotland in Borders region *pop* 2249

Du·que de Ca·xi·as \,dü-kə-də-kə-'shē-əs\ city SE Brazil in Rio de Janeiro state N of city of Rio de Janeiro *pop* 575,533

Du·ran·go \d(y)ù-'raŋ-(,)gō\ 1 state NW *cen* Mexico *area* 42,272 *sq mi* (109,907 *sq km*), *pop* 1,160,196 2 city, its ✻ *pop* 182,633

Dur·ban \'dər-bən\ city & port E Republic of S. Africa in E Natal on Natal Bay *pop* 736,852

Durg \'dů(ə)rg\ *or formerly* **Drug** \'drüg\ city E *cen* India in SE Madhya Pradesh E of Nagpur *pop* 64,132

Dur·ham \'dər-əm, 'də-rəm, 'důr-əm\ 1 city NE *cen* N.C. NW of Raleigh *pop* 100,831 2 county N England bordering on North sea *area* 911 *sq mi* (2369 *sq km*), *pop* 606,400 3 city, its ✻, S of Newcastle *pop* 26,422

Dur·res \'důr-əs\ *or It* **Du·raz·zo** \dù-'rät-(,)sō\ *or anc* **Ep·i·dam·nus** \,ep-ə-'dam-nəs\ *or* **Dyr·ra·chi·um** \də-'rā-kē-əm\ city & port Albania on Adriatic sea W of Tiranë *pop* 65,900

Du·shan·be \d(y)ü-'sham-bə, -'shäm-\ *or formerly* **Sta·lin·abad** \,stäl-i-nə-'bäd, ,stal-i-nə-'bad\ city U.S.S.R. in Soviet Central Asia ✻ of Tadzhik Republic *pop* 494,000

Düs·sel·dorf \'d(y)üs-əl-,dôrf, 'düs-\ city W W. Germany on the Rhine N of Cologne ✻ of N. Rhine-Westphalia *pop* 590,479

Dutch Borneo — see KALIMANTAN

Dutch East Indies NETHERLANDS EAST INDIES

Dutch Guiana — see SURINAME

Dutch New Guinea NETHERLANDS NEW GUINEA

Dvi·na \də-,vē-'nä\ 1 river 630 *mi* (1014 *km*) U.S.S.R. rising in Valdai hills & flowing W into Gulf of Riga 2 — see NORTHERN DVINA

Dvina Gulf *or* **Dvina Bay** *or formerly* **Gulf of Arch·an·gel** \'är-,kān-jəl\ arm of White sea U.S.S.R. in N Soviet Russia, Europe

Dvinsk — see DAUGAVPILS

Dyf·ed \'dəv-ed, -əd\ county SW Wales ✻ Carmarthen *area* 2226 *sq mi* (5788 *sq km*), *pop* 332,300

Dzaudzhikau — see ORDZHONIKIDZE

Dzer·zhinsk \dər-'zhin(t)sk\ city U.S.S.R. in *cen* Soviet Russia, Europe, on Oka river W of Gorki *pop* 257,000

Dzun·gar·ia \,(d)zəŋ-'gar-ē-ə, (d)zůŋ-, -'ger-\ *or* **Jung·gar** \'zhůŋ-'gär\ *or* **Dzun·gar·ian Basin** \,(d)zəŋ-'gar-ē-ən, (d)zůŋ-, -,ger-\ region W China in N Sinkiang Uighur N of the Tien Shan

E¹ — see LHOTSE

Ea·gan \'ē-gən\ city SE Minn. *pop* 20,700

Ea·gle \'ē-gəl\ lake 13 *mi* (21 *km*) long N Calif. ENE of Lassen Peak

Eagle Pass city SW Tex. on Rio Grande *pop* 21,407

Ea·ling \'ē-liŋ\ borough of W Greater London, England *pop* 284,000

East An·glia \'aŋ-glē-ə\ region E England including Norfolk & Suffolk; one of kingdoms in Anglo-Saxon heptarchy *pop* 1,224,400 — **East An·gli·an** \-ən\ *adj or n*

East Antarctica — see ANTARCTICA

East Bengal the part of Bengal now in Bangladesh

East Beskids — see BESKIDS

East·bourne \'ēs(t)-,bō(ə)rn, -,bô(ə)rn\ borough S England in E. Sussex on English channel *pop* 77,608

East Cape — see DEZHNEV, CAPE

East Chicago city NW Ind. SE of Chicago, Ill. *pop* 39,786

East China sea W Pacific between China (on W), S. Korea (on N), Japan & Ryukyu islands (on E), & Taiwan (on S)

East Cleveland city NE Ohio NE of Cleveland *pop* 36,957

East Detroit city SE Mich. NE of Detroit *pop* 38,280

Eas·ter \'ē-stər\ *or* **Ra·pa Nui** \,räp-ə-'nü-ē\ *or Sp* **Is·la de Pas·cua** \,ēz-lä-də-'päs-kwə\ island Chile in SE Pacific 2000 *mi* (3200 *km*) W of coast *area* 50 *sq mi* (130 *sq km*)

Eastern Ghats \'gôts\ chain of mountains SE India extending SW & S from near delta of the Mahanadi in Orissa to W Tamil Nadu; highest point Mt. Dodabetta (in Nilgiri hills) 8640 *ft* (2633 *m*) — see WESTERN GHATS

Eastern Rumelia region S Bulgaria including Rhodope mountains & the Maritsa valley

Eastern Samoa — see AMERICAN SAMOA

Eastern Shore region E Md. & E Va. E of Chesapeake Bay; sometimes considered as including Del. — see DELMARVA

Eastern Thrace — see THRACE

East Flanders province NW *cen* Belgium ✻ Ghent *area* 1147 *sq mi* (2982 *sq km*), *pop* 1,331,192

East Frisian — see FRISIAN

East Germany the German Democratic Republic — see GERMANY

East Ham \'ēst-'ham\ former county borough SE England in Essex, now part of Newham

East Hartford town *cen* Conn. *pop* 52,563

East Haven \'ēst-,hā-vən\ town S Conn. SE of New Haven *pop* 25,028

East Indies 1 *or* **East India** southeastern Asia including India, Indochina, Malaya, & Malay archipelago — a chiefly former name 2 the Malay archipelago — **East Indian** *adj or n*

East·lake \'ēst-,lāk\ city NE Ohio NE of Cleveland *pop* 22,104

East Lansing city S Mich. *pop* 51,392

East Liverpool city E Ohio on the Ohio *pop* 16,687

East London city & port S Republic of S. Africa in SE Cape of Good Hope on Indian ocean *pop* 119,727

East Lo·thi·an \'lō-thē-ən\ *or* **Had·ding·ton** \'had-iŋ-tən\ *or* **Had·ding·ton·shire** \-,shi(ə)r, -shər\ former county SE Scotland ✻ Haddington — see LOTHIAN

East·main \'ēst-,mān\ river 375 *mi* (604 *km*) Canada in W Que.

East Malaysia the parts of Malaysia on the island of Borneo, comprising Sabah and Sarawak

East Moline city NW Ill. on Mississippi river *pop* 20,907

Eas·ton \'ē-stən\ 1 city SE Mass. SW of Brockton *pop* 16,623 2 city E Pa. NE of Allentown *pop* 26,027

East Orange city NE N.J. NW of Newark *pop* 77,690

East Pakistan the former E division of Pakistan comprising the E portion of Bengal — see BANGLADESH

East Paterson — see ELMWOOD PARK 2

East Peoria city N *cen* Ill. *pop* 22,385

East Point \'ēst-,pôint\ city NW *cen* Ga. SW of Atlanta *pop* 37,486

East Providence city E R.I. *pop* 50,980

East Prussia region N Europe bordering on the Baltic E of Pomerania; formerly a province of Prussia, for a time (1919–39) separated from rest of Prussia by Polish Corridor; since 1945 in Poland & U.S.S.R.

East Punjab — see PUNJAB

East Ridge \'ēst-,rij\ town SE Tenn. SE of Chattanooga *pop* 21,236

East Riding — YORK

East river strait SE N.Y. connecting Upper New York Bay with Long Is. Sound & separating Manhattan Is. from Long Is.

East Saint Louis city SW Ill. *pop* 55,200

East Siberian sea arm of Arctic ocean N of Yakut Republic, U.S.S.R., extending from New Siberian islands to Wrangel Is.

East Strouds·burg \-'straůdz-,bərg\ borough E Pa. *pop* 8039

East Suffolk — see SUFFOLK

East Sus·sex \-'səs-iks, *US also* -,eks\ county SE England ✻ Lewes *area* 693 *sq mi* (1802 *sq km*), *pop* 666,700

Eastview — see VANIER

East York borough Canada in SE Ont. near Toronto *pop* 101,974

Eau Claire \ō-'klā(ə)r, -'klē(ə)r\ city W Wis. *pop* 51,509

Eb·bw Vale \'eb-ü-'väl\ town SE Wales in W Gwent *pop* 24,422

Eboracum — see YORK

Ebro \'ā-(,)brō\ river 480 *mi* (772 *km*) NE Spain flowing from Cantabrian mountains ESE into the Mediterranean

Ecbatana — see HAMADAN

Ec·ua·dor \'ek-wə-,dô(ə)r\ country W S. America bordering on the Pacific; a republic ✻ Quito *area* 104,510 *sq mi* (271,726 *sq km*), *pop* 6,521,710 — **Ec·ua·dor·an** \,ek-wə-'dôr-ən, -'dōr-\ *adj or n* — **Ec·ua·dor·ean** *or* **Ec·ua·dor·ian** \-ē-ən\ *adj or n*

Edam \'ēd-əm, 'ē-,dam, *D* ā-'däm\ commune NW Netherlands on the IJsselmeer NNE of Amsterdam *pop* 23,853

Ede 1 \'äd-ə\ commune E Netherlands NW of Arnhem *pop* 85,892 2 \'ā-,dā\ city SW Nigeria NE of Ibadan *pop* 216,400

Edes·sa \i-'des-ə\ 1 *or* **Vo·de·na** \,vō-the-'nä\ city N Greece in W Macedonia; ancient ✻ of Macedonian kings *pop* 15,980 2 — see URFA

Edi·na \i-'dī-nə\ village SE Minn. SW of Minneapolis *pop* 46,073

Ed·in·boro \'ed-ən-,bər-ə, -,bə-rə\ borough NW corner of Pa *pop* 6324

Edin·burg \'ed-'n-,bərg\ city S Tex. NW of Brownsville *pop* 24,075

Ed·in·burgh \'ed-'n, -bər-ə, -,bə-rə, -b(ə-)rə\ 1 *or ScGael* **Dun·edin** \,də-'nēd-²n\ city W ✻ of Scotland & of Lothian region on Firth of Forth *pop* 419,187 2 *or* **Ed·in·burgh·shire** \-,shi(ə)r, -shər\ — see MIDLOTHIAN

Edir·ne \ā-'dir-nə\ *or formerly* **Adri·a·no·ple** \,ā-drē-ə-'nō-pəl\ city Turkey in Europe on the Maritsa *pop* 71,927

Ed·is·to \'ed-ə-,stō\ river 150 *mi* (241 *km*) S S.C. flowing SE into the Atlantic

Edith Ca·vell, Mount \-'kav-əl, -kə-'vel\ mountain 11,033 *ft* (3363 *m*) Canada in SW Alta. in Jasper National Park

Ed·mond \'ed-mənd\ city *cen* Okla. N of Oklahoma City *pop* 34,637

Ed·monds \'ed-mən(d)z\ city W Wash. N of Seattle *pop* 27,679

Ed·mon·ton \'ed-mən-tən\ **1** city Canada ✲ of Alta. on the N. Saskatchewan *pop* 532,246 **2** former municipal borough SE England in Middlesex, now part of Enfield

Edo — see TOKYO

Edom \'ēd-əm\ *or* **Id·u·maea** *or* **Id·u·mea** \,ij-ə-'mē-ə\ ancient country SW Asia S of Judea & the Dead sea

Ed·ward, Lake \'ed-wərd\ lake E Africa SW of Lake Albert on boundary bet. NE Zaire & SW Uganda *area* 830 *sq mi* (2158 *sq km*)

Ed·wards \'ed-wərdz\ plateau 2000–5000 *ft* (610–1524 *m*) SW Tex.

Efa·te \ā-'fä-,tä\ *or* **F Va·te** \vä-tā\ island SW Pacific in *cen* Vanuatu; chief town Vila (✲ of Vanuatu) *area* 200 *sq mi* (520 *sq km*)

Effigy Mounds National Monument site NE Iowa on Mississippi river NW of Dubuque including prehistoric mounds

Ega·di \'eg-əd-ē\ *or anc* **Ae·ga·tes** \ē-'gāt-ēz\ islands Italy off W coast of Sicily *area* 15 *sq mi* (6 *sq km*)

Eger \'ā-gər\ *or Czech* **Ohře** \'or-zhə\ river 193 *mi* (311 *km*) E W. Germany & W Czechoslovakia flowing NE into the Elbe

Eg·mont, Mount \'eg-,mänt\ *or* **Ta·ra·na·ki** \,tar-ə-'nak-ē, ,tär-\ mountain 8260 *ft* (2518 *m*) New Zealand in W *cen* North Is.

Egorevsk — see YEGOR'YEVSK

Egypt \'ē-japt\ *or Ar* **Misr** \'misr'\ country NE Africa bordering on Mediterranean & Red seas ✲ Cairo *area* 386,198 *sq mi* (1,004,115 *sq km*), *pop* 36,626,204 — see UNITED ARAB REPUBLIC

Ei·fel \'ī-fəl\ plateau region W W. Germany NW of the Moselle & NE of Luxembourg

Ei·ger \'ī-gər\ mountain 13,025 *ft* (3970 *m*) W *cen* Switzerland NE of the Jungfrau

Eind·ho·ven \'īnt-,hō-vən, 'ānt-\ commune S Netherlands in N. Brabant *pop* 194,641

Eire — see IRELAND

Ei·se·nach \'īz-ə'n-,äk, -,äk\ city SW E. Germany in Thuringia W of Erfurt *pop* 50,754

Ekaterinburg — see SVERDLOVSK

Ekaterinodar — see KRASNODAR

Ekaterinoslav — see DNEPROPETROVSK

El Aiún — see AAIÚN, EL

El Alamein — see ALAMEIN

Elam \'ē-ləm\ *or* **Su·si·ana** \,sü-zē-'an-ə, -'än-ə, -'ā-nə\ ancient kingdom SW Asia at head of Persian gulf E of Babylonia ✲ Susa — **Elam·ite** \'ē-lə-,mīt\ *adj or n*

Elatea — see CITHAERON

Elath \'ē-,lath\ **1** — see 'AQABA **2** *or* **Ei·lat** \ā-'lät\ town & port S Israel at head of Gulf of 'Aqaba

Ela·zig \,el-ə-'zig\ city E *cen* Turkey in valley of the upper Murat *pop* 142,787

El·ba \'el-bə\ island Italy in the Mediterranean bet. Corsica & mainland; chief town Portoferraio *area* 86 *sq mi* (224 *sq km*), *pop* 27,602

El Bahnasa — see OXYRHYNCHUS

El·be \'el-bə, 'elb\ *or Czech* **La·be** \'lä-be\ river 720 *mi* (1159 *km*) NW Czechoslovakia, *cen* E. Germany & N W. Germany flowing NW into North sea

El·bert, Mount \'el-bərt\ mountain 14,431 *ft* (4398 *m*) *cen* Colo. in Sawatch mountains; highest in Colo. & Rocky mountains

El·blag \'el-,blȯŋ\ *or G* **El·bing** \'el-biŋ\ city & port N Poland near the Frisches Haff *pop* 112,136

El·brus \el-'brüz\ *or* **El·bo·rus** \,el-bə-'rüz\ mountain 18,481 *ft* (5633 *m*) U.S.S.R. in Kabardin-Balkar Republic; highest in the Caucasus & in Europe

El·burz \el-'bu̇(ə)rz\ mountains N Iran parallel with S shore of Caspian sea — see DAMAVAND

El Ca·jon \,el-kə-'hōn\ city SW Calif. E of San Diego *pop* 73,892

El Cen·tro \el-'sen-(,)trō\ city S Calif. in Imperial valley *pop* 23,996

El Cer·ri·to \,el-sə-'rēt-(,)ō\ city W Calif. on San Francisco Bay N of Berkeley *pop* 22,731

El·che \'el-(,)chā\ city SE Spain SW of Alicante *pop* 164,779

El Do·ra·do \,el-də-'räd-(,)ō, -'rād-ə\ city S Ark. *pop* 25,270

Electric Peak mountain 11,155 *ft* (3400 *m*) S Mont. in Yellowstone National Park; highest in Gallatin range

El·e·phan·ta \,el-ə-'fant-ə\ *or* **Gha·ra·pu·ri** \,gär-ə-'pu̇(ə)r-ē\ island W India in Bombay harbor

El·e·phan·ti·ne \,el-ə-,fan-'tī-nē, -fən-, -'tē-\ island S Egypt in the Nile opposite Aswân *pop* 1814

Eleu·sis \i-'lü-səs\ ancient deme W Attica NW of Athens; ruins at modern town of **Elev·sis** \,el-əf-'sēs\ in E Greece — **Eleu·sin·i·an** \,el-yü-'sin-ē-ən\ *adj or n*

Eleu·thera \i-'lü-thə-rə\ island Bahamas E of New Providence Is. *area* 164 *sq mi* (426 *sq km*)

El Fai·yûm \,el-fī-'(y)üm, -(,)fī-\ city N Egypt SSW of Cairo *pop* 166,910

El Fa·sher \el-'fash-ər\ city W Sudan in Darfur

El Fer·rol \el-fə-'rȯl\ *or* **El Ferrol del Cau·di·llo** \-,del-kau̇-'thē-(,)yō, -'thēl-(,)yȯ\ city & port NW Spain on the Atlantic *pop* 87,736

El Gezira — see GEZIRA, EL

El·gin 1 \'el-jən\ city NE Ill. *pop* 63,798 **2** \'el-gən\ *or* **El·gin·shire** \-,shi(ə)r, -shər\ — see MORAY **3** \'el-gən\ royal burgh NE Scotland in Moray district of Grampian region *pop* 18,905

El·gon, Mount \'el-,gän\ extinct volcano 14,178 *ft* (4321 *m*) E Africa on boundary bet. Uganda & Kenya NE of Lake Victoria

El Hasa — see HASA

Elis \'ē-ləs\ *or NGk* **Ília** \ē-'lē-ə\ region S Greece in NW Peloponnisos S of Achaea bordering on Ionian sea

Elisabethville — see LUBUMBASHI

Elisavetgrad — see KIROVOGRAD

Elisavetpol — see KIROVABAD

Eliz·a·beth \i-'liz-ə-bəth\ **1** short river SE Va. flowing between cities of Norfolk & Portsmouth into Hampton Roads **2** islands SE Mass. bet. Buzzards Bay & Vineyard Sound **3** city & port NE N.J. SW of Newark on Newark Bay *pop* 106,201

Elk Grove Village village NE Ill. NW of Chicago *pop* 28,907

Elk·hart \'el-,kärt\ city N Ind. E of S. Bend *pop* 41,305

Elk Island National Park reservation Canada in E *cen* Alta.

Ellás — see GREECE

Elles·mere \'elz-,mi(ə)r\ island Canada in Northwest Territories W of NW Greenland — see COLUMBIA (Cape)

Ellice — see TUVALU

El·liot Lake \'el-ē-ət-, 'el-yət-\ town Canada in SE Ont. *pop* 16,723

El·lis \'el-əs\ island SE N.Y. in Upper New York Bay; served as immigrant station 1892–1954

El·lo·ra \e-'lōr-ə, -'lȯr-\ *or* **Elu·ra** \-'lu̇r-ə\ village W India in *cen* Maharashtra NW of Aurangabad; caves

Ells·worth Land \'elz-(,)wərth\ region W Antarctica on Bellingshausen sea

El Maghreb al Aqsa — see MAGHREB

El Mansûra — see MANSÛRA

Elm·hurst \'elm-,hərst\ city NE Ill. W of Chicago *pop* 44,276

El Minya — see MINYA, AL

El·mi·ra \el-'mī-rə\ city S N.Y. *pop* 35,327

El Misti — see MISTI

El Mon·te \el-'mänt-ē\ city SW Calif. E of Los Angeles *pop* 79,494

El Mor·ro National Monument \el-'mȯr-(,)ō, -'mȯr-\ reservation W N.Mex. SE of Gallup; rock carvings, pueblo

Elm·wood Park \,elm-,wu̇d-\ **1** village NE Ill. *pop* 24,016 **2** *or formerly* **East Pat·er·son** \'pat-ər-sən\ borough NE N.J. *pop* 18,377

El Obeid \,el-ō-'bād\ city *cen* Sudan in Kordofan *pop* 66,270

El Paso \el-'pas-(,)ō\ city S Tex. at W tip on Rio Grande *pop* 425,259 — **El Paso·an** \-'pas-ə-wən\ *n*

El Sal·va·dor \el-'sal-və-,dó(ə)r, ,sal-və-'\ country Central America bordering on the Pacific; a republic ✲ San Salvador *area* 8236 *sq mi* (21,414 *sq km*) *pop* 4,813,000

Elsass — see ALSACE

Elsene — see IXELLES

El Uqsor — see LUXOR

Elu·ru \e-'lu̇(ə)r-(,)ü\ *or formerly* **El·lore** \e-'lȯ(ə)r, -'lȯ(ə)r\ city SE India in E Andhra Pradesh *pop* 168,148

Ely \'ē-lē\ town E England in N *cen* Cambridgeshire

Ely, Isle of district & former administrative county (✲ Ely) E England in Cambridgeshire — see CAMBRIDGESHIRE

Elyr·ia \i-'lir-ē-ə\ city NE Ohio SW of Cleveland *pop* 57,538

Em·bar·ras *or* **Em·bar·rass** \'am-,brȯ\ river 150 *mi* (241 *km*) E Ill. flowing SE into the Wabash

Em·den \'em-dən\ city & port NW W. Germany at mouth of Ems river *pop* 51,186

Emesa — see HOMS

Emi·lia \ā-'mēl-yə\ **1** district N Italy comprising the W part of Emilia-Romagna region **2** — see EMILIA-ROMAGNA

Emi·lia-Ro·ma·gna \ā-,mēl-yə-rō-'män-yə\ *or formerly* **Emilia** *or anc* **Ae·mil·ia** \ē-'mil-yə\ region N Italy bounded by the Po, the Adriatic, & the Apennines ✲ Bologna *area* 8546 *sq mi* (22,220 *sq km*), *pop* 4,039,388

Em·men \'em-ən\ commune NE Netherlands *pop* 90,816

Em·men·tal *or* **Em·men·thal** \'em-ən-,täl\ valley of the upper **Em·me** \'em-ə\ (river 45 *mi* or 72 *km*) *cen* Switzerland in E Bern canton

Em·po·ria \em-'pōr-ē-ə, -'pȯr-\ city E *cen* Kans. *pop* 25,287

Empty Quarter RUB' AL KHALI

Ems \'emz, 'em(p)s\ **1** river 200 *mi* (322 *km*) NW W. Germany flowing N into North sea **2** *or* **Bad Ems** \'bät-\ town *cen* W. Germany SE of Koblenz *pop* 10,358

Enchanted Mesa sandstone butte W N.Mex. NE of Acoma

En·der·bury \'en-dər-,ber-ē\ island (atoll) *cen* Pacific in the Phoenix islands chain of Kiribati

En·di·cott \'en-di-kət, -də-,kät\ mountains N Alaska, the central range of Brooks range

En·field \'en-,fēld\ **1** town N Conn. *pop* 42,695 **2** borough N Greater London, England *pop* 261,100

En·ga·dine \,eŋ-gə-'dēn\ valley of upper Inn river 60 *mi* (96 *km*) long E Switzerland in Graubünden

En·gland \'iŋ-glənd, 'iŋ-lənd\ **1** *or LL* **An·glia** \'aŋ-glē-ə\ country S Great Britain; a division of the United Kingdom of Great Britain and Northern Ireland ✲ London *area* 50,331 *sq mi* (130,861 *sq km*), *pop* 46,220,955 **2** England & Wales **3** UNITED KINGDOM

En·gle·wood \'eŋ-gəl-,wu̇d\ **1** city N *cen* Colo. S of Denver *pop* 30,021 **2** city NE N.J. on the Hudson *pop* 23,701

English channel *or F* **La Manche** \lä-mä̇nsh\ strait between S England & N France connecting North sea & Atlantic ocean

Enid \'ē-nəd\ city N Okla. *pop* 50,363

Eni·we·tok \,en-i-'wē-,täk\ island (atoll) W Pacific in the NW Marshalls

En·na \'en-ə\ commune Italy in *cen* Sicily *pop* 27,705

En·nis \'en-əs\ urban district W Ireland ✲ of County Clare

En·nis·kil·len \,en-ə-'skil-ən\ *or* **In·nis·kil·ling** \,in-ə-'skil-iŋ\ municipal borough SW Northern Ireland in *cen* Fermanagh district

Enns \'enz, 'en(t)s\ river 160 *mi* (257 *km*) *cen* Austria flowing E & N from Styria into the Danube

En·sche·de \'en(t)-ska-,dā\ commune E Netherlands in Overijssel near German frontier *pop* 144,897

En·se·na·da \,en(t)-sə-'näd-ə\ city & port NW Mexico in Baja California Norte on the Pacific SE of Tijuana *pop* 113,320

En·teb·be \en-'teb-ə, -ē\ town S Uganda N on shore of Lake Victoria; former ✲ of Uganda *pop* 21,096

En·ter·prise \'ent-ər-,prīz\ city SE Ala. *pop* 18,033

Eph·e·sus \'ef-ə-səs\ ancient city W Asia Minor in Ionia near Aegean coast; its site SSE of Izmir — **Ephe·sian** \i-'fē-zhən\ *adj or n*

Ephra·im \'ē-frē-əm\ **1** *or* **Mount Ephraim** hilly region *cen* Palestine in N Jordan E of Jordan river **2** — see ISRAEL

Epidamnus — see DURRES

Ep·i·dau·rus \,ep-ə-'dȯr-əs\ ancient town S Greece in Argolis on Saronic Gulf

Épi·nal \,ā-pi-'nal\ commune NE France on the Moselle *pop* 39,000

Epi·rus *or* **Epei·rus** \i-'pī-rəs\ *or NGk* **Ípi·ros** \'ē-,pē-,rȯs\ region N Greece bordering on Ionian sea — **Epi·rote** \i-'pī-,rōt, -rət\ *n*

Ep·ping Forest \'ep-iŋ\ forested region SE England in Essex NE of London & S of town of **Epping**

Ep·som and Ew·ell \,ep-sə-mən-'(d)yü-əl\ borough SE England in Surrey SW of London *pop* 69,230

Equatorial Guinea country W Africa on Bight of Biafra comprising former Spanish Guinea; an independent republic since 1968 ✲ Malabo *area* 10,831 *sq mi* (28,161 *sq km*), *pop* 300,000 — see SPANISH GUINEA

Erbil — see ARBIL
Er·ci·yas Da·gi \ˌer-jē-ˌ(y)äs-dä-ˈ(g)ē\ mountain 12,848 *ft* (3916 *m*) *cen* Turkey; highest in Asia Minor
Er·e·bus, Mount \ˈer-ə-bəs\ volcano 12,450 *ft* (3795 *m*) E Antarctica on Ross Is. in SW Ross sea
Ere·gli \ˌer-ā-ˈ(g)lē\ **1** city S Turkey SSE of Ankara *pop* 38,362 **2** town & port NW Turkey in Asia on Black sea *pop* 18,978
Er·furt \ˈe(ə)r-fərt, -ˌfu̇(ə)rt\ city SW E. Germany WSW of Leipzig *pop* 212,035
Erie \ˈi(ə)r-ē\ **1** city & port NW Pa. on Lake Erie *pop* 119,123 **2** canal 363 *mi* (584 *km*) long N N.Y. from Hudson river at Albany to Lake Erie at Buffalo; built 1817–25; superseded by **New York State Barge Canal** (*ab* 525 *mi* or 840 *km* long)
Erie, Lake lake E *cen* N. America on boundary bet. the U.S. & Canada; one of the Great Lakes *area* 9940 *sq mi* (25,844 *sq km*)
Eriha — see JERICHO
Er·in \ˈer-ən\ poetic name for Ireland
Er·i·trea \ˌer-ə-ˈtrē-ə, -ˈtrā-\ former country NE Africa bordering on Red sea ✻ Asmara; incorporated (1962) into Ethiopia *area* 46,000 *sq mi* (119,600 *sq km*) — **Er·i·tre·an** \-ən\ *adj or n*
Er·lang·en \ˈe(ə)r-ˌläŋ-ən\ city SE W. Germany in Bavaria NNW of Nuremberg *pop* 101,845
Er·mou·po·lis *or* **Her·mou·po·lis** \er-ˈmü-pə-ləs\ *or* **Sy·ros** \ˈsī-ˌräs\ town & port Greece on Síros; chief town of the Cyclades *pop* 14,115
Er Rif *or* **Rif** \(er-)ˈrif\ mountain range N Morocco on the Mediterranean
Erz·ge·bir·ge \ˈerts-gə-ˌbir-gə\ mountain range SE E. Germany & NW Czechoslovakia on boundary bet. Saxony & Bohemia; highest Klínovec (in Czechoslovakia) 4081 *ft* (1244 *m*)
Er·zin·can \ˌer-zin-ˈjän\ city E *cen* Turkey on the Euphrates *pop* 73,335
Er·zu·rum \ˌerz-(ə-)ˈrüm, ˌərz-\ city NE Turkey in mountains of W Turkish Armenia *pop* 190,121
Es·bjerg \ˈes-bē-ˌe(ə)r(g)\ city & port SW Denmark in SW Jutland peninsula on North sea *pop* 79,694
Escaut — see SCHELDT
Es·con·di·do \ˌes-kən-ˈdēd-(ˌ)ō\ city SW Calif. N of San Diego *pop* 64,355
Es·dra·e·lon, Plain of \ˌez-drə-ˈē-lən\ *or* **Plain of Jez·re·el** \ˈjez-rē-ˌel, -ˌrē(ə)l\ plain N Israel NE of Mt. Carmel in valley of the upper Qishon
Es·fa·hān \ˌes-fə-ˈhän, -ˈhan\ *or* **Is·fa·han** \ˌis-\ *or* **Is·pa·han** \ˌis-pə-\ city W *cen* Iran; former ✻ of Persia *pop* 424,045
Esher \ˈē-shər\ town S England in N Surrey *pop* 61,446
Es·kils·tu·na \ˈes-kəl-ˌstü-nə\ city SE Sweden *pop* 90,354
Es·ki·se·hir \ˌes-ki-shə-ˈhi(ə)r\ *or* **Es·ki·shehr** \-ˈshe(ə)r\ city W *cen* Turkey on tributary of the Sakarya *pop* 309,335
España — see SPAIN
Española — see HISPANIOLA
Es·pí·ri·to San·to \ə-ˌspir-ə-ˌtü-ˈsan-(ˌ)tü\ state E Brazil bordering on the Atlantic ✻ Vitória *area* 16,543 *sq mi* (43,012 *sq km*), *pop* 2,063,679
Es·pi·ri·tu San·to \ə-ˌspir-ə-ˌtü-ˈsan-(ˌ)tü\ island SW Pacific in NW Vanuatu largest in the group *area* 1875 *sq mi* (4875 *sq km*)
Es·qui·line \ˈes-kwə-ˌlīn, -lən\ hill in Rome, Italy, one of seven on which the ancient city was built — see AVENTINE
Es·sa·oui·ra \ˌes-ə-ˈwir-ə\ *or* **Mog·a·dor** \ˈmäg-ə-ˌdō(ə)r\ city & port W Morocco on the Atlantic W of Marrakech *pop* 30,061
Es·sen \ˈes-ᵊn\ city W W. Germany in the Ruhr *pop* 647,643
Es·se·qui·bo \ˌes-ə-ˈkē-(ˌ)bō\ river 600 *mi* (966 *km*) Guyana flowing N into the Atlantic through a wide estuary
Es·sex \ˈes-iks\ county SE England bordering on North sea & N shore of Thames river; one of kingdoms in Anglo-Saxon heptarchy ✻ Chelmsford *area* 1419 *sq mi* (3689 *sq km*), *pop* 1,480,100
Ess·ling·en \ˈes-liŋ-ən\ city S W. Germany on the Neckar *pop* 90,835
Es·te·rel \ˌes-tə-ˈrel\ forested mountain region SE France on coast bet. Fréjus & Cannes; highest point 2020 *ft* (616 *m*)
Es·tes Park \ˌes-tēz-\ valley N Colo. in Front range of the Rocky mountains at E border of Rocky Mountain National Park
Es·to·nia \e-ˈstō-nē-ə, -nyə\ *or* **Es·tho·nia** \e-ˈstō-, es-ˈthō-\ country N Europe bordering on Baltic sea; one of the Baltic Provinces of Russia 1721–1917, an independent republic 1918–40, since 1940 a constituent republic (**Estonian Republic**) of the U.S.S.R. ✻ Tallin *area* 18,361 *sq mi* (47,739 *sq km*), *pop* 1,466,000
Es·to·ril \ˌesh-tə-ˈril\ resort town Portugal on coast W of Lisbon *pop* 15,740
Es·tre·ma·du·ra \ˌes-trə-mə-ˈdu̇r-ə\ **1** region & old province W *cen* Portugal ✻ Lisbon; SW part included in present Estremadura province **2** *or* **Ex·tre·ma·du·ra** \ˌek-strə-\ region & old province W Spain bordering on Portugal; area included in present Cáceres & Badajoz provinces
Ethi·o·pia \ˌē-thē-ˈō-pē-ə\ **1** ancient country NE Africa S of Egypt bordering on Red sea **2** *or* **Ab·ys·sin·ia** \ˌab-ə-ˈsin-yə, -ˈsin-ē-ə\ country E Africa; formerly an empire, since 1975 a republic ✻ Addis Ababa *area* 471,776 *sq mi* (1,226,618 *sq km*), *pop* 32,775,000
Et·na \ˈet-nə\ volcano 10,902 *ft* (3323 *m*) Italy in NE Sicily
Eto·bi·coke \e-ˈtō-bi-ˌkō—*sic*\ borough Canada in SE Ont. *pop* 298,713
Eton \ˈēt-ᵊn\ town SE *cen* England in Berkshire
Etru·ria \i-ˈtru̇r-ē-ə\ ancient country *cen* Italy coextensive with modern Tuscany & part of Umbria; home of the Etruscans
Et·trick Forest \ˌe-trik-\ region, formerly a forest & hunting ground, in SE Scotland in Borders region
Euboea — see ÉVVOIA — **Eu·boe·an** \yu̇-ˈbē-ən\ *adj or n*
Eu·clid \ˈyü-kləd\ city NE Ohio NE of Cleveland *pop* 59,999
Eu·ga·ne·an \yü-ˈgā-nē-ən, ˌyü-gə-ˈnē-\ hills NE Italy in SW Veneto bet. Padua & the Adige
Eu·gene \yü-ˈjēn\ city W Oreg. on the Willamette *pop* 105,624
Eu·less \ˈyü-ləs\ village NE Tex. NE of Fort Worth *pop* 24,002
Eu·pen \ˈȯi-pən; ˌə(r)-ˈpen, œ̄-\ commune E Belgium E of Liège; formerly in Germany, transferred (with Malmédy) to Belgium 1919
Eu·phra·tes \yu̇-ˈfrāt-(ˌ)ēz\ river 1700 *mi* (2736 *km*) SW Asia flowing from E Turkey SW & SE to unite with the Tigris forming the Shatt-al-Arab — see KARA SU — **Eu·phra·te·an** \-ˈfrāt-ē-ən\ *adj*
Eur·asia \yu̇-ˈrā-zhə, -shə\ name given to Asia & Europe as one continent
Eure \ˈər\ river 140 *mi* (225 *km*) NW France flowing N into the Seine
Eu·re·ka \yu̇-ˈrē-kə\ city & port NW Calif. *pop* 24,153
Eu·rope \ˈyu̇r-əp\ **1** continent of the E hemisphere bet. Asia & the Atlantic *area ab* 3,800,000 *sq mi* (9,880,000 *sq km*) **2** the European continent as distinguished from the British Isles
European Economic Community *or* **Common Market** economic community consisting of Belgium, France, Italy, Luxembourg, Netherlands, West Germany, Denmark, Greece, Ireland, United Kingdom, Spain, & Portugal
Ev·ans, Mount \ˈev-ənz\ mountain 14,264 *ft* (4348 *m*) N *cen* Colo. in Front range WSW of Denver
Ev·ans·ton \ˈev-ən(t)-stən\ city NE Ill. N of Chicago *pop* 73,706
Ev·ans·ville \ˈev-ənz-ˌvil\ city SW Ind. on Ohio river *pop* 130,496
Ev·er·est, Mount \ˈev-(ə-)rəst\ *or Tibetan* **Cho·mo·lung·ma** \ˌchō-mə-ˈlu̇ŋ-mə\ mountain 29,028 *ft* (8848 *m*) S Asia on border bet. Nepal & Tibet in the Himalayas; highest in the world
Ev·er·ett \ˈev-(ə-)rət\ **1** city E Mass. N of Boston *pop* 37,195 **2** city NW *cen* Wash. on Puget Sound N of Seattle *pop* 54,413
Ev·er·glades \ˈev-ər-ˌglādz\ swamp region S Fla. S of Lake Okeechobee; now partly drained; SW part forms **Everglades National Park**
Evergreen Park village NE Ill. S of Chicago *pop* 22,260
Eve·sham \ˈēv-shəm\ borough W *cen* England in Hereford and Worcester S of Birmingham in **Vale of Evesham** *pop* 15,271
Évian *or* **Évian–les–Bains** \ā-vyäⁿ-le-baⁿ\ commune E France on Lake Geneva; health resort *pop* 5765
Évo·ra \ˈev-ə-rə\ city S *cen* Portugal *pop* 50,545
Évreux \āv-ˈrə(r)\ commune N France WNW of Paris *pop* 46,181
Ev·ri·pos \ˈev-ri-ˌpȯs\ *or* **Eu·ri·pus** \yu̇-ˈrī-pəs\ *or NGk* **Ev·rí·pou Porth·mós** \ˈev-ri-pü-ˈpȯrth-ˌmȯs\ narrow strait E Greece bet. Évvoia & mainland
Évros — see MARITSA
Év·voia \ˈev-(ˌ)yä\ *or* **Eu·boea** \yu̇-ˈbē-ə\ island 90 *mi* (145 *km*) long E Greece in the Aegean NE of Attica & Boetia ✻ Chalcis *area* 1457 *sq mi* (3788 *sq km*)
Ex·e·ter \ˈek-sət-ər\ city SW England ✻ of Devon *pop* 95,621
Ex·moor \ˈek-ˌsmu̇(ə)r, -ˌsmō(ə)r, -ˌsmȯ(ə)r\ moorland SW England in Somerset & Devonshire *area* 32 *sq mi* (83 *sq km*)
Ex·u·ma \ik-ˈsü-mə, ig-ˈzü-\ islands in *cen* Bahamas S of **Exuma Sound** (SE of New Providence Is.); chief island **Great Exuma**
Eyre \ˈa(ə)r, ˈe(ə)r\ peninsula Australia in S S. Australia W of Spencer Gulf
Eyre, Lake intermittent lake *cen* Australia in NE S. Australia
Eyzies, Les — see LES EYZIES
Fa·en·za \fä-ˈen-zə, -ˈen(t)-sə\ commune N Italy *pop* 55,003
Faer·oe *or* **Far·oe** \ˈfa(ə)r-(ˌ)ō, ˈfe(ə)r-\ islands Denmark in the NE Atlantic NW of the Shetlands ✻ Thorshavn *area* 540 *sq mi* (1404 *sq km*), *pop* 44,000
Fa·ial \fə-ˈyäl, fī-ˈäl\ island *cen* Azores *area* 64 *sq mi* (166 *sq km*)
Fair·banks \ˈfa(ə)r-ˌbaŋ(k)s, ˈfe(ə)r-\ city E *cen* Alaska *pop* 22,645
Fair·born \ˈfa(ə)r-ˌbȯ(ə)rn, ˈfe(ə)r-\ city SW *cen* Ohio *pop* 29,702
Fair·fax \ˈfa(ə)r-ˌfaks, ˈfe(ə)r-\ city NE Va. *pop* 19,390
Fair·field \ˈfa(ə)r-ˌfēld, ˈfe(ə)r-\ **1** city W Calif. NE of Berkeley *pop* 58,099 **2** city SW Conn. SW of Bridgeport *pop* 54,849 **3** city SW Ohio *pop* 30,777
Fair Lawn borough NE N.J. NE of Paterson *pop* 32,229
Fair·mont \ˈfa(ə)r-ˌmänt, ˈfe(ə)r-\ city N W.Va. *pop* 23,863
Fair·view Park \ˌfa(ə)r-ˌvyü-, ˌfe(ə)r-\ city NE Ohio *pop* 19,311
Fair·weath·er, Mount \ˈfa(ə)r-ˌweth-ər, ˈfe(ə)r-\ mountain 15,300 *ft* (4663 *m*) on boundary between Alaska & B.C.; highest in **Fairweather range** of the Coast ranges
Fai·sa·la·bad \ˌfī-ˌsäl-ə-ˈbäd, -ˌsal-ə-ˈbad\ *or formerly* **Lyall·pur** \lē-ˌäl-ˈpu̇(ə)r\ city NE Pakistan W of Lahore *pop* 1,092,000
Faiyûm, El — see EL FAIYÛM
Faiz·abad \ˈfī-zə-ˌbad\ **1** city NE Afghanistan *pop* 70,871 **2** *or* **Fyz·abad** \ˈfī-\ city N India in Uttar Pradesh *pop* 141,714
Fa·jar·do \fə-ˈhärd-(ˌ)ō\ town NE Puerto Rico *pop* 26,298
Fa·ka·ra·va \ˌfäk-ə-ˈräv-ə\ island (atoll) S Pacific, principal island of the Tuamotu archipelago
Fako — see CAMEROON
Fa·laise \fa-ˈlāz\ town NW France SSE of Caen *pop* 8133
Fal·kirk \ˈfȯl-(ˌ)kərk\ royal burgh *cen* Scotland in Central region ENE of Glasgow *pop* 36,875
Falk·land \ˈfȯ(l)-klənd\ *or Sp* **Is·las Mal·vi·nas** \ˌēz-läz-mäl-ˈvē-näs\ islands SW Atlantic E of S end of Argentina; a Brit. crown colony ✻ Stanley *area* 4618 *sq mi* (12,007 *sq km*)
Falkland Islands Dependencies islands & territories in the S Atlantic & in Antarctica administered by the British from Falkland islands, including S. Orkney, S. Sandwich, & S. Shetland islands, S. Georgia Is., Antarctic peninsula, & Antarctic archipelago
Fall River \ˈfȯl\ city & port SE Mass. *pop* 92,574
Fal·mouth \ˈfal-məth\ town SE Mass. on Cape Cod *pop* 23,640
False Bay \ˈfȯls\ inlet Republic of S. Africa in SW Cape Province E of Cape of Good Hope
Fal·ster \ˈfȯl-stər, ˈfäl-\ island Denmark in Baltic sea S of Sjælland
Fa·ma·gus·ta \ˌfäm-ə-ˈgüs-tə, ˌfam-\ city & port E Cyprus on **Famagusta Bay** (inlet of the Mediterranean) *pop* 42,500
Fanning — see TABUAERAN
Far·al·lon \ˈfar-ə-ˌlän\ islands in the Pacific W *cen* Calif. W of San Francisco
Far East the countries of E Asia & the Malay archipelago — usu. considered as comprising the Asian countries bordering on the Pacific but sometimes as including also India, Sri Lanka, Bangladesh, Tibet, & Burma — **Far Eastern** *adj*
Fare·well, Cape \ˈfa(ə)r-ˌwel, ˈfe(ə)r-\ cape Greenland at S tip
Far·go \ˈfär-(ˌ)gō\ city E N.Dak. on Red river *pop* 61,383
Farm·ers Branch \ˈfär-mərz\ city NE Tex. *pop* 24,863
Far·ming·ton \ˈfär-miŋ-tən\ city NW N.Mex. *pop* 31,222
Farmington Hills city SE Mich. *pop* 58,056

Far·quhar \\'fär-k(w)ər\ island group NW Indian ocean NE of Madagascar belonging to Seychelles

Far·rukh·abad \fə-'rü-kə-,bad, -,bäd\ city N India in Uttar Pradesh on the Ganges WNW of Lucknow pop 160,927

Fársala — see PHARSALUS

Fashoda — see KODOK

Fá·ti·ma \'fat-ə-mə\ village cen Portugal NNE of Lisbon

Fatshan — see FO-SHAN

Fay·ette·ville \'fā-ət-,vil, -vəl; 2 is also 'fed-vəl\ 1 city NW Ark. pop 36,608 2 city SE cen N.C. on Cape Fear river pop 59,507

Fear, Cape \'fi(ə)r\ cape SE N.C. at mouth of Cape Fear river

Feath·er \'feth-ər\ river 100 mi (161 km) N cen Calif. flowing S into Sacramento river

Federal Capital Territory — see AUSTRALIAN CAPITAL TERRITORY

Federal District 1 or Pg Dis·tri·to Fe·de·ral \dish-'trē-tü-,feth-ə-'räl\ district E cen Brazil including ✳ city of Brasília area 2260 sq mi (5876 sq km) 2 — see DISTRITO FEDERAL 3 3 — see DISTRITO FEDERAL 4

Federated Malay States former Brit. protectorate (1895–1945) comprising the Malay states of Negri Sembilan, Pahang, Perak, & Selangor ✳ Kuala Lumpur

Federated Shan States — see SHAN STATE

Fen \'fen, 'fən\ river 300 mi (483 km) N China in cen Shansi flowing SSE into the Hwang

Fengtien 1 — see LIAONING 2 — see MUKDEN

Fer·ga·na or **Fer·gha·na** \fər-'gän-ə\ valley U.S.S.R. in the Tien Shan in Kirghiz, Tadzhik, & Uzbek republics SE of Tashkent

Fer·gu·son \'fər-gə-sən\ city E Mo. N of St. Louis pop 24,740

Fer·man·agh \fər-'man-ə\ district SW Northern Ireland, established 1974 area 724 sq mi (1882 sq km), pop 51,008

Fer·nan·do de No·ro·nha \fər-'nan-(,)dō-də-nə-'rōn-yə\ island Brazil in the Atlantic NE of city of Natal area 7 sq mi (18 sq km)

Fernando Po or **Fernando Poo** — see BIOKO

Fern·dale \'fərn-,dāl\ city SE Mich. N of Detroit pop 26,227

Fer·ra·ra \fə-'rär-ə\ commune N Italy in Emilia-Romagna NE of Bologna near the Po pop 150,265

Ferro — see HIERRO

Ferrol, El — see EL FERROL

Ferryville — see MENZEL-BOURGUIBA

Fertile Crescent semicircle of fertile land stretching from SE coast of Mediterranean around Syrian desert N of Arabia to Persian Gulf

Fez \'fez\ or **Fès** \'fes\ city N cen Morocco pop 448,823

Fez·zan \fe-'zan\ region SW Libya, chiefly desert

Fich·tel·ge·bir·ge \'fik-t'l-gə-,bir-gə\ mountains E W. Germany in NE Bavaria; highest Schneeberg 3448 ft (1051 m)

Fie·so·le \fē-'ā-zə-lē, -,lā\ or anc **Fae·su·lae** \'fē-zə-,lē\ commune cen Italy in Tuscany NE of Florence pop 14,486

Fife \'fīf\ or **Fife·shire** \-,shi(ə)r\ region, formerly a county E Scotland between firths of Tay & Forth ✳ Cupar area 504 sq mi (1310 sq km), pop 326,480

Fi·ji \'fē-(,)jē\ islands SW Pacific E of Vanuatu constituting (with Rotuma Is.) an independent dominion of the Commonwealth ✳ Suva (on Viti Levu) area 7083 sq mi (18,416 sq km), pop 588,068 — **Fi·ji·an** \-ən\ adj or n

Filch·ner Ice Shelf \'filk-nər\ area of shelf ice Antarctica in Weddell sea

Filipinas, República de — see PHILIPPINES

Finch·ley \'finch-lē\ former municipal borough SE England in Middlesex, now part of Barnet

Find·lay \'fin-(d)lē\ city NW Ohio pop 35,594

Fin·gal's Cave \'fiŋ-gəlz-\ sea cave W Scotland on Staffa Is.

Fin·ger Lakes \'fiŋ-gər-\ group of long narrow lakes W cen N.Y. comprising Cayuga, Seneca, Keuka, Canandaigua, Skaneateles, Owasco, & several smaller lakes

Fin·is·terre, Cape \,fin-ə-'ste(ə)r, -'ster-ē\ cape NW Spain on coast of La Coruña province; westernmost point of Spanish mainland, at 9°18′W

Fin·land \'fin-lənd\ or **Finn Suo·mi** \'swō-mē\ country N Europe bordering on Gulf of Bothnia & Gulf of Finland; a rep. ✳ Helsinki area 130,165 sq mi (338,429 sq km), pop 4,717,724 — **Fin·land·er** n

Finland, Gulf of arm of Baltic sea between Finland & Estonia

Fin·lay \'fin-lē\ river 250 mi (402 km) Canada in N cen B.C. flowing SE to unite with **Pars·nip** \,pär-snəp\ river (145 mi or 232 km) forming Peace river

Fins·bury \'finz-,ber-ē, -b(ə-)rē\ former metropolitan borough E cen London, England, now part of Islington

Fin·ster·aar·horn \,fin(t)-stər-'är-,hô(ə)rn\ mountain 14,022 ft (4274 m) S Switzerland; highest of the Berner Alpen

Fiord·land \fē-'ô(ə)rd-,land\ mountain region S New Zealand in SW South Is.

Fitch·burg \'fich-,bərg\ city N cen Mass. pop 39,580

Fiume — see RIJEKA

Fiu·mi·ci·no \,fyü-mə-'chē-(,)nō\ town cen Italy on Tyrrhenian sea SW of Rome & WNW of Ostia pop 13,180

Flag·staff \'flag-,staf\ city N cen Ariz. pop 34,743

Flam·bor·ough Head \,flam-,bər-ə-, -,bə-rə-, -b(ə-)rə-\ promontory NE England on Humberside coast

Flan·ders \'flan-dərz\ or F **Flan·dre** \fläⁿdr^ə\ or Flem **Vlaan·de·ren** \'vlän-də-rə(n)\ 1 medieval county along coast of what is now Belgium and adjacent parts of France & Netherlands ✳ Lille 2 semiautonomous region W Belgium — see EAST FLANDERS, WEST FLANDERS

Flat·head \'flat-,hed\ river 250 mi (402 km) SE B.C. & NW Mont. flowing S through Flathead Lake (reservoir in Mont.) into Clark Fork

Flat·tery, Cape \'flat-ə-rē\ cape NW Wash. at entrance to Strait of Juan de Fuca

Flens·burg \'flenz-,bərg, 'flen(t)s-,bürk\ city & port N W. Germany on inlet of the Baltic near Danish border pop 87,862

Fletsch·horn \'flech-,hô(ə)rn\ or **Ross·bo·den·horn** \'rôs-'bōd-'n-,hô(ə)rn\ mountain 13,127 ft (4001 m) S Switzerland in Pennine Alps S of Simplon pass

Flevo·land \'flev-ō-,land\ province cen Netherlands ✳ Lelystad area 548 sq mi (1420 sq km)

Flin·ders \'flin-dərz\ 1 river 500 mi (805 km) Australia in cen Queensland flowing NW into Gulf of Carpentaria 2 mountain ranges Australia in E S. Australia E of Lake Torrens

Flint \'flint\ 1 river 265 mi (426 km) W Ga. flowing S & SW into Lake Seminole 2 city SE cen Mich. NNW of Detroit pop 159,611 3 or **Flint·shire** \-,shi(ə)r, -shər\ former county NE Wales ✳ Mold

Flod·den \'fläd-'n\ hill N England in N Northumberland near Scottish border

Floral Park village SE N.Y. on E Long Is. pop 16,805

Flor·ence \'flōr-ən(t)s, 'flär-\ 1 city NW Ala. on Tennessee river pop 37,029 2 city E S.C. pop 30,062 3 or It **Fi·ren·ze** \fē-'rent-sā\ commune cen Italy on the Arno ✳ of Tuscany pop 453,293 — **Flor·en·tine** \'flōr-ən-,tēn, 'flär-, -,tīn\ adj or n

Flo·res \'flōr-əs, 'flór-\ 1 island NW Azores area 57 sq mi (148 sq km) 2 island Indonesia in Lesser Sunda islands area 5509 sq mi (14,323 sq km), pop 6556

Flo·ri·a·nó·po·lis \,flōr-ē-ə-'näp-ə-ləs, ,flór-\ city S Brazil ✳ of Santa Catarina state on island off coast pop 187,800

Flor·i·da \'flōr-əd-ə, 'flär-\ 1 state SE U.S. ✳ Tallahassee area 58,560 sq mi (152,256 sq km), pop 9,746,324 2 \'flōr-əd-ə, 'flär-; flə-'rēd-ə\ island W Pacific in SE Solomons N of Guadalcanal — **Flo·rid·i·an** \flə-'rid-ē-ən\ adj or n — **Flor·i·dan** \'flōr-əd-ən, 'flär-\ adj or n

Florida, Straits of channel bet. Florida Keys (on NW) & Cuba & Bahamas (on S & E) connecting Gulf of Mexico with the Atlantic

Florida Keys chain of islands S Florida extending SW from S tip of the peninsula

Flo·ris·sant \'flōr-ə-sənt, 'flór-\ city E Mo. NNW of St. Louis pop 55,372

Flo·ris·sant Fossil Beds National Monument \'flōr-ə-sənt, ,flór-\ reservation cen Colo.

Flush·ing \'fləsh-iŋ\ 1 section of New York City on Long Is. in Queens 2 — see VLISSINGEN

Fly \'flī\ river 650 mi (1046 km) S New Guinea flowing SE into Gulf of Papua

Foc·sa·ni \fōk-'shän-(ē)\ city E Romania in S Moldavia pop 62,275

Fog·gia \'fó-jə, -(,)jä\ commune SE Italy in Apulia pop 157,126

Foggy Bottom section of Washington, D.C., near the Potomac where the State Department building is located

Foix \'fwä\ region & former province S France in the Pyrenees SE of Gascony

Folke·stone \'fōk-stən, US also -,stōn\ borough SE England in Kent on Strait of Dover pop 43,742

Fond du Lac \'fän-d'l-,ak, 'fän-jə-,lak\ city E Wis. on Lake Winnebago pop 35,863

Fon·se·ca, Gulf of \fän-'sā-kə\ or **Fonseca Bay** inlet of the Pacific in Central America in El Salvador, Honduras, & Nicaragua

Fon·taine·bleau \'fänt-'n-,blō\ commune N France pop 16,436

Fon·tana \fän-'tan-ə\ city SW Calif. E of Los Angeles pop 37,111

Foo·chow \'fü-'jō, -'chau\ or **Fu·zhou** \'fü-'jō\ or **Fu–chou** \-'jō\ or formerly **Min·how** \'min-'hō\ city & port SE China ✳ of Fukien on Min river pop 623,000

For·a·ker, Mount \'fór-i-kər, 'fär-\ mountain 17,400 ft (5304 m) S Alaska in Alaska range SW of Mt. McKinley

Forest Park 1 city N Ga. SE of Atlanta pop 18,782 2 city SW Ohio N of Cincinnati pop 18,675

For·far \'fór-fər\ 1 or **For·far·shire** \-,shi(ə)r, -shər\ — see ANGUS 2 royal burgh E Scotland in Tayside pop 12,742

Fo·ril·lon National Park \,fór-ē(l)-'yōⁿ-\ reservation E Canada in Gaspé peninsula

For·lì \fór-'lē\ commune N Italy in Emilia-Romagna SE of Bologna pop 109,815

For·mo·sa \fór-'mō-sə, fər-, -zə\ 1 — see TAIWAN 2 strait between Taiwan & China mainland connecting E. China & S. China seas — **For·mo·san** \-'mōs-'n, -'mōz-\ adj or n

For·ta·le·za \,fórt-'l-'ā-zə\ city & port NE Brazil on the Atlantic ✳ of Ceará pop 1,308,919

Fort Col·lins \'käl-ənz\ city N Colo. pop 65,092

Fort–de–France \,fórd-ə-'fräⁿs\ city French W. Indies ✳ of Martinique on W coast pop 93,598

Fort de Kock — see BUKITTINGGI

Fort Dodge \'däj\ city NW cen Iowa pop 29,423

Fort Erie \'i(ə)r-ē\ town Canada in SE Ont. on Niagara river pop 24,096

Fort Fred·er·i·ca National Monument \,fred-ə-'rē-kə, fre-'drē-\ reservation SE Ga. on W shore of St. Simons Is. containing site of fort built by Oglethorpe 1736

Fort George \'jó(ə)rj\ river 480 mi (772 km) Canada in cen Que. flowing W into James Bay

Forth \'fō(ə)rth, 'fó(ə)rth\ river 114 mi (183 km) S cen Scotland flowing E into **Firth of Forth** (estuary 48 mi or 77 km long, inlet of North sea)

Fort Jefferson National Monument — see DRY TORTUGAS

Fort Knox \'näks\ military reservation N cen Ky. SSW of Louisville; location of U.S. Gold Bullion Depository

Fort–Lamy — see N'DJAMENA

Fort Lau·der·dale \'lód-ər-,dāl\ city SE Fla. on the Atlantic pop 153,279

Fort Lee \'lē\ borough NE N.J. on the Hudson pop 32,449

Fort Mc·Hen·ry National Monument \mə-'ken-rē\ site in Baltimore, Md., of a fort bombarded 1814 by the British

Fort Ma·tan·zas National Monument \mə-'tan-zəs\ reservation SSE of St. Augustine, Fla., containing fort built ab 1736 by the Spanish

Fort Mc·Mur·ray \mak-'mər-ē\ city Canada in NE Alta. pop 31,000

Fort My·ers \'mi(-ə)rz\ city SW Fla. pop 36,638

Fort Nel·son \'nel-sən\ river 260 mi (418 km) Canada in NE B.C. flowing NW into the Liard

Fort Peck Reservoir \'pek\ reservoir ab 130 mi (209 km) long NE Mont. formed in Missouri river by **Fort Peck Dam**

Fort Pierce \'pi(ə)rs\ city E Fla. on the Atlantic pop 33,802

Fort Pu·las·ki National Monument \pə-'las-kē, pyü-\ reservation E Ga. comprising island in mouth of Savannah river, site of a fort built 1829–47 to replace Revolutionary Fort Greene

Fort Smith \'smith\ city NW Ark. on Arkansas river pop 71,626

Fort Stan·wix National Monument \'stan-(,)wiks\ historic site E cen N.Y. in Rome

Fort Sum·ter National Monument \'səm(p)-tər\ reservation S.C. at entrance to Charleston harbor containing site of Fort Sumter

Fort Union National Monument reservation NE N.Mex. ENE of Santa Fe containing site of military post 1851–91

Fort Wal·ton Beach \'wólt-'n\ city NW Fla. E of Pensacola pop 20,829

Fort Wayne \'wän\ city NE Ind. pop 172,196

Fort William — see THUNDER BAY
Fort Worth \\'wərth\\ city N Tex. W of Dallas *pop* 385,164
Fos \\'fôs\\ port S France on Gulf of Fos in Rhône delta *pop* 2693
Fo–shan *or* **Fo·shan** \\'fō-'shän\\ *or* **Fat·shan** \\'fäch-'än\\ city SE China in *cen* Kwangtung SW of Canton *pop* 120,000
Fossil Butte National Monument reservation SW Wyo. containing aquatic fossils
Fountain Valley city SW Calif. SE of Los Angeles *pop* 55,080
Four Forest Cantons the cantons of Uri, Schwyz, Unterwalden, & Lucerne in *cen* Switzerland surrounding Vierwaldstätter See
Fou·ta Djal·lon *or* **Fu·ta Jal·lon** \\'füt-ə-jə-'lōn\\ mountain region W Guinea; highest point *ab* 4200 *ft* (1280 *m*)
Fox \\'fäks\\ **1** islands SW Alaska in the E Aleutians — see UMNAK, UNALASKA, UNIMAK **2** river 220 *mi* (354 *km*) SE Wis. & NE Ill. flowing S into Illinois river **3** river 175 *mi* (282 *km*) E Wis. flowing NE & N through Lake Winnebago into Green Bay
Foxe Basin \\'fäks-\\ inlet of the Atlantic N Canada in E Northwest Territories W of Baffin Is.; connected with Hudson bay by **Foxe Channel**
Foyle \\'fói(ə)l\\ river *ab* 20 *mi* (32 *km*) N Ireland flowing NE past city of Derry to **Lough Foyle** (inlet of the Atlantic 18 *mi or* 29 *km* long)
Fra·ming·ham \\'frā-miŋ-,ham\\ town E Mass. WSW of Boston *pop* 65,113
France \\'fran(t)s\\ country W Europe bet. English channel & the Mediterranean; a republic ✻ Paris *area* 212,659 *sq mi* (552,913 *sq km*), *pop* 52,655,802
Franche–Com·té \\fränsh-kōⁿ-tā\\ region & former county & province E France E of the Saône ✻ Besançon — see BURGUNDY
Fran·cis Case, Lake \\-,fran(t)-səs-'käs\\ reservoir *ab* 100 *mi* (161 *km*) long S S.Dak. formed in Missouri river by **Fort Ran·dall Dam** \\'ran-d²l\\
Fran·co·nia \\fraŋ-'kō-nē-ə, -nyə\\ former duchy in Austrasia, now included chiefly in Baden-Wurtemburg, Bavaria, & Hesse states, W. Germany — **Fran·co·ni·an** \\-nē-ən, -nyən\\ *adj or n*
Francs Peak *or* **Franks Peak** \\'fraŋ(k)s-\\ mountain 13,140 *ft* (4005 *m*) NW Wyo; highest in Absaroka range
Frank·fort \\'fraŋk-fərt\\ city ✻ of Ky., on Kentucky river E of Louisville *pop* 25,973
Frank·furt \\'fraŋk-fərt, 'fräŋk-,fú(ə)rt\\ *or* **Frankfurt an der Oder** \\-,än-də-'rōd-ər\\ city E Germany on the Oder *pop* 70,817
Frank·furt am Main \\'fraŋk-fərt-, 'fräŋ-,fú(ə)rt-(,)äm-'mīn\\ *or* **Frankfurt** city *cen* W. Germany on Main river *pop* 629,375
Frank·lin \\'fraŋ-klən\\ **1** town E *cen* Mass. SW of Boston *pop* 18,217 **2** city SE Wis., a SSW suburb of Milwaukee *pop* 16,871 **3** former district Canada in N Northwest Territories including Arctic islands & Boothia & Melville peninsulas
Franklin D. Roosevelt Lake reservoir 151 *mi* (243 *km*) long NE Wash. formed in Columbia river by Grand Coulee Dam
Franklin Park village NE Ill. W of Chicago *pop* 17,507
Franz Jo·sef Land \\fran(t)s-'jō-zəf-,land *also* -saf-; fran(t)s-'yō-zəf-,länt\\ archipelago U.S.S.R. in Soviet Russia, Europe, in Arctic ocean N of Novaya Zemlya
Fras·ca·ti \\fra-'skät-ē, frä-\\ commune *cen* Italy in Latium SE of Rome *pop* 18,728
Fra·ser \\'frā-zər, -zhər\\ river 850 *mi* (1368 *km*) Canada in S *cen* B.C. flowing into Strait of Georgia
Frau·en·feld \\'fraú-(ə)n-,felt\\ commune NE Switzerland ✻ of Thurgau canton *pop* 18,607
Fred·er·ick \\'fred-(ə-)rik\\ city N Md. *pop* 28,086
Fred·er·ic·ton \\'fred-(ə-)rik-tən\\ city Canada ✻ of N.B. on St. John river *pop* 43,723
Fred·er·iks·berg \\'fred-(ə-)riks-,bərg\\ city Denmark on Sjælland Is., a W suburb of Copenhagen *pop* 88,167
Free·man \\'frē-mən\\ city SE S. Dak. *pop* 1462
Free·port \\'frē-,pō(ə)rt, -,pó(ə)rt\\ **1** city N Ill. W of Rockford *pop* 26,266 **2** village SE N.Y. on Long Is. *pop* 38,272 **3** city NW Bahamas on *cen* Grand Bahama Is. *pop* 22,301
Free·town \\'frē-,taún\\ city & port ✻ of Sierra Leone on the Atlantic *pop* 178,600
Frei·burg \\'frī-,bú(ə)rg, -,bərg\\ *or* **Freiburg im Breis·gau** \\-im-'brīs-,gaú\\ city SW W. Germany at W foot of Black Forest *pop* 175,106
Fréjus — see CENIS, MONT 2
Fré·jus, Mas·sif du \\ma-,sēf-də-frā-'zhüs, -'zhūēs\\ mountain on border bet. France & Italy at SW end of Graian Alps
Fre·man·tle \\'frē-,mant-²l\\ city Australia in SW Western Australia at mouth of Swan river; port for Perth *pop* 22,484
Fre·mont \\'frē-,mänt\\ **1** city W Calif. SE of Oakland *pop* 131,945 **2** city E Nebr. *pop* 23,979 **3** city N Ohio *pop* 17,834
French Broad \\'bród\\ river 210 *mi* (338 *km*) flowing from W N.C. to E Tenn.
French Community *or* **F Com·mu·nau·té fran·çaise** \\kō-mūē-nō-tā-fräⁿ-sez\\ former federation comprising metropolitan France, its overseas departments & territories, & the former French territories in Africa that on becoming republics chose to maintain their ties with France
French Equatorial Africa *or* **French Congo** former country W *cen* Africa N of Congo river comprising a federation of Chad, Gabon, Middle Congo, & Ubangi-Shari territories ✻ Brazzaville
French Guiana country N S. America; an overseas department of France ✻ Cayenne *area* 34,740 *sq mi* (90,324 *sq km*), *pop* 73,022
French Guinea — see GUINEA
French India former French possessions in India including Chandernagore (ceded to India 1950) & Pondicherry, Karikal, Yanaon, & Mahé (ceded to India 1954) ✻ Pondicherry
French Indochina — see INDOCHINA
French Morocco — see MOROCCO
French Polynesia *or formerly* **French Oceania** islands in S Pacific belonging to France & including Society, Marquesas, Tuamotu, Gambier, & Tubuai groups ✻ Papeete (on Tahiti) *pop* 137,382
French Somaliland — see DJIBOUTI
French Sudan — see MALI
French Territory of the Afars and the Issas — see DJIBOUTI
French Togo — see TOGOLAND
French Union former federation (1946–58) comprising metropolitan France & its overseas departments, territories, & associated states — see FRENCH COMMUNITY

French West Africa former federation of French dependencies W Africa consisting of Dahomey, French Guinea, French Sudan, Ivory Coast, Mauritania, Niger, Senegal, & Upper Volta
French West Indies islands of the W. Indies belonging to France & including Guadeloupe, Martinique, Désirade, Les Saintes, Marie Galante, St. Barthélemy, & part of St. Martin
Fres·no \\'frez-(,)nō\\ city S *cen* Calif. SE of San Francisco *pop* 218,202
Fria, Cape \\'frē-ə\\ cape NW Namibia on the Atlantic
Fri·bourg \\frē-'bú(ə)r\\ **1** canton W *cen* Switzerland *area* 647 *sq mi* (1682 *sq km*), *pop* 185,246 **2** commune, its ✻, SW of Bern *pop* 37,400
Frid·ley \\'frid-lē\\ city SE Minn. N of St. Paul *pop* 30,228
Fries·land \\'frēz-land, 'frēs-, -,land\\ **1** old region N Europe bordering on North sea **2** province N Netherlands ✻ Leeuwarden *area* 1431 *sq mi* (3721 *sq km*), *pop* 595,131
Frio, Cape \\'frē-(,)ō\\ cape SE Brazil E of Rio de Janeiro
Fri·sches Haff \\'frish-əs-,häf\\ lagoon N Poland & E Soviet Russia, Europe; inlet of Gulf of Gdansk
Fri·sian \\'frizh-ən, 'frē-zhən\\ islands NW Europe in North sea including **West Frisian** islands (off N Netherlands), **East Frisian** islands (off NW W. Germany), & **North Frisian** islands (off W. Germany & Denmark, including Helgoland & Sylt)
Fri·u·li \\'frē-ə-(,)lē, frē-'ü-lē\\ district N Italy in Friuli-Venezia Giulia on Yugoslav border — **Fri·u·li·an** \\frē-'ü-lē-ən\\ *adj or n*
Friuli–Ve·ne·zia Giu·lia \\-və-,net-sē-ə-'jül-yə\\ region N Italy E of Veneto ✻ Udine *area* 6223 *sq mi* (16,180 *sq km*), *pop* 1,229,929
Fro·bi·sher Bay \\,frō-bi-shər-\\ inlet of the Atlantic N Canada in E Northwest Territories on SE coast of Baffin Is.
Front \\'frənt\\ range of the Rockies extending from *cen* Colo. N into SE Wyo. — see GRAYS PEAK
Fro·ward, Cape \\'frō-(w)ərd\\ headland S Chile N of Strait of Magellan; southernmost point of mainland of S. America at *ab* 53°54′S
Frun·ze \\'frün-zə\\ *or formerly* **Pish·pek** \\pish-'pek\\ city U.S.S.R. on Chu river ✻ of Kirghiz Republic *pop* 431,000
Fu–chou — see FOOCHOW
Fu·jai·ra \\fü-'jī-rə\\ sheikhdom, member of United Arab Emirates
Fu·ji \\'fü-jē\\ *or* **Fu·ji·ya·ma** \\,fü-jē-'(y)äm-ə\\ *or* **Fu·ji–san** \\-'sän\\ mountain 12,388 *ft* (3776 *m*) Japan in S *cen* Honshu; highest in Japan
Fu·kien \\'fü-'kyen, -kē-'en\\ *or* **Fu·jian** \\'fü-'jän, -jē-'än\\ province SE China bordering on Formosa strait ✻ Foochow *area* 47,529 *sq mi* (123,575 *sq km*), *pop* 25,931,106
Fu·ku·o·ka \\,fü-kə-'wō-kə\\ city & port Japan on N Kyushu on inlet of Tsushima strait *pop* 1,104,483
Ful·da \\'fúl-də\\ city E W. Germany *pop* 57,035
Ful·ham \\'fúl-əm\\ former metropolitan borough SW London, England, now part of Hammersmith
Ful·ler·ton \\'fúl-ərt-²n\\ city SW Calif. NE of Long Beach *pop* 102,034
Fu·na·fu·ti \\,f(y)ü-nə-'f(y)üt-ē\\ island (atoll) S Pacific in *cen* Tuvalu islands; contains ✻ of the group *pop* 1328
Fun·chal \\fün-'shäl, ,fən-\\ city & port Portugal ✻ of Madeira Is. *pop* 119,022
Fun·dy, Bay of \\'fən-dē\\ inlet of the Atlantic SE Canada bet. N.B. & N.S.
Fundy National Park reservation SE Canada in N.B. on upper Bay of Fundy
Fur·neaux \\'fər-(,)nō\\ islands Australia off NE Tasmania
Fur·ness \\'fər-nəs\\ district N England comprising peninsula in Irish sea in SW Cumbria
Fürth \\'fú(ə)rt, 'fuert\\ city SE W. Germany NW of Nuremberg *pop* 99,088
Fu·se \\'fü-(,)sä\\ city Japan in S Honshu E of Osaka
Fu·shun \\'fü-'shún\\ city NE China in NE Liaoning E of Mukden *pop* 1,019,000
Fu·sin *or* **Fu·xin** \\'fü-'shin\\ city NE China in NE Liaoning
Futa Jallon — see FOUTA DJALLON
Fu·tu·na \\fə-'tü-nə\\ **1** *or* **Hoorn** \\'hō(ə)rn, 'hó(ə)rn\\ islands SW Pacific NE of Fiji; formerly a French protectorate, since 1959 part of Wallis & Futuna islands territory *pop* 2689 **2** island SW Pacific in Futuna group **3** island SW Pacific in SE Vanuatu
Fuzhou — see FOOCHOW
Fyn \\'fin\\ island Denmark in the Baltic bet. Sjælland & Jutland; chief city Odense *area* 1149 *sq mi* (2987 *sq km*), *pop* 389,404
Fyzabad — see FAIZABAD
Ga·bès \\'gäb-əs, -,es\\ city & port SE Tunisia on Gulf of Gabès *or anc* **Syr·tis Mi·nor** \\'sirt-əs-\\ (arm of the Mediterranean) *pop* 40,585
Ga·bon \\ga-'bōⁿ\\ **1** *or* **Ga·boon** *or* **Ga·bun** \\gə-'bün, ga-\\ river NW Gabon flowing into the Atlantic through long wide estuary **2** country W Africa on the Atlantic; formerly a territory of French Equatorial Africa, since 1958 a republic ✻ Libreville *area* 103,089 *sq mi* (268,031 *sq km*), *pop* 1,206,000 — **Ga·bo·nese** \\,gab-ə-'nēz, -'nēs\\ *adj or n*
Ga·bo·rone \\,gab-ə-'rōn\\ *or formerly* **Ga·be·ro·nes** \\-'rō-nəs\\ town SE Botswana, its ✻ *pop* 59,000
Gad·a·ra \\'gad-ə-rə\\ ancient town Palestine SE of Sea of Galilee — **Gad·a·rene** \\'gad-ə-,rēn, ,gad-ə-'\\ *adj or n*
Gades *or* **Gadir** — see CÁDIZ — **Gad·i·tan** \\'gad-ə-tən\\ *adj or n*
Gads·den \\'gadz-dən\\ city NE Ala. on the Coosa *pop* 47,565
Gadsden Purchase tract of land S of Gila river in present Ariz. & N.Mex. purchased 1853 by the U.S. from Mexico *area* 29,640 *sq mi* (77,064 *sq km*)
Ga·e·ta \\gä-'ät-ə\\ city & port *cen* Italy in Latium on Gulf of Gaeta (inlet of Tyrrhenian sea N of Bay of Naples) *pop* 22,605
Gaf·sa \\'gaf-sə\\ *or anc* **Cap·sa** \\'kap-sə\\ oasis W *cen* Tunisia
Ga·han·na \\gə-'han-ə\\ city *cen* Ohio NE of Columbus *pop* 18,001
Gaines·ville \\'gānz-,vil, -vəl\\ city N *cen* Fla. *pop* 81,371
Gaird·ner, Lake \\'ga(ə)rd-nər, 'ge(ə)rd-\\ salt lake Australia in S. Australia W of Lake Torrens *area* 1840 *sq mi* (4784 *sq km*)
Ga·lá·pa·gos Islands \\gə-'läp-ə-gəs, -'lap-\\ *or* **Ar·chi·pié·la·go de Co·lón** \\,är-chē-'pyel-ə-gō-thā-kə-'lōn\\ island group Ecuador in the Pacific W

---

of mainland ✻ on San Cristóbal Is. *area* 3029 *sq mi* (7875 *sq km*), *pop* 4037 — see ISABELA

Gal·a·ta \'gal-ət-ə\ port & commercial section of Istanbul, Turkey

Ga·la·ti \gə-'läts(-ē)\ city E Romania on the Danube *pop* 260,898

Ga·la·tia \gə-'lā-sh(ē-)ə\ ancient country & Roman province *cen* Asia Minor in region centered on modern Ankara, Turkey — **Ga·la·tian** \-shən\ *adj or n*

Gald·hö·pig·gen \'gäl-,hə(r)-,pig-ən\ mountain 8100 *ft* (2469 *m*) S *cen* Norway in Jotunheim mountains

Gales·burg \'gā(ə)lz-,bərg\ city NW Ill. WNW of Peoria *pop* 35,305

Ga·li·cia \gə-'lish-(ē-)ə\ **1** region E *cen* Europe including N slopes of the Carpathians & valleys of the upper Vistula, Dniester, Bug, & Seret rivers; former Austrian crown land; belonged to Poland between the two world wars; now divided between Poland & Ukrainian Republic **2** region & ancient kingdom NW Spain bordering on the Atlantic — **Ga·li·cian** \-'lish-ən\ *adj or n*

Gal·i·lee \'gal-ə-,lē\ hill region N Israel N of Esdraelon plain — **Gal·i·le·an** \,gal-ə-'lē-ən\ *adj or n*

Galilee, Sea of *or bib* **Lake of Gen·nes·a·ret** \gə-'nes-ə-,ret, -rət\ *or* **Sea of Ti·be·ri·as** \tī-'bir-ē-əs\ *or* **Sea of Chin·ne·reth** \'kin-ə-,reth\ *or Heb* **Yam Kin·ne·ret** \'yäm-'kin-ə-,ret\ lake 14 *mi* (22 *km*) long & 8 *mi* (13 *km*) wide N Israel on Syrian border traversed by Jordan river; 686 *ft* (209 *m*) below sea level

Gal·la·tin \'gal-ət-ᵊn\ **1** city N Tenn. *pop* 17,191 **2** mountain range S Mont. — see ELECTRIC PEAK **3** river 125 *mi* (201 *km*) SW Mont. — see THREE FORKS

Ga·lli·nas, Point \gə-'yē-nəs\ cape N Colombia; northernmost point of S. America, at 12°15′ N

Gal·lip·o·li \gə-'lip-ə-lē\ *or* **Ge·li·bo·lu** \,gel-ə-bə-'lü\ peninsula Turkey in Europe bet. the Dardanelles & Saros gulf — see CHERSONESE

Gal·lo·way \'gal-ə-,wā\ former district SW Scotland comprising area formerly in counties of Wigtown & Kirkcudbright — see DUMFRIES AND GALLOWAY — **Gal·we·gian** \gal-'wē-j(ē-)ən\ *adj or n*

Gal·lup \'gal-əp\ city NW N.Mex. near Indian reservations *pop* 18,161

Galt \'gölt\ former city, Ont., Canada — see CAMBRIDGE

Gal·ves·ton \'gal-və-stən\ city SE Tex. on **Galveston Island** (30 *mi or* 48 *km* long) at entrance to **Galveston Bay** (inlet of Gulf of Mexico) *pop* 61,902 — **Gal·ves·to·nian** \,gal-və-'stō-nē-ən, -nyən\ *n*

Gal·way \'gȯl-,wā\ **1** county W Ireland in Connacht bordering on the Atlantic *area* 2293 *sq mi* (5962 *sq km*), *pop* 172,018 **2** municipal borough & port, its ✻, on **Galway Bay** (inlet) *pop* 37,835

Gam·bia \'gam-bē-ə\ **1** river 460 *mi* (740 *km*) W Africa flowing from Fouta Djallon in W Guinea W through Senegal into the Atlantic in Gambia **2** *or* **The Gambia** country W Africa; a republic in the Commonwealth ✻ Banjul *area* 3977 *sq mi* (10,340 *sq km*), *pop* 695,886 — **Gam·bi·an** \-bē-ən\ *adj or n*

Gam·bier \'gam-,bi(ə)r\ islands S Pacific SE of Tuamotu archipelago belonging to France — see MANGAREVA

Gan — see KAN

Gana — see GHANA

Gand — see GHENT

Gan·dhi·na·gar \'gən-də-,nəg-ər\ town W India ✻ of Gujarat

Gandzha — see KIROVABAD

Gan·ges \'gan-,jēz\ river 1550 *mi* (2494 *km*) N India flowing from the Himalayas SE & E to unite with the Brahmaputra & empty into Bay of Bengal through the vast **Ganges delta** — see HOOGHLY — **Gan·get·ic** \gan-'jet-ik\ *adj*

Gang·tok \'gaŋ-'täk, 'gəŋ-\ town NE India ✻ of Sikkim *pop* 12,000

Gan·nett Peak \,gan-ət-\ mountain 13,785 *ft* (4202 *m*) *cen* Wyo.; highest in Wind River range & in the state

Gansu — see KANSU

Gar — see KAERH

Gar·da, Lake \'gärd-ə\ lake 35 *mi* (56 *km*) long N Italy bet. Lombardy & Veneto draining through the Mincio into the Po

Gar·de·na \gär-'dē-nə\ city SW Calif. S of Los Angeles *pop* 45,165

Garden City **1** city W Kans. on Arkansas river *pop* 18,256 **2** city SE Mich. SW of Detroit *pop* 35,640 **3** village SE N.Y. on Long Is. *pop* 22,927

Garden Grove city SW Calif. SW of Los Angeles *pop* 123,351

Gard·ner \'gärd-nər\ city N *cen* Mass. *pop* 17,900

Gar·field \'gär-,fēld\ **1** mountain 10,961 *ft* (3341 *m*) SW Mont. near Idaho border; highest in Beaverhead & Bitterroot ranges **2** city NE N.J. N of Newark *pop* 26,803

Garfield Heights city NE Ohio SSE of Cleveland *pop* 34,938

Ga·ri·glia·no \,gär-ēl-'yän-(,)ō\ river 100 *mi* (161 *km*) *cen* Italy in Latium flowing SE & SW into Gulf of Gaeta

Gar·land \'gär-lənd\ city NE Tex. NNE of Dallas *pop* 138,857

Gar·misch–Par·ten·kir·chen \'gär-mish-'pärt-ᵊn-,ki(ə)r-kən\ city S W. Germany in Bavaria SW of Munich in foothills of the Alps *pop* 27,828

Ga·ronne \gə-'rän, -'rȯn\ river 355 *mi* (571 *km*) SW France flowing NW to unite with the Dordogne forming Gironde estuary

Gar·ri·son Dam \'gar-ə-sən-\ dam 210 *ft* (64 *m*) high in Missouri river W *cen* N. Dak. — see SAKAKAWEA (Lake)

Gary \'ga(ə)r-ē, 'ge(ə)r-\ city NW Ind. on Lake Michigan *pop* 151,953

Gas·co·nade \,gas-kə-'nād\ river 250 *mi* (402 *km*) S *cen* Mo. flowing NE into Missouri river

Gas·co·ny \'gas-kə-nē\ *or F* **Gas·cogne** \gȧ-skȯnʸ\ region & former province SW France ✻ Auch

Ga·sher·brum \'gəsh-ər-,brüm, -,brüm\ mountain 26,470 *ft* (8068 *m*) N Kashmir in Karakoram range SE of K^2

Gas·pé \gas-'pā, 'gas-,\ **1** peninsula Canada in SE Que. between mouth of St. Lawrence river & Chaleur Bay **2** city Canada in E Que. *pop* 17,261 — **Gas·pe·sian** \ga-'spē-zhən\ *adj*

Gas·ti·neau \'gas-tə-,nō\ channel SE Alaska between Douglas Is. & mainland; Juneau is situated on it

Gas·to·nia \ga-'stō-nē-ə, -nyə\ city S N.C. *pop* 47,333

Gates·head \'gāts-,hed\ borough N England in Tyne and Wear county on the Tyne opposite Newcastle *pop* 181,367

Gates of the Arctic National Park wilderness area N *cen* Alaska in Brooks range N of the Arctic Circle

Gath \'gath\ city of ancient Philistia ENE of Gaza

Gat·i·neau \,gat-ᵊn-'ō\ **1** river 240 *mi* (386 *km*) Canada in SW Que. flowing S into Ottawa river at Hull **2** town Canada in SW Que. *pop* 74,988

Ga·tun \gə-'tün\ lake *cen* Panama formed by the **Gatun Dam** in the Chagres; formerly in Canal Zone

Gaul \'gȯl\ *or L* **Gal·lia** \'gal-ē-ə\ ancient country W Europe comprising chiefly the region occupied by modern France & Belgium & at one time including also the Po valley in N Italy — see CISALPINE GAUL, TRANSALPINE GAUL

Ga·var·nie \,gav-ər-'nē\ waterfall 1385 *ft* (422 *m*) SW France S of Lourdes in the **Cirque de Gavarnie** \,si(ə)rk-də-\ (natural amphitheater at head of Gave de Pau) — see PAU

Gave de Pau — see PAU

Gav·ins Point Dam \,gav-ənz-\ dam SE S.Dak. & NE Nebr. in Missouri river — see LEWIS AND CLARK

Gäv·le \'yev-lə\ city & port E Sweden on Gulf of Bothnia NNW of Stockholm *pop* 87,378

Ga·ya \gə-'yä\ city NE India in *cen* Bihar *pop* 246,778

Ga·za *or Ar* **Ghaz·ze** \'gäz-ə\ city S Palestine near the Mediterranean; with surrounding coastal district (**Gaza Strip,** adjoining Sinai peninsula), administered 1949–67 by Egypt, since 1967 by Israel *pop* 118,300

Ga·zi·an·tep \,gäz-ē-(,)än-'tep\ *or formerly* **Ain·tab** \īn-'tab\ city S Turkey N of Aleppo, Syria *pop* 371,000

Gdansk \gə-'dän(t)sk, -'dan(t)sk\ *or G* **Dan·zig** \'dan(t)-sig, 'dän(t)-\ city & port N Poland on Gulf of Gdansk *pop* 458,874

Gdansk, Gulf of *or* **Gulf of Danzig** inlet of S Baltic sea in N Poland & W U.S.S.R.

Gdyn·ia \gə-'din-ē-ə\ city & port N Poland on Gulf of Gdansk NNW of Gdansk *pop* 237,150

Gebel Katherina — see KATHERINA (Gebel)

Gebel Musa — see MUSA (Gebel)

Ge·diz \gə-'dēz\ *or* **Sa·ra·bat** \,sär-ə-'bät\ river 200 *mi* (322 *km*) W Turkey in Asia flowing W into Gulf of Izmir

Gee·long \jə-'lȯŋ\ city & port SE Australia in S Victoria on Port Phillip Bay SW of Melbourne *pop* 14,471

Geelvink Bay — see SARERA BAY

Gejiu — see KO-CHIU

Gel·der·land \'gel-dər-,land\ province E Netherlands bordering on IJsselmeer ✻ Arnhem *area* 1965 *sq mi* (5109 *sq km*), *pop* 1,727,500

Gelibolu — see GALLIPOLI

Gel·sen·kir·chen \,gel-zən-'ki(ə)r-kən\ city W W. Germany in the Ruhr W of Dortmund *pop* 304,386

General San Martín — see SAN MARTÍN

Gen·e·see \,jen-ə-'sē\ river 144 *mi* (232 *km*) W N.Y. flowing N into Lake Ontario

Ge·ne·va \jə-'nē-və\ *or F* **Ge·nève** \zhə-'nev\ *or G* **Genf** \'genf\ **1** canton SW Switzerland *area* 107 *sq mi* (278 *sq km*), *pop* 349,040 **2** city, its ✻ , at SW tip of Lake of Geneva on the Rhône *pop* 156,505 — **Gen·e·vese** \,jen-ə-'vēz, -'vēs\ *adj or n*

Geneva, Lake of *or* **Lake Le·man** \'lē-mən, 'lem-ən, lə-'man\ lake 45 *mi* (72 *km*) long on border between SW Switzerland & E France; traversed by the Rhône

Gennesaret, Lake of — see GALILEE (Sea of)

Gen·oa \'jen-ə-wə\ *or It* **Ge·no·va** \'je-nō-vä\ *or anc* **Gen·ua** \'jen-yə-wə\ commune & port NW Italy ✻ of Liguria at foot of the Apennines & at head of **Gulf of Genoa** (arm of Ligurian sea) *pop* 760,300 — **Gen·o·ese** \,jen-ə-'wēz, -'wēs\ *adj or n* — **Gen·o·vese** \-ə-'vēz, -'vēs\ *adj or n*

Gen·tof·te \'gen-,təf-tə\ city Denmark on Sjælland Is., N suburb of Copenhagen *pop* 66,782

George \'jȯ(ə)rj\ river 345 *mi* (555 *km*) Canada in NE Que. flowing N into Ungava Bay

George, Lake **1** lake 14 *mi* (22 *km*) long NE Fla. in course of St. Johns river WNW of Daytona Beach **2** lake 33 *mi* (53 *km*) long E N.Y. S of Lake Champlain

Georg·es Bank \'jȯ(ə)r-jəz-\ submerged sandbank E of Mass.

George·town \'jȯ(ə)rj-,taůn\ **1** section of Washington, D.C., in W part of the city **2** city & port ✻ of Guyana on the Atlantic *pop* 162,000

George Town \'jȯ(ə)rj-,taůn\ **1** town ✻ of Cayman islands on Grand Cayman Is. **2** *or* **Pi·nang** \pi-'naŋ\ *or* **Pe·nang** \pə-\ city & port Malaysia ✻ of Penang on Penang Is. *pop* 234,930

George Washington Birthplace National Monument historic site E Va.

George Washington Carver National Monument historic site SW Mo. SE of Joplin

Geor·gia \'jȯr-jə\ **1** state SE U.S. ✻ Atlanta *area* 58,876 *sq mi* (153,078 *sq km*), *pop* 5,463,105 **2** *or* **Geor·gian Republic** \,jȯr-jən-\ constituent republic of the U.S.S.R. S of Caucasus mountains bordering on Black sea; an ancient & medieval kingdom ✻ Tbilisi *area* 26,875 *sq mi* (69,875 *sq km*), *pop* 5,015,000

Georgia, Strait of channel 150 *mi* (241 *km*) long NW Wash. & SW B.C. bet. S Vancouver Is. & mainland NW of Puget Sound

Georgian Bay inlet of Lake Huron, Canada, in SE Ont.

Georgian Bay Islands National Park reservation SE Canada including Flowerpot Is. SE of Manitoulin Is. & a group of small islands N of Midland, Ont.

Ge·ra \'ger-ə\ city S E. Germany ESE of Erfurt *pop* 126,069

Ger·la·chov·ka \'ge(ə)r-lə-,kóf-kə, -,kȯv-\ *or* **Ger·la·chov·sky** \-skē\ mountain 8711 *ft* (2655 *m*) E Czechoslovakia in Tatry mountains; highest in Carpathians

German East Africa former country E Africa comprising Tanganyika & Ruanda-Urundi (now Rwanda & Burundi); a German protectorate 1885–1920

Ger·ma·nia \(,)jər-'mā-nē-ə, -nyə\ **1** region of ancient Europe E of the Rhine & N of the Danube **2** region of Roman Empire just W of the Rhine in what is now NE France & part of Belgium & the Netherlands

German Southwest Africa — see NAMIBIA

Ger·man·town \'jər-mən-,taůn\ **1** city SW Tenn. *pop* 20,459 **2** a NW section of Philadelphia, Pa.

Ger·ma·ny \'jərm-(ə-)nē\ *or G* **Deutsch·land** \'dȯich-,länt\ former country *cen* Europe bordering on North & Baltic seas, since 1949 divided into two republics: **Federal Republic of Germany** *or* **Bun·des·re·pu·blik Deutschland** \,bün-dəs-,rā-pü-'blēk-\ to the W (✻ Bonn, *area* 96,000 *sq mi or* 249,600 *sq km, pop* 59,576,000) & **German Democratic Republic** *or* **Deutsche De·mo·krat·ische Re·pu·blik** \,dȯi-chə-,dā-mō-'krät-ish-ə-,rā-pü-'blēk\ to the E (✻ East Berlin *area* 41,804 *sq mi or* 108,690 *sq km, pop* 16,705,635)

Ger·mis·ton \'jər-mə-stən\ city NE Republic of S. Africa in S Transvaal E of Johannesburg *pop* 221,972

Ge·ro·na \hā-'rō-nə, jə-\ 1 province NE Spain in NE Catalonia *area* 2264 *sq mi* (5886 *sq km*), *pop* 466,992 2 commune, its ✱ *pop* 116,477

Ge·zi·ra, El \,el-jə-'zir-ə\ *or* Al Ja·zi·rah \,al-jə-'zir-ə\ district E *cen* Sudan bet. Blue Nile & White Nile rivers

Gha·da·mes *or* Gha·da·mis \gə-'dam-əs, -'däm-\ oasis & town NW Libya in Tripolitania near Algerian border *pop* 6172

Gha·gha·ra \'gäg-ə,-,rä\ *or* Ghagh·ra \'gäg-rə, -,rä\ river 570 *mi* (1207 *km*) S *cen* Asia flowing S from SW Tibet through Nepal into the Ganges in N India

Gha·na \'gän-ə, 'gan-ə\ 1 *or* Ga·na ancient empire W Africa in what is now W Mali; flourished 4th–13th centuries ✱ *or formerly* Gold Coast country W Africa bordering on Gulf of Guinea; a republic within the Commonwealth; formerly (as Gold Coast) a Brit. territory comprising Gold Coast colony, Ashanti, Northern Territories, & Togoland trust territory ✱ Accra *area* 91,843 *sq mi* (238,792 *sq km*), *pop* 12,244,000 — Gha·na·ian *or* Gha·ni·an \gän-ē-ən, 'gän-yən, 'gan-\ *adj or n* — Gha·nese \gä-'nēz, ga-, -'nēs\ *adj*

Gharapuri — see ELEPHANTA

Ghar·da·ïa \gär-'dī-ə\ commune N *cen* Algeria *pop* 70,500

Ghats — see EASTERN GHATS, WESTERN GHATS

Ghazal, Bahr el — see BAHR EL GHAZAL

Ghaz·ni \'gäz-nē\ city E *cen* Afghanistan; once ✱ of a Muslim kingdom extending from the Tigris to the Ganges *pop* 30,425

Ghazze — see GAZA

Ghent \'gent\ *or* Flem Gent \'gent\ *or* F Gand \gän\ city NW *cen* Belgium ✱ of E. Flanders *pop* 148,860

Giant's Causeway formation of prismatic basaltic columns Northern Ireland on N coast of Moyle

Gib·e·on \'gib-ē-ən\ city of ancient Palestine NW of Jerusalem — Gib·e·on·ite \-ə-,nīt\ *n*

Gi·bral·tar \jə-'brol-tər\ town & port on Rock of Gibraltar; a Brit. colony *area* 2.5 *sq mi* (6.5 *sq km*), *pop* 29,760 — Gi·bral·tar·i·an \jə-,brol-'ter-ē-ən, ,jib-,rol-, -'tar-\ *n*

Gibraltar, Rock of *or anc* Calpe \'kal-(,)pē\ headland on S coast of Spain at E end of Strait of Gibraltar; highest point 1396 *ft* (426 *m*) — see PILLARS OF HERCULES

Gibraltar, Strait of passage bet. Spain & Africa connecting the Atlantic & Mediterranean *ab* 8 *mi* (12.8 *km*) wide at narrowest point

Gies·sen \'gēs-ᵊn\ city *cen* W. Germany N of Frankfurt am Main *pop* 76,374

Gi·fu \'gē-(,)fü\ city Japan in *cen* Honshu *pop* 410,399

Gi·jón \hē-'hōn\ city & port NW Spain in Oviedo province on Bay of Biscay *pop* 256,433

Gi·la \'hē-lə\ river 630 *mi* (1014 *km*) N.Mex. & Ariz. flowing W into Colorado river

Gila Cliff Dwellings National Monument reservation SW N.Mex. including cliff-dweller ruins

Gil·bert \'gil-bərt\ islands Kiribati in *cen* Pacific — Gil·bert·ese \,gil-bər-'tēz, -tēs\ *n or adj*

Gilbert and El·lice \'el-əs\ island group W Pacific; until 1976 a Brit. colony; now divided into the independent countries of Kiribati and Tuvalu

Gil·boa, Mount \gil-'bō-ə\ mountain 1631 *ft* (497 *m*) N Palestine W of Jordan river & S of Valley of Jezreel

Gil·e·ad \'gil-ē-əd\ mountainous region of Palestine E of Jordan river; now in Jordan — Gil·e·ad·ite \-ē-ə-,dīt\ *n*

Gil·git \'gil-gət\ 1 district NW Kashmir 2 town NW Kashmir on Gilgit river *pop* 4671

Gil·ling·ham \'jil-iŋ-əm\ borough SE England in Kent *pop* 93,741

Gil·roy \'gil-,roi\ city W Calif. SE of San Jose *pop* 21,641

Gin·za \'gin-zə\ shopping street & entertainment district in downtown Tokyo, Japan

Gi·re·sun \gir-ə-'sün\ *or* Ke·ra·sun \,ker-ə-\ city & port NE Turkey on Black sea W of Trabzon *pop* 46,068

Girgenti — see AGRIGENTO

Gi·ronde \jə-'ränd, zhə-; zhē-rōⁿd\ estuary 45 *mi* (72 *km*) W France formed by junction of the Garonne & the Dordogne & flowing NW into Bay of Biscay

Gis·borne \'giz-bərn, -,bó(ə)rn\ borough & port New Zealand on E North Is. *pop* 29,986

Gi·za \'gēz-ə\ city N Egypt on W bank of the Nile near Cairo *pop* 1,230,446

Gju·he·zes, Cape \jü-'hə-,zəs\ *or formerly* Cape Lin·guet·ta \liŋ-'gwet-ə\ *or* Cape Glos·sa \'gläs-ə, 'glós-ə\ cape SW Albania projecting into Strait of Otranto

Glace Bay \'gläs\ town Canada in NE N.S. on Cape Breton Is. *pop* 21,466

Gla·cier Bay \glā-shər\ inlet SE Alaska at S end of St. Elias range in Glacier Bay National Park

Glacier National Park 1 — see WATERTON-GLACIER INTERNATIONAL PEACE PARK 2 reservation W Canada in SE B.C. in Selkirk mountains W of Yoho National Park

Glad·beck \'glät-,bek, 'glad-\ city W W. Germany in the Ruhr *pop* 79,747

Glades \'glādz\ EVERGLADES

Glad·stone \'glad-,stōn\ city W Mo. N of Kansas City *pop* 24,990

Gla·mor·gan \glə-'mór-gən\ *or* Gla·mor·gan·shire \-,shi(ə)r, -,shər\ former county SE Wales ✱ Cardiff — see MID GLAMORGAN, SOUTH GLAMORGAN, WEST GLAMORGAN

Gla·rus \'glär-əs\ *or* F Gla·ris \glä-'rēs\ 1 canton E *cen* Switzerland *area* 267 *sq mi* (694 *sq km*), *pop* 36,718 2 commune, its ✱ *pop* 5969

Glas·gow \'glas-(,)kō, 'glas-(,)gō, 'glaz-(,)gō\ city & port S Scotland on the Clyde ✱ of Strathclyde *pop* 762,288 — Glas·we·gian \glas-'wē-jən\ *n or adj*

Glas·ton·bury \'glas-tən-,ber-ē\ 1 town *cen* Conn. SE of Hartford *pop* 24,327 2 borough SW England in Somerset *pop* 6773

Glen Canyon Dam \'glen\ Dam N Ariz. in Glen Canyon of Colorado river forming Lake Pow·ell \'pau(-ə)l\ (chiefly in SE Utah)

Glen·coe \glen-'kō\ valley W Scotland SE of Loch Leven

Glen Cove \'glen-'kōv\ city SE N.Y. on NW Long Is. *pop* 24,618

Glen·dale \'glen-,dāl\ 1 city *cen* Ariz. NW of Phoenix *pop* 97,172 2 city SW Calif. NE of Los Angeles *pop* 139,060

Glen·dale Heights \,glen-,dāl-'hīts\ city NE Ill. *pop* 23,163

Glen·do·ra \glen-'dōr-ə, -'dór-\ city SW Calif. *pop* 38,654

Glen El·lyn \gle-'nel-ən\ village NE Ill. W of Chicago *pop* 23,649

Glen More \glen-'mó(ə)r, -'mó(ə)r\ valley *ab* 50 *mi* (80 *km*) long N Scotland running SW to NE & connecting Loche Linnhe & Moray firth — see CALEDONIAN CANAL

Glen·view \'glen-,vyü\ village NE Ill. NNW of Chicago *pop* 32,060

Glit·ter·tind \'glit-ər-,tin\ mountain 8110 *ft* (2472 *m*) S *cen* Norway in Jotunheim mountains; highest in Scandinavia

Gli·wi·ce \gli-'vēt-sə\ *or* G Glei·witz \'glī-(,)vits\ city SW Poland in Silesia W of Katowice *pop* 202,238

Glom·ma \'glô-,mä, 'gläm-ə\ river 185 *mi* (298 *km*) E Norway flowing S into the Skagerrak

Glouces·ter \'gläs-tər, 'glós-\ 1 city NE Mass. on Cape Ann *pop* 27,768 2 city Canada in SE Ont. near Ottawa *pop* 72,859 3 borough SW *cen* England ✱ of Gloucestershire

Glouces·ter·shire \'gläs-tər-,shi(ə)r, -,shər, -'glós-\ *or* Glouces·ter \'gläs-tər, 'glós-\ county SW *cen* England *area* 1020 *sq mi* (2652 *sq km*), *pop* 503,800

Glov·ers·ville \'gləv-ərz-,vil\ city E N.Y. *pop* 17,836

Gnossus — see KNOSSOS

Goa *or* Pg Gôa \'gō-ə\ state W India on Malabar Coast; before 1962 belonged to Portugal; with Daman & Diu constituted a union territory 1962–1987; ✱ Panaji *area* 1301 *sq mi* (3383 *sq km*), *pop* 626,978 — see PORTUGUESE INDIA — Go·an \'gō-ən\ *adj or n* — Goa·nese \,gō-ə-'nēz, -'nēs\ *adj or n*

Go·bi \'gō-(,)bē\ desert E *cen* Asia in Mongolia & China *area ab* 500,000 *sq mi* (1,300,000 *sq km*)

Go·da·va·ri \gə-'däv-ə-rē\ river 900 *mi* (1448 *km*) *cen* India flowing SE across the Deccan into Bay of Bengal

Go·des·berg \'gōd-əs-,bərg, -,be(ə)rg\ *or* Bad Godesberg \'bät-\ commune W W. Germany on the Rhine S of Bonn *pop* 73,512

Godt·haab \'gót-,hōb, 'gät-\ town ✱ of Greenland on SW coast

Godwin Austen — see K2

Go·ge·bic \gō-'gē-bik\ iron range N Wis. & NW Mich.

Goi·â·nia *or formerly* Goy·a·nia \gói-'an-ē-ə\ city SE *cen* Brazil ✱ of Goiás *pop* 717,948

Goi·ás *or* Goi·az *or* Goy·az \gói-'äs\ state SE *cen* Brazil ✱ Goiânia *area* 244,330 *sq mi* (635,258 *sq km*), *pop* 3,967,907

Gök·çe·ada \,goek-jä-ə-'dä\ *or formerly* Im·roz \im-'róz\ island Turkey in NE Aegean *area* 110 *sq mi* (286 *sq km*)

Go·lan Heights \gō-,län-, -lən-\ hilly region NE of Sea of Galilee; annexed by Israel 1981

Gol·con·da \gäl-'kän-də\ ruined city *cen* India in W Andhra Pradesh W of Hyderabad ✱ (1512–1687) of Golconda kingdom

Gold Coast 1 region W Africa on N shore of Gulf of Guinea bet. the Ivory Coast (on W) & the Slave Coast (on E) 2 — see GHANA 3 former Brit. colony in S Gold Coast region ✱ Accra; now part of Ghana

Golden Chersonese — see CHERSONESE

Golden Gate strait 2 *mi* (3.2 *km*) wide W Calif. connecting San Francisco Bay with Pacific ocean

Golden Horn inlet of the Bosporus, Turkey; harbor of Istanbul

Golden Valley village E Minn. W of Minneapolis *pop* 22,775

Golds·boro \'gōl(d)z-,bər-ə, -,bə-rə\ city E *cen* N.C. *pop* 31,871

Golgotha — see CALVARY

Go·mel \'gō-məl, 'gó-\ city U.S.S.R. in SE Belorussia *pop* 383,000

Go·mor·rah \gə-'mór-ə, -'mär-\ city of ancient Palestine in the plain of Jordan river

Go·nâve, Gulf of \gō-'näv\ arm of Caribbean sea on W coast of Haiti

Gon·dar \'gän-dər, -,där\ city NW Ethiopia N of Lake Tana ✱ of Amhara & former ✱ of Ethiopia *pop* 85,941

Gond·wa·na·land \gän-'dwän-ə-,land\ *or* Gond·wa·na \-'dwän-ə\ hypothetical land area believed to have once connected the Indian subcontinent & the landmasses of the southern hemisphere

Gongga — see MINYA KONKA

Good Hope, Cape of \,gúd-'hōp\ cape S Republic of S. Africa in SW Cape Province W of False Bay, at 34°21′S — see CAPE OF GOOD HOPE

Good·win Sands \,gúd-wən-\ shoals SE England in Strait of Dover off E coast of Kent — see DOWNS

Goose Creek \gü-'skrēk, -skrik\ city SE S.C. *pop* 17,811

Go·rakh·pur \'gór-ək-,pú(ə)r, 'gór-\ city NE India in E Uttar Pradesh N of Banaras *pop* 306,399

Gor·gān \gór-'gän\ *or formerly* As·ter·a·bad \,äs-t(ə)rə-'bäd, 'as-\ city N Iran near SE coast of Caspian sea *pop* 88,348

Go·ri·zia \gə-'rēt-sē-ə\ commune NE Italy in Venetia *pop* 41,325

Gor·ki *or* Gor·ky *or* Gor·kii \'gór-kē\ *or formerly* Nizh·ni Nov·go·rod \nizh-nē-'näv-gə-,räd\ city U.S.S.R. in *cen* Soviet Russia, Europe, at confluence of Oka & Volga rivers *pop* 1,344,000

Gör·litz \'gór-,lits, -ləts\ city SE E. Germany on Neisse river *pop* 81,003

Gor·lov·ka \gor-'lóf-kə, -'lôv-\ city U.S.S.R. in E Ukrainian Republic in the Donets basin N of Donetsk *pop* 335,000

Gor·no-Al·tai \,gór-(,)nō,al-'tī\ *or formerly* Oi·rot \'ói-rət\ autonomous region U.S.S.R. in S Soviet Russia, Asia, in SE Altai Territory in Altai mountains ✱ Gorno-Altaisk (formerly Oirot-Tura) *area* 35,800 *sq mi* (93,080 *sq km*), *pop* 168,000

Gor·no-Ba·dakh·shan \,gór-(,)nō-,bäd-,äk-'shän\ autonomous region U.S.S.R. in Soviet Central Asia in SE Tadzhik Republic in the Pamirs ✱ Khorog *area* 25,784 *sq mi* (67,038 *sq km*), *pop* 98,000

Go·shen \'gō-shən\ 1 city N Ind. *pop* 19,665 2 district of ancient Egypt E of the Nile delta

Gos·port \'gäs-,pō(ə)rt, -,pó(ə)rt\ borough S England in Hampshire on Portsmouth harbor *pop* 77,276

Gö·te·borg \,yə(r)t-ə-'bór-ē\ *or* Goth·en·burg \'gäth-ən-,bərg\ city & port SW Sweden on the Kattegat *pop* 431,273

Go·tha \'gōt-ə, 'gō-thə\ city SW E. Germany W of Erfurt *pop* 57,847

Got·land \'gät-,land, -lənd\ island Sweden in the Baltic off SE coast; chief town Visby *area* 1167 *sq mi* (3034 *sq km*), *pop* 54,093

Göt·ting·en \'gə(r)t-iŋ-ən, 'get-\ city E W. Germany SSW of Brunswick *pop* 129,656

Gott·wal·dov \\'gät-vəl-ˌdȯf, -ˌdȯv\ *or formerly* **Zlin** \zə-'lēn\ city *cen* Czechoslovakia in SE Moravia *pop* 83,983

Gou·da \'gaúd-ə, 'güd-\ commune SW Netherlands *pop* 59,179

Gow·er \'gaú(-ə)r\ peninsula S Wales W of Swansea

Gra·ham Land \'grā-əm-, 'gra(-ə)m-\ **1** — see ANTARCTIC **2** the N section of the Antarctic peninsula

Gra·hams·town \'grā-əmz-ˌtaún, 'gra(-ə)mz-\ city S Republic of S. Africa in SE Cape Province ENE of Port Elizabeth *pop* 41,302

Gra·ian Alps \ˌgrā-(y)ən-, ˌgrī-ən-\ section of W Alps S of Mont Blanc on border between France & Italy — see GRAN PARADISO

Grain coast \'grān\ region W Africa in Liberia on Gulf of Guinea

Gram·pi·an \'gram-pē-ən\ **1** hills *cen* Scotland between the Lowlands & the Highlands — see BEN NEVIS **2** region NE *cen* Scotland, established 1975 ✵ Aberdeen *area* 3360 *sq mi* (8736 *sq km*), *pop* 470,596

Gra·na·da \grə-'näd-ə\ **1** city SW Nicaragua on NW shore of Lake Nicaragua *pop* 56,232 **2** medieval Moorish kingdom S Spain **3** province S Spain in Andalusia bordering on the Mediterranean *area* 4928 *sq mi* (12,813 *sq km*), *pop* 724,299 **4** city, ✵ of Granada province, Spain, in the Sierra Nevada *pop* 246,642

Gran·by \'gran-bē\ city Canada in S Que. *pop* 38,069

Gran Chaco — see CHACO

Grand 1 river 260 *mi* (418 *km*) SW Mich. flowing N & W into Lake Michigan **2** river 300 *mi* (483 *km*) NW Mo. flowing SE into Missouri river **3** river 140 *mi* (225 *km*) W Mo. flowing SE into Lake of the Ozarks **4** river 200 *mi* (322 *km*) N S.Dak. flowing E into Missouri river **5** the Colorado river from its source to junction with Green river in SE Utah — a former name **6** — see NEOSHO **7** *or* **Da** \'dä\ canal *ab* 1000 *mi* (1609 *km*) long E China from Hangchow to Tientsin

Grand Atlas — see ATLAS

Grand Bahama island Bahamas, NW island of group *area* 430 *sq mi* (1118 *sq km*)

Grand Bank *or* **Grand Banks** shoals in W Atlantic SE of Newfoundland

Grand Canary *or Sp* **Gran Ca·na·ria** \ˌgrän-kə-'när-yä\ island Spain in the Canaries; chief city Las Palmas *area* 523 *sq mi* (1360 *sq km*)

Grand Canyon gorge of the Colorado NW Ariz. extending from mouth of the Little Colorado W to the Grand Wash Cliffs; over 1 *mi* (1.6 *km*) deep; area largely comprised in **Grand Canyon National Park** — see MARBLE CANYON

Grand Canyon of the Snake — see HELLS CANYON

Grand Cayman — see CAYMAN

Grand Cou·lee \'kü-lē\ valley E Wash. extending SSW from S wall of canyon of Columbia river where it turns W in forming the Big Bend

Grand Coulee Dam dam NE *cen* Wash. in Columbia river — see FRANKLIN D. ROOSEVELT LAKE

Grande, Rio 1 \ˌrē-ō-'grand(-ē)\ *also* \ˌrī-ō-'grand\ river U.S. & Mexico — see RIO GRANDE **2** \ˌrē-ō-'gran-də, -dē\ river 680 *mi* (1094 *km*) E Brazil in Minas Gerais flowing W to unite with Paranaíba river forming Paraná river

Grande–Terre \gran-'te(ə)r\ island French W. Indies constituting the E portion of Guadeloupe *area* 220 *sq mi* (572 *sq km*)

Grand Falls — see CHURCHILL FALLS

Grand Forks city E N.Dak. on Red river *pop* 43,765

Grand Island city SE *cen* Nebr. near Platte river *pop* 33,180

Grand Junction city W Colo. on Colorado river *pop* 28,144

Grand Lac — see TONLE SAP

Grand Ma·nan \mə-'nan\ island 20 *mi* (32 *km*) long Canada in N.B. at entrance to Bay of Fundy

Grand Mesa mountain *ab* 10,000 *ft* (3048 *m*) W Colo. near junction of Colorado & Gunnison rivers; summit *area ab* 53 *sq mi* (138 *sq km*)

Grand Portage National Monument historic site NE Minn. on Lake Superior

Grand Prairie city NE *cen* Tex. W of Dallas *pop* 71,462

Grand Rapids city SW Mich. on Grand river *pop* 181,843

Grand Te·ton \'tē-ˌtän, 'tēt-ʰn\ mountain 13,766 *ft* (4196 *m*) W Wyo. in Grand Teton National Park; highest in Teton range

Grand Teton National Park reservation NW Wyo. including Jackson Lake & main part of Teton range

Grand Tra·verse Bay \-ˌtrav-ərs-\ inlet of Lake Michigan in Mich. on NW coast of lower peninsula

Grand Turk — see TURKS AND CAICOS

Grand·view \'grand(ˌ)vyü\ city W Mo. *pop* 24,502

Grange·mouth \'grānj-məth, -ˌmaúth\ burgh & port *cen* Scotland in Central region on Firth of Forth *pop* 21,666

Granicus — see KOCABAS

Granite City city SW Ill. on Mississippi river *pop* 36,815

Granite Peak mountain 12,799 *ft* (3901 *m*) S Mont. NE of Yellowstone National Park in Beartooth range (spur of Absaroka range); highest point in state

Gran Pa·ra·di·so \ˌgran-ˌpar-ə-(ˌ)dē-(ˌ)zō\ mountain 13,323 *ft* (4061 *m*) NW Italy in NW Piedmont; highest in Graian Alps

Gras·mere \'gras-ˌmi(ə)r\ lake 1 *mi* (1.6 *km*) long NW England in Cumbria in Lake District

Grasse \'gras, 'gräs\ commune SE France W of Nice *pop* 24,260

Grass·lands National Park \'gras-ˌlan(d)z-, -ˌlən(d)z-\ reservation Canada in SW Sask.

Grau·bün·den \graú-'bün-dən, -'bʉen-\ *or F* **Gri·sons** \grē-zōⁿ\ canton E Switzerland ✵ Chur *area* 2744 *sq mi* (7134 *sq km*), *pop* 164,641

Graudenz — see GRUDZIADZ

Gravenhage, 's — see HAGUE (The)

Graves·end \ˌgräv-'zend\ borough SE England in Kent on Thames estuary *pop* 52,963

Grays Harbor \'grāz\ inlet of the Pacific W Wash.

Grays Peak mountain 14,270 *ft* (4349 *m*) *cen* Colo., highest in Front range

Graz \'gräts\ city S Austria ✵ of Styria on the Mur *pop* 243,405

Great Abaco — see ABACO

Great Australian Bight wide bay on S coast of Australia; part of Indian ocean

Great Barrier Reef coral reef 1250 *mi* (2012 *km*) long Australia in Coral sea off NE coast of Queensland; in part comprises a marine park

Great Basin region W U.S. between Sierra Nevada & Wasatch mountains including most of Nev. & parts of Calif., Idaho, Utah, Wyo. & Oreg. & having no drainage to ocean; contains many isolated mountain ranges (the **Basin ranges**)

Great Basin National Park reservation E Nev. including Wheeler Peak & Lehman Caves

Great Bear lake Canada in W Northwest Territories *area* 12,000 *sq mi* (31,200 *sq km*)

Great Bend city W *cen* Kans. *pop* 16,608

Great Brit·ain \'brit-ʰn\ *or* **Britain 1** island W Europe comprising England, Scotland, & Wales *area* 88,745 *sq mi* (230,737 *sq km*), *pop* 54,397,000 **2** UNITED KINGDOM

Great Crosby — see CROSBY

Great Dismal — see DISMAL

Great Divide — see CONTINENTAL DIVIDE

Great Dividing Range mountain system E Australia extending from Cape York Peninsula to S Victoria, & interrupted by Bass strait, into Tasmania — see KOSCIUSKO (Mount)

Greater An·til·les \-ˌan-'til-ēz\ group of islands in the W. Indies including Cuba, Hispaniola, Jamaica, & Puerto Rico

Greater London metropolitan county SE England comprising London (city) & 32 surrounding boroughs *area* 620 *sq mi* (1612 *sq km*), *pop* 6,851,400

Greater Manchester metropolitan county NW England ✵ Manchester *area* 498 *sq mi* (1295 *sq km*), *pop* 2,624,400

Greater Sunda — see SUNDA

Greater Walachia — see MUNTENIA

Great Exuma — see EXUMA

Great Falls 1 *or* **Great Falls of the Potomac** waterfall 35 *ft* (11 *m*) in the Potomac N of Washington **2** city W *cen* Mont. on Missouri river WSW of the **Great Falls of the Missouri** (waterfall, now in modified form) *pop* 56,725

Great Inagua — see INAGUA

Great Indian — see THAR

Great Kabylia — see KABYLIA

Great Karroo — see KARROO

Great Lakes 1 chain of five lakes (Superior, Michigan, Huron, Erie, & Ontario) *cen* N. America in the U.S. & Canada draining through St. Lawrence river into the Atlantic **2** group of lakes E *cen* Africa including Lakes Rudolf, Albert, Victoria, Tanganyika, & Malawi

Great Namaqualand — see NAMAQUALAND

Great Ouse — see OUSE

Great Plains elevated plains region W *cen* U.S. & W Canada E of Rocky mountains & chiefly W of 100th meridian extending from NE B.C. & NW Alta. SE & S to include the Llano Estacado of N.Mex. & Tex.

Great Rift valley \-'rift-\ depression SW Asia & E Africa extending with several breaks from valley of Jordan river S to *cen* Mozambique

Great Saint Ber·nard \-ˌsänt-bər-(ˌ)närd\ mountain pass 8111 *ft* (2472 *m*) through Pennine Alps bet. Switzerland & Italy

Great Salt Lake lake *ab* 70 *mi* (113 *km*) long N Utah having strongly saline waters & no outlet

Great Salt Lake desert flat barren region NW Utah

Great Sand Dunes National Monument reservation S Colo. on W slope of Sangre de Cristo mountains

Great Slave Lake lake NW Canada in S Northwest Territories receiving Slave river on S & draining into Mackenzie river on W *area* 11,170 *sq mi* (29,042 *sq km*)

Great Smoky mountains on N.C.-Tenn. boundary partly in **Great Smoky Mountains National Park** — see CLINGMANS DOME

Great Yarmouth — see YARMOUTH

Greece \'grēs\ *or Gk* **Hel·las** \'hel-əs\ *or NGk* **El·lás** \e-'läs\ country S Europe at S end of Balkan peninsula; a republic ✵ Athens *area* 50,147 *sq mi* (130,382 *sq km*), *pop* 9,706,687

Gree·ley \'grē-lē\ city N Colo. *pop* 53,006

Green \'grēn\ **1** river 730 *mi* (1175 *km*) W U.S. flowing from Wind River range in W Wyo. S into Colorado river in SE Utah **2** mountains E N. America in the Appalachian system extending from S Que. S through Vt. into W Mass. — see MANSFIELD (Mount)

Green Bay 1 inlet of NW Lake Michigan 120 *mi* (193 *km*) long in NW Mich. & NE Wis. **2** city NE *cen* Wis. on Green Bay *pop* 87,899

Green·belt \'grēn-ˌbelt\ city *cen* Md. NE of Washington, D.C. *pop* 17,332

Green·dale \'grēn-ˌdāl\ village SE Wis. SW of Milwaukee *pop* 16,928

Green·field \'grēn-ˌfēld\ **1** town NW Mass. on Connecticut river *pop* 18,436 **2** city SE Wis. near Milwaukee *pop* 31,467

Greenfield Park town Canada in S Que. E of Montreal *pop* 18,527

Green·land \'grēn-lənd, -ˌland\ **1** island N Atlantic off NE N. America belonging to Denmark ✵ Godthaab *area* 839,800 *sq mi* (2,183,480 *sq km*), *pop* 54,000 **2** sea arm of Arctic ocean between Greenland and Spitsbergen — **Green·land·er** \-lən-dər, -ˌlan-\ *n*

Gree·nock \'grēn-ək\ burgh & port SW Scotland in Strathclyde on Firth of Clyde *pop* 57,324

Greens·boro \'grēnz-ˌbər-ə, -ˌbə-rə\ city N *cen* N.C. *pop* 155,642

Greens·burg \'grēnz-ˌbərg\ city SW Pa. *pop* 17,558

Green·ville \'grēn-ˌvil, -vəl\ **1** city W Miss. on Mississippi river *pop* 40,613 **2** city E N.C. *pop* 35,740 **3** city NW S.C. *pop* 58,242 **4** city NE Tex. NE of Dallas on the Sabine *pop* 22,161

Green·wich 1 \'gren-ich, 'grēn-, -wich, 'grin-ˌwich\ town SW Conn. on Long Is. Sound *pop* 59,578 **2** \'grin-ij, 'gren-, -ich\ borough of E Greater London, England *pop* 214,900

Green·wich Village \ˌgren-ich-\ section of New York City in Manhattan on lower W side

Green·wood \'grēn-ˌwúd\ **1** city *cen* Ind. *pop* 19,327 **2** city W Miss. *pop* 20,115 **3** city W S.C. *pop* 21,613

Gre·na·da \grə-'näd-ə\ island Brit. W. Indies in S Windward islands; with S Grenadines, independent member of the Commonwealth since 1974 ✵ St. George's *area* 133 *sq mi* (346 *sq km*), *pop* 89,088 — **Gre·na·dan** \-'näd-ʰn\ *adj or n* — **Gre·na·di·an** \-'näd-ē-ən\ *adj or n*

Gren·a·dines \ˌgren-ə-'dēnz\ islands Brit. W. Indies in *cen* Windward islands between Grenada & St. Vincent; divided administratively between Grenada & St. Vincent and the Grenadines

Gre·no·ble \grə-'nō-bəl, -'nȯbl\ city SE France on the Isère *pop* 165,431

Gresh·am \'gresh-əm\ city NW Oreg. E of Portland *pop* 33,005

Gret·na \'gret-nə\ city SE La. S of New Orleans *pop* 20,615

Grey·lock, Mount \'grā-ˌläk\ mountain 3491 *ft* (1064 *m*) NW Mass.; highest in Berkshire hills & in state

Grif·fin \'grif-ən\ city W *cen* Ga. *pop* 20,728

Grif·fith \'grif-əth\ town NW Ind. S of Hammond *pop* 17,026

Grims·by \'grimz-bē\ borough E England in Humberside near mouth of the Humber *pop* 92,147

Grin·del·wald \'grin-d'l-ˌwóld, -ˌvält\ valley & village *cen* Switzerland in Bern canton in the Berner Alpen E of Interlaken

Gri·qua·land West \'grik-wə-ˌland\ district NW Republic of S. Africa in N Cape of Good Hope N of Orange river; chief town Kimberley

Gris–Nez, Cape \grē-nā\ headland N France projecting into Strait of Dover

Grisons — see GRAUBÜNDEN

Grod·no \'gräd-(ˌ)nō, 'gród-\ city U.S.S.R. in W Belorussia on the Neman *pop* 195,000

Gro·ning·en \'grō-niŋ-ən\ **1** province NE Netherlands *area* 866 *sq mi* (2252 *sq km*), *pop* 560,614 **2** city, its ✳ *pop* 166,951

Gros Morne National Park \grō-mórn-\ reservation Canada in Newfoundland island

Grosse Pointe Woods \ˌgrōs-ˌpóint-\ city SE Mich. *pop* 18,886

Gross·glock·ner \'grōs-ˌgläk-nər\ mountain 12,457 *ft* (3797 *m*) SW Austria, highest in the Hohe Tauern & in Austria

Gros Ventre \'grō-ˌvänt\ river 100 *mi* (161 *km*) W Wyo. flowing W into Snake river

Grot·on \'grät-ᵊn\ town SE Conn. E of New London *pop* 41,062

Grove City \'grōv\ city Ohio *pop* 16,816

Groves \'grōvz\ city SE Tex. NE of Port Arthur *pop* 17,090

Groz·ny or **Groz·nyy** \'gróz-nē, 'gräz-\ city U.S.S.R. in S Soviet Russia, Europe, N of Caucasus mountains *pop* 375,000

Gru·dziadz \'grü-ˌjó(n)ts\ or *G* **Grau·denz** \'graú-ˌden(t)s\ city N Poland on the Vistula NE of Bydgoszcz *pop* 91,081

Gua·da·la·ja·ra \ˌgwäd-ə-lə-'här-ə\ **1** city W *cen* Mexico ✳ of Jalisco *pop* 2,343,034 **2** province E *cen* Spain in NE New Castile *area* 4676 *sq mi* (12,158 *sq km*), *pop* 125,834 **3** commune ✳ of Guadalajara province, Spain *pop* 64,334

Gua·dal·ca·nal \ˌgwäd-ᵊl-kə-'nal, ˌgwäd-ə-kə-\ island W Pacific in the SE Solomons *area* 2500 *sq mi* (6500 *sq km*), *pop* 23,922 — see HONIARA

Gua·dal·qui·vir \ˌgwäd-ᵊl-'kwiv-ər, -ki-'vi(ə)r\ river 374 *mi* (602 *km*) S Spain flowing W & SW into Gulf of Cádiz

Gua·da·lupe \'gwäd-ᵊl-ˌüp\ **1** mountains S N.Mex. & W Tex., the S extension of Sacramento mountains; highest point **Guadalupe Peak**, 8751 *ft* (2667 *m*) in **Guadalupe Mountains National Park** (in Tex.) **2** river 300 *mi* (483 *km*) SE Tex. flowing SE into San Antonio river

Gua·da·lupe Hi·dal·go \ˌgwäd-ᵊl-ˌüp-(ē)-hi-'dal-(ˌ)gō\ former city *cen* Mexico N of Mexico City now part of city of Gustavo A. Madero **2**
GUSTAVO A. MADERO

Gua·de·loupe \ˌgwäd-ᵊl-ˌüp\ two islands, Basse-Terre (or Guadeloupe proper) & Grande-Terre, in French W. Indies in *cen* Leeward islands; an overseas department of France ✳ Basse-Terre (on Basse-Terre Is.) *area* 583 *sq mi* (1516 *sq km*), *pop* 327,002

Gua·di·a·na \ˌgwäd-ē-'än-ə, -'an-\ river 515 *mi* (829 *km*) Spain & Portugal flowing W & S into Gulf of Cádiz

Guairá Falls — see SETE QUEDAS

Guam \'gwäm\ island W Pacific in S Marianas belonging to U.S. ✳ Agana *area* 212 *sq mi* (551 *sq km*), *pop* 105,979 — **Gua·ma·ni·an** \gwä-'mä-nē-ən\ *adj or n*

Gua·na·ba·coa \ˌgwän-ə-bə-'kō-ə\ city W Cuba E of Havana *pop* 89,741

Gua·na·ba·ra Bay \ˌgwän-ə-'bar-ə, -'bär-ə\ inlet of Atlantic ocean SE Brazil

Gua·na·jua·to \ˌgwän-ə-'(h)wät-(ˌ)ō\ **1** state *cen* Mexico *area* 11,804 *sq mi* (30,690 *sq km*), *pop* 3,044,402 **2** city, its ✳ *pop* 65,258

Guangdong — see KWANGTUNG

Guangxi Zhuangzu — see KWANGSI CHUANG

Guangzhou — see CANTON

Guan·tá·na·mo \gwän-'tän-ə-ˌmō\ city SE Cuba NW of **Guantánamo Bay** (inlet of the Caribbean; site of U.S. naval station) *pop* 204,268

Gua·po·ré \ˌgwäp-ə-'rā\ **1** or **Ité·nez** \ē-'tā-nəs\ river 950 *mi* (1529 *km*) W Brazil & NE Bolivia flowing NW to the Mamoré **2** — see RONDÔNIA

Guar·da·fui, Cape \ˌg(w)ärd-əf-'wē, -ə-'fü-ē\ cape NE Somalia at entrance to Gulf of Aden

Guá·ri·co \'gwär-i-ˌkō\ river 225 *mi* (362 *km*) W Venezuela flowing SW & S into the Apure

Gua·te·ma·la \ˌgwät-ə-'mäl-ə\ **1** country Central America S of Mexico bordering on the Pacific & the Caribbean; a republic *area* 42,042 *sq mi* (109,309 *sq km*), *pop* 6,043,559 **2** or **Guatemala City** city, its ✳ *pop* 749,784 — **Gua·te·ma·lan** \-'mäl-ən\ *adj or n*

Gua·via·re \ˌgwäv-ē-'yär-ē\ river 650 *mi* (1046 *km*) Colombia flowing E into the Orinoco

Gua·ya·ma \gwə-'yäm-ə\ town SE Puerto Rico *pop* 21,097

Gua·ya·quil \ˌgwī-ə-'kē(ə)l, -'kil\ city & port W Ecuador on Guayas river 40 *mi* (64 *km*) from **Gulf of Guayaquil** (inlet of the Pacific) *pop* 823,219

Gua·yas \'gwī-əs\ river *ab* 100 *mi* (161 *km*) W Ecuador forming delta in Gulf of Guayaquil

Guay·mas \'gwī-məs\ city & port NW Mexico in Sonora on Gulf of California *pop* 57,492

Guay·na·bo \gwī-'näb-(ˌ)ō\ city NE *cen* Puerto Rico *pop* 65,075

Guelph \'gwelf\ city Canada in SE Ont. *pop* 71,207

Guern·sey \'gərn-zē\ island English channel in the Channel islands ✳ St. Peter Port *area* 25 *sq mi* (65 *sq km*), *pop* 46,182

Guer·re·ro \gə-'re(ə)r-(ˌ)ō\ state S Mexico bordering on the Pacific ✳ Chilpancingo *area* 24,885 *sq mi* (64,701 *sq km*), *pop* 2,174,162

Gui — see KUEI

Gui·a·na \gē-'an-ə, -'än-ə; gī-'an-ə\ region N S. America bordering on the Atlantic & bounded on W & S by Orinoco, Negro, & Amazon rivers; includes Guyana, French Guiana, Suriname, & adjoining parts of Brazil & Venezuela — **Gui·a·nan** \-ən\ *adj or n* — **Gui·a·nese** \ˌgī-ə-'nēz, ˌgē-ə-, -'nēs\ *adj or n*

Gui·enne or **Guy·enne** \gwē-'(y)en\ region & former province SW France bordering on Bay of Biscay ✳ Bordeaux — see AQUITAINE

Guil·ford \'gil-fard\ city S Conn. on Long Is. Sound *pop* 17,375

Guilin — see KUEI-LIN

Gui·nea \'gin-ē\ or *F* **Gui·née** \gē-nā\ **1** region W Africa bordering on the Atlantic from Gambia (on N) to Angola (on S) **2** or *formerly* **French Guinea** republic W Africa bordering on the Atlantic; formerly a territory of French West Africa ✳ Conakry *area* 108,455 *sq mi* (281,983 *sq km*), *pop* 5,781,014 — **Guin·ean** \'gin-ē-ən\ *adj or n*

Guinea, Gulf of arm of the Atlantic W *cen* Africa; includes bights of Benin & Biafra

Guin·ea–Bis·sau \ˌgin-ē-bis-'aú\ or *formerly* **Por·tu·guese Guinea** \ˌpōr-chə-ˌgēz-, ˌpór-, -ˌgēs-\ republic W Africa S of Senegal; until 1974 a Portuguese colony ✳ Bissau *area* 13,948 *sq mi* (36,265 *sq km*), *pop* 767,739

Gui·púz·coa \gē-'püs-kə-wə\ province N Spain; one of the Basque provinces ✳ San Sebastian *area* 728 *sq mi* (1893 *sq km*), *pop* 733,042

Guiyang — see KUEI-YANG

Guizhou — see KWEICHOW

Gu·ja·rat or **Gu·je·rat** \ˌgüj-ə-'rät, ˌgúj-ə-\ **1** region W India where Gujarati is spoken **2** state W India N & E of Gulf of Cambay ✳ Gandhinagar *area* 72,226 *sq mi* (187,788 *sq km*), *pop* 33,960,905

Guj·ran·wala \ˌgüj-rən-'wäl-ə, ˌgúj-\ city NE Pakistan N of Lahore *pop* 785,000

Gulf·port \'gəlf-ˌpō(ə)rt, -ˌpó(ə)rt\ city & port SE Miss. *pop* 39,676

Gulf Stream warm current in N Atlantic flowing from Gulf of Mexico NE along U.S. coast to Nantucket & thence eastward

Gulja — see KULDJA

Gum·ti \'gúm(p)-tē\ river 500 *mi* (805 *km*) N India flowing SE into the Ganges

Gun·ni·son \'gən-ə-sən\ river 150 *mi* (241 *km*) W *cen* Colo. flowing W & NW into Colorado river — see BLACK

Gun·tur \gùn-'tú(ə)r\ city E India in *cen* Andhra Pradesh W of Machilipatnam *pop* 367,219

Gus·ta·vo A. Ma·de·ro \gə-'stäv-(ˌ)ō-'ä-mə-'de(ə)r-(ˌ)ō\ city *cen* Mexico in Distrito Federal N of Mexico City *pop* 1,182,895

Guy·ana \gī-'an-ə\ or *formerly* **British Guiana** country N S. America on Atlantic coast; a republic within the Commonwealth since 1970 ✳ Georgetown *area* 83,000 *sq mi* (215,800 *sq km*), *pop* 758,619 — **Guy·a·nese** \ˌgī-ə-'nēz, -'nēs\ *adj or n*

Gwa·dar or **Gwa·dur** \'gwäd-ər\ town & port SW Pakistan on Arabian sea; until 1958 belonged to Sultan of Oman *pop* 17,000

Gwa·li·or \'gwäl-ē-ˌó(ə)r\ **1** former state N *cen* India ✳ Lashkar; part of Madhya Pradesh since 1956 **2** city N *cen* India in NW Madhya Pradesh SSE of Agra *pop* (including adjacent city of **Lash·kar** \'läsh-kər\) 559,776

Gwent \'gwent\ county SE Wales ✳ Cwmbran *area* 531 *sq mi* (1381 *sq km*), *pop* 440,100

Gwyn·edd \'gwin-eth\ county NW Wales ✳ Caernarvon *area* 1493 *sq mi* (3882 *sq km*), *pop* 234,100

Gyor \'jər\ city NW Hungary WNW of Budapest *pop* 123,618

Haar·lem \'här-ləm\ city W Netherlands ✳ of N. Holland *pop* 154,423

Haar·lem·mer·meer \ˌhär-lə-mər-'me(ə)r\ commune W Netherlands *pop* 82,250

Habana — see HAVANA

Hack·en·sack \'hak-ən-ˌsak\ city NE N.J. *pop* 36,039

Hack·ney \'hak-nē\ borough of N Greater London, England *pop* 187,000

Had·ding·ton \'had-iŋ-tən\ **1** or **Had·ding·ton·shire** \-shi(ə)r, -shər\ — see EAST LOTHIAN **2** royal burgh Scotland in Lothian *pop* 8117

Ha·dhra·maut or **Ha·dra·maut** \ˌhäd-rə-'maút\ region S Arabia bordering on Arabian sea E of Aden in Yemen; chief city Mukalla *area* 58,500 *sq mi* (152,100 *sq km*)

Hadrumetum — see SOUSSE

Hae·ju \'hī-(ˌ)jü\ city SW N. Korea on inlet of Yellow sea S of Pyongyang *pop* 140,000

Ha·erh–pin \'hä-'er-'bin\ or **Har·bin** \'här-bən, här-'bin\ or *formerly* **Pin·kiang** \'bin-jē-'äŋ\ city NE China ✳ of Heilungkiang on Sungari river *pop* 2,624,000

Ha·gen \'häg-ən\ or **Hagen in West·fa·len** \-in-ˌvest-'fäl-ən\ city W *cen* W. Germany ENE of Düsseldorf *pop* 218,927

Ha·gers·town \'hä-gərz-ˌtaún\ city N Md. *pop* 34,132

Hague, The \thə-'häg\ or *D* **'s Gra·ven·ha·ge** \s(k)räv-ən-'häg-ə\ city SW Netherlands in S. Holland near coast of North sea; de facto ✳ of the Netherlands *pop* 449,700

Haidarabad — see HYDERABAD

Hai·fa \'hī-fə\ city & port NW Israel at foot of Mt. Carmel *pop* 227,800

Hai·kou \'hī-'kō\ city & port SE China ✳ of Hainan *pop* 402,000

Hai·nan \'hī-'nän\ **1** island SE China in S. China sea; a province ✳ Haikou *area* 13,000 *sq mi* (33,800 *sq km*) **2** or **Qiong·zhou** \chē-'úŋ-'jō\ or **Chiung·chou** \jē-'úŋ-'jō\ or **Kiung·chow** \kē-'úŋ-'jō\ strait bet. Hainan Is. & Lei-chou peninsula connecting Gulf of Tonkin with S. China sea

Hai·naut \(h)ā-'nō\ **1** medieval county in Low Countries SE of Flanders in modern SW Belgium & N France **2** province SW Belgium ✳ Mons *area* 1436 *sq mi* (3734 *sq km*), *pop* 1,301,477

Hai·phong \'hī-'fóŋ\ city & port N Vietnam in Tonkin in delta of Red river *pop* 812,000

Hai·ti or *formerly* **Hay·ti** \'hät-ē\ **1** — see HISPANIOLA **2** country W. Indies on W Hispaniola; a republic ✳ Port-au-Prince *area* 10,714 *sq mi* (27,856 *sq km*), *pop* 5,053,792

Ha·ko·da·te \ˌhäk-ə-'dät-ē\ city & port Japan in SW Hokkaido on Tsugaru strait *pop* 319,244

Hal·ber·stadt \'häl-bər-ˌs(h)tät\ city W E. Germany SE of Brunswick *pop* 47,713

Hal·di·mand \'hól-də-mən(d)\ town Canada in SE Ont. *pop* 16,866

Ha·le·a·ka·la Crater \ˌhäl-ē-ˌäk-ə-'lä\ crater of dormant volcano 10,023 *ft* (3055 *m*) Hawaii on E Maui; 2720 *ft* (829 *m*) deep, 20 *mi* (32 *km*) in circumference; in **Haleakala National Park**

Hal·fa·ya Pass \hal-ˌfī-ə-\ pass NW Egypt through hills near Mediterranean coast

Hal·i·car·nas·sus \ˌhal-ə-kär-'nas-əs\ ancient city SW Asia Minor in SW Caria on Aegean sea

Hal·i·fax \'hal-ə-ˌfaks\ **1** city & port Canada ✳ of N.S. *pop* 114,594 **2** borough N England in W. Yorkshire *pop* 87,488

Hal·lan·dale \'hal-ən-ˌdāl\ city SE Fla. S of Fort Lauderdale *pop* 36,517

Hal·le \'häl-ə\ city SW E. Germany on the Saale NW of Leipzig *pop* 232,396

\ə\ abut \ᵊ\ kitten, F table \ər\ further \a\ ash \ā\ ace \ä\ cot, cart
\aú\ out \ch\ chin \e\ bet \ē\ easy \g\ go \i\ hit \ī\ ice \j\ job
\ŋ\ sing \ō\ go \ó\ law \ói\ boy \th\ thin \t͟h\ the \ü\ loot \ú\ foot
\y\ yet \zh\ vision \á, ḳ, ⁿ, œ, œ, ɶ, ɨɛ, ᵛ\ *see* Guide to Pronunciation

Hall·statt \'hȯl-,stat, 'häl-,s(h)tät\ village W *cen* Austria on shore of **Hall·stät·ter Lake** \,hȯl-,stet-ər, ,häl-,s(h)tet-\

Hal·ma·he·ra \,hal-mə-'her-ə, ,häl-\ island E Indonesia in Moluccas; largest in group *area* 6928 *sq mi* (18,013 *sq km*), *pop* 54,000

Halm·stad \'hälm-,stä(d)\ city & port SW Sweden *pop* 76,042

Häl·sing·borg \'hel-siŋ,bȯ(ə)rg, ,hel-siŋ-'bȯr-ē\ city & port SW Sweden on Öresund opposite Helsingör, Denmark *pop* 101,956

Hal·tom City \'hȯl-təm-\ village N Tex. NE of Fort Worth *pop* 29,014

Hal·ton Hills \'hȯlt-ᵊn-\ town Canada in S Ont. *pop* 35,190

Halys — see KIZIL IRMAK

Ha·ma \'ham-ä\ *or bib* **Ha·math** \'hā-,math\ city W Syria on the Orontes *pop* 176,640

Ha·mad, Al \,al-hə-'mad\ the SW portion of Syrian desert

Ha·ma·dan \,ham-ə-'dan, -'dän\ *or anc* **Ec·bat·a·na** \ek-'bat-ᵊn-ə\ city W Iran WSW of Tehran *pop* 124,167

Ha·ma·ma·tsu \,häm-ə-'mät-(,)sü\ city Japan in S Honshu SE of Nagoya near Pacific coast *pop* 496,073

Ham·burg \'ham-,bərg; 'häm-,bü(ə)rg\ city & port N W. Germany on the Elbe 90 *mi* (145 *km*) from its mouth; since 1948 a state of the Federal Republic of Germany *area* 288 *sq mi* (749 *sq km*), *pop* 1,645,095 — **Ham·burg·er** \-gər, -,bür-\ *n*

Ham·den \'ham-dən\ town S Conn. N of New Haven *pop* 51,071

Ha·meln \'häm-əln\ city N *cen* W. Germany in Lower Saxony SW of Hannover *pop* 58,390

Ham·hung \'häm-,hů\ city E *cen* N. Korea near coast *pop* 420,000

Ham·il·ton \'ham-əl-tən, -ᵊlt-ᵊn\ **1** *or now officially* **Hamilton!** city SW Ohio N of Cincinnati *pop* 63,189 **2** town & port ✳ of Bermuda *pop* 1617 **3** — see CHURCHILL **4** city & port Canada in SE Ont. on Lake Ontario *pop* 306,434 **5** borough New Zealand on *cen* North Is. *pop* 91,109

Hamilton, Mount mountain 4261 *ft* (1299 *m*) W Calif. E of San Jose

Hamilton Inlet inlet of the Atlantic 150 *mi* (241 *km*) long (with Lake Melville) Canada in SE Labrador

Hamm \'häm, 'ham\ city W *cen* W. Germany on Lippe river *pop* 171,869

Ham·mer·fest \'ham-ər-,fest, 'häm-\ town & port N Norway on island in Arctic ocean; northernmost town in Europe, at 70°38′N

Ham·mer·smith \'ham-ər-,smith\ borough of SW Greater London, England *pop* 153,800

Ham·mond \'ham-ənd\ city NW Ind. SE of Chicago *pop* 93,714

Hamp·shire \'ham(p)-,shi(ə)r, -shər\ *or* **Hants** \'han(t)s\ county S England on English channel ✳ Winchester *area* 1457 *sq mi* (3788 *sq km*), *pop* 1,479,500

Hamp·stead \'ham(p)-stəd, -,sted\ former metropolitan borough NW London, England, now part of Camden

Hamp·ton \'ham(p)-tən\ city & port SE Va. E of Newport News on Hampton Roads *pop* 122,617

Hampton Roads channel SE Va. through which James & Elizabeth rivers flow into Chesapeake Bay

Ham·tramck \ham-'tram-ik\ city SE Mich. within city of Detroit *pop* 21,300

Han \'hän\ **1** river 900 *mi* (1448 *km*) E *cen* China in Shensi & Hupeh flowing SE into the Yangtze **2** river 220 *mi* (354 *km*) N *cen* S. Korea flowing W & NW into Yellow sea

Han Cities WUHAN

Han·ford \'han-fərd\ city S *cen* Calif. SE of Fresno *pop* 20,958

Hang·chow \'haŋ-'chaů, 'hä ŋ-\ *or* **Hang·zhou** \'häŋ-'jō\ *or* **Hang·chou** \-'jō\ city E China ✳ of Chekiang at head of **Hangchow Bay** (inlet of E. China sea) *pop* 784,000

Han·ko \'haŋ-,kō\ *or Sw* **Hangö** \'häŋ-,ə(r)\ city & port SW Finland on Hanko (Hangö) peninsula in the Baltic SE of Turku

Han·kow \'haŋ-'kaů, -'kō; 'hän-'kō\ former city E *cen* China — see WU-HAN

Han·ni·bal \'han-ə-bəl\ city NE Mo. on Mississippi river *pop* 18,811

Han·no·ver *or* **Han·o·ver** \'han-,ō-vər, 'han-ə-vər, *G* hä-'nō-vər, -'nō-fər\ city N W. Germany WNW of Brunswick *pop* 534,451

Ha·noi \ha-'nȯi, hə-, hä-\ city ✳ of Vietnam in Tonkin on Red river; formerly ✳ of French Indochina & of N. Vietnam *pop* 414,600

Han·o·ver Park \'han-,ō-vər\ village NE Ill. *pop* 28,850

Han·yang \'hän-'yäŋ\ former city E *cen* China — see WUHAN

Ha·rap·pa \hə-'rap-ə\ locality W Pakistan in Indus valley NE of Multan; center of a prehistoric civilization

Ha·rar \'här-ər\ city E Ethiopia E of Addis Ababa *pop* 70,289

Ha·ra·re \hə-'rä-(,)rä\ *or formerly* **Salisbury** city ✳ of Zimbabwe *pop* 654,000

Harbin — see HA-ERH-PIN

Ha·ri Rud \,har-ē-'rüd\ *or anc* **Ari·us** \'ar-ē-əs, 'er-; ə-'rī-əs\ river 700 *mi* (1126 *km*) NW Afghanistan, NE Iran, & S Turkmen Republic flowing W & N into Kara Kum desert

Har·lem \'här-ləm\ **1** river channel SE N.Y. NE of Manhattan Is.; with Spuyten Duyvil Creek, connects Hudson & East rivers **2** section of New York City in NE Manhattan bordering on Harlem & East rivers **3** HAARLEM — **Har·lem·ite** \-lə-,mīt\ *n*

Har·lin·gen \'här-lən-jən\ **1** city S Tex. NNW of Brownsville *pop* 43,543 **2** \-liŋ-ən\ town & port N Netherlands in Friesland

Har·ney Lake \'här-nē\ intermittent salt lake SE Oreg. in **Harney basin** (depression, *area* 2500 *sq mi* or 6500 *sq km*)

Harney Peak mountain 7242 *ft* (2207 *m*) SW S.Dak.; highest in Black Hills & in state

Harris — see LEWIS WITH HARRIS

Har·ris·burg \'har-əs-,bərg\ city ✳ of Pa. *pop* 53,264

Har·ri·son·burg \'har-ə-sən-,bərg\ city N Va. *pop* 19,671

Har·ro·gate \'har-ə-gət, -,gāt\ borough N England in N. Yorkshire N of Leeds *pop* 66,475

Har·row \'har-(,)ō\ borough of NW Greater London, England *pop* 199,200

Hart·ford \'härt-fərd\ city N *cen* Conn., its ✳ *pop* 136,392

Hart·le·pool \'härt-lē-,pül\ borough N England in Cleveland on North sea *pop* 94,359

Har·vard, Mount \'här-vərd\ mountain 14,420 *ft* (4395 *m*) *cen* Colo. in Collegiate range of Sawatch mountains SE of Mt. Elbert

Har·vey \'här-vē\ city NE Ill. S of Chicago *pop* 35,810

Har·wich \'har-ij, -ich, *US also* 'här-(,)wich\ borough SE England in Essex on North sea *pop* 15,076

Ha·ry·a·na *or* **Ha·ri·a·na** \,hə-rē-'än-ə\ state NW India in E Punjab formed 1966 from southern part of former state of Punjab ✳ Chandigarh *area* 17,010 *sq mi* (44,226 *sq km*), *pop* 12,850,902

Harz \'härts\ mountains E W. Germany & W E. Germany bet. the Elbe & the Leine — see BROCKEN

Ha·sa *or* **El Hasa** \(el-)'has-ə\ region NE Saudi Arabia in E Nejd bordering on Persian gulf

Has·selt \'häs-əlt\ commune NE Belgium ✳ of Limburg *pop* 64,613

Has·tings \'hā-stiŋz\ **1** city S Nebr. *pop* 23,045 **2** borough SE England in E. Sussex on Strait of Dover *pop* 74,803

Ha·tay \hä-'tī\ district S Turkey E of Gulf of Iskenderun

Hat·ter·as \'hat-ə-rəs, 'ha-trəs\ island N.C. bet. Pamlico Sound & Atlantic ocean; a long barrier island

Hatteras, Cape cape N.C. on SE Hatteras Is.

Hat·ties·burg \'hat-ēz-,bərg\ city SE Miss. *pop* 40,829

Hau·ra·ki Gulf \haů-,rak-ē-, -,räk-\ inlet of the S Pacific N New Zealand on N coast of North Is.

Haute–Vol·ta \ōt-vȯl-tà\ French name for Upper Volta

Ha·va·na *or* **Ha·ba·na** \hə-'van-ə *or Sp* **La Ha·ba·na** \lä-(ä-)'vän-ə\ city & port ✳ of Cuba on Gulf of Mexico *pop* 990,000 — **Ha·van·an** \hə-'van-ən\ *adj or n*

Hav·ant and Wa·ter·loo \'hav-ənt-ᵊn-,wȯt-ər-'lü, -,wät-\ town S England in Hampshire NE of Portsmouth *pop* 116,649

Ha·vel \'häf-əl\ river 225 *mi* (362 *km*) N E. Germany flowing SW through Berlin into the Elbe

Have·lock \'hav-,läk, -lək\ city SE N.C. *pop* 17,718

Hav·er·ford·west \,hav-ər-fərd-'west, ,här-fərd-\ borough & port SW Wales in Dyfed *pop* 9936

Ha·ver·hill \'hāv-(ə-)rəl\ city NE Mass. *pop* 46,865

Ha·ver·ing \'hāv-(ə-)riŋ\ borough of NE Greater London, England *pop* 241,800

Havre — see LE HAVRE

Ha·waii \hə-'wä-(y)ē, -'wī-(,)(y)ē, -'wȯ-(,)(y)ē, -'wä-yə, -'wȯ-yə, -'wi-(y)ə\ **1** *or* **Ha·wai·ian islands** \hə-'wä-yən-, -,wi-(y)ən-, -,wȯ-yən-\ *or formerly* **Sand·wich islands** \,san-(,)dwich\ group of islands *cen* Pacific belonging to U.S. **2** island SE Hawaii, largest of the group; chief city Hilo *area* 4021 *sq mi* (10,455 *sq km*) **3** state of the U.S. comprising Hawaiian islands except Midway islands; annexed 1898, a territory 1900–59 ✳ Honolulu *area* 6450 *sq mi* (16,770 *sq km*), *pop* 964,691

Hawaii Volcanoes National Park reservation Hawaii including Mauna Loa & Kilauea volcanoes on Hawaii (island)

Hawke Bay \'hȯk\ inlet of the S Pacific N New Zealand on SE coast of North Is.

Haw·thorne \'hȯ-,thō(ə)rn\ **1** city SW Calif. SW of Los Angeles *pop* 56,447 **2** borough NE N.J. N of Paterson *pop* 18,200

Hay \'hā\ river 530 *mi* (853 *km*) Canada in N Alta. & SW Mackenzie district flowing NE into Great Slave Lake

Hayes \'hāz\ **1** river 300 *mi* (483 *km*) Canada in E Man. flowing NE into Hudson bay **2** *or* **Hayes and Har·ling·ton** \'här-liŋ-tən\ former urban district SE England in Middlesex, now part of Hillingdon

Hayti — see HAITI

Hay·ward \'hā-wərd\ city W Calif. SE of Oakland *pop* 94,167

Ha·zel Park \,hā-zəl-\ city SE Mich. N of Detroit *pop* 20,914

Ha·zle·ton \'hā-zəl-tən\ city E Pa. S of Wilkes-Barre *pop* 27,318

Heard \'hərd\ island S Indian ocean SE of Kerguelen, at 53°10′S, 74°10′E; claimed by Australia

Hebei — see HOPEH

Heb·ri·des \'heb-rə-,dēz\ *or* **Western** islands W Scotland in the Atlantic divided by Little Minch into **Inner Hebrides** (near the mainland) & **Outer Hebrides** (to NW) *area* 2900 *sq mi* (7540 *sq km*), *pop* 60,000 — see LEWIS WITH HARRIS, WESTERN ISLES — **Heb·ri·de·an** \,heb-rə-'dē-ən\ *adj or n*

He·bron \'hē-brən\ *or anc* **Kir·jath–ar·ba** \,kir-,jath-'är-bə, ,ki(ə)r-\ city *cen* Palestine SSW of Jerusalem in modern Jordan *pop* 38,348

Hec·ate \'hek-ət\ strait Canada in W B.C., inlet of the Pacific bet. Queen Charlotte islands & the coast

Heer·len \'he(ə)r-lən\ commune SE Netherlands in Limburg NE of Maastricht *pop* 92,158

Hefei — see HOFEI

Hei·del·berg \'hīd-ᵊl-,bərg, -,be(ə)rg\ city S W. Germany on the Neckar SE of Mannheim *pop* 133,227

Heil·bronn \'hi(ə)l-,brän, hīl-'brȯn\ city S W. Germany on the Neckar N of Stuttgart *pop* 111,938

Hei·lung·kiang *or* **Hei·long Jiang** \'hā-'lůŋ-jē-'äŋ\ province NE China in N Manchuria bordering on the Amur ✳ Harbin *area* 178,996 *sq mi* (465,390 *sq km*), *pop* 32,665,546

He·jaz \hej-'az, hi-jäz\ *or* **Al Hi·jäz** \,al-hi-'jaz\ region W Saudi Arabia on Red sea; a viceroyalty ✳ Mecca *area* 150,000 *sq mi* (390,000 *sq km*), *pop* 1,400,000

Hek·la \'hek-lə\ volcano 4892 *ft* (1491 *m*) SW Iceland

Hel·e·na \'hel-ə-nə\ city W *cen* Mont., its ✳ *pop* 23,938

Hel·go·land \'hel-gō-,land\ *or* **Hel·i·go·land** \'hel-i-gō-,land, -,länt\ island NW W. Germany in North sea, in N. Frisian islands

Hel·i·con \'hel-ə-,kän, -i-kən\ mountain 5735 *ft* (1748 *m*) E *cen* Greece in SW Boeotia near Gulf of Corinth

He·li·op·o·lis \,hē-lē-'äp-ə-ləs\ **1** — see BAALBEK **2** ancient ruined city N Egypt S of modern Cairo **3** ancient ruined city NE of modern Cairo

Hellas — see GREECE

Hel·les, Cape \'hel-(,)ēz\ headland Turkey in Europe at S tip of Gallipoli peninsula

Hellespont, Hellespontus — see DARDANELLES

Hell Gate a narrow part of East river in New York City between Long Is. & Manhattan Is.

Hells Canyon \'helz\ *or* **Grand Canyon of the Snake** canyon of Snake river on Idaho-Oreg. border

Hel·mand \'hel-mənd\ river 650 *mi* (1046 *km*) SW Afghanistan flowing SW & W into a morass on Iran border

Hel·mond \'hel-,mȯnt\ commune S Netherlands *pop* 59,345

Helm·stedt \'helm-,s(h)tet\ city E W. Germany E of Brunswick near E. German border *pop* 26,718

Hel·sing·ör \,hel-siŋ-'ər\ city & port Denmark on N Sjælland Is. *pop* 56,280

Hel·sin·ki \'hel-,siŋ-kē, hel-'\ *or Sw* **Hel·sing·fors** \'hel-siŋ-,fȯ(ə)rz\ city & port ✳ of Finland on Gulf of Finland *pop* 483,051

Hel·vel·lyn \hel-'vel-ən\ mountain 3118 *ft* (950 *m*) NW England in Cumbria SW of Ullswater

Helvetia — see SWITZERLAND — **Hel·ve·tian** \hel-'vē-shən\ *adj or n*

Hem·et \'hem-ət\ city SE Calif. SE of San Bernardino *pop* 22,454

Hemp·stead \'hem(p)-,sted, -stəd\ village SE N.Y. on Long Is. *pop* 40,404

Henan — see HONAN

Hen·der·son \'hen-dər-sən\ **1** city NW Ky. *pop* 24,834 **2** city S Nev. *pop* 24,363

Hen·der·son·ville \'hen-dər-sən-,vil, -vəl\ city N Tenn. NE of Nashville *pop* 26,561

Hen·don \'hen-dən\ former urban district SE England in Middlesex, now part of Barnet

Heng·e·lo \'heŋ-ə-,lō\ commune E Netherlands in Overijssel *pop* 76,535

Heng·yang \'həŋ-'yäŋ\ city *cen* China in SE Hunan on the Hsiang *pop* 240,000

Hen·ley \'hen-lē\ *or* **Henley on Thames** borough SE *cen* England in Oxfordshire W of London *pop* 31,744

Hen·lo·pen, Cape \hen-'lō-pən\ headland SE Del. at entrance to Delaware Bay

Hen·ry, Cape \'hen-rē\ headland SE Va. S of entrance to Chesapeake Bay

He·rat \he-'rät, hə-\ *or anc* **Aria** \'ar-ē-ə, 'er-; ə-'rī-ə\ city NW Afghanistan on the Hari Rud *pop* 163,960

Her·cu·la·ne·um \,hər-kyə-'lā-nē-əm\ ancient city S Italy in Campania on Tyrrhenian sea; destroyed A.D. 79 by eruption of Mt. Vesuvius

Her·e·ford \'her-ə-fərd, *US also* 'här-fərd\ **1** *or* **Her·e·ford·shire** \-,shi(ə)r, -shər\ former county W England on Welsh border **2** borough W England in Hereford and Worcester *pop* 47,652

Hereford and Wor·ces·ter \'wus-tər\ county W England ✳ Worcester *area* 1516 *sq mi* (3942 *sq km*), *pop* 634,700

Her·ford \'he(ə)r-fȯ(ə)rt\ city N *cen* W. Germany in N. Rhine-Westphalia NE of Bielefeld *pop* 62,881

Her·i·sau \'her-ə-,zaú\ commune NE Switzerland ✳ of Appenzell Outer Rhodes canton *pop* 14,600

Her·mon, Mount \'hər-mən\ mountain 9232 *ft* (2814 *m*) on border bet. Syria & Lebanon; highest in Anti-Lebanon mountains

Her·mo·sa Beach \(,)hər-,mō-sə-\ city SW Calif. SW of Los Angeles *pop* 18,070

Her·mo·si·llo \,er-mə-'sē-(,)(y)ō\ city NW Mexico ✳ of Sonora on Sonora river *pop* 232,691

Hermoúpolis — see ERMOÚPOLIS

Her·ne \'he(ə)r-nə\ city W W. Germany in the Ruhr *pop* 182,542

Her·ten \'he(ə)rt-ᵊn\ city W W. Germany in N. Rhine-Westphalia N of Essen *pop* 69,247

Hert·ford \'här-fərd *also* 'härt-, *US also* 'hȯrt-\ borough SE England ✳ of Hertfordshire *pop* 21,412

Hert·ford·shire \'här-fərd-,shi(ə)r, -shər, *also* 'härt-, *US also* 'hȯrt-\ *or* **Hert·ford** \'här-fərd *also* 'härt-, *US also* 'hȯrt-\ county SE England *area* 654 *sq mi* (1699 *sq km*), *pop* 964,800

Hertogenbosch, 's — see 'S HERTOGENBOSCH

Her·ze·go·vi·na \,hert-sə-gō-'vē-nə, -'gō-və-nə *or Serb* **Her·ce·go·vi·na** \'kert-sə-gō-vē-nä\ region W *cen* Yugoslavia S of Bosnia & NW of Montenegro; now part of Bosnia and Herzegovina republic — **Her·ze·go·vi·nian** \,hert-sə-gō-'vē-nē-ən, ,hərt-, -nyən\ *n*

Hesse \'hes, 'hes-ə\ *or G* **Hes·sen** \'hes-ᵊn\ **1** region *cen* W. Germany N of Baden-Württemberg divided into **Hesse–Darmstadt** (in the S) & **Hes·se–Cas·sel** \'kas-əl, 'käs-\ (in the N), the latter being united with Prussia in 1866 as part of the province of **Hesse–Nassau** along with the duchy of Nassau & the city of Frankfurt am Main **2** state of the Weimar Republic, equivalent to Hesse-Darmstadt **3** state of W. Germany including larger part of Hesse-Darmstadt & part of Hesse-Nassau ✳ Wiesbaden *area* 8148 *sq mi* (21,185 *sq km*), *pop* 5,601,031

Hes·ton and Isle·worth \,hes-tə-nə-'nī-zəl-(,)wərth, ,hes-ᵊn-ə-'nī-\ former municipal borough SE England in Middlesex, now part of Hounslow

Hetian — see HO·TIEN

Hi·a·le·ah \,hī-ə-'lē-ə\ city SE Fla. N of Miami *pop* 145,254

Hib·bing \'hib-iŋ\ village NE Minn. *pop* 21,193

Hibernia — see IRELAND

Hi·bok·hi·bok \,hē-,bȯk-'hē-,bȯk\ volcano 5620 *ft* (1713 *m*) S Philippines on Camiguin Is.

Hick·o·ry \'hik-(ə-)rē\ city W *cen* N.C. *pop* 20,757

Hi·dal·go \hid-'al-(,)gō\ state *cen* Mexico ✳ Pachuca *area* 8057 *sq mi* (20,948 *sq km*), *pop* 1,516,511

Hierosolyma — see JERUSALEM

Hier·ro \'ye(ə)r-(,)ō\ *or formerly* **Fer·ro** \'fe(ə)r-(,)ō\ island Spain, westernmost of the Canary islands *area* 107 *sq mi* (278 *sq km*)

Hi·ga·shi·ōsa·ka \hē-,gä-shē-ō-'säk-ə\ city Japan in S Honshu; suburb of Osaka *pop* 522,359

High Atlas — see ATLAS

High·land \'hī-lənd\ **1** town NW Ind. S of Hammond *pop* 25,935 **2** region N Scotland, established 1975 ✳ Inverness *area* 9813 *sq mi* (25,514 *sq km*), *pop* 200,030

Highland Park **1** city NE Ill. N of Chicago *pop* 30,611 **2** city SE Mich. within city of Detroit *pop* 27,909

High·lands \'hī-lən(d)z\ the chiefly mountainous N part of Scotland N of a line connecting Firth of Clyde & Firth of Tay

Highlands of Navesink — see NAVESINK (Highlands of)

Highlands of the Hudson hilly region SE N.Y. on both sides of Hudson river; includes Storm King (W of the Hudson) 1340 *ft* (408 *m*)

High Plains the Great Plains esp. from Nebr. southward

High Point \'hī-,pȯint\ city N *cen* N.C. SW of Greensboro *pop* 63,380

High Sierra the Sierra Nevada (in Calif.)

High Wyc·ombe \'wik-əm\ borough SE *cen* England in Buckinghamshire WNW of London *pop* 60,516

Hii·u·maa \'hē-ə-,mä\ island U.S.S.R. in Estonia in Baltic sea N of Sarema Is. *area* 371 *sq mi* (965 *sq km*)

Hijaz, Al — see HEJAZ

Hil·des·heim \'hil-dəs-,hīm\ city N W. Germany SSE of Hannover *pop* 102,619

Hil·ling·don \'hil-iŋ-dən\ borough of W Greater London, England *pop* 232,800

Hills·boro \'hilz-,bər-ə, -,bə-rə, -brə\ city NW Oreg. W of Portland *pop* 27,664

Hi·lo \'hē-(,)lō\ city & port Hawaii in E Hawaii (island) *pop* 35,269

Hil·ver·sum \'hil-vər-səm\ city *cen* Netherlands in N. Holland SE of Amsterdam *pop* 89,510

Hi·ma·chal Pra·desh \hi-,mäch-əl-prə-'desh, -'däsh\ state NW India NW of Uttar Pradesh ✳ Simla *area* 21,629 *sq mi* (56,235 *sq km*), *pop* 4,237,569

Hi·ma·la·ya \,him-ə-'lā-ə, hə-'mäl-(ə-)yə\ mountains S Asia on border bet. India & Tibet & in Kashmir, Nepal, & Bhutan — see EVEREST — **Hi·ma·la·yan** \,him-ə-'lā-ən, hə-'mäl-(ə-)yən\ *adj*

Hi·me·ji \hi-'mej-ē\ city Japan in W Honshu *pop* 448,111

Hindenburg — see ZABRZE

Hin·du Kush \,hin-(,)dü-'kúsh, -'kəsh\ *or anc* **Cau·ca·sus In·di·cus** \,kȯ-kə-sə-'sin-di-kəs\ mountain range *cen* Asia SW of the Pamirs on border of Kashmir & in Afghanistan — see TIRICH MIR

Hin·du·stan *or* **Hin·do·stan** \,hin-(,)dü-'stan, -də-, -'stän\ **1** region N India N of the Deccan including the plain drained by the Indus, the Ganges, & the Brahmaputra **2** the subcontinent of India **3** the Republic of India

Hing·ham \'hiŋ-əm\ town E Mass. SE of Boston *pop* 20,339

Hins·dale \'hinz-,dāl\ village NE of Chicago *pop* 16,726

Hip·po \'hip-(,)ō\ *or* **Hippo Re·gi·us** \-'rē-j(ē-)əs\ ancient city N Africa S of modern Bône, Algeria; chief town of Numidia

Hi·ro·sa·ki \hi-'rō-sə-kē, ,hir-ə-'säk-ē\ city Japan in N Honshu SW of Aomori *pop* 175,909

Hi·ro·shi·ma \his-'pän-ē-ə, -'pän-yə, hə-'rō-shə-mə\ city & port Japan in SW Honshu on Inland sea *pop* 910,768

His·pa·nia \his-'pän-ē-ə, -'pän-yə\ the Iberian peninsula

His·pan·io·la \,his-pən-'yō-lə\ *or Sp* **Es·pa·ño·la** \,es-,pän-'yō-lə\ *or formerly* **Hai·ti** \'hāt-ē\ *or* **San·to Do·min·go** \,sant-əd-ə-'miŋ-(,)gō\ *or* **San Domingo** \,san-də-\ island W. Indies in the Greater Antilles; divided between Haiti (on W) & Dominican Republic (on E) *area* 29,979 *sq mi* (77,945 *sq km*)

His·sar·lik \,his-ər-'lik\ site of ancient Troy NW Turkey in Asia 4 *mi* (6.4 *km*) SE of mouth of the Dardanelles

Hi·va Oa \,hē-və-'ō-ə\ island S Pacific in SE Marquesas *area* 154 *sq mi* (400 *sq km*)

Hi·was·see \hī-'wäs-ē\ river 150 *mi* (241 *km*) E U.S. flowing from NE Ga. WNW through W N.C. into Tennessee river in Tenn.

Ho·bart **1** \'hō-bərt\ city NW Ind. *pop* 22,987 **2** \-,bärt\ city & port Australia ✳ of Tasmania *pop* (with suburbs) 47,920

Hobbs \'häbz\ city SE corner of N.Mex. *pop* 29,153

Ho·bo·ken \'hō-,bō-kən\ **1** city NE N.J. N of Jersey City *pop* 42,460 **2** commune N Belgium, suburb of Antwerp *pop* 34,563

Ho Chi Minh City \,hō-(,)chē-,min-, -(,)shē-\ *or formerly* **Sai·gon** \sī-'gän, 'sī-,\ city & port S Vietnam; formerly (as Saigon) ✳ of S. Vietnam

Ho·dei·da \hō-'dād-ə\ city & port W Yemen *pop* 40,000

Hod·me·zo·va·sar·hely \'hȯd-mə-,zə(r)-'väsh-ər-,āl\ city SE Hungary NE of Szeged near the Tisza *pop* 54,481

Hof \'hȯf, 'hōf\ city E W. Germany in Bavaria on the Saale *pop* 53,180

Ho·fei *or* **He·fei** \'hə-'fā\ *or formerly* **Lu·chow** \'lü-'jō\ city E China ✳ of Anhwei W of Nanking *pop* 360,000

Hoff·man Estates \'häf-mən, 'hȯf-\ village NE Ill. *pop* 37,272

Ho·fuf \hú-'füf, hō-\ city NE Saudi Arabia in E Nejd; chief town of Hasa region *pop* 85,000

Hoggar — see AHAGGAR

Ho·hen·zol·lern \'hō-ən-,zäl-ərn\ region SW W. Germany, formerly a province of Prussia — see WÜRTTEMBERG

Ho·he Tau·ern \,hō-ə-'taú-ə)rn\ range of the E Alps W Austria between Carinthia & Tirol — see GROSSGLOCKNER

Hohhot — see HUHEHOT

Ho·ho·kam Pi·ma National Monument \hō-,hō-kəm-'pē-mə-\ reservation SE of Phoenix, Ariz.; not open to the public

Hok·kai·do \hä-'kīd-(,)ō\ *or formerly* **Ye·zo** \'yez-(,)ō\ island N Japan N of Honshu *area* 30,077 *sq mi* (78,200 *sq km*)

Hol·guín \hȯl-'gēn\ city E Cuba in plateau region *pop* 239,641

Hol·land \'häl-ənd\ **1** city W Mich. on Lake Michigan *pop* 26,281 **2** medieval county of Holy Roman Empire bordering on North sea, now forming N. & S. Holland provinces of the Netherlands **3** — see NETHERLANDS — **Hol·land·er** \-ən-dər\ *n*

Holland, Parts of district & former administrative county E England in SE Lincolnshire ✳ Boston *area* 420 *sq mi* (1092 *sq km*)

Hollandia — see DJAJAPURA

Hol·ly·wood \'häl-ē-,wúd\ **1** section of Los Angeles, Calif. NW of the downtown district **2** city SE Fla. N of Miami *pop* 121,323

Hol·stein \'hōl-,stīn, -,stēn\ region N W. Germany S of Jutland peninsula adjoining Schleswig; once a duchy of Denmark, became a part of Prussia 1866 — see SCHLESWIG-HOLSTEIN

Hol·ston \'hōl-stən\ river 140 *mi* (225 *km*) E Tenn. flowing SW to unite with French Broad river forming the Tennessee river

Ho·ly \'hō-lē\ **1** *or* **Lin·dis·farne** \'lin-dəs-,färn\ island N England off NE coast of Northumberland; connected to mainland at low tide *pop* 190 **2** *or* **Holy·head** \'häl-ē-,hed\ island NW Wales in St. George's Channel off W coast of Anglesey

Holy Cross, Mount of the mountain 14,005 *ft* (4269 *m*) NW *cen* Colo. in Sawatch range

Holy·head \'häl-ē-,hed\ urban area & port NW Wales in Gwynedd on Holy Is.

Holy Land a name for Palestine first used in Zech. 2:12

Holy Loch inlet of Firth of Clyde W Scotland on NW shore of the firth opposite mouth of the Clyde

Hol·yoke \'hōl-,yōk\ city SW Mass. N of Springfield *pop* 44,678

Hom·burg \'häm-,bərg, -,bú(ə)rg\ *or* **Bad Homburg** \(')bät-\ city W W. Germany N of Frankfurt am Main *pop* 41,847

Home·stead \'hōm-,sted\ city SE Fla. SW of Miami *pop* 20,668

\ə\ abut \ᵊ\ kitten, F table \ər\ further \a\ ash \ā\ ace \ä\ cot, cart
\aú\ out \ch\ chin \e\ bet \ē\ easy \g\ go \i\ hit \ī\ ice \j\ job
\ŋ\ sing \ō\ go \ȯ\ law \ȯi\ boy \th\ thin \th\ the \ü\ loot \ú\ foot
\y\ yet \zh\ vision \á, k̲, ⁿ, œ, œ̄, ue, ūe, ᵞ\ see Guide to Pronunciation

Homestead National Monument site SE Nebr. (W of Beatrice) of first homestead entered under General Homestead Act of 1862
Home·wood \'hōm-,wu̇d\ **1** city *cen* Ala. *pop* 21,412 **2** village NE Ill. S of Chicago *pop* 19,724
Homs \'hȯmz, 'hu̇ms\ **1** *or formerly* **Leb·da** \'leb-də\ town & port Libya ESE of Tripoli **2** *or anc* **Em·e·sa** \'em-ə-sə\ city W Syria on the Orontes *pop* 354,508
Ho·nan \'hō-'nan\ *or* **He·nan** \'hə-'nän\ province E *cen* China ✱ Chengchou *area* 64,479 *sq mi* (167,645 *sq km*), *pop* 74,422,739
Hon·du·ras \hän-'d(y)u̇r-əs\ country Central America bordering on the Caribbean & the Pacific; a republic ✱ Tegucigalpa *area* 59,160 *sq mi* (153,816 *sq km*), *pop* 4,372,000 — **Hon·du·ran** \-ən\ *adj or n* — **Hon·du·ra·ne·an** *or* **Hon·du·ra·ni·an** \,hän-d(y)u̇-'rā-nē-ən\ *adj or n*
Honduras, Gulf of inlet of the Caribbean bet. S Belize, E Guatemala, & N Honduras
Hon·fleur \ōⁿ-'flər\ town & port N France on Seine estuary *pop* 8995
Hong — see RED
Hong Kong \'häŋ-,käŋ, -'käŋ; 'hȯŋ-,kȯŋ, -'kȯŋ\ **1** Brit. crown colony on SE coast of China E of mouth of Chu river including Hong Kong Is., Kowloon peninsula & adjacent area (New Territories) on mainland, & nearby islands ✱ Victoria *area* 391 *sq mi* (1017 *sq km*), *pop* 4,986,560 **2** — see VICTORIA
Hongshui — see HUNGSHUI
Ho·ni·a·ra \,hō-nē-'är-ə\ town W Pacific ✱ of Solomon islands on Guadalcanal Is. *pop* 14,942
Ho·no·lu·lu \,hän-ᵊl-'ü-(,)lü, ,hōn-ᵊl-\ city & port ✱ of Hawaii on Oahu *pop* 365,048 — **Ho·no·lu·lan** \-'ü-lən\ *n*
Hon·shu \'hän-(,)shü\ *or* **Hon·do** \-(,)dō\ island Japan, chief island of the group *area* 88,000 *sq mi* (228,800 *sq km*)
Hood, Mount \'hu̇d\ mountain 11,245 *ft* (3427 *m*) NW Oreg. in Cascade range; highest point in state
Hood Canal inlet of Puget Sound 80 *mi* (129 *km*) long W Wash. along E shore of Olympic peninsula
Hoo·ghly \'hü-glē\ river 120 *mi* (193 *km*) E India flowing S into Bay of Bengal; most westerly channel of the Ganges in its delta
Hook of Holland \,hu̇k-\ headland SW Netherlands in S. Holland on coast SW of The Hague
Hoorn — see FUTUNA
Hoo·sac \'hü-sak\ mountain range NW Mass. & SW Vt., a southern extension of Green mountains
Hoo·ver \'hü-vər\ city *cen* Ala. *pop* 19,792
Hoo·ver Dam \,hü-vər-\ *or* **Boul·der Dam** \,bōl-dər-\ dam 726 *ft* (221 *m*) high in Colorado river bet. Nev. & Ariz. — see MEAD (Lake)
Ho·pat·cong, Lake \hə-'pat-,kän, -,käŋ\ lake 8 *mi* (13 *km*) long N N.J.
Ho·peh \'hō-'bā\ *or* **He·bei** \'hə-'bā\ *or* **Ho·pei** \'hō-\ *or formerly* **Chih·li** \'chē-'lē\ province NE China ✱ Shih-chia-chuang *area* 84,865 *sq mi* (220,649 *sq km*), *pop* 53,005,875
Hope·well \'hōp-,wel, -wəl\ city SE Va. *pop* 23,397
Hop·kins·ville \'häp-kənz-,vil\ city SW Ky. *pop* 27,318
Ho·reb \'hōr-,eb, 'hȯr-\ *or* **Si·nai** \'sī-,nī *also* -nē-,ī\ mountain where according to the Bible the Law was given to Moses; thought to be in the Gebel Musa on Sinai peninsula
Hor·muz *or* **Or·muz** \'(h)ȯr-,məz, (h)ȯr-'müz\ **1** ancient town S Iran on **Strait of Hormuz** (strait connecting Persian Gulf & Gulf of Oman) **2** island SE Iran in Strait of Hormuz *pop* 2410
Horn \'hȯ(ə)rn\ *or* **North Cape** cape NW Iceland
Horn, Cape headland S Chile on **Horn** island in Tierra del Fuego; southernmost point of S. America, at 55°59′S
Horn·church \'hȯ(ə)rn-,chərch\ former urban district SE England in Essex, now part of Havering
Horn of Africa the easternmost projection of Africa; variously used of Somalia, SE or all of Ethiopia & sometimes Djibouti; its E tip is Cape Guardafui
Hor·sens \'hȯrs-ᵊnz, -ᵊn(t)s\ city & port Denmark *pop* 54,684
Hos·pi·ta·let \,(h)äs-,pit-ᵊl-'et\ city NE Spain in Barcelona province, SW suburb of Barcelona *pop* 295,074
Ho–t'ien \'hō-tē-'en\ *or* **He·tian** \'hə-tē-'än\ *or* **Kho·tan** \'kō-'tän\ town & oasis W China in SW Sinkiang Uighur on S edge of the Takla Makan
Hot Springs city W *cen* Ark. adjoining **Hot Springs National Park** (reservation containing hot mineral springs) *pop* 35,781
Hou·ma \'hō-mə, 'hü-\ city SE La. *pop* 32,602
Houns·low \'hau̇nz-(,)lō\ borough of SW Greater London, England *pop* 204,300
Hou·sa·ton·ic \,hü-sə-'tän-ik, ,hü-zə-\ river 148 *mi* (238 *km*) W Mass. & W Conn. flowing from Berkshire hills S into Long Is. Sound
Hous·ton \'(h)yü-stən\ city & port SE Tex. connected with Galveston Bay by ship canal *pop* 1,595,138 — **Hous·to·nian** \(h)yü-'stō-nē-ən, -nyən\ *n* — **Hous·ton·ite** \'(h)yü-stə-,nīt\ *n*
Hove \'hōv\ borough S England in E. Sussex *pop* 66,612
Ho·ven·weep National Monument \'hō-vən-,wēp\ site SE Utah & SW Colo. of prehistoric pueblos & cliff dwellings
How·rah \'hau̇-rə\ city E India in W. Bengal on the Hooghly opposite Calcutta *pop* 599,740
Hra·dec Kra·lo·ve \,(h)räd-,ets-'kräl-ə-,vā\ *or G* **Kö·nig·grätz** \'kā-nig-,grāts, 'kə(r)n-ig-\ city W Czechoslovakia *pop* 95,588
Hsi *or* **Si** *or* **Xi** \'shē\ river 300 *mi* (483 *km*) SE China in Kwangsi & Kwantung formed by confluence of the Hungshui & the Yü & flowing E into S. China sea
Hsia–men *or* **Xia·men** \shē-'ä-'mən\ *or* **Amoy** \ä-'mȯi, a-, ə-\ city & port SE China in S Fukien on Amoy & Ku-lang islands *pop* 308,000
Hsiang *or* **Xiang** \shē-'äŋ\ river 350 *mi* (560 *km*) SE *cen* China flowing from N Kwangsi N into Hunan
Hsiang–t'an *or* **Xiang·tan** *or* **Siang·tan** \shē-'äŋ-'tän\ city SE China in E Hunan on the Hsiang S of Changsha *pop* 281,523
Hsin·chu \'shin-'chü\ city & port China in NW Taiwan on coast SW of Taipei *pop* 125,814
Hsin–hsiang *or* **Sin·siang** *or* **Xin·xiang** \'shin-shē-'äŋ\ city E China in N Hunan N of Cheng-chou *pop* 203,000
Hsi–ning *or* **Xi·ning** *or* **Si·ning** \shē-'niŋ\ city NW China WNW of Lanchow ✱ of Tsinghai *pop* 300,000
Hsinkao — see YÜ SHAN
Hsüan–hua *or* **Xuan·hua** \shü-'än-'hwä\ city NE China in NW Hopeh near Kalgan *pop* 114,000
Huai \hü-'ī\ river 600 *mi* (966 *km*) E China flowing from S Honan E into Hungtse lake
Huai·nan \hü-'ī-'nän\ city E China in N *cen* Anhwei SW of Pengpu *pop* 685,000
Hua·lla·ga \wä-'yäg-ə\ river 700 *mi* (1126 *km*) N *cen* Peru flowing N into the Marañón
Huam·bo \'(h)wäm-(,)bō\ *or formerly* **No·va Lis·boa** \'nō-və-lēzh-'bō-ə\ city Angola in W *cen* highlands *pop* 49,823
Huangpu — see WHANGPOO
Huas·ca·rán \,wäs-kə-'rän\ mountain 22,205 *ft* (6768 *m*) W Peru; highest in the country
Huber Heights \'hyü-bər, 'yü-\ city W Ohio *pop* 35,480
Hu·bli–Dhar·war \,hu̇b-lē-,där-'wär\ city SW India in W Karnataka
Hud·ders·field \'həd-ərz-,fēld\ borough N England in W. Yorkshire NE of Manchester *pop* 123,888
Hud·son \'həd-sən\ **1** river 306 *mi* (492 *km*) E N.Y. flowing from Adirondack mountains S into New York Bay **2** bay inlet of the Atlantic in N Canada; an inland sea 850 *mi* (1368 *km*) long **3** strait 450 *mi* (724 *km*) long NE Canada bet. S Baffin Is. & N Que. connecting Hudson bay with the Atlantic — **Hud·so·ni·an** \,həd-'sō-nē-ən\ *adj*
Hue *or F* **Hué** \'(h)wā, h(y)ü-'ā\ city & port *cen* Vietnam in Annam; formerly ✱ of Annam *pop* 209,043
Huel·va \'(h)wel-və\ **1** province SW Spain in Andalusia on Gulf of Cádiz *area* 3913 *sq mi* (10,174 *sq km*), *pop* 392,954 **2** city, its ✱ *pop* 127,822
Hues·ca \'(h)wes-kə\ **1** province NE Spain in Aragon *area* 5848 *sq mi* (15,205 *sq km*), *pop* 199,211 **2** commune, its ✱ *pop* 41,593
Hu·he·hot \'hü-(,)hā-'hōt\ *or* **Hoh·hot** \'hō-'hōt\ *or* **Hu–ho–hao–t'e** \'hü-'hō-'hau̇-'tə\ city N China ✱ of Inner Mongolia *pop* 320,000
Hui·la \'(h)wē-(,)lä\ volcano 18,865 *ft* (5750 *m*) SW *cen* Colombia
Hull \'həl\ **1** city Canada in SW Que. on Ottawa river opposite Ottawa, Ont. *pop* 56,225 **2** *or* **Kings·ton upon Hull** \'kiŋ(k)-stən\ city & borough & port N England in Humberside *pop* 285,472
Hu·ma·cao \,ü-mə-'kau̇\ town E Puerto Rico *pop* 19,147
Hum·ber \'həm-bər\ estuary 40 *mi* (64 *km*) E England formed by Ouse & Trent rivers & flowing E & SE into North sea
Hum·ber·side \'həm-bər-,sīd\ county E England; area formerly in Yorkshire ✱ Kingston upon Hull *area* 1356 *sq mi* (3526 *sq km*), *pop* 852,400
Hum·boldt \'həm-,bōlt\ **1** river 290 *mi* (467 *km*) N Nev. flowing W & SW into Rye Patch reservoir & formerly into Humboldt Lake **2** glacier NW Greenland **3** bay NW Calif. on which Eureka is situated
Humboldt Lake *or* **Humboldt Sink** intermittent lake W Nev. formerly receiving Humboldt river; has no outlet
Hum·phreys Peak \'həm(p)-frēz\ mountain peak 12,633 *ft* (3851 *m*) N *cen* Ariz. — see SAN FRANCISCO PEAKS
Hu·nan \'hü-'nän\ province SE *cen* China ✱ Changsha *area* 81,274 *sq mi* (211,312 *sq km*), *pop* 54,008,851
Hun·ga·ry \'həŋ-g(ə-)rē\ *or Hung* **Ma·gyar·or·szag** \,mäj-,är-'ȯr-,säg\ country *cen* Europe; formerly a kingdom, since 1946 a republic ✱ Budapest *area* 35,912 *sq mi* (93,371 *sq km*), *pop* 10,709,463
Hung·nam \'hu̇ŋ-,näm\ city & port *cen* N. Korea on Sea of Japan *pop* 143,600
Hung·shui *or* **Hong·shui** \'hu̇ŋ-'shwā\ river 800 *mi* (1287 *km*) S China flowing from E Yunnan E to unite with the Yü in E Kwangsi Chuang forming the Hsi
Hung·tse *or* **Hong·ze** \'hu̇ŋ-'(d)zə\ lake 65 *mi* (105 *km*) long E China in W Kiangsu; traversed by the Hwang
Hun·ter \'hənt-ər\ river 287 *mi* (462 *km*) SE Australia in E New S. Wales flowing E into the Pacific
Hun·ting·don \'hənt-iŋ-dən\ **1** *or* **Hun·ting·don·shire** \-,shi(ə)r, -shər\ *or* **Huntingdon and Pe·ter·bor·ough** \'pēt-ər-,bər-ə, -,bə-rə, -b(ə-)rə\ *or* **Hunts** \'hən(t)s\ former county E *cen* England ✱ Huntingdon and Godmanchester; since 1974 part of Cambridgeshire **2** *or* **Huntingdon and God·man·ches·ter** \'gäd-mən-,ches-tər\ borough E *cen* England in Cambridgeshire *pop* 17,467
Hun·ting·ton \'hənt-iŋ-tən\ city W W.Va. on Ohio river *pop* 63,684
Huntington Beach city SW Calif. SE of Los Angeles *pop* 170,505
Huntington Park city SW Calif. S of Los Angeles *pop* 46,223
Hunts·ville \'hən(t)s-,vil, -vəl\ **1** city N Ala. *pop* 142,513 **2** city E Tex. N of Houston *pop* 23,936
Hu·on Gulf \'hyü-,än\ inlet of Solomon sea on SE coast of North-East New Guinea S of Huon peninsula
Hu·peh \'hü-'be\ *or* **Hu·bei** \'hü-'bā\ *or* **Hu·pei** \'hü-'bā, -'pā\ province E *cen* China ✱ Wuhan *area* 72,394 *sq mi* (188,224 *sq km*), *pop* 47,804,150
Hu·ron, Lake \'hyu̇r-ən, 'hyu̇(ə)r-,än, *or without* h\ lake E *cen* N. America between the U.S. & Canada; one of the Great Lakes *area* 23,010 *sq mi* (59,826 *sq km*)
Hurst \'hərst\ city NE Tex. NE of Fort Worth *pop* 31,420
Hutch·in·son \'həch-ə(n)-sən\ city *cen* Kans. *pop* 40,284
Hutt \'hət\ urban area New Zealand on S North Is. *pop* 122,000
Huy \'(h)wē\ commune E Belgium SW of Liège *pop* 17,331
Huy·ton with Ro·by \,hīt-ᵊn-with-'rō-bē, -with-\ town NW England in Lancashire E of Liverpool *pop* 57,671
Hwaining — see AN-CH'ING
Hwang *or* **Huang** \'hwäŋ\ *or* **Yellow** river 3000 *mi* (4828 *km*) N China flowing from Kunlun mountains in Tsinghai E into Po Hai
Hy·bla \'hī-blə\ ancient town in Sicily on S slope of Mt. Etna
Hydaspes — see JHELUM
Hy·der·abad \'hīd-(ə-)rə-,bad, -,bäd\ **1** former state S *cen* India in the Deccan ✱ Hyderabad **2** *or* **Hai·dar·abad** city S *cen* India ✱ of Andhra Pradesh *pop* 2,528,198 **3** city S Pakistan in Sind on the Indus *pop* 795,000
Hy·dra \'hī-drə\ *or NGk* **Ídhra** \'ēth-rə\ island Greece in S Aegean sea off E coast of Peloponnisos *area* 20 *sq mi* (52 *sq km*), *pop* 2794 — **Hy·dri·ot** \'hī-drē-ət, -drē-,ät\ *or* **Hy·dri·ote** \-,ōt, -ət\ *n*
Hydraotes — see RAVI
Hy·ères \ē-'e(ə)r, 'ye(ə)r\ **1** *or F* **Îles d'Hyères** \,ēl-dē-'e(ə)r, ēl-'dye(ə)r\ islands in the Mediterranean off SE coast of France **2** commune SE France on Côte d'Azur E of Toulon *pop* 29,366
Hy·met·tus \hī-'met-əs\ mountain ridge 3370 *ft* (1027 *m*) *cen* Greece E & SE of Athens — **Hy·met·ti·an** \-'met-ē-ən\ *adj*
Hyr·ca·nia \(,)hər-'kā-nē-ə\ province of ancient Persia on SE coast of Caspian NE of Media & NW of Parthia — **Hyr·ca·ni·an** \-nē-ən\ *adj*
Ia·si \'yäsh(-ē)\ *or* **Jas·sy** \'yäs-ē\ city NE Romania *pop* 271,441

Iba·dan \i-'bäd-ᵊn, -'bad-\ city SW Nigeria NNE of Lagos *pop* 1,009,000
Ibe·ria \ī-'bir-ē-ə\ **1** ancient Spain **2** the Iberian peninsula **3** ancient region S of the Caucasus W of Colchis in modern Georgia (republic)
Ibe·ri·an \-ē-ən\ peninsula SW Europe between the Mediterranean & the Atlantic occupied by Spain & Portugal
Ibi·cuí \ˌē-bi-'kwē\ river 400 *mi* (644 *km*) S Brazil in Rio Grande do Sul flowing W into Uruguay river
Ibi·za *or* **Ivi·za** \ē-'vē-thə, -'bē-\ island Spain in the Balearics SW of Majorca *area* 230 *sq mi* (598 *sq km*)
Içá — see PUTUMAYO
Icar·ia \ī-'ker-ē-ə, -'kar-; ik-'er-, -'ar-\ *or NGk* **Ika·ria** \ˌē-kə-'rē-ə\ island Greece in Southern Sporades WSW of Samos *area* 99 *sq mi* (257 *sq km*) — **Icar·i·an** \ī-'ker-ē-ən, -'kar-; ik-'er-, -'ar-\ *adj or n*
Ice·land \'ī-slənd, 'ī-ˌsland\ *or Dan* **Is·land** \'ē-ˌslän\ *or Icelandic* **Ís·land** \'ē-ˌslänt\ island bet. the Arctic & the Atlantic SE of Greenland; a republic formerly (1380–1944) belonging to Denmark, later (1918–44) an independent kingdom in personal union with Denmark ✻ Reykjavik *area* 39,709 *sq mi* (103,243 *sq km*), *pop* 235,000 — **Ice·land·er** \'ī-ˌslan-dər, 'ī-slən-\ *n*
I–ch'ang \'ē-'chäŋ\ *or* **Yi·chang** \'yē-'chäŋ\ city *cen* China in W Hupeh *pop* 110,000
Ichi·ka·wa \i-'chē-ˌkä-wə\ city Japan in SE Honshu E of Tokyo *pop* 372,478
Iconium — see KONYA
Ida — see KAZ DAGI
Ida·ho \'īd-ə-ˌhō\ state NW U.S. ✻ Boise *area* 83,557 *sq mi* (217,248 *sq km*), *pop* 943,935 — **Ida·ho·an** \ˌīd-ə-'hō-ən\ *adj or n*
Idaho Falls city SE Idaho on Snake river *pop* 39,590
Id·fu \'id-(ˌ)fü\ city S Egypt on the Nile *pop* 34,858
Idhi \'ē-thē\ *or* **Ida** \'īd-ə\ mountain 8058 *ft* (2456 *m*) Greece in *cen* Crete; highest on island
Idumaea *or* **Idumea** — see EDOM — **Id·u·mae·an** *or* **Id·u·me·an** \ˌij-ə-'mē-ən\ *adj or n*
Ie·per \'yā-pər\ *or F* **Ypres** \'ēprᵊ\ commune NW Belgium in W. Flanders *pop* 20,825
Ife \'ē-(ˌ)fā\ city SW Nigeria NE of Ibadan *pop* 209,100
If·ni \'if-nē\ former territory SW Morocco; administered by Spain 1934–69 ✻ Sidi Ifni
Igua·çú \ˌē-gwə-'sü\ river 380 *mi* (612 *km*) S Brazil in Paraná state flowing W into Alto Paraná river; contains **Iguaçú Falls** (waterfall over 2 *mi or* 3.2 *km* wide composed of numerous cataracts averaging 200 *ft or* 61 *m* in height)
IJs·sel \'ī-səl\ river 70 *mi* (113 *km*) E Netherlands flowing out of the Rhine N into IJsselmeer
IJs·sel·meer \ˌī-səl-'me(ə)r\ *or* **Lake Ijs·sel** \'ī-səl\ freshwater lake N Netherlands separated from North sea by a dike & bordered by reclaimed lands; part of former Zuider Zee (inlet of North sea)
Île–de–France \ēl-də-fräⁿs\ region & former province N *cen* France bounded on N by Picardy, on E by Champagne, on S by Orléanais, & on W by Normandy ✻ Paris
Ile des Pins \ˌēl-dā-'paⁿ\ *or* **Isle of Pines** \'pīnz\ island SW Pacific in New Caledonia territory SE of New Caledonia Is. *area* 58 *sq mi* (151 *sq km*)
Île du Diable — see DEVIL'S ISLAND
Îles de la Société — see SOCIETY
Îles du Vent — see WINDWARD
Îles sous le Vent — see LEEWARD
Il·ford \'il-fərd\ former municipal borough SE England in Essex, now part of Redbridge
Il·fra·combe \'il-frə-ˌküm\ town SW England in Devon on Bristol channel *pop* 10,133
Ili \'ē-'lē\ river 800 *mi* (1287 *km*) *cen* Asia flowing from W Sinkiang Uighur, China, W & NW into Lake Balkhash in Kazakhstan
Ilía — see ELIS
Il·i·am·na \ˌil-ē-'am-nə\ **1** lake 80 *mi* (129 *km*) long SW Alaska NE of Bristol Bay **2** volcano 10,016 *ft* (3053 *m*) NE of Iliamna Lake
Ilion *or* **Ilium** — see TROY — **Il·i·an** \'il-ē-ən\ *adj or n*
Illam·pu \ē-'(y)äm-(ˌ)pü\ **1** *or* **So·ra·ta** \sə-'rät-ə\ massif in the Andes W Bolivia E of Lake Titicaca — see ANCOHUMA **2** peak 20,873 *ft* (6325 *m*) in the Illampu massif
Illi·ma·ni \ˌē-(y)ə-'män-ē\ mountain 21,201 *ft* (6462 *m*) Bolivia E of La Paz
Il·li·nois \ˌil-ə-'nȯi *also* -'nȯiz\ **1** river 273 *mi* (439 *km*) Ill. flowing SW into Mississippi river **2** state *cen* U.S. ✻ Springfield *area* 56,400 *sq mi* (146,640 *sq km*), *pop* 11,426,518 — **Il·li·nois·an** \ˌil-ə-'nȯi-ən, -'nȯiz-ᵊn\ *adj or n*
Il·lyr·ia \il-'ir-ē-ə\ ancient region S Europe in Balkan peninsula bordering on the Adriatic — **Il·lyr·ic** \-'lir-ik\ *adj*
Il·lyr·i·cum \il-'ir-i-kəm\ province of Roman Empire in Illyria, roughly coextensive with what is now W Yugoslavia
Il·men \'il-mən\ lake U.S.S.R. in NW Soviet Russia, Europe, S of Ladoga Lake
Ilo·ilo \ˌē-lə-'wē-(ˌ)lō\ city Philippines on Panay Is. *pop* 244,827
Im·pe·ria \im-'pir-ē-ə, -'per-\ commune & port NW Italy in Liguria SW of Genoa *pop* 41,838
Im·pe·ri·al \im-'pir-ē-əl\ valley U.S. & Mexico in SE Calif. & NE Baja California in Colorado desert; most of area below sea level
Imperial Beach city SW Calif. S of San Diego *pop* 22,689
Imp·hal \'imp-ˌhəl\ city NE India ✻ of Manipur *pop* 155,639
Imroz — see GÖKÇEADA
Ina·gua \in-'äg-wə\ two islands in the SE Bahamas: **Great Inagua** (50 *mi or* 80 *km* long) & **Little Inagua** (8 *mi or* 13 *km* long)
In·chon \'in-ˌchän\ *or* **Che·mul·po** \jə-'mül-(ˌ)pō\ city & port NW S. Korea W of Seoul *pop* 1,084,730
In·de·pen·dence \ˌin-də-'pen-dən(t)s\ city W Mo. E of Kansas City *pop* 111,806
In·dia \'in-dē-ə\ **1** peninsula region (often called a subcontinent) S Asia S of the Himalayas bet. Bay of Bengal & Arabian sea occupied by India, Pakistan & Bangladesh & formerly often considered as also including Burma (but not Ceylon) **2** those parts of India until 1947 under Brit. rule or protection together with Baluchistan & the Andaman & Nicobar islands &, prior to 1937, Burma **3** country comprising major portion of peninsula; a republic within the Commonwealth; until 1947 a part of the Brit. Empire ✻ New Delhi *area* 1,265,093 *sq mi* (3,289,242 *sq km*), *pop* 685,184,692
In·di·an \'in-dē-ən\ ocean E of Africa, S of Asia, W of Australia & Tasmania, & N of Antarctica *area* 28,925,000 *sq mi* (75,205,000 *sq km*)
In·di·ana \ˌin-dē-'an-ə\ state E *cen* U.S. ✻ Indianapolis *area* 36,291 *sq mi* (94,357 *sq km*), *pop* 5,490,224 — **In·di·an·an** \-'an-ən\ *adj or n* — **In·di·an·i·an** \-'an-ē-ən\ *adj or n*
Indiana Harbor harbor district in E. Chicago, Ind., on Lake Michigan
In·di·a·nap·o·lis \ˌin-dē-ə-'nap-(ə-)ləs\ city *cen* Ind., its ✻ *pop* 700,807
Indian River lagoon 165 *mi* (266 *km*) long E Fla. bet. mainland & coastal islands
Indian States *or* **Native States** former semi-independent states of the Indian Empire ruled by native princes subject to varying degrees of Brit. authority — see BRITISH INDIA
Indian Territory former territory S U.S. in present state of Okla.
In·dies \'in-(ˌ)dēz\ **1** EAST INDIES **2** WEST INDIES
In·di·gir·ka \ˌin-də-'gi(ə)r-kə\ river 850 *mi* (1368 *km*) U.S.S.R. in NE Yakut Republic flowing N into E. Siberian sea
In·dio \'in-dē-ˌō\ city SE Calif. SE of San Bernardino *pop* 21,611
In·do·chi·na \'in-(ˌ)dō-'chī-nə\ **1** peninsula SE Asia; includes Myanmar, Cambodia, Laos, Malay peninsula, Thailand, & Vietnam **2** *or* **French Indochina** former country SE Asia comprising Annam, Cambodia, Cochin China, Laos, & Tonkin ✻ Hanoi
In·do·ne·sia \ˌin-də-'nē-zhə, -shə\ **1** country SE Asia in Malay archipelago comprising Sumatra, Java, S & E Borneo, Celebes, Timor, W New Guinea, the Moluccas, & many adjacent smaller islands; a republic since 1949; formerly (as **Netherlands East Indies**) an overseas territory of the Netherlands ✻ Djakarta *area* 575,450 *sq mi* (1,496,170 *sq km*), *pop* 147,490,298 **2** the Malay archipelago
In·dore \in-'dō(ə)r, -'dȯ(ə)r\ **1** former state *cen* India in Narbada valley ✻ Indore; area now in Madhya Pradesh **2** city NW *cen* India in W Madhya Pradesh *pop* 827,071
In·dus \'in-dəs\ river 1800 *mi* (2897 *km*) S Asia flowing from Tibet NW & SSW through Pakistan into Arabian sea
In·gle·wood \'iŋ-gəl-ˌwu̇d\ city SW Calif. SW of Los Angeles *pop* 94,245
In·gol·stadt \'iŋ-gəl-ˌs(h)tät\ city S W. Germany in *cen* Bavaria *pop* 90,490
I–ning \'ē-'niŋ\ *or* **Yi·ning** \'yē-'niŋ\ KULDJA
Ink·ster \'iŋ(k)-stər\ village SE Mich. W of Detroit *pop* 35,190
In·land \'in-ˌland, -lənd\ sea inlet of the Pacific 240 *mi* (386 *km*) long SW Japan bet. Honshu on E & N, Kyushu on W, & Shikoku on S
Inland Empire region NW U.S. bet. Cascade range & Rocky mountains in E Wash., N Idaho, NW Mont., & NE Oreg.
Inn \'in\ river 320 *mi* (515 *km*) flowing from SE Switzerland NE through Austria into the Danube in W. Germany — see ENGADINE
Inner Hebrides — see HEBRIDES
Inner Mon·go·lia \män-'gōl-yə, mäŋ-, -'gō-lē-ə\ *or* **Nei Mong·gol** \'nā-'män-ˌgōl, -'mäŋ-\ region N China in SE Mongolia & W Manchuria ✻ Huhehot *area* 454,633 *sq mi* (1,182,046 *sq km*), *pop* 19,274,279
Inniskilling — see ENNISKILLEN
Inns·bruck \'inz-ˌbru̇k, 'in(t)s-\ city W Austria *pop* 116,100
Inside Passage *or* **Inland Passage** protected shipping route from Puget Sound, Wash., to Skagway, Alaska, following channels bet. mainland & coastal islands
In·ter·la·ken \'int-ər-ˌläk-ən\ commune W *cen* Switzerland in Bern canton on the Aare bet. Thuner See & Lake of Brienz *pop* 4852
International Zone — see MOROCCO
In·ver·car·gill \ˌin-vər-'kär-gəl\ borough New Zealand on S coast of South Is. *pop* 49,446 — see BLUFF
In·ver Grove Heights \ˌin-vər-\ city SE Minn. *pop* 17,171
In·ver·ness \ˌin-vər-'nes\ **1** *or* **In·ver·ness–shire** \-'nes(h)-ˌshi(ə)r, -shər\ former county NW Scotland **2** burgh NW Scotland ✻ of Highland region *pop* 39,736
Io·an·ni·na \yō-'än-ē-(ˌ)nä\ city NW Greece in N Epirus *pop* 44,362
Io·na \ī-'ō-nə\ island Scotland in S Inner Hebrides off SW tip of Mull Is. *area* 6 *sq mi* (16 *sq km*), *pop* 120
Io·nia \ī-'ō-nē-ə\ ancient region W Asia Minor bordering on the Aegean W of Lydia & Caria — **Io·ni·an** \-nē-ən\ *adj or n*
Ionian **1** sea arm of the Mediterranean bet. SE Italy & W Greece **2** islands W Greece in Ionian sea
Io·wa \'ī-ə-wə\ **1** river 291 *mi* (468 *km*) Iowa flowing SE into Mississippi river **2** state *cen* U.S. ✻ Des Moines *area* 56,290 *sq mi* (146,354 *sq km*), *pop* 2,913,808 — **Io·wan** \-wən\ *adj or n*
Iowa City city E Iowa *pop* 50,508
I–pin \'ē-'bēn\ *or* **Yi·bin** \'yē-'bēn\ *or formerly* **Süi·chow** \'s(h)ü-'jō, 'sü-'chau̇\ city *cen* China in S Szechwan *pop* 190,000
Ipiros — see EPIRUS
Ipoh \'ē-(ˌ)pō\ city Malaysia (federation) in Perak *pop* 125,766
Ipsambul — see ABU SIMBEL
Ips·wich \'ip-(ˌ)swich\ **1** city E Australia in SE Queensland *pop* 68,297 **2** borough SE England ✻ of Suffolk *pop* 120,447
Iqui·que \i-'kē-kē\ city & port N Chile on the Pacific *pop* 65,288
Iqui·tos \i-'kēt-(ˌ)ōs\ city NE Peru on the Amazon *pop* 203,568
Irák·li·on \i-'rak-lē-ən\ *or* **Can·dia** \'kan-dē-ə\ city & port Greece on N coast of Crete *pop* 77,783
Iran \i-'rän, -'ran; ī-'ran\ *or esp formerly* **Per·sia** \'pər-zhə, *esp Brit* -shə\ country SW Asia bordering in N on Caspian sea & in S on Persian Gulf & Gulf of Oman; an Islamic republic since 1979, formerly an empire ✻ Tehran *area* 628,000 *sq mi* (1,632,800 *sq km*), *pop* 33,591,875 — **Irani** \-'rän-ē, -'ran-\ *adj or n*
Iraq \i-'räk, -'rak\ country SW Asia in Mesopotamia; a republic since 1958, formerly a kingdom ✻ Baghdad *area* 171,555 *sq mi* (446,043 *sq km*), *pop* 12,000,497 — **Iraqi** \-'räk-ē, -'rak-\ *adj or n*
Irbil — see ARBIL
Ire·land \'ī(ə)r-lənd\ **1** *or L* **Hi·ber·nia** \hī-'bər-nē-ə\ island W Europe in the Atlantic, one of the British Isles *area* 32,375 *sq mi* (84,175 *sq km*); divided bet. Ireland (republic) & Northern Ireland **2** *or* **Ei·re**

\'ar-ə, 'ar-ē, 'er-, 'ār-, 'ir-\ country occupying major portion of the island; a republic since 1949; a division of the United Kingdom of Great Britain and Ireland 1801–1921 & (as **Irish Free State**) a dominion of the Commonwealth 1922–37 ✱ Dublin *area* 26,602 *sq mi* (69,165 *sq km*), *pop* 3,443,405 **3** — see NORTHERN IRELAND
Irian Jaya — see WEST IRIAN
Irish Sea arm of the Atlantic between Great Britain & Ireland
Ir·kutsk \i(ə)r-'kütsk, ˌər-\ city U.S.S.R. in E *cen* Soviet Russia, Asia, on the Angara near Lake Baikal *pop* 550,000
Iron Gate \'ī(-ə)rn-\ gorge 2 *mi* (3.2 *km*) long of the Danube where it cuts around Transylvanian Alps on border bet. Romania & Yugoslavia
Ir·ra·wad·dy \ˌir-ə-'wäd-ē\ river 1350 *mi* (2173 *km*) Myanmar flowing S into Bay of Bengal through several mouths
Ir·tysh \i(ə)r-'tish, ˌər-\ river 2200 *mi* (3541 *km*) *cen* Asia flowing from Altai mountains in China, NW & N into the Ob in U.S.S.R.
Irún \ē-'rün\ commune N Spain in Guipúzcoa *pop* 45,060
Ir·ving \'ər-viŋ\ city NE Tex. W of Dallas *pop* 109,943
Ir·ving·ton \-tən\ town NE N.J. WSW of Newark *pop* 61,493
Is·a·bela \ˌiz-ə-'bel-ə\ *or* **Al·be·marle** \'al-bə-ˌmärl\ island Ecuador; largest of the Galápagos *area* 1650 *sq mi* (4290 *sq km*), *pop* 336
Isar \'ē-ˌzär\ river 219 *mi* (352 *km*) W Europe flowing from Tirol, Austria, NW through Bavaria, W. Germany, into the Danube
Isau·ria \ī-'sȯr-ē-ə\ ancient district in E Pisidia S Asia Minor on N slope of W Taurus mountains — **Isau·ri·an** \-ē-ən\ *adj or n*
Is·chia \'is-kē-ə\ island Italy in Tyrrhenian sea WSW of Naples *area* 18 *sq mi* (47 *sq km*)
Ise Bay \ˌē-ˌsā-\ inlet of the Pacific S Japan on S coast of Honshu
Iseo, Lake \ē-'zā-(ˌ)ō\ lake 14 *mi* (22 *km*) long N Italy in Lombardy
Isère \ē-'ze(ə)r\ river 150 *mi* (241 *km*) SE France flowing from Graian Alps WSW into the Rhône
Iser·lohn \ˌē-zər-'lōn, 'ē-zər-ˌ\ city *cen* W. Germany *pop* 93,823
Isfahan — see ESFAHĀN
Ishim \i-'shim\ river 1330 *mi* (2140 *km*) U.S.S.R. flowing from N Kazakhstan N into the Irtysh
Isis \'ī-səs\ the Thames river, England, at & upstream from Oxford
Is·ken·de·run \(ˌ)is-ˌken-də-'rün\ *or* **Is·ken·de·ron** \-'rän\ *or formerly* **Al·ex·an·dret·ta** \ˌal-ig-(ˌ)zan-'dret-ə, ˌel-\ city & port S Turkey on **Gulf of Iskenderun** (inlet of the Mediterranean) *pop* 69,382
Is·lam·abad \is-'läm-ə-ˌbäd, iz-'lam-ə-ˌbad\ city ✱ of Pakistan in NE Pakistan in Murree hills NE of Rawalpindi *pop* 250,000
Island *or* **Ísland** — see ICELAND
Is·lay \'ī-(ˌ)lā, -lə\ island Scotland in S Inner Hebrides *area* 234 *sq mi* (608 *sq km*), *pop* 3855
Isle au Haut \ˌī-lə-'hō(t), ˌē-lə-'hō\ island Maine at entrance to Penobscot Bay — see ACADIA NATIONAL PARK
Isle of Av·a·lon \'av-ə-lən, -ˌlän\ district, orig. an island, SW England in Somerset including Glastonbury
Isle of Ely — see ELY (Isle of)
Isle of Man — see MAN (Isle of)
Isle of Pines — see YOUTH (Isle of)
Isle of Wight — see WIGHT (Isle of)
Isle Roy·ale \(')ī(ə)l-'rȯi(-ə)l\ island Mich. in NW Lake Superior in **Isle Royale National Park**
Is·ling·ton \'iz-liŋ-tən\ borough of N Greater London, England *pop* 167,400
Is·ma·ilia \ˌiz-mā-ə-'lē-ə\ city NE Egypt on the Suez canal *pop* 145,930
Isole Eolie — see LIPARI
Ison·zo \ē-'zȯn(t)-(ˌ)sō\ *or* **So·ca** \'sȯ-kə\ river 75 *mi* (121 *km*) NW Yugoslavia & NE Italy flowing S into Gulf of Trieste
Ispahan — see ESFAHĀN
Is·par·ta \ˌis-(ˌ)pär-'tä\ city SW Turkey N of Antalya *pop* 91,544
Is·ra·el \'iz-rē-əl, -rā-əl, -rəl *also* 'is-\ **1** ancient kingdom Palestine comprising the lands occupied by the Hebrew people; established *ab* 1025 B.C.; divided *ab* 933 B.C. into a S kingdom (Judah) & a N kingdom (Israel) **2** *or* **Northern Kingdom** *or* **Ephra·im** \'ē-frē-əm\ the N portion of the Hebrew kingdom after the division ✱ Samaria **3** country Palestine bordering on the Mediterranean; a republic established 1948 ✱ Jerusalem *area* 7993 *sq mi* (20,782 *sq km*), *pop* 4,037,620 — see PALESTINE
Is·sus \'is-əs\ ancient town S Asia Minor N of modern Iskenderun
Is·syk Kul \ˌis-ik-'kəl\ lake 115 *mi* (185 *km*) long U.S.S.R. in Soviet Central Asia in NE Kirghiz Republic *area* 2250 *sq mi* (5850 *sq km*)
Is·tan·bul \ˌis-təm-'bül, -ˌtäm-, -ˌtam-, -ˌtän-\ *or formerly* **Con·stan·ti·no·ple** \ˌkän-ˌstant-ᵊn-'ō-pəl\ *or anc* **By·zan·ti·um** \bə-'zan-sh(ē-)əm, -'zant-ē-əm\ city NW Turkey on the Bosporus & Sea of Marmara; former ✱ of Turkey & of Ottoman Empire *pop* 2,853,539
Ister — see DANUBE
Is·tria \'is-trē-ə\ peninsula NW Yugoslavia in Croatia & Slovenia projecting into the N Adriatic — **Is·tri·an** \-trē-ən\ *adj or n*
Itai·pu \ē-'tī-pü\ dam in Paraná river between Brazil & Paraguay
Italian East Africa former territory E Africa comprising Eritrea, Ethiopia, & Italian Somaliland
Italian Somaliland former Italian colony E Africa bordering on Indian ocean ✱ Mogadishu; since 1960 part of Somalia
It·a·ly \'it-ᵊl-ē\ *or It* **Ita·lia** \ē-'täl-yə\ *or L* **Ita·lia** \ə-'tal-yə, i-\ **1** peninsula 760 *mi* (1223 *km*) long S Europe projecting into the Mediterranean bet. Adriatic & Tyrrhenian seas **2** country comprising the peninsula of Italy, Sicily, Sardinia, & numerous other islands; a republic since 1946, formerly a kingdom ✱ Rome *area* 119,764 *sq mi* (311,386 *sq km*), *pop* 56,243,935
Ita·na·gar \ˌēt-ə-'nəg-ər\ town NE India ✱ of Arunachal Pradesh
Itas·ca, Lake \ī-'tas-kə\ lake NW *cen* Minn.; generally considered as source of Mississippi river
Iténez — see GUAPORÉ
Ith·a·ca \'ith-i-kə\ **1** city S *cen* N.Y. on Cayuga Lake *pop* 28,732 **2** *or NGk* **Ithá·ki** \ē-'thä-kē\ island W Greece in the Ionian islands NE of Cephalonia *area* 36 *sq mi* (94 *sq km*) — **Ith·a·can** \'ith-i-kən\ *adj or n*
Itsu·ku·shi·ma \it-ˌsü-kə-'shē-mə\ *or* **Mi·ya·ji·ma** \ˌmē-(y)ə-'jē-mə\ island *ab* 5 *mi* (8 *km*) long Japan in Inland sea SW of Hiroshima
It·u·raea *or* **It·u·rea** \ˌich-ə-'rē-ə\ ancient country NE Palestine S of Damascus — **It·u·rae·an** *or* **It·u·re·an** \-'rē-ən\ *adj or n*
Iva·no–Fran·kovsk \i-ˌvän-ə-frän-'kȯfsk\ *or formerly* **Sta·ni·slav** \ˌstan-ə-'släf, -'släv\ city U.S.S.R. in SW Ukrainian Republic *pop* 134,000
Iva·no·vo \i-'vän-ə-və\ *or formerly* **Ivanovo Voz·ne·sensk** \-ˌväz-nə-'sen(t)sk\ city U.S.S.R. in *cen* Soviet Russia, Europe, WNW of Gorki *pop* 419,000
Iviza — see IBIZA
Ivory Coast *or* **Côte d'Ivoire** \ˌkōt-dēv-'wär\ **1** region W Africa bordering on the Atlantic W of the Gold Coast **2** country W Africa including the Ivory Coast & its hinterland; a republic; formerly a territory of French W. Africa ✱ Abidjan *area* 127,520 *sq mi* (331,552 *sq km*), *pop* 9,300,000 — **Ivo·ry Coast·er** \ˌīv-(ə-)rē-'kō-stər\ *n*
Iwo \'ē-(ˌ)wō\ city SW Nigeria NE of Ibadan *pop* 255,100
Iwo Ji·ma \ˌē-(ˌ)wō-'jē-mə\ island Japan in W Pacific in the Volcano islands *area* 8 *sq mi* (21 *sq km*)
Ix·elles \ēk-'sel\ *or Flem* **El·se·ne** \'el-sə-nə\ commune *cen* Belgium in Brabant; suburb of Brussels *pop* 75,723
Ix·tac·ci·huatl *or* **Ix·ta·ci·huatl** *or* **Iz·tac·ci·huatl** \ˌēs-(ˌ)tä-'sē-ˌwät-ᵊl\ extinct volcano 17,343 *ft* (5286 *m*) S Mexico N of Popocatepetl
Iza·bal \ˌē-zə-'bäl, -sə-\ lake 25 *mi* (40 *km*) long E Guatemala
Izal·co \i-'zal-(ˌ)kō, ē-'säl-\ volcano 7828 *ft* (2386 *m*) W El Salvador
Izhevsk \'ē-ˌzhefsk\ *or 1985–1987* **Usti·nov** \'üs-ti-ˌnȯv\ city U.S.S.R. in E Soviet Russia, Europe ✱ of Udmurt Republic *pop* 422,000
Iz·ma·il *or Romanian* **Is·ma·il** \ˌiz-mā-'ē(ə)l\ city U.S.S.R. in SW Ukrainian Republic on the Danube delta *pop* 63,000
Iz·mir \iz-'mi(ə)r\ city & port W Turkey in Asia on an inlet of the Aegean *pop* 753,749
Iz·mit *or* **Iz·mid** \iz-'mit\ *or anc* **As·ta·cus** \'as-tə-kəs\ *or* **Nic·o·me·dia** \ˌnik-ə-'mēd-ē-ə\ city & port NW Turkey in Asia on **Gulf of Izmit** (E arm of Sea of Marmara) *pop* 191,340
Iz·nik \iz-'nik\ lake 14 *mi* (22 *km*) long NW Turkey in Asia
Jabal Katrinah — see KATHERINA, GEBEL
Ja·bal·pur \'jəb-əl-ˌpu̇(ə)r\ city *cen* India in *cen* Madhya Pradesh *pop* 757,726
Jack·son \'jak-sən\ **1** city S Mich. *pop* 39,739 **2** city ✱ of Miss. on Pearl river *pop* 202,895 **3** city W Tenn. *pop* 49,131
Jackson Hole valley NW Wyo. E of Teton range & partly in Grand Teton National Park; contains **Jackson Lake** (reservoir)
Jack·son·ville \'jak-sən-ˌvil\ **1** city *cen* Ark. NE of Little Rock *pop* 27,589 **2** city NE Fla. near mouth of St. Johns river *pop* 540,920 **3** city W *cen* Ill. *pop* 20,284 **4** city E N.C. *pop* 17,056
Jadotville — see LIKASI
Ja·én \hä-'ān\ **1** province S Spain in N Andalusia *area* 5203 *sq mi* (13,528 *sq km*), *pop* 611,655 **2** commune, its ✱ *pop* 86,001
Jaf·fa \'jaf-ə, 'yaf-ə\ *or* **Jop·pa** \'jäp-ə\ *or* **Ya·fo** \yä-'fō\ former city W Israel, since 1950 a S section of Tel Aviv
Jaff·na \'jäf-nə\ **1** peninsula N extremity of Sri Lanka extending into Palk strait **2** city N Sri Lanka on Jaffna penin. *pop* 118,215
Jain·tia \'jīnt-ē-ə\ hills E India in N *cen* Assam E of Khasi hills
Jai·pur \'jī-ˌpu̇(ə)r\ **1** former state NW India; now part of Rajasthan **2** city, its ✱, now ✱ of Rajasthan *pop* 1,004,669
Jakarta — see DJAKARTA
Ja·la·pa \hə-'läp-ə\ city E Mexico ✱ of Veracruz *pop* 151,419
Ja·lis·co \hə-'lis-(ˌ)kō\ state W *cen* Mexico ✱ Guadalajara *area* 31,149 *sq mi* (80,987 *sq km*), *pop* 4,293,549
Jal·u·it \'jal-(y)ə-wət\ island (atoll) W Pacific, in Ralik chain of the Marshalls
Ja·mai·ca \jə-'mā-kə\ island W. Indies in the Greater Antilles; a dominion of the Commonwealth since 1962; formerly a Brit. colony ✱ Kingston *area* 4411 *sq mi* (11,469 *sq km*), *pop* 2,095,878 — **Ja·mai·can** \-kən\ *adj or n*
Jamaica Bay inlet of Atlantic ocean SE N.Y. in SW Long Is.
Jambi — see TELANAIPURA
James \'jāmz\ **1** river 710 *mi* (1143 *km*) N.Dak. & S.Dak. flowing S to Missouri river **2** river 340 *mi* (547 *km*) Va. flowing E into Chesapeake Bay at Hampton Roads
James Bay the S extension of Hudson bay 280 *mi* (448 *km*) long & 150 *mi* (240 *km*) wide Canada bet. NE Ont. & W Que.
James·town \'jām-ˌstau̇n\ **1** city SW N.Y. *pop* 35,775 **2** ruined village E Va. SW of Williamsburg on James river; first permanent English settlement in America (1607)
Jam·mu \'jəm-(ˌ)ü\ **1** district N India (subcontinent) S of Kashmir in valley of the upper Chenab **2** city S of Srinagar, winter ✱ of Jammu & Kashmir *pop* 135,522
Jammu and Kashmir — see KASHMIR
Jam·na·gar \jäm-'nəg-ər\ city W India in W Gujarat on Gulf of Kutch *pop* 317,037
Jam·shed·pur \'jäm-ˌshed-ˌpu̇(ə)r\ city E India in S Bihar SE of Ranchi *pop* 669,984
Ja·mu·na \'jəm-ə-nə\ the lower Brahmaputra
Janes·ville \'jānz-ˌvil\ city S Wis. SE of Madison *pop* 51,071
Ja·nic·u·lum \jə-'nik-yə-ləm\ hill in Rome, Italy, on right bank of the Tiber opposite the seven hills on which the ancient city was built — see AVENTINE
Jan Ma·yen \yän-'mī-ən\ island in Arctic ocean E of Greenland & NNE of Iceland belonging to Norway *area* 147 *sq mi* (382 *sq km*)
Ja·pan \jə-'pan, ja-\ *or Jp* **Nip·pon** \nip-'än\ *or* **Ni·hon** \'nē-'hȯn\ country E Asia comprising Honshu, Hokkaido, Kyushu, Shikoku, & other islands in the W Pacific; a constitutional monarchy ✱ Tokyo *area* 146,690 *sq mi* (381,394 *sq km*), *pop* 117,057,485
Japan, Sea of arm of the N Pacific W of Japan
Ja·pu·rá \ˌzhäp-ə-'rä\ river 1750 *mi* (2816 *km*) S Colombia & NW Brazil flowing SE into the Amazon
Jar·vis \'jär-vəs\ island *cen* Pacific in the Line islands; claimed by the U.S.
Jas·per National Park \'jas-pər-\ reservation W Canada in W Alta. on E slopes of the Rockies NW of Banff National Park
Jassy — see IASI
Ja·va \'jäv-ə, 'jav-ə\ *or Indonesian* **Dja·wa** **1** island Indonesia SE of Sumatra; chief city Djakarta *area* 51,007 *sq mi* (132,618 *sq km*), *pop* 78,201,001 **2** sea, arm of the Pacific bounded on S by Java, on W by Sumatra, on N by Borneo, & on E by Celebes
Java Head cape Indonesia at W end of Java on Sunda strait
Ja·va·ri \ˌzhäv-ə-'rē\ *or Sp* **Ya·va·rí** \ˌyäv-ə-'rē\ *or formerly* **Ya·ca·ra·na** \ˌyäk-ə-'rän-ə\ river 650 *mi* (1046 *km*) Peru & Brazil flowing NE on the boundary & into the Amazon
Jaxartes — see SYR DARYA

Jazirah, Al — see GEZIRA, EL
Jebel, Bahr el — see BAHR EL GHAZAL
Je·bel ed Druz \\jeb-ə-,led-'drüz\\ or Jebel Druz region S Syria E of Sea of Galilee on border of Jordan
Jebel Musa — see MUSA (Jebel)
Jebel Toubkal — see TOUBKAL (Jebel)
Jed·burgh \\'jed-b(ə-)rə\\ royal burgh SE Scotland in Borders region
Jef·fer·son \\'jef-ər-sən\\ river 250 mi (402 km) SW Mont. — see THREE FORKS
Jefferson, Mount mountain 10,495 ft (3199 m) NW Oreg. in Cascades
Jefferson City city * of Mo. on Missouri river pop 33,619
Jef·fer·son·ville \\'jef-ər-sən-,vil\\ city S Ind. pop 21,220
Je·hol \\jə-'hōl, 'rō-'hō\\ former province NE China * Chengteh; divided 1955 among Hopeh, Liaoning, & Inner Mongolia
Je·mappes \\zhə-'map\\ commune SW Belgium W of Mons
Je·na \\'yā-nə, -,(,)nä\\ city SW E. Germany E of Erfurt pop 104,282
Jen·nings \\'jen-inz\\ city S Mo., N suburb of St. Louis pop 17,026
Je·qui·ti·nho·nha \\zhə-,kēt-ə-'n(y)ōn-yə\\ river 500 mi (805 km) E Brazil flowing NE into the Atlantic
Jerba — see DJERBA
Je·rez \\hə-'räs\\ or Je·rez de la Fron·te·ra \\hə-'rez-də-lə-,frən-'ter-ə\\ or formerly Xe·res \\'sher-ēz\\ city SW Spain NE of Cádiz pop 175,653
Jer·i·cho \\'jer-i-,kō\\ 1 or Ar Eri·ha \\ə-'rē-ə\\ town W Jordan 5 mi (8 km) NW of Dead sea 2 ancient Palestinian city near site of modern Jericho
Jer·sey \\'jər-zē\\ 1 island English channel in the Channel islands * St. Helier area 45 sq mi (117 sq km) 2 NEW JERSEY — Jer·sey·an \\-ən\\ n — Jer·sey·ite \\-,īt\\ n
Jersey City city & port NE N.J. pop 223,532
Je·ru·sa·lem \\jə-'rü-s(ə-)ləm, -'rüz-(ə-)ləm\\ or anc Hi·ero·sol·y·ma \\,hī-(ə-)rō-'säl-ə-mə\\ city cen Palestine NW of Dead sea; divided 1948-67 bet. Jordan (old city) & Israel (new city) * of Israel since 1950 & formerly * of ancient kingdoms of Israel & Judah; old city under Israeli control since 1967 pop 376,000 — Je·ru·sa·lem·ite \\-,īt\\ n
Jer·vis Bay \\'jär-vəs-\\ inlet of the Pacific SE Australia on SE coast of New S. Wales on which is situated district (area 28 sq mi or 73 sq km) that is part of Australian Capital Territory
Jesselton — see KOTA KINABALU
Jewel Cave National Monument limestone cave SW S.Dak.
Jewish Autonomous Oblast autonomous region U.S.S.R. in E Soviet Russia, Asia, bordering on the Amur * Birobidzhan area 14,085 sq mi (36,621 sq km), pop 173,000
Jez·re·el \\,jez-rē-,el, -,rē(ə)l\\ ancient town cen Palestine in Samaria NW of Mt. Gilboa in Valley of Jezreel; now in N Israel
Jezreel, Plain of the Plain of Esdraelon
Jezreel, Valley of the the E end of the Plain of Esdraelon
Jhan·si \\'jän(t)-sē\\ city N India in S Uttar Pradesh pop 281,332
Jhe·lum \\'jā-ləm\\ or anc Hy·das·pes \\hī-'das-(,)pēz\\ river 450 mi (724 km) NW India (subcontinent) flowing from Kashmir S & SW into the Chenab
Jiamusi — see CHIA-MU-SSU
Jiangsu — see KIANGSU
Jiangxi — see KIANGSI
Jibuti — see DJIBOUTI
Jid·da \\'jid-ə\\ or Jed·da \\'jed-ə\\ city W Saudi Arabia in Hejaz on Red sea; port for Mecca pop 561,104
Jih–k'a–tse — see SHIGATSE
Jinan — see TSINAN
Jin·ja \\'jin-jə\\ city & port SE Uganda on Lake Victoria pop 228,520
Jinzhou — see CHIN-CHOU
João Pes·soa \\zhwaün(m)-pə-'sō-ə\\ or formerly Pa·ra·í·ba \\,par-ə-'ē-bə\\ city NE Brazil * of Paraíba pop 330,176
Jodh·pur \\'jäd-pər, -,pù(ə)r\\ 1 or Mar·war \\'mär-,wär\\ former state NW India bordering on Thar desert & Rann of Kutch; since 1949 part of Rajasthan state 2 city, its * pop 493,609
Jod·rell Bank \\,jäd-rəl-\\ locality W England in NE Cheshire near Macclesfield
Jogjakarta — see YOGYAKARTA
Jo·han·nes·burg \\jō-'han-əs-,bərg, -'hän-\\ city NE Republic of S. Africa in S Transvaal in cen Witwatersrand pop 654,232
John Day \\'jän-'dā\\ river 281 mi (452 km) N Oreg. flowing W & N into Columbia river
John Day Fossil Beds National Monument reservation N cen Oreg.
John o' Groat's \\,jän-ə-'grōts\\ or John o' Groat's House locality N Scotland; popularly considered the northernmost point of mainland of Scotland & Great Britain — see DUNNET HEAD
John·son City \\'jän(t)-sən-\\ 1 village S N.Y. NW of Binghamton pop 17,126 2 city NE Tenn. S of Va. border pop 39,753
John·ston \\'jän(t)-stən, -sən\\ 1 island (atoll) mid Pacific SW of Honolulu, Hawaii; belongs to the U.S. 2 town N R.I. SW of Providence pop 24,907
Johns·town \\'jän-,staùn\\ city SW cen Pa. pop 35,496
Jo·hore \\jə-'hō(ə)r, -'hó(ə)r\\ state Malaysia in Peninsular Malaysia at S end of Malay peninsula * Johore Bahru 7321 sq mi (19,035 sq km), pop 1,601,504
Johore Bah·ru \\-'bär-(,)ü\\ city S Malaysia (federation) * of Johore on an inlet opposite Singapore Is. pop 135,936
Join·ville \\'join-,vil\\ or formerly Join·vil·le \\zhóin-'vē-əl\\ city S Brazil NNW of Florianópolis pop 235,612
Jo·li·et \\,jō-lē-'et, chiefly by outsiders ,jäl-ē-\\ city NE Ill. pop 77,956
Jo·liette \\,zhō-lē-'et\\ city Canada in S Que. pop 16,987
Jo·lo \\hō-'lō\\ island S Philippines, chief island of Sulu archipelago area 345 sq mi (897 sq km)
Jones·boro \\'jōnz-,bər-ə, -,bə-rə\\ city NE Ark. pop 31,530
Jön·kö·ping \\'yə(r)n-,chə(r)p-in\\ city S Sweden at S end of Vättern lake pop 107,561
Jon·quière \\,zhón-'kē-'e(ə)r\\ city Canada in S cen Que. pop 60,354
Jop·lin \\'jäp-lən\\ city SW Mo. pop 38,893
Joppa — see JAFFA
Jor·dan \\'jórd-ʰn\\ 1 river 45 mi (72 km) cen Utah flowing from Utah Lake N into Great Salt Lake 2 river 200 mi (322 km) NE Palestine flowing from Anti-Lebanon mountains S through Sea of Galilee into Dead sea 3 or formerly Trans·jor·dan \\(')tran(t)s-, (')tranz-\\ country

SW Asia in NW Arabia * Amman area 37,737 sq mi (98,116 sq km), pop 2,152,273 — Jor·da·ni·an \\jór-'dā-nē-ən\\ adj or n
Josh·ua Tree National Monument \\'jäsh-(ə-)wə\\ reservation S Calif. N of Salton sea containing unusual desert flora
Jo·tun·heim \\'yōt-ʰn-,häm\\ or Norw Jo·tun·hei·men \\-,hā-mən\\ mountains S cen Norway — see GLITTERTIND
Juan de Fu·ca, Strait of \\,(h)wän-də-'fyü-kə\\ strait 100 mi (161 km) long bet. Vancouver Is., B.C., & Olympic peninsula, Wash.
Juan Fer·nán·dez \\,(h)wän-fər-'nan-dəs\\ group of three islands SE Pacific W of Chile; belongs to Chile area 70 sq mi (182 sq km)
Juan–les–Pins \\,zhwän-lā-'paⁿ\\ town SE France on Cap d'Antibes
Juárez — see CIUDAD JUÁREZ
Ju·ba \\'jü-bə\\ river 1000 mi (1609 km) E Africa flowing from S Ethiopia S through Somalia into Indian ocean
Ju·by, Cape \\'jü-bē, 'yü-\\ cape NW Africa on NW coast of Western Sahara
Jú·car \\'hü-,kär\\ river 300 mi (483 km) E Spain flowing S & E into the Mediterranean S of Valencia
Ju·daea or Ju·dea \\jü-'dē-ə, -'dä-\\ ancient region Palestine constituting the S division (Judah) of the country under Persian, Greek, & Roman rule; bounded on N by Samaria, on E by Jordan river & Dead sea, on SW by Sinai peninsula, & on W by the Mediterranean — Ju·dae·an or Ju·dean \\-ən\\ adj or n
Ju·dah \\'jüd-ə\\ ancient kingdom S Palestine * Jerusalem — see ISRAEL
Jugoslavia — see YUGOSLAVIA — Ju·go·sla·vian adj or n
Juiz de Fo·ra \\zhwēzh-də-'fōr-ə, -'fór-\\ city E Brazil in S Minas Gerais pop 307,820
Ju·juy \\hü-'hwē\\ city NW Argentina N of Tucumán pop 44,188
Julian Alps \\jül-yən-\\ section of E Alps NW Yugoslavia N of Istrian peninsula; highest peak Triglav 9393 ft (2863 m)
Julian Venetia — see VENEZIA GIULIA
Jul·lun·dur \\'jəl-ən-dər\\ city NW India in Punjab pop 405,700
Jum·na \\'jəm-nə\\ river 860 mi (1384 km) N India in Uttar Pradesh flowing from the Himalayas S & SE into the Ganges
Junction City city NE cen Kans. pop 19,305
Ju·neau \\'jü-(,)nō, jü-'\\ city & port * of Alaska in SE coastal strip pop 19,528
Jung·frau \\'yùn,fraù\\ mountain 13,642 ft (4158 m) SW cen Switzerland in Berner Alpen bet. Bern & Valais cantons
Junggar — see DZUNGARIA
Ju·ni·ata \\,jü-nē-'at-ə\\ river 150 mi (241 km) S cen Pa. flowing E into the Susquehanna
Ju·nín \\hü-'nēn\\ 1 city E Argentina W of Buenos Aires pop 62,080 2 town cen Peru at S end of Lake Junín (25 mi or 40 km long)
Ju·pi·ter \\'jü-pət-ər\\ island SE Fla. in the Atlantic
Ju·ra \\'jùr-ə\\ 1 canton W Switzerland 2 mountains France & Switzerland extending 200 mi (322 km) along the boundary; highest Crête de la Neige (in France) 5652 ft (1723 m) 3 island 24 mi (39 km) long W Scotland in the Inner Hebrides S of Mull
Juramento — see SALADO
Ju·ruá \\,zhùr-(ə-)'wä\\ river 1200 mi (1931 km) NW cen S. America flowing from E cen Peru NE into the Solimões in NW Brazil
Ju·rue·na \\,zhùr-(ə-)'wā-nə\\ river 600 mi (966 km) W cen Brazil flowing N to unite with the São Manuel forming the Tapajoz
Jut·land \\'jət-lənd\\ or Dan Jyl·land \\'yùel-,än, 'yœl-\\ 1 peninsula N Europe projecting into North sea & comprising mainland of Denmark & N portion of Schleswig-Holstein, W. Germany 2 the mainland of Denmark
Kaapland — see CAPE OF GOOD HOPE
Kab·a·le·ga Falls \\,käb-ə-'lēg-ə, -'läg-ə\\ or formerly Mur·chi·son Falls \\'mər-chə-sən\\ waterfall 120 ft (36 m) W Uganda in the Victoria Nile in Kabalega National Park
Kab·ar·din–Bal·kar Republic \\,kab-ər-'dēn-'bòl-,kär-, -'bal-\\ or Kab·ar·di·no–Balkar Republic \\-'dē-(,)nō-\\ or Kabardino–Bal·kar·ska·ya Republic \\-'bòl-'kär- skə-yə, -bal-\\ autonomous republic U.S.S.R. in S Soviet Russia, Europe, on N slopes of the Caucasus * Nalchik area 4600 sq mi (11,960 sq km), pop 539,000 — Kab·ar·din·ian \\,kab-ər-'dē-nē-ən\\ adj or n
Kabia — see SELAJAR
Ka·bul \\'käb-əl\\ 1 river 360 mi (579 km) Afghanistan & N Pakistan flowing E into the Indus 2 city * of Afghanistan on Kabul river pop 913,164 — Ka·buli \\'käb-ə-(,)lē, kə-'bü-lē\\ adj or n
Kab·we \\'käb-(,)wā\\ or formerly Bro·ken Hill \\,brō-kən-\\ city cen Zambia pop 143,635
Ka·by·lia \\kə-'bī-lē-ə, -'bil-ē-ə\\ mountainous region N Algeria on coast E of Algiers; comprises two areas: Great Kabylia (to W) & Little Kabylia (to E)
Ka·desh–bar·nea \\,kā-,desh-'bär-nē-ə\\ ancient town S Palestine SW of Dead sea; exact location uncertain
Ka·di·koy \\,käd-i-'kói\\ or anc Chal·ce·don \\'kal-sə-,dän, kal-'sēd-ʰn\\ former city Asia on the Bosporus; now a district of Istanbul
Kadiyevka — see STAKHANOV
Ka·erh \\'kä-'e(ə)r\\ or Gar \\'gär\\ town China in SW Tibet
Kae·song \\'kä-,sòn\\ city N. Korea SE of Pyongyang pop 140,000
Kaf·fe·klub·ben \\'käf-ə-,klüb-ən, -,kləb-\\ island in Arctic ocean off N coast of Greenland; northernmost point of land in the world, at 83°40'N
Kaf·frar·ia \\kə-'frar-ē-ə, ka-, -'frer-\\ region Republic of S. Africa in E Cape Province S of Natal & bordering on Indian ocean
Kafiristan — see NURISTAN
Ka·fue \\kə-'fü-ē\\ river 500 mi (805 km) Zambia flowing into the Zambezi
Ka·ge·ra \\kə-'ger-ə\\ river 430 mi (692 km) Burundi, Rwanda, & NW Tanganyika flowing N & E into Lake Victoria on Uganda border
Ka·go·shi·ma \\,käg-ə-'shē-mə, kä-'gō-shə-\\ city & port S Japan in S Kyushu on Kagoshima Bay (inlet of the Pacific) pop 510,882

Ka·hoo·la·we \,kä-hō-'lä-vē, -wē\ island Hawaii SW of Maui *area* 45 *sq mi* (117 *sq km*)

Kai·bab \'ki-,bab\ plateau N Ariz. & SW Utah N of Grand Canyon

Kai·e·teur Falls \,kī-ǝ-,tú(ǝ)r-, ,kī-,chü(ǝ)r-\ waterfall 741 *ft* (226 *m*) high & 350 *ft* (107 *m*) wide *cen* Guiana

Kai·feng \'kī-'fǝŋ\ city E *cen* China in NE Honan *pop* 318,000

Kai·lua \kī-'lü-ǝ\ city Hawaii in NE Oahu *pop* 35,812

Kair·ouan \ker-'wän\ city NE Tunisia *pop* 54,546

Kai·sers·lau·tern \,kī-zǝrz-'laút-ǝrn\ city SW W. Germany W of Ludwigshafen *pop* 98,745

Ka·ki·na·da \,käk-ǝ-'näd-ǝ\ city & port E India in NE Andhra Pradesh on Bay of Bengal *pop* 226,642

Ka Lae \kä-'lä-ä\ *or* South Cape headland Hawaii, southernmost point of Hawaii (island)

Kalaeloa Point — see BARBERS POINT

Kal·a·ha·ri \,kal-ǝ-'här-ē\ desert region S Africa N of Orange river & S of Lake Ngami in Botswana & NW Republic of S. Africa

Ka·la·ma·ta \,kal-ǝ-'mät-ǝ\ *or NGk* Ka·lá·mai \kǝ-'läm-ē\ city & port S Greece in SW Peloponnisos *pop* 41,998

Kal·a·ma·zoo \,kal-ǝ-mǝ-'zü\ city SW Mich. *pop* 79,722

Ka·lat *or* Khe·lat \kǝ-'lät\ region N Pakistan including S & *cen* Baluchistan; a former princely state ✻ Kalat

Ka·le·mie \kǝ-'lä-mē\ *or formerly* Al·bert·ville \,al-,ber-'vē(ǝ)l, 'al-bǝrt-,vil\ city & port E Zaire on Lake Tanganyika *pop* 27,500

Kal·gan \'kal-'gan\ *or* Zhang·jia·kou \'jäŋ-zhē-'ä-'kō\ *or* Ch'ang-chia-k'ou \'chäŋ-jē-'ä-'kō\ city NE China in NW Hopeh NW of Peking *pop* 229,300

Kal·goor·lie \kal-'gú(ǝ)r-lē\ town Australia in S *cen* W. Australia

Kalhu — see CALAH

Ka·li·man·tan \,käl-ǝ-'man-,tan, ,käl-ǝ-'män-,tän\ 1 BORNEO — its Indonesian name 2 the S & E part of Borneo belonging to Indonesia; formerly (as **Dutch Borneo**) part of Netherlands India

Ka·li·nin \kǝ-'lē-nǝn, -'lēn-,yēn\ *or formerly* Tver \tǝ-'ve(ǝ)r\ city U.S.S.R. in W *cen* Soviet Russia, Europe, on the Volga *pop* 412,000

Ka·li·nin·grad \kǝ-'lē-nǝn-(y)ǝn-,grad\ *or* G Kö·nigs·berg \'kā-nigz-'bǝrg, *Ger* 'kœ-niks-,berk\ city & port U.S.S.R. in W Soviet Russia, Europe, near the Frisches Haff; formerly ✻ of E. Prussia *pop* 355,000

Ka·lisz \'käl-ish\ commune *cen* Poland W of Lodz *pop* 100,340

Kal·mar \'käl-,mär, 'kal-\ city & port SE Sweden *pop* 52,846

Kal·myk Republic \(,)käl-,mik-\ autonomous republic of the U.S.S.R. in S Soviet Russia, Europe, on NW shore of Caspian sea W of the Volga ✻ Elista *area* 29,417 *sq mi* (76,484 *sq km*), *pop* 268,000

Ka·lu·ga \kǝ-'lü-gǝ\ city U.S.S.R. in W *cen* Soviet Russia, Europe, on Oka river WNW of Tula *pop* 265,000

Ka·ma \'käm-ǝ\ river 1200 *mi* (1931 *km*) U.S.S.R. in E Soviet Russia, Europe, flowing SW into the Volga S of Kazan

Ka·ma·ku·ra \kä-'mäk-ǝ-,rä, ,käm-ǝ-'kúr-ǝ\ city Japan in SE Honshu on Sagami sea S of Yokohama *pop* 173,392

Kam·chat·ka \kam-'chat-kǝ\ peninsula 750 *mi* (1207 *km*) long U.S.S.R. in NE Soviet Russia, Asia, bet. Sea of Okhotsk & Bering sea

Ka·met \'kǝm-ǝt\ mountain 25,447 *ft* (7756 *m*) N India in Uttar Pradesh in the NW Himalayas

Kam·loops \'kam-,lüps\ city Canada in S B.C. *pop* 64,048

Kam·pa·la \käm-'päl-ǝ\ city ✻ of Uganda N of Lake Victoria *pop* 458,423

Kampuchea — see CAMBODIA

Kan *or* Gan \'gän\ river 350 *mi* (563 *km*) SE China in Kiangsi flowing N through Poyang Lake into the Yangtze

Ka·nan·ga \kǝ-'näŋ-gǝ\ *or formerly* Lu·lua·bourg \lü-'lü-ǝ-,bù(ǝ)r(g)\ city S *cen* Zaire *pop* 285,470

Kananur — see CANNANORE

Ka·na·ta \kǝ-'nät-ǝ\ city Canada in SE Ont. *pop* 19,728

Ka·na·wha \kǝ-'nó-(w)ǝ\ river 97 *mi* (156 *km*) W W.Va. flowing NW into Ohio river

Ka·na·za·wa \kǝ-'näz-ǝ-wǝ, ,kän-ǝ-'zä-wǝ\ city & port Japan in W *cen* Honshu near Sea of Japan *pop* 419,971

Kan·chen·jun·ga \,kan-chǝn-'jǝŋ-gǝ, -'jùŋ-\ mountain 28,208 *ft* (8598 *m*) Nepal & Sikkim in the Himalayas; 3d highest in world

Kan·chi·pu·ram \,kän-'chē-pǝ-rǝm\ city SE India in N Tamil Nadu SW of Madras *pop* 145,329

Kan·da·har \'kan-dǝ-,här\ city SE Afghanistan *pop* 130,212

Kand·la \'kǝn-dlǝ\ port W India in Gujarat on Gulf of Kutch

Kan·dy \'kan-dē\ city W *cen* Sri Lanka ENE of Colombo *pop* 101,281 — Kan·dy·an \-dē-ǝn\ *adj*

Kane Basin \'kān\ section of the passage between NW Greenland & Ellesmere Is. N of Baffin Bay

Ka·ne·o·he \,kä-nē-'ō-ē, -'ō-(,)hä\ city Hawaii in E Oahu on **Kaneohe Bay** (inlet) *pop* 29,919

Kan·i·a·pis·kau \,kan-ē-ǝ-'pis-(,)kō\ river 575 *mi* (925 *km*) Canada in N Que. flowing N to unite with the Larch forming the **Kok·so·ak** \'käk-sǝ-,wak\ river (85 *mi* or 136 *km* flowing into Ungava Bay)

Kan·ka·kee \,kaŋ-kǝ-'kē\ 1 river Ind. & Ill. flowing SW & W to unite with Des Plaines river forming Illinois river 2 city NE Ill. on Kankakee river *pop* 30,141

Ka·no \'kän-(,)ō\ city N *cen* Nigeria *pop* 475,000

Ka·noya \kä-'nói-ǝ\ city Japan in S Kyushu *pop* 73,242

Kan·pur \'kän-,pú(ǝ)r\ city N India in S Uttar Pradesh on the Ganges *pop* 1,688,242

Kan·sas \'kan-zǝs\ 1 *or* Kaw \'kó\ river 169 *mi* (272 *km*) E Kans. flowing E into Missouri river — see SMOKY HILL 2 state *cen* U.S. ✻ Topeka *area* 82,264 *sq mi* (213,886 *sq km*), *pop* 2,363,679 — Kan·san \'kan-zǝn\ *adj or n*

Kansas City 1 city NE Kans. adjacent to Kansas City, Mo. *pop* 161,087 2 city W Mo. on Missouri river *pop* 448,159

Kan·su *or* Gan·su \'gän-'sü\ province N *cen* China ✻ Lanchow *area* 137,104 *sq mi* (356,470 *sq km*), *pop* 19,569,261

Kan·ton \'kant-ʳn\ island (atoll) *cen* Pacific in Phoenix islands

Kan·to Plain \,kan-(,)tō-\ region Japan in E *cen* Honshu; Tokyo is situated on it

Kao·hsiung \'kaú-shē-'úŋ, 'gaú-\ city & port SW Taiwan *pop* 1,227,454

Ka·pi·da·gi \,käp-ē-dä-'(g)ē\ *or anc* Cyz·i·cus \'siz-i-kǝs\ peninsula NW Turkey in Asia projecting into Sea of Marmara

Ka·ra \'kär-ǝ\ sea arm of Arctic ocean off coast of N U.S.S.R. E of Novaya Zemlya

Ka·ra·cha·ye·vo–Cher·kess \,kär-ǝ-'chī-ǝ-,vō-cher-'kes\ autonomous region U.S.S.R. in SE Soviet Russia, Europe, in N Caucasus *area* 5442 *sq mi* (14,149 *sq km*) ✻ Cherkessk

Ka·ra·chi \kǝ-'räch-ē\ city & port S Pakistan ✻ of Sind *pop* 5,103,000

Karafuto — see SAKHALIN

Ka·ra·gan·da \,kär-ǝ-gǝn-'dä\ city U.S.S.R. in *cen* Kazakhstan *pop* 572,000

Ka·ra–Kal·pak Republic \,kär-ǝ-kal-'pak-\ autonomous republic U.S.S.R. in NW Uzbek Republic SE of Aral sea ✻ Nukus *area* 61,600 *sq mi* (160,160 *sq km*), *pop* 829,000

Kar·a·ko·ram \,kär-ǝ-'kōr-ǝm, -'kòr-\ 1 mountain system S *cen* Asia in N Kashmir & NW Tibet on Sinkiang Uighur border; westernmost system of the Himalaya complex, connecting the Himalayas with the Pamirs — see K2 2 mountain pass 18,290 *ft* (5575 *m*) NE Kashmir through Karakoram range

Kar·a·ko·rum \-ǝm\ ruined city Mongolia on the upper Orkhon ✻ of Mongol Empire

Ka·ra Kum \,kär-ǝ-'küm\ desert U.S.S.R. in Turkmen Republic S of Lake Aral between the Caspian sea & the Amu Darya *area* 110,000 *sq mi* (286,000 *sq km*)

Kara Shahr — see YEN-CH'I

Ka·ra Su \,kär-ǝ-'sü\ the Euphrates above its junction with the Murat in E *cen* Turkey

Kar·ba·lā \,kär-bǝ-'lä\ city *cen* Iraq SSW of Baghdad *pop* 83,301

Ka·re·lia \kǝ-'rē-lǝ-ǝ, -'rēl-yǝ\ region NE Europe bet. Gulf of Finland & White sea in the U.S.S.R. & Finland

Ka·re·lian Isthmus \-,rē-lē-ǝn-, -,rēl-yǝn-\ isthmus U.S.S.R. in Karelia bet. Gulf of Finland & Lake Ladoga

Ka·re·lian Republic \kǝ-'rē-lē-ǝn-, -,rēl-yǝn-\ *or* Ka·rel'·ska·ya Republic \-,kär-,yel-skǝ-yǝ-\ autonomous republic U.S.S.R. in NW Soviet Russia, Europe, in Karelia region; formerly (1940-56), as the Ka·re·lo–Finn·ish Republic \kǝ-,rē-(,)lō-,fin-ish-\ constituent republic of the U.S.S.R. ✻ Petrozadovsk *area* 68,900 *sq mi* (179,140 *sq km*), *pop* 738,000

Ka·ri·ba \kǝ-'rē-bǝ\ lake 165 *mi* (266 *km*) long SE Zambia & N Zimbabwe formed in the Zambezi by **Kariba Dam**

Ka·ri·kal \,kär-ǝ-'käl\ 1 territory of former French India S of Pondicherry; incorporated 1954 in India *area* 52 *sq mi* (135 *sq km*) 2 city & port, its ✻, on Bay of Bengal *pop* 22,252

Kar·kheh \,kǝr-'kä\ *or anc* Cho·as·pes \kō-'as-(,)pēz\ river 340 *mi* (547 *km*) flowing from W Iran S & W into marshlands E of the Tigris in SE Iraq

Karl–Marx–Stadt \(')kärl-'märk-,s(h)tät\ *or formerly* Chem·nitz \'kem-,nits, -nǝts\ city S E. Germany SE of Leipzig *pop* 317,696

Kar·lo·vy Va·ry \,kär-lǝ-vē-'vär-ē\ city NW Czechoslovakia in NW Bohemia NNW of Plzen *pop* 60,950

Karls·kro·na \kärl-'skrü-nǝ\ city & port SE Sweden on Baltic sea *pop* 60,141

Karls·ru·he \'kärlz-,rü-ǝ\ city SW W. Germany in Baden-Württemberg on the Rhine *pop* 271,892 — Karls·ru·her \-,rü-ǝr\ *n*

Karl·stad \'kär(ǝ)l-,stä(d)\ city SW Sweden *pop* 74,068

Kar·nak \'kär-,nak\ town S Egypt on the Nile N of Luxor on N part of site of ancient Thebes

Kar·na·ta·ka \kǝr-'nät-ǝ-kǝ\ *or formerly* My·sore \mī-'sō(ǝ)r, -'sò(ǝ)r\ state SW India ✻ Bangalore *area* 74,326 *sq mi* (193,248 *sq km*), *pop* 37,034,451

Kár·pa·thos \'kär-pǝ-,thäs\ island Greece in the S Dodecanese *area* 118 *sq mi* (307 *sq km*), *pop* 8129

Kar·roo *or* Ka·roo \kǝ-'rü\ plateau region W Republic of S. Africa W of Drakensberg mountains divided into **Little Karroo** or **Southern Karroo** (in S Cape Province); **Great Karroo** or **Central Karroo** (in S *cen* Cape Province); and **Northern Karroo** or **Upper Karroo** (in N Cape Province, Orange Free State, & W Transvaal)

Kars \'kärz, 'kärs\ city NE Turkey *pop* 58,651

Karst — see KRAS

Ka·run \kǝ-'rün\ river 450 *mi* (724 *km*) W Iran flowing into Shatt-al-Arab

Ka·sai \kǝ-'sī\ 1 river 1200 *mi* (1931 *km*) N Angola & W Zaire flowing N & W into Congo river 2 region S *cen* Zaire

Ka·shan \kǝ-'shän\ city *cen* Iran N of Esfahan *pop* 84,545

Kash·gar \'kash-,gär, 'käsh-\ *or* Kashi \'kash-ē, 'käsh-\ city W China in SW Sinkiang Uighur *pop* 100,000

Kash·mir \'kash-,mi(ǝ)r, 'kazh-, kash-', kazh-'\ *or formerly* Cash·mere 1 mountainous region N India (subcontinent) W of Tibet & SW of Sinkiang Uighur; includes valley (**Vale of Kashmir**) watered by the Jhelum 2 *or* Jam·mu and Kashmir \'jǝm-(,)ü\ state N India including Kashmir region & Jammu (to the S); claimed also by Pakistan; summer ✻ Srinagar, winter ✻ Jammu *area* 92,780 *sq mi* (241,228 *sq km*), *pop* 5,981,600

Kas·kas·kia \kǝ-'skas-kē-ǝ\ river 300 *mi* (483 *km*) SW Ill. flowing SW into Mississippi river

Kas·sa·la \'kas-ǝ-lǝ\ city NE Sudan *pop* 99,000

Kas·sel \'kas-ǝl, 'käs-\ city E W. Germany WNW of Erfurt *pop* 195,912

Kas·ser·ine Pass \,kas-ǝ-,rēn-\ mountain pass *cen* Tunisia

Ka·stel·lór·i·zon \,käs-tǝ-'lór-ǝ-,zòn\ *or* Ca·stel·lo·ri·zo \käs-tǝ-'lòr-ǝ-,zō\ *or It* Cas·tel·ros·so \,käs-,tel-'rós-(,)ō\ island Greece in the E Dodecanese off SW coast of Turkey *area* 4 *sq mi* (10 *sq km*)

Ká·stron \'käs-,tròn\ 1 town Greece on Lemnos 2 — see CHIOS

Kastrop–Rauxel — see CASTROP-RAUXEL

Ka·tah·din, Mount \kǝ-'täd-ʳn\ mountain 5268 *ft* (1606 *m*) N *cen* Maine; highest point in state

Katanga — see SHABA

Ka·tan·gese \kǝ-,täŋ-'gēz, -,taŋ-, -'gēz\ *adj*

Kath·er·i·na, Ge·bel \,jeb-ǝl-,kath-ǝ-'rē-nǝ\ *or* Ja·bal Kat·ri·nah \'jäb-ǝl-,kä-'trē-nǝ\ mountain 8652 *ft* (2637 *m*) NE Egypt on Sinai peninsula; highest in the Gebel Musa

Ka·thi·a·war \,kät-ē-ǝ-'wär\ peninsula W India in Gujarat between Gulf of Kutch & Gulf of Cambay

Kath·man·du *or* Kat·man·du \,kat-,man-'dü\ city ✻ of Nepal *pop* 235,211

Kat·mai, Mount \'kat-,mī\ volcano 6715 *ft* (2047 *m*) S Alaska in Aleutian range at NE end of Alaska peninsula

Katmai National Park reservation S Alaska including Mt. Katmai & Valley of Ten Thousand Smokes

Ka·to·wi·ce \,kät-ǝ-'vēt-sǝ\ city S Poland in Silesia *pop* 363,523

Kat·rine, Loch \'ka-trǝn\ lake 9 *mi* (14 *km*) long *cen* Scotland in Central region E of Loch Lomond

Ka·tsi·na \'kät-si-nə\ city N Nigeria * of old kingdom of Katsina *pop* 145,500

Kat·te·gat \'kat-i-ˌgat\ arm of North sea between Sweden & Jutland peninsula of Denmark

Kau·ai \'kaù-ˌi\ island Hawaii WNW of Oahu *area* 551 *sq mi* (1433 *sq km*)

Kau·nas \'kaù-nəs, -ˌnäs\ *or Russ* Kov·no \'kóv-(ˌ)nō\ city U.S.S.R. in *cen* Lithuania on the Neman; a former (1918–40) * of Lithuania *pop* 370,000

Ka·vál·la \kə-'val-ə, -'väl-\ city & port NE Greece in Macedonia *pop* 56,260

Kaveri — see CAUVERY

Kaw — see KANSAS

Ka·wa·gu·chi \ˌkä-wə-'gü-chē, kä-'wäg-ù-(ˌ)chē\ city Japan in E Honshu N of Tokyo *pop* 386,633

Ka·war·tha Lakes \kə-ˌwór-thə-\ group of lakes Canada in SE Ont. E of Lake Simcoe; traversed by Trent canal system

Ka·wa·sa·ki \ˌkä-wə-'säk-ē\ city Japan in E Honshu on Tokyo Bay, S suburb of Tokyo *pop* 1,045,244

Kay·se·ri \ˌkī-zə-'rē\ *or anc* Cae·sa·rea \ˌsē-zə-'rē-ə, ˌsez-ə-, ˌses-ə-\ *or* Maz·a·ca \'maz-ə-kə\ *or* Caesarea Mazaca city *cen* Turkey in Asia at foot of Erciyas Dagi; chief city of ancient Cappadocia *pop* 273,362

Ka·zakh·stan \ˌkä-ˌzak-'stan; kə-ˌzäk-'stän, ˌkä-\ *or* Ka·zakh Republic \ˌkä-ˌzak-, -ˌzäk-\ constituent republic of the U.S.S.R. in Soviet Central Asia extending from Caspian sea to Altai mountains * Alma-Ata *area* 1,047,930 *sq mi* (2,724,618 *sq km*), *pop* 14,684,000

Ka·zan 1 \kə-'zan\ river 455 *mi* (732 *km*) Canada flowing through a series of lakes into Baker Lake 2 \kə-'zan, -(ˈan-)yə\ city U.S.S.R. in E Soviet Russia, Europe * of Tatar Republic *pop* 993,000

Kazan Retto — see VOLCANO

Kaz·bek \käz-'bek\ mountain 16,558 *ft* (5047 *m*) U.S.S.R. in S Soviet Russia, Europe, in *cen* Caucasus mountains

Kaz Da·gi \ˌkäz-dä-'(g)ē\ *or* Ida \'īd-ə\ mountain 5797 *ft* (1767 *m*) NW Turkey in Asia SE of ancient Troy

Kazvin — see QAZVIN

Ke·a·la·ke·kua Bay \kä-ˌäl-ə-kə-ˌkü-ə-\ inlet of the Pacific Hawaii in W Hawaii (island) on Kona coast W of Mauna Loa

Kear·ney \'kär-nē\ city S *cen* Nebr. on Platte river *pop* 21,158

Kear·ny \'kär-nē\ town NE N.J. N of Newark *pop* 35,735

Kecs·ke·met \'kech-kə-ˌmāt\ city *cen* Hungary *pop* 91,929

Ked·ah \'ked-ə\ state Malaysia in N Peninsular Malaysia bordering on Strait of Malacca * Alor Star *area* 3660 *sq mi* (9516 *sq km*), *pop* 1,102,200

Keeling — see COCOS

Kee·lung \'kē-'lùŋ\ city & port N Taiwan *pop* 347,828

Keene \'kēn\ city SW N.H. *pop* 21,449

Kee·wa·tin \kē-'wāt-ʔn\ former district Canada in E Northwest Territories N of Man. & Ont. & including the islands in Hudson bay

Kefallinía — see CEPHALONIA

Kef·la·vík \'kyeb-lə-ˌvēk, 'kef-\ town SW Iceland WSW of Reykjavík

Keigh·ley \'kēth-lē—*sic*\ borough N England in W. Yorkshire, NW of Leeds *pop* 57,451

Kej·im·ku·jik National Park \ˌkej-(ə)mə-'kü-jik\ reservation Canada in SW N.S.

Ke·lan·tan \kə-'lan-ˌtan\ state Malaysia in N Peninsular Malaysia on S. China sea * Kota Bharu *area* 5746 *sq mi* (14,940 *sq km*), *pop* 877,575

Ke·low·na \kə-'lō-nə\ city Canada in S B.C. *pop* 59,196

Keltsy — see KIELCE

Ke·me·ro·vo \'kem-ə-rə-və, -ˌrō-və, -rə-ˌvó\ city U.S.S.R. in S Soviet Russia, Asia, in Kuznetsk basin on Tom river *pop* 471,000

Ke·nai \'kē-ˌnī\ peninsula S Alaska E of Cook inlet; site of Kenai Fjords National Park (ice field)

Ken·dal \'ken-dʔl\ borough NW England in Cumbria *pop* 23,411

Ken·il·worth \'ken-ʔl-ˌwərth\ town *cen* England in Warwickshire *pop* 19,315

Ke·ni·tra \kə-'nē-trə\ *or formerly* Port Lyau·tey \ˌpór-lē-ˌō-'tā, -'ō-\ city N Morocco NE of Rabat *pop* 139,206

Ken·more \'ken-ˌmō(ə)r, -ˌmó(ə)r\ village W N.Y. *pop* 18,474

Ken·ne·bec \'ken-i-ˌbek, ken-i-'\ river 164 *mi* (264 *km*) S Maine flowing S from Moosehead lake into the Atlantic

Kennedy, Cape — see CANAVERAL (Cape)

Ken·ne·dy, Mount \'ken-əd-ē\ mountain 13,905 *ft* (4238 *m*) NW Canada in Yukon Territory in St. Elias range near Alaska border

Ken·ner \'ken-ər\ city SE La. W of New Orleans *pop* 66,382

Ken·ne·saw Mountain \ˌken-ə-ˌsó-\ mountain 1809 *ft* (551 *m*) NW Ga. NW of Atlanta

Ken·ne·wick \'ken-ə-ˌwik\ city SE Wash. *pop* 34,397

Ke·no·sha \kə-'nō-shə\ city SE Wis. S of Racine *pop* 77,685

Ken·sing·ton and Chel·sea \ˌken-zin-tən-ən-'chel-sē, 'ken(t)-siŋ-\ royal borough of W Greater London, England *pop* 146,900; includes former boroughs of Kensington & Chelsea

Kent \'kent\ 1 island Md. in Chesapeake Bay 15 *mi* (25 *km*) long; largest island in the bay 2 city NE Ohio SE of Cleveland *pop* 26,164 3 city W Wash. S of Seattle *pop* 23,152 4 county SE England bordering on Strait of Dover; one of kingdoms in Anglo-Saxon heptarchy * Maidstone *area* 1441 *sq mi* (3747 *sq km*), *pop* 1,482,900 — Kent·ish \'kent-ish\ *adj*

Ken·tucky \kən-'tək-ē\ 1 river 259 *mi* (417 *km*) N *cen* Ky. flowing NW into Ohio river 2 state E *cen* U.S. * Frankfort *area* 40,395 *sq mi* (105,027 *sq km*), *pop* 3,661,433 — Ken·tuck·i·an \-ē-ən\ *adj or n*

Kent·wood \'kent-ˌwùd\ city SW Mich. *pop* 30,438

Ke·nya \'ken-yə, 'kēn-\ 1 extinct volcano 17,058 *ft* (5199 *m*) *cen* Kenya near equator 2 republic E Africa S of Ethiopia bordering on Indian ocean; member of the Commonwealth, formerly Brit. crown colony & protectorate * Nairobi *area* 224,960 *sq mi* (584,896 *sq km*), *pop* 15,327,061 — Ke·nyan \-yən\ *adj or n*

Ke·os \'kē-ˌäs\ *or* Kea \'kē-ə\ *or anc* Ce·os \'sē-ˌäs\ island Greece in NW Cyclades; chief town Kea *area* 67 *sq mi* (174 *sq km*), *pop* 6315

Ker·a·la \'ker-ə-lə\ state SW India bordering on Arabian sea * Trivandrum *area* 15,035 *sq mi* (39,091 *sq km*), *pop* 25,403,217

Kerasun — see GIRESUN

Kerch \'ke(ə)rch\ 1 peninsula U.S.S.R. in S Soviet Russia, Europe, projecting E from the Crimea 2 strait between Kerch peninsula &

Taman peninsula connecting Sea of Azov & Black sea 3 city & port in the Crimea on Kerch strait *pop* 149,000

Ker·gue·len \'kər-gə-lən, ˌker-gə-'len\ 1 archipelago S Indian ocean belonging to France *area* 7000 *sq mi* (18,200 *sq km*) 2 island in the archipelago

Ke·rin·tji \kə-'rin-chē\ volcano 12,484 *ft* (3805 *m*) Indonesia in W *cen* Sumatra; highest on the island

Kérkira *or* Kérkyra — see CORFU

Kerk·ra·de \'ke(ə)r-ˌkräd-ə\ commune SE Netherlands *pop* 53,353

Ker·mad·ec \(ˌ)kər-'mad-ək\ islands SW Pacific NE of New Zealand; belong to New Zealand *area* 13 *sq mi* (34 *sq km*), *pop* 9

Ker·man \kər-'män, ker-\ 1 *or anc* Car·ma·nia \kär-'mā-nē-ə, -nyə\ region SE Iran bordering on Gulf of Oman & Persian Gulf S of ancient Parthia 2 *or anc* Car·ma·na \kär-'män-ə, -'man-, -'män-\ city SE *cen* Iran in NW Kerman region *pop* 88,000

Kermanshah — see BAKHTARAN

Kern \'kərn\ river 150 *mi* (241 *km*) S *cen* Calif. flowing SW into Buena Vista reservoir

Ker·ry \'ker-ē\ county SW Ireland in Munster * Tralee *area* 1815 *sq mi* (4719 *sq km*), *pop* 122,770

Ker·u·len \'ker-ə-lən\ river 650 *mi* (1046 *km*) E Mongolia flowing S & E into the Argun in Manchuria

Kes·te·ven, Parts of \ke-'stē-vən\ district & former administrative county E England in SW Lincolnshire * Sleaford *area* 724 *sq mi* (1882 *sq km*)

Kes·wick \'kez-ik\ town NW England in Cumbria in Lake District

Ket·ter·ing \'ket-ə-riŋ\ city SW Ohio S of Dayton *pop* 61,186

Keu·ka \'kyü-kə, kā-'yü-\ lake 18 *mi* (29 *km*) long W *cen* N.Y.; one of the Finger Lakes

Kew \'kyü\ 1 city SE Australia in S Victoria, NE suburb of Melbourne *pop* 28,870 2 parish S England in Surrey, now in the Greater London borough of Richmond upon Thames

Ke·wee·naw \'kē-wə-ˌnó\ peninsula NW Mich. projecting from upper Mich. peninsula into Lake Superior W of Keweenaw Bay

Key Lar·go \-'lär-(ˌ)gō\ island S Fla. in the Florida Keys

Key West \-'west\ city SW Fla. on Key West (island) at W end of Florida Keys *pop* 24,382 — Key West·er \-ər\ *n*

Kha·ba·rovsk \kə-'bär-əfsk\ 1 territory U.S.S.R. in E Soviet Russia, Asia, bordering on Sea of Okhotsk & Bering sea *area* 965,400 *sq mi* (2,510,040 *sq km*), *pop* 1,346,000 2 city, its *, on the Amur *pop* 437,000

Kha·kass \kə-'kas\ autonomous region U.S.S.R. in S Soviet Russia, Asia, in SW Krasnoyarsk Territory N of the Sayan mountains * Abakan *area* 24,000 *sq mi* (62,400 *sq km*), *pop* 446,000

Khalkidikí — see CHALCIDICE

Khal·kis \käl-'kēs\ *or* Chal·cis \'kal-səs, -kəs\ city *cen* Greece * of Évvoia on Evripos strait *pop* 44,774

Khaniá — see CANEA

Khan·ka \'kaŋ-kə\ lake E Asia bet. Maritime Territory, U.S.S.R., & Heilungkiang, China *area* 1700 *sq mi* (4420 *sq km*)

Khan Ten·gri \ˌkän-'teŋ-(g)rē\ mountain 22,949 *ft* (6995 *m*) on border bet. Kirghiz Republic (U.S.S.R.) & Sinkiang Uighur (China) in Tien Shan

Kha·rag·pur \'kär-əg-ˌpú(ə)r, 'kər-\ city E India in SW W. Bengal WSW of Calcutta *pop* 234,931

Khar·kov \'kär-ˌkóf, -ˌkóv, -kəf\ city U.S.S.R. in NE Ukrainian Republic, its * 1921–34, on edge of Donets Basin *pop* 1,444,000

Khar·toum *or* Khar·tum \kär-'tüm\ city * of Sudan at junction of White Nile & Blue Nile rivers *pop* 1,089,339

Khartoum North city *cen* Sudan *pop* 151,000

Kha·si \'käs-ē\ hills E India in NW *cen* Assam

Kha·tan·ga \kə-'taŋ-gə\ river 800 *mi* (1287 *km*) U.S.S.R. in N Soviet Russia, Asia, in NE Krasnoyarsk Territory flowing N into Laptev sea

Khelat — see KALAT

Kher·son \ker-'són\ city & port U.S.S.R. in S Ukrainian Republic on the Dnieper near its mouth *pop* 319,000

Khí·os \'kē-ˌós\ 1 — see CHIOS 2 city & port Greece on E coast of Chios Is. *pop* 24,074

Khirbat Qumran — see QUMRAN

Khi·va \'kē-və\ *or* Kho·rezm \kə-'rez-əm\ oasis U.S.S.R. in Uzbek Republic on the lower Amu Darya 2 *or* Khwa·razm \kwə-'raz-əm, kwä-\ former khanate *cen* Asia including Khiva oasis 3 city in the oasis, * of the khanate *pop* 24,139

Khmer Republic — see CAMBODIA

Khor·a·san \ˌkór-ə-'sän, ˌkór-\ *or* Khu·ra·san \ˌkùr-ə-'sän, ˌkùr-\ region NE Iran; chief city Meshed

Khor·ram·shahr \ˌkór-əm-'shä(-h)ə)r, ˌkór-\ city & port W Iran in Khuzistan on Shatt-al-Arab NNW of Abadan *pop* 146,709

Khotan — see HO-T'IEN

Khu·zi·stan \ˌkü-zi-'stän, -'stan\ region SW Iran bordering on Persian gulf; chief city Khorramshahr

Khy·ber \'kī-bər\ mountain pass 33 *mi* (53 *km*) long on border bet. Afghanistan & Pakistan in Safed Koh range WNW of Peshawar

Kiamusze — see CHIA-MU-SSU

Kiang·si *or* Jiang·xi \jē-'äŋ-'shē\ province SE China * Nanchang *area* 63,629 *sq mi* (165,435 *sq km*), *pop* 33,184,827

Kiang·su *or* Jiang·su \jē-'äŋ-'sü\ province E China bordering on Yellow sea * Nanking *area* 41,699 *sq mi* (108,417 *sq km*), *pop* 60,521,114

Kiao·chow Bay \jē-'aù-'jō\ inlet of Yellow sea E China in E Shantung *area* 200 *sq mi* (520 *sq km*)

Ki·bo \'kē-(ˌ)bō\ mountain peak 19,340 *ft* (5895 *m*) Tanzania in NE Tanganyika; highest peak of Kilimanjaro & highest point in Africa

Kid·der·min·ster \'kid-ər-ˌmin(t)-stər\ borough W *cen* England in Hereford and Worcester SW of Birmingham *pop* 51,261

Kid·ron \'kid-rən, 'ki-drən\ valley *cen* Palestine bet. Jerusalem & Mount of Olives; source of stream (Kidron) flowing E to Dead sea

---

\ə\ abut \ʔ\ kitten, F table \ər\ further \a\ ash \ā\ ace \ä\ cot, cart \aù\ out \ch\ chin \e\ bet \ē\ easy \g\ go \i\ hit \ī\ ice \j\ job \ŋ\ sing \ō\ go \ó\ law \ói\ boy \th\ thin \t̶h\ the \ü\ loot \ù\ foot \y\ yet \zh\ vision \à, ḵ, ⁿ, œ, œ̄, ue, ūe, ᵊ\ *see* Guide to Pronunciation

Kiel \'kē(ə)l\ **1** city & port N W. Germany ✻ of Schleswig-Holstein on SE coast of Jutland peninsula *pop* 250,062 **2** ship canal 61 *mi* (98 *km*) N W. Germany across base of Jutland peninsula connecting Baltic sea & North sea
Kiel·ce \kē-'elt-(,)sä\ *or Russ* **Kelt·sy** \'kelt-sē\ city S Poland S of Warsaw *pop* 188,822
Ki·ev *or* **Ki·yev** \'kē-,(y)ef, -,(y)ev, -(y)əf\ city U.S.S.R. ✻ of Ukrainian Republic on the Dnieper *pop* 2,144,000 — **Ki·ev·an** \-ən\ *adj*
Ki·ga·li \ki-'gäl-ē\ city *cen* Rwanda, its ✻ *pop* 117,749
Kikládhes — see CYCLADES
Ki·lau·ea \,kē-,lau̇-'ā-ə\ volcanic crater 2 *mi* (3.2 *km*) wide Hawaii on Hawaii (island) in Hawaii Volcanoes National Park on E slope of Mauna Loa
Kil·dare \kil-'da(ə)r, -'de(ə)r\ county E Ireland in Leinster ✻ Naas *area* 654 *sq mi* (1700 *sq km*), *pop* 104,122
Kil·i·man·ja·ro \,kil-ə-mən-'jär-(,)ō, -'jar-\ mountain Tanzania on NE mainland near Kenya border — see KIBO
Kil·ken·ny \kil-'ken-ē\ **1** county SE Ireland in Leinster *area* 796 *sq mi* (2070 *sq km*), *pop* 70,806 **2** municipal borough, its ✻
Kil·lar·ney, Lakes of \kil-'är-nē\ three lakes SW Ireland in County Kerry
Kill Dev·il \'kil-,dev-əl\ hill E N.C. near village of **Kit·ty Hawk** \'kit-ē-,hȯk\ on sand barrier opposite Albemarle sound
Kil·leen \kil-'ēn\ city *cen* Tex. N of Austin *pop* 46,296
Kil·lie·cran·kie \,kil-ē-'kraŋ-kē\ mountain pass *cen* Scotland in Tayside in the SE Grampians NW of Pitlochry
Kill Van Kull \,kil-(,)van-'kəl, -vən-\ channel between N.J. & Staten Is., N.Y., connecting Newark Bay & Upper New York Bay
Kil·mar·nock \kil-'mär-nək\ burgh SW Scotland in Strathclyde *pop* 52,080
Kim·ber·ley \'kim-bər-lē\ city Republic of S. Africa in N Cape of Good Hope WNW of Bloemfontein *pop* 105,258
Kim·ber·leys \-lēz\ plateau region N Western Australia N of 19°30'S lat.
Kin·a·ba·lu *or* **Kin·a·bu·lu** \,kin-ə-bə-'lü\ mountain 13,455 *ft* (4101 *m*) N *cen* N. Borneo in Crocker range; highest in Borneo Is.
Kin·car·dine \kin-'kärd-ᵊn\ *or* **Kin·car·dine·shire** \-,shi(ə)r, -shər\ *or* **The Mearns** \'mərnz, 'me(ə)rnz\ former county E Scotland ✻ Stonehaven
Ki·nesh·ma \'kē-nish-mə\ city U.S.S.R. in *cen* Soviet Russia, Europe, NE of Moscow *pop* 94,000
King George's Falls — see AUGHRABIES FALLS
King·man \'kiŋ-mən\ reef *cen* Pacific at N end of Line islands
King's — see OFFALY
Kings Canyon National Park \'kiŋz-\ reservation SE *cen* Calif. in the Sierra Nevada N of Sequoia National Park
King's Lynn \'kiŋz-'lin\ *or* **Lynn** *or* **Lynn Re·gis** \-'rē-jəs\ borough E England in Norfolk near The Wash *pop* 33,340
Kings Mountain ridge N.C. & S.C. SW of Gastonia, N.C.
Kings Peak mountain 13,528 *ft* (4123 *m*) NE Utah in Uinta mountains; highest point in state
Kings·port \'kiŋz-,pō(ə)rt, -,pȯ(ə)rt\ city NE Tenn. on the Holston *pop* 32,027
Kings·ton \'kiŋ-stən\ **1** city SE N.Y. on the Hudson *pop* 24,481 **2** city Canada in SE Ont. on Lake Ontario near head of St. Lawrence river; ✻ of Canada 1841–44 *pop* 52,616 **3** *or* **Kingston upon** (*or* **on**) **Thames** royal borough of SW Greater London, England ✻ of Surrey *pop* 135,000 **4** city & port ✻ of Jamaica on **Kingston Harbor** (inlet of the Caribbean) *pop* 117,400
Kingston upon Hull — see HULL
Kings·town \'kiŋ-,stau̇n\ **1** town & port ✻ of St. Vincent and the Grenadines on St. Vincent Is. at head of Kingstown Bay **2** — see DUN LAOGHAIRE
Kings·ville \'kiŋz-,vil, -vəl\ city S Tex. *pop* 28,808
Kinneret, Yam — see GALILEE (Sea of)
Kin·ross \kin-'rȯs\ *or* **Kin·ross–shire** \-'rȯs(h)-,shi(ə)r, -shər\ former county E *cen* Scotland ✻ Kinross
Kin·sha·sa \kin-'shäs-ə\ *or formerly* **Lé·o·pold·ville** \'lē-ə-,pōld-,vil, 'lā-\ city ✻ of Zaire on Congo river at outlet of Stanley Pool *pop* 2,242,297
Kin·ston \'kin(t)-stən\ city E N.C. *pop* 25,234
Kin·tyre \kin-'tī(ə)r\ peninsula 40 *mi* (64 *km*) long SW Scotland bet. the Atlantic & Firth of Clyde; terminates in **Mull of Kintyre** \,məl-\ (cape in N. channel)
Kioga — see KYOGA
Kir·ghiz Republic *or* **Kir·giz Republic** \(,)ki(ə)r-,gēz-\ *or* **Kir·ghi·zia** \ki(ə)r-'gē-z(h)ē-ə, -zhə\ constituent republic of the U.S.S.R. in Soviet Central Asia on China border NE of Tadzhik Republic ✻ Frunze *area* 76,100 *sq mi* (197,860 *sq km*), *pop* 3,529,000
Ki·ri·bati \'kir-ə-,bas—*sic*\ island nation W Pacific SSE of the Marshalls comprising Ocean island and the Gilbert, Line, & Phoenix groups ✻ Tarawa *area* 102 *sq mi* (265 *sq km*), *pop* 63,848
Ki·rik·ka·le \kə-'rik-ə-,lā\ city *cen* Turkey E of Ankara
Ki·rin \'kē-'rin\ *or* **Ji·lin** \'jē-'lin\ **1** province NE China in E Manchuria ✻ Changchun *area* 72,201 *sq mi* (187,723 *sq km*), *pop* 22,560,053 **2** *or formerly* **Yung·ki** \'yu̇ŋ-'jē\ city NE China in E *cen* Kirin *pop* 583,000
Ki·riti·mati \kə-'ris-məs—*sic*\ *or formerly* **Christ·mas** \'kris-məs\ island (atoll) in the Line islands *area* 234 *sq mi* (608 *sq km*), *pop* 674
Kirjath–arba — see HEBRON
Kirk·caldy \(,)kər-'kȯ(l)d-ē, -'käd-\ royal burgh & port E Scotland in Fife on Firth of Forth N of Edinburgh *pop* 46,314
Kirk·cud·bright \(,)kər-'kü-brē\ *or* **Kirk·cud·bright·shire** \-,shi(ə)r, -shər\ former county S Scotland ✻ Kirkcudbright (*pop* 2574)
Kirk·land \'kər-klənd\ city W Wash. NE of Seattle *pop* 18,779
Kirk·pat·rick, Mount \,kərk-'pa-trik\ mountain 14,856 *ft* (4528 *m*) E Antarctica in Queen Alexandra Range S of Ross sea
Kirks·ville \'kərks-,vil\ city NE Mo. *pop* 17,167
Kir·kuk \ki(ə)r-'kük\ city NE Iraq SE of Mosul *pop* 175,303
Kirk·wall \'kər-,kwȯl\ burgh & port N Scotland ✻ of Orkney, on Mainland Is. *pop* 5947
Kirk·wood \'kər-,kwu̇d\ city E Mo. W of St. Louis *pop* 27,987
Ki·rov \'kē-,rȯf, -,rȯv, -rəf\ *or formerly* **Vyat·ka** \vē-'at-kə, -'ät-\ city U.S.S.R. in E Soviet Russia, Europe *pop* 390,000
Ki·ro·va·bad \ki-'rō-və-,bad\ *or formerly* **Gan·dzha** \'gän-jə\ *or* **Eli·sa·vet·pol** \i-,liz-ə-'vet-,pȯl\ city U.S.S.R. in W Azerbaijan *pop* 232,000
Ki·ro·vo·grad \ki-'rō-və-,grad\ *or formerly* **Zi·nov·ievsk** \zə-'nȯv-,yefsk\ *or* **Eli·sa·vet·grad** \i-,liz-ə-'vet-,grad\ city U.S.S.R. in S *cen* Ukrainian Republic *pop* 237,000
Ki·ru·na \'kē-rə-,nä\ city N Sweden in Lapland *pop* 29,705
Ki·san·ga·ni \,kē-sən-'gän-ē\ *or formerly* **Stan·ley·ville** \'stan-lē-,vil\ city NE Zaire on Congo river *pop* 291,888
Kish \'kish\ ancient city of Sumer & Akkad E of site of Babylon
Ki·shi·nev \'kish-ə-,nef, -,nev\ *or Romanian* **Chi·si·nau** \,kē-shi-'nau̇\ city U.S.S.R. ✻ of Moldavia *pop* 503,000
Kis·ka \'kis-kə\ island SW Alaska in Rat group of the Aleutians
Kis·ma·yu \kis-'mī-(,)ü\ city & port S Somalia *pop* 30,115
Kis·sim·mee \kis-'im-ē\ river 150 *mi* (241 *km*) S *cen* Fla. flowing SSE from Lake Tohopekaliga through **Lake Kissimmee** (12 *mi or* 19 *km* long) into Lake Okeechobee
Kistna — see KRISHNA
Ki·su·mu \ki-'sü-(,)mü\ city W Kenya on Lake Victoria *pop* 152,643
Ki·ta·kyu·shu \kē-'tä-kē-'ü-(,)shü\ city & port Japan in N Kyushu formed 1963 by amalgamation of former cities of Kokura, Moji, Tobata, Wakamatsu, & Yahata *pop* 1,065,038
Kitch·e·ner \'kich-(ə-)nər\ city Canada in SE Ont. *pop* 139,734
Kithairón — see CITHAERON
Kí·thi·ra \'kē-thə-(,)rä\ *or It* **Ce·ri·go** \'cher-i-,gō\ island W Greece, southernmost of the Ionian islands ✻ Kíthira *area* 110 *sq mi* (286 *sq km*)
Kit·i·mat \'kit-ə-,mat\ river *ab* 50 *mi* (80 *km*) W Canada in NW B.C. flowing to Douglas channel (inlet of the Pacific)
Kit·ta·tin·ny Mountain \,kit-ə-,tin-ē-\ ridge E U.S. in the Appalachians extending from SE N.Y. through NW N.J. into E Pa.
Kit·tery Point \,kit-ə-rē-\ cape Maine at S tip
Kitt Peak \'kit\ mountain 6875 *ft* (2096 *m*) S Ariz. SW of Tucson
Kitty Hawk — see KILL DEVIL
Kitz·bü·hel \'kits-,byü(-ə)l, -,bu̅e(-ə)l\ resort town W Austria in the Tirol
Kiungchow — see HAINAN 2
Ki·vu, Lake \'kē-(,)vü\ lake 60 *mi* (96 *km*) long & 30 *mi* (48 *km*) wide E Zaire in Great Rift valley N of Lake Tanganyika *area* 1025 *sq mi* (2665 *sq km*)
Ki·zil Ir·mak \kə-,zil-i(ə)r-'mäk\ *or anc* **Ha·lys** \'hā-ləs\ river 600 *mi* (966 *km*) N *cen* Turkey flowing W & NE into Black sea
Kjö·len \'chə(r)l-ən\ mountains on border bet. NE Norway & NW Sweden; highest Kebnekaise (in Sweden) 6965 *ft* (2123 *m*)
Kla·gen·furt \'kläg-ən-,fu̇(ə)rt\ city S Austria ✻ of Carinthia WSW of Graz *pop* 86,303
Klai·pe·da \'klī-pəd-ə\ *or* **Me·mel** \'mā-məl\ city & port U.S.S.R. in W Lithuania on the Baltic *pop* 176,000
Klam·ath \'klam-əth\ **1** river 250 *mi* (402 *km*) S Oreg. & NW Calif. flowing from Upper Klamath Lake SW into the Pacific **2** mountains S Oreg. & NW Calif. in the Coast ranges; highest Mt. Eddy (in Calif.) 9038 *ft* (2755 *m*)
Klamath Falls city SW Oreg. *pop* 16,661
Kle·ve \'klā-və\ city W W. Germany WSW of Münster *pop* 44,026
Klon·dike \'klän-,dīk\ **1** river 90 *mi* (145 *km*) Canada in *cen* Yukon Territory flowing W into the Yukon **2** the Klondike river valley
Klu·ane National Park \klü-,ȯn-ē-, -,än-\ reservation Canada in SW Yukon Territory
Kly·az·ma \klē-'az-mə\ river 425 *mi* (684 *km*) U.S.S.R. in W *cen* Soviet Russia, Europe, flowing E to join the Oka W of Gorki
Knok·ke \kə-'näk-ə\ town NW Belgium NNE of Bruges
Knos·sos *or* **Cnos·sus** \(kə-)'näs-əs\ *or* **Gnos·sus** \(gə-)'näs-əs\ ruined city ✻ of ancient Crete near N coast SE of modern Candia
Knox·ville \'näks-,vil, -vəl\ city E Tenn. on Tennessee river *pop* 175,030
Knud Ras·mus·sen Land \'nüd-'räs-,mu̇s-ᵊn, -'ras-mə-sən\ region N & NW Greenland NE of Baffin Bay
Ko·ba·rid \'kō-bə-,rēd\ *or It* **Ca·po·ret·to** \,kap-ə-'ret-(,)ō, ,käp-\ village NW Yugoslavia on the Isonzo NE of Udine, Italy
Ko·be \'kō-bē, -,bā\ city & port Japan in S Honshu on Osaka Bay *pop* 1,375,006
København — see COPENHAGEN
Ko·blenz *or* **Co·blenz** \'kō-,blen(t)s\ city W *cen* W. Germany SSE of Cologne at confluence of the Rhine & the Moselle *pop* 113,676
Ko·buk Valley National Park \kō-'bu̇k-\ reservation W Alaska N of the arctic circle along **Kobuk River**
Ko·ca \kō-'jä\ river 75 *mi* (121 *km*) S Turkey flowing SW & S into the Mediterranean
Ko·ca·bas \,kȯ-jə-'bäsh\ *or anc* **Gra·ni·cus** \grə-'nī-kəs\ river *ab* 30 *mi* (48 *km*) NW Turkey in Asia flowing NE to Sea of Marmara
Ko·chi \'kō-chē\ city & port Japan in S Shikoku *pop* 302,524
Ko–chiu \'gō-jē-'ü\ *or* **Ge·jiu** \'gəj-ē-'ü\ city S China in SE Yunnan S of Kunming *pop* 180,000
Ko·di·ak \'kōd-ē-,ak\ island S Alaska in Gulf of Alaska E of Alaska peninsula *area* 3465 *sq mi* (9009 *sq km*)
Ko·dok \'kōd-,äk\ *or formerly* **Fa·sho·da** \fə-'shōd-ə\ town SE Sudan on White Nile river
Ko·fu \'kō-(,)fü\ city Japan in S *cen* Honshu *pop* 199,430
Ko·ha·la \kō-'häl-ə\ mountains Hawaii in N Hawaii (island); highest *ab* 5500 *ft* (1676 *m*)
Ko·hi·ma \kō-'hē-mə\ town NE India ✻ of Nagaland
Koil — see ALIGARH
Ko·kand \kō-'kand\ **1** region & former khanate U.S.S.R. in Soviet Central Asia in E Uzbek Republic **2** city in Kokand region SE of Tashkent *pop* 153,000
Ko·ko·mo \'kō-kə-,mō\ city N *cen* Ind. *pop* 47,808
Ko·ko Nor \,kō-(,)kō-'nȯ(ə)r\ *or* **Qing·hai** \'chiŋ-'hī\ *or* **Ch'ing Hai** shallow saline lake W *cen* China in NE Tsinghai province S of Nan Shan mountains at altitude of *ab* 10,000 *ft* (3048 *m*) *area* 2300 *sq mi* (5980 *sq km*)
Koksoak — see KANIAPISKAU
Ko·la \'kō-lə\ peninsula 250 *mi* (402 *km*) long & 150 *mi* (241 *km*) wide U.S.S.R. in NW Soviet Russia, Europe, bet. Barents & White seas
Ko·lar Gold Fields \kō-'lär\ city S India in SE Karnataka *pop* 144,406
Kol·ha·pur \'kō-lə-,pu̇(ə)r\ city W India in SW Maharashtra SSE of Bombay *pop* 351,073
Kolmar — see COLMAR
Köln — see COLOGNE

Ko·ly·ma or **Ko·li·ma** \kə-'lē-mə\ **1** river 1110 *mi* (1786 *km*) U.S.S.R. in NE Soviet Russia, Asia, flowing from Kolyma range NE into E. Siberian sea **2** mountain range Soviet Russia, Asia, in NE Khabarovsk Territory parallel to coast of Penzhinskaya Bay

Ko·man·dor·skie \,käm-ən-'dor-skē\ or **Com·man·der** \kə-'man-dər\ islands U.S.S.R. in E Soviet Russia, Asia, in Bering sea E of Kamchatka peninsula *area* 850 *sq mi* (2210 *sq km*)

Ko·ma·ti \kə-'mät-ē\ river 500 *mi* (805 *km*) S Africa flowing from N Drakensberg mountains in NE Republic of S. Africa E & N into Delagoa Bay in S Mozambique

Ko·mi Republic \'kō-mē\ autonomous republic U.S.S.R. in NE Soviet Russia, Europe, W of N Ural mountains * Syktyvkar *area* 145,221 *sq mi* (377,575 *sq km*), *pop* 965,000

Kommunizma, Pik — see COMMUNISM PEAK

Ko·mo·do \kə-'mōd-(,)ō\ island Indonesia in the Lesser Sundas E of Sumbawa Is. & W of Flores Is. *area* 185 *sq mi* (481 *sq km*)

Kom·so·molsk \,käm(p)-sə-'mólsk\ city U.S.S.R. in E Soviet Russia, Asia, in S Khabarovsk Territory on the Amur

Ko·na \'kō-nə\ coast region Hawaii in W Hawaii (island)

Konakry — see CONAKRY

Königgrätz — see HRADEC KRALOVE

Königsberg — see KALININGRAD

Kon·kan \'kän-kən\ region W India in W Maharashtra bordering on Arabian sea & extending from Bombay S to Goa

Konstanz — see CONSTANCE

Kon·ya \'kōn-yä\ or anc **Ico·ni·um** \ī-'kō-nē-əm\ city SW cen Turkey on edge of cen plateau *pop* 325,850

Ko·o·lau \,kō-ə-'laú\ mountains Hawaii in E Oahu

Koo·te·nai or (in Canada) **Koo·te·nay** \'küt-ⁿn-,ā, -ⁿn-ē\ river 407 *mi* (655 *km*) SW Canada & NW U.S. in B.C., Mont., & Idaho flowing through **Kootenay Lake** (65 *mi* or 104 *km* long, in B.C.) into Columbia river

Kootenay National Park reservation Canada in SE B.C. including section of the upper Kootenay

Ko·per \'kō-,pe(ə)r\ or **Ko·par** \-,pär\ or It **Ca·po·dis·tria** \,kap-ə-'distrē-ə, ,käp-ə-'dēs-\ town & port Yugoslavia at N end of Istrian peninsula SSW of Trieste *pop* 16,683

Ko·peysk or **Ko·peisk** \kō-'päsk\ city U.S.S.R. in W Soviet Russia, Asia, SE of Chelyabinsk *pop* 146,000

Kor·do·fan \,kórd-ə-'fan\ region cen Sudan W & N of White Nile river; chief city El Obeid

Ko·rea \kə-'rē-ə, esp South (')kō-\ **1** peninsula 600 *mi* (966 *km*) long & 135 *mi* (217 *km*) wide E Asia bet. Yellow sea & Sea of Japan **2** strait 120 *mi* (193 *km*) wide bet. S. Korea & SW Japan connecting Sea of Japan & Yellow sea **3** or Jp **Cho·sen** \'chō-'sen\ country coextensive with Korea peninsula; once a kingdom & (1910–1945) a Japanese dependency * Seoul; divided 1948 at 38th parallel into republics of **North Korea** (* Pyongyang *area* 47,839 *sq mi* or 124,381 *sq km, pop* 18,747,000) & **South Korea** (* Seoul *area* 37,427 *sq mi* or 97,310 *sq km, pop* 37,436,315)

Korea Bay arm of Yellow sea bet. Liaotung peninsula & N. Korea

Kórinthos — see CORINTH

Kort·rijk \'kórt-,rīk\ or **Cour·trai** \kúr-'trä\ commune NW Belgium in W. Flanders on the Lys NNE of Lille *pop* 44,961

Kos or **Cos** \'käs, 'kós\ **1** island Greece in the Dodecanese *area* 111 *sq mi* (289 *sq km*), *pop* 19,987 **2** chief town on the island

Kos·ci·us·ko, Mount \,käz-ē-'əs-(,)kō\ mountain 7316 *ft* (2230 *m*) SE Australia in SE New S. Wales; highest in Great Dividing range & in Australia

Ko·si·ce \'kó-shət-,sä\ city E Czechoslovakia *pop* 202,368

Ko·stro·ma \,käs-trə-'mä\ city U.S.S.R. in N cen Soviet Russia, Europe, on the Volga *pop* 255,000

Kotabaru — see DJAJAPURA

Ko·ta Bha·ru \,kōt-ə-'bär-(,)ü\ city Malaysia in N Peninsular Malaysia * of Kelantan *pop* 281,161

Ko·ta Kin·a·ba·lu \,kōt-ə-,kin-ə-bə-'lü\ or formerly **Jes·sel·ton** \'jes-əltən\ city & port Malaysia * of Sabah *pop* 112,758

Ko·tor \'kō-,tó(ə)r\ or It **Cat·ta·ro** \'kät-ə-,rō\ town & port SE Yugoslavia in Montenegro on an inlet of the Adriatic

Kottbus — see COTTBUS

Kot·ze·bue Sound \'kät-si-,byü-\ arm of Chuckchee sea NW Alaska NE of Bering strait

Kou·chi·bou·guac National Park \kü-,shē-bü-'gwäk-\ reservation SE Canada in E N.B.

Kovno — see KAUNAS

Kow·loon \'kaú-'lün\ **1** peninsula SE China in Hong Kong colony opposite Hong Kong Is. **2** city on Kowloon peninsula

Koy·u·kuk \'kī-ə-,kək\ river 425 *mi* (684 *km*) N cen Alaska flowing from Brooks range SW into Yukon river

Kozhikode — see CALICUT

Kra, Isthmus of \'krä\ isthmus S Thailand in N cen Malay peninsula; 40 *mi* (64 *km*) wide at narrowest part

Krak·a·tau or **Krak·a·toa** \,krak-ə-'taú\ or **Krak·a·toa** \-'tō-ə\ island & volcano Indonesia bet. Sumatra & Java

Kra·ków or **Cra·cow** \'kräk-,aú, 'krak-, 'krāk-, -(,)ō, Pol 'kräk-,üf\ city S Poland on the Vistula *pop* 722,903

Kras \'kräs\ or G **Karst** \'kärst\ or It **Car·so** \'kär-(,)sō\ limestone plateau NW Yugoslavia NE of Istrian peninsula

Kras·no·dar \'kras-nə-,där\ **1** territory U.S.S.R. in S Soviet Russia, Europe, in N Caucasus region *area* 32,800 *sq mi* (85,280 *sq km*), *pop* 4,511,000 **2** or formerly **Eka·te·ri·no·dar** \i-,kat-ə-'rē-nə-,där\ city, its *, on the Kuban *pop* 560,000

Kras·no·yarsk \,kras-nə-'yärsk\ **1** territory U.S.S.R. in W cen Soviet Russia, Asia, extending along valley of the Yenisey from Arctic ocean to Sayan mountains *area* 928,000 *sq mi* (2,412,800 *sq km*), *pop* 2,962,000 **2** city, its *, on the upper Yenisey *pop* 796,000

Kre·feld \'krā-,felt\ or formerly **Krefeld–Uer·din·gen** \'ürd-in-ən, -'uer-\ city W W. Germany on the Rhine WSW of Essen *pop* 223,969

Krim — see CRIMEA

Krish·na \'krish-nə\ or formerly **Kist·na** \'kist-nə\ river 800 *mi* (1287 *km*) S India flowing from Western Ghats E into Bay of Bengal

Kristiania — see OSLO

Kris·tian·sand \'kris(h)-chən-,san(d)\ city & port SW Norway on the Skagerrak SW of Oslo *pop* 60,945

Kris·tian·sund \-,sün(d)\ city & port W Norway *pop* 17,936

Kríti — see CRETE

Kri·voy Rog or **Kri·voi Rog** \,kriv-,ói-'rōg, -'rók\ city U.S.S.R. in SE cen Ukrainian Republic NE of Odessa *pop* 650,000

Kru·ger National Park \'krü-gər\ game reserve NE Republic of S. Africa in E Transvaal on Mozambique border

Kru·gers·dorp \'krü-gərz-,dórp, 'krū̄-ərz-\ city NE Republic of S. Africa in S Transvaal W of Johannesburg *pop* 92,725

Krung Thep — see BANGKOK

K2 \'kā-'tü\ or **God·win Aus·ten** \,gäd-wə-'nós-tən, -'näs-\ mountain 28,250 *ft* (8611 *m*) N Kashmir in Karakoram range; 2d highest in the world

Kua·la Lum·pur \,kwäl-ə-'lüm-,pú(ə)r, -'ləm-\ city * of Malaysia in Peninsular Malaysia *pop* 937,875

Kuang–chou — see CANTON

Ku·ban \kü-'bän, -'bän\ river 512 *mi* (824 *km*) U.S.S.R. flowing from the Caucasus N & W into Sea of Azov

Ku·ching \'kü-chiŋ\ city & port Malaysia * of Sarawak *pop* 231,490

Ku·dus \-,üs\ city Indonesia in cen Java NE of Semarang

Kuei \'gwä\ or **Gui** \'gwē\ river 200 *mi* (322 *km*) SE China in E Kwangsi Chuang flowing S into the Hsi

Kuei–lin \'gwā-'lin\ or **Gui·lin** \'gwē-'lin\ or **Kwei·lin** \'gwä-\ city S China in NE Kwangsi Chuang on the Kuei *pop* 170,000

Kuei–yang \'gwā-'yäŋ\ or **Gui·yang** \gə-'wē-'yäŋ, 'gwē-'yäŋ\ or **Kwei·yang** \'gwā-\ city S China * of Kweichow *pop* 530,000

Kufra — see AL KUFRAH

Kui·by·shev or **Kuy·by·shev** \'kwē-bə-,shef, 'kü-ē-bə-, -,shev\ or formerly **Sa·ma·ra** \sə-'mär-ə\ city U.S.S.R. in SE Soviet Russia, Europe, in valley of the Volga *pop* 1,047,000

Ku·la Gulf \,kü-lə-\ body of water 17 *mi* (27 *km*) long in the Solomons bet. New Georgia & adjacent islands

Kul·dja \'kúl-(,)jä\ or **Gul·ja** \'gúl-\ city W China in NW Sinkiang Uighur *pop* 85,000

Kum \'küm\ river 247 *mi* (398 *km*) cen S. Korea flowing into Yellow sea

Ku·ma·mo·to \,kü-mə-'mōt-(,)ō\ city Japan in W Kyushu *pop* 532,590

Ku·ma·si \kü-'mäs-ē, -'mas-\ city S cen Ghana in Ashanti *pop* 415,280

Kum·chon \'küm-,chän\ city cen S. Korea NW of Taegu

Kumgang — see DIAMOND

Kunene — see CUNENE

Kun·lun \'kün-'lün\ mountains W China extending from the Pamirs & Karakoram range E along N edge of Tibetan plateau to SE Tsinghai — see ULUGH MUZTAGH

Kun·ming \'kún-'miŋ\ or formerly **Yun·nan** \yü-'nän\ or **Yun·nan·fu** \-'fü\ city S China * of Yunnan *pop* 900,000

Kun·san \'gün-,sän\ city & port W S. Korea on Yellow sea at mouth of the Kum *pop* 165,318

Kun·tse·vo \'kün(t)-sə-,vō\ city U.S.S.R. in Soviet Russia, Europe, SW suburb of Moscow

Ku·pre·a·nof \'kü-prē-'an-,óf\ island SE Alaska in E Alexander archipelago

Ku·ra \kə-'rä, 'kúr-ə\ river 825 *mi* (1328 *km*) W Asia in Transcaucasia flowing from NE Turkey ESE through Georgia & Azerbaijan, U.S.S.R., into Caspian sea

Kur·di·stan \,kúrd-ə-'stan, ,kərd-\ region SW Asia chiefly in E Turkey, NW Iran, & N Iraq

Ku·re \'k(y)ú(ə)r-ē, 'kü-(,)rä\ **1** or **Ocean** island cen Pacific in Hawaii, westernmost of the Leewards **2** city & port Japan in SW Honshu on Inland sea SSE of Hiroshima *pop* 233,315

Kurg — see COORG

Kur·gan \kú(ə)r-'gan, -'gän\ city U.S.S.R. in W Soviet Russia, Asia, E of Chelyabinsk *pop* 310,000

Ku·ria Mu·ria \,k(y)úr-ē-ə-'m(y)úr-ē-ə\ islands in Arabian sea off SW Oman belonging to Oman *area* 28 *sq mi* (73 *sq km*), *pop* 85

Ku·ril or **Ku·rile** \'kyü(ə)r-,ēl, kyü-'rē(ə)l\ islands U.S.S.R. in the Pacific bet. S Kamchatka & NE Hokkaido, Japan; belonged 1875–1945 to Japan *area* 3960 *sq mi* (10,296 *sq km*)

Kur·isch·es Haff \,kúr-ish-əs-'häf\ or **Cour·land Lagoon** \,kúr-lənd-\ or **Kur·skiy Za·liv** \,kúr-skyē-'zäl-if\ inlet of the Baltic W U.S.S.R. on border bet. Lithuania & Soviet Russia *area* 625 *sq mi* (1625 *sq km*)

Kur·land or **Cour·land** \'kú(ə)r-lənd\ region U.S.S.R. in W Latvia bordering on the Baltic & Gulf of Riga

Kur·nool \kər-'nül\ city S India in W Andhra Pradesh SSW of Hyderabad *pop* 206,661

Kursk \'kú(ə)rsk\ city U.S.S.R. in SW Soviet Russia, Europe, on the Seym *pop* 375,000

Ku·saie \kü-'sī-,ā\ island E Carolines, part of Federated States of Micronesia

Kush — see CUSH

Kus·ko·kwim \'kəs-kə-,kwim\ river 550 *mi* (885 *km*) SW Alaska flowing SW into Kuskokwim Bay (inlet of Bering sea)

Kut \'küt\ or **Al–kut** \al-\ or **Kut–al–Ima·ra** \,al-ē-'mär-ə\ city SE cen Iraq on the Tigris SE of Baghdad *pop* 42,116

Ku·tah·ya \kü-'tä-yə\ city W cen Turkey *pop* 101,087

Kutch or **Cutch** \'kəch\ former principality & state W India N of Gulf of Kutch * Bhuj; now part of Gujarat

Kutch, Gulf of inlet of Arabian sea W India N of Kathiawar

Kutch, Rann of \,rən-\ salt marsh in S Pakistan & W India stretching in an arc from the mouths of the Indus to the head of Gulf of Kutch

Ku·wait \kü-'wät\ **1** country SW Asia in Arabia at head of Persian Gulf; a sheikhdom, before 1961 under Brit. protection *area* 6178 *sq mi* (16,063 *sq km*), *pop* 1,355,827 **2** city & port, its * *pop* 181,774 — **Ku·waiti** \-'wät-ē\ adj or n

Kuz·netsk \küz-'netsk\ city U.S.S.R. in SE cen Soviet Russia, Europe

Kuznetsk Basin or **Kuz·bass** or **Kuz·bas** \'küz-,bas\ basin of the Tom U.S.S.R. in W cen Soviet Russia, Asia, extending from Novokuznetsk to Tomsk

---

Kwa·ja·lein \'kwäj-ə-lən, -,län\ island (atoll) 78 *mi* (126 *km*) long W Pacific in Ralik chain of the Marshalls; encloses lagoon (*area* 650 *sq mi* or 1690 *sq km*)
Kwan·do \'kwän-(,)dō\ river 600 *mi* (966 *km*) S Africa flowing from *cen* Angola SE & E into the Zambezi just above Victoria Falls
Kwang·cho·wan \'gwäŋ-'jō-'wän, 'kwäŋ-\ former territory SE China in Kwangtung on Lei-chou peninsula; leased 1898–1946 to France ✻ Fort Bayard *area* 325 *sq mi* (845 *sq km*)
Kwang·ju \'gwäŋ-(,)jü, 'kwäŋ-\ city SW S. Korea *pop* 726,627
Kwang·si Chuang \'gwäŋ-'shē-'wäŋ\ *or* **Guang·xi Zhuang·zu** \-'wäŋ-zü\ region & former province S China W of Kwangtung ✻ Nanning *area* 85,096 *sq mi* (221,250 *sq km*)
Kwang·tung \'gwäŋ-'dùŋ, 'kwäŋ-, -'tùŋ\ *or* **Guang·dong** \'gwäŋ-'dùŋ\ province SE China bordering on S. China sea & Gulf of Tonkin ✻ Canton *area* 76,344 *sq mi* (198,494 *sq km*), *pop* (with Hainan) 59,299,220
Kwan·tung \'gwän-'dùŋ, 'kwän-, -'tùŋ\ former territory NE China in S Manchuria at tip of Liaotung peninsula; leased to Russia 1898–1905, to Japan 1905–45, & to Russia again 1945–55; included cities of Port Arthur & Dairen
Kwei·chow \'gwā-'jō, 'kwā-\ *or* **Gui·zhou** \'gwē-'jō\ province S China S of Szechwan ✻ Kuei-yang *area* 67,181 *sq mi* (174,671 *sq km*), *pop* 28,552,997
Kweilin — see KUEI-LIN
Kyo·ga *or* **Kio·ga** \kē-'ō-gə\ lake *cen* Uganda N of Lake Victoria traversed by the Victoria Nile *area* 1000 *sq mi* (2600 *sq km*)
Kyo·to \kē-'ōt-(,)ō\ city Japan in W *cen* Honshu NNE of Osaka; formerly (794–1869) ✻ of Japan *pop* 1,480,278
Kyu·shu \kē-'ü-(,)shü\ island S Japan S of W end of Honshu *area* 16,240 *sq mi* (42,224 *sq km*)
Laaland — see LOLLAND
La Baie \lä-'bā\ city Canada in S *cen* Que. *pop* 20,935
Labe — see ELBE
Lab·ra·dor \'lab-rə-,dò(ə)r\ **1** peninsula E Canada bet. Hudson bay & the Atlantic; divided bet. Que. & Nfld. **2** the section of the peninsula belonging to Nfld. *area* 101,881 *sq mi* (264,891 *sq km*) **3** sea, arm of the Atlantic bet. Labrador & Greenland — **Lab·ra·dor·ean** *or* **Lab·ra·dor·ian** \,lab-rə-'dòr-ē-ən, -'dōr-\ *adj or n*
La·bu·an \lə-'bü-ən\ island Malaysia off W coast of Sabah *pop* 14,904
Lac·ca·dive \'lak-ə-,dēv, -,dīv\ *or* **Can·na·nore** \'kan-ə-,nōr\ islands India in Arabian sea N of Maldive islands
Lacedaemon — see SPARTA — **Lac·e·dae·mo·nian** \,las-əd-i-'mō-nē-ən, -nyən\ *adj or n*
La Chaux–de–Fonds \lä-,shōd-ə-'fōⁿ\ commune W Switzerland in Neuchâtel canton in Jura mountains WNW of Bern *pop* 37,234
La·chine \lə-'shēn\ city Canada in S Que. above the **Lachine Rapids** on St. Lawrence river SW of Montreal *pop* 37,521
La·chish \'lā-kish\ ancient city S Palestine W of Hebron
Lach·lan \'läk-lən\ river 800 *mi* (1287 *km*) SE Australia in *cen* New S. Wales flowing W into the Murrumbidgee
Lack·a·wan·na \,lak-ə-'wän-ə\ city W N.Y. *pop* 22,701
La·co·nia \lə-'kō-nē-ə, -nyə\ ancient country S Greece in SE Peloponnisos bordering on the Aegean & the Mediterranean ✻ Sparta — **La·co·nian** \-nē-ən, -nyən\ *adj or n*
Laconia, Gulf of inlet of the Mediterranean on S coast of Greece in Peloponnisos bet. capes Matapan & Malea
La Co·ru·ña \,lä-kə-'rün-yə\ **1** province NW Spain in Galicia bordering on the Atlantic *area* 3051 *sq mi* (7933 *sq km*), *pop* 1,068,088 **2** *or* **Co·run·na** \kə-'rən-ə\ commune & port, its ✻ *pop* 231,721
La Crosse \lə-'kròs\ city W Wis. *pop* 48,347
La·dakh \lə-'däk\ district N India in E Kashmir on border of Tibet ✻ Leh *area* 45,762 *sq mi* (118,981 *sq km*) — **La·dakhi** \-'däk-ē\ *adj or n*
Lad·o·ga \'lad-ə-gə, 'läd-\ lake U.S.S.R. in NW Soviet Russia, Europe, near Leningrad *area* 7000 *sq mi* (18,200 *sq km*); largest in Europe
Ladrone — see MARIANA
La·dy·smith \'lād-ē-,smith\ city E Republic of S. Africa in W Natal *pop* 28,920
Lae \'lä-,ā\ city Papua New Guinea on Huon Gulf *pop* 61,617
La·fay·ette \,laf-ē-'et, ,läf-\ **1** city W Calif. E of Berkeley *pop* 20,879 **2** city W *cen* Ind. *pop* 43,011 **3** city S La. *pop* 81,961
La·gash \'lā-,gash\ ancient city of Sumer bet. the Euphrates & the Tigris at modern village of Telloh \te-'lō\ in S Iraq
Lagoa dos Patos — see PATOS (Lagoa dos)
La·gos \'lā-,gäs\ city & port ✻ of Nigeria on an offshore island in Bight of Benin & on mainland opposite the island *pop* 1,060,848
La Gou·lette \,lä-gù-'let\ city N Tunisia on Bay of Tunis; port for Tunis *pop* 41,912
La Grange \lə-'grānj\ city W Ga. *pop* 24,204
La Granja — see SAN ILDEFONSO
La Guai·ra \lə-'gwī-rə\ city N Venezuela on the Caribbean; port for Caracas *pop* 20,344
La·gu·na Beach \lə-,gü-nə-\ city SW Calif. SE of Long Beach *pop* 17,901
Laguna Madre — see MADRE (Laguna)
La Habana — see HAVANA
La Ha·bra \lə-'häb-rə\ city SW Calif. SE of Los Angeles *pop* 45,232
La Hague, Cape \lə-'hāg, -'häg\ *or F* **Cap de la Hague** \kàp-də-là-àg\ headland NW France at tip of Cotentin peninsula
La Hogue \lə-'hōg\ roadstead NW France in English channel off E coast of Cotentin peninsula
La·hore \lə-'hō(ə)r, -'hò(ə)r\ city Pakistan in E Punjab province near the Ravi *pop* 2,922,000
Lah·ti \'lät-ē\ city S Finland NNE of Helsinki *pop* 94,875
La Jol·la \lə-'hòi-ə\ a NW section of San Diego, Calif.
Lake Charles \-'chär(ə)lz\ city SW La. *pop* 75,226
Lake Clark National Park \-'klärk-\ reservation S *cen* Alaska WSW of Anchorage
Lake District area NW England in S Cumbria & NW Lancashire containing many lakes & peaks
Lake Jack·son \-'jak-sən\ city SE Tex. *pop* 19,102
Lake·land \'lā-klənd\ city *cen* Fla. E of Tampa *pop* 47,406
Lake Os·we·go \-ä-'swē-(,)gō\ city NW Oreg. S of Portland *pop* 22,868
Lake·wood \'lā-,kwùd\ **1** city SW Calif. NE of Long Beach *pop* 74,654 **2** city N *cen* Colo. W of Denver *pop* 112,860 **3** city NE Ohio on Lake Erie W of Cleveland *pop* 61,963
Lake Worth \-'wərth\ city SE Fla. on Lake Worth (lagoon) S of W. Palm Beach *pop* 27,048
Lak·shad·weep \lək-'shäd-,wēp\ *or formerly* **Lac·ca·dive, Min·i·coy, and Admin·di·vi Islands** \'lak-ə-,dēv, -,dīv; 'min-i-,kòi; ,əm-ən-'dē-vē\ union territory India comprising the Laccadive group ✻ Kavaratti *area* 11 *sq mi* (29 *sq km*), *pop* 40,237
La Lí·nea \lä-'lē-nē-ə\ commune SW Spain on Bay of Algeciras *pop* 51,021
La Man·cha \lə-'män-chə, -'man-\ region S *cen* Spain in S New Castile — **Man·che·gan** \man-'chē-gən\ *adj or n*
La Mau·ri·cie National Park \lä-,mò-rē-'sē-\ reservation SE Canada in S Quebec
Lam·ba·ré·né \,läm-bə-'rā-nē, -rə-'nā\ city W Gabon *pop* 17,770
Lam·beth \'lam-bəth, -,beth\ borough of S Greater London, England *pop* 256,200
La Me·sa \lə-'mā-sə\ city SW Calif. NE of San Diego *pop* 50,308
La·mia \lə-'mē-ə\ city E *cen* Greece NW of Thermopylae *pop* 42,019
La Mi·ra·da \,läm-ə-'räd-ə\ city SW Calif. SE of Los Angeles *pop* 40,986
Lam·mer·muir \'lam-ər-,myù(ə)r\ *or* **Lam·mer·moor** \-,mù(ə)r\ hills SE Scotland in Lothian & Borders regions
Lam·pe·du·sa \,lam-pə-'dü-sə, -zə\ island Italy in the Pelagians *pop* 4387
La·nai \lə-'nī\ island Hawaii W of Maui *area* 141 *sq mi* (367 *sq km*)
Lan·ark \'lan-ərk\ **1** *or* **Lan·ark·shire** \-,shi(ə)r, -shər\ former county S *cen* Scotland; chief city Glasgow **2** burgh *cen* Scotland in Strathclyde SE of Glasgow *pop* 9778
Lan·ca·shire \'laŋ-kə-,shi(ə)r, -shər\ *or* **Lan·cas·ter** \'laŋ-kə-stər\ county NW England bordering on Irish Sea ✻ Preston *area* 1174 *sq mi* (3052 *sq km*), *pop* 1,382,200
Lan·cas·ter \'laŋ-kə-stər; 'lan-,kas-tər, 'laŋ-\ **1** city S *cen* Ohio SE of Columbus *pop* 34,953 **2** city SE Pa. *pop* 54,725 **3** city NW England in Lancashire *pop* 46,321 — **Lan·cas·tri·an** \laŋ-'kas-trē-ən, lan-\ *adj or n*
Lan–chou *or* **Lan·zhou** \'län-'jō\ city N *cen* China ✻ of Kansu *pop* 1,500,000
Landes \'läⁿ(n)d\ coastal region SW France on Bay of Biscay bet. Gironde estuary & the Adour
Land's End \'lan(d)-'zend\ cape SW England at SW tip of Cornwall; extreme W point of England, at 5°41'W
Lang·dale Pikes \,laŋ-,dāl-\ two mountain peaks NW England in Cumbria in Lake District
Lan·gue·doc \,laŋ-gə-'däk, ,läⁿ(ŋ)-gə-'dòk\ region & former province S France extending from Auvergne to the Mediterranean
Lanka — see CEYLON
Lans·dale \'lanz-,dāl\ borough SE Pa. NW of Philadelphia *pop* 16,526
Lan·sing \'lan(t)-siŋ\ **1** village NE Ill. SSE of Chicago *pop* 29,039 **2** city S Mich., its ✻ *pop* 130,414
Lan·tao \'län-'daù\ island Hong Kong colony W of Hong Kong Is. *area* 58 *sq mi* (151 *sq km*)
La·nús \lə-'nüs\ city E Argentina S of Buenos Aires *pop* 465,891
La·od·i·cea \(,)lā-,äd-ə-'sē-ə\ **1** ancient city W *cen* Asia Minor in Phrygia **2** — see LATAKIA — **La·od·i·ce·an** \-'sē-ən\ *adj or n*
Laoighis \'lāsh, 'lēsh\ *or* **Leix** \'lāsh, 'lēsh\ *or formerly* **Queen's** county *cen* Ireland in Leinster ✻ Portlaoighise *area* 664 *sq mi* (1726 *sq km*), *pop* 51,171
Laon \läⁿ\ commune N France NE of Paris *pop* 27,420
Laos \'laùs, 'lä-(,)ōs, 'lā-,äs\ country SE Asia; a republic, until 1975 a kingdom; formerly a state of French Indochina; ✻ Vientiane *area* 91,482 *sq mi* (237,853 *sq km*), *pop* 4,104,000
La Pal·ma \lə-'päl-mə\ island Spain in Canary islands; chief town Santa Cruz de la Palma *area* 280 *sq mi* (728 *sq km*)
La Paz \lə-'paz, -'päz, -'päs\ **1** city, administrative ✻ of Bolivia E of Lake Titicaca at altitude of 11,910 *ft* (3630 *m*), *pop* 635,283 **2** town W Mexico ✻ of Baja California Sur on **La Paz Bay** (inlet of Gulf of California) *pop* 46,011
Lap·land \'lap-,land, -lənd\ region N Europe above the arctic circle in N Norway, N Sweden, N Finland, & Kola peninsula of the U.S.S.R. — **Lap·land·er** \-,lan-dər, -lən-\ *n*
La Pla·ta \lə-'plät-ə\ city E Argentina SE of Buenos Aires *pop* 454,884
La Plata Peak \lə-,plat-ə-\ mountain 14,336 *ft* (4370 *m*) *cen* Colo. in Sawatch mountains
La Porte \lə-'pō(ə)rt, -'pò(ə)rt\ city N Ind. *pop* 21,796
Lap·tev \'lap-,tef, -,tev\ *or formerly* **Nor·den·skjöld** \'nórd-ᵊn-,shəld, -,shùld, -,sheld\ sea, arm of Arctic ocean U.S.S.R. bet. Taimyr peninsula & New Siberian islands
La Pu·en·te \lä-'pwent-ē\ city SW Calif. ESE of Los Angeles *pop* 30,882
L'Aqui·la \'läk-wi-lə, 'lak-\ commune *cen* Italy NE of Rome ✻ of Abruzzi *pop* 63,465
Lar·a·mie \'lar-ə-mē\ **1** river 200 *mi* (322 *km*) N Colo. & SE Wyo. flowing N & NE into N. Platte river **2** city SE Wyo. *pop* 24,410
Larch \'lärch\ river 270 *mi* (434 *km*) Canada in W Que. flowing NE to unite with the Kaniapiskau forming Koksoak river
La·re·do \lə-'rād-(,)ō\ city S Tex. on Rio Grande *pop* 91,449
Lar·go \'lär-(,)gō\ town W Fla. S of Clearwater *pop* 58,977
La Rio·ja \,lä-rē-'ō-hä\ *or* **the Rioja** region N Spain along the upper Ebro
La·ris·sa \lə-'ris-ə\ city N *cen* Greece in E Thessaly *pop* 103,263
Lar·i·stan \,lar-ə-'stan\ region S Iran bordering on Persian Gulf
Larne \'lärn\ district NE Northern Ireland, established 1974 *area* 131 *sq mi* (341 *sq km*), *pop* 28,929
La Ro·chelle \,lär-ə-'shel\ city & port W France *pop* 72,936
Lar·vik \'lär-vik\ town & port SE Norway *pop* 8133
La·Salle \lə-'sal\ city Canada in S Que. on the St. Lawrence *pop* 76,299
Las·caux \la-'skō\ cave SW *cen* France near town of Montignac
Las Cru·ces \läs-'krü-sās\ city S N.Mex. *pop* 45,086
La Se·re·na \,läs-ə-'rā-nə\ city N *cen* Chile *pop* 99,908
La·shio \lə-'shō\ town E *cen* Burma
Lashkar — see GWALIOR
Las Pal·mas \läs-'päl-məs\ **1** province Spain comprising the E Canary islands *area* 1279 *sq mi* (3325 *sq km*), *pop* 767,912 **2** city & port, its ✻, in NE Grand Canary Is. *pop* 360,098
La Spe·zia \lä-'spet-sē-ə\ city & port NW Italy in Liguria *pop* 115,215
Las·sen Peak \'las-ᵊn-\ volcano 10,457 *ft* (3187 *m*) N Calif. at S end of Cascade range; central feature of **Lassen Volcanic National Park**
Las Ve·gas \läs-'vā-gəs\ city SE corner of Nev. *pop* 164,674

Lat·a·kia \‚lat-ə-'kē-ə\ **1** region NW Syria bordering on the Mediterranean **2** or anc **La·od·i·cea** \(‚)lā-‚äd-ə-'sē-ə\ city & port, its chief town, on the Mediterranean pop 196,791
Latin America 1 Spanish America & Brazil **2** all of the Americas S of the U.S. — **Latin–American** adj — **Latin American** n
La·tium \'lā-sh(ē-)əm\ or It **La·zio** \'lät-sē-‚ō\ region cen Italy bordering on Tyrrhenian sea & traversed by the Tiber ✳ Rome
Lat·via \'lat-vē-ə\ country N Europe bordering on the Baltic; an independent republic 1918–40, since 1940 a constituent republic (**Lat·vi·an Republic** \‚lat-vē-ən-\) of the U.S.S.R. ✳ Riga area 25,200 sq mi (65,520 sq km), pop 2,521,000
Lau·der·dale Lakes \‚lòd-ər-‚dāl-\ city SE Fla. pop 25,426
Lau·der·hill \'lòd-ər-‚hil\ city SE Fla. pop 37,271
Laun·ces·ton \'lòn(t)-sə-stən, 'län(t)-\ city & port Australia in N Tasmania pop (with suburbs) 31,273
Lau·ra·sia \lòr-'ā-zhə, -shə\ hypothetical land area believed to have once connected the landmasses of the northern hemisphere except for the Indian subcontinent
Lau·rel \'lòr-əl, 'lär-\ city SE Miss. pop 21,897
Lau·ren·tian \lò-'ren-chən\ hills Canada in S Que. N of the St. Lawrence on S edge of Canadian Shield
Laurentian Shield — see CANADIAN SHIELD
Lau·ri·um \'lòr-ē-əm, 'lär-\ mountain SE Greece at SE tip of Attica
Lau·sanne \lō-'zän, -'zan\ commune W Switzerland ✳ of Vaud canton on Lake of Geneva pop 127,349
Lausitz — see LUSATIA
Lava Beds National Monument reservation N Calif. SE of Lower Klamath Lake
La·val \lə-'val\ city Canada in S Que. NW of Montreal pop 246,243
La Vendée — see VENDÉE
La Verne \lə-'vərn\ city SW Calif. E of Los Angeles pop 23,508
Lawn·dale \'lòn-‚dāl, 'län-\ city SW Calif. SSW of Los Angeles pop 23,460
Law·rence \'lòr-ən(t)s, 'lär-\ **1** town cen Ind. NE of Indianapolis pop 25,591 **2** city NE Kans. WSW of Kansas City pop 52,738 **3** city NE corner of Mass. pop 63,175
Law·ton \'lòt-ᵊn\ city SW Okla. pop 80,054
Lay·san \'lī-‚sän\ island Hawaii in the Leewards NW of Niihau
Lay·ton \'lāt-ᵊn\ city N Utah N of Salt Lake City pop 22,862
League City \'lēg-\ city SE Tex. pop 16,578
Leam·ing·ton \'lem-iŋ-tən\ or **Royal Leamington Spa** borough S cen England in Warwickshire pop 44,989
Leav·en·worth \'lev-ən-‚wərth\ city NE Kans. on Missouri river NW of Kansas City pop 33,656
Leb·a·non 1 \'leb-ə-nən\ city SE cen Pa. E of Harrisburg pop 25,711 **2** \-nən, -‚nän\ or anc **Lib·a·nus** \'lib-ə-nəs\ mountains Lebanon running parallel to coast W of Bekaa valley **3** \-nən, -‚nän\ country SW Asia bordering on the Mediterranean; a republic since 1944, formerly (1920–44) a French mandate ✳ Beirut area 4105 sq mi (10,673 sq km), pop 2,707,000 — **Leb·a·nese** \‚leb-ə-'nēz, -'nēs\ adj or n
Lebda — see HOMS
Le Bour·get \lə-‚bùr-'zhā\ commune N France, NE suburb of Paris
Lec·ce \'lā-chē, 'lech-ē\ commune SE Italy in Apulia pop 91,265
Lec·co \'lā-(‚)kō, 'lek-(‚)ō\ commune N Italy in Lombardy on SE arm (**Lake Lecco**) of Lake Como pop 51,349
Lech \'lek, 'lek\ river 177 mi (285 km) Austria & W. Germany flowing from Vorarlberg N into the Danube
Le·do \'lēd-‚ō, 'lād-\ town NE India in NE Assam
Leeds \'lēdz\ city N England in W. Yorkshire pop 448,528
Lee's Summit \'lēz-\ city W Mo. SE of Kansas City pop 28,741
Leeu·war·den \'lā-‚värd-ᵊn\ commune N Netherlands ✳ of Friesland pop 85,058
Lee·ward \'lē-wərd\ **1** island chain cen Pacific extending 1250 mi (2012 km) WNW from main islands of the Hawaiian group; includes Nihoa, Necker, Laysan, Midway, & Kure islands **2** or F **Îles sous le Vent** \‚ēl-sü-lə-'väⁿ\ islands S Pacific, W group of the Society islands **3** islands W. Indies in the N Lesser Antilles extending from Virgin islands (on N) to Dominica (on S) ✳ former colony Brit. W. Indies in the Leewards including Antigua, St. Kitts-Nevis, & Montserrat
Leg·horn \'leg-‚(h)ò(ə)rn\ or It **Li·vor·no** \li-'vòr-(‚)nō\ commune & port cen Italy in Tuscany on Tyrrhenian sea pop 175,371
Leh \'lā\ town India in E Kashmir on the Indus ✳ of Ladakh
Le Ha·vre \lə-'hävr\ or **Havre** or formerly **Le Ha·vre–de–Grâce** \lə-‚häv-rəd-ə-'gräs, -‚häv-də-\ city & port N France on English channel on N side of Seine estuary pop 216,917
Le·high \'lē-‚hī\ river 100 mi (161 km) E Pa. flowing SW & SE into Delaware river
Leh·man Caves \‚lē-mən-\ limestone caverns E Nev. on E slope of Wheeler Peak in Great Basin National Park
Leices·ter \'les-tər\ city cen England ✳ of Leicestershire pop 279,791
Leices·ter·shire \'les-tər-‚shi(ə)r, -shər\ or **Leicester** \'les-tər\ county cen England ✳ Leicester area 986 sq mi (2564 sq km), pop 857,700
Lei·chou or **Lei·zhou** \'lā-'jō\ or **Lui·chow** \lə-'wē-‚jō\ peninsula SE China in Kwangtung bet. S. China sea & Gulf of Tonkin
Lei·den or **Ley·den** \'līd-ᵊn, D usu 'lā-yə\ city W Netherlands in S. Holland on a branch of the lower Rhine pop 103,678
Leie — see LYS
Lei·ne \'lī-nə\ river 119 mi (192 km) E W. Germany & W E. Germany
Lein·ster \'len(t)-stər\ province E Ireland area 7580 sq mi (19,708 sq km), pop 1,494,544
Leip·zig \'līp-sig, -sik\ city S cen E. Germany in Saxony pop 561,867
Lei·ria \lā-'rē-ə\ town W cen Portugal SSW of Coimbra
Leith \'lēth\ port section of Edinburgh, Scotland, on Firth of Forth
Lei·tha \'lī-(‚)tä\ river 112 mi (180 km) E Austria & NW Hungary flowing SE into the Raba
Lei·trim \'lē-trəm\ county NW Ireland in Connacht ✳ Carrick on Shannon area 589 sq mi (1531 sq km), pop 27,609
Leix — see LAOIGHIS
Lei·xões \lā-'shōiⁿsh\ town NW Portugal on the Atlantic; port for Porto
Lek \'lek\ river 40 mi (64 km) Netherlands flowing W into the Atlantic; the N branch of the lower Rhine
Lely·stad \'lel-ē-‚stät\ commune cen Netherlands ✳ of Flevoland
Le Maine — see MAINE
Leman, Lake — see GENEVA (Lake of)

Le Mans \lə-'mäⁿ\ city NW France on the Sarthe pop 150,289
Le Marche — see MARCHES
Lemberg — see LVOV
Lem·nos \'lem-‚näs, -nəs\ or NGk **Lím·nos** \'lēm-‚nòs\ island Greece in the Aegean ESE of Chalcidice peninsula; chief town Kástron area 175 sq mi (455 sq km)
Le·na \'lē-nə, 'lā-\ river 3000 mi (4828 km) U.S.S.R. in W Soviet Russia, Asia, flowing from mountains W of Lake Baikal NE & N into Laptev sea through wide delta
Le·nexa \lə-'nek-sə\ city E Kans. SW of Kansas City pop 18,639
Len·in·grad \'len-ən-‚grad\ or formerly (1703–1914) **Saint Pe·ters·burg** \sänt-'pēt-ərz-‚bərg, sant-\ or (1914–24) **Pet·ro·grad** \'pe-trə-‚grad\ city U.S.S.R. in NW Soviet Russia, Europe, at E end of Gulf of Finland; ✳ of Russian Empire 1712–1917, pop 3,513,000 — **Len·in·grad·er** \'len-ən-‚grad-ər\ n
Le·nin Peak \‚len-ən-, ‚lān-, -‚ēn-\ mountain 23,405 ft (7134 m) on border bet. Kirghiz & Tadzhik republics; highest in Trans Alai range
Lens \'läⁿs\ city N France SW of Lille pop 39,973
Leom·in·ster \'lem-ən-stər\ city N Worcester pop 34,508
Le·ón \lā-'ōn\ **1** or **León de los Al·da·mas** \-də-‚lò-‚sal-'däm-əs\ city cen Mexico in Guanajuato pop 453,976 **2** city W Nicaragua pop 90,897 **3** region & ancient kingdom NW Spain W of Old Castile **4** province NW Spain in N León region area 5936 sq mi (15,434 sq km), pop 491,911 **5** city, its ✳ pop 127,095
Le·o·ne, Mon·te \‚mòn-tē-lā-'ō-nē\ mountain 11,657 ft (3553 m) on border bet. Switzerland & Italy SW of Simplon pass; highest in Lepontine Alps
Le·o·pold II, Lake \'lē-ə-‚pōld, 'lā-\ lake 90 mi (145 km) long W Zaire
Léopoldville — see KINSHASA
Lepanto, Gulf of — see CORINTH (Gulf of)
Le·pon·tine Alps \li-‚pän-‚tīn-, ‚lep-ən-\ range of cen Alps on border bet. Switzerland & Italy — see LEONE (Monte)
Lep·tis Mag·na \‚lep-tə-'smag-nə\ ancient seaport N Africa near present-day Homs
Lé·ri·da \'lā-rəd-ə, 'ler-əd-\ **1** province NE Spain in NW Catalonia area 4690 sq mi (12,194 sq km) pop 340,167 **2** commune, its ✳ pop 106,814
Ler·wick \'lər-(‚)wik, 'le(ə)r-\ burgh & port N Scotland ✳ of Shetland on Mainland Is. pop 7223
Les Ey·zies \lā-zā-'zē\ commune SW cen France SE of Périgueux
Le·so·tho \lə-'sō-(‚)tō, -'süt-(‚)ü\ or formerly **Ba·su·to·land** \bə-'süt-ə-‚land\ country S Africa surrounded by Republic of S. Africa; a constitutional monarchy, in the Commonwealth ✳ Maseru area 11,716 sq mi (30,462 sq km), pop 1,528,000
Lesser An·til·les \an-'til-‚ēz\ islands in the W. Indies including Virgin, Leeward, & Windward islands, Trinidad, Barbados, Tobago, & islands in the S Caribbean N of Venezuela
Lesser Armenia region S Turkey corresponding to ancient Cilicia
Lesser Slave Lake \'släv\ lake Canada in cen Alta. draining through the **Lesser Slave** river to Athabasca river area 461 sq mi (1199 sq km)
Lesser Sunda — see SUNDA
Lés·vos \'lez-‚vòs\ or **Les·bos** \'lez-‚bäs, -bəs\ island Greece in the Aegean off NW Turkey area 623 sq mi (1620 sq km)
Leth·bridge \'leth-(‚)brij\ city Canada in S Alta. pop 54,072
Le·ti·cia \lā-'tē-sē-ə\ town SE Colombia on the Amazon
Leuc·tra \'lük-trə\ ancient village Greece in Boeotia SW of Thebes
Leuven — see LOUVAIN
Le·val·lois–Per·ret \lə-‚val-‚wä-pə-'rā\ commune N France on the Seine, NW suburb of Paris pop 52,460
Levant \lə-'vant\ the countries bordering on the E Mediterranean — **Le·van·tine** \'lev-ən-‚tīn, -‚tēn, lə-'van-\ adj or n
Levant States — see SYRIA
Le·ven, Loch \'lē-vən\ **1** inlet of Loch Linnhe W Scotland in Highland region **2** lake 4 mi (6.4 km) long E Scotland SSE of Perth
Le·ver·ku·sen \'lā-vər-‚küz-ᵊn\ city W W. Germany on the Rhine SE of Düsseldorf pop 160,825
Lé·vis \lā-'vəs\ city Canada in S Que. pop 17,895
Lev·kás \lev-'käs\ island Greece in the Ionians at entrance to Ambracian Gulf area 111 sq mi (289 sq km)
Lew·es 1 \'lü-əs\ the upper Yukon river S of its junction with the Pelly **2** borough S England ✳ of E. Sussex on Ouse river S of London
Lewis and Clark \‚lü-ə-sən-'klärk\ **1** lake 30 mi (48 km) long SE S.Dak. & NE Nebr. formed by Gavins Point Dam **2** or **Mor·ri·son Cave** \‚mòr-ə-sən-, 'mär-\ cavern cen Mont. WNW of Bozeman
Lew·i·sham \'lü-ə-shəm\ borough of SE Greater London, England pop 238,600
Lew·is·ton \'lü-ə-stən\ **1** city NW Idaho on Wash. border pop 27,986 **2** city SW Maine on the Androscoggin opposite Auburn pop 40,481
Lew·is·ville \'lü-əs-‚vil, -vil\ city N Tex. pop 24,273
Lewis with Har·ris \‚lü-əs-with-'har-əs\ island NW Scotland in the Outer Hebrides divided administratively into **Lewis** (in the N; chief town & port Stornoway) & **Harris** (in the S); largest of the Hebrides, in Western Isles regional division area 770 sq mi (2002 sq km)
Lex·ing·ton \'lek-siŋ-tən\ **1** city N cen Ky. ESE of Frankfort pop 204,165 **2** town NE Mass. NW of Boston pop 29,479
Leyden — see LEIDEN
Ley·te \'lāt-ē\ island Philippines in the Visayans W of **Leyte Gulf** (inlet of the Pacific); chief town Tacloban area 2785 sq mi (7241 sq km)
Ley·ton \'lāt-ᵊn\ former municipal borough SE England in Essex, now part of Waltham Forest
Lha·sa \'läs-ə, 'las-\ city SW China ✳ of Tibet pop 175,000
Lho·tse \'(h)lòt-'sā\ mountain 27,923 ft (8511 m) in Mt. Everest massif S of Mt. Everest; 4th highest in the world
Liao \lē-'aü\ river 700 mi (1126 km) NE China flowing into Gulf of Liaotung
Liao·ning \lē-'aü-niŋ\ or formerly **Feng·tien** \'fəŋ-tē-'en\ province NE China in S Manchuria ✳ Mukden area 58,301 sq mi (151,583 sq km), pop 35,721,693

Liao·si \lē-'aú-'shē\ former province (1948–54) NE China in S Manchuria bordering on Gulf of Liaotung ✻ Chin-chou

Liao·tung or Liao·dong \lē-'aú-'dún\ peninsula NE China in S Liaoning bet. Korea Bay & Gulf of Liaotung (arm of Po Hai)

Liao·yang \lē-'aú-'yän\ city NE China in cen Liaoning NE of Anshan pop 200,000

Liao·yüan \lē-'aú-yü-'än\ city NE China in W Kirin S of Changchun on the Liao pop 177,000

Li·ard \'lē-ərd\ river 755 mi (1215 km) W Canada flowing from Stikine mountains in Yukon Territory E & N into Mackenzie river

Libanus — see LEBANON

Li·be·rec \'lib-ə-,rets\ city W Czechoslovakia in N Bohemia pop 97,474

Li·be·ria \lī-'bir-ē-ə\ country W Africa, a republic ✻ Monrovia area 43,000 sq mi (111,800 sq km), pop 1,503,368 — Li·be·ri·an \-ē-ən\ adj or n

Lib·er·ty \'lib-ərt-ē\ or formerly Bed·loe's \'bed-,lōz\ island SE N.Y. in Upper New York Bay; comprises Statue of Liberty National Monument

Lib·er·ty·ville \'lib-ərt-ē-,vil, -vəl\ city NE Ill. pop 16,520

Li·bre·ville \'lē-brə-,vil, -,vē(ə)l\ city & port ✻ of Gabon at mouth of Gabon river pop 105,080

Lib·ya \'lib-ē-ə\ 1 the part of Africa N of the Sahara between Egypt & Syrtis Major (Gulf of Sidra) — an ancient name 2 N Africa W of Egypt — an ancient name 3 country N Africa bordering on the Mediterranean; a colony of Italy 1912–43, an independent kingdom 1951–69, a republic since 1969 ✻ Tripoli area 679,358 sq mi (1,766,331 sq km), pop 3,224,000

Lib·y·an \'lib-ē-ən\ desert N Africa W of the Nile in Libya, Egypt, & Sudan

Lich·field \'lich-,fēld\ city W cen England in Staffordshire pop 25,600

Lick·ing \'lik-iŋ\ river 350 mi (563 km) NE Ky. flowing NW into Ohio river

Li·di·ce \'lid-ə(t)-sē, -,sä\ village W Czechoslovakia in W cen Bohemia

Li·do \'lēd-(,)ō\ island Italy in the Adriatic separating Lagoon of Venice & Gulf of Venice

Liech·ten·stein \'lik-tən-,s(h)tīn\ country W Europe bet. Switzerland & Austria bordering on the Rhine; a principality ✻ Vaduz area 62 sq mi (161 sq km), pop 26,130 — Liech·ten·stein·er \-,s(h)tī-nər\ n

Liège \lē-'ezh, -'āzh\ or Flem Luik \'lik\ 1 province E Belgium area 1525 sq mi (3965 sq km), pop 999,413 2 city, its ✻ pop 214,119

Lien–yün–kang \lē-'ən-'yün-'gän\ or Lian·yun·gang \lē-'än-\ or formerly Tung·hai \'tuŋ-,hī\ city E China in N Kiangsu pop 210,000

Lie·pa·ja \lē-'ep-ə-yə, -'ep-,ä-yə\ or G Li·bau \'lē-,baú\ city & port U.S.S.R. in W Latvia on the Baltic pop 108,000

Lif·fey \'lif-ē\ river 50 mi (80 km) E Ireland flowing into Dublin Bay

Lif·ford \'lif-ərd\ town NW Ireland (republic) in Ulster ✻ of county Donegal

Li·gu·ria \lə-'gyúr-ē-ə\ region NW Italy bordering on Ligurian sea ✻ Genoa — Li·gu·ri·an \-ē-ən\ adj or n

Ligurian sea arm of the Mediterranean N of Corsica

Li·ka·si \li-'käs-ē\ or formerly Ja·dot·ville \,zhad-ō-'vē(ə)l, zha-'dō-,vil\ city SE Zaire in SE Shaba pop 146,394

Lille \'lē(ə)l\ or formerly Lisle \'lē(ə)l, 'lī(ə)l\ city N France; medieval ✻ of Flanders pop 171,010

Li·long·we \li-'lóŋ-(,)wä\ city ✻ of Malawi pop 102,924

Li·ma 1 \'lī-mə\ city NW Ohio pop 47,381 2 \'lē-mə\ city ✻ of Peru, on the Rimac pop 3,968,972

Lim·a·vady \,lim-ə-'vad-ē\ district N Northern Ireland, established 1974 area 226 sq mi (588 sq km), pop 26,270

Li·may \lē-'mī\ river 250 mi (402 km) W Argentina flowing out of Lake Nahuel Huapí & joining the Neuquén forming Negro river

Lim·burg \'lim-,bərg\ 1 region W Europe E of the Meuse including parts of present Limburg province, Netherlands, & Limburg province, Belgium 2 province NE Belgium ✻ Hasselt area 929 sq mi (2415 sq km), pop 716,888 3 province SE Netherlands ✻ Maastricht area 851 sq mi (2213 sq km), pop 1,080,309

Lime·house \'līm-,haús\ district E London, England, in Tower Hamlets on N bank of Thames river

Lim·er·ick \'lim-(ə-)rik\ 1 county SW Ireland in Munster area 1037 sq mi (2696 sq km), pop 161,661 2 city & county borough & port, its ✻, on the Shannon pop 60,736

Limnos — see LEMNOS

Li·moges \lē-'mōzh, -'mózh\ city SW cen France pop 136,059

Li·món or Puer·to Limón \(,)pwert-ō-)li-'mōn\ city & port E Costa Rica on the Caribbean pop 29,621

Li·mou·sin \,lē-mü-'za^n\ region & former province S cen France W of Auvergne ✻ Limoges

Lim·po·po \lim-'pō-(,)pō\ or Croc·o·dile \'kräk-ə-,dīl\ river 1000 mi (1609 km) S Africa flowing from Transvaal, Republic of S. Africa, into Indian ocean in Mozambique

Li·na·res \li-'när-əs\ commune S Spain N of Jaén pop 45,330

Lin·coln \'liŋ-kən\ 1 city SE Nebr., its ✻ pop 171,932 2 town N R.I. pop 16,949 3 city E England ✻ of Lincolnshire pop 76,660

Lincoln Park city SE Mich. SW of Detroit pop 45,105

Lin·coln·shire \'liŋ-kən-,shi(ə)r, -shər\ or Lincoln county E England ✻ Lincoln area 2272 sq mi (5907 sq km), pop 547,700

Lin·den \'lin-dən\ city NE N.J. SSW of Elizabeth pop 37,836

Lin·den·hurst \'lin-dən-,hərst\ village SE N.Y. in cen Long Is. pop 26,919

Lin·den·wold \'lin-dən-,wōld\ city SW N.J. pop 18,196

Lin·des·nes \'lin-də-,snäs\ cape Norway ✻ S tip on North sea

Lindisfarne — see HOLY

Lind·sey, Parts of \'lin-zē\ district & former administrative county E England in N Lincolnshire ✻ Lincoln area 1520 sq mi (3952 sq km)

Line \'līn\ islands Kiribati in cen Pacific S of Hawaii formerly divided bet. the U.S. (Kingman Reef & Palmyra) & Great Britain (Teraina, Tabuaeran & Kiritimati) pop 1180

Lin·ga·yen Gulf \,liŋ-gə-,yen-\ inlet of S. China sea Philippines in NW Luzon

Linguetta, Cape — see GJUHEZES, CAPE

Lin·kö·ping \'lin-,chə(r)p-iŋ\ city SE Sweden pop 112,600

Lin·lith·gow \lin-'lith-(,)gō\ 1 or Lin·lith·gow·shire \-,shi(ə)r, -shər\ — see WEST LOTHIAN 2 burgh SE Scotland in Lothian region W of Edinburgh pop 9524

Linn·he, Loch \'lin-ē\ inlet of the Atlantic on W coast of Scotland extending NE from head of Firth of Lorne

Linz \'lints, 'linz\ city N Austria on the Danube pop 197,962

Li·ons, Gulf of \'lī-ənz\ or F Golfe du Lion \gólf-dü-lyō^n\ arm of the Mediterranean on S coast of France

Lip·a·ri \'lip-ə-rē\ 1 or It Iso·le Eo·lie \'ē-zə-,lā-ā-'ó-lē-,ā\ islands Italy in SE Tyrrhenian sea off NE Sicily area 45 sq mi (117 sq km) — see STROMBOLI 2 or anc Lip·a·ra \'lip-ə-rə\ island, chief of the Lipari group

Li·petsk \'lē-,petsk\ city U.S.S.R. in S cen Soviet Russia, Europe, N of Voronezh pop 396,000

Lip·pe \'lip-ə\ 1 river 150 mi (241 km) cen W. Germany flowing from Teutoburger Wald W into the Rhine 2 former principality & state W Germany between Teutoburger Wald & the Weser ✻ Detmold

Li·ri \'lir-ē\ river 100 mi (161 km) cen Italy flowing into Gulf of Gaeta

Lis·bon \'liz-bən\ or Pg Lis·boa \lēzh-'vō-ə\ city & port ✻ of Portugal on Tagus estuary pop 812,385 — Lis·bo·an \liz-'bō-ən\ n

Lis·burn \'liz-(,)bərn\ district E Northern Ireland, established 1974 area 171 sq mi (445 sq km), pop 82,091

Lis·burne, Cape \'liz-bərn\ cape NW Alaska projecting into Arctic ocean near W end of Brooks range

Li·sieux \lēz-'yə(r), -'yœ\ city NW France E of Caen pop 24,972

Li·ta·ni \li-'tä-nē\ river 90 mi (144 km) S Lebanon flowing into Mediterranean

Lith·u·a·nia \,lith-(y)ə-'wā-nē-ə, -nyə\ or Lith Lie·tu·va \lē-ə-tü-'vä\ country N cen Europe bordering on the Baltic; remnant of a medieval principality extending from Baltic sea to Black sea; a republic 1918–40, since 1940 a constituent republic (Lithuanian Republic) of the U.S.S.R. ✻ Vilnius area 31,200 sq mi (81,120 sq km), pop 3,398,000

Little Abaco — see ABACO

Little Bighorn river 80 mi (129 km) N Wyo. & S Mont. flowing N into Bighorn river

Little Colorado river 300 mi (483 km) NE Ariz. flowing NW into Colorado river

Little Diomede — see DIOMEDE

Little Inagua — see INAGUA

Little Kabylia — see KABYLIA

Little Karroo — see KARROO

Little Minch — see MINCH

Little Missouri river 560 mi (901 km) W U.S. flowing from NE Wyo. N into Missouri river in W N.Dak.

Little Namaqualand — see NAMAQUALAND

Lit·tle Rock \'lit-'l-,räk\ city ✻ of Ark. on Arkansas river pop 158,461

Little Saint Bernard mountain pass 7177 ft (2188 m) over Savoy Alps bet. France & Italy S of Mont Blanc

Lit·tle·ton \'lit-əl-tən\ town N cen Colo. S of Denver pop 28,631

Little Walachia — see OLTENIA

Liu·chou or Liu·zhou or Liu·chow \lē-'ü-'jō\ city S China in cen Kwangsi Chuang pop 190,000

Liv·er·more \'liv-ər-,mō(ə)r, -,mó(ə)r\ city W Calif. SE of Oakland pop 48,349

Liv·er·pool \'liv-ər-,pül\ city & port NW England in Merseyside on Mersey estuary pop 510,306 — Liv·er·pud·li·an \,liv-ər-'pəd-lē-ən\ adj or n

Liv·ing·stone \'liv-iŋ-stən\ city S Zambia on the Zambezi pop 71,987

Livingstone Falls rapids in lower Congo river W equatorial Africa below Stanley Pool; a series of cascades dropping ab 900 ft (273 m) in 220 mi (352 km)

Li·vo·nia \lə-'vō-nē-ə, -nyə\ 1 region cen Europe bordering on the Baltic in Latvia & Estonia 2 city SE Mich. W of Detroit pop 104,814 — Li·vo·nian \-nē-ən, -nyən\ adj or n

Livorno — see LEGHORN

Lizard Head or Lizard Point headland SW England in S Cornwall at S tip of the Lizard (peninsula projecting into English channel); extreme S point of Great Britain, at 49°57′30″N, 5°12′W

Lju·blja·na \lē-,ü-blē-'än-ə\ city NW Yugoslavia ✻ of Slovenia on the Sava pop 169,064

Llan·ber·is \(h)lan-'ber-əs\ village NW Wales in Gwynedd near Snowdon at entrance to Pass of Llanberis (1169 ft or 354 m)

Llan·drin·dod Wells \(h)lan-'drin-,dòd\ town E Wales ✻ of Powys

Llan·dud·no \(h)lan-'did-(,)nō, -'dəd-\ town NW Wales on coast of Gwynedd pop 18,991

Lla·nel·li or Lla·nel·ly \hla-'ne-hlē, (h)la-'nel-ē\ borough & port S Wales in Dyfed pop 24,079

Llan·gef·ni \(h)lan-'gev-nē\ town NW Wales in Gwynedd on Anglesey Is. pop 4265

Lla·no Es·ta·ca·do \'län-(,)ō-,es-tə-'käd-(,)ō, 'län-\ or Staked Plain \'stāk(t)-\ plateau region SE N.Mex. & NW Tex.

Llu·llai·lla·co \,yü-,yī-'yäk-(,)ō\ volcano 22,057 ft (6723 m) N Chile in Andes on Argentina border SE of Antofagasta

Lo·an·ge \lō-'an-gə\ or Pg Lu·an·gue \lü-'aŋ-gə\ river 425 mi (684 km) NE Angola & SW Congo flowing N into Kasai river

Lo·bi·to \lō-'bēt-(,)ō\ city & port W Angola pop 59,528

Lo·bos, Point \'lō-bəs\ 1 promontory Calif. in San Francisco S side of entrance to the Golden Gate 2 promontory Calif. on the Pacific SW of Monterey

Lo·car·no \lō-'kär-(,)ō\ commune SE cen Switzerland pop 14,103

Loch·gilp·head \,läk-'gilp-,hed\ burgh W Scotland on Loch Fyne

Lock·port \'läk-,pō(ə)rt, -,pó(ə)rt\ city W N.Y. NE of Buffalo pop 24,844

Lo·cris \'lō-krəs, 'läk-rəs\ region of ancient Greece N of Gulf of Corinth — Lo·cri·an \'lō-krē-ən, 'läk-rē-\ adj or n

Lod \'lōd\ or Lyd·da \'lid-ə\ city cen Israel pop 30,500

Lo·di 1 \'lōd-,ī\ city cen Calif. SSE of Sacramento pop 35,221 2 \'lōd-,ī\ borough NE N.J. SE of Paterson pop 23,956 3 \'lòd-(,)ē\ commune N Italy in Lombardy SE of Milan pop 42,873

Lodz \'lüj, 'lädz\ city cen Poland WSW of Warsaw pop 843,027

Lo·fo·ten \'lō-,fōt-'n\ island group Norway off NW coast SW of Vesterålen area 475 sq mi (1235 sq km)

Lo·gan \'lō-gən\ city N Utah pop 26,844

Logan, Mount mountain 19,850 ft (6050 m) Canada in SW Yukon Territory; highest in St. Elias & Coast ranges & in Canada & 2d highest in N. America

Lo·gans·port \'lō-gən-,spō(ə)rt, -,spó(ə)rt\ city N cen Ind. pop 17,899

Lo·gro·ño \lə-'grōn-(ˌ)yō\ 1 province N Spain in NE Old Castile *area* 1946 *sq mi* (5060 *sq km*), *pop* 241,957 2 commune, its ✻, on the Ebro *pop* 109,536

Loire \lə-'wär\ river 625 *mi* (1006 *km*) *cen* France flowing from the Massif Central NW & W into Bay of Biscay

Lol·land \'läl-ənd\ island Denmark in the Baltic S of Sjælland *area* 477 *sq mi* (1240 *sq km*), *pop* 81,760

Lo·ma·mi \lō-'mäm-ē\ river 900 *mi* (1448 *km*) *cen* Zaire flowing N into Congo river

Lo·mas \'lō-məs\ *or* Lo·mas de Za·mo·ra \-ˌmäz-də-zə-'mōr-ə, -'mȯr-\ city E Argentina SW of Buenos Aires *pop* 508,620

Lom·bard \'läm-ˌbärd\ village NE Ill. W of Chicago *pop* 37,295

Lom·bar·dy \-ˌbärd-ē, -bȯrd-\ *or It* Lom·bar·dia \ˌläm-bȯr-'dē-ə\ region N Italy chiefly N of the Po ✻ Milan

Lom·blen \'läm-ˌblen\ island Indonesia in the Lesser Sundas E of Flores *area* 468 *sq mi* (1217 *sq km*)

Lom·bok \'läm-ˌbäk\ island Indonesia in the Lesser Sundas E of Bali; chief town Mataram *area* 1825 *sq mi* (4745 *sq km*), *pop* 1,300,234

Lo·mé \lō-'mā\ city & port ✻ of Togo *pop* 229,400

Lo·mi·ta \lō-'mēt-ə\ city SW Calif. S of Los Angeles *pop* 18,807

Lo·mond, Ben \ben-'lō-mənd\ mountain 3192 *ft* (973 *m*) S *cen* Scotland on E side of Loch Lomond

Lomond, Loch lake 24 *mi* (39 *km*) long S *cen* Scotland in Strathclyde & Central regions; largest in Scotland

Lom·poc \'läm-ˌpōk\ city SW Calif. W of Santa Barbara *pop* 26,267

Lon·don \'lən-dən\ 1 city Canada in SE Ont. on Thames river *pop* 254,280 2 city & port SE England formerly constituting an administrative county ✻ of United Kingdom; comprises City of London & 12 inner boroughs of Greater London *pop* 2,395,200 3 *or* City of London *or anc* Lon·din·i·um \län-'din-ē-əm, ˌlən-\ city within Greater London, England, on Thames river *area* 675 *acres* (270 *hectares*) 4 GREATER LONDON — Lon·don·er \-də-nər\ n

Londonderry — see DERRY

Long Beach 1 city & port SW Calif. SE of Los Angeles *pop* 361,334 2 city SE N.Y. on island S of Long Is. *pop* 34,073

Long Branch city E *cen* N.J. on the Atlantic *pop* 29,819

Long·ford \'lȯŋ-fərd\ 1 county E *cen* Ireland in Leinster *area* 403 *sq mi* (1048 *sq km*), *pop* 31,140 2 urban district, its ✻ *pop* 3998

Long Island island 118 *mi* (190 *km*) long SE N.Y. S of Conn. *area* 1401 *sq mi* (3643 *sq km*)

Long Island City section of New York City in NW Queens

Long Island Sound inlet of the Atlantic between Conn. & Long Is.

Long·mont \'lȯŋ-ˌmänt\ city N Colo. N of Denver *pop* 42,942

Longs Peak \'lȯŋz-\ mountain 14,255 *ft* (4345 *m*) N *cen* Colo. in Front range in Rocky Mountain National Park

Lon·gueuil \lȯŋ-'gā(ə)l\ city Canada in S Que. E of Montreal *pop* 124,320

Long·view \'lȯŋ-ˌvyü\ 1 city NE Tex. *pop* 62,762 2 city SW Wash. on Columbia river *pop* 31,052

Long Xuy·en \lȯŋ-'swē-ən\ city S Vietnam in SW Cochin China on S side of Mekong delta

Lookout, Cape cape E N.C. on the Atlantic SW of Cape Hatteras

Lookout Mountain ridge 2126 *ft* (648 *m*) SE Tenn., NW Ga., & NE Ala. near Chattanooga, Tenn.

Lo·rain \lə-'rān, lō-\ city N Ohio on Lake Erie W of Cleveland *pop* 75,416

Lor·ca \'lȯr-kə\ commune SE Spain SW of Murcia *pop* 60,609

Lord Howe \lō(ə)rd-'hau̇\ island Australia in Tasman sea ENE of Sydney belonging to New S. Wales *area* 5 *sq mi* (13 *sq km*)

Lo·re·to \lə-'rāt-(ˌ)ō, -'ret-\ commune *cen* Italy in the Marches S of Ancona

Lo·ri·ent \ˌlȯr-ē-'än\ commune & port NW France in Brittany on Bay of Biscay *pop* 68,653

Lorne, Firth of \'lō(ə)rn\ *or* Firth of Lorn strait W Scotland between E Mull Is. & mainland

Lor·raine \lə-'rān, lȯ-\ *or G* Lo·thring·en \'lō-triŋ-ən\ region & former duchy NE France around the upper Moselle & the Meuse; remnant (Upper Lorraine) of medieval kingdom of Lo·tha·rin·gia \ˌlō-thə-'rin-j(ē)ə\ including also territory to N (Lower Lorraine) bet. the Rhine & the Scheldt — see ALSACE-LORRAINE

Los Al·tos \lȯs-'sal-təs\ city W Calif. SSE of Palo Alto *pop* 25,769

Los An·ge·les \lȯ-'san-jə-ləs *also* -'san-g(ə-)ləs\ city & port SW Calif. on the Pacific *pop* 2,966,763 — Los An·ge·le·no \-ˌsan-jə-'lē-(ˌ)nō, -ˌsan-gə-'lē-\ n

Los An·ge·les \lȯs-ˌäŋ-hā-ˌläs\ city S *cen* Chile *pop* 41,719

Los Gat·os \lȯs-'gat-əs\ city W Calif. S of San José *pop* 26,593

Lot \'lät, 'lōt\ river 300 *mi* (483 *km*) S France flowing W into the Garonne

Lo·thi·an \'lō-thē-ən\ region S Scotland bordering on Firth of Forth, established 1975 ✻ Edinburgh *area* 678 *sq mi* (1755 *sq km*), *pop* 735,892; formerly divided into three counties (the Lothians): East Lothian, Midlothian, & West Lothian

Lough·bor·ough \'ləf-ˌbər-ə, -ˌbə-rə, -b(ə-)rə\ borough *cen* England in Leicestershire S of Nottingham *pop* 47,647

Lou·ise, Lake \lü-'ēz\ lake W Canada in SW Alta. in Banff National Park

Lou·i·si·ade \lü-ˌē-zē-'äd, -'ad\ archipelago in Solomon sea SE of New Guinea; belongs to Papua New Guinea *pop* 14,599

Lou·i·si·ana \lü-ˌē-zē-'an-ə, ˌlü-zē-\ state S U.S. ✻ Baton Rouge *area* 48,523 *sq mi* (126,160 *sq km*), *pop* 4,205,900 — Lou·i·si·an·an \-'an-ən\ *adj or n* — Lou·i·si·an·ian \-'an-ē-ən, -'an-yən\ *adj or n*

Louisiana Purchase region W *cen* U.S. bet. Mississippi river & the Rockies purchased 1803 from France *area* 885,000 *mi* (2,301,000 *sq km*)

Lou·is·ville \'lü-i-ˌvil, -vəl\ city N Ky. on Ohio river *pop* 298,451

Loup \'lüp\ river 290 *mi* (467 *km*) with longest headstream (the Middle Loup) E *cen* Nebr. flowing E into Platte river

Lourdes \'lu̇(ə)rd(z)\ commune SW France on the Gave de Pau SSW of Tarbes *pop* 17,685

Lourenço Marques — see MAPUTO

Louth \'lau̇th\ county E Ireland in Leinster bordering on Irish sea ✻ Dundalk *area* 317 *sq mi* (824 *sq km*), *pop* 88,514

Lou·vain \lü-'van\ *or Flem* Leu·ven \'lə(r)v-ə(n)\ city *cen* Belgium in Brabant E of Brussels *pop* 85,076

Love·land \'ləv-lənd\ 1 mountain pass N *cen* Colo. in Front range of Rocky mountains 2 city N Colo. N of Denver *pop* 30,244

Low Countries region W Europe bordering on North sea & comprising modern Belgium, Luxembourg, & the Netherlands

Low·ell \'lō-əl\ city NE Mass. NW of Boston *pop* 92,418

Lower Canada the province of Canada 1791–1841 corresponding to modern Que. — see UPPER CANADA

lower 48 the continental states of the U.S. excluding Alaska

Lower Klamath lake N Calif. on Oreg. border SSE of Upper Klamath Lake (in Oreg.)

Lower Saxony *or G* Nie·der·sach·sen \ˌnēd-ər-'zäk-sən\ state of W. Germany bordering on North sea ✻ Hannover *area* 18,289 *sq mi* (47,551 *sq km*), *pop* 7,256,386 — see SAXONY

Lowes·toft \'lō-stəf(t), -ˌstȯft\ borough & port E England in E. Suffolk on North sea *pop* 55,231

Low·lands \'lō-lən(d)z, -ˌlan(d)z\ the *cen* & E part of Scotland lying bet. the Highlands & the Southern Uplands

Loyalty islands SW Pacific E of New Caledonia; a dependency of New Caledonia *area* 800 *sq mi* (2080 *sq km*), *pop* 12,248

Lo·yang \'lō-'yäŋ\ *or* Luo·yang \lə-'wō-'yäŋ\ city E China in N Honan in the Hwang basin *pop* 171,200

Lu·a·la·ba \ˌlü-ə-'läb-ə\ river 400 *mi* (640 *km*) SE Zaire flowing N to join the Lu·a·pu·la \-'pü-lə\ (outlet of Lake Bangweulu) forming Congo river

Lu·an·da \lü-'an-də\ city & port ✻ of Angola *pop* 475,328

Luang Pra·bang \lü-ˌäŋ-prə-'bäŋ\ city NW Laos on the Mekong NNW of Vientiane *pop* 44,244

Luangue — see LOANGE

Lub·bock \'ləb-ək\ city NW Tex. *pop* 173,979

Lü·beck \'lü-ˌbek, 'lüe-\ city & port NE W. Germany NE of Hamburg *pop* 220,588

Lu·blin \'lü-blən, -ˌblēn\ city E Poland SE of Warsaw *pop* 308,805

Lu·bum·ba·shi \ˌlü-büm-'bäsh-ē\ *or formerly* Elis·a·beth·ville \i-'liz-ə-bəth-ˌvil\ city SE Zaire in SE Shaba *pop* 588,307

Lucania — see BASILICATA

Lu·ca·nia, Mount \lü-'kä-nē-ə, -nyə\ mountain 17,147 *ft* (5226 *m*) Canada in SW Yukon Territory in St. Elias range N of Mt. Logan

Luc·ca \'lü-kə\ commune *cen* Italy in Tuscany NW of Florence *pop* 90,097

Lu·cerne \lü-'sərn\ *or G* Lu·zern \lüt-'se(ə)rn\ 1 canton *cen* Switzerland *area* 579 *sq mi* (1505 *sq km*), *pop* 296,159 2 commune, its ✻, on Vierwaldstätter See *pop* 63,278

Lucerne, Lake of — see VIERWALDSTÄTTER SEE

Luchow — see HOFEI

Luck·now \'lək-ˌnau̇\ city N India ESE of Delhi ✻ of Uttar Pradesh *pop* 1,006,538

Lüda — see DAIREN

Lü·de·ritz \'lüd-ə-rəts\ town & port SW Namibia

Lu·dhi·a·na \ˌlüd-ē-'än-ə\ city NW India in Punjab SE of Amritsar *pop* 606,250

Lud·low \'ləd-(ˌ)lō\ town SW Mass. NE of Springfield *pop* 18,150

Lud·wigs·burg \'lüt-vigz-ˌbu̇(ə)rg, 'lüd-\ city S W. Germany in Baden-Württemberg N of Stuttgart *pop* 81,589

Lud·wigs·ha·fen \ˌlüt-vigz-'häf-ən, ˌlüd-\ city S W. Germany on the Rhine opposite Mannheim *pop* 159,399

Luf·kin \'ləf-kən\ city E Tex. NNE of Houston *pop* 28,562

Lu·ga·no \lü-'gän-(ˌ)ō\ commune S Switzerland in Ticino canton on Lake Lugano *pop* 27,815

Lugano, Lake lake on border between Switzerland & Italy E of Lake Maggiore *area* 19 *sq mi* (49 *sq km*)

Lu·gansk \lü-'gän(t)sk\ *or Alternately since 1935* Vo·ro·shi·lov·grad \ˌvȯr-ə-'shē-ləf-ˌgrad, ˌvär-, -ˌləv-\ city U.S.S.R. in E Ukrainian Republic in Donets basin *pop* 463,000

Lu·go \'lü-(ˌ)gō\ 1 province NW Spain in NE Galicia on Bay of Biscay *area* 3814 *sq mi* (9916 *sq km*), *pop* 384,365 2 commune, its ✻ *pop* 71,299

Luichow — see LEI-CHOU

Luik — see LIÈGE

Lu·lea \'lü-lə-ˌō, -lē-ˌō\ city & port N Sweden near head of Gulf of Bothnia *pop* 66,834

Lu·le·bur·gaz \ˌlü-lə-bûr-'gäz\ city *cen* Turkey in Europe

Luluabourg — see KANANGA

Lum·ber·ton \'ləm-bərt-ᵊn\ city S N.C. *pop* 18,241

Lund \'lu̇nd, 'lùnd\ city SW Sweden NE of Malmö *pop* 78,487

Lun·dy \'lən-dē\ island SW England at mouth of Bristol channel off coast of Devon *area* 2 *sq mi* (5.2 *sq km*)

Lü·ne·burg \'lü-nə-ˌbu̇(ə)rg\ city N W. Germany SE of Hamburg & NE of Lüneburg Heath *or G* Lü·ne·bur·ger Hei·de \-ˌbûr-gər-ˌhīd-ə\ (tract of moorland 50 *mi* or 80 *km* long) *pop* 62,225

Lü·nen \'lü-nən, 'lüe-\ city W *cen* W. Germany S of Münster *pop* 85,872

Lu·né·ville \'lü-nə-ˌvil\ city NE France on the Meurthe SE of Nancy *pop* 22,438

Lungki — see CHANG-CHOU

Lu·ray \'lü-ˌrā, lü-'\ caverns N Va. in Blue Ridge mountains

Lu·ri·stan \ˌlu̇r-ə-ˌstan, -ˌstän\ region W Iran; chief town Burujird

Lu·sa·ka \lü-'säk-ə\ city ✻ of Zambia *pop* 538,469

Lu·sa·tia \lü-'sā-sh(ē-)ə\ *or G* Lau·sitz \'lau̇-(ˌ)zits\ region SE E. Germany NW of Silesia E of the Elbe

Lü–shun — see PORT ARTHUR

Lusitania — see PORTUGAL — Lu·si·ta·ni·an \ˌlü-sə-'tā-nē-ən, -nyən\ *adj or n*

Lü–ta — see DAIREN

Lutetia — see PARIS

Lu·ton \'lüt-ᵊn\ borough SE *cen* England in SE Bedfordshire *pop* 164,049

Lüt·zen \'lüt-sən, 'lüet-\ town S E. Germany in Saxony SW of Leipzig

---

Lux·em·bourg or **Lux·em·burg** \'lək-səm-,bərg, 'lùk-səm-,bú(ə)rg\ **1** province SE Belgium ✻ Arlon area 1705 sq mi (4433 sq km), pop 221,926 **2** country W Europe bet. Belgium, France, & W. Germany; a grand duchy area 999 sq mi (2597 sq km), pop 364,606 **3** city, its ✻ pop 79,596 — **Lux·em·bourg·er** or **Lux·em·burg·er** \-,bər-gər, -,bùr-\ n — **Lux·em·bourg·ian** or **Lux·em·burg·ian** \,lək-səm-'bər-gē-ən, ,lùk-səm-'bùr-\ adj
Lux·or \'lək-,só(ə)r, 'lùk-\ or Ar **El Uq·sor** \e-'lùk-,sù(ə)r\ city S Egypt on the Nile on S part of site of ancient Thebes pop 92,748
Lu·zon \lü-'zän\ island N Philippines, chief island of the group area 40,420 sq mi (105,092 sq km), pop 16,669,724
Lvov \lə-'vóv\ or \'vóv\ or Pol **Lwów** \lə-'vüf, -'vüv\ or G **Lem·berg** \'lem-,bərg, -,be(ə)rg\ city U.S.S.R. in W Ukrainian Republic pop 238,600
Lyallpur — see FAISALABAD
Ly·ca·bet·tus or Gk **Ly·ka·bet·tos** \,lik-ə-'bet-əs, ,lī-kə-\ mountain 909 ft (277 m) in NE part of Athens, Greece
Ly·ca·o·nia \,lik-ā-'ō-nē-ə, ,lī-kā-, -nyə\ ancient region & Roman province SE cen Asia Minor N of Cilicia
Ly·cia \'lish-(ē-)ə\ ancient region & Roman province SW Asia Minor on coast SE of Caria — **Ly·cian** \-(ē-)ən\ adj or n
Lydda — see LOD
Lyd·ia \'lid-ē-ə\ ancient country W Asia Minor bordering on the Aegean ✻ Sardis — **Lyd·i·an** \-ən\ adj or n
Lyn·brook \'lin-,brúk\ village SE N.Y. on Long Is. pop 20,424
Lynch·burg \'linch-,bərg\ city S cen Va. on James river pop 66,743
Lynd·hurst \'lind-,hərst\ city NE Ohio E of Cleveland pop 18,092
Lynn \'lin\ **1** city NE Mass. NE of Boston pop 78,471 **2** or **Lynn Regis** — see KING'S LYNN
Lynn Canal narrow inlet of the Pacific 80 mi (129 km) long SE Alaska extending N from Juneau
Lynn·wood \'lin-,wúd\ city W Wash. N of Seattle pop 22,641
Lyn·wood \'lin-,wùd\ city SW Calif. S of Los Angeles pop 48,548
Ly·on·nais or **Ly·o·nais** \,lē-ə-'nā\ former province SE cen France NE of Auvergne & W of the Saône & the Rhône ✻ Lyons
Ly·ons \lē-'ōⁿ, 'lī-ənz\ or **Lyon** \lyōⁿ\ or anc **Lug·du·num** \lùg-'dü-nəm, ,ləg-\ city SE cen France at confluence of the Saône & the Rhône pop 462,841
Lys \lēs\ or **Leie** \'lā-ə, 'lī-ə\ river 120 mi (193 km) France & Belgium flowing NE into the Scheldt
Lyt·tel·ton \'lit-ᵊl-tən\ borough New Zealand on South Is.; port for Christchurch, on **Port Lyttelton** (inlet) pop 3184

Maarianhamina — see MARIEHAMN
Maas — see MEUSE
Maas·tricht or **Maes·tricht** \'mäs-,trikt\ commune SE Netherlands on the Meuse ✻ of Limburg pop 112,598
Ma·cao or **Ma·cau** \mə-'kaú\ **1** island SE China in Kwangtung in Hsi delta W of Hong Kong **2** Portuguese overseas territory comprising peninsula on SE Macao Is. & adjacent islands area 6 sq mi (16 sq km), pop 323,000 **3** city & port, its ✻ pop 161,252 — **Mac·a·nese** \,mak-ə-'nēz, -'nēs\ n
Ma·ca·pá \,mak-ə-'pä\ city & port N Brazil ✻ of Amapá pop 137,698
Macassar — see MAKASSAR — **Ma·cas·sar·ese** \mə-,kas-ə-'rēz, -'rēs\ n
Mac·cles·field \'mak-əlz-,fēld\ borough W England in E Cheshire SSE of Manchester pop 46,832
Mac·don·nell Ranges \mək-'dän-ᵊl\ series of mountain ridges cen Australia S Northern Territory; highest point Mt. Ziel 4955 ft (1510 m)
Mac·e·do·nia \,mas-ə-'dō-nyə, -nē-ə\ **1** region S Europe in Balkan peninsula in NE Greece, SE Yugoslavia, & SW Bulgaria including territory of ancient kingdom of Macedonia (or **Mac·e·don** \'mas-əd-ən, -ə-,dän\ ✻ Pella) **2** the Yugoslav section of Macedonia; a federated republic ✻ Skopje area 10,229 sq mi (26,595 sq km), pop 1,623,598
Ma·ceió \,mas-ā-'ō\ city NE Brazil ✻ of Alagoas pop 400,041
Mac·gil·li·cud·dy's Reeks \mə-,gil-ə-,kəd-ēz-'rēks\ mountain range SW Ireland in County Kerry — see CARRANTUOHILL
Ma·chi·li·pat·nam \,məch-ə-li-'pət-nəm\ or formerly **Mich·i·li·mack·i·nac** \,mish-ə-lē-\ island N Mich. in Straits of Mackinac
Mac·ki·nac, Straits of \'mak-ə-,nó\ channel N Mich. connecting Lake Huron & Lake Michigan; 4 mi (6.4 km) wide at narrowest point
Ma·comb \mə-'kōm\ city W Ill. SW of Peoria pop 19,863
Ma·con \'mā-kən\ city cen Ga. on the Ocmulgee pop 116,896
Mâ·con \mä-kōⁿ\ city E cen France pop 39,130
Mac·quar·ie \mə-'kwär-ē\ river 750 mi (1200 km) SE Australia in E cen New S. Wales flowing NNW to Darling river
Mac·tan \mäk-'tän\ island S cen Philippines off E coast of Cebu
Mad·a·gas·car \,mad-ə-'gas-kər\ island W Indian ocean off SE Africa; formerly a French territory; became (1958) a republic of the French Community as the **Mal·a·gasy Republic** \,mal-ə-,gas-ē-\ or F **Ré·pu·blique Mal·gache** \rā-pū-blēk-mál-gäsh\ or since 1975 **Democratic Republic of Madagascar** ✻ Antananarivo area 226,657 sq mi (589,308 sq km), pop 9,985,000 — **Mad·a·gas·can** \,mad-ə-'gas-kən\ adj or n
Ma·dei·ra \mə-'dir-ə, -'der-ə\ **1** river 2100 mi (3380 km) W Brazil formed at Bolivian border by confluence of the Mamoré & the Beni & flowing NE to the Amazon **2** islands in N Atlantic N of the Canaries belonging to Portugal ✻ Funchal area 302 sq mi (785 sq km), pop 257,822 **3** island, chief of group area 285 sq mi (741 sq km) — **Ma·dei·ran** \-'dir-ən, -'der-\ adj or n
Ma·de·ra \mə-'der-ə\ city S cen Calif. NW of Fresno pop 21,732
Ma·dhya Bha·rat \,mäd-yə-'bär-ət\ former state cen India; a union of 20 states including Gwalior, Indore, & Malwa formed 1948; became part of Madhya Pradesh 1956

Madhya Pra·desh \-prə-'desh, -'dāsh\ state cen India ✻ Bhopal area 171,201 sq mi (445,123 sq km), pop 52,131,717 — see CENTRAL PROVINCES AND BERAR, MADHYA BHARAT
Mad·i·son \'mad-ə-sən\ **1** river 180 mi (290 km) SW Mont. — see THREE FORKS **2** city S Wis., its ✻ pop 170,616
Madison Heights city SE Mich. N of Detroit pop 35,375
Mad·i·son·ville \'mad-ə-sən-,vil\ city W Ky. pop 16,979
Ma·dras \mə-'dras, -'dräs\ **1** — see TAMIL NADU **2** city & port ✻ of Tamil Nadu pop 4,276,635 — **Ma·drasi** \-ē\ n
Ma·dre, La·gu·na \lə-,gü-nə-'mäd-rē\ inlet of Gulf of Mexico S Tex. between Padre Is. & mainland
Ma·dre de Dios \,mäd-rā-,dād-ē-'ōs\ river 900 mi (1448 km) rising in SE Peru & flowing E into the Beni in Brazil
Ma·drid \mə-'drid\ **1** province cen Spain in NW New Castile area 3084 sq mi (8018 sq km), pop 5,024,549 **2** city, its ✻ & ✻ of Spain pop 3,158,818 — **Mad·ri·le·nian** \,mad-rə-'lē-nē-ən, -nyən\ adj or n — **Ma·dri·le·no** \,mä-drə-'lā-(,)nō\ n
Ma·du·ra or D **Ma·doe·ra** \mə-'dùr-ə\ island Indonesia off coast of NE Java area (with adjacent islands) 2113 sq mi (5494 sq km), pop 1,858,183 — **Mad·u·rese** \,mad-ə-'rēz, ,maj-, -'rēs\ adj or n
Ma·du·rai \,mäd-ə-'rī\ city S India in S Tamil Nadu pop 904,362
Maeander — see MENDERES
Maf·e·king \'maf-ə-kiŋ\ town S Republic of S. Africa in N Cape Province near W Transvaal border pop 6515
Ma·fia \'mäf-ē-ə, 'maf-\ island Tanzania in Indian ocean S of Zanzibar area 170 sq mi (442 sq km), pop 16,748
Ma·ga·dan \,mäg-ə-'dan, -'dän\ city & port U.S.S.R. in E Soviet Russia, Asia, on N shore of Sea of Okhotsk pop 121,000
Magallanes — see PUNTA ARENAS
Mag·da·la \'mag-də-lə\ **1** ancient N Palestine on W shore of Sea of Galilee N of Tiberias **2** town N cen Ethiopia
Mag·da·len \'mag-də-lən\ or F **Îles de la Ma·de·leine** \ēl-də-lá-mäd-(ə-)len\ islands Canada in Que. in Gulf of St. Lawrence bet. Newfoundland & P.E.I. area 102 sq mi (265 sq km), pop 13,151
Mag·da·le·na \,mag-də-'lā-nə, -'lē-\ river 1000 mi (1609 km) Colombia flowing N into the Caribbean
Mag·de·burg \'mag-də-,bú(ə)rg, 'mag-də-,bərg\ city W E. Germany on the Elbe WSW of Berlin pop 289,292
Ma·ge·lang \,mäg-ə-'läŋ\ city Indonesia in cen Java pop 123,484
Ma·gel·lan, Strait of \mə-'jel-ən, chiefly Brit -'gel-\ strait 370 mi (595 km) long at S end of S. America between mainland & Tierra del Fuego archipelago
Mageröy — see NORTH CAPE
Mag·gio·re, Lake \mə-'jōr-ē, -'jòr-\ lake 40 mi (64 km) long N Italy & S Switzerland traversed by Ticino river
Magh·er·a·felt \'mär-ə-,felt, 'mak-ə-rə-,felt\ district cen Northern Ireland, established 1974 area 221 sq mi (575 sq km), pop 30,825
Ma·ghreb or **Ma·ghrib** \'mäg-rəb\ **1** NW Africa &, at time of the Moorish occupation, Spain; now considered as including Morocco, Algeria, Tunisia, & sometimes Libya **2** or **El Ma·ghreb al Aq·sa** \el-'mäg-rəb-äl-'äk-sä\ MOROCCO — **Ma·ghre·bi** or **Ma·ghri·bi** \'mäg-rə-bē\ adj or n — **Ma·ghreb·i·an** \mə-'greb-ē-ən\ or **Ma·ghrib·i·an** \-'grib-\ adj or n
Mag·na Grae·cia \,mag-nə-'grē-shə\ the ancient Greek colonies in S Italian peninsula including Tarentum, Sybaris, Crotona, Heraclea, & Neapolis
Magnesia — see MANISA
Mag·ni·to·gorsk \mag-'nēt-ə-,gòrsk\ city U.S.S.R. in W Soviet Russia, Asia, on Ural river pop 406,000
Magyarorszag — see HUNGARY
Ma·hal·la el Ku·bra \mə-,hal-ə-el-'kü-brə\ city N Egypt in Nile delta NE of Tanta pop 292,114
Ma·ha·na·di \mə-'hän-əd-ē\ river 512 mi (1331 km) E India flowing into Bay of Bengal in Orissa through several mouths
Ma·ha·rash·tra \,mä-hə-'räsh-trə\ **1** region W cen India S of the Narbada; the original home of the Marathas **2** state W India bordering on Arabian sea formed 1960 from SE part of former Bombay state ✻ Bombay area 118,717 sq mi (308,664 sq km), pop 62,093,898
Ma·hé \ma-'hā\ **1** island in Indian ocean, chief of the Seychelles group **2** or formerly **May·ya·li** \,mī-'yäl-ē\ city SW India in N Kerala NW of Kozhikode; a settlement of French India until 1954 pop 8972
Ma·hón \mə-'hōn\ or **Port Ma·hon** \-mə-'hōn\ city & port Spain on Minorca Is. pop 17,802
Ma·hone Bay \mə-,hōn-\ inlet of the Atlantic E Canada in S N.S.
Maid·en·head \'mād-ᵊn-,hed\ borough S England in Berkshire on Thames river W of London pop 49,038
Maid·stone \'mād-stən, -,stōn\ borough SE England ✻ of Kent on the Medway ESE of London pop 72,311
Mai·kop \mī-'kóp\ city U.S.S.R. in S Soviet Russia, Europe ✻ of Adygei autonomous region pop 111,000
Main \'mīn, 'mān\ river 305 mi (491 km) S W. Germany rising in N Bavaria in the Fichtelgebirge & flowing W into the Rhine
Maine \'mān\ **1** state NE U.S. ✻ Augusta area 33,215 sq mi (86,359 sq km), pop 1,124,660 **2** or **Le Maine** \lə-\ region & former province NW France S of Normandy ✻ Le Mans **3** — see MAYENNE — **Main·er** \'mā-nər\ n
Main·land \'mān-,land, -lənd\ **1** Honshu, the chief island of Japan **2** island S Scotland, largest of the Orkneys **3** island N Scotland, largest of the Shetlands
Mainz \'mīnts\ or F **Ma·yence** \má-yäⁿs\ city S W. Germany on the Rhine ✻ of Rhineland-Palatinate pop 187,392
Ma·jor·ca \mə-'jór-kə, -'yór-\ or Sp **Ma·llor·ca** \mä-'yor-kə\ island Spain, largest of the Balearic islands; chief city Palma area 1405 sq mi (3653 sq km) — **Ma·jor·can** \mə-'jòr-kən, -'yòr-\ adj or n
Ma·jun·ga \mə-'jəŋ-gə\ or **Ma·ha·jan·ga** \mə-hə-'jəŋ-gə\ city & port NW Madagascar pop 65,864
Ma·ka·lu \'mək-ə-,lü\ mountain 27,824 ft (8481 m) in the Himalayas in NE Nepal SE of Mt. Everest; 5th highest in world
Ma·kas·sar \mə-'kas-ər\ **1** or **UJUNG PANDANG 2** or **Ma·kas·ar** or **Ma·cas·sar** strait Indonesia bet. E Borneo & W Celebes
Ma·ka·téa \,mä-kə-'tā-ə\ island S Pacific in NW Tuamotu archipelago area 8 sq mi (21 sq km)
Ma·ke·yev·ka \mə-'kā-(y)əf-kə\ city U.S.S.R. in E Ukrainian Republic in Donets basin NE of Donetsk pop 393,000
Ma·kga·di·kga·di \mä-,käd-ē-'käd-ē\ large salt basin NE Botswana

Ma·khach·ka·la \mə-ˌkäch-kə-'lä\ *or formerly* Pe·trovsk \pə-'trófsk\ city U.S.S.R. in SE Soviet Russia, Europe, on the Caspian ✹ of Dagestan *pop* 251,000

Ma·kin \'mäk-ən, 'mä-kən\ *or* Bu·ta·ri·ta·ri \bù-ˌtär-ē-'tär-ē\ island (atoll) W Pacific at N end of Kiribati *area* 4 *sq mi* (10 *sq km*), *pop* 2714

Mal·a·bar \'mal-ə-ˌbär\ coast region SW India on Arabian sea in Karnataka & Kerala states

Ma·la·bo \mä-'lä-(ˌ)bō\ *or formerly* San·ta Isabel \ˌsan-tə-'iz-ə-ˌbel\ city ✹ of Equatorial Guinea on Bioko Is. *pop* 37,237

Ma·lac·ca \mə-'lak-ə, -'läk-\ 1 state Malaysia on W coast of Peninsular Malaysia *area* 633 *sq mi* (1646 *sq km*), *pop* 453,153 2 *or* Me·laka city, its ✹ *pop* 250,635 — Ma·lac·can \-ən\ *adj*

Malacca, Strait of channel 500 *mi* (805 *km*) long between S Malay peninsula & island of Sumatra

Má·la·ga \'mal-ə-gə\ 1 province S Spain in Andalusia *area* 2812 *sq mi* (7311 *sq km*), *pop* 958,967 2 city & port, its ✹, NE of Gibraltar *pop* 502,232

Malagasy Republic — see MADAGASCAR

Ma·lai·ta \mə-'lät-ə\ island SW Pacific in the SE Solomons NE of Guadalcanal *area* 2500 *sq mi* (6500 *sq km*), *pop* 50,661

Ma·lang \mä-'län\ city Indonesia in E Java S of Surabaja *pop* 341,452

Mä·lar·en \'mä-ˌlär-ən\ lake SE Sweden extending from Baltic sea 70 *mi* (113 *km*) inland

Ma·la·tya \ˌmäl-ə-'tyä\ *or anc* Mel·i·te·ne \ˌmel-ə-'tē-nē\ city E Turkey NE of Gaziantep *pop* 184,390

Ma·la·wi \mə-'lä-wē, -'laù-ē\ *or formerly* Ny·asa·land \nī-'as-ə-ˌland, nē-\ country SE Africa bordering on Lake Malawi; formerly a Brit. protectorate; independent member of the Commonwealth since 1964; a republic since 1966 ✹ Lilongwe *area* 37,374 *sq mi* (97,172 *sq km*), *pop* 5,547,460 — Ma·la·wi·an \-ən\ *adj or n*

Malawi, Lake *or* Lake Ny·asa \nī-'as-ə, nē-\ lake SE Africa in Great Rift valley in Malawi, Mozambique, & Tanzania

Ma·lay \mə-'lā, 'mā-(ˌ)lā\ 1 archipelago SE Asia including Sumatra, Java, Borneo, Celebes, Moluccas, & Timor; usu. considered as including also the Philippines & sometimes New Guinea 2 peninsula 700 *mi* (1126 *km*) long SE Asia divided bet. Thailand & Malaysia 3 sea SE Asia surrounding the Malay archipelago

Ma·la·ya \mə-'lā-ə, mä-\ 1 the Malay peninsula 2 *or* BRITISH MALAYA 3 *or* Federation of Malaya former country SE Asia; a Brit. dominion 1957–63, since 1963 a territory (now called Peninsular Malaysia) of Malaysia ✹ Kuala Lumpur *area* 50,690 *sq mi* (131,794 *sq km*)

Ma·lay·sia \mə-'lā-zh(ē-)ə, -sh(ē-)ə\ 1 the Malay archipelago 2 *or* Federation of Malaysia country SE Asia, a union of Malaya, Sabah (N. Borneo), Sarawak, & (until 1965) Singapore; a limited constitutional monarchy in the Commonwealth ✹ Kuala Lumpur *area* 128,703 *sq mi* (334,628 *sq km*), *pop* 13,700,000 — Ma·lay·sian \mə-'lā-zhən, -shən\ *adj or n*

Mal·den \'mól-dən\ 1 city E Mass. N of Boston *pop* 53,386 2 island *cen* Pacific, one of the Line islands

Mal·dives \'mól-ˌdēv, -ˌdīv- *also* 'mal-, -ˌdiv\ islands in Indian ocean S of the Laccadives; a sultanate under Brit. protection until 1965; now an independent member of the Commonwealth as Republic of Maldives ✹ Male *area* 115 *sq mi* (299 *sq km*), *pop* 143,046 — Mal·div·i·an \mól-'div-ē-ən, mal-\ *adj or n*

Ma·le \'mäl-ē\ island (atoll), chief of the Maldives

Ma·lea, Cape \mə-'lē-ə\ cape S Greece at extremity of E peninsula of the Peloponnisos

Ma·le·bo Pool \mä-'lā-ˌbō-\ *or* Stanley Pool expansion of Congo river *ab* 20 *mi* (32 *km*) long 300 *mi* (483 *km*) above its mouth between Congo & Zaire

Malgache, République — see MADAGASCAR

Mal·heur \'mal-ˌhú(ə)r\ lake SE Oreg. in Harney basin

Ma·li \'mäl-ē, 'mal-ē\ 1 federation 1959–60 of Senegal & Sudanese Republic 2 *or formerly* Sudanese Republic country W Africa in W Sahara & Sudan regions; a republic; before 1958 constituted French Sudan (a territory of France) ✹ Bamako *area* 461,389 *sq mi* (1,199,611 *sq km*), *pop* 6,524,650 — Ma·li·an \-ē-ən\ *adj or n*

Malines — see MECHLIN

Mal·in Head \ˌmal-ən-\ cape Ireland (republic) in county Donegal; northernmost tip of Ireland

Mal·mé·dy \ˌmal-mə-'dē\ commune E Belgium SE of Liège; formerly in Germany, transferred (with Eupen) to Belgium 1919 *pop* 10,036

Malmö \'mal-ˌmə(r)\ city & port SW Sweden on Öresund opposite Copenhagen, Denmark *pop* 258,311

Mal·ta \'mól-tə\ *or anc* Mel·i·ta \'mel-ət-ə\ 1 *or* Maltese islands \ˌmól-ˌtēz-, -ˌtēs-\ group of islands in the Mediterranean S of Sicily; a dominion of the Commonwealth since 1964 ✹ Valletta *area* 122 *sq mi* (317 *sq km*), *pop* 366,000 2 island, chief of the group *area* 95 *sq mi* (247 *sq km*)

Maluku — see MOLUCCAS

Mal·vern \'mól(-)vərn\ hills W England in Hereford and Worcester

Malvinas, Islas — see FALKLAND

Ma·mar·o·neck \mə-'mar-ə-ˌnek, -nik\ village SE N.Y. *pop* 17,616

Mam·be·ra·mo \ˌmam-bə-'räm-(ˌ)ō\ river 500 *mi* (805 *km*) W. New Guinea flowing NW into the Pacific

Mammoth Cave \ˌmam-əth-\ limestone caverns SW *cen* Kentucky in Mammoth Cave National Park

Ma·mo·ré \ˌmäm-ə-'rā\ river 1200 *mi* (1931 *km*) Bolivia flowing N to unite with the Beni on Brazilian border forming Madeira river

Man, Isle of \'man\ *or anc* Mo·na·pia \mō-'nä-pē-ə\ *or* Mo·na \'mō-nə\ island British Isles in Irish sea; a possession of the Brit. Crown; has own legislature & laws ✹ Douglas *area* 221 *sq mi* (575 *sq km*), *pop* 60,496 — Manx·man \'maŋ(k)-smən\ *n*

Ma·na·do \mə-'näd-(ˌ)ō\ city & port Indonesia on NE Celebes Is. on Celebes sea *pop* 217,159

Ma·na·gua \mə-'näg-wə\ 1 lake 38 *mi* (61 *km*) long W Nicaragua draining S to Lake Nicaragua 2 city ✹ of Nicaragua on Lake Managua *pop* 552,900

Ma·na·ma \mə-'nam-ə\ city ✹ of Bahrain *pop* 108,684

Ma·na·tí \ˌmän-ə-'tē\ town N Puerto Rico *pop* 17,347

Ma·naus \mə-'naus\ city W Brazil ✹ of Amazonas on Negro river 12 *mi* (19 *km*) from its junction with the Amazon *pop* 634,659

Mancha, La — see LA MANCHA

Manche, La — see ENGLISH CHANNEL

Man·ches·ter \'man-ˌches-tər, -chə-stər\ 1 town *cen* Conn. E of Hartford *pop* 49,761 2 city S N.H. on the Merrimack *pop* 90,936 3 city NW England ENE of Liverpool *pop* 448,934 — see GREATER MANCHESTER — Man·cu·nian \man-'kyü-nē-ən, -nyən\ *adj or n*

Man·chu·kuo \'man-ˌchü-'kwō, man-'chü-\ former country (1931–45) E Asia in Manchuria & E Inner Mongolia ✹ Changchun

Man·chu·ria \man-'chúr-ē-ə\ region NE China S of the Amur including Heilungkiang, Kirin, & Liaoning provinces & part of Inner Mongolia — Man·chu·ri·an \-ē-ən\ *adj or n*

Man·da·lay \ˌman-də-'lā\ city *cen* Myanmar *pop* 453,000

Man·ga·ia \mäŋ-'(g)ī-ə\ island S Pacific in SE Cook islands; completely encircled by reef *area* 25 *sq mi* (65 *sq km*)

Man·ga·lore \ˌmäŋ-gə-ˌlō(ə)r, -ˌló(ə)r\ city S India in Karnataka on Malabar coast W of Bangalore *pop* 305,513

Man·ga·re·va \ˌmäŋ-gə-'rā-və\ island S Pacific, chief of the Gambier islands *area* 7 *sq mi* (18 *sq km*)

Man·hat·tan \man-'hat-²n, mən-\ 1 city NE *cen* Kans. on Kansas river *pop* 32,644 2 island 13 *mi* (21 *km*) long SE N.Y. on New York Bay 3 borough of New York City comprising Manhattan Is., several small adjacent islands, & a small area (Marble Hill) on mainland *pop* 1,524,541 — Man·hat·tan·ite \-ˌīt\ *n*

Manhattan Beach city SW Calif. S of Los Angeles *pop* 31,542

Ma·ni·hi·ki \ˌmän-ə-'hē-kē\ 1 — see NORTHERN COOK 2 island, chief of the Northern Cook group; an atoll *pop* 408

Ma·nila \mə-'nil-ə\ city & port ✹ of the Philippines on W coast of Luzon on Manila Bay (inlet of S. China sea) *pop* 1,630,485

Man·i·pur \ˌman-ə-'pú(ə)r, -mən-\ 1 river 210 *mi* (338 *km*) NE India & W Myanmar flowing into the Chindwin 2 state NE India bet. Assam & Myanmar ✹ Imphal *area* 8628 *sq mi* (22,433 *sq km*)

Ma·ni·sa *or* Ma·nis·sa \ˌmän-ə-'sä\ *or anc* Mag·ne·sia \mag-'nē-shə, -zhə\ city W Turkey NE of Izmir *pop* 93,970

Man·i·to·ba \ˌman-ə-'tō-bə\ province S *cen* Canada ✹ Winnipeg *area* 251,000 *sq mi* (652,600 *sq km*), *pop* 1,026,241 — Man·i·to·ban \-bən\ *adj or n*

Manitoba, Lake lake 120 *mi* (193 *km*) long Canada in S Man. *area* 1817 *sq mi* (4724 *sq km*)

Man·i·tou·lin \ˌman-ə-'tü-lən\ island 80 *mi* (129 *km*) long Canada in Ont. in Lake Huron *area* 1068 *sq mi* (2777 *sq km*)

Man·i·to·woc \'man-ət-ə-ˌwäk\ city E Wis. *pop* 32,547

Ma·ni·za·les \ˌman-ə-'zäl-əs, -'zal-\ city W *cen* Colombia in Cauca valley *pop* 267,543

Man·ka·to \man-'kāt-(ˌ)ō\ city S Minn. *pop* 28,651

Man·nar, Gulf of \mə-'när\ inlet of Indian ocean between Sri Lanka & S tip of India S of Palk strait

Mann·heim \'man-ˌhīm, 'män-\ city S W. Germany at confluence of the Rhine & the Neckar *pop* 304,303

Mans·field \'man(t)s-ˌfēld, 'manz-\ 1 town *cen* Conn. *pop* 20,634 2 city N *cen* Ohio *pop* 53,927 3 borough N England in Nottinghamshire N of Nottingham *pop* 58,949

Mansfield, Mount mountain 4393 *ft* (1339 *m*) N Vt.; highest in Green mountains & in state

Man·sû·ra *or* El Mansûra \(ˌel-)man-'sûr-ə\ city N Egypt in Nile delta *pop* 212,300

Man·te·ca \man-'tē-kə\ city *cen* Calif. S of Stockton *pop* 24,925

Man·tua \'manch-(ə-)wə, 'mant-ə-wə\ *or* Man·to·va \'män-tə-və\ commune N Italy in Lombardy WSW of Venice *pop* 60,932 — Man·tu·an \'manch-(ə-)wən, 'mant-ə-wən\ *adj or n*

Ma·nua \mə-'nü-ə\ islands SW Pacific in American Samoa E of Tutuila *area* 22 *sq mi* (57 *sq km*)

Ma·nus \'män-əs\ island SW Pacific in Admiralty islands; largest of group *area* 600 *sq mi* (1560 *sq km*)

Man·za·la, Lake \man-'zäl-ə\ *or anc* Ta·nis \'tä-nəs\ lagoon N Egypt in Nile delta W of N entrance of Suez canal

Man·za·ni·llo \ˌman-zə-'nē-(ˌ)(y)ō\ 1 city & port E Cuba on the Caribbean *pop* 124,537 2 city & port SW Mexico in Colima *pop* 29,347

Mao·ke \'maù-kā\ *or formerly* Snow \'snō\ mountains W. Irian; include Sudirman & Djajawidjaja ranges — see DJADJA (Mount)

Maple Grove city SE *cen* Minn. *pop* 20,525

Maple Heights city NE Ohio SE of Cleveland *pop* 29,735

Ma·ple·wood \'mā-pəl-ˌwúd\ village SE Minn. *pop* 26,990

Ma·pu·to \mä-'pü-(ˌ)tō\ *or formerly* Lou·ren·ço Mar·ques \lə-ˌren(t)-(ˌ)sō-ˌmär-'kes, -'märk(s)\ city & port ✹ of Mozambique on Delagoa Bay *pop* 755,300

Ma·quo·ke·ta \mə-'kō-kət-ə\ river 150 *mi* (241 *km*) E Iowa flowing SE into Mississippi river

Mar·a·cai·bo \ˌmar-ə-'kī-(ˌ)bō\ city NW Venezuela on channel between Lake Maracaibo & Gulf of Venezuela *pop* 929,000

Maracaibo, Lake the S extension of Gulf of Venezuela in NW Venezuela *area* 6300 *sq mi* (16,380 *sq km*)

Maracanda — see SAMARKAND

Ma·ra·cay \ˌmär-ə-'kī\ city N Venezuela WSW of Caracas *pop* 185,655

Marais des Cygnes \'mard-ə-ˌzēn\ river 150 *mi* (241 *km*) E Kans. & W Mo. flowing into the Osage

Ma·ra·nhão \ˌmar-ən-'yaùⁿ\ state NE Brazil bordering on the Atlantic ✹ São Luis *area* 133,674 *sq mi* (347,552 *sq km*), *pop* 4,097,231

Ma·ra·ñón \ˌmar-ən-'yōn\ river 800 *mi* (1287 *km*) N Peru flowing from the Andes NNW & E to join the Ucayali forming the Amazon

Ma·ras *or* Ma·rash \mə-'räsh\ city S *cen* Turkey *pop* 63,284

Mar·a·thon \'mar-ə-ˌthän, -thən\ 1 plain E Greece in Attica NE of Athens on the Aegean 2 ancient town on the plain

Marble Canyon canyon of Colorado river N Ariz. just above the Grand Canyon, sometimes considered its upper portion

Mar·ble·head \'mär-bəl-ˌhed, ˌmär-bəl-'\ town E Mass. *pop* 20,126

Mar·burg \'mär-ˌbú(ə)rg, -ˌbərg\ city *cen* W. Germany in Hesse N of Frankfurt am Main *pop* 76,419

Marche \'märsh\ region & former province *cen* France NW of Auvergne

---

\ə\ abut \ᵊ\ kitten, F table \ər\ further \a\ ash \ā\ ace \ä\ cot, cart \aù\ out \ch\ chin \e\ bet \ē\ easy \g\ go \i\ hit \ī\ ice \j\ job \ŋ\ sing \ō\ go \ò\ law \òi\ boy \th\ thin \th\ the \ü\ loot \ù\ foot \y\ yet \zh\ vision \à, k̲, ⁿ, œ, œ̄, ս̈, ᵞ\ *see* Guide to Pronunciation

March·es \'mär-chəz\ *or* **Le Mar·che** \lā-'mär-(,)kā\ region *cen* Italy on the Adriatic NW of Abruzzi ✻ Ancona
Mar·cus \'mär-kəs\ island W Pacific E of the Bonin islands, belonging to Japan; occupied 1945–68 by U.S. *area* 1 *sq mi* (2.6 *sq km*)
Mar·cy, Mount \'mär-sē\ mountain 5344 *ft* (1629 *m*) NE N.Y.; highest in Adirondack mountains & in state
Mar del Pla·ta \,mär-,del-'plät-ə\ city & port E Argentina SSE of Buenos Aires *pop* 407,024
Mare \'ma(ə)r, 'me(ə)r\ island W Calif. in San Pablo Bay
Ma·rem·ma \mə-'rem-ə\ low-lying district W Italy on Tyrrhenian coast in SW Tuscany; formerly swampland
Ma·ren·go \mə-'reŋ-(,)gō\ village NW Italy in SE Piedmont
Mar·eo·tis, Lake \,mar-ē-'ōt-əs\ *or Ar* **Mar·yût** \mər-'yüt\ lake N Egypt in Nile delta; Alexandria is situated bet. it & the Mediterranean
Ma·reth \'mär-əth, 'mar-\ town SE Tunisia SSE of Gabes
Mar·ga·ri·ta \,mär-gə-'rēt-ə\ island N Venezuela in the Caribbean, chief of the **Nue·va Es·par·ta** \nü-,ā-və-es-'pärt-ə\ group; chief town & port Porlamar *area* 444 *sq mi* (1154 *sq km*)
Mar·gate \'mär-,gāt\ **1** city SE Fla. *pop* 36,044 **2** \-,gāt, -gət\ borough SE England in Kent on coast of Isle of Thanet *pop* 53,280
Mar·i·ana \,mar-ē-'an-ə, ,mer-\ *or formerly* **La·drone** \lə-'drōn\ islands W Pacific S of Bonin islands; comprise commonwealth of Northern Mariana islands & Guam
Ma·ri·a·nao \,mär-ē-ə-'naü\ city W Cuba, W suburb of Havana *pop* 127,563
Ma·ri·an·ske Laz·ne \,mär-ē-,än(t)-skə-'läz-nə\ *or G* **Ma·ri·en·bad** \mə-'rē-ən-,bad, -,bät\ town W Czechoslovakia in NW Bohemia NE of Plzeň
Ma·ri·as \mə-'rī-əs, -əz\ **1** river 250 *mi* (402 *km*) NW Mont. flowing SE to Missouri river **2** mountain pass 5213 *ft* (1589 *m*) NW Mont. in Lewis range at SE corner of Glacier National Park
Ma·ri·bor \'mär-i-,bȯ(ə)r\ city NW Yugoslavia *pop* 97,167
Ma·rie Byrd Land \mə-,rē-'bərd-\ region W Antarctica E of Ross Ice Shelf & Ross sea
Ma·rie Ga·lante \mə-,rē-gə-'länt\ island E W. Indies in the Leewards; a dependency of Guadeloupe *area* 60 *sq mi* (156 *sq km*), *pop* 15,912
Ma·rie·hamn \mə-,rē-'ham-ən\ *or* **Maa·rian·ha·mi·na** \'mär-yan-,ham-ə-,nä\ seaport SW Finland ✻ of Ahvenanmaa *pop* 9638
Mar·i·et·ta \,mar-ē-'et-ə, ,mer-\ city NW Ga. NW of Atlanta *pop* 30,829
Ma·rin·du·que \,mar-ən-'dü-(,)kā, ,mär-\ island Philippines in Sibuyan sea S of Luzon; chief town Boac *area* 355 *sq mi* (923 *sq km*), *pop* 173,715
Mar·i·on \'mer-ē-ən, 'mar-\ **1** city N *cen* Ind. *pop* 35,874 **2** city E Iowa NE of Cedar Rapids *pop* 19,474 **3** city *cen* Ohio *pop* 37,040
Ma·ri Republic \'mär-ē\ autonomous republic U.S.S.R. in E *cen* Soviet Russia, Europe ✻ Ioshkar Ola *area* 8900 *sq mi* (23,140 *sq km*), *pop* 685,000
Maritime Alps section of the W Alps SE France & NW Italy extending to the Mediterranean; highest point Punta Argentera 10,817 *ft* (3297 *m*)
Maritime Provinces *or* **Maritimes** the Canadian provinces of N.B., N.S., P.E.I. & sometimes thought to include Nfld. — see ATLANTIC PROVINCES
Maritime Territory *or Russ* **Pri·mor·ye** \prē-'mȯr-yə\ territory U.S.S.R. in E Soviet Russia, Asia, bordering on Sea of Japan ✻ Vladivostok *area* 64,900 *sq mi* (168,740 *sq km*), *pop* 1,722,000
Ma·ri·tsa \mə-'rēt-sə\ *or NGk* **Év·ros** \'ev-,rȯs\ *or Turk* **Me·ric** \mə-'rēch\ river 320 *mi* (515 *km*) S Europe flowing from W Rhodope mountains in S Bulgaria E & S through Thrace into the Aegean
Ma·ri·u·pol \,mar-ē-'ü-,pȯl\ *or 1949–1989* **Zhda·nov** \zhə-'dän-əf, 'shtän-\ city U.S.S.R. in E Ukrainian Republic *pop* 417,000
Mark·ham \'mär-kəm\ **1** town Canada in SE Ont. NE of Toronto *pop* 77,037 **2** river 200 *mi* (322 *km*) E New Guinea flowing S & SE into Solomon sea
Markham, Mount mountain 14,275 *ft* (4351 *m*) Antarctica in Queen Elizabeth Range W of Ross Ice Shelf
Marl \'mär(ə)l\ city W W. Germany in the Ruhr *pop* 89,082
Marl·bor·ough *or* **Marl·boro** \'märl-,bər-ə, 'mȯl-, -,bə-rə, -brə\ city E Mass. E of Worcester *pop* 30,617
Mar·ma·ra, Sea of \'mär-mə-rə\ *or anc* **Pro·pon·tis** \prə-'pänt-əs\ sea NW Turkey connected with Black Sea by the Bosporus & with Aegean sea by the Dardanelles *area* 4250 *sq mi* (11,050 *sq km*)
Mar·mo·la·da \,mär-mə-'läd-ə\ mountain 10,965 *ft* (3342 *m*) NE Italy; highest in the Dolomites
Marne \'märn\ river 325 *mi* (523 *km*) NE France flowing W into the Seine
Ma·ro·ni \mə-'rō-nē\ *or D* **Ma·ro·wij·ne** \,mär-ə-'vī-nə\ river 420 *mi* (676 *km*) on border between Suriname & French Guiana flowing N into the Atlantic
Maros — see MURES
Mar·que·sas \mär-'kā-zəz, -zəs, -səz, -səs\ *or F* **Îles Mar·quises** \,ē(ə)l-mär-'kēz\ islands S Pacific N of Tuamotu archipelago in French Polynesia *area* 480 *sq mi* (1248 *sq km*), *pop* 5147
Mar·quette \mär-'ket\ city NW Mich. in upper peninsula on Lake Superior *pop* 23,288
Mar·ra·kech *or* **Mar·ra·kesh** \mə-'räk-ish, ,mar-ə-'kesh\ *or formerly* **Mo·roc·co** \mə-'räk-(,)ō\ city *cen* Morocco in foothills of the Grand Atlas *pop* 439,728
Mar·sa·la \mär-'säl-ə\ city & port Italy on W coast of Sicily S of Trapani *pop* 79,093
Mar·seilles \mär-'sā, -'sā(ə)lz\ *or* **Mar·seille** \mär-'sā\ *or anc* **Mas·sil·ia** \mə-'sil-ē-ə\ city & port SE France on Gulf of Lions *pop* 908,600
Mar·shall \'mär-shəl\ **1** city NE Tex. *pop* 24,921 **2** islands E Trust Territory of the Pacific Islands ✻ Majuro; internally self-governing since 1980 — **Mar·shall·ese** \,mär-shə-'lēz, -'lēs\ *adj or n*
Mar·shall·town \'mär-shəl-,taün\ city *cen* Iowa *pop* 26,938
Marsh·field \'märsh-,fēld\ **1** town E Mass. N of Plymouth *pop* 20,916 **2** city N *cen* Wis. *pop* 18,290
Mar·ston Moor \,mär-stən-\ locality N England in N. Yorkshire W of York
Mar·ta·ban, Gulf of \,märt-ə-'ban\ arm of Andaman sea S Myanmar
Mar·tha's Vineyard \,mär-thəz-\ island 20 *mi* (32 *km*) long SE Mass. in the Atlantic off SW coast of Cape Cod WNW of Nantucket — **Vine·yard·er** \'vin-yərd-ər\ *n*
Mar·ti·nez \mär-'tē-nəs\ city W Calif. NE of Oakland *pop* 22,582
Mar·ti·nique \,märt-ᵊn-'ēk\ island W. Indies in the Windwards; department of France ✻ Fort-de-France *area* 385 *sq mi* (1001 *sq km*), *pop* 326,717
Mar·tins·ville \'märt-ᵊnz-,vil, -vəl\ city S Va. *pop* 18,149
Marwar — see JODHPUR
Mary·land \'mer-ə-lənd\ state E U.S. ✻ Annapolis *area* 10,577 *sq mi* (27,500 *sq km*), *pop* 4,216,975 — **Mary·land·er** \-lən-dər, -,lan-\ *n*
Mary·le·bone \'mar-(ə-)lə-bən, 'mar-i-bən\ *or* **Saint Marylebone** former metropolitan borough W *cen* London, England; now part of Westminster
Mary·ville \'mer-ē-,vil, 'mar-ē-, 'mā-rē-, -vəl\ city E Tenn. *pop* 17,480
Ma·sa·da \mə-'säd-ə\ fortress town of ancient Palestine, site in SE Israel W of Dead sea
Ma·san \'mäs-,än\ *or formerly* **Ma·sam·po** \'mäs-,äm-,pō\ city & port SE S. Korea on an inlet of Korea strait E of Pusan *pop* 386,773
Mas·ba·te \mäz-'bät-ē\ island *cen* Philippines in the Visayans NE of Panay *area* 1571 *sq mi* (4085 *sq km*)
Mas·ca·rene \,mas-kə-'rēn\ islands W Indian ocean E of Madagascar including Mauritius, Réunion, and Rodrigues
Mas·couche \mas-'küsh\ town Canada in S Que. N of Montreal *pop* 20,345
Mas·e·ru \'maz-ə-,rü\ city ✻ of Lesotho *pop* 71,500
Mash·had \mə-'shad\ *or* **Me·shed** \mə-'shed\ city NE Iran *pop* 667,770
Ma·son City \,mās-ᵊn-\ city N Iowa *pop* 30,144
Ma·son–Dix·on line \,mās-ᵊn-'dik-sən-\ the boundary line from the SW corner of Del. N to Pa. & W to approximately the SW corner of Pa. & often considered the boundary bet. the N & S states
Mas·sa·chu·setts \,mas(-ə)-'chü-səts, -zəts\ state NE U.S. ✻ Boston *area* 8257 *sq mi* (21,468 *sq km*), *pop* 5,737,037
Massachusetts Bay inlet of the Atlantic E Mass.
Mas·sa·nut·ten Mountain \,mas-ə-'nət-ᵊn\ ridge N Va. in Blue Ridge mountains
Mas·sa·pe·qua Park \,mas-ə-'pē-kwə\ village SE N.Y. on Long Is. *pop* 19,779
Mas·sa·wa \mə-'sä-wə, -'saü-ə\ city & port N Ethiopia in Eritrea on an inlet of Red sea *pop* 18,490
Mas·sif Cen·tral \ma-,sēf-,sen-'träl, -,säⁿ-\ plateau *cen* France rising sharply just W of the Rhône-Saône valley & sloping N to the Paris basin & W to the basin of Aquitaine
Mas·sil·lon \'mas-ə-lən, -,län\ city NE Ohio *pop* 30,557
Mas·sive, Mount \'mas-iv\ mountain 14,421 *ft* (4396 *m*), *cen* Colo. in Sawatch mountains N of Mt. Elbert
Ma·su·ria \mə-'zür-ē-ə, -'sür-\ *or G* **Ma·su·ren** \mə-'zür-ən\ region NE Poland SE of Gulf of Gdansk; formerly in E. Prussia, Germany — **Ma·su·ri·an** \mə-'zür-ē-ən, -'sür-\ *adj*
Mat·a·be·le·land \,mat-ə-'bē-lē-,land\ region SW Zimbabwe between the Limpopo & the Zambezi; chief town Bulawayo
Ma·ta·di \mə-'täd-ē\ town & port W Zaire *pop* 140,475
Mat·a·gor·da Bay \,mat-ə-'gȯrd-ə\ inlet of Gulf of Mexico 30 *mi* (48 *km*) long SE Tex.
Mat·a·mo·ros \,mat-ə-'mōr-əs, -'mȯr-\ city NE Mexico in Tamaulipas on Rio Grande opposite Brownsville, Tex. *pop* 182,887
Mat·a·nus·ka \,mat-ə-'nü-skə\ river 90 *mi* (145 *km*) S Alaska flowing SW to head of Cook inlet
Ma·tan·zas \mə-'tan-zəs\ city & port W Cuba on Straits of Florida E of Havana *pop* 109,747
Matapan — see TAÍNARON
Ma·thu·ra \'mət-ə-rə\ *or* **Mut·tra** \'mə-trə\ city N India in W Uttar Pradesh NW of Agra *pop* 160,995
Mat·lock \'mat-,läk\ town N England ✻ of Derbyshire *pop* 20,610
Ma·to Gros·so *or formerly* **Mat·to Gros·so** \,mat-ə-'grō-(,)sō\ **1** state SW Brazil ✻ Cuiabá *area* 475,504 *sq mi* (1,236,310 *sq km*), *pop* 1,169,812 **2** plateau region in E *cen* Mato Grosso state
Ma·to Gros·so do Sul \-dō-'sül\ state SW Brazil ✻ Campo Grande *area* 140,219 *sq mi* (350,548 *sq km*), *pop* 1,401,151
Mato Tepee — see DEVILS TOWER
Ma·trûh \mə-'trü\ *or* **Mer·sa Matrûh** \(,)mər-,sä-\ town NW Egypt
Mat·su \'mät-'sü, 'mat-, -(,)sü\ island off SE China in Formosa strait; administered by Taiwan *pop* 11,002
Ma·tsue \'mät-sə-,wā, -sü-,yā\ city of Japan in W Honshu NW of Hiroshima *pop* 136,662
Ma·tsu·mo·to \,mät-sə-'mōt-(,)ō\ city Japan in *cen* Honshu NE of Nagoya *pop* 192,769
Ma·tsu·shi·ma \,mät-sü-'shē-mə, mät-'sü-shi-mə\ group of over 200 islets Japan off N Honshu NE of Sendai
Mat·su·ya·ma \,mät-sə-'yäm-ə\ city & port Japan in W Shikoku *pop* 407,969
Mat·tag·a·mi \mə-'tag-ə-mē\ river 275 *mi* (442 *km*) Canada in E Ont.
Mat·ta·po·ni \,mat-ə-pə-'nī\ river 125 *mi* (201 *km*) E Va.
Mat·ter·horn \'mat-ər-,hȯ(ə)rn, 'mät-\ *or F* **Mont Cer·vin** \mōⁿ-ser-'vaⁿ\ mountain 14,690 *ft* (4478 *m*) in Pennine Alps on border between Switzerland & Italy
Mat·toon \mə-'tün, ma-\ city SE *cen* Ill. *pop* 19,055
Ma·tu·rín \,mät-ə-'rēn\ city NE Venezuela *pop* 97,257
Maui \'maü-ē\ island Hawaii NW of Hawaii (island) *area* 728 *sq mi* (1893 *sq km*)
Mau·mee \(ˈ)mȯ-'mē\ river 175 *mi* (282 *km*) NE Ind. & NW Ohio flowing NE into Lake Erie at Toledo
Mau·na Kea \,maü-nə-'kā-ə\ extinct volcano 13,796 *ft* (4205 *m*) Hawaii in N *cen* Hawaii (island)
Mauna Loa \-'lō-ə\ volcano 13,680 *ft* (4170 *m*) Hawaii in S *cen* Hawaii (island) in Hawaii Volcanoes National Park — see KILAUEA
Maures, Monts des \,mōⁿ-dā-'mō(ə)r, -'mȯ(ə)r\ mountains SE France along the Riviera SW of Fréjus
Mau·re·ta·nia *or* **Mau·ri·ta·nia** \,mȯr-ə-'tā-nē-ə, ,mär-, -nyə\ ancient country N Africa W of Numidia in modern Morocco & W Algeria — **Mau·re·ta·nian** *or* **Mau·ri·ta·nian** \-nē-ən, -nyən\ *adj or n*
Mauritania *or F* **Mau·ri·ta·nie** \mȯ-rē-tà-nē\ country NW Africa bordering on the Atlantic N of Senegal river; a republic within the French Community, formerly a territory ✻ Nouakchott *area ab* 432,000 *sq mi* (1,123,200 *sq km*), *pop* 1,419,939 — **Mau·ri·ta·nian** \mȯr-ə-'tā-nē-ən, ,mär-, -nyən\ *adj or n*
Mau·ri·ti·us \mȯ-'rish-(ē-)əs\ island in Indian ocean in *cen* Mascarenes; constitutes with Rodrigues & other dependencies a dominion of the

Commonwealth ✳ Port Louis *area* 720 *sq mi* (1872 *sq km*), *pop* 993,000
— **Mau·ri·tian** \-'rish-ən\ *adj or n*
May, Cape \'mā\ cape S N.J. at entrance to Delaware Bay
May·a·gua·na \,mä-ə-'gwän-ə\ island in the SE Bahamas NNE of Great Inagua Is. *area* 96 *sq mi* (250 *sq km*)
Ma·ya·güez \,mī-ə-'gwez, -'gwes\ city & port W Puerto Rico *pop* 82,968
Ma·ya·pán \,mī-ə-'pän\ ruined city ✳ of the Mayas SE Mexico in Yucatán SSE of Mérida
Mayence — see MAINZ
Ma·yenne \mä-'yen\ river 125 *mi* (201 *km*) NW France uniting with the Sarthe to form the **Maine** \'män\ (8 *mi* or 13 *km* long, flowing into the Loire)
May·fair \'mā-,fa(ə)r, -,fe(ə)r\ district of W London, England, in Westminster borough
May·field Heights \,mā-,fēld\ city NE Ohio E of Cleveland *pop* 21,550
May·nooth \mā-'nüth\ town E Ireland in County Kildare
Mayo 1 \'mī-(,)ō\ river 250 *mi* (402 *km*) NW Mexico in Sonora flowing SW into Gulf of California 2 \'mā-(,)ō\ county NW Ireland in Connacht ✳ Castlebar *area* 2084 *sq mi* (5418 *sq km*), *pop* 114,766
Ma·yon \mä-'yōn\ volcano 7943 *ft* (2421 *m*) Philippines in SE Luzon
Ma·yotte \mä-'yät\ island of the Comoro group; a French dependency *area* 144 *sq mi* (374 *sq km*) — see COMORO ISLANDS
May·wood \'mā-,wud\ 1 city SW Calif. W of Whittier *pop* 21,810 2 village NE Ill. W of Chicago *pop* 27,998
Mayyali — see MAHÉ
Mazaca — see KAYSERI
Ma·za·tlán \,mä-zə-'tlän, ,mäs-\ city & port W Mexico in Sinaloa on the Pacific *pop* 147,010
Mba·bane \,em-bə-'bän\ town ✳ of Swaziland *pop* 23,109
Mban·da·ka \,em-,bän-'däk-ə\ or formerly **Co·qui·lhat·ville** \,kō-kē-'at-,vil\ city W Zaire on Congo river *pop* 137,484
Mbi·ni \em-'bē-nē\ or formerly **Río Mu·ni** \,rē-ō-'mü-nē\ mainland portion of Equatorial Guinea bordering on Gulf of Guinea ✳ Bata *area* 10,040 *sq mi* (26,104 *sq km*)
Mbomou — see BOMU
Mbu·ji-Ma·yi \em-,bü-jē-'mī-,ē\ or formerly **Ba·kwan·ga** \bə-'kwän-gə\ city S Zaire *pop* 285,470
Mc·Al·es·ter \mə-'kal-ə-stər\ city E *cen* Okla. *pop* 17,255
Mc·Al·len \mə-'kal-ən\ city S Tex. WNW of Brownsville *pop* 66,281
Mc·Kees·port \mə-'kēz-,pō(ə)rt, -,pó(ə)rt\ city SW Pa. S of Pittsburgh *pop* 31,012
Mc·Kin·ley, Mount \mə-'kin-lē\ or **De·na·li** \də-'näl-ē\ mountain 20,320 *ft* (6194 *m*) *cen* Alaska in Alaska range; highest in U.S. & N. America; in Denali National Park
M'·Clure Strait \mə-,klü(ə)r-\ channel N Canada between Banks Is. & Melville Is. opening on the W into Arctic ocean
Mc·Mur·do Sound \mək-,mərd-ō-\ inlet of W Ross sea Antarctica bet. Ross Is. & coast of Victoria Land
Mead, Lake \'mēd\ reservoir NW Ariz. & SE Nev. formed by Hoover Dam in Colorado river
Mearns, The — see KINCARDINE
Meath \'mēth, 'mēth\ county E Ireland in NE Leinster ✳ Trim *area* 903 *sq mi* (2348 *sq km*), *pop* 95,419
Meaux \'mō\ commune N France ENE of Paris *pop* 41,831
Mec·ca \'mek-ə\ city Saudi Arabia ✳ of Hejaz *pop* 366,801 — **Mec·can** \'mek-ən\ *adj or n*
Mech·lin \'mek-lən\ or Flem **Me·che·len** \'mek-ə-lə(n)\ or F **Ma·lines** \mə-'lēn\ commune N Belgium *pop* 65,466
Meck·len·burg \'mek-lən-,bərg\ region N E. Germany SE of Jutland peninsula & E of the Elbe; in 18th & 19th centuries divided into duchies of **Mecklenburg–Schwe·rin** \-shfä-'rēn\ & **Mecklenburg–Stre·litz** \-'s(h)trä-ləts\ which became grand duchies 1815 & states of Weimar Republic 1919
Me·dan \mā-'dän\ city Indonesia in NE Sumatra *pop* 1,378,955
Me·del·lín \,med-ᵊl-'ēn, ,mä-thə-'yēn\ city NW Colombia NW of Bogotá *pop* 1,163,862
Med·ford \'med-fərd\ 1 city E Mass. N of Boston *pop* 58,076 2 city SW Oreg. *pop* 39,603
Me·dia \'mēd-ē-ə\ ancient country & province of Persian Empire SW Asia in NW modern Iran — **Me·di·an** \-ē-ən\ *adj or n*
Media Atropatene — see AZERBAIJAN
Medicine Bow \'med-ə-sən\ 1 river 120 *mi* (193 *km*) S Wyo. flowing into N. Platte river 2 mountains N Colo. & S Wyo. in the Rockies; highest **Medicine Bow Peak** (in Wyo.) 12,013 *ft* (3662 *m*)
Medicine Hat city Canada in SE Alta. *pop* 40,380
Me·di·na \mə-'dē-nə\ city W Saudi Arabia *pop* 198,186
Medina as–Shaab \-,ash-'shäb\ city People's Democratic Republic of Yemen; formerly a national ✳ & (as **Al It·ti·had** \,al-,it-i-'had, -'häd\) ✳ of Federation of S. Arabia
Mediolanum — see MILAN
Med·i·ter·ra·nean \,med-ə-tə-'rā-nē-ən, -nyən\ sea 2330 *mi* (3750 *km*) long bet. Europe & Africa connecting with the Atlantic through Strait of Gibraltar & with Red sea through Suez canal
Mé·doc \mā-'däk\ district SW France N of Bordeaux
Med·way \'med-,wā\ river 60 *mi* (97 *km*) SE England in Kent flowing NE into Thames river
Mee·rut \'mā-rət, 'mir-ət\ city N India in NW Uttar Pradesh NE of Delhi *pop* 538,461
Meg·a·ra or NGk **Mé·ga·ra** \'meg-ə-rə\ city & port Greece on Saronic Gulf W of Athens *pop* 17,294; chief town of ancient **Meg·a·ris** \'meg-ə-rəs\ (district between Saronic Gulf & Gulf of Corinth) — **Me·gar·i·an** \mə-'gar-ē-ən, me-, -'ger-\ *adj or n*
Me·gha·la·ya \,mä-gə-'lä-yə\ state NE India ✳ Shillong *area* 8666 *sq mi* (22,532 *sq km*), *pop* 1,327,824
Megh·na \'meg-nə\ the lower course of the Surma, India
Me·gid·do \mi-'gid-(,)ō\ ancient city N Palestine N of Samaria
Meis·sen \'mīs-ᵊn\ city S E. Germany NW of Dresden *pop* 43,561
Méjico — see MEXICO
Mek·nes \mek-'nes\ city N Morocco WSW of Fez; former ✳ of Morocco *pop* 248,369
Me·kong \'mā-'koŋ, -'käŋ\ river 2600 *mi* (4184 *km*) SE Asia flowing from Tsinghai (China) S & SE into S. China sea in S Vietnam
Melaka — see MALACCA 2

Mel·a·ne·sia \,mel-ə-'nē-zhə, -shə\ the islands in the Pacific NE of Australia & S of Micronesia including Bismarck archipelago, the Solomons, Vanuatu, New Caledonia, & the Fijis
Mel·bourne \'mel-bərn\ 1 city E Fla. SSW of Cape Kennedy *pop* 46,536 2 city & port SE Australia ✳ of Victoria on Port Phillip Bay *pop* 139,678 — **Mel·bur·ni·an** \mel-'bər-nē-ən\ *n*
Me·li·lla \mə-'lē-(y)ə\ city & port NE Morocco on coast NE of Fez; a Spanish presidio *pop* 60,843
Melita — see MALTA
Melitene — see MALATYA
Me·li·to·pol \,mel-ə-'tó-pəl\ city U.S.S.R. in S Ukrainian Republic near Sea of Azov *pop* 137,000
Melos — see MILOS
Mel·rose \'mel-,rōz\ city E Mass. N of Boston *pop* 30,055
Melrose Park village NE Ill. W of Chicago *pop* 20,735
Mel·ville \'mel-,vil\ 1 island Canada in N Northwest Territories in Parry islands *area* 16,141 *sq mi* (41,967 *sq km*) 2 peninsula Canada in E Northwest Territories between Foxe Basin & an arm of Gulf of Boothia
Melville, Lake lake Canada in Nfld. in Labrador; the inner basin of Hamilton inlet *area* 1133 *sq mi* (2946 *sq km*)
Memel — see KLAIPEDA
Mem·phis \'mem(p)-fəs\ 1 city SW Tenn. on Mississippi river *pop* 646,356 2 ancient city N Egypt on the Nile S of modern Cairo; once ✳ of Egypt — **Mem·phi·an** \-fē-ən\ *adj or n* — **Mem·phite** \'mem-,fīt\ *adj or n*
Mem·phre·ma·gog, Lake \,mem(p)-fri-'mä-,gäg\ lake 30 *mi* (48 *km*) long on border between Canada & the U.S. in Que. & Vt.
Men·ai \'men-,ī\ strait 14 *mi* (22 *km*) long N Wales between Anglesey Is. & mainland
Me Nam — see CHAO PHRAYA
Men·den·hall \'men-dən-,hól\ glacier SE Alaska N of Juneau
Men·de·res \,men-də-'res\ 1 or anc **Mae·an·der** \mē-'an-dər\ river 240 *mi* (386 *km*) W Turkey in Asia flowing SW & W into the Aegean 2 or anc **Sca·man·der** \skə-'man-dər\ river 60 *mi* (96 *km*) NW Turkey in Asia flowing from Mt. Ida W & NW across the plain of ancient Troy into the Dardanelles
Men·dip \'men-,dip, -dəp\ hills SW England in NE Somerset; highest Blackdown 1068 *ft* (326 *m*)
Men·do·ci·no, Cape \,men-də-'sē-(,)nō\ headland NW Calif. SSW of Eureka; extreme W point of Calif., at 124°8'W
Men·do·ta \men-'dōt-ə\ lake 6 *mi* (9.6 *km*) long S Wis. NW of Madison
Men·do·za \men-'dō-zə\ city W Argentina SE of Aconcagua *pop* 109,122
Men·lo Park \,men-(,)lō-\ city S of San Francisco *pop* 25,673
Me·nom·i·nee \mə-'näm-ə-nē\ 1 river 125 *mi* (201 *km*) NE Wis. flowing SE on Mich.–Wis. border into Green Bay 2 iron range NE Wis. & NW Mich. in upper peninsula
Me·nom·o·nee Falls \mə-,näm-ə-nē-\ village SE Wis. *pop* 27,845
Menorca — see MINORCA
Men·ton \mä⁻-tō⁻\ or It **Men·to·ne** \men-'tō-nē\ city SE France on the Mediterranean ENE of Nice *pop* 24,736
Men·tor \'ment-ər\ city NE Ohio NE of Cleveland *pop* 42,065
Men·zel–Bour·gui·ba \men-,zel-búr-'gē-bə\ or formerly **Fer·ry·ville** \'fer-ē-,vil\ city N Tunisia on Lake Bizerte *pop* 42,111
Me·ra·no \mə-'rän-(,)ō\ commune N Italy in Trentino-Alto Adige NW of Bolzano *pop* 33,508
Mer·ced \mər-'sed\ 1 river 150 *mi* (241 *km*) *cen* Calif. flowing W through Yosemite valley into the San Joaquin 2 city *cen* Calif. in San Joaquin valley *pop* 36,499
Mer·cer Island \,mər-sər-\ city W Wash. E of Seattle *pop* 21,522
Mer·cia \'mər-sh(ē-)ə\ ancient Anglian kingdom *cen* England; one of kingdoms in the Anglo-Saxon heptarchy
Mer·gent·heim \'mer-gənt-,hīm\ or **Bad Mergentheim** \(')bät-\ town S *cen* W. Germany in Baden-Württemberg NNE of Stuttgart
Meric — see MARITSA
Mé·ri·da \'mer-əd-ə\ 1 city SE Mexico ✳ of Yucatán *pop* 233,912 2 city W Venezuela S of Lake Maracaibo *pop* 74,214
Mer·i·den \'mer-əd-ᵊn\ city S *cen* Conn. S of Hartford *pop* 57,118
Me·rid·i·an \mə-'rid-ē-ən\ city E *cen* Miss. *pop* 46,577
Merin — see MIRIM
Mer·i·on·eth \,mer-ē-'än-əth\ or **Mer·i·on·eth·shire** \-,shi(ə)r, -shər\ former county NW Wales ✳ Dolgellau
Mer·o·ë \'mer-ə-,wē\ ancient city, site in N *cen* Sudan on the Nile — **Me·ro·ite** \'mer-ə-,wīt\ *n* — **Me·ro·it·ic** \,mer-ə-'wit-ik\ *adj*
Meroë, Isle of ancient region E Sudan between the Nile & Blue Nile river & the Atbara
Mer·rill·ville \'mer-əl-,vil, -,vəl\ town NW Ind. *pop* 27,677
Mer·ri·mack \'mer-ə-,mak\ river 110 *mi* (177 *km*) S N.H. & NE Mass. flowing S & NE into the Atlantic
Mer·ritt \'mer-ət\ island 40 *mi* (64 *km*) long E Fla. W of Canaveral peninsula between Indian & Banana rivers
Mersa Matrûh — see MATRÛH
Mer·sey \'mər-zē\ river 70 *mi* (113 *km*) NW England flowing NW & W into Irish sea through a large estuary
Mer·sey·side \'mər-zē-,sīd\ metropolitan county NW England ✳ Liverpool *area* 250 *sq mi* (650 *sq km*), *pop* 1,524,700
Mer·sin \me(ə)r-'sēn\ city & port S Turkey on the Mediterranean WSW of Adana *pop* 215,300
Mer·thyr Tyd·fil \,mər-thər-'tid-,vil\ borough SE Wales in Mid Glamorgan *pop* 53,843
Mer·ton \'mərt-ᵊn\ borough of SW Greater London, England *pop* 168,100
Me·ru \'mā-(,)rü\ mountain 14,979 *ft* (4566 *m*) NE Tanzania
Me·sa \'mā-sə\ city SW *cen* Ariz. E of Phoenix *pop* 152,453
Me·sa·bi \mə-'säb-ē\ range of hills NE Minn. NW of Duluth containing large deposits of iron

---

Me·sa Verde National Park \\,mä-sə-'vərd(-ē)-\ reservation SW Colo. containing prehistoric cliff dwellings

Me·se·ta \mə-'sät-ə\ the central plateau of Spain

Meshed — see MASHHAD

Me·so·amer·i·ca \,mez-ō-ə-'mer-i-kə, ,mēz-, ,mēs-, ,mes-\ region of S N. America that was occupied during pre-Columbian times — **Me·so·amer·i·can** \-kən\ adj

Me·so·lón·gi·on \,mes-ə-'lóŋ-gē(-,ȯn)\ town SW cen Greece pop 11,275

Mes·o·po·ta·mia \,mes-(ə-)pə-'tä-mē-ə, -myə\ 1 region SW Asia bet. the Tigris & the Euphrates extending from the mountains of E Asia Minor to the Persian Gulf 2 the entire Tigris-Euphrates valley — **Mes·o·po·ta·mian** \-mē-ən, -myən\ adj or n

Mes·quite \mə-'skēt, me-\ city NE Tex. E of Dallas pop 67,053

Mes·se·ne or NGk **Mes·sí·ni** \mə-'sē-nē\ town S Greece in SW Peloponnisos, ancient ✳ of Messenia

Mes·se·nia \mə-'sē-nē-ə, -nyə\ region S Greece in SW Peloponnisos bordering on Ionian sea

Messenia, Gulf of inlet of the Mediterranean S Greece on S coast of Peloponnisos

Mes·si·na \mə-'sē-nə\ or anc **Mes·sa·na** \mə-'sän-ə\ or **Zan·cle** \'zaŋ-(,)klē\ city & port Italy in NE Sicily pop 255,890

Messina, Strait of channel between S Italy & NE Sicily

Mes·ta \me-'stä\ or Gk **Nés·tos** \'nes-,täs\ river 130 mi (209 km) SW Bulgaria & NE Greece flowing from W end of Rhodope mountains SE into the Aegean

Me·ta \'mät-ə\ river 685 mi (1102 km) NE Colombia flowing into the Orinoco on Venezuela-Colombia boundary

Met·air·ie \'met-ə-rē\ populated place SE La. pop 164,160

Me·tau·rus \mə-'taú(ə)r-(,)ō\ or anc **Me·tau·rus** \-'tȯr-əs\ river 70 mi (113 km) E cen Italy flowing E into the Adriatic

Me·thu·en \mə-'th(y)ü-ən\ town NE Mass. pop 36,701

Metz \'mets, F mes\ city NE France on the Moselle pop 110,939

Meurthe \'mərt\ river 100 mi (161 km) NE France flowing NW from Vosges mountains to the Moselle

Meuse \'myüz, 'mə(r)z\ or D **Maas** \'mäs\ river 575 mi (925 km) W Europe flowing from NE France through S Belgium into North sea in the Netherlands

Mewar — see UDAIPUR

Mex·i·cali \,mek-si-'kal-ē\ city NW Mexico ✳ of Baja California Norte state on Mexico–Calif. border pop 281,333

Mex·i·co \'mek-si-,kō\ or Sp **Mé·ji·co** \'me-hē-(,)kō\ or MexSp **Mé·xi·co** \'me-hē-(,)kō\ 1 country S N. America S of the U.S.; a republic ✳ Mexico area 761,830 sq mi (1,980,758 sq km), pop 67,395,826 2 state S cen Mexico ✳ Toluca area 8267 sq mi (21,494 sq km), pop 7,545,692 3 or Mexico City ✳ of Mexico (republic) in Federal District (area surrounded on three sides by state of Mexico) district pop 9,373,353 — see TENOCHTITLÁN

Mexico, Gulf of inlet of the Atlantic on SE coast of N. America

Mé·zenc \mä-'zaŋk\ mountain 5755 ft (1754 m) S France; highest in the Cévennes

Mez·zo·gior·no \,met-sō-'jȯr-(,)nō, ,med-zō-\ the Italian peninsula S of ab the latitude of Rome

Mfumbiro — see VIRUNGA

Mi·ami \mī-'am-ē, -'am-ə\ city & port SE Fla. on Biscayne Bay pop 346,865 — **Mi·ami·an** \-'am-ē-ən\ n

Miami Beach city SE Fla. pop 96,298

Mich·i·gan \'mish-i-gən\ state N U.S. in Great Lakes region including an upper (NW) & a lower (SE) peninsula ✳ Lansing area 58,216 sq mi (151,362 sq km), pop 9,262,078 — **Mich·i·gan·der** \,mish-i-'gan-dər\ n — **Mich·i·gan·ite** \'mish-i-gə-,nīt\ n

Michigan, Lake lake N cen U.S.; one of the Great Lakes area 22,400 sq mi (58,240 sq km)

Michigan City city N Ind. on Lake Michigan pop 36,850

Michilimackinac — see MACKINAC

Mi·cho·a·cán \,mē-chə-wä-'kän\ state SW Mexico bordering on the Pacific ✳ Morelia area 23,200 sq mi (60,320 sq km), pop 3,048,704

Mi·cro·ne·sia \,mī-krə-'nē-zhə, -shə\ the islands of the W Pacific E of the Philippines & N of Melanesia including the Caroline, Kiribati, Mariana, & Marshall groups

Micronesia, Federated States of islands in the Carolines forming an internally self-governing district of Trust Territory of the Pacific Islands & comprising Kusaie, Pohnpei, Truk, & Yap

Mid·del·burg \'mid-ᵊl-,bərg\ city SW Netherlands on Walcheren Is. ✳ of Zeeland pop 38,697

Middle Congo former French territory W cen Africa — see CONGO, FRENCH EQUATORIAL AFRICA

Middle East or **Mid·east** \'mid-'ēst\ the countries of SW Asia & N Africa — usu. considered as including the countries extending from Libya on the W to Afghanistan on the E — **Middle Eastern** or **Mid·east·ern** \'mid-'ē-stərn\ adj

Mid·dles·brough \'mid-ᵊlz-brə\ town N England ✳ of Cleveland on Tees river pop 149,770

Mid·dle·sex \'mid-ᵊl-,seks\ former county SE England, now absorbed in Greater London

Mid·dle·town \'mid-ᵊl-,taún\ 1 city cen Conn. S of Hartford pop 39,040 2 city SE N.Y. pop 21,454 3 city SW Ohio SW of Dayton pop 43,719 4 town S R.I. N of Newport pop 17,216

Middle West or **Mid·west** \'mid-'west\ region N cen U.S. including area around Great Lakes & in upper Mississippi valley from Ohio & sometimes Ky. on the E to N.Dak., S.Dak., Nebr., & Kans. on the W — **Middle Western** or **Mid·west·ern** \'mid-'wes-tərn\ adj — **Middle Westerner** or **Mid·west·ern·er** \'mid-'wes-tə(r)-nər\ n

Mid Gla·mor·gan \,mid-glə-'mȯr-gən\ county SE Wales area 393 sq mi (1022 sq km), pop 537,000

Mi·di \mē-'dē\ the south of France

Mid·i·an \'mid-ē-ən\ ancient region NW Arabia E of Gulf of 'Aqaba

Mid·land \'mid-lənd\ 1 city cen Mich. NW of Saginaw pop 37,250 2 city W Tex. NE of Odessa pop 70,525

Mid·lands \'mid-lən(d)z\ the central counties of England usu. considered as comprising Bedfordshire, Buckinghamshire, Cambridgeshire, Derbyshire, Leicestershire, Lincolnshire, Northamptonshire, Nottinghamshire, Oxfordshire, Staffordshire, Warwickshire, W. Midlands, & part of Hereford and Worcester

Mid·lo·thi·an \mid-'lō-thē-ən\ or earlier **Ed·in·burgh** \'ed-ᵊn-,bər-ə, -,bə-rə, -b(ə-)rə\ or **Ed·in·burgh·shire** \-,shi(ə)r, -shər\ former county SE Scotland ✳ Edinburgh — see LOTHIAN

Mid·way \'mid-,wā\ islands (atoll) cen Pacific 1300 mi (2092 km) WNW of Honolulu, Hawaii, belonging to the U.S., in Hawaiian group but not incorporated in state of Hawaii area 2 sq mi (5.2 sq km)

Midwest City city cen Okla. E of Oklahoma City pop 49,559

Mie·res \mē-'er-əs\ commune NW Spain in Oviedo province pop 64,552

Mikonos — see MYKONOS

Mi·lan \mə-'lan, -'län\ or It **Mi·la·no** \mi-'län-(,)ō\ or anc **Me·dio·la·num** \,med-ē-ō-'lä-nəm\ commune N Italy ✳ of Lombardy pop 1,634,638 — **Mil·a·nese** \,mil-ə-'nēz, -'nēs\ adj or n

Mi·laz·zo \mi-'lät-(,)sō\ or anc **My·lae** \'mī-(,)lē\ city & port Italy in NE Sicily W of Messina pop 30,399

Mi·le·tus \mi-'lēt-əs, mə-\ ancient city on W coast of Asia Minor in Caria near mouth of Maeander river

Mil·ford \'mil-fərd\ 1 city S Conn. on Long Is. Sound pop 50,898 2 town E Mass. SE of Worcester pop 23,390

Milford Haven town & port SW Wales in Dyfed on Milford Haven (inlet of St. George's channel) pop 13,194

Milk \'milk\ river 625 mi (1006 km) Canada & U.S. in Alta. & Mont. flowing SE into Missouri river

Mill·brae \'mil-,brā\ city W Calif. on San Francisco Bay S of San Francisco pop 20,058

Mille Lacs \mil-'lak(s)\ lake 20 mi (32 km) long E cen Minn.

Mil·ling·ton \'mil-iŋ-tən\ town SW Tenn. N of Memphis pop 20,236

Mill·ville \'mil-,vil\ city S N.J. pop 24,815

Mi·los or **Me·los** \'mē-,läs\ island Greece in SW Cyclades area 57 sq mi (148 sq km)

Mil·pi·tas \mil-'pēt-əs\ city W Calif. N of San José pop 37,820

Mil·ton \'milt-ᵊn\ 1 town E Mass. S of Boston pop 25,860 2 town Canada in SE Ont. SW of Toronto pop 28,067

Mil·wau·kee \mil-'wȯ-kē\ city & port SE Wis. on Lake Michigan pop 636,212 — **Mil·wau·kee·an** \-kē-ən\ n

Mil·wau·kie \mil-'wȯ-kē\ city NW Oreg. S of Portland pop 17,931

Min \'min\ 1 river 350 mi (563 km) cen China in Szechwan flowing SE into the Yangtze 2 river 250 mi (402 km) SE China in Fukien flowing SE into E. China sea

Mi·nas Basin \,mī-nəs-\ landlocked bay E Canada in cen N.S.; the NE extension of Bay of Fundy; connected with it by **Minas Channel**

Mi·nas de Rí·o·tin·to \,mē-nəs-(,)dä-,rē-ə-'tin-(,)tō\ commune SW Spain in Huelva province NE of Huelva

Mi·nas Ge·rais \,mē-nə-zhə-'rīs\ state E Brazil ✳ Belo Horizonte area 226,179 sq mi (588,065 sq km), pop 13,651,852

Minch \'minch\ channel NW Scotland comprising **North Minch** & **Little Minch** between Outer Hebrides & NW coast of Scotland

Min·cio \'mēn-(,)chō, 'min-chē-,ō\ or anc **Min·cius** \'min-sh(ē-)əs, 'min(t)-sē-əs\ river 115 mi (185 km) N Italy issuing from Lake Garda & emptying into the Po

Min·da·nao \,min-də-'nä-,ō, -'naú\ 1 island S Philippines area (including adjacent islands) 36,537 sq mi (94,996 sq km), pop 7,292,691 2 sea S Philippines N of Mindanao

Min·do·ro \min-'dōr-(,)ō, -'dȯr-\ island cen Philippines SW of Luzon area 3759 sq mi (9773 sq km), pop 473,940

Minhow — see FOOCHOW

Min·i·coy \'min-i-,kȯi\ island India, southernmost of the Laccadives

Min·ne·ap·o·lis \,min-ē-'ap-(ə-)ləs\ city SE Minn. on Mississippi river pop 370,951 — **Min·ne·apol·i·tan** \-ē-ə-'päl-ət-ᵊn\ n

Min·ne·so·ta \,min-ə-'sōt-ə\ 1 river 332 mi (534 km) S Minn. flowing from Big Stone Lake to Mississippi river 2 state N U.S. ✳ St. Paul area 84,068 sq mi (218,577 sq km), pop 4,075,970 — **Min·ne·so·tan** \-'sōt-ᵊn\ adj or n

Min·ne·ton·ka \,min-ə-'täŋ-kə\ village SE Minn. E of **Lake Minnetonka** (12 mi or 19 km long) pop 38,683

Minni — see ARMENIA

Mi·nor·ca \mə-'nȯr-kə\ or Sp **Me·nor·ca** \mā-\ island Spain in the Balearic islands ENE of Majorca; chief city Mahón area 264 sq mi (686 sq km) — **Mi·nor·can** \mə-'nȯr-kən\ adj or n

Mi·not \'mī-,nät\ city N N.Dak. pop 32,843

Minsk \'min(t)sk\ city U.S.S.R. ✳ of Belorussia pop 907,000

Min·yā, Al \al-'min-yə\ or **El Minya** \el-\ city cen Egypt on the Nile pop 146,366

Min·ya Kon·ka \,min-yə-'kän-kə\ or **Gong·ga** \'gäŋ-gə\ mountain 24,900 ft (7590 m) W China in SW cen Szechwan; highest in China

Mi·que·lon \'mik-ə-,län, ,mēk-\ island off S coast of Newfoundland, Canada, belonging to France — see SAINT PIERRE

Mi·ra·mar \'mir-ə-,mär\ city SE Fla. pop 32,813

Mi·rim \mə-'rim\ or Sp **Me·rín** \mā-'rēn\ lake 108 mi (174 km) long on boundary bet. Brazil & Uruguay near Atlantic coast

Mir·za·pur \'mi(ə)r-zə-,pú(ə)r\ city N India in SE Uttar Pradesh on the Ganges SW of Banaras pop 128,179

Mi·se·num \mī-'sē-nəm\ ancient port & naval station S Italy at NW corner of Bay of Naples

Mish·a·wa·ka \,mish-ə-'wȯ-kə, -'wäk-ə\ city N Ind. pop 40,201

Mis·kolc \'mish-,kōlts\ city NE Hungary NE of Budapest pop 206,727

Misr — see EGYPT

Mis·sion \'mish-ən\ city S Tex. pop 22,589

Missionary Ridge mountain SE Tenn. & NW Ga. SE of Chattanooga

Mis·sis·sau·ga \,mis-ə-'sȯ-gə\ town Canada in S Ont. SW of Toronto pop 250,017

Mis·sis·sip·pi \,mis-(ə-)'sip-ē\ 1 river 2470 mi (3975 km) cen U.S. flowing from N cen Minn. to Gulf of Mexico — see ITASCA (Lake) 2 river 105 mi (169 km) Canada in SE Ont. flowing NE & N into Ottawa river 3 sound, inlet of Gulf of Mexico E of Lake Pontchartrain 4 state S U.S. ✳ Jackson area 47,716 sq mi (124,062 sq km), pop 2,520,638

Mis·sou·la \mə-'zü-lə\ city W Mont. pop 33,388

Mis·sou·ri \mə-'zú(ə)r-ē, -'zúr-ə\ 1 river 2700 mi (4345 km) W U.S. flowing from SW Mont. into Mississippi river in E Mo. — see THREE FORKS 2 state cen U.S. ✳ Jefferson City area 69,686 sq mi (181,184 sq km), pop 4,916,686 — **Mis·sou·ri·an** \-'zúr-ē-ən\ adj or n

Missouri City city SE Tex. pop 24,533

Mis·tas·si·ni \ˌmis-tə-'sē-nē\ **1** lake Canada in S cen Que. draining W to James Bay area 840 sq mi (2184 sq km) . **2** river 185 mi (298 km) Canada in S Que. flowing S into Lake St. John

Mis·ti, El \el-'mēs-tē, 'mis-\ dormant volcano 19,101 ft (5822 m) S Peru

Mitch·am \'mich-əm\ former municipal borough S England in Surrey, now part of Merton

Mitch·ell, Mount \'mich-əl\ mountain 6684 ft (2037 m) W N.C. in Black mountains of the Blue Ridge mountains; highest point in U.S. E of Mississippi river

Miyajima — see ITSUKUSHIMA

Mi·ya·za·ki \mē-ˌ(y)äz-'äk-ē, mē-'(y)äz-ə-ˌ)kē\ city & port Japan in Kyushu on SE coast pop 268,786

Mi·zo·ram \mi-'zōr-əm\ state NE India area 8142 sq mi (21,169 sq km), pop 487,774

Mma·ba·tho \mä-'bä-ˌ)tō\ town ✳ of Bophuthatswana

Mo·ab \'mō-ˌab\ region Jordan E of Dead sea; in biblical times a kingdom between Edom & the country of the Amorites

Mo·bile \mō-'bē(ə)l, 'mō-ˌbēl\ **1** river 38 mi (61 km) long SW Ala. formed by Alabama & Tombigbee rivers & flowing S into **Mobile Bay** (inlet of Gulf of Mexico) **2** city & port SW Ala. pop 200,452

Moçambique — see MOZAMBIQUE

Moçâmedes — see NAMIBE

Mo·cha \'mō-kə\ or Ar **Mu·khā** \mù-'kä\ town & port SW Yemen on the Red sea

Mod·der \'mäd-ər\ river 180 mi (290 km) Republic of S. Africa in Orange Free State; a tributary of the Vaal

Mo·de·na \'mōd-ʰn-ə, -ʰn-ˌä\ or anc **Mu·ti·na** \'myüt-ʰn-ə\ commune N Italy in Emilia SW of Venice pop 179,933 — **Mod·e·nese** \ˌmōd-ʰn-'ēz, -'ēs\ n

Mo·des·to \mə-'des-ˌ)tō\ city cen Calif. on the Tuolumne pop 106,105

Moe·sia \'mē-sh(ē-)ə\ ancient country & Roman province SE Europe in modern Serbia & Bulgaria S of the Danube from the Drina to Black sea

Mog·a·di·shu \ˌmäg-ə-'dish-ˌ)ü, -'dēsh-\ or **Mog·a·di·scio** \-ˌ)ō\ city & port ✳ of Somalia on Indian ocean pop 349,245

Mogador — see ESSAOUIRA

Mo·gi·lev \ˌmäg-ə-ˌlef, -ˌlev\ city U.S.S.R. in E Belorussia on the Dnieper pop 202,000

Mo·go·llon \ˌməg-ē-'ōn, ˌmōg-\ **1** mountains SW N.Mex.; highest Whitewater Baldy 10,892 ft (3320 m) **2** plateau ab 8000 ft (2438 m) cen Ariz.

Mo·hacs \'mō-ˌhach, -ˌhäch\ town S Hungary pop 21,385

Mo·hawk \'mō-ˌhòk\ river 148 mi (238 km) E cen N.Y. flowing E into Hudson river

Mo·hen·jo–Da·ro \mō-ˌhen-(ˌ)jō-'där-(ˌ)ō\ prehistoric city Pakistan in Indus valley NE of modern Karachi

Mo·ja·ve or **Mo·ha·ve** \mō-'häv-ē\ desert S Calif. SE of S end of the Sierra Nevada

Mo·ji \'mō-(ˌ)jē\ former city Japan in N Kyushu on Shimonoseki strait — see KITAKYUSHU

Mok·po \'mäk-(ˌ)pō\ city & port SW S. Korea on Yellow sea SW of Kwangju pop 221,816

Mold \'mōld\ town NE Wales in Clwyd

Mol·da·via \mäl-'dā-vē-ə, -vyə\ **1** region Europe in NE Romania & SE U.S.S.R. bet. the Carpathians & Transylvanian Alps on the W & the Dniester on the E **2** or **Moldavian Republic** constituent republic of the U.S.S.R. in E Moldavia region ✳ Kishinev area 13,100 sq mi (34,060 sq km), pop 3,858,000 — **Mol·da·vian** \-vē-ən, -vyən\ adj or n

Mo·len·beek \'mō-lən-ˌbäk\ or **Sint–Jans–Molenbeek** \ˌsint-'yän(t)s-\ or **Molenbeek–Saint–Jean** \-san-'zhän\ commune cen Belgium in Brabant W of Brussels pop 70,850

Mo·line \mō-'lēn\ city NW Ill. on Mississippi river pop 45,709

Mo·li·se \'mō-li-ˌzā\ region cen Italy bet. the Apennines & the Adriatic S of Abruzzi ✳ Campobasso pop 328,402 — see ABRUZZI

Mo·lo·kai \ˌmäl-ə-'kī, ˌmō-lə-\ island cen Hawaii area 259 sq mi (673 sq km)

Mo·lo·po \mə-'lō-(ˌ)pō\ river 600 mi (966 km) S Africa flowing W along border between Botswana & Republic of S. Africa & thence S into Orange river; now usu. dry

Molotov — see PERM

Mo·luc·cas \mə-'lək-əz\ or Indonesian **Ma·lu·ku** \mə-'lü-(ˌ)kü\ islands Indonesia in Malay archipelago bet. Celebes & New Guinea area 32,300 sq mi (83,980 sq km), pop 995,000 — see HALMAHERA — **Mo·luc·ca** \mə-'lək-ə\ or **Mo·luc·can** \-ən\ adj

Mom·ba·sa \mäm-'bäs-ə\ **1** island Kenya on coast N of Pemba **2** city & port on Mombasa Is. & adjacent mainland pop 341,148

Mona 1 — see ANGLESEY **2** or **Monapia** — see MAN (Isle of)

Mo·na·co \'män-ə-ˌkō also mə-'näk-(ˌ)ō\ **1** country S Europe on the Mediterranean coast of France; a principality area 368 acres (147 hectares), pop 27,063 **2** commune, its ✳ — **Mo·na·can** \'män-ə-kən, mə-'näk-ən\ adj or n — **Mon·e·gasque** \ˌmän-i-'gask\ adj or n

Mo·nad·nock, Mount \mə-'nad-ˌnäk\ mountain 3166 ft (965 m) SW N.H.

Mon·a·ghan \'män-ə-hən, -ˌhan\ **1** county NE Ireland (republic) in Ulster area 498 sq mi (1295 sq km), pop 51,192 **2** urban district, its ✳

Mo·na Passage \ˌmō-nə-\ strait W. Indies between Hispaniola & Puerto Rico connecting the Caribbean & the Atlantic

Monastir — see BITOLA

Mön·chen·glad·bach \ˌmœ(r)n-kən-'glät-ˌbäk, ˌmœn-kən-'glät-ˌbäk\ or formerly **Mün·chen–Glad·bach** \ˌm(y)ün-, ˌmœn-\ city W W. Germany W of Düsseldorf pop 258,424

Monc·ton \'məŋ(k)-tən\ city Canada in E N.B. pop 57,743

Mon·go·lia \män-'gōl-yə, mäŋ-, -'gō-lē-ə\ **1** region E Asia E of Altai mountains; includes Gobi desert **2** or **Outer Mongolia** country E Asia comprising major portion of Mongolia region; a republic ✳ Ulan Bator area 580,158 sq mi (1,508,411 sq km), pop 1,594,800 **3** INNER MONGOLIA

Mon·he·gan \män-'hē-gən\ island Maine E of Portland

Mon·mouth \'män-məth, 'mən-\ or **Mon·mouth·shire** \-ˌshi(ə)r, -shər\ former county SE Wales, often regarded as part of England ✳ Newport

Mo·no \'mō-(ˌ)nō\ saline lake 14 mi (22 km) long E Calif.

Mo·noc·a·cy \mə-'näk-ə-sē\ river 60 mi (96 km) S Pa. & N Md. flowing S into the Potomac

Mo·non·ga·he·la \mə-ˌnän-gə-'hē-lə, -ˌnäŋ-gə-, -'hä-lə\ river 128 mi (206 km) N W.Va. & SW Pa. flowing N to unite with Allegheny river at Pittsburgh forming Ohio river

Mon·roe \(ˌ)mən-'rō\ **1** city N La. pop 57,597 **2** city SE Mich. SSW of Detroit on Lake Erie pop 23,531

Mon·roe·ville \(ˌ)mən-'rō-ˌvil\ borough SW Pa. E of Pittsburgh pop 30,977

Mon·ro·via \(ˌ)mən-'rō-vē-ə\ **1** city SW Calif. E of Pasadena pop 30,531 **2** city & port ✳ of Liberia, on the Atlantic pop 243,243

Mons \'mōⁿs\ or Flem **Ber·gen** \'ber-kə(n)\ commune SW Belgium ✳ of Hainaut pop 94,417

Mon·tana \män-'tan-ə\ state NW U.S. ✳ Helena area 147,138 sq mi (382,559 sq km), pop 786,690 — **Mon·tan·an** \-'tan-ən\ adj or n

Mont·au·ban \ˌmänt-ō-'bäⁿ, mōⁿ-tō-bäⁿ\ city SW France on the Tarn N of Toulouse pop 35,344

Mon·tauk Point \ˌmän-ˌtòk-\ headland SE N.Y. at E tip of Long Is.

Mont Blanc \mōⁿ-'bläⁿ\ **1** mountain peak 15,771 ft (4807 m) SE France on Italian border in Savoy Alps; highest of the Alps **2** tunnel 7¹⁄₂ mi (12 km) long France & Italy under Mont Blanc

Mont·clair \mänt-'kla(ə)r, -'kle(ə)r\ **1** city SW Calif. E of Los Angeles pop 22,628 **2** town NE N.J. SSW of Paterson pop 38,321

Mon·te Al·bán \ˌmänt-ē-äl-'bän\ ruined city of the Zapotecs S Mexico in Oaxaca state SW of Oaxaca

Mon·te·bel·lo \ˌmänt-ə-'bel-(ˌ)ō\ city SW Calif. pop 52,929

Mon·te Car·lo \ˌmänt-i-'kär-(ˌ)lō\ commune Monaco pop 13,154

Mon·te·go Bay \män-ˌtē-(ˌ)gō-\ city & port NW Jamaica on Montego Bay (inlet of the Caribbean) pop 42,800

Mon·te·ne·gro \ˌmänt-ə-'nē-(ˌ)grō, -'nā-\ federated republic S Yugoslavia on the Adriatic; formerly a kingdom (✳ Cetinje) ✳ Titograd area 5343 sq mi (13,892 sq km), pop 530,361 — **Mon·te·ne·grin** \-grən\ adj or n

Mon·te·rey \ˌmänt-ə-'rā\ city W Calif. on Monterey peninsula at S end of **Monterey Bay** (inlet of the Pacific) pop 27,558

Monterey Park city SW Calif. E of Los Angeles pop 54,338

Mon·ter·rey \ˌmänt-ə-'rā\ city NE Mexico ✳ of Nuevo León pop 830,336

Mon·te·vi·deo \ˌmänt-ə-'dā-(ˌ)ō, -vid-ē-ˌō\ city & port ✳ of Uruguay on N shore of Río de la Plata pop 1,260,753

Mon·te·zu·ma Castle National Monument \ˌmänt-ə-'zü-mə\ reservation cen Ariz. containing prehistoric cliff dwellings

Mont·gom·ery \(ˌ)mən(t)-'gəm-(ə-)rē, män(t)-, -'gäm-\ **1** city ✳ of Ala. on Alabama river pop 177,857 **2** or **Mont·gom·ery·shire** \-ˌshi(ə)r, -shər\ former county E Wales ✳ Welshpool

Mont·mar·tre \mōⁿ-'märtrʰ\ section of Paris, France, on a hill in N cen part of the city

Mont·mo·ren·cy \ˌmänt-mə-'ren(t)-sē, mōⁿ-mó-räⁿ-sē\ commune N France, N suburb of Paris pop 20,927

Mont·mo·ren·cy Falls \ˌmänt-mə-ˌren(t)-sē-\ waterfall 270 ft (82 m) Canada in S Que. NE of Quebec city in **Montmorency** (60 mi or 96 km flowing S into St. Lawrence river)

Mont·par·nasse \ˌmōⁿ-(ˌ)pär-'näs, -'nas\ section of Paris, France, in S cen part of the city — **Mont·par·nas·sian** \-'nash-ən, -'nas-ē-ən\ adj

Mont·pe·lier \mänt-'pēl-yər, -'pil-\ city ✳ of Vt. pop 8241

Mont·pel·lier \mōⁿ-pe-lyā\ city S France WNW of Marseilles pop 178,136

Mon·tre·al \ˌmän-trē-'òl, ˌmən-\ or **Mont·ré·al** \mōⁿ-rā-ál\ city & port Canada in S Que. on **Montreal Island** (32 mi or 51 km long, in St. Lawrence river) pop 980,354 — **Mon·tre·al·er** \ˌmän-trē-'ò-lər, ˌmən-\ n

Montreal North or **Montréal–Nord** \-'nòr\ town Canada in S Que. on Montreal Is. pop 94,914

Mon·treuil \mōⁿ-'trəi\ or **Montreuil–sous–Bois** \-ˌsü-'bwä\ commune N France, E suburb of Paris pop 96,684

Mon·treux \mōⁿ-'trœ\ group of villages W Switzerland in Vaud canton at E end of Lake Geneva pop 20,421

Mont–Roy·al \mōⁿ-rā-yál\ or **Mount Roy·al** \maùnt-'ròi(-ə)l\ height 769 ft (234 m) in Montreal, Que.

Mont–Saint–Mi·chel \mōⁿ-saⁿ-mē-shel\ small island NW France in Gulf of St-Malo

Mont·ser·rat \ˌmän(t)-sə-'rat\ island Brit. W. Indies in the Leewards SW of Antigua ✳ Plymouth area 40 sq mi (104 sq km), pop 11,606

Monument Valley region NE Ariz. & SE Utah containing red sandstone buttes, mesas, & arches

Mon·za \'mōn(t)-sə, 'män-zə\ commune N Italy in Lombardy SE of Milan pop 122,103

Moore \'mō(ə)r, 'mò(ə)r\ city cen Okla. S of Oklahoma City pop 35,063

Mo·o·rea \ˌmō-ə-'rā-ə\ island S Pacific in Society Islands NW of Tahiti area 51 sq mi (133 sq km)

Moor·head \'mō(ə)r-ˌhed, 'mò(ə)r-, 'mù(ə)r-\ city W Minn. on Red river opposite Fargo, N.Dak. pop 29,998

Moose \'müs\ river 50 mi (80 km) Canada in NE Ont. flowing NE into James Bay; estuary of Abitibi, Mattagami, & other rivers

Moose·head \'müs-ˌhed\ lake 35 mi (56 km) long NW cen Maine

Moose Jaw city Canada in S Sask. W of Regina pop 33,941

Mo·rad·abad \mə-'räd-ə-ˌbäd\ city N India in NW Uttar Pradesh ENE of Delhi pop 347,983

Mo·ra·tu·wa \mə-'rät-ə-wə\ city W Sri Lanka on Indian ocean S of Colombo pop 135,610

Mo·ra·va \'mōr-ə-və\ **1** river 180 mi (290 km), cen Czechoslovakia in Moravia flowing S into the Danube **2** river 134 mi (216 km) E Yugoslavia in Serbia flowing N into the Danube

Mo·ra·via \mə-'rā-vē-ə\ or **Mo·ra·va** \'mōr-ə-və\ region cen Czechoslovakia S of Silesia traversed by Morava river; chief city Brno

Mo·ra·vi·an Gate \mə-ˌrā-vē-ən-\ mountain pass cen Europe bet. Sudeten & Carpathian mountains

Moravska Ostrava — see OSTRAVA

Mor·ay \'mər-ē, 'mə-rē\ or **Mor·ay·shire** \-ˌshi(ə)r, -shər\ or **El·gin** \'el-gən\ or **El·gin·shire** \-ˌshi(ə)r, -shər\ former county NE Scotland bordering on North sea ✳ Elgin

---

Moray firth inlet of North sea N Scotland
Mor·do·vi·an Republic \(,)mȯr-ˈdō-vē-ən-\ *or* **Mord·vin·i·an Republic** \(,)mȯrd-ˌvin-ē-ən-\ autonomous republic U.S.S.R. in *cen* Soviet Russia, Europe, S & W of the middle Volga ✱ Saransk *area* 10,100 *sq mi* (26,260 *sq km*), *pop* 1,030,000
Mo·reau \ˈmōr-(ˌ)ō, ˈmȯr-\ river 250 *mi* (402 *km*) NW S.Dak. flowing E into Missouri river
More·cambe and Hey·sham \ˌmōr-kəm-ən(d)-ˈhē-shəm, ˌmȯr-\ borough NW England in N Lancashire on **Morecambe Bay** (inlet of Irish Sea) *pop* 41,187
Mo·re·lia \mə-ˈrāl-yə\ city SW Mexico ✱ of Michoacán *pop* 209,507
Mo·re·los \mə-ˈrā-ləs\ state S *cen* Mexico ✱ Cuernavaca *area* 1916 *sq mi* (4982 *sq km*), *pop* 931,675
More·ton Bay \ˌmōrt-ᵊn-, ˌmȯrt-\ inlet of the Pacific Australia in SE Queensland at mouth of Brisbane river
Mor·gan·town \ˈmȯr-gən-ˌtau̇n\ city N W.Va. *pop* 27,605
Mo·ri·ah \mə-ˈrī-ə\ hill *cen* Palestine in E part of Jerusalem
Mo·ri·o·ka \ˌmȯr-ē-ˈō-kə, ˌmȯr-\ city Japan in N Honshu *pop* 230,787
Mo·roc·co \mə-ˈräk-(ˌ)ō\ **1** country NW Africa bordering on the Atlantic & the Mediterranean; a kingdom ✱ Rabat, summer ✱ Tangier *area ab* 240,881 *sq mi* (626,291 *sq km*), *pop* 21,392,000; formerly (1911–56) divided into **French Morocco** (protectorate ✱ Rabat), **Spanish Morocco** (protectorate ✱ Tetuán), **Southern Morocco** (Spanish protectorate, chief town Cabo Yubi), & the **International Zone** of Tangier **2** — see MARRAKECH — **Mo·roc·can** \-ˈräk-ən\ *adj or n*
Mo·ro Gulf \ˌmōr-(ˌ)ō-, ˌmȯr-\ arm of Celebes sea S Philippines off SW coast of Mindanao
Mo·ro·ni \mȯ-ˈrō-nē\ city ✱ of Comoro Islands *pop* 20,112
Mor·ris Jes·up, Cape \ˌmȯr-əs-ˈjes-əp, ˌmär-\ headland N Greenland in Peary Land on Arctic ocean; is world's northernmost dry land
Morrison, Mount — see YÜ SHAN
Morrison Cave — see LEWIS AND CLARK
Mor·ris·town \ˈmȯr-ə-ˌstau̇n, ˈmär-\ **1** town NE *cen* N.J. *pop* 16,614 **2** city E Tenn. ENE of Knoxville *pop* 19,683
Mor·ton Grove \ˌmȯrt-ᵊn-\ village NE Ill. W of Evanston *pop* 23,747
Mos·cow \ˈmäs-(ˌ)kō, -ˌkau̇\ *or Russ* **Mos·kva** \mäsk-ˈvä\ **1** river 315 *mi* (507 *km*) U.S.S.R. in W *cen* Soviet Russia, Europe, flowing E into Oka river **2** city NW Idaho *pop* 16,513 **3** city ✱ of U.S.S.R. & of Soviet Russia on Moscow river *pop* 7,061,000 — see MUSCOVY
Mo·selle \mō-ˈzel\ *or G* **Mo·sel** \ˈmō-zəl\ river 320 *mi* (515 *km*) E France & W W. Germany flowing from Vosges mountains into the Rhine at Koblenz
Mosquito coast *or* **Mos·qui·tia** \mə-ˈskēt-ē-ə\ region Central America bordering on the Caribbean in E Honduras & E Nicaragua
Mos·sel Bay \ˌmȯ-səl-\ city & port S Republic of S. Africa in S Cape of Good Hope on Mossel Bay (inlet of Indian ocean) *pop* 17,574
Moss Point city SE Miss. E of Gulfport *pop* 18,998
Mos·tag·a·nem \mə-ˈstag-ə-ˌnem\ city & port NW Algeria *pop* 101,600
Mo·sul \mō-ˈsül, ˈmō-səl\ city N Iraq on the Tigris *pop* 264,146
Moth·er·well and Wish·aw \ˈməth-ər-ˌwel-ən-ˈwish-ˌȯ, -wə-lən-\ burgh *cen* Scotland in Strathclyde SE of Glasgow *pop* 73,116
Moul·mein \mül-ˈmān, mōl-, -ˈmīn\ city S Myanmar on Gulf of Martaban at mouth of the Salween *pop* 171,977
Mound City Group National Monument reservation S Ohio N of Chillicothe containing prehistoric mounds
Mountain Brook city N *cen* Ala. E of Birmingham *pop* 19,718
Mountain View city W Calif. NW of San Jose *pop* 58,655
Mount Clem·ens \-ˈklem-ənz\ city SE Mich. *pop* 18,806
Mount De·sert \-də-ˈzərt, -ˈdez-ərt\ island S Maine in the Atlantic E of Penobscot Bay *area* 100 *sq mi* (260 *sq km*)
Mount·lake Terrace \ˌmau̇nt-ˌlāk-\ city W Wash. N of Seattle *pop* 16,534
Mount Pleasant city *cen* Mich. NW of Saginaw *pop* 23,746
Mount Pros·pect \-ˈpräs-ˌpekt\ village NE Ill. *pop* 52,634
Mount Rainier National Park — see RAINIER (Mount)
Mount Rev·el·stoke National Park \-ˈrev-əl-ˌstōk-\ reservation Canada in SE B.C. on a plateau including Mt. Revelstoke W of Selkirk mountains
Mount Royal — see MONT-ROYAL
Mount Saint Helens National Volcanic Monument — see SAINT HELENS (Mount)
Mount Ver·non \-ˈvər-nən\ **1** city S Ill. *pop* 17,193 **2** city SE N.Y. N of New York City *pop* 66,713
Mourne \ˈmō(ə)rn, ˈmȯ(ə)rn\ **1** mountains SE Northern Ireland **2** district S Northern Ireland, established 1974 *area* 345 *sq mi* (897 *sq km*), *pop* 72,243
Moyle \ˈmȯi(ə)l\ district N Northern Ireland, established 1974 *area* 191 *sq mi* (497 *sq km*), *pop* 14,252
Mo·zam·bique \ˌmō-zəm-ˈbēk\ *or Pg* **Mo·çam·bi·que** \ˌmü-səm-ˈbē-kə\ **1** channel 950 *mi* (1529 *km*) long SE Africa bet. Madagascar & Mozambique **2** *or formerly* **Portuguese East Africa** country SE Africa bordering on Mozambique channel; a republic, until 1975 a dependency of Portugal ✱ Maputo *area* 297,654 *sq mi* (773,900 *sq km*), *pop* 11,673,725 — **Mo·zam·bi·can** \ˌmō-zəm-ˈbē-kən\ *adj or n*
Mtwa·ra \em-ˈtwär-ə\ city & port Tanzania in SE mainland
Mu·gu, Point \mə-ˈgü\ cape SW Calif. W of Los Angeles
Muir Woods National Monument \ˈmyu̇(ə)r\ reservation N Calif. NW of San Francisco containing a redwood grove
Mui·zen·berg \ˈmīz-ᵊn-ˌbərg\ town Republic of S. Africa on False Bay, SSE suburb of Cape Town
Mu·kal·la \mu̇-ˈkal-ə\ city & port Yemen on Gulf of Aden; chief town of the Hadhramaut
Muk·den \ˈmu̇k-dən, ˈmək-; mu̇k-ˈden\ *or* **Shen·yang** \ˈshən-ˈyäŋ\ *or formerly* **Feng·tien** \ˈfəŋ-tē-ˈen\ city NE China ✱ of Liaoning; chief city of Manchuria *pop* 4,012,000
Mukhā — see MOCHA
Mül·heim \ˈm(y)ül-ˌhīm, ˈmᵫl-\ *or* **Mülheim an der Ruhr** \-än-də(r)-ˈru̇(ə)r\ city W W. Germany on Ruhr river *pop* 181,279
Mul·house \mə-ˈlüz\ commune NE France in Alsace *pop* 116,494
Mull \ˈməl\ island W Scotland in the Inner Hebrides *area* 351 *sq mi* (913 *sq km*), *pop* 1499
Mul·lin·gar \ˌməl-ən-ˈgär\ town N *cen* Ireland ✱ of Westmeath
Mul·tan \mu̇l-ˈtän\ city NE Pakistan SW of Lahore *pop* 742,000
Mult·no·mah Falls \ˌməlt-ˈnō-mə\ waterfall 620 *ft* (189 *m*) NW Oreg. E of Portland in a tributary of Columbia river
München–Gladbach — see MÖNCHENGLADBACH
Mun·cie \ˈmən(t)-sē\ city E *cen* Ind. *pop* 77,216
Mun·de·lein \ˈmən-də-ˌlīn\ village NE Ill. NW of Chicago *pop* 17,053
Mu·nich \ˈmyü-nik\ *or G* **Mün·chen** \ˈmᵫn-k̲ən\ city SE W. Germany ✱ of Bavaria on the Isar *pop* 1,298,941
Mun·ster \ˈmən(t)-stər\ **1** town NW Ind. SW of Hammond *pop* 20,671 **2** province S Ireland *area* 9317 *sq mi* (24,224 *sq km*), *pop* 880,000
Mün·ster \ˈmən(t)-stər, ˈm(y)ün(t)-, ˈmᵫn-\ city W W. Germany; formerly ✱ of Westphalia *pop* 203,300
Mun·te·nia \ˌmən-ˈtē-nē-ə, mün-ˈten-ē-ə\ *or* **Greater Walachia** region SE Romania in E part of Walachia
Mur \ˈmu̇(ə)r\ *or* **Mu·ra** \ˈmu̇r-ə\ river 230 *mi* (370 *km*) Austria & N Yugoslavia flowing into the Drava
Mu·ra·no \mü-ˈrän-(ˌ)ō\ town NE Italy on islands in Lagoon of Venice
Mu·rat \mü-ˈrät\ *or anc* **Ar·sa·ni·as** \är-ˈsā-nē-əs\ river 380 *mi* (612 *km*) E Turkey flowing WSW into the Euphrates
Mur·chi·son \ˈmər-chə-sən\ river 400 *mi* (644 *km*) Australia in W Western Australia flowing W into Indian ocean
Murchison Falls — see KABALEGA FALLS
Mur·cia \ˈmər-sh(ē-)ə\ **1** region & ancient kingdom SE Spain bordering on the Mediterranean **2** province SE Spain bordering on the Mediterranean *area* 4453 *sq mi* (11,578 *sq km*), *pop* 922,866 **3** commune, its ✱ & ✱ of ancient kingdom of Murcia *pop* 284,585
Mu·res \ˈmü-ˌresh\ *or Hung* **Ma·ros** \ˈmȯr-ˌōsh\ river 400 *mi* (644 *km*), *cen* Romania & E Hungary flowing W into the Tisza
Mur·frees·boro \ˈmər-f(r)ēz-ˌbər-ə, -ˌbə-rə\ city *cen* Tenn. *pop* 32,845
Mur·mansk \mu̇r-ˈman(t)sk, -ˈmän(t)sk\ city & port U.S.S.R. in NW Soviet Russia, Europe, on an inlet of Barents sea *pop* 381,000
Mu·ro·ran \ˌmu̇r-ə-ˈrän\ city & port Japan in SW Hokkaido on an inlet of the Pacific *pop* 157,005
Mur·ray \ˈmər-ē, ˈmə-rē\ **1** city N Utah *pop* 25,750 **2** river 1200 *mi* (1931 *km*) SE Australia flowing from near Mt. Kosciusko in E Victoria W into Indian ocean in SE S. Australia
Mur·rum·bidg·ee \ˌmər-əm-ˈbij-ē, ˌmə-rəm-\ river 1000 *mi* (1609 *km*) SE Australia in New S. Wales flowing W into Murray river
Murviedro — see SAGUNTO
Mu·sa, Ge·bel \ˌjeb-əl-ˈmü-sə\ mountain group NE Egypt in S Sinai peninsula — see HOREB, KATHERINA (Gebel)
Mu·sa, Je·bel \ˌjeb-əl-ˈmü-sə\ *or anc* **Ab·i·la** *or* **Ab·y·la** \ˈab-ə-lə\ mountain 2775 *ft* (846 *m*) N Morocco opposite Rock of Gibraltar — see PILLARS OF HERCULES
Mus·cat \ˈməs-ˌkat, -kət\ town & port ✱ of Oman on Gulf of Oman *pop* 50,000
Muscat and Oman — see OMAN
Mus·ca·tine \ˌməs-kə-ˈtēn\ city E Iowa *pop* 23,467
Mus·co·vy \(ˌ)mə-ˈskō-vē; ˈməs-kə-, -ˌkō-\ **1** the principality of Moscow (founded 1295) which in 15th century came to dominate Russia **2** RUSSIA — a former name
Mus·ke·gon \mə-ˈskē-gən\ **1** river 200 *mi* (322 *km*) W *cen* Mich. flowing SW into Lake Michigan **2** city & port SW Mich. *pop* 40,823
Mus·kin·gum \mə-ˈskiŋ-(g)əm\ river 120 *mi* (193 *km*) E Ohio flowing SSE into Ohio river
Mus·ko·gee \mə-ˈskō-gē\ city E Okla. *pop* 40,011
Mus·ko·ka, Lake \mə-ˈskō-kə\ lake Canada in SE Ont. E of Georgian Bay & N of Lake Simcoe *area* 54 *sq mi* (140 *sq km*)
Mus·sel·shell \ˈməs-əl-ˌshel\ river 300 *mi* (483 *km*) *cen* Mont. flowing E & N into Missouri river
Mu·tan–chiang *or* **Mu·dan·jiang** *or* **Mu·tan·kiang** \ˈmü-ˈdän-jē-ˈäŋ\ city NE China in S Heilungkiang on the **Mu·tan (Mu·dan)** \ˈmü-ˈdän\ river (310 *mi or* 496 *km* flowing NE into Sungari river) *pop* 251,000
Mutina — see MODENA
Mu·tsu Bay \ˌmüt-(ˌ)sü-\ inlet N Japan on NE Honshu on Tsugaru strait
Muttra — see MATHURA
Muztag — see ULUGH MUZTAGH
Mwe·ru \mə-ˈwe(ə)r-(ˌ)ü\ lake 80 *mi* (129 *km*) long on border bet. Zaire & Zambia SW of Lake Tanganyika
Myan·mar \ˈmyän-ˌmär\ *or* **Myan·ma** \-ˌmä\ *or formerly* **Bur·ma** \ˈbər-mə\ country SE Asia on Bay of Bengal; a federal republic ✱ Yangon *area* 261,789 *sq mi* (680,651 *sq km*), *pop* 35,313,905
Myc·a·le \ˈmik-ə-(ˌ)lē\ promontory W Turkey opposite Samos Is.
My·ce·nae \mī-ˈsē-(ˌ)nē\ ancient city S Greece in NE Peloponnisos
Myk·o·nos \ˈmik-ə-ˌnäs, -nəs\ *or NGk* **Mí·ko·nos** \ˈmē-kə-ˌnȯs\ island Greece in the Aegean in NE Cyclades *area* 35 *sq mi* (91 *sq km*)
Mylae — see MILAZZO
My·men·singh \ˌmī-mən-ˈsiŋ\ city N Bangladesh *pop* 182,153
My·ra \ˈmī-rə\ ancient city S Asia Minor on coast of Lycia
Myr·tle Beach \ˌmərt-ᵊl-\ city E S.C. on the Atlantic *pop* 18,446
My·sia \ˈmish-(ē-)ə\ ancient country NW Asia Minor bordering on the Propontis — **My·sian** \-(ē-)ən\ *adj or n*
My·sore \mī-ˈsō(ə)r, -ˈsȯ(ə)r\ **1** — see KARNATAKA **2** city S India in S Karnataka *pop* 476,446
Mys·tic \ˈmis-tik\ river E Mass. flowing SE into Boston harbor
Naas \ˈnās\ urban district E Ireland in Leinster ✱ of Kildare
Nab·a·taea *or* **Nab·a·tea** \ˌnab-ə-ˈtē-ə\ ancient Arab kingdom SE of Palestine — **Nab·a·tae·an** *or* **Nab·a·te·an** \-ˈtē-ən\ *adj or n*
Na·be·rezh·nye Chel·ny \ˌnä-bə-ˈrezh-n(y)ə-ˈchel-nē\ city U.S.S.R. in E Soviet Russia, Europe in Tatar Republic *pop* 301,000
Nab·lus \ˈnab-ləs, ˈnäb-\ *or anc* **She·chem** \ˈshē-kəm, -ˌkem\ *or* **Ne·ap·o·lis** \nē-ˈap-ə-ləs\ city *cen* Palestine in Samaria; now in W Jordan *pop* 44,223
Nac·og·do·ches \ˌnak-ə-ˈdō-chəz, -chəs\ city E Tex. *pop* 27,149
Na·fūd, An \an-nə-ˈfüd\ *or* **Ne·fud** \nə-ˈfüd\ desert N Saudi Arabia in N Nejd
Na·ga \ˈnäg-ə\ hills E India & N Myanmar SE of the Brahmaputra; highest Saramati 12,553 *ft* (3826 *m*)
Na·ga·land \ˈnäg-ə-ˌland\ state E India N of Manipur in Naga hills ✱ Kohima *area* 6336 *sq mi* (16,474 *sq km*), *pop* 773,231
Na·ga·o·ka \ˌnäg-ə-ˈō-kə, nä-ˈgä-ō-(ˌ)kä\ city Japan in N *cen* Honshu SSW of Niigata *pop* 180,835
Na·ga·sa·ki \ˌnäg-ə-ˈsäk-ē, ˌnag-ə-ˈsak-ē\ city & port Japan in W Kyushu on E. China sea *pop* 449,321
Na·gor·no–Ka·ra·bakh Region \nə-ˌgȯr-(ˌ)nō-ˈkär-ə-ˌbäk-\ autonomous region U.S.S.R. in SW Azerbaijan ✱ Stepanakert *area* 1700 *sq mi* (4420 *sq km*), *pop* 149,000

Na·go·ya \nə-'gȯi-ə, 'näg-ə-(ˌ)yä\ city Japan in S *cen* Honshu *pop* 2,092,183

Nag·pur \'näg-ˌpür\ city E *cen* India in NE Maharashtra *pop* 1,297,977

Na·ha \'nä-(ˌ)hä\ city & port Ryukyu islands in SW Okinawa Is. ✳ of Okinawa *pop* 296,982

Na·han·ni National Park \nä-ˌhän-ē-\ reservation W Canada in SW Northwest Territories

Na·huel Hua·pí \nä-ˌwəl-wä-'pē\ lake SW Argentina in the Andes in **Nahuel Huapi National Park**

Nairn \'na(ə)rn, 'ne(ə)rn\ **1** *or* **Nairn·shire** \-ˌshi(ə)r, -shər\ former county NE Scotland **2** burgh, its ✳, on Moray firth *pop* 7721

Nai·ro·bi \nī-'rō-bē\ city S *cen* Kenya, its ✳ *pop* 827,775

Najd — *see* NEJD — **Najdi** \'naj-dē\ *adj or n*

Na·khi·che·van \ˌnäk-i-chə-'vän\ **1** *or* **Nakhichevan Republic** autonomous republic U.S.S.R.; part of Azerbaijan *area* 2100 *sq mi* (5460 *sq km*), *pop* 202,000 **2** city, its ✳, on the Araks *pop* 33,000

Nak·tong \'näk-ˌtȯŋ\ river 260 *mi* (418 *km*) S & E S. Korea flowing S & E into Korea strait near Pusan

Na·ma·qua·land \nə-'mäk-wə-ˌland\ *or* **Na·ma·land** \'näm-ə-\ region SW Africa; divided by Orange river into **Great Namaqualand** (in Namibia) & **Little Namaqualand** (in Cape Province, Republic of S. Africa, chief town Springbok)

Na·mi·be \nä-'mē-bä\ *or formerly* **Mo·çâ·me·des** \mə-'säm-əd-ish\ town & port SW Angola

Na·mib·ia \nə-'mib-ē-ə\ *or formerly* **South–West Africa** *or 1884–1919* **German Southwest Africa** country SW Africa on the Atlantic; until 1990 a territory administered by Republic of S. Africa which captured it from Germany in World War I ✳ Windhoek *area* 318,099 *sq mi* (827,057 *sq km*), *pop* 1,184,000 — **Na·mib·ian** \-mib-ē-ən, -'mib-yən\ *adj*

Nam·pa \'nam-pə\ city SW Idaho W of Boise *pop* 25,112

Nam·po \'näm-(ˌ)pō\ *or formerly* **Chin·nam·po** \'chē(n)-ˌnäm-(ˌ)pō\ city & port SW N. Korea SW of Pyongyang *pop* 130,000

Na·mur \nə-'m(y)ü(ə)r\ **1** province S Belgium *area* 1413 *sq mi* (3674 *sq km*), *pop* 407,400 **2** commune, its ✳ *pop* 102,321

Nan \'nän\ river 350 *mi* (563 *km*) N Thailand flowing S to join the Ping forming the Chao Phraya

Nan·chang *or* Nan·zhang \'nän-'jän\ city SE China ✳ of Kiangsi on the Kan SW of Poyang Lake *pop* 520,000

Nan·chung *or* Nan·chong \'nän-'chüŋ\ city *cen* China in E *cen* Szechwan *pop* 206,000

Nan·cy \'nan(t)-sē, näⁿ-sē\ city NE France on the Meurthe *pop* 106,906

Nan·da De·vi \ˌnən-də-'dā-vē\ mountain 25,645 *ft* (7816 *m*) N India in the Himalayas in Uttar Pradesh

Nan·di *or* Na·di \'nän-(ˌ)dē\ village Fiji on W Viti Levu Is.

Nan·ga Par·bat \ˌnəŋ-gə-'pər-bət\ mountain 26,660 *ft* (8126 *m*) NW Kashmir in the W Himalayas

Nan·king \'nan-'kiŋ, 'nän-\ *or* Nan·jing \'nän-'jiŋ\ city E China on the Yangtze ✳ of Kiangsu & (1928–37 & 1946–49) ✳ of China *pop* 1,419,000

Nan Ling \'nän-'liŋ\ mountain system SE China roughly separating Kwangtung & Kwangsi Chuang from Hunan & Kweichow

Nan·ning \'nän-'niŋ\ *or formerly* Yung·ning \'yüŋ-'niŋ\ city S China ✳ of Kwangsi Chuang on the Yü *pop* 260,000

Nansei — *see* RYUKYU

Nan·shan \'nän-'shän\ mountain range W China extending E from Kunlun mountains along NE edge of Tibetan plateau

Nan·terre \nän-'ter\ commune N France W of Paris *pop* 94,441

Nantes \'nan(t)s\ city NW France on the Loire *pop* 252,537

Nan·ti·coke \'nant-i-ˌkōk\ city Canada in SE Ont. *pop* 19,816

Nan·tuck·et \nan-'tək-ət\ island Mass. S of Cape Cod on **Nantucket Sound** (inlet of the Atlantic) *pop* 5660 — **Nan·tuck·et·er** \-ər\ *n*

Nan·tung *or* Nan·tong \'nän-'tüŋ\ city & port E China in SE Kiangsu on Yangtze estuary NW of Shanghai *pop* 240,000

Napa \'nap-ə\ city W Calif. N of Vallejo *pop* 50,879

Na·per·ville \'nā-pər-ˌvil\ city NE Ill. W of Chicago *pop* 42,330

Na·pi·er \'nā-pē-ər\ borough & port New Zealand in E North Is. on Hawke Bay *pop* 48,314

Na·ples \'nā-pəlz\ **1** city SW Fla. *pop* 17,581 **2** *or* It **Na·po·li** \'näp-ə-lē\ *or anc* **Ne·ap·o·lis** \nē-'ap-ə-ləs\ city & port Italy on **Bay of Naples** (inlet of Tyrrhenian sea) ✳ of Campania *pop* 1,210,503

Na·po \'näp-(ˌ)ō\ river 550 *mi* (885 *km*) N S. America rising near Mt. Cotopaxi in *cen* Ecuador & flowing E & SE into the Amazon

Na·ra \'när-ə\ city Japan in W *cen* Honshu E of Osaka; an early ✳ of Japan *pop* 305,210

Nar·ba·da \nər-'bad-ə\ river 800 *mi* (1287 *km*) *cen* India flowing W bet. Vindhya mountains & Satpura range into Gulf of Cambay

Nar·bonne \när-'bän, -'bən\ city S France *pop* 36,525

Na·rew \'när-ˌef, -ˌev\ *or Russ* Na·rev \när-'yȯf, -'yȯv\ river 285 *mi* (459 *km*) NE Poland flowing W & SW into Bug river

Nar·ra·gan·sett Bay \ˌnar-ə-'gan(t)-sət\ inlet of the Atlantic SE R.I.

Nar·vik \'när-vik\ town & port N Norway *pop* 19,326

Nash·ua \'nash-ə-wə, -ˌwä\ city N N.H. *pop* 67,865

Nash·ville \'nash-ˌvil, -vəl\ city N *cen* Tenn., its ✳ *pop* 446,027

Nas·sau \'nas-ˌȯ, *G* 'näs-ˌaú\ **1** city & port ✳ of the Bahamas on New Providence Is. *pop* 101,182 **2** region *cen* W. Germany N & E of the Rhine; chief city Wiesbaden **3** — *see* SUDIRMAN

Nasser, Lake — *see* ASWAN

Na·tal \nə-'tal, -'täl\ **1** city & port NE Brazil ✳ of Rio Grande do Norte *pop* 416,906 **2** province E Republic of S. Africa bet. Drakensberg mountains & Indian ocean ✳ Pietermaritzburg *area* 35,284 *sq mi* (91,738 *sq km*), *pop* 5,723,215

Natchez \'nach-əz\ city SW Miss. on Mississippi river *pop* 22,015

Natchez Trace pioneer road bet. Natchez, Miss., & Nashville, Tenn., used in the early 19th century

Natch·i·toches \'nak-ə-ˌtäsh, 'nak-(ə-)tȯsh\ city NW *cen* La. *pop* 16,664

Na·tick \'nāt-ik\ town E Mass. W of Boston *pop* 29,461

National City city SW Calif. S of San Diego *pop* 48,772

Native States — *see* INDIAN STATES

Natural Bridges National Monument reservation SE Utah

Nau·cra·tis \'nȯ-krət-əs\ ancient Greek city N Egypt in Nile delta

Nau·ga·tuck \'nȯ-gə-ˌtək\ borough SW *cen* Conn. *pop* 26,456

Nau·plia \'nȯ-plē-ə\ *or NGk* Náv·pli·on \'näf-plē-ˌȯn\ town & port S Greece in E Peloponnisos near head of Gulf of Argolis

Nauplia, Gulf of — *see* ARGOLIS (Gulf of)

Na·u·ru \nä-'ü-(ˌ)rü\ *or formerly* **Pleas·ant** \'plez-ᵊnt\ island (atoll) W Pacific 26 *mi* (42 *km*) S of the equator; formerly a joint Brit., New Zealand, & Australian trust territory; since 1968 an independent republic *area* 8 *sq mi* (21 *sq km*), *pop* 7254

Nav·a·jo National Monument \'nav-ə-ˌhō-, 'näv-\ reservation N Ariz. SW of Monument Valley near Utah boundary containing cliff dwellings

Na·varre \nə-'vär\ *or Sp* Na·var·ra \nə-'vär-ə\ **1** region & former kingdom N Spain & SW France in W Pyrenees **2** province N Spain ✳ Pamplona *area* 4055 *sq mi* (10,543 *sq km*), *pop* 497,223

Nav·e·sink, Highlands of \'nav-ə-ˌsiŋk, 'nev-ə(r)-\ *or* Navesink Highlands range of hills E N.J. from near Sandy Hook to Raritan Bay

Navigators — *see* SAMOA

Náv·pak·tos \'näf-ˌpäk-təs\ town & port Greece on N shore of strait connecting Gulf of Corinth & Patraïkós Kólpos

Nax·os \'nak-səs, -ˌsäs\ **1** *or NGk* Ná·xos \'näk-ˌsȯs\ island Greece, largest of the Cyclades *area* 171 *sq mi* (445 *sq km*) **2** oldest Greek colony in Sicily; ruins SW of Taormina

Na·ya·rit \ˌnī-ə-'rēt\ state W Mexico bordering on the Pacific ✳ Tepic *area* 10,444 *sq mi* (27,154 *sq km*), *pop* 730,024

Naz·a·reth \'naz-(ə-)rəth\ city N Israel in Galilee SE of Haifa *pop* 33,300

Naze, The \'näz\ headland SE England on E coast of Essex

Na·zil·li \ˌnäz-ə-'lē\ city SW Turkey SE of Izmir

N'Dja·me·na \en-'jäm-ə-nə\ *or formerly* **Fort–La·my** \ˌfȯr-lə-'mē\ city on the Chari ✳ of Chad *pop* 179,000

Neagh, Lough \'nā\ lake *cen* Northern Ireland *area* 153 *sq mi* (398 *sq km*); largest in British Isles

Neapolis **1** — *see* NABLUS **2** — *see* NAPLES

Near \'ni(ə)r\ islands SW Alaska at W end of the Aleutians — *see* ATTU

Near East **1** the Ottoman Empire at its greatest extent — a former usage **2** the countries of SW Asia & NE Africa — **Near Eastern** *adj*

Ne·bo, Mount \'nē-(ˌ)bō\ mountain 2631 *ft* (802 *m*) Palestine in Jordan E of N end of Dead sea

Ne·bras·ka \nə-'bras-kə\ state *cen* U.S. ✳ Lincoln *area* 77,227 *sq mi* (200,790 *sq km*), *pop* 1,569,825 — **Ne·bras·kan** \-kən\ *adj or n*

Ne·chako \ni-'chak-(ˌ)ō\ river 287 *mi* (462 *km*) Canada in *cen* B.C. flowing N & E into the Fraser

Ne·ches \'nā-chəz\ river 280 *mi* (451 *km*) E Tex. flowing S & SE into Sabine Lake

Neck·ar \'nek-ər, -ˌär\ river 246 *mi* (396 *km*) SW W. Germany rising in the Black Forest & flowing N & W into the Rhine

Neck·er \'nek-ər\ island Hawaii in Leewards NW of Niihau island

Ne·der·land \'nēd-ər-lənd\ city SE Tex. SE of Beaumont *pop* 16,855

Need·ham \'nēd-əm\ town E Mass. WSW of Boston *pop* 27,901

Nee·nah \'nē-nə\ city E Wis. on Lake Winnebago *pop* 22,432

Nefud — *see* NAFŪD, AN

Neg·ev \'neg-ˌev\ *or* Neg·eb \-ˌeb\ region S Israel, a triangular wedge of desert touching Gulf of 'Aqaba in S

Ne·gri Sem·bi·lan \nə-ˌgrē-səm-'bē-lən\ state Malaysia in Peninsular Malaysia on Strait of Malacca ✳ Seremban *area* 2550 *sq mi* (6630 *sq km*), *pop* 563,955

Ne·gro \'nā-(ˌ)grō\ **1** river 630 *mi* (1014 *km*) S *cen* Argentina flowing E into the Atlantic **2** river 1400 *mi* (2253 *km*) E Colombia & N Brazil flowing into the Amazon **3** river 290 *mi* (467 *km*) *cen* Uruguay flowing SW into Uruguay river

Ne·gros \'nā-(ˌ)grōs\ island S *cen* Philippines in the Visayans SE of Panay Is. *area* 4905 *sq mi* (12,753 *sq km*)

Nei·chiang *or* Nei·jiang \'nā-jē-'äŋ\ city *cen* China in S *cen* Szechwan SE of Ch'eng-tu *pop* 180,000

Nei Monggol — *see* INNER MONGOLIA

Neis·se \'nī-sə\ **1** *or* Lau·sitz·er Neisse \'laù-zət-sər-,\ river 140 *mi* (225 *km*) N Europe flowing from N Czechoslovakia N into the Oder **2** — *see* NYSA

Nejd \'nejd, 'nezhd\ *or* Najd \'najd, 'nazhd\ region *cen* & E Saudi Arabia; a viceroyalty ✳ Riyadh *area* 447,000 *sq mi* (1,162,200 *sq km*), *pop* 1,200,000 — **Nejdi** \'nej-dē, 'nezh-\ *adj or n*

Nel·son \'nel-sən\ **1** river 400 *mi* (644 *km*) Canada in Man. flowing from N end of Lake Winnipeg to Hudson bay **2** city & port New Zealand on N coast of South Is. *pop* 33,304

Ne·man \'nem-ən\ *or* Ne·mu·nas \'nem-ə-ˌnäs\ river 500 *mi* (805 *km*) W U.S.S.R. flowing from *cen* Belorussia N & W into Kurland Gulf

Ne·mea \'nē-mē-ə\ valley & town Greece in NE Peloponnisos W of Corinth — **Ne·me·an** \'nē-mē-ən, ni-'mē-\ *adj*

Ne·o·sho \nē-'ō-(ˌ)shō, -shə\ *or in Okla* Grand river 460 *mi* (740 *km*) SE Kans. & NE Okla. flowing SE & S into Arkansas river; now largely submerged in its lower course

Ne·pal \nə-'pȯl, -'päl, -'pal\ country Asia on NE border of India in the Himalayas; a kingdom ✳ Kathmandu *area* 54,000 *sq mi* (140,400 *sq km*), *pop* 15,020,451 — **Nep·a·lese** \ˌnep-ə-'lēz, -'lēs\ *adj or n*

Ne·pe·an \'nē-pē-ən\ city Canada in SE Ont. SW of Ottawa *pop* 84,361

Ness, Loch \'nes\ lake 23 *mi* (37 *km*) long NW Scotland in Highland region

Nestos — *see* MESTA

Neth·er·lands \'neth-ər-lən(d)z\ **1** LOW COUNTRIES — an historical usage **2** *or* Hol·land \'häl-ənd\ *or D* Ne·der·land \'nād-ər-ˌlänt\ country NW Europe on North sea; a kingdom, official ✳ Amsterdam, de facto ✳ The Hague *area* 15,785 *sq mi* (41,041 *sq km*), *pop* 14,386,000 — **Neth·er·land** \-lənd\ *adj* — **Neth·er·land·er** \-ˌlan-dər, -lən-\ *n* — **Neth·er·land·ic** \-ˌlan-dik\ *adj* — **Neth·er·land·ish** \-ˌlan-dish, -lən-\ *adj*

Netherlands An·til·les \an-'til-ēz\ Dutch overseas territory, W. Indies comprising Bonaire, Curaçao, Saba, St. Eustatius, & S part of St. Martin ✳ Willemstad (on Curaçao) *area* 403 *sq mi* (1048 *sq km*), *pop* 246,000

Netherlands East Indies — *see* INDONESIA

Netherlands Guiana — *see* SURINAME

Netherlands India *or* **Netherlands Indies** NETHERLANDS EAST INDIES
Netherlands New Guinea — see WEST IRIAN
Netherlands Timor — see TIMOR
Néthou, Pic de — see ANETO (Pico de)
Net·tu·no \nä-'tü-(,)nō\ commune Italy on Tyrrhenian sea SSE of Rome adjoining Anzio *pop* 28,872
Neu·châ·tel \,n(y)ü-shə-'tel, ,nə(r)sh-ə-, nœ-shä-tel\ *or G* **Neu·en·burg** \'nòi-ən-,bərg\ **1** canton W Switzerland in Jura mountains *area* 312 *sq mi* (811 *sq km*), *pop* 158,368 **2** commune, its ✱, on **Lake of Neuchâtel** (*area* 84 *sq mi or* 218 *sq km*), *pop* 34,428
Neuil·ly–sur–Seine \,nə(r)-,yē-,sü(ə)r-'sān\ commune N France NW of Paris near the Bois de Boulogne *pop* 65,941
Neu·mün·ster \nòi-'mu̇en-stər\ city N W. Germany SSW of Kiel *pop* 80,145
Neu·quén \nyü-'kān, neù-\ river 375 *mi* (604 *km*) W Argentina flowing from the Andes E to join the Limay forming Negro river
Neuse \'n(y)üs\ river 260 *mi* (418 *km*) E *cen* N.C. flowing SE into Pamlico Sound
Neuss \'nòis\ city W W. Germany W of Düsseldorf *pop* 149,334
Neus·tria \'n(y)ü-strē-ə\ **1** the western part of the dominions of the Franks after the conquest by Clovis in 511, comprising the NW part of modern France bet. the Meuse, the Loire, & the Atlantic **2** a name for Normandy used after 912 — **Neus·tri·an** \-ən\ *adj or n*
Ne·va \'nē-və, 'nā-\ river 40 *mi* (64 *km*) U.S.S.R. in NW Soviet Russia, Europe, flowing from Lake Ladoga to Gulf of Finland at Leningrad
Ne·va·da \nə-'vad-ə, -'väd-ə\ state W U.S. ✱ Carson City *area* 110,540 *sq mi* (287,404 *sq km*), *pop* 800,493 — **Ne·va·dan** \-'vad-ᵊn, -'väd-ᵊn\ *or* **Ne·va·di·an** \-'vad-ē-ən, -'väd-\ *adj or n*
Ne·vers \nə-'ve(ə)r\ city *cen* France SE of Orléans *pop* 45,122
Ne·ves \'nā-vəs\ city SE Brazil on Guanabara Bay *pop* 53,052
Ne·vis \'nē-vəs\ island Brit. W. Indies, part of St. Kitts-Nevis, in the Leewards; chief town Charlestown *area* 50 *sq mi* (130 *sq km*)
New Al·ba·ny \'òl-bə-nē\ city S Ind. on Ohio river *pop* 37,103
New Am·ster·dam \'am(p)-stər-,dam\ town founded 1625 on Manhattan Is. by the Dutch; renamed New York 1664 by the British
New·ark \'n(y)ü-ərk, 'n(y)ù(-ə)rk; *esp 2 & 4* 'n(y)ü-,ärk\ **1** city W Calif. SE of San Francisco *pop* 32,126 **2** city NE Del. W of Wilmington *pop* 25,247 **3** city & port NE N.J. on **Newark Bay** (W extension of Upper New York Bay) *pop* 329,248 **4** city *cen* Ohio *pop* 41,200
New Bed·ford \'bed-fərd\ city & port SE Mass. on W side of Buzzards Bay *pop* 98,478
New Ber·lin \'bər-lən\ city SE Wis. W of Milwaukee *pop* 30,529
New Braun·fels \'braùn-fəlz\ city SE *cen* Tex. *pop* 22,402
New Brigh·ton \'brīt-ᵊn\ village SE Minn. N of St. Paul *pop* 23,269
New Brit·ain \'brit-ᵊn\ **1** city *cen* Conn. *pop* 73,840 **2** island Bismarck archipelago; largest of group *area* 14,000 *sq mi* (36,400 *sq km*), *pop* 198,456
New Bruns·wick \'brənz-(,)wik\ **1** city N *cen* N.J. *pop* 41,442 **2** province SE Canada bordering on Gulf of St. Lawrence & Bay of Fundy ✱ Fredericton *area* 27,985 *sq mi* (72,761 *sq km*), *pop* 696,403
New·burgh \'n(y)ü-,bərg\ city SE N.Y. on Hudson river S of Poughkeepsie *pop* 23,438
New Cal·e·do·nia \,kal-ə-'dō-nyə, -nē-ə\ island SW Pacific SW of Vanuatu; with nearby islands, constitutes an overseas department of France ✱ Nouméa *area* 8548 *sq mi* (22,225 *sq km*), *pop* 118,715
New Ca·naan \'kā-nən\ town SW Conn. NW of Norwalk *pop* 17,931
New Castile — see CASTILE
New·cas·tle \'n(y)ü-,kas-əl, *3 is locally* n(y)ü-'\ **1** city & port SE Australia in E New S. Wales at mouth of Hunter river *pop* 135,207 **2** town Canada in SE Ont. ENE of Toronto *pop* 32,229 **3** *or* **Newcastle upon Tyne** \'tīn\ city & port N England ✱ of Tyne and Wear *pop* 192,454 **4** *or* **Newcastle under Lyme** \-'līm\ borough W *cen* England in Staffordshire *pop* 72,853
New Cas·tle \'n(y)ü-,kas-əl\ **1** city E Ind. S of Muncie *pop* 20,056 **2** city W Pa. ESE of Youngstown, Ohio *pop* 33,621
New Delhi city ✱ of India in Delhi Territory S of city of (old) Delhi *pop* 324,283
New England **1** the NE U.S. comprising the states of Maine, N.H., Vt., Mass., R.I., & Conn. **2** mountain range & plateau SE Australia in NE New S. Wales; part of Great Dividing range — **New En·gland·er** \-'iŋ-glən-dər *also* -'iŋ-lən-\ *n* — **New En·glandy** \-dē\ *adj*
New Forest forested area S England in Hampshire bet. the Avon & Southampton Water; once a royal hunting ground
New·found·land \'n(y)ü-fən-(d)lənd, -,(d)land; ,n(y)ü-fən-'(d)land\ **1** island Canada in the Atlantic E of Gulf of St. Lawrence *area* 42,734 *sq mi* (111,108 *sq km*) **2** province E Canada comprising Newfoundland (island) & part of Labrador ✱ St. John's *area* 154,734 *sq mi* (402,308 *sq km*), *pop* 597,681 — **New·found·land·er** \-(d)lən-dər, -'(d)lan-dər\ *n*
New France the possessions of France in N. America before 1763
New Geor·gia \'jòr-jə\ **1** island group W Pacific in *cen* Solomon islands **2** island 50 *mi* (80 *km*) long, chief island of the group
New Gra·na·da \grə-'näd-ə\ Spanish viceroyalty in NW S. America 1717–1819 comprising area included in modern Panama, Colombia, Venezuela, & Ecuador
New Guin·ea \-'gin-ē\ **1** island in Malay archipelago N of E Australia divided bet. W. Irian on W & Papua New Guinea on E *area* 306,600 *sq mi* (797,160 *sq km*) **2** the NE portion of the island of New Guinea with the Bismarck archipelago, Bougainville, Buka, & adjacent small islands; part of Papua New Guinea — see NORTH-EAST NEW GUINEA — **New Guin·ean** \-'gin-ē-ən\ *adj or n*
New·ham \'n(y)ü-əm\ borough of E Greater London, England *pop* 214,700
New Hamp·shire \'ham(p)-shər, -,shi(ə)r\ state NE U.S. ✱ Concord *area* 9304 *sq mi* (24,190 *sq km*), *pop* 920,610 — **New Hamp·shire·man** \-mən\ *n* — **New Hamp·shir·ite** \-,īt\ *n*
New Ha·ven \'hā-vən\ city & port S Conn. *pop* 126,109
New Hebrides — see VANUATU
New Hope \'n(y)ü-,hōp\ village E Minn. N of Minneapolis *pop* 23,087
New Ibe·ria \ī-'bir-ē-ə\ city S La. SE of Lafayette *pop* 32,766
New·ing·ton \'nyü-iŋ-tən\ town *cen* Conn. SW of Hartford *pop* 28,841
New Ire·land \'ī(ə)r-lənd\ island W Pacific in Bismarck archipelago N of New Britain ✱ Kavieng *area* 3340 *sq mi* (8684 *sq km*), *pop* (with adjacent islands) 48,774
New Jer·sey \'jər-zē\ state E U.S. ✱ Trenton *area* 7836 *sq mi* (20,374 *sq km*), *pop* 7,364,823 — **New Jer·sey·an** \-'jər-zē-ən\ *n* — **New Jer·sey·ite** \-,īt\ *n*
New Ken·sing·ton \'ken-ziŋ-tən\ city SW Pa. NE of Pittsburgh on Allegheny river *pop* 17,660
New Lon·don \'lən-dən\ city & port SE Conn. on Long Is. Sound at mouth of Thames river *pop* 28,842
New·mar·ket \'n(y)ü-,mär-kət\ **1** town Canada in SE Ont. N of Toronto *pop* 29,753 **2** town E England in Suffolk *pop* 16,235
New Mex·i·co \'mek-si-,kō\ state SW U.S. ✱ Santa Fe *area* 121,666 *sq mi* (316,332 *sq km*), *pop* 1,302,894 — **New Mex·i·can** \-si-kən\ *adj or n*
New Mil·ford \'mil-fərd\ **1** city W Conn. *pop* 19,420 **2** borough NE N.J. *pop* 16,876
New Neth·er·land \'neth-ər-lənd\ Dutch colony in N. America 1613–64 occupying lands bordering on Hudson river & later also on lower Delaware river ✱ New Amsterdam
New Or·leans \'òr-lē-ənz, 'òrl-(y)ənz, (,)òr-'lēnz\ city & port SE La. bet. Lake Pontchartrain & Mississippi river *pop* 557,515 — **New Or·lea·nian** \(,)òr-'lē-nyən, -nē-ən\ *n*
New Philadelphia city E Ohio *pop* 16,883
New·port \'n(y)ü-,pō(ə)rt, -,pò(ə)rt\ **1** city N Ky. on Ohio river opposite Cincinnati, Ohio *pop* 21,587 **2** city & port SE R.I. on Narragansett Bay *pop* 29,259 **3** borough S England ✱ of Isle of Wight *pop* 23,570 **4** borough SE Wales in Gwent WNW of Bristol *pop* 105,374 — **New·port·er** \-ər\ *n*
Newport Beach city SW Calif. SE of Long Beach *pop* 62,556
Newport News \,n(y)ü-,pōrt-'n(y)üz, -,pòrt-, -pərt-\ city & port SE Va. on James river & Hampton Roads *pop* 144,903
New Prov·i·dence \'präv-əd-ən(t)s, -ə-,den(t)s\ island in NW *cen* Bahamas E of Andros; site of Nassau *area* 58 *sq mi* (151 *sq km*)
New Quebec region Canada in N Que. N of the Eastmain between Hudson bay & Labrador — see UNGAVA
New Quebec Crater *or* **Chubb Crater** \'chəb\ lake-filled meteoric crater Canada in N Que., in N Ungava peninsula; 3 *mi* (4.8 *km*) in diameter
New Ro·chelle \,n(y)ü-rə-'shel\ city SE N.Y. on Long Is. Sound E of Mount Vernon *pop* 70,794
New Siberian islands U.S.S.R. in N Soviet Russia, Asia, in Arctic ocean bet. Laptev & E. Siberian seas *area* 11,000 *sq mi* (28,600 *sq km*)
New South Wales state SE Australia bordering on the Pacific ✱ Sydney *area* 309,432 *sq mi* (804,523 *sq km*), *pop* 5,126,217
New Spain Spanish viceroyalty 1521–1821 including territory now in SW U.S., Mexico, Central America N of Panama, much of the W. Indies, & the Philippines ✱ Mexico City
New Sweden Swedish colony in N. America 1638–55 bordering on W bank of Delaware river from modern Trenton, N.J., to its mouth
New·ton \'n(y)üt-ᵊn\ city E Mass. W of Boston *pop* 83,622
New·town \'n(y)ü-,taùn\ town SW Conn. E of Danbury *pop* 19,107
New·town·ab·bey \,n(y)üt-ᵊn-'ab-ē\ district E Northern Ireland, established 1974 *area* 58 *sq mi* (151 *sq km*), *pop* 71,631
Newtown Saint Bos·wells \-sənt-'bäz-wəlz, -sānt-\ village S Scotland W of Kelso ✱ of Borders region
New West·min·ster \wes(t)-'min(t)-stər\ city Canada in SW B.C. on the Fraser ESE of Vancouver *pop* 38,550
New Windsor — see WINDSOR
New York \'yò(ə)rk\ **1** state NE U.S. ✱ Albany *area* 49,576 *sq mi* (121,898 *sq km*), *pop* 17,558,072 **2** *or* **New York City** city & port SE N.Y. at mouth of Hudson river; includes boroughs of Bronx, Brooklyn, Manhattan, Queens, & Staten Is. *pop* 7,071,639 **3** the borough of Manhattan in New York City — **New York·er** \'yòr-kər\ *n*
New York Bay inlet of the Atlantic SE N.Y. & NE N.J. at mouth of Hudson river forming harbor of metropolitan New York & consisting of **Upper New York Bay** & **Lower New York Bay** connected by the **Narrows** (strait separating Staten Is. & Long Is.)
New York State Barge Canal — see ERIE
New Zea·land \'zē-lənd\ country SW Pacific ESE of Australia comprising chiefly North Is. & South Is.; a dominion of the Commonwealth ✱ Wellington *area* 103,736 *sq mi* (269,714 *sq km*), *pop* 3,175,737 — **New Zea·land·er** \-lən-dər\ *n*
Ngaliema, Mount — see STANLEY (Mount)
Nga·mi, Lake \eŋ-'gäm-ē\ marshy depression NW Botswana N of Kalahari desert; formerly a large lake
Ngau·ru·hoe \eŋ-,gaù-rə-'hō-ē\ volcano 7515 *ft* (2291 *m*) New Zealand in *cen* North Is. in Tongariro National Park
Ni·ag·a·ra Falls \(,)nī-'ag-(ə-)rə\ **1** waterfalls on border bet. N.Y. & Ont. in the **Niagara** river (36 *mi or* 58 *km* flowing from Lake Erie N into Lake Ontario); divided by Goat Is. into Horseshoe, or Canadian, Falls (158 *ft or* 48 *m* high, 3010 *ft or* 917 *m* wide at crest) & American Falls (167 *ft or* 51 *m* high, 1060 *ft or* 323 *m* wide) **2** city W N.Y. at the falls *pop* 71,384 **3** city Canada in SE Ont. *pop* 70,960
Nia·mey \nē-'äm-(,)ā, nyä-'mā\ city ✱ of Niger *pop* 225,314
Ni·as \'nē-,äs\ island Indonesia in Indian ocean off W coast of Sumatra *area* 1569 *sq mi* (4079 *sq km*), *pop* 314,829 — **Ni·as·san** \'nē-ə-sən\ *n*
Ni·caea \nī-'sē-ə\ *or* **Nice** \'nīs\ ancient city of Byzantine Empire, site at modern village of Iznik in NW Turkey in Asia at E end of Iznik lake — **Ni·cae·an** \nī-'sē-ən\ *adj*
Nic·a·ra·gua \,nik-ə-'räg-wə\ **1** lake 100 *mi* (161 *km*) long S Nicaragua **2** country Central America bordering on the Pacific & the Caribbean; a republic ✱ Managua *area* 57,143 *sq mi* (148,572 *sq km*), *pop* 2,824,000 — **Nic·a·ra·guan** \-'räg-wən\ *adj or n*
Nice \'nēs\ *or anc* **Ni·caea** \nī-'sē-ə\ city & port SE France on the Mediterranean *pop* 331,002
Nic·o·bar \'nik-ə-,bär\ islands India in Indian ocean S of Andaman islands *area* 635 *sq mi* (1651 *sq km*), *pop* 14,563 — see ANDAMAN AND NICOBAR
Nicomedia — see IZMIT
Ni·cop·o·lis \nə-'käp-ə-ləs, nī-\ ancient city NW Greece in Epirus
Nic·o·sia \,nik-ə-'sē-ə\ city *cen* Cyprus, its ✱ *pop* 145,900
Nidwald, Nidwalden — see UNTERWALDEN
Niedersachsen — see LOWER SAXONY
Nieuw·poort *or* **Nieu·port** \'n(y)ü-,pō(ə)rt, -,pò(ə)rt, *F* nyœ-pòr\ commune NW Belgium in W. Flanders on the Yser *pop* 8195
Ni·ger \'nī-jər\ **1** river 2600 *mi* (4184 *km*) W Africa flowing from Fouta Djallon NE, SE, & S into Gulf of Guinea **2** country W Africa; a republic, until 1958 a territory of French W. Africa ✱ Niamey *area*

458,874 sq mi (1,193,072 sq km), *pop* 5,098,427 — **Ni·ger·ois** \‚nē-zhər-'wä, -zher-\ *n*

Ni·ge·ria \nī-'jir-ē-ə\ country W Africa bordering on Gulf of Guinea; a republic within the Commonwealth, formerly a colony & protectorate ✶ Lagos *area* 356,669 *sq mi* (927,339 *sq km*), *pop* 86,126,000 — **Ni·ge·ri·an** \-ē-ən\ *adj or n*

Nihon — see JAPAN

Nii·ga·ta \nē-'gät-ə, 'nē-gə-‚tä\ city & port Japan in N Honshu on Sea of Japan *pop* 462,445

Nii·hau \'nē-‚haů\ island Hawaii WSW of Kauai *area* 72 *sq mi* (187 *sq km*)

Nij·me·gen \'nī-‚mā-gən\ commune E Netherlands in Gelderland on the Waal S of Arnhem *pop* 147,150

Nik·ko \'nik-(‚)ō\ city Japan in E *cen* Honshu *pop* 23,885

Ni·ko·la·yev \‚nik-ə-'lī-əf\ city & port U.S.S.R. in S Ukrainian Republic *pop* 440,000

Ni·ko·pol \'nik-ə-pəl\ city U.S.S.R. in E *cen* Ukrainian Republic on the Dnieper *pop* 125,000

Nile \'nī(ə)l\ river 4037 *mi* (6497 *km*) E Africa flowing from Lake Victoria in Uganda N into the Mediterranean in Egypt; in various sections called specifically: **Vic·to·ria Nile** \vik-'tōr-ē-ə, -'tòr-\ *or* **Som·er·set Nile** \'sam-ər-sət, -‚set\ bet. Lake Victoria & Lake Albert; **Al·bert Nile** \'al-bərt\ bet. Lake Albert & Lake No; & **White Nile** from Lake No to Khartoum — see BLUE NILE

Niles \'nī(ə)lz\ **1** village NE Ill. NW of Chicago *pop* 30,363 **2** city NE Ohio SE of Warren *pop* 23,088

Nil·gi·ri \'nil-gə-rē\ hills S India in W Tamil Nadu; highest point Mt. Dodabetta 8640 *ft* (2633 *m*)

Nîmes \'nēm\ city S France NE of Montpellier *pop* 123,914

Nimrud — see CALAH

Nin·e·veh \'nin-ə-və\ *or* L **Ni·nus** \'nī-nəs\ ancient city ✶ of Assyria; ruins in Iraq on the Tigris opposite Mosul

Ninghsia — see YINCHUAN

Ning·po *or* **Ning·bo** \'niŋ-'bō\ *or formerly* **Ning·hsien** \'niŋ-shē-'en\ city E China in N Chekiang ESE of Hangchow *pop* 280,000

Ningsia — see YINCHUAN

Ning·sia Hui \'niŋ-shē-'ä-'hwē\ *or* **Ning·xia Hui·zu** \-'hwēd-'zü\ region N China; formerly a province ✶ Yinchuan *area* 30,039 *sq mi* (78,101 *sq km*)

Ni·o·bra·ra \‚nī-ə-'brar-ə, -'brer-\ river 431 *mi* (694 *km*) E Wyo. & N Nebr. flowing E into Missouri river

Niort \nē-'ô(ə)r\ city W France ENE of La Rochelle *pop* 59,297

Nip·i·gon, Lake \'nip-ə-‚gän\ lake Canada in W Ont. N of Lake Superior *area* 1870 *sq mi* (4862 *sq km*)

Nip·is·sing, Lake \'nip-ə-siŋ\ lake Canada in SE Ont. NE of Georgian Bay *area* 330 *sq mi* (858 *sq km*)

Nippon — see JAPAN

Nip·pur \nip-'ú(ə)r\ ancient city of Sumer SSE of Babylon

Nis *or* **Nish** \'nish\ city E Yugoslavia in E Serbia *pop* 128,231

Ni·shi·no·mi·ya \‚nish-ə-'nō-mē-‚(y)ä\ city Japan in *cen* Honshu on Osaka Bay E of Kobe *pop* 410,413

Ni·te·rói *or formerly* **Nic·the·roy** \‚nit-ə-'ròi\ city SE Brazil on Guanabara Bay opposite Rio de Janeiro *pop* 400,140

Ni·u·a·foo \‚nē-ü-ə-‚fōō\ island SW *cen* Pacific in the N Tongas *pop* 599

Ni·ue \nē-'ü-(‚)(w)ä\ island S *cen* Pacific; a self-governing territory of New Zealand (*area* 100 *sq mi* (260 *sq km*), *pop* 4048

Ni·velles \nē-'vel\ commune *cen* Belgium *pop* 21,580

Ni·ver·nais \‚nē-vər-'nā\ region & former province *cen* France E of the upper Loire ✶ Nevers

Nizhni Novgorod — see GORKI

Nizh·ni Ta·gil \‚nizh-nē-tə-'gil\ city U.S.S.R. in W Soviet Russia, Asia, on E slope of the Urals *pop* 398,000

No, Lake \'nō\ lake S *cen* Sudan where Bahr el Jebel & Bahr el Ghazal join to form White Nile *area* 40 *sq mi* (104 *sq km*)

No·ga·les \nō-'gal-əs, -'gäl-\ city NW Mexico in Sonora *pop* 14,254

No·ga·ta \nō-'gät-ə\ city Japan in N Kyushu *pop* 62,595

Nome, Cape \'nōm\ cape W Alaska on S side of Seward peninsula

Noot·ka Sound \‚nut-kə-, ‚nüt-\ inlet of the Pacific Canada in SW B.C. on W coast of Vancouver Is.

Nor·co \'nô(ə)r-(‚)kō\ city SE Calif. W of Palm Springs *pop* 21,126

Nordenskjold — see LAPTEV

Nord·kyn, Cape \'nô(ə)r-kən, 'nür-kuen\ cape NE Norway on Barents sea E of N. Cape; northernmost point of European mainland, at 71°8'N

Nor·folk \'nôr-fək, *US also* -‚fók\ **1** city NE Nebr. *pop* 19,449 **2** city & port SE Va. on Elizabeth river S of Hampton Roads *pop* 266,979 **3** island S Pacific bet. New Caledonia & New Zealand; administered by Australia *area* 13 *sq mi* (34 *sq km*) **4** county E England bordering on North sea ✶ Norwich *area* 2067 *sq mi* (5374 *sq km*), *pop* 619,500

Norfolk Broads — see BROADS

Norge — see NORWAY

Nor·i·cum \'nòr-i-kəm, 'när-\ ancient country & Roman province S *cen* Europe S of the Danube in modern Austria & S W. Germany

No·rilsk \nə-'rēlsk\ city U.S.S.R. in NW Soviet Russia, Asia, N of arctic circle near mouth of the Yenisey *pop* 180,000

Nor·mal \'nòr-məl\ town *cen* Ill. N of Bloomington *pop* 35,672

Nor·man \'nòr-mən\ city *cen* Okla. on Canadian river *pop* 68,020

Nor·man·dy \'nòr-mən-dē\ *or* F **Nor·man·die** \nòr-mä^n-dē\ region & former province NW France NE of Brittany ✶ Rouen

Nor·ris·town \'nòr-ə-‚staůn, 'när-\ borough SE Pa. *pop* 34,684

Norr·kö·ping \'nô(ə)r-‚chə(r)p-iŋ\ city & port SE Sweden SW of Stockholm at head of an inlet of the Baltic *pop* 120,300

North island N New Zealand *area* 44,280 *sq mi* (115,128 *sq km*), *pop* 1,956,411

North Ad·ams \-'ad-əmz\ city NW Mass. *pop* 18,063

North·al·ler·ton \nôr-'thal-ərt-ᵊn\ town N England ✶ of N. Yorkshire

North America continent of the western hemisphere NW of S America bounded by Atlantic, Arctic, & Pacific oceans *area* 9,385,000 *sq mi* (24,401,000 *sq km*) — **North American** *adj or n*

North·amp·ton \north-'(h)am(p)-tən\ **1** city W *cen* Mass. on Connecticut river N of Holyoke *pop* 29,286 **2** borough *cen* England ✶ of Northamptonshire *pop* 145,421

North·amp·ton·shire \north-'(h)am(p)-tən-‚shi(ə)r, -shər\ *or* **Northampton** county *cen* England ✶ Northampton *area* 914 *sq mi* (2376 *sq km*), *pop* 532,400

North Andover town NE Mass. E of Lawrence *pop* 20,129

North Arlington borough NE N.J. NE of Newark *pop* 16,587

North At·tle·boro \-'at-ᵊl-‚bər-ə, -‚bər-ə\ town SE Mass. *pop* 21,095

North Bay \'nò(ə)rth-‚bā\ city Canada in SE Ont. *pop* 51,268

North Borneo — see SABAH

North Brabant *or* D **Noord–Bra·bant** \‚nòrt-brä-'bänt\ province S Netherlands ✶ 's Hertogenbosch *area* 1965 *sq mi* (5109 *sq km*), *pop* 2,093,929

North·brook \'nòrth-‚brůk\ village NE Ill. NW of Chicago *pop* 30,778

North Canadian river 760 *mi* (1223 *km*) S *cen* U.S. flowing ESE from NE N.Mex. into Canadian river in E Okla. — see BEAVER

North Cape **1** cape New Zealand at N tip of North Is. **2** cape NE Norway on **Ma·ger·öy** \‚mäg-ə-'ròi\ island (*area* 111 *sq mi* or 289 *sq km*) at 71°10'20"N **3** — see HORN

North Car·o·li·na \-‚kar(-ə)-'lī-nə\ state E U.S. ✶ Raleigh *area* 52,586 *sq mi* (136,724 *sq km*), *pop* 5,881,766 — **North Car·o·lin·ian** \-'lin-ē-ən, -'lin-yən\ *adj or n*

North Cas·cades National Park \-kas-‚kādz, -'kas-‚\ reservation N *cen* Wash. on Canadian border

North channel strait bet. NE Ireland & SW Scotland connecting Irish sea & the Atlantic

North Chicago city NE Ill. S of Waukegan *pop* 38,774

North Da·ko·ta \-də-'kōt-ə\ state NW *cen* U.S. ✶ Bismarck *area* 70,665 *sq mi* (183,729 *sq km*), *pop* 652,717 — **North Da·ko·tan** \-'kōt-ᵊn\ *adj or n*

North Down district E Northern Ireland, established 1974 *area* 28 *sq mi* (73 *sq km*), *pop* 65,849

North Downs hills S England chiefly in Kent & Surrey

North East Frontier Agency — see ARUNACHAL PRADESH

North–East New Guinea the NE part of mainland Papua New Guinea

Northern Cir·cars \-(‚)sär-'kärz\ historic name for the coast region of E India now in E Andhra Pradesh

Northern Cook \-'kůk\ *or* **Ma·ni·hi·ki** \‚män-ə-'hē-kē\ islands S *cen* Pacific N of Cook islands; belong to New Zealand

Northern Dvi·na \-də-‚vē-'nä\ *or Russ* **Se·ver·na·ya Dvina** \'sä-vər-nə-yə-\ river 1100 *mi* (1770 *km*) U.S.S.R. in N Soviet Russia, Europe, flowing NW into White sea

Northern Ireland country N Ireland; a division of the United Kingdom of Great Britain and Northern Ireland ✶ Belfast *area* 5461 *sq mi* (14,199 *sq km*), *pop* 1,543,000 — see ULSTER

Northern Karroo — see KARROO

Northern Kingdom — see ISRAEL

Northern Mar·i·ana \-‚mar-ē-'an-ə\ islands W Pacific; in Trust Territory of the Pacific Islands 1947–76 & a U.S. commonwealth since 1986; *area* 184 *sq mi* (478 *sq km*), *pop* 16,780

Northern Rhodesia — see ZAMBIA

Northern Sporades — see SPORADES

Northern Territory territory *cen* & N Australia bordering on Arafura sea ✶ Darwin *area* 523,620 *sq mi* (1,361,412 *sq km*), *pop* 123,324

Northern Yukon National Park reservation NW Canada

North·glenn \'nō(ə)rth-‚glen\ city N *cen* Colo. N of Denver *pop* 29,847

North Ha·ven \'nō(ə)rth-‚hā-vən\ town S Conn. *pop* 22,080

North Holland *or* D **Noord–Hol·land** \'nōrt-‚hò-‚länt\ province NW Netherlands ✶ Haarlem *area* 1163 *sq mi* (3024 *sq km*), *pop* 2,308,590

North Kings·town \-'kiŋ-stən\ town S R.I. *pop* 21,938

North Korea — see KOREA

North Las Vegas city SE Nev. *pop* 42,739

North Lau·der·dale \-'lòd-ər-‚dāl\ city SE Fla. *pop* 18,479

North Little Rock city *cen* Ark. *pop* 64,288

North Miami city SE Fla. *pop* 42,566

North Miami Beach city SE Fla. *pop* 36,553

North Minch — see MINCH

North Olm·sted \-'əm-‚sted\ city NE Ohio *pop* 36,486

North Os·se·tian Republic \-ō-‚sē-shən-\ autonomous republic U.S.S.R. in SE Soviet Russia, Europe, on the N slopes of Caucasus mountains ✶ Dzaudzhikau *area* 3500 *sq mi* (9100 *sq km*)

North Plainfield borough NE N.J. SW of Elizabeth *pop* 19,108

North Platte **1** river 618 *mi* (994 *km*) W U.S. flowing from N Colo. N & E through Wyo. into Nebr. to unite with the S. Platte forming Platte river **2** city SW *cen* Nebr. *pop* 24,479

North Providence town NE R.I. *pop* 29,188

North Rhine–Westphalia *or* G **Noord–Rhein–West·fa·len** \'nòrt-‚rīn-‚vest-'fä-lən\ state W W. Germany formed 1946 by union of former Westphalia province, Lippe state, & N Rhine Province ✶ Düsseldorf *area* 13,107 *sq mi* (34,078 *sq km*), *pop* 17,058,193

North Rich·land Hills \-‚rich-lən(d)-\ town N Tex. *pop* 30,592

North Ridge·ville \-'rij-‚vil\ village N Ohio *pop* 21,522

North Riding — see YORK

North river estuary of Hudson river between SE N.Y. & NE N.J.

North Roy·al·ton \-'ròi(-ə)l-tən\ city N Ohio *pop* 17,671

North Saskatchewan — see SASKATCHEWAN

North sea arm of the Atlantic 600 *mi* (966 *km*) long & 350 *mi* (563 *km*) wide E of Great Britain

North Slope region N Alaska bet. Brooks range & Arctic ocean

North Tonawanda city W N.Y. N of Buffalo *pop* 35,760

North Truchas Peak — see TRUCHAS PEAK

North·um·ber·land \nòr-'thəm-bər-lənd\ **1** strait 180 *mi* (290 *km*) long Canada in Gulf of St. Lawrence bet. P.E.I. & the mainland **2** county N England ✶ Newcastle upon Tyne *area* 1943 *sq mi* (5052 *sq km*), *pop* 301,100

North·um·bria \nòr-'thəm-brē-ə\ ancient country Great Britain bet. the Humber & Firth of Forth; one of kingdoms in Anglo-Saxon heptarchy

North Vancouver city Canada in SW B.C. *pop* 33,952

North Vietnam — see VIETNAM

North–West Frontier Province province of Pakistan & formerly of Brit. India on Afghanistan border ✶ Peshawar *pop* 10,885,000

Northwest Passage a passage by sea bet. the Atlantic & the Pacific along the N coast of N. America

Northwest Territories territory N Canada comprising the arctic islands, the mainland N of 60° bet. Yukon Territory & Hudson bay, & the islands in Hudson bay; ❋ Yellowknife *area* 1,253,438 *sq mi* (3,258,939 *sq km*), *pop* 45,741

North York city Canada in SE Ont. N of Toronto *pop* 559,521

North Yorkshire county N England ❋ Northallerton *area* 3211 *sq mi* (8349 *sq km*), *pop* 673,900

Nor·ton Shores \nórt-ʔn-\ city W Mich. S of Muskegon *pop* 22,025

Norton Sound arm of Bering sea W Alaska bet. Seward peninsula & the mouths of Yukon river

Nor·walk \'nó(ə)r-‚wòk\ **1** city SW Calif. SE of Los Angeles *pop* 85,286 **2** city SW Conn. on Long Is. Sound *pop* 77,767

Nor·way \'nó(ə)r-‚wā\ *or Norw* **Nor·ge** \'nòr-gə\ country N Europe in Scandinavia bordering on Atlantic & Arctic oceans; a kingdom ❋ Oslo *area* 119,085 *sq mi* (309,621 *sq km*), *pop* 4,091,142

Nor·we·gian \nòr-'wē-jən\ sea, arm of the N Atlantic W of Norway

Nor·wich \'nò(ə)r-(‚)wich; 'nòr-ich, 'när-\ **1** city SE Conn. *pop* 38,074 **2** \'när-ij, -ich\ city E England ❋ of Norfolk *pop* 121,688

Nor·wood \'nó(ə)r-‚wud\ **1** town E Mass. SW of Boston *pop* 29,711 **2** city SW Ohio within city of Cincinnati *pop* 26,342

Not·ta·way \'nät-ə-‚wā\ river 400 *mi* (644 *km*) Canada in SW Que. flowing NW into James Bay

Not·ting·ham \'nät-iŋ-əm, *US also* -‚ham\ borough N *cen* England ❋ of Nottinghamshire *pop* 271,080

Not·ting·ham·shire \'nät-iŋ-əm-shi(ə)r, -shər, *US also* -‚ham-\ *or* **Nottingham** *or* **Notts** \'näts\ county N *cen* England ❋ Nottingham *area* 836 *sq mi* (2174 *sq km*), *pop* 991,900

Nouak·chott \nù-'äk-‚shät\ city ❋ of Mauritania near coast in SW *pop* 134,986

Nou·méa \nü-'mā-ə\ city & port ❋ of New Caledonia *pop* 56,078

No·va Igua·çu \‚nò-və-‚ē-gwə-'sü\ city SE Brazil in Rio de Janeiro state NW of Rio de Janeiro *pop* 1,094,650

Nova Lisboa — see HUAMBO

No·va·ra \nō-'vär-ə\ commune NW Italy in Piedmont *pop* 101,635

No·va Sco·tia \‚nò-və-'skō-shə\ province SE Canada comprising a peninsula (375 *mi or* 600 *km* long) & Cape Breton Is. ❋ Halifax *area* 21,103 *sq mi* (54,868 *sq km*), *pop* 847,442 — see ACADIA — **No·va Scotian** \-shən\ *adj or n*

No·va·to \nō-'vät-(‚)ō\ city W Calif. N of San Francisco *pop* 43,916

No·va·ya Zem·lya \‚nō-və-yə-‚zem-lē-'ä\ two islands U.S.S.R. in NE Soviet Russia, Europe, in Arctic ocean bet. Barents sea & Kara sea *area* 36,000 *sq mi* (93,600 *sq km*), *pop* 400

Nov·go·rod \'näv-gə-‚räd\ **1** medieval principality E Europe extending from Lake Peipus & Lithuania to the Urals **2** city U.S.S.R. in NW Soviet Russia, Europe *pop* 128,000

No·vi Sad \‚nò-vē-'säd\ city NE Yugoslavia on the Danube; chief city of Vojvodina *pop* 162,000

No·vo·kuz·netsk \‚nò-(‚)vō-kúz-'netsk\ *or formerly* **Sta·linsk** \'stäl-(y)ən(t)sk, 'stal-\ city U.S.S.R. in SW Soviet Russia, Asia, at S end of Kuznetsk Basin *pop* 499,000

No·vo·si·birsk \‚nò-(‚)vō-sə-'bi(ə)rsk\ *or formerly* **No·vo·ni·ko·la·evsk** \-‚nik-ə-'lī-əfsk\ city U.S.S.R. in SW Soviet Russia, Asia, on the Ob *pop* 1,221,000

Nu·bia \'n(y)ü-bē-ə\ region & ancient kingdom NE Africa along the Nile in S Egypt & N Sudan

Nu·bi·an \'n(y)ü-bē-ən\ desert NE Sudan E of the Nile

Nu·e·ces \n(y)ù-'ā-səs\ river 338 *mi* (544 *km*) S Tex. flowing S & SE into Nueces Bay at head of Corpus Christi Bay

Nueva Esparta — see MARGARITA

Nue·vo La·re·do \nü-‚ā-(‚)vō-lə-'räd-(‚)ō\ city N Mexico in Tamaulipas on Rio Grande opposite Laredo, Tex. *pop* 175,750

Nue·vo Le·ón \-lā-'ōn\ state N Mexico in the Sierra Madre Oriental ❋ Monterrey *area* 25,134 *sq mi* (65,348 *sq km*), *pop* 2,463,298

Nu·ku·a·lo·fa \‚nü-kə-wə-'lō-fə\ town ❋ of Tonga on Tongatapu Is. *pop* 18,312

Nu·ku Hi·va \‚nü-kə-'hē-və\ island S Pacific in the Marquesas; largest in group *area* 186 *sq mi* (484 *sq km*), *pop* 1216

Null·ar·bor Plain \‚nəl-ə-‚bò(ə)r-\ treeless plain SW Australia in Western Australia & S. Australia bordering on Great Australian Bight

Num·foor \'nüm-‚fō(ə)r, -‚fò(ə)r\ island W. Irian in W Schouten islands *area* 28 *sq mi* (73 *sq km*)

Nu·mid·ia \n(y)ü-'mid-ē-ə\ ancient country N Africa E of Mauretania in modern Algeria; chief city Hippo — **Nu·mid·i·an** \-ē-ən\ *adj or n*

Nun·ea·ton \‚nə-'nēt-ʔn\ borough *cen* England in Warwickshire E of Birmingham *pop* 71,530

Nu·ni·vak \'nü-nə-‚vak\ island 50 *mi* (80 *km*) long W Alaska in Bering sea *pop* 225

Nu·rem·berg \'n(y)ùr-əm-‚bərg\ *or G* **Nürn·berg** \'nuərn-‚berk\ city SE W. Germany in N *cen* Bavaria *pop* 484,403

Nu·ri·stan \‚nùr-i-'stan\ *or formerly* **Kaf·i·ri·stan** \‚kaf-ə-ri-'stan\ district E Afghanistan S of the Hindu Kush ❋ Puchal

Nut·ley \'nət-lē\ town NE N.J. N of Newark *pop* 28,998

Nyasa, Lake — see MALAWI (Lake)

Nyasaland — see MALAWI

Nyi·ra·gon·go \‚nē-ir-ə-'gòŋ-(‚)gō, -'gän-\ volcano *ab* 11,400 *ft* (3475 *m*) E Zaire in Virunga mountains NE of Lake Kivu

Nysa \'nis-ə\ *or* **Neis·se** \'nī-sə\ river 120 *mi* (193 *km*) SW Poland flowing NE into the Oder

Oa·he Reservoir \ə-'wä-(‚)hē\ reservoir *ab* 225 *mi* (362 *km*) long N S.Dak. & S N.Dak. formed in Missouri river by **Oahe Dam**

Oa·hu \ə-'wä-(‚)hü\ island Hawaii, site of Honolulu *area* 589 *sq mi* (1531 *sq km*)

Oak Creek city SE Wis. *pop* 16,932

Oak Forest village NE Ill. S of Chicago *pop* 26,096

Oak·ham \'ō-kəm\ town E *cen* England in E Leicestershire; ❋ of former county of Rutlandshire *pop* 7996

Oak·land \'ō-klənd\ city & port W Calif. on San Francisco Bay opposite San Francisco *pop* 339,288

Oakland Park city SE Fla. N of Fort Lauderdale *pop* 23,035

Oak Lawn village NE Ill. SW of Chicago *pop* 60,590

Oak Park **1** village NE Ill. W of Chicago *pop* 54,887 **2** city SE Mich. N of Detroit *pop* 31,537

Oak Ridge city E Tenn. W of Knoxville *pop* 27,662

Oak·ville \'ōk-‚vil\ town Canada in SE Ont. SW of Toronto *pop* 75,773

Oa·xa·ca \wə-'häk-ə\ **1** state SE Mexico bordering on the Pacific *area* 36,371 *sq mi* (94,565 *sq km*), *pop* 2,518,157 **2** city, its ❋ *pop* 116,826 — **Oa·xa·can** \-ən\ *adj*

Ob \'äb, 'òb\ river 2500 *mi* (4023 *km*) U.S.S.R. in W Soviet Rus·ia, Asia, flowing NW & N into **Gulf of Ob** (inlet of Arctic ocean 500 *mi or* 800 *km* long)

Ober·am·mer·gau \‚ō-bər-'äm-ər-‚gaú\ town S W. Germany in Bavaria SSW of Munich *pop* 4906

Ober·hau·sen \'ō-bər-‚haúz-ʔn\ city W W. Germany in the Ruhr WNW of Essen *pop* 228,947

Oberland — see BERNER ALPEN

Oberpfalz — see PALATINATE

Obwald *or* **Obwalden** — see UNTERWALDEN

Oca·la \ō-'kal-ə\ city N *cen* Fla. S of Gainesville *pop* 37,170

Ocean **1** island W Pacific ESE of Nauru Is.; belongs to Kiribati islands *area* 2 *sq mi* (5.2 *sq km*), *pop* 2314 **2** — see KURE

Oce·a·nia \‚ō-shē-'an-ē-ə, -'ā-nē-ə\ *or* **Oce·an·i·ca** \-'an-i-kə\ the lands of the *cen* & S Pacific including Micronesia, Melanesia, Polynesia (including New Zealand), often Australia, & sometimes the Malay archipelago — **Oce·a·ni·an** \-'an-ē-ən, -'ā-nē-\ *adj or n*

Ocean·side \'ō-shən-‚sīd\ city SW Calif. NNW of San Diego *pop* 76,698

Oc·mul·gee \ōk-'məl-gē\ river 255 *mi* (410 *km*) *cen* Ga. flowing SE to join the **Oco·nee** \ō-'kō-nē\ (250 *mi or* 402 *km*) forming the Altamaha

Ocmulgee National Monument reservation *cen* Ga. at Macon containing Indian mounds & other remains

Ocra·coke \'ō-krə-‚kōk\ island off *cen* N.C. coast bet. Pamlico Sound & the Atlantic — see CROATAN

Oden·se \'ōd-ʔn-sə, 'ü-ən-zə\ city Denmark in N Fyn Is. *pop* 169,183

Oder \'ōd-ər\ *or* **Odra** \'ō-drə\ river 563 *mi* (906 *km*) *cen* Europe rising in the mountains of Silesia, Czechoslovakia, & flowing N to join Neisse river & thence N into the Baltic sea

Odes·sa \ō-'des-ə\ **1** city W Tex. *pop* 90,027 **2** city & port U.S.S.R. in S Ukrainian Republic on Black sea *pop* 892,000

Oea — see TRIPOLI

Oe·ta \'ēt-ə\ mountains *cen* Greece, E spur of Pindus mountains; highest point 7060 *ft* (2152 *m*)

Of·fa·ly \'òf-ə-lē, 'äf-\ *or formerly* **King's** county *cen* Ireland in Leinster ❋ Tullamore *area* 771 *sq mi* (2005 *sq km*), *pop* 58,312

Of·fen·bach \'òf-ən-‚bäk, -‚bäk\ city *cen* W. Germany on Main river E of Frankfurt am Main *pop* 110,993

Oga·den \ō-'gäd-‚ən\ plateau region SE Ethiopia

Ogasawara — see BONIN

Og·bo·mo·sho \‚äg-bə-'mō-(‚)shō\ city W Nigeria *pop* 514,400

Og·den \'äg-dən, 'äg-\ city N Utah *pop* 64,407

Ogee·chee \ō-'gē-chē\ river 250 *mi* (402 *km*) E Ga. flowing SE into the Atlantic

Ohio \ō-'hī-(‚)ō, ə-, -ə\ **1** river 981 *mi* (1579 *km*) E U.S. flowing from junction of Allegheny & Monongahela rivers in W Pa. into Mississippi river **2** state E *cen* U.S. ❋ Columbus *area* 41,222 *sq mi* (107,177 *sq km*), *pop* 10,797,630 — **Ohio·an** \-'hī-ə-wən\ *n*

Ohře — see EGER

Oirot — see GORNO-ALTAI

Oise \'wäz\ river 186 *mi* (299 *km*) N France flowing SW into the Seine

Oi·ta \'òi-‚tä, ō-'ē-tä\ city & port Japan in NE Kyushu *pop* 368,079

Oji·na·ga \‚ō-hē-'näg-ə\ town N Mexico on Rio Grande

Ojos del Sa·la·do \‚ō-(‚)hōz-‚del-sə-'läd-(‚)ō\ mountain 22,539 *ft* (6870 *m*) NW Argentina in the Andes W of Tucumán

Oka \ō-'kä\ **1** river 530 *mi* (853 *km*) U.S.S.R. in S *cen* Soviet Russia, Asia, flowing N from the Sayan mountains into the Angara **2** river 950 *mi* (1529 *km*) U.S.S.R. in *cen* Soviet Russia, Europe, flowing into the Volga

Oka·nog·an *or in* Canada **Oka·na·gan** \‚ō-kə-'näg-ən\ river 300 *mi* (483 *km*) U.S. & Canada flowing from **Okanagan Lake** (70 *mi or* 112 *km* long, in SE B.C.) into Columbia river in NE Wash.

Okavango — see CUBANGO

Oka·ya·ma \‚ō-kə-'yäm-ə\ city & port Japan in W Honshu on Inland sea *pop* 550,767

Oka·za·ki \‚ō-kə-'zäk-ē, ō-'käz-ə-kē\ city Japan in S *cen* Honshu SE of Nagoya *pop* 267,540

Okee·cho·bee, Lake \‚ō-kə-'chō-bē\ lake 37 *mi* (60 *km*) long S *cen* Fla.

Oke·fe·no·kee \‚ō-kə-fə-'nō-kē\ swamp 40 *mi* (64 *km*) long SE Ga. & NE Fla.

Okhotsk, Sea of \ō-'kätsk\ inlet of the Pacific U.S.S.R. in E Soviet Russia, Asia, W of Kamchatka peninsula & Kuril islands

Oki \'ō-(‚)kē\ archipelago Japan in Sea of Japan off SW Honshu

Oki·na·wa \‚ō-kə-'nä-wə, -'naú-ə\ **1** island group Japan in *cen* Ryukyu islands ❋ Naha; occupied by the U.S. 1945–1972 **2** island in the group; largest in the Ryukyus *area* 579 *sq mi* (1505 *sq km*) — **Oki·na·wan** \-'nä-wən, -'naú-ən\ *adj or n*

Okla·ho·ma \‚ō-klə-'hō-mə\ state S *cen* U.S. ❋ Oklahoma City *area* 69,919 *sq mi* (181,789 *sq km*), *pop* 3,025,290 — **Okla·ho·man** \-mən\ *adj or n*

Oklahoma City city ❋ of Okla. on the N. Canadian *pop* 403,213

Öland \'ə(r)l-‚änd\ island Sweden in Baltic sea off SE coast; chief town Borgholm *area* 519 *sq mi* (1349 *sq km*)

Ola·the \ō-'lä-thə\ city NE Kans. SW of Kansas City *pop* 37,258

Old Castile — see CASTILE

Ol·den·burg \'ōl-dən-‚bərg\ **1** former state NW Germany bordering on North sea **2** city N W. Germany W of Bremen *pop* 136,764

Old·ham \'ōl-dəm\ borough NW England in Greater Manchester *pop* 95,467

Old Point Comfort cape SE Va. on N shore of Hampton Roads

Old Sar·um \-'sar-əm\ *or anc* **Sor·bi·o·du·num** \‚sòr-bē-ə-'d(y)ü-nəm\ ancient city S England in Wiltshire N of Salisbury

Ol·du·vai Gorge \'ōl-də-‚vī-\ canyon Tanzania in N mainland SE of Serengeti Plain; fossil beds

Ole·an \‚ō-lē-‚an, ‚ō-lē-'\ city SW N.Y. *pop* 18,207

Olek·ma \ō-'lek-mə\ river 700 *mi* (1126 *km*) U.S.S.R. in E Soviet Russia, Asia, rising in Yablonovy mountains & flowing N into the Lena

Ole·nek \ˌäl-ən-'yok\ river 1325 mi (2132 km) U.S.S.R. in N cen Soviet Russia, Asia, flowing NE into Laptev sea W of the Lena

Ol·i·fants \'äl-ə-fən(t)s\ river 350 mi (563 km) S Africa in Republic of S. Africa & Mozambique flowing from Transvaal into the Limpopo

Olives, Mount of or **Ol·i·vet** \'äl-ə-ˌvet, ˌäl-ə-'\ mountain ridge 2680 ft (817 m) W Jordan running N & S on E side of Jerusalem

Olo·mouc \'o-lə-ˌmots\ or G **Ol·mütz** \'ol-ˌm(y)üts\ city Czechoslovakia in cen Moravia pop 102,112

Olsz·tyn \'olsh-tən\ or G **Al·len·stein** \'al-ən-ˌs(t)īn, 'äl-\ city N Poland NNW of Warsaw pop 140,011

Olt \'olt\ river 308 mi (496 km) S Romania flowing S through the Transylvanian Alps into the Danube

Ol·te·nia \äl-'tē-nē-ə\ or **Little Walachia** region S Romania W of the Olt; the W division of Walachia

Olym·pia \ə-'lim-pē-ə, ō-\ 1 city ✻ of Wash. on Puget Sound pop 27,447 2 plain S Greece in NW Peloponnisos along the Alpheus —
Olym·pi·an \-pē-ən\ adj or n — **Olym·pic** \-pik\ adj

Olympic 1 mountains NW Wash. in cen Olympic peninsula — see OLYMPUS (Mount) 2 peninsula NW Wash. W of Puget Sound

Olympic National Park reservation NW Wash. including part of Olympic mountains & strip of land along coast to W

Olym·pus \ə-'lim-pəs, ō-\ 1 mountains NE Greece in Thessaly near coast of Gulf of Salonika; highest peak 9550 ft (2911 m) 2 — see ULU DAG

Olympus, Mount mountain 7965 ft (2428 m) NW Wash.; highest in Olympic mountains

Olyn·thus \ō-'lin(t)-thəs\ ancient city NE Greece in Macedonia on Chalcidice peninsula

Om \'om\ river 450 mi (724 km) U.S.S.R. in SW Soviet Russia, Asia, flowing into the Irtysh

Omagh \'o-mə\ 1 district W Northern Ireland, established 1974 area 436 sq mi (1134 sq km), pop 41,159 2 town W Northern Ireland in cen Omagh district pop 14,627

Oma·ha \'o-mə-ˌho, -ˌha\ city E Nebr. on Missouri river pop 314,255

Oman \ō-'män, -'man\ or formerly **Muscat and Oman** country SW Asia in SE Arabia bordering on Arabian sea; a sultanate ✻ Muscat area 82,000 sq mi (213,200 sq km), pop 1,079,000 — **Omani** \ō-'män-ē, -'man-\ adj or n

Oman, Gulf of arm of Arabian sea bet. Oman & SE Iran

Om·dur·man \ˌäm-dər-'man, -'män\ city cen Sudan on the Nile opposite Khartoum & Khartoum North pop 299,000

Omo·lon \ˌäm-ə-'lon\ river 600 mi (966 km) U.S.S.R. in NE Soviet Russia, Asia, flowing from the Kolyma range N into Kolyma river

Omsk \'om(p)sk, 'am(p)sk\ city U.S.S.R. in SW Soviet Russia, Asia, at confluence of the Irtysh & the Om pop 1,014,000

Omu·ra \ō-mə-rə\ city & port Japan in NW Kyushu on **Omura Bay** (inlet of E. China sea) NNE of Nagasaki pop 65,538

Omu·ta \ō-mə-ˌta\ city & port Japan in NW Kyushu pop 163,000

One·ga \ō-'neg-ə\ lake U.S.S.R. in NW Soviet Russia, Europe, in S Karelian Republic area 3764 sq mi (9786 sq km)

Onei·da \ō-'nīd-ə\ lake ab 22 mi (35 km) long cen N.Y. NE of Syracuse

On·tar·io \än-'ter-ē-ˌo, -'tar-\ 1 city SW Calif. NW of Riverside pop 88,820 2 province E Canada bet. Great Lakes & Hudson bay * Toronto area 363,282 sq mi (944,533 sq km), pop 8,625,107 — **On·tar·i·an** \-ē-ən\ adj or n

Ontario, Lake lake U.S. & Canada in N.Y. & Ont.; easternmost of the Great Lakes area 7540 sq mi (19,604 sq km)

Ope·li·ka \ˌo-pə-'lī-kə\ city E Alabama pop 21,896

Op·e·lou·sas \ˌäp-ə-'lü-səs\ city S La. N of Lafayette pop 18,903

Opo·le \o-'po-lə\ or G **Op·peln** \'o-pəln\ city SW Poland on the Oder pop 118,196

Oporto — see PORTO

Oquirrh \'o-kər\ mountain range N cen Utah S of Great Salt Lake; highest ab 11,000 ft (3353 m)

Ora·dea \o-'räd-ē-ə\ city NW Romania in Transylvania near Hungarian border pop 184,871

Oran \o-'rän\ city & port NW Algeria pop 491,900

Or·ange \'or-inj, 'är-, -ənj\ 1 city SW Calif. N of Santa Ana pop 91,788 2 city NE N.J. NW of Newark pop 31,136 3 city E Tex. E of Beaumont on the Sabine pop 23,628 4 river 1300 mi (2092 km) S Africa flowing from the Drakensbergs in Lesotho W into the Atlantic

Orange \'or-änzh\ city SE France N of Avignon pop 19,847

Orange Free State \'or-inj, 'är-, -ənj\ or **Oran·je Vry·staat** \o-ˌrän-yə-'froi-ˌstät\ province E cen Republic of S. Africa bet. Orange & Vaal rivers ✻ Bloemfontein area 49,647 sq mi (129,082 sq km), pop 1,988,293

Orasul Stalin — see BRASOV

Or·dzho·ni·kid·ze \ˌor-jän-ə-'kid-zə\ or formerly **Dzau·dzhi·kau** \(d)zau-'jē-ˌkau\ city U.S.S.R. in SE Soviet Russia, Europe ✻ of N. Ossetian Republic pop 279,000

Öre·bro \ˌər-ə-'brü\ city S cen Sweden pop 116,969

Or·e·gon \'or-i-gən, 'är-, chiefly by outsiders -ˌgän\ 1 the Columbia river — an old name used esp. prior to discovery of mouth & renaming of river (1791) by Capt. Robert Gray 2 state NW U.S. ✻ Salem area 96,981 sq mi (252,151 sq km), pop 2,633,105 3 city NW Ohio E of Toledo pop 18,675 — **Or·e·go·nian** \ˌor-i-'go-nē-ən, ˌär-, -nyən\ adj or n

Oregon Caves limestone caverns SW Oreg. SW of Medford in **Oregon Caves National Monument**

Oregon Country region W N. America bet. Pacific coast & the Rockies and bet. N Calif. & Alaska — often so called ab 1818–46

Oregon Trail pioneer route to the Pacific Northwest ab 2000 mi (3219 km) long from vicinity of Independence, Mo., to Fort Vancouver, Wash.; used esp. 1842–60

Orel \o-'rel, o-'ryol\ city U.S.S.R. in S Soviet Russia, Europe

Orem \'or-əm, 'or-\ city N cen Utah N of Provo pop 52,399

Oren·burg \'or-ən-ˌbərg, 'or-, -ˌbu(ə)rg\ or formerly **Chka·lov** \chə-'käl-əf\ city U.S.S.R. in E Soviet Russia, Europe, on Ural river pop 459,000

Oren·se \o-'ren(t)-ˌsä\ 1 province NW Spain area 2694 sq mi (7004 sq km), pop 413,627 2 city, its ✻ pop 86,951

Øre·sund \'ər-ə-ˌsən\ strait bet. Sjælland Is., Denmark, & S Sweden connecting Kattegat with Baltic sea

Organ Pipe Cactus National Monument reservation S Ariz. on Mexican border

Oril·lia \o-'ril-yə\ city Canada in SE Ont. on Lake Simcoe pop 23,955

Ori·no·co \ˌor-ə-'no-(ˌ)ko, ˌor-\ river 1600 mi (2575 km) Venezuela flowing from Brazilian border to Colombia border & thence into the Atlantic through wide delta

Oris·sa \o-'ris-ə\ state E India bordering on Bay of Bengal ✻ Bhubaneswar area 60,136 sq mi (156,354 sq km), pop 26,272,064

Ori·za·ba \ˌor-ə-'zäb-ə, ˌor-\ 1 — see CITLALTEPETL 2 city E Mexico in Veracruz state pop 105,150

Or·khon \'or-ˌkän\ river 450 mi (724 km) N Mongolia flowing NE from N edge of the Gobi into the Selenga

Ork·ney \'ork-nē\ islands N Scotland constituting a region ✻ Kirkwall (on Mainland Is.) area 376 sq mi (978 sq km), pop 18,906 — **Ork·ney·an** \'ork-nē-ən, ork-'\ adj or n

Or·lan·do \or-'lan-(ˌ)do\ city E cen Fla. NE of Tampa pop 128,291

Or·land Park \'o(ə)r-lənd\ city NE Ill. SW of Chicago pop 23,045

Or·lé·a·nais \ˌor-lē-ə-'nä\ region & former province N cen France ✻ Orléans

Or·lé·ans \or-lā-äⁿ\ commune N cen France pop 88,503

Or·ly \'or-lē, or-'lē\ commune France, SSE suburb of Paris

Or·moc Bay \or-'mäk\ inlet of Camotes sea Philippines in NW Leyte Is.

Or·mond Beach \'o(ə)r-mənd\ city E Fla. pop 21,378

Ormuz — see HORMUZ

Orne \'o(ə)rn\ river 95 mi (153 km) NW France flowing N into Bay of the Seine

Oron·tes \o-'ränt-ēz, -'rän-ˌtēz\ river 246 mi (396 km) Syria & Turkey rising in Lebanon in the Bekaa & flowing into the Mediterranean

Or·ping·ton \'or-pin-tən\ former urban district SE England in Kent, now part of Bromley

Or·re·fors \ˌor-ə-'forz, -'fosh\ town S Sweden NW of Kalmar

Orsk \'o(ə)rsk\ city U.S.S.R. in SE Soviet Russia, Europe, on Ural river S of Magnitogorsk pop 247,000

Or·te·gal, Cape \ˌort-i-'gäl\ cape NW Spain

Or·tles \'ort-ˌläs\ or G **Ort·ler** \-lər\ mountain range of E Alps N Italy bet. Venezia Tridentina & Lombardy; highest peak Ortles 12,792 ft (3899 m)

Oru·ro \o-'rü(ə)r-(ˌ)o\ city W Bolivia pop 124,213

Or·vie·to \ˌor-vē-'ät-(ˌ)o\ or anc **Vel·su·na** \vel-'sü-nə\ or **Vol·sin·ii** \väl-'sin-ē-ˌī\ commune cen Italy WNW of Terni pop 22,509

Osage \o-'säj, 'o-ˌ\ river E Kans. & Mo. flowing E into Missouri river; now partly submerged in Lake of the Ozarks

Osa·ka \o-'säk-ə\ city & port Japan in S Honshu on **Osaka Bay** (inlet of the Pacific) pop 2,625,624

Osh·a·wa \'äsh-ə-ˌwä\ city Canada in SE Ont. on Lake Ontario ENE of Toronto pop 117,519

Osh·kosh \'äsh-ˌkäsh\ city E Wis. on Lake Winnebago pop 49,620

Osi·jek \'o-sē-ˌ(y)ek\ city N Yugoslavia in Slavonia pop 94,989

Os·lo \'äz-(ˌ)lo, 'äs-\ or formerly **Chris·ti·a·nia** \ˌkris(h)-chē-'an-ē-ə, ˌkris-tē-, -'än-\ city ✻ of Norway at N end of **Oslo Fjord** (inlet of the Skagerrak) pop 451,789

Os·na·brück \'äz-nə-ˌbrük\ city NW W. Germany in Lower Saxony pop 157,367

Osor·no \o-'sor-(ˌ)no\ 1 volcano 8727 ft (2644 m) S cen Chile in lake district 2 city S cen Chile S of Valdivia pop 69,220

Os·sa \'äs-ə\ mountain 6490 ft (1967 m) NE Greece in E Thessaly

Os·se·tia \ä-'sē-sh(ē-)ə\ region U.S.S.R. in SE Soviet Russia, Europe, in cen Caucasus — see NORTH OSSETIAN REPUBLIC, SOUTH OSSETIA

Os·si·ning \'äs-ⁿn-iŋ, 'äs-nin\ village SE N.Y. pop 20,196

Ost·end \äs-'tend, 'äs-ˌ\ or Flem **Oost·en·de** \o-'sten-də\ or F **Os·tende** \o-stäⁿd\ city & port NW Belgium pop 68,915

Österreich — see AUSTRIA

Os·tia \'äs-tē-ə\ town cen Italy at mouth of the Tiber E of site of ancient town of the same name which was the port for Rome

Ostrasia — see AUSTRASIA

Ostra·va \'o-strə-və\ or formerly **Mo·rav·ska Ostrava** \ˌmor-əf-skə-\ city cen Czechoslovakia in Moravia pop 322,073

Osu·mi \'o-sə-(ˌ)mē\ island group Japan in N Ryukyus

Os·we·go \ä-'swē-(ˌ)go\ city N N.Y. on Lake Ontario pop 19,793

Oś·wię·cim \ˌosh-vē-'en(t)-səm\ or **Ausch·witz** \'aush-ˌvits\ commune S Poland W of Kraków pop 45,245

Ota·go Harbor \o-'täg-o\ inlet of the Pacific S New Zealand on E coast of South Is.; Dunedin is situated on it

Ota·ru \o-'tär-(ˌ)ü\ city & port Japan on W coast of Hokkaido pop 183,635

Otran·to \o-'tran-(ˌ)to, 'o-trən-ˌto\ commune & port S Italy on coast at SE tip of Apulia pop 4811

Otranto, Strait of strait bet. SE Italy & W Albania

Otsu \'ot-(ˌ)sü\ city Japan in W cen Honshu pop 220,096

Ot·ta·wa \'ät-ə-ˌwä, -ˌwo\ 1 city N cen Ill. pop 18,166 2 river 696 mi (1120 km) E Canada in SE Ont. & S Que. flowing E into St. Lawrence river 3 city ✻ of Canada in SE Ont. pop 295,163

Ot·to·man Empire \ˌät-ə-mən-\ former Turkish sultanate (✻ Constantinople) in SE Europe, W Asia, & N Africa including at greatest extent Turkey, Syria, Mesopotamia, Palestine, Arabia, Egypt, Barbary States, Balkans, & parts of Russia & Hungary

Ot·tum·wa \o-'təm-wə, o-'tam-\ city SE Iowa pop 27,381

Oua·chi·ta \'wäsh-ə-ˌto\ 1 mountains W Ark. & SE Okla. S of Arkansas river 2 river 605 mi (974 km) SW Ark. & E La. flowing into Black river

Oua·ga·dou·gou \ˌwäg-ə-'dü-(ˌ)gü\ city cen Burkina Faso, its ✻ pop 172,661

Ouar·gla \'wor-glə, 'wär, -ˌglä\ town & oasis Algeria in the Sahara pop 77,400

Oubangui — see UBANGI

Oubangui–Chari — see UBANGI-SHARI

Ou·den·aar·de \ˌaud-ⁿn-'ärd-ə, ˌod-\ or F **Au·de·narde** \ˌod-ⁿn-'ärd\ commune Belgium in E Flanders on the Scheldt pop 27,318

Oudh \'aud\ region N India in E cen Uttar Pradesh ✻ Lucknow

\ə\ abut \ᵊ\ kitten, F table \ər\ further \a\ ash \ā\ ace \ä\ cot, cart
\au̇\ out \ch\ chin \e\ bet \ē\ easy \g\ go \i\ hit \ī\ ice \j\ job
\ŋ\ sing \ō\ go \o̊\ law \o̊i\ boy \th\ thin \th\ the \ü\ loot \u̇\ foot
\y\ yet \zh\ vision \ä, k̲, ⁿ, œ, œ̄, ue, ūe, ᵜ\ see Guide to Pronunciation

Oudts·hoorn \'ōts-,hȯ(ə)rn\ city S Republic of S. Africa in S Cape Province E of Cape Town *pop* 26,907
Oues·sant, Île d' \el-dwā-säⁿ\ *or* **Ush·ant** \'əsh-ənt\ island NW France off tip of Brittany *pop* 1814
Ouj·da \üzh-'dä\ city NE Morocco near Algerian border *pop* 260,082
Ou·lu \'au̇-(,)lü, 'ō-\ *or Sw* **Ulea·borg** \'ü-lē-ō-,bȯr-ē\ city N *cen* Finland on Gulf of Bothnia *pop* 87,224
Ou·ro Prê·to \,ō-,rü-'prāt-(,)ü\ city E Brazil in Minas Gerais *pop* 53,434
Ouse \'üz\ **1** *or* **Great Ouse** river 160 *mi* (257 *km*) *cen* & E England flowing into The Wash **2** river 57 *mi* (92 *km*) NE England flowing SE to unite with Trent river forming the Humber
Outer Banks chain of sand islands & peninsulas along N.C. coast
Outer Hebrides — see HEBRIDES
Outer Mongolia — see MONGOLIA — **Outer Mongolian** *adj or n*
Out islands islands of the Bahamas group excepting New Providence
Ou·tre·mont \'ü-trə-,mänt, *F* ü-trə-mōⁿ\ city Canada in S Que. on Montreal Is. *pop* 24,338
Ova·lle \ō-'vī-,ā, -'vä-,yā\ city N *cen* Chile
Over·ijs·sel \,ō-və-'rī-səl\ province E Netherlands * Zwolle *area* 1318 *sq mi* (3427 *sq km*), *pop* 1,038,341
Over·land \'ō-vər-lənd\ city E Mo. NW of St. Louis *pop* 19,620
Overland Park city NE Kans. S of Kansas City *pop* 81,784
Ovie·do \,ō-vē-'ā-(,)thō\ **1** province NW Spain on Bay of Biscay *area* 4025 *sq mi* (10,465 *sq km*), *pop* 1,140,239 — see ASTURIAS **2** city * of Oviedo province *pop* 184,473
Owas·co \ō-'wäs-(,)kō\ lake 11 *mi* (18 *km*) long *cen* N.Y.; one of the Finger Lakes
Owa·ton·na \,ō-wə-'tän-ə\ city SE Minn. *pop* 18,632
Ow·en Falls \,ō-ən-\ former waterfall E Africa in Uganda in the Nile N of Lake Victoria; now submerged by **Owen Falls Dam**
Ow·ens \'ō-ənz\ river E Calif. formerly flowing into **Owens Lake** (now dry), now supplying water to city of Los Angeles by way of Los Angeles Aqueduct
Ow·ens·boro \'ō-ənz-,bər-ə, -,bə-rə\ city NW Ky. *pop* 54,450
Owen Sound city Canada in SE Ont. on Georgian Bay *pop* 19,883
Owen Stan·ley \'stan-lē\ mountain range E New Guinea; highest peak Mt. Victoria 13,363 *ft* (4073 *m*)
Owy·hee \ō-'wī-(,)(h)ē\ river 250 *mi* (402 *km*) SW Idaho & SE Oreg. flowing N into Snake river
Ox·ford \'äks-fərd\ **1** village SW Ohio *pop* 17,655 **2** *or ML* **Ox·o·nia** \äk-'sō-nē-ə\ city S *cen* England * of Oxfordshire *pop* 98,521 — **Ox·ford·ian** \äks-'fōrd-ē-ən, -'fȯrd-\ *adj or n*
Ox·ford·shire \'äks-fərd-,shi(ə)r, -shər\ *or* **Oxford** county S *cen* England * Oxford *area* 1009 *sq mi* (2623 *sq km*), *pop* 455,200
Ox·nard \'äk-,snärd\ city S Calif. SE of Santa Barbara *pop* 108,195
Oxus — see AMU DARYA
Oxy·rhyn·chus \,äk-si-'riŋ-kəs\ *or Ar* **El Bah·na·sa** \el-'ban-ə-sə\ archaeological site Egypt N of Al Minyā & S of El Faiyûm
Ozark plateau \'ō-,zärk-\ *or* **Ozark mountains** eroded tableland 1500–2500 *ft* (457–762 *m*) high *cen* U.S. N of Arkansas river in N Ark., S Mo., & NE Okla. with E extension in S Ill. — **Ozark·er** \'ō-,zär-kər\ *n* — **Ozark·ian** \ō-'zär-kē-ən\ *adj or n*
Ozarks, Lake of the reservoir 130 *mi* (209 *km*) long *cen* Mo. formed in Osage river by Bagnell Dam
Pa·bia·ni·ce \,päb-yə-'nēt-sə\ commune *cen* Poland *pop* 70,968
Pa·chu·ca \pə-'chü-kə\ city *cen* Mexico * of Hidalgo *pop* 83,892
Pa·cif·ic \pə-'sif-ik\ ocean extending from the arctic circle to the antarctic regions & from W N. America & W S. America to E Asia & Australia *area* 69,375,000 *sq mi* (180,375,000 *sq km*)
Pa·cif·i·ca \pə-'sif-i-kə\ city W Calif. S of San Francisco on the Pacific *pop* 36,866
Pacific Islands, Trust Territory of the islands in W Pacific in association with U.S. comprising the Carolines & the Marshalls; with the Marianas (except Guam) constituted a Japanese mandate 1919–45
Pacific Rim National Park reservation SW Canada in Vancouver island
Pac·to·lus \pak-'tō-ləs\ river Asia Minor in ancient Lydia flowing into the Hermus (modern Gediz) near Sardis
Pa·dang \'päd-,äŋ\ city & port Indonesia in W Sumatra *pop* 480,922
Pad·ding·ton \'pad-iŋ-tən\ former metropolitan borough NW London, England, now part of Westminster
Pa·dre \'päd-rē, 'pad-\ island 100 *mi* (161 *km*) long S Tex. bet. Laguna Madre & Gulf of Mexico
Pad·ua \'paj-ə-wə, 'pad-ə-wə\ *or It* **Pa·do·va** \'päd-ə-,vä\ commune NE Italy W of Venice *pop* 231,337 — **Pad·u·an** \'paj-ə-wən, 'pad-ə-\ *adj or n*
Pa·du·cah \pə-'d(y)ü-kə\ city W Ky. on Ohio river *pop* 29,315
Padus — see PO
Paes·tum \'pēs-təm, 'pes-\ *or earlier* **Po·sei·do·nia** \,päs-,ī-'dō-nē-ə, ,pō-,sī-\ ancient city S Italy in W Lucania on Gulf of Salerno (ancient **Bay of Paestum**)
Pa·go Pa·go \,päŋ-(,)(g)ō-'päŋ-(,)(g)ō, ,päg-(,)ō-'päg-(,)ō\ town & port * of American Samoa on Tutuila Is. *pop* 2451
Pa·hang \pə-'haŋ\ state E Malaysia (federation) bordering on S. China sea * Kuala Lipis *area* 13,873 *sq mi* (36,070 *sq km*), *pop* 770,644
Painted desert region NE Ariz. E of the Little Colorado
Pais·ley \'pāz-lē\ burgh SW Scotland in Strathclyde *pop* 84,789
Pa·ki·stan \'pak-i-,stan, ,päk-i-'stän\ country S Asia orig. comprising an E division & a W division; a dominion 1947–56 & a republic 1956–72 of the Commonwealth, formed from parts of former Brit. India; * Islamabad *area* 310,403 *sq mi* (807,048 *sq km*), *pop* 83,782,000 — see EAST PAKISTAN, WEST PAKISTAN — **Pa·ki·stani** \-'stan-ē, -'stän-ē\ *adj or n*
Pa·lat·i·nate \pə-'lat-ᵊn-ət\ *or G* **Pfalz** \'(p)fälts\ either of two districts SW Germany once ruled by counts palatine of the Holy Roman Empire: **Rhenish Palatinate** *or* **Rhine Palatinate** *or G* **Rheinpfalz** \'rīn-,(p)fälts\ (on the Rhine E of Saarland) & **Upper Palatinate** *or G* **Oberpfalz** \'ō-bər-,(p)fälts\ (on the Danube around Regensburg) — see RHINELAND-PALATINATE
Pal·a·tine \'pal-ə-,tīn\ **1** hill in Rome, Italy, one of seven on which the ancient city was built — see AVENTINE **2** village NE Ill. NW of Chicago *pop* 32,166
Palau *or* **Pelew** — see BELAU
Pa·la·wan \pə-'lä-wən, -,wän\ island 278 *mi* (445 *km*) long W Philippines W of the Visayans *area* 4550 *sq mi* (11,830 *sq km*), *pop* (with adjacent islands) 232,322
Pa·lem·bang \,päl-əm-'bäŋ\ city & port Indonesia in SE Sumatra *pop* 787,187
Pa·len·cia \pə-'len-ch(ē-)ə\ **1** province N Spain *area* 3256 *sq mi* (8466 *sq km*), *pop* 165,215 **2** city, its *, NNE of Valladolid *pop* 66,496
Pa·len·que \pə-'leŋ-(,)kā\ ruined Mayan city S Mexico in N Chiapas SW of modern town of Palenque
Pa·ler·mo \pə-'lər-(,)mō, -'le(ə)r-\ *or anc* **Pan·or·mus** \pa-'nȯr-məs\ *or* **Pan·hor·mus** \pan-'hȯr-\ city & port Italy * of Sicily *pop* 699,691 — **Pa·ler·mi·tan** \pə-'lər-mət-ᵊn, -'ler-\ *adj or n*
Pal·es·tine \'pal-ə-,stīn\ *or L* **Pal·aes·ti·na** \,pal-ə-'stē-nə, -'stī-\ **1** ancient region SW Asia bordering on E coast of the Mediterranean & extending E of Jordan river **2** former country bordering on the Mediterranean on W & Dead sea on E; a part of the Ottoman Empire 1516–1917, a Brit. mandate 1923–48; now divided bet. Israel & Jordan — **Pal·es·tin·ian** \,pal-ə-'stin-ē-ən, -'stin-yən\ *adj or n*
Pal·i·sades \,pal-ə-'sādz\ line of cliffs 15 *mi* (24 *km*) long SE N.Y. & NE N.J. on W bank of Hudson river
Palk \'pȯ(l)k\ strait 40 *mi* (64 *km*) wide bet. N Sri Lanka & SE India connecting Gulf of Mannar & Bay of Bengal
Pal·ma \'päl-mə\ *or* **Palma de Ma·llor·ca** \-,dā-mə(l)-'yȯr-kə\ commune & port Spain * of Baleares province on Majorca *pop* 310,421
Pal·mas, Cape \'päl-məs\ cape Liberia on extreme SE coast
Palm Bay city E Fla. *pop* 18,560
Palmer archipelago, Palmer peninsula — see ANTARCTIC
Palm·er Land \'päm-ər, 'päl-mər\ the S section of Antarctic peninsula
Palm·er·ston \'päm-ər-stən, 'päl-mər-\ island (atoll) *cen* Pacific NW of Rarotonga Is.; belongs to New Zealand *area* 1 *sq mi* (2.6 *sq km*)
Palmerston North city New Zealand on S North Is. NE of Wellington *pop* 60,105
Palm Springs city SW Calif. E of Los Angeles *pop* 32,271
Pal·my·ra \pal-'mī-rə\ **1** island *cen* Pacific in Line islands *area* 1 *sq mi* (2.6 *sq km*) **2** *or bib* **Tad·mor** \'tad-,mȯ(ə)r\ *or* **Ta·mar** \'tā-,mär, -mər\ ancient city Syria on N edge of Syrian desert NE of Damascus — **Pal·my·rene** \,pal-mə-'rēn, -mī-\ *adj or n*
Palo Al·to \,pal-ə-'wal-(,)tō\ city W Calif. SE of San Francisco on San Francisco Bay *pop* 55,225
Pal·o·mar, Mount \'pal-ə-,mär\ mountain 6140 *ft* (1871 *m*) S Calif. NNE of San Diego
Pa·los \'pä-,lōs\ *or* **Palos de la Fron·te·ra** \-,lōz-,dā-lə-,frən-'ter-ə\ town & former port SW Spain SE of Huelva
Pa·los Hills \'pā-ləs-\ city NE Ill. *pop* 16,654
Pa·louse \pə-'lüs\ **1** river 150 *mi* (241 *km*) NW Idaho & SE Wash. flowing W & S into Snake river **2** fertile hilly region E Wash. & NW Idaho N of Snake & Clearwater rivers
Pa·mirs \pə-'mi(ə)rz\ *or* **Pa·mir** \-'mi(ə)r\ mountain region *cen* Asia in Tadzhik Republic & on borders of Sinkiang Uighur, Kashmir, & Afghanistan from which radiate Tien Shan to N, Kunlun & Karakoram to E, & Hindu Kush to W; has many peaks over 20,000 *ft* (6096 *m*)
Pam·li·co \'pam-li-,kō\ river E N.C., estuary of Tar river, flowing E into **Pamlico Sound** (inlet of the Atlantic bet. the mainland & offshore islands)
Pam·pa \'pam-pə\ city NW Tex. ENE of Amarillo *pop* 21,396
Pam·phyl·ia \pam-'fil-ē-ə\ ancient district & Roman province S Asia Minor on coast S of Pisidia — **Pam·phyl·i·an** \-ē-ən\ *adj or n*
Pam·plo·na \pam-'plō-nə\ *or formerly* **Pam·pe·lu·na** \,pam-pə-'lü-nə\ city N Spain * of Navarra province & once * of Navarre kingdom *pop* 177,906
Pan·a·ji \'pən-ə-jē\ town & port W India * of Goa & formerly * of Portuguese India *pop* 34,953
Pan·a·ma *or Sp* **Pa·na·má** \'pan-ə-,mä, -,mȯ, ,pan-ə-'\ **1** country S Central America; a republic; before 1903 part of Colombia *area* (including Canal Zone) 29,129 *sq mi* (75,735 *sq km*), *pop* 1,824,796 **2** *or* **Panama City** city & port, its *, on Gulf of Panama *pop* 386,393 **3** ship canal 51 *mi* (82 *km*) *cen* Panama connecting the Atlantic (Caribbean sea) & the Pacific (Gulf of Panama) — **Pan·a·ma·ni·an** \,pan-ə-'mā-nē-ən\ *adj or n*
Panama, Gulf of inlet of the Pacific on S coast of Panama
Panama, Isthmus of *or formerly* **Isthmus of Dar·i·en** \-,dar-ē-'en, -,der-\ isthmus Central America connecting N. America & S. America & comprised in Panama (republic)
Panama Canal Zone — see CANAL ZONE
Panama City **1** city & port NW Fla. on Gulf of Mexico *pop* 33,346 **2** — see PANAMA
Pan·a·mint \'pan-ə-,mint, -mənt\ mountains E Calif. W of Death Valley — see TELESCOPE PEAK
Pa·nay \pə-'nī\ island Philippines in the Visayans; chief town Iloilo *area* 4446 *sq mi* (11,560 *sq km*)
Pan·gaea \pan-'jē-ə\ hypothetical land area believed to have once connected the landmasses of the S hemisphere with those of the N hemisphere — see GONDWANALAND, LAURASIA
Pa·ni·pat \'pän-i-,pət\ city NW India in SE Haryana state *pop* 137,953
Panjab — see PUNJAB
Panj·nad \,pənj-'näd\ river 50 *mi* (80 *km*) Pakistan, the combined stream of the Chenab & the Sutlej, flowing SW into the Indus
Pan·kow \'päŋ-(,)kō\ NE suburb of Berlin, Germany; seat of E. German government
Pan·mun·jom \,pän-,mu̇n-'jəm\ village N S. Korea SE of Kaesong
Pan·no·nia \pə-'nō-nē-ə\ Roman province SE Europe including territory W of the Danube now in Hungary & N Yugoslavia
Pantar — see ALOR
Pan·tel·le·ria \,pan-,tel-ə-'rē-ə\ island Italy in the Mediterranean bet. Sicily & Tunisia
Pá·nu·co \'pän-ə-,kō\ river 240 *mi* (386 *km*) *cen* Mexico flowing from Hidalgo state NE into Gulf of Mexico
Pao–chi *or* **Bao·ji** \'bau̇-'jē\ city N *cen* China in SW Shensi on the Wei W of Sian *pop* 180,000
Pão de Açú·car \,pau̇ⁿ(n)-dē-ə-'sü-kər\ *or* **Sugarloaf Mountain** peak 1296 *ft* (395 *m*) SE Brazil in city of Rio de Janeiro on W side of entrance to Guanabara Bay
Paoking — see SHAOYANG
Pao·ting *or* **Bao·ding** \'bau̇-'diŋ\ or formerly **Tsing·yuan** \'chiŋ-yü-'än\ city NE China SW of Peking *pop* 250,000
Pao–t'ou *or* **Bao·tou** \'bau̇-'tō\ city N China in SW Inner Mongolia on the Hwang W of Huhehot *pop* 1,400,000

Papal States — see STATES OF THE CHURCH

Pa·pee·te \ˌpäp-ē-ˈät-ē; pə-ˈpāt-ē, -ˈpēt-\ commune & port Society islands on Tahiti ✱ of French Polynesia *pop* 22,967

Paph·la·go·nia \ˌpaf-lə-ˈgō-nē-ə, -nyə\ ancient country & Roman province N Asia Minor bordering on Black sea — **Paph·la·go·nian** \-nē-ən, -nyən\ *adj or n*

Pa·phos \ˈpā-ˌfäs\ town SW Cyprus on coast 10 *mi* (16 *km*) WNW of site of ancient city of Paphos

Pa–Pien Chiang — see BLACK 4

Pa·pua \ˈpap-yə-wə, ˈpäp-ə-wə\ the SE portion of the island of New Guinea; part of Papua New Guinea

Papua, Gulf of arm of Coral sea SE New Guinea

Papua New Guinea country comprising territories of Papua & New Guinea; independent from 1975, formerly a U.N. trust territory administered by Australia ✱ Port Moresby *area* 182,700 *sq mi* (475,020 *sq km*), *pop* 3,010,727

Pa·rá \pə-ˈrä\ **1** river 200 *mi* (322 *km*) N Brazil, the E mouth of the Amazon **2** state N Brazil S of the Amazon ✱ Belém *area* 470,752 *sq mi* (1,223,955 *sq km*), *pop* 3,507,312 **3** — see BELÉM

Par·a·guay \ˈpar-ə-ˌgwī, -ˌgwā\ **1** river 1500 *mi* (2414 *km*) *cen* S. America flowing from Mato Grosso plateau in Brazil S into Paraná river in Paraguay **2** country *cen* S. America traversed by Paraguay river; a republic ✱ Asunción *area* 157,006 *sq mi* (408,216 *sq km*), *pop* 3,026,165 — **Par·a·guay·an** \ˌpar-ə-ˈgwī-ən, -ˈgwā-\ *adj or n*

Pa·ra·í·ba \ˌpar-ə-ˈē-bə\ **1** *or* **Paraíba do Nor·te** \-də-ˈnȯrt-ē\ river 240 *mi* (386 *km*) NE Brazil flowing E into the Atlantic **2** *or* **Paraíba do Sul** \-ˈsül\ river 660 *mi* (1062 *km*) SE Brazil flowing NE into the Atlantic **3** state NE Brazil bordering on the Atlantic ✱ João Pessoa *area* 21,591 *sq mi* (56,137 *sq km*), *pop* 2,810,032

Par·a·mar·i·bo \ˌpar-ə-ˈmar-ə-ˌbō\ city & port ✱ of Suriname on Suriname river *pop* 110,867

Par·a·mount \ˈpar-ə-ˌmau̇nt\ city SW Calif. N of Long Beach *pop* 36,407

Pa·ram·us \pə-ˈram-əs\ borough NE N.J. *pop* 26,474

Pa·ra·ná \ˌpar-ə-ˈnä\ **1** *or in upper course* **Al·to Paraná** \ˌal-(ˌ)tō-\ river 2040 *mi* (3283 *km*) *cen* S. America flowing from junction of Rio Grande & Paraíba river in Brazil SSW into the Río de la Plata in Argentina **2** state S Brazil E of Paraná river ✱ Curitiba *area* 82,741 *sq mi* (215,127 *sq km*), *pop* 7,749,752 **3** city NE Argentina on Paraná river *pop* 159,581

Pa·ra·na·í·ba *or formerly* **Pa·ra·na·hi·ba** \ˌpar-ə-nə-ˈē-bə\ river 530 *mi* (853 *km*) S Brazil flowing SW to unite with the Rio Grande forming Paraná river

Par·du·bi·ce \ˈpärd-ə-ˌbit-sə\ city Czechoslovakia in Bohemia on the Elbe E of Prague *pop* 91,855

Pa·ria \ˈpär-ē-ə\ peninsula NE Venezuela

Paria, Gulf of inlet of the Atlantic bet. Trinidad & Venezuela

Pa·rí·cu·tin \pə-ˈrē-kə-ˌtēn\ volcano 7451 *ft* (2271 *m*) SW Mexico in NW Michoacán; first eruption 1943

Parida, La — see BOLÍVAR (Cerro)

Par·is \ˈpar-əs\ **1** city NE Tex. *pop* 25,498 **2** *or anc* **Lu·te·tia** \lü-ˈtē-sh(ē-)ə\ city ✱ of France on the Seine *pop* 2,299,830 — **Pa·ri·sian** \pə-ˈrizh-ən, -ˈrēzh-\ *adj or n*

Par·kers·burg \ˈpär-kərz-ˌbərg\ city NW W.Va. *pop* 39,967

Park Forest village NE Ill. S of Chicago *pop* 26,222

Park Ridge city NE Ill. NW of Chicago *pop* 38,704

Par·ma \ˈpär-mə\ **1** city NE Ohio S of Cleveland *pop* 92,548 **2** commune N Italy in Emilia-Romagna *pop* 176,750

Parma Heights city NE Ohio S of Cleveland *pop* 23,112

Par·na·í·ba *or formerly* **Par·na·hy·ba** \ˌpär-nə-ˈē-bə\ river 900 *mi* (1448 *km*) NE Brazil flowing NE into the Atlantic

Par·nas·sus \pär-ˈnas-əs\ *or NGk* **Par·nas·sós** \ˌpär-nə-ˈsȯs\ mountain 8061 *ft* (2457 *m*), *cen* Greece N of Gulf of Corinth

Par·os \ˈpar-ˌäs, ˈper-\ *or NGk* **Pá·ros** \ˈpär-ˌȯs\ island Greece in *cen* Cyclades W of Naxos *area* 81 *sq mi* (211 *sq km*)

Par·ra·mat·ta \ˌpar-ə-ˈmat-ə\ city SE Australia, W suburb of Sydney, on Parramatta river (estuary, W arm of Port Jackson) *pop* 130,943

Par·ris \ˈpar-əs\ island S S.C. in Port Royal sound

Par·ry \ˈpar-ē\ islands Canada in N Northwest Territories in Arctic ocean N of Victoria Is.

Parsnip — see FINLAY

Par·thia \ˈpär-thē-ə\ ancient country SW Asia in NE modern Iran

Pas·a·de·na \ˌpas-ə-ˈdē-nə\ **1** city SW Calif. E of Glendale *pop* 119,374 **2** city SE Tex. E of Houston *pop* 112,560 — **Pas·a·de·nan** \-nən\ *n*

Pa·sar·ga·dae \pə-ˈsär-gə-ˌdē\ city of ancient Persia built by Cyrus the Great; ruins NE of site of later Persepolis

Pa·say \ˈpäs-ˌī\ municipality Philippines in Luzon on Manila Bay S of Manila *pop* 287,770

Pas·ca·gou·la \ˌpas-kə-ˈgü-lə\ city & port SE Miss. *pop* 29,318

Pas·co \ˈpas-(ˌ)kō\ city SE Wash. *pop* 17,944

Pasco, Cerro de — see CERRO DE PASCO

Pascua, Isla de — see EASTER

Pas de Calais — see DOVER (Strait of)

Pa·sig \ˈpäs-ig\ river 12 *mi* (19 *km*) Philippines in Luzon flowing from the Laguna de Bay through Manila into Manila Bay

Pas·sa·ic \pə-ˈsā-ik\ **1** river 100 *mi* (161 *km*) NE N.J. flowing into Newark Bay **2** city NE N.J. SSE of Paterson *pop* 52,463

Pas·sa·ma·quod·dy Bay \ˌpas-ə-mə-ˈkwäd-ē\ inlet of Bay of Fundy bet. E Maine & SW N.B. at mouth of St. Croix river

Pas·se·ro, Cape \ˈpäs-ə-ˌrō, ˈpas-\ headland Italy at SE tip of Sicily

Pas·sy \pa-ˈsē\ section of Paris, France, on right bank of the Seine near the Bois de Boulogne

Pas·ta·za \pə-ˈstäz-ə, -ˈstäs-\ river 400 *mi* (644 *km*) Ecuador & Peru flowing S into the Marañón

Pat·a·go·nia \ˌpat-ə-ˌgō-nyə, -nē-ə\ region S. America in S Argentina & S Chile between the Andes & the Atlantic S of *ab* 40° S lat.; sometimes considered as including Tierra del Fuego — **Pat·a·go·nian** \-nyən, -nē-ən\ *adj or n*

Pa·tan \ˈpä-ˌtən\ city E *cen* Nepal adjoining Kathmandu *pop* 48,577

Pa·tap·sco \pə-ˈtap-(ˌ)skō, -si-ˌkō\ river 80 *mi* (129 *km*) N *cen* Md. flowing SE into Chesapeake Bay

Pat·er·son \ˈpat-ər-sən\ city NE N.J. N of Newark *pop* 137,970

Pa·ti·a·la \ˌpət-ē-ˈäl-ə\ **1** former state NW India, now part of Punjab state **2** city, its ✱, SW of Simla *pop* 205,849

Pat·mos \ˈpat-məs\ island Greece in the NW Dodecanese

Pat·na \ˈpət-nə\ city NE India on the Ganges, winter ✱ of Bihar

Pa·tos, La·goa dos \lə-ˌgō-əd-ə-ˈspat-əs\ lagoon 124 *mi* (200 *km*) long S Brazil in Rio Grande do Sul

Pa·tra·ïkós Kól·pos \ˌpät-rī-ˈkȯs-ˈkȯl-(ˌ)pȯs\ *or* **Gulf of Pa·tras** \pə-ˈtras, ˈpa-trəs\ inlet of Ionian sea W Greece W of Gulf of Corinth

Pa·tras \pə-ˈtras, ˈpa-trəs\ *or NGk* **Pa·trai** \ˈpä-trā\ *or anc* **Pa·trae** \ˈpā-(ˌ)trē\ city & port W Greece in N Peloponnisos on Patraïkós Kólpos *pop* 140,878

Patrimony of St. Peter — see ROME (Duchy of)

Pa·tux·ent \pə-ˈtək-sənt\ river 100 *mi* (161 *km*) *cen* Md. flowing S & SE into Chesapeake Bay

Pau \ˈpō\ **1** *or F* **Gave de Pau** \gȧv-də-pō\ river 100 *mi* (161 *km*) SW France rising in the Pyrenees SW of Pau & flowing to the Adour — see GAVARNIE **2** commune SW France on Pau river *pop* 81,560

Pa·via \pə-ˈvē-ə\ commune N Italy S of Milan *pop* 85,056

Pav·lof, Mount \ˈpav-ˌlȯf\ volcano 8261 *ft* (2518 *m*) SW Alaska on SW Alaska peninsula in Aleutian range

Paw·tuck·et \pə-ˈtək-ət, pȯ-\ city NE R.I. *pop* 71,204

Pay·san·dú \ˌpī-ˌsän-ˈdü\ city & port W Uruguay *pop* 62,412

Pea·body \ˈpē-ˌbäd-ē, -bəd-ē\ city NE Mass. N of Lynn *pop* 45,976

Peace \ˈpēs\ river 945 *mi* (1521 *km*) W Canada flowing E & NE in N B.C. & N Alta. into Slave river — see FINLAY

Pearl \ˈpər(-ə)l\ **1** river 490 *mi* (788 *km*) S Miss. flowing S into Gulf of Mexico **2** — see CHU 1

Pearl City city Hawaii in S Oahu *pop* 42,575

Pearl Harbor inlet Hawaii on S coast of Oahu W of Honolulu

Pea·ry Land \ˈpi(ə)r-ē\ region N Greenland on Arctic ocean

Pe·chen·ga \ˈpech-ən-gə\ *or Finn* **Pet·sa·mo** \ˈpet-sə-ˌmō\ town & port U.S.S.R. in NW Soviet Russia, Europe, on inlet of Barents sea in district that belonged to Finland 1920–44 *pop* 3500

Pe·cho·ra \pə-ˈchōr-ə, -ˈchȯr-\ river 1125 *mi* (1811 *km*) U.S.S.R. in NE Soviet Russia, Europe, flowing N into Barents sea

Pe·cos \ˈpā-kəs\ river 735 *mi* (1183 *km*) E N.Mex. & W Tex. flowing SE into the Rio Grande

Pe·cos National Monument \ˈpā-kəs\ archaeological site N *cen* N.Mex. SE of Santa Fe containing Indian villages & a Spanish mission

Pecs \ˈpāch\ city S Hungary W of the Danube *pop* 168,788

Ped·er·nal·es \ˌpərd-ᵊn-ˈal-əs\ river 150 *mi* (241 *km*) *cen* Tex. flowing E into Colorado river

Pee·bles \ˈpē-bəlz\ **1** *or* **Pee·bles·shire** \ˈpē-bəl-ˌshi(ə)r, -shər\ *or* **Tweed·dale** \ˈtwēd-ˌdāl\ former county SE Scotland including upper course of the Tweed **2** burgh SE Scotland in Borders region

Pee Dee \ˈpē-ˌdē\ river 233 *mi* (375 *km*) N.C. & S.C. flowing SE into Winyah Bay — see YADKIN

Peeks·kill \ˈpēk-ˌskil\ city SE N.Y. N of Yonkers *pop* 18,236

Peel \ˈpē(ə)l\ river 425 *mi* (684 *km*) NW Canada rising in W Yukon Territory & flowing E & N into the Mackenzie

Pee·ne \ˈpā-nə\ river 70 *mi* (113 *km*) NE E. Germany flowing E through Pomerania and forming **Peene Estuary** which flows N–S between Stettiner Haff and the Baltic

Pee·ne·mün·de \ˌpā-nə-ˈm(y)ün-də, -ˈmɶn-\ village NE E. Germany on island at mouth of Peene Estuary

Pei·pus \ˈpī-pəs\ *or Estonian* **Peip·si** \ˈpāp-sē\ *or Russ* **Chud·skoe** \ˈchüt-skə-yə\ lake U.S.S.R. in E Estonia & NW Soviet Russia, Europe *area* 1357 *sq mi* (3528 *sq km*)

Pe·ka·long·an \ˌpek-ə-ˈlȯŋ-ˌän\ city Indonesia in *cen* Java on N coast *pop* 132,558

Pe·kin \ˈpē-kən, -ˌkin\ city N *cen* Ill. SSW of Peoria *pop* 33,967

Pe·king \ˈpē-ˈkiŋ\ *or* **Bei·jing** \ˈbā-ˈjiŋ\ *or formerly* **Pei·ping** \ˈpā-ˈpiŋ, ˈbā-\ municipality NE China, its ✱ *pop* 9,230,687

Pe·la·gian \pə-ˈlā-j(ē-)ən\ islands Italy in the Mediterranean S of Sicily bet. Malta & Tunisia

Pe·lee \ˈpē-lē\ island SE Canada in W Lake Erie SW of Point Pelee, Ont. *area* 18 *sq mi* (47 *sq km*), *pop* 275

Pe·lée, Mount \pə-ˈlā\ volcano French W. Indies in N Martinique; erupted 1902

Pelee, Point — see POINT PELEE NATIONAL PARK

Pel·e·liu \ˌpel-ə-ˈlē-(ˌ)ü\ island W Pacific at S end of Belau islands

Pelew — see BELAU

Pe·li·on \ˈpē-lē-ən\ *or NGk* **Pí·lion** \ˈpēl-ˌyȯn\ mountain 5089 *ft* (1551 *m*) NE Greece in E Thessaly SE of Mt. Ossa

Pel·la \ˈpel-ə\ ancient city NE Greece, ancient ✱ of Macedonia

Pel·ly \ˈpel-ē\ river 330 *mi* (531 *km*) NW Canada in Yukon Territory flowing W into Yukon river

Pel·o·pon·ni·sos *or* **Pel·o·pon·ne·sus** \ˌpel-ə-pə-ˈnē-səs\ *or* **Pel·o·pon·nese** \ˈpel-ə-pə-ˌnēz, -ˌnēs\ peninsula forming S part of mainland of Greece — **Pel·o·pon·ne·sian** \ˌpel-ə-pə-ˈnē-zhən, -shən\ *adj or n*

Pe·lo·tas \pə-ˈlōt-əs\ city S Brazil in SE Rio Grande do Sul at S end of Lagoa dos Patos *pop* 260,190

Pem·ba \ˈpem-bə\ island Tanzania in Indian ocean N of island of Zanzibar *pop* 207,919

Pem·broke \ˈpem-ˌbru̇k, *US also* -ˌbrōk\ *or* **Pem·broke·shire** \-ˌshi(ə)r, -shər\ former county SW Wales ✱ Haverfordwest

Pem·broke Pines \ˈpem-ˌbrōk\ city SE Fla. *pop* 35,776

Pe·nang \pə-ˈnaŋ\ **1** island SE Asia at N end of Strait of Malacca *area* 108 *sq mi* (281 *sq km*) **2** state Malaysia (federation) comprising Penang island & mainland opposite: until 1948 one of the Straits Settlements ✱ George Town *area* 400 *sq mi* (1040 *sq km*), *pop* 911,586 **3** — see GEORGE TOWN

Pen–ch'i \ˈbən-ˈchē\ *or* **Ben·xi** \ˈbən-ˈshē\ *or* **Pen·ki** \-ˈjē\ *or* **Pen–hsi** \-ˈshē\ city NE China in E *cen* Liaoning *pop* 449,000

Pen·del·i·kón \ˌpen-de-li-ˈkȯn\ mountain 3638 *ft* (1109 *m*) E Greece in Attica NE of Athens

Pend Oreille \ˌpän-də-ˈrā\ river 100 *mi* (161 *km*) N Idaho & NE Wash. flowing from **Pend Oreille Lake** (35 *mi* or 56 *km* long, in Idaho) W & N into Columbia river in B.C.

Penedos de São Pedro e Sao Paulo — see SAINT PAUL'S ROCKS

\ə\ abut \$^{ə}$\ kitten, F table \ər\ further \a\ ash \ā\ ace \ä\ cot, cart
\au̇\ out \ch\ chin \e\ bet \ē\ easy \g\ go \i\ hit \ī\ ice \j\ job
\ŋ\ sing \ō\ go \ȯ\ law \ȯi\ boy \th\ thin \t͟h\ the \ü\ loot \u̇\ foot
\y\ yet \zh\ vision \ȧ, k̟, ^{n}, œ, œ̄, ue, ue̅, ^{y}\ *see* Guide to Pronunciation

Pe·ne·us \pə-'nē-əs\ *or NGk* **Pi·niós** \pēn-'yòs\ *or formerly* **Sa·lam·bria** \sə-'lam-brē-ə\ river 125 *mi* (201 *km*) N Greece in Thessaly flowing E into Gulf of Salonika

P'eng-hu \'pəŋ-'hü\ *or* **Pes·ca·do·res** \pes-kə-'dōr-ēz, -'dȯr-, -əs\ islands E China in Formosa strait, attached to Taiwan; chief town Makung (on P'eng-hu, chief island) *area* 49 *sq mi* (127 *sq km*)

Peng·pu \'pəŋ-'pü\ *or* **Peng·bu** \-'bü\ city E China in N Anhwei *pop* 253,000

Peninsular Malaysia — see MALAYA

Pen·nine Alps \'pen-,īn\ section of Alps on border bet. Switzerland & Italy NE of Graian Alps — see ROSA (Monte)

Pennine Chain mountains N England extending S from Scotland border to Derbyshire & Staffordshire; highest Cross Fell 2930 *ft* (893 *m*)

Penn·syl·va·nia \,pen(t)-səl-'vā-nyə, -nē-ə\ state NE U.S. ❋ Harrisburg *area* 45,333 *sq mi* (117,866 *sq km*), *pop* 11,863,895

Pe·nob·scot \pə-'näb-,skät, -skət\ river 101 *mi* (162 *km*) cen Maine flowing S into **Penobscot Bay** (inlet of the Atlantic)

Pen·rhyn \pen-'rin, 'pen-\ *or* **Ton·ga·reva** \,täŋ-(g)ə-'rē-və\ island S Pacific in the Manihiki islands

Pen·sa·co·la \,pen(t)-sə-'kō-lə\ city & port NW Fla. on **Pensacola Bay** (inlet of Gulf of Mexico) *pop* 57,619

Pen·tap·o·lis \pen-'tap-ə-ləs\ any one of several groups of five ancient cities in Italy, Asia Minor, & Cyrenaica

Pen·tic·ton \pen-'tik-tən\ city Canada in S B.C. *pop* 23,181

Pent·land \'pent-lənd\ 1 firth, channel bet. Orkneys & mainland of Scotland 2 hills S Scotland in Borders, Lothian, & Strathclyde regions; highest peak Scald Law 1898 *ft* (578 *m*)

Pen·za \'pen-zə\ city U.S.S.R. in S Soviet Russia, Europe, W of Kuibyshev *pop* 374,000

Pen·zance \pen-'zan(t)s, pən-\ borough & port SW England in Cornwall on English channel *pop* 19,521

Pen·zhin·ska·ya \,pen-'zhin(t)-skə-yə\ *or* **Pen·zhi·na** \'pen-zhə-nə\ bay, arm of Sea of Okhotsk, U.S.S.R., bet. Kamchatka peninsula & mainland

People's Democratic Republic of Yemen — see YEMEN

People's Republic of China China exclusive of Taiwan

Pe·o·ria \pē-'ōr-ē-ə, -'ȯr-\ city N cen Ill. on Illinois river *pop* 124,160

Pe·pin, Lake \'pip-ən, 'pep-\ expansion of upper Mississippi river 34 *mi* (55 *km*) long bet. SE Minn. & W Wis.

Pera — see BEYOGLU

Pe·raea *or* **Pe·rea** \pə-'rē-ə\ ancient region of Palestine E of Jordan river

Pe·rak \'per-ə, 'pir-ə, 'per-,ak\ state Malaysia in W Peninsular Malaysia on Strait of Malacca ❋ Kuala Kangsar *area* 7980 *sq mi* (20,748 *sq km*), *pop* 1,762,288

Per·di·do \pər-'dēd-(,)ō\ river 60 *mi* (96 *km*) rising in SE Ala. & flowing S into Gulf of Mexico forming part of Ala.-Fla. boundary

Per·ga \'pər-gə\ ancient city S Asia Minor in Pamphylia

Per·ga·mum \'pər-gə-məm\ *or* **Per·ga·mus** \-məs\ *or* **Per·ga·mos** \-məs, -,mäs\ 1 ancient Greek kingdom covering most of Asia Minor; at its height 263–133 B.C. 2 *or modern* **Ber·ga·ma** \bər-'gäm-ə\ city W Turkey NNE of Izmir ❋ of ancient Pergamum

Pé·ri·gord \,per-ə-'gȯ(ə)r\ old division of N Guienne in SW France ❋ Périgueux

Pé·ri·gueux \-'gə(r), -'gœ\ commune SW France NE of Bordeaux *pop* 34,779

Pe·rim \pə-'rim, -'rēm\ island in Bab el Mandeb strait at entrance to Red sea; belongs to Yemen

Per·lis \'per-ləs\ state Malaysia bordering on Thailand & Andaman sea ❋ Kangar *area* 310 *sq mi* (806 *sq km*), *pop* 147,726

Perm \'pərm, 'pe(ə)rm\ *or formerly* **Mo·lo·tov** \'mäl-ə-,tȯf, 'mȯl-, 'mōl-, -,tȯv\ city U.S.S.R. in E Soviet Russia, Europe *pop* 901,000

Per·nam·bu·co \,pər-nəm-'b(y)ü-(,)kō, ,per-nəm-'bü-\ 1 state NE Brazil ❋ Recife *area* 38,315 *sq mi* (99,619 *sq km*), *pop* 6,242,933 2 — see RECIFE

Per·nik \'pe(ə)r-nik\ *or formerly* **Di·mi·tro·vo** \də-'mē-trə-,vō\ city W Bulgaria S of Sofia *pop* 87,432

Per·pi·gnan \,per-pē-nyⁿ\ city S France SE of Toulouse near Mediterranean coast *pop* 101,198

Per·sep·o·lis \pər-'sep-ə-ləs\ city of ancient Persia, site in SW Iran NE of Shiraz

Persia — see IRAN

Persian Gulf arm of Arabian sea between SW Iran & Arabia

Persian Gulf States Kuwait, Bahrain, Qatar, & United Arab Emirates

Persis ancient region SW Iran

Perth \'pərth\ 1 city ❋ of Western Australia on Swan river *pop* 79,398 — see FREMANTLE 2 *or* **Perth·shire** \-,shi(ə)r, -shər\ former county cen Scotland 3 burgh cen Scotland *pop* 41,998

Perth Am·boy \-'am-,bȯi\ city & port NE N.J. on Raritan Bay at mouth of Raritan river *pop* 38,951

Pe·ru \pə-'rü\ country W S. America; a rep. ❋ Lima *area* 482,257 *sq mi* (1,253,868 *sq km*), *pop* 17,031,221 — **Pe·ru·vi·an** \-'rü-vē-ən\ *adj or n*

Pe·ru·gia \pə-'rü-jē-ə\ pā-\ commune cen Italy between Lake Trasimeno & the Tiber ❋ of Umbria *pop* 142,522

Pe·sa·ro \'pā-zə-,rō\ commune & port cen Italy on the Adriatic NW of Ancona *pop* 90,147

Pe·sca·ra \pe-'skär-ə\ commune & port cen Italy on the Adriatic *pop* 131,345

Pe·sha·war \pə-'shä-wər, -'shaů-(ə)r\ city N Pakistan ESE of Khyber pass *pop* 555,000

Pe·tah Tiq·wa \,pet-ə-'tik-(,)vä, ,pät-\ city W Israel *pop* 112,000

Pet·a·lu·ma \,pet-ʾl-'ü-mə\ city W Calif. N of San Francisco *pop* 33,834

Pe·ter·bor·ough \'pēt-ər-,bər-ə, -,bȯr-ə, -b(ə-)rə\ 1 city Canada in SE Ont. *pop* 60,620 2 borough E cen England *pop* 88,346

Peterborough, Soke of \'sōk\ former administrative county E cen England in Northamptonshire; later part of Huntingdonshire & since 1974 in Cambridgeshire

Pe·ters·burg \'pēt-ərz-,bərg\ 1 city SE Va. *pop* 41,055 2 SAINT PETERSBURG — see LENINGRAD

Pet·it·co·di·ac \,pet-ē-'kōd-ē-,ak\ river 60 *mi* (96 *km*) SE Canada in SE N.B. flowing to head of Bay of Fundy

Pe·ti·tot \'pet-i-,tō\ river 295 *mi* (475 *km*) W cen Canada flowing W into the Liard

Pe·tra \'pē-trə, 'pe-trə\ ancient city of NW Arabia on slope of Mt. Hor, site now in SW Jordan; ❋ of the Edomites & Nabataeans

Petrified Forest National Park reservation E Ariz. in Painted desert containing natural exhibit of petrified wood

Pe·tro·dvo·rets \,pe-trəd-və-'rets\ *or formerly* **Pe·ter·hof** \'pēt-ər-,hȯf, -,häf\ town U.S.S.R. in NW Soviet Russia, Europe, W of Leningrad

Petrograd — see LENINGRAD

Pet·ro·pav·lovsk \,pe-trə-'pav-,lȯfsk\ city U.S.S.R. in Soviet Central Asia in N Kazakhstan *pop* 173,000

Petropavlovsk–Kam·chat·ski \-kam-'chat-skē\ city & port U.S.S.R. in E Soviet Russia, Asia, on Kamchatka peninsula *pop* 154,000

Pe·tró·po·lis \pə-'träp-ə-ləs\ city SE Brazil in Rio de Janeiro state *pop* 241,884

Petrovsk — see MAKHACHKALA

Pe·tro·za·vodsk \,pe-trə-zə-'vätsk\ city U.S.S.R. in NW Soviet Russia, Europe ❋ of Karelian Republic on Lake Onega *pop* 216,000

Petsamo — see PECHENGA

Pfalz — see PALATINATE

Pforz·heim \'(p)fȯrts-,hīm\ city S W. Germany SE of Karlsruhe *pop* 106,500

Pha·ros \'fa(ə)r-,äs, 'fe(ə)r-\ peninsula N Egypt in city of Alexandria; formerly an island

Pharr \'fär\ city S Tex. E of McAllen *pop* 21,381

Phar·sa·lus \fär-'sā-ləs\ *or modern* **Phar·sa·la** \'fär-sə-lə\ *or NGk* **Fár·sa·la** \'fär-'säl-yə, -'sál-yə\ town NE Greece in E Thessaly in ancient district of **Phar·sa·lia** \fär-'sāl-yə, -'sál-yə\

Phe·nix City \,fē-niks-\ city E Ala. *pop* 26,928

Phe·rae \'fi(ə)r-ē\ ancient town SE Thessaly

Phil·a·del·phia \,fil-ə-'del-fyə, -fē-ə\ 1 city & port SE Pa. on Delaware river *pop* 1,688,210 2 — see ALASEHIR 3 — see AMMAN — **Phil·a·del·phian** \-fyən, -fē-ən\ *adj or n*

Phi·lae \'fī-(,)lē\ former island S Egypt in the Nile above Aswān; now submerged

Philippeville — see SKIKDA

Phi·lip·pi \'fil-ə-,pī *also* fə-'lip-,ī\ ancient town NE Greece in N cen Macedonia — **Phi·lip·pi·an** \fə-'lip-ē-ən\ *adj or n*

Phil·ip·pine \'fil-ə-,pēn, 'fil-ə-,\ 1 islands of the Malay archipelago NE of Borneo — see PHILIPPINES 2 sea comprising the waters of the W Pacific E of & adjacent to the Philippine islands

Phil·ip·pines \-'pēnz, -,pēnz\ *or Sp* **Fil·i·pi·nas** \re-'püb-lē-kä-thä-fē-lē-'pē-(,)näs\ *or Pilipino* **Re·pu·bli·ka ng Pi·li·pi·nas** \-näŋ-,pē-lē-'pē-(,)näs\ country E Asia comprising the Philippine islands; a republic; once a Spanish possession & (1898–1945) a U.S. possession ❋ Manila *land area* 114,830 *sq mi* (298,558 *sq km*), *pop* 48,098,460 — **Philippine** *adj*

Philippopolis — see PLOVDIV

Phi·lis·tia \fə-'lis-tē-ə\ ancient country SW Palestine on the coast; land of the Philistines

Phil·lips·burg \'fil-əps-,bərg\ town W N.J. on Delaware river *pop* 16,647

Phnom Penh \pə-'näm-'pen, (pə-)'nȯm-\ city ❋ of Cambodia, on the Mekong *pop* 300,000

Pho·caea \fō-'sē-ə\ ancient city of Asia Minor on Aegean sea in N Ionia — **Pho·cae·an** \-ən\ *adj or n*

Pho·cis \'fō-səs\ region cen Greece N of Gulf of Corinth

Phoe·ni·cia *or* **Phe·ni·cia** \fi-'nish-(ē-)ə, -'nēsh-\ *or* **Phe·ni·ce** \-'nī-sē\ ancient country SW Asia at E end of the Mediterranean in modern Syria & Lebanon

Phoe·nix \'fē-niks\ 1 city ❋ of Ariz. on Salt river *pop* 789,704 2 islands cen Pacific belonging to Kiribati

Phryg·ia \'frij-ē-ə\ ancient country W cen Asia Minor divided *ab* 400 B.C. into **Greater Phrygia** (the inland region) & **Lesser Phrygia** (region along the Hellespont)

Pia·cen·za \pyä-'chen(t)-sə, ,pē-ə-\ *or anc* **Pla·cen·tia** \plə-'sen-ch(ē-)ə\ commune N Italy on the Po SE of Milan *pop* 108,177

Pi·auí *or formerly* **Pi·au·hy** \pyaů-'ē, pē-,aů-\ state NE Brazil bordering on the Atlantic E of Parnaíba river ❋ Teresina *area* 94,819 *sq mi* (246,529 *sq km*), *pop* 2,188,150

Pia·ve \'pyäv-(,)ä, pē-'äv-\ river 137 *mi* (220 *km*) NE Italy flowing S & SE into the Adriatic

Pic·ar·dy \'pik-ərd-ē\ *or F* **Pi·car·die** \pē-kàr-dē\ region & former province N France bordering on English channel N of Normandy ❋ Amiens — **Pi·card** \'pik-,ärd, -ərd; pik-'ärd\ *adj or n*

Pi·ce·num \pi-'sē-nəm\ district of ancient Italy on the Adriatic SE of Umbria

Pi·co Ri·ve·ra \,pē-(,)kō-rə-'vir-ə\ city SW Calif. *pop* 53,459

Pied·mont \'pēd-,mänt\ 1 plateau E U.S. lying E of the Appalachian mountains between N. Y. & cen Ala. 2 *or It* **Pie·mon·te** \pyä-'mȯn-(,)tä\ region NW Italy bordering on France & Switzerland W of Lombardy ❋ Turin — **Pied·mon·tese** \,pēd-mən-'tēz, -(,)män-, -'tēs\ *adj or n*

Pie·dras Ne·gras \pē-ä-drəs-'nä-grəs\ city N Mexico in Coahuila on the Rio Grande opposite Eagle Pass, Tex. *pop* 65,883

Pi·e·ria \pī-'ir-ē-ə, -'er-\ ancient region NE Greece in Macedonia N of Thessaly

Pierre \'pi(ə)r\ city ❋ of S.Dak. on Missouri river *pop* 11,973

Pierre·fonds \pē-,e(ə)r-'fōⁿ\ city Canada in S Que. W of Montreal *pop* 35,402

Pie·ter·mar·itz·burg \,pēt-ər-'mar-əts-,bərg\ city E Republic of S. Africa ❋ of Natal *pop* 128,598

Pigs, Bay of — see COCHINOS (Bahia de)

Pikes Peak \'pīks\ mountain 14,110 *ft* (4301 *m*) E cen Colo. at S end of Front range

Pik Pobedy — see POBEDA PEAK

Pi·la·tus \pi-'lät-əs\ mountain 6983 *ft* (2128 *m*) cen Switzerland in Unterwalden SW of Lucerne

Pil·co·ma·yo \,pil-kə-'mī-(,)ō\ river 1000 *mi* (1609 *km*) S cen S. America rising in Bolivia & flowing SE on Argentina-Paraguay boundary into Paraguay river

Pilion — see PELION

Pillars of Her·cu·les \'hər-kyə-,lēz\ the two promontories at E end of Strait of Gibraltar: Rock of Gibraltar (in Europe) & Jebel Musa (in Africa)

Pí·los \'pē-,lòs\ town & port SW Greece in SW Peloponnisos

Pim·li·co \'pim-li-,kō\ district of W London, England, in SW Westminster

Pinang — see GEORGE TOWN

Pi·nar del Río \pi-,när-,del-'rē-(,)ō\ city & port W Cuba *pop* 148,112

Pin·dus \'pin-dəs\ mountains N Greece bet. Epirus & Thessaly; highest point over 7500 *ft* (2286 *m*)

Pine Bluff \'pīn-,bləf, -,bləf\ city SE *cen* Ark. *pop* 56,636

Pi·nel·las \pī-'nel-əs\ peninsula W Fla. W of Tampa Bay

Pinellas Park city W Fla. NW of St. Petersburg *pop* 32,811

Pines, Isle of **1** — see YOUTH (Isle of) **2** — see ILE DES PINS

Ping \'piŋ\ river 360 *mi* (579 *km*) W Thailand flowing SSE to join Nan river forming the Chao Phraya

Piniós — see PENEUS

Pinkiang — see HA-ERH-PIN

Pinnacles National Monument reservation W *cen* Calif. in Coast range SSE of Hollister

Pinsk \'pin(t)sk\ city U.S.S.R. in SW Belorussia *pop* 73,000

Pinsk Marshes — see PRIPET

Pio·tr·ków Try·bu·nal·ski \'pyòt-ər-,küf-,trib-ü-'näl-skē, pē-'òt-, -,küv-\ commune *cen* Poland SSE of Lodz *pop* 73,691

Pipe Spring National Monument reservation NW Ariz. on Kaibab plateau containing old Mormon fort

Pipe·stone National Monument \'pīp-,stōn\ reservation SW Minn. containing quarry once used by Indians

Piq·ua \'pik-(,)wä, -wə\ city W Ohio N of Dayton *pop* 20,480

Pi·rai·évs \,pē-re-'efs\ *or* **Pi·rae·us** \pī-'rē-əs\ city E Greece on Saronic Gulf; port of Athens *pop* 183,957

Pirineos — see PYRENEES

Pir·ma·sens \,pi(ə)r-mə-'zen(t)s\ city SW W. Germany near French border E of Saarbrücken *pop* 49,615

Pir·na \'pi(ə)r-nə\ city SE E. Germany SE of Dresden *pop* 48,001

Pi·sa \'pē-zə, *It* -sä\ commune W *cen* Italy in Tuscany on the Arno *pop* 104,334 — **Pi·san** \'pēz-ˀn\ *adj or n*

Pis·ca·ta·qua \pis-'kat-ə-,kwò\ river 12 *mi* (19 *km*) Maine & N.H. formed by junction of Cocheco & Salmon Falls rivers & flowing SE on Maine-N.H. boundary into the Atlantic

Pishpek — see FRUNZE

Pi·sid·ia \pə-'sid-ē-ə, pī-\ ancient country S Asia Minor N of Pamphylia — **Pi·sid·i·an** \-ē-ən\ *adj*

Pi·sto·ia \pi-'stòi-ə, -'stò-yə\ commune *cen* Italy NW of Florence *pop* 93,516

Pit \'pit\ river 280 *mi* (451 *km*) N Calif. flowing SW into the Sacramento

Pit·cairn \'pit-,ka(ə)rn, -,ke(ə)rn\ island S Pacific SE of Tuamotu archipelago; a Brit. colony, with several smaller islands

Pitts·burg \'pits-,bərg\ **1** city W Calif. NE of Oakland on San Joaquin river *pop* 33,034 **2** city SE Kans. *pop* 18,770

Pitts·burgh \'pits-,bərg\ city SW Pa. at confluence of the Allegheny & the Monongahela where they form the Ohio *pop* 423,938

Pitts·field \'pits-,fēld\ city W Mass. *pop* 51,974

Piz Bernina — see BERNINA

Pla·cen·tia \plə-'sen-chə\ city SW Calif. SE of Los Angeles *pop* 35,041

Placentia Bay inlet of the Atlantic E Canada in SE Newfoundland

Plac·id, Lake \'plas-əd\ lake 5 *mi* (8 *km*) long NE N. Y. in the Adirondacks

Plain·field \'plān-,fēld\ city NE N. J. *pop* 45,555

Plains of Abra·ham \'ā-brə-,ham\ plateau Canada in W part of city of Quebec

Plain·view \'plān-vyü\ city NW Tex. N of Lubbock *pop* 22,187

Pla·no \'plā-(,)nō\ city NE Tex. N of Dallas *pop* 72,331

Plantation city SE Fla. W of Fort Lauderdale *pop* 48,501

Plant City \'plant-\ city W *cen* Fla. E of Tampa *pop* 19,270

Plas·sey \'plas-ē\ village NE India in W. Bengal N of Calcutta

Pla·ta, Rio de la \,rē-ō-,del-ə-'plät-ə\ *or* **River Plate** \'plāt\ estuary of Paraná & Uruguay rivers S. America bet. Uruguay & Argentina; 225 *mi* (362 *km*) long

Pla·taea \plə-'tē-ə\ *or* **Pla·tae·ae** \-'tē-,ē\ ancient city Greece in SE Boeotia S of Thebes — **Pla·tae·an** \-'tē-ən\ *adj or n*

Platte \'plat\ river 310 *mi* (499 *km*) cen Nebr. formed by junction of the N. Platte & S. Platte & flowing E into the Missouri **2** river 300 *mi* (483 *km*) SW Iowa & NW Mo. flowing into the Missouri

Plattensee — see BALATON

Platts·burgh *or* **Platts·burg** \'plats-,bərg\ city NE N.Y. on Lake Champlain *pop* 21,057

Plau·en \'plaú-ən\ *or* **Plauen im Vogt·land** \,plaú-ə-,nim-'fōk-,tlänt\ city S E. Germany on the Weisse Elster *pop* 78,632

Pleasant — see NAURU

Pleasant Hill city W Calif. ENE of Oakland *pop* 25,124

Pleas·an·ton \'plez-ˀn-tən\ city W Calif. SE of Oakland *pop* 35,160

Plenty, Bay of inlet of the S. Pacific N New Zealand on NE coast of North Is.

Ple·ven \'plev-ən\ city NW Bulgaria *pop* 107,567

Plo·es·ti \plò-'(y)esht(-ē)\ city SE Romania *pop* 211,505

Plov·div \'plóv-,dif, -,div\ *or Gk* **Phil·ip·pop·o·lis** \,fil-ə-'päp-ə-ləs\ city S Bulgaria on the Maritsa N of the Rhodope mountains *pop* 299,638

Plum \'pləm\ city SW Pa. *pop* 25,390

Plym·outh \'plim-əth\ **1** town SE Mass. *pop* 35,913 **2** village SE Minn. NW of Minneapolis *pop* 31,615 **3** city & port SW England in Devon *pop* 243,895

Plzeň \'pəl-,zen(-yə)\ city Czechoslovakia in Bohemia WSW of Prague *pop* 170,701

Po \'pō\ *or anc* **Pa·dus** \'pād-əs\ river 418 *mi* (673 *km*) N Italy flowing from slopes of Mt. Viso E into the Adriatic through several mouths

Po·be·da Peak \pō-'bed-ə, pə-\ *or Russ* **Pik Po·be·dy** \,pēk-pə-'bed-ē\ mountain 24,406 *ft* (7439 *m*) U.S.S.R. in S Soviet Russia, Asia; highest in Tien Shan

Po·ca·tel·lo \,pō-kə-'tel-(,)ō, -'tel-ə\ city SE Idaho *pop* 46,340

Po·co·no \'pō-kə-,nō\ mountains E Pa. NW of Kittatinny Mountain; highest point *ab* 1600 *ft* (488 *m*)

Podgorica *or* **Podgoritsa** — see TITOGRAD

Po·do·lia \pə-'dō-lē-ə, -'dōl-yə\ *or Russ* **Po·dolsk** \pə-'dólsk\ region U.S.S.R. in W Ukrainian Republic N of middle Dniester river

Po·dolsk \pə-'dólsk\ city U.S.S.R. in S *cen* Soviet Russia, Europe, S of Moscow *pop* 169,000

Po Hai *or* **Bo·hai** \'bō-'hī\ *or* **Gulf of Chih·li** \'chē-'lē, 'ji(ə)r-\ arm of Yellow sea NE China bounded on NE by Liaotung peninsula & on SE by Shantung peninsula

Po·hang \'pō-,häŋ\ *or* **Pohang–dong** \-'dòŋ\ city & port SE S. Korea on Sea of Japan *pop* 201,355

Pohn·pei \'pòn-,pā\ *or* **Po·na·pe** \'pō-nə-,pā\ island E Carolines, part of Federated States of Micronesia

Pointe–à–Pi·tre \,pwant-ə-'pētrˀ\ city & port French W. Indies in Guadeloupe on Grande-Terre *pop* 25,312

Pointe–aux–Trem·bles \,point-ō-'trem-bəlz\ city Canada in S Que. N of Montreal *pop* 36,270

Pointe–Claire \,point-'kla(ə)r, -'kle(ə)r\ city Canada in S Que. on St. Lawrence river SW of Montreal *pop* 24,571

Pointe–Noire \,pwant-nə-'wär\ city & port SW Congo on the Atlantic; formerly ✳ of Middle Congo *pop* 135,000

Point Pe·lee National Park \'point-'pē-lē\ reservation Canada in SE Ont. on **Point Pelee** (cape projecting into Lake Erie)

Point Pleasant borough E N.J. SSW of Asbury Park *pop* 17,747

Poi·tiers *or formerly* **Poic·tiers** \pwä-'tyā, 'pwät-ē-,ā\ city W *cen* France SW of Tours *pop* 78,739

Poi·tou \pwä-'tü\ region & former province W France SE of Brittany ✳ Poitiers

Po·land \'pō-lənd\ *or Pol* **Pol·ska** \'pòl-skä\ country E *cen* Europe bordering on Baltic sea; in medieval period a kingdom, at one time extending to the lower Dnieper; partitioned 1772, 1793, 1795 among Russia, Prussia, & Austria; again a kingdom 1815–30; lost autonomy 1830–1918; since 1918 a republic ✳ Warsaw *area* 120,355 *sq mi* (312,923 *sq km*), *pop* 35,061,450

Polish Corridor strip of land N Europe in Poland that bet. World War I & World War II separated E. Prussia from main part of Germany; area was before 1919 part of Germany

Pol·ta·va \pəl-'täv-ə\ city U.S.S.R. in *cen* Ukrainian Republic on Vorskla river WSW of Kharkov *pop* 220,000

Poltoratsk — see ASHKHABAD

Pol·y·ne·sia \,päl-ə-'nē-zhə, -shə\ the islands of the *cen* & S Pacific including Hawaii, the Line, Phoenix, Tonga, Cook, & Samoa islands, Tuvalu, Easter Is., French Polynesia, & often New Zealand

Pom·er·a·nia \,päm-ə-'rā-nē-ə, -nyə\ *or G* **Pom·mern** \'pò-mərn\ *or Pol* **Po·mo·rze** \pò-'mò-zhe\ **1** region N Europe on Baltic sea; formerly in Germany, now mostly in Poland **2** former province of Prussia

Pom·er·e·lia \,päm-ə-'rē-lē-ə, -'rēl-yə\ *or G* **Pom·me·rel·len** \,pò-mə-'rel-ən\ region E Europe on the Baltic W of the Vistula & E of Pomerania; orig. part of Pomerania

Po·mo·na \pə-'mō-nə\ city SW Calif. E of Los Angeles *pop* 92,742

Pom·pa·no Beach \'päm-pə-,nò, 'pəm-\ city SE Fla. on the Atlantic N of Fort Lauderdale *pop* 52,618

Pom·pe·ii \päm-'pā, -'pā-ē\ ancient city S Italy SE of Naples destroyed A.D. 79 by eruption of Mt. Vesuvius — **Pom·pe·ian** *or* **Pom·pei·ian** \-'pā-ən\ *adj or n*

Pon·ca City \,pän-kə-\ city N Okla. on Arkansas river *pop* 26,238

Pon·ce \'pòn(t)-(,)sä\ city & port S Puerto Rico *pop* 161,739

Pon·di·cher·ry \,pän-də-'cher-ē, -'sher-\ *or F* **Pon·di·ché·ry** \pòn-dē-shā-rē\ **1** union territory SE India SSW of Madras surrounded by Tamil Nadu; a settlement of French India before 1954, *area* 112 *sq mi* (291 *sq km*), *pop* 604,136 **2** city & port, its ✳ *pop* 251,471

Pon·ta Del·ga·da \,pänt-ə-del-'gäd-ə, -'gad-\ city & port Azores on São Miguel Is. *pop* 66,654

Pont·char·train, Lake \'pän-chər-,trān, ,pän-chər-'\ lake SE La. E of the Mississippi & N of New Orleans *area* 600 *sq mi* (1560 *sq km*)

Pon·te·fract \'pänt-i-,frakt\ borough N England in W. Yorkshire, SE of Leeds *pop* 31,971

Pon·te·ve·dra \,pänt-ə-'vā-drə\ **1** province NW Spain in SW Galicia on the Atlantic *area* 1695 *sq mi* (4407 *sq km*), *pop* 915,152 **2** commune & port, its ✳, NW of Vigo *pop* 68,645

Pon·ti·ac \'pänt-ē-,ak\ city SE Mich. NW of Detroit *pop* 76,715

Pon·ti·a·nak \,pänt-ē-'än-,äk\ city Indonesia on SW coast of Borneo ✳ of W. Kalimantan *pop* 304,778

Pon·tine \'pän-,tīn, -,tēn\ islands Italy in Tyrrhenian sea W of Naples; chief islands **Pon·za** \'pòn(t)-sä\ & **Pon·ti·ne** \pòn-'tē-nē\

Pontine marshes district *cen* Italy in SW Latium, separated from sea by low sand hills that prevent natural drainage; now reclaimed

Pon·tus \'pänt-əs\ **1** ancient country NE Asia Minor; a kingdom 4th century B.C. to 66 B.C. later a Roman province **2** *or* **Pontus Euxinus** — see BLACK SEA

Pon·ty·pool \,pänt-ə-'pül\ town SE Wales in Gwent *pop* 36,761

Pon·ty·pridd \,pänt-ə-'prēth\ town SE Wales in Mid Glamorgan *pop* 32,992

Poole \'pül\ borough S England in Dorset on English channel *pop* 118,922

Poo·na \'pü-nə\ city W India in Maharashtra ESE of Bombay *pop* 1,685,300

Po·o·pó \,pō-ə-'pō, (ˀ)pō-'pō\ lake 60 *mi* (96 *km*) long W *cen* Bolivia S of Lake Titicaca at altitude of 12,000 *ft* (3658 *m*)

Pop·lar \'päp-lər\ former metropolitan borough E London, England, on N bank of the Thames, now part of Tower Hamlets

Poplar Bluff city SE Mo. *pop* 17,139

Po·po·ca·te·petl \,pō-pə-,kat-ə-'pet-ˀl\ volcano 17,887 *ft* (5452 *m*) SE *cen* Mexico in Puebla

Porcupine river 590 *mi* (950 *km*) in N Yukon Territory & NE Alaska flowing N & W into the Yukon

Po·ri \'pōr-ē\ city & port SW Finland *pop* 72,938

Pork·ka·la \'pòr-kə-lä, -,lä\ peninsula S Finland W of Helsinki

Por·la·mar \,pòr-lə-'mär\ city & port NE Venezuela on Margarita Is.

Port Ade·laide \'ad-ˀl-,ād\ city SE S. Australia on Gulf of St. Vincent at mouth of Torrens river; port for Adelaide *pop* 35,407

Por·tage \'pōrt-ij, 'pòrt-\ **1** city NW Ind. E of Gary *pop* 27,409 **2** city SW Mich. S of Kalamazoo *pop* 38,147

Port Al·ber·ni \al-'bər-nē\ city Canada in SW B.C. on Vancouver Is. *pop* 19,892

Port An·ge·les \'an-jə-ləs\ city NW Wash. on Strait of Juan de Fuca WNW of Seattle *pop* 17,311
Port Ar·thur \-'är-thər\ **1** city & port SE Tex. on Sabine Lake *pop* 61,251 **2** — see THUNDER BAY **3** *or* **Lü–shun** \'lü-'shün\ city & port NE China in S Liaoning at tip of Liaotung peninsula *pop* 200,000
Port–au–Prince \,pōrt-ō-'prin(t)s, ,pȯrt-; ,pȯr(t)-ō-'pra^{n}s\ city & port * of Haiti on SE shore of Gulf of Gongave *pop* 763,188
Port Blair \-'ble(ə)r\ town & port India on S. Andaman Is. * of Andaman and Nicobar islands union territory
Port Ches·ter \'pōrt-,ches-tər, 'pȯrt-\ village SE N.Y. NE of New Rochelle on Long Is. Sound *pop* 23,565
Port Col·borne \-'kōl-bərn\ city Canada in SE Ont. W of Buffalo, N.Y. *pop* 19,225
Port Co·quit·lam \-kō-'kwit-ləm\ city Canada in SW B.C. E of Vancouver *pop* 27,535
Port Eliz·a·beth \-ᵊl-'iz-ə-bəth, -i-'liz-\ city & port S Republic of S. Africa in SE Cape Province on Algoa Bay *pop* 468,797
Por·ter·ville \'pōrt-ər-,vil, 'pȯrt-\ city S *cen* Calif. *pop* 19,707
Port Ev·er·glades \-'ev-ər-,glādz\ seaport SE Fla. on the Atlantic S of Fort Lauderdale
Port Hed·land \-'hed-lənd\ port Western Australia
Port Hue·ne·me \-wī-'nē-mē\ city S Calif. near Oxnard *pop* 17,803
Port Hu·ron \-'(h)yür-ən\ city E Mich. on Lake Huron & St. Clair river *pop* 33,981
Port Jack·son \-'jak-sən\ inlet of S Pacific SE Australia in New S. Wales; the harbor of Sydney
Port·land \'pōrt-lənd, 'pȯrt-\ **1** city & port SW Maine on Casco Bay *pop* 61,572 **2** city & port NW Oreg. at confluence of Columbia & Willamette rivers *pop* 366,383
Portland Canal inlet of the Pacific *ab* 80 *mi* (129 *km*) long Canada & U.S. bet. B.C. & SE tip of Alaska
Port·laoigh·i·se \pōrt-'lā-ə-shə\ town *cen* Ireland * of County Laoighis
Port Lou·is \-'lü-əs, -'lü-ē\ city & port * of Mauritius *pop* 148,389
Port Lyautey — see KENITRA
Port Mahon — see MAHÓN
Port Mores·by \-'mō(ə)rz-bē, -'mȯ(ə)rz-\ city & port SE New Guinea in Papua * of Papua New Guinea *pop* 123,624
Por·to \'pōr-tü\ *or* **Opor·to** \ō-'pōrt-(,)ō, -'pȯrt-\ city & port NW Portugal on the Douro *pop* 329,104 — see LEIXÕES
Pôr·to Ale·gre \,pōrt-(,)ō-ə-'leg-rə, ,pȯrt-\ city & port S Brazil * of Rio Grande do Sul state at N end of Lagoa dos Patos *pop* 1,125,901
Por·to·be·lo \,pōrt-ə-'bel-(,)ō, ,pȯrt-\ town & port Panama on Caribbean coast; the great emporium of S. American trade in 17th & 18th centuries
Por·to·fi·no \,pōrt-ə-'fē-(,)nō, ,pȯrt-\ village N Italy in Liguria on the coast SE of Genoa
Port of Spain city & port * of Trinidad and Tobago, on NW Trinidad Is. *pop* 47,300
Por·to–No·vo \,pōrt-ə-'nō-(,)vō, ,pȯrt-\ city & port * of Benin *pop* 192,000
Port Or·ange \-'är-inj, -'är(-ə)nj; *chiefly Northern & Midland* 'ȯr- inj, 'ȯr(-ə)nj\ city E Fla. *pop* 18,756
Porto Rico — see PUERTO RICO
Port Phil·lip Bay \-'fil-əp-\ inlet of Bass strait SE Australia in Victoria; the harbor of Melbourne
Port Roy·al \-'rȯi(-ə)l\ town Jamaica at entrance to Kingston Harbor; early * of Jamaica, destroyed by earthquakes 1692 & 1907 & partly engulfed by the sea
Port Royal Sound inlet of the Atlantic S S.C.
Port Said \-sä-'ēd, -'sīd\ city & port NE Egypt on the Mediterranean at N end of Suez canal *pop* 262,760
Ports·mouth \'pōrt-sməth, 'pȯrt-\ **1** city & port SE N.H. on the Atlantic *pop* 26,254 **2** city S Ohio at junction of Ohio & Scioto rivers *pop* 25,943 **3** city & port SE Va. on Elizabeth river opposite Norfolk *pop* 104,577 **4** city S England in Hampshire on **Port·sea** \'pōrt-sē, 'pȯrt-\ (island in English channel) *pop* 179,419
Port Stanley — see STANLEY
Port Sudan city & port NE Sudan on Red sea *pop* 100,700
Por·tu·gal \'pōr-chi-gəl, 'pȯr-\ *or anc* **Lu·si·ta·nia** \,lü-sə-'tā-nē-ə, -nyə\ country SW Europe in W Iberian peninsula bordering on the Atlantic; a republic before 1910 a kingdom * Lisbon *area* (not including Azores & Madeira) 34,240 *sq mi* (89,024 *sq km*), *pop* 9,784,200
Portuguese East Africa — see MOZAMBIQUE
Portuguese Guinea — see GUINEA-BISSAU
Portuguese India former Portuguese possessions on W coast of India peninsula, annexed 1962 by India; comprised territory of Goa & districts of Damão & Diu
Portuguese Timor — see TIMOR
Portuguese West Africa — see ANGOLA
Porz am Rhein \,pȯrt-säm-'rīn\ city W W. Germany ESE suburb of Cologne *pop* 76,762
Poseidonia — see PAESTUM
Potch·ef·stroom \'päch-əf-,strōm\ city NE Republic of S. Africa in S Transvaal SW of Johannesburg *pop* 51,800
Po·to·mac \pə-'tō-mək, -mik\ river 287 *mi* (462 *km*) E U.S. flowing from W.Va. into Chesapeake Bay & forming S boundary of Md.
Po·to·sí \,pōt-ə-'sē\ city S Bolivia *pop* 77,397
Pots·dam \'päts-,dam\ city *cen* E. Germany SW of Berlin *pop* 132,005
Potts·town \'pät-,staün\ borough SE Pa. ESE of Reading *pop* 22,729
Potts·ville \'päts-,vil\ city E *cen* Pa. NNW of Reading *pop* 18,195
Pough·keep·sie \pə-'kip-sē, pō-\ city SE N.Y. *pop* 29,757
Pow·der \'paüd-ər\ **1** river 150 *mi* (241 *km*) E Oreg. flowing into the Snake **2** river 375 *mi* (604 *km*) N Wyo. & SE Mont. flowing N into the Yellowstone
Powell, Lake — see GLEN CANYON DAM
Po·wys \'pō-əs\ county E *cen* Wales * Llandrindod Wells *area* 1960 *sq mi* (5096 *sq km*), *pop* 111,300
Po·yang \'pō-'yäŋ\ lake 90 *mi* (145 *km*) long E China in N Kiangsi
Poz·nan \'pōz-,nan(-yə), 'pōz-, -,nän(-yə)\ *or G* **Po·sen** \'pōz-ᵊn\ city W *cen* Poland on the Warta *pop* 557,992
Poz·zuo·li \pöt-'swȯ-lē\ *or anc* **Pu·te·o·li** \p(y)ü-'tē-ə-,lī\ commune & port S Italy in Campania W of Naples *pop* 70,350
Prague \'präg\ *or Czech* **Pra·ha** \'prä-(,)hä\ city * of Czechoslovakia in Bohemia on Vltava river *pop* 1,182,186
Praia \'prī-ə\ town * of Cape Verde on São Tiago Is. *pop* 37,480
Prairie Provinces the Canadian provinces of Man., Sask., & Alta.
Prairie Village city NE Kans. S of Kansas City *pop* 24,657
Pra·to \'prät-ō\ commune *cen* Italy in Tuscany *pop* 158,797
Pratt·ville \'prat-,vil, -vəl\ city *cen* Ala. NW of Montgomery *pop* 18,647
Pres·cott \'pres-kət, -,kät\ city *cen* Ariz. *pop* 20,055
Presque Isle \pre-'skī(ə)l\ peninsula NW Pa. in Lake Erie forming **Presque Isle Bay** (harbor of Erie, Pa.)
Pressburg — see BRATISLAVA
Pres·ton \'pres-tən\ **1** former town, Ont., Canada — see CAMBRIDGE **2** borough NW England NNW of Liverpool * of Lancashire *pop* 86,913
Prest·wich \'pres-(,)twich\ borough NW England in Greater Manchester NNW of Manchester *pop* 31,198
Prest·wick \'pres-(,)twik\ burgh SW Scotland in Strathclyde N of Ayr *pop* 13,532
Pre·to·ria \pri-'tōr-ē-ə, -'tȯr-\ city, administrative * of Republic of S. Africa & * of Transvaal *pop* 303,684
Prib·i·lof \'prib-ə-,lȯf\ islands Alaska in Bering sea
Prich·ard \'prich-ərd\ city SW Ala. N of Mobile *pop* 39,541
Primorye — see MARITIME TERRITORY
Prince Al·bert \-'al-bərt\ city Canada in *cen* Sask. *pop* 31,380
Prince Albert National Park reservation Canada in *cen* Sask. in watershed area
Prince Ed·ward Island \-,ed-wərd-\ island SE Canada in Gulf of St. Lawrence off E N.B. & N N.S.; a province * Charlottetown *area* 2184 *sq mi* (5678 *sq km*), *pop* 122,506
Prince Edward Island National Park reservation Canada on N coast of P.E.I.
Prince George \-'jȯ(ə)rj\ city Canada in E *cen* B.C. *pop* 67,559
Prince of Wales \-'wā(ə)lz\ **1** island SE Alaska, largest in Alexander archipelago *area* 1500 *sq mi* (3900 *sq km*) **2** island N Canada bet. Victoria Is. & Somerset Is. *area* 12,830 *sq mi* (33,358 *sq km*)
Prince of Wales, Cape cape Alaska at W tip of Seward peninsula; most westerly point of mainland of N. America, at 168°W
Prince Ru·pert's Land \-'rü-pərts-\ historical region N & W Canada comprising drainage basin of Hudson Bay granted 1670 by King Charles II to Hudson's Bay Company; purchased 1869 by the Dominion
Prince Wil·liam Sound \-,wil-yəm-\ inlet of Gulf of Alaska S Alaska E of Kenai peninsula
Prín·ci·pe \'prin(t)-sə-pə\ island W Africa in Gulf of Guinea N of São Tomé *area* 58 *sq mi* (151 *sq km*) — see SÃO TOMÉ
Prip·et \'prip-,et, -ət\ *or Russ* **Pri·pyat** \'prip-yət\ river 500 *mi* (805 *km*) E *cen* Europe in the U.S.S.R. in NW Ukrainian Republic & S White Russia flowing E through the **Pripet,** *or* **Pinsk, marshes** to the Dnieper
Pro·gre·so \prə-'gres-(,)ō\ city SE Mexico on Yucatán peninsula; port for Mérida *pop* 22,100
Pro·ko·pyevsk \prə-'kȯp-yəfsk\ city U.S.S.R. in SW Soviet Russia, Asia, at S end of Kuznetsk basin NW of Novokuznetsk *pop* 275,000
Propontis — see MARMARA (Sea of)
Pro·vence \prə-'vä^{n}s\ region & former province SE France bordering on the Mediterranean * Aix-en-Provence
Prov·i·dence \'präv-əd-ən(t)s, -ə-,den(t)s\ city & port N R.I., its * *pop* 156,804
Pro·vo \'prō-(,)vō\ city N *cen* Utah on Utah Lake *pop* 73,907
Prud·hoe Bay \'prüd-(,)(h)ō, 'prəd-\ inlet of Beaufort sea N Alaska
Prus·sia \'prəsh-ə\ *or G* **Preus·sen** \'prȯis-ᵊn\ **1** historical region N Germany bordering on Baltic sea **2** former kingdom & state of Germany * Berlin — see EAST PRUSSIA, WEST PRUSSIA — **Prus·sian** \'prəsh-ən\ *adj or n*
Prut \'prüt\ river 500 *mi* (805 *km*) E Europe flowing from the Carpathians SSE into the Danube & since World War II forming the boundary bet. Romania & the U.S.S.R.
Pskov \pə-'skȯf, -'skȯv\ city U.S.S.R. in Soviet Russia, Europe, near **Lake Pskov** (S arm of Peipus lake) *pop* 127,000
Ptol·e·ma·ïs \,täl-ə-'mā-əs\ **1** ancient town in upper Egypt on left bank of the Nile NW of Thebes **2** ancient town in Cyrenaica NW of Barca; site at modern village of Tolmeta **3** — see ACRE
Pueb·la \'pweb-lə\ **1** state SE *cen* Mexico *area* 13,124 *sq mi* (34,122 *sq km*), *pop* 3,279,960 **2** *or* **Puebla de Za·ra·go·za** \-dā-,zar-ə-'gō-zə\ city, its *, SE of Mexico (City) *pop* 521,885
Pueb·lo \'pweb-,lō\ city SE *cen* Colo. on the Arkansas *pop* 101,686
Puer·to Bar·rios \,pwert-ō-'bär-ē-,ōs\ city & port E Guatemala on Gulf of Honduras *pop* 46,782
Puerto Ca·be·llo \-kə-'bā-(,)(y)ō\ city & port N Venezuela 70 *mi* (113 *km*) W of Caracas *pop* 70,598
Puerto La Cruz \-lə-'krüz, -'krüs\ city NE Venezuela NE of Barcelona *pop* 82,059
Puerto Limón — see LIMÓN
Puerto Montt \-'mȯnt\ city & port S *cen* Chile *pop* 119,059
Puer·to Ri·co \,pōrt-ə-'rē-(,)kō, ,pȯrt-, ,pwert-\ *or formerly* **Por·to Rico** island W. Indies E of Hispaniola; a self-governing commonwealth in union with the U.S. * San Juan *area* 3435 *sq mi* (8931 *sq km*), *pop* 3,196,520 — **Puerto Ri·can** \-'rē-kən\ *adj or n*
Pu·get Sound \,pyü-jət-\ arm of the Pacific extending 80 *mi* (129 *km*) S into W Wash. from E end of Strait of Juan de Fuca
Puglia *or* **Le Puglie** — see APULIA
Pu·ka·pu·ka \,pü-kə-'pü-kə\ *or* **Dan·ger islands** \'dān-jər-\ atoll *cen* Pacific N of Cook islands; chief island Pukapuka; administered with Cook islands by New Zealand
Pu·la \'pü-lə\ city & port NW Yugoslavia at tip of Istrian peninsula *pop* 45,000
Pul·ko·vo \'pül-kə-və, -,vō\ village U.S.S.R. in Soviet Russia, Europe, S of Leningrad
Pull·man \'pül-mən\ city SE Wash. *pop* 23,579
Pu·log \'pü-,lȯg\ mountain 9606 *ft* (2928 *m*) Philippines in N Luzon at S end of Cordillera Central; highest in Luzon
Pu·na de Ata·ca·ma \'pü-nə-,dā-,at-ə-'käm-ə, -,ät-\ high plateau region NW Argentina NW of San Miguel de Tucumán
Pun·jab *or* **Pan·jab** \,pən-'jäb, -'jab, 'pən-,\ **1** region NW Indian subcontinent in Pakistan & NW India occupying valleys of the Indus & its five tributaries; formerly a province of Brit. India * Lahore **2** *or* **East Punjab** former state NW India in E Punjab divided 1966 into two states of Punjabi Suba & Haryana **3** *or formerly* **West Punjab** province NE

Pakistan ✻ Lahore   4 *or* Pun·ja·bi Su·ba \‚pən-‚jäb-ē-'sü-bə, -‚jab-\ state NW India formed from N part of former state of Punjab ✻ Chandigarh *area* 19,495 *sq mi* (50,687 *sq km*), *pop* 16,669,755

Punt \'pùnt\ — ancient Egyptian name for a part of Africa not certainly identified, probably Somaliland

Pun·ta Are·nas \‚pün-tə-ə-'rā-nəs\ *or formerly* Ma·ga·lla·nes \‚mäg-ə-'yän-əs\ city & port S Chile on Strait of Magellan *pop* 67,514

Punta del Es·te \-‚del-'es-tē\ town S Uruguay E of Montevideo *pop* 5272

Pu·ra·cé \‚pùr-ə-'sā\ volcano 15,604 *ft* (4756 *m*) SW *cen* Colombia

Pur·beck, Isle of \'pər-‚bek\ peninsula region S England in Dorset extending E into English channel

Pur·ga·to·ire \'pər-gə-‚twär, 'pik-ət-‚wī(ə)r\ river 190 *mi* (306 *km*) SE Colo. flowing into the Arkansas

Pu·ri \'pùr-ē\ city & port E India in SE Orissa on Bay of Bengal *pop* 101,089

Pu·rus \pə-'rüs\ river 2000 *mi* (3219 *km*) NW *cen* S. America rising in the Andes in SE Peru & flowing NE into the Amazon in Brazil

Pu·san \'pü-‚sän\ city & port SE S. Korea on Korea strait *pop* 3,160,276

Push·kin \'pùsh-kən\ *or formerly* Tsar·skoe Se·lo \‚(t)sär-skə-yə-sə-'lò\ *or* Det·skoe Selo \‚det-skə-yə-\ city U.S.S.R. in NW Soviet Russia, Europe, S of Leningrad *pop* 73,000

Puteoli — *see* POZZUOLI

Put-in-Bay \‚pùt-‚in-\ inlet of Lake Erie in Ohio on S. Bass Is. N of Sandusky Bay; site of Perry's Victory and International Peace Memorial National Monument

Pu·tu·ma·yo \‚pùt-ə-'mī-(‚)ò\ *or in Brazil* Içá \ē-'sä\ river 980 *mi* (1577 *km*) NW S. America flowing from SW Colombia into the Amazon in NW Brazil

Puy·al·lup \pyü-'al-əp\ city W *cen* Wash. *pop* 18,251

Puy de Dôme — *see* DÔME (Puy de)

Puy de Sancy — *see* SANCY (Puy de)

Pya·ti·gorsk \pē-‚at-i-'gò(ə)rsk\ city U.S.S.R. in S Soviet Russia, Europe, in N Caucasus SE of Stavropol *pop* 130,000

Pyd·na \'pid-nə\ ancient town Macedonia on W shore of Gulf of Salonika

Pyong·yang \pē-'òn-‚yän, pē-'əŋ-, -‚yaŋ\ city ✻ of N. Korea on the Taedong *pop* 1,250,000

Pyramid lake 30 *mi* (48 *km*) long NW Nev. NE of Reno

Pyr·e·nees \'pir-ə-‚nēz\ *or F* Py·ré·nées \pē-rā-nā\ *or Sp* Pi·ri·ne·os \‚pē-rē-'nā-(‚)òs\ mountains along French-Spanish border from Bay of Biscay to Gulf of Lions — *see* ANETO (Pico de) — Pyr·e·ne·an \‚pir-ə-'nē-ən\ *adj or n*

Qa·tar \'kät-ər, 'gät-, 'gət-\ country E Arabia on peninsula projecting into Persian Gulf; an independent emirate ✻ Doha *area* 6000 *sq mi* (15,600 *sq km*), *pop* 270,000

Qat·ta·ra Depression \kə-‚tär-ə\ region NW Egypt, a low area 40 *mi* (64 *km*) from coast; lowest point 440 *ft* (134 *m*) below sea level

Qaz·vin *or* Kaz·vin \käz-'vēn\ city NW Iran S of Elburz mountains & NW of Tehran *pop* 138,527

Qe·na \'ken-ə, 'kā-nə\ city S Egypt N of Luxor *pop* 93,680

Qeshm \'kesh-əm\ island S Iran in Strait of Hormuz *pop* 15,000

Qingdao — *see* TSINGTAO

Qinghai   1 — *see* KOKO NOR   2 — *see* TSINGHAI

Qinhuangdao — *see* CH'IN-HUANG-TAO

Qiongzhou — *see* HAINAN 2

Qiqihar — *see* TSITSIHAR

Qi·shon \'kē-‚shòn, kē-\ river 50 *mi* (80 *km*) N Israel flowing NW through Plain of Esdraelon to the Mediterranean

Quanzhou — *see* CH'ÜAN-CHOU

Qu'Ap·pelle \kwə-'pel\ river 270 *mi* (434 *km*) Canada in S Sask. flowing E into the Assiniboine

Quathlamba — *see* DRAKENSBERG

Que·bec \kwi-'bek, ki-\ *or* Qué·bec \kā-bek\   1 province E Canada extending from Hudson bay to Gaspé peninsula *area* 523,860 *sq mi* (1,362,036 *sq km*), *pop* 6,438,403   2 city & port, its ✻, on the St. Lawrence *pop* 177,082 — Que·bec·er *or* Que·beck·er \kwi-'bek-ər, ki-\ *n*

Queen·bor·ough-in-Shep·pey \'kwēn-‚bər-ə-in-'shep-ē, -‚bə-rə-, -b(ə-)rə-\ borough SE England in Kent at mouth of the Thames *pop* 33,362

Queen Char·lotte \'shär-lət\   1 islands Canada in W B.C. in Pacific ocean *area* 3970 *sq mi* (10,322 *sq km*), *pop* 4747   2 sound S of Queen Charlotte islands

Queen Eliz·a·beth \-ʼl-'iz-ə-bəth, -i-'liz-\ islands N Canada N of water passage extending from M'Clure strait to Lancaster Sound; include Parry, Sverdrup, Devon, & Ellesmere islands

Queen Maud Land \'mòd\ section of Antarctica on the Atlantic

Queens \'kwēnz\ borough of New York City on Long Is. E of Brooklyn *pop* 1,891,325

Queen's — *see* LAOIGHIS

Queens·land \'kwēnz-‚land, -lənd\ state NE Australia ✻ Brisbane *area* 670,500 *sq mi* (1,743,300 *sq km*), *pop* 2,295,123 — Queens·land·er \-ər\ *n*

Queenstown — *see* COBH

Quelpart — *see* CHEJU

Que·moy \k(w)i-'mòi, 'kwē-\ island SE China in Formosa strait 15 *mi* (24 *km*) E of Amoy; garrisoned by Taiwan since 1950 *pop* 60,544

Que·ré·ta·ro \kə-'ret-ə-‚rò\   1 state *cen* Mexico *area* 4432 *sq mi* (11,523 *sq km*), *pop* 726,054   2 city, its ✻, *pop* 140,379

Quet·ta \'kwet-ə\ city Pakistan in N Baluchistan *pop* 285,000

Que·zal·te·nan·go \ke(t)-‚säl-tə-'näŋ-(‚)gò\ city SW Guatemala *pop* 72,745

Que·zon City \'kā-‚sòn\ city Philippines in Luzon NE of Manila; former (1948–76) official ✻ of the Philippines *pop* 1,165,865

Quil·mes \'kē(ə)l-‚mäs, -‚mes\ city E Argentina SE of Buenos Aires *pop* 445,662

Quim·per \ka^n(m)-'pe(ə)r\ commune NW France W of Rennes near Bay of Biscay *pop* 50,856

Qui·nault \kwin-'òlt\ river 65 *mi* (105 *km*) W Wash. flowing to the Pacific

Quin·cy   1 \'kwin(t)-sē\ city W Ill. on the Mississippi *pop* 42,554   2 \'kwin-zē\ city E Mass. SE of Boston *pop* 84,743

Quin·ta·na Roo \kēn-‚tän-ə-'rò\ state SE Mexico in E Yucatán ✻ Chetumal *area* 19,438 *sq mi* (50,539 *sq km*), *pop* 209,858

Quin·te, Bay of \'kwint-ē\ inlet of Lake Ontario in Canada in SE Ont.; connected with Georgian Bay by Trent canal

Quir·i·nal \'kwir-ən-ʼl\ hill in Rome, Italy, one of seven on which the ancient city was built — *see* AVENTINE

Qui·to \'kē-(‚)tò\ city ✻ of Ecuador *pop* 599,828

Qum \'kùm\ city NW *cen* Iran *pop* 246,831

Qum·ran \‚kùm-'rän\ *or* Khir·bat Qumran \kir-‚bät-\ site Palestine in NW Jordan on Wadi Qumran near NW shore of Dead sea of an Essene community (*ab* 100 B.C. – A.D. 68) near a series of caves in which the Dead Sea Scrolls were found

Quoddy Bay PASSAMAQUODDY BAY

Ra·ba \'räb-ə\ river 160 *mi* (257 *km*) SE Austria & W Hungary flowing E & NE into the Danube

Ra·bat \rə-'bät\ city ✻ of Morocco on Atlantic coast *pop* 518,616

Ra·baul \rä-'baù(ə)l\ city Bismarck archipelago at E end of New Britain; formerly ✻ of Territory of New Guinea *pop* 14,973

Rabbah, Rabbath — *see* AMMAN

Race, Cape \'rās\ headland, SE point of Newfoundland, Canada

Ra·ci·bórz \rät-'sē-‚bùsh\ *or G* Ra·ti·bor \'rät-ə-‚bò(ə)r\ city SW Poland in Silesia on the Oder *pop* 57,182

Ra·cine \rə-'sēn, rā-\ city SE Wis. S of Milwaukee *pop* 85,725

Rad·nor \'rad-nər, -‚nò(ə)r\ *or* Rad·nor·shire \-‚shi(ə)r, -shər\ former county E Wales ✻ Llandrindod Wells

Ra·dom \'räd-‚òm\ commune Poland NE of Kielce *pop* 194,381

Raetia — *see* RHAETIA — Rae·tian \'rē-shən\ *adj or n*

Rages — *see* RHAGES

Ra·gu·sa \rə-'gü-zə\ commune Italy in SE Sicily *pop* 63,898

Rah·way \'rò-‚wā\ city NE N.J. SW of Elizabeth *pop* 26,723

Ra·ia·téa \‚rī-ə-'tā-ə\ island S Pacific in Leeward group of the Society islands WNW of Tahiti *area* 75 *sq mi* (195 *sq km*)

Rainbow Bridge National Monument reservation S Utah near Ariz. boundary containing Rainbow Bridge (large natural bridge)

Rai·nier, Mount \rə-'ni(ə)r, rā-\ *or formerly* Mount Ta·co·ma \tə-'kō-mə\ mountain 14,410 *ft* (4392 *m*) W *cen* Wash., highest in the Cascade range & in Wash.; in Mount Rainier National Park

Rainy \'rā-nē\   1 river 80 *mi* (129 *km*) on Canada-U.S. boundary bet. Ont. & Minn. flowing from Rainy lake into Lake of the Woods   2 lake Canada & U.S. bet. Ont. & Minn. *area* 366 *sq mi* (952 *sq km*)

Rai·pur \'rī-‚pù(ə)r\ city E India in SE Madhya Pradesh E of Nagpur *pop* 338,973

Rai·sin \'rāz-ʼn\ river 150 *mi* (241 *km*) SE Mich. flowing into Lake Erie

Ra·jah·mun·dry \‚räj-ə-'mùn-drē\ city E India in E Andhra Pradesh on Godavari river W of Kakinada *pop* 267,749

Ra·ja·sthan \'räj-ə-‚stän\ state NW India bordering on Pakistan ✻ Jaipur *area* 132,077 *sq mi* (343,400 *sq km*), *pop* 34,102,912

Raj·kot \'räj-‚kòt\   1 former state W India in N *cen* Kathiawar peninsula   2 city, its ✻, now in Gujarat *pop* 444,156

Raj·pu·ta·na \‚räj-pə-'tän-ə\ *or* Rajasthan region NW India bordering on Pakistan & including part of Thar desert

Ra·leigh \'ròl-ē, 'räl-ē\ city E *cen* N.C., its ✻ *pop* 150,255

Ra·lik \'räl-ik\ the W chain of the Marshall islands

Ram·a·po \'ram-ə-‚pò\ mountains of the Appalachians N N.J. & S N.Y.; highest point 1164 *ft* (355 *m*)

Ra·mat Gan \rə-'mät-‚gän\ city W Israel E of Tel Aviv *pop* 120,900

Ram·bouil·let \‚rän-bü-'yä\ town N France SW of Paris *pop* 18,446

Ram·gan·ga \räm-'gəŋ-gə\ river 370 *mi* (595 *km*) N India in Uttar Pradesh flowing S into the Ganges

Ram·pur \'räm-‚pù(ə)r\   1 former state N India NW of Bareilly, now in Uttar Pradesh   2 city, its ✻, ENE of Delhi *pop* 203,491

Rams·gate \'ramz-‚gāt, -gət\ borough SE England in Kent on North sea N of Dover *pop* 39,642

Ran·chi \'rän-chē\ city E India in Bihar NW of Calcutta *pop* 500,593

Ran·ders \'rän-ərs\ city & port NE Denmark *pop* 62,232

Ran·dolph \'ran-‚dälf\ town E Mass. S of Boston *pop* 28,218

Range·ley Lakes \'ranj-lē\ chain of lakes W Maine & N N.H.

Ran·goon \ran-'gün, raŋ-\   1 *or* Yangon river 185 *mi* (298 *km*) S Myanmar, the E outlet of the Irrawaddy   2 — *see* YANGON

Ran·noch, Loch \'ran-ək, -ok\ lake 9 *mi* (14 *km*) long *cen* Scotland

Rann of Kutch — *see* KUTCH (Rann of)

Ran·toul \ran-'tül\ village E Ill. NNE of Champaign *pop* 20,161

Ra·pa \'räp-ə\ island S Pacific in SE Tubuai group *area* 15 *sq mi* (39 *sq km*)

Ra·pal·lo \rə-'päl-(‚)ò\ commune NW Italy in Liguria ESE of Genoa on Gulf of Rapallo (inlet of Ligurian sea) *pop* 28,318

Rapa Nui — *see* EASTER

Rap·i·dan \‚rap-ə-'dan\ river 70 *mi* (113 *km*) N Va. rising in Blue Ridge mountains & flowing E into the Rappahannock

Rap·id City \‚rap-əd-\ city W S.Dak. in Black hills *pop* 46,492

Rap·pa·han·nock \‚rap-ə-'han-ək\ river 185 *mi* (298 *km*) NE Va. flowing into Chesapeake bay

Rap·ti \'räp-tē\ river 400 *mi* (644 *km*) Nepal & N India flowing SE into the Gogra

Rar·i·tan \'rar-ət-ʼn\ river 75 *mi* (121 *km*) N *cen* N.J. flowing E into Raritan Bay (inlet of the Atlantic S of Staten Is., N.Y.)

Rar·o·ton·ga \‚rar-ə-'tän-(g)ə\ island S Pacific in SW part of Cook islands; site of Avarua, ✻ of the group

Ras al Khai·mah \‚räs-äl-'kī-mə, -'ki-\ sheikhdom, member of United Arab Emirates

Ras Da·shan \‚räs-də-'shän\ mountain 15,158 *ft* (4260 *m*) N Ethiopia NE of Lake Tana; highest in Ethiopia

Ras el Tib — *see* BON (Cape)

Rashid — *see* ROSETTA

Rasht \'rasht\ city NW Iran near the Caspian *pop* 187,203

Rat \'rat\ islands SW Alaska in W Aleutians — *see* AMCHITKA, KISKA

Ra·tak \'rä-‚täk\ the E chain of the Marshall islands

Rath·mines and Rath·gar \rath-ˈmīn-zən-(ˌ)rath-ˈgär\ town E Ireland, S suburb of Dublin

Ra·ton \ra-ˈtōn, rə-, -ˈtün; *usu* -ˈtōn *in N Mex*, -ˈtün *in Colo*\ pass 7834 *ft* (2388 *m*) SE Colo. just N of Colo.-N.Mex. border in **Raton range** (E spur of Sangre de Cristo mountains)

Ra·ven·na \rə-ˈven-ə\ commune N Italy NE of Florence *pop* 137,597

Ra·vi \ˈräv-ē\ *or anc* **Hy·dra·o·tes** \ˌhī-drə-ˈōt-(ˌ)ēz\ river 450 *mi* (724 *km*) N India flowing SW to the Chenab & forming part of boundary bet. E. Punjab (India) & W. Punjab (Pakistan)

Ra·wal·pin·di \ˌrä-wəl-ˈpin-dē, raụl-ˈ, rōl-ˈ\ city NE Pakistan NNW of Lahore *pop* 966,000

Ray·town \ˈrā-ˌtaụn\ city W Mo. SE of Kansas City *pop* 31,759

Read·ing \ˈred-iŋ\ **1** town E Mass. N of Boston *pop* 22,678 **2** city SE Pa. on the Schuylkill *pop* 78,686 **3** borough S England ✱ of Berkshire *pop* 123,731

Re·bild \ˈrā-ˌbil\ village N Denmark in N Jutland S of Ålborg in **Rebild hills** (site of **Rebild National Park**)

Re·ci·fe \rə-ˈsē-fə\ *or formerly* **Per·nam·bu·co** \ˌpər-nəm-ˈb(y)ü-(ˌ)kō, ˌper-nəm-ˈbü-\ city & port NE Brazil ✱ of Pernambuco state *municipal area pop* 1,204,738

Reck·ling·hau·sen \ˌrek-liŋ-ˈhauz-ᵊn\ city W W. Germany SW of Münster *pop* 119,418

Red \ˈred\ **1** sea 1450 *mi* (2334 *km*) long bet. Arabia & NE Africa **2** river 1018 *mi* (1638 *km*) flowing E on Okla.-Tex. boundary & into the Atchafalaya & Mississippi in La. **3** river 310 *mi* (499 *km*) N *cen* U.S. & S *cen* Canada flowing N on Minn.-N.Dak. boundary & into Lake Winnipeg in Man. **4** — see ARCTIC RED **5** *or* **Hong** \ˈhȯŋ\ *or* (*in China*) **Yuan** \yü-ˈän\ river 500 *mi* (805 *km*) SE Asia rising in *cen* Yunnan, China, & flowing SE across N Vietnam into Gulf of Tonkin

Red·bridge \ˈred-(ˌ)brij\ borough of NE Greater London, England *pop* 229,800

Red Deer **1** river 385 *mi* (620 *km*) Canada in S Alta. flowing E & SE into the S. Saskatchewan **2** city Canada in S *cen* Alta. S of Edmonton *pop* 46,393

Red·ding \ˈred-iŋ\ city N Calif. *pop* 41,995

Red Lake lake 38 *mi* (61 *km*) long N Minn. divided into **Upper Red Lake** & **Lower Red Lake**; drained by **Red Lake river** (135 *mi or* 216 *km* flowing W into Red river)

Red·lands \ˈred-lən(d)z\ city S Calif. SE of San Bernardino *pop* 43,619

Re·don·do Beach \ri-ˈdän-dō\ city SW Calif. *pop* 57,102

Red Volta river 200 *mi* (322 *km*) S Upper Volta & N Ghana flowing into Lake Volta

Red·wood City \ˈred-ˌwu̇d\ city W Calif. SE of San Francisco *pop* 54,951

Redwood National Park reservation NW Calif.; groves of redwoods

Reel·foot \ˈrē(ə)l-ˌfu̇t\ lake NW Tenn. near the Mississippi

Re·gens·burg \ˈrā-gənz-ˌbərg, -ˌbu̇(ə)rg\ city SE W. Germany in Bavaria on the Danube NNE of Munich *pop* 132,604

Reg·gane \re-ˈgän, -ˈgan\ oasis *cen* Algeria in Tanezrouft SSE of Béchar

Reg·gio \ˈrej-(ē-)(ˌ)ō\ **1** *or* **Reggio di Ca·la·bria** \-ˌdē-kə-ˈläb-rē-ə\ *or* **Reggio Calabria** *or anc* **Rhe·gi·um** \ˈrē-jē-əm\ commune & port S Italy on Strait of Messina *pop* 171,324 **2** *or* **Reggio nel·l'Emi·lia** \-ˌnel-ə-ˈmēl-yə\ *or* **Reggio Emilia** commune N Italy in Emilia-Romagna NW of Bologna *pop* 129,893

Re·gi·na \ri-ˈjī-nə\ city Canada ✱ of Sask. *pop* 162,613

Reims *or* **Rheims** \ˈrēmz, *F* raⁿs\ city NE France ENE of Paris *pop* 177,320

Reindeer lake Canada on Man.-Sask. border *area* 2444 *sq mi* (6354 *sq km*)

Re·ma·gen \ˈrā-ˌmäg-ən\ town W W. Germany on W bank of the Rhine NW of Koblenz

Rem·scheid \ˈrem-ˌshīt\ city W W. Germany in N. Rhine-Westphalia ESE of Düsseldorf *pop* 129,082

Ren·do·va \ren-ˈdō-və\ island W Pacific in *cen* Solomon islands off SW *cen* coast of New Georgia Is.

Ren·frew \ˈren-ˌfrü\ *or* **Ren·frew·shire** \-ˌshi(ə)r, -shər\ former county SW Scotland ✱ Paisley

Rennes \ˈren\ city NW France N of Nantes *pop* 194,094

Re·no \ˈrē-(ˌ)nō\ city W Nev. NNE of Lake Tahoe *pop* 100,756

Ren·ton \ˈrent-ᵊn\ city W Wash. SE of Seattle *pop* 30,612

Re·pen·ti·gny \rə-ˌpäⁿ-tēn-ˈyē\ town Canada in S Que. N of Montreal *pop* 34,419

Republican river 445 *mi* (716 *km*) Nebr. & Kans. rising in E Colo. & flowing E to unite with the Smoky Hill forming Kansas river

Re·si·ta \ˈresh-ət-ˌsä\ *or* **Re·ci·ta** \ˈrech-\ commune SW Romania SE of Arad *pop* 90,698

Re·thondes \rə-tōⁿd\ village N France E of Compiègne

Ré·union \rē-ˈyün-yən\ island W Indian ocean in the W Mascarenes ✱ St.-Denis; an overseas department of France *area* 970 *sq mi* (2522 *sq km*), *pop* 476,675

Reut·ling·en \ˈrȯit-liŋ-ən\ city S W. Germany in Baden-Württemberg S of Stuttgart *pop* 95,456

Revel — see TALLIN

Re·vere \ri-ˈvi(ə)r\ city E Mass. NE of Boston *pop* 42,423

Re·vil·la·gi·ge·do \ri-ˌvil-ə-gə-ˈgēd-(ˌ)ō\ island SE Alaska in SE Alexander archipelago E of Prince of Wales Is.

Re·vi·lla Gi·ge·do \ri-ˌvē-(y)ə-hi-ˈhād-(ˌ)ō\ islands Mexico in the Pacific SW of S end of Baja California

Reyes, Point \ˈrāz\ cape W Calif. at S extremity of peninsula extending into the Pacific NW of Golden Gate

Reyk·ja·vík \ˈrāk-(y)ə-ˌvik, -ˌvēk\ city & port ✱ of Iceland *pop* 83,766

Reyn·olds·burg \ˈren-ᵊl(d)z-ˌbərg\ village *cen* Ohio *pop* 20,661

Rey·no·sa \rā-ˈnō-sə\ city NE Mexico in Tamaulipas on the Rio Grande *pop* 181,646

Re·zā·ˈīyeh \rə-ˈzī-(y)ə\ **1** *or* **Lake Ur·mia** \ˈu̇r-mē-ə\ shallow saline lake NW Iran **2** — see URMIA

Rhae·tia *or* **Rae·tia** \ˈrē-sh(ē-)ə\ ancient Roman province *cen* Europe S of the Danube including most of modern Tirol & Vorarlberg region of Austria & Graubünden canton of E Switzerland — **Rhae·tian** \-shən\ *adj or n*

Rhaetian Alps section of Alps E Switzerland in E Graubünden — see BERNINA

Rha·ges \ˈrā-jəz\ *or* **Rha·gae** \-(ˌ)jē\ *or bib* **Ra·ges** \ˈrā-jəz\ city of ancient Media; ruins at modern village of **Rai** \ˈrī\ S of Tehran, Iran

Rhein·fall \ˈrīn-ˌfäl\ waterfall in the Rhine N Switzerland 370 *ft* (113 *m*) wide, with two principal falls 50 *ft* (15 *m*) & 60 *ft* (18 *m*) high

Rheinpfalz — see PALATINATE

Rhenish Palatinate *or* **Rhine Palatinate** — see PALATINATE

Rheydt \ˈrīt\ city W W. Germany S of München-Gladbach *pop* 100,300

Rhine \ˈrīn\ *or G* **Rhein** \ˈrīn\ *or F* **Rhin** \raⁿ\ *or D* **Rijn** \ˈrīn\ river 820 *mi* (1320 *km*) W Europe flowing from SE Switzerland to North sea in the Netherlands; forms W boundary of Liechtenstein & Austria & SW boundary of W. Germany — **Rhe·nish** \ˈren-ish, ˈrē-nish\ *adj*

Rhine·land \ˈrīn-ˌland, -lənd\ *or G* **Rhein·land** \ˈrīn-ˌlänt\ **1** the part of W. Germany W of the Rhine **2** RHINE PROVINCE — **Rhine·land·er** \ˈrīn-ˌlan-dər, -lən-\ *n*

Rhineland–Palatinate *or G* **Rheinland–Pfalz** \-ˈ(p)fälts\ state of W. Germany chiefly W of the Rhine ✱ Mainz *area* 7654 *sq mi* (19,900 *sq km*), *pop* 3,642,482

Rhine Province *or* **Rhenish Prussia** former province of Prussia, Germany, bordering on Belgium ✱ Koblenz

Rhode Is·land \rō-ˈdī-lənd\ **1** *or officially* **Rhode Island and Providence Plantations** state NE U.S. ✱ Providence *area* 1214 *sq mi* (3156 *sq km*), *pop* 947,154 **2** — see AQUIDNECK — **Rhode Is·land·er** \-lən-dər\ *n*

Rhodes \ˈrōdz\ *or NGk* **Ró·dhos** \ˈrō-ˌt͟hȯs\ **1** island Greece in the SE Aegean, chief island of the Dodecanese *area* 545 *sq mi* (1417 *sq km*) **2** city, its ✱ *pop* 40,656 — **Rho·di·an** \ˈrōd-ē-ən\ *adj or n*

Rho·de·sia \rō-ˈdē-zh(ē-)ə\ **1** region *cen* S Africa S of Zaire comprising Zambia & Zimbabwe; contains rich archaeological findings **2** — see ZIMBABWE 2 — **Rho·de·sian** \-zh(ē-)ən\ *adj or n*

Rhodesia and Nyasaland, Federation of former country S Africa comprising S. Rhodesia, N. Rhodesia, & Nyasaland; a federal state within the Commonwealth; dissolved 1963

Rhod·o·pe \ˈräd-ə-(ˌ)pē\ mountains S Bulgaria & NE Greece; highest Musala 9596 *ft* (2925 *m*)

Rhon·dda \ˈrän-də, ˈ(h)rän-t͟hə\ borough SE Wales in Mid Glamorgan *pop* 81,725

Rhône \ˈrōn\ river 500 *mi* (805 *km*) Switzerland & France rising in the Alps and flowing through Lake of Geneva into Gulf of Lions inlet of the Mediterranean

Rhyl \ˈril\ town & port NE Wales in Clwyd at mouth of the Clwyd *pop* 22,714

Ri·al·to \rē-ˈal-(ˌ)tō\ **1** city SW Calif. W of San Bernardino *pop* 37,474 **2** island & district of Venice, Italy

Ri·au *or formerly* **Ri·ouw** \ˈrē-ˌaụ\ archipelago Indonesia S of Singapore; chief island Bintan *area* 2279 *sq mi* (5925 *sq km*), *pop* 278,966

Ri·bei·rão Prê·to \ˌrē-və-ˈraụⁿ-ˈprā-(ˌ)tü\ city SE Brazil in N *cen* São Paulo state *pop* 318,375

Rich·ard·son \ˈrich-ərd-sən\ city NE Tex. N of Dallas *pop* 72,496

Rich·e·lieu \ˈrish-ə-ˌlü\ river 210 *mi* (338 *km*) Canada in S Que. flowing N from Lake Champlain to head of Lake St. Peter in the St. Lawrence

Rich·field \ˈrich-ˌfēld\ village SE Minn.; a S suburb of Minneapolis *pop* 37,851

Rich·land \ˈrich-lənd\ city SE Wash. at confluence of Yakima & Columbia rivers *pop* 33,578

Rich·mond \ˈrich-mənd\ **1** city W Calif. NNW of Oakland on San Francisco Bay *pop* 74,676 **2** city E Ind. *pop* 41,349 **3** city *cen* Ky. *pop* 21,705 **4** borough of New York City — see STATEN ISLAND **5** city ✱ of Va. on the James *pop* 219,214 **6** *or* **Richmond upon Thames** royal borough of SW Greater London, England *pop* 163,000 — **Rich·mond·er** \-mən-dər\ *n*

Richmond Hill town Canada in SE Ont. N of Toronto *pop* 37,778

Ri·deau \ri-ˈdō\ canal system Canada 126 *mi* (203 *km*) long in SE Ont. connecting Lake Ontario & Ottawa river & including **Rideau Lake** (20 *mi or* 32 *km* long) & **Rideau River** (flowing into the Ottawa)

Ridge·field \ˈrij-ˌfēld\ town SW Conn. NW of Norwalk *pop* 20,120

Ridge·wood \ˈrij-ˌwu̇d\ village NE N.J. NNE of Paterson *pop* 25,208

Rid·ing Mountain National Park \ˌrīd-iŋ-\ reservation Canada in SW Man.; has game preserve

Rif — see ER RIF

Rift valley GREAT RIFT VALLEY

Ri·ga \ˈrē-gə\ city & port U.S.S.R. ✱ of Latvia at S extremity of the Gulf of Riga *pop* 835,000

Riga, Gulf of inlet of Baltic sea bordering on Estonia & Latvia

Ri·je·ka *or* **Ri·e·ka** \rē-ˈ(y)ek-ə\ *or It* **Fiu·me** \ˈfyü-(ˌ)mā, fē-ˈü-\ city & port NW Yugoslavia in Croatia *pop* 128,883

Rijs·wijk \ˈrīs-ˌvīk\ commune SW Netherlands *pop* 50,514

Ri·mac \ˈrē-ˌmäk\ river 80 *mi* (129 *km*) W Peru flowing SW through Lima into the Pacific

Ri·mi·ni \ˈrim-ə-(ˌ)nē, ˈrē-mə-\ *or anc* **Arim·i·num** \ə-ˈrim-ə-nəm\ commune & port N Italy on the Adriatic ESE of Ravenna *pop* 126,949

Ri·mou·ski \rim-ˈü-skē\ city Canada in E Que. on Gaspé peninsula *pop* 29,120

Rio \ˈrē-(ˌ)ō\ RIO DE JANEIRO

Rio Bran·co \ˌrē-(ˌ)ō-ˈbraŋ-(ˌ)kō\ **1** — see BRANCO **2** city W Brazil, ✱ of Acre *municipal area pop* 117,113

Rio de Ja·nei·ro \ˈrē-(ˌ)ō-ˌdā-zhə-ˈne(ə)r-(ˌ)ō, -ˌdē-, -də-, -jə-ˈne(ə)r-, -ˈni(ə)r-\ **1** state SE Brazil *area* 16,832 *sq mi* (43,763 *sq km*), *pop* 11,489,797 **2** city, its ✱ & port on Guanabara Bay; former ✱ of Brazil *pop* 5,093,232

Río de la Plata — see PLATA (Río de la)

Río de Oro \ˌrē-(ˌ)ōd-ē-ˈōr-(ˌ)ō, -ˈȯr-\ territory NW Africa comprising the S zone of Western Sahara

Rio Grande \ˌrē-(ˌ)ō-ˈgrand(-ē) *also* ˌrī-ō-ˈgrand\ **1** *or MexSp* **Río Bravo** \ˌrē-(ˌ)ō-ˈbräv-(ˌ)ō\ river 1885 *mi* (3034 *km*) SW U.S. forming part of Mexico-U.S. boundary & flowing from San Juan mountains in SW Colo. to Gulf of Mexico **2** *or* **Rio Gran·de do Sul** \ˌrē-ō-ˌgrand-ē-də-ˈsül\ city S Brazil in Rio Grande do Sul state W of entrance to Lagoa dos Patos *pop* 146,214 **3** — see GRANDE (Rio)

Rio Grande de Cagayan — see CAGAYAN

Rio Gran·de do Nor·te \ˌrē-ō-ˌgrand-ē-də-ˈnȯrt-ə\ state NE Brazil ✱ Natal *area* 20,236 *sq mi* (52,614 *sq km*), *pop* 1,933,126

Rio Grande do Sul \-ˈsül\ state SE Brazil bordering on Uruguay ✱ Pôrto Alegre *area* 100,150 *sq mi* (260,390 *sq km*), *pop* 7,942,722

Rioja, the — see LA RIOJA

Río Muni — see MBINI

Río Pie·dras \ˌrē-(ˌ)ō-pē-ˈā-drəs\ former city, since 1951 part of San Juan, Puerto Rico

Rip·on Falls \ˌrip-ən-, -ˌän-\ former waterfall in the Victoria Nile N of Lake Victoria; submerged by Owen Falls Dam
Riv·er·side \ˈriv-ər-ˌsīd\ city S Calif. *pop* 170,876
Riv·i·era \ˌriv-ē-ˈer-ə\ coast region SE France & NW Italy bordering on the Mediterranean — see CÔTE D'AZUR
Riviera Beach city SE Fla. N of W. Palm Beach *pop* 26,489
Ri·yadh \rē-ˈ(y)äd\ city ✻ of the Nejd & of Saudi Arabia *pop* 666,840
Rju·kan \rē-ˈü-ˌkän\ town S Norway W of Oslo near **Rjukan Falls** (waterfall 780 *ft or* 238 *m*)
Ro·a·noke \ˈrō-(ə-)ˌnōk\ **1** river 380 *mi* (612 *km*) S Va. & NE N.C. flowing E & SE into Albemarle Sound **2** island N.C. S of entrance to Albemarle Sound **3** city W *cen* Va. *pop* 100,220
Rob·erts, Point \ˈräb-ərts\ cape NW Wash., tip of a peninsula extending S into Strait of Georgia from B.C. & separated from U.S. mainland by Boundary Bay
Rob·son, Mount \ˈräb-sən\ mountain 12,972 *ft* (3954 *m*) W Canada in E B.C.; highest in Canadian Rockies
Ro·ca, Cape \ˈrō-kə\ *or Pg* **Ca·bo da Ro·ca** \ˌkä-vü-thə-ˈrō-kə\ cape Portugal; westernmost point of continental Europe, at 9°30′W
Roch·dale \ˈräch-ˌdāl\ borough NW England in Greater Manchester NNE of Manchester *pop* 92,704
Roche·fort \rȯsh-ˈfō(ə)r, ˈrōsh-fərt\ *or* **Rochefort–sur–Mer** \-ˌsu̇r-ˈme(ə)r\ city W France SSE of La Rochelle *pop* 27,264
Roch·es·ter \ˈräch-ə-stər, -ˌes-tər\ **1** city SE Minn. *pop* 57,890 **2** city SE N.H. *pop* 21,560 **3** city W N.Y. on the Genesee *pop* 241,741 **4** city SE England in Kent *pop* 52,505
Rock \ˈräk\ river 300 *mi* (483 *km*) S Wis. & N Ill. flowing S & SW into the Mississippi at Rock Island
Rock·all \ˈräk-ˌȯl\ islet N Atlantic NW of Ireland, at 57°36′ N, 13°41′ W
Rock·ford \ˈräk-fərd\ city N Ill. NW of Chicago *pop* 139,712
Rock·hamp·ton \räk-ˈ(h)am(p)-tən\ city & port E Australia in E Queensland on Fitzroy river *pop* 52,383
Rock Hill city N S.C. SSW of Charlotte, N.C. *pop* 35,344
Rock Island city NW Ill. on the Mississippi *pop* 47,036
Rock Springs city SW Wyo. near Utah border *pop* 19,458
Rock·ville \ˈräk-ˌvil, -vəl\ city SW Md. *pop* 43,811
Rockville Centre village SE N.Y. in W *cen* Long Is. *pop* 25,412
Rocky \ˈräk-ē\ mountains W N. America extending from N Alaska SE to N.Mex. — see ELBERT (Mount), ROBSON (Mount)
Rocky Mount city NE *cen* N.C. *pop* 41,283
Rocky Mountain National Park reservation N Colo.
Rocky River city NE Ohio on Lake Erie W of Cleveland *pop* 21,084
Ródhos — see RHODES
Ro·dri·gues *or* **Ro·dri·guez** \rō-ˈdrē-gəs\ island Indian ocean in the Mascarenes; a dependency of Mauritius; chief town Port Mathurin *area* 40 *sq mi* (104 *sq km*), *pop* 18,335
Rog·ers \ˈräj-ərz\ **1** city NW Ark. *pop* 17,429 **2** mountain pass Canada in SE B.C. in Selkirk mountains
Rogue \ˈrōg\ river 220 *mi* (354 *km*) SW Oreg. rising in Crater Lake National Park & flowing W & SW into the Pacific
Ro·hil·khand \ˈrō-ˌhil-ˌkənd\ *or* **Ba·reil·ly** \bə-ˈrā-lē\ region N India in Uttar Pradesh; chief city Bareilly
Rolling Meadows city NE Ill. NW of Chicago *pop* 20,167
Ro·ma·gna \rō-ˈmän-yə\ district N Italy on the Adriatic comprising the E part of Emilia-Romagna region
Roman Campagna — see CAMPAGNA DI ROMA
Ro·ma·nia \rō-ˈmā-nē-ə, -nyə\ *or* **Ru·ma·nia** \ru̇-\ country SE Europe bordering on Black sea ✻ Bucharest *area* 91,934 *sq mi* (239,028 *sq km*), *pop* 21,559,910
Rom·blon \räm-ˈblōn\ **1** islands Philippines in N Visayan islands in Sibuyan sea *area* 512 *sq mi* (1331 *sq km*) **2** island in the group
Rome \ˈrōm\ **1** city NW Ga. NW of Atlanta *pop* 29,654 **2** city E *cen* N.Y. NW of Utica *pop* 43,826 **3** *or It* **Ro·ma** \ˈrō-mä\ *or anc* **Ro·ma** \ˈrō-mə\ city ✻ of Italy on the Tiber *pop* 2,830,569 **4** the Roman Empire
Rome, Duchy of division of Byzantine Empire 6th to 8th century *cen* Italy comprising most of modern Latium; later a province of the States of the Church called **Patrimony of Saint Pe·ter** \ˈpēt-ər\
Rom·ford \ˈräm(p)-fərd, ˈrəm(p)-\ former municipal borough SE England in Essex, now part of Havering
Rom·u·lus \ˈräm-yə-ləs\ city SE Mich. *pop* 24,857
Ron·ces·va·lles \ˌrōn(t)-səs-ˈvī-əs\ *or F* **Ron·ce·vaux** \rō^{n}s-(ə-)vō\ commune N Spain 5 *mi* (8 *km*) from French boundary in the Pyrenees near **Pass of Roncesvalles**
Ron·dô·nia \rō^{n}(n)-ˈdōn-yə\ *or formerly* **Gua·po·ré** \ˌgwäp-ə-ˈrā\ state W Brazil ✻ Porto Velho *area* 96,986 *sq mi* (252,164 *sq km*), *pop* 503,125
Rong·er·ik \ˈräŋ-ə-ˌrik, ˈrȯŋ-\ island W *cen* Pacific in the Marshalls in Ratak chain E of Bikini
Ron·ne Ice Shelf \ˈrō-nə, ˈrən-ə\ area of shelf ice Antarctica in Weddell sea
Roo·de·poort–Ma·rais·burg \ˈrōd-ə-ˌpō(ə)rt-mə-ˈrā-ˌbərg, ˈrō-i-ˌpō(ə)rt, -ˌpō(ə)rt\ city Republic of S. Africa in Transvaal W of Johannesburg
Roo·se·velt \ˈrō-zə-ˌvelt, -vəlt *also* ˈrü-\ river 200 *mi* (322 *km*) W *cen* Brazil flowing from W Mato Grosso state N into the Aripuanã
Ro·rai·ma \rō-ˈrī-mə\ mountain 9094 *ft* (2772 *m*) N S. America in Serra Pacaraima on boundary bet. Venezuela, Guyana, & Brazil; has flat top
Ror·schach \ˈrō(ə)r-ˌshäk, ˈrō(ə)r-, -ˌshäk\ commune NE Switzerland on S shore of Lake Constance *pop* 9878
Ro·sa, Mon·te \ˌmōnt-ē-ˈrō-zə\ mountain 15,203 *ft* (4634 *m*) on Swiss-Italian border; highest in Pennine Alps
Ro·sa·rio \rō-ˈzär-ē-ˌō, -ˈsär-\ city E *cen* Argentina on the Paraná *pop* 591,428
Ros·com·mon \rä-ˈskäm-ən\ **1** county *cen* Ireland in Connacht *area* 951 *sq mi* (2473 *sq km*), *pop* 54,543 **2** town, its ✻ *pop* 1673
Rose, Mount \ˈrōz\ mountain 10,788 *ft* (3285 *m*) W Nev. in Carson range SW of Reno
Ro·seau \rō-ˈzō\ seaport ✻ of Dominica *pop* 10,157
Rose·burg \ˈrōz-ˌbərg\ city SW Oreg. E of Coos Bay *pop* 16,644
Ro·selle \rō-ˈzel\ **1** city NE Ill. *pop* 16,948 **2** borough NE N.J. W of Elizabeth *pop* 20,641
Rose·mead \ˈrōz-ˌmēd\ city SW Calif. E of Los Angeles *pop* 42,604
Ro·sen·berg \ˈrōz-ᵊn-ˌbərg\ city SE Tex. *pop* 17,995
Ro·set·ta \rō-ˈzet-ə\ *or* **Ra·shid** \rä-ˈshēd\ *or anc* **Bol·bi·ti·ne** \ˌbäl-bə-ˈtī-nē\ **1** river 146 *mi* (235 *km*) N Egypt forming W branch of the Nile in its delta **2** city N Egypt on the Rosetta *pop* 36,711
Rose·ville \ˈrōz-ˌvil\ **1** city W Calif. NE of Sacramento *pop* 24,347 **2** city SE Mich. NE of Detroit *pop* 54,311 **3** village SE Minn. N of St. Paul *pop* 35,820
Ross \ˈrȯs\ sea, arm of S Pacific extending into Antarctica E of Victoria Land
Ross and Crom·ar·ty \ˈkräm-ərt-ē\ former county N Scotland ✻ Dingwall
Rossbodenhorn — see FLETSCHHORN
Ross Dependency section of Antarctica lying bet. 160°E and 150°W long.; claimed by New Zealand
Ross Ice Shelf area of shelf ice Antarctica in S Ross sea
Ros·tock \ˈräs-ˌtäk, ˈrō-ˌstȯk\ city & port N E. Germany on Warnow river near the Baltic coast *pop* 234,475
Ros·tov \rə-ˈstȯf, -ˈstȯv\ *or* **Rostov–on–Don** \-ˌȯn-ˈdän, -ˌän-\ city U.S.S.R. in SE Soviet Russia, Europe, on the Don *pop* 789,000
Ros·well \ˈräz-ˌwel, -wəl\ **1** city NW *cen* Ga. N of Atlanta *pop* 23,337 **2** city SE N.Mex. *pop* 39,676
Ro·ta \ˈrōt-ə\ **1** island W Pacific at S end of the Marianas *area* 35 *sq mi* (91 *sq km*) **2** town & port SW Spain on the Atlantic NW of Cádiz
Roth·er·ham \ˈräth-ə-rəm\ borough N England in S. Yorkshire NE of Sheffield *pop* 81,988
Rothe·say \ˈräth-sē\ royal burgh SW Scotland on island of Bute in Strathclyde *pop* 5408
Ro·to·rua \ˌrōt-ə-ˈrü-ə\ city New Zealand in N *cen* North Is. *pop* 38,157
Rot·ter·dam \ˈrät-ər-ˌdam\ city & port SW Netherlands on the Nieuwe Maas *pop* 558,814 — **Rot·ter·dam·mer** \-ər\ *n*
Ro·tu·ma \rō-ˈtü-mə\ island SW Pacific N of Fiji islands *area* 14 *sq mi* (36 *sq km*); belongs to Fiji
Rou·baix \rü-ˈbā\ city N France NE of Lille *pop* 109,473
Rou·en \rü-ˈä^{n}(n)\ city & port N France on the Seine *pop* 113,536
Rous·sil·lon \ˌrü-sē-ˈ(y)ō^{n}\ region & former province S France bordering on the Pyrenees & the Mediterranean ✻ Perpignan
Rou·yn \ˈrü-ən, ru̇-ˈa^{n}\ city Canada in SW Que. *pop* 17,224
Rox·burgh \ˈräks-ˌbər-ə, -ˌbə-rə, -b(ə-)rə\ *or* **Rox·burgh·shire** \-ˌshi(ə)r, -shər\ former county SE Scotland ✻ Jedburgh
Roy \ˈrȯi\ city NE Utah SW of Ogden *pop* 19,694
Royal Gorge section of the canyon of Arkansas river S *cen* Colo.
Royal Leamington Spa — see LEAMINGTON
Royal Oak city SE Mich. N of Detroit *pop* 70,893
Royal Tun·bridge Wells \-ˌtən-brij-\ borough SE England in Kent *pop* 44,506
Ruad — see ARWAD
Ru·an·da–Urun·di \ru̇-ˌän-də-u̇-ˈrün-dē\ *or* **Belgian East Africa** former country E *cen* Africa bordering on Lake Tanganyika & comprising two districts, **Ruanda** (✻ Kigali) & **Urundi** (✻ Usumbura), administered by Belgium under League of Nations mandate 1919–45 & under U.N. trusteeship 1946–62 ✻ Usumbura — see BURUNDI, RWANDA
Ru·a·pe·hu \ˌrü-ə-ˈpā-(ˌ)hü\ volcano 9175 *ft* (2796 *m*) New Zealand, highest peak in North Is., in Tongariro National Park
Rub' al Kha·li \ˌru̇b-al-ˈkäl-ē, *Ar* -ˈkäl-\ desert region S Arabia extending from Nejd S to Hadhramaut *area* 300,000 *sq mi* (780,000 *sq km*)
Ru·bi·con \ˈrü-bi-ˌkän\ river 15 *mi* (24 *km*) N *cen* Italy flowing E into the Adriatic
Ru·dolf, Lake \ˈrü-ˌdälf\ *or* **Lake Tur·kana** \tər-ˈkan-ə\ lake N Kenya in Great Rift valley *area* 3500 *sq mi* (9100 *sq km*)
Ru·fisque \rü-ˈfēsk\ city & port W Senegal *pop* 47,000
Rug·by \ˈrəg-bē\ borough *cen* England in Warwick on the Avon *pop* 59,564
Rü·gen \ˈrü-gən, ˈrue̅-\ island N E. Germany in Baltic sea off coast of Pomerania *area* 374 *sq mi* (972 *sq km*); chief town Bergen
Ruhr \ˈru̇(ə)r\ **1** river 144 *mi* (232 *km*) *cen* W. Germany flowing NW & W to the Rhine **2** industrial district in valley of the Ruhr
Ruis·lip North·wood \ˌrī-sləp-ˈnȯrth-ˌwu̇d\ former urban district S England in Middlesex, now part of Hillingdon
Ru·me·lia *or* **Rou·me·lia** \ru̇-ˈmēl-yə, -ˈmē-lē-ə\ a division of the old Ottoman Empire including Albania, Macedonia, & Thrace
Run·ny·mede \ˈrən-ē-ˌmēd\ meadow S England in Surrey at Egham on S bank of the Thames
Ru·pert \ˈrü-pərt\ river 380 *mi* (612 *km*) Canada in W Que. flowing W into James Bay
Rupert's Land PRINCE RUPERT'S LAND
Ru·se \ˈrü-(ˌ)sā\ *or Turk* **Rus·chuk** \ru̇s-ˈchük\ city NE Bulgaria on the Danube S of Bucharest *pop* 159,578
Rush·more, Mount \ˈrəsh-ˌmō(ə)r, -ˌmȯ(ə)r\ mountain 5600 *ft* (1707 *m*) W S.Dak. in Black hills on which are carved faces of Washington, Jefferson, Lincoln, Theodore Roosevelt; a national memorial
Rus·sell Cave National Monument \ˌrəs-əl-\ reservation NE Ala. including cavern where remains of early pre-Columbian humans have been found
Rus·sia \ˈrəsh-ə\ *or Russ* **Ros·si·ya** \rä-ˈsē-(y)ə\ **1** former empire E Europe & N Asia coextensive (except for Finland & Kars region) with the present U.S.S.R. ✻ Petrograd **2** RUSSIAN REPUBLIC **3** the U.S.S.R.
Russian Republic — see SOVIET RUSSIA
Russian Turkestan region comprising the republics of Soviet Central Asia
Rus·ton \ˈrəs-tən\ city N La. *pop* 20,585
Ru·the·nia \ru̇-ˈthē-nyə, -nē-ə\ *or* **Carpathian Ruthenia** *or* **Za·kar·pat·ska·ya** \ˌzäk-ər-ˈpät-skə-yə\ region U.S.S.R. in W Ukrainian Republic S of the Carpathian mountains; part of Hungary before 1918 & 1939–45; a province of Czechoslovakia 1918–38 ✻ Uzhgorod — **Ru·thene** \-ˈthēn\ *n* — **Ru·the·nian** \-ˈthē-nyən, -nē-ən\ *adj or n*
Ruth·er·ford \ˈrəth-ə(r)-fərd, ˈrəth-\ borough NE N.J. SSE of Paterson on Passaic river *pop* 19,068

\ə\ abut \ᵊ\ kitten, F table \ər\ further \a\ ash \ā\ ace \ä\ cot, cart
\au̇\ out \ch\ chin \e\ bet \ē\ easy \g\ go \i\ hit \ī\ ice \j\ job
\ŋ\ sing \ō\ go \ȯ\ law \ȯi\ boy \th\ thin \th\ the \ü\ loot \u̇\ foot
\y\ yet \zh\ vision \á, k, ^{n}, œ, œ̄, ue, ue̅, ʸ\ *see* Guide to Pronunciation

Rut·land \'rət-lənd\ 1 city W *cen* Vt. *pop* 18,436 2 *or* **Rut·land·shire** \-lən(d)-,shi(ə)r, -shər\ former county E *cen* England ✱ Oakham

Ru·vu·ma *or Pg* **Ro·vu·ma** \rü-'vü-mə\ river 400 *mi* (644 *km*) SE Africa rising in S Tanganyika & flowing E into Indian ocean

Ru·wen·zo·ri \,rü-(w)ən-'zōr-ē, -'zȯr-\ mountain group E *cen* Africa bet. Lake Albert & Lake Edward, on boundary bet. Uganda & Zaire — see STANLEY (Mount)

Rwan·da \rü-'än-də\ *or formerly* **Ru·an·da** country E *cen* Africa; a republic ✱ Kigali *area* 10,166 *sq mi* (26,432 *sq km*), *pop* 4,819,317 — see RUANDA-URUNDI — **Rwan·dan** \-dən\ *adj or n*

Rya·zan \,rē-ə-'zan(-yə)\ city U.S.S.R. in *cen* Soviet Russia, Europe, on Oka river SE of Moscow *pop* 351,000

Ry·binsk \'rib-ən(t)sk\ *or 1946–57* **Shcher·ba·kov** \,sh(ch)er-bə-'kȯf\ *or 1984–89* **An·dro·pov** \an-'drō-,pȯf\ city U.S.S.R. in N *cen* Soviet Russia, Europe

Rye \'rī\ borough SE England in E. Sussex *pop* 4293

Ryu·kyu \rē-'(y)ü-(,)k(y)ü\ islands W Pacific extending bet. Kyushu, Japan, & Taiwan; belonged to Japan 1895–1945; occupied by U.S. 1945; returned to Japan in 1953 (N islands) and 1972 (S islands) *area* 1803 *sq mi* (4688 *sq km*) — see AMAMI, OKINAWA, OSUMI, SAKISHIMA, TOKARA — **Ryu·kyu·an** \-,(y)ü-'k(y)ü-ən\ *adj or n*

Saa·le \'zäl-ə, 'säl-\ river 226 *mi* (364 *km*) SW E. Germany rising in NE Bavaria in the Fichtelgebirge & flowing N into the Elbe

Saar \'sär, 'zär\ 1 *or F* **Sarre** \sär\ river 84 *mi* (135 *km*) Europe flowing from Vosges mountains in France N to the Moselle in W. Germany 2 *or* **Saar·land** \'sär-,land, 'zär-\ region W Europe in basin of Saar river bet. France & W. Germany; once part of Lorraine, became part of Germany in 19th century; administered by League of Nations 1919–35; became a state of Germany 1935; came under control of France after World War II; to W. Germany by a plebiscite Jan. 1, 1957, as a state **(Saarland)** ✱ Saarbrücken *area* 898 *sq mi* (2335 *sq km*), *pop* 1,066,299

Saar·brück·en \zär-'brük-ən, sär-, -'brœk-\ city SW W. Germany ✱ of Saarland *pop* 193,554

Saaremaa — see SAREMA

Sa·ba 1 \'sā-bə, 'säb-ə\ island SE W. Indies in Leeward islands; part of Netherlands Antilles ✱ The Bottom *area* 5 *sq mi* (13 *sq km*), *pop* 972 2 — see SHEBA

Sa·ba·dell \,sab-ə-'del\ commune NE Spain NW of Barcelona *pop* 186,123

Sa·bah \'säb-ə\ *or formerly* **North Borneo** state Malaysia in NE Borneo, formerly a Brit. colony ✱ Kota Kinabalu *area* 29,388 *sq mi* (76,409 *sq km*), *pop* 1,002,608

Sa·bar·ma·ti \,säb-ər-'mət-ē\ river 200 *mi* (322 *km*) W India flowing S into head of Gulf of Cambay

Sa·bi \'säb-ē\ *or in Mozambique* **Sa·ve** \'säv-ə\ river 400 *mi* (644 *km*) SE Africa rising in *cen* Zimbabwe & flowing E across S Mozambique to Indian ocean

Sa·bine \sə-'bēn\ river 380 *mi* (612 *km*) E Tex. & W La. flowing SE through **Sabine Lake** (15 *mi or* 24 *km* long) & **Sabine Pass** (channel) into Gulf of Mexico

Sa·ble \'sā-bəl\ island Canada 20 *mi* (32 *km*) long in the Atlantic SE of Cape Canso; belongs to N.S.

Sable, Cape 1 cape at SW tip of Fla., southernmost point of U.S. mainland, at *ab* 25°7'N 2 headland E Canada on an islet S of **Cape Sable Island** (7 *mi or* 11 *km* long, at S end of N.S.)

Sab·ra·tha \'sab-rə-thə\ *or anc* **Sab·ra·ta** \-rət-ə\ town Libya on the coast WNW of Tripoli *pop* 30,836

Sachsen — see SAXONY

Sa·co \'sȯ-(,)kō\ river 104 *mi* (167 *km*) E N.H. & SW Maine flowing SE into the Atlantic

Sac·ra·men·to \,sak-rə-'ment-(,)ō\ 1 mountains S N.Mex. — see GUADALUPE, SIERRA BLANCA PEAK 2 river 382 *mi* (615 *km*) N Calif. flowing S into Suisun Bay 3 city ✱ of Calif. on Sacramento river NE of San Francisco *pop* 275,741

Sa·fed Koh \sə-,fed-'kō\ mountain range E Afghanistan on Pakistan border; a S extension of the Hindu Kush

Sa·fi \'saf-ē\ city & port W Morocco SW of Casablanca *pop* 129,113

Sa·ga·mi \sə-'gäm-ē\ sea, inlet of the Pacific Japan in *cen* Honshu SW of Tokyo Bay

Saghalien — see SAKHALIN

Sag·i·naw \'sag-ə-,nȯ\ city E *cen* Mich. NNW of Flint *pop* 77,508

Saginaw Bay inlet of Lake Huron in E Mich.

Sa·gres \'sag-rēsh\ village SW Portugal E of Cape St. Vincent

Sa·gua·ro National Monument \sə-'wär-ə, -'(g)wär-(,)ō\ reservation SE Ariz. E of Tucson

Sag·ue·nay \'sag-ə-,nā, ,sag-ə-'\ river 125 *mi* (201 *km*) Canada in S Que. flowing from Lake St. John E into the St. Lawrence

Sa·guia el Ham·ra \sə-,gē-ə-,el-'ham-rə\ territory NW Africa, the N zone of Western Sahara

Sa·gun·to \sə-'gün-(,)tō\ *or formerly* **Mur·vie·dro** \,mür-vē-'ā-(,)drō\ commune E Spain NNE of Valencia *pop* 17,052

Sa·ha·ra \sə-'har-ə, -'her-, -'här-\ desert region N Africa N of the Sudan region extending from the Atlantic coast to Red sea or, as sometimes considered, to the Nile — **Sa·ha·ran** \-ən\ *adj*

Sa·ha·ran·pur \sə-'här-ən-,pü(ə)r\ city N India in NW Uttar Pradesh NNE of Delhi *pop* 294,391

Sa·hel \'sa-hil, sə-'hil\ the semidesert S fringe of the Sahara that stretches from Mauritania to Chad

Saida — see SIDON

Saigon — see HO CHI MINH CITY — **Sai·gon·ese** \,sī-gə-'nēz, -'nēs\ *adj or n*

Sai·maa \'sī-,mä\ lake SE Finland, largest of the **Saimaa Lakes**

Saint Al·bans \-'ȯl-bənz\ borough SE England in Hertfordshire *pop* 50,888

Saint Al·bert \-'al-bərt\ town Canada in *cen* Alta. *pop* 31,996

Saint Bar·thé·le·my \sa^n-bär-tā-lə-mē\ island French W. Indies in department of Guadeloupe; chief town Gustavia *pop* 2351

Saint Ber·nard \,sānt-bə(r)-'närd\ two Alpine passes — see GREAT SAINT BERNARD, LITTLE SAINT BERNARD

Saint–Bru·no–de–Mon·tar·ville \sānt-'brü-,nō-də-'mänt-ər-,vil, sənt-\ town Canada in S Que. E of Montreal *pop* 22,880

Saint Cath·a·rines \-'kath-(ə-)rənz\ city Canada in SE Ont. NW of Niagara Falls on Welland ship canal *pop* 124,018

Saint Charles \-'chär(-ə)lz\ 1 city NE Ill. *pop* 17,492 2 city E Mo. on the Missouri *pop* 37,379

Saint Clair, Lake \-'kla(ə)r, -'kle(ə)r\ lake SE Mich. & SE Ont. *area* 460 *sq mi* (1196 *sq km*), connected by **Saint Clair river** (40 *mi or* 64 *km*) with Lake Huron & draining through Detroit river into Lake Erie

Saint Clair Shores city SE Mich. NE of Detroit *pop* 76,210

Saint–Cloud \sant-'klaủd, sənt-; sa^n-klü\ commune France, WSW suburb of Paris *pop* 28,052

Saint Cloud \-'klaủd\ city *cen* Minn. on the Mississippi *pop* 42,566

Saint Croix \sānt-'krȯi, sənt-\ 1 river 75 *mi* (121 *km*) Canada & U.S. bet. N.B. & Maine 2 river 164 *mi* (264 *km*) NW Wis. & E Minn. flowing into the Mississippi 3 *or* **San·ta Cruz** \,sant-ə-'krüz\ island, W. Indies, largest of the Virgin Islands of the U.S. *area* 80 *sq mi* (208 *sq km*); chief town Christiansted

Saint Croix Island International Historic Site reservation E Maine on Canada border on island in Saint Croix river

Saint–Cyr–l'École \sa^n-'si(ə)r-lā-'kəl\ commune N France W of Versailles *pop* 17,795

Saint–De·nis \,sa^n(t)-də-'nē\ 1 commune N France NNE of Paris *pop* 95,808 2 commune ✱ of Réunion Is. *pop* 94,104

Sainte–Foy \sānt-'fȯi, sənt-; sa^{n}t-(ə-)fwä\ city Canada in SE Que. SW of Quebec city *pop* 68,883

Saint Eli·as \,sānt-^{ə}l-'ī-əs\ mountain range of the Coast ranges SW Yukon Territory & E Alaska — see LOGAN (Mount)

Saint Elias, Mount mountain 18,008 *ft* (5489 *m*) on Alaska-Canada boundary in St. Elias range

Sainte–Thé·rèse \,sānt-ə-'rāz\ city Canada in S Que. *pop* 18,750

Saint–Étienne \sa^n-tā-tyen\ city SE *cen* France *pop* 218,289

Saint Eus·tache \,sa^n-tyü-'stash\ town Canada in S Que. *pop* 29,716

Saint Eu·sta·ti·us \,sānt-yü-'stā-sh(ē-)əs\ *or* **Sta·tia** \'stā-shə\ island W. Indies in Netherlands Antilles NW of St. Kitts *area* 7 *sq mi* (18 *sq km*)

Saint Fran·cis \sānt-'fran(t)-səs, sənt-\ 1 river 425 *mi* (684 *km*) SE Mo. & E Ark. flowing S into the Mississippi 2 *or* **Saint Fran·çois** \sa^n-frä^n-swä\ river 165 *mi* (266 *km*) Canada in S Que. flowing NW into the St. Lawrence

Saint Francis, Lake expansion of St. Lawrence river Canada above Valleyfield, Que.

Saint Gall \sānt-'gȯl, sənt-; sa^n-'gäl\ *or G* **Sankt Gal·len** \zäŋ(k)t-'gäl-ən\ 1 canton NE Switzerland *area* 800 *sq mi* (2080 *sq km*), *pop* 391,995 2 commune, its ✱ *pop* 75,847

Saint George's Channel \-,jȯr-jəz-\ strait British Isles bet. SW Wales & Ireland

Saint–Ger·main \,sa^n-zhər-'ma^n\ *or* **Saint–Ger·main–en–Laye** \-,ma^n-,ä^n-'lā\ commune N France WNW of Paris *pop* 35,351

Saint–Gilles \sa^n-'zhē(ə)l\ *or Flem* **Sint–Gil·lis** \sənt-'gil-əs\ commune *cen* Belgium near Brussels *pop* 46,076

Saint Gott·hard \sānt-'gät(h)-ərd, sənt-; ,sa^n-gə-'tär\ 1 mountains Switzerland in Lepontine Alps bet. Uri & Ticino cantons 2 mountain pass 6935 *ft* (2114 *m*) in St. Gotthard range

Saint He·le·na \,sānt-^{ə}l-'ē-nə, ,sānt-hə-'lē-\ island S Atlantic; a Brit. colony ✱ Jamestown *area* 47 *sq mi* (122 *sq km*), *pop* 4829

Saint Hel·ens \sānt-'hel-ənz, sənt-\ borough NW England in Merseyside ENE of Liverpool *pop* 98,769

Saint Helens, Mount mountain 8364 *ft* (2534 *m*) SW Wash. in Cascades; in **Mount Saint Helens National Volcanic Monument**

Saint Hel·ier \-'hel-yər\ town Channel islands ✱ of Jersey *pop* 28,135

Saint–Hu·bert \sānt-'hyü-bərt, sənt-\ town Canada in S Que. E of Montreal *pop* 60,573

Saint–Hy·a·cinthe \sānt-'hī-ə-(,)sin(t)th, sənt-; ,sant-yə-'sant\ city Canada in S Que. E of Montreal *pop* 38,246

Saint Jean \sa^n-zhä^n\ *or* **Saint Johns** \sānt-'jänz, sənt-\ city Canada in S Que. SE of Montreal *pop* 35,640

Saint–Jean–Cap–Fer·rat \sa^n-'zhä^n-,kap-fə-'rä\ commune SE France on coast E of Nice

Saint–Jean–de–Luz \sa^n-,zhä^n-də-'lüz, -'lūez\ town SW France on Bay of Biscay SW of Biarritz *pop* 10,921

Saint–Jé·rôme \,sa^n-zhā-'rōm, ,sānt-jə-'rōm\ city Canada in S Que. NW of Montreal *pop* 25,123

Saint John \sānt-'jän, sənt-\ 1 river 450 *mi* (724 *km*) NE U.S. & SE Canada flowing from N Maine into Bay of Fundy in N.B. 2 city & port Canada in S N.B. at mouth of the St. John *pop* 80,521 3 island W. Indies, one of the Virgin Islands of the U.S. *area* 20 *sq mi* (52 *sq km*)

Saint John, Lake *or* **Lac Saint–Jean** \läk-sa^n-zhä^n\ lake Canada in S Que. draining through the Saguenay to the St. Lawrence *area* 350 *sq mi* (910 *sq km*)

Saint Johns \sānt-'jänz, sənt-\ 1 river 276 *mi* (444 *km*) NE Fla. flowing N & E into the Atlantic 2 town Brit. W. Indies ✱ of Antigua on Antigua Is. *pop* 24,359 3 — see SAINT JEAN

Saint John's \sānt-'jänz, sənt-\ city & port Canada ✱ of Nfld. *pop* 83,770

Saint Jo·seph \'jō-zəf *also* -səf\ city NW Mo. *pop* 76,691

Saint Kitts \-'kits\ *or* **Saint Chris·to·pher** \-'kris-tə-fər\ island Brit. W. Indies in the Leewards; chief town Basseterre *area* 68 *sq mi* (177 *sq km*); with Nevis, forms independent state of **Saint Kitts–Nevis** (✱ Basseterre *area* 152 *sq mi or* 395 *sq km, pop* 44,404) — **Kit·ti·tian** \kə-'tish-ən\ *n*

Saint–Lam·bert \sānt-'lam-bərt, sənt-\ city Canada in S Que. E of Montreal *pop* 20,557

Saint–Lau·rent \,sa^n-lȯ-'rä^n, ,sant-lȯ-'rent\ city Canada in S Que. on Montreal Is. *pop* 64,404

Saint Law·rence \sānt-'lȯr-ən(t)s, sənt-, -'lär-\ 1 island 95 *mi* (153 *km*) long W Alaska in N Bering sea 2 river 760 *mi* (1223 *km*) E Canada in Ont. & Que. bordering on the U.S. in N.Y., flowing from Lake Ontario NE into the Atlantic, & forming at its mouth a wide bay (the **Gulf of Saint Lawrence**) 3 seaway Canada & U.S. in & along the St. Lawrence bet. Lake Ontario & Montreal

Saint Lawrence, Lake expansion of St. Lawrence river Canada & U.S. WSW of Cornwall, Ont.

Saint Lawrence Islands National Park reservation SE Canada in SE Ont.

Saint–Lé·o·nard \,sa^n-,lā-ə-'när; sānt-'len-ərd, sənt-\ city Canada in S Que. N of Montreal *pop* 74,429

Saint–Lô \sānt-'lō, sənt-; sa^n-lō\ commune NW France *pop* 21,670

Saint–Lou·is \,sa^n-lü-'ē\ 1 city & port Senegal on island at mouth of Senegal river; formerly ✱ of Senegal *pop* 88,404 2 city & port Réunion

Saint Lou·is \sänt-'lü-əs, sənt-\ **1** river 220 *mi* (354 *km*) NE Minn. flowing to W tip of Lake Superior **2** city E Mo. on the Mississippi *pop* 453,085 — **Saint Lou·i·san** \-'lü-ə-sən\ *n*

Saint Lou·is, Lake \sänt-'lü-ē, sənt-\ expansion of St. Lawrence river Canada above Lachine rapids

Saint Louis Park \-'lü-əs-\ city SE Minn. *pop* 42,931

Saint Lu·cia \sänt-'lü-shə, sənt-\ island Brit. W. Indies in the Windwards S of Martinique; an independent member of the Commonwealth since 1979 ✻ Castries *area* 233 *sq mi* (606 *sq km*), *pop* 122,000

Saint–Ma·lo \saⁿ-mə-'lō\ city & port NW France in Brittany on island in Gulf of Saint-Malo *pop* 43,277

Saint–Malo, Gulf of arm of English channel NW France between Cotentin peninsula & Brittany

Saint Mar·tin \sänt-'märt-ᵊn, sənt-\ *or D* Sint Maar·ten \sint-\ island W. Indies in the N Leewards; divided bet. France & Netherlands *area* 33 *sq mi* (86 *sq km*)

Saint Marylebone — see MARYLEBONE

Saint Mar·ys \'me(ə)r-ēz, 'ma(ə)r-ēz, 'mä-rēz\ **1** river 175 *mi* (282 *km*) on Fla.-Ga. border flowing from Okefenokee swamp to the Atlantic **2** river 63 *mi* (101 *km*) bet. Canada & U.S. in Ont. & upper peninsula of Mich. flowing from Lake Superior into Lake Huron; descends 20 *ft* (6.1 *m*) in a mile at **Saint Marys Falls** — see SAULT SAINTE MARIE CANALS

Saint–Maur–des–Fos·sés \saⁿ-mòr-dā-fō-sā\ commune N France SE of Paris on the Marne *pop* 80,797

Saint Mau·rice \saⁿt-'mòr-əs, sənt-, -'mär-; ,saⁿ-mə-'ris\ river 325 *mi* (523 *km*) Canada in S Que. flowing S into the St. Lawrence

Saint–Mi·hiel \saⁿ-mē-yel\ town NE France on the Meuse *pop* 5544

Saint Mo·ritz \sänt-mə-'rits, sənt-mə-\ *or G* Sankt Mo·ritz \,zän(k)t-mə-'rits\ town E Switzerland in Graubünden canton SSE of Chur *pop* 5900

Saint–Na·zaire \,saⁿ-nə-'za(ə)r, -'ze(ə)r\ commune & port NW France at mouth of the Loire *pop* 65,228

Sain·tonge \saⁿ-tōⁿzh\ region & former province of France on Bay of Biscay N of the Gironde ✻ Saintes

Saint–Ouen \saⁿ-twaⁿ\ commune France, N suburb of Paris *pop* 43,569

Saint Pan·cras \sänt-'paŋ-krəs, sənt-\ former metropolitan borough NW London, England, now part of Camden

Saint Paul \'pȯl\ city E Minn., its ✻ *pop* 270,230 — **Saint Paul·ite** \'pȯ-līt\ *n*

Saint Paul's Rocks *or Pg* Pe·ne·dos de São Pe·dro e São Pau·lo \pə-,nā-thüs-thə-,saúⁿ(m)-'päth-rü-ä-,saúⁿ(m)-'paú-lü\ rocky islets in the Atlantic 600 *mi* (966 *km*) NE of Natal, Brazil; belong to Brazil

Saint Pe·ter, Lake \sänt-'pēt-ər, sənt-\ expansion of St. Lawrence river Canada between Sorel & Trois-Rivières, Que.

Saint Pe·ters·burg \'pēt-ərz-,bərg\ **1** city W Fla. on Pinellas peninsula SW of Tampa *pop* 238,647 **2** — see LENINGRAD

Saint Pierre and Mi·que·lon \saⁿ-'pyer-ənd-,mēk-ə-'lōⁿ\ French islands in the Atlantic off S Newfoundland ✻ St. Pierre, *area* 93 *sq mi* (242 *sq km*), *pop* 6051

Saint–Quen·tin \sänt-'kwent-ᵊn, sənt-, *F* saⁿ-kän-taⁿ\ commune N France on the Somme NW of Laon *pop* 69,956

Saint Si·mons \sänt-'sī-mənz, sənt-\ island SE Ga. in the Atlantic

Saint Thom·as \'täm-əs\ **1** island W. Indies, one of the Virgin Islands of the U.S. *area* 32 *sq mi* (83 *sq km*) **2** — see CHARLOTTE AMALIE **3** city Canada in SE Ont. S of London *pop* 28,165

Saint–Tro·pez \saⁿ-trò-pā\ commune SE France on the Mediterranean SW of Cannes *pop* 4484

Saint Vin·cent \saⁿt-'vin(t)-sənt, sənt-\ island Brit. W. Indies in *cen* Windwards; with N Grenadines became independent 1979 as **Saint Vincent and the Grenadines** ✻ Kingstown *area* 150 *sq mi* (390 *sq km*), *pop* 124,000

Saint Vincent, Cape *or Pg* Ca·bo de São Vi·cen·te \'kä-vü-thə-saúⁿ-vē-'sän(t)-tə\ cape SW Portugal

Saint Vincent, Gulf inlet of Indian ocean Australia in S. Australia E of Yorke peninsula

Sai·pan \sī-'pan, -'pän, 'sī-,\ island W Pacific in S *cen* Marianas *area* 70 *sq mi* (182 *sq km*), *pop* 7967 — **Sai·pa·nese** \,sī-pə-'nēz, -'nēs\ *adj or n*

Sa·is \'sā-əs\ ancient city Egypt in Nile delta

Sa·ja·ma \sə-'häm-ə\ mountain 21,391 *ft* (6520 *m*) W Bolivia near Chilean boundary

Sa·kai \(')sä-'kī\ city Japan in S Honshu on Osaka Bay *pop* 815,291

Sak·a·ka·wea, Lake \,sak-ə-kə-'wē-ə\ reservoir 140 *mi* (225 *km*) long W N.Dak. formed in the Missouri by the Garrison Dam

Sa·kar·ya \sä-'kär-yə\ river 300 *mi* (483 *km*) NW Turkey in Asia flowing into the Black sea E of the Bosporus

Sa·kha·lin \'sak-ə-,lēn, -lən; ,sak-ə-'lēn\ *or formerly* Sa·gha·lien \'sag-ə-,lēn, ,sag-ə-\ *or Jp* Ka·ra·fu·to \kə-'räf-ə-,tō\ island U.S.S.R. in Sea of Okhotsk N of Hokkaido; formerly (1905–45) divided bet. Russia & Japan *area* 24,560 *sq mi* (63,856 *sq km*)

Sa·ki·shi·ma \,säk-i-'shē-mə, sä-'kish-ə-mə\ island group Japan in S Ryukyus off E coast of N Taiwan; occupied 1945–72 by the U.S. *area* 343 *sq mi* (892 *sq km*)

Sakkara — see SAQQÂRA

Sa·kon·net River \sə-'kän-ət\ inlet of the Atlantic SE R.I., E of Aquidneck Is.

Salaberry–de–Valleyfield — see VALLEYFIELD

Sa·la·do \sə-'läd-(,)ō\ **1** *or in upper course* Ju·ra·men·to \,hür-ə-'men-(,)tō\ river 1120 *mi* (1802 *km*) N Argentina flowing from the Andes SE into the Paraná **2** *or in upper course* Des·agua·de·ro \dā-,säg-wə-'de(ə)r-(,)ō\ river 850 *mi* (1368 *km*) W *cen* Argentina flowing S into the Colorado

Salajar — see SELAJAR

Sal·a·man·ca \,sal-ə-'maŋ-kə, ,säl-ə-'mäŋ-\ **1** province W Spain *area* 4829 *sq mi* (12,555 *sq km*), *pop* 319,137 **2** commune, its ✻, WNW of Madrid *pop* 153,981

Sal·a·maua \,sal-ə-'maú-ə\ town Papua New Guinea on Huon Gulf

Salambria — see PENEUS

Sal·a·mis \'sal-ə-məs\ **1** ancient city Cyprus on E coast **2** island Greece in Saronic Gulf off Attica

Sal·da·nha Bay \,sal-'dan-yə\ inlet of the Atlantic on SW coast of Cape Province, Republic of S. Africa

Sa·le·la \sa-'lā\ *or formerly* Sal·lee \'sal-ē\ city & port NW Morocco, N suburb of Rabat *pop* 289,391

Sa·lem \'sā-ləm\ **1** city & port NE Mass. NE of Lynn *pop* 38,220 **2** town SE N.H. E of Nashua *pop* 24,124 **3** city ✻ of Oreg. on Willamette river *pop* 89,233 **4** town W *cen* Va. WNW of Roanoke *pop* 23,958 **5** city S India in N Tamil Nadu SW of Madras *pop* 515,021

Sa·ler·no \sə-'ler-(,)nō, -'le(ə)r-\ commune & port S Italy on Gulf of Salerno (inlet of Tyrrhenian sea) ESE of Naples *pop* 157,243 — **Sa·ler·ni·tan** \-'ler-nə-tən\ *adj or n*

Sal·ford \'sȯl-fərd\ urban area NW England in Greater Manchester *pop* 98,024

Sa·li·na \sə-'lī-nə\ city *cen* Kans. on Smoky Hill river *pop* 41,843

Sa·li·nas \sə-'lē-nəs\ **1** river 150 *mi* (241 *km*) W Calif. flowing NW into Monterey Bay **2** city W Calif. near Monterey Bay *pop* 80,479

Salinas National Monument reservation *cen* N. Mex. containing archaeological ruins

Salis·bury \'sȯlz-,ber-ē, -b(ə-)rē\ **1** city W *cen* N.C. SSW of Winston=Salem *pop* 22,677 **2** — see HARARE **3** city & borough S England in Wiltshire on the Avon *pop* 35,355

Salisbury Plain plateau S England in Wiltshire NW of Salisbury

Salm·on \'sam-ən\ river 420 *mi* (676 *km*) *cen* Idaho flowing into Snake river

Salmon River mountains *cen* Idaho; many peaks over 9000 *ft* (2743 *m*)

Sa·lo·ni·ka \sə-'län-i-kə, ,sal-ə-'nē-kə\ *or NGk* Thes·sa·lo·ní·ki \,thes-ə-lə-'nē-kē\ *or* Sa·lo·ní·ki \,sal-ə-'nē-kē\ city & port N Greece in Macedonia *pop* 402,443

Salonika, Gulf of — see THERMAÏKÓS KÓLPOS

Sal·op \'sal-əp\ *or formerly* Shrop·shire \'shräp-,shi(ə)r, -shər\ **1** county S England bordering on Wales ✻ Shrewsbury *area* 1347 *sq mi* (3502 *sq km*), *pop* 382,100 **2** — see SHREWSBURY — **Sa·lo·pi·an** \sə-'lō-pē-ən\ *adj or n*

Salt \'sȯlt\ **1** river 200 *mi* (322 *km*) Ariz. flowing W into the Gila **2** river 100 *mi* (161 *km*) N *cen* Ky. flowing into Ohio river **3** river 200 *mi* (322 *km*) NE Mo. flowing SE into Mississippi river

Sal·ta \'säl-tə\ city NW Argentina *pop* 260,323

Sal·ti·llo \säl-'tē-(,)ō, sal-\ city NE Mexico ✻ of Coahuila *pop* 200,712

Salt Lake City city N Utah, its ✻ *pop* 163,033

Sal·to \'sal-(,)tō\ city & port NW Uruguay on Uruguay river *pop* 74,881

Sal·ton Sea \,sȯlt-ᵊn-\ saline lake *ab* 235 *ft* (72 *m*) below sea level SE Calif. at N end of Imperial valley formed by diversion of water from Colorado river into depression formerly called **Salton sink**

Salt sea — see DEAD SEA

Sa·lu·da \sə-'lüd-ə\ river 200 *mi* (322 *km*) W *cen* S.C. flowing SE to unite with Broad river forming the Congaree

Sal·va·dor \'sal-və-,dò(ə)r, ,sal-və-'\ **1** EL SALVADOR **2** *or formerly* São Salvador \saúⁿ-\ *or* Ba·hia \bä-'ē-ə\ port NE Brazil ✻ of Bahia *pop* 1,506,502 — **Sal·va·dor·an** \,sal-və-'dòr-ən, -'dòr-\ *adj or n* — **Sal·va·dor·ean** *or* **Sal·va·dor·ian** \-ē-ən\ *adj or n*

Sal·ween \'sal-,wēn\ river 1750 *mi* (2816 *km*) SE Asia flowing from Tibet S into Gulf of Martaban in Myanmar

Salz·burg \'sȯlz-,bərg, 'sälz-, 'salz-, 'sòlts-, -,bú(ə)rg, *G* 'zälts-,búrk\ city W Austria ESE of Munich, W. Germany *pop* 138,213

Salz·git·ter \'zälts-,git-ər\ *or formerly* Wa·ten·stedt–Salzgitter \'vät-ᵊn-,s(h)tet-\ city E W. Germany SW of Brunswick *pop* 113,600

Salz·kam·mer·gut \'zälts-,käm-ər-,güt\ district N Austria E of Salzburg; chief town Bad Ischl

Samanala — see ADAM'S PEAK

Sa·mar \'säm-,är\ island *cen* Philippines in the Visayans N of Leyte *area* 5050 *sq mi* (13,130 *sq km*)

Samara — see KUIBYSHEV

Sa·mar·ia \sə-'mer-ē-ə, -'mar-\ **1** district of ancient Palestine W of the Jordan bet. Galilee & Judaea **2** city, its ✻ & ✻ of the Northern Kingdom (Israel); rebuilt by Herod the Great & renamed Se·bas·te \sə-'bas-tē\; site in Jordan at modern village of Sebastye

Sam·ar·kand \'sam-ər-,kand\ *or anc* Mar·a·can·da \,mar-ə-'kan-də\ city U.S.S.R. in E Uzbek Republic *pop* 477,000

Sam·ni·um \'sam-nē-əm\ ancient country *cen* Italy E & SE of Latium

Sa·moa \sə-'mō-ə\ *or formerly* Navigators islands SW *cen* Pacific N of Tonga islands; divided at long. 171°W into American, or Eastern, Samoa & Western Samoa *area* 1209 *sq mi* (3143 *sq km*)

Sa·mos \'sä-,mäs\ island Greece in the Aegean off coast of Turkey N of the Dodecanese *area* 171 *sq mi* (445 *sq km*) — **Sa·mi·an** \-mē-ən\ *adj or n*

Sam·o·thrace \'sam-ə-,thrās\ *or NGk* Sa·mo·thrá·ke \,säm-ə-'thräk-ē\ island Greece in the NE Aegean — **Sam·o·thra·cian** \,sam-ə-'thrā-shən\ *adj or n*

Sam·sun \säm-'sün\ city & port N Turkey on Black sea NW of Ankara *pop* 107,510

San·'a \sän-'ä, 'san-,ä\ city S Arabia ✻ of Yemen & formerly ✻ of Yemen Arab Republic *pop* 125,093

San An·dre·as Fault \san-an-,drā-əs-,\ zone of faults Calif. extending from N coast toward head of Gulf of California

San An·ge·lo \sa-'nan-jə-,lō\ city W *cen* Tex. *pop* 73,240

San An·to·nio \,san-ən-'tō-nē-,ō\ **1** river 200 *mi* (322 *km*) S Tex. flowing SE into Gulf of Mexico **2** city S Tex. on San Antonio river *pop* 785,880 — **San An·to·ni·an** \-nē-ən\ *n*

San Be·ni·to \,san-bə-'nēt-(,)ō\ city S Tex. NW of Brownsville *pop* 17,988

San Ber·nar·di·no \,san-,bər-nə(r)'-dē-(,)nō\ **1** mountains S Calif. S of Mojave desert; highest San Gorgonio Mountain 11,502 *ft* (3506 *m*) **2** city SW Calif. E of Los Angeles *pop* 117,490

San Bru·no \san-'brü-(,)nō\ city W Calif. S of San Francisco *pop* 35,417

San Buenaventura — see VENTURA

San Car·los \san-'kär-ləs\ city W Calif. SE of San Francisco *pop* 24,710

San Carlos de Bariloche — see BARILOCHE

San Cle·men·te \,san-klə-'ment-ē\ **1** island S Calif., southernmost of the Channel islands **2** city SW Calif. NW of San Diego *pop* 27,325

San Cris·to·bal \,san-kris-'tō-bəl\ island W Pacific in SE Solomons

San Cris·tó·bal \ˌsan-kris-ˈtō-bəl\ 1 island Ecuador in the Galápagos *pop* 1404 2 city W Venezuela SSW of Lake Maracaibo *pop* 151,717

Sanc·ti Spí·ri·tus \ˌsäŋ(k)-tē-ˈspir-ə-ˌtüs\ city W *cen* Cuba SE of Santa Clara *pop* 103,116

San·cy, Puy de \ˌpwēd-ə-ˌsäⁿ-ˈsē\ mountain 6188 *ft* (1886 *m*) S *cen* France; highest in the Monts Dore & Auvergne mountains

San·da·kan \san-ˈdäk-ən\ city & port Malaysia in Sabah on Sulu sea; former ✱ of N. Borneo *pop* 118,417

Sand·hurst \ˈsand-ˌhərst\ village S England in E Berkshire SE of Reading *pop* 6445

San·dia \san-ˈdē-ə\ mountains N *cen* N.Mex. E of Albuquerque; highest **Sandia Crest** 10,678 *ft* (3255 *m*)

San Di·ego \ˌsan-dē-ˈā-(ˌ)gō\ city & port SW Calif. on **San Diego Bay** (inlet of the Pacific) *pop* 875,538 — **San Di·egan** \-gən\ *adj or n*

San Di·mas \san-ˈdē-məs\ city SW Calif. NW of Pomona *pop* 24,014

San Domingo 1 — see HISPANIOLA 2 — see DOMINICAN REPUBLIC 3 — see SANTO DOMINGO

San·dring·ham \ˈsan-driŋ-əm\ village E England in NW Norfolk

San·dus·ky \sən-ˈdəs-kē, san-\ 1 river 150 *mi* (241 *km*) N Ohio flowing N into Lake Erie 2 city N Ohio at entrance to **Sandusky Bay** (inlet of Lake Erie) *pop* 31,360

Sand·wich \ˈsan-(ˌ)(d)wich\ 1 islands — see HAWAII 2 borough SE England in Kent on Stour river *pop* 4227

Sandy Hook peninsula E N.J. extending N toward New York Bay

San Fer·nan·do \ˌsan-fər-ˈnan-(ˌ)dō\ 1 valley S Calif. NW of Los Angeles; partly within Los Angeles city limits 2 city SW Calif. in San Fernando valley *pop* 17,731

San·ford \ˈsan-fərd\ 1 city NE Fla. *pop* 23,176 2 town SW Maine *pop* 18,020

Sanford, Mount mountain 16,237 *ft* (4949 *m*) S Alaska at W end of Wrangell mountains

San Fran·cis·co \ˌsan-frən-ˈsis-(ˌ)kō\ city & port W Calif. on **San Francisco Bay** & the Pacific *pop* 678,974 — **San Fran·cis·can** \-kən\ *adj or n*

San Francisco Peaks mountain N *cen* Ariz. N of Flagstaff; includes three peaks: Mt. Humphreys 12,633 *ft* (3851 *m*), highest point in the state; Mt. Agassiz 12,340 *ft* (3761 *m*); & Mt. Fremont 11,940 *ft* (3639 *m*)

San Ga·bri·el \san-ˈgā-brē-əl\ 1 mountains S Calif. SW of Mojave desert & NE of Los Angeles; highest San Antonio Peak 10,080 *ft* (3072 *m*) 2 city SW Calif. S of Pasadena *pop* 30,072

San·ga·mon \ˈsaŋ-gə-mən\ river 225 *mi* (362 *km*) *cen* Ill. flowing SW & W into Illinois river

San·gay \säŋ-ˈgī\ volcano 17,159 *ft* (5230 *m*) SE *cen* Ecuador

San·gi·he \ˌsäŋ-gē-ˈā\ *or* **San·gi** \ˈsäŋ-gē\ 1 islands Indonesia NE of Celebes *area* 134 *sq mi* (348 *sq km*), *pop* 194,253 2 island, chief of the group

San Gi·mi·gna·no \ˌsän-jē-mēn-ˈyän-(ˌ)ō\ commune Italy NW of Siena

San·gre de Cris·to \ˌsaŋ-grēd-ə-ˈkris-(ˌ)tō\ mountains S Colo. & N N.Mex. in Rocky mountains — see BLANCA PEAK

San·i·bel \ˈsan-ə-bəl, -ˌbel\ island SW Fla. SW of Fort Myers

San Il·de·fon·so \ˌsan-ˌil-də-ˈfän(t)-(ˌ)sō\ *or* **La Gran·ja** \lə-ˈgräŋ-(ˌ)hä\ commune *cen* Spain SE of Segovia

San Isi·dro \ˌsan-ə-ˈsē-(ˌ)drō\ city E Argentina *pop* 287,048

San Ja·cin·to \ˌsan-jə-ˈsint-ə, -hə-ˈsint-\ river 100 *mi* (161 *km*) SE Tex. flowing S into Galveston Bay

San Joa·quin \ˌsan-wä-ˈkēn, -wò-\ river 350 *mi* (563 *km*) *cen* Calif. flowing from the Sierra Nevada SW & then NW into Sacramento river

San Jo·se \ˌsan-ə-ˈzā *also* ˌsan-(h)ō-ˈzā\ city W Calif. SSE of San Francisco *pop* 636,550

San Jo·sé \ˌsan-ə-ˈzā, ˌsan-(h)ō-ˈzā\ city *cen* Costa Rica, its ✱ *pop* 203,148

San Juan \san-ˈ(h)wän\ 1 river 360 *mi* (579 *km*) SW Colo., NW N.Mex., & SE Utah flowing W into Colorado river 2 mountains SW Colo. in the Rocky mountains — see UNCOMPAHGRE PEAK 3 islands NW Wash. bet. Vancouver Is. & the mainland 4 city & port NE Puerto Rico, its ✱ *pop* 424,600 5 city W Argentina N of Mendoza *pop* 106,564 6 hill E Cuba near Santiago de Cuba — **San Jua·ne·ro** \ˌsan-(h)wä-ˈne(ə)r-(ˌ)ō\ *n*

Sankt An·ton am Arl·berg \zäŋ(k)-ˈtän-ˌtōn-ˌäm-ˈär(ə)l-ˌbərg, -ˌbe(ə)rg\ village W Austria in Tirol W of Innsbruck

Sankt Gallen — see SAINT GALL

Sankt Moritz — see SAINT MORITZ

San Le·an·dro \ˌsan-lē-ˈan-(ˌ)drō\ city W Calif. SE of Oakland *pop* 63,952

San Lu·cas, Cape \san-ˈlü-kəs\ headland NW Mexico, the S extremity of Baja California

San Lu·is \san-ˈlü-əs\ valley S Colo. & N N.Mex. along the upper Rio Grande bet. San Juan & Sangre de Cristo mountains

San Luis Obis·po \san-ˌlü-ə-sə-ˈbis-(ˌ)pō\ city W Calif. NW of Santa Barbara *pop* 34,252

San Lu·is Po·to·sí \ˌsän-lù-ˌē-ˌspōt-ə-ˈsē\ 1 state *cen* Mexico *area* 24,415 *sq mi* (63,479 *sq km*), *pop* 1,670,637 2 city, its ✱, NE of León *pop* 274,320

San Mar·cos \san-ˈmär-kəs\ city S Tex. NE of San Antonio *pop* 23,420

San Ma·ri·no \ˌsan-mə-ˈrē-(ˌ)nō\ 1 country S Europe on Italian peninsula SSW of Rimini; a republic *area* 24 *sq mi* (62 *sq km*), *pop* 19,149 2 town, its ✱ — **San Mar·i·nese** \san-ˌmar-ə-ˈnēz, -ˈnēs\ *adj or n*

San Mar·tín \ˌsan-mär-ˈtēn\ *or* **Ge·ne·ral San Martín** \ˌhā-nā-ˈräl-\ city E Argentina, NW suburb of Buenos Aires *pop* 384,306

San Ma·teo \ˌsan-mə-ˈtā-(ˌ)ō\ city W Calif. SSE of San Francisco *pop* 77,561

San Mi·guel de Tu·cu·mán \ˌsan-mig-ˌel-də-ˌtü-kə-ˈmän\ *or* **Tucumán** city NW Argentina at foot of E ranges of the Andes *pop* 271,546

San Pab·lo \san-ˈpab-(ˌ)lō\ city W Calif. N of Oakland on **San Pablo Bay** (N extension of San Francisco Bay) *pop* 19,750

San Pe·dro \san-ˈpē-(ˌ)drō, -ˈpā-\ channel SW Calif. bet. Santa Catalina Is. & the mainland

San Ra·fael \ˌsan-rə-ˈfel\ city W Calif. N of San Francisco on San Pablo Bay *pop* 44,700

San Re·mo \sän-ˈrā-(ˌ)mō, san-ˈrē-\ city & port NW Italy in Liguria near French border *pop* 60,787

San Sal·va·dor \san-ˈsal-və-ˌdò(ə)r\ 1 island *cen* Bahama islands *area* 60 *sq mi* (156 *sq km*) 2 city W *cen* El Salvador, its ✱ *pop* 349,333

San Se·bas·tián \ˌsan-si-ˈbas-chən, ˌsän-ˌseb-əs-ˈchän\ city & port N Spain ✱ of Guipúzcoa on Bay of Biscay *pop* 172,303

San Stefano — see YESILKOY

San·ta Ana \ˌsant-ə-ˈan-ə\ 1 city SW Calif. ESE of Long Beach *pop* 203,713 2 city NW El Salvador NW of San Salvador *pop* 168,047

Santa Bar·ba·ra \-ˈbär-b(ə-)rə\ 1 channel SW Calif. bet. the N Channel islands & mainland 2 — see CHANNEL 3 city S Calif. *pop* 74,542

Santa Catalina — see CATALINA

San·ta Ca·ta·ri·na \ˌsant-ə-ˌkat-ə-ˈrē-nə\ state S Brazil bordering on the Atlantic ✱ Florianópolis *area* 31,118 *sq mi* (80,907 *sq km*), *pop* 3,687,652

Santa Clara \-ˈklar-ə, -ˈkler-\ 1 city W Calif. NW of San Jose *pop* 87,746 2 city W *cen* Cuba *pop* 189,092

Santa Cruz \-ˈkrüz\ 1 island SW Calif. in NW Channel islands 2 city W Calif. S of San Jose on Monterey Bay *pop* 41,483 3 — see SAINT CROIX 4 river 250 *mi* (402 *km*) S Argentina flowing E into the Atlantic 5 city E Bolivia *pop* 254,682 6 islands SW Pacific in SE Solomons N of Vanuatu, chief island Ndeni; until 1978 administratively attached to Brit. Solomon islands *area* 380 *sq mi* (988 *sq km*)

Santa Cruz de Te·ne·ri·fe \-də-ˌten-ə-ˈrē-(ˌ)fā, -ˈrēf, -ˈrif\ 1 province Spain comprising W Canary islands *area* 1528 *sq mi* (3973 *sq km*), *pop* 762,503 2 city & port, its ✱, on NE Tenerife Is. *pop* 185,899

San·ta Fe \ˌsant-ə-ˈfā\ 1 city ✱ of N.Mex. *pop* 48,953 2 city *cen* Argentina on Salado river *pop* 287,240 — **San·ta Fe·an** \-ˈfā-ən\ *n*

Santa Fe Trail pioneer route to the Southwest used esp. 1821–80 from vicinity of Kansas City, Mo., to Santa Fe, N.Mex.

San·ta Is·a·bel \ˌsant-ə-ˈiz-ə-ˌbel\ 1 island W Pacific in the E *cen* Solomons NE of Guadalcanal *area* 1500 *sq mi* (3900 *sq km*) 2 — see MALABO

Santa Ma·ria \-mə-ˈrē-ə\ city W Calif. NW of Santa Barbara *pop* 39,685

Santa Ma·ría \-mə-ˈrē-ə\ volcano 12,362 *ft* (3768 *m*) W Guatemala

Santa Mar·ta \-ˈmärt-ə\ city & port N Colombia on the Caribbean E of Barranquilla *pop* 137,474

Santa Mon·i·ca \-ˈmän-i-kə\ city SW Calif. adjacent to Los Angeles on **Santa Monica Bay** (inlet of the Pacific) *pop* 88,314

San·tan·der \ˌsän-ˌtän-ˈde(ə)r, ˌsan-ˌtan-\ 1 province N Spain in N Old Castile bordering on Bay of Biscay *area* 2108 *sq mi* (5481 *sq km*), *pop* 507,489 2 city & port, its ✱, on Bay of Biscay *pop* 179,694

San·ta Pau·la \ˌsant-ə-ˈpò-lə\ city SW Calif. NW of Los Angeles *pop* 20,552

San·ta·rém \ˌsant-ə-ˈrem\ city N Brazil in W Pará at confluence of the Tapajoz & the Amazon *pop* 192,203

San·ta Ro·sa \ˌsant-ə-ˈrō-zə\ 1 island SW Calif. in NW Channel islands 2 city W Calif. N of San Francisco *pop* 83,205

San·tee \(ˈ)san-ˈtē, ˈsan-ˌ\ river 143 *mi* (230 *km*) S.C. flowing SE into the Atlantic — see CONGAREE

San·ti·a·go \ˌsant-ē-ˈäg-(ˌ)ō, ˌsänt-\ 1 city *cen* Chile, its ✱ *metropolitan area pop* 3,614,947 2 *or* **Santiago de los Ca·ba·lle·ros** \-də-ˌlòs-ˌkäb-ə-ˈye(ə)r-(ˌ)ōs\ city N *cen* Dominican Republic *pop* 382,244 3 *or* **Santiago de Com·pos·te·la** \-də-ˌkäm-pə-ˈstel-ə\ commune NW Spain *pop* 70,893 — **San·ti·a·gan** \ˌsant-ē-ˈäg-ən, ˌsänt-\ *n*

Santiago de Cu·ba \-də-ˈkyü-bə\ city & port SE Cuba *pop* 403,604

Santiago del Es·te·ro \-ˌdel-ə-ˈste(ə)r-(ˌ)ō\ city N Argentina SE of San Miguel de Tucumán *pop* 148,357

San·to Do·min·go \ˌsant-əd-ə-ˈmiŋ-(ˌ)gō\ 1 *or* **Santo Domingo de Guz·mán** \-də-gü-ˈsmän\ *or formerly* **Tru·ji·llo** \trü-ˈhē-(ˌ)(y)ō\ *or* **Ci·u·dad Trujillo** \ˌsē-ü-ˌthä-, ˌsē-ü-ˌdad-\ city & port ✱ of Dominican Republic on Caribbean sea *pop* 654,757 2 — see HISPANIOLA 3 — see DOMINICAN REPUBLIC — **San·to Do·min·gan** \ˌsant-əd-ə-ˈmiŋ-gən\ *adj or n*

San·to·rin \ˌsant-ə-ˈrēn, -ˈrin\ *or NGk* **San·to·ri·ni** \-ˈrē-nē\ *or* **Thí·ra** \ˈthir-ə\ *or anc* **The·ra** \ˈthir-ə\ island Greece in S Cyclades *area* 30 *sq mi* (78 *sq km*)

San·tos \ˈsant-əs\ city & port SE Brazil in SE São Paulo state SSE of São Paulo on an island in a tidal inlet *pop* 416,784

San·tur·ce \san-ˈtù(ə)r-(ˌ)sā\ a NE section of San Juan, Puerto Rico

São Fran·cis·co \ˌsaùⁿ(m)-frən-ˈsis-(ˌ)kō\ river 1800 *mi* (2897 *km*) E Brazil flowing from S *cen* Minas Gerais NE & E into the Atlantic

São Luís \ˌsaùⁿ-lù-ˈēs\ city & port NE Brazil ✱ of Maranhão state on Maranhão Is. *pop* 449,877

São Ma·nuel \ˌsaùⁿ-mən-ˈwel\ river 600 *mi* (966 *km*), *cen* Brazil flowing NW to join the Juruena forming the Tapajoz

São Mi·guel \ˌsaùⁿ-mi-ˈgel\ island Portugal in E Azores; chief town Ponta Delgada *area* 297 *sq mi* (772 *sq km*)

Saône \ˈsōn\ river 275 *mi* (442 *km*) E France flowing SSW into the Rhône

São Pau·lo \saùⁿ(m)-ˈpaù-(ˌ)lü, -(ˌ)lō\ 1 state SE Brazil *area* 95,459 *sq mi* (248,193 *sq km*), *pop* 25,375,199 2 city, its ✱ *pop* 8,493,598

São Ro·que, Cape \saùⁿ-ˈrò-kə\ headland NE Brazil N of Natal

São Salvador — see SALVADOR

São Tia·go \ˌsaùⁿ(n)t-ē-ˈäg-(ˌ)ü, -(ˌ)ō\ island Cape Verde islands, largest of the group; chief town Praia *area* 359 *sq mi* (933 *sq km*)

São To·mé \ˌsaùⁿ(n)t-ə-ˈmā\ island W Africa in Gulf of Guinea; with Príncipe Is., forms the republic (until 1975 a Portuguese territory) of **Sao Tome and Principe** (✱ São Tomé *area* 377 *sq mi or* 980 *sq km, pop* 89,000)

São Vicente, Cabo de — see SAINT VINCENT (Cape)

Sap·po·ro \ˈsäp-ə-ˌrō; sə-ˈpōr-(ˌ)ō, -ˈpòr-\ city Japan on W Hokkaido *pop* 1,433,355

Saq·qâ·ra *or* **Saq·qā·rah** *or* **Sak·ka·ra** \sə-ˈkär-ə\ village N Egypt SW of ruins of Memphis

Sarabat — see GEDIZ

Saragossa — see ZARAGOZA

Sa·ra·je·vo \ˈsär-ə-ye-ˌvò\ city *cen* Yugoslavia ✱ of Bosnia and Herzegovina *pop* 223,000

Sar·a·nac \ˈsar-ə-ˌnak\ river 100 *mi* (161 *km*) NE N.Y. flowing NE from **Saranac Lakes** (three lakes in the Adirondacks: Upper Saranac, Middle Saranac, & Lower Saranac) into Lake Champlain

Sa·ransk \sə-ˈrän(t)sk, -ˈran(t)sk\ city U.S.S.R. in *cen* Soviet Russia, Europe ✱ of Mordvinian Republic *pop* 190,000

Sar·a·so·ta \ˌsar-ə-ˈsōt-ə\ city W Fla. S of Tampa *pop* 48,868

Sar·a·to·ga \ˌsar-ə-ˈtō-gə\ 1 lake 7 *mi* (11 *km*) long E N.Y. S of Lake George 2 city W Calif. SW of San Jose *pop* 29,261

Saratoga Springs *or* **Saratoga** city NE N.Y. *pop* 23,906

Sa·ra·tov \sə-'rät-əf\ city U.S.S.R. in SE Soviet Russia, Europe, on a reservoir of the Volga *pop* 758,000

Sa·ra·wak \sə-'rä-(,)wä(k\ -,wak\ state Malaysia in N Borneo, formerly a Brit. colony ✻ Kuching *area* 47,000 *sq mi* (122,200 *sq km*), *pop* 1,294,753

Sardica — see SOFIA

Sar·din·ia \sär-'din-ē-ə, -'din-yə\ *or It* **Sar·de·gna** \sär-'dän-yə\ island Italy S of Corsica; with surrounding smaller islands, constitutes a region of Italy ✻ Cagliari *area* 9283 *sq mi* (24,136 *sq km*), *pop* 1,488,008

Sar·dis \'särd-əs\ *or* **Sar·des** \'särd-,ēz\ ancient city W Asia Minor ✻ of ancient kingdom of Lydia; site E of Izmir — **Sar·di·an** \'särd-ē-ən\ *adj or n*

Sa·re·ma *or Estonian* **Saa·re·maa** \'sär-ə-,mä\ island U.S.S.R. in Estonia at mouth of Gulf of Riga *area* 1010 *sq mi* (2626 *sq km*)

Sa·re·ra Bay \sə-'re-rə-\ *or formerly* **Geel·vink Bay** \'gä(ə)l-(,)viŋk-\ inlet Indonesia in N W. Irian

Sar·gas·so sea \sär-,gas-(,)ō-\ tract of comparatively still water N Atlantic lying chiefly between 25° & 35° N & 40° & 70° W

Sark \'särk\ island in the English channel, one of the Channel islands; a dependency of Guernsey *area* 2 *sq mi* (5.2 *sq km*)

Sar·ma·tia \sär-'mä-sh(ē-)ə\ ancient region E Europe in modern Poland & Russia bet. the Vistula & the Volga — **Sar·ma·tian** \-shən\ *adj or n*

Sar·nia \'sär-nē-ə\ city Canada in SE Ont. on St. Clair river opposite Port Huron, Mich. *pop* 50,892

Sa·ron·ic Gulf \sə-,rän-ik-\ inlet of the Aegean SE Greece bet. Attica & the Peloponnisos

Sa·ros, Gulf of \'sa(ə)r-,äs, 'se(ə)r-\ inlet of the Aegean SW Turkey in Europe N of Gallipoli peninsula

Sarre — see SAAR

Sarthe \'särt\ river 175 *mi* (282 *km*) NW France flowing S to unite with the Mayenne forming Maine river

Sarum OLD SARUM

Sa·se·bo \'säs-ə-,bō\ city & port Japan in NW Kyushu on an inlet of E. China sea *pop* 251,717

Sas·katch·e·wan \sə-'skach-ə-wən, sa-, -,wän\ **1** river 340 *mi* (547 *km*) S *cen* Canada formed by confluence in *cen* Sask. of two branches rising in the Rockies in Alta., the **North Saskatchewan** (760 *mi or* 1216 *km*) & the **South Saskatchewan** (865 *mi or* 1384 *km*), & flowing E into Lake Winnipeg **2** province SW Canada ✻ Regina *area* 237,975 *sq mi* (618,735 *sq km*), *pop* 968,313 — **Sas·katch·e·wan·ian** \-,skach-ə-'wän-ē-ən\ *adj or n*

Sas·ka·toon \,sas-kə-'tün\ city Canada in *cen* Sask. on S. Saskatchewan river *pop* 154,210

Sas·sa·ri \'säs-ə-(,)rē\ commune Italy in NW Sardinia *pop* 118,158

Sa·til·la \sə-'til-ə\ river 220 *mi* (354 *km*) SE Ga. flowing E into the Atlantic

Sat·pu·ra \'sät-pə-rə\ range of hills W *cen* India between the Narbada & the Tapti

Sa·tu–Ma·re \,sä-(,)tü-'mär-(,)ā\ city NW Romania in Transylvania on the Somes *pop* 78,812

Sau·di Arabia \,saúd-ē-, ,saúd-ē-, ,sòd-ē-, sä-,üd-ē-\ country SW Asia occupying most of Arabian peninsula; a kingdom, comprising former kingdoms of Nejd & Hejaz & principality of Asir ✻ Riyadh *area* 870,000 *sq mi* (2,262,000 *sq km*), *pop* 10,025,000 — **Saudi** *adj or n* — **Saudi Arabian** *adj or n*

Sau·gus \'sò-gəs\ town NE Mass. W of Lynn *pop* 24,746

Sault Sainte Ma·rie \,sü-(,)sänt-mə-'rē\ city Canada in Ont., across the St. Marys from Michigan *pop* 82,697

Sault Sainte Marie Canals *or* **Soo Canals** \,sü-\ three ship canals, two in the U.S. & one in Canada, at rapids in St. Marys river connecting Lake Superior & Lake Huron

Sau·mur \sō-'m(y)ú(ə)r, -'mūēr\ commune NW France on the Loire SE of Angers *pop* 30,984

Sau·rash·tra \saú-'räsh-trə\ former state (1948–56) W India on Kathiawar peninsula; in Bombay state 1956–60 & since 1960 in Gujarat

Sa·va \'säv-ə\ river 450 *mi* (724 *km*) N Yugoslavia flowing from Italian border E into the Danube at Belgrade

Sa·vaii \sə-'vī-,ē\ island SW *cen* Pacific, largest in Samoa, in W. Samoa

Sa·van·nah \sə-'van-ə\ **1** river 314 *mi* (505 *km*) E Ga. flowing SE to the Atlantic & forming Ga.–S.C. boundary **2** city & port E Ga. at mouth of Savannah river *pop* 141,390

Save — see SABI

Sa·vo \'säv-(,)ō\ island W Pacific in SE Solomons N of W Guadalcanal

Sa·vo·na \sə-'vō-nə\ commune & port NW Italy SW of Genoa *pop* 75,069

Sa·voy \sə-'vòi\ *or F* **Sa·voie** \sà-vwà\ *or It* **Sa·voia** \sä-'vò-yä\ region SE France in Savoy Alps SW of Switzerland & bordering on Italy; duchy 1416–1720, part of kingdom of Sardinia 1720–1860; became part of France 1860 — **Sa·voy·ard** \sə-'vòi-,ärd, ,sav-,òi-'ärd, ,sav-,wä-'yär(d)\ *adj or n*

Savoy Alps section of W Alps SE France — see MONT BLANC

Sa·watch \sə-'wäch, 'sə-wäsh\ mountain range *cen* Colo. in Rocky mountains — see ELBERT (Mount)

Saxe \'saks\ SAXONY — its French form, used in English chiefly in names of former duchies in Thuringia: **Saxe–Al·ten·burg** \-'ält-ᵊn-,bú(ə)rg\, **Saxe–Co·burg** \-'kō-,bərg\, **Saxe–Go·tha** \-'gòt-ə, -'gō-thə\, **Saxe–Mei·ning·en** \-'mī-niŋ-ən\, & **Saxe–Wei·mar–Ei·se·nach** \-'vī-,mär-'īz-ᵊn-,äk, -,äk\

Sax·o·ny \'sak-s(ə-)nē\ *or G* **Sach·sen** \'zäk-sən\ **1** region & former duchy N W. Germany S of Jutland peninsula between the Elbe & the Rhine — see LOWER SAXONY **2** region & former state SE E. Germany N of the Erzgebirge — see SAXE

Sa·yan \sə-'yän\ mountains U.S.S.R. in S Soviet Russia, Asia, on border of Tuva N of Altai mountains

Sayre·ville \'sa(ə)r-,vil, 'se(ə)r-\ borough E *cen* N.J. *pop* 29,969

Sa·zan \sä-'zän\ *or It* **Sa·se·no** \sə-'zä-(,)nō, sä-\ island Albania in N Strait of Otranto

Sca·fell \'skò-'fel\ mountain 3162 *ft* (964 *m*) NW England in Cumbrians SW of Keswick; second highest peak in England

Scafell Pike mountain 3210 *ft* (978 *m*) NW England in Cumbria NE of Scafell; highest in the Cumbrians & in England

Scamander — see MENDERES

Scan·di·na·via \,skan-də-'nā-vē-ə, -vyə\ **1** peninsula N Europe occupied by Norway & Sweden **2** Denmark, Norway, Sweden, & sometimes also Iceland, the Faeroe islands, & Finland

Scapa Flow \,skap-ə-'flō\ sea basin N Scotland in the Orkneys

Scar·bor·ough \'skär-,bər-ə, -,bə-rə, -b(ə-)rə\ **1** borough Canada in SE Ont. near Toronto *pop* 443,353 **2** borough & port NE England in N. Yorkshire *pop* 43,103

Scars·dale \'skärz-,dāl\ village SE N.Y. NE of Yonkers *pop* 17,650

Schaer·beek *or* **Schaar·beek** \'skär-,bāk\ commune *cen* Belgium, NE suburb of Brussels *pop* 106,754

Schaff·hau·sen \'shäf-'haúz-ᵊn\ **1** canton N Switzerland bordering on W. Germany *area* 114 *sq mi* (296 *sq km*), *pop* 69,413 **2** commune, its ✻ *pop* 34,250

Schaum·burg \'shäm-(,)bərg\ village NE Ill. NW of Chicago *pop* 53,305

Schaum·burg–Lip·pe \,shaúm-,bú(ə)rg-'lip-ə\ state of Germany 1918–33 in NW bet. Westphalia & Hannover

Scheldt \'skelt\ *or* **Schel·de** \'skel-də\ *or F* **Es·caut** \es-kō\ river 270 *mi* (434 *km*) W Europe flowing from N France through Belgium into North sea in Netherlands

Sche·nec·ta·dy \skə-'nek-təd-ē\ city E N.Y. *pop* 67,972

Sche·ve·ning·en \'skā-və-,niŋ-ən\ town SW Netherlands on North sea W of The Hague

Schie·dam \skē-'däm\ commune SW Netherlands *pop* 71,281

Schles·wig \'s(h)les-(,)wig, -(,)vik\ **1** *or Dan* **Sles·vig** \'slis-vē\ region N W. Germany & S Denmark in Jutland peninsula **2** city N W. Germany *pop ab* 29,798

Schleswig–Hol·stein \-'hōl-,stīn\ state N W. Germany consisting of Holstein & part of Schleswig ✻ Kiel *area* 6052 *sq mi* (15,735 *sq km*), *pop* 2,611,285

Scho·field Barracks \'skō-,fēld\ city Hawaii in *cen* Oahu *pop* 18,851

Schou·ten \'skaút-ᵊn\ islands Indonesia in N W. Irian at mouth of Sarera Bay *area* 1230 *sq mi* (3198 *sq km*)

Schuyl·kill \'skül-,kil, 'skü-kəl\ river 131 *mi* (211 *km*) SE Pa. flowing SE into Delaware river at Philadelphia

Schwaben — see SWABIA

Schwarzwald — see BLACK FOREST

Schwein·furt \'shfīn-,fú(ə)rt\ city E W. Germany on Main river *pop* 52,445

Schweiz — see SWITZERLAND

Schwe·rin \shfä-'rēn\ city NW E. Germany E of Hamburg *pop* 122,179

Schwyz \'shfēts\ **1** canton E *cen* Switzerland *area* 351 *sq mi* (913 *sq km*), *pop* 97,354 **2** town, its ✻, E of Lucerne *pop* 12,100

Scil·ly \'sil-ē\ island group SW England off Land's End comprising 140 islands ✻ Hugh Town (on St. Mary's, largest island) *area* 6 *sq mi* (16 *sq km*), *pop* 2428 — see CORNWALL AND ISLES OF SCILLY — **Scil·lo·ni·an** \sil-'ō-nē-ən\ *adj or n*

Sci·o·to \sī-'ōt-ə\ river 237 *mi* (381 *km*) Ohio flowing S into Ohio river

Scit·u·ate \'sich-ə-wət\ town E Mass. SE of Boston *pop* 17,317

Scone \'skün\ locality E Scotland N of Perth *pop* 3713

Sco·pus, Mount \'skō-pəs\ mountain Palestine in W Jordan in small area belonging to Israel

Scores·by Sound \'skō(ə)rz-bē, 'skó(ə)rz-\ inlet of Norwegian sea E Greenland N of 70°N

Sco·tia \'skō-shə\ sea part of the S Atlantic SE of Falkland islands, W of S. Sandwich islands, & N of S. Orkney islands

Scot·land \'skät-lənd\ *or L* **Cal·e·do·nia** \,kal-ə-'dō-nyə, -nē-ə\ ML **Sco·tia** \'skō-shə\ country N Great Britain; a division of United Kingdom of Great Britain and Northern Ireland ✻ Edinburgh *area* 29,794 *sq mi* (77,464 *sq km*), *pop* 5,116,000

Scotts Bluff National Monument \'skäts\ reservation W Nebr. on N. Platte river including **Scotts Bluff** (high butte that was a landmark on the Oregon Trail)

Scotts·dale \'skäts-,dāl\ city SW *cen* Ariz. E of Phoenix *pop* 88,412

Scran·ton \'skrant-ᵊn\ city NE Pa. *pop* 88,117

Scun·thorpe \'skən-,thó(ə)rp\ borough E England in Humberside WSW of Hull *pop* 66,353

Scu·ta·ri, Lake \'sküt-ə-rē\ *or* **Ska·dar·sko Je·ze·ro** \skä-'där-(,)skō-'jä-zə-(,)rò\ lake NW Albania & S Yugoslavia *area* 130 *sq mi* (338 *sq km*)

Scyth·ia \'sith-ē-ə, 'sith-\ the country of the ancient Scythians comprising parts of Europe & Asia now in U.S.S.R. in regions N & NE of Black sea & E of Aral sea

Sea Islands islands SE U.S. in the Atlantic off coast of S.C., Ga., & Fla. bet. mouths of Santee & St. Johns rivers

Seal Beach city SW Calif. SE of Los Angeles *pop* 25,975

Sea·side \'sē-,sīd\ city W Calif. on Monterey Bay *pop* 36,567

Se·at·tle \sē-'at-ᵊl\ city & port W Wash. bet. Puget Sound & Lake Washington *pop* 493,846 — **Se·at·tle·ite** \-ᵊl-,īt\ *n*

Se·ba·go \sə-'bä-(,)gō\ lake 13 *mi* (21 *km*) long SW Maine

Sebaste \-\ *or* **Sebastia** *or* **Sivas** — see SAMARIA

Se·cun·der·abad \si-'kən-də-rə-,bad, -,bäd\ city S *cen* India in Andhra Pradesh, NE suburb of Hyderabad *pop* 345,052

Se·da·lia \si-'dāl-yə\ city W *cen* Mo. *pop* 20,927

Se·dan \si-'dan, *F* sə-däⁿ\ city NE France on the Meuse NE of Reims *pop* 23,867

Sedge·moor \'sej-,mú(ə)r, -,mó(ə)r, -,mò(ə)r\ tract of moorland SW England in *cen* Somerset

Se·dom \sə-'dóm\ town Israel near S end of Dead sea

Se·go·via \sā-'gō-vyə, -vē-ə\ **1** — see COCO **2** province N *cen* Spain in Old Castile *area* 2635 *sq mi* (6851 *sq km*), *pop* 132,467 **3** commune, its ✻, NW of Madrid *pop* 53,366

Se·guin \sə-'gēn\ city SE *cen* Tex. *pop* 17,854

Seim — see SEYM

Seine \'sān, 'sen\ river 480 *mi* (772 *km*) N France flowing NW into **Bay of the Seine** (inlet of English channel)

Sek·on·di–Ta·ko·ra·di \,sek-ən-'dē-,täk-ə-'räd-ē\ city & port SW Ghana *pop* 161,071

\ə\ abut \ᵊ\ kitten, F table \ər\ further \a\ ash \ā\ ace \ä\ cot, cart \aú\ out \ch\ chin \e\ bet \ē\ easy \g\ go \i\ hit \ī\ ice \j\ job \ŋ\ sing \ō\ go \ò\ law \òi\ boy \th\ thin \t͟h\ the \ü\ loot \ú\ foot \y\ yet \zh\ vision \à, k̟, ⁿ, œ, œ̄, ᵫ, ᵬ, � see Guide to Pronunciation

Se·la·jar *or* Sa·la·jar \sə-'lä-,yär\ *or* Ka·bia \'käb-ē-ə\ island Indonesia off SW Celebes Is. *area* 256 *sq mi* (666 *sq km*), *pop* 87,278

Se·lang·or \sə-'laŋ-ər, -,ó(ə)r\ state *cen* Malaysia (federation) on Strait of Malacca ✻ Shah Alam *area* 3072 *sq mi* (7987 *sq km*), *pop* 1,467,441

Se·lat Sun·da \sə-'lät-sún-'dä\ strait bet. Java & Sumatra

Sel·en·ga \sel-ən-'gä\ river 750 *mi* (1207 *km*) N *cen* Asia rising in W Mongolia & flowing to Lake Baikal

Se·leu·cia \sə-'lü-sh(ē-)ə\ **1** *or* Seleucia Tra·che·o·tis \,trä-kē-'ōt-əs\ ancient city SE Asia Minor in Cilicia SW of Tarsus **2** ancient city, chief city of the Seleucid Empire; ruins now in Iraq on the Tigris SSE of Baghdad **3** *or* Seleucia Pi·eria \pī-'ir-ē-ə, -'er-\ ancient city Asia Minor N of mouth of the Orontes; port for Antioch

Sel·kirk \'sel-,kərk\ **1** mountains SW Canada in SE B.C. W of the Rockies; highest Mt. Sir Sandford 11,590 *ft* (3533 *m*) **2** *or* Sel·kirk·shire \-,shi(ə)r, -shər\ former county SE Scotland **3** burgh *cen* Borders region SE of Edinburgh *pop* 5417

Sel·ma \'sel-mə\ city *cen* Ala. W of Montgomery *pop* 26,684

Se·ma·rang \sə-'mär-,äŋ\ city & port Indonesia in *cen* Java on N coast *pop* 1,026,671

Sem·i·nole, Lake \'sem-ə,nōl\ reservoir SW Ga. & NW Fla. formed by confluence of Chattahoochee & Flint rivers & emptying by the Apalachicola

Sem·i·pa·la·tinsk \,sem-i-pə-'lä-,tin(t)sk\ city U.S.S.R. in Soviet Central Asia in NE Kazakhstan on the Irtysh *pop* 283,000

Sen·dai \(')sen-'dī\ city Japan in NE Honshu *pop* 645,331

Sen·e·ca \'sen-i-kə\ lake 35 *mi* (56 *km*) long W *cen* N.Y.; one of the Finger lakes

Sen·e·gal \,sen-i-'gól\ **1** river 1050 *mi* (1690 *km*) W Africa flowing from Fouta Djallon NW & W into the Atlantic **2** country W Africa on the Atlantic; a republic of the French Community, formerly a territory of French W. Africa ✻ Dakar *area* 81,081 *sq mi* (210,811 *sq km*), *pop* 5,811,000 — Sen·e·ga·lese \,sen-i-gə-'lēz, -'lēs\ *adj or n*

Sen·e·gam·bia \,sen-ə-'gam-bē-ə\ **1** region W Africa around Senegal & Gambia rivers **2** confederation of Senegal & Gambia; formed 1982 — Sen·e·gam·bi·an \-ən\ *adj or n*

Sen·lac \'sen-,lak\ hill SE England in Sussex NW of Hastings

Sen·lis \sän-'lēs\ commune N France NNE of Paris *pop* 13,481

Sen·nar *or* Sen·naar \sə-'när\ region E Sudan chiefly bet. White Nile & Blue Nile rivers; an ancient kingdom

Sens \säⁿs\ city NE *cen* France WSW of Troyes *pop* 25,621

Seoul \'sōl\ city NW S. Korea on Han river; formerly W of Korea, since 1948 ✻ of S. Korea *pop* 8,366,756

Se·pik \sä-pik\ river 600 *mi* (966 *km*) N Papua New Guinea

Sept–Îles \se-'tē(ə)l\ *or* Seven Islands city Canada in E Que. at the mouth of the St. Lawrence river *pop* 30,617

Se·quoia National Park \si-'kwói-ə\ reservation SE *cen* Calif.; includes Mt. Whitney

Seram — see CERAM

Ser·bia \'sər-bē-ə\ *or formerly* Ser·via \-vē-ə\ federated republic SE Yugoslavia traversed by Morava river; once a kingdom ✻ Belgrade *area* 34,080 *sq mi* (88,608 *sq km*), *pop* 11,596,572

Serbs, Croats, and Slovenes, Kingdom of the — see YUGOSLAVIA

Serdica — see SOFIA

Serendib — see CEYLON

Ser·en·geti Plain \,sər-ən-'get-ē\ area N Tanzania including Serengeti National Park (wild game reserve)

Ser·gi·pe \sər-'zhē-pə\ state NE Brazil ✻ Aracajú *area* 8321 *sq mi* (21,635 *sq km*), *pop* 1,156,642

Se·rin·ga·pa·tam \,sə-,riŋ-gə-pə-'tam\ town S India N of city of Mysore

Se·rowe \sə-'rō-ē\ city E Botswana *pop* 15,723

Ser·ra da Es·tre·la \,ser-ə-dä-e-'strel-ə\ mountain range Portugal; highest point Malhão da Estrela (highest in Portugal) 6532 *ft* (1991 *m*)

Serra do Mar \-də-'mär\ mountain range S Brazil along coast; highest point 7323 *ft* (2232 *m*)

Serra Pa·ca·rai·ma \-,pak-ə-'rī-mə\ *or* Si·er·ra Pacaraima \sē-,er-ə-\ mountain range N S. America in SE Venezuela, N Brazil, & W Guyana — see RORAIMA

Ser·ra Pa·ri·ma \,ser-ə-pə-'rē-mə\ mountain range N S. America on Venezuela-Brazil border SW of Serra Pacaraima; source of the Orinoco; highest peak *ab* 8000 *ft* (2438 *m*)

Ses·tos \'ses-təs\ ruined town Turkey in Europe on the Dardanelles (Hellespont) at narrowest point

Sète \'set\ *or formerly* Cette \'set\ commune & port S France SSW of Montpellier *pop* 39,075

Se·te Que·das \,sät-ə-'kā-thəsh\ *or* Guai·ra Falls \gwī-'rä-\ cataract (now submerged) in Alto Paraná river on Brazil-Paraguay boundary

Sé·tif \sā-'tēf\ commune NE Algeria *pop* 144,200

Se·tú·bal \sə-'tü-bəl, -,bäl\ city & port SW Portugal *pop* 64,531

Se·van \sə-'vän\ lake U.S.S.R. in N Armenia *area* 540 *sq mi* (1404 *sq km*)

Se·vas·to·pol \sə-'vas-tə-,pōl, -,pól, -pəl; ,sev-ə-'stō-pəl, -'stō-\ *or formerly* Se·bas·to·pol \-'bas-; ,seb-ə-\ city & port U.S.S.R. in Soviet Russia, Europe, in SW Crimea *pop* 301,000

Sev·ern \'sev-ərn\ **1** inlet (Severn River) of Chesapeake Bay, in Md., on which Annapolis is situated **2** river 610 *mi* (982 *km*) Canada in NW Ont. flowing NE into Hudson bay **3** river 210 *mi* (338 *km*) Great Britain flowing from E *cen* Wales into Bristol channel in England

Severnaya Dvina — see NORTHERN DVINA

Se·ver·na·ya Zem·lya \'sev-ər-nə-,yä-,zem-lē-'ä\ islands U.S.S.R. in N Soviet Russia, Asia, N of Taimyr peninsula in Arctic ocean bet. Kara & Laptev seas *area* 14,300 *sq mi* (37,180 *sq km*)

Se·vier \sə-'vi(ə)r\ river 280 *mi* (451 *km*) SW *cen* Utah flowing into Sevier Lake (25 *mi or* 40 *km* long; saline)

Se·ville \sə-'vil\ *or Sp* Se·vi·lla \sā-'vē-(,)(y)ä\ **1** province SW Spain *area* 5428 *sq mi* (14,113 *sq km*), *pop* 1,397,534 **2** city, its ✻, on the Guadalquiver *pop* 645,817

Sè·vres \'sevr'\ commune N France SW of Paris *pop* 21,100

Sew·ard \'sü-ərd\ peninsula 180 *mi* (290 *km*) long & 130 *mi* (209 *km*) wide W Alaska projecting into Bering sea between Kotzebue & Norton sounds — see PRINCE OF WALES (Cape)

Sey·chelles \sā-'shel(z)\ island group W Indian ocean NE of Madagascar; formerly a Brit. colony, a republic in the Commonwealth since 1976 ✻ Victoria (on Mahé Is.) *area* 178 *sq mi* (462 *sq km*), *pop* 61,898

Sey·han \sā-'hän\ **1** *or* Sei·hun \-'hün\ river 300 *mi* (483 *km*) Turkey flowing SSW into the Mediterranean **2** — see ADANA

Seym *or* Seim \'säm\ river 435 *mi* (700 *km*) U.S.S.R. in SW *cen* Soviet Russia, Europe, flowing W into the Desna

Sfax \'sfaks\ city & port Tunisia on Gulf of Gabes *pop* 171,297

's Gravenhage — see HAGUE (The)

Sha·ba \'shäb-ə\ *or formerly* Ka·tan·ga \kə-'täŋ-gə, -'taŋ-\ region SE Zaire; chief city Lubumbashi

Shache — see SO-CH'E

Shah·ja·han·pur \,shäj-ə-'hän-,pú(ə)r\ city N India in *cen* Uttar Pradesh NNW of Kanpur *pop* 205,325

Shah·pur \shä-'pú(ə)r\ ancient city SW Iran W of Shiraz

Sha·ker Heights \,shā-kər-\ city NE Ohio E of Cleveland *pop* 32,487

Shakh·ty \'shäk-tē\ *or formerly* Ale·ksan·drovsk Gru·shev·ski \,al-ik-'san-drəfsk-grü-'shef-skē, ,el-, -ig-'zan-, -'shev-\ city U.S.S.R. in SE Soviet Russia, Europe, NE of Rostov *pop* 209,000

Shang–ch'iu \'shäŋ-chē-'ü\ *or* Shang·qiu \-chē-'ü\ *or* Shang·kiu \-jē-'ü\ city E China in E Honan *pop* 165,000

Shang·hai \'shaŋ-'hī\ municipality & port E China in SE Kiangsu on the Whangpoo near the Yangtze estuary *pop* 11,859,748

Shan·non \'shan-ən\ river 240 *mi* (386 *km*) W Ireland flowing S & W into the Atlantic

Shan·si \'shän-'sē\ *or* Shan·xi \-'shē\ province N China bordering on the Hwang ✻ Taiyuan *area* 60,656 *sq mi* (157,706 *sq km*), *pop* 25,291,389

Shan State \'shän, 'shan\ *or formerly* Federated Shan States province E Burma comprising a mountainous region (the Shan hills) ✻ Taunggyi *pop* 3,178,000

Shantou — see SWATOW

Shan·tung \'shan-'təŋ\ *or* Shan·dong \-'dəŋ\ **1** peninsula E China projecting ENE bet. Yellow sea & Po Hai **2** province E China including Shantung peninsula ✻ Tsinan *area* 59,189 *sq mi* (153,891 *sq km*), *pop* 74,419,054

Shao–hsing *or* Shao·xing \'shaú-'shiŋ\ city E China in N Chekiang SE of Hangchow *pop* 160,000

Shao·yang \'shaú-'yaŋ\ *or formerly* Pao·king \'baú-'chiŋ\ city SE China in *cen* Hunan W of Hengyang *pop* 170,000

Shari — see CHARI

Shar·ja \'shär-jə\ sheikhdom, member of the United Arab Emirates

Shark Bay inlet of Indian ocean 150 *mi* (241 *km*) long W Western Australia, at *ab* 25°S

Shar·on \'shar-ən, 'sher-\ city NW Pa. on Ohio border *pop* 19,057

Sharon, Plain of region Israel on coast bet. Mt. Carmel & Jaffa

Sha–shih \'shä-'shi(ə)r\ *or* Sha·shi \-'shē\ *or* Shasi \'shē\ city E *cen* China in S Hupeh on the Yangtze *pop* 120,000

Shas·ta, Mount \'shas-tə\ mountain 14,162 *ft* (4316 *m*) N Calif. in Cascade range; an isolated volcanic cone

Shatt–al–Ar·ab \,shät-al-'ar-əb\ river 120 *mi* (193 *km*) SE Iraq formed by the Tigris & the Euphrates & flowing SE into Persian Gulf

Shaw·an·gunk Mountains \,shäŋ-gəm-, shə-,wän-(,)gəŋk-\ mountain ridge SE N.Y.; part of Kittatinny Mountain

Sha·win·i·gan \shə-'win-i-gən\ city Canada in S Que. on the St. Maurice NW of Trois-Rivières *pop* 23,011

Shaw·nee \shó-'nē, 'shó-,; shä-'nē, 'shä-\ **1** city NE Kans. S of Kansas City *pop* 29,653 **2** city *cen* Okla. *pop* 26,506

Shcherbakov — see ANDROPOV

She·ba \'shē-bə\ *or* Sa·ba \'sä-bə\ ancient country S Arabia, probably Yemen

She·boy·gan \shi-'bói-gən\ city & port E Wis. *pop* 48,085

Shechem — see NABLUS

Sheer·ness \shi(ə)r-'nes\ former urban district & port SE England in Kent at mouth of Thames river; now part of Queenborough-in-Sheppey

Shef·field \'shef-,ēld\ city N England in S. Yorkshire *pop* 477,142

Shel·i·kof \'shel-ə-,kóf\ strait S Alaska bet. Alaska peninsula & islands of Kodiak & Afognak

Shel·ton \'shelt-ⁿn\ city SW Conn. *pop* 31,314

Shen·an·do·ah \,shen-ən-'dō-ə, ,shan-ə-'dō-ə\ river 55 *mi* (88 *km*) N Va. flowing NE bet. Allegheny & Blue Ridge mountains across NE tip of W.Va. & into the Potomac; forms Shenandoah Valley

Shenandoah National Park reservation N Va. in Blue Ridge mountains

Shen·si \'shen-'sē\ *or* Shaan·xi \-'shē\ province N *cen* China bordering on the Hwang ✻ Sian *area* 75,598 *sq mi* (196,555 *sq km*), *pop* 28,904,423

Shenyang — see MUKDEN

Sher·brooke \'shər-,brúk\ city E Canada in S Que. *pop* 74,075

Sher·man \'shər-mən\ city NE Tex. N of Dallas *pop* 30,413

's Her·to·gen·bosch \,ser-,tō-gən-'bós\ city S Netherlands ✻ of N. Brabant *pop* 81,471

Sher·wood Forest \,shər-,wúd- *also* ,she(ə)r-\ ancient royal forest *cen* England chiefly in Nottinghamshire

Shet·land \'shet-lənd\ **1** islands N Scotland NE of the Orkneys **2** *or* Zet·land \'zet-\ region comprising the Shetlands ✻ Lerwick (on Mainland Is.) *area* 550 *sq mi* (1430 *sq km*), *pop* 26,716 — Shet·land·er \'shet-lən-dər\ *n*

Shey·enne \shī-'an, -'en\ river 325 *mi* (523 *km*) SE *cen* N.Dak. flowing into Red river

Shi·bin el Kôm \shib-ē-,nel-'kōm\ city N Egypt *pop* 100,000

Shi·ga·tse \shi-'gät-sə\ *or* Xi·ga·zê \'shē-'gäd-ze\ *or* Jih-k'a·tse \'zhi(ə)r-'käd-zə\ town W China in SE Tibet on the Tsangpo W of Lhasa

Shih–chia–chuang *or* Shi·jia·zhuang *or* Shih·kia·chwang \,shi(ə)r-jē-'äj-'wäŋ, ,shē-jē-\ city NE China ✻ of Hopeh *pop* 1,500,000

Shi·kar·pur \shi-'kär-,pú(ə)r\ city S *cen* Pakistan in Sind *pop* 88,000

Shi·ko·ku \shi-'kō-(,)kü\ island S Japan E of Kyushu *area* 7246 *sq mi* (18,840 *sq km*)

Shil·ka \'shil-kə\ river 300 *mi* (483 *km*) U.S.S.R. in SE Soviet Russia, Asia, flowing NE to unite with the Argun forming the Amur

Shil·long \'shil-'óŋ\ city NE India ✻ of Meghalaya *pop* 173,064

Shi·loh \'shī-(,)lō\ ancient village Palestine W of Jordan river on slope of Mt. Ephraim

Shi·mi·zu \shi-'mē-(,)zü, 'shē-mi,zü\ city & port Japan in *cen* Honshu on Suruga Bay; port for Shizuoka *pop* 241,390

Shi·mo·da \shi-'mōd-ə, -'mō-,dä\ city & port Japan in S Honshu SW of Yokohama on Sagami slope *pop* 31,007

Shi·mo·no·se·ki \shim-ə-nō-'sek-ē\ **1** strait Japan bet. Honshu & Kyushu connecting Inland sea & Korea strait **2** *or formerly* Ba·kan \'bäk-än\ city & port Japan in SW Honshu on Shimonoseki strait *pop* 268,630

Shi·nar \'shī-nər, -ˌnär\ a country known to the early Hebrews as a plain in Babylonia; prob. Sumer

Ship Rock isolated mountain 7178 *ft* (2188 *m*) N.Mex. in NW corner

Shi·raz \shi-'räz\ city SW *cen* Iran *pop* 416,408

Shi·re \'shē-(ˌ)rā\ river 370 *mi* (595 *km*) S Malawi & *cen* Mozambique flowing from Lake Malawi S into the Zambezi

Shi·shal·din \shish-'al-dən\ volcano 9387 *ft* (2861 *m*) SW Alaska on Unimak Is.; highest in Aleutian range

Shive·ly \'shīv-lē\ city N Ky. SW of Louisville *pop* 16,819

Shi·zu·o·ka \shiz-ə-'wō-kə, shē-zə-'ō-kə\ city Japan in *cen* Honshu near Suruga Bay SW of Shimizu *pop* 459,392

Shko·dër \'shkòd-ər\ city NW Albania *pop* 64,700

Sho·la·pur \'shō-lə-ˌpù(ə)r\ city W India in SE Maharashtra SE of Bombay *pop* 514,461

Shore·ditch \'shō(ə)r-ˌdich, 'shò(ə)r-\ former metropolitan borough N *cen* London, England, now part of Hackney

Shore·view \'shō(ə)r-ˌvyü, 'shò(ə)r-\ city E Minn. *pop* 17,300

Short·land \'shòrt-lənd\ islands W Pacific in the Solomons off S end of Bougainville

Sho·sho·ne \shə-'shō-nē, shə-'shōn\ river 120 *mi* (193 *km*) NW Wyo. flowing NE into Bighorn river

Shoshone Falls waterfall 210 *ft* (64 *m*) S Idaho in Snake river

Shreve·port \'shrēv-ˌpō(ə)rt, -ˌpò(ə)rt, *esp South* 'srēv-\ city NW La. on Red river *pop* 205,820

Shrews·bury **1** \'sh(r)üz-ˌber-ē, -b(ə-)rē, *esp South* 'srüz-\ town E Mass. E of Worcester *pop* 22,674 **2** *Brit often* 'shrōz-\ *or* **Sal·op** \'sal-əp\ borough W England * of Salop *pop* 59,826

Shropshire — see SALOP

Shu·ma·gin \'shü-mə-gən\ islands SW Alaska S of Alaska peninsula; largest Unga

Shushan — see SUSA

Si — see HSI

Si·al·kot \sē-'äl-ˌkōt\ city NE Pakistan NNE of Lahore *pop* 308,000

Siam — see THAILAND

Siam, Gulf of *or* **Gulf of Thailand** arm of S. China sea bet. Indochina & Malay peninsula

Si·an *or* **Xi·an** \'shē-'än\ *or formerly* **Chang·an** \'chän-'än\ city E *cen* China * of Shensi on the Wei *pop* 1,900,000

Siang — see YÜ

Siangtan — see HSIANG-T'AN

Si·be·ria \sī-'bir-ē-ə\ region N Asia in U.S.S.R. extending from the Urals to the Pacific; roughly coextensive with Soviet Russia, Asia — **Si·be·ri·an** \-ē-ən\ *adj or n*

Si·biu \sē-'byü\ city W *cen* Romania in Transylvania *pop* 161,049

Si·bu·yan \sē-bü-'yän\ sea *cen* Philippines bounded by Mindoro, S Luzon, & the Visayans

Sic·i·ly \'sis-(ə-)lē\ *or* **It Si·ci·lia** \sē-'chēl-yä\ *or anc* **Si·cil·ia** \sə-'sil-yə\ *or* **Tri·nac·ria** \trə-'nak-rē-ə, trī-\ island S Italy in the Mediterranean; a region * Palermo *area* 9926 *sq mi* (25,808 *sq km*), *pop* 4,867,650 — **Si·cil·ian** \sə-'sil-yən\ *adj or n*

Si·cy·on \'sis(h)-ē-ˌän\ *or Gk* **Sik·y·on** \'sik-ē-\ ancient city S Greece in NE Peloponnisos NW of Corinth

Si·di Bar·râ·ni \ˌsēd-ē-bə-'rän-ē\ village NW Egypt on coast

Si·di–bel–Ab·bès \-ˌbel-ə-'bes\ commune NW Algeria *pop* 116,000

Sid·ney \'sid-nē\ city W Ohio *pop* 17,657

Si·don \'sīd-ᵊn\ *or* **Ar Sai·da** \'sīd-ə\ city & port SW Lebanon; a chief city of ancient Phoenicia — **Si·do·ni·an** \sī-'dō-nē-ən\ *adj or n*

Si·dra, Gulf of \'sid-rə\ *or* **Gulf of Sir·te** \-'sirt-ə\ *or anc* **Syr·tis Ma·jor** \ˌsərt-ə-'smä-jər\ inlet of the Mediterranean on coast of Libya

Sie·ben·ge·bir·ge \'zē-bən-gə-ˌbi(ə)r-gə\ hills W W. Germany on right bank of the Rhine SSE of Bonn — see DRACHENFELS

Si·ena *or* **Si·en·na** \sē-'en-ə\ commune *cen* Italy in Tuscany *pop* 65,966 — **Sienese** *or* **Sien·nese** \ˌsē-ə-'nēz, -'nēs\ *adj or n*

Si·er·ra Blan·ca Peak \sē-ˌer-ə-ˌblaŋ-kə\ mountain 12,003 *ft* (3658 *m*) S *cen* N.Mex. in Sierra Blanca range of the Sacramento mountains

Sierra de Cór·do·ba \sē-ˌer-ə-'kòrd-ə-bə\ mountain range *cen* Argentina chiefly in Córdoba province; highest peak Cerro Champaquí 9350 *ft* (2850 *m*)

Sierra de Gre·dos \-də-'gräd-(ˌ)ōs\ mountain range W *cen* Spain, SW extension of Sierra de Guadarrama; highest peak Plaza de Almanzor 8504 *ft* (2592 *m*)

Sierra de Gua·dar·ra·ma \-də-ˌgwäd-ə-'räm-ə\ mountain range *cen* Spain; highest peak Pico de Peñalara 7972 *ft* (2430 *m*)

Sier·ra Le·one \sē-ˌer-ə-lē-'ōn, ˌsir-ē-\ country W Africa on the Atlantic; a dominion of the Commonwealth * Freetown *area* 27,925 *sq mi* (72,605 *sq km*), *pop* 2,735,159 — **Sier·ra Le·on·ean** \-'ō-nē-ən\ *adj or n*

Sier·ra Ma·dre del Sur \sē-ˌer-ə-ˌmäd-rā-ˌdel-'sù(ə)r\ mountain range S Mexico along Pacific coast in Guerrero & Oaxaca

Sierra Madre Oc·ci·den·tal \-ˌäk-sə-ˌden-'täl\ mountain range NW Mexico parallel to the Pacific coast

Sierra Madre Ori·en·tal \-ˌōr-ē-ˌen-'täl, -ˌòr-\ mountain range E Mexico parallel to coast of Gulf of Mexico

Sierra Mo·re·na \-mə-'rā-nə\ mountain range SW Spain bet. the Guadiana & the Guadalquivir; highest peak Estrella 4339 *ft* (1322 *m*)

Sierra Ne·va·da \-nə-'vad-ə, -'väd-\ **1** mountain range E Calif. — see WHITNEY (Mount) **2** mountain range S Spain; highest peak Mulhacén 11,411 *ft* (3478 *m*)

Sierra Nevada de Mérida — see CORDILLERA MÉRIDA

Sierra Nevada de San·ta Mar·ta \-ˌsant-ə-'märt-ə\ mountain range N Colombia on Caribbean coast; highest peak 19,030 *ft* (5800 *m*)

Sierra Pacaraima — see SERRA PACARAIMA

Sierra Vis·ta \-'vis-tə\ city SE Ariz. *pop* 24,937

Si·kang \'shē-'käŋ\ former province S China * Yaan

Sikes·ton \'sīk-stən\ city SE Mo. *pop* 17,431

Si·kho·te Alin \ˌsē-kə-ˌtā-ə-'lēn\ mountain range U.S.S.R. in Soviet Russia, Asia in Maritime Territory; highest point 6814 *ft* (2004 *m*)

Sik·kim \'sik-əm, -ˌim\ former country SE Asia on S slope of the Himalayas bet. Nepal & Bhutan; since 1975 a state of India * Gangtok *area* 2818 *sq mi* (7327 *sq km*), *pop* 315,682 — **Sik·kim·ese** \ˌsik-ə-'mēz, -'nēs\ *adj or n*

Si·le·sia \sī-'lē-zh(ē-)ə, sə-, -sh(ē-)ə\ region E *cen* Europe in valley of the upper Oder bordering on Sudeten mountains; formerly chiefly in Ger-

many, now chiefly in N Czechoslovakia & SW Poland — **Si·le·sian** \-zh(ē-)ən, -sh(ē-)ən\ *adj or n*

Simbirsk — see ULYANOVSK

Sim·coe, Lake \'sim-(ˌ)kō\ lake E Canada in SE Ont. SE of Georgian Bay *area* 280 *sq mi* (725 *sq km*)

Sim·fe·ro·pol \ˌsim(p)-fə-'rō-pəl, -'rō-\ city U.S.S.R. in S Soviet Russia, Europe, in the Crimea *pop* 250,000

Si·mi Valley \si-'mē\ city SW Calif. W of Los Angeles *pop* 77,500

Sim·la \'sim-lə\ city N India N of Delhi * of Himachal Pradesh & former summer * of India *pop* 55,368

Si·mons·town \'sī-mənz-ˌtaùn\ town & port SW Republic of S. Africa in Cape Province on False Bay S of Cape Town

Sim·plon \'sim-ˌplän\ **1** mountain pass 6589 *ft* (2008 *m*) in Lepontine Alps bet. Switzerland & Italy in Valais & Piedmont **2** tunnel *ab* 12 *mi* (19 *km*) long through Monte Leone near the pass

Sims·bury \'simz-ˌber-ē, -b(ə-)rē\ town N Conn. *pop* 21,161

Si·nai \'sī-ˌnī *also* -nē-ˌī\ **1** peninsula extension of continent of Asia NE Egypt bet. Red sea & the Mediterranean **2** — see HOREB — **Si·na·it·ic** \ˌsī-nē-'it-ik\ *adj*

Si·na·loa \ˌsē-nə-'lō-ə, ˌsin-ə-\ state W Mexico bordering on Gulf of California * Culiacán *area* 22,580 *sq mi* (58,708 *sq km*), *pop* 1,880,098

Sind \'sind\ province S Pakistan in lower Indus valley * Karachi

Sin·ga·pore \'siŋ-(g)ə-ˌpō(ə)r, -ˌpò(ə)r\ **1** island Malay archipelago in S. China sea off S end of Malay peninsula; formerly a Brit. crown colony, from 1963 to 1965 a state of Malaysia (federation), an independent republic in the Commonwealth since 1965, *area* 225 *sq mi* (585 *sq km*), *pop* 2,413,945 **2** city & port, its *, on Singapore Strait *pop* 206,500 — **Sin·ga·por·ean** \ˌsiŋ-(g)ə-'pōr-ē-ən, -'pòr-\ *adj or n*

Singapore Strait channel SE Asia bet. Singapore Is. & Riau archipelago connecting Strait of Malacca & S. China sea

Sining — see HSI-NING

Sin·kiang Ui·ghur *or* **Xin·jiang Uy·gur** \'shin-jē-'äŋ-ˌwē-gər\ region W China bet. Kunlun & Altai mountains; formerly a province * Urumchi *area* 635,829 *sq mi* (1,653,154 *sq km*), *pop* 13,081,681

Si·nop \sə-'nòp\ *or anc* **Si·no·pe** \-'nō-pē\ town & port N Turkey on peninsula in Black sea NW of Ankara *pop* 18,381

Sinsiang — see HSIN-HSIANG

Sint–Gillis — see SAINT-GILLES

Sint–Jans–Molenbeek — see MOLENBEEK

Sint Maarten — see SAINT MARTIN

Sin·tra *or* **Cin·tra** \'sēn-trə\ city W Portugal NW of Lisbon *pop* 224,763

Sin·ui·ju \'shin-ē-ˌjü\ city W N. Korea on the Yalu opposite Antung, China *pop* 165,000

Sion **1** \sē-'ōⁿ\ *or G* **Sit·ten** \'zit-ᵊn, 'sit-\ commune SW *cen* Switzerland * of Valais *pop* 22,877 **2** — see ZION

Sioux City \'sü\ city NW Iowa on Missouri river *pop* 82,003

Sioux Falls city SE S.Dak. on the Big Sioux *pop* 81,343

Siping — see SSU-P'ING

Sip·par \sip-'är\ ancient city of Babylonia on the Euphrates SSW of modern Baghdad; Sargon's capital

Siracusa — see SYRACUSE

Si·ret \si-'ret\ river 270 *mi* (434 *km*) E Romania flowing from the Carpathians SE into the Danube

Si·ros \'sē-ˌrós\ island Greece in the Cyclades S of Andros

Sis·ki·you \'sis-kē-ˌ(y)ü\ mountains N Calif. & SW Oreg., a range of Klamath mountains; highest Mt. Ashland (in Oreg.) 7530 *ft* (2295 *m*)

Sit·tang \'si-ˌtäŋ\ river 350 *mi* (563 *km*) E *cen* Myanmar flowing S into Gulf of Martaban

Sit·twe \'si-ˌtwā\ *or* **Akyab** \'ak-ˌyab\ city & port W Myanmar; chief town of Arakan coast *pop* 42,329

Si·vas \si-'väs\ *or anc* **Se·bas·te** \sə-'bas-tē\ *or* **Se·bas·tia** \sə-'basch(ē-)ə, -tē-ə\ city E *cen* Turkey on the upper Kizil Irmak *pop* 173,831

Si·wa \'sē-wə\ *or anc* **Am·mo·ni·um** \ə-'mō-nē-əm\ oasis & town NW Egypt W of Qattara Depression *pop* 4999

Si·wa·lik \si-'wäl-ik\ range of foothills of the Himalayas N India extending SE from N Punjab into Uttar Pradesh

Sjæl·land \'shel-ˌän\ island, largest of islands of Denmark; site of Copenhagen *area* 2709 *sq mi* (7043 *sq km*)

Skadarsko Jezero — see SCUTARI, LAKE

Skag·er·rak \'skag-ə-ˌrak\ arm of the North sea bet. Norway & Denmark

Skag·it \'skaj-ət\ river 200 *mi* (322 *km*) SW B.C. & NW Wash. flowing S & W into Puget Sound

Skan·eat·e·les \ˌskan-ē-'at-ləs, ˌskin-\ lake 16 *mi* (26 *km*) long *cen* N.Y. SW of Syracuse; one of the Finger Lakes

Skaw, The \'skò\ *or* **Ska·gens Od·de** \'skäg-ən-ˌzòd-ə\ cape Denmark at N extremity of Jutland

Skee·na \'skē-nə\ river 360 *mi* (579 *km*) Canada in W B.C. flowing S & W into Hecate strait

Skid·daw \'skid-ˌò\ mountain 3054 *ft* (931 *m*) NW England in NW *cen* Cumbria

Skik·da \'skik-(ˌ)dä\ *or formerly* **Phi·lippe·ville** \'fil-əp-ˌvil, fi-ˌlēp-'vē(ə)l\ city & port NE Algeria N of Constantine *pop* 107,700

Ski·ros \'skē-ˌrós\ island Greece in the Northern Sporades E of Évvoia

Sko·kie \'skō-kē\ village NE Ill. N of Chicago *pop* 60,278

Skop·je \'skóp-ˌyä\ city S Yugoslavia * of Macedonia on the Vardar *pop* 308,117

Skunk river 264 *mi* (425 *km*) SE Iowa flowing SE into Mississippi river

Skye \'skī\ island Scotland, one of the Inner Hebrides *area* 670 *sq mi* (1742 *sq km*)

Slave river 258 *mi* (415 *km*) Canada flowing from W end of Lake Athabasca N into Great Slave Lake

Slave Coast region W Africa bordering on Bight of Benin bet. Benin & Volta rivers

Slav·kov \'släf-ˌkóf, 'släv-ˌkóv\ *or* **Aus·ter·litz** \'ò-stər-ˌlits, 'aù-\ town *cen* Czechoslovakia ESE of Brno

---

\ə\ abut \ᵊ\ kitten, F table \ər\ further \a\ ash \ā\ ace \ä\ cot, cart \aù\ out \ch\ chin \e\ bet \ē\ easy \g\ go \i\ hit \ī\ ice \j\ job \ŋ\ sing \ō\ go \ò\ law \òi\ boy \th\ thin \t̲h̲\ the \ü\ loot \ù\ foot \y\ yet \zh\ vision \à, k̲, ⁿ, œ, œ̄, ᵫ, ᵫ̄, ᵜ\ see Guide to Pronunciation

Sla·vo·nia \slə-'vō-nē-ə, -nyə\ region N Yugoslavia in E Croatia bet. the Sava, the Drava, & the Danube
Slea·ford \'slē-fərd\ town E England in SW Lincolnshire SSE of Lincoln
Slesvig — see SCHLESWIG
Sli·dell \slī-'del\ town SE La. NE of New Orleans *pop* 26,718
Slide Mountain \'slīd\ mountain 4204 *ft* (1281 *m*) SE N.Y. W of Kingston; highest in the Catskills
Sli·go \'slī-(,)gō\ **1** county N Ireland (republic) in N Connacht *area* 694 *sq mi* (1804 *sq km*), *pop* 55,474 **2** municipal borough & port, its ✱, on **Sligo Bay** (inlet of Atlantic ocean) *pop* 17,232
Slough \'slau̇\ borough SE *cen* England in Berkshire *pop* 87,005
Slo·va·kia \slō-'väk-ē-ə, -'vak-\ *or* **Slo·ven·sko** \slȯ-'ven(t)-skȯ\ region E Czechoslovakia E of Moravia; chief city Bratislava
Slo·ve·nia \slō-'vē-nē-ə, -nyə\ federated republic NW Yugoslavia N & W of Croatia ✱ Ljubljana *area* 7708 *sq mi* (20,041 *sq km*), *pop* 1,697,068
Smith·field \'smith-,fēld\ city N R.I. NW of Providence *pop* 16,886
Smoky Hill river 540 *mi* (869 *km*) *cen* Kans. flowing E to unite with Republican river forming the Kansas
Smo·lensk \smō-'len(t)sk\ city U.S.S.R. in W Soviet Russia, Europe, on the upper Dnieper WSW of Moscow *pop* 276,000
Smyr·na \'smər-nə\ town NW Ga. NW of Atlanta *pop* 20,312
Snake \'snāk\ **1** river 1038 *mi* (1670 *km*) NW U.S. flowing from NW Wyo. across S Idaho & into Columbia river in Wash. **2** mountain range E Nevada
Sno·qual·mie \snō-'kwäl-mē\ **1** mountain pass 3004 *ft* (916 *m*) W *cen* Wash. in Cascade range SE of Seattle **2** waterfall 268 *ft* (82 *m*) W *cen* Wash. in Snoqualmie river
Snow — see MAOKE
Snow·don \'snōd-ᵊn\ massif 3560 *ft* (1085 *m*) NW Wales in Gwynedd; highest point in Wales
Snow·do·nia \snō-'dō-nē-ə, -nyə\ mountain region NW Wales centering around Snowdon
Snowy **1** mountains SE Australia in SE New S. Wales **2** river 240 *mi* (386 *km*) SE Australia flowing from Snowy mountains to the Pacific in SE Victoria
So·bat \'sō-,bat\ river 460 *mi* (740 *km*) W Ethiopia & SE Sudan flowing W into White Nile river
Soca — see ISONZO
So–ch'e \'sō-'chə\ *or* **Sha·che** \'shä-'chə\ *or* **Yar·kand** \yär-'kand\ city W China in SW Sinkiang Uighur at oasis on Yarkand river
So·chi \'sō-chē\ city & port U.S.S.R. in S Soviet Russia, Europe, on NE coast of Black sea *pop* 224,000
So·ci·ety Islands \sə-'sī-ət-ē-\ *or F* **Îles de la So·cié·té** \ēl-də-lȧ-sȯ-syā-tā\ islands S Pacific belonging to France ✱ Papeete (on Tahiti) *area* 650 *sq mi* (1690 *sq km*), *pop* 81,424
So·co·tra \sə-'kō-trə\ island Indian ocean E of Gulf of Aden in Yemen ✱ Tamrida (Hadibu) *area* 1400 *sq mi* (3640 *sq km*), *pop* 8000
Sod·om \'säd-əm\ city of ancient Palestine in plain of Jordan river
So·fia \'sō-fē-ə, 'sȯ-, sō-'\ *or Bulg* **So·fi·ya** \'sȯ-fē-(y)ə\ *or anc* **Ser·di·ca** \'sərd-i-kə\ *or* **Sar·di·ca** \'särd-\ city W Bulgaria, its ✱ *pop* 967,214
Sog·di·a·na \,säg-dē-'an-ə, -'än-ə, -'ā-nə\ province of ancient Persian Empire bet. the Jaxartes (Syr Darya) & Oxus (Amu Darya) ✱ Maracanda (Samarkand)
Sog·ne Fjord \,sȯŋ-nə-\ inlet of Norwegian sea SW Norway; longest fjord in Norway
So·hâg \sō-'haj\ city *cen* Egypt on the Nile SE of Asyût *pop* 85,300
So·ho \'sō-,hō\ district of *cen* London, England, in Westminster
Sois·sons \swä-'sōⁿ\ commune N France NW of Paris *pop* 29,694
So·lent, The \'sō-lənt\ channel S England bet. Isle of Wight & the mainland
So·li·hull \,sō-li-'həl\ borough *cen* England in W. Midlands SE of Birmingham *pop* 111,541
So·li·mões \,sü-lē-'mōiⁿsh\ the upper Amazon, Brazil, from Peruvian border to the mouth of Negro river
So·ling·en \'zō-liŋ-ən, 'sō-\ city W W. Germany in the Ruhr ESE of Düsseldorf *pop* 166,085
Sol·na \'sōl-,nä\ city E Sweden, N suburb of Stockholm *pop* 50,441
Solo — see SURAKARTA
Sol·o·mon \'säl-ə-mən\ **1** islands W Pacific E of New Guinea divided bet. Papua New Guinea & the independent country of the Solomon islands (former Brit. protectorate) *area* 16,120 *sq mi* (41,912 *sq km*), *pop* 249,000 **2** sea arm of Coral sea W of Solomon islands
So·lo·thurn \'zō-lə-,tu̇(ə)rn, 'sō-\ *or F* **So·leure** \sō-'lər\ **1** canton NW Switzerland *area* 306 *sq mi* (796 *sq km*), *pop* 218,102 **2** commune, its ✱, on the Aare *pop* 15,778
Sol·way firth \,säl-,wā-\ inlet of Irish Sea in Great Britain on boundary bet. England & Scotland
So·ma·lia \sō-'mäl-ē-ə, sə-, -'mäl-yə\ country E Africa bordering on Gulf of Aden & Indian ocean; formed 1960 by union of Brit. Somaliland & Italian Somaliland ✱ Mogadishu *area* 262,000 *sq mi* (681,200 *sq km*), *pop* 4,760,000 — **So·ma·lian** \-'mäl-ē-ən, -'mäl-yən\ *adj or n*
So·ma·li·land \sō-'mäl-ē-,land, sə-\ region E Africa comprising Somalia, Djibouti, & Ogaden region of E Ethiopia
Som·er·set \'səm-ər-,set, -sət\ **1** town SE Mass. N of Fall River *pop* 18,813 **2** island N Canada in Northwest Territories N of Boothia peninsula *area* 9370 *sq mi* (24,362 *sq km*) **3** *or* **Som·er·set·shire** \-,shi(ə)r, -shər\ county SW England ✱ Taunton *area* 1620 *sq mi* (4212 *sq km*), *pop* 428,900
Somerset Nile — see NILE
Som·er·ville \'səm-ər-,vil\ city E Mass. N of Cambridge *pop* 77,372
So·mes \sō-'mesh\ *or Hung* **Sza·mos** \'sȯm-,ōsh\ river 200 *mi* (322 *km*) NE Hungary & NW Romania flowing NW into the Tisza
Somme \'säm, 'səm\ river 147 *mi* (236 *km*) N France flowing NW into the English channel
Songhua — see SUNGARI
So·no·ra \sə-'nōr-ə, -'nȯr-\ **1** river 300 *mi* (483 *km*) NW Mexico flowing SW into upper Gulf of California **2** state NW Mexico bordering on U.S. & Gulf of California ✱ Hermosillo *area* 70,477 *sq mi* (183,240 *sq km*), *pop* 1,498,931 — **So·no·ran** \-ən\ *adj or n*
Sonoran *or* **Sonora** desert SW U.S. & NW Mexico in S Ariz., SE Calif., & N Sonora
Soo Canals — see SAULT SAINTE MARIE CANALS
Soo·chow \'sü-'jō, -'chau̇\ *or* **Su·zhou** \-'jō\ *or formerly* **Wu·hsien** \'wü-shē-'en\ city E China in SE Kiangsu W of Shanghai *pop* 633,000
So·pot \'sȯ-,pȯt\ city N Poland NNW of Gdansk *pop* 51,085
Sop·ron \'shō-,prōn\ city W Hungary *pop* 53,930
Sorata — see ILLAMPU
Sorbiodunum — see OLD SARUM
So·rel \sə-'rel\ city Canada in S Que. on St. Lawrence river *pop* 20,347
So·ria \'sōr-ē-ə, 'sȯr-\ **1** province N *cen* Spain *area* 3983 *sq mi* (10,356 *sq km*), *pop* 88,772 **2** commune, its ✱, W of Zaragoza *pop* 30,558
So·ro·ca·ba \,sōr-ə-'kab-ə, ,sȯr-\ city SE Brazil in SE São Paulo state *pop* 269,880
Sor·ren·to \sə-'ren-(,)tō\ *or anc* **Sur·ren·tum** \sə-'rent-əm\ commune & port S Italy on S side of Bay of Naples *pop* 17,301
Sos·no·wiec \sä-'snōv-,yets\ *or* **Sos·no·wi·ce** \,sȯs-nə-'vēt-sə\ city SW Poland NE of Katowice *pop* 251,916
Sou·fri·ère \,sü-frē-'e(ə)r\ **1** volcano 4813 *ft* (1467 *m*) French W. Indies in S Basse-Terre, Guadeloupe **2** volcano 4048 *ft* (1234 *m*) Brit. W. Indies on St. Vincent Is.
Sou·ris \'su̇r-əs\ river 450 *mi* (724 *km*) Canada & U.S. flowing from SE Sask. SE into N N.Dak. & N into the Assiniboine in SW Man.
Sousse \'süs\ *or anc* **Had·ru·me·tum** \,had-rə-'mēt-əm\ city & port NE Tunisia *pop* 69,530
South island S New Zealand *area* 58,092 *sq mi* (151,039 *sq km*), *pop* 798,681
South Africa, Republic of country S Africa S of the Limpopo, Molopo, & Orange rivers bordering on Atlantic & Indian oceans; a republic, until 1961 (as **Union of South Africa**) a Brit. dominion; administrative ✱ Pretoria, legislative ✱ Cape Town, judicial ✱ Bloemfontein *area* 472,359 *sq mi* (1,228,133 *sq km*), *pop* 26,129,000
Sou·thall \'sau̇-,thȯl\ former municipal borough S England in Middlesex, now part of Ealing
South America continent of the W hemisphere lying bet. the Atlantic & Pacific oceans SE of N. America & chiefly S of the equator *area* 7,035,357 *sq mi* (18,291,928 *sq km*) — **South American** *adj or n*
South·amp·ton \sau̇th-'(h)am(p)-tən\ **1** island N Canada in Northwest Territories, bet. Hudson bay & Foxe channel *area* 15,700 *sq mi* (40,820 *sq km*) **2** city & port S England in Hampshire on **Southampton Water** (estuary of Test river) *pop* 204,406
South Arabia, Federation of former Brit. protectorate comprising crown colony of Aden & numerous semi-independent Arab sultanates & emirates; made part of People's Democratic Republic of Yemen 1967
South Australia state S Australia ✱ Adelaide *area* 380,070 *sq mi* (988,182 *sq km*), *pop* 1,285,033
South Bend \-'bend\ city N Ind. NW of Fort Wayne *pop* 109,727
South·bridge \'sau̇th-(,)brij\ town S Mass. *pop* 16,665
South Canadian — see CANADIAN
South Cape — see KA LAE
South Car·o·li·na \-,kar-(ə-)'lī-nə\ state SE U.S. ✱ Columbia *area* 31,055 *sq mi* (80,743 *sq km*), *pop* 3,121,820 — **South Car·o·lin·ian** \-'lin-ē-ən, -'lin-yən\ *adj or n*
South China sea W Pacific enclosed by SE China, Taiwan, Philippines, Indochina, Malaya, & Borneo
South Da·ko·ta \-də-'kōt-ə\ state NW *cen* U.S. ✱ Pierre *area* 77,047 *sq mi* (200,322 *sq km*), *pop* 690,768 — **South Da·ko·tan** \-'kōt-ᵊn\ *adj or n*
South Downs \-'dau̇nz\ hills S England chiefly in Sussex
South El Monte city SW Calif. SE of Los Angeles *pop* 16,623
South·end on Sea \,sau̇-,thend-\ borough SE England in Essex at mouth of Thames estuary *pop* 156,683
Southern Alps mountain range New Zealand in W South Is. extending almost the length of the island — see COOK (Mount)
Southern Morocco *or* **Southern Protectorate of Morocco** former Spanish protectorate W Africa S of former French Morocco
Southern ocean the Antarctic ocean
Southern Rhodesia — see ZIMBABWE
Southern Uplands elevated moorland region S Scotland extending from English border to a line joining Girvan & Dunbar
Southern Yemen — see YEMEN
South Euclid city NE Ohio E of Cleveland *pop* 25,713
South·field \'sau̇th-,fēld\ city SE Mich. NW of Detroit *pop* 75,568
South·gate \'sau̇th-,gāt\ city SE Mich. S of Detroit *pop* 32,058
South Gate \-,gāt\ city SW Calif. SE of Los Angeles *pop* 66,784
South Georgia island S Atlantic E of Tierra del Fuego in Falkland Islands Dependencies *area* 1450 *sq mi* (3770 *sq km*)
South Glamorgan county SE Wales ✱ Cardiff *area* 161 *sq mi* (419 *sq km*), *pop* 390,400
South Holland **1** village NE Ill. S of Chicago *pop* 24,977 **2** *or D* **Zuid–Hol·land** \zit-'hō-,länt\ province SW Netherlands ✱ Rotterdam *area* 1212 *sq mi* (3151 *sq km*), *pop* 3,130,426
South·ing·ton \'səth-iŋ-tən\ town W *cen* Conn. *pop* 36,879
South Kingstown town S R.I. *pop* 20,414
South Korea — see KOREA
South Lake Tahoe city E Calif. on Lake Tahoe *pop* 20,681
South Milwaukee city SE Wis. on Lake Michigan *pop* 21,069
South Mountain ridge S Pa. & W Md. at N end of Blue Ridge
South Na·han·ni \-nə-'han-ē\ river 350 *mi* (563 *km*) Canada in SW Northwest Territories flowing SE into the Liard
South Orkney islands S Atlantic SE of the Falklands in Falkland Islands Dependencies *area* 400 *sq mi* (1040 *sq km*)
South Ossetia *or* **South Ossetian Region** autonomous region U.S.S.R. in N Georgia ✱ Tskhinvali *area* 1500 *sq mi* (3900 *sq km*), *pop* 100,000
South Pasadena city SW Calif. *pop* 22,681
South Pass broad level valley SW *cen* Wyo. crossing Continental Divide
South Plainfield borough NE N.J. SW of Elizabeth *pop* 20,521
South Platte river 424 *mi* (682 *km*) Colo. & Nebr. flowing E to join N. Platte river forming the Platte river
South·port \'sau̇th-,pō(ə)rt, -,pȯ(ə)rt\ borough NW England in Merseyside on coast N of Liverpool *pop* 89,745
South Portland city SW Maine *pop* 22,712
South Saint Paul city SE Minn. on Mississippi river *pop* 21,235
South Sandwich islands S Atlantic SE of S. Georgia Is. in Falkland Islands Dependencies *area* 120 *sq mi* (312 *sq km*)
South San Francisco city W Calif. *pop* 49,393
South Saskatchewan — see SASKATCHEWAN
South Seas the areas of the Atlantic, Indian, & Pacific oceans in the southern hemisphere, esp. the S Pacific

South Shetland islands S Atlantic SE of Cape Horn off tip of Antarctic peninsula in Falkland Islands Dependencies

South Shields \'shē(ə)l(d)z\ borough N England in Tyne and Wear at mouth of the Tyne E of Newcastle *pop* 87,203

South Tirol — see ALTO ADIGE

South Vietnam — see VIETNAM

South·wark \'səth-ərk, 'saúth-wərk\ borough of S London, England *pop* 221,300

South–West Africa — see NAMIBIA

South Windsor town N Conn. NE of Hartford *pop* 17,198

South Yemen SOUTHERN YEMEN

South Yorkshire metropolitan county N England * Barnsley *area* 602 *sq mi* (1565 *sq km*), *pop* 1,315,100

So·vetsk \səv-'yetsk\ *or G* Til·sit \'til-sət, -zət\ city U.S.S.R. in W Soviet Russia, Europe, on the Neman *pop* 36,000

So·vet·ska·ya Ga·van \səv-,yet-skə-yə-'gäv-ən(-yə)\ city & port U.S.S.R. in SE Soviet Russia, Asia, on Tatar strait *pop* 26,000

Soviet Central Asia the portion of *cen* Asia belonging to the U.S.S.R. & comprising the Kirghiz, Tadzhik, Turkmen, & Uzbek republics & sometimes Kazakhstan

Soviet Russia **1** *or* **Russian Republic** constituent republic of the U.S.S.R. in E Europe (**Soviet Russia, Europe**) & N Asia (**Soviet Russia, Asia**) bordering on Arctic & Pacific oceans & on Baltic & Black seas * Moscow *area* 6,501,500 *sq mi* (16,903,900 *sq km*), *pop* 137,551,000 **2** the U.S.S.R.

Soviet Union — see UNION OF SOVIET SOCIALIST REPUBLICS

So·we·to \sə-'wā-tō, -tü\ township NE Republic of S. Africa in S Transvaal adjoining SW Johannesburg; a black residential complex

Spa \'spä\ town E Belgium SE of Liège *pop* 9619

Spain \'spān\ *or Sp* Es·pa·ña \ä-'spän-yä\ country SW Europe in the Iberian peninsula; a kingdom * Madrid *area* 193,144 *sq mi* (502,174 *sq km*), *pop* 37,746,260

Span·dau \'s(h)pän-,daú\ a W section of W. Berlin, W. Germany

Spanish America **1** the Spanish-speaking countries of the Americas **2** the parts of America settled & formerly governed by the Spanish

Spanish Guinea former Spanish colony W Africa bordering on Gulf of Guinea including Río Muni (Mbini), Fernando Po (Bioko) & other islands — see EQUATORIAL GUINEA

Spanish Main **1** the mainland of Spanish America esp. along N coast of S. America **2** the Caribbean sea & adjacent waters esp. at the time when region was infested with pirates

Spanish Morocco — see MOROCCO

Spanish Peaks two mountains (**East Spanish Peak** 12,683 *ft or* 3866 *m* & **West Spanish Peak** 13,623 *ft or* 4152 *m*) S Colo.

Spanish Sahara former Spanish possessions Río de Oro & Saguia el Hamra — see WESTERN SAHARA

Spanish Town town SE *cen* Jamaica W of Kingston; former * of Jamaica

Sparks \'spärks\ city W Nev. E of Reno *pop* 40,780

Spar·ta \'spärt-ə\ *or* **Lac·e·dae·mon** \,las-ə-'dē-mən\ ancient city S Greece in Peloponnisos * of Laconia

Spar·tan·burg \'spärt-ªn-,bərg\ city NW S.C. *pop* 43,968

Spen·cer Gulf \,spen(t)-sər-\ inlet of Indian ocean SE S. Australia

Spey \'spā\ river 110 *mi* (177 *km*) NE Scotland flowing into Moray firth

Spey·er \'s(h)pī(-ə)r\ *or* **Spires** \'spī(ə)rz\ city SW W. Germany on W bank of the Rhine SW of Heidelberg *pop* 43,864

Spezia, La — see LA SPEZIA

Spits·ber·gen \'spits-,bər-gən\ group of islands in Arctic ocean N of Norway; belongs to Norway *area* 24,280 *sq mi* (63,128 *sq km*) — see SVALBARD

Split \'split\ city & port W Yugoslavia in Croatia on Dalmatian coast *pop* 150,739

Spo·kane \spō-'kan\ **1** river 120 *mi* (193 *km*) N Idaho & E Wash. flowing from Coeur d'Alene Lake W into Columbia river **2** city E Wash. at Spokane Falls in Spokane river *pop* 171,300

Spo·le·to \spō-'lāt-(,)ō\ commune *cen* Italy SE of Perugia *pop* 36,839

Spor·a·des \'spór-ə-,dēz, 'spär-\ two island groups Greece in the Aegean: the **Northern Sporades** (chief island Skíros, N of Évvoia & E of Thessaly) & the **Southern Sporades** (chiefly Samos, Icaria, & the Dodecanese, off SW Turkey)

Sprat·ly \'sprat-lē\ islands *cen* S. China sea SE of Cam Ranh Bay, Vietnam; claimed by several countries

Spree \'s(h)prā\ river 220 *mi* (354 *km*) E E. Germany flowing N into the Havel

Spree·wald \-,vält\ marshy district E E. Germany in Spree valley

Spring·dale \'spriŋ-,dāl\ city NW Ark. *pop* 23,458

Spring·field \'spriŋ-,feld\ **1** city * of Ill. on the Sangamon *pop* 99,637 **2** city SW Mass. on Connecticut river *pop* 152,319 **3** city SW Mo. *pop* 133,116 **4** city W *cen* Ohio NE of Dayton *pop* 72,563 **5** city W Oreg. on the Willamette E of Eugene *pop* 41,621

Springs \'spriŋz\ city NE Republic of S. Africa in S Transvaal *pop* 142,812

Spring Valley village SE N.Y. N of New York City *pop* 20,537

Spuy·ten Duy·vil Creek \,spīt-ªn-'dī-vəl-\ channel New York City N of Manhattan Is. connecting Hudson & Harlem rivers

Sri Lan·ka \(')srē-'läŋ-kə, (')shrē-\ *or formerly* Cey·lon \si-'län, sā-\ country coextensive with island of Ceylon; an independent republic in the Commonwealth * Colombo *area* 25,332 *sq mi* (65,863 *sq km*), *pop* 14,850,001 — **Sri Lan·kan** \-'läŋ-kən\ *adj or n*

Sri·na·gar \sri-'nəg-ər\ city India, summer * of Jammu and Kashmir, in W Kashmir on the Jhelum NNE of Lahore *pop* 423,253

Ssu–p'ing \'sü-'piŋ\ *or* **Si·ping** \'sē-'piŋ\ *or formerly* Sze·ping·kai \'sü-'piŋ-'gī\ city NE China in Kirin SW of Changchun *pop* 150,000

Staf·fa \'staf-ə\ islet W Scotland in the Inner Hebrides W of Mull — see FINGAL'S CAVE

Staf·ford \'staf-ərd\ borough W *cen* England * of Staffordshire *pop* 55,497

Staf·ford·shire \'staf-ərd-,shi(ə)r, -shər\ *or* **Stafford** county W *cen* England * Stafford *area* 1049 *sq mi* (2727 *sq km*), *pop* 1,015,700

Staked Plain — see LLANO ESTACADO

Sta·kha·nov \stə-'kän-əf\ *or formerly* Ka·di·yev·ka \kə-'dē-(y)əf-kə\ city U.S.S.R. in E Ukrainian Republic *pop* 108,000

Stalin 1 — see BRASOV **2** — see DONETSK **3** — see VARNA

Stalinabad — see DUSHANBE

Stalingrad — see VOLGOGRAD

Stalino — see DONETSK

Stalinsk — see NOVOKUZNETSK

Stam·boul *or* **Stam·bul** \stam-'bül\ **1** the older part of Istanbul S of the Golden Horn **2** ISTANBUL

Stam·ford \'stam(p)-fərd\ city SW Conn. *pop* 102,453

Stanislav — see IVANO-FRANKOVSK

Stan·ley \'stan-lē\ *or* **Port Stanley** town * of the Falklands

Stanley, Mount *or in Zaire* **Mount Nga·lie·ma** \-,en-gäl-'yä-mə\ mountain with two peaks (higher Margherita Peak 16,763 *ft or* 5109 *m*) E *cen* Africa; highest of Ruwenzori

Stanley Falls — see BOYOMA FALLS

Stanley Pool — see MALEBO POOL

Stanleyville — see KISANGANI

Stan·o·voi \,stan-ə-'vói\ mountain range U.S.S.R. in E Soviet Russia, Asia, N of the Amur; highest point 8143 *ft* (2482 *m*)

Stan·ton \'stant-ªn\ city SW Calif. SE of Los Angeles *pop* 23,723

Sta·ra Za·go·ra \,stär-ə-zə-'gör-ə, -'gór-\ city *cen* Bulgaria *pop* 122,200

State College borough *cen* Pa. NE of Altoona *pop* 36,130

Stat·en Island \'stat-ªn-\ **1** island SE N.Y. SW of mouth of Hudson river **2** *or formerly* Rich·mond \'rich-mənd\ borough of New York City including Staten Is. *pop* 352,121

States of the Church *or* **Papal States** temporal domain of the popes in *cen* Italy 755–1870

States·ville \'stāts-,vil, -vəl\ city W *cen* N.C. *pop* 18,622

Statia — see SAINT EUSTATIUS

Statue of Liberty National Monument — see LIBERTY

Staun·ton \'stant-ªn\ city NW *cen* Va. *pop* 21,857

Sta·vang·er \stə-'väŋ-ər, -'vaŋ-\ city & port SW Norway *pop* 90,732

Stav·ro·pol \stav-'rö-pəl, -'rö-\ **1** territory U.S.S.R. in S Soviet Russia, Europe, N of the Caucasus *area* 29,600 *sq mi* (76,960 *sq km*), *pop* 2,306,000 **2** city, its * *pop* 198,000 **3** — see TOLYATTI

Ste·bark \'ste(ⁿ)m-,bärk\ *or G* Tan·nen·berg \'tan-ən-,bərg, 'tän-ən-,berk\ village NE Poland SW of Olsztyn

Steens \'stenz\ mountains SE Oreg.; highest **Steens Mountain** (massif) 9354 *ft* (2851 *m*)

Stel·len·bosch \'stel-ən-,bäs(h), *Afrik* ,stel-əm-'bós\ city SW Republic of S. Africa in SW Cape Province *pop* 29,955

Step·ney \'step-nē\ former metropolitan borough E London, England, on N bank of Thames river, now part of Tower Hamlets

Sterling Heights city SE Mich. N of Detroit *pop* 108,999

Stet·ti·ner Haff \s(h)te-'tē-nər-,häf\ lagoon on Baltic coast between NE E. Germany & NW Poland at mouth of the Oder

Steu·ben·ville \'st(y)ü-bən-,vil\ city E Ohio *pop* 26,400

Ste·vens Point \,stē-vənz-\ city *cen* Wis. *pop* 22,970

Stew·art \'st(y)ü-ərt, 'st(y)ü(-ə)rt\ **1** river 320 *mi* (515 *km*) Canada in *cen* Yukon Territory flowing W into Yukon river **2** island New Zealand S of South Is. *area* 670 *sq mi* (1742 *sq km*)

Sti·kine \stik-'ēn\ river 335 *mi* (539 *km*) Canada & Alaska flowing from **Stikine mountains** (in B.C. & Yukon Territory) into the Pacific

Still·wa·ter \'stil-,wót-ər, -,wät-\ city N *cen* Okla. *pop* 38,268

Stir·ling \'stər-liŋ\ **1** *or* **Stir·ling·shire** \-,shi(ə)r, -shər\ former county *cen* Scotland **2** burgh *cen* Scotland * of Central region *pop* 38,638

Stock·holm \'stäk-,hō(l)m\ city & port * of Sweden on Mälaren lake *pop* 647,214 — **Stock·holm·er** \-,hō(l)-mər\ *n*

Stock·port \'stäk-,pō(ə)rt, -,pó(ə)rt\ borough NW England in Greater Manchester S of Manchester *pop* 136,496

Stock·ton \'stäk-tən\ city *cen* Calif. on the San Joaquin *pop* 149,779

Stockton–on–Tees \-'tēz\ borough N England in Cleveland *pop* 81,274

Stoke New·ing·ton \-'n(y)ü-iŋ-tən\ former metropolitan borough N London, England, now part of Hackney

Stoke on Trent \-stō-,kón-'trent, -,kän-\ city W *cen* England in Staffordshire *pop* 252,351

Stone·ham \'stō-nəm, 'stōn-,(h)am\ town E Mass. *pop* 21,424

Stone·ha·ven \'stōn-'hā-vən, ,stōn-'hā\ burgh & port E Scotland in Grampian region *pop* 7885

Stone·henge \'stōn-,henj, (')stōn-'\ assemblage of megaliths S England in Wiltshire on Salisbury Plain erected by prehistoric peoples

Stone Mountain mountain 1686 *ft* (514 *m*) NW *cen* Ga. E of Atlanta

Stones \'stōnz\ river 60 *mi* (96 *km*) *cen* Tenn. flowing NW into Cumberland river

Ston·ey Creek \'stō-nē-\ town Canada in SE Ont. *pop* 36,762

Stor·mont \'stór-mənt\ E suburb of Belfast, Northern Ireland; site of Parliament House

Stor·no·way \'stór-nə-,wā\ burgh NW Scotland in Lewis * of Western Isles region *pop* 8660

Stough·ton \'stōt-ªn\ town E Mass. NW of Brockton *pop* 26,710

Stour 1 \'stü(ə)r\ river 60 *mi* (96 *km*) SE England flowing E bet. Essex & Suffolk into the North sea **2** \'staú(ə)r, 'stü(ə)r\ river 55 *mi* (88 *km*) S England in Dorset & Hampshire flowing into Avon river **3** \'stü-(ə)r *also* 'staú(ə)r\ river 40 *mi* (64 *km*) SE England in Kent flowing NE into the North sea **4** \'staú(ə)r, 'stó(ə)r\ river 20 *mi* (32 *km*) *cen* England in Oxfordshire & Warwickshire flowing NW into Avon river **5** *same as* 4 \ river 20 *mi* (32 *km*) W *cen* England in Staffordshire & Hereford and Worcester flowing S into Severn river

Stour·bridge \'staú(ə)r-(,)brij, 'stó(ə)r-\ borough W *cen* England in W. Midlands W of Birmingham *pop* 54,661

Stow \'stō\ city NE Ohio NE of Akron *pop* 25,303

Stra·bane \strə-'ban\ district W Northern Ireland, established 1974 *area* 336 *sq mi* (874 *sq km*), *pop* 35,028

Straits Settlements former country SE Asia bordering on Strait of Malacca & comprising Singapore Is., Penang, & Malacca; now divided between Singapore (republic) & Malaysia (federation) *area* 1242 *sq mi* (3229 *sq km*)

Stral·sund \'s(h)träl-,zúnt, -,súnt\ city & port N E. Germany on the Baltic opposite Rügen Is. *pop* 75,070

Stras·bourg \'sträs-,bü(ə)rg, 'sträz-, -,bərg\ *or G* **Strass·burg** \'shträs-,bürk\ city NE France on Ill river *pop* 251,520
Strat·ford \'strat-fərd\ **1** town SW Conn. *pop* 50,541 **2** city Canada in SE Ont. W of Kitchener *pop* 26,262
Stratford–upon–Avon \-ā-vən\ borough *cen* England in Warwickshire SSE of Birmingham *pop* 20,858
Strath·clyde \strath-'klīd\ **1** Celtic kingdom of 6th to 11th centuries S Scotland & NW England ✻ Dumbarton; its S part called **Cum·bria** \'kəm-brē-ə\ **2** region SW Scotland, established 1975; ✻ Glasgow *area* 5348 *sq mi* (13,905 *sq km*), *pop* 2,397,827
Strath·more \strath-'mō(ə)r, -'mò(ə)r\ great valley of E *cen* Scotland S of the Grampians
Stream·wood \'strēm-,wùd\ village NE Ill. E of Elgin *pop* 23,456
Stre·sa \'strā-zə\ town NW Italy in Piedmont on Lake Maggiore
Stret·ford \'stret-fərd\ borough NW England in Greater Manchester SW of Manchester *pop* 47,600
Stri·món, Gulf of \strē-'mòn\ *or* **Stri·mon·i·kós Kól·pos** \stri-'män-i-,kòs-'kòl-pòs\ *or* **Stry·mon·ic Gulf** \strī-,män-ik-\ inlet of the Aegean NE Greece NE of Chalcidice peninsula
Strom·bo·li \'sträm-bə-(,)lē\ *or anc* **Stron·gy·le** \'strän-jə-,lē\ **1** island Italy in Lipari islands *pop* 469 **2** volcano 3038 *ft* (926 *m*) on the island
Strom·lo, Mount \'sträm-(,)lō\ hill 2500 *ft* (758 *m*) SE Australia in Australian Capital Territory W of Canberra
Strongs·ville \'strȯŋz-,vil\ city NE Ohio SW of Cleveland *pop* 28,577
Stry·mon \'strī-,män\ *or NGk* **Stri·món** \strē-'mòn\ *or Bulg* **Stru·ma** \'strü-mə\ river 225 *mi* (362 *km*) W Bulgaria & NE Greece flowing SE into Gulf of Strimón
Stutt·gart \'s(h)tùt-,gärt, 'stət-\ city SW W. Germany ✻ of Baden-Württemberg on the Neckar *pop* 580,648
Styr \'sti(ə)r\ river 300 *mi* (483 *km*) U.S.S.R. in NW Ukrainian Republic flowing N into the Pripet in the Pripet marshes
Styr·ia \'stir-ē-ə\ *or Ger* **Stei·er·mark** \'s(h)tī(-ə)r-,märk\ region *cen* & SE Austria; chief city Graz — **Styr·i·an** \'stir-ē-ən\ *adj or n*
Sua·kin \'swäk-ən\ town & port NE Sudan on Red sea
Su·bic \'sü-bik\ town Philippines in W Luzon at head of **Subic Bay** (inlet of S. China sea NW of Bataan peninsula) *pop* 30,340
Su·bo·ti·ca \'sü-bə-,tēt-sə\ city NE Yugoslavia in N Vojvodina near Hungarian border *pop* 88,787
Sü·chow **1** *or* **Xu·zhou** *or* **Hsü–chou** \'s(h)ü-'jō, 'sü-'chaù\ city E China in NW Kiangsu N of Pengpu *pop* 1,500,000 **2** — see I-PIN
Su·cre \'sü-(,)krā\ city, constitutional ✻ of Bolivia, SE of La Paz *pop* 63,625
Su·dan \sü-'dan, -'dän\ **1** region N Africa bet. the Atlantic & the upper Nile S of the Sahara including basins of Lake Chad & Niger river & the upper Nile **2** country NE Africa S of Egypt; a republic, until 1956 a territory (**Anglo–Egyptian Sudan**) under joint Brit. & Egyptian rule ✻ Khartoum *area* 967,500 *sq mi* (2,515,500 *sq km*), *pop* 20,564,364 — **Su·da·nese** \,süd-ᵊn-'ēz, -'ēs\ *adj or n*
Sudanese Republic — see MALI
Sud·bury \'səd-,ber-ē, -b(ə-)rē\ city Canada in SE Ont. N of Georgian Bay *pop* 91,829
Sudd \'səd\ swamp region S Sudan drained by White Nile river
Su·de·ten·land \sü-'dāt-ᵊn-,land, -,länt\ region N Czechoslovakia in Sudety mountains
Su·de·ty *Czech* 'sù-det-yē, *Polish* sù-'det-ē\ *or* **Su·de·ten** \sü-'dāt-ᵊn\ mountains *cen* Europe W of the Carpathians bet. Czechoslovakia & Poland — **Sudeten** *adj or n*
Su·dir·man \sü-'di(ə)r-mən\ *or formerly* **Nas·sau** \'nas-,ò\ mountain range *cen* W. Irian — see DJAJA (Mount)
Su·ez \sü-'ez, 'sü-,ez, *chiefly Brit* 'sü-iz\ **1** city & port NE Egypt at S end of Suez canal on **Gulf of Suez** (arm of Red sea) *pop* 193,282 **2** canal 92 *mi* (148 *km*) long NE Egypt traversing Isthmus of Suez
Suez, Isthmus of isthmus NE Egypt between Mediterranean & Red seas connecting Africa & Asia
Suf·folk \'səf-ək, *US also* -,òk\ **1** city SE Va. W of Chesapeake *pop* 47,621 **2** county E England bordering on North sea ✻ Ipswich *area* 1462 *sq mi* (3800 *sq km*), *pop* 604,900; formerly divided into administrative counties of **East Suffolk** (✻ Ipswich) & **West Suffolk** (✻ Bury St. Edmunds)
Suffolk Broads — see BROADS
Sugarloaf Mountain — see PÃO DE AÇÚCAR
Suisse — see SWITZERLAND
Sui·sun Bay \sə-'sün\ the E extension of San Pablo Bay *cen* Calif.
Sukarnapura — see DJAJAPURA
Su·khu·mi \'sùk-ə-mē\ city & port U.S.S.R. in NW Georgia ✻ of Abkhaz Republic on Black sea *pop* 102,000
Suk·kur city Pakistan in N Sind on the Indus *pop* 193,000
Sulawesi — see CELEBES
Sul·grave \'səl-,grāv\ village England in S Northamptonshire
Sul·phur \'səl-fər\ city SW La. *pop* 19,709
Su·lu \'sü-(,)lü\ **1** archipelago SW Philippines SW of Mindanao **2** sea W Philippines N of Celebes sea
Su·ma·tra \sù-'mä-trə\ island W Indonesia S of Malay peninsula *area* 166,789 *sq mi* (433,651 *sq km*) — **Su·ma·tran** \-trən\ *adj or n*
Sum·ba \'süm-bə\ island Indonesia in the Lesser Sundas *area* 4306 *sq mi* (11,196 *sq km*), *pop* 251,126
Sum·ba·wa \süm-'bä-wə\ island Indonesia in the Lesser Sundas *area* 5693 *sq mi* (14,802 *sq km*), *pop* 195,554
Su·mer \'sü-mər\ the S division of ancient Babylonia — see AKKAD, SHINAR
Sum·ga·it \,sùm-gä-'ēt\ city & port U.S.S.R. in Azerbaijan on the Caspian NW of Baku *pop* 124,000
Sum·mit \'səm-ət\ city NE N.J. W of Newark *pop* 21,071
Sum·ter \'səm(p)-tər\ city E *cen* S.C. E of Columbia *pop* 24,890
Sun City city SW *cen* Ariz. *pop* 40,505
Sun·da \'sün-də\ **1** islands Malay archipelago comprising the **Greater Sunda** islands (Sumatra, Java, Borneo, Celebes, & adjacent islands) & the **Lesser Sunda** islands (extending E from Bali to Timor); with exception of N Borneo, belongs to Indonesia **2** SELAT SUNDA
Sun·der·land \'sən-dər-lənd\ borough N England in Tyne and Wear on North sea *pop* 196,152
Sunds·vall \'sən(t)s-,väl, 'sün(t)s-\ city & port E Sweden on Gulf of Bothnia *pop* 94,742
Sun·ga·ri \'sùŋ-gə-rē\ *or* **Song·hua** \'sùŋ-'hwä\ **1** river 800 *mi* (1287 *km*) NE China in E Manchuria flowing from Chang Pai Shan on N. Korea border NW & NE into the Amur **2** reservoir formed by dam in upper Sungari river
Sun·ny·vale \'sən-ē-,vāl\ city W Calif. WNW of San Jose *pop* 106,618
Sun·rise \'sən-,rīz\ city SE Fla. *pop* 39,681
Sunset Crater volcanic crater N *cen* Ariz. in **Sunset Crater National Monument**
Suomi — see FINLAND
Su·pe·ri·or \sù-'pir-ē-ər\ city & port NW Wis. on Lake Superior *pop* 29,571
Superior, Lake lake U.S. & Canada; largest, northernmost, & westernmost of the Great Lakes *area* 31,820 *sq mi* (82,732 *sq km*)
Superstition mountain range S *cen* Ariz. E of Phoenix; highest point **Superstition Mountain** 5057 *ft* (1541 *m*)
Sur \'sù(ə)r\ *or* **Tyre** \'tī(ə)r\ *or* **Tyr** \'ti(ə)r\ town S Lebanon on the coast; ancient ✻ of Phoenicia
Sur, Point \'sər\ promontory Calif. on the Pacific SSW of Monterey — see BIG SUR
Su·ra·ba·ja *or* **Su·ra·ba·ya** \,sùr-ə-'bī-ə\ city & port Indonesia in NE Java on **Surabaja strait** (bet. Java & W end of Madura) *pop* 2,027,913
Su·ra·kar·ta \,sùr-ə-'kärt-ə\ *or* **So·lo** \'sō-(,)lō\ city Indonesia in *cen* Java *pop* 469,888
Su·rat \'sùr-ət, sə-'rat\ city W India in SE Gujarat *pop* 912,568
Sur·bi·ton \'sər-bət-ᵊn\ former municipal borough S England in Surrey WSW of London, now part of Kingston upon Thames
Su·ri·ba·chi, Mount \,sùr-ə-'bäch-ē\ volcano 548 *ft* (167 *m*) in the Volcano islands at S end of Iwo Jima
Su·ri·na·me \,sùr-ə-'näm-ə\ **1** *or formerly* **Dutch Guiana** *or* **Netherlands Guiana** country N S. America bet. Guyana & French Guiana; a republic, until 1975 territory of the Netherlands ✻ Paramaribo *area* 55,142 *sq mi* (143,369 *sq km*), *pop* 352,041 **2** river 400 *mi* (644 *km*) N Suriname flowing N into the Atlantic — **Su·ri·nam·er** \'sùr-ə-,nam-ər, ,sùr-ə-'näm-\ *n* — **Su·ri·nam·ese** \,sùr-ə-,nə-'mēz, -'mēs\ *adj or n*
Sur·ma \'sù(ə)r-mə\ river 560 *mi* (901 *km*) NE India (subcontinent) in Manipur & Bangladesh — see MEGHNA
Surrentum — see SORRENTO
Sur·rey \'sər-ē, 'sə-rē\ county SE England S of London ✻ Kingston upon Thames *area* 648 *sq mi* (1685 *sq km*), *pop* 1,014,800
Surts·ey \'sərt-,sā, 'sù(ə)rt-\ island Iceland off S coast *area* 1 *sq mi* (2.6 *sq km*); formed 1963 by volcanic eruption
Su·ru·ga Bay \'sùr-ə-gə\ inlet of the Pacific Japan on coast of SE Honshu W of Sagami sea
Su·sa \'sü-zə\ *or bib* **Shu·shan** \'shü-shən, -,shan\ ancient city ✻ of Elam; ruins in SW Iran
Susiana — see ELAM
Sus·que·han·na \,səs-kwə-'han-ə\ river 444 *mi* (714 *km*) E U.S. flowing from *cen* N.Y. S through Pa. & into Chesapeake Bay in N Md.
Sus·sex \'səs-iks, *US also* -,eks\ former county SE England bordering on English channel; one of kingdoms in Anglo-Saxon heptarchy — see EAST SUSSEX, WEST SUSSEX
Suth·er·land \'sət͟h-ər-lənd\ *or* **Suth·er·land·shire** \-lən(d)-,shi(ə)r, -shər\ former county N Scotland ✻ Dornoch
Sutherland Falls waterfall 1904 *ft* (580 *m*) New Zealand in SW South Is.
Sut·lej \'sət-,lej\ river 900 *mi* (1448 *km*) N India (subcontinent) flowing from Tibet W & SW through the Punjab to join the Chenab
Sut·ton \'sət-ᵊn\ borough of S Greater London, England *pop* 169,900
Sut·ton Cold·field \'kōl(d)-,fēld\ borough *cen* England in W. Midlands NE of Birmingham *pop* 86,494
Sutton–in–Ash·field \-'ash-,fēld\ town N *cen* England in Nottinghamshire N of Nottingham *pop* 41,270
Su·va \'sü-və\ city & port ✻ of Fiji, on Viti Levu Is. *pop* 63,628
Su·wał·ki \sù-'väl-kē\ **1** district NE Poland **2** city in the district
Su·wan·nee \sə-'wän-ē\ river 240 *mi* (386 *km*) SE Ga. & N Fla. flowing SW into Gulf of Mexico
Su·won \'sü-,wän\ city NW S. Korea S of Seoul *pop* 310,757
Suzhou — see SOOCHOW
Sval·bard \'sfäl-,bär\ islands in the Arctic ocean including Spitsbergen, Bear Is., & other small islands *area* 25,000 *sq mi* (65,000 *sq km*); under Norwegian administration
Sverd·lovsk \sferd-'lòfsk\ *or formerly* **Eka·te·rin·burg** \i-'kat-ə-rən-,bərg\ city U.S.S.R. in W Soviet Russia, Asia, in *cen* Ural mountains *pop* 1,026,000
Sver·drup \'sfer-drəp\ islands N Canada W of Ellesmere Is. including Axel Heiberg, Ellef Ringnes, & Amund Ringnes Islands
Swa·bia \'swā-bē-ə\ *or G* **Schwa·ben** \'shfäb-ən\ region and medieval county SW Germany chiefly in area comprising modern Baden-Wurttemberg & W Bavaria in W. Germany — **Swa·bi·an** \'swā-bē-ən\ *adj or n*
Swan \'swän\ **1** two islands in the Caribbean NE of Honduras **2** *or in its upper course* **Av·on** \'av-ən\ river 150 *mi* (241 *km*) SW Western Australia flowing W into Indian ocean
Swan·sea \'swän-zē (*usual Brit pron*), 'swän(t)-sē\ city & port SE Wales ✻ of W. Glamorgan *pop* 167,796
Swat \'swät\ river 400 *mi* (644 *km*) Pakistan flowing into Kabul river
Swa·tow \'swä-'taù\ *or* **Shan·tou** \'shän-'tō\ city & port SE China in E Kwangtung on S. China sea *pop* 250,000
Swa·zi·land \'swäz-ē-,land\ country SE Africa N of Natal bet. Transvaal & Mozambique; a former Brit. protectorate, an independent kingdom since 1968 ✻ Mbabane *area* 6705 *sq mi* (17,433 *sq km*), *pop* 494,534
Swe·den \'swēd-ᵊn\ *or Sw* **Sve·ri·ge** \'sfer-yə\ country N Europe on Scandinavian peninsula W of Baltic sea; a kingdom ✻ Stockholm *area* 173,349 *sq mi* (450,707 *sq km*), *pop* 8,208,544
Swin·don \'swin-dən\ borough S England in NE Wiltshire *pop* 91,136
Swi·no·ujś·cie \,shfē-nō-'üish-(,)chā\ city & port NW Poland on N coast of Uznam (Usedom) Is. NNW of Szczecin *pop* 48,292
Swin·ton and Pen·dle·bury \,swint-ᵊn-ən-'pen-dᵊl-,ber-ē, -b(ə-)rē\ borough NW England in Greater Manchester NW of Manchester *pop* 39,621
Swit·zer·land \'swit-sər-lənd\ *or F* **Suisse** \swʸēs\ *or G* **Schweiz** \'shfīts\ *or It* **Sviz·ze·ra** \'zvēt-tsä-rä\ *or L* **Hel·ve·tia** \hel-'vē-sh(ē-)ə\ country W Europe in the Alps; a federal republic ✻ Bern *area* 15,940 *sq mi* (41,444 *sq km*), *pop* 6,365,960

Syb·a·ris \'sib-ə-rəs\ ancient Greek city S Italy on Gulf of Tarentum; destroyed 510 B.C.

Syd·ney \'sid-nē\ **1** city & port SE Australia on Port Jackson ✻ of New S. Wales *metropolitan area pop* 3,021,982 **2** city Canada in NE N.S. on Cape Breton Is. *pop* 29,444 — **Syd·ney·ite** \-,īt\ *n*

Syene — see ASWĀN

Sylt \'zilt, 'silt\ island N W. Germany, chief of the N. Frisian islands *area* 36 *sq mi* (94 *sq km*)

Syr·a·cuse \'sir-ə-,kyüs, -,kyüz\ **1** city *cen* N.Y. near Oneida lake *pop* 170,105 **2** or It **Si·ra·cu·sa** \,sē-rə-'kü-zə\ *or anc* **Syr·a·cu·sae** \,sir-ə-'kyü-(,)sē, -,(,)zē\ city & port Italy in SE Sicily *pop* 117,689 — **Syr·a·cu·san** \,sir-ə-'kyüs-'n, -'kyüz-\ *adj or n*

Syr Dar·ya \si(ə)r-'där-yə\ *or anc* **Jax·ar·tes** \jak-'särt-(,)ēz\ river 1500 *mi* (2414 *km*) U.S.S.R. in Soviet Central Asia flowing from Tien Shan W & NW into Lake Aral

Syr·ia \'sir-ē-ə\ **1** ancient region SW Asia bordering on the Mediterranean & covering modern Syria, Lebanon, Israel, & Jordan **2** former French mandate (1920–44) comprising the **Le·vant States** \li-'vant\ (Syria, Lebanon, Latakia, & Jebel ed Druz), administrative ✻ Beirut, legislative ✻ Damascus **3** country SW Asia bordering on the Mediterranean; a republic 1944–58 & since 1961; a province of United Arab Republic 1958–61 ✻ Damascus *area* 72,234 *sq mi* (187,808 *sq km*), *pop* 9,171,622 — **Syr·i·an** \'sir-ē-ən\ *adj or n*

Syrian desert W Asia bet. Mediterranean coast & the Euphrates covering N Saudi Arabia, NE Jordan, SE Syria, & W Iraq

Syrtis Major — see SIDRA (Gulf of)

Syrtis Minor — see GABES (Gulf of)

Szamos — see SOMES

Szcze·cin \'shchet-,sēn\ city & port NW Poland *pop* 335,400

Sze·chwan \'sech-'wän\ *or* **Si·chuan** \'sēch-'wän\ province SW China ✻ Ch'eng-tu *area* 219,691 *sq mi* (571,197 *sq km*), *pop* 99,713,310

Sze·ged \'seg-,ed\ city S Hungary on Yugoslav border *pop* 171,342

Sze·kes·fe·her·var \'sā-,kesh-,fe-ər-,vär\ city W *cen* Hungary *pop* 103,197

Szepingkai — see SSU-P'ING

Szom·bat·hely \'sōm-,bot-,hā\ city W Hungary *pop* 82,830

Ta·bas·co \tə-'bas-(,)kō\ state SE Mexico on the Caribbean SW of Yucatán peninsula ✻ Villahermosa *area* 9782 *sq mi* (25,433 *sq km*), *pop* 1,149,756

Ta·blas \'täb-ləs\ island *cen* Philippines in Romblon group

Table Bay harbor of Cape Town, Republic of S. Africa

Table Mountain mountain 3563 *ft* (1086 *m*) Republic of S. Africa S of Cape Town

Ta·bor, Mount \'tā-bər, -,bó(ə)r\ mountain 1929 *ft* (588 *m*) N Palestine E of Nazareth

Ta·briz \tə-'brēz\ *or anc* **Tau·ris** \'tór-əs\ city NW Iran in Azerbaijan *pop* 597,976

Ta·bua·er·an \tə-,bü-ə-'er-ən\ *or formerly* **Fan·ning** \'fan-iŋ\ island *cen* Pacific in the Line islands *area* 15 *sq mi* (39 *sq km*), *pop* 376

Ta·bun Bog·do \'täb-,ün-'bóg-(,)dō\ mountain 15,266 *ft* (4653 *m*) W Mongolia; highest in Altai mountains

Tac·na \'tak-nə\ city S Peru near Chilean border *pop* 97,108; in region (**Tacna–Ari·ca** \-ə-'rē-kə\) occupied 1884–1930 by Chile & now divided bet. Chile & Peru

Ta·co·ma \tə-'kō-mə\ city & port W Wash. on Puget Sound S of Seattle *pop* 158,501

Tacoma, Mount — see RAINIER (Mount)

Ta·con·ic \tə-'kän-ik\ mountains along N part of Conn.-N.Y. boundary, entire Mass.-N.Y. boundary & in SW Vt.; highest Mt. Equinox (in Vt.) 3816 *ft* (1163 *m*)

Ta·djou·ra, Gol·fe de \,gól-fə-thä-tə-'jür-ə\ *or* **Gulf of Tadjoura** inlet of Gulf of Aden in E Djibouti

Tadmor — see PALMYRA

Ta·dzhik Republic \tä-'jik, -jēk\ *or* **Ta·dzhik·i·stan** \tä-jik-i-'stan, tə-, -jēk-, -'stän\ constituent republic of the U.S.S.R. in Soviet Central Asia bordering on China (Sinkiang Uighur) & Afghanistan ✻ Dushanbe *area* 54,900 *sq mi* (142,740 *sq km*), *pop* 3,801,000

Tae·dong \,tä-'dúŋ, tī-\ river 200 *mi* (322 *km*) cen N. Korea flowing SW into Korea Bay

Tae·gu \,tä-'gü, tī-\ city SE S. Korea NNW of Pusan *pop* 1,607,458

Tae·jon \,tä-'jón, tī-\ city *cen* S. Korea NW of Taegu *pop* 651,642

Ta·gan·rog \'tag-ən-,räg\ city U.S.S.R. in Soviet Russia, Europe, on **Gulf of Taganrog** (NE arm of Sea of Azov) *pop* 276,000

Ta·gus \'tā-gəs\ *or Sp* **Ta·jo** \'tä-(,)hō\ *or Pg* **Te·jo** \'tā-(,)zhü\ river 566 *mi* (911 *km*) Spain & Portugal flowing W into the Atlantic

Ta·hi·ti \tə-'hēt-ē\ island S Pacific in Windward group of the Society Islands; chief town Papeete *area* 402 *sq mi* (1045 *sq km*), *pop* 61,519

T'ai·chou *or* **Tai·zhou** \'tī-'jō\ city E China in *cen* Kiangsu

Tai·chung \'tī-'chúŋ\ city W Taiwan *pop* 607,238

T'ai Hu \'tī-'hü\ lake 40 *mi* (64 *km*) long & 35 *mi* (56 *km*) wide E China in Kiangsu

Tai·myr *or* **Tai·mir** \tī-'mi(ə)r\ peninsula U.S.S.R. in NW Soviet Russia, Asia, bet. the Yenisey & the Khatanga — see CHELYUSKIN (Cape)

Tai·nan \'tī-'nän\ city SW Taiwan *pop* 594,739

Tai·na·ron \'tä-nə-,rón\ *or* **Mat·a·pan** \,mat-ə-'pan\ cape S Greece at S tip of Peloponnisos bet. gulfs of Laconia & Messenia

Tai·pei \'tī-'pā, -'bā\ city ✻ of (Nationalist) China, on Taiwan *pop* 2,270,983

T'ai Shan \'tī-'shän\ mountain 5069 *ft* (1545 *m*) E China in W Shantung

Tai·wan \'tī-'wän\ *or* **For·mo·sa** \fór-'mō-sə, fər-, -zə\ island China off SE coast of Fukien; belonged to Japan 1895–1945; since 1949 seat of (Nationalist) Republic of China (✻ Taipei) *area* 13,900 *sq mi* (36,140 *sq km*) — **Tai·wan·ese** \,tī-wə-'nēz, -'nēs\ *adj or n*

Tai·yu·an \'tī-yü-'än\ *or formerly* **Yang·ku** \'yäŋ-'kü\ city N China ✻ of Shansi *pop* 1,053,000

Ta·ju·mul·co \,tä-hü-'mül-(,)kō\ mountain 13,845 *ft* (4220 *m*) W Guatemala; highest in Central America

Ta·ka·mat·su \,täk-ə-'mät-(,)sü, tä-'käm-ət-,sü\ city & port Japan in NE Shikoku on Inland sea *pop* 318,815

Ta·ka·o·ka \tə-'kaú-kə\ city Japan in *cen* Honshu *pop* 175,299

Ta·kat·su·ki \tə-'kät-sü-(,)kē\ city Japan in S Honshu *pop* 340,508

Tak·ka·kaw \'tak-ə-,kó\ waterfall 1650 *ft* (503 *m*) Canada in SE B.C. in Yoho National Park; highest in Canada

Ta·kla Ma·kan *or* **Ta·kli·ma·kan** \,täk-lə-mə-'kän\ desert W China in *cen* Sinkiang Uighur bet. Tien Shan & Kunlun mountains

Ta·la·ud \'täl-,ä-,üd\ *or* **Ta·laur** \-,ä-,ü(ə)r\ islands Indonesia NE of Celebes *area* 494 *sq mi* (1284 *sq km*), *pop* 194,253

Tal·ca \'täl-kə\ city *cen* Chile S of Santiago *pop* 133,160

Tal·ca·hua·no \,tal-kə-'(h)wän-(,)ō\ city & port S *cen* Chile NW of Concepción *pop* 112,087

Tal·la·de·ga \,tal-ə-'dē-gə, -'dig-ə\ city E *cen* Ala. *pop* 19,128

Tal·la·has·see \,tal-ə-'has-ē\ city ✻ of Fla. *pop* 81,548

Tal·la·hatch·ie \,tal-ə-'hach-ē\ river 301 *mi* (484 *km*) N Miss. flowing SW

Tal·la·poo·sa \,tal-ə-'pü-sə\ river 268 *mi* (431 *km*) NW Ga. & E Ala. flowing SW to join the Coosa forming Alabama river

Tal·linn \'tal-ən, 'täl-\ *or formerly* **Re·vel** \'rā-vəl\ city & port U.S.S.R. ✻ of Estonia *pop* 430,000

Tam·al·pais, Mount \,tam-əl-'pī-əs\ mountain 2604 *ft* (794 *m*) W Calif. NW of San Francisco

Ta·man \tə-'män\ peninsula U.S.S.R. in S Soviet Russia, Europe, in Ciscaucasia bet. Sea of Azov & Black sea

Tam·an·ras·set \,tam-ən-'ras-ət\ wadi & oasis SE Algeria

Ta·mar \'tä-mər\ **1** river 40 *mi* (64 *km*) Australia in N Tasmania flowing N to Bass strait **2** river 60 *mi* (96 *km*) SW England flowing SE from NW Devon into English channel **3** — see PALMYRA

Tam·a·rac \'tam-ə-,rak\ city SE Fla. *pop* 29,376

Tamatave — see TOAMASINA

Ta·mau·li·pas \,täm-,aú-'lē-pəs, təm-\ state NE Mexico bordering on Gulf of Mexico ✻ Ciudad Victoria *area* 30,731 *sq mi* (79,901 *sq km*), *pop* 1,924,934

Tam·bo·ra \täm-'bór-ə, -'bór-\ volcano 9350 *ft* (2850 *m*) Indonesia on Sumbawa Is.

Tam·bov \täm-'bóf, -'bóv\ city U.S.S.R. in *cen* Soviet Russia, Europe, SE of Moscow *pop* 270,000

Tam·il Na·du \,tam-əl-'näd-(,)ü\ *or formerly* **Madras** state SE India bordering on Bay of Bengal ✻ Madras *area* 50,110 *sq mi* (130,286 *sq km*), *pop* 48,297,456

Tamiš — see TIMIS

Tam·pa \'tam-pə\ city W Fla. on **Tampa Bay** (inlet of Gulf of Mexico) *pop* 271,523 — **Tam·pan** \-pən\ *adj or n*

Tam·pe·re \'tam-pə-,rä, 'täm-\ city SW Finland *pop* 167,028

Tam·pi·co \tam-'pē-(,)kō\ city & port E Mexico in S Tamaulipas on the Pánuco 7 *mi* (11 *km*) from its mouth *pop* 212,188

Ta·na \'tän-ə\ *or* **Tsa·na** \'(t)sän-ə\ **1** lake NW Ethiopia; source of Blue Nile river *area* 1418 *sq mi* (3687 *sq km*) **2** river 500 *mi* (805 *km*) E Africa in Kenya flowing into Indian ocean

Ta·na·gra \'tan-ə-grə, tə-'nag-rə\ village E *cen* Greece E of Thebes; an important town of ancient Boeotia

Tan·a·na \'tan-ə-,nó\ river 475 *mi* (764 *km*) E & *cen* Alaska flowing NW into Yukon river

Tananarive, Tananarivo — see ANTANANARIVO

Tan·ga \'taŋ-gə\ city & port Tanzania on NE mainland *pop* 103,409

Tan·gan·yi·ka \,tan-gən-'yē-kə, ,taŋ-gən-, -gə-'nē-\ former country E Africa bet. Lake Tanganyika & Indian ocean; administered by Britain 1920–61; became an independent member of the Commonwealth 1961 ✻ Dar es Salaam; since 1964 united with Zanzibar as Tanzania — see GERMAN EAST AFRICA — **Tan·gan·yi·kan** \-kən\ *adj or n*

Tanganyika, Lake lake E Africa in Great Rift valley bet. Zaire & Tanzania *area* 12,700 *sq mi* (32,893 *sq km*)

Tan·gier \tan-'ji(ə)r\ *or* **Tan·giers** \-'ji(ə)rz\ **1** city & port N Morocco on Strait of Gibraltar; summer ✻ of Morocco *pop* 187,894 **2** the International Zone of Tangier — see MOROCCO — **Tan·ger·ine** \,tan-jə-'rēn\ *adj or n*

Tang·shan \'däŋ-'shän, 'täŋ-\ city NE China in E Hopeh *pop* 1,200,000

Ta·nim·bar \tə-'nim-,bär, tä-\ islands Indonesia in SE Moluccas ENE of Timor *pop* 50,000

Ta·nis \'tä-nəs\ *or bib* **Zo·an** \'zō-,an\ ancient city N Egypt in E Nile delta near Lake Tanis

Tanis, Lake — see MANZALA (Lake)

Tan·jung·pri·ok \,tän-,jüŋ-prē-'ók\ port of Djakarta, Indonesia

Tannenberg — see STEBARK

Tan·ta \'tänt-ə\ city N Egypt in *cen* Nile delta *pop* 283,240

Tan–tung *or* **Dan·dong** \'dän-'dúŋ\ *or* **An·tung** \'än-'túŋ\ city & port NE China in SE Liaoning at mouth of the Yalu *pop* 420,000

Tan·za·nia \,tan-zə-'nē-ə, ,tän-\ republic E Africa formed 1964 by union of Tanganyika & Zanzibar ✻ Dar es Salaam *area* 362,844 *sq mi* (943,394 *sq km*), *pop* 17,527,564 — **Tan·za·ni·an** \-'nē-ən\ *adj or n*

Taor·mi·na \,taúr-'mē-nə\ *or anc* **Tau·ro·me·ni·um** \,tór-ə-'mē-nē-əm\ commune Italy in NE Sicily *pop* 10,085

Ta·pa·joz \,tap-ə-'zhós\ river 500 *mi* (805 *km*) N Brazil flowing NE into the Amazon — see JURUENA

Tap·pan Zee \,tap-ən-'zē\ expansion of Hudson river SE N.Y.

Taprobane — see CEYLON

Tap·ti \'täp-tē\ river 436 *mi* (702 *km*) W India S of Satpura range flowing W into Gulf of Cambay

Ta·qua·ri \,tak-wə-'rē\ river 450 *mi* (724 *km*) S *cen* Brazil rising in S *cen* Mato Grosso & flowing WSW into Paraguay river

Tar \'tär\ river 215 *mi* (346 *km*) NE N.C. — see PAMLICO

Tara \'tar-ə\ village Ireland in County Meath NW of Dublin near **Hill of Tara** (seat of ancient Irish kings)

Tarabulus — see TRIPOLI

Taranaki — see EGMONT

Ta·ran·to \'tär-ən-,tō, tə-'rant-(,)ō\ *or anc* **Ta·ren·tum** \tə-'rent-əm\ city & port SE Italy on **Gulf of Taranto** (inlet of Ionian sea) *pop* 242,774

Ta·ra·wa \tə-'rä-wə, 'tar-ə-,wä\ island *cen* Pacific ✻ of Kiribati *area* 8 *sq mi* (21 *sq km*), *pop* 20,203

Tarbes \'tärb\ city SW France ESE of Pau *pop* 54,286

Ta·ri·fa, Cape \tä-ˈrē-fə\ cape S Spain; southernmost point of continental Europe, at 36°01′N

Ta·rim \ˈdä-ˈrēm, ˈtä-\ river 1250 *mi* (2012 *km*) W China in Sinkiang Uighur in the Takla Makan flowing E & SE into Lop Nor (marshy depression)

Tar·lac \ˈtär-ˌläk\ city Philippines in *cen* Luzon *pop* 688,457

Tarn \ˈtärn\ river 233 *mi* (375 *km*) S France flowing W into the Garonne

Tar·nów \ˈtär-ˌnüf\ city S Poland E of Kraków *pop* 107,139

Tar·qui·nia \tär-ˈkwēn-yə, -ˈkwēn-ē-ə, -ˈkwin-\ *or formerly* **Cor·ne·to** \kȯr-ˈnāt-(ˌ)ō\ *or anc* **Tar·quin·ii** \tär-ˈkwin-ē-ˌī\ town *cen* Italy in N Latium NW of Viterbo *pop* 13,097

Tar·ra·go·na \ˌtar-ə-ˈgō-nə\ **1** province NE Spain on the Mediterranean *area* 2505 *sq mi* (6513 *sq km*), *pop* 537,617 **2** commune & port, its *, SW of Barcelona *pop* 132,164

Tar·ra·sa \tə-ˈräs-ə\ commune NE Spain NNW of Barcelona *pop* 155,614

Tar·shish \ˈtär-(ˌ)shish\ ancient maritime country referred to in the Bible, by some located in S Spain & identified with Tartessus

Tar·sus \ˈtär-səs\ city S Turkey near the Cilician Gates * of ancient Cilicia *pop* 57,035

Tar·tes·sus *or* **Tar·tes·sos** \tär-ˈtes-əs\ ancient kingdom on SW coast of Spanish peninsula — see TARSHISH

Tar·tu \ˈtär-(ˌ)tü\ *or G* **Dor·pat** \ˈdȯ(ə)r-ˌpät\ city E Estonia, U.S.S.R. W of Lake Peipus *pop* 105,000

Tash·kent \tash-ˈkent\ city U.S.S.R. in Soviet Central Asia E of the Syr Darya * of Uzbek Republic *pop* 1,780,000

Tas·man \ˈtaz-mən\ sea comprising the part of the S Pacific between SE Australia & W New Zealand

Tasman, Mount mountain 11,475 *ft* (3498 *m*) New Zealand in South Is. in Southern Alps NE of Mt. Cook

Tas·ma·nia \taz-ˈmā-nē-ə, -nyə\ *or formerly* **Van Die·men's Land** \van-ˈdē-mənz\ island SE Australia S of Victoria; a state * Hobart *area* 26,215 *sq mi* (68,159 *sq km*), *pop* 418,957 — **Tas·ma·nian** \taz-ˈmā-nē-ən, -nyən\ *adj or n*

Ta·tar \ˈtät-ər\ strait between Sakhalin Is. & mainland of Asia

Tatar Republic autonomous republic U.S.S.R. in E Soviet Russia, Europe * Kazan *area* 26,100 *sq mi* (67,860 *sq km*), *pop* 3,131,000

Ta·ta·ry \ˈtät-ə-rē\ *or* **Tar·ta·ry** \ˈtärt-ə-\ an indefinite historical region in Asia & Europe extending from Sea of Japan to the Dnieper

Ta·try \ˈtä-trē\ *or* **Ta·tra** \ˈtä-trə\ mountains E Czechoslovakia & S Poland in *cen* Carpathian mountains — see GERLACHOVKA

Ta·tung *or* **Da·tong** \ˈdä-ˈtu̇ŋ\ city NE China in N Shansi *pop* 243,000

Tau·ghan·nock Falls \tə-ˌgan-ək-\ waterfall 215 *ft* (66 *m*) S *cen* N.Y. NW of Ithaca

Taung·gyi \ˈtau̇n-ˈjē\ town E Burma * of Shan State *pop* 8652

Taun·ton \ˈtȯnt-^{ə}n, ˈtänt-, ˈtant-\ city SE Mass. *pop* 45,001

Tau·nus \ˈtau̇-nəs\ mountain range *cen* W. Germany E of the Rhine & N of lower Main river; highest peak Grosser Feldberg 2887 *ft* (880 *m*)

Tauric Chersonese — see CHERSONESE

Tauris — see TABRIZ

Tau·rus \ˈtȯr-əs\ *or Turk* **To·ros** \tō-ˈrōs\ mountains S Turkey parallel to Mediterranean coast; highest Ala Dag 12,251 *ft* (3734 *m*)

Tax·co \ˈtäs-(ˌ)kō\ *or* **Taxco de Alar·cón** \-(ˌ)dā-ˌäl-ˌär-ˈkōn\ city S Mexico in Guerrero SSW of Mexico City *pop* 27,089

Tay \ˈtā\ river 120 *mi* (193 *km*) E *cen* Scotland flowing into North sea through **Loch Tay** and **Firth of Tay**

Tay·lor \ˈtā-lər\ city SE Mich. SW of Detroit *pop* 77,568

Tay·side \ˈtā-ˌsīd\ region E *cen* Scotland, established 1975 * Dundee *area* 2928 *sq mi* (7613 *sq km*), *pop* 391,529

Tbi·li·si \tə-ˈbil-ə-sē\ *or* **Tif·lis** \ˈtif-ləs, tə-ˈflēs\ city U.S.S.R. * of Georgia on the Kura *pop* 1,066,000

Tchad — see CHAD

Teche, Bayou \ˈtesh\ stream 175 *mi* (282 *km*) S La. flowing SE into the Atchafalaya

Tees \ˈtēz\ river 70 *mi* (113 *km*) N England flowing E into North sea

Tees·side \ˈtē(z)-ˌsīd\ former county borough (1968–74) N England; since 1974 part of Cleveland

Te·gu·ci·gal·pa \tə-ˌgü-sə-ˈgal-pə\ city * of Honduras *pop* 273,894

Te·hach·a·pi \ti-ˈhach-ə-pē\ **1** mountains SE Calif. N of Mojave desert running E–W between S end of Sierra Nevada & the Coast ranges; highest Double Mountain 7988 *ft* (2435 *m*) **2** pass 3793 *ft* (1156 *m*) at E end of the mountains

Teh·ran *or* **Te·he·ran** \ˌtā-ə-ˈran, -ˈrän\ city * of Iran at foot of S slope of Elburz mountains *pop* 4,530,223

Teh·ri \ˈtā-rē\ *or* **Tehri Garh·wal** \-(ˌ)gər-ˈwäl\ district N India in NW Uttar Pradesh on Tibet border; chief town Tehri

Te·huan·te·pec, Isthmus of \tə-ˈwänt-ə-ˌpek\ the narrowest section of Mexico, between **Gulf of Tehuantepec** (on Pacific side) & Bay of Campeche; 130 *mi* (209 *km*) wide at narrowest point

Tejo — see TAGUS

Te·jon \tē-ˈhōn\ pass 4183 *ft* (1275 *m*) SW Calif. in Tehachapi mountains NW of Los Angeles

Tel·a·nai·pura \ˌtel-ə-ˈnī-ˌpu̇r-ə\ *or formerly* **Djam·bi** *or* **Jam·bi** \ˈjäm-bē\ city & port Indonesia in SE *cen* Sumatra *pop* 113,080

Tel Aviv \ˌtel-ə-ˈvēv\ city W Israel on the Mediterranean *pop* 386,612 — see JAFFA — **Tel Avi·van** \-ˈvē-vən\ *n*

Tel el Amar·na \ˌtel-ˌel-ə-ˈmär-nə\ locality *cen* Egypt on E bank of the Nile NW of Asyût; site of ruins

Tel·e·mark \ˈtel-ə-ˌmärk\ mountain region SW Norway

Telescope Peak mountain 11,045 *ft* (3366 *m*) E Calif., highest in Panamint mountains

Te·ma \ˈtē-mə\ city & port Ghana E of Accra *pop* 60,767

Tem·pe **1** \tem-ˈpē\ city S *cen* Ariz. SE of Phoenix *pop* 106,743 **2** \ˈtem-pē\ *or NGk* **Tém·bi** \ˈtem-bē\ valley (**Vale of Tempe**) in NE Thessaly bet. Mounts Olympus & Ossa

Tem·ple \ˈtem-pəl\ city NE *cen* Tex. SSW of Waco *pop* 42,483

Temple City city SW Calif. SE of Pasadena *pop* 28,972

Te·mu·co \tā-ˈmü-(ˌ)kō\ city S *cen* Chile *pop* 197,232

Tenedos — see BOZCAADA

Te·ne·ri·fe \ˌten-ə-ˈrē-(ˌ)fā, -ˈrēf, -ˈrif\ *or formerly* **Ten·er·iffe** \ˌten-ə-ˈrif, -ˈrēf\ island Spain, largest of the Canary islands; chief town Santa Cruz de Tenerife *area* 782 *sq mi* (2033 *sq km*)

Ten·nes·see \ˌten-ə-ˈsē, ˈten-ə-ˌ\ **1** river 652 *mi* (1049 *km*) E U.S., in Tenn., Ala., & Ky. flowing into Ohio river **2** state SE *cen* U.S. * Nashville *area* 42,244 *sq mi* (109,834 *sq km*), *pop* 4,591,120 — **Ten·nes·se·an** *or* **Ten·nes·see·an** \ˌten-ə-ˈsē-ən\ *adj or n*

Te·noch·ti·tlán \tā-ˌnȯch-tē-ˈtlän\ MEXICO CITY — its name when capital of the Aztec Empire

Ten·sas \ˈten-ˌsȯ\ river 250 *mi* (402 *km*) NE La. uniting with Ouachita river to form Black river

Ten·saw \ˈten-ˌsȯ\ river 40 *mi* (64 *km*) SW Ala. formed by Tombigbee & Alabama rivers & flowing S into Mobile Bay

Te·o·ti·hua·cán \ˌtā-ō-ˌtē-wə-ˈkän\ city S *cen* Mexico in Mexico state NE of Mexico City; once * of the Toltecs *pop* 2238

Te·pic \tā-ˈpēk\ city W Mexico * of Nayarit *pop* 108,924

Te·quen·da·ma Falls \ˌtā-kən-ˈdäm-ə\ waterfall 475 *ft* (145 *m*) *cen* Colombia S of Bogotá

Te·rai·na \ter-ˈī-nə\ *or formerly* **Washington** island *cen* Pacific in the Line islands *pop* 437

Ter·cei·ra \tər-ˈser-ə, -ˈsir-\ island *cen* Azores *area* 233 *sq mi* (606 *sq km*)

Te·re·si·na \ˌter-ə-ˈzē-nə\ city NE Brazil * of Piauí *pop* 378,026

Termonde — see DENDERMONDE

Ter·na·te \tər-ˈnä-(ˌ)tā\ **1** island Indonesia in N Moluccas off W Halmahera *pop* 33,964 **2** city & port, chief city of Ternate Is. *pop* 24,287

Ter·ni \ˈte(ə)r-nē\ commune *cen* Italy NNE of Rome *pop* 111,401

Ter·ra·ci·na \ˌter-ə-ˈchē-nə\ city & port *cen* Italy in Latium SE of Pontine marshes *pop* 36,795

Ter·ra No·va National Park \ˌter-ə-ˈnō-və\ reservation E Canada in E Newfoundland (island)

Ter·re Haute \ˌter-ə-ˈhōt *also* -ˈhət, *rapid* ter-ˈhōt, -ˈhət\ city W Ind. on the Wabash *pop* 61,125

Te·ruel \ˌter-ə-ˈwel\ **1** province E Spain in S Aragon *area* 5720 *sq mi* (14,872 *sq km*), *pop* 133,068 **2** commune, its *, S of Zaragoza *pop* 25,532

Teschen — see CIESZYN

Tessin — see TICINO

Te·ton \ˈtē-ˌtän, ˈtēt-^{ə}n\ mountain range NW Wyo. — see GRAND TETON

Té·touan \tā-twä^{n}\ *or Sp* **Te·tuán** \te-ˈtwän, ˌtet-ə-ˈwän\ city & port N Morocco on the Mediterranean *pop* 139,105

Teu·to·burg Forest \ˈt(y)üt-ə-ˌbərg\ *or G* **Teu·to·bur·ger Wald** \ˈtȯit-ə-ˌbu̇r-gər-ˌvält\ range of forested hills NW W. Germany in region bet. Ems & Weser rivers; highest point 1530 *ft* (466 *m*)

Tewkes·bury \ˈt(y)üks-ˌber-ē, ˈtu̇ks-, -b(ə-)rē\ borough SW *cen* England in Gloucestershire on Avon & Severn rivers *pop* 9554

Tewks·bury \ˈt(y)üks-ˌber-ē, ˈtu̇ks-, -b(ə-)rē\ town NE Mass. *pop* 24,635

Tex·ar·kana \ˌtek-sər-ˈkan-ə\ **1** city SW Ark. *pop* 21,459 **2** city NE Tex. adjacent to Texarkana, Ark. *pop* 31,271

Tex·as \ˈtek-səs, -siz\ state S U.S. * Austin *area* 267,339 *sq mi* (695,081 *sq km*), *pop* 14,229,191 — **Tex·an** \-sən\ *adj or n*

Texas City city & port SE Tex. on Galveston Bay *pop* 41,403

Tex·co·co \tes-ˈkō-(ˌ)kō\ city *cen* Mexico in Mexico state E of Mexico City *pop* 18,044

Thai·land \ˈtī-ˌland, -lənd\ *or formerly* **Si·am** \sī-ˈam\ country SE Asia on Gulf of Siam; a kingdom * Bangkok *area* 198,247 *sq mi* (515,442 *sq km*), *pop* 44,278,000 — **Thai·land·er** \-ˌlan-dər, -lən-\ *n*

Thailand, Gulf of — see SIAM (Gulf of)

Thames **1** \ˈtemz, ˈthāmz, ˈtāmz\ river 15 *mi* (24 *km*) SE Conn., an estuary flowing S into Long Is. Sound **2** \ˈtemz\ river 135 *mi* (217 *km*) Canada in SE Ont. flowing S & SW into Lake St. Clair **3** \ˈtemz\ river 209 *mi* (336 *km*) S England flowing from the Cotswolds in Gloucestershire E into the North sea — see ISIS

Than·et, Isle of \ˈthan-ət\ tract of land SE England in NE Kent cut off from mainland by arms of Stour river *area* 42 *sq mi* (109 *sq km*)

Thar \ˈtär\ *or* **Great Indian** desert NW India (subcontinent) in Pakistan & India (republic) bet. Aravalli range & the Indus

Thá·sos \ˈthäs-ˌȯs\ island Greece in the N Aegean E of Chalcidice peninsula *area* 152 *sq mi* (395 *sq km*)

The·ba·id \thi-ˈbā-əd, ˈthē-bā-ˌid\ ancient district surrounding Thebes in Egypt or in Greece

Thebes \ˈthēbz\ **1** *or anc* **The·bae** \ˈthē-(ˌ)bē\ *or* **Di·os·po·lis** \dī-ˈäs-pə-ləs\ ancient city S Egypt on the Nile S of modern Qena — see KARNAK, LUXOR **2** ancient city E Greece in Boeotia NNW of Athens — **The·ban** \ˈthē-bən\ *adj or n*

The Hague — see HAGUE (The)

The·lon \ˈthē-ˌlän\ river *ab* 550 *mi* (885 *km*) N Canada in E Northwest Territories flowing NE to Baker Lake

The·o·dore Roo·se·velt National Park \ˌthē-ə-ˌdō(ə)r-, -ˌdȯ(ə)r-, -əd-ər-\ reservation W N.Dak. comprising three areas in badland region on the Little Missouri

Thera — see SANTORIN

Ther·ma·ï·kós Kól·pos \ther-ˌmä-i-ˌkȯs-ˈkōl-(ˌ)pōs\ *or* **Gulf of Sa·lo·ni·ka** \sə-ˈlän-i-kə, ˌsal-ə-ˈnē-kə\ arm of Aegean sea N Greece W of Chalcidice

Ther·mop·y·lae \(ˌ)thər-ˈmäp-ə-(ˌ)lē\ locality E Greece bet. Mt. Oeta & Gulf of Lamia; once a narrow pass along the coast, now a rocky plain 6 *mi* (9.6 *km*) from the sea

Thessaloníki — see SALONIKA

Thes·sa·ly \ˈthes-ə-lē\ *or Gk* **Thes·sa·lía** \ˌthā-sə-ˈlē-ə\ region E Greece bet. Pindus mountains & the Aegean — **Thes·sa·lian** \the-ˈsā-lē-ən, -ˈsāl-yən\ *adj or n*

Thet·ford Mines \ˌthet-fərd-\ city Canada in S Que. *pop* 19,965

Thim·bu \ˈthim-(ˌ)bü\ city W *cen* Bhutan, its *

Thíra — see SANTORIN

Tho·hoy·an·dou \tō-ˌhȯi-an-ˈdü\ town * of Venda

Thom·as·ville \ˈtäm-əs-ˌvil, -vəl\ city S Ga. *pop* 18,463

Thomp·son \ˈtäm(p)-sən\ **1** river 304 *mi* (489 *km*) Canada in S B.C. flowing S (as the **North Thompson**) & thence W & SW into the Fraser; joined by a branch, the **South Thompson** **2** city Canada in *cen* Man. *pop* 17,291

Thorn·ton \ˈthȯ(ə)rnt-^{ə}n\ city NE *cen* Colo. N of Denver *pop* 40,343

Thors·havn *or* **Tórs·havn** \ˈtȯrs-ˈhau̇n\ town & port * of the Faeroe islands, on Strömö Is. *pop* 11,618

Thousand Islands island group Canada & U.S. in St. Lawrence river in Ont. & N.Y.

Thousand Oaks city SW Calif. W of Los Angeles *pop* 77,072

Thrace \ˈthrās\ region SE Europe in Balkan peninsula N of the Aegean; as ancient country (**Thra·ce** \ˈthrā-(ˌ)sē\ *or* **Thra·cia** \ˈthrā-sh(ē-)ə\), extended to the Danube; modern remnant divided bet. Greece (**West-**

ern Thrace) & Turkey (**Eastern Thrace,** constituting Turkey in Europe) — **Thra·cian** \'thrā-shən\ *adj or n*

Thracian Chersonese — see CHERSONESE

Three Forks locality SW Mont. where Missouri river is formed by confluence of Gallatin, Jefferson, & Madison rivers *pop* 1247

Three Rivers TROIS-RIVIÈRES

Thu·le \'tü-lē\ settlement & district NW Greenland N of Cape York

Thunder Bay city & port Canada in SW Ont. on Lake Superior, formed 1970 by consolidation of Fort William & Port Arthur *pop* 112,486

Thun·er See \'tü-nər-,zā\ *or* **Lake of Thun** \'tün\ lake 10 *mi* (16 *km*) long *cen* Switzerland; an expansion of Aare river

Thur·gau \'tu̇(ə)r-,gau̇\ *or F* **Thur·go·vie** \tu̅e̅r-gȯ-vē\ canton NE Switzerland ✻ Frauenfeld *area* 397 *sq mi* (1032 *sq km*), *pop* 183,795

Thu·rin·gia \th(y)u̇-'rin-j(ē-)ə\ *or G* **Thü·ring·en** \'tu̅e̅-riŋ-ən\ region SW E. Germany including the **Thu·rin·gian Forest** \th(y)u̇-'rin-j(ē-)ən\ *or G* **Thü·ring·er Wald** \'tu̅e̅-riŋ-ər-,vält\ (wooded mountain range bet. the upper Werra & the Czech border)

Thur·rock \'thər-ək, 'thə-rək\ former urban district SE England in Essex

Thursday island NE Australia off N Queensland in Torres strait

Thyatira — see AKHISAR

Ti·a·hua·na·co \,tē-ə-wə-'näk-(,)ō\ locality W Bolivia near SE end of Lake Titicaca; site of prehistoric ruins

Ti·ber \'tī-bər\ *or It* **Te·ve·re** \'tā-vā-rā\ river 224 *mi* (360 *km*) *cen* Italy flowing through Rome into Tyrrhenian sea

Ti·be·ri·as \tī-'bir-ē-əs\ city N Palestine in Galilee on W shore of Sea of Galilee; now in NE Israel *pop* 23,900

Tiberias, Sea of — see GALILEE (Sea of)

Ti·bes·ti \tə-'bes-tē\ mountains N *cen* Africa in the Sahara in NW Chad; highest Emi Koussi 11,204 *ft* (3415 *m*)

Ti·bet \tə-'bet\ *or* **Xi·zang** \'shēd-'zäŋ\ region SW China on high plateau (average altitude 16,000 *ft or* 4877 *m*) N of the Himalayas ✻ Lhasa *area* 471,660 *sq mi* (1,226,316 *sq km*), *pop* 1,892,393

Ti·bu·rón \,tē-bə-'rōn\ island 34 *mi* (55 *km*) long NW Mexico in Gulf of California off coast of Sonora

Ti·ci·no \ti-'chē-(,)nō\ **1** river 154 *mi* (248 *km*) Switzerland & Italy flowing from slopes of St. Gotthard range SE & SW through Lake Maggiore into the Po **2** *or F* **Tes·sin** \tā-sa^n\ canton S Switzerland bordering on Italy ✻ Bellinzona *area* 1085 *sq mi* (2821 *sq km*), *pop* 265,899

Tien Shan *or* **Tian Shan** \tē-'en-'shän, tē-'än-\ mountain system *cen* Asia extending from the Pamirs NE into Sinkiang Uighur — see POBEDA PEAK

Tien·tsin \tē-'en(t)-'sin, 'tin(t)-\ *or* **Tian·jin** \tē-'än-'jin\ city & port NE China in Hopeh SE of Peking *pop* 7,764,141

Tier·ra del Fue·go \tē-'er-ə-,del-f(y)u̇-'ā-(,)gō\ **1** archipelago off S S. America S of Strait of Magellan; in Argentina & Chile *area* 27,600 *sq mi* (71,760 *sq km*) **2** chief island of the archipelago; divided bet. Chile and Argentina *area* 18,530 *sq mi* (48,178 *sq km*)

Tif·fin \'tif-ən\ city N Ohio on Sandusky river *pop* 19,549

Tiflis — see TBILISI

Ti·gre **1** \'tē-(,)grā\ city E Argentina, NW suburb of Buenos Aires, on islands in Paraná delta *pop* 199,366 **2** \ti-'grā, 'tig-(,)rā\ region N Ethiopia bordering on Eritrea

Ti·gris \'tī-grəs\ river 1150 *mi* (1851 *km*) Iraq & SE Turkey flowing SSE & uniting with the Euphrates to form the Shatt-al-Arab

Ti·jua·na \tē-(ə-)'wän-ə\ city NW Mexico on U.S. border in Baja California Norte *pop* 335,125

Ti·kal \ti-'käl\ ancient Mayan city N Guatemala

Til·burg \'til-,bərg\ commune S Netherlands SE of Rotterdam *pop* 153,889

Til·bury \'til-,ber-ē, -b(ə-)rē\ town & port SE England in Essex on Thames river E of London

Til·la·mook Bay \'til-ə-,mək, -,mu̇k\ inlet of the Pacific NW Oreg.

Tilsit — see SOVETSK

Ti·ma·ga·mi, Lake \tə-'mäg-ə-mē\ lake Canada in Ont. N of Lake Nipissing

Timbuktu — see TOMBOUCTOU

Tim·gad \'tim-,gad\ ancient Roman city NE Algeria

Ti·miş \'tē-mish\ *or* **Ta·miš** \'tä-mish\ river 270 *mi* (434 *km*) Romania & Yugoslavia flowing W & S into the Danube downstream from Belgrade

Ti·mi·soa·ra \,tē-mish-(ə-)'wär-ə\ city W Romania near Yugoslav border *pop* 287,143

Tim·mins \'tim-ənz\ town Canada in E Ont. N of Sudbury *pop* 46,114

Ti·mor \'tē-,mȯ(ə)r, tē-'\ **1** island E Indonesia in Lesser Sunda islands *area* 13,094 *sq mi* (34,044 *sq km*), *pop* 3,000,000; W part (formerly **Netherlands Timor**) belonged to the Dutch until 1946, E part (formerly **Portuguese Timor**) to Portugal until 1975 **2** sea bet. Timor Is. & Australia — **Ti·mor·ese** \(,)tē-,mȯ-'rēz, -'rēs\ *adj or n*

Tim·pa·no·gos, Mount \,tim-pə-'nō-gəs\ mountain 12,008 *ft* (3660 *m*) N *cen* Utah N of Provo; highest in Wasatch mountains

Timpanogos Cave National Monument series of limestone caverns N *cen* Utah on N slope of Mt. Timpanogos

Ti·ni·an \,tin-ē-'an\ island W Pacific in the S Marianas

Tin·ley Park \,tin-lē-\ city NE Ill. *pop* 26,171

Tí·nos \'tē-,nȯs\ island Greece in N Cyclades SE of Andros

Tin·tag·el Head \tin-,taj-əl-\ headland SW England in NW Cornwall

Tip·pe·ca·noe \,tip-ē-kə-'nü\ river 200 *mi* (322 *km*) N Ind. flowing SW into the Wabash

Tip·per·ary \,tip-ə-'re(ə)r-ē\ **1** county S Ireland in Munster ✻ Clonmel *area* 1643 *sq mi* (4272 *sq km*), *pop* 135,261 **2** urban district in SW County Tipperary *pop* 4984

Ti·ra·në *or* **Ti·ra·na** \ti-'rän-ə\ city *cen* Albania, its ✻ *pop* 190,200

Tir·gu–Mu·res \,ti(ə)r-(,)gü-'mü-,resh\ city NE *cen* Romania ESE of Cluj-Napoca *pop* 134,297

Ti·rich Mir \,tir-ich-'mi(ə)r\ mountain 25,230 *ft* (7690 *m*) Pakistan on Afghan border; highest in the Hindu Kush

Ti·rol *or* **Ty·rol** \tə-'rōl; 'tī-,rōl, tī-'; 'tir-əl\ *or It* **Ti·ro·lo** \tē-'rō-(,)lō\ region Europe in E Alps chiefly in Austria; the section S of Brenner pass has belonged since 1919 to Italy — **Ti·ro·le·an** \tə-'rō-lē-ən, tī-; ,tir-ə-', ,tī-rə-'\ *adj or n* — **Ti·ro·lese** \,tir-ə-'lēz, ,tī-rə-, -'lēs\ *adj or n*

Ti·ruch·chi·rap·pal·li *or* **Ti·ru·chi·ra·pal·li** \,tir-ə-chə-'räp-ə-lē\ city S India in *cen* Tamil Nadu *pop* 607,815

Ti·ryns \'tir-ənz, 'tī-rənz\ city of pre-Homeric Greece; ruins in E Peloponnisos SE of Argos

Ti·sza \'tis-,ȯ\ river 800 *mi* (1287 *km*) E Europe flowing from the Carpathians in W Ukrainian Republic W & SW into the Danube

Ti·ti·ca·ca \,tit-i-'käk-ə\ lake on Peru-Bolivia boundary at altitude of 12,500 *ft* (3810 *m*), *area* 3200 *sq mi* (8320 *sq km*)

Ti·to·grad \'tēt-(,)ō-,grad\ *or formerly* **Pod·go·ri·ca** *or* **Pod·go·ri·tsa** \'päd-gə-,rēt-sə\ city S Yugoslavia ✻ of Montenegro *pop* 54,509

Ti·tus·ville \'tīt-əs-,vil, -vəl\ city E Fla. E of Orlando *pop* 31,910

Tiv·o·li \'tiv-ə-lē\ *or anc* **Ti·bur** \'tī-bər\ commune *cen* Italy in Latium ENE of Rome *pop* 50,969

Tji·la·tjap \chi-'läch-,äp\ city & port Indonesia in S Java ESE of Bandung *pop* 55,333

Tjir·e·bon \,chir-ə-'bȯn\ *or* **Cher·i·bon** \,cher-ə-\ city Indonesia in W Java on N coast E of Djakarta *pop* 223,776

Tlax·ca·la \tlä-'skäl-ə\ **1** state *cen* Mexico *area* 1555 *sq mi* (4043 *sq km*), *pop* 547,261 **2** city, its ✻, E of Mexico City *pop* 21,421

Tlem·cen \tlem-'sen\ *or* **Ti·lim·sen** \tə-lim-'sen\ city NW Algeria *pop* 109,400

To·a·ma·si·na \,tō-ə-mə-'sē-nə\ *or* **Ta·ma·tave** \,təm-ə-'täv, ,täm-\ city & port E coast of Madagascar *pop* 77,395

To·ba·go \tə-'bā-(,)gō\ island SE W. Indies, a territory of Trinidad and Tobago; chief town Scarborough *area* 116 *sq mi* (302 *sq km*), *pop* 39,500

To·bol \tə-'bȯl\ river 800 *mi* (1287 *km*) U.S.S.R. flowing from SE foothills of the Urals NNE into the Irtysh

To·bruk \'tō-,bru̇k\ city & port NE Libya *pop* 34,200

To·can·tins \,tō-kən-'tēnz, ,tü-kən-'tē^{n}s\ river 1700 *mi* (2736 *km*) E *cen* & NE Brazil rising in S *cen* Goiás & flowing N into Pará river

To·go \'tō-(,)gō\ republic W Africa ✻ Lomé *area* 21,893 *sq mi* (56,922 *sq km*), *pop* 2,703,000 — **To·go·land·er** \'tō-(,)gō-,lan-dər\ *n* — **To·go·lese** \,tō-gə-'lēz, -'lēs\ *adj or n*

To·go·land \'tō-(,)gō-,land\ region W Africa on Gulf of Guinea bet. Benin & Ghana; until 1919 a German protectorate, then divided into two trust territories: **British Togoland** (in W; since 1957 part of Ghana) & **French Togo** (in E; since 1958 Togo)

To·ho·pe·kal·i·ga \tə-,hō-pi-'kal-i-gə\ lake *cen* Fla. S of Orlando

To·ka·ra \tō-'kär-ə\ island group Japan in N Ryukyus

To·ke·lau \'tō-kə-,lau̇\ islands *cen* Pacific N of Samoa belonging to New Zealand — **To·ke·lau·an** \,tō-kə-'lau̇-ən\ *n*

To·ku·shi·ma \,tō-kə-'shē-mə\ city & port Japan on E coast of Shikoku Is. *pop* 251,032

To·kyo \'tō-kē-,ō\ *or formerly* **Edo** \'ed-(,)ō\ *or* **Ye·do** \'yed-(,)ō\ city ✻ of Japan in SE Honshu on **Tokyo Bay** (inlet of the Pacific) *pop* 8,340,177 — **To·kyo·ite** \'tō-kē-(,)ō-,īt\ *n*

To·le·do \tə-'lēd-(,)ō, -'lēd-ə\ **1** city & port NW Ohio on the Maumee river *pop* 354,635 **2** province *cen* Spain in W New Castile *area* 5919 *sq mi* (15,389 *sq km*), *pop* 445,326 **3** commune, its ✻ *pop* 60,133 — **To·le·dan** \-'lēd-^{ə}n\ *adj or n* — **To·le·do·an** \-'lēd-ə-wən\ *adj or n*

To·li·ma \tə-'lē-mə\ dormant volcano W *cen* Colombia 17,110 *ft* (5215 *m*)

To·lu·ca \tə-'lü-kə\ *or* **Toluca de Ler·do** \-də-'le(ə)r-(,)dō\ city *cen* Mexico ✻ of Mexico state *pop* 220,195

To·lu·ca, Ne·va·do de \nə-'väd-ō-,dāt-^{ə}l-'ü-kə\ extinct volcano 15,016 *ft* (4577 *m*) S *cen* Mexico in Mexico state

Tol·yat·ti \tȯl-'yät-ē\ *or formerly* **Stav·ro·pol** \stav-'rȯ-pəl, -'rō-\ city U.S.S.R. in SE Soviet Russia, Europe, NW of Kuibyshev *pop* 251,000

Tom \'täm, 'tȯm\ river 450 *mi* (724 *km*) U.S.S.R. in W Soviet Russia, Asia, rising in NW Altai mountains & flowing into the Ob

Tom·big·bee \täm-'big-bē\ river 300 *mi* (483 *km*) NE Miss. & W Ala. flowing S to Mobile & Tensaw rivers

Tom·bouc·tou \tō^n-bük-tü\ *or* **Tim·buk·tu** \,tim-,bək-'tü, tim-'bək-(,)tü\ town W Africa in Mali near Niger river *pop* 20,483

Tomsk \'täm(p)sk, 'tȯm(p)sk\ city U.S.S.R. in W *cen* Soviet Russia, Asia, on Tom river near its junction with the Ob *pop* 339,000

Ton·a·wan·da \,tän-ə-'wän-də\ city W N.Y. *pop* 18,693

Ton·ga \'täŋ-(g)ə\ islands SW Pacific E of Fiji; a kingdom in the Commonwealth ✻ Nukualofa *area* 270 *sq mi* (702 *sq km*), *pop* 90,085

Tongareva — see PENRHYN

Ton·ga·ri·ro \,täŋ-(g)ə-'ri(ə)r-(,)ō\ volcano 6516 *ft* (1986 *m*) New Zealand in *cen* North Is. in **Tongariro National Park**

Tonghua — see T'UNG-HUA

Tongue \'təŋ\ river 240 *mi* (386 *km*) N Wyo. & S Mont. flowing N into Yellowstone river

Ton·kin \'täŋ-kən; 'tän-'kin, 'täŋ-\ *or* **Tong·king** \'täŋ-'kiŋ\ region N Indochina bordering on China, since 1946 forming N part of Vietnam; chief city Hanoi — **Ton·kin·ese** \,täŋ-kə-'nēz, ,tän-, -'nēs\ *or* **Tong·king·ese** \,täŋ-kiŋ-'ēz, -'ēs\ *adj or n*

Tonkin, Gulf of arm of S. China sea E of N Vietnam

Ton·le Sap \,tän-,lā-'sap\ *or F* **Grand Lac** \grä^n-lák\ lake 87 *mi* (140 *km*) long SW Indochina in W Cambodia

Ton·to National Monument \'tän-(,)tō\ reservation S *cen* Ariz. E of Phoenix containing cliff-dweller ruins

Too·woom·ba \tə-'wu̇m-bə\ city E Australia in SE Queensland *pop* 66,698

To·pe·ka \tə-'pē-kə\ city ✻ of Kans. on Kansas river *pop* 115,266

To·po·lo·bam·po \tə-,pō-lə-'bäm-(,)pō\ town & port NW Mexico in Sinaloa on Gulf of California

Tor·bay \(')tȯr-'bā\ former county borough SW England in Devonshire on **Tor Bay** (inlet of English channel); included Brixham, Paignton, & Torquay

Tor·cel·lo \tȯr-'chel-(,)ō\ island Italy in Lagoon of Venice

Tor·de·si·llas \,tȯrd-ə-'sē-(y)əs\ village NW Spain SW of Valladolid

Torino — see TURIN

Tor·ne \'tȯr-nə\ *or Finn* **Tor·nio** \'tȯr-nē-,ō\ river 250 *mi* (400 *km*) NE Sweden flowing S, forming part of Finnish-Swedish border, to head of Gulf of Bothnia

To·ron·to \tə-ˈränt-(ˌ)ō, -ˈränt-ə\ city & port Canada ✱ of Ont. on Lake Ontario *pop* 599,217 — **To·ron·to·ni·an** \tə-ˌrän-ˈtō-nē-ən; ˌtȯr-ən-, ˌtär-ən-\ *adj or n*
Toros — see TAURUS
Tor·rance \ˈtȯr-ən(t)s, ˈtär-\ city SW Calif. SSW of Los Angeles *pop* 131,497
Tor·re An·nun·zi·a·ta \ˈtȯr-ē-ə-ˌnün(t)-sē-ˈät-ə\ commune S Italy on Bay of Naples SE of Naples *pop* 57,097
Torre de Cerredo — see CERREDO
Tor·re del Gre·co \ˈtȯr-ē-ˌdel-ˈgrek-(ˌ)ō, -ˈgräk-\ commune S Italy on Bay of Naples *pop* 102,890
Tor·rens, Lake \ˈtȯr-ənz, ˈtär-\ salt lake Australia in E S. Australia N of Spencer Gulf; 25 *ft* (8 *m*) below sea level
Tor·re·ón \ˌtȯr-ē-ˈōn\ city N Mexico in Coahuila *pop* 257,045
Tor·res \ˈtȯr-əs\ strait 80 *mi* (129 *km*) wide bet. island of New Guinea & N tip of Cape York peninsula, Australia
Tor·res Ve·dras \ˌtȯr-əs-ˈvā-drəs\ town W Portugal N of Lisbon
Tor·ring·ton \ˈtȯr-iŋ-tən, ˈtär-\ city NW Conn. *pop* 30,987
Tórshavn — see THORSHAVN
Tor·to·la \tȯr-ˈtō-lə\ island Brit. W. Indies, chief of the Brit. Virgin islands; site of Road Town *area* 24 *sq mi* (62 *sq km*), *pop* 9730
Tor·tu·ga \tȯr-ˈtü-gə\ island Haiti off N coast *area* 70 *sq mi* (182 *sq km*); a resort of pirates in 17th century *pop* 13,723
To·ruń \ˈtȯr-ˌün(-yə)\ city N Poland on the Vistula *pop* 180,053
Toscana — see TUSCANY
Tot·ten·ham \ˈtät-ᵊn-əm, ˈtät-nəm\ former municipal borough SE England in Middlesex, now part of Haringey
Toub·kal, Je·bel \ˌjeb-əl-tüb-ˈkäl\ mountain 13,665 *ft* (4165 *m*) W *cen* Morocco; highest in Atlas mountains
Toug·gourt \tə-ˈgu̇(ə)rt\ town & oasis NE Algeria S of Biskra *pop* 75,600
Tou·lon \tü-ˈlō^n\ commune & port SE France on the Mediterranean *pop* 180,508
Tou·louse \tu̇-ˈlüz\ city SW France on the Garonne *pop* 373,796
Tou·raine \tu̇-ˈrān, -ˈren\ region & former province NW *cen* France ✱ Tours
Tourane — see DA NANG
Tour·coing \tu̇(ə)r-ˈkwa^n\ city N France NE of Lille *pop* 102,092
Tour·nai *or* **Tour·nay** \tu̇(ə)r-ˈnā\ *or Flem* **Door·nik** \ˈdōr-nik, ˈdȯr-\ commune SW Belgium on the Scheldt *pop* 67,906
Tours \ˈtu̇(ə)r\ city NW *cen* France *pop* 139,560
Tower Hamlets borough of E Greater London, England *pop* 146,300
Towns·ville \ˈtau̇nz-ˌvil, -vəl\ city & port NE Australia in NE Queensland *pop* 81,172
To·ya·ma \tō-ˈyäm-ə\ city Japan in *cen* Honshu near **Toyama Bay** (inlet of Sea of Japan) *pop* 306,866
To·yo·ha·shi \ˌtȯi-ə-ˈhäsh-ē\ city Japan in S Honshu SE of Nagoya *pop* 308,776
Trab·zon \trab-ˈzän\ *or* **Treb·i·zond** \ˈtreb-ə-ˌzänd\ *or anc* **Trap·e·zus** \ˈtrap-i-zəs\ city & port NE Turkey on Black sea *pop* 107,412
Tra·cy \ˈtrā-sē\ city *cen* Calif. SSW of Stockton *pop* 18,428
Tra·fal·gar, Cape \trə-ˈfal-gər, *Sp* ˌträ-fäl-ˈgär\ cape SW Spain SE of Cádiz at W end of Strait of Gibraltar
Tra·lee \trə-ˈlē\ urban district & port SW Ireland ✱ of Kerry
Trans Alai \ˌtran(t)s-ə-ˈlī, ˌtranz-\ mountain range U.S.S.R. in NW Pamirs in Kirghiz & Tadzhik republics — see LENIN PEAK
Transalpine Gaul the part of Gaul included chiefly in modern France & Belgium
Transcaucasia — see CAUCASUS 2 — **Trans·cau·ca·sian** \ˌtran(t)s-kȯ-ˈkā-zhən, -ˈkazh-ən\ *adj or n*
Transjordan — see JORDAN — **Transjordanian** *adj or n*
Trans·kei \(ˈ)tran(t)s-ˈkī\ black enclave in the Republic of S. Africa; granted independence 1976; ✱ Umtata — **Trans·kei·an** \-ən\ *adj or n*
Trans·vaal \tran(t)s-ˈväl, tranz-\ province NE Republic of S. Africa bet. the Vaal & the Limpopo; in 19th century a Boer republic (**South African Republic**) ✱ Pretoria *area* 110,450 *sq mi* (287,170 *sq km*), *pop* 10,350,345
Tran·syl·va·nia *or Romanian* **Tran·sil·va·nia** \ˌtran(t)s-əl-ˈvā-nyə, -nē-ə\ region W Romania bounded on the N, E, & S by the Carpathians & the Transylvanian Alps; part of Hungary 1867–1918 — **Tran·syl·va·nian** \-nyən, -nē-ən\ *adj or n*
Transylvanian Alps a S extension of the Carpathian mountains in *cen* Romania
Tra·pa·ni \ˈträp-ə-nē\ commune & port Italy at NW tip of Sicily *pop* 71,430
Tra·si·me·no, Lake \ˌtraz-ə-ˈmen-(ˌ)ō\ lake 10 *mi* (16 *km*) wide *cen* Italy W of Perugia
Trav·an·core \ˈtrav-ən-ˌkō(ə)r, -ˌkȯ(ə)r\ region & former state SW India on Malabar coast extending N from Cape Comorin; included (1949–56) in former **Travancore and Co·chin** \ˈkō-chən\ state (✱ Trivandrum) — see KERALA
Trav·erse, Lake \ˈtrav-ərs\ lake NE S.Dak. & W Minn.; drained by the Bois de Sioux (headstream of Red river)
Treb·bia \ˈtreb-ē-ə\ *or anc* **Tre·bia** \ˈtrē-bē-ə\ river 71 *mi* (114 *km*) NW Italy flowing N into the Po
Treb·i·zond \ˈtreb-ə-ˌzänd\ **1** — see TRABZON **2** Greek empire 1204–1461, an offshoot of Byzantine Empire; at greatest extent included Georgia, Crimea, & S coast of Black sea E of the Sakarya
Trem·blant, Mont \mō^n-trän-ˈblä^n\ mountain 3150 *ft* (960 *m*) Canada in S Que. in Laurentian hills NW of Montreal
Treng·ga·nu \treŋ-ˈgän-(ˌ)ü\ state Malaysia in NE Peninsular Malaysia on S. China sea ✱ Kuala Trengganu *area* 5050 *sq mi* (13,130 *sq km*)
Trent \ˈtrent\ **1** river 150 *mi* (241 *km*) Canada in SE Ont. flowing from Kawartha Lakes through Rice Lake into Lake Ontario (Bay of Quinte) **2** *or* **Trent–Sev·ern** \-ˈsev-ərn\ canal system Canada 224 *mi* (360 *km*) long in SE Ont. connecting Lake Huron (Georgian Bay) with Lake Ontario (Bay of Quinte) **3** river 170 *mi* (274 *km*) *cen* England flowing NNE & uniting with Ouse river to form the Humber
Tren·ti·no \tren-ˈtē-(ˌ)nō\ district N Italy in S Tirol; with Alto Adige, forms **Trentino–Alto Adige** region (✱ Trento *area* 6327 *sq mi or* 16,450 *sq km*, *pop* 870,475)
Tren·ton \ˈtrent-ᵊn\ **1** city SE Mich. on Detroit river *pop* 22,762 **2** city ✱ of N.J. on Delaware river *pop* 92,124
Tre·vi·so \trā-ˈvē-(ˌ)zō\ commune NE Italy NW of Venice *pop* 87,069
Trier \ˈtri(ə)r\ city W W. Germany on the Moselle near Luxembourg border *pop* 104,100
Tri·este \trē-ˈest, -ˈes-tē\ *or Serbo-Croatian* **Trst** \ˈtərst\ city & port NE Italy on **Gulf of Trieste** (inlet at head of the Adriatic NW of the Istrian peninsula) *pop* 251,380; once belonged to Austria; part of Italy 1919–47; in 1947 made with surrounding territory the **Free Territory of Trieste** under administration of the United Nations; city with N part of Free Territory returned to Italy 1953, S part of territory having previously been absorbed into Yugoslavia — **Tri·es·tine** \trē-ˈes-tən, -ˌtēn\ *adj*
Trim \ˈtrim\ urban district E Ireland ✱ of County Meath
Trinacria — see SICILY — **Tri·nac·ri·an** \trə-ˈnak-rē-ən, trī-\ *adj*
Trin·co·ma·lee \ˌtriŋ-kō-mə-ˈlē, triŋ-ˈkəm-ə-lē\ city & port NE Sri Lanka on Bay of Bengal *pop* 44,913
Trin·i·dad \ˈtrin-ə-ˌdad\ island SE W. Indies off coast of NE Venezuela; with Tobago, a dominion (**Trinidad and Tobago**) of the Commonwealth since 1962; formerly a Brit. colony ✱ Port of Spain *area* 1864 *sq mi* (4846 *sq km*), *pop* 1,059,825 — **Trin·i·da·di·an** \ˌtrin-ə-ˈdād-ē-ən, -ˈdad-\ *adj or n*
Trin·i·ty \ˈtrin-ət-ē\ river 360 *mi* (579 *km*) E Tex. flowing SE into Galveston Bay
Trip·o·li \ˈtrip-ə-lē\ **1** *or Ar* **Ṭa·rā·bu·lus** \tə-ˈräb-ə-ləs\ *or anc* **Trip·o·lis** \ˈtrip-ə-ləs\ city & port NW Lebanon NNE of Beirut *pop* 127,611 **2** *or Ar* **Ṭarābulus** *or anc* **Oea** \ˈē-ə\ city & port NW Libya, a ✱ of Libya *pop* 247,365 **3** Tripolitania when it was one of the Barbary States — **Tri·pol·i·tan** \trip-ˈäl-ət-ᵊn\ *adj or n*
Tri·po·li·ta·nia \trip-ˌäl-ə-ˈtān-yə, ˌtrip-ə-lə-\ *or anc* **Trip·o·lis** \ˈtrip-ə-ləs\ region & former province NW Libya bordering on the Mediterranean — **Tri·po·li·ta·nian** \trip-ˌäl-ə-ˈtān-yən, ˌtrip-ə-lə-\ *adj or n*
Tri·pu·ra \ˈtrip-ə-rə\ state E India bet. Bangladesh & Assam ✱ Agartala *area* 4032 *sq mi* (10,483 *sq km*), *pop* 2,060,189
Tris·tan da Cu·nha \ˌtris-tən-də-ˈkü-nə\ island S Atlantic, chief of the Tristan da Cunha islands attached to Brit. colony of St. Helena *area* 42 *sq mi* (109 *sq km*), *pop* 251; volcanic eruptions 1961
Tri·van·drum \triv-ˈan-drəm\ city & port S India NW of Cape Comorin ✱ of Kerala *pop* 519,766
Tro·as \ˈtrō-ˌas\ **1** *or* **Tro·ad** \-ˌad\ territory surrounding the ancient city of Troy in NW Mysia, Asia Minor **2** ancient city of Mysia S of site of Troy — **Tro·ad·ic** \trō-ˈad-ik\ *adj*
Tro·bri·and \ˈtrō-brē-ˌänd\ islands SW Pacific in Solomon sea; attached to Papua New Guinea *area* 170 *sq mi* (442 *sq km*) — **Tro·bri·and·er** \ˌtrō-brē-ˈän-dər\ *n*
Trois–Ri·vières \ˌt(r)wä-riv-ˈye(ə)r\ city Canada in S Que. NE of Montreal on N bank of St. Lawrence river *pop* 50,466
Trom·sö \ˈträm-ˌsō, -ˌsə(r)\ city & port N Norway *pop* 46,444
Trond·heim \ˈträn-ˌhām\ city & port *cen* Norway on **Trondheim Fjord** (80 *mi or* 128 *km* long), *pop* 134,983
Tros·sachs \ˈträs-əks, -ˌaks\ valley *cen* Scotland bet. Loch Katrine & Loch Achray
Trou·ville \trü-ˈvē(ə)l\ *or* **Trouville–sur–Mer** \-(ˌ)su̇r-ˈme(ə)r\ town & port N France on English channel S of Le Havre *pop* 5718
Trow·bridge \ˈtrō-(ˌ)brij\ town S England ✱ of Wiltshire *pop* 22,984
Troy \ˈtrȯi\ **1** city SE Mich. N of Detroit *pop* 67,102 **2** city E N.Y. on Hudson river NNE of Albany *pop* 56,638 **3** city W Ohio *pop* 19,086 **4** *or* **Il·i·um** \ˈil-ē-əm\ *or* **Il·i·on** \ˈil-ē-ˌän, -ē-ən\ *or* **Troia** \ˈtrȯi-ə, ˈtrō-yə\ *or* **Tro·ja** \ˈtrō-jə, -yə\ ancient city NW Asia Minor in Troas SW of the Dardanelles
Troyes \trə-ˈwä\ city NE France SE of Paris *pop* 71,600
Tru·chas Peak \ˌtrü-chəs-\ *or* **North Truchas Peak** mountain 13,110 *ft* (3996 *m*) N N.Mex. in Sangre de Cristo mountains NE of Santa Fe; highest of three peaks forming **Truchas Peaks**
Trucial Oman, Trucial States — see UNITED ARAB EMIRATES
Truck·ee \ˈtrək-ē\ river 120 *mi* (193 *km*) E Calif. & W Nev. flowing from Lake Tahoe into Pyramid lake
Tru·ji·llo \trü-ˈhē-(ˌ)(y)ō\ **1** city NW Peru NW of Lima *pop* 193,528 **2** — see SANTO DOMINGO
Trujillo Al·to \-ˈäl-(ˌ)tō\ town NE *cen* Puerto Rico *pop* 41,141
Truk \ˈtrək, ˈtru̇k\ islands *cen* Carolines, part of Federated States of Micronesia
Trum·bull \ˈtrəm-bəl\ town SW Conn. N of Bridgeport *pop* 32,989
Tru·ro \ˈtru̇(ə)r-(ˌ)ō\ city & borough SW England, a ✱ of Cornwall and Isles of Scilly *pop* 16,277
Tsana — see TANA
Tsang·po \ˈ(t)säŋ-ˈpō\ the upper Brahmaputra in Tibet
Tsaritsyn — see VOLGOGRAD
Tsarskoe Selo — see PUSHKIN
Tsi·nan *or* **Ji·nan** *or* **Chi·nan** \ˈjē-ˈnän\ city E China ✱ of Shantung *pop* 1,500,000
Tsing·hai *or* **Qing·hai** \ˈchiŋ-ˈhī\ province W China ✱ Hsi-ning *area* 278,378 *sq mi* (723,783 *sq km*), *pop* 3,895,706
Tsing·tao \ˈchiŋ-ˈdau̇, ˈ(t)siŋ-ˈtau̇\ *or* **Qing·dao** \ˈchiŋ-ˈdau̇\ city & port E China in E Shantung on Kiaochow Bay *pop* 1,900,000
Tsi·tsi·har \ˈ(t)sēt-sē-ˌhär, ˈchē-chē-\ *or* **Qi·qi·har** \ˈchē-ˈchē-ˈhär\ *or* **Ch'i–ch'i–ha–erh** \ˈchē-ˈchē-ˈhä-ˈər\ city NE China in W Heilungkiang *pop* 1,500,000
Tskhin·va·li \ˈ(t)skin-və-lē\ town N Georgia, U.S.S.R., NW of Tbilisi ✱ of S. Ossetia *pop* 30,000
Tsu·ga·ru \ˈ(t)sü-gə-ˌrü\ strait Japan bet. Honshu & Hokkaido
Tsu·shi·ma \(t)sü-ˈshē-mə\ islands Japan in Korea strait separated from Kyushu and Honshu by **Tsushima strait** (the SE part of Korea strait) *area* 271 *sq mi* (705 *sq km*)
Tu·a·mo·tu \ˌtü-ə-ˈmō-(ˌ)tü\ archipelago S Pacific E of Society islands; belongs to France *area* 330 *sq mi* (858 *sq km*)
Tü·bing·en \ˈt(y)ü-biŋ-ən, ˈtue-\ city SW W. Germany on the Neckar S of Stuttgart *pop* 73,132
Tu·buaï \tüb-ˈwä-ˌē\ *or* **Aus·tral** \ˈȯs-trəl, ˈäs-\ islands S Pacific S of Tahiti belonging to France *area* 115 *sq mi* (299 *sq km*), *pop* 5208
Tuc·son \tü-ˈsän, ˈtü-ˌ\ city SE Ariz. *pop* 330,537
Tucumán — see SAN MIGUEL DE TUCUMÁN
Tu·ge·la \tü-ˈgā-lə\ river 300 *mi* (483 *km*) E Republic of S. Africa in *cen* Natal flowing E to Indian ocean; near its source on Mont Aux Sources are the **Tugela Falls** (3110 *ft or* 948 *m*)
Tu·la \ˈtü-lə\ **1** *or* **Tula de Allen·de** \-ˌdä-ä-ˈyen-dē\ city *cen* Mexico in SW Hidalgo N of Mexico City; ancient ✱ of the Toltecs *pop* 36,460 **2**

city U.S.S.R. in *cen* Soviet Russia, Europe, S of Moscow on a tributary of Oka river *pop* 462,000
Tu·la·gi \tü-'läg-ē\ island S Pacific in S *cen* Solomons
Tu·lare \tü-'la(ə)r(-ē), -'le(ə)r(-ē)\ **1** former lake S *cen* Calif. S of Fresno; now drained for farmland **2** city S *cen* Calif. SE of Fresno *pop* 22,475
Tul·la·more \,təl-ə-'mō(ə)r, -'mȯ(ə)r\ urban district *cen* Ireland ✱ of County Offaly *pop* 7901
Tul·sa \'təl-sə\ city NE Okla. on Arkansas river *pop* 360,919
Tu·ma·ca·co·ri National Monument \,tü-mə-'käk-ə-rē\ historic site S Ariz. S of Tucson; contains remains of Franciscan mission
Tu·men \'tü-'mən\ river 220 *mi* (354 *km*) E Asia on border bet. N. Korea, China, & the U.S.S.R. flowing NE & SE into Sea of Japan
Tu·muc–Hu·mac *or Pg* **Tu·mu·cu·maque** \tə-,mü-kə-'mäk\ range of low mountains NE Brazil on Suriname-French Guiana boundary
Tunbridge Wells ROYAL TUNBRIDGE WELLS
Tunghai — see LIEN-YÜN-KANG
T'ung–hua *or* **Tong·hua** *or* **Tung·hwa** \'tůŋ-'(h)wä\ city NE China in SW Kirin *pop* 158,000
Tun·gu·ska \tůŋ-'gü-skə, tən-\ any of three rivers in Soviet Russia, Asia, tributaries of the Yenisey: **Lower Tunguska, Stony Tunguska, & Upper Tunguska** (lower course of the Angara)
Tu·nis \'t(y)ü-nəs\ **1** city ✱ of Tunisia near site of ancient Carthage *pop* 550,404 **2** TUNISIA — used esp. of the former Barbary state
Tu·ni·sia \t(y)ü-'nē-zh(ē-)ə, -'nizh-(ē-)ə\ country N Africa bordering on the Mediterranean; formerly one of the Barbary states; a French protectorate 1881–1956, a monarchy 1956–57, & a republic since 1957 ✱ Tunis *area* 48,300 *sq mi* (125,580 *sq km*), *pop* 6,966,173 — **Tu·ni·sian** \-'nē-zh(ē-)ən, -'nizh-(ē-)ən\ *adj or n*
Tu·ol·um·ne \tů-'äl-ə-mē\ river 155 *mi* (249 *km*) *cen* Calif. flowing W from Yosemite National Park into the San Joaquin
Tu·pe·lo \'t(y)ü-pə-,lō\ city NE Miss. *pop* 23,905
Tu·pun·ga·to \,tü-pən-'gät-(,)ō\ mountain 22,310 *ft* (6800 *m*) in the Andes on Argentina-Chile boundary ENE of Santiago, Chile
Tu·rin \'t(y)ůr-ən, t(y)ů-'rin\ *or It* **To·ri·no** \tō-'rē-(,)nō\ commune NW Italy on the Po ✱ of Piedmont *pop* 1,103,520 — **Tu·rin·ese** \,t(y)ůr-ə-'nēz, -'nēs\ *adj or n*
Turkana, Lake — see RUDOLF, LAKE
Tur·ke·stan \,tər-kə-'stan, -'stän\ region *cen* Asia bet. Iran & Siberia; now divided bet. U.S.S.R., China, & Afghanistan — see CHINESE TURKESTAN, RUSSIAN TURKESTAN
Tur·key \'tər-kē\ country W Asia & SE Europe bet. Mediterranean & Black seas; formerly center of an empire (✱ Constantinople), since 1923 a republic ✱ Ankara *area* 301,302 *sq mi* (783,385 *sq km*), *pop* 50,664,458 — see OTTOMAN EMPIRE
Turk·men Republic \,tərk-mən-\ constituent republic U.S.S.R. in *cen* Asia bordering on Afghanistan, Iran, & the Caspian sea ✱ Ashkhabad *area* 187,200 *sq mi* (486,720 *sq km*), *pop* 2,759,000 — **Turk·man** \'tərk-mən\ *n, pl* **Turk·men** \-mən\ — **Turkmen** *adj* — **Turk·me·ni·an** \,tərk-'mē-nē-ən\ *adj*
Turks and Cai·cos \,tərk-sən-'kā-kəs\ two groups of islands (Turks islands & Caicos islands) Brit. W. Indies at SE end of the Bahamas; a Brit. colony; seat of government Grand Turk on **Grand Turk** island (7 *mi or* 11 *km* long) *area* 166 *sq mi* (432 *sq km*), *pop* 7436
Tur·ku \'tů(ə)r-(,)kü\ city & port SW Finland *pop* 163,526
Tur·lock \'tər-,läk\ city *cen* Calif. SE of Modesto *pop* 26,287
Turn·hout \'tů(ə)rn-,haůt, tůr-'nüt\ commune N Belgium *pop* 37,453
Tur·tle Bay \,tərt-ᵊl-\ section of New York City in E *cen* Manhattan on East river; site of United Nations headquarters
Tus·ca·loo·sa \,təs-kə-'lü-sə\ city W *cen* Ala. on Black Warrior river SW of Birmingham *pop* 75,211
Tus·ca·ny \'təs-kə-nē\ *or It* **To·sca·na** \tō-'skän-ə\ region NW *cen* Italy bordering on Ligurian & Tyrrhenian seas ✱ Florence *area* 8861 *sq mi* (23,039 *sq km*), *pop* 3,570,926
Tus·cu·lum \'təs-k(y)ə-ləm\ ancient town Italy in Latium SE of Rome
Tus·tin \'təs-tən\ city SW Calif. E of Santa Ana *pop* 32,317
Tu·tu·ila \,tüt-ə-'wē-lə\ island, chief of American Samoa group *area* 52 *sq mi* (135 *sq km*), *pop* 30,626 — **Tu·tu·ilan** \-lən\ *adj or n*
Tu·va \'tü-və\ autonomous republic U.S.S.R. in S Soviet Russia, Asia, N of Mongolia *area* 65,810 *sq mi* (171,106 *sq km*)
Tu·va·lu \tü-'väl-(,)ü, -'vär-\ *or formerly* **El·lice** \'el-əs\ islands W Pacific N of Fiji; a Brit. territory 1976–78; became an independent member of the Commonwealth 1978 ✱ Funafuti *area* 9 *sq mi* (23 *sq km*), *pop* 7300 — see GILBERT AND ELLICE
Tux·tla \'tüst-lə\ *or* **Tuxtla Gu·tiér·rez** \-gü-'tyer-əs\ city SE Mexico ✱ of Chiapas *pop* 66,851
Tu·zi·goot National Monument \'tü-zi-,güt\ reservation *cen* Ariz. SW of Flagstaff containing ruins of prehistoric pueblo
Tver — see KALININ
Tweed \'twēd\ river 96 *mi* (154 *km*) SE Scotland & NE England flowing E into North sea
Tweeddale — see PEEBLES
Twick·en·ham \ 'twik-(ə-)nəm \ former municipal borough SE England in Middlesex, now part of Richmond upon Thames
Twin Cities the cities of Minneapolis & St. Paul, Minn.
Twin Falls city S Idaho SW of Twin Falls (waterfall 125 *ft or* 38 *m* in Snake river) *pop* 26,209
Ty·ler \'tī-lər\ city E Tex. ESE of Dallas *pop* 70,508
Tyn·dall, Mount \'tin-dᵊl\ **1** mountain 14,025 *ft* (4275 *m*) S *cen* Calif. in Sierra Nevada NW of Mt. Whitney **2** mountain 8280 *ft* (2524 *m*) New Zealand in *cen* South Is. in Southern Alps
Tyne \'tīn\ river 35 *mi* (56 *km*) N England flowing E into North sea
Tyne and Wear \-'wi(ə)r\ metropolitan county N England ✱ Newcastle upon Tyne *area* 208 *sq mi* (541 *sq km*), *pop* 1,161,100
Tyne·mouth \'tīn-,maůth\ borough N England in Tyne and Wear on North sea at mouth of the Tyne *pop* 60,022
Tyr, Tyre — see SUR — **Tyr·i·an** \'tir-ē-ən\ *adj or n*
Ty·ree, Mount \tī-'rē\ mountain 16,290 *ft* (4965 *m*) W Antarctica in Ellsworth mountains NW of Vinson Massif
Tyrol — see TIROL — **Tyrolean** *adj or n* — **Tyrolese** *adj or n*
Ty·rone \tir-'ōn\ former county W *cen* Northern Ireland ✱ Omagh *area* 1218 *sq mi* (3167 *sq km*)
Tyr·rhe·ni·an \tə-'rē-nē-ən\ sea, the part of the Mediterranean W of Italy, N of Sicily, & E of Sardinia & Corsica
Tyu·men \tyü-'men\ city U.S.S.R. in W Soviet Russia, Asia, on the **Tura** \tů-'rä\ (a tributary of the Tobol) *pop* 359,000
Tzu–kung \'(d)zə-'gůŋ\ *or* **Zi·gong** \'zē-'gůŋ\ *or* **Tze·kung** \'(d)zə-'gůŋ\ city S *cen* China in S *cen* Szechwan *pop* 280,000
Tzu–po \'(d)zə-'bō\ *or* **Zi·bo** \'dzē-'bō\ city E China in *cen* Shantung *pop* 806,000
Uap — see YAP
Uau·pés \waů-'pes\ *or Sp* **Vau·pés** \vaů-\ river 700 *mi* (1126 *km*) Colombia & Brazil flowing ESE into Negro river
Uban·gi \(y)ü-'baŋ-(g)ē\ *or F* **Ou·ban·gui** \ü-bä^{n}-gē\ river 700 *mi* (1126 *km*) W *cen* Africa on NW border of Zaire flowing W & S into Congo river — see UELE
Ubangi–Sha·ri \-'shär-ē\ *or F* **Oubangui–Cha·ri** \-shȧ-rē\ former French territory N *cen* Africa — see CENTRAL AFRICAN REPUBLIC
Ube \'ü-(,)bā\ city & port Japan in SW Honshu *pop* 170,142
Uca·ya·li \,ü-kə-'yäl-ē\ river 1200 *mi* (1931 *km*) *cen* & N Peru flowing N to unite with the Marañón forming the Amazon
Uc·cle \'üklᵊ, 'ᵫklᵊ\ *or Flem* **Uk·kel** \'ək-əl\ commune *cen* Belgium *pop* 76,004
Udai·pur \ů-'dī-,pů(ə)r\ **1** *or* **Me·war** \mā-'wär\ former state NW India, now part of Rajasthan state **2** city, its ✱, *pop* 229,762
Udi·ne \'üd-i-,nā\ commune NE Italy NE of Venice ✱ of Friuli-Venezia Giulia region *pop* 101,264
Ud·murt Republic \'ůd-,mů(ə)rt\ autonomous republic U.S.S.R. in E Soviet Russia, Europe, in W foothills of the Urals ✱ Izhevsk *area* 16,200 *sq mi* (42,120 *sq km*), *pop* 1,417,000
Ue·le \'wel-ē\ river 700 *mi* (1126 *km*) *cen* Africa flowing W in N Zaire to unite with the Bomu forming Ubangi river
Ufa \ü-'fä\ **1** river 430 *mi* (692 *km*) U.S.S.R. in E Soviet Russia, Europe, in S Urals flowing NW & SW into the Belaya **2** city U.S.S.R. in E Soviet Russia, Europe ✱ of Bashkir Republic *pop* 969,000
Ugan·da \(y)ü-'gan-də, -'gän-\ republic E Africa N of Lake Victoria; member of the Commonwealth ✱ Kampala *area* 93,981 *sq mi* (244,351 *sq km*), *pop* 12,630,076 — **Ugan·dan** \-dən\ *adj or n*
Uga·rit \,ü-gə-'rēt\ ancient city, Syria on Mediterranean coast
Uin·ta \yü-'int-ə\ mountain range NE Utah — see KINGS PEAK
Uj·jain \'ü-,jīn\ city NW *cen* India in W Madhya Pradesh NNW of Indore *pop* 281,878
Ujung Pan·dang \ü-,jůŋ-(,)pän-'däŋ\ *or formerly* **Ma·kas·sar** \mə-'kas-ər\ city & port Indonesia in SW Celebes *pop* 709,038
Ukrai·ni·an Republic \yü-,krā-nē-ən-\ *or* **Ukraine** \yü-'krān, *also* -'krīn, 'yü-,\ constituent republic of the U.S.S.R. in E Europe on N coast of Black sea ✱ Kiev *area* 222,600 *sq mi* (578,760 *sq km*), *pop* 49,755,000
Ulan Ba·tor \,ü-,län-'bä-,tȯ(ə)r\ *or formerly* **Ur·ga** \'ů(ə)r-gə\ city N *cen* Mongolia (republic), its ✱ *pop* 418,700
Ulan–Ude \,ü-,län-ů-'dā\ *or formerly* **Verkh·ne·udinsk** \,verk-nə-'ü-,din(t)sk\ city U.S.S.R. in E Soviet Russia, Asia ✱ of Buryat Republic on the Selenga *pop* 300,000
Uleåborg — see OULU
Ulls·wa·ter \'əlz-,wȯt-ər, -,wät-\ lake 7 *mi* (11 *km*) long NW England in Cumbria
Ulm \'ůlm\ city S W. Germany in E Baden-Württemberg *pop* 100,671
Ul·ster \'əl-stər\ **1** region N Ireland (island) comprising Northern Ireland & N Ireland (republic); ancient kingdom, later a province comprising nine counties, three of which in 1921 joined Irish Free State (now Ireland) while the rest remained with United Kingdom **2** province N Ireland (republic) comprising counties Cavan, Donegal, & Monaghan *area* 3093 *sq mi* (8042 *sq km*) **3** Northern Ireland comprising counties Antrim, Armagh, Down, Fermanagh, Londonderry, & Tyrone ✱ Belfast — **Ul·ster·ite** \-stə-,rīt\ *n* — **Ul·ster·man** \-stər-mən\ *n*
Ulu Dag \,ü-lə-'dä(g)\ *or anc* **Olym·pus** \ə-'lim-pəs, ō-\ mountain 8343 *ft* (2543 *m*) NW Turkey in Asia SE of Bursa
Ulugh Muz·tagh \,ü-lə-məz-'tä(g)\ *or* **Muz·tag** \məz-'tä(g)\ mountain 25,340 *ft* (7724 *m*) W China in S Sinkiang Uighur; highest in Kunlun mountains
Ul·ya·novsk \ül-'yän-əfsk\ *or formerly* **Sim·birsk** \sim-'bi(ə)rsk\ city U.S.S.R. in E *cen* Soviet Russia, Europe, on the Volga *pop* 464,000
Uma·til·la \,yü-mə-'til-ə\ river 80 *mi* (129 *km*) NE Oreg. flowing W & N into Columbia river
Um·bria \'əm-brē-ə\ region *cen* Italy in the Apennines ✱ Perugia
Umm al Qai·wain \'ům-äl-kī-'wīn\ sheikhdom, member of United Arab Emirates
Um·nak \'üm-,nak\ island SW Alaska in Fox islands
Ump·qua \'əm(p)-,kwȯ\ river 200 *mi* (322 *km*) SW Oreg. flowing into the Pacific
Um·ta·ta \ům-'tät-ə\ city ✱ of Transkei
Un·alas·ka \,ən-ə-'las-kə\ island SW Alaska in Fox islands
Unalaska Bay bay SW Alaska on N coast of Unalaska Is.
Un·com·pah·gre Peak \,ən-kəm-'päg-rē\ mountain 14,309 *ft* (4361 *m*) SW Colo.; highest in San Juan mountains
Uncompahgre Plateau tableland W Colo. SW of the Gunnison
Un·gava \,ən-'gav-ə\ **1** peninsula Canada in N Que. bet. Hudson Bay & Ungava Bay **2** region Canada N of the Eastmain & W of Labrador including Ungava peninsula, divided 1927 bet. Que. & Nfld. — see NEW QUEBEC
Ungava Bay inlet of Hudson strait Canada in N Que.
Uni·mak \'yü-nə-,mak\ island SW Alaska in Fox islands
Union City **1** city W Calif. S of Oakland *pop* 39,406 **2** city NE N.J. N of Jersey City *pop* 55,593
Union of South Africa — see SOUTH AFRICA (Republic of)
Union of Soviet Socialist Republics *or* **Soviet Union** country E Europe & N Asia bordering on the Arctic & Pacific oceans & Baltic & Black seas; a union of 15 constituent republics ✱ Moscow *area* 8,662,400 *sq mi* (22,522,240 *sq km*), *pop* 262,436,227 — see RUSSIA
United Arab Emirates *or formerly* **Tru·cial States** \'trü-shəl-\ *or* **Trucial Oman** \-ō-'män, -'man\ country NE Arabia on Persian Gulf between Qatar & Oman; a republic composed of seven sheikdoms (Abu Dhabi,

\ə\ abut \ᵊ\ kitten, F table \ər\ further \a\ ash \ā\ ace \ä\ cot, cart \aů\ out \ch\ chin \e\ bet \ē\ easy \g\ go \i\ hit \ī\ ice \j\ job \ŋ\ sing \ō\ go \ȯ\ law \ȯi\ boy \th\ thin \t̲h̲\ the \ü\ loot \ů\ foot \y\ yet \zh\ vision \ȧ, k̲, ⁿ, œ, ᵫ, ue, ᵫ̄, ʸ\ *see* Guide to Pronunciation

Ajman, Dubai, Fujaira, Ras al Khaimah, Sharja, & Umm al Qaiwain) formerly under Brit. protection ✻ Abu Dhabi *area* 32,000 *sq mi* (83,200 *sq km*), *pop* 1,043,225
United Arab Republic former name (1961–71) of republic of Egypt & previously (1958–61) of union of Egypt & Syria
United Kingdom 1 *or* **United Kingdom of Great Britain and Northern Ireland** country W Europe in British Isles comprising Great Britain & Northern Ireland ✻ London *area* 89,034 *sq mi* (231,488 *sq km*), *pop* 55,671,000 2 *or* **United Kingdom of Great Britain and Ireland** country 1801–1921 comprising Great Britain & all of Ireland
United Nations international territory, a small area in New York City in E *cen* Manhattan overlooking East river; seat since 1951 of permanent headquarters of the United Nations political organization — see TURTLE BAY
United Provinces *or* **United Provinces of Agra and Oudh** former province N India formed 1902 ✻ Allahabad; as Uttar Pradesh, became a state of India (republic) 1950
United States of America *or* **United States** \yu̇-ˌnīt-əd-ˈstāts, *esp Southern* ˈyü-\ 1 country N. America bordering on Atlantic, Pacific, & Arctic oceans; a federal republic ✻ Washington *area* 3,615,123 *sq mi* (9,399,320 *sq km*), *pop* 226,504,825 2 the United States of America with dependencies & possessions
University City city E Mo. WNW of St. Louis *pop* 42,738
University Park city NE Tex. within city of Dallas *pop* 22,254
Un·ter·wal·den \ˈu̇nt-ər-ˌväl-dən\ former canton *cen* Switzerland, now divided into two cantons (formerly half cantons): **Nid·wal·den** \ˈnēt-ˌväl-dən\ *or F* **Nid·wald** \nēd-vält\ (✻ Stans *area* 112 *sq mi or* 291 *sq km, pop* 28,617) & **Ob·wal·den** \ˈōp-ˌväl-dən\ *or F* **Ob·wald** \ōb-vält\ (✻ Sarnen *area* 183 *sq mi or* 476 *sq km, pop* 25,865)
Up·land \ˈəp-lənd\ city SW Calif. W of San Bernardino *pop* 47,647
Upo·lu \ü-ˈpō-(ˌ)lü\ island S Pacific in Western Samoa
Upper Adige — see ALTO ADIGE
Upper Arlington city *cen* Ohio W of Columbus *pop* 35,648
Upper Canada the Canadian province 1791–1841 corresponding to modern Ont. — see LOWER CANADA
Upper Karroo — see KARROO
Upper Klamath lake 30 *mi* (48 *km*) long S Oreg. SSE of Crater Lake National Park drained by Klamath river — see LOWER KLAMATH
Upper Palatinate — see PALATINATE
Upper Peninsula the N part of Mich. bet. Lakes Superior & Michigan
Upper Volta — see BURKINA FASO — **Upper Vol·tan** \-ˈvält-ᵊn, -ˈvōlt-, -ˈvȯlt-\ *adj or n*
Upp·sa·la \ˈəp-sə-ˌlä, -ˌsäl-ə; ˌəp-ˈsäl-ə\ city E Sweden NNW of Stockholm *pop* 146,192
Ur \ˈər, ˈu̇(ə)r\ city of ancient Sumer; site in S Iraq NW of Basra
Ural \ˈyu̇r-əl\ 1 river 1400 *mi* (2253 *km*) U.S.S.R. rising at S end of Ural mountains & flowing S into the Caspian 2 mountain system U.S.S.R. extending from Kara sea to steppes N of Lake Aral; usu. considered the dividing line bet. Asia & Europe; highest Narodnaya 6214 *ft* (1894 *m*)
Uralsk \yu̇-ˈralsk\ city U.S.S.R. in Soviet Central Asia in W Kazakhstan on Ural river *pop* 167,000
Ura·ri·coe·ra \ü-ˌrär-i-ˈkwer-ə\ river 360 *mi* (579 *km*) N Brazil, a headstream of the Branco
Ura·wa \u̇-ˈrä-wə\ city Japan in Honshu N of Tokyo *pop* 363,041
Ur·bana \ˌər-ˈban-ə\ city E *cen* Ill. *pop* 35,978
Ur·ban·dale \ˈər-bən-ˌdāl\ city S *cen* Iowa *pop* 17,869
Ur·bi·no \u̇(ə)r-ˈbē-(ˌ)nō\ commune *cen* Italy *pop* 15,918
Ur·fa \u̇r-ˈfä\ *or anc* **Edes·sa** \i-ˈdes-ə\ city SE Turkey *pop* 148,434
Urga — see ULAN BATOR
Uri \ˈu̇(ə)r-ē\ canton *cen* Switzerland S of Vierwaldstätter See ✻ Altdorf *area* 415 *sq mi* (1079 *sq km*), *pop* 33,883
Ur·mia \ˈu̇(ə)r-mē-ə\ *or formerly* **Re·zāi·yeh** \rə-ˈzī-(y)ə\ city NW Iran *pop* 163,991
Urmia, Lake — REZAIYEH
Uru·bam·ba \ˌu̇r-ə-ˈbäm-bə\ river 450 *mi* (724 *km*) *cen* Peru flowing NNW to unite with the Apurímac forming the Ucayali
Uru·guay \ˈ(y)u̇r-ə-ˌgwī, ˈyu̇r-ə-ˌgwā\ 1 river 980 *mi* (1577 *km*) SE S. America rising in Brazil & flowing into the Río de la Plata 2 *or* **Re·pú·bli·ca Ori·en·tal del Uru·guay** \re-ˈpü-bli-(ˌ)kä-ˌōr-ē-ˌen-ˈtäl-ˌdel-ˌu̇r-ə-ˈgwī, -ˌȯr-\ country SE S. America bet. the lower Uruguay & the Atlantic; a republic ✻ Montevideo *area* 72,172 *sq mi* (187,647 *sq km*), *pop* 2,788,429 — see BANDA ORIENTAL — **Uru·guay·an** \ˌ(y)u̇r-ə-ˈgwī-ən, ˌyu̇r-ə-ˈgwā-\ *adj or n*
Urum·chi \ü-ˈrüm-chē, ˌu̇r-əm-ˈ\ *or* **Ürüm·qi** \ˈue-ˈruem-ˈchē\ *or* **Wu-lu-mu-ch'i** \ˈwü-ˈlü-ˈmü-ˈchē\ city NW China ✻ of Sinkiang Uighur on N side of Tien Shan *pop* 320,000
Urundi — see BURUNDI
Ushant — see OUESSANT, ÎLE D'
Us·hua·ia \ü-ˈswī-ə\ town S Argentina on S coast of Tierra del Fuego Is., at 54°48′S; southernmost city in the world *pop* 10,998
Usk \ˈəsk\ river 60 *mi* (96 *km*) S Wales & W England flowing E & S into Severn estuary
Üs·kü·dar \ˌu̇s-kə-ˈdär\ suburb of Istanbul, Turkey, on Asian side of the Bosporus
Us·pal·la·ta \ˌü-spə-ˈyät-ə, -ˈzhät-\ *or* **La Cum·bre** \lə-ˈküm-(ˌ)brā\ mountain pass (12,572 *ft or* 3832 *m*) & tunnel S S. America in the Andes bet. Mendoza, Argentina & Santiago, Chile
Us·su·ri \u̇-ˈsu̇(ə)r-ē\ river 450 *mi* (724 *km*) E Asia on border bet. U.S.S.R. & China flowing N into the Amur
Usti nad La·bem \ˈü-stē-ˈnäd-lä-ˌbem\ city W Czechoslovakia in N Bohemia on the Elbe *pop* 87,909
Ustinov — see IZHEVSK
Usumbura — see BUJUMBURA
Utah \ˈyü-ˌtȯ, -ˌtä\ 1 lake 30 *mi* (48 *km*) long N *cen* Utah drained by Jordan river 2 state W U.S. ✻ Salt Lake City *area* 84,916 *sq mi* (220,782 *sq km*), *pop* 1,461,037 — **Utah·an** \-ˌtȯ(-ə)n, -ˌtä(-ə)n\ *adj or n* — **Utahn** \-ˌtȯ(-ə)n, -ˌtä(-ə)n\ *n*
Uti·ca \ˈyüt-i-kə\ 1 city E *cen* N.Y. on Mohawk river *pop* 75,632 2 ancient city N Africa on Mediterranean coast NW of Carthage
Utrecht \ˈyü-ˌtrekt\ 1 province *cen* Netherlands S of the IJsselmeer *area* 535 *sq mi* (1391 *sq km*), *pop* 922,821 2 city, its ✻ *pop* 231,600
Utsu·no·mi·ya \ˌüt-sə-ˈnō-mē-ˌ(y)ä\ city Japan in *cen* Honshu N of Tokyo *pop* 383,246
Ut·tar Pra·desh \ˌu̇t-ər-prə-ˈdesh, -ˈdāsh\ state N India bordering on Tibet & Nepal ✻ Lucknow *area* 113,409 *sq mi* (294,863 *sq km*), *pop* 110,358,019 — see UNITED PROVINCES
Ux·bridge \ˈəks-(ˌ)brij\ former municipal borough SE England in Middlesex, now part of Hillingdon
Ux·mal \üsh-ˈmäl\ site of ancient Maya city SE Mexico in W Yucatán
Uz·bek Republic \ˈu̇z-ˌbek, ˈəz-, u̇z-ˈ\ *or* **Uz·bek·i·stan** \(ˌ)u̇z-ˌbek-i-ˈstan, ˌəz-, -ˈstän\ constituent republic U.S.S.R. in W *cen* Asia E of the Amu Darya ✻ Tashkent *area* 171,070 *sq mi* (444,782 *sq km*), *pop* 15,391,000
Vaal \ˈväl\ river 700 *mi* (1126 *km*) Republic of S. Africa rising in SE Transvaal & flowing W into Orange river in N Cape Province
Vaa·sa *or Sw* **Va·sa** \ˈväs-ə\ city & port W Finland *pop* 44,316
Vaca·ville \ˈvak-ə-ˌvil\ city W Calif. SW of Sacramento *pop* 43,367
Va·duz \vä-ˈdüts\ commune ✻ of Liechtenstein on the upper Rhine
Vah \ˈvä(k)\ *or Hung* **Vag** \ˈväg\ river 210 *mi* (338 *km*) Czechoslovakia rising in Tatry mountains & flowing W & S into the Danube
Va·lais \va-ˈlā\ *or G* **Wal·lis** \ˈväl-əs\ canton SW *cen* Switzerland bordering on France & Italy ✻ Sion *area* 2026 *sq mi* (5268 *sq km*), *pop* 218,707
Val·dai \väl-ˈdī\ hills U.S.S.R. in W Soviet Russia, Europe, SE of Lake Ilmen; highest point 1053 *ft* (321 *m*)
Val·di·via \val-ˈdē-vē-ə\ city & port S *cen* Chile *pop* 115,536
Val d'Or \ˈval-ˌdȯ(ə)r\ town Canada in SW Que. *pop* 21,371
Val·dos·ta \val-ˈdäs-tə\ city S Ga. *pop* 37,596
Va·lence \va-ˈläⁿs\ commune SE France S of Lyons *pop* 67,101
Va·len·cia \və-ˈlen-ch(ē-)ə, -ˈlen(t)-sē-ə\ 1 region & ancient kingdom E Spain bet. Andalusia & Catalonia 2 province E Spain *area* 4150 *sq mi* (10,790 *sq km*), *pop* 2,112,921 3 commune & port on the Mediterranean, its ✻ *pop* 744,748 4 city N Venezuela WSW of Caracas *pop* 523,000
Va·len·ci·ennes \və-ˌlen(t)-sē-ˈen(z)\ city N France *pop* 41,976
Va·len·tia *or* **Va·len·cia** \və-ˈlen-ch(ē-)ə\ island SW Ireland in County Kerry in the Atlantic S of entrance to Dingle Bay
Val·la·do·lid \ˌval-əd-ə-ˈlid, -ˈlē\ 1 province NW *cen* Spain *area* 2922 *sq mi* (7597 *sq km*), *pop* 488,373 2 commune, its ✻, NNW of Madrid *pop* 320,293
Val·lau·ris \ˌval-ō-ˈrēs\ village SE France NE of Cannes
Va·lle·cas \vä-ˈyā-kəs, vī-ˈā-\ commune *cen* Spain, SE suburb of Madrid
Valle d'Ao·sta \ˌväl-ā-dä-ˈōs-tə\ *or* **Val d'Ao·sta** \ˌväl-dä-\ autonomous region NW Italy bordering on France & Switzerland NW of Piedmont ✻ Aosta *area* 1260 *sq mi* (3276 *sq km*), *pop* 112,662
Val·le·jo \və-ˈlā-(ˌ)ō\ city W Calif. on San Pablo Bay *pop* 80,303
Val·let·ta *or* **Va·let·ta** \və-ˈlet-ə\ city & port ✻ of Malta *pop* 14,042
Valley East town Canada in S Ont. N of Sudbury *pop* 20,433
Val·ley·field \ˈval-ē-ˌfēld\ *or* **Sal·a·ber·ry–de–Valleyfield** \ˈsal-ə-ˌber-ē-də-\ city Canada in S Que. SW of Montreal *pop* 29,574
Valley of Ten Thousand Smokes volcanic region SW Alaska in Katmai National Monument
Valley Stream village SE N.Y. on Long Is. *pop* 35,769
Va·lois \ˈval-ˌwä\ medieval county & duchy N France in NE Île-de-France ✻ Crépy-en-Valois
Valona — see VLORË
Val·pa·rai·so 1 \ˌval-pə-ˈrā-(ˌ)zō\ city NW Ind. SE of Gary *pop* 22,247 2 \-ˈrī-(ˌ)zō, -ˈrā-\ *or Sp* **Val·pa·ra·í·so** \ˌväl-pä-rä-ˈē-sō\ city & port *cen* Chile WNW of Santiago *pop* 266,428
Van \ˈvan\ salt lake E Turkey in Armenia *area* 1425 *sq mi* (3705 *sq km*)
Van·cou·ver \van-ˈkü-vər\ 1 island W Canada in B.C. off SW coast; chief city Victoria *area* 12,408 *sq mi* (32,261 *sq km*) 2 city SW Wash. on Columbia river opposite Portland, Oreg. *pop* 42,834 3 city & port Canada in SW B.C. on Burrard Inlet *pop* 414,281 — **Van·cou·ver·ite** \-və-ˌrīt\ *n*
Vancouver, Mount mountain 15,700 *ft* (4785 *m*) on Alaska-Yukon boundary in St. Elias range
Van Die·men \van-ˈdē-mən\ gulf, inlet of Arafura sea N Australia in N Northern Territory
Van Diemen's Land — see TASMANIA
Vä·nern \-nərn\ lake SW Sweden *area* 2141 *sq mi* (5567 *sq km*)
Va·nier \ˈvan-ˌyā\ *or formerly* **East·view** \ˈēst-ˌvyü\ city Canada in SE Ont. NE of Ottawa on Ottawa river *pop* 10,725
Va·nua Le·vu \və-ˌnü-ə-ˈlev-(ˌ)ü\ island S Pacific in the Fijis NE of Viti Levu *area* 2128 *sq mi* (5533 *sq km*)
Van·u·atu \ˌvan-ə-ˈwät-(ˌ)ü\ *or formerly* **New Heb·ri·des** \ˈheb-rə-ˌdēz\ islands SW Pacific NE of New Caledonia & W of Fiji; formerly under joint Brit. & French administration, a republic since 1980 ✻ Vila (on Efate) *area* 5700 *sq mi* (14,820 *sq km*), *pop* 112,304
Varanasi — see BANARAS
Var·dar \ˈvär-ˌdär\ river 200 *mi* (322 *km*) SE Yugoslavia & N Greece flowing S into Thermaïkós Kólpos
Va·re·se \və-ˈrā-sē\ commune N Italy NW of Milan *pop* 90,285
Var·na \ˈvär-nə\ *or formerly* **Sta·lin** \ˈstäl-ən, ˈstal-, -ˌēn\ city & port E Bulgaria on Black sea *pop* 252,525
Väs·ter·ås \ˌves-tə-ˈrōs\ city E Sweden on Mälaren lake NW of Stockholm *pop* 117,487
Vaté — see EFATE
Vat·i·can City \ˌvat-i-kən-\ *or It* **Cit·tà del Va·ti·ca·no** \chēt-ˈtä-del-ˌvä-tē-ˈkä-nō\ independent papal state within commune of Rome, Italy; created Feb. 11, 1929 *area* 109 *acres* (43 *hectares*), *pop* 736
Vät·tern \-ərn\ lake S Sweden *area* 733 *sq mi* (1906 *sq km*)
Vaud \ˈvō\ *or G* **Waadt** \ˈvät\ canton W Switzerland N of Lake of Geneva ✻ Lausanne *area* 1256 *sq mi* (3266 *sq km*), *pop* 528,747
Vaughan \ˈvȯn, ˈvän\ town Canada in SE Ont. N of Toronto *pop* 17,782
Vaupés — see UAUPÉS
Ve·ga Ba·ja \ˌvā-gə-ˈbä-(ˌ)hä\ town N Puerto Rico *pop* 18,233
Vegas LAS VEGAS
Ve·ii \ˈvē-ˌ(y)ī\ ancient city of Etruria in *cen* Italy NNW of Rome
Vel·bert \ˈfel-bərt\ city W W. Germany in N. Rhine-Westphalia in Ruhr valley NE of Düsseldorf *pop* 93,056
Vel·la La·vel·la \ˌvel-ə-lə-ˈvel-ə\ island SW Pacific in *cen* Solomons
Vel·lore \və-ˈlō(ə)r, ve-, -ˈlȯ(ə)r\ city SE India in N Tamil Nadu WSW of Madras *pop* 246,937
Vel·sen \ˈvel-zən, -sən\ commune W Netherlands; outer port for Amsterdam *pop* 59,117
Velsuna — see ORVIETO
Vence \väⁿs\ commune SE France W of Nice *pop* 7332

Ven·da \'ven-də\ black enclave in the Republic of S. Africa; granted independence 1979; ✻ Thohoyandou

Ven·dée \vä(n)-'dā\ or **La Vendée** \lä-\ region W France bordering on Bay of Biscay S of Brittany

Ven·dôme \vä(n)-'dōm\ town N cen France WSW of Orléans

Ve·ne·tia \və-'nē-sh(ē-)ə\ or It **Ve·ne·zia** \və-'net-sē-ə\ **1** area NE Italy & NW Yugoslavia including territory bet. the lower Po & the Alps **2** VENEZIA EUGANEA — **Ve·ne·tian** \-'nē-shən\ adj

Ve·ne·to \'ven-ə-,tō, 'vā-nə-\ region NE Italy comprising most of Venezia Euganea ✻ Venice area 7092 sq mi (18,439 sq km), pop 4,309,427

Ve·ne·zia Eu·ga·nea \və-,net-sē-ə-,eü-'gän-ē-ə\ the S portion of Venetia

Venezia Giu·lia \-'jül-yə\ the E portion of Venetia including Julian Alps & Istria; now mainly in Yugoslavia

Venezia Tri·den·ti·na \,trē-,den-'tē-nə\ the NW portion of Venetia N of Lake Garda; included in Trentino-Alto Adige region

Ven·e·zu·e·la \,ven-əz-(ə-)'wā-lə, -'wē-\ country N S. America; a republic ✻ Caracas area 352,141 sq mi (915,567 sq km), pop 14,516,735 — **Ven·e·zu·e·lan** \-lən\ adj or n

Venezuela, Gol·fo de \,gōl-fō-,thä-\ or **Gulf of Venezuela** inlet of the Caribbean NW Venezuela N of Lake Maracaibo

Ven·iam·i·nof Crater \ven-'yam-ə-,nȯf\ volcano 8225 ft (2507 m) SW Alaska on cen Alaska peninsula in Aleutian range

Ven·ice \'ven-əs\ or It **Ve·ne·zia** \və-'net-sē-ə\ or L **Ve·ne·tia** \vi-'nē-sh(ē-)ə\ city & port NE Italy ✻ of Veneto, on islands in **Lagoon of Venice** (inlet of Gulf of Venice) pop 332,775 — **Ve·ne·tian** \və-'nē-shən\ adj or n

Venice, Gulf of arm of the Adriatic bet. Po delta & Istria

Ven·lo or formerly **Ven·loo** \'ven-(,)lō\ commune SE Netherlands on Maas river near W. German border pop 62,564

Ven·ta \'vent-ə\ river 200 mi (322 km) U.S.S.R. in Lithuania & Latvia flowing into the Baltic

Ven·ti·mi·glia \,venti-'mēl-yə\ commune NW Italy on Ligurian sea W of San Remo near Menton, France pop 26,373

Vents·pils \'ven(t)-,spils, -,spilz\ or G **Win·dau** \'vin-,daü\ city & port Latvia at mouth of the Venta pop 37,000

Ven·tu·ra \ven-'t(y)ür-ə\ or officially **San Buen·a·ven·tu·ra** \(,)san-,bwen-ə-,ven-\ city & port SW Calif. on Santa Barbara channel ESE of Santa Barbara pop 74,474

Ve·nue, Ben \ben-və-'n(y)ü\ mountain 2393 ft (729 m) cen Scotland S of Loch Katrine

Ve·ra·cruz \,ver-ə-'krüz, -'krüs\ **1** state E Mexico ✻ Jalapa area 27,736 sq mi (72,114 sq km), pop 5,264,611 **2** or **Vera Cruz Lla·ve** \-'yä-(,)vä\ city & port E Mexico in Veracruz state on Gulf of Mexico pop 242,351

Ver·cel·li \ver-'chel-ē, (,)ver-\ commune NW Italy pop 51,975

Verde, Cape \'vərd\ or **Cap Vert** \kap-'vərt\ or **Cape Vert** \'vərt\ promontory W Africa in Senegal; westernmost point in Africa at 17° 30' W

Ver·di·gris \'vərd-ə-grəs\ river 280 mi (451 km) SE Kans. & NE Okla. flowing into Arkansas river

Ver·dun \(,)vər-'dən, ver-\ **1** city Canada in S Que. on Montreal Is. pop 61,287 **2** or **Verdun–sur–Meuse** \-,sü(ə)r-\ city NE France on the Meuse ESE of Reims pop 22,889

Ver·ee·ni·ging \fə-'rā-nə-giŋ, -nək-əŋ\ city NE Republic of S. Africa in S Transvaal on the Vaal S of Johannesburg pop 94,500

Verkhneudinsk — see ULAN-UDE

Ver·mont \vər-'mänt\ state NE U.S. ✻ Montpelier area 9609 sq mi (24,983 sq km), pop 511,456 — **Ver·mont·er** \-ər\ n

Ver·non \'vər-nən\ town N cen Conn. NE of Hartford pop 27,974

Vernyi — see ALMA-ATA

Vé·roia \'ve(ə)r-yə\ or anc **Be·rea** or **Be·roea** \bə-'rē-ə\ town NE Greece in Macedonia W of Salonika

Ve·ro·na \və-'rō-nə\ commune NE Italy on the Adige pop 261,208 — **Ver·o·nese** \,ver-ə-'nēz, -'nēs\ adj or n

Ver·sailles \(,)vər-'sī, ver-\ city N France, WSW suburb of Paris pop 93,359

Ver·viers \ver-'vyā\ commune E Belgium E of Liège pop 55,371

Ves·ter·ålen \'ves-tə-,rô-lən\ island group Norway off NW coast NE of Lofoten islands pop 56,696

Ve·su·vi·us \və-'sü-vē-əs\ or It **Ve·su·vio** \vā-'züv-yō\ volcano 4190 ft (1277 m) Italy in Campania on Bay of Naples

Vet·lu·ga \vet-'lü-gə\ river 500 mi (805 km) U.S.S.R. in cen Soviet Russia, Europe, flowing S into the Volga

Ve·vey \və-'vā\ commune W Switzerland in Vaud on NE shore of Lake Geneva pop 16,139

Viatka — see VYATKA

Vi·cen·te Ló·pez \və-,sent-ə-'lō-,pez\ city E Argentina, N suburb of Buenos Aires, on Río de la Plata pop 289,815

Vi·cen·za \vi-'chen(t)-sə\ commune NE Italy W of Venice pop 113,931

Vi·chu·ga \vi-'chü-gə\ city U.S.S.R. in cen Soviet Russia, Europe, NE of Moscow pop 53,000

Vi·chy \'vish-ē, 'vē-shē\ commune cen France on the Allier pop 32,107

Vicks·burg \'viks-,bərg\ city W Miss. pop 25,434

Vic·to·ria \vik-'tōr-ē-ə, -'tȯr-\ **1** city SE Tex. on Guadalupe river pop 50,695 **2** city Canada ✻ of B.C. on SE Vancouver Is. pop 64,379 **3** island N Canada SE of Banks Is. area 81,930 sq mi (213,018 sq km) **4** river 350 mi (563 km) Australia in NW Northern Territory flowing N & NW to Timor sea **5** state SE Australia ✻ Melbourne area 87,884 sq mi (228,498 sq km), pop 3,832,443 **6** lake E Africa in Tanzania, Kenya, & Uganda area 26,200 sq mi (68,120 sq km) **7** or **Hong Kong** \'häŋ-,käŋ, -'käŋ; 'hȯŋ-,kȯŋ, -'kȯŋ\ city & port ✻ of Hong Kong colony on NW Hong Kong Is. pop 1,026,870 — **Vic·to·ri·an** \vik-'tōr-ē-ən, -'tȯr-\ adj or n

Victoria Falls waterfall 200 to 350 ft (61 to 107 m) high & 5580 ft (1701 m) wide S Africa in the Zambezi on border bet. Zambia & Zimbabwe

Victoria Land region E Antarctica S of New Zealand on W shore of Ross sea & Ross Ice Shelf

Victoria Nile — see NILE

Vic·to·ria·ville \vik-'tōr-ē-ə-,vil, -'tȯr-\ town Canada in S Que. pop 21,838

Vied·ma \'vyäd-mä\ town S cen Argentina pop 24,338

Vi·en·na \vē-'en-ə\ or G **Wien** \'vēn\ city ✻ of Austria on the Danube pop 1,515,666 — **Vi·en·nese** \,vē-ə-'nēz, -'nēs\ adj or n

Vi·enne \vē-'en\ **1** river 217 mi (349 km) SW cen France flowing NW into the Loire **2** city SE France on the Rhône pop 25,981

Vien·tiane \(')vyen-'tyän\ city ✻ of Laos, near Thailand border pop 132,253

Vie·ques \vē-'ā-kəs\ island W. Indies off E Puerto Rico, belonging to Puerto Rico; chief town Isabel Segunda

Vier·wald·stät·ter See \fi(ə)r-'vält-,s(h)tet-ər-,zä\ or **Lake of Lu·cerne** \lü-'sərn\ lake 24 mi (39 km) long cen Switzerland area 44 sq mi (114 sq km)

Viet·nam \vē-'et-'näm, vyet-, -ət-, vēt-, -'nam\ country SE Asia in Indochina; state, including Tonkin & N Annam, set up 1945–46; with S Annam & Cochin China, an associated state of French Union 1950–54; after civil war, divided 1954–75 at 17th parallel into republics of **North Vietnam** (✻ Hanoi) & **South Vietnam** (✻ Saigon) reunited 1975 (✻ Hanoi) area 127,207 sq mi (330,738 sq km), pop 52,741,766

Vi·go \'vē-(,)gō\ city & port NW Spain on **Vigo Bay** (inlet of the Atlantic) pop 261,331

Viipuri — see VYBORG

Vi·ja·ya·na·gar \,vij-ə-yə-'nəg-ər\ or **Bi·ja·na·gar** \,bij-ə-'nəg-\ Hindu kingdom (1336–1565) S India S of the Krishna

Vi·ja·ya·wa·da \,vij-ə-yə-'wäd-ə\ or formerly **Bez·wa·da** \bez-'wäd-ə\ city SE India in E Andhra Pradesh on the Krishna, at head of its delta pop 544,958

Vi·la \'vē-lə\ town & port ✻ of Vanuatu in SW Efate Is. pop 4729

Villa Cisneros — see DAKHLA

Vi·lla·her·mo·sa \,vē-(y)ə-,er-'mō-sə\ city SE Mexico ✻ of Tabasco state pop 78,034

Vil·la Park \,vil-ə-\ village NE Ill. W of Chicago pop 23,185

Ville·franche \vēl-(ə-)'fränsh\ **1** or **Villefranche–sur–Mer** \-sür-'me(ə)r\ commune & port SE France E of Nice pop 6600 **2** or **Villefranche–sur–Saône** \-'sōn\ commune E cen France NNW of Lyons pop 29,996

Vil·leur·banne \(,)vē-,yər-'ban, -'bän\ commune E France, E suburb of Lyons pop 115,913

Vil·ni·us \'vil-nē-əs\ city U.S.S.R. ✻ of Lithuania pop 372,000

Vi·lyui \vil-'yü-ē\ river 1500 mi (2414 km) U.S.S.R. in cen Soviet Russia, Asia, flowing E into the Lena

Vim·i·nal \'vim-ən-°l\ hill in Rome, Italy, one of seven upon which the ancient city was built — see AVENTINE

Vi·my Ridge \,vē-mē-, vi-,mē-\ ridge near Vimy commune N France N of Arras

Vi·ña del Mar \,vēn-ə-(,)del-'mär\ city & port cen Chile E of Valparaiso pop 281,389

Vin·cennes \(')vin-'senz; for 2, F van-'sen\ **1** city SW Ind. pop 20,857 **2** commune N France, E suburb of Paris pop 44,256

Vin·dhya \'vin-dyə, -dē-ə\ mountain range N cen India N of & parallel to the Narbada

Vindhya Pra·desh \pra-'desh, -'däsh\ former state NE cen India ✻ Rewa; became (1956) part of Madhya Pradesh

Vine·land \'vīn-lənd\ city S N.J. pop 53,753

Vin·land \'vin-lənd\ a portion of the coast of N. America visited & so called by Norse voyagers ab A.D. 1000; perhaps N tip of Newfoundland

Vin·ni·tsa \'vin-ət-sə\ city U.S.S.R. in W cen Ukrainian Republic pop 211,000

Vin·son Massif \'vin(t)-sən\ mountain 16,864 ft (5140 m) W Antarctica S of Ellsworth Land in Ellsworth mountains; highest in Antarctica

Vir·gin \'vər-jən\ **1** river 200 mi (322 km) SW Utah & SE Nev. flowing to Lake Mead **2** islands W. Indies E of Puerto Rico — see BRITISH VIRGIN ISLANDS, VIRGIN ISLANDS OF THE UNITED STATES

Vir·gin·ia \vər-'jin-yə, -'jin-ē-ə\ state E U.S. ✻ Richmond area 40,817 sq mi (106,124 sq km), pop 5,346,818 — **Vir·gin·ian** \-yən, -ē-ən\ adj or n

Virginia Beach city SE Va. on the Atlantic pop 262,199

Virginia Capes Cape Charles & Cape Henry in Va. forming entrance to Chesapeake Bay

Virgin Islands National Park reservation W. Indies in Virgin Islands of the U.S. on St. John Is.

Virgin Islands of the United States the W islands of the Virgin islands group including St. Croix, St. John, & St. Thomas; a territory ✻ Charlotte Amalie (on St. Thomas Is.) area 132 sq mi (343 sq km), pop 96,569 — see DANISH WEST INDIES

Vi·run·ga \və-'rüŋ-gə\ or **Mfum·bi·ro** \em-'füm-bə-,rō\ volcanic mountain range E cen Africa in Z Zaire & SW Uganda N of Lake Kivu; highest peak Karisimbi 14,780 ft (4505 m)

Vi·sa·lia \vī-'säl-yə\ city S cen Calif. SE of Fresno pop 49,729

Vi·sa·yan \və-'sī-ən\ or **Bi·sa·yas** \bə-'sī-əz\ islands cen Philippines bet. Luzon & Mindanao — see BOHOL, CEBU, LEYTE, MASBATE, NEGROS, PANAY, ROMBLON, SAMAR

Vis·by \'viz-bē\ city & port Sweden on Gotland Is. in the Baltic pop 19,319

Vish·a·kha·pat·nam \vi-,shäk-ə-'pət-nəm\ or **Vi·sa·kha·pat·nam** \vi-,säk-\ city & port E India in NE Andhra Pradesh pop 594,259

Vi·so \'vē-(,)zō\ mountain 12,602 ft (3841 m) NW Italy in Piedmont SW of Turin near French border; highest in Cottian Alps

Vis·ta \'vis-tə\ city SW Calif. N of San Diego pop 35,834

Vis·tu·la \'vis(h)-chə-lə, 'vis-tə-\ or Pol **Wis·ła** \'vē-(,)slä\ river 630 mi (1014 km) Poland flowing N from the Carpathians into Gulf of Gdansk

Vistula Lagoon FRISCHES HAFF

Vi·tebsk \'vē-,tepsk, -,tebsk, və-\ city U.S.S.R. in NE Belorussia on Dvina river pop 231,000

Vi·ter·bo \vi-'te(ə)r-(,)bō\ commune cen Italy in Latium pop 57,830

Vi·ti Le·vu \,vēt-ē-'lev-(,)ü\ island SW Pacific, largest of the Fiji group area 4053 sq mi (10,538 sq km)

Vi·tim \və-'tēm\ river 1100 mi (1770 km) U.S.S.R. in S Soviet Russia, Asia, flowing NE & N into the Lena

Vi·to·ria \vi-'tōr-ē-ə, -'tȯr-\ city N Spain ✻ of Álava province SSE of Bilbao pop 189,533

Vi·tó·ria \vi-'tōr-ē-ə, -'tȯr-\ city & port E Brazil ✻ of Espírito Santo state on Espírito Santo Is. pop 207,560

Vi·try–sur–Seine \vi-ˌtrē-ˌsů(ə)r-'sän, -'sen\ commune N France, SSE suburb of Paris *pop* 87,119

Viz·ca·ya \vis-'ki-ə\ *or* **Bis·ca·ya** \bis-\ *or* **Bis·cay** \'bis-(ˌ)kā, -kē\ province N Spain on Bay of Biscay; one of the Basque provinces ✸ Bilbao *area* 836 *sq mi* (2174 *sq km*), *pop* 1,280,018

Vlaanderen — *see* FLANDERS

Vlaar·ding·en \'vlär-diŋ-ən\ commune & port SW Netherlands W of Rotterdam *pop* 77,069

Vla·di·mir \'vlad-ə-ˌmi(ə)r, vlə-'dē-ˌmi(ə)r\ city U.S.S.R. in *cen* Soviet Russia, Europe, on the Klyazma E of Moscow *pop* 234,000

Vlad·i·vos·tok \ˌvlad-ə-və-'stäk, -'väs-ˌtäk\ city & port U.S.S.R. in SE Soviet Russia, Asia ✸ of Maritime Territory *pop* 442,000

Vlis·sing·en \'vlis-iŋ-ən\ *or* **Flush·ing** \'fləsh-iŋ\ city & port SW Netherlands on Walcheren Is. *pop* 46,379

Vlo·rë \'vlȯr-ə, 'vlȯr-\ *or* **Va·lo·na** \və-'lō-nə\ *or formerly* **Avlo·na** \av-'lō-nə\ city & port S Albania *pop* 56,400

Vlta·va \'vəl-tə-və\ river 270 *mi* (434 *km*) W Czechoslovakia in Bohemia flowing N into the Elbe

Vodena — *see* EDESSA

Vogelkop — *see* DOBERAI

Voiotía — *see* BOEOTIA

Voj·vo·di·na \'vȯi-və-ˌdē-nə, -di-ˌnä\ autonomous region NE Yugoslavia N of the Danube; chief city Novi Sad *area* 8683 *sq mi* (22,576 *sq km*), *pop* 1,950,268

Volcano *or Jp* **Ka·zan Ret·to** \'käz-ˌän-'ret-(ˌ)ō\ islands W Pacific S of Bonin islands; belong to Japan; under U.S. control 1945–68 *area* 11 *sq mi* (29 *sq km*) — *see* IWO JIMA

Vo·len·dam \'vō-lən-ˌdam, ˌvō-lən-'däm\ village NW Netherlands on IJsselmeer SE of Edam *pop* 10,123

Vol·ga \'väl-gə, 'vȯl-, 'vōl-\ river 2325 *mi* (3742 *km*) U.S.S.R. in Soviet Russia, Europe, rising in Valdai hills & flowing into the Caspian

Vol·go·grad \'väl-gə-ˌgrad, 'vȯl-, 'vōl-\ *or formerly* **Sta·lin·grad** \'stäl-ən-ˌgrad, 'stal-\ *or* **Tsa·ri·tsyn** \(t)sə-'rēt-sən\ city U.S.S.R. in S Soviet Russia, Europe, on the Volga *pop* 929,000

Vo·log·da \'vȯ-ləg-də\ city U.S.S.R. in N *cen* Soviet Russia, Europe, NNE of Moscow *pop* 237,000

Vo·los \'vō-ˌläs\ *or NGk* **Vó·los** \'vȯ-ˌlȯs\ city & port E Greece on **Gulf of Volos** (inlet of the Aegean) *pop* 70,967

Volsinii — *see* ORVIETO

Vol·ta \'väl-tə, 'vȯl-, 'vōl-\ river *ab* 100 *mi* (161 *km*) W Africa flowing from **Lake Volta** (reservoir *area* 3275 *sq mi or* 8515 *sq km* receiving the **Black Volta** & **White Volta**) in N *cen* Ghana & flowing S into Bight of Benin — *see* RED VOLTA

Vol·ta Re·don·da \ˌväl-tə-ri-'dän-də, ˌvōl-, ˌvȯl-\ city E Brazil on Paraíba river NW of city of Rio de Janeiro *pop* 183,917

Vol·ter·ra \väl-'ter-ə, vōl-, vȯl-\ *or anc* **Vo·la·ter·rae** \ˌvō-lə-'te(ə)r-ˌī, -(ˌ)ē\ commune *cen* Italy in Tuscany SE of Pisa *pop* 14,080

Vol·tur·no \väl-'tů(ə)r-(ˌ)nō, vȯl-, vōl-\ river 110 *mi* (177 *km*) S *cen* Italy flowing from the Apennines SE & SW into Gulf of Gaeta

Vor·arl·berg \'fō(ə)r-ˌärl-ˌbərg, 'fȯ(ə)r-\ province W Austria W of Tirol bordering on Switzerland ✸ Bregenz *pop* 305,615

Vo·ro·nezh \və-'rō-nish\ city U.S.S.R. in S *cen* Soviet Russia, Europe, near Don river *pop* 783,000

Voroshilovgrad — *see* LUGANSK

Vosges \'vōzh\ mountains NE France on W side of Rhine valley; highest Ballon de Guebwiller 4672 *ft* (1424 *m*)

Voy·a·geurs National Park \ˌvȯi-ə-'zhərz\ reservation N Minn. on Canadian border S of Rainy lake

Vrangelya — *see* WRANGEL

Vyat·ka *or* **Viat·ka** \vē-'ät-kə\ **1** river 800 *mi* (1287 *km*) U.S.S.R. in E Soviet Russia, Europe, flowing into the Kama **2** — *see* KIROV

Vy·borg \'vē-ˌbō(ə)rg, -ˌbȯr-ē\ *or Finn* **Vii·pu·ri** \'vē-pə-rē\ city & port U.S.S.R. in NW Soviet Russia, Europe, on arm of Gulf of Finland; belonged to Finland 1917–40 *pop* 76,000

Vy·cheg·da \'vich-ig-də\ river 700 *mi* (1120 *km*) U.S.S.R. in N Soviet Russia, Europe, flowing W to the Northern Dvina

Waadt — *see* VAUD

Waal \'väl\ river Netherlands, the S branch of the lower Rhine

Wa·bash \'wȯ-ˌbash\ river 475 *mi* (764 *km*) Ind. & Ill. flowing into Ohio river

Wa·co \'wā-(ˌ)kō\ city NE *cen* Tex. on the Brazos *pop* 101,261

Wad·den Zee \ˌväd-ᵊn-'zā\ inlet of North sea N Netherlands bet. W. Frisian islands & IJsselmeer

Wad·ding·ton, Mount \'wäd-iŋ-tən\ mountain 13,260 *ft* (4042 *m*) W Canada in SW B.C. in Coast mountains; highest in the province

Wad Me·da·ni \ˌwäd-'med-ᵊn-ē\ city E *cen* Sudan on the Blue Nile *pop* 106,715

Wa·gram \'vä-ˌgräm\ village Austria NE of Vienna

Wa·hi·a·wa \ˌwä-hē-ə-'wä\ city Hawaii in *cen* Oahu *pop* 16,911

Wai·a·le·ale \wī-ˌäl-ē-'äl-ē\ mountain 5080 *ft* (1548 *m*) Hawaii in *cen* Kauai

Wai·ka·to \wī-'kät-(ˌ)ō\ river 220 *mi* (354 *km*) New Zealand in NW North Is. flowing NW into Tasman sea

Wai·ki·ki \ˌwī-kə-'kē\ resort section of Honolulu, Hawaii NW of Diamond Head on **Waikiki Beach**

Wai·mea Canyon \wī-ˌmā-ə-\ gorge Hawaii on SW coast of Kauai

Wai·pa·hu \wī-'pä-(ˌ)hü\ city Hawaii in SW Oahu *pop* 29,139

Wai·ta·ki \wī-'täk-ē\ river 135 *mi* (217 *km*) New Zealand in SE *cen* South Is. flowing ESE into the Pacific

Wa·ka·ya·ma \ˌwäk-ə-'yäm-ə\ city & port Japan SW Honshu on Inland sea *pop* 362,000

Wake \'wāk\ island N Pacific N of Marshall islands belonging to the U.S.

Wake·field \'wāk-ˌfēld\ **1** town E Mass. N of Boston *pop* 24,895 **2** city & borough N England ✸ of W. Yorkshire *pop* 60,540

Wa·la·chia *or* **Wal·la·chia** \wä-'lā-kē-ə\ region S Romania bet. the Transylvanian Alps & the Danube; includes Muntenia & Oltenia; chief city Bucharest — **Wa·la·chi·an** *or* **Wal·la·chi·an** \-kē-ən\ *adj or n*

Wal·deck \'väl-ˌdek\ former county, principality, & state of Germany between Westphalia & Hesse-Nassau ✸ Arolsen

Wal·den Pond \ˌwȯl-dən-\ pond NE Mass. S of Concord

Wales \'wā(ə)lz\ *or W* **Cym·ru** \'kəm-ˌrē\ *or ML* **Cam·bria** \'kam-brē-ə\ principality SW Great Britain; a division of the United Kingdom of Great Britain and Northern Ireland ✸ Cardiff *area* 7469 *sq mi* (19,419 *sq km*), *pop* 2,790,462

Wal·la·sey \'wäl-ə-sē\ borough NW England in Merseyside on coast W of Liverpool *pop* 90,057

Wal·la Wal·la \ˌwäl-ə-'wäl-ə, 'wäl-ə-\ city SE Wash. *pop* 25,618

Wal·ling·ford \'wäl-iŋ-fərd\ town S Conn. NNE of New Haven *pop* 37,274

Wal·lis \'wäl-əs\ **1** islands SW Pacific NE of Fiji islands; with Futuna islands, constitute a French overseas territory (**Wallis and Futuna Islands** *pop* 8546) **2** — *see* VALAIS

Wal·lops \'wäl-əps\ island E Va. in the Atlantic SW of Chincoteague Bay

Wal·lowa \wä-'laů-ə\ mountains NE Oreg. E of Blue mountains; highest Sacajawea Peak 9833 *ft* (2997 *m*)

Walnut Canyon National Monument reservation N *cen* Ariz. ESE of Flagstaff containing cliff dwellings

Walnut Creek city W Calif. E of Berkeley *pop* 53,643

Wal·pole \'wȯl-ˌpōl, 'wäl-\ town E Mass. SW of Boston *pop* 18,859

Wal·sall \'wȯl-ˌsȯl, -sál\ borough W *cen* England in W. Midlands NNW of Birmingham *pop* 178,909

Wal·tham \'wȯl-ˌtham, *chiefly by outsiders* -thəm\ city E Mass. W of Boston *pop* 58,200

Wal·tham Forest \ˌwȯl-thəm\ borough of NE Greater London, England *pop* 217,400

Wal·tham·stow \'wȯl-thəm-ˌstō\ former municipal borough SE England in Essex, now part of Waltham Forest

Wal·vis Bay \ˌwȯl-vəs-\ town, port, & district SW Africa on Walvis Bay (inlet) W of Windhoek; an exclave of Republic of S. Africa in Namibia *area* (of district) 374 *sq mi* (972 *sq km*)

Wands·worth \'wän(d)z-(ˌ)wərth\ borough of SW Greater London, England *pop* 265,200

Wang·a·nui \ˌwäŋ-(g)ə-'nü-ē\ **1** river 150 *mi* (241 *km*) New Zealand in SW *cen* North Is., flowing into Tasman sea **2** city & port New Zealand in North Is. on Tasman sea *pop* 37,012

Wan·ne·Eick·el \ˌvän-ə-'ī-kəl\ city W W. Germany in the Ruhr N of Bochum *pop* 100,300

Wan·stead and Wood·ford \ˌwän-stəd-ᵊn-'wůd-fərd\ former municipal borough S England in Essex, now part of Redbridge

Wap·si·pin·i·con \ˌwäp-si-'pin-i-kən\ river 225 *mi* (362 *km*) SE Minn. & E Iowa flowing SE into Mississippi river

Wa·ran·gal \wə-'raŋ-gəl\ city S *cen* India in N Andhra Pradesh NE of Hyderabad *pop* 336,018

War·bur·ton, The \(ˌ)wȯr-(ˌ)bərt-ᵊn\ watercourse 275 *mi* (442 *km*) Australia in NE S. Australia flowing SW into Lake Eyre

Ware·ham \'war-əm, 'wer-, 'wa(ə)r-ˌham, 'we(ə)r-\ city SE Mass. ENE of New Bedford *pop* 18,457

War·ley \'wȯr-lē\ town W *cen* England, a NW suburb of Birmingham *pop* 152,455

War·ner Rob·ins \ˌwȯr-nər-'räb-ənz\ city *cen* Ga. *pop* 39,893

War·ren \'wȯr-ən, 'wär-\ **1** city SE Mich. N of Detroit *pop* 161,134 **2** city NE Ohio NW of Youngstown *pop* 56,629

War·ren·ville Heights \ˌwȯr-ən-ˌvil\ city NE Ohio *pop* 16,565

War·ring·ton \'wȯr-iŋ-tən, 'wär-\ borough NW England in Cheshire on the Mersey E of Liverpool *pop* 57,389

War·saw \'wȯr-ˌsȯ\ *or Pol* **War·sza·wa** \vär-'shäv-ə\ city ✸ of Poland on the Vistula *pop* 1,611,565

War·ta \'värt-ə\ *or G* **War·the** \'värt-ə\ river 445 *mi* (716 *km*) Poland flowing NW & W into the Oder

War·wick \'wär-ik, *US also* 'wȯr-ik, 'wȯr-(ˌ)wik\ **1** city *cen* R.I. S of Providence on Narragansett Bay *pop* 87,123 **2** borough *cen* England ✸ of Warwickshire *pop* 21,936

War·wick·shire \'wär-ik-ˌshi(ə)r, -shər, *US also* 'wȯr-ik-, 'wȯr-(ˌ)wik-\ *or* **Warwick** county *cen* England ✸ Warwick *area* 765 *sq mi* (1989 *sq km*), *pop* 474,500

Wa·satch \'wȯ-ˌsach\ mountain range SE Idaho & N & *cen* Utah — *see* TIMPANOGOS (Mount)

Wash, The \'wȯsh, 'wäsh\ inlet of North sea E England bet. Norfolk & Lincoln

Wash·ing·ton \'wȯsh-iŋ-tən, 'wäsh-, *chiefly Midland also* 'wȯr-shiŋ- *or* 'wär-shiŋ-\ **1** state NW U.S. ✸ Olympia *area* 68,192 *sq mi* (177,299 *sq km*), *pop* 4,132,156 **2** city ✸ of the U.S., coextensive with District of Columbia *pop* 637,651 **3** city SW Pa. *pop* 18,363 **4** — *see* TERAINA —

Wash·ing·to·nian \ˌwȯsh-iŋ-'tō-nē-ən, ˌwäsh-, -nyən\ *adj or n*

Washington, Lake lake 20 *mi* (32 *km*) long W Wash. E of Seattle

Washington, Mount mountain 6288 *ft* (1916 *m*) N N.H.; highest in White mountains

Wash·i·ta \'wäsh-ə-ˌtȯ\ river 500 *mi* (805 *km*) NW Tex. & SW Okla. flowing SE into Red river

Wa·tau·ga \wä-'tȯ-gə\ river 60 *mi* (96 *km*) NW N.C. & NE Tenn. flowing into S fork of the Holston

Watenstedt–Salzgitter — *see* SALZGITTER

Wa·ter·bury \'wȯt-ə(r)-ˌber-ē, 'wät-\ city W *cen* Conn. *pop* 103,266

Wa·ter·ee \'wȯt-ə-ˌrē, 'wät-\ river S.C., lower course of the Catawba — *see* CONGAREE

Wa·ter·ford \'wȯt-ər-fərd, 'wät-\ **1** town SE Conn. SW of New London *pop* 17,843 **2** county S Ireland in Munster *area* 710 *sq mi* (1846 *sq km*), *pop* 88,591 **3** city & port, its ✸ *pop* 38,473

Wa·ter·loo \ˌwȯt-ər-'lü, ˌwät-\ **1** city NE *cen* Iowa *pop* 75,985 **2** town *cen* Belgium S of Brussels *pop* 24,755 **3** city Canada in SE Ont. W of Kitchener *pop* 49,428

Wa·ter·ton–Gla·cier International Peace Park \ˌwȯt-ərt-ᵊn-'glā-shər, ˌwät-\ reservation comprising **Glacier National Park** (reservation NW Mont.) & **Waterton Lakes National Park** (reservation Canada in Rocky mountains in S Alta.)

Wa·ter·town \'wȯt-ər-ˌtaůn, 'wät-\ **1** town SW Conn. NW of Waterbury *pop* 19,489 **2** town E Mass. W of Boston *pop* 34,384 **3** city N *cen* N.Y. SE of Kingston, Ont. *pop* 27,861 **4** city SE Wis. *pop* 18,113

Wa·ter·ville \'wȯt-ər-ˌvil, 'wät-\ city S *cen* Maine *pop* 17,779

Wat·ford \'wät-fərd\ borough SE England in Hertfordshire NW of London *pop* 78,117

Wat·son·ville \'wät-sən-ˌvil\ city W Calif. *pop* 23,543

Wat·ten·scheid \'vät-ᵊn-ˌshīt\ city W W. Germany E of Essen *pop* 80,527

Watts \'wäts\ section of Los Angeles, Calif. S of the downtown district *pop ab* 34,420

Wau·ke·gan \wȯ-'kē-gən\ city NE Ill. N of Chicago *pop* 67,653
Wau·ke·sha \'wȯ-kə-‚shȯ\ city SE Wis. *pop* 50,319
Wau·sau \'wȯ-‚sȯ, -sə\ city N *cen* Wis. *pop* 32,426
Wau·wa·to·sa \‚wȯ-wə-'tō-sə\ city SE Wis. *pop* 51,308
Way·cross \'wā-‚krȯs\ city SE Ga. *pop* 19,371
Wayne \'wān\ village SE Mich. SW of Detroit *pop* 21,159
Wa·zir·i·stan \wə-‚zir-i-'stan, -'stän\ region W Pakistan on border of Afghanistan NE of Baluchistan
Weald \'wē(ə)ld\ region SE England in Kent, Surrey, & Sussex, bet. N. Downs & S. Downs; once heavily forested
Wear \'wi(ə)r\ river 67 *mi* (108 *km*) N England flowing into North sea at Sunderland
Web·ster Groves \‚web-stər-\ city E Mo. *pop* 23,097
Wed·dell \wə-'del, 'wed-ᵊl\ sea, arm of the S Atlantic E of Antarctic peninsula
Wei \'wā\ river 400 *mi* (644 *km*) N *cen* China flowing E to join the Hwang
Wei·fang \'wā-'fäŋ\ city E China in E *cen* Shantung *pop* 190,000
Wei·hai \'wā-'hi\ *or formerly* Wei·hai·wei \‚wā-‚hi-'wā\ city & port E China in NE Shantung on Yellow sea *pop* 175,000
Wei·mar \'vi-‚mär, 'wi-\ city SW E. Germany E of Erfurt *pop* 64,000
Weimar Republic the German republic 1919–33
Weir·ton \'wi(ə)rt-ᵊn\ city N W.Va. on Ohio river *pop* 24,736
Wel·land \'wel-ənd\ 1 city Canada in SE Ont. SW of Niagara Falls *pop* 45,448 2 ship canal 28 *mi* (45km) Canada in SE Ont. connecting Lake Erie & Lake Ontario
Welles·ley \'welz-lē\ town E Mass. WSW of Boston *pop* 27,209
Wel·ling·ton \'wel-iŋ-tən\ city & port ✳ of New Zealand in SW North Is. on Port Nicholson (Wellington Harbor) on Cook strait *pop* 135,688
Wells \'welz\ city & borough SW England in Somerset *pop* 8374
Welsh·pool \'welsh-‚pül\ town E Wales in Powys *pop* 7317
Wel·wyn Garden City \'wel-ən\ urban district SE England in Hertfordshire N of London *pop* 40,369
Wem·bley \'wem-blē\ former municipal borough SE England in Middlesex, now part of Brent
We·natch·ee \wə-'nach-ē\ city *cen* Wash. *pop* 17,257
Wen·chow *or* Wen·zhou *or* Wen–chou \'wən-'jō\ city & port E China in S Chekiang on E. China sea *pop* 210,000
Wer·ra \'ver-ə\ river 180 *mi* (290 *km*), E W. Germany & SW E. Germany flowing N
We·ser \'vā-zər, 'wē-\ river 280 *mi* (451 *km*) N *cen* W. Germany flowing into North sea
Wes·la·co \'wes-li-‚kō\ city S Tex. W of Harlingen *pop* 19,331
Wes·sex \'wes-iks\ ancient Anglian kingdom S England ✳ Winchester; one of kingdoms in Anglo-Saxon heptarchy
West Al·lis \'al-əs\ city SE Wis. *pop* 63,982
West Antarctica — see ANTARCTICA
West Bank area Palestine W of Jordan river; occupied by Israel since 1967
West Bend \'bend\ city SE Wis. NNW of Milwaukee *pop* 21,484
West Bengal state E India comprising the W third of former Bengal province ✳ Calcutta *area* 33,945 *sq mi* (88,257 *sq km*), *pop* 54,485,560
West Beskids — see BESKIDS
West Brom·wich \'brəm-ij, 'bräm-, -ich\ borough W *cen* England in W. Midlands NW of Birmingham *pop* 154,930
West·ches·ter \'wes(t)-‚ches-tər\ village NE Ill. *pop* 17,730
West Ches·ter \'wes(t)-‚ches-tər\ borough SE Pa. *pop* 17,435
West Co·vi·na \kō-'vē-nə\ city SW Calif. *pop* 80,291
West Des Moines city S *cen* Iowa *pop* 21,894
Wes·ter·ly \'wes-tər-lē\ town SW R.I. *pop* 18,580
Western — see HEBRIDES
Western Australia state W Australia on Indian ocean ✳ Perth *area* 975,920 *sq mi* (2,537,392 *sq km*), *pop* 1,273,624
Western Ghats \'gȯts\ chain of mountains SW India extending SSE parallel to coast from mouth of the Tapti to Cape Comorin; highest Anai Mudi 8842 *ft* (2695 *m*) — see EASTERN GHATS
Western Isles the Outer Hebrides, constituting since 1975 a region of W Scotland ✳ Stornoway *area* 1120 *sq mi* (2912 *sq km*), *pop* 31,766
Western Reserve tract of land NE Ohio on S shore of Lake Erie; part of W lands of Conn., ceded 1800 *area ab* 5470 *sq mi* (14,222 *sq km*)
Western Sahara *or* Spanish Sahara former Spanish possessions Río de Oro & Saguia el Hamra in NW Africa, divided 1975 bet. Mauritania, which gave up its claim in Aug. 1979, & Morocco, which subsequently occupied the entire territory
Western Samoa group of islands of Samoa W of 171°W; until 1962 a territory administered by New Zealand; became an independent member of the Commonwealth 1962 ✳ Apia (on Upolu Is.) *area* 1133 *sq mi* (2946 *sq km*), *pop* 156,349
Western Thrace — see THRACE
Wes·ter·ville \'wes-tər-‚vil, -vəl\ city *cen* Ohio *pop* 23,414
West·field \'wes(t)-‚fēld\ 1 city SW Mass. WNW of Springfield *pop* 36,465 2 town NE N.J. WSW of Elizabeth *pop* 30,447
West Flanders province NW Belgium bordering on North sea ✳ Bruges *area* 1248 *sq mi* (3245 *sq km*), *pop* 1,079,253
West Frisian — see FRISIAN
West Germany the Federal Republic of Germany — see GERMANY
West Glamorgan county SE Wales ✳ Swansea *area* 315 *sq mi* (819 *sq km*), *pop* 369,700
West Ham \'ham\ former county borough SE England in Essex, now part of Newham
West Hartford town *cen* Conn. *pop* 61,301
West Ha·ven \'west-‚hā-vən\ city S Conn. *pop* 53,184
West Indies 1 the islands lying bet. SE N. America & N S. America bordering the Caribbean & comprising the Greater Antilles, Lesser Antilles, & Bahamas 2 *or* West Indies Federation former country including all of the Brit. W. Indies except the Bahamas & the Brit. Virgin islands; established 1958, dissolved 1961 — West Indian *adj or n*
West Indies Associated States the self-governing states of Antigua, Dominica, St. Kitts-Nevis, St. Lucia, & St. Vincent, associated with United Kingdom in foreign relations & defense
West Iri·an \‚ir-ē-'än\ *or* Irian Ja·ya \'jä-yə, 'ji-ə\ *or formerly* Netherlands New Guinea territory of Indonesia comprising the W half of New

Guinea & adjacent islands; belonged to the Netherlands until 1963 ✳ Djajapura *area* 164,159 *sq mi* (426,813 *sq km*), *pop* 1,173,875
West Jordan city N *cen* Utah *pop* 27,192
West Lafayette city W *cen* Ind. *pop* 21,247
West·lake \'west-‚lāk\ city N Ohio W of Cleveland *pop* 19,483
West·land \'wes-(t)lənd\ city SE Mich. W of Detroit *pop* 84,603
West Lo·thi·an \'lō-thē-ən\ *or earlier* Lin·lith·gow \lin-'lith-(‚)gō\ *or* Lin·lith·gow·shire \-‚shi(ə)r, -shər\ former county SE Scotland bordering on Firth of Forth ✳ Linlithgow — see LOTHIAN
West Malaysia the peninsular part of Malaysia — see MALAYA 3
West·meath \(')wes(t)-'mēth, -'mēth\ county E *cen* Ireland in Leinster ✳ Mullingar *area* 681 *sq mi* (1771 *sq km*), *pop* 61,523
West Memphis city E Ark. on Mississippi river *pop* 28,138
West Midlands metropolitan county W *cen* England ✳ Birmingham *area* 347 *sq mi* (902 *sq km*), *pop* 2,674,000
West Miff·lin \'mif-lən\ borough SW Pa. SE of Pittsburgh *pop* 26,279
West·min·ster \'wes(t)-‚min(t)-stər\ 1 city SW Calif. E of Long Beach *pop* 71,133 2 city N *cen* Colo. NW of Denver *pop* 50,211 3 borough of W *cen* Greater London, England *pop* 194,900
West·mont \'wes(t)-‚mänt\ city NE Ill. *pop* 16,718
West·mor·land \'wes(t)-mər-lənd, *US also* wes(t)-'mō(ə)r- *or* -'mȯ(ə)r-\ former county NW England ✳ Kendal
West·mount \'wes(t)-‚maȯnt\ city Canada in S Que. within city of Montreal *pop* 20,480
West New York town NE N.J. on Hudson river *pop* 39,194
Wes·ton–su·per–Mare \'wes-tən-‚sü-pər-'ma(ə)r, -'me(ə)r\ borough SW England in Avon on Bristol channel *pop* 57,980
West Orange town NE N.J. NW of Newark *pop* 39,510
West Pakistan the former W division of Pakistan, now coextensive with Pakistan
West Palm Beach city SE Fla. on Lake Worth inlet *pop* 63,305
West·pha·lia \wes(t)-'fāl-yə, -'fā-lē-ə\ *or G* West·fa·len \vest-'fäl-ən\ region W W. Germany bordering on the Netherlands E of the Rhine; includes Ruhr valley; a province of Prussia 1816–1945 ✳ Münster — see NORTH RHINE-WESTPHALIA — West·pha·lian \wes(t)-'fāl-yən, -'fā-lē-ən\ *adj or n*
West·port \'wes(t)-‚pō(ə)rt, -‚pȯ(ə)rt\ town SW Conn. *pop* 25,290
West Prussia region N Europe bordering on the Baltic bet. Pomerania & E. Prussia; since 1945 in Poland
West Punjab — see PUNJAB
West Quod·dy Head \‚kwäd-ē\ cape NE Maine at entrance to Passamaquoddy Bay
Wes·tra·lia \we-'sträl-yə, -'strä-lē-ə\ WESTERN AUSTRALIA
West Riding — see YORK
West Saint Paul city SE Minn. S of St. Paul *pop* 18,527
West Spitsbergen island in Arctic ocean, largest of the Spitsbergen group *area* 14,600 *sq mi* (37,960 *sq km*) — see SVALBARD
West Springfield town SW Mass. on Connecticut river *pop* 27,042
West Suffolk — see SUFFOLK
West Sus·sex \-'səs-iks, *US also* -‚eks\ county S England ✳ Chichester *area* 769 *sq mi* (1999 *sq km*), *pop* 666,000
West Virginia state E U.S. ✳ Charleston *area* 24,181 *sq mi* (62,871 *sq km*), *pop* 1,949,644 — West Virginian *adj or n*
West Warwick town *cen* R.I. *pop* 27,026
West Yorkshire metropolitan county NW England ✳ Wakefield *area* 787 *sq mi* (2046 *sq km*), *pop* 2,065,400
Weth·ers·field \'weth-ərz-‚fēld\ town *cen* Conn. *pop* 26,031
Wex·ford \'weks-fərd\ 1 county SE Ireland in Leinster *area* 908 *sq mi* (2361 *sq km*), *pop* 99,081 2 municipal borough & port, its ✳
Wey·mouth \'wā-məth\ town E Mass. SE of Boston *pop* 55,601
Whales, Bay of inlet of Ross sea Antarctica in Ross Ice Shelf
Whang·poo *or* Huang·pu \'hwäŋ-'pü\ river 70 *mi* (113 *km*) E China flowing E & N past Shanghai into the Yangtze
Whea·ton \'hwēt-ᵊn, 'wēt-\ city NE Ill. W of Chicago *pop* 43,043
Wheat Ridge city N *cen* Colo. W of Denver *pop* 30,293
Whee·ler Peak \‚hwē-lər-, ‚wē-\ 1 mountain 13,063 *ft* (3982 *m*) E Nev. in Snake range 2 mountain 13,161 *ft* (4011 *m*) N N.Mex. in Sangre de Cristo mountains; highest in the state
Whee·ling \'hwē-liŋ, 'wē-\ 1 village NE Ill. NNE of Chicago *pop* 23,266 2 city N W. Va. on Ohio river *pop* 43,070
Whid·bey \'hwid-bē, 'wid-\ island 40 *mi* (64 *km*) long NW Wash. at N end of Puget Sound E of Admiralty inlet
Whit·by \'hwit-bē, 'wit-\ town Canada in S Ont. *pop* 36,698
White 1 river 690 *mi* (1110 *km*) N Ark. & SW Mo. flowing SE into Mississippi river 2 river 160 *mi* (257 *km*) NW Colo. & E Utah flowing W into Green river 3 river 50 *mi* (80 *km*) SW Ind. flowing W into the Wabash 4 river 325 *mi* (523 *km*) S S.Dak. flowing E into Missouri river 5 river 75 *mi* (121 *km*) NW Tex. 6 mountains N N.H. in the Appalachians — see WASHINGTON (Mount) 7 mountain pass 2885 *ft* (879 *m*) SE Alaska N of Skagway 8 *or Russ* Be·loye Mo·re \‚bel-ə-yə-'mȯr-yə\ sea, inlet of Barents sea U.S.S.R. on N coast of Soviet Russia, Europe, enclosed on the N by Kola peninsula
White Bear Lake city E Minn. NE of St. Paul *pop* 22,538
White·chap·el \'hwit-‚chap-əl, 'wit-\ district of E London, England, N of Thames river in Tower Hamlets
White·friars \'hwit-‚fri(ə)rz, 'wit-\ district of *cen* London, England, on Thames river
White·hall \-‚hȯl\ city *cen* Ohio, E suburb of Columbus *pop* 21,299
White·horse \'hwit-‚hȯ(ə)rs, 'wit-\ town NW Canada ✳ of Yukon Territory on upper Yukon river *pop* 14,814
White Nile — see NILE
White Plains city SE N.Y. NE of Yonkers *pop* 46,999
White Russian Republic — see BELORUSSIA
White Sands National Monument reservation S N.Mex. SW of Alamogordo comprising an area of gypsum sand dunes
White Volta — see VOLTA

Whit·ney, Mount \ˈhwit-nē, ˈwit-\ mountain 14,494 *ft* (4418 *m*) SE *cen* Calif. in Sierra Nevada in Sequoia National Park; highest in the U.S. outside of Alaska

Whit·ti·er \ˈhwit-ē-ər, ˈwit-\ city SW Calif. SE of Los Angeles *pop* 69,717

Wich·i·ta \ˈwich-ə-ˌtȯ\ 1 city S *cen* Kans. on Arkansas river *pop* 279,272 2 river 230 *mi* (370 *km*) N Tex. flowing ENE into Red river 3 mountains SW Okla.; highest Mt. Scott 2464 *ft* (751 *m*)

Wichita Falls city N Tex. on Wichita river *pop* 94,201

Wick·liffe \ˈwik-ləf, -(ˌ)lif\ city NE Ohio *pop* 16,790

Wick·low \ˈwik-(ˌ)lō\ 1 county E Ireland in Leinster *area* 782 *sq mi* (2033 *sq km*), *pop* 87,449 2 urban district & port, its ✱, SSE of Dublin 3 mountains Ireland along E coast; highest Lugnaquilla 3039 *ft* (926 *m*)

Wien — see VIENNA

Wies·ba·den \ˈvēs-ˌbäd-ᵊn, ˈvis-\ city *cen* W. Germany on the Rhine W of Frankfort am Main ✱ of Hesse *pop* 274,464

Wig·an \ˈwig-ən\ borough NW England in Greater Manchester W of Manchester *pop* 79,535

Wight, Isle of \ˈwīt\ island S England in English channel constituting **Isle of Wight** county (✱ Newport *area* 147 *sq mi or* 382 *sq km*, *pop* 116,300)

Wig·town \ˈwig-tən, -ˌtau̇n\ *or* **Wig·town·shire** \-ˌshi(ə)r, -shər\ former county SW Scotland ✱ Wigtown

Wilderness Road trail from SW Va. to *cen* Ky. through Cumberland Gap blazed to site of Boonesborough by Daniel Boone 1775 & later extended to falls of the Ohio at Louisville

Wil·helms·ha·ven \ˌvil-ˌhelmz-ˈhäf-ən, ˈvil-əmz-ˌ\ city & port N W. Germany NW of Bremen *pop* 99,230

Wilkes–Barre \ˈwilks-ˌbar-ə, -ˌbar-ē, -ˌba(ə)r\ city NE Pa. on the Susquehanna SW of Scranton *pop* 51,551

Wilkes Land \ˈwilks-\ coast region E Antarctica extending along Indian ocean S of Australia

Wil·kins·burg \ˈwil-kənz-ˌbərg\ borough SW Pa. *pop* 23,669

Wil·lam·ette \wə-ˈlam-ət\ river 190 *mi* (306 *km*) NW Oreg. flowing N into Columbia river

Wil·la·pa Bay \ˈwil-ə-ˌpȯ, -ˌpä\ inlet of the Pacific SW Wash.

Wil·lem·stad \ˈvil-əm-ˌstät\ city ✱ of Netherlands Antilles on Curaçao Is. *pop* 43,547

Willes·den \ˈwilz-dən\ former municipal borough SE England in Middlesex, now part of Brent

Wil·liams·burg \ˈwil-yəmz-ˌbərg\ city SE Va. NNW of Newport News; site of large-scale restoration project, Colonial Williamsburg

Wil·liam·son, Mount \ˈwil-yəm-sən\ mountain 14,375 *ft* (4382 *m*) SE *cen* Calif. in Sierra Nevada NNW of Mt. Whitney

Wil·liams·port \ˈwil-yəmz-ˌpō(ə)rt, -ˌpȯ(ə)rt\ city N *cen* Pa. on W branch of the Susquehanna *pop* 33,401

Wil·lough·by \ˈwil-ə-bē\ city NE Ohio NE of Cleveland *pop* 19,329

Wil·lo·wick \ˈwil-ə-ˌwik\ city NE Ohio E of Cleveland *pop* 17,834

Wil·mette \wil-ˈmet\ village NE Ill. N of Chicago *pop* 28,229

Wil·ming·ton \ˈwil-miŋ-tən\ 1 city & port N Del. *pop* 70,195 2 town NE Mass. SE of Lowell *pop* 17,471 3 city & port SE N.C. *pop* 44,000

Wil·son \ˈwil-sən\ city E *cen* N.C. E of Raleigh *pop* 34,424

Wilson, Mount mountain 5710 *ft* (1740 *m*) SW Calif. NE of Pasadena

Wilt·shire \ˈwilt-ˌshi(ə)r; ˈwil-chər, ˈwilt-shər\ county S England ✱ Trowbridge *area* 1345 *sq mi* (3497 *sq km*), *pop* 521,300

Wim·ble·don \ˈwim-bəl-dən\ former municipal borough SE England in Surrey, now part of Merton

Win·ches·ter \ˈwin-ˌches-tər, -chə-stər\ 1 town E Mass. NW of Boston *pop* 20,701 2 city N Va. *pop* 20,217 3 city & borough S England ✱ of Hampshire *pop* 30,642

Wind \ˈwind\ river W *cen* Wyo., the upper course of Bighorn river

Windau — see VENTSPILS

Wind Cave limestone cavern SW S.Dak. in Black Hills in **Wind Cave National Park**

Win·der·mere \ˈwin-də(r)-ˌmi(ə)r\ lake 10 *mi* (16 *km*) long NW England in Cumbria; largest in England

Wind·ham \ˈwin-dəm\ town E *cen* Conn. *pop* 21,062

Wind·hoek \ˈvint-ˌhu̇k\ city ✱ of Namibia *pop* 36,051

Wind River mountain range W *cen* Wyo. — see GANNETT PEAK

Wind River Canyon gorge of Bighorn river W *cen* Wyo.

Wind·sor \ˈwin-zər\ 1 town N *cen* Conn. N of Hartford *pop* 25,204 2 city Canada in SE Ont. on Detroit river opposite Detroit, Mich. *pop* 192,083 3 *or* **New Windsor** royal borough S England in Berkshire on Thames river W of London *pop* 30,065

Wind·ward \ˈwin-dwərd\ 1 islands W. Indies in the S Lesser Antilles extending S from Martinique but not including Barbados, Tobago, or Trinidad 2 former colony Brit. W. Indies comprising territories of St. Lucia, St. Vincent, & Grenada in the Windward group & Dominica in the Leewards 3 *or F* **Iles du Vent** \ēl-dü̅e-väⁿ\ islands S Pacific, E group of the Society islands, including Tahiti

Windward Passage channel bet. Cuba & Hispaniola

Win·ne·ba·go, Lake \ˌwin-ə-ˈbā-(ˌ)gō\ lake 30 *mi* (48 *km*) long E Wis.

Win·ni·peg \ˈwin-ə-ˌpeg\ 1 river 200 *mi* (322 *km*) Canada in W Ont. & SE Man. flowing from Lake of the Woods to Lake Winnipeg 2 city Canada ✱ of Man. *pop* 564,473 — **Win·ni·peg·ger** \-ˌpeg-ər\ *n*

Winnipeg, Lake lake 275 *mi* (442 *km*) long Canada in S *cen* Man. drained by Nelson river *area* 9460 *sq mi* (24,596 *sq km*)

Win·ni·pe·go·sis, Lake \ˌwin-ə-pə-ˈgō-səs\ lake Canada in W Man. W of Lake Winnipeg *area* 2086 *sq mi* (5424 *sq km*)

Win·ni·pe·sau·kee, Lake \ˌwin-ə-pə-ˈsȯ-kē\ lake *cen* N.H. *area* 71 *sq mi* (185 *sq km*)

Wi·no·na \wə-ˈnō-nə\ city SE Minn. *pop* 25,075

Wi·noo·ski \wə-ˈnü-skē\ river 100 *mi* (161 *km*) N *cen* Vt. flowing into Lake Champlain

Win·ston–Sa·lem \ˌwin(t)-stən-ˈsā-ləm\ city N N.C. *pop* 131,885

Winter Haven city *cen* Fla. E of Lakeland *pop* 21,119

Winter Park city E Fla. N of Orlando *pop* 22,339

Win·ter·thur \ˈvint-ər-ˌtu̇(ə)r\ commune N Switzerland in Zurich canton NE of Zurich *pop* 86,758

Win·throp \ˈwin(t)-thrəp\ town E Mass. *pop* 19,294

Win·yah Bay \ˈwin-ˌyȯ-\ inlet of the Atlantic E S.C.

Wis·con·sin \wis-ˈkän(t)-sən\ 1 river 430 *mi* (692 *km*) *cen* Wis. flowing S & W into Mississippi river 2 state N *cen* U.S. ✱ Madison *area* 56,164 *sq mi* (146,026 *sq km*), *pop* 4,705,767 — **Wis·con·sin·ite** \-sə-ˌnīt\ *n*

Wisconsin Dells — see DELLS OF THE WISCONSIN

Wisconsin Rapids city *cen* Wis. *pop* 17,995

Wisła — see VISTULA

Wis·mar \ˈvis-ˌmär, ˈwiz-ˌmär\ city & port NW E. Germany *pop* 57,586

Wis·sa·hick·on \ˌwis-ə-ˈhik-ən\ creek SE Pa. flowing into the Schuylkill at Philadelphia

With·la·coo·chee \ˌwith-lə-ˈkü-chē\ 1 river 110 *mi* (177 *km*) S Ga. & NW Fla. flowing SE into the Suwannee 2 river 120 *mi* (193 *km*) NW *cen* Fla. flowing NW into Gulf of Mexico

Wit·ten \ˈvit-ᵊn\ city W *cen* W. Germany SW of Dortmund *pop* 105,876

Wit·ten·berg \ˈwit-ᵊn-ˌbərg\ city *cen* E. Germany E of Dessau *pop* 54,094

Wit·wa·ters·rand \ˈwit-ˌwȯt-ərz-ˌrand, -ˌwät-, -ˌränd, -ˌränt\ ridge of auriferous rock 62 *mi* (100 *km*) long & 23 *mi* (37 *km*) wide NE Republic of S. Africa in S Transvaal

Wło·cła·wek \vlȯt-ˈsläv-ˌek\ commune N *cen* Poland on the Vistula *pop* 109,997

Wo·burn \ˈwü-bərn, ˈwō-\ city E Mass. NW of Boston *pop* 36,626

Wolds, The \ˈwōl(d)z\ chalk hills NE England in N. Yorkshire, Humberside, & N Lincolnshire

Wolfs·burg \ˈwu̇lfs-ˌbərg, ˈvȯlfs-ˌbu̇(ə)rg\ city E W. Germany *pop* 125,935

Wol·lon·gong \ˈwu̇l-ən-ˌgän, -ˌgȯŋ\ city SE Australia in E New S. Wales S of Sydney *pop* (with suburbs) 208,651

Wol·ver·hamp·ton \ˈwu̇l-vər-ˌham(p)-tən\ borough W *cen* England in W. Midlands NW of Birmingham *pop* 252,447

Won·san \ˈwən-ˌsän\ city & port N. Korea on E coast *pop* 215,000

Wood Buffalo National Park reservation W Canada in N Alta. & S Northwest Territories

Wood Green former municipal borough SE England in Middlesex, now part of Haringey

Wood·land \ˈwu̇d-lənd\ city W Calif. NW of Sacramento *pop* 30,235

Wood·lark \ˈwu̇d-ˌlärk\ island W Pacific in Solomon sea off SE end of New Guinea; attached to Papua New Guinea *area* 400 *sq mi* (1040 *sq km*)

Wood·ridge \ˈwu̇d-(ˌ)rij\ city NE Ill. *pop* 22,322

Woods, Lake of the lake S Canada & N U.S. in Ont., Man., & Minn. SE of Lake Winnipeg *area* 1485 *sq mi* (3861 *sq km*)

Wood·stock \ˈwu̇d-ˌstäk\ city Canada in SE Ont. *pop* 26,603

Wool·wich \ˈwu̇l-ij, -ich\ former metropolitan borough E London, England, now part of Greenwich

Woom·era \ˈwu̇m-ə-rə\ town S. Australia W of Lake Torrens

Woon·sock·et \wün-ˈsäk-ət, ˈwün-ˌ\ city N R.I. *pop* 45,914

Woos·ter \ˈwu̇s-tər\ city N *cen* Ohio SW of Akron *pop* 19,289

Worces·ter \ˈwu̇s-tər\ 1 city E *cen* Mass. W of Boston *pop* 161,799 2 *or* **Worces·ter·shire** \-tə(r)-ˌshi(ə)r, -shər\ former county W *cen* England — see HEREFORD AND WORCESTER 3 city, ✱ of Hereford and Worcester *pop* 73,445

Worms \ˈwərmz, ˈvȯrm(p)s\ city S W. Germany on the Rhine NNW of Mannheim *pop* 73,603

Worth, Lake \ˈwərth\ inlet (lagoon) of the Atlantic SE Fla.

Wor·thing \ˈwər-t͟hiŋ\ borough S England in W. Sussex on English channel *pop* 91,668

Wound·ed Knee \ˌwün-dəd-ˈnē\ creek *ab* 50 *mi* (80 *km*) SW S.Dak. flowing NNW into White river S of Badlands National Park

Wran·gel \ˈraŋ-gəl\ *or Russ* **Vran·ge·lya** \ˈvrän-gəl-yə\ island U.S.S.R. off NE Soviet Russia, Asia, in Arctic ocean

Wran·gell \ˈraŋ-gəl\ 1 island SE Alaska NE of Prince of Wales Is. 2 mountain range S Alaska NW of St. Elias range — see BLACKBURN (Mount)

Wrangell, Cape cape on Attu Is. in Aleutians, Alaska

Wrangell, Mount active volcano 14,163 *ft* (4317 *m*) S Alaska in Wrangell mountains NW of Mt. Blackburn

Wran·gell–Saint Eli·as National Park \ˈraŋ-gəl-sānt-ᵊl-ˈī-əs-\ reservation S *cen* Alaska; largest park in the world covering 12,318,000 *acres* (4,927,200 *hectares*)

Wrath, Cape \ˈrath, *Sc* ˈrȯth *or* ˈräth\ extreme NW point of Scotland, at 58°35′N

Wrex·ham \ˈrek-səm\ borough NE Wales in Clwyd *pop* 40,272

Wro·cław \ˈvrȯt-ˌsläf, -ˌsläv\ city SW Poland, chief city of Silesia *pop* 621,865

Wu \ˈwü\ river 500 *mi* (805 *km*) *cen* China rising in W Kweichow & flowing through Szechwan into the Yangtze

Wu·chang \ˈwü-ˈchäŋ\ former city E *cen* China — see WUHAN

Wu·chow *or* **Wu·zhou** *or* **Wu–chou** \ˈwü-ˈjō\ city S China in E Kwangsi Chuang at junction of the Kuei and the Hsi *pop* 120,000

Wu·han \ˈwü-ˈhän\ city E *cen* China ✱ of Hupeh at junction of Han & Yangtze rivers; formed from the former separate cities of Hankow, Hanyang, & Wuchang *pop* 4,250,000

Wu–hsi *or* **Wu·xi** *or* **Wu·sih** \ˈwü-ˈshē\ city E China in S Kiangsu NW of Soochow

Wuhsien — see SOOCHOW

Wu·hu \ˈwü-ˈhü\ city E China in E Anhwei *pop* 300,000

Wu–lu–mu–ch'i — see URUMCHI

Wu·pat·ki National Monument \wü-ˈpat-kē\ reservation N Ariz. NNE of Flagstaff containing prehistoric Indian dwellings

Wup·per·tal \ˈvu̇p-ər-ˌtäl\ city W W. Germany in Ruhr valley ENE of Düsseldorf *pop* 393,381

Würt·tem·berg \ˈwərt-əm-ˌbərg, ˈwu̇rt-; ˈvuert-əm-ˌberk\ region SW W. Germany bet. Baden & Bavaria; chief city Stuttgart; once a duchy, kingdom 1813–1918, state 1918–45; divided 1945–51, S part being joined to Hohenzollern forming **Württemberg–Hohenzollern** state & N part to N Baden forming **Württemberg–Baden** state; since 1951 part of Baden–Württemberg state

Würz·burg \ˈwərts-ˌbərg, ˈwu̇rts-; ˈvuerts-ˌbu̇rk\ city S W. Germany on Main river in N Bavaria NW of Nuremberg *pop* 128,652

Wutsin — see CH'ANG-CHOU

Wu–t'ung–ch'iao *or* **Wu·tong·qiao** \ˌwü-ˌtu̇ŋ-chē-ˈau̇\ city SW *cen* China in S Szechwan S of Ch'eng-tu *pop* 140,000

Wy·an·dotte \ˈwī-ən-ˌdät *also* ˈwīn-ˌ\ city SE Mich. *pop* 34,006

Wye \ˈwī\ river 130 *mi* (209 *km*) E Wales & W England flowing into Severn river

Wy·o·ming \wī-ˈō-miŋ\ 1 state NW U.S. ✱ Cheyenne *area* 97,914 *sq mi* (254,576 *sq km*), *pop* 469,557 2 valley NE Pa. along the Susquehanna 3 city SW Mich. *pop* 59,616 — **Wy·o·ming·ite** \-miŋ-ˌīt\ *n*

Xan·thus \\'zan(t)-thəs\\ city of ancient Lycia; its site near mouth of Koca river in SW Turkey

Xe·nia \\'zē-nyə, -nē-ə\\ city SW *cen* Ohio *pop* 24,653

Xeres — see JEREZ

Xi — see HSI

Xiamen — see HSIA-MEN

Xi'an — see SIAN

Xiang — see HSIANG

Xiangtan — see HSIANG-T'AN

Xigazê — see SHIGATSE

Xin·gu \\shēŋ-'gü\\ river 1300 *mi* (2092 *km*) *cen* & N Brazil rising on Mato Grosso plateau & flowing N into the Amazon near its mouth

Xining — see HSI-NING

Xinjiang Uygur — see SINKIANG UIGHUR

Xinxiang — see HSIN-HSIANG

Xizang — see TIBET

Xo·chi·mil·co \\‚sō-chi-'mēl(‚)-kō, ‚sō-shi-, -'mil-\\ city S *cen* Mexico, SE suburb of Mexico City *pop* 116,493

Xuanhua — see HSÜAN-HUA

Xuzhou — see SÜCHOU

Ya·blo·no·vy *or* **Ya·blo·no·vyy** \\‚yäb-lə-nə-'vē\\ mountain range U.S.S.R. in S Soviet Russia, Asia, on E border of Buryat Republic

Yacarana — see JAVARI

Yad·kin \\'yad-kən\\ river 202 *mi* (325 *km*) *cen* N.C., the upper course of the Pee Dee

Yafo — see JAFFA

Ya·ha·ta \\yə-'hät-ə\\ *or* **Ya·wa·ta** \\-'wät-\\ former city Japan in N Kyushu — see KITAKYUSHU

Yak·i·ma \\'yak-ə-‚mò\\ 1 river 200 *mi* (322 *km*) S Wash. flowing SE into Columbia river   2 city S *cen* Wash. *pop* 49,826

Yak·u·tat Bay \\'yak-ə-‚tat-\\ inlet of the Pacific SE Alaska

Ya·kut Republic \\yə-'küt-\\ autonomous republic U.S.S.R. in E *cen* Soviet Russia, Asia ✱ Yakutsk *area* 1,182,300 *sq mi* (3,073,980 *sq km*), *pop* 664,000

Ya·kutsk \\yə-'kütsk\\ city U.S.S.R. in E *cen* Soviet Russia, Asia ✱ of Yakut Republic *pop* 152,000

Yal·ta \\'yòl-tə\\ city & port U.S.S.R. in S Ukrainian Republic on S coast of Crimea *pop* 57,000

Ya·lu \\'yäl-(‚)ü\\ river 300 *mi* (483 *km*) SE Manchuria & NW N. Korea flowing N, W, & SW into Korea Bay

Ya·lung *or* **Ya·long** \\'yä-'lùŋ\\ river 725 *mi* (1167 *km*) SW China in W Szechwan flowing S into the Yangtze

Ya·mal \\yə-'mäl\\ peninsula U.S.S.R. in NW Soviet Russia, Asia, at N end of Ural mountains bet. Gulf of Ob & Kara sea

Ya·mous·sou·kro \\‚yäm-ə-'sü-krō\\ town *cen* Ivory Coast

Yam·pa \\'yam-pə\\ river 200 *mi* (322 *km*) NW Colo. flowing W into Green river in Dinosaur National Monument

Ya·na \\'yän-ə\\ river 750 *mi* (1207 *km*) U.S.S.R. in N Soviet Russia, Asia, flowing N into Laptev sea

Yang–chou *or* **Yang·zhou** *or* **Yang·chow** \\'yäŋ-'jō\\ city E China in SW Kiangsu NW of Nanking *pop* 160,000

Yang·chüan *or* **Yang·quan** \\'yäŋ-chü-'än\\ city N China in E Shansi E of Taiyuan *pop* 200,000

Yangku — see TAIYUAN

Yan·gon \\‚yän-'gòn\\ 1 — see RANGOON 1   2 *or formerly* **Rangoon** city & port ✱ of Myanmar on Rangoon river 21 *mi* (34 *km*) from its mouth *pop* 1,717,649

Yang·tze \\'yaŋ-'sē, 'yaŋ(k)t-'sē\\ *or* **Ch'ang** \\'chäŋ\\ river 3100 *mi* (4989 *km*) *cen* China flowing from Kunlun mountains in SW Tsinghai E into E. China sea

Yantai — see CHEFOO

Yaoun·dé *or* **Yaun·de** \\yaún-'dā\\ city S *cen* Cameroon, its ✱ *pop* 435,892

Yap \\'yap, 'yäp\\ *or* **Uap** \\'wäp\\ islands W Carolines, part of Federated States of Micronesia — **Yap·ese** \\yä-'pēz, yä-, -'pēs\\ *adj*

Ya·quí \\'yä-‚kē\\ river 420 *mi* (676 *km*) NW Mexico in Sonora flowing SW into Gulf of California

Yar·kand \\'yär-'kand\\ 1 river 500 *mi* (805 *km*) Kashmir & China flowing from Karakoram range N & W to join the Khotan in Sinkiang Uighur forming the Tarim   2 — see SO-CH'E

Yar·mouth \\'yär-məth\\ 1 city SE Mass. E of Barnstable *pop* 18,449   2 *or* **Great Yarmouth** borough & port E England in Norfolk on North sea *pop* 50,152

Ya·ro·slavl \\‚yär-ə-'släv-əl\\ city U.S.S.R. in W *cen* Soviet Russia, Europe, on the Volga NE of Moscow *pop* 597,000

Yavarí — see JAVARI

Yazd \\'yazd\\ *or* **Yezd** \\'yezd\\ city *cen* Iran *pop* 98,000

Yaz·oo \\'ya-‚zü, 'yaz-(‚)ü\\ river 188 *mi* (302 *km*) Miss. flowing SW into Mississippi river

Yedo — see TOKYO

Ye·gor'·yevsk \\yə-'gòr-(y)əfsk\\ city U.S.S.R. W *cen* Soviet Russia, Europe, SE of Moscow *pop* 65,000

Yellow 1 — see HWANG   2 sea, inlet of E. China sea bet. N China, N. Korea, & S. Korea

Yel·low·knife \\'yel-ə-‚nīf\\ town Canada ✱ of Northwest Territories on Great Slave Lake *pop* 9483

Yel·low·stone \\'yel-ə-‚stōn\\ river 671 *mi* (1080 *km*) NW Wyo. & S & E Mont. flowing N through **Yellowstone Lake** (*area* 140 *sq mi* or 364 *sq km*) & **Grand Canyon of the Yellowstone** in Yellowstone National Park & NE into Missouri river in NW N.Dak. near Mont. border

Yellowstone Falls two waterfalls NW Wyo. in Yellowstone river at head of Grand Canyon of the Yellowstone; upper fall 109 *ft* (33 *m*), lower fall 308 *ft* (94 *m*)

Yellowstone National Park reservation NW Wyo., E Idaho, & S Mont. including plateau region notable for numerous geysers & hot springs

Ye·men \\'yem-ən\\ country S Arabian peninsula bordering on Red sea & Gulf of Aden; a republic formed 1990 by merger of **Yemen Arab Republic** (✱ San'a) with **People's Democratic Republic of Yemen** *or* **Southern Yemen** (✱ Aden) ✱ San'a *area* 186,074 *sq mi* (483,792 *sq km*), *pop* 7,395,893 — **Ye·me·ni** \\'yem-ə-nē\\ *adj or n* — **Ye·men·ite** \\-ə-‚nīt\\ *n or adj*

Yen·an \\'yen-'än\\ *or* **Yan'·an** \\'yän-'än\\ city NE China in *cen* Shensi *pop* 45,000

Yen–ch'i \\'yen-'chē\\ *or* **Yan·qi** \\'yän-'chē\\ *or* **Ka·ra Shahr** \\‚kär-ə-'shär\\ city W China in *cen* Sinkiang Uighur on N edge of Takla Makan desert *pop* 80,000

Yen·i·sey \\‚yen-ə-'sā\\ river *ab* 2300 *mi* (3701 *km*) U.S.S.R. in Soviet Russia, Asia, flowing N into Arctic ocean

Yen–t'ai — see CHEFOO

Ye·re·van \\‚yer-ə-'vän\\ city U.S.S.R. ✱ of Armenia *pop* 767,000

Ye·ru·pa·ja \\‚yer-ə-'pä-(‚)hä\\ mountain 21,765 *ft* (6634 *m*) W *cen* Peru

Ye·sil Ir·mak \\yə-'shē(ə)l-ir-'mäk\\ river *ab* 250 *mi* (402 *km*) N Turkey in Asia flowing N into Black sea

Ye·sil·koy \\‚yesh-(‚)ēl-'kói\\ *or formerly* **San Ste·fa·no** \\san-'stef-ə-‚nō\\ town Turkey in Europe on Sea of Marmara W of Istanbul

Yezo — see HOKKAIDO

Yibin — see I-PIN

Yichang — see I-CH'ANG

Yin·chuan \\'yin-chü-'än\\ *or formerly* **Ning·sia** *or* **Ning·hsia** \\'niŋ-shē-'ä\\ city N China ✱ of Ningsia Hui on the Hwang *pop* 91,000

Ying·kow \\'yiŋ-‚kaù, -'kō\\ *or* **Ying·kou** \\'yiŋ-‚kō\\ city & port NE China in *cen* Liaoning on Gulf of Liaotung *pop* 161,000

Yog·ya·kar·ta \\‚yòg-yə-'kärt-ə\\ *or* **Jog·ja·kar·ta** \\‚jòg-jə-\\ *or* **Djok·ja·kar·ta** \\‚jòk-jə-\\ city Indonesia in S Java *pop* 398,727

Yo·ho National Park \\'yō-(‚)hō-\\ reservation W Canada in SE B.C. on Alta. border

Yok·kai·chi \\yō-'kī-chē\\ city & port Japan in S Honshu SW of Nagoya *pop* 257,131

Yo·ko·ha·ma \\‚yō-kə-'häm-ə\\ city & port Japan in SE Honshu on Tokyo Bay S of Tokyo *pop* 2,841,170

Yo·ko·su·ka \\yō-'kō-s(ə-)kə\\ city & port Japan in Honshu W of entrance to Tokyo Bay *pop* 424,077

Yo·ne·za·wa \\‚yō-nə-'zä-wə\\ city Japan in N Honshu *pop* 92,823

Yon·kers \\'yäŋ-kərz\\ city SE N.Y. N of New York City *pop* 195,351

Yonne \\'yän\\ river 120 *mi* (193 *km*) NE *cen* France flowing NNW into the Seine

York \\'yó(ə)rk\\ 1 city SE Pa. SE of Harrisburg *pop* 44,619   2 borough Canada in SE Ont. near Toronto *pop* 134,617   3 *or* **York·shire** \\-‚shi(ə)r, -shər\\ former county N England bordering on North sea comprising city of York & (former) administrative counties of **East Riding** (✱ Beverley), **North Riding** (✱ Northallerton), & **West Riding** (✱ Wakefield) — see HUMBERSIDE, NORTH YORKSHIRE, SOUTH YORKSHIRE, WEST YORKSHIRE   4 *or anc* **Ebo·ra·cum** \\i-'bòr-ə-kəm, -'bär-\\ city N England in N. Yorkshire on Ouse river *pop* 99,787

York, Cape — see CAPE YORK PENINSULA

Yorke \\'yó(ə)rk\\ peninsula Australia in SE S. Australia bet. Spencer Gulf and Gulf of St. Vincent

York River estuary 40 *mi* (64 *km*) E Va. flowing SE into Chesapeake Bay

Yo·sem·i·te \\yō-'sem-ət-ē\\ 1 waterfall E *cen* Calif. descending from rim of Yosemite valley in two falls (upper fall 1430 *ft* or 436 *m*, lower fall 320 *ft* or 98 *m* connected by a cascade)   2 glaciated valley of Merced river E *cen* Calif. on W slope of Sierra Nevada in **Yosemite National Park**

Yo·su \\'yō-(‚)sü\\ city & port S S. Korea on Korea strait *pop* 161,009

Yough·io·ghe·ny \\‚yäk-ə-'gā-nē, ‚yō-hə-, -'gen-ē\\ river 135 *mi* (217 *km*) NE W.Va., NW Md., & SW Pa. flowing N & NW into the Monongahela

Youngs·town \\'yəŋ-‚staún\\ city NE Ohio E of Akron *pop* 115,436

Youth, Isle of *or formerly* **Isle of Pines** island W Cuba in the Caribbean *area* 1180 *sq mi* (3068 *sq km*)

Ypres — see IEPER

Yp·si·lan·ti \\‚ip-sə-'lant-ē\\ city SE Mich. *pop* 24,031

Yser \\ē-'ze(ə)r\\ river 55 *mi* (88 *km*) France & Belgium flowing into North sea

Yü *or* **You** \\'yü\\ *or* **Siang** \\shē-'ä\\ river 400 *mi* (644 *km*) SE China in Yunnan & Kwangsi flowing E to unite with the Hungshui forming the Hsi

Yu·an \\yù-'än\\ 1 river 500 *mi* (805 *km*) SE *cen* China flowing from Kweichow NE to NE Hunan   2 — see RED

Yu·ba City \\'yü-bə-\\ city N Calif. N of Sacramento *pop* 18,736

Yu·ca·tán \\‚yü-kə-'tan, -'tän\\ 1 peninsula SE Mexico & N Central America including Belize & part of Guatemala   2 channel bet. Yucatán & W end of Cuba   3 state SE Mexico at N end of Yucatán peninsula ✱ Mérida *area* 23,926 *sq mi* (62,208 *sq km*), *pop* 1,034,648

Yuc·ca House National Monument \\'yək-ə-\\ reservation SW Colo.; contains prehistoric ruins

Yu·go·sla·via *or* **Ju·go·sla·via** \\‚yü-gō-'släv-ē-ə\\ country S Europe bordering on the Adriatic; established 1918 as a kingdom (**Kingdom of the Serbs, Croats, and Slo·venes** \\'sərbz-'kròt-sən-'slō-‚vēnz *also* -'krō-‚at-sən-\\), became a federal republic 1945 ✱ Belgrade *area* 99,044 *sq mi* (257,514 *sq km*), *pop* 22,839,000 — **Yu·go·slav** \\‚yü-gō-'släv, -'slav\\ *or* **Yu·go·sla·vi·an** \\-'släv-ē-ən\\ *adj or n*

Yu·kon \\'yü-‚kän\\ 1 city *cen* Okla. *pop* 17,112   2 river 1979 *mi* (3185 *km*) Yukon Territory & Alaska flowing NW & SW into Bering sea — see LEWES   3 *or* **Yukon Territory** territory NW Canada bet. Alaska & B.C. bordering on Arctic ocean ✱ Whitehorse *area* 205,346 *sq mi* (533,900 *sq km*), *pop* 21,836

Yu·ma \\'yü-mə\\ city SW Ariz. on Colorado river *pop* 42,433

Yungki — see KIRIN

Yungning — see NANNING

Yun·nan \\yü-'nän\\ 1 province SW China bordering on Indochina & Burma ✱ Kunming *area* 168,417 *sq mi* (437,884 *sq km*), *pop* 32,553,817   2 *or* **Yunnanfu** — see KUNMING — **Yun·nan·ese** \\‚yü-nə-'nēz, -'nēs\\ *adj or n*

Yun·que, El \\el-'yüŋ-(‚)kā\\ mountain 3494 *ft* (1065 *m*) E Puerto Rico

Yü Shan \\'yü-'shän\\ *or* **Hsin·kao** \\'shin-'kaú\\ *or* **Mount Mor·ri·son** \\'mòr-ə-sən\\ mountain 13,113 *ft* (3997 *m*) *cen* Taiwan; highest on island

Yuzovka — see DONETSK

Yver·don \ē-ver-dōⁿ\ commune W Switzerland N of Lausanne *pop* 20,802

Zaan·dam \zän-'dam, -'däm\ commune W Netherlands *pop* 129,341

Zab·rze \'zäb-(,)zhä\ *or G* **Hin·den·burg** \'hin-dən-bərg, -,bủ(ə)rg\ city SW Poland in Silesia *pop* 196,841

Za·ca·te·cas \,zak-ə-'tā-kəs, -'tek-əs\ **1** state N *cen* Mexico *area* 28,122 *sq mi* (73,117 *sq km*), *pop* 1,145,327 **2** city, its ✱ *pop* 56,829

Za·dar \'zäd-,är\ *or It* **Za·ra** \'zär-ə\ city & port W Yugoslavia in Croatia; held by Italy 1920–47 *pop* 43,588

Zag·a·zig \'zag-ə-,zig\ *or* **Az Za·qā·zīq** \,az-zə-,kä-'zēk\ city N Egypt NNE of Cairo *pop* 202,637

Za·greb \'zäg-,reb\ city NW Yugoslavia ✱ of Croatia *pop* 561,773

Zag·ros \'zag-rəs, -,rós\ mountains W & S Iran bordering on Turkey, Iraq, & Persian Gulf; highest over 14,000 *ft* (4267 *m*)

Zaire \'zī(ə)r, zä-'i(ə)r\ **1** river in Africa — see CONGO **2** *or formerly* **Congo** *or* **Democratic Republic of the Congo** *or earlier* **Belgian Congo** country *cen* Africa comprising most of Congo river basin E of lower Congo river; a republic ✱ Kinshasa *area* 893,000 *sq mi* (2,321,800 *sq km*), *pop* 30,261,000 — **Zair·ian** \'zī-rē-ən, zä-'ir-ē-\ *adj or n*

Zakarpatskaya — see RUTHENIA

Zá·kin·thos \'zäk-ən-,thōs\ *or* **Zan·te** \'zant-ē\ *or anc* **Za·cyn·thus** \zə-'sin(t)-thəs\ **1** island W Greece, one of the Ionian islands, SSE of Cephalonia *area* 156 *sq mi* (406 *sq km*) **2** its chief town

Za·ko·pa·ne \,zäk-ə-'pän-(,)ā\ city S Poland in Tatry mountains S of Krakow *pop* 28,930

Za·ma \'zä-mə, 'zäm-ə\ ancient town N Africa SW of Carthage

Zam·be·zi *or* **Zam·be·si** \zam-'bē-zē\ river 1650 *mi* (2655 *km*) SE Africa flowing from NW Zambia into Mozambique channel

Zam·bia \'zam-bē-ə\ *or formerly* **Northern Rhodesia** country S Africa; formerly a Brit. protectorate; independent republic within the Commonwealth since 1964 ✱ Lusaka *area* 290,410 *sq mi* (755,066 *sq km*), *pop* 5,679,808 — **Zam·bi·an** \'zam-bē-ən\ *adj or n*

Zam·bo·an·ga \,zam-bə-'wäŋ-gə\ city & port Philippines on SW coast of Mindanao *pop* 176,800

Za·mo·ra \zə-'mōr-ə, -'mór-\ **1** province NW Spain in *cen* León *area* 4097 *sq mi* (10,652 *sq km*), *pop* 201,869 **2** city, its ✱ *pop* 54,299

Zancle — see MESSINA

Zanes·ville \'zānz-,vil\ city E *cen* Ohio *pop* 28,655

Zan·zi·bar \'zan-zə-,bär\ **1** island E Africa off NE Tanzania mainland *area* 640 *sq mi* (1664 *sq km*), *pop* 122,004; formerly a sultanate, with Pemba & adjacent islands forming a Brit. protectorate; became independent 1963; united 1964 with Tanganyika to form Tanzania **2** city & port ✱ of the island & protectorate *pop* 110,669 — **Zan·zi·bari** \,zan-zə-'bär-ē\ *n or adj*

Za·po·rozh'·ye \,zäp-ə-'ró-zhə\ *or formerly* **Ale·ksan·drovsk** \,al-ik-'sandrəfsk, ,el-\ city U.S.S.R. in SE Ukrainian Republic *pop* 658,000

Za·ra·go·za \,zar-ə-'gō-zə\ *or* **Sar·a·gos·sa** \,sar-ə-'gäs-ə\ **1** province NE Spain in W Aragon *area* 6726 *sq mi* (17,488 *sq km*), *pop* 828,692 **2** city, its ✱, on the Ebro *pop* 571,855

Zee·brug·ge \'zā-,brag-ə\ town NW Belgium; port for Bruges

Zee·land \'zē-lənd, 'zā-; 'zā-,länt\ province SW Netherlands ✱ Middelburg *area* 1040 *sq mi* (2704 *sq km*), *pop* 354,816

Zeist \'zīst\ commune *cen* Netherlands E of Utrecht *pop* 61,332

Zem·po·al·te·pec \,zem-pə-'wäl-tə-,pek\ *or* **Zem·po·al·te·petl** \-,wäl-'tä-,pet-'l, -,wäl-tə-'\ mountain 11,138 *ft* (3395 *m*) SE Mexico in Oaxaca

Zer·matt \(t)ser-'mät\ village SW *cen* Switzerland in Valais in Pennine Alps NE of the Matterhorn

Zetland — see SHETLAND

Zhangdu — see CHANGTU

Zhangjiakou — see KALGAN

Zhangzhou — see CHANG-CHOU

Zhao'an — see CH'AO-AN

Zhdanov — see MARIUPOL

Zhejiang — see CHEKIANG

Zhengzhou — see CHENG-CHOU

Zhenjiang — see CHEN-CHIANG

Zhi·to·mir \zhi-'tó-,mi(ə)r\ city U.S.S.R. in W Ukrainian Republic *pop* 161,000

Zhoushan — see CHOU-SHAN

Zhu — see CHU 1

Zhuzhou — see CHU-CHOU

Zibo — see TZU-PO

Zigong — see TZU-KUNG

Zim·ba·bwe \zim-'bäb-wē, -(,)wā\ **1** archaeological site NE Zimbabwe (2) **2** *or formerly* **Southern Rhodesia** *or 1970-79* **Rhodesia** country S Africa S of the Zambezi; a self-governing Brit. colony which declared itself a republic 1970; adopted majority rule 1979 ✱ Harare *area* 150,333 *sq mi* (390,866 *sq km*), *pop* 7,550,000 — **Zim·ba·bwe·an** \-ən\ *adj or n*

Zinovievsk — see KIROVOGRAD

Zi·on \'zī-ən\ city NE Ill. N of Waukegan *pop* 17,861

Zi·on \'zī-ən\ *or* **Si·on** \'sī-\ **1** the stronghold of Jerusalem conquered by David **2** JERUSALEM **3** ISRAEL

Zion, Mount hill E Jerusalem, Israel; occupied in ancient times by the Jewish Temple

Zi·on National Park \'zī-ən\ reservation SW Utah centering around Zion Canyon of Virgin river

Zi·pan·gu \zə-'paŋ-(,)gü\ JAPAN — the name used by Marco Polo

Zi·pa·qui·rá \,sē-pə-ki-'rä\ town *cen* Colombia N of Bogotá

Zla·to·ust \,zlät-ə-'üst\ city U.S.S.R. in W Soviet Russia, Asia, in the S Urals *pop* 181,000

Zlin — see GOTTWALDOV

Zoan — see TANIS

Zom·ba \'zäm-bə\ city SE Malawi S of Lake Malawi *pop* 21,000

Zon·gul·dak \,zóŋ-gəl-'däk\ city & port NW Turkey *pop* 108,661

Zug \'(t)sük, 'züg\ *or F* **Zoug** \'züg\ **1** canton N *cen* Switzerland *area* 92 *sq mi* (239 *sq km*), *pop* 75,930 **2** commune, its ✱, on Lake of Zug *pop* 21,609

Zug, Lake of lake N *cen* Switzerland in Zug & Schwyz cantons N of Vierwaldstätter See *area* 15 *sq mi* (39 *sq km*)

Zug·spit·ze \'(t)sük-,s(h)pit-sə, 'züg-\ mountain 9721 *ft* (2963 *m*) S W. Germany; highest in Bavarian Alps & in W. Germany

Zui·der Zee \,zīd-ər-'zā, -'zē\ former inlet of North sea N Netherlands — see IJSSELMEER

Zuidholland — see SOUTH HOLLAND

Zu·lu·land \'zü-(,)lü-,land\ territory E Republic of S. Africa in NE Natal bordering on Indian ocean N of the Tugela *area* 10,427 *sq mi* (27,110 *sq km*), *pop* 570,160

Zu·rich \'zủ(ə)r-ik\ *or G* **Zü·rich** \'tsǖ-rik\ **1** canton N Switzerland *area* 665 *sq mi* (1729 *sq km*), *pop* 1,122,839 **2** city, its ✱, at NW end of Lake of Zurich *pop* 369,522 — **Zü·rich·er** \-ər\ *n*

Zurich, Lake of lake 25 *mi* (40 *km*) long N *cen* Switzerland

Zut·phen \'zət-fən\ commune E Netherlands on the IJssel *pop* 31,495

Zwick·au \'tsfik-,aủ, 'zwik-\ city S E. Germany S of Leipzig *pop* 121,787

Zwol·le \'zvòl-ə, 'zwól-\ city E Netherlands ✱ of Overijssel *pop* 86,388

Colleges and Universities

United States

Abilene Christian U. Abilene, Tex. 79601; 1906
Abraham Baldwin Agricultural C. Tifton, Ga. 31794; junior, 1907
Adams State C. of Colorado Alamosa, Colo. 81101; 1921
Adelphi U. Garden City, N.Y. 11530; 1896
Adirondack Comm. C. Glens Falls, N.Y. 12801; junior, 1961
Adrian C. Adrian, Mich. 49221; 1845
Aeronautics, Acad. of Flushing, N.Y. 11371; junior, 1932
Agnes Scott C. Decatur, Ga. 30030; 1889
Aiken Technical C. Aiken, S.C. 29801; junior, 1969
Aims Comm. C. Greeley, Colo. 80631; junior, 1967
Air Force, Comm. C. of the Montgomery, Ala. 36112; junior, 1972
Air Force Inst. of Tech. Wright-Patterson AFB, Ohio 45433; 1919
Akron, U. of Akron, Ohio 44325; 1870
Alabama, U. of Tuscaloosa, Ala. 35486; 1831
Alabama A. & M. U. Normal, Ala. 35762; 1873
Alabama Christian C. Montgomery, Ala. 36109; junior, 1942
Alabama in Birmingham, U. of 35294; 1966
Alabama in Huntsville, U. of 35807; 1966
Alabama State U. Montgomery, Ala. 36104; 1874
Alamance Comm. C. Haw River, N.C. 27258; junior, 1959
Alameda, C. of Alameda, Calif. 94501; junior, 1964
Alaska, U. of Anchorage, Alaska 99504; 1970
Alaska, U. of Fairbanks, Alaska 99701; 1917
Alaska Pacific U. Anchorage, Alaska 99504; 1957
Albany Junior C. Albany, Ga. 31705; 1966
Albany State C. Albany, Ga. 31705; 1903
Albemarle, C. of the Elizabeth City, N.C. 27909; junior, 1960
Albertus Magnus C. New Haven, Conn. 06511; 1925
Albion C. Albion, Mich. 49224; 1835
Albright C. Reading, Pa. 19604; 1856
Albuquerque, U. of Albuquerque, N.Mex. 87120; 1940
Alcorn State U. Lorman, Miss. 39096; 1871
Alderson–Broaddus C. Philippi, W.Va. 26416; 1871
Alfred U. Alfred, N.Y. 14802; 1836
Alice Lloyd C. Pippa Passes, Ky. 48144; junior, 1923
Allan Hancock C. Santa Maria, Calif. 93454; junior, 1920
Allegany Comm. C. Cumberland, Md. 21502; junior, 1961
Allegheny C. Meadville, Pa. 16335; 1815
Allegheny County, Comm. C. of Pittsburgh, Pa. 15212; junior, 1965
Allen County Comm. C. Iola, Kans. 66749; junior, 1923
Allentown C. of St. Francis de Sales Center Valley, Pa. 18034; 1965
Allen U. Columbia, S.C. 29204; 1870
Alma C. Alma, Mich. 48801; 1886
Alpena Comm. C. Alpena, Mich. 49707; junior, 1952
Alvernia C. Reading, Pa. 19607; 1958
Alverno C. Milwaukee, Wis. 53215; 1887
Alvin Comm. C. Alvin, Tex. 77511; junior, 1949
Amarillo C. Amarillo, Tex. 79105; junior, 1929
American Baptist C. Nashville, Tenn. 37207; 1924
American Conservatory of Music Chicago, Ill. 60605; 1886
American International C. Springfield, Mass. 01109; 1885
American River C. Sacramento, Calif. 95841; junior, 1955
American Samoa Comm. C. Pago Pago, American Samoa 96799; junior, 1970
American Technological U. Killeen, Tex. 76541; 1973
American U. Washington, D.C. 20016; 1893
Amherst C. Amherst, Mass. 01002; 1821
Ancilla Domini C. Donaldson, Ind. 46513; junior, 1937
Anderson C. Anderson, S.C. 29621; junior, 1911
Anderson U. Anderson, Ind. 46012; 1917
Andrew C. Cuthbert, Ga. 31740; junior, 1854
Andrews U. Berrien Springs, Mich. 49104; 1874
Angelina C. Lufkin, Tex. 75901; junior, 1968
Angelo State U. San Angelo, Tex. 76901; 1928
Anna Maria C. Paxton, Mass. 01612; 1946
Anne Arundel Comm. C. Arnold, Md. 21012; junior, 1961
Anoka–Ramsey Comm. C. Coon Rapids, Minn. 55433; junior, 1965
Anson Technical C. Ansonville, N.C. 28007; junior, 1962
Antelope Valley C. Lancaster, Calif. 93534; junior, 1929
Antioch U. Yellow Springs, Ohio 45387; 1852
Appalachian Bible C. Bradley, W.Va. 25818; 1950
Appalachian State U. Boone, N.C. 28607; 1903
Aquinas C. Grand Rapids, Mich. 49506; 1886
Aquinas Junior C. Milton, Mass. 02186; 1956
Aquinas Junior C. Nashville, Tenn. 37205; 1961
Arapahoe Comm. C. Littleton, Colo. 80120; junior, 1965
Arizona, U. of Tucson, Ariz. 85721; 1885
Arizona C. of the Bible Phoenix, Ariz. 85021; 1971
Arizona State U. Tempe, Ariz. 85287; 1885

Arizona Western C. Yuma, Ariz. 85364; junior, 1963
Arkansas, U. of Fayetteville, Ark. 72701; 1871
Arkansas at Little Rock, U. of 72204; 1927
Arkansas at Monticello, U. of 71655; 1909
Arkansas at Pine Bluff, U. of 71601; 1873
Arkansas Baptist C. Little Rock, Ark. 72202; 1884
Arkansas C. Batesville, Ark. 72501; 1872
Arkansas Medical Sciences, U. of Little Rock, Ark. 72201; 1879
Arkansas State U. State University, Ark. 72467; 1909
Arkansas Tech U. Russellville, Ark. 72801; 1909
Armstrong C. Berkeley, Calif. 94704; 1918
Armstrong State C. Savannah, Ga. 31406; 1935
Art Center C. of Design Pasadena, Calif. 91103; 1930
Art Inst. of Chicago, Sch. of the Chicago, Ill. 60603; 1866
Asbury C. Wilmore, Ky. 40390; 1890
Asheville–Buncombe Technical C. Asheville, N.C. 28801; junior, 1959
Ashland C. Ashland, Ohio 44805; 1878
Ashland Comm. C. Ashland, Ky. 41101; junior, 1937
Asnuntuck Comm. C. Enfield, Conn. 06082; junior, 1972
Assumption C. Worcester, Mass. 01609; 1904
Assumption C. for Sisters Mendham, N.J. 07945; junior, 1953
Athens State C. Athens, Ala. 35611; 1822
Atlanta Christian C. East Point, Ga. 30344; 1937
Atlanta C. of Art Atlanta, Ga. 30309; 1928
Atlanta Junior C. Atlanta, Ga. 30310; 1974
Atlanta U. Atlanta, Ga. 30314; 1865
Atlantic, C. of the Bar Harbor, Me. 04609; 1969
Atlantic Christian C. Wilson, N.C. 27893; 1902
Atlantic Comm. C. Mays Landing, N.J. 08330; junior, 1964
Atlantic Union C. South Lancaster, Mass. 01561; 1882
Auburn U. Auburn, Ala. 36830; 1856
Augsburg C. Minneapolis, Minn. 55404; 1869
Augusta C. Augusta, Ga. 30904; 1925
Augustana C. Rock Island, Ill. 61201; 1860
Augustana C. Sioux Falls, S.Dak. 57102; 1860
Aurora U. Aurora, Ill. 60506; 1893
Austin C. Sherman, Tex. 75090; 1849
Austin Comm. C. Austin, Minn. 55912; junior, 1940
Austin Comm. C. Austin, Tex. 78768; junior, 1972
Austin Peay State U. Clarksville, Tenn. 37040; 1927
Averett C. Danville, Va. 24541; 1859
Avila C. Kansas City, Mo. 64145; 1866
Azusa Pacific U. Azusa, Calif. 91702; 1899
Babson C. Babson Park, Mass. 02157; 1919
Bacone C. Bacone, Okla. 74420; junior, 1880
Bainbridge Junior C. Bainbridge, Ga. 31717; 1970
Baker C. Baker, Oreg. 97814; junior, 1957
Baker U. Baldwin City, Kans. 66006; 1858
Bakersfield C. Bakersfield, Calif. 93305; junior, 1913
Baldwin–Wallace C. Berea, Ohio 44017; 1845
Ball State U. Muncie, Ind. 47306; 1918
Baltimore, Comm. C. of Baltimore, Md. 21215; junior, 1947
Baltimore, U. of Baltimore, Md. 21201; 1925
Baltimore Hebrew C. Baltimore, Md. 21215; 1919
Bangor Theol. Sem. Bangor, Me. 04401; 1814
Baptist Bible C. Springfield, Mo. 65802; 1925
Baptist Bible C. of Pennsylvania Clarks Summit, Pa. 18411; 1932
Baptist C. at Charleston S.C. 29411; 1960
Barat C. Lake Forest, Ill. 60045; 1857
Barber–Scotia C. Concord, N.C. 28025; 1867
Bard C. Annandale-on-Hudson, N.Y. 12504; 1860
Barnard C. New York, N.Y. 10027; 1889
Barrington C. Barrington, R.I. 02806; 1900
Barry C. Miami, Fla. 33161; 1940
Barstow C. Barstow, Calif. 92311; junior, 1960
Bartlesville Wesleyan C. Bartlesville, Okla. 74003; 1910
Barton County Comm. C. Great Bend, Kans. 67530; junior, 1965
Bassist C. Portland, Oreg. 97205; junior, 1963
Bates C. Lewiston, Me. 04240; 1864
Bayamon Central U. Bayamon, Puerto Rico 00619; 1961
Bay de Noc Comm. C. Escanaba, Mich. 49829; junior, 1963
Baylor U. Waco, Tex. 76703; 1845
Bay Path Junior C. Longmeadow, Mass. 01106; 1897
Bay State Junior C. of Business Boston, Mass. 02116; 1946
Beal C. Bangor, Me. 04401; junior, 1891
Beaufort County Comm. C. Washington, N.C. 27889; junior, 1967
Beaufort Technical C. Beaufort, S.C. 29902; junior, 1968
Beaver C. Glenside, Pa. 19038; 1853
Beaver County, Comm. C. of Monaca, Pa. 15061; junior, 1966

Becker Junior C.–Leicester Campus Leicester, Mass. 01524; junior, 1784
Becker Junior C.–Worcester Campus Worcester, Mass. 01609; 1887
Beckley C. Beckley, W.Va. 25801; junior, 1933
Bee County C. Beeville, Tex. 78102; junior, 1966
Belhaven C. Jackson, Miss. 39202; 1894
Bellarmine C. Louisville, Ky. 40205; 1950
Belleville Area C. Belleville, Ill. 62221; junior, 1946
Bellevue C. Bellevue, Nebr. 68005; 1965
Bellevue Comm. C. Bellevue, Wash. 98007; junior, 1966
Belmont Abbey C. Belmont, N.C. 28012; 1878
Belmont C. Nashville, Tenn. 37203; 1951
Beloit C. Beloit, Wis. 53511; 1846
Bemidji State U. Bemidji, Minn. 56601; 1913
Benedict C. Columbia, S.C. 29204; 1870
Benedictine C., The Atchison, Kans. 66002; 1857
Bennett C. Greensboro, N.C. 27420; 1873
Bennington C. Bennington, Vt. 05201; 1925
Bentley C. Waltham, Mass. 02154; 1917
Berea C. Berea, Ky. 40403; 1855
Bergen Comm. C. Paramus, N.J. 07652; junior, 1965
Berklee C. of Music Boston, Mass. 02215; 1945
Berkshire Christian C. Lenox, Mass. 01240; 1897
Berkshire Comm. C. Pittsfield, Mass. 01201; junior, 1960
Bernard M. Baruch C. New York, N.Y. 10010; 1919
Berry C. Mount Berry, Ga. 30149; 1902
Bethany Bible C. Santa Cruz, Calif. 95066; 1919
Bethany C. Lindsborg, Kans. 67456; 1881
Bethany C. Bethany, W.Va. 26032; 1840
Bethany Lutheran C. Mankato, Minn. 56001; 1911
Bethel C. Mishawaka, Ind. 46544; 1947
Bethel C. North Newton, Kans. 67117; 1887
Bethel C. St. Paul, Minn. 55112; 1871
Bethel C. McKenzie, Tenn. 38201; 1842
Bethune–Cookman C. Daytona Beach, Fla. 32015; 1872
Beulah Heights C. Atlanta, Ga. 30316; 1928
Big Bend Comm. C. Moses Lake, Wash. 98837; junior, 1962
Biola U. La Mirada, Calif. 90639; 1908
Birmingham–Southern C. Birmingham, Ala. 35204; 1856
Biscayne C. Miami, Fla. 33054; 1962
Bismarck Junior C. Bismarck, N.Dak. 58501; 1939
Blackburn C. Carlinville, Ill. 62626; 1835
Black Hawk C. Moline, Ill. 61265; junior, 1946
Black Hills State C. Spearfish, S.Dak. 57783; 1883
Bladen Technical C. Dublin, N.C. 28332; junior, 1967
Blinn C. Brenham, Tex. 77833; junior, 1883
Bloomfield C. Bloomfield, N.J. 07003; 1868
Bloomsburg U. of Pennsylvania Bloomsburg, Pa. 17815; 1839
Bluefield C. Bluefield, W.Va. 24605; 1922
Bluefield State C. Bluefield, W.Va. 24701; 1895
Blue Mountain C. Blue Mountain, Miss. 38610; 1873
Blue Mountain Comm. C. Pendleton, Oreg. 97801; junior, 1962
Blue Ridge Comm. C. Weyers Cave, Va. 24486; junior, 1967
Blue Ridge Technical C. Flat Rock, N.C. 28731; junior, 1969
Bluffton C. Bluffton, Ohio 45817; 1899
Bob Jones U. Greenville, S.C. 29614; 1927
Boca Raton, C. of Boca Raton, Fla. 33432; junior, 1963
Boise State U. Boise, Idaho 83707; 1932
Borough of Manhattan Comm. C. New York, N.Y. 10020; junior, 1963
Borromeo C. of Ohio Wickliffe, Ohio, 44092; 1953
Boston C. Chestnut Hill, Mass. 02167; 1863
Boston Conservatory of Music Boston, Mass. 02115; 1867
Boston State C. Boston, Mass. 02115; 1852
Boston U. Boston, Mass. 02215; 1869
Bowdoin C. Brunswick, Me. 04011; 1794
Bowie State C. Bowie, Md. 20715; 1867
Bowling Green State U. Bowling Green, Ohio 43402; 1910
Bradford C. Bradford, Mass. 01830; 1803
Bradley U. Peoria, Ill. 61606; 1897
Brainerd Comm. C. Brainerd, Minn. 56401; junior, 1938
Brandeis U. Waltham, Mass. 02154; 1947
Brandywine C. Wilmington, Del. 19803; junior, 1967
Brazosport C. Lake Jackson, Tex. 77566; junior, 1968
Brenau C. Gainesville, Ga. 30501; 1878
Brescia C. Owensboro, Ky. 42301; 1874
Brevard C. Brevard, N.C. 28712; junior, 1853
Brevard Comm. C. Cocoa, Fla. 32922; junior, 1960
Brewer State Junior C. Fayette, Ala. 35555; 1968
Brewton–Parker C. Mt. Vernon, Ga. 30445; junior, 1904
Briar Cliff C. Sioux City, Iowa 51104; 1930
Bridgeport, U. of Bridgeport, Conn. 06602; 1927
Bridgeport Engineering Inst. Bridgeport, Conn. 06603; 1924
Bridgewater C. Bridgewater, Va. 22812; 1880
Bridgewater State C. Bridgewater, Mass. 02324; 1840
Brigham Young U. Provo, Utah 84601; 1875
Bristol Comm. C. Fall River, Mass. 02720; junior, 1966
Bronx Comm. C. Bronx, N.Y. 10468; junior, 1957
Brookdale Comm. C. Lincroft, N.J. 07738; junior, 1967
Brookhaven C. Farmers Branch, Tex. 75234; junior, 1965
Brooklyn C. Brooklyn, N.Y. 11210; 1930
Brooks C. Long Beach, Calif. 90804; junior, 1971
Brooks Inst. Santa Barbara, Calif. 93103; 1945
Broome Comm. C. Binghamton, N.Y. 13902; junior, 1946
Broward Comm. C. Fort Lauderdale, Fla. 33314; junior, 1960
Brown U. Providence, R.I. 02912; 1764
Brunswick Junior C. Brunswick, Ga. 31520; 1964
Bryan C. Dayton, Tenn. 37321; 1930
Bryant C. Smithfield, R.I. 02917; 1863
Bryn Mawr C. Bryn Mawr, Pa. 19010; 1880
Bucknell U. Lewisburg, Pa. 17837; 1846
Bucks County Comm. C. Newtown, Pa. 18940; junior, 1965
Buena Vista C. Storm Lake, Iowa 50588; 1891
Buffalo County Teachers C. Alma, Wis. 54610; junior, 1902
Bunker Hill Comm. C. Charlestown, Mass. 02129; junior, 1973

Burlington County C. Pemberton, N.J. 08068; junior, 1966
Butler County Comm. C. Butler, Pa. 16001; junior, 1965
Butler County Comm. Junior C. El Dorado, Kans. 67042; 1927
Butler U. Indianapolis, Ind. 46208; 1850
Butte C. Oroville, Calif. 95965; junior, 1967
Cabrillo C. Aptos, Calif. 95003; junior, 1959
Cabrini C. Radnor, Pa. 19087; 1957
Caldwell C. Caldwell, N.J. 07006; 1939
Caldwell Comm. C. and Technical Inst. Lenoir, N.C. 28645; junior, 1964
California, Berkeley, U. of 94720; 1868
California, Davis, U. of 95616; 1908
California, Irvine, U. of 92717; 1965
California, Los Angeles, U. of 90024; 1881
California, Riverside, U. of 92502; 1907
California, San Diego, U. of 92037; 1901
California, San Francisco, U. of 94143; 1873
California, Santa Barbara, U. of 93106; 1891
California, Santa Cruz, U. of 95060; 1965
California Baptist C. Riverside, Calif. 92504; 1950
California Christian C. Fresno, Calif. 93703; 1955
California C. of Arts and Crafts Oakland, Calif. 94618; 1907
California C. of Podiatric Medicine San Francisco, Calif. 94115; 1914
California Inst. of Tech. Pasadena, Calif. 91125; 1891
California Inst. of the Arts Valencia, Calif. 91355; 1961
California Lutheran C. Thousand Oaks, Calif. 91360; 1959
California Maritime Acad. Vallejo, Calif. 94590; 1929
California Polytechnic State U., San Luis Obispo 93410; 1901
California State C., Bakersfield 93309; 1965
California State C., San Bernardino 92407; 1960
California State C., Stanislaus Turlock, Calif. 95380; 1957
California State Polytechnic U., Pomona 91766; 1938
California State U., Chico 95929; 1887
California State U., Dominguez Hills Carson, Calif. 90747; 1960
California State U., Fresno 93710; 1911
California State U., Fullerton 92631; 1957
California State U., Hayward 94542; 1957
California State U., Long Beach 90801; 1949
California State U., Los Angeles 90032; 1947
California State U., Northridge 91330; 1958
California State U., Sacramento 95819; 1947
California U. of Pennsylvania California, Pa. 15419; 1852
Calumet C. Whiting, Ind. 46394; 1951
Calvary Bible C. Kansas City, Mo. 64147; 1932
Calvin C. Grand Rapids, Mich. 49506; 1876
Camden County C. Blackwood, N.J. 08012; junior, 1966
Cameron U. Lawton, Okla. 73501; 1908
Campbellsville C. Campbellsville, Ky. 42718; 1906
Campbell U. Buies Creek, N.C. 27506; 1887
Cañada C. Redwood City, Calif. 94061; junior, 1968
Canisius C. Buffalo, N.Y. 14208; 1870
Canyons, C. of the Valencia, Calif. 91355; junior, 1969
Cape Cod Comm. C. West Barnstable, Mass. 02668; junior, 1961
Cape Fear Technical Inst. Wilmington, N.C. 28401; junior, 1958
Capital U. Columbus, Ohio 43209; 1850
Capitol Inst. of Tech. Kensington, Md. 20795; 1964
Cardinal Glennon C. St. Louis, Mo. 63119; 1900
Cardinal Newman C. St. Louis, Mo. 63121; 1976
Cardinal Stritch C. Milwaukee, Wis. 53217; 1932
Caribbean U. C. Bayamon, Puerto Rico 00619; 1969
Carl Albert Junior C. Poteau, Okla. 74953; 1934
Carleton C. Northfield, Minn. 55057; 1866
Carlow C. Pittsburgh, Pa. 15213; 1929
Carl Sandburg C. Galesburg, Ill. 61401; junior, 1967
Carnegie Mellon U. Pittsburgh, Pa. 15213; 1900
Carroll C. Helena, Mont. 59601; 1909
Carroll C. Waukesha, Wis. 53186; 1840
Carson–Newman C. Jefferson City, Tenn. 37760; 1851
Carteret Technical C. Morehead City, N.C. 28557; junior, 1963
Carthage C. Kenosha, Wis. 53141; 1847
Carver Bible Inst. and C. Atlanta, Ga. 30302; 1943
Casco Bay C. Portland, Me. 04101; junior, 1863
Case Western Reserve U. Cleveland, Ohio 44106; 1826
Casper C. Casper, Wyo. 82601; junior, 1945
Castleton State C. Castleton, Vt. 05735; 1787
Catawba C. Salisbury, N.C. 28144; 1851
Catawba Valley Technical C. Hickory, N.C. 28601; junior, 1958
Cathedral C. of the Immaculate Conception Douglaston, N.Y. 11362; 1914
Catholic U. of America Washington, D.C. 20017; 1887
Catholic U. of Puerto Rico Ponce, Puerto Rico 00731; 1948
Catonsville Comm. C. Catonsville, Md. 21228; junior, 1957
Cayuga County Comm. C. Auburn, N.Y. 13021; junior, 1953
Cazenovia C. Cazenovia, N.Y. 13035; junior, 1824
Cecil Comm. C. North East, Md. 21901; junior, 1968
Cedar Crest C. Allentown, Pa. 18104; 1867
Cedar Valley C. Lancaster, Tex. 75134; junior, 1974
Cedarville C. Cedarville, Ohio 45314; 1887
Centenary C. Hackettstown, N.J. 07840; 1867
Centenary C. of Louisiana Shreveport, La. 71104; 1825
Center for Creative Studies Detroit, Mich. 48202; 1926
Center for Early Ed. Los Angeles, Calif. 90048; 1939
Central Alabama Comm. C. Alexander City, Ala. 35010; junior, 1965
Central Arizona C. Coolidge, Ariz. 85228; junior, 1969
Central Arkansas, U. of Conway, Ark. 72032; 1907
Central Baptist C. Conway, Ark. 72032; 1950
Central Bible C. Springfield, Mo. 65802; 1922
Central Carolina Comm. C. Sanford, N.C. 27330; junior, 1961
Central City Business Inst. Syracuse, N.Y. 13203; junior, 1904
Central C. McPherson, Kans. 67460; junior, 1914
Central Comm. C.–Grand Island Campus Grand Island, Nebr. 68802; junior, 1976
Central Comm. C.–Hastings Campus Hastings, Nebr. 68901; junior, 1966

Central Comm. C.–Platte Campus Columbus, Nebr. 68601; junior, 1968
Central Connecticut State U. New Britain, Conn. 06050; 1849
Central Florida, U. of Orlando 32816; 1963
Central Florida Comm. C. Ocala, Fla. 32670; junior, 1958
Centralia C. Centralia, Wash. 98531; junior, 1925
Central Methodist C. Fayette, Mo. 65248; 1854
Central Michigan U. Mount Pleasant, Mich. 48858; 1892
Central Missouri State U. Warrensburg, Mo. 64093; 1871
Central New England Colleges, The Worcester, Mass. 01608; 1905
Central Ohio Technical C. Newark, Ohio 43055; junior, 1971
Central Oregon Comm. C. Bend, Oreg. 97701; junior, 1949
Central Pennsylvania Business Sch. Summerdale, Pa. 17093; junior, 1922
Central Piedmont Comm. C. Charlotte, N.C. 28204; junior, 1963
Central State U. Conway, Ark. 72032; 1907
Central State U. Wilberforce, Ohio 45384; 1887
Central State U. Edmond, Okla. 73034; 1890
Central Texas C. Killeen, Tex. 76541; junior, 1967
Central U. of Iowa Pella, Iowa 50219; 1853
Central Virginia Comm. C. Lynchburg, Va. 24502; junior, 1966
Central Washington U. Ellensburg, Wash. 98926; 1891
Central Wesleyan C. Central, S.C. 29630; 1906
Central Wyoming C. Riverton, Wyo. 82501; junior, 1966
Central YMCA Comm. C. Chicago, Ill. 60606; junior, 1960
Centre C. of Kentucky Danville, Ky. 40422; 1819
Cerritos C. Norwalk, Calif. 90650; junior, 1955
Cerro Coso Comm. C. Ridgecrest, Calif. 93555; junior, 1973
Chabot C. Hayward, Calif. 94545; junior, 1961
Chadron State C. Chadron, Nebr. 69337; 1911
Chaffey C. Alta Loma, Calif. 91701; junior, 1883
Chamberlayne Junior C. Boston, Mass. 02116; 1892
Chaminade U. of Honolulu Honolulu, Hawaii 96816; 1955
Champlain C. Burlington, Vt. 05401; junior, 1861
Chapman C. Orange, Calif. 92666; 1861
Charles County Comm. C. La Plata, Md. 20646; junior, 1958
Charles S. Mott Comm. C. Flint, Mich. 48503; junior, 1923
Charleston, C. of Charleston, S.C. 29401; 1770
Charleston, U. of Charleston, W.Va. 25304; 1888
Chatfield C. Saint Martin, Ohio 45170; junior, 1959
Chatham C. Pittsburgh, Pa. 15232; 1869
Chattahoochee Valley Comm. C. Phenix City, Ala. 36867; junior, 1974
Chattanooga State Technical Comm. C. Chattanooga, Tenn. 37406; junior, 1963
Chemeketa Comm. C. Salem, Oreg. 97303; junior, 1954
Chesapeake C. Wye Mills, Md. 21679; junior, 1967
Chesterfield–Marlboro Technical C. Cheraw, S.C. 29520; junior, 1969
Chestnut Hill C. Philadelphia, Pa. 19118; 1871
Cheyney U. of Pennsylvania Cheyney, Pa. 19319; 1837
Chicago, U. of Chicago, Ill. 60637; 1891
Chicago, City Colleges of Chicago, Ill. 60601; junior, 1931
Chicago State U. Chicago, Ill. 60628; 1869
Chipola Junior C. Marianna, Fla. 32446; 1947
Chippewa Valley Technical C. Eau Claire, Wis. 54701; junior, 1912
Chowan C. Murfreesboro, N.C. 27855; junior, 1848
Christian Brothers C. Memphis, Tenn. 38104; 1871
Christopher Newport C. Newport News, Va. 23606; 1960
Cincinnati, U. of Cincinnati, Ohio 45221; 1819
Cincinnati Bible C. Cincinnati, Ohio 45204; 1924
Cincinnati Technical C. Cincinnati, Ohio 45223; junior, 1966
Circleville Bible C. Circleville, Ohio 43113; 1948
Cisco Junior C. Cisco, Tex. 76437; 1940
Citadel, The Charleston, S.C. 29409; 1842
Citrus C. Azusa, Calif. 91702; junior, 1915
City C. New York, N.Y. 10031; 1847
City C. Seattle, Wash. 98104; 1973
City C. of San Francisco San Francisco, Calif. 94112; junior, 1935
City U. of New York New York, N.Y. 10021; 1961
Clackamas Comm. C. Oregon City, Oreg. 97045; junior, 1966
Claflin C. Orangeburg, S.C. 29115; 1869
Claremont McKenna C. Claremont, Calif. 91711; 1946
Clarendon C. Clarendon, Tex. 79226; junior, 1927
Clarion U. of Pennsylvania Clarion, Pa. 16214; 1866
Clark C. Atlanta, Ga. 30314; 1869
Clark C. Vancouver, Wash. 98663; junior, 1933
Clark County Comm. C. Las Vegas, Nev. 89101; junior, 1971
Clarke C. Dubuque, Iowa 52001; 1843
Clarke C. Newton, Miss. 39345; junior, 1908
Clarkson U. Potsdam, N.Y. 13676; 1896
Clark Technical C. Springfield, Ohio 45505; junior, 1966
Clark U. Worcester, Mass. 01610; 1887
Clatsop Comm. C. Astoria, Oreg. 97103; junior, 1958
Clayton Junior C. Morrow, Ga. 30260; 1965
Clearwater Christian C. Clearwater, Fla. 33519; 1966
Cleary C. Ypsilanti, Mich. 48197; 1883
Clemson U. Clemson, S.C. 29631; 1889
Cleveland Inst. of Art Cleveland, Ohio 44106; 1882
Cleveland Inst. of Music Cleveland, Ohio 44106; 1920
Cleveland State Comm. C. Cleveland, Tenn. 37311; junior, 1967
Cleveland State U. Cleveland, Ohio 44115; 1923
Cleveland Technical C. Shelby, N.C. 28150; junior, 1965
Clinton Comm. C. Clinton, Iowa 52732; junior, 1946
Clinton Comm. C. Plattsburgh, N.Y. 12901; junior, 1966
Clinton Junior C. Rock Hill, S.C. 29730; 1894
Cloud County Comm. C. Concordia, Kans. 66901; junior, 1965
Coahoma Junior C. Clarksdale, Miss. 38614; 1926
Coastal Carolina Comm. C. Jacksonville, N.C. 28540; junior, 1964
Coastline Comm. C. Fountain Valley, Calif. 92708; junior, 1976
Cochise C. Douglas, Ariz. 85607; junior, 1962
Coe C. Cedar Rapids, Iowa 52402; 1851
Coffeyville Comm. C. Coffeyville, Kans. 67337; junior, 1923
Cogswell C. San Francisco, Calif. 94110; 1930
Coker C. Hartsville, S.C. 29550; 1894
Colby C. Waterville, Me. 04901; 1813
Colby Comm. C. Colby, Kans. 67701; junior, 1964

Colby–Sawyer C. New London, N.H. 03257; 1837
Coleman C. San Diego, Calif. 92110; 1963
Colgate U. Hamilton, N.Y. 13346; 1819
Colorado, U. of Boulder, Colo. 80302; 1861
Colorado Christian C. Lakewood, Colo. 80226; 1914
Colorado C. Colorado Springs, Colo. 80903; 1874
Colorado Mountain C. Glenwood Springs, Colo. 81601; junior, 1967
Colorado Northwestern Comm. C. Rangely, Colo. 81648; junior, 1962
Colorado Sch. of Mines Golden, Colo. 80401; 1874
Colorado State U. Fort Collins, Colo. 80521; 1870
Colorado Technical C. Colorado Springs, Colo. 80907; 1965
Colorado Women's C. Denver, Colo. 80220; 1909
Columbia Basin C. Pasco, Wash. 99301; junior, 1955
Columbia Bible C. Columbia, S.C. 29230; 1923
Columbia Christian C. Portland, Oreg. 97220; 1956
Columbia C. Columbia, Calif. 95310; junior, 1968
Columbia C. Chicago, Ill. 60605; 1890
Columbia C. Columbia, Mo. 65201; 1851
Columbia C. Columbia, S.C. 29203; 1854
Columbia–Greene Comm. C. Hudson, N.Y. 12534; junior, 1967
Columbia State Comm. C. Columbia, Tenn. 38401; junior, 1966
Columbia Union C. Takoma Park, Md. 20012; 1904
Columbia U. New York, N.Y. 10027; 1754
Columbus C. Columbus, Ga. 31907; 1958
Columbus State Comm. C. Columbus, Ohio 43215; junior, 1963
Compton Comm. C. Compton, Calif. 90221; junior, 1927
Conception Sem. C. Conception, Mo. 64433; 1883
Concord C. Athens, W.Va. 24712; 1872
Concordia C. River Forest, Ill. 60305; 1864
Concordia C. Ann Arbor, Mich. 48105; 1962
Concordia C. Moorhead, Minn. 56560; 1891
Concordia C. St. Paul, Minn. 55104; 1893
Concordia C. Bronxville, N.Y. 10708; 1881
Concordia C. Portland, Oreg. 97211; 1905
Concordia C. Milwaukee, Wis. 53208; 1881
Concordia Lutheran C. Austin, Tex. 78705; junior, 1926
Concordia Sem. St. Louis, Mo. 63105; 1839
Concordia Teachers C. Seward, Nebr. 68434; 1894
Connecticut, U. of Storrs, Conn. 06268; 1881
Connecticut C. New London, Conn. 06320; 1911
Connors State C. Warner, Okla. 74469; junior, 1908
Conservatory of Music of Puerto Rico Santurce, Puerto Rico 00936; 1959
Contra Costa C. San Pablo, Calif. 94806; junior, 1949
Converse C. Spartanburg, S.C. 29301; 1889
Cooke County C. Gainesville, Tex. 76240; junior, 1924
Cooper Union New York, N.Y. 10003; 1859
Copiah–Lincoln Junior C. Wesson, Miss. 39191; 1915
Coppin State C. Baltimore, Md. 21216; 1900
Cornell C. Mount Vernon, Iowa 52314; 1853
Cornell U. Ithaca, N.Y. 14853; 1865
Corning Comm. C. Corning, N.Y. 14830; junior, 1956
Cornish Inst. Seattle, Wash. 98102; 1915
Corpus Christi State U. Corpus Christi, Tex. 78412; 1973
Cosumnes River C. Sacramento, Calif. 95823; junior, 1969
Cottey C. Nevada, Mo. 64772; junior, 1884
County C. of Morris Randolph, N.J. 07801; junior, 1965
Covenant C. Lookout Mountain, Tenn. 37350; 1955
Cowley County Comm. C. Arkansas City, Kans. 67005; junior, 1922
Crafton Hills C. Yucaipa, Calif. 92399; junior, 1972
Cranbrook Acad. of Art Bloomfield Hills, Mich. 48013; 1927
Craven Comm. C. New Bern, N.C. 28560; junior, 1965
Creighton U. Omaha, Nebr. 68178; 1878
Crosier Sem. Onamia, Minn. 56359; junior, 1922
Crowder C. Neosho, Mo. 64850; junior, 1963
Crowley's Ridge C. Paragould, Ark. 72450; junior, 1964
Cuesta C. San Luis Obispo, Calif. 93401; junior, 1963
Cullman C. Cullman, Ala. 35055; junior, 1940
Culver–Stockton C. Canton, Mo. 63435; 1853
Cumberland C. Williamsburg, Ky. 40769; 1888
Cumberland C. of Tennessee Lebanon, Tenn. 37087; junior, 1842
Cumberland County C. Vineland, N.J. 08360; junior, 1964
Curry C. Milton, Mass. 02186; 1879
Curtis Inst. of Music Philadelphia, Pa. 19103; 1924
Cuyahoga Comm. C. Cleveland, Ohio 44115; junior, 1963
Cypress C. Cypress, Calif. 90630; junior, 1966
Dabney S. Lancaster Comm. C. Clifton Forge, Va. 24422; junior, 1964
Daemen C. Amherst, N.Y. 14226; 1947
Dakota State C. Madison, S.Dak. 57042; 1881
Dakota Wesleyan U. Mitchell, S.Dak. 57301; 1883
Dallas, U. of Irving, Tex. 75060; 1956
Dallas Baptist C. Dallas, Tex. 75211; 1891
Dallas Christian C. Dallas, Tex. 75234; 1950
Dalton Junior C. Dalton, Ga. 30720; 1966
Dana C. Blair, Nebr. 68008; 1884
Daniel Webster C. Nashua, N.H. 03060; 1965
Danville Area Comm. C. Danville, Ill. 61832; junior, 1946
Danville Comm. C. Danville, Va. 24541; junior, 1936
Dartmouth C. Hanover, N.H. 03755; 1769
Davenport C. of Business Grand Rapids, Mich. 49502; junior, 1910
David Lipscomb C. Nashville, Tenn. 37203; 1891
Davidson C. Davidson, N.C. 28036; 1837
Davidson County Comm. C. Lexington, N.C. 27292; junior, 1961
Davis and Elkins C. Elkins, W.Va. 26241; 1903
Davis Junior C. Toledo, Ohio 43624; 1858
Dawson Comm. C. Glendive, Mont. 59330; junior, 1940
Dayton, U. of Dayton, Ohio 45469; 1850
Daytona Beach Comm. C. Daytona Beach, Fla. 32015; junior, 1958
Dean Junior C. Franklin, Mass. 02038; 1865
De Anza C. Cupertino, Calif. 95014; junior, 1967
Deep Springs C. Deep Springs, Calif. 89010; junior, 1917
Defiance C. Defiance, Ohio 43512; 1850
DeKalb Comm. C. Clarkston, Ga. 30021; junior, 1963
Delaware, U. of Newark, Del. 19711; 1743

Delaware County Comm. C. Media, Pa. 19063; junior, 1967
Delaware State C. Dover, Del. 19901; 1891
Delaware Technical and Comm. C. Dover, Del. 19901; junior, 1967
Delaware Valley C. of Science and Agric. Doylestown, Pa. 18901; 1896
Delgado Comm. C. New Orleans, La. 70119; junior, 1921
Del Mar C. Corpus Christi, Tex. 78404; junior, 1935
De Lourdes C. Des Plaines, Ill. 60016; 1951
Delta C. University Center, Mich. 48710; junior, 1961
Delta State U. Cleveland, Miss. 38732; 1924
Denison U. Granville, Ohio 43023; 1831
Denmark Technical C. Denmark, S.C. 29042; junior, 1948
Denver, U. of Denver, Colo. 80210; 1864
Denver Auraria Comm. C. Denver, Colo. 80204; junior, 1970
De Paul U. Chicago, Ill. 60604; 1898
DePauw U. Greencastle, Ind. 46135; 1837
Desert, C. of the Palm Desert, Calif. 92260; junior, 1961
Des Moines Area Comm. C. Ankeny, Iowa 50021; junior, 1927
Detroit, U. of Detroit, Mich. 48221; 1877
Detroit C. of Business Administration Dearborn, Mich. 48126; 1936
DeVry Inst. of Tech. Phoenix, Ariz. 85016; 1967
DeVry Inst. of Tech. Atlanta, Ga. 30341; 1969
DeVry Inst. of Tech. Chicago, Ill. 60618; 1931
DeVry Inst. of Tech. Columbus, Ohio 43209; 1952
DeVry Inst. of Tech. Irving, Tex. 75062; 1969
Diablo Valley C. Pleasant Hill, Calif. 94523; junior, 1949
Dickinson C. Carlisle, Pa. 17013; 1773
Dickinson State C. Dickinson, N.Dak. 58601; 1918
Dillard U. New Orleans, La. 70122; 1869
District of Columbia, U. of the Washington, D.C. 20009; 1851
Divine Word C. Epworth, Iowa 52045; 1913
Dixie C. St. George, Utah 84770; junior, 1911
Doane C. Crete, Nebr. 68333; 1872
Dodge City Comm. Junior C. Dodge City, Kans. 67801; 1935
Dominican C. Orangeburg, N.Y. 10962; 1952
Dominican C. of San Rafael San Rafael, Calif. 94901; 1890
Don Bosco C. Newton, N.J. 07860; 1929
Don Bosco Technical Inst. Rosemead, Calif. 91790; junior, 1955
Donnelly C. Kansas City, Kans. 66102; junior, 1949
Dordt C. Sioux Center, Iowa 51250; 1955
Dowling C. Oakdale, N.Y. 11769; 1959
D–Q U. Davis, Calif. 95616; junior, 1971
Drake U. Des Moines, Iowa 50311; 1881
Drew U. Madison, N.J. 07940; 1866
Drexel U. Philadelphia, Pa. 19104; 1891
Dr. Martin Luther C. New Ulm, Minn. 56073; 1884
Drury C. Springfield, Mo. 65802; 1873
Dubuque, U. of Dubuque, Iowa 52001; 1852
Duke U. Durham, N.C. 27706; 1838
Dundalk Comm. C. Baltimore, Md. 21222; junior, 1970
DuPage, C. of Glen Ellyn, Ill. 60137; junior, 1966
Duquesne U. Pittsburgh, Pa. 15219; 1878
Durham Technical Inst. Durham, N.C. 27703; junior, 1958
Dutchess Comm. C. Poughkeepsie, N.Y. 12601; junior, 1957
Dyersburg State Comm. C. Dyersburg, Tenn. 38024; junior, 1967
Dyke C. Cleveland, Ohio 44114; 1848
D'Youville C. Buffalo, N.Y. 14201; 1909
Earlham C. Richmond, Ind. 47374; 1847
East Arkansas Comm. C. Forrest City, Ark. 72335; junior, 1973
East Carolina U. Greenville, N.C. 27834; 1907
East Central C. Union, Mo. 63084; junior, 1968
East Central Junior C. Decatur, Miss. 39327; 1914
East Central Oklahoma State U. Ada, Okla. 74820; 1909
Eastern Arizona C. Thatcher, Ariz. 85552; junior, 1891
Eastern C. St. Davids, Pa. 19087; 1952
Eastern Connecticut State U. Willimantic, Conn. 06226; 1889
Eastern Illinois U. Charleston, Ill. 61920; 1895
Eastern Kentucky U. Richmond, Ky. 40475; 1906
Eastern Mennonite C. Harrisonburg, Va. 22801; 1917
Eastern Michigan U. Ypsilanti, Mich. 48197; 1849
Eastern Montana C. Billings, Mont. 59101; 1927
Eastern Nazarene C. Wollaston, Mass. 02170; 1900
Eastern New Mexico U. Portales, N.Mex. 88130; 1934
Eastern Oklahoma State C. Wilburton, Okla. 74578; junior, 1909
Eastern Oregon State C. La Grande, Oreg. 97850; 1929
Eastern Shore Comm. C. Melfa, Va. 23410; junior, 1971
Eastern Utah, C. of Price, Utah 84501; junior, 1937
Eastern Washington U. Cheney, Wash. 99004; 1890
Eastern Wyoming C. Torrington, Wyo. 82240; junior, 1948
Eastfield C. Mesquite, Tex. 75150; junior, 1970
East Georgia C. Swainsboro, Ga. 30401; 1970
East Los Angeles C. Monterey Park, Calif. 91754; junior, 1945
East Mississippi Junior C. Scooba, Miss. 39358; 1927
East Stroudsburg U. of Pennsylvania East Stroudsburg, Pa. 18301; 1893
East Tennessee State U. Johnson City, Tenn. 37601; 1909
East Texas Baptist C. Marshall, Tex. 75670; 1914
East Texas State U. Commerce, Tex. 75428; 1889
East Texas State U. at Texarkana Texarkana, Tex. 75501; 1971
East–West U. Chicago, Ill. 60605; junior, 1978
Eckerd C. St. Petersburg, Fla. 33733; 1960
Edgecombe Technical C. Tarboro, N.C. 27886; junior, 1967
Edgewood C. Madison, Wis. 53711; 1927
Edinboro U. of Pennsylvania Edinboro, Pa. 16444; 1859
Edison Comm. C. Fort Myers, Fla. 33901; junior, 1962
Edison State Comm. C. Piqua, Ohio 45356; junior, 1973
Edmonds Comm. C. Lynnwood, Wash. 98036; junior, 1967
Edward Waters C. Jacksonville, Fla. 32209; 1866
El Camino C. Torrance, Calif. 90506; junior, 1946
El Centro C. Dallas, Tex. 75202; junior, 1965
Elgin Comm. C. Elgin, Ill. 60120; junior, 1949
Elizabeth City State U. Elizabeth City, N.C. 27909; 1891
Elizabeth Seton C. Yonkers, N.Y. 10701; junior, 1961
Elizabethtown C. Elizabethtown, Pa. 17022; 1899
Elizabethtown Comm. C. Elizabethtown, Ky. 42701; junior, 1963

Ellsworth Comm. C. Iowa Falls, Iowa 50126; junior, 1890
Elmhurst C. Elmhurst, Ill. 60126; 1871
Elmira C. Elmira, N.Y. 14901; 1853
Elon C. Elon College, N.C. 27244; 1889
El Paso County Comm. C. El Paso, Tex. 79904; junior, 1969
El Reno Junior C. El Reno, Okla. 73036; 1938
Embry–Riddle Aeronautical U. Bunnell, Fla. 32010; 1926
Emerson C. Boston, Mass. 02116; 1880
Emmanuel C. Franklin Springs, Ga. 30639; junior, 1919
Emmanuel C. Boston, Mass. 02115; 1919
Emmaus Bible Sch. Oak Park, Ill. 60301; 1941
Emory and Henry C. Emory, Va. 24327; 1838
Emory U. Atlanta, Ga. 30322; 1836
Emporia State U. Emporia, Kans. 66801; 1863
Endicott C. Beverly, Mass. 01915; junior, 1939
Enterprise State Junior C. Enterprise, Ala. 36330; 1965
Erie Comm. C. Williamsville, N.Y. 14221; junior, 1946
Erskine C. and Sem. Due West, S.C. 29639; 1839
Essex Agricultural and Technical Inst. Hathorne, Mass. 01937; junior, 1912
Essex Comm. C. Baltimore, Md. 21237; junior, 1957
Essex County C. Newark, N.J. 07102; junior, 1968
Eureka C. Eureka, Ill. 61530; 1855
Evangel C. Springfield, Mo. 65802; 1955
Evansville, U. of Evansville, Ind. 47702; 1854
Everett Comm. C. Everett, Wash. 98201; junior, 1941
Evergreen State C., The Olympia, Wash. 98505; 1967
Evergreen Valley C. San Jose, Calif. 95121; junior, 1975
Fairfield U. Fairfield, Conn. 06430; 1942
Fairleigh Dickinson U. Rutherford, N.J. 07070; 1942
Fairmont State C. Fairmont, W.Va. 26554; 1867
Faith Baptist Bible C. Ankeny, Iowa 50021; 1924
Fashion Inst. of Tech. New York, N.Y. 10001; junior, 1944
Faulkner State Junior C. Bay Minette, Ala. 36507; 1965
Fayetteville State U. Fayetteville, N.C. 28301; 1867
Fayetteville Technical Inst. Fayetteville, N.C. 28303; junior, 1961
Feather River C. Quincy, Calif. 95971; junior, 1968
Federal City C. Washington, D.C. 20001; 1966
Felician C. Lodi, N.J. 07644; 1942
Felician C., The Chicago, Ill. 60645; junior, 1926
Fergus Falls Comm. C. Fergus Falls, Minn. 56537; junior, 1960
Ferris State U. Big Rapids, Mich. 49307; 1884
Ferrum C. Ferrum, Va. 24088; 1914
Findlay C. Findlay, Ohio 45840; 1882
Finger Lakes, Comm. C. of the Canandaigua, N.Y. 14424; junior, 1965
Fisher Junior C. Boston, Mass. 02116; 1903
Fisk U. Nashville, Tenn. 37203; 1866
Fitchburg State C. Fitchburg, Mass. 01420; 1894
Five Towns C. Merrick, N.Y. 11566; junior, 1972
Flagler C. St. Augustine, Fla. 32084; 1963
Flathead Valley Comm. C. Kalispell, Mont. 59901; junior, 1967
Florence–Darlington Technical C. Florence, S.C. 29501; junior, 1962
Florida, U. of Gainesville, Fla. 32601; 1853
Florida A. & M. U. Tallahassee, Fla. 32307; 1887
Florida Atlantic U. Boca Raton, Fla. 33432; 1964
Florida C. Temple Terrace, Fla. 33617; junior, 1944
Florida Inst. of Tech. Melbourne, Fla. 32901; 1958
Florida International U. Miami, Fla. 33199; 1965
Florida Junior C. at Jacksonville 32205; 1963
Florida Keys Comm. C. Key West, Fla. 33040; junior, 1965
Florida Memorial C. Miami, Fla. 33054; 1879
Florida Southern C. Lakeland, Fla. 33802; 1885
Florida State U. Tallahassee, Fla. 32306; 1857
Floyd Junior C. Rome, Ga. 30161; 1968
Fontbonne C. St. Louis, Mo. 63105; 1923
Foothill C. Los Altos Hills, Calif. 94022; junior, 1957
Fordham U. Bronx, N.Y. 10458; 1841
Forsyth Technical Inst. Winston-Salem, N.C. 27103; junior, 1960
Fort Hays State U. Hays, Kans. 67601; 1902
Fort Lauderdale C. of Business and Finance Fort Lauderdale, Fla. 33301; 1940
Fort Lewis C. Durango, Colo. 81301; 1911
Fort Scott Comm. C. Fort Scott, Kans. 66701; junior, 1919
Fort Valley State C. Fort Valley, Ga. 31030; 1895
Fort Wayne Bible C. Fort Wayne, Ind. 46807; 1904
Fort Wright C. of the Holy Names Spokane, Wash. 99204; 1907
Framingham State C. Framingham, Mass. 01701; 1839
Francis Marion C. Florence, S.C. 29501; 1970
Franklin and Marshall C. Lancaster, Pa. 17604; 1787
Franklin C. of Indiana Franklin, Ind. 46131; 1834
Franklin Inst. of Boston Boston, Mass. 02116; junior, 1908
Franklin Pierce C. Rindge, N.H. 03461; 1962
Franklin U. Columbus, Ohio 43215; 1902
Frank Phillips C. Borger, Tex. 79007; junior, 1946
Frederick Comm. C. Frederick, Md. 21701; junior, 1957
Freed–Hardeman C. Henderson, Tenn. 38340; 1869
Freeman Junior C. Freeman, S.Dak. 57029; 1900
Free Will Baptist Bible C. Nashville, Tenn. 37205; 1942
Fresno City C. Fresno, Calif. 93741; junior, 1910
Fresno Pacific C. Fresno, Calif. 93702; 1944
Friends Bible C. Haviland, Kans. 67059; 1917
Friends U. Wichita, Kans. 67213; 1898
Friends World C. Huntington, N.Y. 11743; 1965
Front Range Comm. C. Westminster, Colo. 80030; junior, 1968
Frostburg State C. Frostburg, Md. 21532; 1898
Fullerton C. Fullerton, Calif. 92634; junior, 1913
Fulton–Montgomery Comm. C. Johnstown, N.Y. 12095; junior, 1963
Furman U. Greenville, S.C. 29613; 1825
Gadsden State Comm. C. Gadsden, Ala. 35999; junior, 1965
Gainesville Junior C. Gainesville, Ga. 30501; 1965
Gallaudet U. Washington, D.C. 20002; 1856
Galveston C. Galveston, Tex. 77550; junior, 1967
Gannon U. Erie, Pa. 16501; 1933
Garden City Comm. Junior C. Garden City, Kans. 67846; 1919

Gardner–Webb C. Boiling Springs, N.C. 28017; 1905
Garrett Comm. C. McHenry, Md. 21541; junior, 1971
Gaston C. Dallas, N.C. 28034; junior, 1963
Gateway Comm. C. Phoenix, Ariz. 85034; junior, 1968
Gateway Technical Inst. Kenosha, Wis. 53140; junior, 1912
Gavilan C. Gilroy, Calif. 95020; junior, 1919
General Motors Inst. Flint, Mich. 48502; 1919
Genesee Comm. C. Batavia, N.Y. 14020; junior, 1966
Geneva C. Beaver Falls, Pa. 15010; 1848
George Corley Wallace State Comm. C. at Selma Ala. 36701; junior, 1963
George C. Wallace State Comm. C. at Dothan Ala. 36301; junior, 1949
George Fox C. Newberg, Oreg. 97132; 1891
George Mason U. Fairfax, Va. 22030; 1960
Georgetown C. Georgetown, Ky. 40324; 1787
Georgetown U. Washington, D.C. 20057; 1789
George Washington U. Washington, D.C. 20052; 1821
Georgia, U. of Athens, Ga. 30601; 1785
Georgia C. at Milledgeville Milledgeville, Ga. 31061; 1889
Georgia Inst. of Tech. Atlanta, Ga. 30332; 1885
Georgia Military C. Milledgeville, Ga. 31061; junior, 1879
Georgian Court C. Lakewood, N.J. 08701; 1908
Georgia Southern C. Statesboro, Ga. 30458; 1908
Georgia Southwestern C. Americus, Ga. 31709; 1906
Georgia State U. Atlanta, Ga. 30303; 1913
Germanna Comm. C. Locust Grove, Va. 22508; junior, 1969
Gettysburg C. Gettysburg, Pa. 17325; 1832
Glassboro State C. Glassboro, N.J. 08028; 1923
Glendale Comm. C. Glendale, Ariz. 85302; junior, 1965
Glendale Comm. C. Glendale, Calif. 91208; junior, 1927
Glen Oaks Comm. C. Centreville, Mich. 49032; junior, 1965
Glenville State C. Glenville, W.Va. 26351; 1872
Gloucester County C. Sewell, N.J. 08080; junior, 1968
Goddard C. Plainfield, Vt. 05667; 1938
Gogebic Comm. C. Ironwood, Mich. 49938; junior, 1932
Golden Gate U. San Francisco, Calif. 94105; 1901
Golden West C. Huntington Beach, Calif. 92647; junior, 1966
Goldey Beacom C. Wilmington, Del. 19899; 1886
Gonzaga U. Spokane, Wash. 99202; 1887
Gordon C. Wenham, Mass. 01984; 1889
Gordon Junior C. Barnesville, Ga. 30204; 1852
Goshen C. Goshen, Ind. 46526; 1894
Goucher C. Towson, Md. 21204; 1885
Governors State U. Park Forest South, Ill. 60466; 1969
Grace Bible C. Grand Rapids, Mich. 49509; 1946
Grace C. Winona Lake, Ind. 46590; 1948
Grace C. of the Bible Omaha, Nebr. 68108; 1943
Graceland C. Lamoni, Iowa 50140; 1895
Grambling State U. Grambling, La. 71245; 1929
Grand Canyon C. Phoenix, Ariz. 85017; 1949
Grand Rapids Baptist C. Grand Rapids, Mich. 49505; 1941
Grand Rapids Junior C. Grand Rapids, Mich. 49502; 1914
Grand Valley State C. Allendale, Mich. 49401; 1963
Grand View C. Des Moines, Iowa 50316; 1896
Gratz C. Philadelphia, Pa. 19141; 1895
Grays Harbor C. Aberdeen, Wash. 98520; junior, 1930
Grayson County C. Denison, Tex. 75020; junior, 1963
Greater Hartford Comm. C. Hartford, Conn. 06106; junior, 1967
Great Falls, C. of Great Falls, Mont. 59401; 1932
Great Lakes Bible C. Lansing, Mich. 48901; 1949
Greenfield Comm. C. Greenfield, Mass. 01301; junior, 1962
Green Mountain C. Poultney, Vt. 05764; 1834
Green River Comm. C. Auburn, Wash. 98002; junior, 1965
Greensboro C. Greensboro, N.C. 27402; 1838
Greenville C. Greenville, Ill. 62246; 1855
Greenville Technical C. Greenville, S.C. 29606; junior, 1962
Grinnell C. Grinnell, Iowa 50112; 1846
Grossmont C. El Cajon, Calif. 92020; junior, 1961
Grove City C. Grove City, Pa. 16127; 1876
Guam, U. of Mangilao, Guam 96913; 1952
Guilford C. Greensboro, N.C. 27410; 1834
Guilford Technical Inst. Jamestown, N.C. 27282; junior, 1958
Gulf Coast Bible C. Houston, Tex. 77008; 1953
Gulf Coast Comm. C. Panama City, Fla. 32401; junior, 1957
Gustavus Adolphus C. St. Peter, Minn. 56082; 1862
Gwynedd–Mercy C. Gwynedd Valley, Pa. 19437; 1948
Hagerstown Junior C. Hagerstown, Md. 21740; 1946
Halifax Comm. C. Weldon, N.C. 27890; junior, 1967
Hamilton C. Clinton, N.Y. 13323; 1793
Hamline U. St. Paul, Minn. 55104; 1854
Hampden–Sydney C. Hampden-Sydney, Va. 23943; 1776
Hampshire C. Amherst, Mass. 01002; 1970
Hampton U. Hampton, Va. 23668; 1868
Hannibal–LaGrange C. Hannibal, Mo. 63401; junior, 1858
Hanover C. Hanover, Ind. 47243; 1827
Harcum Junior C. Bryn Mawr, Pa. 19010; 1915
Harding U. Searcy, Ark. 72143; 1924
Hardin–Simmons U. Abilene, Tex. 79601; 1891
Harford Comm. C. Bel Air, Md. 21014; junior, 1957
Harrisburg Area Comm. C. Harrisburg, Pa. 17110; junior, 1964
Harris–Stowe State C. St. Louis, Mo. 63103; 1857
Harry M. Ayers State Technical C. Anniston, Ala. 36201; junior, 1966
Hartford, U. of West Hartford, Conn. 06117; 1877
Hartford C. for Women Hartford, Conn. 06105; junior, 1933
Hartford State Technical C. Hartford, Conn. 06106; junior, 1946
Hartnell C. Salinas, Calif. 93901; junior, 1920
Hartwick C. Oneonta, N.Y. 13820; 1928
Harvard U. Cambridge, Mass. 02138; 1636
Harvey Mudd C. Claremont, Calif. 91711; 1955
Hastings C. Hastings, Nebr. 68901; 1882
Haverford C. Haverford, Pa. 19041; 1833
Hawaii at Hilo, U. of Hilo, Hawaii 96720; 1947
Hawaii at Manoa, U. of Honolulu, Hawaii 96822; 1907
Hawaii Loa C. Kaneohe, Hawaii 96744; 1963

Hawaii Pacific C. Honolulu, Hawaii 96813; 1965
Hawkeye Inst. of Tech. Waterloo, Iowa 50704; junior, 1966
Hawthorne C. Antrim, N.H. 03440; 1962
Haywood Technical C. Clyde, N.C. 28721; junior, 1965
Hazard Comm. C. Hazard, Ky. 41701; junior, 1968
Heald Inst. of Tech. San Francisco, Calif. 94109; 1863
Hebrew C. Brookline, Mass. 02146; 1918
Hebrew Theol. C. Skokie, Ill. 60076; 1922
Hebrew Union C. Cincinnati, Ohio 45220; 1875
Heidelberg C. Tiffin, Ohio 44883; 1850
Hellenic C. Brookline, Mass. 02146; 1937
Henderson Comm. C. Henderson, Ky. 42420; junior, 1960
Henderson County Junior C. Athens, Tex. 75751; 1946
Henderson State U. Arkadelphia, Ark. 71923; 1929
Hendrix C. Conway, Ark. 72032; 1876
Henry Ford Comm. C. Dearborn, Mich. 48128; junior, 1938
Herbert H. Lehman C. Bronx, N.Y. 10468; 1931
Herkimer County Comm. C. Herkimer, N.Y. 13357; junior, 1966
Herron Sch. of Art Indianapolis, Ind. 46202; 1878
Hesston C. Hesston, Kans. 67062; junior, 1909
Hibbing Comm. C. Hibbing, Minn. 55746; junior, 1916
Highland Comm. C. Freeport, Ill. 61032; junior, 1961
Highland Comm. C. Highland, Kans. 66035; junior, 1858
Highland Park Comm. C. Highland Park, Mich. 48203; junior, 1918
Highline Comm. C. Midway, Wash. 98031; junior, 1961
High Point C. High Point, N.C. 27262; 1924
Hilbert C. Hamburg, N.Y. 14075; junior, 1928
Hill Junior C. Hillsboro, Tex. 76645; 1962
Hillsborough Comm. C. Tampa, Fla. 33622; junior, 1968
Hillsdale C. Hillsdale, Mich. 49242; 1844
Hinds Junior C. Raymond, Miss. 39154; 1917
Hiram C. Hiram, Ohio 44234; 1850
Hiwassee C. Madisonville, Tenn. 37354; junior, 1849
Hobart and William Smith Colleges Geneva, N.Y. 14456; 1822
Hocking Technical C. Nelsonville, Ohio 45764; junior, 1968
Hofstra U. Hempstead, N.Y. 11550; 1935
Hollins C. Hollins College, Va. 24020; 1842
Holmes Junior C. Goodman, Miss. 39079; 1911
Holy Apostles C. Cromwell, Conn. 06416; 1956
Holy Cross, C. of the Worcester, Mass. 01610; 1843
Holy Cross Junior C. Notre Dame, Ind. 46556; 1966
Holy Family C. Mission San Jose, Calif. 94538; 1946
Holy Family C. Philadelphia, Pa. 19114; 1954
Holy Names C. Oakland, Calif. 94619; 1868
Holyoke Comm. C. Holyoke, Mass. 01040; junior, 1946
Holy Redeemer C. Waterford, Wis. 53185; 1965
Hood C. Frederick, Md. 21701; 1893
Hope C. Holland, Mich. 49423; 1851
Hopkinsville Comm. C. Hopkinsville, Ky. 42240; junior, 1965
Horry–Georgetown Technical C. Conway, S.C. 29526; junior, 1965
Hostos Comm. C. Bronx, N.Y. 10451; junior, 1970
Houghton C. Houghton, N.Y. 14744; 1883
Housatonic Regional Comm. C. Bridgeport, Conn. 06608; junior, 1966
Houston, U. of Houston, Tex. 77004; 1927
Houston Baptist U. Houston, Tex. 77074; 1960
Howard Comm. C. Columbia, Md. 21044; junior, 1966
Howard C. at Big Spring Tex. 79720; junior, 1945
Howard Payne U. Brownwood, Tex. 76801; 1889
Howard U. Washington, D.C. 20059; 1867
Hudson Valley Comm. C. Troy, N.Y. 12180; junior, 1953
Humboldt State U. Arcata, Calif. 95521; 1913
Humphreys C. Stockton, Calif. 95207; junior, 1896
Hunter C. New York, N.Y. 10021; 1870
Huntingdon C. Montgomery, Ala. 36106; 1854
Huntington C. Huntington, Ind. 46750; 1897
Huron C. Huron, S.Dak. 57350; 1883
Husson C. Bangor, Me. 04401; 1898
Huston–Tillotson C. Austin, Tex. 78702; 1877
Hutchinson Comm. C. Hutchinson, Kans. 67501; junior, 1928
Idaho, C. of Caldwell, Idaho 83605; 1891
Idaho, U. of Moscow, Idaho 83843; 1889
Idaho State U. Pocatello, Idaho 83201; 1901
Illinois, U. of Urbana, Ill. 61801; 1867
Illinois Benedictine C. Lisle, Ill. 60532; 1887
Illinois Central C. East Peoria, Ill. 61611; junior, 1966
Illinois C. Jacksonville, Ill. 62650; 1829
Illinois C. of Optometry Chicago, Ill. 60616; 1872
Illinois Inst. of Tech. Chicago, Ill. 60616; 1892
Illinois State U. Normal, Ill. 61761; 1857
Illinois Valley Comm. C. Oglesby, Ill. 61348; junior, 1924
Illinois Wesleyan U. Bloomington, Ill. 61701; 1850
Immaculata C. Immaculata, Pa. 19345; 1920
Immaculate Conception Sem. Mahwah, N.J. 07430; 1856
Immaculate Conception Sem. Troy, N.Y. 12180; 1959
Imperial Valley C. Imperial, Calif. 92251; junior, 1922
Incarnate Word C. San Antonio, Tex. 78209; 1881
Independence Comm. C. Independence, Kans. 67301; junior, 1925
Indiana Central U. Indianapolis, Ind. 46227; 1902
Indiana Inst. of Tech. Fort Wayne, Ind. 46803; 1930
Indiana State U. Terre Haute, Ind. 47809; 1865
Indiana U. at Bloomington Ind. 47401; 1820
Indiana U. at Kokomo Ind. 46902; 1945
Indiana U. at South Bend Ind. 46615; 1940
Indiana U. East Richmond, Ind. 47374; junior, 1946
Indiana U. Northwest Gary, Ind. 46408; 1921
Indiana U. of Pennsylvania Indiana, Pa. 15701; 1875
Indiana U.–Purdue U. at Fort Wayne Ind. 46805; 1917
Indiana U.–Purdue U. at Indianapolis Ind. 46202; 1916
Indiana U. Southeast New Albany, Ind. 47150; 1941
Indian Hills Comm. C. Ottumwa, Iowa 52501; junior, 1930
Indian River Comm. C. Fort Pierce, Fla. 33450; junior, 1960
Indian Valley C. Novato, Calif. 94947; junior, 1971
Insurance, C. of New York, N.Y. 10038; 1962

Inter American U. of Puerto Rico San Germán, Puerto Rico 00753; 1912
Interboro Inst. New York, N.Y. 10003; junior, 1888
International Inst. of the Americas of World U. Hato Rey, Puerto Rico 00917; 1965
International Training, Sch, for Brattleboro, Vt. 05301; 1964
Inver Hills Comm. C. Inver Grove Heights, Minn. 55075; junior, 1969
Iona C. New Rochelle, N.Y. 10801; 1940
Iowa, U. of Iowa City, Iowa 52242; 1847
Iowa Central Comm. C. Fort Dodge, Iowa 50501; junior, 1921
Iowa Lakes Comm. C. Estherville, Iowa 51334; junior, 1924
Iowa State U. of Science and Tech. Ames, Iowa 50010; 1858
Iowa Wesleyan C. Mount Pleasant, Iowa 52641; 1842
Iowa Western Comm. C. Council Bluffs, Iowa 51501; junior, 1923
Isothermal Comm. C. Spindale, N.C. 28160; junior, 1966
Itasca Comm. C. Grand Rapids, Minn. 55744; junior, 1922
Itawamba Junior C. Fulton, Miss. 38843; 1948
Ithaca C. Ithaca, N.Y. 14850; 1892
Jackson C. Honolulu, Hawaii 96822; 1949
Jackson Comm. C. Jackson, Mich. 49201; junior, 1928
Jackson State Comm. C. Jackson, Tenn. 38301; junior, 1965
Jackson State U. Jackson, Miss. 39217; 1877
Jacksonville C. Jacksonville, Tex. 75766; junior, 1899
Jacksonville State U. Jacksonville, Ala. 36265; 1883
Jacksonville U. Jacksonville, Fla. 32211; 1934
James Madison U. Harrisonburg, Va. 22801; 1908
James Sprunt Technical C. Kenansville, N.C. 28349; junior, 1964
Jamestown C. Jamestown, N.Dak. 58401; 1884
Jamestown Comm. C. Jamestown, N.Y. 14701; junior, 1934
Jarvis Christian C. Hawkins, Tex. 75765; 1912
Jefferson C. Hillsboro, Mo. 63050; junior, 1963
Jefferson Comm. C. Louisville, Ky. 40202; junior, 1967
Jefferson Comm. C. Watertown, N.Y. 13601; junior, 1963
Jefferson Davis State Junior C. Brewton, Ala. 36426; junior, 1963
Jefferson State Junior C. Birmingham, Ala. 35215; 1963
Jefferson Technical C. Steubenville, Ohio 43952; junior, 1966
Jersey City State C. Jersey City, N.J. 07305; 1927
Jewish Theol. Sem. of America New York, N.Y. 10027; 1886
J. F. Drake State Technical C. Huntsville, Ala. 35881; junior, 1961
John A. Gupton C. Nashville, Tenn. 37203; junior, 1946
John A. Logan C. Carterville, Ill. 62918; junior, 1967
John Brown U. Siloam Springs, Ark. 72761; 1919
John Carroll U. Cleveland, Ohio 44118; 1886
John C. Calhoun State Comm. C. Decatur, Ala. 35601; junior, 1965
John F. Kennedy U. Orinda, Calif. 94563; 1964
John Jay C. of Criminal Justice New York, N.Y. 10003; 1965
Johns Hopkins U. Baltimore, Md. 21218; 1876
Johnson and Wales C. Providence, R.I. 02903; 1914
Johnson Bible C. Knoxville, Tenn. 37920; 1893
Johnson C. Smith U. Charlotte, N.C. 28216; 1867
Johnson County Comm. C. Overland Park, Kans. 66210; junior, 1967
Johnson State C. Johnson, Vt. 05656; 1867
Johnston Technical C. Smithfield, N.C. 27577; junior, 1969
Johnstown C. Johnstown, Pa. 15902; junior, 1927
John Tyler Comm. C. Chester, Va. 23831; junior, 1967
Joliet Junior C. Joliet, Ill. 60436; 1902
Jones C. Jacksonville, Fla. 33211; 1918
Jones County Junior C. Ellisville, Miss. 39437; 1911
Jordan C. Cedar Springs, Mich. 49319; 1967
J. Sargeant Reynolds Comm. C. Richmond, Va. 23230; junior, 1972
Judaism, U. of Los Angeles, Calif. 90028; 1947
Judson Baptist C. Portland, Oreg. 97220; 1956
Judson C. Marion, Ala. 36756; 1838
Judson C. Elgin, Ill. 60120; 1913
Juilliard Sch., The New York, N.Y. 10023; 1905
Juniata C. Huntingdon, Pa. 16652; 1876
Kalamazoo C. Kalamazoo, Mich. 49001; 1833
Kalamazoo Valley Comm. C. Kalamazoo, Mich, 49001; junior, 1966
Kankakee Comm. C. Kankakee, Ill. 60901; junior, 1966
Kansas, U. of Lawrence, Kans. 66044; 1863
Kansas City Art Inst. Kansas City, Mo. 64111; 1885
Kansas City Kansas Comm. C. Kansas City, Kans. 66101; junior, 1923
Kansas Newman C. Wichita, Kans. 67213; 1933
Kansas State U. of Agric. and Applied Science Manhattan, Kans. 66502; 1863
Kansas Wesleyan U. Salina, Kans. 67401; 1886
Kaskaskia C. Centralia, Ill. 62801; junior, 1940
Kean C. of New Jersey Union, N.J. 07083; 1855
Kearney State C. Kearney, Nebr. 68847; 1905
Keene State C. Keene, N.H. 03431; 1909
Kellogg Comm. C. Battle Creek, Mich. 49016; junior, 1956
Kemper Military Sch. and C. Boonville, Mo. 65233; junior, 1844
Kendall C. Evanston, Ill. 60204; 1934
Kennesaw C. Marietta, Ga. 30061; 1966
Kent State U. Kent, Ohio 44242; 1910
Kentucky, U. of Lexington, Ky. 40506; 1866
Kentucky Christian C. Grayson, Ky. 41143; 1919
Kentucky State U. Frankfort, Ky. 40601; 1886
Kentucky Wesleyan C. Owensboro, Ky. 42301; 1866
Kenyon C. Gambier, Ohio 43022; 1824
Kettering C. of Medical Arts Kettering, Ohio 45429; junior, 1967
Keuka C. Keuka Park, N.Y. 14478; 1890
Keystone Junior C. La Plume, Pa. 18440; 1868
Kilgore C. Kilgore, Tex. 75662; junior, 1935
King C. Bristol, Tenn. 37620; 1867
Kingsborough Comm. C. Brooklyn, N.Y. 11235; junior, 1963
King's C. Wilkes-Barre, Pa. 18711; 1946
King's C., The Briarcliff Manor, N.Y. 10510; 1938
King's River Comm. C. Reedley, Calif. 93654; junior, 1926
Kirkwood Comm. C. Cedar Rapids, Iowa 52406; junior, 1966
Kirtland Comm. C. Roscommon, Mich. 48653; junior, 1966
Kishwaukee C. Malta, Ill. 60150; junior, 1967
Knox C. Galesburg, Ill. 61401; 1837
Knoxville C. Knoxville, Tenn. 37921; 1863

Kutztown U. of Pennsylvania Kutztown, Pa. 19530; 1860
Labette Comm. C. Parsons, Kans. 67357; junior, 1923
Laboratory Inst. of Merchandising New York, N.Y. 10022; junior, 1939
Laboure Junior C. Boston, Mass. 02124; 1971
Lackawanna Junior C. Scranton, Pa. 18503; 1894
Lafayette C. Easton, Pa. 18042; 1826
LaGrange C. LaGrange, Ga. 30240; 1831
LaGuardia Comm. C. Long Island City, N.Y. 11101; junior, 1970
Lake City Comm. C. Lake City, Fla. 32055; junior, 1947
Lake County, C. of Grayslake, Ill. 60030; junior, 1967
Lake Erie C. Painesville, Ohio 44077; 1856
Lake Forest C. Lake Forest, Ill. 60045; 1857
Lake Land C. Mattoon, Ill. 61938; junior, 1966
Lakeland C. Sheboygan, Wis. 53081; 1862
Lakeland Comm. C. Mentor, Ohio 44060; junior, 1967
Lake Michigan C. Benton Harbor, Mich. 49022; junior, 1946
Lake Region Comm. C. Devils Lake, N.Dak. 58301; junior, 1941
Lakeshore Technical Inst. Cleveland, Wis. 53015; junior, 1912
Lake–Sumter Comm. C. Leesburg, Fla. 32748; junior, 1962
Lake Superior State C. Sault Ste. Marie, Mich. 49783; 1946
Lake Tahoe Comm. C. South Lake Tahoe, Calif. 95702; junior, 1975
Lakewood Comm. C. White Bear Lake, Minn. 55110; junior, 1967
Lamar Comm. C. Lamar, Colo. 81052; junior, 1937
Lamar U. Beaumont, Tex. 77710; 1923
Lambuth C. Jackson, Tenn. 38301; 1843
Lancaster Bible C. Lancaster, Pa. 17601; 1933
Lander C. Greenwood, S.C. 29646; 1872
Lane C. Jackson, Tenn. 38301; 1882
Lane Comm. C. Eugene, Oreg. 97405; junior, 1965
Laney C. Oakland, Calif. 94606; junior, 1927
Langston U. Langston, Okla. 73050; 1897
Lansing Comm. C. Lansing, Mich. 48914; junior, 1957
Laramie County Comm. C. Cheyenne, Wyo. 82001; junior, 1968
Laredo Junior C. Laredo, Tex. 78040; 1946
Laredo State U. Laredo, Tex. 78040; 1947
La Roche C. Pittsburgh, Pa. 15237; 1963
La Salle U. Philadelphia, Pa. 19141; 1863
Lasell Junior C. Newton, Mass. 02166; 1851
Lassen C. Susanville, Calif. 96130; junior, 1925
Latter–day Saints Business C. Salt Lake City, Utah 84111; junior, 1886
La Verne, U. of La Verne, Calif. 91750; 1891
Lawrence Inst. of Tech. Southfield, Mich., 48075; 1932
Lawrence U. Appleton, Wis. 54911; 1847
Lawson State Comm. C. Birmingham, Ala. 35221; junior, 1965
Lebanon Valley C. Annville, Pa. 17003; 1866
Lee C. Cleveland, Tenn. 37311; 1918
Lee C. Baytown, Tex. 77520; junior, 1934
Lees Junior C. Jackson, Ky. 41339; 1883
Lees–McRae C. Banner Elk, N.C. 28604; junior, 1900
Lehigh County Comm. C. Schnecksville, Pa., 18078; junior, 1966
Lehigh U. Bethlehem, Pa. 18015; 1865
Le Moyne C. Syracuse, N.Y. 13214; 1946
LeMoyne–Owen C. Memphis, Tenn. 38126; 1870
Lenoir Comm. C. Kinston, N.C. 28501; junior, 1960
Lenoir–Rhyne C. Hickory, N.C. 28601; 1891
Lesley C. Cambridge, Mass. 02138; 1909
LeTourneau C. Longview, Tex. 75601; 1946
Lewis and Clark C. Portland, Oreg. 97219; 1867
Lewis and Clark Comm. C. Godfrey, Ill. 62035; junior, 1970
Lewis–Clark State C. Lewiston, Idaho 83501; 1955
Lewis U. Romeoville, Ill. 60441; 1930
Lexington Technical Inst. Lexington, Ky. 40506; junior, 1965
Liberty U. Lynchburg, Va. 24506; 1971
L.I.F.E. Bible C. Los Angeles, Calif. 90026; 1925
Lima Technical C. Lima, Ohio 45804; junior, 1971
Limestone C. Gaffney, S.C. 29340; 1845
Lincoln Christian C. Lincoln, Ill. 62656; 1944
Lincoln C. Lincoln, Ill. 62656; junior, 1865
Lincoln Land Comm. C. Springfield, Ill. 62703; junior, 1967
Lincoln Memorial U. Harrogate, Tenn. 37752; 1897
Lincoln Trail C. Robinson, Ill. 62454; junior, 1969
Lincoln U. Jefferson City, Mo. 65101; 1866
Lincoln U. Lincoln University, Pa. 19352; 1854
Lindenwood C. St. Charles, Mo. 63301; 1827
Lindsey Wilson C. Columbia, Ky. 42728; junior, 1903
Linfield C. McMinnville, Oreg. 97128; 1849
Linn–Benton Comm. C. Albany, Oreg. 97321; junior, 1966
Livingstone C. Salisbury, N.C. 28144; 1879
Livingston U. Livingston, Ala. 35470; 1840
Lock Haven U. of Pennsylvania Lock Haven, Pa. 17745; 1870
Loma Linda U. Loma Linda, Calif. 92354; 1905
Long Beach City C. Long Beach, Calif. 90808; junior, 1913
Long Island U., Brooklyn Center Brooklyn, N.Y. 11201; 1926
Long Island U., C. W. Post Center Greenvale, N.Y. 11548; 1954
Long Island U., Southampton C. Southampton, N.Y. 11968; 1963
Longview Comm. C. Lee's Summit, Mo. 64063; junior, 1969
Longwood C. Farmville, Va. 23901; 1884
Lon Morris C. Jacksonville, Tex. 75766; junior, 1873
Lorain County Comm. C. Elyria, Ohio 44035; junior, 1963
Loras C. Dubuque, Iowa 52001; 1839
Lord Fairfax Comm. C. Middletown, Va. 22645; junior, 1969
Los Angeles Baptist C. Newhall, Calif. 91321; 1927
Los Angeles City C. Los Angeles, Calif. 90029; junior, 1929
Los Angeles Harbor C. Wilmington, Calif. 90744; junior, 1949
Los Angeles Mission C. San Fernando, Calif. 91340; junior, 1974
Los Angeles Pierce C. Woodland Hills, Calif. 91371; junior, 1947
Los Angeles Southwest C. Los Angeles, Calif. 90047; junior, 1967
Los Angeles Trade–Technical C. Los Angeles, Calif. 90015; junior, 1949
Los Angeles Valley C. Van Nuys, Calif. 91401; junior, 1949
Los Medanos C. Pittsburg, Calif. 94565; junior, 1973
Louisburg C. Louisburg, N.C. 27549; junior, 1787

Louisiana C. Pineville, La. 71360; 1906
Louisiana State U. and A. & M. C. Baton Rouge, La. 70803; 1860
Louisiana State U. at Alexandria 71301; junior, 1959
Louisiana State U. at Eunice 70535; junior, 1964
Louisiana State U. at Shreveport 71105; 1965
Louisiana Tech U. Ruston, La. 71270; 1894
Louisville, U. of Louisville, Ky. 40208; 1798
Lourdes C. Sylvania, Ohio 43560; junior, 1957
Lowell, U. of Lowell, Mass. 01854; 1894
Lower Columbia C. Longview, Wash. 98632; junior, 1934
Loyola C. Baltimore, Md. 21210; 1852
Loyola Marymount U. Los Angeles, Calif. 90045; 1865
Loyola U. in New Orleans La. 70118; 1849
Loyola U. of Chicago Ill. 60611; 1870
Lubbock Christian C. Lubbock, Tex. 79407; 1957
Lurleen B. Wallace State Junior C. Andalusia, Ala. 36420; 1968
Lutheran Bible Inst. of Seattle Issaquah, Wash. 98027; 1944
Luther C. Decorah, Iowa 52101; 1861
Luther Theol. Sem. St. Paul, Minn. 55108; 1876
Luzerne County Comm. C. Nanticoke, Pa. 18634; junior, 1966
Lycoming C. Williamsport, Pa. 17701; 1812
Lynchburg C. Lynchburg, Va. 24504; 1903
Lyndon State C. Lyndonville, Vt. 05851; 1911
Macalester C. St. Paul, Minn. 55105; 1853
MacCormac C. Chicago, Ill. 60604; junior, 1904
MacMurray C. Jacksonville, Ill. 62650; 1846
Macomb County Comm. C. Warren, Mich. 48093; junior, 1953
Macon Junior C. Macon, Ga. 31206; 1968
Madison Area Technical C. Madison, Wis. 53703; junior, 1912
Madison Business C. Madison, Wis. 53703; junior, 1856
Madisonville Comm. C. Madisonville, Ky. 42431; junior, 1968
Madonna C. Livonia, Mich. 48150; 1937
Maine at Augusta, U. of 04330; junior, 1965
Maine at Farmington, U. of 04938; 1864
Maine at Fort Kent, U. of 04743; 1878
Maine at Machias, U. of 04654; 1909
Maine at Orono, U. of 04473; 1865
Maine at Presque Isle, U. of 04769; 1903
Maine Maritime Acad. Castine, Me. 04421; 1941
Mainland, C. of the Texas City, Tex. 77590; junior, 1966
Mallinckrodt C. Wilmette, Ill. 60091; junior, 1918
Malone C. Canton, Ohio 44709; 1892
Manatee Junior C. Bradenton, Fla. 33505; 1958
Manchester C. North Manchester, Ind. 46962; 1889
Manchester Comm. C. Manchester, Conn. 06040; junior, 1963
Manhattan Christian C. Manhattan, Kans. 66502; 1927
Manhattan C. Bronx, N.Y. 10471; 1853
Manhattan Sch. of Music New York, N.Y. 10027; 1917
Manhattanville C. Purchase, N.Y. 10577; 1841
Mankato State U. Mankato, Minn. 56001; 1866
Mannes C. of Music New York, N.Y. 10021; 1916
Manor Junior C. Jenkintown, Pa. 19046; 1947
Mansfield U. of Pennsylvania Mansfield, Pa. 16933; 1857
Maple Woods Comm. C. Kansas City, Mo. 64156; junior, 1969
Maria C. of Albany N.Y. 12208; junior, 1958
Marian C. Indianapolis, Ind. 46222; 1851
Marian C. of Fond du Lac Fond du Lac, Wis. 54935; 1936
Maria Regina C. Syracuse, N.Y. 13208; junior, 1934
Marietta C. Marietta, Ohio 45750; 1835
Marin, C. of Kentfield, Calif. 94904; junior, 1926
Marion C. Marion, Ind. 46952; 1920
Marion Military Inst. Marion, Ala. 36756; junior, 1842
Marion Technical C. Marion, Ohio 43302; junior, 1971
Marist C. Poughkeepsie, N.Y. 12601; 1946
Marlboro C. Marlboro, Vt. 05344; 1946
Marquette U. Milwaukee, Wis. 53233; 1857
Marshalltown Comm. C. Marshalltown, Iowa 50158; junior, 1927
Marshall U. Huntington, W.Va. 25701; 1837
Mars Hill C. Mars Hill, N.C. 28754; 1856
Martin Comm. C. Williamston, N.C. 27892; junior, 1967
Martin Methodist C. Pulaski, Tenn. 38478; junior, 1870
Mary Baldwin C. Staunton, Va. 24401; 1842
Mary, U. of Bismarck, N.Dak. 58501; 1959
Marycrest C. Davenport, Iowa 52804; 1939
Marygrove C. Detroit, Mich. 48221; 1906
Mary Hardin–Baylor, U. of Belton, Tex. 76513; 1845
Mary Holmes C. West Point, Miss. 39773; junior, 1892
Maryland at Baltimore, U. of Baltimore 21201; 1807
Maryland Baltimore County, U. of Catonsville 21228; 1963
Maryland College Park, U. of 20742; 1856
Maryland Eastern Shore, U. of Princess Anne, Md. 21853; 1886
Maryland Inst. C. of Art Baltimore, Md. 21217; 1826
Maryland University C., U. of College Park, Md. 20742; 1947
Marylhurst C. for Lifelong Learning Marylhurst, Oreg. 97036; 1893
Marymount C. Tarrytown, N.Y. 10591; 1907
Marymount C. of Kansas Salina, Kans. 67401; 1922
Marymount Manhattan C. New York, N.Y. 10021; 1948
Marymount Palos Verdes C. Rancho Palos Verdes, Calif. 90274; junior, 1932
Marymount U. Arlington, Va. 22207; 1950
Maryville C. Maryville, Tenn. 37801; 1819
Maryville C.–Saint Louis St. Louis, Mo. 63141; 1872
Mary Washington C. Fredericksburg, Va. 22401; 1908
Marywood C. Scranton, Pa. 18509; 1915
Massachusetts–Amherst, U. of 01003; 1863
Massachusetts–Boston, U. of 02125; 1964
Massachusetts Bay Comm. C. Wellesley, Mass. 02181; junior, 1961
Massachusetts C. of Art Boston, Mass. 02215; 1873
Massachusetts C. of Pharmacy and Allied Health Sciences Boston, Mass. 02115; 1823
Massachusetts Inst. of Tech. Cambridge, Mass. 02139; 1861
Massachusetts Maritime Acad. Buzzards Bay, Mass. 02532; 1891
Massasoit Comm. C. Brockton, Mass. 02402; junior, 1966
Mater Dei C. Ogdensburg, N.Y. 13669; junior, 1960

Mattatuck Comm. C. Waterbury, Conn. 06702; junior, 1967
Mayland Technical C. Spruce Pine, N.C. 28777; junior, 1971
Maysville Comm. C. Maysville, Ky. 41056; junior, 1968
Mayville State C. Mayville, N.Dak. 58257; 1889
McDowell Technical C. Marion, N.C. 28752; junior, 1964
McHenry County C. Crystal Lake, Ill. 60014; junior, 1967
McKendree C. Lebanon, Ill. 62254; 1828
McLennan Comm. C. Waco, Tex. 76703; junior, 1966
McMurry C. Abilene, Tex. 79605; 1923
McNeese State U. Lake Charles, La. 70601; 1939
McPherson C. McPherson, Kans. 67460; 1887
Medaille C. Buffalo, N.Y. 14214; 1937
Medgar Evers C. Brooklyn, N.Y. 11225; 1969
Medical C. of Georgia Augusta, Ga. 30901; 1828
Medical C. of Pennsylvania Philadelphia, Pa. 19129; 1850
Medical U. of South Carolina Charleston, S.C. 29401; 1824
Meharry Medical C. Nashville, Tenn. 37208; 1876
Memphis Acad. of Arts Memphis, Tenn. 38112; 1936
Memphis State U. Memphis, Tenn. 38152; 1912
Menlo C. Menlo Park, Calif. 94025; 1915
Merced C. Merced, Calif. 95340; junior, 1963
Mercer County Comm. C. Trenton, N.J. 08608; junior, 1947
Mercer U. Macon, Ga. 31207; 1833
Mercy C. Dobbs Ferry, N.Y. 10522; 1950
Mercy C. Cumberland, R.I. 02864; 1957
Mercy C. of Detroit Detroit, Mich. 48219; 1941
Mercyhurst C. Erie, Pa. 16501; 1871
Mercy Inst. Portland, Me. 04103; junior, 1956
Meredith C. Raleigh, N.C. 27602; 1891
Meridian Junior C. Meridian, Miss. 39301; 1937
Merrimack C. North Andover, Mass. 01845; 1947
Merritt C. Oakland, Calif. 94609; junior, 1953
Mesabi Comm. C. Virginia, Minn. 55792; junior, 1918
Mesa C. Grand Junction, Colo. 81501; 1925
Mesa Comm. C. Mesa, Ariz. 85202; junior, 1965
Messiah C. Grantham, Pa. 17027; 1909
Methodist C. Fayetteville, N.C. 28301; 1956
Metropolitan State C. Denver, Colo. 80204; 1963
Metropolitan Technical Comm. C. Omaha, Nebr. 68137; junior, 1974
Miami, U. of Coral Gables, Fla. 33124; 1925
Miami Christian U. Miami, Fla. 33167; 1946
Miami–Dade Comm. C. Miami, Fla. 33156; junior, 1960
Miami–Jacobs Junior C. of Business Dayton, Ohio 45402; 1860
Miami U. Oxford, Ohio 45056; 1809
Michael J. Owens Technical C. Toledo, Ohio 43699; junior, 1966
Michigan, U. of Ann Arbor, Mich. 48109; 1817
Michigan Christian C. Rochester, Mich. 48063; junior, 1955
Michigan State U. East Lansing, Mich. 48823; 1855
Michigan Technological U. Houghton, Mich. 49931; 1885
Mid–America Nazarene C. Olathe, Kans. 66061; 1966
Middlebury C. Middlebury, Vt. 05753; 1800
Middle Georgia C. Cochran, Ga. 31014; junior, 1920
Middlesex Comm. C. Middletown, Conn. 06457; junior, 1966
Middlesex Comm. C. Bedford, Mass. 01730; junior, 1970
Middlesex County C. Edison, N.J. 08817; junior, 1964
Middle Tennessee State U. Murfreesboro, Tenn. 37132; 1909
Midland C. Midland, Tex. 79701; junior, 1972
Midland Lutheran C. Fremont, Nebr. 68025; 1883
Midlands Technical C. Columbia, S.C. 29250; junior, 1962
Mid Michigan Comm. C. Harrison, Mich. 48625; junior, 1965
Mid Plains Comm. C. at McCook Nebr. 69001; junior, 1926
Mid Plains Comm. C. at North Platte Nebr. 69101; junior, 1941
Mid–South Bible C. Memphis, Tenn. 38112; 1944
Midway C. Midway, Ky. 40347; junior, 1847
Midwest Christian C. Oklahoma City, Okla. 73111; 1946
Midwestern State U. Wichita Falls, Tex. 76308; 1922
Miles C. Birmingham, Ala. 35208; 1907
Miles Comm. C. Miles City, Mont. 59301; junior, 1939
Millersville U. of Pennsylvania Millersville, Pa. 17551; 1854
Milligan C. Milligan College, Tenn. 37682; 1882
Millikin U. Decatur, Ill. 62522; 1901
Millsaps C. Jackson, Miss. 39210; 1890
Mills C. Oakland, Calif. 94613; 1852
Milton C. Milton, Wis. 53563; 1844
Milwaukee Area Technical C. Milwaukee, Wis. 53203; junior, 1923
Milwaukee Sch. of Engineering Milwaukee, Wis. 53201; 1903
Mineral Area C. Flat River, Mo. 63601; junior, 1922
Minneapolis C. of Art and Design Minneapolis, Minn. 55404; 1886
Minneapolis Comm. C. Minneapolis, Minn. 55403; junior, 1965
Minnesota at Duluth, U. of 55812; 1947
Minnesota at Minneapolis St. Paul, U. of 55455; 1851
Minnesota at Morris, U. of 56267; 1960
Minnesota Bible C. Rochester, Minn. 55901; 1913
Minnesota Technical C. at Crookston, U. of 56716; junior, 1966
Minnesota Technical C. at Waseca, U. of 56093; junior, 1969
Minot State U. Minot, N.Dak. 58701; 1913
Mira Costa C. Oceanside, Calif. 92054; junior, 1934
Misericordia, C. Dallas, Pa. 18612; 1923
Mississippi, U. of University, Miss. 38677; 1844
Mississippi C. Clinton, Miss. 39056; 1826
Mississippi County Comm. C. Blytheville, Ark. 72315; junior, 1974
Mississippi Delta Junior C. Moorhead, Miss. 38761; 1911
Mississippi Gulf Coast Junior C. Perkinston, Miss. 39573; 1911
Mississippi Industrial C. Holly Springs, Miss. 38635; 1905
Mississippi State U. Mississippi State, Miss. 39762; 1878
Mississippi U. for Women Columbus, Miss. 39701; 1884
Mississippi Valley State U. Itta Bena, Miss. 38941; 1946
Missouri, U. of Columbia, Mo. 65201; 1839
Missouri at Kansas City, U. of 64110; 1933
Missouri at Rolla, U. of 65401; 1870
Missouri at St. Louis, U. of 63121; 1960
Missouri Baptist C. St. Louis, Mo. 63141; 1963
Missouri Inst. of Tech. Kansas City, Mo. 64108; 1937
Missouri Southern State C. Joplin, Mo. 64801; 1937

Missouri Valley C. Marshall, Mo. 65340; 1888
Missouri Western State C. St. Joseph, Mo. 64507; 1915
Mitchell C. New London, Conn. 06320; junior, 1938
Mitchell Comm. C. Statesville, N.C. 28677; junior, 1852
Moberly Junior C. Moberly, Mo. 65270; 1927
Mobile C. Mobile, Ala. 36613; 1961
Modesto Junior C. Modesto, Calif. 95350; 1921
Mohawk Valley Comm. C. Utica, N.Y. 13501; junior, 1946
Molloy C. Rockville Centre, N.Y. 11570; 1955
Monmouth C. Monmouth, Ill. 61462; 1853
Monmouth C. West Long Branch, N.J. 07764; 1933
Monroe Comm. C. Rochester, N.Y. 14623; junior, 1961
Monroe County Comm. C. Monroe, Mich. 48161; junior, 1964
Montana, U. of Missoula, Mont. 59801; 1893
Montana C. of Mineral Science and Tech. Butte, Mont. 59701; 1893
Montana State U. Bozeman, Mont. 59715; 1893
Montcalm Comm. C. Sidney, Mich. 48885; junior, 1965
Montclair State C. Upper Montclair, N.J. 07043; 1908
Monterey Inst. of International Studies Monterey, Calif. 93940; 1955
Monterey Peninsula C. Monterey, Calif. 93940; junior, 1947
Montevallo, U. of Montevallo, Ala. 35115; 1896
Montgomery C. Rockville, Md. 20850; junior, 1946
Montgomery County Comm. C. Blue Bell, Pa. 19422; junior, 1964
Montreat–Anderson C. Montreat, N.C. 28757; junior, 1916
Moody Bible Inst. Chicago, Ill. 60610; 1886
Moore C. of Art Philadelphia, Pa. 19103; 1844
Moorhead State U. Moorhead, Minn. 56560; 1885
Moorpark C. Moorpark, Calif. 93021; junior, 1963
Moraine Park Technical Inst. Fond du Lac, Wis. 54935; junior, 1967
Moraine Valley Comm. C. Palos Hills, Ill. 60465; junior, 1967
Moravian C. Bethlehem, Pa. 18018; 1807
Morehead State U. Morehead, Ky. 40351; 1922
Morehouse C. Atlanta, Ga. 30314; 1867
Morgan State U. Baltimore, Md. 21239; 1867
Morningside C. Sioux City, Iowa 51106; 1889
Morris Brown C. Atlanta, Ga. 30314; 1881
Morris C. Sumter, S.C. 29150; 1908
Morristown C. Morristown, Tenn. 37814; junior, 1881
Morton C. Cicero, Ill. 60650; junior, 1924
Motlow State Comm. C. Tullahoma, Tenn. 37388; junior, 1967
Mountain Empire Comm. C. Big Stone Gap, Va. 24219; junior, 1972
Mountain View C. Dallas, Tex. 75211; junior, 1970
Mount Aloysius Junior C. Cresson, Pa. 16630; 1848
Mount Angel Sem. St. Benedict, Oreg. 97373; 1887
Mount Carmel Junior C. New Orleans, La. 70124; 1924
Mount Holyoke C. South Hadley, Mass. 01075; 1837
Mount Hood Comm. C. Gresham, Oreg. 97030; junior, 1965
Mount Ida Junior C. Newton Centre, Mass. 02159; 1899
Mount Marty C. Yankton, S.Dak. 57078; 1922
Mount Mary C. Milwaukee, Wis. 53222; 1913
Mount Mercy C. Cedar Rapids, Iowa 52402; 1875
Mount Olive C. Mount Olive, N.C. 28365; junior, 1951
Mount Sacred Heart C. Hamden, Conn. 06514; junior, 1954
Mount St. Clare C. Clinton, Iowa 52732; 1895
Mount St. Joseph on–the–Ohio, C. of Mount St. Joseph, Ohio 45051; 1920
Mount St. Mary C. Newburgh, N.Y. 12550; 1930
Mount St. Mary's C. Los Angeles, Calif. 90049; 1925
Mount St. Mary's C. Emmitsburg, Md. 21727; 1808
Mount St. Vincent, C. of Riverdale, N.Y. 10471; 1847
Mount San Antonio C. Walnut, Calif. 91789; junior, 1945
Mount San Jacinto C. San Jacinto, Calif. 92383; junior, 1963
Mount Senario C. Ladysmith, Wis. 54848; 1962
Mount Union C. Alliance, Ohio 44601; 1846
Mount Vernon C. Washington, D.C. 20007; 1875
Mount Vernon Nazarene C. Mount Vernon, Ohio 43050; 1966
Mount Wachusett Comm. C. Gardner, Mass. 01440; junior, 1963
Muhlenberg C. Allentown, Pa. 18104; 1848
Multnomah Sch. of the Bible Portland, Oreg. 97220; 1936
Mundelein C. Chicago, Ill. 60660; 1930
Murray State C. Tishomingo, Okla. 73460; junior, 1908
Murray State U. Murray, Ky. 42071; 1922
Muscatine Comm. C. Muscatine, Iowa 52761; junior, 1929
Muskegon Business C. Muskegon, Mich. 49442; junior, 1885
Muskegon Comm. C. Muskegon, Mich. 49443; junior, 1926
Muskingum Area Technical C. Zanesville, Ohio 43701; junior, 1969
Muskingum C. New Concord, Ohio 43762; 1837
Napa C. Napa, Calif. 94558; junior, 1941
Nash Technical Inst. Rocky Mount, N.C. 27801; junior, 1967
Nashville State Technical Inst. Nashville, Tenn. 37209; junior, 1969
Nassau Comm. C. Garden City, N.Y. 11533; junior, 1959
Nasson C. Springvale, Me. 04083; 1912
National Business C. Roanoke, Va. 24009; junior, 1886
National C. of Ed. Evanston, Ill. 60201; 1886
National Technical Schools Los Angeles, Calif. 90037; junior, 1905
National U. San Diego, Calif. 92108; 1971
Navajo Comm. C. Tsaile, Ariz. 86503; junior, 1969
Navarro C. Corsicana, Tex. 75110; junior, 1946
Nazarene Bible C. Colorado Springs, Colo. 80935; junior, 1964
Nazareth C. Nazareth, Mich. 49074; 1924
Nazareth C. of Rochester Rochester, N.Y. 14610; 1924
Nebraska at Lincoln, U. of 68508; 1869
Nebraska at Omaha, U. of 68101; 1908
Nebraska Wesleyan U. Lincoln, Nebr. 68504; 1887
Nebraska Western C. Scottsbluff, Nebr. 69361; junior, 1926
Neosho County Comm. C. Chanute, Kans. 66720; junior, 1936
Ner Israel Rabbinical C. Baltimore, Md. 21215; 1933
Neumann C. Aston, Pa. 19014; 1965
Nevada at Las Vegas, U. of 89154; 1957
Nevada at Reno, U. of 89507; 1874
Newberry C. Newberry, S.C. 29108; 1856
Newbury Junior C. Boston, Mass. 02115; 1962
New Church, Acad. of the Bryn Athyn, Pa. 19009; 1876
New C. of Calif. San Francisco, Calif. 94110; 1971

New C. of the U. of South Florida Sarasota, Fla. 33580; 1960
New England, U. of Biddeford, Me. 04005; 1953
New England C. Henniker, N.H. 03242; 1946
New England C. of Optometry Boston, Mass. 02116; 1894
New England Conservatory of Music Boston, Mass. 02115; 1867
New Hampshire, U. of Durham, N.H. 03824; 1866
New Hampshire C. Manchester, N.H. 03104; 1932
New Hampshire Technical Inst. Concord, N.H. 03301; junior, 1961
New Haven, U. of West Haven, Conn. 06516; 1920
New Jersey Inst. of Tech. Newark, N.J. 07102; 1881
New Mexico, U. of Albuquerque, N.Mex. 87106; 1889
New Mexico Highlands U. Las Vegas, N.Mex. 87701; 1893
New Mexico Inst. of Mining and Tech. Socorro, N.Mex. 87801; 1889
New Mexico Junior C. Hobbs, N.Mex. 88240; 1965
New Mexico Military Inst. Roswell, N.Mex. 88201; junior, 1891
New Mexico State U. Las Cruces, N.Mex. 88003; 1888
New Orleans, U. of New Orleans, La. 70122; 1958
Newport C.–Salve Regina Newport, R.I. 02840; 1934
New River Comm. C. Dublin, Va. 24084; junior, 1966
New Rochelle, C. of New Rochelle, N.Y. 10801; 1904
New Sch. for Social Research New York, N.Y. 10011; 1919
New Sch. of Music Philadelphia, Pa. 19103; 1945
Newton Junior C. Newtonville, Mass. 02160; 1946
New York Agricultural and Technical, State U. of Alfred, N.Y. 14802; junior, 1908
New York Agricultural and Technical C., State U. of Canton, N.Y. 13617; junior, 1907
New York Agricultural and Technical C., State U. of Cobleskill, N.Y. 12043; junior, 1911
New York Agricultural and Technical C., State U. of Delhi, N.Y. 13753; junior, 1913
New York Agricultural and Technical C., State U. of Farmingdale, N.Y. 11735; junior, 1912
New York Agricultural and Technical C., State U. of Morrisville, N.Y. 13408; junior, 1908
New York at Albany, State U. of 12203; 1844
New York at Binghamton, State U. of 13901; 1946
New York at Buffalo, State U. of 14214; 1846
New York at Stony Brook, State U. of 11790; 1957
New York City Comm. C. of Applied Arts and Sciences Brooklyn, N.Y. 11201; junior, 1946
New York C. at Brockport, State U. of 14420; 1841
New York C. at Buffalo, State U. of 14222; 1867
New York C. at Cortland, State U. of 13045; 1863
New York C. at Fredonia, State U. of 14063; 1866
New York C. at Geneseo, State U. of 14454; 1867
New York C. at New Paltz, State U. of 12561; 1828
New York C. at Old Westbury, State U. of 11771; 1966
New York C. at Oneonta, State U. of 13820; 1889
New York C. at Oswego, State U. of 13126; 1861
New York C. at Plattsburgh, State U. of 12901; 1889
New York C. at Potsdam, State U. of 13676; 1816
New York C. at Purchase, State U. of 10577; 1967
New York C. of Environmental Science and Forestry, State U. of Syracuse 13210; 1911
New York C. of Podiatric Medicine New York, N.Y. 10035; 1911
New York C. of Tech. at Utica/Rome, State U. of Utica 13502; 1966
New York Downstate Medical Center, State U. of Brooklyn, N.Y. 11203; 1930
New York Empire State C., State U. of Saratoga Springs 12866; 1971
New York Inst. of Tech. Old Westbury, N.Y. 11568; 1910
New York Maritime C., State U. of Bronx, N.Y. 10465; 1874
New York U. New York, N.Y. 10003; 1831
New York Upstate Medical Center, State U. of Syracuse, N.Y. 13210; 1834
Niagara County Comm. C. Sanborn, N.Y. 14132; junior, 1962
Niagara U. Niagara University, N.Y. 14109; 1856
Nicholls State U. Thibodaux, La. 70301; 1948
Nichols C. Dudley, Mass. 01570; 1815
Norfolk State U. Norfolk, Va. 23504; 1935
Normandale Comm. C. Bloomington, Minn. 55431; junior, 1968
North Adams State C. North Adams, Mass. 01247; 1894
North Alabama, U. of Florence, Ala. 35630; 1872
North American Baptist Sem. Sioux Falls, S.Dak. 57105; 1850
Northampton County Area Comm. C. Bethlehem, Pa. 18017; junior, 1966
North Arkansas Comm. C. Harrison, Ark. 72601; junior, 1974
North Carolina Agricultural and Technical State U. Greensboro, N.C. 27411; 1891
North Carolina at Asheville, U. of 28804; 1927
North Carolina at Chapel Hill, U. of 27514; 1789
North Carolina at Charlotte, U. of 28213; 1946
North Carolina at Greensboro, U. of 27412; 1891
North Carolina at Wilmington, U. of 28401; 1947
North Carolina Central U. Durham, N.C. 27707; 1909
North Carolina Sch. of the Arts Winston-Salem, N.C. 27107; 1965
North Carolina State U. at Raleigh 27607; 1887
North Carolina Wesleyan C. Rocky Mount, N.C. 27801; 1956
North Central Bible C. Minneapolis, Minn. 55404; 1930
North Central C. Naperville, Ill. 60540; 1861
North Central Michigan C. Petoskey, Mich. 49770; junior, 1958
North Central Missouri C. Trenton, Mo. 64683; junior, 1925
North Central Technical C. Mansfield, Ohio 44906; junior, 1961
North Central Technical Inst. Wausau, Wis. 54401; junior, 1912
North Country Comm. C. Saranac Lake, N.Y. 12983; junior, 1967
North Dakota, U. of Grand Forks, N.Dak. 58201; 1883
North Dakota, Williston, U. of 58801; junior, 1957
North Dakota State C. of Science Wahpeton, N.Dak. 58076; junior, 1903
North Dakota State U. Fargo, N.Dak. 58102; 1890
Northeast Alabama State Junior C. Rainsville, Ala. 35986; 1963
Northeastern Bible C. Essex Fells, N.J. 07021; 1950
Northeastern Christian Junior C. Villanova, Pa. 19085; 1959
Northeastern Illinois U. Chicago, Ill. 60625; 1961

Northeastern Junior C. of Colorado Sterling, Colo. 80751; 1941
Northeastern Oklahoma A. & M. C. Miami, Okla. 74354; junior, 1919
Northeastern Oklahoma State U. Tahlequah, Okla. 74464; 1846
Northeastern U. Boston, Mass. 02115; 1898
Northeast Louisiana U. Monroe, La. 71201; 1931
Northeast Mississippi Junior C. Booneville, Miss. 38829; 1948
Northeast Missouri State U. Kirksville, Mo. 63501; 1867
Northeast Technical Comm. C. Norfolk, Nebr. 68701; junior, 1927
Northern Arizona U. Flagstaff, Ariz. 86001; 1899
Northern Colorado, U. of Greeley, Colo. 80639; 1889
Northern Essex Comm. C. Haverhill, Mass. 01830; junior, 1961
Northern Illinois U. De Kalb, Ill. 60115; 1895
Northern Iowa, U. of Cedar Falls, Iowa 50613; 1876
Northern Kentucky U. Highland Heights, Ky. 41076; 1968
Northern Maine Vocational Technical Inst. Presque Isle, Me. 04769; junior, 1961
Northern Michigan U. Marquette, Mich. 49855; 1899
Northern Montana C. Havre, Mont. 59501; 1913
Northern Nevada Comm. C. Elko, Nev. 89801; junior, 1967
Northern Oklahoma C. Tonkawa, Okla. 74653; junior, 1901
Northern State C. Aberdeen, S.Dak. 57401; 1901
Northern Virginia Comm. C. Annandale, Va. 22003; junior, 1965
North Florida, U. of Jacksonville, Fla. 32216; 1965
North Florida Junior C. Madison, Fla. 32340; 1958
North Georgia C. Dahlonega, Ga. 30533; 1873
North Greenville C. Tigerville, S.C. 29688; junior, 1892
North Harris County C. Houston, Tex. 77037; junior, 1972
North Hennepin Comm. C. Minneapolis, Minn. 55428; junior, 1966
North Idaho C. Coeur d'Alene, Idaho 83814; junior, 1939
North Iowa Area Comm. C. Mason City, Iowa 50401; junior, 1918
Northlake C. Irving, Tex. 75062; junior, 1965
Northland C. Ashland, Wis. 54806; 1892
Northland Comm. C. Thief River Falls, Minn. 56701; junior, 1965
Northland Pioneer C. Holbrook, Ariz. 86025; junior, 1973
North Park C. Chicago, Ill. 60625; 1891
North Platte Comm. C. North Platte, Nebr. 69101; junior, 1964
Northrop U. Inglewood, Calif. 90306; 1942
North Seattle Comm. C. Seattle, Wash. 98103; junior, 1969
North Shore Comm. C. Beverly, Mass. 01915; junior, 1965
North Texas State U. Denton, Tex. 76203; 1890
Northwest Alabama State Junior C. Phil Campbell, Ala. 35581; 1963
Northwest Bible C. Minot, N.Dak. 58701; 1934
Northwest Christian C. Eugene, Oreg. 97401; 1895
Northwest C. of the Assemblies of God Kirkland, Wash. 98033; 1934
Northwest Comm. C. Powell, Wyo. 82435; junior, 1946
Northwestern C. Orange City, Iowa 51041; 1882
Northwestern C. Roseville, Minn. 55113; 1902
Northwestern C. Watertown, Wis. 53094; 1865
Northwestern Connecticut Comm. C. Winsted, Conn. 06098; junior, 1965
Northwestern Michigan C. Traverse City, Mich. 49684; junior, 1951
Northwestern Oklahoma State U. Alva, Okla. 73717; 1897
Northwestern State U. of Louisiana Natchitoches, La. 71457; 1884
Northwestern U. Evanston, Ill. 60201; 1851
Northwest Mississippi Junior C. Senatobia, Miss. 38668; 1915
Northwest Missouri State U. Maryville, Mo. 64468; 1905
Northwest Nazarene C. Nampa, Idaho 83651; 1913
Northwest Technical C. Archbold, Ohio 43502; junior, 1968
Northwood Inst. Midland, Mich. 48640; 1959
Norwalk Comm. C. Norwalk, Conn. 06854; junior, 1961
Norwalk State Technical C. Norwalk, Conn. 06854; junior, 1961
Norwich U. Northfield, Vt. 05663; 1819
Notre Dame, C. of Belmont, Calif. 94002; 1851
Notre Dame, U. of Notre Dame, Ind. 46556; 1842
Notre Dame C. Manchester, N.H. 03104; 1950
Notre Dame C. Cleveland, Ohio 44121; 1922
Notre Dame of Maryland, C. of Baltimore, Md. 21210; 1848
Notre Dame Sem. New Orleans, La. 70118; 1923
Nova U. Fort Lauderdale, Fla. 33314; 1964
Nyack C. Nyack, N.Y. 10960; 1882
Oakland City C. Oakland City, Ind. 47560; 1885
Oakland Comm. C. Bloomfield Hills, Mich. 48013; junior, 1964
Oakland U. Rochester, Mich. 48063; 1959
Oakton Comm. C. Des Plaines, Ill. 60016; junior, 1969
Oakwood C. Huntsville, Ala. 35806; 1896
Oberlin C. Oberlin, Ohio 44074; 1833
Oblate C. Washington, D.C. 20017; 1904
Occidental C. Los Angeles, Calif. 90041; 1887
Ocean County C. Toms River, N.J. 08753; junior, 1964
Odessa C. Odessa, Tex. 79760; junior, 1946
Oglethorpe U. Atlanta, Ga. 30319; 1835
Ohio C. of Podiatric Medicine Cleveland, Ohio 44106; 1916
Ohio Dominican C. Columbus, Ohio 43219; 1911
Ohio Northern U. Ada, Ohio 45810; 1871
Ohio State U. Columbus, Ohio 43210; 1870
Ohio U. Athens, Ohio 45701; 1804
Ohio Valley C. Parkersburg, W.Va. 26101; junior, 1960
Ohio Wesleyan U. Delaware, Ohio 43015; 1842
Ohlone C. Fremont, Calif. 94537; junior, 1966
Okaloosa–Walton Junior C. Niceville, Fla. 32578; 1963
Oklahoma, U. of Norman, Okla. 73069; 1890
Oklahoma, U. of Science and Arts of Chickasha, 73018; 1908
Oklahoma Baptist U. Shawnee, Okla. 74801; 1906
Oklahoma Christian C. Oklahoma City, Okla. 73111; 1950
Oklahoma City U. Oklahoma City, Okla. 73106; 1911
Oklahoma Panhandle State U. Goodwell, Okla. 73939; 1909
Oklahoma Sch. of Business Tulsa, Okla. 74119; junior, 1919
Oklahoma State U. of Agric. and Applied Science Stillwater, Okla. 74074; 1890
Oklahoma State U. Technical Inst. Oklahoma City 73107; junior, 1961
Old Dominion U. Norfolk, Va. 23508; 1930
Olivet C. Olivet, Mich. 49076; 1844
Olivet Nazarene U. Kankakee, Ill. 60901; 1907
Olney Central C. Olney, Ill. 62450; junior, 1963

Olympic C. Bremerton, Wash. 98310; junior, 1946
Onondaga Comm. C. Syracuse, N.Y. 13210; junior, 1961
Open Bible C. Des Moines, Iowa 50321; 1931
Oral Roberts U. Tulsa, Okla. 74105; 1963
Orangeburg–Calhoun Technical C. Orangeburg, S.C. 29115; junior, 1966
Orange Coast C. Costa Mesa, Calif. 92626; junior, 1947
Orange County Comm. C. Middletown N.Y. 10940; junior, 1950
Oregon, U. of Eugene, Oreg. 97403; 1872
Oregon Health Sciences U. Portland, Oreg. 97201; 1974
Oregon Inst. of Tech. Klamath Falls, Oreg. 97601; 1947
Oregon State U. Corvallis, Oreg. 97331; 1868
Otero Junior C. La Junta, Colo. 81050; 1941
Ottawa U. Ottawa, Kans. 66067; 1865
Otterbein C. Westerville, Ohio 43081; 1847
Ouachita Baptist U. Arkadelphia, Ark. 71923; 1886
Our Lady of Holy Cross C. New Orleans, La. 70114; 1916
Our Lady of the Elms, C. of Chicopee, Mass. 01013; 1928
Our Lady of the Lake U. of San Antonio Tex. 78285; 1911
Oxnard C. Oxnard, Calif. 93030; junior, 1975
Ozark Bible C. Joplin, Mo. 64801; 1942
Ozarks, C. of the Clarksville, Ark. 72830; 1834
Ozarks, Sch. of the Point Lookout, Mo. 65726; 1906
Pace U. New York, N.Y. 10038; 1906
Pacific, U. of the Stockton, Calif. 95204; 1851
Pacific Christian C. Fullerton, Calif. 92631; 1928
Pacific Lutheran U. Tacoma, Wash. 98447; 1890
Pacific Northwest C. of Art Portland, Oreg. 97205; 1909
Pacific Oaks C. Pasadena, Calif. 91105; 1945
Pacific Union C. Angwin, Calif. 94508; 1882
Pacific U. Forest Grove, Oreg. 97116; 1849
Paducah Comm. C. Paducah, Ky. 42001; junior, 1932
Paine C. Augusta, Ga. 30901; 1882
Palm Beach, U. of West Palm Beach, Fla. 33402; 1926
Palm Beach Atlantic C. West Palm Beach, Fla. 33401; 1968
Palm Beach Junior C. Lake Worth, Fla. 33460; 1933
Palomar C. San Marcos, Calif. 92069; junior, 1946
Palo Verde C. Blythe, Calif. 92225; junior, 1947
Pamlico Technical C. Grantsboro, N.C. 28529; junior, 1962
Panama Canal C. Balboa, Republic of Panama; 1934
Pan American U. Edinburg, Tex. 78539; 1927
Panola Junior C. Carthage, Tex. 75633; 1947
Paris Junior C. Paris, Tex. 75460; 1924
Park C. Parkville, Mo. 64152; 1875
Parkersburg Comm. C. Parkersburg, W.Va. 26101; junior, 1971
Parkland C. Champaign, Ill. 61820; junior, 1965
Pasadena City C. Pasadena, Calif. 91106; junior, 1924
Pasco–Hernando Comm. C. Dade City, Fla. 33525; junior, 1972
Patrick Henry Comm. C. Martinsville, Va. 24112; junior, 1971
Patrick Henry State Junior C. Monroeville, Ala. 36460; 1965
Paul D. Camp Comm. C. Franklin, Va. 23851; junior, 1971
Paul Quinn C. Waco, Tex. 76703; 1881
Paul Smith's C. Paul Smiths, N.Y. 12970; junior, 1937
Peabody Inst. of Johns Hopkins U. Baltimore, Md. 21202; 1857
Peace C. Raleigh, N.C. 27602; junior, 1857
Pearl River Junior C. Poplarville, Miss. 39470; 1909
Peirce Junior C. Philadelphia, Pa. 19102; 1865
Pembroke State U. Pembroke, N.C. 28372; 1887
Peninsula C. Port Angeles, Wash. 98362; junior, 1961
Pennsylvania, U. of Philadelphia, Pa. 19104; 1740
Pennsylvania C. of Optometry Philadelphia, Pa. 19141; 1919
Pennsylvania State U. University Park, Pa. 16802; 1855
Penn Valley Comm. C. Kansas City, Mo. 64111; junior, 1915
Pensacola Junior C. Pensacola, Fla. 32504; 1948
Pepperdine U. Malibu, Calif. 90265; 1937
Peru State C. Peru, Nebr. 68421; 1867
Pfeiffer C. Misenheimer, N.C. 28109; 1887
Philadelphia, Comm. C. of Philadelphia, Pa. 19107; junior, 1965
Philadelphia C. of Art Philadelphia, Pa. 19102; 1876
Philadelphia C. of Bible Langhorne, Pa. 19047; 1913
Philadelphia C. of the Performing Arts Philadelphia, Pa. 19102; 1870
Philadelphia C. of Pharmacy and Science Philadelphia, Pa. 19104; 1821
Philadelphia C. of Textiles and Science Philadelphia, Pa. 19144; 1884
Philander Smith C. Little Rock, Ark. 72203; 1868
Phillips County Comm. C. Helena, Ark. 72342; junior, 1965
Phillips U. Enid, Okla. 73701; 1906
Phoenix C. Phoenix, Ariz. 85013; junior, 1920
Piedmont Bible C. Winston-Salem, N.C. 27101; 1945
Piedmont C. Demorest, Ga. 30535; 1897
Piedmont Technical C. Roxboro, N.C. 27573; junior, 1970
Piedmont Technical C. Greenwood, S.C. 29646; junior, 1963
Piedmont Virginia Comm. C. Charlottesville, Va. 22901; junior, 1972
Pierce C. Tacoma, Wash. 98498; junior, 1967
Pikes Peak Comm. C. Colorado Springs, Colo. 80906; junior, 1967
Pikeville C. Pikeville, Ky. 41501; 1889
Pima Comm. C. Tucson, Ariz. 85709; junior, 1967
Pinebrook Junior C. Coopersburg, Pa. 18036; 1950
Pine Manor C. Chestnut Hill, Mass. 02167; 1911
Pioneer Comm. C. Kansas City, Mo. 64111; junior, 1976
Pitt Comm. C. Greenville, N.C. 27834; junior, 1961
Pittsburgh, U. of Pittsburgh, Pa. 15260; 1787
Pittsburgh Bradford, U. of Bradford, Pa. 16701; 1963
Pittsburgh Greensburg, U. of Greensburg, Pa. 15601; junior, 1963
Pittsburgh Johnstown, U. of Johnstown, Pa. 15902; 1927
Pittsburgh Titusville, U. of Titusville, Pa. 16354; junior, 1963
Pittsburg State U. Pittsburg, Kans. 66762; 1903
Pitzer C. Claremont, Calif. 91711; 1963
Platte Technical Comm. C. Columbus, Nebr. 68601; junior, 1969
Plymouth State C. Plymouth, N.H. 03264; 1871
Point Loma C. San Diego, Calif. 92106; 1902
Point Park C. Pittsburgh, Pa. 15222; 1933
Polk Comm. C. Winter Haven, Fla. 33880; junior, 1964
Polytechnic Inst. of New York Brooklyn, N.Y. 11201; 1854
Pomona C. Claremont, Calif. 91711; 1887

Pontifical C. Josephinum Columbus, Ohio 43085; 1888
Porterville C. Porterville, Calif. 93257; junior, 1927
Portland, U. of Portland, Oreg. 97203; 1901
Portland Comm. C. Portland, Oreg. 97201; junior, 1961
Portland Sch. of Art Portland, Me. 04101; 1882
Portland State U. Portland, Oreg. 97207; 1946
Post C. Waterbury, Conn. 06708; 1890
Potomac State C. of West Virginia U. Keyser, W.Va. 26726; junior, 1901
Prairie State C. Chicago Heights, Ill. 60411; junior, 1958
Prairie View A. & M. U. Prairie View, Tex. 77445; 1876
Pratt Comm. C. Pratt, Kans. 67124; junior, 1938
Pratt Inst. Brooklyn, N.Y. 11205; 1887
Prentiss Normal and Industrial Inst. Prentiss, Miss. 39474; junior, 1907
Presbyterian C. Clinton, S.C. 29325; 1880
Presbyterian Sch. of Christian Ed. Richmond, Va. 23227; 1914
Presentation C. Aberdeen, S.Dak. 57401; junior, 1922
Prestonburg Comm. C. Prestonburg, Ky. 41653; junior, 1964
Prince George's Comm. C. Largo, Md. 20870; junior, 1958
Princeton U. Princeton, N.J. 08540; 1746
Principia C., The Elsah, Ill. 62028; 1898
Providence C. Providence, R.I. 02918; 1917
Pueblo Vocational Comm. C. Pueblo, Colo. 81004; junior, 1979
Puerto Rico, U. of Río Piedras, Puerto Rico 00931; 1900
Puerto Rico Junior C. Río Piedras, Puerto Rico 00928; 1949
Puget Sound, U. of Tacoma, Wash. 98416; 1888
Puget Sound C. of the Bible Edmonds, Wash. 98020; 1950
Purdue U. West Lafayette, Ind. 47907; 1869
Queensborough Comm. C. Bayside, N.Y. 11364; junior, 1960
Queens C. Flushing, N.Y. 11367; 1937
Queens C. Charlotte, N.C. 28274; 1857
Quincy C. Quincy, Ill. 62301; 1860
Quincy Junior C. Quincy, Mass. 02169; 1958
Quinnipiac C. Hamden, Conn. 06518; 1929
Quinsigamond Comm. C. Worcester, Mass. 01606; junior, 1963
Rabbinical C. of Telshe Wickliffe, Ohio 44092; 1876
Radford U. Radford, Va. 24142; 1910
Rainy River Comm. C. International Falls, Minn. 56649; junior, 1967
Ramapo C. of New Jersey Mahwah, N.J. 07430; 1971
Rancho Santiago C. Santa Ana, Calif. 92706; junior, 1915
Randolph–Macon C. Ashland, Va. 23005; 1830
Randolph–Macon Woman's C. Lynchburg, Va. 24503; 1891
Randolph Technical C. Asheboro, N.C. 27203; junior, 1962
Ranger Junior C. Ranger, Tex. 76470; 1926
Rappahannock Comm. C. Glenns, Va. 23149; junior, 1971
Raritan Valley Comm. C. Somerville, N.J. 08876; junior, 1965
Redlands, U. of Redlands, Calif. 92373; 1907
Red Rocks Comm. C. Golden, Colo. 80401; junior, 1967
Redwoods, C. of the Eureka, Calif. 95501; junior, 1964
Reed C. Portland, Oreg. 97202; 1904
Reformed Bible C. Grand Rapids, Mich. 49506; 1940
Regis C. Denver, Colo. 80221; 1877
Regis C. Weston, Mass. 02193; 1927
Reinhardt C. Waleska, Ga. 30183; junior, 1883
Rend Lake C. Ina, Ill. 62846; junior, 1956
Rensselaer Polytechnic Inst. Troy, N.Y. 12181; 1824
Rhode Island, Comm. C. of Warwick, R.I. 02886; junior, 1964
Rhode Island, U. of Kingston, R.I. 02881; 1892
Rhode Island C. Providence, R.I. 02908; 1854
Rhode Island Sch. of Design Providence, R.I. 02903; 1877
Rhodes C. Memphis, Tenn. 38112; 1848
Rice U. — see WILLIAM MARSH RICE U.
Richard Bland C. Petersburg, Va. 23803; junior, 1960
Richland C. Dallas, Tex. 75231; junior, 1972
Richmond, U. of Richmond, Va. 23173; 1840
Richmond C. Staten Island, N.Y. 10301; 1965
Richmond Technical C. Hamlet, N.C. 28345; junior, 1964
Ricks C. Rexburg, Idaho 83440; junior, 1888
Rider C. Lawrenceville, N.J. 08648; 1865
Ringling Sch. of Art and Design Sarasota, Fla. 33580; 1931
Rio Grande C. Rio Grande, Ohio 45674; 1876
Rio Hondo C. Whittier, Calif. 90608; junior, 1963
Ripon C. Ripon, Wis. 54971; 1851
Rip Reagan C. and Music Conservatory Ama, La. 70031; 1974
Riverside City C. Riverside, Calif. 92506; junior, 1916
Rivier C. Nashua, N.H. 03060; 1933
Roane State Comm. C. Harriman, Tenn. 37748; junior, 1970
Roanoke Bible C. Elizabeth City, N.C. 27909; 1948
Roanoke–Chowan Technical C. Ahoskie, N.C. 27910; junior, 1967
Roanoke C. Salem, Va. 24153; 1842
Robert Morris C. Coraopolis, Pa. 15108; 1921
Roberts Wesleyan C. Rochester, N.Y. 14624; 1866
Robeson Technical C. Lumberton, N.C. 28358; junior, 1965
Rochester, U. of Rochester, N.Y. 14627; 1850
Rochester Comm. C. Rochester, Minn. 55901; junior, 1915
Rochester Inst. of Tech. Rochester, N.Y. 14623; 1829
Rockford C. Rockford, Ill. 61101; 1847
Rockingham Comm. C. Wentworth, N.C. 27375; junior, 1964
Rockland Comm. C. Suffern, N.Y. 10901; junior, 1959
Rock Valley C. Rockford, Ill. 61101; junior, 1964
Rocky Mountain C. Billings, Mont. 59102; 1878
Rogers State C. Claremore, Okla. 74017; junior, 1909
Roger Williams C. Bristol, R.I. 02809; 1919
Rogue Comm. C. Grants Pass, Oreg. 97526; junior, 1970
Rollins C. Winter Park, Fla. 32789; 1885
Roosevelt U. Chicago, Ill. 60605; 1945
Rosary C. River Forest, Ill. 60305; 1848
Rosary Hill C. Buffalo, N.Y. 14226; 1948
Rose–Hulman Inst. of Tech. Terre Haute, Ind. 47803; 1874
Rosemont C. Rosemont, Pa. 19010; 1921
Rose State C. Midwest City, Okla. 73110; junior, 1971
Rowan Technical C. Salisbury, N.C. 28144; junior, 1961

Roxbury Comm. C. Roxbury, Mass. 02186; junior, 1973
Russell Sage C. Troy, N.Y. 12180; 1916
Rust C. Holly Springs, Miss. 38635; 1866
Rutgers–The State U. New Brunswick, N.J. 08903; 1766
Rutledge C. Fayetteville, N.C. 28301; junior, 1973
Sacramento City C. Sacramento, Calif. 95822; junior, 1916
Sacred Heart, U. of the Santurce, Puerto Rico 00914; 1935
Sacred Heart C. Belmont, N.C. 28012; 1892
Sacred Heart Sem. C. Detroit, Mich. 48206; 1919
Sacred Heart U. Bridgeport, Conn. 06604; 1963
Saddleback C. Mission Viejo, Calif. 92692; junior, 1967
Saginaw Valley State C. University Center, Mich. 48710; 1963
Saint Alphonsus C. Suffield, Conn. 06078; 1963
Saint Ambrose U. Davenport, Iowa 52803; 1882
Saint Andrews Presbyterian C. Laurinburg, N.C. 28352; 1857
Saint Anselm C. Manchester, N.H. 03102; 1889
Saint Augustine's C. Raleigh, N.C. 27602; 1867
Saint Basil's C. Stamford, Conn. 06902; 1939
Saint Benedict, C. of St. Joseph, Minn. 56374; 1913
Saint Bernard C. St. Bernard, Ala. 35138; 1892
Saint Bonaventure U. St. Bonaventure, N.Y. 14778; 1859
Saint Catharine C. St. Catharine, Ky. 40061; junior, 1932
Saint Catherine, C. of St. Paul, Minn. 55116; 1906
Saint Charles Borromeo Sem. Philadelphia, Pa. 19151; 1832
Saint Clair County Comm. C. Port Huron, Mich. 48060; junior, 1923
Saint Cloud State U. St. Cloud, Minn. 56301; 1866
Saint Edward's U. Austin, Tex. 78704; 1876
Saint Elizabeth, C. of Convent Station, N.J. 07961; 1899
Saint Francis, C. of Joliet, Ill. 60435; 1874
Saint Francis C. Fort Wayne, Ind. 46808; 1890
Saint Francis C. Brooklyn, N.Y. 11201; 1884
Saint Francis C. of Pennsylvania Loretto, Pa. 15940; 1847
Saint Francis de Sales C. Milwaukee, Wis. 53207; 1856
Saint Gregory's C. Shawnee, Okla. 74801; junior, 1915
Saint Hyacinth C. and Sem. Granby, Mass. 01033; 1927
Saint John Fisher C. Rochester, N.Y. 14618; 1952
Saint John's C. Camarillo, Calif. 93010; 1939
Saint John's C. Winfield, Kans. 67156; 1893
Saint John's C. Annapolis, Md. 21404; 1696
Saint John's C. Santa Fe, N. Mex. 87501; 1964
Saint Johns River Comm. C. Palatka, Fla. 32077; junior, 1958
Saint John's Sem. Brighton, Mass. 02135; 1884
Saint John's U. Collegeville, Minn. 56321; 1857
Saint John's U. Jamaica, N.Y. 11432; 1870
Saint John Vianney C. Sem. Miami, Fla. 33165; 1960
Saint Joseph C. West Hartford, Conn. 06117; 1932
Saint Joseph's C. Rensselaer, Ind. 47978; 1889
Saint Joseph's C. North Windham, Me. 04062; 1915
Saint Joseph's C. Brooklyn, N.Y. 11205; 1916
Saint Joseph Sem. C. St. Benedict, La. 70457; 1891
Saint Joseph's Sem. and C. Yonkers, N.Y. 10704; 1839
Saint Joseph's U. Philadelphia, Pa. 19131; 1851
Saint Joseph the Provider, C. of Rutland, Vt. 05701; 1957
Saint Lawrence U. Canton, N.Y. 13617; 1856
Saint Leo C. St. Leo, Fla. 33574; 1959
Saint Louis Christian C. Florissant, Mo. 63033; 1956
Saint Louis C. of Pharmacy St. Louis, Mo. 63110; 1864
Saint Louis Comm. C. at Florissant Valley St. Louis, Mo. 63135; junior, 1962
Saint Louis Comm. C. at Forest Park St. Louis, Mo. 63110; junior, 1962
Saint Louis Comm. C. at Meramec St. Louis, Mo. 63122; junior, 1964
Saint Louis Conservatory of Music Saint Louis, Mo. 63130; 1924
Saint Louis U. St. Louis, Mo. 63103; 1818
Saint Martin's C. Lacey, Wash. 98503; 1895
Saint Mary, C. of Omaha, Nebr. 68124; 1923
Saint Mary C. Leavenworth, Kans. 66048; 1882
Saint Mary of the Plains C. Dodge City, Kans. 67801; 1952
Saint Mary–of–the–Woods C. Saint Mary-of-the-Woods, Ind. 47876; 1840
Saint Mary's C. Notre Dame, Ind. 46556; 1844
Saint Mary's C. Orchard Lake, Mich. 48033; 1885
Saint Mary's C. Winona, Minn. 55987; 1912
Saint Mary's C. Raleigh, N.C. 27602; junior, 1842
Saint Mary's C. of California Moraga, Calif. 94575; 1863
Saint Mary's C. of Maryland St. Marys City, Md. 20686; 1839
Saint Mary's C. of O'Fallon O'Fallon, Mo. 63366; junior, 1929
Saint Mary's C. Sem. St. Mary, Ky. 40063; 1821
Saint Mary's Dominican C. New Orleans, La. 70118; 1910
Saint Mary's Junior C. Minneapolis, Minn. 55406; 1964
Saint Mary's Sem. Cleveland, Ohio 44108; 1848
Saint Mary's Sem. and C. Perryville, Mo. 63775; 1818
Saint Mary's Sem. and U. Baltimore, Md. 21210; 1791
Saint Mary's U. of San Antonio San Antonio, Tex. 78284; 1852
Saint Meinrad C. St. Meinrad, Ind. 47577; 1854
Saint Michael's C. Winooski, Vt. 05404; 1903
Saint Norbert C. De Pere, Wis. 54115; 1898
Saint Olaf C. Northfield, Minn. 55057; 1874
Saint Patrick's C. Mountain View, Calif. 94040; 1898
Saint Paul Bible C. St. Bonifacius, Minn. 55375; 1916
Saint Paul's C. Concordia, Mo. 64020; junior, 1883
Saint Paul's C. Lawrenceville, Va. 23868; 1888
Saint Paul Sem. St. Paul, Minn. 55101; 1895
Saint Petersburg Junior C. St. Petersburg, Fla. 33733; 1927
Saint Peter's C. Jersey City, N.J. 07306; 1872
Saint Philip's C. San Antonio, Tex. 78203; junior, 1898
Saint Pius X Sem. Garrison, N.Y. 10524; 1956
Saint Rose, C. of Albany, N.Y. 12203; 1920
Saint Scholastica, C. of Duluth, Minn. 55811; 1912
Saints C. Lexington, Miss. 39095; junior, 1918
Saint Teresa, C. of Winona, Minn. 55987; 1907
Saint Thomas, C. of St. Paul, Minn. 55101; 1885
Saint Thomas, U. of Houston, Tex. 77006; 1947
Saint Thomas Aquinas C. Sparkill, N.Y. 10976; 1952

Saint Thomas Sem. Denver, Colo. 80210; 1906
Saint Vincent C. Latrobe, Pa. 15650; 1846
Saint Xavier C. Chicago, Ill. 60655; 1846
Salem C. Winston-Salem, N.C. 27108; 1772
Salem C. Salem, W.Va. 26426; 1888
Salem Comm. C. Penns Grove, N.J. 08069; junior, 1972
Salem State C. Salem, Mass. 01970; 1854
Salisbury State U. Salisbury, Md. 21801; 1925
Salt Lake Comm. C. Salt Lake City, Utah 84130; junior, 1947
Samford U. Birmingham, Ala. 35209; 1841
Sam Houston State U. Huntsville, Tex. 77340; 1879
Sampson Technical C. Clinton, N.C. 28328; junior, 1965
San Antonio C. San Antonio, Tex. 78284; junior, 1925
San Bernardino Valley C. San Bernardino, Calif. 92403; junior, 1926
Sandhills Comm. C. Carthage, N.C. 28327; junior, 1963
San Diego, U. of San Diego, Calif. 92110; 1949
San Diego City C. San Diego, Calif. 92101; junior, 1914
San Diego Mesa C. San Diego, Calif. 92111; junior, 1962
San Diego Miramar C. San Diego, Calif. 92126; junior, 1969
San Diego State U. San Diego, Calif. 92182; 1897
San Francisco, U. of San Francisco, Calif. 94117; 1855
San Francisco Art Inst. San Francisco, Calif. 94133; 1874
San Francisco C. of Mortuary Science San Francisco, Calif. 94109;
    junior, 1930
San Francisco Conservatory of Music San Francisco, Calif. 94122; 1917
San Francisco State U. San Francisco, Calif. 94132; 1899
Sangamon State U. Springfield, Ill. 62703; 1969
San Jacinto C. Pasadena, Tex. 77505; junior, 1961
San Joaquin Delta C. Stockton, Calif. 95204; junior, 1935
San Jose Bible C. San Jose, Calif. 95108; 1939
San Jose City C. San Jose, Calif. 95114; junior, 1921
San Jose State U. San Jose, Calif. 95192; 1857
San Juan Technological Comm. C. Hato Rey, Puerto Rico 00918; ju-
    nior, 1972
San Mateo, C. of San Mateo, Calif. 94402; junior, 1922
Santa Barbara City C. Santa Barbara, Calif. 93105; junior, 1946
Santa Clara, U. of Santa Clara, Calif. 95053; 1851
Santa Fe, C. of Santa Fe, N.Mex. 87501; 1947
Santa Fe Comm. C. Gainesville, Fla. 32601; junior, 1965
Santa Monica C. Santa Monica, Calif. 90406; junior, 1929
Santa Rosa Junior C. Santa Rosa, Calif. 95401; 1918
Sarah Lawrence C. Bronxville, N.Y. 10708; 1926
Sauk Valley C. Dixon, Ill. 61021; junior, 1965
Savannah State C. Savannah, Ga. 31404; 1890
Sayre Junior C. Sayre, Okla. 73662; 1938
Scarritt C. for Christian Workers Nashville, Tenn. 37203; 1924
Schenectady County Comm. C. Schenectady, N.Y. 12305; junior,
    1967
Schoolcraft C. Livonia, Mich. 48151; junior, 1961
Schreiner C. Kerrville, Tex. 78028; junior, 1923
Scott Comm. C. Bettendorf, Iowa 52722; junior, 1966
Scottsdale Comm. C. Scottsdale, Ariz. 85253; junior, 1969
Scranton, U. of Scranton, Pa. 18510; 1888
Scripps C. Claremont, Calif. 91711; 1926
S. D. Bishop State Junior C. Mobile, Ala. 36603; 1965
Seat of Wisdom C. Litchfield, Conn. 06759; 1958
Seattle Central Comm. C. Seattle, Wash. 98122; junior, 1966
Seattle Pacific U. Seattle, Wash. 98119; 1891
Seattle U. Seattle, Wash. 98122; 1892
Selma U. Selma, Ala. 36701; 1878
Seminole Comm. C. Sanford, Fla. 32771; junior, 1965
Seminole Junior C. Seminole, Okla. 74868; 1931
Sequoias, C. of the Visalia, Calif. 93277; junior, 1926
Seton Hall U. South Orange, N.J. 07079; 1856
Seton Hill C. Greensburg, Pa. 15601; 1883
Seward County Comm. C. Liberal, Kans. 67901; junior, 1967
Shasta C. Redding, Calif. 96001; junior, 1949
Shaw C. at Detroit Detroit, Mich. 48202; 1962
Shaw U. Raleigh, N.C. 27602; 1865
Shawnee C. Ullin, Ill. 62956; junior, 1967
Shawnee State U. Portsmouth, Ohio 45662; junior, 1975
Shelby State Comm. C. Memphis, Tenn, 38104; junior, 1969
Sheldon Jackson C. Sitka, Alaska 99835; 1878
Shelton C. Cape Canaveral, Fla. 32920; 1907
Shelton State Comm. C. Tuscaloosa, Ala. 35404; junior, 1953
Shenandoah C. and Conservatory of Music Winchester, Va. 22601; 1875
Shepherd C. Shepherdstown, W.Va. 25443; 1871
Sheridan C. Sheridan, Wyo. 82801; junior, 1948
Shimer C. Waukegan, Ill. 60085; 1853
Shippensburg U. of Pennsylvania Shippensburg, Pa. 17257; 1871
Shoreline Comm. C. Seattle, Wash. 98133; junior, 1964
Shorter C. North Little Rock, Ark. 72114; 1884
Shorter C. Rome, Ga. 30161; 1873
Siena C. Loudonville, N.Y. 12211; 1937
Siena Heights C. Adrian, Mich. 49221; 1919
Sierra C. Rocklin, Calif. 95677; junior, 1914
Sierra Nevada C. Incline Village, Nev. 89450; 1969
Silver Lake C. Manitowoc, Wis. 54220; 1869
Simmons C. Boston, Mass. 02115; 1899
Simon's Rock of Bard C. Great Barrington, Mass. 01230; 1964
Simpson C. San Francisco, Calif. 94134; 1921
Simpson C. Indianola, Iowa 50125; 1860
Sinclair Comm. C. Dayton, Ohio 45402; junior, 1887
Sinte Gleska C. Rosebud, S.Dak. 57570; 1970
Sioux Empire C. Hawarden, Iowa 51023; junior, 1967
Sioux Falls C. Sioux Falls, S.Dak. 57101; 1883
Siskiyous, C. of the Weed, Calif. 96094; junior, 1959
Skagit Valley C. Mount Vernon, Wash. 98273; junior, 1926
Skidmore C. Saratoga Springs, N.Y. 12866; 1911
Skyline C. San Bruno, Calif. 94066; junior, 1969
Slippery Rock U. of Pennsylvania Slippery Rock, Pa. 16057; 1889
Smith C. Northampton, Mass. 01063; 1875
Snead State Junior C. Boaz, Ala. 35957; 1898
Snow C. Ephraim, Utah 84627; junior, 1888

Solano Comm. C. Suisun City, Calif. 94585; junior, 1945
Somerset Comm. C. Somerset, Ky. 42501; junior, 1965
Sonoma State U. Rohnert Park, Calif. 94928; 1960
South, U. of the Sewanee, Tenn. 37375; 1857
South Alabama, U. of Mobile, Ala. 36688; 1963
South Carolina, U. of Columbia, S.C. 29208; 1801
South Carolina State C. Orangeburg, S.C. 29115; 1896
South Central Comm. C. New Haven, Conn. 06511; junior, 1967
South Dakota, U. of Vermillion, S.Dak. 57069; 1862
South Dakota Sch. of Mines and Tech. Rapid City, S.Dak. 57701; 1885
South Dakota State U. Brookings, S.Dak. 57006; 1881
Southeast Comm. C. Cumberland, Ky. 40823; junior, 1960
Southeastern Baptist C. Laurel, Miss. 39440; 1948
Southeastern Bible C. Birmingham, Ala. 35256; 1934
Southeastern C. of the Assemblies of God Lakeland, Fla. 33801; 1935
Southeastern Comm. C. West Burlington, Iowa 52655; junior, 1920
Southeastern Comm. C. Whiteville, N.C. 28472; junior, 1964
Southeastern Illinois C. Harrisburg, Ill. 62946; junior, 1961
Southeastern Louisiana U. Hammond, La. 70401; 1925
Southeastern Massachusetts U. North Dartmouth, Mass. 02747; 1895
Southeastern Oklahoma State U. Durant, Okla. 74701; 1909
Southeastern U. Washington, D.C. 20024; 1879
Southeast Missouri State U. Cape Girardeau, Mo. 63701; 1873
Southern Arkansas U. Magnolia, Ark. 71753; 1909
Southern Baptist C. Walnut Ridge, Ark. 72476; junior, 1941
Southern Bible C. Houston, Tex. 77015; 1958
Southern California, U. of Los Angeles, Calif. 90007; 1880
Southern California C. Costa Mesa, Calif. 92626; 1920
Southern California C. of Optometry Fullerton, Calif. 92631; 1904
Southern C. of Optometry Memphis, Tenn. 38104; 1932
Southern Colorado, U. of Pueblo, Colo. 81005; 1933
Southern Connecticut State U. New Haven, Conn. 06515; 1893
Southern Idaho, C. of Twin Falls, Idaho 83301; junior, 1964
Southern Illinois U. at Carbondale 62901; 1874
Southern Illinois U. at Edwardsville 62026; 1971
Southern Indiana, U. of Evansville, Ind. 47712; 1965
Southern Maine, U. of Portland, Me. 04103; 1878
Southern Maine Vocational Technical Inst. South Portland, Me. 04106;
    junior, 1946
Southern Methodist U. Dallas, Tex. 75222; 1910
Southern Missionary C. Collegedale, Tenn. 37315; 1893
Southern Mississippi, U. of Hattiesburg, Miss. 39401; 1910
Southern Nazarene U. Bethany, Okla. 73008; 1899
Southern Ohio C. Cincinnati, Ohio 45202; junior, 1927
Southern Oregon State C. Ashland, Oreg. 97520; 1926
Southern Sem. Junior C. Buena Vista, Va. 24416; 1868
Southern State Comm. C. Wilmington, Ohio 45177; junior, 1975
Southern Technical Inst. Marietta, Ga. 30060; 1948
Southern Union State Junior C. Wadley, Ala. 36276; 1934
Southern U. and A. & M. C. Baton Rouge, La. 70813; 1880
Southern Utah State C. Cedar City, Utah 84720; 1897
Southern Vermont C. Bennington, Vt. 05201; 1926
Southern Vocational C. Tuskegee, Ala. 36083; junior, 1969
Southern West Virginia Comm. C. Williamson, W.Va. 25661; junior,
    1971
South Florida, U. of Tampa, Fla. 33620; 1956
South Florida Junior C. Avon Park, Fla. 33825; 1965
South Georgia C. Douglas, Ga. 31533; junior, 1906
South Oklahoma City Junior C. Oklahoma City, Okla. 73159; 1969
South Plains C. Levelland, Tex. 79336; junior, 1958
South Puget Sound Comm. C. Olympia, Wash. 98502; junior, 1970
Southside Virginia Comm. C. Alberta, Va. 23821; junior, 1969
South Suburban C. South Holland, Ill. 60473; junior, 1927
Southwest, C. of the Hobbs, N.Mex. 88240; 1957
Southwest Baptist U. Bolivar, Mo. 65613; 1878
Southwestern Adventist C. Keene, Tex. 76059; 1893
Southwestern Assemblies of God C. Waxahachie, Tex. 75165; 1927
Southwestern Baptist Bible C. Phoenix, Ariz. 85032; 1960
Southwestern Christian C. Terrell, Tex. 75160; junior, 1950
Southwestern C. Chula Vista, Calif. 92010; junior, 1961
Southwestern C. Winfield, Kans. 67156; 1885
Southwestern C. of Christian Ministries Bethany, Okla. 73008; 1946
Southwestern Comm. C. Creston, Iowa 50801; junior, 1926
Southwestern Louisiana, The U. of Lafayette, La. 70501; 1900
Southwestern Michigan C. Dowagiac, Mich. 49047; junior, 1964
Southwestern Oklahoma State U. Weatherford, Okla. 73096; 1901
Southwestern Oregon Comm. C. Coos Bay, Oreg. 97420; junior, 1961
Southwestern Technical C. Sylva, N.C. 28779; junior, 1964
Southwestern U. Georgetown, Tex. 78626; 1840
Southwest Mississippi Comm. C. Summit, Miss. 39666; 1918
Southwest Missouri State U. Springfield, Mo. 65804; 1905
Southwest State U. Marshall, Minn. 56258; 1963
Southwest Texas Junior C. Uvalde, Tex. 78801; 1946
Southwest Texas State U. San Marcos, Tex. 78666; 1899
Southwest Virginia Comm. C. Richlands, Va. 24641; junior, 1968
Southwest Wisconsin Vocational Technical Inst. Fennimore, Wis.
    53805; junior, 1967
Spalding U. Louisville, Ky. 40203; 1829
Spartanburg Methodist C. Spartanburg, S.C. 29301; junior, 1911
Spartanburg Technical C. Spartanburg, S.C. 29303; junior, 1961
Spelman C. Atlanta, Ga. 30314; 1881
Spertus C. of Judaica Chicago, Ill. 60605; 1925
Spokane Comm. C. Spokane, Wash. 99202; junior, 1963
Spokane Falls Comm. C. Spokane, Wash. 99204; junior, 1963
Spoon River C. Canton, Ill. 61520; junior, 1959
Spring Arbor C. Spring Arbor, Mich. 49283; 1873
Springfield C. Springfield, Mass. 01109; 1885
Springfield C. in Illinois Springfield, Ill. 62702; junior, 1929
Springfield Technical Comm. C. Springfield, Mass. 01105; junior,
    1965
Spring Garden C. Philadelphia, Pa. 19118; 1850
Spring Hill C. Mobile, Ala. 36608; 1830
Standing Rock Comm. C. Fort Yates, N.Dak. 58538; junior, 1971
Stanford U. Stanford, Calif. 94305; 1885

Stanly Technical C. Albemarle, N.C. 28001; junior, 1971
Stark Technical C. Canton, Ohio 44720; junior, 1970
State Fair Comm. C. Sedalia, Mo. 65301; junior, 1966
Staten Island, C. of Staten Island, N.Y. 10301; 1956
State Technical Inst. at Memphis Tenn. 38134; junior, 1967
Steed C. Johnson City, Tenn. 37601; 1940
Stephen F. Austin State U. Nacogdoches, Tex. 75961; 1917
Stephens C. Columbia, Mo. 65201; 1833
Sterling C. Sterling, Kans. 67579; 1887
Stetson U. De Land, Fla. 32720; 1883
Steubenville, U. of Steubenville, Ohio 43952; 1946
Stevens Inst. of Tech. Hoboken, N.J. 07030; 1867
Stillman C. Tuscaloosa, Ala. 35401; 1876
Stockton State C. Pomona, N.J. 08240; 1969
Stonehill C. North Easton, Mass. 02356; 1948
Strayer C. Washington, D.C. 20005; 1904
Sue Bennett C. London, Ky. 40741; junior, 1896
Suffolk County Comm. C. Selden, N.Y. 11784; junior, 1960
Suffolk U. Boston, Mass. 02114; 1906
Sullins C. Bristol, Va. 24201; junior, 1870
Sullivan County Comm. C. Loch Sheldrake, N.Y. 12759; junior, 1963
Sul Ross State U. Alpine, Tex. 79830; 1920
Sumter Area Technical C. Sumter, S.C. 29105; junior, 1961
Suomi C. Hancock, Mich. 49930; junior, 1896
Surry Comm. C. Dobson, N.C. 27017; junior, 1965
Susquehanna U. Selinsgrove, Pa. 17870; 1858
Swarthmore C. Swarthmore, Pa. 19081; 1864
Sweet Briar C. Sweet Briar, Va. 24595; 1901
Syracuse U. Syracuse, N.Y. 13210; 1870
Syracuse U., Utica C. of Utica, N.Y. 13502; 1946
Tabor C. Hillsboro, Kans. 67063; 1908
Tacoma Comm. C. Tacoma, Wash. 98465; junior, 1965
Taft C. Taft, Calif. 93268; junior, 1922
Tahoe C. Tahoe Paradise, Calif. 95705; 1967
Talladega C. Talladega, Ala. 35160; 1867
Tallahassee Comm. C. Tallahassee, Fla. 32304; junior, 1965
Tampa, U. of Tampa, Fla. 33606; 1931
Tampa C. Tampa, Fla. 33614; 1890
Tarkio C. Tarkio, Mo. 64491; 1883
Tarleton State U. Stephenville, Tex. 76401; 1899
Tarrant County Junior C. Fort Worth, Tex. 76102; 1965
Taylor U. Upland, Ind. 46989; 1846
Teachers C. New York, N.Y. 10027; 1888
Temple Junior C. Temple, Tex. 76501; 1926
Temple U. Philadelphia, Pa. 19122; 1884
Tennessee at Chattanooga, U. of 37403; 1886
Tennessee at Knoxville, U. of 37916; 1794
Tennessee at Martin, U. of 38237; 1900
Tennessee State U. Nashville, Tenn. 37203; 1912
Tennessee Technological U. Cookeville, Tenn. 38501; 1915
Tennessee Temple U. Chattanooga, Tenn. 37404; 1946
Tennessee Wesleyan C. Athens, Tenn. 37303; 1857
Terra Technical C. Fremont, Ohio 43420; junior, 1968
Texarkana Comm. C. Texarkana, Tex. 75501; junior, 1927
Texas A&I U. Kingsville, Tex. 78363; 1925
Texas A&M U. College Station, Tex. 77843; 1876
Texas at Arlington, U. of 76019; 1895
Texas at Austin, U. of 78712; 1881
Texas at Dallas, U. of Richardson, Tex. 75080; 1969
Texas at El Paso, U. of 79999; 1913
Texas at San Antonio, U. of 78285; 1969
Texas at Tyler, U. of 75701; 1972
Texas Christian U. Fort Worth, Tex. 76129; 1873
Texas C. Tyler, Tex. 75701; 1894
Texas Health Science Center at Dallas, U. of 75235; 1943
Texas Health Science Center at Houston, U. of 77025; 1972
Texas Health Science Center at San Antonio, U. of 78284; 1959
Texas Lutheran C. Seguin, Tex. 78155; 1891
Texas Med. Branch at Galveston, U. of 77550; 1881
Texas of the Permian Basin, U. of Odessa, Tex. 79762; 1970
Texas Southern U. Houston, Tex. 77004; 1947
Texas Southmost C. Brownsville, Tex. 78520; junior, 1926
Texas State Technical Inst. Waco, Tex. 76705; junior, 1965
Texas Tech U. Lubbock, Tex. 79409; 1923
Texas Wesleyan C. Fort Worth, Tex. 76105; 1890
Texas Woman's U. Denton, Tex. 76204; 1901
Thames Valley State Technical C. Norwich, Conn. 06360; junior, 1963
Thiel C. Greenville, Pa. 16125; 1866
Thomas A. Edison C. Trenton, N.J. 08608; 1972
Thomas Aquinas C. Santa Paula, Calif. 93060; 1971
Thomas C. Waterville, Me. 04901; 1894
Thomas Jefferson U. Philadelphia, Pa. 19107; 1825
Thomas More C. Fort Mitchell, Ky. 41017; 1921
Thomas Nelson Comm. C. Hampton, Va. 23366; junior, 1967
Three Rivers Comm. C. Poplar Bluff, Mo. 63901; junior, 1966
Tidewater Comm. C. Portsmouth, Va. 23703; junior, 1958
Tiffin U. Tiffin, Ohio 44883; 1924
Toccoa Falls C. Toccoa Falls, Ga. 30577; 1911
Toledo, U. of Toledo, Ohio 43606; 1872
Tomlinson C. Cleveland, Tenn. 37311; junior, 1966
Tompkins–Cortland Comm. C. Dryden, N.Y. 13053; junior, 1967
Tougaloo C. Tougaloo, Miss. 39174; 1869
Touro C. New York, N.Y. 10036; 1970
Towson State U. Baltimore, Md. 21204; 1866
Transylvania U. Lexington, Ky. 40508; 1780
Treasure Valley Comm. C. Ontario, Oreg. 97914; junior, 1962
Trenton State C. Trenton, N.J. 08625; 1855
Trevecca Nazarene C. Nashville, Tenn. 37210; 1901
Tri–County Comm. C. Murphy, N.C. 28906; junior, 1964
Tri–County Technical C. Pendleton, S.C. 29670; junior, 1962
Trident Technical C. Charleston, S.C. 29411; junior, 1964
Trinidad State Junior C. Trinidad, Colo. 81082; 1925
Trinity Bible Inst. Ellendale, N.Dak. 58436; 1948

Trinity Christian C. Palos Heights, Ill. 60463; 1959
Trinity C. Hartford, Conn. 06106; 1823
Trinity C. Washington, D.C. 20017; 1897
Trinity C. Deerfield, Ill. 60015; 1897
Trinity C. Burlington, Vt. 05401; 1925
Trinity U. San Antonio, Tex. 78284; 1869
Tri–State U. Angola, Ind. 46703; 1884
Triton C. River Grove, Ill. 60171; junior, 1964
Trocaire C. Buffalo, N.Y. 14220; junior, 1958
Troy State U. Troy, Ala. 36081; 1887
Truett McConnell C. Cleveland, Ga. 30528; junior, 1947
Tufts U. Medford, Mass. 02155; 1852
Tulane U. of Louisiana New Orleans, La. 70118; 1834
Tulsa, U. of Tulsa, Okla. 74104; 1894
Tulsa Junior C. Tulsa, Okla. 74119; 1970
Tunxis Comm. C. Farmington, Conn. 06032; junior, 1970
Tusculum C. Greeneville, Tenn. 37743; 1794
Tuskegee Inst. Tuskegee Institute, Ala. 36088; 1881
Tyler Junior C. Tyler, Tex. 75701; 1926
Ulster County Comm. C. Stone Ridge, N.Y. 12484; junior, 1963
Umpqua Comm. C. Roseburg, Oreg. 97470; junior, 1964
Union C. Barbourville, Ky. 40906; 1879
Union C. Lincoln, Nebr. 68506; 1891
Union C. Cranford, N.J. 07016; junior, 1933
Union C. Schenectady, N.Y. 12308; 1795
Union County Technical Inst. Scotch Plains, N.J. 07076; junior, 1959
Union U. Jackson, Tenn. 38301; 1834
United States Air Force Acad. Colorado Springs, Colo. 80840; 1954
United States Coast Guard Acad. New London, Conn. 06320; 1876
United States International U. San Diego, Calif. 92131; 1952
United States Merchant Marine Acad. Kings Point, N.Y. 11024; 1938
United States Military Acad. West Point, N.Y. 10996; 1802
United States Naval Acad. Annapolis, Md. 21402; 1845
United States Naval Postgraduate Sch. Monterey, Calif. 93940; 1909
United Wesleyan C. Allentown, Pa. 18103; 1921
Unity C. Unity, Me. 04988; 1966
Upper Iowa U. Fayette, Iowa 52142; 1857
Upsala C. East Orange, N.J. 07019; 1893
Urbana U. Urbana, Ohio 43078; 1850
Ursinus C. Collegeville, Pa. 19426; 1869
Ursuline C. Cleveland, Ohio 44124; 1871
Utah, U. of Salt Lake City, Utah 84112; 1850
Utah State U. Logan, Utah 84322; 1888
Utah Valley Comm. C. Orem, Utah 84058; junior, 1941
Utica Junior C. Utica, Miss. 39175; 1903
Valdosta State C. Valdosta, Ga. 31601; 1906
Valencia Comm. C. Orlando, Fla. 32802; junior, 1967
Valley City State U. Valley City, N.Dak. 58072; 1890
Valley Forge Christian C. Phoenixville, Pa. 19460; 1938
Valley Forge Military Junior C. Wayne, Pa. 19087; 1928
Valparaiso Technical Inst. Valparaiso, Ind. 46383; 1934
Valparaiso U. Valparaiso, Ind. 46383; 1859
Vanderbilt U. Nashville, Tenn. 37203; 1872
VanderCook C. of Music Chicago, Ill.; 60616; 1928
Vassar C. Poughkeepsie, N.Y. 12601; 1861
Vennard C. University Park, Iowa 52595; 1910
Ventura C. Ventura, Calif. 93003; junior, 1925
Vermilion Comm. C. Ely, Minn. 55731; junior, 1922
Vermont, Comm. C. of Montpelier, Vt. 05602; junior, 1970
Vermont, U. of Burlington, Vt. 05401; 1791
Vermont Technical C. Randolph Center, Vt. 05061; junior, 1957
Vernon Regional Junior C. Vernon, Tex. 76384; 1970
Victoria C. Victoria, Tex. 77901; junior, 1925
Victor Valley C. Victorville, Calif. 92392; junior, 1961
Villa Julie C. Stevenson, Md. 21153; junior, 1947
Villa Maria C. Erie, Pa. 16505; 1925
Villa Maria C. of Buffalo Buffalo, N.Y. 14225; junior, 1960
Villanova U. Villanova, Pa. 19085; 1842
Vincennes U. Vincennes, Ind. 47591; junior, 1801
Virginia, U. of Charlottesville, Va. 22903; 1819
Virginia C. Lynchburg, Va. 24501; junior, 1888
Virginia Commonwealth U. Richmond, Va. 23284; 1838
Virginia Highlands Comm. C. Abingdon, Va. 24210; junior, 1967
Virginia Intermont C. Bristol, Va. 24201; 1884
Virginia Military Inst. Lexington, Va. 24450; 1839
Virginia Polytechnic Inst. and State U. Blacksburg, Va. 24061; 1872
Virginia State U. Petersburg, Va. 23803; 1882
Virginia Union U. Richmond, Va. 23220; 1865
Virginia Wesleyan C. Norfolk, Va. 23502; 1961
Virginia Western Comm. C. Roanoke, Va. 24015; junior, 1966
Virgin Islands, C. of the St. Thomas, Virgin Islands 00802; 1963
Visual Arts, Sch. of New York, N.Y. 10010; 1947
Viterbo C. La Crosse, Wis. 54601; 1931
Volunteer State Comm. C. Gallatin, Tenn. 37066; junior, 1970
Voorhees C. Denmark, S.C. 29042; 1897
Wabash C. Crawfordsville, Ind. 47933; 1832
Wabash Valley C. Mt. Carmel, Ill. 62863; junior, 1961
Wadhams Hall Sem. and C. Ogdensburg, N.Y. 13669; 1924
Wagner C. Staten Island, N.Y. 10301; 1883
Wake Forest U. Winston-Salem, N.C. 27109; 1834
Wake Technical C. Raleigh, N.C. 27603; junior, 1958
Waldorf C. Forest City, Iowa 50436; junior, 1903
Walker C. Jasper, Ala. 35501; junior, 1938
Walla Walla C. College Place, Wash. 99324; 1892
Walla Walla Comm. C. Walla Walla, Wash. 99362; junior, 1967
Walsh C. Canton, Ohio 44720; 1960
Walters State Comm. C. Morristown, Tenn. 37814; junior, 1970
Warner Pacific C. Portland, Oreg. 97215; 1937
Warren Wilson C. Swannanoa, N.C. 28778; 1893
Wartburg C. Waverly, Iowa 50677; 1852
Washburn U. of Topeka Topeka, Kans. 66621; 1865
Washington, U. of Seattle, Wash. 98195; 1861
Washington and Jefferson C. Washington, Pa. 15301; 1780
Washington and Lee U. Lexington, Va. 24450; 1749

Washington Bible C. Lanham, Md. 20801; 1938
Washington C. Chestertown, Md. 21620; 1782
Washington State U. Pullman, Wash. 99163; 1890
Washington Technical C. Marietta, Ohio 45750; junior, 1971
Washington U. St. Louis, Mo. 63130; 1853
Washtenaw Comm. C. Ann Arbor, Mich. 48107; junior, 1965
Waterbury State Technical C. Waterbury, Conn. 06708; junior, 1964
Waubonsee Comm. C. Sugar Grove, Ill. 60554; junior, 1966
Wayland Baptist C. Plainview, Tex. 79072; 1909
Wayne Comm. C. Goldsboro, N.C. 27530; junior, 1957
Wayne County Comm. C. Detroit, Mich. 48201; junior, 1968
Waynesburg C. Waynesburg, Pa. 15370; 1850
Wayne State C. Wayne, Nebr. 68787; 1891
Wayne State U. Detroit, Mich. 48202; 1868
Weatherford C. Weatherford, Tex. 76086; junior, 1869
Webber C. Babson Park, Fla. 33827; 1927
Webb Inst. of Naval Architecture Glen Cove, N.Y. 11542; 1889
Weber State C. Ogden, Utah 84408; 1889
Webster C. St. Louis, Mo. 63119; 1915
Wellesley C. Wellesley, Mass. 02181; 1870
Wells C. Aurora, N.Y. 13026; 1868
Wenatchee Valley C. Wenatchee, Wash. 98801; junior, 1939
Wentworth Inst. of Tech. Boston, Mass. 02115; 1904
Wentworth Military Acad. Lexington, Mo. 64067; junior, 1880
Wesleyan C. Macon, Ga. 31201; 1836
Wesleyan U. Middletown, Conn. 06457; 1831
Wesley C. Dover, Del. 19901; 1873
Wesley C. Florence, Miss. 39073; 1972
Westark Comm. C. Fort Smith, Ark. 72901; junior, 1928
Westbrook C. Portland, Me. 04103; junior, 1831
Westchester Business Inst. White Plains, N.Y. 10606; junior, 1915
Westchester Comm. C. Valhalla, N.Y. 10595; junior, 1946
West Chester U. of Pennsylvania West Chester, Pa. 19380; 1812
West Coast Christian C. Fresno, Calif. 93710; 1944
West Coast U. Los Angeles, Calif. 90005; 1909
Western Baptist C. Salem, Oreg. 97302; 1946
Western Carolina U. Cullowhee, N.C. 28723; 1889
Western Connecticut State U. Danbury, Conn. 06810; 1903
Western Illinois U. Macomb, Ill. 61455; 1899
Western Iowa Tech Comm. C. Sioux City, Iowa 51106; junior, 1966
Western Kentucky U. Bowling Green, Ky. 42101; 1906
Western Maryland C. Westminster, Md. 21157; 1867
Western Michigan U. Kalamazoo, Mich. 49001; 1903
Western Montana C. Dillon, Mont. 59725; 1893
Western Nevada Comm. C. Carson City, Nev. 89701; junior, 1971
Western New England C. Springfield, Mass. 01119; 1919
Western New Mexico U. Silver City, N.Mex. 88061; 1893
Western Oklahoma State C. Altus, Okla. 73521; junior, 1926
Western Oregon State C. Monmouth, Oreg. 97361; 1856
Western Piedmont Comm. C. Morganton, N.C. 28655; junior, 1964
Western State C. of Colorado Gunnison, Colo. 81230; 1901
Western States C. of Engineering Inglewood, Calif. 90301; 1946
Western Texas C. Snyder, Tex. 79549; junior, 1969
Western Washington U. Bellingham, Wash. 98225; 1893
Western Wisconsin Technical Inst. La Crosse, Wis. 54601; junior, 1912
Western Wyoming Comm. C. Rock Springs, Wyo. 82901; junior, 1959
Westfield State C. Westfield, Mass. 01085; 1839
West Florida, U. of Pensacola, Fla. 32504; 1967
West Georgia C. Carrollton, Ga. 30117; 1933
West Hills Comm. C. Coalinga, Calif. 93210; junior, 1932
West Liberty State C. West Liberty, W.Va. 26074; 1837
West Los Angeles C. Culver City, Calif. 90230; junior, 1968
Westmar C. Le Mars, Iowa 51031; 1900
Westminster Choir C. Princeton, N.J. 08540; 1926
Westminster C. Fulton, Mo. 65251; 1851
Westminster C. New Wilmington, Pa. 16142; 1852
Westminster C. Salt Lake City, Utah 84105; 1875
Westmont C. Santa Barbara, Calif. 93103; 1940
West Shore Comm. C. Scottville, Mich. 49454; junior, 1967
West Texas State U. Canyon, Tex. 79015; 1910
West Valley C. Saratoga, Calif. 95070; junior, 1963
West Virginia Inst. of Tech. Montgomery, W.Va. 25136; 1895
West Virginia Northern Comm. C. Wheeling, W.Va. 26003; junior, 1972
West Virginia State C. Institute, W.Va. 25112; 1891
West Virginia U. Morgantown, W.Va. 26506; 1867
West Virginia Wesleyan C. Buckhannon, W.Va. 26201; 1890
Wharton County Junior C. Wharton, Tex. 77488; 1946
Whatcom Comm. C. Bellingham, Wash. 98225; junior, 1970
Wheaton C. Wheaton, Ill. 60187; 1860
Wheaton C. Norton, Mass. 02766; 1834
Wheeling C. Wheeling, W.Va. 26003; 1954
Wheelock C. Boston, Mass. 02215; 1889
White Pines C. Chester, N.H. 03036; junior, 1965
Whitman C. Walla Walla, Wash. 99362; 1859
Whittier C. Whittier, Calif. 90608; 1901
Whitworth Bible C. Brookhaven, Miss. 39601; 1818
Whitworth C. Spokane, Wash. 99251; 1890
Wichita State U. Wichita, Kans. 67208; 1892
Widener U. Chester, Pa. 19013; 1821
Wilberforce U. Wilberforce, Ohio 45384; 1856
Wiley C. Marshall, Tex. 75670; 1873
Wilkes C. Wilkes-Barre, Pa. 18703; 1933
Wilkes Comm. C. Wilkesboro, N.C. 28697; junior, 1965
Willamette U. Salem, Oreg. 97301; 1842
William and Mary, C. of Williamsburg, Va. 23185; 1693
William Carey C. Hattiesburg, Miss. 39401; 1911
William Jewell C. Liberty, Mo. 64068; 1849
William Marsh Rice U. Houston, Tex. 77001; 1891
William Paterson C. Wayne, N.J. 07470; 1855
William Penn C. Oskaloosa, Iowa 52577; 1873
William Rainey Harper C. Palatine, Ill. 60067; junior, 1965
Williamsburg Technical C. Kingstree, S.C. 29556; junior, 1969

Williams C. Williamstown, Mass. 01267; 1793
Williamsport Area Comm. C. Williamsport, Pa. 17701; junior, 1920
William Tyndale C. Farmington Hills, Mich. 48018; 1945
William Woods C. Fulton, Mo. 65251; 1870
Willmar Comm. C. Willmar, Minn. 56201; junior, 1961
Wilmington C. New Castle, Del. 19720; 1967
Wilmington C. Wilmington, Ohio 45177; 1870
Wilson C. Chambersburg, Pa. 17201; 1869
Wilson County Technical Inst. Wilson, N.C. 27893; junior, 1958
Wingate C. Wingate, N.C. 28174; 1896
Winona State U. Winona, Minn. 55987; 1858
Winston-Salem State U. Winston-Salem, N.C. 27102; 1892
Winthrop C. Rock Hill, S.C. 29730; 1886
Wisconsin Conservatory of Music Milwaukee, Wis. 53202; 1899
Wisconsin-Eau Claire, U. of 54701; 1916
Wisconsin-Green Bay, U. of 54302; 1969
Wisconsin-La Crosse, U. of 54601; 1909
Wisconsin-Madison, U. of 53706; 1836
Wisconsin-Milwaukee, U. of 53201; 1908
Wisconsin-Oshkosh, U. of 54901; 1871
Wisconsin-Parkside, U. of Kenosha, Wis. 53140; 1969
Wisconsin-Platteville, U. of 53818; 1866
Wisconsin-River Falls, U. of 54022; 1875
Wisconsin-Stevens Point, U. of 54481; 1894
Wisconsin-Stout, U. of Menomonie, Wis. 54751; 1893
Wisconsin-Superior, U. of 54880; 1896
Wisconsin-Whitewater, U. of 53190; 1868
Wittenberg U. Springfield, Ohio 45501; 1845
Wofford C. Spartanburg, S.C. 29301; 1854
Woodbury U. Los Angeles, Calif. 90017; 1884
Woodcrest C. and Conference Center Lindale, Tex. 75771; 1940
Wood Junior C. Mathiston, Miss. 39752; 1886
Wood Sch., The New York, N.Y. 10017; junior, 1879
Wooster, C. of Wooster, Ohio 44691; 1866
Worcester Junior C. Worcester, Mass. 01608; 1905
Worcester Polytechnic Inst. Worcester, Mass. 01609; 1865
Worcester State C. Worcester, Mass. 01620; 1871
World C. West San Rafael, Calif. 94912; 1973
Worthington Comm. C. Worthington, Minn. 56187; junior, 1936
Wright State U. Dayton, Ohio 45431; 1964
Wyoming, U. of Laramie, Wyo. 82070; 1886
Wytheville Comm. C. Wytheville, Va. 24382; junior, 1963
Xavier U. Cincinnati, Ohio 45207; 1831
Xavier U. of Louisiana New Orleans, La. 70125; 1915
Yakima Valley Comm. C. Yakima, Wash. 98902; junior, 1928
Yale U. New Haven, Conn. 06520; 1701
Yavapai C. Prescott, Ariz. 86301; 1966
Yeshiva U. New York, N.Y. 10033; 1886
York C. York, Nebr. 68467; junior, 1890
York C. Jamaica, N.Y. 11451; 1967
York C. of Pennsylvania York, Pa. 17405; 1941
York Technical C. Rock Hill, S.C. 29730; junior, 1962
Young Harris C. Young Harris, Ga. 30582; junior, 1886
Youngstown State U. Youngstown, Ohio 44503; 1908
Yuba C. Marysville, Calif. 95901; junior, 1927

Canada

Acadia U. Wolfville, N.S., 1838
Alberta, U. of Edmonton, Alta., 1906
Aldersgate C. Moose Jaw, Sask., 1940
Algoma U. C. Sault Ste. Marie, Ont., 1965
Amos, Sém. d' Amos, Que., 1940
André-Grasset, C. Montreal, Que., 1927
Angèle Mérici, C. Quebec, Que., 1936
Assumption U. Windsor, Ont., 1857
Athabasca U. Athabasca, Alta., 1970
Atlantic Inst. of Ed. Halifax, N.S., 1970
Basile-Moreau, C. St. Laurent, Que., 1929
Bishop's U. Lennoxville, Que., 1843
Bon Pasteur, C. du Chicoutimi, Que., 1947
Bourget, C. Rigaud, Que., 1850
Brandon U. Brandon, Man., 1899
Brescia C. London, Ont., 1919
British Columbia, U. of Vancouver, B.C., 1890
Brock U. St. Catharines, Ont., 1962
Bruyère, C. Ottawa, Ont., 1925
Calgary, U. of Calgary, Alta., 1945
Campion C. Regina, Sask., 1917
Camrose Lutheran C. Camrose, Alta., junior, 1911
Canadian Bible C. Regina, Sask., 1941
Canadian Mennonite Bible C. Winnipeg, Man., 1947
Canadian Nazarene C. Winnipeg, Man., 1920
Canadian Theological C. Regina, Sask., 1941
Canadian Union C. Lacombe, Alta., junior, 1907
Canterbury C. Windsor, Ont., 1957

Cape Breton, C. of Sydney, N.S., 1974
Carey Hall Vancouver, B.C., 1960
Carleton U. Ottawa, Ont., 1942
Chicoutimi, Sém. de Chicoutimi, Que., 1873
Christian Training Inst. Edmonton, Alta., 1939
Christ the King, Sem. of Mission City, B.C., 1932
Concordia Lutheran C. Edmonton, Alta., junior, 1921
Concordia U. Montreal, Que., 1974
Confederation C. Thunder Bay, Ont., 1967
Conrad Grebel C. Waterloo, Ont., 1961
Cornwall, C. Classique de Cornwall, Ont., 1949
Dalhousie U. Halifax, N.S., 1818
Emmanuel and Saint Chad, C. of Saskatoon, Sask., 1879
Gardes–Malades, École des Edmundston, N.B., 1946
Gaspé, Sém. de Gaspé, Que., 1926
Grande Prairie Regional C. Grande Prairie, Alta., junior, 1966
Grant Macewan Comm. C. Edmonton, Alta., junior, 1971
Gravelbourg, C. Catholique de Gravelbourg, Sask., 1917
Guelph, U. of Guelph, Ont., 1964
Hautes Études Commerciales, École des Montreal, Que., 1907
Hearst, U.C. of Hearst, Ont., 1953
Holy Heart Sem. Halifax, N.S., 1895
Holy Names C. Windsor, Ont., 1934
Holy Redeemer C. Windsor, Ont., 1956
Huntington U. Sudbury, Ont., 1960
Huron C. London, Ont., 1863
Ignatius C. Guelph, Ont., 1913
Iona C. Windsor, Ont., 1964
Jean–de–Brébeuf, C. Montreal, Que., 1928
Jean–Jacques Olier C. Verdun, Que., 1951
Jésuites, C. des Quebec, Que., 1635
Jésus–Marie de Sillery, C. Quebec, Que., 1857
Jésus–Marie d'Outremont, C. Outremont, Que., 1933
Joliette, Sém. de Joliette, Que., 1846
Journalism, Sch. of Halifax, N.S., 1945
King's C. London, Ont., 1912
King's C., U. of Halifax, N.S., 1789
Knox C. Toronto, Ont., 1844
Kootenay Sch. of Art Nelson, B.C., 1961
Lakehead U. Thunder Bay, Ont., 1946
Lambton C. of Allied Arts and Tech. Sarnia, Ont., junior, 1966
L'Assomption, C. Moncton, N.B., 1943
L'Assomption, C. de L'Assomption, Que., 1832
Laurentian U. of Sudbury Sudbury, Ont., 1960
Laval, U. Quebec, Que., 1852
Lethbridge, U. of Lethbridge, Alta., 1967
Lethbridge Comm. C. Lethbridge, Alta., junior, 1957
Lévis, C. de Levis, Que., 1853
London C. of Bible and Missions London, Ont., 1935
Longueuil, Externat Classique de Ville Jacques-Cartier, Que., 1950
Loyola C. Montreal, Que., 1896
Lutheran Theol. Sem. Saskatoon, Sask., 1913
Luther C. Regina, Sask., 1921
McGill U. Montreal, Que., 1821
McMaster Divinity C. Hamilton, Ont., 1957
McMaster U. Hamilton, Ont., 1887
Manitoba, U. of Winnipeg, Man., 1877
Manitoba Law Sch. Winnipeg, Man., 1914
Marguerite–Bourgeoys, C. Montreal, Que., 1908
Marguerite d'Youville, C. Hull, Que., 1945
Marguerite d'Youville, Inst. Montreal, Que., 1934
Marianopolis C. Montreal, Que., 1943
Marie–Anne, C. Ahuntsic, Montreal, Que., 1932
Marie de France, C. Montreal, Que., 1939
Marie–de–la–Présentation, C. Drummondville, Que., 1955
Marie de l'Incarnation, C. Trois-Rivières, Que., 1697
Marie–Immaculée, Sém. Oblat de Chambly, Que., 1926
Marie–Médiatrice, C. Hull, Que., 1938
Maritime C. of Pharmacy Halifax, N.S., 1911
Maritime Sch. of Social Work Halifax, N.S., 1941
Médecine Vétérinaire, L'École St. Hyacinthe, Que., 1886
Medicine Hat C. Medicine Hat, Alta., junior, 1965
Memorial U. of Newfoundland St. John's, Nfld., 1925
Mennonite Brethren C. of Arts Winnipeg, Man., 1944
Moncton, U. de Moncton, N.B., 1864
Montréal, C. de Montreal, Que., 1767
Montréal, U. de Montreal, Que., 1876
Montreal Diocesan Theol. C. Montreal, Que., 1873
Mont–St.–Louis, C. Montreal, Que., 1888
Mount Allison U. Sackville, N.B., 1839
Mount Royal C. Calgary, Alta., junior, 1910
Mount St. Bernard C. Antigonish, N.S., 1883
Mount St. Vincent U. Halifax, N.S., 1914
Musique, École de Edmundston, N.B., 1950
New Brunswick, U. of Fredericton, N.B., 1785
New Brunswick in Saint John, U. of Saint John, N.B., 1964
Nicolet, Sém. de Nicolet, Que., 1801
Nipissing C. North Bay, Ont., 1967
Normale Secondaire, École Montreal, Que., 1941
North American Baptist C. South Edmonton, Alta., 1939
Notre–Dame, C. Prince Albert, Sask., 1958
Notre Dame C. Wilcox, Sask., 1933
Notre–Dame d'Acadie, C. Moncton, N.B., 1943
Notre–Dame de Bellevue, C. Quebec, Que., 1937
Notre–Dame de Grâce, Scolasticat Hull, Que., 1940
Notre–Dame de l'Assomption, C. Nicolet, Que., 1937
Notre–Dame du Perpétuel Secours, Sém. Moncton, N.B., 1956
Notre–Dame du St.–Rosaire, Scolasticat Rimouski, Que., 1957
Notre Dame of Canada C. Wilcox, Sask., 1933
Notre Dame U. of Nelson Nelson, B.C., 1950
Nova Scotia Agricultural C. Truro, N.S., junior, 1905
Nova Scotia C. of Art and Design Halifax, N.S., 1887
Nova Scotia Technical C. Halifax, N.S., 1907
Oka, Inst. Agricole d' La Trappe, Que., 1893

Ontario Agricultural C. Guelph, Ont., 1874
Ontario Bible C. Willowdale, Ont., 1935
Ontario Inst. for Studies in Ed. Toronto, Ont., 1965
Ontario Veterinary C. Guelph, Ont., 1862
Optométrie, École d' Montreal, Que., 1910
Ottawa, Grand Sém. d' Ottawa, Ont., 1847
Ottawa, Petit Sém. d' Ottawa, Ont., 1925
Ottawa, U. d' Ottawa, Ont., 1848
Pédagogie Familiale, Inst. de Montreal, Que., 1943
Pédagogique, Inst. Montreal, Que., 1926
Pédagogique St.–Georges, Inst. Laval des Rapides, Que., 1929
Philosophie, Sém. de Montreal, Que., 1876
Pine Hill Divinity Hall Halifax, N.S., 1820
Polytechnique, École Montreal, Que., 1873
Presbyterian C. Montreal, Que., 1865
Prince Edward Island, U. of Charlottetown, P.E.I., 1969
Provincial Inst. of Tech. and Art Calgary, Alta., junior, 1916
Québec, Acad. de Quebec, Que., 1862
Québec, Sém. de Quebec, Que., 1663
Québec à Chicoutimi, U. du Que., 1969
Québec à Montréal, U. du Que., 1969
Québec à Rimouski, U. du Que., 1969
Québec à Trois-Rivières, U. du Que., 1969
Queen's C. St. John's, Nfld., 1841
Queen's Theol. C. Kingston, Ont., 1912
Queen's U. at Kingston Kingston, Ont., 1841
Red Deer C. Red Deer, Alta., junior, 1964
Regina, U. of Regina, Sask., 1974
Regis C. Toronto, Ont., 1930
Renison C. Waterloo, Ont., 1959
Rimouski, C. de Rimouski, Que., 1855
Rouyn, C. Classique de Rouyn, Que., 1948
Royal Conservatory of Music Toronto, Ont., 1886
Royal Military C. of Canada Kingston, Ont., 1876
Royal Roads Military C. Victoria, B.C., 1942
Ryerson Polytechnical Inst. Toronto, Ont., 1948
Sacré–Coeur, C. du Sherbrooke, Que., 1945
Sacré–Coeur, Scolasticat du Lebret, Sask., 1926
Sacré–Coeur, Sém. du St. Victor, Que., 1910
Sacred Heart, Convent of the Halifax, N.S., junior, 1849
Saint–Alexandre, C. Limbour, Que., 1912
Saint–Alphonse, Sém. Aylmer, Que., 1896
Saint Andrew's C. Winnipeg, Man., 1946
Saint Andrew's C. Saskatoon, Sask., 1912
Saint Andrew's Hall Vancouver, B.C., 1957
Saint–Antoine, Sém. Quebec, Que., 1902
Saint–Augustin, Sém. Cap-Rouge, Que., 1965
Saint Augustine's Sem. Scarborough, Ont., 1913
Saint–Boniface, C. universitaire de Saint-Boniface, Man., 1818
Saint Bride's C. Littledale, Nfld., 1884
Saint Charles Scholasticate Battleford, Sask., 1939
Saint–Denis, C. Montreal, Que., 1950
Sainte–Anne, U. Pointe-de-l'Eglise, N.S., 1890
Sainte–Anne–de–la–Pocatière, C. Ste. Anne de la Pocatière, Que., 1827
Sainte–Croix, C. Montreal, Que., 1929
Sainte–Croix, Sém. St. Laurent, Que., 1899
Sainte–Marie, C. Montreal, Que., 1848
Sainte–Marie, Sém. Shawinigan, Que., 1947
Sainte–Thérèse, Sém. de Sainte-Thérèse-de-Blainville, Que., 1825
Saint Francis Xavier U. Antigonish, N.S., 1853
Saint–Georges, Sém. de Saint-Georges, Que., 1946
Saint–Hyacinthe, Sém. de St. Hyacinthe, Que., 1811
Saint–Jean, C. Edmonton, Alta., 1908
Saint–Jean, C. de Saint-Jean, Que., 1911
Saint–Jean, C. Militaire Royal de Saint Jean, Que., 1952
Saint–Jean, Scolasticat Ottawa, Ont., 1902
Saint–Jean–Eudes, Externat Classique Quebec, Que., 1937
Saint Jerome's C., U. of Waterloo, Ont., 1864
Saint John's C. Winnipeg, Man., 1849
Saint–Joseph, C. Moncton, N.B., 1864
Saint–Joseph, Sém. Mont Laurier, Que., 1915
Saint–Joseph, Sém. Trois-Rivières, Que., 1663
Saint Joseph's C. Edmonton, Alta., 1927
Saint Joseph's C. Yorkton, Sask., junior, 1919
Saint–Laurent, C. de St. Laurent, Que., 1847
Saint–Louis–Maillet, Centre U. Edmundston, N.B., 1946
Saint Mark's C. Vancouver, B.C., 1965
Saint Martha's Sch. of Nursing Antigonish, N.S., 1933
Saint Mary's U. Halifax, N.S., 1802
Saint–Maurice, C. St. Hyacinthe, Que., 1935
Saint Michael's C., U. of Toronto, Ont., 1852
Saint Patrick's C. Ottawa, Ont., 1932
Saint–Paul, C. Montreal, Que., 1957
Saint Paul's C. Winnipeg, Man., 1926
Saint Paul's United C. Waterloo, Ont., 1961
Saint Paul U. Ottawa, Ont., 1848
Saint Peter's C. Muenster, Sask., junior, 1922
Saint–Sacrement, Sém. des Pères du Terrebonne, Que., 1902
Saints–Apôtres, Sém. des Côte Sainte-Catherine, Comté de Laprairie, Que., 1952
Saint Stephen's C. Edmonton, Alta., 1903
Saint Thomas C. North Battleford, Sask., 1932
Saint Thomas More C. Saskatoon, Sask., 1936
Saint Thomas U. Fredericton, N.B., 1910
Saint–Viateur, C. Montreal, Que., 1951
Saskatchewan, U. of Saskatoon, Sask., 1907
Saskatchewan Indian Federated C. Regina, Sask., 1976
Sciences Domestiques, École des Sherbrooke, Que., 1956
Sherbrooke, Sém. de Sherbrooke, Que., 1875
Sherbrooke, U. de Sherbrooke, Que., 1954
Shippegan, Centre U. Shippegan, N.B., 1960
Simon Fraser U. Burnaby, B.C., 1963
Sir George Williams U. Montreal, Que., 1929
Spiritain de Sainte–Foy, Sém. Ste.-Foy, Que., 1940

Stanislas, C. Montreal, Que., 1938
Sudbury, U. de Sudbury, Ont., 1913
Technologie Supérieure, École de Montreal, Que., 1974
Thomas More Inst. for Adult Ed. Montreal, Que., 1948
Thorneloe U. Sudbury, Ont., 1961
Toronto, U. of Toronto, Ont., 1827
Toronto Bible C. Toronto, Ont., 1894
Trent U. Peterborough, Ont., 1963
Trinity C., U. of Toronto, Ont., 1851
United C. Winnipeg, Man., 1871
United Theol. C. of Montreal Montreal, Que., 1926
Ursulines, C. des Rimouski, Que., 1906
Valleyfield, Sém. de Valleyfield, Que., 1893
Vancouver Sch. of Theology Vancouver, B.C., 1912

Victoria, U. of Victoria, B.C., 1902
Victoria Conservatory of Music Victoria, B.C., 1964
Victoria U. Toronto, Ont., 1836
Victoriaville, C. de Victoriaville, Que., 1872
Vincent–d'Indy, École de musique Montreal, Que., 1932
Vocations Tardives, Sém. des Nicolet, Que., 1956
Waterloo, U. of Waterloo, Ont., 1959
Western Ontario, U. of London, Ont., 1878
Wilfrid Laurier U. Waterloo, Ont., 1973
Windsor, U. of Windsor, Ont., 1963
Winnipeg, U. of Winnipeg, Man., 1871
Winnipeg Bible C. Winnipeg, Man., 1925
Wycliffe C. Toronto, Ont., 1877
York U. North York, Ont., 1959

Signs and Symbols

Astronomy

SUN, GREATER PLANETS, ETC.

☉	the sun; Sunday
●, ☾, or ☽	the moon; Monday
●	new moon
☽, ●, ☽,)	first quarter
○ or ☽	full moon
☾, ●, ☾, (	last quarter
☿	Mercury; Wednesday
♀	Venus; Friday
⊕, ⊖, or ♁	the earth
♂	Mars; Tuesday
♃	Jupiter; Thursday
♄ or ♄	Saturn; Saturday
♁, ♅, or ♅	Uranus
♆, ♆, or ♆	Neptune
♇	Pluto

☄	comet
✴ or ✳	fixed star

ASPECTS AND NODES

☌	conjunction—indicating that the bodies have the same longitude, or right ascension
☐	quadrature—indicating a difference of 90° in longitude, or right ascension
△	trine—indicating a difference of 120° in longitude, or right ascension
☍	opposition—indicating a difference of 180° in longitude, or right ascension; as, ☍ ♆ ☉ opposition of Neptune to the sun
☊	ascending node
☋	descending node

Biology

○	an individual, specif., a female—used chiefly in inheritance charts
☐	an individual, specif., a male—used chiefly in inheritance charts
♀	female
♂ or ♂	male

×	crossed with; hybrid
+	wild type
F_1	offspring of the first generation
F_2	offspring of the second generation
F_3, F_4, F_5	offspring of the third, fourth, fifth, etc., generation

Business and Finance

a/c	account ⟨in a/c with⟩
@	at; each ⟨4 apples @ 5¢=20¢⟩
P	principal; present value
i,r	rate of interest
n	number of periods (as of interest) and esp. years
/ or ℔	per
c/o	care of
#	number if it precedes a numeral ⟨track #3⟩; pounds if it follows ⟨a 5# sack of sugar⟩
℔	pound; pounds

%	percent
‰	per thousand
$	dollars
¢	cents
£	pounds
/	shillings
	(for other currency symbols see MONEY table)
©	copyrighted
®	registered trademark

Chemistry

+   signifies "plus", "and", "together with", and is used between the symbols of substances brought together for, or produced by, a reaction; placed to the right of a symbol above the line it signifies a unit charge of positive electricity: Ca^{++} denotes the ion of calcium, which carries two positive charges; the plus sign is used also to indicate dextrorotation [as (+)tartaric acid]

—   signifies a single "bond", or unit of attractive force or affinity, and is used between the symbols of elements or groups which unite to form a compound: H—Cl for HCl, H—O—H, for H_2O; placed to the right of a symbol above the line, it signifies a unit charge of negative electricity: Cl^- denotes a chlorine ion carrying a negative charge; the dash indicates levorotation [as (–)quinine]; it is used also to indicate the removal of a part from a compound (as $-CO_2$)

·   is used: (1) sometimes to indicate a single bond (as H·Cl for H—Cl) or (2) to denote the presence of a single unpaired electron (as H·) or (3) to separate parts of a compound regarded as loosely joined (as $CuSO_4 \cdot 5H_2O$)

⬡ or ⬡   denotes the benzene ring

=   indicates a double bond; placed to the right of a symbol above the line, it signifies two unit charges of negative electricity (as $SO_4{=}$, the negative ion of sulfuric acid, carrying two negative charges)

≡   signifies a triple bond or a triple negative charge

:   is used to indicate an unshared pair of electrons (as : NH_3) or sometimes a double bond

⋮   is used sometimes to indicate a triple bond

( )   marks groups within a compound [as in $C_6H_4(CH_3)_2$, the formula for xylene which contains two methyl groups (CH_3)]

⌐ or ⌐   join attached atoms or groups in structural formulas for cyclic compounds, as that for glucose

$$CH_2OHCH(CHOH)_3CHOH$$

=	give or form
→	gives, leads to, or is converted to
⇌	forms and is formed from, is in equilibrium with
↓	indicates precipitation of the substance

↑ indicates that the substance passes off as a gas
≡ is equivalent—used in statements to show how much of one substance will react with a given quantity of another so as to leave no excess of either
1-, 2-, etc. used initially in names, referring to the positions of substituting groups, attached to the first, etc., of the numbered atoms of the parent compound

²H *also* H² deuterium
³H *also* H³ tritium
R group—used esp. of a univalent hydrocarbon group
X halogen atom
Z atomic number
(for element symbols see ELEMENT table)

Flowchart symbols

⊃ TERMINAL. Marks the beginning and the end of the flowchart.
▭ PROCESSING. Indicates the performance of a given task
▽ MANUAL OPERATION.
◇ DECISION. Indicates a juncture at which a choice must be made.
⊏ ANNOTATION. Connected to the flowchart proper by a dotted line.
○ CONNECTOR. Used to indicate common points in the flow when connecting lines cannot be drawn.
▱ INPUT/OUTPUT. This is the general symbol for input/output. It may be replaced by one of the more specific symbols below.
▭ PUNCHED CARD.
▱ PUNCHED TAPE.

○ MAGNETIC TAPE.
◁ MANUAL INPUT. Usually indicates a keyboard device.
○ DISPLAY OUTPUT. Indicates a video display.
◻ DOCUMENT. Indicates output from a printing device (as a line printer).
α ON-LINE STORAGE. Indicates a mass storage unit (as a drum or disk).
▽ *or* ∇ OFF-LINE STORAGE. Indicates data storage that cannot be accessed directly by a computer.
↑← DIRECTION OF FLOW. Arrowheads need not be used when direction of flow is from top to bottom or from left to right.
⌐ COMMUNICATION LINK. Indicates a transfer of data from one location to another (as by a telephone connection).

Mathematics

+ plus; positive $\langle a+b=c \rangle$ —used also to indicate omitted figures or an approximation
− minus; negative
± plus or minus ⟨the square root of $4a^2$ is $\pm 2a$⟩
× multiplied by; times $\langle 6 \times 4 = 24 \rangle$—also indicated by placing a dot between the factors $\langle 6 \cdot 4 = 24 \rangle$ or by writing factors other than numerals without signs
÷ *or* : divided by $\langle 24 \div 6 = 4 \rangle$—also indicated by writing the divisor under the dividend with a line between $\langle \frac{24}{6} = 4 \rangle$ or by writing the divisor after the dividend with an oblique line between $\langle 3/8 \rangle$
= equals $\langle 6+2=8 \rangle$
≠ *or* ≢ is not equal to
> is greater than $\langle 6 > 5 \rangle$
≫ is much greater than
< is less than $\langle 3 < 4 \rangle$
≪ is much less than
≥ *or* ≧ is greater than or equal to
≤ *or* ≦ is less than or equal to
≯ is not greater than
≮ is not less than
≈ is approximately equal to
≡ is identical with
∼ is similar to; the negation of; the negative of
≅ is congruent to
∝ varies directly as; is proportional to
: is to; the ratio of
∴ therefore
∞ infinity
∠ angle; the angle $\langle \angle \text{ABC} \rangle$
∟ right angle $\langle \llcorner \text{ABC} \rangle$
⊥ the perpendicular; is perpendicular to $\langle \text{AB} \perp \text{CD} \rangle$
∥ parallel; is parallel to $\langle \text{AB} \parallel \text{CD} \rangle$
⊙ *or* ○ circle
⌢ arc of a circle
△ triangle
▢ square
▭ rectangle
√ root—used without a figure to indicate a square root (as in $\sqrt{4}=2$) or with an index above the sign to indicate another degree (as in $\sqrt[3]{3}$, $\sqrt[5]{7}$); also denoted by a fractional index at the right of a number whose denominator expresses the degree of the root $\langle 3^{1/3} = \sqrt[3]{3} \rangle$
( ) parentheses
[ ] brackets } indicate that the quantities enclosed by them are to be taken together
{ } braces
— (above the quantities) vinculum
Δ the operation of finding the difference between two nearby values of a variable (as y) or of a function (as f) for two values of its independent variable (as x)

differing by a small nonzero amount (as h) $\langle \Delta y = y_2 - y_1 \rangle$ $\langle \Delta f(x) = f(x+h) - f(x) \rangle$
∫ integral; integral of $\langle \int 2x dx = x^2 + C \rangle$
$\int_b^a$ the integral taken between the values a and b of the variable
δ_j^i Kronecker delta
s standard deviation of a sample taken from a population
σ standard deviation of a population
Σ sum; summation
$\bar{x}$ arithmetic mean of a sample of a variable x
μ arithmetic mean of a population
μ_2 *or* σ^2 variance
χ^2 chi-square
P the probability of obtaining a result as great as or greater than the observed result in a statistical test if the null hypothesis is true
r correlation coefficient
$E(x)$ expected value of the random variable x
π pi; the number $3.14159265+$; the ratio of the circumference of a circle to its diameter
Π product
! factorial
e *or* ϵ (1) the number $2.7182818+$; the base of the natural system of logarithms (2) the eccentricity of a conic section
i the positive square root of minus one; $\sqrt{-1}$
n an unspecified number (as an exponent) esp. when integral
° degree $\langle 60° \rangle$
′ minute; foot $\langle 30' \rangle$—used also to distinguish between different values of the same variable or between different variables (as a', a'', a''', usually read a prime, a double prime, a triple prime)
″ second, inch $\langle 30'' \rangle$
², ³, etc. —used as exponents placed above and at the right of an expression to indicate that it is raised to a power whose degree is indicated by the figure $\langle a^2$, the square of $a \rangle$
⁻², ⁻³, etc. —used as exponents placed above and at the right of an expression to indicate that the reciprocal of the expression is raised to the power whose degree is indicated by the figure $\langle a^{-2}$ equals $1/a^2 \rangle$
$\sin^{-1}x$ arc sine of x
$\cos^{-1}x$ arc cosine of x
$\tan^{-1}x$ arc tangent of x
$\cot^{-1}x$ arc cotangent of x
$\sec^{-1}x$ arc secant of x
$\operatorname{cosec}^{-1}x$ arc cosecant of x
f function
f^{-1} the inverse of the function f
$|z|$ the absolute value of z
⊕ an operation in a mathematical system (as a group or ring) with $A \oplus B$ indicating the sum of the two elements A and B

⊗   an operation in a mathematical system (as a group or ring) with $A \otimes B$ indicating the product of the two elements A and B

[x]   the greatest integer not greater than x

(a,b)   the open interval $a < x < b$

[a,b]   the closed interval $a \leqq x \leqq b$

ℵ₀   aleph-null

ω   the ordinal number of the positive integers

∪   union of two sets

∩   intersections of two sets

⊂   is included in, is a subset of

⊃   contains as a subset

∈ or ε   is an element of

∉   is not an element of

∧ or 0   empty set, null set
or φ or { }

Medicine

ĀĀ , Ā, or āā   ana; of each

℞   take—used on prescriptions; prescription; treatment

☠   poison

APOTHECARIES' MEASURES

℥   ounce

f℥   fluidounce

f℈   fluidram

min or ♏   minim

APOTHECARIES' WEIGHTS

℔   pound

℥   ounce (as ℥ i or ℥ j, one ounce; ℥ ss, half an ounce; ℥ iss or ℥ jss, one ounce and a half; ℥ ij, two ounces)

℈   dram

℈   scruple

Miscellaneous

&   and

&c   et cetera; and so forth

" or "   ditto marks

/   diagonal or slant or solidus or virgule; used to mean "or" (as in and/or), "and/or" (as in dead/wounded), "per" (as in feet/second), indicates end of a line of verse; separates the figures of a date (4/4/73)

☞   index or fist

<   derived from

>   whence derived ⎱ used in

+   and   ⎰ etymologies

*   assumed

†   died—used esp. in genealogies

✝   cross (for variations see CROSS illustration)

☧   monogram from Greek XP signifying Christ

卐   swastika

✡   Magen David

☥   ankh

℣   versicle

℟   response

✳   —used in Roman Catholic and Anglican service books to divide each verse of a psalm, indicating where the response begins

✠   or +—used in some service books to indicate where the sign of the cross is to be made; also used by certain Roman Catholic and Anglican prelates as a sign of the cross preceding their signatures

LXX   Septuagint

f/ or ƒ: relative aperture of a photographic lens

⊕   civil defense

⊕   peace

Ⓤ   kosher certification

x   by ⟨3x5 cards⟩

Physics

α   alpha particle

β   beta ray

γ   gamma, photon, surface tension

ε   electromotive force, permittivity

η   efficiency, viscosity

λ   wavelength

μ   magnetic moment, micro-, permeability

ν   frequency, neutrino

ρ   density, resistivity

σ   conductivity, cross section, surface tension

φ   luminous flux, magnetic flux

Ω   ohm

B   magnetic induction, magnetic field

c   velocity of light

e   electronic charge

E   electric field, illumination

G   conductance, weight

h   Planck's constant

H   enthalpy

L   inductance

n   index of refraction

P   momentum of a particle

S   entropy

T   absolute temperature, period

V   electrical potential, frequency

W   energy

X   power of magnification, reactance

Y   admittance

Z   impedance

Reference marks

*   asterisk or star

†   dagger

‡   double dagger

§   section or numbered clause

‖   parallels

¶ or ⸿   paragraph

Stamps and stamp collecting

★   unused

⊙ or ○   used

⊞   block of four or more

⊠   entire cover or card

barometer, changes of
/ Rising, then falling
/ Rising, then steady; or rising, then rising more slowly
/ Rising steadily, or unsteadily
✓ Falling or steady, then rising; or rising, then rising more quickly
— Steady, same as 3 hours ago
\ Falling, then rising, same or lower than 3 hours ago
\ Falling, then steady; or falling, then falling more slowly
\ Falling steadily, or unsteadily
\ Steady or rising, then falling; or falling, then falling more quickly
◎ calm
○ clear
◐ cloudy (partly)
● cloudy (completely overcast)
+ drifting or blowing snow
, drizzle
≡ fog

∾ freezing rain
⊶ front, cold
⊷ warm
⊷ occluded
⌁ stationary
)(funnel clouds
∞ haze
⚫ hurricane
⌀ tropical storm
↔ ice needles
• rain
⁚ rain and snow
⋎ rime
⌇ sandstorm or dust storm
▽ shower(s)
▿ shower of rain
⍀ shower of hail
△ sleet
✳ snow
ℝ thunderstorm
⌇ visibility reduced by smoke

A Handbook of Style

Punctuation

The English writing system uses punctuation marks to separate groups of words for meaning and emphasis; to convey an idea of the variations of pitch, volume, pauses, and intonations of speech; and to help avoid contextual ambiguity. English punctuation marks, together with general rules and bracketed examples of their use, follow.

Apostrophe ,

1. indicates the possessive case of nouns and indefinite pronouns

< Mrs. Cenacci's office >
< the boy's mother >
< the boys' mothers >
< It is anyone's guess how much it will cost. >
< her mother-in-law's car >

NOTE: The use of an 's with words ending in \s\ or \z\ sounds usually depends on whether a pronounceable final syllable is thus formed: if the syllable is pronounced, the 's is usually used; if no final pronounceable syllable is formed, the apostrophe is retained but the s is usually not added.

< Knox's products >
< Aristophanes' play >
< for righteousness' sake >

2. marks omissions in contracted words

< didn't >   < o'clock >

3. marks omission of numerals

< class of '83 >

4. often forms plurals of letters, figures, and words referred to as words

< You should dot your *i*'s and cross your *t*'s. >
< His *l*'s and his *7*'s looked alike. >
< She has trouble pronouncing her *the*'s. >

Brackets [ ]

1. set off extraneous data such as editorial interpolations especially within quoted material

< He wrote, "I ain't [sic] going." >

2. function as parentheses within parentheses

< Bowman Act (22 Stat., ch. 4, § [or sec.] 4, p. 50) >

3. set off phonetic symbols

< [t] in British *duty* >

Colon :

1. introduces a clause or phrase that explains, illustrates, amplifies, or restates what has gone before

< The sentence was poorly constructed: it lacked both unity and coherence. >

2. directs attention to an appositive

< He had only one pleasure: eating. >

3. introduces a series

< Three countries were represented: England, France, and Belgium. >

4. introduces lengthy quoted material set off from the rest of a text by indentation but not by quotation marks

< I quote from the text of Chapter One: >

5. separates elements in page references, bibliographical and biblical citations, and in set formulas used to express ratios and time

< *Journal of the American Medical Association* 48:356 >
< Springfield, Mass.: Merriam-Webster Inc. >
< John 4:10 >
< 8:30 a.m. >
< a ratio of 3:5 >

6. separates titles and subtitles (as of books)

< *The Tragic Dynasty: A History of the Romanovs* >

7. follows the salutation in formal correspondence

< Dear Sir: >   < Gentlemen: >

8. punctuates memorandum and government correspondence headings, and some subject lines in general business letters

< TO: >   < VIA: >
< SUBJECT: >
< REFERENCE: >

, Comma

---

1. separates main clauses joined by a coordinating conjunction (as *and, but, or, nor,* or *for*) and very short clauses not so joined

< She knew very little about him, and he volunteered nothing. >
< I came, I saw, I conquered. >

2. sets off an adverbial clause (or long phrase) that precedes or interrupts the main clause

< When she discovered the answer, she reported it to us. >
< The report, after being read aloud, was put up for consideration. >

3. sets off from the rest of the sentence transitional words and expressions (as *on the contrary, on the other hand*), conjunctive adverbs (as *consequently, furthermore, however*), and expressions that introduce an illustration or example (as *namely, for example*)

< Your second question, on the other hand, remains unanswered. >
< He will travel through two countries, namely, France and England. >
< He responded as completely as he could; that is, he answered each of the individual questions specifically. >

4. sets off contrasting and opposing expressions within sentences

< The cost is not $65.00, but $56.65. >
< He changed his style, not his ethics. >

5. separates words, phrases, or clauses in series

< He was young, eager, and restless. >
< It requires one to travel constantly, to have no private life, and to need no income other than living expenses.—Sara Davidson >

NOTE: Commas separate coordinate adjectives modifying a noun.

< The harsh, cold wind was strong. >

6. sets off from the rest of the sentence parenthetical elements (as nonrestrictive modifiers and nonrestrictive appositives)

< Our guide, who wore a blue beret, was an experienced traveler. >
< We visited Gettysburg, the site of a famous battle. >
< The author, Marie Jones, was an accomplished athlete. >

7. introduces a direct quotation, terminates a direct quotation that is neither a question nor an exclamation, and encloses split quotations

< Mary said, "I am leaving." >
< "I am leaving," Mary said. >
< "I am leaving," Mary said with determination, "even if you want me to stay." >

NOTE: If the quotation is used as a subject or predicate nominative or if it is not being presented as actual dialogue, a comma is not used.

< "The computer is down" was the reply she feared. >
< The fact that he said he was about to "leave this instant" doesn't mean he actually left. >

8. sets off words in direct address, absolute phrases, and mild interjections

< You may go, John, if you wish. >
< I fear their encounter, his temper being what it is. >
< Ah, that's my idea of an excellent dinner. >

9. separates a tag question from the rest of the sentence

< It's a fine day, isn't it? >

10. indicates the omission of a word or words, and especially a word or words used earlier in the sentence

    < Common stocks are preferred by some investors; bonds, by others. >

    NOTE: When the meaning of the sentence is quite clear without the comma, the comma is omitted.

    < He was in love with her and she with him. >

11. is used to avoid ambiguity and also to emphasize a particular phrase

    < To Mary, Jane was someone special. >
    < The more embroidery on a dress, the higher the price. >

12. is used to group numbers into units of three in separating thousands, millions, etc; however, it is generally not used in numbers of four figures, in pagination, in dates, or in street numbers

    < Smithville, pop. 100,000 >
        but
    < 3600 rpm >   < the year 1983 >
    < page 1411 >   < 4507 Main Street >

13. punctuates an inverted name

    < Morton, William A. >

14. separates a proper name from a following corporate, academic, honorary, governmental, or military title

    < Sandra H. Cobb, Vice President >

15. sets off geographical names (as state or country from city), items in dates, and addresses from the rest of a text

    < Shreveport, Louisiana, is the site of a large air base. >
    < On Sunday, June 23, 1940, he was wounded. >
    < Number 10 Downing Street, London, is a famous address. >

    NOTE: When just the month and the year are given, the comma is usually omitted.

    < She began her career in April 1983 at a modest salary. >

16. follows the salutation in informal correspondence and follows the complimentary close of a formal or informal letter

    < Dear Mark, >
    < Affectionately, >
    < Very truly yours, >

Dash   —

1. usually marks an abrupt change or break in the continuity of a sentence

   < When in 1960 the stockpile was sold off—indeed, dumped as surplus—natural rubber sales were hard hit.—Barry Commoner >

2. is sometimes used in place of other punctuation (as the comma) when special emphasis is required

   < The presentations—and especially the one by Ms. Dow—impressed the audience. >

3. introduces a summary statement that follows a series of words or phrases

   < Oil, steel, and wheat—these are the sinews of industrialization. >

4. often precedes the attribution of a quotation

   < My foot is on my native heath . . .—Sir Walter Scott >

5. may be used with the exclamation point or the question mark

   < The faces of the crash victims—how bloody!—were shown on TV. >
   < Your question—it was *your* question, wasn't it, Mr. Jones?—just can't be answered. >

6. removes the need for a comma if the dash falls where a comma would ordinarily separate two clauses

   < If we don't succeed—and the critics say we won't—then the whole project is in jeopardy. >

Ellipsis   . . .   .

1. indicates the omission of one or more words within a quoted passage

   < The head is not more native to the heart . . . than is the throne of Denmark to thy father.—Shak. >

2. indicates the omission of one or more sentences within a quoted passage or the omission of words at the end of a sentence by using four dots the first of which represents the period

   < That recovering the manuscripts would be worth almost any effort is without question. . . . The monetary value of a body of Shakespeare's manuscripts would be almost incalculable—Charlton Ogburn >
   < It will take scholars years to determine conclusively the origins, the history, and, most importantly, the significance of the finds. . . .—Robert Morse >

3. usually indicates omission of one or more lines of poetry when ellipsis is extended the length of the line

< It little profits that an idle king,
. . . .
Matched with an aged wife, I mete and dole
Unequal laws unto a savage race,
That hoard, and sleep, and feed,
         and know not me.
         —Alfred Tennyson >

4. indicates halting speech or an unfinished sentence in dialogue

< "I'd like to . . . that is . . . if you don't mind. . . ." >

! Exclamation Point

1. terminates an emphatic phrase or sentence

< Get out of here! >

2. terminates an emphatic interjection

< Encore! >

- Hyphen

1. marks separation or division at the end of a line terminating with a syllable of a word that is to be carried over to the next line

< mill-
stone >
< pas-
sion >

2. is used between some prefix and root combinations, as

    prefix + proper name;
    prefix ending with a vowel + root word beginning often with the same vowel;
    stressed prefix + root word, especially when this combination is similar to a different word

< pre-Renaissance >
< co-opted > < re-ink >
< re-cover a sofa >
    but
< recover from an illness >

3. is used in some compounds, especially those containing prepositions

< president-elect >
< sister-in-law >
< attorney-at-law >
< good-for-nothing >

4. is often used between elements of a compound modifier in attributive position in order to avoid ambiguity

< traveling in a fast-moving van >
< She has gray-green eyes. >
< He looked at her with a know-it-all expression. >

5. suspends the first part of a hyphenated compound when used with another hyphenated compound

< a six- or eight-cylinder engine >

6. is used in writing out compound numbers between 21 and 99

< thirty-four >
< one hundred and thirty-eight >

7. is used between the numerator and the denominator in writing out fractions especially when they are used as modifiers; however, fractions used as nouns are often styled as open compounds especially when either the numerator or the denominator already contains a hyphen

< a two-thirds majority of the vote >
< one seventy-second of an inch >

8. serves as an arbitrary equivalent of the phrase "(up) to and including" when used between numbers and dates

< pages 40–98 >
< the decade 1980–89 >

9. is used in the compounding of capitalized names

< the New York-Paris flight >

Hyphen, Double   ⹀

is used at the end-of-line division of a hyphenated compound
to indicate that the compound is hyphenated and not closed

self⹀[end of line] seeker
           but
self- [end of line] same

The styling of compounds varies: they may be open, closed, or hyphenated. When in doubt, one should consult the main
vocabulary of this dictionary for the most commonly used styling.

Parentheses   ( )

1. set off supplementary, parenthetic, or explanatory mate-
    rial when the interruption is more than that indicated by
    commas and when the inclusion of such material does
    not essentially alter the meaning of the sentence

    < Three old destroyers (all now out of commission) will be
    scrapped. >

2. enclose Arabic numerals which confirm a written num-
    ber in a text

    < Delivery will be made in thirty (30) days. >

3. enclose numbers or letters in a series

    < We must set forth (1) our long-term goals, (2) our immedi-
    ate objectives, and (3) the means at our disposal. >

4. enclose abbreviations synonymous with spelled-out
    forms and occurring after those forms or may enclose
    the spelled-out form occurring after the abbreviation

    < a ruling by the Federal Communications Commission
    (FCC) >
    < the manufacture and disposal of PVC (polyvinyl chloride) >

5. indicate alternative terms and omissions (as in form
    letters)

    < Please indicate the lecture(s) you would like to attend. >

6. are used with other punctuation marks in the following
    ways:

    if the parenthetic expression is an independent sentence
    standing alone, its first word is capitalized and a period
    is included *inside* the last parenthesis; however, if the
    parenthetic expression, even if it could stand alone as a
    sentence, occurs within a sentence, it needs neither
    capitalization nor a final period but may have an excla-
    mation point or question mark

    < The discussion was held in the boardroom. (The results are
    still confidential.) >
    < Although we liked the restaurant (their Italian food was the
    best), we seldom went there. >
    < After waiting in line for an hour (why do we do these
    things?), we finally left. >

    parenthetic material within a sentence may be inter-
    nally punctuated by a question mark, a period after an
    abbreviation only, an exclamation point, or a set of
    quotation marks

    < Years ago, someone (who was it?) told me about it. >
    < The conference was held in Vancouver (that's in B.C.). >
    < He was depressed ("I must resign") and refused to do any-
    thing. >

    no punctuation mark should be placed directly before
    parenthetical material in a sentence; if a break is re-
    quired, punctuation should be placed *after* the final
    parenthesis

    < I'll get back to you tomorrow (Friday), when I have more
    details. >

Period   .

1. terminates sentences or sentence fragments that are nei-
    ther interrogatory nor exclamatory

    < Give it your best. >
    < I gave it my best. >
    < He asked if she had given it her best. >

2. follows some abbreviations and contractions

    < Dr. >   < A.D. >   < ibid. >   < i.e. >
    < Jr. >   < etc. >   < cont. >

3. is used with an individual's initials

    < F. Scott Fitzgerald >
    < T.S. Eliot >

4. is used after Roman and Arabic numerals and after letters when they are used in outlines and enumerations

< I. Objectives
   A. Economy
      1. low initial cost
      2. low maintenance cost
   B. Ease of operation >
< Required skills are:
   1. Shorthand
   2. Typing
   3. Transcription >

?   Question Mark

1. terminates a direct question

< How did she do it? >
< "How did she do it?" he asked. >

2. terminates an interrogative element that is part of a sentence; however, indirect questions should not be followed by a question mark

< How did she do it? was the question on each person's mind. >
< He wondered, will it work? >
< He wondered whether it would work. >

3. punctuates each element of an interrogative series that is neither numbered nor lettered; however, only one such mark punctuates a numbered or lettered interrogative series

< Can you give us a reasonable forecast? back up your predictions? compare them with last quarter's earnings? >
< Can you (1) give us a reasonable forecast, (2) back up your predictions, (3) compare them with last quarter's earnings? >

4. indicates the writer's ignorance or uncertainty

< Geoffrey Chaucer, English poet (1340?–1400) >

"   "   Quotation Marks, Double

1. enclose direct quotations in conventional usage, but not indirect quotations

< He said, "I am leaving." >
< He said that he was leaving. >

2. enclose words or phrases borrowed from others, words used in a special way, and often slang words when introduced into formal writing

< As the leader of a gang of "droogs," he is altogether frightening, as is this film.—Liz Smith >
< He called himself "emperor," but he was really just a dictator. >
< He was arrested for smuggling "smack." >

3. enclose titles of poems, short stories, articles, lectures, chapters of books, short musical compositions, and radio and TV programs

< Robert Frost's "Dust of Snow" >
< Katherine Anne Porter's "That Tree" >
< The third chapter of *Treasure Island* is entitled "The Black Spot." >
< "America the Beautiful" >
< Ravel's "Bolero" >
< NBC's "Today Show" >

4. are used with other punctuation marks in the following ways:

the period and the comma fall *within* the quotation marks

< "I am leaving," he said >
< Her camera was described as "waterproof," but "moisture-resistant" would have been a better description. >

the colon and semicolon fall *outside* the quotation marks

< There was only one thing to do when he said, "I may not run": promise him a large campaign contribution. >
< He spoke of his "little cottage in the country"; he might better have called it a mansion. >

the dash, the question mark, and the exclamation point fall *within* the quotation marks when they refer to the quoted matter only; they fall *outside* when they refer to the whole sentence

< He asked, "When did she leave?" >
< What is the meaning of "the open door"? >
< The sergeant shouted "Halt!" >
< Save us from his "mercy"! >

5. are not used with *yes* or *no* except in direct discourse

< She said yes to all our requests. >

6. are not used with lengthy quotations set off from the text

<He took the title for his biography of Thoreau from a passage in *Walden*:

> I long ago lost a hound, a bay horse, and a turtle-dove, and am still on their trail. . . . I have met one or two who had heard the hound, and the tramp of the horse, and even seen the dove disappear behind a cloud, and they seemed as anxious to recover them as if they had lost them themselves.

However, the title *A Hound, a Bay Horse, and a Turtle-Dove* probably puzzled some readers.>

Quotation Marks, Single   ' '

1. enclose a quotation within a quotation in American usage

<The witness said, "I distinctly heard him say, 'Don't be late,' and then heard the door close.">

2. are sometimes used in place of double quotation marks especially in British usage

<The witness said, 'I distinctly heard him say, "Don't be late," and then heard the door close.'>

NOTE: When both single and double quotation marks occur at the end of a sentence, the period typically falls *within* both sets of marks.

<The witness said, "I distinctly heard him say, 'Don't be late.' ">

Semicolon   ;

1. links main clauses not joined by a coordinating conjunction

<Some people have the ability to write well; others do not.>

2. links main clauses joined by conjunctive adverbs (as *consequently, furthermore, however*)

<Speeding is illegal; furthermore, it is very dangerous.>

3. separates phrases and clauses which themselves contain commas

<The country's resources consist of large ore deposits; lumber, waterpower, and fertile soils; and a strong, rugged people.>
<Send copies to our offices in Portland, Maine; Springfield, Illinois; and Savannah, Georgia.>

4. often occurs before phrases or abbreviations (as *for example, for instance, that is, that is to say, namely, e.g.,* or *i.e.*) that introduce expansions or series

<As a manager she tried to do the best job she could; that is, to keep her project on schedule and under budget.>

Virgule   /

1. separates alternatives

<. . . designs intended for high-heat and/or high-speed applications—F. S. Badger, Jr.>
<. . . sit hour after hour . . . and finally year after year in a catatonic/frenzied trance rewriting the Bible—William Saroyan>

2. separates successive divisions (as months or years) of an extended period of time

<the fiscal year 1983/1984>

3. serves as a dividing line between run-in lines of poetry

<Say, sages, what's the charm on earth/Can turn death's dart aside?—Robert Burns>

4. often represents *per* in abbreviations

<9 ft/sec> <20 km/hr>

5. sets off phonemes and phonemic transcription

</b/ as in *but*>

Italicization

The following are usually italicized in print and underlined in manuscript and typescript.

1. titles of books, magazines, newspapers, plays, movies, works of art, and long musical compositions (but not musical compositions identified by the nature of the musical form in which they were written)

< Eliot's *The Waste Land* >
< *Saturday Review* >
< *Christian Science Monitor* >
< Shakespeare's *Othello* >
< the movie *High Noon* >
< Gainsborough's *Blue Boy* >
< Mozart's *Don Giovanni* >
but
< Fantasy in C Minor >

NOTE: Plurals of such italicized titles have roman-type inflectional endings.

< hidden under a stack of *Saturday Review*s >

2. names of ships and aircraft, and often spacecraft

< M. V. *West Star* >
< Lindbergh's *Spirit of St. Louis* >
< *Apollo 13* >

3. words, letters, and figures when referred to as words, letters, and figures

< The word *receive* is often misspelled. >
< The *g* in *align* is silent. >
< You should dot your *i*'s and cross your *t*'s. >
< The first *2* and the last *0* are barely legible. >

4. foreign words and phrases that have not been naturalized in English

< *aere perennius* >
< *che sarà, sarà* >
< *sans peur et sans reproche* >
< *ich dien* >
but
< pasta > < ad hoc >
< ex officio >

NOTE: The decision as to whether or not a word or phrase has been naturalized in English will vary according to the subject matter and the expected audience of the passage in which it appears. In general, any word entered in the main A–Z vocabulary of this dictionary need not be italicized.

5. New Latin scientific names of genera, species, subspecies, and varieties (but not groups of higher rank, as phyla, classes, or orders) in botanical or zoological names

< a thick-shelled American clam *(Mercenaria mercenaria)* >
< a cardinal *(Richmondena cardinalis)* >
but
< the family Hominidae >

6. case titles in legal citations, both in full and shortened form ("v" for "versus" is set in roman, though)

< *Jones* v. *Massachusetts* >
< the *Jones* case > < *Jones* >

Capitalization

Capitals are used for two broad purposes in English: they mark a beginning (as of a sentence) and they signal a proper noun, pronoun, or adjective. The following principles, each with bracketed examples, describe the most common uses of capital letters.

Beginnings

1. The first word of a sentence or sentence fragment is capitalized.

   < The play lasted nearly three hours. >
   < How are you feeling? >
   < Bravo! >
   < "Have you hand grenades?"
   "Plenty."
   "How many rounds per rifle?"
   "Plenty."
   "How many?"
   "One hundred fifty. More maybe."
   —Ernest Hemingway >

2. The first word of a sentence contained within parentheses is capitalized if it does not occur within another sentence; however, a parenthetical sentence occurring in the midst of another sentence does not begin with a capital.

   < The discussion was held in the boardroom. (The results are still confidential.) >
   < Although we liked the restaurant (their Italian food was the best), we seldom ate there. >
   < After waiting in line for an hour (why do we do these things?), we finally left. >

3. The first word of a direct quotation is capitalized; however, if the quotation is interrupted in the middle of a sentence, the second part does not begin with a capital.

   < The President said, "We have rejected this report entirely." >
   < "We have rejected this report entirely," the President said, "and we will not comment on it further." >

   NOTE: When a quotation, whether a sentence fragment or a complete sentence, is syntactically dependent on the sentence in which it occurs, the quotation does not begin with a capital.

   < The President made it clear "that there is no room for compromise." >

4. The first word of a direct question within a sentence is capitalized.

   < That question is: Is man an ape or an angel?
   —Benjamin Disraeli >
   < My first thought was, How can I avoid this assignment? >

5. The first word of a line of poetry is capitalized.

   < The best lack all conviction,
           while the worst
   Are full of passionate
           intensity.
   —W. B. Yeats >

6. The first word following a colon may be lowercased or capitalized if it introduces a complete sentence; while the former is the more usual styling, the latter is common when the sentence introduced by the colon is fairly lengthy and distinctly separate from the preceding clause.

   < The advantage of this particular system is clear: it's inexpensive. >
   < The situation is critical: This company cannot hope to recoup the fourth-quarter losses that were sustained in five operating divisions. >

7. The first words of run-in enumerations that form complete sentences are capitalized, as are the first words of phrasal lists and enumerations blocked beneath running texts; however, phrasal enumerations run in with the introductory text are lowercased.

   < Do the following tasks at the end of the day: 1. Clean your typewriter. 2. Clear your desktop of papers. 3. Cover office machines. 4. Straighten the contents of your desk drawers, cabinets, and bookcases. >

   < This is the agenda:
       Call to order
       Roll call
       Minutes of the previous
          meeting
       Treasurer's report >

< On the agenda will be (1) call to order, (2) roll call, (3) minutes of the previous meeting, (4) treasurer's report. . . . >

8. The first word in an outline heading is capitalized.

< I. Editorial tasks
II. Production responsibilities
    A. Cost estimates
    B. Bids >

9. The first word of the salutation of a letter and the first word of a complimentary close are capitalized.

< Dear Mary, >
< Gentlemen: >
< Sincerely yours, >
< Yours sincerely, >

Proper Nouns, Pronouns, and Adjectives

The essential distinction in the use of capitals and lowercase letters beginning words lies in the particularizing or individualizing significance of capitals as against the generic or generalizing significance of lowercase. A capital is used with proper nouns, that is, nouns that distinguish some individual person, place, or thing from others of the same class, and with proper adjectives, that is, adjectives that take their descriptive meaning from what is named by the noun.

ARMED FORCES

1. Branches and units of the armed forces are capitalized, as are easily recognized short forms of full branch and unit designations; however, the words *army, navy,* etc., are lowercased when standing alone, when used collectively in the plural, or when they are not part of an official title.

< United States Army >
< a contract with the Army >
< Corps of Engineers >
< a bridge built by the Engineers >
< allied armies >

AWARDS

2. The names of awards and prizes are capitalized.

< the Nobel Prize in medicine >
< Distinguished Service Cross >
< Academy Award >

DERIVATIVES OF PROPER NAMES

3. Derivatives of proper names are capitalized when used in their primary sense.

< Roman customs >
< Shakesparean comedies >
< Edwardian era >
    but
< manila envelope >
< quixotic > < herculean >
< bohemian tastes >

GEOGRAPHICAL REFERENCES

4. Divisions of the earth's surface and names of distinct areas, regions, places, or districts are capitalized, as are derivative adjectives and some derivative nouns and verbs.

< The Eastern Hemisphere >
< Midwest > < Tropic of Cancer >
< Springfield, Massachusetts >
< the Middle Eastern situation >
< an Americanism >
    but
< a japan finish >
< sovietize >

5. Popular names of localities are capitalized.

< the Corn Belt > < the Loop >
< The Big Apple >
< the Gold Coast >
< the Eastern Shore >

6. Words designating global, national, regional, or local political divisions are capitalized when they are essential elements of specific names; however, they are usually lowercased when they precede a proper name or stand alone.

< the British Empire >
< Washington State >
< Bedford County >
< New York City >
< Ward 1 >
    but
< the fall of the empire >
< the state of Washington >

< the county of Bedford >
< the city of New York >
< fires in three wards >

NOTE: In legal documents, these words are often capitalized regardless of position.

< The State of New York >
< the County of Bedford >
< the City of New York >

7. Generic geographical terms (as *lake, mountain, river, valley*) are capitalized if they are part of a specific proper name.

< Hudson Bay >   < Long Island >
< Niagara Falls >   < Crater Lake >

8. Generic terms preceding names are usually capitalized.

< Lakes Michigan and Superior >
< Mounts Whitney and Rainier >

9. Generic terms following names are usually lowercased, as are singular or plural generic terms that are used descriptively or alone.

< the Himalaya and Andes mountains >
< the Missouri and Platte rivers >
< the Atlantic coast of Labrador >
< the Hudson valley >
< the Arizona desert >
< the river valley >   < the valley >

10. Compass points are capitalized when they refer to a geographical region or when they are part of a street name, but they are lowercased when they refer to simple direction.

< up North >   < back East >
< the Northwest >
< West Columbus Avenue >
but
< west of the Rockies >
< the west coast of Florida >

11. Adjectives derived from compass points and nouns designating the inhabitants of some geographical regions are capitalized; when in doubt consult the main vocabulary portion of this dictionary.

< a Southern accent >
< Northerners >

12. Terms designating public places are capitalized if they are part of a proper name.

< Brooklyn Bridge >   < Lincoln Park >
< the Dorset Hotel >
< Independence Hall >
but
< Fifth and Park avenues >
< the Dorset and Drake hotels >

GOVERNMENTAL AND JUDICIAL BODIES

13. Full names of legislative, deliberative, executive, and administrative bodies are capitalized, as are easily recognized short forms of these names; however, nonspecific noun and adjective references to them are usually lowercased.

< the U.S. House of Representatives >
< the House >
< the Federal Bureau of Investigation >
but
< both houses of Congress >
< a federal agency >

14. Names of international courts, the U.S. Supreme Court, and other higher courts are capitalized; however, names of city and county courts are usually lowercased.

< The International Court of Arbitration >
< the Supreme Court of the United States >   < the Supreme Court >
< the United States Court of Appeals for the Second Circuit >
< the Michigan Court of Appeals >
< Lawton municipal court >
< Newark night court >

HISTORICAL PERIODS AND EVENTS

15. The names of congresses, councils, and expositions are capitalized.

< the Yalta Conference >
< the Republican National Convention >

16. The names of historical events, some historical periods, and some cultural periods and movements are capitalized; when in doubt, consult the main vocabulary portion of this dictionary.

< the Boston Tea Party >
< Renaissance >
< Prohibition >
< Augustan Age >
< the Enlightenment >
but
< space age >   < cold war >
< neoclassicism >

17. Numerical designations of historical time periods are capitalized when they are part of a proper name; otherwise they are lowercased.

< the Third Reich >
< Roaring Twenties >
but
< eighteenth century >
< the eighties >

18. Names of treaties, laws, and acts are capitalized.

< Treaty of Versailles >
< The Controlled Substances Act of 1970 >

ORGANIZATIONS

19. Names of firms, corporations, schools, and organizations and their members are capitalized; however, common nouns used descriptively and occurring after the names of two or more organizations are lowercased.

< Merriam-Webster Inc. >
< University of Wisconsin >
< European Economic Community >
< Rotary International >
< Kiwanians >
< American and United airlines >

NOTE: The word *the* at the beginning of such names is only capitalized when the legal name is referred to.

20. Words such as *group, division, department, office,* or *agency* that designate corporate and organizational units are capitalized when used with a specific name.

< while working for the Editorial Department of this company >
but
< a notice to all department heads >

PEOPLE

21. The names of persons are capitalized.

< Noah Webster >
< Sir Arthur Thomas Quiller-Couch >
< Thomas De Quincey >
< Werner Von Braun >
< Gerald ter Hoerst >

NOTE: The capitalization of particles (as *de, della, der, du, l', la, ten, van*) varies widely especially in names of people in English-speaking countries.

22. Titles preceding the name of a person and epithets used instead of a name are capitalized; however, titles following a name or used alone are usually lowercased.

< President Roosevelt >
< Professor Harris >
< Queen Elizabeth >
< Old Hickory >   < the Iron Chancellor >
but
< Henry VIII, king of England >

23. Corporate titles are capitalized when referring to specific individuals; when used in general or plural contexts, they are lowercased.

< Laura Jones, Vice President >
< The sales manager called me. >

24. Words of family relationship preceding or used in place of a person's name are capitalized; however, these words are lowercased if they are part of a noun phrase that is being used in place of a name.

< Cousin Julia >
< Grandfather Jones >
< I know when Mother's birthday is. >
but
< I know when my mother's birthday is. >

25. Words designating peoples, tribes, races, and languages are capitalized.

< Canadians >   < Iroquois >
< Ibo >   < Afro-American >
< Latin >   < Indo-European >
< black >   < white >
< highlander >   < bushman >

NOTE: Designations based on color or local usage are variously capitalized or lowercased by different writers; however, style manuals usually recommend lowercasing such words.

PERSONIFICATIONS

26. Personifications are capitalized.

< She dwells with Beauty—Beauty, that must die;
And Joy, whose hand is ever at his lips
Bidding adieu.
—John Keats >

< obey the commands of Nature >

PRONOUNS

27. The pronoun I is capitalized. For pronouns referring to the Deity, see rule 29 below.

< . . . no one but I myself had yet printed any of my work—Paul Bowles >

RELIGIOUS TERMS

28. Words designating the Deity are capitalized.

< An anthropomorphic, vengeful Jehovah became a spiritual, benevolent Supreme Being.—A. R. Katz >

29. Pronouns and pronominal adjectives referring to the Deity are capitalized by some authors only when such words are not closely preceded by their antecedents; other writers capitalize these words regardless of their distance from their antecedents.

< The principal group that disagreed with them . . . did so only in an even greater faith—that when God chose to save the heathen He could do it by Himself.—Elmer Davis >
< Allah will not subject any believer to eternal punishment because of His readiness to yield to the Prophet's intercession.—G. E. Grunebaum >
< The Almighty has his own purposes.—Abraham Lincoln >
< so lonely 'twas, that God himself scarce seemed there to be. —S.T. Coleridge >
< all Thy works, O Lord, shall bless Thee.—*Oxford Amer. Hymnal* >
< God's in His heaven—all's right with the world!—Robert Browning >

30. Traditional designations of revered persons, as prophets, apostles, and saints are often capitalized.

< our Lady >
< the Prophet >
< the Lawgiver >

31. Names of creeds and confessions, religious denominations, and monastic orders are capitalized, as is the word *Church* when used to designate a specific body or edifice.

< Apostles' Creed >
< the Thirty-nine Articles of the Church of England >
< Society of Jesus >
< Hunt Memorial Church >
    but
< the Baptist church >

32. Names for the Bible or parts, versions, or editions of it and names of other sacred books are capitalized.

NOTE: Adjectives derived from the names of sacred books are irregularly capitalized or lowercased; when in doubt, consult the main vocabulary portion of this dictionary.

< Authorized Version >   < New English Bible >   < Old Testament >
< Pentateuch >   < Apocrypha >
< Gospel of Saint Mark >   < Talmud >
< Koran >

SCIENTIFIC TERMS

33. Names of planets and their satellites, asteroids, stars, constellations, and groups of stars and other unique celestial objects are capitalized; however, the words *sun*, *earth*, and *moon* are usually lowercased unless they occur with other astronomical names.

< Venus >
< Ganymede >
< Sirius >
< Pleiades >
< the Milky Way >
< probes heading for the Moon and Mars >

34. Genera in binomial scientific names in zoology and botany are capitalized; names of species are not.

< a cabbage butterfly *(Pieris rapae)* >
< a common buttercup *(Ranunculus acris)* >
< a robin *(Turdus migratorius)* >

35. New Latin names of classes, families, and all groups above genera in zoology and botany are capitalized; however, their derivative adjectives and nouns are not.

< Gastropoda > *but* < gastropod >
< Thallophyta > *but* < thallophyte >

36. Geological eras, periods, epochs, strata, and names of prehistoric divisions are capitalized.

< Silurian period >
< Pleistocene epoch >
< Age of Reptiles >
< Neolithic age >

TIME PERIODS AND ZONES

37. The names of days of the week, months of the year, and holidays and holy days are capitalized.

< Tuesday >   < June >   < Thanksgiving >
< Independence Day >   < Easter >
< Yom Kippur >

38. The names of time zones are capitalized when abbreviated but usually lowercased when spelled out except for words that are proper names.
See also rules 16 and 17 above.

< CST >
< central standard time >
< Pacific standard time >

TITLES OF PRINTED MATTER

39. Words in titles are capitalized with the exception of internal conjunctions, prepositions, and articles.

NOTE: In some publications, prepositions of five or more letters (as *about, toward*) are capitalized also.

< *The Lives of a Cell* >
< *Of Mice and Men* >
< "The Man Who Would Be King" >
< "To His Coy Mistress" >
< "Acquainted with the Night" >

40. Major sections (as a preface, introduction, or index) of books, long articles, or reports are capitalized when they are specifically referred to within the same material; however, the word *chapter* is lowercased and spelled out in text.

   < See the Appendix for further information. >
   < The Introduction explains the scope of this book. >
   < discussed later in chapter 4 >

   Capitalization of the titles of movies, plays, and musical compositions follows similar conventions. For more details, see the Italicization section above.

TRADEMARKS

41. Registered trademarks and service marks are capitalized.

   < Dubonnet > < Orlon > < Air Express >
   < Laundromat >

VEHICLES

42. The names of ships, aircraft, and spacecraft are capitalized.

   < M.V. *West Star* > < Lindbergh's *Spirit of St. Louis* >
   < *Apollo 13* >

Plurals

The plurals of English words are regularly formed by the addition of the suffix -s or -es to the singular, as

< dog → dogs >
< race → races >
< guy → guys >
< monarch → monarchs >

< grass → grasses >
< dish → dishes >
< buzz → buzzes >
< branch → branches >

The plurals of words that follow other patterns, as

< army → armies >
< duo → duos >
< ox → oxen >
< foot → feet >
< p. → pp. >
< sheep → sheep >

< phenomenon → phenomena >
< libretto → librettos or libretti >
< curriculum → curricula also curriculums >
< alga → algae >
< corpus delicti → corpora delicti >
< sergeant major → sergeants major or sergeant majors >

are given at the appropriate vocabulary entries in the main body of the dictionary.

Additional information on the treatment of plurals in this dictionary may be found in the Explanatory Notes section of the front matter.

Documentation of Sources

Authors and editors use various methods to indicate the source of a given quotation or piece of information. In works related to the humanities, the footnote form traditionally has been preferred. In this form, full bibliographical information including author, title, publisher, date, and page is keyed to specific text passages through notes set aside from the rest of the text. In works related to the social and natural sciences, a system relying on parenthetical notes that appear in the text and that refer the reader to a list of sources elsewhere in the work has been used. Details relating to both these systems of documentation, as well as to a modified system utilizing elements of each, are explained in the following pages. For more detailed information, *The Chicago Manual of Style*, 13th edition, and the *MLA Style Sheet* may be consulted.

Footnotes

Footnotes to a text are indicated by superscript Arabic numerals placed immediately after the material to be footnoted, with no intervening space. The numbering may be consecutive throughout a paper, article, or book, or, especially in longer works, may start over with each new chapter or other section of the text. The footnotes may appear at the end of the complete text, at the end of each chapter, or at the bottom of each page. Notes appearing at the end of the chapter or the work are often called endnotes, and they are generally preferred over notes appearing at the bottom of the page because they are easier to handle when preparing manuscript or printed pages. Authors and editors should be aware that statements in *The Chicago Manual of Style*, 13th edition, and in *PMLA [Publications of the Modern Language Association]* 97 (1982): 318-24 encourage the use of parenthetical references even for texts related to the humanities. The following samples exemplify the basic types of footnotes.

Sample Footnotes

BOOKS

one author
[1]Albert H. Marckwardt, *American English* (New York: Oxford University Press, 1958), 94.

multiple authors
[2]De Witt T. Starnes and Gertrude E. Noyes, *The English Dictionary from Cawdrey to Johnson 1604-1775* (Chapel Hill: University of North Carolina Press, 1946), 119.

translation and/or edition
[3]Simone de Beauvoir, *The Second Sex*, trans. and ed. H. M. Parshley (New York: Alfred A. Knopf, 1953), 600.

[4]William Shakespeare, *The Complete Works of Shakespeare,* ed. George Lyman Kittredge (Boston: Ginn and Company, 1936), 801.

second or later edition
[5]Albert C. Baugh, *A History of the English Language,* 2nd ed. (New York: Appleton-Century-Crofts, 1957), 300.

a work in a festschrift or collection
[6]Kemp Malone, "The Phonemes of Current English," *Studies for William A. Read,* ed. Nathaniel M. Caffee and Thomas A. Kirby (Baton Rouge: Louisiana State University Press, 1940), 133-65.

corporate author
[7]President's Commission on Higher Education, *Higher Education for American Democracy* (Washington, D.C.: GPO, 1947), I:26.

book without publisher, date, or pagination
[8]*Photographic View Album of Cambridge* [England], n.d., n.p., n. pag.

ARTICLES

from a journal with pagination throughout the annual volume
[9]James M. Kusack and John S. Bowers, "Public Microcomputers in Public Libraries," *Library Journal* 107 (1982): 2137-41.

from a journal paging each issue separately
[10]Roseann Duenas Gonzalez, "Teaching Mexican American Students to Write: Capitalizing on the Culture," *English Journal* 71.7 (November 1982): 22-24.

from a monthly magazine
[11]Shirley Abbott, "Southern Women," *Harper's,* July 1982, 44-47.

from a weekly magazine
[12]Walter Clemons, "Cheever's Triumph," *Newsweek,* 14 March 1977, 61-67.

from a newspaper [13]Nancy Bauer, "Housing and the Native: A Sore Spot on Nantucket," *Boston Globe*, 20 June 1982, News section, p. 29, col. 2–4.

letter to the editor [14]Charles H. Percy, "Letters to the Editor," *The Wall Street Journal*, 4 November 1982, 31.

a signed review [15]Jane H. Hill, rev. of *Language and Learning: The Debate between Jean Piaget and Noam Chomsky*, ed. Massimo Piattelli-Palmarini, *Language* 57 (1981): 948–53.

Parenthetical References

Parenthetical references are highly abbreviated bibliographical citations that are set off from the rest of the text by parentheses. Such references direct readers to a bibliography or list of references with full information that is usually placed at the end of the work. The parenthetical references usually include the name of the author, the date of the work, and a page reference. If an entire work in the list of references is being cited, the page reference may be omitted. To distinguish among works published by the same author in a single year, an additional designation in the form of a lowercase letter (as 1980a or 1980b) is used. The following parenthetical references are keyed to the list of references that follows them and refer to some of the same sources used in the Footnotes section. The two different versions of the list of references show how such a list might be styled, respectively, in the humanities and in the social and natural sciences; however, numerous variations of these basic forms are in use throughout the academic disciplines and professional specialty fields.

Sample References

one author (Chapman 1969)

multiple authors (Starnes and Noyes 1946, 119)

translation and/or edition (Beauvoir 1953, 600)

second or later edition (Baugh 1957, 300)

a work in festschrift or collection (Malone 1940) [entire article being cited]

corporate author (President's Commission on Higher Education 1947, I:26)

journal article (Webb 1977) [entire article being cited]

signed review (Hill 1981) [entire review being cited]

Sample Lists of References

representative style for the humanities

Baugh, Albert C. *A History of the English Language*, 2nd ed. New York: Appleton-Century-Crofts, 1957.

Beauvoir, Simone de. *The Second Sex*. Translated and edited by H. M. Parshley. New York: Alfred A. Knopf, 1953.

Chapman, R. F. *The Insects*. New York: American Elsevier, 1969.

Hill, Jane H. Review of *Language and Learning: The Debate between Jean Piaget and Noam Chomsky*, ed. Massimo Piattelli-Palmarini. *Language* 57 (December 1981): 948–53.

Malone, Kemp. "The Phonemes of Current English." In *Studies for William A. Read*, edited by Nathaniel M. Caffee and Thomas A. Kirby, 133–65. Baton Rouge: Louisiana State University Press, 1940.

President's Commission on Higher Education. *Higher Education for American Democracy*. Washington, D.C.: GPO, 1947.

Starnes, De Witt T., and Gertrude E. Noyes. *The English Dictionary from Cawdrey to Johnson 1604–1775*. Chapel Hill: University of North Carolina Press, 1946.

Webb, Karen E. "An Evolutionary Aspect of Social Structure and a Verb 'Have.'" *American Anthropologist* 79 (1977): 42–49.

representative style for the social and natural sciences

Baugh, Albert C. 1957. *A history of the English language*. 2nd ed. New York: Appleton-Century-Crofts.

Beauvoir, Simone de. 1953. *The second sex.* Trans and ed. H. M. Parshley. New York: Alfred A. Knopf.

Chapman, R. F. 1969. *The insects.* New York: American Elsevier.

Hill, Jane H. 1981. Review of *Language and Learning: The Debate between Jean Piaget and Noam Chomsky,* ed. Massimo Piattelli-Palmarini. *Language* 57: 948–53.

Malone, Kemp. 1940. The phonemes of current English. In *Studies for William A. Read,* ed. Nathaniel M. Caffee and Thomas A. Kirby, 133–65. Baton Rouge: Louisiana State University Press.

President's Commission on Higher Education. 1947. *Higher education for American democracy.* Washington, D.C.: GPO.

Starnes, De Witt T., and Gertrude E. Noyes. 1946. *The English dictionary from Cawdrey to Johnson 1604–1775.* Chapel Hill: University of North Carolina Press.

Webb, Karen E. 1977. An evolutionary aspect of social structure and a verb "have." *American Anthropologist* 79: 42–49.

A Modified System

There are many modifications and combinations of the two basic documentation methods outlined above that are followed by various publishing houses and professional journals and societies. The modified system described here is fairly common among scholarly publications. The first reference to a work gives complete bibliographical information in the form of a footnote either at the bottom of the page or in a notes section. Such a note can also include an author's comment on the work cited and may indicate a shortened form by which the work will be cited elsewhere in the text. Subsequent references to that work are given in the form of parenthetical references which may rely on the shortened form indicated in the first note or may include the name of the author, a shortened form of the title, and a page reference. Even if no shortened form is indicated in the first note, subsequent parenthetical references need not repeat any element of the reference that is clear from the context.

first reference　　[1]Albert H. Marckwardt, *American English* (New York: Oxford University Press, 1958), 94.

[2]De Witt T. Starnes and Gertrude E. Noyes, *The English Dictionary from Cawdrey to Johnson 1604–1775* (Chapel Hill: University of North Carolina Press, 1946), 119; hereafter cited parenthetically in the text as *English Dictionary.*

subsequent references　　(Marckwardt 101) [appropriate if only one of Marckwardt's works will be cited in text]

(*American English 101*) [appropriate if more than one of Marckwardt's works will be cited and if the author's name is clear from the context]

(101) [appropriate if both author and title can be easily established]

(*English Dictionary* 201)

Forms of Address

Since the relationship between correspondents affects the form of address used in letters, no rigid guidelines can be set down for all occasions. It is to be understood in the following examples of generally accepted form that when two salutations are shown, the formal styling precedes the informal; that if the formal address shown for a man is "Sir," the formal address for a woman is "Madam," and vice versa; and that if the informal address shown for a man is "Mr.," the informal address for a woman is "Mrs.," "Miss," or "Ms.," and vice versa.

Addressee	Form of Address	Salutation
clerical and religious orders		
abbot	The Right Reverend John R. Smith, O.S.B. Abbot of —	Right Reverend and dear Father:
archbishop	The Most Reverend Archbishop of — or The Most Reverend John R. Smith Archbishop of —	Your Excellency: Dear Archbishop Smith:
archdeacon	The Venerable the Archdeacon of —	Venerable Sir:
bishop, Catholic	The Most Reverend John R. Smith Bishop of —	Your Excellency: Dear Bishop Smith:
bishop, Episcopal	The Right Reverend John R. Smith Bishop of —	Right Reverend Sir: Dear Bishop Smith:
bishop, other denomination(s)	The Reverend John R. Smith	Reverend Sir: Dear Bishop Smith:
brotherhood, Catholic, member of	Brother James, S.J.	Dear Brother James:
brotherhood, Catholic, superior of	Brother Michael, S.J., Superior	Dear Brother Michael:
cardinal	His Eminence John Cardinal Smith	Your Eminence: Dear Cardinal Smith:
clergyman, Protestant	The Reverend John R. Smith or The Reverend Dr. John R. Smith (if having a doctor's degree)	Dear Sir: Dear Mr. Smith: or Dear Dr. Smith:
dean (of a cathedral)	The Very Reverend John R. Smith or Dean John R. Smith	Very Reverend Sir: Dear Dean Smith:
monsignor	The Right Reverend Monsignor John R. Smith	Dear Monsignor Smith:
patriarch (of an Eastern church)	His Beatitude the Patriarch of —	Most Reverend Lord:
pope	His Holiness Pope — or His Holiness the Pope	Your Holiness: or Most Holy Father:
priest	The Reverend Father Smith or The Reverend John R. Smith	Dear Father Smith: Dear Father:
rabbi	Rabbi John R. Smith or Rabbi John R. Smith, D.D. (if having a doctor's degree)	Dear Rabbi Smith: or Dear Dr. Smith:

Addressee	Form of Address	Salutation
sisterhood, member of	Sister Mary Angelica, S.C.	Dear Sister Mary Angelica: Dear Sister:
sisterhood, superior of	The Reverend Mother Superior, S.C.	Reverend Mother: Dear Reverend Mother:

college and university officials

Addressee	Form of Address	Salutation
chancellor of a university	Dr. Amelia R. Smith Chancellor	Dear Dr. Smith:
dean of a college or university	Dean John R. Smith	Dear Dean Smith:
president of a college or university	President Amelia R. Smith *or* Dr. Amelia R. Smith	Dear President Smith: *or* Dear Dr. Smith:
professor, assistant or associate	Mr. John R. Smith *or* Dr. John R. Smith Assistant/Associate Professor of —	Dear Mr. Smith: *or* Dear Dr. Smith: *or* Dear Professor Smith:
professor, full	Professor Amelia R. Smith *or* Dr. Amelia R. Smith Professor of —	Dear Professor Smith: *or* Dear Dr. Smith:

diplomats

Addressee	Form of Address	Salutation
ambassador, American	The Honorable John R. Smith American Ambassador *or if in Canada or Latin America* The Ambassador of the United States of America	Sir: Dear Mr. Ambassador:
ambassador, foreign	Her Excellency Amelia R. Smith Ambassador of — *or if from Great Britain* Her Excellency The Right Honorable Amelia R. Smith British Ambassador	Excellency: Dear Madame Ambassador:
chargé d'affaires, American	John R. Smith, Esq. American Chargé d'Affaires *or if in Canada or Latin America* The United States Chargé d'Affaires	Sir: Dear Mr. Smith:
chargé d'affaires, foreign	Ms. Amelia R. Smith Chargé d'Affaires of —	Madame: Dear Ms. Smith:
consul, American	The American Consul *or if in Canada or Latin America* The Consul of the United States of America *or if individual name is known* John R. Smith, Esq. American Consul *or if in Canada or Latin America* Consul of the United States of America	Sir: Sir: Dear Mr. Smith:

Addressee	Form of Address	Salutation
consul, foreign	The Consul of — *or if individual name is known* The Honorable Amelia R. Smith — Consul *or* Consul of —	Sir: Madame: Dear Ms. Smith:
minister, American	The Honorable John R. Smith American Minister *or if in Canada or Latin America* Minister of the United States of America	Sir: Dear Mr. Minister:
minister, foreign	The Honorable Amelia R. Smith Minister of —	Madame: Dear Madame Minister:
secretary-general, U.N.	His Excellency John R. Smith Secretary-General of the United Nations	Excellency: Dear Mr. Secretary-General: *or* Dear Mr. Smith:

foreign heads of state

Addressee	Form of Address	Salutation
premier	Her Excellency Amelia R. Smith Premier of —	Excellency: Dear Madame Premier:
president of a republic	His Excellency John R. Smith President of —	Excellency: Dear Mr. President:
prime minister	Her Excellency Amelia R. Smith	Excellency: Dear Madame Prime Minister:

government officials, federal

Addressee	Form of Address	Salutation
attorney general	The Honorable John R. Smith The Attorney General	Sir: Dear Mr. Attorney General:
cabinet officer addressed as "Secretary"	The Honorable Amelia R. Smith Secretary of — *or* The Secretary of —	Madam: Dear Madam Secretary:
chairman of a (sub)committee, U.S. Congress (stylings shown apply to House of Representatives and Senate)	The Honorable John R. Smith Chairman Committee on — United States Senate	Dear Mr. Chairman: Dear Senator Smith:
commissioner	*if appointed* The Honorable Amelia R. Smith Commissioner *if career* Ms. Amelia R. Smith Commissioner	Dear Madam Commissioner: Dear Ms. Smith: Dear Ms. Smith:
director (as of an independent federal agency)	The Honorable John R. Smith — Agency	Dear Mr. Smith:
former elected government official	The Honorable Amelia R. Smith	Madam: Dear Ms. Smith:
judge	The Honorable John R. Smith Judge of the United States District Court for — District of —	Sir: Dear Judge Smith:
president	The President The White House *or*	Madam President: Dear Madam President:

Addressee	Form of Address	Salutation
	The Honorable Amelia R. Smith President of the United States The White House	
representative, United States Congress	The Honorable John R. Smith United States House of Representatives *or for local address* The Honorable John R. Smith Representative in Congress	Dear Sir: Dear Representative Smith: Dear Mr. Smith:
senator, United States Senate	The Honorable Amelia R. Smith United States Senate	Madam: Dear Senator Smith:

speaker,
United States House
of Representatives
	The Honorable Speaker of the House of
	    Representatives
	    or
	The Honorable John R. Smith
	Speaker of the House of Representatives
		Sir:
		Dear Mr. Speaker:
		Dear Mr. Smith:

supreme court, associate justice	Madam Justice Smith The Supreme Court of the United States	Madam: Dear Madam Justice: Dear Madam Justice Smith:
supreme court, chief justice	The Chief Justice of the United States The Supreme Court of the United States *or* The Chief Justice The Supreme Court	Sir: Dear Mr. Chief Justice:
special assistant to the President	Ms. Amelia R. Smith	Dear Ms. Smith:
undersecretary of a department	The Honorable John R. Smith Undersecretary of —	Dear Mr. Smith:
vice president	The Vice President of the United States United States Senate *or* The Honorable Amelia R. Smith Vice President of the United States	Madam: Dear Madam Vice President:

government officials, state and local

alderman	The Honorable John R. Smith Alderman *or* Alderman John R. Smith	Dear Mr. Smith: Dear Alderman Smith:
assemblyman	— see REPRESENTATIVE, STATE	
city attorney	The Honorable Amelia R. Smith	Dear Ms. Smith:
clerk of a court	John R. Smith, Esq. Clerk of the Court of —	Dear Mr. Smith:
councilman	— see ALDERMAN	
county clerk	The Honorable Amelia R. Smith Clerk of — County	Dear Ms. Smith:
county treasurer	— see COUNTY CLERK	
delegate	— see REPRESENTATIVE, STATE	
governor	The Honorable Amelia R. Smith *or* The Honorable John R. Smith Governor of —	Sir: Dear Governor Smith:

Addressee	Form of Address	Salutation
judge, local	The Honorable Amelia R. Smith Judge of the — Court of —	Dear Judge Smith:
judge, state	The Honorable John R. Smith Judge of the — Court	Dear Judge Smith:
lieutenant governor	The Honorable Lieutenant Governor of — *or* The Honorable Amelia R. Smith Lieutenant Governor of —	Madam: Dear Ms. Smith:
mayor	The Honorable John R. Smith Mayor of —	Sir: Dear Mayor Smith:
representative, state	The Honorable Amelia R. Smith House of Representatives	Madam: Dear Ms. Smith:
secretary of state	The Honorable Secretary of State of — *or* The Honorable John R. Smith Secretary of State of —	Sir: Dear Mr. Secretary:
selectman	— see ALDERMAN	
senate, state, president of	The Honorable Amelia R. Smith President of the Senate of the State (or Commonwealth) of —	Madam: Dear Ms. Smith: Dear Senator Smith:
senator, state	The Honorable John R. Smith The Senate of —	Sir: Dear Senator Smith:
speaker, state assembly, house of delegates, or house of representatives	The Honorable Amelia R. Smith Speaker of —	Madam: Dear Ms. Smith:
supreme court, state, associate justice	The Honorable John R. Smith Associate Justice of the Supreme Court of —	Sir: Dear Justice Smith:
supreme court, state, chief justice	The Honorable Amelia R. Smith Chief Justice of the Supreme Court of —	Madam: Dear Madam Chief Justice:

military ranks — a typical but not exhaustive list

admiral vice admiral rear admiral	*(full rank + full name + comma + abbreviation of branch of service)*	Sir: Dear Admiral Smith:
airman	*(same as above)*	Dear Airman Smith:
cadet	Cadet John R. Smith United States Military Academy	Dear Mr. Smith:
captain (air force, army, coast guard, marine corps, or navy)	*(full rank + full name + comma + abbreviation of branch of service)*	Dear Captain Smith:
colonel lieutenant colonel (air force, army, or marine corps)	*(same as above)*	Dear Colonel Smith:
commander (coast guard or navy)	*(same as above)*	Dear Commander Smith:
corporal	*(same as above)*	Dear Corporal Smith:

Addressee   Form of Address   Salutation

Addressee	Form of Address	Salutation
first lieutenant second lieutenant (air force, army, or marine corps)	*(same as above)*	Dear Lieutenant Smith:
general lieutenant general major general brigadier general (air force, army, or marine corps)	*(same as above)*	Sir: Dear General Smith:
lieutenant commander lieutenant lieutenant (jg) ensign (coast guard or navy)	*(same as above)*	Dear Mr. Smith:
major (air force, army, or marine corps)	*(same as above)*	Dear Major Smith:
master sergeant [a typical example for other enlisted ranks having compound titles not shown here]	*(same as above)*	Dear Sergeant Smith:
midshipman	Midshipman Amelia R. Smith United States Naval Academy	Dear Midshipman Smith:
petty officer *and* chief petty officer ranks	*(full rank + full name + comma + branch* *of service)*	Dear Mr. Smith: Dear Mr. Smith: *or* Dear Chief Smith:
private	*(same as above)*	Dear Private Smith:
seaman	*(same as above)*	Dear Seaman Smith:
specialist	*(same as above)*	Dear Specialist Smith:
warrant officer	*(same as above)*	Dear Mr. Smith:
other ranks not here listed	*(same as above)*	Dear + rank + surname:

miscellaneous professional ranks and titles

Addressee	Form of Address	Salutation
attorney	Mr. John R. Smith Attorney-at-Law *or* John Smith, Esq.	Dear Mr. Smith: *or if having JD degree* Dear Dr. Smith:
dentist	Amelia R. Smith, D.D.S. (office address) *or* Dr. Amelia R. Smith (home address)	Dear Dr. Smith:
physician	John R. Smith, M.D. (office address) *or* Dr. John Smith (home address)	Dear Dr. Smith:
veterinarian	John Smith, D.V.M. (office address) *or* Dr. John Smith (home address)	Dear Dr. Smith:

Index

Merriam-Webster's Language Research Service

The Language Research Service offers owners of Webster's Ninth New Collegiate Dictionary a unique privilege. With the Language Research Service, readers can take advantage of the unparalleled editorial resources of America's foremost dictionary publisher — *at no cost*.

The Language Research Service will answer *your* questions about words and their usage. Word origins and pronunciations, shades of meaning, variants and slang, new coinages, changes in usage over the centuries — *specific* questions about any of these will be answered promptly, accurately, and concisely. Please note, however, that only written inquiries accompanied by a stamped, self-addressed envelope will be accepted.

The largest dictionary staff in America will handle your inquiry. Resources include a library of more than 13 million word citations and a data collection program that produces hundreds of thousands of new citations every year. As a Collegiate owner you are offered personal access to these vast resources and assured of current, carefully researched replies.

You don't have to be a scholar to benefit from the Language Research Service. It makes Merriam-Webster's experience and resources available to professionals, students, and laymen alike in a way no other dictionary publisher has ever attempted.

Take advantage of this unique offer. Send your questions to Language Research Service, Merriam-Webster Inc., P.O. Box 281, Springfield, Massachusetts 01102. *Be sure to enclose a stamped, self-addressed envelope.*

Other Fine Dictionaries and Reference Books
Published by
Merriam-Webster Inc.

Webster's Third New International Dictionary, Unabridged
12,000 Words: A Supplement to Webster's Third New
    International Dictionary
Webster's School Dictionary (high school level)
Webster's Intermediate Dictionary (junior high level)
Webster's Elementary Dictionary
Webster's New Ideal Dictionary
Webster's Vest Pocket Dictionary
Webster's Dictionary of English Usage
Webster's Collegiate Thesaurus
Webster's School Thesaurus
Webster's New Dictionary of Synonyms
Webster's Word Histories
Webster's American Biographies
Webster's New Biographical Dictionary
Webster's New Geographical Dictionary
Webster's Secretarial Handbook, Second Edition
Webster's Instant Word Guide
Webster's Medical Desk Dictionary
Webster's Medical Secretaries Handbook
Webster's Medical Speller, Second Edition
Webster's Legal Secretaries Handbook
Webster's Legal Speller
Webster's Standard American Style Manual
Webster's Guide to Business Correspondence
Webster's Guide to Abbreviations
Webster's Compact Rhyming Dictionary
The Official Scrabble® Players Dictionary
Webster's Official Crossword Puzzle Dictionary
Webster's Sports Dictionary
Webster's Beginning Book of Facts
A Pronouncing Dictionary of American English